DIRECTORY OF AMERICAN SCHOLARS

DIRECTORY OF AMERICAN SCHOLARS

TENTH EDITION

VOLUME IV

PHILOSOPHY, RELIGION, & LAW

Caryn E. Klebba, Editor

GALE GROUP

THOMSON LEARNING

Detroit • New York • San Diego • San Francisco
Boston • New Haven, Conn. • Waterville, Maine
London • Munich

ISBN: 0-7876-5008-0 (Volume 1)
ISBN: 0-7876-5009-9 (Volume 2)
ISBN: 0-7876-5010-2 (Volume 3)
ISBN: 0-7876-5011-0 (Volume 4)
ISBN: 0-7876-5012-9 (Volume 5)
ISBN: 0-7876-5013-7 (Volume 6)
ISBN: 0-7876-5007-2 (set)
ISSN: 0070-5101

Printed in the United States of America
Published in the United States by Gale Group

CONTENTS

PREFACE

First published in 1942 under the auspices of the American Council of Learned Societies, the *Directory of American Scholars* remains the foremost biographical reference to American humanities scholars. With the tenth edition, the Gale Group has added social science scholars, recognizing the close relationship of the social sciences to the humanities.

The directory is arranged for convenient use in five subject volumes: Volume I: History, Archaeology, and Area Studies; Volume II: English, Speech, and Drama; Volume III: Foreign Languages, Linguistics, and Philology; Volume IV: Philosophy, Religion, and Law; Volume V: Psychology, Sociology, and Education. Each volume of biographical listings contains a geographic index. Volume VI contains an alphabetical index, a discipline index, an institutional index and a cumulative geographic index of scholars listed in the first five volumes.

The tenth edition of the *Directory of American Scholars* profiles more than 30,000 United States and Canadian scholars currently active in teaching, research, and/or publishing. The names of entrants were obtained from a variety of sources, including former entrants, academic deans, or citations in professional journals. In most cases, nominees received a questionnaire to complete, and selection for inclusion was made based on the following criteria:

1. Achievement, by reason of experience and training, of a stature in scholarly work equivalent to that associated with the doctoral degree, coupled with current activity in such work;

or

2. Achievement as evidenced by publication of scholarly works;

or

3. Attainment of a position of substantial responsibility by reason of achievement as outlined in (1) and (2).

Enhancements to the tenth edition include the addition of the fifth subject volume, Volume V: Psychology, Sociology, and Education, and the renaming of Volume I to better reflect the disciplines covered within. An outline of the major disciplines within the social sciences and humanities has been added to each volume to assist in locating scholars associated with disciplines related to, but not named outright in the titles of the individual volumes. Please see page ix for this information. Those individuals involved in multiple fields are listed in all appropriate volumes.

The tenth edition of the *Directory of American Scholars* is produced by fully automated methods. Limitations in the printing method have made it necessary to omit most diacritics.

Individual entries can include: place and year of birth, *primary discipline(s), vital statistics, education, honorary degrees, past and present professional experience, concurrent positions, *membership in international, national and regional societies, honors and awards, *research interest, *publications, postal mailing and electronic mailing addresses. Elements preceded by an asterisk are limited as to the number of items included. If an entrant exceeded these limitations, the editors selected the most recent information. Biographies received in the offices of the Gale Group after the editorial deadline were included in an abbreviated manner whenever possible.

The editors have made every effort to include material as accurately and completely as possible within the confines of format and scope. However, the publishers do not assume and hereby disclaim any liability to any party for any loss or damage caused by errors or omissions in the *Directory of American Scholars*, whether such errors or omissions result from negligence, accident, or any other cause.

Thanks are expressed to those who contributed information and submitted nominations for the new edition. Many societies provided membership lists for the research process and published announcements in their journals or newsletters, and their help is appreciated.

Comments and suggestions regarding any aspect of the tenth edition are invited and should be addressed to The Editors, *Directory of American Scholars*, Gale Group, 27500 Drake Road, Farmington Hills, MI 48333-3535.

MAJOR HUMANITIES & SOCIAL SCIENCE DISCIPLINES

Volume I: History, Archaeology, & Area Studies

Aesthetics
Architecture
Archaeology
Area Studies
Art
Art History
Assyriology
Community Studies
Community Planning
Demography
Geography
History
International Studies
Urban Studies
Western Civilization

Volume II: English, Speech, & Drama

Advertising
Audiology
Bibliography
Cinema
Classical Literature
Communications
Composition (Language Arts)
Creative Writing
Drama
English Literature
Film Studies
Journalism
Library Science
Literary Theory
Literature
Marketing
Mass Communication
Media Studies
Music
Music History
Musicology
Performing Arts
Poetry
Rhetoric
Speech Communication
Speech-Language Pathology
Theater Studies

Volume III: Foreign Languages, Linguistics, & Philology

Classical Languages
Comparative Literature
Foreign Languages
Foreign Literature Studies
Linguistics
Modern Languages
Philology
Romance Languages
Translation

Volume IV: Philosophy, Religion, & Law

Accounting
Business Administration
Corrections
Criminal Justice
Criminology
Economics
Epistemology
Ethics
Evangelism
Forensic Sciences
Government
Homiletics
International Relations
Missiology
Philosophy
Political Science
Public Affairs
Religious Studies
Statistics

Volume V: Psychology, Sociology, & Education

Adult Education
Anthropology
Behavioral Sciences
Child Development
Clinical Psychology
Counseling
Culture Studies
Education
Ethnology
Folklore
Gender Studies
Gerontology
Health Studies
Human Development
Language Education
Psychology
Social Work
Sociology
Women's Studies

ABBREVIATIONS

AAAS American Association for the Advancement of Science
AAUP American Association of University Professors
abnorm abnormal
acad academia, academic, academica, academie, academique, academy
accad accademia
acct account, accountant, accounting
acoust acoustical, accounstic(s)
adj adjunct, adjutant
actg acting
activ activities, activity
addn addition(s), additional
AID Agency for International Development
adjust adjust
admin administration, administrative
adminr administrator(s)
admis admissions
adv advisor(s), advisory
advan advance(d), advancement
advert advertisement, advertising
aerodyn aerodynamic(s)
aeronaut aeronautic(s), aeronautical
aesthet aesthetics
affil affiliate(s), affiliation
agr agricultural, agriculture
agt agent
AFB Air Force Base
AHA American Historical Association
akad akademi, akademia
Ala Alabama
Algem algemeen, algemen
allergol allergological, allergology
allgem allgemein, allgemeine, allgemeinen
Alta Alberta
Am America, Americain, American, Americana, Americano, Amerika, Amerikaansch, Amerikaner, Amerikanisch, Amerikansk
anal analysis, analytic, analytical
analog analogue
anat anatomic, anatomical, anatomy
ann annal(s)
anthrop anthropological, anthropology
anthropom anthropometric, anthropometrical, anthropometry
antiq antiquaire(s), antiquarian, antiquary(ies), antiquities
app appoint, appointed, appointment
appl applied
appln application
approx approximate, approximately
Apr April
apt apartment(s)
arbit arbitration
arch archiv, archiva, archive(s), archivio, archivo
archaeol archaeological, archaeology
archaol archaologie, archaologisch
archeol archeological, archeologie, archeologique, archeology
archit architectural, architecture
Arg Argentina, Argentine
Ariz Arizona
Ark Arkansas
asn association
asoc asociacion
assoc(s) associate(s), associated
asst assistant
Assyriol Assyriology
astrodyn astrodynamics
astron astronomical, astronomy
astronaut astronautical, astronautics
astronr astronomer
attend attendant, attending
atty attorney
audiol audiology
Aug August
auth author(s)
AV audiovisual
ave avenue

b born
BC British Columbia
bd board
behav behavior, behavioral, behaviour, behavioural
Bibl Biblical, Biblique
bibliog bibliografia, bibliographic, bibligraphical, bibliography(ies)
bibliogr bibliographer
bibliot biblioteca, bibliotec, bibliotek, bibliotheca, bibliothek, bibliothequeca
biog biographical, biography
biol biological, biology
bk(s) books
bldg building
blvd boulevard
bol boletim, boletin
boll bollettino
bor borough
bot botanical, botany
br branch
Brit Britain, British
Bro(s) Brother(s)
bull bulletin
bur bureau
bus business
BWI British West Indies

c children
Calif California
Can Canada, Canadian, Canadien, Canadienne
cand candidate
cartog cartografic, cartographical, cartography
cartogra cartographer
Cath Catholic, Catholique
CBS Columbia Broadcasting System
cent central
Cent Am Central America
cert certificat, certificate, certified
chap chapter
chem chermical, chemistry
chg charge
chemn chairman
Cie Compagnie
cient cientifica, cientifico
class classical
clin(s) clinic(s)
Co Companies, Company, County
coauth coauth
co-dir co-director
co-ed co-editor
co-educ co-educational
col(s) colegio, college(s), collegiate
collab collaboration, collaborative, collaborating, collaborator
Colo Colorado
Comdr Commander
com commerce, commercial
commun communication(s)
comn(s) commission(s)
comnr commissioner
comp comparative, comparee
compos composition(s)
comput computer, computing
comt committee
conf conference
cong congress
Conn Connecticut

conserv conservacion,conservation, conservatoire, conservatory
consol consolidated, consolidation
const constitution, constitutional
construct construction
consult consultant, consulting
contemp contemporary
contrib contribute, contribution
contribur contributor
conv convention
coop cooperation, cooperative
coord coordinating, coordination
coordr coordinator
corresp corresponding
Corp Corporation
coun council, counsel, counseling
counr councillor, counselor
criminol criminology
Ct Court
ctr center
cult cultra, cultural, culturale, culture
cur curator
curric curriculum
cybernet cybernetics
CZ Canal Zone
Czeck Czechoslovakia

DC District of Columbia
Dec December
Del Delaware
deleg delegate, delegations
demog demographic, demography
demonstr demonstrator
dent dental, dentistry
dep deputy
dept department
Deut Deutsch, Deutschland
develop development
diag diagnosis, diagnostic
dialectol dialectology
dig digest
dipl diploma, diploma, diplomate, diplome
dir director(s), directory directory
Diss Abstr Dissertation Abstracts
dist district
distrib distributive
distribr distributors
div division, divorced
doc document, documentation
Dom Dominion
Dr Doctor, Drive
Drs Doctroandus

e east
ecol ecological, ecology
econ economic(s), economical, economy
ed edicion, edition, editor, editorial, edizione
educ education, educational
educr educator(s)
Egyptol Egyptology
elec electric, electrical, electricity electrical
elem elementary
emer emeriti, emeritus
encour encouragement
encycl encyclopedia
employ employment
Eng England
environ environment, environmental
EPDA Education Professions Development Act
equip equipment
ERIC Educational Resources Information Center
ESEA Elementary & Secondary Education Act

espec especially
estab established, establishment
estud estudante, estudas, estudianet, estudio(s), estudo(s)
ethnog ethnographical, ethnography
ethnol ethnological, ethnology
Europ European
eval evaluation
evangel evangelical
eve evening
exam examination
examr examiner
except exceptional
exec executive(s)
exeg exegesis(es), exegetic, exegetical, exegetics
exhib exhibition(s)
exp experiment, experimental, experimentation
exped expedition(s)
explor exploration(s)
expos exposition
exten extension

fac faculties, faculty
facil facilities, facility
Feb February
fed federal
fedn federation
fel(s) fellow(s), fellowship(s)
filol filologia, filologico
filos filosofia, filosofico
Fla Florida
FLES Foreign Languages in the Elementary Schools
for foreign
forsch forschung, forschungen
found foundation
Fr Francais(s), French
Ft Fort

Ga Georgia
gen general, generale
geneal genealogical, genealogy
genoot genootschap
geod geodesy, geodetic
geog geografia, geografico, geographer(s), geographic,
geographie, geographical, geography
geogr geographer
geol geologic, geological, geology
geophys geophysical
Ger German, Germanic, Germanisch, Germany
Ges gesellschaft
gov governing, governors
govt government
grad graduate
Gr Brit Great Britain
guid guidance
gym gymnasium

handbk(s) handbooks
Hawaii
Hisp Hispanic, Hispanico, Hispano
hist historie, historia, historial, historic, historica,
historical, historique, historische, history
histol histology, histological
Hoshsch Hoshschule
hon honorable, honorary
hosp(s) hospital(s)
hq headquarters
HumRRO Human Resources Research Office
hwy highway

Ill Illinois

illum illuminating, illumination
illus illustrate, illustration
illusr illustrator
imp imperial
improv improvement
Inc Incorporated
incl include, included, includes, including
Ind Indiana
indust(s) industrial, industry(ies)
infor information
inst institut, institute(s), institution(s), instituto
instnl institutional, institutionalized
instr instruction, instructor(s)
instruct instructional
int internacional, international, internazionale
intel intelligence
introd introduction
invest investigacion, investiganda, investigation, investigative
investr investigator
ist istituto
Ital Italia, Italian, Italiana, Italiano, Italica, Italien, Italienisch, Italienne, Italy

J Journal
Jan January
jour journal, journalism
jr junior
jurisp jurisprudence
juv juvenile(s)

Kans Kansas
Koninki koninklijk
Ky Kentucky

La Louisiana
lab laboratorie, laboratorio, laboratorium, laboratory(ies)
lang language(s)
lect lecture(s)
lectr lecturer
legis legislacion, legislatief, legislation, legislative,
legislativo, legislature, legislazione
lett letter(s), lettera, letteraria, letterature, lettere
lib liberal
libr libary(ies), librerio
librn librarian(s)
lic license, lecencia
ling linguistic(s), linguistica, linguistique
lit liteary, literatur, literatura, literature, littera,
literature
Ltd Limited

m married
mach machine(s), machinery
mag magazine
Man Manitoba
Mar March
Mariol Mariological, Mariology
Mass Massachusetts
mat matematica, matematiche, matematico, matematik
math mathematics, mathematical, mathematics, mathematik,
mathematique(s), mathematisch
Md Maryland
mech mechanical
med medical, medicine
Mediter Mediterranean
mem member, memoirs, memorial
ment mental, mentally

metrop metropolitan
Mex Mexican, Mexicano, Mexico
mfg manufacturing
mfr manufacture, manufacturer
mgr manager(s)
mgt management
Mich Michigan
mid middle
mil military
Minn Minnesota
Miss Mississippi
mitt mitteilung
mkt market, marketing
MLA Modern Language Association of America
Mo Missouri
mod modern,moderna, moderne, moderno
monatsh monatsheft(e)
monatsschr monatsschrift
monogr monograph
Mont Montana
morphol morphologica, morphologie, morphology
mt mount, mountain(s)
munic municipal
mus museum(s)
musicol musicological, musicology

n north
nac nacional
NASA National Aeronautics & Space Administration
nat nationaal, national, nationale, nationalis, naturalized
NATO North Atlantic Treaty Organization
naz nazionale
NB New Brunswick
NC North Carolina
MCTE National Council of Teachers of English
NDak North Dakota
NDEA National Defense Education Act
NEA National Education Association
Nebr Nebraska
Ned Nederland, Nederlandsch
Nev Nevada
Neth Netherlands
Nfld Newfoundland
NH New Hampshire
NJ New Jersey
NMex New Mexico
no number
nonres nonresident
norm normal, normale
Norweg Norwegian
Nov November
NS Nova Scotia
NSW New South Wales
NT Northwest Territories
numis numismatic, numismatico, numismatique
NY New York
NZ New Zealand

occas occasional
occup occupation, occupational
Oct October
Ohio
OEEC Organization for European Economic Cooperation
off office, officer(s), official(s)
Okla Oklahoma
Ont Ontario
oper operation(s), operational, operative
ord ordnance
Ore Oregon
orgn organization, organizational
orient oriental, orientale, orientalist, orientalia
ornithol ornithological, ornithology

Pa Pennsylvania
Pac Pacific
paleontol paleontological, paleontology
PanAm Pan American
pedag pedagogia, pedagogic, pedagogical, pedagogico,
pedagogoie, pedagogik, pedagogique, pedagogy
Pei Prince Edward Island
penol penological, penology
phenomenol phenomenological, phenomenologie, phenomenology
philol philologica, philological, philologie, philologisch, philology
philos philosophia, philosophic, philosophical, philosophie,
philosophique, philosophisch, philosophical, philosohpy,
philosozophia
photog photographic, photography
photogr photographer(s)
phys physical
pkwy parkway
pl place
polit politica, political, politicas, politico, politics,
politek, politike, politique, politsch, politisk
polytech polytechnic
pop population
Pontif Pontifical
Port Portugal, Portuguese
postgrad postgraduate
PR Puerto Rico
pract practice
prehist prehistoric
prep preparation, preparatory
pres president
Presby Presbyterian
preserv preservation
prev prevention, preventive
prin principal(s)
prob problem(s)
probtn probation
proc proceding
prod production
prof professional, professor, professorial
prog program(s), programmed, programming
proj project, projective
prom promotion
prov province, provincial
psychiat psychiatria, psychiatric, psychiatrica, psychiatrie,
psychiatrique, psychiatrisch, psychiatry
psychol psychological
pt point
pub pub, publique
publ publication(s), published, publisher(s), publishing
pvt private

qm quartermaster
quad quaderni
qual qualitative, quality
quart quarterly
Que Quebec

rd road
RD Rural Delivery, Rural Free Delivery
Rural Free Delivery
rec record(s), recording
rech recherche
redevelop redevelopment
ref reference
regist register, registered, registration
registr registrar
rehabil rehabilitation
rel(s) relacion, relation(s), relative, relazione
relig religion, religious
rep representative
repub republic
req requirement(s)
res research, reserve
rev review, revised, revista, revue
rhet rhetoric, rhetorical
RI Rhode Island
Rt Right
Rte Route
Russ Russian
rwy railway

s south
SAfrica South Africa
SAm South America, South American
Sask Saskatchewan
SC South Carolina
Scand Scandinavian
sch(s) school(s)
scholar scholarship
sci science(s), scientia, scientific, scientifico, scientifique,
scienza
SDak South Dakota
SEATO Southeast Asia Treaty Organization
sec secondary
sect section
secy secretary
sem seminaire, seminar, seminario, seminary
sen senator, sneatorial
Sept September
ser serial, series
serv service(s)
soc social, sociedad, sociedade, societa, societas, societate,
societe, societet, society(ies)
soc sci social science(s)
sociol sociological, sociology
Span Spanish
spec special
sq square
sr senior
sr sister
St Saint, Street
sta station
statist statistical, statistics
Ste Sainte, Suite
struct structural, structure(s)
subcomt subcommittee
subj subject
substa substa
super superieur, superior, superiore
suppl supplement, supplementary
supt superintendent
supv supervising, supervision
supvr supervisor
supvry supervisory
surg surgical, surgery
surv survey
Swed Swedish
Switz Switzerland
symp symposium
syst system, systematic

tech technic(s), technica, technical, technicky, techniczny,
techniek, technik, technika, technikum, technique, technisch
technol technologic, technological, technologicke,
technologico, technologiczny, technologie, technologika,

technologique, technologisch, technology
tecnol technologia, technologica, technologico
tel telegraph(s), telephone
temp temporary
Tenn Tennessee
Terr Terrace
teol teologia, teologico
Tex Texas
textbk textbook(s)
theol theological, theologie, theologique, theologisch, theology
theoret theoretic(al)
ther therapy
trans transactions
transp transportation
transl translation, translator(s)
treas treasurer, treasury
trop tropical
TV television
twp township

u und
UAR United Arab Republic
UK United Kingdom
UN United Nations
unemploy unemployment
UNESCO United Nations Educational, Scientific & Cultural Organization
UNICEF United Nations Children's Fund
univ(s) universidad, universite, university(ies)
UNRRA United Nations Relief & Rehabilitation Administration
UNRWA United Nations Relief & Works Agency
USA United States of America
US United States
USPHS United States Public Health Service
USSR Union of Soviet Socialist Republics
Utah

Va Virginia
var various
veg vegetable(s), vegetation
ver vereeniging, verein, vereingt, vereinigung
vet veteran, veterinarian, veterinary
VI Virgin Islands
vis visiting
voc vocational
vocab vocabulary
vol(s) volume(s), voluntary, volunteer(s)
vchmn vice chairman
vpres vice president
Vt Vermont

w west
Wash Washington
wetensch wetenschappelijk, wetenschappen
WHO World Health Organization
WI West Indies
wid widow, widowed, widower
Wis Wisconsin
wiss wissenschaft(en), wissenschaftliche(e)
WVa West Virginia
Wyo Wyoming

yearbk yearbook(s)
YMCA Young Men's Christian Association
YMHA Young Men's Hebrew Association
YWCA Young Women's Christian Association
YWHA Young Women's Hebrew Association

z zeitschrift

Biographies

A

AAGESON, JAMES W.
PERSONAL Born 11/24/1947, Havre, MT, m, 1970, 3 children **DISCIPLINE** NEW TESTAMENT STUDIES; HISTORY OF EARLY CHRISTIANITY **EDUCATION** MDiv, 76, MTh, 77, D Phil, 84. **CAREER** Prof Relig, Concordia,Col. **MEMBERSHIPS** Soc Bibl Lit; Cath Bibl Asn **RESEARCH** Pauline Studies; New Testament Socio-linguistics; Jewish-Christian relations. **SELECTED PUBLICATIONS** Auth, Written Also for Our Sake: Paul and the Art of Biblical Interpretation, John Knox Press, 93; Paul's Gospel and the Language of Control: A Summary, Teaching at Concordia, 93; Judaizing and Lectionary, Early Jewish, Anchor Bible Dictionary; Typology, Correspondence, and the Application of Scripture in Romans 9-11, The Pauline Writings: A Sheffield Reader, Sheffield Acad Press, 95; Control in Pauline Language and Culture: A Study of Rom 6; New Testament Studies, 96; A Theoretical Context for Understanding I Cor 1:18-2:16, Teaching at Concordia, 96; 2 Timothy and Its Theology: In Search of a Theological Pattern, Soc of Bibl Lit Sem Papers, 97; Paul and Judaism: The Apostle in the Context of Recent Interpretation, World and World, 00; In the Beginning: Critical Concepts for the Study of the Bible, Westview Pr, 01. **CONTACT ADDRESS** 901 S Eight St., Moorhead, MN 56562. **EMAIL** aageson@cord.edu

AARONS, LESLIE ANN
PERSONAL Born 06/18/1964, New York, NY **DISCIPLINE** PHILOSOPHY **EDUCATION** Duquesne Univ, MA, 87, PhD, 95. **CAREER** Lectr, Calif State Univ, Bakersfield, 97-98; Consultant & part-time Instr in Philosophy at Cabrillo College, Aptos, CA **HONORS AND AWARDS** NEH summer grant, 96. **MEMBERSHIPS** APA; SWIP. **RESEARCH** Gender studies; history of Western civilization. **CONTACT ADDRESS** Dept of Philosophy, California State Univ, Bakersfield, 19538 Mallory Canyon Rd., Prunedale, CA 93907. **EMAIL** dr_aarons@yahoo.com

ABADINSKY, HOWARD
PERSONAL Born Brooklyn, NY, m, 2 children **DISCIPLINE** CRIMINAL JUSTICE **EDUCATION** Queens Col, CUNY, BA, 63; Fordham Univ, MSW, 70; New York Univ, PhD, 83. **CAREER** Inspector, Cook County, Ill, Sheriff (part-time), 82-90; Parole Officer, State of New York Div of Parole, 64-72, Sr Parole Officer, 72-78; asst prof, Western Carolina Univ, NC, 78-81; prof, Saint Xavier Univ, Chicago, 81-. **HONORS AND AWARDS** Consult, President's Commission on Organized Crime. **MEMBERSHIPS** Am Soc of Criminology, Acad of Criminal Justice Scis. **RESEARCH** Organized crime. **SELECTED PUBLICATIONS** Auth, Social Service in Criminal Justice, Prentice Hall (79); auth, The Mafia in America: An Oral History, Praeger (81); auth, The Criminal Elite: Professional and Organized Crime, Greenwood Press (83); coauth with L. Thomas Winfree, Understanding Crime: An Introduction to Crime Theory, Nelson-Hall (96); auth, Law and Justice: An Introduction to the American Legal System, 4th ed, Nelson-Hall (98); auth, Drug Abuse: An Introduction, 4th ed, Wadsworth (2000); auth, Probation and Parole: Theory and Practice, 7th ed, Prentice Hall (2000); auth, Organized Crime, 6th ed, Wadsworth (2000). **CONTACT ADDRESS** Dept Sociol & Anthropol, Saint Xavier Univ, 3700 W 103rd St, Chicago, IL 60655. **EMAIL** abadinsky@worldnet.att.net

ABBOTT, W. R.
DISCIPLINE PHILOSOPHY **EDUCATION** Ohio State Univ, PhD, 66. **RESEARCH** Epistemology; Philos of Mind; Spinoza; Rationalists; Philos of Lang; Hume. **SELECTED PUBLICATIONS** Auth, pub(s) on epistemology, philosophy of mind, Spinoza, rationalists, and philosophy of language. **CONTACT ADDRESS** Dept of Philosophy, Univ of Waterloo, 200 University Ave W, Waterloo, ON, Canada N2L 3G1. **EMAIL** wrabbott@watarts.uwaterloo.ca

ABDUL-MASIH, MARGUERITE
PERSONAL Born 11/14/1956, Egypt **DISCIPLINE** THEOLOGY **EDUCATION** Bryn Mawr Col, BA, 78; Johns Hopkins Univ, MA, 81, PhD, 85; Univ St Michael's Col, Mdiv, 89, PhD, 95; Regis Col, STL, 95. **CAREER** Asst Prof, 96-, St Mary's Univ. **MEMBERSHIPS** CTSA, AAR, Sabul ecumenical center for peace & justice in Palestine. **RESEARCH** Religion & science, inter-regional dialogue, peace in middle east. **SELECTED PUBLICATIONS** Auth, Experience and Christology in the Thoughts of Haus Frie and Edward Schillebeecks, Can Corp for the Study of Relig, forthcoming. **CONTACT ADDRESS** Dept of Rel Studies, Saint Mary's Univ, 923 Robie St, Halifax, NS, Canada B3H 3C3. **EMAIL** magi.abdul-masih@stmarys.ca

ABE, NOBUHIKO
PERSONAL Born 10/26/1941, Utsunomiya, Japan, m, 1978, 1 child **DISCIPLINE** THEOLOGY **EDUCATION** Northwest Univ, PhD, 72; Harvard Univ, ThD, 93. **CAREER** Res Assoc, Harvard Div Sch, 93-97; evening/weekend supervisor, Public Services Dept, Yenching Libr, Harvard Div Sch, 98-. **MEMBERSHIPS** Am Acad of Relig; Assoc of Asian Studies **RESEARCH** Constructive Theology; Comparative Theology **SELECTED PUBLICATIONS** Rev, The Social Self in Zen and American Pragmatism, The Eastern Budhist, 97 **CONTACT ADDRESS** 2 Divinity Ave., Cambridge, MA 02138. **EMAIL** nabe@fas.harvard.edu

ABEGG, MARTIN G., JR.
PERSONAL Born 03/06/1950, Peoria, IL, m, 1975, 2 children **DISCIPLINE** RELIGIOUS STUDIES **EDUCATION** Bradley Univ, BS, 72; Northwestern Baptist Sem, MDiv, 83; Hebrew Univ, Jerusalem, MA Studies, 84-87; Hebrew Union Col, MA, 90, PhD, 92. **CAREER** Instr, 82-84, Northwestern Bap Sem; res Fel, 88-91, Hebrew Union Coll; vis Lectr, 90-91, Univ of Cincinnati; co-Dir Dead Sea Scrolls Project, 91-96, Institute of Mediterranean Studies & Biblical Arch Stud; Assoc Prof, 92-95, Grace Theo Sem, IL; co-Dir, 95-, Dead Sea Scrolls Institute, Trinity Western Univ; Asst Prof, Religious Studies, 95-, Trinity Western Univ, Langley BC. **HONORS AND AWARDS** Who's Who in Biblical Studies & Archaeology. **MEMBERSHIPS** BAS **RESEARCH** Dead Sea Scrolls **SELECTED PUBLICATIONS** Co-auth, The Fragmentary Remains of 11QTorah Temple Scroll, 11QTb, 11QTc and 4QparaTorah, in: Hebrew Union College Annual, 91; auth, Messianic Hope and 4Q285, A Reassessment, in: J of Bib Lit, 94; The Messiah at Qumran, Are We Still Seeing Double? in: Dead Sea Discoveries 2, 95; co-auth, The Dead Sea Scrolls, A New Translation, San Fran, HarperCollins, 96; Qumran and Exile, in: Exile Old Testament, Jewish and Christian Conceptions, ed, J Scott, Leiden, E J Brill, 97; review, The Complete Dead Sea Scrolls in English, by Geza Vermes, in: J of Semitic Studies, forthcoming. **CONTACT ADDRESS** Dept of Religious Studies, Trinity Western Univ, 7600 Glover Rd., Langley, BC, Canada V2Y 1Y1. **EMAIL** abegg@twu.ca

ABEL, DONALD C.
PERSONAL Born 06/26/1948, Pomeroy, WA, m, 1988 **DISCIPLINE** PHILOSOPHY **EDUCATION** Gonzaga Univ, BA, 71; Tulane Univ, MA, 73; St Michael's Inst, PhL, 75; Loyola Univ Chicago, MDiv, 79; Northwestern Univ, PhD, 83. **CAREER** Instr, Gonzaga Univ, 73-75; instr, Northwestern Univ, 81-83; ed, Great Books Found, 83-84; asst prof, St Norbert Col, 84-91; assoc prof, Norbert Col, 91-00; prof St. Norbert Col, 00-. **HONORS AND AWARDS** Univ Fel, Northwestern Univ, 78-79; Diss Year Fel, Northwestern Univ, 81; Sasser Young Prof Awd, 86; Ledvina Awd for Excellence in Teaching, 88; King Distinguished Scholar Awd, 93. **MEMBERSHIPS** Am Philos Asn; Am Cath Philos Asn; Soc for Ancient Greek Philos; Soc for Philos and Psychol. **RESEARCH** Philosophy of human nature; Ethics; Medieval philos. **SELECTED PUBLICATIONS** Auth, Freud on Instinct and Morality, 89; ed, Theories of Human Nature, 93; Fifty Readings in Philosophy, 94; Discourses: A Database of Philosophy Readings. 94-; Human Nature, Philos of Educ, An Encycl, 96; Aquinas and Freud on the Human Soul, Aquinas on Mind and Intellect, 96. **CONTACT ADDRESS** St. Norbert Col, 100 Grant St, De Pere, WI 54115. **EMAIL** abeldc@mail.snc.edu

ABELA, PAUL R.
DISCIPLINE PHILOSOPHY **EDUCATION** Univ Toronto, BA; Queen's Univ, Ont, MA; Oxford Univ, Balliol Col, PhD. **CAREER** Asst prof, Loyola Univ, 96-; 2yr postdr res fel, Univ Toronto. **RESEARCH** Kant; early modern philosophy; metaphysics; epistemology. **SELECTED PUBLICATIONS** Articles in, Idealistic Stud & Philos Quart. **CONTACT ADDRESS** Dept of Philosophy, Loyola Univ, Chicago, 820 N. Michigan Ave., Chicago, IL 60611.

ABELE, ROBERT P.
PERSONAL Born 03/20/1955, Dayton, OH **DISCIPLINE** PHILOSOPHY **EDUCATION** Univ Dayton, BA, 76; Mt St Mary, MDiv, 83; Athenaeum of Ohio, MA, 85; Marquette Univ, PhD, 95. **CAREER** Lectr, philos, 88-90, 91-94, adj fac, 95, Marquette Univ; lectr philos, Carthage Col, 91; adj fac, Milwaukee Area Tech Col, 95; adj fac, Oakton Col, 96; adj fac, Col of DuPage, 96; asst prof, Silver Lake Col, 96- . **HONORS AND AWARDS** Scholar, Archdiocese of Cincinnati, 79-82, Marquette Univ, 85-92; fac development award, 97-98. **MEMBERSHIPS** C G Jung Inst; Concerned Philos for Peace; APA; Joseph Campbell Found; Greenpeace. **SELECTED PUBLICATIONS** Auth, Moral Questions on the Bombing of Libya, Milwaukee Sentinel, 96; auth, The Just War Theory and the Persian Gulf War, Milwaukee J, 91. **CONTACT ADDRESS** 2313 3rd St, Peru, IL 61354-3249.

ABELL, JENNIE
DISCIPLINE LAW **EDUCATION** Queen's Univ, BA; Univ Saskatchewan, LLB; York Univ, LLM. **CAREER** Assoc prof, Univ of Ottawa, 88-. **RESEARCH** Criminal law and procedure; law, poverty and social change; feminist theory and law; women and human rights: international perspectives; women in Central and South America; women's interests. **SELECTED PUBLICATIONS** Auth, Criminal Law and Procedure: Cases, Context and Critique and Criminal Law; Procedure: Proof, Defences and Beyond; pubs on legal aid, feminist theory, women and violence, and human rights. **CONTACT ADDRESS** Fac Common Law, Univ of Ottawa, 57 Louis Pasteur, Ottawa, ON, Canada K1N 6N5. **EMAIL** jabell@uottawa.ca

ABERBACH, JOEL D.
PERSONAL Born 06/19/1940, New York, NY, m, 1962, 4 children **DISCIPLINE** POLITICAL SCIENCE **EDUCATION** Cornell Univ, AB, 61; Ohio State Univ, MA, 63; Yale Univ, MA, 65; PhD, 67. **CAREER** Teaching Asst, Yale Univ, 65-67; Res Assoc, Univ Mich, 71-72; Vis Prof, Univ Stockholm, 77; Sen Fel, Brookings Inst, 77-80; Lectr to Prof, Univ Mich, 67-88; Prof and Dir, UCLA, 88-. **HONORS AND AWARDS** Fel, Nat Sci Found, 69-73, 78-81, 86-89; Fel, Brookings Inst, 77-80; Fel, Ctr for Adv Study in Beh Sci, 83-84; Fel, Nat Sci Found, 93-00; Fel, Swedish Col for Adv Study in the Soc Sci, 97; Phi Beta Kappa. **MEMBERSHIPS** Am Polit Sci Asn; Midwest Polit Sci Asn; Intl Polit Sci Asn. **SELECTED PUBLICA-**

TIONS Auth, Keeping a Watchful Eye: The Politics of Congressional Oversight, Brookings Inst, 90; co-auth, "The Political Views of Senior Federal Executives, 1970-1992," J of Politics, 95; auth, "Sharing isn't Easy: When Separate Institutions Clash," Governance, 98; auth, "Reinventing Government: Problems and Prospects," Gestion y Analisis de Politicas, 99; co-auth, In the Web of Politics: Three decades of the U.S. Federal Executive, Brookings Inst, 00; co-auth, "Senior Executives in a Changing Political Environment," in The Future of Merit: Twenty Years After the Civil Service Reform Act, (Johns Hopkins Univ Press, 00); co-auth, "Radical Reform in New Zealand: Crisis, Windows of Opportunity, and Rational Actors," Public Administration, 01. **CONTACT ADDRESS** Center for Am Polit and Pub Policy, Univ of California, Los Angeles, 4250 Public Policy Bldg, Los Angeles, CA 90095-1484. **EMAIL** Aberbach@polisci.ucla.edu

ABOU EL FADL, KHALED M.
PERSONAL Born 10/23/1963, Kuwait, m, 1995, 1 child **DISCIPLINE** LAW **EDUCATION** Yale Univ, BA, 86; Univ Pa, JD, 89; Princeton Univ, PhD, 96. **CAREER** Lectr, Yale Law Sch, 94-95; Asst Prof, Univ Tex, 95-98; Acting Prof, UCLA Sch of Law, 98-. **HONORS AND AWARDS** Whitting Fel; Omar and Azmeralda Alfi Distinguished Fel in Islamic Law. **MEMBERSHIPS** NJ Law Bar; PA Law Bar; Am Bar Asn; Asn of Law and Relig; Asn of Law and Soc. **RESEARCH** Islamic law; Jurisprudence and Legal History. **SELECTED PUBLICATIONS** Auth, Rebellion and Violence in Islamic Law, Cambridge Univ Press, 01; auth, Conference of the Books: The Search for Beauty in Islam, Univ Press of Am, 01; auth, Speaking in God's Name: Islamic Law, Authority and Women, Oneworld Press, 01; auth, And God Knows the Soldiers, Univ Press of Am, 01. **CONTACT ADDRESS** Sch of Law, Univ of California, Los Angeles, 405 Hilgard Ave, Rm 1242, Los Angeles, CA 90095. **EMAIL** abouelfa@mail.law.ucla.edu

ABRAHAM, GERALD
DISCIPLINE CRIMINAL LAW, CRIMINAL PROCEDURE, FAMILY LAW, CHILDREN AND THE LAW **EDUCATION** NYork Univ, AB, 51; NYork Univ Sch Law, JD, 53. **CAREER** Prof; fac, Villanova Univ, 62-; aasoc dean acad aff, 77-92; clerked for, Honorable Charles Froessel, NY Ct Appeals; past tchg fel, Harvard Univ Law Sch; taught at, Duquesne Law Sch, Univ Gottingen, Ger. **MEMBERSHIPS** Past pres, Mental Health Asn Southwestern Pa; chem, Chester Co Mental Health Retardation Bd & chp, Haverford State Hosp Patients Rights Rev Comt. **RESEARCH** Family law, children and the law. **SELECTED PUBLICATIONS** Coauth, Amram's Pennsylvania Practice, 70. **CONTACT ADDRESS** Law School, Villanova Univ, 800 Lancaster Ave, Villanova, PA 19085-1692. **EMAIL** abraham@law.vill.edu

ABRAHAMSEN, VALERIE
PERSONAL Born 10/05/1954, Norwood, MA **DISCIPLINE** RELIGION **EDUCATION** Univ S Carolina, BA, 75; Harvard Div Sch, MTS, 79; ThD, 86. **CAREER** Inst Registrar, Dir, 98-99, Lasell College; Registrar, 93-98, MGH Inst Hlth Professions; adj fac, 95-, Bunker Hill Comm College; Ethics/Prof admin, 86-89, Harvard Univ; registrar, Roxbury Community Col, 00-. **HONORS AND AWARDS** Who's Who in Biblical Studies and Archaeol; Who's Who of Am Women. **MEMBERSHIPS** SBL; AAR; AIA; AACRAO. **RESEARCH** Women in Early Christianity; Women in Greco-Roman antiquity; New Testament archaeology; Philippi. **SELECTED PUBLICATIONS** Auth, Women and Worship at Philippi: Diana/Artemis and Other Cults in the Early Christian Era, Portland ME, Astarte Shell Press, 95; auth, "Burials from Greek Macedonia: Possible Evidence for Same-Sex Committed Relationships in Early Christianity," J Higher Criticism, 97; auth, "Art Ancient," in Historical Encyc of World Slavery, ed. Junius P Rodriguez (Santa Barbara, ABC-CLIO, 97); auth, "Essays in Honor of Marija Gimbutas: A Response," J Feminist studies in Religion (97); auth, "The Goddess and Healing: Nursing's Heritage from Antiquity," J Holistic Nursing, (97); auth, Jesus According to Barbara Walker, J Higher Criticism, in press; auth, Women in the Proseuche at Philippi, Women in Scripture: A Dictionary of Named and Unnamed Women in the Hebrew Bible, Apocrypha, and New Testament, Houghton-Mifflin Co, in press. **CONTACT ADDRESS** 47 Seaverns Ave #1R, Jamaica Plain, MA 02130. **EMAIL** vabrahamse@aol.com

ABRAMS, DOUGLAS EDWARD
PERSONAL Born 05/16/1951, New York, NY **DISCIPLINE** LAW **EDUCATION** Wesleyan Univ, BA, 73; Columbia Univ, JD, 76. **CAREER** Law clerk, NY Ct Appeals, 76-78; atty, Kaye, Scholer, Fierman, Hays & Handler, New York, 78-81; Vis Assoc Prof Law, Fordham Univ, 81, Adj instr law, New York Law Sch, 79-81; assoc prof, Univ Mo Columbia, 81- . **RESEARCH** Securities regulation; administrative law. **SELECTED PUBLICATIONS** Coauth, Pass-on under the antitrust laws, NY Law J, 5/80; Intent in criminal prosecutions, Nat Law J, 12/80. **CONTACT ADDRESS** Sch of Law, Univ of Missouri, Columbia, 310 Watson Pl, Columbia, MO 65201-5006.

ABRAMSON, HAROLD I.
DISCIPLINE LAW **EDUCATION** Univ MI, BBA, 71; Syracuse Univ, JD, 74; Harvard Univ, MPA, 82, LLM, 83. **CAREER** Prof Law, Touro Col; spec coun and dir, Utility Intervention Off of the NY State Consumer Protection Bd; staff atty, Monroe County Legal Assistance Corp; arbitrator, Compulsory Arbitration Prog, Rochester, NY; dir, summer law prog, Moscow State Univ. **MEMBERSHIPS** Ch, NY State Bar Asn Comt on Alternative Dispute Resolution. **RESEARCH** Legal (dispute resolution) **SELECTED PUBLICATIONS** Written a number of articles on administrative law, government regulation, and dispute resolution. **CONTACT ADDRESS** Touro Col, New York, 300 Nassau Rd, Huntington, NY 11743. **EMAIL** HalA@tourolaw.edu

ABRAMSON, HENRY
PERSONAL Born 16/25/1963, Iroquois falls, ON, Canada **DISCIPLINE** JEWISH STUDIES **EDUCATION** Univ Toronto, PhD. **CAREER** Asst prof. **HONORS AND AWARDS** Awd for Outstanding Teaching, Life Long learning Soc, Florida Arlantic Univ, 99; Louis Wolfsohn II Hist Media Center Awd, 00; Videographer Awd of Distintion for Relig Documentary, Videographer's Society, 00; Third Place for Creative Excellence, US Inter Film and Video Festival, 00; Who's Who Among America's Teach Listing, 00; Fel, Center for Advanced Holocaust Studies, United States Holocaust Mem Museum, 00; 1999/2000 Awd for Excellecnce in Undergrad Teaching, Florida Atlantic Unvi, 00; Nat Endowment ofr the Humanities (NEH) summer Stipend, 00; Excellance in the Academy Awd (Teach), National Education Association, 01. **RESEARCH** Jewish history and culture with an emphasis on Russian and East European Jews. **SELECTED PUBLICATIONS** Auth, Historiography on the Jews and the Ukrainian Revolution, Jour Ukrainian Studies, 90; auth, The Scattering of Amalek: A Model for Understanding the Ukrainian-Jewish Conflict, 94; auth, A Ready Hatred: Depictions of the Jewish Woman in Medieval Antisemitic Art and Caricature, 96; auth, "Foreword to the turei Zhav of rabbi david ben Shumuel," Ukraine: Developing a Democratic Polity, Edmonton: CIUS, (96), 97-108; auth, "The Prince in captivity: Reading hasidic Disourses from the Warsaw Ghetto as sources for Social and Inteellectual History," J of Gencide Res 1:2, London, (99), 213-225; auth, " A Prayer for the Government: Jews and Ukrainins in Revolutionary Times," Harvard Judaic Texts and Studies, Cambridge, MA: Harvard Unvi Press, 99; auth, "Communal Trauma among Hasidim in the Holocaust," Transcultural Psychiatry 37:3, Montreal, (00), 321-335; auth, "Four Hundred Repetions and the Divine Voice: Aspects of Talmudic Pedagogy and the University Setting," Thougth and Action, Forthcoming 01. **CONTACT ADDRESS** Florida Atlantic Univ, 777 Glades Rd, Boca Raton, FL 33431. **EMAIL** habramso@fau.edu

ABU-NIMER, MOHAMMED
DISCIPLINE PEACE AND CONFLICT RESOLUTION **EDUCATION** George Mason Univ, PhD. **CAREER** Prof, Am Univ. **HONORS AND AWARDS** USIP, 92. **RESEARCH** Religion and Peace, Research on conflict resolution and dialogue for peace among Palestinians and Jews in Israel, Israeli-Palestinian conflict. **SELECTED PUBLICATIONS** Auth, Recouciliation, 01. **CONTACT ADDRESS** American Univ, 4400 Massachusetts Ave, Washington, DC 20016. **EMAIL** abunim@american.edu

ACAMPORA, CHRISTA DAVIS
DISCIPLINE PHILOSOPHY **EDUCATION** Emory Univ, PhD, 97; MA, 95; Hollins Col, BA, 90. **CAREER** Asst prof Philos, Univ Maine, present. **MEMBERSHIPS** Amer Philos Assoc; Soc for Philos Sport; N Amer Niezsche Soc; Soc of Women in Philos. **RESEARCH** 19th & 20th Century Continental Philosophy. **SELECTED PUBLICATIONS** Re/ Introducting Nietzsche's Homer's Contest: A New Translation with Notes and Commentary, in Nietzscheana, 95. **CONTACT ADDRESS** Dept of Philosophy, Univ of Maine, Orono, ME 04469-5776. **EMAIL** christa.acampora@umit.maine.edu

ACHINSTEIN, PETER
PERSONAL Born 06/30/1935, New York, NY, 3 children **DISCIPLINE** PHILOSOPHY **EDUCATION** Harvard Univ, BA, 56; AM, 58; PhD, 61. **CAREER** Asst prof, Univ Iowa, 61-62; from asst prof to assoc prof, 62-68, prof philos, Johns Hopkins Univ, 68; vis prof, Mass Inst Technol, 65-66; mem US nat comt, Int Union Hist & Philos Sci, 68-72; adv panel, div hist & philos sci, Nat Sci Found, 68-69 & 79-81; vis prof grad center, City Univ New York, 73; mem Steering Comt of Prog Comt 6th Int Cong Logic, Methodology, & Philos of Sci, 76-; Lady Davis vis prof, Hebrew Univ, Jerusalem, 76. **HONORS AND AWARDS** Guggenheim fel, 66; Lakatos Award, 93; NEH fel; NSF fel. **MEMBERSHIPS** Am Philos Assn; Philos Sci Assn. **RESEARCH** Philosophy of science. **SELECTED PUBLICATIONS** Auth, The Problem of Theoretical Terms, 65; auth, Concepts of Science, 68; coed, The Legacy of Logical Positivism, Johns Hopkins Univ, 69; auth, Law and Explanation, Oxford Univ, 71; auth, "What is an Explanation?," Am Philos Quart, (77); auth, "Concepts of Evidence," Mind (78); auth, The Nature of Explanation, Oxford Univ Press, 82; auth, Particles and Waves, Oxford Univ Press, 91. **CONTACT ADDRESS** Dept of Philosophy, Johns Hopkins Univ, Baltimore, 3400 N Charles St, 347 Gilman Hall, Baltimore, MD 21218. **EMAIL** phl_zpa@jhuvms.hcf.jhu.edu

ACHTEMEIER, PAUL JOHN
PERSONAL Born 09/03/1927, Lincoln, NE, m, 1952, 2 children **DISCIPLINE** NEW TESTAMENT **EDUCATION** Elmhurst Col, AB, 49; Union Theol Sem(NYork), BD, 52, ThD(New Testament), 58. **CAREER** Instr Greek & Bibl lit, Elmhurst Col, 56-57; asst prof New Testament, Lancaster Theol Sem, 57-59, assoc prof, 59-61, prof, 61-73; Prof New Testament, Union Theol Sem, Va, 73-97; emeritus, 97; Bk rev ed, Theol & Life, 58-65; recording secy, NAm Area Coun, World Alliance Reformed & Presby Churches, 63-70; tutpr, grad scj eci, emoca; stidoes, World Coun Churches, Univ Geneva, 63-64; vis prof, Pittsburgh Theol Sem, 67-68; participant, Int Greek New Testament Proj, 68-69; vis prof New Testament, Lutheran Theol Sem, Gettysburg, 70-72; sem assoc, Columbia Univ, 72-; mem, Roman Cath-Reformed & Presbyterian Bilateral Consult, 72-80; assoc ed, Interpretation, 80-82; Cath Bibl Quart, 81-89, 95-; ed, Interpretation 83-89; New Testament ed, Interpretation: Biblical commentaries for teaching and preaching, 79-; coed Biblical scholarship in North America, 78-80; ed Soc of Bib Lit Abstracts 77-80, ed. Soc of Bib Lit Seminar Papers 77-80; gen ed, Harpers Bible Dic 85; rev ed 96. **HONORS AND AWARDS** Elmhurst col Distinguished Alumni Awd, 84; Bibl Archaeol Soc special publication award for Harpers Bible Dictionary, 86; Distinguished New Testament Lecturer, Andover Newton Theol School, 93; Bibl Archaeol Soc Publication Awd for 1 Peter Commentary as Best Book Relating to the New Testament, 95-96; Academy of Parish Clergy 10 best books award for Inspiration and Authority, 99. **MEMBERSHIPS** Soc Bibl Lit (exec secy, 77-80; pres 85); Soc Studies New Testament; Am Theol Soc; Am Coun Learned Soc. **RESEARCH** Gospel of Mark; Espistle to the Romans, 1 Peter, form and function of miracle stories in hellenistic world, theology of St. Paul. **SELECTED PUBLICATIONS** Coauth, The Old Testament Roots of our Faith, Abingdon, 62; re-issued Fortress, 79; auth, An Introduction to the New Hermeneutic, Westminster, 69; auth, Mark, Fortress, 75, 2nd rev ed, 94; auth, Invitation to Mark Doubleday, 78; auth, The Inspiration of Scripture Westminster 80, (French trans Ed Fides, 85); auth, Romans A Bible Commentary, John Knox 84; auth, The Quest For Unity in the New Testament Church, Fortress, 87; Rev ed Hendrickson, 95; auth, Commentary on 1 Peter, Fortress 96; auth, Inspiration and Authority, Hendrickson 98. **CONTACT ADDRESS** Union Theol Sem, Virginia, 3401 Brook Rd., Richmond, VA 23227. **EMAIL** pachtemr@utsva.edu

ACHTENBERG, DEBORAH
DISCIPLINE HISTORY OF PHILOSOPHY, ANCIENT PHILOSOPHY **EDUCATION** New Schl for Soc Res, PhD, 82. **CAREER** Assoc prof, Univ Nev, Reno. **RESEARCH** Aristotle; ethics; political philosophy. **SELECTED PUBLICATIONS** Essays on Aristotle's ethics were recently published in Crossroads of Norm and Nature: Essays on Aristotle's 'Ethics' and 'Metaphysics' (Rowman & Littlefield Press), Essays in Ancient Greek Philosophy IV (SUNY) and Feminism and Ancient Philosophy (Routledge). **CONTACT ADDRESS** Univ of Nevada, Reno, Reno, NV 89557. **EMAIL** achten@scs.unr.edu

ACKELSBERG, MARTHA A.
PERSONAL Born 06/05/1946, New York, NY **DISCIPLINE** POLITICAL SCIENCE **EDUCATION** Radcliffe Col, BA, 68; Princeton Univ, MA, 70, PhD, 76. **CAREER** From lectr to asst and assoc prof, and prof, Smith Col, 72- ; vis lectr, Sch of Soc Sci, Univ Sussex, UK, 77; vis prof, Soc Thought and Polit Econ, Univ Mass, Amherst, 89. **HONORS AND AWARDS** Phi Beta Kappa; NDEA Fel; AAUW post-doctoral res fel, fel, Mary Ingraham Bunting Inst, Radcliffe Col, 83-84; vis fel, Ctr for Europ Stud, Harvard Univ, 83-84; vis fel, Walt Whitman Ctr for Culture and Polit of Democracy, Rutgers Univ, 92-93. **MEMBERSHIPS** Am Polit Sci Asn; Western Polit Sci Asn. **RESEARCH** Democratic theory; feminist political theory; women's activism; Spanish anarchism. **SELECTED PUBLICATIONS** Co-ed, Women, Welfare and Higher Education: Toward Comprehensive Policies, Smith, 88; auth, Free Women of Spain: Anarchism and the Struggle for the Emancipation of Women, Indiana, 91; auth, Models of Revolution: Rural Women and Anarchist Collectivisation in Civil War Spain, J of Peasant Stud, 93; auth, Dependency or Mutuality: A Feminist Perspective on Dilemmas of Welfare Policy, Rethinking Marxism, 94; coauth, Report of the Committee on the Status of Lesbians and Gays in the Political Science Profession, PS: Polit Sci and Polit, 95; auth, Identity Politics, Political Identities: Thoughts Toward a Multicultural Politics, Frontiers: J of Women's Stud, 96; auth, Toward a Multicultural Politics: A Jewish Feminist Perspective, in Brettschneider, ed, The Narrow Bridge: Jewish Views on Multiculturalism, Rutgers, 96; auth, Rethinking Anarchism/Rethinking Power: A Contemporary Feminist Perspective, in Shanley, ed, Reconstructing Political Theory: Feminist Perspectives, Polity, 97; coauth, Privacy, Publicity and Power: A Feminist Rethinking of the Public-Private Distinction, in Hirschmann, ed, Revisioning the Political: Feminist Reconstructions of Traditional Concepts in Western Political Theory, Westview, 96. **CONTACT ADDRESS** Dept of Government, Smith Col, Northampton, MA 01063. **EMAIL** mackelsb@smith.edu

ACKERMAN, FELICIA
PERSONAL Born 06/23/1947, Brooklyn, NY, s **DISCIPLINE** PHILOSOPHY **EDUCATION** Cornell Univ, AB, 68;

Univ Mich, PhD, 76. **CAREER** Prof philos, Brown Univ, 91-; vis fac mem, St Andrews Univ and Hebrew Univ of Jerusalem. **HONORS AND AWARDS** Phi Beta Kappa, 67; St Fulbright lectr, Hebrew Univ of Jerusalem, 85; fel, Center for the Advanced Study in the Behavioral Sci/NEH fel, 88-89; O. Henry award for short story, 90. **MEMBERSHIPS** Am Philos Asn, Modern Lang Asn, Int Arthurian Soc. **RESEARCH** Philosophical themes in Malory, biomedical ethics. **SELECTED PUBLICATIONS** Auth, "Assisted Suicide, Terminal Illness, Severe Disability, and the Double Standard," in M. Battin, et al, eds, Physician-Assisted Suiucide: Expanding the Debate, Routledge (98); auth, "Flourish Your Heart in This World," in M. Nussbaum and C. Sunste, eds, Clones and Clones: Facts and Fantasies About Human Cloning, Norton (98); auth, "Late in the Quest: The Study of Malory's 'Morte Darthur' as a New Direction in Philosophy," in H. K. Wettstein and P. A. French, eds, Midwest Studies in Philosophy XXIII: New Directions in Philosophy, Blackwell (99); auth, "'The More He is of Worshyp the More Shall Be My Worshyp to Have Add With Hym': Jousting with Scott Hess About Malory," Arthuriana 10:1 (2000). **CONTACT ADDRESS** Dept Philos, Brown Univ, PO Box 1918, Providence, RI 02912-9100. **EMAIL** Felicia_Ackerman@Brown.edu

ACKERMAN, JAMES S.
DISCIPLINE RELIGIOUS STUDIES **EDUCATION** Harvard Univ, PhD, 66. **CAREER** Prof emer, Ind Univ Bloomington. **RESEARCH** Religion and literature of Israel and the Ancient Near East; Bible as literature. **SELECTED PUBLICATIONS** Auth, articles on Numbers and Jonah, in Literary Guide to the Bible; auth, 2 Samuel in Journal of Bilical Lit, 90; auth, 1 Samuel, Prooftexts, 91. **CONTACT ADDRESS** Dept of Religious Studies, Indiana Univ, Bloomington, Sycamore Hall 230, Bloomington, IN 47405. **EMAIL** ackerman@indiana.edu

ACKERMAN, ROBERT M.
PERSONAL Born 03/26/1951, Yonkers, NY, m, 1978, 2 children **DISCIPLINE** ALTERNATIVE DISPUTE RESOLUTION, TORTS, LEGISLATION; LEGAL PROFESSION **EDUCATION** Colgate Univ, BA, 73; Harvard Univ, JD, 76. **CAREER** Assoc, Holme, Roberts & Owen, Denver, Colo, 76-80; asst profr, Dickinson School of Law, 80- 83; assoc prof, 83-85; prof, 85; vis lectr, Leicester Polytechnic Sch Law, Eng, 87; vis prof, Pa State Univ, 89; vis prof, Univ Vienna, 94; dean-; Willamette Univ College of Law, 96-99; prof, Dickinson School of Law of Penn State Univ, 99-. **MEMBERSHIPS** Mem, Phi Beta Kappa; Soc Prof(s) in Dispute Resolution. **SELECTED PUBLICATIONS** Auth, Instructor's Manual with Simulation and Problem Materials to Accompany Riskin Westbrook's Dispute Resolution and Lawyers; contrib, To Promote the General Welfare, Carney, ed. 99. **CONTACT ADDRESS** The Dickirson School of Law of the Pennsylvania State Univ, Willamette Univ, 150 S. College St., Carlisle, PA 17013. **EMAIL** bxa9@psu.edu

ACKLEY, JOHN B.
PERSONAL Born 09/24/1948, Dayton, OH, m, 1974 **DISCIPLINE** SYSTEMATIC THEOLOGY **EDUCATION** Wittenberg Univ, BA, 71; Lutheran Theol Sem, MDiv, 75; Catholic Univ Amer, PhD, 88. **CAREER** Dir mus organ, Emanuel Lutheran Church, 75-8; dir music organ, Church Good Shep VA, 81-85; chaplain's asst, Hospice N VA, 87-90; assoc mus dir, St Timothy's Episcopal Church VA, 88-; exec board, Leadership Program for Musicians Serving Small Congregations, Virginia. **HONORS AND AWARDS** Lutheran Honor Awd; Eliza-Catherine Smith Fel; AGO, Exceptional Ser Awd; Who's Who in the South and SW; Intl Who's Who. **MEMBERSHIPS** AAR; Hymn Soc; AGO. **RESEARCH** Ecclesiology; Clergy-Musician relations. **SELECTED PUBLICATIONS** Auth, The Church of the Word: A Comparative Study of Word, Church and Office of the Thought of Karl Rahner and Gerhard Ebeling, NY, Peter Lang Pub, 93; auth, Professionally Speaking: Clergy-Musician Relations II, Amer Organist, 91, 92. **CONTACT ADDRESS** 10401 Monterosa Place, Manassas, VA 20110.

ACKLEY-BEAN, HEATHER ANN
PERSONAL Born 01/22/1966, Massilon, OH, m, 1993, 1 child **DISCIPLINE** PHILOSOPHY **EDUCATION** Mount Union Col, BA, 89; Claremont Sch Theol, MA, 91; Claremont Grad Univ, PhD, 97. **CAREER** Asst dir, Center for Process Studies, 91-93; res asst, Inst for Antiquity and Christianity, 93-94; prog asst, Bavrier Free Prog, Los Angeles County Museum of Art, 95; adj prof, Scholars Bible Col, 97-99; from lectr to asst prof, Azusa Pacific Univ, 98-. **HONORS AND AWARDS** Nat Merit Scholar, 84; full tuition merit fels, Claremont Grad Univ, 91-93; Prof of the Year, Scholars Bible Col, 98; Creative Educ Grant, Fac Development Coun of Azusa Pacific Univ, 99-00; Lilly/Luce Teaching Grant, Am Acad of Relig, 00-01. **MEMBERSHIPS** Am Acad of Relig, Am Studies Asn, Appalachian Studies Asn, Weslyan Theol Soc, Christian Theol Reflection Soc, Pacific Southwest Mennonite Confr. **RESEARCH** Service Learning in Religious Studies, American Religious Movements, Appalachian Religion, Women's Studies in Religion, Religion and Culture, Religion and Film. **SELECTED PUBLICATIONS** Rev, of "Out on the Edge: Ministry on the Edge of the Media Reformation," by Michael Slaughter, J of the Wesleyan Theol Soc 34.2 (99): 287-290; auth, "Goals and Methods for Teaching & Service Learning Course in Religious Studies," Acad Exchange Quart (00); auth, "The Anabaptist/Mennonite Environmental Ethic: An Evaluation," in The Environment and Creation: An Anabaptist Perspective on a Sustainable World, ed. Calvin Redekop (MA: Johns Hopkins Univ Pub, 00). **CONTACT ADDRESS** Dept Relig & Philos, Azusa Pacific Univ, PO Box 7000, Azusa, CA 91702-7000. **EMAIL** hbean@apu.edu

ADAMEK, WENDI
PERSONAL Born 11/25/1959, Honolulu, HI, m, 1998 **DISCIPLINE** RELIGION **EDUCATION** Stanford Univ, PhD, 98. **CAREER** Asst Prof, 98-, Univ of IA. **HONORS AND AWARDS** Fulbright Fel, Javits Fel, Bukkyo Dendo Kyokai. **MEMBERSHIPS** AAR, AAS. **RESEARCH** Tang Buddhism, Dunhuang Studies. **CONTACT ADDRESS** School of Religion, The Univ of Iowa, 314 Gilmore Hall, Iowa City, IA 52242. **EMAIL** wendi-adamek@uiowa.edu

ADAMS, DOUGLAS GLENN
PERSONAL Born 04/12/1945, DeKalb, IL, m, 1968 **DISCIPLINE** THEOLOGY & ARTS **EDUCATION** Duke Univ, BA, 67; Pac Sch Relig, MDiv & MA, 70; Grad Theol Union, ThD, 74. **CAREER** Asst prof Am relig & art, Univ Mont, 75-76; asst prof liturgy & arts, 76-79, assoc prof to prof Christianity & Arts, Pac Sch Relig, 79-84; Smithsonian fel art hist, 74-75; doctoral fac relig & arts, Grad Theol Union, 77-. **MEMBERSHIPS** Int Sacred Dance Guild; Am Acad Relig; fel N Am Acad Liturgy; Polanyi Soc; Col Art Assn; Soc for the Arts, Rel, and Contemporary Culture. **RESEARCH** Early American liturgy; American art history; theology and dance. **SELECTED PUBLICATIONS** Auth, Transcendence with the Human body in Art: Segal, De Staebler, Johns, and Christo, Crossroads, 91; auth, Eyes To See Wholeness: Visual Arts as Biblical and Theological Studies, EMI Press, 95; auth, The Prostitute in the Family Tree: Discovering Humor and Irony in the Bible, Westminster, John Knox, 97. **CONTACT ADDRESS** Pacific Sch of Religion, 1798 Scenic Ave, Berkeley, CA 94709-1323. **EMAIL** dadams@psr.edu

ADAMS, E. MAYNARD
PERSONAL Born 12/29/1919, Clarkton, VA, m, 1942, 2 children **DISCIPLINE** PHILOSOPHY **EDUCATION** Univ Richmond, BA, 41; MA, 44; Colgate-Rochester Div Sch, BD, 44; Harvard Univ, MA, 47; PhD, 48. **CAREER** Asst prof, Ohio Univ, 47-48; asst prof to prof, Univ of NC, 48-; Kenan Prof Emeritus, 90-. **HONORS AND AWARDS** Alpha Mu Omicron; Colgate-Rochester Scholar, 44-45; Frances Wayland Ayer Fel, 45-47; James H Woods Fel, 45-46; Kenan Res Leave, 65, 79; Thomas Jefferson Awd, 71; Outstanding Educator of Am Awd, 71; Kenan Distinguished Prof, 71; Doctor of Humane Letters, Wake Forest Univ, 69; Festschrift, Ridgeview Pub Co, 89; Doctor of Humanities Hon Degree, Univ of Richmond, 92; E Maynard Adams Prof, 92; E Maynard Adams Annual Lectue, 98; Outstanding Scholar of the Twentieth Century. **MEMBERSHIPS** NC Philos Soc; Southern Soc for Philos and Psych; Am Assoc for Philos. **RESEARCH** Value Theory, Ethics, Epistemology, Metaphysics, Philosophy of Culture, with a focus on Western Cilvilization. **SELECTED PUBLICATIONS** Auth, Ethical Naturalism and the Modern World-View, UNC Pr, 60; auth, Philosophy and the Modern Mind, UNC Pr, 75; auth, Metaphysics of Self and World, Temple Univ Pr, 91; Religion and Cultural Freedom, Temple Univ Pr, 93; A Society Fit for Human Beings, SUNY Pr, 97. **CONTACT ADDRESS** Dept Philos, Univ of No Carolina, Chapel Hill, Caldwell hal CB#3125, Chapel Hill, NC 27599-2319. **EMAIL** eadams@email.unc.edu

ADAMS, FREDERICK R., JR.
PERSONAL Born 07/20/1950, Belleville, IL, m, 1972, 1 child **DISCIPLINE** PHILOSOPHY **EDUCATION** Southern IL Univ, Edwardsville, BA, 72, MA , 74; Univ Wis, PhD, 82. **CAREER** Instr, , 80-81, Lawrence Univ, Appleton, WI; lect,82, Univ WI-Madison; asst prof, 82-86, Augustina Col, Rock Island, IL; asst prof, 86-88, chr, dept of philos, 88-97, Cent Mich Univ; chr, dept of philos, Univ Del, 97-. **HONORS AND AWARDS** Fulbright Res fel, Univ Bristol, UK, 78; Dean's Fel, Univ WI, 79-80; NEH fel, Univ NE, 83, 84, Rutgers Univ, 92; vis scholar, Stanford Univ, Ctr for Stud of Lang & Info, 92; 20th Fritz Marti Lect, Southern Ill Univ, Edwardsville, 95; Univ Tchng Excel Awd, Cent Mich Univ, 95. **MEMBERSHIPS** Aristotelian Soc; Fulbright Alumni Asn; Am Philos Asn; Soc for Philos and Psychol; Southern Soc for Philos and Psychol; Phi Sigma Tau Nat Honor Soc; Phi Kappa Phi Nat Honor Soc. **RESEARCH** Cognitive science; epistemology; philos of mind. **SELECTED PUBLICATIONS** Auth, Goal-Directed Systems, Univ Microfilms Int, 92; coauth, Reflections on Philosophy, St Martin's, 93; auth, Simon Says, Stanford Hum Rev Sup, 94; auth, Trying: You've Got to Believe, Philos Res, 95; coauth, Rock Beats Scissors: Historicalism Fights back, Analysis, 97; auth, Cognitive Trying, Contemp Action Theory, vol 1, Kluwer, 97; coauth, The Semantics of Fictional Names, Pacific Philos Quart, 97;coauth, Fodor's Asymmetric Causal Dependency Theory and Proximal Projections, So J of Philos, 97;coauth, Functions and Goal-Directedness, Nature's Purposes, MIT/Adams, 98; coauth, Object Dependent Thoughts, Perspectival Thoughts, and Psychological Generalizations, Dialectica, forthcoming. **CONTACT ADDRESS** Dept Philosophy, Univ of Delaware, Newark, DE 19716. **EMAIL** Fa@udel.edu

ADAMS, GEORGE
DISCIPLINE LAW **EDUCATION** McMaster Univ, BA; Osgoode Hall Law Sch, LLB; Harvard Univ, LLM. **CAREER** Prof, 71- **HONORS AND AWARDS** Walter Owen Bk Prize, 87. **SELECTED PUBLICATIONS** Auth, Canadian Labour Law; pubs on labour law treatise. **CONTACT ADDRESS** Fac of Law, Univ of Toronto, 78 Queen's Park, Toronto, ON, Canada M5S 1A1. **EMAIL** george.adams@utoronto.ca

ADAMS, GREGORY B.
DISCIPLINE ANTITRUST, CONTRACTS AND CORPORATE LAW, AND PROFESSIONAL RESPONSIBILITY **EDUCATION** La State Univ, BS, 77, JD, 73; Columbia Univ, LLM, 79, JSD, 86. **CAREER** Assoc prof, Univ of SC. **MEMBERSHIPS** SCar Bar Asn. **RESEARCH** Advanced Legal Profession, business coporations, contracts, close corporation and partnership planning, law firm entity workshop, professional responsibility. **SELECTED PUBLICATIONS** Coauth, SC Corporate Practice Manual; co-reporter, SC Bus Corp Act. **CONTACT ADDRESS** School of Law, Univ of So Carolina, Columbia, Law Center Main & Greene St, Columbia, SC 29208. **EMAIL** gbadams@law.law.sc.edu

ADAMS, JOHN OSCAR
PERSONAL Born 04/03/1937, Chatanooga, TN **DISCIPLINE** LAW; PHOTOGRAPHY **EDUCATION** Wayne State Univ, BS 1962; Loyola Univ, JD 1970. **CAREER** Detroit Publ School, instr 1962-64; Pasadena City Col, lectr 1964-65; IBM LA, mgr, sys engr, instr 1964-70; IBM Corp Hdqtr, atty antitrust 1970-72; US Senate Small bus Comm, minor coun 1972-75; City of Los Angeles, dep city atty 1975-76; Wallace & Wallace, special counsel 1975-80; Adams Industries Inc of CA, president, bd chmn 1978-82; atty at law 1982-; art dealer 1985-; Mediator, 96; Photographer, 00-. **HONORS AND AWARDS** Special Achievement Awd Los Angeles Urban League 1970; Saturday Rev Commen Issue 1975; Men of Achievement; "Future Hope for the US"; **MEMBERSHIPS** Former chairman and mem of bd of dirs Hollywood Chamber of Commerce; bd dirs Hollywood Arts Coun; mem Supreme Court, CA, NY, Wash DC Bar Asns; former mem Hollywood Kiwanis. **SELECTED PUBLICATIONS** "Notes of an Afro-Saxon." **CONTACT ADDRESS** Adams & Alexander, 8383 Wilshire Blvd #919, Beverly Hills, CA 90211. **EMAIL** johnoadams@aol.com

ADAMS, LOUIS JEROLD
PERSONAL Born 06/01/1939, Logan, UT, m, 1963, 2 children **DISCIPLINE** POLITICAL SCIENCE, ASIAN POLITICS AND INTERNATIONAL LAW **EDUCATION** Univ Wa., Seattle, PhD, 72. **CAREER** Asst prof, Central Mo State Univ, 72-80; assoc prof, 80-90; prof, 90-. **MEMBERSHIPS** Amer Polit Sci Asn; Assoc for Asian Studies; Intl Studies Assoc. **RESEARCH** US-Japan trade relations. **SELECTED PUBLICATIONS** Auth, United States - Japan Trade Relations: The Function of Treaties, Chuo Law Rev, vol CIV, no 10-11, Aug, 98; The Law of United States - Japan Trade Relations, Jour of World Trade, Apr, 90. **CONTACT ADDRESS** Political Science Dept., Central Missouri State Univ, Warrensburg, MO 64093. **EMAIL** jadams@cmsu1.cmsu.edu

ADAMS, MARILYN M.
DISCIPLINE HISTORICAL THEOLOGY **EDUCATION** Univ Ill, AB, 64; Cornell Univ, PhD, 67; Princeton Theol Sem, ThM, 84; ThM, 85. **HONORS AND AWARDS** NEH, Younger Humanist fel, 74-75; Am Coun Learned Soc fel, 88-89; UC Pres Coun Hum fel, 88-89; Guggenheim fel, 89-90. **SELECTED PUBLICATIONS** Auth, Ockham's Treatise on Predestination, God's Foreknowledge, and Future Contingents, Century-Crofts, 69; Paul of Venice: On the Truth and Falsity of Propositions and On the Significatum of a Proposition, Oxford Univ Press, 77; William Ockham, Notre Dame Univ Press, 87; Ed, The Philosophical Theology of John Duns Scotus: A Collection of Essays by Allan B. Wolter, Oxford Univ Press, 90; Couth, The Problem of Evil, Oxford Univ Press, 90. **CONTACT ADDRESS** Yale Univ, 409 Prospect St., New Haven, CT 06511-2167.

ADAMS, ROBERT MERRIHEW
PERSONAL Born 09/08/1937, Philadelphia, PA, m, 1966 **DISCIPLINE** PHILOSOPHY **EDUCATION** Princeton Univ, AB, 59; Oxford Univ, Mansfield Col, BA, 61, MA, 65; Princeton Theol Sem, BD, 62; Cornell Univ, MA, 67, PhD, 69. **CAREER** Pastor, Montauk Community Church (Presbyterian), L.I., NY, 62-65; lectr to asst prof, Univ Mich, Ann Arbor, 68-72; assoc prof, Univ Calif, Los Angeles, 72-76, prof, 76-93, chair, Dept of Philos, 75-79, chair, Prog in the Study of Relig, 78-79, 85-87, 89-93; vis prof, Yale Divinity Sch, spring 88; prof and chair, Yale Univ, 93-, Clark Prof of Moral Philos and Metaphysics, 95-. **HONORS AND AWARDS** Nat Endowment of the Humanities, Younger Humanist Awd, 74-75; fel, Ctr of Theol Inquiry, Princeton, NJ, fall 83 and fall 84; Univ Calif Pres's Res Fel in the Humanities, 88-89; Wilde Lectr in Natural Relig, Oxford Univ, spring 89; fel, Am Acad of Arts & Scis,

91-; The Fac Awd for 1992, Univ Calif, Los Angeles, Col of Letters & Sci; Trustee, The Charlotte W. Newcombe Found, 79-; Bd of trustees, Princeton Theol Sem, mem(80-), secy (82-91), vice chair (91-96), chair (96-); Exec Comt, Am Philos Asn, Eastern Div, 95-98; Exec Comt, Soc of Christian Philosophers, 78-85, Pres, 81-83; Pres, Leibniz Soc, 94-98. **MEMBERSHIPS** Am Acad of Relig; Soc of Christian Ethics; Soc for the Scientific Study of Relig; Am Asn of Univ Profs; Presbytery of the Pacific, The Presbyterian Church (U.S.A.). **RESEARCH** Philosophy of religion, history of early modern philosophy, ethical theory, metaphysics. **SELECTED PUBLICATIONS** Auth, The Virtue of Faith and Other Essays in Philosophical Theology, New York: Oxford Univ Press (87); auth, Leibniz: Determinist, Theist, Idealist, New York: Oxford Univ Press (94); auth, Finite and Infinite Goods: A Framework for Ethics, New York: Oxford Univ Press (99). **CONTACT ADDRESS** Dept Philos, Yale Univ, PO Box 208306, New Haven, CT 06520-8306. **EMAIL** Robert.Adams@Yale.edu

ADDAMS, ROBERT DAVID

PERSONAL Born 02/12/1957, Chicago, IL **DISCIPLINE** LAW **EDUCATION** Princeton University, AB, 1978; Columbia University Graduate School of Journalism, MSJ, 1980; Columbia University School of Law, JD, 1982. **CAREER** Goodman, Eden, Millender & Bedrosian, associate attorney, 82-86; National Conference of Black Lawyers, associate director, 86; City Coll of NY, Revson Prof, 86-87; Association of Legal Aid Attorneys, executive director, 86-92; Institute for Mediation and Conflict Resolution, president/chief executive officer, currently; Brooklyn Coll, visiting prof, currently. **HONORS AND AWARDS** Princeton University Department of Afro-American Studies, Sr Thesis Prize, 1978; Revson Fellowship City College of New York Center for Legal Education, 1986-87; Brooklyn Coll, Belle Zeller, Visiting Distinguished Professorship, 1994-. **MEMBERSHIPS** National Conference of Black Lawyers, board of directors, 1985-87; Metropolitan Black Bar Association, 1992; State Bar of Michigan, 1982-92; National Lawyers Guild, 1982-86; American Bar Association, 1982-84; National Bar Association, 1982-84; Wolverine Bar Association, 1982-86; NY State Mediation Assn, bd of dirs, 1993-94. **CONTACT ADDRESS** President/CEO, Institute for Mediation and Conflict Resolution, PO Box 15, New York, NY 10031.

ADDIS, LAIRD CLARK

PERSONAL Born 03/25/1937, Bath, NY, m, 1962, 2 children **DISCIPLINE** PHILOSOPHY **EDUCATION** Univ Iowa, BA, 59, PhD, 64 Brown Univ, MA, 60. **CAREER** Instr, 63-64, from asst prof to prof, 64-74, Prof Philos, Univ Iowa, 74-, Chmn Dept, 77-85; Sr Fulbright lectr, Univ Groningen, 70-71. **HONORS AND AWARDS** Sr Humanities Fel. **MEMBERSHIPS** Am Philos Asn; Philos Sci Asn; Am Soc for Aesthetics, and others. **RESEARCH** Philosophy of mind; philosophy of the human sciences; metaphysics; aesthetics. **SELECTED PUBLICATIONS** Auth, The Logic of Society: A Philosophical Study, Univ Minn, 75; Natural Signs: A Theory of Intentionality, Temple Univ, 89; Of Mind and Music, Cornell Univ Press, 99. **CONTACT ADDRESS** Dept of Philos, The Univ of Iowa, 269 English Phil Bld, Iowa City, IA 52242-1408. **EMAIL** laird-addis@uiowa.edu

ADELMAN, HOWARD

PERSONAL Born 01/07/1938, Toronto, ON, Canada **DISCIPLINE** PHILOSOPHY **EDUCATION** Univ Toronto, BA, 60, MA, 63, PhD, 71. **CAREER** Lectr, Univ Toronto, 63-64; asst prof, 66-70, assoc prof, 70-80, Prof Philos, York Univ, 80-, assoc & acting dean, Atkinson Col, 69-71, ch philos dept, 74-77, dir grad prog philos, 80-83, 95-96. **RESEARCH** Internationa ethics, refugee studies, nationalism, and genocide. **SELECTED PUBLICATIONS** ed, The Indochinese Refugee Movement in Canada, 80; auth, Canada and the Indochinese Refugees, 82; co-ed, Refuge or Asylum? A Choice for Canada, 90; ed, Refugee Policy: Canada and the United States, 91; ed, Hungarian Refugees, 93; co-ed, African Refugees, 93; ed, Legitimate and Illegitimate Discrimination, 95; coauth, Early Warnings and Conflict Management: Genocide in Rwanda, 96; auth, Multiculturalism, Jews and Canadian Identity, 96; coed, Early Warning and Conflict Manangement: Genocide in Rawanda; co-ed, The Path of Genocied: The Rawnadan Crisis from Uganda to Zaire. **CONTACT ADDRESS** Dept of Philosophy, York Univ, 4700 Keele St, Downsview, ON, Canada M3J 1P3. **EMAIL** hadelman@yorku.ca

ADELMAN, MARTIN JEROME

PERSONAL Born 02/22/1937, Detroit, MI, m, 1961 **DISCIPLINE** LAW **EDUCATION** Univ Mich, AB, 58, MS, 59, JD, 62. **CAREER** The Antitrust Bull, 47-79; Prof of Law and Dir of the Intellectual Property Program, George Washington Univ Law School; Law Prof and Dir, Fed Dist Ct, Mich, 62-63; assoc, Honigman, Miller, Schwartz & Cohn, 63-64; patent atty, Burroughs Corp, 64-65; assoc, Barnard, McGlynn & Reising, 65-68, partner, 68-73; book rev ed, Actg dean, 74-75, Prof Law, Sch of Law, Wayne State Univ, 73-99; vis prof law, Sch of Law, Univ Mich, 82. **RESEARCH** Patent law; antitrust law; law and economics. **SELECTED PUBLICATIONS** Auth, Territorial restraints in international technology agreements after Topco, Antitrust Bull, 72 & Patent Law Rev, 73; The integrity of the administrative process, Sherman Section 2 and Per Se Rules-Lessons of fraud on the Patent Office, Wayne Law Rev, 72, J Patent Off Soc, 73 & Patent Law Rev, 73; Secrecy and patenting: Some proposals for resolving the conflict, Am Patent Law Asn Quart, 73 & Patent Law Rev, 73; Patent-antitrust: Patent dynamics and field of use licensing, NY Univ Law Rev, 75, Patent Law Rev, 495 & J of Reprints for Antitrust Law & Econ 429; Property rights theory and patent-antitrust: The role of compulsory licensing, NY Univ Law Rev, 77, Intellectual Property Law Rev 77 & J of Reprints for Antitrust Law & Econ 287; The relevant market paradox - attempted and completed patent fraud monopolization, Ohio State Law J, 77, Intellectual Property Law Rev 115 & J of Reprints for Antitrust Law & Econ 709; Use of industrial property as a Clandestine Cartel, Am J Comp Law, 82; The Supreme Court, market structure and innovation: Chakrabarty, Rohm & Haas, Antitrust Bull, 82; Patent Law Perspectives, 8 vol, updated continuously; co-auth, Cases and materials on Patent Law, West Group, 98. **CONTACT ADDRESS** Law Prog, The George Washington Univ, Center for Intellectual Property Studies, Washington, DC 20052. **EMAIL** madelman@main.nlc.gwu.edu

ADKINS, ARTHUR WILLIAM HOPE

PERSONAL Born 10/17/1929, Leicester, England, m, 1961, 2 children **DISCIPLINE** CLASSICS; PHILOSOPHY **EDUCATION** Oxford Univ, BA, 52, MA, 55, DPhil, 57. **CAREER** Asst lectr Latin humanities, Univ Glasgow, 54-56; lectr Greek, Bedford Col, Univ London, 56-61; fel class lang & lit, Exeter Col, Oxford, 61-65; prof classics, Univ Reading, 66-74; chmn, Dept Classics, 75-80, prof Greek, philos & early Christian lit, Univ Chicago, 74- ; vis sr fel classics Soc Humanities, Cornell Univ, 69-70. **MEMBERSHIPS** Soc Promotion Hellenic Studies; Class Asn Gt Brit; Am Philol Asn; Am Philos Asn; Asn Ancient Historians. **RESEARCH** Greek philosophy; Greek thought and religion; Greek literature. **SELECTED PUBLICATIONS** Auth, Merit and Responsibility: A Study in Greek Values, Clarendon, Oxford, 60; contribr, Greek religion, In: Historia Religionum Handbook for the History of Religions, Leiden, Brill, 69; auth, From the Many to the One: A Study of Personality and Views of Human Nature in the Context of Ancient Greek Society, Values and Beliefs, Constable, London & Cornell Univ, 70; Moral Values and Political Behavior in Ancient Greece, Chatto & Windus, London & Clark Irwin, Toronto, 72; Paralysis and Akrasia in Eth Nic 1102b16 ff, Am J Philos, Vol 97, 62-64; Polupragmosune and minding one's own business: A study in Greek social and political values, CP, 76; Callinus 1 and Tyrtaeus 10 as poetry, HSCP, 77; Lucretius I, 137 ff and the problems of writing Versus Latini, Phoenix, 77; auth, Poetic Craft in the Early Greek Elegists, Univ Chicago, 85; Ethics with Aristotle, Classical Philol, Vol 0088, 93; rev, Hybris- A Study in the Values of Honor and Shame in Ancient Greece, Class Jour, Vol 0090, 95; rev, Aidos - The Psychology and Ethics of Honor and Shame in Ancient Greek Literature, Class Jour, Vol 0090, 95. **CONTACT ADDRESS** Dept of Classics, Univ of Chicago, 1050 E 59th St, Chicago, IL 60637. **EMAIL** eadkins@midway.chicago.edu

ADLER, JACOB

DISCIPLINE SOCIAL AND POLITICAL PHILOSOPHY **EDUCATION** Harvard Univ, PhD. **CAREER** Philos, Univ Ark **SELECTED PUBLICATIONS** Auth, The Urgings of Conscience, Temple Univ Press, 92. **CONTACT ADDRESS** Univ of Arkansas, Fayetteville, Fayetteville, AR 72701. **EMAIL** jadler@comp.uark.edu

ADLER, JOSEPH A.

PERSONAL Born 03/14/1948, Suffern, NY, m, 1982, 1 child **DISCIPLINE** RELIGIOUS STUDIES **EDUCATION** Univ Rochester, BA, 70; Univ Calif, Santa Barbara, MA, 77, PhD, 84. **CAREER** Vis asst prof, Univ S Calif, 86-87; from asst prof to assoc prof, 87-, Kenyon Col. **MEMBERSHIPS** Am Acad Religion; Asn Asian Stud; Society Stud Chinese Religions. **RESEARCH** Neo-Confucianism **SELECTED PUBLICATIONS** Auth, Descriptive and Normative Principle(li) in Confucian Moral Metaphysics: Is/Ought from the Chinese Perspective, 81; coauth, Sung Dynasty Uses of the I Ching, 90; auth, art, Response and Responsibility: Chow Tun-I and Neo-Confucian Resources for Environmental Ethics, 98; auth, art, Zhou Dunyi: The Metaphysics and Practice of Sagehood, 98. **CONTACT ADDRESS** Dept of Religious Studies, Kenyon Col, Gambier, OH 43022. **EMAIL** adlerj@kenyon.edu

AGICH, GEORGE J.

PERSONAL Born 05/27/1947, Rochester, PA, m, 1980, 1 child **DISCIPLINE** PHILOSOPHY **EDUCATION** Duquesne Univ, BA, eng & philos, 69; Univ Tex Austin, MA, philos, 71, PhD, philos, 76. **CAREER** Asst prof to prof, med humanities and psychiat, Southern Ill Univ Sch of Med, 76-96; F. J. O'Neill chair, clinical bioethics, chair, dept of bioethics, Cleveland Clinic Found, 97-. **RESEARCH** Bioethics; Philosophy of medicine; Philosophy of psychiatry. **SELECTED PUBLICATIONS** Article, Ethical Issues in Managed Care, Oncology Issues, 13, no 3, 25-27, May/Jun, 98; article, Can the Patient Make Treatment Decisions? Evaluating Decisional Capacity, Cleveland Clinic Jour of Med, 64, 461-464, Oct, 97; article, Ethics Expert Testimony: Against the Skeptics, Jour of Med and Philos, 22, 381-403, 97; article, Consent in Patients with Mental Illness, Current Opinion in Psychiat, 10, 423-26, 97; article, Maladie Chronique et Autonomie: Des Lecons pour Comprehension Schizophrenie, L'Evolution Psychiatrique, 62, 401-409, 97; article, Ethics Committees and Consultants in the United States, Gesundheits-Oeconomica, 89-100, 95; article, Disease, Functions, Values, and Psychiatric Classification, Philos, Psychiat, and Psychol, 2, 219-231, 95; article, Authority in Ethics Consultation, Jour of Law, Med and Ethics, 23, 273-283, 95; article, Key Concepts: Autonomy, Philos, Psychiat, and Psychol, I, 267-269, Dec, 94; article, Expertise in Ethics Consultation: Reaction to Fox and Stocking, HEC Forum 6, 379-383, Nov, 94; article, Consent in Children and at the End of Life, Current Opinion in Psychiat, 7, 426-429, 94; article, On Values in Recent American Psychiatric Classification, Jour of Med and Philos, 19, 261-277, 94; article, Privacy and Medical Record Information, Jour of the Amer Med Info Asn, 1, 323-324, Jul-Aug, 94. **CONTACT ADDRESS** Dept. of Bioethics, Cleveland Clinic Foundation, 9500 Euclid Av., Cleveland, OH 44195. **EMAIL** agichg@cesmtp.ccf.org

AHLERS, ROLF

PERSONAL Born 06/22/1936, Hamburg, Germany, m, 1965, 2 children **DISCIPLINE** THEOLOGY **EDUCATION** Breco Univ, BA, 56; Princeton Theol Sem, MDiv, 61; Univ Hamburg, PhD, 66. **CAREER** Asst Prof, Seminar fur Systematische Theologie v. Sozialethik, Hamburg, Ger, 61-66; Asst Prof, Ill Col, 66-72; Prof, Russell Sage Col, Tray NY, 73-. **HONORS AND AWARDS** NEH Awd, 70-71. **MEMBERSHIPS** Hegel Soc of Am, New Heaven Theol Discussion Group, Am Acad of Relig. **RESEARCH** German Idealism, Hegel. **SELECTED PUBLICATIONS** Auth, The Batmen Theological Declaration, 1934, Mellen Press, 86. **CONTACT ADDRESS** Dept Soc Studies, Russell Sage Col, 65 N 1st St, Troy, NY 12180-1538.

AHLSTROM, GOSTA WERNER

PERSONAL Born 08/27/1918, Sandviken, Sweden, m, 1952, 2 children **DISCIPLINE** OLD TESTAMENT **EDUCATION** Univ Uppsala, Teol Lic, 54, Teol Dr, 59, Fil Kand, 61. **CAREER** From instr to asst prof Old Testament, Univ Uppsala, 54-63; vis assoc prof, 62-63, assoc prof, 63-76, Prof Old Testament & Ancient Palestinian Studies, Univ Chicago, 76- ; Ann prof, W F Albright Inst Archaeol Res, Jerusalem, 69-70, staff mem, Am excavations in Israel, Cyprus & Tuninsia, 69-77; trustee, 70-74. **MEMBERSHIPS** Am Orient Soc; Am Schs Orient Res; Archaeol Inst Am; Soc Bibl Lit; Der Deutsche Verein zur Erforschung Palastinas (pres, 76-78). **RESEARCH** Syro-Palestinian history and religions; Palestinian archaeology. **SELECTED PUBLICATIONS** Auth, Psalm 89 Eine Liturgie aus dem Ritual des leidenden Konigs, 59 & Aspects of Syncretism in Israelite Religion, 63, CWK Gleerup, Lund; Joel and the Temple Cult of Jerusalem, Brill, Leiden, 71; An Israelite God figurine from Hazor, Orient Suecana, 72; Prophecy, In: Encyclopedia Britannica, 74; Winepresses and cup-marks of the Jenin-Megiddo survey, Bull Am Schs Oreint Res, No 231, 78; Another Moses tradition, J Near Eastern Studies, No 39, 80; Royal administration and national religion in ancient Palestine, Brill Leiden, 81; Palestine in Prehellenic Time, Jour of Near Eastern Studies, Vol 0053, 94. **CONTACT ADDRESS** Univ of Chicago, Swift Hall, Chicago, IL 60637.

AHN, TIMOTHY MYUNGHOON

PERSONAL Born 05/21/1953, Korea, m, 1978, 2 children **DISCIPLINE** CHRISTIAN EDUCATION **EDUCATION** Boston Univ, ThD, 94. **CAREER** Sr Pastor, Arcola Korean United Methodist Church. **CONTACT ADDRESS** S-62 Paramus Rd, Paramus, NJ 07652. **EMAIL** Wonseop@aol.com

AICHELE, GEORGE

PERSONAL Born 06/12/1944, Washington, DC, m, 1968, 2 children **DISCIPLINE** THEOLOGY **EDUCATION** Univ Ill, BA, 65; Garrett Theol Sem, BD, 69; Northwest Univ, PhD, 74. **CAREER** Chaplain, Northwest Univ, 74-75; instr, N Iowa Community Coll, 76-77; instr Upper Iowa Univ, 77-78; Adrian Coll Mich, 78-; prof Adrian Coll Mich, 90-. **MEMBERSHIPS** Am Acad Rel; Soc Bibl Lit; Int Asn For Fantasy in Art and Lit; Internet discussions gropus. **SELECTED PUBLICATIONS** Auth, Jesus Framed, 96; Sign, Text, Scripture: Semiotics and the Bible, 97; co-ed, Semeia:69/70: Intertextuality and the Bible, 95; The Bible and fantasy. Journal for the Fantastic in the Arts, 97; The Monstrous and the Unspeakable: the Bible as Fantastic Literature, 97; Violence, Utopia, and the Kingdom of God, 98; ed, Culture, Entertainment, and the Bible, 00; auth, The Control of Biblical Meaning, 01. **CONTACT ADDRESS** Dept of Philosophy and Religion, Adrian Col, Adrian, MI 49221. **EMAIL** gaichele@adrian.edu

AIKEN, JANE HARRIS

PERSONAL Born 04/12/1955, Greenville, SC, m, 1991, 3 children **DISCIPLINE** LAW **EDUCATION** Hollins Col, BA, 77; NYork Univ, JD, 83; Georgetown Univ, LLM, 85. **CAREER** Clin Instr, Georgetown Univ Law Center, 83-85; Assoc Prof to Prof and Clin Dir, Ariz State Univ, 85-91; Prof, Univ SCar School of Law, 92-97; Prof, Wash Univ, 97-. **HONORS AND AWARDS** Congressional Fel; Root-Tilden Scholar, NY Univ; Order of the Coif; Burlington-Northern Teaching Awd; Outstanding Prof, Ariz State Univ; Carnegie Fel; Fulbright Sen Res Fel, Katmandu. **MEMBERSHIPS** Am Bar Asn; Am Asn of Am Law Sch; Nat Lawyer's Guild. **RESEARCH** Evidence;

Intimate Violence; Justice Education. **SELECTED PUBLICATIONS** Auth, "Ex Post Facto in the Civil Context: Unbridled Punishment," Ky Law J, 92; co-auth, "Why Have-Nots Win in the HIV Litigation Arena: Sociolegal Dynamics of Extreme Cases," 94; auth, "A Citizens' AIDS Task Force: Overcoming Obstacles," in Activism and Marginalization in the AIDS Crisis, 97; auth, "Intimate Violence: The Problem of Consent: An Essay, SC Law Rev, 97; auth, "Striving to Teach 'Justice, Fairness and Morality," Clin Law Rev, 97; auth, "Sexual Character Evidence in Civil Actions: Refining the Propensity Rule," Wis Law Rev, 97; co-auth, "Developing Genetic Privacy Legislation: The South Carolina Experience," Genetic Testing, 98; co-auth, "Evidence Issues in Domestic Violence Civil Cases," Family Law Quart, 00. **CONTACT ADDRESS** School of Law, Washington Univ, One Brookings Dr, Saint Louis, MO 63130. **EMAIL** Aiken@wulaw.wustl.edu

AIRHART, PHYLLIS
PERSONAL Born 06/24/1953, Moncton, NB, Canada, m, 1979 **DISCIPLINE** RELIGION **EDUCATION** Univ Manitoba, BA, 77; Univ Chicago, MA, 81, PhD, 85. **CAREER** Asst prof, 85-90, assoc prof, 90-, hist of christianity, Emmanuel College, Victoria Univ, cross-appointed to religion, 94-, Univ of Toronto. **HONORS AND AWARDS** Victoria Univ Awd for Excellence in Tchng, 91. **MEMBERSHIPS** Amer Hist Soc; Amer Soc of Church history; Can Catholic Hist Soc; Can Methodist Hist Soc; Can Soc of Church History. **RESEARCH** Religion in N America; gender & religion; religion and social reform; revivalism. **SELECTED PUBLICATIONS** Auth, Serving the Present Age Revivalism Progressivism and the Methodist Tradition in Canada, McGill-Queen Univ Press, 92; coed, Faith Traditions and the Family, Westminster John Knox Press, 96; coed, Christianizing the Social Order a Founding Vision of the United Church of Canada, Toronto J of Theology, 96; art, Art, Christianizing the Social Order and Founding Myths Double Vision, Christianizing the Social Order A Founding Vision of the United Church of Canada, Toronto Jour of Theology, 96; art, Condensation and Heart Religion Canadian Methodists as Evangelicals 1884-1925, Aspects of the Canadian Evangelical Exper, McGill-Queen Univ Press, 97; art, As Canadian as Possible under the Circumstances Reflections on the Study of North American Protestantism, New Directions in Amer Rel History, Oxford Univ Press, 97; art, Ecumenical Theological Education and Denominational Relationships The Emmanuel College Case 1960-1985, Theological Ed in Canada, United Church Pub House, 98. **CONTACT ADDRESS** Univ of Toronto, 75 Queens Park Cr, Toronto, ON, Canada M5S 1K7. **EMAIL** pairhart@chass.utoronto.ca

AKIN, DANIEL L.
PERSONAL Born 01/02/1957, Atlanta, GA, m, 1978, 4 children **DISCIPLINE** THEOLOGY **EDUCATION** Criswell Col, BA; Southwestern Baptist Theol Sem, MDiv; Univ Tex, PhD. **CAREER** Assoc prof, Southeastern Baptist Theol Sem; dean, Sch of Theol, S Baptist Theol Sem. **MEMBERSHIPS** Mem, S Baptist Hist Soc; Soc Sci Stud of Rel; Evangel Theol Soc. **SELECTED PUBLICATIONS** Ed, Believer's Study Bible. **CONTACT ADDRESS** Sch Theol, So Baptist Theol Sem, 2825 Lexington Rd, Louisville, KY 40280. **EMAIL** dakin@sbts.edu

AKRAM, SUSAN M.
PERSONAL Born 11/24/1956, Lahore, Pakistan, m, 1986 **DISCIPLINE** LAW **EDUCATION** Univ Mich, BA, 79; Georgetown Univ, JD, 82. **CAREER** Vis prof, Fulbright Scholar, Al Quds Univ, 97, 99; assoc prof, Boston Univ, 93-. **HONORS AND AWARDS** Fulbright Sr Scholar, Teach Fel, 99-00, Al-Quds Univ; Adv Awd, Polit Asyl/Immig Represent Proj, 93; IMMACT 90 Adv Awd, AILA, 90; Secret Evidence Litigat Awd, Nat Immig Proj, NLG, 98. **MEMBERSHIPS** Grassroots Intl; Boston Cen Refugee Hlth Hum Rts; AALS; American-Arab Anti-Discrimination Comm; Peace Edu Comm; Am Friends Ser Comm; Gov Adv Coun on Refugee Immig; Att Gen Civil Rts Task Force; AILA; MBA; CBA; CTLA; SFTLA; NLG. **RESEARCH** Immigration law, particularly deportation defense, family immigration, civil and constitutional rights of immigrants; Comparative refugee law, and US asylum law: issues related to international migration, the interpretation of international refugee law and policies, and a comparative approach to the interpretation of international refugee principles; Human rights law relating to refugees: refugees in and from the Middle East and Asia; the Palestinian refugee problem; issues relating to refugee women from the Middle East and the Muslim world, and stereotypes through which they are viewed. **SELECTED PUBLICATIONS** Auth, "Orientalism Revisited in Asylum and Refugee Claims," Intl J Ref Law 1 (00); auth, "Scheherezade Meets Kafka: Two Dozen Sordid Tales of Ideological Exclusion," Georgetown Imm Law J 51 (99); co-auth, "Brief Amicus Curiae on the Status of Palestinian Refugees Under International Law," Pales Yearbook Intl Law (forthcoming); co-auth, "Durable Solutions for Palestinian Refugees: A Challenge to the Oslo Process," Pales Yrbk of Intl Law (forthcoming); auth, "Traps for the Unwary, or Major Issues on Judicial Review of Deportation Decisions Under the Immigration & Nationality Act, Section 106," Imm Nat Law Hbk, Vol. II, Advanced Topics, 95-96; auth, "Medical Testimony on Victims of Torture: A Physician's Guide to Political Asylum Cases" (91); auth, "Reinterpreting Palestinian Refugee Rights Under International Law," in Palestinian Refugees and the Right of Return, ed. Naseer Aruri (Pluto Press, UK, forthcoming). **CONTACT ADDRESS** Sch of Law, Boston Univ, Boston, MA 02215. **EMAIL** sakram@gbls.org

AL'UQDAH, WILLIAM MUJAHID
PERSONAL Born 10/29/1953, Cincinnati, OH, m, 1976 **DISCIPLINE** LAW **EDUCATION** University of Cincinnati, BS, 1982; Salmon P Chase Col of Law, JD, 1987. **CAREER** Hamilton County Prosecutors Office, asst district Attorney, 88-94; WCIN 1480 AM Radio, sports dir and on air personality, 92-; Harmon, Davis and Keys Co, LPA, senior assoc, 94-96; Lawson and Gaines, Attorney, 96-. **HONORS AND AWARDS** Black Professionals, Scholarship, 1986. **MEMBERSHIPS** Black Male Coalition, first exec dir, 1988-89; Black Law Student Assn of America, president, 1985-86. **SELECTED PUBLICATIONS** The Good, The Bad, and The Ugly, Criminal Justice State of Cincinnati, sponsored by Cincinnati Urban League, 1995; When Going Gets Tough, Central State University Symposium, Welfare Reform, 1982. **CONTACT ADDRESS** Harmon, Davis & Keys Co, 1014 Vine Street, Cincinnati, OH 45202.

AL-MARAYATI, ABID AMIN
PERSONAL Born 10/14/1931, Baghdad, Iraq, 1 child **DISCIPLINE** POLITICAL SCIENCE, SOCIOLOGY, INTERNATIONAL LAW **EDUCATION** Bradley Univ, BA, 49-52, MA, 52-54; New York Univ, PhD, 54-59. **CAREER** Secy, Delegation Iraq, UN Gen Assembly, 55; secy, Delegation Yemen, UN Gen Assembly, 56-60; Instr, Govt, Univ Mass, 60; tech asst off, Int Atomic Energy Agency, Vienna, 60-62; assoc prof, SUNY, 62-64; res fel, Harvard Univ, 64-65; assoc prof, Ariz State Univ, 65-68; lectr & int educ consult, Am Inst For Trade, 65-68; PROF EMER, POLIT SCI, UNIV TOLEDO, 68-; vis prof, Univ Kuwait, 82-83; vis prof, Inst Public Admin, Riyadh, Saudi Arabia, 85-86; guest lectr, 90; vis prof, Beijing Stud Univ, 91. **MEMBERSHIPS** Assoc Student Educ; Middle East Studies Assoc N Amer; Phi Kappa Phi **RESEARCH** Psychological and Cultural Factors in the Iraq/Iran War; Shiism: A Study in Religion and Politics **CONTACT ADDRESS** Dept Polit Sci, Univ of Toledo, 2109 Terr View West, Toledo, OH 43607. **EMAIL** a_almarayati@yahoo.com

ALAIMO, KATHLEEN
PERSONAL Born 12/21/1956, Brooklyn, NY, m, 1983, 2 children **DISCIPLINE** HISTORY, POLITICAL SCIENCE **EDUCATION** Brooklyn Col, BA, 78; Univ Chicago, MA, 79; Univ Wis, PhD, 89. **CAREER** Asst Prof, Xavier Univ, 87-92; From Asst Prof to Assoc Prof, St Xavier Univ, 93-. **HONORS AND AWARDS** Summer Inst Grant, Nat Endowment Humanities, 91; Writing Coun Grant, St Xavier Univ, 93; Excellence in Teaching Awd, St Xavier Univ, 95, 97; Fac Develop Grant, St Xavier Univ, 96; Who's Who in America's Teachers, 99; Res Sabbatical, St Xavier Univ, 00. **MEMBERSHIPS** AHA, SFHS, Coord Coun for Women in Hist, WHA, HES, AAUP. **RESEARCH** European social history, women's history, history of adolescence, history of child rights. **SELECTED PUBLICATIONS** Rev, "Childhood and Adolescence in Modern European History," J of Soc Hist 24:3 (91): 591-602; auth, "Shaping Adolescence in the Popular Milieu: Social Policy, Reformers and French Youth 1870-1920," J of Family Hist 17:4 (92): 419-438; auth, "Adolescence, Gender and Class in Education Reform in France: The Development of Enseignement Primaire Superieur 1880-1910," Fr Hist Studies 18:4 (94): 1025-1055; co-ed, Children as Equals: Exploring the Rights of the Child, UP of Am, forthcoming; auth, "Juvenile Delinquency and Hooliganism in Europe from the Renaissance to the Present," in The Encycl of European Soc Hist (Scribners, forthcoming). **CONTACT ADDRESS** Dept Hist & Polit Sci, Saint Xavier Univ, 3700 W 103rd St, Chicago, IL 60655-3105. **EMAIL** alaimo@sxu.edu

ALARID, LEANNE F.
PERSONAL Born 09/16/1967, Niskiyuna, NY, m **DISCIPLINE** CRIMINAL JUSTICE **EDUCATION** Univ N Colo, BA, 89; Sam Houston State Univ, MA, 93; PhD, 96. **CAREER** Asst Prof, Univ Mo, 96-. **HONORS AND AWARDS** Teaching Grant, Univ Mo; Fac Res Grant, Univ Mo, 97-99; Res Grant, Kan City Police Dept, 98-00; Res Grant, Kan City Police Dept, 99-01; Conf Travel Grant Awds, Univ Mo, 96-00. **MEMBERSHIPS** ASC, ACJS. **RESEARCH** Corrections, policing, women and crime. **SELECTED PUBLICATIONS** Coauth, "HIV/AIDS Knowledge and Risk Perception of Adult Women in an Urban Area Jail," J of Correctional Health Care 6-1 (99): 97-127; auth, "Along Racial and Gender Lines: Jail Subcultures in the Midst of Racial Disproportionality," Corrections Management Quart 4-1 (00): 8-19; coauth, "Cultural Influences on Taiwanese Police Management and Patrol Practices: An Exploratory Investigation of Ouchi's Theory Z," Int J of the Soc of Law 28-2 (forthcoming); auth, "Sexual Orientation Perspectives of Incarcerated Bisexual and Gay men: The County Jail Protective Custody Experience," The Prison J (forthcoming); coauth, "Gender and Crime Among Felony Offenders: Assessing the Generality of Social Bond and Differential Association Theories," J of Res in Crime and Delinquency 37-2 (forthcoming): 171-199; auth, "Law Enforcement Departments as Learning Organizations: Argyris' Theory as a Framework for Implementing Community-Oriented Policing," Police Quart (forthcoming); **CONTACT ADDRESS** Dept Criminal Justice, Univ of Missouri, Kansas City, 5120 Rockhill Rd, 208 Hoag Hall, Kansas City, MO 64110.

ALBERS, ROBERT H.
DISCIPLINE PASTORAL CARE **EDUCATION** Wartburg Sem, MDiv, 66; S Calif Sch Theol, PhD, 82. **CAREER** Vis lectr, Dana Col, 76-78; grad res asst, S Calif Sch, 79-81; vis lectr, S Calif Sch of Theol, 80-81; asst prof, 81; dir, Ministry in Pastoral Care and Soc Change prog, 85-91; act dean of students, 82-83; prof, 91-; dir, doctoral prog in Pastoral Care and Counseling, 87-; Lutheran World Federation Fel, 67-68. **HONORS AND AWARDS** Lutheran World Fedn Fel, 67-68; ed, jour of ministry in addiction and recovery. **MEMBERSHIPS** Mem, Minn Chem Dependency Assn; Interfaith Network for Chem Dependency. **SELECTED PUBLICATIONS** Auth, A Life of Prayer, ALC confirmation material, 84; Healing the Hurts: Separation and Loss, 91; Why Do People Suffer?, Responding to Evil and Suffering, 92; Shame: A Faith Perspective, 95; Caring and Community, 95. **CONTACT ADDRESS** Dept of PastoralCare, Luther Sem, 2481 Como Ave, Saint Paul, MN 55108. **EMAIL** ralbers@luthersem.edu

ALBERT, SIDNEY PAUL
PERSONAL Born 04/11/1914, Syracuse, NY, d, 3 children **DISCIPLINE** PHILOSOPHY **EDUCATION** Syracuse Univ, AB, 34; Yale Univ, PhD, 39. **CAREER** Instr philos, Univ Conn, 46; asst prof, Triple Cities Col, Syracuse, 46-50 & Harpur Col, 50-53; from asst prof to assoc prof, 56-64, chmn dept, 60-63, prof, 64-79, Emer Prof Philos, Calif State Univ, Los Angeles, 79- **MEMBERSHIPS** Am Philos Asn; Am Soc Aesthetics; MLA; AAUP; Am Soc Theatre Res; Theatre Lib Asn; Shaw Soc (London); Bernard Shaw Soc (NYork); Shaw Soc of Jap; Cal State Univ Emer & Ret Fac Asn. **RESEARCH** Philos and dramatic art of George Bernard Shaw; philos in drama; aesthetics in drama. **SELECTED PUBLICATIONS** Auth, "Bernard Shaw: The Artist as Philosopher," J of Aesthetics and Art Crit 14, no 4 (June 56): 419-38; auth, "'In More Ways Than One': 'Major Barbara's' Debt to Gilbert Murray," in Bernard Shaw's Plays, ed Warren S. Smith, (NY: Norton, 70), 375-3697; auth, "Shaw's Advice to the Players of 'Major Barbara'," Theatre Survey: The Am J of Theatre Hist 10, no 1 (May 69), 1-17; auth, "More Shaw Advice to the Players of 'Major Barbara'," Theatre Survey: The Am J of Theatre Hist 11, no 1 (May 70), 66-85; auth, "Reflections on Shaw and Psychoanalysis," Mod Drama 14, no 2 (Spet 71), 169-94; auth, "The Price of Salvation: Moral Economics in 'Major Barbara'," Mod Drama 14, no 3 (Dec 71), 307-23; auth, "The Lord's Prayer and 'Major Barbara'," in Shaw and Religion, ed Charles A. Berst [Vol 1 of Shaw: The Annual of Bernard Shaw Studies] (81), 107-28; auth, "Gilbert Murray," in Dictionary of Literary Biography Vol 10, ed Stanley Weintraub (Detroit: Gale Res, 82), 61-71; auth, "Evangelizing the Garden City?" in Shaw: The Annual of Bernard Shaw Studies, Vol 19 (99), 41-77; auth, "Barbara's Progress," in Shaw: The Annual of Bernard Shaw Studies, ed Gale Larson, Vol 21 (forthcoming). **CONTACT ADDRESS** 847 Eaton Dr, Pasadena, CA 91107-1837.

ALBIN, THOMAS R.
PERSONAL Born 05/10/1951, Wakeeney, KS, m, 1971, 3 children **DISCIPLINE** CHURCH HISTORY **EDUCATION** Oral Roberts Univ, BA, 73, MA, 76; Fuller Theol Sem, MA, 77; Univ Cambridge, PhD, 00. **CAREER** Vis lect, 87-88, Boston Univ School of Theol, adj fac, 89; asst prof, 88-92, Univ Dubuque Theol Sem, dir, contextual ed & instr in spiritual formation, 92-99, Univ Dubuque Theol Sem. **HONORS AND AWARDS** BA, magna cum laude, 73; MA, 78; G. Lemuel Fenn Ministerial Scholar; John Wesley Fel, a Fund for Theol Ed, ATFE, 78-82; Bethune-Baker grant, fac of Div, Cambridge Univ; Pasadena Methodist Found Scholar; Charis Awd for Excel in Tchng, UDTS, 90-91, 92-93. **MEMBERSHIPS** Am Academy of Relig; Charles Wesley Soc; Oxford Inst for Methodist Theol Stud: Spiritual Dirs Int; Wesley Hist Soc, Eng. **RESEARCH** Wesleyan Hist & Spiritual Formation. **SELECTED PUBLICATIONS** Auth, Spiritual Formation and Contextual Education, in the Report of the Proceedings of the Asn of Theol Field Ed, 93; auth, John and Charles Wesley, The Dict of Christian Ethics & Pastoral Theol, IVP, 95; auth, What We Believe and Why We Believe It: Understanding Our Doctrinal Standards and Our Theological Task, a 6 wk stud, pvtly printed, local United Methodist Churches, 96; rev, Of Laughter in the Amen Corner: The Life of Evangelist Sam Jones by Kathleen Minnix, 93, pub in Missiology: An Int Rev, vol XXV, no 2, 97; auth, One week of devotions in Disciplines 1999, Upper Room, 98; auth, The Charles Wesley Family in Bristol, Proceed of the Charles Wesley Soc, vol 4, 97, 98; auth, The Role of Small Groups in Early Methodist Spiritual Formation, in The Role of the Heart in N Amer Methodism, Scarecrow Press. **CONTACT ADDRESS** 4116 Helena Bay Ct., Hermitage, TN 37076-3105. **EMAIL** talbin@univ.dbq.edu

ALBRECHT, GLORIA H.
DISCIPLINE RELIGION AND ETHICS **EDUCATION** Univ Md, BA; Johns Hopkins Univ, MLA; St Mary's Sem, STM; Temple Univ, PhD. **CAREER** Assoc prof; Univ Detroit Mercy, 92-. **RESEARCH** Business and economic ethics, feminist eth-

ics and theology, and women's studies. **CONTACT ADDRESS** Dept of Religious Studies, Univ of Detroit Mercy, 4001 W McNichols Rd, PO Box 19900, Detroit, MI 48219-0900. **EMAIL** ALBRECGH@udmercy.edu

ALDRICH, MARK
PERSONAL Born 10/16/1941, Northhampton, MA, m, 1965 **DISCIPLINE** ECONOMIC HISTORY **EDUCATION** Middlebury Col, BA 63; Univ Calif Berk, MA 64; Univ Texas, PhD 69. **CAREER** Smith Col, asst prof, assoc prof, prof, 68 to 83-, Marilyn Carlson Nelson Prof of Econ, 95-. **MEMBERSHIPS** EHA; SHT. **RESEARCH** History of workplace safety. **SELECTED PUBLICATIONS** Auth, Safety First: Technology Business and Labor in the Transformation of Work Safety in America, Bal, John Hopkins Univ Press, 97; auth, The Peril of the Broken Rail: the Carriers the Steel Companies and Rail Technology, 1900-1945, Technology and Culture, forthcoming; Energy Conservation on Steam Railroads: Institutions Markets Technology, 1889-1943, Railroad History, 97; auth, The Perils of Mining Authracite: Regulation Technology and Safety, 1870-1945, Penn History, 97; auth, The Cherry Mine Disaster of 1909: The Rest of the Story as told by George S. Rice, Mining History Jour, 97; auth, The Last Run of Engineer Peake: Work safety on the Rio Grande Southern Around the Time of World War I, Jour of the West, 97; Locomotive Inspection Materials at the National Archives, Railroad History, 96; auth, Preventing the Needless Peril of the Coal Miner: The Bureau of Mines and the Campaign to Prevent Coal Mine Explosions, Technology and Culture, 95; auth, Does Comparable Worth Correct for Discrimination?, David Saunders, ed, New Approaches to Employee Management, Greenwich CT, JAI, 94. **CONTACT ADDRESS** Smith Col, 10 Prospect St, Northampton, CT 01063. **EMAIL** maldrich@smith.edu

ALEXAKIS, ALEXANDER
DISCIPLINE RELIGION **EDUCATION** Oxford Univ, PhD, 92. **CAREER** Asst prof. **RESEARCH** History of the Byzantine church and theology; relations between Constantinople and Rome; patristics; hagiography; Byzantine literature and epistolography; Byzantine ecclesicastic procedural law; paleography. **SELECTED PUBLICATIONS** Auth, Codex Parisinus Graecus 1115 and its Archetype, pubs on iconoclasm and Byzantine hagiography. **CONTACT ADDRESS** Dept of Religion, Columbia Col, New York, 2960 Broadway, New York, NY 10027-6902. **EMAIL** aa177@columbia.edu

ALEXAKOS, PANOS D.
DISCIPLINE PHILOSOPHY **EDUCATION** Villanova Univ, MA, 85; Pa State Univ, PhD, 95. **CAREER** Instr, Philos, Univ Tenn. **RESEARCH** Contemporary continental philosophy; history of philosophy. **SELECTED PUBLICATIONS** Auth, "Metamorphoses: On the Limits of Thought," Thought (March 91); co-auth, "A Case of Mistaken Identity: The Censorship of American Psycho," Liberty (Nov 91); rev, Thomas Busch's "The Power of Consciousness and the Force of Circumstance in Sartre's Philosophy," Thought (March 91); rev, Maudemarie Clark's "Nietzsche on Truth and Philosophy," Int Philos Quart, 93; auth, "Nietzsche's Understanding of Persons," forthcoming; auth, "The Darkness Beckons," forthcoming. **CONTACT ADDRESS** Dept of Philos, Univ of Tennessee, Knoxville, 801 McClung Tower, Knoxville, TN 37996-0480. **EMAIL** palexako@utk.edu

ALEXANDER, BOBBY C.
PERSONAL Born 12/03/1950, Shreveport, LA **DISCIPLINE** ANTHROPOLOGY, RELIGIOUS STUDIES **EDUCATION** Baylor Univ, BA, 73; Union Theol Sem, M.Div, 76; Columbia Univ, MPhil, 81, & Union Theol Sem, PhD, 85. **CAREER** Tchng asst, 79-81, Barnard Col; adj lectr, 81-85, adj asst prof, 85-86, Hunter Col, CUNY; asst prof, 86-93, Southern Methodist Univ; lectr, 93-97, sr lectr, 97-, Univ Texas, Dallas; col master and asst dean for undergraduate studies,Sch of Social Sciences, 99-. **HONORS AND AWARDS** Student Choice Tchng Awd, schl of soc sci, Univ Texas Dallas, 96; Jr Scholar Awd SW Comm on Relig Stud, SW region of Amer Acad of Relig, 89-90; Res Asst Grant, AAR, 88-89; grant, US Department of Educ Fund for the Improvement of Post-secondary Educ, 99-002. **MEMBERSHIPS** Amer Anthrop Assn; AAR, Soc for Sci Stud of Relig. **RESEARCH** Relig & polit culture; religion in contemp Amer soc; religious community & its role as social network and adaptation in Mexican migrant workers in the US global economy. **SELECTED PUBLICATIONS** Ed asst, The Encycl of Relig, 84-86; auth, "Ceremony", Encycl of Relig, Macmillan, 87; art, Pentecostal Ritual Reconsidered: 'Anti-structural' Dimension of Possession, J of Ritual Stud, 351:109, 89; art, Turner's Definition of Ritual Reconsidered: Grotowski's Experimental Theater as Secular Rituals of Spiritual Healing, Method & Theory in Stud of Relig, 3,1,31:62, 91; art, Correcting Misinterpretations of Turner's Theory: An African-American Pentecostal Illustration, J for Sci Stud of Relig, 30,1: 26, 91; auth, Victor Turner Revisited: Ritual As Social Change, Scholars Press, AAR, 91; auth, Televangelism Reconsidered: Ritual in the Search for Human Community, Scholars Press, AAR, 91; auth, An Afterward on Ritual in Biblical Studies, Semeia, 67:209, 95; ed, Listening: J of Religion and Culture, vol 33; ed, sect on ritual, Anthrop of Relig: A Handbk; auth, Ritual and Current Studies of Ritual: Overview, Anthrop of Relig: A Handbk, Greenwood Press, 97; auth, Televangelism Reconsidered: Ritual Within a Larger Social Drama, Rethinking Media, Relig, & Culture, Sage Pub, 97; auth, "A Pentecostal styled Mexican Mission in Dallas: An Illustration of Religious Diversity among New Latino Immigrants," Listeing, vol. 33, no. 3, pp 175-187. **CONTACT ADDRESS** School of Social Sciences, Univ of Texas, Dallas, PO Box 830688, Richardson, TX 75083. **EMAIL** bcalex@utdallas.edu

ALEXANDER, GEORGE
PERSONAL Born 05/20/1958, Manhattan, NY **DISCIPLINE** PHILOSOPHY **EDUCATION** Columbia Col, BA, 79; Harvard Univ, MA, 81; PhD, 86. **CAREER** Asst Prof to Assoc Prof, Amherst Col, 88-. **HONORS AND AWARDS** Fulbright Fel, 83; Fel, NEH, 00. **MEMBERSHIPS** Am Philos Asn. **RESEARCH** Philosophy of Language; Philosophy of Mathematics. **SELECTED PUBLICATIONS** Ed, Western State Terrorism, Polity/Routledge, 91; ed, Mathematics and Mind, Oxford Univ Press, 94; co-auth, Philosophies of Mathematics, Blackwell, 01. **CONTACT ADDRESS** Dept Philos, Amherst Col, Amherst, MA 01002. **EMAIL** ageorge@amherst.edu

ALEXANDER, GEORGE J.
PERSONAL Born 03/08/1931, Berlin, Germany, m, 1958, 2 children **DISCIPLINE** LAW **EDUCATION** Univ PA, AB, 53, JD, 59; Yale Univ, LLM, 65, JSD, 69. **CAREER** Instr law, Univ Chicago, 59-60; from asst prof to prof, Syracuse Univ, 60-67, prof & assoc dean, 67-70; dean sch law and prof law, 70-85, Sutro Prof Law, 96-, Univ Santa Clara, 70-; consult, US Comn Civil Rights, 62-63, Educ Policies Res Ctr, 68- & Syracuse Res Corp Policy Inst, 69-; mem, Int Inst Space Law; consult, US Comptroller Gen, 77- **HONORS AND AWARDS** Order of the Coif, Justinian Hon Soc, Ralph E Kharas Civil Liberty Awd. **MEMBERSHIPS** Am Bar Asn; Soc Am Law Teachers; Int Inst Space Law; Int Comt Human Rights. **RESEARCH** Antitrust and trade regulation law; constitutional law; psychiatry and law. **SELECTED PUBLICATIONS** Auth, Civil Rights, USA, Public Schools . . . Buffalo, New York, US Govt Printing Off, 63; chaps, In: World Unfair Competition Law, M Nijoff, The Hague, 65; Jury Instructions on Medical Issues, Allen Smith, 66; Honesty and Competition: False Advertising Law and Policy Under FTC Administration, Syracuse Univ, 67; chap, In: Changing Aspects of Business Law, Heath, 67; coauth, The Aged and the Need for Surrogate Management, Syracuse Univ, 72; auth, Commercial Torts, Allen Smith, 73; Ed Int Perspectives on Aging; auth Law and Mental Disorder, Carolina Acad, 98. **CONTACT ADDRESS** Sch Law, Santa Clara Univ, 500 El Camino Real, Santa Clara, CA 95053-0001. **EMAIL** GJAlexander@scu.edu

ALEXANDER, JAMES
PERSONAL Born 09/04/1956, Chicago, IL, m, 1977, 2 children **DISCIPLINE** RELIGION, EDUCATION **EDUCATION** Central Mo Univ, BSE, 77, MSE, 82; St Thomas Theol Sem, MA, 85; Univ Ark, PhD, 95. **CAREER** Elementary teacher, 77-81; minister, 83-87; Chapter 1 Reading Teacher, 87-90; instr, ABE/GED, Dept of Corrections, 90-92; parochiol sch teacher, 92-95; asst prof, Lincoln Univ, 96-98; asst prof, Ky Wesleyan Col, 98-. **HONORS AND AWARDS** Theology Merit Scholar. **MEMBERSHIPS** IRA; Ky Reading Asn. **RESEARCH** Brain based teaching strategies, religion and public education. **SELECTED PUBLICATIONS** Auth, "A Strategy for Meaningful Phonics Instruction," The Mo Reader (spring 97); auth,"Multiple Intelligences Theory Applied to Reading Instruction," ERIC Document Reproduction Services ED402563; auth,"Religion Epistemology and the Public School," Relig and Ed (fall 97) and Relig and Politics, Am Political Sci Asn (summer 97); auth, "Reading Skill and Context Facilitation: A Classic Study Revisited," J of Ed Res (May/Jume 97); auth,"Reading and Postmodernism," Balanced Reading Instruction and ERIC/REC (in press). **CONTACT ADDRESS** Dept Ed, Kentucky Wesleyan Col, PO Box 1039, Owensboro, KY 42302. **EMAIL** jamesal@kwc.edu

ALEXANDER, LARRY
PERSONAL Born 09/23/1943, Fort Worth, TX, m, 3 children **DISCIPLINE** PHILOSOPHY **EDUCATION** Williams Col, BA, 65; Yale Univ, LLB, 68. **CAREER** Res Atty, Calif Court Appeal, 68-70; Asst Prof to Prof, 70-95, Warren Distinguished Prof Law, Univ San Diego, 95-; Vis Prof, Univ Calif, 89; Vis Prof, Univ Pa, 95. **HONORS AND AWARDS** Phi Beta Kappa, 64; Summer Stipend, NEH, 73; Summer Fel, Inst Humane Studies, 79. **MEMBERSHIPS** Am Soc Polit & Legal Philos; Am Philos Asn. **RESEARCH** Constitutional law; criminal law; legal and moral philosophy. **SELECTED PUBLICATIONS** Coauth, Whom Does the Constitution Command?, Greenwood Press, 88; auth, Contract Law, Dartmouth Publ Co, 91; Constitutionalism: Philosophical Foundations, Cambridge Univ Press, 98; coauth, Past Imperfect: Rules, Principles, and the Dilemnas of Law, Duke Univ Press (forthcoming); auth, Legal Rules and Legal Reasoning, Dartmouth Publ Co (forthcoming); Freedom of Speech, Dartmouth Publ Co (forthcoming); author of numerous articles. **CONTACT ADDRESS** School of Law, Univ of San Diego, 5998 Alcala Rd., San Diego, CA 92110. **EMAIL** larrya@acurd.edu

ALEXANDER, LAURENCE BENEDICT
PERSONAL Born 10/31/1959, New Orleans, LA, m, 1988 **DISCIPLINE** LAW **EDUCATION** University of New Orleans, BA, 1981; University of Florida, MA, 1983; Tulane University, School of Law, JD, 1987. **CAREER** The Times-Picayune, New Orleans, staff writer, 81; The Houma Courier, staff writer, 82; The Times Picayune, staff writer, 82-85; University of New Orleans, director of journalism program, assistant professor of journalism, 87-88; Temple University, director of news editorial sequence, assistant professor of communications, 88-91; The Philadelphia Inquirer, summer copy editor, 89-92; University of Florida, assistant professor of journalism, 91-94, chair of journalism, 94-98, associate professor, 94-. **HONORS AND AWARDS** AEJMC/ACEJMC Baskett Mosse Awd, 1994; AEJMC, AHANA Research Grant, 1990; The Poynter Institute, Selected Teaching Fellow, 1989; Press Club of New Orleans, Deadline News Writing Awd, 1985. **MEMBERSHIPS** Assn for Education in Journalism and Mass Communication, 1989-; International Communications Association, 1992-; Society of Professional Journalists, 1989-; Natl Assn of Black Journalists, 1989-; American Bar Association, 1987-; Louisiana State Bar Association, 1987-. **SELECTED PUBLICATIONS** Major works published in: The Tulane Maritime Lawyer, 1987; The Black Law Journal, 1989; Newspaper Research Journal, 1992, 1994, 1995, 1996; Western Journal of Black Studies, 1992; Communications and the Law, 1993, 1996; Journalism Educator, 1994, Notre Dame Journal of Legislation, 1997; Editor and Publisher, 1990, 1993, 1996. **CONTACT ADDRESS** Dept of Journalism, Univ of Florida, 3052 Weimer Hall, Gainesville, FL 32611.

ALEXANDER, RALPH H.
PERSONAL Born 09/03/1936, Tyler, TX, m, 1964, 3 children **DISCIPLINE** SEMITICS AND OLD TESTAMENT; ARCHAEOLOGY **EDUCATION** Rice Univ, AB, 59; Dallas Theol Sem, ThM, 63, ThD, 68. **CAREER** Instr, S Bible Training School, 63-64, 65-66; asst prof of Bible and Archaeology, Wheaton Col, 66-72; prof Hebrew Scripture, dir summer quart Israel Prog, 74 & 78, W Baptist Sem, 73-87; assoc archaeologist, Albright Inst Archaeology, 77-78; dir, Advan Trng Studies Coordr Old Testament Concentration Bibl Educ Exten Int Austria, 87-95; dir, educ develop & advan trng studies, cis, bibl educ exten int, Moscow, 95-. **HONORS AND AWARDS** US Govt Fulbright grant, Israel, 64-65; Henry Thiessen Awd New Testament; Outstanding Young Men Amer, 70; Outstanding Educ Amer; Who's Who Relig. **MEMBERSHIPS** Amer Schools Oriental Res; Archeol Inst Amer; Evangel Theol Soc; Fel Evangel Europ Tchrs; Inst Bibl Res; Israel Explor Soc; Nat Asn Hebrew Prof; Near East Archeol Soc; Soc Bibl Lit. **RESEARCH** Psalms; Old Testament Archaeology; Old Testament Law & Prophets. **SELECTED PUBLICATIONS** Contribur, New Commentary on the Whole Bible, Tyndale, 94; auth, Marriage and Divorce, Dictionary of Old Testament Ethics, Baker, 96; A New Covenant and An Eternal People, Israel: The Land and the People, Kregel, 98. **CONTACT ADDRESS** Box 3366, Gresham, OR 97030. **EMAIL** ralphmyrna@earthlink.net

ALEXANDER, SCOTT C.
DISCIPLINE RELIGIOUS STUDIES **EDUCATION** Columbia Univ, PhD, 93. **CAREER** Asst prof. **RESEARCH** History and comparative study of religions; Islamic religion and society; medieval studies. **SELECTED PUBLICATIONS** Auth, Islamic heresiography, Jour Mid E Studies, 87. **CONTACT ADDRESS** Dept of Religious Studies, Indiana Univ, Bloomington, Sycamore Hall 230, Bloomington, IN 47405. **EMAIL** scalexan@indiana.edu

ALEXANDER, THOMAS
PERSONAL Born 09/08/1952, Albuquerque, NM, m, 1983, 2 children **DISCIPLINE** PHILOSOPHY **EDUCATION** Univ New Mexico, BA, 74; Emory Univ, MA, 76, PhD, 84. **CAREER** Asst prof, assoc prof, prof S Ill Univ, Carbondale, 85-. **MEMBERSHIPS** APA; Soc for the Advanc Am Philos. **RESEARCH** American philosophy; John Dewey. **SELECTED PUBLICATIONS** Auth, John Dewey's Theory of Art Experience and Nature, SUNY, 87. **CONTACT ADDRESS** Dept of Philosophy, So Illinois Univ, Carbondale, Carbondale, IL 62901. **EMAIL** talex@siu.edu

ALEXANDER, WILLIAM M.
PERSONAL Born 12/05/1928, Jacksonville, FL, m, 1953, 3 children **DISCIPLINE** PHILOSOPHY OF RELIGION **EDUCATION** Davidson Col, AB, 50; Louisville Presby Sem, BD, 53; Harvard Univ, STM; 57; Princeton Theol Sem, PhD, 61. **CAREER** Teach fel, PTS, 59-61; from asst prof to distinguished prof, St Andrews Col, 61-. **HONORS AND AWARDS** NEH; Res Gnt, Coun Philo Stud; Dist Prof, St Andrews Coll; Vis Fac Mem, Univ North Carolina. **MEMBERSHIPS** APA; MSA. **RESEARCH** John Philoponos (sixth c.); Kant and 18th century philosophy. **SELECTED PUBLICATIONS** Auth, Johann Georg Hamann: Philosophy and Faith, Nijhoff, 66; contr, Encyclopedia of Philosophy, Macmillan. **CONTACT ADDRESS** Dept Humanities and Fine Arts, St. Andrews Presbyterian Col, 1700 Dogwood Mile, Laurinburg, NC 28352.

ALEXANDRAKIS, APHRODITE
PERSONAL m, 3 children **DISCIPLINE** PHILOSOPHY **EDUCATION** Rutgers Univ, BA, 68; Univ Miami, MA, 76, PhD, 86. **CAREER** Adjunct lectr, Barry Univ, 81-91, asst prof, 92-94, assoc prof, 94-97, prof, 98-. **HONORS AND AWARDS** Barry Univ: Prof Achievement Awds: 91-; NEH Summer Sem Awd, 96, 97; Outstanding Fac Awd, Barry Univ, 97; Barry Univ Min-grant, 98; Greek Ministry of Culture grant, 98; Sister Jean O'Laughlin Scholar's Awd, Nov 99. **MEMBERSHIPS** Am Philos Asn, Int Soc for Neoplatonic Studies, Soc for Ancient Greek Philos, Am Soc for Aesthetics, Int Asn for Aesthetics, Southern Soc for Philos and Psychol, Am Cath Philos Asn, Int Center of Interdisciplinary Res, Int Asn for Greek Philos, Int Congress of Medieval Studies, Inst of Global Culture Studies. **RESEARCH** Ancient philosophy (aesthetics). **SELECTED PUBLICATIONS** Auth, "The Classical Notion of Beauty in Byzantine Art," Diotima, 23 (95): 157-161; auth, "Plotinian Influence on Psellus' Dialectic," Soc for Ancient Greek Philos, Univ of NY, SUNY Press (95); auth, "Sensual Beauty Ideal Beauty and Works of Art," Alexandria The J of the Western Cosmological Traditions, (July 00); auth, "Animal Images in Greek Thought and Art," Prima Philsophia (July 98); auth, "Plotinus' Aesthetic Approach to the One," Philosophia The Acad of Athens (April 98); auth, "Neopythagoreanizing Influences on Plotinus Mystical Notion of Numbers," Philos Inquiry, Vol XXI (98); auth, "Does Modern Art Reflect Plotinus' Notion of Beauty?," J of Neoplatonic Studies; auth, "Neoplatonic Influences on Iconoclasm: A Greek-Rooted Tradition," SUNY Press (forthcoming). **CONTACT ADDRESS** Continuing Educ, Barry Univ, 11300 NE 2nd Ave, Miami Shores, FL 33161. **EMAIL** aalexandrakis@mail.barry.edu

ALEXANIAN, JOSEPH M.
DISCIPLINE NEW TESTAMENT TEXTUAL CRITICISM **EDUCATION** Wheaton Col, AB, 52; Fuller Theol Sem, Mdiv, 55; Univ Chicago, PhD, 82. **CAREER** Prof emer, Trinity International Univ. **CONTACT ADDRESS** Col of Arts and Sciences, Trinity Intl Univ, Col of Arts and Sciences, 2065 Half Day Road, Deerfield, IL 60015.

ALFORD, HAILE LORRAINE
PERSONAL Born 07/00/1949, Brooklyn, NY **DISCIPLINE** LAW **EDUCATION** Herbert H Lehman, BA 1971; Rutgers Univ School of Law Camden, JD, 76. **CAREER** Jr HS, teacher, 71; Wiltwyck School for Boys, teacher, 72-73; Lincoln Univ, adj lecturer, 81-; Hercules Inc, attny, 76-92; assoc Judge, DE Superior Ct, 92- . **HONORS AND AWARDS** First African-American Female on Superior Court in Delaware. **MEMBERSHIPS** Mem ABA Labor Law Sect, NBA Corp Sect, PA Bar Assoc, DE Bar Assoc, Rodney Inn of Court, Judicial Council of the National Bar Assoc, Philadelphia Judicial Council, Court Interpreters Advisory Committee and The Judical Education Committee. **CONTACT ADDRESS** Daniel L. Hermann Courthouse, Superior Court, 1020 N King St, Mezzanine Fl, Wilmington, DE 19801.

ALI-JACKSON, KAMIL
PERSONAL Born 03/04/1959, El Paso, TX, m, 1985 **DISCIPLINE** LAW **EDUCATION** Princeton Univ, AB, 1981; Harvard Law School, JD, 1984. **CAREER** McCarter & English, associate, 84-86; Pepper, Hamilton & Scheetz, associate, 86-90; Merck & Co Inc, director, Corporate Licensing, 90-. **HONORS AND AWARDS** Princeton Univ, Ralph G Treen Memorial Scholarship, 1980. **MEMBERSHIPS** National Bar Association, 1986-92; Philadelphia Bar Association, 1986-92; Pennsylvania Bar Association, 1986-. **SELECTED PUBLICATIONS** The Experienced Hand, How to Make the Most of an Internship, 1980. **CONTACT ADDRESS** Merck & Co Inc, One Merck Dr, Whitehouse Station, NJ 08889-0100.

ALISTAIR, MACLEOD
DISCIPLINE PHILOSOPHY **EDUCATION** Univ Glasgow, MA; Queen's Univ, PhD. **CAREER** Dept Philos, Queen's Univ **RESEARCH** Doctrine of instrumental rationality and the ideal of efficiency and the relation in which they stand to each other and to Paretianism **SELECTED PUBLICATIONS** Auth, Paul Tillich: An Essay on the Role of Ontology in his Philosophical Theology, Allen and Unwin, 73; Freedom and Equality: A False Antithesis, Univ Kans, 97. **CONTACT ADDRESS** Philos Dept, Queen's Univ at Kingston, Kingston, ON, Canada K7L 3N6. **EMAIL** macleoda@post.queensu.ca

ALLEN, ANITA
DISCIPLINE PHILOSOPHY **EDUCATION** Harvard Univ, BA; Univ Mich, PhD, 79. **CAREER** Asst prof, Carnegie Mellon Univ, 78-80; asst prof, Univ Pittsburgh, 85-87, adj prof, 87-. **RESEARCH** Race relations policy; law and literature **SELECTED PUBLICATIONS** Auth, Uneasy Access: Privacy for Women in a Free Society, 88; co-auth, Cases and Materials on Privacy Law, 92. **CONTACT ADDRESS** Dept of Philosophy, Georgetown Univ, 37th and O St, Washington, DC 20057.

ALLEN, BERNARD LEE
PERSONAL Born 07/19/1937, Weston, WV, m, 1964, 2 children **DISCIPLINE** HISTORY, PHILOSOPHY **EDUCATION** WVa Univ, BS, 59; Southern Ill Univ, MA, 64; WVa Univ, PhD(hist), 71. **CAREER** Instr hist & philos, WVa Univ, Parkersburg, 66-68 & WVa Univ, 70-71; asst prof hist & philos, 71-74, actg asst dean arts & sci, 75-76; assoc prof, 74-81, dean arts & sci & actg dean occup tech, 76, asst dean instr, 79-80, Prof Hist & Philos, Parkersburg Community Col;adj instr, Wheeling Jesuit Univ, 93-98; adj instr, Washington St Comm Coll, 93-98. **HONORS AND AWARDS** Bd of Dir, WV Hum Fnd, Outstand Svc to Higher Edu, WV Prof of the Yr. **MEMBERSHIPS** Appalachian Stud Assn, WV Hist Assn of Col and Univ Tchrs of Hist; Oil, Gas, and Indus Hist Assn. **RESEARCH** John Dewey's philosophy of history; mid-Ohio valley; women of the Ohio valley; U.S. social and ideological history; the Virginias and the Carolinas. **SELECTED PUBLICATIONS** Auth, John Dewey's Views on History, 1859-1971, Univ Microfilms, 71; Oarkersburg: A Bicentennial History, Parkersburg Bicentennial Commission, 85; Lessons, Data Day, 90; Compassion: A History of the Harry Logan Children's Home, Harry Logan Children's Home Fnd, 92; co-auth, Where It All Began, 94. **CONTACT ADDRESS** Dept of Hist, West Virginia Univ, Parkersburg, 300 Campus Dr, Parkersburg, WV 26101. **EMAIL** BALLEN@ALPHA.WVUP.WVNET.EDU

ALLEN, COLIN
DISCIPLINE PHILOSOPHY **EDUCATION** Univ Calif, Los Angeles, PhD. **CAREER** Prof, Texas A&M Univ. **HONORS AND AWARDS** Phi Kappa Phi. **MEMBERSHIPS** Am Philos Asn, Philos of Science Asn. **RESEARCH** Philosophy of Mind, Animal Cognition. **SELECTED PUBLICATIONS** Auth, Belief and Concept Attribution in Non-human Animals, Philos Sci, 91; Mental Content, Brit J for the Philos Sci, 92; It Isn't What You Think: A New Idea About Intentional Causation, Nous, 95 & Function, Adaptation, and Design, Philos Sci, 95; coauth, Intentionality, Social Play, and Definition, Biology and Philosophy, 94; coauth, Species of Mind, MIT Pr, 97; coed, Nature's Purposes, MIT Pr, 98; coed, The Evolution of Mind, Oxford Univ Pr, 98. **CONTACT ADDRESS** Dept of Philosophy, Texas A&M Univ, Col Station, 314 Bolton Hall, College Station, TX 77843-4237. **EMAIL** colin-allen@tamu.edu

ALLEN, DIOGENES
PERSONAL Born 10/17/1932, Lexington, KY, m, 1958, 4 children **DISCIPLINE** PHILOSOPHICAL THEOLOGY **EDUCATION** Univ Ky, BA, 54; Oxford Univ, BA, 57, MA, 61; Yale Univ, BD, 59, MA, 61, PhD, 65. **CAREER** Asst prof to assoc prof, York Univ, 64-67; assoc prof, prof, Stuart prof of philos, Princeton Theol Sem, 67-. **HONORS AND AWARDS** Rhodes scholar, Rockefeller fel; res fel ATS; PEW scholarship; Templeton award in science & theol; Center of Theol Inquiry fel. **MEMBERSHIPS** Am Phil Assn; Am Theol Soc; Am Weil Soc; Leibniz Gesellschaft; Am Acad Relig. **RESEARCH** Science & relig, spirituality, Simone Weil, 17th cen philos. **SELECTED PUBLICATIONS** Auth, Mechanical Explanations and the Ultimate Origin of the Universe According to Leibniz, 83, Steiner; auth, Philosophy for Understanding Theology, 85, John Knox Press, and German translation Philosophie fuer das Theologiestudium, 95, Chr. Kaiser; auth, Christian Belief in a Postmodern World: The Full Wealth of Conviction, 89, John Knox Press; coauth, Nature, Spirit, and Community: Issues in the Thought of Simone Weil, 94, SUNY; auth, Spiritual Theology: the Theology of Yesterday for Help Today, 97, Cowley Publications; auth, "Intellectual Inquiry and Spiritual Formation," in Essentials of Christian Community, 96, T & T Clark; auth, "Christian Spirituality and Psychology," in Linning to the Psyche: Explorations into Christian Psychology, 97, Eerdmans; auth, "Jesus and Human Experience," in The Truth about Jesus, 98, Eerdmans; auth, "Natural Evil and the Love of God," Relig Studies, Dec 80; auth, "George Herbert and Simone Weil," Relig and Lit, Aug 85; auth, "Mozart's Don Giovanni and Love of Neighbor," Theol Today, Oct 88; auth, "The Issues Posed by the Order of the Universe," Proceedings of the V Leibniz Kongress, 88; auth, "Incarnation in the Gospels and the Bhagavad-Gita," Faith and Philos, Jan 89; auth, "The End of the Modern World," Christian Scholars Rev, July 83; auth, "Manifestations of the Supernatural according to Simone Weil: An Essay in Theological Reasoning," Cahiers Simone Weil, Sept 94. **CONTACT ADDRESS** Princeton Theol Sem, Princeton, NJ 08542. **EMAIL** diogenes.allen@ptsem.edu

ALLEN, LAYMAN E.
PERSONAL Born 06/09/1927, Turtle Creek, PA, m, 4 children **DISCIPLINE** LAW **EDUCATION** Turtle Creek High Sch, 45; Wash & Jefferson Col, 46-47; Princeton Univ, AB, 51; Harvard Univ, MPA, 52; Yale Univ, LLB, 56. **CAREER** United States Naval Reserves, 45-46; from instr to assoc prof, Yale Law Sch, 58-66; res scientist, Univ of Mich, 66-; from assoc prof to prof, Univ of Mich Law Sch, 66-. **HONORS AND AWARDS** Fel, Ctr for Advanced Study in the Behav Sci; Ford Found Fel; Soc Sci Res Coun Fel; Felix S. Cohen Prize, Yale Law Sch; Frances Kellor Prize, Yale Law Sch; Benjamin Scharps Prize, Yale Law Sch; Pioneer in Computers and Law, Norwegian Res Ctr for Computers and Law. **MEMBERSHIPS** Am Bar Asn, Asn for Symbolic Logic, Conn Bar Asn, AMINTAPHIL, Soc and Law, Am Asn for the Advancement of Sci, Nat Asn of Teachers of Mathematics, Am Orthopsychiatric Asn, Am Educ Res Asn, N Am Simulation and Gaming Asn, Coun of the Secy on Sci and Technol of the Am Bar Asn, Test Development and Res Comn of the Law Sch Admissions Coun, Test Question Rev Comt of the Law Sch Admissions Coun, Rackham Gaming/Simulation Studies Prog Comt, Nat Academic Games Tournament, Mich League of Acad Games, Int Asn for Artificial Intelligence and Law, Centro Interdipartimentale di Ricerca in Filosofia del Diritto e Informatica Guiridica dell Univ degli Studi di Bologna. **SELECTED PUBLICATIONS** Auth, The Real Numbers Game, Autotelic Instructional materials Pub, 66; coauth, On-Words: The Game of Word Structures, Autotelic Instructional materials Pub, 71; auth, Thinkers League Handbook, 86-87; coauth, "Better Language, Better Thought, Better Communication: The A-HOHFELD Language for Legal Analysis," Proceedings of the Fifth International Conference on Artificial Intelligence and Law, Univ of Md, 95; auth, "From the Fundamental Legal Conceptions of Hohfeld to LEGAL RELATIONS: Refining the Enrichment of Solely Deontic LEGAL RELATIONS," DEONTIC LOGIC AGENCY AND NORMATIVE SYSTEMS, 96; auth, "Achieving Fluency in Modernized and Formalized Hohfeld: Puzzles and Games for the LEGAL RELATIONS Language," Proceedings of the Sixth International Conference on Artificial Intelligence and Law, Univ of Melbourne, 97; **CONTACT ADDRESS** Sch of Law, Univ of Michigan, Ann Arbor, 625 S State St, Ann Arbor, MI 48109-1215.

ALLEN, O. WESLEY, JR.
PERSONAL Born 06/16/1965, Sylacavoa, AL, m, 1995, 1 child **DISCIPLINE** NEW TESTAMENT **EDUCATION** Yale Divinity School, Mdiv, 90; Birmingham, Southern Col, BA, 87; Emory Univ, PhD, 96. **CAREER** Dean of the Chapel, 98-, DePaul Univ. **MEMBERSHIPS** Soc Biblical Lit. **RESEARCH** Synoptic Gospels. **SELECTED PUBLICATIONS** Auth, The Death of Herod: The narrative and theological function of retribution in Like-Acts, 97; Good News from Thinville: Stories of heart and hope, spring, 99; Interpreting the Synoptic Gospels, Fall, 99. **CONTACT ADDRESS** DePaul Univ, 209 E Seminary St, Greencastle, IN 46135. **EMAIL** wallen@depauw.edu

ALLEN, ROBERT F.
PERSONAL Born 02/09/1959, Detroit, MI, m, 1990, 2 children **DISCIPLINE** PHILOSOPHY **EDUCATION** Univ Michigan, BA, Wayne State Univ, PhD. **CAREER** Central Michigan Univ Detroit, adj prof, 94-. **MEMBERSHIPS** APA **RESEARCH** Metaphysics **CONTACT ADDRESS** Dept of Philosophy, Central Michigan Univ, 9901 Marion, Redford, MI 48239-2015. **EMAIL** RAllen8219@aol.com

ALLEN, RONALD J.
PERSONAL Born 04/26/1949, Poplar Bluff, MO, m, 1975, 5 children **DISCIPLINE** NEW TESTAMENT, HOMILETICS **EDUCATION** Phillips Univ, AB, 71; Union Theol Sem, MDiv, 74; Drew Univ, PhD, 77. **CAREER** Co-pastor, First Christian Church, Grand Is, Nebr, 77-82; Nettie Sweeny and Hughth Miller prof of Preaching and New Test, Christian Theol Sem, Indianapolis, 82- . **MEMBERSHIPS** SBL; Acad Homiletics; Relig Speech Commun Asn. **RESEARCH** Preaching **SELECTED PUBLICATIONS** Auth, The Teaching Sermon, Abingdon, 95; coauth, Holy Root, Holy Branches, Abingdon, 96; coauth, Theology for Preaching, Abingdon, 97; Interpreting the Gospel, Chalice, 98; Patterns for Preaching, Chalice, 98; coauth, The Vital Church, Chalice 98; coauth, Preaching Verse by Verse, 99; auth, Preaching Luke-Acts, 00; co-ed, Preaching in Context of Worship, 00; auth, Preaching and Practical Ministry, forthcoming. **CONTACT ADDRESS** Dept of New Testament, Christian Theol Sem, 1000 W 42nd St, Indianapolis, IN 46208. **EMAIL** roniallen@cts.edu

ALLEN, WILLIAM BARCLAY
PERSONAL Born 03/18/1944, Fernandina Beach, FL, m **DISCIPLINE** POLITICAL SCIENCE **EDUCATION** Pepperdine Col, BA 1967; Claremont Grad School, MA 1968, PhD 1972. **CAREER** From asst prof to prof, Govt, Harvey Mudd Col, 83-92; dean & prof, James Madison Col, Mich State Univ, 93-98; dir, State Counc of High Educ for Va, 98-99; prof, poli sci, 98- . **HONORS AND AWARDS** Fulbright Fel, 70-71; Kellogg Natl Fel, WK Kellogg Found, 84-87; Prix Montesquieu Academic France, 86; Pi Sigma Alpha, Sigma Alpha; LID, Pepperdine University, 88. **RESEARCH** Am founding; 18th century enlightenment; polit philos; education; lit & politics; moral fables. **SELECTED PUBLICATIONS** Auth, Let the Advice Be Good: A Defense of Madison's Democratic Nationalism, 93; ed, George Washington: A Collection; ed, The Works of Fisher Ames; ed, The Essential Antifederalist; auth, The Federalist Papers, 00. **CONTACT ADDRESS** Dept of Poli Sci, Michigan State Univ, 303 S Kedzie Hall, East Lansing, MI 48824-1032. **EMAIL** allenwi@msu.edu

ALLIN, CRAIG WILLARD
PERSONAL Born 10/03/1946, Two Harbors, MN, m, 1977 **DISCIPLINE** POLITICAL SCIENCE **EDUCATION** Grinnell Col, BA, 68; Princeton Univ, MA, 70, PhD, 76. **CAREER** Asst prof, Polit Sci, Cornell Coll, 72-79; assoc prof, Cornell Coll, 79-85; Prof, Polit Sci, Cornell Coll 85-. **HONORS AND AWARDS** Phi Beta Kappa, Grinnell College, 68; Charles Grosvenor Osgood Fellow, Princeton Univ, 69-72; Univ House Fellow, Univ of Iowa, 82-83; Presidential Fellow, Cornell College, 89-90; Richard and Norma Small Distinguished Professor, Cornell College, 96-98. **MEMBERSHIPS** Am Political Science Assoc; Policy Studies Organization. **RESEARCH** Envi-

ronmental politics; Management of wilderness areas & federal conservation lands **SELECTED PUBLICATIONS** Auth, The Leopold Legacy and American Wilderness in Thomas Tanner, ed.: Aldo Leopold: the Man and His Legacy Soil Conservation Society of America, 87; auth, Agency Values in Wilderness Management in John D. Hutcheson, Jr. ed.: Outdoor Recreation Policy, Westport, Connecticut: Greenwood Press, 90; auth, Four Theses on Wilderness Management: From Aldo Leopold to the Wilderness Resource, St. Paul: University of Minnesota, 90; auth, Congress or the Agencies: Who'll Rule Wilderness in the 21st Century? In Patrick C. Reed, ed.: Preparing to Manage Wilderness in the 21st Century, Athens: University of Georgia, 90; auth, Conservation Movement in Robert Paehlke, ed.: Conservation and Environmentalism: an Encyclopedia, New York: Garland Publishing, 95; auth, Sierra Club in Robert ed.: Conservation and Environmentalism: an Encyclopedia New York: Garland Publishing, 95; auth, The Gila Wilderness Area Is Designated in Frank N. Magill, ed.: Great Events from History II: Ecology and the Environment, Pasadena, California: Salem Press, 95; auth, Congress Creates Eastern Wilderness areas, in Frank N. Magill, ed.: Great Events from History II: Ecology and the Environment, Pasadena, California: Salem Press, 95; auth, National Parks and Nature Reserves of the World in The World Book Encyclopedia, Chicago: World Book Publishing, 96. **CONTACT ADDRESS** Dept Polit, Cornell Col, 600 First St W, Mount Vernon, IA 52314-1098. **EMAIL** callin@cornell-iowa.edu

ALLISON, DALE C., JR.
PERSONAL Born 11/25/1955, Wichita, KS, m, 1982, 3 children **DISCIPLINE** BIBLICAL STUDIES **EDUCATION** Wichita State Univ, BA, 77; Duke Univ, MA, 79, PhD, 82. **CAREER** Res assoc, TX Christian Univ, 82-86; res scholar, Saint Paul School of Theology, 86-89; res fel, Friends Univ, 89-97; assoc prof of New Testament and Early Christianity, Pittsburgh Theol Sem, 97-. **HONORS AND AWARDS** Recipient of Pew Charitable Trust grant, 97-98. **MEMBERSHIPS** Studiorum Novi Testamenti Societas; Soc of Biblical Lit. **RESEARCH** Ancient Judaism and early Christianity. **SELECTED PUBLICATIONS** Auth, The End of the Ages has Come: An Early Interpretation of the Passion and Resurrection of Jesus, Fortress, 85, T & T Clark, 87; with W D Davies, An Exegetical and Critical Commentary on the Gospel according to St Matthew, T & T Clark, 88, vol 2, T & T Clark, 91, vol 3, T & T Clark, 97; with W D Davies, The New Moses: A Matthean Typology, Fortress and T & T Clark, 93; The Silence of Angels, Trinity Press Int, 95; The Jesus Tradition in Q, Trinity Press Int, 97; Jesus of Nazareth: Millenarian Prophet, Fortress, 98; The Sermon on the Mount: Inspiring the Moral Imagination, Crossroad, 99; auth, The Intertextual Jesus: Scripture in Q, Trinity Press Intl, 00. **CONTACT ADDRESS** Pittsburgh Theol Sem, 616 N Highland Ave, Pittsburgh, PA 15206. **EMAIL** dallison@pts.edu

ALMEDER, ROBERT F.
DISCIPLINE THEORY OF KNOWLEDGE, PHILOSOPHY OF SCIENCE, ETHICAL THEORY, AMERICAN PHILOS **EDUCATION** Univ Pa, PhD, 69. **CAREER** Prof, Ga State Univ; ed, Am Philos Quart. **SELECTED PUBLICATIONS** Auth, Blind Realism: An Essay on Human Knowledge and Natural Science; Death and Personal Survival; The Philosophy of Charles S. Peirce; Harmless Naturalism. **CONTACT ADDRESS** Georgia State Univ, Atlanta, GA 30303. **EMAIL** phlrra@panther.gsu.edu

ALMEIDA, ONESIMO
PERSONAL Born 12/18/1946, Azores, Portugal, m, 1992, 3 children **DISCIPLINE** PHILOSOPHY **EDUCATION** Portuguese Cath Univ, Lisbon, BA, 72; Brown Univ, MA, 77, PhD, 80. **CAREER** Prof and chemn Dept of Portuguese and Brazilian Stud, Brown Univ, 91- . **HONORS AND AWARDS** Srec Essay Prize, 86; officer, Order of Prince Henry, Pres of Portugal. **MEMBERSHIPS** APA; Soc for the Study of European Ideas; Am Portuguese Stud Asn. **RESEARCH** Sixteenth century Portugal; world views, values and ideologies. **SELECTED PUBLICATIONS** Auth, Que Nome e Esse, O Nezimo? 94; ed, Y.R. Migueis, Aforismos Edesaforismos De Aparicio, 96; auth, Rio Atlantico, 97. **CONTACT ADDRESS** Brown Univ, PO Box 0, Providence, RI 02912. **EMAIL** onesimo_almeida@brown.edu

ALPERSON, PHILIP A.
DISCIPLINE PHILOSOPHY **EDUCATION** Univ Toronto, PhD. **CAREER** Dept Philos, Univ Louisville **HONORS AND AWARDS** Ed, The Jour of Aesthet and Art Criticism. **RESEARCH** Aesthetics. **SELECTED PUBLICATIONS** Auth, articles on musical performance and improvisation, the philos of art and mus edu, value theory, and the aesthet theories of Hegel and Schopenhauer; ed, The Philosophy of the Visual Arts, Oxford, 92; What Is Music?, An Introduction to the Aesthetics of Music, Penn State UP, 94; Musical Worlds: New Directions in the Philosophy of Music, Penn State UP, 98. **CONTACT ADDRESS** Dept of Philos, Univ of Louisville, 2301 S 3rd St, Louisville, KY 40292-0001. **EMAIL** paalpe01@homer.louisville.edu

ALPERT, REBECCA T.
PERSONAL Born 04/12/1950, Brooklyn, NY, 2 children **DISCIPLINE** RELIGION **EDUCATION** Temple Univ, PhD, 78. **CAREER** Dean of Students, Reconstructionist Rabbinical Col, 79-88; Dir of Adult Progs, Temple Univ, 89-92, co-dir, Women's Studies Prog, 92-, asst prof, Religion, Temple Univ, 96-. **HONORS AND AWARDS** Lambda Literary Awd for Religion/Spirituality, 98. **MEMBERSHIPS** Am Academy of Relig; Nat Women's Studies Asn; Reconstructionist Rabbinical Asn. **RESEARCH** Relig and sexuality; women in Judaism. **SELECTED PUBLICATIONS** Auth, Joshua Loth Liebman: The Peace of Mind Rabbi, in Faith and Freedom: Essays in Honor of Franklin Littell, ed R Libowitz, Pergamon Press, 87; The Quest for Economic Justice: Kaplan's Response to the Challenge of Communism 1929-1940, in The American Judaism of Mordecai Kaplan, ed M Scult, E Goldsmith and R Seltzer, NY Univ Press, 90; Challenging Male/Female Complementarity: Jewish Lesbians and the Jewish Tradition, in People of the Body: Jews and Judaism from an Embodied Perspective, ed Howard Eilberg-Schwartz, SUNY Press, 92; Sometimes the Law is Cruel: The Construction of a Jewish Anti-Abortion Position in the Writings of Immanuel Jakobovits in J of Feminist Studies in Relig, fall 95; with Goldie Milgram, Women in the Reconstructionist Rabbinate in Religious Institutions and Women's Leadership: New Roles Inside the Mainstream, ed Catherine Wessinger, Univ SC Press, 96; On Seams and Seamlessness, in Judaism Since Gender, eds Laura Levitt and Miriam Peskowitz, Routledge, 96, reprinted from Shofar: An Interdisciplinary Journal of Jewish Studies, fall 95; Like Bread on the Seder Plate: Jewish Lesbians and the Transformation of Tradition, Columbia Univ Press, 97, Lambda Literary Award, 98; with J Staub, Exploring Judaism: A Reconstructionist Approach, Reconstructionist Press, 85, rev ed, 00; ed, Voices of the Religious Left, Temple Univ Press, 00. **CONTACT ADDRESS** 6817 Milton St, Philadelphia, PA 19119. **EMAIL** ralpert@nimbus.temple.edu

ALSCHULER, ALBERT W.
PERSONAL Born 09/24/1940, Aurora, IL, d **DISCIPLINE** LAW **EDUCATION** Harvard, AB, 62; LLB, 65. **CAREER** Prof, Univ of Tex, 66-75; prof, Univ of Colo, 76-84; prof, Univ of Pa, 84; Wilson-Dickinson Prof, Univ of Chicago, 85-. **HONORS AND AWARDS** Sutherland Prize, Am Soc of Legal Hist, 97; Guggenheim Fel, 97-98. **RESEARCH** Criminal law, criminal procedure, American legal theory. **SELECTED PUBLICATIONS** Auth, Law Without Values: The Life, Work, and Legacy of Justice Holmes; auth, Rediscovering Blackstone; auth, Alternatives to the Plea Bargaining System; auth, The Privilege Against Self-Incrimination. Its Origin and Development. **CONTACT ADDRESS** School of Law, Univ of Chicago, 1111 E 60th St, Chicago, IL 60637-2776. **EMAIL** al_alschuler@law.uchicago.edu

ALTER, TORIN
PERSONAL Born 06/08/1963, New York, NY, m, 1998 **DISCIPLINE** PHILOSOPHY **EDUCATION** Hampshire Col, BA, 85; UCLA, MA, 87; PhD, 95. **CAREER** Asst Prof, The Univ of Alabama, 95-97, 98-99; Asst Prof, The College of New Jersey, 97-98; Teaching Fellow, UCLA, 92-94; Teaching Assoc, UCLA, 88-92; Teaching Asst, UCLA, 87-88. **HONORS AND AWARDS** Research Advisory Committee Grant, The Univ of Alabama, 99; Research Advisory Committee Grant, The Univ of Alabama, 97; Arts and Sciences Teaching Grant, The Univ of Alabama, 96; Carnap Prize, UCLA, 94; UCLA Philosphy Department Fellowship, 86; **MEMBERSHIPS** Amer Philosophical Assoc. **RESEARCH** Philosophy of Mind; Philosophy of Language. **SELECTED PUBLICATIONS** Auth, "Teleportation: A Fast Way to Travel or a Fast Way to Die?" Presentation, Philosophy Club, The University of Alabama, Fall 95; auth, "Moral Paradox?" Presentation, Philosophy Club, The College of New Jersey, Fall 97; auth, "Genuine De Re Belief," Collouium, Department of Philosophy, Texas A&M University, Spring 98; auth, "Commentator on "Immunity to Error in First Person Memory Reports," Colloquium, American Philosophical Association, Pacific Division Meeting, Spring 98; auth, "E.O. Wilson on Ethics and Religion," Presentation, The Dean's Colloquium, The University of Alabama, Fall 98; auth, "Emotions, Belief, and the Knowledge Argument," Presentation, Emotions, Consciousness, and Qualia, interdisciplinary conference, Fall 98; auth, "The Knowledge Argument," survey article, in a Field Guide to the Philosophy of Mind, edited by M. Nani and M. Marraffa, June 99; auth, "On Racist Symbols and Reparations," review essay fortcoming in Social Theory and Practice 26, Spring 00, auth, "Schedler on Racism and the Confederate Battle Flag," Colloquium, American Philosophical Association, Pacific Division Meeting, Spring 00; auth, "Sensations, Brain Processes, and Essence," Presentation, Toward a Science of Consciousness: Tucson 2000, interdisciplinary conference, Spring 00. **CONTACT ADDRESS** Philos Dept, Univ of Alabama, Tuscaloosa, Box 870218, Tuscaloosa, AL 35487-0218. **EMAIL** talter@philos.as.ua.edu

ALTMAN, IRA
PERSONAL Born 03/17/1944, Kzyl-kya, Russia, m, 1969, 1 child **DISCIPLINE** SOCIOLOGY, PHILOSOPHY **EDUCATION** City Col of NY, BA, 66; Graduate School the City University of NY, MA, 74; PhD, 78. **CAREER** Instr-adjunct assoc prof, Queens's Col, 68; Hunter Col, 68; Lehman Col, 69-71; Brooklyn Col, 69-78; Long Island Univ, 70-71; Stevens Inst of Tech, 74-78; NY Inst Tech, 78-84; Pace Univ, 85-91; Yeshiva Univ, 90-92; Touro Col, 90-; Queensborough Community Col, 93-; Suffolk Community Col, 90-; ed, The City College Philosophy Journal, Logos, 65-67. **HONORS AND AWARDS** Special honors in theSocial Sciences (Social Sciences Honors Degree); the Marc Showitz Memorial Scholarship for Graduate Studies; univ fellowship; teaching assistantship; pres, The City Col Philos Soc (65); presented paper at the 18th annual spring meeting of the Long Island Philos Asn (82); invited to join a select delegation of philosophers to visit the Russian Republic and Hungary (95), China (96), India (96); invited paper based on his book "The Concept of Intelligence" at the Twentieth World Congress of Philosophy (98). **MEMBERSHIPS** Am Philos Asn, Long Island Philos Soc. **RESEARCH** Epistemology, critical thinking, ordinary language analysis, the philosophy of science, the philosophy of mind, **SELECTED PUBLICATIONS** Auth, The Concept of Intelligence: A Philosophical Analysis, Univ Press Am (97); Lectures in Philosophy, Am Heritage (96); Readings in Philosophy, McGraw-Hill (97); Lectures in Critical Thinking: A Beginner's Guide to Informal and Formal Logic, Copley (98); Exercise Manual for Lectures in Critical Thinking, McGraw-Hill (99). **CONTACT ADDRESS** Dept Social Sciences, Queensborough Comm Col, CUNY, 22205 56th Ave., Oakland Gardens, NY 11364-1432. **EMAIL** ialman@freewweb.com

ALTMAN, SCOTT A.
DISCIPLINE FAMILY LAW **EDUCATION** Univ Wis, BA, 83; Harvard Univ, JD,87. **CAREER** Virginia S.& Fred H. Bice prof & assoc dean, Univ Southern Calif;clerked, Honorable Dorothy Nelson, Judge US Ct Appeals 9th Circuit. **RESEARCH** Jurisprudence & family law. **SELECTED PUBLICATIONS** Auth, Should Child Custody Rules Be Fair; Divorcing Threats and Offers; Child Custody and Justice,; Beyond Candor & A Patchwork Theory of Blackmail. **CONTACT ADDRESS** School of Law, Univ of So California, University Park Campus, Los Angeles, CA 90089. **EMAIL** saltman@law.usc.edu

ALWARD, LORI L.
PERSONAL Born 12/31/1957, Tacoma, WA, s **DISCIPLINE** PHILOSOPHY **EDUCATION** Univ North Carolina, Chapel Hill, MA, 87, PhD, 97. **CAREER** Vis asst prof, Univ Puget Sound, 96- . **HONORS AND AWARDS** Javits fel, 86-90; Kennan fel, 85-86. **MEMBERSHIPS** APA; Soc for the Study of Women Philos. **RESEARCH** Ethics; social and political philosophy; feminst theory; Kant. **CONTACT ADDRESS** 2911 N 12 St, Tacoma, WA 98406. **EMAIL** lalward@ups.edu

AMAKER, NORMAN CAREY
PERSONAL Born 01/15/1935, New York, NY, m, 1962 **DISCIPLINE** LAW **EDUCATION** Amherst Clg, BA (cum laude) 1956; Columbia U, JD 1959. **CAREER** NAACP Legal Def Fund NYC, atty, 60-68, first asst cnsl, 68-71; Nbrh Legal Serv Prog Wash DC, exec dir, 71-73; Natl Comm Agnst Dscrmntn in Housing, gen cnsl; 73; Rutgers Univ, prof of law, 73-76; Loyola Univ of Chicago Law Sch, prof of law, 76-. **HONORS AND AWARDS** IBPOE of W Awd 1965; BALSA Awd 1973. **MEMBERSHIPS** Sch bd mem Dist 202 Evanston Twnshp H S 1980-87, pres pro-tem 1983-84; pres Chicago Forum Chicago 1982-83; bd of gov Soc of Am Law Tchrs 1979-87. **SELECTED PUBLICATIONS** Auth, Civil Liberties & Civil Rghts Oceana 1967; Civil Rights and the Reagan Adm, Urban Inst Wash DC, 988. **CONTACT ADDRESS** Loyola Univ, Chicago, 1 E Pearson St, 526, Chicago, IL 60611.

AMAN, ALFRED C., JR.
PERSONAL Born 07/07/1945, Rochester, NY, m, 1976 **DISCIPLINE** POLITICAL SCIENCE, LAW **EDUCATION** Univ Rochester, AB, 67; Univ Chicago, JD, 70. **CAREER** Intern, 67, exec comm Econ devel, NY St Constitutional Convention; assoc, 69, Covington & Burling, Wash, DC, and Sullivan & Cromwell, NY; law clerk, 70-72, Hon Elbert P. Tuttle, US Court of Appeals, Fifth Circuit; adj prof, 71-75, Law, Emory Univ; assoc, 72-75, Sutherland, Asbill & Brennan, Atlanta, Wash, DC, 75-77; vis fel, 83-84, 90-91, Wolfson Col, Cambridge Univ; assoc prof, 77-83, prof of Law, 83-91, Cornell Law School; res fel, 93, Bellagio Study & Conf Ctr, Rockefeller Found; vis prof Law, 97, Univ Paris (II), Inst of Comparative Law, 98, 99; Fulbright Dist Chr in Comparative Constitutional and Administrative Law, Trento Univ School of Law, Italy, 98; dean, prof, Ind Univ School of Law, 91-. **HONORS AND AWARDS** Phi Beta Kappa; Univ Scholar; William E. Townsend fel Awd for Achievement in Polit Sci; Exec ed, Univ Chicago Law Rev; Nat Honor Scholar. **MEMBERSHIPS** DC Bar; GA Bar; NY Bar; IN Bar; Am Bar Asn; IN State Bar Asn; Federal Bar Asn. **RESEARCH** Globalization; administrative law; comparative constitutional law. **SELECTED PUBLICATIONS** Auth, Administrative Law In A Global Era, Cornell Univ Press, 93; coauth, Administrative Law Treatise, West Pub Co, 93; auth, Administrative Law and Process, Matthew-Bender Corp, 93, supp, 97, 2nd ed; ed, The Globalization of Law, Politics and Markets, 1 Indiana J. Global Legal Stud, 93; auth, Preserving the Eggshell Planet: A Global Perspective on Domestic Regulation, 102 Yale Law J, 2107, 93; auth, Administrative Law for a New Century, The Province of Administra-

tive Law, Hart Pub, Oxford, 97; auth, The Globalizing State: A Future-Oriented Perspective on the Public/Private Distinction, Federalism and Democracy, 32 Vand J trans L, 98. **CONTACT ADDRESS** School of Law, Indiana Univ, Bloomington, 211 S Indiana Ave, Bloomington, IN 47405. **EMAIL** Fredaman@law.indiana.edu

AMARU-HALPERN, BETSY
PERSONAL Born 09/07/1939, Ahoona, PA, d, 4 children **DISCIPLINE** RELIGION **EDUCATION** Barnard BA, 61; Brandeis Univ, MA, 63; Harvard Univ, MAT 63; Univ MA, PhD, 69. **CAREER** Prof 81-, Vassar College. **MEMBERSHIPS** SBL **RESEARCH** Judaism. **SELECTED PUBLICATIONS** Rev, The Land of Israel in Judaism, W D Davies's, The Territorial Dimension of Judaism, Midstream, 93; auth, Rewriting the Bible: Land and Covenant in Post-Biblical Jewish Literature, Philadelphia, Trinity Press Intl, 94; The First Women Wives and Mothers in Jubilees, J Biblical Lit, 94; Teaching Judaism in a Christian Academic Setting, in: A Global Approach to Higher Education, ed, Moshe Davis, NY, NY U Press, 94; rev, Christopher Wright's God's People in God's Land, Hebrew Studies, 95; Jewish Civilization in Christian Academic Settings, Teaching Jewish Civilization, ed, Moshe Davis, Jerusalem, Magnes 96, Hebrew Edition; Exile and Return in the Book of Jubilees, Exile: Old Testament Jewish Christian Conceptions, ed James M Scott, Leiden, EJ Brill, 97; The Portrait of Sarah in Jubilees, Jewish Studies in a New Europe, eds U Haxen, H Trautner-Kromann, K Goldschmidt Salamon, Copenhagen Reitzel A/S, 98; auth, The Empowerment of Women in the Book of Jubilees, Leiden, EJ Brill, 99; The Renaming of Levi, Pseudepigraphic Perspectives: The Apocrypha and the Pseudepigrapha in Light of the Dead Sea Scrolls, eds M Stone, E Chazon, Leiden, EJ Brill, 99; auth, "The Empowerment of Rachel in the Book of Jubilees," The Bible and Its World, ed. R. Margolin, (Jerusalem: Hebrew Univ), 99. **CONTACT ADDRESS** Vassar Col, Box 555, Poughkeepsie, NY 12604. **EMAIL** amaru@vassar.edu

AMBROSIO, FRANCIS J.
PERSONAL Born New York, NY **DISCIPLINE** PHILOSOPHY **EDUCATION** Fordham Univ, BA, PhD. **CAREER** Asst prof, St Joseph's Univ, 76-79; assoc prof, 81-. **RESEARCH** Existentialism; Christian philosophy. **SELECTED PUBLICATIONS** Auth, Fra Angelico at San Marco: The Place of Art; co-ed, Text and Teaching, Georgetown; The Question of Christian Philosophy Today, Fordham Univ. **CONTACT ADDRESS** Dept of Philosophy, Georgetown Univ, 37th and O St, Washington, DC 20057.

AMBROZIC, ALOYSIUS M.
PERSONAL Born 01/27/1930, Gabrje, Slovenia **DISCIPLINE** THEOLOGY **EDUCATION** St Augustine's Sem; Univ San Tommaso, STL, 58; Pontificio Inst Biblico, SSL, 60; Univ Wurzburg, ThD, 70. **CAREER** Prof, 60-67, dean stud, St Augustine's Sem, 71-76; prof, Toronto Sch Theol, 70-76; aux bishop, Roman Cath Archdiocese Toronto, 76-86; Coadjutor Archbishop Toronto, 86-90; ARCHBISHOP, ROMAN CATHOLIC ARCHDIOCESE OF TORONTO, 90-. **MEMBERSHIPS** Cath Bibl Asn Am; ACEBAC. **SELECTED PUBLICATIONS** Auth, The Hidden Kingdom, 72; auth,Remarks on the Canadian Catechism, 74; auth, Oce, posveceno bodi tvoje ime, 80; auth, Oce, zgodi se tvoja volja, 96. **CONTACT ADDRESS** Roman Catholic Archdiocese of Toronto, 1155 Yonge St, Toronto, ON, Canada M4T 1W2.

AMERIKS, KARL
DISCIPLINE PHILOSOPHY **EDUCATION** Yale Univ, PhD. **CAREER** Prof. **RESEARCH** European philosophy from the 17th century to the present. **SELECTED PUBLICATIONS** Auth, Kant's Theory of Mind, 82; Understanding Apperception Today, Kant Cont Epistemol, 94; The Ineliminable Subject: From Kant to Frank, 95; Kant's Lectures on Metaphysics, 96; Probleme der Moralitat bei Kant und Hegel, 95; New Views on Kant's Judgment of Taste, 97. **CONTACT ADDRESS** Philosophy Dept, Univ of Notre Dame, 336/7 O'Shaughnessy, Notre Dame, IN 46556. **EMAIL** ameriks.2@nd.edu

AMES, FRANK
PERSONAL Born 04/14/1955, Denver, CO, m, 1974, 2 children **DISCIPLINE** BIBLICAL STUDIES, HEBREW BIBLE, LIBRARY SCIENCE **EDUCATION** Western Bible Col, BS, 77; Denver Sem, MDiv, 80; Univ Denver, MA, 81; PhD, 98. **CAREER** Adj instr, Denver Sem, 81-83; lib, Western Bib Col, 83-85; act dean, 85-89; asst dean, Colo Christ Col, 89-92; dean, assoc prof, Sch Bib Stud, Colo Christ Univ, 92-97; lib, prof, 97-. **HONORS AND AWARDS** Student Gov Asn Awd; Hebrew Fel. **MEMBERSHIPS** SBL; AAR. **RESEARCH** Social world of the Bible. **SELECTED PUBLICATIONS** Auth, "Levirate Marriage," in the New Intl Dictionary of Old Testament Theology and Exegesis, Zondervan, 97. **CONTACT ADDRESS** Dept Bible Studies, Colorado Christian Univ, 180 S Garrison St, Denver, CO 80226-1053. **EMAIL** fames@ccu.edu

AMICO, ROBERT P.
PERSONAL Born 04/03/1947, Dorchester, MA, m, 1982, 1 child **DISCIPLINE** PHILOSOPHY **EDUCATION** Univ Rochester, PhD, 86. **CAREER** Prof philos, St. Bonaventure Univ. **MEMBERSHIPS** APA; AAUP. **RESEARCH** Epistemology. **SELECTED PUBLICATIONS** Auth, The Problem of the Criterion, Rowman & Littlefield, 93. **CONTACT ADDRESS** St. Bonaventure Univ, PO Box 101, Saint Bonaventure, NY 14778. **EMAIL** ramico@sbu.edu

AMINRAZAVI, MEHDI
PERSONAL Born 09/22/1957, Mashhad, Iran, m, 1982, 2 children **DISCIPLINE** RELIGION, PHILOSOPHY **EDUCATION** Temple Univ, PhD 89; Univ Washington, MA 81, BA 79. **CAREER** Mary Washington College, assoc prof, dir, 90-. **HONORS AND AWARDS** Kabbani Awd; Mahvi Foun Awd; Outstanding Yng Fac Awd; Kut F Leidecker Ch. **MEMBERSHIPS** APA; AAR. **RESEARCH** Islamic philo; medieval philo; philo religion. **SELECTED PUBLICATIONS** Auth, An Anthology of Philosophy In Persia, co-ed, vol 2, OUP, 2000; An Anthology of Philosophy of Persia, co-ed, vol 1, OUP, 1999; Philosophy Religion and the Question of Intolerance, co-ed, NY, SUNY Press, 97; The Islamic Intellectual tradition in Persia, ed, London, Curzon Press, 96; Suhrawardi and the School of Illumination, London, Curzon Press, 96; The Complete Bibliography of the Works of Seyyed Hossein Nasr: From 1958-1993, coauth, Malaysia, Islamic Acad of Sci Press, 94; Ibn Sina's Theory Knowledge by Presence, in: Proceedings of the Mulla Sadra Conference, forthcoming; Avicenna and Suhrawardi on Knowledge, Jour of Islamic Sci and Philo, forthcoming; Ontological and Metaphysical Perspectives of SH Nasr, in Living Lib of Philosophers, ed L.E. Hahn, forthcoming; Mystical and Philosophical Poetry of Suhrawardi, in: Treatises on Islamic philosophy, ed, Z Morris, Kazi Press, 99. **CONTACT ADDRESS** Dept of Classics Philosophy and Religion, Mary Washington Col, Fredericksburg, VA 22401. **EMAIL** maminraz@mwc.edu

AMMON, THEODORE G.
DISCIPLINE HISTORY OF PHILOSOPHY, EPISTEMOLOGY, PHILOSOPHY AND LITERATURE **EDUCATION** Miss State Univ, BA; Wash Univ, MA, PhD. **CAREER** Dept Philos, Millsaps Col **SELECTED PUBLICATIONS** Publ on, ethical duties of teachers; philos underpinnings of lit of Jorge Luis Borges; teaching strategies for moral develop. **CONTACT ADDRESS** Dept of Philosophy, Millsaps Col, 1701 N State St, Jackson, MS 39210. **EMAIL** ammontg@okra.millsaps.edu

AMORE, ROY C.
PERSONAL Born 09/10/1942, Newark, OH **DISCIPLINE** RELIGIOUS STUDIES **EDUCATION** Ohio Univ, BA, 64; Drew Univ (NJ), BD, 67; Columbia Univ, PhD, 70. **CAREER** Lectr, Drew Univ, 68-69; vis lectr, Upsala Univ (NJ), 69; instr, Bard Col, 69-70; asst to assoc prof, 70-81, coordr Asian stud prog, 80-81, 82-86, PROF RELIGIOUS STUDIES, UNIV WINDSOR, 81-, dept head, 86-88; Wilson-Craven prof, Southwestern Univ, 78-79. **MEMBERSHIPS** Can Coun Southeast Asian stud (pres, 80-82); Can Asian Stud Asn (vice pres 80-82); Can Soc Stud Relig. **SELECTED PUBLICATIONS** Auth, Two Masters, One Message, 78, Asian ed 85; coauth, Lustful Maidens and Ascetic Kings: Buddhist and Hindu Stories of Life, 81; coauth, Buddhism, in World Religions: Eastern Traditions, 96; ed, Developments in Buddhist Thought: Canadian Contributions to Buddhist Studies, 79; co-ed, Culture and Development in Southeast Asia, 87. **CONTACT ADDRESS** Dept of Political Science, Univ of Windsor, 401 Sunset Ave, Windsor, ON, Canada N9B 3P4. **EMAIL** amore@server.uwindsor.ca

AMSTERDAM, ANTHONY G.
PERSONAL Born 09/12/1935, Philadelphia, PA, m **DISCIPLINE** LEGAL STUDIES, CRIMINOLOGY **EDUCATION** Haverford Col, AB, 57; Univ Pa, LLB, 60. **CAREER** Prof, Univ of Pa Law Sch, 62-69; Prof, Stanford Univ Law Sch, 69-81; Judge Edward Weinfeld Prof, NYork Univ Law Sch, 81-. **HONORS AND AWARDS** Fel, Am Acad of Arts and Sci, 77; John D. and Catherine T. MacArthur fel, 89; August Vollmer Awd, Am Soc of Criminol, 86. **MEMBERSHIPS** Am Acad of Arts and Sci. **RESEARCH** Civil rights and civil liberties, Constitutional Law, Criminal Procedure. **SELECTED PUBLICATIONS** Auth, "Race and the Death Penalty," 7 Criminal Justice Ethics 1-2 (88); auth, Trial Manual 5 for Defense of Criminal Cases, Am Law Inst - Am Bar Asn (Philadelphia), 89; auth, "Equality as an Enforceable Right: Problems and Prospects Ahead," 135 Proceedings of the Am Philos Soc 13 (91); coauth, Trial Manula for Defense Attorneys in Juvenile Court, Am Law Inst - Am Bar Asn (Philadelphia), 91-92; coauth, "An Analysis of Closing Arguments to a Jury," 37 NY Law Sch Law Rev 55 (92); auth, "Thurgood Marshall's image of the Blue-Eyed Child in 'Brown'," NY Univ Law Rev 226 (93); auth, "Telling Stories and Stories About Them," 1 Clinical Law Rev 9 (94); auth "Selling a Quick Fix for Boot Hill: The Myth of Justice in Delayed Death Cases," in The Killing State: Capital Punishment, Politics, and Culture 148, ed. Austin Sarat (NY and Oxford: Oxford Univ Press, 99)); coauth, Minding the Law, Harvard Univ Press (Cambridge, MA), 00. **CONTACT ADDRESS** Sch of Law, New York Univ, 249 Sullivan St, New York, NY 10012. **EMAIL** amsterdam@juris.law.nyu.edu

ANAWALT, HOWARD C.
DISCIPLINE LAW **EDUCATION** Stanford, BA; Univ Calif-Boalt Hall, JD. **CAREER** Prof & dir, Santa Clara Univ; NASA legal consultant; Special Coun, ACLU; legal experience in litigations, transactions, legal planning, and legislative work. **HONORS AND AWARDS** Vis Schol, Stanford; vis schol, Univ Calif at Boalt Hall; vis schol, Univ Wash. **MEMBERSHIPS** UNESCO consultation on the right to communicate; **SELECTED PUBLICATIONS** Coauth, 1991 Licensing Law Handbook; coauth, I P Strategy: Complete Intellectual Property Planning, Access, and Protection, West Group, 96-99; auth, Ideas in the Workplace. **CONTACT ADDRESS** Sch of Law, Santa Clara Univ, 500 El Camino Real, Santa Clara, CA 95053-0001.

ANCHUSTEGUI, ANN-MARIE
PERSONAL Born 08/28/1962, Twin Falls, ID **DISCIPLINE** PHILOSOPHY **EDUCATION** Univ Wisconsin Madison, MA, 88; Wayne State Univ, PhD, 97. **CAREER** Adj fac, 94-, Wayne State Univ. **HONORS AND AWARDS** Grad tchg assistantship, 88-89. **MEMBERSHIPS** APA. **RESEARCH** Aesthetics; Philosophy of Mind. **CONTACT ADDRESS** Dept of Philos, Wayne State Univ, Detroit, MI 48201. **EMAIL** ad5846@wayne.edu

ANDERSEN, ROGER WILLIAM
PERSONAL Born 10/20/1948, Chicago, IL, m, 1975, 2 children **DISCIPLINE** LAW **EDUCATION** Knox Col, BA, 70; Univ Iowa, JD, 73; Univ Ill, LLM, 78. **CAREER** Legal Writing instr, Col of Law, Univ Ill, 76-77; asst prof, Sch of Law, Oklahoma City Univ, 77-79; from assoc prof to prof Law, Col of Law, Univ Toledo, 79-83; vis prof, Univ Richmond, 83-84; vis scholar, Wolfson College, Cambridge, England, 90. **HONORS AND AWARDS** Phi Beta Kappa. **SELECTED PUBLICATIONS** Coauth (with Dr LeRoy Rogers), Time-limited water rights: Legal and economic considerations, Gonz Law Rev, 77; auth, The resource conservation and Recovery Act of 1976: Closing the gap, Wis Law Rev, 78 & Solid & Hazardous Waste Management in Wis, Clew, 4/79; Stating objectives for a legal writing course, J Legal Educ, 79; Accessible private housing: A suggested agenda, Notre Dame Law, 80; Understanding Trusts and Estates, 2nd ed, Matthew Bender, 99; auth, The Impact of USLTA's Articles 4 & 5 on Ohio Lien Law, U Toledo L Rev, 84; auth, auth, The Influence of te Uniform Probate Code in Non-adopting States, U. Puget Sound L Rev, 85; auth, Informed Discisionmaking in an Office Pratice, B.C.L., Rev, 87; coauth, Ohio's College Savings Plan: Buyer Beware, with Douglas Chapman, U Toledo L Rev, 89; auth, Cnveyancing Reform: A Great Place to Start, Real Prop Porb & Tr. J, 91; auth, Architectural Barriers Legislation and the Range of Human Abilities: of Civil Rights, Missed Opportunities, and Building Codes, Williamette L. Rev, 92; auth, Will Executions: A Modern Guide, Am J. Trial Advc, 94; auth, Present & Future Interests: A Graphic Explanation, Seattle U.L. Rev, 95; Fundamentals of Trusts and Estates, Matthew Bender, 96, with John Gaubatz, Ira Bloom, Lewis Solomon, with Teachers Guide. **CONTACT ADDRESS** Col of Law, Univ of Toledo, 2801 W Bancroft St, Toledo, OH 43606-3391. **EMAIL** roger.andersen@utoledo.edu

ANDERSON, ALEXIS J.
PERSONAL Born 07/11/1951, Philadelphia, PA, m, 1984, 2 children **DISCIPLINE** LAW **EDUCATION** Wake Forest, BA; Univ Va, JD; MA. **CAREER** Atty, Philadelphia, 78-83; adj prof, Villanova Univ, 81-83; asst prof to assoc prof, Boston Col, 83-. **HONORS AND AWARDS** Fulbright Fel, Boston Col. **MEMBERSHIPS** Am Soc of Legal History; Clinical Legal Educ Asn; Pa Bar Asn; Mass Bar Asn. **RESEARCH** Development of Free Speech Theory. **SELECTED PUBLICATIONS** auth, "New England's Experiences with Punishing Political Speech During World War I: A Study in Prosecutorial Discretion," Mass J of Legal Hist, 98. **CONTACT ADDRESS** Sch of Law, Boston Col, Newton Ctr, 885 Center St, Newton, MA 02459. **EMAIL** andersoa@bc.edu

ANDERSON, CHARLES SAMUEL
PERSONAL Born 03/04/1930, Madison, WI, m, 1951, 2 children **DISCIPLINE** HISTORICAL THEOLOGY **EDUCATION** St Olaf Col, BA, 51; Univ Wis, MA, 54; Luther Theol Sem, BD, 57; Union Theol Sem, NYork, PhD (Hist Theol & Reformation Studies), 62. **CAREER** Teaching asst English, Univ Wis, 53-54; from asst prof to prof Hist Theol, Luther Theol Sem, 61-77, dir Grad Studies, 68-72, vpres Acad Affairs & dean, 77-80, pres, Augsburg Col, 80-97, clergyman, Am Lutheran Church, 57-; mem, Rockefeller Scholar Area Selection Comt, 63, 69; comn Inter Church Affairs, Am Lutheran Church, 64; vis lectr, Northwestern Lutheran Theol Sem, 64; Am Asn Theol Sch sabbatical studies grant, 67-68; vis lectr, Concordia Theol Sem, 68; Bush Found fel, 71-; chmn div Theol Studies, Lutheran Coun USA, 72-. **HONORS AND AWARDS** Phi Betta Kappa, Rockefeller & Martin Luther fell; Bush Leadership fell. **MEMBERSHIPS** Am Soc Church Hist; Renaissance Soc Am; Soc Reformation Res. **RESEARCH** Reformation theology; the military aspects of the Reformation; improvement of education for ministry. **SELECTED PUBLICATIONS** Auth, International Luther studies, Ecumenist, 66; Will the real Luther please stand up, Dialog, 67; The Reformation Then and Now,

67; The Augsburg Historical Atlas of Christianity in the Middle Ages and Reformation, 67, 72 & ed, Readings in Luther for Laymen, 67, Augsburg; auth, Robert Barnes, In: Interpretors of Luther, 68 & ed, Facet Books Reformation Series, 69-, Fortress; auth, Faith and Freedom: The Christian Faith According to the Lutheran Confessions, Augsburg, 78. **CONTACT ADDRESS** 1377 Grantham St, Saint Paul, MN 55108. **EMAIL** andersoc@visi.com

ANDERSON, CHARLES W.
PERSONAL Born 06/28/1934, Maniiowoc, WI, m, 1955 **DISCIPLINE** POLITICAL SCIENCE **EDUCATION** Grinnell Col, BA, 55; Johns Hopkins Univ, MA, 57; Univ Wisconsin, PhD, 60. **CAREER** Asst prof, prof, prof emer, polit sci, Univ Wisconsin, Madison, 60-96. **HONORS AND AWARDS** LLD, Grinnell Col, 88; Spitz Prize, 92. **RESEARCH** Political philosophy; political economy. **SELECTED PUBLICATIONS** Auth, The Political Economy of Mexico, 63; auth, Politics and Economic Change in Latin America, 67; auth, The Political Economy of Modern Spain, 70; auth, Issues of Political Development, 74; auth, Statecraft, 77; auth, Value Judgment and Income Distribution, 81; auth, Pragmatic Liberalism, 90; auth, Prescribing the Life of the Mind, 93; auth, A Deeper Freedom, 02. **CONTACT ADDRESS** Dept of Political Science, Univ of Wisconsin, Madison, 1304 Nishishin Trl, Monona, WI 53716.

ANDERSON, DAVID LEECH
DISCIPLINE PHILOSOPHY **EDUCATION** Whitman Col, BA; Regent Col, DCS; Harvard Univ, MTS, PhD. **CAREER** Assoc prof. **SELECTED PUBLICATIONS** Auth, A Dogma of Metaphysical Realism, Am Philos Quarterly, 95. **CONTACT ADDRESS** Dept of Philosophy, Illinois State Univ, Normal, IL 61761. **EMAIL** dlanders@ilstu.edu

ANDERSON, DAVID M.
PERSONAL Born 12/15/1958, Atlantic City, NJ **DISCIPLINE** PHILOSOPHY **EDUCATION** George Wash Univ, BA, 81; Univ MI, PhD, 90. **CAREER** Asst prof lect, 96-98, Philos, George Wash Univ; lectr, Univ Cincinnati & Col of Charleston; assoc prof lect, 96-97, adj assoc prof, Grad School of Polit Management, George Wash Univ, 97-. **HONORS AND AWARDS** Charlotte Newcombe Found fel, 87-88; Phi Beta Kappa, 82. **MEMBERSHIPS** APA; Soc for the Advancement of Socio-Economics; Commentaria Network. **RESEARCH** Ethics; social and political philos; business ethics; ethics and political management. **SELECTED PUBLICATIONS** Auth, False Stability and Defensive Justification in Rawlsian Liberalism: A Feminist Critique, in The Ethics of Liberal Democracy: Morality and Democracy in Theory and Practice, Berg Pubs, 94, Contemporary Philos, vol XIV, no 5, 92; auth, Scholars Roundtable: Remarks on Dr. Martin Luther King Jr's Concept of the Beloved Community, Inst for Conflict Analysis and Resolution Newsl, vol 7, no 3, 95, & The First Annual Scholars Roundtable on Peace & Conflict Stud: A Report to the Wash Area Consortium of Univ, 96; auth, A Few Questions for Communitarians, The Responsive Community, vol 6, no 2, 96; auth, Communitarian Approaches to the Economy, Merits and Limits of Markets, Springer-Verlag, 98; A Viable Strategy for Women's Progress, Women's Progress: Perspectives on the Past: Blueprint for the Future, Conf Proceed, Inst for Women's Policy Res 98; auth, Part of the Project of Building a Progressive Coalition: Uniting Working Mothers and Welfare Mothers Behind a National Family Policy, Inherent and Instrumental Value: An Excursion of Value Inquiry, Intentional Scholars Pubs, 99. **CONTACT ADDRESS** Grad School of Polit Management, The George Washington Univ, 805 21st St, NW Ste 401, Washington, DC 20052. **EMAIL** davidand@gwu.edu

ANDERSON, DENNIS A.
DISCIPLINE CHURCH ADMINISTRATION **EDUCATION** Gustavus Adolphus Col, BA, 59; Augustana Theol Sem, MDiv, 63; Austin Presbyterian Sem, Grad Stud, 64-65; Gustavus Adolphus Col, DD, 78; Midland Lutheran Col, DHL, 80; Wittenberg Univ, DD, 90. **CAREER** Sec Interpretation/Regional dir Amer Missions, Lutheran Church Am, 71-73; Bishop, Nebraska Synod, Lutheran Church Am, 78-87; Bishop, Nebraska Synod, Evangel Lutheran Church Am, 88-90; president, 90-. **SELECTED PUBLICATIONS** Auth, Mission90 Bible Study/Witness, Augsburg, 91; co-auth, The Many Faces of Pastoral Ministry, Augsburg, 89; contrib, Sacraments and Daily Life - Homiletical Helps, Div Parish Svc, Lutheran Church Am, 87. **CONTACT ADDRESS** Ministry Dept, Trinity Lutheran Sem, 2199 E Main St, Columbus, OH 43209-2334. **EMAIL** danderso@trinity.capital.edu

ANDERSON, DOUGLAS R.
PERSONAL Born 05/17/1953, Keene, NH, m, 1976, 2 children **DISCIPLINE** PHILOSOPHY **EDUCATION** Penn State Univ, PhD, 84. **CAREER** Wittenburg Univ, 84-90; Penn State Univ, 90-. **RESEARCH** Am philos; hist of philos. **SELECTED PUBLICATIONS** Auth, Creativity and the Philosophy of C. S. Pierce, Martinus Nijhoff Pubs, The Hague, 87; auth, Strands of System: The Philosophy of Charles Pierce, Purdue Univ Press, 95; co-ed, Philosophy in Experience: American Philosophy in Transition, Fordham Univ Press, 97; chap, intros, & 1 chap auth, "Pierce and Representative Persons". **CONTACT ADDRESS** Dept of Philosophy, Pennsylvania State Univ, Univ Park, University Park, PA 16802. **EMAIL** dra3@psu.edu

ANDERSON, ELIZABETH S.
PERSONAL Born 12/05/1959, Boston, MA, m, 1992, 2 children **DISCIPLINE** PHILOSOPHY **EDUCATION** Swarthmore Col, BA, 81; Harvard Univ, MA, 87, PhD, 87. **CAREER** Tchg fel, Harvard Univ, 83-85; vis instr philos, Swarthmore Col, 85-86; asst prof philos, 87-93, assoc prof philos and women's stud, 93-99, Univ Michigan. **HONORS AND AWARDS** Humanities Inst Fel, Univ Michigan, 89-90; Univ Mich Col of LS&A excellence in educ award, 91; selected by The Philos Asn, one of ten best philos papers in 91; Arthur F. Thurnau prof, awarded for excellence in undergrad tchg, 94; Mich Humanities Awd, 99. **MEMBERSHIPS** APA; Soc for Analytic Feminism. **RESEARCH** Ethics; social and political philosophy; philosophy of the social sciences; feminist theory; epistemology. **SELECTED PUBLICATIONS** Auth, Value in Ethics and in Economics, Harvard, 93; auth, The Democratic University: The Role of Justice in The Production of Knowledge, Social Philos and Policy, 95; auth, Feminist Epistemology: An Interpretation and Defense, Hypatia, 95; auth, Knowledge, Human Interests, and Objectivity in Feminist Epistemology, Philos Topics, 95; auth, Reasons, Attitudes, and Values: Replies to Sturgeon and Piper, Ethics, 96; auth, Practical Reason and Incommensurable Goods, in Chang, ed, Incommensurability, Incomparability, and Practical Reason, Harvard, 97; auth, Pragmatism, Science, and Moral Inquiry, in Fox, ed, In Face of the Facts: Moral Inquiry in American Scholarship, Cambridge, 98; auth, John Stuart Mill on Democracy as Sentimental Education, in Rorty, ed, Philosophy of Education, Chicago, 98; auth, What Is The Point of Equality? Ethics, 99; co-auth, Expressive Theories of Law: A General Restatement, Univ of PA, Law Rev, 00; auth, The Ethical Limitations of the Market, Economics and Philosophy 6, 90; auth, Is Women's Labor a Commodity? Philosophy and Public Affairs 19, 90; auth, Beyond Homo Economicus, Philosophy and Public Affairs 29, 00; auth, John Stuart Mill and Experiments in Living, Ethics 102, 91. **CONTACT ADDRESS** Dept of Philosophy, Univ of Michigan, Ann Arbor, 435 South State St, Angell Hal, Ann Arbor, MI 48109-1003. **EMAIL** eandersn@umich.edu

ANDERSON, JAMI L.
DISCIPLINE PHILOSOPHY **EDUCATION** Ariz State Univ, BA, 89; Univ Southern Calif, PhD, 95. **CAREER** Tchg Asst, Univ Southern Calif, 95; Instr, Otis Liberal Arts Col, 95; Asst prof, Univ Central Ark, 95-. **MEMBERSHIPS** Am Philos Asn; Ark Philos Asn; North Am Socy Soc Philos; Hegel Soc Am; Soc Study Women Philos. **RESEARCH** Social & political theory; legal theory; ethical theory. **SELECTED PUBLICATIONS** Rev, State Punishment, by Nicola Lacey, Philos Today, 96; auth, "Reciprocity as a Justification for Retribution," Crim Just Ethics vol 16, no 1, 97; auth, "Understanding Punishment as Annulment," in Technology, Morality, and Social Policy, 97; auth, "Annulment Retributivism: A Hegelian Theory of Punishment," in Legal Theory, forthcoming. **CONTACT ADDRESS** Dept of Philos, Univ of Michigan, Flint, 544 French Hall, Flint, MI 48502-1950.

ANDERSON, MICHELLE J.
PERSONAL Born 01/30/1967, Valdosta, GA **DISCIPLINE** FEMINIST LEGAL THEORY, CRIMINAL LAW, CRIMINAL PROCEDURE, CHILDREN AND THE LAW **EDUCATION** Univ Calif at Santa Cruz, BA, 88; Yale Law Sch, JD, 94; Georgetown Univ Law Ctr, LLM, 97. **CAREER** Asst prof; clerk to, Honorable William A. Norris, US Ct Appeals 9th Circuit; past tchg fel and Adjprof in Appellate Litigation Prog, Georgetown Univ Law Ctr; past vis prof, Georgetown's Ins for Public Repr. **HONORS AND AWARDS** Orville H. Schell Ctr, Int Human Rights fel; Ford Found fel in Public Int Law. **RESEARCH** Feminist legal theory, rape law. **SELECTED PUBLICATIONS** Auth, Silencing Women's Speech, in The Price We Pay: The Case Against Racist Speech, Hate Propaganda, and Pornography 122, 95 & A License To Abuse: The Impact of Conditional Status on Female Immigrants, 102 Yale L.J. 1401, 93; auth, Reviving Resistance in Rape Law, Univ Il, Rev 953, 98. **CONTACT ADDRESS** Law School, Villanova Univ, 800 Lancaster Ave, Villanova, PA 19085-1692. **EMAIL** anderson@law.vill.edu

ANDERSON, MYRON GEORGE
PERSONAL Born 05/05/1930, Minneapolis, MN, m, 1957, 1 child **DISCIPLINE** PHILOSOPHY **EDUCATION** Univ Minn, BA, 51, MA, 54; Brown Univ, PhD, 59. **CAREER** Instr, Trinity Col, Conn, 56-60, asst prof, 60-65; assoc prof, 65-70, Prof Philos, St Cloud State Univ, 70-, Chairperson Dept, 73-80. **MEMBERSHIPS** Am Philos Asn. **RESEARCH** Epistemology; hist of modern philos; social and political philos. **CONTACT ADDRESS** Dept of Philosophy, St. Cloud State Univ, 720 4th Ave S, Saint Cloud, MN 56301-4498. **EMAIL** manderson@stcloudstate.edu

ANDERSON, NEIL D.
PERSONAL Born 04/19/1952, Newcastle, PA, m, 1975, 3 children **DISCIPLINE** THEOLOGY **EDUCATION** Asbury Col, BA, 88; Asbury Theol Sem, MDiv, 91; Drew Univ, MA, 94, PhD, 99. **CAREER** Zarephath Bible Inst, 94-96; Asbury Col, asst prof, 96-. **MEMBERSHIPS** AAR, WHS, WTS, NAPS. **RESEARCH** Systematics, patristics, John Wesley; new testament. **CONTACT ADDRESS** Dept of Bible and Theology, Asbury Col, 1 Macklem Dr, Wilmore, KY 40390. **EMAIL** neil.anderson@asbury.edu

ANDERSON, R. LANIER
PERSONAL Born 10/14/1965, Macon, GA, m, 1996 **DISCIPLINE** PHILOSOPHY **EDUCATION** Yale Univ, BA, 87; Univ Pa, MA, 93; PhD, 93. **CAREER** Lectr, Univ Pa, 93-95; Vis Asst Prof, Bryn Mawr Col, 95-96; Asst Prof, Stanford Univ, 96-. **MEMBERSHIPS** APA, HSS. **RESEARCH** Kant, Neo-Kantianism, Nietzsche, 19th Century philosophy. **SELECTED PUBLICATIONS** Auth, "Nietzsche's Will to Power as a Doctrine of the Unity of Science," Studies in Hist and Philos of Sci 25 (94): 729-750; auth, "'Putnam' and 'Quine'," in The Dict of Cult and Critical Theory (Oxford: Blackwell, 96); auth, "Overcoming Charity: The Case of Maudemarie Clark's 'Nietzsche on Truth and Philosophy'," Nietzsche-Studien 25 (96): 307-341; auth, "Truth and Objectivity in Perspectivism," Syntheses 115 (98): 1-32; auth, "Nietzsche's Views on Truth and the Kantian Background of his Epistemology," in Nietzsche, Epistemology and Philos of Sci: Nietzsche and the Sci II (London: Kluwer Publ, 99), 47-59. **CONTACT ADDRESS** Dept Philos, Stanford Univ, Building 90, Stanford, CA 94305.

ANDERSON, ROBERT MAPES
PERSONAL Born 04/06/1929, New York, NY **DISCIPLINE** AMERICAN SOCIAL HISTORY & AMERICAN RELIGIOUS HISTORY **EDUCATION** Wagner Col, BA, 59; Columbia Univ, MA, 62, PhD, 69. **CAREER** Hist ed, Monarch Press, New York, 62-64; lectr hist, 64-65, from instr to assoc prof, 65-77, chmn, Dept Hist & Polit Sci, 70-75, prof hist, Wagner Col, 77-. **MEMBERSHIPS** AHA; Orgn Am Historians; AAUP. **RESEARCH** American religious history. **SELECTED PUBLICATIONS** Ed, United States Since 1865, Monarch, 63; Vision of the Disinherited: The Making of American Pentecostalism, Oxford Univ Press, 79, 2nd ed, Hendrickson Press, 92. **CONTACT ADDRESS** Wagner Col, 631 Howard Ave, Staten Island, NY 10301-4428. **EMAIL** rmander877@aol.com

ANDERSON, STANLEY DANIEL
PERSONAL Born 06/27/1937, Gary, IN, m, 1963, 3 children **DISCIPLINE** PHILOSOPHY **EDUCATION** Wheaton Col, Ill, BA, 59, MA, 62; Gordon Divinity Sch, BD, 62; Boston Univ, MA, 72; Univ Minn, PhD, 80. **CAREER** Instr, 68-70, asst prof, 72-76, assoc prof, 76-80, Prof Philos, Bethel Col, 80-. **MEMBERSHIPS** Am Philos Asn; Soc Christian Philosophers. **RESEARCH** Ethical theory; social philosophy; philosophy of higher education. **CONTACT ADDRESS** Dept of Philos, Bethel Col, Minnesota, 3900 Bethel Dr, Saint Paul, MN 55112-6999. **EMAIL** andsta@bethel.edu

ANDERSON, SUSAN LEIGH
PERSONAL Born 11/13/1944, Portland, OR, m, 1974, 1 child **DISCIPLINE** PHILOSOPHY **EDUCATION** Vassar Col, AB, 66; Univ Calif, Los Angeles, MA, 71; PhD, 74. **CAREER** Teaching assoc philos, Univ Calif, Los Angeles, 68-70; instr, Calif State Univ, Northridge, 70-71; asst prof, 72-80, Assoc Prof Philos, 80-91, Prof, Univ Conn, Stamford, 91-; rev & panelist, Nat Endowment for Humanities; vis asst Prof, Mt Holyoke Col, 77. **HONORS AND AWARDS** Nat Endowment for Humanities fel, Princeton Univ, 75 & Brown Univ, 78; Lilly fel, Yale Univ, 76; Yale vis fac fel, 90- 91. **MEMBERSHIPS** Am Philos Asn. **RESEARCH** The self; applied ethics; 19th century philosophy; philosophy in literature. **SELECTED PUBLICATIONS** Auth, Coconsciousness and numerical identity of the person, Philos Studies, 76; The substantive center theory versus the bundle theory, Monist, 78; Chisholm's argument that a person cannot be an Ens Successivum, Philos Studies, 80; The Libertarian conception of freedom, Int Philos Quart, 81; Plantinga and the Free Will Defense, 81; auth, Criticism of Liberal/Feminist Views on Abortion, Public Affairs Q, 87; auth, Evil, J Value Inquiry, 90; auth, The Status of Frozen Embryos, Public Affairs Q, 90; auth, A Picture of the Self which Supports Moral Responsibility, The Monist, 91; auth, Equal Opportunity, Freedom and Sex- Stereotyping, J Philos Res, 91; auth, Philosophy and Fiction, Metaphilosophy, 92; auth, Being Held Morally Responsible for an Actions versus Acting Responsibly/Irresponsibly, J Philos Res, 95; auth, Natural Rights and the Individualism vs Collectivism Debate, J Value Inquiry, 95; auth, Problems in Developing a Practical Theory of Moral Responsibility, J Value Inquiry, 96; auth, On Mill, wadsworth Philosophers Series, 00; auth, On Kierkegaard, Wadsworth Philosophers Series, 00; auth, On Dostoevsky, Wadsworth Philosophers Series, 00; auth, "Do We Ever Have a Duty to Die?," in Is There a Duty to Die?, edited by Humber and almeger, Biomedical Ethics Reviews, Humana Press, 00; auth, "We Are Our Values," in Questioning Matters, edited by Daniel Kolak, Mayfield, 00. **CONTACT ADDRESS** Dept of Philos, Univ of Connecticut, Stamford, 1 University Pl, Stamford, CT 06901-2315. **EMAIL** Susan.Anderson@uconn.edu

ANDERSON, THOMAS C.
PERSONAL Born 10/06/1935, Britton, SD, m, 1960, 7 children **DISCIPLINE** PHILOSOPHY **EDUCATION** Loyola Univ, BS, 58; Marquette Univ, MA, 62, PhD, 66. **CAREER** From Instr to Asst Prof, St Michael's Col, 63-67; Asst Prof to Prof, Marquette Univ, 67-. **HONORS AND AWARDS** NEH Grant; Grant, Am Coun of Learned Soc; Fac Awd for Teaching Excellence, Marquette Univ. **MEMBERSHIPS** Soc for Phenomenology & Existential Philos, ACPA, Soc for Philos & Technol, AAUP, Sartre Soc, Marcel Soc. **RESEARCH** French

existentialism, Soren Kierkegaard, philosophy of technology. **SELECTED PUBLICATIONS** Auth, "Technics and Atheism in Gabriel Marcel," Bulletin de la Societe Americaine de Langue Francaise, VII (95); auth, "Sartre and Human Nature," Am Cath Philos Quart (96); auth, "Technology and the Decline of Leisure," Proceedings of the Am Cath Philos Asn (96); auth, "Kierkegaard and Approximation Knowledge," in Int Kierkegaard Commentary: Concluding Unscientific Postscript (Mercer UP, 97); auth, "Authenticity, Conversion and the City of Ends in Sartre's 'Notebooks for an Ethics'," in Existentialist Ethics (New York: Garland Publ, 97). **CONTACT ADDRESS** Dept Philos, Marquette Univ, PO Box 1881, Milwaukee, WI 53201-1881. **EMAIL** thomas.anderson@marquette.edu

ANDERSON, VINTON RANDOLPH
PERSONAL Born 07/11/1927, Somerset, Bermuda, m, 1952 **DISCIPLINE** THEOLOGY **EDUCATION** Wilberforce University, BA (with honors); Payne Theological Seminary, MDiv, 1952; Kansas University, MA, philosophy; Yale University Divinity School, continuing education; Urban Training Center for Christian Missions. **CAREER** St Mark AME Church, pastor, 52-53; Brown Chapel AME Church, pastor, 53-55; St Luke AME Church, Lawrence, pastor, 55-59; St Paul AME Church, Wichita, pastor, 59-64; St Paul AME Church, St Louis, pastor, 64-72; presiding bishop, chief pastor: 9th Episcopal District, Alabama, 72-76; 3rd Episcopal District, Ohio, West Virginia, West Pennsylvania, 76-84; Office of Ecumenical Relations and Development, 84-88; 5th Episcopal District, 14 states including 255 Churches west of the Mississippi River, 88-. **HONORS AND AWARDS** Ebony Magazine, Religion Awd, 1988, 1991; American Black Achievement Awds, 1991; National Association for Equal Opportunity in Higher Education, Distinguished Alumni Honoree, 1988; Honorary Doctorate Degrees: Eden Theological Seminary; Paul Quinn College; Wilberforce University; Payne Theological Seminary; Temple Bible College; Morris Brown College. **MEMBERSHIPS** World Council of Churches, numerous committees and delegations; World Methodist Council, North American Region, first vice pres, executive committee; World Methodist Council and Conference, delegate, 1961-; National Council of Churches, governing board, Faith & Order Commission, chairperson; Congress of National Black Churches, vice pres, charter member; Consultation on Church Union, vice pres; United Methodist Church, General Commission of Christian Unity and Interreligious Concern; Schomburg Center for Research in Black Culture, national advisory board; NAACP, life member; Urban League, St Louis dialogue group. **SELECTED PUBLICATIONS** Developed: church hymnal, The Bicentennial Edition; first AME Book of Worship; established, edited: The Connector; produced, edited: A Syllabus For Celebrating The Bicentennial; numerous articles in publications of the AME Church. **CONTACT ADDRESS** African Methodist Episcopal Church, 4144 Lindell Blvd, Suite 222, Saint Louis, MO 63108.

ANDERSON, WILLIAM P.
DISCIPLINE RELIGIOUS STUDIES **EDUCATION** Princeton Univ, PhD. **CAREER** Res scholar, Inst d'histoire de la Reformatiabout Univ de Geneve; vis, prof, Inst Oecumenique, Univ de Geneve, World Coun Churches and The United Theolog Sem; past vis lect, Grad Sch for Religion and Philosophy, St Petersburg Asn of Scholars, St. Petersburg, Russ; prof, Univ Dayton. **RESEARCH** Historical theology, early Christian church, Protestant Christianity. **SELECTED PUBLICATIONS** Auth, Aspects of the Theology of Karl Barth and Basic Issues in Christian Philosophy. **CONTACT ADDRESS** Dept of Religious Studies, Univ of Dayton, 300 College Park, 321 Humanities, Dayton, OH 45469-1679. **EMAIL** anderson@checkov.hm.udayton.edu

ANDERSON-GOLD, SHARON
DISCIPLINE PHILOSOPHY **CAREER** Assoc prof to prof, Philos, Rensselaer Polytech Inst. **RESEARCH** History and moral progress; the relationship between international law and human rights. **SELECTED PUBLICATIONS** Auth, Unnecessary Evil: History and Moral Progress in the Philosophy of Immanual Kant; auth, Cosmopolitanism and Human Rights. **CONTACT ADDRESS** Sci & Tech Studies, Rensselaer Polytech Inst, Troy, NY 12180. **EMAIL** anders@rpi.edu

ANDREEN, WILLIAM L.
PERSONAL Born 02/02/1953, Pittsburgh, PA, m, 2 children **DISCIPLINE** LAW **EDUCATION** Col Wooster, BA, 75; Columbia Univ Sch Law, JD, 77. **CAREER** Prof, Univ Ala. **HONORS AND AWARDS** Phi Beta Kappa. **MEMBERSHIPS** Ala Rives Alliance; Exec comt, Env Law Sec Asn Amer Law Schools; Commission on EnvironmentalLaw, IUCN. **RESEARCH** Environmental Law, Administrative Law, Int'l Assistance. **SELECTED PUBLICATIONS** Auth, "Environmental Law and International Assistance: The Challenge of Strengthening Environmental Law in the Developing World," 25 Col of Environmental Law, (00): 17-69. **CONTACT ADDRESS** Law Dept, Univ of Alabama, Tuscaloosa, Box 870382, Tuscaloosa, AL 35487-0382. **EMAIL** wandreen@law.ua.edu

ANDRESEN, JENSINE
PERSONAL Born 02/06/1964, Flint, MI, m, 2000 **DISCIPLINE** THEOLOGY, BIOETHICS **EDUCATION** Princeton Univ, BSE, 86; Columbia Univ, MA, 89; Harvard Univ, MA, 92; PhD, 97. **CAREER** Vis asst prof, 97-98, Univ Vt; asst prof, 98- , Boston Univ. **MEMBERSHIPS** Am Acad Relig. **RESEARCH** Religion and Science; Embodiment; Bioethics; Social Ethics. **SELECTED PUBLICATIONS** Auth; "Course Syllabus for 'Religion and Science: Divergence and Convergence," Religion and Education 26(2) (99): 43-47; auth, "Crisis and Kuhn," Isis 90 (99):s43-s67; auth, "Review Article: Science and Technology in Non-Western Cultures," Zygon: Journal of Religion and Science 34(2) (99): 345-352; auth, "Tibetan Monks of the Gaden Monastery," Boston Univ School of Theology's Focus journal, (99); auth, "Book Review: Tower of Babel: The Evidence against the New Creationism by Robert T. Pennock," The Journal of Religion 80(4) (00): 688-689; coed, Cognitive Models and Spiritual Maps: Interdisciplinary Explorations of Religious Experience, Imprint Academic (Thorverton, UK), 00; auth, "Vajrayana Art and Iconography," Zygon: Journal of Religion and Science 35(2) (00): 357-370; ed, Religion in Mind: Cognitive Perspectives on Religious Belief, Ritual, and Experience, Cambridge Univ Press (Cambridge, UK), 01; coauth, "Impact of Attachment Styles on Dream Recall and Dream Content: A Test of the Attachment Hypothesis of REM Sleep," in Journal of Sleep Research (forthcoming). **CONTACT ADDRESS** School of Theology, Boston Univ, 745 Commonwealth Ave, Boston, MA 02215. **EMAIL** jensine@bu.edu

ANDREW, SCOTT
PERSONAL Born 10/23/1950, CT, m, 1973 **DISCIPLINE** PHILOSOPHY **EDUCATION** Southwestern Baptist Theol Sem, PhD, 92. **MEMBERSHIPS** APA **RESEARCH** War theory. **CONTACT ADDRESS** 4016 32nd St, Mount Rainier, WA 20712.

ANDREWS, KRISTIN
PERSONAL Born 03/16/1971, Nashville, TN **DISCIPLINE** PHILOSOPHY **EDUCATION** Antioch Col, BA, 92; Western Mich Univ, MA, 95; Univ Minn, PhD, 00. **HONORS AND AWARDS** Phi Kappa Phi. **MEMBERSHIPS** Am Philos Asn; Europ Soc of Philos and Psychol; Southern Soc of Philos and Psychol. **RESEARCH** Philosophy and Psychology; Philosophy and Language. **SELECTED PUBLICATIONS** Auth, The First Step, the case for Great Ape equality: The Argument for Other Minds, Etica and Animali: The Great Ape Project, 96; auth, Our Understanding of Other Minds: Theory of Mind and the Intentional Stance, Jour of Consciousness Studies, forthcoming. **CONTACT ADDRESS** Philosophy Dept, Appalachian State Univ, Boone, NC 28608. **EMAIL** andrewsk@appstate.edu

ANDRUS, KAY L.
PERSONAL Born 04/05/1953, Idaho Falls, ID, m, 1977, 2 children **DISCIPLINE** LEGAL RESEARCH **EDUCATION** Brigham Young Univ, BA, MLS, JD. **CAREER** Prof & dir, Law Libr; Creighton Univ, 90-; past assoc law lib dir, Northwestern Univ Sch Law; Reader Sevc(s) libn, asst prof, Southern Ill Univ; past sr ref libn, Southern Methodist Univ; past asst law lib dir, Okla City Univ. **SELECTED PUBLICATIONS** Pub(s) in, J Air Law and Commerce; Syllabus; Libr J & Southern Ill Univ Law J. **CONTACT ADDRESS** Klutznick Law Libr, Creighton Univ, 2500 California Plaza , Omaha, NE 68178-0056. **EMAIL** andrus@culaw.Creighton.edu

ANGELELLI, IGNAZIO ALFREDO
PERSONAL Born 04/03/1933, Rome, Italy, m, 1959, 3 children **DISCIPLINE** PHILOSOPHY **EDUCATION** Univ Fribourg, PhD(philos), 65. **CAREER** Instr, Univ Notre Dame, 66-67; from asst prof to assoc prof, 67-72, Prof Philos, Univ Tex, Austin, 72-. **RESEARCH** History of logic; logic; history of philosophy, 1500-1900. **SELECTED PUBLICATIONS** Auth, Studies on G Frege and traditional philosophy, Reidel, Holland, 67. **CONTACT ADDRESS** Dept of Philosophy, Univ of Texas, Austin, Austin, TX 78712-1026. **EMAIL** plac565@utxvms.cc.utexas.edu

ANGELL, RICHARD B.
PERSONAL Born 10/14/1918, Scarsdale, NY, m, 1949, 5 children **DISCIPLINE** PHILOSOPHY **EDUCATION** Swarthmore, BA, 40; Univ PA, MGA , 48; Harvard, MA, 48, PhD, 54. **CAREER** Asst prof to full prof, 54-68, Ohio Wesleyan; prof, 68-89, chmn philos dept, 68-73, 76-78, emeritus prof, 89-, Wayne State Univ. **MEMBERSHIPS** APA. **RESEARCH** Logic. **SELECTED PUBLICATIONS** Auth, Reasoning and Logic, 64; auth, Analytic Logic, forthcoming. **CONTACT ADDRESS** 150 Kendal Dr, Kennett Square, PA 19348. **EMAIL** rbangell@bellatlantic.net

ANGLIN, DOUGLAS G.
PERSONAL Born 12/16/1923, Toronto, ON, Canada **DISCIPLINE** POLITICAL SCIENCE, HISTORY **EDUCATION** Univ Toronto, BA, 48; Corpus Christi Col & Nuffield Col, Univ Oxford, BA, 50, MA, 54, DPhil, 56. **CAREER** Asst to assoc prof polit sci, Univ Man, 51-58; assoc prof to prof, 58-89, PROF EMER, CARLETON UNIV, 93-; assoc res fel, Nigerian Inst Soc Econ Res, Univ Ibadan, 62-63; vice chancellor, Univ Zambia, 65-69; res assoc, Ctr Int Stud, Princeton Univ, 69-70. **MEMBERSHIPS** African Stud Asn (US); Can Inst Int Affairs; Can Polit Sci Asn; Can Asn African Stud (pres 73-74). **SELECTED PUBLICATIONS** Auth, The St Pierre and Miquelon Affaire of 1941, 66; auth, Zambia Crisis Behaviour: Confronting Rhodesia's Unilateral Declaration of Independence 1965-1966, 94; coauth, Zambia's Foreign Policy: Studies in Diplomacy and Dependence, 79; co-ed, Africa: The Political Pattern, 61; co-ed, Canada, Scandinavia and Southern Africa, 79; co-ed, Conflict and Change in Southern Africa, 79. **CONTACT ADDRESS** Dept of Political Science, Carleton Univ, 1125 Colonel By Dr, Ottawa, ON, Canada K1S 5B6. **EMAIL** d_anglin@carleton.ca

ANISE, LADUN OLADUNJOYE E.
PERSONAL Born 03/24/1940 **DISCIPLINE** POLITICAL SCIENCE **EDUCATION** Albion Col, BA, 1967; Syracuse Univ, MA 1968, PhD Political Science 1970; Univ of Pittsburgh, MA 1975. **CAREER** Syracuse Univ, African Studies-Minority Studies, lecturer, 68-70; Educ Policy & Resource Devel Center, Syracuse Univ, rsch assoc, 69-70; Univ of Pittsburgh, asst prof, 70-75; Univ of Ife Nigeria, visiting sr lecturer, 79-83; Hill Dist Catholic School System & Educ Devel Center, Pittsburgh PA, consultant, 72-75; Univ of Pittsburgh, assoc prof, 75-, African Studies Group, coord, 82-88, Black Studies Dept, chmn (summers) 87, 89. **HONORS AND AWARDS** ASPAU Achievement & Scholastic Awd 1967; Omicron Delta Kappa 1967; Maxwell Fellow 1967-70; Woodrow Wilson Doctoral Fellow 1970; Meritorious Achievement Awd Univ of Pittsburgh 1974. **MEMBERSHIPS** Mem Current Issues Comm African Studies Assoc 1968-, Amer Political Science Assoc, Natl Org of Black Political Science, African Heritage Studies Assoc, Natl Acad of Social Science. **CONTACT ADDRESS** Dept of Political Science, Univ of Pittsburgh, 4T25 Forbes Quad, Pittsburgh, PA 15260.

ANKENY, RACHEL A.
PERSONAL Born 04/13/1967, Detroit, IL **DISCIPLINE** HISTORY, PHILOSOPHY **EDUCATION** St. John's Col, BA, 88; Univ Pittsburgh, MA, 95; MA, 96; PhD, 97. **CAREER** Asst prof, Univ of Pittsburgh, 97-98; asst prof, Connecticut Col, 98-. **HONORS AND AWARDS** Javits Fel, 92-96; Mellon Fel, 96-97; Davis Ctr Fel, Princeton Univ, 99-00. **MEMBERSHIPS** Am Philos Assoc; Philos of Sci Assoc; Hist of Sci Soc; Am Soc of Bioethics and Humanities; Sigma Xi. **RESEARCH** History and Philosophy of biomedical sciences, bioethics. **CONTACT ADDRESS** History and Philosophy of Science, Connecticut Col, 270 Mohegan Ave, Box 5548, New London, CT 06320. **EMAIL** raank@conncoll.edu

ANKERSEN, THOMAS T.
DISCIPLINE LAW **EDUCATION** Univ S Fla, BA, MA; Univ Fla, JD. **CAREER** Atty, asst in Law, Ctr for Govt Responsibility, Univ Fla Col Law; dir, Center's Mesoamerican Env Law Prog; aff fac mem, Univ Florida's Ctr for Latin Amer Stud; guest ed, Span lang jour Mesoamerica; Fla Law Rev; past atty, Denver and Tallahassee off,; past sr litigation assoc, Peeples, Earl and Blank, Miami. **HONORS AND AWARDS** Dean Frank Maloney env law writing awd. **MEMBERSHIPS** Pres bd Dir, Env and Natural Resources Law Ctr; Tropical Ecosystems Directorate US Dept of State Man and the Biosphere Prog; bd dir, Forest Mgt Trust; bd adv, Fla Defenders of the Env. **RESEARCH** Coastal law and policy, water law, and legal issues associated with protection of biological diversity. **SELECTED PUBLICATIONS** Auth, Law, Sci and Little Old Ladies: The Many Hands That Made a Movement, J Fla Humanities Coun, 95; coauth, The Environmental Impacts of Intl Finance Corporation Lending and Proposals for Reform: A Case Study of Conservation and Oil Development in the Guatemalan Peten, J Env Law, 99; Ecosystem Management and the Everglades: A Legal and Institutional Analysis, J Land Use and Env Law 473, 96. **CONTACT ADDRESS** School of Law, Univ of Florida, PO Box 117629, Gainesville, FL 32611-7629. **EMAIL** ankersen@law.ufl.edu

ANSBRO, JOHN J.
PERSONAL Born 11/16/1932, New York, NY, s **DISCIPLINE** PHILOSOPHY **EDUCATION** St. Joseph's Sem, BA, 55; Fordham Univ, MA, 57, PhD, 64. **CAREER** Lectr, Manhattan Col, 58-59, instr, 59-63, asst prof, 63-68, assoc prof, 68-79, full prof, 79-93, chmn dept of philos, 77-81. **HONORS AND AWARDS** Ford Found Grant, 85; Am Can Company (Primerica) grant, 85; ford found grant, 73; samuel rubin found grant, 85. **MEMBERSHIPS** Am Asn of Univ Prof; Am Philos Asn; Soc for Ancient Greek Philos; Hegel Soc of Am; Soren Kierkegaard Soc; Soc for the Advan of Am Philos. **RESEARCH** History of philosophy; philosophy of nonviolence; African-American studies. **SELECTED PUBLICATIONS** Auth, Martin Luther King, Jr.: The Making of a Mind, 82; "Martin Luther King's Debt to Hegel," 94; "The Credo of Marcus Garvey," 94; "The Credo of Malcolm X," 95; "The Credo of W.E.B. Du-Bois," 95; "President Nelson Mandela's Appreciation of the Power of the Negative," 97; "Martin Luther King's Appreciation of the Power of the Negative," 97; "Frederick Douglass's Appreciation of the Power of the Negative," 97; "Malcolm X's Appreciation of the Power of the Negative," 98; "Marcus Garvey's Appreciation of the Power of the Negative," 98; auth, "The Credo of Frederick Douglass," 99; auth, "The Credo of

Booker T Washington," 00; auth, "Martin Luther King, Jr: Nonviolent Strategies and Tactics for Social Change," Madison Books. **CONTACT ADDRESS** 65 Greenvale Ave, Yonkers, NY 10703.

ANSON, RICHARD
PERSONAL Born 08/29/1945, Jacksonville, FL, m, 1990, 3 children **DISCIPLINE** CRIMINAL JUSTICE **EDUCATION** Iowa State Univ, MS, 70; PhD, 73. **CAREER** Asst Prof, S Dak State Univ, 73-76; Prof, Fla Jr Col, 77; Asst Prof, Memphis State Univ, 78-81; Chair, Albany State Univ, 81-. **HONORS AND AWARDS** Liberty Bell Awd, Dougherty Bar Asn, 89; Researcher of the Year, Albany State Univ, 90; Elected, Dougherty County Board of Educ, 96. **MEMBERSHIPS** Am School Board Asn. **RESEARCH** Police Officer Stress. **SELECTED PUBLICATIONS** Co-auth, Intro to Criminal Justice System, Harper Collins, 90. **CONTACT ADDRESS** Dept Criminal Justice, Albany State Univ, 504 Col Dr, Albany, NY 31705.

ANTHONY, WILLIAM PHILIP
PERSONAL Born 01/30/1943, Chicago, IL, m, 1968, 2 children **DISCIPLINE** MANAGEMENT **EDUCATION** BBA, 65, Ohio Univ; MBA, 67, PhD, 71, OH State Univ. **CAREER** Prof of Mgt, FL State Univ, 70-. **HONORS AND AWARDS** Beta Gamma Sigma; DeSantis Professorship. **MEMBERSHIPS** Acad of Mgt; Southern Mgt Assoc. **RESEARCH** Top Mgt Teams, Hum Res. **SELECTED PUBLICATIONS** Books with Pam Perrewe and Micki Kacmar, Strategic Human Resource Management, 3rd ed Ft Worth, HBJ/Dryden, 93, 96, 99; B.J. Hodge and Larry Gales, Organization Theory, 5th ed, Boston MA, Allyn and Bacon Inc, 79, 84, 88, 91, 96; Articles with Erich Brockman, The Influence of Tacit Knowledge and Collective Mind on Strategic Planning, Journal of Managerial Issues, Vol X No2 pp204-222, 98; Marc street, A Conceptual Framework Establishing the Relationship Between Groupthink and Escalating Commitment Behavior, Small Group Research Vol23 No2, pp267-293, 97; Nick Maddox, Robert Bennett and Walt Wheatley, The Mind's Eye and the Practice of Management, Envisioning the Ambiguous, Management Decision Vol 32 No2, pp21-29,94. **CONTACT ADDRESS** Coll of Bus, Florida State Univ, Tallahassee, FL 32306-1110. **EMAIL** banthon@cob.fsu.edu

ANTOCI, PETER
PERSONAL Born 05/06/1963, NY **DISCIPLINE** RELIGIOUS STUDIES **EDUCATION** Catholic Univ of Am, PhD 95. **CAREER** UMBC Shriver Peaceworker Prog, assoc dir; George Mason Univ, adj prof. **HONORS AND AWARDS** Leadershp Washington. **MEMBERSHIPS** AAR **RESEARCH** Religion and Culture Hermeneutics. **SELECTED PUBLICATIONS** Auth, Scandal and Marginality in the Vitae of Holy Fools, in: Christianity and Lit, 95. **CONTACT ADDRESS** 1810 Calvert St NW #3, Washington, DC 20009.

ANTON, JOHN P.
PERSONAL Born 11/02/1920, Canton, OH, m, 1955, 3 children **DISCIPLINE** PHILOSOPHY **EDUCATION** Columbia Univ, BS, 49, MA, 50, PhD, 54. **CAREER** Asst prof Philos, Univ NE, 55-58; assoc prof Philos, Ohio Wesleyan Univ, 58-62; prof Philos, State Univ NY/Buffalo, 62-69; Calloway Prof Philos, Emory Univ, 69-82; Distinguished Prof Philos, Univ South FL, 82-. **HONORS AND AWARDS** Honorary member, Phi Beta Kappa; honorary doctorate of Philos, Univ of Athens; Corresp member, Academy of Athens; honorary member, Parnassus Literary Soc; honorary citizen of Olympia; honorary pres, Int Assoc Greek Philos. **MEMBERSHIPS** Am Philos Asn; Soc Ancient Greek Philos; Am Soc Aesthetics; Int Soc Neoplatonic Studies. **RESEARCH** Ancient Greek philos and culture; Aristotle; Plato; Plotinus; Metaphysics; philos of art; classical political theories; modern Greek poetry. **SELECTED PUBLICATIONS** Ed and intro & notes, Upward Panic: The Autobiography of Eva Palmer Sikelianos, London: Gordon and Breach Science Pubs, Harwood Academic Pubs, 93; auth, The Poetry and Poetics of Constantine P. Cavafy, London: Harwood Academic Pubs, 95; Categories and Experience: Essays on Aristotelian Themes, Dowling Col Press, 96; Aristotle's On the Nature of Logos, in The Philos of Logos, ed K. Boudouris, vol I, Athens, 96, reissued with additions in Philos Inquiry, vol XVIII, nos 1-2, winter/spring 96; Plotinus and Augustine on Cosmic Alienation: Proodos and Epistrophe, in J of Neoplatonic Studies, vol IV/2, spring 96; ed and intro, Twenty Letters on the Ancient Drama by Eva Palmer-Sikelianos, bylingual ed, trans into Greek by Loukia Tsokopoulou, Athens: A Livanis Pub, 97; auth, Arcadia in the Poetry of Kostis Palamas, in Nea Estia, vol 141, no 1672, 3/1/97; Neoplatonic Elements in Arethas' Scholia on Aristotle and Porphyry, in Neoplatonisme et Philosophie Medieval, Actes du Colloque international, Societe Int pour l'Etude de la Philosophie Medieval (Oct 95), ed Linos G. Benakis, Brepols, 97; Plato as Critic of Democracy: Ancient and Modern, in Platonic Political Philos, proceedings of the VIII Conference of the Int Assoc Greek Philos, vol I, ed K. Boudouris, Athens, 97. **CONTACT ADDRESS** Dept Philos, Univ of So Florida, Tampa, FL 33620. **EMAIL** hanton1@tampabay.rr.com

ANTONELLI, GIAN ALDO
PERSONAL Born 02/10/1962, Torino, Italy, m, 1987, 2 children **DISCIPLINE** PHILOSOPHY **EDUCATION** Univ Torino, Laurea, 86; Univ Pittsburgh, PhD, 92. **CAREER** Lectr, Yale Univ, 93-96; vis asst prof, Stanford Univ, 96-97; asst prof, Mich State Univ, 97-98; asst prof, Univ Calif Irvine, 98-00, assoc prof, 00-. **HONORS AND AWARDS** Fulbrigth Scholar, 87; Rotary Int Scholar, 87. **MEMBERSHIPS** Asn for Symbolic Logic; Am Philos Asn. **RESEARCH** Pure and Applied Logic; Philosophy of Mathematics. **SELECTED PUBLICATIONS** Auth, The Complexity of Revision, Notre Dame J of Formal Logic, 94; Non-Well-Founded Sets via Revision Rules, J of Philos Logic, 94; A Revision-Theoretic Analysis of the Arithmetical Hierarchy, Notre Dame J of Formal Logic, 94; What's in a Function?, Synthese, 96; Defeasible Inheritance on Cyclic Networks, Artificial Intelligence, 97; Godel, Penrose, e I fondamenti dell'intelligenza artificiale, Sistemi Intelligenti, 97; Extensional Quotients for Type Theory and the Consistency Problem for NF, J of Symbolic Logic, 98; coauth, Backwards Forward Induction, TARK, 94; Games Servers Play: A Procedural Approach, Intelligent Agents II, 96; Game-Theoretic Axioms for Local Rationality and Bounded Knowledge, J of Logic, Lang, and Information, 95. **CONTACT ADDRESS** Dept of Logic & Phil Science, Univ of California, Irvine, Irvine, CA 92697-5100. **EMAIL** aldo@uci.edu

ANZALONE, FILIPPA M.
PERSONAL Born 09/27/1953, Cambridge, MA, m, 1983, 2 children **DISCIPLINE** LAW **EDUCATION** Smith Col, AB, 75; Simmons Col, SM, 77; Suffolk Univ, JD, 85. **CAREER** Libr, Medford Pub Libr, 75-79; Dir, Cambridge Pub Libr, 79-80; Res Libr, Dike, Bronstein, Cushman & Pfund, Boston, 80-81; Dir to Libr and Acting Dean, Northeastern Univ, 91-. **MEMBERSHIPS** AALL; ABA; ALA; SLA **RESEARCH** Teaching and learning; Legal education; Library management. **SELECTED PUBLICATIONS** Auth, "Il Project Management nelle biblioteche," in La Biblioteca Pubblica: Manuale ad Uso del Bibliotecario, Deizione Unicoplie, 99; auth, "Project Management: A Technique for Coping with Change," Law Libr J, 00; auth, KeyCite Research Guide, West Group, 00. **CONTACT ADDRESS** Sch of Law, Northeastern Univ, 400 Huntington Ave, Boston, MA 02115. **EMAIL** f.anzalone@neu.edu

APPEL, FREDERICK
PERSONAL Born, Canada **DISCIPLINE** POLITICAL SCIENCE; POLITICAL PHILOSOPHY **EDUCATION** McGill Univ, PhD, 95. **CAREER** Postdoctoral fel, Ctr for Europ Studies, 96-98; lectr, Prog for Degrees in Social Studies, Harvard Univ, 98-99; **HONORS AND AWARDS** Les Fords FCAR Postdoctoral Fel, 96-98. **MEMBERSHIPS** Amer Philos Asn; Amer Polit Sci Asn **RESEARCH** History of social and political thought (esp 19th Century); Contemporary political philosophy. **SELECTED PUBLICATIONS** Auth, Nietzsche contra Democracy, Cornell Univ Press, 98. **CONTACT ADDRESS** Social Studies Program, Harvard Univ, 59 Shepard St, Hilles Lib, Cambridge, MA 02138. **EMAIL** appel@fas.harvard.edu

APPELL, ANNETTE RUTH
DISCIPLINE INDIVIDUAL LIBERTIES, JUVENILE AND FAMILY LAW AND TRIAL PRACTICE **EDUCATION** Northwestern Univ JD, 86. **CAREER** Ed bd, Northwestern J of Int Law and Bus; atty, Sonnenschein Nath & Rosenthal, Meites, Frackman, Mulder & Burgerin, Off of the Pub Guardian of Cook County, Chicago; clin instr, atty, Northwestern Univ, 92-96; asst prof, Univ SC, Columbia, 96-98; assoc prof, mem, clin fac, Univ Nev, Las Vegas. **SELECTED PUBLICATIONS** Published extensively in the area of children's rights and family law. **CONTACT ADDRESS** Univ of Nevada, Las Vegas, Las Vegas, NV 89154.

APPIAH, KWAME ANTHONY
DISCIPLINE AFRO-AMERICAN STUDIES AND PHILOSOPHY **EDUCATION** Cambridge Univ, England, BA, PhD. **CAREER** Prof. **MEMBERSHIPS** Past pres, Socr African Philos in NAm & is an ed of Transition. **RESEARCH** Epistemology and philosophy of language; African philosophy; philosophical problems of race and racism; Afro-American and African literature and literary theory. **SELECTED PUBLICATIONS** Auth, My Father's House: Africa in the Philosophy of Culture, 92 & Color Conscious: The Political Morality of Race, 96. **CONTACT ADDRESS** Dept of Philosophy, Harvard Univ, 8 Garden St, Cambridge, MA 02138. **EMAIL** appiah@fas.harvard.edu

APPLEGATE, JUDITH K.
PERSONAL Born 10/01/1948, KS, s, 3 children **DISCIPLINE** THEOLOGY **EDUCATION** Portland State Univ, BA, 71; Western Evangel Sem, MA, 81; Earlham Sch Relig, MDiv, 82; Vanderbilt Univ, PhD, 89. **CAREER** Western Evangel Sem, adj fac, 79-81; George Fox Col, adj fac, 83; Earlham Sch of Relig, asst prof, 87-96; Center for the Prevention of Sexual and Violence, prog specialist, 96-. **HONORS AND AWARDS** Ordained Quaker Minister. **RESEARCH** New Testament; feminist studies; justice issues for women; spirituality; domestic violence; Ministerial ethics. **SELECTED PUBLICATIONS** Auth, And she wet his feet with her tears: A Feminist Interpretation of Luke 7:36-50, Marking Boundaries, Sheffield: Sheffield Acad Press, 98; auth, The Bible as Friend, Foe and Elder, Pendle Hill Study Center, Wallingford, PA, 96; auth, Women in the Gospels, Ohio Northern Univ, Ada, OH, 93; auth, The Co-Elect Woman of 1 Peter, in: New Testament Studies, 92. **CONTACT ADDRESS** PO Box 21641, Seattle, WA 98111. **EMAIL** 76677.1403@compuserve.com

APPLETON, SHELDON L.
PERSONAL Born 09/17/1933, New York, NY, m, 1956, 4 children **DISCIPLINE** POLITICAL SCIENCE **EDUCATION** New York Univ, BA, 54; MA, 86; Univ Minn, PhD, 61. **CAREER** Newswriter, Int Cooperation Admin, 55-56; officer, US Foreign Serv, 56-57; asst prof to prof, Oakland Univ 60-; assoc dean, 79-87; assoc provost, 87-93. **HONORS AND AWARDS** Regents Scholar, NY State Univ, 51-54; Ford Found Fel, 58-60; Fulbright-Hays Fel, Taiwan, 67; Teaching Excellence Awd, Oakland Univ, 82. **MEMBERSHIPS** Midwest Polit Sci Assoc; Am Polit Sci Assoc. **RESEARCH** American and Chinese Political Culture, Public Opinion and Political Psychology. **SELECTED PUBLICATIONS** Auth, The Eternal Triangle: Communist China, the U.S. and the U.N., Mich State Univ Pr, 61; auth, United States Foreign Policy, Little Brown, 68. **CONTACT ADDRESS** Dept Polit Sci, Oakland Univ, Rochester, MI 48309. **EMAIL** appleton @oakland.edu

AQUILA, RICHARD E.
PERSONAL Born 08/20/1944 **DISCIPLINE** PHILOSOPHY **EDUCATION** Harvard Univ, AB, 65; Northwestern Univ, MA, 67; PhD, 68. **CAREER** Instr, Northwestern Univ, 68; asst prof, Duke Univ, 68-74; vis asst prof, Univ Iowa, 70; from asst prof to prof, Philos, Univ Tenn, 70- . **RESEARCH** Hist of modern philos; philos of mind. **SELECTED PUBLICATIONS** Auth, Intentionality: A Study of Mental Acts, Pa State Univ Pr, 77; auth, Rhyme or Reason: A Limerick History of Philosophy, Univ Pr of Am, 81; auth, Representational Mind: A Study of Kant's Theory of Knowledge, Ind Univ Pr, 83; auth, Matter in Mind: A Study of Kant's Transcendental Deduction, Ind Univ Pr, 89; auth, "The Content of Cartesian Sensation and the Intermingling of Mind and Body," Hist Philos Quart 12 (95); auth, "Unity of Apperception and the Division of Labor in the Transcendental Anlytic," Kantian Review, 1, (98), 17-52; auth, "Sartre's Other and the Field of Consciousness: A Husserlian Reading," Eruopean Journal of Philosophy, 6, (98), 53-76. **CONTACT ADDRESS** Dept of Philos, Univ of Tennessee, Knoxville, 801 McClung Tower, Knoxville, TN 37996-0480. **EMAIL** raquila@utk.edu

AQUINO, MARIA PILAR
DISCIPLINE LIBERATION THEOLOGY AND CHRISTIAN SOCIAL ETHICS **EDUCATION** Pontifical Cath Univ of Salamanca, Spain, STD. **CAREER** Dept Theo, Univ San Diego **RESEARCH** Cath soc thought; Cath theology; feminist theologies. **SELECTED PUBLICATIONS** Ed 1 bk & auth, 2 bks and numerous articles on, the contrib of women to theol, soc, and the Church. **CONTACT ADDRESS** Dept of Theological and Relig Studies, Univ of San Diego, 5998 Alcal Park, Maher 297, San Diego, CA 92110-2492. **EMAIL** aquino@acusd.edu

ARAI, PAULA K. R.
PERSONAL Born 08/20/1960, Detroit, MI **DISCIPLINE** RELIGIOUS STUDIES **EDUCATION** Kalamazoo Col, BA, 83; Harvard Univ, MA, 87; PhD, 93. **CAREER** Asst prof, Vanderbilt Univ, 94-. **HONORS AND AWARDS** Fulbright Sen Res grant, Fulbright Dissertation grant, Am Coun of Learned Soc Res grant. **MEMBERSHIPS** Am Acad of Relig. **RESEARCH** Japanese Buddhist healing rituals, Japanese women's religious experiences, Japanese Buddhist nuns. **SELECTED PUBLICATIONS** Auth, Women Living Zen: Japanese Soto Buddhist Nuns, Oxford Univ Press, 99. **CONTACT ADDRESS** Dept Religious Studies, Vanderbilt Univ, Box 97, Station B, Nashville, TN 37235-0001. **EMAIL** p.arai@vanderbilt.edu

ARAIZA, WILLIAM
DISCIPLINE LAW **EDUCATION** Columbia Univ, BA, 83; Georgetown Univ, MS, 85; Yale Univ, JD, 90. **CAREER** Clerk, hon William Norris, US Ct of Appeals, 9th Circuit; clerk, hon David Souter, US Supreme Ct; adj, Univ Calif, LA Law Sch; vis prof, Univ Calif, Hastings Col Law, 97. **SELECTED PUBLICATIONS** Auth & coauth texts on, administrative and constitutional law. **CONTACT ADDRESS** Law School, Loyola Marymount Univ, 919 S. Albany St., Burns 310, Los Angeles, CA 90015. **EMAIL** william.araiza@lls.edu

ARAND, CHARLES P.
PERSONAL Born 04/27/1957, Amarillo, TX, m, 1980, 2 children **DISCIPLINE** THEOLOGY **EDUCATION** Concordia Col, BA, 80; Concordia Sem, MDiv, 84, STM, 87, ThD, 89. **CAREER** Pastor, St. John, New Minden & St. Luke, Covington, Ill, 84-87; asst prof, 89-95, assoc prof, systematic theol, 95-, chemn dept, 95- , asst dean fac, 96-98, fac marshall, 97- , actg dean of fac, 97, Concordia Sem; assoc vpres for acad aff, 98-. **MEMBERSHIPS** Am Acad Relig; Sixteenth-Century Stud Conf; Soc for Reformation Res. **RESEARCH** Catechisms, Luther's and Lutheran; creeds and Reformation confessions; trini-

tarian studies; Christology. **SELECTED PUBLICATIONS** Auth, Testing the Boundaries: Windows to Lutheran Identity, Concordia, 95; auth, Apology as Polemical Commentary, in Wengert, ed, Philip Melanchthon (1497-1560) and the Commentary, Sheffield, 97; auth, The Small Catechism within the Catechumenate, Lutheran Forum, 98; auth, The Life of Faith: A Theological Overview of the Small Catechism, in, Arkkila, ed, The Gospel is the Power of God: The Third International Confessional Lutheran Conference, Sley-Kirjat, 98; auth, That I May Be His Own: An Overview of Luther's Catechisms, Concordia Academic Press (St Louis, MO), 00; transl, Apology of the Augsburg Confession, in The Book of Concord: The Confessions of the Evangelical Lutheran Church, (Philadelphia: Fortress Press, 00). **CONTACT ADDRESS** Concordia Sem, 801 DeMun Ave, Saint Louis, MO 63105. **EMAIL** arandc@csl.edu

ARAV, RAMI
PERSONAL Born 10/21/1947, Israel, m, 1980, 3 children **DISCIPLINE** RELIGION **EDUCATION** Tel Aviv Univ, MA 80; New York Univ, PhD 86. **CAREER** Univ Nebraska Omaha, vis prof, 94-98; and Dir of excavations at Bethsaida. **MEMBERSHIPS** SBL; ASOR. **RESEARCH** Archaeology of the Land of Israel. **SELECTED PUBLICATIONS** Co-auth, Jesus and His World, an Archaeological and Cultural Dictionary, Fortress Pr, 95; co-ed, Bethsaida a City by the Northern Shores of the Sea of Galille, vol 1 & 2, Harry Truman Univ Pr (Mo). **CONTACT ADDRESS** Dept of Philosophy and Religion, Univ of Nebraska, Omaha, 4814 Capitol Ave, Omaha, NE 68182. **EMAIL** rarav@mail.unomaha.edu

ARBAUGH, GEORGE E.
PERSONAL Born 10/31/1933, Hartford, WI, m, 1955, 3 children **DISCIPLINE** PHILOSOPHY **EDUCATION** Augustana Col, BA, 55; State Univ Iowa, MA, 58, PhD, 59. **CAREER** From asst prof to assoc prof, 59-67, prof philos, 59-, Pac Lutheran Univ. **MEMBERSHIPS** Am Philos Assn; Soren Kierkegaard Soc. **RESEARCH** Ethics and theory of value; metaphysics and epistemology; Kierkegaard and existentialism. **SELECTED PUBLICATIONS** Coauth, Kierkegaard's Authorship, Allen & Unwin, 68. **CONTACT ADDRESS** Dept of Philosophy, Pacific Lutheran Univ, 12180 Park Ave S, Tacoma, WA 98447-0014. **EMAIL** arbaugge@plu.net

ARBINO, GARY P.
PERSONAL Born 01/16/1960, North Hollywood, CA, m **DISCIPLINE** ARCHAEOLOGY, OLD TESTAMENT INTERPRETATION **EDUCATION** Humboldt State Univ, BA; Golden Gate Baptist Theol Sem, MDiv, PhD. **CAREER** Asst curator, design dir, Marian Eakins Archaeol Col, 91-98, Curator, 98-; from adj prof to assoc prof, Golden Gate Baptist Theol Sem, 92-. **HONORS AND AWARDS** Will Edd Langford Memorial scholar, 92; Who's Who Among Students In Amer Univ(s) and Col(s), 89, 92; Broadman Seminarian Awd, 89; National Dean's List, 87, 92; supvr, sem library's audio-visual dept and video production studio, 90-96; lib circulation svc, 94-96. **MEMBERSHIPS** Mem, Am Sch(s) of Oriental Res; Soc Biblical Lit; member adv bd, Nat Asn prof(s)of Hebrew; Am Inst of Archaeol. **RESEARCH** Tel Miqne/Ekron Excavations; Bet Shemesh Excavations; Tel Rehov. **SELECTED PUBLICATIONS** Auth, New Eerdmans Dictionary of the Bible, 00. **CONTACT ADDRESS** Golden Gate Baptist Theol Sem, 201 Sem Dr, Mill Valley, CA 94941-3197. **EMAIL** garyarbino@ggbts.edu

ARCHIE, LEE C.
PERSONAL Born 06/20/1944, Houston, TX, d, 1 child **DISCIPLINE** PHILOSOPHY **EDUCATION** Austin Col, BS, 67; Univ Arkansas, MA, 72, PhD, 77. **CAREER** Lectr, Univ Arkansas, 77-78; prof, Lander Univ, 78-. **HONORS AND AWARDS** Redia essay prize, 78; prof of the year, 84. **MEMBERSHIPS** APA; Philos of Sci Assn. **RESEARCH** Philosophy of science. **SELECTED PUBLICATIONS** Auth, The No-Alternative Paradox and the Possibility of Metaphysics, Contemp Philos, 95; auth, An Analysis of the Hobbes' Game, Tchg Philos, 95. **CONTACT ADDRESS** Dept of Philosophy, Lander Univ, PO Box 6031, Greenwood, SC 29649. **EMAIL** larchie@lander.edu

ARDREY, SAUNDRA CURRY
PERSONAL Born 08/26/1953, Louisville, GA, m **DISCIPLINE** POLITICAL SCIENCE **EDUCATION** Winston-Salem State University, BA, 1975; Ohio State University, MA, 1976, PhD, 1983. **CAREER** University of North Carolina Chapel Hill, visting lecturer 1979-80; Jefferson Community College, University of Kentucky, instructor, 80-81; Furman University, asst prof 1983-88; Western Kentucky University, Dept of Government, Professor, 88-. **HONORS AND AWARDS** Western Kentucky University, Outstanding Achievement in Service Awd, 1990; Outstanding Paper Awd, National Conference of Black Political Scientists, Annual Conference, 1994; Elections Analyst for Kentucky Public TV, 1995-; campaign consultant, 1995-. **MEMBERSHIPS** American Political Science Assn, 1975-87; Natl Conference of Black Political Science, 1978-; Southern Political Science Assn, 1983-87; American Assn of University Professor, 1983-85; bd mem, Greenville City Urban League, 1983-87; Greenville City United Way, 1983-84; exec comm, Greenville City Democratic Party, 1984-85; pres, Greenville City Young Democrats, 1984-85; pres, Bowling Green NOW; NAACP, Bowling Green Branch, 1990-; Alpha Kappa Alpha Sorority, 1989-. **CONTACT ADDRESS** Dept of Govt, Western Kentucky Univ, Grise Hall, Bowling Green, KY 42101.

ARGALL, RANDALL A.
DISCIPLINE RELIGION **EDUCATION** Univ Iowa, PhD, 92. **CAREER** Asst prof, chaplain, Jamestown Col, 98- . **MEMBERSHIPS** Soc Bibl Lit. **CONTACT ADDRESS** 808 19th St NE, Jamestown, ND 58401. **EMAIL** argall@acc.jc.edu

ARGEN, RALPH J., III
PERSONAL Born 07/26/1958, Buffalo, NY, m, 1983, 3 children **DISCIPLINE** GEOLOGY; LAW; PHILOSOPHY **EDUCATION** Syracuse Univ, BS, 81; State Univ NYork Buffalo, MS, 88, MA, 89, JD, 93, PhD, 94. **CAREER** Construction mgt, Claims Consultant. **MEMBERSHIPS** PA Bar Asn; Wash DC Bar Asn. **RESEARCH** Construction law; Ethics; Environmental Ethics and Value Theory. **SELECTED PUBLICATIONS** Auth, The Commensurability of Environmental Geology and Petroleum Geology, AAPG Bulletin, vol 74, 600, May 90. **CONTACT ADDRESS** 17711 Crystal Cove Pl, Tampa, FL 33549. **EMAIL** rargenl@tampabay.rr.com

ARGRETT, LORETTA COLLINS
PERSONAL m **DISCIPLINE** LAW **EDUCATION** Howard Univ, BS, 1958; Institute Fur Organische Chemie, Technische Hochschule; Harvard Law School, JD, 1976. **CAREER** US Congress, Joint Committee on Taxation, attorney; Wald, Harkrader and Ross, attorney, partner; Howard Univ School of Law, professor; US Justice Dept, Tax Div, asst attorney general, 93-. **HONORS AND AWARDS** Greenwood Voters League, Outstanding Service and Achievement in the Field of Law, 1994. **MEMBERSHIPS** Harvard Law School, visiting committee mem, 1987-93; American Bar Foundation, fellow, 1993-; District of Columbia Bar, legal ethics committee mem, 1993-97; Univ of Baltimore Law School, Graduate Tax Program, advisory committee mem, 1986-; American Bar Assn, standing comm on ethics and professional responsibility, 1998-. **SELECTED PUBLICATIONS** Auth, Tax treatment of higher education expenditures: an unfair investment disincentive, 41 Syracuse Law Rev 621, 90 & Proposed tax incentives for education - a critique and counterproposal, 41 Tax Notes 461, 88; coauth, Settlement Reference Manual, Wash, DC, US Dept Justice, Tax Div, 96. **CONTACT ADDRESS** Assistant Attorney General, US Justice Department, 950 Pennsylvania Ave NW, Rm 4143, Washington, DC 20530.

ARKWAY, ANGELA
DISCIPLINE PHILOSOPHY **EDUCATION** Graduate Center, City Univ NYork, PhD, 95. **CAREER** Adj asst prof, 95-96, Pace Univ NY; vis asst prof, 96-97, Univ Cincinnati; adj asst prof, 97- NY Univ. **HONORS AND AWARDS** Recipient of a stipend from the NEH to participate in the Summer Seminar. **MEMBERSHIPS** APA; Soc for Phil & Psychl. **RESEARCH** Philosophy of mind; the simulation theory; the theory theory of our folk psychological practices. **SELECTED PUBLICATIONS** Art, The Simulation Theory the Theory Theory and Folk Psychological Exploration, Phil Stud, 99. **CONTACT ADDRESS** 54 Riverside Dr, Apt 7C, New York, NY 10024. **EMAIL** aarkway@nyc.rr.com

ARLEN, JENNIFER H.
PERSONAL Born Berkeley, CA **DISCIPLINE** LAW **EDUCATION** Harvard Univ, BA, 82; NYork Univ, JD, 86; Nyork Univ, PhD, 92. **CAREER** Ivadelle & Theodore Johnson prof Law & Bus, Univ Southern Calif; dir, Olin Prog in Law and Rational Choice; clerked, Honorable Phyllis Kravitch, Judge US Ct Appeals 11th Circuit; past ch, Torts Section & past ch, Law and Econ Sect Asn Amer Law Sch; dir, USC; vis prof, Calif Institute of Technology, 01. **MEMBERSHIPS** Am Law Inst; Bd of Dir Am Law & Economics Asn, 91-93. **RESEARCH** Corporate civil & criminal liability, particularly securities fraud; tort liability for death & injury; law & economics. **SELECTED PUBLICATIONS** Auth, The Potentially Perverse Effects of Corporate Criminal Liability; Vicarious Liability for Fraud in Securities Markets: Theory and Evidence; A Political Theory of Corporate Taxation. **CONTACT ADDRESS** School of Law, Univ of So California, University Park Campus, Los Angeles, CA 90089. **EMAIL** jarlen@law.usc.edu

ARMENTROUT, DONALD S.
PERSONAL Born 04/22/1959, Harrisonburg, PA, m, 1967, 3 children **DISCIPLINE** THEOLOGY **EDUCATION** Roanoke Col, BA, 61; Lutheran Theol Sem, BD, 64; Vanderbilt Univ, PhD, 70. **CAREER** From Asst Prof to Prof, Sch of Theol, 70-. **HONORS AND AWARDS** Res Excellence Awd, Concordi Hist Inst, 77; Commendation, Am Asn of St and Local Hist, 85. **MEMBERSHIPS** Am Asn of Univ Profs, Am Soc for Reformation Res, Am Soc of Church Hist, Conf of Anglican Church Historians. **RESEARCH** History of the Episcopal Church with Robert Slocum. **SELECTED PUBLICATIONS** Auth, Documents of Witness: A History of the Episcopal Church 1782-1985, Church Hymnal Corp (New York, NY), 94; auth, An Episcopal Dictionary of the Church: A User Friendly Reference for Episcopalians, Church Publ, Inc (New York, NY), 99. **CONTACT ADDRESS** Dept Theol, Sch of Theol, 335 Tennessee Ave, Sewanee, TN 37383-0001. **EMAIL** darmentr@sewanee.edu

ARMOUR, JODY D.
DISCIPLINE LAW **EDUCATION** Harvard Univ, AB,82; Univ Calif, Berkeley,86, JD. **CAREER** Prof; Univ Southern Calif; private practice; taught at, Univ Calif, Berkeley; Ind Univ & Univ Pittsburgh. **RESEARCH** Race issues in legal decision-making. **SELECTED PUBLICATIONS** Auth, Just Desserts: Narrative, Perspective, Choice & Blame; Stereotypes & Prejudice: Helping Legal Decisionmakers Break the Prejudice Habit & Negrophobia & Reasonable Racism: The Hidden Costs of Being Black in America. **CONTACT ADDRESS** School of Law, Univ of So California, University Park Campus, Los Angeles, CA 90089. **EMAIL** jarmour@law.usc.edu

ARMSTRONG, JOHN M.
PERSONAL Born 10/29/1967, Washington, DC, m, 1989, 2 children **DISCIPLINE** PHILOSOPHY **EDUCATION** Brigham Young Univ, BA, 92; Univ Ariz, MA, 95, PhD, 98. **CAREER** Asst prof, S Va Col, 98-. **HONORS AND AWARDS** William H Fink Prize for Outstanding PhD student, Dept of Philos, Univ Ariz, 96-97; Summer Scholarship, Center for the Hellenic Studies, Washington, DC, 00. **MEMBERSHIPS** Amer Philos Assoc. **RESEARCH** Ancient Greek philos; ethics. **SELECTED PUBLICATIONS** Auth, "Epicurean Justice," Phronesis, 97; auth, "Aristotle on the Philosophical Nature of Poetry," Classical Quarterly, 98. **CONTACT ADDRESS** Philos Dept, So Virginia Univ, Buena Vista, VA 24416. **EMAIL** jarmstrong@southernvirginia.edu

ARMSTRONG, SUSAN JEAN
PERSONAL Born 05/23/1941, Minneapolis, MN, 4 children **DISCIPLINE** PHILOSOPHY **EDUCATION** Bryn Mawr Col, AB, 63, PhD(philos), 76. **CAREER** Asst prof philos, Univ the Pac, 69-70; asst prof Philos, 72-76, chemn dept, 73-75, 77, assoc prof, 76-80, prof philos, Humboldt State Univ, 81-. **MEMBERSHIPS** Am Philos Asn; Soc for Women in Philos; Intl Soc for Environmental Ethics. **RESEARCH** Environmental ethics; process philosophy; feminist theory. **SELECTED PUBLICATIONS** Ed, with Richard Botzler, Environmental Ethics, McGraw-Hill, 93, 98. **CONTACT ADDRESS** Dept Philos, Humboldt State Univ, Arcata, CA 95521-6861. **EMAIL** sja@axe.humboldt.edu

ARNELLE, HUGH JESSE
PERSONAL Born 12/30/1933, New Rochelle, NY, m **DISCIPLINE** LAW **EDUCATION** PA State Univ, BA 1955; Dickinson School of Law, JD 1962; admitted to practice CA, PA, United States Supreme Court. **CAREER** AU State Univ All-Amer Basketball, 52-54; PA State Univ, honorable mention All-Amer Football 1953-54; NBA Ft Wayne Piston, 55-56; NFL Baltimore Colts, 57-58; Dept of Labor, atty 1962-63; Peace Corps, assoc dir 1963-65, dir 1965-66, staff 1966-67; FPC, asst to gen counsel 1967-68; IDEA Inc Chas F Kettering Found 1968-69; Morrison Foerster Holloway, atty 1971-73; US Dist Ct, asst federal public defender, sr partner, 85-; private practice 1973-85; Arnelle & Hastie, civil litigation & public finance atty, senior partner, 85-. **MEMBERSHIPS** Mem Coll of Civil Trial Advocacy 1976; faculty Hastings Law School Criminal Trial Advocacy 1977; mem Hall of Fame NY 1977; commissioner San Francisco Redevelopment Agency 1981-; bd of dir SF Boys Club 1981-; mem Amer Bd of Criminal Trial Lawyers 1982-; exec commissioner, bd of trustees San Francisco World Affairs Council 1983-; bd of trust PA State Univ; PA State Board of Trustees, vice chairman, 1993-; PA State Univ; dir Renaissance Fund PA State Univ; mem Charles Houston Bar Assn; life mem Natl Bar Assn, Bar of PA, CA, Bar of US Supreme Court; diplomate Hastings Law School; mem Natl Panel of Arbit, Amer Trial Lawyers Assn, Westchester County Hall of Fame; National Football Foundation Hall of Fame, 1993; adj prof Hastings Law School Coll of Advocacy; former pres Afro-American Hist Society; board of directors San Francisco Op; bd of dir Bay Area UNICEF; Corporate BoardS, Wells Fargo Bank and Wells Fargo & Co, director, 1991, FPL Groups Inc, director, 1990, Waste Management, Inc, director, 1992, University Governance, Pennsylvania State University Board of Trustees, vice-chairman, 1993. **CONTACT ADDRESS** Arnelle & Hastie, 455 Market St, San Francisco, CA 94105.

ARNESON, RICHARD J.
DISCIPLINE POLITICAL AND SOCIAL PHILOSOPHY **EDUCATION** Univ Calif-Berkeley, PhD, 75. **CAREER** Prof, Philos, Univ Calif, San Diego. **RESEARCH** Polit and social philos; Applied philos. **SELECTED PUBLICATIONS** Auth, "Democratic Rights at National and Workplace Levels," The Idea of Democracy, Cambridge Univ Press, 93; "Autonomy and Preference Formation," In Harm's Way, Cambridge Univ Press, 94; "Cracked Foundations of Liberal Equality," Dworkin and His Critics, Basil Blackwell, 95; "Against 'Complex Equality', Pluralism, Justice, and Equality," Oxford Univ Press, 95. **CONTACT ADDRESS** Dept of Philos, Univ of California, San Diego, 9500 Gilman Dr, La Jolla, CA 92093.

ARNOLD, BARRY
PERSONAL Born 09/29/1951, Mooresville, NC, m, 1984 **DISCIPLINE** PHILOSOPHY **EDUCATION** Davidson Col, AB, 73; Rice Univ, Grad Fel, 73-75; Emory Univ, M.Div, 76, PhD, 86; Univ Glasgow, Postgraduate Fel, 76. **CAREER** Prof, Andrew Col, 83-84; from asst to assoc to acting chemn to chair, 86-, Univ W Fla; Private Practice Counseling, Pace, 96-. **HONORS AND AWARDS** Phi Beta Kappa; Phi Kappa Phi; Who's Who Among Am Tchrs; Who's Who in Am.,; dist tchg award, univ w fla, 88, 90,95. **MEMBERSHIPS** Am Conseling Asn; Nat Asn Cognitive Behavorial Therapists; Am Acad Rel; Am Col Counselors. **RESEARCH** Psychoanalysis and religion; bio-ethics; alternative medicine. **SELECTED PUBLICATIONS** Auth, The Pursuit of Virtue, 88; coauth, Essays in American Ethics, 91; ed, The Reshaping of Psychoanalysis, 11 volumes. **CONTACT ADDRESS** Dept of Philosophy, Univ of West Florida, 11000 University Pky, Pensacola, FL 32514.

ARNOLD, BILL T.
PERSONAL Born 09/01/1955, Lancaster, KY, m, 1977, 3 children **DISCIPLINE** OLD TESTAMENT AND ANCIENT NEAR EASTERN STUDIES **EDUCATION** Asbury Col, BA, 77; Asbury Theol Sem, M Div, 80; Hebrew Union Col, PhD, 85. **CAREER** Assoc prof, old testament and bibl lang, Wesley Bibl Sem, 85-89; prof, old testament and bibl lang, Wesley Bible Sem, 89-91; assoc prof, old testament and semitic lang, Ashland Theol Sem, 91-93; prof, old testament and semitic lang, Ashland Theol Sem, 93-95; prof, old testament and semitic lang, Asbury Theol Sem, 95-. **HONORS AND AWARDS** Lykins Found Scholar, 77-78; Magee Christ Educ Found Scholar, 73-79; Intl Hon Soc of Theta Phi, 79; Joseph and Helen Regenstein Found fel, 80-81; S. H. and Helen R. Scheuer grad fel, 82-84; Nat Endow for the Humanities, summer stipend, 88; Eta Beta Rho, Nat Hon Soc of Students of Hebrew Lang and Culture, 92. **MEMBERSHIPS** Amer Oriental Soc; Amer Sch of Orient Res; Inst for Bibl Res; Nat Asn of the Prof of Hebrew; Soc of Bibl Lit; Wesleyan Theol Soc. **RESEARCH** Genesis; History of Israelite religion; Israelite historiography. **SELECTED PUBLICATIONS** Auth, What Has Nebuchadnezzar to do with David? On the Neo-Babylonian Period and Early Israel, Syria-Mesopotamia and the Bible, Sheffield Acad Press, 98; articles, The New Intl Dict of Old Testament Theol and Exegesis, Zondervan Publ House, 97; auth, The Use of Aramaic in the Hebrew Bible: Another Look at Bilingualism in Ezra and Daniel, Jour of Northwest Semitic Lang, 22, 2, 1-16, 96; auth, Luke's Characterizing Use of the Old Testament in the Book of Acts, 300-323, Hist, Lit, and Soc in the Book of Acts, Cambridge Univ Press, 96; auth, Age, Old (the Aged), Daniel, Theology of Manna Vision, Evang Dict of Bibl Theol, Baker Book House, 96; auth, Forms of Prophetic Speech in the Old Testament: A Summary of Claus Westermann's Contributions, Ashland Theol Jour, 27, 30-40, 95; auth, Babylonians, 43-75, Peoples of the Old Testament World, Baker Book House, 94; auth, The Weidner Chronicle and the Idea of History is Israel and Mespotamia, 129-148, Faith, Tradition, and History: Old Testament Historiography in Its Near Eastern Context, Eisenbrauns, 94. **CONTACT ADDRESS** Asbury Theol Sem, 204 N Lexington Ave, Wilmore, KY 40390-1199. **EMAIL** Bill_Arnold@ats.wilmore.ky.us

ARNOLD, CRAIG ANTHONY
PERSONAL Born 05/22/1965, Montreal, QC, Canada, m, 2000 **DISCIPLINE** LAW **EDUCATION** Univ Kans, BA, 87; Stanford Law Sch, JD, 90. **CAREER** Adj prof, Trinity Univ, 95; teaching fel, Stanford Law Sch, 95-96; asst to assoc prof, Chapman Univ, 96-. **HONORS AND AWARDS** Phi Beta Kappa; Time Mag Col Achievement Awd, 86; Harry S Truman Scholar, 85; Fel, Stanford Law Sch, 95-96; Hagman Conf Scholar, 00; Outstanding Prof of the Year, Chapman Univ, 99-00. **MEMBERSHIPS** Am Bar Assoc; Assoc of Am Law Sch; Urban Land Inst; Am Planning Assoc; Orange County Bar Assoc. **RESEARCH** Land use regulation and planning, the environmental regulation of land use and development, environmental justice, property rights, property theory, empirical analysis of land use legal problems, legal pragmatism, regulation of religious land uses and free exercise of religion, ecosystem protections and land development, property law pedagogy. **SELECTED PUBLICATIONS** Auth, "Beyond Self-Interest: Policy Entrepreneurs and Aid to the Homeless", 18 Policy Studies J 47, (89); auth, "Ignoring the Rural Underclass: The Biases of Federal Housing Policy", 2 Stanford Law and Policy Rev 191, (90): auth, "Conserving Habitats and Building Habitats: The Emerging Impact of the Endangered Species Act on Land Use Development", 10 Stanford Environ Law J 1 (91); auth, "Religious Freedom as a Civil Rights Struggle", 2 Nexus 149 (97); auth, "Planning Milagros: Environmental Justice and Land Use Regulation", 76 Denver Univ Law Rev 1 (98); auth, "Introduction and Tribute to the Honorable Deanell Reece Tacha, Inaugural Distinguished Jurist in Residence", 2 Chapman L Rev 1 (99); auth, "How Do Law Students Really Learn? Problem-Solving, Modern Pragmatism, and Property Law", 22 Seattle Univ Law Rev 891 (99); auth, "Land Use Regulation and Environmental Justice", Environ Law Reporter, (00); auth, Environmental Justice: Lessons Learned, Environ Law Inst, (forthcoming). **CONTACT ADDRESS** Sch of Law, Chapman Univ, One University Dr, Orange, CA 92866. **EMAIL** caarnold@chapman.edu

ARNOLD, PHILIP P.
DISCIPLINE RELIGION **EDUCATION** Univ Colo, BA, 85; Univ London, Inst Archaeol, MA, 86; Univ Chicago, PhD, 92. **CAREER** Asst prof, Univ Mo, Columbia, 92-95; ASST PROF AM RELIGS, SYRACUSE UNIV, 96-. **CONTACT ADDRESS** Dept of Relig, Syracuse Univ, 501 Hall Langs, Syracuse, NY 13244. **EMAIL** pparnold@syr.edu

ARNOLD, RUDOLPH P.
PERSONAL Born 05/24/1948, Harlem, NY, m **DISCIPLINE** LAW **EDUCATION** Howard Univ, BA 1970; Univ of CT, JD 1975; NYork Univ, LLM 1976. **CAREER** Aetna Life & Casualty 1971-72; Legal Aid Soc of Hartford Cty, attny 1976-81; Arnold & Hershinson, attny 1982-84; Arnold & Assoc, atty 1985-; Society for Savings Bancorp Inc, chmn, 91-93. **HONORS AND AWARDS** Natl Bar Assn, 1980-; Hartford County Bar, Pro Bond Awd, 1991. **MEMBERSHIPS** CT Bar Assn, Hartford Bar Assn; bd of dir, Urban League 1977-79; deputy mayor Hartford City Council 1979-83; bd of dir World Affairs Ctr 1983-88; chmn, Hartford Comm TV 1986-89; bd dir Soc for Savings 1987-93; Natl Bar Assn; Amer Bar Assn; lifetime mem, NAACP; dir, Natl Council for Intl Visitors 1989-92; Hartford Public Library, board of directors, 1994-; National Association Bond Lawyer; Natl Assn Securities Prof. **SELECTED PUBLICATIONS** What You Should Know About Evictions, 1981 **CONTACT ADDRESS** Arnold & Assoc, 80 Cedar Street, Hartford, CT 06106.

ARNOLD, SCOTT
PERSONAL Born 07/14/1952, York, PA, m, 1985, 2 children **DISCIPLINE** PHILOSOPHY **EDUCATION** Univ Penn, BA, 73; Univ Mass at Amherst, PhD, 79. **CAREER** Prof, Univ Ala at Birmingham, 82-; vis scholar, Social Philos and Policy Ctr, Bowling Green State Univ, 87-88; Title VIII fel, US State Dept, Hoover Inst at Stanford Univ, 90-91; vis scholar, Social Philos and Policy Ctr at Bowling Green State Univ, 92. **RESEARCH** History of philosophy; contemporary political philosophy. **SELECTED PUBLICATIONS** Auth, Marx's Radical Critique of Capitalist Society, Oxford UP, 90; The Philosophy and Economic of Market Socialism, Oxford UP, 94; co-ed, Philosophy Then and Now, Basil Blackwell; Affirmative Action and the Demands of Justice, Social Philosophy & Policy 16, 1998; The Monitoring Problem for Market Socialist Firms, in Advances in Austrian Economics, JAI Press, 1996; Capitalism, Socialism, and Equity Ownership, in Liberty for the 21st Century, Rowman & Littlefield, 1995; Market Socialism, Critical Review 6, 1993. **CONTACT ADDRESS** Dept of Philosophy, Univ of Alabama, Birmingham, 1400 University Blvd, Birmingham, AL 35294-1150. **EMAIL** sarnold@uab.edu

ARNOLD, STEVEN H.
DISCIPLINE INTERNATIONAL DEVELOPMENT THEORY **EDUCATION** Occidental Col, BA; John Hopkins Sch Adv Int Studies, MA, PhD. **CAREER** Prof, Am Univ. **HONORS AND AWARDS** Dir, Int Develop Div, dir, Hubert H. Humphrey North-South Fel Prog. **RESEARCH** International Development Theory & Institutions, Development Management, and Development Education. **SELECTED PUBLICATIONS** Auth, Responsibility Without Resources: The Dilemmas of Grassroots Managers, Grassroots Develop, 96; Our Global Vision: Development as Transformation, Educ Global Change, 91. **CONTACT ADDRESS** American Univ, 4400 Massachusetts Ave, Washington, DC 20016.

ARONOFF, MYRON J.
PERSONAL Born 03/01/1940, Kansas City, MO, m, 1962, 2 children **DISCIPLINE** ANTHROPOLOGY, POLITICAL SCIENCE **EDUCATION** Miami Univ, BA, 62; UCLA, MA, 65, PhD, 76; Manchester Univ, PhD, 69. **CAREER** Res fel, Manchester Univ, 65-69; lectr, 70-73, sr lectr, 73-76, assoc prof, 76-77, Tel Aviv Univ; assoc prof, 77-81, prof, 81-90, prof II of political science & anthropology, 90-, Rutgers Univ. **HONORS AND AWARDS** SSRC-UK 1969-71; Ford Found, 72-73; ACLS & SSRC, 82-83; Neth Inst Advan Stud fel, 74-75 & 96-97. **MEMBERSHIPS** Int Union Anthrop & Ethnol (vpres 93-2003); Am Polit Sci Asn; Am Anthrop Asn; Asn Polit & Legal Anthrop (pres 85-87); Asn Israel Stud (pres 85-87). **RESEARCH** Political culture; collective identity-ethnicity & nationalism; literature & politics; politics of espionage; Israeli culture & politics; Israel-Palestinian relations. **SELECTED PUBLICATIONS** Auth, The Spy Novels of John le Carre: Balancing Ethics and Politics, St. Martins, 99; auth, Power and Ritual in the Israel Labor Party, M E Sharpe, 93; coauth, Explaining Domestic Influences on Current Israeli Foreign Policy: The Peace Negotiations, The Brown Jour World Affairs, 96; The Peace Process and Competing Challenges to the Dominant Zionist Discourse, The Middle East Peace Process, SUNY Press, 98; Domestic Determinants of Israeli Foreign Policy: The Peace Process from the Declaration of Principles to the Oslo II Interim Agreement, The Middle East and the Peace Process: The Impact of the Oslo Accords, Univ Press Fla, 98. **CONTACT ADDRESS** Political Studies Dept, Rutgers, The State Univ of New Jersey, New Brunswick, Hickman Hall-Douglas Campus, PO Box 270, New Brunswick, NJ 08903-0270. **EMAIL** maronoff@rci.rutgers.edu

ARONOWICZ, ANNETTE
PERSONAL Born 03/09/1952, Poland **DISCIPLINE** RELIGIOUS STUDIES **EDUCATION** UCLA, PhD, 82. **CAREER** Assoc Prof, Dept of Rel Studies, Franklin and Marshall Col. **HONORS AND AWARDS** Jerusalem Fellows. **MEMBERSHIPS** AAR; ASSR; AJS. **RESEARCH** Post-war Jewish thought in France; modern religious thought. **SELECTED PUBLICATIONS** Auth, Nine Talmudic Readings by Emmanuel Uvinas, IN Univ Press, 91; Jews and Christians on Time and Eternity, Stanford, 98. **CONTACT ADDRESS** Religious Studies Dept., Franklin and Marshall Col, Box 3003, Lancaster, PA 17604. **EMAIL** A_Aronowicz@ACAD.FandM.edu

ARONSON, JAY RICHARD
PERSONAL Born 08/26/1937, New York, NY, m, 1959, 3 children **DISCIPLINE** ECONOMICS **EDUCATION** Clark Univ, AB, 59, PhD, 64; Stanford Univ, MA, 61. **CAREER** Asst prof, Worcester Polytech Inst, 61-65; asst prof to assoc prof Economics, 65-73, prof Economics, 73-84, Master of Taylor Residential Col, 84-88, Dir Martindale Ctr Study Pvt Enterprise & William L Clayton Prof Bus & Econ, Lehigh Univ, 80-; Rockefeller fel, Stanford Univ, 59-61; hon fel, 62, vis lectr Clark Univ, 64-66; vis scholar, 73, Fulbright scholar, 78 & 96, vis scholar, 91, Hon Prof, Dept Economics, 96-99, Univ York. **HONORS AND AWARDS** Lindback Awd, 68, Stabler Awd, 74, Deming Lewis Awd, 84, Hillman Serv Awd, 86, Lehigh Univ. **MEMBERSHIPS** Int Bus Asn; Asn Can Studies US; Fulbright Alumni Asn; Public Choice Soc; Royal Econ Soc; Nat Tax Asn; Am Fin Asn; Am Econ Asn. **SELECTED PUBLICATIONS** coauth "Inequality Decomposition Analysis and the Gini Coefficient Revisited," Econ Jour, 93; "Redistributial Effect and Unequal Income Tax Treatment," Econ Jour, 94; "Decomposing the Gini Coefficient to Reveal Vertical, Horizontal and Reranking Effects of Income Taxation," Nat Tax Jour, 94; Non equivalence in a Ferderalism: Dual Tax Shares, Flypaper Effects and Leviathan, Public Choice, 96; ed Management Policies in Local Government Finance, ICMA, Wash, 96. **CONTACT ADDRESS** Dept of Economics, Lehigh Univ, Bethlehem, PA 18015. **EMAIL** JRA1@lehigh.edu

ARONSON, JONATHAN DAVID
PERSONAL Born 10/28/1949, St Louis, MO, m, 1984, 2 children **DISCIPLINE** INTERNATIONAL RELATIONS **EDUCATION** Harvard AB, 71; Stanford Univ, PhD. **CAREER** Prof, Univ of Southern CA; dir School of International Relations; prof, Annenberg School for Communication. **MEMBERSHIPS** Council on Foreign Relations, Asia Society, Pacific on International Policy. **RESEARCH** International intellectual property protection; how the globalization of telecommunications networks is transforming international financial activities; International trade, international communications policy. **SELECTED PUBLICATIONS** Auth, Money and Power: Banks and the World Monetary System, Sage, 77; Debt and the Less Developed Countries, Westview, 79 & Trade in Services: Case for Open Markets, Amer Enterprises Inst, 84; coauth, Trade Talks: America Better Listen, Coun For Rel(s), 85; When Countries Talk: Trade in Telecommunication Services, Ballinger, 88; Changing Networks: Mexico's Telecommunications Options, UCSD, 89 & Managing the World Economy: The Consequences of Corporate Alliances, Coun For Rel(s), 93. **CONTACT ADDRESS** Annenberg School for Commun, Univ of So California, University Park Campus, Los Angeles, CA 90089-0281. **EMAIL** aronson@usc.edu

ARP, KRISTANA
PERSONAL Born 08/12/1951, CA, d, 1 child **DISCIPLINE** PHILOSOPHY **EDUCATION** Univ Chicago, BA, 75; Univ Calif, PhD, 87. **CAREER** Asst prof, Long Island Univ, 90-96; assoc prof, Long Island Univ, 96-; chair Philos Dept, Long Island Univ, 97-. **HONORS AND AWARDS** Univ Calif Dissertation Fel, 86-86; Univ Calif Regents' Fel, 80-81. **MEMBERSHIPS** Beauvor Circle, Ed of Newsletter, 95-97; Soc Phenomenol & Existential Philos; Am Philos Asn; Editorial board, Assoc of the Center for Advanced Res in Phenomenology; Board of Dirs of the Simone de Beauvoir Circle; New York City for Women in Philosophy 98-99. **RESEARCH** Simone de Beauvoir; Edmund Husserl; Existentialist Ethics; Phenomenology; Feminism. **SELECTED PUBLICATIONS** Auth, "Conceptions of Freedom in Beauvoir's The Ethics of Ambiguity," International Studies in Philosophy, Vol 31, No 2, 99; auth, "Beauvoir's Existentialist Ontology," Philosophy Today, Vol 43, No 3 , 99; Rev, " Elizabeth Fallaize, ed, Simone de Beauvoir: A Critical Reader," Hypatia, Vol 14, No 4, 99; auth, "Moral Obligation in Simone de Beauvoirs's The Ethics of Amiguity," Labyrinth, International Journal for Philosophy, Feminist Theory and Cultural Hermeneutics, Vol 1, No 1, 00. **CONTACT ADDRESS** Dept of Philosophy, Long Island Univ, Brooklyn, Brooklyn, NY 11201. **EMAIL** ksarp@aol.edu

ARP, ROBERT
PERSONAL Born 03/20/1970, Chicago, IL, m, 1996 **DISCIPLINE** PHILOSOPHY **EDUCATION** Catholic Univ Am, BA, 92; MA, 93. **HONORS AND AWARDS** Who's Who of Am Teachers, 00; Fel, St Louis Univ, 96-01; Basselin Scholarship, Catholic Univ, 90-93. **MEMBERSHIPS** Am Philos Asn; Hume Soc. **RESEARCH** Early Modern Philosophy; Metaphysics; Hobbes. **SELECTED PUBLICATIONS** Auth, "Hegel's

Prospect of Perpetual Peace," Dialogos, 99; auth, "Hume's Mitigated Skepticism and the Design Argument," American Catholic Philosophical Quarterly, 99; auth, "A Humean Analysis of Scotus's Conception of Infinite Being," Ideas y Valores, 99; auth, "The Quinque Viae of Thomas Hobbes," in History of Philosophy Quarterly, 99; auth, "Freud's Wretched Makeshift and Scheler's Religious Act," Journal of Philosophical Research, forthcoming; auth, "The Double Life of Justice and Injustice in Thrasymachus's Account," Polis, forthcoming. **CONTACT ADDRESS** Dept Philos, St. Louis Univ, 221 N Grand Blvd, Saint Louis, MO 63103-2006. **EMAIL** arpr@slu.edu

ARRINGTON, ROBERT LEE
PERSONAL Born 10/19/1938, Bainbridge, GA, m, 1961, 2 children **DISCIPLINE** PHILOSOPHY **EDUCATION** Vanderbilt Univ, BA, 60; Tulane Univ, MA, 62, PhD(philos), 66. **CAREER** Asst prof philos, Univ Southern Miss, 63-66; asst prof, 66-69, assoc prof, 69-79, prof philos & chmn dept, Ga State Univ, 79-, Am Coun Learned Socs fel, 74-75. **MEMBERSHIPS** Am Philos Asn; Southern Soc Philos & Psychol. **RESEARCH** Wittgenstein; philosophy of psychology; ethics. **SELECTED PUBLICATIONS** Can there be a linguistic phenomenology?, Philos Quart, 75; Rationalism, Realism, and Relativisim, Cornell Univ Press, 89; Western Ethics, Blackwell, 97; A Companion to the Philosophers, Blackwell, 98; ed, Wittgenstein ans Quine, co-ed, Routledge, 96; Criteria and entailment, Ratio, 6/79; Mechanism and calculus, Wittgenstein: Sources & Perspectives, 79; Practical reason, responsibility, and the psychopath, J Theory Social Behav, 3/79; Advertising and behavior control, J Bus Ethics, 2/82. **CONTACT ADDRESS** Dept of Philosophy, Georgia State Univ, 33 Gilmer St S E, Atlanta, GA 30303-3080. **EMAIL** phlrla@panther.gsu.edu

ARROW, DENNIS WAYNE
PERSONAL Born 07/27/1949, Chicago, IL, m **DISCIPLINE** CONSTITUTIONAL & AMERICAN INDIAN LAW **EDUCATION** George Washington Univ, BA, 70; CA Western Sch Law, JD, 74; Harvard Law Sch, LLM, 75. **CAREER** PROF LAW, OKLA CITY UNIV, 75-. **MEMBERSHIPS** OK Constitutional Rev Study Commission, 88-91; Assoc Justice, Supreme Court of the Cheyenne-Arapaho Tribes, 95-. **RESEARCH** Constitutional and Am Indian law. **SELECTED PUBLICATIONS** Auth, The Propsed Regime for the Unilateral Exploitation of the Deep Seabed, Harvard Int Law J, 80; The Customary Norm Process and the Deep Seabed, Ocean Develop & Int Law J, 81; The Dimensions of the Newly-Emergent Quasi-fundamental Right to Ballot Access, OK City Univ Law Rev, 81; The Alternative Seabed Mining Regime: 1981, Fordham Int Law J, 81 & 82; Prospective Impacts of the Draft Sea Convention, Int Property Invest J, 83; Seabeds, Sovereignty, and Objective Regimes, Fordham Inst Law J, 84; Contemporary Tensions in Constitutional Indian Law, OK City Univ Law Rev, 87; Federal Question Jurisdiction and American Indian Law, OK City Univ Law Rev, 89; The Indian Free Exercise Clause, Sovereignty Symposium, 91; Representative Government and Popular Distrust, OK City Univ Law Rev, 92; Bankruptcy Relief Against Governmental Entities, Consumer Finance Law Quart Report, 93; Oklahoma's Tribal Courts: A Prologue, The First Fifteen Years of the Modern Era, and a Glimpse of the Road Ahead, OK City Univ Law Rev, 94; Oklahoma Tribal Court Reports, vols 1-5, Native Am Legal Resource Center, 94-99; Pomobable: Postmodern Newspeak and Constitutional "Meaning" for the Uninitiated, MI Law Rev, 97; auth, Rich, Textured, and Nuanced, Constitutional Scholarship and Constitutional Messianism at the Millennium, Texas Law Rev, 99. **CONTACT ADDRESS** Sch Law, Oklahoma City Univ, 2501 N Blackwelder, Oklahoma City, OK 73106-1493.

ASCOUGH, RICHARD S.
PERSONAL Born 08/27/1962, Darlington, United Kingdom, m, 1985, 1 child **DISCIPLINE** THEOLOGY **EDUCATION** Univ of St. Michael's Col, Toronto Sch of Theol, PhD, 97. **CAREER** Asst prof, Inst of Pastoral Stud, Loyola Univ, 97- . **HONORS AND AWARDS** John M Kelly Awd, Toronto Sch of Theol, 96; Gov Gen Acad Gold Medal, Univ of St Michael's Col, 97. **MEMBERSHIPS** Chicago Soc of Bibl Res; Am Soc of Greek and Latin Epigraphy; Catholic Bibl Asn; Can Soc of Bibl Stud; Soc of Bibl Lit. **RESEARCH** New Testament; early Christianity and its social context; voluntary associations in antiquity. **SELECTED PUBLICATIONS** Auth, Rejection and Repentance: Peter and the Crowds in Luke's Passion Narrative, Biblica, 93; auth, An Analysis of the Baptismal Ritual of the Didache, Studia Liturgica, 94; auth, Narrative Technique and Generic Designation: Crowd Scenes in Luke-Acts and in Chariton, Catholic Bibl Q, 96; auth, The Completion of a Religious Duty: The Background of 2 Cor 8.1-15, New Testament Stud, 96; auth, Translocal Relationships Among Voluntary Associations and Early Christianity, J of Early Christian Stud, 97; auth, Civic Pride at Philippi: The Text-Critical Problem of Acts 16. 12, New Testament Stud, 98; auth, What Are They Saying About the Formation of Pauline Churches? Paulist, 98. **CONTACT ADDRESS** Inst of Pastoral Studies, Loyola Univ, Chicago, 6525 N Sheridan Rd, Chicago, IL 60626. **EMAIL** rascoug@luc.edu

ASHANIN, CHARLES B.
PERSONAL Born 11/15/1920, Montenegro, Yugoslavia, m, 1953, 4 children **DISCIPLINE** RELIGION HISTORY **EDUCATION** Church Col, Yugoslavia, AB, 43; Univ Glasgow, BD, 52, PhD, 55. **CAREER** Asst prof relig, Univ Col Ghana, 55-60; from assoc prof to prof relig & philos, Allen Univ, 60-65; prof, Claflin Univ, 65-67; assoc prof early church hist, 67-76, Prof Early Church Hist, Christian Theol Sem, 76-; Guest scholar, Princeton Theol Sem, 57; vis scholar & Lilly fel, Harvard Divinity Sch, 64-65; assoc ed, The Logas, 68-; fel, Woodbrooke Col, Eng, 73-74; mem, Patristic Cong Am Acad Relig. **MEMBERSHIPS** Am Soc Church Hist; Orthodox Theol Soc Am. **RESEARCH** Roman Empire and Christian Church in the IV century; history of Christian humanism from the beginning until AD 1536; philosophy of religion; religion and culture; Emperor Constantine and his age. **SELECTED PUBLICATIONS CONTACT ADDRESS** Christian Theol Sem, 1000 W 42nd St, Indianapolis, IN 46208.

ASHBURN, JOHNNY
PERSONAL Born 12/12/1945, Fayetteville, TN, m, 1970, 4 children **DISCIPLINE** BIBLICAL STUDIES, THEOLOGY **EDUCATION** Trinity Theol Sem, ThM; BA; Assemblies God Theol Sem, ThD; Belmont Univ, M Min. **CAREER** Instr, Christian Life Col, 83-. **HONORS AND AWARDS** Fel of the Sem, 87. **RESEARCH** Biblical theology, apologetics. **SELECTED PUBLICATIONS** Auth, Paradigm Shift; Left Turn from Orthodoxy, 95. **CONTACT ADDRESS** Dept Rel, Christian Life Col, 400 E Gregory St, Mount Prospect, IL 60056-2522. **EMAIL** f5mando@mindspring.com

ASHE, MARIE
DISCIPLINE LAW **EDUCATION** Clark Univ, BA, 66; Tufts Univ, MA, 71; Univ Nebr, 79. **CAREER** Law Sch, Suffolk Univ **RESEARCH** Constitutional law; criminal law; jurisprudence. **SELECTED PUBLICATIONS** Auth, Mind's Opportunity: Birthing a Poststructuralist Feminist Jurisprudence, 95; The Bell Jar and the Ghost of Ethel Rosenberg, Routlege, 95; Postmodernism, Legal Ethics, and Representation of 'Bad Mothers', Routlege, 95; Poststructuralist Feminist Jurisprudence, Univ Ca, 95; co-auth, Child Abuse: A Problem for Feminist Theory, 94. **CONTACT ADDRESS** Sch of Law, Suffolk Univ, 120 Tremont St., Boston, Boston, MA 02108-4977. **EMAIL** mashe@acad.suffolk.edu

ASHLEY, BENEDICT M.
PERSONAL Born 05/03/1915, Neodesha, KS **DISCIPLINE** PHILOSOPHY, THEOLOGY **EDUCATION** Univ Chicago, MA, 38; Univ Notre Dame, PhD(polit sci), 41; Aquinas Inst, PhD(philos), 50. **CAREER** Pres, Aquinas Inst, IL, 62-69; prof moral theol, Inst Relig & Human Develop, Univ TX Med Sch, Houston, 69-72; Prof Moral Theol, Aquinas Inst Theol, 73-, Dir, Albertus Magnus Lyceum, 62-; regent of studies, St Albert Great Prov, Dominican Fathers, 72-. **RESEARCH** Philosophy of nature and education; moral theology; medical ethics. **SELECTED PUBLICATIONS** Auth, Catholicism as a Sign System, 3 Religious Languages, Am J of Semiotics, vol 10, 93. **CONTACT ADDRESS** Aquinas Inst of Theol, 2570 Asbury Rd, Dubuque, IA 52001.

ASHLEY, JAMES MATTHEW
DISCIPLINE PHILOSOPHY OF SCIENCE **EDUCATION** St. Louis Univ, BS 82; Weston Sch of Theol, MTS, 88; Univ Chicago, PhD, 93. **CAREER** Asst prof, 93-. **RESEARCH** Science and theology; liberation theology. **SELECTED PUBLICATIONS** Auth, Interruptions: Mysticism, Theology and Politics in the Work of Johannes Baptist Metz, 98; The Turn to Spirituality? The Relationship Between Theology and Spirituality, 95; A Post-Einsteinian Settlement? On Spirituality as a Possible Border-Crossing Between Religion and the New Science, 98; ed, A Passion for God: The Mystical-Political Dimension of Christianity, 98. **CONTACT ADDRESS** History and Philosophy of Science Dept, Univ of Notre Dame, Notre Dame, IN 46556. **EMAIL** James.M.Ashley.2@nd.edu

ASHTON, DIANNE C.
PERSONAL Born 06/21/1949, Buffalo, NY, m, 1988 **DISCIPLINE** RELIGIOUS STUDIES **EDUCATION** Adelphi Univ, BA, 71; Univ MA, graduate studies, 74; Temple Univ, PhD, 86. **CAREER** Instr/grad asst, Temple Univ, 82-83, 86; instr, Col of Gen Studies, Univ PA, 87; instr, LaSalle Univ, 86-88; instr, Netyzky Inst, Gratz Col, 86-88; instr, Rutgers Univ, 88; Prof Relig (early tenure), Rowan Univ, 86-. **HONORS AND AWARDS** Nat Merit Scholarship, 67; Scholarship Awds, Temple Univ Relig Dept, 78-85; America-Holy Land Studies Int Conference, Nat Archives, Washington, DC, full stipend, 83; Franklin fel for extended res, Amer Jewish Archives, 84; PhD awarded with distinction, Temple Univ, 87; Rapoport Post Doctoral fel, Amer Jewish Archives, 88; Separately Budgeted Res Grants, Rowan Univ, 91, 92, 93, 94, 95, 96, 98; Margerite R. Jacobs Post Doctoral fel, Amer Jewish Archives, 98. **MEMBERSHIPS** Nat Assoc for Multicultural Ed, 91-94; Amer Academy Relig; Amer Studies Assoc; Assoc for Jewish Studies; Israeli Anthropology Assoc; Org of Amer Hist; Soc for the Scientific Study of Relig; Relig Res Assoc. **RESEARCH** Women in Amer Judaism and in Amer Jewish history. **SELECTED PUBLICATIONS** Auth, Four Centuries of Jewish Women's Spirituality: A Sourcebook , ed and intros with Ellen M. Umansky: Beacon Press, 92; The Feminization of Jewish Education, Transformations, v 3, no 2, fall 92; Souls Have No Sex: Philadelphia Women Who Shaped American Jewish Life, in Murray Friedman, ed When Philadelphia Was the Capital of Jewish America, Assoc Univ Presses, 93; The Philadelphia Group: A Guide to Archival and Bibliographic Collections, compiled for the Center for Amer Jewish Hist: Temple Univ, 93; Grace Aguilar and the Matriarchal Theme in Jewish Women's Spirituality, in Maurie Sacks, ed, Active Voices: Women in Jewish Culture, Univ IL Press, 95; Crossing Boundaries: The Career of Mary M. Cohen, in Amer Jewish Hist, vol 83, no 2, June 95; Recent Scholarship on American Jewry, Relig Studies Rev, vol 21, no 2, April 95; Rebecca Gratz, Amer Nat Biography, Amer Council of Learned Socs and Oxford Univ Press, 96; Rebecca Gratz, Jewish Women in America: An Historical Encyclopedia, Carlson Pubs, 97; Jewish Life in Pennsylvania, PA Hist Assoc, Ethnic Hist Series, 98; Rebecca Gratz: Women and Judaism in Antebellum America, Detroit: Wayne State Univ Press, 98. **CONTACT ADDRESS** Dept of Philos and Relig, Rowan Univ, Bruce Hall, Glassboro, NJ 08028. **EMAIL** ashtond@rowan.edu

ASHWORTH, E. JENNIFER
PERSONAL Born 10/06/1939, Sevenoaks, England **DISCIPLINE** PHILOSOPHY **EDUCATION** Cambridge Univ, BA, 60, MA, 64; Bryn Mawr Col, PhD, 65. **CAREER** From lectr to asst prof philos, Univ Man, 64-69; from asst prof to assoc prof, 69-75, Prof Philos, Univ Waterloo, 75-. **HONORS AND AWARDS** Killam Res Fel, 88-90; Fel, Royal Soc Can. **RESEARCH** Medieval and Post-Medieval Logic; Medieval Philosophy; Aquinas. **SELECTED PUBLICATIONS** Auth, Language and Logic in the Post-Medieval Period, D. Reidel, 74; The Tradition of Medieval Logic and Speculative Grammar from Anselm to the End of the Seventeenth Century: A Bibliography from 1836 Onwards, PIMS, 78; Studies in Post-Medieval Semantics, Variorum, 85; ed, Paul of Venice, Logica Magna Part II, Fascicule 8, Oxford, 88; The Routledge Encycl of Philos, 98. **CONTACT ADDRESS** Dept of Philosophy, Univ of Waterloo, Waterloo, ON, Canada N2L 3G1. **EMAIL** ejashwor@uwaterloo.ca

ASKIN, FRANK
PERSONAL Born 01/08/1932, Baltimore, MD, m, 1960, 4 children **DISCIPLINE** LAW **EDUCATION** City Col New York, BA, 66; Rutgers Univ, JD, 66. **CAREER** From asst prof to assoc prof, 66-71, prof law, Rutgers Univ, Newark, 71-, gen coun & Mem, nat bd, Am Civil Liberties Union, 69-; mem, bd gov, Soc Am Law Teachers, 73-76; spec counsel, Comt Educ & Labor, US House Rep, 76-77, special counsel, Govt Ops Comm, U.S. House Rep, 87-92. **MEMBERSHIPS** Soc Am Law Teachers; Am Civil Liberties Union. **RESEARCH** Constitutional litigation; federal courts and procedure; law and social science. **SELECTED PUBLICATIONS** Auth, The Case for Compensatory Treatment, Rutgers Law Rev, 69; Police Dossiers and Emerging Principles of First Amendment Adjudication, Stanford Law Rev, 70; Surveillance: The Social Science Perspective, Columbia Human Rights Law Rev, 72; ;Defending Rights: A Life in Law and Politics, Humanities Press, 97. **CONTACT ADDRESS** Sch of Law, Rutgers, The State Univ of New Jersey, Newark, 123 Washington St, Newark, NJ 07102-3192. **EMAIL** faskin@uinoy.rutgers.edu

ASKLAND, ANDREW
PERSONAL Born 08/16/1951, New York, NY **DISCIPLINE** PHILOSOPHY **EDUCATION** Univ of Maryland, JD, 78; Univ of Col-Boulder, PhD, 95. **CAREER** Instr, Arizona St Univ. **MEMBERSHIPS** Am Philos Asn; CO Bar Asn; MD Bar Asn; DC Bar Asn. **RESEARCH** Philosophy of law; Philosophy of economics; Professional ethics; Environmental philosophy. **SELECTED PUBLICATIONS** Auth The Tardy Berry Picker: A Criticism of the Market Metaphor for Civil Society, Publ Affairs Quart, 94; Conflicting Accounts of Equal Opportunity, Int Jour Appl Philos, 96; Fostering Market Competence, Jour of Thought, 97; The Sin of Inequality, Jour Philos Res, 98; A Justification of Compensation to the Descendants of Wrong Parties: An Intended Analogy, Pub Affairs Quart, 98. **CONTACT ADDRESS** Colllege of Law, Arizona State Univ, Box 877906, Tempe, AZ 85287-7906. **EMAIL** sandy.askland@law.asu.edu

ASPELL, PATRICK JOSEPH
PERSONAL Born 06/21/1930, Boston, MA, m, 1979, 1 child **DISCIPLINE** PHILOSOPHY, PSYCHOLOGY **EDUCATION** Oblate Col, BA, 56; Cath Univ Am, STL & MA, 57, Ph-D(philos), 59; Univ Redlands, MA, 79; US Int Univ, PhD(psychol), 82. **CAREER** From instr to assoc prof philos, Oblate Col, 59-70, chmn dept, 68-81, prof, 70-81; Lectr philos, Cath Univ Am, 61-63; vis asst prof, Univ Tex, San Antonio, 80-81; publisher, Lfewings, Ltd.; vice pres, Aspell Empowerment Enter, Inc. **MEMBERSHIPS** Christian Asn Psychol Stud. **RESEARCH** History of philosophy; theories of knowledge; metapsychol; psychol. **SELECTED PUBLICATIONS** Auth, A critique of Santayana's epistemology, Mod Schoolman, 61; Objective knowledge according to Ralph Barton Perry, New Scholasticism, 62; Plato and Anaxagoras, In: The New Cath Encycl, McGraw, 67; History of Philosophy, coauth, Readings in Ancient Western Philosophy, 70, Ancient Western Philosophy,

71, auth, Medieval Western Philosophy, 78 & Readings in Medieval Western Philosophy, 78, Appleton; auth, The Enneagram Personality Portraits: Enhancing Professional Relationships; The Enneagram Inventory and Profile, Enhancing Team Performance, Improving Problem-Solving Skills, Leadership Styles and the Enneagram, Jossey Bass; auth, What Drives You Crazy?, Human Resource Dev Press. **CONTACT ADDRESS** 247 Barbara Dr, San Antonio, TX 78216. **EMAIL** pat@aspell.com

ASUAGBOR, GREG
DISCIPLINE POLITICAL SCIENCE **EDUCATION** Univ Nev-Reno, BA (2), 87; MA, 90; PhD, 94. **CAREER** Instr-lectr, Univ Nev-Reno, 92-94; assoc prof polit sci, Bluffton Col, 96-. **HONORS AND AWARDS** Ford Found Res grant, 97. **MEMBERSHIPS** Am Polit Asn; African Student Asn; N Am Asn Cameroon Scholars. **RESEARCH** Human rights, Democratization in Africa, American foreign policy in Africa. **SELECTED PUBLICATIONS** Auth, Democratization and Modernization in a Multilingual Cameroon, Edwin Mellen Press; auth, The Anglophone Minority in Cameroon Politics: Struggles for Inclusion, (98); auth, Scandinavian Jnal of Development Alternatives and Area Studies, (99). **CONTACT ADDRESS** Dept Hist & Philos, Bluffton Col, PO Box 5619, Lima, OH 45802. **EMAIL** asuagbor@bluffton.edu

ATKINS, ROBERT
DISCIPLINE PHILOSOPHY **EDUCATION** City Col NYork, BS; Univ Calif Berkeley, MA; JD; PhD. **CAREER** Prof. **SELECTED PUBLICATIONS** Auth, pubs on philosophical and legal issues. **CONTACT ADDRESS** Philosophy Dept, Union Inst, 440 E McMillan St, Cincinnati, OH 45206-1925.

ATKINS, ROBERT A., JR.
PERSONAL Born 10/07/1949, Dallas, TX, m, 1971, 2 children **DISCIPLINE** BIBLICAL STUDIES **EDUCATION** Elmhurst Col, BA; Northwestern Univ, MDiv, PhD. **CAREER** Instr, Northwestern Univ, 73-76; Lectr, Loyola Univ, 76-78; pastor, 80-. **MEMBERSHIPS** SBL; AAR; CBA; CSBR; AACC. **RESEARCH** Psychology; Biblical studies. **SELECTED PUBLICATIONS** Auth, Egalitarian Community, Alabama, 91. **CONTACT ADDRESS** Trinity United Methodist Church, 1024 Lake Ave, Wilmette, IL 60091. **EMAIL** bobatkins@iname.com

ATKINS, STEPHEN E.
PERSONAL Born 01/29/1941, Columbia, MO, m, 1966, 2 children **DISCIPLINE** POLITICAL SCIENCE, LIBRARY SCIENCE **EDUCATION** Univ Missouri, Columbia, BA, 63, MA, 64; Univ Iowa, PhD, 76, MA, 83. **CAREER** Monograph cataloger, Library, Univ Iowa, 74-89; polit sci subject specialist, Library, Univ Ill, Urbana-Champaign, 83-89; head, collection dev, 89-97, Asst Univ Librn, 97- Texas A & M Univ. **HONORS AND AWARDS** Phi Eta Sigma; Peace Awd, ALA, 92; **MEMBERSHIPS** ALA; ACRL; LAMA. **RESEARCH** International security issues; arms control and disarmament; terrorism; atomic energy; academic library history. **SELECTED PUBLICATIONS** Auth, The Academic Library in the American University, ALA, 91; auth, Terrorism: A Reference Handbook, ABC-CLIO, 92; auth, A Historical Encyclopedia of Atomic Energy, Greenwood, 99. **CONTACT ADDRESS** 716 Royal Adelaide Dr, College Station, TX 77845. **EMAIL** s-atkins@tamu.edu

ATKINSON, CAMILLE
PERSONAL Born 05/28/1960, CA **DISCIPLINE** PHILOSOPHY **EDUCATION** New Sch for Soc Res, PhD, 98. **CAREER** Vis Asst Prof, Manhattan Col, 98-. **HONORS AND AWARDS** New Sch Fel, 96-97. **MEMBERSHIPS** APA. **RESEARCH** Hermenentics, political theory and ethics. **SELECTED PUBLICATIONS** Auth, Women, Ethics and the Workplace, Praeger (Westport, CT), 97. **CONTACT ADDRESS** Dept Philos, Manhattan Col, 4513 Manhattan Col Pkwy, Bronx, NY 10471-4004. **EMAIL** catkinso@manhattan,edu

ATKINSON, HARLEY
PERSONAL Born 06/08/1951, Grand Prarie, Canada, m, 1995, 2 children **DISCIPLINE** RELIGIOUS EDUCATION **EDUCATION** Trinity Western Univ, AA, 75; Can Bible Col, BRE, 80; Biola Univ Talbot Sch Theol, MA, 85; EdD, 89. **CAREER** Minister of Youth, Red Deer Alliance Church, 80-83; assoc prof of Christian Educ, Toccoa Falls Col, 89-. **MEMBERSHIPS** North Am Professors of Christian Educ, Youth Ministry Educators. **SELECTED PUBLICATIONS** Auth, "Dewey's Process of Reflective Thinking and Christian Education," Christian Educ J vol IX, 3 (89); auth, "Identifying Reasons for Non participation in CE Classes in CMA Churches of the South Pacific District," Christian Educ J vol XIII, 3 (93); auth, "Reinforcement in Learning: Integrating Skinner and Scripture," Christian Educ J vol XIV, 1 (93); auth, "Factors Motivating Participation in Adult Christian Education Opportunities in C & MA Churches of the South Pacific District," Christian Educ J vol XIV, 2 (94); ed, Handbook of Young Adult Religious Education, Relig Education Press (Birmingham, AL), 95; auth, Ministry With Youth In Crisis, Relig Educ Press (Birmingham, AL), 97; auth, Teaching Youth With Confidence, Evangelical Training Asn (Wheaton, IL), 00. **CONTACT ADDRESS** Dept Christian Educ, Toccoa Falls Col, PO Box 800-157, Toccoa, GA 30577.

ATLAS, JAY DAVID
PERSONAL Born 02/01/1945, Houston, TX **DISCIPLINE** PHILOSOPHY & LINGUISTICS **EDUCATION** Amherst Col, AB, 66; Princeton Univ, PhD, 76. **CAREER** Asst prof, 76-80, assoc prof Philos, 81-88, prof philos, Pomona Col, 89-, Mem common rm, Wolfson Col, Oxford, 78 & 80; vis fel, Princeton Univ, 79; sr assoc, JurEcon, Inc, 81-; res assoc, Inst Advan Study School Hist, Princeton, NJ, 82-84, 86; vis lectr, Dept Philos, Univ Hong Kong, 86; vis prof, Dept Philos, UCLA, 89-95; vis prof, Dept Dutch Ling, Univ Groningen, The Netherlands, spring 95; vis scholar, Max Planck Inst for Psycolinguistics, nijmegen, The Netherlands, 97. **MEMBERSHIPS** Am Philos Asn; Asn Symbolic Logic. **RESEARCH** Philos of lang; metaphysics; linguistics and lit theory. **SELECTED PUBLICATIONS** Auth, Frege's polymorphous concept of presupposition and its role in theory of meaning, Semantikos, 1: 29-44; Presupposition: A sematico-pragmatic account, Pragmatics Microfiche, 1.4, D13-G9, 75; Negation, ambiguity, and presupposition, Ling & Philos, 1: 321-336; On presupposing, Mind, 87: 396-411; Reference, meaning, and translation, Philos Books, 21: 129-140; coauth, It-clefts, informativeness, and logical form: Radical pragmatics, In: Radical Pragmatics, Acad Press, 81; auth, Is not logical?, Proc 11th Int Symposium on Multiple-Valued Logic, Inst Elec & Electronics Engrs, 81; Comparative adjectives and adverbials of degree, Ling & Philos, 84; Whate are negative existence statements about?, Ling & Philos, 88; Philosophy without Ambiguity: A Logico-Linguistic Essay, Clarendon Press, Oxford, 89; Only noun phrases, pseudo-negative generalized quantitatives, negative plarity items, and monotanacity, J Semantics, 96. **CONTACT ADDRESS** Dept Philos, Pomona Col, 333 N College Way, Claremont, CA 91711-6319. **EMAIL** jatlas@pomona.edu

ATLESON, JAMES B.
PERSONAL Born 09/24/1938, Akron, OH, m, 1961, 2 children **DISCIPLINE** LAW **EDUCATION** Ohio State Univ, BA, 60, JD, 62; Stanford Univ, LLM, 64. **CAREER** Asst prof, 64-69, Prof Law, Fac Law, State Univ NY Buffalo, 69-, NY Fac fels, State Univ NY, 68 & 70; Baldy fel, 74. **MEMBERSHIPS** Labor Law Group; Indust Rel Res Asn; Am Arbitration Asn; Union Dem Asn; Law & Soc Asn. **RESEARCH** Labor law; internal union democracy. **SELECTED PUBLICATIONS** Auth, NLRB & Jurisdictional Disputes, Georgetown Law Rev, 64; Union Members Right to Free Speech and Assembly, Minn Law Rev, 67; Workmen's Compensation: Third Party Actions and Apportionment of Attorneys Fees, Buffalo Law Rev, 70; Union Fines & Picket Lines, Univ Calif, Los Angeles Law Rev, 70; Disciplinary Discharges, Arbitration and NLRB Deference, Buffalo Law Rev, 71; Work Group Behavior and Wildcat Strikes, Ohio State Law J, 73; Threats to Health and Safety, Minn Law Rev, 75; coauth, & Collective Bargaining in Private Employment, Bur Not Affairs, spring 78, 2nd ed, 84; The Law of Collective Bargaining and Wartime Labor Regulation, in Miller & Cornford, eds, American Labor in the Era of World War II, Praeger, 95; Labor and the Wartime State, University of Illinois, 98. **CONTACT ADDRESS** Fac of Law, SUNY, Buffalo, J L O Hall, Buffalo, NY 14260-0001. **EMAIL** atleson@buffalo.edu

ATTERTON, PETER C.
PERSONAL Born 06/22/1961, London, England **DISCIPLINE** PHILOSOPHY **EDUCATION** Univ Essex, Colchester Eng, PhD, 86-90. **CAREER** San Diego State Univ Cal, lectr, 95-. **HONORS AND AWARDS** Brit Acad Awd **MEMBERSHIPS** APA **RESEARCH** Cont philo; Kantian ethics; hist ethics. **SELECTED PUBLICATIONS** Auth, Levinas's Skeptical Critique of Metaphysics and Anti-humanism, Philo Today, 1997, Power's Blind Struggle for Existence: Foucault, Genealogy and Darwinism, Hist of the Human Sciences Jour, 1994, Levinas and the Language of Peace: A Response to Derrida, Philo Today, 1992. **CONTACT ADDRESS** Dept of Philosophy, San Diego State Univ, 1566 Missouri St, San Diego, CA 92109-3038. **EMAIL** atterton@rohen.sdsu.edu

ATTRIDGE, HAROLD WILLIAM
PERSONAL Born 11/24/1946, New Bedford, MA, m, 1968, 2 children **DISCIPLINE** NEW TESTAMENT, PATRISTICS **EDUCATION** Boston Col, BA, 67; Cambridge Univ, BA, 69, MA, 73; Harvard Univ, PhD(New Testament), 75. **CAREER** Asst prof, 77-80, assoc Prof New Teatament, Perkins Sch Theol, Southern Methodist Univ, 80-, Harvard Univ jr fel, 74-77. **MEMBERSHIPS** Soc Bibl Lit; Cath Bibl Asn; Int Asn Coptic Studies; Am Philol Asn. **SELECTED PUBLICATIONS** Auth, P Oxy 1081 and the Sophia Jesu Christi, Enchoria, 75; co-ed, The Syrian Goddess (De Dea Syria) attributed to Lucian, 76, auth, The Interpretation of Biblical History in the Antiquitates Judaicae of Josephus, 76 & First-Century Cynicism in the Epistles of Heraclitus, 76, Scholars; contribr, Translations of the Tripartite Tractate and the Dialogue of the Savior in the Nag Hammadi Library in English, Harper, 77; co-ed, Philo of Byblos, The Phoenician History, Cath Bibl Asn, 81; The Apocalypse of Elijah, Scholars, 81. **CONTACT ADDRESS** Univ of Notre Dame, Notre Dame, IN 46556.

ATWOOD, CRAIG D.
PERSONAL Born 12/02/1960, NC, m, 4 children **DISCIPLINE** RELIGION **EDUCATION** Univ NC Chapel Hill, BA, 83; Moravian Sem, M Div, 87; Princeton Sem, PhD, 95. **CAREER** Chaplain, Moravian Col, 86-88; asst dean, Moravian Sem, 88-89; prof, relig, Salem Col, 95-. **HONORS AND AWARDS** Salem Col Summer Sabbatical grant, 97; Aldridge fel grant, Jan, 97; PTS merit scholar, 89-93; Lilly Endow grant, 88-89; David Bishop award, MTS, 87; Streetman award, 94; Magna Cum Laude grad, MTS, 87; Rotary scholar, Univ NC, 79. **MEMBERSHIPS** Amer Acad of Relig; Amer Soc of Church Hist. **RESEARCH** Moravian history; Zinzendorf. **SELECTED PUBLICATIONS** Article, Mother of All Souls: Zinzendorf's Doctrine of the Holy Spirit, Koinonia, 4, no 2, Fall, 92; article, Zinzendorf's 1749 Reprimand to the Brudergemeine, Transactions of the Moravian Hist Soc, 29, Fall, 96; Article, The Joyfulness of Death in Eighteenth Century Moravian Communities, Communal Soc, Fall, 97; article, Sleeping in the Arms of Christ: Sanctifying Sexuality in the Eighteen Century Moravian Church, Jour of the Hist of Sex, 8, no 2, Summer, 97; article, Zinzendorf's Litany of the Wounds of the Husband, Lutheran Quart, Spring, 97; article, Moravian Community and American Discommunity, The Hinge, Fall, 97; auth, "The Mother of God's People: the Adoration fo the Holy Spirit in the Eighteenth-Century Brudergemien," Church Hist, 68, (99), 886-909; auth, Always Reforming: a History of Christianity since 1300, Mercer Press, 01; ed, Handbook of Denominations in the Unitied States, 11th ed, Abingdon Press, 01; ed, Zinzendorf's Pennsylvania Sermons, Morvian Church Pub, 01. **CONTACT ADDRESS** PO Box 10548, Winston-Salem, NC 27108. **EMAIL** atwood@salem.edu

AUBLE, JOEL
DISCIPLINE PHILOSOPHY **EDUCATION** Northwestern Univ, PhD. **CAREER** Assoc prof. **RESEARCH** Critical thinking; world religions; philosophy and literature; existentialism. **SELECTED PUBLICATIONS** Auth, pubs on obligation theory and critical thinking. **CONTACT ADDRESS** Philosophy Dept, State Univ of West Georgia, Carrollton, GA 30118. **EMAIL** jauble@westga.edu

AUDI, ROBERT
DISCIPLINE ETHICS, EPISTEMOLOGY, AND PHILOSOPHY OF MIND **EDUCATION** Univ Mich, PhD, 67. **CAREER** Charles J Mach Distinguished Prof, Univ Nebr, Lincoln. **MEMBERSHIPS** Past pres, Ctr Div, Am Philos Asn. **SELECTED PUBLICATIONS** Auth, The Structure of Justification, Cambridge, 93; Acting from Virtue, Mind 104, 95; Perceptual Experience, Doxastic Practice, and the Rationality of Religious Commitment, J of Philos Res XX, 95; Ed-in-Ch, The Cambridge Dictionary of Philosophy, 95. **CONTACT ADDRESS** Univ of Nebraska, Lincoln, Lincoln, NE 68588-0417.

AUNE, BRUCE ARTHUR
PERSONAL Born 11/07/1933, Minneapolis, MN, m, 1955, 1 child **DISCIPLINE** PHILOSOPHY **EDUCATION** Univ Minn, BA, 55, MA, 57, PhD, 60. **CAREER** Prof, Univ of Mass at Amherst, 66-; prof and acting head, Univ of Mass at Amherst, 75-76; visiting prof, Mt. Holyoke Col, 76; visiting prof, Amherst Col, 83; graduate program didr, Umass, Amherst, 93-94. **HONORS AND AWARDS** John Simon Guggenheim Fel, 63-64; Resident Fel, 74-75; Dir, NEH Summer Seminar for Col Teachers, 77; Delivered Chancellor's Lecturer and awarded Chancellor's Medal, 81; Fulbright Lectr on Am Philosophy, 82; Distinguished Teacher Awd, 90. **MEMBERSHIPS** Am Philos Asn; Mind Asn. **RESEARCH** Epistemology, philosophy of mind, and ancient Greek philosophy. **SELECTED PUBLICATIONS** Auth, Knowledge, Mind, and Nature, New York: Random House, 67; auth, Rationalsim, Empiricism, and Pragmatism, New York: Random House, 70; auth, Reason and Action, Dordrecht, Holland: Reidel, 78; auth, Kant's Theory of Morals, Princeton Univ Press, 80; auth, Metaphysics: The Elements, Univ of Minn Press, 85; auth, Knowledge of the External World, London: Routledge, 90; auth, "Speaking of Selves," philosophical quarterly, 44, (94): 279-293; auth, "Haack's Evidence and Inquiry," invited critical article, Philos, and Phen, Res, LVI, No 3, 96; auth, "Chisholm on States of Affairs and Reference," in Lewis E. Hahn, ed., The Philosophy of Roderick Chisholm, LaSalle, Illinois: Open Court, Library of Living Philosophers, (97): 343-360; auth, "The Unity of Plato's Republic," Ancient Philosophy, 17, (97): 1-18. **CONTACT ADDRESS** Dept of Philosophy, Univ of Massachusetts, Amherst, 360 Bartlett Hall, Amherst, MA 01002. **EMAIL** aune@philos.umass.edu

AUNE, JAMES ARNT
DISCIPLINE PHILOSOPHY **EDUCATION** Northwestern Univ, PhD. **CAREER** Assoc prof, Texas A&M Univ. **SELECTED PUBLICATIONS** Auth, Rhetoric and Marxism; contribur, At the Intersection: Rhetoricand Cultural Studies; Refiguring Realism: International Relations and Rhetorical Practices; Argumentation and the Rhetoric of Assent; Rhetoric and Philosophy; Texts in Context; assoc ed, Commun Stud; ed, Argumentation and Advocacy. **CONTACT ADDRESS** Dept of Speech Communication, Texas A&M Univ, Col Station, College Station, TX 77843-4234.

AUNE, MICHAEL B.
PERSONAL Born 09/20/1944, Bemidji, MN, 2 children **DISCIPLINE** WORSHIP **EDUCATION** St. Olaf Col, AB; Luther

Theol Sem, MDiv; Univ Notre Dame, MA, PhD. **CAREER** Vis scholar, Linguistic Soc Am Summer Inst; instr, Cook Training Sch for Ministry, 83; prof, 78-; PLTS Dean of the Chapel, 79-82; PLTS Acad Dean, 98-. **HONORS AND AWARDS** GTU Core Doctoral fac; Dean's soc of Doctoral fel(s), GTU, 89-90; co-org, GTU Interdisciplinary Workshop on Ritual; adv coun, Word and World; exec comm, Ctr for Hermeneutical Stud, GTU. **MEMBERSHIPS** North Am Acad of Liturgy; Norwegian-Am Historical Asn. **RESEARCH** Ritual theory, liturgical theology, theological method. **SELECTED PUBLICATIONS** Auth, Religious and Social Ritual, State U of New York P, 96; To Move the Heart: Rhetoric and Ritual in the Theology of Philip Melanchthon, Christian UP, 94; rev, To Move the Heart: Rhetoric and Ritual, Theol of Philip Melanchthon. **CONTACT ADDRESS** Dept of Worship, Pacific Lutheran Theol Sem, 2770 Marin Ave, Berkeley, CA 94708-1597. **EMAIL** aune@plts.edu

AUSTIN, SCOTT
PERSONAL Born 03/10/1953, New York, NY **DISCIPLINE** ANCIENT PHILOSOPHY **EDUCATION** Yale Univ, BA, 74; Univ Tex at Austin, PhD, 79. **CAREER** Asst prof, Texas A&M Univ, 88-91 to assoc prof, 91-. **HONORS AND AWARDS** App vis fel, Princeton Univ, 99-2000; Golden Key Honor Soc, Tex A&M Asn of Former Students Fac Distinguished Tchg Awd, 95; Univ Honors Prog Awd to develop new course, 90; Univ Mini-grant, 89; Dept Res Grant, 89; Fulbright Fel, to Christ's Col, Cambridge, 83-84, Dining Rights at Christ's Col; Danforth Fel, 75-79. **SELECTED PUBLICATIONS** Auth, Parmenides: Being, Bounds, Logic, Yale UP, 86; Genesis and Motion in Parmenides: B8 12-13, Harvard Stud in Classical Philos 87, 83; Parmenides and Ultimate Reality, Ultimate Reality and Meaning 7, 84; The Paradox of Socratic Ignorance, Philosophical Topics 15, 87 & Parmenides' Reference, Classical Quart, 90; auth, "Parmenides and the Closure of the West," Am Catholic Philos Quarterly 74(00). **CONTACT ADDRESS** Dept of Philosophy, Texas A&M Univ, Col Station, 309E Bolton Hall, College Station, TX 77843-4237. **EMAIL** s-austin@tamu.edu

AUSTIN, WILLIAM H.
PERSONAL Born 04/10/1936, Peru, IN, d **DISCIPLINE** PHILOSOPHY **EDUCATION** Wesleyan Univ, BA, 57; Yale Univ, BD, 60; PhD, 66. **CAREER** Instr to Asst Prof, Rice Univ, 64-73; Assoc Prof to Prof, Univ of Houston, 74-. **HONORS AND AWARDS** NEH Younger Humanist Fel, 72-73; Course Awd, Templeton Sci & Relig Course Prog, 96. **MEMBERSHIPS** Am Philos Asn, Am Acad of Relig. **RESEARCH** Philosophy and History of Science, Philosophy and History of Religion. **SELECTED PUBLICATIONS** Auth, Waves, Particles, and Paradoxes, Rice Univ Studies LIII,2, 67; auth, "Isaac Newton on Science and Religion," J of the Hist of Ideas XXXI (70): 521-542; auth, "Paradigms, Rationality, and Partial Communication," J for Gen Philos of Sci III (72): 203-218; auth, "Religious Commitment and the Logical Status of Doctrines," Relig Studies IX (73): 39-48; auth, The Relevance of Natural Science to Theology, Barnes and Noble (NY) and Macmillan (London), 76; auth, "Rational Credibility and Causal Explanations of Belief," Neue Zeitschrift fur Systematische Theologie und Religionsphilosophie XXVI (84): 116-133; auth, "Evolutionary Explanations of Religion and Morality: Explaining Religion Away?," in Evolution and Creation, ed. Ernan McMullin (Notre Dame: Univ of Notre Dame Press, 85), 252-272; auth, "Explanatory Pluralism," J of Am Acad of Rel LXVI (98): 13-37. **CONTACT ADDRESS** Dept Philos, Univ of Houston, Houston, TX 77204-3785. **EMAIL** waustin@uh.edu

AVAKUMOVIC, IVAN
PERSONAL Born 08/22/1926, Belgrade, Yugoslavia, m, 1957, 1 child **DISCIPLINE** MODERN HISTORY, POLITICAL SCIENCE **EDUCATION** Cambridge Univ, BA, 47, MA, 52; Univ London, MA, 54; Oxford Univ, DPhil(soc sci), 58. **CAREER** Asst lectr polit, Aberdeen Univ, 57-58; from asst prof to assoc prof polit sci & int rels, Univ Man, 58-63; from assoc prof to prof polit sci, 63-69, Prof Hist, Univ BC, 69-, Can Coun leave fel, 68-69; Killam Sr Fel, Killam Found, 76-77. **MEMBERSHIPS** AHA; Am Asn Advan Slavic Studies; Am Polit Sci Asn; Can Hist Asn. **RESEARCH** Movements of social dissent; East European politics and history; international relations. **SELECTED PUBLICATIONS** Coauth, The Anarchist Prince--A Biographical Study of Peter Kropotkin, Boardman, London & NY, 50; auth, The Communist Party in Canada: a history, by Ivan Avakumovic; coauth, Peter Kropotkin: From Prince to Rebel, by George Woodcock, Ivan Avakumovic, 90. **CONTACT ADDRESS** Dept of Hist, Univ of British Columbia, 1873 E Mall, Ste 1297, Vancouver, BC, Canada V6T 1Z1.

AVERILL, EDWARD W.
DISCIPLINE PHILOSOPHY **EDUCATION** Harvard Univ, BA; UCLA, Santa Barbara, MS, PhD. **CAREER** Prof, TX Tech Univ, 80-. **RESEARCH** Philosophical psychol; philos of lang. **SELECTED PUBLICATIONS** Auth, Are Physical Properties Dispositions?, The Philos of Sci; Color and the Anthropocentric Problem, The J of Philos; The Primary-Secondary Quality Distinction, The Philos Rev; The Relational Nature of Color, The Philos Rev. **CONTACT ADDRESS** Texas Tech Univ, Lubbock, TX 79409-5015. **EMAIL** avewa@ttacs.ttu.edu

AVERY, MICHAEL
PERSONAL Born 12/05/1944, Chicago, IL, m, 3 children **DISCIPLINE** LEGAL STUDIES **EDUCATION** Yale, BA, 66, LLB, 70. **CAREER** Staff lawyer, ACLU, 70-71; private law practice, 71-98; assoc prof, Suffolk Law, 98-. **MEMBERSHIPS** Nat Lawyers Guild. **RESEARCH** Civil rights, evidence, forensic science. **SELECTED PUBLICATIONS** Auth, "Police chases: More Deadly than a Speeding Bullet?," Trial Magazine (Sept 97); coauth with Avery, Rudovsky & Blum, Police misconduct law and litigation, West Group; coauth with Liacos and Brodiil, Handbook of Massachusetts Evidence, Aspen; auth, "Laudry vs Attorney General: DNA Databanks Hold a Mortgage on Property Rights," Boston B J 18 (Jan 2000): 44. **CONTACT ADDRESS** Sch Law, Suffolk Univ, 41 Temple St, Boston, MA 02114-4241. **EMAIL** mavery@acad.suffolk.edu

AVERY-PECK, ALAN
PERSONAL Born 06/26/1953, Chicago, IL, m, 1981, 3 children **DISCIPLINE** RELIGION **EDUCATION** Univ Ill, BA, 75; Brown Univ, PhD, 81. **CAREER** Visiting Asst Prof to Prof, Tulane Univ, 81-93; Prof, Col of the Holy Cross, 93-. **HONORS AND AWARDS** Eta Beta Rho, 75; Brown Univ Fel, 77-78; Summer Res Grant, Brown Center, 81; Hewlett-Mellon Grant, Col of the Holy Cross, 96; Mellon Grant, Col of the Holy Cross, 97. **MEMBERSHIPS** Am Acad of Relig, Soc of Biblical Literature **RESEARCH** Hist and Lit of Early Rabbinic Judaism. **SELECTED PUBLICATIONS** Auth, The Talmud of Babylonia. An American Translation. Vol VII. Tractate Besah, Scholars Press, 86; auth, The Talmud of the Land of Israel. A Preliminary Translation and Explanation. Vol V. Tractate Besah, Univ Chicago Press, 99; auth, The Talmud of Babylonia. An American Translation. Vol V. Tractate Rosh Hashanah, Scholars Press, 95; ed, The annual of Rabbinic Judaism: Ancient, Medieval, and Modern Vol, Brill Pub, 99; co-ed, The Encyclopedia of Judaism, Continuum Intl Pub, 00; co-ed, Judaism in Late Antiquity. Vol four. Special Topics: death, Afterlife, Resurrection, and the world to Come, Brill Pub, 00; auth, "The Politics of the Mishnah in its Contemporary Context," in Religion and the Political Order: Politics in Classical and contemporary Christianity, Islam and Judaism, Scholars Press, 96; auth, "The Exodus in Jewish Faith: The Problem of God's Intervention in History," in The annual of rabbinic Judaism: Ancient, Medieval, and Modern, Brill Pub, 98, vol. 2, 99, vol. 3, 00. **CONTACT ADDRESS** Dept Relig Studies, Col of the Holy Cross, 1 College St, Worcester, MA 01610-2322. **EMAIL** aavery@holycross.edu

AWN, PETER
DISCIPLINE RELIGION **EDUCATION** Harvard Univ, PhD, 78. **CAREER** Prof. **HONORS AND AWARDS** Phillip and Ruth Hettleman Awd. **MEMBERSHIPS** Am Council Learned Soc. **SELECTED PUBLICATIONS** Auth, Satan's Tragedy and Redemption: Ibls in Sufi Psychology. **CONTACT ADDRESS** Dept of Religion, Columbia Col, New York, 2960 Broadway, New York, NY 10027-6902. **EMAIL** awn@columbia.edu

AXINN, SIDNEY
PERSONAL Born 01/30/1923, New York, NY, m, 1947, 2 children **DISCIPLINE** PHILOSOPHY **EDUCATION** Univ PA, AB, 47, PhD(philos), 55. **CAREER** From instr to assoc prof, 49-63, chmn dept, 52-67, Prof Philos, Temple Univ, 63-, Adj Prof Psychiat Philos, Sch Med, Temple Univ, 65-. **MEMBERSHIPS** Am Philos Asn; Asn Polit & Legal Philos; Asn Philos Law & Soc Philos. **RESEARCH** Philosophy of science; social ethics; history of philosophy. **SELECTED PUBLICATIONS** Auth, Two Concepts of Optimism, Philos Sci, 54; Kant, Logic, and the Concept of Mankind, Ethics, 58; Fallacy of the Single Risk, Philos Sci, 66; Kant and the Moral Antinomy, Ottawa Kant Cong, Ottawa Univ, 76; coauth, On the Logic of the Ignorance Relations, Am Philos Quart, 76; auth, Kant and Goodman on Possible Individuals, Monist, 78; Philip P. Wiener, 1905-1992-Obituary, J of the History of Ideas, Vol 54, 93. **CONTACT ADDRESS** Dept of Philos, Temple Univ, 728 Anderson Hall, Philadelphia, PA 19122. **EMAIL** axinn@chuma.cas.usf.edu

AXTELL, G. S.
PERSONAL Born 06/05/1957, Oakland, CA, m, 1994 **DISCIPLINE** PHILOSOPHY **EDUCATION** Univ Hawaii, PhD, 91 **CAREER** Univ Nevada, 92- **HONORS AND AWARDS** NEH Fel; Board of Ed Consultants, Amer Philos Quarterly, 1997-2000; Certificate Merit, Ntl Judicial Col, 93 **MEMBERSHIPS** Amer Philos Assoc; Soc Advancement Amer Philos; Philos Sci Assoc; 4S Soc; Hist Sci Soc; Amer Soc Value Inquiry; N Amer Soc Social Philos; Int Soc Chinese Philos; Soc Asian Comparative Philos **RESEARCH** American Philosophy; Dewey; James; Epistemology; Philosophy of Religion; Asian Traditions of India; China & Japan; Social & Political Thought **SELECTED PUBLICATIONS** Auth, "The Role of the Intellectual Virtues in the Reunification of Epistemology," Monist, 98; auth, "Recent Work on Virtue Epistemology," Amer Philos Quarterly, 97; auth, "Epistemic Virtue-Talk: The Reemergence of American Axiology?," Jrnl Speculative Philos, 96; auth, Knowledge, Belief, and Character: Readings in Contemporary Virtue Epistemology, Rowman & Littlefield, 00; auth, "Teaching James" "The Will to Believe" in Teaching Philosophy, 01; ed, "Epistemic Luck in Light of the Virtues" in Virtue Epistmology, Linda Zagzebski, Oxford Univ Press, 01. **CONTACT ADDRESS** Dept Philos/102, Univ of Nevada, Reno, Reno, NV 89557-0056. **EMAIL** axtell@unr.nevada.edu

AYDEDE, MURAT
PERSONAL Born 08/18/1961, Ankara, Turkey, m, 1982, 1 child **DISCIPLINE** PHILOSOPHY **EDUCATION** Bogazici Univ, BA, 86; Univ MD Col Park, PhD, 93. **CAREER** Stanford Univ, vis Scholar, 93-94; Xerox PARC Consult, 93-94; Univ Chicago, asst prof 94-. **MEMBERSHIPS** APA, SPP, SSPP **RESEARCH** Philo of Mind; Psych; Philo Lang. **SELECTED PUBLICATIONS** Auth, Language of Thought Hypothesis, in: Stanford Encycl of Philo, ed E. Zalta, Stanford: CSLI Pub, 98; Aristotle on Episteme and Nous: The Posterior Analytics, South Jour of Philo 98; Has Fodor Really Changed His Mind on Narrow Content, Mind and Lang, 97; Pure Informational Semantics and the Broad; Narrow Dichotomy, in Maribor Papers in Nat Sem, ed Dunja Jutronic, Maribor Univ Press, 97; Language of Thought: The Connectionist Contribution, Mind and Lang, 97; On the Relation Between Phenomenal and Representational Properties, Brain and Behav Sciences, 97. **CONTACT ADDRESS** Dept of Philosophy, Univ of Chicago, 1050 E 59th St, Chicago, IL 60637. **EMAIL** m-aydede@uchicago.edu

AYERS, JAMES R.
PERSONAL Born 01/06/1953, Hanover, PA, m, 1972, 3 children **DISCIPLINE** RELIGION **EDUCATION** Lancaster Bible Col, BS, 80; Rider Col, MA, 85; Oxford Grad Sch, MLitt, 91, DPhil, 92. **CAREER** Dir, Phila Col of Bible, 80-86; Sen Pastor, Easton Union Church, 86-93; chemn, 93-, dir, 94-, Lancaster Bible Col; Chairman, Pastoral Dept, Dir Center for Church Leadership. **HONORS AND AWARDS** Oxford Chalice Awd, 92; Who's Who Among Am Tchrs, 95. **MEMBERSHIPS** Evangelical Theol Society **RESEARCH** AIDS; church ministries **SELECTED PUBLICATIONS** Auth, Confronting the Youth Crisis, 85; auth, The Quagmire of HIV/AIDS Related Issues Which Haunt the Church, 95; auth, Focus on Fatherhood, 95; auth, Revitalizing the Church, 96. **CONTACT ADDRESS** 5842 Clarkson Dr, East Petersburg, PA 17520. **EMAIL** jayers@lbc.edu

B

BAADE, HANS WOLFGANG
PERSONAL Born 12/16/1929, Berlin, Germany, m, 1957, 2 children **DISCIPLINE** LAW **EDUCATION** Syracuse Univ, AB, 49; Univ Kiel, Dr iur, 51; Duke Univ, LLB & LLM, 55; Hague Acad Int Law, dipl, 56. **CAREER** Res assoc int law, Univ Kiel, 55-60; from assoc prof to prof law, Duke Univ, 60-70; prof, Univ Toronto, 70-71; Albert Sidney Burleson prof, 71-75, Hugh Lamar Stone Chair Civil Law, Univ TX, Austin, 75-, Ed secy, Jahrbuch Int Recht, 56-60; Privatdozent, Univ Kiel, 60; ed, Law & Contemp Problems, 61-65; dir, Am Asn Comp Studies Law, 61-; chmn, comt regional affairs, Am Soc Int Law, 67-68; consult, proj group on govt reform, WGer Fed Ministry of Interior, 69; consult, Spanish & Mexican water law, State of TX, 80. **MEMBERSHIPS** Am Asn Comp Studies Law; Am Foreign Law Asn; Am Soc Int Law. **RESEARCH** Public international and comparative law; Southwestern legal history; conflict of laws; Roman Law in the Water, Mineral and Public Land Law of the Southwestern United-States, Am J of Comparative Law, Vol 40, 92; Time and Meaning-Notes on the Intertemporal La of Statutory Construction and Constitutional Interpretation, Am J of Comparative Law, Vol 43, 95. **CONTACT ADDRESS** School of Law, Univ of Texas, Austin, Austin, TX 78712.

BABBITT, SUSAN
DISCIPLINE PHILOSOPHY **EDUCATION** Univ Ottawa, BA; Cornell Univ, MA; PhD. **CAREER** Dept Philos, Queen's Univ **RESEARCH** Contemporary moral philosophy; philosophy of science. **SELECTED PUBLICATIONS** Auth, Impossible Dreams: Rationality, Integrity and Moral Imagination, Westview, 96. **CONTACT ADDRESS** Philosophy Dept, Queen's Univ at Kingston, Kingston, ON, Canada K7L 3N6. **EMAIL** babbitts@post.queensu.ca

BABCOCK, BARBARA ALLEN
PERSONAL Born 07/06/1938, Washington, DC, m, 1979, 0 child **DISCIPLINE** LAW **EDUCATION** Univ PA, AB, 60; Yale Law Sch, LLB, 63. **CAREER** Law clerk to Judge Henry W Edgerton, US Ct Appeals, Washington, DC, 63; assoc, Edward Bennet Williams, Washington, DC, 64-66; staff atty, Legal Aid Agency, Washington, DC, 66-68; dir, Pub Defender Serv, Washington, DC, 68-72; assoc prof, prof law, 72-77, Stanford Law Sch; Asst atty gen, Civil Div, Dept Justice, Washington, DC, 77-79; Ernest W. McFarland Prof of Law, 79-98; Judge John Crown Prof of Law, Stanford Law Sch, 98-. **HONORS AND AWARDS** Mcfarland Prof, 77-96; Judge John Crown Prof, 96-;Margaret Brent Women Lawyers of Achievement Awd; J.D., Honora Causa, Univ of Pudget Sound School of Law; J.D., Honora causa, Univ of Sand Diego School of

Law; Soc of Am Law Teachers Ward for Distinguished Teaching and Service; Hurlbut Awd for Excellence in Teaching, Stanford Law Sch, 80, 84, 98; Associated Students of Stanford Teaching Awd for Excellence in Teaching; Phi Beta Kappa, 60; Woodrow Wilson scholar, 60; Harlan Fiske Stone prize, 63; Order of the Coif, 63. **RESEARCH** Women's Legal History. **SELECTED PUBLICATIONS** Coauth, Civil Procedure: Cases and Comments on the Process of Adjudication, Little, Brown, & Co, 76, 83; coauth, Sex Discrimination and the Law: History, Practice and Theory, Little, Brown & Co, 76, 96; auth, "Reconstructing the Person: The Case of Clara Shortridge Foltz," in Revealing Lives: Autobiography, Biography, and Gender, ed. Susan Groag Bell and Marilyn Yalom (90); auth, "Jury Service and Community Representation," in Verdict, ed. Robert E. Litan (The Brookings Institution, 93); auth, "In Defense of the Criminal Jury," in Postmortem: the O.J. Simpson Case, ed. Jeffrey Abramson (96); coauth, Civil Procedure: Cases and Problems, Little, Brown & Co., 97; auth, "Feminist Lawyers," Standford Law Review 50, 98; coauth, Civil Procedure: Cases and Problems, Aspen Law and Business, 01; auth, "Women Defenders," Univ of Nebraska L.V.L. Review (forthcoming); auth, biography of Clara Shortridge Foltz (forthcoming). **CONTACT ADDRESS** Stanford Law Sch, Stanford Univ, Stanford, CA 94305-1926.

BABCOCK, WILLIAM SUMMER
PERSONAL Born 06/18/1939, Boston, MA, m, 1960, 2 children **DISCIPLINE** CHURCH HISTORY **EDUCATION** Brown Univ, AB, 61; Yale Univ, MA, 65, PhD(relig studies), 71. **CAREER** From instr to asst prof, 67-91; Am Coun Learned Socs studies fel, 73-74; Dir, graduate program in religious studies, 90-; Assoc Prof Church Hist, Perkins Sch Theol, Southern Methodist Univ, 91-; Provost ad interim and VP for Academic Affairs, 95-96. **MEMBERSHIPS** Am Soc Church Hist; Mediaeval Acad Am; NAm Patristics Soc; Am Cath Hist Asn. **RESEARCH** Augustine; Latin Patristics; history of Christian theology. **SELECTED PUBLICATIONS** Auth, Grace, Freedom and Justice: Augustine and the Christian Tradition, summer 73 & Patterns of Roman Selfbood: Marcus Aurelius and Augustine of Hippo, fall 74, Perkins Sch Theol J; Augustine's Interpretation of Romans (AD 394-396), Augustinian Studies 19, 79; Agustin y Ticonio: sobre la appropriacion latina de Pablo, Augustinus, 7-12/81; Art and Architecture, Christian, In: Abingdon Dict of Living Religions, 81; auth, Augustine on Sin and Moral Agency, J Religious Ethics 16, 88; Tyconius: The Book of Rules, 89; ed, Paul and the Legacies of Paul, 90; auth, Cupiditas and Caritas: The Early Augustine on Love and Human Fulfillment, In: The Ethics of st. Augustine, 91; auth, Augustine and the Spirituality of Desire, Augustinian Studies 25 (94); Is There Only One True Religion or Are There Many, with S. M. Ogden, Theology Today, Vol 50, 94; auth, Sin and Punishment: The early Augustine on Evil, In: Augustine: Presbyter Factus Sum, 94. **CONTACT ADDRESS** Perkins Sch of Theol, So Methodist Univ, Dallas, TX 75275. **EMAIL** wbabcock@mail.smu.edu

BABER, HARRIET ERICA
PERSONAL Born 01/06/1950, Paterson, NJ, m, 1972, 3 children **DISCIPLINE** PHILOSOPHY **EDUCATION** Lake Forest Col, BA, 71; Johns Hopkins Univ, MA, 76, PhD, 80. **CAREER** Instr philos, Northern IL Univ, 80-81; from asst prof to assoc prof, 81-92, prof philos, Univ San Diego, 92. **MEMBERSHIPS** Am Philos Asn; Soc Christian Philosophers. **RESEARCH** Metaphysics; philos of mind; philosophical theol. **SELECTED PUBLICATIONS** Auth, The lifetime language, Philos Studies. **CONTACT ADDRESS** Dept of Philos, Univ of San Diego, 5998 Alcala Park, San Diego, CA 92110. **EMAIL** baber@acusd.edu

BABICH, BABETTE E.
PERSONAL Born 11/14/1956, New York, NY, s **DISCIPLINE** PHILOSOPHY **EDUCATION** SUNY - Stonybrook, BA; Boston Col, PhD, 87. **CAREER** Vis Asst Prof, Denison Univ, 87-88; Asst Prof, Marquette Univ, 88-89; Assoc Prof, Fordham Univ, 89-; Adj Res Prof, Georgetown Univ, 97-. **HONORS AND AWARDS** Fulbright Fel, 83-85; Fulbright Prof, 91-91. **MEMBERSHIPS** Am Philos Asn; Soc Philos and Eng. **RESEARCH** Philosophy of science and technology; aesthetics; antiquity. **SELECTED PUBLICATIONS** Auth, Nietzsche's Philosophy of Science: Reflecting Science on the Ground of Art and Life, SUNY Press, 94; ed, From Phenomenology to Thought, Errancy, and Desire: Essays in Honor of William J. Richardson, S.J., Dordrecht, 95; co-ed, Continental and Postmodern Perspectives in the Philosophy of Science, Avebury, 95; Nietzsche and the Sciences, Boston Studies in the Philosophy of Science, Kluwer (forthcoming 97); Heidegger's Philosophy of Science (in prep); author of numerous articles. **CONTACT ADDRESS** Dept Philosophy, Fordham Univ, 113 W. 60th St., New York, NY 10023. **EMAIL** babich@mary.fordham.edu

BABLER, JOHN
PERSONAL Born Dallas, TX, m, 8 children **DISCIPLINE** SOCIAL WORK AND MINISTRY-BASED EVANGELISM **EDUCATION** UT Dallas, BGS, 83; Southwestern Baptist Theol Sem, MACSS, 89, PhD, 95; UTA, MSSW, 89. **CAREER** Adj prof, 92-95; asst prof, Southwestern Baptist Theol Sem, 95-. **HONORS AND AWARDS** Who's Who Among Am Col Univ Students; Who's Who Among Am Teachers; soc work coord, huguley hospice; prog dir, childrens's home. **MEMBERSHIPS** National Assoc of Nouthetic Counselors; North Am Assoc of Christians in Social Work. **RESEARCH** Ministry based Evangolism, Hospice, Biblical Cnslg. **SELECTED PUBLICATIONS** Auth, Hospice: An Opportunity for Truly Wholistic Social Work, Christianity and Soc Work, NACSW, 98; A Comparison of Spiritual Care Provided by Hospice Social Workers, Nurses, and Spiritual Care Professionals, Hospice Jour, 97. **CONTACT ADDRESS** Sch Edu Ministries, Southwestern Baptist Theol Sem, PO Box 22000, Fort Worth, TX 76122-0297. **EMAIL** jeb@swbts.edu

BACCHIOCCHI, SAMUELE
PERSONAL Born Rome, Italy **DISCIPLINE** THEOLOGY AND CHURCH HISTORY **EDUCATION** Newbold Col, Eng, BA; Andrews Univ, BD, MA; Pontifical Gregorian Univ, Ital, PhD, summa cum laude, 74. **CAREER** Prof, Andrews Univ. **HONORS AND AWARDS** Gold medal, Pope Paul VI. **SELECTED PUBLICATIONS** Auth, Immortality or Resurrection? A Biblical Study on Human Nature and Destiny; From Sabbath to Sunday: A Historical Investigation of the Rise of Sunday Observance in Early Christianity; Divine Rest for Human Restlessness: A Theological Study of the Good News of the Sabbath for Today; The Sabbath in the New Testament. Answers to Questions; God's Festivals in Scripture and History, Vol I: The Spring Festivals; God's Festivals in Scripture and History, Vol 2: The Fall Festivals; Wine in the Bible: A Biblical Study on the Use of Alcoholic Beverages; The Advent Hope for Human Hopelessness. A Theological Study of the Meaning of the Second Advent for Today; Women in the Church: A Biblical Study on the Role of Women in the Church; Christian Dress and Adornment; Hal Lindsey's Prophetic Jigsaw Puzzle: Five Predictions that Failed!; The Time of the Crucifixion and the Resurrection; The Marriage Covenant: A Biblical Study on Marriage, Divorce, and Remarriage. **CONTACT ADDRESS** Andrews Univ, Berrien Springs, MI 49104-0180.

BACH, KENT
PERSONAL Born 07/10/1943, San Francisco, CA, m, 1984, 2 children **DISCIPLINE** PHILOSOPHY **EDUCATION** Harvard, AB, 64; UC-Berkeley, PhD, 68. **CAREER** Tchg asst, UC-Berkeley, 64-67; asst prof, Univ Nebraska, 68-69; asst to assoc to full prof, San Francisco State Univ, 69-. **MEMBERSHIPS** Am Philos Asn; Soc Philos & Psychol; AAUP. **RESEARCH** Philosophy of language; Theory of knowledge, Philosophy of mind. **SELECTED PUBLICATIONS** Auth Meaning, speech acts, and communication, Basic Topics in the Philosophy of Language, Prentice-Hall, 94; Emotional disorder and attention, Philosophical Psychopathy, MIT Press, 94; Semantic slack: What is said and more, Foundations of Speech Act Theory, Routledge, 94; Conversational impliciture, Mind & Language, 94; Terms of agreement, Ethics, 95; Do belief reports report beliefs?, Pac Philos Quart, 97; assorted entries Cambridge Dictionary of Philos, Oxford Companion to Philoso, Routledge Encyclo of Philos, MIT Encyclo of Cognitive Sci; auth, "Apparent paradoxes of self-deception," in Self-Deception and Paradoxes of Rationality, ed. by J.P. Dupuy, (CSLI Publications, Stanford Univ, 99); auth, "The semantics-pragmatics distinction: What it is and why it matters," in The Semantics-Pragmatics Interface from Different Points of View, Elsevier, (99); auth, "The myth of conventional implicature," Linguistics and Philosohy, 99; auth, "Quantificaiton, qualifiction, and context," Mind & Language, 00; auth, "You don't say?," Synthese, 01. **CONTACT ADDRESS** Dept of Philosophy, San Francisco State Univ, San Francisco, CA 94132. **EMAIL** kbach@sfsu.edu

BACH, SHIRLEY
DISCIPLINE PHILOSOPHY **EDUCATION** Univ Wis, PhD. **CAREER** Prof, W Mich Univ. **SELECTED PUBLICATIONS** Auth, Social Biology, Kendall/Hunt. **CONTACT ADDRESS** Philos Dept, Western Michigan Univ, 320 Moore Hall, 1903 W Michigan Ave, Kalamazoo, MI 49008-5328. **EMAIL** shirley.bach@wmich.edu

BACHE, CHRISTOPHER MARTIN
PERSONAL Born 07/04/1949, Vicksburg, MS, d, 3 children **DISCIPLINE** PSYCHOLOGY & PHILOSOPHY OF RELIGION **EDUCATION** Univ Notre Dame, AB, 71; Cambridge Univ, MA, 73; Brown Univ, PhD(philos relig), 78. **CAREER** Dir of Transformative Learning, Institute of Noetic Sciences. **HONORS AND AWARDS** Distinguished Prof, Youngstown State Univ, 82. **MEMBERSHIPS** Am Acad Relig; Asn Transpersonal Psychol; Soc Sci Study Relig; Am Philos Asn. **RESEARCH** LSD psychotherapy and the critical study of mysticism; the philosophical implications of nonordinary states of consciousness. **SELECTED PUBLICATIONS** Auth, Lifecycles: Reincarnation & the Web of Life, 90; Dark Night, Early Dawn: Steps to The Deep Ecology of Mind. **CONTACT ADDRESS** Dept of Philos & Relig Studies, Youngstown State Univ, 475 Gate Five Rd., Sansalito, CA 94961. **EMAIL** cbache@noetic.og

BACHMAN, JAMES V.
PERSONAL Born 06/14/1946, Council Bluffs, IA **DISCIPLINE** PHILOSOPHY AND THEOLOGY **EDUCATION** Math and philos, Valparaiso Univ, BS, 64-68; Fulbright grantee, BA, theol, Cambridge Univ, 68-70; Concordia Sem, ministry, M Div, 70-72; theol, Cambridge Univ, England, MA, 74; philos, Fla State Univ Tallahassee, PhD, 86. **CAREER** Pastor, Our Redeemer Luth Church, Lake City, Fla, 71-81; full-time facul, philos and world relig, Lake City Community Col, 71-81; dept chair, comp educ, Lake City Community Col, 79-81; pastor/dir, Univ Luth Ctr, Tallahassee, 81-89; asst prof, philos, Fla State Univ Tallahassee, 86-89; occasional visiting prof, Concordia Theol Sem, Ft Wayne, Ind, 95-96; occasional visiting prof, Concordia Sem, St Louis, Mo, 92-; coord of curric and prog planning, dept of philos, Valparaiso Univ, 89-92, 94-95; John R. Eckrich chair, relig and the healing arts, prof of philos, Valparaiso Univ, 89-. **HONORS AND AWARDS** Fulbright grantee, Cambridge Univ, England, 68-70; col teaching fel, Fla State Univ, 82-83; univ fel, Fla State Univ Tallahassee, 83-86; Phi Kappa Phi, 84-; Fla State Univ Coun of Instr grant, 89; visiting scholar, The Hastings Ctr, mar, 89; Who's Who in Relig, 85 & 91; Dict of Intl Bio, 93; grant for supporting and mentoring Health Ethics Fellows, 95-97. **MEMBERSHIPS** Amer Philos Asn; Chicago Clinical Ethics Prog; The Park Ridge Ctr; The Fla-Ga District; Luth Church- Mo Synod. **SELECTED PUBLICATIONS** Auth, Christians and Procreative Choices: How Do God's Chosen Choose?, CTCR, 97; auth, Witnessing in a Culture of Choice, GEM Module Course, Luth Church Mo Synod, 96; auth, Christian Care at Life's End, CTCR doc, 93; co-auth, What If..? Toward Excellence in Reasoning, 91; auth Teacher's Manual for What If..? Toward Excellence in Reasoning, 91; auth, chap, The Appeal to Authority, Fallacies: Classical and Contemporary Readings, The Penn State Univ Press, 95; article, Religious Voices in Secular Settings, Invited Papers of the Austrian Ludwig Wittgenstein Society, aug, 98; article, Two Sermon Studies, Concordia Jour, apr, 98; article, The Ten Suggestions: Putting Theology into Practice, Concordia Jour, apr, 98; article, Putting Theories into Practice, Proceedings of the Austrian Ludwig Wittgenstein Society, aug, 97; article, Ministry in a Culture of Choice, Concordia Jour, jan, 97; article, Ethics at VU, Valpo, 96; article, Here I Stand, a Reformation Homily, The Cresset, nov, 95; article, Compassion, Maximal vs. Minimal Ethics, Ready Reference: Ethics, Salem Press, 175-176, 536-537, 94. **CONTACT ADDRESS** Concordia Univ, California, 1530 Concordia West, Irvine, CA 92612-3299.

BACK, ALLAN
DISCIPLINE PHILOSOPHY **EDUCATION** Univ Tex Austin, PhD, 79. **CAREER** Asst prof, Rice Univ, 83-84; asst prof, Wayne State Univ, 84-85; asst prof, Dickinson Coll, 85-86; Prof, Kutztown Univ, 87-. **HONORS AND AWARDS** Phi Beta Kappa; Humboldt Forschangspreis, 99. **MEMBERSHIPS** Am Philos Asn, Soc for Greek Philos. **RESEARCH** History and Philosophy of Logic; Ancient Philosophy; Medieval Philosophy; Comparative Philosophy. **SELECTED PUBLICATIONS** Auth, Avicena and Averroes: The Islamic Background, Individuation in Scholasticism, 94; Aristotelian Necessities, Hist and Philos of Logic, 95; On Reduplication, 96; The Triplex Status Naturae and its Justification, Studies in the Hist of Logic, 96; rev, Geneerische Kennzeichungen, Nous, 96; Avicenna and Descartes on the Wax Example, Proceedings of the SIEPM Conference, 96; Aristole's Theory of Predication, 00; The Way To Go, 00. **CONTACT ADDRESS** Dept of Philosophy, Kutztown Univ of Pennsylvania, Kutztown, PA 19530. **EMAIL** Back@kutztown.edu

BACKHOUSE, CONSTANCE B.
DISCIPLINE LAW **EDUCATION** Osgoode Hall Law Sch, LLB, 75; Harvard Univ, LLM, 79. **CAREER** Prof. **HONORS AND AWARDS** Willard Hurst Prize, 92; Outstanding Bk Human Rights, 93. **RESEARCH** Sex discrimination; human rights; labour law; criminal law. **SELECTED PUBLICATIONS** Auth, Petticoats and Prejudice: Women and Law in Nineteenth Century Canada, 92; The Secret Oppression: Sexual Harassment of Working Women and Challenging Times: The Women's Movement in Canada and the United States, 93. **CONTACT ADDRESS** Fac of Law, Univ of Western Ontario, London, ON, Canada N6A 3K7. **EMAIL** cbbackho@julian.uwo.ca

BAEHR, AMY R.
PERSONAL Born 04/15/1966, Livingston, NJ, m, 1998 **DISCIPLINE** PHILOSOPHY **EDUCATION** State Univ of New York at Stony Brook, PhD. **CAREER** Asst Prof and Chr Dept of Philosophy, 97-, Moravian Col. **MEMBERSHIPS** Amer Phil Assoc; Soc for Women in Phil. **RESEARCH** Contemporary political philosophy; liberalism; feminist philosophy **SELECTED PUBLICATIONS** Auth, Towards a New Feminist Liberalism: Okin, Rawls, and Habermas, Hyapatia 11, 96, and The Philosophy of Rawls, 98; Feminists Reconsider the Self and Families, Constellations, 97. **CONTACT ADDRESS** Dept of Philosophy, Moravian Col, 1200 Main St., Bethlehem, PA 18018. **EMAIL** mearb01@moravian.edu

BAER, EUGEN SILAS
PERSONAL Born 08/19/1937, Klosters, Switzerland, m, 1988, 3 children **DISCIPLINE** PHILOSOPHY **EDUCATION** Univ

Fribourg, Lic, 65; Yale Univ, PhD(Philos), 71. **CAREER** Asst prof, 71-77, chmn dept, 73-74, assoc prof to prof Philos, Hobart & William Smith Cols, 77-, semi-sabbatical leave, Univ Aix-en-Provence, France, 74-75; fel, Nat Humanities Inst, Univ Chicago, 76-77. **MEMBERSHIPS** Am Philos Asn; AAUP; Semiotic Soc Am; Int Asn Semiotic Studies. **RESEARCH** Semiotics; psychoanalysis. **SELECTED PUBLICATIONS** Auth, The language of the unconscious according to Jacques Lacan, 71, Semiotic approaches to psychiatry, 72 & Semiotic approaches to human behavior, 73, Semiotica; Semiotic Approaches to Psychotherapy, Ind Univ, Bloomington, 75; Ideas and archetypes--a synopsis of Kant and Jung, Philosophy Today, 76; Myth and illness: Identity and difference, Contemp Psychoanal, 76; "Semiotic model theory in psychoanalysis," Semiotica, 77; "Things are stories--a manifesto for a reflexive semiotics," Semiotica, 78; auth, Medical Semiotics, 88; auth, Lacan's Theory of Language, 98. **CONTACT ADDRESS** Dept of Philosophy, Hobart & William Smith Cols, 300 Pulteney St, Geneva, NY 14456-3382. **EMAIL** baer@hws.edu

BAER, JUDITH A.
PERSONAL Born 04/05/1945, New York, NY **DISCIPLINE** POLITICAL SCIENCE **EDUCATION** Univ Chicago, PhD, 74. **CAREER** Asst prof, SUNY Albany, 76-83; asst prof to assoc prof, Calif State Polytech Univ, 85-88; assoc prof, to prof, Texas A&M Univ, 88- . **HONORS AND AWARDS** Fel, Woodrow Wilson Int Ctr for Scholars, 95-96; roving Fulbright sr lectr, Turkey, 97-98. **MEMBERSHIPS** Am Polit Sci Asn; Pi Sigma Alpha. **RESEARCH** Public law; feminist theory. **SELECTED PUBLICATIONS** Auth, Women in American Law, 2d ed, Holmes & Meier, 96; auth, Our Lives before The Law: Constructing a Feminist Jurisprudence, Princeton, 99. **CONTACT ADDRESS** Dept of Political Science, Texas A&M Univ, Col Station, College Station, TX 77843-4348. **EMAIL** j_baer@tamu.edu

BAERGEN, RALPH
DISCIPLINE PHILOSOPHY **EDUCATION** Syracuse Univ, PhD, 90. **CAREER** Assoc prof. **RESEARCH** Medical ethics; epistemology. **SELECTED PUBLICATIONS** Auth, Contemporary Epistemology. **CONTACT ADDRESS** Dept of English and Philosophy, Idaho State Univ, Pocatello, ID 83209. **EMAIL** baerralp@isu.edu

BAGBY, DANIEL G.
PERSONAL Born 05/30/1941, Porto Alegre, Brazil, m, 1965, 2 children **DISCIPLINE** RELIGIOUS STUDIES **EDUCATION** Baylor Univ, BA, 62; MA, 64; Southern Baptist Theol Seminary, MDiv, 67; PhD, 73. **CAREER** Prof, Baptist Theol Seminary, 94-. **HONORS AND AWARDS** Who's Who in Religion. **MEMBERSHIPS** AAMFT, AAPC, Am Orthopsychiatric Asn. **RESEARCH** Marriage and Family Counseling, Crisis Care, Conflict Resolution. **SELECTED PUBLICATIONS** Auth, Understanding Anger in the Church; Auth, Transition and Newness; auth, Before You Marry; auth, The Church: The Power to Help and to Hurt; auth, Seeing Through our Tears. **CONTACT ADDRESS** Dept Relig, Baptist Theol Sem, 3400 Brook Rd, Richmond, VA 23227-4536.

BAGLEY, STANLEY B.
PERSONAL Born 09/07/1935, Trenton, NJ, m **DISCIPLINE** THEOLOGY **EDUCATION** Morehouse Coll, BA 1958; Crozer Theol Sem, BD 1961; Ashland Theol Sem, MDiv 1973; Univ of OK, grad study, 1967; Century University, PhD, 1994; Association Mental Health Clergy, certified professional mental health clergy, 1976; Department of VA National Black Chaplin Association, certified clinical chaplain, 1996. **CAREER** Galilee Bapt Ch Trenton NJ, asst pastor 1961-65; Calvary Bapt Ch, pastor 1965-67; Bapt Campus Ministry Langston Univ, dir 1967-70; Hough Ch, minister of educ comm 1970-71; VA Medical Center Brecksville OH, chaplain 1971-; Lakeside Bapt Ch E Cleveland OH, pastor 1972-1979. **HONORS AND AWARDS** Christian Leadership Citation Bapt Student Union Langston Univ 1969; Outstanding Young Man, Outstanding Amer Found, 1970; 33 Degree Free Mason; United Supreme Council 33 Degree Ancient and Accepted Scottish Rite of Freemasonry Prince Hall Affiliation; loaned executive from VAMC to the Combined Federal Campaign, 1988; Crozer Theological Seminary, Crozer Scholar, 1989, 1995. **MEMBERSHIPS** E Cleveland Ministerial Alliance 1975; Assn of Mental Health Clergy, bd certified chaplain, 1974; Ohio Health Care Chaplains; Amer Protestant Hosp Assn; College of Chaplains; chmn, Evangelism Com Bapt Minister's Conf Cleveland OH; Dept of Metropolitan Ministry Cleveland Baptist Assn; life mem and golden heritage life mem, NAACP; Omega Psi Phi Fraternity Inc; American Association of Christian Counselors; Associations of Christian Marriage Counselors; Dept of Veterans Affairs, Natl Black Chaplains Assn, certified clinical chaplain, 1996. **CONTACT ADDRESS** VA Medical Ctr, 10000 Brecksville Rd, Brecksville, OH 44141.

BAILEY, ALISON
DISCIPLINE PHILOSOPHY **EDUCATION** Dickinson Col, BA, 83; Colo State Univ, MA, 86; Univ Cincinnati, PhD, 93. **CAREER** Assoc prof. **SELECTED PUBLICATIONS** Auth, Posterity and Strategic Policy: A Moral Assessment of Nuclear Policy Options, Univ Am, 89; auth, "Mothering, Diversity and Peace: Comments on Sara Ruddick's Feminist Maternal Peace Politics," Jour Soc Philos XXVI.1 (95): 162-182; auth, "Mothers, Birthgivers and Peacemakers: A Critical Reflection on Maternal Peace Politics," in Perspectives on Power and Domination, ed. Lawrence Bone and Laura Duhan Kaplan (Rodophi, New York, 97), 263-275; auth, "Greenham Common" and "White Women," in A Reader's Guide to Women's Studies, ed. Eleanor B. Amico (Fitzroy Dearborn Publishers, Chicago, 98); auth, "Locating Traitorous Identities: Toward a Theory of White Character Formation," Hypatia 13.3 (98): 27-42; auth, "Privilege: Expanding on Marilyn Frye's 'Oppression,'" The Jour of Social Philos 29.3 (98): 104-119; auth, "Despising an Identity They Taught Me to Claim: Exploring a Dilemma of White Priviledge Awareness," in Whiteness: Feminist Philosophical Narratives, ed. Chris J. Cuomo and Kim Q. Hall (Rowman and Littlefield, Totowa, NJ, 99); auth, "Race-making as the Process of Enimification," in Peacemaking: Lessons From the Past, Visions for the Future, ed. Judith Presler and Sally Scholtz (Rodophi, New York, 99); coed, Community, Diversity, and Difference: Implications for Peace, Rodophi (New York), forthcoming; "Privilege" and "White Privilege," in Encyclopedia of Feminist Theories, ed. Lorraine Code (Routledge, New York, forthcoming). **CONTACT ADDRESS** Dept of Philosophy, Illinois State Univ, Normal, IL 61790-4540. **EMAIL** baileya@ilstu.edu

BAILEY, CHARLES E.
PERSONAL Born 09/29/1940, Logan, WV, m, 1968, 3 children **DISCIPLINE** HISTORY, RELIGION **EDUCATION** Bob Jones Univ, BA, 62; MA, 63; Roosevelt Univ, MA, 69; Univ Va, PhD, 78. **CAREER** Teacher, Adirondack Col, 72-; adj prof, Plattsburgh Univ at ACC, 76-. **HONORS AND AWARDS** Listed in Who's Who Among Scholars in Am Community, Technical and Junior Colleges, 86-; Phi Alpha Theta; President's Awd for Excellence, Adirondack Col, 89; Distinguished Prof, Adirondack Col, 90. **RESEARCH** World War I. **SELECTED PUBLICATIONS** Auth, "The British Protestant Theologians and the First World War," Harvard Theol Rev 77.2 (84): 195-221; auth, "The Verdict of French Protestantism Against Germany in the First World War," Church Hist 58.1 (89): 66-82; auth, "Nietzsche: Moralist or Immoralist?--The Verdict of the European Theologians," Hist of European Ideas (89): 799-814. **CONTACT ADDRESS** Dept Soc Sci, Adirondack Comm Col, 439 Bay Rd, Queensbury, NY 12804-1408.

BAILEY, JAMES L.
PERSONAL Born 03/16/1938, Columbus, OH, m, 1963, 2 children **DISCIPLINE** THEOLOGY **EDUCATION** Capital Univ, BA, 60; Trinity Lutheran Sem, BD, 64; Univ of St Andrews, PhD, 67. **CAREER** Pastor, 67-70, Hope Lutheran Church Cincinnati; Asst Prof, 70-74, Trinity Lutheran Sem; Asst Prof, Assoc Prof, 75-85, Concordia Coll; Assoc Prof, Prof, 85-, Wartburg Theo Sem. **HONORS AND AWARDS** Trinity Luth Sem, dist alumnus Awd. **MEMBERSHIPS** SBL. **RESEARCH** New Testament, sermon on the mount. **SELECTED PUBLICATIONS** Co-auth, Literary Texts in the New Testament A Handbook, Louisville John Knox/Westminster Press, 92; auth, The Sermon on the Mount, Model for Contrast Community, forthcoming; Mark, Men's Bible Study Series, Augsburg, 87; auth, Experiencing the Kingdom as a Little Child, A Rereading of Mark 10:13-16, in: Word and World, 95; auth, A Pattern for Interpreting Biblical Texts, in: Currents in Theology and Mission, 95; The Bible, As We Become Open to God's Word, We Shall Be Changed, in: Parish Teacher, 90; auth, "Gene Analysis," in Hearing the New Testament, ed Joel B. Green (Eerdmaus, 95) 197-221. **CONTACT ADDRESS** Wartburg Theol Sem, 333 Wartburg Pl, Dubuque, IA 52004-5004. **EMAIL** jbailey@wartburgseminary.edu

BAILEY, LEE
PERSONAL Born 11/21/1943, FL, m, 1974, 2 children **DISCIPLINE** RELIGION, PHILOSOPHY **EDUCATION** Univ IL, BFA, 65; Columbia Univ, Mdiv, 70; Syracuse Univ, PhD, 83. **CAREER** Assoc prof, Ithaca Col, 83-. **HONORS AND AWARDS** Who's Who in the East, 95-99; res grants, Ithaca Col, Syracuse Univ. **MEMBERSHIPS** Am Acad Relig. **RESEARCH** Western religions, Jungarian psychology, near-death experiences, technology and culture. **SELECTED PUBLICATIONS** Auth, "Preface " to Religious Projection by Fokke Sierksma, Ann Arbor, Mich, UMI (90); auth, "Preface " to Envisioning the Invisible by Han Fortmann, Ann Arbor, UMI, (91); rev of Robert Ackerman's The Myth and Ritual School: J. G. Frazier and the Cambridge Riualists, in J of the Am Acad of Relig, LX1/4: 813-815 (93); auth, ""The No-Thing-ness of Near-Death Experience," in The Near Death Experience: A Reader, NY: Routledge (96); auth, "Unknown Well-Known Near-Death Experiences," in The Near-Death Experience: A Reader, NY: Routledge (96); coauth with Jenny Yates, "The Near-Death Experience: A Reader, NY:Routledge (96); auth, "The Titanic Enchantment and Education," Voice of the Liberal Arts at Ithaca Col, vol 1, no 1:1-4 (spring 98); rev of Maureen Korp's Sacred Art of the Earth: Ancient and Contemporaty Earthworks, NY:Continuum (97), in Studies in Religion/ Sciences Religieuses, 27/2: 242 (98); coauth with Mary Pat Fisher, Anthology of Living Religions, London: Calmann-King Ltd./Upper Saddle River, NJ: Prentice-Hall (99); auth, "A Little Death: Tibetan Delogs and the Near-Death Experience," J of Near-Death Studies (in press). **CONTACT ADDRESS** Dept Rel & Philos, Ithaca Col, 953 Danbury Rd, Ithaca, NY 14850-7000. **EMAIL** Bailey@ithaca.edu

BAILEY, RANDALL CHARLES
PERSONAL Born 05/26/1947, Malden, MA, m, 1973 **DISCIPLINE** RELIGION **EDUCATION** Brandeis Univ, Waltham, MA, BA (cum laude), 1969; Univ of Chicago, IL, AM, Social Serv Admin, 1972; Candler School of Theology, Atlanta, GA, MDiv (cum laude), 1979; Emory Univ, Atlanta, GA, PhD, Religion, 1987. **CAREER** PCSAP Loop College, Chicago, IL, dir of educ prog, 72-73; Shelby Co Devel Coord Dept, Memphis, TN, assoc dir, 73; Atlanta Univ School of Social Work, Atlanta, GA, asst prof, 73-81; First Cong Church, UCC, Atlanta, GA, asst minister, 80-81; Interdenominational Theological Center, Atlanta, GA, instructor, 81-87, asst prof, 87-90, Assoc Prof, 90-; Andrew W Mellon, Assoc Prof, 98-. **HONORS AND AWARDS** Distinguished Serv Awd, Atlanta Natl Assn of Black Social Workers, 1978; Fellow, Black Doctoral Prog/FTE, 1979-81, 1984-85; "Litany for Beginning," Inauguration of Mayor Andrew Young, 1981; Fellow, United Negro Coll Fund, 1984-85. **MEMBERSHIPS** Mem, Black Theology Project, 1986-; co-chair, Afro-Amer Theology & Biblical Hermeneutics Soc of Biblical Lit, 1987-94; co-chair, Unity/Renewal Study, COFO/NCCCUSA, 1988-92; mem, Div Educ & Min/ NCCCUSA, 1988-91, Bible Translation & Utilization Comm DEM/NCCCUSA, 1988-, Soc for the Study of Black Religion, 1988-; mem exec bd, NCCCUSA. **SELECTED PUBLICATIONS** Author: "Wash Me White as Snow: When Bad is Turned to Good, Race, Class and the Politics of Bible Translation," Seneia 76, 1996; "The Redemption of Yhwh: A Literary Critical Function of the Songs of Hannah and David," Biblical Interpretation, 1995; "'Is That Any Name for a Nice Hebrew Boy?' - Exodus 2:1-10: The De-Africanization of an Israelite Hero," The Recover of Black Presence: An Interdisciplinary Exploration, Abingdon, 1995; "They're Nothing but Incestuous Bastards: The Polemical Use of Sex and Sexuality in Hebrew Canon Narrative," Reading From This Place: Social Location and Biblical Interpretation in the United States, Fortress, 1994; "And Then They Will Know That I Am YHWH: The P Recasting of the Plague Narratives," JITC, 1994; "What Price Inclusivity?: An Afrocentric Reading of Dangerous Biblical Texts," Voices from the Third World, 1994; "Cobb Clergy's Gay Stance Loses Punch in Biblical Debate," Atlanta Journal/ Constitution, p F2, June 26, 1994; "A De-politicized Gospel: Reflections on Galatians 5:22-23," Ecumenical Trends, 22 No 1, Jan 1993; "Doing the Wrong Thing: Male-Female Relationships in the Hebrew Canon," We Belong Together: The Churches in Solidarity with Women, Friendship Press, 1992; David in Love and War: The Pursuit of Power in a Samuel 10-12, Sheffield, 1990; numerous other publications. **CONTACT ADDRESS** Old Testament and Hebrew, Interdenominational Theol Ctr, 700 MLK Jr Dr, SW, Atlanta, GA 30314.

BAILEY, STORM M.
PERSONAL Born Columbia, SC, m, 1981, 5 children **DISCIPLINE** PHILOSOPHY **EDUCATION** Wheaton Col, Ba, 87; Univ Wisc, Madison, MA, PhD, 97. **CAREER** Asst prof philos, Luther Col. **CONTACT ADDRESS** Luther Col, 700 College Dr, Decorah, IA 52101. **EMAIL** baileyst@luther.edu

BAILIFF, JOHN
PERSONAL Born 03/24/1936, San Pedro, CA, d, 3 children **DISCIPLINE** PHILOSOPHY **EDUCATION** Stanford Univ, AB, 58; Penn State Univ, MA, 61, PhD, 66. **CAREER** Instr, Penn State Univ, 61-63; instr, Univ Nev Las Vegas, 63-66; asst prof, 66-69, assoc prof, 69-74, prof, philos, 74-94, prof emer, philos, 94-, Univ Wisc Stevens Point. **HONORS AND AWARDS** Stanford Club scholar, 54-56; Crossett scholar in philos, Stanford Univ, 56-58; NDEA fel, philos, Penn State Univ, 60-63; Phi Kappa Phi, Penn State Univ, 63. **MEMBERSHIPS** Amer Philos Asn; Heidegger Conf; Soc for Phenomenol & Existential Philos; Intl Asn for Philos & Lit. **RESEARCH** Heidegger studies; Philosophy and fiction. **SELECTED PUBLICATIONS** Rev, Gibt es auf Erden ein Mass? and Ethos und Lebenswelt, Man and World, 88; auth, Truth and Power, Man and World, 87; auth, The Essence of Teaching, Teaching Forum, 87; auth, Elementary Logics, 2nd ed, Univ Wisc, 73; auth, Elementary Logics, Univ Wisc, 69; auth, Religious Discourse and Existence, Philos Forum, 67; auth, On the Ideal Observer, Philos and Phenomenol Res, 64. **CONTACT ADDRESS** 932 Bukolt Ave., Stevens Point, WI 54481-1733. **EMAIL** jbailiff@uwsp.edu

BAILLY, CONSTANTINA RHODES
DISCIPLINE RELIGIOUS STUDIES **EDUCATION** Columbia Univ, PhD. **CAREER** Asst prof. **RESEARCH** Kashmir Shaiva Hinduism; Goddess traditions of India. **SELECTED PUBLICATIONS** Auth, Shaiva Devotional Songs of Kashmir: The Shivastotravali of Utpaladeva; co-auth, God Dwells within You As You. **CONTACT ADDRESS** Religious Studies Dept, Eckerd Col, 54th Ave S, PO Box 4200, Saint Petersburg, FL 33711. **EMAIL** baillycr@eckerd.edu

BAIRD, DAVIS
PERSONAL Born 04/12/1954, Boston, MA, m, 1994, 1 child **DISCIPLINE** PHILOSOPHY **EDUCATION** Brandeis Univ, AB, 76; Stanford Univ, AM, 78; PhD, 81. **CAREER** Vis asst

prof, Univ Ariz, 81-82; from asst prof to prof, 82-, chair, 92-, Univ SCar. **HONORS AND AWARDS** NEH Conference Grant, 93-95; GTE Conference Grant, 94. **MEMBERSHIPS** Am Philos Asn; Philos of Sci Asn; Brit Asn for Philos of Sci; Int Soc for Philos of Chem; Soc for Philos and Technol. **RESEARCH** Philosophy of scientific instrumentation; philosophy of analytical chemistry, instructive logic. **SELECTED PUBLICATIONS** Auth, Inductive Logic: Probability and Statistics, Prentice-Hall, 92; coed, "Heinrich Hertz: Classical Physicist, Modern Philosopher," in Boston Studies in the Philosophy of Science (Kluwer Acad Publ, 97); coed, "Philosophy of Chemistry: Synthesis of a New Discipline," in Boston Studies in the Philosophy of Science (Kluwer Acad Publ, 01); auth, Thing Knowledge: A Philosophy of Scientific Instruments, Univ of Calif Press, 01. **CONTACT ADDRESS** Dept of Philos, Univ of So Carolina, Columbia, Columbia, SC 29208. **EMAIL** db@sc.edu

BAIRD, FORREST
DISCIPLINE PHILOSOPHY **EDUCATION** Westmont, BA; Fuller, Mdiv; Claremont Grad Sch, MA, PhD. **CAREER** Instr, Fuller Theol Sem; prof, 78-. **HONORS AND AWARDS** Res fel, Inst Ecumenical and Cult Res, St John's Univ; selected, three graduating classes, most influential prof; voted, tch yr (3). **RESEARCH** Chinese philosophy; the problem of evil. **SELECTED PUBLICATIONS** Ed, Human Thought and Action: Readings in Western Intellectual History; co-auth, Introduction to philosophy: A Case Study Approach, HarperCollins. **CONTACT ADDRESS** Dept of Rel/Philos, Whitworth Col, 300 West Hawthorne Rd, Spokane, WA 99251. **EMAIL** fbaird@whitworth.edu

BAIRD, ROBERT DAHLEN
PERSONAL Born 06/29/1933, Philadelphia, PA, m, 1954, 4 children **DISCIPLINE** RELIGION **EDUCATION** Houghton Col, BA, 54; Fuller Theol Sem, BD, 57; Southern Methodist Univ, STM, 59; Univ Iowa, PhD(Relig), 64. **CAREER** From instr to asst prof Philos & Relig, Univ Omaha, 62-65; from asst prof to assoc prof Hist Relig, 66-73, prof Hist Relig, Univ Iowa, 74-01; dir School of Relg, Univ Iowa, 95-00; Soc Relig Higher Educ fel, 65-66; Am Inst Indian Studies fac fel, India, 71-72; book rev ed, J Am Acad Relig, 80-; Prof Emeritus, Univ of Iowa, 01-; Goodwin -Philpot Sr Eminent Chair in Religion, Auburn Univ, 01. **HONORS AND AWARDS** Fel, Am Inst of Indian Studies, Sr Short Term, 92. **MEMBERSHIPS** Am Acad Relig; Asn Asian Studies. **RESEARCH** History of religious methodology; religion in India, Religion and law in Modern India. **SELECTED PUBLICATIONS** Auth, Category Formation and the History of Religions, Mouton, The Hague, 71; coauth, Indian and Far Eastern Religious Traditions, Harper, 72; auth, The Symbol of Emptiness and the Emptiness of Symbols, Humanitas, Spring 72; Mr Justice Gajendragadkar and the Religion of the Indian Secular State, J Const & Parliamentary Studies, 12/72; ed, Methodological Issues in Religious Studies, New Horizons, 75; auth, Religion and the Secular: Categories for Religious Conflict and Religious Change in Independent India, In: Religion and Social Conflict in South Asia, 76 & Religion and the Legitimation of Nehru's Concept of the Secular State, In: Religion and the Legitimation of Power in South Asia, 78, Brill; ed & contribr, Religion in Modern India, Manohar, New Delhi, 81; auth, Essays in the History of Religions, Peter Lang, New York, 91; auth, Religion and Law in Independent India, Manohar, New Delhi, 93. **CONTACT ADDRESS** Sch of Relig, Univ of Iowa, 308 Gilmore Hall, Iowa City, IA 52242-1376. **EMAIL** robert-baird@uiowwa.eud

BAIRD, ROBERT MALCOLM
PERSONAL Born 05/30/1937, Memphis, TN, m, 1959, 3 children **DISCIPLINE** PHILOSOPHY **EDUCATION** Baylor Univ, BA, MA, 61; Southern Baptist Theol Sem, BD, 64; Emory Univ, PhD(philos), 67. **CAREER** Instr philos, Baylor Univ, 60-61; asst prof, Oglethorpe Col, 66-67 & NE Wesleyan Univ, 67-68; asst prof, 68-70, assoc prof, 70-78, Prof Philos, Baylor Univ, 79-. **MEMBERSHIPS** Am Philos Asn; AAUP. **RESEARCH** Existentialism; history of modern philosophy; contemporary ethics. **SELECTED PUBLICATIONS** Auth, John Dewey's Two Meta-ethical Views, Southwestern J Philos, fall 70; Philosophy, Southern Baptist Convention Press, spring 71; Existentialism, Death, and Caring, J Relig & Health, 4/76; The Sixties, the Students, the Conflict with Authority: Lessons in Retrospect, J Thought, 4/77; coauth, Thomas Reid's Criticisms of Adam Smith's Theory of the Moral Sentiments, J Hist Ideas, 9/77; Leibniz and Locke: On the Relationship Between Metaphysics and Science, Sci, Faith, & Revelation: An Approach Christian Philos, 79; The Creative Role of Doubt in Religion, J Relig Health, fall 80; Reasoned Commitment in the Face of Uncertainty, Contemp Philos: Philos Res Anal, fall, 81. **CONTACT ADDRESS** Dept of Philos Col of Arts & Sci, Baylor Univ, Waco, Waco, TX 76703.

BAIRD, WILLIAM R.
PERSONAL Born 03/27/1924, Santa Cruz, CA, m, 1946, 2 children **DISCIPLINE** BIBLICAL STUDIES **EDUCATION** Northwest Christian Col, BTh, 46; Univ Ore, BA, 47; Yale Divinity Sch, BD, 50; Yale Univ, MA, 52; PhD, 55; post-doctoral, Marburg, Heidelberg, Univ Chicago. **CAREER** Assoc prof, Phillips Theol Sem, 52-56; prof, Lexington Theol Sem, 56-67; prof, Tex Christian Univ Brite Divinity Sch, 67-92; prof Emeritus, Tex Christian Univ Brite Divinity Sch. **HONORS AND AWARDS** Phi Beta Kappa; Failing-Beekman Oratory, Univ Ore; Tew Prize, Yale Divinity Sch; Two Brothers Fel, Yale Univ; Fac Fel, Asn of Theol Schs; Chancellor's Awd for Distinguished Teaching, Tex Christian Univ. **MEMBERSHIPS** Soc of Biblical Lit, Studiorom Novi Testamenti Soc, Asn of Disciple for Theol Discussion, Theta Phi. **RESEARCH** History of Research about the New Testament; Life, Letters, & Theology of Paul. **SELECTED PUBLICATIONS** Auth, History of New Testament Research; auth, 1 and 2 Corinthians; auth, The Quest of the Christ of Faith; auth, The Corinthian Church; auth, Paul's Message and Mission. **CONTACT ADDRESS** Brite Divinity Sch, Texas Christian Univ, Fort Worth, TX 76129.

BAKAN, JOEL
DISCIPLINE LAW **EDUCATION** Simon Fraser Univ, BA, 81; Oxford Univ, BA, 83; Dalhousie Univ, LLB, 84; Harvard Univ, LLM, 87. **CAREER** Law Clerk, Justice Brian Dickson, Supreme Court Can, 85; asst prof, Osgoode Hall Law, 87-90; assoc prof, Univ of British Columbia, 90-. **HONORS AND AWARDS** Tchg Excellence Awd; UBC Killam Res Prize; Rhodes Scholar. **RESEARCH** Constitutional law; legal theory; socio legal studies. **SELECTED PUBLICATIONS** Coauth, "Getting to the Bottom of Meech Lake," Ottawa Law Rev 21 (90): 247-261; auth, "Politics, the Charter and the State: A Review Essay," J of Human Justice (90): 117-124; auth, "Constitutional Interpretation and Social Change: You Can't Always Get What You Want (Nor What You Need)," Can Bar Rev, 70 (91): 307-328; coauth, "Spatial Boundaries, Legal Categories and the Judicial Mapping of the Worker," Environment and Planning 24 (92): 629-644; auth, "Against Constitutional Property Rights," in Constitutional Politics, ed. D. Cameron (Toronto: Lorimer, 92): 117-126; coed, Social Justice and the Constitution: Perspectives on a Social Union for Canada, Carleton Univ Press, 92; auth, "Some Hard Questions About the Hard Cases Question," Univ of Toronto Law J 42 (92): 504-516; coauth, "Spacing Out: Towards a Critical Geography of Law," Osgoode Hall Law J (92): 661-690; coauth, "Developments in Constitutional Law, 1993-1994 Term," Supreme Court Law Rev 6 (95): 67-126; auth, Just Words: Constitutional Rights and Social Wrongs, Univ of Toronto Press, 97. **CONTACT ADDRESS** Fac of Law, Univ of British Columbia, 1822 East Mall, Vancouver, BC, Canada V6T 1Z1. **EMAIL** bakan@law.ubc.ca

BAKER, BEVERLY POOLE
PERSONAL Born 01/14/1944, Birmingham, AL, m, 1968, 3 children **DISCIPLINE** LAW **EDUCATION** Univ of Alabama at Birmingham, BA (summa cum laude), 1982; Cumberland School of Law, Birmingham AL, JD, 1985. **CAREER** McMillan & Spratling, Birmingham, AL, atty, 85-86; Haskell Slaughter & Young, Birmingham, AL, atty, 86-. **HONORS AND AWARDS** Dean's Awd, Univ of Alabama at Birmingham, 1981, 1982; Fellow, Amer Assn of Univ Women, 1984. **MEMBERSHIPS** American Bar Assn, Standing Committee on Lawyers' Public Service Responsibility; co-chair, Equal Opportunity Committee of the Litigation Section; Natl Bar Assn; Natl Assn of Bond Lawyers; Magic City Bar Assn; Birmingham Bar Assn; Leadership Alabama, board of directors, alumni council; Leadership Birmingham; Jefferson County Medical Examiners Comm; Research Council of Alabama; Cumberland School of Law, advisory board; University of Alabama in Birmingham Leadership Council. **SELECTED PUBLICATIONS** "Perceptions and Propinquity on Police Patrol," SE Sociological Assn, 1982; "Privacy in a High-Tech World," seminar, 1985; "The Age Discrimination in Employment Act and Termination of the Public Sector Employee," Alabama Bar Inst Seminar, 1989; "Basic Wage and Hour Law in AL," NBI, 1996. **CONTACT ADDRESS** 1901 Sixth Ave N, Ste 1200, Birmingham, AL 35203. **EMAIL** BPB@HSY.COM

BAKER, C. EDWIN
PERSONAL Born 05/28/1947, Nashville, TN **DISCIPLINE** CONSTITUTIONAL LAW, LEGAL PHILOSOPHY, MASS MEDIA **EDUCATION** Stanford Univ, BA, 69; Yale Univ, JD, 72. **CAREER** Asst prof, Univ Toledo, 72-75; asst prof, Univ Ore, 75-79, assoc prof, 79-81 & prof, 81-82; Prof Law, Univ Pa, 82-, Fel, Harvard Univ, 74-75; vis prof law, Univ Tex, 80 & Univ Pa, 81-82; Staff Atty, ACLU, NY, 87-88; Fel, Shorentein Barone Ctr, Kennedy Sch Govt, Harvard, 92; vis prof, Cornell Univ, 93; Vis Lombard Prof, Kennedy Sch Govt, Harvard Univ, 93; vis prof, Univ of Chicago, 00. **RESEARCH** Mass media; constitutional law. **SELECTED PUBLICATIONS** Auth, Human Liberty and Freedom of Speech, Oxford Univ 89; Advertising and a Democratic Press, Princeton, 94; author of numerous journal articles. **CONTACT ADDRESS** Law Sch, Univ of Pennsylvania, 3400 Chestnut St, Philadelphia, PA 19104-6204. **EMAIL** ebaker@law.upenn.edu

BAKER, DONALD W.
DISCIPLINE LAW **EDUCATION** Southern Methodist Univ, BA, 67; Univ Tex, JD 70. **CAREER** Ira Drayton Pruitt sr prof, Univ Ala. **RESEARCH** Commercial transactions,.bankruptcy, and contracts. **SELECTED PUBLICATIONS** Auth, A Lawyer's Basic Guide to Secured Transactions, Amer Law Inst. **CONTACT ADDRESS** Law Dept, Univ of Alabama, Tuscaloosa, Box 870000, Tuscaloosa, AL 35487-0000. **EMAIL** dbaker@law.ua.edu

BAKER, JOHN ARTHUR
PERSONAL Born 01/15/1937, Liverpool, England, m, 1964, 2 children **DISCIPLINE** PHILOSOPHY, ETHICS **EDUCATION** Oxford Univ, MA, 63, BPhil, 63, DPhil, 69. **CAREER** Lectr. Balliol Col, Oxford Univ, 63-64, Exeter & Trinity Col, 64-67; asst prof, 67-72, assoc prof Philos, Univ Calgary, 72-, Vis lectr, Trinity Col, Oxford Univ, 76. **MEMBERSHIPS** Can Philos Asn; Humanities Asn Can. **RESEARCH** Decision theory; philosophy of language; classical Greek philosophy. **SELECTED PUBLICATIONS** Auth, A Select Bibliography of Moral Philosophy: Oxford Study Aids in Philosophy Series, Vol IX, Oxford Univ, 77. **CONTACT ADDRESS** Dept of Philos, Univ of Calgary, Calgary, AB, Canada T2N 1N4. **EMAIL** baker@uclgary.ca

BAKER, JOHN M.
PERSONAL m, 1975, 1 child **DISCIPLINE** PHILOSOPHY **EDUCATION** Oxford Univ, BA, 71; Univ Toronto, MA, 72, Oxford Univ, B Phil, 74. **CAREER** Bradford Univ, lectr, 76-77; Nat Univ Ireland Dublin, lectr 77-. **HONORS AND AWARDS** Birkbeck Col, Hon Res fel, SUNY Stony Brook, res assoc, Yale, vis fel. **MEMBERSHIPS** APA, APSA, PSA, PSAI. **RESEARCH** Equality; egalitarian theory and democratic theory. **SELECTED PUBLICATIONS** Auth, Utilitarianism and Secondary Principles, Philos Quart, 71; auth, An Egalitarian Case for Basic Income, Arguing for Basic Income, ed., P. Van Parijs, Verso, 92; auth, Fair Representation and the Concept of Proportionality Political Studies, 96; auth, Studying Equality, Imprints, 97; auth, Equality, Social Policy in Ireland: Principles, Practice and Problems, ed., S. Healy & B. Reynolds, Dublin: Oak Tree Pr, 98; coauth, Responsibility for Needs, Necessary Goods: Our Responsibilities to Meet Others Needs, ed., G. Brock, Lanham, MD: Rowman and Littlefield, 98. **CONTACT ADDRESS** Dept of Politics, Univ Col of Dublin, Dublin, Ireland. **EMAIL** john.baker@ucd.ie

BAKER, JOHN R.
DISCIPLINE LOGIC, PHILOSOPHY OF RELIGION **EDUCATION** Hardin-Simmons Univ, BA, 61; Southwestern Baptist Theol Sem, BD, PhD, 69; Vanderbilt Univ, MA, PhD, 73. **CAREER** Assoc prof, La State Univ. **RESEARCH** Metaphysical areas related to identity and to Christian theology. **SELECTED PUBLICATIONS** Published in the areas of analytic metaphysics, theistic proofs, and Whiteheadian studies. **CONTACT ADDRESS** Dept of Philos and Relig Stud, Louisiana State Univ and A&M Col, 106 Coates Hall, Baton Rouge, LA 70803.

BAKER, LYNNE R.
DISCIPLINE PHILOSOPHY **EDUCATION** Vanderbilt Univ, PhD, 72. **CAREER** Asst prof, Mary Baldwin Coll, 72-76; asst prof, assoc prof, prof, Middlebury Coll, 76-94; prof, Univ Mass Amherst, 89-. **HONORS AND AWARDS** Phi Beta Kappa; Fel Nat Humanities Center; Fel Woodrow Wilson Int Center for Scholars. **MEMBERSHIPS** Am Philos Asn; Soc for Philos and Psychol; Soc of Christian Philos. **RESEARCH** Philosophy of Mind; Metaphysics; Nature of the material world; Nature of Human Persons. **SELECTED PUBLICATIONS** Auth, Saving Belief: A Critique of Physicalism, 87; Content Meets Consciousness, Philos Topics, 94; auth, Explaining Attitudes: A Practical Approach to the Mind, 95; auth, Attitudes as Nonentities, Philos Studies, 95; Need a Christian be a Mind-Body Dualist?, Faith and Philos, 95; Science and the Attitudes: A Replay to Sanford, Behavior and Philos, 96; Why Constitution is Not Identity, J of Philos, 97; auth, Persons and Bodies: A Constitution View, 00. **CONTACT ADDRESS** Univ of Massachusetts, Amherst, Bartlett Hall 352, PO Box 30525, Amherst, MA 01003-0525. **EMAIL** lrbarker@philos.umass.edu

BAKER, ROBERT B.
PERSONAL Born 12/05/1937, New York, NY, m, 1958, 2 children **DISCIPLINE** PHILOSOPHY **EDUCATION** CUNY, BA, 59; Univ Minn, PhD, 67. **CAREER** Instr, 64-65, Univ Minn; from instr to asst prof, 65-69, Univ Iowa; asst prof, 69-73, adj prof biomed ethics, 73-74,, Wayne St Univ Med Sch, Wayne State Univ; asst prof, 73-80, coord, Med Term Abroad, 76-, co-dir, Health & Human Values, 79-, assoc prof, 80-88, chmn, 82-95, Human Subj Res Comm, dir, 84-88, CHUC, prof, 89-, chmn, 91-96, phil dept, Union Col, NY; vis assoc prof, 81, NYU Med Ctr; vis prof, 96-, Ctr Bioethics, Univ Penn. **HONORS AND AWARDS** NEH jr res fel, 69; Coun of Philos Stud Sum Stud Grant, Rochefeller Bros Fund, 74; Natl Endow for Humanities Sel Fields Fel, 74-75; Melon Fel, 76-77; Inst of Health & Human Values Fel, 77-78; Ethical Values in Sci & Tech, NEH-NSF, 81-82; Computers in Humanities Undergrad Curriculum, CHUC, 84-86; Amer Philos Soc travel grant, 94-95; Wood Inst Fel, 96-97; NEH Collaborative Res grant (History of Medical Ethics), 99-02. **MEMBERSHIPS** APA, ASBH, Pres Hist med Ethics Affinity Group. **RESEARCH** Bioethics, hist of medical ethics, social and political philosophy; philosophy of medicine; philosophy of sex. **SELECTED PUBLICATIONS** Art, Resistance to Medical Ethics Reform in the Nineteenth Century, Malloch Rm Newsl of NY Acad of Med, 96; art, The Impact of Legislation Requiring DNR Orders: New York State Compared to Neighboring States, J of Intensive Care Med 11, 96; art, Recent Works in the History of Medical Ethics and Its Relevance to Bioethics, APA Newsl, 96; art, The Kappa

Lambda Society of Hippocrates: The Secret Origins of the American Medical Association, Fugitive Leaves, Col of Phys of Phil, 97; coauth, Crisis, Ethics and the American Medical Association: 1847 and 1997, J of Amer Med Assn, 97; art, Multiculturalism, Postmodernism and the Bankruptcy of Fundamentalism, Kennedy Inst Ethics J, 98; art, A Theory of International Bioethics, Kennedy Inst Ethics J, 98; coauth, The American Medical Ethics Revolution, John Hopkins, 99. **CONTACT ADDRESS** Dept of Philosophy, Union Col, New York, 807 Union St, Schenectady, NY 12308-3107. **EMAIL** bakerr@union.edu

BAKER, THOMAS E.
PERSONAL Born 02/25/1953, Youngstown, OH, m, 1974, 2 children **DISCIPLINE** LAW **EDUCATION** Fla St Univ, BS, 74; Univ Fla, JD, 77. **CAREER** Law Clerk, Hon James C Hill, U S Ct of Appeals, 5th Dist, 77-79; Fed Judicial Fel, Supreme Court of the United States, 85-86; Acting Admin Asst, Hon Chief Justice William H. Rehnquist, 86-87; Fel Prof, Univ Athens, 92-93; Vis Prof, Univ Fla, 94; From Asst Prof to Prof, Tex Technol Univ, 79-98; Prof, Drake Univ, 98-. **HONORS AND AWARDS** Judicial Fel, U S Supreme Ct. **MEMBERSHIPS** Am Law Inst, Am Judicature Soc, ABA. **RESEARCH** U S Constitution and Supreme Court. **SELECTED PUBLICATIONS** Auth, The Good Judge, Priority Pr, 89; auth, A Primer on the Jurisdiction of the United States Courts of Appeals, Fed Judicial Ctr, 89; auth, Rationing Justice on Appeal --- The Problems of the U S Courts of Appeals, West Publ Co, 94; auth, The Most Wonderful Work---Our Constitution Interpreted, West Publ Co, 96; co-ed, Can a Good Christian Be A Good Lawyer? Homilies, Witnesses and Reflections, Univ Notre Dame Pr, 98. **CONTACT ADDRESS** Law Sch, Drake Univ, 2507 University Ave, Des Moines, IA 50311-4505. **EMAIL** thomas.baker@drake.edu

BAKER, THOMAS E.
PERSONAL Born 06/15/1941, New York, NY, m, 1969, 1 child **DISCIPLINE** SOCIOLOGY, CRIMINAL JUSTICE **EDUCATION** Va Commonwealth Univ, AA, MS; East Stroudsburg Univ, Med, MS; Marywood Univ, CAGS Psychology and Counseling; PA State Univ, Advanced Study Adult Ed; Temple Univ, Educational Leadership. **CAREER** Assoc prof, Univ Scranton, 75-; Lt. Col. (Ret.) US Army Reserve Military Police Corps; Special Agent and Commander , US Army Criminal Investigation Command; police consultant to local law enforcement agencies, police administration, police testing, and COPPS grants. **HONORS AND AWARDS** Phi Epsilon Kappa; Kappa Delta Pi; Pi Gamma Mu; Scholarship Awd, Mich State Univ, Police Community Relations; Outstanding Honor Academic Graduate, Montgomery County Police Acad, Md; Dean's list student, Va Commonwealth Univ; Who's Who in Am Law Enforcement; Directory of Distinguished Americans; Who's Who in America; Who's Who in the East; Outstanding Young Men of America; Who's Who in the Northeast. **MEMBERSHIPS** Police and Criminal Psychology; Nat Asn of Chiefs of Police; Southern Criminal Justice Asn; The American Legion; Disabled American Veterans. **RESEARCH** Psychological personality profiling; police administration; criminal investigation; crime prevention; organized crime; community-oriented and problem-solving policing; police grantsmanship; crime analysis. **SELECTED PUBLICATIONS** Author of more than 40 articles in professional journals. **CONTACT ADDRESS** Dept Sociol, Univ of Scranton, 800 Linden St, Scranton, PA 18510.

BAKER-KELLY, BEVERLY
PERSONAL Born 11/02/1942, Detroit, MI, m, 1966, 2 children **DISCIPLINE** LAW **EDUCATION** Howard Univ, 1961-62; Univ of Mich, BA, 1964; Columbia Univ, MA, 1966, MEd, 1970, School of International Affairs, Certificate of African Studies, 1970, EdD, 1973; Univ of California, Berkeley, JD, 1976; Harvard Univ, MA, 1977, PhD, 1978; Johns Hopkins Univ, 1984-86; London School of Economics, 1991-92. **CAREER** Columbia Univ, co-dir of African-American Summer Studies Program, 70; Univ of Windsor, sociology instructor, 71-73; Greenberg and Glusker, law clerk, 74; Dunn and Cruthcer, law clerk, 75; Legal Aid Society, law clerk, 76; California State Univ, assoc prof, 76-82; Mayr, Galle, Weiss-Tessback, und Ben Ibler, Attorneys at Law, stagiaire, 78-79; UNESCO, stagiaire, 79-80; Univ of Maryland, US Army Bases, lecturer and facilitator, 80; Southern Poverty Law Cent, assoc, 81; Univ of Calif, dir of Academic Support Program, lecturer, 82-84; Research Management Services, partner and director of Intl Law Div, 84-86; Focus Intl Consultancy, dir, 86-93; Private Immigration Law Practice, 91-93; Howard Univ, visiting assoc prof, 93-; Golden Gate University, School of Law, 96, 97. **HONORS AND AWARDS** Natl Bar Assn, Presidential Awd for Outstanding Service, 1992, 1993, 1995. **MEMBERSHIPS** Natl Bar Assn, Intl Law Section, Chair, 1994-96; Union Internationale Des Avocats; Boalt Hall Fund for Diversity, VP/Bd of Dir, 1988-91. **SELECTED PUBLICATIONS** Assoc Ed, California Law Review; Articles Editor, Black Law Journal; Coauthor, The African-American Encyclopedia of Education, 1994; A Study of the Degree of Transnationalization of College and Non-College Educated Blacks, Columbia Univ; Housing Conceptions and Satisfactions of Residents in Federally Subsidized Lower-Middle Income Housing, Harvard Univ; "US Immigration: A Wake up Call," Howard Law Journal, 1995. **CONTACT ADDRESS** Attorney, 2983 Burdeck Dr, Oakland, CA 94602. **EMAIL** bbakerkelly@yahoo.com

BAKHURST, DAVID J.
DISCIPLINE PHILOSOPHY **EDUCATION** Keele Univ, BA, 82; Oxon, MA; DPhil. **CAREER** Prof, Communication, Univ Cal, San Diego; dept philos, Queen's Univ, 90- **HONORS AND AWARDS** Junior Research Fellow, Exeter College, 85-88. **RESEARCH** Russian philosophy; metaethics; the social self. **SELECTED PUBLICATIONS** Auth, "Consciousness and Revolution in Soviet Philosophy: From the Bolsheviks to Evald Ilyenkov. Modern European Philosophy Series," Cambridge University Press, 91; co-ed, "The Social Self," Sage, 95; auth, "Social Memory in Soviet Thought," Routledge, 96; auth, "Activity, Consciousness and Communication," Mind, Culture and Activity, Cambridge University Press, 97; auth, "Pragmatism and Moral Knowledge," Pragmatism, Canadian Journal of Philosophy Supplementary, 98 **CONTACT ADDRESS** Dept of Philosophy, Queen's Univ at Kingston, Kingston, ON, Canada K7L 3N6. **EMAIL** bakhurst@post.queensu.ca

BAKKEN, GORDON MORRIS
PERSONAL Born 01/10/1943, Madison, WI, d, 1964, 2 children **DISCIPLINE** AMERICAN HISTORY, LAW **EDUCATION** Univ Wis-Madison, BS, 66, MS, 67, PhD(Am hist), 70, JD, 73. **CAREER** From asst prof to assoc prof Am hist, 69-76, Prof Hist, CA State Univ, Fullerton, 76-, Dir Fac Affairs & Records, 74- . **HONORS AND AWARDS** Penrose Fund/Am Philos Soc fel, 74 **MEMBERSHIPS** AHA; Orgn Am Historians; Western Hist Asn. **RESEARCH** American legal history. **SELECTED PUBLICATIONS** Auth, The Development of Law on the Rocky Moutain Frontier, 1850-1912, Westport CT, Greenwood Press, 83; auth, The Development of Law in Frontier California: Civil Law and Society, 1850-1890, Westport, CT, Greenwood Press, 85; auth, Rocky Mountain Constitution Making, 1850-1912, Westport CT, Greenwood Press, 87; auth, California Legal History Manuscripts in the Huntington Library: A Guide, San Marino, CA, Huntington Library Publications, 89; auth, Practicing Law in Frontier California, Lincoln, Nebraska, Univ of Nebraska Press, 91; auth, Surviving the North Dakota Depression, Pasadena, CA, Wood & Jones, 92; coauth, Learning California History , Wheaton, IL, Harlan Davidson, Inc, 99; ed, Law in the Western United States, Norman: Univ of Oklahoma Press, in press, 00; coauth, The American West, six volumes, Garland Publishing, Inc, New York, 01; auth, ed, California History: A Topical Approach, Harlan Davidson, Inc, est, 01. **CONTACT ADDRESS** Dept of Hist, California State Univ, Fullerton, Fullerton, CA 92834-6846. **EMAIL** gbakken@fullerton.edu

BALAS, DAVID L.
PERSONAL Born 08/06/1929, Kispest, Hungary **DISCIPLINE** THEOLOGY, PHILOSOPHY **EDUCATION** Pontif Univ St Anselm, Rome, LicTheol, 56, LicPhilos, 58, STD, 63. **CAREER** From instr to assoc prof, 59-72, chmn dept theol, 67-74 & 79-80, Prof Theol, Univ Dallas, 77-, Grad Dean & Dir, Inst Philos Studies, 80-, Pres, Coun Southwestern Theol Schs, 72-74; prof extraordinarius theol fundamentalis et dogmaticae, Pontif Athenaeum Anselmianum, Rome, 75-77. **MEMBERSHIPS** Am Acad Relig; Am Cath Philos Asn; Cath Theol Soc Am; NAm Patristic Soc (vpres, 75 & 81-83); Int Asn Patristic Studies. **RESEARCH** Hellenistic philosophy and patristic thought, especially Gregory of Nyssa; philosophy of religion; theological anthropology. **SELECTED PUBLICATIONS** **CONTACT ADDRESS** Univ of Dallas, Irving, TX 75060.

BALCOMB, RAYMOND
PERSONAL Born 02/08/1923, San Bernardino, CA, m, 1944, 5 children **DISCIPLINE** NEW TESTAMENT **EDUCATION** San Jose St Col, AB, 44; Boston Univ Sch of Theol, STB, 47; Boston Univ Grad Sch, PhD, 51. **CAREER** Ordain Meth Clergy, 48; Adj Faculty, 98-pres, Claremont Sch of Theol. **HONORS AND AWARDS** Lucinda Bidwell Beebe Fel, 47 **RESEARCH** Church History; Archaeology of Middle East. **SELECTED PUBLICATIONS** Auth, Stir What You've Got, Abingdon Press; Auth, Try Reading the Bible This Way, Westminster. **CONTACT ADDRESS** 868 SW Troy, Portland, OR 97219. **EMAIL** rbalcomb@uswest.net

BALDNER, KENT
PERSONAL Born 08/08/1956, Breckenridge, MN, m, 1999, 4 children **DISCIPLINE** MODERN PHILOSOPHY **EDUCATION** Univ Calif, Irvine, PhD. **CAREER** Dept Chair and Assoc prof, Philos, W Mich Univ. **MEMBERSHIPS** Am Philos Asn. **RESEARCH** Immanuel Kant. **SELECTED PUBLICATIONS** Auth, "Transcendental Idealism and the Fact/Value Dichotomy," Electronic J of Analytic Philos, 3 (Spring 95), auth, Kant Society, Synthese, Between the Species; articles in Philos Quart and Electronic Jour Analytic Philos. **CONTACT ADDRESS** Philos Dept, Western Michigan Univ, 1903 W Michigan Ave, Kalamazoo, MI 49008-5201. **EMAIL** baldner@wmich.edu

BALDWIN, CYNTHIA A.
PERSONAL Born 02/08/1945, McKeesport, PA, m, 1967 **DISCIPLINE** LAW **EDUCATION** Pennsylvania State Univ, University Park PA, BA, English, 1966, MA, English, 1974; Duquesne Univ School of Law, Pittsburgh PA, JD, 1980. **CAREER** Pennsylvania State Univ, McKeesport PA, asst dean student affairs, 76-77; Neighborhood Legal Serv, McKeesport PA, staff atty, 80-81; Office of Attorney Gen, PA, deputy atty gen, 81-83, atty-in-charge, 83-86; Palkovitz and Palkovitz, McKeesport PA, atty; Duquesne Univ of Law, Pittsburgh PA, adjunct professor, 84-86, visiting professor, 86-87, Adj Prof, 89-; Allegheny County, Court of Common Pleas, Adult/Family Division, and Civil Division Judge, 90-. **HONORS AND AWARDS** Susan B Anthony Awd, Women's Bar Assoc 1998; Distinguished Daughters of Pennsylvania Awd, Governor Tom Ridge, 1996; Tribute to Women Awd in the Professions, YWCA, 1987; Humanitarian Service Awd, Penn State Forum on Black Affairs, 1989; Whitney M Young Jr Service Awd, Boy Scouts of America, 1991; Women's Equality Day Recognition Plaque, Greater Pittsburgh Comm on Women, 1990; Inducted into MCK School Hall of Fame, 1990; first black woman elected to the Allegheny County, PA, bench for a ten-year term; first black woman installed as president of Penn State Alumni Assn. **MEMBERSHIPS** Penn State, bd of trustees, Gubernational Appointee, 1995-97; exec comm, Homer S Brown Law Assn, 1980-97; vice pres, bd of dir, Neighborhood Legal Serv Assn, 1986-88; pres-elect, 1987-88, Penn State Alumni Assn; president 1989-91; bd of dir, Greater Pittsburgh YMCA, 1987-; mem, Allegheny County Bar Assn, 1980-, Greater Pittsburgh Commn on Women, 1987-, Pennsylvania Bar Assn, 1988-, Pennsylvania Bar Assn House of Delegates, 1988-; member, Pennsylvania Commission on Crime and Delinquency. **CONTACT ADDRESS** 820 City-County Building, 414 Grant St., Pittsburgh, PA 15219.

BALDWIN, DONALD E.
PERSONAL Born 07/24/1936, Hardin, MT, m, 1960, 5 children **DISCIPLINE** THEOLOGY **EDUCATION** Univ Calif, BA, 62; Fuller Theology Sem, M.Div, 66; Univ Colo, MA, 72; Univ Mo, PhD, 78. **CAREER** Asst prof, Evangel Univ, 66-77; teaching fel, Univ Mo, 71-73; adj prof, Fuller Sem, 82; adj prof, Center Theological Studies, 85; vis prof, Continental Sem, 90. **HONORS AND AWARDS** Nat Teaching Fel, Univ Mo; Teaching Awd, Nat Science Found; Fuller Sem Auxillary Awd; Prof of the Year. **MEMBERSHIPS** APA; Int Berkley Society; Society of Christian Philos. **RESEARCH** Philosophy of religion; ethics. **SELECTED PUBLICATIONS** Auth, Introduction to Philosophy; coauth, The Complete Biblical Library; auth, Power, Ethics and Team Building; auth, Leadership and Team Building. **CONTACT ADDRESS** Vanguard Univ of So California, 55 Fair Dr, Costa Mesa, CA 92626. **EMAIL** dbaldwin@vanguard.edu

BALDWIN, FLETCHER N., JR.
DISCIPLINE LAW **EDUCATION** Univ Ga, AB, JD; Univ Ill, LLM; Yale Univ, LLM. **CAREER** Prof, Univ Fla, 62-. **HONORS AND AWARDS** Cofounder and lect, Human Rights Peace Inst, Makerere Univ; Cofounder and dir, Ctr Intl Financial Crimes Stud. **MEMBERSHIPS** Ga Bar; Amer Law Inst; Order of the Coif; Phi Beta Kappa; Phi Kappa Phi. **RESEARCH** Constitutional law, political and civil rights, criminal procedure, international financial crimes. **SELECTED PUBLICATIONS** Coauth, Money Laundering, Asset Forfeiture and Intl Financial Crimes. **CONTACT ADDRESS** School of Law, Univ of Florida, PO Box 117625, Gainesville, FL 32611-7625. **EMAIL** baldwin.f@law.ufl.edu

BALDWIN, GORDON BREWSTER
PERSONAL Born 09/03/1929, Binghamton, NY, m, 1958, 2 children **DISCIPLINE** LAW **EDUCATION** Haverford Col, BA, 50; Cornell Univ, LLB, 53. **CAREER** Pvt pract law, Rochester, NY, 53; lawyer int law, Judge Advocate Gen Sch, US Army, 54-57; from asst prof to assoc prof law, 57-64, assoc dean law sch, 60-63 & 68-70, Prof Law, Univ Wis-Madison, 64-, Consult, US Naval War Col, 60-65, vis prof int law, 63-64; vis prof law, Ain Shams Univ, Cairo, 66-67 & Tehran Univ, Iran, 70-71; lectr, US Dept State Cult Affairs Prog, Cyprus & Iran, 69; dir, Off Educ Prog, Univ Wis, 71-; mem adv screening comt law, Fulbright-Hays Prog, 72-75. **MEMBERSHIPS** Am Bar Asn; Am Law Sch Asn; Am Soc Int Law. **RESEARCH** Constitutional, international and military law. **SELECTED PUBLICATIONS** Auth, Justice Fortas on dissent, Wis Law Rev, 69; Administration of justice by laymen in Iran, World Asn Judges, 72; The Iranian legal system, Int Lawyer, 73; The foreign affairs advice privilege, Wis Law Rev, 76. **CONTACT ADDRESS** Law Sch, Univ of Wisconsin, Madison, 975 Bascom Mall, Madison, WI 53706-1301. **EMAIL** gbaldwin@facstaff.wisc.edu

BALDWIN, JOHN R.
DISCIPLINE COMMUNICATION; RELIGIOUS STUDIES **EDUCATION** Abilene Christian Univ, Masters, 91; Ariz State Univ, PhD, 94. **CAREER** Asst prof, Ill State Univ, 94-. **HONORS AND AWARDS** Ralph E. Cooley Awd, top intercultural paper, nat conf of the Speech Commun Assn. **MEMBERSHIPS** Nat Commun Assn, Cent States Commun Assn, Int Network on Personal Rels, Soc for Int Educ, Training and Res. **RESEARCH** Intergroup/Intercultural commun; relationships; issues of tolerance. **SELECTED PUBLICATIONS** Co-auth, An African American communication perspective, Intercultural

communication: A reader, Wadsworth, 7th ed, 140-147, 94; co-auth, Definitions of culture: Conceptualizations from five disciplines, Urban Studies Ctr, Ariz State Univ, 94; auth, Lost and Found: Ethics in intercultural/interethnic communication studies, Seeking understanding of communication, language and gender, CyberSpace, 94; co-auth, The layered perspective of cultural (in)tolerance(s): The roots of a multidisciplinary approach, Intercultural Communication Theory, Sage, 59-90, 95; Book review, Understudied relationships: Off the beaten track, ISSPR Bulletin: Official News Journal of the International Society for the Study of Personal Relationships, 16-18, 96; co-auth, An African American Communication Perspective, Intercultural communication: A reader, Wadsworth, 8th ed, 147-154, 97; co-auth, Family culture and relationship differences as a source of intercultural communication, Readings in cultural contexts, Mayfield, 335-344, 98; co-auth, Layers and holograms: A new look at prejudice, Communication of Prejudice, Sage, 57-84, 98; Auth, Tolerancee/intolerance: A historical and multidisciplinary view of prejudice, Communication of Prejudice, Sage, 24-56, 98. **CONTACT ADDRESS** Dept of Commun, Illinois State Univ, Ill State Univ, PO Box 4480, Normal, IL 61790-4480. **EMAIL** jrbaldw@ilstu.edu

BALDWIN, LEWIS V.
PERSONAL Born 09/17/1949, Camden, AL, m, 1979 **DISCIPLINE** THEOLOGY **EDUCATION** Talladega Col, BA, history, 1971; Colgate-Rochester, Bexley Hall, Crozer Seminary, MA, black church studies, 1973, MDiv, theology, 1975; Northwestern University, PhD, history of Christianity, 1980. **CAREER** Wooster College, visiting assistant professor of religion, 81-92; Colgate University, assistant professor of philosophy and religion, 82-84, visiting assistant professor of church history, 83-84, Colgate-Rochester Divinity School; Vanderbilt University, assistant professor of religious studies, 84-90, associate professor, 91-. **HONORS AND AWARDS** US Jaycees, Outstanding Young Man of America, 1975, 1980, 1985, 1990; American Theological Library Association, Book Awd, 1981; Mid-West Publishers' Association, MBA Book Awd, 1992. **MEMBERSHIPS** Society for the Study of Black Religion, 1981-; American Academy of Religion, 1981-; American Society of Church History, 1981-; NAACP, 1980-; Southern Christian Leadership Conference, financial supporter, 1986-. **SELECTED PUBLICATIONS** Books published: Freedom is Never Free: A Biographical Profile of E D Nixon Sr, 1992; To Make the Wounded Whole: The Cultural Legacy of M L King Jr, 1992; There is a Balm in Gilead: The Cultural Roots of M L King Jr, 1991; The Mark of a Man: Peter Spencer and the African Union Methodist Tradition, 1987; Invisible Strands in African Methodism: The AUMP and UAME Churches, 1805-1980, 1983; Toward the Beloved Community: Martin Luther King Jr and South Africa, 1995. **CONTACT ADDRESS** Vanderbilt Univ, Garland Hall, Rm 305, 21st Ave S, Nashville, TN 37235.

BALESTRA, DOMINIC JOSEPH
PERSONAL Born 05/21/1947, Philadelphia, PA, m, 1974, 3 children **DISCIPLINE** PHILOSOPHY OF SCIENCE, CLASSICAL MODERN PHILOSOPHY **EDUCATION** Saint Francis Col, BS, 68; Saint Louis Univ, PhD, 77. **CAREER** Instr, 75-76, asst prof, 76-82, asst chmn, 79-82, assoc prof philos, ch dept philos, 89-95, and 99-02, pres fac sen, 92-94, prof philos, 98, Fordham Univ, 82-, asst dir honors prog, Saint Louis Univ, 73-75, lectr philos, 73-75; bd gov, Manchester Col, Oxford Univ, 93-96; ed consult, Thought. **HONORS AND AWARDS** Phi Beta Kappa; Sigma Xi. **MEMBERSHIPS** Am Cath Philos Asn, Treas; Am Philos Asn. **RESEARCH** Rationality and historicity of the scientific enterprise; classical modern philosophy; science and religion. **SELECTED PUBLICATIONS** Auth, The centrality of perception: A phenomenol'l perspective in Leibniz, Dialogue, 10/76; Non-falsifiability: An inductivist perspective, Int Logic Rev, 12/79; The mind of Piaget: Its philosophical roots, Thought, 12/80; Dueling Ambitions, Franklin Bacon: The Temper of a Man, Fordham Univ, 93; Galileo's Unfinished Case and Its Cartesian Product: Method, History, and Rationality, Intl Philos Quart, 94; Rev of F Wormald, Francis Bacon: History, Politics, and Science, 1561-1626, Sixteenth Century J, 95; Rev of L Lampert, Nietzsche and Modern Times: A Study of Bacon, Descartes, and Nietzsche, Intl Philos Quart, 97; Science and Religion, Philosophy of Religion: A Guide to the Subject, O P London, 98; At the Origins of Modern Science: Demythologizing Pythagoreanism, The Modern Schoolman, 99. **CONTACT ADDRESS** Dept of Philosophy, Fordham Univ, 501 E Fordham Rd, Bronx, NY 10458-5191. **EMAIL** balestra@fordham.edu

BALL, DAVID T.
PERSONAL Born 08/15/1960, Cincinnati, OH, m, 1997, 3 children **DISCIPLINE** THEOLOGY, LAW **EDUCATION** Ohio Wesleyan Univ, BA, 82; Boston Univ Sch Theology, MDiv, 86; Sch Law, Univ Calif, Berkeley, JD, 91; Graduate Theol Union, PhD, 98. **CAREER** Assoc, Farello, Braun, and Martel, San Francisco, Calif, 91-94; assoc pastor, First United Methodist Church, Wapakeneta, Ohio, 95-96; Dir of Religious Life and Service-Learning, Denison Univ, Granville, Ohio, 96-; adjunct fac, Methodist Theol Sch in Ohio, Delaware, 99-2000. **HONORS AND AWARDS** Paul Harris fel, Jackson & Lowstuter Fel. **MEMBERSHIPS** Am Acad of Relig, State Bar of Calif, Nat Asn of Col and Univ Chaplains. **RESEARCH** Constitutional history, constitutional law, service-learning. **SELECTED PUBLICATIONS** Book rev, L'Ecologie et la loi: le statut juridique de l'environment, 17, Ecology Law Quart 227 (90); auth, "Rabbinic Rhetoric and the Tribute Passage," Novum Testamentum, 25 (93): 1-14; auth, "In House Termination Is at Issue," The Nat Law J (May 30, 94); auth, "The Things That Are God's': Reflections on Caesar's Coin," The Christian Century, 115 (Nov 11, 98): 1046-47; auth, "The Displacement and Recovery of Self and Spirit in the Practice of Law," in The Ohio State Bar Asn and Continuing Legal Ed Inst, Faith and Law: The Religious and Ethical Dimensions of Zealous Advocacy, Reference Manual, Vol 99-76 (99). **CONTACT ADDRESS** Alford Center for Service-Learning, Denison Univ, Office of Religious Life, Granville, OH 43023-1372. **EMAIL** ball@denison.edu

BALL, TERENCE
PERSONAL Born 07/18/1944, Independence, KS, m, 1967, 2 children **DISCIPLINE** POLITICAL SCIENCE **EDUCATION** Univ Calif Santa Cruz, BA, 67; Univ Calif Berkeley, PhD, 73. **CAREER** Asst prof to prof, Univ Minn, 72-98; vis prof, Univ Calif San Diego, 84; prof, Ariz State Univ, 98-. **HONORS AND AWARDS** Phi Beta Kappa; Vis Fel, Oxford Univ, 78-7, 93, 95, 98; Fel, Woodrow Wilson Intl Ctr for Scholars; NEH Fel; Bush Found Fel. **MEMBERSHIPS** Am Polit Sci Asn; Conf for the Study of Polit Thought. **RESEARCH** Political theory: political philosophy, history of political thought, green political theory; History and philosophy of the social sciences. **SELECTED PUBLICATIONS** Ed, James Mill: Political Writings, Cambridge, 92; auth, Reappraising Political Theory, Oxford, 95; auth, Rousseau's Ghost: A Novel, New York, 98; co-ed, Thomas Jefferson: Political Writings, Cambridge, 99. **CONTACT ADDRESS** Dept Polit Sci, Arizona State Univ, MC 2001, Tempe, AZ 85287. **EMAIL** terence.ball@asu.edu

BALL, WILLIAM BATTEN
PERSONAL Born 08/28/1928, San Antonio, TX, m, 1956 **DISCIPLINE** LAW; TAX LAW SPECIALIST; INSURANCE COMPANY TAX LAW SPECIALIST **EDUCATION** Woodrow Wilson Jr Coll, Chicago IL, 1944-45; Roosevelt Univ, Chicago IL, BS, Commerce, 1955, MBA, 1960; Chicago Kent Coll of Law of IL Inst of Technology, Chicago IL, JD, 1968. **CAREER** IRS, revenue officer 1955-57; Supreme Life Insurance Co, accountant, jr exec 1957-59; State of IL Dept of Labor, auditor 1959; IRS, agent 1959-67, appellate appeals officer 1967-86; management coordinator, 72-73; Attorney, private practice, 86-. **HONORS AND AWARDS** Various Awds & Honors, BSA; Outstanding Performance Awd, IRS; master's thesis, "Insurance Co Annual Statement Preparation/ Instructions," Roosevelt Univ, 1960. **MEMBERSHIPS** Member, Chicago & Cook Co Bar Assoc, IL State Bar Assn, Amer Bar Assn, Natl Bar Assn; chmn admin bd St Mark United Meth Ch 1973-77; troop committeeman BSA; member Order of the Arrow Natl Fraternity of Scout Honor Campers; member Order of Brotherhood; life member, Kappa Alpha Psi Fraternity Inc; member, bd of dir, Community Mental Health Council, 1982-87; Chicago Board of Education, mem of: Westcott Local School Council, 1989-93, chairman, Bylaws Committee, Subdistrict 8 Council Representative, 1989-93. **CONTACT ADDRESS** 8355 S Perry Ave, Chicago, IL 60620.

BALLARD, HAROLD WAYNE, JR.
PERSONAL Born 09/16/1963, Wooster, OH, m, 1985, 2 children **DISCIPLINE** THEOLOGY **EDUCATION** Okla Baptist Univ, BA, 85; Golden Gate Baptist Theol Sem, MDiv, 90; S Baptist Theol Sem, PhD, 95. **CAREER** Instr, S Baptist Theol Sem, 94; instr, Boyce Bible Col, 95-97; asst prof Relig, Campbell Univ, 97-. **HONORS AND AWARDS** Outstanding Young Men of Am, 96, 98. **MEMBERSHIPS** Soc Bibl Lit; Nat Asn Baptist Prof Relig; Am Acad Relig; NAPH. **RESEARCH** Psalms and wisdom literature; Hebrew Bible. **SELECTED PUBLICATIONS** Auth, The Divine Warrior Motif in the Psalms, 98; co-ed, An Introduction to Wisdom Literature and the Psalms, 00. **CONTACT ADDRESS** PO Box 603, Buies Creek, NC 27506. **EMAIL** ballard@mailcenter.campbell.edu

BALLOT, MICHAEL
PERSONAL Born 01/08/1940, New York, NY, m, 1963, 3 children **DISCIPLINE** BUSINESS ADMINISTRATION **EDUCATION** Cornell Univ, BME, 62; Univ Santa Clara, MBA, 65; Stanford Univ, MA, 68, PhD, 73. **CAREER** Engineer, 62-64, Lockheed Missiles & Space; mfg eng, 64-65, Beckman Instruments; Asst Prof econ, 68-71, Cal State Univ, Chico; Asst, Assoc, Prof, 71-, Univ Pacific. **HONORS AND AWARDS** Stanford U Fel. **MEMBERSHIPS** AEA; IRRA; DSI; SCS; AAPSS. **RESEARCH** Labor Mgmt Relations; Comparative IR; Forecasting for Business. **SELECTED PUBLICATIONS** Auth, Decision-Making Models in Production and Operations Management, Krieger, 86; auth, Labor Relations in Russia and Eastern Europe, Labor and L J 95; coauth, Where will all the Workers Go? Chinese Labor Relations in Transition, Labor L J, 95; coauth, Labor Relations in Pacific Asia's Four Little Tigers, Govt Union Rev, 95; coauth, The Iron Rice Bowel: Labor Turmoil in China, Research & Practice in Human Resource Mgmt, 95; Auth, British Labor Relations and the Law, Labor L J96; auth, Labor-Management Relations in a Changing Environment, Wiley, 96. **CONTACT ADDRESS** Eberhardt Sch of Business, Univ of the Pacific, Stockton, Stockton, CA 95211. **EMAIL** mballot@uop.edu

BALMER, RANDALL
PERSONAL Born 10/22/1954, Chicago, IL, m, 1998, 3 children **DISCIPLINE** RELIGION **EDUCATION** Princeton Univ, PhD 85. **CAREER** Columbia Univ, asst prof, assoc prof, assoc prof Barnard, prof Barnard, 85-. **HONORS AND AWARDS** Sidney E Mead Prize; Nominated for Emmy Awd Acad Tele Arts and Sciences, 93-94. **MEMBERSHIPS** AAR; ATAS; ASCH. **RESEARCH** Evangelicalism; Acadian History and Culture. **SELECTED PUBLICATIONS** Auth, Grant Us Courage: Travels Along the Mainland of American Protestantism, NY Oxford Univ Press, 96; The Presbyterians, coauth, Denominations in Amer Series, ed Henry Warner Bowden, NY and Westport CT, Greenwood Press, 93, pbk 94; Mine Eyes Have Seen the Glory: A Journey into the Evangelical Subculture in America, NY, Oxford Univ Press, 89, expanded 93, 3rd ed 99; Modern Christian Revivals, coed, Urbana and Chicago, Univ IL Press, 93; In the Beginning: The Creationist Controversy, writer and presenter for PBS, produced by WTTW-Television, Chicago, produced by Kay Weibel, dir by Jack Ginay; Crusade: The Life of Billy Graham, exec prod, writer and presenter for PBS, produced by WTTW-Television, Chicago and Cutting Edge Prod, London, dir by Julian Norridge, recut for broadcast in A&E Biography Series, 95; Mine Eyes Have Seen the Glory, writer and presenter for PBS, Prod by WTTW-Television, Chicago and Isis Prod, London, dir by Julie Norridge; auth, Blessed Assurance: A History of Evangelicalism in America, Beacon Press (Boston), 99. **CONTACT ADDRESS** Dept of Religion, Columbia Univ, 3009 Broadway, New York, NY 10027-6598. **EMAIL** rb281@columbia.edu

BANCHETTI-ROBINO, MARINA P.
PERSONAL Born 11/07/1963, Montevideo, Uruguay **DISCIPLINE** PHILOSOPHY **EDUCATION** Univ Miami, BA, 85; MA, 90; PhD, 91. **CAREER** Adj prof, Fla A&M Univ, 91-93; vis asst prof, 93-95; asst prof, 95-, Fla Atlantic Univ. **HONORS AND AWARDS** NSF travel grant 10th Intl Cong of Logic, Methodology and Philos of Sci, presentation of lect; Col Res Yr, 97-98, asst prof. **MEMBERSHIPS** Intl Asn Philos & Lit; Philos of Sci Asn; Husserl Cir; Am Philos Asn; So Soc Philos and Psych, Fla Philos Asn; Soc for Phenomenology and Existential Philosophy. **RESEARCH** Phenomenology; philosophy of science; philosophy of language, philosophy of mind. **SELECTED PUBLICATIONS** "Follesdal on the Notion of the Noema," in Husserl Stud, 93; "On the Use of Fictional Works in Eng Ethics Courses," APA Newsl on Tchg Philos, 96; "Husserl's Theory of Language as Calculus Ratiocinator," Synthese, 97; author, "A Wittgensteinian Approach to Scientific Instrumentalism," Role of Pragmatics in Contemporary Philosophy, Austrian Ludwig Wittgenstein Society, 97. **CONTACT ADDRESS** Dept of Philosophy, Florida Atlantic Univ, PO Box 3091, Boca Raton, FL 33431-0991. **EMAIL** banchett@fau.edu

BANDMAN, BERTRAM
PERSONAL m **DISCIPLINE** BIOETHICS, PHILOSOPHY OF LAW, PHILOSOPHY OF RELIGION **EDUCATION** Columbia Univ, BS, MA, PhD. **CAREER** Prof, Long Island Univ; exec comt, Conf on Methods in Philos and the Sci. **HONORS AND AWARDS** Trustee Awd, Long Island Univ; Human Rights fel, Columbia Univ. **RESEARCH** Children's rights; the moral development of health care providers. **SELECTED PUBLICATIONS** Auth, The Child's Right to Inquire, in Thinking Children and Education, Kendall/Hunt, 93; The Adolescent's Right to Freedom, Care and Enlightenment, in Thinking Children and Education, Kendall/Hunt, 93; coauth, Nursing Ethics Through The Life Span, Appelton-Lange, 95; Critical Thinking, Appelton-Lange, 95; coed, Philosophical Essays on Teaching, Lippincott, 69; Philosophical Essays on Curriculum, Lippincott, 69; Bioethics and Human Rights: A Reader for Health Professionals, Little Brown, 78. **CONTACT ADDRESS** Dept of Philos, Long Island Univ, Brooklyn, Brooklyn, NY 11201-8423. **EMAIL** bertram.bandman@liu.edu

BANDSTRA, BARRY L.
PERSONAL Born 04/05/1951, Chicago, IL, m, 1971, 3 children **DISCIPLINE** RELIGIOUS STUDIES **EDUCATION** Yale Univ, PhD, 82. **CAREER** Prof, 83-. **HONORS AND AWARDS** Mellon Fel, 85-86. **MEMBERSHIPS** Soc of Bibl Lit; Chicago Soc for Bibl Res. **RESEARCH** Hebrew grammar and syntax. **SELECTED PUBLICATIONS** Auth, Reading the Old Testament, 99. **CONTACT ADDRESS** Dept of Religion, Hope Col, 126 E 10th St, Holland, MI 49423. **EMAIL** bandstra@hope.edu

BANGERT, MARK PAUL
DISCIPLINE PASTORAL THEOLOGY; WORSHIP AND MUSIC **EDUCATION** Concordia Sem; Univ Minn, PhD. **CAREER** John H. Tietjen prof; dir, Pub events at LSTC; dir, LSTC Chorus, 83-93; dir, Adult Mus, St. Luke Lutheran Church. **HONORS AND AWARDS** Bd mem, Paul Manz Inst. **MEMBERSHIPS** Mem, intl study group on Bach res. **CONTACT ADDRESS** Dept of Pastoral Theology, Worship and Music, Lutheran Sch of Theol at Chicago, 1100 E 55th St, Chicago, IL 60615. **EMAIL** mbangert@lstc.edu

BANGS, CARL
PERSONAL Born 04/05/1922, Seattle, WA, m, 1942, 3 children **DISCIPLINE** THEOLOGY **EDUCATION** Pasadena

Col, AB, 45; Nazarene Theol Sem, BD, 49; Univ Chicago, PhD(theol), 58. **CAREER** From asst prof to assoc prof relig & philos, Olivet Nazarene Col, 53-61; assoc prof, 61-66, Prof Hist of Theol, St Paul Sch Theol, 66-, Kansas City Coun Higher Educ res grant, 63; Fulbright prof theol, State Univ Leiden, 68-69, guest prof, 75. **HONORS AND AWARDS** Christian Res Found Prize, 62. **MEMBERSHIPS** Am Soc Church Hist (pres, 72); Am Theol Soc (pres Midwest Div, 66-67); Am Soc Reformation Res; Dutch Church Hist Soc. **RESEARCH** Dutch Reformation; Arminianism; Mennonite history. **SELECTED PUBLICATIONS** Auth, The Communist Encounter, Beacon Hill, 63; De herstructering van de theologische opleiding, Theol en Praktijk, 7/69; Arminius: A Study in the Dutch Reformation, 71; All the best Bishoprics and Deaneries: The enigma of Arminian politics, Church Hist, 3/73. **CONTACT ADDRESS** Saint Paul Sch of Theol, 5123 Truman Rd, Kansas City, MO 63127.

BANKS, SHARON P.
PERSONAL Born 09/21/1942, Washington, DC **DISCIPLINE** LAW **EDUCATION** Morgan State Coll, BA 1964; Howard Univ Law Sch, JD 1967. **CAREER** Neighborhood Legal Serv Program, 67-72; Private Practice, attorney, 72-; Howard Univ, part-time teacher, 69-72, full-time teacher, 72-. **MEMBERSHIPS** Mem Natl, Amer, DC Bar Assns; Howard Univ Law Alumni Assn; bd dir DC ACIU; Kappa Beta Pi Legal Sor. **CONTACT ADDRESS** Dept of Pol Sci, Howard Univ, 112 Douglass Hall, Washington, DC 20001.

BANNAN, JOHN F.
DISCIPLINE PHILOSOPHY **EDUCATION** Catholic Univ America, AB, MA; Univ Louvain, Belgium, PhD. **CAREER** Prof, Loyola Univ Chicago, 57-; chp & dir, grad Stud; fac, New Rochelle Col, NY. **RESEARCH** Descartes; French phenomenology; Merleau-Ponty; Sartre; Levi-Strauss. **SELECTED PUBLICATIONS** Auth, Among his publications are The Philosophy of Merleau-Ponty,Harcourt, Brace, & World, 67; coauth, Law, Morality, and Vietnam: The Peace Militants and the Courts, Ind UP, 74. **CONTACT ADDRESS** Dept of Philosophy, Loyola Univ, Chicago, 820 N. Michigan Ave., Chicago, IL 60611.

BAR-ON, DORIT
PERSONAL Born Tel Aviv, Israel, m, 1988, 1 child **DISCIPLINE** PHILOSOPHY **EDUCATION** Tel Aviv Univ, BA, 79; UCLA, MA, 80, PhD, 87. **CAREER** Asst prof, Univ Rochester, 87-89; vis prof, 88, asst prof, 89-94, assoc prf, 94-, Univ North Carolina, Chapel Hill; vis scholar, Tel Aviv Univ, 93. **HONORS AND AWARDS** Cum Laude, 79; NEH stipend, 92; Tanner Awd for Excellence in Undergrad Tchg, 94; Max Chapman Fac Fel, 95; ACLS Grant, 96; Cognitive Sci Course Dev grant, 97; res and study assignment, 97. **MEMBERSHIPS** APA. **RESEARCH** Philosophy of mind; philosophy of language and of linguistics; twentieth-century analytic philosophy, especially Quine, Davidson, Dummett and Wittgenstein. **SELECTED PUBLICATIONS** Auth, Conceptual Relativism and Translation, in Preyer, ed, Language, Mind, and Epistemology, Kluwer, 94; auth, Indeterminacy of Translation: Theory and Practice, Philos and Phenomenol Res, 95; auth, Meaning Reconstructed: Grice and the Naturalization of Semantics, Pacific Philos Quart, 97; auth, Anti-Realism and Speaker Knowledge, Synthese, 96; auth, Natural Semantic Facts--Between Eliminativism and Hyper-Realism, in Jutronic, ed, The Maribor Papers in Naturalized Semantics, 97; auth, "Avowals and First-Person Privilege," in Philosophy and Phenomenological Research; auth, "Deflationism and Truth-Condition Theories of Meaning," in Philosophical Studies; auth, "Speaking My Mind," in Philosophical Topics. **CONTACT ADDRESS** Philosophy Dept, Univ of No Carolina, Chapel Hill, 202-A Caldwell Hall, Chapel Hill, NC 27599-3125. **EMAIL** dbar@email.unc.edu

BARAD, JUDITH A.
PERSONAL Born 02/09/1944, Chicago, IL, m, 1985, 1 child **DISCIPLINE** PHILOSOPHY **EDUCATION** Oakton Community Col, AA, 78; Loyola Univ of Chicago, BA, 80; Northwestern Univ, Evanston, MA, 82, PhD, 84. **CAREER** Adjunct prof, Oakton Community Col, 84-85; instr, Barat Col, 84-85; asst prof, Indiana State Univ, 85-89, assoc prof, 89-94, prof, 94-, acting chair, Philos Dept, 93-94, chair, 94-. **HONORS AND AWARDS** The John B. Lavezzorio Scholarship, Loyola, 78-80; nominee for the Danforth Fel, Loyola, 79; Northwestern Scholarship, 80; Teaching Assistantship, Northwestern, 81-84; Nat Endowment for the Humanities grant, 85; Indiana State Univ Summer Res grant, 88; "Excellence in Education" Awd from Blue Key, 96; Individual Fac Development grant, ISU, 96; Proposal Incentive Fund Awd, 96. **MEMBERSHIPS** Am Cath Philos Asn, Am Philos Asn, Int Thomas Aquinas Soc, Soc for Medieval and Renaissance Philos, Indiana Philos Asn, The Int Soc for Neoplatonic Studies. **RESEARCH** Thomas Aquinas, medieval philosophy, philosophy of religion. **SELECTED PUBLICATIONS** Auth, Consent: The Means to an Active Faith According to St. Thomas Aquinas, New York: Peter Lang Pub Co (92); auth, Aquinas on the Nature and Treatment of Animals, Bethesda, Md: Int Scholars Pub (95); auth, The Ethics of Star Trek, New York: Harper Collins (2000). **CONTACT ADDRESS** Dept Philos--Root Hall, Indiana State Univ, 210 N 7th St, Terre Haute, IN 47809-0001. **EMAIL** pibarad@root.indstate.edu

BARANOWSKI, SHELLEY
PERSONAL Born 06/14/1946, Columbus, OH, m, 1969 **DISCIPLINE** RELIGION **EDUCATION** Wells Col, BA, 68; Princeton Univ, MA, 78; Princeton Univ, PhD, 80. **CAREER** Part-time positions, Princeton Univ, Douglass Col, Ohio State Univ, 80-84; vis asst prof, Kenyon Col, 85-89; asst prof hist, Univ Akron, 89-91; assoc prof hist, Univ Akron, 91-95; prof hist, Univ Akron, 95-. **HONORS AND AWARDS** ACLS Grant-in-Aid; Fel for Independent Study and Res, Nat Endowment for the Humanities; Fulbright-Hays Fel; DAAD Fel. **MEMBERSHIPS** AHA; German Studies Asn; Conf Group on Central European Hist; German Hist Soc; Ohio Acad of Hist. **RESEARCH** Twentieth century Germany; social and religious history. **SELECTED PUBLICATIONS** Auth, The Confessing Church, Conservative Elites and the Nazi State, Edwin Mellen Press, 86; auth, "Consent and Dissent: The Confessing Church and Conservative Oppositions to National Socialism", in Journal of Modern History 59 no.1, 87; auth, "The Sanctity of Rural Life: Protestantism, Agrarian Politics and the Rise of Nazism in Pomerania during the Weimar Republic", in German History 9 no. 1, 91; auth, "Convergence on the Right: Agrarian Elite Radicalism and Nazi Populism in Pomerania, 1928-33", in Between Reform, Reaction, and Resistance: Essays in the History of German Conservatism, 1789-1945, Berg Publishers, 93; auth, The Sanctity of Rural Life. Nobility, Protestantism, and Nazism in Weimar Prussia, Oxford Univ Press, 95; auth, "East Elbian Landed Elites and Germany's Turn to Fascism: The Sonderweg Controversy Revisited", in European History Quart 26 no. 2, 96; auth, "Conservative Antisemitism from Weimar to the Third Reich", in German Studies Review 19 no. 3, 96; auth, "Continuity and Contingency: Agrarian Elites, Conservative Institutions and East Elbia in Modern German History", in Social History 12 no. 3, 97; auth, "Nazism and Polarization: The Left and the Third Reich," Historical J 43 (00); co-ed, Being Elsewhere: Tourism, Consumer Culture and Identity in Modern Europe and North America, Univ Mich Pr, 01. **CONTACT ADDRESS** Department of Akron, Univ of Akron, Akron, OH 44325-1902. **EMAIL** sbarano@uakron.edu

BARASH, CAROL ISAACSON
PERSONAL Born 10/22/1955, Detroit, MI, m, 1986, 2 children **DISCIPLINE** PHILOSOPHY **EDUCATION** Univ of Chicago, PhD. **CAREER** Founder, prin, Genetics, Ethics & Policy Consulting, 94- . **HONORS AND AWARDS** MCHB grant; SPRANS grant, Triggering Need to Know: Barriers to Learning Genetics, 97- . **MEMBERSHIPS** APA. **RESEARCH** Medical genetics; education. **SELECTED PUBLICATIONS** Auth, Consultation on Human Rights and Bioethics, Genetic Resource, 94; auth, Genetic Discrimination and What Consumers Can Do to Protect Themselves, Genetic Connections, Sonters Publ INK, 95; auth, Facing History and Ourselves Teaches ELSI Issues as Civics, Genetic Resource, 95; auth, Commentary: Genetic Testing in Children and Adolescents: Parental Authority, The Rights of Children and the Duties of Geneticists, Univ Chicago Law School Roundtable J, 96; auth,Genetic Privacy or Piracy, Global Insights, 96; auth, What is a Cost? What is a Benefit? Genetic Resource, 97; auth, The Need for Moral Leadership in Applying HGP Advances, 97; auth, Genetic Screening Under Ethically Defensible Conditions, conf proc, Int Bioethics Assn, 97. **CONTACT ADDRESS** Genetics, Ethics & Policy Consulting, 317 Lamartine St, No 2, Boston, MA 02130. **EMAIL** cbarash@tiac.net

BARBEE, LLOYD AUGUSTUS
PERSONAL Born 08/17/1925, Memphis, TN, d **DISCIPLINE** LAW **EDUCATION** LeMoyne Coll, BA 1949; Univ of Wis Madison, JD 1956. **CAREER** Industrial Commn of WI UC Dept, law examiner I 1957-62; Gov's Comm on Human Rights, legal consul 1959; NAACP, pres 1962-64; Milwaukee United Sch Integration Comm, chmn 1964; WI Legislature, state representative 1965-77; Univ of Wisconsin, Law Sch, teacher 1968-69, 72; Univ of Wisconsin at Milwaukee, adjunct prof 1976-88; Bronx Community Coll, adjunct prof, 90-92; private practice, Attorney, 56-. **HONORS AND AWARDS** Milwaukee Man of the Yr Alpha Phi Alpha Frat Inc 1965; Medgar Evers Awd Milwaukee Br NAACP 1969; Outstanding & Continuing Contrib to Milwaukee Black Business Comm 1976; Disting Civil Serv Milwaukee Frontiers 1978; Lawyer Scholar Pub Serv Milwaukee Theological Inst 1978; Serv in Education Law & Govern St Mark AME Church 1979; Outstanding Serv as Law Sch Tchr Univ WI Madison Law Sch 1984; Univ of WI at Milwaukee, Coll of Letters & Sci Amer Studies Dept Faculty Awd; Madison West HS, award for outstanding services toward improving civil rights in WI 1986; Wisconsin Black Political and Economic Development Council Awd, 1987; Rufus King Education Awd, 1989; Wisconsin Assn of Minority Attorneys Awd, 1993; Milwaukee Homeless Project Inc, Awd, 1993; Milwaukee Times, Black Excellence Awd, 1994; Amer Civil Liberties Union, Wisconsin, Lifetime Civil Liberties Achievement Awd, 1995; Annual James H Baker Awd, 1996; Malcolm X Commemoration Mount Freedom Awd, 1997; Dedication of West Barbee St, Milwaukee, WI; Mayor John Norquist Proclamation of Lloyd A Barbee Day, Sept 6, 1997. **MEMBERSHIPS** Mem State Bar of WI 1956-; chmn Enrolled Bills comm 1965-66; mem Comm on Joint Finance 1965-73; chmn Assembly Judiciary Comm 1973-77; mem Comm on Transportation 1969-77; pres/pres emeritus WI Black Lawyers Assn 1965-80; chmn WI Black Elected & Apptd Officials 1972-76; minister Political Empowerment Comm Natl Black Assembly 1973-75; Milwaukee Symphony Orchestra, bd of dirs, 1994-96; Natl Bar Assn; Wisconsin Bar Assn; American Bar Assn. **CONTACT ADDRESS** 231 W Wisconsin Ave, Milwaukee, WI 53203.

BARBIERI, WILLIAM A., JR.
PERSONAL Born 06/30/1965, Concord, MA, m, 2 children **DISCIPLINE** ETHICS; RELIGIOUS STUDIES **EDUCATION** Yale Grad Sch, PhD, 92. **CAREER** Vis Assoc Prof, Holy Cross, 92-93; Vis Prof, Hebrew Univ of Jerusalem, 93-94; Asst Prof, Cath Univ Am, 94-. **HONORS AND AWARDS** Humboldt Fel, 99. **MEMBERSHIPS** Am Acad Relig. **RESEARCH** Ethics & political theory; comparative ethics. **SELECTED PUBLICATIONS** Auth, Ethics of Community: Citizenship & Group Rights in Germany, Duke, 98; Ethics and the Narrated Life, J Relig, 7/98. **CONTACT ADDRESS** School of Religious Studies, Catholic Univ of America, Washington, DC 20064. **EMAIL** barbieri@cua.edu

BARBONE, STEVEN
PERSONAL Born 08/17/1960 **DISCIPLINE** PHILOSOPHY **EDUCATION** Marquette Univ, PhD, 97. **CAREER** Asst prof philos, San Diego State Univ, 97-. **HONORS AND AWARDS** Res grant, Marquette Univ, 92; Fulbright nominee, 93-94, 94-95; travel fel, 94-95, 95-96; NEH publ award, 95; Charles M Ross Trust fel award, 96. **MEMBERSHIPS** APA; Phi Sigma Tau; Soc for Philos of Sex and Love, N Am Spinoza Soc; AAUP; Soc for Lesbian and Gay Philos; Am Soc of Aesthet; Int Soc of Aesthet. **SELECTED PUBLICATIONS** Auth, Virtue and Sociality in Spinoza, Ivyun, 93; auth, Plato on the Beautiful, Lyceum V, 93; auth, Frugalitas in St. Augustine, Augustiniana, 94; coauth, Spinoza and the Problem of Suicide, Int Philos Quart, 94; coauth, Coming Out, Being Out, and Acts of Virtue, Jour of Homosexuality, 94; auth, Nothingness and Sartre's Fundamental Project, Philos Today, 94; auth, The Is/Ought Question in Hume, Indian Philos Quart, 94; auth, Infinity in Descartes, Philos Inquiry, 95; introd and notes in, Spinoza, Baruch. The Letters, Hackett, 95; coauth, Spinoza and Human Sexuality, and, Hatching Your Genes Before They're Counted, in Soble, ed, Sex, Love, & Friendship, Rodopi, 96; auth, Natural Law in William Ockham, Int Stud in Philos, 96; auth, Schlick on Aesthetics, Indian Philos Quart, 97. **CONTACT ADDRESS** Dept of Philosophy, San Diego State Univ, 5500 Campanile Dr, San Diego, CA 92182. **EMAIL** barbone@rohan.sdsu.edu

BARBOUR, HUGH
PERSONAL Born 08/07/1921, Peking, China, m, 1959, 3 children **DISCIPLINE** CHURCH HISTORY **EDUCATION** Harbard Univ, AB, 42; Union Theol Sem, NYork, BD, 45; Yale Univ, PhD(relig), 52. **CAREER** Pastor, Congregational Church, Coventry, CT, 45-47; instr Bible & relig, Syracuse Univ, 47-49; instr Bible, Wellesley Col, 50-53; from asst prof to assoc prof relig, 53-67, Prof Relig, Earlham Col, 67-, Mem gov bd, Nat Coun Churches, 72-. **MEMBERSHIPS** Soc Bibl Theol; Soc Bibl Lit. **RESEARCH** Theological writings of William Penn. **SELECTED PUBLICATIONS** Auth, The Quakers in Puritan England, Yale Univ, 64; Step by Step in Reading the Old Testament, Asn Press, 64; Programmed teaching for Old Testament, Relig Educ, 11-12/67; Protestant Quakerism, 71 & The God of peace, 72, Quaker Relig Thought; co-ed, Early Quaker Writings, 1650-1700, Eerdmans, 73; Margaret Fell and the Rise of Quakerism, with B. Y. Kunze, J of Relig, Vol 76, 96; Gentle Invaders-Quaker Women Educators and Racial Issues During the Civil-War and Reconstruction, with L. B. Selleck, Church History, Vol 66, 97. **CONTACT ADDRESS** 1840 SW E St., Richmond, IN 47374.

BARBOUR, IAN GRAEME
PERSONAL Born 11/05/1923, Peking, China, m, 1947, 4 children **DISCIPLINE** RELIGION, PHYSICS **EDUCATION** Swarthmore Col, BA, 43; Duke Univ, MA, 46; Univ Chicago, PhD(physics), 49; Yale Univ, BD, 56. **CAREER** Asst prof physics, Kalamazoo Col, 49-51, assoc prof & chmn dept, 51-53; Ford fel, Yale Univ, 53-54; from asst prof to assoc prof relig, 55-65, Prof Relig & Physics, Carleton Col, 65-, Fels, Am Coun Learned Socs, 63-64, Guggenheim & Fulbright, 67-68, Nat Endowment Humanities, 76-77 & Nat Humanities Ctr, 80-81; Lilly vis prof, Purdue Univ, 73-74. **HONORS AND AWARDS** Templeton Prize for Progress in Religion, 99. **MEMBERSHIPS** Am Acad Relig; AAAS. **RESEARCH** Contemporary theology; philosophy of science. **SELECTED PUBLICATIONS** Auth, Issues in Science and Religion, Prentice-Hall, 66; ed, Science and Religion, 68 & auth, Science and Secularity: The Ethics of Technology, 70, Harper; ed, Earth Might be Fair, Prentice-Hall, 72; Western Man and Environmental Ethics, Addison-Wesley, 73; auth, Myths, models and paradigms, SCM, 73; Technology, Environment and Human Values, Praeger, 80; auth, Religion in an Age of Science, Harper Collins, 90; auth, Ethics in an Age of Technology, Harper Collins, 93; auth, Religion and Science: Historical and Contemporary Issues, Harper Collins, 97; auth, When Science Meets Religion, Harper Collins, 00. **CONTACT ADDRESS** Dept of Relig, Carleton Col, Northfield, MN 55057. **EMAIL** ibarbour@carleton.edu

BARBOUR, JOHN D.
PERSONAL Born 08/08/1951, Kalamazoo, MI, m, 1978, 2 children **DISCIPLINE** RELIGION AND LITERATURE **ED-**

UCATION Oberlin Col, BA, 73; Univ Chicago Divinity Sch, MA, 75; PhD, 81. **CAREER** Prof & Chemn of Dept of Relig, St Olaf Col. **SELECTED PUBLICATIONS** Auth, Tragedy as a Critique of Virtue, 84; auth, The Conscience of the Autobiographer, 92; auth, Versions of Deconversion: Autobiography and the Loss of Faith, 94. **CONTACT ADDRESS** Dept Relig, St. Olaf Col, 1520 Saint Olaf Ave, Northfield, MN 55057-1574.

BARKER, EVELYN M.
PERSONAL Born 02/16/1927, Franklin, MA, m, 1961, 2 children **DISCIPLINE** PHILOSOPHY **EDUCATION** Wheaton Col , BA, 48; Vassar Col , MA, 49; Harvard Univ, PhD, 56. **CAREER** Instr, Wells Coll, 50-51; lect, asst prof, Mount Holyoke Coll, 56-61; vis prof, Ohio Wesleyan Univ, 62-63; vis prof, McCoy Coll, Johns Hopkins, 64-65; vis prof, Univ Md Evening Coll, 65-66; lect, assoc prof, Emerita, Univ MD, Baltimore County, 66-. **HONORS AND AWARDS** Phi Beta Kappa. **MEMBERSHIPS** Am Philos Asn; Soc for Ancient Greek Philos. **RESEARCH** Aristotle; Personal Relations, Bioethics, Phenomenology. **SELECTED PUBLICATIONS** Auth, Everyday Reasoning, Prentice Hall, 81; auth, "Personal Relationships," in Ready Reference Ethics, vol 2; auth, "Rethinking Family Loyalties," in Aging and Ethics, ed. N. Jecker (91); auth, Aristotle's Logic: Techne of Episteme?, The Philos of Logos, 96; Socratic Intolerance and Aristotelian Toleration, Philos, Rel and the Question of Intolerance, 97. **CONTACT ADDRESS** 4003 Keswick Rd, Baltimore, MD 21211. **EMAIL** Kesbarkers@aol.com

BARKER, JEFFREY
DISCIPLINE PHILOSOPHY **EDUCATION** CA St Univ, BA, 78; Purdue Univ, MA, 80, PhD 83 **CAREER** Chair & Prof, Albright Col **CONTACT ADDRESS** Dept of Philos, Albright Col, Reading, PA 19612-5234.

BARKER, LANCE R.
PERSONAL Born 03/29/1938, Sidney, NE, m, 1995, 1 child **DISCIPLINE** SOCIAL ETHICS **EDUCATION** Univ Wyoming, BA, 60; San Francisco Theol Sem, BD, 64; Univ Chicago Div Sch, MA, 69; PhD, 76. **CAREER** United Theol Sem, 69-. **HONORS AND AWARDS** Nat Presby Grad Fel; San Francisco Theol Sem Grad Fel. **MEMBERSHIPS** RRA; RSS; SCE. **RESEARCH** Congregational studies; alternative models of theological education; rural churches. **SELECTED PUBLICATIONS** Auth, "Crossing Boundaries - Building Bridges," 91; auth, Alternative Theological Education, 00. **CONTACT ADDRESS** Dept Religion, United Theol Sem of the Twin Cities, 3000 5th Street, Saint Paul, MN 55112-2507.

BARKER, PETER
PERSONAL Born 11/27/1949 **DISCIPLINE** PHILOSOPHY **EDUCATION** Univ Oxford, Eng, BA, 71; SUNY, Buffalo, PhD, 75. **CAREER** Instr, 72-75, SUNY-Buf; asst prof, 75-81, assoc prof, 81-84, Memphis St Univ; dir, grad prog, sci & tech, 85-87, assoc prof, 84-95, Va Polytechnic Inst & St Univ; prof, 95-, chmn, 97-, hist of sci dept, Univ Okla. **HONORS AND AWARDS** NEH: Sum Sem Col Tchrs, 84, Div Res Conf Grants, 84 & 89, Interpretive Res, Hum, Sci & Tech, Res Grant 92-94; Natl Sci Found, res grant, 92-94; vis fel, 92-93 Centrum Phil und Wissenschaftstheorie, Univ Konstanz Germany; vis scholar, Ctr Appl Psychol, Memphis St Univ, 90. **MEMBERSHIPS** Hist of Sci Soc; Phil Sci Assn; APA; So Soc for Phil & Psych. **SELECTED PUBLICATIONS** Co-ed, After Einstein: Proceedings of the Memphis State Einstein Centenary Conference, Mem St Press, 81; coauth, Pierre Duhem: Historian and Philosopher of Science, Synthese 83; 90; co-ed, Revolution and Continuity: Essays in the History and Philosophy of Early Modern Science, Cath Univ Amer Press, 91; coauth, Distance and Velocity in Kepler's Astronomy, Annals of Sci 51, 94; coauth, The Role of Rothmann in the Dissolution of the Celestial Spheres, British J Hist of Sci 28, 95; auth, Understanding Change and Continuity: Transmission and Appropriation in Sixteenth Century Natural Philosophy, Tradition, Transmission, Transformation, Brill, 96; coauth, Kuhn's Mature Philosophy of Science and Cognitive Science, Phil Psych 9, 96; auth, Kepler's Epistemology, Method & Order in Renaissance Natural Phil, Kluwer, 97; auth, Kuhn and the Sociological Revolution, Configurations 6:21, 98; coauth, Kuhn's Theory of Scientific Revolutions and Cognitive Psychology, Phil Psych 11:5, 98; coauth Realism and Instrumentalism in Sixteenth Century Astronomy: A Reappraisal, Persp on Sci, 98; co-trs, Pierre Duhem: Essays in History and Philosophy of Science, 96. **CONTACT ADDRESS** Dept of History of Science, Univ of Oklahoma, 601 Elm, Rm 622, Norman, OK 73019-0315. **EMAIL** BarkerP@ou.edu

BARKER, WILLIAM SHIRMER, II
PERSONAL Born 12/15/1934, St. Louis, MO, m, 1957, 2 children **DISCIPLINE** CHURCH HISTORY **EDUCATION** Princeton Univ, BA, 56; Cornell Univ, MA, 59; Covenant Theol Sem, BD, 60; Vanderbilt Univ, PhD, 70. **CAREER** Instr, Covenant Col, 58-64; asst prof, 64-70; assoc prof, dean of fac, 70-72; assoc prof, dean of fac, Covenant Theol Sem, 72-77; assoc prof, pres, 77-84; prof, Westminster Theol Sem, 87-, vice pres for acad affairs, 91-00. **HONORS AND AWARDS** Phi Beta Kappa. **MEMBERSHIPS** Am Soc of Ch Hist; Ev Theol Soc; Coal on Faith and Hist; 16th-Cent Soc. **RESEARCH** American Presbyterianism; English Puritans. **SELECTED PUBLICATIONS** Ed, Presbyterian Jour, 84-87; auth, Puritan Profiles: 54 Influential Puritans at the Time When the Westminster Confession of Faith Was Written; The Hemphill Case, Benjamin Franklin, and Subscription to the Westminster Confession, Amer Presbyterians, 91. **CONTACT ADDRESS** 508 Sunnyside Ave., Webster Groves, MO 63119.

BARKSDALE, LEONARD N., III
PERSONAL Born 11/11/1948, Galveston, TX, m, 1974 **DISCIPLINE** LAW **EDUCATION** University of Houston, BA, 1971; Thurgood Marshall School of Law, JD, 1974. **CAREER** Legal Aid Society of Louisville, attorney, 74; Houston Legal Foundation, attorney, 75; Houston Community Col, law instructor, 75-85; private practice of law, senior attorney, 76-; Fifth Ward Missionary Baptist Church, minister, 92-; Fifth Ward Missionary Baptist Church, pastor, currently. **HONORS AND AWARDS** Boys Scouts of America, Eagle Scout, 1964; Reginald Heber Smith Fellow, 1974-75; legal intern, United States Judge Advocate Gen, Pentagon, Washington, DC, 1972; Boy Scouts of America, Leadership Awd, 1987; Sigma Gamma Rho Sorority, Men on the Move in the 90's, 1992. **MEMBERSHIPS** State Bar of Texas, 1974-; The National Bar Association, 1975-; Houston Lawyers Association, secretary, 1975-; Omega Psi Phi, 1970-; Central High School Alumni Association, vice pres, 1988-; Phi Alpha Delta, 1974; NAACP, 1990-; Houston Habitat for Humanity, board of directors, 1988-92. **CONTACT ADDRESS** Senior Attorney, Barksdale, Ray, Elmore, Robinson-Wallace, Fitzgerald, 2626 S Loop W, Ste 330, Houston, TX 77054.

BARLOW, BRIAN C.
DISCIPLINE RELIGION, PHILOSOPHY **EDUCATION** Anderson Univ, AB, 78; MA, 83; MDiv, 84; Emory Univ, PhD, 92. **CAREER** Vis asst prof, Emory Univ, 92-96; asst prof, Brenau Univ, 96-. **HONORS AND AWARDS** Hodge Awd, 84; Robert T. Jones Scholar, 89-90. **MEMBERSHIPS** Am Acad of Relig, Am Philos Asn. **RESEARCH** Soren Kierkegaard, Psychoanalysis, Karl Barth, Ludwig Witgenstein. **SELECTED PUBLICATIONS** Auth, "Absence and Presence: The Religious and Psychological Meaning of 'The Lily in the Field and the Bird of the Air,'" Relig Studies and Theol 17,2 (98). **CONTACT ADDRESS** Dept Humanities, Brenau Univ, 1 Centennial Cir, Gainesville, GA 30501-3697.

BARLOW, J. STANLEY
PERSONAL Born 08/25/1924, Johnson City, TN, m, 1951, 4 children **DISCIPLINE** PHILOSOPHY, RELIGION AND PSYCHOLOGY **EDUCATION** Wheaton, AB, 47; Princeton Theol Sem, BD, 50; Univ of St. Andrews, Scotland, PhD, 61; Vanderbilt, 43, 44, Harvard, 59-60; Univ Mich, 62-64. **CAREER** Admin, 64-66, Univ Minn; relig, admin, 66-71, Columbia Univ; Phil, CUNY-Col Staten Island, 72-95. **HONORS AND AWARDS** Robinson fel, 50; Danforth CCW grant, 59; Mich Scholar in Higher Ed Admin, 62-64; Columbia Univ. Sem Assoc, Higher Ed, 73-. **MEMBERSHIPS** APA. **RESEARCH** Mythopoeia and rationality, religion and culture. **SELECTED PUBLICATIONS** Auth, The Fall into Consciousness, Fortress, 73. **CONTACT ADDRESS** 107 Gladwin Ave, Leonia, NJ 07605. **EMAIL** JBarlow31Z@aol.com

BARLOW, JERRY N.
PERSONAL Born 06/13/1945, Waco, TX, m, 1970, 1 child **DISCIPLINE** PASTORAL STUDIES, HOMILETICS **EDUCATION** William Carey Col, BS, 67; New Orleans Baptist Theol Sem, M Div, 78, Th D, 82. **CAREER** Pastor, First Baptist Church, Franklinton, LA, 81-96; chemn, Dept of General Ed, New Orleans Baptist Theol Sem, 96-98, Dir, Commun Center, 98-, assoc prof, 98-. **HONORS AND AWARDS** Petroleum Res Fel, Rice Univ, 67-69; Outstandinmg Young Man in the South, 68; Outstanding Young Men of America, 82; Paul Harris Fel, Rotary Int, 95. **MEMBERSHIPS** Evangelical Homiletics Soc, Evangelical Theol Soc. **RESEARCH** Homiletics, pastoral ministry, communication. **SELECTED PUBLICATIONS** Auth, A Critical Study of the Homiletics of Joseph Parker, New Orleans: NOBTS (82); contribur, Toolbox and Busy Pastors, Nashville: Convention Press (98); auth, Studying with Success: Integrating Acacdemics and Ministry, Gretna: Pelican Pub Co (99). **CONTACT ADDRESS** Grad Sch, New Orleans Baptist Theol Sem, 3939 Gentilly Blvd, New Orleans, LA 70126-4858.

BARLOW, PHILIP L.
PERSONAL Born Salt Lake City, m, 6 children **DISCIPLINE** AMERICAN THEOLOGY & THEOLOGY **EDUCATION** Weber State Col, BA, 75; MTS, 80, ThD, 88, Harvard Univ. **CAREER** Assoc Ed, Journ for the Scientific Study of Religion, 88-90; Asst Prof, 90-94, Assoc Prof, 94-, Chair, 97-99, Hanover Col. **RESEARCH** The concept of time; theology, evil, & suffering; mormonism; religion & space. **SELECTED PUBLICATIONS** Auth, Mormons and the Bible, Oxford, 91; auth, New Historical Atlas of Religion in America, Oxford, 00. **CONTACT ADDRESS** Dept of Theological Studies, Hanover Col, Box 890, Hanover, IN 47243-0890. **EMAIL** barlow@hanover.edu

BARMANN, LAWRENCE F.
PERSONAL Born 06/09/1932, s **DISCIPLINE** HISTORY, HISTORICAL THEOLOGY **EDUCATION** St Louis Univ, BA, 54; PhL, 57; STL, 64; Fordham Univ, MA, 60; Cambridge Univ, ENG, PhD, 70. **CAREER** Teach, St Louis Univ HS, 57-59; from asst prof to prof, St Louis Univ, 70-. **HONORS AND AWARDS** Nancy McNair Ring Awd, SLU, 75; Outstand Teach, Human, SLU, 98; Outstand Teach, Emerson Elec Awd, 99. **MEMBERSHIPS** AAR; ACHA. **RESEARCH** Baron Friedrich von Hugel; Roman Catholic Modernism; Nineteenth Century and Early Twentieth Century European (esp English) Religious History. **SELECTED PUBLICATIONS** Auth, Baron Friedrich von Hugel and the Modernist Crisis in England, Cambridge Univ Press (72); auth, the Letters of Baron Friedrich von Hugel and Professor Norman Kemp Smith, Fordham Univ Press (81); auth, "Confronting Secularization: Origins of the London Society for the Study of Religion," Church Hist (93): 22-40; auth, "Theological Inquiry in an Authoritarian Church: Newman and Modernism," in Discourse and Context: An Interdisciplinary Study of John Henry Newman, ed. Gerard Magill (SW Univ Press, 93), 181-206; auth, "The Modernist As Mystic: Baron Friedrich von Hugel," Zeitschrift fur Neuere Theologicgeschichte (97): 221-250; co-ed, Sanctity and Secularity During the Modernist Period, Soc Bollandistes (Brussels), 99. **CONTACT ADDRESS** Dept American Studies, Saint Louis Univ, 221 N Grand Blvd, Saint Louis, MO 63103. **EMAIL** barmann@slu.edu

BARNBAUM, DEBORAH
PERSONAL Born 04/22/1967, Los Angeles, CA **DISCIPLINE** PHILOSOPHY **EDUCATION** Univ of Calif, LA, BA, 90; Univ of Mass, MA, 93; PhD, 96. **CAREER** TA, assoc prof, Univ of Mass, 91-94; instr, Univ of NH, 94-97; asst prof, Kent State Univ, 97-. **HONORS AND AWARDS** Faculty Summer Institute on Teaching the Ethical, Legal, and Social Implications of the Human Genome Project, NIH; Distinguished Honors Faculty Awd Nominee, Kent State Univ; Puryear Fellowship, Univ of Mass. **MEMBERSHIPS** Am Philos Assoc; Ohio Philos Assoc; The Hastings Center; Bioethics Network of OH. **RESEARCH** Biomedical Ethics, Research Ethics, Ethical Theory. **SELECTED PUBLICATIONS** Auth, "The Harms of Disease and Disability", BioQuarterly 6.4 (98): 4-9; auth, "Why Tamagotchis Are Not Pets", Thinking: The J of Philos for Children 13.4 (98): 41-43; auth, "Early-Onset Diseases, Late-Onset Diseases, and Immortality", Proceedings of the OH Philos Assoc, (98): 27-38; auth, "Viagra, Contraception, and Justice", BioQuarterly 8.1, (99): 1-5; "Interpreting Surrogate Consent Using Counterfactuals", J of Applied Philos 16.2 (99): 167-172; coauth, Ethical Issues in Research: Text and Readings, Prentice Hall (forthcoming). **CONTACT ADDRESS** Dept Philos, Kent State Univ, PO Box 5190, Kent, OH 44242-0001. **EMAIL** dbarnbaum@kent.edu

BARNES, GERALD
DISCIPLINE PHILOSOPHY OF MIND **EDUCATION** Harvard Univ, PhD, 68. **CAREER** Philos, Col NJ. **SELECTED PUBLICATIONS** Auth, Some Remarks on Belief and Desire, Philos Rev, 77; The Conclusion of Practical Reasoning, Analysis, 83. **CONTACT ADDRESS** The Col of New Jersey, PO Box 7718, Ewing, NJ 08628-0718.

BARNES, JOSEPH NATHAN
PERSONAL Born 11/29/1950, Hermondale, MO **DISCIPLINE** LAW **EDUCATION** Ibadan Univ Nigeria, Certificate in Intl Economics, 71; Antioch Col, BA Finance & Commerce, 73; Univ of PA, MBA, 77; Univ of PA Sch of Law, JD, 77. **CAREER** Spearman & Sterling, assoc atty, 77-81; Zimet Haines Moss & Friedman, assoc atty, 81-82; Barnes & Williams, partner, 82-85; Barnes & Darby, partner, 85; Barnes, McGhee, Neal, Poston & Segue, founding partner, currently. **HONORS AND AWARDS** Rockefeller Grant 68, 73; Natl Fellowship Foundation Fel, 73, 74; First Black NY Law firm listed in Dir of Municipal Bond Dealers, 87. **MEMBERSHIPS** Mem Natl Bar Assoc; 81-87; dir Black Entertainment & Sports Lawyers Asn, 83-88; bd mem Urban League Manhattan Branch, 85-87; mem Metro Black Bar Asn, 86-87; Natl Asn of Securities Profs, 86-87; NY chmn telethon United Negro Col Fund, 86, 87, 88; mem NAACP. **CONTACT ADDRESS** Barnes, McGhee, Neal, Poston & Segue, 888 7th Ave #1809, New York, NY 10019-3201.

BARNES, MICHAEL HORTON
DISCIPLINE RELIGIOUS STUDIES **EDUCATION** Marquette Univ, PhD, Religious Studies, 76. **CAREER** Prof of Religious Studies, Univ of Dayton. **HONORS AND AWARDS** Teacher of the Year, 92; Templeton Awd for course in Religion & Science, 97; Templeton Awd for Quality in Excellence in Tchg, 99. **MEMBERSHIPS** AAR; CTS; CTSA; SSSR. **RESEARCH** Evolution of religious thought; science & religion. **SELECTED PUBLICATIONS** Auth, In the Presence of Mystery, Twenty-Third Pub, 84 & 90; Rationality in Religion, Religion, 97; Community, Clannishness, and the Common Good, Vol 41 of The Annual Pub of the Col Theology Soc, XXIII Publications, 96; The Presence and Absence of God, Praying, 96; Parallels in Cultural and Individual Development, Ethnicity, Nationality, and Religious Experience, Vol 37, Univ Press of Am, 95; A Reply to Michael Raschko, Theological Studies, 95;

The Evolution of the Soul from Matter and the Role of Science in the Theology of Karl Rahner, Horizons, 94; Demythologization in the Theology of Karl Rahner, Theological Studies, 94; Having Faith, Being Critical, and Seeking Truth: A Response to Dale W. Cannon, Method and Theory in the Study of Religion, 94; auth, Stages of Thought, Oxford Univ Pr, 00. **CONTACT ADDRESS** Univ of Dayton, Dayton, OH 45469-1530. **EMAIL** barnes@udayton.edu

BARNES, WILLIE R.
PERSONAL Born 12/09/1931, Dallas, TX, m **DISCIPLINE** LAW **EDUCATION** UCLA, BA, political science, 1953; UCLA School of Law, JD, 1959. **CAREER** State of California, Dept of Corps, various Attorney positions, 60-68, supvr corps counsel 1968-70, asst commr, 70-75, commr of corps, 75-79; UCLA Alumni Assn, general counsel, dir, 83-86; Manatt Phelps Rothenberg & Phillips, sr partner, 79-88; Wyman Bautzer, Kuchel & Silbert, sr partner, 89-91; Katten, Muchin, Zavis & Weitzman, sr partner, 91-92; Musick, Peeler & Garrett, sr partner, 92-. **HONORS AND AWARDS** Practicing Law Institute, Certificate of Appreciation, 1973; UCLA Law School, Alumnus of the Year, 1976; California State Senate & Assembly, Resolutions of Commendation, 1979. **MEMBERSHIPS** Exec comm, Business & Corps Sec 1970-86; vp, dir UCLA Law Alumni Assn 1973; Comm Real Estate Franchises Mutual Funds; chmn SEC Liaison Comm 1974-78; chmn Real Estate Investment Comm 1974-78; president Midwest Securities Commission Assn 1978-79; 1st vice pres N Amer Securities Administration Assn 1978-79; co-managing ed, CA Bus Law Reporter 1983; exec comm Corp & Commercial Law Sec, Beverly Hills Bar Assn; board of governors Century City Bar Assn, 1982-84; vice chmn, Comm on Corp; vice chmn, Oil Investment Comm; active leadership in directing the Securities Reg Prog of CA; vice chair, exec committee Business Law Sec, California State Bar, 1983-86; Corp Banking & Bus Law, Fed Regulation of Securities, Commodities, Franchises & State Regulation Committees, Amer Bar Assn; chmn, bd of trustees, Wilshire United Methodist Church986-91; chmn Knox Keene Health Care Service Plan Comm 1976-79; chmn Leveraged Real Estate Task Force 1985-86; CA Senate Commission on Corporate Governance; Independent Commission to Review the Los Angeles Police Dept; advsry bd Institute of Corporate Counsel. **SELECTED PUBLICATIONS** Major role in developing uniform standards for real estate progs on nationwide basis; Acknowledged expert in real estate & oil & gas securities. **CONTACT ADDRESS** Musick, Peeler & Garrett, 1 Wilshire Blvd, Ste 200, Los Angeles, CA 90017.

BARNETTE, HENLEE HULIX
PERSONAL Born 08/14/1911, Taylorsville, NC, w, 1956, 4 children **DISCIPLINE** ETHICS **EDUCATION** Wake Forest Col, BA, 40, DD, 98; Southern Baptist Theol Sem, ThM, 43, ThD, 48, PhD, 75. **CAREER** Asst prof sociol, Howard Col, 46-47; prof relig & sociol, Stetson Univ, 47-51; prof ethics, Southern Baptist Theol Sem, 51-77; Clin Prof Psychiat, Univ Louisville Sch Med, 77-; vis prof, dept environeng, Univ Fla, 72; consult, Christian Life Comn Southern Baptist Convention, 77-; ed counc, Baylor Univ, Journal of Church and State, 59-00; mem bd dirs, DeLand Convalescent Ctr Inc, 77- **HONORS AND AWARDS** Carnegie grant, 49-50; Am Asn Theol Schs fel, Harvard Univ, 59-60; **MEMBERSHIPS** Inst Soc, Ethics & Life Sci. **RESEARCH** Biomedical ethics; ethical conflicts of psychiatric patients; Martin Luther King Jr; Religious fundamentalism. **SELECTED PUBLICATIONS** Auth, Introducing Christian Ethics, Broadman, 61; Introduction to Communism, Baker Bk, 64; The New Theology and Morality, 67, Crucial Problems in Christian Perspective, 70, The Drug Crisis and the Church, 71 & The Church and the Ecological Crisis, 72, Westminster Col; Bioethics, Stetson Univ Press, 81; Exploring Medical Ethics, Mercer Univ Press, 82; Clarence Jordan: Turning Dreams into Deeds, Smyth and Helwys, 92. **CONTACT ADDRESS** 2909 Meadowlark Ave, Louisville, KY 40206.

BARNHART, JOE EDWARD
PERSONAL Born 11/01/1931, Knoxville, TN, m, 1953, 2 children **DISCIPLINE** PHILOSOPHY **EDUCATION** Carson-Newman Col, BA, 53; Southern Baptist Theol Sem, MDiv, 56; Boston Univ, PhD(philos), 64. **CAREER** Asst prof philos, Carson-Newman Col, 57-58; instr, Western Carolina Univ, 61-64; asst prof, Univ Redlands, 64-66; assoc prof, Parsons Col, 66-67; assoc prof, 67-74, Prof Philos, N Tex State Univ, 74-; Chmn, Univ of North Texas, 90. **MEMBERSHIPS** SWestern Philos Soc; Am Philos Asn; Southern Soc Philos & Psychol; Am Acad Relig; Soc Sci Study Relig. **RESEARCH** Philosophy of religion; philosophy of literature. **SELECTED PUBLICATIONS** Auth, The Billy Graham Religion, Philadelphia: Pilgrim Press, 72, Published also in England (Mowbrays, 74) and in Germany Claudius Verlang, 73; auth, Religion and Challenge of Philosophy (Totowa, NJ: Littlefield, Adams and Co, 1975); auth, The Study of Religion and Its Meaning: New Explorations in Light of Karl Popper and Emile Durkheim, The Hague/Paris: Mouton, 77; auth, The Warren-Barnhart Debate, with Thomas Warren, Jonesboro, ARK: National Christian Press, 81; auth, The New Birth: A Naturalistic View of Religious Conversion, with Mary Ann Barnhart, Macon, GA: Mercer Univ Press, 81; auth, The Southern Baptist Holy War, Austin, TX: Texas Monthly Press, 86; auth, Jim And Tammy: Charismatic Intrigue Inside PTL, Buffalo: Prometheus Books, 88; auth, Dostoevsky on Evil and Atonement: The Ontology of Personalism in His Major Fiction, with Linda Kraeger, Lewiston, NY: Edwin Mellen Press, 93; auth, In Search of First-Century Christianity, Hampshire, England: Ashgate International Publishing, with Linda Kraeger, 99. **CONTACT ADDRESS** Dept of Philosophy, Univ of No Texas, PO Box 310920, Denton, TX 76203. **EMAIL** barnhart@unt.edu

BARNHART, MICHAEL G.
PERSONAL Born 03/22/1956, Sewanee, TN, m, 1983, 2 children **DISCIPLINE** PHILOSOPHY **EDUCATION** Haverford Col, BA, 79; Temple Univ, PhD, 91. **CAREER** Assoc prof, 92-, Kingsborough Comm Col, CUNY. **HONORS AND AWARDS** Phi Beta Kappa, hon phil, Haverford; Univ fel, Temple; 2 NEH sum sem; PSC-CUNY res fel. **MEMBERSHIPS** APA, Soc for Asian & Comp Phil; AAR, Asn for Asian Stud. **RESEARCH** Comparative philosophy; comparative ethics; metaphysics and epistemology; Buddhist philosophy; theories of rationality. **CONTACT ADDRESS** Dept of Hist, Philos, and Polit Sci, Kingsborough Comm Col, CUNY, 2001 Oriental Blvd, Brooklyn, NY 11235. **EMAIL** mbarnhart@kbcc.cuny.edu

BARON, CHARLES HILLEL
PERSONAL Born 08/18/1936, Philadelphia, PA, m, 1958, 3 children **DISCIPLINE** LEGAL MEDICINE & PHILOSOPHY **EDUCATION** Univ PA, AB, 58, PhD(philos), 72; Harvard Univ, LLB, 61. **CAREER** Teaching fel philos, Univ PA, 62-64, instr law, 64-65, asst prof, 65-66; assoc prof, 70-74, Prof Law, Boston Col, 74-, Vis prof, Cath Univ Am, 77; adj prof, Antioch Univ, 77; instr, Univ Southern CA, summer, 78 & Univ OR, summer, 79; scholar in residence, Hebrew Univ Jerusalem, 81. **MEMBERSHIPS** Am Soc Law & Med. **RESEARCH** Medical decision making for incompetent patients; blame as deterrent to effective use of legal sanction; human responsibility as a function of distinction between acts and omissions to act. **SELECTED PUBLICATIONS** Coauth, Real freedom of choice for the consumer of legal services: Mr Dooley and the closed panel option, Mass Law Quart, 73; Live organ and tissue transplants from minor donors in Massachusetts, Boston Univ Law Rev, 75; auth, Voluntary sterilization of the mentally retarded, Genetics and the Law, 76; Assuring detached but passionate investigation and decision making, 78 & Medical paternalism and the rule of law, 79, Am J Law & Med; The open society and its enemies: Growing professional secrecy in Massachusetts, Medicolegal News, 80; co-ed, Use/Nonuse/Misuse of Applied Social Research in the Courts, ABT Books, 80. **CONTACT ADDRESS** Law Sch, Boston Col, Newton Ctr, 885 Centre St, Newton, MA 02159-1100.

BARON, MARCIA
PERSONAL Born 09/10/1955, Akron, OH, m, 1981, 1 child **DISCIPLINE** PHILOSOPHY **EDUCATION** Oberlin Col, BA, 76; MA, 78, PhD, 82, UNC-Chapel Hill. **CAREER** Instr, 81-82, Asst Prof, 82-83, Virginia Polytech Inst and State Univ; Visiting Asst Prof, 85, Stanford Univ; Visiting Asst Prof, 87, Univ Michigan; Visiting Assoc Prof, 90, Univ Chicago; Visting Asst Prof, 82-83, Asst Prof, 83-89, Assoc Prof, 89-96, Prof, 96-, Univ Illinois at Urbana-Champaign. **HONORS AND AWARDS** Outstanding Acad Book Awd, 96. **MEMBERSHIPS** Amer Phil Assoc; Illinois Phil Assoc; Intl Hume Soc; North Amer Kant Soc. **RESEARCH** Ethics and the philosophy of criminal law **SELECTED PUBLICATIONS** Auth, "Freedom, Frailty and Impurity," Inquiry 36 (93); Kantian Ethics Almost Without Apology, 95; Kantian Ethics and Claims of Detachment, Feminist Interpretations of Immanuel Kant, 97; Coauth, Three Methods of Ethics: A Debate, 97; Auth, Love and Respect in the Doctrine of Virtue, The Southern Journal of Philosophy; Supererogatory Acts and Imperfect Duties, Jahrbuch fur Recht und Ethik, 98; "Crimes, Genes, and Responsibility," in Genetics and Criminal Behavior: Methods, Meanings and Morals, 00; auth, "Character, Immorality, and Punishment," in Rationality, Impartiality, and Morality: Essays on Bernard Gert's Moral Theory (forthcoming). **CONTACT ADDRESS** Dept of Philosophy, Univ of Illinois, Urbana-Champaign, 810 S. Wright St., 105 Greg H, Urbana, IL 61801. **EMAIL** m-barron@uiuc.edu

BARR, DAVID LAWRENCE
PERSONAL Born 04/24/1942, Belding, MI, m, 1966, 3 children **DISCIPLINE** BIBLICAL STUDIES, HISTORY OF RELIGIONS **EDUCATION** Ft Wayne Bible Col, BA, 65; FL State Univ, MA, 69, PhD, 74. **CAREER** Consult relig pub educ, Relig Instr Asn, 67-71; instr relig, FL A&M Univ, 72-74; asst prof, Univ Northern IA, 74-75; asst prof, 75-80, assoc prof, 80-88, prof relig, Wright State Univ, 88, Chmn, Relig Dept, Wright State Univ, 80-86, Dir, Honors Prog 87-94. **HONORS AND AWARDS** Pres, Eastern Grt Lakes Bible Soc; Pres, Mideast Honors Asn; Phi Kappa Phi; Pres Fac. **MEMBERSHIPS** Soc Bibl Lit; Cath Bibl Asn, Am Acad Relig. **RESEARCH** Apocalypse of John; Narrative analysis; Soc world of early Christianity. **SELECTED PUBLICATIONS** Co-ed (with Nicholas Piediscalzi), The Bible in American Education, a centennial volume prepared for the Soc of Bibl Lit, Fortress Press and Scholars Press, 82; New Testament Story: An Introduction, Wadsworth Publ Co, 87, 2nd ed, 95; Co-ed (with Linda Bennett Elder and Elizabeth Struthers Malbon), Biblical and Humane: A Festschrift for John Priest; Tales of the End: A Narrative Commentary on the Book of Revelation, Polebridge Press, 98. **CONTACT ADDRESS** Dept of Relig, Wright State Univ, Dayton, 3640 Colonel Glenn, Dayton, OH 45435-0002. **EMAIL** david.barr@wright.edu

BARRETT, J. EDWARD
PERSONAL Born 12/18/1932, Philadelphia, PA, m, 1959, 2 children **DISCIPLINE** RELIGION, PHILOSOPHY **EDUCATION** Susquehanna Univ, AB, 55; Princeton Theol Sem, BD, 58, ThM, 60; Univ St Andrews, PhD(philos theol), 65. **CAREER** Pastor, Presby church, Glassboro, NJ, 58-62; from asst prof to prof philos & relig, 64-77, Prof Relig, Muskingum Col, 77-, Prof humanities, Tunghai Univ, Taiwan, 72-73. **MEMBERSHIPS** Am Acad Relig. **RESEARCH** Religious experience; philosophical theology. **SELECTED PUBLICATIONS** Auth, Tragedy, God and Thanksgiving, Presby Life, 11/67; The Christian Conspiracy, Christian Century, 2/68; A Theology of the Meaning of Life, Zygon, J Sci & Relig, 6/68; How Are You Programmed?, John Knox, 71; Pilgrims Progress, From Catechism to Pantheism, Religious Humanism, Vol 29, 95. **CONTACT ADDRESS** Dept of Relig & Philos, Muskingum Col, New Concord, OH 43762.

BARRETT, JOHN A.
DISCIPLINE LAW **EDUCATION** Amherst Col, BA; Harvard Univ, JD. **CAREER** Assoc prof. **SELECTED PUBLICATIONS** Auth, The U.S. Approach to Resolving the Tension Between Environmental Liabilities and Bankruptcy Debt Forgiveness, Kluwer, 98; International Legal Education in the United States: Being Educated for Domestic Practice While Living in a Global Society, Am Univ J Int Law Policy, 97; The Status of International Legal Education in U.S. Law Schools: Plenty of Offerings but Too Few Students, Int Lawyer, 97; Crimes Involving Art, J Criminal Law Criminology, 96; Mexican Insolvency Law, Pace Int Law Rev, 95; The Effect of NAFTA on the Energy Industry of Third-Party Countries, Oil & Gas Law Tax Rev, 94; co-auth, International Sales Agreements: An Annotated Drafting and Negotiating Guide, Kluwer, 98. **CONTACT ADDRESS** Col Law, Univ of Toledo, Toledo, OH 43606. **EMAIL** jbarret@pop3.utoledo.edu

BARRICK, WILLIAM D.
PERSONAL Born 01/05/1946, Hayden, CO, m, 1966, 4 children **DISCIPLINE** OLD TESTAMENT, HEBREW **EDUCATION** Denver Baptist Bible Col, Ba, 68; San Francisco Baptist Theol Sem, MDiv 71, ThM, 72; Grace Theol Sem, ThD, 81. **CAREER** Prof, Denver Baptist Theol Sem, 72-78; exegetical consult for Bible transl, Chittagong, Bangladesh, 81-96; assoc prof, 97-98, prof, 98- , The Master's Sem, Sun Valley, Calif. **HONORS AND AWARDS** Denver Baptist Bible Col alumnus of the year, 80. **MEMBERSHIPS** Evangel Theol Soc; Soc of Bibl Lit; Natl Asn of Profs of Hebrew. **RESEARCH** Hebrew; Old Testament textual criticism; Leviticus; Job; Bible translation. **SELECTED PUBLICATIONS** Auth, William Carey: Memorable Man, Respected Personality, in Weber, ed, Mahan Sadhak William Carey, Bangladesh: Literature Division, 93, in Bengali; auth, the FACTS of Witnessing to People Outside Our Culture, Gospel Herald and the Sunday Sch Times, 94; auth, In the Folds of God's Garment, in 100 Meditations for Advent and Christmas, Upper Room Books, 94; consult, Holy New Testament, Bangladesh Bible Soc, 96; auth, 1 Samuel 1-17 Introduction and Meseges, Living Life, 97; auth, 1 Samuel 18-31 Messages, Living Life, 97; auth, 2 Samuel 1-14 Introduction and Messages, Living Life, 97; auth, 2 Samuel 14-24 Messages, Living Life, 97; auth, Hosea Introduction and Messages, Living Life, 97; auth, 1 Kings 1-4.28 Introduction and Messages and Proverbs 3:21-4:27 Messages, Living Life, 98; auth, Ancient Manuscripts and Biblical exposition, Master's Sem J, 98; auth, Isaiah 53 and 1 Kings 4:29-10:29 and Proverbs 5:1-23 Messages, Living Life, 98; auth, 1 Kings 19:1-22:53 and Proverbs 8:1-36 Messages, Living Life, 98; auth, Daniel 1:1-4:27 Introduction and Messages and Proverbs 10:22-12:8 Messages, Living Life, 98; auth, Daniel 4:28-12:13 and Proverbs 12:9-13:16 Messages, Living Life, 98; consult, Book of Psalms, Bangladesh Bible Soc, 98; consult, Pentateuch, Bangladesh Bible Soc, 98; consult, Holy Bible, Bangladesh Bible Soc, 98; auth, The Mosaic Covenant, Master's Sem J, 99; auth, Living a New Life: Old Testament Teaching about Conversion, Master's Sem J, 00. **CONTACT ADDRESS** Master's Col and Sem, Sun Valley, 13248 Roscoe Blvd, Sun Valley, CA 91352. **EMAIL** bbarrick@tms.edu

BARRON, DAVID J.
PERSONAL Born 07/07/1967, Washington, DC, m, 1996 **DISCIPLINE** LAW **EDUCATION** Harvard Col, BA, 89; Harvard Law Sch, JD, 94. **CAREER** Asst Prof, Harvard Law Sch, 99-. **MEMBERSHIPS** NY Bar, Am Assoc of Law Schs. **RESEARCH** Constitutional Law, Local Government Law. **SELECTED PUBLICATIONS** Auth, "The Promise of Cooley's CXiy: Tracxes of Local Constitutionalism," Univ Pa Law Rev, (99); auth, "Constitutionalism in the Shadow of Doctrine: The President's Nonenforcement Power," Jour of Law and Contemp Problems, (00); coed, Local Government Law, 3rd Edition, West Publ, 01. **CONTACT ADDRESS** Harvard Univ, Cambridge, MA 02138. **EMAIL** dbarron @law.harvard.edu

BARRY, ROBERT M.
DISCIPLINE PHILOSOPHY **EDUCATION** Iona Col, BA; Fordham Univ, MA, PhD. **CAREER** Prof, Loyola Univ, 63-. **RESEARCH** American pragmatism, especially James and Dewey; philosophy of soc science. **SELECTED PUBLICATIONS** Auth, The Medieval: New Dimensions, 74. **CONTACT ADDRESS** Dept of Philosophy, Loyola Univ, Chicago, 820 N. Michigan Ave., Chicago, IL 60611.

BARRY, WILLIAM ANTHONY
PERSONAL Born 11/22/1930, Worcester, MA **DISCIPLINE** PASTORAL THEOLOGY, CLINICAL PSYCHOLOGY **EDUCATION** Boston Col, AB, 56; Fordham Univ, MA, 60; Weston Col, STL, 63; Univ Mich, Ann Arbor, PhD(psychol), 68. **CAREER** Teacher Latin, English & Ger, Fairfield Prep Sch, Conn, 56-58; lectr psychol & staff psychologist, Univ Mich, Ann Arbor, 68-69; asst prof pastoral theol, Weston Sch Theol, 69-73, assoc prof, 73-78, dir, Ctr Relig Develop, 71-75, mem staff, 75-78; VProvincial, 78-84, asst nov dir, 85-88, Provincial, 91-97, Co-Dir, Tertianship, 97-, Soc Jesus New England; Rector, Boston Col, 88-91; Staff psychologist, Ecumenical Career Coun Serv, Melrose, Mass, 70-71; consult, New Eng Prov Soc Jesus, 72-78; adj prof, Boston col, 88-91. **HONORS AND AWARDS** Ph.D. Honoris Causa, Anna Maria College, 92. **MEMBERSHIPS** Am Psychol Asn **RESEARCH** Personality and religious development; prayer and religious experience; pastoral counseling. **SELECTED PUBLICATIONS** Coauth, Personality development and the vocational choice of the ministry, J Coun Psychol, 67; auth, Marriage research and conflict: An integrative review, Psychol Bull, 70; The experience of the first and second weeks of the spiritual exercises, Rev Relig, 73; coauth, Communication, Conflict, and Marriage: Explorations in the Theory and Study of Relationships, Jossey-Bass, 74; auth, Prayer in pastoral care, J Pastoral Care, 77; Spiritual direction and pastoral counseling, Pastoral Psychol, 77; co-auth, The Practice of Spiritual Direction, Seabury, 82; auth, God's Passionate Desire and Our Response, Ave Maria, 93; auth, Allowing the Creator to Deal with the Creature: An Approach to the Spiritual Exercises of Ignatius of Loyola, Paulist, 94; auth, What Do I Want in Prayer? Paulist, 94; auth, Who Do You Say I Am? Meeting the Historical Jesus in Prayer, Ave Maria, 96; auth, Our Way of Proceeding: To Make the Constitutions of the Society of Jesus and Their Complementary Norms Our Own; Institute of Jesuit Sources, 97; auth, With an Everlasting Love: Developing an Intimate Relationship with God, Paulist, 99, auth, God and You, Paulist, 87; auth, Seek my Face, Paulist, 89; auth, Paying Attention to God, Ave Maria, 90; auth, Now Choose Life, 90; auth, Finding God in All Things, Ave Maria, 91; auth, Spiritual Direction and the Encounter with God, Paulist, 92. **CONTACT ADDRESS** Campion Center, 319 Concord Rd, Weston, MA 02493-1398. **EMAIL** frbarry@bc.edu

BARTELT, ANDREW H.
PERSONAL Born 08/04/1949, Milwaukee, WI, m, 1979, 3 children **DISCIPLINE** THEOLOGY **EDUCATION** Concordia Sr Col, BA, 71; Cambridge Univ, England, Hon Degree, 73, MA, 77; Concordia Sem, MDiv, 76; Univ Mich, PhD, 91. **CAREER** From instr to assoc prof, 78-97, prof exegetical theol, 97- , asst acad advisor, 84-95, chemn dept, 94-98, Concordia Sem, dean of admin, 95-98, exec asst to pres, 95- , acting pres, 96, Vpres for Acad Affairs, 98- . **MEMBERSHIPS** Soc of Bibl Lit; Cath Bibl Soc; Bibl Archaeol Soc. **RESEARCH** Old Testament interpretation; preaching on Old Testament texts; Isaiah. **SELECTED PUBLICATIONS** Auth, Isaiah, Concordia, 94; auth, Isaiah Five and Nine: In-or Interdependence? in, Fortunate the Eyes That See: Essays in Honor of David Noel Freedman in Celebration of His 70th Birthday, Eerdmans, 95; auth, The Book Around Immanuel: Style and Structure of Isaiah 1-12, Eisenbrauns, 96; auth, Fundamental Biblical Hebrew, Concordia, 00. **CONTACT ADDRESS** Concordia Sem, 801 DeMun Ave, Saint Louis, MO 63105. **EMAIL** bartelta@csl.edu

BARTHOLET, ELIZABETH
PERSONAL Born 09/09/1940, New York, NY, d, 3 children **DISCIPLINE** LAW **EDUCATION** Radcliffe Col, BA, 62; Harvard Univ, LLB, 65. **CAREER** Atty, 65-77; prof of Law, Harvard Univ, 77- . **HONORS AND AWARDS** Mass Appleseed Ctr, Awd for Advocacy on Behalf of Foster Children; Radcliffe Col Alumnae Recognition Awd, 97; Morris Wasserstein Public Interest Ch at Harvard Law Sch, 96; Open Door Soc, Friends of Adoption Awd, 94; Catholic Adoptive Parents Asn, Media Achievement Awd, 94; Adoptive Parents Comm, Friends of Adoption Awd for Adoption Literature, 93. **MEMBERSHIPS** NAACP Legal Defense & Ed Fund, Inc. Am Acad Adoption Attys; US State Dept Advisory Com on Intercountry Adoption; Legal Action Ctr; Int Concerns Comt for Children; Appleseed Found Adv Coun; Brigham and Women's Hosp; Boston IVF Ethics Advisory Committees. **RESEARCH** Child welfare; adoption; reproductive technology. **SELECTED PUBLICATIONS** Auth, International Adoption: Current Status and Future Prospects, in The Future of Children, No. 1, 93; auth, Blood Knots, in American Prospect, 93; auth, Family Matters, in Vogue, 93; auth, What's Wrong with Adoption Law, in Trial, 94; auth, Adoption Rights and Reproductive Wrongs, in Power & Decision: the social Control of Reproduction, 94; auth, Race Separatism in the Family: More on the Transracial Adoption Debate, in 2 Duke J. Gender L. & Pol'y, 95; auth, Beyond Biology: The Politics of Adoption & Reproduction, in 2 Duke J. Gender L. & Pol'y, 95; coauth, Debate: Best Interests of the Child?, in Prospect, no. 11, 96; auth, What's Wrong with Adoption Law?, in The International Journal of Children's Rights, 96; auth, International Adoption: Propriety, Prospects and Pragmatics, J. Am. Acad. Matrim. Law, 96; auth, Private Race Preferences in Family Formation, Yale L.J., 98; auth, Nobody's Children: Abuse and Neglect, Foster Drift, and the Adoption Alternative, Beacon, 99; auth, Family Bonds: Adoption, Infertility, & the New World of Child Production, Beacon, 99. **CONTACT ADDRESS** Dept of Law, Harvard Univ, Cambridge, MA 02138. **EMAIL** ebarthol@law.harvard.edu

BARTKOWIAK, JULIA
PERSONAL Born 10/12/1957, Detroit, MI, m, 1978, 1 child **DISCIPLINE** PHILOSOPHY **EDUCATION** Wayne State Univ, BA, 83; Univ Rochester, MA, 86, PhD, 90. **CAREER** Kent State Univ, temp asst prof, 89-92; Clarion Univ, asst prof, 92-95, assoc prof, 95-99, prof, 99-. **HONORS AND AWARDS** Univ Rochester, Rush Rhees Fel, 84-87, Univ Fel, 84-88 **MEMBERSHIPS** APA, NASSP **RESEARCH** Ethics; social philo. **SELECTED PUBLICATIONS** Auth, The Role of Internalism in Moral Theory, in: Auslegung, 93; Trends Toward Part-Time Employment: Ethical Issues, in: Jour of Business Ethics, 93; Intellectual Walls, in: Frauen und Wissenschaftspolitik, Zurich: Philosophisches Institut, 94; The U.S. Media and the Liberal Tradition, in: Jour of Social Philo, 94; Contingent Work, in: The Blackwell Encycl Dictionary of Business Ethics, ed by Patricia H. Werhane, and R. Edward Freeman, Oxford: Blackwell Pub, 97; Religious Education in the Public Schools, Proceedings of the Twentieth World Congress of Philosophy, Philo Doc Center, 98; auth, Having and Raising Children: Unconventional Families, Hard Choices, and the Social Good, Penn State Univ Press, 99. **CONTACT ADDRESS** Dept of Philosophy, Clarion Univ of Pennsylvania, Clarion, PA 16214-1232. **EMAIL** bartkowi@mail.clarion.edu

BARTKY, SANDRA
PERSONAL Born 05/05/1935, USA, m, 1971 **DISCIPLINE** PHILOSOPHY **EDUCATION** Univ Ill, Urbana-Champaign, BA, MA, PhD, 63. **CAREER** Univ Ill at Chicago, 65-, full prof since 1990. **HONORS AND AWARDS** Honorary Degree, Dr of Humanities, New England Col, 98. **MEMBERSHIPS** APA, SWIP, RPA, SPEP. **RESEARCH** Critical theory, feminist theory, ethics, political philosophy. **SELECTED PUBLICATIONS** Auth, Femininity and Domination, Routledge (90); ed with Nancy Freser, Revaluing French Feminism, Indiana Univ Press (97). **CONTACT ADDRESS** Dept Philos, Univ of Illinois, Chicago, 601 S Morgan St, M/C 267, Chicago, IL 60607.

BARTLETT, BETH
PERSONAL Born 05/21/1952, Akron, OH, m, 1988, 1 child **DISCIPLINE** WOMEN'S STUDIES AND POLITICAL PHILOSOPHY **EDUCATION** Col Wooster, BA, 74; Kent St, MA, 75; Univ Minn, PhD, 81. **CAREER** Instr, 80-81, asst prof, 81-87, assoc prof, 87-, Univ Minn - Duluth; prof, 00-. **MEMBERSHIPS** Nat Women's Studies Asn; Am Academy of Religion. **RESEARCH** Feminist theory, spirituality; Albert Camus. **SELECTED PUBLICATIONS** Ed, Sarah Grime's Letters on the Equality of the Sexes and other Essays, New Haven: Yale Univ Press, 88; auth, Liberty, Equality, Sorority: Origins and Interpretation of American Feminist Thought: Frances Wright, Sarah Grime, and Margaret Fuller, NY: Carbon Publishing, 96; auth, Journey of the Heart, Duluth: Pfeifer-Hamilton, 97. **CONTACT ADDRESS** Univ of Minnesota, Duluth, 475 Humanities, Duluth, MN 55812. **EMAIL** bbartlet@d.umn.edu

BARTLETT, ROBERT V.
PERSONAL Born 05/02/1953, Portland, IN, m, 1973, 2 children **DISCIPLINE** POLITICAL SCIENCE **EDUCATION** BA 74; MPA 76; PhD 84. **CAREER** IN Univ, res assoc 79-82; TX Tech Univ asst prof 82-85; Purdue Univ asst prof 85-89, assoc prof 89. **HONORS AND AWARDS** Phi Beta Kappa; Univ Canterbury and Lincoln Univ NZ, Fulbright Sch 90; Lincoln Univ Vis Sch 92; Trinity Col, Dublin, Fulbright Sch. **MEMBERSHIPS** APSA; ASEH; PSO; Intl Assn for Impact Assess. **RESEARCH** Environmental Politics and Safety **SELECTED PUBLICATIONS** Environmental Policy: Transnational Issues and National Trends, ed with Lynton K Caldwell, Westport Ct, Quorum Books, 97; Environment as a Focus for Public Policy, ed with James N Gladden, Essays by Lynton K Caldwell, Coll Stn, TX, TX A&M Univ Press, 95; From Rationality to Reasonableness in Environmental Administration: Moving Beyond Proverbs, with Walter F Baber, Journal of Management History, 99; numerous other articles and bks. **CONTACT ADDRESS** Dept of Polit Sci, Purdue Univ, West Lafayette, West Lafayette, IN 47907.

BARTLETT, STEVEN J.
PERSONAL Born 05/15/1945, Mexico, m **DISCIPLINE** PHILOSOPHY **EDUCATION** Raymond Col, BA, 65; Univ Calif, Santa Barbara, MA, 68; Univ Paris, PhD, 71. **CAREER** Res fel, Ctr for Stud of Democratic Inst, 69-70; vis asst prof, Univ Fla, 71-72; asst prof, Univ Hartford, 72-74; res fel, Max Planck Inst, 74-75; prof St Louis Univ, 75-84; res prof, Oregon State Univ, 89- ; vis scholar, Willamette Univ, 89- . **HONORS AND AWARDS** NSFR grant; AAAS grant; Lilly Found grant; Max Planck Gesellschaft fel; Alliance Francaise fel. **MEMBERSHIPS** APA. **RESEARCH** Epistemology; reflexivity. **SELECTED PUBLICATIONS** Auth, Validity, LeBon Press, 72; auth, Metalogic of Reference: A Study in the Foundations of Possibility, Max Planck Inst, 75; auth, Conceptual Therapy: An Introduction to Framework-Relative Epistemology, Studies in Theory and Behavior, 83; coauth, Self-Reference: Reflections on Reflexivity, Martinus Nijhoff, 87; auth, When You don't Know Where to Turn, Contemporary Books, 87; auth, Reflexivity: A Source Book in Self-Reference, Elsevier Science, 92. **CONTACT ADDRESS** 5550 Bethel Heights NW, Salem, OR 97304. **EMAIL** sbartlet@willamette.edu

BARTON, CHARLES K. B.
PERSONAL Born 11/20/1959 **DISCIPLINE** PHILOSOPHY **EDUCATION** Victoria Univ, BA, 87; Massey Univ, MA, 90; Australian Nat Univ, PhD, 96. **CAREER** Consult, Australian Nat Univ, 95-96; Dir, Facilitation Serv Australia, 95-97; Mediator, Conflict Resolution Serv, 91-97; Res Scholar, Australian Nat Univ, 90-96; Lectr, Charles Sturt Univ, 97-01; Vis Prof, Univ Colo, 01-. **HONORS AND AWARDS** Fel, Massey Univ, 97-99; Fel, ARC Key Centre Australia, 99; Res Scholar, Australian Nat Univ, 90; Prince of Wales Trust Scholar, Cambridge Univ, 90; Scholar, New Zealand Univ, 90. **RESEARCH** Professional and Applies Ethics; Philosophy of Law and Punishment; Conflict Resolution; Restorative Justice. **SELECTED PUBLICATIONS** Auth, Getting Even: Revenge as a Form of Justice, Open Court, 99; auth, "Empowerment and Retribution in Criminal Justice," Prof Ethics, (99): 111-135; co-auth, "Personal Identity, Reductionism, and the Necessity of Origins," Erkenntnis, (99): 277-294; co-auth, "Restorative Justice Conferencing and the Ethic of Care," Ethics and Justice, (99): 55-65; auth, "Getting Even Again: A Reply to Davis," Intl J of App Philos, (00): 129-142; auth, "Theories of Restorative Justice," Australian J of Prof and App Ethics, (00): 41-53; auth, "Restorative Justice Empowerment," Australian J of Prof and App Ethics, forthcoming; auth, "Victim - Offender and Community Empowerment: A New Paradigm in Criminal Justice," Intl J of App Philos, forthcoming; auth, Restorative Justice: The Empowerment Model, Fed Press of Australia, forthcoming. **CONTACT ADDRESS** Dept Philos, Univ of Colorado, Boulder, 169 Helems, Boulder, CO 80309. **EMAIL** bartonc@colorado.edu

BARTON, JOHN HAYS
PERSONAL Born 10/27/1936, Chicago, IL, m, 1959, 5 children **DISCIPLINE** INTERNATIONAL LAW **EDUCATION** Marquette Univ, BS, 58; Stanford Univ, JD, 68. **CAREER** Engr, Sylvania, 61-68; assoc, Wilmer, Cutler & Pickering, Washington, DC, 68-69; Prof Law, Law Sch, Stanford Univ, 69-, Res assoc, Int Inst Strategic Studies, London, 76-77; Vis Prof law, Univ MI, fall, 81. **MEMBERSHIPS** Am Soc Int Law. **RESEARCH** International; international technology; biotechnology. **SELECTED PUBLICATIONS** Auth, The Economic Basis of Damages for Breach of Contract, J Legal Studies, 72; Behind the Legal Explosion, Stanford Law Rev, 75; The Developing Nations and Arms Control, Studies in Comp Int Develop, 75; co-ed, International Arms Control: Issues and Agreements, Stanford Univ Press, 76; contribr, Nuclear Weapons and World Politics, McGraw Hill, 77; The Politics of Human Rights, NY Univ Press, 80; auth, The Politics of Peace, Stanford Univ Press, 81; The International Breeder's Rights System and Crop Plant Innovation, Science, 6/4/82; International- Law and Institutions For a New Age, Georgetown Law J, Vol 81, 93; Patent Scope in Biotechnology, IIC-International Review of Industrial Property and Copyright Law, Vol 26, 95; Patents and Antitrust-A Rethinking in Light of Patent Breadth and Sequential Innovation, Antitrust Law J, Vol 65, 97. **CONTACT ADDRESS** Law Sch, Stanford Univ, Stanford, CA 94027. **EMAIL** jbarton@lelaud.stanford.edu

BARTON, MARCELLA BIRO
PERSONAL Born 08/24/1936, Bedford, OH, d, 2 children **DISCIPLINE** INTELLECTUAL AND RELIGIOUS HISTORY **EDUCATION** Univ Calif, BA, 70; Univ Akron, MA, 73; Univ Chicago, PhD(hist), 81. **CAREER** Prof Hist, Univ of Rio Grande, OH, 80-. **HONORS AND AWARDS** Edwin A Jones, Excellence in Teaching Awd, Univ, of Rio Grande 86; National Endowment for the Humanities Summer grant, Harvard Univ, 88; Honors Students Distinguished Teaching Awd, Univ of Rio Grande, 96; Distinguished Service Awd, Gallipolis of Rio Grande, 93; Distinguished Service Awd, Welsh-American Heritage Museum, 99-00; Ohio Academy of History Distinguished Service Awd, 00. **MEMBERSHIPS** AHA; Am Soc Church Hist; Am Cath Hist Asn; OH Acad Hist. **RESEARCH** Intellectual and religious history with an emphasis on Britain, Europe, and America. **SELECTED PUBLICATIONS** Rev, Calvinists Incorporated: Welsh Immigrants on Ohio's Industrial Frontier, by Anne Kelly Knowles, The Historian Vol 60, no 4, (98): 866-867; review, Dublins Merchant-Quaker: Anthony Sharp and the Community of Friends, 1643-1707, Richard L Greaves, Church History, vol 68 no 1, (99), 189-191; auth, "Rio Grande Univ in Ohio site of Welsh music premiere," Y Drych, April 98, p 17; auth, " Hillary Tann's 'The Moor' Premiers at Rio Grande," Ninnau, 98; auth, " Saint Theresa of Avila: Did She Have Epilepsy?" The Catholic Historical Review, Vol 68. No 4, 82; " The Welsh Errand Into the Wilderness," Pathways to Savoring the Past and Shaping the Future: An Ohio Appalachia Source book, (97), 56-63; auth, " The Welsh Errand Into the Wilderness,"

Ninnau, vol 22 no 3, (97): 2-3; ed and intro, Catalogue of Books, Welsh-American Heritage Museum Oak Hill; ed and intro, Welsh-Americans, The Manuscript Collection the Historical Society of Pennsylvania; gen ed, Welsh-American Reference Series, The Madog Center for Welsh Studies, The Univ of Rio Grande and Univ Press of American, New York, **CONTACT ADDRESS** Univ of Rio Grande, 4201 Springdale Rd, Rio Grande, OH 45674. **EMAIL** mbarton@rio.edu

BARTON, PETER G.
DISCIPLINE LAW **EDUCATION** Univ Toronto, BS, 63; Queen's Univ, LLB, 67; Harvard Univ, LLM, 68. **CAREER** Prof, Univ of Western Ontario, 72-; co-ed, Can J of Law and Jurisprudence, 72. **RESEARCH** Civil and criminal procedure; criminal law. **CONTACT ADDRESS** Fac of Law, Univ of Western Ontario, London, ON, Canada N6A 3K7. **EMAIL** pgbarton @julian.uwo.ca

BARWICK, DANIEL
PERSONAL Born 06/21/1968, Utica, NY, m, 1997 **DISCIPLINE** PHILOSOPHY **EDUCATION** SUNY Buffalo, PhD, 97. **CAREER** Alfred Stal. **MEMBERSHIPS** APA; Nat Asn of Scholars. **RESEARCH** Philosophy of education. **CONTACT ADDRESS** 62 Cottage St. #1, Dansville, NY 14437-1320.

BASCH, NORMA
PERSONAL Born Norwich, CT **DISCIPLINE** AMERICAN HISTORY, LAW **EDUCATION** Columbia Univ, BA, 56; NYork Univ, PhD(Am civilization), 79. **CAREER** Prof Hist, Rutgers Univ, 79-. **HONORS AND AWARDS** NEH Res fel, 85-86; ACLS fel, 88-89; Am Antiquarian fel, 91; Berkshire Article Prize, 94; Binkley Stevenson Prize, 98; Scribes Bk award for legal writing, 00. **MEMBERSHIPS** AHA; Orgn Am Historians; Am Studies Asn; Soc Historians Early Am Repub. **RESEARCH** Women's history; cultural history; legal history. **SELECTED PUBLICATIONS** Auth, "Invisible Women: The Legal Fiction of Marital Unity in Antebellum America," Feminist Studies (79); auth, In the Eyes of the Law: Women, Marriage and Property in 19th Century New York, Cornell Univ Press, 82; auth, "Marriage, Morals, and Politics in the Election of 1828," J of Am Hist 80 (93); auth, "Equity is Equality: Emerging Concepts of Women's Political Status in the Age of Jackson," Journal of the Early Republic (83): 297; auth, "Relief in the Premises: Divorce as a Women's Remedy, 1815-1870," Lawaud History Review 8 (90): 1; auth, Framing American Divorce: From the Revolutionary Generation to the Victorians, Univ of Calif Press, 99. **CONTACT ADDRESS** Dept of Hist, Rutgers, The State Univ of New Jersey, Newark, Newark, NJ 07102. **EMAIL** nbasch@mindspring.com

BASCOM, ROBERT
PERSONAL Born 09/25/1951, Glendale, CA, m, 1976, 1 child **DISCIPLINE** RELIGIOUS STUDIES **EDUCATION** Claremont Grad Sch, PhD, 86. **CAREER** Transl consult, United Bible Soc, 86- . **MEMBERSHIPS** SBL. **RESEARCH** Anthropology; linguistics; Biblical studies. **SELECTED PUBLICATIONS** Auth, Adaptable for Translation, in Weis, ed, A Gift of God in Due Season, Sheffield, 96. **CONTACT ADDRESS** 2448 N Mar Vista Ave, Altadena, CA 91001-2510. **EMAIL** bascom@sprynet.com

BASHIR, SHAHZAD
PERSONAL Born 03/12/1968, Bahawalpur, Pakistan, m, 1994 **DISCIPLINE** RELIGIOUS STUDIES **EDUCATION** Amherst Col, BA, 91; Yale Univ, PhD, 97. **CAREER** Instr, 96-97; Asst prof, 97- , Holy Cross Coll. **HONORS AND AWARDS** Best dissertation in Iranian Studies, 98. **MEMBERSHIPS** Am Acad Relig; Mid E Studies Asn; Soc Iranian Studies; Mid E Medievalists **RESEARCH** Islamic studies; Shi ism; Sufism; history of religions. **SELECTED PUBLICATIONS** Auth, Between Mysticism and Messianism: The Life and Thought of Mohammad Nurbakhsh (d.1464), Yale Univ, 97. **CONTACT ADDRESS** 28 Westfield St., Worcester, MA 01602. **EMAIL** sbashir@holycross.edu

BASKIN, JUDITH R.
PERSONAL Born 07/03/1950, Hamilton, ON, Canada, m, 1973, 2 children **DISCIPLINE** JUDAIC STUDIES **EDUCATION** Antioch Col, BA, 71; Yale Univ, PhD, 76. **CAREER** Prof, Univ of Oregon, 00-; Assoc Prof, Prof, Ch, 88-, SUNY Albany; vis Asst Prof, 81-83, Yale Univ; Asst, Assoc Prof, 76-88, Univ Mass. **HONORS AND AWARDS** Danforth Fel; Woodrow Wilson; ACLS Gnt; Dist Teach Awd. **MEMBERSHIPS** AJS; AAR; MA. **RESEARCH** Rabbinic and Medieval Judaism; History of Jewish Women; Comparative Jewish and Christian Exegesis in Late Antiquity. **SELECTED PUBLICATIONS** Ed, Jewish Women in Historical Perspective, Wayne State Univ, 91, 98; ed, Women of the World: Jewish Women and Jewish Writing, Wayne State Univ Press, 94; coed, Gender and Jewish Studies: A Curriculum Guide, Biblio Press, 94; ed, Jewish Women in Historical Perspective, Wayne State Univ Press, 91; auth, Woman as Other in Rabbinic Literature: Where We Stand: Issues and Debates in Ancient Judaism, ed, Jacob Neusner, Alan J Avery-Peck, Brill, 99; auth, Women Saints in Judaism: Dolce of Worms, in: Women Saints in World Religions, ed, Arvind Sharma, State Univ NY Press, 00; Rabbinic Judaism and the Creation of Woman, in: Judaism Since Gender, ed, Miriam Peskowitz, Laura Levitt, Routledge, 97; Silent Partners: Women as Wives in Rabbinic Lit, in: Active Voices: Women in Jewish Culture, ed, Maurie Sacks, Univ IL Press, 95. **CONTACT ADDRESS** 1910 Fairmount Ave, Eugene, OR 97403. **EMAIL** jbaskin@oregon.uoregon.edu

BASS, DOROTHY C.
PERSONAL Born 05/02/1949, m, 2 children **DISCIPLINE** PRACTICAL THEOLOGY **EDUCATION** Wellesley Col, BA, 70; Union Theol Sem and Columbia Univ, MA, 72; Brown Univ, PhD, 80. **CAREER** William Rainey Harper instr, humanities, Univ Chicago, 80-82; asst prof to assoc prof, church hist, Chicago Theol Sem, 82-95; dir, Valparaiso Project on Educ and Formation of People in Faith, Valparaiso Univ, 91-. **HONORS AND AWARDS** Union Theol Sem Distinguished Alum Awd, 96. **MEMBERSHIPS** Amer Acad of Relig; Amer Soc for Church Hist. **RESEARCH** Practical theology; American religion; Spirituality; Church history. **SELECTED PUBLICATIONS** Ed, Practicing Our Faith: A Way of Life for a Searching People, San Francisco, Jossey-Bass, 97; co-auth, Protestant, Catholic, Jew: The Transformative Possibilities of Educating across Religious Boundaries, Relig Educ, 90, 255-276, spring, 95; co-auth, Academic Soul-Searching: Christians and the University, Christ Century, 112, 9, 292-295, mar 15, 95; auth, Congregations and the Bearing of Traditions, Amer Congregations, vol 2, Chicago, Univ of Chicago Press, 94; auth, Receiving the Day: Christian Practices for Opening the Gift of Time, Jossey-Bass (San Francisco), 00; coauth, "Christian Practices and Congregational Education in Faith," Changing Churches: The Local Church and the Structures of Change, Pastoral Press (Portland, OR), 00. **CONTACT ADDRESS** Valparaiso Univ, Linwood House, Valparaiso, IN 46383.

BASSETT, WILLIAM W.
PERSONAL Born 12/18/1932, Peoria, IL, m, 1973, 3 children **DISCIPLINE** LAW; LEGAL HISTORY **EDUCATION** S.T.L. St. Mary of the Lake (IL), MA, 58; Gregorian Univ (Rome), JCD, 65; Cath Univ Am (Wash), JD, 72. **CAREER** Asst to assoc prof, 67-73, Cath Univ Am, 67-73; scholar in res, 73-74, Ludwig-Maximilians Universitat (Munich); vis prof 82-83, Univ Calif; Prof Law, 74-, Univ San Francisco, 74-. **MEMBERSHIPS** Seldon Soc; Canon Law Soc Am; Asn Iuris Canonici Int; Am Soc Legal Hist **RESEARCH** Law of Religious Organizations; Legal History. **SELECTED PUBLICATIONS** California Commmunity Property Law, Bancroft Whitney, 95; Religious Organizations and the Law, West, 98. **CONTACT ADDRESS** School of Law, Univ of San Francisco, 2150 Fulton St., San Francisco, CA 94117. **EMAIL** Bassettw@usfca.edu

BASU, ANANYO
PERSONAL Born 04/04/1966, Calcutta, India, m, 1991, 1 child **DISCIPLINE** PHILOSOPHY **EDUCATION** Dartmouth Col, BA, 89; Duke Univ, PhD, 95. **CAREER** Vis asst prof, Mt Holyoke Col, 94-95; vis asst prof, philos, West Virginia Univ, 96, 97; asst prof philos, Univ Mass, Boston, 95-. **HONORS AND AWARDS** Francis Gramlich philos prize, Dartmouth Univ; Katherine Gilbert fel, Duke Univ. **MEMBERSHIPS** APA; Assoc for Asian Stud. **RESEARCH** Political theory; philosophy of science; Asian and African philosophy. **SELECTED PUBLICATIONS** Auth, Reducing Concern with Self: Parfit and the Ancient Buddhist Schools, in Allen, ed, Culture and Self: Philosophical and Religious Perspectives, East and West, Westview, 97; auth, Communitarianism and Individualism in African Thought, Int Stud in Philos, 98; auth, Response to Prof Huey-Li Li's Paper: Multicultural Foundations for Philosophy of Education: A Propaedeutic, Philos of Educ Proc, 98; auth, The Violence Initiative: Race, Class and Reductionist Biology, Race, Gender and Class, 00. **CONTACT ADDRESS** Dept of Philosophy, Univ of Massachusetts, Boston, 761 Northwest Dr, Morgantown, WV 26505. **EMAIL** abasu@wvu.edu

BATEMAN, HERBERT W.
PERSONAL Born 05/06/1955, Camden, NJ, m, 1979, 1 child **DISCIPLINE** THEOLOGY AND THE NEW TESTAMENT **EDUCATION** Philadelphia Col of Bible, BS, 82; Dallas Theol Sem, ThM, 87, PhD, 93. **CAREER** Prof, new testament, Grace Theol Sem, 95-. **HONORS AND AWARDS** Outstanding Young Men of Amer, 88; Gold Heart Awds, Med City Hospital, 93; William M. Anderson Scholar Awd, Dallas Theol Sem, apr, 93; Who's Who among America's Teachers, 88. **MEMBERSHIPS** Soc of Bibl Lit; Evang Theol Sem; Institute for Biblical Research. **RESEARCH** The use of the Old Testament in the New Testament; Intertestamental history; The book of Hebrews. **SELECTED PUBLICATIONS** Book rev, A Guide to the Study of Greco-Roman and Jewish and Christian History and Literature, Bibliotheca Sacra, 152, 242-43, apr-jun, 95; book rev, Colossians & Philemon, Bibliotheca Sacra, 152, 118-19, jan-mar, 95; jour article, Were The Opponents at Philippi Necessarily Jewish, Bibliotheca Sacra, 155, 39-62, jan-mar, 98; jour article, World Missions, Bible Expositor and Illuminator, 69, dec 96-feb 97; jour article, Two First Century Messianic Uses of the Old Testament: Hebrews 1:5-13 and 4qflorilegium 1:1-19, Jour of the Evang Theol Soc, 38, 11-27, 95; jour article, The Use of Psalm 110:1 in the New Testament, Bibliotheca Sacra 149, 438-53, oct-dec 92; auth, Early Jewish Hermeneutics and Hebrews 1:5-13: The Impact of Early Jewish Exegesis on the Interpretation of a Significant New Testament Passage, New York: Peter Lang Publishing Company, 97; ed., "three Central Issues in Contemporary Dispensationalism," Grand Rapids, Kregel Publishing, 99. **CONTACT ADDRESS** 200 Seminary Dr., Winona Lake, IN 46590. **EMAIL** hwbiv@aol.com

BATEMAN, PAUL E.
PERSONAL Born 02/28/1956, Highland Park, IL, m, 1978 **DISCIPLINE** LAW **EDUCATION** Illinois State University, BS, 1976; University of Michigan, JD, 1980. **CAREER** National Labor Relations Board, trial Attorney, 80-84; Friedman & Koven, associate, 84-86; Sachnoff & Weaver, shareholder, 86-93; Burke, Warren & MacKay, shareholder, 93-. **MEMBERSHIPS** American Bar Association, 1980-; University of Michigan Black Law Alumni, regional liasion, 1991-; Civic Federation of Chicago, advisory board, 1989-; Boy Scouts of America, cubmaster, 1992-. **SELECTED PUBLICATIONS** Illinois Institute of Continuing Legal Education, Age Discrimination, 1996; Investigations, Testing & Privacy, 1990. **CONTACT ADDRESS** Burke, Warren & MacKay, PC, 330 N Wabash, 22nd Fl, Chicago, IL 60611.

BATES, GEORGE ALBERT
PERSONAL Born 05/30/1954, Charlottesville, VA **DISCIPLINE** LAW **EDUCATION** Princeton Univ, BA, 1976; Univ of VA, JD, 1980; Mediate Tech, Inc, General Mediation Cert, 1994. **CAREER** Princeton Univ Food Service, asst mgr, 72-76; Univ of VA, grad asst track coach, 76-80; State Farm Ins Co, automobile liability underwriter, 76-77; US Dept of Labor, law clerk-judge Roy P Smith, 80-81; Univ of VA, assoc dean/off afro-amer affairs, 87; General Counsel North Amer Van Lines, norcross trans, 90-94; Law Office of George A Bates, sole proprietor, 83-; EEO/Diversity consultant, mediator. **HONORS AND AWARDS** Princeton Univ, Co-Captain Track Team, 1976; Track Team Keene-Fitzpatrick Awd, 1975; Heptagonal Track Meet All-Ivy, Triple Jump, 1975; NJ State College Champion Triple Jump Winner, 1973-76; Univ of VA Office of Afro-Amer, Affairs Warrior Awd, 1987; Saint Paul's College, Humanitarian Service Awd, 1988; VA State Univ, Cooperative Extension Service, Humanitarian Service Awd, 1987. **MEMBERSHIPS** Alpha Phi Alpha Fraternity, 1977-; Central VA Minority Bus Assn, 1987-; Old Dominion Bar Assn, past bd mem, 1985-; Cooperative Extension Srvc Bd VA State Univ, 1985-; Albemarle Co, NAACP, 1981-; UVA Black Law Alumni Assn, president, 1985-96. **SELECTED PUBLICATIONS** Co-editor w/Prof Kenneth R Redden, "Punitive Damages" Michie Co, 1980; Journalist for five local newspapers & manuscript in progress on "The History of Bid Whist"; mem of the Ministerial Training Program, Charlottesville Church of Christ-Worldwide Bible Way, 1997. **CONTACT ADDRESS** 644 Maxfield Rd, Keswick, VA 22947.

BATES, JENNIFER
DISCIPLINE PHILOSOPHY **EDUCATION** Univ Toronto, BA, MA, PhD. **CAREER** Vis asst prof. **RESEARCH** Hegel and post-Kantian idealism; philosophy of the imagination and Aristotle. **SELECTED PUBLICATIONS** Pub(s), Bulletin of Hegel Soc of Great Brit; Philos in Rev. **CONTACT ADDRESS** Dept of Philosophy, Univ of Victoria, PO Box 3045, Victoria, BC, Canada V8W 3P4. **EMAIL** jbates@uvic.ca

BATES, STANLEY P.
PERSONAL Born 01/21/1940, Los Angeles, CA, m, 1964, 2 children **DISCIPLINE** PHILOSOPHY **EDUCATION** Dartmouth Col, BA, 61; Oxford Univ, BA, 63; MA, 68; Harvard Univ, PhD, 72. **CAREER** Asst prof, Univ Chicago, 66-71; from asst prof to prof, Middlebury Col, 71-. **RESEARCH** Philosophy; Aesthetics. **CONTACT ADDRESS** Dept of Philos, Middlebury Col, Middlebury, VT 05753-6200. **EMAIL** bates@middlebury.edu

BATEY, RICHARD A.
PERSONAL Born 01/19/1933, TN, m, 1953, 3 children **DISCIPLINE** RELIGION **EDUCATION** David Lipscomb Col, BA, 55; Vanderbilt Univ, BD, 58, PhD, 61. **CAREER** Asst prof New Testament theol, Harding Grad Sch Bible & Relig, 60-65; from asst prof to assoc prof Bible & relig, 65-72 , Prof Relig, Southwestern at Memphis, 72-; Fulbright res scholar, Univ Tubingen, 63-64; jr fel humanities, Memphis Acad Arts, 68-71; vis prof, St Mary's Col, Univ St Andrews, Scotland; W J Millard Chair Relig, 76- . **MEMBERSHIPS** Soc Bibl Lit; Am Acad Relig; Soc Study New Testament. **RESEARCH** New Testament theology; linguistic philosophy. **SELECTED PUBLICATIONS** Auth, So all Israel Will be Saved, Interpretation, 4/66; The One Flesh Union of Christ and the Church, New Testament Studies, 4/67; The Letter of Paul to the Romans, Sweet, 69; ed, New Testament Issues, SCM, England & Harper, 70; auth, New Testament Nuptial Imagery, Brill, Holland, 71; Jesus and the Poor, Harper, 72 & Ed Morcelliana, Italy, 73; Guidelines for Professional Ethics, J Am Col Dentists, 10/74; Thank God I'm OK, Abingdon. **CONTACT ADDRESS** Dept of Relig, Rhodes Col, 2000 N Pkwy, Memphis, TN 38112-1690.

BATTAGLIA, JACK M.
DISCIPLINE LAW **EDUCATION** Fordham Univ, BA, 68; Columbia Univ, JD, 71. **CAREER** Staff atty, Legis Drafting Res Fund, Columbia Univ, 71-73; pvt pract, NYC, 73-82; assoc prof Law, Touro Col, 82-84; pvt pract, San Francisco Bay Area, Calif, 84-92. **HONORS AND AWARDS** Harlan Fiske Stone scholar and tchg fel; Robert Noxan Toppan Prize in Const Law. **SELECTED PUBLICATIONS** Auth, Regulation of Hate Speech By Educational Institutions: A Proposed Policy, Santa Clara Law Rev. **CONTACT ADDRESS** Touro Col, New York, Brooklyn, NY 11230. **EMAIL** jackb@tourolaw.edu

BATTENFIELD, JAMES R.
PERSONAL Born 12/13/1935, Lexington, KY **DISCIPLINE** RELIGIOUS STUDIES **EDUCATION** San Diego State Univ, BA, 58; Talbot Theol Sem, BD, 67, ThM, 69; Grace Theol Sem, ThD, 76; **CAREER** Instr, Talbot Theol Sem, 67-70; asst prof, prof, Grace Theol Sem, 70-90; lectr, Calif State Univ, Long Beach, 90-92; expeditions and study tours Near East, 93-94. **HONORS AND AWARDS** Magna Cum Laude, 69; Zion res travel grant, 74; Univ Calif Los Angeles Syriac Dict project grant, 78. **MEMBERSHIPS** Am School of Oriental Res; Bibl Archaeol Soc. **RESEARCH** Old Testament Pentateuch; ancient Near Eastern language and archaeology; Bible and science issues. **SELECTED PUBLICATIONS** Coauth, Madaba Plains Project: A Preliminary Report of the 1987 Season at Tell el-Umeiri and Vicinity, Bul of Am Schools Orient Res, 90; auth, Field C: The Northern Suburb, and, Field E: The Water System, in Madaba Plains Project 2, Andrews Univ, 91; auth, Archaeology, in LaSor, ed, Old Testament Survey, Eerdmans, 96; auth, Some Onomastic Considerations Concerning Sites in the Tall al- Umayri Region, Central Jordan, 1989, in Herr, ed, Madaba Plains Project 3: The 1989 Season at Tell el-Umeiri and Vicinity and Subsequent Studies, Andrews Univ, 97; contrib, Ancient Ammonites and Modern Arabs, Am Ctr of Orient Res, Jordan, 98. **CONTACT ADDRESS** 3356 Elm Ave, Long Beach, CA 90807-4435. **EMAIL** jjbat@msn.com

BATTIN, MARGARET PABST
DISCIPLINE PHILOSOPHY **EDUCATION** Bryn Mawr Col, BA, 63; Univ Calif, Irvine, MFA, 73, PhD(philos), 76. **CAREER** Asst prof, 75-80, assoc prof, 80-88, Prof Philos, Univ Utah, 88-; Nat Endowment Humanities fel independent study & res philos issues in suicide, 77-78; distinguished prof, 00-. **HONORS AND AWARDS** Distinguished res award, Univ Utah, 97; Named Distinguished Prof, 00; Rosenblatt Prize, 00. **MEMBERSHIPS** Am Philos Asn; Am Soc Aesthet; Am Soc Bioethics and Humanities; Int Asn Bioethics **RESEARCH** Philosophical issues in suicide; fiction and philosophy; aesthetics; bioethics: ethical issues in end of life, esp. suicide and euthanasia; population and other large-scale reprodctive issues; ethical issues in organized relig; hist issues in suicide. **SELECTED PUBLICATIONS** Co-ed, Suicide: The philosophical issues, St Martin's Press, 81; John Donne's Biathanatos, Garland Publ Co, 82; auth, Ethical Issues in Suicide, Prentice-Hall, 82; co-ed, Puzzles about Art, St Martin's Press, 89; co-ed, Ethical Issues in the Professions, Prentice-Hall, 89; auth, Ethics in the Sanctuary, Yale Univ Press, 90; auth, The Least Worst Death, Oxford Univ Press, 94; co-ed, Physician-Assisted Suicide: Expanding the Debate, Routledge, 98; auth, Praying for a Cure, Rowman & Littlefield, 99; Auth, Population, In singer and Kuhse, Blackwells, 99; ed, the Ethics of Suicide: A Historical Sourcebook, 01. **CONTACT ADDRESS** Dept of Philos, Univ of Utah, 260 Central Campus Dr, Rm 341, Salt Lake City, UT 84112-9156. **EMAIL** mp.battin@m.cc.utah.edu

BATTLE, MICHAEL
PERSONAL Born 12/12/1963, New Orleans, LA, m, 1996, 1 child **DISCIPLINE** RELIGIOUS STUDIES **EDUCATION** Duke Univ, BA, 86; PhD, 95; Princeton Sem, Mdiv, 89. **CAREER** Asst prof, Univ of the S, 95-99; asst prof, Duke Univ Divinity School, 99-. **HONORS AND AWARDS** Doctoral Fel, Fund for Theol Educ, 91-92; Duke Univ Grad Award, 92; Res Fel, Univ of Cape Town, 97. **MEMBERSHIPS** ATLA; Soc for the Study of African Relig; Soc for the Study of Black Relig; Soc for the Study of Christian Spirituality; Peace Studies Asn. **RESEARCH** Spirituality; Theology; Ethics; South Africa. **SELECTED PUBLICATIONS** Auth, "Canberra Journal," Linkage (92); auth, "Ubuntu Ungamntu Ngabanye Abantu: Tutu's Ethics and the New South Africa," Linkage (93); auth, "A Response to Dr. Okorocha's Address," Anglican Theol Rev 77 (95); auth, The Wisdom of Desmond Tutu, Lion Press, 99; auth, "A Theology of Community," Interpretation 54 (00). **CONTACT ADDRESS** Divinity School, Duke Univ, Box 90968, Durham, NC 27708. **EMAIL** mbattle@duke.edu

BAUDER, MARK
PERSONAL Born 12/31/1958, Albuquerque, NM **DISCIPLINE** PHILOSOPHY **EDUCATION** Univ Wisc, PhD, 91. **MEMBERSHIPS** Am Philos Asn. **RESEARCH** Realism; Philosophy of science; Philosophy of mind; Philosophy of language; Philosophy of mathematics. **CONTACT ADDRESS** 108 W 45th, #110, Austin, TX 78751. **EMAIL** mbauder@math.utexas.edu

BAUER, JOSEPH P.
PERSONAL Born 11/03/1945, New York, NY, m, 1969, 2 children **DISCIPLINE** ANTITRUST & TRADE REGULATION LAW **EDUCATION** Univ Pa, BA, 65; Harvard Law Sch, JD, 69. **CAREER** Supvr & tchr, Univ Mich Law Sch, 72-73; vis prof, Univ NCar, 81-82; assoc dean, Notre Dame Law Sch, 85-88, 91, 96; prof, Notre Dame Law Sch, 73-. **HONORS AND AWARDS** Co-winner Teacher of the Year Awd, 77; Winner, Teacher of the Year Awd, 81; Spec Pres Awd, Univ Notre Dame, 96. **MEMBERSHIPS** Am Bar Asn, ABA Antitrust Sect **RESEARCH** Antitrust; civil procedure; trade regulation; intellectual property; conflict of laws; business associations; appellate advocacy; administrative law. **SELECTED PUBLICATIONS** Auth, "May a Federal Court Remand a Case to state Court After Federal Claims Have Been Deleted?," Preview of US Supreme Ct Cases, 1987-88 Term, Issue 4 (87); coauth, "Competition at the Teller's Window?: Altered Antitrust Standards for Banks and Other Financial Institutions," 35 Univ Kans Law Rev (87), 657-95; auth, "'Schiavone': An Un-'Fortune'-Ate Illustration of the Supreme Court's Role As Interpreter of the Federal Rules of Civil Procedure," 63 Notre Dame Law Rev (88), 720-32; auth, "A Judicial Clerkship Twenty-Four Years After Graduation: Or, How I Spent my Sabbatical Last Spring," 42 J of Legal Educ (92), 427-31; auth, "Antitrust and Sports: Must Competition on the Field Displace Competition in the Market?," 60 Tenn Law Rev (93), 263-94; auth, "South Bend, Indiana: A Case Study of the Possibilities and Realities of Hospital Cooperation," 8 Loyola Consumer Law Reporter (96) 143-52; auth, "The 'Erie' Doctrine Revisited: How a Conflicts Perspective Can Aid the Analysis," 74 Notre Dame Law Rev (99), 1235-1300. **CONTACT ADDRESS** Sch of Law, Univ of Notre Dame, Notre Dame, IN 46556.

BAUER, NANCY
PERSONAL Born 06/12/1960, Phildadelphia, PA, m, 1989, 2 children **DISCIPLINE** PHILOSOPHY AND RELIGION **EDUCATION** Harvard and Radcliffe Col, AB, 82; Harvard Divinity Sch, Master of Theol Studies, 86; Harvard Univ, PhD, 97. **CAREER** Teacher, epistemol, 93, hist of philos, fall, 93, Commonwealth Sch; teaching fel, prob in med ethics, 86, Harvard Divinity Sch; tutorial leader, lit and relig, 87, sr thesis adviser, 94, teaching fel, 87-94, grp tutorial leader, spring, 91, 92, 96, Harvard Univ; asst prof, 97, Bentley Col; lectr, 98, 97, 95, vis asst prof, 98, Tufts Univ. **HONORS AND AWARDS** Cert of Distinction in Teaching, deductive logic, 88, facts and ethics, 89, intro to the prob of philos, 89, moral perfectionism, 90, autonomy and alienation, 93, moral perfectionism, 94, Harvard Univ; dissertation fel, Harvard Grad Soc, 94-95. **RESEARCH** Feminism and feminist philosophy; Continental philosophy, especially 19th century German and 20th century French; history of philosophy, especially Descarts and Kant; Social and political philosophy; Moral philosophy; Ancient philosophy; Aesthetics; Introductory logic. **SELECTED PUBLICATIONS** Rev, Feminist Interpretations of Simone de Beauvoir, Hypatia, 96; auth, Advaita Vedanta and Contemporary Western Ethics, Philos East and West, 87. **CONTACT ADDRESS** Dept. of Philosophy, Tufts Univ, Medford, Miner Hall, Medford, MA 02155. **EMAIL** nbauer01@tufts.edu

BAUERSCHMIDT, FREDERICK CHRISTIAN
PERSONAL Born 09/21/1961 **DISCIPLINE** THEOLOGY AND ETHICS **EDUCATION** Univ South, BA, 84; Yale Divinity Sch, MAR, 89; Duke Univ, PhD, 96. **CAREER** Asst prof, Loyola Col, 94-; lectr, Duke Univ, 93. **HONORS AND AWARDS** Jr fac Sabbatical, Loyola Col Center Humanities, 97; Summer res grant, dean of Arts and Sci, Loyola Col, 95; dept fel, Duke Univ, 89-94; Dept Honors in Rel, Univ South, 84. **MEMBERSHIPS** Amer Acad Rel; Col Theol Soc; Soc Catholic Liturgy. **RESEARCH** Theology and Ethics. **SELECTED PUBLICATIONS** Essays in Refereed Journals, auth, Seeing Jesus: Julian of Norwich and the Text of Christ's Body, J Medieval and Early Modern Studies 27:2, 97; Julian of Norwich C Incorporated, Modern Theol 13:1, 97; Walking in the Pilgrim City, New Blackfriars 77:909, 96; The Abrahamic Voyage: Michel de Certeau and Theology, Modern Theol 12:1, 96; coauth, Eruditio without Religio The Dilemma of Catholics in the Academy, Communio: Int Catholic Rev 22:2, 95; essays in books, The Politics of the Little Way: Dorothy Day Reads Therese of Lisieux, In American Catholic Traditions: Resources for Renewal, Orbis Books, 97; unrefereed publ, Liturgical Rites and Wrongs: The Temptation to be Relevant, Commonweal, 95; Liturgy of the World C Liturgy of the Church, Publ of the Soc for Catholic Liturgy 2:2, 97; rev, P J Fitzpatrick, In Breaking of Bread, in Pro Ecclesia, 95; Grace Jantzen, Power, Gender and Christian Mysticism in Modern Theol 13:3, 97; papers presented, Not Without: Michel de Certeau and a Future for Christian Theology, Amer Acad Rel, Critical Theory section, Washington DC, 93; The Politics of the Little Way: Dorothy Day Reads Therese of Lisieux, The Col Theol Soc, Consultation on Mysticism and Politics, Dayton OH, 96; Neoplatonic Elements in the Christology of Julian of Norwich, Amer Acad Rel, Platonism and Neoplatonism section, New Orleans LA, 96; The Threefold Body: Theology After Suspicion, Christian Theol Res Fel, San Francisco, CA, 97. **CONTACT ADDRESS** Dept of Theology, Loyola Col, 4501 N Charles St, Baltimore, MD 21210. **EMAIL** fcb@loyola.edu

BAUM, ROBERT J.
PERSONAL Born 10/19/1941, Chicago, IL **DISCIPLINE** PHILOSOPHY **EDUCATION** Northwestern Univ, BA, 63; Ohio State Univ, PhD(philos), 69. **CAREER** From asst to prof philos, Rensselaer Polytech Inst, 69-82; prog dir, Nat Sci Found, 74-76; Prof Philos, Univ Fla, 81-, Dir, Ctr Study Human Dimensions Sci Technol, 76-81 & Ctr Appl Philos & Ethics in Professions, 81-; ed, Bus Prof Ethics J, 81-; ed, Prof Ethics: A Multidisciplinary J, 91-. **HONORS AND AWARDS** Distinguished Services Awd, NSF, 96; Mellon-Aspen Institute Fel, 77; Rockefeller Fel, 90. **MEMBERSHIPS** Am Philos Asn; Soc for Bus Ethics; Asn for Practical and Prof Ethics. **RESEARCH** Ethics; applied philosophy. **SELECTED PUBLICATIONS** Auth & ed Philosophy and Mathematics, Freeman, Cooper & Co, 73; ed, Ethical Arguments for Analysis, 73, 2nd ed, 77 & auth, Logic, 74, 2nd ed 80, 3rd ed 89, 4th ed 96, Harcourt Brace & Co; ed, Ethical Problems in Engineering, RPI, 78, 2nd ed, 80; auth, Ethics and Engineering Curricula, Hastings Ctr, 80. **CONTACT ADDRESS** Dept of Philosophy, Univ of Florida, P O Box 118545, Gainesville, FL 32611-8545. **EMAIL** rbaum@ufl.edu

BAUMANN, CAROL EDLER
PERSONAL Born 08/11/1932, Plymouth, WI, m, 1959, 2 children **DISCIPLINE** INTERNATIONAL RELATIONS **EDUCATION** BA Univ of Wis-Madison, 54; PhD-LSE, Univ of London, 57. **CAREER** Dir Emeritus Inst of Workd Affairs, Prof Emeritus, Dept Poli Sci, Dir Intl Studies and Prog, Univ of WI-Milwaukee, 82-88; Deputy Asst Sec for Assessments and Res, Bureau of Intelligence and Res, Dept of State, 79-81; Chm Intl Rel Major, Univ of WI_Milwaukee, 62-79. **HONORS AND AWARDS** Phi Beta Kappa; Phi Kappa Phi; Phi Eta Sigma; Marshall Scholar; Hon Woodrow Wilson Fel; Wisconsin Common Cause. **MEMBERSHIPS** China Council of the Asia Soc,Inc; Comm on Atlantic Studies; Council on Foreign Rel NY; Intl Studies Assoc; Natl Comm on US-China Rel; Natl Council of World Affairs Org; Pres, Bd of Dir, VP; Bd of Dirs, Foreign Policy Assoc; Bd, Eastern Shores Library System; Bd, Wis., World Trade Assoc. **SELECTED PUBLICATIONS** Auth, Program Planning about World Affairs, The American Forum for Global Education, NY, 91; ed, Europe in NATO: Deterrence, Defense, and Arms Control, Praeger, NY, 87; auth, The Diplomatic Kidnappings, Martinus-Nijhoff, The Hague, 73; ed, Western Europe: What Path to Integration, DC Heath & Co, Boston, 67; co-auth, Great Decisions, 68, Institute of World Affairs, Milwaukee, WI, 69; auth, Political Co-Operation in NATO, National Security Studies Group, Univ WI, Madison, 60. **CONTACT ADDRESS** Inst World Affairs, Univ of Wisconsin, Milwaukee, Milwaukee, WI 53201. **EMAIL** cbaumann@excel.net

BAUMBACH, GERARD
PERSONAL Born 03/29/1946, Jackson Heights, NY, m, 1968, 3 children **DISCIPLINE** THEOLOGY **EDUCATION** St Michael's Col , BA, 68; Univ Md MEd, 75; NYork Univ, EdD, 89. **CAREER** US Air Force Officer, 68-72; Dir Rel Educ, Church of Saint Clare, Albany NY, 72-78; William H Sadlier Inc, 78-; Executive Vice Pres, William H Sadlier Inc, 95-. **MEMBERSHIPS** Asn of Prof and Res in Rel Educ; Rel Educ Asn; Rel Edu Fel NY Univ; Albany Suburban Rel Educ Coord Asn; Com for Adult and Home Educ; Phi Delta Kappa; Kappa Delta Pi, Boy Scouts Of Am. **SELECTED PUBLICATIONS** Auth, Symposium Examines Catechetical Empowerment By Parish Priests, Momentum, 94; Symposium Examines Priests' Empowering Role in Catechesis, Caravan, 94; The Priest as Empowerer of Catechetical Ministry, 95; Experiencing Mystagogy: The Sacred Pause of Easter, 96; A Never-Ending Relationship: Catechesis and Catholic Social Teaching, Catechetical Leadership, 97; Spirituality for Lent and Easter: A Guide for Bridging the Mysteries, 98; auth, Letters from a Wounded Heart: Reflections to Strengthen and Comfort Your Soul, forthcoming. **CONTACT ADDRESS** William H. Sadlier Inc, 9 Pine St, New York, NY 10005.

BAUMGARTEN, ELIAS
PERSONAL Born 07/15/1945, New York, NY **DISCIPLINE** PHILOSOPHY **EDUCATION** Brandeis Univ, AB, 67; Northwestern Univ, MA, 71, PhD, 75. **CAREER** Instr, 72-75, asst prof, 75-80, Assoc Prof Philos, Univ Mich-Dearborn, 80-, Vis fel, Ctr Study Values & Social Policy, Univ Colo, fall, 81 & summer, 82 & vis assoc prof philos, spring, 82; bioethecist consultant, Univ MI Health System, 85-; res assoc, Center for Mid Eastern african Studies, Univ MI, 89-; Board Adv, Med Updates on Theory diag & prevention, 96-; Board Adv, Jewish Peace Lobby, 96-00. **HONORS AND AWARDS** Distinguished Teaching Awd, Univ MI-Dearborn, 77. **MEMBERSHIPS** Am Philol Asn; Am Asn of Philol Teachers, 78-80, 82-86; Am Asn for Bioethics and Humanities, World Congress of Bioethics, Concerned Philosphers for Peace. **RESEARCH** Ethics; bioethics; philos war peace and nationalism. **SELECTED PUBLICATIONS** Auth, The Ethical and Social Responsibilities of Philosophy Teachers, Metaphilos, 4/80; Wittgenstein's Conception of the Willing Subject, Man & World, 81; Ethics in the Academic Profession-A Socratic View, J Higher Educ, 5-6/82; The Right of Psychiatric Patients to Refuse Psychotropic Medication, Ethics, Humanism and Med; auth, " Conflicting Afairs," series of Ethical Case Studies in Teaching Philosophy, Teaching Philosophy, 86; rev, Health Care Ethics: Critical Issues for the 21st Century, American Family Physician, 99; auth, "Should Physicans Help Patients Die? A Philosophical Perspective," Medical Updates on Therapy Diagnosis

and Prevention, quarterly J of the Am International Health Council, Vol 1, No 1, 97; auth, "The Concept of Patient Autonomy, Part 1," Medical Updates, Vol 2 , No 3, 99; auth, " The Concept of Patient Autonomy, Part 2," Medical Updates, 99; auth, " Zionism, Nationalism and Morality," in Nationalism and Ethic Conflict: Philoisophical Perspectives," Open Court Publishing Company, 00. **CONTACT ADDRESS** Dept of Hum, Univ of Michigan, Dearborn, 4901 Evergreen Rd, Dearborn, MI 48128-1491. **EMAIL** elias@umich.edu

BAUMRIN, BERNARD HERBERT
PERSONAL Born 01/07/1934, New York, NY, m, 1953, 3 children **DISCIPLINE** PHILOSOPHY **EDUCATION** Ohio State Univ, AB, 56; Johns Hopkins Univ, PhD, 60; Columbia Univ, JD, 70. **CAREER** Dir forensics, Johns Hopkins Univ, 57-59; vis asst prof philos, Butler Univ, 60-61 & Antioch Col, 61; asst prof philos & chm Del sem philos sci, Univ Del, 61-64; asst prof philos, Wash Univ, 64-67; assoc prof, Hunter Col, 67-68; assoc prof, 68-73, prof Philos, Lehman Col & Grad Sch, City Univ New York, 73- ; adj prof med educ, Mt Sinai Sch of Med, 90- . **HONORS AND AWARDS** AEC; CUNY; Mellon; ACLS; NEH. **MEMBERSHIPS** Am Philos Asn; Am Bar Asn; Mind Asn; AAAS; AAUP. **RESEARCH** Philosophy of science; ethical theory; medical ethics jurisprudence. **SELECTED PUBLICATIONS** Auth, Preventive Detention, In: Dismantling the Criminal Law System: Decriminalization and Divestment, Wayne Law Rev, 3/73; Is There a Freedom Not to Speak?, Metaphilosophy, 1/75; Sexual Immorality Delineated, In: Philosophy and Sex, Prometheus, 75; Autonomy in Rawls and Kant, 76 & Autonomy Interest and the Kantian Interpretation, 77, Midwest Studies Philos; Towards Unravelling the Abortion Problem, In: Bioethics and Human Rights, Little, 78; Foundations of Academic Freedom and Tenure, Annals Scholar, fall 81; Two Concepts of Justice, Midwest Studies Philos, Vol VII, spring 82; auth, Moral Blindnes, in Metaphilosophy, 86; auth, Hobbes' Egalitarianiam, Nantes, 89; auth, The Ethics of Pandemics, APA Newsl, 89; auth, Chronic Illness, J of Med and Philos, 91; auth, Waste, J of Social Philos, 93; auth, Immorality, Midwest Stud, 96; auth, Divorce, In: Encyclopedia of Applied Ethics, 98; Security in Encyclops of Philosophy of Law, 00. **CONTACT ADDRESS** 590 West End Ave, New York, NY 10024. **EMAIL** bbaumrin@tiac.net

BAUR, MICHAEL
PERSONAL Born 11/13/1963, Los Angeles, CA, m, 1999 **DISCIPLINE** PHILOSOPHY, LAW **EDUCATION** Loyola Univ, BA, 85; Univ Toronto, MA, 86, PhD, 91; Harvard Law School, JD, 98. **CAREER** Asst prof, Catholic Univ, 91-95; asst prof, Fordham Univ, 98- . **HONORS AND AWARDS** Fulbright Scholar, Heidelberg, Ger, 88-89. **RESEARCH** German, Kant and Idealism, Epistemology, legal Philosophy. **CONTACT ADDRESS** Dept of Philosophy, Fordham Univ, Bronx, NY 10458. **EMAIL** mbaur@fordham.edu

BAXTER, DONALD
PERSONAL Born 11/16/1954, New York, NY, m **DISCIPLINE** PHILOSOPHY **EDUCATION** Oberlin Col, BA, 76; Univ Pittsburgh, MA, 80; PhD, 84. **CAREER** Instructor to asst prof, Princeton Univ, 83-90; asst prof to assoc prof, Univ Conn, 90-. **HONORS AND AWARDS** N Am Leibniz Soc Essay competition, 94. **MEMBERSHIPS** Am Philos Asn, Hume soc, Leibniz soc. **RESEARCH** Metaphysics, Early Modern Philosophy. **SELECTED PUBLICATIONS** Auth, "Hume's Puzzle about Identity," Philosophical Studies, (00): 179-193; auth, "The discernibility of Identicals," Journal of Philosophical Research, (99): 37-55; auth, "Hume's Labyrinth Concerning the Idea of Personal Identity," Hume Studies, 98; auth, "Abstraction, Inseparability, and Identity," Philosophy and Phenomenological Research, (97): 307-330; auth, "Bradley on Substantive and Adjective: The Complex-Unity Problem," Perspectives on the Logic and Metaphysics of FH Bradley, (96): 1-24; auth, "Corporeal Substances and True Unities," Studia Leibnitiana, (95): 157-184; auth, "Continuity and common Sense," International Studies in Philosophy, (92): 93-97; auth, "Berkeley, Perception, and Identity," Philosophy and Phenomenological Research, (91): 85-98; auth, "Hume on virtue, Beauty, composites, and Secondary Qualities," pacific Philosophical Quarterly, (90): 103-118. **CONTACT ADDRESS** Dept Philos, Univ of Conecticut, Storrs, Manchester Hall, Unit 2054, Storrs, CT 06269-0001. **EMAIL** donald.baxter@uconn.edu

BAXTER, LAURIE RAE
DISCIPLINE EDUCATIONAL PHILOSOPHY **EDUCATION** Holland Col Sch Art & Design, AA; Fairhaven Col, BA; W Wash Univ, Med; Ohio State Univ, PhD. **CAREER** Instr, Univ Brit Columbia; Univ Ariz; Ohio State Univ; prof. **RESEARCH** Cross-cultural aesthetics media and film studies. **SELECTED PUBLICATIONS** Past sr ed, contrib, Can Rev of Art Edu: Research and Issues; pub(s), Jour Aesthetic Edu; Stud in Edu; Jour Multi-Cult and Cross-Cult Res in Art Edu. **CONTACT ADDRESS** Dept of Commun and Soc Found(s), Univ of Victoria, PO Box 3045, Victoria, BC, Canada V8W 3P4. **EMAIL** lbaxter@uvic.ca

BAYCROFT, JOHN A.
PERSONAL Born 06/02/1933, Redcar, England **DISCIPLINE** RELIGION **EDUCATION** Christ Col, Cambridge (Synge sch), BA, 54, MA, 58; Ripon Hall, Oxford (GOE), 55; Trinity Col, Toronto, BD, 59; DD(hon), Montreal Diocesan Theol Col; DSLitt(jur dig), Thornloe Univ; DD(hon), Huron Col. **CAREER** Rector, Loughborough, 55-57; asst rector, St. Matthew's Church, Ottawa, 57-62; rector, Perth, Ont, 62-67; rector, St. Matthias Church, Ottawa, 67-84; rector, Christchurch Cathedral, dean, Ottawa, 84-86; suffragan bishop, Ottawa, 85-93; BISHOP OF OTTAWA, ANGLICAN CHURCH OF CANADA, 93-; lectr, Carleton Univ; mem fac theol, St. Paul Univ. **MEMBERSHIPS** Anglican/Roman Cath Int Comm; Anglican/Roman Cath Dialogue Can; Am Acad Relig; Soc Bible Lit; Can Church Hist. **SELECTED PUBLICATIONS** Auth, The Anglican Way, 80; auth, The Eucharistic Way, 82; auth, The Way of Prayer, 83. **CONTACT ADDRESS** Anglican Church of Canada, 71 Bronson Ave, Ottawa, ON, Canada K1R 6G6.

BAYER, GREG
PERSONAL Born 06/03/1954, PA **DISCIPLINE** PHILOSOPHY **EDUCATION** St John's Col, BA, 78; Univ Toronto, MA, 81; Univ Tex, PhD, 95. **CAREER** Teaching asst, Univ Toronto, 80-81; teaching asst, Univ Tex Austin, 91-94; asst instr, Univ Tex Austin, 95; asst prof, SMU, 95-96; asst prof, William and Mary, 96-97; asst prof, College of Wooster, 97-98; staff, sch Historical Stud, Princeton; asst prof, St. John's Col. **MEMBERSHIPS** Am Philos Asn. **RESEARCH** Philosophy; Ancient Philosophy; Aristotle. **SELECTED PUBLICATIONS** Auth, Definition through Demonstration: Aristotle's two Syllogisms in Posterior Analytics II.8, Phronesis, 95; Mackie, Kripke and Causal Necessity, Southwest Philos Rev, 96; Coming to Know Principles in Posterior Analytics II.19, Aperion, 97; Aristotelian Inquiry in the Posterior Analytics: The What-IS-X? Question, Ancient Philos, 97; Classification and Explanation in Aristotle's Theory of Definition, J of the Hist of Philos; rev, of Analysis and Science in Aristotle, 97. **CONTACT ADDRESS** Dept of Philos, St. John's Col, New Mexico, 1160 Camino Cruz Blanca, Sante Fe, NM 87501. **EMAIL** gbayer@mail.sjcsf.edu

BAYER, HANS F.
PERSONAL Born 10/27/1954, Stuttgart, Germany, m, 1976, 3 children **DISCIPLINE** NEW TESTAMENT EXEGESIS **EDUCATION** Ashland Theol Sem, MA, 77, MDiv, 79; Univ Aberdeen, Scotland, PhD, 84. **CAREER** Dozent, German Theol Sem, Giessen, Ger, 84-94; assoc prof Covenant Theol Sem, 94- ; Dir ThM program, 96- . **HONORS AND AWARDS** Tyndale fel scholar, Cambridge, 83; AfeT Scholar, Germany, 82. **MEMBERSHIPS** Soc Bibl Lit; Evangelical Theol soc; Tyndale fel; AfeT/FEET. **RESEARCH** The Gospel of Mark; Acts. **SELECTED PUBLICATIONS** Auth, Jesus' Predictions of Vindication and Resurrection, Their Provenance, Meaning and Correlation, WUNT, 2/20, O. Hofius, M. Hengel, Tuebingen, JCB Mohr (Paul Siebeck), 86, X + 289 S, (monograph); Rober Yarbrough, O. Cullmanns Progressiv-heilsgeschichtliche Konzeption, in Glaube und Geschichte, ed, Helge Stadelmann, TVG, GieBen/Wuppertal: Brunnen/Brockhaus, 88, 86, 319-347; Verstockung, Weissagen/Weissagung, Verziehen/ Verzoegerung, in Das Grosse Bibellexikon, Bd 3, ed (s), H. Burkhardt, G. Maier, F. Grunzweig, F. Laubach, Wuppertal/ Giessen: Brockhaus/Brunnen, 89, 1641, 1645, 1681, 1682; Jesus-Interpretationen in der Sachliteratur: Franz Alts Jesus-der erste neue Mann, in Christlicher Glaube und Literatur, 5, ed (s) C.P. Thiede, Wuppertal: R. Brockhaus, 1991, 55-71; Predictions of Jesus' Passion and Resurrection, in Dictionary of Jesus and the Gospels, ed (s), J.B. Green, S. McKnight, Downers Grove, IL/Leicester, IVP, 92, 630-633; Christ-Centered Eschatology in Acts 3:17-26, in J.B. Green/M. Turner's Jesus of Nazareth, Lord and Christ, Essays on the Historical Jesus and New Testament Christology, Grand Rapids/Carlisle, Eerdmans/ Paternoster, 96, 236-250; The Preaching of Peter in Acts in I.H. Marshall/ E. Peterson's, Witness to the Gospel: The Theology of Acts, Grand Rapids/Cambridge, W.B. Eerdmans/The Paternoster Press, 98, 257-274. **CONTACT ADDRESS** Dept of Theology, Covenant Theol Sem, 12330 Conway Rd, Saint Louis, MO 63141.

BAYER, RICHARD C.
PERSONAL Born 07/13/1956, Philadelphia, PA, m, 1998, 3 children **DISCIPLINE** SOCIAL ETHICS **EDUCATION** Univ TX AT Arlington, BA, 77, MA, 79; Univ Dallas, MA, 84; Graduate Theological Union, PhD, 90. **CAREER** Chief Operating Officer of The Five O'Clock Club. **MEMBERSHIPS** Soc of Christian Ethics; Amer Acad of Religion; Catholic Theological Soc of Amer; Gabriel Marcel Soc. **RESEARCH** Ethics and economics; political theory **SELECTED PUBLICATIONS** Auth, Ryan's Living Wage: A Reinterpretation and Constructive Proposal, Journal for Peace and Justice Studies, 94; auth, Christian Personalism and Democratic Capitalism, Horizons, 94; auth, Christian Perspectives on A theory of Justice by John Rawls, Journal; auth, Capitalism and Christianity, The Possibility of Christian Personalism Georgetown Univ Press, 99. **CONTACT ADDRESS** America's Premier Career, The Five O'Clock Club, Inc., 300 E 40th St., Apt. 6-L, New York, NY 10016-2147. **EMAIL** rcbyr@prodigy.net

BAYLIS, FRANCOISE
DISCIPLINE MEDICAL PHILOSOPHY **EDUCATION** McGill Univ, BA, 83; W Ontario Univ, MA, 84, PhD, 89. **CAREER** Prof. **RESEARCH** Medical ethics. **SELECTED PUBLICATIONS** Co-ed, Health Care Ethics in Canada, 95; "Errors in Medicine: Nurturing Truthfulness," Jour of Clinical Ethics, 97; "Health Care Ethics Consultation: Training in Virtue," Hum Stud, 98; Codes of Ethics, 98; auth, Informed Consent-New Reproductive Technioligies, Encycl of Reproductive Tech, 98; co-auth, Nat Coun on Bioethics in Human Res, Facilitating Ethical Research: Promoting Informed Choice, Discussion Document, NCBHR Communique, 96; "Women and Health Research: Working for Change," Jour of Clinical Ethics, 96; Child Abuse and Neglect: Cross-Cultural Considerations, Feminism and Families, 97; Medical Ethics and the Pediatric Surgeon, Surgery of Infants and Children, 97; "Bioethics for Clinicians: Ethical Dilemmas that Arise in the Care of Pregnant Women Can," Med Assoc Jour, 97; "Bioethics for Clinicians: Confidentiality," Can Med Assoc Jour, 97; Moral Residue: The Problem of Moral Compromise, Margin of Error, 98; Women and Health Research, Embodying Bioethics: Feminist Advances, 98; Reframing Research Involving Humans, The Politics of Women's Health: Exploring Agency and Autonomy, 98. **CONTACT ADDRESS** Dept of Philos, Dalhousie Univ, Halifax, NS, Canada B3H 3J5. **EMAIL** francoise.baylis@dal.ca

BAYNES, LEONARD M.
PERSONAL Born 06/30/1957, Queens, NY, s **DISCIPLINE** LAW **EDUCATION** New York Univ, BS, 79; Columbia Univ, JD, 82; MBA, 83. **CAREER** Law clk, 83-84; assoc, Gaston Snow, 84-86; att, NYNEX, 86-91. **HONORS AND AWARDS** Omicron Della Epsilon; Hon Soc. **MEMBERSHIPS** AALS; NPCLSC. **SELECTED PUBLICATIONS** Auth, "Derailed From The Information Superhighway: A Case Study of the Bell Atlantic Telephone Company," Dayton Law Rev 418 (96); auth, "The White Man's Burden and FCC Affirmative Action for Minority Ownership," Rutgers Law J 731 (99); auth, "WHITE OUT: The Absence and Stereotyping of People of Color by the Modern Media," Tex Sports Ent Law Rev (forthcoming); auth, "The Paradox of Minority Media Stereotypes and FCC Minority Ownership Affirmative Action Programs Post-Adarand," (work-in-progress); auth, "Life After Adarand: What Happened to the Metro Broadcasting Diversity Rationale for Minority Telecommunications Ownership," J Law Ref (forthcoming); coauth, "The Digital Divide: Discrimination in the Wireless Auctions," (forthcoming); auth, "Who Is Black Enough For You? The Stories Of One Black Man and His Family's Pursuit of the American Dream," Geo Immig Law J 97 (96); auth, "If It's Not Black And White Anymore, Why Does Darkness Cast A Longer Discriminatory Shadow Lightness? An Analysis Of The Color Hierarchy," Denver Law Rev 131(97). **CONTACT ADDRESS** School of Law, Western New England Col, 1215 Wilbraham Rd, Springfield, MA 01119-2612. **EMAIL** lbaynes@law.wnec.edu

BAZAN, BERNARDO C.
PERSONAL Born 10/26/1939, Mendoza, Argentina **DISCIPLINE** PHILOSOPHY **EDUCATION** Univ Cuyo (Arg), MA, 62; Univ Louvain (Belgium), LPhil, 65, PhD Phil, 67, PhD Medieval Stud, 72. **CAREER** Prof, Univ Cuyo (Arg), 69; assoc prof, 77, prof, 79-97, ch dept philos, 89-91, dean arts, 91-95, prof emer, Univ of Ottawa, 97-; vis prof, Catholic Univ Am, 83-84. **HONORS AND AWARDS** Fel, Royal Soc Can. **SELECTED PUBLICATIONS** Auth, Siger de Brabant: Quaestiones in tertium De Anima, De Anima intellectiva, De aeternitate mundi, 72; auth, Siger de Brabant: ecrits de logique, de morale et de physique, 74; auth, S. Thomas Quaestiones disputatae de anima, 96; coauth, Trois commentaires anonymes sur le Traite de l'ame d'Aristote, 71; coauth, Les questions disputees dans les Facultes de theologie, de droit et de medecine, 85; co-ed, Political Philosophies in the Middle Ages, 95. **CONTACT ADDRESS** 8 Birch Ave, Toronto, ON, Canada K1K 3G6.

BAZAN, CARLOS
DISCIPLINE PHILOSOPHY **EDUCATION** Univ Mendoza, BA, MA; Univ Louvain, MA, Dipl Sc Mediev, PhD. **CAREER** Prof, Univ Ottawa. **RESEARCH** Medieval and moral philosophy. **SELECTED PUBLICATIONS** Co-auth, Trois commentaires anonymes sur le Traite de l'ame d'Aristote, Paris, 71; Les Questions disputees et les questions quodlibetiques dans les Facultes de Theologie, de droit et de Medicine, Turnhout, Belgique, 85; auth, Siger de Brabant: Quaestiones in tertium De anima; De anima intellectiva; De aeternitate mundi, edition critique, Louvain-Paris, 72; Siger de Brabant: ecrits de logique, de morale et de physique, edition critique, Louvain-Paris, 74; S. Thomae de Aquino Quaes tinones disputatae de anima, dans Opera Omnia iussu Leonis XII P.M. edita, Rome-Paris, 96; ed, Moral and Political Philosophies in the Middle Ages, Actes du IXe Congres international de Philosophie medievale, Ottawa, 96. **CONTACT ADDRESS** Dept of Philosophy, Univ of Ottawa, 70 Laurier Ave, PO Box 450, Ottawa, ON, Canada K1N 6N5.

BEAL, TIMOTHY K.
DISCIPLINE RELIGIOUS STUDIES **EDUCATION** Emory Univ, PhD. **CAREER** Asst prof, Eckerd Col. **RESEARCH** Biblical studies. **SELECTED PUBLICATIONS** Auth, The Book of Hiding: Gender, Ethnicity, Annihilation, and Esther; co-auth, Reading Bibles, Writing Bodies: Identity and The Book; God in the Fray: Divine Ambivalence in the Hebrew Bible. **CONTACT ADDRESS** Religious Studies Dept, Eckerd Col, 4200 54th Ave S, Saint Petersburg, FL 33711. **EMAIL** bealtk@eckerd.edu

BEALE, DAVID OTIS
PERSONAL Born, VA, m, 3 children **DISCIPLINE** CHURCH HISTORY, THEOLOGY **EDUCATION** Bob Jones Univ, BA, 73, MA, 75, PhD(church hist), 80. **CAREER** Grad asst hist & church hist, 73-78, prof Church Hist, Theology & Bible, Bob Jones Univ, 78-. **HONORS AND AWARDS** Certificate of Award, Society for the Advancement and Preservation of Fundamental Studies of the Christian Faith, 95. **MEMBERSHIPS** Society for the Advancement and Preservation of Fundamental Studies. **RESEARCH** Historical Theology; Church Fathers; Colonial American churches; American Christianity since 1800; Baptist History; continued on-site research in British Isles and Holland tracing roots of Puritans, Pilgrims, Methodists, and Baptists. **SELECTED PUBLICATIONS** Auth, A Pictorial History of Our English Bible, Bob Jones Univ Press, 82; In Pursuit of Purity: American Fundamentalism Since 1950, Bob Jones Univ Press, 86; Ancient Attitudes towards Abortion, 1/82; A Family Travel and Tour Guide: Role of Protestant Churches in Early American History, 7-8/82; Fundamentalism: Past and Present, 10/82; The Purgatory Myth, 1/83; Francis Makemie: Champion of Religious Liberty, 5-6/83; Peter Muhlenberg: from the Pulpit to the Battlefield, 7-8/83; Lessons from the Catacombs, 12/83; The Pilgroms and God's Providence, 11/84; The Log College, 3/85; Faith for Family; The Revelation of Jesus Christ, Rev 19:1-21, Bibl Viewpoint, 11/82; auth, The Mayflower Pilgrims: Roots of Puritan, Presbyterian, Congregationalist, and Baptist Heritage (Belfast, Northern Ireland and Greenville, SC: Ambassador-Emerald International, 00). **CONTACT ADDRESS** Relig Dept, Bob Jones Univ, 1700 Wade Hampton, Greenville, SC 29614-0001. **EMAIL** davidbeale@home.com

BEALE, GREGORY
PERSONAL m, 3 children **DISCIPLINE** NEW TESTAMENT **EDUCATION** Southern Methodist Univ Dallas, BA, 71, MA, 76; Dallas Theol Sem, ThM, 76; Univ Cambridge, PhD, 80. **CAREER** Guest asst, asst prof, Grove City Col, 80-84; prof, Gordon-Conwell Theol Sem, 84 -; dir, ThM Prog in Biblical Theol. **MEMBERSHIPS** Mem, Evangel Theol Soc; Soc Biblical Lit; Inst Biblical Res; Tyndale Fel for Biblical and Theol Res. **RESEARCH** New Testament interpretative methodology, eschatology. **SELECTED PUBLICATIONS** Auth, The Use of Daniel in Jewish Apocalyptic Literature and in the Revelation of St John; ed, The Right Doctrine From the Wrong Text?, Essays on the Use of the Old Testament in the New, 94. **CONTACT ADDRESS** Gordon-Conwell Theol Sem, 130 Essex St, South Hamilton, MA 01982.

BEANBLOSSOM, RONALD EDWIN
PERSONAL Born 11/24/1941, Des Moines, IA, m, 1998, 2 children **DISCIPLINE** HISTORY OF MODERN PHILOSOPHY **EDUCATION** Morningside Col, BA, 64; Union Theol Sem, NYork, BD, 67; Univ Rochester, PhD(philos), 71. **CAREER** Asst prof philos, Northern Ill Univ, 70-77; Univ Chaplain, Ohio Northern Univ, 79-; assoc prof Philos & relig, Ohio Northern Univ, 82-87; chemn dept Philos & relig, 88-91; prof Philos & relig, 87-. **HONORS AND AWARDS** Sara A Ridenour Endowed Chair for Humanities, 89-90. **MEMBERSHIPS** Am Philos Asn. **RESEARCH** British empiricism; theories of perception; problems of knowledge; Quarterly, 88; Natural Reason: Essays in Honor of Joseph Norio Uemura, Hamline, 92; Reid and Hume, On the Nature of Belief, Reid Studies, 98. **SELECTED PUBLICATIONS** Auth, Walton on rational action, Mind, 71; Thomas Reid's Inquiry & Essays, LLA, 75; Russel's indebtedness to Reid, Monist, 78; A new foundation for human scepticism, Philos Studies, 76. **CONTACT ADDRESS** Dept of Philos & Relig, Ohio No Univ, 525 S Main St, Ada, OH 45810-1555.

BEANE, DOROTHEA ANNETTE
PERSONAL Born 03/30/1952, Plainfield, NJ, s **DISCIPLINE** LAW **EDUCATION** Spelman Col, 1971-72; Drew University, BA, 1974; Rutgers-Newark Col of Law, JD, 1977. **CAREER** US Department of Justice, Civil Division, Torts Branch, trial attorney, 77-81; Law Firm of Robinson and Geraldo, associate attorney, 81-82; US Department of Justice, assistant US attorney; Stetson University College of Law, assistant professor, 90-. **HONORS AND AWARDS** US Department of Justice, Attorney General's Special Achievement Awd, 1986; Women's Singles Table Tennis Championship of Jacksonville, FL, 1988-89; US Marshal's Service Letter of Appreciation, 1990; US Postal Service Letter of Appreciation, 1990. **MEMBERSHIPS** American Bar Association, 1990-; Black Law Students Association, faculty advisor, 1990-; Sarasota County American Inns of Court, academic master, 1990-; Association of American Law School, house of representatives, 1991; Stetson University Senate, representative, 1992-; American College of Legal Medicine, 1992-. **CONTACT ADDRESS** Col of Law, Stetson Univ, St. Petersburg, 1401-61st St South, Rm 211, Saint Petersburg, FL 33707.

BEARD, JAMES WILLIAM, JR.
PERSONAL Born 09/16/1941, Chillicothe, OH, m **DISCIPLINE** LAW **EDUCATION** Hardin-Simmons Univ, BS 1967; TX So Univ, JD 1973; Univ of TX, LLM 1976. **CAREER** Thurgood Marshall Law School, TX Southern Univ, assoc prof of law, assoc dean for academic affairs & programs, dir fed tax clinic. **HONORS AND AWARDS** Outstanding Young Amer for 1977. **MEMBERSHIPS** Mem Amer Bar Assn, State Bar of TX; bd of govs Natl Bar Assn; chmn Sect of Taxation NBA; mem NAACP; past trust Houston Legal Found. **CONTACT ADDRESS** Thurgood Marshall Law Sch, Texas So Univ, 3100 Cleburne, Houston, TX 77004.

BEARDSLEY, RUTH E.
PERSONAL Born 06/14/1936, El Paso, TX, d, 2 children **DISCIPLINE** PHILOSOPHY **EDUCATION** Univ Utah, BSN, 53; Univ Colorado, MA, 75, PhD, 85. **CAREER** Univ So Col, 83-86; adj instr, 82-92, chemn, philos dept, 92 -, Pikes Peak Commun Col; Two-year Co-chair/philosophy, State of CO, 82-92. **HONORS AND AWARDS** NEH co-grantee, 82; Fulbright-Hays fel, 93; Fulbright-Hays, NEH, East-West Ctr field study, 94; NEH workshop, 96. **MEMBERSHIPS** APA; Soc Int Universalism. **RESEARCH** Problems with loyalty; undergraduate education; Asian philosophy. **SELECTED PUBLICATIONS** Auth, Don't Let Tactics Trip You Up, Am Jour of Nurs, 83; auth, dir, producer, video, Language Distortion and Propaganda Techniques, 83; auth, Meta-ethics of Commitment, Dialectics and Humanism, 90; auth, Meta-ethics of Commitment II, Conf notes, Western Social Sci Asn, 92; Loyalty and Commitment With Special Emphasis on China, Univ Chicago, 95. **CONTACT ADDRESS** Dept of Communications, Humanities and Social Scie, Pikes Peak Comm Col, 5675 S Academy Blvd, Colorado Springs, CO 80906-5498. **EMAIL** ruth.beardsley@ppcc.cccoes.edu

BEASLEY, A.
PERSONAL Born 04/27/1945, Tuskegee, AL **DISCIPLINE** LAW **EDUCATION** Marygrove Coll Detroit, MI, BA 1966; Univ of CA Berkeley, JD 1973. **CAREER** San Francisco Chronicle, writer 1970; Howard Prim Rice Nemerovski et al, atty 1973-74; Legal Aid Soc of Alameda Co, atty 1974-76; NAACP Legal Def & Educ Fund Inc, atty 1977-78; Erickson Beasley & Hewitt, atty/partner 1978-. **MEMBERSHIPS** Bd mem San Francisco Lawyer's Com for Urban Affairs 1978-; bd mem Legal Aid Soc of Alameda Co 1978-; mem Litigation com Equal rights Adv; mem CA State & Fed Bar Assns 1973-; bd mem Stiles Hall Univ YMCA 1978-; mem Black Women Lawyers Assn; mem Charles Houston Bar Assn; mem & assoc editor CA Law Review 1972-73; lectr Civil Rights Practice for Pract Law Inst/Equal Oppty Employment Commn/CA Continuing Educ of the Bar. **CONTACT ADDRESS** Paralegal Studies, Merritt Col, 12500 Campus Dr, Oakland, CA 94619-3196.

BEATTY, JOHN
DISCIPLINE PHILOSOPHY **CAREER** Univ Ind, PhD. **RESEARCH** Philosophy of science; science and society. **SELECTED PUBLICATIONS** Auth, Dobzhansky and the Biology of Democracy: The Moral and Political Significance of Genetic Variation, Princeton, 94; Speaking of Species: Darwin's Strategy, MIT, 92; co-auth, The Propensity Interpretation of Fitness, MIT, 93. **CONTACT ADDRESS** Philosophy Dept, Univ of Minnesota, Twin Cities, 355 Ford Hall, 224 Church St SE, Minneapolis, MN 55455. **EMAIL** jbeatty@tc.umn.edu

BEATTY, JOSEPH
PERSONAL Born 06/04/1941, Philadelphia, PA, m, 1990, 2 children **DISCIPLINE** ETHICS, SOCIAL, POLITICAL PHILOSOPHY, GREEK PHILOSOPHY **EDUCATION** LaSalle Col, BA(English), 63; Johns Hopkins Univ, MA(Writing), 64; Haverford Col, MA(Philosophy), 66; Northwestern Univ, PhD(Philosophy), 72. **CAREER** Lectr, asst prof, Williams Col, 70-78; vis assoc prof, Duke Univ, 79-81; assoc prof, Davidson Col, 81-83; assoc prof, 83-, prof, philos, 88-, Randolph-Macon Col; Kent fel, Danforth, 70; Nat Hum Ctr fel, 78-79; NEH summer sem, 89. **HONORS AND AWARDS** Kent Fel, Danforth Foundation, 70; Nat Humanities Ctr Fel, 78-79; NEH Summer Seminar for Col Teachers, 89; Thomas Branch Awd for Excellence in Teaching (Randolph-Macon Col, 93. **RESEARCH** History of philosophy (ancient, medieval, modern), nineteenth-century, philosophy, twentieth-century, continental philosophy, existentialism, philosophy in literature, philosophy east-west, the philosophy of education, the philosophy of law. **SELECTED PUBLICATIONS** Auth, "The New Rhetoric, Practical Reason, and Justification: The Communicative Relativism of Chaim Perelman," The Journal of Value Inquiry 17, 93; auth, "The Rationality of the 'Orginal Postion': A Defense," Ethics 93, 83; auth, "The Complexities of Moral Education in a Librerал, Pluralistic Soceitry: The Cases of Socrates, Mrs. Pettit, and Adolf Eichmann," Soundings, 84; auth, "The Incoherence of Universal Prescriptivism," in The Gerogetown Symposium on Ethics: Essays in Honor of Henry Babcock Veatch, ed. By R. Porreco, Univ Pr of Am, 84; auth, "Him or Me?" American Philosophical Quarterly 23, 86; auth, "For Honor's Sake: Moral Education, Honor Systems, and the Informer-Rule," Educational Theory 42, 92; auth, "Thinking amd Moral Considerations: Socrates and Arendt's Eichmann," Hannah Arendt: Critical Essays, ed. By L.P. Hinchman and S.K. Hinchman, Albany: State Univ of New York Pr, 94; auth, "Honor and the Informer-Rule," Perspectives on the Professions 14, 95; auth, "Good Listening," Educational Theoru 49, 99; auth, "For Honor's Sake," in Ethics in Education, 99. **CONTACT ADDRESS** Dept of Philosophy, Randolph-Macon Col, Ashland, VA 23005. **EMAIL** jbeatty@rmc.edu

BEATTY, OTTO, JR.
PERSONAL Born 01/26/1940, Columbus, OH, d **DISCIPLINE** LAW **EDUCATION** Howard University, Washington, DC, BA, business administration, 1961; Ohio State University, Columbus, OH, JD, 1965. **CAREER** Ohio House of Representatives, state representative, 80-; Beatty & Roseboro, Columbus, OH, founder/senior partner, currently. **HONORS AND AWARDS** Citizens for Jesse Jackson Special Achievement Awd; Outstanding Leadership Awd, Columbus State Community College; Outstanding Service, Family Missionary Baptist Church; Outstanding Services Awd, Franklin County Children's Services; 10 Outstanding Young Men Awd, Junior Chamber of Commerce of Ohio; Meritorious Service Awd, The Ohio Academy of Trial Lawyers; Community Service Awd, Ohio Minority Businesses; Certificate of Appreciation for Dedicated Services, Upward Bound Program; Outstanding Legislator Awd; Outstanding Local Trial Bar Association, Continuing Legal Education; Outstanding Worksites Awd. "Damages in Soft Tissue Cases," Ohio Academy of Trial Lawyers; "Judgments under Ohio Tort Reform Law," "Proving Damages after Tort Reform," Ohio Legal Center. **MEMBERSHIPS** American Arbitration Assn; American Bar Assn; American Trial Lawyers Assn; Black Elected Democrats of Ohio; Columbus Area Black Elected Officials; Ohio State Consumer Education Assn; Natl Bar Assn; NAACP; Operation PUSH; Natl Conference of Black Lawyers, Columbus Chapter; Columbus Apartment Assn; Chamber of Commerce; Hunger Task Force of Ohio; Ohio Alliance of Black School Educators; Natl Black Programming Consortium; Black Chamber of Commerce; Columbus Assn of Black Journalists; Ohio Assn of Real Estate Brokers; Eastern Union Missionary Baptist Assn. **SELECTED PUBLICATIONS** "Damages in Soft Tissue Cases," Ohio Academy of Trial Lawyers; "Judgments under Ohio Tort Reform Law," "Proving Damages after Tort Reform," Ohio Legal Center. **CONTACT ADDRESS** Beatty & Roseboro Co, 233 S High St, Suite 300, Columbus, OH 43205.

BEATY, JAMES M.
PERSONAL Born 01/30/1925, m, 1948, 1 child **DISCIPLINE** RELIGION **EDUCATION** Atlantic Christian Col, AB, 45; Vanderbilt School Relig, BD, 49; Vanderbilt Univ, PhD, 63. **CAREER** Secretary, Church of God, 46-47; Missionary, Dominican Republic, 49-52; Educ Director, Church of God in Haiti, 52-59; Superintendent, Church of God in South America, 62-67; Assoc Prof, Lee Col, 67-74; President, Spanish Inst of Ministry, 74-80; Dean, Church of God Theol Sem, 80-92; Prof, Director of the Extension in Puerto Rico, 92-. **HONORS AND AWARDS** Who's Who in Relig, Distinguished Educator's Awd, 92. **MEMBERSHIPS** Soc of Biblical Studies, Soc for Pentecostal Studies. **RESEARCH** Theological bibliography in French and Spanish. **CONTACT ADDRESS** Dept Bible Studies, Church of God Sch of Theol, PO Box 3330, Cleveland, TN 37320-3330. **EMAIL** jbeaty@cogts.edu

BEAUCHAMP, RICHARD A.
PERSONAL Born 09/29/1938, Richmond, VA, m, 1977, 2 children **DISCIPLINE** PHILOSOPHY **EDUCATION** Randolph-Macon Col, BA, 61; Yale Divinity Sch, Mdiv, 64; Duke Univ, PhD, 70. **CAREER** Instr, Duke Univ, 68-69; lectr, Mary Baldwin Col, 71-73; adjunct prof, Christopher Newport Col/St. Leo Col, 73-76; assoc prof, Thomas Nelson Community Col, 76-81; vis prof, Col of William and Mary, 89; asst prof, Christopher Newport Col, 89-92; asst prof, Col of William and Mary, 89-92; assoc prof, Christopher Newport Univ, 92-98. **MEMBERSHIPS** Am Philos Asn, Va Philos Asn; Am Acad of Relig; Am Asn of Col and Univ; Asn of General and Liberal Studies. **RESEARCH** Philosophy; Theology. **SELECTED PUBLICATIONS** Auth, "Peirce, Thirdness, and Pedagogy: Reforming the Paideia," 99; "A Naturalist in Spite of Himself: A Dialogue with E.S. Brightman," 99; "Ethics and Metaethics in Bowne's Philosphy," 97; "Persons and Time: A Habermasian Corrective to Heidegger," 99; "Essay Questions Without Essays: Relief for Bleary-Eyed Professors," 96; "Moral Theory and Moral Education: The Neglected Connection," 95. **CONTACT ADDRESS** Dept of Philosophy & Religious Studies, Christopher Newport Univ, 1 University Pl, Newport News, VA 23606. **EMAIL** Beaucham@cnu.edu

BEAUCHAMP, TOM
PERSONAL Born Austin, TX **DISCIPLINE** PHILOSOPHY **EDUCATION** Yale Univ, BA; Johns Hopkins Univ, PhD, 70. **CAREER** Prof. **RESEARCH** History of modern philosophy and practical ethics; biomedical ethics; business ethics. **SELECTED PUBLICATIONS** Auth, Hume and the Problem of Causation, Oxford, 81; Principles of Biomedical Ethics, Oxford, 79; A History and Theory of Informed Consent, Oxford, 86; Philosophical Ethics, McGraw-Hill, 82. **CONTACT ADDRESS** Dept of Philosophy, Georgetown Univ, 37th and O St, Washington, DC 20057.

BEAUCHESNE, RICHARD J.
DISCIPLINE RELIGIOUS STUDIES **EDUCATION** Oblate Col & Sem, BA, MA; Boston Univ, PhD. **CAREER** Relig, Emmanuel Col. **SELECTED PUBLICATIONS** Coauth, The Eucharist as Sacrifice: Ethics that Enlightens Doctrine and Cult (An Ecumenical Praxis), 91; The Supernatural Existential as Desire: Karl Rahner & Emmanuel Levinas Revisited, Eglise et

Theologie, 92; Attention in Simone Weil and Dying as Supreme Attention, Univ St Paul, 95; Scriptural; Theological Arguments Against Women's Ordination (Simply Stated) and Responses in Journal of Ecumenical Studies, 95; Yves Congar Leaves Rich Legacy, Nat Catholic Reporter, 95; Simone Weil: Judaism, Christianity, and Islam, and Today's Feminist Critique of Patriarchy, The Religions of the Book, Univ Press Am, 96. **CONTACT ADDRESS** Emmanuel Col, Massachusetts, 400 The Fenway, Boston, MA 02115.

BEAUDOIN, JOHN M.
PERSONAL Born 07/18/1968, Chicago, IL, s **DISCIPLINE** PHILOSOPHY **EDUCATION** Univ IA, PhD , 97. **CAREER** Adj asst prof, 97-., Univ Iowa **MEMBERSHIPS** APA; Philos of Sci Asn. **RESEARCH** Philos of relig, of science, and of hist. **SELECTED PUBLICATIONS** Auth, Evil, The Human Cognitive Condition, and Natural Theology, Relig Studes 34, 98; auth, "On Some Criticisms of Hume's Principle of Proportioning Cause to Effect," Philo vol. 2, 99; auth, "Inscrutable Evil and Scepticism," Heythrop Journal, vol. 41, 00. **CONTACT ADDRESS** Dept of Philosophy, The Univ of Iowa, Iowa City, IA 52240. **EMAIL** beaudoin@uiowa.edu

BEBIS, GEORGE S.
PERSONAL Born 11/28/1926, Crete, Greece, s **DISCIPLINE** THEOLOGY **EDUCATION** Holy Cross Greek Orthodox School Theol, BA, 54; BDiv, 57; Harvard Div School, MTheol, 57; Univ Athens, Lisc Theol, 62; Dr Theol, 64. **HONORS AND AWARDS** Archbishop Lakovos Fac Awd, 89; Vis prof, Univ of Athens, 94. **MEMBERSHIPS** AAUP; Am Acad of Relig; Am Soc of Church Hist; Medieval Acad of Am; N Patristic Soc; Orthodox Theol Soc of Am; Boston Patristic Soc. **RESEARCH** Patristics and Liturgics. **SELECTED PUBLICATIONS** Auth, Mind of the Fathers: Essays in Patristic Studies, Holy Cross Orthodox Pr, 94. **CONTACT ADDRESS** Dept Theol, Hellenic Col, 50 Goddard Ave, Brookline, MA 02445-7415.

BECHARD, DEAN P.
PERSONAL Born 12/23/1959, Plattsburg, NY, m **DISCIPLINE** THEOLOGY **EDUCATION** Le Moyne Col, BA, 81; W Sch Theol MD, 91; STL, 93; Yale Univ, MA, 94; M Philos, 95; PhD, 98. **CAREER** Asst Prof, Fordham Univ, 97-. **MEMBERSHIPS** Soc of Bibl Lit, Cath Bibl Asn. **RESEARCH** History and Literature of The New Testament (Luke-Acts). **SELECTED PUBLICATIONS** Rev, of "Joseph Barnabas. Leben und Wirkungsgeschichte," by Bernd Kollman, Relig Studies Rev 25/4 (99): 424; rev, of "The Acts of the Apostles: A Socio-Rhetorical Commentary," by Ben Witherington, Cath Bibl Quart 61/2 (99): 388-390; auth, "The Theological Significance of 'Judaea' in Luke-Acts," in The Unity of Luke-Acts, ed. J. Verheyden (Leuven: Leuven Univ Press, 99), 675-691; rev, of "Die Christologie der Pastoralbriefe," by Hanna Stettler, Cath Bibl Quart 62/1 (00); auth, "Paul Among the Rustics: The Lystran Episode and Lucan Apologetic, " Cath Bibl Quart (forthcoming); auth, "Paul Among the Rustics: A Study of Luke's Socio-Geographical Universalism in Acts 14:8-20, Pontifical Bibl Inst (Rome), in press; auth, The Scripture Documents: An Anthology of Official Catholic Teachings, Liturgical Press (Collegeville, MN), forthcoming. **CONTACT ADDRESS** Dept Theol, Fordham Univ, 441 E Fordham Rd, Bronx, NY 10458-5149. **EMAIL** bechard@fordham.edu

BECHTEL, CAROL M.
PERSONAL Born 05/23/1959, Savannah, IL, d, 2 children **DISCIPLINE** THEOLOGY **EDUCATION** Yale Univ, PhD, 93. **CAREER** Presbyterian Sch of Christian Ed, assoc prof, 91-94; Western Theol Sem, assoc prof, 94-. **MEMBERSHIPS** SBL; Reformed Church in America--General Synod Prof of Theol. **RESEARCH** Psalms; Esther; intersection of Bible and music. **SELECTED PUBLICATIONS** Auth, Glimpses of Glory, Westminster John Knox Press, 98; auth, Sowing Tears Reaping Joy: The Bible and Brahms's Requiem, Kerygma, 97; auth, Hallelujah!: The Bible and Handel's Messiah, Kerygma, 95. **CONTACT ADDRESS** Dept of Old Testament, Western Theol Sem, 101 E. 13th St, Holland, MI 49423-3622. **EMAIL** carol@westernsem.org

BECHTEL, LYN
PERSONAL Born 09/01/1939, NJ, m, 1990, 2 children **DISCIPLINE** BIBLICAL STUDIES **EDUCATION** Drew Univ Grad Sch, PhD, 83. **CAREER** Assoc prof of Hebrew Bible, Moravian Theol Sem, 89-98; vis assoc prof of Hebrew Bible, Drew Theol Sem, 98- . **MEMBERSHIPS** SBL. **RESEARCH** Feminist hermeneutics; Genesis; Deuteronomic theology; postmodern Biblical interpretation. **SELECTED PUBLICATIONS** Auth, The Perception of Shame Within the Divine/Human Relationship in Biblical Israel, in Hopfe, ed, Uncovering Ancient Stones: Essays in Memory of H. Neil Richardson, Eisenbrauns, 94; auth, What If Dinah Is Not Raped? (Genesis 34), J of the Stud of the Old Testament, 94; auth, Adam and Eve: A Myth about Human Maturation, 1994 Annual of Hermeneutics and Social Concern, Continuum, 94; auth, Genesis 2.4b-3.24: A Myth about Human Maturation, J for the Study of Old Testament, 95; auth, A Feminist Approach to the Book of Job, in Brenner, ed, Feminist Companion to Wisdom Literature, Sheffield, 95; auth, A Symbolic Level of Meaning of the Mariage in Cana Story, in Brenner, Feminist Companion to the Hebrew Scriptures in the new Testament, Sheffield, 95; auth, Shame, in Russell, ed, Dictionary of Feminist Theologies, 96; auth, Genesis 34 Revisited, in Rogerson, ed, Pentateuch, Sheffield, 97; auth, The Sanction of Shame in Biblical Israel, in Social-Scientific Old Testament Criticism, Sheffield, 97; auth, Sex, in Freedman, ed, Eerdmans Dictionary of the Bible, Eerdmans, 97; auth, A Feminist Reading of Genesis 19, in Brenner, ed, Feminist Companion to Genesis II, Sheffield, 98; auth, Dinah, Daughters and Wife of Lot, Woman Who Miscarries or Is Barren, Fruitful Wife, Daughters of the Region, Daughters of Jacob, in Meyers, ed, Women in Scripture: A Dictionary of Named and Unnamed Women in the Hebrew Bible, Apocrypha, and New Testament, Houghton Mifflin, 98; auth, Boundary Issues in Genesis 19, in Graham, ed, Marking Boundaries: Essays on/in Feminist Theological Hermeneutics, Sheffield, forthcoming. **CONTACT ADDRESS** 480 Raubsville Rd, Easton, PA 18042. **EMAIL** lkdey@aol.com

BECHTEL, WILLIAM
PERSONAL Born 12/01/1951, Detroit, MI **DISCIPLINE** PHILOSOPHY, PHILOSOPHY OF SCIENCE **EDUCATION** Kenyon Coll, AB, 73; Univ Chicago, PhD, 77. **CAREER** Asst prof, Northern Ky Univ, 77-80; Asst prof; Univ Ill Med Center, 80-83; asst prof and full prof, Ga State Univ, 83-94; PROF, Wash Univ St Louis, 94-. **MEMBERSHIPS** Philos of Sci Asn; Soc for Philos and Psychol; Southern Soc for Philos and Psychol; Cognitive Sci Soc; Cognitive Neuroscience Soc; Am Philos Asn. **RESEARCH** Philosophy of neuroscience and cognitive science; history and philosophy of biology. **SELECTED PUBLICATIONS** Auth, pubs on philosophy of neuroscience and cognitive science, history and philosophy of biology; coauth, Discovering Complexity: decomposition and localization as strategies in scientific research, 93; How to do things with logic, 94; A companion to cognitive science, 98; Connectionism and the mind II: Parallel processing, dynamics, and evolution, in press. **CONTACT ADDRESS** Dept of Philosophy, Washington Univ, Campus Box 1073, Saint Louis, MO 63130. **EMAIL** bill@twinearth.wastl.edu

BECK, GUY
PERSONAL Born 08/03/1948, New York, NY, m, 1979 **DISCIPLINE** HISTORY OF RELIGION **EDUCATION** Syracuse Univ, PhD, MA; Univ FL, MA. **CAREER** Asst Prof, 95-97, Loyola Univ; Act Asst Prof, 90-95, LSU; Vis Asst Prof, 97-99, College of Charleston; ; **HONORS AND AWARDS** Fulbright Schshp; AIIS SR Res Fel. **MEMBERSHIPS** AAR; SE. **RESEARCH** Sacred sound, Hindu Music; Phenomenology of Ethno musicology. **SELECTED PUBLICATIONS** Auth, Seven entries for Encarta Encyclopedia on CD-ROM by Microsoft Inc, including, Om, Bhagavata Purana, Sutra, Mudra, Prayer Wheel, Satori, Ahura Mazda; auth, Religious Music of Northern Areas, in: Garland Encyc of World Music: South Asia Volume, Alison Arnold, ed; Bhajan/Devotional Music, Music Festivals and Music Academies, for the Encyc of Hinduism; auth, Devotional Hymns from Sanskrit, in: Religions In India, DS Lopez Jr ed, Princeton Univ Press, 95; Fire in the Atman: Repentance in Hinduism, in: Repentance: A Comparative Perspective, Amitai Etzioni, David Carney, ed, Lanham MD, Rowman and Littlefield, 97. **CONTACT ADDRESS** Liberal Arts & Sciences, Tulane Univ, 200 Gibson Hall, New Orleans, LA 70118. **EMAIL** beckg@tulane.edu

BECK, JOHN A.
DISCIPLINE OLD TESTAMENT **EDUCATION** Nortwest Col Wis, BA, 78; Wis Lutheran Sem, M.Div, 82; Trinity Ev Divinity School Ill, ThM, 93; PhD, 97. **CAREER** Pastor of St Paul's Ev Lutheran Church Wis, 82-87; Chief flight Instr Northstar Aviation Wis, 87-91; Bible Transl Rev, God's Word to the Nat Bibl Soc Ohio, 92-94; Dir, Freshman Year Experience, 90-; Assoc Prof; Concordia Univ Wis, 91-. **RESEARCH** The Rhetorical Function of Geography in Hebrew Narrative of the Old Testament. **SELECTED PUBLICATIONS** Auth, Translator's As Storytellers, A Study in Septuagint Translation Technique, Peter Lang Press (New York), 00; auth, "Geography and the Narrative Shape of Numbers 13," Bibliotheca Sacra 157 (00): 270-79; auth, "Peer Leadership Beyond the Classroom," Peer Leadership, National Resource Center on the Freshman Year Experience, (00); auth, On The Edge of Success, Wadsworth Publishing Company, forthcoming. **CONTACT ADDRESS** Dept Hebrew & Old Testament, Concordia Univ, Wisconsin, 12800 N Lake Shore Dr, Mequon, WI 53097. **EMAIL** jack_beck@cuw.edu

BECK, MARTHA CATHERINE
PERSONAL Born 04/03/1953, Minneapolis, MN, 3 children **DISCIPLINE** PHILOSOPHY **EDUCATION** Hamline Univ, BA; Bryn Mawr Col, MA, PhD. **CAREER** Asst prof, Lyon Col. **RESEARCH** Plato; Aristotle; Ethics; polit philos. **SELECTED PUBLICATIONS** Auth, Purdah and Human Rights. **CONTACT ADDRESS** Dept of Philos, Lyon Col, PO Box 2317, Batesville, AR 72503. **EMAIL** mbeck@lyon.edu

BECK, NORMAN ARTHUR
PERSONAL Born 02/27/1933, Oak Harbor, OH, m, 1959, 3 children **DISCIPLINE** BIBLICAL THEOLOGY **EDUCATION** Capital Univ, BA, 58; Lutheran Theol Sem, BD, 62; Princeton Theol Sem, PhD, 67; Trinity Lutheran Sem, DD, 90. **CAREER** Instr New Testament, Princeton Theol Sem, 65-66; pastor, Good Shepherd Lutheran Church, 66-70 & King of Kings Lutheran Church, Ann Arbor, 70-75; asst prof, 75-80, assoc prof theol, 80-85, prof theology and classical lang, 85- , TX Lutheran Univ, 75-. **MEMBERSHIPS** Soc Bibl Lit; Am Acad Relig; Am Schs Orient Res. **RESEARCH** The anti-Jewish polemic of the New Testament; Anti-Roman cryptograms in the New Testament. **SELECTED PUBLICATIONS** Auth, The Last Supper as an efficacious symbolic act, J Bibl Lit, 70; Letters to Young Churches (teacher's guide & student's bk), 74 & Hope in Disguise (teacher's guide & student's bk), 78 Augsburg; Four kinds of learning, Parish Teacher, 2/78; Why should we have church schools?, Church Teachers 8, 80; A new statement of faith for a new church, Dialog 20, 81; Reclaiming a Biblical text: The Mark 8:14-21 discussion about bread in the boat, Catholic Bibl Quart 43, 81; Scripture Notes A; Scripture Notes B; Scripture Notes C; Mature Christianity in the 21st Century; Anti-Roman Cryptograms in the New Testament. **CONTACT ADDRESS** Texas Lutheran Univ, 1000 W Court St, Seguin, TX 78155-5999. **EMAIL** nbeck@txlutheran.edu

BECK, ROSALIE
PERSONAL Born 01/28/1949, Amarillo, TX **DISCIPLINE** RELIGION **EDUCATION** Univ Calif, BA, 71; Southwestern Baptist Theol Sem, MDiv, 79; Baylor Univ, PhD, 84. **CAREER** Lectr, Baylor Univ, 84-86; From Asst Prof to Assoc Prof, Baylor Univ, 86-. **HONORS AND AWARDS** Mellen Fel; Carr P Collins Awd; Robert Baker Awd. **MEMBERSHIPS** Southern Asn of Women Historians, Southern Baptist Hist Soc, Am Soc of Church Hist, Nat Asn of Baptist Profs of Relig, Tex Baptist Hist Soc, Whitsitt Soc. **RESEARCH** Missiology, women in Christian history, Baptist history, gender and Christian history. **SELECTED PUBLICATIONS** Auth, "A Community of Scholars."; Chapters in "With Steadfast Purpose," "Stories That Won't Go Away," "A Cloud of Witnesses."; Articles in "Church History: Perspectives," "Baptist History and Heritage." **CONTACT ADDRESS** Dept Religion, Baylor Univ, Waco, PO Box 97284, Waco, TX 76798-7284. **EMAIL** rosalie_beck@baylor.edu

BECK, W. DAVID
PERSONAL Born 07/08/1947, Lancaster, PA, m, 1969, 4 children **DISCIPLINE** PHILOSOPHY **EDUCATION** Houghton Col, BA, 69; Trinity Evangelical Divinity School, MA, 71; Boston Univ, PhD, 80. **CAREER** Teaching Asst, 71-72, Univ Rhode Island; Instr, 73-74, Rhode Island Jr Col; Instr, 74-75, Boston Univ; Instr, 76-78, Bridgewater State Col; Asst/Assoc/Prof, 78-, Chr, Philosophy Dept, 81-88, Asst Dean, Graduate School of Religion, 87-89, Assoc VP for Faculty Devel, 88-97, Dean of Graduate Studies, 89-97, Assoc VP for Academic Affairs and Dean of Graduate School, 97-, Liberty Univ. **HONORS AND AWARDS** Pres, Evangelical Phil Soc. **MEMBERSHIPS** Amer Phil Assoc; Evangelical Phil Soc; Virginia Phil Assoc; Soc of Christian Philosophers; Assoc of Virginia Graduate Deans **RESEARCH** Cosmological argument for God's existence; faculty evaluation and development **SELECTED PUBLICATIONS** Auth, Designing a Christian University, Opening the American Mind, 91; God's Existence, Miracles: Has God Acted in History, 97. **CONTACT ADDRESS** School of Religion, Liberty Univ, Lynchburg, VA 24506. **EMAIL** dbeck@liberty.edu

BECKER, CHARLES M.
PERSONAL Born 10/31/1954, Staten Island, NY, m, 1977, 2 children **DISCIPLINE** ECONOMICS **EDUCATION** Grinnell Col, BA, 76; Princeton Univ, MA, 79; PhD, 81. **CAREER** Instr, Princeton Univ, 79-81; asst prof, Vanderbilt Univ, 81-86; assoc prof to prof, president, Univ of Colo Boulder Economics Inst, 87-; sr econ, IMCC, 98-. **HONORS AND AWARDS** Phi Beta Kappa; Thomas J Watson Found Fel, 76-77. **MEMBERSHIPS** Am Econ Assoc, Population Assoc of Am, Southern Econ Assoc, Western Econ Assoc Int, Reg Sci Assoc Int, Assoc of Comparative Econ Systems. **RESEARCH** Forecasting pension systems, demographic change in former Soviet Union, migration and urbanization in developing countries, fertility transition in developing countries. **SELECTED PUBLICATIONS** Coauth, Studies in Indian Urban Development, Oxford Univ Pr, (NY), 86; auth, "Economic Sanctions Against South Africa," World Politics 34.2 (87): 147-173; auth, "The Demo-Economic Impact of the AIDS Pandemic in Sub-Saharan African," World Develop 18.2 (90): 1599-1619; coauth, The Impact of Sanctions on South Africa, Part I: The Economy, Investor Responsibility Res Center (Washington, DC), 90; coauth, Indian Urbanization and Economic Growth Since 1960, Johns Hopkins Univ, (Baltimore), 92; coauth, Beyond Urban Bias: African Cities in an Age of Structural Adjustment, Heinemann and James Currey, (London), 94; coauth, "Rural-Urban Migration in Africa: Do Age-Gender Cohorts Matter?" Jour of African Econ 5.2, (96): 228-270; coauth, "Demographic Change in the Former Soviet Union during the Transition Period," World Develop 26.11, (98): 1957-1976; coauth, "Urbanization in Transforming Economies," North-Holland Handbook on Applied Urban Economics, eds Paul Cheshire and Edwin S Mills, (Amsterdam: Elsevier North-Holland, 99): 1173-1290; coauth, "Speculative Price Bubbles in the Rice Market and the 1974 Bangladesh Famine," Jour of Econ Develop, forthcoming. **CONTACT ADDRESS** Dept Economics, Univ of Colorado, Denver, Campus Box 181, Denver, CO 80217-3364. **EMAIL** cbecker@carbon.cudenver.edu

BECKER, EDWARD
PERSONAL 2 children **DISCIPLINE** ANALYTIC PHILOSOPHY AND PHILOSOPHY OF LANGUAGE **EDUCATION** Johns Hopkins Univ, PhD, 70. **CAREER** Assoc prof, Univ Nebr, Lincoln. **RESEARCH** Quine. **SELECTED PUBLICATIONS** Quine and the Problem of Significance, Proc of the 7th Int Wittgenstein Symp, 83; Holistic Behaviorism, Proc of the 9th Int Wittgenstein Symp, 85. **CONTACT ADDRESS** Univ of Nebraska, Lincoln, Lincoln, NE 68588-0321. **EMAIL** ebecker@unlserve.unl.edu

BECKER, LAWRENCE C.
PERSONAL Born 04/26/1939, Lincoln, NB, m, 1967 **DISCIPLINE** PHILOSOPHY **EDUCATION** Midland Col, BA, 61; Univ Chicago, MA, 63, PhD, 65. **CAREER** Instr, 65-67, asst prof, 67-71, assoc prof, 71-78, prof, 78-89, fel, 89- , Hollins Col; prof, Col of William and Mary, 89- . **HONORS AND AWARDS** Nat Endowment Hum Fel, 71-72, 93-94; Rockefeller Found Hum Fel, 82-83; Ctr for Advanced Stud in the Behavioral Sci, 83-84. **RESEARCH** Ethics. **SELECTED PUBLICATIONS** Auth, On Justifying Moral Judgements, 73; auth, Property Rights: Philosophic Foundations, 77; auth, Reciprocity, 86. **CONTACT ADDRESS** Dept of Philosophy, Col of William and Mary, PO Box 8795, Williamsburg, VA 23187. **EMAIL** lcbeck@facstaff.wm.edu

BECKER, LEWIS
DISCIPLINE FEDERAL SECURITIES REGULATION, SALES, CONSUMER TRANSACTIONS, FAMILY LAW **EDUCATION** Temple Univ, BS, 58; Univ Pa Sch Law, LLB, 61. **CAREER** Prof; Villanova Univ, 72-. **MEMBERSHIPS** ABA Family Law Section's Marital Property Comt, Alimony Committee, Ethics Comt. **RESEARCH** Family law, securities regulation. **SELECTED PUBLICATIONS** Contrib auth, Alimony, Child Support and Counsel Fees--awd, Modification and Enforcement, 88; Valuation and Distribution of Marital Property, 90, 91 and 94 ed; co-ed and contrib auth, Premarital and Marital Contracts: A Lawyer's Guide to Drafting and Negotiating Enforceable Marital and Cohabitation Agreements, 93. **CONTACT ADDRESS** Law School, Villanova Univ, 800 Lancaster Ave, Villanova, PA 19085-1692. **EMAIL** becker@law.vill.edu

BECKER, WILLIAM HENRY
PERSONAL Born 03/28/1943, New York, NY, m, 1965, 2 children **DISCIPLINE** AMERICAN BUSINESS & ECONOMIC HISTORY **EDUCATION** Muhlenberg Col, BA, 64; Johns Hopkins Univ, PhD, 69. **CAREER** Asst prof, Univ MD Baltimore County, 69-73, assoc prof, 73-80; vis assoc prof, 80-82, assoc prof, 82-83, prof hist, George Washington Univ, 83-; Vis Prof Hist, Johns Hopkins Univ, 96 & Nat Univ Singapore, 98. **HONORS AND AWARDS** Newcomen Awd, Outstanding Bk Bus Hist, 79-82. **MEMBERSHIPS** AHA; Orgn Am Historians; Econ Hist Asn; Econ Hist Asn; Bus Hist Conf. **RESEARCH** Hist of business; comp business hist; business-government rel. **SELECTED PUBLICATIONS** Auth, The Dynamics of Business-Government Relations: Industry and Exports, 1893-1921, Univ Chicago Press, 82; co-ed (with Samuel F Wells), Economics and Diplomacy: An Assessment of American Diplomacy Since 1789, Columbia Univ Press, 84; gen ed, The Encyclopedia of American Business History & Biography, 9 vol, Broccoli Clark Layman, 86-92. **CONTACT ADDRESS** Dept of Hist, The George Washington Univ, 2035 H St N W, Washington, DC 20052. **EMAIL** whbecker@gwu.edu

BECKERMAN, PAUL
PERSONAL Born 08/23/1948, Denver, CO, m, 1983, 1 child **DISCIPLINE** ECONOMICS **EDUCATION** Princeton Univ, PhD 79. **CAREER** World Bank, 88-; Federal Reserve Bank, 85-88. **RESEARCH** Economics of Development; Stabilization. **CONTACT ADDRESS** World Bank, 1818 H St., N W, Washington, DC 20433. **EMAIL** pbeckerman@worldbank.org

BECKERMAN-RODAU, ANDREW
PERSONAL Born New York, NY **DISCIPLINE** LAW **EDUCATION** Hofstra Univ, BS, 76; W New Eng Col, JD, 81; Temple Univ, LLM, 86. **CAREER** Vis asst prof to prof, Ohio N Univ, 86-00; vis prof to prof, Suffolk Univ, 00-. **HONORS AND AWARDS** Teacher of the Year, Ohio N Univ Pettit Col of Law. **MEMBERSHIPS** Am Intellectual Property Law Asn; Am Bar Asn; Mass Bar Asn; Boston Bar Asn; Boston Patent Law Asn; Ohio State Bar Asn; Mass Bar Asn. **RESEARCH** Intellectual property law. **SELECTED PUBLICATIONS** Auth, "Are Ideas Within the Traditional Definition of Property?: A Jurisprudential Analysis," Ark L Rev, 94; auth, Business Associations: Cases and Materials on Agency, Partnership and the Legal Problems of Business Enterprises, LUPUS Pub, 95; auth, Business Organizations: Cases and Materials on Partnerships, Limited Liability Companies and Corporations, LUPUS Pub, 98; auth, "A Jurisprudential Approach to Common Law Legal Analysis," Rutgers L Rev, 99. **CONTACT ADDRESS** Sch of Law, Suffolk Univ, 120 Tremont St, Boston, MA 02108-4977. **EMAIL** arodau@acad.suffolk.edu

BECKETT, STEVEN J.
DISCIPLINE LAW **EDUCATION** Univ Ill, BA, JD. **CAREER** Founder, Beckett & Assoc; adj prof, Univ Ill Urbana Champaign **HONORS AND AWARDS** Awd, Ill pub defender asn, Champaign Co ACLU. **SELECTED PUBLICATIONS** Auth, Whatever Happened to the Bill of Rights? A Criminal Defense Lawyer's Perspective, Univ Ill Law Rev, 92; co-auth, Preparing For Your Deposition. **CONTACT ADDRESS** Law Dept, Univ of Illinois, Urbana-Champaign, 52 E Gregory Dr, Champaign, IL 61820. **EMAIL** sbeckett@law.uiuc.edu

BECKWITH, FRANK
DISCIPLINE APOLOGETICS **EDUCATION** Univ Nev, BA; Fordham Univ, MA, PhD; Simon Greenleaf Univ, MA. **CAREER** Adj prof. **SELECTED PUBLICATIONS** Co-auth, Relativism, Feet Firmly Planted in Mid Air, Baker Bk House, 98; See The Gods Fall: Four Rivals To Christianity, Col Press, 97; co-ed, The Abortion Controversy 25 Years After Roe V. Wade: A Reader, Wadsworth, 98; Affirmative Action: Social Justice Or Reverse Discrimination, Prometheus Bk(s), 97. **CONTACT ADDRESS** So Evangelical Sem, 4298 McKee Rd, Charlotte, NC 28270.

BEDAU, HUGO ADAM
PERSONAL Born 09/23/1926, Portland, OR, m, 1990, 4 children **DISCIPLINE** PHILOSOPHY **EDUCATION** Univ Redlands, BA, 49; Boston Univ, MA, 51; Harvard Univ, MA, 53, PhD, 61. **CAREER** Instr philos, Dartmouth Col, 53-54; instr, Princeton Univ, 54-57, lectr, 58-61; Danforth teacher, Danforth Found, 57-58; Carnegie fel law & philos, Harvard Law Sch, 61-62; assoc prof philos, Reed Col, 62-66; prof, 66-70, chmn dept, 66-76, Austin Fletcher Prof Philos, Tufts Univ, 70-99, Grant-in-aid, Soc Sci Res Coun, 62; Russell Sage Found res grant, 73; dir, Nat Endowment for Humanities summer sem, 75 & 80; Nat Endowment for Humanities summer res, 77; vis fel, Cambridge Univ, 80. **HONORS AND AWARDS** Phi Beta Kappa. **MEMBERSHIPS** Am Philos Asn; Am Soc Polit & Legal Philos; Soc Philos & Pub Affairs. **RESEARCH** Ethics; social, legal and political philosophy. **SELECTED PUBLICATIONS** Ed, The Death Penalty in America, Doubleday, 64, rev ed, 67, 3rd ed, 82; Civil Disobedience, Pegasus, 68; Justice and Equality, Prentice-Hall, 71; coauth, Victimless Crimes, Prentice-Hall, 74; co-ed, Capital Punishment in the US, AMS, 76; coauth, Inspite of Innocense; auth, The Courts, the Constitution, and Capital Punishment, D C Heath, 77; Social Justice and Social Institutions, Midwest Studies Philos, 78; How to Argue about Prisoners' Rights, Rutgers Law Rev, 81; auth, Death Is Different, 87; coauth, Current Issues and Ending Questions, 87; coauth, Critical Thinking, Reading and Writing, 93. **CONTACT ADDRESS** Dept of Philos, Tufts Univ, Medford, Medford, MA 02155-5555.

BEDELL, GEORGE CHESTER
PERSONAL Born 05/13/1928, Jacksonville, FL, m, 1952, 3 children **DISCIPLINE** RELIGION **EDUCATION** Univ of the South, BA, 50; Va Theol Sem, BD, 53; Univ NC, Chapel Hill, MA, 66; Duke Univ, PhD(relig), 69. **CAREER** Rector, Episcopal parishes, FL, 53-64; asst prof, 67-73, Courtesy Assoc Prof Relig, FL State Univ, 73-, Mem Staff, Bd Regents, 71-; exec vice chancellor, 81. **MEMBERSHIPS** Am Acad Relig; Soc Sci Studies Relig; MLA; S Atlantic Mod Lang Asn. **SELECTED PUBLICATIONS** Auth, The Technique of Fiction Revisited, 7/68 & The Prayer Scene in Hamlet, 4/69, Anglican Theol Rev; Kierkegaard's Conception of Time, J Am Acad Relig, 9/69; Kierkegaard and Faulkner: Modalities of Existence, LA State Univ, 73; Religion in America, Macmillan, 75, 2nd ed, 82; Florida-Now, A Kinder, Gentler Press, Scholarly Pub, Vol 25, 93. **CONTACT ADDRESS** Bd of Regents, Florida State Univ, 107 W Gaines St, Tallahassee, FL 32304.

BEDESKI, ROBERT E.
PERSONAL Born 11/03/1937, Detroit, MI **DISCIPLINE** POLITICAL SCIENCE, ASIAN STUDIES, HISTORY **EDUCATION** Univ Calif Berkeley, BA, 64, MA, 65, PhD, 69. **CAREER** Asst prof, Ohio State Univ, 69-73; asst prof, 73-75, assoc prof, Carleton Univ, 75-89; prof Political Science, Univ Victoria, 89-; vis prof, Meiji Univ (Tokyo), 93-94. **HONORS AND AWARDS** Nat Defense Foreign Lang fel in Japanese, 65-67; sr res fel, Ctr Chinese Stud, Univ Calif Berkeley, 67-69; Social Sci Res Coun grant contemporary China, 71-72; SSHRC leave grant, 80-81; Japan Found res fel, 80-81; Pacific Cultur Found grant 82-83; Bilateral Exchange Grant SSHRC & Chinese Acad Soc Sci, 83-84, 86; res fel, Kyungnam Univ Inst Far Eastern Stud (Korea), 88; res fel, Int Cultur Soc Korea, 90; Japan Found fel, 93-94. **MEMBERSHIPS** Can Soc Chinese Stud (bd dir); Can Polit Sci Asn; Can Asian Stud Asn; Int Polit Sci Asn; Can Inst Strategic Stud; Japanese Stud Asn Can (pres 95-96). **SELECTED PUBLICATIONS** Auth, State-Building in Modern China: The Kuomintang in the Prewar Period, 81; auth, The Fragile Entente: the 1978 Japan-China Peace Treaty in a Global Context, 83; auth, The Transformation of South Korea: Reform and Reconstitution in the Sixth Republic Under Roh Tae Woo 1987-93, 94; ed, Confidence Building in the North Pacific: New Approaches to the Korean Peninsula, 96. **CONTACT ADDRESS** Dept of Political Science, Univ of Victoria, Victoria, BC, Canada V8W 3P5. **EMAIL** rbedeski@uvic.ca

BEER, FRANCIS A.
PERSONAL Born 02/05/1939, New York, NY, m, 1965, 3 children **DISCIPLINE** POLITICAL SCIENCE **EDUCATION** Harvard Univ, AB, 60; Berkeley Univ, MA, 63, PhD, 67. **CAREER** Asst Prof to Assoc Prof, Dept Govt, Univ Tex, 67-75; Prof Polit Sci, Univ Colo, 75-. **HONORS AND AWARDS** Undergrad Scholarship, Harvard Col, 57-58; Fulbright Fel, Fondation nationale des sciences politiques, Paris, 65-66; Doctoral Fel, Mershon Prog Educ Nat Security, Ohio State Univ, 66-67; Postdoctoral Schol, Inter-University Consortium for Polit Res, Univ Mich, 78; Fulbright Res Prof, John F. Kennedy Inst, Cath Univ, The Netherlands, 71; Vis Fel, Ctr Int Studies, Univ Cambridge, 82; Univ Colo, Col Arts & Sci, Dean's Writing Prize for Best Article, 87; Outstanding Prof, Univ Colo, Int Affairs Prog, 97; recipient of numerous grants. **MEMBERSHIPS** Am Polit Sci Asn; Int Polit Sci Asn; Int Soc Polit Psychol; Int Soc Study Europ Ideas; Int Soc Study Argumentation; Int Studies Asn. **SELECTED PUBLICATIONS** Auth, Integration and Disintegration in NATO: Processes of Alliance Cohesion and Prospects for Atlantic Community, Ohio State Univ Press, 69; Alliances: Latent War Communities in the Contemporary World, Holt, Rinehart, Winston, 70; The Political Economy of Alliances: Benefits, Costs, and Institutions in NATO, Sage, 75; How Much War in History: Definitions, Estimates Extrapolations, and Trends, Sage, 75; Peace Against War: The Ecology of International Violence, W. H. Freeman, 91; co-ed, Post-Realism: The Rhetorical Turn in International Relations, Mich State Univ Press, 96; author of numerous articles and other publications. **CONTACT ADDRESS** Political Science Dept, Univ of Colorado, Boulder, Boulder, CO 80309. **EMAIL** beer@spot.colorado.edu

BEERMAN, JACK
PERSONAL Born 04/18/1958, Chicago, IL, m, 1989, 4 children **DISCIPLINE** LAW **EDUCATION** Univ Wisc Madison, BA; Univ Chicago, JD, 83. **CAREER** Assoc prof to prof and assoc dean, Boston Univ, 84-. **HONORS AND AWARDS** Fac Res Scholar, 00-01. **MEMBERSHIPS** Am Bar Asn. **RESEARCH** Administrative law; Civil Rights Litigation. **SELECTED PUBLICATIONS** Auth, "The Economic Theory of Politics and Legal Interpretation in the United States," Rechtstheorie, 91; co-auth, "The Social Origins of Property," Can J of Law and Jurisprudence, 93; auth, "The Supreme Court's Narrow View on Civil Rights," Supreme Court Rev, 93; auth, "The Reach of Administrative Law in the United States," in The Province of Administrative Law, 97; auth, "The common Law and Section 1983 Litigation," Chicago-Kent L Rev, (97): 695-746; auth, "Holme's Good Man: A Comment on Levinson and Balkin," BUL Rev, (98): 937-945; co-auth, Administrative Law: Cases and Materials, Aspen L and Bus, 98. **CONTACT ADDRESS** Sch of Law, Boston Univ, 765 Commonwealth Ave, Boston, MA 02215. **EMAIL** beermann@bu.edu

BEFORT, STEPHEN
PERSONAL Born 09/29/1948, Preston, MN, m, 1992, 2 children **DISCIPLINE** LEGAL STUDIES **EDUCATION** Univ Minn, BA, 70, JD, 74. **CAREER** Prof, Univ Minn Law, 82-; assoc dean, 00-. **HONORS AND AWARDS** Teach of Yr Awd, 93; Davis Chmn Excel in Teach and scholar, 94-95; Fesler res Fel, 97. **MEMBERSHIPS** ABA; MBA; AALS; ISSSLL. **RESEARCH** Labor and employment law. **SELECTED PUBLICATIONS** Co-auth, Employment Law and Practice, west Pub, 95, supp, 97, 98, 99, 00, 01; co-auth, "Reassignment Under the Americans with Disabilities Act: Reasonable Accommodation, Affirmative Action, or Both," Wash Lee Rev (01); co-auth, "BFOQ Revisited: Johnson Controls Halts the Expansion of the Defense to International Sex Discrimination," Oh State Law J 5 (91); auth, "Employee Handbooks and the Legal Effect of Disclaimers," Rel Law J 601 (92); co-auth, "Beyond the Rhetoric of the NAFTA Treaty Debate: A Comparative Analysis of Labor and Employment Law in Mexico and the United States," Lab Law J269 (96); auth, "Pre-employment Screening and Investigation: Navigating Between a Rock and a Hard Place," HOFSTRA Lab Law J 365 (97), repr Defense Law J 467 (98); co-auth, "The ADA in Turmoil: Judicial Dissonance, Supreme Court Response, and the Future of Disability Discrimination Law, "Ore Law Rev 27 (99); auth, "Demystifying Federal Labor and Employment Law Preemption," Lab Law 429 (98); co-auth, "Mental Illness and Long-term Disability Plans Under the Americans with Disabilities Act," J Labor and Emp 287 (99); co-auth, "The Sounds of Silence: The Libertarian Ethos of ERISA Preemption," Univ Fl Rev 1 (00). **CONTACT ADDRESS** Law Sch, Univ of Minnesota, Twin Cities, 22919th Ave S, Rm 285, Law 7911, Minneapolis, MN 55455. **EMAIL** befor001@tc.umn.edu

BEGLEITOR, MARTIN D.
PERSONAL Born 10/31/1945, Middletown, CT, m, 2 children **DISCIPLINE** LAW **EDUCATION** Univ Rochester, BA, 67; Cornell Law Sch, JD, 70. **CAREER** Atty, New York, 70-77; assoc prof to prof, Drake Univ, 77-. **HONORS AND AWARDS** Prof of the Year, Drake Univ, 80. **MEMBERSHIPS** Am Law Inst; Am Bar Asn; Iowa State Bar Asn. **RESEARCH** Estate planning; Federal estate and gift taxation; Wills and trusts; Malpractice in estate planning. **SELECTED PUBLICATIONS** Auth, "Attorney Malpractice in Estate Planning - You've Got to Know When to Hold Up, Know When to Fold Up," Kans L Rev, 90; auth, "Article II of the Uniform Pro-

bate Code and the Malpractice Revolution," Tenn L Rev, 91; auth, "Estate Planning in the Nineties: Friday the Thirteenth, Chapter 14: Jason Goes to Washington - Part I," Ky L J, 93; auth, "Anticontest Clauses: When You Care Enough to Send the Final Threat," Ariz State L J, 94; auth, "Estate Planning in the Nineties: Friday the Thirteenth, Chapter 14: Jason Goes to Washington - Part II," DePaul L Rev, 97; auth, "Does the Prudent Investor Need the Uniform Prudent Investor Act - An Empirical Study of Trust Investment Practices," Maine L Rev, 99; auth, "First Let's Sue all the Lawyers - What Will We Get: Damages for Estate Planning Malpractice," Hastings L J, 00. **CONTACT ADDRESS** Sch of Law, Drake Univ, 2507 University Ave, Des Moines, IA 50311. **EMAIL** martin.begleiter@drake.edu

BEIL, RICHARD O.
PERSONAL Born 02/19/1955, Fort Worth, TX, m, 1977, 1 child **DISCIPLINE** ECONOMICS **EDUCATION** N Tex State Univ, MS, 82; Tex A and M Univ, PhD, 88. **CAREER** Vis lectr, Tex A and M Univ, 87-88; asst prof to assoc prof, Auburn Univ, 88-. **HONORS AND AWARDS** Outstanding Fac Teacher, Dept of Econ and the Col of Bus, 00-01; Outstanding Prof, Auburn Univ Panhellenic Coun, 98-99; Outstanding Fac Member, Col of Bus, 98-99; Mortar Board's Favorite Prof, Auburn Univ, 97-98; Outstanding Prof Award, Auburn Univ Panhellenic Coun, 97; William and Kay McCartney Teaching Excellence Award, 96-97; Outstanding Teaching Award, Auburn Univ, 96-97; Outstanding Fac Member, Auburn Student Govt Asn, 95-96; Lynde and Harry Bradley Found Res Grant, Tex A and M Univ, 86-87. **MEMBERSHIPS** Am Econ Asn; Econ Sci Asn; Public Choice Soc; S Econ Asn. **RESEARCH** Coordination failure; Cooperative behavior; Game theory; Teaching of economics. **SELECTED PUBLICATIONS** Co-auth, "Tacit Coordination Games, Strategic Uncertainty, and Coordination Failure," Am Econ Rev, (90): 234-248; co-auth, "Strategic Uncertainty, Equilibrium Selection Principles, and Coordination Failure," Quart J of Econ, (91): 885-910; co-auth, "Asset Markets as an Equilibrium Selection Mechanism: Coordination Failure, Game Form Auctions, and Tacit Communication," Games and Econ Beh, (93): 485-804; co-auth, "Competition and the Price of Municipal Cable Television Services: An Empirical Study," J Regulatory Econ, (93): 401-415; co-auth, "do People Rely on the Self-Interested Maximization of Others? An Experimental Test," Management Sci, (94): 252-262; co-auth, "Entry and Product Quality Under Price Regulation," Rev of Industrial Org, (95): 361-372; co-auth, "The American Economic Association Dues Structure," J of Econ Perspectives, (96): 179-186; co-auth, "The Economics of Prohibition-Related Crime: Contests with Externalities," JAI Advances in Microecon, 98; co-auth, "Are Economists More Selfish Than Other 'Social' Scientists?" Public Choice, (99): 85-101; co-auth, "Cultural Determinants of Economic Success: Reliant Behavior in the U.S. And Japan," Econ Inquiry, (01): 270-279. **CONTACT ADDRESS** Dept of Econ, Auburn Univ, 415 W Magnolia Ave, Auburn, AL 36849-5247. **EMAIL** RBEIL@business.auburn.edu

BELL, DERRICK ALBERT, JR.
PERSONAL Born 11/06/1930, Pittsburgh, PA, m, 1992, 3 children **DISCIPLINE** LAW **EDUCATION** Duquesne Univ, AB, LLB, 52; Univ Pittsburgh Law School, 57 (Assoc ed-in-chief, Pittsburgh Law Rev). **CAREER** Staff Attorney, US Dept of Justice, 57-59; Exe Secretary, Pitts Branch of NAACP, 59-60; First Asst Counsel, NAACP Legal Defense and Ed Found, Inc, 60-66; Depury Dir, Office for Civil Rights, Dept of Health, Education, and Welfare, 66-67; Exe Dir, Western Center on Law and Poverty, Univ Southern CA Law School, 67-69; lect of Law, 69-71, Prof of Law, Harvard Univ, 71-80; Dean and Law Prof, Univ OR Law School, 81-85; Weld Prof of Law, Harvard Univ, 86-92; vis prof, NYU Law School, 91-93; Scholar-in-residence, NY Univ Law School, 93-94; vis prof, New York Univ Law School, 94-98. **HONORS AND AWARDS** Honorary degrees from Pace Law School, 66; Northeastern Law School, 84; Tougalso Col, 83; Mercy Col, 88; Allegheny Col, 89; Teacher of the Year Awd presented by Am Law Schools, 85. **MEMBERSHIPS** Admitted to bars by examination in District of Columbia, 57; PA, 60; NY, 66; CA, 69; admitted to practice in US Supreme Court and in Federal Courts of Appeal in the Fourth, Fifth, Sixth, Eighth, and Tenth Circuits. **SELECTED PUBLICATIONS** Auth, Confronting Authority: Reflections of an Ardent Protester, 94; Constitutional Conflicts, 97; Gospel Choirs: Psalms of Survival in an Alien Land Called Home, 96; Afrolantica Legacies, 98. **CONTACT ADDRESS** 444 Central Park W, Apt 14B, New York, NY 10025-4358. **EMAIL** dbell1930@aol.com

BELL, JOHN L.
DISCIPLINE PHILOSOPHY **EDUCATION** Exeter Col Oxford, BA, 65; Christ Church Oxford, DPhil, 69. **CAREER** Prof. **RESEARCH** Mathematical logic; philosophy of mathematics; set theory; Boolean algebras; lattice theory; category theory. **SELECTED PUBLICATIONS** Coauth, "Elementary Propositions and Independence," Notre Dame J. of Formal Logic, 37, no. 1, 96; auth, "Polymodal Lattices and Polymodal Lobic," Math Logic Quarterly 42, 96; coauth, "Precovers, Modalities, and Universal Closure Operators in a Topos," Math Logic Quarterly 42, 96; auth, "Zorn's Lemma and Complete Booleana Algebras in Intuitionistic Type Theories," Journal of Symbolic Logic 62, no. 4, 97; auth, "Boolean Algebras," Routledge Encyclopedia of Philosophy, 98; auth, A Primer of Infinitesimal Analysis, Cambridge Univ Press, 98; auth, "Boolean Algebras and Distributive Lattices Treated Constructively," Math Logic Quarterly 45, 99; auth, "Frege's Theorem in a Constructive Setting," Journal of Symbolic Logic, 64, no. 2, 99; auth, The Art of the Intelligible: An Elementary Survey of Mathematics in its Conceptual Development, Kluwer, 99. **CONTACT ADDRESS** Dept of Philosophy, Univ of Western Ontario, London, ON, Canada N6A 5B8. **EMAIL** jbell@atsjulian.uwo.ca

BELL, LINDA A.
PERSONAL Born 08/06/1940, Daytona Beach, FL **DISCIPLINE** FEMINIST THEORY, EXISTENTIALISM, ETHICS, CONTINENTAL PHILOSOPHY **EDUCATION** Emory Univ, PhD, 73. **CAREER** Prof, Ga State Univ. **SELECTED PUBLICATIONS** Auth, Visions of Women; Sartre's Ethics of Authenticity; Rethinking Ethics in the Midst of Violence: A Feminist Approach to Freedom. **CONTACT ADDRESS** Georgia State Univ, Atlanta, GA 30303. **EMAIL** wsilab@langate.gsu.edu

BELL, NORA KIZER
PERSONAL Born Charleston, WV, m, 3 children **DISCIPLINE** PHILOSOPHY, BIOETHICS **EDUCATION** Randolph-Macon Woman's Col, BA; Univ So Carolina, MA; Univ N Carolina, PhD. **CAREER** Mem fac, 77- , chemn Dept Philos, 87-92, dir, Ctr for Bioethics, 92-93, Univ So Carolina; Dean, Col of Arts & Sci, Univ N Texas, 93-97; pres, Wesleyan Col, 97- . **HONORS AND AWARDS** Phi Beta Kappa; Omicron Delta Kappa; Mortar Board Woman of the Year, 88; J. Marion Sims Awd, So Carolina Public Health Asn for advancing public health, 88; gubernatorial appointee, Comnr, So Carolina Comn on Aging, 89-93; So Carolina Woman of Achievement Awd, 92; order of the Palmetto, So Carolina, 93; elected vis res fel, Inst for Adv Stud in Hum, Univ Edinburgh, 94; Tau Alpha Pi. **MEMBERSHIPS** Nat Acad Academic Leadership; Coun of Col of Arts and Sci. **SELECTED PUBLICATIONS** Ed and contribur, Who Decides? Conflicts of Rights in Health Care, Humana, 82; auth, Ethical Issues Involving Nutrition in the Critically Ill, in, Zaloga, ed, Nutrition in Critical Care, Mosby, 94; auth, Women and Children with AIDS: A Public Health Challenge for Metropolitan Universities, Metropolitan Univ, 95; auth, Responsibilities and Rights in the Promotion of Health: The Individual and the State, Social Sci and Medicine, 96; auth, Protocol 076: A New Look at Women and Children with AIDS, in Umeh, ed, Cross-Cultural Perspectives on HIV/AIDS Education, Africa World Press, forthcoming. **CONTACT ADDRESS** Office of the President, Wesleyan Col, 4760 Forsyth Rd, Macon, GA 31210-4462. **EMAIL** nora_bell@post.wesleyan-college.edu

BELL, RICHARD H.
DISCIPLINE PHILOSOPHY **EDUCATION** Vanderbilt Col, BA, 60; Yale Univ, BD, 64, MA, 66, PhD, 68. **CAREER** Frank Halliday Ferris prof. **RESEARCH** Wittgenstein; Kierkegaard; Simone Weil; African Philosophy; Contemporary Spirituality. **SELECTED PUBLICATIONS** Auth, Sensing the Spirit, The Westminster Press, 84; ed, The Grammar of the Heart: New Essays in Moral Philosophy and Theology, Harper & Row, 88; Simone Weil's Philosophy of Culture, Cambridge UP, 93; auth, Seeds of The Spirit: Wisdom of The Twentieth Century Westminster John Knox Press, with Barbara L. Battin, 95; auth, Simone Weil: The Way of Justice as Compassion, Rowman & Littlefield, 98. **CONTACT ADDRESS** Dept of Philos, The Col of Wooster, Wooster, OH 44691. **EMAIL** rbell@acs.wooster.edu

BELL, SHEILA TRICE
PERSONAL Born 08/25/1949, Pittsburgh, PA, m, 1971 **DISCIPLINE** LAW **EDUCATION** Wellesley Coll, BA 1971; Harvard Law Sch, JD 1974. **CAREER** Pine Manor Jr Coll, faculty mem 1972-74; Hutchins & Wheeler, assoc lawyer 1973-77; Private Legal Practice, Attorney 1977-79; Fisk Univ, univ counsel 1979-83; Northern KY Univ, acting univ counsel/affirmative action officer 1984-85, univ legal counsel 1985-. **HONORS AND AWARDS** Equal Rights Amendment Commn for the Commonwealth of MA 1976; editorial bd The Journal of College and University Law 1982-83; Mayor's Special Task Force on Union Station Nashville TN 1982-83; **MEMBERSHIPS** Bd mem Family and Children's Services Nashville TN 1981-83; The Links Inc Cincinnati Chap, mem 1984-, vp 1986-89; mem Jack and Jill Inc Cincinnati Chap 1984-90; mem MA, TN, KY Bars, Amer Bar Assns; mem US Dist Courts of MA, the Middle Dist of TN and the Eastern Dist of KY, US Court of Appeals for the Sixth Circuit; bd mem Natl Assn of Coll and Univ Attys 1985-88; bd mem The Program for Cincinnati 1986-88; bd mem, Bethesda Hospital, Inc, 1990-. **SELECTED PUBLICATIONS** "Protection and Enforcement of College and University Trademarks" co-author w/Martin F Majestic in the Journal of College and Univ Law, Vol 10, No 1 1983-84. **CONTACT ADDRESS** Univ Legal Counsel, No Kentucky Univ, 834 Administrative Ctr, Highland Heights, KY 41076.

BELLAMY, DONNIE DUGLIE
PERSONAL Born 09/13/1938, Jacksonville, NC, m, 1959, 2 children **DISCIPLINE** POLITICAL SCIENCE, AMERICAN HISTORY **EDUCATION** NC Cent Univ, AB, 62, MA, 64; Univ Mo-Columbia, PhD, 70. **CAREER** Instr soc sci, Lincoln Univ, Mo, 63-64; instr soc sci, 64-67, from asst prof to assoc prof hist, 67-75, chmn dept hist, 73-, chmn div soc sci, 74-, prof hist, 75, Regents prof hist, 81-, Fort Valley State Col. **HONORS AND AWARDS** Ford Found fel hist, 68-70. **MEMBERSHIPS** Southern Hist Assn; Assn Study Afro-Am Life & Hist; Gd Assn of Historians. **RESEARCH** Education of Blacks; slavery; Antebellum. **SELECTED PUBLICATIONS** Art, Legal Status of Black Georgians during the Colonial and Revolutionary Eras, Journal of Negro History; auth, Light in the Valley: A Pictorial History of Fort Valley State College Since 1985, Donning Company Publishers, 96; auth, From Slavery to Freedom: A Pictorial History of Shish Missionary Baptist Church Since 1863, Donning Company Publishers, 98. **CONTACT ADDRESS** Fort Valley State Univ, 1005 State Univ Dr, Box 4456, Fort Valley, GA 31030-3298.

BELLINZONI, ARTHUR J.
PERSONAL Born 02/21/1936, Brooklyn, NY, s **DISCIPLINE** HISTORY AND PHILOSOPHY OF RELIGION **EDUCATION** Princeton Univ, AB; Harvard Univ, MA, PhD. **CAREER** PROF RELIG, DIR PLANNED AND LEADERSHIP GIVING, WELLS COL **HONORS AND AWARDS** Exxon Educational Found Travel Grant for study in Israel; Ruth and Albert Koch Prof of Humananities, Wells Coll **MEMBERSHIPS** Soc Bibl Lit; Am Acad Relig; Am School Orient Res; Novi Testamenti Studiorum Soc. **RESEARCH** Old Testament; New Testament; Second Century Christianity; Middle East; Major Gift Fund Development. **SELECTED PUBLICATIONS** The Sayings of Jesus in the Writings of Justin Martyr, Brill; Intellectual Honesty and Religious Commitment, Fortress Press; The Two Source Hypothesis: A Critical Appraisal, Mercer University Press; The Influence of the Gospel of Matthew on Christian Literature Before Saint Irenaeus, Mercer Univ Press; "The Source of the Agraphon in Justin Martyr's Dialogue with Trypho 47:5," in Virgilae Christianae. **CONTACT ADDRESS** PO Box 5, Aurora, NY 13026. **EMAIL** ajb@wells.edu

BELLIOTTI, RAYMOND A.
PERSONAL Born 06/17/1948, Dansville, NY, m, 1986, 2 children **DISCIPLINE** PHILOSOPHY; LAW **EDUCATION** Union Col, BA (cum laude), 70; Univ Miami, MA, 76, PhD, 77; Harvard Univ, JD (cum laude), 82. **CAREER** Attorney, Barrett Smith Schapiro Simon and Armstrong, NY City, 82-84; Distinguished Teaching Professor of Philosophy, SUNY Fredonia, 84-. **HONORS AND AWARDS** Kasling Awd for Excellence in Scholarship; Hagan Young Scholar Awd for Excellence in Scholarship. **MEMBERSHIPS** SUNY Chancellor's Board for Excellence in Teaching. **SELECTED PUBLICATIONS** Auth, Justifying Law, Temple Univ Press, 92; Good Sex, Univ Press Kans, 93; Seeking Identity, Univ Press Kans, 95; Stalking Nietzsche, Greenwood Press, 99. **CONTACT ADDRESS** Philosophy, SUNY, Col at Fredonia, 2109 Fenton Hall, Fredonia, NY 14063. **EMAIL** belliotti@fredonia.edu

BELSLEY, DAVID A.
PERSONAL Born 05/24/1939, Chicago, IL, m, 1961, 2 children **DISCIPLINE** ECONOMICS; ECONOMETRICS **EDUCATION** Haverford Col, BA, 61; Mass Inst of Tech, PhD, 65. **CAREER** Asst Prof, 65-66, 66-69, Assoc Prof, 69-74, Prof, 74-, Boston Col. **HONORS AND AWARDS** Grad Honors, Haverford Col, 65; Phi Beta Kappa; Grad Fellow, NSF, 61-65; Fellow, J of Econometrics, 88; Adv Coun, Soc for Computational Econ. **MEMBERSHIPS** Am Econ Asn; Soc for Computational Econ. **RESEARCH** Computational economics & econometrics. **SELECTED PUBLICATIONS** Auth, Conditioning Diagnostics: Collinearity and Weak Data in Regression, John Wiley & Sons, 91; coed, Computational Economics and Econometrics, Vol I, Amsterdam, 92; ed. CSEM Proceedings, special issue of Computational Science in Economics and Management, 5, 92; auth, Computational Techniques for Econometrics and Economic Analysis, Academic Publishers, Amsterdam, 94; auth, Computational Economics and Statistics at the Certosa, special issue in Computational Economics, 9,96; auth, Computational Economics in Geneva: Vol 1, special issue in Computational Economics, 10, 97; auth, Computational Economics in Geneva Vol 2, special issue in Computational Economics. 11. 98; auth, Computational Economics in Stanford, special issue in Computational Economics, forthcoming; auth, Computational Economics in Cambridge, special issue in Computational Economics, forthcoming; auth, Computational Economics and Finance at Boston College, special issue in Computational Economics, forthcoming. **CONTACT ADDRESS** Dept of Economics, Boston Col, Chestnut Hill, Chestnut Hill, MA 02467. **EMAIL** belsley@bc.edu

BELTON, ROBERT
PERSONAL Born 09/19/1935, High Point, NC, m **DISCIPLINE** LAW **EDUCATION** Univ of CT, BA 1961; Boston Univ, JD 1965. **CAREER** NAACP, Legal Defense & Educ Fund Inc, civil rights atty asst counsel, 65-70; Chambers Stein & Ferguson Charlotte NC, atty, 70-75; Vanderbilt Univ School of Law, dir fair employment clinical law program, 75-77, assoc prof of law, 77-82; prof of law, 82-; visiting prof of law, Harvard Law School, 86-87; UNC School of Law, Chapel Hill NC, visiting prof of law 90-91; NCCU Law School, Charles Hamil-

ton Houston Distinguished Visiting Prof, 97. **HONORS AND AWARDS** Awded NC Legal Defense Fund Dinner Comm Plaque for successful litigation in area of employment discrimination 1973; counsel for plaintiffs in Harris v Forklift Sys, 1993; Griggs v. Duke Power Co., 401 US 424 (1971); Albemarle Paper Co vs. Moody, 422 US 405 (1975); **MEMBERSHIPS** American Association of Law Schools, executive committee, 1991-1994; Consultant TN Commn for Human Devel 1976-; editoral bd Class Action Reports 1978-89; consult Equal Employment Opportunity Commn Trial Advocacy Training Programs 1979-; consultant Pres Reorganization Proj Civil Rights 1978; consultant Office of Fed Contracts Compliance Programs Dept of Labor 1979-80; NC Assn of Black Lawyers; Amer Bar Assn; TN Bar Assn, NBA; Amer Law Institute, 1996-. **RESEARCH** Employment discrimination, law, labor law, civil rights. **SELECTED PUBLICATIONS** Auth, Remedies in Employment Discirmination Law, Wiley, 1992; Discrimination in Employment , West, 1999; "Mr Justice Marshall and the Sociology of Affirmative Action" 1989; Reflections on Affirmative Action after Johnson and Paradise, 1988. **CONTACT ADDRESS** Sch of Law, Vanderbilt Univ, Nashville, TN 37203-1181.

BENCE, CLARENCE
DISCIPLINE RELIGIOUS STUDIES **EDUCATION** Houghton Col, BA, 66; Emory Univ, PhD, 81. **CAREER** Prof, 92-. **RESEARCH** Church history. **SELECTED PUBLICATIONS** Auth, Romans, Wesley. **CONTACT ADDRESS** Dept of Religion and Philosophy, Indiana Wesleyan Univ, 4201 S Wash St, Marion, IN 46953. **EMAIL** bbence@indwes.edu

BENDER, ROSS THOMAS
PERSONAL Born 06/25/1929, Tavistock, ON, Canada, m, 1950, 5 children **DISCIPLINE** RELIGION **EDUCATION** Goshen Col, BA, 54, BD, & MRE, 56; Yale Univ, MA, 61, PhD(relig), 62. **CAREER** Asst prof, 62-64, dean, 64-69, Prof Christian Educ, Bibl Sem, Goshen Col, 64-, Dean, Mennonite Bibl Sem, 64-79; Nat Inst Mental Health fel, Div Family Stud, Univ Pa, 79-71; studies in religion & educ, Univ Geneva, Switzerland, 79-80; clin mem, Am Asn Marriage & Family Therapy, 71- **MEMBERSHIPS** Relig Educ Asn. **SELECTED PUBLICATIONS** Auth, The Knowledge of God in Primitive, Partial, or Profound--Essays on the Theory of Christian Education in Honor of Langdon,Alan, Relig Educ, Vol 0089, 94. **CONTACT ADDRESS** 1725 Juniper Pl, Apt 221, Goshen, IN 46526.

BENDITT, THEODORE MATTHEW
PERSONAL Born 10/23/1940, Philadelphia, PA, m, 1968, 1 child **DISCIPLINE** PHILOSOPHY **EDUCATION** Univ of Penn, BA, 62, JD, 65, MA, 67; Univ of Pittsburgh, PhD, 71. **CAREER** Instr, 70-72, Asst Prof, 72-75, Duke Univ; Asst Prof, 75-78, USC; vis Assoc Prof, 79, Univ of Pittsburgh; Assoc Prof, 78-83, Prof, 83-, dean arts & humanities, 84-98, Univ of Alabama, Birmingham. **RESEARCH** Political, legal & moral philosophy. **SELECTED PUBLICATIONS** Auth, Law as Rule and Principle, Stanford Univ Press, 78; Rights, Rowman & Littlefield, 82; co-ed & contrib, Philosophy Then and Now, Basil Blackwell, 98. **CONTACT ADDRESS** Dept of Philosophy, Univ of Alabama, Birmingham, 407E Humanities Bldg, Birmingham, AL 35294-1260. **EMAIL** tbenditt@uab.edu

BENFIELD, DAVID WILLIAM
PERSONAL Born 01/12/1941, Des Moines, IA, m, 1980, 1 child **DISCIPLINE** PHILOSOPHY **EDUCATION** St John's Col, Md, BA, 62; Brown Univ, BA, 66, PhD, 73. **CAREER** Asst prof philos, State Univ NY Stony Brook, 67-73; asst prof, 73-80, assoc prof, 80-91, Prof Philos, Montclair State Univ, 92-, Consult, Nat Endowment for Humanities, 75-77; Nat Endowment for Hum, summer, 74, 77 & 81; vis prof, Univ MI, summer, 76 & 80; mem, Am Philos Asn Comt Tchg, 81-84; vch, Conf Methods Philos & Sci, 82-83. **MEMBERSHIPS** Am Philos Asn; Soc Advan Am Philos; Soc Phenomenol & Existential Philos; Soc Philos & Pub Policy; Leibniz Soc. **RESEARCH** Metaphysics; epistemology; professional ethics. **SELECTED PUBLICATIONS** Auth, Johnstone on the truth of philosophical statements, Philos & Phenomenol Res, 9/71, Kant and uncaused events, Proc 4th Int Kant Cong, Part 2, 1: 179-185; The a priori a posteriori distinction, Philos & Phenomenol Res, 12/74; coauth, Identity, schmidentity--it's not all the same, Philos Studies, 2/75; auth, The a priori and the self-evident: A reply to Mr Casullo, Philos & Phenomenol Res, 12/77; Roderick M Chisholm, In: Routledge Encyclopedia of Philosophy, Routledge, 98. **CONTACT ADDRESS** Dept of Philos & Relig, Montclair State Univ, 1 Normal Ave, Upper Montclair, NJ 07043-1699. **EMAIL** benfield@mail.montclair.edu

BENHABIB, SEYLA
PERSONAL Born 09/09/1950, Istanbul, Turkey, d, 1 child **DISCIPLINE** PHILOSOPHY **EDUCATION** Yale, MPhil, 72, PhD, 72. **CAREER** Prof, 93, Harvard Univ. **HONORS AND AWARDS** AAUW, Humboldt & Fel; Lauss Mem Lectr. **MEMBERSHIPS** APSA; APAP. **RESEARCH** 19th & 20th century continental political triumph; feminist theory/social theory. **SELECTED PUBLICATIONS** Auth, Critique, Norm and Utopia: A Study of the Foundations of Critica Theory, Columbia Univ Press, 86; auth, Situating the Self: Gender, Community and Post-Modernism in Contemporary Ethics, Polity Press, Routledge, 93; coauth, Der Streit um Differenz, Fischer Verlag, 93; coauth, Feminist Contentions: A Philosophical Exchange; Routledge, 96; auth, The Reluctant Modernism of Hannah Arendt, Sage Pub, 96; auth, Kulturelle Vielfelt und Demokratische Gleichheit, Fischer Verlag, 98; auth, Hannah Arendt: Die Melancholische Denkerin der Moderne, Rotbuch Verlag, 98. **CONTACT ADDRESS** European Studies, Harvard Univ, 27 Kirkland St, Cambridge, MA 02138. **EMAIL** benhabib@jss.harvard.edu

BENHAM, PRISCILLA
PERSONAL Born 01/30/1950, Berkeley, CA, m, 1986, 1 child **DISCIPLINE** THEOLOGY **EDUCATION** Patten Col, BS, 69; Holy Names, BA, 70; Wheaton Col, MA, 72; Drew Univ, PhD, 76. **CAREER** Prof, 75-, Pres, 83-, Patten Col. **SELECTED PUBLICATIONS** Coauth, The World of the Early Church, 90; Auth, A Comparison of the Counseling Techniques of Christ and Carl Rogers, 91; The Secret of the Parables in Mark Light of Apocalyptic Literature, 92. **CONTACT ADDRESS** Patten Col, 2433 Coolidge Rd., Oakland, CA 94601.

BENIDICKSON, JAMIE
DISCIPLINE LAW **EDUCATION** Trent Univ, BA; Univ Toronto, LLB, 81; Harvard Univ, LLM, 83. **CAREER** Assoc prof. **RESEARCH** Legal history; administrative and environmental law. **SELECTED PUBLICATIONS** Auth, The Temagami Experience, Idleness, Water and a Canoe and the Environmental Law. **CONTACT ADDRESS** Fac Common Law, Univ of Ottawa, Fauteux Hall, 57 Louis Pasteur, Ottawa, ON, Canada K1N 6N5. **EMAIL** jbenidi@uottawa.ca

BENJAMIN, DON C., JR.
DISCIPLINE BIBLICAL AND ANCIENT NEAR EASTERN STUDIES **EDUCATION** St. Bonaventure Univ, BA, 64; Wash Theol Union, MDiv, Ordained, Roman Catholic, 67; Catholic Univ of Amer, MA, 69; Claremont Grad Univ, PhD, 81. **CAREER** Rice Univ, lectr, 78-81; Univ of Houston, vis scholar, 86,88; Univ of S. Thomas, vis scholar, 80-83,94; Rice Univ, Scholar in Res, 81-96; Kino Institute of Theol, exec dir, 97-. **RESEARCH** OT; Hebrew bible; ancient near east studies. **SELECTED PUBLICATIONS** Coauth, Old Testament Parallels: Laws and Stories from the Ancient Near East, Mahwah: Paulist, 97; Honor and Shame in the World of the Bible, in: Semeia: an Experimental Jour for Bib Crit, Atlanta; Scholars, 96; The Social World of Ancient Israel, 1250 - 587 BCE, Peabody: Hendrickson, 93; Deuteronomy and City Life: a Form Criticism of Texts with the Word City Hebrew: ir, in Deuteronomy 4:41-26:19, Univ Press of Amer, 93. **CONTACT ADDRESS** Kino Inst of Theol, 1224 E Northern Ave, Phoenix, AZ 85020-4295. **EMAIL** dcben@worldnet.att.net

BENJAMIN, PAUL
PERSONAL Born 04/20/1940, Murunkan, Sri Lanka, m, 1968, 2 children **DISCIPLINE** OLD TESTAMENT **EDUCATION** Lutheran Sch of Theol, Chicago, PhD, 86. **CAREER** Prof, Pres and Prof, 86-91, Theol Coll of Lanka, Sri Lanka; Vis Intl Prof, 91-92, Wartburg Theol Sem, Bubuave, IA; Pastor, 93-98, Iowa Annual Conf of the United Methodist Church. **HONORS AND AWARDS** Confessor of Christ Awd for Distinguished Ministry Lutheran Sch of Theol Stud. **MEMBERSHIPS** SBL. **RESEARCH** Old Testament Theology. **SELECTED PUBLICATIONS** Auth, articles to The Anchor Bible Dictionary, 92. **CONTACT ADDRESS** 905 Easy St, Burlington, IA 52601. **EMAIL** PSRBEnjoz@aol.com

BENKO, STEPHEN
PERSONAL Born 06/13/1924, Budapest, Hungary, m, 1952, 4 children **DISCIPLINE** RELIGION, ANCIENT HISTORY **EDUCATION** Reformed Theol Sem Budapest, BD, 47; Univ Basel, PhD(relig), 51. **CAREER** Res fel, Divinity Sch, Yale Univ, 53-54; instr, Sch Theol, Temple Univ, 57-59 & lectr, Grad Sch Philos & Relig, 59-61; prof Bibl studies & patristics, Conwell Sch Theol, 60-69; Prof Ancient Hist, Calif State Univ, Fresno, 69-. **MEMBERSHIPS** Am Hist Asn; Am Philol Asn; Am Soc Church Hist; Soc Bibl Lit. **RESEARCH** Ancient church history; ecumenical relations. **SELECTED PUBLICATIONS** Auth, Education, Culture and the Arts Transylvanian Cultural Hist, Hungarian Quart, Vol 0035, 94. **CONTACT ADDRESS** Dept of Hist, California State Univ, Fresno, Fresno, CA 93740.

BENNETT, GERALD T.
DISCIPLINE LAW **EDUCATION** St Bernard's Col, BA; Barry Col, MA; Univ Fla, JD. **CAREER** Prof emer,Univ Fla, 68-. **HONORS AND AWARDS** Fla Bar Selig Goldin awd; L. Clayton Nance awd, Fla Public Defender's Asn; drafted in fla, aba standards on trial by jury, discovery and incompetency to stand trial. **MEMBERSHIPS** Fla Criminal Rules Comt, 74-; Fla Bar; Order of the Coif; Phi Kappa Phi. **RESEARCH** Criminal law, procedure and litigation skills. **CONTACT ADDRESS** School of Law, Univ of Florida, PO Box 117625, Gainesville, FL 32611-7625. **EMAIL** bennett@law.ufl.edu

BENNETT, JAMES O.
DISCIPLINE PHILOSOPHY **EDUCATION** Univ La, BA, 66; Tulane Univ, MA, 69, PhD, 72. **CAREER** Assoc prof. **RESEARCH** Existentialism, with a secondary interest in American Pragmatism, and a tertiary interest in process philosophy. **SELECTED PUBLICATIONS** Auth, A Venn-Euler Hybrid Test for Categorical Syllogisms, Tchg Philos, 94; coauth, Karl Jaspers and Scientific Philosophy, Jour Hist Philos, 93. **CONTACT ADDRESS** Dept of Philosophy, Univ of Tennessee, Knoxville, Knoxville, TN 37996. **EMAIL** jobennet@utk.edu

BENNETT, PATRICIA W.
PERSONAL Born 08/31/1953, Forest, MS, s **DISCIPLINE** LAW **EDUCATION** Tougaloo Col, BA, 1975; Mississippi Col School of Law, JD, 1979. **CAREER** Small Business Administration, attorney, 79-80; Mississippi Attorney General, special asst attorney general, 80-82; District Attorney of Hinds County, asst district attorney, 82-87; US Attorney, asst US attorney, 87-89; Mississippi College School of Law, professor, currently. **HONORS AND AWARDS** Women for Progress, Woman Achiever, 1988. **MEMBERSHIPS** Smith Robertson Museum Board, 1992; Central Mississippi Legal Services Corp Board, secretary, 1989-; YMCA Board of Directors, 1991-; Mississippi Board of Bar Commissioners, commissioner, 1992. **CONTACT ADDRESS** Professor, Mississippi Col, Jackson, 151 E Griffith St, Jackson, MS 39201.

BENNETT, PHILIP W.
DISCIPLINE PHILOSOPHY **EDUCATION** Rutgers Univ, BA, 64; NYork Univ, MA, 66, PhD, 72. **CAREER** Assoc prof, SUNY, Cortland, 70-87; Instr, La State Univ, 97-99; Adminr, Eugene Lang Col, New School Univ, 99-. **CONTACT ADDRESS** 1226 Park Ave, Hoboken, NJ 07030. **EMAIL** p.bennett@att.net

BENNETT-ALEXANDER, DAWN DEJUANA
PERSONAL Born 01/02/1951, Washington, DC, d **DISCIPLINE** LAW **EDUCATION** The Defiance Col, 1968-70; Federal City Col, BA, 1972; Howard University, School of Law, JD, 1975. **CAREER** The DC Court of Appeals, law clerk to Honorable Julia Cooper Mack, 75-76; The White House Domestic Council, asst to assoc dir & counsel, 76-77; US Federal Trade Commission, law clerk, 77-78; Antioch School of Law, instructor, 79-80; Federal Labor Relations Authority, attorney, advisor, 81-82; University of North Florida, assoc prof of business & employment law, 82-87; Univ of GA, Assoc Prof Legal Studies, 88-. **HONORS AND AWARDS** Selig Foundation, Selig Fellowship for Excellence in Research & Teaching, 1992; Terry Foundation, Terry Fellowship for Excellence in Research & Teaching, 1991; Consortium on Multi-Party Dispute Resolution, Seed Grant Awd, 1992; Beta Gamma Sigma National Honor Society, selection to membership, 1992; McKnight Foundation, Florida Endowment Fund, McKnight Jr Faculty Awd, Fellowship, 1984. **MEMBERSHIPS** Southeastern Academy of Legal Studies in Business, president, 1992-93; American Academy of Legal Studies in Business, co-chair, Employment Law Section, 1992-94; Georgia Political Action Committee PAC, 1993-94; National Council of Negro Women, 1983-; National Organization for Women, 1985-; treasurer, GA Now, 1993-95; DC Bar, 1979-; Friends of Athens Creative Theater, board member, 1990; Consumer Credit Counseling Services of NE Florida, board member, 1983-84; Girls Clubs of Jacksonville, Inc, board member, 1983-85. **SELECTED PUBLICATIONS** Employment Law for Business, Irwin Pub, 1995; The Legal, Ethical & Regulatory Environment of Business, South-Western Pub, 1996; "Hostile Environment Sexual Harassment: A Clearer View," Labor Law Journal, vol 42, no 3, p 131-143, March 1991; "The State of Affirmative Action in Employment: A Post Stotts Retrospective," American Business Law Journal, vol 27/4, p 565-597, winter 1990; "Sexual Harassment in the Office," Personnel Administrator, vol 33, no 6, p 174-88, June 1988. **CONTACT ADDRESS** Terry Col of Business, Univ of Georgia, 202 Brooks Hall, Athens, GA 30602-6255.

BENSEL, RICHARD F.
PERSONAL Born 11/13/1949, Pendleton, OR, m, 1979, 1 child **DISCIPLINE** POLITICAL SCIENCE **EDUCATION** Univ Chicago, Ba, 71; Cornell Univ, PhD, 78. **CAREER** Instr, 77-78, asst prof, 78-82, Texas A&M Univ; asst prof, Univ Texas, Dallas, 82-84; ass prof and prof, Grad Fac, New School for Soc Res, 84-93; prof, Cornell Univ, 93- . **HONORS AND AWARDS** Mark H Ingraham Prize, 84. **MEMBERSHIPS** Am Polit Sci Asn; Am Hist Asn; Social Sci Hist Asn; Economic Hist Asn; Org of Am Hist; Agr Hist Asn; AAAS. **RESEARCH** Political development in America; history of Congress; theories of political economy. **SELECTED PUBLICATIONS** Auth, "Creating the Statutory State: Implications of a Rule of Law Standard in American Politics," Amer Polit Sci Rev (80); auth, Sectionalism and American Political Development, 1880-1980, Wisconsin, 84; auth, Yankee Leviathan: The Origins of Central State Authority in America, 1859-1877, Cambridge, 90; auth, Congress, Sectionalism, and Public Policy Formation since 1870, in Silbey, ed, Encyclopedia of the American Legislative System, Scribner's, 94; auth, Confederate Cabinet, in Current, ed, Encyclopedia of the Confederacy, Simon & Schuster, 93; auth, Sectionalism, in Bacon, ed, Encyclopedia of the United

States Congress, Simon & Schuster, 94; auth, The Political Economy of American Industrialization, 1877-1900, Cambridge, 00. **CONTACT ADDRESS** Government Dept, Cornell Univ, McGraw Hall, Ithaca, NY 14853. **EMAIL** rfb2@cornell.edu

BENSON, LEGRACE
PERSONAL Born 02/23/1930, Richmond, VA, w, 1952, 3 children **DISCIPLINE** ART; PHILOSOPHY; PERCEPTUAL PSYCHOLOGY **EDUCATION** Meredith Coll, AB, 51; Univ Georgia Athens, MFA, 56; Cornell Univ, PhD, 74. **CAREER** Asst prof, Cornell Univ, 68-71; assoc prof/assoc dean for special programs, Wells Coll, 71-77; assoc dean, SUNY-Empire State Coll, 77-80; coordinator of arts, humanities and communications study, center for distance learning, SUNY-Empire State Coll, 81-92. **HONORS AND AWARDS** Empire State Coll Excellence in Scholarship, 92. **MEMBERSHIPS** Natl Coalition of Independent Scholars; Haitian Studies Assn; Coll Art Assn; Latin Amer Studies Assn; Arts Council African Studies Assn; African Studies Assn; Canadian Assn Latin Amer and Caribbean Studies. **RESEARCH** Arts and Culture of Haiti; adult distance learning **SELECTED PUBLICATIONS** Auth, The Utopian Vision in Haitian Painting, Callaloo, Spring 92; Journal of Caribbean Studies, Observations on Islamic Motifs in Haitian Visual Arts, Winter 92/Spring 93; The Arts of Haiti Considered Ecologically, Paper for Culture Change and Technology in the Americas conference, Nov 95; Three Presentations of the Arts of Haiti, Journal of Haitian Studies, Autumn 96; Habits of Attention: Persistence of Lan Ginee in Haiti, in The African Diaspora African Origins and New-world Self-fashioning, 98; How Houngans Use the Light from Distant Stars; Muslim and Breton Survivals in Haitian Voudou Arts, 99; The Artists and the Arts of Haiti in Their Geographical and Conversational Domains, 99. **CONTACT ADDRESS** 314 E. Buffalo St., Ithaca, NY 14850-4227. **EMAIL** legracebenson@clarityconnect.com

BENSON, LENNI B.
PERSONAL Born 09/27/1958, Superior, AZ, m, 1991, 1 child **DISCIPLINE** LAW, LEGAL STUDIES **EDUCATION** Ariz State Univ, BS, 80, JD, 83. **CAREER** Adjunct prof, Ariz State Univ, 87-88; assoc, Sacks Tierney and Kasen, Phoenix, Ariz, 83-86; assoc attorney, Daughton, Hawkins, and Bacon, Phoenix, Ariz, 86-88; partner and assoc, Bryan Cave, 880-94; assoc prof, NYork Law School, 94-. **HONORS AND AWARDS** Elmer Freed Excellence in the Teaching of Immigration Law, 99 (Nat Awd); various scholarships, dean's lists, Awds and memberships in honorary societies. **MEMBERSHIPS** Am Immigration Lawyers Asn. **RESEARCH** Immigration law: jurisdictional and due process rights of aliens; business immigration. **SELECTED PUBLICATIONS** Auth, "INS Undercover Operations," 74 Interpreter Releases 777 (June 13, 94); auth, "By Hook or By Crook: Exploring the Legality of an INS Sting Operation," 31 San Diego Law Rev 813 (94); auth, "Exclusion Alert: Your Client May Be a Smuggler," Immigration and Nationality Law Handbook 1994-1995, Vol II, 456-462, R. Murphy, ed; auth, "Surviving to Fight Another Day: Preserving Issues for Appeal," Immigration and Nationality Law Handbook 1995-1996, Vol II, 353-366, R. Murphy, ed; auth, "Preparing a Successful Application for Political Asylum," 29th Annual Practicing Law Inst on Immigration and Nationality Law, 7-18 (96); auth, "Fundamentals of Judicial Review of Deportation and Exclusion Proceedings," Immigration and Nationality Law Handbook 1996-1997, Vol I, R. Murphy, ed; auth, "Back to the Future: Congress Attacks Judicial Review of Immigration Proceedings," 29 Conn Law Rec 1411 (Nov 97); auth, "The 'New World' of Judicial Review of Removal Orders," 12 Georgetown Immigration Law J 233 (98); auth, "Unresolved Issues and Unintended Consequences of IIRIRA of 1996: Effects Upon Immigrants' Rights," Ch 3 in In Defense of the Alien, Vol XVI, R. Tomasi, ed (99); auth, "Navigating the Maze of Judicial Review of Immigration Proceedings," NY Law J, 9, 12 (June 14, 99). **CONTACT ADDRESS** New York Law Sch, 57 Worth St, New York, NY 10013-2926. **EMAIL** lbenson@nyls.edu

BENSON, P. JANN
DISCIPLINE PHILOSOPHY **EDUCATION** Univ Colo, PhD, 71. **CAREER** Assoc prof. **RESEARCH** Ethics; history of philosophy. **SELECTED PUBLICATIONS** Co-auth, Strutting and Fretting. **CONTACT ADDRESS** Philosophy Dept, Colorado State Univ, Fort Collins, CO 80523.

BENSON, PAUL H.
DISCIPLINE PHILOSOPHY **EDUCATION** Princeton Univ, PhD, 84. **CAREER** Dept Philos, Univ Dayton **RESEARCH** Action theory, soc philos. . **SELECTED PUBLICATIONS** Auth, Freedom and Value, Jour Philos, 87; Moral Worth, Philos Stud, 87; Free Agency and Self-worth, Jour Philos, 94; auth, "Autonomy and Oppressive Socialization," social Theory and Practice, 91; auth, Feeling Crazy, in Relational Autonomy, ed, Mackenzie and Stoljar, 00. **CONTACT ADDRESS** Dept of Philos, Univ of Dayton, 300 Col Park, Dayton, OH 45469-1546. **EMAIL** paul.benson@notes.udayton.edu

BENSON, ROBERT W.
DISCIPLINE LAW **EDUCATION** Columbia Univ, AB, 64; Univ Calif, Berkeley, JD, 68. **CAREER** Prof Loyola, 73-; dir, Loyola summer prog Cent Am; Boalt Hall-Ford Found Int Legal Stud(s) fel, Brazil; worked in, Conn dept commun aff; private practice, Washington DC. **SELECTED PUBLICATIONS** Auth, City of Los Angeles' plain English law. **CONTACT ADDRESS** Law School, Loyola Marymount Univ, 7900 Loyola Blvd, Burns 416, Los Angeles, CA 90045. **EMAIL** rbenson@lmulaw.lmu.edu

BENTON, CATHERINE
PERSONAL m, 1944 **DISCIPLINE** HISTORY OF RELIGION **EDUCATION** Columbia Univ, PhD, 91. **CAREER** LECTR, RELIG, LAKE FOREST COL, 87-. **MEMBERSHIPS** AAR; AAS; Asia Network. **CONTACT ADDRESS** Dept of Relig, Lake Forest Col, 555 N Sheridan Rd, Saint Louis, MO 60045. **EMAIL** benton@lfc.edu

BEOUGHER, TIMOTHY K.
PERSONAL Born 06/24/1959, St. Francis, KS, m, 1982, 4 children **DISCIPLINE** EVANGELISM **EDUCATION** Kans State Univ, BS; Southwestern Baptist Theol Sem, MDiv; Trinity Evangel Divinity Sch, ThM, PhD. **CAREER** Asst prof, Wheaton Col Grad Sch; assoc dir, Billy Graham prof, 96, assoc dean, Billy Graham Sch Missions, Evangel and Church Growth, S Baptist Theol Sem. **SELECTED PUBLICATIONS** Auth, Overcoming Walls to Witnessing; Disciplemaking: Training Leaders to Make Disciples; Evangelism for a Changing World; and Accounts of a Campus Revival: Wheaton Col 95. **CONTACT ADDRESS** So Baptist Theol Sem, 2825 Lexington Rd, Louisville, KY 40280. **EMAIL** tbeougher@sbts.edu

BEPKO, GERALD L.
PERSONAL Born 04/21/1940, Chicago, IL, m, 1968, 2 children **DISCIPLINE** LAW **EDUCATION** Northern Ill Univ, BS, 62; Chicago-Kent Col Law, JD, 65; Yale Univ, LLM, 72. **CAREER** Spec agent, Fed Bur Invest, 65-69; asst prof corp legal writing, Chicago-Kent Col Law, 69-72; assoc prof, 72-75, Prof Law, Ind Univ, Indianapolis, 75-, Dean, 81-86; vpres, Ind Univ, Chancellor, Ind Univ-Purdue Univ, Indianapolis (IUPUI), 86-94; VPres Long Range Planning, Ind Univ, Chancellor, IUPUI, 94-; Consult & reporter, Fed Judicial Ctr, Washington, DC, 73-74; vis prof Univ Ill, 76-77, Ohio State Univ, 78-79 & Ind-Bloomington, summers 76-80. **HONORS AND AWARDS** Ford Fdn fel **MEMBERSHIPS** Perm Editorial Bd, Uniform Commercial Code **RESEARCH** Contract, commercial and related consumer law. **CONTACT ADDRESS** Indiana Univ-Purdue Univ, Indianapolis, 425 Univ Blvd, Indianapolis, IN 46202-5143. **EMAIL** gbepko@iupui.edu

BERENBAUM, MICHAEL
PERSONAL Born 07/31/1945, Newark, NJ, m, 1995, 4 children **DISCIPLINE** RELIGION **EDUCATION** Queens Col, BA, 67; Jewish Theol Sem, 63-67; Heb Univ, 65-66; Boston Univ, MA, 69; FL State Univ, PhD, 75. **CAREER** Colby-Sawyer Col, instr, 69-71; Wesleyan Univ, adj asst prof and chaplain 73-80; Zachor: The Holocaust Resource Cent, 78; Pres Comm on the Holocaust, 79-80; George Wash Univ, assoc prof, 81-83; Jew Comm Coun of Great Wash, exec dir, 80-83; Univ Maryland, vis prof, 83; Amer Univ, adj prof 87; Relig Act Center, sen scholar 86-88; Georgetown Univ, adj prof, 83-97; US Holocaust Mem Museum, research fel 87-88, proj dir, 88-93, dir, of research institute 93-97; Univ of Judaism, adj prof, 98-, Survivors of the Shoah Visual Hist Foundation, pres & CEO, 97-00. **HONORS AND AWARDS** Dennison University Dhl, Honors Causa, 00; Nazareth Col Rochester, PhD (Honoris Causa), 95; Emmy, Cableace and Academy Awds for One Survivor Remembers: The Gerda Weissman Klein Story, 95-96, FL State Univ, Charles E. Merrill Fel, 72-73; Yale Univ, Ezera Styles Fel, 79; Amer Jew Press Assoc, Simon Rockower Awd, 86- 87. **MEMBERSHIPS** SSVHF **SELECTED PUBLICATIONS** Auth, The Vision of the Void: Theological Reflections on the Works of Elie Wiesel, Wesleyan Univ Press, 79; After Tragedy and Triumph: Modern Jewish Thought and the American Experience, Cambridge Univ Press, 90; The World Must Know: The History of the Holocaust, Little Brown and Co, 93; Witness to the Holocaust: An Illustrated Documentary History of the Holocaust in the Words of Its Victims, Perpetrators and Bystanders, Harper Collins, 97, The Holocaust and History: The Known, the Unknown, the Disputed and the Reexamined, Indiana Univ Press, 98; articles, Women, Blacks and Jews: Theologians of Survival, Relig in Life, 76; What We Should Tell Our Children About the Holocaust, Sh'ma, 81; The Paradox of Prayer, Reform Judaism, 86; American Jews Opt Out, New Outlook, 88; ed, Reflections on the Uniqueness of the Holocaust, in: A Mosaic of Victims: Non-Jews Persecuted and Murdered by the Nazis, New York Univ Press, 90; The Mystifying Burden of Goodness, in: Dimensions, 90; Questions for the Unredeemed, Tikkun, 93; The Holocaust, World Book Encycl, 96; Eleanor Roosevelt and the Holocaust, in: The Eleanor Roosevelt Encycl, ed. Maurine H. Beasley and Holly Shulman, Greenwood Pub Group, Inc, 98. **CONTACT ADDRESS** Survivors of the Shoah Visual Hist Foundation, 5757 West Century Blvd., PO Box 3168, Los Angeles, CA 90045. **EMAIL** mberenbaum@eastpointcom.com

BERGANT, DIANNE
PERSONAL Born 08/07/1936, Milwaukee, WI **DISCIPLINE** BIBLE; FIRST TESTAMENT **EDUCATION** St Louis Univ, PhD, 75. **CAREER** Teach, St Louis Univ, 72; Marian College of Fond du Lac, WI, 72-78; Catholic Theological Union, 78-; Regional Seminary, Trindad, West Indies, 86; Regional Seminary, Trindad, West Indies, 98. **HONORS AND AWARDS** Gamma Pi Epsilon (Natl Jesuit Women's Honor Soc), 72; Who's Who in Biblical Studies and Archaeology, 86-87; While editor of The Bible Today, won Natl Catholic Press 1st place award in bible & devotion category, 87, 88, 90. **MEMBERSHIPS** Catholic Biblical Assn, 70; General Council of Congregation of Saint Agnes, 73-77; Soc of Biblical lit, 75; Chicago Soc of Biblical research, 79-; North Amer Conf on Relig and ecology, 85-95. **RESEARCH** Biblical interpretation; Integrity of creation; Feminism; Justice works in progress include commentaries on Song of Songs; Lamentations; Three-volume commentary on lectionary readings using a liturgical interpretive method. **SELECTED PUBLICATIONS** Auth, Il Cantico Dei Cantici, 98; The Earth is the Lord's: The Bible, Ecology, and Worship, Liturgical, 98; auth, Song of Songs: The Love Poetry of Scripture, New City, 98; auth, Response to Vincent L. Wimbush, Black and Catholic: The Challenge and the Gift of Black Folk, Marquette Univ, 98; auth, Biblical Foundation for Christian Ministry, Together in God's Service: Toward a Theology of Ecclesial Ministry, US Cath Conf, 98. **CONTACT ADDRESS** Catholic Theol Union at Chicago, 5401 S Cornell Ave, Chicago, IL 60615. **EMAIL** dbergant@ctu.edu

BERGE, PAUL S.
DISCIPLINE NEW TESTAMENT **EDUCATION** Luther Sem, BD, 63; Union Theol Sem, ThM, 64, ThD, 73. **CAREER** Instr, 73; tchg fel, Union Theol Sem, 72-73; dir the master of arts degree prog, 84; vis prof, Lutheran Theol Sem, Madagascar, 86-87; res fel, Yale Divinity Sch, 79-80; prof, 84-. **HONORS AND AWARDS** Pres, Como Park Lutheran Church; pastor, Our Savior's Lutheran Church, Montevideo, Minn, 64-66; US Air Force Chaplain, 66-70. **SELECTED PUBLICATIONS** Auth, Servants and Stewards of the Gospel: A Stewardship Bible Study from Paul's Letter to the Philippians, 83; Now You Are God's People: A Study in I Peter, 80; contrib, Toward Full Communion and Concordat of Agreement, 91; Implications of the Gospel, 88; The Hist Episcopate, 85. **CONTACT ADDRESS** Dept of New Testament, Luther Sem, 2481 Como Ave, Saint Paul, MN 55108. **EMAIL** pberge@luthersem.edu

BERGEN, ROBERT D.
PERSONAL Born 05/18/1954, Lawrence, KS, m, 1979, 1 child **DISCIPLINE** OLD TESTAMENT, BIBLICAL HEBREW **EDUCATION** Hardin Simmons Univ, BA, 76; Southwestern Baptist Theol Sem, MD, 80, PhD, 86. **CAREER** Assoc Prof of OT and Biblical Lang, 86-98, Hannibal-LaGrange Coll. **MEMBERSHIPS** SBL, ETS, Inst of Biblical Res. **RESEARCH** Discourse Linguistics. **SELECTED PUBLICATIONS** Auth, 1,2 Samuel, New American Commentary, vol 7, 96; 1,2, Samuel, Shepherd's Notes, 98; Ed of Biblical Hebrew and Discourse Linguistics, 94. **CONTACT ADDRESS** Hannibal-LaGrange Col, 2800 Palmyra Rd, Hannibal, MO 63401. **EMAIL** bbergen@hlg.edu

BERGER, ALAN L.
PERSONAL Born 11/16/1939, Highland Park, NJ, m, 1971, 3 children **DISCIPLINE** RELIGION **EDUCATION** Univ of Chicago, MA; Syracuse Univ, PhD. **CAREER** From lectr to prof, Syracuse Univ, 73-95; dir, Holocaust & Jewish Studies, Fla Atlantic Univ, 95-. **MEMBERSHIPS** Am Acad of Rel, Asn for Jewish Studies, Am Jewish Hist Soc. **RESEARCH** Literature and theology, post-holocaust Jewish thought. **SELECTED PUBLICATIONS** Auth, Crisis and Covenant, SUNY Press, 85; ed, Judaism in the Modern World, NYU Press, 94; auth, Children of Job, SUNY Press, 97; co-ed, Second Generation Voices, Syracuse Univ Press (forthcoming). **CONTACT ADDRESS** Dept Holocaust & Judaic Studies, Florida Atlantic Univ, PO Box 3091, Boca Raton, FL 33431-0991. **EMAIL** alanberger@aol.com

BERGER, LAWRENCE
PERSONAL Born 05/21/1928, Newark, NJ, m, 1952, 3 children **DISCIPLINE** LAW **EDUCATION** Univ Pa, BS; Rutgers Univ, JD. **CAREER** Prof **RESEARCH** Property; real estate transactions; accounting. **SELECTED PUBLICATIONS** Auth, pubs on real property. **CONTACT ADDRESS** Law Dept, Univ of Nebraska, Lincoln, 103 Ross McCollum Hall, PO Box 830902, Lincoln, NE 68588-0420. **EMAIL** lberger1@unl.edu

BERGER, MARK
DISCIPLINE LAW **EDUCATION** Columbia Univ, BA; Yale Univ, JD. **CAREER** Prof **RESEARCH** Criminal law; criminal procedure; labor law. **SELECTED PUBLICATIONS** Auth, Taking the Fifth: The Supreme Court and the Privilege Against Self-Incrimination, 80; co-auth, Missouri Criminal Practice and Procedure, 86. **CONTACT ADDRESS** Law Dept, Univ of Missouri, Kansas City, 5100 Rockhill Rd, Kansas City, MO 64110-2499. **EMAIL** bergerm@umkc.edu

BERGER, MORRIS I.
PERSONAL Born 08/05/1928, New York, NY, d, 1 child **DISCIPLINE** PHILOSOPHY OF EDUCATION, PHILOSOPHY **EDUCATION** NYork State Col Teachers, BA, 50, MA, 52;

Columbia Univ, PhD, 56. **CAREER** Assoc prof, 56-63, prof philos of educ, State Univ NY Albany, 63-, chemn dept found, 69-; Res fels, State Univ NY Res Found, 62, State Univ NY, 69-70. **MEMBERSHIPS** Philos Educ Soc; Am Philos Asn. **RESEARCH** Immigration and social settlements; existentialism; conceptual analysis. **SELECTED PUBLICATIONS** Coauth, Public Education in America, Harper, 58; John Dewey: Master Educator, Soc Advan Educ, 59; auth, Doing things with the concept of teaching, Proc Philos Educ Soc, 68; Teaching as Act & Enterprise: Some Reconsiderations, Studies Philos & Educ, fall 68; The Settlement, the Imigrant and the Public School, Arno Press, 80. **CONTACT ADDRESS** Dept of Ed Admin & Policy Studies, SUNY, Albany, 1400 Washington Ave, Albany, NY 12222. **EMAIL** m.berger@albany.edu

BERGER, VIVIAN O.
PERSONAL Born 07/22/1944, New York, NY, w, 1973 **DISCIPLINE** LAW **EDUCATION** Harvard Univ, BA, 66; Columbia Law Sch, JD, 73. **CAREER** Prof, Columbia Univ, 94-. **HONORS AND AWARDS** Young B Smith Prize Best Paper; Jane Marks Murphy Prize Most Proficient Woman; Robert N Toppan Prize; Kent Scholar, 70-73; Jr Phi Beta Kappa; Woodrow Wilson Fel. **MEMBERSHIPS** ACLU, AAI, SCHR, CDRC, ABA, ALI, NYWBA. **RESEARCH** Death penalty, Habeas Corpus, rape, general criminal law and procedure, mediation. **SELECTED PUBLICATIONS** Coauth, "Academic Discipline: A Guide to Fair Process for the University Student," 99 Colum L Rev 289 (99); auth, "Quit Drugging Prisoners," Nat L J (99); auth, "Flawed Law on 'Predators'," Nat L J (00); auth, "The Reality of Capital Punishment in the U S A: Shoddy Lawyering, Political Justice and Danger of Executing Innocent People," (forthcoming); auth, "Rape Law reform at the Millennium: Remarks on Professor Bryden's Non-Millennial Approach," 3 Buffalo Crim L Rev (forthcoming); auth, "Capital Punishment," and "Payne v Tennessee," in Encycl of the Am Constitution, Suppl II (forthcoming). **CONTACT ADDRESS** Dept Law, Columbia Univ, 435 W 116th St, New York, NY 10027-7201. **EMAIL** vberger@law.columbia.edu

BERGMAN, PAUL
PERSONAL Born 09/22/1943, New York, NY, m, 1967, 2 children **DISCIPLINE** LAW **EDUCATION** Univ Calif Los Angeles, BA, 65; Univ Calif Berkeley, JD, 68. **HONORS AND AWARDS** Univ Distinguished Teaching Awd; Am Trial Lawyers Awd. **MEMBERSHIPS** Asn of Am Law Sch. **RESEARCH** Evidence; Trial Techniques; Law and Popular Culture. **SELECTED PUBLICATIONS** Auth, Lawyers as Counselors, 91; auth, Reel Justice: The Courtroom Goes to the Movies, 96; auth, Trial Advocacy: Inferences, Arguments and Techniques, 96; auth, Trial Advocacy in a Nutshell, 3rd ed, 97; auth, Evidence Law & Practice, 00; auth, Represent Yourself in Court, 3rd ed, 00; auth, Nolo's Deposition Handbook 00. **CONTACT ADDRESS** Dept Law, Univ of California, Los Angeles, Box 951476, Los Angeles, CA 90095-1476. **EMAIL** bergman@mail.law.ucla.edu

BERGMANN, MICHAEL
PERSONAL Born 09/08/1964, Revelstoke, Canada, m, 1986, 2 children **DISCIPLINE** PHILOSOPHY **EDUCATION** Univ of Waterloo, BA, 91; MA, 92; Univ Notre Dame, PhD, 97. **CAREER** Asst prof, Perdue Univ, 97- . **HONORS AND AWARDS** Doc fel, Soc Sci hum res coun of Canada, 93-96. **MEMBERSHIPS** Amer Philos Asn; Soc Christian Philos. **RESEARCH** Epistemology; Metaphysics; Philosophy of Religion. **SELECTED PUBLICATIONS** Auth, A New Argument from Actualism to Serious Actualism, Nous 30, 96, 366-359; Review of R. Douglas Geivett's Evil and the Evidence for God, Faith and Philos 13, 436-441, 96; Internalism, Externalism and the No-Defeater Condition, Synthese 110, (97): 399-417; auth, "Might-Counterfactuals, Transworld Untrustworthiness and Plantinga's Free Will Defense," Faith and Philosophy 16, (99): 336-51; auth, "Serious Actualism and Serious Presentism," Nous 33, (99): 118-132; auth, "Deontology and Defeat,' Philosophy and Phenomenological Res 60, (00): 87-102; auth, "Eternalism and Skepticism," The Philosophical Rev 109, (00): 159-94. **CONTACT ADDRESS** Dept of Philosophy-1360 LAEB, Purdue Univ, West Lafayette, West Lafayette, IN 47906. **EMAIL** bergmann@purdue.edu

BERGO, BETTINA
PERSONAL Born 03/31/1957, Zurich, Switzerland, s **DISCIPLINE** PHILOSOPHY **EDUCATION** Georgetown Univ, BA, 80; Catholic Inst, Paris, MA, 84; Boston Univ, MA, 91; PhD, 96. **CAREER** Teach, Boston Univ, 87-92; vis asst prof, Worcester Poly Inst, 93-97; asst prof, Loyola Col, 97-00. **MEMBERSHIPS** APA; SPEP; Phil Soc, Brock U; Merleau Ponty Cir; IAWP. **RESEARCH** Philosophy in the "Continental" tradition (since Hegel); phenomenology (Levinas, Husserl); contemporary French philosophy. **SELECTED PUBLICATIONS** Auth, Levinas between Ethics and Politics: For The Beauty that Adorns the Earth, Martinus Nijhoff Pub (The Hague), 99; co-ed, "New School for Social Research," Grad Fac Philo J 20(98); auth, 'Glory in Levinas and Derrida," in Feeling the Difference: Studies in Continental Philosophy, eds. in James E. Swearingen (NJ: Humanities Press, forthcoming); auth, "Levinas's New Spatio-Temporality" in Joyful Wisdom: Studies in Postmodern Ethics, eds. D Goicoechea, M Zlomislic, Thought House Pub Gp (St CatherineÛs, ON, 99); auth, "The God of Abraham and the God of the Philosophers: A Reading of Emmanuel Levinas's Dieu et la philosophie," New Sch Soc Res Grad Fac Philo J 16 (93): 111-164; transl, Emmanuel Levinas, God, Death, and Time Stanford Univ Press, forthcoming. **CONTACT ADDRESS** Dept Philosophy, Loyola Col, 4501 North Charles St, Baltimore, MD 21210. **EMAIL** bbergo@loyola.edu

BERITELA, GERARD F.
PERSONAL Born 12/07/1954, Rochester, NY **DISCIPLINE** RELIGION **EDUCATION** John Fisher Col, BA, 77; Nashotah House, MDiv, 83; Syracuse Univ, MPhil, 99. **CAREER** Adjunct prof, Le Moyne Col, 94-. **HONORS AND AWARDS** Zelda Lyons Awd: Sr Most Proficient in Humanities, 77. **MEMBERSHIPS** Am Acad of Relig, Soc of Biblical Lit. **RESEARCH** Gender issues in religion, historical Jesus studies, non-canonical (nag hammadi) writings, Hinduism, Freud. **CONTACT ADDRESS** Dept Relig, Le Moyne Col, 1419 Salt Springs Rd, Syracuse, NY 13214-1302. **EMAIL** GFBeritela@aol.com

BERKEY, ROBERT FRED
PERSONAL Born 06/30/1930, Barberton, OH, m, 1957, 2 children **DISCIPLINE** RELIGION **EDUCATION** Otterbein Col, AB, 52; Oberlin Grad Sch Theol, BD, 55, STM, 56; Hartford Sem Found, PhD, 58. **CAREER** From instr to assoc prof, 58-72, prof relig, Mt Holyokde Col, 72-, lectr, Hartford Sem Found, 57-58; vis lectr, Smith Col, 62-63; vis lectr, Trinity Col, 63-64; Eli Lilly Found res fel & sr assoc, Westminster & Cheshunt Cols, Eng, 71-72; vis lectr, Smith Col, spring semester, 87; lectr, Ecumenical Christian Centre, Bongalore, India, July 94; vis scholar, member, Senior Common Room, St Cross Col, Oxford, and also Oxford Centre for Hebrew and Christian Studies, semester, 94; vis scholar, Univ of Tubingen, fall and spring, 90-91; Visting Lecturer, Smith Col, 00; Prof Emeritus, MT Holyoke Col, 00-. **MEMBERSHIPS** Soc Bibl Lit; Am Acad Relig. **RESEARCH** New and Old Testament. **SELECTED PUBLICATIONS** Auth, Eggidzein, Phthanein and Realized Eschatology, J Bibl Lit, 6/63; co-reviser, Essentials of Bible History, Ronald, 66; Realized Eschatology and the post-Bultmannians, Expository Times, 12/72; co-ed & contribr, Christological Perspectives, Pilgrim Press, 82; co-ed and contributor, Christology in Dialogue, 93; with Harvey H. McArthur, The Quest of the Historical Jesus, in Dictionary of Biblical Interpretation, Abingdon Press, summer/fall 98. **CONTACT ADDRESS** Dept of Relig, Mount Holyoke Col, 50 College St, South Hadley, MA 01075-1461. **EMAIL** rberkey@mtholyoke.edu

BERKMAN, JOHN
PERSONAL Born Ottawa, Canada **DISCIPLINE** RELIGIOUS STUDIES **EDUCATION** Duke Univ, PhD, 94 **CAREER** Dir, Hersher Inst Applied Ethics, 93-97; asst prof, Sacred Heart Univ, 93-97; Asst Prof, Dept Theol, Catholic Univ Am, 97-. **RESEARCH** Catholic moral theology; biomedical ethics. **SELECTED PUBLICATIONS** Auth, "The Chief End of All Flesh," with Stanley Hauerwas, Theology Today, vol. XLIX, No. 2, July 92, Reprinted in Stanley Hauerwas, In Good Company, UNDP, South Bend, 96; auth, Truth and Martyrdom: The Structure of Discipleship in Veritatis Splendor," New Blackfriars, November 94; auth, "Absolutely Fabulous and Civil: Milbank's Post-Critical Augustinianism," with Frederick Bauerschmidt, Theology and Philosophy, vol. 9 (3&4), 96; auth, "How Important is the Doctrine of Double Effect? Contextualizing the Controversy," Christian Bioethics, 3:2, 97; auth, "Prophetically Pro-Life: John Paul II's Gospel of Life and Evangelical Concern for Animals," Josephinum Journal of Theology, Vol. 6, No. 1, Winter/Spring 99; auth, "An Analysis and Future Direction for Catholic Biomedical Ethics," The Thomist, 63, 3, July 99; "Has the Message of Evanglieum vitae Been Missed?; coed, The Hauerwas Reader, Duke University Press, Durham, 01. **CONTACT ADDRESS** Dept Theol, Catholic Univ of America, Washington, DC 20064. **EMAIL** berkman@cua.edu

BERLEANT, ARNOLD
PERSONAL Born 03/04/1932, Buffalo, NY, m, 1958, 3 children **DISCIPLINE** PHILOSOPHY **EDUCATION** Eastman Sch Music, Univ Rochester, BMus, 53, MA, 55; Univ Buffalo, PhD (philos), 62. **CAREER** From instr to lectr philos, Univ Buffalo, 60-62; from asst profto assoc prof, 62-70, Prof Philos, C W Post Ctr, Long Island Univ, 70-, Vis prof, Sarah Lawrence Col, 66-68; Am Coun Learned Soc travel grant, 72, 76; Bingham Prof of Humanities, Univ of Louisville, 94. **HONORS AND AWARDS** Pres, Int Asn for Aesthetics, 95-98; hon member, Sydney Soc for lit and Aesthetics; hon member, Finnish Soc of Aesthetics; Membre du Comite d'Honneur de la Societe francaise d' Esthetique; Long Island Univ Trustees Awd for Scholarly Achievement, 92 **MEMBERSHIPS** Am Soc Aesthet (secy-treas, 78-88); Am Soc Value Inquiry; AAUP; Int Inst for Applied Aesthetics; pres, Int Advisory Committee. **RESEARCH** Aesthetics; existentialism and phenomenology; ethics; social philosophy. **SELECTED PUBLICATIONS** Auth, Aestetic Paradigms for an Urban Society, Diogenes, 78; auth, Subsidization of Art as Social Policy, J Behav Econ, 78; auth, Art and Engagement, Temple, 91; auth, The Aesthetics of Environment, 92; auth, Living in the Landscape, Kansas, 97; ed, Environment and the Arts, Ashgate, 01. **CONTACT ADDRESS** P.O. Box 52, Castine, ME 04421. **EMAIL** berleant@acadia.uet

BERLIN, ADELE
PERSONAL Born 05/23/1943, Philadelphia, PA, m, 2 children **DISCIPLINE** BIBLICAL STUDIES, ANCIENT NEAR EASTERN STUDIES **EDUCATION** Univ PA, PhD, 76. **CAREER** Robert H Smith prof of Hebrew Bible, Univ MD. **HONORS AND AWARDS** Guggenheim fel; ACLS fel; NEH translation fel; fel, Am Academy of Jewish Res. **MEMBERSHIPS** Soc of Biblical Lit; Asn for Jewish Studies; Am Oriental Soc. **RESEARCH** Biblical literature. **SELECTED PUBLICATIONS** Auth, Zephaniah, Anchor Bible; The Dynamics of Biblical Parallelism; Poetics and Interpretation of Biblical Narrative. **CONTACT ADDRESS** Dept of English, Univ of Maryland, Col Park, College Park, MD 20742. **EMAIL** aberlin@deans.umd.edu

BERLIN, CHARLES
PERSONAL Born 03/17/1936, Boston, MA, m, 1965, 2 children **DISCIPLINE** HEBRAIC AND JUDAIC LITERATURE **EDUCATION** Hebrew Teachers Col, BJEd, 56, MHL, 59; Harvard Univ, AB, 58, AM, 59, PhD, 63; Simmons Col, MS, 64. **CAREER** Lectr mod Hebrew, 62-65, Lee M Friedman Bibliogr in Judaica, Col Libr, Harvard Univ, 62-, Consult, Univ Fla Libr, 73, Univ Tex Libr, 74, New York Pub Libr, 75 and Emory Univ Libr, 76. **MEMBERSHIPS** Asn Jewish Libr (vpres, 67-68, pres, 68-69); Asn Jewish Studies (treas, 70-72, exec secy, 72-). **RESEARCH** Bibliography of Hebraica and Judaica; Jewish history. **SELECTED PUBLICATIONS** Auth, Digital Imaging at the Harvard Library--The Judaica Divisions Israeli Poster Image Database, Harvard Libr Bull, Vol 0005, 94. **CONTACT ADDRESS** Harvard Col Libr, Harvard Univ, Cambridge, MA 02138.

BERLING, JUDITH
PERSONAL Born 09/08/1945, Jacksonville, FL **DISCIPLINE** THEOLOGY **EDUCATION** Carleton Col, BA, 67; MPhil, 74, PhD, 75, Columbia Univ. **CAREER** Asst/Assoc Prof, 74-87, Indiana Univ; Dean and VP for Academic Affairs, 87-95, Prof, 95-, Graduate Theological Union, Berkeley. **HONORS AND AWARDS** Phi Beta Kappa; Kent Fel; NDFL Fel; Woodrow Wilson Fel, NEH Summer Fellowship. **MEMBERSHIPS** Amer Acad of Religion; Amer Soc for the Study of Religion **RESEARCH** East Asian languages and cultures **SELECTED PUBLICATIONS** Auth, A Pilgrim in Chinese Culture: Understanding Religious Neighbors, 97. **CONTACT ADDRESS** Graduate Theol Union, 2400 Ridge Rd., Berkeley, CA 94709.

BERMAN, BRUCE J.
PERSONAL Born 04/14/1942, New York, NY, m, 1967, 2 children **DISCIPLINE** POLITICAL SCIENCE **EDUCATION** Dartmouth Col, AB, 63; London Sch Econ, MA, 65; Yale Univ, PhD, 73. **CAREER** Res Assoc, Univ Nairobi, 68-69; Lectr to Prof, Queen's Univ, 71-; Recurrent Vis scholar, Univ Cambridge, 77-78, 89-; Vis Prof, Univ Pa, 84; Vis Fel, Australian Nat Univ, 95; Vis Res Fel, Univ Cape Town, 99; Vis Prof, Univ Melbourne, 01. **HONORS AND AWARDS** Reynolds Fel, Dartmouth Col, 63-64; Fel, Nat Sci Found, 64-65; Kent Fel, Danforth Found, 68-70; Fel, Soc Sci and Humanities Res Coun, 77-78, 84-85; Joel Gregory Prize in African Studies, Can Asn of African Studies, 91; Trevor Reese Prize, Inst of Commonwealth Studies, 95. **MEMBERSHIPS** Can Asn of African Studies; African Studies Asn of the U.S.; Hist of Sci Soc. **RESEARCH** Political economy of development, with special reference to Africa Ethnicity; Nationalism and democratic development Science; Technology and industrialization. **SELECTED PUBLICATIONS** Auth, Control and Crisis in Colonial Kenya, James Currey and Ohio Univ Press, 90; auth, "Nationalism , Ethnicity and Modernity: The Paradox of Mau Mau," Can J of African Studies; co-auth, "Louis Leakey's Mau Mau: A Study in the Politics of Knowledge," History and Anthropology, 91; auth, "The State, Computers and African Development," in Microcomputers in African Development, 92; co-auth, Unhappy Valley: Conflict in Kenya and Africa, James Currey and Ohio Univ Press, 92; co-ed, African Capitalists in African Development, Lynne Rienner, 94; auth, "Ethnicity, Patronage and the African State," African Affairs, 98. **CONTACT ADDRESS** Dept Polit Sci, Queen's Univ at Kingston, 331 Union St W, Kingston, ON, Canada K7L 3N6. **EMAIL** bermanb@qsilver.queensu.ca

BERMAN, ELI
PERSONAL Born Ottawa, ON, Canada, m, 1985, 2 children **DISCIPLINE** ECONOMICS **EDUCATION** Hebrew Univ, BA, 87; MA, 89; Harvard Univ, PhD, 93. **CAREER** Asst prof to assoc prof, Boston Univ, 93-01; vis prof, Rice Univ, 01-02; fac res fel, Nat Bureau of Econ Res, 93-. **HONORS AND AWARDS** Nat Bureau of Econ Res Sloan Fel, 99; Loan Doc Dissertation Fel, 92-93; Perlman Scholar, 91-92; Harvard Prize Fel, 89-91; Foerder Scholar, 87-89. **MEMBERSHIPS** Am Econ Asn; Soc of Labor Econ. **RESEARCH** Applied Economics; Labor Economics; Environmental Economics; Fertility; Skill-Biased Technological Change; Economic Growth and Development Applied Microeconomics; Economics of Reli-

gion. **SELECTED PUBLICATIONS** Co-auth, "Changes in the Demand for Skilled Labor within U.S. Manufacturing Industries: Evidence from the Annual Survey of Manufactures," Quart J of Econ, 94; auth, "Help Wanted, Job Needed: Estimates of a Matching Function from Employment Service Data," J of Labor Econ, (97): 251-292; co-auth, "Implications of Skill-Biased Technological Change: International Evidence," Quart J of Econ, 98; auth, "Subsidized Sacrifice: State Support of Religion in Israel," Contemporary Jewry, 99; auth, "Korbanot Mesubsadot: Tmichat HaMedina beDat beYisrael," The Econ Quart, 00; auth, "A Sect, Subsidy and Sacrifice: An Economist's View of Ultra-Orthodox Jews," Quart J of Econ, 00; co-auth, "Skill-Biased Technology Transfer Around the World," Oxford Rev of Econ Policy, 00; co-auth, "Environmental Regulation and Labor Demand: Evidence from the South Coast Air Basin," J of Public Econ, 01 co-auth, "Environmental Regulation and Productivity: Evidence from Oil Refineries," Rev of Econ and Statistics, (forthcoming). **CONTACT ADDRESS** Dept Econ, Boston Univ, 270 Bay State Rd, Boston, MA 02215.

BERMAN, HAROLD J.
PERSONAL Born 02/13/1918, Hartford, CT, m, 1941, 4 children **DISCIPLINE** LAW **CAREER** Asst Prof, Stanford Law School, 47-48; Asst Prof, Story Prof, Ames Prof of Law, Harvard Law School, 48-85; Emory Law School, Woodruff Prof of Law, Harvard Law School, Ames Prof of Law, emeritus, 85-. **HONORS AND AWARDS** Harvard Univ, MA, 52; Catholic Univ of America, LLD, 91; Virginia Theological Seminar, DHL, 95; Univ of Ghent, D, 97. **MEMBERSHIPS** Ameri Academy of Arts and Sciences; Amer Assoc for the Advancement of Slavic Studies; Amer Society for Legal History; Amer Societty of Comparative Law. **RESEARCH** Impact of Belief Systems on the Development of Law; World Law Supporting; The World Economy; World Communications; and The Emerging World Society. **SELECTED PUBLICATIONS** Auth, "Law and Revolution: The Formation of the Western Legal Tradition," 83, Scribes Book Award); auth, Faith and Order: The Reconciliation of Law and Religion," 93; auth, "The Nature and Functions of Law: An Introduction for students of the Arts and Sciences," 96; auth, "Justice in the USSR: An Interpretationof Soviet Law, 2nd ed. Rev. 1963. **CONTACT ADDRESS** Dept Law, Emory Univ, 1301 Clifton Rd., Atlanta, GA 30322-1061. **EMAIL** hberman@law.emory.edu

BERMAN, JEFFREY B.
DISCIPLINE LAW **EDUCATION** City Univ NYork, BS; Univ Denver, MS; Brooklyn Law Sch, JD. **CAREER** Prof **RESEARCH** Trial advocacy. **SELECTED PUBLICATIONS** Auth, Trial Advocacy Teacher's Manual; co-auth, Missouri Civil Procedure Form Book; The Story of a Civil Suit: Dominquez v. Scott's Food Stores Inc. **CONTACT ADDRESS** Law Dept, Univ of Missouri, Kansas City, 5100 Rockhill Rd, Kansas City, MO 64110-2499. **EMAIL** bermanj@umkc.edu

BERMAN, SCOTT
PERSONAL Born 09/19/1962, Baltimore, MD, m, 1985, 2 children **DISCIPLINE** PHILOSOPHY **EDUCATION** Tulane Univ, BA, 84; Univ Wisc, Madison, MA, 87, PhD, 90. **CAREER** Vis asst prof, philos, Univ Neb, Lincoln, 90-91; asst prof, 91-97, assoc prof, 97- , philos, Saint Louis Univ. **HONORS AND AWARDS** Mellon Fac Development Grant, 92, 93, 94, 95, 96; Teacher of the Month, 93. **MEMBERSHIPS** Soc for Ancient Greek Philos; Int Asn for Greek Philos; Int Plato Soc; APA. **RESEARCH** Ancient Greek philosophy; contemporary analytic metaphysics. **SELECTED PUBLICATIONS** Auth, How Polus Was Refuted: Reconsidering Plato's Gorgias 474c-465c, Ancient Philos, 91; auth, Socrates and Callicles on Pleasure, Phronesis, 91; auth, Plato's Refutation of Constructivism in the Cratylus, J of Neoplatonic Stud, 94; auth, Plato's Explanation of False Belief in the Sophist, Apeiron, 96. **CONTACT ADDRESS** Dept of Philosophy, Saint Louis Univ, 3800 Lindell Blvd, PO Box 56907, Saint Louis, MO 63156-0907. **EMAIL** bermansj@slu.edu

BERNIER, PAUL
DISCIPLINE COGNITIVE SCIENCE AND PHILOSOPHY OF MIND **EDUCATION** Univ Montreal, PhD. **CAREER** Prof. **RESEARCH** Philosophy of language. **SELECTED PUBLICATIONS** Pub(s), in Mind and Lang; Quebec Stud; Philos of Sci. **CONTACT ADDRESS** Dept of Philos, Concordia Univ, Montreal, 1455 de Maisonneuve W, Montreal, QC, Canada H3G 1M8. **EMAIL** pbernie@vax2.concordia.ca

BERNSTEIN, JERRY
DISCIPLINE PHILOSOPHY **EDUCATION** Univ Cambridge, UK, MPh, 91. **CAREER** Investment advisor, 20 years. **MEMBERSHIPS** Am Soc for Aesthetics; APA. **RESEARCH** Aesthetics; value theory. **CONTACT ADDRESS** 432 S Curson Ave, #6-H, Los Angeles, CA 90036.

BERNSTEIN, MARK H.
PERSONAL Born 03/19/1948, New York, NY, s **DISCIPLINE** CLASSICS, PHILOSOPHY **EDUCATION** CUNY, 69; Univ Calif, Santa Barbara, PhD, 82. **CAREER** Cis Asst Prof, Wesleyan Univ, 82-83; From Asst Prof to Prof, Univ Tex, 83-. **HONORS AND AWARDS** 2 NEH Fels, Res Develop Awd. **MEMBERSHIPS** APA, SSPP **RESEARCH** Applied ethics, animal ethics, metaphysics, free will. **SELECTED PUBLICATIONS** Auth, Fatalism, Univ Nebr Pr, 92; auth, On Moral Considerability, Oxford UP, 98. **CONTACT ADDRESS** Dept Classics & Philos, Univ of Texas, San Antonio, 6900 N Loop 1604 W, San Antonio, TX 78249-1130. **EMAIL** markb@10.com

BERNSTEIN, RICHARD J.
PERSONAL Born 05/14/1932, Brooklyn, NY, m, 1955, 4 children **DISCIPLINE** PHILOSOPHY **EDUCATION** Univ Chicago, BA, 51; Columbia Univ, BS, 53; Yale Univ, MA, 55, PhD, 58. **CAREER** Instr, 54-57, asst prof, 58-63, assoc prof philos, 63-65, Yale Univ; Fulbright lectr, Hebrew Univ, 57-58; vis prof philos, Hebrew Univ, 65-66; prof philos, 66-78, chemn dept, 66-78, T. Wistar Brown Prof of Philos, 79-89, Haverford Col; vis adj prof, 81-83, Vera List Prof, Grad Fac, chemn Dept of Philos, 89- , New School for Social Res; pres, Adirondack Work/Study Inc., 90- . **HONORS AND AWARDS** Summa cum Laude, 53; Phi Beta Kappa, 53; Tew Prize, 54; Pres, Charles S. Peirce Soc, 69; exec comm E Div APA, 68-70; ed, Rev of Metaphysics, 64-71; Harbison Awd for Gifted Tchg, 70; sr fel NEH, 72-73; ACLS fel, 78-79; ed, Praxis Int, 80-84; NEH fel, 85-86; vpres & pres APA, E Div, & Metaphysical Soc of Am, 87-88; Robert Foster Cherry Awd for Great Tchrs, 91; John Dewey Soc Awd for Outstanding Achievement, 95. **MEMBERSHIPS** APA; Metaphysical Soc of Am. **SELECTED PUBLICATIONS** Auth, An Allegory of Modernity/Postmodernity: Habermas and Derrida, in Madison, ed, Working Through Derrida, Northwestern Univ, 93; auth, Hans Jonas: Rethinking Responsibility, Soc Res, 94; auth, American Pragmatism: The Conflict of Narratives, in Saatkamp, ed, Rorty and Pragmatism, Vanderbilt Univ, 95; auth, Are We Beyond the Enlightenment Horizon? in Shea, ed, Knowledge and Belief in America, Cambridge Univ, 95; auth, Hannah Arendt and the Jewish Question, MIT, 96; auth, The Banality of Evil Reconsidered, in Calhoun, ed, Hannah Arendt and the Meaning of Politics, Univ Minn, 96; auth, The Hermeneutics of Cross-Cultural Understanding, in Balslev, ed, Cross-Cultural Conversation, Scholars, 96; auth, Hans Jonas' Mortality and Morality, Grad Fac Philos J, 97; auth, Provocation and Appropriation: Hannah Arendt's Response to Martin Heidegger, Constellations, 97; auth, Freud & The Legacy of Moses, Cambridge Univ, 98. **CONTACT ADDRESS** Philosophy/Graduate Faculty, New Sch for Social Research, 85 Fifth Ave, New York, NY 10003.

BERNSTEIN-NAHAR, AVI K.
PERSONAL Born 10/24/1963, Orlando, FL, m, 1993, 2 children **DISCIPLINE** RELIGION, PHILOSOPHY **EDUCATION** Brown Univ BA; Stanford Univ PhD. **CAREER** Univ of Toronto Ray D Wolfe fel, 97-98; Dir of Comm educ; Asst Prof of Jewish Thought, Hebrew Col, 99-. **HONORS AND AWARDS** Ray D Wolfe Fel; Mem Foun Jewish Culture Fel; Ntl Foun Jewish Fel; Lady Davis Trust Fell **MEMBERSHIPS** AAR; AJS **RESEARCH** Modern Jewish Thought, Philos of Educ, Transformational Adult Learning. **SELECTED PUBLICATIONS** Auth, Das einzige Herz der Sache: Hermann Cohen's Teaching Concerning Modern Jewish Identity, Yearbook of the Leo Baeck Inst, 98; auth, "The New Learning ," Adult Jewish Education: Modern Judaism out of its Biblical and Philosophical Sources. **CONTACT ADDRESS** Hebrew Col, 43 Hawes St, Brookline, MA 02446. **EMAIL** abernstein@hebrewcollege.edu

BERNSTINE, DANIEL O.
PERSONAL Born 09/07/1947, Berkeley, CA, s, 2 children **DISCIPLINE** LAW **EDUCATION** Univ of CA, BA 1969; NW Univ Sch of Law, JD 1972; Univ of Wis Law Sch, LLM 1975. **CAREER** US Dept of Labor, staff atty, 72-73; Univ of WI Law Sch, teaching fellow, 74-75; Howard Univ Law Sch, asst prof, 75-78; Howard Univ, asst vice pres for legal affairs, 84-87, general counsel, 87-90; Univ of WI Law Sch, prof, 78-97, dean, 90-97; Portland State University, president, currently. **SELECTED PUBLICATIONS** Various publications. **CONTACT ADDRESS** Portland State Univ, PO Box 751, Portland, OR 97207. **EMAIL** bernstined@pdx.edu

BEROFSKY, BERNARD A.
PERSONAL Born 07/05/1935, Jersey City, NJ, m, 1962, 2 children **DISCIPLINE** PHILOSOPHY **EDUCATION** NYork Univ, BA, 56; Columbia Univ, MA, 59, PhD, 63. **CAREER** Instr philos, Vassar Col, 63-64; asst prof, Univ MI, 64-67; from asst to assoc prof, 67-69, Prof Philos, Columbia Univ, 69-, Am Philos Soc grant, 67-; Am Coun Learned Soc fel, 72-73; Fulbright research fel, 87-88. **MEMBERSHIPS** Am Philos Asn. **RESEARCH** Determinism; autonomy; views on free will. **SELECTED PUBLICATIONS** Auth, Causality and general laws, J Philos, 3/66; The regularity theory, Nous, 11/68; Purposive action, Am Philos Quart, 10/70; Determinism, Princeton Univ, 71; co-ed, Introductory Philosophy, Harper, 2nd ed, 71; auth, Freedom from necessity, RKP, 87; Liberation from self, Cambridge, 95. **CONTACT ADDRESS** Dept of Philos, Columbia Univ, 2960 Broadway, New York, NY 10027-6900. **EMAIL** beberofsky@aol.com

BERQUIST, JON L.
PERSONAL Born 12/19/1963, s **DISCIPLINE** RELIGION **EDUCATION** Northwest Christian Col, BA, 85; Vanderbilt Univ, MA, 88, PhD, 89. **CAREER** Phillips Grad Sem, asst prof, assoc prof, 89-94; Westminster John Knox Press, Acquisitions ed, 94-97; Chalice Press, Acad ed, 97-. **HONORS AND AWARDS** Vanderbilt Grad Fel, SCRS jr scholar. **MEMBERSHIPS** AAAR, CBA, SBL, SSSR. **RESEARCH** Social world of ancient Israel; Persian Period Judah; Achaemenid Dynasty. **SELECTED PUBLICATIONS** Auth, Ancient Wine, New Wineskins: The Lord's Supper in Old Testament Perspective, St. Louis: Chalice Press, 91; auth, Reclaiming Her Story: The Witness of Women in the Old Testament, St. Louis, Chalice Press, 92; Surprises by the River: The Prophecy of Ezekiel, St. Louis Press, 93; auth, Judaism in Persia's Shadow: A Social and Historical Approach, Minneapolis: Fortress Press, 95; auth, Incarnations, Chalice Press (St. Louis), 00; auth, Who Do You Say That I Am? Biblical Images and Ministerial Identity, Lexington Theol Quart, 94; auth, The Shifting Frontier: The Achaemenid Empire's Treatment of Western Colonies, Jour World Sys Res, 95; Postcolonization and Imperial Motives for Canonization, Semeia, 96. **CONTACT ADDRESS** 7012 Tholozan Ave, Saint Louis, MO 63109-1131.

BERRIDGE, JOHN MACLENNAN
PERSONAL Born 05/23/1938, Bridgewater, NS, Canada, m, 1966 **DISCIPLINE** THEOLOGY **EDUCATION** Mt Allison Univ, BA, 59; Pine Hill Divinity Hall, BD, 63; Univ Basel, DTheol, 67. **CAREER** Asst prof, 68-73, Assoc Prof Theol;, St Francis Xavier Univ, 73-, Can Coun leave fel, 75-76. **MEMBERSHIPS** Soc Bibl Lit; Am Acad Relig. **RESEARCH** Old Testament; prophecy in the Old Testament; religion in modern India. **SELECTED PUBLICATIONS** Auth, Prophet, People, and the Word of Yahweh: An Examination of Form and Content in the Proclamation of the Prophet Jeremiah; ed, The One and the Many, Readings from the Work of Rabindranath Taagore, Bayeux Arts, Inc, 97. **CONTACT ADDRESS** Dept of Religeous Studies, Francis Xavier Univ, PO Box 5000, Antigonish, NS, Canada B2G 2W5. **EMAIL** jberridg@stfx.ca

BERRY, DONALD K.
PERSONAL Born 04/29/1953, Gary, IN, m, 1972, 2 children **DISCIPLINE** RELIGION **EDUCATION** Ky Wesleyan Col, BA, 75; Southern Theol Sem, MDiv, 78; PhD, 87 **CAREER** Prof, Univ Mobile, 87-. **HONORS AND AWARDS** Garrett Fel, Southern Sem, 84; Megginson Res Awd, Univ Mobile, 95-96, 91-92. **MEMBERSHIPS** Soc of Biblical Lit, Nat Asn of Baptist Prof of Relig, Catholic Biblical Asn, Christian Theol Inst, Am Asn of Univ Prof, Celebration 2000, Ala Holocaust Commission. **RESEARCH** Hebrew poetry and wisdom, Christian worship, Interfaith relations. **SELECTED PUBLICATIONS** Auth, The Psalms and Their Readers: Interpretative Strategies for Psalm 18, Sheffield Press, 94; auth, Introduction to Wisdom and Poetry of the Old Testament, Broadman & Holman, 96. **CONTACT ADDRESS** Dept Relig, Univ of Mobile, PO Box 13220, Mobile, AL 36663-0220. **EMAIL** donaldkberry@hotmail.com

BERSOFF, DONALD N.
DISCIPLINE CRIMINAL LAW **EDUCATION** NYork Univ, BS, 58, MA, 60, PhD, 65; Yale Univ Law Sch, JD, 76. **CAREER** Prof & dir, Law/Psychology Prog; Villanova Univ,90-. **HONORS AND AWARDS** Distinguished Alumni awd, NY Univ Sch Educ, Health, Nursing, and Arts Prof, 81; Who's Who in Am, 82-; **MEMBERSHIPS** Bd dir, Amer Psychol Asn, 94-97, and a Comn mem on, 3rd Circuit Task Force for Equal Treatment in the Courts, Commission on Race and Ethnicity, 95-97; Past ch, Educ and Training in Law and Psychology, 94-95; ed bd(s), J Legal Educ, Behavioral Sci and the Law & Ethics and Behavior; assoc ed, Law and Human Behavior. **RESEARCH** Mental health, social science and the law. **SELECTED PUBLICATIONS** Auth, Ethical Conflicts in Psychology, 95; sr coauth, Legal Issues in Computerized Psychological Testing, The Computer and the Decision-Making Process, 91; Explicit Ambiguity: The 1992 Ethics Code as an Oxymoron, 25 Prof Psychology: Res and Practice 382, 94 & Legal Issues in the Assessment and Treatment of Individuals with Dual Diagnoses, 62 J Consulting and Clinical Psychology 55, 94. **CONTACT ADDRESS** Law School, Villanova Univ, 800 Lancaster Ave, Villanova, PA 19085-1692. **EMAIL** bersoffd@law.vill.edu

BERTHOLD, GEORGE CHARLES
PERSONAL Born 03/01/1935, Lawrence, MA **DISCIPLINE** THEOLOGY, BYZANTINE STUDIES **EDUCATION** St John's Sem, BA, 59, MA, 63; Cath Inst, Paris, STD, 75; Villanova Univ, BA, 77. **CAREER** Asst prof, 76-80, Assoc Prof Theol, St Anselm's Col, 80- **MEMBERSHIPS** Cath Theol Soc Am; Col Theol Soc. **RESEARCH** Patristic studies, chiefly of the later Greek period; ecumenics. **SELECTED PUBLICATIONS CONTACT ADDRESS** Dept of Theol, Saint Anselm Col, Manchester, NH 03102.

BERTOCCI, ROSEMARY
PERSONAL Born 02/22/1964, Pittsburgh, PA, m, 1993 **DISCIPLINE** THEOLOGY **EDUCATION** Duquesne Univ, 95. **CAREER** Seton Hill Col, 91-92; St Francis Col, 92-. **HON-**

ORS AND AWARDS Teaching Fel, Grad Sch; Teacher of the year, 95, 99; Teacher of the Year, St Francis Nat Honor Soc. **MEMBERSHIPS** AAR. **RESEARCH** Science and Religion. **SELECTED PUBLICATIONS** Auth, "A Whiteheadian Theory of Being and Becoming," in A Whiteheadian - Rahnerian Theory of Symbol. **CONTACT ADDRESS** Dept Relig and Philos, Saint Francis Col, Pennsylvania, PO Box 600, Loretto, PA 15940-0600. **EMAIL** rbertocci@aol.com

BERTOLET, ROD
PERSONAL Born 03/22/1949, Allentown, PA **DISCIPLINE** PHILOSOPHY **EDUCATION** Franklin & Marshall Col, BA, 71; Univ Wi Madison, PhD, 77. **CAREER** Asst prof to assoc prof to prof, dept head, Purdue Univ, 77- . **HONORS AND AWARDS** Fel, Center for Humanistic Stud, Purdue Univ, 87, 91. **MEMBERSHIPS** Amer Philos Assoc, Ind Philos Assoc. **RESEARCH** Philos of lang, philos of mind. **SELECTED PUBLICATIONS** Auth, What is Said: A Theory of Indirect Speech Reports, Philos Stud Series, Kluwer Acad Publ, 90; Demonstratives and Intentions, Ten Years Later, Commun & Cognition, 93; Hasker on Middle Knowledge, Faith & Psychol, 94; Saving Eliminativism, Philos Psychol, 94; Conventions and Coreferentiality, J of Philos Res, 94; auth, "Recanati, Descriptive Names, and the Prospect of New Knowledge," Journal of Philosophical Res, 01. **CONTACT ADDRESS** Dept of Philosophy, Purdue Univ, West Lafayette, West Lafayette, IN 47907. **EMAIL** bertolet@purdue.edu

BERTON, PETER
DISCIPLINE INTERNATIONAL RELATIONS **EDUCATION** Columbia Univ, PhD, 56. **CAREER** Prof emer,Univ Southern Calif. **RESEARCH** International relations of Asia and the Pacific; US foreign policy in Asia; Japanese political parties. **SELECTED PUBLICATIONS** Auth, The Psychological Dimension of Japanese Negotiating Behavior; Japan and Russia in the Post-Cold War Era. **CONTACT ADDRESS** East Asian Studies Center, Univ of So California, University Park Campus, Los Angeles, CA 90089.

BESCHLE, D. L.
PERSONAL Born 10/15/1957, CT, s **DISCIPLINE** LAW **EDUCATION** Fordham Univ, BA, 73; New York Univ School of Law, JD, 76; Temple Univ School of Law, LLM, 83. **CAREER** Teaching fel, Temple Univ School of Law, 79-81; ASST PROF, 81-85, ASSOC PROF, 85-97, PROF, 98-, JOHN MARSHALL LAW SCHOOL. **MEMBERSHIPS** Order of the Coif. **RESEARCH** Constitutional law; law and religion; antitrust law. **SELECTED PUBLICATIONS** Auth, "The Juvenile justice Counterevolution: Responding to Cognitive Dissonance in the Laws View of the Deciner-Making Capacity of Minors," 48 Emory L.J.GS, 99; auth, What's Guilt (Or Deterrence) Got To Do With It?: The Death Penalty, Ritual, and Mimetic Violence, William & Mary Law Rev, 97; auth, You've Got To Be Carefully Taught: Justifying Affirmative Action After Croson and Adarand, NC Law Rev, 96; auth, The Role of Courts in the Debate On Assisted Suicide: A Communitarian Approach, Ethics & Public Politics, 95; auth, Defining the Scope of the Constitutional Right to Marry: More Than Tradition, Less Than Unlimited Autonomy, Notre Dame Law Rev, 94; auth, The Use of Religion as Part of the Best Interests Test in Child Custody Disputes, Child, Family & State: Law and Policy Reader, Temple Univ Press, 94; auth, Catechism or Imagination: Is Justice Scalia's Judicial Style Typically Catholic, Villanova Law Rev, 92; auth, Conditional Spending and the First Amendment: Maintaining the Commitment to Rational Liberal Dialogue, Mo Law Rev, 92. **CONTACT ADDRESS** John Marshall Law Sch, 315 S Plymouth Ct, Chicago, IL 60604. **EMAIL** 7beschle@jmls.edu

BESSNER, RONDA
DISCIPLINE LAW **EDUCATION** McGill Univ, BA, 77, BCL, 81, LLB, 81; Harvard Univ, LLM, 86. **CAREER** Adj fac; Senior Legal Analyst, Commission of Inquiry on the Blood System in Canada; asst prof, Univ of Western. **RESEARCH** Young offenders, institutional child abuse, and issues related to AIDS. **SELECTED PUBLICATIONS** Auth, pubs on criminal law, evidence, constitutional law and family law. **CONTACT ADDRESS** Fac of Law, Univ of Toronto, 78 Queen's Park, Toronto, ON, Canada M5S 2C5.

BESSON, PAUL SMITH
PERSONAL Born 05/11/1953, New York, NY, s **DISCIPLINE** LAW **EDUCATION** Cornell Univ, BS labor relations 1975, MBA marketing/finance 1976; Northwestern Univ, JD 1980; Georgetown University Law Center, LLM, 1995. **CAREER** Cummins Engine Co, market planning analyst 1976-77; Jewel Companies, Inc, labor relations counsel 1980-82, mgr personnel/labor relations 1982-83; NBC, Inc, mgr labor relations, 84-88, dir employee relations, 88-1998; Director, Talent Negotiations and Labor Relations; American Commercial Lines, LLC, Sr VP Human Resources 1998-. **MEMBERSHIPS** Mem Amer, IL, Chicago, DC Bar Assn; mem IL, NY, & DC Bars; bd of dir Cornell Club Assn 1982; pres Cornell Black Alumni Assn Chicago 1982-83; Amer Arbitration Assn panel commercial arbitrations; hearing officer, Civil Serv Commn IL; bd of dir ABE Credit Union; pres, Cornell Black Alumni Assn, Washington, DC, 1989-91; Capital Press Club; Washington Association of Black Journalists; mediator, US District Court, Dist of Columbia; Advisor Council GE African American Forum. **SELECTED PUBLICATIONS** Contributing writer Black Enterprise Magazine; **CONTACT ADDRESS** 1710 E. Market St., Jeffersonville, IN 47130.

BEST, ERNEST E.
PERSONAL Born 12/26/1919, Toronto, ON, Canada, m, 1945, 3 children **DISCIPLINE** RELIGION, PHILOSOPHY **EDUCATION** Univ Toronto, BA, 40, MA, 42, BD, 49; Drew Univ, PhD, 58. **CAREER** Assoc prof hist relig and soc ethics, Lafayette Col, 60-65; prof soc ethics, Methodist Theol Sch, Ohio, 65-70; Prof Relig Studies, Victoria Col, Univ Toronto, 70-, Am Asn Theol Schs fel, 68-69; Am Philos Soc res grant, 68-69. **MEMBERSHIPS** Can Soc Studies Relig; Can Soc Asian Studies; Asn Asian Studies; Am Soc Christian Ethics. **RESEARCH** Contemporary Japanese society since 1859; history and sociology of religions; social value theory. **SELECTED PUBLICATIONS** Auth, Christian Faith and Cultural Crisis: The Japanese Case, Brill (Leiden), 66; auth, Religion and Society in Transition, E. Mellen (NY), 82; auth, Essays on Ephesians, T & T Clark (Edinburgh), 97; auth, A critical and Exegetical Commentary on Ephesians, T & T Clark (Edinburgh), 98. **CONTACT ADDRESS** 33 Elmhurst Ave., Toronto, ON, Canada M1B 1A1.

BEST, JUDITH A.
PERSONAL Born Chicago, IL **DISCIPLINE** POLITICAL SCIENCE **EDUCATION** Cornell Univ, PhD, 71. **CAREER** Dist Teach Prof Pol Sci, SUNY, Cortland, 84-. **HONORS AND AWARDS** NY Chanc Awd Excell Teaching, 77; Am High Edu & Carnegie Found, Salute for Edu Leadershp, 86. **MEMBERSHIPS** Bd Editors, Pres Stud Quart, Cent for the Study of the Pres. **RESEARCH** Elect Col, Pol Theory, Found Period. **SELECTED PUBLICATIONS** The Choice of the People?, Debating the Electoral College, Rowman and Littlefield, 96; The Mainstream of Western Political Thought, Univ Free Press, 97; National Representation for the District of Columbia, 84. **CONTACT ADDRESS** SUNY, Col at Cortland, Dept Political Science, Cortland, NY 13045.

BEST, STEVEN
PERSONAL Born 12/20/1955, IL, S **DISCIPLINE** PHILOSOPHY **EDUCATION** Univ Ill, Urbana-Champaign, BA; Univ Chicago, MA; Univ Tex, Austin, PhD. **CAREER** Asst prof **RESEARCH** Cultural criticism; mass media; social theory; postmodern theory. **SELECTED PUBLICATIONS** Auth, The Politics of Historical Vision: Marx, Foucault, and Habermas, Guilford Press, NY; Murray Bookchin: Philosopher of Freedom, Guilford Press, NY, 99; coauth, Postmodern Theory: Critical Interrogations, Guilford Press, NY; The Postmodern Turn: Paradigm Shifts in Art, Theory, and Science, Guilford Press, NY; The Postmodern Adventure: Science, Technology, and Cultural Studies, Guilford Press, NY. **CONTACT ADDRESS** Dept of Philosophy, Univ of Texas, El Paso, 500 W University Ave, El Paso, TX 79968. **EMAIL** sbest1@utep.edu

BETHEL, ARTHUR CHARLES WALTER
PERSONAL Born 12/13/1940, Los Angeles, CA, m, 1970, 1 child **DISCIPLINE** ETHICS, ACTION THEORY **EDUCATION** Univ Calif, Santa Barbara, BA, 64, MA, 68, PhD(philos), 74. **CAREER** Prof Philos, Calif Polytech State Univ, 68- **MEMBERSHIPS** Am Philos Asn. **RESEARCH** Action and responsibility. **SELECTED PUBLICATIONS** Auth, Traditional Logic, Univ Press of Am, 82; Wanting to want, Philos Res Archives ; Logic: A Traditional Approach, Kendall-Hunt, 90. **CONTACT ADDRESS** Philos Dept, California Polytech State Univ, San Luis Obispo, 1 Grand Ave, San Luis Obispo, CA 93407-0001. **EMAIL** abethel@calpoly.edu

BETHEL, LEONARD LESLIE
PERSONAL Born 02/05/1939, Philadelphia, PA, m, 1962, 2 children **DISCIPLINE** THEOLOGY **EDUCATION** Lincoln Univ, BA 1961; Johnson C Smith Univ Sch of Theology, MDiv 1964; New Brunswick Theological Sem, MA 1971; Rutgers Univ, DEd 1975. **CAREER** Washington United Presbyterian Church, pastor 1964-67; Lincoln Univ, asst chaplain & dir counseling 1967-79; Bethel Presbyterian Church, pastor 1982-92; Rutgers Univ Dept Africana Studies, faculty & staff 1969-, assoc prof 1980-. **HONORS AND AWARDS** Phi Delta Kappa Rutgers Univ 1975; Paul Robeson Faculty Awd Rutgers Univ 1978; NAFEO Pres Citation Lincoln Univ 1981; Woodrow Wilson Fellow Princeton Univ 1984. **MEMBERSHIPS** Mem Bd of Trustees Rutgers Prep Sch 1971-84; fellow Rutgers Coll Rutgers Univ 1980-; mem Amer Assn Univ Profs Rutgers Univ 1980-; mem board of directors Plainfield Branch, Union County Coll, 1980-86; mem Frontiers Intl 1980-; mem Presbytery of Elizabeth 1982-; bd of trustees, Bloomfield Coll, 1980-86; bd of trustees, Lincoln Univ, 1996-; bd of dirs, VCC, 1980-87. **SELECTED PUBLICATIONS** Co-author, Advancement Through Service: A History of The Frontiers International, Lanham, University Press of America, 1991, Plainfield's African American: Northern Slavery to Church Freedom, University Press of America, 1997; author, Educating African Leaders: Missionism in America, Edwin Mellon Press, 1997; auth, Africana: An Introduction and Study, Kendell/Hunt Pr. **CONTACT ADDRESS** Rutgers, The State Univ of New Jersey, New Brunswick, Beck Hall #112, New Brunswick, NJ 08903. **EMAIL** bethel@rci.rutgers.edu

BETT, RICHARD
PERSONAL Born 06/10/1957, London, England, m, 1986 **DISCIPLINE** CLASSICS AND PHILOSOPHY **EDUCATION** Oxford Univ, BA, 80; UC Berkley, PhD, 86. **CAREER** Asst Prof, Univ TX at Arlington, 86-91; Asst Prof, Johns Hopkins Univ, 00; 91-94; Assoc Prof, 94-, Sec Appt in Classics, 96-; Acting Exec Dir, APA, 00; Prof, 00-. **HONORS AND AWARDS** Fel Center for Hellenic Stud, Washington DC 94-95. **MEMBERSHIPS** APA; Soc for Ancient Greek Phil; North Amer Nietzsche Soc **RESEARCH** Ancient Greek philosophy, especially Greek skepticism. **SELECTED PUBLICATIONS** Art, Scepticism and Everyday Attitudes in Ancient and Modern Philosophy, Metaphilosophy, 93; art, What Did Pyrrho Think about the Nature of the Divine and the Good, Phronesis, 94; art, Aristocleson Timon on Pyrrho the Text it Logic and its Credibility, Oxford Stud in Ancient Phil, 94; auth, Sextus Against the Ethicists Scepticism, Relativisim or Both, Apeiron, 94; art, Hellenistic Essays Translated, Papers in Hellenistic Phil, 96; Entries in Encyl of Class Philos, 97; auth, Sextus Empiricus, Against the Ethicists (Adversus Mathematicos XI): Introduction, Translation and Commentary, (Oxford: Clarendon Press, 97); auth, Pyrrho, his Antecedents and his Legacy (Oxford: Clarendon Press) forthcoming. **CONTACT ADDRESS** Dept of Philosophy, Johns Hopkins Univ, Baltimore, Gilman Hall, Baltimore, MD 21218-2890. **EMAIL** bett_r@jhunix.hcf.jhu.edu

BETTS, RICHARD KEVIN
PERSONAL Born 08/15/1947, Easton, PA, m, 1987, 3 children **DISCIPLINE** GOVERNMENT **EDUCATION** Harvard Univ, BA, 69, MA, 71, PhD, 75. **CAREER** Lectr, Harvard Univ, Govt, 75-76; res assoc, Brookings Inst, 76-81,sr fel, 81-90; adj lectr, Johns Hopkins School Advanced Int Stud, 78-85; vis prof, Harvard Univ, 85-88; Johns Hopkins, 88-90; PROF, POLIT SCI, DIR, INST WAR & PEACE STUD, COLUMBIA UNIV, 90-. **HONORS AND AWARDS** APSA Woodrow Wilson Awd, 80; IUS Lasswell Awd, 78; Harvard A. Sumner Prize, 76; NISC Intelligene Article Awd, 78,80. **MEMBERSHIPS** Am Polit Sci Asn; Int Inst Strategis Stud; Coun For Relations; Int Stud Asn; Consortium Stud Intell **RESEARCH** War; Strategy; National Security; Military Affairs; International relations; Intelligence Analysis. **SELECTED PUBLICATIONS** Military Readiness: Concepts, Choices, Consequences, Brookings Inst, 95; auth, Soldiers, Statesmen, and Cold War Crises, 2nd ed, Columbia U Press, 91; 1st ed, Harrvard U Press, 77; auth, Surrprise Attack, (Brookings, 82); auth, Nuclear Blackmail and Nuclear Balance, (Brookings, 87); edr, Conflict After the Cold War: Arguments on Causes of War and Peace, MacMillan/Allyn & Bacon, 94. **CONTACT ADDRESS** Inst War & Peace Stud, Columbia Univ, 420 W 118th St, New York, NY 10027. **EMAIL** rkb4@columbia.edu

BETTY, STAFFORD
PERSONAL Born 12/31/1942, Mobile, AL, m, 2000, 5 children **DISCIPLINE** RELIGIOUS STUDIES **EDUCATION** Univ Detroit, MA, 66; Fordham Univ, PhD, 75. **CAREER** Cal State Univ Bakersfield, 72-. **RESEARCH** Philosophy of Religion. **SELECTED PUBLICATIONS** Auth, Thomas, Penguin Book, 98. **CONTACT ADDRESS** Dept Relig and Philos, California State Univ, Bakersfield, 9001 Stockdale Hwy, Bakersfield, CA 93311-1022. **EMAIL** sbetty@csubak.edu

BETZ, HANS DIETER
PERSONAL Born 05/21/1931, Lemgo, Germany, m, 1957, 3 children **DISCIPLINE** RELIGION **EDUCATION** Gymnasium Leopoldinum in Detmold, BA, 51; Theologische Hochschule Bethel, 51-52; Johannes Gutenberg, Univ Mainz, PhD, 57. **CAREER** Prof, Claremont Grad Sch, 63-78; Univ Chicago, 78-. **HONORS AND AWARDS** Humboldt Research Prize, 86-87; Shailer Mathews prof, 90-; johannes gutenberg stipendium, univ mainz, 53-55; fel, world coun of churches, 55-56. **MEMBERSHIPS** Int Soc for New Testament Studies; Soc of Bibl Lit; Chicago Soc of Bibl Res; Inst for Antiquity and Christianity; Int Plutarch Soc; Alexander von Humboldt Asn of Am. **RESEARCH** Religion; New Testament Studies; Greco-Roman Religions. **SELECTED PUBLICATIONS** Auth, Antike und Christentum: Gesammlte Aufsatze IV, 98; The Sermon on the Mount, 95; Paulinische Studien: Gesammelte Aufsatze III, 94. **CONTACT ADDRESS** Divinity School, Univ of Chicago, 1025 E 58th St, Chicago, IL 60637. **EMAIL** hansbetz@midway.uchicago.edu

BETZ, JOSEPH M.
PERSONAL Born 02/13/1940, Philadelphia, PA, m, 1963, 4 children **DISCIPLINE** PHILOSOPHY **EDUCATION** St Joseph's Col, BS, 61; Univ Chicago, MA, 64; Villanova Univ, MA, 66; Univ Chicago, PhD(ideas & methods), 73. **CAREER** Assoc Prof Philos, Villanova Univ, 66-. **HONORS AND AWARDS** Pres, SAAP, 95-97; Pres, NASSP, 97-00. **MEMBERSHIPS** Soc Advan Am Philos; N Am Society for Soc Philosophy; Charles S Peirce Soc; Am Philos Asn. **RESEARCH** Ethics; social philosophy; American philosophy. **SELECTED PUBLICATIONS** Auth, Can civil disobedience be justified?, Social Theory & Pract, fall 70; The relation between love and justice, J Value Inquiry, fall 70; George Herbert Mead on human rights, Trans Charles S Peirce Soc, fall 74; John Dewey on natural rights, Bicentennial Sym Philos: Contrib Papers, 76;

Violence: Garver's definition and a Deweyan correction, Ethics, 7/77; John Dewey on human rights, Trans Charles S Peirce Soc, winter 78; Sandinista Nicaragua as a Deweyan Social Experiment, Trans Charles S Pierce Soc, winter, 00. **CONTACT ADDRESS** Dept of Philosophy, Villanova Univ, 845 E Lancaster Ave, Villanova, PA 19085. **EMAIL** joseph.betz@atsvillanovs.edu

BEVANS, STEPHEN
PERSONAL Born 04/14/1944, Baltimore, MD, s **DISCIPLINE** THEOLOGY **EDUCATION** Divine Word Col, BA, 67; Univ Notre Dame, PhD, 86. **CAREER** Prof, Immaculate Conception Sch Theol, Philippines, 73-81; Luzbetak Prof Mission & Culture, Cath Theol Union, 86-. **MEMBERSHIPS** AAR, ASM, CTSA. **RESEARCH** Inculturation; mission; ecclesiology. **SELECTED PUBLICATIONS** Auth, John Oman and his Doctrine of God, Cambridge Univ Press, 92; auth, Models of Contextual Theology, Orbis Books, 92; auth, Cultural Expressions of Our Faith: Church Teachings and Pastoral Responses, USCC, 93; ed, Dictionary of Mission: Theology, History, Perspectives, Orbis Books, 97; ed, Word Remembered, Word Proclaimed: Selected Papers from the SVD Centennial in North America, Steyler Verlag, 97; ed, New Directions in Mission and Evangelization, Orbis Books, Vol 1, 92, Vol 2, 94, Vol 3, 99. **CONTACT ADDRESS** 5401 S Cornell, Chicago, IL 60615. **EMAIL** sbevans@ctu.edu

BEYER, BRYAN E.
DISCIPLINE BIBLE **EDUCATION** Hebrew Union Col, 85; Denver Sem, 80; Colo St Univ, 76. **CAREER** Assoc prof of Bibl , Columbia Int Univ, 85-; asst dean of the col, Columbia Int Univ, 93-94; academic dean of the col, Columbia Int Univ, 94-. **MEMBERSHIPS** Natl Assoc of Profs of Hebrew. **RESEARCH** Bible. **SELECTED PUBLICATIONS** Coauth, Encountering the Old Testament, Baker Book House, 99; coauth, Reading in the Ancient Near East, Baker Book House, 01. **CONTACT ADDRESS** Columbia Intl Univ, PO Box 3122, Columbia, SC 29230-3122. **EMAIL** bbeyer@ciu.edu

BEZANSON, RANDALL P.
PERSONAL Born 11/17/1946, Cedar Rapids, IA, m, 1968, 2 children **DISCIPLINE** LAW **EDUCATION** Northwestern Univ, BS BA, 68; Univ Iowa, JD, 71. **CAREER** Law clerk, U.S. Court of Appeals, 71-72; law clerk, U.S. Supreme Court, 72-73; asst prof to prof and vp, Univ Iowa; prof, Wash and Less Univ, 94-96. **HONORS AND AWARDS** Fel, Open Soc Inst, 98; Nat Res Award, Sigma Delta Chi, 88; Burlington Northern Teaching Award, Univ Iowa, 87. **MEMBERSHIPS** Order of the Coif; Am Bar Asn; Omicron Delta Kappa; Iowa Bar Asn. **RESEARCH** Constitutional law; Freedom of speech; Freedom of the press; Law and technology; Administrative law. **SELECTED PUBLICATIONS** Co-ed, Reforming Libel Law, Guilford Commun Series, 92; auth, "The Right to Privacy Revisited," Calif L Rev, 92; auth, Taxes on Knowledge in America, Univ Pa Press, 94; auth, "Institutional Speech," Iowa L Rev, 95; auth, Speech Stories: How Free Can Speech Be?, NY Univ Press, 98; co-auth, "Government Speech," Iowa L Rev, 01; coauth, Taking Stock: Journalism in the Publicly Traded Newspaper Company, ISU Press, 01. **CONTACT ADDRESS** Col of Law, Univ Iowa, Melrose and Bylington, Iowa City, IA 52242. **EMAIL** randy-bezanson@uiowa.edu

BHANDARI, JAGDEEP S.
PERSONAL Born 11/09/1953, United Kingdom, s **DISCIPLINE** LAW **EDUCATION** Univ Delhi, BA, 73, MA, 75; Univ Rochester, MS, 77; SMU, PhD, 79; Duquesne, JD, 87; Georgetown, LLM, 89. **CAREER** Prof, econ, W Va Univ, 83-93; econ, Int Monetary Fund, 87-91; prof law, Fla Coastal School Law, 91- . **HONORS AND AWARDS** Best Res Awd, W Va Univ. **RESEARCH** Commercial law, International law, International economics, Bankruptcy, Antitrust, Immigration. **SELECTED PUBLICATIONS** Auth, Corporate Bankruptcy, Cambridge Univ Press, (95) ; auth, Economic Dimensions of International Law, Cambridge Univ Press, (97); auth, Analytical Methods in International Law, Kluwer, (00). **CONTACT ADDRESS** School of Law, Fla Coastal School Law, 7555 Beach Blvd, Jacksonville, FL 32216-3003. **EMAIL** jbhandari@Fcsl.edu

BIALLAS, LEONARD JOHN
PERSONAL Born 05/03/1939, Pontiac, MI, m, 1974 **DISCIPLINE** THEOLOGY, RELIGIOUS STUDIES **EDUCATION** Univ Notre Dame, AB, 61; Holy Cross Col, MA, 65; Inst Cath, Paris, STD, 70. **CAREER** Asst prof relig, Am Col Paris, 67-70; asst prof theol, Univ Notre Dame, 70-73; assoc prof, 73-80, Prof Theol & Relig Studies, Quincy Univ, 80-, Consult relig studies, Nat Endowment Humanities, 77-79; ed, Bull Coun Study Relig, 77-85. **HONORS AND AWARDS** NEH Grant, Yale Univ, 79, Univ Calif, 76; Fac Development Fel Awd, Quincy Univ (6 different years); Awd for Outstanding Teaching and Nominee for the Council For Advancement and Support of Education, Quincy Univ, 78, 85, 86; Excellence in Teaching Awd, Quincy Univ, 94; Trustees Awd for Scholarly Achievement, Quincy Univ, 98; Goodwin-Philpott Eminent Scholar in Religion, Auburn Univ, 99-00. **MEMBERSHIPS** Coun Study Relig; Am Acad Relig; Cath Theol Soc Am; Col Theol Soc (vpres, 80-82). **RESEARCH** Christology; North American Indian religions; mythology. **SELECTED PUBLICATIONS** Auth, The psychological origins of violence and revolution, in Liberation, Revolution and Freedom, Seabury, 75; America: The myth of the Hunter, in America in Theological Perspective, Seabury, 76; Myths: Gods, Heroes, and Saviors, XXIII Publ, 86; World Religions: A Story Approach, XXIII Publ, 91; Dogmatic Theology, in The New Handbook of Christian Theology, 92; author of other articles and book chapters. **CONTACT ADDRESS** Quincy Univ, 1800 College Ave, Quincy, IL 62301-2670. **EMAIL** biallas@quincy.edu

BIANCHI, EUGENE CARL
PERSONAL Born 05/05/1930, Oakland, CA **DISCIPLINE** RELIGION **EDUCATION** Gonzaga Univ, BA, 54, MA, 55; Col St Albert, Louvain, STL, 62; Columbia Univ, PhD, 66. **CAREER** Asst ed, Am Magazine, NY, 63-66; asst prof theol, Univ Santa Clara, 66-68; asst prof relig, 68-72, assoc prof relig, 72-82, prof relig, 82-, Emory Univ, 72-, pres, Soc Priests for Free Ministry, 69-71; Danforth Found Underwood fel, 72-73; distinguished vis prof, Calif State Univ, Sacramento, 75. **MEMBERSHIPS** Am Acad Relig. **RESEARCH** Spirituality of aging; religion and ecology; study of American Jesuits. **SELECTED PUBLICATIONS** Auth, John XXiii and American Protestants, Corpus, 68; Reconciliation: The function of the Church, Sheed, 69; The Religious Experience of Revolutionaries, Doubleday, 72; Aging as a Spiritual Journey, Crossroad, 82; On Growing Older, Crossroad, 85; Elder Wisdom, Crossroad, 94; coauth, From Machismo to Mutuality, Paulist, 75; ed, A Democratic Catholic Church, Crossroad, 91. **CONTACT ADDRESS** Dept of Religion, Emory Univ, 1364 Clifton Rd NE, Atlanta, GA 30322-0001. **EMAIL** releb@emory.edu

BIBZA, JAMES
PERSONAL Born 02/18/1950, Tarenton, PA, m, 5 children **DISCIPLINE** THEOLOGY **EDUCATION** C. W. Post Col, BA, 72; Gorden Cornwell Sem, MDiv, 75; Princeton Theol Sem, PhD, 85. **CAREER** Prof, Grove City Col, 77-. **HONORS AND AWARDS** ODK; Who's Who in Am Teachers, 98, 2000. **MEMBERSHIPS** Evangel Theol Soc. **RESEARCH** Biblical and theological research. **SELECTED PUBLICATIONS** Auth, chapters in Building a Christian World View, ed A. Hoffecker. **CONTACT ADDRESS** Dept Rel & Philos, Grove City Col, 100 Campus Dr, Grove City, PA 16127-2101. **EMAIL** jbibza@gcc.edu

BICA, CAMILLO C.
PERSONAL Born 01/07/1947, New York, NY, m, 1980, 2 children **DISCIPLINE** PHILOSOPHY **EDUCATION** NYork Univ, MA, 88, CUNY, PhD, 95. **CAREER** Prof, 9 yrs, School of Visual Arts; advisor, Ethics Committee, 7 yrs, Dept of Veterans Affairs. **MEMBERSHIPS** APA **RESEARCH** Ethics & war, art & social responsibility. **SELECTED PUBLICATIONS** Auth, Interpreting Just War Theory's Jus in Bello Criterion of Discrimination, in: Pub Affairs Qtly, 98; Establishing Liability in War, Pub Affairs Qtly, 97; Collateral Violence and the Doctrine of Double Effect, in: Pub Affairs Qtly, 97; Social Responsibility and the Artist, in: Art & Academe, 95; Through a Philosopher's Eyes, The Observations and Cynical Rantings of a Vietnam Survivor, in: Words, 94. **CONTACT ADDRESS** 10 Belmont Dr, Smithtown, NY 11787. **EMAIL** DrMiloB@aol.com

BICE, SCOTT H.
PERSONAL Born, CA, m, 1968 **DISCIPLINE** CONSTITUTIONAL LAW **EDUCATION** Univ Southern Calif, BS,65; JD,68. **CAREER** Robert C. Packard Prof of Law, USC; Carl Mason Franklin prof & dean, Univ Southern Calif; clerked, Honorable Earl Warren, Ch Justice US; app by, Ch Justice Calif Supreme Ct to serve on the Calif Judicial Council's Comn on the Future of the Courts. **HONORS AND AWARDS** Amer Bar Found, fel. **MEMBERSHIPS** Pres and dir, Asn Amer Law Deans; Amer Law Inst. **RESEARCH** Constitutional theory; federal jurisdiction. **SELECTED PUBLICATIONS** Auth, Standards of Judicial Review in Constitutional Law & Rationality Analysis in Constitutional Law. **CONTACT ADDRESS** School of Law, Univ of So California, Los Angeles, CA 90089-0071. **EMAIL** sbice@law.usc.edu

BIEGANOWSKI, RONALD
PERSONAL Born 05/23/1941, Milwaukee, WI **DISCIPLINE** ENGLISH, THEOLOGY **EDUCATION** St Louis Univ, AB, 65, MA, 66, PhL, 66; Jesuit Sch Theol, Berkeley, STM, 72; Fordham Univ, PhD (English), 77. **CAREER** Instr English, Marquette High Sch, Milwaukee, 66-69; lectr, Univ of San Francisco; Asst Prof English, Marquette Univ, 76-81, Dir, Honors Prog, 81-93; Dir, Alumni Ministry, 93-96; Adjunct Asst Prof of English, 97-. **HONORS AND AWARDS** NDEA, Univ of the Pacific, 68; NDEA, Univ of New Hampshire, 68; NDEA, Loyola Col, Baltimore, 68; Am Philos Soc (Frost's Reading of Bergson's Creative Evolution), 81. **MEMBERSHIPS** Mod Lang Asn; Am Lit Secion/Mod Lang Asn; Christianity and Lit; Robert Frost Soc. **RESEARCH** Robert Frost; modern American poetry; modern American fiction. **SELECTED PUBLICATIONS** Auth, "Robert Frost's New Hampshire: Realm Not Region," Literature and Belief 2 (82): 83-92; auth, "Robert Frost's Annotations to Henri Bergson's Creative Evolution," Resources for American Literary Study 13 (83): 184-93; auth, "Robert Frost's Sense of Choice in Mountain Interval," College Literature 11 (84): 258-68; auth, "James Baldwin's Vision of Otherness in 'Sonny's Blues' and Giovanni's Room," College Language Association Journal 32 (88): 69-80; auth, "The Self-Consuming Narrator in Poe's Ligeia and Usher," American Literature 60 (88): 175-87; auth, "Robert Frost's A Boy's Will and Henri Bergson's Creative Evolution," The South Carolina Review 21 (88): 9-16; rev, "Robert Frost's Emergent Design: The Truth of The Self In-between Belief and Unbelief Johannes Kjorven," in Journal of Modern Literature 15 (Fall 88): 332-3; rev, "Bergson and American Culture: The Worlds of Willa Cather and Wallace Stevens Tom Quirk," in International Studies in Philosophy 23 (91): 141-2; rev, Robert Frost's "Star in a Stone Boat: A Grammar of Belief," Edward Ingebretsen, S.J. in Theological Studies 57 (March 96): 194; rev, Robert Frost's "Road Taken," Robert F. Fleissner in The Robert Frost Review, (97): 87-8. **CONTACT ADDRESS** Dept of English, Marquette Univ, Milwaukee, WI 53201. **EMAIL** ron.bieganowski@marquette.edu

BIEN, JOSEPH J.
PERSONAL Born 05/22/1936, Cincinnati, OH, m, 1965 **DISCIPLINE** PHILOSOPHY **EDUCATION** Xavier Univ, BS & MA, 58; Univ Paris, DTC, 68. **CAREER** Lectr, Ecole des Arts et Manufacteurs, 65-68; asst prof. Univ Texas-Austin, 68-73; assoc prof & Prof, Univ Missouri-Columbia, 73- ; Dir Social Philos Course, Dubrovnik, 90- . **MEMBERSHIPS** Am Philos Asn; Soc Soc & Polit Philos; Cent States Philos Asn, SW Philos Soc. **RESEARCH** Political philosophy; post-war French thought; 19th Century philosophy. **SELECTED PUBLICATIONS** Ed, Political and Social Essays by Paul Ricoeur, Ohio Univ Press, 74; Phenomenology and the Social Sciences: A Dialogue, The Hague, 78; auth, History, Revolution, and Human Nature: Marx's Philosophical Anthropology, B R Gruner Publ Co, 84; ed, Leviathan, Klare Ltd, 86; Contemporary Social Thought, Klare Ltd, 89; Ethics and Politics, Klare Ltd, 92; Philosophical Issues and Problems, Simon & Schuster, 98. **CONTACT ADDRESS** 100 W Brandon Rd., Columbia, MO 65203. **EMAIL** philjjb@showme.missouri.edu

BIERNAT, LEONARD F.
PERSONAL Born 11/24/1946, Minneapolis, MN, m, 1981, 3 children **DISCIPLINE** LAW **EDUCATION** Manka State Univ, BS, 68; Hamline Sch Law, JD, 75; Univ St Thom, MA, 78; New York Univ, LLM, 85. **CAREER** Assoc dean, 78-84; asst prof, assoc prof, 75-90; prof, 90-, Hamline Sch Law. **RESEARCH** Family law; professional responsibility; education law. **SELECTED PUBLICATIONS** Coauth, Legal Ethics for Management and Their Counsel, Lexis Law Pub, 99; auth, West's Federal Administrative Practice: The Federal Role in Education, 99. **CONTACT ADDRESS** School of Law, Hamline Univ, 1536 Hewitt Ave, Saint Paul, MN 55104-1205. **EMAIL** lbiernat@gw.hamline.edu

BIJLEFELD, WILLEM A.
PERSONAL Born 05/08/1925, Tobelo, Indonesia, m, 1950, 4 children **DISCIPLINE** ISLAMIC STUDIES, HISTORY OF RELIGIONS **EDUCATION** Univ Groningen, BD, 46, Drs Theol, 50; Univ Utrecht, Dr Theol, 59. **CAREER** Chaplain to overseas studies, Univ Leiden, 50-55; consult, Islam in Africa Proj, Northern Nigeria, 59-64; asst prof Arabic and Islamic studies, Univ Ibadan, 64-66; assoc prof, 66-68, acad dean, 69-74, Prof Islamics, Hartford Sem Found, 68-90, Dir, Duncan Black Macdonald Ctr, 74-88, Dir, Pierre Benignus Studies Ctr, Islam in Africa Proj, Ibadan, 64-66; ed, Muslim World, 67-90 **RESEARCH** Qur'anic studies; history of the discipline of history of religions; Muslim-Christian relations, past and present. **SELECTED PUBLICATIONS** Auth, A Century of Arabic and Islamic Studies at Hartford Seminary, Muslim World, Vol 0083, 93. **CONTACT ADDRESS** D B Macdonald Ctr, Hartford Sem, 110 Sherman St, Hartford, CT 06105. **EMAIL** wablfld@sover.net

BILANIUK, PETRO BORYS T.
PERSONAL Born 08/04/1932, Zalishyky, Ukraine, m, 1960, 4 children **DISCIPLINE** THEOLOGY, RELIGION **EDUCATION** Univ Montreal, BTh, 55; Univ Munich, Dr Theol, 61; Ukrainian Free Univ, PhD (hist, philos), 72. **CAREER** Lectr relig knowledge and theol, 62-65, from asst prof to assoc prof theol and relig studies, 65-74, Prof Theol and Relig Studies, Univ St Michael's Col, Univ Toronto, 74-, Can Coun leave fel, 71-72, 78-79; vis prof Ukrainian theol, Ukrainian Free Univ, 72-, vis prof Church history, 73-; consultor, J Ecumenical Studies; mem, Nat Exec and Head Publ Comt, Shevchenko Sci Soc Can, 74-; vis prof Eastern Christian Theol, John XXIII Inst Eastern Christian Studies, 78- **HONORS AND AWARDS** Gold Commemorative Medal of St Peter and Paul from Pope Paul VI in private audience, 66; Diploma for Distinguished Achievement, Men of Achievement, Cambridge, Eng, 76; Certificate in recognization of distinguished achievements, Int Who's Who of Intellectuals, Cambridge, Eng, 76. **MEMBERSHIPS** Can Theol Soc; Theol Soc Am; Col Theol Soc; N Am Acad Ecumenists; Soc Sci Study Relig. **RESEARCH** Systematic theology; Eastern Christianity; Teilhard de Chardin. **SELECTED PUBLICATIONS** Auth, Imperial Unity and Christian Divisions, Cath Hist Rev, Vol 0079, 93; Orientalis Varietas --The Roman Church and the Eastern Churches, J Ecumenical

Stud, Vol 0033, 96; Eros and Transformation--Sexuality and Marriage--An Eastern Orthodox Perspective, Stud Rel Sci Religieuses, Vol 0023, 94; One Orthodoxy, J Ecumenical Stud, Vol 0033, 96. **CONTACT ADDRESS** Fac of Theol Univ, St. Michael's Col, Toronto, ON, Canada M5S 1J4.

BILLINGS, JOHN R.
PERSONAL m **DISCIPLINE** PHILOSOPHY **EDUCATION** Syracuse Univ, PhD, 67. **CAREER** Assoc prof; Univ Wis-SP, 66-; ordained presby clergy, McCormick Theol Sem, 84; McCormick Theol Sem; Fac Senate, 74-76, 87-88, 95-; ch, Stud Conduct Hearing bd, 91-92; ch, NCent Accreditation Study, 86-89; Salary Subcomt Fac Aff, 85-86; L & S Adv Comt, 83-87. **SELECTED PUBLICATIONS** Auth, The Empty Universe, Int Logic Rev, 77. **CONTACT ADDRESS** Dept of Religious Studies, Univ of Wisconsin, Stevens Point, Stevens Point, WI 54481.

BILODEAU, LORRAINE
PERSONAL Born 12/09/1935, Holyoke, MA **DISCIPLINE** ELEMENTARY EDUCATION; RELIGIOUS EDUCATION; LIBRARY SCIENCE AND INFORMATION **EDUCATION** Catholic Teachers Col; BS, 69; Fairfield Univ, MA, 75; Dominican Univ, MLS, 88. **CAREER** Tchr, Rhode Island Catholic Sch; DRE dir, St. Leo the Great; librn, dir, Anna Maria Col. **MEMBERSHIPS** ALA; NEACRL; CLA; NECLA. **RESEARCH** Geneology and icons. **CONTACT ADDRESS** Mondor-Eagen Library, Anna Maria Col, Paxton, MA 01612-1198. **EMAIL** lbilodeau@annamaria.edu

BILSKER, RICHARD L.
PERSONAL Born 04/02/1965, New Brunswick, NJ, m, 1995 **DISCIPLINE** PHILOSOPHY **EDUCATION** Florida Atlantic Univ, BA, 89, PhD 94. **CAREER** Tchg asst, 90-93, instr, 93-94, Fl State Univ Dept of Philos; instr, Univ Fl Div of Continuing Educ, 92-94; adj prof Community Col RI Dept Social Sci, 94-95; adj prof, Prince George's Community Col Dept of Philos, 96-97; asst prof philos, Charles County Community Col, 95- ; vis asst prof of philos, St. Mary's Col of Maryland, 97-. **HONORS AND AWARDS** Outstanding Service and Contribution Awd, 97. **MEMBERSHIPS** APA; N Am Div Schopenhauer Soc; Asn for Advan of Community Col Tchg; E Sociol Soc; Asn for Humanist Soc. **RESEARCH** History of modern philosophy; nineteenth-century philosophy; Schopenhauer. **SELECTED PUBLICATIONS** Auth, Freud and Schopenhauer: Consciousness, the Unconscious, and the Drive Towards Death, Idealistic Stud, v 27; auth, rev of Peter Worsley's Knowledges: Culture, Counterculture, Subculture, in Humanity and Soc, v 22; auth, Crossing Disciplines: A Philosopher Teaches Sociology, Tchg Soc in Two-Year Col, 99. **CONTACT ADDRESS** Dept of Fine Arts and Humanities, Charles County Comm Col, 8730 Mitchell Rd, PO Box 910, La Plata, MD 20646-0910. **EMAIL** richardb@charles.cc.md.us

BILSON, BETH
DISCIPLINE LAW **EDUCATION** Univ Saskatchewan, BA, 67, MA, 70, LLB, 77; Univ London, PhD, 82. **CAREER** Prof, 79-. **RESEARCH** Labour law; administrative law; Canadian legal history. **SELECTED PUBLICATIONS** Auth, The Canadian Law of Nuisance, Butterworths, 91; Workplace Equity: A Seat at the Policy Picnic, Good Jobs Bad Jobs No Jobs, 95. **CONTACT ADDRESS** Col of Law, Univ of Saskatchewan, 15 Campus Dr, Saskatoon, SK, Canada S7N 5A6. **EMAIL** Bilson@law.usask.ca

BINAU, BRAD A.
DISCIPLINE PASTORAL THEOLOGY **EDUCATION** Capital Univ, BA, 77; Trinity Lutheran Sem, MDiv, 81; Princeton Theol Sem, ThM, 82, PhD, 87. **CAREER** Assoc staff, Trinity Couns Svc, Princeton, 85-86; asst prof, 93-96; dir, Ministry in Context Prog, 93-; assoc prof, Trinity Lutheran Sem, 96-. **HONORS AND AWARDS** Bk rev ed, Pastoral Psychol. **MEMBERSHIPS** Soc Pastoral Theol; Amer Acad Rel. **SELECTED PUBLICATIONS** Rev(s), Review of The Child's Son, by Donald Capps, Pastoral Psychol, 96; Review of The Helper's Journey, by Dale Larson, Jour Pastoral Care, 95; auth, Trusting our Way to Blessedness, Selected Sermons, 91-92. **CONTACT ADDRESS** Ministry Dept, Trinity Lutheran Sem, 2199 E Main St, Columbus, OH 43209-2334. **EMAIL** bbinau@trinity.capital.edu

BINDER, DAVID A.
PERSONAL Born Los Angeles, CA, m, 1957, 3 children **DISCIPLINE** LAW **EDUCATION** UCLA, AB, 56; Stanford Univ, LLB, 59. **CAREER** Lawyer, Private Practice, 60-70; Prof, UCLA, 70-. **HONORS AND AWARDS** Luckman Dist Teaching Awd, UCLA; Rutter Awd for Excellence in Teaching, UCLA; Teacher of the Year, UCLA, 72. **RESEARCH** Deposition Practice; Nature and Structure of Legal Arguments. **SELECTED PUBLICATIONS** Co-auth, Lawyers as Counselors: A Client Centered Approach, West Pub Co, 91; co-auth, Trial Advocacy: Inferences, Arguments and Trial Techniques, West Pub, 96; co-auth, Deposition Questioning Strategy and Technique, West Group, 01. **CONTACT ADDRESS** Law Dept, Univ of California, Los Angeles, Box 951476, Los Angeles, CA 90095-1476. **EMAIL** binder@law.ucla.edu

BINDER, LEONARD
PERSONAL Born 08/20/1927, Boston, MA, m, 1947, 2 children **DISCIPLINE** POLITICAL SCIENCE **EDUCATION** Harvard Col, BA, 52; Harvard Univ, PhD, 56. **CAREER** Asst prof, UCLA, 56-61; assoc prof to prof and dept chair, Univ Chicago, 61-85; prof and dept chair, UCLA, 85-. **HONORS AND AWARDS** John Harvard Fel; Detur Prize; Woodrow Wilson Fel; Ford Found Fel; Rockefeller Fel; Soc Sci Res Coun Fel; Am Res Ctr in Cairo Fel; Adv Study in the Beh Sci Fel; Albert Einstein Vis Prof Hebrew Univ; Distinguished Vis Prof Am Univ Cairo. **MEMBERSHIPS** Am Polit Sci Asn; Middle E Studies Asn. **RESEARCH** Comparative Politics of the Middle East; International relations of the Middle East; Islamic Political Theory; Political Philosophy. **SELECTED PUBLICATIONS** Ed, Ethnic Conflict and International Politics in the Middle East, Univ Press Fla, 99. **CONTACT ADDRESS** Dept Polit Sci, Univ of California, Los Angeles, 4289 Bunche, Box 951472, Los Angeles, CA 90095-1472.

BING, ROBERT
PERSONAL Born Tampa, FL, m, 1 child **DISCIPLINE** CRIMINOLOGY AND CRIMINAL JUSTICE **EDUCATION** Fla State Univ, PhD. **CAREER** Assoc prof & dir, Criminol & Criminal Justice prog; serves as, Interim Grad Adv; bd, several criminal justice agencies within Dallas-Fort Worth metroplex. **MEMBERSHIPS** Acad Criminal Justice Serv; Am Soc Criminol. **RESEARCH** Corrections; plea-bargaining; sentencing; criminal justice educ. **SELECTED PUBLICATIONS** Auth, Recreational Programs in Prison, in McShane and Wiliams' Encycl of Prisons, Garland Press, 95; coauth, Race, Delinquency and Discrimination: A Look at the Literature for Unanswered Questions Challenge, 6 2, 95; auth, The Experiences of African-Americans and Whites in Criminal Justice Education: Do Race and Gender Differences Exist, J Criminal Justice Educ, 6 1, 95; Race and Homicide: The Routine Treatment of Blacks, J Commun and Minority Issues, 2 1, 95; coauth, Race and Crime. **CONTACT ADDRESS** Dept of Criminology and Criminal Justice, Univ of Texas, Arlington, 301 Univ Hall, PO Box 19595, Arlington, TX 76019-0595. **EMAIL** rbing@uta.edu

BIRCH, ADOLPHO A., JR.
DISCIPLINE LAW **EDUCATION** Lincoln Univ, 1950-52; Howard Univ, BA, 1956, JD, 1956. **CAREER** Private law practice, 58-69; Meharry Medical Coll, adjunct prof of legal medicine, 59-69; Davidson County, asst public defender, 64-66, asst district attorney general, 66-69; Davidson County Part 1, Court of General Sessions, judge, 69-78; Fisk Univ, lecturer in law, 70-72; Tennessee State Univ, lecturer in law, 70-72; Criminal Court of Davidson County, Div III, judge, 78-87; Tennessee Court of Criminal Appeals, assoc judge, 87-93; Supreme Court of Tennessee, justice, chief justice, currently; Nashville School of Law, instructor in law, currently. **CONTACT ADDRESS** Chief Justice, Tennessee Supreme Court, 304 Supreme Court Bldg, Nashville, TN 37219.

BIRCH, BRUCE CHARLES
PERSONAL Born 12/03/1941, Wichita, KS, m, 1990, 4 children **DISCIPLINE** OLD TESTAMENT, ANCIENT NEAR EASTERN STUDIES **EDUCATION** Southwestern Col, BA, 62; Southern Methodist Univ, BD, 65; Yale Univ, MA, 67, MPhil, 68, PhD, 70. **CAREER** Asst prof relig, Iowa Wesleyan Col, 68-70; asst prof Bible & relig, 70-71, Erskine Col; assoc prof Old Testament, 71-77, prof Old Testament, 77-, dean, 98-, Wesley Theol Sem; Chmn Nat Intersem Coun, 64-67; mem bd dir, Washington Int Col, 71-74; dir & chmn bd, Int Prog Human Resources Develop, 75-; res fel, Asn Theol Schs, 77-78; vis prof, Sch Theol, summer 82, Claremont. **MEMBERSHIPS** Soc Bibl Lit. **RESEARCH** Deuteronomic history; Biblical theology; Biblical ethics. **SELECTED PUBLICATIONS** Auth, Let Justice Roll Down: Old Testament, Ethics, and Christian Life, Westminster, 91; auth, Hosea, Joel, Amos: Westminster Bible Companion, Westminster, 97; auth, 1 and 2 Samuel: The New Interpreter's Bible, v.2, Abingdon, 98. **CONTACT ADDRESS** Wesley Theol Sem, 4500 Mass Ave N W, Washington, DC 20016-5632. **EMAIL** bbirch@wesleysem.edu

BIRD, FREDERICK
DISCIPLINE RELIGION **EDUCATION** Harvard Col, BA, 61; Harvard Divinity school, 64; Grad Theol Union, PhD, 73. **CAREER** Asst Prof, Concordia Univ Montreal, 71-75; Assoc Prof, Concordia Univ, 75-89; Prof, Concordia Univ, 89-. **HONORS AND AWARDS** Rockerfeller Fel, 61-62; ch, concordia univ consultative comm on a proposed univ code of ethics, 93-94. **RESEARCH** Comparative ethics, business ethics, sociology of religion. **SELECTED PUBLICATIONS** Auth, "Good Conversations: a Practical Role for Ethics in Business," in Good Conversations: a Practical A Practical Role for Ethics in Business, ed George Aragon, Boston Col, (91), 13-96; auth, Frederick Bird and Jeffery Gandz, Good Management: Business Ethics in Action, Scarborough: Prenctice Hall, 5-8, (91), 1-460; auth, "Moral Universals," the J of Rel and Culture, vol 3, (93), 75-92; auth, "Religion" with Frances Westley, in Introd to Soc, ed J Teevan, Prentic Hall, (94), chap 10; co auth, "Power and Ethical Aciton," in Managing Strrategic Action, Cynthia hardy, London: Sage, (94), Chap 16; coauth, Religion and ethnic Identity: a Comparative study of Lturgical Ritual in Synagoues, Waterloo, Ontario: Wilfrid Laurier Press, 95; auth, "The Muted Conscience: Moral Silence and the Practice of Ethics on Business," Quorom Books, Greenwood Press, 7-9, (96), 1-268; coauth, "The Ethics of Empowerment," J of Business ethics, vol 15, (96), 383-392; auth, "Moral Universals as cultural Realities," in Ethical Univ in International Business, ed N Brady, Berlin: Verlag, (96), 97-149; auth, "Empowerment and Justice," in The Ethics of Empowerment, ed(s) John Quinn ans Peter Davies, England: MacMillan Press, 99. **CONTACT ADDRESS** Dept of Rel, Concordia Univ, Montreal, 1455 de Maisonneuve W, Montreal, QC, Canada H3G 1M8. **EMAIL** birdfb@vax2.concordia.ca

BISHOP, MICHAEL
PERSONAL Born 09/09/1961, Washington, DC **DISCIPLINE** PHILOSOPHY **EDUCATION** UCSD, PhD, 90. **CAREER** Asst Prof, 90-96, Assoc Prof, 96-, Iowa State Univ. **HONORS AND AWARDS** Who's Who Among Amer Tchr, NEH Summer Seminar, Methodological Debates in 19th c Physics. **MEMBERSHIPS** APA, PSA, SPP. **RESEARCH** Philosophy of science, Epistemology. **SELECTED PUBLICATIONS** Auth, Why the Semantic Incommensurability Thesis is Self-Defeating. Philosophical Studies, 91; The Possibility of Conceptual Clarity in Philosophy, American Philosophical Quarterly, 92; Theory-Ladenness of Perception Arguments, eds, M Forbes & D Hull, PSA, 92; Conceptual Change in Science: The Newton-Hooke Controversy, Scientific Methods: Conceptual and Historical Problems, Krieger Press, 94; auth, "Why Thought Experiments are Not Arguments," Philosophy of Science, 99; auth, "In Praise of Epistemic Irresponsibility: How Lazy and Ignorant Can you Be?" Synthese, 00. **CONTACT ADDRESS** Iowa State Univ of Science and Tech, 402 Catt Hall, Ames, IA 50011. **EMAIL** mikebish@iastate.edu

BITTNER, THOMAS
PERSONAL Born 11/09/1952, Pasadena, CA, s **DISCIPLINE** PHILOSOPHY **EDUCATION** Univ California-Berkeley, BA, 86; MA, 89, PhD, 94, Univ Washington. **CAREER** Lectr, Pacific Lutheran Univ, 95-96; Visiting Lectr, Univ Nevada, Las Vegas, 96-97; Lectr, visiting Asst Prof, Univ Maryland Baltimore County, 97-. **MEMBERSHIPS** Amer Phil Assoc **RESEARCH** Philosophy of the mind **SELECTED PUBLICATIONS** Auth, Probability and Infinite Sets, Cogito, 93; Consciousness and the Act of Will, Philosophical Studies, 96. **CONTACT ADDRESS** Dept of Philo, Univ of Maryland, Baltimore County, 1000 Hilltop Circle, Baltimore, MD 21250. **EMAIL** bittner@research.umbc.edu

BIX, BRIAN
PERSONAL Born 08/01/1962, Minneapolis, MN, s **DISCIPLINE** PHILOSOPHY; LAW **EDUCATION** Wash Univ, BA, 83; Harvard Univ, JD, 86; Balliol Col, Oxford Univ, DPhil, 91. **CAREER** Lect, jurisprudence and legal reasoning, Kings Col, Univ of London, 91-93; assoc prof law, 95-98, vis prof, George Wash Law Sch, 99, Georgetown Law Sch, 00; Prof Law, Quinnipiac Law Sch, 98-. **RESEARCH** Jurisprudence; family law; contract law; philos of language; Wittgenstein. **SELECTED PUBLICATIONS** Auth, Law, Language, and Legal Determinacy, Oxford Univ Press, 93; Physician Assisted Suicide and the American Constitution, 58 Modern Law Review 404, 95; Questions in Legal Interpretation, in Law and Interpretation 137, A. Marmor, ed, Oxford Univ Press, 95; Conceptual Questions and Jurisprudence, 1 Legal Theory 415, 95; Jules Coleman, Legal Postivism, and Legal Authority, Quinnipiac Law Review 16 (96): 241; Natural Law Theory, in A Companion to the Philosophy of Law and Legal Theory 223-240, D. Patterson, ed, Blackwell Press, 96; Jurisprudence: Theory and Context, Westview Press, 96, 2nd ed, Carolina Acad Press, 99; Consent, Sado-Masochism and the English Common Law, 17 Quinnipiac Law Review 157, 97; Dealing with Incommensurability for Dessert and Desert: Comments on Chapman and Katz, 146 Univ PA Law Review 1651, 98; H. L. A. Hart and the Hermeneutic Turn in Legal Theory, 52 SMU Law Review, 98; On Description and Legal Reasoning, in Rules and Reasoning, L. Meyer, ed, Hart Pub, 98; Bargaining in the Shadow of Love: Premarital Agreements and How We Think About Marriage, 40 William and Mary Law Review, 98; ed, Analyzing Law: New Essays in Legal Theory, Oxford Univ Press, 98; Patrolling the Boundaries: Inclusive Legal Postivism and the Nature of Jurisprudential Debate, 12 Canadian J of Law and Jurisprudence, 99. **CONTACT ADDRESS** Law Sch, Quinnipiac Col, 275 Mt Carmel Ave, Hamden, CT 06518. **EMAIL** brian.bix@quinnipac.edu

BLACHOWICZ, JAMES
DISCIPLINE PHILOSOPHY **EDUCATION** Loyola Univ, BS, 66; Northwestern Univ, MA, 70 PhD, 70. **CAREER** Philos, Loyola Univ. **HONORS AND AWARDS** Prof, Loyola Univ, 71-. **RESEARCH** Philosophy of science; history of metaphysics; Hegel's Logic; contemporary epistemology; theories of discovery and inquiry. **SELECTED PUBLICATIONS** Auth, Of Two Minds: The Nature of Inquiry, SUNY Press, 98; essays in, Philos Sci, J Philos, Int Stud in the Philos Sci, Synthese, Idealistic Stud, Erkenntnis, Southern J Philos. **CONTACT ADDRESS** Dept of Philosophy, Loyola Univ, Chicago, 820 N. Michigan Ave., Chicago, IL 60611.

BLACK, C. CLIFTON
PERSONAL Born 05/05/1955, High point, NC, m, 1978, 1 child **DISCIPLINE** BIBLICAL STUDIES **EDUCATION** Wake Forest Univ, BA, 77; Univ Bristol, MA, 80; Emory Univ, MDiv, 81; Duke Univ, PhD, 86. **CAREER** W. D. Davis Instr in Relig, Duke Univ, 84-85; asst prof, Univ Rochester, 86-89; from asst prof to prof, Southern Methodist Univ, 89-99; Otto A. Piper Prof of Biblical Theol, Princeton Theol Sem, 99-. **HONORS AND AWARDS** Carswell Scholar, Wake Forest Univ, 73-77; Phi Beta Kappa, Wake Forest Univ, 76; Kearns Fel, Duke Univ, 81-84; Dempster Fel, Duke Univ, 84-86; Mellon Fac Fel, Univ Rochester, 88-89; Karp Teaching Awd, Univ Rochester, 89; Otto A. Piper Professorship in Biblical Theol, Princeton Theol Sem, 99-. **MEMBERSHIPS** Soc of Biblical Lit, Catholic Biblical Asn of Am, Soc for New Testament Studies. **RESEARCH** Testament Studies, New Testament and Christian Origins: The Gospels, Greco-Roman Rhetoric, Patristic Exegesis. **SELECTED PUBLICATIONS** Auth, Mark: Images of an Apostolic Interpreter, Univ SC Press, 94; co-ed, Exploring the Gospel of John, Westminster John Knox, 96; auth, 1 John, 2 John, 3 John: The New Interpreter's Bible, 98. **CONTACT ADDRESS** Princeton Theol Sem, PO Box 821, Princeton, NJ 08542-0803. **EMAIL** clifton.black@ptsem.edu

BLACK, KENNETH, JR.
PERSONAL Born 01/30/1925, Norfolk, VA, m, 1948, 2 children **DISCIPLINE** INSURANCE, BUSINESS ADMINISTRATION **EDUCATION** Univ NC, BA, 48, MS, 51; Univ Pa, PhD, 53. **CAREER** Instr, Univ Pa, 52-53; Lecturer, Swiss Insurance Training Ctr, 67; Ch, Dept of Insurance, Ga State Univ, 53-69; Dean, Col of Bus Admin, Ga State Univ, 59-92; Holder, CV Starr Ch of Int Insurance, Ga State Univ, 84-92; Regents' Prof Emeritus of Insurance & Dean Emeritus, Ga State Univ. **HONORS AND AWARDS** Phi Beta Kappa, Univ NC, 46; Order of the Golden Fleece, Univ NC, 48; Beta Gamma Sigma, Ga State Univ, 61; Kenneth Black Jr Special Lib Collection in Risk & Insurance, Old Dominion Univ, 5/78; Solomon S Huebner Gold Medal, The Am Col, 85; Kenneth Black Jr Ch of Insurance, Ga State Univ, 88; 1st Ann Distinguished Svc Awd, Life Insurers Conf, 90; Kenneth Black Jr Wing dedicated in Gregg Hall Conf Ctr, Am Col, 6/92; Dr Kenneth Black Jr Distinguished Service Awd est by Int Insurance Soc, Inc, 92; Laureate, Insurance Hall of Fame, Int Insurance Soc, Inc, Tokyo, Japan, 93; pres commission on rr retirement, v ch, 71-72. **MEMBERSHIPS** Southern Risk & Insurance Asn; Am Risk & Insurance Asn; Soc of Chartered Property & Casualty Underwriters; Alpha Kappa Psi; Soc of Financial Service Professionals; Risk & Insurance Management Soc, Inc. **RESEARCH** Int Risk & Insurance/Life Insurance. **SELECTED PUBLICATIONS** Co-auth, Human Behavior and Life Insurance, rev ed, Ga State Univ Bus Press, 93; co-auth, Life and Health Insurance, 13th ed, Prentice-Hall, Inc, 99; auth, The Social Value of Life Insurance, Insurance Soc of ROC, Proceedings, Taipei, Taiwan, 1/95; co-auth, Property and Liability Insurance, 4th ed, Prentice-Hall, Inc, 96; auth, The Future of the Life Insurance Business, J of the Am Soc of CLU & ChFC, vol L, no 1, 1/96. **CONTACT ADDRESS** Dept of Risk Mgt & Insurance, Georgia State Univ, 35 Broad Street, Atlanta, GA 30303-4036. **EMAIL** k.black@gsu.edu

BLACK, NAOMI
PERSONAL Born 02/13/1935, Newcastle-upon-Tyne, England **DISCIPLINE** POLITICAL SCIENCE, HISTORY **EDUCATION** Cornell Univ, AB, 55; Yale Univ, MA, 57, PhD, 64. **CAREER** Instr, polit sci, Brown Univ, 63-64; instr, govt, Ind Univ, 64-65; asst prof, 65-71, assoc prof, 71-84, PROF POLITICAL SCIENCE, YORK UNIV, 85-. **SELECTED PUBLICATIONS** Auth, Social Feminism, 89; coauth, Canadian Women: A History, 88, 2nd ed, 96. **CONTACT ADDRESS** Dept of Polit Sci, York Univ, 4700 Keele St, North York, ON, Canada M3J 1P3.

BLACKBURN, SIMON
PERSONAL Born 07/12/1944, United Kingdom, m, 1968, 2 children **DISCIPLINE** PHILOSOPHY **EDUCATION** Cambridge Univ, BA, 65, PhD, 70. **CAREER** Fel, tutor, Pembroke Col, Oxford, 70-90; Edna J. Koury distinguished prof, philos, Univ North Carolina, Chapel Hill, 90-01; Prof of Philos, Univ of Cambridge, 01. **HONORS AND AWARDS** Hon LLD, Univ Sunderland. **MEMBERSHIPS** APA; Mind Assoc. **RESEARCH** Philosophy. **SELECTED PUBLICATIONS** Auth, Spreading the Word, Oxford, 84; ed, Essays in Quasi-Realism, Oxford, 93; ed, The Oxford Dictionary of Philosophy, Oxford, 94; auth, Practical Tortoise Raising, Mind, 95; auth, Ruling Passions, Oxford, 98; autor, Think, Oxford, 99; auth, Being Good, 00. **CONTACT ADDRESS** Dept of Philosophy, Univ of No Carolina, Chapel Hill, 3152 Caldwell Hall, Chapel Hill, NC 27599. **EMAIL** simon_blackburn@unc.edu

BLACKBURN, TERENCE L.
PERSONAL Born Pittsburgh, PA, m, 2 children **DISCIPLINE** LAW **EDUCATION** Duquesne Univ, BA; Columbia Univ, JD. **CAREER** From adj prof to full prof, Seton Hall Univ, 81-00; prof, dean, Detroit Col of Law, Mich State Univ, 00-. **HONORS AND AWARDS** Charles Evans Hughes fel, Columbia Univ. **RESEARCH** Business associations, corporate finance, business planning, international business. **CONTACT ADDRESS** Detroit Col of Law, Michigan State Univ, 364 Law Col Bldg, East Lansing, MI 48824-1300. **EMAIL** blackb14@msu.edu

BLACKMAN, RODNEY J.
PERSONAL Born 06/29/1936, Chicago, IL, s **DISCIPLINE** LAW, PHILOSOPHY **EDUCATION** Univ Mich, BA, 57; Harvard Univ JD, 60; Univ Chicago, MA, 66; Univ Wisconsin, PhD, 76. **CAREER** Prof, DePaul Col of Law, 1971-. **MEMBERSHIPS** ABA Illinois and California Bars. **RESEARCH** Legal, Philosophy, Constitutions, Law, History, Religion **SELECTED PUBLICATIONS** Auth, Procedural Natural Law labook, Carolina Academic Press. **CONTACT ADDRESS** College of Law, DePaul Univ, 25 E Jackson Blvd, Chicago, IL 60604-2289. **EMAIL** rblackma@wppost.edu

BLACKSTONE, THOMAS L.
PERSONAL Born 08/03/1962, Bangor, ME, m, 1986, 3 children **DISCIPLINE** NEW TESTAMENT **EDUCATION** Albrigh Col, BA, 84; Princeton Theological Sem, M Div, 87; Emory Univ, PhD, 95. **CAREER** Adj faculty, 96- , Bongor Theolog Seminary. **MEMBERSHIPS** Soc of Biblical Lit **RESEARCH** Interpretation; Intertextuality; New Testament models for homiletics **CONTACT ADDRESS** PO Box 992, Presque Isle, ME 04769. **EMAIL** tlbphd@yahoo.com

BLACKWELL, RICHARD JOSEPH
PERSONAL Born 07/31/1929, Cleveland, OH, m, 1954 **DISCIPLINE** PHILOSOPHY **EDUCATION** John Carroll Univ AB 50; St Louis Univ, MA, 52, PhD, 54. **CAREER** Instr philos, John Carroll Univ, 54-61; assoc prof, 61-66, Prof Philos, St Louis Univ, 66-. **MEMBERSHIPS** Am Cath Philos Asn; Philos Sci Asn. **RESEARCH** Philosophy of Aristotle; modern philosophy; philosophy of science. **SELECTED PUBLICATIONS** Co-transl, St Thomas Aquinas, Commentary on Aristotle's Physics, Yale Univ, 63; transl, Christian Wolff, Preliminary Discourse on Philosophy in General, Bobbs, 63; auth, Descartes' laws of motion, Isis, summer 66; Discovery in the Physica Sciences, Univ Notre Dame, 69; Adaptation theory of science, Int Philos Quart, 9/73; The inductivist model of science, Mod Schoolman, 74; Scientific discovery and laws of logic, New Scholasticism, 76; A structuralist account of scientific theories, Int Philos Quart, 76. **CONTACT ADDRESS** Dept of Philos, Saint Louis Univ, 221 N Grand Blvd, Saint Louis, MO 63103-2097.

BLAIR, GEORGE ALFRED
PERSONAL Born 01/13/1934, Watertown, MA, m, 1963, 2 children **DISCIPLINE** PHILOSOPHY **EDUCATION** Boston Col, AB, 58, MA, 59; Weston Col, PhL, 59: Fordham Univ, PhD(philos), 64. **CAREER** From instr to asst prof philos, Xavier Univ, 63-65; from asst prof to assoc prof, 65-75, Prof Philos, Thomas More Col, 75-, Chmn Dept, 68-, Fulbright exchange lectr, Argentina, 64. **MEMBERSHIPS** Am Cath Philos Asn. **RESEARCH** Aristotle; ethics; philosophy of science. **SELECTED PUBLICATIONS** Auth, Aristotle on Entelecheia - A Reply to Graham,Daniel, Am J of Philol, Vol 0114, 93. **CONTACT ADDRESS** Dept of Philos, Thomas More Col, 333 Thomas More Pky, Covington, KY 41017-3495.

BLAISING, CRAIG A.
DISCIPLINE SYSTEMATIC THEOLOGY **EDUCATION** B.S., University of Texas, Austin; Th.M., Dallas Theological Seminary; Th.D., Dallas Theological Seminary; Ph.D., University of Aberdeen, Scotland **CAREER** Act dept ch, Dallas Theol Sem; act assoc dean-. **SELECTED PUBLICATIONS** Auth, Progressive Dispensationalism. **CONTACT ADDRESS** Sch Theol, So Baptist Theol Sem, 2825 Lexington Rd, Louisville, KY 40280. **EMAIL** cblaising@sbts.edu

BLAKE, DEBORAH
DISCIPLINE RELIGIOUS STUDIES, CHRISTIAN ETHICS, HEALTHCARE ETHICS **EDUCATION** Univ Calif, Santa Barbara, BA, 74; Franciscan Sch of Theol, MA, 81; Grad Theol Un, PhD, 89. **CAREER** Assoc prof Relig Stud, Regis Col, 88-. **MEMBERSHIPS** Catholic Theol Soc of Am; Colo Health Care Ethics Comt Network; Soc of Christian Ethics; Soc of Health and Human Values. **RESEARCH** Cultural diversity and health care ethics; environmental issues in the context of culture. **SELECTED PUBLICATIONS** Auth, bk rev of Genetics, Creation and Creationism, by Lloyd Bailey, in The Catholic World, 237, 94; Revolution, Revision, or Reversal: Genetics-Ethics Curriculum, Sci and Educ, 3, 94; Voices, Values and Healthcare Reform in Colorado,Voices (Rocky Mountain Ctr for Healthcare Ethics), 1(1), 94; 'I Don't Speak Principles Only': The Language of Ethics Committees and the Language of Communities, Healthcare Ethics Comt Forum 7(5), 95; Toward a Sustainable Ethic: Virtue and the Environment, in And God Saw it was Good: Catholic Theology and the Environment, Drew Christiansen, S.J. and Walt Grazerm eds, US Catholic Conf, 96; coauth, Safe Sex or Love Lost, in Christian Perspectives on Sexuality and Gender, Adrian Thatcher and Elizabeth Stuart, eds, Gracewing and WB Eerdmans Publ Co, 96. **CONTACT ADDRESS** Dept of Relig Stud, Regis Univ, 3333 Regis Blvd, Denver, CO 80221. **EMAIL** ddblake@regis.edu

BLAKESLEY, CHRISTOPHER L.
PERSONAL Born 02/28/1945, Torrance, CA, m, 1968, 3 children **DISCIPLINE** CRIMINAL LAW, INTERNATIONAL LAW, FAMILY LAW, COMPARATIVE LAW **EDUCATION** Univ Utah, BA, 69; Tufts Univ, 70; Fletcher Sch Law & Dipl, MA, 70; Univ Utah, JD, 73; Columbia Univ, LLM, 76, JSD, 85. **CAREER** Prof, McGeorge Sch Law, Univ Pacific; US Dept State, Off Legal Adviser; PROF & CH, LAW, PAUL M HERBERT LAW CENTRE, LA STATE UNIV. **MEMBERSHIPS** Am Law Inst; Utah Bar Asn; Wash DC Bar Asn; Am Jour Compar Law; Asn Int de Droit Penal; Revue Int de Droit Penal; Am Bar Asn; Am Soc Int Law **RESEARCH** Comparative law; International law; Family law; Foreign law; Comparative criminal law & procedure. **SELECTED PUBLICATIONS** Terrorism, Drugs, International Law and the Protection of Human Liberty, "Innovations in International Law" series, Princeton Univ; Louisiana (and Comparative) Family Law, Lexis Law Publ, 97; The International Legal system: Documentary Supplement, 5th Ed., 99; The International Legal System, 5th ed, Blakesley, Firmage, Scott & Williams, 99. **CONTACT ADDRESS** Paul M Herbert Law Center, Louisiana State Univ and A&M Col, Baton Rouge, LA 70803. **EMAIL** cblake@slu.edu

BLANCHETTE, OLIVA
PERSONAL Born 05/06/1929, Berlin, NH, m, 1975, 2 children **DISCIPLINE** PHILOSOPHY **EDUCATION** Boston Col, AB, 53; St Albert de Louvain, PhL, 54; Boston Col, MA, 58; Weston Col, STL, 61; Univ Laval, PhD, 66. **CAREER** Prof, Boston Col HS, 54-57; from instr to prof, 64-, dean, 68-73, Boston Col. **HONORS AND AWARDS** Pres, MSA; Who's Who in Am, 85, 89, 91, 95, 96, 00, in East, 85, in Society, 88, Authors, 83; Men of Ach, 78, 88; Dict Intl Bio, 81, 89, 00; Intl Who's Who Auth, 79, 86, Intell 88, Am Cath 79. **MEMBERSHIPS** MSA; HAS; ISM; SPT. **RESEARCH** Metaphysics; philosophy of religion; ethics. **SELECTED PUBLICATIONS** Auth, For a Fundamental Social Ethic: A Philosophy of Social Change, Philo Lib (NY), 73; transl of Action (1893) by Maurice Blondel (Notre Dame: Univ Notre Dame Press, 84); auth, Perfection of the Universe According to Aquinas: A Teleological Cosmology, Penn State Univ Press (Coll Pk), 92; auth, Philosophy of Being: A Reconstructive Essay in Metaphysics, forthcoming; auth, "The Wisdom of God in Isaiah," Am Eccle Rev (61): 413-23; auth, "Does the CHEIROGRAPHON of Col 2, 14 Represent Christ Himself?" Cath Bib Quart (61): 306-12; auth, "Saint Cyril of Alexandria's Idea of the Redemption," Sci Eccle (64): 455-80;auth, "The Order of Generation and Time in the Philosophy of Saint Thomas Aquinas," Laval Theol Philo (66): 45-72. **CONTACT ADDRESS** Dept of Philos, Boston Col, Chestnut Hill, 140 Commonwealth Ave, Chestnut Hill, MA 02467-3800. **EMAIL** oliva.blanchette@bc.edu

BLANCHETTE, PATRICIA
DISCIPLINE PHILOSOPHY **EDUCATION** Univ, Calif, BA, 83; Stanford Univ, PhD, 90. **CAREER** Assoc prof. **RESEARCH** Philosophy of logic; philosophy of language; philosophy of mathematics. **SELECTED PUBLICATIONS** Auth, Frege's Reduction, Hist Philos Logic, 94; Frege and Hilbert on Consistency, J Philos, 96; Realism in the Philosophy of Mathematics, Routledge, 98. **CONTACT ADDRESS** Philosophy Dept, Univ of Notre Dame, 336/7 O'Shaughnessy, Notre Dame, IN 46556. **EMAIL** blanchette.1@nd.edu

BLAND, KALMAN PERRY
PERSONAL Born 03/04/1942, Chicago, IL, m, 1964, 2 children **DISCIPLINE** JEWISH PHILOSOPHY **EDUCATION** Columbia Univ, BS, 64; Jewish Theol Sem Am, BRE, 64, MHL, 67; Brandeis Univ, PhD(Medieval Jewish-Islamic philos), 72. **CAREER** Asst prof Judaic relig, Ind Univ, Bloomington, 72-73; asst prof relig and Jewish studies, 73-76, Assoc Prof Relig and Jewish Studies, Duke Univ, 76-, Chmn Dept of Relig, 81-. **MEMBERSHIPS** Am Acad Relig; Asn Jewish Studies; Int Asn Neo-Platonic Studies; Am Oriental Soc. **RESEARCH** Medieval Jewish philosophy; Jewish mysticism; Medieval Jewish-Christian polemics. **SELECTED PUBLICATIONS** Auth, Rabbinic method and literary Criticism, literary interpretations of Biblical narratives, Abingdon, 74; Neo-Platonic and Gnostic themes in Rabbi Moses Cordovero's Doctrine of Evil, Bull Inst Jewish Studies, 75; The Epistle on Conjunction by Ibn Rushd with the commentory of Moses Narboni, KTAV/Jewish Theol Sem, 78 & 81; Moses and the Law According to Maimonides, In: Mystics Philosohers and Politicans: Essays in Honor of Alexander Altman, Duke Univ, 79 & 82; thirty-five entries, In: Abingdon Dict of Living Religion, Abingdon Press, 81. **CONTACT ADDRESS** Dept of Relig, Duke Univ, PO Box 4735, Durham, NC 27706.

BLANKEMEYER, KENNETH JOSEPH
PERSONAL Born 08/07/1946, Cincinnati, OH, m, 1976 **DISCIPLINE** PHILOSOPHY, LOGIC **EDUCATION** Xavier Univ, BS, 68; Southern IL Univ, MA, 71, PhD, 74. **CAREER** Instr to Prof Philos, Tulsa Com Col, 76-. **MEMBERSHIPS** Am Philos Asn; Southwestern Philos Soc. **RESEARCH** Ethics; religion. **SELECTED PUBLICATIONS** Auth, Can reliance on quasi-dependent meaning save Stevenson's ethics, J Thought, 1/77. **CONTACT ADDRESS** Liberal Arts Division, Tulsa Comm Col, 909 S Boston Ave, Tulsa, OK 74119-2011. **EMAIL** kblankem@tulsa.cc.ok.us

BLASIUS, MARK
DISCIPLINE POLITICAL SCIENCE **EDUCATION** New York Univ, BA; MA; Princeton Univ, MA; PhD. **CAREER** Asst Prof to Prof, CUNY, 90-. **RESEARCH** Political theory and philosophy; Lesbian/gay. **CONTACT ADDRESS** Dept Polit Sci, Graduate Sch and Univ Ctr, CUNY, 365 5th Ave, New York, NY 10016.

BLATTNER, WILLIAM
DISCIPLINE PHILOSOPHY **EDUCATION** Univ Pittsburgh, PhD, 89. **CAREER** Prof. **RESEARCH** Modern German philosophy; American pragmatism. **SELECTED PUBLICATIONS** Auth, The Concept of Death in Being and Time, Man and World, 94; Is Heidegger a Kantian Idealist?, Inquiry, 94; Existence and Self-Understanding in Being and Time, Philos Phenomenological Res, 96. **CONTACT ADDRESS** Dept of Philosophy, Georgetown Univ, 37th and O St, Washington, DC 20057.

BLECKER, ROBERT A.
PERSONAL Born 11/17/1956, Philadelphia, PA, m, 1982, 2 children **DISCIPLINE** ECONOMICS **EDUCATION** Stanford Univ, PhD 87, MA 83; Yale univ, BA 78. **CAREER** Am Univ, prof econ 98, assoc prof 92-98, asst prof 85-92. **HONORS AND AWARDS** Fulbright Schl; NSF Fell. **MEMBERSHIPS** AEA; Union of Radical Political Econ **RESEARCH** Intl Econ; macroeconomics; polit econ. **SELECTED PUBLICATIONS** Fundamentals of U S Foreign Trade Policy, co auth Stephen D Cohen, Joel R Paul, Boulder, Westview, 96; U S Trade Policy and Global Growth: New Directions in the Intl Economy, ed Armonk, NY, ME Sharpe Inc, 96; Kaleckian Macro Models for Open Economies, in: Foundations of Intl Econ, ed by John Y Harvey Johan Deprez, London, Routledge, forthcoming; Policy Implications of the International Saving-Investment Correlation, in: The Macroeconomics of Finance, Saving and Investment, ed by Robert Pollin, Ann Arbor, Univ MI Press, 97; auth, "Taming Global Finance: A Better Architecture for Growth and Equity," Economic Policy Inst (99). **CONTACT ADDRESS** Dept of Economics, American Univ, 4400 Massachusetts Ave, Washington, DC 20016. **EMAIL** blecker@american.edu

BLEICH, J. DAVID
DISCIPLINE LAW **EDUCATION** Brooklyn Col, BA, 60; Columbia Univ, MA, 68; NYork Univ, PhD, 74. **CAREER** Instructor, Rutgers Univ, 62-63; Instructor, Hunter Col, 62-69; Instructor, Bar Ilan Univ, 70; Instructor to Asst Prof, Stern Col for Women, 65-78; Adj Prof, Univ Haifa, 74-75; Assoc Prof, Yeshiva Univ, 78-79; Visiting Assoc Prof to Assoc Prof, Benjamin N. Cardozo School of Law, 79-86; Visiting Gruss Prof, Univ Penn, 91-93; Director of Inst for Adv Study of Jurisprudence and Family Law, Rabbi Isaac Elchanan Theol Sem 87-; Prof, Rabbi Isaac Elchanan Theol Sem, 69-; Prof, Yeshiva Univ, 81-. **HONORS AND AWARDS** Woodrow Wilson Nat Fel, 60-61; NY Regents Col Teaching Fel, 60-61; Nat Foundation for Jewish Culture, 61-62. **SELECTED PUBLICATIONS** Auth, "Modern Psychiatric Treatment: Halakhic Perspectives," in Medicine Ethics and Jewish Law, Holte, Denmark, 99; auth, "Prenatal Diagnosis and preimplantation Genetics: Jewish Viewpoints," in Medicine Ethics and Jewish Law, Holte, Denmark, 99; auth, "Rabbinic Confidentiality," Spring 99; auth, "Can There Be Marriage Without Marriage?", winter, 99; auth, Bioethical Dilemmas: A Jewish Perspective, Ktav Pub House, Hoboken, NJ, 98; auth, Be-Netivot ha-Halakhah Vol II, Yeshiva Univ Press, Hoboken, NJ, 98; auth, "Surrogate Motherhood," Jerusalem City of Law and Justice, Jerusalem, 98; auth, "Insurance-Related Halakhic Questions," Summer 97; auth, "Medical and Life Insurance: A Halakhic Mandate," Spring 97; auth, "The Ketubah," Fall 96; auth, "Conjoined Twins," Summer 96; auth, "Treatment of the Terminally Ill," Spring 96; auth, Be-Netivot ha-Halakhah Vol I, Yeshiva Univ Press, Hoboken, NJ, 96; auth, Contemporary Halakhic Problems Vol IV, Ktav Pub House, Hoboken, NJ, 95. **CONTACT ADDRESS** School of Law, Yeshiva Univ, 55 5th Ave, New York, NY 10003-4301.

BLENKINSOPP, JOSEPH
PERSONAL Born 04/03/1927, Durham, England, m, 2 children **DISCIPLINE** BIBLICAL STUDIES **EDUCATION** London Univ, BA, 48; Oxford Univ, PhD, 67. **CAREER** Prof, bibl stud, then John A O'Brien Prof Bibl Stud, Univ Notre Dame, 72- . **HONORS AND AWARDS** NEH res grant, 82-83; rector of Ecumenical Inst, Israel; pres, Catholic Bibl Asn, 89-90. **MEMBERSHIPS** Soc of Bibl Lit; Am Acad of Relig; Soc of Old Testament Stud (UK); Asn of Jewish Stud. **RESEARCH** Biblical literature and theology; history of Israel. **SELECTED PUBLICATIONS** Auth, Ezra-Nehemiah: A Commentary, Westminster, 88; auth, A Jewish Sect of the Persian Period, Catholic Bibl Q, 90; auth, The Judge of All the Earth: Theodicy in the Midrash on Genesis 18:22-33, J of Jewish Stud, 90; auth, The Social Context of the Outsider Woman in Proverbs 1-9, Biblica, 91; auth, The Pentateuch: An Introduction to the First Five Books of the Bible, Doubleday, 92; auth, Ecclesiastes 3.1-15: Another Interpretation, J for the Stud of the Old Testament, 95; auth, Deuteronomy and the Politics of Post-Mortem Existence, Vetus Testamentum, 95; auth, Sage, Priest, Prophet: Religious and Intelectual Leadership in Ancient Israel, Westminster, 95; auth, Wisdom and Law in the Old Testament: The Ordering of Life in Israel and Early Judaism, Oxford, 2d ed, 95; coauth, The Family in Ancient Israel, Westminster, 96; auth, A History of Prophecy in Israel, rev ed, Westminster, 96; auth, Th Judean Priesthood during the Neo-Babylonian and Early Achemenid Period: A Hypothesis, Cath Bibl Q, forthcoming; auth, An Assessment of the Alleged Pre-Exilic Date of the Priestly Material in the Pentateuch, in Zeitschrift fur die Alttestamentliche Wissenschaft, forthcoming. **CONTACT ADDRESS** Dept of Theology, Univ of Notre Dame, Notre Dame, IN 46556.

BLESSING, KAMILA
PERSONAL Born 12/12/1948, Pittsburgh, PA, s **DISCIPLINE** RELIGION **EDUCATION** Carnegie-Mellon Univ, BS, 71; Univ Pitts, MSIS, 76, PhD, 77; Pitts Theol Sem, MA, 84; Duke Univ, PhD, 96. **CAREER** Campus Min, Carnegie-Mellon Univ, 78-83; Pastoral Min, Church of Ascension, 83-85; Rector, St Andrews Church, 85-86; Vicar, St Peters Church, 86-89; Int Rector, St. Pauls Church, 89-90; Priest Assoc, St Philips Church, 90-93; Priest in charge, Christ Church, 93-98; priest in charge, St Johns, 93-98; Adj instr, Hermeneutics, Grace Sem, 85; res asst, 92-93, tchg asst, 94-96, Divinity School, Duke Univ; vp for Congregational Ministries, 00-. **HONORS AND AWARDS** Am Soc Infor Sci Doctoral Forum Awd, 77. **MEMBERSHIPS** Soc Bibl Lit; Am Acad Relig; Asn Jewish Studies. **RESEARCH** Techniques of interpretation; Paul and the Covenant; Paul's conceptuality of Covenant and the ways in which it relates to Gentiles and Jews; Communities of understanding and the way they define truth, scripture, and covenant as reflected in the New Testament text; Christian-Jewish relations; Impact of authoritative religious texts on the roles of women. **SELECTED PUBLICATIONS** Auth, "Drinking in the Spirit," Sharing, March, 90; auth, "Positively, in His Image," Sharing, June-July, 90; auth, "Mericful Laughing," Sharing, Oct, 90; auth, The Lost Coin: Parables of Women, Work, and Wisdom, Sheffield, ed, Mary Ann Beavis, "Gospel of Thomas," 97; auth, "Desolate Jerusalem and Barren Matriarch: Two Distinct Figures in the Pseudepigrapha," Journal for the Study of the Pseudepigrapha 18, Oct, (98): 47-69; auth, It was a Miracle - Stories of Ordinary People and Extraordinary Healing, Minneapolis: Augsburg Fortress, 99; Rev, of Second Chance: A Life after Death by Marvin Barrett, in Episcopal Life, 28, Oct, 99; auth, "Enveloping Warmth," Sharing, March, (00): 15-16; auth, "Murray Bowen's Family Systems Theory as Bible Hermeneutic Using the Family of the Prodigal, Luke 15:11-32," Journal of Psychology and Christianity, Spring, (00): 38-46; auth, "John," in InterVarsity Press Women's Bible Commentary, in press, due out 2001. **CONTACT ADDRESS** Congregational Ministries, Christian Board of Publication, 7821 Delmar Blvd, PO Box 179, Saint Louis, MO 63166. **EMAIL** kblessing@cbp21.com

BLEVINS, JAMES LOWELL
PERSONAL Born 08/25/1936, m, 1961, 3 children **DISCIPLINE** RELIGION **EDUCATION** Duke Univ, AB, 58; Eastern Baptist, MDV, 61; Southeastern Bap Sem, THN, 62; Southern Bap, Louisville, PhD, 65. **CAREER** Southern Bap Sem, prof new test, 76-; Mars Hill Col, prof Rel, 68-76. **MEMBERSHIPS** SNTS; SBL **RESEARCH** New Testament **SELECTED PUBLICATIONS** Revelation as Drama, 80; Greek Hymn Book; Revelation; 83; Messianic Secret, 1901-1965. **CONTACT ADDRESS** Dept New Testament, So Baptist Theol Sem, 2825 Lexington Rd, Louisville, KY 40241.

BLEVINS, KENT
PERSONAL Born 11/01/1954, Columbia, SC, m, 1975, 3 children **DISCIPLINE** THEOLOGY **EDUCATION** Wake Forest Univ, BA, 75; Southern Baptist Theol Sem, MDiv, 78, PhD, 82. **CAREER** Assoc prof relig, Gardner-Webb Univ, 98-; assoc prof ethics practical theol, 94-98, asst prof systematic practical theol, 91-94, Int Baptist Theol Sem, Prague, Czech Rep; lectr, Portuguese Baptist Theol Sem, Portugal, 84-91. **RESEARCH** Ethics. **CONTACT ADDRESS** Dept of Theology, Gardner-Webb Univ, PO Box 7252, Boiling Springs, NC 28017. **EMAIL** kblevins@gardner-webb.edu

BLIZEK, WILLIAM L.
PERSONAL Born Chicago, IL **DISCIPLINE** ETHICS, SOCIAL PHILOSOPHY, THE PHILOSOPHY OF RELIGION **EDUCATION** Southern Ill Univ, BA, 65, MA, 66; Univ Mo, Columbia, PhD, 70. **CAREER** Prof, Univ Nebr, Omaha, 70-; ed, Hum and Pub Life; coed, J of Relig and Film. **SELECTED PUBLICATIONS** Published articles in such journals as Brit J of Aesthet, Philos Exchange, Southern J of Philos, Metaphilosophy, Nebr Med J, Urban Rev, Criminal Justice and Ethics, and J of Commun Develop soc. **CONTACT ADDRESS** Univ of Nebraska, Omaha, Omaha, NE 68182.

BLOCK, JOHN MARTIN
PERSONAL Born 01/23/1940, Chicago Heights, IL, m, 1963, 2 children **DISCIPLINE** LAW **EDUCATION** Furman Univ, BA, 63; Univ Wis-Madison, MA, 65, PhD, 69. **CAREER** Asst prof, 68-75, Assoc Prof, Furman Univ, 75-. **MEMBERSHIPS** AHA; Conf Group Cent Europ Hist; AAUP. **RESEARCH** Nineteenth and twentieth century European diplomatic history, British press history, modern Germany. **SELECTED PUBLICATIONS** Auth, Limiting The Use Of Heightened Scrutiny To Land-Use Exactions, NY Univ Law Rev, Vol 0071, 96. **CONTACT ADDRESS** Dept of Hist, Furman Univ, 3300 Poinsett Hwy, Greenville, SC 29613-0002. **EMAIL** john.block@furman.edu

BLOCK, NED
DISCIPLINE PHILOSOPHY **EDUCATION** M.I.T., SB, 64; St John's Col, Oxford Univ, DPhil, 66; Harvard Univ, PhD, 71. **CAREER** Asst prof, M.I.T., 71-77, assoc prof, 77-83; chemn, 89-95, prof, 83-96; prof, New York Univ, 96-. **HONORS AND AWARDS** U.S. Nat Comt for the Int Union of the Hist and Philos of Sci, Travel Grant, 79; Sloan Found Fel, Univ Calif, Berkeley, 80-81; Guggenheim Fel, 84-85; Nat Sci Found Grant, 85-86, 88-89; Am Coun of Learned Socs Fel, 88-89. **SELECTED PUBLICATIONS** Auth, "Is Experiencing Just Representing?," Philos and Phenomenological Res (Sept 98); coauth, "Holism," "Conceptual Role Semantics," and "Computational Models of the Mind," in The Routledge Encyclopedia of Philosophy (98); auth, "Functional Role Semantics," in MIT Encyclopedia of Cognitive Sci (99); coauth, "Conceptual Analysis, Dualism and the Explanatory Gap," Philos Rev (Jan 99); auth, "Ridiculing Social Constructivism about Phenomenal Consciousness," in Behavioral and Brain Scis (99); auth, "Jack and Jill have Shifted Spectra," Behavioral and Brain Scis, 22, 6 (99); auth, "Sexism, Racism, Ageism and the Nature of Consciousness," in The Philosophy of Sydney Shoemaker, Philosophical Topics, 26 (1 & 2), ed by Richard Moran, Jennifer Whiting, and Alan Sidelle (forthcoming); auth, "Is the Content of Experience the Same as the Content of Thought?," Cognition (forthcoming). **CONTACT ADDRESS** Dept Philos, New York Univ, 100 Washington Sq E, New York, NY 10003-6688.

BLODGETT, BARBARA
DISCIPLINE RELIGION **EDUCATION** Yale Univ, PhD, 00. **CAREER** Dir, Supervised Ministries. **MEMBERSHIPS** Am Acad Relig; Soc Christian Ethics; Asn Practical & Professional Ethics; Feminist Approaches Bioethics. **RESEARCH** Feminist theological ethics. **CONTACT ADDRESS** Yale Univ, 409 Prospect St, New Haven, CT 06511. **EMAIL** barbara.blodgett@yale.edu

BLOESCH, DONALD G.
PERSONAL Born 05/03/1928, Bremen, IN, m, 1962 **DISCIPLINE** THEOLOGY **EDUCATION** Elmhurst Col, BA, 50; Chicago Theological Seminary, BD, 53; Univ of Chicago, PhD, 56; Oxford Univ, post-doctoral studies, 56-67; Basel Univ, post-doctoral studies, 63-64; Tubingen Univ, post-doctoral studies, 63-64. **CAREER** From prof theology to prof emeritus, Univ Dubuque Theological Seminary, 57-. **HONORS AND AWARDS** Alumni Merit Awd, Elmhurst Col, 79; Doane Col, Dr Div, 83. **MEMBERSHIPS** Am Theological Soc; Karl Barth Soc. **RESEARCH** Theology; spirituality. **SELECTED PUBLICATIONS** Auth, Essentials of Evangelical Theology, Harper & row, 78; auth, Freedom for Obedience, Harper & Row, 87; A Theology of Word & Spirit, InterVarsity Press, 92; Holy Scripture, InterVarsity Press, 94; God the Almighty, InterVarsity Press, 95; Jesus Christ: Savior & Lord, InterVarsity Press, 97. **CONTACT ADDRESS** 2185 St John Dr, Dubuque, IA 52002.

BLOM, JOOST
DISCIPLINE LAW **EDUCATION** Univ British Columbia, BA, 67; LLB, 70; Oxford Univ, BCL, 72. **CAREER** Asst prof, 72-76; assoc prof, 76-81; prof, 81-; assoc dean, 82-85; vis prof, Osgoode Hall Law Sch, 81; lectr, Univ Victoria, 79-81. **RESEARCH** Contracts; torts; conflict of law; intellectual property; comparative law. **SELECTED PUBLICATIONS** Auth, pubs about contracts, torts, and conflict of laws and taxation. **CONTACT ADDRESS** Fac of Law, Univ of British Columbia, 1822 East Mall, Vancouver, BC, Canada V6T 1Z1. **EMAIL** blom@law.ubc.ca

BLOMBERG, CRAIG L.
PERSONAL Born 08/03/1955, Rock Island, IL, m, 2 children **DISCIPLINE** RELIGION **EDUCATION** Augustana Col, BA, 77; Trinity Evangel Divinity Sch, MA, 79; Univ Aberdeen, PhD, 82. **CAREER** Asst prof relig, Palm Beach Atlantic Col, 82-85; sr res fel, Tyndale House, Cambridge Univ, 85-86; from asst prof to assoc prof to prof, Denver Sem, 86-. **HONORS AND AWARDS** Paul Harris Rotary Fel. **MEMBERSHIPS** Evangel Theol Soc; Inst Bibl Res; Soc Bibl Lit; Studiorum Novi Testamenti Societas. **RESEARCH** New Testament; Greek. **SELECTED PUBLICATIONS** Coauth, The Image of God in Humanity: A Biblical-Psychological Perspective, Themelios, 93; auth, To What Extent is John Historically Reliable?, Perspective on John: Method and Interpretation in the Fourth Gospel, 93; coauth, Introduction to Biblical Interpretation, 93; auth, The Implications of Globalization for Biblical Understanding, The Globalization of Bibl Educ, 93; auth, Your Faith Has Made You Whole: The Evangelical Liberation Theology of Jesus, Jesus of Nazareth, Lord and Christ, 94; auth, the Parables of Jesus: Current Trends in Needs and Research, Studying the Historical Jesus: Evaluation of the State of Current Research, 94; auth, Dream Job, Jour Case Tchg, 93; auth, Historical Criticism of the New Testament, Found Bibl Interpretation, 94; auth, The Historical Reliability of the New Testament, Reasonable Faith, 94; auth, The Seventy-Four Scholars: Who Does the Jesus Seminar Really Speak For?, Christian Res Jour, 94; auth, Critical Issues in New Testament Studies for Evangelicals Today, Path-

way into Holy Scripture, 94; auth, Where Do We Start Studying Jesus?, Jesus Under Fire, 95; auth, 1 Corinthians, 94; auth, Interpreting the Synoptic Gospels for Preaching, Faith & Mission, 94; auth, The Kingdom of God and Evangelical Theological Education, Didaskalia, 95; auth, The Globalization of Biblical Hermeneutics, Evangel Hermeneutics, 95; auth, Poetic Fiction, Subversive Speech, and Proportional Analogy in the Parables, Horizons Bibl Theol, 96; coauth, How Wide the Divide? A Mormon and Evangelical in Conversation, 97; auth, Jesus and the Gospels: An Introduction and Survey, 97; auth, When God's Word Comes to Me, What Happens Next?, Decision, Jan, 98; auth, Neither Poverty Nor Riches, 99. **CONTACT ADDRESS** Dept of Religion, Denver Conservative Baptist Sem, PO Box 100000, Denver, CO 80250-0100. **EMAIL** craig@densem.edu

BLOOM, ALFRED
PERSONAL Born 11/09/1926, Philadelphia, PA, m, 1951, 2 children **DISCIPLINE** RELIGION **EDUCATION** Eastern Baptist Sem, AB & ThB, 51; Andover-Newton Theol Sch, BD & STM, 53; Harvard Univ, PhD, 63. **CAREER** Assoc prof relig, Univ Ore, 61-70; Prof Relig, Univ Hawaii, Manoa, 80-. **MEMBERSHIPS** Assn Asian Stud; Soc Sci Stud Rel; Amer Acad Rel. **RESEARCH** Old Testament, Japanese Buddhism. **SELECTED PUBLICATIONS** Auth, Shinran's Gospel of Pure Grace, Univ Ariz, 65; Life of Shinran Shonin, EJ Brill, 68; Tannisho: Resource for Modern Living, 81. **CONTACT ADDRESS** Dept of Rel, Univ of Hawaii, Manoa, Honolulu, HI 96822.

BLOOM, IRENE
PERSONAL Born 04/03/1939, New York, NY, m, 1963, 1 child **DISCIPLINE** PHILOSPHY **EDUCATION** Swarthmore Col, BA, 60; Columbia Univ, MA, 72; MPhil, 74; PhD, 76. **CAREER** From Asst Prof to Prof, Barnard Col, 89-. **MEMBERSHIPS** Asn for Asian Studies, Am Acad of Relig. **RESEARCH** Chinese philosophy and religion. **SELECTED PUBLICATIONS** Co-ed, Approaches to the Asian Classics, Columbia Univ Pr, 90; auth, Knowledge Painfully Acquired, Columbia Univ Pr, 2nd Ed, 95; co-ed, Eastern Canons: Approaches to the Asian Classics, Columbia Univ Pr, 95; co-ed, Religious Diversity and Human Rights, Columbia Univ Pr, 96; co-ed, Meeting of Minds: Intellectual and Religious Thought, Columbia Univ Pr, 97; co-ed, Sources of Chinese Tradition, vol 1, Columbia Univ Pr, 99. **CONTACT ADDRESS** Dept Philos, Barnard Col, New York, NY 10027. **EMAIL** ibloom@barnard.edu

BLOOM, JOHN A.
PERSONAL Born 05/25/1952, WI, m, 1977, 1 child **DISCIPLINE** PHYSICS, BIBLICAL STUDIES **EDUCATION** Grinnell Col, BA, 74; Cornell Univ, MS, 77, PhD, 80; Biblical Theol Sem, MA, 83, MDiv, 83; Dropsie Col, MA, 86, PhD, 92. **CAREER** Postdoctoral res assoc, Cornell Univ, 81-82; fel, Interdisciplinary Bibl Res Inst, Hatfield Penn, 88- ; lectr physics, Ursinus Col, 84-89, 92; consult, computer software and hardware, 86- ; asst prof, 93-95, assoc prof, physics, 95- , Biola Univ. **HONORS AND AWARDS** Grinnell Col Honors Scholar, 70-74; Chem Sr Honors Awd, 74; Honors scholar, 80-83; Honors prog, Bibl Theol Sem, 82-83; Honors scholar, Dropsie Col, 83-86; Elise Bohstedt Scholar, 86-91; John Templeton Found, Sci and Relig Course Prog, 97; Provost Awd for Excellence in Bibl Integration, Biola Univ, 98. **MEMBERSHIPS** Am Assoc Physics Tchrs; Am Soc for Engg Educ; Am Sci Affil; Biophysical Soc; Evangel Theol Soc; Sigma Xi; Soc of Bibl Lit. **RESEARCH** Cross cultural comparative study of creation accounts and of prophetic material; exegetical/historical problems in Israelite prehistory and history through the First Temple period; membrane biology; evolution; ancient technologies and science (medicine and mathematics); ancient document preservation via computer technology; use of computer image enhancement techniques in the study of ancient cuneiform and papyrus documents. **SELECTED PUBLICATIONS** Auth, Hosea's Adulterous Wife: A Portrayal of Israel, in Newman, ed, The Evidence of Prophecy: Fulfilled Prediction as a Testimony to the Truth of Christianity, Interdisciplinary Biblical Research Inst, 90; auth, Truth Via Prophecy, and, Why Isn't the Evidence Clearer, in Montgomery, ed, Evidence for Faith: Deciding the God Question, Word, 91; auth, Ancient Near Eastern Temple Assemblies: A Survey and Prolegomena, Annenberg Research Inst, 92 (PhD thesis); auth, On Human Origins : A Survey, Christian Scholar's Review, 97. **CONTACT ADDRESS** Physical Science Dept., Biola Univ, 13800 Biola Ave., La Mirada, CA 90639. **EMAIL** john@drjbloom.com

BLOOM, ROBERT M.
PERSONAL Born 03/17/1946, Brookline, MA, m, 1971, 2 children **DISCIPLINE** LEGAL STUDIES **EDUCATION** Boston Col Law Sch, Juris Doctor. **CAREER** Prof, Boston Col Law Sch, 94-. **MEMBERSHIPS** Am Bar Asn. **RESEARCH** Criminal justice. **SELECTED PUBLICATIONS** Coauth, Criminal Procedure, Little, Brown (2nd ed, 96, 3rd ed, 2000); coauth, Constitutional Criminal Procedure, Little Brown (92); auth, "Automobiles and the Fourth Amendment," in Criminal Defense Technique, ed. Matthew Bender (97); auth, "Suppression of Illegally Obtained Evidence: Pretext Searches," in Criminal Defense Technique, ed. Matthew Bender (97); coauth, "Federal Rules of Civil Procedure. Rule 3- Commencement of Action," in Moore's Federal Practice, Vol 1, 3rd ed, ed. Matthew Bender (97); auth, "Federal Rules of Civil Procedure. Rule 6- Time," in Moore's Federal Practice, Vol 1, 3rd ed, ed. Matthew Bender (97); auth, "Federal Rules of Civil Procedure. Rule 81- Applicability in General," in Moore's Federal Practice, Vol 14, 3rd ed, ed. Matthew bender (97); auth, Informants, Greenwood Pub Group (2001); auth, Searches, Seizures, and Warrants: A Reference Guide to the United States Constitution, Greenwood Pub Group (2002). **CONTACT ADDRESS** Sch of Law, Boston Col, Newton Ctr, 885 Centre St, Newton, MA 02459-1148. **EMAIL** Bloom@bc.edu

BLOSSER, PHILIP
PERSONAL Born 09/14/1950, Chengdu, China, m, 1972, 4 children **DISCIPLINE** PHILOSOPHY **EDUCATION** Sophia Univ, BA, 76; Westminster Theol Sem, MAR, 79; Villanova Univ, MA, 80, Duquesne Univ, PhD, 85. **CAREER** Instr, Duquesne Univ, 82-83; asst prof to prof, Lenoir-Rhyne Col, 84-; vis prof, Harlaxton Col, 99. **HONORS AND AWARDS** NEH Inst, Purdue Univ, 86; Raymond Morris Bost Distinguished Prof Awd, Lenoir Rhyne Col, 90; Teaching Sabbatical, Harlaxton Col, England, 99. **MEMBERSHIPS** Am Philos Assoc; Am Cath Philos Assoc, Soc for Phenomenology and Existential Philos; Max Scheler Gesellschaft. **RESEARCH** Philosophy of Religion, moral philosophy, phenomenology and theory of values, Max Scheler, Japanese and Asian philosophy and religion. **SELECTED PUBLICATIONS** Auth, Japanese and Western Phenomenology, 93; auth, Scheler's Critique of Kant's Ethics, 95; auth, Of Friendship, 97; Scheler's Ethics, 97; The Encyclopedia of Phenomenology, 97. **CONTACT ADDRESS** Dept Relig and Philos, Lenoir-Rhyne Col, 743 6th St NE, Hickory, NC 28601-3904.

BLOWERS, LAVERNE P.
PERSONAL Born 05/16/1940, Rochester, NY, m, 1967, 2 children **DISCIPLINE** THEOLOGY **EDUCATION** Seattle Pacific Univ, BA, 62; Asbury Theolog Sem, Mdiv, 67; Fuller Theolog Sem, ThM, 71; Trinity Evangelical Divinity Sch, Dmiss, 89. **CAREER** Prof, dean, Faculdade de Teologia da lgreja Metodista Lirre, 72-80; asst prof, dir, Seattle Pacific Univ, 80-82; asst prof, dir, Roberts Wesleyan Col, 82-86; assoc prof, chemn, Bethel Col, 86-. **HONORS AND AWARDS** Missionary educator; Who's Who in Relig; Who's Who in the Midwest; Fac Stud Grant, Seattle Pacific, Roberts Wesleyan, Bethel Col. **MEMBERSHIPS** AAR; Am Society Missiology; Wesleyan Theolog Society; Evangelical Missiological Society. **RESEARCH** Theology and history of mission; systematic theology. **CONTACT ADDRESS** 1001 W McKinley Ave, Mishawaka, IN 46545. **EMAIL** blowerl1@bethel-in.edu

BLUM, JOHN D.
PERSONAL Born 12/12/1948, Buffalo, NY, m, 1981, 2 children **DISCIPLINE** LAW **EDUCATION** Camsius Col, BA, 70; Notre Dame Law Sch, JD, 73; Harvard Univ, MHS, 74. **CAREER** Res Atty, Boston Univ Health Policy Ctr, 74-82; assoc prof, Penn State Univ Dept Health Policy Admin, 82-86; prof, dir, Loyala Univ Chicago Inst for Health Law, 86-. **HONORS AND AWARDS** Governance Found Fel, Modern Healthcare; U.S./Canada Fulbright Scholar; Malaysia/U.S. Fulbright Scholar. **MEMBERSHIPS** Am Health Lawyers Asn; Am Soc of Law Medicine and Ethics; Am Public Health Assn. **RESEARCH** Health policy and law. **SELECTED PUBLICATIONS** Auth, Evaluation of Medical Staff Using Fiscal Factors: Economic Credentialing, Jour of Health and Hospital Law Vol 26 No 3, 93; auth, Ontario Health Care: A Model To Be Emulated or Avoided?, National Forum, 93; auth, Universality, Quality & Economics: Finding a Balance in Ontario and British Colombia, Am Jour of Law and Med, Vol 20 No 1&2, 94; auth, Economic Credentialing Moves From the Hospital to Managed Care, Jour of Health Care Finance, 95; auth, The Evolution of Physician Credentialing into Managed Care Selective Contracting, Am Jour of Law and Med, Vol 22, No 2&3, 96; auth Legal Assessment: When Credentialing Becomes Selective Contracting, Cost & Quality Jour, Vol 3 No 3, 97; coauth, Credentialing Mandates and the Telemedical Doctor, New Medicine, Vol 1 No 4, 97; auth, North American Perspectives on Balancing Regional Government Health Mandates in Nova Scotia and Illinois with Federal Economic Imperatives, Dalhousie Law Jour, Vol 20 No 2, 97; auth, Safeguarding the Interests of People with AIDS in Managed Care Settings, Albany Law Review, Vol 61 No 3, 98; auth, "Telemedicine Poses New Challenges for the Law," Health Law in Canada, vol. 20 no. 1, Aug 99; auth, "Credentialing the Cyber Physician," Health Care Law monthly, March 00. **CONTACT ADDRESS** Inst for Health Law, Loyola Univ, Chicago, 1 E Pearson St, Chicago, IL 60611. **EMAIL** jblum@luc.edu

BLUM, KAREN M.
DISCIPLINE LAW **EDUCATION** Wells Col, BA, 74; Suffolk, JD, 76; Harvard Univ, LLM. **CAREER** Instr, 74-76; asst prof, 76-78; assoc prof, 78-83; prof, 83-. **RESEARCH** Affirmative action; civil procedure; civil rights; complex litigation; federal courts; police misconduct litigation. **SELECTED PUBLICATIONS** Auth, Section 1983 Hot Topics, Boston, 98; Justices Revisit Issue of Imposing Municipal Liability Under Section 1983 for Single Decision of Final Policymaker, 96; Local Government Liability Under Section 1983, 96; Qualified Immunity: Interlocutory Appeals, 96. **CONTACT ADDRESS** Law School, Suffolk Univ, Beacon Hill, Boston, MA 02114. **EMAIL** kblum@acad.suffolk.edu

BLUM, LAWRENCE A.
PERSONAL Born 04/16/1943, Baltimore, MD, m, 1975, 3 children **DISCIPLINE** PHILOSOPHY; EDUCATION **EDUCATION** Princeton Univ, BA, 64; Harvard Univ, PhD, 74. **CAREER** Prof, Univ of Mass at Boston, 73- ; vis assoc prof, Univ of Calif, 84; vis prof, Stanford School of Educ, 90; vis prof, Columbia Univ, 90. **HONORS AND AWARDS** Chancellor's Distinguished Scho Awd, Univ of Mass, 81, 94; NEH fel for Col Tchrs, 86-87; Fel in Harvard Prog in Ethics and the Professions, 92-93. **MEMBERSHIPS** Am Philos Asn; Asn for Moral Educ; Philos of Educ Soc; Am Soc for Polit & Legal Philos. **RESEARCH** Moral philosophy; Multicultural education; Race studies; Moral education. **SELECTED PUBLICATIONS** Auth, Friendship, Altruism, and Morality, 80; Moral Perception and Particularity, 94; Community and Virtue, How Should One Live?, ed R. Crisp, 96; Altruism and Egoism, Dictionnaire de philosophie morale, 96; Community, Philos of Educ: An Encyclopedia, ed J.J. Chambliss, 96; Race, Racism, and Pan-African Identity: Thoughts on K. Anthony Appiah's In My Father's House, New Polit Sci, double issue 38/39, 97; Multicultural Education as Values Education, Harvard Proj on Schooling and Children Working Paper, 97; Altruism and Benevolence, Encyclopedic Dictionary of Bus Ethics, eds P. Werhane and R.E. Freeman, 97; Schindler's Motives, Psychoculture: Rev of Psychology and Cult Studies, vol 1, no 2, 97; Recognition, Value, and Equality: A Critique of Charles Taylor's and Nancy Fraser's Accounts of Multiculturalism, Theorizing Multiculturalism: A Guide to the Current Debate, ed C. Willett, 98; Racial Integration Revisited, Norms and Values: Essays In Honor of Virginia Held, eds J. Graf Habera and M. Halfon, 98; coauth, A Truer Liberty: Simone Weil and Marxism, 89. **CONTACT ADDRESS** Dept of Philosophy, Univ of Massachusetts, Boston, 100 Morrissey Blvd., Boston, MA 02125. **EMAIL** lawrence.blum@umb.edu

BLUMBERG, GRACE GANZ
PERSONAL Born 02/16/1940, New York, NY, m, 1959, 1 child **DISCIPLINE** LAW **EDUCATION** Univ Colo, BA, 60; State Univ NYork, Buffalo, JD, 71; Harvard Univ, Llm, 74. **CAREER** Law clerk, NY State Appelate Div, 71-72; teaching fel law, Harvard Law Sch, 72-74; asst prof, Sch Law, State Univ NY Buffalo, 74-77, assoc prof, 77-79, prof, 79-81; Prof, Law Sch, Univ Calif, Los Angeles, 81-. **HONORS AND AWARDS** Distinguished Teaching Awd, UCLA, 99; Rutter Awd for Excellence in Teaching, 89. **MEMBERSHIPS** Asn Am Law Sch. **RESEARCH** Social legislation; family law; women and the law. **SELECTED PUBLICATIONS** Auth, The Relationship Between Property Division and Spousal and Child Support, a 71-page chapter in Valuation and Distribution of Marital Property, a three-volume treatise, Matthew Bender, 90; auth, Community Property in California 2d ed., a casebook, Little, Brown 93; auth, Women and the Law: Taking Stock After Twenty-Five Years, 6 UCLA Women's Law J 279, 96; auth, Child Support Chapter, American Law and Institute, Principles of The Law of Family Dissolution: Analysis and Recommendations, Tentative Draft No. 3, 98, Part II, approved by the membership in May, 98, Council Draft No. 4, 97, Vol II, Preliminary Draft No. 7, 97; co-auth, Domestic Partners Chapter, American Law Institute, Principles of the Law of Family Dissolution: Analysis and Recommendations, Council Draft No. 5, 98; Preliminary Draft No. 8, 98; auth, Sections of Child Support Chapter in Ira Ellman, Paul Kurtz and Elizabeth Scott, Family Law: Cases, Texts, Problems 510-539 3d ed. 98; co-auth, Agreements Chapter, Am Law Inst, Principles of the Law of Family Dissolution: Analysis and Recommendations, Council Draft No. 6, 99, Preliminary Draft No. 9, 99; auth, Blumberg's California Family Code Annotated, West published annually 94-99; auth, Community Property in California 3d ed., a casebook, Aspen 99. **CONTACT ADDRESS** Law Sch, Univ of California, Los Angeles, Box 951476, Los Angeles, CA 90095-1476. **EMAIL** blumberg@law.ucla.edu

BLUMBERG, PHILLIP IRVIN
PERSONAL Born 09/06/1919, Baltimore, MD, m, 1979, 4 children **DISCIPLINE** LAW **EDUCATION** Harvard Univ, AB, 39, JD, 42; Univ Conn, LLD, 94. **CAREER** Assoc, Willkie, Owen, Otis, Farr & Gallagher, 42-43; partner & assoc, Szold, Brandwen, Meyers & Blumberg, NYork, 46-62; pres, Federated Develop Co, 62-68; prof law, Sch Law, Boston Univ, 68-74; Mem, White House Conf Indust World Ahead, 72; Gov O'Neill's Comt Adv Judicial Nominations; trustee, Conn Bar Found; Dean, Sch Law, Univ Conn, 74-84; Prof, Sch Law, Univ Conn, 84-89; Prof Emeritus, 89-. **MEMBERSHIPS** Am Bar Asn; Am Law Inst. **RESEARCH** Corporate social responsibility; corporate power and institutional investors; corporate power and worker participation in corporate ownership and management; corporate groups. **SELECTED PUBLICATIONS** Auth, Corporate Responsibility in a Changing Society, 72; auth, The Megacorporation in American Society, 75; auth, The Law of Corporate Groups: Procedure, 83; auth, The Law of Corporate Groups: Bankruptcy, 85; auth, The Law of Corporate Groups: Substantive Common Law, 87; auth, The Law of Corporate Groups: General Statutuory Law, 89; auth, The Law of Corporate Groups: Specific Statutory Law, 92; auth, The Multination-

al Challenge to Corporation Law, 93; auth, The Law of Corporate Groups: State Statutory Law, 95; auth, The Law of Corporate Groups: Enterprise Liability, 98. **CONTACT ADDRESS** Sch of Law, Univ of Connecticut, Hartford, West Hartford, CT 06117.

BLUMENFELD, DAVID
DISCIPLINE HISTORY OF MODERN PHILOSOPHY, METAPHYSICS, ETHICS, ANALYTIC PHILOSOPHY **EDUCATION** Univ Calif, Berkeley, PhD, 66. **CAREER** Prof, assoc dean, Hum and Fine Arts, Ga State Univ. **SELECTED PUBLICATIONS** Author of over twenty-five articles, including two recent ones in The Cambridge Companion to Leibniz, and an article on free will in Am Philos Quart; co-ed; Overcoming Racism and Sexism. **CONTACT ADDRESS** Georgia State Univ, Box 4038, Atlanta, GA 30303-4038. **EMAIL** dblumenfeld@gsu.edu

BLUMENSON, ERIC D.
PERSONAL Born 02/23/1948, New York, NY, m, 1 child **DISCIPLINE** LAW **EDUCATION** Wesleyan Univ, BA, 68; Harvard Univ, JD, 72. **CAREER** Prof. **RESEARCH** Criminal law; criminal procedure; human rights, evidence; trial and appellate advocacy; clinical teaching, Moral and Legal Philosophy. **SELECTED PUBLICATIONS** Auth, Policing for Profit: The Drug War's Hidden Economic Agenda, Univ Chicago, 98; The Drug War's Hidden Economic Agenda, Nation, 98; Mapping the Limits of Skepticism in Law and Morals, Tex Law Rev, 96. **CONTACT ADDRESS** Sch of Law, Suffolk Univ, 120 Tremont St., Boston, Boston, MA 02108-4977. **EMAIL** eblumens@acad.suffolk.edu

BLUMENTHAL, DAVID REUBEN
PERSONAL Born 12/28/1938, Houston, TX, m, 1967, 3 children **DISCIPLINE** RELIGION, JUDAIC STUDIES **EDUCATION** Univ Pa, BA, 60; Jewish Theol Sem, MA, 61; Columbia Univ, PhD, 72. **CAREER** Vis asst prof Mid Eastern lang, Univ Minn, 72-73; vis asst prof relig, Brown Univ, 73-74, asst prof, 74-76; Assoc Prof Relig & Jay & Leslie Cohen Chmn Prog Judaic Studies, Emory Univ, 76-; NEH fel independent study, 78. **MEMBERSHIPS** Asn Jewish Studies; Am Acad Relig; Mediaeval Acad Am; Am Acad Jewish Res. **RESEARCH** Medieval Jewish philosophy; modern Judaism; Jewish mysticism. **SELECTED PUBLICATIONS** Auth, The Commentary of Hoter ben Shelomo to the Thirteen Principles of Maimonides, Brill, 74; A comparative table of the Bombay, Cairo & Beirut editions of the Rasa'il Ikhwan al-Safa, Arabica, 74; Maimonides' intellectualist mysticism and the superiority of the prophecy of Moses, Studies Medieval Cult, 76; Revelation: A modern dilemma, Conserv Judaism, 77; Understanding Jewish Mysticism, Ktav, 78; Some methodological reflections on the field of Jewish mysticism, Religion, 78; The Philosophic Questions and Answers of Hoter ben Shelomo, Brill, 79; co-ed & contribr, History, Religion & Spiritual Democracy: Essays in Honor of Joseph C Blau, Columbia Univ, 79. **CONTACT ADDRESS** Dept of Relig, Emory Univ, 537 Kilgo Circle, Atlanta, GA 30322-0001. **EMAIL** reldrb@emory.edu

BLUMHOFER, EDITH L.
PERSONAL Born 09/13/1975, Brooklyn, NY, m, 1975, 3 children **DISCIPLINE** AMERICAN RELIGIOUS HISTORY, AMERICAN HISTORY **EDUCATION** Hunt Col, BA, 71; MA; Harv Univ, PhD, 77. **CAREER** Adj prof, Hunt Col, 79-82; asst prof, SW Missou Univ, 82-84; assoc prof, Wheat Col, 87-95; assoc dir, Univ Chic, 96-99; prof, dir, Wheat Col, 99-. **HONORS AND AWARDS** Phi Beta Kappa; Danforth Fel. **MEMBERSHIPS** AHA; ASCH; AAR. **RESEARCH** American religious history; Protestant hymnody; Pentecostalism. **SELECTED PUBLICATIONS** Auth Restoring the Faith: The Assemblies of God, Pentecostalism, and American Culture, Univ Ill Press, 93; auth, Aimee Semple McPherson: Everybody's Sister, W B Erdmans, 93. **CONTACT ADDRESS** Dept History, Wheaton Col, Illinois, 501 College St, Wheaton, IL 60187-5501.

BLUMM, MICAHEL C.
PERSONAL Born 03/03/1950, Detroit, MI, m, 1982 **DISCIPLINE** ENVIRONMENTAL AND ENERGY LAW **EDUCATION** Williams Col, BA, 72; George Washington Univ, JD, 76, LLM, 79. **CAREER** Teaching fel Coastal law, Nat Resources Law Inst, 78-79; Assoc Prof Environ, Property, Energy and Fisheries Law, Sch Law, Lewis and Clark Col, 79-, Prin investr, Sea Grant Col Prog, Ore State Univ, 79-; ed, Anadromous Fish Law Memo, Nat Resources Law Inst, 79-; vis prof, Univ San Francisco, 83. **RESEARCH** Hydropower development and anadromous fish protection; Pacific Northwest energy law; aquatic resources protection. **SELECTED PUBLICATIONS** Auth, Renouncing the Public Trust Doctrine--An Assessment Of The Validity Of Idaho House Bill-794, Ecology Law Quart, Vol 0024, 97; Public Choice Theory And The Public Lands--Why Multiple-Use Failed, Harvard Environ Law Rev, Vol 0018, 94. **CONTACT ADDRESS** Law Sch, Lewis and Clark Col, 10015 SW Terwilliger, Portland, OR 97219-7768.

BLUMROSEN, ALFRED W.
PERSONAL Born 12/14/1928, Detroit, MI, m, 1952, 2 children **DISCIPLINE** LAW **EDUCATION** Univ MI, AB, 50, JD, 53. **CAREER** From asst prof to assoc prof labor law, 55-61, actg dean, 74-75, Prof Law, Rutgers Univ, Newark, 61-, Thomas A. Cowan Prof, 86, Mem panel arbitrators, NJ Mediation Bd, 57-; vis prof, Law Sch, La State Univ, 61-; consult, NJ State Civil Rights Comn, 63-65; mem panel arbitrators, Fed Mediation & Conciliation Serv, 64-; chief conciliations, US Equal Employment Opportunity Comn, 65-67, chief liaison & consult, 65-; vis prof, Law Sch, Howard Univ, 65-; mem panel arbitrators, Am Arbit Asn, 65-; spec atty, US Dept Justice, 68-; consult, US Dept Labor, 69-71, chmn, Inter-Agency Staff Coordr Comt Civil Rights, 69-70; consult, US Dept Housing & Urban Develop, 69; exec consult, MI Civil Rights Comn, 72-73; consult to chairperson, US Equal Employment Opportunity Comt, 77-79; couns, Kaye, Scholer, Fierman, Hays & Handler, 79-, adv US Dept of Labor, 95; Dir, International Employment Discrimination Project, Rutgers Law School, 98-. **HONORS AND AWARDS** Am Bar Asn Ross Prize, 83 **MEMBERSHIPS** Am Bar Asn; Int Soc Labor Law & Soc Legis; Indust Rels Res Asn. **RESEARCH** Discrimination in employment; admin process. **SELECTED PUBLICATIONS** Coauth, Labor Relations and the Law, Little, 3rd ed, 65; auth, Black Employment and the Law, Rutgers Univ, 71; Strangers in paradise: Griggs v Duke Power Co and the concept of employment discrimination, Mich Law Rev, 72; Toward effective administration of new regulatory statutes, Admin Law Rev, 77; Affirmative Action in employment after Weber, Rutgers Law Rev, 81; Modern Law: The Law Transmission System and Equal Employment Opportunity, Univ of Wis Press, 93; auth, Downsizing and Employee Rights, Rutgers Law, Rev, 98. **CONTACT ADDRESS** Sch of Law, Rutgers, The State Univ of New Jersey, Newark, 123 Washington St, Newark, NJ 07102-3192.

BLUMSTEIN, JAMES FRANKLIN
PERSONAL Born 04/24/1945, Brooklyn, NY, m, 1971 **DISCIPLINE** LAW **EDUCATION** Yale Univ, BA, 66, MA, 70, LLB, 70. **CAREER** From asst prof to assoc prof, 70-76, Prof Law, Vanderbilt Law Sch, 76-, Vis assoc prof law & policy sci, Duke Law Sch, 74-75; consult health policy, Dartmouth Med Sch, 75- & US Dept Health, Educ & Welfare, 76-, Nat Ctr Health Care Technol, 81 & Pres Comn Study Ethical Problems in Med & Biomed & Behav Res, 81. **MEMBERSHIPS** Am Bar Asn; Hastings Ctr; Inst Soc, Ethics & Life Sci. **RESEARCH** Constitutional law; health policy; civil rights. **SELECTED PUBLICATIONS** Auth, Constitutional safeguards in the selection of delegates to presidential nominating conventions, Yale Law J, 69; The Supreme Court's jurisdiction--reform proposals discretionary review and writ dismissals, Vanderbilt Law Rev, 73; coauth, Perspectives on government policy in the health sector, Milbank Mem Fund Quart: Health & Soc Quart, summer 73; Coping with quality-cost trade-offs in medical care: the role of PSROs, Northwestern Law Rev, 75; coauth, Strategies in underwriting the costs of catastropic disease, autumn Law & Contempo Prob, 76; coauth, State action as a shield and a sword in a medical services antitrust context: Parker v Brown in Constitutional Perspective, Duke Law J, 78; auth, Some intersections of the negative commerce clause and the New Federalism: The case of discriminatory State Income Tax treatment of out-of-state tax-exempt bonds, Vanderbilt Law Rev, 78; Rationing medical resources: A constitutional, legal and policy analysis, Tex Law Rev, 81. **CONTACT ADDRESS** Law Sch, Vanderbilt Univ, 2201 W End Ave S, Nashville, TN 37240-0001.

BLUSTEIN, JEFFREY
PERSONAL Born 05/30/1947, Minneapolis, MN, m, 1970, 2 children **DISCIPLINE** PHILOSOPHY **EDUCATION** Univ of Minnesota, BA, 68; Harvard Univ, PhD, 74. **CAREER** Barnard Col, 74-82; Mercy Col, 82-94; Albert Einstein Col of Medicine Mountefiore Medical Ctr, 92- . **HONORS AND AWARDS** Phi Beta Kappa; Harvard Univ grad prize fel. **MEMBERSHIPS** APA; Hastings Ctr; Soc for Philos and Pub Aff; Inst for Criminal Justice Ethics. **RESEARCH** Ethics; moral psychology; medical ethics; family ethics. **SELECTED PUBLICATIONS** Auth, Ethical Issues in Anesthesiology, Anesthesiology Alert, 93; auth, Doing What the Patient Orders: Maintaining Integrity in the Doctor-Patient Relationship, Bioethics, 93; auth, The Family in Medical Decisionmaking, Hastings Center Report, 93, repr in Thomasma, ed, Clinical Medical Ethics Cases and Readings, Univ Pr of Am, 95; coauth, The Pro-Life Maternal-Fetal Medicine Physician: A Problem of Integrity, Hastings Center Report, 95; coauth, Reproductive Responsibility and Long-Acting Contraceptives, Hastings Center Report, 95; auth, Should Physicians With Strong Pro-Life Views Avoid Specializing in Perinatology? Physicians Weekly, 95; coauth, Abortion and the Maternal-Fetal Medicine Physician: A Reply, Hastings Center Report, 95; auth, Confidentiality and the Adolescent: An Ethical Analysis, in Cassidy, ed, Pediatric Ethics: From Principles to Practice, Harwood Academic, 96; auth, Intervention with Excessively Aggressive Children: Conceptual and Ethical Issues, in Ferris, ed, Understanding Aggressive Behavior in Children, New York Academy of Sciences, 96; coauth, Reproductive Responsibility and Long-Term Contraceptives, in Moskowitz, ed, Coerced Contraception?, Georgetown, 96; auth, A More Equitable Health Care System for Children: The Moral Argument, in Stein, ed, Health Care for Children: What's Right, What's Wrong, What's Next, United Hospital Fund of New York, 97; auth, Character-Principlism and the Particularity Objection, Metaphilosophy, 97; auth, Procreation and Parental Responsibility, J of Social Philos, 97; auth, What Bioethics Needs to Learn about Families, Theoretical Medicine and Bioethics, 98; ed, The Adolescent Alone, Cambridge, 99. **CONTACT ADDRESS** 425 7th St, Brooklyn, NY 11215. **EMAIL** blustein@accom.yu.edu

BOADT, LAWRENCE E.
PERSONAL Born 10/26/1942, Los Angeles, CA, s **DISCIPLINE** BIBLICAL STUDIES (HEBREW SCRIPTURES) **EDUCATION** St. Paul's Col, MA, 67; Cath Univ of Amer, STL, 71, MA, 73; Pontifical Bibl Inst Rome, SSL, 74, SSD, 76. **CAREER** Roman Cath priest, 69-; adjunct asst prof, theol, Forham Univ, 74-76; prof to prof emer, Wash Theol Union, 76-97; publ, Paulist Press, 97- **HONORS AND AWARDS** Best Book of the Year, Bibl Archaeol Soc, 85. **MEMBERSHIPS** Soc of Bibl Lit; Amer Acad of Relig; Amer Sch of Orient Res; Cath Bibl Asn; Col Theol Soc; Cath Theol Soc of Amer. **RESEARCH** Ancient near eastern poetry; Prophetic phenomena. **SELECTED PUBLICATIONS** Auth, Preaching Biblical Texts, 95; auth, Anchor Bible Dictionary, 92; auth, Oxford Catholic Study Bible of the New American Bible, 92, auth, New Jerome Biblical Commentary, 90; auth, Shaping English Liturgy, 90; auth, Old Testament Reading Guide, 88; auth, Wisdom Literature and Book of Proverbs, 88; auth, Ezekiel and His Book, 86; auth, Reading the Old Testament: An Introduction, 85; auth, Jeremiah 26-52, Habakkuk, Zephaniah and Nahum, 83; auth, Jeremiah 1-25, 82; auth, Old Testament Message, 82; auth, Ezekiel's Oracles Against Egypt, 80. **CONTACT ADDRESS** Paulist Press, 997 Macarthur Blvd., Mahwah, NJ 07430.

BOARDMAN, WILLIAM SMITH
PERSONAL Born 11/20/1939, Springfield, IL, 1 child **DISCIPLINE** PHILOSOPHY **EDUCATION** DePauw Univ, BA, 61; Univ Minn, PhD(philos), 67. **CAREER** Instr, 65-68, asst prof, 68-80, assoc, 80-90, Prof Philos, Lawrence Univ, 90-, Nat Endowment for Humanities younger humanist fel, 71-72. **MEMBERSHIPS** Am Philos Asn. **SELECTED PUBLICATIONS** Auth, The Relativity of Perceptual Knowledge, Synthese, Vol 0094, 93; auth, Coordination and the Moral Obligation to Obey the Law, Ethics, 4-87. **CONTACT ADDRESS** Dept of Philos, Lawrence Univ, 115 S Drew St, Appleton, WI 54911-5798. **EMAIL** william.s.boardman@Lawrence.edu

BOBIC, MICHAEL
PERSONAL Born 03/22/1963, Binghampton, NY, m, 1988 **DISCIPLINE** POLITICAL SCIENCE **EDUCATION** Berea Col, BA; Univ Tenn, Knoxville, MA, PhD. **CAREER** Grad teacher, Univ Tenn, Knoxville, 92-96; adjunct fac, ETSU, 95-96; adjunct fac, Southern Ill Univ, 96-97; adjunct fac, Roane State Community Col, 97; adjunct fac, Knoxville Business Col, 98; asst prof, Emmanuel Col, 98-. **MEMBERSHIPS** Pi Sigma Alpha, Phi Kappa Phi, Midwest Polit Sci Asn, Acad of Polit Sci. **RESEARCH** American National Institutions, research methods, public administration. **SELECTED PUBLICATIONS** Auth, "The Kirton Adaptor Inn Index," in Review of Public Personnel Administration (99); auth, "The Silver Party," Encyclopedia of Am Parties (99); auth, "Afghanistani Emerging Government or Civil Rights Tragedy," History Behind the Headlines (forthcoming). **CONTACT ADDRESS** Dept Soc & Behav Sci, Emmanuel Col, Georgia, PO Box 129, Franklin Springs, GA 30639-0129. **EMAIL** mbobic@emmanuel-college.edu

BOBIK, JOSEPH
PERSONAL Born 07/21/1927, Binghamton, NY, m, 1948, 5 children **DISCIPLINE** METAPHYSICS; PHILOSOPHY OF RELIGION **EDUCATION** St Bernard's Col, BA, 47; Univ Notre Dame, MA, 51, PhD, 53. **CAREER** Instr philos, Marymount Col, Calif, 53-54; instr, Marquette Univ, 54-55; asst prof, 55-61; asst chmn dept, 67-72, assoc prof Philos, Univ Notre Dame, 61-98; prof Philos, 98-; Notre Dame scholar on leave grant, 66; O'Brien Fund res grant, 68-69. **MEMBERSHIPS** Am Cath Philos Asn. **RESEARCH** Philos of relig; medieval philos; metaphysics. **SELECTED PUBLICATIONS** Auth, Aquinas on Being and Essence, Univ Notre Dame, 65; Matter and individuation, In: The Concept of Matter, 66; Intuition and God and some new metaphysicians, In: New Themes in Christian Philosophy, 68; ed, The Nature of Philosophical Inquiry, Univ Notre Dame, 70; auth, The Commentary of Conrad of Prussia on the De Ente et Essentia of Aquinas, Nijhoff, 74; The sixth way, Mod Schoolman, 74; A seventh way, New Scholasticism, 76. **CONTACT ADDRESS** Dept of Philos, Univ of Notre Dame, 336/7 O'Shaugnessy Hall, Notre Dame, IN 46556. **EMAIL** bobik.1@nd.edu

BOCHNOWSKI, MICHAEL
PERSONAL Born 08/04/1938, Brooklyn, NY **DISCIPLINE** RELIGIOUS EDUCATION **EDUCATION** New York Univ, PhD, 93. **CAREER** Dir relig educ, Ft Belvoir, Va, 86- . **HONORS AND AWARDS** Res fel, Yale Divinity Sch; U.S. Army Chief of Chaplains Writing Awd Competition, 96. **MEMBERSHIPS** Am Asn Christian Counr; Relig Educ Asn. **RESEARCH** Religion and worship. **CONTACT ADDRESS** 8637 Beerman Pl, Alexandria, VA 22309-1616. **EMAIL** smbphd@aol.com

BOCK, DARRELL L.
PERSONAL Born 12/18/1953, Calgary, AB, Canada, m, 1975, 3 children **DISCIPLINE** NEW TESTAMENT **EDUCATION** Tx Univ, BA, 75; Dallas Theolog Sem, ThM, 79; Aberdeen Univ, PhD, 83. **CAREER** Pres Elect, Evangelical Theol Soc , 00; Trinity Evangel Divinity Sch, 99; Talbot Therm Sem, 98; Prof Spiritual Develop & Culture, Center Christian Leadership, Dallas Theolog Sem, present; vis prof, Seminario Centro Americano, 98; adjunct prof New Testament, Southern Theolog Sem, 98; Evangelical Bibl Sem Lctr, Osaka, Japan, 98; Consultant, SEARCH Ministries, 97; Coord, IBR Jesus Studies Proj, 96; Plenary Speaker, Far West Regional Evangel Theolog Soc, 95; vis lctr, Wstminister West, Escondido, Calif, 95; vis prof, Seminario Teologico Centroamericano, Guatemala City, 94. **HONORS AND AWARDS** David Edwards Awd-Fac Excellence, 99; Fac Tchg Awd, 87; Alexander Hamilton Scholar, 95-96. **MEMBERSHIPS** Studiorum Novi Testament Studies; Inst Bibl Res Treasurer; Amer Col Bibl Theologians; Bulletin for Bibl Res Ed Advisory Brd; Christianity Today Ed; Soc of Bibl Lit; Inst Bibl Res; Evangel Theolog Soc; Tyndale Soc. **RESEARCH** Historical Jesus; Use of Old Testament in New Testament. **SELECTED PUBLICATIONS** Ed, Three Views of the Millennium and Beyond, Zondervan, 99; Blasphemy and Exaltation in Judaism and the Final Examination of Jesus, Mohr/Siebeck, 98; Jesus vs. Sanhedrin: Why Jesus Lost His Trial, CT, 98; The Parable of the Rich Man in Lazarus, Southwestern Jour of Theology, 97. **CONTACT ADDRESS** Dallas Theol Sem, 3909 Swiss Ave, Dallas, TX 75204. **EMAIL** dbockdts@aol.com

BOCK, ROBERT L.
PERSONAL Born 09/05/1925, Macksville, KS, d, 4 children **DISCIPLINE** POLITICAL SCIENCE **EDUCATION** Univ Kansas, AB, 48, BA, 53; Washburn, JD, 53; Amer Univ, PhD, 60. **CAREER** Prof, WNEC/Springfield, 68-. **MEMBERSHIPS** A Political Science Assn **CONTACT ADDRESS** 66 Holly St, Springfield, MA 01151.

BODDEWYN, JEAN J.
PERSONAL Born 02/03/1929, Brussels, Belgium, m, 1979, 3 children **DISCIPLINE** MANAGEMENT AND STRATEGY, BUSINESS AND SOCIETY, AND MARKETING **EDUCATION** Univ Louvain, Belgium, commercial eng, 51; Univ Ore, MBA, 52; Univ Wash, PhD, Bus Admin. **CAREER** Galeries Anspach, Belgian dept store, market res and systems anal, 52-55; Jantzen Inc, time and motion study, 55-57; Univ Portland Ore, asst prof bus admin, 57-64; NY Univ, full prof of intl bus, 64-73; Baruch Col CUNY, full prof of intl bus, 73-. **HONORS AND AWARDS** Fulbright scholar, 51-52; fel, Acad of Mgt, 74; fel, Acad of Intl Bus, 80; fel, Intl Acad Mgt, 81. **MEMBERSHIPS** Acad Intl Bus; Acad Mgt; Europ Intl Bus Acad; Intl Asn for Bus and Soc. **RESEARCH** International regulation and self-regulation of advertising; International standardization of marketing policies; Political behavior of business firms at home and abroad. **SELECTED PUBLICATIONS** Auth, Global Perspectives on Advertising Self-Regulation, Westport, CT, Quorum Books, 92; papers in prof jour, American Marketing in the European Union: Standardization's Uneven Progress in 1973-1993, with Robert Grosse, Europ Jour of Marketing, 29, 12, 23-42, 95; The Legitimacy of International-Business Political Behavior, The Intl Trade Jour, 9, 1, 143-161, spring, 95; articles, Cigarette Advertising Bans and Cigarette Consumption: The Flawed Policy Connection, Intl Jour of Advert, 13, 4, 325-345, 94; The Taxation of Advertising: A Review of Current Issues, Jour of Current Issues & Res in Advert, 16, 1, 1-13, spring, 94; The Domain of International Management, Journal of International Management, 99; International-Business Research: Beyond Deja Vu, Management International Review 39, 99; with Jacques Picard and Robert Grosse, Centralization and Autonomy in International-Marketing Decision Making: A Longitudinal Study (1973-1993) of U.S. MNEs in the European Union, Journal of Global Marketing, 12, 98; chapters in books, Is International Business a Distinct Field of Inquiry?, in B. Toyne and D. W. Nigh, International Business: Institutions and the Dissemination of Knowledge, Columbia, SC, Univ SC Press, 17-23, 97; The Conceptual Domain of International Business: Territory, Boundaries, and Levels, in B. Toyne and D. W. Nigh, International Business Inquiry: An Emerging Vision, Columbia, SC, Univ SC Press, 50-61, 101-102, 97; Political Resources and Markets in International Business: Beyond Porter's Generic Strategies, in A. M. Rugman and A. Verbeke, Global Competition: Beyond the Three Generics, Research in Global Strategic Management, vol 4, Greenwich, CT, JAI Press, 83-99, 93; articles, Centralization and Autonomy in International-Marketing Decision Making: A Longitudinal Study (1973-1993) of U.S. MNEs in the European Union, Journal of Global Marketing, 98, with Jacques Picard and Robert Grosse; The Domain of International Management, Journal of International Management, 5, 99; International Business Research: Beyond Deja Vu, Management International Review, 99. **CONTACT ADDRESS** 372 Fifth Ave., Apt 9K, New York, NY 10018. **EMAIL** jjmsbodde@aol.com

BODIAN, MIRIAM
PERSONAL Born Baltimore, MD **DISCIPLINE** HISTORY, JUDAIC STUDIES **EDUCATION** Harvard Univ, BA, 69; Hebrew Univ, Jerusalem, PhD, 88. **CAREER** Asst prof, Yeshiva Univ, 88-90; asst prof, Univ Mich, 90-97; assoc prof, PaState Univ, 98-2000. **HONORS AND AWARDS** Nat Jewish Book Awd in Hist, 98; Koret Jewish Book Awd in Hist, 98. **SELECTED PUBLICATIONS** Auth, Hebrews of the Portuguese Nation: Conversos and Community in Early Modern Amsterdam, Indiana Univ Press (97). **CONTACT ADDRESS** Dept Hist, Pennsylvania State Univ, Univ Park, 108 Weaver Bldg, University Park, PA 16802-5500. **EMAIL** mxb59@psu.edu

BODLING, KURT A.
DISCIPLINE HISTORICAL THEOLOGY, LIBRARY SCIENCE **EDUCATION** Concordia Col, AA, 74; Concordia Sen Col, BA, 76; Concordia Sem, MDiv, 80, MST, 86; Univ Ill, MS; Fordham Univ, PhD cand. **CAREER** Ref, res asst, 81-86; asst dir, ref svcs, 86-87, Concordia Hist Inst; free-lance ed, Concordia Pub, 88-89; assoc lib, Winterthur Mus, 90-91; dean, spiritual life, 95-96, COL ARCH, 93- , asst prof, 91-98, ASSOC PROF, RELIG, 98-, DIR LIBR SVCS, 91-, CONCORDIA COL. **HONORS AND AWARDS** Beta Phi Mu. **MEMBERSHIPS** Soc of Am Archivists, Am Library Society, Asn of Col and Res Libraries. **RESEARCH** Am Lutheran History; Religious History of Am. **CONTACT ADDRESS** Concordia Col, New York, 171 White Plains Rd., Bronxville, NY 10708.

BOEDEKER, EDGAR
PERSONAL Born 10/03/1968, St. Louis, MO **DISCIPLINE** PHILOSOPHY **EDUCATION** Northwestern Univ, PhD, 98. **CAREER** DAAD Fel, Univ of Freiburg, Germany, 94-96; Belgian Amer Educational Found Fel, Louvain, Belgium, 98-99; Vis Asst Prof, philos, Northern Ill Univ, DeKolb, 99-00; Asst Prof, philos, Univ of Northern Iowa, Cedar Falls, 00-. **HONORS AND AWARDS** Phi Beta Kappa, 90. **MEMBERSHIPS** Am Philos Assoc; Bertrand Russell Soc. **RESEARCH** Phenomenology, Wittgenstein. **CONTACT ADDRESS** Dept of Philosophy, Univ of No Iowa, Cedar Falls, IA 50614. **EMAIL** boedeker@niu.edu

BOETZKES, ELIZABETH
DISCIPLINE PHILOSOPHY **EDUCATION** B.A., M.A., Alberta; Ph.D., Calgary. **CAREER** Assoc prof. **RESEARCH** Reproductive Ethics, Health Care Ethics, Feminist Ethics, Philos of Law, Environmental Philos. **SELECTED PUBLICATIONS** Auth, "Women, Madness and special Defences in the Law," J of Social Philosophy, vol 21, 90; auth, "Autonomy and advace Directives," Can J on Aging, vol 12, 93; auth, "sex Selextion and the Charter'," Can J of Law and Jurisprudence, vol 7, 94; auth, " Symbolic Harms, Equality, and Feminist Bioethics, " Proceedings of the Tenth World Congress on Med Law, vol A, 94; auth, "Gender, risk and Third-Party Interests," Cambridge Quarterly of Health Care Ethics, vol 8, 99; auth, "Equality, autonomy and femicnsit Bioethics," in Donchin and Purdy, Embodying Bioethics: recent Feminist Advances, Lanham: Rowman and Littlefield, 99. **CONTACT ADDRESS** Philos Dept, McMaster Univ, 1280 Main St W, Hamilton, ON, Canada L8S 4L9. **EMAIL** boetzkes@mcmaster.ca

BOGDAN, RADU J.
DISCIPLINE PHILOSOPHY **EDUCATION** Stanford Univ, PhD, 80. **CAREER** Prof, Tulane Univ: dir, Cognitive Stud Prog. **SELECTED PUBLICATIONS** Auth, Grounds for Cognition, Lawrence Erlbaum; Interpreting Minds, MIT Press, 97; auth, Minding Minds, MIT Press, 00. **CONTACT ADDRESS** Dept of Philosophy, Tulane Univ, 6823 St Charles Ave, New Orleans, LA 70118. **EMAIL** bogdan@mailhost.tcs.tulane.edu

BOGEN, DAVID S.
PERSONAL Born 07/24/1941, Los Angeles, CA, m, 1962, 3 children **DISCIPLINE** LAW **EDUCATION** Harvard Univ, BA, 62; LLB, 65; NY Univ, LLM, 67. **CAREER** Asst prof to prof, Univ of Md, 69-. **MEMBERSHIPS** Am Law Inst. **SELECTED PUBLICATIONS** Auth, Bulwark of Liberty. **CONTACT ADDRESS** School of Law, Univ of Maryland, Baltimore, 500 W Baltimore St, Baltimore, MD 21201-1701. **EMAIL** dbogen@law.umaryland.edu

BOGHOSSIAN, PAUL
PERSONAL Born 06/04/1957, Haifa, Israel **DISCIPLINE** PHILOSOPHY **EDUCATION** Trent Univ, BS, 78; Princeton Univ, MA; PhD, 86. **CAREER** Vis assoc prof, 91-, Princeton Univ; asst, assoc, prof, 84-92, Univ Mich; prof, chmn, phil, 92-, NY Univ. **HONORS AND AWARDS** NEH; Magdalen Col, Oxford; Univ J Landon; Australian Natl Univ. **MEMBERSHIPS** APA. **RESEARCH** Philosophy of mind; philosophy of language; epistemology. **SELECTED PUBLICATIONS** Auth, The Rule - Following Conversations, Mind, 89; auth, The Transparency of Mental Content, Phil Persp, 94; auth, What the Sokal Hoax Ought to Teach Us, Times Lit Suppl, 96; auth, Analyticity Reconsidered, Nois, 96. **CONTACT ADDRESS** Dept of Philosophy, New York Univ, 100 Washington Sq, New York, NY 10003. **EMAIL** paul.boghossian@nyu.edu

BOGUS, CARL T.
PERSONAL Born 05/14/1948, Fall River, MA, m, 1988, 3 children **DISCIPLINE** LAW **EDUCATION** Syracuse Univ, AB, 70; JD, 72. **CAREER** From assoc to partner, Steinberg, Greenstein, Gorelick & Price, Philadelphia, PA, 73-83; from assoc to partner, Mesirov Gelman Jaffe Cramer & Jamieson, Philadelphia, PA, 83-91; vis prof, Rutgers Univ Sch of Law-Camden, 92-96; assoc prof, Roger Williams Univ Sch of Law, 96-. **HONORS AND AWARDS** Ross Essay Award, Am Bar Asn, 91. **MEMBERSHIPS** Bd of Dir, 87-89; Bd of Dir, 89-92; Bd of Governors, 92-93; Bd of Dir, 87-89; State Governing Bd, 99-; Bd of Vis, 79-; Nat Advisory Panel, 93-. **RESEARCH** Products liability; torts; gun control; legal profession. **SELECTED PUBLICATIONS** Auth, The Death of an Honorable Profession, in 71 Indiana Law J 911, 96; The Third Revolution in Procucts Liability, in 72 Chicago-Kent Law Rev 3, 96; The Hidden History of the Second Amendment, in 31 U.C. Davis Law Rev 309, 98; Ronald McDonald is a Bully, in The Nation, Nov. 24, 97; ed, Symposium on Generic Products Liability, in 72 Chicago-Kent Law Rev No.1, 96; The Hidden History of the Second Ammendment, 31 U.C. Davis Law Review 309, 98; A Radical Ruling from the R.I. Supreme Court, Rhode Island Bar Journal, Nov. 99, at 13; Why Lawsuits are Good for America: Disciplined Democracy, Big Business and the Common Law, New York University Press, 01; ed, Symposium on the Second Amendment: Fresh Looks, 76 Chicago-Kent Law Review No. 1, 00. **CONTACT ADDRESS** Sch of Law, Roger Williams Univ, Ten Metacom Ave, Bristol, RI 02806. **EMAIL** ctb@rwulaw.rwu.edu

BOH, IVAN
PERSONAL Born 12/13/1930, Dolenji Lazi, Yugoslavia, m, 1957, 2 children **DISCIPLINE** PHILOSOPHY **EDUCATION** Ohio Univ, BA, 54; Fordham Univ, MA, 56; Univ Ottawa, PhD, 58. **CAREER** From instr to assoc prof philos, Clarke Col, 57-66; assoc prof, Mich State Univ, 66-69; Prof Philos, Ohio State Univ, 69-, Instr Russ, Dubuque Community Sch Dist Eve Div, 59-60; vis asst prof, State Univ Iowa, 62-63; Fulbright res fel, Univ Munich, 64-65; mem adv bd, Notre Dame J Formal Logic, 70-; ed consult, New Scholasticism, 70-; consult ed, Franciscan Studies, 73- **MEMBERSHIPS** Am Philos Asn; Am Cath Philos Asn; Int Soc Study Philos. **RESEARCH** Translations from medieval logicians; history of medieval logic; Bergmann's ontology. **SELECTED PUBLICATIONS** Auth, The Logical Structure of Medieval Law-Statements, Proc Am Cath Philos Asn, 64; Latin averroism, plurality of forms and the problem of predication, Encounter of Civilization in Mediaeval Philos; On Grammatical and Logical Relatives, Acts 15th Int Cong Philos; The conditionatimclause: One of the problems of existential import in the history of logic, Notre Dame J Formal Logic, 77. **CONTACT ADDRESS** Dept of Philos, Ohio State Univ, Columbus, Columbus, OH 43210.

BOHMBACH, KARLA G.
PERSONAL Born 09/02/1961, Alexandria, MN **DISCIPLINE** RELIGION **EDUCATION** Duke Univ, PhD, 96 **CAREER** Asst prof, Susquehanna Univ, 94- . **MEMBERSHIPS** Amer Acad Relig; Soc Bibl Lit. **RESEARCH** Feminist Biblical Scholarship. **CONTACT ADDRESS** Dept of Philosophy, Religion and Classical Studies, Susquehanna Univ, 514 University Ave, Selinsgrove, PA 17870. **EMAIL** bohmbach@susqu.edu

BOISCLAIR, REGINA A.
PERSONAL Born 10/09/1944, Lynn, MA, s **DISCIPLINE** BIBLICAL STUDIES **EDUCATION** Anna Maria Col, BA, 66; Simmons Col, MS, 67; Providence Col, MA, 81; Yale Univ, Mdiv, 79, SJM, 82; Ecole Bibl de Jerusalem, Eleve Titulaire, 89; Temple Univ, MA, 86, PhD, 95. **CAREER** Asst prof, Merrimack Col, 81-85; instr, Univ San Diego, 91-95; assoc prof relig student, Cardinal Newman chr Cath theol, Alaska Pac Univ, 97- . **HONORS AND AWARDS** Int Schol Ecole Bibl de Jerusalem, 88-89; Temple Univ Fel, 83-90; Alaska Pac Univ Pres Forum Fac Awd Teaching, 99. **MEMBERSHIPS** Am Acad Relig, Soc Bibl Lit, Cath Bibl Soc Am, Cath Theol Soc Am, Col Theol Soc, Am Theol Libr Asn, Chicago Soc Bibl Res. **RESEARCH** Sunday lectionaries, Jewish-Christian dialogue, Feminist hermeneutics. **SELECTED PUBLICATIONS** Auth, "Amnesia in the Catholic Sunday Lectionary" in Women and Theol, Collegeville: Liturgical Press, 95. **CONTACT ADDRESS** Dept Lib Arts, Alaska Pacific Univ, 4101 Univ Dr, Anchorage, AK 99508-4625. **EMAIL** boiscl@corecom.net

BOISVERT, MATHIEU
DISCIPLINE RELIGION **CAREER** Prof, 92, Universite du Quebec a Montreal, department de sciences religieuses; dir of graduate studies, departement de sciences religieuses, 95. **HONORS AND AWARDS** John McGill Awd, 86. **MEMBERSHIPS** Amer Acad of Relig; Canadian Soc for the study of relig; Societe Quebecoise pour 1 etude de la religion. **RESEARCH** Indian Buddhism; monasticism; asceticism. **SELECTED PUBLICATIONS** Ed and auth, Un Monde de religions, LesPresses, 97-98; auth, Pelerinage et tourisme, activites semblables, orientations distinctes, Teoros, Revue de recherche en tourisme, 97; The Method of interactive writing and university pedagogy, Blackwell, 98. **CONTACT ADDRESS** Dept des sciences religieuses, Univ of Quebec, Montreal, CP 8888 succursale centre-vill, Montreal, QC, Canada H3C 3P8. **EMAIL** boisvert.mathieu@uqam.ca

BOISVERT, RAYMOND
PERSONAL Born 10/04/1947, Lewiston, ME, m, 1970, 2 children **DISCIPLINE** PHILOSOPHY **EDUCATION** Providence

Coll, BA. 69; Univ of Toronto, MA, 74; Emory Univ, PhD, 80. **CAREER** Instr, 78-84, Clark Coll; Asst, Assoc, Full Prof, 84-, Siena Coll. **HONORS AND AWARDS** Fulbright Lectr, France, 91-92. **MEMBERSHIPS** Amer Philos Assoc; Soc for the Advancement of Amer Philos; Soc for Values in Higher Edu; Soc for Phenomenal and Existential Philos Corririum. **RESEARCH** Philosophy of ritual & food, interpretation theory, American Philosophy. **SELECTED PUBLICATIONS** Dowey's Metaphysics, Fordham Univ Press, 88; Beyond the Spectator Theory of Art, The Challenge of Pragmatism, Soundings, 95; Auth, John Dewey, Rethinking Our Time, SUNY Press, 97; From the Biological to the Logical in Classical American Pragmatism, Its Contemporary Vitality, Univ of Illinois Press, 99; Sokal's Hoax: A Pragmatist Response, Journal of Speculative Philosophy, 99; Philosophy: Postmodern or Polytemporal?, International Phil. Quarterly, 2000. **CONTACT ADDRESS** Dept of Philosophy, Siena Col, Loudonville, NY 12211. **EMAIL** Boisvert@siena.edu

BOK, DEREK CURTIS
PERSONAL Born 03/22/1930, Bryn Mawr, PA, m, 1955, 3 children **DISCIPLINE** LAW **EDUCATION** Stanford Univ, BA, 51; Harvard Univ, JD, 54; George Washington Univ, MA, 58. **CAREER** Asst prof, 58-61, dean law sch, 68-71, Prof Law, Harvard Univ, 61-, Pres, 71-, Chmn, Am Coun Educ, 81-82. **HONORS AND AWARDS** AB, Harvard Col, 71; LLD, Univ Ill, Princeton Univ & Yale Univ, 71. **MEMBERSHIPS** Am Philos Soc; Inst Med; fel Am Acad Arts & Sci. **RESEARCH** Labor law. **SELECTED PUBLICATIONS** Auth, The First Three Years of the Schuman Plan, Princeton Univ, 55; co-ed, Cases and Materials on Labor Law, Found Press, 62; coauth, Labor and the American Community, Simon & Schuster, 70; auth, Reflections on the distinctive character of American labor laws, Harvard Law Rev, 4/71; On the Purposes of Undergraduate Education, Daedalus, 74; Can ethics be taught?, Change Mag, 10/76; The Federal Government and the University, The Public Interest, 80; Beyond the Ivory Tower, Harvard Univ Press, 82. **CONTACT ADDRESS** Office of the Pres, Harvard Univ, 79 John F Kennedy St, Cambridge, MA 02138-5801.

BOKENKAMP, STEPHEN R.
DISCIPLINE RELIGIOUS STUDIES **EDUCATION** Univ Ca, PhD, 86. **CAREER** Assoc prof. **RESEARCH** Taoist studies; Mutual borrowing between Buddhism and Taoism; concepts of self and transcendence; meditation practice; messianism; views of script and scripture in Chinese religions. **SELECTED PUBLICATIONS** Auth, Sources of the Ling-pao Scriptures, Brussels, 83; Taoist Literature through the T'ang Dynasty, Univ Ind, 86; Stages of Transcendence: the Bh-mi Concept in Taoist Scripture, Univ Hawaii, 90. **CONTACT ADDRESS** East Asian Languages, Indiana Univ, Bloomington, Goodbody 240, Bloomington, IN 47405.

BOKINA, JOHN
PERSONAL Born 01/06/1948, Chicago, IL, m, 1982, 1 child **DISCIPLINE** POLITICAL THEORY **EDUCATION** Univ Ill-Chicago, AB, 70; MA, 72; Univ Ill-Urbana, PhD, 79. **CAREER** Vis asst prof, inst, asst prof, Univ Detroit, 76-81; Honors Prog Dir, 77-80; asst prof, asoc prof, prof, Univ Tex, 82- . **HONORS AND AWARDS** Pi Sigma Alpha - Polit Sci Asoc Fac Member of the Year, 80-81; NEH Fel for Col Teachers, 81-82; UTPA Distinguished Fac Achievement Awds, 86, 97; Fulbright German Studies Summer Course, 00. **MEMBERSHIPS** PSA; Int PSA; Midwest PSA; Am Hist Asoc; Caucus for New Polit Sci; Conf Group on German Pol; Found of Pol Theory Group; German Studies Asoc. **RESEARCH** History of modern and contemporary political theory; politics of art and mass culture. **SELECTED PUBLICATIONS** Auth, Holocaust at Mount Carmel, Telos, 95; auth, Eros and Revolution: Henze's Bassarids, The Europ Legacy, 96; auth, Viennese Hysteria-Clinical and Operatic, Vienna: The World of Yesterday, 1889-1914, 97; auth, Opera and Politics: From Monteverdi to Henze, 97; auth, Herbert Marcuse, 99. **CONTACT ADDRESS** 303 Austin Blvd., Edinburg, TX 78539. **EMAIL** JB83E8@panam.edu

BOLCHAZY, LADISLAUS J.
PERSONAL Born 06/07/1937, Slovakia, m, 1965, 1 child **DISCIPLINE** CLASSICS AND PHILOSOPHY **EDUCATION** St. Joseph's Col & Sem, NYork, BA, philos, 63; NYork Univ, MA, classics, 67; SUNY Albany, PhD, classics, 73. **CAREER** Latin/eng, Iona Prep, 64-65; Latin/eng, Sacred Heart High Sch, 62-64; instr, Siena Col, 66-67; asst prof, La Salette Col and Sem, 71-75; visiting asst prof, Millersville State Univ, 75-76; visiting asst prof, Loyola Univ of Chicago, 76-77; adjunct prof, Loyola Univ of Chicago, 79-; pres, Bolchazy-Carducci Publ Inc. **HONORS AND AWARDS** NEH summer inst, ancient hist, Univ Mich, 77; NEH summer sem, Sophocles and Thucydides, Cornell Univ, 76; teaching fel, State Univ of NY Albany, 67-71; res grants, Loyola Univ, spring and summer, 77. **MEMBERSHIPS** Amer Philol Asn. **RESEARCH** History of ethical & theological concepts; Stylometric analysis of language. **SELECTED PUBLICATIONS** Auth, Hospitality in Antiquity, Ares Publ, Chicago, 96; auth, A Concordance to Ausonius, George Olms, Hildesheim, 83; auth, The Coin-Iscriptions and Epigraphical Abbreviations of Imperial Rome, Ares Publ, 78; auth, A Concordance to the Utopia of St. Thomas More, Georg Olms, Hildesheim, 78; auth, Hospitality in Early Rome, Ares Publ, Chicago, 77. **CONTACT ADDRESS** Ladislaus J. Bolchazy, PhD, Bolchazy-Carducci Publishers, Inc, 1000 Brown St., No 101, Unit 101, Wauconda, IL 60084. **EMAIL** classics@bolchazy.com

BOLING, ROBERT GORDON
PERSONAL Born 11/24/1930, Terre Haute, IN, m, 1955, 2 children **DISCIPLINE** RELIGION **EDUCATION** Ind State Col, BS, 52; McCormick Theol Sem, BD, 56; Johns Hopkins Univ, Phd, 59. **CAREER** From instr to asst prof relig, Col Wooster, 59-64; assoc prof, 64-67, Prof Old Testament, McCormick Theol Sem, 67-, Fels Fund grant, 58; Thayer fel, Am Schs Orient Res, 68-69; ed, Bibl Res. **MEMBERSHIPS** Am Schs Orient Res; Am Orient Soc; Soc Bibl Lit; Am Acad Relig. **RESEARCH** Old Testament language and literature; textual criticism; Ugaritica. **SELECTED PUBLICATIONS** Auth, Synonymous parallelism in the Psalms, J Semitic Studies, 7/60; Judges, The Elders in Ancient-Israel--A Study of a Biblical Institution, Jour Amer Oriental Soc, Vol 0112, 92; Prologue to History--The Yahwist as Historian in Genesis, Interpretation-Jour Bible and Theol, Vol 0048, 94. **CONTACT ADDRESS** McCormick Theol Sem, 5555 S Woodlawn Ave, Chicago, IL 60637.

BOLT, JOHN
PERSONAL Born 10/07/1947, Netherlands, m, 1971, 3 children **DISCIPLINE** THEOLOGY **EDUCATION** Calvin Col, BS, 70; Calvin Theol Sem, BD, 73; ThM, 77; Univ St. Michael Col, PhD, 82. **CAREER** Minister, Penticton and Kelowna (BC), CRC, 73-76; Lectr, Calvin Col, 80-82; Prof, Redeema Col, 82-89; Prof, Calvin Theol Sem, 89-. **HONORS AND AWARDS** Can Coun Humanities and Soc Sci, 79; Pew Evangel Scholar. **MEMBERSHIPS** Calvin Studies Soc. **RESEARCH** Dutch Neo-Calvinism, Jonathan Edwards. **SELECTED PUBLICATIONS** Auth, Christian and Reformed Today, 84; auth, Christian Story and the Christian School, 94; auth, Stewards of the Word, 98. **CONTACT ADDRESS** Dept Theol, Calvin Theol Sem, 3233 Burton St Southeast, Grand Rapids, MI 49546-4301. **EMAIL** bltj@calvin.edu

BOLTON, MARTHA BRANDT
DISCIPLINE PHILOSOPHY **EDUCATION** Ohio Wesleyan Univ, BA, 65; Univ Mich, PhD(philos), 73. **CAREER** Asst prof, 71-77, assoc prof philos, 77-95, prof, 95-, Rutgers Univ. **HONORS AND AWARDS** Dilworth Fel, Inst for Advanced Study, 86-87; Fel, Center for Philos of Science, Univ Pittsburgh, 78; Council of Philo Studies Stipend, 74. **MEMBERSHIPS** Am Philos Asn; Soc for Women Philos; AAUP. **RESEARCH** Early modern philosophy. **SELECTED PUBLICATIONS** Auth, Substances, substrata and names of substances in Locke's Essay, Philos Rev, 76; Some Aspects of the Philosophy of Catharine Trotter, J Hist of Philos, 93; The Nominalist Argument of the New essays, Leibnig Soc Rev, 96; Universals, Abstractions, and Essences of Kinds, Cambridge His of Seventeenth Century Philos, Cambridge Univ Press, 97. **CONTACT ADDRESS** Dept of Philos Livingston Col, Rutgers, The State Univ of New Jersey, New Brunswick, PO Box 270, New Brunswick, NJ 08903-0270. **EMAIL** mbolton@rci.rutgers.edu

BOLTUC, PIOTR
PERSONAL Born Warsaw, Poland, 1 child **DISCIPLINE** PHILOSOPHY, APPLIED ETHICS **EDUCATION** Bowling Green State Univ, PhD, 98. **CAREER** St Olaf Col, 96-98; asst prof, Univ Ill, Springfield, 98- . **HONORS AND AWARDS** Fulbright fel; Sr Common Room Mem, St Johns Col, Oxford. **MEMBERSHIPS** APA. **RESEARCH** Meta-ethics; European studies; philosophy of mind, philosophy of person. **SELECTED PUBLICATIONS** Transl, Jaki, Stanley: God and the Cosmologists, Wroclaw, Poland, 95; auth, Does Equality Have an Independent Moral Value? Dialogue and Universalism, 95; coauth, Understanding Action, rev of book by Frederick Schick, Econ and Philos, 95; auth, Reductionism and Qualia, Epistemologia, 98; auth, Why Russia is Needed for Regional Stability: An Application of Institutional Economics for Security Issues, in Kanet, ed, Post-Communist States in the World Community, Macmillan, 98; auth, Is There an Inherent Moral Value in the Second-Person Relationships? in Abbarno, ed, Inherent and Instrumental Value, Rodolpi, 99. **CONTACT ADDRESS** Dept of Philosophy, Univ of Illinois, Springfield, PO Box 19243, Springfield, IL 62794-9243. **EMAIL** pboltl@uis.edu

BOMBARDI, RONALD JUDE
DISCIPLINE PHILOSOPHY **EDUCATION** Le Moyne Col, BA, 75; Marquette Univ, PhD, 84. **CAREER** Assoc prof, 91-; asst prof, 84-91 & instr, 85, Middle Tenn State Univ; instr, Marquette Univ, 79-84; Arthur J. Schmitt fel, 78-79; Marquette Univ fel, 77-78. **HONORS AND AWARDS** Commencement Hon in Philos awd, 75. **MEMBERSHIPS** Amer Philos Asn; Philos Sci Asn & Tenn Philos Asn. **RESEARCH** Philosophies of Language and Logic; Philosophy of Science,History of Early Modern Philosophy. **SELECTED PUBLICATIONS** Auth, The Education of Searle's Demon, Idealistic Stud, Vol 23, 93. **CONTACT ADDRESS** Dept of Philosophy, Middle Tennessee State Univ, 1301 E Main St, Murfreesboro, TN 37132-0001.

BOND, EDWARD J.
DISCIPLINE PHILOSOPHY **EDUCATION** Queen's Univ, BA; MA; Cornell Univ, PhD. **CAREER** Dept Philos, Queen's Univ **RESEARCH** Ethics and value theory; aesthetics; epistemology. **SELECTED PUBLICATIONS** Auth, Reason and Value, 83; Ethics and Human Well-being: an Introduction to Moral Philosophy, Garland, 96. **CONTACT ADDRESS** Philos Dept, Queen's Univ at Kingston, Kingston, ON, Canada K7L 3N6. **EMAIL** ejb@post.queensu.ca

BOND, GILBERT I.
DISCIPLINE THEOLOGY AND BLACK STUDIES **EDUCATION** Lawrence Univ, BA, 78; Bethany Theol Sem, MDiv, 88; Emory Univ, PhD, 94. **CAREER** Fac, Holy Rosary High Sch, 79-82; fac, St. Thomas More High Sch, 84-85; Adj prof, Bethany Theol Sem, 87-88; Vis prof, Bethany Theol Sem, 90; Asst instr, Emory Col, 93-94; Asst prof, Emory Col & Grad Inst Lib Arts; 94-96; Asst prof, Yale Univ, 96-. **HONORS AND AWARDS** Martin Luther King, Jr., Awd for Leadership, 78; Fund Theol Educ Doc Fel, 88-90; Patricia Harris Fel, 88-92; Ass instr Awd Tchg, 92-93; Dissertation Year Sch, 93. **SELECTED PUBLICATIONS** Auth, In Christos as Creolization; Anabaptist Liturgy and German Mysticism; Blues as Profane Performance. **CONTACT ADDRESS** Yale Univ, 409 Prospect St., New Haven, CT 0651-2167.

BONDESON, WILLIAM B.
PERSONAL Born 03/30/1938, m, 2000, 1 child **DISCIPLINE** PHILOSOPHY **EDUCATION** Augustana Col, BA, 58; Univ Ill, MA, 62; Univ Chicago, PhD, 65. **CAREER** Prof; Curators' Distinguished tchg prof Family and Commun Med, 92-; adj clin prof Nursing; staff mem, Chicago Coun For Rel, 62-64; instr, Univ Mo-Columbia, 64-; ch, Dept Philos, 67-69; dir, Honors Col, 69-72; Col Gen Stud, 73-79 & Univ Concert Ser, 76-92; co-dir, Prog Hea Care and Human Values, 79-85; spec asst to deen and dir of develop, Col Arts and Sci, 85-87; fac liaison to the Alumni Asn, 87-91; prof Family and Commun Med, 88-; fac assoc to the Provost, 91-94; dir, Chamber Music Ser, 92-94; ACE fel to, Univ Nebr & VP Acad Aff, Univ Mid-Am; univ and publ serv, founding pres, Mus Associates; pres, Friends of the Libr; founding exec VP, Friends of Music;pres, Mo Citizens for the Arts; ch, Campus United Way; ch, City of Columbia Commn on the Arts; ch, Mo Dept of Mental Hea Prof Rev Comt; Dance Adv Comt of the Mo Arts Coun; Touring Adv Comt of the Mo Arts Coun; pres, Columbia Art League; ch, Med Ethics Prog Dir Nat Gp; ch, MU Hos and Clin Ethics Comt; V.A. Hosp Bioethics Comt; Lenoir Home Ethics Comt; pres, Fac/Staff Golf League; Co-founder, Wakonse Foundation for College Teaching; Co-dir, Wakonse Nat Conf on Col Tchg; Amer Mirror Lectr, Mo Humanities Coun, 92, 93, 94, 95, 96 & 97; pres, Univ Club; Amer Cancer Soc, Columbia Chap, Relay for Life Comt; pres, Search Comt, Univ Mo Sys; Chancellor Search and Screening Task Force, Univ Mo Sys. **HONORS AND AWARDS** Danforth Found fel, 58-65; Univ Chicago fel, 58-60; Summer Res fel, 67 & 71; Dean Fac fel, 69 & 70; fel to Harvard Inst for Educ Mgt, 78; ACLS fel, 78; Soc for Values in Higher Educ fel, 82 & Wakonse fel, 89; Phi Beta Kappa, 58; Omicron Delta Kappa, 82; Phi Kappa Phi, 84; Fac Alumni awd, 68; Amoco Tchg awd, 77; Purple Chalk awd, 79 & 84; Union Electric awd, 84; Panhellenic Outstanding Fac awd, 85; Beta Theta Pi Teaching Excellence awd, 86; Maxine Christopher Shutz awd and Lectureship, 89; Coun Advancement and Support Educ, Mo prof Yr, 89; CASE Nat Gold Medalist awd, 89; Coun of Chiefs, Amer Youth Found, 90; Mo Arts Coun awd, 93; MU Friends of the Library Distinguished Friend awd, 93; MU Alumni Asn Distinguished Fac awd, 93; Mo Stud Asn Distinguished Tchg awd, 93; Jefferson Club Distinguished Scholar, 94; Gamma Sigma Delta Outstanding Tchr awd, 94; Outstanding Tchr awd, Sigma Kappa, 95; Tapped for hon mem, Omicron Delta Kappa, 95; Who's Who Among Amer Teachers, 96; MU Excellence in Educ awd, 96; Beta Theta Pi Outstanding Tchr awd, 96; William T. Kemper fel, 97 & Outstanding Greek Fac awd, 97; $3.5 million for res and prog in, med ethics, arts, higher educ; Academy of Missouri Squires, 99; Presidential Awd for Outstanding Teaching, 00; cofounder & co-ed, wakonse j for col tchg and learning, 96. **RESEARCH** Medical Ethics, Ancient Philosophy, Undergraduate Education and Teaching, Arts Administration and Dev. **SELECTED PUBLICATIONS** Auth, Higher Education, the Research University, and the Reaffirmation of Excellence in Teaching, Univ Mo Spectrum, 90; The Cruzan Case and Some Issues of Public Policy, Governmental Affairs Newsletter, Governmental Affairs Program, Univ Mo, vol xxv, 91; Faculty Development and the New American Scholar, in To Improve the Acad, vol 11, 92; The Student Learning Imperative: Possibilities and Problems from a Faculty Point of View, J Col Stud Develop, 95 & Some Reflections on Teaching and Tenure, Wakonse J Col Tchg and Learning, 96; coauth, The Wakonse Conferences on College Teaching, J Counseling and Develop, vol 72, 94; co-ed, issue of Nat Forum, Pi Kappa Phi jour on health care issues, 93; contribur, Reidel Philosophy and Medicine Series: New Knowledge in the Biomedical Sciences, 82; Abortion and the Status of the Fetus, 83; Rights to Health Care, 90 & Reproductive Rights and Responsibilities, 87; Philosophical Issues and Problems, Simon and Schuster, 99; auth, Ethical Issues in managed Care, Reidel Publishing. **CONTACT ADDRESS** Dept of Philosophy, Univ of Missouri, Columbia, 302 Reynolds Ctr, Columbia, MO 65211. **EMAIL** bondesonw@missouri.edu

BONEVAC, DANIEL A.
PERSONAL Born 01/20/1955, Pittsburgh, PA, m, 1976, 1 child **DISCIPLINE** PHILOSOPHY **EDUCATION** Haverford Col, BA, 75; Univ Pitts, MA, 77; PhD, 80. **CAREER** Asst prof, to prof, Univ Tex at Austin, 80-92-; ch, 91-. **HONORS AND AWARDS** Johnsonian Prize. **MEMBERSHIPS** APA; SEP; NAS. **RESEARCH** Metaphysics; philosophical logic. **SELECTED PUBLICATIONS** Auth, Reduction in the Abstract Sciences, 82; auth, Deduction, 87; auth, The Art and Science of Logic, 90; auth, Simple Logic, 99; auth, Worldly Wisdom, 00. **CONTACT ADDRESS** Dept Philosophy, Univ of Texas, Austin, Austin, TX 78712-1013. **EMAIL** dbonevac@la.utexas.edu

BONGMBA, ELIAS KIFON
PERSONAL Born 12/15/1953, Ntumbaw, Cameroon **DISCIPLINE** RELIGIOUS STUDIES **EDUCATION** Univ Denver, PhD. **CAREER** Adj fac, Red Rocks Commun Col, 94-95; asst prof relig stud, Rice Univ, 95- . **MEMBERSHIPS** Soc for African Philos of N Am; Bonhoeffer Soc; African Stud Asn; African Am Acad of Relig. **RESEARCH** African religions; contemporary postmodern thought, **CONTACT ADDRESS** MS 15 Religious Studies, Rice Univ, 6100 S Main St, Houston, TX 77005. **EMAIL** bongmba@rice.edu

BONI, SYLVAIN
PERSONAL Born 11/12/1931, Paris, France, m, 1972, 2 children **DISCIPLINE** PHILOSOPHY **EDUCATION** Bryn Mawr Col, PhD, 81. **CAREER** Mentor, mentally gifted program, Central High Sch, Philadelphia, 12 yrs; adj prof, philos, Beaver Col, 6 yrs; adj prof, philos, LaSalle Univ, 17 years. **MEMBERSHIPS** APA. **RESEARCH** Philosophy of mind. **SELECTED PUBLICATIONS** Auth, The Self and the Other in the Ontologies of Sartre and Buber. **CONTACT ADDRESS** 1370 Lindsay Ln, Meadowbrook, PA 19046. **EMAIL** sboni@home.com

BONISTEEL, ROY
PERSONAL Born 05/29/1930, Ameliasburgh, ON, Canada **DISCIPLINE** RELIGION **EDUCATION** Laurentian Univ, DLitt, 79; Queen's Univ, DD, 80; Univ Windsor, LLD, 82; Mt St Vincent Univ, DHumLitt, 83; St. Francis Xavier Univ, LLD, 85; Univ PEI, LLD, 87. **CAREER** Reporter, Belleville Intelligencer, 48; reporter, Trenton Courier-Advocate, 49-59; announcer, CJBQ Belleville, 51-52; prog dir, CTKB St. Catharines, 53-64; dir broadcasting, United Church Can, 65-66; nat radio coordr, Anglican, Roman Cath & United Churches, 69-70; host, CBC-TV, Man Alive, 67-89. **HONORS AND AWARDS** ACTRA Awd, 79; Christian Cult Awd, Assumption Univ, 82; Gordon Sinclair Awd Excellence Broadcast Jour, 85; Commemorative Medal, 125th Anniversary Can Confed, 92; Distinguished Can, Univ Regina, 94; mem, Order Can, 95. **SELECTED PUBLICATIONS** Auth, In Search of Man Alive, 80; auth, Man Alive: The Human Journey, 83; auth, There was a Time, 90; auth, All Things Considered, 97. **CONTACT ADDRESS** RR 5, Trenton, ON, Canada K8V 5P8.

BONNEAU, NORMAND
PERSONAL Born 10/05/1948, Lewiston, ME, s **DISCIPLINE** BIBLICAL STUDIES **EDUCATION** Institut Catholique de Paris, STD, 83. **CAREER** Vis prof, 83-84, asst prof New Testament stud, 84-93, assoc prof, 93- , St Paul Univ. **MEMBERSHIPS** Catholic Bibl Asn of Am; Soc of Bibl Lit. **RESEARCH** Letters of Paul; the Roman Catholic Sunday lectionary; Synoptic Gospels. **SELECTED PUBLICATIONS** Auth, Images of God(s) in the New Testament World, in Abromaitis, ed, Roots: Finding Strength in Biblical Tradition, CCCB, 93; auth, Reflections on the Mystery of God and the AIDS Crisis, in Bonneau, ed, AIDS and Faith, Novalis, 93; auth, Fulfilled in Our Hearing: The Dynamism of Scripture in Liturgical Proclamation, in Gasslein, ed, Shaping a Priestly People: A Collection in Honour of Archbishop Hayes, Novalis, 94; auth, Preparing the Table of the Word, Liturgical, 97; auth, Bible and Liturgy, in Farmer, ed, The International Bible Commentary, Liturgical, 98; auth, The Sunday Lectionary: Ritual Word, Paschal Shape, Liturgical, 98. **CONTACT ADDRESS** Saint Paul Univ, 223 Main St, Ottawa, ON, Canada K1S 1C4. **EMAIL** nbonneau@ustpaul.uottawa.ca

BONNETTE, DENNIS
PERSONAL Born 02/26/1939, Gardner, MA, m, 1962, 7 children **DISCIPLINE** PHILOSOPHY **EDUCATION** Univ Detroit, AB, 60; Univ Notre Dame, MA, 62, PhD, 70. **CAREER** Instr philos, Univ San Diego, 63-64; asst prof, Loyola Univ, La, 64-65 & Univ Dayton, 65-67; from Asst Prof to Assoc Prof, 67-90, Prof Philos, Niagara Univ, 90-, Dept Chmn, 93. **MEMBERSHIPS** Am Cath Philos Asn. **RESEARCH** Metaphysics; natural theology; ethics; evolution. **SELECTED PUBLICATIONS** Auth, The doctrinal crisis in Catholic higher education, Social Justice Rev, 11/67; Effects of secularism on higher education, Cath Educ Rev, 3/68; Ex umbris in veritatem, Triumph, 12/70; Aquinas' Proofs for God's Existence, Martinus Nijhoff, 73; Is the United States becoming the Fourth Reich?, 7-8/80 & When human life begins, 3-4/81, Social Justice Rev; The infinite being as sole adequate explanation of the phenomenon of inertia: A variation on the First Way of St Thomas Aquinas, Faith & Reason, summer 82; How Creation Implies God, Faith & Reason, 3-4, 85; A Philosophical Critical Analysis of Recent Ape-Language Studies, Faith & Reason 2-3, Fall 93. **CONTACT ADDRESS** Dept of Philos, Niagara Univ, Niagara University, NY 14109-9999. **EMAIL** bonnette@niagara.edu

BONNIE, RICHARD J.
PERSONAL Born 08/22/1945, Richmond, VA, m, 1967, 3 children **DISCIPLINE** LAW **EDUCATION** Johns Hopkins Univ, BA, 66; Univ Va, LLB, 69. **CAREER** Vis Fel, Cambridge Univ, 77; Vis Prof, Cornell Law School, 93-94; Director, Inst of Law, Univ of Va; Prof and Research Prof, Univ Va. **HONORS AND AWARDS** "Z" Society Awd, Virginia Law Review, 69; Isaac Ray Awd, Am Psychiat Asn, 98; Amicus Awd, Am Acad of Psychiat and the Law, 95; Fel, Va Law Foundation, 95; Who's Who in Am. **MEMBERSHIPS** Nat Acad of Sci, Inst of Medicine Board, Inst of Medicine Committee on Assessing the Science Base for Tobacco Harm Reduction, Nat Res Council Committee, Am Psychiat Asn Council. **RESEARCH** Criminal law, Mental health law, Substance abuse, Bioethics and Public health law and ethics. **SELECTED PUBLICATIONS** Ed, Mental Health Law in Evolution: A 25 Year Retrospective 1972-97, in press; auth, The Trial of John W. Hinckley Jr.: A Case Study in the Insanity Defense, Foundation Press, 00; auth, The Marijuana Conviction: The History of Marijuana Prohibition in the United States, Lindesmith Center, 99; ed, Reducing the Burden of Injury: Advancing Prevention and Treatment, Nat Acad Press, 99; auth, " Unraveling Soviet Psychiatry," Journal of Contemporary Legal Issues, (99): 279-298; auth, "A Presidential Commission on Drug Policy: Instrument of Reform or Defender of the Status Quo?," Contemporary Drug Problems, (98): 169-183; auth, "Psychometric Properties of the MacArthur Competence Assessment Tool-Criminal Adjudication (MacCatCA)," Psychological Assessment, (98): 435-443; auth, "The Competence-Related Abilities of Women Criminal Defendants," Journal of the American Academy of Psychiatry and the Law, (98): 215-222; auth, Criminal Law: Cases and Materials, foundation Press, 97; ed, Work Disability, mental Disorder and The Law, Univ Chicago Press, 97. **CONTACT ADDRESS** School of Law, Univ of Virginia, 580 Massie Rd, Charlottesville, VA 22903-1738. **EMAIL** rbonnie@virginia.edu

BONTEKOE, RON
PERSONAL Born 05/31/1954, Toronto, ON, Canada, d **DISCIPLINE** PHILOSOPHY **EDUCATION** Univ Toronto, BA, 77, B Ed, 78, PhD, 88; Queen's Univ, MA, 82; **CAREER** Lectr, Ryerson Polytech Univ, 88-90; asst prof, 90-95, assoc prof, 95-, Univ Hawaii Manoa; liberal arts fel, Harvard Law Sch, 97-98. **MEMBERSHIPS** Amer Philos Asn; Can Philos Asn; Amintaphil. **RESEARCH** Hermeneutics; Epistemology; Philosophy of law. **SELECTED PUBLICATIONS** Auth, Paul Ricoeur, Encycl of Aesthetics, Oxford Univ Press, 98; auth, Friedrich Schleiermacher, Encycl of Aesthetics, Oxford Univ Press, 98; auth, Grounding a Theory of Rights in Fallibilist Epistemology, Justice and Democracy: Cross-Cultural Perspectives, Univ Hawaii Press, 97; co-ed, Justice and Democracy: Cross-Cultural Perspectives, Univ Hawaii Press, 97; co-ed, A Companion to World Philosophies, Blackwell Publ, 97; auth, Dimension of the Hermeneutic Circle, Humanities Press, 96; co-auth, The Interrelationship of Moral and Aesthetic Excellence, The Brit Jour of Aesthetics, 92; auth, Metaphysics: Should It Be Revisionary or Descriptive? Intl Philos Quart, 92; auth, Rorty's Pragmatism and the Pursuit of Truth, Intl Philos Quart, 90; auth, The Function of Metaphor, Philos and Rhetoric, 87; auth, A Fusion of Horizons: Gadamer and Schleiermacher, Intl Philos Quart, 87; auth, "Truth as a Regulative Ideal," Jrnl ofSpeculative Philos (99). **CONTACT ADDRESS** Philosophy Dept., Univ of Hawaii, Honolulu Comm Col, 2530 Dole St., #D304, Honolulu, HI 96822. **EMAIL** bontekoe@hawaii.edu

BOOMER, DENNIS
PERSONAL Born 10/30/1951, Hobbs, NM, m, 1983 **DISCIPLINE** RELIGION **EDUCATION** Hardin-Simmons Univ, BA, 74; Southwestern Baptist Theol Sem, MDiv, 77; Baylor Univ, PhD, 89. **CAREER** Univ of Mary Hardin-Baylor, 81-86; West Virginia Univ, vis assoc prof, 89-92; Reli Res Serv, founder & dir, 92-. **MEMBERSHIPS** AAR, SBL **RESEARCH** Apologetics; cults and new religions. **CONTACT ADDRESS** Evening Col, Albany, Brewton-Parker Col, Highway 280, Mount Vernon, GA 30445-0197. **EMAIL** drboomer@bellsouth.net

BOOTH, RICHARD A.
PERSONAL Born 11/24/1950, Marion, IN, m, 1976, 2 children **DISCIPLINE** LAW **EDUCATION** Univ Mich, AB, 73; Yale Law School, JD, 76. **CAREER** Assoc Attorney, New York, 76-82; Asst Prof, Southern Methodist Univ, 82-86; Prof, Case Western Reserve Univ, 86-89; visiting Prof, Ill Inst of Technol, 89-90; Visiting Prof, George Washington Univ, 98; Prof, Univ Md, 90-. **MEMBERSHIPS** Am Law Inst. **RESEARCH** Corporations and Securities; Financial Markets. **SELECTED PUBLICATIONS** Auth, financing the Corporation, West Group, 93; auth, Business Basics for Law Students - Essential Terms and concepts, Aspen Law & Business, 98; auth, Fundamentals of Modern Business - a Lawyer's Guide, Aspen, 94; auth, Corporation Finance - Cases and Materials, forthcoming; auth, "A Minimalist approach to Corporation Law," Georgia Law Rev, forthcoming; auth, "Investor Diversification and Corporation Law (Or roll Over Berle and Means), Del J Corp, forthcoming; auth, "The Suitability Rule, Investor diversification, and Using Spread to Measure risk," Business Law, 99; auth, "Stockholders, Stakeholders, and Bagholders (Or How Investor Diversification affects fiduciary Duty," Business Law, 98; auth, "The Limited Liability company and the Search for a Bright Line Between Corporations and Partnerships, Wake forest Law Review, 97. **CONTACT ADDRESS** School of Law, Univ of Maryland, Baltimore, 500 W Baltimore St, Baltimore, MD 21201-1701. **EMAIL** rbooth@law.umaryland.edu

BORAAS, ROGER STUART
PERSONAL Born 02/04/1926, Stillwater, MN, m, 1948, 3 children **DISCIPLINE** BIBLICAL STUDIES; OLD TESTAMENT **EDUCATION** Gustavus Adolphus Col, BA, 48; Augustana Theol Sem, BD, 52; Drew Univ, PhD, 65. **CAREER** From instr to assoc prof, 58-69, Prof Relig, Upsala Col, 69-91, Dir Area Studies Prog Ancient Near East, 67-84, Mem, Drew-McCormich exped, Balatah, 62, 64, 66 & 68; chief archaeologist, Andrews Univ exped, Heshbon, 68, 71, 73, 74, 76. **MEMBERSHIPS** Soc Bibl Lit; Am Schs Orient Res. **RESEARCH** Palestinian archaeology. **SELECTED PUBLICATIONS** Coauth, Heshbon, 1968, Andrews Univ Monogr, 69; auth, Rejm ed- Malfuf, Am Schs Orient Res Newslett, 69; coauth, Heshbon, 1971, Andrews Univ Monogr, 73; assoc ed Harpers Bible Dictionary, 85 & 96. **CONTACT ADDRESS** 50 Fernwood Rd, East Orange, NJ 07017.

BORCHERT, GERALD LEO
PERSONAL Born 03/20/1932, Edmonton, AB, Canada, m, 1959, 2 children **DISCIPLINE** RELIGION, LAW **EDUCATION** Univ Alta, BA, 55, LLB, 56; Eastern Baptist Theol Sem, BD, 59; Princeton Theol Sem, ThM, 61, PhD, 67. **CAREER** Lawyer, Calgary, Alta, 56; part-time teaching fel Greek, Princeton Theol Sem, 60-62; from Assoc Prof to Prof, 63-77, acad dean & vpres, 70-77; prof & dean New Testament, Northern Baptist Sem, 77-80; from prof to Coleman Prof New Testament, Southern Baptist Seminary, 80-98; dir Doctoral Studies and Prof New Testament, Northern Baptist Seminary, 98-; Mem bd abstractors, Relig & Theol Abstr, 67-75, 96; civilian retreat master for US Army, 68; bibl lectr, N Am Continental Cong Crusade of Americas, 68-69; comnr, Int Comn Coop Christianity, Baptist World Alliance, 68-95, secy, 69-80, chair, 90-95, chair study and res div, 95-00; consult law & Christianity, Baptist Joint Comt Pub Affairs Can & US, 69-71, mem comt, 71-77, secy, 73-75, vchair, 75-77; dir-trustee, Am Inst Holy Land Studies, Jerusalem, 71-77, vis prof, 74; trustee, Tabor Col, 70-77; co-teacher, Hidden Treasures of the Bible, TV series of Chicago Sunday Evening Club, 78-79; numerous other visiting professorships. **MEMBERSHIPS** Soc Bibl Lit; Am Acad Relig; Am Schs Orient Res; Soc Study New Testament. **RESEARCH** New Testament, particulary studies in Paul, John and history of interpretation; gnosticism including Coptic studies; law, the relationship between justice and order. **SELECTED PUBLICATIONS** Auth, Form criticism, Foundations, 4/65; Great Themes from John, Baptist Life Asn, 66; The Dynamics of Pauline Evangelism, Roger Williams & NAm Baptist Sem, 69; Law, the Christian and the Contemporary Scene, in Emerging Patterns of Rights and Responsibilities Affecting Church and State, Baptist Joint Comt Pub Affairs, 69; Forum, Monthly Column in Baptist Herald, 70-77; Today's Model Church, Roger Williams, 71; Dynamics of Evangelism, Word Books, 76; Paul and His Interpreters, IVP, 85; Discovering Thessalonians, Guideposts, 86; Assurance and Warning, Broadman, 87; coauth, The Crisis of Fear, Broadman, 88; auth, "John," Mercer Commentary on the Bible, 94; auth, John I-II (New American Commentary), Broadman, 96. **CONTACT ADDRESS** No Baptist Theol Sem, 660 E Butterfield Rd, Lombard, IL 60148-5698. **EMAIL** gborchert@northern.seminary.edu

BORELLI, JOHN
PERSONAL Born 07/19/1946, Oklahoma City, OK, m, 1971, 3 children **DISCIPLINE** HISTORY OF RELIGIONS, THEOLOGY **EDUCATION** Fordham Univ, PhD, 76. **CAREER** Instr, Dept Theology, Fordham Univ, Bronx, NY, 75-76; Prof Religious Studies, Col Mount St Vincent, Riverdale, NY, 76-87; dir, Interreligous Relations, US Conference of Catholic Bishops, 87-. **HONORS AND AWARDS** Phi Beta Kappa, St. Louis Univ, 68. **MEMBERSHIPS** Consultor, Pontifical Coun for Interreligous Dialogue, Vatican; Int Buddhist-Christian Theological Encounter Group; Exec Coun, World Conference on Religion and Peace, USA; adv bd, Monastic Interreligous Dialogue; advisory bd, Institute for Interreligious Study and Dialogue, Catholic Univ of Am; ; Soc for Buddhist-Christian Studies; Soc for Hindu-Christian Studies. **RESEARCH** Interreligous relations; theology of religions; the Hindu tradition; Yoga and meditation; ecumenical relations. **SELECTED PUBLICATIONS** Auth, Children of Abraham: Muslim-Christian-Jewish Relations, Mid-Stream 34, 2, April 95; The 1994 International Buddhist-Christian Theological Encounter, with Judith Simmer-Brown, Buddhist-Christian Studies, 15, 95; Interreligous Relations, Annual report, 1994, Pro Dialogo, Bul of the Pontifical Coun for Interreligous Dialogue, 89, 95; The Goal and Fruit of Catholic-Muslim Dialogue, The Living Light, Dept of Ed, US Cath Conference, 32, 2, winter 95; Talking With Muslims, Faith Alive, Cath News Service, Feb 96; Indispensable Resources on the Christian East and Other Important Books, Ecumenical Trends, 25, 6, June 96; Jesus Christ's Challenge to World Religions: A Response, The Continuing Challenge of Jesus Christ to the World, a Symposium on the Coming of the Third Millenium and the Jubilee Year 2000, sponsored by the NCCB Subcommittee on the Millenium, Sept 7-8, 96, Proceedings; The Virgin Mary in the Breadth and Scope of Interreligious Dialogue, Marian Spirituality and Interreligous Di-

alogue, Marian Studies, 47, 96; Introductory Address for Imam Warith Deen Mohammed, Living City, Oct, 97; The Catholic Church and Interreligous Dialogue, in Vatican II: The Continuing Agenda, ed by Anthony J Cernera, Sacred Heart Univ Press, 97; Religous Pluralism in India and the Mission of the Church, Periodic Paper #4, US Cath Mission Asn, in Mission Update 6, 4, Dec 97; Interreligous Relations, 1996, Annual Report, Pro Dialogo, Bul of the Pontifical Coun for Interreligious Dialogue, 96, 97; Islamic-Catholic Relations in the USA: Activities of the National Conference of Catholic Bishops (1996) and Recent Developments, Islamochristiana 23, 97; ed with John H Erickson, The Quest for Unity, Orthodox and Catholics in Dialogue, St Vladimir's Seminary Press/US Cath Conf, 96. **CONTACT ADDRESS** Interreligious Relations, 3211 Fourth St NE, Washington, DC 20017. **EMAIL** seiamail@nccbuscc.org

BORG, DOROTHY

PERSONAL Born 09/04/1902, Elberon **DISCIPLINE** HISTORY, PUBLIC LAW **EDUCATION** Wellesley Col, AB, 23; Columbia Univ, MA, 31, PhD (pub law and govt), 46. **CAREER** Res assoc Am-Chinese rels, Inst Pac Rels, 38-59; res assoc, EAsian Res Ctr, Harvard Univ, 59-61; Sr Res Assoc, Am Far East Policy, East Asian Inst, Columbia Univ, 62-, Lectr, Peking Univ, 47-48. **HONORS AND AWARDS** Bancroft Prize Hist, 65. **MEMBERSHIPS** AHA; Asn Asian Studies, Acad Polit Sci. **SELECTED PUBLICATIONS** Auth, Social Protestantism in the 20th Century--History of the Inner Mission 1914-1945, J Mod Hist, Vol 0064, 92. **CONTACT ADDRESS** 22 Riverside Dr, New York, NY 10023.

BORG, MARCUS J.

PERSONAL Born 03/11/1942, MN, m, 1985, 2 children **DISCIPLINE** THEOLOGY **EDUCATION** Concordia Col, BA, 64; Oxford, PhD, 72; **CAREER** Instr, 66-69, ast prof, 72-74, Concordia Col; ast prof, Carleton Col, 76-79; prof, Oregon St Univ, 79- **HONORS AND AWARDS** Rockefeller Fel; Danforth Fel; NEH Fel; Hundere Dist Prof of Relig and Cult. **MEMBERSHIPS** Soc Bibl Lit; Am Acad Relig. **RESEARCH** Historian of Jesus and Christian origins; religious studies, theology. **SELECTED PUBLICATIONS** Auth, Meeting Jesus again for the First Time, 94; Jesus in Contemporary Scholarship, 94; Jesus at 2000, 96; The God We Never Knew, 97; Conflict, Holiness, and Politics in the Teachings of Jesus, rev., 98; coauth, The Meaning of Jesus, 98. **CONTACT ADDRESS** 4137 SW Stephenson, Portland, OR 97219.

BORJESSON, GARY

DISCIPLINE PHILOSOPHY **EDUCATION** Whitman Col, BA, 87; Emory Univ, MA, 94, PhD, 97. **CAREER** Asst prof, philos, Univ Central Ark, 98-99; tutor, St. John's Col, 99-. **HONORS AND AWARDS** Winner, Rev of Metaphysics dissertation essay competition, 98. **MEMBERSHIPS** APA. **RESEARCH** Metaphysics; ancient philosophy; history of philosophy. **SELECTED PUBLICATIONS** Auth, A Sounding of Walden's Philosophical Depth, Philos and Lit, 94; auth, Not for Their Own Sake: Species and the Riddle of Individuality, Rev of Metaphysics, 99. **CONTACT ADDRESS** St. John's Col, Maryland, Anapolis, MD 21404. **EMAIL** garyb@mail.uca.edu

BORK, ROBERT HERON

PERSONAL Born 03/01/1927, Pittsburgh, PA, m, 1952, 3 children **DISCIPLINE** LAW **EDUCATION** Univ Chicago, BA, 48, JD, 53; LLD, Creighton Univ Sch Law, 75; LHD, Wilkes-Barre Col, 76 and LLD, Notre Dame Law Sch, 82. **CAREER** Managing ed, Chicago Law Rev, 53; res assoc, Univ Chicago, 53-54; private practice, New York, 54-55 and Chicago, 55-62; from assoc prof to prof, Yale Univ, 62-75; Solicitor Gen of US, 72-77; res scholar, Am Enterprise Inst, Wash, 77; Chancellor Kent Prof, Law Sch, Yale Univ, 77-79; Alexander M Bickel prof pub law, 79-81. Actg Atty Gen of the US, 73-74; Solicitor Gen of US, Dept Justice, Washington, DC, 73-77; trustee, Woodrow Wilson Int Ctr for Scholars, 73-78; resident scholar, Am Enterprise Inst, Washington, DC, 77; partner, Kirkland and Ellis, Washington, DC, 81-82; Circuit Judge, US Ct Appeals for DC Circuit, 82-88; sr fel, Am Enterprise Inst. **MEMBERSHIPS** Fel Am Acad Arts and Sci. **RESEARCH** Constitutional law, antitrust, law, cultural issues. **SELECTED PUBLICATIONS** Auth, The Tempting of America: The Political Seduction of the Law, 89; auth, The Antitrust Paradox: A Policy at War with Itself, 2nd ed, 93; auth, Slouching Towards Gomorrah: Modern Liberalism and American Decline, 96. **CONTACT ADDRESS** Am Enterprise Inst, 1150 Seventeenth St, NW, Washington, DC 20036. **EMAIL** rbork@aei.org

BOROWSKI, ODED

PERSONAL Born 08/26/1939, Petakh Tikva, Israel, m, 1964, 2 children **DISCIPLINE** BIBLICAL ARCHAEOLOGY **EDUCATION** Midrasha Col of Jewish Studies, BHL, 68; Wayne State Univ, BA, 70; Univ of Mich, AM, 72; PhD, 79. **CAREER** Instr, Schoolcraft Col, 73-77; lectr, Univ of Mich, 75-77; instr to assoc prof, Emory Univ, 77-. **HONORS AND AWARDS** Ford Found Grant, 72; Mem Found for Jewish Culture Grant, 79; Emory Univ Grant, 79, 82, 84; NEH Grant 82-84; Lilly Found Fel, 85-86; Annual Prof, Albright Inst, 88; Joe Alon Center Grant, 88; Cobb Inst Grant, 88, 90; Dorot Res Prof, AIAR, Jerusalem 91-92; Mem Found for Jewish Culture, 94-95; Annual Prof, AIAR, Jerusalem, 95-96; Assoc Fel, AIAR, Jerusalem, 99. **MEMBERSHIPS** Israel Exploration Soc; Am Schools of Oriental Res; Soc for Bibl Lit; Nat Assoc of Prof of Hebrew; AAUP. **RESEARCH** Ancient agriculture, daily use of animals in ancient Isreael, space utilization in daily life activities, use of ground penetrating radar and global positioning systems in archaeology. **SELECTED PUBLICATIONS** Auth, Agriculture in Iron Age Israel", Eisenbrauns, (Winona Lake), 87; "Agriculture", Anchor Bible Dictionary, Doubleday, (NY, 92): 95-98; auth, "Halif, Tel: The Iron Age Cemetery", New Encycl of Archaeol Excavations in the Holy Land, Israel Exploration Soc (Jerusalem, 93): 559-560; auth, "The Language of the Media and Daily use of Hebrew", Bulletin of Higher Hebrew Educ 6.7 (94-95): 73-77; auth, "The Pomegranate Bowl from Tell Halif", Israel Exploration J 45 (95): 150-154; coauth, "A Penetrating Look: An Experiment in Remote Sensing at Tell Halif", Retrieving the Past: Essays on Archaeological Research and Methodology in Honor of Gus W Van Beek, ed JD Seger, Eisenbrauns, (96): 25-34; auth, "Irrigation", "Granaries and Silos", and "Food Storage", Oxford Encycl of Near Eastern Archaeol, Oxford Univ Pr, (NY, 97); auth, Every Living Thing: the Daily use of Animals in Ancient Israel, AltaMira Pr, (Walnut Creek, CA), 97. **CONTACT ADDRESS** Dept Middle East Studies, Emory Univ, 1364 Clifton Rd NE, Atlanta, GA 30322-1061.

BORRADORI, GIOVANNA

PERSONAL Born 07/24/1963, Milan, Italy, m, 1990, 2 children **DISCIPLINE** PHILOSOPHY **EDUCATION** Univ degli Studi de Milano, PhD, 85. **HONORS AND AWARDS** San Paolo Fel Humanities, 89-90. **RESEARCH** Continental philosophy, philosophy of architecture, aesthetics. **SELECTED PUBLICATIONS** Auth, The American Philosopher, Conversations with Quine, Davidson, Putnam, Nozick, Danto, Rorty, Cavell, MacIntyre and Kuhn, Univ Chicago Pr (Chicago, IL), 94; auth, "Against the Technological Interpretation of Virtuality," in Hypersurface Architecture II, Architectural Design, vol 69/9-10 (99): 26-31; auth, "The Temporalization of Difference: Reflections on Deleuze's Interpretation of Bergson," in Continental Philos Rev, vol 33/4 (00); auth, "Virtuality, Philosophy, Architecture," in D Columbia Dec for Architecture and Theory, vol 7 (00), 57-78; auth, "Architecture and Normativity," The J of Philos Hermeneutics, vol 1 (00); auth, "The Presence of Bergson in Deleuze's Nietzsche," Philos Today (00); auth, "Two Versions of Continental Holism: Derrida and Structuralism," in Philos and Soc Criticism, vol 26 (forthcoming). **CONTACT ADDRESS** Dept Philos, Vassar Col, 124 Raymond Ave, PO Box 136, Poughkeepsie, NY 12604-0001. **EMAIL** giborradori@vassar.edu

BORROWS, JOHN

DISCIPLINE LAW **EDUCATION** British Columbia Univ, BA, 87; Univ Toronto, MA, 96; LLB, 90; LLM, 91; Osgoode Univ, JD, 94. **CAREER** Assoc prof, Osgoode Hall Sch; asst prof, Univ British Columbia, 92-94; assoc prof, 96-. **MEMBERSHIPS** Can Asn Law; Chippewas Nawash First Nation. **RESEARCH** First Nations and the law; Aboriginal Law; Constitutional Law; Natural Resources/Environmental Law. **SELECTED PUBLICATIONS** Auth, pubs about Chippewas Nawash First Nation legal rights and history. **CONTACT ADDRESS** Fac of Law, Univ of Toronto, 78 Queen's Park, Toronto, ON, Canada M5S 2C5.

BORSCH, FREDERICK HOUK

PERSONAL Born 09/13/1935, Chicago, IL, m, 1960, 3 children **DISCIPLINE** ENGLISH LITERATURE, THEOLOGY **EDUCATION** Princeton Univ, AB, 57; Oxford Univ, MA, 63; Univ Birmingham (UK), PhD, 66. **CAREER** Tutor, Queens Coll, Birmingham (UK), 63-66; assoc prof, Seabury-Western Theol Sem, 66-71; prof, General Theol Sem, 71-72; dean, prof, Church Div Sch of the Pacific, 72-81; dean of chapel, prof, Princeton Univ, 81-88; Bishop, Episcopal Diocese of Los Angeles, 00-. **MEMBERSHIPS** Am Acad Rel; Soc Bib Lit; Studiorum Novi Testamenti Soc; Phi Beta Kappa. **RESEARCH** New Testament theology and literature; early church history. **SELECTED PUBLICATIONS** Auth, The Son of Man in Myth and History, Westminster Press, 67; auth, The Christian and Gnostic Son of Man, SCM Press, 70; auth, God's Parable, Westminster Press, 77; auth, Introducing the Lessons of the Church Year, Seabury Press, 78; auth, Power in Weakness, Fortress Press, 83; ed, Anglicanism and the Bible, Morehouse-Barlow, 84; auth, Many Things in Parables, Fortress Press, 88; auth, Outrage and Hope, Trinity Press Int, 96. **CONTACT ADDRESS** Box 512164, Los Angeles, CA 90051-0164. **EMAIL** bishop@ladiocese.org

BOSS, JUDITH A.

PERSONAL Born 11/11/1942, Rochester, NY, d, 2 children **DISCIPLINE** SOCIAL ETHICS **EDUCATION** Boston Univ, PhD, 90. **CAREER** Asst Dir, Office of Curriculum Affairs, Brown Univ, School of Medicine, 99-. **MEMBERSHIPS** Am Philos Asn. **RESEARCH** BioEthics; moral development. **SELECTED PUBLICATIONS** Auth, The Birth Lottery, Loyola Univ Press, 93; The Alien Abduction: a Case Study for Bioethics, Soc for the Study of Ethics and Animals Newsletter, no 7, March 95; The Morality of Prenatal Diagnosis, in Life and Learning, vol 5, ed Joseph W. Koterski, Georgetown Univ, 95; Circumcision, Free Inquiry, fall 97; Paradigm Shifts, Scientific Revolutions, and the Moral Justification of Experimentation on Non-Human Animals, Between the Species: A J of Ethics, summer/fall 95; Francine: A Fairy Tale for Philosophers Young and Old (fiction), Thinking: The J of Philos for Children, vol 12, no 2, 95; Teaching Ethics Through Community Service, The J of Experiential Ed, vol 18, May 95; Treading on Harrowed Ground: The Violence of Agriculture, in Institutional Violence, eds Deane Curtin and Robert Litke, Rodolphi Press, 96; Ethics for Life, Mayfield Pub Co, 97; Throwing Pearls to the Swine: Women, Forgiveness and the Unrepentant Abuser, in Perspectives on Power and Dominance, eds Laurence Bove and Laura D. Kaplan, Rodolphi Press, 97; Adopting an Aristotelian Approach to Teaching College Ethics, in Philos and Community Service Learning, Asn for the Advancement of Higher Ed, spring 98; Perspectives in Ethics, Mayfield Pub Co, 98; Outdoor Education and the Development of Civic Responsibility, ERIC Clearinghouse on Rural Education and Small Schools, 98; Analyzing Moral Issues, Mayfield Pub Co, forthcoming 99; auth, Healthcare Ethics in a Diverse Society, coauth, Michael Brannigan, Mayfield Pub Co, forthcoming, 01. **CONTACT ADDRESS** Sch of Med, Brown Univ, Box G-232, Providence, RI 02912. **EMAIL** judith-boss@brown.edu

BOTEIN, MICHAEL

PERSONAL Born 01/10/1945, New York, NY, m, 1990, 2 children **DISCIPLINE** LAW **EDUCATION** Wesleyan Univ, BA, 66; Cornell Univ, JD, 69; Columbia Univ, LLM, 71; JSD, 78. **CAREER** Asst Prof, Brooklyn Law School, 69-77; Assoc Prof, Rutgers Law School, 74-77; Prof, NYork Law School, 77-. **HONORS AND AWARDS** Ford Fel, Columbia Law Soc, 71-77. **MEMBERSHIPS** NYC Bar Asn, Fed Comm Bar Asn. **SELECTED PUBLICATIONS** Auth, Cases and Materials on Regulation of the Electronic Mass Media, 3rd ed, 98; auth, "Judicial Review of FCC Action," Cardozo Arts & entertainment L.J. 95; auth, "Move Over Bill Gates: The Real Antitrust Menace is the Law professors," New York Law Journal, (95): A-2; auth, "The 1992 Cable Act," in 13 Encyclopedia of Telecommunications, 96; auth, "The Telecom Reform Act: Who Needs It?," New York Law Journal, 96; auth, "Cable/Telco Mergers and Acquisitions: an antitrust Analysis, 25 Southwestern L Rev, 96; auth, "Medieval Bills of attainder and Modern Telecommunications Policy," New York Law Journal , 98; auth, "Sistema de comunicaciones," in el Derecho de la Informacion en el Marco de la Reforma del Estado en Mexico, 98. **CONTACT ADDRESS** New York Law School, 57 Worth St, New York, NY 10013-2926. **EMAIL** michael.botein@cmcnyls.edu

BOTHAM, THAD M.

PERSONAL Born Grand Junction, CO, m, 1997 **DISCIPLINE** PHILOSOPHY **EDUCATION** Texas A&M Univ, MA. **CAREER** Tchg asst, Texas A&M, 98-99. **HONORS AND AWARDS** Fel, Interdisciplinary Group for Hum; Texas A&M Regents Fel. **MEMBERSHIPS** APA. **RESEARCH** Counterfactual conditional semantics; metaphysics; philosophy of religion; logic. **CONTACT ADDRESS** 1013 S 34th St., Ste. 57, South Bend, IN 46615-1923.

BOTTICINI, MARISTELLA

PERSONAL Born Travagliato, Italy, m, 1997 **DISCIPLINE** ECONOMICS **EDUCATION** Univ Bocconi, Laurea, 90; Northwestern Univ, PhD, 97. **CAREER** Asst Prof, Boston Univ, 97-. **HONORS AND AWARDS** Fel, Boston Univ, 98; Fel, Econ Hist Asn, 96, 98; Fel, John M. Olin Found, 00-01; Fel, Nat Sci Found, 99-04; Fel, Nat Sci Found, 99-00; Teaching Awd, Boston Univ, 99. **MEMBERSHIPS** Am Econ Asn; Econ Hist Asn; Econometric Soc. **RESEARCH** Economic and social history of medieval and Renaissance Tuscany; Dowries; Marriage markets; Intergenerational transfers; Credit markets; Agrarian contracts; Jewish history. **SELECTED PUBLICATIONS** Auth, "A Loveless Economy? Intergenerational Altruism and the Marriage Market in a Tuscan Town, 1415-1436," J of Econ Hist, 99; auth, "A Tale of 'Benevolent' Governments: Private Credit Markets, Public Finance, and the Role of Jewish Lenders in Medieval and Renaissance Italy," J of Econ Hist, 00; co-auth, "The Choice of Agrarian Contracts in Early Renaissance Tuscany: Risk Sharing, Moral Hazard, or Capital Market Imperfections?" Explorations in Econ Hist, 00. **CONTACT ADDRESS** Dept Econ, Boston Univ, 270 Bay State Rd, Rm 310, Boston, MA 02215. **EMAIL** maristel@bu.edu

BOTZLER, RICHARD G.

PERSONAL Born 01/27/1942, Detroit, MI, m, 1963, 5 children **DISCIPLINE** ENVIRONMENTAL ETHICS **EDUCATION** Wayne State Univ, BS, 63; Univ Mich, MWM, 67; PhD, 70. **CAREER** Prof, Humboldt State Univ, 70-; chemn of wildlife dept, Humboldt State Univ, 77-80 & 96-98. **HONORS AND AWARDS** Fulbright Fel, 81-82; Meritorious Performance/Professional Promise Awd, Humboldt State Univ, 88; Outstanding prof Awd, Humboldt State Univ, 91-92; Trustee Outstanding Prof Awd, Calif State Univ System, 92. **MEMBERSHIPS** Fulbright Alumni Asn, Asn of Forest Service Employees for Environmental Ethics, Soc for conservation Biology, Int Soc for Environmental Ethics, Humboldt County Human Rights Comn, Community for Common Ground. **RESEARCH** Environmental and scientific ethics, 1983 to present. **SELECTED PUBLICATIONS** Coauth, "Ethical considerations in research on wildlife diseases," J of Wildlife Diseases 21 (85): 341-345; co-ed, Environmental Ethics: Divergence and Convergence, McGraw-Hill, Inc. (New York, NY), 93; ed, "Ethical guidelines to publication in the J of Wildlife Diseases," J of Wildlife Diseases 32 (96): 163-167; co-ed, Environmental Ethics: Divergence and Convergence, McGraw-Hill, Inc. (New York, NY), 98; auth, "Environmental Ethics," in Natural Resources, consulting eds. M. S. Coyne and C. W. Allin (CA: Salem Press, 98), 246-249; auth, "Environmental Ethics," in Encyclopedia of Environmental Issues, ed. C. W. Allin (CA: Salem Press, 00), 285-287. **CONTACT ADDRESS** Dept Wildlife Mgt, Humboldt State Univ, 1 Harpst St, Arcata, CA 95521. **EMAIL** rbg2@humboldt.edu

BOULAD-AYOUB, JOSIANE
PERSONAL Born 02/22/1941, Alexandria, Egypt **DISCIPLINE** PHILOSOPHIE POLITIQUE **EDUCATION** Lyon III (France) LL, 63, DL, 79; Univ Montreal, MS, 78, PhD, 76. **CAREER** Dir, dp de philos, 92, Prof Titulaire De Philosophie Politique, Univ Quebec Montreal, 92-. **HONORS AND AWARDS** Soc royale du Can. **MEMBERSHIPS** Centre de rech en sci cognitives; Soc philos Que; Asn can philos; Soc d'etudes du dix-huitieme siecle; Soc Nord-Am etudes JJ Rousseau. **SELECTED PUBLICATIONS** Auth, Contre nous de la tyrannie, 90; auth, Mimes et parades, 95; auth, Former un nouveau peuple?, 95; contribur & co-ed, Les Comites d'instruction publique de l'Assemblee Legislative et de la Convention, 97; ed, L'Esprit de la Revolution, 89; ed, Philosophie et Droit, 89; ed, Le Systeme de la nature (Baron d'Holbach), 93; ed, Le Systeme social (Baron d'Holbach), 94; L'Amour des lois, 96. **CONTACT ADDRESS** Dep de philosophie, Univ of Quebec, Montreal, CP 8888, Succ Centre-Ville, Montreal, QC, Canada H3C 3P8. **EMAIL** boulad-ayoub.josiane@uqam.ca

BOUMAN, WALTER R.
PERSONAL Born 07/09/1929, Spingfield, MA, m, 1957, 3 children **DISCIPLINE** SYSTEMATIC THEOLOGY **EDUCATION** Concordia Sem, BA, 52, MDiv, 54; Univ Heidelberg, ThD, 63; Gen Theol Sem, DD, 93. **CAREER** Assoc, prof, Concordia Teachers Col, 63-71; vis prof, ELTS, 71-75; joint prof, ELTS/Hamma, 75-78; prof, 78-83; Edward C. Fendt prof, Trinity Lutheran Sem, 83-99; guest prof, Theol Hochschule, Leipzig, 85; vis prof, Gen Theol Sem, 94-95; scholar in residence Luth Theol Sem, Gettysburg, 99-00; vis prof, Gen Theol Sem, 00-01; Eward C. Fendt prof emer, 99-. **HONORS AND AWARDS** DD, Gen Theol Sem, 93; pres, lutheran acad scholar, 75-77. **MEMBERSHIPS** Pres, Lutheran Acad Scholar, 75-77; Amer Acad Rel. **RESEARCH** Church, worship, aplolgetics **SELECTED PUBLICATIONS** Co auth, We Believe, American Lutheran Publicity Bureau, 99; What Shall I Say?, Discerning God's Call to Ministry, Division for Ministry, Evangel Lutheran Church Am, 95; Like Wheat Arising Greeen, Valparaiso, Indiana, 91. **CONTACT ADDRESS** 1360 Millerdale Rd, Columbus, OH 43209-2334. **EMAIL** wrbouman@aol.com

BOURGEOIS, PATRICK LYALL
PERSONAL Born 03/17/1940, Baton Rouge, LA, m, 1968, 2 children **DISCIPLINE** PHILOSOPHY, RELIGION **EDUCATION** Notre Dame Sem, BA, 62, MA, 64; Notre Dame Univ, MA, 65; Duquesne Univ, PhD(philos), 70. **CAREER** Instr relig, Duquesne Univ, 65-67; from instr to asst prof philos, 68-78, Prof Philos, Loyola Univ of The South, 78-, Fac res grants, Loyola Univ, 72 & 73; La Endowment Humanities fels, State of La, 74 & 76-77. **HONORS AND AWARDS** Dux Academicus, 93. **MEMBERSHIPS** Soc Phenomenol & Existential Philos; Am Acad Relig; Southern Soc Philos & Psychol; Soc Advan Am Philos; Int Husserl & Phenomenol Res Soc. **SELECTED PUBLICATIONS** Auth, Existential phenomenology and phenomenology, Paul Ricoeur's Hermeneutical Phenomenology, Philos Today, 72; Extension of Ricoeur's Hermeneutic, Martinus Nijhoff, 75; Kierkegaard: Ethical marriage or aesthetic pleasure, Personalist, 76; coauth, Pragmatism, scientific methodology and phenomenological return to lived experience, Philos & Phenomenol Res, 77; Mead, Merleau-Ponty and the lived perceptual world, Philos Today, 77; auth, From the hermeneutics of symbols to the interpretation of texts, in an anthology, Ohio Univ, 78; coauth, Pragmatism and Phenomenology: A philosophic encounter, Grunner, 80; Fundamental ontology and epistemic foundations, In: New Scholasticism, Vol LX, 81; The Religious Within Experience & Existance, Duequesne Univ Press, 90. **CONTACT ADDRESS** Loyola Univ, New Orleans, 6363 St Charles Ave, New Orleans, LA 70118-6195. **EMAIL** PBB31740@aol.com

BOURGUIGNON, HENRY J.
PERSONAL Born 08/19/1931, Lakewood, OH, m, 1971, 2 children **DISCIPLINE** LEGAL HISTORY; LAW **EDUCATION** Loyola Univ Chicago, AB, 54, MA, 58; Univ Mich, PhD(legal hist), 68, JD, 71. **CAREER** Trial atty, Dept Justice, 71-74; from Assoc Prof to Distinguished Univ Prof Law, Col Law, Univ Toledo, 74-. **HONORS AND AWARDS** Am Coun Learned Soc fel, England, 80-81. **MEMBERSHIPS** Am Soc Legal Hist (secy, 78-83). **RESEARCH** History of international law; constitutional law. **SELECTED PUBLICATIONS** Auth, The First Federal Court: The Federal Appellate Prize Court of the American Revolution, 1775-1787, Am Philos Soc, 77; Incorporation of the law of Nations during the American Revolution -- the case of the San Antonio, Am J of Int Law 71, 77; The Second Justice Harlan - His Principles of Judicial Decision Making, Supreme Ct Rev, 79; A Revisionist Revises Himself - A Review Essay, Tex Law Rev 64, 85; The Articles of Confederation, In: Encyclopedia of the American Judicial System, Charles Scribner's Sons, 87; Sir William Scott, Lord Stowell, Judge of the High Court of Admiralty, 1798-1828, Cambridge Univ Press, 87; The Belilos Case - New Light on Reservations to Multilateral Treaties, Va J of Int Law 29, 89; coauth, Coming to Terms with Death -- The Cruzan Case, Hast L.J. 42, 91; auth, Human Rights Decisions by the United Supreme Court - October Term 1990, Human Rights L.J. 13, 92; Human Rights Decisions by the United Supreme Court - October Term 1991, Human Rights L.J. 13, 92; The United States Supreme Court and Freedom of Expression - October Term 92, Human Rights L.J. 15, 94; Persons with Mental Retardation - The Reality Behind the Label, Cambridge Quart of Healthcare Ethics 3, 94; The Federal Key to the Judiciary Act of 1789, SC Law Rev 46, 95. **CONTACT ADDRESS** Col of Law, Univ of Toledo, 2801 W Bancroft St, Toledo, OH 43606-3391.

BOUSEMAN, JOHN W.
PERSONAL Born 01/08/1928, Mt Vernon, IL, m, 1997, 3 children **DISCIPLINE** PHILOSOPHY **EDUCATION** Anderson Univ, BA & BS, 50; Union Theol Sem, MDiv, 53; Univ Chicago, MA, 57; PhD, 70. **CAREER** Principal to Vice pres, , Central YMCA High School, 56-71; Vice Pres and Prof, Hillsborough Cmty Col, 71-. **HONORS AND AWARDS** John R Mott Fel, 66; Paul Harris Fel, 84. **MEMBERSHIPS** FUSA, FACC. **RESEARCH** Extrasensory perception, The nature reality, Comparative religion. **CONTACT ADDRESS** Dept Beh Sci & Philos, Hillsborough Comm Col, PO Box 30030, Tampa, FL 33630. **EMAIL** jwbouseman@hotmail.com

BOUZARD, WALTER
PERSONAL Born 09/06/1954, Washington, DC, m, 1974, 2 children **DISCIPLINE** RELIGION, PHILOSPHY **EDUCATION** Univ Tx, BA, 76; Luther Northwestern Theol Sem, MDiv, 80; MTh, 88; Princeton Theol Sem, PhD, 96. **CAREER** Assoc Pastor, St Martin's Lutheran Church, 81-84; Pastor, Christus Lutheran Church, 85-89; Instr, Princeton Theol Sem, 89-93; Instr, Lutheran Theol Sem, 93-94; Prof, Wartburg Col, 94-. **HONORS AND AWARDS** G M Bruce Prize, Luther Northwestern Theol Sem, 80; Fel, Princeton Univ, 89-93; Student Awds for Teaching Excellence, 97-98. **MEMBERSHIPS** SBL, CBA, ASOR. **RESEARCH** Old Testament exegesis theology, Israelite history and religion in its ancient Near Eastern context, archeology, Psalms, wisdom literature, Biblical Hebrew, science and religion. **SELECTED PUBLICATIONS** Coauth, "Do Unto Them as They Have Done to Me," (91); auth, We Have Heard with Our Ears, O God: Sources of the Communal Laments in the Psalms, Scholars Pr (Atlanta, GA), 97; rev, "A God of Vengeance," Theol Today 54/1 (97): 144; rev, "Out of Eden: Reading, Rhetoric and Ideology in Genesis 2-3," Lutheran Quart (forthcoming); rev, "Psalm 109 un die Aussagen zur Feindschaedigung in den Psalmen," J of Bibl Lit (forthcoming). **CONTACT ADDRESS** Dept Relig & Philos, Wartburg Col, 222 9th Street NW, Waverly, IA 50677-2215.

BOVON, FRANCOIS
PERSONAL Born 03/13/1938, Lausanne, Switzerland **DISCIPLINE** THEOLOGY **EDUCATION** Gymnase Classique Cantonal, Lausanne, BA, 56; Univ Lausanne, Licence en Theologie, 61; Univ Basel, ThD, 65. **CAREER** Prof, 67-93, dean theol, 76-79, Univ Geneva; Frothingham Prof of the Hist of Relig, Harvard Univ Div Sch, 93- . **HONORS AND AWARDS** Summa cum laude, 65; Dr Honoris Causa, Uppsala, Sweden, 93. **MEMBERSHIPS** SNTS; SBL; AELAC. **RESEARCH** New Testament; Luke-Acts; Christian apocryphal literature; early church. **SELECTED PUBLICATIONS** Auth, Luke the Theilogian, 87; auth, Das Evangelism nach Lukas, 89; L'Evangile et l'Apotre: Le Christ Inseparable de ses Temoins, Le Moulin, 93; auth, The Role of the Scriptures in the Composition of the Gospel Accounts: The Temptations of Jesus (Lk 4:1-13 par.) and the Multiplication of the Loaves (Lk 9:10-17 par.) in O'Collins, ed, Luke and Acts, Paulist, 93; auth, The Gospel and the Apostle, Harvard Divinity Bull, 94; auth, The Words of Life in the Acts of the Apostle Andrew, Harvard Theol Rev, 94; auth, The Church in the New Testament, Ex Auditu, 94; auth, New Testament Traditions and Apocryphal Narratives, 95; auth, New Testament Traditions and Apocryphal Narratives, Pickwick, 95; auth, Ces chretiens qui revent: L'autorite du reve dans les premiers siecles du christianisme, in Hengel, ed, Geschichte-Tradition-Reflexion, Mohr, 96; auth, After Paul after Paul, Harvard Theol Rev, 97; auth, Apocalyptic Traditions in the Lukan Special Material: Reading Luke 18: 1-8, Harvard Theol Rev, 97; auth, The Child and the Beast: Fighting Violence in Ancient Christianity, Harvard Theological Review, 99; auth, The Canonical Structure of the New Testament: The Gospel and the Apostle, in Farmer, ed, International Bible Commentary, Liturgical, 98; auth, Luke: Portrait and Project in Farmer, ed, International Bible Commentary, Liturgical, 98; The Apocryphal Acts of the Apostles, with Ann Graham Brock and Christopher Matthews, 99. **CONTACT ADDRESS** The Divinity School, Harvard Univ, 45 Francis Ave, Cambridge, MA 02138.

BOWDEN, HENRY WARNER
PERSONAL Born 04/01/1939, Memphis, TN, m, 1997, 2 children **DISCIPLINE** HISTORY, RELIGION **EDUCATION** Baylor Univ, AB, 61; Princeton Univ, AM, 64, PhD (relig), 66. **CAREER** From instr to asst prof, 64-71, asst dean col, 69-71, assoc prof, 71-79, Prof Relig, Douglass Col, Rutgers Univ, 79-. **MEMBERSHIPS** Am Soc Church Hist; American Catholic Hist Assn. **RESEARCH** Historiographical studies, chiefly in the United States; religion of American Indians and missionary activities by Europeans. **SELECTED PUBLICATIONS** Ed, Religion in America, Harper, 70; auth, Church History in the Age of Science, Univ NC, 71; Dict of American Religious Biography, 77 & 93 & ed, John Eliot's Indian Dialogues, 80, Greenwood; auth, American Indians and Christian missions, Chicago, 81; auth, Church History in an Age of Uncertainty, Carbondale, 89; auth, Native and Christian--Indigenous Voices on Religious Identity in the United States and Canada, Am Indian Cult Res J, Vol 0021, 97; Historians of the Christian Tradition--Their Methodology and Influence on Western Thought, Church Hist, Vol 0066, 97; Missionary Conquest--The Gospel and Native American Cultural Genocide, Church Hist, Vol 0064, 95; Historians of the Christian Tradition--Their Methodology and Influence on Western Thought, Church Hist, Vol 0066, 97 Choctaws and Missionaries in Mississippi, 1818-1918, Am Hist Rev, Vol 0102, 97; Converting the West--A Biography of Whitman, Narcissa, Pac Hist Rev, Vol 0061, 92. **CONTACT ADDRESS** Dept of Relig Douglass Col, Rutgers, The State Univ of New Jersey, New Brunswick, P O Box 270, New Brunswick, NJ 08903-0270.

BOWDEN, JAMES HENRY
PERSONAL Born 10/28/1934, Louisville, KY, d, 3 children **DISCIPLINE** AMERICAN STUDIES, RELIGION **EDUCATION** Univ Louisville, MA, 59; Univ MN, Minneapolis, PhD, 70; Louisville Presbyterian Theol Sem, MA, 87. **CAREER** Instr Eng, Univ KY, 60-61, Univ MT, 62-64 & Colgate Univ, 65-66; from Instr to Assoc Prof, 66-80, Prof English, 80-98, Prof Emeritus, Ind Univ SE, 98-, Chmn Hum Div, 80-85; Assoc Dir, Am Studies Ctr, Warsaw, 85-86; Prof, Institut Teknologi Mari, Malaysia, 89-91. **HONORS AND AWARDS** Nat Endowment for the Humanities summer fel, Univ MI, 77; fel, Bread Loaf Writers Conf, 80. **RESEARCH** Relig in Am life; imaginative writing; theories of humor. **SELECTED PUBLICATIONS** Auth, The bland leading the bland, New Oxford Rev, 77; Go purple, West Branch, 77; The grief of Terry Magoo, Great River Rev, 77; The Bible and other Novels, Cresset, 78; Don't Lose This, It's My Only Copy, Col English, 79; ICU, Thornleigh Rev, 82; Conwell Lives, New Oxford Rev, 82; Peter DeVries, A Critical Study, G K Hall, 83. **CONTACT ADDRESS** Dept of Hum, Indiana Univ, Southeast, 4201 Grant Line Rd, New Albany, IN 47150-2158. **EMAIL** jhbowden@iusmail.ius.indiana.edu

BOWDEN, MARIE ANN
DISCIPLINE LAW **EDUCATION** Mt. Allison Univ, BA, 76; Queen's Univ, LLB, 79; Osgoode Hall Law Sch, LLM, 81. **CAREER** Assoc prof, 81-. **HONORS AND AWARDS** Ed, Can Jour Environ Law Policy. **RESEARCH** Environmental law, environmental assessment, public interest advocacy and property law. **SELECTED PUBLICATIONS** Co-auth, Understanding Property: A Guide to Canada's Property Law. **CONTACT ADDRESS** Col of Law, Univ of Saskatchewan, 15 Campus Dr, Saskatoon, SK, Canada S7N 5A6. **EMAIL** Bowden@law.usask.ca

BOWDLE, DONALD N.
PERSONAL Born 02/02/1935, Easton, MD, m, 1994, 3 children **DISCIPLINE** THEOLOGY **EDUCATION** Lee Col, BA 53; Bob Jones Univ, MA 59, PhD 61; Princeton Theol Seminary, ThM 62; Union Theol Seminary, ThD 70. **CAREER** Lee Univ, fac, teach admin, 62-; Georgia State Univ, adj fac, 93-97; Yale Univ Div Sch, vis lect, 85; VA Commonwealth Univ, adj fac, 67-69. **HONORS AND AWARDS** Post Doc Fel Yale Univ and Univ Edinburgh. **MEMBERSHIPS** ASCH; ETS; Karl Barth Soc NA. **RESEARCH** John Calvin; Karl Barth; Non-Wesleyan origins of Amer Pentecostalism. **SELECTED PUBLICATIONS** Auth, Holiness in the Highlands: A Profile of the Church of God, in: Christianity in Appalachia: Profiles In Regional Pluralism, ed Bill J. Leonard, Univ Tenn Press, forthcoming 98. **CONTACT ADDRESS** School of Religion, Lee Col, Tennessee, Cleveland, TN 37311. **EMAIL** dbowdle@leeuniversity.edu

BOWEN, DAVID H.
PERSONAL Born 10/28/1964, Virginia, MN **DISCIPLINE** PHILOSOPHY **EDUCATION** Univ Leuven, Belgium, drs, 98. **CAREER** Instr, 97-98, asst prof, 98-, Univ N Fla. **MEMBERSHIPS** APA; Int Asn of Philos & Lit; Soc for the Philos of Love and Sex. **RESEARCH** 19th century German philos; 20th century French philos; aesthetics; psychoanalysis. **SELECTED PUBLICATIONS** Auth, La pensee de Jacques Lacan, 1994-Louvain-Paris: Editions Peeters, 94. **CONTACT ADDRESS** Dept of History and Philosophy, Univ of No Florida, Jacksonville, FL 32224. **EMAIL** Elagabalus@compuserve.com

BOWERS, J. W.
PERSONAL Born 01/09/1942, Billings, MT, m, 1980, 7 children **DISCIPLINE** LAW AND ECONOMICS **EDUCATION** Yale Univ, BA, 64, Law Sch, LLB, 67. **CAREER** Assoc prof; Prof, Byron R Kantrow Prof, 82-, Louisiana State Univ Law

Cen; Texas Tech Univ Law Sch, Assoc Prof, 78-81; Assoc and shhldr, 69-77, Briggs and Morgan MN; USAR, Cpt, 67-69. **MEMBERSHIPS** ABA; ALEA; CLC LA Law Inst. **RESEARCH** Bankruptcy and Commercial Law. **SELECTED PUBLICATIONS** Auth, Security Interests Creditor Priorities and Bankruptcy, title number 1500, in: the Encyclopedia of Law and Economics, De Geest et al, eds, Elgar, forthcoming 98, also pub on the internet by the Univ of Ghent; coauth, Bonds Liens and Insurance, Washington DC, Federal Pub Inc, 78, 79, 80, 81; Rev, Of Bureaucrats' Brothers-in-Law and Bankruptcy Taxes: Article Nine Filing Systems and the Market for Information, Minn L 95; auth, Rehabilitation Redistribution or Dissipation: The Evidence for Choosing Among Bankruptcy Hypotheses, Wash U L Qtly, 94; Kissing Off Economics and Misunderstanding Murphy's Law: Carlson's On the Efficiency Of Secured Lending, A Commentary, VA L Rev, 94; The Fantastic Wisconsylvania Zero-Bureaucratic-Cost School of Bankruptcy Theory: A Comment, Mich L Rev, 93. **CONTACT ADDRESS** Law Center, Louisiana State Univ and A&M Col, Baton Rouge, LA 70803. **EMAIL** lmbowe@lsu.edu

BOWIE, NORMAN
PERSONAL Born 06/06/1942, Biddeford, ME, m, 1987, 2 children **DISCIPLINE** PHILOSOPHY **EDUCATION** Univ Rochester, PhD. **RESEARCH** Ethics and political philosophy; corporate responsibility; ethical issues in management; ethical foundations of capitalism. **SELECTED PUBLICATIONS** Auth, New Direction in Corporate Responsibility, Bus Horizons, 91; Challenging the Egoistic Paradigm, Bus Ethics Quarterly, 91; co-auth, Business Ethics, Prentice-Hall, 90; co-ed, Ethics and Agency Theory, Oxford, 92. **CONTACT ADDRESS** Philosophy Dept, Univ of Minnesota, Twin Cities, 355 Ford Hall, 224 Church St SE, Minneapolis, MN 55455. **EMAIL** nbowie@csom.umn.edu

BOWLAND, TERRY
PERSONAL Born 08/30/1954, St Joseph, MO, m, 1975, 2 children **DISCIPLINE** NEW TESTAMENT, PRACTICAL THEOLOGY **EDUCATION** Neb Christ Col, BA, 76; BTh, 77; Linc Christ Sem, MA, 80; MDiv, 82; Trin Evan Div, Dmin, 89. **CAREER** Sr min, 77-93; vis lectr, Neb Christ Col, 88-93; prof, Ozark Christ Col, 93-. **RESEARCH** Church growth; church administration; Evangelism; sociology; philosophy. **SELECTED PUBLICATIONS** Auth, Make Disciples: Reaching the Post Modern World for Christ, Joplin Coll Press, 99. **CONTACT ADDRESS** Dept Religion, Ozark Christian Col, PO Box 518, Joplin, MO 64802-0518. **EMAIL** tbowland@occ.edu

BOWMAN, LEONARD JOSEPH
PERSONAL Born 02/04/1941, Detroit, MI, m, 2 children **DISCIPLINE** RELIGION; LITERATURE **EDUCATION** Duns Scotus Col MI, BA 63; Univ Detroit, MA 67; Fordham Univ, PhD 73. **CAREER** Marycrest Intl Univ, prof 73-94, vpres acad dean 94-97; Col Notre Dame MD, vpres acd affs, 97-. **MEMBERSHIPS** AAUP **RESEARCH** Medieval Franciscan Spirituality; St. Bonaventure. **SELECTED PUBLICATIONS** Auth, A Retreat With St. Bonaventure, Element Books Ltd, 93. **CONTACT ADDRESS** Dept of Academic Affairs, Notre Dame Col, 4003 Roundtop Rd, Baltimore, MD 21218. **EMAIL** lbowman@udm.edu

BOWNE, DALE RUSSELL
PERSONAL Born 08/19/1934, Pickaway Co, OH, m, 1956, 2 children **DISCIPLINE** RELIGION, PHILOSOPHY **EDUCATION** Washington & Jefferson Col, BA, 56; Pittsburgh Theol Sem, MDiv, 59; Union theol Sem, NYork, ThD, 63. **CAREER** From asst prof to assoc prof, 63-71, Prof Relig, Grove City Col, 71-99. **HONORS AND AWARDS** DD, Washington & Jefferson Col, 81. **MEMBERSHIPS** Am Acad Relig; Soc Bibl Lit. **RESEARCH** New Testament studies; general Bibl studies; philosophical ethics. **SELECTED PUBLICATIONS** Auth, How to Choose a Bible, Griggs Educ Serv, 79; Paradigms and Principal Parts for the Greek New Testament, 87; Harbison Heritage, 89. **CONTACT ADDRESS** Dept Relig, Grove City Col, 100 Campus Dr, Box 2623, Grove City, PA 16127-2104. **EMAIL** drbowne@gcc.edu

BOYARIN, DANIEL
PERSONAL Born 12/06/1946, Asbury Park, NJ, m, 1967, 2 children **DISCIPLINE** TALMUD **EDUCATION** Goddard Col, BA, 68; Jewish Theolog Seminary, Master Hebrew Lit, 71; Columbia Univ, MA, 72; Jewish Theolog Seminary, PhD, 75 **CAREER** Hermann P. and Sophia Taubman prof, Univ California Berkeley, current; visiting prof, Talmud, Jewish Theolog Seminary, 92, 96; adjunct prof, Graduate Theolog Unio, 91; senior lctr, Bar-Ilan Univ, 90; visiting prof, Yeshiva Univ, 88; visiting assoc prof, Yale Univ, 85; **HONORS AND AWARDS** David Baumgardt Memorial Fel, 95; Crompton-Noll Awd, 95; John Simon Guggenheim Found Fel, 93; President's Res Fel, Univ Calif, 93; Res Fel, Ntl Endowment Humanities, 92; Res Grant, Littauer Found, 91; Fel Institute for Advanced Studies of Shalom Hartman Inst, 88-94 **RESEARCH** Women's Studies; Gay and Lesbian Studies; Talmudic Culture **SELECTED PUBLICATIONS** Co-ed, Studies in Rabbinic Literature, Judah Magnes; auth, co-ed, Queer Theory and the Jewish Question, Columbia Univ, 98; auth, "Goyim Naches; or, Modernity and the Manliness of the Mentsh," Modernity, Culture and "the Jew," 98; auth, "The Colonial Masqued Ball," Theory and Crit, 97; **CONTACT ADDRESS** Univ of California, Berkeley, Berkeley, CA 94720.

BOYCE, JAMES
DISCIPLINE NEW TESTAMENT **EDUCATION** Luther Sem, MDiv, 71; Univ NC, PhD, 74. **CAREER** Instr, Univ NC, 68-70; prof, 87-. **HONORS AND AWARDS** Minister of edu, Prince of Peace Lutheran Church, 74-77. **MEMBERSHIPS** Mem, Soc of Biblical Lit; Amer Philol Assn. **SELECTED PUBLICATIONS** Act ed, Word & World, 90-91; assoc ed, 93-94; cotransl, Mark the Evangelist by Willi Marxsen. **CONTACT ADDRESS** Dept of New Testament, Luther Sem, 2481 Como Ave, Saint Paul, MN 55108.

BOYD, J. WESLEY
PERSONAL Born 11/18/1963, Slidell, LA, m, 1991, 4 children **DISCIPLINE** RELIGION **EDUCATION** Yale Univ, BA, 85; Univ NC, MA, 87; PhD, 92; MD, 92. **CAREER** Instr, Harvard Univ, 94-96; Asst Prof, Tufts Univ Sch of Med, 96-99; Vis Lectr Smith Col, 97-; Staff Psychiatrist, Providence/Mercy Hosps, 97-; Vis Lectr, Mt Holyoke Vol, 98-99; Lectr, Harvard Univ, 98-. **HONORS AND AWARDS** Ger Book Awd, Yale Univ, 1984; Henry Horace Williams Fel, Univ NC, 86; Holderness Med Fel, Univ NC, 90-91; Students' Undergrad Teaching Awd, Univ NC, 92; Pfizer Psychiatric Resident of the Year Awd, 96. **MEMBERSHIPS** SHH, ASBH, NANS, SPEP. **RESEARCH** The psychology of religion, philosophical approaches to the study of religion, ethics and values in psychiatry. **SELECTED PUBLICATIONS** Coauth, "The Tobacco/Health Insurance Connection," The Lancet, 346 (95): 64; coauth, "Health Insurance Industry Investments in Tobacco: Is That 'Piece of a Rock' a Granite Headstone?" Managing Employee Health Benefits (96): 94-95; auth, "Narrative Aspects of a Doctor-Patient Encounter," The J of Med Humanities 17 (96): 5-15; auth, "The Human Toll of Managed Care," Pharos 60:1 (97): 32-34; auth, "Stories of Illness: Authorship in Medicine," Psychiat: Interpersonal and Biolog Processes 60 (97): 347-359; auth, "Managed Care Folly--Time to End the Silence," Pharos 61:4 (98): 28-29; auth, "Throwing Up," Iris: The UNC J of Med, Lit and Visual Art (forthcoming). **CONTACT ADDRESS** Dept Relig, Smith Col, 98 Green St, Northhampton, MA 01063-1000. **EMAIL** jwboyd@pol.net

BOYD, JAMES W.
DISCIPLINE PHILOSOPHY **EDUCATION** Northwestern Univ, PhD, 70. **CAREER** Prof. **RESEARCH** Asian studies. **SELECTED PUBLICATIONS** Auth, Satan and Mara, 75; The Lion and the Dragon, 79; Guide to Zoroastrian Religion, 82; A Persian Offering, 91; co-auth, Ritual Art and Knowledge, 93. **CONTACT ADDRESS** Philosophy Dept, Colorado State Univ, Fort Collins, CO 80523. **EMAIL** jwboyd@lamar.colostate.edu

BOYD, ROBERT
PERSONAL Born 02/10/1952, Hillsdale, MI, m, 1974, 2 children **DISCIPLINE** PHILOSOPHY **EDUCATION** Tex Christian Univ, MA, 79. **CAREER** Adj assoc prof, philos, Tex Christ Univ, 93-96; instr, philos, Fresno City Col, 96-. **HONORS AND AWARDS** Who's Who Among Amer Teachers, 98; Who's Who in the South and Southwest, 97. **MEMBERSHIPS** Amer Asn of Philos Teachers; Amer Philos Asn; Soc of Christ Philos. **RESEARCH** Critical reasoning and logic. **SELECTED PUBLICATIONS** Auth, Strawson On Induction, The Philosophy of P.F. Strawson, Open Court Press, 98; auth, Inductive Reasoning and Rhetoric, Korean Jour of Thinking and Problem Solving, 98; auth, Teaching Writing with Logic, Col Teaching, 43, 95; auth, Writing With Logic in Mind, Harcourt Brace Col Publ, 94; auth, Argument Analysis and Critical Thinking, Korean Jour of Thinking and Problem Solving, 93; auth, Critical Reasoning: The Fixation of Belief, Colonial Press, 92; co-auth, Probability and Lycan's Paradox, Southwest Philos 88; co-auth, Semantic Trees and Philosophical Logics, Southwest Philos Studies, 83. **CONTACT ADDRESS** Philosophy, Fresno City Col, 1101 E. University, Fresno, CA 93741. **EMAIL** rboyd@scccd.com

BOYD, TOM WESLEY
PERSONAL Born 07/04/1933, Nashville, TN, m, 4 children **DISCIPLINE** THEOLOGY, PHILOSOPHY **EDUCATION** Bethany Nazarene Col, BA, 56; Univ Okla, MA, 62; Vanderbilt Univ, BD, 63, PhD, 73. **CAREER** Instr theol, Vanderbilt Divinity Sch, 67-69; asst prof, 69-75, Assoc Prof to David Ross Boyd Prof Emer Philos, Univ Okla, 75-98, 97-. **HONORS AND AWARDS** AMACO Outstanding Teaching Awd, 76; Baldwing travel award, 79; Teacher of the Year Awd, Univ Okla, 80. **MEMBERSHIPS** Southwestern Philos Asn; Am Acad Relig. **RESEARCH** Constructive theology; reinterpretation of traditional religious themes and symbols in light of contemporary insight; ethics of ecology with special attention to technology. **SELECTED PUBLICATIONS** Auth, Libri-Confusi--The So-Called Peisistratus Recension of Homer, Class Jour, Vol 0091, 95; A Regular Illustrated Book--Allingham, William and His Pre-Raphaelite Friends Make The Music Master, 1854-55, Publ Hist, Vol 0037, 95. **CONTACT ADDRESS** Dept of Philos, 18832 E Linvale Circle, Aurora, CO 80013. **EMAIL** tom.w.boyd-1@ou.edu

BOYD, WILLARD L.
PERSONAL Born 03/29/1927, St Paul, MN, m, 1954, 3 children **DISCIPLINE** LAW **EDUCATION** Univ Minn, BSL, 49; LLB, 51, Univ Mich, LLM, 52; SJD, 62. **CAREER** Prof, Univ Iowa, 54-; Pres Emer, 81-; Pres Emer, Field Museum of Nat Hist, 96-. **HONORS AND AWARDS** Hon Fel, Consular Law Soc, NY, 62; NEH Frankel Prize, 89; Thomas & Eleanor Wright Awd, 96. **MEMBERSHIPS** Am Bar Assoc; Am Museum Assoc. **RESEARCH** Nonprofit organizations, cultural institutions, cultural property, international law. **SELECTED PUBLICATIONS** Auth, Wanted: An Effective Director, 38 Curator, 95; auth, Museums as Centers of Controversy, 128 Daedalus, 99. **CONTACT ADDRESS** Col Law, Univ Iowa, 1 Boyd Law Bldg, Iowa City, IA 52242-1113. **EMAIL** willard-boyd@uiowa.edu

BOYKIN, KEITH
PERSONAL Born 08/28/1965, St. Louis, MO, s **DISCIPLINE** GOVERNMENT **EDUCATION** Dartmouth Coll, AB, 1987; Harvard Univ, JD, 1992. **CAREER** White House, special asst to the President of the US, 93-95; National Black Gay and Lesbian Leadership Forum, exec dir, 95-98. **HONORS AND AWARDS** Haravard Law Sch, Muhammad Kenyatta Young Alumni Awd, 94; Gay Men of African Descent, Angel Awd, 1998. **RESEARCH** Media and Politics; Race and Sexual Orientation. **SELECTED PUBLICATIONS** One More River To Cross: Black & Gay in America, Doubleday, 1995; Respecting the Soul: Daily Reflections for Black Lesbians & Gays, 1998. **CONTACT ADDRESS** PO Box 73564, Washington, DC 20056-3564. **EMAIL** boykink@aol.com

BOYLAN, MICHAEL A.
DISCIPLINE PHILOSOPHY **EDUCATION** Carleton Col, BA; Univ Chicago, MA; PhD. **CAREER** Vis Prof, Univ Chicago, 83; Asst prof, Marquette Univ, 79-85; Georgetown Univ, 85-87; Prof, Marymount Univ, 87-. **HONORS AND AWARDS** T.J. Watson Fel, 74; British Arts Coun Fel, 75; NIH Biomedical Res Awd, 81; NEH Summer stipend, Germany, 82; Nominated for best book, Pritzer Awd, 85; Am Asn of Higher Educ Awd, 89. **MEMBERSHIPS** Am Philos Asn, Am Catholic Philos Asn, Philos of Sci Asn, Soc of Anc Greek Philos, Soc of applied and Professional Ethics, Soc of Christian Philos, Va Philos Asn, Asn of Bioethics, Concerned Philos for Peace. **RESEARCH** Ethics, Ancient Philosophy. **SELECTED PUBLICATIONS** Auth, Ethics Across the Curriculum, Lexington Books, forthcoming; auth, Genetic engineering, Prentice-Hall, forthcoming; auth, Environmental Ethics, Prentice-Hall, forthcoming; auth, Business Ethics, Prentice-Hall, in press; auth, Basic Ethics, Prentice-Hall, 00; auth, Biomedical Ethics, Prentice-Hall, 00; auth, Slipknot, Mage, 89; auth, When the Elephants Came, Mage, 88; auth, The Dance of Life, Mage, 87; auth, Far Into the Sound, Ecco, 73. **CONTACT ADDRESS** Dept Lib Arts, Marymount Univ, 2807 N Glebe Rd, Arlington, VA 22207-4224. **EMAIL** mboylan@phoenix.marymount.edu

BOYLE, ASHBY D., II
DISCIPLINE RELIGIOUS STUDIES; LAW **EDUCATION** Princeton Univ, BA, 80; Univ Cambridge, M.Phil, 83; Columbia Univ, MA, 84; Yale Univ, MA, M.Phil, PhD, 90. **CAREER** Partner, McConnell Valdes LLP; law clerk, Chambers of Justice Sandra Day O'Connor, US Supreme Ct, 90-91. **HONORS AND AWARDS** Charles Evans Hughes Fel; Columbia Law School. **MEMBERSHIPS** AAR **RESEARCH** Religion and Constitution; Religious Ethics; International Law. **SELECTED PUBLICATIONS** Fear and Trembling at the Court: Dimensions of Understanding in the Supreme Court's Religion Jurisprudence, 3 Const.L.J., 93. **CONTACT ADDRESS** 15 Ballad Ln, New York, NY 11790. **EMAIL** aboyle@hollandhart.com

BOYLE, CHRISTINE
DISCIPLINE LAW **EDUCATION** Queen's, LLB; 71, LLM, 72. **CAREER** Owen vis prof, 90-92; prof, Univ of British Columbia, 92-. **HONORS AND AWARDS** Tchr Awd Acad Excellence, 95. **MEMBERSHIPS** Can Asn Law. **RESEARCH** Criminal law; feminist perpectives as law. **SELECTED PUBLICATIONS** Auth, The Law of Homicide, Thomson, 94; coauth, Contracts: Cases and Commentaries, 5th ed., Carswell, Thomson Professional Publishing, 94; auth, "Sexual Assualt in Abusive Relationships: Common Sense about Sexual History,"Dalhousie Law Journal 223, 19, (96). **CONTACT ADDRESS** Fac of Law, Univ of British Columbia, 1822 East Mall, Vancouver, BC, Canada V6T 1Z1. **EMAIL** boyle@law.ubc.ca

BOYLE, F. LADSON
DISCIPLINE TAXATION **EDUCATION** Col Charleston, BS, 69; Univ SC, JD, 74; NYork Univ, LM, 75. **CAREER** Prof, Univ of SC. **SELECTED PUBLICATIONS** Co-ed, Probate Practice Reporter. **CONTACT ADDRESS** School of Law, Univ of So Carolina, Columbia, Law Center, Columbia, SC 29208. **EMAIL** Lad@law.law.sc.edu

BOYLE, FRANCIS
DISCIPLINE POLITICAL SCIENCE, LAW **EDUCATION** Univ Chicago, BA, 71; Harvard Law School, JD, 76; Harvard Grad Sch of Arts and Sci, MA, 78; PhD, 83. **CAREER** Tchg fel, Harvard Univ Dept of Govt, 76-78; ast prof, assoc prof,

prof, Univ Ill, Champaign, Col of Law, 78- ; **HONORS AND AWARDS** Phi Beta Kappa; Sigma Xi Certificate of Merit; Magna Cum Laude, 76; Jerusalem Fund Awd, 97; Dare to Speak Out Awd, Coun for Natl Interest, 97. **SELECTED PUBLICATIONS** Auth, The Right of Citizen Resistance to State Crimes, in Mahoney, ed, Human Rights in the Twenty-First Century: A Global Challenge,, 93; auth, the Decolonization of Northern ireland, Asian Yearbook Int L, 94; auth, The Restoration of the Independent Nation State of Hawaii under International Law, St Thoms L Rev, 95; auth, The Bosnian People Charge Genocide, Aletheia, 96; auth, Is Bosnia the End of the Road for the United Nations? Periodica Islamica, 96; auth, Foundations of World Order: The Legalist Approach to International Relations, 1898-1921, Duke, 99. **CONTACT ADDRESS** 504 E Pennsylvania Ave, Champaign, IL 61820. **EMAIL** fboyle@law.uiuc.edu

BOYLE, JOHN PHILLIPS
PERSONAL Born 08/23/1931, Iowa City, IA **DISCIPLINE** CATHOLIC THEOLOGY, BIOETHICS **EDUCATION** Ambrose Col, BA, 53; Pontif Gregorian Univ, STB, 55, STL, 57; Fordham Univ, PhD(theol), 72. **CAREER** Asst prof, 72-77, Assoc Prof Relig, Univ Iowa, 77-, Dir, Sch Relig, 79- **MEMBERSHIPS** Cath Theol Soc Am; Am Acad Relig; Soc Health & Human Values; Soc Christian Ethics. **RESEARCH** Church role in moral decisions; religion in public education; fundamental moral theology. **SELECTED PUBLICATIONS** Auth, Lonergan's method and objectivity in morals, Thomist, 7/73; Faith and Christian ethics in Rahner & Lonergan, Thought, 75; Presbyters, pastors, the laity & decision-making in the church, Am Ecclesiastical Rev, 75; The Sterilization Controversy: A New Crisis for the Catholic Hospital?, Paulist Press, 77; The ordinary magisterium: Toward a history of the concept, Heythrop J, 79, 2nd ed, 80; The natural law and the magisterium: Historical perspectives and epistemological problems, Catholic Theol Soc Am, 79; Paradigms for public education religions studies curricula: Some suggestions and critique, In: Public Education Religion Studies: An overview, Chico, Scholars Press, 81. **CONTACT ADDRESS** Sch of Relig, Univ of Iowa, 308 Gilmore Hall, Iowa City, IA 52242-1376.

BOYLE, JOSEPH
PERSONAL Born 07/30/1942, Philadelphia, PA, m, 1966, 4 children **DISCIPLINE** PHILOSOPHY **EDUCATION** LaSalle Univ, AB, 65; Georgetown Univ, PhD, 70. **CAREER** Asst Prof, Aquinas Col; Asst Prof to Assoc Prof, Col of St Thomas; Assoc Prof to Prof, Univ St Thomas; Prof, Univ Toronto, 86-; Prin, St. Michael's Col, 91-. **MEMBERSHIPS** APA; ACPA; CPA. **RESEARCH** Moral Philosophy; Natural Law; Aquinas' ethics; Bioethics; International ethics. **SELECTED PUBLICATIONS** Auth, "Who is Entitled to Double Effect?," J of Medicine and Philosophy, (91): 475-494; auth, "A Case for Sometimes Tube-Feeding Patients in Persistent Vegetative State," in Euthanasia Examined, (Cambridge Univ Press, 95), 189-199; auth, "The Place of Religion in the Practical Reasoning of Individuals and Groups," Am J of Jurisprudence, (98): 1-24; auth, "The Absolute Prohibition of Lying and the Origins of the Casuistry of Mental Reservation: Augustinian Arguments and Thomistic Developments," The Am J of Jurisprudence, (99): 43-65; auth, "Fairness in Holdings: A Natural Law Account of Property and Welfare Rights," Social Philosophy and Policy, (01): 206-226; co-auth, "'Direct' and 'Indirect': A Reply to Critics of Our Action Theory," The Thomist, (01): 1-44. **CONTACT ADDRESS** Off of the Prin, St. Michael's Col, 81 St. Mary St, Toronto, ON, Canada M5S 1J4. **EMAIL** jboyle@chass.utoronto.ca

BOYLE, ROBIN A.
PERSONAL Born 09/30/1958, Amityville, NY, m, 2 children **DISCIPLINE** LEGAL STUDIES **EDUCATION** Vassar Col, Poughkeepsie, NY, BA, 80; Fordham Law Sch, NY, NY, JD, 89. **CAREER** Practiced law at large law firms and clerked for a judge, 89-94; asst Legal Writing prof, St John's Univ Sch of Law, 94-. **MEMBERSHIPS** Asn of the Bar of the City of NY. **RESEARCH** Learning styles, women's and children's issues. **SELECTED PUBLICATIONS** Coauth with Kathryn Lazar and Laura Zeisel, Community Serv. Admin., Studies in Community Action: A Chronology and Bibliography (81); coauth with Kathryn Lazar and Laura Zeisel, Community Serv. Admin., Studies in Community Action: A Legislative and Administrative History (81); coauth with Rita Dunn, "Teaching Law Students Through Individual Learning Styles," 62 Ala Law Rev, 213 (98); auth, "Women, the Law, and Cults: Three Avenues of Legal Recourse- New Rape Laws, VAWA, and Anti-Stalking Laws, 15 (1) Cultic Studies J, 1 (98); auth, "How Children in Cults May Use Emancipation Laws to Free Themselves," 16, 1 Cultic Studies J, 1 (99); auth, "Bringing Learning Styles Instructional Strategies to Law School," in Practical Approaches to Using Learning Stylers Application in Higher Education, R. Dunn and S. A. Griggs, eds (forthcoming). **CONTACT ADDRESS** Sch of Law, St. John's Univ, 8150 Utopia Pkwy, Jamaica, NY 11439-0001. **EMAIL** Boyler@stjohns.edu

BOYS, SAMUEL A.
PERSONAL Born 07/07/1961, Plymouth, IN **DISCIPLINE** RELIGION, PSYCHOLOGY, ETHICS **EDUCATION** DePauw Univ, Greencastle, IN, BA, 84; Eden Theol Sem, St Louis, MDiv, 88. **CAREER** Ordained Minister, United Methodist Church; Chaplain: Bashor Children's Home; Prof of Ethics and Biblical Stud, Ancilla Coll. **HONORS AND AWARDS** Edu of the Ys, Ancilla Coll, 98. **MEMBERSHIPS** SBL, AAR. **RESEARCH** Biblical Ethics. **SELECTED PUBLICATIONS** Auth, The Messenger of the United Church, Where Have All the Morals Gone?, Biblical Ethics for the Next Generation. **CONTACT ADDRESS** 10955 Edison Rd, Osceola, IN 46561-9729.

BOZEMAN, THEODORE D.
PERSONAL Born 01/27/1942, Gainesville, FL, m, 1973 **DISCIPLINE** AMERICAN RELIGIOUS HISTORY **EDUCATION** Eckerd Col, BA, 64; Union Theol Sem, NYC, BD, 68; Univ Theol Sem, Richmond, ThM, 70; Duke Univ, PhD, 74. **CAREER** Instr to prof, Univ Iowa, 73- . **HONORS AND AWARDS** NEH fel, 84, 92. **MEMBERSHIPS** Orgn Am Hist; Am Hist Asn; Am Soc Church Hist. **RESEARCH** Puritanism, American religious thought. **SELECTED PUBLICATIONS** Auth, Protestants in an Age of Science, Chapel Hill, (78); auth, To Live Ancient Lives, Chapel Hill, (88). **CONTACT ADDRESS** Dept Hist, Univ Iowa, 205 Schaeffer Hall, Iowa City, IA 52242-1409. **EMAIL** d-bozeman@uiowa.edu

BRAATEN, LAURIE
DISCIPLINE OLD TESTAMENT **EDUCATION** Eastern Nazarene Col, BA; Nazarene Theol Sem, Mdiv; Boston Univ, PhD. **CAREER** Ch, dept hist, Eastern Nazarene Col. **SELECTED PUBLICATIONS** Area: Old Testament. **CONTACT ADDRESS** Eastern Nazarene Col, 23 East Elm Ave, Quincy, MA 02170-2999.

BRABANT, JOZEF M.
PERSONAL Born 11/05/1942, Hasselt, Belgium, m, 1968, 2 children **DISCIPLINE** ECONOMICS **EDUCATION** Yale Univ, PhD 73, MPhil 68, MA 67; Cath Univ, Louvain Belgium, 65, Tchr(s), Math, Economics and Thomistic Philo Degrees, with Distinction or Great Distinction. **CAREER** United Nations Secretariat, Dept of Econ and Soc Affairs, NY, 75-98-; Isituto Univ Europeo, Italy, vis prof, 87. **HONORS AND AWARDS** Bel Nat Found Sci Res Fellow; Sch of Econ Warsaw Fel; Fulbright-Hays Gnt; Yale Fellow; Belgian Fellowships. **MEMBERSHIPS** ACES **RESEARCH** Eastern Europ Transformation. **SELECTED PUBLICATIONS** The 1996 IGC, in: The Europ Union, ed, Boulder CO, Rowman and Littlefield, 99; Managing Globalization, One Europe Mag; The Implications of Widening and Third Countries, in: The Euro Union, ed, Boulder Co, Rowman and Littlefield, 99; Eastern Europe and the World Trade Organization, in: Eastern Europe and the World Economy, ed by Iliana Zloch-Christy, Chelt, Northampton, MA, Edward Elgar, 98; numerous articles, conf papers, rev. **CONTACT ADDRESS** United Nations, DC 2 2150, New York, NY 10163-0020. **EMAIL** brabant@un.org

BRACEY, WILLIE EARL
PERSONAL Born 12/21/1950, Jackson, MS, m, 1987 **DISCIPLINE** LAW **EDUCATION** Wright Jr Coll, AA 1970; Mt Senario Coll, BS 1973; Eastern IL Univ, MS 1976; Southern IL Univ, JD 1979. **CAREER** Southern IL Univ, law clerk 1978-79; Southern IL Univ Ctr for Basic Skill, instr 1977-78; Southern IL Univ Law School, rsch asst 1977-78; Notre Dame Law School, teaching asst 1977; Western IL Univ, dir, student legal serv, 79-87, asst vice pres for student affairs support servs; adj prof, college student personnel grad program, 87- 99; Assoc Vice Pres for Student Services, W Ill Univ, 99-. **MEMBERSHIPS** Mem NAACP, 1979-, ATLA 1979-90, ABA 1979-90, IBA 1979-, McDonough City Bar Assn 1979-, Natl Assn of Student Personnel Admin 1987-; faculty mem Blue Key Honor Soc; Housing Commissoner, McDonough County Housing Authority, appointment ends 1998; Illinois Attorney General Date Rape Drugs Steering Committee, 1999. **CONTACT ADDRESS** Western Illinois Univ, One University Cir, Macomb, IL 61455.

BRACKEN, J. A.
PERSONAL Born 03/22/1930, Chicago, IL, s **DISCIPLINE** THEOLOGY **EDUCATION** Xavier Univ, Litt B, 53; Loyola Univ, MA, 60; Univ Freiburg, PhD, 68. **CAREER** Asst and Assoc Prof of Theology, St Mary of the Lake Seminary, 68-74; Assoc Prof of Theology, Marquette Univ, 74-82; Prof of Theology, Xavier Univ, 82-. **HONORS AND AWARDS** Book Awd, College Theology Society, 95. **MEMBERSHIPS** American Academy of Religion, Catholic Theological Society of America, College Theology Society, Metaphysical Society of America. **RESEARCH** Trinitarina Theology, Process Philosophy and Theology, Comparative Religions, Religion and Science. **SELECTED PUBLICATIONS** Auth, The Triune Symbol, 85; auth, Society and Spirit, 91; auth, The Divine Matrix, 97; auth, Trinity in Process, 97. **CONTACT ADDRESS** Dept Theology, Xavier Univ, Ohio, 3800 Victory Parkway, Cincinnati, OH 45207-1035. **EMAIL** bracken@xavier.xu.edu

BRACKEN, W. JEROME
PERSONAL Born 04/13/1940, Baltimore, MD **DISCIPLINE** THEOLOGY **EDUCATION** St Michael's Sem, MA, 68; Fordham Univ, PhD, 78. **CAREER** Assoc prof, St. Charles Borromeo Sem, 89. **MEMBERSHIPS** Cath Theol Soc of Am; Fel of Cath Scholars. **RESEARCH** Sexual ethics; health care ethics; Christology; cognitive and affective learning. **SELECTED PUBLICATIONS** Auth, Roman Catholic Case Study, J of Ecumenical Stud, 90; auth, Roman Catholic Deliberations, J of Ecumenical Stud, 90; auth, Is the Early Embryo A Person?, Linacre Q, forthcoming. **CONTACT ADDRESS** Seton Hall Univ, So Orange, South Orange, NJ 07079. **EMAIL** brackeje@shu.edu

BRACKENRIDGE, ROBERT DOUGLAS
PERSONAL Born 08/06/1932, Youngstown, OH, m, 1954, 5 children **DISCIPLINE** HISTORY, CHURCH HISTORY **EDUCATION** Muskingum Col, BA, 54; Pittsburgh Theol Sem, BD, 57, ThM, 59; Glasgow Univ, PhD(church hist), 62. **CAREER** Pastor, Cross Rd United Presby Church, 58-60; from asst prof to assoc prof, 62-72, Prof Relig, Trinity Univ, Tex, 72-, Assoc, Danforth Found, 72- **HONORS AND AWARDS** Thornwell Awd, 68; Piper Prof, Minnie Stevens Piper Found, 73; Distinguished Serv Awd, Presby Hist Soc, 81. **MEMBERSHIPS** Presby Hist Soc (pres, 76-); Am Soc Church Hist; Am Acad Relig; Scottish Church Hist Soc. **SELECTED PUBLICATIONS** Auth, The Sabbath War 1865-1866, Records Scottish Church Hist Soc, Part I, 66; The Growth and Development of Sabbatarianism in Scotland 1560-1650, 10 & 12/67 & Sumner Bacon, the Apostle of Texas, 10 & 12/67, J Presby Hist; Voice in the Wilderness, 68 & Beckoning Frontiers, 76, Trinity Univ; Eugene Carson Blake: Prophet With Portfolio, Seabury, 78. **CONTACT ADDRESS** Dept of Relig, Trinity Univ, San Antonio, TX 78287.

BRADIE, MICHAEL
PERSONAL Born 08/02/1940, Detroit, MI, m, 1969 **DISCIPLINE** PHILOSOPHY **EDUCATION** Mass Inst Technol, BS, 62; Boston Univ, MA, 65; Univ Hawaii, PhD(philos), 70. **CAREER** From instr to asst prof, 68-76, assoc prof, 76-81, Prof Philos, Bowling Green State Univ, 81-, Nat Endowment Humanities fel-in-residence philos, 76-77. **MEMBERSHIPS** Philos Sci Asn; AAAS; Am Philos Asn; Brit Soc Philos Sci. **RESEARCH** Philosophy of science; epistemology; analytic philosophy. **SELECTED PUBLICATIONS** Auth, The causal theory of perception, Synthese, 76; Russell and Ayer on naive realism, Philos Sci Asn, 76; The development of Russell's Structural Postulates, Philos Sci, 77; Pragmatism and internal realism, Analysis, 79; On doing without events, Philos Studie, 79; Models, metaphors and scientific realism, nature & Syst, 80; Adequacy conditions and event identity, Synthese, 81; The status of the principle of natural selection, Nature & Syst, 81. **CONTACT ADDRESS** Bowling Green State Univ, 1001 E Wooster St, Bowling Green, OH 43403-0001.

BRADLEY, CRAIG M.
PERSONAL Born 12/05/1945, Downers Grove, IL, m, 1978, 2 children **DISCIPLINE** LAW **EDUCATION** Univ NC, AB, 67; Univ Va, JD, 70. **CAREER** Asst US Atty, Washington DC, 72-75; Law Clerk, Justice Rehnquist, US Supreme Court, 75-76; Sr Trial Atty, Public Integrity, US Dept Justice, 76-78; Vis Assoc Prof, Univ NC Law Sch, 78-79; James Louis Calamaras Prof Law, Ind Univ Sch Law, 79-; Vis Schol, Stanford Univ Law Sch, 85; Vis Lectr, Inst Int Law, 92. **HONORS AND AWARDS** Fulbright Sr Schol, Australian Nat Univ, 88-89; Alexander von Humboldt Schol, 82, 92. **MEMBERSHIPS** Am Bar Asn; AALS; Am Soc Comp Law. **RESEARCH** Criminal procedure; federal criminal law; comparative criminal law and procedure. **SELECTED PUBLICATIONS** Auth, The Failure of the Criminal Procedure Revolution, Univ Pa Press, 93; The Supreme Court's Two Models of the Fourth Amendment: Carpe Diem!, J Criminal Law and Criminol, 93; N.O.W. v Scheidler: When RICO Meets the First Amendment, Supreme Court Rev, 95; coauth, Public Perception, Justice, and The Search for Truth in Criminal Cases, Southern Calif Law Rev, 96; auth, The Rule of Law in an Unruly Age, Ind Law J, 96; ed and contribr, Criminal Procedure: A Worldwide Study, Carolina Acad Press, 98. **CONTACT ADDRESS** School of Law, Indiana Univ, Bloomington, Bloomington, IN 47405. **EMAIL** bradleyc@indiana.edu

BRADLEY, DENIS J. M.
DISCIPLINE PHILOSOPHY **EDUCATION** Assumption Univ Windsor, BA; Univ Toronto. **CAREER** Prof. **HONORS AND AWARDS** Woodrow Wilson, 63-64; Canada Coun, 67-69; Fel Am Acad in Rome, 70-72; A.C.L.S., 75, 83; **RESEARCH** Romistic Ethics **SELECTED PUBLICATIONS** Auth, pubs on history of the faith-reason problematic in the Middle Ages, Aquinas's metaphysics and its relationship to post-Kantian transcendental philosophy, and Thomistic implications of philosophical pluralism; auth, Aquinas on the Two Fold Human Good, Catholic Univ Am Press, 97. **CONTACT ADDRESS** Dept of Philosophy, Georgetown Univ, 37th and O St, Washington, DC 20057. **EMAIL** bradleyd@gunet.georgetown.edu

BRADLEY, MARSHELL C.
DISCIPLINE PHILOSOPHY **EDUCATION** Midwestern State Univ, BA, 79; Duquesne Univ, MA, 81; PhD, 84. **CAREER** Lectr, Duquesne Univ, 82; asst prof, Alderson-Broaddus Col, 84-86; Akademischer Rat auf Zeit, Technische Universitat

Carolo wilhelmina zu Braunschweig, Ger, 86-87; asst prof to assoc prof, Sam Houston State Univ, 90-. **HONORS AND AWARDS** Outstanding Philos Student, Midwestern State Univ, 79; Vinson Creative Writing Awd, Woods Found, 79; Phi sigma Tau, 90; Teaching Excellence Awd, Sam Houston State Univ, 92; Delta Phi Alpha, 96; Excellence in Res Finalist, Sam Houston State Univ, 00. **RESEARCH** Philosophy, Historical Drama, Biblical Studies. **SELECTED PUBLICATIONS** Auth, "The Significance of the Name in The Name of the Rose", Lang and Lit, X Spring 85; auth, "Nietzxche's Critique of Pure Reason", Neophilogus, 72 88; auth, "Caska: Stoic, Cynic, Christian", Lit and Theol, Oxford Univ Pr, 8, (Nov 94); auth, Of Friendship, Second Edition, Univ Pr of Am, 97; auth, The Brothers Booth, Sam Houston State Univ Pr, 00. **CONTACT ADDRESS** Dept Psychol and Philos, Sam Houston State Univ, PO Box 2447, Huntsville, TX 77341-2447. **EMAIL** bradley@shsu.edu

BRADSHAW, DENNY
PERSONAL Born 04/05/1960, Estherville, IA **DISCIPLINE** PHILOSOPHY **EDUCATION** Mankato State Univ, BA, 82; Univ of Iowa, PhD, 88. **CAREER** Vis asst prof, Memphis State univ, 88-91; vis asst prof, Univ Ky, 91-92; asst prof, 92-98, assoc prof, 98- , Univ Texas, Arlington. **HONORS AND AWARDS** Summa Cum Laude, 82; fel, Phi Kappa Phi, 82-83; tchg-res fel, 82-83; grad col fel, 83-84; res grant, 96. **MEMBERSHIPS** AAUP; Texas Fac Asn; APA; Soc for Philos and Psych; Soc for Philos and Psych; Metroplex Inst for Neural Dynamics; N Texas Philos Asn. **RESEARCH** Metaphysics; epistemology; philosophy of mind; philosophy of language. **SELECTED PUBLICATIONS** Auth, Connectionism and the Specter of Representationalism, in Horgan, ed, Connectionism and the Philosophy of Mind, Kluwer, 91; auth, On the Need for A Metaphysics of Justification, Metaphilosophy, 92; auth, The Nature of Concepts, Philos Papers, 92; auth, The Non-Logical Basis of Metaphysics, Idealistic Stud, 96; auth, Meaning, Cognition, and the Philosophy of Thought: Vindicating Traditional Ontology, Jour of Philos Res, 98; auth, Patterns and Descriptions, Philos papers, 98. **CONTACT ADDRESS** Dept of Philosophy and Humanities, Univ of Texas, Arlington, Arlington, TX 76019-0527. **EMAIL** bradshaw@uta.edu

BRADY, JAMES B.
PERSONAL Born 08/30/1939, Harlingen, TX, m **DISCIPLINE** PHILOSOPHY, LAW **EDUCATION** Southern Methodist Univ, BA, 61; Univ Tex, JD, 64, PhD, 70. **CAREER** From lectr to asst prof, 67-73, assoc chmn, Dept Philos & dir undergrad studies, 70-72, assoc provost fac soc sci & admin, 72-75, co-dir, Baldy Ctr Law & Social Policy, 78-81, Assoc Prof Philos, State Univ NY Buffalo, 73-, Assoc ed, Tex Law Rev; res asst, State Bar Tex Comt Penal Code Rev, 66-67; vis mem, Linacre Col, Oxford Univ, 75. **SELECTED PUBLICATIONS** Auth, Recklessness, Law Philos, vol 0015, 96. **CONTACT ADDRESS** Dept of Philos, SUNY, Buffalo, Buffalo, NY 14222.

BRADY, JULES M.
PERSONAL Born 02/17/1919, St. Louis, MO **DISCIPLINE** PHILOSOPHY **EDUCATION** St Louis Univ, PhD, 49. **CAREER** Instr, 55-58, assoc prof, 68-70, Prof Philos, Rockhurst Col, 70. **MEMBERSHIPS** Am Cath Philos Asn. **SELECTED PUBLICATIONS** Auth, St Augustine's theory of seminal reasons, New Scholasticism, 4/64; Seminal reasons, In: New Catholic Encyclopedia, McGraw, 67; Note on the Fourth Way, spring, 74 & A contemporary approach to God's existence, winter, 77, New Scholasticism; An Augustine Treasury, Daughters of St Paul Press, 81; A Philospher's Search for the Infinite, Philos Libr, 82; An Aquinas Treasury, Publ Assoc, 88; New Approaches to God, Genesis Publ Co, 92; Newman for Everyone, Alba House, 96. **CONTACT ADDRESS** Dept of Philos, Rockhurst Col, 1100 Rockhurst Rd, Kansas City, MO 64110-2561.

BRADY, MICHELLE E.
PERSONAL Born 01/15/1970, Lawrence, KS, s **DISCIPLINE** PHILOSOPHY **EDUCATION** BA, Haverford Col, 91; MA, 95, PhD, 98, Emory Univ. **CAREER** Teaching Instr, Emory Univ, 95-96, 98; Part-time Instr, 95-98, Georgia State Univ; Adjunct Faculty, Oglethorpe Univ, 98-. **HONORS AND AWARDS** Phi Betta Kappa, 91 **MEMBERSHIPS** Amer Phil Assoc **RESEARCH** Moral and Political Philosophy, Philosophical Antropology, Ancient Philosophy **CONTACT ADDRESS** Philosophy Dept, Emory Univ, Atlanta, GA 30322. **EMAIL** mbrady@emory.edu

BRAITHWAITE, JOHN
DISCIPLINE LAW **CAREER** Vis prof. **SELECTED PUBLICATIONS** Auth, pubs on business regulation and criminal justice. **CONTACT ADDRESS** Fac of Law, Univ of Toronto, 78 Queen's Park, Toronto, ON, Canada M5S 1A1.

BRAITHWAITE, WILLIAM T.
DISCIPLINE LAW **EDUCATION** Windsor Univ, BA, 73; Univ Western Ontario, LLB, 76, LLM, 77. **CAREER** Law clerk, Justice Bora Laskin, Supreme Court Can; assoc dean, Osgoode Hall Law Sch, 82-83; prof. **MEMBERSHIPS** Chairman, Ontario Securities Commission Advisory Committee, 91-93 **SELECTED PUBLICATIONS** Auth, pubs on securities law. **CONTACT ADDRESS** Sch of Law, Loyola Univ, Chicago, 1 E Pearson St, Chicago, IL, Canada 60611-2055.

BRAKAS, JURGIS GEORGE
PERSONAL Born 11/14/1944, Copenhagen, Denmark, m, 1996, 0 child **DISCIPLINE** PHILOSOPHY **EDUCATION** Princeton Univ, BA, 68; Columbia Univ, MA, 74; MPhil, 79; PhD, 84. **CAREER** Assoc prof, New York Univ, 88-90; asst prof, Marist Col, 90-. **HONORS AND AWARDS** Columbia Univ Pres Fel; Woodrow Wilson Nominee, 68; Marist Sabbatical leave awarded, 94; Tenure granted, 94. **MEMBERSHIPS** Am Philos Asn, Soc for Ancient Greek Philos, Any Rand Soc. **RESEARCH** Aristotle, Logic, Ethics. **SELECTED PUBLICATIONS** Auth, Aristotle's Concept of the Universal, Hildesheim, 88; auth, "Macdonald, Aristotle, and the Good," Journal of Neoplatonic Studies, (88): 77-114. **CONTACT ADDRESS** Dept Philos, Marist Col, 290 North Rd, Poughkeepsie, NY 12601-1326. **EMAIL** jurgis.brakas@marist.edu

BRAKKE, DAVID
PERSONAL Born 05/10/1961, Long Beach, CA, s **DISCIPLINE** RELIGIOUS STUDIES **EDUCATION** Univ Va, BA, 83; Harvard Univ, M Div, 86; Yale Univ, MA, 87, M Phil, 89, PhD, 92. **CAREER** Visiting asst prof, relig, Concordia Col, 92-93; asst prof, relig, Ind Univ, 93-. **HONORS AND AWARDS** Mellon Fel in the Humanities; Ind Univ Outstanding Jr Facul. **MEMBERSHIPS** North Amer Patristic Soc; Amer Acad of Relig; Amer Soc of Church Hist; Intl Asn of Coptic Studies; Soc of Bibl Lit; Chicago Soc of Bibl Res. **RESEARCH** Early Christianity. **SELECTED PUBLICATIONS** Auth, Outside the Places, Within the Truth, Athanasius of Alexandria and the Localization of the Holy, Pilgrimage and Holy Space in Late Antique Egypt, Relig in the Graeco-Roman World, Leiden, Brill, 457-93, 98; co-reviser, Introduction to Christianity, 3rd ed, Belmont, Calif, Wadsworth, 97; auth, Athanasius of Alexandria and the Cult of the Holy Dead, Studia Patristica,32, 12-18, 97; auth, The Problematization of Nocturnal Emissions in Early Christian Syria, Egypt, and Gaul, Jour of Early Christ Studies, 3, 419-60, 95; auth, Athanasius and the Politics o Asceticism, Oxford Early Christian Studies, Clarendon Press, NY, Oxford Univ Press, 95; auth, The Greek and Syriac Versions of the Life of Antony, Le Museon, 107, 29-53, 94; auth, Canon Formation and Social Conflict in Fourth-Century Egypt: Athanasius of Alexandria's Thirty-Ninth Festal Letter, Harvard Theol Rev, 87, 395-419, 94; auth, The Authenticity of the Ascetic Athanasiana, Orientalia, 63, 17-56, 94. **CONTACT ADDRESS** Dept. of Religious Studies, Indiana Univ, Bloomington, Sycamore Hall 230, Bloomington, IN 47405-2601. **EMAIL** dbrakke@indiana.edu

BRAKMAN, SARAH-VAUGHAN
DISCIPLINE PHILOSOPHY **EDUCATION** Mt Holyoke Col, BA, 86; Rice Univ, MA, 90, PhD, 94. **CAREER** Asst prof; ethics consult & voting mem, Ethics Comt, The Devereux Found, Devon, Pa, Jan 95-; Ethics Comt, The Grad Hosp, Philadelphia, Pa, Jan 94-; invited lect(s), papers & grand rounds; Ethical Traditions and Contemporary Life (joint), Nat Conf on Ethics and Popular Cult, The Ethics Ctr, Univ South Fa, Apr 96; Integenerational Responsibilities in Families: Who Owes What to Whom, Luncheon Lecture Series, The Ctr for Bioethics, Univ Pa, Apr 96; Moderator, Bioethics Symposium, Ethical Issues in Scientific Research, The Grad Hosp, Philadelphia, Pa, Mar 96; Filial Responsibilities and Gender: Who Owes What to Whom, Humanities Grand Rounds, Med Humanities Div, Med Col Pa and Hahnemann Univ, Sept 95; Intergeneraltional Responsibilities in Families: Who Owes What to Whom, Grand Rounds of the Dept Psychiat and Human Behavior, Jefferson Med Col, Thomas Jefferson Univ, June 95; Moderator Bioethics Symposium, Genetic Engineering: an Ethical Perspective, Grad Hosp, Philadelphia, Pa, Mar 95. **SELECTED PUBLICATIONS** Auth, The Case of the Golden Years: An Ethicist's Perspecitive, Bioethics Bul, 96; Adult Daughter Caregivers: Philosophical Analysis and Implications for Health Care Policy, A World Growing Old: The Coming Health Care Challenges, Washington, DC: Georgetown Univ Press, 95; Filial Responsibility and Long-Term Care Decision Making, Long-Term Care Decisions: Ethical and Conceptual Dimensions, Johns Hopkins Univ Press, 95: Daughter Caregivers: Philosophical Analysis and Implications for Health Care Policy, A World Growing Old: The Coming Health Care Challenges, Georgetown Univ Press, 95; Adult Daughter Caregivers, Hastings Ctr Report 24, 94; rev, Life and Death: Philosophical Essays in Biomedical Ethics, Cambridge Quart of Healthcare Ethics, 94; Teaching Tips, SHHV Stud Bul, 91. **CONTACT ADDRESS** Dept of Philosophy, Villanova Univ, 800 Lancaster Ave., Villanova, PA 19085-1692.

BRAMANN, JORN
PERSONAL Born 12/21/1938, Wuppertal, Germany, s **DISCIPLINE** PHILOSOPHY **EDUCATION** Univ Wyo, MA, 65; Univ Ore, PhD, 71. **CAREER** Assoc Prof, Frostburg St Univ, 77-. **HONORS AND AWARDS** Fulbright Travel Grant, 64-65; Nat Endowment Humanities Fel, Princeton Univ, 75-76; NEH Summer Fel, Univ Calif, 81; NEH Summer Fel, Univ S Calif, 75; NEH Summer Fel, Univ Calif, 89. **RESEARCH** Ethics, social philosophy, aesthetics, philosophy and humanistic studies, philosophical films. **SELECTED PUBLICATIONS** Auth, Capital as Power: A Concise Summary of the Marxist Analysis of Capitalism, Adler Publ Co, 84; auth, Self-Determination: An Anthology of Philosophy and Poetry, 2nd ed, Adler Publ Co, 87; auth, Phantom Doors: A Mystery, G Aston Nelson Books, 88; auth, Taking Cover: The Role of the Uniform in Films of the Weimar Republic, Video presented at 16th Colloguium on Lit and Film, WV Univ (91). **CONTACT ADDRESS** Dept Philos, Frostburg State Univ, 101 Braddock Rd, Frostburg, MD 21532-2303. **EMAIL** jornfsu@hotmail.com

BRAME, GRACE ADOLPHSEN
PERSONAL m **DISCIPLINE** THEOLOGY; SPIRITUALITY **EDUCATION** Wittenberg Univ, Bmus; Union Theol Sem, MSM; Temple Univ, MA, PhD 88. **CAREER** Villanova Univ, lectr 86-92; LaSalle Univ, grad, und grad 92-98. **HONORS AND AWARDS** Ezcell Ach Awd; Rep to APATS Conf; Delaware Women Rem; Legacy frm Del Women; Friends Cen Comm Res Gnt. **MEMBERSHIPS** CTSA; LSA; SSCS; CTS. **RESEARCH** Contemplation and action; Lutheran spirituality; Comparative spirituality between Catholics Orthodox and Protestants; comparative spirituality between religions.... **SELECTED PUBLICATIONS** Auth, Receptive Prayer, Chalice Press; auth A Manual of Receptive Prayer, Charis Enterprises; editor, intro, Ways of the Spirit, by Evelyn Underhill,, Crossroad; auth, Faith: The Yes of the Heart, a theology of spirituality based on Luther's Theology of the Heart, Augsburg/Fortress Press, 99; Capacity for God: Evelyn Underhill's Theology of Spirituality, in progress; articles in over 40 jrnls/mags: The Lutheran, Worship; Patristic and Byzantine Review, Spirituality Today, Sisters Today, Lutheran Women, etc. **CONTACT ADDRESS** Dept of Theology, La Salle Univ, 13 North Cliffe Dr, Wilmington, DE 19809-1623. **EMAIL** ebramejr@aol.com

BRAMER, PAUL G.
PERSONAL Born 02/09/1952, Canada, m **DISCIPLINE** THEOLOGY **EDUCATION** Univ Toronto, BA, 78; BEd, 80; Brock Univ, MEd, 85; Trinity Evangelical Div School, PhD, 95. **CAREER** Adj Fac, Tyndale Sem, 93-95; Asst Prof, North Park Theol Sem, 95-. **HONORS AND AWARDS** Res Grant, N Am Prof of Christian Educ, 93; Prof Wedell Christian Educ Awd, 90; Procor Acad Proficiency Awd, 71. **MEMBERSHIPS** Am Psychol Asn, Asn for Psychol Type, Asn of Prof and Res in Relig Educ, Asn for Theol Field Educ, N Am Prof of Christian Educ, Soc for the Study of Christian Spirituality, Spiritual Directors Intl. **RESEARCH** Christian spirituality; Christian community; Psychological type: group dynamics and small group ministry; Teaching methodologies; Leadership and administration; History and theory of Christian education. **CONTACT ADDRESS** Dept Theol, No Park Theol Sem, 3225 W Foster Ave, Chicago, IL 60625-4823. **EMAIL** pbramer@northpark.edu

BRAND, EUGENE L.
DISCIPLINE THEOLOGY **EDUCATION** Capital Univ, BA, 53; Lutheran Theol Sem, BD, 57; Heidelberg Univ, ThD; Lutheran Theol Sem, DD, 78; Christ Sem-Seminex, DHL, 81. **CAREER** Prof, Lutheran Theol Sem, 60-71; dir, Commn on Worship, Lutheran Church Am, 71-73; coord, Worship, LCA, 73-75; proj dir, Inter-Lutheran Commn on Worship, 75-78; dir, Office of Stud, Lutheran World Ministries, 77-81; Sec for Worship, Lutheran World Fed, 82-83; assoc dir, Dept Stud, sec, Interconfessional Dialogue and Ecclesiological Res, LWF, 84-90; asst gen sec, Ecumenical Aff, LWF, 90-96; distinguished intl prof in residence, 97-98. **HONORS AND AWARDS** Berakah Awd, N Amer Acad Liturgy, 84; J. Sittler Awd, Trinity Lutheran Sem, 91. **SELECTED PUBLICATIONS** Auth, Living Water and Sealing Spirit, Collegeville, 95; The Episcopal Office in the Nordic Lutheran Churches Seen from the Worldwide Perspective, Biskopsambetet, Nordisk Ekumenisk Skriftserie 23, Uppsala, 94; The Lutheran Common Service: Heritage and Challenge, Studia Liturgica 19, 89. **CONTACT ADDRESS** Hist, Theol, Soc Dept, Trinity Lutheran Sem, 2199 E Main St, Columbus, OH 43209-2334. **EMAIL** ebrand@trinity.capital.edu

BRAND, MYLES
PERSONAL Born 05/17/1942, New York, NY, m, 1964, 1 child **DISCIPLINE** PHILOSOPHY **EDUCATION** Rensselaer Polytech Inst, BS, 64; Univ Rochester, PhD(philos), 67. **CAREER** Asst chm, philos dept, Univ Pitt, 71-72; Chmn, philos dept, Univ Ill Chi, 72-81; Prof, Univ Arizona, 81-86; Prof & Vice Pres, Acad Affairs, Ohio State Univ, 86-89; Pres, Univ of Oregon, 89-94; Pres & Prof, Indiana Univ, 94-. **MEMBERSHIPS** Am Philos Asn; Philos Sci Asn; Soc Philos & Psyhchol. **RESEARCH** Analytical metaphysics; philosophy of mind. **SELECTED PUBLICATIONS** Ed, The nature of human action, Glenview, 70; ed, The Nature of causation, Urbana: Univ of Illinois Press, 76; auth, Intending and acting; toward a naturalized action theroy, Cambridge, Mass: MIT Press, 84; coed, The Representation of knowledge and belif, Univ of Arzona Press, 86. **CONTACT ADDRESS** Office of the Pres, Indiana Univ, Bloomington, 107 S. Indiana Ave., Bloomington, IN 47405-7000. **EMAIL** pres@indiana.edu

BRANDOM, ROBERT BOYCE
PERSONAL Born 03/13/1950, m, 1998, 2 children **DISCIPLINE** PHILOSOPHY **EDUCATION** Yale Univ, BA, 72; Princeton Univ, PhD, 77. **CAREER** Distinguished Service Prof, 76-, Univ of Pittsburgh. **HONORS AND AWARDS** Fel, Am Academy of Arts and Sciences, 00. **SELECTED PUBLICATIONS** Auth, Making It Explicit: Reasoning, Representing

and Discursive Commitment, Harvard Univ Press, 74; Study Guide to Sellars, Empiricism and the Philosophy of Mind, in: Empiricism and the Philosophy of Mind, Harvard Univ Press, 97; The Significance of Complex Numbers for Frege's Philosophy of Mathematics, Proceedings of the Aristotelian Society, 96; Knowledge and the Social Articulation of the Space of Reasons, Philosophy and Phenomenological Research, 95; Unsuccessful Semantics, Analysis, 94; auth, Articulating Reasons, Harvard Univ Press, 00; ed, Rorty and his Critics, Blackwell's Publishers, 00. **CONTACT ADDRESS** Dept of Philosophy, Univ of Pittsburgh, Pittsburgh, PA 15260. **EMAIL** rbrandom@pitt.edu

BRANDON, ROBERT N.
DISCIPLINE PHILOSOPHY **EDUCATION** Harvard Univ, PhD, 77. **CAREER** Prof, Duke Univ. **RESEARCH** Logic. **SELECTED PUBLICATIONS** Auth, Adaptation and Environment, Princeton Univ, 90; co-ed, Genes, Organisms, Populations: Controversies over the Units of Selection, MIT, 84; publ(s) on philos sci. **CONTACT ADDRESS** Philos Dept, Duke Univ, West Duke Bldg, Durham, NC 27706. **EMAIL** rbrandon@acpub.duke.edu

BRANDT, ERIC A.
PERSONAL Born Bloomington, IL **DISCIPLINE** RELIGIOUS STUDIES **EDUCATION** Univ Chicago, MA, 80; Columbia Univ, PhD, 90. **HONORS AND AWARDS** Res Grant from Amer Acad of Religion, 98. **MEMBERSHIPS** Amer Acad of Religion; Amer Phil Asn. **RESEARCH** Christianity and indigenous religions. **SELECTED PUBLICATIONS** Auth, Dangerous Liaisons Minorities in Conflict, NY New Press, 99. **CONTACT ADDRESS** 3856 19th St, No 4, San Francisco, CA 94114. **EMAIL** brandtesf@aol.com

BRANDT, GREGORY J.
DISCIPLINE LAW **EDUCATION** Univ Saskatchewan, BA, 59; LLB, 61; Oxford Univ, BA, 64, MA, 68. **CAREER** Adj prof; fac, 64; prof emer. **HONORS AND AWARDS** Rhodes Scholar. **RESEARCH** Public law. **SELECTED PUBLICATIONS** Auth, pubs on constitutional law and labour law; co-auth, Evidence and Procedure in Canadian Labour Arbitration. **CONTACT ADDRESS** Fac of Law, Univ of Western Ontario, London, ON, Canada N6A 3K7. **EMAIL** gjbradt@julian.uwo.ca

BRANICK, VINCENT P.
PERSONAL Born 04/26/1941, San Francisco, CA, m, 1996, 3 children **DISCIPLINE** THEOLOGY, SCRIPTURE, BUSINESS ETHICS **EDUCATION** Pontifical Bibl Inst, SSD, 75; Univ Freiburg, PhilD, 71. **CAREER** Assoc prof of Relig & Philos, Chaminade Col of Honolulu, 73-78; prof Relig Studies, Univ Dayton, 77-; Woodrow Wilson fel. **MEMBERSHIPS** Cath Bibl Asn; Soc Bibl Lit. **RESEARCH** Biblical theology; Business ethics. **SELECTED PUBLICATIONS** Auth Wonder in a Technical World, An Introduction to Method and Writers of Philosophy, Univ Press Am, 80; The House Church in the Writing of Paul, Michael Glazier, 89; Understanding the New Testament and its Message, Paulist Press, 98. **CONTACT ADDRESS** Dept of Relig Studies, Univ of Dayton, Dayton, OH 45469-1530. **EMAIL** branick@checkov.hm.udayton.edu

BRANSON, DOUGLAS M.
PERSONAL Born 10/06/1945, Cleveland, OH, d, 2 children **DISCIPLINE** LAW **EDUCATION** Univ Notre Dame, BA, 65; Northwestern Univ, JD, 70; Univ Va, LLM, 74. **CAREER** Vis Assoc Prof, Ariz State Univ, 77; Vis Senior Lecturer, Univ E Anglia, 81; Vis Prof, Cornell Univ, 85; Vis prof, Univ Oregon, 87-88; Vis Prof, Univ Ala, 93; Chair, Univ Pittsburgh. **MEMBERSHIPS** ABA, ALI. **RESEARCH** Corporate Governance, Securities Law, Multinational Corporations. **SELECTED PUBLICATIONS** Auth, "Teaching Comparative corporate Governance: The significance of 'Soft Law' and International Institutions," Georgia Law Review, forthcoming; auth, Forensic Social Work 2nd ed, 99; auth, Understanding corporate Law, Matthew Bender & co., 99; auth, "Securities Litigation in State courts--Something Old, something New, Something Borrowed," Wash ULO, (98): 509-536; auth, Corporate Governance Problems, Cathedral Press, 97; auth, "Chasing the rogue Professional After the Private Securities Litigation Reform Act of 1995," SMUL Review, (96): 91-125; auth, "Running the Gauntlet: A Description of the Arduous (And Now Often Fatal) Journey for Plaintiffs in Federal Securities Law Actions," U Cinn L Rev, (96): 3-41; auth, "Pragmatist or Prairie Populist? The corporate and Securities Law Opinions of Mr. Justice John Paul Stevens," Rutgers Law Journal, (96): 605-626; auth, auth, "Recent changes to the Model Business corporation Act: Death Knells for Main Street Corporation Law," Nebraska L Rev, (93): 258; auth, Corporate Governance, Michie & Co, 93; auth, Forensic Social Work, Haworth Press, 92. **CONTACT ADDRESS** School of Law, Univ of Pittsburgh, 512 Law Bldg, Pittsburgh, PA 15260-7102. **EMAIL** branson@law.pitt.edu

BRANT, DALE
DISCIPLINE PHILOSOPHY **EDUCATION** Univ CA Irvine, BS, 86; BA, 86; MA, 91; PhD, 96. **CAREER** Philos, Valparaiso Univ. **HONORS AND AWARDS** Outstanding Hum tchg asst, Univ CA, 95; Regents Irvine Fel, Univ CA, 86-89; grad res fel, Univ CA, 86. **MEMBERSHIPS** Am Philos Asn. **RESEARCH** Metaphysics and epistemology; medieval philos; philos of relig; formal and informal logic, philos of lang; ancient philos and mod philos; ethics and soc/polit philos; philos of mind. **SELECTED PUBLICATIONS** Auth, On Plantinga's Way Out, Faith and Philos, 97. **CONTACT ADDRESS** Valparaiso Univ, 1500 E Lincoln Way, Valparaiso, IN 46383-6493.

BRASSARD, FRANCIS
PERSONAL Born 02/16/1961, St. Hyacinthe, Canada, m, 1992, 1 child **DISCIPLINE** RELIGIOUS STUDIES **EDUCATION** McGill Univ, Phd, 97. **CAREER** Lectr, McGill Univ **HONORS AND AWARDS** Deans Honour List **RESEARCH** Mahayana Buddhism; South Asian religions. **SELECTED PUBLICATIONS** Forthcoming, The Concept of Bodhicitta in Shantidevas Bodhicarjauatara **CONTACT ADDRESS** Dept of Relig and Philos, Berry Col, 1 Mount Berry Sta, Rome, GA, Canada 30165-7736. **EMAIL** CYFB@musica.mcgill.CA

BRAUCH, MANFRED T.
PERSONAL Born 03/10/1940, Germany, m, 3 children **DISCIPLINE** BIBLICAL THEOLOGY **EDUCATION** Houghton Col, BA; N Amer Baptist Sem, BD; Univ Hamburg, grad stud; Princeton Theol Sem, ThM; McMaster Univ, PhD. **CAREER** Prof, E Baptist Theol Sem. **HONORS AND AWARDS** Honorary Doctorates, Eastern College and Houghton College. **MEMBERSHIPS** Mem, Inst for Biblical Res and Evangelicals for Soc Action. **RESEARCH** Pauline Studies **SELECTED PUBLICATIONS** Auth, Hard Sayings of Paul, IVP, 89. **CONTACT ADDRESS** Eastern Baptist Theol Sem, 6 Lancaster Ave, Wynnewood, PA 19096. **EMAIL** mbrauch@ebts.edu

BRAUER, JAMES L.
PERSONAL Born 09/29/1938, Julesburg, CO, m, 1964, 2 children **DISCIPLINE** THEOLOGY, MUSIC **EDUCATION** Concordia Col, AA, 58; Concordia Sr Col, BA, 60; Concordia Sem, MDiv, 64, STM, 67; Union Theol Sem, SMM, 72; CUNY, PhD, 83. **CAREER** Instr, Concordia Col, 65-71; from asst prof to prof, 71-87, exec dir, 87-91, Commission on Worship, Lutheran Church, Missouri Synod; guest instr, 90, asst prof practical theol, 91-98, prof, 98- chaplain, 91-92, dean of the chapel, 92- , Concordia Seminary. **MEMBERSHIPS** No Am Acad of Liturgy; Asn of Lutheran Musicians; Am Guild of Organists; Hymn Soc of N Am; Societas Liturgica; Sixteenth Century Music Soc; Int Heinrich Schulz Soc. **RESEARCH** Music in the church; liturgy; the adult catechumenate. **SELECTED PUBLICATIONS** Composer, Trios on Four Advent/Christmas Carols for Strings, Winds or Organ, Concordia, 91; composer, When He Returns, SATB and Organ, Morning Star Music, 91; auth, The Church Year, in Lutheran Worship: History and Practice, Concordia, 91; auth, Meaningful Worship: A Guide to the Lutheran Service, Concordia, 94; auth, Does the Church Really Need the Adult Catechumenate Process, Lutheran Forum, 98; auth, Musica Contrafacta; Can Secular Music be Recycled for New Hymn Texts? Missio Apostolica, 98; auth, "The Role of Music in Seeker Services," Concordia J, 98. **CONTACT ADDRESS** Concordia Sem, 801 DeMun Ave, Saint Louis, MO 63105. **EMAIL** brauerj@csl.edu

BRAUER, JERALD
PERSONAL Born 09/16/1921, Fond du Lac, WI, m, 1945, 3 children **DISCIPLINE** HISTORY OF CHRISTIANITY **EDUCATION** Carthage Col, AB, 43; Northwestern Lutheran Theol Sem, BD, 45; Univ Chicago, PhD, 48. **CAREER** Instr church hist & hist Christian thought, Union Theol Sem, NY, 48-50; from asst prof to prof church hist, 50-69, dean federated theol fac, 55-60, dean divinity sch, 60-70, Prof Hist Christianity, Univ Chicago, 69-, Naomi Shenstone Donnelley Prof, 69-, Kessler lectr, Hamma Divinity Sch & Wittenberg Col, 54; Merrick lectr, Ohio Wesleyan, 58; mem bd dirs, Rockefeller Theol Fel Prog & Inst Advan Pastoral Studies; trustee, Carthage Col; pres bd theol educ, Lutheran Church in Am, 62-68; deleg observer, Vatican Coun II, session 3, 64, session 4, 65; vis lectr, Univ Tokoyo & Kokagokuin Univ, 66; consult, NY State Dept Educ, 70-; vis fel, Ctr Studies Democratic Insts, 72 & 74; pres bd gov, Int House, 73-; Am Asn Theol Schs grant; fel, Ctr Policy Study, 74-79; Nat Endowment for Humanities fel, 77-78; chmn bd, Coun Relig & Int Affairs, 79- **HONORS AND AWARDS** DD, Miami Univ, 56; LLD, Carthage Col, 57; STD, Ripon Col, 61; LHD, Gettysburg Col, 63. **MEMBERSHIPS** Am Soc Church Hist (pres, 60). **RESEARCH** Puritanism influence in the United States and England; revivalism; religion in America. **SELECTED PUBLICATIONS** Auth, Protestantism in America, Westminster, 53; coauth, Luther and the Reformation, 53 & auth, Basic questions for the Christian scholar, 54, Nat Lutheran Coun; ed, Essays in Divinity (7 vols), Univ Chicago, 67-69; Reinterpretation in American Church History, Univ Chicago, 69; Paul Tillich, My Travel Diary, Harper, 70; Westminster Dictionary of Church History, Westminster, 71; Religion and the American Revolution, Fortress, 76. **CONTACT ADDRESS** Divinity Sch, Univ of Chicago, 207 Swift Hall, Chicago, IL 60637.

BRAUNGARDT, JURGEN
PERSONAL Born 03/02/1959, Coburg, Germany **DISCIPLINE** PHILOSOPHY **EDUCATION** Univ Munich, BA, 86; Jesuit Univ of Munich, MA, 87; Prof Sch of Psych, MA, 95; Grad Theol Union, Berkeley, PhD candidate. **CAREER** Author **MEMBERSHIPS** APA; Am Psych Assoc. **RESEARCH** Psychoanalysis, Frankfurt School. **CONTACT ADDRESS** 271 Vernon St, #303, Oakland, CA 94610. **EMAIL** jurgen@autobahn.org

BRAUTIGAM, DEBORAH
PERSONAL Born 11/28/1954, WI, s **DISCIPLINE** INTERNATIONAL DEVELOPMENT **EDUCATION** Ohio Wesleyan Univ, BA; Tufts Univ, MALD, PhD. **CAREER** Asst Prof, Columbia Univ, 87-94; Assoc Prof, Am Univ, 94-. **HONORS AND AWARDS** Fulbright Fel; Council on Foreign Relations Fel. **RESEARCH** Political economy of foreign aid and economic reform. **SELECTED PUBLICATIONS** Auth, Chinese Aid and African Development, St Martin's Press, 98. **CONTACT ADDRESS** American Univ, 4400 Massachusetts Ave, Washington, DC 20016. **EMAIL** dbrauti@american.edu

BRAXTON, EDWARD KENNETH
PERSONAL Born 06/28/1944, Chicago, IL, s **DISCIPLINE** THEOLOGY **EDUCATION** BA, 1966; MA, 1968; M, Div, 1969; STB, 1968; PhD, 1975; STD, 1976; Univ of Chicago, Postdoctoral Fellowship. **CAREER** Harvard Univ, 76-77; Notre Dame Univ, visiting prof, 77-78; Diocese of Cleveland, chancellor for theological affairs & personal theology; Archdiocese ofWashington, DC, chancellor for theological affairs, 78-81; Rome North Amer Coll, scholar in residence, 82-83; Univ of Chicago, Catholic Student Center, dir; William H Sadlier Inc, official theological cons; 88 winter school lecturer, South Africa. **MEMBERSHIPS** Mem, Amer Acad of Religion; Catholic Theological Soc of Amer; Black Catholic Clergy Caucus; Catholic Bishop's Committee on Liturgy & Doctrine; bd of dir, St Mary of the Lake Seminary, Chicago; keynote speaker, 43 Intl Eucharistic Congress, Nairobi, Kenya; theological advisor to bishops of Africa & Madagascan, 1984; del, writer & speaker for Historic Natl Black Catholic Congress, Washington, DC 1987. **SELECTED PUBLICATIONS** Auth, The Wisdom Comm; numerous articles on Catholic Theological Religion; One Holy Catholic and Apostolic: Essays for the Community of Faith. **CONTACT ADDRESS** William H Sadlier Inc, 11 Park Place, New York, NY 10007.

BRAY, GERALD L.
PERSONAL Born 11/16/1948, Montreal, QC, Canada, s **DISCIPLINE** THEOLOGY **EDUCATION** McGill Univ, BA, 69; Sorbonne, Doctorat es Lettres, 73. **CAREER** Tutor, Oak Hill Col, 80-92; Prof, Samford Univ, 93-. **HONORS AND AWARDS** Visiting Fel, Cambridge, 99-00. **RESEARCH** Church History. **SELECTED PUBLICATIONS** Auth, Documents of the English Reformation, 94; auth, Biblical Interpretation, 96; auth, The Anglican Canons, 1529-1947, 98; auth, "Romans", 98, "I & II Corinthians", 99, "James", 00, Ancient Christian Commentary on Scripture; auth, Tudor Church Reform, 00. **CONTACT ADDRESS** Beeson Divinity School, Samford Univ, 800 Lakeshore Dr, Birmingham, AL 35229-0001. **EMAIL** glbray@samford.edu

BRAYBROOKE, DAVID
PERSONAL Born 10/18/1924, Hackettstown, NJ, m, 1994, 3 children **DISCIPLINE** PHILOSOPHY **EDUCATION** Harvard Univ, BA, 48; Cornell Univ, MA, 51; PhD, 53. **CAREER** Instr, Hobart, 48-50; instr, Univ Mich, 53-54; instr, Bowdouin, 54-56; asst prof, Yale Univ, 56-63; prof, Dalhousie Univ, 63-90; prof, Centennial Commission Chair, Univ of Tex Austin, 90-. **HONORS AND AWARDS** Guggenheim Fel; Rockefeller Found Grant; Res Fel, Canada Coun and Soc Sci and Humanities Res Coun of Can; Fel, Royal Soc of Can. **MEMBERSHIPS** Can Philos Assoc; Can Polit Sci Assoc; Am Philos Assoc; Am Polit Sci Assoc. **RESEARCH** Ethical theory, especially utilitarianism; deliberation in democracy; logic of rules; philosophy of social science and history. **SELECTED PUBLICATIONS** Coauth, A Strategy of Decision; coauth, Three Tests for Democracy - Meeting Needs; auth, Philosophy of Social Science; coauth, Logic on the Track of Social Change; auth, Moral Objectives, Rules and the Forms of Social Change. **CONTACT ADDRESS** Dept Gov, Univ of Texas, Austin, Campus Mail Code A1800, Austin, TX 78712-1013. **EMAIL** braeburn@mail.la.utexas.edu

BRECHT, ALBERT O.
DISCIPLINE LAW **EDUCATION** North Tex State Univ, BA,69 ; Univ Houston, JD,72; Univ Wash, MLL,73. **CAREER** John Stauffer prof Univ Southern California , assoc dean & Ch inf off. **MEMBERSHIPS** Past pres, Amer Asn Law Libraries. **RESEARCH** Computerized legal research and the expanding role of law librarians in the scholarly mission of the faculty. **SELECTED PUBLICATIONS** Auth, The Impact of Automation on Academic Libraries & Changes in Legal Scholarship and Their Impact on Law School Library Reference Service. **CONTACT ADDRESS** School of Law, Univ of So California, University Park Campus, Los Angeles, CA 90089. **EMAIL** abrecht@law.usc.edu

BRECKENRIDGE, JAMES
PERSONAL Born 06/30/1935, St. Louis, MO, m, 1969, 2 children **DISCIPLINE** HISTORY OF RELIGIONS, CHURCH HISTORY **EDUCATION** Biola Col, BA, 57; Calif Baptist theol Sem, BD, 60; Univ Southern Calif, MA, 65, PhD(relig), 68. **CAREER** Lectr church hist & world relig hist, Am Baptist Sem the West, 67-74; Assoc Prof Hist Relig, Baylor Univ, 74-, Lectr philos, Calif State Polytech Univ, 69-74. **MEMBERSHIPS** Am Acad Relig. **SELECTED PUBLICATIONS** Auth, Pelagius, Evangel Quart,70; Julian and Athanasius, theology, 73; Augustine and the Donatists, Foundations, 76; Religion and the problem of death, J Dharma, 79. **CONTACT ADDRESS** Dept of Relig, Baylor Univ, Waco, Waco, TX 76703.

BREDECK, MARTIN JAMES
PERSONAL Born 11/05/1933, St. Louis, MO **DISCIPLINE** RELIGIOUS STUDIES, AMERICAN CATHOLICISM **EDUCATION** St Louis Univ, AB, 57, PhL, 58, MA, 58, STB, 66; Cath Univ Am, PhD, 77. **CAREER** Instr class lang, St Louis Univ High Sch, 58-61; instr theol, St Joseph's Col, Pa, 71-74; lectr, Rockhurst Col, 74-76; asst prof relig studies, Mount St Mary's Col, Los Angeles, 76-78; asst prof, 78-81, assoc prof, 81-89; prof Theol & Relig Studies, Rockhurst Col, 89-. **HONORS AND AWARDS** Disting Serv Awd 95; Exec Com MO St Conf AAUP; Who's Who Midwest, 26th Ed; Who's Who Wrld, 16th Ed. **MEMBERSHIPS** Am Acad Relig; Col Theol Soc; Am Assoc of Univ Profs. **RESEARCH** Cultural impact on Christianity; American pluralistic thought and Catholicism; space-age religious thought. **SELECTED PUBLICATIONS** Auth, The Question of Survival Revisited, Explorations, winter, 87; Imperfect Apostles, 88, Garland; auth, Jesuit Theater in Italy: A Bibliography, AHSI, 97. **CONTACT ADDRESS** Dept of Theology, Rockhurst Col, 1100 Rockhurst Rd, Kansas City, MO 64110-2561. **EMAIL** Martin.Bredeck@rockhurst.edu

BREEDEN, JAMES PLEASANT
PERSONAL Born 10/14/1934, Minneapolis, MN **DISCIPLINE** THEOLOGY **EDUCATION** Dartmouth Coll, BA 1956; Union Theological Seminary NYork City, MDiv 1960; Harvard Grad Sch of Educ, EdD 1972. **CAREER** Canon St Paul's Cathedral Episc Diocese of MA, 63-65; Comm on Religion & Race Natl Council of Churches, asst dir, 65-67; Comm on Church & Race MA Council of Churches, dir 1967-69; Harvard Grad Sch of Educ, assoc prof 1972-76; Univ of Das Salaam Tanzania, prof in ed 1973-75; Boston Public Schs, sr officer planning policy 1978-82; Ctr for Law & Ed, dir 1983-84; Dartmouth Coll, dean Wm Jewett Tucker Found 1984-. **HONORS AND AWARDS** Annual Awd MA Soc Worker Assn 1964; The Young Men of Boston Boston Jr Chamber of Commerce 1965; Alper Awd Civil Liberties Union MA 1978. **CONTACT ADDRESS** Wm Jewett Tucker Foundation, Dartmouth Col, Hanover, NH 03755.

BREGMAN, LUCY
PERSONAL Born 12/18/1944, New York, NY, s **DISCIPLINE** RELIGION **EDUCATION** Brown Univ, BA, 66; Univ of Chicago, MA, 70; PhD, 73. **CAREER** Ind, Univ, 72-74; Temple Univ, 74-. **MEMBERSHIPS** Am Acad of Relig; Soc for the Sci Study of Relig; Assoc for Death Educ and Counseling. **RESEARCH** Religion and psychology, death, dying and spirituality. **SELECTED PUBLICATIONS** Auth, Death in the Midst of Life: Perspectives on Death from Christianity and Depth Psychology, Baker Book House, 92; coauth, First Person Mortal: Personal Narratives of Illness, Grief and Dying, Paragon House, 95; auth, Beyond Silence and Denial: Death and Dying Reconsidered, Westminster John Knox Pr, 99. **CONTACT ADDRESS** Dept Relig, Temple Univ, 1114 W Berks St, Philadelphia, PA 19122-6007. **EMAIL** bregman@vm.temple.edu

BREHM, H. ALAN
PERSONAL m, 3 children **DISCIPLINE** NEW TESTAMENT **EDUCATION** Howard Payne Univ, BA, 83; Southwestern Baptist Theol Sem, MDiv, 86; PhD, 92. **CAREER** Adj tchr, 90-92; asst prof, 92-. **HONORS AND AWARDS** President's Scholar, Southwestern Sem, 83-84; Fulbright Scholar, Univ Tuebingen, 89-90; pastor, naruna baptist church, 81-83; vaughan baptist church, 86-89. **MEMBERSHIPS** Soc Biblical Lit; Inst Biblical Res. **SELECTED PUBLICATIONS** Auth, Will the Real Jesus Please Stand? Evaluating the 'Third Quest of the Historical Jesus', Southwestern Jour Theol, 96; The Meaning of Hellenistes in Acts in Light of a Diachronic Analysis of Hellenizein, JSOT Press, 95; Paul's Relationship with the Jerusalem Apostles in Galatians 1 and 2, Southwestern Jour Theol, 94; The Significance of the Summaries for Interpreting Acts, Southwestern Jour Theol, 90. **CONTACT ADDRESS** Pastor, First Baptist Church, 512 E Huron St, Ann Arbor, MI 48104. **EMAIL** fbca2@prodigy.net

BREIT, WILLIAM LEO
PERSONAL Born 02/13/1933, New Orleans, LA, s **DISCIPLINE** ECONOMICS **EDUCATION** Univ TX, BA, 55, MA, 56; Mich State Univ, PhD, 61. **CAREER** Adjunct scholar, Am Enterprise Inst for Public Policy Res, 77-; E.M. Stevens Distinguished Prof of Econ, Trinity Univ, 83-99; Vernon F. Taylor Distinguished Prof of Econ, Trinity Univ, 99-. **HONORS AND AWARDS** Distinguished Alumni Awd, Mich State Univ, 98; Phi Beta Kappa. **MEMBERSHIPS** Am Economic Asn; Mystery Writers of Am; Southern Economic Asn; Southwestern Social Sci Asn; Mont Pelerin Soc. **RESEARCH** History of economic thought; antitrust economics. **SELECTED PUBLICATIONS** Auth, Stone, Sire John Richard N., An Encycl of Keynesian Economics, Edward Elgar, 97; coauth, Discrimination and Diversity: Market and Non-Market Settings, Public Choice, 95; A Deadly Indifference, Carrol & Graf, 95, Princeton Univ Press, 98; The Academic Scribblers, Princeton Univ Press, 98; The Antitrust Casebook: Milestones in Economic Regulation, The Dryden Press, 96; The Yeager Mystique: The Polymath as Teacher, Scholar and Colleague, Eastern Economic J, spring 96; Reputation versus Influence: The Evidence from Textbook References, Eastern Economic J, fall 97; co-ed, Lives of the Laureates: Thirteen Nobel Economists, MIT Press, 95 & 97. **CONTACT ADDRESS** Dept of Economics, Trinity Univ, 715 Stadium Dr., San Antonio, TX 78212-7200. **EMAIL** wbreit@trinity.edu

BRENNAN, JAMES FRANKLIN
PERSONAL Born 07/05/1932, Peoria, IL **DISCIPLINE** LAW **EDUCATION** Georgetown Univ, BS, 55; Univ Calif, Berkeley, MA, 60, PhD(hist), 63. **CAREER** Teaching asst Europ hist, Univ Calif, Berkeley, 60-62; asst prof, Ripon Col, 63-66; asst prof, 66-67, Assoc Prof Europ Hist, Cent Wash Univ, 67-. **MEMBERSHIPS** AHA; Am Asn Advan Slavic Studies. **RESEARCH** History of the labor and socialist movements in Russia; eighteenth century Russia. **SELECTED PUBLICATIONS** Auth, The origin and nature of economism in St Petersburg, Can Slavic Studies, summer 70. **CONTACT ADDRESS** Dept of Hist, Central Washington Univ, Ellensburg, WA 98926.

BRENNAN, MARY ALETHEA
PERSONAL Born 06/11/1909, Larksville, PA **DISCIPLINE** PHILOSOPHY, CLASSICS **EDUCATION** Col Mt St Vincent, BA, 30; Cath Univ Am, MA, 44, PhL, 48, PhD(philos), 50; Univ Freiburg & Univ Dublin, 62. **CAREER** Instr chem & math, Cathedral High Sch, New York, NY, 34-35, chem, 35-41, head dept, 41-43; instr chem & Latin, 44-45, asst prof Latin, 45-47, from instr to assoc prof philos, 50-76, Adj Assoc Prof Philos, Col Mt St Vincent, 76- **MEMBERSHIPS** Am Philos Soc; Am Cath Philos Asn; Metaphys Soc Am; Cath Class Asn (pres, 43-44). **RESEARCH** Science, especially chemistry. **SELECTED PUBLICATIONS** Auth, Religion, Law, and Power, the Making of Protestant Ireland, 1660-1760, Albion, Vol 0025, 93; Neither Kingdom Nor Nation in the Irish Quest For Constitutional-Rights, 1698-1800, Albion, Vol 0027, 95. **CONTACT ADDRESS** Dept of Philos, Col of Mount Saint Vincent, Mount View, CA 94039.

BRENNAN, PAULINE G.
PERSONAL Born 06/30/1967, Rochester, NY, s **DISCIPLINE** CRIMINAL JUSTICE **EDUCATION** SUNY, PhD, 99. **CAREER** Res Analyst, NYC Criminal Justice Agency, 91-97; Asst Prof, Univ NCar, 97-. **HONORS AND AWARDS** Elliot M Lumbard Awd, 99; First Prize, Am Soc of Criminology Stud Paper Competition; 97; Grad Fel, SUNY, 88-89; Phi Beta Kappa, 88. **MEMBERSHIPS** Am Soc of Criminol; Acad of Criminal Justice Sci. **RESEARCH** Sentencing; Corrections; Female Studies. **CONTACT ADDRESS** Dept Criminal Justice, Univ of No Carolina, Charlotte, 9201 Univ City, Charlotte, NC 28223. **EMAIL** pkbrenna@email.uncc.edu

BRENNAN, TIMOTHY J.
PERSONAL Born 12/26/1952, Washington, DC, d **DISCIPLINE** ECONOMICS **EDUCATION** Univ Wis, PhD, 78. **CAREER** Economist, Antitrust div, US Dept Justice, 78-98; Assoc prof Pul Policy, Commun (s), and Econ (s), Grad Sch Arts and Sci, George Washington Univ, 86-89; Gilber White fel, resources for the futures, Wash, DC, 95; sr Econ Industrial org and reg, coun Econ Adv (s), Exec Office Pres, Wash DC, 96-97; sr fel, res for the futures, Wash DC, 95- ; Prof Policy Sci and Econ (s), Univ Md, 93- . **HONORS AND AWARDS** Gilbert White fel, res for the futures, Wash DC; Wis Alumni res found grad fel: Math, 74-75, Econ (s), 76-77, doct diss Econ (s), 77-78; Valedictorian, Univ Md, Dec 73; Who's Who in the East, 92-95; Dept Justice merit awd, 82, 84; Dept Justice Antitrust Div awd of merit, 85. **MEMBERSHIPS** Amer Econ (s) Assn; Amer Philos Assn; Amer Bar Assn; Amer Law Econ (s) Assn; Assn Pub Policy Analysis and Mgt; Assn Environ Res Econ (s); Indust org soc; Assn Ed Jour and Mass Commun; Broadcast Ed Asn; Assn Soc Econ; Hist Econ Soc; Assn Evolutionary Econ (s); S Econ Assn. **RESEARCH** Ethics and public policy; First Amendment policy; regulation, antitrust, intellectual property law; methodology of economics. **SELECTED PUBLICATIONS** Auth, A Methodological Assessment of Multiple Utility frameworks, in The Philosophy and Methodology of Economics, Aldershot, Edward Elgar, 93, vol 1, 405-424; The Futility of Multiple Utility, Economics and Philosophy, 9,1, 93, 155-164; Copyright, Property, and the Right to Deny, Chicago-Kent Law Rev, 68,2, 93, 675-714; Comparing the Costs and Benefits of Diversification by Regulated Firms, Jour Regulatory Econ, 6, 2, 94, 115-136; Economic Theory in Industrial Policy: Lessons from U.S. vs AT&T, Res in the Hist Econ Thought and Methodology, 11, 94, 49-72; Talking to One's Selves: The Social Science of Jon Elster, Jour Communication, 44, 1, 94, 73-81; Markets, Information, and Benevolence, Econ and Philos, 10, 2, 94, 151-168; Game Theory and the First Amendment: Strategic Implications of Freedom of the Press, in Toward a Competitive Telecommunication Industry: Selected Papers from the 1994 Telecommunications Policy Research Conference, New York, Lawrence erlbaum, 95, 309-331; Does the Theory Behind U.S. v AT&T Still Apply Today?, Antitrust Bulletin, 40, 3, 95, 455-482; Remote sensing Satellites and Privacy: a Framework for Policy Assessment, Jour of Law, Computers, and Artificial Intel, 4, 3, 95, 233-248; Ed, Symposium: Recent Competition Issues in Telecommunications, Antitrust Bulletin, 40, 3, 95; Balancing Present Costs and Future Benefits, in National Res Counc, Financing Tomorrow's Infrastructure: Challenges and Issues, Washington, National Acad Press, 96, 7-20; Does the theory Behind U.S. v AT&T Still Apply Today?, in The Internet and Telecommunications Policy: Selected Papers from the 1995 Telecommunications Policy Research Conference, New York, Lawrence Erlbaum, 96, 13-33; Additional Considerations in the Electricity Competition Debate, in Natl Res Coun, Competition in the electricity Industry: Emerging Issues, Opportunities and Risks for Facility Operators, Washington, Natl Acad Press, 96; Is Cost-of Service Regulation Worth the Cost?, Intl Jour Econ Bus, 3, 1, 96, 25-42; Methodology-Abstract Philosophy or Criticism of Diminishing Returns, Res in Hist Econ Thought and Method, 14, 96, 329-342; Making Sense of the Telecommunications Act of 1996, Industrial and Corp Change, 5, 96, 941-961; A Shock to the System: Restructuring America's Electricity Industry, Wash DC, Resources for the Future, 96; Die okonomische Analyse des Rechts aus philosopher Sicht: Gesellschaftspolitsche Ziele im Kontext des Rechts, in effiziente Verhaltenssteuerung und Kooperation im Zivilrecht, Tubingen, Mohr Siebeck, 97, 283-309; Stranded Costs, Takings, and the Law and Economics of Implicit Contracts, Jour Regulatory Econ, 11, 97, 41-54; Technology and Coordination: Antitrust Implications of Remote Sensing Satellites, Antitrust Bulletin, 42, 97, 477-502; Industry Parallel Interconnection Agreements, Info Econ and Policy, 9, 97, 133-149; American Democratic Institutions and Social Values, in Democracy, Social Values, and Pub Policy, Westport, CT, Greenwood, 98, 37-55. **CONTACT ADDRESS** Dept of Economics, Univ of Maryland, Baltimore, 1000 Hilltop Cir, Baltimore, MD 21250. **EMAIL** brennan@umbc.edu

BRENNEMAN, WALTER L., JR.
PERSONAL Born 12/05/1936, Harrisburg, PA, m, 1963, 6 children **DISCIPLINE** HISTORY OF RELIGION **EDUCATION** Gettysburg Col, BA; Univ Chicago, BA; Union Inst, PhD. **CAREER** Prof relig, Univ Vt, 69-99. **MEMBERSHIPS** Am Acad Relig; Am Comt Irish Stud. **RESEARCH** Irish Celtic religion; Irish Celtic Christianity; phenomenological method. **SELECTED PUBLICATIONS** Auth, Spirals: A study in Symbol, Myth and Ritual, Univ Press Am, 78; coauth, The Seeing Eye: Hermeneutical Phenomenology in the Study of Religion, Penn State, 82; coauth, Crossing the Circle at the Holy Walls of Ireland, Univ Press of Vir, 95. **CONTACT ADDRESS** 1853 County Rd, PO Box 760, Montpelier, VT 05602. **EMAIL** wbrennem@zoo.uvm.edu

BRENNEN, BONNIE S.
DISCIPLINE MEDIA ETHICS **EDUCATION** Calif State Univ, BA; Univ Iowa, PhD. **CAREER** Asst prof, 96-; **RESEARCH** Mass communications, communications history, media, society and popular culture. **SELECTED PUBLICATIONS** Co-ed, Newsworkers: Toward a History of the Rank and File, Univ Minn Press, 95; contribu, Jour Am Hist; Comm Theory; Comm Quart; Studies Popular Cult; Jour Comm Inquiry. **CONTACT ADDRESS** Sch Mass Commun, Virginia Commonwealth Univ, PO Box 842034, Richmond, VA 23284-2034.

BRENNER, WILLIAM H.
PERSONAL Born 08/29/1941, Bay City, MI, M, 1995, 2 children **DISCIPLINE** PHILOSOPHY **EDUCATION** Univ Va, PhD, 70. **CAREER** Philos, Old Dominion Univ. **RESEARCH** Wittgenstein, logic, philosophy of religion. **SELECTED PUBLICATIONS** Auth, Logic and Philosophy ;Elements of Modern Philosophy; auth, Wittgen Steins Philosophical Investigations. **CONTACT ADDRESS** Philosophy Dept., Old Dominion Univ, Norfolk, VA 23058. **EMAIL** WBrenner@odu.edu

BRESHEARS, RUSSELL
PERSONAL Born 12/15/1962, Little Rock, AR, m, 1989, 2 children **DISCIPLINE** THEOLOGY **EDUCATION** Onachiat Baptist Univ, BA; Vanderbilt Univ, MA; Union Theol Sem, MDiv; Univ Ark, PhD. **CAREER** Instr & dir of Int Programs, Univ of Ark Community Col at Hope, 97-. **HONORS AND AWARDS** NEH, Yale Univ, 99; Fulbright Teaching Exchange, 00. **MEMBERSHIPS** MLA, Ark Philo Asn. **RESEARCH** Oral History, Bible as Literature. **SELECTED PUBLICATIONS** Auth, Entering the Garden of Delights: Song of Songs Revisited, Ark Philol Asn. **CONTACT ADDRESS** Dept Commun, Univ of Ark Community Col at Hope, PO Box 140, Hope, AR 71802-0140. **EMAIL** rbreshears@mail.uacch.cc.ar.us

BREST, PAUL
PERSONAL Born 08/09/1940, Jacksonville, FL, m, 1962, 2 children **DISCIPLINE** LAW **EDUCATION** Swarthmore Col,

AB, 62; Harvard Univ, LLB, 65. **CAREER** Prof Law, Stanford Univ, 69-, Vis prof law, Yale Univ, 77-78. **HONORS AND AWARDS** DL, Northeastern Univ, 80. **MEMBERSHIPS** Am Acad Arts & Sci. **RESEARCH** Legal theory; legal education. **SELECTED PUBLICATIONS** Auth, Palmer versus Thompson: An approach to the problem of unconstitutional motivation, Supreme Court Rev, No 95; The conscientious legislator's guide to constitutional interpretation, Stanford Law Rev, 27: 585; Processes of Constitutional Decisionmaking, Little, Brown, 75 & 2nd ed, Sanford Levinson, 82; foreword to Harvard Law Rev, 90: 1; The misconceived quest for the original understanding, Boston Univ Law Rev, 60: 204; The fundamental rights controversy: The essential contradictions of normative constitutional scholarship, Yale Law J, 90: 1063. **CONTACT ADDRESS** Law Sch, Stanford Univ, Stanford, CA 94305-1926.

BRETT, NATHAN C.
DISCIPLINE PHILOSOPHY OF LAW **EDUCATION** Univ New Hampshire, BA, 64; Univ Waterloo, MA, 68, PhD, 72. **CAREER** Assoc prof, Dalhousie Univ. **RESEARCH** Ethics, theories of justice, modern philosophy. **SELECTED PUBLICATIONS** Auth, "Hume's Causal Account of the Self," Man and Nature 9 (90): 23-32; auth, "Language Laws and Collective Rights," The Can J of Law and Jurisp 9 (91): 347-360; auth, "Mercy and Criminal Justice: A Plea for Mercy," The Can J of Law and Jurisp 5 (92): 347-360; auth, "Sexual Offenses and Consent," The Can J of Law and Jurisp 11 (98): 69-88; auth, "Forgiveness and Mercy," in The Philosophy of Law: An Encyclopedia, ed. C. Gray (NY: Garland, 99), 548-550; auth, "Dementia, Critical Interests and Euthanasia," in Moral Issues in Global Perspective, ed. C. Koggel (Peterborough: Broadview, 99), 45-56. **CONTACT ADDRESS** Dept of Philos, Dalhousie Univ, Halifax, NS, Canada B3H 4P9. **EMAIL** nathan.brett@dal.ca

BRETTSCHNEIDER, MARLA
PERSONAL Born 05/16/1965, New York, NY **DISCIPLINE** POLITICS **EDUCATION** SUNY, Binghamton, BA, 86; NYork Univ, MA, 88, PhD, 93. **CAREER** Asst prof, 93-96, Bloomsburg Univ; asst prof, 96-, Univ NH. **HONORS AND AWARDS** Gustavus Meyers Human Rights Awd. **MEMBERSHIPS** APSA; AJS; SWIP; AAR; APA. **RESEARCH** Democratic theory; feminist theory; multicultural theory; Jewish politics. **SELECTED PUBLICATIONS** Auth, Cornerstones of Peace: Jewish Identity Politics & Democratic Theory, Rutgers, 96; auth, The Narrow Bridge: Jewish Views on Multiculturalism, Rutgers, 96; auth, Race, Gender, & Class: Jewish Persp, 98. **CONTACT ADDRESS** Univ of New Hampshire, Durham, Durham, NH 03824. **EMAIL** marlab@cisunix.unh.edu

BRETZKE, JAMES T.
PERSONAL Born 02/22/1952, Milwaukee, WI, s **DISCIPLINE** MORAL THEOLOGY **EDUCATION** Pontifical Gregorian Univ, STD, 89 **CAREER** Asst Prof, 90-93, Pont Greg Univ; Asst Prof, 93-pres, Jesuit Sch of Theol. **HONORS AND AWARDS** Reference Book Category, 2nd Place Awd for 99, Cathlolic Press Assoc. **MEMBERSHIPS** SCE, CTSA, CTS, AAR, PCTS. **RESEARCH** Cross Cultural Ethics, Scripture and Ethics; Korean Confucianism & Christianity. **SELECTED PUBLICATIONS** Auth, Bibliography on Scripture and Christian Ethics, Edwin Mellen Press, 97; Auth, Consecrated Phrases, A Latin Dictionary of Theological Terms, Liturgical Press, 98 **CONTACT ADDRESS** Grad Theolog Union, Jesuit Sch of Theol, Berkeley, 1735 LeRoy Ave, Berkeley, CA 94709-1193. **EMAIL** jbretzke@jstb.edu

BREWBAKER, WILLIAM S., III
DISCIPLINE LAW **EDUCATION** Vanderbilt Univ, 81; Univ Va, 86; Duke Univ, LLM, 93. **CAREER** Asst prof, 93; assoc prof, Univ Ala, 96-. **RESEARCH** Health care law, antitrust law, and property. **CONTACT ADDRESS** Law Dept, Univ of Alabama, Tuscaloosa, Box 870000, Tuscaloosa, AL 35487-0383. **EMAIL** wbrewbak@law.ua.edu

BREYER, STEPHEN GERALD
PERSONAL Born 08/15/1938, San Francisco, CA, m, 1967, 2 children **DISCIPLINE** LAW **EDUCATION** Stanford Univ, AB, 59; Oxford Univ, BA, 61; Harvard Univ, LLB, 64. **CAREER** Law clerk to Justice Goldberg, US Supreme Court, 64-65; spec asst to Asst US Atty Gen for Antitrust, US Dept Justice, 65-67; from asst prof to assoc prof, 67-75, Prof Law, Law Sch, Harvard Univ, 75-, Consult, Econ Coun of Can, 68-; mem, White House Task Force on Common Policy, 68-; Senate Commerce Comt, 70-; mem, Kennedy inst Polit, 71-; asst spec prosecutor, Watergate Spec Prosecution Force, 73; mem, Spec Coun, US Senate Judiciary Comn, 74-75, chief coun, 79-81; prof govt, J F Kennedy Sch, 78-81; judge, US Court Appeals for Ist Circuit, 81-; judicial rep, Admin Conf of US. **RESEARCH** Economic regulation; antitrust. **SELECTED PUBLICATIONS** Auth, The Federal Judicial Law Clerk Hiring Problem and the Modest March One Solution, Yale Law J, Vol 0104, 94. **CONTACT ADDRESS** Law Sch, Yale Univ, New Haven, CT 06520-8306.

BRICKER, DANIEL P.
PERSONAL Born 08/15/1954, Little Rock, AR, s **DISCIPLINE** RELIGION **EDUCATION** Moody Bib Inst, BA, 77; Talbot Theol Sem, MDiv, 80; Fuller Theol Sem, PhD, 98. **CAREER** Azus Pacific Univ, adj prof, 98-. **HONORS AND AWARDS** Honors and Awds graduated are laud from Talbot. **MEMBERSHIPS** ETS, SBL **RESEARCH** OT wisdom lit; Hebrew poetry; ancient near east studies and languages; Hebrew prophets; archaeology. **SELECTED PUBLICATIONS** Auth, The Doctrine of the Two Ways in the Book of Proverbs, Jour of the Evan Theo Society, 95; rev, The Book of Proverbs: A Survey of Modern Study, by R.N. Whybray, in: Jour of the Evan Theol Society, 97. **CONTACT ADDRESS** 1725 N Sierra Bonita, Pasadena, CA 91104. **EMAIL** dbricker@apu.edu

BRICKEY, KATHLEEN F.
DISCIPLINE LAW **EDUCATION** Univ Ky, AB, 65; JD, 68. **CAREER** Asst to assoc prof, Univ of Louisville, 72-76; assoc to prof, Wash Univ, 76-. **HONORS AND AWARDS** John C. Vance Awd, TRB, 91; Wash Univ Alumni Distinguished Teaching Awd, 91; Wash Univ Treiman Fac Fel, 00-01. **MEMBERSHIPS** Am Law Inst, Soc for the Reform of the Criminal Law, Assoc of Am Law Sch. **RESEARCH** Environmental Crime, White Collar Crime, Federal Criminal Law. **SELECTED PUBLICATIONS** Auth, "Criminal Liability of Corporate Officers for Strict Liability Offenses - Another View," 35 Vand Law Rev 1337, (82); auth, Corporate Criminal Liability, Clark Boardman Callaghan, 84; auth, "Forfeiture of Attorneys' Fees: The Impact of RICO and CCE Forfeitures on the Right to Counsel," 72 Va L Rev 493, (86); auth, "Rethinking Corporate Liability Under the Model Penal Code," 19 Rutgers LJ 593, (88); auth, Corporate and White Collar Crime, Cases and Materials, Little, Brown and Co. 90; auth, "The Rhetoric of Environmental Crime: Culpability, Discretion and Structural Reform," 84 Iowa L Rev 115, (98); auth, "Charging Practices in Hazardous Waste Prosecutions," 62 Ohio State LJ 1007, (01). **CONTACT ADDRESS** Sch of Law, Washington Univ, One Brookings Dr, Anheuser-Busch Hall, Saint Louis, MO 63130. **EMAIL** brickey@wulaw.wustl.edu

BRICKMAN, LESTER
PERSONAL Born 09/04/1940, New York, NY, m, 1977, 1 child **DISCIPLINE** LAW **EDUCATION** Carnegie inst Technol, BS, 61; Univ Fla, LLB, 64; Yale Univ, LLM, 65. **CAREER** From asst prof to prof law, Univ Toledo, 65-76; actg dean, 80-82, Prof Law, Cardozo Sch Law, Yeshiva Univ, 76-, Dep dir, Asn Am Law Schs Study Wave Surv, 66-67; vis res prof, Coun Legal Educ for Prof Responsibility, 69-70, consult, 69-78; consult, Legal Serv, 67-75, hearing examr, Ohio Civil Rights Comn, 67-70; consult, Toledo Model Cities Prog, 68-69, Ford Found, 70-71, NCent Asn, 72, Law Enforcement Assistance Admin, 74, Nat Sci Found, 75-, Am Bar Asn Spec Comt on Specialization, 75 & US office Educ, 78. **RESEARCH** Legal services delivery systems; legal paraprofessionals. **SELECTED PUBLICATIONS** Auth, Expansion of the lawyering process through a new delivery system: The emergence and state of legal paraprofessionalism, Columbia Law Rev, 71 & In: The Lawyer's Secretary, 72; auth, Of arterial passageways through legal process: The right of universal access to courts and lawyering services, NY Univ Law Rev, 73; co-ed, The Role of Research in Delivery of Legal Services, 76 & Law & Soc Rev, 76; auth, "Nonrefundable Retainers: Impermissible Under Fiduciary, Statutory and Contract Law," 57 Fordham Law Rev (88): 149-190; auth, "Contingent Fees Without Contingencies: 'Hamlet' Without the Prince of Denmark?", 37 UCLA Law Rev (89): 29-137; auth, "The Asbestos Litigation Crisis: Is There a Need for An Administrative Alternative?", 13 Cardozo Law Rev (92): 1819-1889; auth, "Nonrefundable Retainers Revisited," 72 NCar Law Rev (93): 1-54; co-auth, Rethinking Contingency Fees: A Proposal to Align the Contingency Fee System with its Policy Roots and Ethical Mandates, 94; auth, "Contingency Fee Abuses, Ethical Mandates and the Disciplinary System: The Case Against Cases-by-Case Enforcement," 53 Wash & Lee Law Rev (96): 1339-1379; auth, "ABA Regulation of Contingency Fees: Money Talks, Ethics Walks," 65 Fordham Law Rev (96): 247-335 **CONTACT ADDRESS** Benjamin N Cardozo Sch of Law, Yeshiva Univ, 55 5th Ave, New York, NY 10033-4301. **EMAIL** brickman@ymail.yu.edu

BRIDWELL, R. RANDAL
DISCIPLINE ADMIRALTY, LEGAL HISTORY, AND CONFLICTS **EDUCATION** Midwestern Univ, BA, 67; Southern Methodist Univ, JD, 70; Harvard Univ, LLM, 71. **CAREER** Strom Thurmond prof, Univ of SC. **SELECTED PUBLICATIONS** Publ on, legal hist and admiralty issues. **CONTACT ADDRESS** School of Law, Univ of So Carolina, Columbia, Law Center, Columbia, SC 29208. **EMAIL** Randall@law.law.sc.edu

BRIER, BOB
PERSONAL Born 12/13/1943, New York, NY, 3 children **DISCIPLINE** PHILOSOPHY **EDUCATION** Hunter Col, BA, 64; Univ NC, Chapel Hill, PhD(philos), 70. **CAREER** From asst prof to assoc prof, 71-80, Prof Philos, C W Post Col, Long Island Univ, 80-. **HONORS AND AWARDS** David Newton Awd for Teaching Excellence. **MEMBERSHIPS** AAAS; Parapsychol Asn, Egypt Exploration Soc, Am Res Ctr in Egypt. **RESEARCH** Ancient Egyptian philosophy. **SELECTED PUBLICATIONS** Auth, The use of Natron in Human Mummification in a Modern Experiment--Zeitschrift fur Agyptische Sprache und Altertumskunde, Vol 0124, 97; auth, "The Murder of Tutankhamen," Putnam, 98; auth, "Encyclopedia of Mummies," Facts on File, 99. **CONTACT ADDRESS** CW Post Campus, Long Island Univ, C.W. Post, Coll Arts & Sci, Greenvale, NY 11548. **EMAIL** mammy123@aol.com

BRIETZKE, PAUL H.
PERSONAL Born 07/30/1944, Chicago, IL, m, 1970, 1 child **DISCIPLINE** LAW **EDUCATION** Lake Forest Col, BA, 66; Univ Wis, JD, 69; Univ London, PhD(law), 79. **CAREER** Lectr law, Univ Malawi, 70-73; asst prof, Addis Abeba Univ, 73-75; lectr, Brunel Univ, England, 75-78; prof law, Valparaiso Univ, 78-, Nat Endowment for the Humanities fel, 80. **HONORS AND AWARDS** Phi Beta Kappa. **MEMBERSHIPS** Int Third World Legal Studies Asn; Soc Pub Teachers Law; Am Soc Political & Legal Philos. **RESEARCH** Comparative law; antitrust law; law and economics. **SELECTED PUBLICATIONS** Coauth, Traditional Courts Manual, Malawi Govt Printer, 72; auth, Murder & Manslaughter in Malawi's Traditional Courts, J African Law, 74; The Childbwe Murders Trials, African Studies Rev, 74; co-ed, Legal Analysis Teaching Materials, Addis Abeba Univ Press, 74; coauth, Ethiopia, Weltforum-Verlag, Munich, 76; auth, The Rightness of the Rightness of Things, Valparaiso Univ Law Rev, 79; Socialism & Law in the Ethopian Revolution, Rev Socialist Law, 81; Law, Development & the Ethiopian Revolution, Bucknell Univ Press, 82. **CONTACT ADDRESS** Sch of Law, Valparaiso Univ, Wesemann Hall, Valparaiso, IN 46383-6493. **EMAIL** Paul.Brietzke@valpo.edu

BRIGHAM, JOHN
PERSONAL Born 08/27/1945, San Francisco, CA, m, 1982, 2 children **DISCIPLINE** POLITICAL SCIENCE **EDUCATION** Univ Calif Berkeley, BA, 67; Univ W Madison, MA, 69; Univ Calif Santa Barbara, PhD, 75. **CAREER** Vis prof, Univ Chicago, Syracuse, SUNY-Albany, CSU Chico; Prof, Political Science Dept, Univ Mass Amherst, 76-. **HONORS AND AWARDS** Fel Int Inst Sociol Law; Trustee, Law & Soc Asn. **MEMBERSHIPS** APSA; Law Soc Asn. **RESEARCH** Law; Social movements; Gender; Property. **SELECTED PUBLICATIONS** Auth, Property and the Politics of Entitlement, Temple Univ Press, 90; The Constitution of Interests: Beyond the Politics of Rights, NY Univ Press, 96; The Other Countries of American Law, Social Identities: Jour for the Study of Race, Nation and Cult, 96; Institutional Authority and Political Momentum: Constitutional Equal Protection in American Politics, Critic of Auth, Institutions Series: Horizons of Justice, Peter Lang Publ, 96; Law in Politics: Struggles Over Property and Public Space on New York Citys Lower East Side, Law and Social Inquiry, 96; From the Matz Patrol to the Free Speech Movement, States, Citizens and Questions of Significance, Peter Lang, 97; Staates, Citizens and Questions of Significance: Proceedings of the Tenth Roundtable on Law and Semiotics, Peter Lang, 97. **CONTACT ADDRESS** Political Science Dept, Univ of Massachusetts, Amherst, Amherst, MA 01003. **EMAIL** brigham@polsci.umass.edu

BRIGHOUSE, M. H.
PERSONAL Born 06/14/1963, Stockport, OK, m, 1991, 1 child **DISCIPLINE** PHILOSOPHY **EDUCATION** USC, PhD, 92 **CAREER** Asst Prof, UC Davis, 91-92; assoc prof, Univ of Wis, 98-00; prof, Univ of Wis, 00-. **HONORS AND AWARDS** Cornell Univ, Inst for Ethics and Pub Life, Young Scholar, 98 **MEMBERSHIPS** APA. **RESEARCH** Political Philosophy; Philosophy of Education. **SELECTED PUBLICATIONS** Auth, "Neutrality, Publicity, and State Funding of the Arts," Philosophical and Public Affairs, 95; auth, "Political Equality in Justice as Fairness," Philosophical Studies, 97; auth, "Why Should States Fund Schools?", British Journal of Educational Studies, 98; auth, "Civic Education and Liberal Legitimacy," Ethics, 98; auth, School Choice: Some Theoretical Considerations, Verso, 98; Auth, Civic Education and Liberal Legitimacy, Ethics vol 108 no 4, 98, 719-745; Auth, Why Should States Fund Schools, British Journal of Educational Studies, 98; auth, Educational Equality and the New Selective Schooling (IMPACT Pamphlet #3: Philosophy of Education Society of Great Britain, 00; auth, School of Choice and Social Justice, Oxford Univ Pr, 00. **CONTACT ADDRESS** Dept of Philos, 5119, Univ of Wisconsin, Madison, 600 N Park St, Madison, WI 53706. **EMAIL** mhbrigho@facstaff.wisc.edu

BRINDLE, WAYNE
PERSONAL Born 09/21/1947, Concordia, KS, m, 1967, 2 children **DISCIPLINE** RELIGIOUS STUDIES **EDUCATION** Kans Wesleyan Univ, BA, 69; Dallas Theol Sem, ThM, 73; ThD, 88. **CAREER** Dir, Seminario por Extension, 75-79; prof, Liberty Univ, 81-; ed of ETS Newsletter, Evangelical Theol Soc, 94-. **HONORS AND AWARDS** Magna cum Laude, 69; listed in Who's Who Among America's Teachers, 98 & 00. **MEMBERSHIPS** Soc of Biblical Lit, Evangelical Theol Soc. **RESEARCH** Greek and New Testament Exegesis. **SELECTED PUBLICATIONS** Auth, "Righteousness and Wickedness in Ecclesiastes 7:15-18," in Reflecting with Solomon: Selected Studies on the Book of Ecclesiastes, Baker Book

House, 94; rev, of "The Beloved Disciple," by James H. Charlesworth, J of the Evangelical Theol Soc 42.4 (99): 751-752; auth, "I Finally Understood," Decision (99); rev, of "Revelation," by J. Ramsey Michaels, J of the Evangelical Theol Soc 43.1 (00): 160-161; rev, of "The Gospel of Luke," by Joel B. Green, J of the Evangelical Theol Soc 43.1 (00): 140-142; auth, "Looking for the Blessed Hope: An Analysis of Biblical Evidence for the Imminence of the Rapture," Bibliotheca Sacra 158 (forthcoming). **CONTACT ADDRESS** Dept Relig, Liberty Univ, 1971 University Blvd, Lynchburg, VA 24502-2269. **EMAIL** wabrindl@liberty.edu

BRINGHURST, NEWELL G.
PERSONAL Born 04/03/1942, Salt Lake City, UT, m, 1969, 1 child **DISCIPLINE** HISTORY, POLITICAL SCIENCE **EDUCATION** Univ Ut, BS, 65; MS, 67; Univ Calif Davis, PhD, 75. **CAREER** Lectr, San Jose State Univ, 72-75; instr, Bosie State Univ, 75-76; asst prof, Ind univ at Kokomo, 77-81; instr, Col of the Sequoias, 81-. **HONORS AND AWARDS** Fac Recognition Awd, Col of the Sequoias, 86-87; Best Article Awd, Mormon Hist Asn, 79 & 90; Dale L. Morgan Awd, Ut Hist Asn, 90. **MEMBERSHIPS** Western Hist Asn, Am Hist Asn, Mormon Hist Asn. **RESEARCH** U.S. political, social, and cultural history, the American West, American religious history with a focus on Mormonism. **SELECTED PUBLICATIONS** Auth, Mormonism, 81; Saints, Slaves, and Blacks: The Changing Place of Black People within Brigham Young and the Expanding American Frontier, 86; auth, Fawn McKay Brodie: A Biographer's Life, 99. **CONTACT ADDRESS** Dept Soc Sci, Col of the Sequoias, 915 S Mooney Blvd, Visalia, CA 93277-2214. **EMAIL** newellb@giant.sequoias.cc.ca.us

BRINK, DAVID O.
PERSONAL Born 01/16/1958, Minneapolis, MN, m, 2 children **DISCIPLINE** PHILOSOPHY **EDUCATION** Univ Minn, BA, 80; Cornell Univ, MA, 83; PhD, 85. **CAREER** Instr, Cornell Univ, 84; vis asst prof, Stanford Univ, 86; asst prof, Case W Res Univ, 85-87; asst prof, Mass Inst Technol, 87-91; asn prof, Mass Inst Technol, 91-94; Univ Calif, San Diego, asn prof, 94-96; Univ Calif, San Diego, full prof, 96-. **HONORS AND AWARDS** Old Dominion Fel, 90; Nat Endowment Humanities, 90-91; Andrew W Mellon, 90-91; Fel Center Advan Study Behav Scis, 90-91; Univ Calif Pres Fel, 98. **MEMBERSHIPS** Am Philos Asn. **RESEARCH** Ethical Theory; History of Ethics; Political Philosophy; Jurisprudence. **SELECTED PUBLICATIONS** Auth, Moral Realism and the Foundations of Ethics, 89; The Separateness of Persons, Distributive Norms, and Moral Theory, Value, Welfare and Morality, 93; Common Sense and First Principles, Sidgwick's Methods, Social Philosphy & Policy and Cultural Pluralism and Moral Knowledge, 94; A Reasonable Morality, Ethics, 94; Moral Conflict and Its Structure, The Philos Rev, 94,, Moral Dilemmas and Moral Theory, 95; Le Realisme Moral, Dictionaire de Philosphie Morale, 96; Rational Egoism and the Separateness of Persons, Reading Parfit, 97; Kantian Rationalism: Inescapability, Authority, and Supremacy, Ethics and Practical Reasons, 97; Self-love and Altruism, Soc Philos and Policy, 97; Moral Motivation, Ethics, 97; Eudaimonism, Love and Friendship, and Political Community, Soc Philos and Policy, 99; Legal Interpretation, Objectivity, and Morality, Objectivity in LAward and Morals, 99. **CONTACT ADDRESS** Philosophy Dept, Univ of California, San Diego, 9500 Gilman Dr, La Jolla, CA 92093-0119. **EMAIL** dbrink@ucsd.edu

BRINKLEY, GEORGE A.
PERSONAL Born 04/20/1931, Wilmington, NC, m, 1959, 1 child **DISCIPLINE** INTERNATIONAL RELATIONS, RUSSIAN AND EAST EUROPEAN STUDIES **EDUCATION** Davidson Col, BA, 53; Columbia Univ, MA, 55, PhD, 64. **CAREER** Instr, Columbia Univ, 57-58; Instr to prof emer, 58-91, dir, 69-87, Prog of Soviet and East European Stud, Univ of Notre Dame. **HONORS AND AWARDS** Phi Beta Kappa, 52; Ford Found Fel, 54-57; Beer Prize, Am Hist Asn, 67; Fel Coun on For Rel, 68. **MEMBERSHIPS** Am Asn for Advan of Slavic Stud. **RESEARCH** Soviet/Russian government and foreign relations. **SELECTED PUBLICATIONS** Auth, The Volunteer Army and Allied Intervention in South Russia, 1917-1921, Univ Notre Dame Pr, 66. **CONTACT ADDRESS** 19539 Cowles Ave, South Bend, IN 46637.

BRINKMAN, JOHN T.
DISCIPLINE HISTORY OF RELIGION **EDUCATION** Fordham Univ, PhD, 88. **CAREER** Inst of Asian Stud, St John's Univ, 89-97. **MEMBERSHIPS** AAAS; AAR. **RESEARCH** Ecological dimension of world religion; East Asian thought; history of religions with refined focus in the sequence; Japan; Chiina; India; **SELECTED PUBLICATIONS** Auth, The Simplicity of Dogen, Eastern Buddhist, 94; auth, Harmony, Attribute of the Sacred and Phenomenal in Aquinas and Kukai, Buddhist-Christian Stud, 95; auth, The Simplicity of Nichiren, Eastern Buddhist, 95; auth, Simplicity: A Distinctive Quality of Japanese Spirituality, Peter Land, 96; auth, Cosmology and Consciousness, Buddhist-Christian Studies, 98; auth, The Kyoto Protocol and Exigent Ecological Vision, Int Shinto Found Symp Proc, 98-99. **CONTACT ADDRESS** 2 Darthouth Rd, Shoreham, NY 11786.

BRINKMANN, KLAUS
PERSONAL Born 09/21/1944, Germany, m, 1974, 2 children **DISCIPLINE** PHILOSOPHY **EDUCATION** Univ Tubingen, PhD. **CAREER** Lectr, Univ Bonn, 79-82 & 84-88; Asst Prof, Philosophy, Boston Univ, 82-83; Asst Prof, Univ Tubingen, 84-89; Assoc Prof, Philosophy, Boston Univ. **MEMBERSHIPS** Allgemeine Gesellschaft fur Philos; Amer Philos Asn; Hegel Soc N Amer; N Amer Fichte Soc; Soc Ancient Greek Philos. **RESEARCH** Aristotle; German idealism; Hegel. **SELECTED PUBLICATIONS** Auth, Kurswissen Politische Philosophie: Staat-Recht-Politik, Stuttgart-Dresden, 95; The Consistency of Aristotles Thought on Substance, Artistotles Philosophical Development, Problems and Prospects, Rowman & Littlefield, 95; Le platonisme de l Eudeme reexamine, L Aristote perdu, Roma-Atene, 95; Hegel on the Animal Organism, Laval theologique et philosophique, 96; Zenon fut-il meterialiste et nominaliste?, Diotima, 97; Hegel sur le cogito cartesien, Laval theologique et philosophique, 98; Egalite politique et inegalite factuelle: La reponse aristotelicienne a un dilemme politique, La Societa Civile et la Societa Politica nel Pensiero di Aristotele, Roma, 98; Jaspers and Arendt on Communication and Politics, Jahrbuch der Osterreichischen Karl-Jaspers-Gesellschaft, 98; auth, "The Natural and the Supernatural in Human Nature: Hegel on the Soul," in Philosophies of Nature: The Human Dimension (Kluwer, 98); ed, The Proceedings of the Twentieth World Congress of Philosophy, vol 1, 99. **CONTACT ADDRESS** Philosophy Dept, Boston Univ, 745 Commonwealth Ave., Boston, MA 02215. **EMAIL** brinkman@bu.edu

BRINNER, WILLIAM MICHAEL
PERSONAL Born 10/06/1924, Alameda, CA, m, 1951, 3 children **DISCIPLINE** PHILOLOGY, ISLAMIC HISTORY **EDUCATION** Univ Calif, Berkeley, AB, 48, MA, 50, PhD, 56. **CAREER** From instr to assoc prof, 56-64, chmn dept & dir Near Eastern Lang & Area Ctr, 65-70, dir Ctr Arabic Studies Abroad, 67-70, Prof Near Eastern Lang, Univ Calif, Berkeley, 64-, Lectr Arabic, Ctr Mid Eastern Studies, Harvard Univ, 61; Visiting Prof, Hebrew Univ of Jerusalem, 70-71; 73-75; Univ of San Francisco, 85; Univ of Washington, 91. Am Coun Learned Soc-Soc Sci Res Coun grant Near Eastern studies, 61-62; mem, Am Res Ctr Egypt, 68-70; consult, US off Educ, 65-68; Guggenheim fel, 65-66; mem joint comt Near & Mid E, Am Coun Learned Soc-Soc Sci Res Coun, 66-70 & chmn, 69-70; mem exec comt, Am inst Iranian Studies, 68; Founder and U.S. Director, Center for Arabic Studies Abroad, Amer Univ in Cairo, 66-70; Fulbright-Hays fac res award, 70-71 & sr consult, Comt int Exchange Persons, 72-73; Member, Evaluation Panels, Natl Endowmen for the Humanities, 78-81; 85-91; dir, Univ Calif Studies Ctr, Jerusalem, 73-75; Visiting Committee, Dept of Near Eastern Langs. And Lit, Harvard Univ, 84-90; Acting Dir, Annenberg Research Institute, Philadelphia, 92-93. **HONORS AND AWARDS** Berkeley Citation for Academic Achievement and Distinguished Service, 91; Hebrew Union College, Los Angeles, Doctor of Human Letters, 92; Honoree, International Interdisciplinary Conference, Bridging the Worlds of Judaism and Islam, Berkeley, 93. **MEMBERSHIPS** Am Orient Soc (pres, 76-77); Mediaeval Acad Am; Mid E Studies Asn (pres, 69-70); Am Asn Teachers Arabic (pres, 68-69); Soc for Judaco -Arabic Studies; Am Acad for Jewish Research; Association for Jewish Studies. **RESEARCH** Arabic and Hebrew language and literature; Islamic and Jewish history. **SELECTED PUBLICATIONS** Auth, "A Chronicle of Damascus, 1389-97 2 vols, Univ of Cal of Press, 63; auth, "Sutro Library Hebraica: A Handlist," Cal State Library, 67; auth, "Readings in Modern Arabic Literature," E.J. Brill, Leiden, 72; auth, "An Elegant Composition Concerning Relief After Adversity," Yak Univ Press, 78-, reprint by Jason Aronson Inc., 96; auth, "Studies in Islamic and Judaic Traditions," vol 1 86, vol 11 89, Atlanta Scholars Press; auth, "Prophets and Patriarchs," History of al-/ Tabari, vol 11, Suny Press, 87; auth, "The Children of Israel," History of al-Tabari, vol 111, Suny Press, 91. **CONTACT ADDRESS** Dept of Near Eastern Studies, Univ of California, Berkeley, 250 Barrows Hall, Berkeley, CA 94720-1940. **EMAIL** zebrin@socrates.berkeley.edu

BRISCO, THOMAS V.
PERSONAL m, 2 children **DISCIPLINE** BIBLICAL BACKGROUNDS AND ARCHAELOLOGY **EDUCATION** Ouachita Baptist Univ, BA, 69; Southwestern Baptist Theol Sem, MDiv, 73; Southwestern Baptist Theol Sem, PhD, 81; advan stud, Cambridge Univ, 86. **CAREER** Tchg fel, Southwestern Baptist Theol Sem, 75-76; instr, Ouachita Baptist Univ, 77-80; instr to prof, Southwestern Baptist Theol Sem, 80-; assoc dean, Spec Masters Degrees. **HONORS AND AWARDS** David Meier Intl Stud League Awd, Southwestern Baptist Theol Sem, 74; Outstanding Young Men of Am, 78, 79; Who's Who Among Students in Amer Univ(s) and Col(s), 76; Who's Who Among Biblical Archaeol; interim pastor, kingsland baptist church, 96-97; first baptist church, 95-96; first baptist church, humble, 94-95; intl baptist church, 93; first baptist church, arkadelphia, 92-93; vp, amer sch(s) oriental res, 82-83; president, 83-84; vp, nat assn bapti **SELECTED PUBLICATIONS** Auth, Biblical Illustrator, Baptist Sunday Sch Bd, 79; Intl Standard Bible Encycl, Eerdmans, 88; contribur, Holman Bible Dictionary, Broadman & Holman, 91; auth, Holman Bible Atlas; contribur, Eerdmans Dictionary of the Bible; contribur, New Int Dictionary of Old Testament Theol. **CONTACT ADDRESS** Sch Theol, Southwestern Baptist Theol Sem, PO Box 22000, Fort Worth, TX 76122-0418. **EMAIL** tvb@swbts.swbts.edu

BRISTER, C. W.
PERSONAL Born, LA, m, 1946, 1 child **DISCIPLINE** PASTORAL STUDIES, THEOLOGY **EDUCATION** La Col, BA, 47; New Orleans Baptist Sem, BD, 52; MDiv, 73; Southwestern Baptist Theol Sem, ThD, 57; PhD, 74. **CAREER** Chair, Southwestern Baptist Theol Sem, 57-. **HONORS AND AWARDS** Who's Who in Society, 88; Who's Who in Relig, 92; Who's Who in the South and Southwest, 97-98. **MEMBERSHIPS** Baptist World Alliance Comm; Am Assoc of Marriage and Family Therapy; Assoc for Clinical Pastoral Educ; Soc for Pastoral Theol; Family Systems Ministries Int. **SELECTED PUBLICATIONS** Auth, Becoming You; auth, Take Care; auth, The Promise of Counseling; auth, Life Under Pressure: Dealing With Stress in Marriage; auth, It's Tough Growing Up; auth, Dealing with Doubt; auth, People Who Care: auth, Pastoral Care in the Church, 92; auth, Caring for the Caregivers, 97; auth, Change Happens: Finding Your Way Through Life's Transitions, 97. **CONTACT ADDRESS** Dept of Pastoral Care, Southwestern Baptist Theol Sem, PO Box 22036, Fort Worth, TX 76122-0036. **EMAIL** cwb@swbts.edu

BRISTOW, CLINTON, JR.
PERSONAL Born 03/15/1949, Montgomery, AL, m, 1975 **DISCIPLINE** LAW **EDUCATION** Northwestern University, Evanston, IL, BS, 1971, JD, 1974, PhD, 1977; Governors State University, University Park, IL, MBA, 1984 **CAREER** Roosevelt University, Chicago, IL, professor, 76-79; Olive-Harvey College, Chicago, IL, vice-president, 79-81; Chicago State University, Chicago, IL, professor, chairperson, dean, 81-; Alcorn State Univ, pres, 81-95, 95-. **HONORS AND AWARDS** Legal Opportunity Scholarship Awdee, Northwestern Univ, 1971; Urban Affairs Fellow, Northwestern Univ, 1976; Top Ladies of Distinction Role Model, TLOD Inc, 1987; Outstanding Educator Awd, City of Chicago, Department of Human Services, 1991. **MEMBERSHIPS** President, Chicago Bd of Education, 1990-92. **CONTACT ADDRESS** President, Alcorn State Univ, 1000 ASU Dr, #359, Lorman, MS 39096.

BRISTOW, EDWARD
DISCIPLINE JEWISH HISTORY **EDUCATION** Yale Univ, PhD. **CAREER** Dean, prof, Fordham Univ. **HONORS AND AWARDS** Grants, NEH; Am Philos Soc. **RESEARCH** Mod Britain. **SELECTED PUBLICATIONS** Auth, Profit-Sharing, Socialism and Labor Unrest, Essays in Anti-Labor Hist, 75; Vice and Vigilance: Purity Movements in Britain Since 1700, Rowan and Littlefield, 78; Prostitution and Prejudice: The Jewish Fight Against White Slavery, 1875-1939, Clarendon Press, 82; Individualism Versus Socialism in Britain, 1880-1914, Garland Publ, 87. **CONTACT ADDRESS** Dept of Hist, Fordham Univ, 113 W 60th St, New York, NY 10023.

BRITT, BRIAN M.
PERSONAL Born 08/28/1964, Omaha, NE, m, 1989, 2 children **DISCIPLINE** RELIGION **EDUCATION** Oberlin Col, BA, 86; Univ Chicago, MA, 87, PhD, 92. **CAREER** Asst prof, relig & phil, 92-96, Wesleyan Col; asst prof, relig, 96-, Virginia Tech. **HONORS AND AWARDS** Dean's Grant, Ed Tech, 97; Vulcan Co Tchng Awd, Wesleyan Col, 96; Phi Kappa Phi, 96; Natl Found Jew Culture Res Grant, 91; Inst Advan Stud of Relig, Jr Fel, 91-92; Divinity Schl Fel, 89-91; Divinity Schl Milo Jewett Prize, 89, 91; Phi Beta Kappa, Zeta of OH, 86. **MEMBERSHIPS** AAR; Soc of Bibl Lit; SE Conf Stud of Relig; Intl Walter Benjamin Assn. **SELECTED PUBLICATIONS** Art, The Aura of Benjamin's Untimely Death: An Interview With Lisa Fittko, Continuum 2, 93; art, Archive of Pure Language: Language and Scared Text in Benjamin's Philosophy, Continuum 3, 91; auth, Georgia Rallies 'Round the Flag', The Nation, 93; auth, Walter Benjamin and the Bible, Continuum, 96; art, The Veil of Allegory in Hawthorne's The Blithedale Romance, Lit & Theol 10, 96; art, Snapshots of Belief: Apparitions of the Virgin Mary in Conyers, Georgia, Nova Religio, 98. **CONTACT ADDRESS** Religious Studies Program, Virginia Polytech Inst and State Univ, Blacksburg, VA 24061-0135. **EMAIL** bbritt@vt.edu

BROAD, ROBIN
DISCIPLINE POLITICAL ECONOMY AND INTERNATIONAL DEVELOPMENT **EDUCATION** Williams Col, BA; Princeton Univ, MA, PhD. **CAREER** Prof, Am Univ. **HONORS AND AWARDS** Grants, John D. and Catherine T. MacArthur Found, Asn Asian Studies; Coun For Rel; int econ, carnegie endowment int peace, u.s. house representatives, u.s. dept treasury. **SELECTED PUBLICATIONS** Coauth, Plundering Paradise: The Struggle for the Environment in the Philippines, Univ Calif Press, 93; Auth, Unequal Alliance: The World Bank, the International Monetary Fund, and the Philippines,Univ Calif Press, 88. **CONTACT ADDRESS** American Univ, 4400 Massachusetts Ave, Washington, DC 20016.

BROADIE, SARAH
DISCIPLINE PHILOSOPHY **EDUCATION** Oxford Univ, MA, 64; Edinburgh Univ, PhD, 78. **CAREER** Lectr, Univ Edinburgh, 67-84; prof, Univ Tex Austin, 84-86; prof, Yale Univ, 86-91; prof, Rutgers Univ, 91-93; prof, 93-. **HONORS AND AWARDS** Guggenheim Found fel; Fel of the Acad of Arts and Sci. **MEMBERSHIPS** Am Philos Asn; Am Asn for Univ Prof; Soc for Ancient Greek Philos. **SELECTED PUBLI-**

CATIONS Auth, Ethics with Aristotle, 93. **CONTACT ADDRESS** Dept of Philosophy, Princeton Univ, 1879 Hall, Princeton, NJ 08540.

BROCK, DAN W.
PERSONAL Born 12/05/1937, Mineola, NY, m, 1969, 1 child **DISCIPLINE** PHILOSOPHY **EDUCATION** Cornell Univ, BA, 60; Columbia Univ, PhD(philos), 70. **CAREER** Asst prof, 69-75, assoc prof, 75-79. **MEMBERSHIPS** Am Philos Asn; Am Soc Polit & Legal Philos. **RESEARCH** Ethics; political philosophy; biomedical ethics. **SELECTED PUBLICATIONS** **CONTACT ADDRESS** Ctr Biomed Eth, Brown Univ, Providence, RI 02912.

BROCKELMAN, PAUL
DISCIPLINE PHILOSOPHY **EDUCATION** Northwestern Univ, PhD, 68. **CAREER** Prof, Univ NH, 63-. **RESEARCH** Existential phenomenology; phenomenology of religion; philosophy of religion; environmental theology; cosmology. **SELECTED PUBLICATIONS** Auth, The Inside Story: A Narrative Approach to Religious Understanding and Truth, SUNY, 92. **CONTACT ADDRESS** Philosophy Dept, Univ of New Hampshire, Durham, Hamilton Smith Hall, Durham, NH 03824. **EMAIL** ptb@hopper.unh.edu

BROCKOPP, JONATHAN E.
PERSONAL Born 09/11/1962, Valparaiso, IN, m, 1990, 1 child **DISCIPLINE** RELIGIOUS STUDIES **EDUCATION** Valparaiso Univ, BA, 84; Yale Univ, MPhil, 92, PhD, 95; Am Univ in Cairo; Bourguiba Inst (Tunisia); Tubingen Univ (Germany). **CAREER** Adj asst prof, Fairfield Univ, 91; teach asst, Yale Univ, 91-92; vis lect, Amherst Col, 92-93; teach asst, Yale Univ, 94; Asst Prof Rel, Bard Coll. **HONORS AND AWARDS** Fulbright fel, 90-91; Yale Univ fel, 82-83, 88-93; Am Res Ctr in Egypt grant, 95; Bard Col Fac Res Travel grant, 96; Inst Adv Study, Hebrew Univ, 99; Fulbright Fel, 00. **MEMBERSHIPS** Am Acad Rel; Am Inst Maghrib Stud; Am Oriental Soc; Am Res Ctr Egypt; Middle East Stud Asn. **RESEARCH** Islamic law; women and Islam; Arabic lang and lit; rel ethics. **SELECTED PUBLICATIONS** Auth, Early Islamic Jursiprudence in Egypt: Two Scholars and their Mukhtasars, Int J Middle East Studies, 98; auth, Re-reading the History of Early Maliki jurisprudence, J Am Oriental Soc, 98; auth, Islam, in The Pilgrim Library of World Religions, Pilgrim Press, 97; auth, Sources for Studying Islam, in The Pilgrim Library of World Religions, Pilgrim Press, 97; auth, "Literary Geneologies from the Mosque-Library of Kairovan," Islamic Law and Soc (99); coauth, Judaism and Islam in Practice, Routledge, 00; auth, Early Maliki Law: Ibn Abd Al-Hokam and His Large Compendium of Jurisprudence, Brill, 00. **CONTACT ADDRESS** Dept of Religion, Bard Col, Annandale, NY 12504. **EMAIL** brockopp@bard.edu

BROD, HARRY
PERSONAL Born 02/01/1951, Berlin, Germany, m, 1980, 2 children **DISCIPLINE** PHILOSOPHY **EDUCATION** Univ Cal SD, PhD 81, MA 75; Ruhr Univ Germany, Fulbright Gnt, 76-77; NYork Univ, BA 68-72. **CAREER** Univ of Northern Iowa, Assoc Prof of Philosophy and Humanities; Temple Univ, asst prof; Univ Delaware, asst prof 94; Mount St Mary's College LA lecrt, Univ Cal LA lectr, Antioch Univ LA adj fac, Los Angeles Pasadena Sch Dist inst/edu, 92-94; Kenyon College, vis assoc prof 88-92; Harvard Law Sch, fel 87-88; Univ S Cal, lectr, sr lect, asst prof, 82-87; Cal State SB, lect 81-82; Palomar College, inst 78-80; Univ Cal SD, tch asst 73-78. **HONORS AND AWARDS** Fulbright Fel; Choice Outstanding Acad Book. **RESEARCH** Gender studies; political philosophy; Hegal. **SELECTED PUBLICATIONS** Auth, Theorizing Masculinity's, coed, Sage Pub, 94; Hegal's Philosophy of Politics: Idealism Identity and Modernity, Westview Press, 92; Who's Afraid of Lorena Bobbitt?, Second Thoughts: Critical Thinking from a Multicultural Perspective, ed Wanda Teays, Mayfield, 96; Of Mice and Supermen: Images of the Jewish Masculinity, gender and Judaism, ed, Tamar M. Rudavsky, NY Univ Press, 95, reprint, in: Redeeming Men: Essays on Men Masculinity's and Religion, eds, Stephen B Boyd, Merle Longwood, Mark W Muesse, Westminster; John Knox Press, 96; Gender Violence: Interdisciplinary Perspectives, eds, Laura O'Toole, Jessica R. Schiffman, reprinted, NYU Press, 96. **CONTACT ADDRESS** Dept of Philosophy and Religion, Univ of No Iowa, 1818 Timberledge Dr, Cedar Falls, IA 50613-1741.

BRODIN, MARK S.
PERSONAL Born 05/09/1959, New York, NY, m **DISCIPLINE** LAW **EDUCATION** Columbia Col, BA, 69; Columbia Univ, JD, 72. **CAREER** Assoc prof to prof and assoc dean, Boston Col Law Sch, 85-. **SELECTED PUBLICATIONS** Auth, "Accuracy, Efficiency, and Accountability in the Litigation Process - The Case for the Verdict," Univ Cincinnati L Rev, (90): 15-111; auth, "The Demise of Circumstantial Proof in Employment discrimination Litigation: St Mary's Honor Center v. Hicks, Pretext, and the 'Personality' Excuse," Berkeley J of Employment and Labor L, (97): 183-239; co-auth, Handbook of Massachusetts Evidence, Aspen, 99; co-auth, Criminal Procedure: Examples and Explanations, Aspen, 00; co-auth, Civil Procedure: Doctrine, Practice and Context, 00. **CONTACT ADDRESS** Sch of Law, Boston Col, Newton Ctr, 885 Center St, Newton, MA 02459.

BRODLEY, JOSEPH F.
PERSONAL Born 09/22/1926, Washington, DC, m, 1960, 2 children **DISCIPLINE** LAW **EDUCATION** UCLA, BA, 49; Yale Univ, LLB, 52; Harvard Univ, LLM, 53. **CAREER** JAG, US Air Force, 53-56; atty, 56-68; prof, Ind State Univ, 68-79; vis prof, Univ of Southern Calif, 73-74; prof, Boston Univ, 80-; vis prof, Univ of Mich, 82; vis fel, Oxford Univ, 85, vis fel, Univ of Cambridge, 93, vis fel, Tilburg Univ, Netherlands, 97, vis scholar, Fed Trade Comm, 01. **HONORS AND AWARDS** Phi Beta Kappa **MEMBERSHIPS** Am Bar Assoc. **RESEARCH** Antitrust and Industrial Organization, Use of modern strategic analysis and game theory in application. **SELECTED PUBLICATIONS** Auth, "Oligopoly Power Under the Sherman and Clayton Acts: From Economic Theory to Legal Policy," 19 Stanford Law Rev 285, (67); auth "Massive Industrial Size, Classical Economics and the Search for Humanistic Value," 24 Stanford Law Rev 1155, (72); auth, "Potential Competition Mergers: A Structural Synthesis," 87 Yale Law Jour 1 (77); coauth, "Predatory Pricing: Competing Economic Theories and the Evolution of Legal Standards," 66 Cornell Law Rev 738, (81); auth, "Joint Ventures and the Antitrust Policy," 95 Harvard Law Rev 1521, (82); auth, "The Economic Goals of Antitrust: Efficiency, Consumer Welfare and Technological Progress," 62 NYU Law Rev, 801, (88); auth, "Antitrust, Innovation, and Collaboration," 4 Jour of Econ Perspectives 87, (90); coauth, "Contract Penalties, Monopolizing Strategies and Antitrust Policy," 45 Stanford Law Rev 1161, (93); auth, "Antitrust Standing in Private Merger Cases: Reconciling Private Incentives and Public Enforcement Goals," 94 Mich Law Rev 1, (95); coauth, "Predatory Pricing, Strategic Theory and Legal Policy," 88 Georgetown Law Rev 2239, (00). **CONTACT ADDRESS** Sch of Law and Dept of Econ, Boston Univ, 765 Commonwealth Ave, Boston, MA 02215. **EMAIL** jbrodley@bu.edu

BRODSKY, GARRY
PERSONAL Born 11/06/1932, Brooklyn, NY, m, 1982, 1 child **DISCIPLINE** ETHICS, SOCIAL AND POLITICAL PHILOSOPHY **EDUCATION** Brooklyn Col, BA, 54; Yale Univ, MA, 58; PhD, 61. **CAREER** Dept Philos, Univ Conn **HONORS AND AWARDS** BA with hon(s), 54. **RESEARCH** Nietzsche, Modernity and Postmodernity; ethics; social and politcal philosophy. **SELECTED PUBLICATIONS** Co-auth, Contemporary Readings in Social and Political Ethics, Prometheus Bk(s), 84; auth, A Way Of Being A Jew, A Way Of Being A Person, Goldberg and Krausz, Culture and Jewish Identity, Temple Univ Press, 93; West's Evasion of Pragmatism, Praxis Intl, 94; auth, Nietzsche's Motion of Amor Fati, Continental Philosophy Review, 98. **CONTACT ADDRESS** 22 Cooke St., Pautucket, RI 02860. **EMAIL** gmb@netway.com

BRODY, BORUCH ALTER
PERSONAL Born 04/21/1943, New York, NY, m, 1965 **DISCIPLINE** PHILOSOPHY **EDUCATION** Brooklyn Col, BA, 62; Princeton Univ, MA, 65, PhD(philos), 67. **CAREER** Lectr philos, Hunter Col, 66-67; from asst prof to assoc prof, Mass inst Technol, 67-75; Prof Philos, Rice Univ, 75-, Prof Medicine & Dir, Ctr Ethics, Med, Pub Issues, Baylor Col Med, 82-. **RESEARCH** Metaphysics; philosophy of law, philosophy & medicine. **SELECTED PUBLICATIONS** Coauth, Science: Men, Methods, Goals, W A Benjamin, 68; ed, Words of Thomas Reid, MIT, 70; Readings in the Philosophy of Science, 70, auth, Logic: Theoretical and Applied, 73 & Readings in the Philosophy of Religion, 74, Prentice-Hall; Abortion and the Sanctity of Human Life, MIT, 75; Beginning Philosophy, Prentice-Hall, 76; ed, Mental Health, Reidel, 78; Identity and essence, Princeton, 81. **CONTACT ADDRESS** Baylor Col of Med, Houston, TX 77030.

BROGAN, DORIS DELTOSTO
DISCIPLINE LAW **EDUCATION** Rowan/Glassboro State Col, BA, 74; Villanova Univ Sch Law, JD, 81. **CAREER** Prof; Villanova Univ, 83-; assoc dean, Acad Aff, 92-. **HONORS AND AWARDS** Distinguished Alumna awd, Rowan/Glassboro St Col, 87. **MEMBERSHIPS** Amer Bar Asn; Pa and Philadelphia Bar Asn; bd dir, Del Co Legal Asst Asn. **RESEARCH** Ethics, domestic relations, abuse; conflict of laws. **SELECTED PUBLICATIONS** Auth, Attorney Client Privilege and Conflicts of Interest & Legal Ethics for Trial Lawyers, Pa Trial Lawyers Ass'n Course Text, 92; Lawyers' Responses to Client Perjury Under the New Pennsylvania Rules of Professional Conduct-What Judges Can Expect, 34 Vill L. Rev 63, 89; Divorce Settlement Agreements: The Problem of Merger or Incorporation and the Status of the Agreement in Relation to the Decree, 67 Neb L. Rev 235, 88 & The Domestic Relations Exceptions to Fed Diversity Jurisdiction, Matrimonial Litigation: Across State Lines, PBI Program Course Text, 85. **CONTACT ADDRESS** Law School, Villanova Univ, 800 Lancaster Ave, Villanova, PA 19085-1692. **EMAIL** brogan@law.vill.edu

BROGAN, WALTER A.
DISCIPLINE PHILOSOPHY **EDUCATION** Catholic Univ, BA, 68; Northern Ill Univ, MA; Duquesne Univ, PhD, 81. **CAREER** Prof. **SELECTED PUBLICATIONS** Auth, Is Plato's Drama the Death of Tragedy, Int Stud in philos, 91; The Decentered Self: Nietzsche's Transgression of Metaphysical Subjectivity, The Southern J of Philos, 91; Haunting Resonances at the Threshold of Contemporary Philosophy, a rev article on Echoes After Heidegger by John Sallis, Research in Phenomenology, XXIII, 93; Twisting out of Metaphysics in John Sallis and the Path of Archaic Thinking, SUNY Press, 95; The Place of Aristotle in the Development of Heidegger's Phenomenology, Reading Heidegger from the Start SUNY Press, 94; The Tragic Figure of the Last Philosopher, Res in Phenomenol, 94; Heidegger's Aristotelian Reading of Plato: The Discovery of the Philosopher, Res in Phenomenol, 95; coauth, The Socratic Method: A Philosophical Assessment of Outcome-Based Education, Educ Forum, 95; co transl, Martin Heidegger, Aristotle's Metaphysics IX, 1-3: On the Essence and Actuality of Force, Ind Univ Press, 94. **CONTACT ADDRESS** Dept of Philosophy, Villanova Univ, 800 Lancaster Ave., Villanova, PA 19085-1692.

BRONIAK, CHRISTOPHER
PERSONAL Born 04/05/1957, Detroit, MI, s **DISCIPLINE** PHILOSOPHY **EDUCATION** Loyla Univ, PhD, 97. **CAREER** Sr lectr, Loyola Univ, 89-94; adjunct, Roosevelt Univ, 97. **HONORS AND AWARDS** Summer fel, Loyola Univ, 89; tchg fel, Loyola Univ, 88-89, 90-91. **MEMBERSHIPS** APA; Am Cath Philos Asn; SAAP; SPEP; IAPL. **RESEARCH** Phenomenology; American pragmatism. **SELECTED PUBLICATIONS** auth, "Duty or Virtue as a Metaethical Question," Dialogos, 90; rev, Eugene Taylor's "William James on Consciousness Beyond the Margin," Trans of the Charles S. Peirce Soc, 96; auth, "James' Theory of Fringes," Trans of the Charles S. Peirce Soc, 96. **CONTACT ADDRESS** 6807 N Sherican Rd, Apt 612, Chicago, IL 60626. **EMAIL** cbroniak@aon.com

BRONSTEIN, HERBERT
PERSONAL Born 03/01/1930, Cincinnati, OH, m, 1954, 3 children **DISCIPLINE** RELIGIOUS HISTORY, JUDAISM **EDUCATION** Univ Cincinnati, BA, 52; MA, 54; Hebrew Union Col, MAHL, 56; DD, 82. **CAREER** Univ of Rochester; Univ of IL Chicago; Northwestern Univ; Lake Forest Col. **HONORS AND AWARDS** Taft Teaching Fel, 53, 54; Hirsch Fel, 55-56; Vis Scholar, Oxford Univ, 76, 93. **MEMBERSHIPS** Central Conf of Am Rabbis; Assoc of Jewish Studies; Midwest Assoc of Jewish Studies; Am Acad of Relig. **RESEARCH** Liturgy, Judaism and modernity, issues in comparative religion. **SELECTED PUBLICATIONS** Auth, Passover Haggadah, CCAR, (NY), 74; auth, The Five Scrolls, CCAR (NY), 84; Auth, "Time-Schemes, Order and Chaos: Periodization and History", Time Order Chaos, eds Fraser and Soulsby, Int Univ Pr, 98; auth, "Mitzvah and Autonomy", Duties of the Soul, UAHC, 99; auth, "Autonomy and Mitzvah: The Oxymoron of Reform Judaism", Tikkun, Summer 99; auth, "Social Action and Spirituality", Tikkun, May 00. **CONTACT ADDRESS** Dept Relig, Lake Forest Col, 555 N Sheridan Rd, Lake Forest, IL 60045-2338. **EMAIL** bronstein@lfc.edu

BROOK, ANDREW
DISCIPLINE PHILOSOPHY **EDUCATION** Univ of Alberta and Oxford, PhD, 73. **CAREER** Vis scholar, Queen's Univ, 95; vis tutor, Univ Oxford, 95; fac, Toronto Inst of Contemp Psychoanalysis, 92-; assoc dean of grad stud, 79-80; Wexler vis prof, Bryn Mawr Col, 98-99; dir, Inst Interdisciplinary Stud, 91-; ch, Cognitive Sci Mgt Comm; prof, Carleton Univ. **HONORS AND AWARDS** Lorne J Calhoun scholar for extracurricular act, Univ Alberta, 65; Francis J Reeves grad scholar, Univ Alberta, 65-66; Woodrow Wilson fel, 65; Rhodes scholar, Alberta, 66; Carleton Univ Merit award, 77-78; SSHRC Leave fel and res grant, 79-80; Carleton Univ Scholarly Achievement award, 86; Levin prize, Can Psychoanalytic Soc, 91; Marston Lafrance res fel, Carleton Univ, 91-92; Prado Prize (joint winner), Can Psychoanalytic Soc, 94; treasurer, can philos assn; ch, ed comm, can lib philos, 77-79; assoc ed, intl jour/rev of psychoanalysis, 90-92; ed bd, can jour of psychoanalysis, , 94-. **MEMBERSHIPS** Can Psychoanalytic Soc, Canadian Philos Asn. **RESEARCH** The project of interdisciplinary cognitive research, Kant; consciousness; psychoogical and psychoanalytic explanation; environmental ethics. **SELECTED PUBLICATIONS** Auth, "Neuroscience versus Psychology in Freud," Ann N.Y. Acad Sci, vol. 843, (98): 66-79; auth, "ritical Notice of L. Falkenstein, Knats Intuitionism: A Commentary on the Transcedental Aesthetic," Canadian Jouranl of Philsophy, 29, 98; auth, Report on Panel, Castration as an Organizer of Bisexuality International Journal of Psychonalysis, no. 1, (98): 380-4; auth, "CSS Panel on Education, Introduction," New York: LEA, 98; auth, "Unified Consciousness and the Self," Journal of Consciousness Studies 5, (98): 583-91; auth, "Does Philosophy Have Distinctive Methods to Offer Cognitive Science?," New York: LEA, (98): 102-8; auth, "Kant", MIT Encyclopedia of the Cognitive Sciences, Cambridge MA: MIT Press, 99; auth, "Kant", MIT Encyclopaedia of the Cognitive Sciences, Cambridge MA: MIT Press, 99; auth, "Unity of Consciousness," stanford Electronic Encyclopedia of Philosophy, 99; coauth, Knowledge and Mind, Cambridge, MA: MIT Press, 00. **CONTACT ADDRESS** Dept of Philos, Carleton Univ, 1125 Colonel By Dr, Ottawa, ON, Canada K1S 5B6. **EMAIL** a_brook@carleton.ca

BROOKS, CATHERINE M.
PERSONAL Born 09/27/1956, New York City, NY, m, 1986, 1 child **DISCIPLINE** LAW **EDUCATION** Thomas More Col Fordham Univ, BA; Fordham Univ, MA; Univ VA, JD. **CA-**

REER Prof Creighton Univ; past vis asst prof, Seton Hall Univ Sch Law; served pvt pract; asst dep Public Defender, NJ Dept Pub Advocate, 83-88; app, Nebr Gov Comn on County Atty Studies, 97- 99. **HONORS AND AWARDS** Named 1 of 10 Outstanding Young Omahans, 94; co-founder and former dir Ctr for the Study Children's Issues, Creighton Univ; dir and co-founder, ctr for the study childrens issues, creighton univ. **MEMBERSHIPS** Nebr Permanency Plan Task Force; NACC. **SELECTED PUBLICATIONS** Auth, The Law's Response to Child Abuse and Neglect, Law, Mental Health, and Mental Disorder; ed & coauth, Nebr Juvenile Ct Procedures Manual; publ in, Lawyers for Children; Behavioral Sci and the Law; Criminal Behavior and Mental Health & Creighton Law Rev. **CONTACT ADDRESS** Sch of Law, Creighton Univ, 2500 California Plaza , Omaha, NE 68178. **EMAIL** brooks@culaw.Creighton.edu

BROOKS, JOHN
PERSONAL Born 09/06/1957, Chapel Hill, NC, m, 1994 **DISCIPLINE** HISTORY, GOVERNMENT **EDUCATION** Duke Univ, BA, 79; Univ Chicago, MA, 82; PhD, 90. **CAREER** Vis Asst Prof, Austin Col, 90-91; Asst Prof, Teikyo Loretto Heights Univ, 91-98; Asst Prof, Fayetteville State Univ, 98-. **HONORS AND AWARDS** Searle Fel, Univ Chicago, 71-84; George Lurcy Fel for Diss Res in France, 85-86; Tocqueville Awd and Soc Sci Res Coun Fel, 86-87; Phi Alpha Theta. **MEMBERSHIPS** AHA, Int Soc for the Hist of the Behav Sci, Forum for Hist of Human Sci, Hist of Sci Soc, Soc for Fr Hist Studies, World Hist Asn. **RESEARCH** History of human sciences, modern French history, modern European intellectual history. **SELECTED PUBLICATIONS** Auth, "Analogy and Argumentation in an Interdisciplinary Context: Durkheim's Individual and Collective Representations," Hist of the Human Sci 4 (91): 223-259; auth, "Philosophy and Psychology at the Sorbonne 1885-1913," J of the Hist of the Behav Sci 29 (93): 123-145; auth, "The Definition of Sociology and the Sociology of Definition: Durkheim's Rules of Sociological Method and High School Philosophy in France," J of the Hist of the Behav Sci 32 (96): 379-407; auth, The Eclectic Legacy: Academic Philosophy and the Human Sciences in Nineteenth-Century France, Univ Del Pr (Newark, NJ), 98. **CONTACT ADDRESS** Dept Hist, Fayetteville State Univ, 1200 Murchison Rd, Fayetteville, NC 28301-4252.

BROOKS, ROY LAVON
PERSONAL Born 03/07/1950, New Haven, CT, m **DISCIPLINE** LAW **EDUCATION** University of Connecticut, BA, 72; Yale University, JD, 75. **CAREER** United States District Court, law clerk, 75-77; Yale Law Journal, editor, 75; Cravath, Swaine, & Moore, corporate attorney, 77-79; University of San Diego, School of Law, professor, 79-. **HONORS AND AWARDS** Gustavus Meyers Outstanding Book Awd. **MEMBERSHIPS** NAACP San Diego Chapter, Am Law Inst. **SELECTED PUBLICATIONS** Foreign Currency Translations, 1980; Small Business Financing, 1981; Affirmative Action in Law Teaching, 1982; auth, Rethinking the American Race Problem, University of California Press; auth, Integration or Separation? A Strategy for Racial Equality, Harvard University Press. **CONTACT ADDRESS** School of Law, Univ of San Diego, San Diego, CA 92110-2492. **EMAIL** rbrooks@sandiego.edu

BROPHY, ALFRED L.
PERSONAL Born 09/06/1966, Champaign, IL, s **DISCIPLINE** LAW **EDUCATION** Univ Pa, AB, 87; Columbia Univ, JD, 90; Harvard Univ, AM, 93. **CAREER** Law clerk, U.S. Court of Appeals, 90-91; assoc attorny, Skadden, Arps, Slate, Meagler, and Flow, 91-92; prof, Okla City Univ, 94-; vis prof, Ind Univ, 99; vis prof, Boston Col, 00-01. **HONORS AND AWARDS** Mellon Fel, Harvard Univ, 92-94. **MEMBERSHIPS** Am Soc for Legal Hist. **RESEARCH** Antebellum America, Legal History, Slavery, Race and Law. **SELECTED PUBLICATIONS** Auth, "Humanity, Utility, and Logic in Southern Legal Thought," Boston Univ Law Rev, 98; auth, "Reason and Sentiment: The Moral Worlds and Masks of Reasoning of Antebellum Junits," Boston Univ Law Rev, 99. **CONTACT ADDRESS** Sch of Law, Oklahoma City Univ, 2501 N Blackwelder Ave, Oklahoma City, OK 73106-1402. **EMAIL** abrophy@okcu.edu

BROSS, JAMES BEVERLEY
PERSONAL Born 11/21/1938, Knoxville, TN, m, 1959, 4 children **DISCIPLINE** RELIGION; HISTORY **EDUCATION** Cent Wesleyan Col, AB, 59; Univ Ill, MA, 65; Univ Iowa, PhD(relig), 72. **CAREER** Teacher math, Tenn Pub Schs, 59-60, 62-63 & All Tribes Indian Mission Sch, 60-62; instr, Southern Wesleyan Univ, 63-64; asst prof, Iowa Wesleyan Col, 65-68; teacher, Iowa Publ Schs, 72-73; Prof Relig, Southern Wesleyan Univ, 73-. **MEMBERSHIPS** Wesleyan Theol Soc; Am Soc Church Hist; Conf Faith & Hist; Evangelical Theol Soc. **RESEARCH** Puritanism in England; American religion. **CONTACT ADDRESS** So Wesleyan Univ, P O Box 1020, Central, SC 29630-1020. **EMAIL** jbbross@hotmail.com

BROUDY, HARRY S.
PERSONAL Born 07/27/1905, Filipowa, Poland, m, 1947, 1 child **DISCIPLINE** PHILOSOPHY OF EDUCATION **EDUCATION** Boston Univ, AB, 29; Harvard Univ, MA, 33, PhD, 35. **CAREER** Supvr adult educ, Mass Dept Educ, 36-37; prof philos educ, Mass State Col North Adams, 37-49, Framingham, 39-57; Prof Philos, Univ Ill, Urbana, 57-, Lectr, Cornell Univ, 62; Boyd H Bode lectr, Ohio State Univ, 63; ed, Educ Forum, 64-73; fel Ctr Advan Study Behav Sci, 67-68; consult, Educ Res Coun Am, Cleveland, 66-80; distinguished vis prof, Mem Univ, St John's Nfld, 74, Calif State Univ, Los Angeles, 78; Emens distinguished prof, Ball State Univ, 82. **HONORS AND AWARDS** DH, Oakland Univ, 69, Mass State Col, 81; DHL, Eastern Ky State Univ, 79. **MEMBERSHIPS** Philos Educ Soc (pres, 54); Asn Realistic Philos (pres, 55-56); Am Philos Asn; Metaphys Soc; Am Soc Aesthet. **RESEARCH** Aesthetic education; uses of schooling in nonschool situations; Polanyi's tacit knowing. **SELECTED PUBLICATIONS** Auth, Thoughts on Art Education, J Aesthetic Educ, Vol 0027, 93. **CONTACT ADDRESS** Col of Educ, Univ of Illinois, Chicago, Chicago, IL 60680.

BROUGHTON, JANET SETZER
PERSONAL Born 08/23/1948, New York, NY, m, 1972 **DISCIPLINE** PHILOSOPHY **EDUCATION** Univ Calif, Davis, AB, 72; Princeton Univ, PhD(philos), 77. **CAREER** Instr Philos, Harvard Univ, 76-77, asst prof, 77-79; asst prof Philos, Univ Calif, Berkeley, 79-83; Assoc Prof. 83-; dept chmn, 89-94. **RESEARCH** History of seventeenth and eighteenth century philosophy. **CONTACT ADDRESS** Dept of Philosophy, Univ of California, Berkeley, 314 Moses Hall, Berkeley, CA 94720-2391. **EMAIL** broughtn@socrates.berkeley.edu

BROWER, BRUCE W.
DISCIPLINE PHILOSOPHY **EDUCATION** Univ Pittsburgh, PhD, 85. **CAREER** Assoc prof, Tulane Univ. **SELECTED PUBLICATIONS** Auth, The Limits of Public Reason, J Philos; pub(s) in, Ethics; J Philos. **CONTACT ADDRESS** Dept of Philosophy, Tulane Univ, 6823 St Charles Ave, New Orleans, LA 70118. **EMAIL** bbrower@mailhost.tcs.tulane.edu

BROWN, ALEXANDRA
PERSONAL Born 08/01/1955, Erwin, TN, s **DISCIPLINE** RELIGION, BIBLICAL STUDIES, NEW TESTAMENT **EDUCATION** Duke Univ, AB, 77; Yale Divinity Sch, MDIV, 80; Columbia Univ, Union Theol Seminary, PhD, 90. **CAREER** Assoc prof of relig, dept head, Washington & Lee Univ. **MEMBERSHIPS** Soc of Biblical Lit **RESEARCH** Pauline letters; early christianity **SELECTED PUBLICATIONS** Auth, The Cross and Human Transformation: Paul's Apocalyptic word in 1 Corinthians, 95; Putting Body and Soul Together: Essays in Honor of robin Scrogg, 97; The Word of the Cross: Pattern for Moral Discernment, Doctrine and Life, 97; The Gospel Takes Place: Paul's Theology of Power-in-Weakness in 2 Corinthians, Interpretation, July 98; Essays on Regeneration, Latter Days, and Judgement for the Eerdman's Dictionary of the Bible, forthcoming 98; Review of Joost Holleman, Resurrection and Parousia: A Traditio-Historical Study of Paul's Eschatology in 1 Corinthians 15, for the Journal of Biblical Literature, forthcoming 98. **CONTACT ADDRESS** Dept of Relig, Washington and Lee Univ, Newcomb Hall, Lexington, VA 24450. **EMAIL** brown.a@wlu.edy

BROWN, ALISON L.
PERSONAL Born 01/28/1959, Champagne, IL, s, 1 child **DISCIPLINE** PHILOSOPHY **EDUCATION** Univ Utah, BA, 81, MA, 84; Univ Mass Amherst, PhD, 89. **CAREER** Author **HONORS AND AWARDS** Honorary mem, Iota Iota Iota, 96; Northern Ariz Univ res grants, 95, 94, 91, 90; Northern Ariz Univ Assoc Women Students Outstanding Woman Facul of the Year, 91; NEH summer inst, Univ Calif Santa Cruz, 90. **MEMBERSHIPS** Amer Philos Asn. **SELECTED PUBLICATIONS** Auth, Subjects of Deceit: A Phenomenology of Lying, State Univ of NY Press, 98; auth, Foucault's Play, Symploke, 96; auth, Hegelian Silences and the Politics of Communication: A Feminist Appropriation, Rethinking the Canon: Hegel, Pa State Press, 96; auth, Anxiety, God and the Feminine Divine, Kierkegaard in Post/Modernity, Studies in Continental Thought series, Univ Ind Press, 95; auth, Truth, Fear, and Writing: From Paper Village to Electronic Community, Postmodern Culture Series, State Univ of NY Press, 95; auth, Grave Voices: A Discussion about Praxis, Man and World, 25, 5-19, 92; co-auth, On the Rational Rejection of Utilitarianism and the Limitations of Moral Principles, Jour of Value Inquiry, 84. **CONTACT ADDRESS** 523 N. Agassiz, Flagstaff, AZ 86001. **EMAIL** alison.brown@nau.edu

BROWN, AMOS CLEOPHILUS
PERSONAL Born 02/20/1941, Jackson, MS, m **DISCIPLINE** THEOLOGY **EDUCATION** Morehouse Coll, BA 1964; Crozer Seminary, MDiv 1968; VA Seminary & Coll, DD 1984; United Theological Seminary; Doctor of Ministry, 1990. **CAREER** NAACP, field sec 60-62; St Paul Bapt Church Westchester PA, pastor 65-70; Pilgrim Baptist St Paul MN, pastor 70-76; Third Baptist San Francisco CA, pastor 76-. **HONORS AND AWARDS** Outstanding Young Man of Amer Jr Chamber of Commerce 1974-76; Martin Luther King Jr Ministerial Awd Colgate-Rochester Div School 1984; Man of the Yr San Francisco Business & Professional Women Inc 1985. **MEMBERSHIPS** Pres MS Youth Council NAACP 1956-59, Hi-Y Clubs MS 1958-59; natl chmn NAACP Youth Dept 1960-62; chmn Amer Baptist Black Caucus 1972-80, chmn, Natl Baptist Civil Rights Comm 1982-; mem Comm Coll Gov Bd 1982-88; founding mem bd Black Amer Resp to African Crisis 1984; life member, NAACP; mem San Francisco City County Board of Supervisors, 1996-. **CONTACT ADDRESS** Third Baptist Church, 1399 McAllister, San Francisco, CA 94115.

BROWN, BARRY
PERSONAL Born 10/20/1946, Newton, MA **DISCIPLINE** LAW **EDUCATION** Harvard Univ, BA, 68, EdM, 69; JD, 72. **CAREER** Prof. **RESEARCH** Bioethics; land transfer and finance; legal profession; real property. **SELECTED PUBLICATIONS** Auth, Reconciling Property Law with Advances in Reproductive Science, 95; When a Disposition is Not a Disposition, 90; co-auth, Massachusetts Condominium Law, 92; "Genetic Testing, Access to Genetic Data and Discrimination: Conceptual Legislative Models," Suffolk Univ Law Review 27, (93). **CONTACT ADDRESS** Sch of Law, Suffolk Univ, 120 Tremont St., Boston, Boston, MA 02108-4977. **EMAIL** bbrown@acad.suffolk.edu

BROWN, BRYSON
DISCIPLINE PHILOSOPHY **EDUCATION** Trent Univ, BA; MA; Univ Pittsburgh, PhD, 85. **CAREER** Prof of Philos, Univ of Lethbridge, 86. **RESEARCH** Philosophical logic; philosophy of science, philosophy of time. **SELECTED PUBLICATIONS** Auth, "Yes, Virginia, There Really are Paraconsistent Logics," Journal of Philosophical Logic, 99; auth, "Adjunction and Aggregation," Nous, 99. **CONTACT ADDRESS** Dept of Philosophy, Univ of Lethbridge, 4401 University Dr W, Lethbridge, AB, Canada T1K 3M4. **EMAIL** brown@uleth.ca

BROWN, COLIN
PERSONAL Born 02/26/1932, Bradford, United Kingdom, m, 1958, 3 children **DISCIPLINE** RELIGION **EDUCATION** Univ Liverpool, BA, 53; Univ London, BD, 58; Univ Nottingham, MA, 61; Univ Bristol, PhD, 70; Univ Nottingham, DD, 94. **CAREER** Anglican / Episcopal Church, ordained min, 58-; Tyndale Hall / Trinity Col, Bristol, fac, 61-78; Univ Bristol, rec tchr, 61-72; Fuller Theol Sem, prof, 78-, assoc dean 88-97. **HONORS AND AWARDS** ECBPA, Gold Medallion, 85; C. Davis Weyerhaeuser Awd for Excellence, 88 **MEMBERSHIPS** Tyndale Fel, AAR, SBL, SCP, IBR **RESEARCH** Quest of the hist Jesus. **SELECTED PUBLICATIONS** Auth, Karl Barth and the Christian Message, InterVarsity Press, 67; Philosophy and the Christian Faith, InterVarsity Press, [69], 19th printing, 98; ed, History, Criticism and Faith, InterVarsity Press, 76, Fr trans, 82; Miracles and the Critical Mind, Paternoster Press, 85; Jesus in European Protestant Thought, 1778-1860, Labyrinth Press, 85, pbk ed Baker Book House, 88; That You May Believe, Paternoster Press, 85; History and Faith, InterVarsity Press, 87; Christianity and Western Thought, vol 1, From the Ancient World to the Age of Enlightenment, Downer Grove: InterVarsity Press, Apollos Press, 90. **CONTACT ADDRESS** Dept of Systematic Theology, Fuller Theol Sem, 135 N Oakland Ave, Pasadena, CA 91182. **EMAIL** colbrn@fuller.edu

BROWN, CRAIG
DISCIPLINE LAW **EDUCATION** Otago Univ, LLB, 73; Univ Ill, LLM, 77; Otago Univ, LLD, 94. **CAREER** Prof. **RESEARCH** Insurance; torts; public international law. **SELECTED PUBLICATIONS** Auth, Insurance Law in Canada; No Fault Automobile Insurance in Canada, the Encyclopedia of Insurance Law; Canadian Insurance Contract Law in a Nutshell. **CONTACT ADDRESS** Fac of Law, Univ of Western Ontario, London, ON, Canada N6A 3K7. **EMAIL** cbrown3@julian.uwo.ca

BROWN, DALE W.
PERSONAL Born 01/12/1926, Wichita, KS, m, 1947, 3 children **DISCIPLINE** THEOLOGY **EDUCATION** McPherson Col, AB, 46; Bethany Bibl Sem, BD, 49; Northwestern Univ, PhD(church hist), 62. **CAREER** Asst prof philos & relig & dir relig life, McPherson Col, 58-62; assoc prof, 62-70, Prof theol, Bethany theol Sem, 70- **MEMBERSHIPS** Am theol Soc; Am Soc Church Hist. **RESEARCH** German pietism; theology of revolution; Brethren beliefs and practices. **SELECTED PUBLICATIONS** Auth, Four Words for World, 68 & Brethren and Pacifism, 70, Brethren; So Send I You, Faith & Life, 69; The Christian Revolutionary, 71 & Understanding Pietism, 78, Eerdmans; Flamed by the Spirit, Brethren, 78. **CONTACT ADDRESS** Dept of theol, Bethany Theol Sem, Butterfield & Meyers Rds, Oak Brook, IL 60521.

BROWN, DANIEL ALOYSIUS
PERSONAL Born 07/13/1940, Chicago, IL **DISCIPLINE** RELIGIOUS STUDIES **EDUCATION** Marianum, Rome, STB, 63, STL, 65; Vatican Libr, dipl libr sci, 63; Cath Univ, PhD(relig & relig educ), 73. **CAREER** Teacher relig, Notre Dame High Sch, 65-66; chaplain, the Claremont Cols, 69-71 & Univ Southern Calif, 71-72; assoc prof, 72-78, Prof Relig, Calif State Univ, Fullerton, 78-, Vis lectr relig, Marianum Pontifical Fac theol, 74; Nat Endowment for Humanities fel, Univ Calif, Los Angeles-African Humanities inst, 78 & summer fel, Dumbarton

Oaks, 78; Henry Luce fel, Univ Southern Calif, 79; Fulbright res fel, Italy, 82-83. **MEMBERSHIPS** Col theol Soc; Am Acad Relig; Soc Sci Study Relig. **RESEARCH** Religion and social issues; Medieval religious movements; religions in America. **SELECTED PUBLICATIONS** Auth, Maria Luisa Maurizei, la venerabile dalla morte ad oggi 183-1966, Moniales Ordinis Servorum, 66; Teaching the Old Testament to American students, Living Light, 68-69; The Need For a Sane Public Ritual, Worship, 73; Prayer, fasting and almsgiving, Communio, 74, reprinted Relig Teacher's J, 76; coauth, Is Mary a sign of unity among Christians? An empirical study, Mirianum, 75; auth, the clothes people wear, Way, 76; the mythical Shaman of Ames, Iowa as religious educator, Living Light, 77; Brothers and Service, Berwyn, 81. **CONTACT ADDRESS** Dept of Relig, California State Univ, Fullerton, Fullerton, CA 92634.

BROWN, ERIC
DISCIPLINE PHILOSOPHY **EDUCATION** Univ Chicago, AB, 91; AM, 93; PhD, 97. **CAREER** Instr, Univ Chicago, 95; Asst Prof, Wash Univ, 97-. **HONORS AND AWARDS** Phi Beta Kappa, 91; Mellon Found Fel, Univ Chicago, 94; Mrs Giles Whiting Fel, Univ Chicago, 96-97. **MEMBERSHIPS** Am Philol Asn, Am Philos Asn, SAGP. **RESEARCH** Ancient philosophy, ethics, moral psychology, metaethics, normative moral theory, social and political philosophy. **SELECTED PUBLICATIONS** Auth, "A Defense of Plato's Argument for the Immortality of the Soul at 'Republic'," Apeiron 30 (97): 211-238; auth, "Justice and Compulsion for Plato's Philosopher-Rulers," Ancient Philos 20 (00): 1-17. **CONTACT ADDRESS** Dept Philos, Washington Univ, 1 Brookings Dr, Campus Box 1073, Saint Louis, MO 63130-4899. **EMAIL** eabrown@twinearth.wustl.edu

BROWN, GEORGE, JR.
PERSONAL Born 12/19/1942, Philadelphia, PA, m, 1965, 3 children **DISCIPLINE** THEOLOGY **EDUCATION** Central Col, Pella IA, BA, 65; Western Theol Sem, BD, ordained, 69; Princeton Theol Sem, MTh, 71; Michigan State Univ, PhD, 89. **CAREER** Pottersville Reformed Church, minr, 69-73; Cent Reformed Church Grand Rapids, min, 73-88; Western Theol Sem Holland, MI, Dean of Fac, 88-96; assoc dean, prof, 96-. **HONORS AND AWARDS** RC in Am, Educator of the Yr, 96; Humanitarian Svc Awd, 85. **MEMBERSHIPS** APRRE, ASCD. **RESEARCH** Religious Education Circiculum. **SELECTED PUBLICATIONS** Coauth, Religious Education, 1960-1993: An Annotated Bibliography, Greenwood Press, 95; auth, Reformed Education in: Harper's Encycl of Relig Edu, ed, I.V. Cully and K.B. Cully, Harper & Row, 90; Selected Resources on Mentoring, CERCA RCA Educator, 95; Gospel and Culture Themes in Christian Religious Educational Literature, The Gospel and Our Culture, 90; Resource of Highest Value: Tapping the Experience of Adult Learners, Options MAACE Scholarly Jour, 90. **CONTACT ADDRESS** Dept of Christian Education, Western Theol Sem, 101 E 13th St, Holland, MI 49423-3622. **EMAIL** georgeb@westernsem.org

BROWN, HAROLD I.
PERSONAL Born 12/04/1940, Brooklyn, NY, d, 2 children **DISCIPLINE** PHILOSOPHY **EDUCATION** The Cooper Union, BCE, 62; City Col of New York, MA, 65; Northwestern Univ, PhD, 70. **CAREER** Asst prof, Simpson Col, 68-69; from asst prof to prof, Northern Ill Univ, 69-. **HONORS AND AWARDS** Younger Humanist Fel, NEH, 72-73; Winner, Am Philos Quart Essay Competition, 78; Res Grant, Nat Sci Found, 88; Summer Res Stipend, NEH, 90; Pres Res Prof, Northern Ill Univ, 96; STS Res Grant, Nat Sci Found, 99. **MEMBERSHIPS** Am Asn for the Advancement of Sci, Am Philos Asn, British Asn for the Philos of Sci, Hist of Sci Soc, Philos of Sci Asn. **RESEARCH** Philosophy of Science, Theory of Knowledge, History of Philosophy, History of Science. **SELECTED PUBLICATIONS** Auth, Observation and Objectivity, Oxford Univ Press, 87; auth, Rationality, Routledge, 88; auth, "Reason, Judgment, and Bayes' Law," Philos of Sci 64 (94); auth, "Circular Justifications," PSA 1994 Vol 1, ed. D. Hull, M. Forbes, and R. M. Burian (The Philos of Sci Asn, 94), 406-414; auth, "The methodological Roles of Theory in Science," in The Scientific Basis of Geomorphology," ed. B. L. Rhoads and C. E. Thorn (John Wiley and Sons, 96), 3-20; auth, "Psychology, Naturalized Epistemology and Rationality," in Philosophy and Psychology, ed. Richard Kitchener and William O'Donohue (Sage Pub, 96), 19-32; auth, "Why do Conceptual Analysts Disagree?" Metaphilosophy 30 (99): 33-59; auth, "The Role of Judgment in Science," in A Companion to the Philosophy of Science, ed. W. H. Newton-Smith (Blackwell Pub, 00), 194-202. **CONTACT ADDRESS** Dept Philos, No Illinois Univ, 1425 W Lincoln Hwy, Dekalb, IL 60115-2828. **EMAIL** hibrown@niu.edu

BROWN, HAROLD O. J.
PERSONAL Born 07/06/1933, Tampa, FL, m, 1962, 2 children **DISCIPLINE** SYSTEMATIC THEOLOGY **EDUCATION** Harvard Univ, BA; Harvard Divinity Sch, BDiv, ThM, PhD. **CAREER** Vis prof, Trinity prof, Trinity Univ, 76-83, 87; prof; Reformed Theological Seminary, Charlotte, 98-. **HONORS AND AWARDS** American Theological Society Fellowship, 82-83; co-founder, ch, christian action coun,; dir, ctr rel and soc, howard center instr, intl sem on jurisprudence and human rights, strasbourg; **MEMBERSHIPS** Mem, Fullbright, Danforth awards; Evangelical Theological Society; Stewards' Enclosure of the Henley Royal Regatta; Harvard Club NYC; Swiss Alpine Club, American Alpine Club; Turnerschaft Saxonia Marburg. **RESEARCH** Right-to-life issues, ethics, especially medical and family values; Reformation history and Theology. **SELECTED PUBLICATIONS** Ed, Religion and Society Report; auth, Protest of a Troubled Protestant, Zondervan, 69; Christianity and the Class Struggle, Arlington House, 70; Death Before Birth, Thomas Nelson, 77; Reconstruction of the Republic, Arlington House, 77; Before the crash: a Biblical basis for economics, Christian Stud Ctr, 78; War: Four Christian Views, BMH Bk(s), 81; Heresies: The Image of Christ in the Mirror of Heresy and Orthodoxy from the Apostles to the Present, Doubleday 84; rep. Hendrickson, 98; Christian Vision: Man & State: Religion, Society & the Constitution, Hillsdale Col Press, 89; Sensate Culture, Word, 96. **CONTACT ADDRESS** Dept of Systematic Theology, Reformed Theol Sem, No Carolina, 2101 Carmel Rd, Charlotte, NC 28226. **EMAIL** hrborwn@rts.edu

BROWN, J. DANIEL
PERSONAL Born 01/27/1934, Cabarrus Co, NC, m, 1957, 2 children **DISCIPLINE** RELIGION, PHILOSOPHY **EDUCATION** Lenoir-Rhyne Col, BA, 56; Lutheran Southern Sem, MDiv, 59; Princeton Theol Sem, ThM, 60; Drew Univ PhD(theol & cult), 70. **CAREER** Instr relig, Converse Col, 65-67; from asst prof to assoc prof, 67-74, Prof Relig & Philos, Catawba Col, 74-, Vis mem grad fac relig, Wake Forest Univ, 69-70. **MEMBERSHIPS** Am Acad Relig. **RESEARCH** Religion and literature; language. **SELECTED PUBLICATIONS** Auth, The absurd drama of Eugene Ionesco as religious ritual, Drew Gateway, 70; The comic, In: Echoes of the Wordless Word, Univ Mont, 73; Notes on Philosophy, Hunter, 76. **CONTACT ADDRESS** Catawba Col, Salisbury, NC 28144.

BROWN, JAMES J.
PERSONAL Born 12/22/1937, Cleveland, OH, m, 1963, 3 children **DISCIPLINE** LAW **EDUCATION** Univ Pa, BS, 60; Cleveland State Univ, JD, 64; Washington Univ, LLM, 70. **CAREER** Asst prof, Sch Law, Univ Mo-Kansas City, 70-73, assoc prof, 74-76; assoc prof, Nova Univ Law Ctr, Ft Lauderdale, 76-78, prof, 78-81; vis prof, 81-82, Prof, Col Law, Stetson Univ, 82-, Assoc ed, Urban Lawyer, 70-74; consult & proj dir, Mo Dept Community Affairs, 72-74; vis prof, Col Law, Univ Ky, spring, 73; dir, Scribes, Am Soc Writers Legal Subj, 75-80; appointee, Governor Robert Grahams Adv Comt, 80-81. **MEMBERSHIPS** Am Planning Asn; Real Estate Educr Asn; Am Real Estate & Urban Econ Asn; Scribes, Am Soc Writers Legal Subj (pres, 74-75). **RESEARCH** Land use planning and zoning; environmental law; real property. **SELECTED PUBLICATIONS** **CONTACT ADDRESS** Col of Law, Stetson Univ, St. Petersburg, 1401 61st St S, Saint Petersburg, FL 33707-3299. **EMAIL** brownj@hermes.law.stetson.edu

BROWN, JAMES R.
PERSONAL Born Montreal, PQ, Canada **DISCIPLINE** PHILOSOPHY **EDUCATION** Univ Guelph, BA, 73, MA, 75; Univ W Ont, PhD, 81. **CAREER** Prof Philos, Univ Toronto, 81-. **RESEARCH** Philos of Sci; Thought Experiments; Scientific Realism; Philos of Mathematics; Foundations of Physics; Sci and Soc. **SELECTED PUBLICATIONS** Auth, The Rational and the Social, 89; auth, The Laboratory of the Mind, 91; auth, Smoke and Mirrors, 94; auth, Philosophy of Mathematics, 99; auth, Who Should Rule?: A Guide to the Epistemology and Politics of the Science Wars, 00. **CONTACT ADDRESS** Dept of Philosophy, Univ of Toronto, 215 Huron St, Toronto, ON, Canada M5S 1A1. **EMAIL** jrbrown@chass.utoronto.ca

BROWN, JERRY WAYNE
PERSONAL Born 02/24/1936, Frederick, OK, m, 1958, 1 child **DISCIPLINE** RELIGION, HISTORY **EDUCATION** Harvard Univ, AB, 58; Eastern Baptist Theol Sem, BD, 61; Univ Pa, MA, 61; Princeton Univ, MA, 63, PhD(relig), 64. **CAREER** Teaching fel relig, Princeton Univ, 63-64; asst prof, Bowdoin Col, 64-69, actg chmn dept, 64-65, resident prof, Sr Ctr, 65-66, dean students, 66-69; Assoc Prof Hist, Rider Col 69-, VPres Acad Affairs, 70-;, Provost, 75-. **RESEARCH** Religion in America. **SELECTED PUBLICATIONS** The Rise of Biblical Criticism in American, 1800-1870, Wesleyan Univ, 69. **CONTACT ADDRESS** Dept of Hist, Rider Univ, Lawrenceville, NJ 08648.

BROWN, JONATHAN CHARLES
PERSONAL Born 10/02/1942, Fond du Lac, WI, m, 1965, 1 child **DISCIPLINE** ECONOMIC HISTORY **EDUCATION** Univ Wis, Madison, BA, 66; Univ Ariz, MA, 68; Univ Tex, Austin, PhD(hist), 76. **CAREER** Lectr hist, Univ Calif, Santa Barbara, 76-77; Lectr Hist, Univ Calif, Los Angeles, 77-. **MEMBERSHIPS** AHA; Conf Latin Am Hist; Econ Hist Asn; Can Econ Asn. **RESEARCH** Argentina; Latin American economic history; Venezuela. **SELECTED PUBLICATIONS** Auth, Dynamics and autonomy of a traditional marketing system: Buenos Aires, 1810-1860, Hisp Am Hist Rev, 76; A nineteenth century Argentine cattle empire, Agr Hist, 78; The genteel tradition of nineteenth century Colombian culture, Americas, 78; A Socioeconomic History of Argentina, Cambridge Univ, 79. **CONTACT ADDRESS** Dept of Hist, Univ of California, Los Angeles, Los Angeles, CA 90024.

BROWN, KENNETH
PERSONAL Born 03/05/1943, Chicago, IL, 2 children **DISCIPLINE** BIBLE, THEOLOGY, HISTORY **EDUCATION** Asbury Theol Sem, BA Theol, 66; Mdiv 76; Drew Univ, PhD, 88. **CAREER** Pastor/Minister, 66-; Prof, Vennard Coll, 76-79. **MEMBERSHIPS** Amer Acad Rel; ATLA; Wesleyan Theol Soc; Christian Holiness Partnership. **RESEARCH** Camp Meeting History; History of the Holiness Movement; Biographical Studies. **SELECTED PUBLICATIONS** Auth, Holy Ground, Too, The Camp Meeting Family Tree, Hazleton, Holiness Archives, 98; co-auth, "Wholly and Forever Thine," Leadership in the Early Natl Camp Meeting Assoc for the Promotion of Holiness, Holiness Archives (Hazleton), 99. **CONTACT ADDRESS** 243 S Pine St, Hazleton, PA 18201. **EMAIL** cmbooks@ptdprolog.net

BROWN, KENNETH LEE
PERSONAL Born 06/15/1933, Wichita, KS, m, 1960, 3 children **DISCIPLINE** PEACE STUDIES, RELIGION **EDUCATION** McPherson Col, AB, 55; Bethany Theol Sem, BD, 58; Duke Univ, PhD, 65. **CAREER** From instr to assoc prof, 61-73, Prof Relig & Philos, Manchester Col, 73-, Lilly Endowment Open Fel, Fel of Reconciliation, Inst for World Order, NYC, 78-79; dir, Peace Studies Inst & Prog in Conflict Resolution, 80. **HONORS AND AWARDS** COPRED, Peace educator fo the Year, 95; Who's Who Among Am Teachers, 98; Am Fel of Reconciliation, Martin Luther King Award, 98; Peace Studies Assoc, Peacemaker Award, 99. **MEMBERSHIPS** Am Acad Relig; Am Soc Christian Ethics. **RESEARCH** Soc ethics; polit philos; pacifism. **SELECTED PUBLICATIONS** Ed, Bull of the Peace Studies Inst, 80-; Auth, Christian's relationship to the state, In: Six Papers on Peace, Brethren, 69; The flow children, In: Life Styles, Scott, 71. **CONTACT ADDRESS** Peace Studies Inst, Manchester Col, 601 E College Ave, North Manchester, IN 46962-1226. **EMAIL** klbrown@manchester.edu

BROWN, KRISTEN M.
DISCIPLINE 19TH CENTURY GERMAN PHILOSOPHY, ANCIENT PHILOSOPHY **EDUCATION** Stanford Univ, BA; Vanderbilt Univ, MA, PhD. **CAREER** Dept Philos, Millsaps Col **SELECTED PUBLICATIONS** Publ on, Embodiment and Feminine Other in Nietzsche & Form as Logos in Aristotle's Metaphysics Z and Politics. **CONTACT ADDRESS** Dept of Philosophy, Millsaps Col, 1701 N State St, Jackson, MS 39210. **EMAIL** brownkm@okra.millsaps.edu

BROWN, LEE BATEMAN
PERSONAL Born 01/14/1932, Milton, IA, 1 child **DISCIPLINE** PHILOSOPHY **EDUCATION** Univ Utah, BA, 56; Northwestern Univ, MA, 58, PhD(philos), 66. **CAREER** Instr Philos, Northwestern & Roosevelt Univs, 60-61; from instr to asst prof, 61-71, Assoc Prof Philos, Ohio State Univ, 71-. **MEMBERSHIPS** Am Philos Asn; AAUP; Hegel Soc Am. **RESEARCH** Aesthetics; metaphysics. **SELECTED PUBLICATIONS** Auth, Definitions in art theory & Traditional aesthetics revisited, J Aesthet & Art Criticism; World interpretations and lived experience, Monist, Vol 55, No 2; Adorno Aesthetic Theory - The Redemption of Illusion - Zuidervaart,l/, J Aesthet Educ, Vol 27, 1993; Notes to Literature, Vol 1 - Adorno,TW/, J Aesthet Educ, Vol 27, 1993; Notes to Literature, Vol 2 - Adorno,TW/, J Aesthet Educ, Vol 28, 1994. **CONTACT ADDRESS** Dept of Philos, Ohio State Univ, Columbus, 230 N Oval Mall, Columbus, OH 43210. **EMAIL** brown68@osu.edu

BROWN, MARK A.
PERSONAL Born 10/31/1939, Little Falls, NY, m, 1962, 2 children **DISCIPLINE** PHILOSOPHY **EDUCATION** Syracuse Univ, BA, 61; PhD, 71. **CAREER** Asst/Assoc Prof, Syracuse Univ, 71-; Asst/Assoc Dean, Col of Arts and Sci, Syracuse Univ, 72-80. **MEMBERSHIPS** Am Philos Asn, Asn for Symbolic Logic, Soc for Exact Philos, Creighton Club. **RESEARCH** Model logic, quantifiers, metaphysics, action. **SELECTED PUBLICATIONS** Auth, "Some Remarks on Zawadowski's Theory of Preordered Quantifier's," in Quantifiers, ed. Michal Krynicki, Marcin Mostowski and Leslaw W. Szczerba (Kluwer, 95), 255-264; auth, "Operators on Branched Quantifiers," n Quantifiers, ed. Michal Krynicki, Marcin Mostowski and Leslaw W. Szcserba (Kluwer, 95), 21-61; auth, "A Logic of Comparative Obligation," Studia Logica 57 (96): 117-137; auth, "Doing As We Ought: Towards a Logic of Simply Dischargeable Obligations," in Deontic Logic, Agency and Normative Systems (EON '96), ed. Mark A. Brown and Jose Carmo (Spriner-Verlag, 96), 47-65; co-ed, Deontic Logic, Agency and Normative Systems (EON '96), Spriner-Verlag, 96; coauth, "An Extended Branching-time Ockhamist Temporal Logic," in Verslagreeks van die Deprtment Wiskunde, Rand Afrikaans Univ, Safr (98), and J of Logic, Lang and Infor 8 (99): 143-166; auth, "Agents with Changing and Conflicting Commitments: A Preliminary Study," in New Studies in Deontic Logic and Computer Science, ed. H. Prakken, and P.F. McNamara (IOS Press, 99), 109-125; auth, "Conditional and Uncoditional Obligation For Agents in Time," in Advances in Modal Logic II, ed. M. de Rijke, Krister Segerberg, Heinrich Wansing, and Michael Zakharyaschev (CSLI Press, forthcoming). **CONTACT ADDRESS** Dept Philos, Syracuse Univ, 541 Hall of Lang, Syracuse, NY 13244-1170. **EMAIL** mabrown@syr.edu

BROWN, MURRAY
PERSONAL Born 07/04/1929, Alden, NY, m, 1954, 1 child **DISCIPLINE** ECONOMICS **EDUCATION** Univ Buff, BA, 52; Grad fac The New Sch, PhD, 56. **CAREER** Prof, SUNY, Buff, 67-; res assoc, Cen econo stud, 64-84; Prof econo George Wash Univ, 62-65; Asst prof, Univ Penn, 56-61. **HONORS AND AWARDS** Fulbright, 87; Guggenheim fel, 66; Ford Fac fel, 62. **MEMBERSHIPS** AEA **RESEARCH** Coalition formation; game theory **SELECTED PUBLICATIONS** Essays in Modern Capitol Theory, ed with Kazuo Sato, Paul Zarembka, N Holl, NY, 76; many numerous articles in books and journals. **CONTACT ADDRESS** 80 Fairlawn Rd, Amherst, NY 14260. **EMAIL** mbrown@acsu.buffalo.edu

BROWN, PAUL LLEWELLYN
PERSONAL Born 11/19/1920, Sutersville, PA, w, 1 child **DISCIPLINE** PHILOSOPHY, RELIGION **EDUCATION** Maryville Col, BA, 41; Western Theol Sem, STB, 44; Victoria Univ, Ont, ThD(philos relig), 53. **CAREER** Asst minister, First Presby Church, Wilkinsburg, Pa, 44-45; minister, Artesia, NMex, 45-47; from asst prof to assoc prof relig & philos, 49-68, Prof Philos, Univ Tulsa, 68-90; Chair, Philos Dept, 83-90; Dir Univ of Tulsa Honors Prog, 85-90; McFarlin Prof of Philos, 87-90; Prof Emer Philos, Univ Tulsa, 90-. **MEMBERSHIPS** Am Philos Asn; Asn Symbolic Logic; Charles S Peirce Soc; Southwestern Philos Asn; AAUP. **SELECTED PUBLICATIONS** Coauth, Elementary Modern Logic, Ronald, 65; auth, Omnicredulity and Religious Beliefs, Crane Rev, spring 61; Religion and Truth, Perspective, fall 72; Is God a person or personal being, Personalist. **CONTACT ADDRESS** Dept of Philos, Univ of Tulsa, 1224 S Delaware Place, Tulsa, OK 74104.

BROWN, PETER G.
PERSONAL Born 01/15/1940, 3 children **DISCIPLINE** PHILOSOPHY **EDUCATION** Haverford Col, BA, 61; Columbia Univ, MA, Union Theological Seminary, 64, PhD, 69. **CAREER** Teacher social & polit philos, Univ Md, College Park, 69-70; reseacher, Urban Inst, 70-73; prof philos, Univ Wash, 73-74; fel, Off Acad Contemp Prob, 74-76; founder & dir, Ctr Philos & Pub Policy, 76-81, actg dean, 80-81, Assoc Dean, Sch Pub Affairs to grad sch fac, Univ Md, College Park, 81-, Vis fel, Battelle Seattle Res Ctr, 73-74. **HONORS AND AWARDS** Founded the Inst for Philos and Pub policy, the School of Pub Affairs, Eastern Shore Land Conservancy; Established the Environmental Policy Programs, Univ of Maryland's School of Public Affairs; Tree Farmer of the Year, Garrett County, Md, 95; Steward of Walker Pond, Hancock County Ma; Chair of the Rural Legacy Advisory Committee, Md. **MEMBERSHIPS** Hastings Center, Cosmos Club. **RESEARCH** Governance and Protection of the Environment. **SELECTED PUBLICATIONS** Urban Inst, 75; The place of informed consent in social experiments: Some cautionary notes, In: Ethical and Legal Issues of Social Experimentation, Brookings Inst, 75; ed, Food Policy: The Responsibility of the United States in the Life and Death Choices, Free Press, 77 & 79; co-ed, Human Rights and US Foreign Policy: Principles and Applications, Lexington Bks, 79 & 80; Income Support: Conceptual and Policy Issues & Boundaries: National Autonomy and its Limits, Rowman & Littlefield, 81; auth, Ethics and policy research, Policy Anal, spring 76, Restoring the Public Trust: A Fresh Vision for Progressive Govt in Am, Beacon Press, 94; Ethics economics and international relations, for Edinburgh Univ Press; Assessing the behavior of public officials from a moral point of view, In: Public Duties: The Moral Obligations of Public Officials, Harvard Univ Press. **CONTACT ADDRESS** Office of Grad Studies and Res, Univ of Maryland, Col Park, Lee Bldg., College Park, MD 20742-5121. **EMAIL** pbrown@puafmail.umd.edu

BROWN, R. L.
PERSONAL Born Baltimore, MD, m, 1995, 3 children **DISCIPLINE** CONSTITUTIONAL LAW; CONSTITUTIONAL THEORY; EVIDENCE **EDUCATION** St Johns Col, BA, 78; Georgetown Univ Law Ctr, JD, 82. **CAREER** Judicial clerk, Hon Spottswood W Robinson, III Chief Justice, US Court Appeals District of Columbia Circle, 82-83 & Chambers of Hon Thurgood Marshall, Assoc Justice, US Supreme Court, 85 Term; atty adv, Off Legal Coun US Dept Justice, 83-85; assoc atty, Onek, Klein, & Farr, Wash DC, 86-88; asst prof, 88-91, assoc prof, 91-94, PROF, 94- , Vanderbilt Univ School of Law, 88- . **HONORS AND AWARDS** Asn Am Law Schools Scholar Papers Awd, 93 **MEMBERSHIPS** Dist Columbia, US Court Appeals, 83; US Supreme Court, 86; ALI, 96. **RESEARCH** Separation of powers; Judicial review; Constitutional interpretation. **SELECTED PUBLICATIONS** Auth, Separated Powers and Ordered Liberty, Univ Penn Law Rev, 91; A Tribute to Justice Thurgood Marshall, or: How I Learned to Stop Worrying and Love Formalism, Temple Polit & Civil Rights Law Rev, 92; Tradition and Insight, Yale Law Jour, 93; When Political Questions Affect Individual Rights: The Other Nixon v. United States, Supreme Court Rev, 93; rev, The Interpretable Constitution, Constitutional Commentary, 94-95; Formal Neutrality in the Warren and Rehnquist Courts: Illusions of Similarity, Vanderbilt Law Rev, 97; Constitutional Tragedies: The Dark Side of Judgement, Constitutional Stupidities, Constitutional Tragedies, 98; Accountability, Liberty, and the Constitution, Columbia Law Rev, 98. **CONTACT ADDRESS** Law Sch, Vanderbilt Univ, 131 21st Ave S, Ste 207, Nashville, TN 37203-1181. **EMAIL** rebecca.brown@law.vanderbilt.edu

BROWN, ROBERT FATH
PERSONAL Born 06/06/1941, St. Louis, MO, m, 1997, 3 children **DISCIPLINE** PHILOSOPHY OF RELIGION **EDUCATION** DePauw Univ, BA, 63; Columbia Univ, MA, 67; PhD, 71. **CAREER** From instr to assoc prof, 70-86, prof, philos, Univ Del, 86-; Vis lectr philos, Hull Univ, England, 80-81; dir Univ Honrs Prog, Univ Del, 89-98. **MEMBERSHIPS** Am Acad Relig; Am Philos Asn; Hegel Soc Am; Soc Chr Phil; Soc Phil Rel. **RESEARCH** German idealism; history of western religious thought; problem of evil. **SELECTED PUBLICATIONS** Auth, The Later Philosophy of Schelling, Bucknell Univ, 77; cotrans, Hegel: Lectures on the Philosophy of Religion, Univ Calif, 84-87; ed, cotrans, Hegel: Lectures on the History of Philosophy, Vol 3, Univ Calif, 90, Vols 1-2 forthcoming. **CONTACT ADDRESS** Dept of Philos, Univ of Delaware, Newark, DE 19716. **EMAIL** rfbrown@udel.edu

BROWN, SCOTT KENT
PERSONAL Born 10/01/1940, Murray, UT, m, 1966, 5 children **DISCIPLINE** EARLY CHRISTIAN HISTORY & LITERATURE **EDUCATION** Univ Calif, Berkeley, BA, 67; Brown Univ, PhD (Bibl studies), 72. **CAREER** Asst prof, 71-76, Assoc Prof to prof, Ancient Scripture, Brigham Young Univ, 76-; Mem, Inst Ancient Studies, Brigham Young Univ, 73-; corresp mem, Inst Antiquity & Christianity, Calif, 73-. **MEMBERSHIPS** Soc Bibl Lit. **RESEARCH** New Testament; New Testament apocrypha. **SELECTED PUBLICATIONS** Auth, James the Just and the question of Peter's leadership in the light of new sources, In: Sperry Lectr Series, Brigham Young Univ, 73; The book of Lehi: A lost record?, spring 74 & The Apocalypse of Peter (CG VII, 3): A translation, spring 74, Brigham Young Univ Studies; Masada + Excavations and Discoveries from the World of the New-Testament - Herod Fortress and the Zealots Last Stand - a Brigham-Young-University forum address, Brigham Young Univ Studies, Vol 36, 1997. **CONTACT ADDRESS** Dept of Ancient Scripture, Brigham Young Univ, 5435 HBLL, Provo, UT 84602. **EMAIL** skb@byu.edu

BROWN, STEPHEN G.
DISCIPLINE RELIGIOUS STUDIES **EDUCATION** Univ Calif at Los Angeles, BA, 65; Talbot Sch of Theol, BD, 68; Western Sem, ThM, 70; Brandeis Univ, MA, 72; PhD, 74. **CAREER** Asst prof, Biola Col, 73-76; assoc prof, Los Angeles Baptist Col (now the Master's Col), 76-84; business mgr, Kenneth B. Jacques Enterprises, 84-91; independent res & scholar, The Lookman Found, 84-91; acad dean, Shasta Bible Col, 91-00; adj prof, Simpson Col, 91-00. **HONORS AND AWARDS** NEH Fel, 83. **MEMBERSHIPS** Soc of Biblical Lit, Inst of Biblical Res, Evangelical Theol Soc. **RESEARCH** Wisdom Literature, Discourse Analysis, Hebrew Semantics. **SELECTED PUBLICATIONS** Auth, "Prophecy," "Prophets," "Prophetesses," and "Maccobees," in Nelson's Illustrated Bible Dictionary (Thomas Nelson, 86); auth, "The Structure of Ecclesiastes," Evangelical Rev of Theol, 91; auth, "The Intertextuality of Isa 66:17 and 2 Thess 2:7: A Solution for the 'Restrainer' Problem," in Paul and the Scriptures of Israel, eds. Chris A. Evans and James A. Sanders (93). **CONTACT ADDRESS** Dept Relig, Shasta Bible Col, 2980 Hartnell Ave, Redding, CA 96002-2312. **EMAIL** sbrown@shasta.edu

BROWN, STEVEN M.
PERSONAL Born Philadelphia, PA, m, 1975, 2 children **DISCIPLINE** JEWISH EDUCATION AND STUDIES **EDUCATION** Jewish Theol Sem Am, BA, BHL; Columbia Univ, MA, EdD. **CAREER** Prin, Cent Hebrew HS Long Island, NY; head tchr to headmaster, N Brch Solomon Schechter Day School, 73-75; educ dir, Adath Jeshurun, Elkins Park, Pa; dir, Melton Res Ctr Jewish Educ, 96; dean William Davidson Grad Schl Jewish Educ, Jewish Theol Sem Am. **HONORS AND AWARDS** Jewish educ workshops, Israel and Argentina; exec bd, Jewish Educ Assembly; pres, Solomon Schechter Day Schl Principals Coun; bd dir, Jewish Comm Rel Coun Philadelphia; bd dir, Adath Jeshurun. **MEMBERSHIPS** Asn Supervision and Curr Devel; Jewish Fed Greater Philadelphia. **SELECTED PUBLICATIONS** Auth, L'Ela--L'Ela: Higher and Higher--Making Jewish Prayer Part of Us; Reclaiming Our Legacy.* Marbeh Torah, Marbeh Chaim-The More Torah, The More Life; Willing, Leaming, and Striving, A Course for Teaching Jewish Youth Based on Emet Ve-Emunah; Approaches to the Numinous, Learn Torah With.Dr Brown. **CONTACT ADDRESS** Jewish Theol Sem of America, 3080 Broadway, New York, NY 10027. **EMAIL** stbrown@jtsa.edu

BROWN, WILLIAM H., III
PERSONAL Born 01/19/1928, Philadelphia, PA, m, 1975 **DISCIPLINE** LAW **EDUCATION** Temple Univ, BS, 1952; Univ of PA Law School, JD, 1955. **CAREER** Schnader, Harrison, Segal & Lewis, partner, Attorney, 74-; Norris, Brown & Hall, partner, 64-68; Norris, Green, Harris & Brown, partner, 62-64; Norris, Schmidt, Green, Harris & Higginbotham, assoc, 56-62; EEOC, chmn, 69-73; EEOC, commr, 68-69; Deputy Dist Attorney, chief of frauds, 68; chmn, Philadelphia Special Investigation Commn, 85-86. **HONORS AND AWARDS** Awd of Recognition, Alpha Phi Alpha, 1969; Handbook of Modern Personnel Admin, 1972; Philadelphia NAACP President's Awd; Fidelity Awd, Philadelphia Bar Assn, 1990; Legal Defense & Education Fund, Judge William H Haste Awd, 1992; American Heart Association, Dr Edward S Cooper Awd, 1995; The Urban League of Philadelphia, Whitney M Young Jr, Leadership Awd, 1996; Lawyers' Committee for Civil Rights Under Law, The Whitney North Seymoure Awd, 1996. **MEMBERSHIPS** Bd of dir, United Parcel Serv, 1983-; mem, Regional Bd of Dir, First PA Banking & Trust Co, 1968-73; co-chair, bd dir, mem exec comm, Lawyers Comm for Civil Rights Under Law; founding mem, World Association of Lawyers; permanent mem, 3rd Cir Judicial Conference; mem, Alpha Phi Alpha; Philadelphia, Am Fed & PA Bar Assn; life member, Nat Bar Assn; Am Arbitration Association; Am Law Inst; Inter-Am Bar Assn; mem, Commn on Higher Educ, Middle States Association of Coll; mem, National Sr Citizen's Law Center; faculty mem, Natl Inst Trial Advocacy, 1980-; faculty mem, Practicing Law Inst, 1970-85; pres, mem, bd of dir, National Black Child Devel Institute, 1986-; mem, bd of dir, Community Legal Services; board of directors, NAACP Legal Defense & Educ Fund; fellow, American Bar Foundation; member, board of directors, Philadelphia Diagnostic and Rehabilitation Center; National Senior Citizens Law Center, board of directors, 1988-94. **SELECTED PUBLICATIONS** numerous articles **CONTACT ADDRESS** Schnader Harrison Segal Lewis, 1600 Market St, Ste 3600, Philadelphia, PA 19103.

BROWN, WILLIAM P.
PERSONAL Born 10/19/1958, Washington, DC, m, 1990, 2 children **DISCIPLINE** BIBLE STUDIES **EDUCATION** Emory Univ, PhD 91; Princeton Theol Sem, MDiv, honors, 85; Whitman Col, BA 81. **CAREER** Union Theol Sem, asst prof, assoc prof, 91 to 95-; full prof, 98-. **MEMBERSHIPS** SBL; ASOR; AAR. **RESEARCH** Wisdom Lit of Hebrew Bible; Creation Theology; Ethics. **SELECTED PUBLICATIONS** Auth, Society of Biblical Literature Dissertation Series, Atlanta: Scholars Press, 93; auth, The Character of Covenant in the Old Testament: A Theocentric Probe, The Annual of the Soc of Christian Ethics, 96; Character in Crisis: A Fresh Approach to the Wisdom Literature of the Old Testament, Grand Rapids, Eerdmans, 96; auth, Obadiah-Malachi: Westminster Bible Companion, Louisville, Westminster/John Knox, 96; auth, Psalm 139: The Pathos of Praise, Interpretation, 96; Genesis The Book Of, in: Harper's Bible Dictionary, 2nd ed, San Francisco, Harper and Row, 96; auth, A Royal Performance: Critical Notes on Psalm 110:3ag-b, Jour of Biblical Lit, 98; auth, The Ethos of the Cosmos: The Genesis of Moral Imagination in the Bible, Grand Rapids, Eerdmans, 99; auth, Creation, and Judith The Book of in: The Eerdmans Dictionary of the Bible, ed DN Freedman, Grand Rapids, Eerdmans, forthcoming; Judith of, in: Dict of Biblical Interpretation, ed JH Hayes, Nashville, Abingdon, forthcoming; auth, Ecclesiastes, Interpretation series, 00; auth, Structure, Role, and Ideology in the Hebrew and Greek Manuscripts of Genesis 1:1-2:3. **CONTACT ADDRESS** Dept of Old Testament, Union Theol Sem, Virginia, 3401 Brook Rd, Richmond, VA 23227. **EMAIL** wbrown@union-psce.edu

BROWN WEISS, EDITH
PERSONAL Born, OR, m, 2 children **DISCIPLINE** LAW **EDUCATION** Stanford Univ, AB, 63; Harvard Law School, LLB, 66; Univ Calif, PhD, 73. **CAREER** Asst prof, Princeton Univ, 74-78; prof, Georgetown Univ, 78-; assoc gen coun, US Environmental Protection Agency, 90-92. **HONORS AND AWARDS** Chicago-Kent Col of Law; Elizabeth Haub Awd, Brussels, 95; Cert of Merit, Am Soc of Intl Law, 90; Prominent Woman in Intl Law Awd, 96. **MEMBERSHIPS** Am Soc Intl Law, Am Law Inst, Coun on For Relations. **RESEARCH** International Law, Environment and trade, Water law, International Environmental Law. **SELECTED PUBLICATIONS** Auth, In Fairness to Future Generations, 89; auth, Engaging Countries: Strengthening Compliance with International Accords, 98; auth, International Environmental Law and Police, 98; auth, Environmental change and International Law, 92. **CONTACT ADDRESS** School of Law, Georgetown Univ, 600 New Jersey Ave NW, Washington, CD 20001-2022. **EMAIL** weiss@law.georgetown.edu

BROWNE, GREGORY M.
PERSONAL Born 07/05/1957, Bluffton, OH, s **DISCIPLINE** PHILOSOPHY **EDUCATION** Mich State Univ, MA, 84, PhD, 94. **CAREER** Adj instr, Macomb Commun Col, 94-97, 98-; instr, Central Mich Univ, 00-. **MEMBERSHIPS** Am Philos Asn **RESEARCH** Necessary truth; A Prior knowledge; Philosophy of language; Causality; Natural kinds; Freewill; Theories of justice. **SELECTED PUBLICATIONS** Auth, Necessary Factual Truth, forthcoming. **CONTACT ADDRESS** 4667 Crow's Nest Ct., Brighton, MI 48114. **EMAIL** greg.blufton@prodigy.net

BROWNE, STANLEY M.
PERSONAL Born 06/18/1948, Birmingham, AL, d, 4 children **DISCIPLINE** PHILOSOPHY **EDUCATION** Howard Univ, BA, 69, MA, 74; Univ Ottawa, PhD, 83. **CAREER** Mellon fel, 81; asst prof, Howard Univ, 86-89; asst rpof, Tuskegee Univ, 78-83; Talladega Col, 77-78; asst prof, Youngstown Univ, 89-95; prof, Ala A&M Univ, 95-. **HONORS AND AWARDS** Nat Writing Project Teacher Fel, Ala A&M Univ, 97-99; Andew Mellow Found and United Negro Col Fund, 81. **MEMBERSHIPS** Am Philos Asn; Ala Philos Soc; Southern Soc for Philos

and Psychol; Alabama Counc of Teachers of Eng; Nat Education Asn; Ala Education Asn. **RESEARCH** African Am Philos; Epistemology; Metaphysics; Hist of Philos; Applied Philos; Drug Addiction. **SELECTED PUBLICATIONS** Auth, "Problems of Knowings and Being in Public Humanities Projects," Federation Reports: The Journal of State Humanities Councils, Vol II, No. 4, (84); auth, "A Contribution to the Theory of Reasoning," Behaviorism, Vol. 16, No. 1, (98); auth, "Crack House Blues," Proceedings of the National Asn of African Am Studies, Vol. I, (98): 214-228; auth, "Selective Prosecution and Punishment of Black Female Drug Addicts," (99); auth, "Race and Racist Reconstructions of Black Motherhod,' (00): 96-134; auth, "The World of Philosophers: Introductory Readings in Philosophy," Harcourt Brace College Publishers, 00; auth, "Point, Counterpoint: Introductory Readings in Philosophy," Harcourt Brace College Publishers, 01. **CONTACT ADDRESS** Dept Behavioral Sciences, Alabama A&M Univ, PO Box 1926, Normal, AL 35762. **EMAIL** SBrowne@aamu.edu

BROWNING, DANIEL C.
PERSONAL Born 10/26/1956, Albany, GA, m, 1982, 2 children **DISCIPLINE** ARCHAEOLOGY; BIBLICAL BACKGROUNDS **EDUCATION** Univ Alabama Huntsville, BSE, 80; MDiv, 84, PhD, 88, Southwestern Baptist Theological Seminary. **CAREER** Instr, Texas Christian Univ, 87-89; Teaching Fel, 85-87, Adjunct Instr, 87-89, Southwestern Baptist Theological Seminary; Instr, 88-90, Tarrant County Jr. Col; Asst Prof, 90-93, Assoc Prof, 93-, William Carey Col. **HONORS AND AWARDS** Endowment for Biblical Research/American Schools of Oriental Research Travel Grant, 84; Research Fel, Albright Inst of Archaeological Research, Jerusalem, 88; Outstanding Faculty Member 95/96, William Carey Col (Student Govt Assoc Awd), 96; Teaching Excellence Grants William Carey Col, 93-97. **MEMBERSHIPS** Amer Schools of Oriental Research; Israel Exploration Soc; Soc of Biblical Lit. **RESEARCH** Biblical backgrounds; culture of New Testament times; archaeological field work **SELECTED PUBLICATIONS** Auth, Land of Goshen, Biblical Illustrator 19, 93; The Other Side of the Sea of Galilee, Biblical Illustrator, 20, 94; Standards of Greatness in the First Century, Biblical Illustrator 21, 95; Coauth, Of Seals and Scrolls, Biblical Illustrator 22, 96; Auth, The Strange Search for the Ashes of the Red Hefer, Biblical Archaeologist, 96; The Hill Country is not Enough for Us: Recent Arcaheology and the Book of Joshua, Southwestern Journal of Theology, 98; Jesus as Carpenter, Biblical Illustrator, 98; Iron Age Loom Weights from Timnah, Tell Batash (Timnah) II: The Finds from the Iron Age II, forthcoming. **CONTACT ADDRESS** William Carey Col, Hattiesburg, MS 39401. **EMAIL** browning@wmcarey.edu

BROWNING, DON S.
PERSONAL Born 01/13/1934, Trenton, MO, m, 1958, 2 children **DISCIPLINE** THEOLOGY, PSYCHOLOGY OF RELIGION **EDUCATION** Univ Chicago, BD, 59, MA, 62, PhD, 64. **CAREER** Asst prof theol & pastoral care, Grad Sem, Phillips Univ, 63-65; from instr to assoc prof relig & psychol studies, 65-77, prof & dean, Disciples Divinity House, 77-80, Alexander Campbell Prof Relig & Psychol Studies, Divinity Sch, Univ Chicago, 80-, Asn Theol Sch res grant relig & psychol, 69-70 & 82; Guggenheim fel, 75-76. **HONORS AND AWARDS** Hon Dr of Divinity, Univ Glasgow, 98. **MEMBERSHIPS** Am Acad Relig; Soc Sci Study Relig; Am Asn of Practical Theol; Int Acad of Practical Theol. **RESEARCH** The relation of theology to the social sciences; practical theology; religious ethics. **SELECTED PUBLICATIONS** Auth, Atonement and Psychotheraphy, Westminster, 66; Generative man, Westminster, 73; Moral Context of Care, Westminster, 76; Pluralism and Personality, Bucknell Univ, 80; Religious Ethics and Pastoral Care, Fortress, 83; Religious Thought and the Modern Psychologies, Fortress, 87; A Fundamental Practical Theology, 91; coauth, From Culture Wars to Common Ground: Religion and the American Family Debate, Westminster, 97. **CONTACT ADDRESS** Divinity Sch, Univ of Chicago, 1025-35 E 58th St., Chicago, IL 60637-1577. **EMAIL** dsbrowni@midwat.uchicago.edu

BROWNING, PETER
DISCIPLINE PHILOSOPHY **EDUCATION** Univ Chicago, PhD. **CAREER** Prof, Drury Col. **RESEARCH** Med ethics; relig(s) studies; feminist theology. **SELECTED PUBLICATIONS** Auth, Review of A Matter of Principles? Ferment in U.S. Bioethics, Trinity Intl, 95; Review of The Craft of Theology by Avery Dulles, Crossroad, 92; Homosexuality, Ordination and Polity, Quarterly Review, 94; ed, Proceedings of the Ethics, Higher Education and Church Relations Conference, 94. **CONTACT ADDRESS** Relig and Philos Dept, Drury Col, N Benton, PO Box 900, Springfield, MO 65802.

BROWNMILLER, SARA N.
PERSONAL Born 03/11/1952, San Antonio, TX, m, 1975, 2 children **DISCIPLINE** POLITICAL SCIENCE **EDUCATION** Incarnate Word Col, BA, 74; Univ of AZ, MLS, 78 **CAREER** Ref Librn, 79-82, Univ of N IA; Cent Ref Librn, 82-87, Univ of AZ, Coord, 87-89, 89-94, Prof, 94-, Univ of OR **HONORS AND AWARDS** Beta Phi Mu; IAC **MEMBERSHIPS** Am Lib Asn **RESEARCH** Women's studies **SELECTED PUBLICATIONS** Coauth, Index to Women's Studies Anthologies: Research Across the Disciplines, 1980-1984, Boston: GK Hall, 94; Index to Women's Studies Anthologies: Research Across the Disciplines, 1985-1989, Boston: GK Hall, 96 **CONTACT ADDRESS** Libr Sys Dept, Univ of Oregon, Eugene, OR 97403-1299. **EMAIL** snb@darkwing.uoregon.edu

BROWNSON, JAMES
PERSONAL Born 02/06/1955, Hackensack, NJ, m, 1979, 3 children **DISCIPLINE** NEW TESTAMENT STUDIES **EDUCATION** Univ Michigan, BA, 77; Western Theol Sem, MDiv, 80; Princeton Theol Sem, PhD, 90. **CAREER** Asst prof, Calvin Col, 89-90; James and Jean Cook prof of New Testament, 90- , acad dean, 96- , Western Theol Sem. **MEMBERSHIPS** Soc Bibl Lit. **RESEARCH** Gospel of John; hermeneutics; gospel studies. **SELECTED PUBLICATIONS** Auth, The Odes of Solomon and the Johannine Tradition, J for the Stud of the Pseudepigrapha 2, 88; auth, Pastor, Which Bible? Reformed Rev, 90; auth, Selecting a Translation of the Bible for Public Reading, Reformed Liturgy and Music, 90; auth, How to Read a Parable, the Church Herald, 91; auth, The Virtuous Interpreter, Perspectives, 91; auth, What is The Gospel? Reformed Rev, 91; auth, Thoughts on God-Language, Perspectives, 93; auth, Reflections on El Salvador, Perspectives, 93; auth, Speaking the Truth in Love: Elements of a Missional Hermeneutic, Int Rev of Mission, 94; auth, Narrow Gate, Wide Horizons, Perspectives, 94; auth, Only Grace, Perspectives, 95; auth, Speaking the Truth in Love: New Testament Resources for a Missional Hermeneutic, Trinity Press. **CONTACT ADDRESS** 101 E 13th St, Holland, MI 49423. **EMAIL** Jim@westernsem.org

BROYLES, JAMES EARL
PERSONAL Born 12/24/1931, Spokane, WA, m, 1956, 4 children **DISCIPLINE** PHILOSOPHY **EDUCATION** Univ Idaho, BS, 54; Univ Wash, MA, 59, DPhil, 64. **CAREER** Teaching asst philos, Univ Wash, 59-61; from instr to asst prof, 61-72, chmn dept, 70-75, assoc prof, 72-77, prof philosophy, Wash State Univ, 77-; Vis prof, Univ Guam, 73-74. **MEMBERSHIPS** Northwestern Conf Philos (pres, 67); Am Philos Asn. **RESEARCH** British analytic philosophy; appraisal of argument; philosophical psychology. **SELECTED PUBLICATIONS** Auth, Logical and Empirical Factors in Conceptual Change, Proc Seventh Inter-Am Cong Philos, 68; Knowledge and mistake, Mind, 4/69; Language and common sense, Am Philos Quart, 7/69; An observation on Wittgenstein's use of fantasy, Metaphilos, 10/74; The fallacies of composition and division, Philos & Rhet, 75; The intellectural respectability of religion, Relig Humanist, autumn 77; Ryle: The category and location of mind, Personalist, 4/78; Talk about space: Wittgestein and Newton, Philos Invest, 81. **CONTACT ADDRESS** Dept of Philosophy, Washington State Univ, PO Box 645130, Pullman, WA 99164-5130.

BRUANT, REES
PERSONAL Born 09/12/1930, Memphis, TN, m, 1952, 4 children **DISCIPLINE** MISSIOLOGY **EDUCATION** Harding Univ, BA, 52; MA, 53; Fuller Theol Sem, MA, 80; DMiss, 90. **CAREER** Assoc prof, Lubbock Christian Univ, 63-64, 67-76; prof, Lincoln Christian Sem, 90-00; prof, Fla Christian Col, 00-. **HONORS AND AWARDS** Distinguished Alumnus, Harding Univ, 83. **MEMBERSHIPS** Evangelical Theol Soc; Evangelical Missiological Soc. **RESEARCH** Missions, Theology, Anthropology. **SELECTED PUBLICATIONS** Auth, Baptism: Why Wait? (Faith's Response to Conversion), College Pr, (Joplin, MO), 99. **CONTACT ADDRESS** Florida Christian Col, 1011 Bill Beck Blvd, Kissimmee, FL 34744.

BRUCH, C. S.
PERSONAL Born 06/11/1941, d, 2 children **DISCIPLINE** LAW **EDUCATION** Shimer Col, BA, 60; Univ Calif Sch of Law, JD, 72. **CAREER** Actg prof, 73-78, prof of Law, 78- , Univ Calif, Davis School of Law; mem, Grad Gp in Human Develop, 79- . **HONORS AND AWARDS** Regents' Fac Fel in Humanities, Univ of Calif, 74; Max Rheinstein Sr Res Fel, Alexander von Humboldt Foundation, 78-79; Davis, Acad Senate: 1st Annual Distinguished Public Service Awd, 90; Vis Fel, Fitzwilliam Col, 90; Western European Regional Fulbright Scholar, in residence at the Univs of Cologne and Cambridge, 90; Sr Res Fel, Alexander von Humboldt Foundation, 92; Fulbright Sr Scholar, in residence as Vis Fulbright Prof at The Hebrew Univ of Jerusalem, for research in Israel, Jordan and Egypt, 97; Fel, Univ of Calif Humanities Res Inst, 99. **MEMBERSHIPS** Am Law Inst; U.S. Supreme Court Bar; Calif State Bar. **SELECTED PUBLICATIONS** Auth, International Child Abduction Cases: Experience Under the 1980 Hague Convention, in Eekelaar, ed, Parenthood in Modern Society, Martinus Nijhoff, 93; auth, The Central Authority's Role Under the Hague Child Abduction Convention: A Friend in Deed, Family Law Q, 94; auth, Statutory Reform of Constitutional Doctrine: Fitting International Shoe to Family Law, UC Davis L Rev, 95; auth, Family Support Across Frontiers--New Ideas from the Americas, in, Families Across Frontiers, Martinus Nijhoff, 95; auth, How to Draft a Successful Family Law Convention: Lessons from the Child Abduction Conventions, in, Children on the Move, Martinus Nijhoff, 95; auth, "The Relocation of Children and Custodial Parents: Public Policy, Past and Present," 30 Family Law Quarterly, 96; auth, "Providing Justice for Family Law Litigants," The Family Justice System 46, ed. Ludwig Salgo, 97; auth, "The Hague Child Abduction Convention: Past Accomplishments, Future Challenges," The Globalization of Child Law 33, eds. Sharon Dietrick & Paul Vlaardingerbroek, Kluwer, 99; auth, "Public Policy and The Relocation of Custodial Households in the United States," in Family Law and Social Policy, 99; auth, "Family Law and Women's Human Rights: The Cases of Israel and Jordan," in Human Rights in Muslim Communities, ed. Suad Joseph, 99. **CONTACT ADDRESS** Univ of California, Davis, 1013 Stanford Dr, Davis, CA 95616. **EMAIL** csbruch@ucdavis.edu

BRULAND, ESTHER
PERSONAL m, 1 child **DISCIPLINE** RELIGION **EDUCATION** Drew Univ, PhD, 90. **CAREER** Adj prof, Col of Wooster, 87; adj prof, Fuller Theol Sem, 88; vis asst prof, Oberlin Col, 90; adj prof, Youngstown State Univ, 93-95; adj prof, Wiliam Tyndale Col, 96-; adj prof, Eastern Mich Univ, 96-98. **HONORS AND AWARDS** Phi Beta Kappa, 90. **MEMBERSHIPS** AAR; Soc of Christian Ethics. **RESEARCH** Social change; women and religion; nineteenth century reform movements; ecumenism; religion and culture. **SELECTED PUBLICATIONS** Coauth, A Passion for Jesus, A Passion for Justice, Judson, 83; auth, Evangelical and Feminist Ethics: Complex Solidarities, J of Relig Ethics, 89; auth, Regathering, Eerdmans, 95. **CONTACT ADDRESS** 420 W Caledonia, Howell, MI 48843-1118.

BRUMBAUGH, JOHN MAYNARD
PERSONAL Born 02/09/1927, Annapolis, MD **DISCIPLINE** LAW **EDUCATION** Swarthmore Col, BA, 48; Harvard Univ, LLB, 51. **CAREER** Teaching fel law sch, Harvard Univ, 55-56; from asst prof to assoc prof, 56-63, Prof Law, Sch Law, Univ MD, Baltimore, 63-96, prof emer, 96-, Reporter, Comn Md Criminal Law, 65-81. **MEMBERSHIPS** Am Law Inst. **CONTACT ADDRESS** Sch of Law, Univ of Maryland, Baltimore, 500 W Baltimore St, Baltimore, MD 21201. **EMAIL** jbrumb@umaryland.law.edu

BRUNK, CONRAD
PERSONAL Born 10/04/1945 **DISCIPLINE** PHILOSOPHY **EDUCATION** Wheaton Col, BA, 67; Northwestern Univ, MA, 68; PhD, 74. **CAREER** Asst prof, Oakland Univ, 74-76; Asst prof, Univ Waterloo, 76-80, Assoc prof, 80-97, Prof of Philos, 97-. **HONORS AND AWARDS** Danforth Found Kent Fel, 73-74; Woodrow Wilson Fel, 67-68; SSHRC Strategic Grant in Applied Ethics, 91-93; Can Tri-Coun Green Plan Grant, Univ of Guelph, 93-96; Res Fel, Centre for Applied Ethics, Univ of British Columbia, 94; Res fel, Centre for Studies in Relig and Soc, Univ of Victoria, 97; SSHRC Strategic Grant in Applied Ethics, 97-99. **RESEARCH** Applied and Professional Ethics; Values and Technology; Philosophy of Law; Social & Political Philosophy; Conflict Analysis and Conflict Resolution. **SELECTED PUBLICATIONS** Co-auth, Value Assumptions in Risk Assessment: The Alachlor Controversy, Wilfrid Laurier Univ Press, 91; auth, "The Breast Implant Controversy: Did Dow Corning Meet Its Ethical Responsibility To Women?" in Liberalism and Responsibility, Wilfrid Laurier Univ Press, (96); auth, "Restorative Justice and Punishment," Dialogue: Canadian J of Philosophy (96): 593-98; co-auth, "A Conceptual and Normative Analysis of Agroecosystem Health Research Projects," Eco-Research Program of the Tri-Council Secretariat (96); auth, "Silicone Breasts: Dow Corning and the Implant Controversy," Mad Cows and Mothers Milk, McGill-Queen's Univ Press, (97); co-auth, "A Dual-Perspective Model of Agroecosystem Health: System Functions and System Goals," J of Agricultural Ethics (98); auth, "Managing Risks in the Restructured Corporation: The Case of Dow Corning and Silicone Breast Implants," The Ethics of the New Economy: Restructuring and Beyond, Wilfrid Laurier Univ Press (98): 189-201; auth, "Peace Studies: An Integrated Approach to the Study of Conflict," Patterns of Conflict, Paths to Peace, McGill-Queens Univ Press (99). **CONTACT ADDRESS** Dept of Philos, Univ of Waterloo, 200 University Ave W, Waterloo, ON, Canada N2L 3G1. **EMAIL** cbrunk@watservl.uwaterloo.ca

BRUNNEE, JUTTA
DISCIPLINE LAW **EDUCATION** Dalhousie Univ, LLM; Johannes Gutenberg Univ, JD. **CAREER** Asst prof, McGill Univ, 90-95; assoc prof, Univ of British Columbia, 95-. **HONORS AND AWARDS** Ed, Yearbook Int Environ Law. **MEMBERSHIPS** World Conserv Union's. **RESEARCH** International environmental law; European and Canadian environmental law; comparative law. **SELECTED PUBLICATIONS** Auth, "Toward Effective International Environment Law, Trends and Developments," in Law and Process in Environmental Management, ed. Steven A. Kennett, (Calgary: Canadian Institute of Resources Law, 93): 217-236; auth, "Environmental Security in the Twenty-First Century: New Momentum for the Development of International Environmental Law?, 18, (Fordham International Law Journal, 95): 2201-2206; auth, "Toward International Ecosystem Law? A Legal and Policy Framework for Freshwater Resources," Ecosystem Health, 1, (95): 31-41; auth, "A Conceptual Framework for an International Forest Convention: Customary Law and Engineering Principles," in Canadian Council of International Law, ed., Global Forests and International Environmental Law 41-77, (London: Graham & Trotman, 95); auth, "Environmental Security and Freshwater Re-

sources: A Case for International Ecosystem Law," 5 Yearrbook of International Environmental Law, 41-76; auth, "Between the Forests and the Trees - An Emerging International Foroest Law,' Environmental Conservation, (97): 307-314; auth, "From a Black Hole Into a Greener Future? Comparative Perspectives on Environmental Liability Law in Quebec and Its Reform," in Melanges Paul - Andre Crepeau, (Cowansville: Editions Yvon Blais, 97): 155-197; auth, "Environmental Security and Freshwater Resources: Ecosystem Regime Building," Am Journal of International Law, (97): 26-59; auth, "Freshwater Regimes: The Madate of the International Joint Commission," Arzona Journal of International and Corporate Law, (98): 273-287; auth, "International Environmental Law in National Courts," Review of European Community and International Environmental Law, (98): 48-57. **CONTACT ADDRESS** Fac of Law, Univ of British Columbia, 1822 East Mall, Vancouver, BC, Canada V6T 1Z1. **EMAIL** brunnee@law.ubc.ca

BRUNO, JAMES EDWARD
PERSONAL Born 12/12/1940, Brooklyn, NY, m, 1980, 2 children **DISCIPLINE** EDUCATION, ECONOMICS, ENGINEERING **EDUCATION** UCLA, PhD, 68. **CAREER** Prof Education, UCLA. **HONORS AND AWARDS** EUCLAN Res Awd. **MEMBERSHIPS** AERA; ORSA. **RESEARCH** Temporal orientation and human behavior; Decision analysis-operations research; Information referenced testing and assessment. **SELECTED PUBLICATIONS** Coauth, Item Banking: Interactive Testing and Self Assessment, Springer-Verlag, Berling, 93; auth, Time in the Lifetime of a Teacher: Educational Leadership in an Era of Time Scarcity, Corwin Press, 97. **CONTACT ADDRESS** Dept of Education, Univ of California, Los Angeles, 1032A Moore Hall, Los Angeles, CA 90095. **EMAIL** jbruno@ucla.edu

BRYANT, ALAN W.
DISCIPLINE LAW **EDUCATION** McGill, BC, 65; Univ Toronto, LLB, 68. **CAREER** Prof. **HONORS AND AWARDS** Tchg Awd, 76; Owen Bk Prize, 95. **SELECTED PUBLICATIONS** Auth, pubs on criminal law, evidence and advocacy; co-auth, The Law of Evidence in Canada, 94. **CONTACT ADDRESS** Fac of Law, Univ of Western Ontario, London, ON, Canada N6A 3K7. **EMAIL** awbryant@julian.uwo.ca

BRYANT, DAVID J.
DISCIPLINE RELIGIOUS STUDIES **EDUCATION** Princeton Theological Sem, PhD. **CAREER** Prof. **MEMBERSHIPS** AAR **RESEARCH** Christian thought; interaction of religion and Western culture; influence of religion on our treatment of the natural environment; religion and the arts. **SELECTED PUBLICATIONS** Auth, Faith and the Play of Imagination: On the Role of Imagination in Religion. **CONTACT ADDRESS** Religious Studies Dept, Eckerd Col, 4200 54th Ave. S., Saint Petersburg, FL 33711. **EMAIL** bryantdj@eckerd.edu

BRYANT, LYNN ROSS
DISCIPLINE RELIGIOUS STUDIES **EDUCATION** Univ Chicago, PhD. **CAREER** Assoc prof. **RESEARCH** Religion and Nature in the U.S., Religious in the U.S. Women and religion. **SELECTED PUBLICATIONS** Auth, Imagination and the Life of the Spirit; The Land in American Religious Experience. **CONTACT ADDRESS** Religious Studies Dept, Univ of Colorado, Boulder, Boulder, CO 80309. **EMAIL** Lynn.Ross-Bryant@Colorado.edu

BRYDEN, PHILIP
DISCIPLINE LAW **EDUCATION** Dalhousie Univ, BA, 75; Oxford Univ, BA; 78, BCL, 79; Harvard Univ, LLM, 85. **CAREER** Law Clerk, Justice Bertha Wilson, Supreme Court Can; asst prof, 85-91; assoc prof, 91-. **HONORS AND AWARDS** Pres, Can Asn Law; pres, Civil Liberties Asn. **MEMBERSHIPS** Can Asn Law; Civil Liberties Asn; Former Pres, Can Assoc Law Teachers; Former Pres B.C. Civil Liberties Assoc **SELECTED PUBLICATIONS** Auth, pubs about administrative law and constitutional law. **CONTACT ADDRESS** Fac of Law, Univ of British Columbia, 1822 East Mall, Vancouver, BC, Canada V6T 1Z1. **EMAIL** bryden@law.ubc.ca

BRYSON, WILLIAM HAMILTON
PERSONAL Born 07/29/1941, Richmond, VA **DISCIPLINE** ENGLISH & AMERICAN LEGAL HISTORY **EDUCATION** Hampden-Sydney Col, BA, 63; Harvard Univ, LLB, 67; Univ Va, LLM, 68; Cambridge Univ, PhD, 72. **CAREER** Max Planck Inst grant, Frankfurt, 72-73; prof law, Univ Richmond, 73-. **HONORS AND AWARDS** Yorke Prize, Cambridge Univ, 73; Am Coun Learned Soc fel, 80. **MEMBERSHIPS** Fel Royal Hist Soc; Selden Soc; Am Soc Legal Hist; Medieval Acad Am. **RESEARCH** English legal history (particularly the history of equity); Virginia legal institutions; Virginia civil procedure. **SELECTED PUBLICATIONS** Auth, Dict of Sigla and Abbreviations to and in Law Books Before 1607, Hein, 96; ed, Legal Education in Virginia, 1779-1979, Univ Press Va, 82; ed, Sir John Randolph's King's Bench Reports, Hein, 96; auth, Legal Education in 19th Century Virginia, essay, Hein, 98; auth, Virgina Law Books, Am Philosophical Soc, 00, auth, samuel Dodd's reports, Carolina Acad Press, 00. **CONTACT ADDRESS** Law School, Univ of Richmond, 28 Westhampton Way, Richmond, VA 23173. **EMAIL** hbryson@richmond.edu

BUB, JEFFREY
PERSONAL Born 02/12/1942, Cape Town, South Africa, m, 1990, 2 children **DISCIPLINE** PHILOSOPHY **EDUCATION** Univ of Cape Town, BSc, 61, 62; London Univ, PhD, 66. **CAREER** Asst prof, philos, phys, Yale Univ, 69-71; asst prof, assoc prof, prof, philos, Univ Western Ontario, 71-86; prof, philos, Univ Maryland, 86-. **MEMBERSHIPS** Philos Sci Asn; APA; Int Quantum Structures Asn. **RESEARCH** The new work in the rapidly developing field of quantum information and quantum computation. **SELECTED PUBLICATIONS** Auth, Von Neumann's Projection Postulate as a Probability Conditionalization Rule in Quantum Mechanics, Journal of Philosophical Logic 6, (77): 381-390; coauth, Curious Properties of Quantum Ensembles which have been both Pre-and Post-Selected, Physical Review Letters 56, (86): 2337-2340; auth, Quantum Mechanics Without the Projection Postulate, Foundations of Physics, 22, (92): 737-754; auth, Quantum auth, Testing Models of Cognition Through the Analysis of Brain-Damaged Performance, Br J for the Philos of Sci, 94; auth, A Uniqueness Theorem for Interpretations of Quantum Mechanics, Stud in the Hist and Philos of Mod Phys, 96; auth, Schutte's Tautology and the Kochen-Specker Theorem, Found of Physics, 96; auth, Schutte's Tautology and the Kochen-Specker Theorem, Foundations of Physics, 26, (96): 787-806; coauth, A Uniqueness Theorem for Interpretations of Quantum Mechanics, Studies in the History and Philosophy of Physics, 26, (96): 181-219; auth, Interpreting the Quantum World, Cambridge, 97; auth, Quantum Mechanics as a Principle Theory, Studies in the History and Philosophy of Modern Physics 31, (00): 75-94. **CONTACT ADDRESS** Philosophy Dept, Univ of Maryland, Col Park, 1318 Wallach Pl, NW, Washington, DC 20742. **EMAIL** jbub@carnap.umd.edu

BUBANY, CHARLES PHILLIP
PERSONAL Born 12/20/1940, Kirksville, MO, m, 1969, 2 children **DISCIPLINE** LAW **EDUCATION** St Ambrose Univ, BA, 62; Washington Univ, St Louis, JD, 65. **CAREER** Grad teaching asst law, Col Law, Univ Ill, 65-66; asst prof, Col Law, WVa Univ, 66-67; asst prof, 71-73, assoc prof, 73-75, prof law, Sch Law, Tex Tech Univ, 75-. **HONORS AND AWARDS** Nat Univ Continuing Educ Assoc, 91, Service to the Professions Awd; George Herman Mahon Prof; Outstanding Law Prof, 94, 97, 98. **RESEARCH** Criminal justice; juvenile process; domestic relations law. **SELECTED PUBLICATIONS** Auth, The Texas Penal Code of 1974 in Annual Survey of Texas Law, Southwestern Law J, 28: 292; Constitutional Question Appellate Jurisdiction of the Missouri Supreme Court: The Albatross Hangs Heavy Still, Mo Law Rev, 39- 299; coauth (with Frank F Skillern), Taming the Dragon: An Adminstrative Law for Prosecutor Decisionmaking, Am Criminal Law Rev, 13: 473; auth, The Texas Confession Statute: Some New Wine in the Same Old Bottle, Tex Tech Law Rev, 10-67; contribr, Preparation and Trial of Criminal Cases, In: Texas Methods of Practice, West Publ Co, Vol 15, 79 & Vol 16, 80; coauth (with Perry Cockerell), Excluding Texas-style: Can Private Searches Poison the Fruit?, Tex Tech Law Rev, 12: 611; auth, Class C Misdemeanor Probation in Texas, South Tex Law J, 22: 249; Commentary to Chapter 21: Uniform Reciprocal Enforcement of Support Act, Tex Tech Law Rev, Vol 13, No 3; auth, Criminal Procedure: Trial and Appeal, Annual Survey of Texas Law, 45 SW Law L 91; Fifth Circuit Survey - Criminal Law, 27 Tex Tech Law Rev, 96; Counseling Clients to Do the Right Thing in Child Custody Cases, Children's Legal Rights J, winter 96; coauth, The Anatomy of a Client Interview, The Practical Lawyer, Dec 96; coauth, Texas Vehicle and Traffic Laws, 2nd ed, 97. **CONTACT ADDRESS** Sch of Law, Texas Tech Univ, Lubbock, TX 79409-0004. **EMAIL** xwcpb@ttacs.ttu.edu

BUCHANAN, GEORGE WESLEY
PERSONAL Born 12/25/1921, Denison, IA, m, 1947, 3 children **DISCIPLINE** NEW TESTAMENT **EDUCATION** Simpson Col, BA, 47; Garrett Theol Sem, MDiv, 51; Northwestern Univ, MA, 52; Drew Univ, PhD, 59. **CAREER** Teacher high sch, Iowa, 43-44; pastor, Methodist church, Shelby, Iowa, 44-45, Wenona, Ill, 47-48, Kaukauna, Wis, 52-54, Towaco, NJ, 54-57 & Cincinnati, Ohio, 59-60; from asst prof to assoc prof, 60-66, prof New Testament, 66-92, prof emeritus, 92-, Wesley Theol Sem. **HONORS AND AWARDS** S H Scheuer Interfaith fel, 59-60; Am Asn Theol Schs fel, 66; Hebrew Union Col Bibl & Archaeol Sch fel, 66-67; Rosenstiel fel, Univ Notre Dame, 73; Claremont-Soc Bibl Lit fel, 80-81; LittD, Simpson Col, 73; DSL, Mellen Univ, 95; littd, simpson col, 73. **MEMBERSHIPS** Soc Bibl Lit; Stud Novi Testamenti Soc; Cath Bibl Soc; AAUP; ed bd, Bibl Archaeol Rev; ed bd, Gospel Stud; adv bd, Arts and Hum Index; adv bd, Int Soc of Poetry. **RESEARCH** Christian origins; the historical Jesus; Jewish, Samaritan, and Christian literature; intertextuality. **SELECTED PUBLICATIONS** Auth, New Testament Eschatology: Historical and Cultural Background, Edwin Mellen, 93; auth, The Book of Revelation: Its Introduction and Prophecy, Edwin Mellen, 93; auth, Introduction to Intertextuality, Edwin Mellen, 95; auth, The Gospel According to Matthew, 2 v, Edwin Mellen, 96; The Consequences of the Covenant, Leiden, Brill, 70; To the Hebrews (Garden City, Doubleday) 72; Revelation and Redemption, Dillsboro, Western N. Congress, 78; Jesus: The King and His Kingdom, Macon, Press, 84; Typology and The Gospel, Lanhan, Univ Press of Am, 87; Biblical and Theological Insights from Ancient and Modern Civil Law Leweston, Edwin Mellen, 92; The Book of Daniel, Edwin Mellen, 99. **CONTACT ADDRESS** Wesley Theol Sem, 4400 Massachusetts Ave NW, Washington, DC 20016-2415. **EMAIL** gwesb@cpcug.org

BUCHER, GLENN R.
PERSONAL Born 05/20/1940, Mechanicsburg, PA, m, 1963, 2 children **DISCIPLINE** RELIGION, HIGHER EDUCATION **EDUCATION** Elizabethtown Col, AB, 62; Union Theol Sem, NYork, MDiv, 65; Boston Univ, PhD(ethics), 68. **CAREER** Asst, Boston Univ, 66-67; instr philos, Emerson Col, 67-68; instr ethics & soc, Howard Univ, 68-70; asst prof, 70-75, assoc prof, 75-80, chmn dept, 78-80, actg dir, Ctr Prog Inst Renewal, 80-82, Lincoln Prof Relig, Col Wooster, 82-. **HONORS AND AWARDS** Distinguished Alumnus Awd for Prof Achievement, Elizabethtown Col, Pa, 77. **MEMBERSHIPS** AAUP; Soc Sci Study Relig; Am Acad Relig; Am Soc Christian Ethics. **RESEARCH** American religious history; liberation theology and ethics; secuality and religion. **SELECTED PUBLICATIONS** Auth, Confusion and Hope: Clergy, Laity, and the Church in Transition, 74 & Straight, White, Male, 76, Fortress Press; The era of the trustees, Presby Surv, Vol 70, 12/80; Seventy futures for Presbyterianism: The Colleges of the Church, Presby Outlook, Vol 163, 4/20/81; The deferred maintenance of the faculty, The Chronicle of Higher Educ, Vol 22, 4/27/81; Worlds of total meaning: An interpretation of cult religion, Soundings, fall 81; Fourteen cases: The study of religion in church-related higher education, Coun Study of Relig Bull, 10/81; Church-related higher education: A review & assessment, Educ Rec, winter 82; Political Incorrectness and Theological Education/, Theol Today, Vol 49, 1993. **CONTACT ADDRESS** Dept of Relig, The Col of Wooster, Beall Ave, Wooster, OH 44691.

BUCK, HARRY MERWYN
PERSONAL Born 11/18/1921, Enola, PA, m, 1943, 2 children **DISCIPLINE** HISTORY OF RELIGIONS **EDUCATION** Albright Col, AB, 42; Evangel Sch Theol, MDiv, 45; Univ Chicago, PhD, 54. **CAREER** Pastor, Evangel United Brethren Church, Md, 42-46, Pa, 46-49; from instr to asst prof Bibl hist, 51-59, assoc prof Bible & relig, 59-68, prof Relig Studies, Wilson Col, 68-; consult, New Testament Greek Text Proj, Am Bible Soc, 55; mem, East-West Philosophers Conf, Honolulu, Hawaii, 59; comt lectionary study, Int Greek New Testament Proj, 59-; seminar Indian Civilization, Hyderabad, India, 61; managing ed, J Am Acad Relig, 61-73; chmn, Am Textual Criticism Sem, 60-62; fac training fel, Am Inst Indian Studies & hist relig fel, Soc Relig Higher Educ, 65-66; partic fel, Int Conf-Sem on Tamil Studies, Univ Malaya, 66; ed, Anima, 74-. **MEMBERSHIPS** Am Acad Relig; Soc Bibl Lit; Soc Study New Testament; Asn Asian Studies; Int Soc Study Relig. **RESEARCH** Epic literature of South Asia; function of sacred tradition; methodology in the history of religions. **SELECTED PUBLICATIONS** Auth, People of the Lord, History, Scriptures and Faith of Ancient Israel, Macmillan, 66; co-ed, Religious Traditions and the Limits of Tolerance, Anima, 88; auth, Rama in Buddhist Cultures, 95; art, Beyond Walls, Fences, and Interreligious Dialogue, J of Ecumenical Stories, 97; auth, Beware the Self Evident, Dharma World, 98. **CONTACT ADDRESS** 1053 Wilson Ave, Chambersburg, PA 17201.

BUCKINGHAM, DON
DISCIPLINE LAW **EDUCATION** Univ Saskatchewan, BA; Liege Univ, LLB, 86. **CAREER** Law clerk, Justice Heald, Federal Court Appeal; assoc prof. **HONORS AND AWARDS** Dir, Westminster Inst Ethics Human Values. **RESEARCH** International trade law; agricultural law. **SELECTED PUBLICATIONS** Auth, Does the WTO Care About Ecosystem Health: The Case of Trade in Agricultural Products, Ecosystem Health; A Recipe for Change: Towards an Integrated Approach to Food in International Law, 94; co-auth, Counting Our Chickens Before They Hatch: New Hope or No Hope for Discipline in Agricultural Trade under the new GATT and the NAFTA?, 94; Understanding the Law and Learning About Law, McGraw-Hill Ryers; co-ed, Law, Agriculture and the Farm Crisis, Purich, 92. **CONTACT ADDRESS** Col of Law, Univ of Saskatchewan, 15 Campus Dr, Saskatoon, SK, Canada S7N 5A6. **EMAIL** Buckingham@abyss.usask.ca

BUCKLEY, FRANCIS J.
PERSONAL Born 08/31/1928, Los Angeles, CA **DISCIPLINE** DOGMATIC THEOLOGY **EDUCATION** Gonzaga Univ, AB, 51, MA, 52; Alma Col, STL, 59; Univ Santa Clara, MA, 59; Gregorian Univ, STD, 64. **CAREER** Mem staff Latin & relig, Bellarmine Col Prep, 52-55; instr New Testament, 60-61, church hist, 61, from asst prof to assoc prof, 63-72, dir, grad prog relig educ, 74-75, actg chemn, dept theol, 71-73, chemn, dept theol & relig studies, 78-79, chemn, dept relig educ & pastoral ministries, 79-82, prof dogmatic theol, Univ San Francisco, 72-; mem, Catechetical Forum, 64-71, co-ed, Nat Catechetical Dir, 74-78; assoc ed, Theol Studies, 68-76; bd trustees, Jesuit Community Univ of San Francisco, 69-76 & 77-82; bd dirs, Coun Study of Relig, 72-75; dir proj renewal sacrament of penance, comt Pastoral Res & Practice, Nat Conf Cath Bishops, 73-76; bd trustees, Loyola Marymount Univ, 74; theol adv, US Bishops at Synod on Catechesis, 77; bd of trustees, Pacific Grad School of Psychology, 84-86, chemn, 86; bd of trustees, School of Applied Theology, 93-; consult, US Cath Conference, Dept

of Ed, evaluation of catechetical texts, 97-; consult, Hispanic Telecommunications Network, 88-; consult, State of CA Coun for private postsecondary and vocational education, 93-. **HONORS AND AWARDS** Doctor of Humane Letters, Pacific Graduate School of Psychology, 88. **MEMBERSHIPS** Am Soc Church Hist; Cath Bibl Asn; Cath Theol Soc Am; Int Soc Jesuit Ecumenists; Asn Prof & Res Relig Educ; Col Theology Soc (pres, 72-74, bd, 69-76, regional chemn, 66-72). **RESEARCH** Pastoral theology; scripture; catechetics. **SELECTED PUBLICATIONS** Auth, Principles of Intercommunion, Proc Cath Theol Soc Am, 69 & Theol Dig, 69; Children and God: Communion, Confession, Confirmation, Corpus, 70, 2nd ed, Dimension Bks, 73; I confess--the Sacrament of Penance today, Ave Maria, 72; Religious Content for Children from Six to Twelve, Catechesis: Realities and Visions, US Cath Conf, 77; Punishment and Penance in a Changing Church and Society, Theology Confronts a Changing World, Twenty-Third Publ, 77; coauth, Lord of life Series, Sadlier, 78; auth, Right to the Sacraments of Initiation, Origins, 78 & Catholic Mind, 79; Reconciling, Ave Maria Press, 81; Team Teaching: What, Why, How, Sage, 98. **CONTACT ADDRESS** Dept Relig, Univ of San Francisco, 2130 Fulton St, San Francisco, CA 94117-1050. **EMAIL** buckley@usfca.edu

BUCKLEY, THOMAS W.
PERSONAL Born 06/11/1929, Abington, MA **DISCIPLINE** BIBLICAL STUDIES **EDUCATION** Harvard Col, BA, 49; Fordham Univ, MA, 52; Catholic Univ Am, STL, 58; Pontifical Bibl Inst, Rome, SSL, 60; Univ St Thomas Aquinas, Rome, STD, 62. **CAREER** Lectr theol, Regis Col, 60-61; prof New Testament, Bibl Greek, St. John's Sem, 63-81; lectr New Testament, St. Paul's House of Studies, 77-87; lectr in New Testament, St Scholastica Priory, 81-84; pastor St John's parish, Essex, MA, 81- . **MEMBERSHIPS** Catholic Bibl Asn; Soc of Bibl Lit. **RESEARCH** New Testament. **SELECTED PUBLICATIONS** Auth, Apostle to the Nations: The Life and Letters of St Paul: A Biblical Course, Daughters of St Paul, 81; auth, Seventy Times Seven: Sin, Judgment, and Forgiveness in Matthew, Liturgical, 91. **CONTACT ADDRESS** PO Box 986, Essex, MA 01929.

BUCKWOLD, TAMARA
DISCIPLINE LAW **EDUCATION** Univ Saskatchewan, LLB, 80, LLM, 95. **CAREER** Asst prof, 87-. **MEMBERSHIPS** Law Soc Saskatchewan. **RESEARCH** Contracts and secured transactions. **SELECTED PUBLICATIONS** Auth, The Rights of Account and Inventory Financers Under the P.P.S.A.: Transamerica Commercial Finance Corp. v. Royal Bank of Canada, Sask Rev, 95; The Treatment of Receiver-Managers in the P.P. S.A.: Conceptual and Practical Implications, Can Bus Law Jour, 97; co-auth, The Personal Property Security Act and the Bankruptcy and Insolvency Act: Two Solitudes or Complementary Systems?, Banking and Finance Rev, 97. **CONTACT ADDRESS** Col of Law, Univ of Saskatchewan, 15 Campus Dr, Saskatoon, SK, Canada S7N 5A6. **EMAIL** Buckwold@law.usask.ca

BUCY, PAMELA H.
PERSONAL Born 07/28/1953, Raymondville, TX **DISCIPLINE** LAW **EDUCATION** Austin Col, BA, 75; Wash Univ Sch Law, JD, 78. **CAREER** Frank M. Bainbridge prof, Univ Ala. **HONORS AND AWARDS** Teaching and Bar awards. **MEMBERSHIPS** Order of the Coif. **RESEARCH** Criminal law; criminal procedure; white-collar crime. **SELECTED PUBLICATIONS** Auth, White Collar Crime, Cases and Materials, West, 91, 2d ed 97; auth, Health Care Fraud, LJSP, 96; coauth, Federal Criminal Law, 97. **CONTACT ADDRESS** Law Dept, Univ of Alabama, Tuscaloosa, Box 870000, Tuscaloosa, AL 35487-0383. **EMAIL** pbucy@law.ua.edu

BUEHLER, ARTHUR
DISCIPLINE FUNDAMENTALISM, NATIONALISM, RELIGION **EDUCATION** Harvard Univ, PhD, 93. **CAREER** Asst prof, Colgate Univ; asst prof, La State Univ. **HONORS AND AWARDS** Fulbright Fel **RESEARCH** Study of Islam; South Asian Religions; Sufism; Shamanism; mysticism; spiritual practice. **SELECTED PUBLICATIONS** Auth, Sufi Heirs of the Prophet: The Indian Naqshbandiyya and the Rise of the Sufi Mediating Shaykh, Univ SC Press, 98; The Naqshbandiyya in Timurid India: The Central Asian Legacy, Jour of Islamic Studies 7:2, 96; Currents of Sufism in Nineteenth- and Twentieth-Century Indo-Pakistan: An Overview, in Muslim World 87/3-4, 97; guest ed, Sufi Illuminations 1:1, 97; ed, Jour of Sufi History. **CONTACT ADDRESS** Dept of Philos and Relig, La State Univ, 106 Coates Hall, Baton Rouge, LA 70803. **EMAIL** abuehl1@lsu.edu

BUEHLER, ARTHUR F.
DISCIPLINE JUDIASM, CHRISTIANITY, ISLAM **EDUCATION** Harvard Univ, PhD, 93. **CAREER** Asst prof, La State Univ, 98-. **RESEARCH** Sufi Shaykh. **SELECTED PUBLICATIONS** Auth, The Naqshbandiyya in Timurid India: The Central Asian Legacy, in J of Islamic Stud 7, 96; Currents of Sufism in Nineteenth-and Twentieth-Century Indo-Pakistan: An Overview, in Muslim World, 97. **CONTACT ADDRESS** Dept of Philos and Relig Stud, Louisiana State Univ and A&M Col, 106 Coates Hall, Baton Rouge, LA 70803.

BUFFORD, EDWARD EUGENE
PERSONAL Born 07/15/1935, Birmingham, AL, m **DISCIPLINE** THEOLOGY **EDUCATION** Miles Coll, BA 1970; M Div Gammon Theol Sem, 1973; D Div Union Bapt Theol Sem, 1974. **CAREER** Centenary Un Meth Ch, minister; St Johns Un Meth Ch LA, 72-74; Morning Star Un Meth Ch AL, 69-72; Mt Moriah Un Meth Ch, 67-69; Powell Chapel Lafayette AL, 63-67; St Paul Jasper AL, 62-63; St James, 59-61; Watts Comm Ministries, dir 1972-74. **HONORS AND AWARDS** Crusade Scholar 1971. **MEMBERSHIPS** Mem NAACP; Masons; Alpha Phi Alpha Frat Inc. **CONTACT ADDRESS** 584 E Mc Lemore Ave, Memphis, TN 38106.

BUFORD, THOMAS O.
PERSONAL Born 11/17/1932, Overton, TX, m, 1954, 3 children **DISCIPLINE** PHILOSOPHY **EDUCATION** NTex State Univ, BA, 55; Southwestern Baptist Theol Sem, BD, 58; Boston Univ, PhD, 63. **CAREER** Coordr of assistants, Dept Philos, Boston Univ, 59-60; asst prof philos, Ky Southern Col, 62-68 & NTex State Univ, 68-69; assoc prof, 69-76, Prof Philos, Furman Univ, 76-, Chmn Dept 70-85. **MEMBERSHIPS** Am Philos Asn; Southern Soc Philos & Psychol; Philos Educ Soc; SAtlantic Philos Educ Soc (pres, 80-82). **RESEARCH** Epistemology; philosophy of education, Ancient Greek philosophy; Louis G. Forqione Prof of Philosophy, 98-; Senior Lilly Fellow, 97-98. **SELECTED PUBLICATIONS** Ed, We Pass This Way But Once, Southern Press, 62; auth, Toward a philosophy of general education, Personalist, fall 67; Some random thoughts on curriculum building for today's students, South Baptist Educator, 12/68; Toward a Philosophy of Education, Holt, 69; Essays on Other Minds, Univ Ill, 70; coauth, Contemporary Studies in Philosophical Idealism, Claude Stark, 75; ed, Philosophy for Adults, Univ Press Am, 81; auth, In Search of a Calling, Mercer Univ Press; ed, Personalism Revisited, Rodopi, 00. **CONTACT ADDRESS** Dept of Philosophy, Furman Univ, Greenville, SC 26913. **EMAIL** tom.buford@Furman.edu

BUGG, CHARLES B.
PERSONAL Born 12/25/1942, Miami, FL, m, 1967, 2 children **DISCIPLINE** THEOLOGY **EDUCATION** Stetson Univ, BA, 65; Southern Baptist Theol Sem, MDiv, 69, PhD, 72. **CAREER** Carl Bates Prof of Preaching, Southern Baptist Theol Sem, 89-93; Kenneth Chafin Prof of Preaching, Baptist Theol Sem of Richmond, 96-; Founder and dir, Chevis Horne Center for Preaching and Worship, BTSR, 97-. **HONORS AND AWARDS** Outstanding Alumnus, Stetson Univ, 84. **MEMBERSHIPS** Acad of Homiletics, Henri Nouwen Soc. **RESEARCH** Pastoral preaching, relationship of lay and clergy. **SELECTED PUBLICATIONS** Auth, Preaching and Intimacy (90); auth, Preaching from the Inside Out (94); auth, Learning to Dream Again (97); auth, Things My Children are Teaching Me; auth, A Faith that Meets Our Fears. **CONTACT ADDRESS** Dept Relig, Baptist Theol Sem, 3400 Brook Rd, Richmond, VA 23227-4536. **EMAIL** cbbugg@aol.com

BUHNEMANN, GUDRUN
PERSONAL Born Goslar **DISCIPLINE** INDIAN AND BUDDHIST STUDIES, SANSKRIT STUDIES **EDUCATION** Vienna Univ, PhD, 80. **CAREER** Prof, Univ Wis Madison. **HONORS AND AWARDS** Nat Endow for the Humanities; Amer Coun of Learned Soc; Japan Soc for the Promotion of Sci. **MEMBERSHIPS** Amer Acad of Relig; Amer Orient Soc; Amer Coun of Southern Asian Art. **RESEARCH** Classical Indian studies; Religions of India. **SELECTED PUBLICATIONS** Auth, Sadhanasataka and Sadhanasatapancasika. Two Buddhist Sadhana Collections in Sanskrit Manuscript, Wien, Univ Wien, 94; auth, Nispannayogavali. Two Sanskrit Manuscripts from Nepal, Tokyo, The Ctr for East Asian Cultural Studies, 91; auth, The Hindu Deities Illustrated according to the Pratisthalaksanasarasamuccaya, Tokyo, The Ctr for East Asian Cultural Studies, 90; auth, Forms of Ganesa. A Study based on the Vidyarnavatantra, Wichtrach, Inst fur Indologie, 89; auth, The Worship of Mahaganapati according to the Nityotsava, Wichtrach, Inst fur Indologie, 88; auth, Puja. A Study in Smarta Ritual, Vienna, Inst fur Indologie, Univ Wien, 88; auth, The Iconography of Hindu Tantric Deities, 2 vols, Egbert Forsten, 00. **CONTACT ADDRESS** Dept of Lang and Cult of Asia, Univ of Wisconsin, Madison, 11220 Lindon Dr., Madison, WI 53706. **EMAIL** gbuhnema@facstaff.wisc.edu

BUICKEROOD, JAMES G.
PERSONAL Born 10/23/1951, Syracuse, NY, m, 1981 **DISCIPLINE** PHILOSOPHY **EDUCATION** Harper Col, BA, 81; Rutgers Univ, PhD, 88. **CAREER** Instr, philos, Rutgers Univ, 81-87; asst prof, San Jose State Univ, 88-89; vis asst prof, philos, College of William & Mary, 89-90; vis asst prof, philos, Washington Univ, 90-92; adj assoc prof, philos, Univ Delaware, 92-93; adj prof of Philosophy, Rochester institute of Technology, 98-99; vis asst prof, Washington University 99-. **MEMBERSHIPS** APA; Am Soc for Eighteenth-Century Stud; Soc for the Hist of Philos. **RESEARCH** Early Modern philosophy; Locke; British materialism. **SELECTED PUBLICATIONS** Auth, The Natural History of the Understanding: Locke and the Rige of Cacultative Logic in The Eighteenth Century, History and Philogsophy of Logic, 85; auth, Logic, in Black, ed, Dictionary of Eighteenth-Century World History, Blackwell, 94; auth, Pursuing the Science of Man: Some Difficulties in Understanding Eighteenth-Century Maps of the Mind, Eighteenth-Century Life, 95; ed, introd, A Philosophick Essay Concerning Ideas, According to Dr. Sherlock's Principles, AMS, 96; ed, introd, annotations, Smith, A Philosophical Discourse of the Nature of Rational and Irrational Souls, AMS, 98; auth, Two Dissertation concerning Sense, and the Imagination, With an Essay on Consciousness: Study in Attribution, 1650 to 1850: Toleas, Aesthetics, and Inquiries in the Modern Era, 00. **CONTACT ADDRESS** Dept of Philosophy, Washington Univ, CB 1073, Saint Louis, MO 63130-4899. **EMAIL** jameina18@yahoo.com

BULBULIA, AHMED I.
DISCIPLINE LAW **EDUCATION** London Sch Econ, LLB; Univ MI, LLM. **CAREER** Prof; Seton Hall Univ, 72-; barrister at law, Middle Temple & advocate before Supreme Ct S Africa; taught at Univ New Brunswick, Can & adj prof, Rutgers and NY Law Sch; dir, Legal Educ Opportunity prog. **RESEARCH** Conflict of laws; contracts; criminal law; business associations; public international law. **SELECTED PUBLICATIONS** Publ on, corporations and professional responsibility. **CONTACT ADDRESS** Law School, Seton Hall Univ, Newark, 1 Newark Center, Newark, NJ 07102. **EMAIL** bulbulah@shu.edu

BULL, BARRY L.
PERSONAL Born 08/29/1947, Billings, Mont, m, 1971, 2 children **DISCIPLINE** PHILOSOPHY, EDUCATION **EDUCATION** Yale Univ, BA, 69; Univ Va, MA, 70; Univ Idaho, MAT, 72; Cornell Univ, PhD, 79. **CAREER** Asst Prof, Wellesley Col, 79-84; Asst Prof to Assoc Prof, Univ Haw, 86-89; Assoc Prof, Univ Minn, 89-90; Assoc Prof to Full Prof, Ind Univ, 90-. **HONORS AND AWARDS** Francis I. Dupont Fel, Univ Va, 69-70; Fel, Univ Idaho, 71-72; Fel, Am Coun of Learned Soc, 82-83; Mellon Fel, 83-84; Phi Kappa Phi; Phi Delta Kappa; Dean's Medallion, Ind Univ, 00. **MEMBERSHIPS** Philos of Educ Soc; Intl Network of Philos of Educ; Am Educ Res Asn. **RESEARCH** The ethics of education policy generally, currently focusing on the adoption and implementation of national curriculum and achievement standards. **SELECTED PUBLICATIONS** Auth, "The limits of teacher professionalization," in The moral dimensions of teaching, Jossey-Bass, 90; co-auth, "The pedagogic nature of subject matter knowledge," Am Educ Res J, 91; co-auth, The Ethics of multicultural and bilingual education, Teachers Col Press, 92; co-auth, Education in Indiana: An overview, Ind Educ Policy Center, 94; co-auth, Professional development and teacher time: Principles, guidelines, and policy options for Indiana, Ind Educ Policy Center, 94; co-auth, Learning together: Professional development for better schools, Ind Educ Policy Center,, 96; co-auth, Planning together: Professional development for teachers of all students, Ind Educ Policy Center,, 97; auth, "School reform in Indiana since 1980," In Hoosier schools: Past and Present, Ind Univ Press, 98; auth, "Political philosophy and the balance between central and local control of schools," in Balancing local control and state responsibility for K-12 Education, 00. **CONTACT ADDRESS** Dept Educ, Indiana Univ, Bloomington, Education 4240, Bloomington, IN 47405. **EMAIL** bbull@indiana.edu

BULL, ROBERT JEHU
PERSONAL Born 10/21/1920, Harrington, DE, m, 1959 **DISCIPLINE** CHURCH HISTORY, ARCHAEOLOGY **EDUCATION** Randolph-Macon Col, BA, 43; Duke Univ, BD, 46; Yale Univ, MA, 51, PhD, 56. **CAREER** Instr philos, Colgate Univ, 54-55; from instr to assoc prof, 55-70, field supvr, Drew Univ-McCormick Archaeol Exped, Jordan, 56-57, 60-62, 64, Prof Church Hist, Drew Univ, 70-, Dir, Inst Archaeol Res, 68-, Mem, Hazen Theol Discussion Group; Am Asn Theol Sch fel, Univ Utrecht, 59-60; Am Sch Orient Res, Jordan, 66-67; field supvr, Wooster Exped, Pella, 66; dir, Tell er Ras Exped, 66, 68; vpres, Comm Arch & Hist, United Methodist Church, 68; dir, Am Sch Orient Res, Jerusalem, 70-71, Joint Exped Khirbet Shemac, 70 & Joint Exped Caesarea, 71; res prof, William Foxwell Albright Inst Archaeol Res, 74. **MEMBERSHIPS** Am Soc Church Hist; Am Sch Orient Res; Albright Inst Archaeol Res; Nat Lectr Archaeol Inst Am. **RESEARCH** Patristics; Palestinian archaeology; early American Methodist history. **SELECTED PUBLICATIONS** Auth, The Making of Our Tradition, Westminster, 67; coauth, The sixth campaign at Balatah, Bull Am Sch Orient Res, 4/68; The excavation of Tell er Ras, Bull Am Sch Orient Res, 4/68; The excavation of Tell er Ras on Mt Gerigim, Bibl Archaeologist, 5/68; Towards a Corpus Inscriptonum Latinarum Britannecarum in Palestina, Blestine Exploration Quart, 70; Tell er Ras, The Pottery, 71 & Tell er Ras, The Coins, 71, Smithsonian; co-ed, Eaesarea, The Preliminary Reports, Vol I, Harvard Univ, 74; auth, The Gold Coin Hoard at Caesarea + Ancient Numismatic Studies/, Bibl Archaeol, Vol 56, 1993; Caesarea and King Herod Magnificent City Plan/, Am J Archaeol, Vol 100, 1996. **CONTACT ADDRESS** Dept of Hist, Drew Univ, Madison, NJ 07940.

BULLARD, EDWARD A., JR.
PERSONAL Born 04/02/1947, Syracuse, NY, m **DISCIPLINE** LAW **EDUCATION** Southern Univ, BS 1969; Syracuse Univ, MBA 1972; Univ of Detroit Law School, JD 1978. **CAREER** Carrier Corp, analyst 1969; Ernst & Young, accountant 1969-72; Univ of MI Flint, prof, 72-93; GMI, assoc prof acctg 1972-1993; Detroit College of Business-Flint, prof, cur-

rently. **HONORS AND AWARDS** CPA NY 1977-; Outstanding Prof Univ of MI Flint 1979; mem Univ of Detroit Law Schl Moot Court Tax Team 1977. **MEMBERSHIPS** Bd mem Urban League Flint 1984, Flint Comm Devel Corp 1984; mem AICPA, Amer Acctg Assoc; adv Flint City Schools Bus Prog 1985; mem City of Flint Cable TV Advisory Panel; Small business consultant and urban analyst; mem Amer Business Law Assoc; board of directors, Urban League of Flint; board of directors, Flint Community Development Coordination; legal regress committee, executive committee, NAACP of Flint; advisory panel, Flint Cable TV; consultant, Junior Achievement, Beecher High School; mem, Congressional Black Caucus-Flint; numerous others. **CONTACT ADDRESS** Professor, Detroit Col of Business-Flint, 3488 N Jennings Rd, Flint, MI 48504. **EMAIL** flebullaro@dcb.edu

BULLARD, JOHN MOORE
PERSONAL Born 05/06/1932, Winston-Salem, NC **DISCIPLINE** BIBLICAL STUDIES; ENGLISH LANGUAGE AND LITERATURE **EDUCATION** AB, 53, AM, 55, UNC- Chapel Hill; Mdiv, 57, PhD, 62, Yale Univ. **CAREER** Asst in Instruction, Yale Univ, 57-62; Asst Prof, 61-65, Assoc Prof, 65-70, Albert C. Outler Prof, 70-, Chmn, Dept of Religion, 62-, Wofford Col. **HONORS AND AWARDS** Fund for the Study of the Great Religions grant to travel around the world and live 6 months in Indian, Colgate, Univ, 70-71; James Graduate Fel at Yale, 57-62; NEH Summer Senimars: Harvard, 82, Upenn, 86, Yale, 87; Dana Fel, Emory Univ, 89-90. **MEMBERSHIPS** Amer Acad of Religion; Soc of Biblical Lit; South Carolina Acad of Religion; New Bach Soc; Moravian Music Fdn. **RESEARCH** The Hymn as Literary form from ancient Sumerians to the Hebrew Psalter and beyond. **SELECTED PUBLICATIONS** Auth, Dictionary of Biblical Interpretation, ed. J.H. Hayes, Abingdon Press, 99; auth, Encyclopedia of the Ancient World, ed. C. Moose, Salem Press, CA, 00. **CONTACT ADDRESS** Dept of Religion, Wofford Col, 429 N. Church St., Spartanburg, SC 29303. **EMAIL** bullardjm@wofford.edu

BULLOCK, ALICE G.
DISCIPLINE TAX LAW **EDUCATION** Howard Univ, BA, 72, JD, 75. **CAREER** Asst prof, 79; assoc dean, 88-90, and actg dean, 90; assoc dean, Acad Aff, 91-92 & interim dean, 96, Howard Univ. **MEMBERSHIPS** Dep dir, Asn Amer Law Sch, 92-94; Amer Law Inst; ABA Comt on Teaching Taxation; bd dir, Coun Legal Educ Opportunity; bd visitors, Brigham Young Univ Law Sch & bd trustees, Inst Independent Educ. **SELECTED PUBLICATIONS** Auth, Taxes, social policy and philanthropy: the untapped potential of low and middle income generosity, Cornell J Law and Public Policy, 97; A dean's role in supporting recruitment of minority faculty, Minority Law Teachers Conf 90, 10 St Louis Univ Public Law Rev 347, 91 & Is there life after safe harbor leasing, 19 New Eng Law Rev 1, 84; bk chap, Legal Issues in Mental Health, in Mental Health and Mental Illness in the Black Community, 90 & Taxes in Horowitz and Davidson, Legal Rights of Children, 84. **CONTACT ADDRESS** Dept of Law, Howard Univ, 2400 Sixth St NW, Washington, DC 20059.

BULLOCK, JAMES
PERSONAL Born 08/22/1926, Charleston, MS, m **DISCIPLINE** LAW **EDUCATION** Texas Southern Univ, BA, JD, 1970. **CAREER** US Postal Service, supvr; TX Southern Univ, assoc dean law, assoc prof law, currently. **HONORS AND AWARDS** Phi Alpha Delta Outstanding Alumnus. **MEMBERSHIPS** Justice Greener Chap Phi Alpha Delta Legal Frat; TX Black Caucus; mem Am Bar Assn; Nat Bar Assn; State Bar TX; Houston Bar Assn; Houston Lawyers Assn; Phi Alpha Delta Legal Frat; mem S & Central YMCA; NAACP; Harris Co Cncl Orgn; TX Assn Coll Tchrs. **CONTACT ADDRESS** Sch of Law, Texas So Univ, 3100 Cleburne Avenue, Houston, TX 77004.

BULLOCK, JOAN R.
DISCIPLINE LAW **EDUCATION** Mich State Univ, BA; Univ Toledo, JD; Univ Mich, MBA. **CAREER** Assoc prof. **SELECTED PUBLICATIONS** Auth, The Pebble in the Shoe: Making the Case for the Government Employee, 93; Abortion Rights in America, 94. **CONTACT ADDRESS** Col Law, Univ of Toledo, Toledo, OH 43606. **EMAIL** joan.bullock@utoledo.edu

BUNGE, MARIO
DISCIPLINE PHILOSOPHY **EDUCATION** Univ Nat de La Plata, PhD, 52. **RESEARCH** Philosophy of the social sciences, philosophy of mind, and social mechanisms. **SELECTED PUBLICATIONS** Auth, Philosophical Problems in Linguistics, In Japanese, Tokyo: Seishin-Shobo, 86; transl, Philosophy of Psychology, with Ruben Ardila, 87; auth, Treatise on Basic Philosophy, 8 vols. on semantics, ontology, epistemology, philosophy of science and technology, and axiology and ethics, Reidel, 84-89; auth, Finding Philosophy in Social Science, Yale Univ Press, 96; auth, Foundations of Biophilosophy, with Martin Mahner, Springer, 97; auth, Philosophy of Science: From Problem to Theroy, vol. 1, Transaction Publishers, 98; auth, Philosophy of Science: From Explanation to Justification, vol. 2, Transaction Publishers, 98; auth, Social Science Under Debate, Univ of Toronto Press, 98; auth, Critical Approaches to Science and Philosophy, Transaction Publishers, 98; auth, Dictionary of Philosophy, Prometheus Books, 98; auth, The Sociology-Philosophy Connection, Transaction Publishers, 99. **CONTACT ADDRESS** Philosophy Dept, McGill Univ, 855 Sherbrooke St, Montreal, QC, Canada H3A 2T5. **EMAIL** czmb@musica.mcgill.ca

BUNGE, WILFRED F.
PERSONAL Born 11/21/1931, Caledonia, MN, m, 1963, 2 children **DISCIPLINE** RELIGION, CLASSICAL LANGUAGES **EDUCATION** Luther Col, BA, 53; Luther Theol Sem, BTh, 58; State Univ Iowa, MA, 55; Harvard Univ, ThD(New Testament), 66. **CAREER** Instr Relig & Classics, Luther Col, 56-57; instr Greek, Luther Theol Sem, 57-58; asst prof Relig, 62-69, assoc prof Relig, 69-74, registrar, 72-79, prof Relig, Luther Col, 74-, head dept, 79-87; Bk ed, Dialog, 66-70, asst prof, St John's Univ, Minn, 67-68; prof emer, Rel and Classics, 99-. **MEMBERSHIPS** Soc Bibl Lit; Am Asn Col Registr & Admin Off; corresp mem Inst Antiq & Christianity. **RESEARCH** Ecumenical Christian dialogue; Greco-Roman religions; Apuleius. **SELECTED PUBLICATIONS** Auth, Critical method and the New Testament, In: Theological Perspectives, Luther Col, 64; transl, God's righteousness in Paul, the Bultmann School of Biblical interpretation: New directions?, 65 & Paul and Nascent Catholicism, Distinctive Protestant and Catholic themes reconsidered, 67, J Theol & Church, Harper Torchbk; coauth (with John Bale), The word and words: Liberal education of the clergy, Dialog, Spring 80; Warmly Weston: A Luther College Life, Decorah: Luther College Press, 98. **CONTACT ADDRESS** Dept of Classics & Relig, Luther Col, 700 College Dr, Decorah, IA 52101-1045. **EMAIL** bungewil@luther.edu

BUNZL, MARTIN
DISCIPLINE PHILOSOPHY OF SCIENCE **EDUCATION** Univ Minn, BA, PhD. **CAREER** Instr, Rutgers, State Univ NJ, Livingston Col. **SELECTED PUBLICATIONS** Auth, The Context of Explanation, Kluwer, 93; Real History, Routledge, 97. **CONTACT ADDRESS** Dept of Philos, Rutgers, The State Univ of New Jersey, Livingston Col, 113 Davison Hall, Douglass, NJ 28342. **EMAIL** bunzl@rci.rutgers.edu

BURBANK, STEPHEN B.
PERSONAL Born 01/08/1947, New York, NY, m, 1970, 1 child **DISCIPLINE** LEGAL STUDIES **EDUCATION** Harvard, AB, 68; JD 73; Univ Pa, AM, 83. **CAREER** Law Clerk to the Chief Justice of the US, 74-75; Gen Coun, Univ of Pa, 75-80; from Asst to Assoc Prof, Univ of Pa, 79-91; Robert Fuller Prof, 91-95; David Berger Prof, Univ of Pa, 95-. **HONORS AND AWARDS** Summa Cum Laude, Harvard; Phi Beta Kappa; John Harvard Scholar; Sheldon Fel; Newhold Rhinelander Landon Fel; Fay Diploma, Univ of Pa Law Sch; Beale Prize, Harvard Law Rev; Mellon Fel, Aspen Inst, 78-79. **MEMBERSHIPS** Am Law Inst, Am Judicature Soc, Am Bar Asoc. **RESEARCH** Administration of Justice, Judicial Independence and Accountability, International Litigation. **SELECTED PUBLICATIONS** Coauth, Rule 11 in Transition: The Report of the Third Circuit Task Force on Federal Rule of Civil Procedure 11 (Am Judicature Soc), 89; auth, "The World in Our Courts," Mich Law Rev 1459 (91); coauth, Report to the National Commission on Judicial Discipline and Removal, 93; coauth, "Foreword: the Law of Federal Judicial Discipline and the Lessons of Social Science," 142 Univ Pa Law Rev 1 (93); auth, "The Reluctant Partner: Making Procedural Law for International Civil Litigation," 57 Law and Contemp Prob 101 (94); auth, "Procedure and Power," 46 J Legal Ed 513 (96); auth, "The Courtroom as Classroom: Independence, Imagination and Ideology in the Work of Jack Weinstein," 97 Columbia Law Rev 1971 (97); auth, "Implementing Procedural Change: Who, How, Why, and When?, " 49 Ala Law Rev 221 (97); coauth, "Civil Procedure Reform in Comparative Context: The United States of America," 45 Am J Comp Law 673 (97); auth, "The Architecture of Judicial Independence," 72 S Calif Law Rev 315 (99). **CONTACT ADDRESS** Sch of Law, Univ of Pennsylvania, 3400 Chestnut St, Philadelphia, PA 19104-6204. **EMAIL** sburbank@law.upenn.edu

BURBIDGE, JOHN WILLIAM
PERSONAL Born 02/29/1936, Hoiryung, Korea, m, 1958, 3 children **DISCIPLINE** PHILOSOPHY **EDUCATION** Univ Toronto, BA, 57, PhD(philos), 71; Yale Univ, MA, 58; Victoria Col, Ont, BD, 62. **CAREER** Lectr philos, Victoria Col, Ont, 58-59; minster in charge, Lakeview United Church, Port Credit, Ont, 63-68; from asst prof to assoc prof philos, 70-80, master, 77-82, Prof Philos, Champlain Col, Trent Univ, 80-. **HONORS AND AWARDS** Trentt Univ Distinguished Res Awd **MEMBERSHIPS** Can Philos Asn; Can Soc Study Relig; Hegel Soc Am; Metaphysical Soc Am; Soc Philos & Relig. **RESEARCH** Hegel and Schelling; logic of religious belief; logic and syntax. **SELECTED PUBLICATIONS** Auth, One in Hope and Doctrine, Ryerson, 68; Concept and time in Hegel, Dialogue, 73; Being and Will, Paulist Press, 77; contribr, The necessity of contingency, In: Art and Logic in Hegel's Philosophy, Humanities, 80; contribr, Peirce on Historical Explanation, In: Pragmatism and Purpose, Univ Toronto Press, 81; auth, On Hegel's Logic, Humanities, 81; Man, God and death in Hegel's Phenomenology, Philos & Phenomenol Res, 81; Religion in Callaghan,Morley 'Such is my Beloved'/, J Can Dtudies-Revue d Etudes Canadiennes, Vol 27, 1992; **CONTACT ADDRESS** Trent Univ, 310 London St., Peterborough, ON, Canada K9H 7P4. **EMAIL** philosophy@trentu.ca

BURCH, FRANCIS FLOYD
PERSONAL Born 05/15/1932, Baltimore, MD **DISCIPLINE** COMPARATIVE LITERATURE, THEOLOGY **EDUCATION** Fordham Univ, AB, 56, MA, 58; Woodstock Col, PhL, 57, STL, 64; Univ Paris, Dr, 67. **CAREER** Teacher English & French, Gonzaga High Sch, Washington, DC, 57-60; ordained priest, Roman Catholic, 63; from asst prof to assoc prof, 67-76, trustee, 71-76, asst acad dean, 72-74, prof English, St Joseph's Univ, PA, 76-, Scholar-in-residence English, Millersville State Col, 78. **HONORS AND AWARDS** Alpha Epsilon Delta; Alpha Sigma Nu; Merit Awds for teaching SJU, 80, 83. **MEMBERSHIPS** Int Soc Neoplatonic Studies; MLA. **RESEARCH** Ironic, Conversational poetry 1850 to the present, French and Anglo-American; the neoplatonic tradition in literature and religion; Tristan Corbiere. **SELECTED PUBLICATIONS** Auth, Corbiere and Verlaine's Romances sans paroles, Mod Lang Rev, 58; Clement Mansfield Ingleby on Poe's Raven, Am Lit, 63; Soirees bretonnes: The first published verse of Alexis and Edouard Corbiere, Romance Notes, 70; Tristan Corbiere: L'originalite des amours jaunes et leur influence sur T S Eliot, Nizet, Paris, 70; co-ed, Tristan Corbiere: Oeuvres completes, Gallimard, Paris, 70; auth, Sur Tristan Corbiere: Lettres inedites adressees au poete et premieres critiques le concernant, Nizet, Paris, 75; Introd & transl, The Path to Transcendence: From Philosophy to Mysticism in Saint Augustine, Pittsburgh Theol Monogr Series, No 37, 81; The Iconography of Tristan Corbiere, Studies in Comparative Literature, 91; A Letter from Laurence Housman concerning A E Housman's Poetry, Notes and Queries, 92; RH Benson, Dictionary of Literary Biography, 95; auth, "Charles Warren Currier," "Louis William Valentine DuBourg," "Joseph Hunter Guthrie," in Am Nat Biography, 99; auth, "Three Unpublished Letters of Robert Frost," Am Notes and Queries, 00. **CONTACT ADDRESS** Saint Joseph's Univ, 5600 City Ave, Philadelphia, PA 19131-1376. **EMAIL** fburch@sju.edu

BURCH, ROBERT W.
PERSONAL Born 03/31/1943, m, 1 child **DISCIPLINE** PHILOSOPHY **EDUCATION** Rice Univ, BA, 65, PhD, 69. **CAREER** Prof, Tex A&M Univ, 80-. **HONORS AND AWARDS** Phi Beta Kappa, 65; James A. and Alice G. Baker Scholar, 63-64; Thomas R. and Julia H. Franklin Scholar, 64-65; National Defense Educ Act Fel, 65-69; Tex A&M Univ Asn Former Students; Distinguished Tchg Awd, 83; Tex A&M Univ col Liberal Arts Fifth Annual Humanities Lectr, 89. **RESEARCH** Logic and the history of logic, American philosophy. **SELECTED PUBLICATIONS** Auth, Study Guide for Hurley/Logic, 5th ed, Belmont, Calif: Wadsworth Publ Co, 94. **CONTACT ADDRESS** Dept of Philosophy, Texas A&M Univ, Col Station, 314 Bolton Hall, College Station, TX 77843-4237.

BURCH, SHARON PEEBLES
PERSONAL Born Monterey, CA, m, 1983 **DISCIPLINE** SYSTEMATIC THEOLOGY; PHILOSOPHY OF RELIGION **EDUCATION** Grad Theolog Union, PhD, 92. **CAREER** Asst prof, Boston Univ, 93-98 **HONORS AND AWARDS** N Amer Paul Tillich Soc Pres, 96 **MEMBERSHIPS** Amer Acad Relig; N Amer Paul Tillich Soc; Assoc Practical Theolog; Assoc of Professors & Researchers in Relig Educ; United Meth Assoc of Christian Educators; Soc of Buddhist-Christian Studies. **RESEARCH** Practical Theology; Religious Education; Congregational Studies; Tillich Studies; Feminism; Postmodern Theology. **SELECTED PUBLICATIONS** Collective Absolute Presuppositions, Peter Lang, 99. **CONTACT ADDRESS** Dept of Theology, Boston Univ, 745 Commonwealth Ave, Boston, MA 02215. **EMAIL** spburch@bu.edu

BURGDORF, ROBERT L., JR.
DISCIPLINE CONSTITUTIONAL LAW, CIVIL PROCEDURE **EDUCATION** Univ Notre Dame, AB, 70, JD, 73. **CAREER** Prof; co-dir, Legis Clin; past mem, Proj Action, Accessible Commun Transp in Our Nation, Nat Coun Handicapped & Nat Ctr for Law and the Handicapped; co-dir, Univ MD Sch of Law's Develop Disabilities Law Proj, 76-81. **HONORS AND AWARDS** Securing equal rights for persons with disabilities, fed Am(s) with Disabilities Act of 91; completed a legal treatise on disability discrimination in employ law for the Bureau of Nat Aff. **SELECTED PUBLICATIONS** Pub, a casebk & articles and reports in his field. **CONTACT ADDRESS** School of Law, Univ of District of Columbia, 4200 Connecticut Ave Northwest, Washington, DC 20008.

BURGER, RONNA C.
DISCIPLINE PHILOSOPHY **EDUCATION** New Sch Soc Res, PhD, 73. **CAREER** Prof, Tulane Univ. **SELECTED PUBLICATIONS** Auth, The Phaedo, Yale; Plato's Phaedrus, Ala; pub(s) in, Rev Metaphysics; Interpretation; Essays in Ancient Greek Philos; auth, "Plato's Phaedo," Yale University Press, reprint with new foreword, St. Augustine's Press, 00. **CONTACT ADDRESS** Dept of Philosophy, Tulane Univ, New Orleans, LA 70118. **EMAIL** rburger@tulane.edu

BURGESS, ANDREW J.
PERSONAL Born 06/16/1936, m, 1994 **DISCIPLINE** RELIGIOUS STUDIES **EDUCATION** St Olaf Col, BA, 58; Yale Univ, PhD, 69; Univ Minn, MA, 94; Luther Theol Sem, MDiv, 95. **CAREER** Asst prof, religion, 69-76, Case Western Reserve Univ; vis assoc prof, religious stud, 76-78, Cleveland St Univ; assoc prof, philosophy, dir, religious studies prog, 78-, Univ of NMex. **MEMBERSHIPS** Amer Acad of Religion; Amer Phil Asn; Soren Kierkegaard Soc. **RESEARCH** Philosophy of religion; history of Christian thought; Kierkegaard. **SELECTED PUBLICATIONS** Auth, Passion Knowing How and Understanding An Essay on the Concept of Faith, Amer Acad of Rel Acad Series 9, Scholars Press, 75; art, Repetition A Story of Suffering, Repetition Intl Kierkegaard Comm Vol VI, 93; art, Forstand in the Swenson-Lowrie Correspondence and in the Metaphysical Caprice, Phil Fragments and Johannes Climacus, Intl Kierkegaard Comm Vol VII, Mercer Univ Press, 94; art, Kierkegaard on Homiletics and the Genre of the Sermon, Jour of Comm and Religion, 94; art, The Bilateral Symmetry of Kierkegaards Postscript, Concluding Unscientific Postscript, Intl Kierkegaard Comm Vol XII, Mercer Univ Press, 97; art, Kierkegaard and Kenneth Burke on the Rhetoric of the Comic, Kierkegaard and Ethics Kierkegaard on the Language of Existence, Nakanishiya, 98. **CONTACT ADDRESS** Religious Studies Prog, Univ of New Mexico, Albuquerque, 302 Hokona-Zuni, Albuquerque, NM 87131-1151. **EMAIL** aburgess@unm.edu

BURGESS, STANLEY M.
PERSONAL Born 11/27/1937, India, m, 1960, 5 children **DISCIPLINE** RELIGIOUS STUDIES **EDUCATION** Univ Michi, BA, 58, MA, 59; Univ Missouri, Columbia, PhD, 71. **CAREER** Tchr, hist, Emerson Jr High Sch, Flint, Mich, 57-58; fac memb, Evangel Univ, 59-76; prof, relig stud, Southwest Missouri State Univ, 76- . **HONORS AND AWARDS** Burlington Northern Found fac achievement award, 89; Christianity Today Critics Choice award, 90; Tantur Scholar, 86. **MEMBERSHIPS** Am Acad Relig. **RESEARCH** Historical pneumatology. **SELECTED PUBLICATIONS** Auth, The Spirit and the Church: Antiquity, Hendrickson, 84, rereleased as The Holy Spirit: Ancient Christian Traditions, 94; auth, Reaching Beyond: Chapters in the History of Perfectionism, Hendrickson, 86; ed, Dictionary of Pentecostal and Charismatic Movements, Zondervan, 88; auth, The Holy Spirit: Eastern Christian Traditions, Hendrickson, 89; auth, The Holy Spirit: Medieval Roman Catholic and Reformation Traditions, Hendrickson, 97; ed, New International Dictionary of Pentecostal and Charismatic Movements, Zondervan, 00. **CONTACT ADDRESS** Dept of Religious Studies, Southwest Missouri State Univ, Springfield, 901 S National, Springfield, MO 65804. **EMAIL** smb209f@mail.smsu.edu

BURGH, RICHARD
PERSONAL Born 03/07/1945, New York, NY, m, 1980, 1 child **DISCIPLINE** PHILOSOPHY **EDUCATION** Rider Univ, BA cum laude; Univ Wis MA, PhD. **CAREER** Dept ch; instr, Rider Univ, 75-; Westminister, 92-. **HONORS AND AWARDS** NEH fel. **RESEARCH** Medical ethics. **SELECTED PUBLICATIONS** Extensive publ(s) on the moral foundation of the law. **CONTACT ADDRESS** Westminster Choir Col, Rider Univ, 101 Walnut, Princeton, NJ 08540. **EMAIL** burgh@rider.edu

BURIAN, RICHARD M.
PERSONAL Born 09/14/1941, Hanover, NH, m, 1987, 3 children **DISCIPLINE** PHILOSOPHY **EDUCATION** Reed Col, BA, 63; Univ Pittsburgh, PhD, 71. **CAREER** Instr, asst prof, lectr, Brandeis Univ, 67-76; vis asst prof of philos, Fla A&M Univ, 68-69; assoc dean of col, Brandeis Univ, 73-76; assoc prof, Drexel Univ, 77-83; res assoc, Mus of Camparative Zoology, Harvard Univ, 76-77; vis assoc prof, Dept Hist and Philos of Sci, Univ Pittsburgh, 78-79; vis assoc prof, Dept of Philos and Hist, Div of Biol Sci, Univ Calif, 81-82; prof philos, Va Polytechnic Inst and State Univ 83-92; adjunct prof, Ctr for the Study of Sci in Society, Va Polytechnic Inst and State Univ, 83-92; head, Dept of Philos, Va Polytechnic Inst and State Univ, 83-92; resident fel, Nat Humanities Ctr, Research Triangle Park, 91-92; vis prof, Univ de Bourgogne, 92; dir, Ctr for the Study of Sci in Society, and the Grad Prog in Sci and Tech Studies, Va Polytechnic Inst and State Univ, 92-97; prof sci studies and philos, Va Polytechnic Inst and State Univ, 92-present. **HONORS AND AWARDS** Res grant, Nat Endowment for the Humanities for work on a Conceptual History of the Gene; Nat Sci Foun Conf Grant, Santa Fe Inst; resident fel, Nat Humanities Ctr; pres, Int Soc for Hist, Philos, and Soc Studies of Biology; resident fel, Ctr. For History of Recent Science, George Washington Univerisity, 99-00. **MEMBERSHIPS** Soc for Integrative and Comparative Biology; Am Asn for the Advan of Sci; Int Soc for Hist, Philos, and Soc Studies of Biology; Am Philos Asn; British Soc for the Hist of Sci; British Soc for the Philos of Sci; Federation of Am Scientists; Genetics Soc of Am; Hist of Sci Soc; Philos of Sci Asn; Sigma Xi, Soc de d'Histoire et d'Epistemologie des Sciences de la Vie; Soc for the Study of Evolution; Soc for Social Studies of Sci; Soc of Systematic Biology; Union of Concerned Scientists. **RESEARCH** Philosophy of biology; philosophy of science; history of 19th and 20th century biology. **SELECTED PUBLICATIONS** Co-ed, Integration in Biology, in Biology and Philosophy, 8(3), 93; co-ed, The Right Organism for the Job, in Jour of the Hist of Biology, 26(2), 93; co-ed, PSA 1994, vol. 1, Philos of Sci Asn, 94; auth, Jean Brachet's Cytochemical Embryology: Connections with the Renovation of Biology in France?, in Les sciences biologiques et medicales en France 1920-1950, vol. 2, CNRS Editions, 94; auth, Dobzhansky on Evoluionary Dynamics, in The Evolution of Theodosius Dobzhansky, Princeton Univ Press, 94; auth, Comments on Hans-Jorg Rheinberger's 'From Experimental Systems to Cultures of Experimentation', in Concepts, Theories, and Rationality in the Biological Sciences: The Second Pittsburgh-Konstanz Colloquium in the Philosophy of Science, Univ Konstanz and Univ Pittsburgh Press, 95; co-ed, PSA 1994, vol. 2, Philos of Sci Asn, 95; auth, Some Epistemological Reflections on Polistes as a Model Organism, in Natural History and Evolution of an Animal Society: The Paper Wasp Case, Oxford Univ Press, 96; auth, Underappreciated Pathways Toward Molecular Genetics as illustrated by Jean Brachet's Chemical Embryology, in The Philosophy and History of Molecular Biology: New Perspectives, Dordrecht: Kluwer, 96; auth, On Conflicts Between Genetic and Developmental Viewpoints - and their Resolution in Molecular Biology, in Structure and Norms in Science, vol. 2 of the 10th Int Congress of Logic, Methodology, and Philosophy of Science, Dordrecht: Kluwer, 95; co-ed, Research Programs of the Rouge Cloitre, in History and Philosophy of the Life Sciences, 19(1), 97. **CONTACT ADDRESS** Dept of Philosophy, Virginia Polytech Inst and State Univ, 2001 Meeting at Quinnipiac University, Blacksburg, VA 24061-0126. **EMAIL** rmburian@vt.edu

BURKE, ALBIE
PERSONAL Born 03/21/1932, Rugby, ND, d, 1960, 2 children **DISCIPLINE** AMERICAN CONSTITUTIONAL & LEGAL HISTORY **EDUCATION** Univ Chicago, BA, 58, MA, 65, PhD, 68. **CAREER** Assoc prof, 72-77, prof hist, Calif State Univ, Long Beach, 77-. **MEMBERSHIPS** Am Civil Liberties Union; Orgn Am Historians; Am Soc Legal Hist. **SELECTED PUBLICATIONS** Auth, Federal regulation of congressional elections in Northern cities 1871-94, Am J Legal Hist, 1/70; ed, The Hist Teacher, 79-85. **CONTACT ADDRESS** Dept Hist, California State Univ, Long Beach, 1250 N Bellflower, Long Beach, CA 90840-0001. **EMAIL** aburke@csucb.edu

BURKE, JOHN
PERSONAL Born 09/15/1928, Washington, DC, s **DISCIPLINE** RELIGIOUS STUDIES **EDUCATION** Dominican House Studies, Licentiate in Sacred Theol, 60; Cath Univ Am, Wash, DC, MA, 65, STD, 69. **CAREER** Prof, St Stephen's Col, Dover, Mass, 61-64; prof, Col of the Immaculate Conception, Washington, DC, 64-68; asst prof, Cath Univ of Am, 64-69; prof, Washington Theol Coalition, 68-70; adjunct prof, Chicago Theol Union, 84; adjunct prof, Va Theol Sem, Alexandria, 79-; adjunct prof, North Am Col, Rome, 91-97; prof, Dominican House of Studies, Washington, DC, 90-. **RESEARCH** Homiletics. **SELECTED PUBLICATIONS** Auth, "Dominicans (Order of Friars Preachers)," in Concise Encyclopedia of Preaching, Willimon, William H. and Richard Lischer, eds, Louisville: Westminster John Knox Press (95): 105-106; auth, Companion to the Prayer of Christians: Reflections and Personal Prayers, Collegeville: The Liturgical Press (95); auth, "The Basics of Prophetic Preaching: What this trendy term really means," Today's Parish, Mystic: Twenty-Third Pubs (April-May 95): 26-28; auth, "Preaching to Secular Humanists at Sunday Mass," Homiletic and Pastoral Rev; auth, "The History of Preaching," in Encyclopedia of Cath Doctrine (96); auth, "The Gift of the Priestly Homilist," Homiletic and Pastoral Rev (Nov 99): 12-20; **CONTACT ADDRESS** Dept Pastoral Ministry, Dominican House of Studies, 487 Michigan Ave NE, Washington, DC 20017-1584. **EMAIL** BURKEOP@aol.com

BURKE, MICHAEL B.
PERSONAL Born 02/16/1943, Quincy, MA, m **DISCIPLINE** PHILOSOPHY **EDUCATION** Univ Va, BA, 64; Univ Wis-Madison, PhD, 76. **CAREER** Asst prof, Bosphorus Univ, Istanbul, 76-79; Prof, Ind Univ, 80- . **HONORS AND AWARDS** Outstanding Mem Sch Liberal Arts, Ind Univ-Indpls, 97; IU Tchg Excellence Awd, 97. **MEMBERSHIPS** Am Philos Asn; Philos Time Soc; Asn for Informal Logic and Critical Thinking. **RESEARCH** Metaphysics; Informal Logic. **SELECTED PUBLICATIONS** Auth, Cohabitation, Stuff, and Intermittent Existence, Mind, vol 355, no 355, July 80, 391-405; The Infinitistic Thesis, The S Jour Philos, vol 22, no 3, Fall 84, 295-305; Hume and Edwards on Why is There Something Rather Than Nothing?, The Australasian Jour Philos, vol 62, no 4, Dec 84, 355-362; Spatial Analogues of 'Annihilation and Re-creation, Analysis, vol 45, no 1, Jan 85, 24-29; Unstated Premises, Informal Logic, vol 7, no 2-3, Spring and Fall 85, 107-118; Copper Statues and Pieces of Copper: A Challenge to the Standard Account, Analysis, vol 52, no 1, Jan 92, 12-17; Dion and theon: An Essentialist Solution to an Ancient Puzzle, the Jour Philos, vol 91, no 3, March 94, 129-139; Preserving the Principle of One Object to a Place: A Novel Account of the Relations Among Objects, Sorts, Sortals, and Persistence Conditions, Philos and Phenomenological Res, vol 54, no 3, Sept 94, 591-624; Denying the Antecedent: A Common Fallacy? Informal Logic, vol 16, no1, Winter 94, 23-30; Sortal Essentialism and the Potentiality Principle, Rev of Metaphysics, vol 49, no 3, March 96, 491-514; Tibbles the Cat: a Modern Sophisma, Philos Stud (s), vol 84, no 1, Oct 96, 63-74; Coinciding Objects: Reply to Lowe and Denkel, Analysis, vol 57, no 1, Jan 97, 11-18; Preserving the Principle of One Object to a Place: A Novel Account of the Relations Among Objects, Sorts, Sortals, and Persistence Conditions, reprinted in Material Constitution: A Reader, Lanham, MD, Rowman, 97, 236-269; Persons and Bodies: How to Avoid the New Dualism, Amer Philos Quart, vol 34, no 4, Oct 97, 457-467; auth, "On the Impossibiliby of Superfeats," The Southern Journal of Philosophy, vol. 38, no. 2, (00): 207-220. **CONTACT ADDRESS** Dept of Philosophy, Indiana Univ-Purdue Univ, Indianapolis, 425 University Blvd, Indianapolis, IN 46202. **EMAIL** mburke@iupui.edu

BURKE, RONALD R.
PERSONAL Born Harlan, IA, m, 1971, 2 children **DISCIPLINE** RELIGIOUS STUDIES **EDUCATION** Univ Notre Dame, BA, 66, MA, 68; Yale Univ, MPhil, 70, PhD, 74. **CAREER** Instr, Univ Nebr, Omaha, 71-; coed, J of Relig and Film. **HONORS AND AWARDS** NEH grant, Univ Calif, Santa Barbara, 78-79; NEH grant, Univ Calif, Berkeley, 92; founder, roman cath modernism gp, am acad of relig, 76. **MEMBERSHIPS** Bd dir, Roman Cath Modernism Gp, Am Acad of Relig. **SELECTED PUBLICATIONS** Ed, John Henry Newman: Theology and Reform, Garland, 92; conribur, Personality and Belief, Lanham, 94. **CONTACT ADDRESS** Univ of Nebraska, Omaha, Omaha, NE 68182.

BURKE, WILLIAM THOMAS
PERSONAL Born 08/17/1926, Brazil, IN, m, 1959, 3 children **DISCIPLINE** LAW **EDUCATION** Ind State Teachers Col, BS, 49; Ind Univ, JD, 53; Yale Univ, JSD, 59. **CAREER** Res assoc & lectr law, law sch, Yale Univ, 56-62; prof, Ohio State Univ, 62-68; fac chmn, Inst Marine Studies, 73, Prof Law, Univ Wash, 68-99, Prof Marine Studies, 76-; Prof Law Emer, 99-. **MEMBERSHIPS** Marine Technol Soc. **RESEARCH** International law of the sea; fisheries law; international regulation of whaling. **SELECTED PUBLICATIONS** Coauth, The Public Order of the Oceans, Yale Univ, 62; auth, Ocean sciences technology and the future international law of the sea, Mershon Ctr Pamphlet, Ohio State Univ, 66; Contemporary legal problems in ocean development, In: Toward a Better Use of the Ocean, SIPRI, Stockholm, Sweden, 69; Straight Base-lines in International Maritime Boundary Delimitation - Reisman,MW, Westerman,GS/, Ocean Development and Int Law, Vol 25, 1994; United-Nations Resolutions on Driftnet Fishing - An Unsustainable Precedent for High Seas and Coastal Fisheries Management/, Ocean Development and Int Law, Vol 25, 94; Implications for Fisheries Management of US Acceptance of the 1982 Convention on the Law of the Sea/, Am J Int Law, Vol 89, 1995; Importance of the 1982 UN Convention on the Law of the Sea and its Future-Development/, Ocean Development and International Law, Vol 27, 1996; Memorandum of Opinion on the Legality of the Designation of the Southern-Ocean Sanctuary by the IWC/, Ocean Development and Int Law, Vol 27, 1996; Legal-Aspects of the IWC Decision on the Southern-Ocean Sanctuary/, Ocean Development and Int Law, Vol 28, 1997; The International Regime of Fisheries - From UNCLOS 1982 to the Presential Sea - Deyturriaga,JA/, Am J Int Law, Vol 91, 1997; auth, The New International Law of Fisheries, Oxford, 94; auth, International Law of the Sea--Documents & Notes, Lupus, 99. **CONTACT ADDRESS** Sch of Law, Univ of Washington, Seattle, WA 98105. **EMAIL** burke@u.washington.edu

BURKETT, DELBERT ROYCE
PERSONAL Born 08/22/1949, Lamesa, TX, s **DISCIPLINE** NEW TESTAMENT; CHRISTIAN ORIGINS **EDUCATION** Abilene Christian Col, BA, 71; Harvard Divinity School, MA, 73; Duke Univ, Phd, 89. **CAREER** Vis asst prof, W Ky Univ, 89-90; vis asst prof, Appalachian St Univ, 90-93; asst prof, Lebanon Valley Col, 93-96; asst prof, La St Univ, 96-. **MEMBERSHIPS** Soc Bibl Lit. **RESEARCH** The canonical gospels and apocalyptic thought. **SELECTED PUBLICATIONS** Auth, "Four Sahidic Songs to St. John the Evangelist," Coptic Church Review 9, (88): 83-86; auth, The Son of the Man in the Gospel of John, Sheffield Academic Press, 91; auth, "The Nontitular Son of Man: A History and Critique," New Testament Studies 40, (94): 504-21; auth, "Two Accounts of Lazarus' Resurrection in John 11." Novum Testamentum 36, (94): 209-32; auth, The Son of Man Debate: A History and Evaluation, New Testament Studies Monograph Series, Cambridge Univ Press, 99. **CONTACT ADDRESS** Dept of Philosophy and Relig Stud, Louisiana State Univ, Baton Rouge, LA 70803-3901. **EMAIL** dburket@lsu.edu

BURKETT, RANDALL KEITH
PERSONAL Born 10/23/1943, Union City, IN, m, 1965 **DISCIPLINE** RELIGION, HISTORY **EDUCATION** Am Univ, AB, 65; Harvard Divinity Sch, MTS, 69; Univ Southern Calif, PhD(social ethics), 75. **CAREER** Admin asst curric develop, Univ Southern Calif, 72-73; assoc dir spec studies, 73-77, assoc coordr grants & res, 76-79, Dir Spec Studies, Col of Holy Cross, 77-, Coordr Grants & Res, 79-, Lectr, Ctr Exp Studies; ed, Afro-Am Relig Hist Group Newsletter, Am Acad of Relig, 76-; Nat Endowment for the Humanities fel, 79-80. **MEMBERSHIPS** Am Acad Relig; Am Soc Church Hist; Asn for Study Afro-Am Life & Hist. **RESEARCH** Afro-American religious history.

SELECTED PUBLICATIONS Auth, Black Redemption: Churchmen Speak for the Garvey Movement, Temple Univ, 78; co-ed, Black Apostles: Afro-American Clergy Confront the Twentieth Century, G K Hall, 78; auth, Garveyism as a Religious Movement: The Institutionalization of a Black Civil Religion, Scarecrow, 78. **CONTACT ADDRESS** Off of Spec Studies, Col of the Holy Cross, Worcester, MA 01610.

BURKEY, JOHN
PERSONAL Born 07/02/1953, Reading, PA, m, 1982, 2 children **DISCIPLINE** PHILOSOPHY **EDUCATION** Villanova, MA, 78; Duquesne, PhD, 85. **CAREER** Assoc Prof, Siena Col, 85-. **RESEARCH** Phenomenology; history of philosophy **CONTACT ADDRESS** Dept of Philosophy, Siena Col, Louisville, NY 12211. **EMAIL** burkey@siena.edu

BURKHARDT, FREDERICK
PERSONAL Born 09/13/1912, New York, NY, m, 1973, 3 children **DISCIPLINE** PHILOSOPHY **EDUCATION** Columbia Univ, PhD, 40. **CAREER** Instr to assoc prof, 36-47, pres, 47-57, Bennington Col; pres, Am Coun of Learned Soc, 57-74; ed, The Works of William James, 75- ; ed, The Correspondence of Charles Darwin, 74- . **HONORS AND AWARDS** LLD, Columbia Univ and Univ Michigan. **MEMBERSHIPS** Phi Beta Kappa; HSS; AAAS; APA; APS; Am Antiq Soc; Mass Hist Soc. **RESEARCH** History and philosophy of science. **SELECTED PUBLICATIONS** Ed, The Works of William James, 18 v, Harvard, 75-88; ed, The Correspondence of Charles Darwin, 11 v, Cambridge Univ, 85-99; ed, The Letters of Charles Darwin: A Selection, Cambridge Univ, 96. **CONTACT ADDRESS** PO Box 1037, Bennington, VT 05201. **EMAIL** fhb@gover.net

BURKHART, JOHN E.
PERSONAL Born 10/25/1927, Riverside, CA, m, 1951, 3 children **DISCIPLINE** THEOLOGY **EDUCATION** Occidental Col, BA, 49; Union Theol Sem, NYork, BD, 52; Univ Southern Calif, PhD(relig), 59. **CAREER** From instr to assoc prof, 59-68, prof syst theol, 68-81, Prof Theol, McCormick Theol Sem, 81-, Roblee lectr, Stephens Col, 63; vis prof theol, Garrett Theol Sem, 66 & DePaul Univ, 70; consult, US Cath Conf, 70; mem coun theol sems, United Presby Church, 73-79. **HONORS AND AWARDS** DD, Occidental Col, 64. **MEMBERSHIPS** Am Theol Soc (pres, 69-70); Am Acad Relig; Cath Theol Soc Am; Soc Values Higher Educ; Royal Anthrop Inst. **RESEARCH** Ecclesiology; liturgies; social anthropology. **SELECTED PUBLICATIONS** **CONTACT ADDRESS** Dept of Theol, McCormick Theol Sem, 5555 S Woodlawn Ave, Chicago, IL 60637.

BURKLE, HOWARD R.
PERSONAL Born 07/15/1925, Monticello, AR, m, 1948, 3 children **DISCIPLINE** PHILOSOPHY, RELIGION **EDUCATION** Cent Mo State Col, AB, 45; Yale Univ, BD, 48, STM, 49, PhD(philos theol), 54. **CAREER** Asst prof relig, Colo Col, 51-54, philos, Dickinson Col, 54-58; assoc prof philos & relig, 58-66, prof philos, 66-68 Prof Philos & Relig Studies & Chmn Dept Relig Studies, Grinnell Col, 68-, Vis prof Christian ethics, Int Christian Univ, Tokyo, 61-62. **MEMBERSHIPS** Soc Phenomenol & Existential Philos; Am Acad Relig; Japanese Asn Studies Am Philos. **RESEARCH** Contemporary Philosophy of religion; social philosophy of Jean Paul Sartre. **SELECTED PUBLICATIONS** **CONTACT ADDRESS** Dept of Relig, Grinnell Col, PO Box 805, Grinnell, IA 50112. **EMAIL** burkle@ac.grin.edu

BURKS, ARTHUR WALTER
PERSONAL Born 10/13/1915, Duluth, MN, m, 1943, 3 children **DISCIPLINE** PHILOSOPHY **EDUCATION** DePauw Univ, BA, 36; Univ Mich, MA, 37, PhD(philos), 41. **CAREER** Teacher, high sch, Mich, 37-38; instr electrical engineering, Univ Pa, 41-46; from asst prof to assoc prof philos, 46-54, chmn dept computer & commun sci, 67-71, Prof Philos, Univ Mich, Ann Arbor, 54-, Prof Computer & Commun Sci, 67-, Dir Logic of Computers Group, 56-, Instr, Swarthmore Col, 45-46; consult MANIAC, Inst Advan Studies, Princeton, 46-48; digital computers, Burroughs Corp, 48-54; res assoc philos, Univ Chicago, 50-51; consult ORACLE, Argonne Nat Lab, 50-51; Guggenheim Mem fel, 53-54; res assoc philos, Harvard, 55; mem ed bd, Philos Sci, 55-; res prof applied mathematics, Univ Ill, Urbana, fall 60; mem comt to advise dir res, Atomic Energy Comn Digital Computers, 60-62; Am Coun Learned Soc fel, 62-63; vis prof, Indian Inst Technol, Kanpur, 65-66; consult ed, Synthese, an Int J Epistemology, Methodology & Philos Sci, 66-; fel, Ctr Advan Studies Behav Sci, Stanford Univ, 71-72. **HONORS AND AWARDS** ScD, DePauw Univ, 73. **MEMBERSHIPS** Am Philos Asn; Asn Computing Machinery; Mind Asn; Charles S Peirce Soc (pres, 54-55); Philos Sci Asn. **RESEARCH** Philosophy of science; inductive logic; computer organization. **SELECTED PUBLICATIONS** Logic, Computers and Men, Proceedings & Addresses Am Philos Asn, 72-73; Chance, Cause, Reason--An Inquiry into the Nature of Scientific Evidence, Univ Chicago Press, 77; Peirces Evolutionary Pragmatic Idealism/, Synthese, Vol 106, 1996; Who Invented the Computer - A Memoir of the 1940s/, Mich Quart Rev, Vol 36, 1997. **CONTACT ADDRESS** 3445 Vintage Valley, Ann Arbor, MI 48105.

BURNEKO, GUY
DISCIPLINE LITERATURE, PHILOSOPHY OF SCIENCE, EVOLUTION OF CONSCIOUSNESS **EDUCATION** Fordham Univ, BA; Univ AK, MA; Emory Univ, PhD. **CAREER** Assoc prof, dir, Grad Liberal Stud, Golden Gate Univ. **HONORS AND AWARDS** NEH fel, Claremont Grad Sch & Stanford Univ. **MEMBERSHIPS** Acad of Consciousness Stud, Princeton Univ. **SELECTED PUBLICATIONS** Auth of articles on intercultural and philosophical interpretation, philosophical hermeneutics, interdisciplinary and transdisciplinary educ, intuition and cult develop, and other topics. **CONTACT ADDRESS** Golden Gate Univ, San Francisco, CA 94105-2968.

BURNETT, DONALD L.
PERSONAL Born 10/01/1946, Pocatello, ID, m, 1969, 2 children **DISCIPLINE** LAW, ECONOMICS **EDUCATION** Harvard Col, AB 68; Univ Chicago, JD, 71; Univ Va, LLM, 90. **CAREER** Law clerk to Chief Justice, Idaho Supreme Court, 71-72; asst atty general, State of Idaho, 72-74; private practice, 75-81; judge, Idaho Court of Appeals, 82-90; dean, Louis D. Brandeis School of Law, Univ of Louisville, 90-00; Prof, 00-. **HONORS AND AWARDS** Pres, Idaho State Bar , 81. **MEMBERSHIPS** Idaho State Bar; Louisville Bar Assn; Am Bar Assn; Kentucky Ctr for Public Issues; Judge Advocate General's Corps, U.S. Army Reserve. **RESEARCH** Judiciary and judicial administration; law and economic theory; legal ethics and professionalism; environmental law and policy. **SELECTED PUBLICATIONS** Auth, "Subject of Native American Law", in Harvard Journal on Legislation, 72; auth, "Subject of Water Law", in Idaho Law Review, 85; auth and ed, Idaho Appellate Handbook, 86, 90; auth, Remand, Am Bar Assn, 86-90; auth, "Subject of Legal Education", in Kentucky Bench & Bar, 96. **CONTACT ADDRESS** Louis D. Brandeis School of Law, Univ of Louisville, Louisville, KY 40292. **EMAIL** don.burnett@louisville.edu

BURNETT, FREDRICK WAYNE
PERSONAL Born 12/18/1944, Birmingham, AL, m, 1995, 2 children **DISCIPLINE** RELIGION **EDUCATION** Anderson Col, Ind, BA, 67, Anderson Theol Sem, MDiv, 70; Vanderbilt Divinity Sch, DMin, 73, Vanderbilt Univ, MA, 76, PhD, 79. **CAREER** From assoc prof to Prof Relig Studies, Anderson Univ, IN, 76. **MEMBERSHIPS** Soc Bibl Lit; Cath Bibl Asn Am; Am Acad Relig. **RESEARCH** The Gospel of Matthew and its community setting; lit criticism and New Testament studies; soc sci methodologies and New Testament studies. **SELECTED PUBLICATIONS** Auth, The Testament of Jesus-Sophia: A Redaction-Critical Study of the Eschatological Discourse in Matthew, Univ Press Am, 81; co-auth, The Postmodern Bible, Yale Univ Press, 95. **CONTACT ADDRESS** Anderson Univ, 1100 E 5th St, Anderson, IN 46012-3495. **EMAIL** fburnett@kirk.anderson.edu

BURNETT, STEPHEN G.
PERSONAL Born 10/06/1956, Madison, WI, m, 1981, 3 children **DISCIPLINE** HISTORY, RELIGIOUS STUDIES **EDUCATION** Univ Wis-Madison, BA, 78; MA, 83; PhD, 90. **CAREER** Vis prof, hist & Judaic studies, 93-96, lectr, hist, classics and Judaic studies, Univ Neb Lincoln, 96-; Asst Prof of Classics/Religious Studies and History, 00-. **HONORS AND AWARDS** Friends of the Univ Wisc libr grant-in-aid, 98; res grant, Amer Philos Soc, 95, Frank S. Elizabeth D. Brewer prize, Amer Soc of Church Hist, 94; Fellow, Center for Advance Judaic Studies, Univ of Pennsylvania, 99; ACLS Research Fellowhip, 99-00. **MEMBERSHIPS** Asn of Jewish Studies; Asn of Jewish Libr; Sixteenth Century Studies Conf. **RESEARCH** Christian Hebrew scholarship; Christian-Jewish relations in early modern Europe. **SELECTED PUBLICATIONS** Auth, From Christian Hebraism to Jewish Studies: Johannes Buxtorf (1564-1629) and Hebrew Learning in the Seventeenth-Century, Studies in the History of Christian Thought, vol 68, Leiden, E. J. Brill, 96; article, From Israel to Germany: A Conference Report, Judaic Studies Newsletter, Univ Neb Lincoln, 97-98; article, The Regulation of Hebrew Printing in Germany, 1555-1630: Confessional Politics and the Limits of Jewish Toleration, 329-348, Infinite Boundaries: Order, Disorder, and Reorder in Early Modern German Culture, Sixteenth Century Jour Publ, 98; article, Jews and Anti-Semitism in Early Modern Germany: A Review Article, Sixteenth Century Jour, 27/4, 1057-1064, 96; article, Hebrew Censorship in Hanau: A Mirror of Jewish-Christian Coextistence in Seventeenth Century Germany, 199-222, The Expulsion of the Jews: 1492 and After, Garland Studies in the Renaissance, vol 2, 94; article, Buxtorf Family Papers, 71-88, Die Handschriften der Universitat Basel: Die hebraische Handschriften, Verlag der Universitatsbibliothek, 94; auth, Christian Hebrew Printing in the Sixteen Century: Printers, humanism and the impact of the Reformation, Helmantica, (00): 13-42. **CONTACT ADDRESS** Dept of Hist, Univ of Nebraska, Lincoln, 612 Old Father Hall, Lincoln, NE 68588-0327. **EMAIL** sburnett1@unl.edu

BURNOR, RICHARD N.
PERSONAL Born 08/26/1952, Cleveland, OH, m, 1979, 4 children **DISCIPLINE** PHILOSOPHY **EDUCATION** Bucknell Univ, BS, 74; MA, 78, PhD, 85, Univ Arizona. **CAREER** Lectr, Univ Arizona, 83-84; Supply Lectr, 84-85, Asst Visiting Prof, 85-86, Univ Wyoming; Asst Prof, Towson State Univ, 86-93; Visiting Asst Prof, 93-96, Univ Toledo; Part time Instr, 96, Washtenaw Comm Col; Visiting Scholar, 96, Part time Instr, 97, Univ Toledo; Asst Prof, 97-, Felician Col. **HONORS AND AWARDS** Riesen Prize for Best Philosophy Paper, Univ Arizona, 83; Teaching Fel, Univ Wyoming Summer High School Inst, 86; Fel NEH Summer Seminar for College Teachers, 91; Felician Col Summer Research Stipend, 98. **MEMBERSHIPS** Amer Phil Assoc; Philosophy of Time Soc; The Soc of Christian Philosophers **RESEARCH** Philosophical interpretations of probability; theory acceptance; philosophy of time; philosophy of technology; new technologies in teaching **SELECTED PUBLICATIONS** Auth, "What's the Matter with 'The Matter of Chance?'," Philosophical Studies, 84; auth, Rethinking Objective Homogeneity: Statistical Versus Ontic Approaches, Philosophical Studies, 93; Review of Le Poidevin and MacBeath, Philosophy of Time, 93, Teaching Philosophy, 94; A Structural Model for Temporal Passage, The Southern Journal of Philosophy, 94; Outlines for Success: Outline Processors and Teaching Philosophy, Teaching Philosophy, 95; auth, "Modal Models of Time," The Southern Journal of Philos. **CONTACT ADDRESS** Dept of Philosophy, Felician Col, 262 S Main St, Lodi, NJ 07644. **EMAIL** RNVBURNOR@AOL.COM

BURNS, J. LANIER
PERSONAL m, 4 children **DISCIPLINE** THEOLOGY **EDUCATION** Davidson Col, AB, 65; Dallas Theolog Sem, ThM, 72, ThD, 79; Univ Tex, Dallas, PhD, 93. **CAREER** Pres, Am Council Asian Christian Acad, Evangelical Theolog Sem, 73-; Comt on Academic Excellence, Highland Park Independent School District, 89-90; Bd Adv, The Providence Sch, 91-; consult, The Damares Project, 98-; Bd Dir, K-Life Ministries, 91-98; Bd Dir, Pine Cove Ministries, 93-96; ed consult, Zondervan Publ House, 88-; relig consult, The Los Angeles Times, 98. **HONORS AND AWARDS** Who's Who in Am, 85, Who's Who in Religion, 85; Who's Who in Leadership Society, 86; Who's Who in Science and Theol, 95; Who's Who among Am tchrs: The Best Tchrs in Am Selected by the Best Stud, 96; Sr Class Award for Fac Excellence, 99. **MEMBERSHIPS** Am Acad Rel; Am Philolog Asn, Evangelical Theolog Society; Renaissance Society Am; Society Biblical Lit; Society Christian Philos; Dist Leadership Society. **SELECTED PUBLICATIONS** Auth, "Hermeneutical Issues and Principles in Hebrews as Exemplified in the Second Chapter," Chicago, Ilinois, 94; published in JETS, 95; auth, "Peace As a Possible Bridge between New-Age Hope and Biblical Promises," Philadelphia, Penn, 95; auth, "The Personality of the Holy Spirit: Biblical and Contemporary," (Jackson, MS), 96; auth, "What's Being Discussed and Who's Discussing It," Faculty Workshop, 97; auth, "Cultural Lies the Church Believes: Our Vlaue Is Vested in the Role We Play," Moody Monthly, 97; auth, The Jiles Brooks Memorial Lectures, Calvary Baptist Churh, New York City, 97; auth, "Not Far from Each of Us," (Santa Clara, CA), 97; auth, "Report on Columbia International University's and Columbia Biblical Seminary's Educational Standing," for SACS, 97; auth, "Clio: Msue of the Past with Clues for Our Present," 98; auth, "Romans 9-11: A Theological Blueprint," with Response" to Dr. Stanley Toussaint, in Three Issues that Concern Dispensationalists, ed. Herb Bateman, (Kregel, 99). **CONTACT ADDRESS** Dept of Theology, Dallas Theol Sem, 3909 Swiss Ave, Dallas, TX 75204-6411.

BURNS, J. PATOUT, JR.
PERSONAL Born 10/14/1939, New Orleans, LA, d **DISCIPLINE** THEOLOGY **EDUCATION** Spring Hill Col, BA, 63, MA, 64; Regis Col Toronto, MDiv, 70; Univ of St Michael's Col Toronto, ThM, 71; Yale Univ, PhD, 74. **CAREER** Jesuit Sch of Theol, asst prof, assoc prof, 74-80; Loyola Univ of Chicago, 80-86; Univ of Fla, prof, 86-90; Washington Univ St Louis, prof, 90-99; Vanderbilt Div Sch, 99-. **MEMBERSHIPS** AAR, NAPS. **RESEARCH** Christianity in Roman Africa. **SELECTED PUBLICATIONS** Auth, The Development of Augustine's Doctrine of Operative Grace, Paris: Etudes Augustiennes, 80; auth, War and its Discontents: Pacifism and Quietism in the Abrahamic Traditions, contrib ed., Washington: Georgetown Univ Pr, 96; auth, The Ethics of Warfare: Muslim, Jewish and Christian Religious Traditions: Conference Report, Jour Relig Pluralism, 93; auth, The Atmosphere of Election: Augustinianism as Common Sense, Jour Early Christian Studies, 93; auth, Delighting the Spirit: Augustine's Practice of Figurative Interpretation, De doctoria christiana: A Classic of Western Culture, ed. D. W. H. Arnold and P. Bright, Notre Dame: Univ Notre Dame Press, 95; auth, The Holiness of the Churches, The Unbounded Community, ed. W. Caferro and D. Fisher, NY: Garland Pub, 96. **CONTACT ADDRESS** Divinity School, Vanderbilt Univ, Nashville, TN 37240. **EMAIL** patout.burns@vanderbilt.edu

BURNS, STEVEN A. M.
DISCIPLINE PHILOSOPHY **EDUCATION** Acadia Univ, BA, 62; Alberta Univ, MA, 66; Univ London, PhD, 70. **CAREER** Prof. **RESEARCH** Wittgenstein, Plato, aesthetics, political philosophy. **SELECTED PUBLICATIONS** Auth, "Reason, Love and Laughter," Dialogue, 89; The Place of Art in a Reasonable Education, Reason in Tchg and Edu, 89; "Otto Weininger's Metaphysics," Jour Philos Res, 90; "If a Lion Could Talk," Wittgenstein Stud, 94; "Ethics and Socialism: Tensions in the Political Philosophy of J. G. Schurman," Jour Can Stud, 96. **CONTACT ADDRESS** Dept of Philos, Dalhou-

sie Univ, Halifax, NS, Canada B3H 3J5. **EMAIL** steven.burns@dal.ca

BURR, JOHN ROY
PERSONAL Born 07/18/1933, Oshkosh, WI, m, 1963, 3 children **DISCIPLINE** PHILOSOPHY **EDUCATION** Univ Wis, Madison, BA, 55; Columbia Univ, MA, 56, Phd, 59. **CAREER** Instr philos, Franklin & Marshall Col, 59-61; asst prof, Hood Col, 61-64; from asst prof to assoc prof, 64-68, chemn dept philos & div humanities, 66-76, prof philos, Univ Wis, Oshkosh, 68-, asst dean Col Lett & Sci, 76-79, pres fac senate, 83-84, 87-88; chemn univ acad policies com, 96-; mem fac senate, 81-96, 97-99; Partic, Hood Col Sem Prog on India, Ford Found, 63-64; chemn, dept philos, 66-76, 00; chemn div, Wis State Univ Oshkosh study grant int educ & Wis State Univ curric, 67; Wis State Univ Regents res grant, 71-72. **HONORS AND AWARDS** John McNRosebush Univ prof, 84; Phi Beta Kappa, Univ Wis, Madison, 54; Phi Kappa Phi, Univ Wis, Madison, 54. **MEMBERSHIPS** Am Philos Asn; Metaphys Soc Am; Asn Asian Studies; AAUP. **RESEARCH** Aesthetics; Indian philosophy; American Philos, William James. **SELECTED PUBLICATIONS** Co-ed, Philosophy and Contemporary Issues, Macmillan, 72, 76, 80, 84, 88, 92 Prentice Hall, 96, 00; auth, H L Mencken: Scientific skeptic, Menckeniana, summer 75; H L Mencken: American scientific skeptic, Bicentennial Symp Philos, CUNY Grad Ctr, 76; ed, Handbook of World Philosophy: Contemporary Developments Since 1945, 80; auth, articles on Clarence Darrow, Joseph McCabe, and H L Mencken, In: Encyc of Unbelief, Prometheus, 85; ed, World Philosophy: A Contemporary Bibliography, Greenwood, 93; co-ed, Philosphy and Contemporary Issues, Macmillan, 72,76, 80,84, 88, 92, Prentice Hall, 96, 00. **CONTACT ADDRESS** Dept of Philosophy, Univ of Wisconsin, Oshkosh, 800 Algoma Blvd, Oshkosh, WI 54901-8617. **EMAIL** burr@vaxa.cis.uwosh.edu

BURRELL, DAVID
PERSONAL Born 03/01/1933, Akron, OH, s **DISCIPLINE** PHILOSOPHY **EDUCATION** Univ Notre Dame, AB, 54; Gregorian Univ, STL, 60; Yale Univ, PhD, 65. **CAREER** Prof. **RESEARCH** Medieval philosophy; philosophical theology; Islamic philosophy; metaphysics. **SELECTED PUBLICATIONS** Auth, Creation or Emanation: Two Paradigms of Reason, 90; auth, Al-Ghazali on Ninety-Nine Beautiful Names of God, 92; auth, Freedom and Creation in Three Traditions, 93; auth, Aquinas and Islamic and Jewish Thinkers, 93; auth, Islamicist as Interpreter, 97; auth, Friendship and Ways to Truth, 00. **CONTACT ADDRESS** Philosophy Dept, Univ of Notre Dame, 336/7 O'Shaughnessy, Notre Dame, IN 46556. **EMAIL** david.b.burrell.1@nd.edu

BURRES, KENNETH LEE
PERSONAL Born 08/12/1934, Topeka, KS, m, 1956, 3 children **DISCIPLINE** BIBLICAL STUDIES, LINGUISTICS **EDUCATION** Baker Univ, AB, 56; Garrett Theol Sem, BD, 60; Northwestern Univ, MA, 61, PhD, 70. **CAREER** Pastor, United Methodist Church, Gary, IN, 64-67; from asst prof to prof religh, Central Methodist Col, 67-; chair, dept of philos & relig, Central Methodist Col, 97-. **MEMBERSHIPS** Soc Bibl Lit; Am Academy of Relig. **RESEARCH** Linguistic analysis of New Testament Greek; New Testament theology; early Christian history. **SELECTED PUBLICATIONS** Auth, Prolegomena to a new biblical lexicography, Soc Bibl Lit Sem Papers, 71; articles in Encyclopedia of the Ancient World, Salem Pr, forthcoming. **CONTACT ADDRESS** Dept of Relig, Central Methodist Col, 411 Central Methodist Sq, Fayette, MO 65248-1198. **EMAIL** ckburres@mcmsys.com

BURRILL, RUSSELL C.
PERSONAL Born 06/19/1941, Haverhill, MA, m, 1963, 2 children **DISCIPLINE** CHURCH GROWTH **EDUCATION** Atlantic Union Col, BA, 63; Andrews Univ, MA, 64; Fuller Seminary, DMin, 97. **CAREER** Pastor, Conn, 64-68; pastor, Cumberland, BD, 68-70; evangelist/pastor, 70-85; prof, Andrews Univ, 85-. **HONORS AND AWARDS** Excellence in Res, 98. **RESEARCH** Church growth, Church planting, Evangelism, Equipping laity. **SELECTED PUBLICATIONS** Auth, Revolution in the Church, HART, 93; auth, Radical Disciples for Revolutionary Churches, 96; auth, Revolutized Church of the 21st Century, 97; auth, Recovering An Adventist Approach to Life and Mission in the Adventist Church, 98; auth, Rekindling the Lost Passion, 99. **CONTACT ADDRESS** Dept of Christian Ministry, Andrews Univ, 100 US Highway 31, Berrien Springs, MI 49104-0001. **EMAIL** russellburrill@cs.com

BURRINGTON, DALE E.
PERSONAL Born 03/27/1930, St. Louis, MO, m, 1976, 5 children **DISCIPLINE** PHILOSOPHY **EDUCATION** Johns Hopkins Univ, PhD, 64. **CAREER** Hartwick Col, prof, 62-96 **MEMBERSHIPS** APA, ALSC **RESEARCH** Philos of mind; moral responsibility; free will. **SELECTED PUBLICATIONS** Auth, The Command and the Orders in Brunner's Ethic, Scottish Jour of Theol, 67; auth, Blameworthiness, Jour Philos Res, 99. **CONTACT ADDRESS** 52 Dietz St, Oneonta, NY 13820. **EMAIL** burringtond@hartwick.edu

BURRIS, JOHN, JR.
PERSONAL Born 02/06/1956, m, 1985 **DISCIPLINE** RELIGION **CAREER** Vist asst prof, 98, Wesleyan Univ; sr lectr, 98-99, Suffolk Univ. **HONORS AND AWARDS** Diss of Year, 96, Univ Calif, Santa Barbara **MEMBERSHIPS** Amer Acad of Religion. **RESEARCH** Amer religion; religion & colonialism **SELECTED PUBLICATIONS** Ed, Reflections in the Mirror of Religion, Macmillan Press, 97. **CONTACT ADDRESS** 79 B Broadmeadow #11, Marlborough, MA 01752-5419. **EMAIL** kathjohn@gte.net

BURRIS, JOHN L.
PERSONAL Born 05/05/1945, Vallejo, CA, m **DISCIPLINE** LAW **EDUCATION** Vallejo Jr Coll, AA 1965; Golden Gate Coll San Francisco, BS 1967; Univ of CA Grad Sch of Bus Berkeley, MBA 1970; Univ of CA Sch of Law, JD 1973. **CAREER** Haskins & Sells San Francisco, acct/auditor 1967-69; Jenner & Block Chicago, assoc atty 1973-74; State Atty Office Cook Co Chicago, asst state atty 1975-76; Alameda Co DA Office Oakland, dep dist atty 1976-79; Harris, Alexander & Burris, atty; Law Office of John L Burris, atty, currently. **HONORS AND AWARDS** Outstanding Leadership Awd CA Assn of Black Lawyers 1980; Omegas Continental Boys Club, Outstanding Leadership Awd, 1986; Second Baptist Church, Martin Luther King Leadership Awd Vallejo, 1985; Clinton White, Outstanding Trial Lawyers, Charles Houston Bar Association, 1987; Loren Miller, Outstanding Civil Rights Lawyer, 1989; Alameda County's Peace Officer for Better Committee Relationship, Outstanding Merit Awd, 1991; NAACP Legal Defense Fund, Bay Area Chapter, Pro Bono Awd, 1992; Special investigation into fatal shooting of 15-year-old youth, & entry into NAACP offices by Oakland police officers. **MEMBERSHIPS** Past pres CA Assn of Black Lawyers; past president Charles Houston Bar Assn; spec consultant to president Natl Bar Assn; American Trial Lawyers Association; Alameda Co Bar Association; Kappa Alpha Psi Fraternity; Lawyers Committee for Urban Affairs - (SF); African-American Lawyers Against Apartheid; 100 Black Men, San Francisco Bay Chapter; Lawyer Delegate to Ninth Circuit, 1992. **CONTACT ADDRESS** Law Office of John L Burris, 1212 Broadway, 12th Floor, Oakland, CA 94612.

BURT, DONALD X.
DISCIPLINE PHILOSOPHY **EDUCATION** Villanova Univ, AB, 52; Catholic Univ Am, MA, 55; PhD, 60. **CAREER** Prof. **SELECTED PUBLICATIONS** Auth, The Rush to Resurrection, Liturgical Press: Collegeville, Minn, 85; Emmanuel: Reflections on God with Us, Liturgical Press, 88; But When You Are Older Reflections on Coming to Age, Liturgical Press, 92; The Pilgrim God, Liturgical Press, 95; Augustine's World: an Introduction to his Speculative Philosophy, Univ Press Am, 96; Augustine On Divine Voluntarism, Angelicum, Angelicum Univ, Rome, Italy, 87; Augustine On The Morality Of Violence: Theoretical Issues And Applications, Atti: Congresso Internazionale Su S. Agostinio Nel XVI Centenario Della Conversion, Stud Ephemeridis Augustinianum, 26, Inst Patristicum Augustinianum, Rome, 87; Facts, Fables, and Moral Rules: An Analysis of the Abortion Debate, New Scholasticism, 88; Augustine on the Authentic Approach to Death, Augustinianum, Inst Patristicum Augustinianum, Rome, 88; Augustine On the State as a Natural Society, Augustiniana, 90; Augustine On The Authentic Approach To Death: A Summary of Research, Stud Patristica, 90; Courageous Optimism: Augustine on the good of Creation, Augustinian Studies, 90; Friendship and Subordination in Earthly Societies, Augustinian Stud(s), 92; Friendship and the State: A Summary of Research, Collectanea Augustiniana II: Presbyter Factus Sum, Peter Lang, 93; auth, Friendship and Society: An Introduction to Augustine's Practical Philosophy, Eerdmans Pub, 99; auth, "Friendly Persuasion,"Augustine on Religious Toleration, American Catholic Philosophical Quarterly, 00. **CONTACT ADDRESS** Dept of Philosophy, Villanova Univ, St. Thomas Monastery, Villanova, PA 19085.

BURT, ROBERT AMSTERDAM
PERSONAL Born 02/03/1939, Philadelphia, PA, m, 1964, 2 children **DISCIPLINE** LAW & PSYCHIATRY **EDUCATION** Princeton Univ, BA, 60; Oxford Univ, MA, 62; Yale Univ, JD, 64. **CAREER** Law clerk, chief judge David L Bazelon, US Court of Appeals, DC, 64-65; asst gen counsel, Off Spec Rep Trade Negotiations, Exec Off of President, 65-66; legis asst, Sen Joseph D Tydings, 66-68; assoc prof law, Univ Chicago, 68-70; from assoc prof to prof law, Univ Mich, Ann Arbor, 70-76, law in psychiat, 74-76; Prof Law, Yale Univ, 76-. **HONORS AND AWARDS** Mem Inst of Med, Nat Res Coun & Nat Acad Sci, 76; Rockefeller Found fel humanities, 76; Guggenheim fel, 97. **RESEARCH** Law and psychological disciplines, especially psychiatry, in regulating family relations and anti-social conduct; constitutional law. **SELECTED PUBLICATIONS** Auth, Taking Care of Strangers: The Rule of Law in Doctor-Patient Relations, Free Press, 79; The constitution of the family, Supreme Ct Rev, 79; auth, Two Jewish Justices, Univ Calif Press, 88; auth, The Constitution in Conflict, Harvard Univ Press, 92. **CONTACT ADDRESS** Law Sch, Yale Univ, PO Box 208215, New Haven, CT 06520-8215. **EMAIL** robert.burt@yale.edu

BURTCHAELL, JAMES T.
DISCIPLINE THEOLOGY **CAREER** Prof Theol, Univ Notre Dame, 75-. **SELECTED PUBLICATIONS** Auth, The Dying of the Light: The Disengagement of Colleges and Universities from Their Christian Churches, Eerdmans, 98; Philemon's Problem: A Theology of Grace, Eerdmans, 98. **CONTACT ADDRESS** Univ of Notre Dame, Corby Hall, Notre Dame, IN 46556. **EMAIL** jtbcsc@worldnet.att.net

BURTNESS, JAMES H.
DISCIPLINE SYSTEMATIC THEOLOGY **EDUCATION** St. Olaf Col, BA, 49; Luther Sem, BTh, 53; Princeton Sem, ThD, 58. **CAREER** Instr, 55; vis prof, Gurukul Theol Col, Madras, India, 63-64; ATS fel, Free Univ Berlin, 66-67; Lutheran tutor, Mansfield Col, Oxford, Eng, 73-74; prof, 72; prof emeri. **HONORS AND AWARDS** Ch, Aus Memorial Lectures Comm; pastor, Faith Lutheran Church, Albany, 58-60. **MEMBERSHIPS** Mem, Task Force on Church and Soc of the Commn for the New Lutheran Church. **RESEARCH** Christian ethics. **SELECTED PUBLICATIONS** Ed, Word & World, 79-81; auth, Shaping the Future: The Ethics of Dietrich Bonhoeffer, 84; Whatever You Do, 67; co-ed, The New Community in Christ; All Things Are Yours, 62. **CONTACT ADDRESS** Dept of Systematic Theology, Luther Sem, 2481 Como Ave, Saint Paul, MN 55108. **EMAIL** jburtnes@luthersem.edu

BURTON, KEITH
PERSONAL Born 08/01/1963, m, 1998, 2 children **DISCIPLINE** NEW TESTAMENT INTERPRETATION **EDUCATION** Northwst Univ, PhD, 94; Oakwood Col, BA, 87 **CAREER** Asst Prof of Relig, Oakwood Col; Res Asst, Garrett Evangel Theol Sem **HONORS AND AWARDS** Whos Who Among Teachers; Amer Bible Soc Greek & Hebrew Awd **MEMBERSHIPS** Am Acad of Relig; Soc Bibl Lit; Cath Bibl Assoc **RESEARCH** Origins of Christianity in Africa; Blacks in Society; Rhetorical Understanding of New Testament **SELECTED PUBLICATIONS** Auth, So That You May be With Another, UMI, 95; We've Come This Far by Faith, A Voice in the Wilderness Publications, 96 **CONTACT ADDRESS** Dept of Relig, Oakwood Col, Huntsville, AL 35896. **EMAIL** burton@oakwood.edu

BUSBY, KAREN
DISCIPLINE LAW **EDUCATION** Univ Manitoba, LLB, 81; Univ Columbia, LLM, 87. **CAREER** Asst prof, 88-93; assoc prof, 93-00; prof, 00-. **HONORS AND AWARDS** Univ of Manitoba Community Outreach Awd, 96; ed, can jour women law, 89-. **MEMBERSHIPS** Law Soc of Manitoba **RESEARCH** Gender and the law; administrative law; civil procedure; research and writing. **SELECTED PUBLICATIONS** Auth, Queen's Bench Act and Rules, Annotated, Univ of Manitoba Legal Research Institute, 89; auth, Equality Issues in Family Law: Considerations for Test Case Litigation, Univ of Manitoba Legal Research Institute, 90; auth, "Discriminatory Uses of Personal Records in Sexual Violence Cases," Canadian Journal of Women and the Law, 97; auth, Class Proceedings (Report #100), Manitoba Law Reform Commission, 98; auth, Manitoba Queen's Bench Rules Annotated, Toronto: Carswell, 1st ed, 92, 2nd ed, 94, 3rd ed, 96, 4th ed, 98; auth, "Not a Victim Until a Conviction is Entered," Fernwood Pr, 99; auth, "LEAF and the Little Sisters Case: Some Issues to Consider," Women's Legal Education and Action Fund, 99; auth, "Legal Truth," Partiality, Incompleteness and Inequality in Sexual Violence Prosecutions, " in Fragment By Fragment: Feminist Perspectives on Memory and Child Abuse, 99; auth, "Raising the Dough: Funding for Lawyers at Public Inquiries," Peppr in Our Eyes, Police/State in Canada, Univ of British Columbia Pr, 00; auth, "Third Party Records Cases Since O'Connor," Manitoba Law Journal, forthcoming. **CONTACT ADDRESS** Fac of Law, Univ of Manitoba, Robson Hall, Winnipeg, MB, Canada R3T 2N2. **EMAIL** busby@cc.umanitoba.ca

BUSCH, THOMAS W.
PERSONAL Born 06/18/1937, Cleveland, OH, m, 1963, 3 children **DISCIPLINE** PHILOSOPHY **EDUCATION** St Joseph Col, BA, 60; Marquette Univ, MA, 62, PhD, 67. **CAREER** From instr to assoc prof, 64-77, Prof Philos, Villanova Univ, 77-. **MEMBERSHIPS** Soc Phenomenol & Existential Philos; Merleau-Ponty Circle. **RESEARCH** Contemporary French philosophy; phenomenology; philosophical anthropology. **SELECTED PUBLICATIONS** Auth, Being and Nothingness: Ontology vs Phenomenology, Southern J Philos, 65; Merleau-Ponty and the problem of origins, Philos Today, 67; From phenomenology to Marxism, Res Phenomenol, 72; Sartre: The phenomenological reduction and human relationships, J Brit Soc Phenomenol, 75; Sartre and the senses of alienation, Southern J Philos, 77; Phenomenology as humanism: The case of Husserl and Sartre, Res Phenomenol, 80; Sartre's use of the reduction: Being and Nothingness revisited, in Existence & Dialectic: Contemporary approaches to the philosophy of Jean-Paul Sartre, Duquesne Univ Press, 80; Coming to terms with Jean-Paul Sartre, Philos Today, fall 80; La Nausee: A lover's quarrel with Husserl, Res Phenomenol, 82; Beyond the cogito: The question of the continuity of Sartre's thought, Mod Schoolman, 3/83; Shifting paradigms: Sartre on critique, language and the role of the intellectual, in Critical and Dialectical Phenomenology, SUNY Press, 87; Gabriel Marcel on the death of man, in

Contributions of Gabriel Marcel to Philosophy, Edwin Mellon, 89; The Power of Consciousness and the Force of Circumstances in Sartre's Philosophy, Ind Univ Press, 90; Sartre on surpassing the given, Philos Today, spring 91; Merleau-Ponty, Hermeneutics and Postmodernism, SUNY Press, 92; Ethics and ontology: Levinas and Merleau-Ponty, Man and World, 92; Secondary reflection as interpretation, Bull de la Societe Francaise de Philosophy de Langue Francaise, fall 95; Sartre and Ricoeur on imagination, Am Cath Philos Quart, autumn 96; Merleau-Ponty and Derrida on the phenomenon, in Ecart and Difference: Merleau-Ponty and Derrida on Seeing and Writing, Humanities, Press, 97; auth, "Circulating Being: From Embodiment to Incorporation," Fradham University Press, 99; auth, "Phenomenology and Communication Ethics: Hamesh, Sartri and Merleau-Bonty," The Ethics of Postmodermity, Northwestern University Press. **CONTACT ADDRESS** Dept of Philos, Villanova Univ, 845 E Lancaster Ave, Villanova, PA 19085. **EMAIL** tbusch@vill.edu

BUSCHART, DAVID
PERSONAL Born Evanston, IL, 2 children **DISCIPLINE** THEOLOGY **EDUCATION** Wheaton Col, BA; Trinity Evangel Divinity Sch, ThM, MDiv; Drew Univ, MPhil, PhD. **CAREER** Prof, Denver Sem, 98-. **HONORS AND AWARDS** Founding mem, Res Sci and Ethics Adv Comm, Wascana Rehabilitation Ctr, Regina, Saskatchewan. **MEMBERSHIPS** Mem, Amer Acad of Rel; Evangel Theol Soc; Soc for the Stud of E Orthodoxy and Evangelicalism. **SELECTED PUBLICATIONS** Auth, Traditions of Protestant Theology. **CONTACT ADDRESS** Denver Conservative Baptist Sem, PO Box 100000, Denver, CO 80250. **EMAIL** davidb@densem.edu

BUSH, L. RUSS
PERSONAL m, 1968, 2 children **DISCIPLINE** RELIGION **EDUCATION** Miss Col, BA, 67; Southwestern Sem, MDiv, 70, PhD, 75. **CAREER** Prof, 72-89, Southwestern Sem; dean, 89-, Southeastern Sem. **MEMBERSHIPS** Am Acad Religion; Society Biblical Lit; Evangelical Theol Society; Evangelical Philos Society; Society Christian Philos. **RESEARCH** Hist of ideas. **SELECTED PUBLICATIONS** Auth, Psalms, 99; Baptists and the Bible, revised edition, 99. **CONTACT ADDRESS** PO Box 1889, Wake Forest, NC 27588. **EMAIL** lrbush@msn.com

BUSH, NATHANIEL
PERSONAL Born 01/19/1949, Washington, DC, m **DISCIPLINE** LAW **EDUCATION** Ripon Coll, BA 1973; Cleveland Marshall Coll of Law, JD 1977; Wharton Sch of Business, certificate 1984. **CAREER** Distinguished visiting Prof of Law Cambridge Univ, grad asst 1976-77; Bureau of ATF Dept of Treas, Attorney 1979-81; Univ of the District of Columbia, adjunct prof criminology 1982-84; DC State Campaign Jesse Jackson for Pres, general counsel 1983-84; DC Bd of Educ, vice pres; Ward VII rep. **HONORS AND AWARDS** Moot Court Bd of Govs Cleveland Marshall Coll of Law; 1st place Third Annual Douglas Moot Court Competition 1975; Jessup Intl Moot Court Competition 1976; Outstanding Young Men of America, 1984. **MEMBERSHIPS** Bd of dir Southeast Neighbors Citizens Assoc; bd of dirs Far East Comm Serv Inc; chmn bd of dirs Concerned Citizens on Alcohol & Drug Abuse; mem Bar of the State of OH 1977; mem Bar of the District of Columbia 1979. **CONTACT ADDRESS** DC Bd of Education, 415 12th St NW, Washington, DC 20019.

BUSS, MARTIN JOHN
PERSONAL Born 11/04/1930, Hunan, China, s **DISCIPLINE** RELIGION **EDUCATION** Bloomfield Col, BA, 51; Princeton Theol Sem, BD, 54, ThM, 55; Yale Univ, PhD, 58. **CAREER** Vis asst prof relig, Macalester Col, 57-58; vis instr, Coe Col, 58-59; from asst prof to assoc prof, 59-77, Prof Relig, Emory Univ, 77-; Am Coun Learned Soc fel, 64-65; assoc ed, J Bibl Lit, 70-74. **MEMBERSHIPS** Soc Bibl Lit. **RESEARCH** Israelite law; hermeneutics; comparative scriptures **SELECTED PUBLICATIONS** Auth, The language of the Divine I, J Bible & Relig, 61; The Psalms of Asaph and Korah, J Bibl Lit, 12/63; The beginning of human life as an ethical problem, J Relig, 7/67; The Prophetic Word of Hosea, Topelmann, Berlin, 69; The Distinction Between Civil and Criminal Law in Ancient Israel, Proc Sixth World Cong Jewish Studies, 77; Understanding communication, In: Encounter With the Text, Fortress Press, 79; Selfhood and biblical eschatology, Zeitschrift fur die alttestamentliche Wissenschaft, 88; Logic and Israelite law, Semeia, 89; Biblical Form Criticism in its Context, Sheffield Acad Press, 98. **CONTACT ADDRESS** Dept of Relig, Emory Univ, S214 Callaway Ctr, Atlanta, GA 30322-0001. **EMAIL** relmjb@emory.edu

BUSSANICH, JOHN
DISCIPLINE GREEK PHILOSOPHY, MEDIEVAL PHILOSOPHY, PHILOSOPHY OF RELIGION **EDUCATION** Stanford Univ, BA, 72, PhD, 82. **CAREER** Assoc prof, Univ NMex. **SELECTED PUBLICATIONS** Auth, The One and its Relation to Intellect in Plotinus: A Commentary on Selected Texts, Brill, 88; Plotinus' Metaphysics of the One, in The Cambridge Companion to Plotinus, ed, Lloyd P Gerson, Cambridge UP, 96; coed, Ancient Philosophy. **CONTACT ADDRESS** Univ of New Mexico, Albuquerque, Albuquerque, NM 87131. **EMAIL** manonash@unm.edu

BUSSEL, DANIEL J.
DISCIPLINE LAW **EDUCATION** Univ Pa, BA, 81; Stanford Law Sch, JD, 85. **CAREER** Prof, UCLA, 91-. **RESEARCH** Bankruptcy; Contracts and Commercial Law. **CONTACT ADDRESS** Dept Law, Univ of California, Los Angeles, Box 951476, Los Angeles, CA 90095-1476. **EMAIL** bussel@mail.law.ucla.edu

BUTCHVAROV, PANAYOT K.
PERSONAL Born 04/02/1933, Sofia, Bulgaria, m, 2 children **DISCIPLINE** PHILOSOPHY **EDUCATION** Robert Coll, BA, 52; Univ of VA, MA, 54, PhD, 55. **CAREER** Instr, 55-57, Univ of Baltimore; Asst Prof, 57-59, Univ of SC; Asst Prof, 59-61, Assoc Prof, 61-66, Prof, 66-68, Syracuse Univ; Prof, 68-, Univ of IA. **HONORS AND AWARDS** Pres, APA. **MEMBERSHIPS** APA **RESEARCH** Epistemology, metaphysics, ethics. **SELECTED PUBLICATIONS** Auth, Resemblance and Identity, IN Univ Press, 66; The Concept of Knowledge, Northwestern Univ Press, 70; Being Qua Being, IN Univ Press, 79; Skepticism in Ethics, IN Univ Press, 89; Skepticism About the External World, Oxford Univ Press, 98. **CONTACT ADDRESS** Dept of Philosophy, The Univ of Iowa, 269 EPB, Iowa City, IA 52242-1408. **EMAIL** panayot-butchvarov@uiowa.edu

BUTLER, CLARK WADE
PERSONAL Born 07/29/1944, Los Angeles, CA, m, 1971, 1 child **DISCIPLINE** PHILOSOPHY **EDUCATION** Univ Southern Calif, BA, 66, PhD(philos), 70. **CAREER** From instr to asst prof, 69-75, assoc prof, 75-80, actg chmn dept, 77-79, Prof Philos, Ind Univ-Purdue Univ, Ft Wayne, 80-, Chmn Dept, 79-83; Co-ed, Clio, 76- & Clio Hegel Studies, 81-; Philosophy Editor, 95-. **HONORS AND AWARDS** Phi Beta Kappa **MEMBERSHIPS** Hegel Soc Am; Am Philos Soc; Int Hegel Vereinigung; Int Hegel Gesellschaft; Brit Hegel Soc. **RESEARCH** Hegel; metaphysics; social philosophy. **SELECTED PUBLICATIONS** Auth, G W F Hegel, G K Hall, 77; cotransl, Hegel: The Letters, Ind Univ Press, 84; auth, Hegelian Panentheism as Joachimite Christianity, In: Hegel's Philosophy of Religion, SUNY Press, 92; Empirical vs. Rational Order in the History of Philosophy, Owl of Minerva, Fall 94; The Reducibility of Ethics to Human Rights, Dialogue and Universalism, Univ Warsaw, vol 5, no 7, 95; Hegel's Logic: Between Dialectic and History, Northwestern Univ Press, 96; History as the Story of Freedom, Editions Rodopi (Amsterdam), 97; author of numerous other journal articles. **CONTACT ADDRESS** Dept of Philos Ind, Indiana Univ-Purdue Univ, Fort Wayne, 2101 Coliseum Blvd E, Fort Wayne, IN 46805-1445. **EMAIL** butler@tpfw.edu

BUTLER, J.
DISCIPLINE PHILOSOPHY **EDUCATION** Yale Univ, BA, 78, MA, 82, M Phil, 82, PhD, 84; Heidelberg Univ, Cert Study, 78-79 **CAREER** Actg instr, 81 & 86, Yale Col; Prize tchg fel, 82-83, Yale Univ; vis instr & asst prof of Letters, 83-85, Andrew W Mellon Postdr fel, 85-86, Wesleyan Univ; asst prof philos, 86-89, George Wash Univ; assoc prof, Hum, 89-91, prof Hum, 91-94, Johns Hopkins Univ; prof of Rhet, 93-94, prof of rhetoric & compartive literature, 94-, chancellors prof, Univ Calif Berkeley; Maxine Elliott Prof, 98-. **HONORS AND AWARDS** Fac, Nat Endowment for Hum, 94 & 97; Donald M Kramer vis scholar Hum Brooklyn Col, 94; invited fac, Dartmouth School Criticism & Theory, 95; Hum res fel Univ Calif Berkeley, 96; invited fac C Europ Univ, 98; invited fac Univ Munich, 98; Guggenheim fel, 99. **MEMBERSHIPS** Amer Philos Asn; Mod Lang Asn; Engish Inst; Soc Critical Exchange; Int Gay & Lesbian Hum Rights Comn; Hum Res Inst. **RESEARCH** Feminist theory and sexuality studies; 19th and 20th Century continental philosophy; Philosophy and literature; Social and political thought. **SELECTED PUBLICATIONS** Auth, Bodies that Matter: On the Discursive Limits of Sex, Routledge, 93; Excitable Speech: A Politics of the Performative, Routledge, 97; The Psychic Life of Power: Theories in Subjection, Stanford Univ Press, 97; ed, Der Streit um Differenz: Feminismus und Postmoderne in der Gegenwart, Fischer Verlag, 93; auth, Feminist Contentions: A Philosophical Exchange, Routledge, 94; Diacritics, Critical Crossings, 94; Atopia, Stanford Univ Press; auth, Merely Cultural, Social Text, 97; Vocabularies of the Censor, Censorship and Silencing, Oxford Univ Press, 98; Sovereign Performatives in the Contemporary Scene of Utterance, Critical Inquiry, 97. **CONTACT ADDRESS** Dept of Rhetoric, Univ of California, Berkeley, 7408 Dwinelle Hall, Berkeley, CA 94720-2670.

BUTLER, J. RAY
PERSONAL Born 08/05/1923, Roseboro, NC, m, 1943, 4 children **DISCIPLINE** THEOLOGY **EDUCATION** Shaw U, BA, BD, MDiv, 74, DD, 73; Friendship Coll, DD, 66; Southeastern Theol Sem, 66-67; McKinley Theol Sem LLD, 76; Southeastern Theol Seminary DTh, 69. **CAREER** Pastor, Ebenezer Bapt Ch Wilmington, 54-70; pastor, First Bapt Ch Creeddmoor; pastor, Mt Olive Bapt Ch Fayeteville; pastor, New Christian Chapel Bapt Ch RoseHill; pastor, Shiloh Bapt Church Winston-Salem, 70-90; founder, pastor, United Cornerstone Baptist Church, Winston-Salem, NC, 90-. **HONORS AND AWARDS** Various tours in foreign countries; Pastor of Yr Awd Midwestern Bapt Laymen's Fellowship Chicago 75, 76; elected Contbng Writer Nat Bapt Sunday Sch Publ Bd. **MEMBERSHIPS** Past pres Interdenom Ministerial All; past pres Interracieal Minist Assn; past pres Wilmington Civic League; past pres PTA; 1st vice pres NAACP; bd of dirARC; mem Man Power Delvel; mem Citizens Coalition Bd; pres-at-large Gen Bapt State Conv; pres Bapt Ministers Conf & Asso; mem Forsyth Clergy Assn Chmn of Gen Bapt St Conv of NC Inc; mem extension tchg staff of Shaw U; exec bd of Lott Carey Bapt Foreign Missions & Conv; appointed bd of licensed gen contractors Gov Jim Hunt of NC; founder, Shilohian/St Peters Day Care; moderator, Rowan Baptist Missionary Association, 1989-. **SELECTED PUBLICATIONS** Auth, The Christian Communion as Related to the Jewish Passover and Monetary Commitment, 87; auth, From Playtime to Pulpit Service, 91. **CONTACT ADDRESS** United Cornerstone Missionary Baptist Church, 2745 Patria St, Winston-Salem, NC 27127.

BUTLER, LEE HAYWARD, JR.
PERSONAL Born 02/15/1959, Harrisburg, PA, m **DISCIPLINE** PASTORAL THEOLOGY **EDUCATION** Eastern Baptist Sem, Mdiv, 86; Princeton Sem, ThM, 88; Drew Univ, MPhil, 92; PhD, 94. **CAREER** Asst prof, Lancaster Theol Sem, 91-96; Chicago Theol Sem, 96-. **MEMBERSHIPS** AAR; Soc for the Study of Black Relig; Asn of Black Psychologists. **RESEARCH** Psychology; Religion; Identity formation; Healing traditions. **CONTACT ADDRESS** Chicago Theol Sem, 5757 S University Ave, Chicago, IL 60637-5213. **EMAIL** lhbutler@compuserve.com

BUTLER, TRENT C.
PERSONAL Born 02/16/1941, Wichita Falls, TX, m, 1999, 2 children **DISCIPLINE** BIBLICAL STUDIES **EDUCATION** Hardin-Simmons Univ, BA, 63; Southern Baptist Theol Sem, BD, 66; Vanderbilt Univ, PhD, 71. **CAREER** Asst prof relig, Atlanta Baptist Col, 70-71; asst prof Old Testament, Int Baptist Theol Sem, Switzerland, 71-81; curric design ed, Baptist Sunday School Bd, 81-83; ed, Holmam Bible Pub, 83- . **MEMBERSHIPS** ETS; IBR; SBL; SSOT; ASOR. **RESEARCH** Old Testament language; Old Testament theology; Book of Joshua and historical Books. **SELECTED PUBLICATIONS** Auth, Isaiauth, Layman's Bible Book Commentary, 82; Joshua, Word Biblical Commentary 7, 83; auth, Piet in the psalm; Review of Expositior, 84; A Forgottenauth, Understanding the Basic Theory of Joshua, Word, 91; Ed, Holman Student Bible Dictionary, Holman, 93; ed, Holman Book of Maps, Charts and Reconstructions, Holman, 93; auth, Experiencing God, revised edition by Henry Blackaby and Claude King, 94; auth, Points for Emphasis, Broadman & Holman, 94, 95, 96, 97, 98; auth, auth, Experiencing God Study Bible, Broadman & Holman, 95; auth, Cracking Old Testament Codes, Broadman & Holman, 95; auth, Experiencing God Calendar, Broadman & Holman, 95; auth, Narrative Form Criticism: Dead or Alive, in A Biblical Itinerary, Sheffield, 97; ed, Holman Bible Atlas, Holman, 98; auth, The Theology of Joshua, Rev and Expositor, 98. **CONTACT ADDRESS** 100 Mimosa Dr., Gullatin, TN 37066. **EMAIL** TButler@lifeway.com

BUXBAUM, RICHARD MANFRED
PERSONAL Born 04/16/1930, Friedberg, Germany, m, 2 children **DISCIPLINE** LAW **EDUCATION** Cornell Univ, AB, 50, LLB, 52; Univ Calif, Berkeley, LLM, 53. **CAREER** Atty, 53-61; dir Earl Warren Legal Inst, 70-75, Prof Law, Univ Calif, Berkeley, 61-; dean, Int & Area Studies, Univ Calif Berkeley, 93-99; ed in chief, Am Journal of Comparative Law, 87-. **HONORS AND AWARDS** Humboldt Research Prize, 92; Order of Merit, FedRepGermany, 93; Dr iur hc Univ Osnabruck, 93, Dr iur hc and Hon prof, Eotvos Lorand Univ, 93; Hon prof Peking Univ, 98; Officier, Arts y Lettres, France; Order of Rio Branco, Brazil. **MEMBERSHIPS** Am Bar Asn. **RESEARCH** Corporation law; government regulation of business; law and economic development; Int Assn Comparative Law; German Soc of Comparative Law. **SELECTED PUBLICATIONS** Auth, Restrictions inherent in the patent monopoly: A comparative critique, Univ Pa Law Rev, 65; co-ed, Corporations--Cases and Materials, Callaghan, 4th ed, 68 & West, 5th ed, 79; auth, Public participation in the enforcement of the antitrust laws, Calif Law Rev, 71; auth, Die Private Klage als Mittel zur Durchsetzung Wirtschaftspolitischer Rechtsnormen, C F Muller, Karlsruhe, 72; co-auth, Legal Harmonization and the Business Enterprise, 88; auth, European Economic and Business Law with Hertig, Hirsch & Hopt, eds, 96; auth, Responsibilities of Transnational Corporations to Host Nations, in Current Legal Issues in the Internationalization of Business Enterprises, Heng et al, eds, 96; auth, Die Rechtsvergleichung zwischen nationalem Staat und internationaler Wirtschaft, in Rabels Zeitschrift, 96; auth, Corporate Governance and Corporate Monitoring -- The Whys and Hows, in Australian Journal of Corporate Law, 96; auth, Back to the Future? In FS Sandrock, 00; auth, Family Law and the Federal System, In Gedaechtnisschrift Alexander Luederitz, 00. **CONTACT ADDRESS** Sch of Law, Univ of California, Berkeley, 220 Boalt Hall, Berkeley, CA 94720-7200. **EMAIL** bux@uclink.berkeley.edu

BYBEE, JAY S.
PERSONAL Born 10/27/1953, Oakland, CA, m, 1986, 4 children **DISCIPLINE** CONSTITUTIONAL LAW **EDUCATION** Brigham Young Univ, JD, cum laude, 80. **CAREER** Bus mngr, Brigham Young Univ Law Rev; assoc, Sidley &

Austin, 81-84; atty, US Dept of Justice Off of Legal Policy and Civil Div, 84-89; assoc coun to the Pres, White House, 89-91; Prof, La State Univ; prof, Univ Nev, Las Vegas. **HONORS AND AWARDS** Phi Kappa Phi. **RESEARCH** Constitutional Law & Hist, Admin Law. **SELECTED PUBLICATIONS** Published articles in various journals, including the Yale Law Journal, Northwestern University Law Review, Vanderbilt Law Review, and George Washington Law Review. **CONTACT ADDRESS** Univ of Nevada, Las Vegas, Las Vegas, NV 89154. **EMAIL** jbybee@ccmail.nevada.edu

BYER, INEZ
PERSONAL Born 03/22/1927, Kansas City, MO, m, 1949, 2 children **DISCIPLINE** PHILOSOPHY, RELIGION **EDUCATION** Univ Mo, Columbia, BA, 48, MA, 49, PhD(Philos), 68. **CAREER** Asst Philos, Univ Mo-Columbia, 63-65; asst prof, 65-73, prof Philos, Cottey Col, 73-. **MEMBERSHIPS** Am Philos Asn. **RESEARCH** Aesthetics. **CONTACT ADDRESS** Div of Humanities, Cottey Col, 1000 W Austin, Nevada, MO 64772-2790. **EMAIL** IByer@Cottey.edu

BYMAN, SEYMOUR DAVID
PERSONAL Born 10/26/1934, Chicago, IL, m, 1956, 3 children **DISCIPLINE** RELIGIOUS HISTORY **EDUCATION** Univ Ill, Urbana, BA, 56; Roosevelt Univ, MA, 67; Northwestern Univ, PhD(hist), 71. **CAREER** Asst prof, 70-75, assoc prof, 75-78, Prof Hist, Winona State Univ, 78-, Assoc, Inst Psychohistory, 77-78. **MEMBERSHIPS** AHA. **RESEARCH** Martyrology. **SELECTED PUBLICATIONS** Auth, Tudor death stands, Moreana, 73; Suicide and alienation: Martyrdom in Tudor England, Psychoanal Rev, 74; Guilt and martyrdom: The case of John Bradford, Harvard Theol Rev, 75; A defense of psychohistory, 78 & Child raising and melancholia in Tudor England, 78, J Psychohistory; Ritualistic acts and compulsive behavior: The pattern of sixteenth century martyrdom, Am Hist Rev, 78; Humanities and the Law School Experience, J of Legal Educ, 85; The Perils of Psychohistory, J of Psychohistory, 88. **CONTACT ADDRESS** Dept of History, Winona State Univ, P O Box 5838, Winona, MN 55987-0838. **EMAIL** sbyman@vax2.winona.msus.edu

BYNAGLE, HANS EDWARD
PERSONAL Born 02/24/1946, Ruurlo, Netherlands, m, 2 children **DISCIPLINE** LIBRARY SCIENCE, PHILOSOPHY **EDUCATION** Calvin Col, BA, 68; Kent State Univ, MLS, 76; Columbia Univ, PhD, 73. **CAREER** Friends Univ, 76-82; Eckerd Col, 82-83; libr dir, Whitworth Col, 83-. **MEMBERSHIPS** Am Libr Asn; Asn Col & Res Libr. **RESEARCH** Philosophical bibliography; Philosophy of history; Philosophy of mind; Idea of progress. **SELECTED PUBLICATIONS** Auth A Friends University Bibliography: Books by Alumni and Faculty, 1898-1979, Friends Univ, 79; Introduction: A Map ofTwentieth-Century Philosophy, Twentieth-Century Philosophy, Prentice-Hall, 96; Philosophy: A Guide to the Reference Literature, Libraries Unlimited, 86, 2nd ed, 96. **CONTACT ADDRESS** Cowles Libr, Whitworth Col, 300 W Hawthorne Road, Spokane, WA 99251. **EMAIL** hbynagle@whitworth.edu

BYRD, JAMES DAVID, JR.
PERSONAL Born 06/05/1972, Fort Campbell, KY, s **DISCIPLINE** PHILOSOPHY **EDUCATION** Univ Central Fla, BA, 96; Univ Calif, Davis, PhD candidate. **CAREER** Tchg asst, Univ Calif, Davis, 97- . **HONORS AND AWARDS** Phi Theta Kappa. **MEMBERSHIPS** APA. **RESEARCH** Philosophy of mind; cognitive science. **CONTACT ADDRESS** 1111 J St, #152, Davis, CA 95616. **EMAIL** jdbyrd@ucdavis.edu

BYRD, JERRY STEWART
PERSONAL Born 12/11/1935, Greenville, SC, m, 1983, 1 child **DISCIPLINE** LAW **EDUCATION** Fisk Univ, BA 1961; Howard Univ, JD 1964; Southeastern Univ, ASBA 1975. **CAREER** atty, Natl Labor Relations Bd Regional Adv Branch, 64-65; managing atty, Neighborhood Legal Serv, 65-69, 74-81, dep dir, 70-71; pol sci instructor, Howard Univ, 71-72; hearing commissioner, Superior Ct of DC, 81-; administrative law judge, social security administration, Sept-Dec 97. **MEMBERSHIPS** Mem Hearing Comm Bd of Professional Responsibility 1982-85; Special Judges Division of the American Bar Association; Washington and National Bar Association; general secretary, Washington Buddhist Vihara Society, Inc; mem bd dir, Hospitality Comm Fed Credit Union; mem DC Consumer Goods Repair Bd 1974-77. **SELECTED PUBLICATIONS** parental Immunity in Negligence Actions Abolished, 9 How L J 183 (1963); Courts, Slums and Feasibility of Adopting the Warranty of Fitness, The DC Housing Research Comm Report 1967; Nix vs Watson, RS-650-80R; 18 Family Law Reporter (Nov 12, 1991); auth, "District of Columbia v. Lederman," 27 Daily Washington Law Reporter, 685, 98. **CONTACT ADDRESS** Hearing Commissioner Magistrate Judge, Superior Court of DC, 500 Indiana Ave NW, Washington, DC 20001.

BYRNE, EDMUND F.
PERSONAL Born 05/30/1933, Kansas City, MO, 2 children **DISCIPLINE** PHILOSOPHY, LAW **EDUCATION** Saint Joseph's Col Ind, BA, 55; Loyola Univ Chicago, MA, 56; Univ Louvain, Belg, PhD(philos), 66; Ind Univ, JD, 78. **CAREER** Asst prof philos, Mich State Univ, 66-69; from asst prof to assoc prof, 69-76, Prof Philos, Ind Univ, Indianapolis, 76-, Chmn Dept, 79-, Prog coordr, Soc Study Philos & Technol, 76-, treas, 81- **MEMBERSHIPS** Am Philos Asn; Am Legal Studies Asn; Popular Cult Asn; Am Bar Asn; Am Legal Studies Asn; Popular Cult Asn; Soc Philos & Technol (treas, 81-). **RESEARCH** Philosophy of technology; philosophy of public policy; philosophy of law. **SELECTED PUBLICATIONS** Auth, Probability and Opinion, Nijhoff, The Hague, 68; coauth, Human Being and Being Human: Man's Philosophies of Man, Appleton-Century-Crofts, 69; auth, The depersonalization of violence, J Value Inquiry, fall 73; contribr, Philosophy and Technology: An Annual Compilation of Research, Vols I & II, JAI Press, 78 & 79; auth, After mental illness what?, In: Action and Responsibility, Bowling Green Univ, 80; Death and aging in technopolis, In: Philosophical Foundations of Gerontology, Human Sci Press, 81; US Domsat policy, In: Papers on Science of Science and Forecasting 1-2, Wroclaw, Poland, 81; The adversary system: Who needs it?, In: Ethics and the Legal Profession, Prometheus (in prep). **CONTACT ADDRESS** Dept of Philos, Indiana Univ-Purdue Univ, Indianapolis, 1100 W Michigan St, Indianapolis, IN 46202-5140. **EMAIL** ebyrne@iupul.edu

BYRNE, JAMES E.
PERSONAL Born 06/12/1945, Detroit, MI, m, 1973, 4 children **DISCIPLINE** LAW **EDUCATION** Univ Notre Dame, BA, 68; Stetson Univ, JD, 77; Univ Pa, LLM, 78. **CAREER** Prof, George Mason Univ, 82-; dir, IIBLP, 92-. **HONORS AND AWARDS** UNCITL, US Del Hd, 88-95; ABA, BLS, Ch, 96-; ISPP, Ch, 94-99. **MEMBERSHIPS** IACCL; ABA. **RESEARCH** Letters of Credit; international banking. **SELECTED PUBLICATIONS** Ed-in-ch, Documentary Credit World, 97-; ed-in-ch, Letter of Credit Update, 85-97; auth, "The Myth of Prime Bank Financial Instruments," En Law Rep 178 (99); coauth, "The ABCs of the UCC, ABA (98); coauth, "Letters of Credit: 1998 Cases, Bus Law 54 (99); auth, "International Standby Practices: New Rules for Standby Letters of Credit, UCCLJ 32 (99); ed, "1999 Annual Survey of Letter of Credit Law and Practice (Inst Intl Bank Law Pract, 99); auth, "Finality in Commercial Law: Some General Reflections," ABA (97); auth, "Why New Draft Rules for Standby are Necessary," Doc Cred Insight (97); auth, "The Original Documents Controversy," (99). **CONTACT ADDRESS** School of Law, George Mason Univ, Arlington, 3401 Fairfax Dr, Arlington, VA 22201. **EMAIL** jbyrne@iiblp.org

BYRNE, PATRICK HUGH
PERSONAL Born 05/16/1947, Syracuse, NY, m, 1971, 1 child **DISCIPLINE** PHILOSOPHY **EDUCATION** Boston Col BS, 69, MA, 73; State Univ NYork, Stony Brook, PhD(philos), 78. **CAREER** Asst prof, 75-80, Assoc Prof Philos, Boston Col, 80-. **RESEARCH** Philosophy of 20th century science; philosophy of logic and mathematics; axiological ethical theory. **SELECTED PUBLICATIONS** Ed, Philosophy and Social Theory, Stony Brook Studies in Philosophy, Vol 1, 74. **CONTACT ADDRESS** Dept of Philos, Boston Col, Chestnut Hill, 140 Commonwealth Ave, Chestnut Hill, MA 02467. **EMAIL** patrick.byrne.1@bc.edu

BYRNES, JOHN
PERSONAL Born 04/06/1970, Valparaiso, IN, m, 1998 **DISCIPLINE** PHILOSOPHY **EDUCATION** Carnegie Mellon Univ, PhD, 99. **MEMBERSHIPS** Asn of Symbolic Logic. **RESEARCH** Automated theorem proofs; Proof theory; Philosophy of mathematics. **SELECTED PUBLICATIONS** Auth, "Peirce's First-Order of Logic of 1885" in Transactions of the Charles S. Peirce Soc, 98; co-auth, "An Abstract Model for Parallel Computations: Gandy's Thesis," in The Monist, 98; co-auth, "Godel, Turing, and K-Graph Machines," in Logic in Florence, 98; co-auth, "Normal Natural Deduction Proofs (in Classical Logic)," in Studiea Logica, 98; auth, "Normal Forms Resulting From Proof Search Strategies," in Bull of Symbolic Logic, 97; co-auth, K-Graph Machines: Generalizing Turing's Machines and Arguments," in Godel, 96; co-auth, "A Graphical Presentation of Gandy's Parallel Machines," in Bul of Symbolic Logic, 96; co-auth, "A Mathematical Explication of Turing's Argument," in Bull of Symbolic Logic, 95. **CONTACT ADDRESS** Dept of Philosophy, Carnegie Mellon Univ, Pittsburgh, PA 15217. **EMAIL** byrnes@cmu.edu

C

CABAL, THEODORE JAMES
PERSONAL Born 12/24/1952, Whittier, CA, m, 1977, 3 children **DISCIPLINE** PHILOSOPHY OF RELIGION **EDUCATION** Swstrn Baptist Theol Sem, PhD, 95 **CAREER** Asst Prof, 93-95, Dallas Baptist Univ; Asst Prof, 95-98, Swstrn Baptist Theol Sem; Dean, 98-pres, Sthrn Bapt Theol Sem. **HONORS AND AWARDS** Dallas Baptist Univ Religion Student of Year, 88; President's Scholar Awd, 89; Who's Who Among Students in Amer **MEMBERSHIPS** Am Acad of Relig; Am Philos Assoc; Baptist Assoc of Philos Teachers; Evangelical Philos Soc; Evangelical Theological Soc; Ntl Assoc of Baptist Professors of Relig; Soc of Christian Philosophers **RESEARCH** Philosophy of Religion; Philosophy of Science **SELECTED PUBLICATIONS** Coauth, Rockamnia, SBC Life, 96; Auth, Shapers of Modern Evangelical Thought, Bullentine, 94 **CONTACT ADDRESS** 2825 Lexington Rd, Louisville, KY 40280. **EMAIL** tcabal@sbts.edu

CADORETTE, CURT R.
PERSONAL Born 12/03/1948, Holyoke, MA **DISCIPLINE** RELIGIOUS STUDIES **EDUCATION** Univ Chicago, BA, 70, MA, 71; Regis Col, Toronto, STD, 85; Univ of St Michael's Col, Toronto, PhD, 85. **CAREER** Mary Knoll School of Theology, 86-94; Marxist Col, 87-88; Thiel Col, 89-91; assoc prof, Univ Rochester, 94-. **HONORS AND AWARDS** Adraham Karp Awd for Teaching Excellence; Golden Key Honor Soc. **MEMBERSHIPS** Am Academy of Religion; Cath Theol Soc; Asn of Relig and Intellectual Life. **RESEARCH** Relig and society in Latin Am; Andean culture and relig. **SELECTED PUBLICATIONS** Auth, From the Heart of the People: The Theology of Gustavo Cutierrez, MeyerStone/Crossroad/Continuum, 88; Liberation from Violence: The Contemporary Catholic Challege, in The Grail: An Ecumenical J, Sept 95; The Church in Peru, in The New Catholic Encyclopedia, vol 19, Dec 95; Liberating Catholicism: Living the Incarnation in a Post-Modern World, in The Month: A Review of Christian Thought and World Affairs, Aug 95; Catholicism in the Social Order of a New Era in Review for Religios, Sept-Oct 95; Liberating Mission: David Bosch and Latin American Christianity, in Mission in Bold Humility: David Bosch's Work Considered, Willem Saayman and Klippies Kritzinger, eds, Orbis Books, 96; Searching for Easter in Peru: Class, Culture and Evangelization, in Cross Currents: A Journal of the Asn for Relig and Intellectual Life, vol 46, no 2, 96; Christs in the Night: The Missiological Challenge of Andean Catholicism, in Missiology: An International Review, vol 25, no 1, Jan 97; Uncanny Grace: Christian Communities and the Survival of Hope, in Small Christian Communities: Imagining Future Church, Robert S Pelton, CSC, ed, Notre Dame Univ Press, 97; Liberation Theology: A Reader, Orbis Books, 92, 6th ed, 98; Legion and the Believing Community: Discipleship in an Imperial Age, in Paths That Lead to Life: The Church as Counterculture, SUNY Press, forthcoming 98; numerous other articles and publications. **CONTACT ADDRESS** Univ of Rochester, 430 Rush Rhees Library, Rochester, NY 14627. **EMAIL** ccrt@troi.cc.rochester.eu

CADY, DUANE LYNN
PERSONAL Born 08/01/1946, Milwaukee, WI, m, 1969, 2 children **DISCIPLINE** PHILOSOPHY **EDUCATION** Hamline Univ, BA, 68; Brown Univ, Am, 70, PhD(Philos), 71. **CAREER** Asst prof Philos, Gustavus Adolphus Col, 71-74; prof philos, Hamline Univ, 74-, ed, Hamline Rev, 80-. **HONORS AND AWARDS** Conger Prize, Humanities Scholarship, 89; Sears-Roebuck Foundation Teaching Excellence & Campus Leadership Awd, 90; Hamline Univ Com Social Action Awd, 98; Grimes Teaching Awd, 99. **MEMBERSHIPS** Am Philos Asn; Concerned Philos for Peace, Pres, 91; Fel of Reconciliation, natl council, 96-02. **RESEARCH** History of philosophy; ethics; soc & polit theory. **SELECTED PUBLICATIONS** Auth, From Warism to Pacifism, 89; co-ed, Just War, Nonviolence & Nuclear Deterrence, 91; co-auth: Humanitarian Intervention: Just War vs Pacifism, 96; Bringing Peace Home: Feminism, Violence & Nature, 96. **CONTACT ADDRESS** Dept of Philosophy, Hamline Univ, 1536 Hewitt Ave, Saint Paul, MN 55104-1284. **EMAIL** dcady@gw.hamline.edu

CAFARO, PHILIP
PERSONAL Born 02/27/1962, New York, NY, m, 2000 **DISCIPLINE** ETHICS, APPLIED ETHICS **EDUCATION** Univ Chicago, BA, 84; Univ Ga, MA, 88; Boston Univ, PhD, 97 **CAREER** Asst prof, Southwest State Univ, 97-; asst prof, Southwest State Univ, 97-99; asst prof, Colorado State Univ, 99-. **HONORS AND AWARDS** Univ fel for acad excellence, 86-88; hon, masters thesis, 88; Pres fel, 90-93; jr vis fel, 95. **RESEARCH** Ethical theory, environmental ethics, philosophy and lit. **SELECTED PUBLICATIONS** Auth, Thoreauvian Patriotism as an Environmental Virtue, Philos in the Contemp World, 2, 95, 1-9; Economic Consumption and the Quarrel Between Ethics and Economics, Acad Inquiry, 1, 95, 39-52; coauth, For Indian Wilderness, Terra Nova, 3(3), 98, 53-58; Virtue Ethics (Not Too) Simplified, Auslegung: A Jour Philos, 22, 98, 49-67; Less is More: Economic Consumption and the Good Life, Philos Today, 22, 98, 49-67; coauth, "Ethical Issues in Biodiversity Protection," with Richard Primack, Encyclopedia of Biodiversity, vol 2, Academic Press, (01): 593-607; coauth, "Environmental Ethics," with Richard Primack, Encyclopedia of Biodiversity, vol 2, Academic Press, (01): 545-555; auth, "Thoreau, Leopold and Carson: Toward an Environmental Virtue Ethics," Environmental Ethics 23, (01): 3-17. **CONTACT ADDRESS** Dept of Philosophy, Colorado State Univ, Fort Collins, CO 80523. **EMAIL** cafaro@lamar.colostate.edu

CAFFENTZIS, C. GEORGE
PERSONAL Born 02/09/1945, Brooklyn, NY, 1 child **DISCIPLINE** PHILOSOPHY **EDUCATION** Princeton Univ, PhD, 78. **CAREER** Assoc prof; coordr, Comt for Acad, Freedom in Africa. **SELECTED PUBLICATIONS** Auth, Clipped Coins, Abused Words and Civil Government: John Locke's Philosophy of Money, 88; coaut, Anti-Samuelson: A Critique of a Rep-

resentative Textbook of Bourgeois Economics, vols 1-4, 73-75; Midnight Oil: Work, Energy, War 1973-1992, 92; auth, Exciting the industry of mankind: George Berkeley, Philosophy of Money, 00. **CONTACT ADDRESS** Dept of Philosophy, Univ of So Maine, 96 Falmouth St, PO Box 9300, Portland, ME 04104-9300. **EMAIL** Caffentz@usm.maine.edu

CAHAN, JEAN
DISCIPLINE JUDAIC STUDIES **EDUCATION** Johns Hopkins Univ, PhD, 83. **CAREER** Asst prof Judaic Stud, Univ Nebr, Lincoln. **RESEARCH** Philosophy of religion; philosophy of history. **SELECTED PUBLICATIONS** Published on Spinoza, modern Jewish philosophy and Marx. **CONTACT ADDRESS** Univ of Nebraska, Lincoln, Lincoln, NE 68588-0417.

CAHILL, ANN J.
PERSONAL Born 08/30/1969, Gloucester, MA, m, 1998 **DISCIPLINE** PHILOSOPHY **EDUCATION** Col Holy Cross, BA, 1991; State Univ NYork, PhD, 98. **CAREER** Asst prof, Elon Col, 98-99. **HONORS AND AWARDS** Am Fel Diss Fel, Am Asn Univ Women, 97. **MEMBERSHIPS** Soc Phenomenol Existential Philos; Am Philos Asn, Society for Women in Philosophy. **RESEARCH** Feminist theory; theory of the body; social and political philosophy. **SELECTED PUBLICATIONS** Auth, "Foucault, Rape, and the Construction of the Feminine Body," Hypatia, Vol 15 (00): 43-63. **CONTACT ADDRESS** Dept of Philosophy, Elon Col, 800 Scott Ave, Greensboro, NC 27403-2119. **EMAIL** cahilla@elon.edu

CAHILL, LISA SOWLE
PERSONAL Born 03/27/1948, Philadelphia, PA, m, 1972, 5 children **DISCIPLINE** CHRISTIAN THEOLOGICAL ETHICS **EDUCATION** Univ Santa Clara, BA, 70; Univ Chicago, MA, 73, PhD(theol), 76. **CAREER** Assoc prof to J. DONALD MONAN, S. J. PROF THEOL, BOSTON COL, 76-; assoc ed, J Relig Ethics; ethics ed, Relig Studies Rev; advisory bd, J of Med and Philos; bd of dirs, Concilium. **HONORS AND AWARDS** Pres, Cath Theological Soc of Am, 92-93; pres, Soc of Christian Ethics, 97-98; Honorary degrees from: Santa Clara Univ, St Peter's Col, St Mary's Col, Moraga, CA, Graduate Theological Union, Lasell Col, Univ Toronto, Providence Col. **MEMBERSHIPS** Am Acad Relig; Soc Christian Ethics; Cath Theol Soc Am;Am Academy of Arts and Sciences; Nat Advisory bd on Ethics and Reproduction; March of Dimes advisory comm; Cath Comm Ground Initiative. **RESEARCH** Bioethics; feminist ethics; sexual ethics; bible and ethics; methodology in Christian ethics. **SELECTED PUBLICATIONS** Auth, Between the Sexes: Toward a Christian Ethics of sexuality, Fortress and Paulist Presses, 85, 7th printing, 97, Fortress Books; auth, Religion and Artificial Reproduction: Inquiry into the Vatican Instruction on Human Life, with Thomas A. Shannon, Crossroad Press, 88; auth, Women and Sexuality, Paulist Press, 92; auth, Love Your Enemies: Discipleship, Pacifism, and Just War Theory, Fortress Press, 94; co-ed, Embodiment, Morality, and Medicine, Kluwer Academic Pubs, 95; auth, Sex, Gender, and Christian Ethics, Cambridge Univ Press, 96; co-ed, Christian Ethics: Problems and Prospects, in honor of James M. Gustafson, Pilgrim Press, 96; auth, Families: A Christian Social Perspective, 00. **CONTACT ADDRESS** Dept of Theol, Boston Col, Chestnut Hill, 140 Commonwealth Ave, Chestnut Hill, MA 02167-3800.

CAHILL, P. JOSEPH
PERSONAL Born 10/29/1923, Chicago, IL **DISCIPLINE** RELIGIOUS STUDIES **EDUCATION** Xavier Univ, Ohio, LittB, 47; Loyola Univ, Ill, MA, 55; Pontif Gregorian Univ, STD, 60. **CAREER** Asst prof theol, Bellarmine Sch Theol, 60-66; assoc dean sch theol, Loyola Univ, Ill, 66-67; assoc prof theol, Univ Notre Dame, 66-70; acting chmn dept relig studies, 70-74, Prof Relig Studies, Univ Alta, 70-, Vis lectr, Beloit Col, 66; mem Jesuit Comn Probs of Belief & Unbelief, 66-; consult, Encycl Britannica, 68-; bd mem, Corp Publ of Acad Studies, Can, 73-; Can Coun leave & res fel, 76-77. **MEMBERSHIPS** Cath Theol Asn; Soc Sci Studies Relig; Soc Bibl Lit. **RESEARCH** Secularization and religious values; theology of Rudolf Bultmann; existentialism and Christian apologetics. **SELECTED PUBLICATIONS** Auth, The Narrative Jesus--A Semiotic Reading of Mark Gospel, Cath Biblical Quart, Vol 0057, 95. **CONTACT ADDRESS** Dept of Relig Stud, Univ of Alberta, Edmonton, AB, Canada T6G 0X7.

CAHN, EDGAR S.
DISCIPLINE EDUCATION LAW AND PROPERTY **EDUCATION** Swarthmore Col, BA, 56; Yale Univ, MA, 57, PhD, 60, JD, 63. **CAREER** Prof; tchs in, Publ Entitlements Clin; codean, Antioch Sch Law, 71-80; a vis scholar, Columbia Univ(s) Ctr, Study of Human Rights; sr res fel, Southeast FL Ctr on Aging, FL Int Univ; distinguished vis scholar, London Sch Econ, 86. **HONORS AND AWARDS** Co-founder, Nat Legal Serv prog; innovative concept of, ser credits or time dollars, as an economic strategy for addressing soc prob(s) is being implemented in 36 states and in Sweden, Japan & Can. **SELECTED PUBLICATIONS** Auth, Hunger; USA; Time Dollars; Our Brothers' Keeper: The Indian in White America; articles on, zoning, int law, public interest law, legal educ. **CONTACT ADDRESS** School of Law, Univ of District of Columbia, 4200 Connecticut Ave Northwest, Washington, DC 20008.

CAHOONE, LAWRENCE
PERSONAL Born 08/31/1954, Providence, RI, m, 1985, 2 children **DISCIPLINE** PHILOSOPHY **EDUCATION** Clark Univ, BA, 76; State Univ of NYork at Stony Brook, PhD, 85. **CAREER** Asst prof Philos, Boston Univ, 87-96; assoc prof Philos, Boston Univ, 96-. **HONORS AND AWARDS** Eugene McKayden Ntl Univ Pr Bk Awd in Humanities, 89. **MEMBERSHIPS** Amer Philos Assoc **RESEARCH** Modernism; Postmodernism; Social and Political Theory; American Philosophy; European Philosophy; Liberalism; Civil Society. **SELECTED PUBLICATIONS** Dilemma of Modernity: Philosophy, Culture, and Anti-Culture, St Univ NY, 88; The Ends of Philosophy, St Univ of NY, 95; From Modernism to Postmodernism: An Anthology, Blackwell Publ, 96. **CONTACT ADDRESS** Dept of Philosophy, Boston Univ, Boston, MA 02215. **EMAIL** lcahoone@bu.edu

CAIDEN, GERALD E.
PERSONAL Born 02/06/1936, London, England, m, 1960, 2 children **DISCIPLINE** PUBLIC ADMINISTRATION, POLITICAL SCIENCE **EDUCATION** London School of Economics & Political Sci, PhD, 59. **CAREER** Australian Nat Univ, 61-66; Hebrew Univ, 66-68; Univ of Calif at Berkeley, 68-71; Haifa Univ, 71-75; Univ Southern Calif, 75-. **RESEARCH** International public administration; public policy; public ethics; administrative reform. **SELECTED PUBLICATIONS** Over 25 books and monographs, and over 240 refereed articles. **CONTACT ADDRESS** School of Policy, Planning, and Development, Univ of So California, Los Angeles, CA 90089-0626. **EMAIL** caiden@usc.edu

CAIN, JAMES
PERSONAL Born 04/21/1951, d, 1 child **DISCIPLINE** PHILOSOPHY **EDUCATION** Univ Penn, PhD, 85. **CAREER** Lectr, res assoc, Princeton Univ, 86-89; vis asst prof, Virginia Tech, 89-90; vis asst prof, Univ Cincinnati, 90-91; vis asst prof, Univ Rochester, 91-92; vis asst prof, Univ Louisville, 92-96; vis lectr, Georgia State Univ, 96-97; asst prof, Oklahoma State Univ, 97- . **MEMBERSHIPS** APA; Soc of Christian Philos. **RESEARCH** Logic; philosophy of religion; metaphysics; ethics. **SELECTED PUBLICATIONS** Auth, Arithmetic with Satisfaction, Notre Dame J of Formal Logic, 95; auth, Infinite Utility, Australasian J of Philos, 95; auth, The Hume-Edwards Principle, Relig Stud, 95. **CONTACT ADDRESS** Dept of Philosophy, Oklahoma State Univ, Stillwater, Stillwater, OK 74078-5064. **EMAIL** jcain@okstate.edu

CAIRNS, ALAN
DISCIPLINE LAW **EDUCATION** Univ Toronto, BA, 53, MA, 57, Univ Oxford, Phol, 63. **CAREER** Prof, 53- **HONORS AND AWARDS** Canadian Council Killam Scholarship, 89; Molson Prize, 82, Governor General's Int Awd, 94; Doctor of Laws degree from the Univ of Toronto, 96, Univ of British Columbia, 98. **MEMBERSHIPS** Royal Soc Can. **RESEARCH** Canadian federalism; Charter and the constitution. **SELECTED PUBLICATIONS** Auth, Constitution, Government and Society in Canada, 98, Disruptions: Constitutional Struggles from the Charter to Meech Lake, 91, Reconfigurations: Canadian Citizenship and Constitutional Change, 95, The Charter Versus Federalism, 92. **CONTACT ADDRESS** Col of Law, Univ of Saskatchewan, 15 Campus Dr, Saskatoon, SK, Canada S7N 5A6. **EMAIL** Cairns@law.usask.ca

CAIRNS, HUGH A. C.
PERSONAL Born 03/02/1930, Galt, ON, Canada **DISCIPLINE** LAW, POLITICAL SCIENCE, HISTORY **EDUCATION** Univ Toronto, BA, 53, MA, 57; St. Antony's Col, Oxford Univ, Dphil, 63. **CAREER** Instr to prof, polit sci, 60-95, chmn, 73-80, PROF EMER, UNIV BC, 95-; vis prof, Memorial Univ Nfld, 70-71; vis prof, Can stud, Univ Edinburgh, 77-78; vis prof, Can stud, Harvard Univ 82-83; Brenda and David McLean ch Can stud, 93-95; John Willis vis prof law, Univ Toronto, 95-96; PROF AND LAW FOUNDATION OF SASK CHAIR, COLLEGE OF LAW, UNIV OF SASKATCHEWAN, 97-. **HONORS AND AWARDS** Gold Medal Polit Sci & Econ, 53; Queen's Silver Jubilee Medal, 77; Pres Medal Univ Western Ont, 77; Molson Prize Can Coun, 82; Killam res fel, 89-91; Gov Gen Int Awd Can Stud, 94; DLaws(hon), Carleton Univ, 94; DLaws(hon), Univ Toronto, 96; DLaws(hon), Univ BC, 98. **MEMBERSHIPS** Can Polit Sci Asn (pres, 76-77); Int Polit Sci Asn (mem coun, 76-79). **SELECTED PUBLICATIONS** Auth, Prelude to Imperialism: British Reactions to Central African Society 1840-1890, 65; coauth, A Survey of the Contemporary Indians of Canada: Economic, Political and Educational Needs and Policies, vol 1, 66; coauth, Constitution, Government and Society in Canada: Selected Essays by Alan C. Cairns, 88; coauth, Disruptions: Constitutional Struggles from the Charter to Meech Lake, 91; coauth, Charter versus Federalism: The Dilemmas of Constitutional Reform, 92; coauth, Reconfigurations: Canadian Citizenship and Constitutional Change, 95. **CONTACT ADDRESS** 1866 Main Mall, Vancouver, BC, Canada V6T 1Z1.

CALABRESI, THE HONORABLE GUIDO
PERSONAL Born 10/18/1932, Milan, Italy, m, 1961, 3 children **DISCIPLINE** LAW **EDUCATION** Yale Col , BS, analytical econ, 53; Oxford Univ, Magdalen Col, BA, politics, philos, econ, 55, MA, politics, philos, econ, 59; Yale Univ Law School, LLB, 58. **CAREER** Asst instr, Dept Econ, Yale Coll, 55-56; Simpson, Thacher & Bartlett (law firm), summer 57; law clerk to Justice Hugo Black, U.S. Supreme Court, 58-59; asst prof law, 59-61, assoc prof law, 61-62, prof law, 62-70, John Thomas Smith Prof Law, 70-78, Sterling Prof Law, 78-95, dean, law school, 85-94, Sterling Prof Law Emeritus, lecturer, 95-, Yale Univ; consult, Dept Trans, Auto Insurance Study, 68-70; consult, Insurance Dept, Auto Insurance Report, State of New York, 69-70; judge, U.S. Court Appeals, Second Circuit, 94-. **HONORS AND AWARDS** Rhodes Scholar, 53; one of Ten Oustanding Young Men in Am, U.S. Jr. Chamber of Commerce, 62; Laetare Medal, Univ Notre Dame, 85; named commendatore (honary knight commander), Republic of Italy, 94; Fellows of Amer Bar Found Awd for Oustanding Research in Law and Government, 98; Thomans Jefferson Medal in Law, 00. **MEMBERSHIPS** American Philosopical Society; American Academy of Arts and Sciences, 83-86; American Law Institute ; Associazione Italiana di Diritto Comparato; Corresponding Fellow, British Academy; Royal Swedish Academy of Sciences; Accademia delle Scienze di Torino; Canadian Institute for Advanced Legal Studies; Connecticut Academy of Arts and Sciences; Institute of Medicine (National Academy of Sciences) 74-76; Accademia Nazionale dei Lincei; Fel, Timothy Dwight Col, Yale Univ. **RESEARCH** Law **SELECTED PUBLICATIONS** Auth, "Altruism and Not for Profits: Ends as Well as Means," Le Organizzazioni Senza Fini di Lucro (nonprofit organizations), Giuffre Editore, 96; coauth, "Directions in Tort Law," Valparaiso Univ Law Review 30 , 96; auth, "Remarks: The Inalienability: A Twenty-Five year Retrospective," Yale Law Journal 106, 97; auth, "Comments on: Is There a Threat to Judicial Independence in the United States Today?," Fordham Urban L J XXVI, 98; auth, "Two Functions of Formalism," U Chi L Rev 67, 00. **CONTACT ADDRESS** U S Court of Appeals, 2nd Circuit, 157 Church St., New Haven, CT 06510.

CALDWELL, HARRY M.
DISCIPLINE CRIMINAL PROCEDURE **EDUCATION** CA State Univ, BA, 72; Pepperdine Univ, JD, 76. **CAREER** Prof; student wrtg ed, Pepperdine Law Rev; dep dist atty, County Riverside, 76-79; dep dist atty, County Santa Barbara, 79-80. **HONORS AND AWARDS** Harriet and Charles Luckman distinguished tchr fel, 91-96. **MEMBERSHIPS** Mem, State Bar CA; Am Bar Assn; Am Trial Lawyers Assn. **SELECTED PUBLICATIONS** Co-auth, California Criminal Trial Book, West, 90. **CONTACT ADDRESS** Sch of Law, Pepperdine Univ, 24255 Pacific Coast Hwy, Malibu, CA 90263.

CALDWELL, L. K.
PERSONAL Born 11/21/1913, Montezuma, IA, m, 1940, 2 children **DISCIPLINE** HISTORY, GOVERNMENT **EDUCATION** Univ Chicago, PhB, 34 PhD, 43; Harvard Univ, MA, 38; Western Mich Univ, LLD, 77. **CAREER** Dir Res, Council of State Governments, 44-47; prof polit sci, Syracuse Univ, 47-53; co-dir, Public Admin Inst for Turkey and Middle East, United Nations, 53-54; vis prof, Univ Calif, Berkeley, 54-55; prof Polit Sci & Public and Environ Affairs to Arthur F. Bentley prof emer , Indiana Univ, 55- . **HONORS AND AWARDS** UN Global 500, 91; John Gaus Awd, Am Polit Sci Asn, 96; Natural Rsrc Coun Awd, 97; Hon Life Member, Int Asn of Impact Assessment; fel, Am Asn for Advanc of Sci; fel, Nat Acad of Public Admin; fel, Royal Soc of the Arts. **MEMBERSHIPS** Am Polit Sci Asn; Am Soc for Public Admin; Asn for Polit and Life Sci. **RESEARCH** Public policy, law, and administration; policy for science, technology, and the environment. **SELECTED PUBLICATIONS** Coauth, Policy for Land: Law and Ethics, Rowman and Littlefield, 93; auth, Environment as a Focus for Public Policy, Texas A & M, 95; co-ed, Environmental Policy: Transnational Issues and National Trends, Quorum, 96; auth, International Environmental Policy, 3d ed, Duke, 96; auth, Scientific Assumptions and Misplaced Certainty in Natural Resources and Environmental problem-Solving, in Lemons, ed, Scientific Uncertainty and Environmental Problem-Solving, Blackwell, 96; auth, Implications for a World Economy for Environmental Policy and Law, in Dasgupta, ed, The Economics of Transnational Commons, Oxford, 97; auth, The national Environmental Policy Act: Agenda for the Future, Indiana, 98; auth, The Concept of Sustainability: A Critical Approach, in Lemons, Ecological Sustainability and Integrity; Concepts and Approaches, Kluwer Academic, 98. **CONTACT ADDRESS** School of Public and Environmental Affairs, Indiana Univ, Bloomington, 1315 E Tenth St, Bloomington, IN 47405. **EMAIL** lkcaldwe@indiana.edu

CALFEE, DENNIS A.
DISCIPLINE LAW **EDUCATION** Gonzaga Univ, BBA, JD; Univ Fla, LLM. **CAREER** Prof; cert public accountant; fac, Acad Int Taxation Rep China, 86, 88-96; past vis prof, Leiden Univ, The Neth; Peking Univ in Beijing, China; Acad Int Tax, Taipei, Taiwan; prof, Univ Fla, 75- ,assoc dean, 88-93; pat law clerk, Div III, Wash State Ct Appeals. **MEMBERSHIPS** Wash Bar. **RESEARCH** Taxation. **SELECTED PUBLICATIONS** Coauth, Federal Estate and Gift Taxation 6th ed. **CONTACT ADDRESS** School of Law, Univ of Florida, PO Box 117625, Gainesville, FL 32611-7625. **EMAIL** calfee@law.ufl.edu

CALIAN, CARNEGIE SAMUEL
PERSONAL Born 07/01/1933, New York, NY, m, 1959, 3 children **DISCIPLINE** THEOLOGY, EASTERN ORTHODOX STUDIES **EDUCATION** Occidental Col, BA, 55; Princeton Theol Sem, BD, 58; Univ Basel, ThD, 62. **CAREER** Asst pastor, Calvary Presby Church, 58-60; vis prof theol, Dubuque Theol Sem, Univ Dubuque, 63-67, assoc prof, 67-72, prof, 72-81; pres & prof theol, Pittsburgh Theol Sem, 81-, consult, Eastern Orthrox affairs, United Presby Church Comn Ecumenical Mission & Rel, 63-; mem nat faith & order colloquium, Nat Coun Churches, 65-; Comt Five Rep the World Alliance N Am Area in Off Schs, 72; J Omar Good distinguished vis prof, Juniata Col, 75-77. **HONORS AND AWARDS** Doctor of Human Letters, Waynesburg College, 92; Doctor of Divinity, Washington and Jefferson College, 95; lld, westminister col, 82. **MEMBERSHIPS** Am Theol Soc; Am Acad Relig; Soc Sci Studies Relig; AAUP; fel Soc Human Values Higher Educ. **RESEARCH** Eastern Christianity; reformed theology; Christian ethics. **SELECTED PUBLICATIONS** Auth, Where's the Passion for Excellence in the Church?, Morehouse Publishing, 89; auth, Theology Without Boundaries: Encounters of Eastern Orthodoxy and Western Tradition, Westminster/John Knox Press, 92; auth, "Survival or Revival: Ten Keys to Church Vitality," Westminster John Knox Press, 99. **CONTACT ADDRESS** Pittsburgh Theol Sem, 616 N Highland Ave, Pittsburgh, PA 15206-2525. **EMAIL** calian@pts.edu

CALKINS, MARTIN
PERSONAL Born 12/01/1952, Cleveland, OH **DISCIPLINE** BUSINESS ADMINISTRATION, BUSINESS ETHICS **EDUCATION** Xavier Univ, BS, 78; Am Grad School Int Mgt, MIM, 79; Western School Theol, MD, 94; ThM, 94; Univ Va, PhD, 98. **CAREER** Int Admin Coordr, Luria Brothers & Co/ Ogden Corp, 80-82; Int Sales Mgr, Perry Div/Affiliated Hospital Products, 83-84; instr, Univ Detroit Mercy, 89-91; instr, Univ Va, 94-98. **HONORS AND AWARDS** Who's Who in Am Univ and Coll, 93-94. **MEMBERSHIPS** Soc for Bus Ethics; Am Philos Asn; Acad of Mgt; Soc of Christian Ethics. **RESEARCH** Casuistry; Virtue ethics; Self-deception. **SELECTED PUBLICATIONS** Auth, The Christian Manager: Dilemmas in the Workplace, Cath World, 94; auth, Tom Moeller, Univ Va, 96; coauth, A Profile of Richard T De George, Bus Ethics, 96; auth, Religion and Business Ethics, Blackwell Encycl Dictionary of Bus Ethics, 97; auth, Post-industrial Fitness, Am Fitness Mag, 98; auth, Adam Smith, Aristotle, and the Virtues of Commerce, J of Value Inquiry, 98; auth, "Recovering Religion's Voice for Business Ethics," Journal of Business Ethics 23 (Feb 00): 339-352; auth, "Business, Justice, and the Withholding Tax," Explore 3 (Winter 00): 22-27; coauth, A CD/ Web-Based Team Project for Undergraduate Business Ethics Students, Ed-Media 2000 Conference Proceedings, forthcoming; auth, "Casuistry and the Case Method," Business Ethics Quarterly, forthcoming. **CONTACT ADDRESS** Santa Clara Univ, St Joseph's Hall Rm 116, Santa Clara, CA 95053-0390. **EMAIL** mcalkins@scu.edu

CALLAHAN, DANIEL FRANCIS
PERSONAL Born 11/28/1939, Boston, MA, m, 1974, 3 children **DISCIPLINE** MEDIEVAL & CHURCH HISTORY **EDUCATION** St John's Sem, Mass, BA, 62; Boston Col, MA, 66; Univ Wis-Madison, PhD(hist), 68. **CAREER** Asst prof to prof hist, Univ Delaware, 68-. **HONORS AND AWARDS** Am Coun Learned Soc grant, 82. **MEMBERSHIPS** Medieval Acad Am; AHA; Am Cath Hist Asn. **RESEARCH** The church in France, 750-1050; Medieval pilgrimages. **SELECTED PUBLICATIONS** Auth, "Ademar of Chabannes, Millennial Fears and the Development of Western Anti-Judaism," The J of Ecclesiastical Hist, 46 (95): 19-35; auth, "When Heaven Came Down to Earth: The Family of St. Martial of Limoges and the 'Terrors of the Year 1000,'" in Portraits of Medieval and Renaissance Living: Essays in Memory of David Herlihy, ed. S. Cohn and S. Epstein (Ann Arbor, 95), 245-258; auth, "Ecclesia Semper Reformanda: Clerical Celibacy and Reform in the Church," in Medieval Piety and Purity, ed. M. Frassetto (New York, 98), 377-388. **CONTACT ADDRESS** Dept of Hist, Univ of Delaware, Newark, DE 19711. **EMAIL** dfcao@udel.edu

CALLAHAN, JAMES P.
PERSONAL Born 03/03/1960, Hinsdale, IL, m, 1982, 4 children **DISCIPLINE** THEOLOGY **EDUCATION** Marquette Univ, PhD, 94. **CAREER** Asst prof theol, Wheaton Col, 94-. **MEMBERSHIPS** Am Acad Relig; Soc of Bibl Lit. **RESEARCH** Hermeneutics; narrative and theology. **SELECTED PUBLICATIONS** Auth, The Convergence of Narrative and Christology: Hans W. Frei on the Uniqueness of Jesus Christ, Jour of Evangel Theol Soc, 95; auth, Claritas Scripturae: The Role of Perspicuity in Protestant Hermeneutics, Jour of Evangel Theol Soc, 96; auth, Reforming Dispensationalism: The Battle for Dispensationalism's History, Fides et Historia, 96; auth, Primitivist Piety: The Ecclesiology of the Early Plymouth Brethren, in Dayton, ed, Studies in Evangelicalism, Scarecrow, 96; auth, The Bible Says: Evangelical and Postliberal Biblicism, Theol Today, 97; auth, articles in Elwell, ed, Evangelical Dictionary of Theology, rev ed, forthcoming. **CONTACT ADDRESS** Dept Bible Studies, Wheaton Col, Illinois, 501 College Ave, Wheaton, IL 60187-5501. **EMAIL** james.p.callahan@wheaton.edu

CALLAN, T.
PERSONAL Born 02/06/1947, Helena, MT, m, 1981, 2 children **DISCIPLINE** RELIGION **EDUCATION** Gonzaga Univ, BA 69; Yale Univ, MPhil 72, PhD 76. **CAREER** Asst prof, Xavier Univ, 75-80; dir rel educ, St. Clement Parish, 80-83; from asst prof to prof, academic dean, Athenaeum of Ohio, 83-. **HONORS AND AWARDS** Woodrow Wilson Fel **MEMBERSHIPS** SBL; CBA; EGLBS **RESEARCH** Paul; New Testament Christology; Luke-Acts; Christianity and Judaism. **SELECTED PUBLICATIONS** Auth, The Origins of Christian Faith, Paulist, 94; The Background of the Apostolic Decree, Catholic Biblical Quart, 93; auth, "Paul the Law and the Jewish People," in Essays on Jews and Judaism in the New Testament, ed, D P Efroymson, E. J. Fisher, L. Klenicki, Collvi MN, Liturgical Press, 93. **CONTACT ADDRESS** Dept of Biblical Studies, Athenaeum of Ohio, 6616 Beechmont Ave, Cincinnati, OH 45230. **EMAIL** tcallan@mtsm.org

CALLAWAY, MARY CHILTON
PERSONAL Born 12/21/1945, RI, m, 1972, 2 children **DISCIPLINE** BIBLICAL STUDIES **EDUCATION** St John's Col, BA, 68; Columbia Univ, PhD, 79. **CAREER** Asst prof, 80-90, chemn theol dept, 95-99, assoc prof, Fordham Univ, 91- . **MEMBERSHIPS** Soc of Bibl Lit; Catholic Bibl Asn; Am Acad Relig. **RESEARCH** Hebrew Bible; Jeremiah; Biblical hermeneutics; literary criticism and the Bible. **SELECTED PUBLICATIONS** Auth, Sing, O Barren One: A Study in Comparative Midrash, Scholars, 86; auth, A Hammer that Breaks Rock in Pieces: prophetic Critique in Ancient Israel, in Evans, ed, Studies in Anti-Semitism and Early Christianity: Polemic and Faith, Augsburg Fortress, 93; auth, Canonical Criticism, in Haynes, ed, To Each its Own Meaning, John Knox, 93; auth, Exegesis as Banquet: Reading Jeremiah with the Rabbis, in Weis, ed, A Gift of God in Due Season, Academic, 96; auth, The Apocryphal/Deuterocanonical Books: An Anglican/ Episcopal View, in Kohlenberger, ed, The Parallel Apocrypha, Oxford, 97; auth, Black Fire on White Fire: Historical Context and Literary Subtext in Jeremiah 37-38, in Papers from the Consultation on the Study of Jeremiah at the Society of Biblical Literature, Sheffield, forthcoming. **CONTACT ADDRESS** Theology Dept, Fordham Univ, 441 E Fordham Rd, Bronx, NY 10458. **EMAIL** callaway@fordham.edu

CALLENDER, CARL O.
PERSONAL Born 11/16/1936, New York, NY, m **DISCIPLINE** LAW **EDUCATION** Brooklyn Comm Col, NYork, 1960-61; Hunter Col, Bronx, NYork, AB 1961-64; Howard Univ Sch Law Washington DC, JD. **CAREER** Housing Litigation Bur NYC, dir 1975-76; Comm Law Ofcs Prgm, dir 1972-75; Comm Law Ofcs, deputy dir 1971-72; Comm Law & Ofcs, assoc dir 1971; CALS Reginald Heber Smith Fellow Prgm NYC, COORD 1970-71; Reginald Heber Smith fellow Harlem Assertion of Rights Inc, 69-70; Harlem Assertion of Rights Inc, staff atty 1968-69; Palystreet NYC, dir 1967; Hunter Coll NYC, asst librn aide 1966; Ebenezer Gospel Tabernacle, ordained minister 1972. **HONORS AND AWARDS** "Student who made most & significant progress in senior year" 1967; Am Jurisprudence Awd for Insurance 1967; half hour film on channel 2 "Eye On New York". **MEMBERSHIPS** Chmn & pres Natl Young People's Christian Assn Inc; chmn & pres Christian Leaders United Inc; mem elec com of Student Bar Assn administrative asst; Housing Research Com; Phi Alpha Delta Legal Fraternity. **SELECTED PUBLICATIONS** Prentice-Hall's Federal Tax Service Bulletins NJ, legal edit; "Attorney For The Defenseless" 1970. **CONTACT ADDRESS** 415 Louis Ave, Floral Park, NY 11001.

CALLENDER, WILFRED A.
PERSONAL Born 03/23/1929, Colon, Panama, m **DISCIPLINE** LAW **EDUCATION** Brooklyn Coll, BA 1954; Brooklyn Coll, MA 1963; Brooklyn Law Sch, JD 1969. **CAREER** Boys High School Brooklyn, educator, 57-69; Dept Real Estate Commerce Labor Industry Corp Kings, asst dir, 69-70; Wade & Callender, atty, 72-; Hostos Community College, prof, 70-91; Wade & Callender ESQS Practice of Law. **MEMBERSHIPS** Mem Brooklyn Bar Assn; Bedford Stuyvesant Lawyers Assn; Natl Conf Black Lawyers; bd Trustees Encampment for Citizenship 1971-; pres Black Caucus Hostos 1972-; mem bd trustees Social Serv; bd NY Soc Ethical Culture. **CONTACT ADDRESS** 1501 No Strand Ave, Brooklyn, NY 11226.

CALLIES, DAVID LEE
PERSONAL Born 04/21/1943, Chicago, IL, m, 1966, 1 child **DISCIPLINE** LAW **EDUCATION** DePauw Univ, AB, 65; Univ Mich, JD, 68; Univ Nottingham, LLM, 69. **CAREER** Adj assoc prof, Sch Archit & Urban Planning, Univ Wis-Milwaukee, 73-78; adj assoc prof, Col Urban Sci, Univ Ill, 76; Prof Law, Sch Law, Univ Hawaii, 78-, Assoc & partner, Attorney at Law, Ross, Hardies, O'heefe, Babcock & Parsons, 69-78; coun, The Conservation Found, 74-76; reporter, Land Use Law & Zoning Digest, 79-; columnist, Sun edition, Honolulu Advertise, 81- **MEMBERSHIPS** Nat Acad Sci. **RESEARCH** Land use management; real property; state and local government. **SELECTED PUBLICATIONS** Auth, The Quiet Revolution Revisited--A Quarter-Century Of Progress, Urban Lawyer, Vol 0026, 94. **CONTACT ADDRESS** 4621 Aukai Ave, Honolulu, HI 96816.

CALVERT-KOYZIS, NANCY
PERSONAL Born 12/14/1959, New York, NY, m, 1996 **DISCIPLINE** BIBLICAL STUDIES; NEW TESTAMENT **EDUCATION** Wheaton Col, BA, 82; Gordon-Conwell Theol Sem, M Div, 86; Univ Sheffield, PhD, 93. **CAREER** Teaching asst, new testament, Univ Sheffield, 89-90; asst prof, new testament, Wheaton Col, 90-96; prof, new testament, Tyndale Sem, Toronto, 96-. **HONORS AND AWARDS** Aldeen Fund Publ grant, Wheaton Col, spring, 96; Overseas res scholar, British govt, 87-89; grant, Tyndale House, Cambridge, 87-89, Parsonage Grad fel, Gordon-Conwell Theol Sem, 86-87. **MEMBERSHIPS** Soc of Bibl Lit; Inst of Bibl Res; Cath Bibl Asn. **RESEARCH** Pauline studies; Women in new testament world; Sociology of new testament world. **SELECTED PUBLICATIONS** Auth, On My Mind, Wheaton Alumni, 15, Spring, 96; auth, Abraham and Ancestors, Dict of the Later New Testament, vol 3, IVP, 97; auth, Galatians: Introduction and Notes, Women's Study New Testament, Harper/Baker, 95; auth, Philo's Use of Jewish Traditions About Abraham, SBL Seminar Papers, Scholar's Press, 94; auth, Abraham and Idolatry: Paul's Comparison of Obedience to the Law to Idolatry in Galatians 4:1-10, Paul and the Scriptures of Israel, Sheffield Acad Press, 93; auth, Abraham, Dict of Paul and his Letters, IVP, 93; auth, Abraham, Dict of Jesus and the Gospels, InterVarsity, 3-7, 92. **CONTACT ADDRESS** Ontario Theol Sem, 25 Ballyconnor Ct., North York, ON, Canada M2M4B3. **EMAIL** ncalkoy@aol.com

CAMERON, DAVID L.
DISCIPLINE FEDERAL TAXATION, INTERNATIONAL TAXATION, STATE AND LOCAL TAXATION **EDUCATION** Mass Inst Tech, BS, 80; Northwestern Univ, JD, 86. **CAREER** Clk, Hon Edward F Hennessey, Chief Justice, Supreme Judicial Court of Mass, 86-87; assoc, Goodwin, Procter & Hoar, Boston, 87-90; asst prof, Willamette Univ, 90-94; assoc prof, 94-97; prof, 97-. **MEMBERSHIPS** Mem, Northwestern Univ Law Rev; Order of the Coif. **SELECTED PUBLICATIONS** Co-auth, Taxation of Intangible Assets, 97. **CONTACT ADDRESS** Sch of Law, Willamette Univ, 900 State St, Salem, OR 97301. **EMAIL** dcameron@willamette.edu

CAMERON, DONALD M.
DISCIPLINE LAW **EDUCATION** Univ Toronto, BA, 75, MA, 76, LLB, 79; Registered Professional Engineer (Ontario), 80. **CAREER** Partner, Smith Lyons; partner, Aird & Berlis; Adjunct Prof of Law, Univ of Victoria. **HONORS AND AWARDS** Fel, Patent and Trademark Inst of Canada. **MEMBERSHIPS** Can Bar Asn; Comput Law Asn; Am Intellectual Property Law Asn; NY Intellectual Property Law Asn; Advocates' Soc; Am Bar Asn; Am Inst Aeronaut Astronaut; Can Aeronaut Space Inst; Licensing Exec Soc. **SELECTED PUBLICATIONS** Co-auth, Computer Contracts, Butterworth's Canadian Forms and Precedents and Eureka! Now What?, CCH. **CONTACT ADDRESS** Fac of Law, Univ of Toronto, 78 Queen's Park, Toronto, ON, Canada M5S 1A1.

CAMP, RODERIC A.
PERSONAL Born 02/19/1945, Colfax, WA, m, 1966, 2 children **DISCIPLINE** GOVERNMENT **EDUCATION** George Washington Univ, BA, 66, MA, 67; Univ Ariz, PhD, 70. **CAREER** Asst to Assoc to Prof, Polit Sci, Cent Univ of Iowa, 70-91, Ch 73-76, 80-82, 85-91, Asst Dean, 78; Ch, Polit Sci Dept, Tulane Univ, 93-96; Adjunct Fellow, Ctr for Strategic & Int Stud, 98-; Prof of Govt, Claremont McKenna Col, 98-. **HONORS AND AWARDS** Winfield Scott Blaney Fellow in Int Aff, GW Univ, 66-67; NEH Grant, 79, 82, Fellow, 77, 81, 91; Tinker Mex Policy Stud Fellow, Mexico, 93, 94, 95, 96; Hewlett Foundation Awd, Latin Am Dem, 98-99, Mexican Dem, 00-01. **MEMBERSHIPS** NE Coun of Latin Am Stud (Exec Coun 90-00); MidW Polit Sci Asn; N Cent Coun of Latin Americanists (pres 83-84); AHA; LASA. **RESEARCH** Mexican politics. **SELECTED PUBLICATIONS** Auth, Generals in the Palacio, the Military in Modern Mexico, Oxford Univ Press, 92; auth, Who's Who in Mexico Today, 2nd ed, Westview Press, 93; auth, The Successor, A Political Thriller, Univ NMex Press, 93; auth, Mexican Political Biographies, 1935-1993, 3rd ed, Univ Tex Press, 95; Political Recruitment Across Two Centuries, Mexico, 1884-1991, Univ Tex Press, 95; auth, Politics in Mexico, Democratizing Authoritarianism, Oxford Univ Press, 3rd ed, 99; auth, Crossing Swords, Politics and Religion in Mexico, Oxford Univ Press, 97. **CONTACT ADDRESS** Dept of Govt, Claremont McKenna Col, Claremont, CA 91711. **EMAIL** roderic-camp@mckenna.edu

CAMPANY, ROBERT F.
PERSONAL Born 04/04/1959, Columbus, MS **DISCIPLINE** RELIGIOUS STUDIES **EDUCATION** BA, Davidson Col, 81; Univ Chicago, MA, 83, PhD, 88, Univ Chicago. **CAREER** Assoc prof, Indiana Univ, 88-. **RESEARCH** Chinese religious history; History and methods of the study of religion. **SELECTED PUBLICATIONS** Auth, Strange Writing: Anomaly Accounts in Early medieval China, SUNY, 95; pubs on Confucian, Buddhist, and Taoist texts dating from the third century B.C.E. to the sixteenth century C.E. **CONTACT ADDRESS** Dept of Religious Studies, Indiana Univ, Bloomington, Sycamore Hall 230, Bloomington, IN 47405. **EMAIL** campanyr@indian.edu

CAMPBELL, COURTNEY S.
DISCIPLINE BIOMEDICAL ETHICS **EDUCATION** Yale Univ, BA; Univ Va, MA, PhD. **CAREER** Philos, Oregon St Univ. **HONORS AND AWARDS** Dir, Prog Ethics, Sci, Environment. **SELECTED PUBLICATIONS** Ed, Duties to Others; What Price Parenthood?. **CONTACT ADDRESS** Dept Philos, Oregon State Univ, Corvallis, OR 97331-4501.

CAMPBELL, GERRY
DISCIPLINE PHILOSOPHY **EDUCATION** University Western Ontario, BA, 64; Univ Laval, PhL, 66; PhD, 72. **CAREER** Ch, St. Jerome's Univ; assoc prof, St. Jerome's Univ; asst prof, St. Jerome's Univ; lectr in philos, St. Jerome's Univ. **HONORS AND AWARDS** Distinguished Tchr Awd, 80. **SELECTED PUBLICATIONS** Auth, Sartre's Absolute Freedom; Taking Issue: With the Case for Ordination. **CONTACT ADDRESS** Dept of Philosophy, St. Jerome's Univ, Waterloo, ON, Canada N2L 3G3. **EMAIL** gcampbel@watarts.uwaterloo.ca

CAMPBELL, JOSEPH GORDON
PERSONAL Born 06/02/1934, Nashville, TN, m, 1958, 2 children **DISCIPLINE** RELIGION PHILOSOPHY **EDUCATION** Vanderbilt Univ, BA, 56; McCormick Theol Sem, BD, 62; Duke Univ, PhD(relig). **CAREER** Instr theol, 65-66, asst prof, 66-71, assoc prof, 71-82, Prof Theol, Hanover Col, 82- **MEMBERSHIPS** Am Acad Relig. **SELECTED PUBLICATIONS** Auth, Are all speech-acts self-involving?, Relig Studies, 6/72. **CONTACT ADDRESS** Dept of Theol, Hanover Col, P O Box 108, Hanover, IN 47243-0108.

CAMPBELL, KEN M.
PERSONAL Born 08/26/1940, Isle of Skye, Scotland, m, 1967, 1 child **DISCIPLINE** THEOLOGY **EDUCATION** Univ Aberdeen, MA, 67; Westminster Theological Seminary, BD, 70; THM, 71; Univ Manchester, PhD, 75. **CAREER** Head of Religious Education, Sandown High School, 78-88; Minister of Covenant Presbyterian Church, 88-94; Assoc Prof of Biblical Studies, Belhaven Col, 94-00. **MEMBERSHIPS** Society of Biblical Literature (SBL); Evangelical Theological Society (ETS); Institute for Biblical Research (IBR); Amer Academy of Religion (AAR). **SELECTED PUBLICATIONS** auth, "The Ugly Emotions," Christian Focus Publications, 96; auth, "Our Awesome God," Christian Focus Publications, 96; auth, "The Credible Church, Bible Press, 99. **CONTACT ADDRESS** Dept Bible Studies, Belhaven Col, 1500 Peachtree St, Jackson, MS 39202-1754.

CAMPBELL, LEE W.
DISCIPLINE LAW **EDUCATION** Westminster Col, BA,66; Univ Southern Calif, JD,74. **CAREER** Clinical prof Univ Southern California; practd law in Los Angeles. **MEMBERSHIPS** Past dir, Calif Inst Trial Advocacy Skills; Los Angeles City Task Force on Family Diversity. **SELECTED PUBLICATIONS** Publ on, clinical education; lawyers' skills training; children's rights & evidence. **CONTACT ADDRESS** School of Law, Univ of So California, University Park Campus, Los Angeles, CA 90089.

CAMPBELL, RICHMOND M.
DISCIPLINE MORAL AND POLITICAL PHILOSOPHY **EDUCATION** Harvard Univ, BA, 64; Cornell Univ, PhD, 70. **CAREER** Prof. **RESEARCH** Philosophy of mind, philosophy of biology, feminism. **SELECTED PUBLICATIONS** Auth, The Virtues of Feminist Empiricism, Hypatia, 94; "Can Biology Make Ethics Objective?," Biol and Philos, 96; Illusions of Paradox: A Feminist Epistemology Naturalized, Roman & Littlefield, 98. **CONTACT ADDRESS** Dept of Philos, Dalhousie Univ, Halifax, NS, Canada B3H 3J5. **EMAIL** richmond.campbell@dal.ca

CAMPBELL, SUSAN
DISCIPLINE PHILOSOPHY **EDUCATION** Univ Alberta, BA, 78, MA, 83; Univ Toronto, PhD, 92. **CAREER** Asst prof. **RESEARCH** Philosophical psychology, feminist theory, aesthetics, ethics. **SELECTED PUBLICATIONS** Auth, "Elegy and Identity," Daimon, 92; "Being Dismissed: The Politics of Emotional Expression," Hypatia, 94; Interpreting the Personal: Expression and the Formation of Feelings, Cornell UP, 97. **CONTACT ADDRESS** Dept of Philos, Dalhousie Univ, Halifax, NS, Canada B3H 3J5. **EMAIL** susan.campbell@dal.ca

CAMPBELL, TED A.
PERSONAL Born 09/03/1953, Beaumont, TX, m, 1975, 2 children **DISCIPLINE** CHURCH HISTORY **EDUCATION** Univ N Tex, BA, 76; Oxford Univ, BA/MA, 79; SMU, PhD, 84 **CAREER** Visiting lctr, Methodist Thelog School, 84-85; asst prof, Duke Divinity, 85-93; prof, Wesley Theolog Seminary, 93 **MEMBERSHIPS** AAR; ASCH; World Methodist Hist Soc **RESEARCH** Wesleyan Studies; History of Christian Doctrine **SELECTED PUBLICATIONS** Auth, Christian Confessions, Westminister John Knox Press, 96; auth, John Wesley and Christian Antiquity, Kingsword Bks, 91; **CONTACT ADDRESS** Wesley Theol Sem, 4500 Massachussettes, Washington, DC 20016. **EMAIL** tcamp@clark.net

CANEDAY, ARDEL B.
PERSONAL Born 01/16/1950, Minneapolis, MN, m, 1972, 2 children **DISCIPLINE** BIBLICAL STUDIES **EDUCATION** Trinity Evangelical Divinity School, PhD, 91. **CAREER** Assoc Prof Northwestern Col, 92- . **MEMBERSHIPS** Soc Bibl Lit; Inst Bibl Studies; Evangelical Theol Soc; Ctr of Am Exp **RESEARCH** Social & cultural issues; New Testament use of the Old Testament. **SELECTED PUBLICATIONS** Contrib, Eerdmans Bible Dictionary; Evangelical Inclusivism and the Exclusivity of the Gospel SBJT, 97. **CONTACT ADDRESS** Northwestern Col, Minnesota, 3003 Snelling Ave. N, Saint Paul, MN 55113. **EMAIL** abc@nwc.edu

CANNON, DALE W.
PERSONAL Born 03/22/1942, Sedro-Woolley, WA, m, 1966, 3 children **DISCIPLINE** PHILOSOPHY; RELIGIOUS STUDIES **EDUCATION** Seattle Pacific Col, BA, 65; Duke Univ, PhD, 69. **CAREER** Skidmore Col, 68-70; Univ Va, 70-73; Western Oregon Univ, 77- . **HONORS AND AWARDS** Magna cum laude, 65; NDEA Title IV fel, 65-66; Duke Scholar, 66-67; Kearns Fel, 67-68; Kent Fellow, 67-69; NEH summer sem, 78; NEH Inst, 88; East-West Center Inst on Infusing Asian Studies into the Curric, 92, res fel, Inst for Ecumenical and Cultural Res, 93, 00. **MEMBERSHIPS** APA; Northwest Conf on Philos; Am Acad Relig; Polanyi Soc. **RESEARCH** Philosophical foundations of the comparative study of religion; phenomenology of religion; the idea of religious common sense; Michael Polanyi; Soren Kierkegaard;the concept of truth in all of its dimensions; the concepts of objectivity, empathy and personal judgment; children's philosophy. **SELECTED PUBLICATIONS** Auth, Haven't You Noticed that Modernity is Bankrupt, Tradition and Discovery, 94-95; auth, Six Ways of Being Religious: A Framework for Comparative Studies of Religion, Wadsworth, 96; auth, Sanders' Analytic Rebuttal to Polanyi's Critics, With Some Musings on Polanyi's Idea of Truth, Tradition and Discovery, 96-97; auth, An Existential Theory of Truth, Personalist Forum, 96; auth, Religious Taxonomy, Academia, and Interreligious Dialogue, Buddhist Christian Stud, 98; auth, A Polanyian Approach to Conceiving and Teaching Introduction to Philosophy, Tradition, and Discovery, 99; auth, "Religious Commonsense and the Comparative Study of Religion", in Issues in Religious Studies, 99; auth, "Polanyi's 'Invitation to Dogmatism'? A Response to Andy Sanders' 'Polanyian Puzzle'," in Polanyiana, 99; auth, "Some Aspects of Polyani's Version of Realism", in Tradition and Discovery, 00; auth, "A Post-Critical Approach to Conceiving and Teaching Introduction to Philosophy", in Teaching Philosophy, 01. **CONTACT ADDRESS** Dept of Philosophy and Religious Studies, Western Oregon Univ, Monmouth, OR 97361. **EMAIL** cannodw@wou.edu

CANNON, JOHN J.
PERSONAL Born Philadelphia, PA **DISCIPLINE** LABOR LAW **EDUCATION** Villanova Univ, AB, 59; Villanova Univ Sch Law, JD, 62; Grad Stud, Georgetown Univ Law Ctr, 63-64. **CAREER** Prof, Villanova Univ. **MEMBERSHIPS** Order of the Coif; Amer Bar Asn. **RESEARCH** Employment and labor law; civil litigation. **CONTACT ADDRESS** Law School, Villanova Univ, 800 Lancaster Ave, Villanova, PA 19085-1692. **EMAIL** cannon@law.vill.edu

CANNON, KATIE GENEVA
PERSONAL Born 01/03/1950, Concord, NC, s **DISCIPLINE** THEOLOGY **EDUCATION** Barber-Scotia Coll, BS, Elementary Education (magna cum laude), 71; Johnson C Smith Seminary, Atlanta, MDiv, 74; Union Theological Seminary, New York, NYork, MPhil, 83, PhD, Christian Ethics, 83. **CAREER** Episcopal Divinity School, asst prof; New York Theological Seminary, admin faculty, 77-80; Ascension Presbyterian Church, first African-American female pastor, 75-77; Yale Divinity School, visiting lecturer, 87; Harvard Divinity School, visiting scholar, 83-84; Wellesley College, visiting professor, 91; Temple University, Department of Religion, assoc prof of Christian ethics, currently. **HONORS AND AWARDS** Isaac R Clark Preaching Awd, Interdenominational Theological Center, 73; Rockfeller Prostestant Fellow Fund for Theological Educ, 72-74; Rockefeller Doctoral Fellow Fund for Theological Educ, 74-76; Ford Found Fellow Natl Fellowships Fund, 76-77; Roothbert Fellow, 81-83; Harvard Divinity School, woman research assoc, Ethics, 83-84; Radcliffe Coll Bunting Inst, 87-88; Episcopal Church's Conant Grant, 87-88; Assn of Theological School Young Scholar Awd, 87-88; **MEMBERSHIPS** Ecumenical dialogue, Third World theologians, editor, Que Pasa, member, Amer Acad of Religion, Assn of Black Women in Higher Educ, bd of dir, Women's Theological Center, member, Soc for the Study of Black Religion. **SELECTED PUBLICATIONS** Auth, Black Womanist Ethics, Scholars Press, 88; coed, Inheriting Our Mothers' Garden, Westminster Press, 88; Katie's Canon: Womanism and the Soul of the Black Community, 95. **CONTACT ADDRESS** Union Theol Sem, Virginia, 3401 Brook Rd, Richmond, VA 23227.

CANTOR, NORMAN FRANK
PERSONAL Born 11/19/1929, Winnipeg, MB, Canada, m, 1957, 2 children **DISCIPLINE** MEDIEVAL & ENGLISH LEGAL HISTORY, HISTORICAL SOCIOLOGY **EDUCATION** Univ Man, BA, 51; Princeton Univ, MA, 53, PhD, 57. **CAREER** From instr to asst prof hist, Princeton Univ, 55-60; vis prof, Johns Hopkins Univ, 60; from assoc prof to prof, Columbia Univ, 60-66; prof, Brandeis Univ, 66-68, Leff prof, 68-70; chmn dept, State Univ NY, Binghamton, 70-74, distinguished prof hist, 70-76, provost for grad studies, 75-76, vpres acad affairs, 75-76; vchancellor acad affairs & prof hist, Ill-Chicago Circle, 76-78; dean fac arts & sci, 78-81, prof hist, 78-81, Prof Hist & Sociol, New York Univ, 81-; Can Coun fel, 60; Am Coun Learned Soc fel, 60; consult, Bar Asn NYC, 63-67; consult, Encycl Britannica, 64-65; consult, Life mag, 66-68; vis prof, Brooklyn Col, 72-73, Adelphi Univ, 87; Fulbright prof, Tel Aviv, 87-88; consult, NEH 73, 89-91. **HONORS AND AWARDS** Nat Book Critics Circle Nomination, 91; NY Public Libr Awd, 97; Fel Royal Hist Soc, 74; lld, univ winnipeg, 73. **MEMBERSHIPS** AHA; AAUP. **RESEARCH** Medieval cultural history; legal history; comparative European history. **SELECTED PUBLICATIONS** Inventing the Middle Ages, Morrow, 91; Civilization of the Middle Ages, HarperCollins, 93; The Sacred Chain, HarperCollins, 94; Medieval Lives, HarperCollins, 94; The Medieval Reader, 95; The Jewish Experience, HarperCollins, 95; The American Century, HarperCollins, 97; Imagining the Law, HarperCollins, 97. **CONTACT ADDRESS** Dept Hist, New York Univ, 53 Washington Sq S, New York, NY 10012-4556.

CAPIZZI, JOSEPH E.
PERSONAL Born 07/24/1967, Staten Island, NY, m, 1995, 2 children **DISCIPLINE** THEOLOGY **EDUCATION** Univ Vir, BA, 89; Emory Univ, MTS, 93; Univ Notre Dame, PhD, 98. **CAREER** Asst Prof, Cath Univ Am, 97-. **MEMBERSHIPS** AAR; SCE; CTSA. **RESEARCH** Political and social thought. **CONTACT ADDRESS** Theology Dept, Catholic Univ of America, Religious Studies School, Washington, DC 20064. **EMAIL** capizzi@cua.edu

CAPLAN, ARTHUR L.
PERSONAL Born 03/31/1950, Boston, MA, d, 1971, 1 child **DISCIPLINE** BIOETHICS **EDUCATION** Brandeis Univ, BA, 71; Columbia Univ, MA, 73; Columbia Univ, M.Phil, 75; Columbia Univ, PhD, 79. **CAREER** Dir, Center Bioethics, Univ Penn, 94-; Trustee Prof Bioethics, Univ Penn, 94-; Chief, Div Bioethics, Univ Penn, 96-; Dir, Center Biomedical Ethics, Univ Minn, 87-94; Prof Philos & Prof Surgery, Univ Minn, 87-94; assoc dir, Hastings Center, 85-87; vis assoc prof Philos, Univ Pitt, 86; assoc Humanities, Hastings Center, 77-84; assoc Social Medicine, Columbia Col of Physicians and Surgeons, 78-81; instr, Columbia Univ Col of Physicians and Surgeons, 77-78. **HONORS AND AWARDS** Hero of Public Health, Columbia Univ; Doctor of Laws, Elizabethtown Col, 98; Commencement Speech, Elizabethtown Col, 98; Univ S Carolina Convocation Address, 97; Beaver Col Doctor Laws, 97; Univ Minn School Medicine Commencement Speaker, 96; Philadelphia Col of Textiles & Design Convocation Speaker, 96; Philadelphia Col of Textiles & Sci Centennial Medal, 95; Brandeis Univ Alumni Achievement Awd, 95; UTNE 100 Visionaries, 95; Col of Physicians of Philadelphia Fel, 94-; Amer Assoc Advancement Sci Fel, 94-; John Morgan Soc, 94-; Omicron Delta Kappa Honor Soc, 94-; Amer Assoc Bioethics Pres, 93-95; Univ Minn Commencement Speaker, 93. **MEMBERSHIPS** AIDS Med Found; Amer Assoc Advancement Sci; Amer Col Cardiology; Battelle Memorial Inst; Carnegie Found; Committee on Sci & Tech, US House of Reps; Consumers' Union; Heinz Fam Found; Labor Resources Committee, US Senate; Amer Acad Neurology Med Task Force; Amer Cancer Soc, Minn Cancer Council; Center for Disease Control; Ntl Inst of Health; Ntl Endowment for Humanities; NY Acad of Medicine; NY Acad of Sci; Dept Health & Human Services; US Congress Office of Tech Assessmet; President's Commission for the Study of Ethical Problems in Medicine and Biomedical and Behavioral Res; United Health Care. **RESEARCH** Medical Ethics; Health Policy; Ethical Issues in Science and Technology; History and Philosophy of Medicine and the Life Sciences. **SELECTED PUBLICATIONS** Ed, The American Medical Ethics Revolution: Sesquicentennial Reflections on the AMA's Code of Medical Ethics, Johns Hopkins Univ Pr, 98; Due Consideration: Controversy in the Age of Medical Miracles, John Wiley & Sons, 98; Am I My Brother's Keeper? The Ethical Frontiers of Biomedicine, Ind Univ Pr, 98; "Paradigms for clinical ethics consultation practice," Cambridge Quarterly of Healthcare Ethics, 98; "Dealing with Dolly: inside the national bioethics advisory commission," Health Affairs, 98. **CONTACT ADDRESS** Dept of Bioethenics, Univ of Pennsylvania, 60 W Mermaid Ln, Philadelphia, PA 19118-4024. **EMAIL** caplan@mail.med.upenn.edu

CAPPS, DONALD E.
PERSONAL Born 01/30/1939, Omaha, NE, m, 1964, 1 child **DISCIPLINE** RELIGION **EDUCATION** Lewis and Clark Col, BA 60; Yale Div Sch, BD 63, STM 65; Univ Chicago, MA 66, PhD 70. **CAREER** Oregon State Univ, inst 69; Univ Chicago Div Sch, inst, asst prof, 69-74; Univ N Carolina, assoc prof, 74-76; Phillips Univ Grad Sem, assoc prof, prof, 76-81; Princeton Theo Seminary, William Harte Felmeth prof of pastoral theol, 81-. **HONORS AND AWARDS** SSSR pres; ThD honors Univ Uppsala. **MEMBERSHIPS** SSSR; SPT; AAR; SBL (Society for Biblical Literature). **RESEARCH** Psychology of religion; psychology of art and selected genres; psychobiography; theory and practice of pastoral counseling; social scientific

study of religion. **SELECTED PUBLICATIONS** Auth, Freud, Freudians, and Religion: A Reader, Yale Univ Press, 01; auth, Jesus: A Psychological Biography, Chalice Press, 00; auth, Living Stories: Pastoral Counseling in Congregational Context, Fortress Press, 98; Men Religion and Melancholia, Yale Univ Press, 97; The Child's Song: The Religious Abuse of Children, Westminster John Knox Press, 95; Agents of Hope: A Pastoral Psychology, Fortress Press, 95; The Poet's Gift: Toward the Renewal of Pastoral care, Westminster/John Knox Press, 93; The Depleted Self: Sin in a Narcissistic Age, Fortress Press, 93; Reframing: A New Method in Pastoral care, Fortress Press, 90. **CONTACT ADDRESS** Dept of Theology, Princeton Theol Sem, 64 Mercer St, PO Box 821, Princeton, NJ 08542-0803.

CAPRA, DANIEL J.
DISCIPLINE CONSTITUTIONAL CRIMINAL PROCEDURE **EDUCATION** Rockhurst, AB, 74; Berkeley, JD, 77. **CAREER** Pvt practice, Lord, Day & Lord, 77-79; asst prof, Tulane Law Sch, 79-81; Philip D Reed prof, 81-; ch, Comm prof resp, Assn Bar NYC, 90-93; ch, Comm fed legis, Assn Bar NYC, 93-96. **MEMBERSHIPS** Mem, exec comm, Assn Bar NYC, 97-. **SELECTED PUBLICATIONS** Auth, Cases and Commentary on American Criminal Procedure, Columns on Evidence, NY Law Jour, 96; co-auth, Basic Criminal Procedure, Evidence: The Objection Method, 97; Federal Rules of Evidence Manual, NY Evidence Handbk, 97. **CONTACT ADDRESS** Law Sch, Fordham Univ, 113 W 60th St, New York, NY 10023. **EMAIL** dcapra@mail.lawnet.fordham.edu

CAPRIOTTI, EMILE
PERSONAL Born 06/28/1950, Chicago Heights, IL **DISCIPLINE** LAW, PHILOSOPHY **EDUCATION** Univ of Southern Calif, PhD, 88; Ind Univ Law School, JD, 90; De Paul Univ College of Law, LLM, 98. **CAREER** Asst State's Attorney, La Beau, Dietchweiler and Assoc. **HONORS AND AWARDS** Claude R Lambe Fellow, 88-89; 89-90. **MEMBERSHIPS** Am Bar Asn; Ill Bar Asn; Chicago Bar Asn; Kankakee County Bar Asn; Justinian Soc; Am Philos Asn; Federalist Soc. **RESEARCH** Medical ethics; Legal philosophy; Political Philosophy: Ethics. **SELECTED PUBLICATIONS** Auth, The Grounds and Limits of Political Obligation, 92. **CONTACT ADDRESS** Box 136, Saint Anne, IL 60964.

CAPRON, ALEXANDER M.
PERSONAL Born 08/16/1944, Hartford, CT, m, 1989, 4 children **DISCIPLINE** ECONOMICS & HISTORY, LAW **EDUCATION** Swarthmore Col, BA, 66; Yale Law Sch, LLB, 69. **CAREER** USC Law School **HONORS AND AWARDS** Fellow, Am Asn for Advan of Sci; Hon Fellow, Am Col of Legal Med. **MEMBERSHIPS** Inst Med; Nat Acad Sci; Int Asn of Bioethics; Am Soc of Law, Med, & Ethics (past pres). **RESEARCH** Ethical & social issues in medical & the life sciences. **CONTACT ADDRESS** USC Law School, Univ of So California, Los Angeles, CA 90089-0071. **EMAIL** acapron@law.usc.edu

CAPUTO, JOHN D.
PERSONAL Born 10/26/1940, Philadelphia, PA, m, 1968, 3 children **DISCIPLINE** PHILOSOPHY **EDUCATION** LaSalle Univ, BA, 62; Villanova Univ, MA, 64; Bryn Mawr Col, PhD, 68. **CAREER** Villanova Univ, David R Cook prof, 92-; prof, 76-; assoc prof, 72-76; asst prof, 68-72; vis prof, New Sch for Soc Res, 94; distinguished adj prof, Fordham Univ Grad Prog, 85-88; vis prof, Fordham Univ, 80 & Duquesne Univ, 78; instr, St Joseph's Univ, 65-68; pres, Phi Kappa Phi, Villanova Univ Chap, 79-80; Univ Rank and Tenure Comt, 81-;Search Comt, VP for Acad Aff, 94-95; ch, Bd of Publ, 89-; chp, Dept Grad Prog, 85-91; dept chp, Bd of Trustees Liason Comt, Acad Aff, 72-80; Search Comt for Grad Dean, 86-87; Search Comt for Dir of Res, 85-86; Search Comt for Dean of Arts & Sci(s), 80-81; chp, Fac Coun, 76-78; exec co-dir, Soc for Phenomenol and Existential Philos, 92-95; ch, Comt on Career Opportunities, Amer Philos Asn, 90-93; mem, ex officio, Nat Bd of Off, Amer Philos Asn, 90-93; pres, Amer Catholic Philos Asn, 87-88; exec comt, Amer Philos Asn, Eastern Div, 86-89; exec co-dir, Greater Philadelphia Philos Consortium, 83-87; ser ed, Perspectives in Continental Philos, Fordham Univ Press; mem bd(s): Heidegger Stud, Man & World, Amer Catholic Philos Quart, Hist of Philos Quart, Stud in Contl Philos-Ind Univ Press; Joyful Wisdom, The J Postmodern Thought, Epoche & Int Adv Bd Handbk for the Philos of Relig in the 20th century; bd trustees, Radnor Township Mem Libr,86-89; Dem Cand for Radnor Township Sch Bd, 91, 93; dir educ, Radnor Township Dem Comt, 91-94. **HONORS AND AWARDS** NEH fel, Col Tchr(s), 91-91; NEHs, Summer stipend, 85; Amer Coun of Learned Soc(s), fel, 83-84; Outstanding Fac Schol Awd, Villanova Univ, 82; Summer Res Grant, Villanova Univ, 82; Distinguished Alumnus, Villanova Univ Grad Sch, 81; Amer Coun of Learned Soc(s), grant, 72. **MEMBERSHIPS** Hon mem, Phi Beta Kappa, Villanova Chap, 89. **SELECTED PUBLICATIONS** Auth, Deconstruction in a Nutshell: A Conversation with Jacques Derrida, Fordham Univ Press, 97; The Prayers and Tears of Jacques Derrida: Religion without Religion, Ind Univ Press, 97; Againsts Ethics: Contributions to a Poetics of Obligation with Constant Reference to Deconstruction, Studies in Continental Thought, Ind Univ Press, 93; Demythologizing Heidegger, Studies in the Philosophy of Religion, Ind Univ Press, 93; Radical Hermeneutics: Repetition, Deconstruction and the Hermeneutic Project, Studies in Phenomenology and Existential Philosophy, Ind Univ Press, 87; Soll die Philosophie das letzte Wort haben, Levinas und der junge Heidegger uber Philosophie und Glauben, Festschrift, Hermann Schafer, Haus der Geschichte, 1996; Instants, Secrets, Singularities: Dealing Death in Kierkegaard and Derrida, Kierkegaard in Post/Modernity, Ind Univ Press, 95; Dark Hearts: Heidegger, Richardson, and Evil., From Phenomenol to Thought, Errancy, and Desire, Kluwer, 96; Infestations: The Religion of the Death of God and Scott's Ascetic Ideal, Res in Phenomenol, 95; Bedevilling the Tradition: Deconstruction and Catholicism, (Dis)continuity and (De)construction: Reflections on the Meaning of the Past in Crisis Situations, Pharos, 95; coaut, Modernity and Its Discontents, Fordham Univ Press, 92; guest ed, J Amer Catholic Philos Quart, 64, 95; Heidegger Issue, Presenting Heidegger, Philos Today, 96; Phenomenology and Beyond, Selected Stud ies in Phenomenol & Existential Philosophy, vol 21; co-ed, Foucault and the Critique of Institut;ions, Pa State Univ Press, 93; auth, More Radical Hermeneutics, Indiana Univ. Press, 00; ed, God, the Gift, and Postmodernism; Indiana Univ. Press, 99. **CONTACT ADDRESS** Dept of Philosophy, Villanova Univ, 800 Lancaster Ave., Villanova, PA 19085-1692. **EMAIL** jcaputo@erols.com

CARANFA, ANGELO
PERSONAL Born 05/24/1942, Rotello, Italy, s **DISCIPLINE** AESTHETICS, PHILOSOPHY **EDUCATION** Stonehill Col, BS, 66; Boston Col, MA, 71; Univ Florence, PhD, 72. **CAREER** Adj instr, Newbury Jr Col, 75-76, Boston State Col, 76-78, Bridgewater State Col, 85-87, Stonehill Col, 78-85, 90-. **MEMBERSHIPS** Am Philos Asn **RESEARCH** 20th Century French aesthetics. **SELECTED PUBLICATIONS** Auth, Obedience, Love and Marriage in the Philosophy of St John, Licacre Quarterly, 83; coed, Western Heritage: Man's Encounter with Himsef and the World, Lanham, Md: Univ Press of Am, 84; auth, Proust and Augustine on Time, Hist of Eurpean Ideas, 86; auth, Claudel: Beauty and Grace, Lewisburg, Penn: Bucknell Unvi Press, 89; auth, Proust: The Creative Silence, Lewisburg, Penn: Bucknell Univ Press, 90; auth, The Interior Life in claudel's Art Criticism of renaissance Dutch Painting, Art Crticism, 97; auth, Toward an Aesthetic Model of Teaching and Writing in the Humanitie, J of Aesthetic Ed, 99; auth, Camille Claudel: A Sculptuer of Interior Solitued, Bucknell Univ Press, 99. **CONTACT ADDRESS** 27 Sprague Ave., Brockton, MA 02302. **EMAIL** acaranfa@stonehill.edu

CARD, CLAUDIA F.
PERSONAL Born 09/30/1940, Madison, WI **DISCIPLINE** PHILOSOPHY **EDUCATION** Univ Wis-Madison, BA, 62; Harvard Univ, Am, 64, PhD, 69. **CAREER** Instr, 66-69, asst prof, 69-72, Assoc Prof Philos, Univ Wis-Madison, 72-, Vis assoc prof philos, Dartmouth Col, 78-79 & Univ Pittsburgh, 80. **HONORS AND AWARDS** Phi Kappa Phi, 61; Phi Beta Kappa, 62; NEH Fel, 74-75; Vilas Assoc, Univ Wis, 89-91; Distinguished Woman Philos of the Year, Soc Women Philos, 96; Am Coun of Learned Soc Senior Fel 99-00; Inst of Res in the Humanities ResidentFel, 00. **MEMBERSHIPS** Am Philos Asn; Soc Women Philos; Nat Women's Study Asn; Soc for Lesbian & Gay Philos; N Am Nietzsche Soc; Soc Philosophic Study of Sport; Int Soc for the Study of Environmental Ethics. **RESEARCH** Ethics; feminist philosophy; social philosophy. **SELECTED PUBLICATIONS** Auth, On mercy, Philos Rev, 72; co-ed, Religious Commitment and Salvation, Charles E Merrill Co, 74; ed, Feminist Ethics, 91; Adventures in Lesbian Philosophy, 94; auth, Lesbian Choices, 95; The Unnatural Lottery, 96; editor of book series, Feminist Ethics, for Univ Press Kans; ed, Philos Book Reviews, J Homosexuality; ed, On Feminist Ethics and Politics, 99. **CONTACT ADDRESS** Dept of Philos, Univ of Wisconsin, Madison, 600 North Park St, Madison, WI 53706-1403. **EMAIL** cfcard@facstaff.wisc.edu

CAREY, JOHN M.
PERSONAL Born 12/15/1964, Arlington, MA, m, 1991, 2 children **DISCIPLINE** POLITICAL SCIENCE **EDUCATION** Harvard Univ, BA, 86; Univ Calif San Diego, PhD, 94. **CAREER** Asst Prof, Univ Rochester, 94-97; Asst Prof to Assoc Prof, Wash Univ, 97-. **HONORS AND AWARDS** NSF, 95-97, 00-02; APSA Harold D. Lasswell Dissertation Awd, 95. **MEMBERSHIPS** Am Polit Sci Asn; Midwest Polit Sci Asn; Latin Am Studies Asn. **RESEARCH** Comparative democratic institutions. **SELECTED PUBLICATIONS** Co-auth, Presidents and Assemblies: Constitutional Design and Electoral Dynamics, Cambridge Univ Press, 92; auth, "Political Shirking and the Last Term Problem: Evidence for a Party-Administered Pension System," Public Choice, 94; co-auth, "Incentives to Cultivate a Personal Vote: A Rank Ordering of Electoral Formulas," Electoral Studies, 95; auth, Term Limits and Legislative Representation, Cambridge Univ Press, 96; co-auth, Executive Decree Authority, Cambridge Univ Press, 98; auth, "Partidos y coaliciones en el Congreso Chileno," Politica y obierno, 99; co-auth, "Presidential Agenda Control and Spending Policy: Lessons from General Pinochet's Constitution," Am J of Polit Sci, 99; co-auth, Term Limits in the State Legislatures, Univ Mich Press, 00; auth, "Parchment, Equilibria, and Institutions," Comparative Polit Studies, 00; co-auth, "Incumbency and the Probability of Reelection in State Legislative Elections," J of Polit, (00): 671-700. **CONTACT ADDRESS** Dept Polit Sci, Washington Univ, Saint Louis, MO 63130. **EMAIL** jmcarey@artsci.wustl.edu

CAREY, PATRICK W.
PERSONAL Born 07/02/1940, m, 2 children **DISCIPLINE** RELIGIOUS STUDIES; HISTORY OF AMERICAN RELIGION **EDUCATION** St John's Univ, BA, 62; St John's Sem, M Div, 66; Union Theol Sem, STM, 71; Fordham Univ, PhD, 75. **CAREER** Asst prof, St Peter's Col, 75-76; Elisabeth Seton Col, 76; Carleton Col, 76-77; Gustavus Adolphus, 77-78; from asst prof to assoc prof, Marquette Univ, 78-. **MEMBERSHIPS** Am Acad of Rel; Am Soc of Church Hist; U.S. Cath. Hist Soc; Am Cath. Hist Asn; Am Cath. Hist Soc of Philadelphia; Col Theol Soc; Cath. Theol Soc of Am. **RESEARCH** Hist of Am Rel. **SELECTED PUBLICATIONS** Auth, Orestes A. Brownson: Selected Writings, 91; The Roman Catholics, 93; The Roman Catholics in America, 96; Orestes A. Brownson: A Bibliography, 1826-1876, 96; Ontologism in American Catholic Thought, 1840-1900, Revue d'Histoire Ecclesiastique 91/3-4, 96; Catholicism, Encycl of the United States in the Twentieth Century, ed S. I. Kutler et al, 96; After Testem Benevolentiae and Pascendi, Catholic Southwest: A Jour of History and Culture 7, 96; ed, The Pastoral Letters of the United States Catholic Bishops, vol 6, 1989-1997, 98; coed, Theological Education in the Catholic Tradition: Contemporary Challenges, 97. **CONTACT ADDRESS** Dept of Theology, Marquette Univ, 100 Coughlin Hall, PO Box 1881, Milwaukee, WI 53233-2295. **EMAIL** careyp@csd.mu.edu

CARL, HAROLD F.
PERSONAL Born 11/18/1958, Marion, IL, m, 1980, 1 child **DISCIPLINE** SYSTEMATIC THEOLOGY **EDUCATION** Westminster Theol Sem, PhD. **CAREER** Assoc prof theol, Houston Grad Sch of Theol, 92-97; chaplain, Berry Col, 97-. **MEMBERSHIPS** Evang Theol Soc; Soc of Bibl Lit. **RESEARCH** Theology; Christology; Historical Theology. **SELECTED PUBLICATIONS** Auth, User Friendly Faith, full text reprint, SirS Renaissance Database, Mar, 98; User Friendly Faith: What liberals believed and why fundamentalists made such a fuss, Christ Hist, 55, vol 16, no 3, Aug, 97; Integrative Theology, vol 3, Lewis and Demarest, Book Rev, JETS, vol 40, no 2, Jun, 97; Jesus's Relational Language in John 14-16: Implications for the Doctrine of the Trinity, paper presented to the Annual Mtg of the Evangel Theol Soc, Nov, 96; Ministry in the Age of Technology, Gospel Monthly Mag, Feb, 96; The NIV and Homosexuality (Part 1 & 2), Gospel Monthly Mag, Dec 95, Jan 96; The Biblical Perspective on the Personhood of the Unborn, http://www.sehlat.com/lifelink/multi/rea1.html, Dec, 95; The Atonement, Gospel Monthly Mag, Oct, 95; What is the Atonement?, Houston Church Mag, Aug, 95; Imitating the Incarnation (Christ-like Self-sacrifice), Gospel Monthly Mag, Oct, 94. **CONTACT ADDRESS** PO Box 490460, Mount Berry, GA 30149-0460. **EMAIL** hcarl@berry.edu

CARLSON, DAVID A.
PERSONAL Born 06/17/1948, Colorado Springs, CO, m, 1982, 5 children **DISCIPLINE** RELIGION **EDUCATION** Claremont Grad Sch, PhD, 88. **CAREER** Assoc Prof, Unification Theol Sem, 88-. **HONORS AND AWARDS** Outstanding Young Man of Am, U S Jr Chamber of Commerce, 80; Cert of Appreciation, Zonta Club of Bacolod, Philippines, 94. **MEMBERSHIPS** AAR. **RESEARCH** World religion and culture. **SELECTED PUBLICATIONS** Auth, "Hak Ja Han: Wife, Mother, Spiritual Leader," Women and Korean Relig," Unification News (91); auth, "Denial of 'Self' as a Religious Principle: Towards a Unity of Religions," in The Establishment of a New Cult and Unification Thought, (Tokyo: UTI Pr, 91); auth, "Ecological Considerations of Unification Thought," in Vol II, Proceedings of the Seventeenth Int Conf on the Unity of the Sci: Absolute Values and the Reassessment of the Contemp world (Los Angeles: ICUS, 91); coauth, Explorations in Unificationism, UTS (New York), 96. **CONTACT ADDRESS** Dept Relig, Unification Theol Sem, 10 Dock St, Barrytown, NY 12507-5000. **EMAIL** k4273843@epix.net

CARLSTON, CHARLES E.
PERSONAL Born 11/14/1923, Lewistown, MT, m, 1945, 5 children **DISCIPLINE** RELIGION **EDUCATION** Harvard Univ, AB, 47, AM, 51, PhD, 58; Fuller Theol Sem, BD, 50. **CAREER** Vis prof church hist, theol sem, Univ Dubuque, 55-56; vis prof New Testament, 56-58, from assoc prof to prof New Testament lit & exeg, 58-64; assoc prof relig, Univ Iowa, 64-69; Prof New Testament, 69-71, Norris Prof New Testament, Andover Newton Theol Sch, 71-, Sealantic fel, Tubingen, 59-60; ed Bibl res, Chicago Soc Bibl Res J, 66-68; Fulbright res grant, Tubingen, 73; Asn Theol Schs & Soc Bibl Lit fel, Claremont, 77-78; ed, Sources Bibl Study, Soc Bibl Lit, 80- **MEMBERSHIPS** Soc Bibl Lit; Studiorum Novi Testamenti Soc; Cath Bibl Asn. **RESEARCH** New Testament. **SELECTED PUBLICATIONS** **CONTACT ADDRESS** Andover Newton Theol Sch, Newton, MA 02159.

CARMAN, TAYLOR
PERSONAL Born 06/19/1965, Boulder, CO, m, 1992, 1 child **DISCIPLINE** PHILOSOPHY **EDUCATION** Stanford Univ, PhD, 93 **CAREER** Asst prof, Barnard Col. **MEMBERSHIPS** APA. **RESEARCH** 19th and 20th century European philoso-

phy. **SELECTED PUBLICATIONS** Auth, "The Body in Husserl and Merleau-Ponty," Philosophical Topics 27, 2 (99): 205-226; auth, "Must We Be Authentic?" in Heidegger, Authenticity, and Modernity: Essays in Honor of Hubert L. Dreyfus, Vol. 1 (Cambridge, the MIT Press, 00). **CONTACT ADDRESS** Dept of Philos, Barnard Col, 3009 Broadway, New York, NY 10027. **EMAIL** Tcarman@barnard.edu

CARMICHAEL, CALUM MACNEILL

PERSONAL Born 04/01/1938, Glasgow, Scotland, m, 1959, 4 children **DISCIPLINE** BIBLICAL AND SEMITIC STUDIES **EDUCATION** Glasgow Univ, BSc, 59; Edinburgh Univ, BD, 62; Oxford Univ, BLitt, 64; Glasgow Univ, UD, 91. **CAREER** Sr res fel Jewish-non-Jewish rel, Univ Southampton, 66-67; asst prof Bibl & Semitic studies, 67-70, assoc prof Semitic lang & lit, 70-75, Prof Comp Lit & Bibl Studies, Cornell Univ, 75-, Am Coun Learned Soc grant-in-aid, 72 & 79; vis fel, Oxford Ctr Postgrad Hebrew Studies, 72, 72 & 82; fel, St Cross Col, Oxford, 82; Guggenheim fel, 82; Adjunct Prof of Law, 92-. **MEMBERSHIPS** Soc Bibl Lit; Jewish Law Asn. **RESEARCH** Biblical and ancient Near Eastern legal and wisdom literature; New Testament and Rabbinic Judaism. **SELECTED PUBLICATIONS** Auth, The Laws of Deuteronomy (Cornell Univ Press, Ithaca), 74; auth, Women, Law, and the Genesis Traditions (Edinburgh Univ Press), 79; auth, Law and Narrative in the Bible (Cornell Univ Press, Ithaca), 85; auth, The Origins of Biblical Law: The Decalogues and the Book of the Covenant (Cornell Univ Press, Ithaca), 92; ed, Studies in Comparative Legal History, Collected Works of David Daube, vol 1 Talmudic Law (Univ of CA, Berkeley), 92; auth, Essays on Law and Religion in Honour of David Daube (Univ of CA, Berkeley), 93; auth, The Story of Creation: Its Origin and Its Interpretation in Philo and the Fourth Gospel (Cornell Univ Press, Ithaca), 96; auth, The Spirit of Biblical Law (Univ of Georgia Press, Athens), 96; auth, Law, Legend, and Incest in the Bible: Leviticus 18-20 (Cornell Univ Press, Ithaca, 97; auth, New Testament Judaism, (Unif of CA, Berkeley), 00. **CONTACT ADDRESS** Dept of Comp Lit, Cornell Univ, 143 Goldwin Smith, Ithaca, NY 14853-0001. **EMAIL** cmc13@cornell.edu

CARNEY, JAMES DONALD

PERSONAL Born 12/27/1930, Evanston, IL, m, 1961, 2 children **DISCIPLINE** PHILOSOPHY **EDUCATION** Northern Baptist Theol Sem, BA, 53; Roosevelt Univ, MA, 53; Univ Nebr-Lincoln, PhD(philos), 59. **CAREER** From instr to asst prof philos, Kenyon Col, 59-63; lectr, Univ Otago, NZ, 63-64, sr lectr, 64-66; assoc prof, 66-67, Prof Philos to Prof emer, Ariz State Univ, 67-. **MEMBERSHIPS** Am Philos Asn. **RESEARCH** Linguistic analysis; logic. **SELECTED PUBLICATIONS** Auth, A Historical Theory of Art Criticism, Jour Aesthetic Edu, Vol 0028, 94. **CONTACT ADDRESS** Dept of Philos, Arizona State Univ, PO Box 872004, Tempe, AZ 85287-2004.

CARNEY, WILLIAM J.

PERSONAL Born 05/10/1937, Chicago, IL, m, 1973, 3 children **DISCIPLINE** LAW, ECONOMICS **EDUCATION** Yale Univ, BA, 59, Llb, 62. **CAREER** Assoc, Holland & Hart, Denver, 62-68, partner, 68-70; pvt pract law, Aspen, CO, 70-73; assoc prof law, Col Law, Univ WY, 73-76, prof, 76-78; Prof Law, Sch Law, Emory Univ, 78-; Sr Mem Acad Staff, Law & Econ Ctr, 81-85. **MEMBERSHIPS** Am Law Inst. **RESEARCH** Law and Economic Analysis; Shareholder Conflicts; the Political Economy of Corporate Law. **SELECTED PUBLICATIONS** Auth, Exemptions from securities registration for small issues: Shifting from full disclosure, Land & Water Law Rev, 76; The Perils of Rule 146, Univ Toledo Law J, 77; Securities Practice: The Law in Georgia, Harrison Co, 80; Fundamental Corporate Changes, Minority Shareholders & Business Purposes, Am Bar Found Res J, 80; coauth, Defining a Security: Georgia's Struggle with the Risk Capital Test, Emory Law J, 81; ed, The Changing Role of the Corporate Attorney, Lexington Books, 82; auth, Shareholder Coordination Costs, Shark Repellants and Takeout Mergers, Am Bar Found Res J, 83; Toward a More Perfect Market for Corporate Control, Del J Corp L, 84; Takeover Tussles: The Courts' Tug-of-war with Corporate Boards, Business & Soc Rev, 85; Two-Tier Tender Offers and Shark Repellants, Midland J Corporate Finance, 86; Signalling and Causation in Insider Trading, Catholic U L Rev, 87; Controlling Management Opportunism in the Market for Corporate Control: An Agency Cost Model, WI L Rev, 88; The Limits of the Fraud on the Market Doctrine, Business Lawyer, 89; Does Defining Constituencies Matter?, Cinn L Rev, 90; coauth, The Theft of Time, Inc? Efficient Law and Efficient Markets, Regulation, 91; coauth, Vicarious Liability for Fraud on the Market: Theory and Evidence, 92; auth, The ALI's Corporate Governance Project: The Death of Property Rights?, Geo Wash L Rev, 93; Limited Liability Companies: Origins and Antecedents, Univ CO L Rev, 95; The Political Economy of Competition for Corporate Charters, J Legal Studies, 97; Large Bank Shareholders: Saviors or Substitutes?, J Applied Corp Finance, 97; The Production of Corporate Law, S CA Law Rev, 98; Explaining the Shape of Corporate Law, Managerial and Decision Econ, 98; auth, Mergers and Acquisitions: Cases and Materials, Foundation Press; auth, The Legacy of The Market for Corporate Control and the Origins of Theory of the Firm, 50 Case Wes. Res. L. Rev. 215; auth, Teaching Problems in Corporate Law: Making It Real 34 Ga. L. Rev. 823. **CONTACT ADDRESS** Sch Law, Emory Univ, 1364 Clifton Rd N E, Atlanta, GA 30322-2770.

CARPENTER, ELIZABETH S.

PERSONAL Born 04/24/1944, Chicago, IL, m, 1967, 3 children **DISCIPLINE** RELIGIOUS STUDIES, PHILOSOPHY **EDUCATION** Randolph Macon Woman's Col, AB, 66; Univ IL, Chicago, AM (philos), 69; Univ VA, MA, 97, PhD (religious studies), 97. **HONORS AND AWARDS** AB with Honors in Philos. **MEMBERSHIPS** Am Academy Relig; Soc Biblical Lit; Soc Christian Ethics. **RESEARCH** Religious ethics; political theory; theology; philosophy. **CONTACT ADDRESS** 5285 Celt Rd, Stanardsville, VA 22973.

CARPENTER, JAMES ANDERSON

PERSONAL Born 04/02/1928, King's Mountain, NC, m, 1954, 2 children **DISCIPLINE** THEOLOGY, PHILOSOPHY **EDUCATION** Wofford Col, BA, 48; Duke Univ, BD, 51; Cambridge Univ, PhD(theol), 59. **CAREER** Asst prof, 63-65, Prof Dogmatic Theol, Gen Theol Sem, 65-, Sub-Dean, 74-, Am Philos Soc res grant, 68. **MEMBERSHIPS** Am Theol Soc; Soc Arts, Relig & Cult; Anglican Theol Soc. **RESEARCH** Nineteenth century theology and philosophy; liberal Catholic movement in England; the religious thought of Samuel Taylor Coleridge. **SELECTED PUBLICATIONS** Auth, A Study in Liberal Catholic Thought, Faith, 60; Christian socialism of Charles Gore, Crucible, 63; New theology and the old religion, Witness, 65; A plea for liberal Catholicism, Living Church, 67; On the Marxist-Christian dialogue, Anglican Theol Rev, 71; Samuel Taylor Coleridge, theologian, St Luke's J, 73; Charles Raven: Prophet not without honor, Anglican Theol Rev, 77; Jews and Christians: Suggestions for dialogue, Forward Movement Press, 81; The priest as theologian, Anglican Theol Rev, 82. **CONTACT ADDRESS** General Theol Sem, 3 Chelsea Sq, New York, NY 10011.

CARR, ANNE E.

PERSONAL Born 11/11/1934, Chicago, IL **DISCIPLINE** THEOLOGY, RELIGIOUS STUDIES **EDUCATION** Mundelein Col, BA, 56; Marquette Univ, MA, 63; Univ Chicago, PhD(theol), 71. **CAREER** Asst prof relig studies, Mundelein Col, 63-73 & Ind Univ, Bloomington, 73-75; asst prof theol, 75-77, assoc dean, 77-81, Assoc Prof Theol, Divinity Sch, Univ Chicago, 77-. **HONORS AND AWARDS** Hon Degree, Doctor of Divinity, Jesuit Sch of Theol, 83; Honorary Degree, Doctor of Humane Letters, Loyola Univ, 95; John Courtney Murray Awd for Excellence in Theology, Cath Theol Soc of Am, 97. **MEMBERSHIPS** Am Acad Relig; Cath Theol Soc Am; Col Theol Soc; Am Theol Soc. **RESEARCH** Contemporary Christology; women's studies; Rahner. **SELECTED PUBLICATIONS** Auth, Theology and experience in Karl Rahner, J Relig, summer 73; The church in process, In: Women and Catholic Priesthood, Paulist, 76; The Theological Method of Karl Rahner, Scholars, 77; contribr, Authentic theology in service of the church, In: Women Priests, Paulist, 77; auth, Seminar on Christology: Hans Kung's On Being a Christian, Proc Cath Theol Soc Am, 77; Women's ordination and Christian thought, Listening, spring 78; contribur, Research Report: Women in church and society, Cath Theol Soc Am, 78; auth, Is a Christian feminist theology possible, Theol Studies, 6/82. **CONTACT ADDRESS** Divinity Sch, Univ of Chicago, 1025-35 E 58th St., Chicago, IL 60637-1577.

CARR, DAVID

PERSONAL Born 02/01/1940, Parkersburg, WV, m, 1995, 3 children **DISCIPLINE** PHILOSOPHY **EDUCATION** Yale Univ, BA, 61; MA, 64; PhD, 66. **CAREER** Charles Howard Candler Prof and Acting Dir of Graduate Studies, Philos, Emory Univ. **HONORS AND AWARDS** Woodrwow Wilson Fel, 61-62; US Gov Grant, 62-63; Morse fel, 69-70; Yale Sr Fac Fel, 75-76; Alexander von Humboldt Fel, 75-76, 79; Soc Sci and Humanities Res Council of Can, Res Grant, 83-84, 90; car acting instr, yale univ, 64-66; asst prof, 66-72; assoc prof, 72-76; vis asst prof, new school for the soc res, 68; vis asst prof, wash univ, 71; assoc prof, univ okla, 76-78; assoc prof, univ ottawa, 78-79; vis prof, ,new school for the soc res, 90; **RESEARCH** Recent continental European philosophy; Husserl, and the Philosophy of history. **SELECTED PUBLICATIONS** Auth, Modernity, Postmodernity and the Philosophy of History, Am Cath Philos Quart, 94; Alfred Schutz and The Project of Phenomenological Social Theory, Phenomenol of the Cultural Disciplines, 94; getting the Story Straight: Narrative and Historical Knowledge, Historiography Between Modernism and Postmodernism, 94; The Question of the Subject: Heidegger and the TranscendentalTradition, Huma n Studies, 95; Kant's Theory of the Subject; Transcendental Philos Everyday Experience, 97; White und Ricoeur: Die Narrative Erzahloform und das Altagliche, Metageschichte: hayden White und Paul Ricoeur, 97; Die Realitat der Geschichte, Historische Sinnbilding, 97; Margolis and Philosphy of History, 97. **CONTACT ADDRESS** Dept Philos, Emory Univ, 1364 Clifton Rd NE, Atlanta, GA 30322-1061. **EMAIL** dcarr@emory.edu

CARR, LOIS GREEN

PERSONAL Born 03/07/1922, Holyoke, MA, m, 1963, 1 child **DISCIPLINE** AMERICAN COLONIAL & LEGAL HISTORY **EDUCATION** Swarthmore Col, AB, 43; Radcliffe Col, AM, 44; Harvard Univ, PhD(hist), 68. **CAREER** Asst ed, Alfred A Knopf, Inc Col Dept, 51-52; jr archivist, Hall of Rec Comn, Annapolis, 56-64; adj prof hist, Historian, Historic St Mary's City Comn, MD, 67-, vis prof hist, St Mary's Col Md, 70; coun mem, omohundro, Inst Early Am Hist & Cult, 80-82; mem, Res Div, AHA, 80-82; adv bd, McNeil Ctr for Early Am Stud, 81- ; adj prof hist, Univ Md, 82- ; sr adj scholar, Md State Archv, 88- ; sr hist, Md Hist Trust, 89- ; pres, Econ Hist Asn, 90-91; publ comt, Md Hist Soc, 90- ; Bd of Trustees, Charles Carroll House of Annapolis, 94- ; Md Hum Coun, 98- . **HONORS AND AWARDS** Phi Beta Kappa; Vis prof hist, St Mary's Col; co-prin investr, Nat Sci Found grant, 72-73 & Nat Endowment for Humanities grant, 76-79; fel, Regional Econ Hist Res Ctr, Eleutherian Mills-Hagley Found, 79-80; sr res assoc, Nat Endowment for Humanities grant, 81-83; proj dir, Am Asn for State and Local Hist grant, 88-89; co-winner, Md Hist Soc Book Prize, 93; co-winner, Econ Hist Asn Alice Hanson Jones Prize, 94; co-winner, Eisenberg Prize for Excellence in the Hum, Md Hum Coun, 96; Woman of the Year, 00; Md Commission on Women, 00. **MEMBERSHIPS** AHA; Orgn Am Historians; Econ Hist Asn; Soc Sci Hist Asn.; So Hist Asn; Am Soc for Legal Hist. **RESEARCH** Colonial Chesapeake society and economy; local government and the courts of colonial Maryland; social analysis of communities. **SELECTED PUBLICATIONS** Auth, The Metropolis of Maryland: A Comment on Town Development Along the Tobacco Coast, Md Hist Mag, summer 74; coauth, Maryland's Revolution of Government, 1689-1692, Cornell Univ, 74; The Planter's Wife: The Experience of White Women in Seventeenth Century Maryland, William & Mary Quart, 10/77; auth, The Development of the Maryland Orphan's Court, 1654-1715, In: Law, Society and Politics in Early Maryland, Johns Hopkins Univ Press, 77; The Foundations of Social Order: Local Government in Colonial Maryland, In: Town and County: Essays on the Structure of Local Government in the American Colonies, Wesleyan Univ Press, 78; coauth, Immigration and Opportunity: The Freedman in early Colonial Maryland, In: The Chesapeake in the Seventeenth Century: Essays on Anglo-American Society and Politics, Univ NC Press, 79; Inventories and the Analysis of Wealth and Consumption Patterns in St Mary's County, Maryland, 1658-1777, Hist Methods, spring 80; The Lords Baltimore and the Colonization of Maryland, In: Maryland in a Wider World, Wayne State Univ Press, 82; Robert Cole's World: Agriculture and Society in Early Maryland, North Carolina, 91; auth, Emigration and the Standard of the Living: The Seventeenth Century Chesapeake, in J of Econ Hist, 92; co-auth, Changing Life Styles and Consumer Behavior in the Colonial Chesapeake, In: Of Consuming Interests: Styles of Life in the Eighteenth Century, Univ Pr of Va, 94; auth, Wealth and Welfare in the Colonial Chesapeake, William and Mary Q, 99. **CONTACT ADDRESS** Maryland State Archives, 350 Rowe Blvd, Annapolis, MD 21401. **EMAIL** loisc@mdmarchives.state.md.us

CARR, THOMAS

PERSONAL Born 04/21/1962, Washington, DC, m, 1996, 1 child **DISCIPLINE** THEOLOGY AND RELIGION **EDUCATION** Princeton Theological Sem, M Div, 90; Oxford Univ, M Phil (theol & philos), 92, D Phil (theol), 95. **CAREER** Junior dean, Oriel Col, Oxford, 93-96; adjunct lect, Westminster Col, Oxford, 94-96; Asst Prof, Mount Union Col, 94-. **MEMBERSHIPS** Am Academy of Relig. **RESEARCH** Hermeneutics; Nietzsche; near death experiences; death & dying. **SELECTED PUBLICATIONS** Auth, A Man for Our Time?: Isaiah Berlin's Magus of the North, in Jof Relig and Public Life, June/July 94; Only a God Can Save Us: a review essay of John Macquarrie's Heidegger and Christianity, in J of Relig and Public Life, Aug/Sept 95; Heidegger and Jaspers, J of the Am Academy of Religion, vol LXIV, no 2, summer 96; Let Being Be (a review of Joanna Hodges' Heidegger and Ethics, Routledge Press, 95), Times Literary Supplement, Jan 16, 96; Newman and Gadamer: Toward a Hermeneutics of Religious Knowledge, Scholars Press, 96; Review of the Cambridge Companion to Nietzsche, in Times Higher Education Supplement, Sept 5, 97; Death and Dying: An Introduction, Simon & Schuster, forthcoming 99; The Truth that We Are: Gadamerian Ethics and the Theological Task, under consideration by Routledge Press; Zarathustra or Zossima: amor fati and the affirmation of life in Nietzsche and Dostoevski, J of the Am Academy of Religion, forthcoming. **CONTACT ADDRESS** Dept Relig & Philos, Mount Union Col, Alliance, OH 44601. **EMAIL** carrtk@muc.edu

CARRASCO, GILBERT P.

DISCIPLINE LAW **EDUCATION** Univ San Diego, BA, 75; Univ Santa Clara, JD, 78; Georgetown Univ Law Ctr, LLM, 79. **CAREER** Vis prof, Univ San Diego Sch Law; Seton Hall Sch Law; legis dir, Equal Justice found, 79; consult, Migrant Legal Aid Prog, Inc, 79; trial atty, US Dept Justice, Civil Rights Div, 80-84; dir atty, Nat Ctr Immigrants' Rt(s), 84-85; dir atty, Legal Aid Soc, 85-86; Nat dir, Immigration Serv, US Cath Conf, 86-88; prof, Villanova Univ Law Sch; prof Williamette Univ, 01. **HONORS AND AWARDS** Hon mem, Order of the Coif; pres, pa hisp bar assn. **MEMBERSHIPS** Mem, Hisp Nat Bar Assn; Latin Amer Law Stud Assn; UNHCR. **RESEARCH** Civil rights and immigration. **SELECTED PUBLICATIONS** Coauth, Civil Rights Litigation, 95; Immigration and Nationality Law: Cases and Materials, 91, 92; auth, Latinos in the United States: Invitation and Exile,The New Nativism, 96. **CONTACT ADDRESS** Sch of Law, Willamette Univ, 900 State St, Salem, OR 97301. **EMAIL** gcarrasco@willamette.edu

CARRIER, DAVID
DISCIPLINE PHILOSOPHY **EDUCATION** Columbia Univ, PhD. **CAREER** Philos, Carnegie Mellon Univ. **SELECTED PUBLICATIONS** Auth, Panofsky, Leo Steinberg, David Carrier. The Problem of Objectivity in Art History, Jour Aesthetics & Art Criticism, 89; Art History in the Mirror Stage. Interpreting Un Bar aux Folies-Bergre, History & Theory, 90; Poussin's Paintings, Pa State Press, 93. **CONTACT ADDRESS** Carnegie Mellon Univ, 5000 Forbes Ave, Pittsburgh, PA 15213.

CARRINGTON, PAUL
PERSONAL Born 06/12/1931, Dallas, TX, m, 1952, 4 children **DISCIPLINE** LAW **EDUCATION** Univ TX, BA, 52; Harvard, LLB, 55 **CAREER** Private practice in Dallas, 55; U.S. Army, 55-57; Teaching Fel, Harvard Univ, 57-58; Asst Prof of Law, Univ of Wyoming, 58-60; Asst Prof Law, Indiana Univ, 60-62; Assoc Prof of Law, Ohio State Univ, 62-64; Prof of Law, Ohio State Univ, 64; Prof of Law, Univ of Mich, 65-78; Prof of Law, Duke Univ, 78-; Dean, 78-88; Chadwick Prof of Law, 89-. **MEMBERSHIPS** Am Law Inst, 66-91, Am Bar Foundation, 85-65, Am Acad of Arts an Sciences, 00. **SELECTED PUBLICATIONS** Auth, The Hague Conference on Private International Law, 57-3 Law and Contemp. Prob, 94; auth, Appeals, Michie & Co., 94; auth, Readings on Judicial Independence and Accountability, American Bar Association, 98; auth, Judicial Independence and Democratic Accountability 61-1 Law and Contemp. Prob., 99; auth, Stewards of Democracy: Law as A Public Profession, Harper Collins Westview, 99; auth, Teaching Civil Procedure: A Retrospective View, 50 J Leg. Ed, 99; auth, Procedure in the Canon, in The Canons of Legal Education, ed, Jack Balkin and Sanford Levinson, New York Univ Pr, 00; auth, Tanking the Rankings: Thoughts on Law Schools Rankings by The Media, The American Lawer, 00; auth, A True Confession, 3 Alibi 19, 00; auth, No Substitute for ED, 3 Alibi 20, 00; auth, The Dark Side of Contract Law, 36-5 Trial 73, 00. **CONTACT ADDRESS** Law Sch, Duke Univ, Durham, NC 27708. **EMAIL** pdc@law.duke.edu

CARROLL, BEVERLEE JILL
PERSONAL Born 07/25/1963, Shreveport, LA **DISCIPLINE** RELIGIOUS STUDIES **EDUCATION** Rice Univ, PhD, 94. **CAREER** Lectr, 92- , Univ Houston; lectr, 96- , Rice Univ. **HONORS AND AWARDS** Charlotte Newcombe Dissertation Grant, 93-94; Research grant, Amer Acad of Relig, 97-98. **MEMBERSHIPS** Amer Acad of Relig **RESEARCH** Philosophy and religion; Religion and world politics. **CONTACT ADDRESS** 1518 Washington Ave, Apt E, Houston, TX 77007-0775. **EMAIL** bjillc@aol.com

CARROLL, JOHN T.
PERSONAL Born 04/22/1954, Buffalo, NY, m, 1977, 2 children **DISCIPLINE** BIBLICAL STUDIES, NEW TESTAMENT **EDUCATION** Univ Tulsa, BA, 76; Oxford Univ, Dipl Theol, 78; Princeton Theol Sem, M Div, 79; PhD, 86. **CAREER** From asst prof to assoc prof, Louisiana State Univ, 86-92; from assoc prof to dean of faculty, Union Theol Sem, 92-; co-ed, Interpretation: A Jal of Bible and Theology, 96-. **HONORS AND AWARDS** ODK Graduate Fel; HS Gehman Prize. **MEMBERSHIPS** Soc of Bibl Lit; Catholic Bibl Asoc; Studiorum Novi Testamenti Soc. **RESEARCH** Luke - Acts; Gospel interpretation; early Christian eschatology. **SELECTED PUBLICATIONS** Auth, The End in the Synoptics, The Bible Today, 92; auth, Sickness and Healing in the New Testament Gospels, Interpretation, 95; co-auth with Joel B. Green, The Death of Jesus in Early Christianity, 95; co-auth with James R. Carroll, Preaching the Hard Sayings of Jesus, 96; Luke-Acts, Reading New Testament Today, 99; auth, The Return of Jesus in Early Christianity, 00. **CONTACT ADDRESS** Union Theol Sem, Virginia, 3401 Brook Rd., Richmond, VA 23227. **EMAIL** jcarroll@union-psee.edu

CARROLL, RAOUL LORD
PERSONAL Born 03/16/1950, Washington, DC, m, 1979 **DISCIPLINE** LAW **EDUCATION** Morgan State Coll, BS 1972; St John's Univ Sch of Law, JD 1975; Georgetown Univ Law Center, 1980-81. **CAREER** Dept of Justice, asst US atty 1979-80; US Bd of Veterans Appeals, assoc mem 1980-81; Hart Carroll & Chavers, partner 1981-86; Bishop Cook Purcell & Reynolds, partner 1986-89; US Dept of Veterans Affairs, Washington, DC, general counsel 1989-91; US Dept of Housing and Urban Development, pres, Government National Mortgage Assn 1991-92; chief operating officer, M.R. Beal & Company, New York, NY, 92-95; Christalex Partners, partner, currently. **MEMBERSHIPS** Washington Bar Assn, 1976-, District of Columbia Bar, 1979-; New York Bar, 1976-; Natl Bar Assn, 1977-; pres Black Asst US Attorney Assoc 1981-83; trustee, Christian Brothers Investment Services, Inc; chmn Amer Ctr for Intl Leadership 1985; trustee, The Enterprise Foundation. **SELECTED PUBLICATIONS** "After the Dust Settles, Other Modes of Relief," The Advocate Vol 10 No 6 1978. **CONTACT ADDRESS** 1420 N St NW, Washington, DC 20005.

CARROLL, ROSEMARY F.
PERSONAL Born 10/15/1935, Providence, RI, s **DISCIPLINE** HISTORY, LAW **EDUCATION** Brown Univ, BA, 57; Wesleyan Univ, MA, 62; Rutgers Univ, PhD, 68; Univ Iowa, JD, 83. **CAREER** Asst prof, Notre Dame Col, 68-70; vis asst prof, Denison Univ, 70-71; asst prof, Coe Col, 71-75, 75-84; prof, 84-. **HONORS AND AWARDS** Radcliffe-Hicks Prize, Brown Univ, 56; teaching assistantship, Rutgers NDEA Summer Inst, 65, 67; res assistantship, Rutgers, 65-66; Squire Fel, Wesleyan Univ, 61-62; Coe Found Fel, Yale Univ, summer 63; General Electric Found Fel, Union Col, summer 64; Fel, Sem for Hist Adminrs, Williamsburg, Va, summer 66; Univ Fel, Rutgers, 66-67; Hoover grant, Hoover Pres Library Asn, 87-88; Olmsted Fel, Hoover Pres Library Asn, 87-92; Edward S. Murray Memorial Res Awd, Coe Col, 87-88; Fac Develop grant, Coe Col, 92-93; NEH travel grant, 92-93; listed in: Phi Kappa Phi, Who's Who in the Midwest, Who's Who of Contemporary Women, Who's Who in Am Law, Who's Who in Am Educ, The Dir of Distinguished Ams, The Int Biography of Women, The World's Who's Who of Women, Community Leaders of the World, The Int Dir of Distinguished Leadership, Two Thousand Notable Am Women, Lexington's Who's Who. **MEMBERSHIPS** Am Bar Asn, Iowa State Bar Asn, Linn Co Bar Asn, Linn Co Women Attorneys, Am Hist Asn, Org of Am Hists, Am Asn of Univ Profs, Southern Hist Asn, Southern Asn of Women Hists. **RESEARCH** U.S. Women's History, U.S. Law. **SELECTED PUBLICATIONS** Auth, "Margaret Clark Griffis: Plantation Teacher," Tenn Hist Quart, fall 67; rev of N. D. Markowitz, The Rise and Fall of the People's Century, The Historian (fall 75); auth, "A Plantation Teacher's Perception of the Impending Crisis," Southern Studies (fall 79); rev of Kent Folmar, This State of Wonders, The Annals of Iowa (fall 88); rev of Tim Purdy, The Journals of Sylvester Daniels, The Annals of Iowa (winter 89); rev of Ruth Dennis, The Homes of the Hoovers, The Annals of Iowa (spring 89); auth, "Lou Henry Hoover: The Emergence of a Leader, 1874-1916," an essay in Dale Mayer, ed, Lou Henry Hoover: Essays on a Busy Life (fall 93); auth, "Lou Henry Hoover: The Early Years," Hoover VII Symposium (forthcoming); auth, "Lou Henry Hoover: The London Years," Hoover VIII Symposium (forthcoming). **CONTACT ADDRESS** Dept Hist, Coe Col, 1220 1st Ave Northeast, Cedar Rapids, IA 52402-5008. **EMAIL** rcarroll@coe.edu

CARROLL, WARREN HASTY
PERSONAL Born 03/24/1932, Minneapolis, MN, m, 1967 **DISCIPLINE** CATHOLIC HISTORY **EDUCATION** Bates Col, BA, 53; Columbia Univ, MA, 54, PhD(hist), 59. **CAREER** Instr hist, Ind Univ, 57-58; asst command historian, Sec Air Force, US Strategic Air Command, 60-61; admin asst, Calif State Senator John G Schmitz, 67-70, legis asst, 70-72; dir, Christian Commonwealth Inst, 73-75; Pres, Christendom Col, 77-85, Contrib ed, Triumph Mag, 73-75; trustee, Seton Sch, Manassas, 76-. **MEMBERSHIPS** Fel Catholic Scholars. **RESEARCH** Church history in the broadest sense; history of the Spanish-speaking peoples; history of modern revolutionary movements, since 1789. **SELECTED PUBLICATIONS** Auth, Law: The Quest for Certainty, Am Bar Asn J, 1/63; The West come to Judgment, Triumph, 5/72; Philip II versus William Cecil: The Cleaving of Christendom, Faith & Reason, winter 75-76; coauth, Reasons for Hope, Christendom Col Press, 78; auth, The dispersion of the Apostles: Overview, Peter, spring 81, The Dispersion of the Apostles: Thomas, summer 81 & The Dispersion of the Apostles: St Jude and the Shroud, fall 81, Faith & Reason; 1917: Red Banners, White Mantle, Christendom Publ, 81; Our Lady of Guadalupe and the Conquest of Darkness, 83; The Founding of Christendom , 85; The Guillotine and the Cross, 86; The Building of Christendom, 87; Isabel of Spain, the Catholic Queen, 91; The Glory of Christendom, 93; The Rise and Fall of the Communist Revolution, 95; The Last Crusade, 96. **CONTACT ADDRESS** Christendom Col, 134 Christendom Dr, Box 87, Front Royal, VA 22630-6534. **EMAIL** Warren.h.carroll@trincomm.org

CARSON, JAMES
DISCIPLINE PHILOSOPHY **EDUCATION** North Carolina at Chapel Hill, BA; Tulane, MA; Kentucky, PhD. **CAREER** Dept Philos, Queen's Univ **RESEARCH** Native American ethnohistory; intercultural contact in North America; antebellum Southern United States; political culture of the late 18th and early 19th century United States. **SELECTED PUBLICATIONS** Auth, pubs on state rights ideology in the American South, Native American cultural change and persistence, and Native American women in the American South; auth, Searching for the Bright Path: The Mississippi Choctaws from Prehistory to Removal, Univ of Nebraska Press, 99. **CONTACT ADDRESS** Dept of Hist, Queen's Univ at Kingston, Kingston, ON, Canada K7L 3N6. **EMAIL** jc35@qsilver.queensu.ca

CARSON, LOGAN
PERSONAL Born 07/12/1932, Marion, NC, m, 1960, 2 children **DISCIPLINE** THEOLOGY **EDUCATION** Shaw Univ, BA, 57; Hartford Sem, BD, 60; Louisville Presby, ThM, 61; Drew Univ, PhD, 80. **CAREER** Bible knowledge master, Waka Tchrs Col, 65-68; instr Relig, Mt. Claire State, 69-73; prof Relig, Gardner-Webb, 73-94; prof theol, Southeastern Baptist Theol Sem, 94-. **HONORS AND AWARDS** Distinguished Service Awd, 95; Outstanding Relig Tchr, Gardner-Webb; Hebrew Prize, Hartford Sem, 59. **MEMBERSHIPS** SBL, ETS, ABPR. **RESEARCH** Books for lay people. **CONTACT ADDRESS** Dept of Theology, Southeastern Baptist Theol Sem, PO Box 1889, Wake Forest, NC 27588-1889. **EMAIL** lcarson@sebts.edu

CARSON, THOMAS L.
PERSONAL Born Chicago, IL, m, 1982, 2 children **DISCIPLINE** PHILOSOPHY **EDUCATION** St Olaf Col, BA, 72; Brown Univ, PhD, 77. **CAREER** Vis lectr, Univ Calif Los Angeles, 76; asst prof, Va Tech, 77-85; assoc prof, 85-94, prof, 94-, Loyola Univ Chicago. **HONORS AND AWARDS** Phi Beta Kappa, 72; NEH fel for col teachers, 80-81. **MEMBERSHIPS** Amer Philos Asn. **RESEARCH** Ethics; Metaethics; Business ethics; Utilitarianism. **SELECTED PUBLICATIONS** Auth, Bribery, Extortion, and The Foreign Corrupt Practices Act, Philos & Public Affairs, 85; auth, Hare's Defense of Utilitarianism, Philos Studies, 86; auth, Perpetual Peace: What Kant Should Have Said, Soc Theory and Practice, 88; auth, Who are We to Judge?, Teaching Philos, 88; auth, Could Ideal Observers Disagree?, Philos and Phenomenol Res, 89; auth, A Note on Hooker's Rule-Consequentialism, Mind, Vol C, 91; auth, Second Thoughts on Bluffing, Bus Ethics Quart, 93; auth, Friedman's Theory of Corporate Social Responsibility, Bus and Prof Ethics Jour, 93; co-auth, Relativism and Normative Nonrealism: Basing Morality on Rationality, Metaphilos, 96; Auth, Morality and the Good Life, Oxford Univ Press, 97; auth, value and the good Life, Nortre Dame, 00; coed, Anthology: Moral Relativism: A Reader, Oxford, 01. **CONTACT ADDRESS** Philosophy Dept., Loyola Univ, Chicago, Chicago, IL 60626. **EMAIL** tcarson@luc.edu

CARTER, BARRY EDWARD
PERSONAL Born 10/14/1942, Los Angeles, CA **DISCIPLINE** INTERNATIONAL AND PROPERTY LAW **EDUCATION** Stanford Univ, AB, 64; Princeton Univ, MPA, 66; Yale Univ, JD, 69. **CAREER** Prog analyst systems, Off Asst Secy Defense, 69-70 & Nat Security Coun Staff, 70-72; res fel, Inst Polit, Harvard Univ, 72; assoc, Wilmer, Cutler & Pickering, 73-75; sr coun, US Sen Select Comt Intelligence Activities, 75; assoc, Morrison & Foerster, 76-79; Assoc Prof Law, Georgetown Univ, 79-, Int affairs fel, Coun Foreign Rels, 72; mem, Soviet-Am Parallel Studies Prog, UN, 77. **MEMBERSHIPS** Coun Foreign Rels; Am Asn Law Schs. **RESEARCH** International economic sanctions; international business law; national security policies. **SELECTED PUBLICATIONS** Auth, International-Law and Institutions aor a New Age, Georgetown Law Jour, Vol 0081, 93. **CONTACT ADDRESS** Law Ctr, Georgetown Univ, 600 New Jersey N W, Washington, DC 20001-2022.

CARTER, CHARLES EDWARD
PERSONAL Born 06/20/1925, Springfield, OH, d **DISCIPLINE** LAW **EDUCATION** Miami Univ OH, AB 1950; OH State Univ, LLB 1957, JD 1967. **CAREER** City of Springfield, OH, law dir 1960-69; Mahoming Co Legal Serv Youngstown, OH, 69-71; NAACP, assoc gen counsel 1971-86; Corporate Counsel 1986-. **SELECTED PUBLICATIONS** "Civil Rights Handbook" NAACP 1979. **CONTACT ADDRESS** Corporate Counsel, NAACP, 4805 Mt Hope Dr, Baltimore, MD 21215.

CARTER, CHARLES MICHAEL
PERSONAL Born 04/18/1943, Boston, MA **DISCIPLINE** LAW **EDUCATION** Univ of CA Berkeley, BS 1967; George Washington Univ Schl of Law, JD 1973. **CAREER** Winthrop, Stimson, Putnam, and Roberts, assc 1973-81; The Singer Comp, div counsel & finance staff and investment counsel 1981-83; RJR Nabisco Inc, sr corporate counsel 1983-87; Concurrent Computer Corporation, vice pres, general counsel & secretary of Corporate Development 1987-. **MEMBERSHIPS** Mem Amer Bar Assn, Natl Bar Assn. **CONTACT ADDRESS** Vice Pres, General Counsel, and Secretary, Concurrent Computer Corp, 2 Crescent Pl, Oceanport, NJ 07757.

CARTER, DAVID K.
PERSONAL Born 06/20/1938, Portland, OR **DISCIPLINE** PHILOSOPHY **EDUCATION** Grinnell Col , AB, 60; Yale Univ, MA, 65; PhD, 82. **CAREER** Asst prof, Univ Denver, 67-69; asst prof, Calif State Univ, 70-78; asst prof, Univ Tex Pan AM, 78-. **MEMBERSHIPS** Am Philos Asn. **RESEARCH** Ethics; American Philosophy. **CONTACT ADDRESS** 1108 Cardinal, McAllen, TX 7854. **EMAIL** dcarter@panam.edu

CARTER, GUY C.
PERSONAL Born 02/21/1951, Austin, TX, m, 1994, 2 children **DISCIPLINE** HISTORICAL THEOLOGY **EDUCATION** Univ St. Thomas, BA, 73; Marquette Univ, MA, 80; Lutheran Sch Theol, MDiv, 86; Marquette Univ, PhD, 87. **CAREER** Pastor, Evangel Lutheran Abbey of St. Boniface, hameln, Ger, 89-91; pastor, Grace Evangel Lutheran Church, NJ, 92-94; pastor, Trinity Evangel Lutheran Church, NJ, 94-89; adj lectr, St. Peter's Col, 92-98, asst prof, 98- . **HONORS AND AWARDS** Magna cum Laude, 73; Arthur J. Schmitt Doctoral Fel, 81-82, 82-83. **MEMBERSHIPS** Am Acad Relig; Soc of Bibl Lit; Int Bonhoeffer Soc for Arch & Res. **RESEARCH** Historical theology of the German Church struggle, 1933-45; Holocaust studies. **SELECTED PUBLICATIONS** Auth, "Walter A. Maier," Twentieth Century Shapers of American Ppular Religion, Greenwood, 89; co-ed, "Bonhoeffer's Ethics," Kok Pharos, 91; auth, "Evangelische Theologie und ihre Didaktik," Damit wir einander nahe sind, Haensel-Hohenhausen, 98. **CONTACT ADDRESS** Theology Dept, Saint Peter's Col, 2641 Kennedy Blvd, Jersey City, NJ 07306. **EMAIL** gcemc@earthlink.net

CARTER, JEFFREY D. R.
PERSONAL Born 04/18/1963, Boston, MA, m, 1996 **DISCIPLINE** THE HISTORY OF RELIGIONS; THE RELIGIONS OF AFRICA **EDUCATION** Univ of Chicago, PhD, 97 **CAREER** Vis asst prof, Davidson Col, 97-98; vis asst prof, Univ S Carolina, 98-99. **HONORS AND AWARDS** Fulbright Dissertation Fel Nigeria; Pre-dissertation Fel Soc Sci Res Coun Nigeria; Inst Advan Study Relig Chicago. **MEMBERSHIPS** Amer Acad Relig **RESEARCH** Comparative religions; Indigenous religious traditions; Religions of Africa; Methods & theories in the study of religion. **SELECTED PUBLICATIONS** rev, Prey into Hunter: The Politics of Religious Experience, Jour Relig, 93; rev, The Social Control of Religious Zeal: A Study of Organizational Contradictions, Jour Relig, 95; rev, A History of Christianity in Africa: From Antiquity to the Present, Jour Relig, 97; Religion and Politics in Nigeria: A Study of Middle Belt Christianity, Jour Relig, 97; auth, Description is not Explanation: A Methodology of Comparison, Method & Theory in the Study of Religion, 98. **CONTACT ADDRESS** Dept of Religious Studies, Univ of So Carolina, Columbia, Columbia, SC 29208. **EMAIL** carterj@garnet.cla.sc.edu

CARTER, JOHN J.
PERSONAL Born 04/28/1955, Weaton, MO, m, 1979, 1 child **DISCIPLINE** POLITICAL SCIENCE **EDUCATION** Westmin Col, 73-75; Univ Missou, AB, 77; Cen Missou State Univ, MA, 79; Univ Missou, PhD, 81. **CAREER** Instr to prof, Cen Meth Col, 80-00. **HONORS AND AWARDS** Who's Who Am Teach; Dr John F Kincaid Edu Ach Awd; Wye Fel, Aspen Inst. **MEMBERSHIPS** APSA. **RESEARCH** The American presidency and congress. **SELECTED PUBLICATIONS** Auth, Covert Operations as a Tool of Presidential Foreign Policy, 1800-1920, Mellon Press (NY), 00; auth, "Secret Democracy: A Historical Analysis of the Roots of Presidential-Congressional Struggles for Control of Covert Operations, SE Polit Rev (00). **CONTACT ADDRESS** Dept Social Science, Central Methodist Col, 411 Central Methodist Sq, Fayette, MO 65248-1129. **EMAIL** jcarter@cmc.edu

CARTER, JOHN ROSS
PERSONAL Born 06/22/1938, Baytown, TX, m, 1960, 2 children **DISCIPLINE** HISTORY OF RELIGIONS, BUDDHIST STUDIES **EDUCATION** Baylor Univ, BA, 60; Southern Baptist Theol Sem, BD, 63; Univ London, MTh, 65; Harvard Univ, PhD(hist relig), 72; D Litt Kelaniya Univ, 98. **CAREER** Asst prof, 72-80, assoc prof, Colgate Univ, 80-, Dir, Fund Study Great Relig & Chapel House, Colgate Univ, 74-; Asst prof of phil and rel, 72-79; assoc prof, 79-83; prof, Colgate Univ, 83-; dir, Chapel House & Fund for the study of the Great rel, 74-; Robert Ho prof, Asian Studies, 96-. **MEMBERSHIPS** Am Acad Relig; Asn Asian Studes. **RESEARCH** History of religion; Buddhist studies. **SELECTED PUBLICATIONS** Auth, Dhamma: Western Academic and Sinhalese Buddhist Interpretations, Hokuseido Press, Tokyo, 78; ed, Religiousness in Sri Lanka, Marga Inst, Colombo, 79; co-ed, Religiousness in Yoga by T K V Desikachar, Univ Press Am, 80; cotranslator, The Dhammapada, Oxford Univ Press, 87; auth, On Outstanding Buddhits, State Univ, NY, 93; ed, Religious Heritage of Japan, Book East, 99. **CONTACT ADDRESS** Colgate Univ, 13 Oak Dr, Hamilton, NY 13346-1379.

CARTER, K. CODELL
PERSONAL Born 12/27/1939, Salt Lake City, UT, m, 1965, 2 children **DISCIPLINE** PHILOSOPHY **EDUCATION** Univ Utah, BS, 63, MA, 64; Cornell Univ, PhD, 68. **CAREER** Asst prof, Rutgers Univ, 67-73; prof, Brigham Young Univ, 73-. **MEMBERSHIPS** Am Philos Asn; Am Asn Hist Medicine; Royal Society Medicine. **RESEARCH** History of medicine. **SELECTED PUBLICATIONS** Auth, Essays of Robert Koch, 87; auth, art, The Development of Pasteur's Concept of Disease Causation and the Emergence of Specific Causes in Nineteenth-Century Medicine, 91; auth, Childbed Fever: A Scientific Biography of Ignaz Semmelweis, 94; auth, art, Toward a Rational History of Medical Science, 95; auth, art, Causes of Disease and Causes of Death, 97. **CONTACT ADDRESS** Brigham Young Univ, 3196 JKHB, Provo, UT 84602. **EMAIL** codell_carter@byu.edu

CARTER, LAWRENCE E., SR.
PERSONAL Born 09/23/1941, Dawson, GA, m **DISCIPLINE** RELIGION **EDUCATION** VA Univ of Lynchburg, BA Soc Studies 1964; Boston Univ, MDiv Theol 1968, STM Pastoral Care 1970, PhD Pastoral Care & Counseling 1978; Andover Newton Theol School, OH State Univ, New York University, Harvard University, Georgia State University, attended; Univ of Wisconsin, George Washington Univ, attended. **CAREER** Roxbury United Presbyterian Church, minister to youth 1965-67; Boston Public Schools, sub teacher 1966-77; Twelfth Baptists Church, minister of counseling 1968-71; Boston Univ Warren Residence Hall, resident counselor & asst dir 1968-71; Boston University MLK Jr African-American Cultural Center, director, 71-73; People's Baptist Church, assoc minister 1971-78; Harvard Univ Divinity School, clergy teaching advisor 1976-77; Marsh Chapel Boston Univ, assoc dean 1978-79; Morehouse Coll, Prof, Dept of Philosophy & Religion 1979-; Martin Luther King Jr Intl Chapel Morehouse Coll, Dean 1979-, archivist/curator, 82-97. **HONORS AND AWARDS** Fulbright Scholar, Brazil, 1994; Citizenship Medal of the Year VA Coll 1964; Recognition of Outstanding Achievement in the field of Religion & Humanitarianism Omega Scroll of Honor Morehouse Coll 1979; Natl Black Christian Student Leadership Consultation Awd in Appreciation for Support & Commitment to Devel of Black Christian Leadership 1980; Delegate to United Nations Spec Committee Against Apartheid 1984; numerous radio & TV appearances including Ebenezer Church Serv WAGA Channel 5 Atlanta GA, "The Role of the Black Church" WAOK Interview Atlanta GA, WCNN Radio Anthony Johnson Commentary 1984, CNN Roy Patterson Interview 1984; Voted Faculty Mem of the Year Morehouse Coll Student Newspaper; Del to the 6th Assembly of the World Council of Churches 1983; Del to the World Baptist Youth Conf in Argentina, 1984; Del to 4thtl Council of Churches Dialogue between the Soviety Union Clergy & Amer Clergy in Moscow; Senate Concurrent Resolution by the State of MI in Honor of Dr Carter, 32nd Degree Mason Prince Hall Lodge, 1985. **MEMBERSHIPS** Mem Atlanta United Nations Assoc; board of directors Natl Council of Chuches of Christ 1983-90; mem Natl Assoc of Coll & Univ Chaplains, ACLU, Amer Acad of Religion, Assoc of Black Prof of Religion, Ministries to Blacks in Higher Ed, NAACP; coord Afro-Amer Studies Prog Simmons Coll, coord 1977-78; mem Soc for the Study of Black Religion, Class of Leadership Atlanta 1986; American Academy of Religion, 1979-. **CONTACT ADDRESS** Dept of Phil and Relig, Morehouse Col, 830 Westview Dr, PO Box 24, Atlanta, GA 30314.

CARTER, MICHELE A.
PERSONAL Born 04/24/1949, Okinawa, Japan **DISCIPLINE** PHILOSOPHY, APPLIED ETHICS, BIOETHICS **EDUCATION** Univ Hawaii, BS, 72; Texas Womens Univ, MS, 82; Univ Tenn, PhD, 89. **CAREER** Postdr fel, Nat Inst Health Clin & Res Ethics Clin Ctr, 89-91; bioethics consult, Wash Hosp, 91-93; MEM INST MED HUM, ASST PROF, DEPT PREVENTIVE MED & COMMUN HEALTH, SCHOOL MED, UNIV TEX MED BRANCH, 93-; DIR, UNIV TEX MED BRANCH ETHICS CONSULT SERV, 93-; Univ Tenn Nat Alumni Asn Grad fel, 88-89; Bacon-Bearc Scholar Philos, 88-89; Rolf-Deiter Hermann Scholar Philos, 83. **MEMBERSHIPS** Am Soc Bioethics and Hum; Am Philos Asn; Kennedy Inst Ethics; Hasting's Ctr. **RESEARCH** Philosophy of trust; Clinical and research ethics; Ethics of health care practice. **SELECTED PUBLICATIONS** Auth Ethical Framework for Care of the Chronically Ill, Holistic Nursing Practice, 93; Patient-Provider Relationship in the Context of Genetic Testing for Hereditary Cancers, Jour Nat Cancer Inst, 95; Mental Health Services: Ethical Issues, Encyclo of Bioethics, Simon & Schuster MacMillan, 95; coauth Experiences of a Nursing Ethics Forum: Case Studies and Outcomes, Critical Care Nursing Clinics of N Am: Ethical Decision Making in the Critical Care Patient, 97; Optimizing Ethics Services and Education in a Teaching Hospital: Rounds vs Consultation, Jour of Clinical Ethics, 97. **CONTACT ADDRESS** 301 University Blvd, Galveston, TX 77555-1311. **EMAIL** mcarter@utmb.edu

CARTER, PERCY A., JR.
PERSONAL Born 07/04/1929, Hampton, VA, m **DISCIPLINE** THEOLOGY **EDUCATION** VA Union U, AB 1949; Harvard Sch of Bus Adminstrn, 1951-52; M Div Andover-Newton, 1953; Boston Univ Sch of Theology, MST 1953; Harvard Divinity Sch, 1953-55; Brown U, 1958-59. **CAREER** Olney St Bapt Ch Providence RI, formerly pastored; Mt Calvary Bapt Ch Mansfield OH; Hosack St Bapt Ch Columbus OH, pastor, currently; Eastern Union Bible College of Columbus, OH, instructor, currently. **MEMBERSHIPS** Mem Bapt Pastor's Conf; mem Ministerial Alliance; mem Interdenom of Ministerial Alliance of Columbus OH; Met Area Church Bd Affiliate; broadcasts on radio weekly; previously served as substitue tchr on secondary level in pub sch; past chmn Mansfield Alliance for Progress; past chmn & founder Opport Indusl Cntr of Mansfield OH. **SELECTED PUBLICATIONS** Contrib "What Jesus Means to Me", "Seven Black Preachers" 1971. **CONTACT ADDRESS** Hosack Street Baptist Church, 1160 Watkins Rd, Columbus, OH 43207.

CARTER, ROBERT EDGAR
PERSONAL Born 07/04/1937, Lawrence, MA, m, 1960, 2 children **DISCIPLINE** PHILOSOPHY **EDUCATION** Tufts Univ, AB, 59; Harvard Univ, MDiv, 62; Univ Toronto, MA, 63, PhD, 69. **CAREER** Asst philos, Tufts Univ, 60-62; instr, Univ Toronto, 62-65; lectr, Mem Univ Nfld, 65-66; assoc prof & chmn dept, Prince of Wales Col, 66-68; spec lectr found educ, McArthur Col, Queen's Univ, 68-69; assoc prof philos, Sir George Williams Univ, 69-73; assoc prof philos & master, Otonabee Col, 73-77, Prof Philos, Trent Univ, 78-, Chmn Dept, 82-. **HONORS AND AWARDS** Billings prize, Harvard Univ, 62; Tom Symons Awd for Excellence in Teaching. **MEMBERSHIPS** Am Philos Asn, Can Philos Asn, Am Soc Value Inquiry; Metaphys Soc; Soc Creative Philos. **RESEARCH** Ethics, East Asian Philosophy, Phenomenology and Hermeneutics, and the Phislosophy of Religion. **SELECTED PUBLICATIONS** Auth, Dimensions of Moral Education, (Univ of Toronto Press); auth, The Nothingness Beyond God and God, the Self, and Nothingness, (Paragon House); auth, Becoming Bamboo, (McGill-Queen's); co-transl, Watsuji Tetsuro's Rinrigaku, (State Univ of New York Press). **CONTACT ADDRESS** Dept of Philosophy, Trent Univ, 310 London St, Peterborough, ON, Canada K9H 7P4. **EMAIL** rcarter@khc.kansai-gaidai-u.ac.jp

CARTER, THEODORE ULYSSES
PERSONAL Born 10/16/1931, Birmingham, AL, m **DISCIPLINE** LAW **EDUCATION** Howard U, BA 1955; JD 1958; NYork Univ, postgrad 1962-63. **CAREER** PA NJ bars, atty; IRS Phila, atty 1961-; Glassboro NJ State Coll, adj prof justice. **MEMBERSHIPS** Vol counsel Camden Legal Servs 1970-; mem Am Jud & Soc; Am Nat PA NJ Bar Assns; Howard Univ Alumni Assn. **CONTACT ADDRESS** Carter & Berry, 1400-02 Mt Ephraim Ave, Camden, NJ 08104.

CARTER, WARREN
PERSONAL Born 01/06/1955, New Zealand, m, 1977, 2 children **DISCIPLINE** BIBLICAL STUDIES OF THE NEW TESTAMENT **EDUCATION** Victoria Univ of Wellington, BA; Melbourne Col of Divinity; Th M, BD; Princeton Theol Sem, PhD. **CAREER** Instr, new testament, 90-91, asst prof, new testament, 91-95, from assoc prof to prof, new testament, 95-, St Paul Sch of Theol, Ks City, Mo. **HONORS AND AWARDS** ATS Facul Fel, 98-99; SBL Reg Scholar Awd, 95; ATS Globalization Awd, 92. **MEMBERSHIPS** Soc of Bibl Lit; Cath Bibl Asn. **RESEARCH** History and literature of early Christian movement, espec Gospel of Matthew. **SELECTED PUBLICATIONS** Coauth, with J. P. Heil, Matthew's Parables: Audience-Oriented Perspectives, CBQMS, 30, Wash, CBA, 98; auth, Matthew: Storyteller, Interpreter, Evangelist, Peabody, Mass, Hendrickson, 96; auth, Discipleship and Households: A Study of Matthew 19-20, JSNTSS, 103, Sheffield, Sheffield Acad, JSOT, 94; auth, What are They Saying About Matthew's Sermon on the Mount?, Mahwah, NJ, Paulist Press, 94; articles, Towards an Imperial-Critical Reading of Matthew, SBL 1998 Sem Papers, Atlanta, Scholars, 98; Jesus I Have come Statements in Matthew's Gospel, Cath Bibl Quart, 60, 44-62, 98; Narrative/Literary Approaches to Matthean Theology: The Reign of the Heavens as an Example, Matthew 4:17-5:12, Jour for the Study of the New Testament, 67, 3-27, 97; Matthew 4: 18-22 and Matthean Discipleship: An Audience-Oriented Perspective, Cath Bibl Quart, 59, 58-75, 97; Community Definition and Matthew's Gospel, ed E. Lovering, SBL 1997 Sem Papers, Atlanta, Scholars, 637-63, 97; auth, "Paying the Tax to Rome as Subversive Praxis: Matthew 17:26-27," Journal for the Study of the New Testament 76 (99) 3-31; auth, Matthew and the Margins: A Socio-Political and Religious Reading, Orbis Books (Maryknoll, NY), 00. **CONTACT ADDRESS** Saint Paul Sch of Theol, 5123 Truman Rd., Kansas City, MO 64127. **EMAIL** wcarter@spst.edu

CARTWRIGHT, HELEN MORRIS
PERSONAL Born 07/18/1931, Ferndale, MI, m, 1959 **DISCIPLINE** PHILOSOPHY **EDUCATION** Univ Mich, AB, 54, MA, 57, PhD, 63. **CAREER** Asst prof, 68-73; assoc prof 73-85, Prof Philos, Tufts Univ, 85-98, Prof Emer, 98-. **MEMBERSHIPS** Am Philos Asn; Clare Hall, Univ Cambridge, life mem. **RESEARCH** Metaphysics; philosophy of language. **SELECTED PUBLICATIONS** Auth, Heraclitus and the Bath Water, Philos Rev, 10/65; Quantities, Philos Rev, 1/70; Amounts and Measure of Amount, Nous, 5/75; Parts and Partitives, Synthese, 84; Parts and Places in Being and Saying, MIT Press, 87; Underterminacy of Personal Identity, Synthese, 93; Some of a Plurality in Philosophical Perspectives, 96; A Note on Plural Pronouns, Synthese, 98. **CONTACT ADDRESS** Dept of Philos, Tufts Univ, Medford, Medford, MA 02155-5555.

CARVALHO, JOHN
DISCIPLINE PHILOSOPHY **EDUCATION** Univ Calif, Santa Cruz, BA, 76; Duquesne Univ, MA, 79; PhD, 87. **CAREER** Asst prof, philos, 87-94, assoc prof, 95- , Villanova Univ; vis lectr, Bryn Mawr Col, 94-95; vis assoc prof, Haverford Col, 97. **HONORS AND AWARDS** Fel NEH Summer Inst, 88, 91, 94, 97; hon mention, Lindback Awd for Teaching Excellence, 91, 93, 94; sum res grant, 93. **MEMBERSHIPS** APA; Am Soc for Aesthetics; Soc for Phenomenology and Existential Philos; Soc for Ancient Greek Philos; Soc for the Philos Study of the Contemp Visual Arts; Greater Phila Philos Consortium. **RESEARCH** Critical and cultural theory; ancient philosophy; nineteenth century philosophy; aesthetics. **SELECTED PUBLICATIONS** Auth, "Terror: The Space of a Savage Exteriority, Philos Today, 98; auth, The Visible and Invisible in Merleau-Ponty and Foucault, Int Stud in Philos, XXV/3; Repetitions: Appropriating Representation in Contemporary Art, Philos Today, 91. **CONTACT ADDRESS** Dept of Philosophy, Villanova Univ, 800 Lancaster Ave., Villanova, PA 19085-1692. **EMAIL** john.carvalho@villanova.edu

CARVER, FRANK G.
PERSONAL Born 05/27/1928, Crookston, NE, m, 1949, 2 children **DISCIPLINE** RELIGION **EDUCATION** Taylor Univ, BA, 50; Nazarene Theol Sem, BD, 54; Princeton Theol Sem, MTh, 58; Univ Edinburgh, PhD, 64. **CAREER** Pastor, Nazarene churches Nebr, NJ, & Scot, 49-59; Olivet Nazarene Col, 72; pastor, Nazarene Theol Col, Johannesburg, RSA, 79; prof Bibl lit & theol, dept ch, dir grad relig stud, Pasadena/Pt Loma Nazarene Col, 61-96; lectr Europ Nazarene Bibl Col, 96-98; prof emer relig, Pt Loma Nazarene Col, 97-. **MEMBERSHIPS** SBL, WTS. **RESEARCH** Classic spirituality. **SELECTED PUBLICATIONS** Auth, Nature of Biblical Prophecy, The Second Coming, Beacon Hill Pr of Ks Cty, 95; When Jesus Said Goodbye, Beacon Hill Pr of Ks Cty, 96; The Essence

of Wesleyanism, The Preacher's Mag, 96; "Growth in Sanctification: John Wesley and John of the Cross," The Tower 3 (99). **CONTACT ADDRESS** 4037 95 Porte De Palmas, San Diego, CA 92122. **EMAIL** fgcarver@ptluma.edu

CARVER, MARC
DISCIPLINE POST-MODERN ETHICS **EDUCATION** Inst Christian Studies, BA, 79; Austin Presbyterian theol sem, Mdiv, 92; Princeton sem, ThM, 93; Claremont Sch Theol, PhD; cont edu, Seton hosp, 91; Princeton sem, 93; Austin Presbyterian sem, 94; Loyola Marymont, 96; Mount St Mary's Col, 96-98. **CAREER** Chaplain, Brackenridge State hosp, 91; adjunct fac, Inst Christian Studies, 93-95; assoc min, Univ Ave Church of Christ, 88-95; therapist, Pepperdine Couns Ctr, 96-97; pastoral couns, 97-; adjunct fac, 96-. **HONORS AND AWARDS** Silver Stallion Awd, Annawakkee Residential Treatment, 85; scholarc awards, Inst Christian Studies, 87-89; Austin Presbyterian theol sem, 89-91; outstanding young man of Am award, 90; scolar awards, Claremont Sch Theol, 95-. **MEMBERSHIPS** Mem, Am Assn Pastoral Counselors; Am Acad Rel Soc Biblical Lit; Soc Pastoral Theol; Soc Sci Relig. **RESEARCH** Interaction of theol and personality theory, psychol of relig. **SELECTED PUBLICATIONS** Auth, Lessons of Job for Ministry: Are We Aiding or Afflicting?, Leaven 4/4, 96. **CONTACT ADDRESS** Dept of Relig, Pepperdine Univ, 24255 Pacific Coast Hwy, Malibu, CA 90263. **EMAIL** mcarver@pepperdine.edu

CARY, PHILLIP
PERSONAL Born 06/10/1958, Buffalo, NY, m, 1983, 3 children **DISCIPLINE** PHILOSOPHY & RELIG STUD **EDUCATION** Wash Univ, St. Louis, BA, 80; Yale Univ, MA, 89, PhD, 94. **CAREER** Adj fac, philos dept,93, Univ CT, Stamford; adj fac, 93-94, Hillier Col, Univ Hartford; Arthur J. Ennis Postdoct Fel, 94-97, Villanova Univ Core Hum Prog; Rocco A. and Gloria C. Postdoct Fel, Villanova Univ Core Hum Prog, 97-98; asst prof, Eastern Col, St. Davids, 98-. **HONORS AND AWARDS** Wash Univ: Mylonas Scholar, Phi Beta Kappa; Yale Univ: Univ Fel, Special Diss Fel. **MEMBERSHIPS** APA; Soc of Christian Philos;AAR. **RESEARCH** Augustine; hist of Christian thought. **SELECTED PUBLICATIONS** Auth, On Behalf of Classical Trinitarianism: an Historical and Systematic Critique of Rahner on the Trinity, The Thomist, 92; auth, God in the Soul: Or, the Residue of Augustine's Manichaean Optimism, Univ of Dayton Rev, 94; auth, The Logic of Trinitarian Doctrine, Relig and Theol Stud Fel Bul, 95; auth, Historical Perspectives on Trinitarian Doctrine, Relig and Theol Stud Fel Bul, 95; auth, Believing the Word: a Proposal about Knowing Other Persons, Faith & Philosophy, 13/1, 96; auth, Augustine: Philosopher and Saint, lect ser, Tchng Co, 97; auth, Philosophy and Religion in the West, lect ser, Tchng Co, 97; auth, What Licentius Learned: A Narrative Reading of the Cassiciacum Dialogues, Augustinian Stud, 29/1, 98; auth, Interiority in St. Augustine Through the Ages: an Encyclopedia, Eerdmans, 00; auth, Augustine's Invention of the Inneer Self, Oxford Univ Press, 00. **CONTACT ADDRESS** Philosophy Dept, Eastern Col, 1300 Eagle Rd, Saint Davids, PA 19087-3696. **EMAIL** pcary@eastern.edu

CASEBIER, ALLAN
PERSONAL Born 10/01/1934, Los Angeles, CA, m, 1994 **DISCIPLINE** PHILOSOPHY; HISTORY **EDUCATION** UCLA, MA, 64; Michigan, PhD, 69. **CAREER** Philos Prof, USC, IL; Cinema/Television, Usc, Miami, FL. **HONORS AND AWARDS** Fulbright, India, 82. **MEMBERSHIPS** Amer Philos Assoc; Amer Soc for Aesthetics; Soc for Cinema Studies. **RESEARCH** Aesthetics; ethics; ontology; film hist. **SELECTED PUBLICATIONS** Auth, Film Appreciation, NY: Harcourt Brace Jovanovich, 76; Social Responsibilities of the Mass Media, Washington, DC: Univ Press Amer, 78; The Phenomenology of Japanese Cinema, Quart Rev Film & Video, 90; Film and Phenomenology, NY: Cambridge Univ Press, 91; Phenomenology and Aesthetics, Encyclopedia of Aesthetics, Oxford Univ Press, 97; A Phenomenology of Motion Picture Experience, Film and Philosophy, vol 4, 98; The Japanese Aesthetic, Journal of Comparative Lit and Art, fall 98; Theorizing the Moving Image, Film and Philos, vol 5, 99; Representation: Cultural Representations and Signifying Practices, World Communication, winter 99; Critical Communication, manuscript in progress. **CONTACT ADDRESS** Philosophy Dept, Univ of Miami, Coral Gables, FL 33124-4670. **EMAIL** acasebie@miami.edu

CASEY, EDWARD S.
PERSONAL Born 02/24/1939, Topeka, KS, m, 1962, 2 children **DISCIPLINE** PHILOSOPHY **EDUCATION** Yale Univ, BA, 61; Northwestern Univ, PhD, 67. **CAREER** Univ Calif, Santa Barbara, 67-68; Yale Univ, 68-78; State Univ New York, Stony Brook, 78- . **HONORS AND AWARDS** Phi Beta Kappa, Magna cum Laude, Yale Univ, 61; Woodrow Wilson fel, 62-63, 66-67; Fulbright fel, Paris, 64-66; Morse fel, Yale Univ, 72-73; ALLS fel, 78; NEH fel, 87-88; Rockefeller fel, Wesleyan Univ, 90. **MEMBERSHIPS** APA; Soc for Phenomenology and Existential Philos. **RESEARCH** Aesthetics; phenomenology; structuralism; poststructuralism; philosophy of psychoanalysis; philosophy of mind; philosophy of perception. **SELECTED PUBLICATIONS** Auth, Spirit and Soul: Essays in Philosophical Psychology, 91; auth, Getting Back into Place: Toward a Renewed Understanding of the Place-World, Indiana, 93; auth, The Fate of Place: A Philosophical History, California, 97. **CONTACT ADDRESS** Dept of Philosophy, SUNY, Stony Brook, Stony Brook, NY 11794.

CASEY, JOHN DUDLEY
PERSONAL Born 01/18/1939, Worcester, MA, m, 1982, 4 children **DISCIPLINE** HISTORY, LAW, AND LITERATURE **EDUCATION** Harvard Col, BA; Harvard Law School, LLB; Univ of Iowa, MFA. **CAREER** Prof of English, Univ of Va, 72-92. **HONORS AND AWARDS** Nat Board Awd for Fiction, 89. **MEMBERSHIPS** P.E.N. **SELECTED PUBLICATIONS** Auth, The Half-life of Happiness, 98; auth, Supper at the Black Pearl, 95; auth, Spartina, 89; auth, Testimony & Demeanor, 79; auth, An American Romance, 77. **CONTACT ADDRESS** Dept of English, Univ of Virginia, Bryant Hall, Charlottesville, VA 22904.

CASEY, KENNETH
PERSONAL Born 10/26/1956, Waco, TX, m, 1987, 3 children **DISCIPLINE** PHILOSOPHY **EDUCATION** Univ of Florida, BA; Southern Bapt Sem, MDiv, Vanderbilt, PhD. **CAREER** Teacher **MEMBERSHIPS** APA **RESEARCH** Ancient and medieval philo; hist of ethics; rhetoric and lit. **CONTACT ADDRESS** 5017 Ridgeview Dr, Bowling Green, KY 42101. **EMAIL** ken.casey@wku.edu

CASEY, TIMOTHY
PERSONAL Born 10/08/1950, Cleveland, OH, m, 1972, 4 children **DISCIPLINE** PHILOSOPHY **EDUCATION** Loras Coll, BA, 72; Duquesne Univ, PhD, 86. **CAREER** Prof, Philos Dept, 87-, Univ of Scranton. **HONORS AND AWARDS** BA Magna Cum Laude; PhD, Honors. **MEMBERSHIPS** Amer Philos Assoc. **RESEARCH** Philosophy of Technology, Philosophy of Architecture, 20th Century Continental Philosophy. **SELECTED PUBLICATIONS** Coed, Lifeworld and Technology, Center for Advanced Research in Phenomenology and Univ Press of America, 90; auth, Architecture as Environmental Philosophy, Research in Philosophy and Technology, 99; Medieval Technology and the Husserlian Critique of Galilean Science, American Catholic Philosophical Quarterly, 97; Technology and Science as Philosophical Problems, CCICA Annual, pub by Catholic Commission on Intellectual and Cultural Affairs, 97; Technology and the Metaphysics of Technique, Research in Philosophy and Technology, 97; Architecture, in: The Encyclopedia of Phenomenology, Kluwer Academic Publishers, 97. **CONTACT ADDRESS** Dept of Philosophy, Univ of Scranton, Scranton, PA 18510. **EMAIL** caseyt1@uofs.edu

CASS, RONALD ANDREW
PERSONAL Born 08/12/1949, Washington, DC, m, 1969, 2 children **DISCIPLINE** LAW **EDUCATION** Univ VA, BA, 70; Univ Chicago, JD, 73. **CAREER** Law clerk, US Court Appeals 3rd Circuit, 73-74; assoc, Arent, Fox, Kintner, Plotkin & Kahn, 74-76; asst prof, Univ VA, 76-81; assoc prof Law, 81-83, prof Law, 83-; Dean, Boston Univ School of Law, 90-, Bigelas Prof, 95-; comm'r, vice-chair, US Int Trade Commn, 88-90. **HONORS AND AWARDS** Fel Am Bar Found; Adj scholar; Am Enterprise Inst; sr fel, Int Center Econ Res, 96-97; Distinguished Lecturer, Univ Francisco Marroquinn, 96. **MEMBERSHIPS** Am Law Inst; Asn Am Law Deans; Mont Pelerin soc; New England Coun; New England Legal Found; Trans-Atlantic Policy Network. **RESEARCH** Administrative law; communications law; international trade law; legal process. **SELECTED PUBLICATIONS** Coauth, Administrative Law: Cases and Materials, Little, Brown & Co, Boston, MA, 94, 2nd ed (teacher's manual 94; Teacher's Update, 96); auth, The How and Why of Law School Accreditation, 45 J of Legal Ed 418, 95; The Optimal Pace of Privatization, 13 Boston Univ Int Law J 413, 95; auth, Judging: Norms and Incentives of Retrospective Decision-making, 75 Boston Univ Law Rev, 95; auth, Economics and International Law, 29 NY Univ J of Int Law & Politics 473, 97; auth,Money, Power, and Politics: Governance Models and Campaign Finance Regulation, 6 Supreme Court Economic Rev 1, 98; coauth, International Trade in Telecommunications, MIT Press, Cambridge, MA & AEI Press, Washington, DC, 98; coauth, Administrative Law: Cases and Materials, Aspen Pubs, NY, NY, 98, 3rd ed (teacher's manual, 98); coauth, Antitrust Intent, 74 Southern California L. Rev., 01. **CONTACT ADDRESS** Sch Law, Boston Univ, 765 Commonwealth Ave, Boston, MA 02215-1401. **EMAIL** roncass@bu.edu

CASSEL, J. DAVID
PERSONAL Born 02/16/1950, Fort Couins, CO, m, 1995, 2 children **DISCIPLINE** THEOLOGY **EDUCATION** Grinnell Coll, BA, 72; Princeton Theo Sem, MDiv, 75; Univ of VA, PhD, 92. **CAREER** Asst Prof, 92-97, Assoc Prof, 98-, Hanover Coll. **MEMBERSHIPS** AAR, NAPS. **RESEARCH** History of Biblical Interpretation, Cyril of Alexandria. **SELECTED PUBLICATIONS** Auth, Stewardship, Experiencing and Expressing God's Nurturing Love, in: Amer Bap Qtly, 98; Defending the Cannibals, in: Christian Hist, 98; Cyril of Alexandria, Champion of Christology, in: Covenant Companion, 94; Athanasius, Advocate for Equality within the Godhead, in: Covenant Companion, 94; Origin of Alexandria, Saint or Heretic, in: Covenant Companion, 94; Justin Martyr, Defending the Faith until Death, in: Covenant Companion, 94. **CONTACT ADDRESS** Dept of Theological Studies, Hanover Col, Hanover, IN 47243. **EMAIL** cassel@hanover.edu

CASSELL, P. G.
PERSONAL Born 06/05/1959, Orange, CA, m, 1988, 3 children **DISCIPLINE** ECONOMICS **EDUCATION** Stanford Univ, BA, JD, 81. **CAREER** Prof 92-, Univ Utah; E Dist VA Asst Us Att, 88-91; US Dept Justice Att Gen, Assoc deputy, 86-88; law clerk, 85-86, Justice W E Burger; law clerk, 84-85, Judge A Scalia. **HONORS AND AWARDS** Order of the Coif. **RESEARCH** Criminal Justice; Rights of Crime Victims. **SELECTED PUBLICATIONS** Coauth, Handcuffing the Cops: A Thirty Year Perspective on Miranda, Effects on Law Enforcement, Stanford L Rev 98; auth, Miranda, Negligible Effect on Law Enforcement: Some Skeptical Observations, Harv J L & Pub 97; The Costs of the Miranda Mandate: A Lesson in the Dangers of Inflexible Prophylactic, Supreme Court Inventions, AZ St L J 96; co auth, Police Interrogation in the 1990's: An Empirical Study of the Effects of Miranda, UCLA L Rev, 96; auth, All Benefits No Costs: The Grand Illusion of Miranda, Defenders, Northwestern U L Rev, 96; Miranda's Social Costs: An Empirical Reassessment Northwestern L Rev, 96; Search and Seizure Law in Utah: The Irrelevance of the Antipolygamy Raids, BYU L Rev 95; Balancing the Scales of Justice: The Case For and the Effects Of Utah's Victim Rights Amendment, Utah L Rev 94; The Rodney King Trials and the Double Jeopardy Clause: Some Observations on Original Meaning and the ACLU's Schizophrenic Views of the Dual Sovereign Doctrine, UCLA L Rev, 94. **CONTACT ADDRESS** Col of Law, Univ of Utah, 332 S 1400 E Fort, Salt Lake City, UT 84112. **EMAIL** cassellp@law.utah.edu

CASSELS, JAMIE
DISCIPLINE LAW **EDUCATION** Carleton Univ, BA, 76; Western Ontario Univ, LLB, 80; Columbia Univ, LLM, 81. **CAREER** Asst prof, 81-93; prof, 93-; assoc dean, 95-98. **RESEARCH** Environmental issues; law and society in India. **SELECTED PUBLICATIONS** Auth, The Uncertain Promise of Law: Lessons from Bhopal; pubs on contracts, legal theory, and remedies; co-auth, Remedies: Cases and Materials. **CONTACT ADDRESS** Fac of Law, Univ of Victoria, PO Box 2400, Victoria, BC, Canada V8W 3H7. **EMAIL** jcassels@uvic.ca

CASSIDY, LAURENCE LAVELLE
PERSONAL Born 06/09/1929, New York, NY **DISCIPLINE** PHILOSOPHY, THEOLOGY **EDUCATION** Bellarmine Col, AB, 54; Woodstock Col, STL, 62; Fordham Univ, MA, 64, PhD(philos), 68. **CAREER** Asst prof philos, Fordham Univ, 67-68; assoc prof, 69-81, prof Philos, St Peter's Col, 81-; chmn Philos Dept, 87-94; pres Chapter AAUP, 97-73; sec, 73-85; Chmn Phil Dept, 00-. **MEMBERSHIPS** Am Philos Asn; Am Cath Philos Asn; AAUP; Soc Christian Philosophers; Astrologers Guild Am (vpres, 80-83); Jesuit Philo Assn, 69-. **RESEARCH** Rational theology; phenomenology and idealism; philosophy and para-science. **SELECTED PUBLICATIONS** Auth, Truth as immediacy, Jesuit Philos Asn, 72; The flat earth fallacy, Astrological Rev, Summer 73; The believing Christian as a dedicated astrologer, Astrological J, UK, Spring 79; Astrology and science, Astrological Rev, Winter 80; Existence and Presence, Univ Press Am, 81; Creationism and academic freedom, Academe, 3/82; The Spiritual World of Astrology, The Astrological Journal, 96; The Thinking Self, Univ Press Am, 97. **CONTACT ADDRESS** Dept of Philosophy, Saint Peter's Col, 2641 Kennedy Blvd, Jersey City, NJ 07306-5997.

CASSWELL, DONALD G.
DISCIPLINE LAW **EDUCATION** Univ Toronto, BS, 72, LLM, 80; York Univ, LLB, 76. **CAREER** Asst prof, 80-83; assoc prof, 83-92; prof, 92-; assoc dean, 90-93. **MEMBERSHIPS** Can Bar Asn. **RESEARCH** Evidence; torts; medical law; trial and appellate advocacy; immigration and refugee law; lesbian and gay rights law. **SELECTED PUBLICATIONS** Auth, pubs on AIDS, ethics and law, lesbians, gay men, and canadian law; co-auth, Fundamentals of Trial Techniques. **CONTACT ADDRESS** Fac of Law, Univ of Victoria, PO Box 2400, Victoria, BC, Canada V8W 3H7. **EMAIL** casswell@uvic.ca

CASTE, NICHOLAS J.
DISCIPLINE POLITICAL PHILOSOPHY, BUSINESS ETHICS **EDUCATION** SUNY, Stony Brook, BA, 72; Emory Univ, MA, 74, PhD, 80. **CAREER** Adj prof, Univ NC, Charlotte. **RESEARCH** The ethics of soc interaction in groups such as corporations and in polit syst such as democracies. **SELECTED PUBLICATIONS** Auth, Corporations and Rights, J of Value Inquiry 26, 92; Drug Testing in the Workplace, J of Bus Ethics 11, 92; auth, "Teaching in Prison: The Big A, APA Newsletter on Teaching Philos, 94; Thinking Critically: Techniques for Logical Reasoning, West Publ Co, 95; auth, "Corporate Democracy," J of Soc Philos. **CONTACT ADDRESS** Dept of Philos, Univ of No Carolina, Charlotte, Charlotte, NC 28223-0001. **EMAIL** njcaste@email.uncc.edu

CASTELLI, ELIZABETH
DISCIPLINE RELIGION **EDUCATION** Brown Univ, BA, 79; Claremont Grad Sch, MA, PhD, 78. **CAREER** Asst prof. **RESEARCH** Feminist interpretation of the Bible; early Christian martyrdom and asceticism; women's history in late antiquity; Bible and contemporary culture. **SELECTED PUBLICATIONS** Auth, Imitating Paul: A Discourse of Power, Westminster John Knox, 91; auth, The Postmodern Bible, 95;

co-ed, Reimagining Christian Origins, Trinity, 96. **CONTACT ADDRESS** Dept of Religion, Columbia Col, New York, 2960 Broadway, New York, NY 10027-6902. **EMAIL** ecastelli@barnard.columbia.edu

CASULLO, ALBERT
DISCIPLINE EPISTEMOLOGY AND METAPHYSICS **EDUCATION** Univ Iowa, PhD, 75. **CAREER** Prof, Univ Nebr, Lincoln. **RESEARCH** A priori knowledge. **SELECTED PUBLICATIONS** Auth, Revisability, Reliabilism, and A Priori Knowledge, Philos and Phenomenol Res 49, 88; Causality, Reliabilism, and Mathematical Knowledge, Philos and Phenomenol Res 52, 92; Analyticity and the A Priori, Can J of Philos, Suppl Vol 18, 93. **CONTACT ADDRESS** Univ of Nebraska, Lincoln, Lincoln, NE 68588-0417.

CATALANO, JOSEPH STELLARIO
PERSONAL Born 10/16/1928, Brooklyn, NY **DISCIPLINE** PHILOSOPHY **EDUCATION** St John's Univ, BA, 50, MA, 56, PhD(philos), 62. **CAREER** From instr to asst prof philos, St John's Univ, 59-65; assoc prof, 65-73, Prpf Philos, Kean Col, NJ, 73-, St John's Univ res grant, 64; adj assoc prof, C W Post Col, Long Island Univ, 65 & New Sch Social Res, 68- **MEMBERSHIPS** Am Philos Asn; Asn Symbolic Logic. **RESEARCH** Existentialism. **SELECTED PUBLICATIONS** Auth, Crafting Marks Into Meanings, Philos and Lit, Vol 0020, 96; The Script Rose, Philos and Lit, Vol 0019, 95. **CONTACT ADDRESS** Dept of Philos, Kean Col of New Jersey, Union, NJ 07083.

CAUCHY, VENANT
PERSONAL Born 05/18/1924, North Bay, Canada, m, 1949, 10 children **DISCIPLINE** PHILOSOPHY **EDUCATION** Col Bourget, Can, BA, 44; Univ Montreal, PhB, 45, PhL, 46, PhD(philos), 47. **CAREER** From instr to asst prof philos, St Louis Univ, 47-51; asst prof, Our Lady of the Lake Col, 51-53 & Fordham Univ, 53-57; from asst prof to assoc prof, 57-63, Prof Philos, Univ Montreal, 63-, Can Coun fel, 68-69; co-ed, Rev Cirpho, 73- **MEMBERSHIPS** Can Philos Asn (pres, 78-79); Soc Philos Fr Lang (vpres). **RESEARCH** Post-Aristotelian Greek philosophy; philosophy of religion. **SELECTED PUBLICATIONS** Auth, Meaning and Knowledge--Proposals for Responsibility and Solidarity in The Modern World, Laval Theol et Philos, Vol 0052, 96; Chinese and Oriental Approaches to Philosophy and Culture, Jour Chinese Philos, Vol 0021, 94; Violence--Biology, History and Christian Morality, Laval Theol et Philos, Vol 0053, 97. **CONTACT ADDRESS** Dept of Philos, Univ of Montreal, Montreal, QC, Canada H3C 3J7.

CAUSEY, ROBERT LOUIS
PERSONAL Born 04/13/1941, Los Angeles, CA, m, 1964, 2 children **DISCIPLINE** LOGIC, PHILOSOPHY, COGNITIVE SCIENCE **EDUCATION** Calif Inst Technol, BS, 63; Univ Calif, Berkeley, PhD(logic & methodology of sci), 67. **CAREER** Asst prof, 67-73, assoc prof, 73-79, prof philos, Univ Tex, Austin, 79-, chmn dept, 80-88, assoc dir, Univ Tx Artificial Intelligence Lab, 84-97, Nat Sci Found res fel, 73-74 & 79-81, consult, 79-81, Philosophical Web Site Review Editor for Am Philos, Asn, Newsletter on Philosoophy and Computers, Consultant to several government agencies and private corporations. **MEMBERSHIPS** ACM; AAAI; AAAS; Philos Sci Asn; Am Philos Asn. **RESEARCH** Cognitive Science; unity of science; applied logic. **SELECTED PUBLICATIONS** Auth, Derived Measurement, Dimensions and Dimensional Analysis, Philos Sci, 69; Attribute--Identities in Microreductions, J Philos, 72; Uniform Microreductions, Synthese, 72; contribr, Formal Methods in Methodology of Empirical Sciences, 76 & auth, Unity of Science, 77, Reidel; contribr, Current Research in Philosophy of Science, 79; Scientific Discovery, Logic, and Rationality, 80; auth, The Use of Microcomputers for Classroom Demonstrations, Issues in Higher Educ, 82; Logic, Sets, and Recursion, Jones & Bartlett, 94; auth, "Evid: A System for Interactive Defeasible Reasoning", Deision Support Systems, Vol. 11, 103-131, (94). **CONTACT ADDRESS** Dept of Philos, Univ of Texas, Austin, Austin, TX 78712-1180. **EMAIL** RLC@cs.utexas.edu

CAVADINI, JOHN C.
PERSONAL Born 11/09/1953, New Haven, CT, m, 1979, 7 children **DISCIPLINE** THEOLOGY **EDUCATION** Wesleyan Univ, BA, 75; Marquette Univ, MA, 79; Yale, MA, 81, MPhil, 83, PhD, 88. **CAREER** Instr, 90-present, U of Notre Dame, Dept of Theology; chair, 97-present. **HONORS AND AWARDS** Phi Beta Kappa **MEMBERSHIPS** AAR; NAPS. **RESEARCH** History of Christian Theology; The early church; Medieval theology. **SELECTED PUBLICATIONS** Auth, Augustine's De Trinitate and the Quest for Truth, Theological Studies, 97; auth, Ambrose and Augustine de bono mortis, in The Limits of Ancient Christianity, Univ Mich, 98; auth, A Note on Gregory's Theology of the Miraculous in The Life and Miracles of St. Benedict, American Benedictine Review, forthcoming. **CONTACT ADDRESS** Dept of Theology, Univ of Notre Dame, Notre Dame, IN 46556. **EMAIL** cavadini.1@nd.edu

CAVALIER, ROBERT
DISCIPLINE ADVANCEMENT OF APPLIED ETHICS **EDUCATION** Duquesne Univ, PhD. **CAREER** Philos, Carnegie Mellon Univ. **SELECTED PUBLICATIONS** Auth, Making MOSAIC Webs Work on the Course Level, Syllabus Magazine, 95; Computers, Philosophy of Education: An Encyclopedia, Garland Publ, 96; Feminism and Pornography: A Dialogical Perspective, Computer-Mediated Communication, 96; Evaluating Evaluation in Light of Discipline-Specific Computational Turns Jour Computing Higher Educ, 96; Multimedia in Philosophy Teaching and Research in The Digital Phoenix: How Computers are Changing Philosophy, Blackwell, 97. **CONTACT ADDRESS** Carnegie Mellon Univ, 5000 Forbes Ave, Pittsburgh, PA 15213.

CAVALLARO, ROSANNA
PERSONAL 2 children **DISCIPLINE** LAW **EDUCATION** Harvard Univ, BA, 83; JD, 86. **CAREER** Prof. **RESEARCH** Criminal law; evidence; legal profession. **SELECTED PUBLICATIONS** Auth, Police & Thieves (rev), Mich Law Rev, 98; A Big Mistake: Eroding the Defense of Mistake of Fact About Consent in Rape, Jour Criminal Law, 96. **CONTACT ADDRESS** Suffolk Univ, 120 Tremont St., Boston, MA 02108. **EMAIL** rcavalla@acad.suffolk.edu

CAVANAUGH, MAUREEN B.
PERSONAL Born 01/07/1955, Minneapolis, MN, m, 1980 **DISCIPLINE** LAW **EDUCATION** Swarthmore Col, BA, 75; Cornell Univ, MA, 75; PhD, 80; Univ Minn, JD, 95. **CAREER** Asst prof, Middlebury Col, 80-82; asst prof, Pomona Col, 82-83; asst prof, Washington and Lee Univ, 98-. **HONORS AND AWARDS** Fel, Am School of Class Studies, Athens, 78-79; Fel, Washington and Lee, 01-02. **MEMBERSHIPS** Am Philog Assoc, Am Bar Assoc. **RESEARCH** Classics, Law, Legal History. **SELECTED PUBLICATIONS** Auth, "Towards a New Kind of Equality," Law and Inequality Jour, (95); auth, Eleusis and Athens, Scholars Pr, 96; auth, "Order in Multiplicy: Aristotle on Text, Context and in the Rule of Law," NCar Law Rev, (01). **CONTACT ADDRESS** Sch of Law, Washington and Lee Univ, 458 Padgetts Hill Rd, Natural Bridge, VA 24578. **EMAIL** cavanaughm@wlu.edu

CAVANAUGH, THOMAS A.
DISCIPLINE PHILOSOPHY **EDUCATION** Thomas Aquinas Col, AB, 85; Univ of Notre Dame, MA; PhD, 95. **CAREER** Asst to assoc prof, Univ of San Francisco, 94-. **HONORS AND AWARDS** Weaver Fel; Fleishhacker Fel. **MEMBERSHIPS** Am Phils Assoc; Am Soc of Bioethics and the Humanities; Int Assoc of Bioethics; Am Cath Philos Assoc. **RESEARCH** Bioethics, Principle of Double Effect, Physican-Assisted Suicide, Genetic Information - Privacy. **SELECTED PUBLICATIONS** Auth, "Aquinas and the Historical Roots of Proportionalism", Aquinas Rev 1.2 (95): 31-44; auth, "The Ethics of Death-Hastening of Death-Causing Palliative Analgesic Administration to the Terminally Ill", J of Pain and Symptom Management 12.4 (96): 1-7; auth, "Aquinas's Account of Double Effect", Thomist 61.1 (97): 107-121; auth, "The Nazi! Accusation and Current US Proposals", Bioethics 11.3-4, (97): 291-297; auth, "Act-Evaluation, Willing, and Double Effect", Am Cath Philos Quarterly 71, (97): 243-253; coauth, To Tell the Truth: Ethical and Practical Issues in Disclosing Medical Mistakes to Patients", J of Gen Internal Med 12, (97): 77-775; auth, "Currently Accepted Practices that are Known to Lead to Death and PAS: Is there an Ethically Relevant Difference?", Cambridge Quarterly of Healthcare Ethics 7, (98): 373-379; auth, "Double Effect and the End-not-means Principle: A Response to Bennett", J of Applied Philos 16.2, (99): 181-185; auth, "Covering Up: To Acknowledge?", Ward Ethics: A Case Approach for Doctors in Training, Cambridge Univ Pr, (forthcoming); auth, "Aquinas's Account of the Ineradicably Social Character of Private Property", Labor, Solidarity and the Common Good, Carolina Acad Pr, (forthcoming). **CONTACT ADDRESS** Dept Philos, Univ of San Francisco, 2130 Fulton St, San Francisco, CA 94117-1080. **EMAIL** cavanaught@usfca.edu

CAVE, ERIC M.
PERSONAL Born 11/12/1965, Lund, Sweden, 2 children **DISCIPLINE** PHILOSOPHY **EDUCATION** Trinity Univ, BA, 88; Univ Calif Irvine, MA, 90; PhD, 94. **CAREER** Vis asst prof, Union Coll, 94-95; asst prof Ark State Univ, 95-00, assoc prof, 00-. **HONORS AND AWARDS** NEH Summer Res Sem Participant, 97. **MEMBERSHIPS** Am Philos Asn; Soc for the Philos of Sex and Love; Phi Beta Kappa. **RESEARCH** Ethics; Political Philosophy. **SELECTED PUBLICATIONS** Auth, A Leibnizian Account of Why Belief in the Christian Mysteries Is Justified, Rel Studies, 95; Would Pluralist Angels (Really) Need Government?, Philos Studies, 96; The Individual Rationality of Maintaining a Sense of Justice, Theory and Decision, 96; Habituation and Rational Preference Revision, Dialogue: Can Philos Rev, 98; Prefering Justice: Rationality, Self-Transformation, and the Sense of Justice, 98. **CONTACT ADDRESS** English and Philosophy, Box 1890, State University, AR 72467-1890. **EMAIL** ecave@toltec.astate.edu

CAWS, PETER JAMES
PERSONAL Born 05/25/1931, Southall, England, m, 1987, 3 children **DISCIPLINE** PHILOSOPHY OF THE SCIENCES **EDUCATION** Univ London, BSc, 52; Yale Univ, MA, 54, PhD, 56. **CAREER** Instr natural sci, Mich State Univ, 56-57; from asst prof to assoc prof philos & chmn dept, Univ Kans, 57-62; exec assoc, Carnegie Corp, New York, 62-65, consult, 65-67; chmn dept philos, Hunter Col, 65-67, prof philos, 65-82; Univ Prof Philos, George Washington Univ, 82-; mem, Coun Philos Studies, 65-; mem, Nat Res Coun, 67-; exec officer, PhD prog philos, City Univ New York, 67-70; Am Coun Learned Soc fel, 72-73; mem, Bd Dir (Comn Int Coop), Am Philos Asn, 74-84; nat lectr, Soc Signma Xi, 75-77; Rockefeller Found fel, 79-80; vis prof, Fr NY Univ, spring, 82; Phi Beta Kappa vis schol, 83-84; vis prof, comp lit Univ Maryland, 85. **HONORS AND AWARDS** Pres medal, CUNY Grad Sch, 78; First Dist Lectr Business and Society Baruch Col, 86; hon mem Phi Beta Kappa, 92. **MEMBERSHIPS** Fel AAAS (vpres, 67-68); Am Philos Asn; Philos Sci Asn; Soc Gen Syst Res (pres, 66-67); Soc Am de Phil de Langue Francaise (pres, 92-94). **RESEARCH** Structure and development of theory and praxis; philosophy and politics; recent European philosophy. **SELECTED PUBLICATIONS** Ed, Two Centuries of Philosophy in America, Blackwell, 80; auth, Structuralism, Humanities, 88; auth, Yorick's World: Science and the Knowing Subject, California, 93; auth, Ethics from Experience, Wadsworth, 96. **CONTACT ADDRESS** Dept of Philosophy, The George Washington Univ, 2035 H St NW, Washington, DC 20052-0001. **EMAIL** pcaws@gwu.edu

CAYARD, W. W.
PERSONAL Born 04/05/1921, Port Arthur, TX, m, 1952, 4 children **DISCIPLINE** RELIGION **EDUCATION** Univ of S CA, PhD, 56 **CAREER** Asst Prof, 56-60; Assoc Prof, 61-65; Prof, 66-86; Chair, 69-86; W Liberty St Col **MEMBERSHIPS** Am Philos Assoc **RESEARCH** Quaker Topics; Historical Jesus **SELECTED PUBLICATIONS** Auth, Berdyaev's Philosophy of Freedom, University of Southern California Press, 56; auth, A Quaker View of Liberation Theology, Friends Journal, (89): 16-18; auth, Interfaith Dialogue and Personal Commitment, Friends Journal, (90): 28-29; auth, Dramatic Changes in World Quaker Membership, Friends Journal, (95): 14-15; auth, A Quaker View of the Bible, Pittsburgh Friends Meeting Newsletter, 98, 10-11 **CONTACT ADDRESS** 100 Norman Dr, Cranberry Township, PA 16066-4232. **EMAIL** cayard@fyi.net

CECIRE, ROBERT C.
DISCIPLINE CHURCH HISTORY **EDUCATION** Wheaton Col, BA; Gordon Divinity Sch, BD; Univ Kans, MA, PhD. **CAREER** Adj prof, Bethel Col; Anoka-Ramsey Community Col; vis lectr, Univ Kans; lectr, Gordon Col; asst prof, Wiinebrenner Theol Sem, 97-; dir, Theol Stud. **MEMBERSHIPS** Mem, Soc Biblical Lit; Conf on Faith and History; Nat Hist Honor Soc. **SELECTED PUBLICATIONS** Rev(s), Jour Evangel Theol Soc; Res Publica Litterarum; pub, article on Encratism, Res Publica Litterarum. **CONTACT ADDRESS** Winebrenner Theol Sem, 701 E Melrose Ave, PO Box 478, Findlay, OH 45839.

CEDERBERG, HERBERT RENANDO
PERSONAL Born 08/11/1933, Spokane, WA, m, 1989, 2 children **DISCIPLINE** UNITED STATES ECONOMIC HISTORY, ART HISTORY, HISTORY OF PHILOSOPHY **EDUCATION** Univ Calif, Berkeley, AB, 59, MA, 63, PhD(hist), 68. **CAREER** From asst prof to prof US colonial hist, 66-78, admin dir minority serv off, 72-73, Prof Hist, Univ Wis-River Falls, 78-; guest prof, Univ Minn, 75-76; Chair, Bd of Dir of Jobs Now Coalition, 98-. **HONORS AND AWARDS** Wis State Legis res fels, 68-69, 75-76; Nat Endowment for Humanities fel in residence, 77; Outstanding Fac Mem of the Yr, Univ Wis-River Falls, Col of Arts & Scis, 99. **MEMBERSHIPS** AHA; Inst Early Am Hist & Cult; Hakluyt Soc. **RESEARCH** Economic analysis of early settlement in colonial America; colonial art history; probate and inventory records in 17th and 18th century Massachusetts. **SELECTED PUBLICATIONS** Auth, An Economic Analysis of English Settlement in North America 1583-1635, Arno, 77; co-auth, The Cost of Living in Minnesota, 2000: A Family Self-Sufficiency Wage Analysis (Part Three of the Job Gap Economic Literacy Project), 01. **CONTACT ADDRESS** Dept of History, Univ of Wisconsin, River Falls, 410 S 3rd St, River Falls, WI 54022-5013. **EMAIL** herbert.cederberg@uwrf.edu

CEDERBLOM, JERRY
PERSONAL Born 10/07/1944, Seattle, WA, m, 1 child **DISCIPLINE** MORAL AND POLITICAL PHILOSOPHY, EPISTEMOLOGY, HISTORY OF PHILOSOPHY **EDUCATION** Whitman Col, BA, 67; Claremont Grad Sch, PhD, 72. **CAREER** Instr to prof Univ Nebr, Omaha; vis prof, Evergreen State Col. **HONORS AND AWARDS** Excellence in Tchg award, Univ Nebr, Omaha, 91. **SELECTED PUBLICATIONS** Coauth, Critical Reasoning; Ethics at Work; coed, Justice and Punishment. **CONTACT ADDRESS** Univ of Nebraska, Omaha, Omaha, NE 68182. **EMAIL** jerryced@unomaha.edu

CEDERMAN, LARS-ERIK
PERSONAL Born 05/27/1963, Storfors, Sweden **DISCIPLINE** POLITICAL SCIENCE **EDUCATION** Uppsala Univ, MS, 88; Grad Sch Intl Studies, MA, 90; Univ Mich, PhD, 94. **CAREER** Lectr, Grad Inst of Intl Studies, 94-95; Univ Lectr, Oxford Univ, 95-97; Asst Prof, UCLA, 97-01; Assoc Prof, Harvard Univ, 01-. **HONORS AND AWARDS** Fulbright Fel, 86-87; Fel, Swiss Confed, 88-90; Fel, Rotary Found, 90-91; Fel, Am-Scandinavian Found, 91-92; Fel, soc Sci Res Coun, 92-94; Fel, Europ Univ Inst, 99-00; Fel, John M. Olin Inst, 00-01; Horace H. Rackham Distinguished Dissertation Awd, 95; Edgar s. Furniss Book Awd, Mershon Ctr, 98. **MEMBERSHIPS** APSA; ISA **RESEARCH** Computational modeling; International relations theory; Nationalism; Integration; State-formation; Ethnic conflict; Security studies. **SELECTED PUBLICATIONS** Auth, Emergent Actors in World Politics, Princeton Univ Press, 97; ed, Constructing Europe's Identity, Lynne Rienner, 01; auth, "Back to Kant: Reinterpreting the Democratic Peace as a Macrohistorical Process," Am Polit Sci Rev, 01; auth, "Nationalism and Bounded Integration," Europ J of Intl Relations, 01. **CONTACT ADDRESS** Weatherhead Center, Harvard Univ, 1737 Cambridge St, Cambridge, MA 02138. **EMAIL** cederman@cfia.harvard.edu

CENKNER, WILLIAM
PERSONAL Born 10/25/1930, Cleveland, OH **DISCIPLINE** HISTORY OF RELIGIONS **EDUCATION** Providence Col, AB, 54; Pontif Fac Theol, STL, 59; Fordham Univ, PhD(hist relig), 69. **CAREER** Assoc prof hist, 69-80, Assoc Prof HistRelig & Relig Educ, CaTh Univ Am, 80-, Chauncey Stillman Found res grant, 69; mem, Nat Coun Relig & Pub Educ, 72-; assoc ed, Col Theol Soc, 73- **MEMBERSHIPS** Col Theol Soc (pres, 78-80); Am Acad Relig; Asn Asian Studies. **RESEARCH** Encounter of world religions; religion and education; Sankaracarya's. **SELECTED PUBLICATIONS** Auth, Rabindranath Tagore and aesthetic man, Int Philos Quart, 73; The emergence of an Indian-Christian theology, Z Missionswissenschaft & Religionswissenchaft, 73; The covergence of religions, Cross Currents, 73; Relgion & education: Models from contemporary Hinduism, Relig Educ, 75; The Hindu Personality in Education, South Asia Bks, 76; Tagore's vision of relationality, Humanitas, 76; Understanding the religious personality, Horizons, 78. **CONTACT ADDRESS** Sch of Relig Studies, Catholic Univ of America, 620 Michigan Ave NE, Washington, DC 20064-0002.

CENTORE, FLOYD
DISCIPLINE PHILOSOPHY **EDUCATION** Canisius Col Buffalo, BA, 59; Univ Md, MA, 62; St John's Univ, PhD, 68. **CAREER** Graduate asst, Univ of Maryland, 59-60; graduate asst, St John's Univ, 62-64, instructor, 64-68; ch, St. Jerome's Univ; vis lectr, Duchesne Residence School, 65-66; asst prof, St. John's Univ, 68-69; asst prof, St Jerome's Univ, 69-73; asst dean, St. Jerome's Univ, 70-73; prof, St. Jerome's Univ; asst prof, St Jerome's Univ, 73-88; prof of philos, St. Jerome's Univ, 88-. **SELECTED PUBLICATIONS** Auth, Being and Becoming: A Critique of Post-Modernism; auth, Life, Atoms, Chance: Three Essays in the Philosophy of Science; auth, Persons: A Comparative Account of the Six Possible Theories; auth, Philosophy Today: A Critical Survey of Current Trends in Philosophy for Layman; auth, Robert Hooke's Contributions to Mechanics: A Study in Seventeenth Century; auth, "A Note on Diversity and Difference"; auth, "A Note on T.G. Smith's 'The Theory of Forms, Relations and Infinite Regress,'"; auth, "A Note on W.J. Hills 'The Doctrine of God After Vatican II,'" auth, "A Note on Wittgenstein as an Unwilling Nominalist,"; auth, "Aquinas on Inner Space". **CONTACT ADDRESS** Dept of Philosophy, St. Jerome's Univ, Waterloo, ON, Canada N2L 3G3.

CESARZ, GARY
PERSONAL Born 10/01/1950, Albuquerque, NM, m, 1998, 2 children **DISCIPLINE** PHILOSOPHY **EDUCATION** Univ of N Mex, BA, 74, MA, 78, PhD, 88. **CAREER** Instr, Chapman Univ, 78-97; from Tchg asst to tchg assoc to adj asst prof, 80-93, Univ N Mex; asst prof, Col Santa Fe, 86-89; instr, Auburn Univ, 97-. **HONORS AND AWARDS** Nat Hon Soc in Philos; Popejoy Dissertation Prize Nominee **MEMBERSHIPS** Am Philos Assoc; Soc for the Advancement of Am Philos; Leibniz Soc; Marcel Soc **RESEARCH** Early Modern Philosophy, 19th Century Philosophy through early 20th century Analytic Philosophy and Phenomenology, Leibniz, Kant, Aristotle, Russell, Frege, Husserl, Metaphysics and epistemology, Idealism (German, British, American), Ancient Greek Philosophy. **SELECTED PUBLICATIONS** Auth, J.M.E. McTaggart in A Companion to the Philosphers; auth, Meaning, Individual and the Problem of Bare Particluars: a Study in Husserl's Ideas, in Husserl Studies; rev, Metaphysics: His Philosophy 9 Course for 1915-16, in Society for the Advancement of American Philosophy Newsletter. **CONTACT ADDRESS** Dept of Philos, Auburn Univ, Auburn, AL 36849-5210. **EMAIL** cesargl@mail.auburn.edu

CHALFANT, WILLIAM Y.
PERSONAL Born 10/03/1928, Hutchinson, KS, m, 1956, 2 children **DISCIPLINE** HISTORY; LAW **EDUCATION** Univ Kans, AB, 50; Univ Mich, Juris Dr, 56. **CAREER** Atty at Law, Branwe, Chalfant, & Hill, 56-. **HONORS AND AWARDS** Various. **MEMBERSHIPS** Kans Bar Asn; Am Bar Asn; SW Bar Asn; W Hist Asn; Santa Fe Trail Asn. **RESEARCH** Spanish Entrada on Western Plains; military history of Southern Plains; Plains Indians. **SELECTED PUBLICATIONS** Auth, Cheyennes and Horse Soldiers, Univ Okla Press, 89; auth, Without Quarter, Univ Okla Press, 91; Dangerous Passage, Univ Okla Press, 94; Cheyennes at Darkwater Creek, Univ Okla Press, 97. **CONTACT ADDRESS** Branine, Chalfant & Hill, 418 First Nat Ctr, PO Box 2027, Hutchinson, KS 67504-2027.

CHALMERS, DAVID
PERSONAL Born 04/20/1966, Sydney, Australia, s **DISCIPLINE** PHILOSOPHY **EDUCATION** Univ Adelaide, Australia, BS; Ind Univ, PhD. **CAREER** Prof, Univ Calif, Santa Cruz; prof, and assoc dir of Center for Consciousness, Univ of Ariz. **HONORS AND AWARDS** McDonnell fel, Wash Univ; Rhodes Scholarship, 87. **MEMBERSHIPS** Asn Sci Stud Consciousness; Soc Philos Psychol; Am Philos Asn. **RESEARCH** Philosophy of mind, related areas of cognitive science and metaphysics. **SELECTED PUBLICATIONS** Auth, The Conscious Mind: In Search of a Fundamental Theory, Oxford Univ Press, 96; auth, Explaining Consciousness: The Hard Problem, MIT Press, 97. **CONTACT ADDRESS** Dept of Philos, Univ of California, Santa Cruz, 1156 High St, Santa Cruz, CA 95064. **EMAIL** chalmers@paradox.ucsc.edu

CHAMBERLAIN, GARY L.
PERSONAL Born 08/21/1938, Denver, CO, m, 1968, 2 children **DISCIPLINE** RELIGIOUS STUDIES **EDUCATION** St Louis Univ, BA, 62; Univ Chicago, MA, 67; Grad Theol Union, PhD, 73. **CAREER** Assoc prof, Webster Univ St Louis, 71-79; assoc prof; chair, 87-91; prof, Seattle Univ, 79-. **HONORS AND AWARDS** NEH Fel, 75-76; Summa cum laude, 62; Gaffney Endowed Chair, 91-94. **MEMBERSHIPS** Am Acad of Rel; Soc of Christian Ethics; Assoc Prof and Res in Rel Educ; Pax Christi; Amnesty Int; Sierra Club. **RESEARCH** Population, Consumption, and the Environment; Human Sexuality; Peace and Justice; Faith Development. **SELECTED PUBLICATIONS** Auth, Learning from the Japanese on Abortion, Am, 94; Catholics as Remnant in Japan, Nat Cath Reporter, 94; Kamagasaki: the Underside of Japan's economic Miracle, Japan Christian Rev, 94; Abortion, Family Life, and Economic Development in Belize, Belize Studies, 95. **CONTACT ADDRESS** Theology and Religious Studies, Seattle Univ, Seattle, WA 98122. **EMAIL** gchamber@seattleu.edu

CHAMBERLAIN, PAUL
PERSONAL Born 12/24/1954, Alberta, BC, Canada, m, 1979, 2 children **DISCIPLINE** ETHICS **EDUCATION** Marquette Univ, PhD, 90 **CAREER** Assoc Prof, 90-pres, Trinity Western Univ **MEMBERSHIPS** Can Philos Assoc; Soc of Christian Philos **RESEARCH** Physician Assisted Suicide; Ethical Foundations **CONTACT ADDRESS** Dept of Philosophy, Trinity Western Univ, 7600 Glover Rd, Langley, BC, Canada V2Y 1Y1. **EMAIL** chamberl@twu.ca

CHAMBERLIN, BILL F.
DISCIPLINE LAW **EDUCATION** Univ Wash, BA, PhD; Univ Wis, Madison, MA. **CAREER** Fac, Univ Ncar, Chapel Hill, 76-87; prof, Univ Fla, 87-; dir, Joseph L. Brechner Ctr for Freedom of Information. **RESEARCH** Mass media law, first amendment theory, media law research. **CONTACT ADDRESS** School of Law, Univ of Florida, PO Box 117625, Gainesville, FL 32611-7625. **EMAIL** chamberlin@law.ufl.edu

CHAMBERS, JAMES
PERSONAL Born 03/30/1940, Colorado Springs, CO, m, 1991, 4 children **DISCIPLINE** PUBLIC ADMINISTRATION **EDUCATION** Portland State Univ, BA, 62; Portland State Univ, MS, 84; Portland State Univ, MPA, 84; Portland State Univ, PhD, 86. **CAREER** Adj Prof, Portland State Univ, 82-86; Vis Prof, Wash State Univ, 86-87; Asst Prof, Mesa State Col, 87-91; Asst Prof, Ind State Univ, 91-96; Adj Prof, Ind State Univ, 91-96; Assoc Prof, Fl Gulf Coast Univ, 96-. **HONORS AND AWARDS** Prof of the Year, 91. **MEMBERSHIPS** Nat Asn of Urban Affairs. **RESEARCH** The theoretical aspects of the phenomenology of crime structures and correction within the public sector, focus on the etiology of the behavior utilizing geographical, economical, political, sociological, historical and psychological factors considered to be criminogenic. **SELECTED PUBLICATIONS** Auth, Police and Community Relations, Ind St Univ Pr, 93; Auth, Hate Crimes, Ind St Univ Pr, 93; Auth, Philosophy, Slavery and Socio-Economic Disorder, IASS Publ, 93; Auth, Introduction to Juvenile Delinquency, Kendall-Hunt Publ, 94; Auth, Introduction to Criminal Justice Systems, Kendall-Hunt Publ, 94; Auth, Dynamics of Delinquent and Criminal Behavior, Kendall-Hunt Publ, 94; Auth, The Police and Community: '"Theory and Practice Alternative Relations, Kendall-Hunt Publ, 94; Auth, "A Reaction to the Reaction," in Representing O.J.: Murder, Criminal Justice and Mass Culture (Harrow and Heston Publ, 96), 185-190. **CONTACT ADDRESS** Dept Pub Admin, Fl Gulf Coast Univ, 10501 FGCU Blvd S, Fort Myers, FL 33965-0001. **EMAIL** jchamber@fgcu.edu

CHAMBERS, JOHN CURRY, JR.
PERSONAL Born 05/22/1956, Newark, NJ, m, 1981 **DISCIPLINE** LAW **EDUCATION** Univ of Pennsylvania, BA; The Washington College of Law, American Univ, JD. **CAREER** American Petroleum Institute, principal RCRA Attorney, 81-84; CONOCO, in-house counsel, 85; McKenna & Cuneo, partner, 86-97; Arent Fox, mem, 97-. **MEMBERSHIPS** DC Bar; ABA, National Bar Assn; Environmental Law Editorial Institute, advisory bd, Journal of Environmental Permitting; advisory committee, ABA Conference on Minority Partners; committee, National Institute for the Environment; vice chair, ABA Teleconference & Video Programs Sonreel; vice chair, ABA Sonreel Diversity Committee; guest commentator, Natl Public Radio; founder, Brownfields Business Information Network; co-chair, ABA Video Teleconferences Committee; mem, EPA NACEPT Title VI Federal Advisory Committee on Implementation of Environmental Justice. **SELECTED PUBLICATIONS** Numerous publications. **CONTACT ADDRESS** Arent Fox, 1050 Connecticut Ave, Washington, DC 20036.

CHAMBERS, JULIUS LEVONNE
PERSONAL Born 10/06/1936, Montgomery Co, NC, m, 1960, 2 children **DISCIPLINE** LAW **EDUCATION** NC Central Univ Durham, BA History (summa cum laude) 1958; Univ of MI, MA 1959; Univ of NC Sch of Law, JD 1962; Columbia Univ Sch of Law ML 1963. **CAREER** Columbia Univ Sch of Law, assoc in law 1962-63; NAACP Legal Def & Educ Fund Inc, legal intern 1963-64; Chambers Stein Ferguson & Becton PA, pres 1964-84; Harvard Univ Law Sch, lecturer 1965; Univ of VA Law Sch, guest lecturer 1971-73; Univ of PA Sch of Law, lecturer 74-90; Columbia University School of Law, adjunct 1978-91; NAACP Legal & Educ Fund Inc, dir counsel 1984-92; University of Michigan Law School, adjunct 1989-92; North Carolina Central University, chancellor 1993-. **HONORS AND AWARDS** WEB DuBois Awd Scotland Co 1973; Hall of Fame Awd NAACP 1975; numerous hon LLD degrees; various distinguished serv awds, frats & Assns. **MEMBERSHIPS** Mem numerous cts of practice 1962-; mem Amer, Natl, 26th Judicial Dist NC Bar Assns; NC Assn of Black Lawyers; mem Amer Bar Assn Section on Indiv Rights & Responsibilities; adv com Natl Bar Assn Equal Employment Oppor; mem NC Bar Assn Com on Rules of Appellate Procedure; mem NC State Bar Assn Const Study Com; mem various NAACP brs; mem various legal assns; bd of dirs Epilepsy Assn of NC; mem various Univ bds; mem various alumni assns; mem various frats; mem Friendship Baptist Church Charlotte. **CONTACT ADDRESS** No Carolina Central Univ, Durham, NC 27707.

CHAMBERS, TIMOTHY
PERSONAL Born 05/04/1971, Milwaukee, WI **DISCIPLINE** PHILOSOPHY **EDUCATION** Univ CT, BS, 93, BA , 93; Tufts Univ, MA, 95; Brown Univ, ABD, 98. **MEMBERSHIPS** APA **RESEARCH** Epistemology; metaphysics; philosophical logic. **SELECTED PUBLICATIONS** Co-auth, Identification of Coumarin in Vanilla Extracts by TLC and HPLC, 65 J of Chem Ed, 88; auth, Quest for Truth Remains an Uncertain Pursuit, Hartford Courant, 90; co-auth, Evidence for Changes in the Alzheimer's Disease Brain Cortical Membrane Structure Mediated by Cholesterol, 13 Neurobiology of Aging, 92; auth, Note On a Contentious Conditional, 6 Lyceum, 94; auth, On Vagueness, Sorites, and Putnam's Intuitionistic Strategy, 81 The Monist, 98; auth, Time Travel: How Not to Defuse The Principal Paradox, 12 Ratio, 99; auth, On Behalf of the Devil: A parady of Anselm Revisited, 100 proceedings of the Aristotelian Society, 00; auth, A Quick Reply to Putnam's Paradox, Mind, 00. **CONTACT ADDRESS** Dept of Philosophy, Brown Univ, Box 1918, Providence, RI 02912. **EMAIL** Timothy_Chambers@brown.edu

CHAMBLISS, PRINCE C., JR.
PERSONAL Born 10/03/1948, Birmingham, AL, m, 1971, 1 child **DISCIPLINE** LAW **EDUCATION** Wesleyan Univ, 1966-68; Univ of Alabama, Birmingham, BA, 1971; Harvard Univ School of Law, JD, 1974. **CAREER** Special asst to pres, Univ of Alabama-Birmingham, 74-75; law clerk, Judge Sam C Pointer Jr, 75-76; Armstrong Allen, et al, law, 76-. **HONORS AND AWARDS** National Bar Assn, Judicial Conference Community Service Awd, 1986; Memphis Legal Secretaries Assn, Boss of the Year, 1983. **MEMBERSHIPS** Tennessee Bd of Law Examiners, vp, 1988-; Tennessee Bar Assn, scy, 1994-97; Memphis Bar Assn, bd of dirs, 1994-, president, 1997-98; Ben F Jones Chapter of the National Bar Assn, chairman, judicial recommendations committee, 1978-; Grant Information Ctr Inc, chairman-elect, 1994-; Memphis Mid-South Chapter, bd of dirs American Red Cross, bd of dirs, 1987-. **SELECTED PUBLICATIONS** "Legal Ethics for Trial Lawyers," The Litigator; "Inconsistent Verdicts: How to Recognize & Cope With," The Litigator. **CONTACT ADDRESS** Armstrong, Allen, Prewitt, Gentry, Johnston & Holmes, 80 Monroe Ave, Ste 700, Memphis, TN 38103. **EMAIL** pchambliss@armstrongallen.com

CHANCE, J. BRADLEY
DISCIPLINE THEOLOGY **EDUCATION** Univ NC, Chapel Hill, AB, 75; Southwestern Baptist Theol Sem, MD, 78; Duke Univ, PhD, 84. **CAREER** PROF, WM JEWELL COL, 82-. **CONTACT ADDRESS** 969 Northwyck Dr, Liberty, MO 64068.

CHANCELLOR, JAMES D.
PERSONAL Born 11/23/1944, St. Louis, MO, m, 1969, 2 children **DISCIPLINE** HISTORY OF RELIGION, ISLAM **EDUCATION** Duke Univ, PhD, 88. **CAREER** Assoc prof Relig, 85-89, Col Baptist Univ; dean, prof Rel, Col Christian Univ, 89-92; prof Rel, S Bapt Theol Sem, 92- . **MEMBERSHIPS** AAR; SSR; CESNUR. **RESEARCH** New Religious Movements; The Family **SELECTED PUBLICATIONS** Auth, The Night of the Cross, The Dividing Edge, Fall, 91; Christ and Religious Pluralism, Rev and Expositor, vol 91, no 4, Fall, 94; Religion in the Middle East, in Introduction to Missions, Broadman and Holman Publ, 98; auth, Life in the Family: An Oral History of the Children of God, Syracuse Univ Press, 00. **CONTACT ADDRESS** Dept of Religion, So Baptist Theol Sem, 2825 Lexington Rd, Louisville, KY 40280. **EMAIL** jchancellor@sbts.edu

CHANDLER, EVERETT A.
PERSONAL Born 09/21/1926, Columbus, OH, d, 4 children **DISCIPLINE** LAW **EDUCATION** Ohio State Univ, BSc in Educ 1955; Howard Univ Law School, JD 1958. **CAREER** Juvenile Ct Cuyahoga County, referee, support dept 1959; City of Cleveland OH, house insp 1960; Cuyahoga County Welfare Dept, legal inv 1960-64; Cuyahoga County OH, asst cty pros 1968-71; City of Cleveland OH, chief police prosecutor 1971-75; private practice, Attorney 1975-. **HONORS AND AWARDS** Main speaker banquet Frontiers Intl Columbus OH 1972; Cleveland Bar Association, Meritorious Service Awd, 1972. **MEMBERSHIPS** Bd mem, Cedar Branch YMCA, 1965; Comm Action Against Addiction, 1975-80, bd chrmn, 1980-87; bd mem, Legal Aid Soc of Cleveland, 1980; polemarch and bd chmn, Kappa Alpha Psi Inc, Cleveland Alumni Chapter, 1976, 1980-83; NAACP; Urban League; bd mem, past bd pres, CIT Mental Health; Excelsior Lodge #11 F&AM; Mt Olive Missionary Baptist Church, 1958-. **SELECTED PUBLICATIONS** Book review vol 21 #2 Cleveland State Law School Law Review. **CONTACT ADDRESS** 16010 Talford Ave, Cleveland, OH 44128.

CHANDLER, HUGH
DISCIPLINE PHILOSOPHY **EDUCATION** Cornell Univ, PhD, 64. **CAREER** Assoc prof, Univ Ill Urbana Champaign. **RESEARCH** Metaphysics; philosophy of mind; philosophy of religion; ethics. **SELECTED PUBLICATIONS** Auth, Theseus' Clothes-Pin; Indeterminate People; Sources of Essence; Some Ontological Arguments. **CONTACT ADDRESS** Philosophy Dept, Univ of Illinois, Urbana-Champaign, 52 E Gregory Dr, Champaign, IL 61820. **EMAIL** hchandle@uiuc.edu

CHANDLER, JAMES P.
PERSONAL Born 08/15/1938, Bakersfield, CA, m **DISCIPLINE** LAW **EDUCATION** Univ CA, AB, JD; Havard U, LLM. **CAREER** The Natl Law Center, George Washington Univ, Prof of Law 1977-; Univ CA, research asst; Boston Univ Law School, instructor 1970-71; Univ of MD Law School, asst assoc prof 1971-75; Univ of MS Law Center, distinguished visiting prof of law 1976; Univ CO Law School, visiting prof of law 1977. **MEMBERSHIPS** DC Bar; Am Soc Intl Law 1969-; Am Assn Univ Profs 1971-; Am Soc Law Profs 1974-; Alpha Phi Alpha Frat 1961-; bd dirs Ch God Evening Light Saints 1972-; Computer Law Assn 1974-; Woodbourne Ctr Inc 1974-76; sect council mem Am Bar Assn; consult Adminstrn Officer Cts St MD 1974-76; US Gen Acctng Office 1973-81. **CONTACT ADDRESS** School of Law, The George Washington Univ, 2000 Pennsylvania Ave, Ste 185, Washington, DC 20006-4211.

CHANDLER, MARTHE ATWATER
PERSONAL Born Chestertown, MD, m, 1982, 2 children **DISCIPLINE** PHILOSOPHY **EDUCATION** Vassar col, AB, magna cum laude, 62; Univ Chicago, MA, 64; Univ Ill-Chicago Cir, PhD, 80. **CAREER** Inst Philos, Central YMCA Commun Col, 71-80; vis asst prof, Philos, Univ Ky, 80-81; asst prof, Philos, DePauw Univ, 81-86; vis scholar, Univ Mich, Inter-Univ Consortium for Polit and Soc res, Summer, 88; vis prof Philos, Northwestern univ, 88-89; assoc prof, Philos, 86-94, prof, 94-, DePauw Univ. **MEMBERSHIPS** Amer Philos Asn; Soc Asian Compar Philos; Philos Sci Asn; Ind Philos Asn; Soc Women Philos. **RESEARCH** Philosophy of Social Science; Chinese Philosophy; Metaphysics of Time. **SELECTED PUBLICATIONS** Auth, Abortion Politics in the United States and Canada: Studies in Public Opinion, Praeger, 94; Coauth, Abortion in the United States and Canada: A Comparative Study of Public Opinion, in Abortion Politics in the United States and Canada: Studies in Public Opinion, Praeger, 94; Coauth, Two Faces of Feminism, in Perspectives on the Politics of Abortion, Paragon House, 95. **CONTACT ADDRESS** Dept of Philosophy, DePauw Univ, Greencastle, IN 46135. **EMAIL** chandler@depauw.edu

CHANG, DAE HONG
PERSONAL Born 01/09/1928, Nara, Japan, m, 1964, 2 children **DISCIPLINE** POLITICAL SCIENCE **EDUCATION** Mich State Univ, BA, Polit Sci, 57, MA, 58, PhD, Soc Sci, 62. **CAREER** Statistical analyst, Sec State, State of Mich, 58-61; grad & tchg asst, Soc Sci, Mich State Univ, 61-62; asst prof, Soc & Anthrop, Olivet Coll, 62-66; asst prof, Soc, Northern Ill Univ, 66-69; prof & ch, Soc & Anthrop, Univ Wis, 69-75; PROF & CH, ADMIN & JUSTICE, WICHITA STATE UNIV, 75-; ch, Asian Stud Prog, Wichita State Univ, 87-. **SELECTED PUBLICATIONS** Juvenile Delinquency and Juvenile Justice: Comparative and International Perspective, Acorn Press, 95; "Organized Crime in South Korea," Comparative Criminal Justice: Traditional and Nontraditional Systems of Law and Control, Waveland press, 96; "Drug and Punishment: An International Survey," International Journal of Comparative and Applied Criminal Justice, 93; "International Judicial Cooperation in Criminal Matters," International Journal of Comparative and Applied Criminal Justice, 94; "A New Form of International Crime: The Human Organ Trade," International Journal of Comparative and Applied Criminal Justice, 95. **CONTACT ADDRESS** Crim Justice, Hugo Wall Sch Urban & Public Affairs, Wichita State Univ, Wichita, KS 67260-0135. **EMAIL** dchang@twsuvm.uc.twsu.edu

CHANG, HOWARD F.
DISCIPLINE LAW **EDUCATION** Harvard Univ, AB, 82; Princeton Univ, MPA,85; Harvard Univ, JD,87; Mass Inst Technol, PhD,92. **CAREER** Prof Univ Southern California; clerked for, Honorable Ruth Bader Ginsburg, Judge US Ct Appeals DC Circuit. **MEMBERSHIPS** Amer Law & Econ Asn. **RESEARCH** International trade regulation; intellectual property; immigration; law & economics. **SELECTED PUBLICATIONS** Auth, Liberalized Immigration as Free Trade: Economic Welfare & the Optimal Immigration Policy; An Economic Analysis of Trade Measures to Protect the Global Environment & Patent Scope, Antitrust Policy, and Cumulative Innovation; coauth, Bargaining & the Division of Value in Corporate Reorganization. **CONTACT ADDRESS** School of Law, Univ of So California, University Park Campus, Los Angeles, CA 90089. **EMAIL** hchang@law.usc.edu

CHANG, RUTH
DISCIPLINE PHILOSOPHY **EDUCATION** Dartmouth Col, AB, 85; Harvard Law School, JD, 88; Oxford Univ, PhD, 97. **CAREER** Asst Prof, Rutgers Univ. **HONORS AND AWARDS** Rockefeller Fel, Princeton Univ. **MEMBERSHIPS** APA, NY & Washington Bar Asn. **RESEARCH** Ethics; Practical reasoning. **CONTACT ADDRESS** Dept Philos, Rutgers, The State Univ of New Jersey, New Brunswick, PO Box 270, New Brunswick, NJ 08903-0270. **EMAIL** changr@rci.rutgers.edu

CHAPMAN, DOUGLAS K.
DISCIPLINE LAW **EDUCATION** Ohio State Univ, BA; Ohio Northern Univ, JD. **CAREER** Prof. **SELECTED PUBLICATIONS** Auth, Enforceability of Settlement Agreement Allocations, Baylor, 95; Ohio's College Savings Plan: Buyer Beware, Univ Toledo, 89; Below Market Loans: From Abuse to Misuse-A Sports Illustration, 87. **CONTACT ADDRESS** Col Law, Univ of Toledo, Toledo, OH 43606. **EMAIL** dchapma@utnet.utoledo.edu

CHAPMAN, ROBERT L.
PERSONAL Born 10/31/1946, White Plains, NY, s **DISCIPLINE** PHILOSOPHY **EDUCATION** Col New Rochelle, BA; Fordham Univ, MA; PhD. **RESEARCH** Relationship between nature and human culture and the philosophical implications for environmental thought; role of religion in the formation of environmental values. **SELECTED PUBLICATIONS** Auth, "No Room at the Inn, or Why Population Problems are not all Economic," Population and Environment, 99; auth, "Settling Westchester: The value of place," Capitalism nature Soc, 99; auth, "The Place of Natural Law in the Greening of Philosophy," Journal of the natural Law Society, 99; auth, "Immigration and Environment: Settling the Moral Boundaries," Environmental Values, 00. **CONTACT ADDRESS** Dept Relig & Philos, Pace Univ, New York, 1 Pace Plaza, New York, NY 10038-1502. **EMAIL** rchapman@pace.edu

CHAPPELL, DAVID WELLINGTON
PERSONAL Born 02/03/1940, St. John, NB, Canada, 2 children **DISCIPLINE** HISTORY OF RELIGIONS **EDUCATION** Mt Allison Univ, BA, 61; McGill Univ, BD, 65; Yale Univ, PhD(Chinese Buddhism), 76. **CAREER** Teaching asst world relig, Yale Univ, 70-71; actg asst prof Chinese relig, Univ Hawaii, 71-77; asst prof, Univ Toronto, 77-78; asst prof, 78-80, Prof Chinese Relig, Univ Hawaii, Manoa, 85- **MEMBERSHIPS** Asn for Asian Studies; Am Acad Relig; Soc Study Chinese Relig; NAm Soc Buddhist Studies; Soc for Buddhist-Christian Stu. **RESEARCH** Formation of Chinese Buddhism; Buddhist-Christian comparisons. **SELECTED PUBLICATIONS** Auth, Introduction to the T'ien-t'ai ssu-chiao-i, Eastern Buddhist, 5/76; A perspective on the Pure Land Doctrine of T'ien-t'ai Chih-i (538-597), (in Japanese), Taisho Daigaku Bukkyo gaku, 76; coed & contribr article, In: Buddhist and Taoist Studies (Vol I), Univ Hawaii, 77; contribr, Early Ch'an in China and Tibet, 82; ed, T'ien-t'ai Buddhism, Dai-ichi-Shobo, 83; auth, Pure Land Buddhism: History, Culture and Doctrine, Univ Calif, 97; ed, Buddhist Peacework, Wisdom, 99. **CONTACT ADDRESS** Dept of Relig, Soka Univ of America, 2530 Dole St, Aliso Viejo, CA 92656. **EMAIL** alohachap@aol.com

CHAPPELL, VERE CLAIBORNE
PERSONAL Born 03/22/1930, Rochester, NY, m, 1951, 8 children **DISCIPLINE** PHILOSOPHY **EDUCATION** Yale Univ, BA, 51, MA, 53, PhD, 58. **CAREER** Instr philos, Yale Univ, 54-57; from instr to prof, Univ Chicago, 57-70; head dept, 70-74, acting assoc provost & dean grad sch, 74-76, assoc provost, 77-78, Prof Philos, Univ Mass, Amherst, 78-, Managing ed, Rev Metaphysics, 54-56; asst ed, Ethics, 58-61; asst treas, Philos Quart, 59-69; consult ed, Random House, Inc-Alfred A Knopf Inc, 63-74; vis prof, Ind Univ, 67, Univ Ill, 68, Univ Notre Dame, 69 & Univ Southern Calif, 69; Nat Endowment for Humanities fel, 70; vis prof, Smith Col, 73-74; mem, Coun Philos Studies, 73-78; Mass Found for Humanities & Pub Policy grant, 81; Univ Mass Inst Advan Study fel, 81-82; vis prof, Mount Holyoke Col, 82. **MEMBERSHIPS** Am Philos Asn; Aristotelian Soc; Royal Inst Philos; Asn Computing Humanities; Soc Bus Ethics. **RESEARCH** History of philosophy, especially 17th and 18th century; metaphysics; theory of knowledge. **SELECTED PUBLICATIONS** Ed, The Philosophy of Mind, Prentice-Hall, 62; The Philosophy of David Hume, Random, 63; auth, Stuff and things, Aristotelian Soc Proc, 70-71; Selected articles on Locke, Philos Res Arch, 81; Locke, Berkeley and Hume, New Trends Philos, Tel Aviv, 82; auth, The Theory of Ideas, Essays on Descartes Meditations, Univ of Calif, 86; coauth, Twenty-five Years of Descartes Scholarships, 1960-1984: A Bibliography, Garland, 87; auth, The Theory of Sensations, The Philosophy of Thomas Reid, Kluwer, 89; auth, Locke and Relative Identity, Hist of Philos Qrt 6, 89; auth, Locke on the Ontology of Matter, Living Things and Persons, Philos Stu 60, 90; auth, Essays on Early Modern Philosophers: From Descartes and Hobbes to Newton and Leibniz, 12 vols, Garland, 92; auth, The Cambridge Companion to Locke, Cambridge Univ, 94; ed, Locke's Theory of Ideas, The Cambridge Companion to Locke, Cambridge Univ, 94; auth, L'homme cartesien, Descartes. Ojecter et repondre, Univ France, 94; auth, Descartes' Compatibilism, Reason, Will, and Sensation: Studies in Cartesian Metaphysics, Oxford Univ, 94; auth, Locke on the Freedom of the Will, Locke's Philodophy: Content and Context, Oxford Univ, 94; auth, Descartes's Ontology, Topoi 16, 97; auth, Locke, Oxford Univ, 98; auth, Hobbes and Bramhall on Libertyand Necessity, Cambridge, 99. **CONTACT ADDRESS** Dept of Philos, Univ of Massachusetts, Amherst, Bartlett Hall, Amherst, MA 01003-0002. **EMAIL** chappell@philos.umass.edu

CHAPPLE, C. K.
PERSONAL Born 09/04/1954, Medina, NY, m, 1974, 2 children **DISCIPLINE** HISTORY OF RELIGION **EDUCATION** SUNY Stony Brook, BA, 76; Fordham Univ, MA, 78, PhD, 80. **CAREER** Prof, 85-, Loyola Marymont Univ; Lectr, 80-85, SUNY Stony Brook; Asst Dir, 80-85, Inst Adv Stud Wld Rel. **HONORS AND AWARDS** 2 NEH Fels; Lily Gnt; College Fel; Chilton Ch Awd; Gannett Schlshp; IAAPEA Res Awd; CWHE Appre Certif; Grant Devel Gnt. **MEMBERSHIPS** AAR; AAS; AIIS. **RESEARCH** Yoga Traditions; Jainism; Hinduism; Buddhism. **SELECTED PUBLICATIONS** Ed, Ecological Prospects: Scientific Religious and Aesthetic Perspectives, Albany, SUNY Press, 94, Intl edition, Delhi, Indian Books Cen, 95; auth, Nonviolence to Animals Earth and Self in Asian Traditions, Albany, NY, SUNY Press, 93, Intl edition, Delhi, Indian Books Cen, 95; ed, Jesuit Tradition in Education and Missions, Scranton, U of Scranton Press, 93; Haribhadra's Analysis of Patanjala and Kula Yoga in the Yogadrstisamuccaya, in: Open Boundaries: Jain Communities and Cultures in Indian History, ed, John E Cort, Albany, SUNY Press, 98; India: The Land of Plentitude, Satya, 98; Animals in the Buddhist Birth Stories, in: Buddhism and Ecology: The Interconnection of Dharma, and Deeds, ed, Mary Evelyn Tucker, Duncan Ryuken Williams, Cambridge MA, Harv Univ Cen Stud Of World Rel, 97; Renouncer Traditions Of India: Jainism and Buddhism, in: Ananya: A Portrait of India, ed, S Sn Sridhar, Nirmal K Mattoo, NY, Assoc of Indians in Amer, 97; co-ed, Hinduism and Ecology, Cambridge, CSWR, Harvard Press, 00. **CONTACT ADDRESS** Dept Theol Studies, Loyola Marymount Univ, 7900 Loyola Blvd, Los Angeles, CA 90045. **EMAIL** cchapple@lmu.edu

CHARETTE, BLAINE
PERSONAL Born Ponoka, AB, Canada, m, 1980, 2 children **DISCIPLINE** NEW TESTAMENT **EDUCATION** Gordon-Conwell Theol Sem, MA, 82; Univ of Sheffield, PhD, 92. **CAREER** Asst prof, Emmanuel Col, Franklin Springs, GA, 91-95; Assoc Prof, Northwest Col, Kirkland, Wa, 95-. **HONORS AND AWARDS** Phi Alpha Chi Honor Soc (Gordon-Conwell). **MEMBERSHIPS** Soc of Bib Lit; Inst for Biblical Res; Soc for Pentecostal Studies. **RESEARCH** Gospel of Matthew. **SELECTED PUBLICATIONS** Auth, The Theme of Recompense in Matthew's Gospel, JSNT Sup 79, Sheffield, JSOT Press,92; A Harvest for the People? An Interpretation of Matthew 9.37f, J for the Study of the New Testament 38 (90); To Proclaim Liberty to the Captives: Matthew 11.28-30 in the Light of OT Prophetic Expectation, New Testament Studies 38 (92); Speaking Against the Holy Spirit: The Correlation Between Messianic Task and National Fortunes in the Gospel of Matthew, J of Pentecostal Theol 3 (93); Never Has Anything Like This Been Seen in Israel: The Spirit as Eschatological Sign in Matthew's Gospel, J of Pentecostal Theol 8 (96). **CONTACT ADDRESS** 14011 53rd Ave. West, Edmonds, WA 98026-3843. **EMAIL** blaine.charette@ncag.edu

CHARITY, RUTH HARVEY
PERSONAL Born Pittsylvania Count, VA, m **DISCIPLINE** LAW **EDUCATION** Howard Univ, BA, JD. **CAREER** Formerly asst to dir President's Cncl on Consumer Affairs; Indust Rel Analyst Wage Stabil Bd; law prof; former Dem Natl Committeewoman. **HONORS AND AWARDS** Founder/President Black Women for Political Action; Charter Mem natl Women's Chamber of Commerce; Natl Fedn of Dem Women Mid-Atlantic Region; Alpha Kappa Alpha Sor; NAACP; listed in Biography of Charlotte Hawkins Brown, Rights on Trial; Lecturer & consultant to political & civil rights & educational groups. **MEMBERSHIPS** Mem Pres's Comm on Civil Rights under the Law; past pres Old Dominion Bar Assn (1st woman to serve this capacity); mem Natl Bar Assn; formerly vice pres of Natl Bar Assn(1st woman to serve as vice pres of NBA at time of election); organiz Women's Sect Natl Bar Assn (1st natl orgn of Black women lawyers); mem Intl Fedn of Women Lawyers; past pres of Natl Assn of Black Women Lawyers; founder/pres VA Assn of Black Women Lawyers; past mem trustee bd Howard Univ;past mem trustee bd Palmer Meml Inst; mem bd of VA Seminary; past chrpsn VA State Adv Com US Civil Rights Comm (1st woman in VA to serve as chrpsn); mem Amer Assn of Univ Women; League of Women Voters; NOW; past mem Legal Staff State Conf NAACP; past natl parliamentarian Natl Cncl of Negro Women; pastgrand legal advisor Grand Templeughters IBPOE of W; past pres Chums Inc. **CONTACT ADDRESS** 514 S Main St, Danville, VA 24543.

CHARLES, J. DARYL
PERSONAL Born 12/09/1950, Lancaster, PA, m, 1980, 3 children **DISCIPLINE** HERMENEUTICS **EDUCATION** Catholic Univ Amer and Westminster Theol Sem, PhD. **CAREER** Lectr, 88-95, Chesapeake Theol Sem; schl in res, 90-95, The Wilberforce Forum; aff fel, 96-97, Princeton Univ CSAR; Assoc Prof, 97-, Taylor Univ. **MEMBERSHIPS** SRS; NAS; IBR; SBL; ETS. **RESEARCH** Religion and Culture; Criminal Justice; New Testament; Ethics. **SELECTED PUBLICATIONS** Auth, 2 Peter, Jude, BCBC, Herald Press, 98; Virtue Amidst Vice, JSNTSS, Sheffield Academic Press, 97; translated, Roots of Wisdom, by Claus Westerman, Westminster/John Knox; auth, The Language and Logic of Virtue in 2 Peter 1:5-7, Bulletin for Biblical Res, 98; A Feisty Fundamentalism, Doing Theology in the Great Tradition, Regeneration Qtly, 98; Wordsmiths as Warriors: The Intellectual Honesty of GK Chesterton and CS Lewis, Parnassus, 98; Crime and the New Consensus, Soc Justice Rev, 98; Suicidal Thought in a Culture of Death, in: T Demy, G Stewart, eds, Suicide and the Christian Community: An Ethical Dilemma, Kregel, 97; Evangelicals and Catholics Together: One Year Later, Pro Ecclesial, 96; Crime the Christian and Capitol Justice, J the Evangelical Theol Soc, 95; auth, Basic Questions in Human Sexuality, Kregel, 00; auth, "What Does the Lord Require? Reflections on Sonlcraft and Statecraft," Social Justice Review, 99; auth, " Pagan Sources in the New Testament" and " Vice an Virtue Lists in the New Testament," Dictionary of New England Backgrounds, Inter-Varsity, 00; auth," Interpreting the General Epistles", New Testament Criticism and Interpretation, Broadman & Holman, 00; auth, " Assessing Recent Pronouncement on Justification Evidence from 'The Gift of Salvation' and the Catholic Catechism," Proecclesta, 99; auth, " The Necessity of Doubt," Regeneration Quarterly, winter 99-00; auth, " Losing Our Moral Theology," First Things, 99. **CONTACT ADDRESS** Dept of Philosophy, Taylor Univ, Upland, Upland, IN 46989. **EMAIL** drcharles@tayloru.edu

CHARLESWORTH, JAMES H.
PERSONAL Born 05/30/1940, St Petersburg, FL, m, 1965, 3 children **DISCIPLINE** RELIGION **EDUCATION** Oh Wesleyan Univ, AB, 62; Duke Div Sch, BD, 65; Duke Grad Sch, PhD, 67. **CAREER** Asst Prof to Assoc Prof and Dir, Duke Univ, 69-84; Prof, Princeton Theol Sem, 84-. **HONORS AND AWARDS** Kappa Kappa Psi; Phi Beta Kappa; Frank Moore Cross Awd, Am Sch of Oriental Res, 97; Biblical Archaeol Soc Pub Awd, 95, 86, 84; Distinguished Achievement Citation, OH Wesleyan Univ, 85; Outstanding Educ of Am, 75. **SELECTED PUBLICATIONS** Ed, Graphic Concordance to the Dead Sea Scrolls, Paul Siebeck, 91; co-ed, Images of Jesus Today, Trinity Press Intl, 94; auth, The Beloved Disciple, Trinity Press Intl, 95; ed, The Dead Sea Scrolls: Rule of the Community, Photographic Multi-Language Edition, New York, 96; co-ed, The Dead Seas Scrolls and Christian Faith, Trinity Press Intl, 98; ed, Pseudepigrapha and Non-Masoretic Psalms, Daily Prayers, and Related documents Vol 4, Paul Siebeck, 98; ed, Angelic Liturgy: Songs of the Sabbath Sacrifice Vol 4, Paul Siebeck, 98; auth, How Barisat Bellowed: folklore, Humor, and Iconography in the Jewish Apocalypses and the Apocalypse of John, BIBAL Press, 98. **CONTACT ADDRESS** Dept Bible Studies, Princeton Theol Sem, PO Box 821, Princeton, NJ 08452-0803. **EMAIL** james.charlesworth@ptsem.edu

CHARLTON, CHARLES HAYES
PERSONAL Born 12/22/1940, Radford, VA, m **DISCIPLINE** THEOLOGY **EDUCATION** Christiansburg Inst, 1959; VA Seminary, attended; E TN State Univ, attended; ETSU, BS 1982, M Ed 1984; Emmaus Bible Institute of Seminary, Elizabeth, TN, ThD, 1986; Cornerstone Univ, PhD Temperament Therapy. **CAREER** Radford City School Bd, 72-74; City of Radford VA, mayor 1974-76; Friendship Bapt Church, pastor; CASA Northeast, Johnson City, TN, coordinator, 87-; CASA, 87-92; ETSU, Johnson City, TN, career counselor, 91-92; City of Johnson City, planning commission, 90-; Northeast State Tech Comm Coll, instructor, beginning 1992, counselor & advisor, 94, Asst Prof, currently; Emmaus Bible Inst & Seminary, Elizabethton, TN, dean of educ, 84-89; Johnson City Board of Directors. **HONORS AND AWARDS** Radfords Outstanding Young Men Radford Jaycees 1973; VA Historical Society, honors for contributions to the State of VA **MEMBERSHIPS** Moderator Schaetter Meml Assoc of SW VA 1974-77; treas Bethel Dist Assoc; vice pres Radford Jaycees; moderator Bethel Dist Assoc of TN 1982-; dean ed Emmaus Bible Inst & Seminary Elizabethton TN 1984-; dir Pastors Conf of the TN BM&E Convention 1984-; pres, Black Ministers Alliance, 1990-91; zone chairman, Washington County Democratic Party, 1994-; City of Johnson City, TN, Board of Education, 1996-. **SELECTED PUBLICATIONS** Published Agony & Ecstasy of the Ministry, Making The Fundamentals Fun, 1993; Love is the Key, To Love And Be Loved, How To Really Love Your Pastor, This We Believe, Meditations on Love, 1994; author of religious columns published in Radford News Journal and Johnson City Press. **CONTACT ADDRESS** PO Box 246, Blountville, TN 37617-0246.

CHARNEY, JONATHAN I.
PERSONAL Born 10/29/1943, New York, NY, m, 1966, 3 children **DISCIPLINE** LAW **EDUCATION** NY Univ, BA, 65; Univ Wis, JD, 68. **CAREER** Attorney, US Dept of Justice, 68-72; asst prof to prof, Vanderbilt Univ, 72-. **HONORS AND AWARDS** Int Maritime Boundaries Cert of Merit, 94; Alexander Heard Distinguished Serv Prof, 99-00. **MEMBERSHIPS** Am Law Inst; Am Soc of Int Law; Am J of Int Law; Ocean Develop and Int Law; Coun on For Relations; Am Soc of Int Law Maritime Boundary Proj. **RESEARCH** Public International Law. **SELECTED PUBLICATIONS** Auth, "The Implications of Expanding International Law", Int Law for Antarctica 51-101, eds F. Francioni and T. Scovazzi, 96; auth, "The Law of the Sea", Encycl of US For Relations 49-51, eds BW Jentleson and TG Paterson, 97; auth, "Third Party Dispute Settlement and International Law", Columbia J of Transnational Law 65-89, 97; coed, International Maritime Boundaries, vol III, Martinus Nijhoff Pub, 98; coauth, "The Facts", 92 Am J of Int Law (98): 666-675; coauth, "Forward", 93 Am J of Int Law, (99): 1-2; auth, "Is International Law Threatened by Multiple International Tribunals?", 271 Recueil Des Cours, (98): 101-382; auth, "Progress in International Criminal Law?", 93 Am J of Int Law, (99): 452-464; auth, "The Impact on the International Legal System of the Growth of International Courts and Tribunals", 31 NY Univ J of Int Law, (99): 697-708; auth, "Rocks that Cannot Sustain Human Habitation", 93 Am J of Int Law, (99): 863-878; auth, "Anticipatory Humanitarian Intervention in Kosovo", 93 Am J of Int Law, (99): 834-841. **CONTACT ADDRESS** Sch of Law, Vanderbilt Univ, 2201 West End Ave, Nashville, TN 37235-0001. **EMAIL** jonathan.charney@law.vanderbilt.edu

CHARRON, WILLIAM C.
PERSONAL Born 02/25/1938, Denver, CO, m, 1962 **DISCIPLINE** PHILOSOPHY **EDUCATION** St Benedict's Col, KS, BA, 59; Univ Detroit, MA, 61; Marquette Univ, PhD, 66. **CAREER** Asst prof philos, St Benedict's Col, KS, 64-67; asst prof, 67-73, assoc prof, 73-80, Prof Philos, St Louis Univ, 80-, Ed, Mod Scholman, 89-. **MEMBERSHIPS** Am Philos Asn; Hume Soc; T S Eliot Society. **RESEARCH** Class mod philos; ethics; philos of mind; mathematical theory of fames. **SELECTED PUBLICATIONS** Auth, The simplicity of conscious experiences: A problem for neural identity theory, Mod Schollman, 5/74; Death: A philosophical perspective on the legal definitions, Wash Univ Law Quart, 12/75; Convention, games of strategy, and Hume's philosophy of law and government, Am Philos Quart, 10/80; Some legal definitions and semiotic: Toward a general theory, Semiotica, 12/80; The Prescriptives of the New Hobbesian Contractarian, In: Law and Semiotics, I, Plenum Press, 87; Mediation and Morality Conflicts, In: Law and Semiotics, II, Plenum Press, 88; On the Self-Refuting Statement There Is No Truth., Vivarium, 93; T S Eliot: Aristotelian Arbiter of Bradleyan Antinomies, The Modern Schoolman, 95; Public Reason, Mediation and Marakets: Kant against Rauls, In: Critic of Institutions: Horizons of Justice, Peter Lang, 96. **CONTACT ADDRESS** Dept of Philos, Saint Louis Univ, 3800 Lindell Blvd, Saint Louis, MO 63156-0907.

CHASTAIN, CHARLES
DISCIPLINE PHILOSOPHY **EDUCATION** Princeton Univ, PhD. **CAREER** Assoc prof, Univ IL at Chicago. **RESEARCH** Epistemology and philos of lang; ethics. **SELECTED PUBLICATIONS** Auth, Reference and Context, MN Univ, 75. **CONTACT ADDRESS** Philos Dept, Univ of Illinois, Chicago, S Halsted St, PO Box 705, Chicago, IL 60607. **EMAIL** cpcronin@uic.edu

CHAUSSE, GILLES
PERSONAL Born 06/06/1931, Montreal, PQ, Canada **DISCIPLINE** THEOLOGY, CHURCH HISTORY **EDUCATION** Univ Montreal, MA, 58, PhD, 73. **CAREER** Prof hist, Col Jean-de-Brebeuf Montreal, 69-85; PROF D'HISTOIRE DE L'EGLISE, FACULTE DE THEOLOGIE, UNIV MONTREAL, 86-. **HONORS AND AWARDS** Collaborateur a l'Institut historique de la Compagnie de Jesus a Rome; recipiendaire du Merite Diocesain 'Monseigneur Ignace Bourger', 86. **MEMBERSHIPS** Societe Canadienne d'Histoire de l'Eglise catholique **SELECTED PUBLICATIONS** Auth, Jean-Jacques Lartigue, premier eveque de Montreal, 80; coauth, Les Ultramontains canadiens-francais, 85; coauth, Le Christianisme d'ici a-t-il un avenir?, 88; coauth, L'Image de la Revolution francaise au Quebec 1789-1989, 89; coauth, Quebec, terre d'Evangile: les defis de l'evangelisation dans la culture contemporaine, 91; coauth, Montreal 1642-1992, 92; coauth, Dictionnaire Biographique du Canada, tomes 4-8; coauth, A Concise History of Christianity in Canada, 96. **CONTACT ADDRESS** Fac de Theologie, Univ of Montreal, CP 6128, Succ Centre Ville, Montreal, QC, Canada H3C 3J7. **EMAIL** chausseg@magellan.umontreal.ca

CHEATHAM, CARL W.
PERSONAL Born 08/04/1940, Lincoln, AR, m, 1961, 4 children **DISCIPLINE** MODERN CHURCH HISTORY **EDUCATION** Harding Univ, BA, 62; Harding Graduate Sch, MTh, 65; Vanderbilt, MA, 79, PhD, 82. **CAREER** Prof, Faulkner Univ, 81-. **MEMBERSHIPS** Am Soc Church Hist; AAR; SBL; ETS. **RESEARCH** Restoration History **CONTACT ADDRESS** Faulkner Univ, 5345 Atlanta Hwy, Box 44, Montgomery, AL 36109. **EMAIL** ccheatha@faulkner.edu

CHEEK, H. LEE, JR.
PERSONAL Born 10/27/1960, Winston-Salem, NC, m, 1994, 1 child **DISCIPLINE** POLITICAL SCIENCE, PHILOSOPHY **EDUCATION** Western Carolina Univ, BA, 83; Duke Univ, MDiv, 86; Western Carolina Univ, MPA, 88; Cath Univ Am, PhD, 98. **CAREER** Vis instr, Western Carolina Univ, 88; editor, Humanitas, 88-92; pastor, Ruffin Methodist Church, 91-94; sr pastor, Bethel United Methodist Church, 94-96; instr, Rockingham Community Col, 96-97; Director of Inst Res, Brewton-parker col, 97-99. **HONORS AND AWARDS** Phi Gamma Mu; Phi Kappa Phi, Who's Who in the World, 01. **MEMBERSHIPS** Am Polit Sci Assoc; Am Soc for Pub Admin; Conf on Faith and Hist; Eric Voeglin Soc; Ga Polit Sci Assoc; Soc of Early Americanists. **RESEARCH** Political Philosophy, American Political Thought, American Government, Politics and Religion, Mass Media and American Politics, Organizational Theory, Public Administration, Campaigns and Elections. **SELECTED PUBLICATIONS** Auth, "A Note on the Platonic and Aristotelian Critique of Democratic Man", Int Soc Sci Rev 66.2, (91): auth, "Patience Against Exuberance: A Meditation on Psalms 29 and 37", Sacramental Life 85. (95): auth, "Politicizing Religion", Winston-Salem J (March 9, 96); auth, "Original Diversity: Bishops Allen, Asbury, and Black Methodists", Methodist Hist XXXV.3, (97); auth, "Articles of Confederation", "Luther Martin", The Supreme Court, Salem Pr, (Pasadena, 00); auth, "Freidrich Engle", Makers of Western Culture, ed John Powell, Greenwood Pr, (Westport, 00); auth, "John C Calhoun", "Secession", Encycl of the Am Civil War, ABC-CLIO, (Oxford, 00); ed, Calhoun: Selected Writings and Speeches, Regnery Books, (forthcoming); coed, Critical Assessments of Calhoun, 1811-2000, Thoemmes Pr, (London), (forthcoming). **CONTACT ADDRESS** Dept Soc and Behav Sci, Brewton-Parker Col, Box 2034, Mount Vernon, GA 30445-0197. **EMAIL** lcheek@bpc.edu

CHEEK, KING VIRGIL, JR.
PERSONAL Born 05/26/1937, Weldon, NC, m **DISCIPLINE** LAW **EDUCATION** Bates Coll ME, BA 1959; Univ of Chicago, MA 1960; Univ of Chicago Law School, JD 1964. **CAREER** Shaw Univ Raleigh, NC, asst econ prof 1964-65, acting dean 1956-66, dean 1966-67; private practice law Raleigh 1965-69; Shaw Univ, vice pres acad affairs 1965-69; Citizenship Lab, lectr 1968-69; Shaw Univ, pres 1969-71; Morgan State Coll, pres 1971-74; Union for Experimenting Colls & Univs, vice pres for planning & devel 1974-76, pres, 76-78; New York Inst of Tech, exec dir ctr for leadership and career develop 1978-85; New York Inst of Tech, Ctr for Leadership and Career Develop, vice pres, dean of grad studies, exec dir 1985-89, vice pres institutional advancement, 89-91, vice pres academic affairs, 91-96. **HONORS AND AWARDS** Grand Commdr of Order of Star Africa 1971; Top Young Leaders in Amer Acad Change Magazine 1978; Disting Civilian Awd AUS 1973; LLD DE State Coll 1970, Bates Coll, Univ of MD 1972; LHD Shaw Coll at Detroit 1983. **MEMBERSHIPS** Bd of dir Baltimore Contractors 1974-; bd of dir Inst for Econ Devel 1978-; bd of trustees Martin Center Coll; bd of trustees Shaw Coll Detroit; bd of visitors Univ of Chicago Law Sch; bd of trustees Warnborough Coll Oxford England. **CONTACT ADDRESS** 409 3rd St SW, Ste 202, Washington, DC 20024.

CHEEVER, FRED
PERSONAL Born 03/09/1957, Rome, Italy, m, 1982, 2 children **DISCIPLINE** ENVIRONMENTAL LAW **EDUCATION** Stanford Univ, BA/MA, 89; UCLA, JD, 86. **CAREER** Judicial Clerk, US Court Appeals, 86-87; Assoc Atty, Sierra Club Legal Defense Fund, 87-89; Res Fel, Natural Resources Law Ctr, 90, Assoc Prof, 90-93, Prof Law, Univ Colo, 93-. **RESEARCH** Environmental law; endangered species law; public land law; property law; Land Trusts and Conservation Easements. **SELECTED PUBLICATIONS** Auth, The Road to Re-

covery: A New Way of Thinking About the Endangered Species Act, Ecol Law Quart 1, 96; Human Population and the Loss of Biological Diversity -- Two Aspects of the Same Problem, Int J Environment & Pollution 62, 97; Public Good and Private Magic in the Law of Land Trusts and Conservation Easements: A Happy Present and a Troubled Future, Univ Denver Law Rev, 96; The Failure of the National Forest Management Act's Substantive Forest Practice Requirements: A Lesson in the Limits of Legislative Power, Oregon Law Rev, 98; auth, "From Population Segregation to Species Zoning: The Evolution of Reintroductioin Law Under Section 10(j) of the Endangered Species Act, 1 Wyo. L. Rev. 287, 01. **CONTACT ADDRESS** College of Law, Univ of Denver, 1900 Olive St., Denver, CO 80220. **EMAIL** fcheever@mail.law.du.edu

CHEHABI, HOUCHANG E.

PERSONAL Born 02/22/1954, Teheran, Iran **DISCIPLINE** INTERNATIONAL RELATIONS, HISTORY **EDUCATION** Univ Caen, Licence, 75; Sciences Po, Paris, Diploma, 77; Yale Univ, MA, 79; PhD, 86. **CAREER** Asst to assoc prof, Harvard Univ, 86-94; vis fel, Oxford Univ, 94-95; vis assoc prof, UCLA, 95-97; prof, Boston Univ, 98-. **HONORS AND AWARDS** Centre for Lebanese Studies Fel, 94-95; Woodrow Wilson Fel, 97-98; Gregory Luebbert Prize, Am Polit Sci Assoc, 99. **MEMBERSHIPS** Middle Eastern Studies Assoc, Soc for Iranian Studies, Center for Iranian Res and Analysis, Assoc for the Study of Persianate Soc. **RESEARCH** Iranian politics and culture, Cultural history of Iran, Turkey, and Afghanistan, the politics of small island states. **SELECTED PUBLICATIONS** Auth, "Self-Determination, Territorial Integrity, and the Falkland Islands," Polit Sci Quart, (85); auth, Iranian Politics and Religious Modernism: The Liberation Movement of Iran under the Shah and Khomeini, Cornell Univ Pr, 90; auth, "Ardabil Becomes a Province: Center-Periphery Relations in the Islamic Republic of Iran," Int Jour of Middle East Studies, (97); coed, Sultanistic Regimes, Johns Hopkins Univ Pr, 98; auth, "The Political Regime of the Islamic Republic of Iran in Comparative Perspective," Govt and Opposition, (01); auth, "US-Iranian Sports Diplomacy," Diplomacy and Statecraft, (01). **CONTACT ADDRESS** Boston Univ, 152 Bay State Rd, Boston, MA 02215. **EMAIL** chehabi@bu.edu

CHEMERINSKY, ERWIN

DISCIPLINE ADMINISTRATIVE LAW **EDUCATION** Northwestern Univ, BS, 75; Harvard Univ, JD,78. **CAREER** Sydney M. Irmas prof Public Interest Law, Legal Ethics and Polit Sci, Univ Southern California; lect, Fed Judicial Ctr; National Judicial Col; Ctr for Civic Educ & Constitutional Rights Found; testified before, US Senate Judiciary Comt; participated in, US Atty General's Prog for Honor Law Graduates;private practice,Wash, DC. **MEMBERSHIPS** Los Angeles City Charter Comn. **RESEARCH** Constitutional law; civil rights. **SELECTED PUBLICATIONS** Auth, Constitutional Law: Principles & Policies; Interpreting the Constitution; Fed Jurisdiction; The Values of Fedism & The First Amendment: When the Government Must Make Content Based Choices. **CONTACT ADDRESS** School of Law, Univ of So California, University Park Campus, Los Angeles, CA 90089.

CHEN, J.

PERSONAL Born 12/17/1966, Taipei, Taiwan, w **DISCIPLINE** LAW **EDUCATION** Harvard Univ, JD 91; Emory Univ, BA summa cum laude, MA 87; Univ Iceland, Fulbright Sch, 87-88. **CAREER** Univ Minnesota, assoc prof, 93-, prof, 99-; Univ de Nantes, vis prof, 95; Justice Clarence Thomas, DC, law clerk, 92-93; Judge J. Michael Luttig, VA, law clerk, 91-92; vis prof, Heinrich-Heine-Universitat, 99. **SELECTED PUBLICATIONS** Auth, DeFunis, Defunct, 16 Const. Commentary 91, 99; auth, The Second Coming of Smyth v. Ames, 77, Tex. L. Rev. 1535, 99; auth, Midnight in the Courtroom of Good and Evil, 16 Const Commentary 499, 99; auth, The Sound of Legal Thunder: The Chaotic Consequences of Crushing Constitutional Butterflies, 16 Const. Commentary 483, 99; auth, The Magnificent Seven; American Telephony's Deregulatory Shootout, 50 Hastings, L.J. 1503, 99; auth, Hope a Better Rate for Me, 17 Yale J. on Reg. 195, 00; auth, Mark My Words, 3 Green Bag 2d 121, 00; auth, The Death of Contra, 52 Stan. L. Rev 889, 00; auth, Globalization and Its Losers, 9 Minn. J. Global Trade 157, 00; auth, Standing in the Shadows of Giants; The Role of Intergenerational Equity in Telecommunications Reform, 71 U. Colo. L. Rev. 921, 00. **CONTACT ADDRESS** Dept of Law, Univ of Minnesota, Twin Cities, 229 19th Ave S, Minneapolis, MN 55455. **EMAIL** chenx064@tc.umn.edu

CHEN, JIE

PERSONAL Born 10/08/1955, Beijing, China, m, 1982, 1 child **DISCIPLINE** POLITICAL SCIENCE **EDUCATION** Inst Intl Politics Beijing, BA, 82; Monterey Inst, MA, 87; Wash State Univ, PhD, 91. **CAREER** Vis Asst Prof, Loretto Heights Univ, 91-93; Asst to Assoc Prof, Univ Wisc, 93-97; Director, Univ Wisc, 97; Acting Dir and Assoc Prof, Old Dominion Univ, 97-. **HONORS AND AWARDS** Who's Who in the World, 96; Featured Fac, Institute on Race and Ethnicity, Univ Wisc, 95; Pi Sigma Alpha, 90; Distinguished Grad Stud, Washington State Univ, 90; Teaching Assistantship, Washington State Univ, 87-91; Scholarship, Monterey Institute of Intl Studies, 85-87. **MEMBERSHIPS** Am Polit Sci Asn, Asn of Chinese Polit Studies, Asn of Asian Studies, Intl Studies Asn, Third World Studies Asn. **RESEARCH** Comparative Politics and Chinese Politics. **SELECTED PUBLICATIONS** Auth, China Since the Cultural Revolution: From Totalitarianism to Authoritarianism, Praeger Pub, 95; auth, Ideology in US Foreign Policy: Case Studies in US China Policy, Praeger Pub, 92; auth, "Valuation of Individual Liberty vs. Social Order among Democratic Supporters: A Cross-Validation," Political Research Quarterly, in press; auth, "Subjective Motivations for Mass Political Participation in Urban China," Social Science Quarterly, (00): 645-662; auth, "Comparing Mass and Elite Subjective Orientations in Urban China," Public Opinion Quarterly, (99): 193-219; auth, "Political Interest (or Apathy) in Urban China," Communist and Post-communist Studies, (99): 281-303; auth, "Mass Political Culture in Beijing: Findings from Two Public Opinion Surveys," Asian Survey, (98): 763-783; auth, "Defining the Political System of Post-Deng China: Emerging Public Support for a Democratic Political System," Problems of Post-Communism, (98): 30-42; auth, "The Cross-Straight Relationship and the Role of the United States in the Unification of Mainland China and Taiwan," in The Cross-Strait Relations toward the Twenty-First Century, 98. **CONTACT ADDRESS** Dept Polit Sci & Geog, Old Dominion Univ, Norfolk, VA 23529. **EMAIL** jchen@odu.edu

CHEN, JIM

PERSONAL Born Taipei, Taiwan, m, 2001 **DISCIPLINE** LAW **EDUCATION** Emory Univ, BA; MA, 87; Harvard Law Sch, JD, 91. **CAREER** Prof, Univ Minn, 93-. **MEMBERSHIPS** Nat Asn of Scholars. **RESEARCH** Telecommunications law and regulated industries; constitutional law; Environmental law; International trade and economic development; Agricultural law. **SELECTED PUBLICATIONS** Auth, "Law as a Species of Language Acquisition," Wash Univ L Quart, 95; auth, "Of Agriculture's First disobedience and Its Fruit," Vanderbilt L Rev, 95; auth, "Diversity and Damnation," UCLA L Rev, 96; auth, "The Last Picture Show (On the Twilight of Federal Mass Communications Law)," Minn L Rev, 96; auth, "Filburn's Forgotten Footnote," Minn L Rev, 97; auth, "The Second Coming of Smyth v. Ames," Tex L Rev, 99; auth, "Globalization and Its Losers," Minn J of Global Trade, 00; auth, "Standing I the Shadows of Giants," Univ Colo L Rev, 00; auth, "The Authority to Regulate Broadband Internet Access over Cable," Berkeley Technol L J, 01; auth, "Reconciling Intellectual Property with Biological Diversity," Univ Ill L Rev, forthcoming. **CONTACT ADDRESS** Sch of Law, Univ of Minnesota, Twin Cities, 229 19th Ave S, Minneapolis, MN 55455. **EMAIL** chenx064@maroon.tc.umn.edu

CHEN, XIANG

DISCIPLINE PHILOSOPHY OF SCIENCE, HISTORY OF SCIENCE **EDUCATION** Zhongshand Univ, BA, 82; MA, 85; Va Polytechnic Inst and State Univ, MS, 88; PhD, 92. **CAREER** Asst prof, Calif Lutheran Univ, 92-98; Sr Residential Fel, Dibner Inst for the Hist of Sci and Tech at MIT, 98-99; assoc prof, Calif Lutheran Univ, 98-. **HONORS AND AWARDS** Fel for Sr Resident Fel, Dibner Inst for the Hist of Sci and Tech at MIT, 98-99; NEH res stipend, Johns Hopkins Univ, 92. **MEMBERSHIPS** Philos of Sci Asn, Hist of Sci Soc, Am Philos Asn. **RESEARCH** Theories of scientific revolutions, cognitive psychology and philosophy of science, history of optics in 19th century. **SELECTED PUBLICATIONS** Auth, "Recent Progress in the Studies of Incommensurability," Sci, Philos, and Culture, Zhongshan Univ Press (96): 169-190; coauth, "Kuhn's Mature Philosophy of Science and Cognitive Psychology," Philos Psychol 9 (96): 347-363; auth, "Thomas Kuhn's Latest Notion of Incommensurability," J for General Philos of Sci 28 (97): 257-273; auth, "The Debate on the Polarity of Light during the Optical Revolution," Archive for Hist of Exact Sci 50 (97): 359-393; coauth, "Kuhn's Theory of Scientific Revolutions and Cognitive Psychology," Philos Psychol 11 (98): 5-28; auth, "Dispersion, Experimental Apparatus, and the Acceptance of the Wave Theory of Light," Annals of Sci 55 (98): 401-420; auth, "Instrumental Unification: Optical Apparatus in the Unification of Dispersion and Selective Absorption," Studies in Hist and Philos of Modern Physics 30 (99): 519-542; coauth, "Continuity through Revolution: A Frame-based Account of Conceptual Change during Scientific Revolutions," Philos of Sci 67 (00): A1-A9; Auth, Instrumental Traditions and Theories of Light: The Uses of Instruments in the Optical Revolution, Kluwer Acad, 00. **CONTACT ADDRESS** Dept Philos, California Lutheran Univ, 60 W Olsen Rd, Thousand Oaks, CA 91360-2700. **EMAIL** Chenxi@clunet.edu

CHENG, CHUNG-YING

PERSONAL Born 09/29/1935, Nanking, China, m, 1964, 4 children **DISCIPLINE** PHILOSOPHY; LINGUISTICS **EDUCATION** Nat Taiwan Univ, BA, 56; Univ Wash, MA, 58; Harvard Univ, PhD, 64. **CAREER** From asst prof to assoc prof, 63-74, prof philos, Univ Hawaii, Manoa, 74-, vis assoc prof, ch dept phil, 70-72, dir grad inst philos, 70-72, Nat Taiwan Univ, fall 65, vis prof, spring 68; prin investigator inquiries into class Chinese logic, Nat Sci Found grant, 65-67; fellow-participant, Summer Inst Ling, Univ Calif, Los Angeles, 66, Summer Inst Philos Sci, Stanford Univ, 67; vis assoc prof, Yale Univ, 68-69; E/W Ctr Commun Inst Sr. Fel, 78-79; pres Far E Inst Advan Studies, 85-92. **HONORS AND AWARDS** Pac Cult Found Grant, 87-88; Jiuli Zhouyi Awd Best Essay Philos, 94; Honoris Doctoris Excellence Study Devel Chinese Philos Inst Far East Stud, 95; guest prof ceremony Wuhan Univ, 96, Jejiang Univ, 96, & Anhui Univ, 96. **MEMBERSHIPS** Eastern Div Am Philos Asn; Am Asn Asian Studies; Am Orient Soc; Soc Asian & Comp Philos (treas-secy, 68-); Charles S Pierce Soc; Int Soc Chinese Philos; Int Soc I Ching; Ctr Advan Studies Chinese Philos; Far E Inst Advanced Studies; Int Found Chines Mgt Contemp Ethics; Int Fed Confucian Studies. **RESEARCH** Chinese philosophy and logic; philosophy of language and logic; contemporary American philosophy and ethics. **SELECTED PUBLICATIONS** Coauth, Ontic commitment and the empty universe, J Philos, 7/65; auth, Classical Chinese logic: A preliminary description, Philos E & W, 65; Requirements for the validity of induction, Philos & Phenomenol Res, 3/68; Peirce's and Lewis' Theories of Induction, Martinus Nijihof, Hague, 69; Tai Chen's Inquiry into Goodness, Orient Soc, Hanover, 69; Chinese Philosophy and Chinese Civilization, 74 & Scientific Knowledge and Human Value, 75, San Min Publ Co, Taipei; The Philosophical Aspects of the Mind-Body Problem, Univ Hawaii, 75; auth C Theory: Yijing Philosophy of Kuanli, Dongda Book, 95; On the Spirits of Philosophy in China and West, E. Publ Ctr, 96; Study on Zhuxi and Neo-Confucianism, Lienking Press; ed Journal of Chinese Philosophy. **CONTACT ADDRESS** Dept Philos, Univ of Hawaii, Manoa, 2530 Dole St, Honolulu, HI 96822-2303. **EMAIL** ccheng@hawaii.edu

CHERMAK, STEVEN

PERSONAL Born 10/30/1964, OH, m, 1997 **DISCIPLINE** CRIMINAL JUSTICE **EDUCATION** Bowling Green State Univ, BS, 87; Univ Albany, MS, 89, PhD, 93. **CAREER** Asst to assoc prof, Indiana Univ, 93-. **HONORS AND AWARDS** Eliot Lumbard Awd for Academic Excellence; Teaching Excellence Recognition Awd, 97, 99. **MEMBERSHIPS** Am Soc of Criminology, Acad of Criminal Justice Services. **RESEARCH** Media coverage of crime, effect of celebrated cases on criminal justice decision-making. **SELECTED PUBLICATIONS** Auth, "Body Count News: How Crime is Presented in the News Media," Justice Quart, 11,4 (94): 561-582; auth, Victims in the News: crime and the American News Media, Boulder, Co: Westview Press (95);auth, "Image Control: How Police Affect the Presentation of Crime News," Am J of Police, 14, 2 (95): 21-43; coauth with Marla Sandys,"A Journey into the Unknown: Pretrial Publicity and Capital Cases," Commun, Law, and Policy, 1, 4 (96): 533-577; auth, "The Presentation of Drugs in the News Media: News Sources Involved in the Construction of Social Problems," Justice Quart, 14, 4 (97): 687-718; coauth with Alexander Weiss, "The Effects of the Media on Federal Criminal Justice Policy," Criminal Justice Policy Rev, 8, 4 (97): 323-341; auth, "Predicting Crime Story Salience: the Effects of Crime, Victim, and Defendant Characteristics," J of Criminal Justice, 26, 1 (98): 670; coauth with A. Weiss,"The News Value of African American Victims: An Examination of the Media's Presentation of Homicide," J of Crime and Justice, XXI 2 (98): 71-88; coauth with A. Weiss, "Activity-Based Learning of Statistics: Using Practical Applications to Improve Students' Learning," J of Criminal Justice Ed, 10, 2 (99): 361-372; auth, "Public Reaction to Crime," in The Encyclopedia of Crime and Delinquency, David Luckenbill and Dennis Peck, eds, Philadelphia: Taylor & Francis (2000). **CONTACT ADDRESS** Dept Criminal Justice, Indiana Univ, Bloomington, 1033 E 3rd St, Bloomington, IN 47405. **EMAIL** schermak@indiana.edu

CHERNUS, IRA

DISCIPLINE RELIGIOUS STUDIES **EDUCATION** Temple Univ, PhD. **CAREER** Prof. **SELECTED PUBLICATIONS** Auth, Nuclear Madness: Religion and Psychology of the Nuclear Age; Order and Disorder in the Definition of Peace; pubs on religious dimensions of nuclear weapons issues. **CONTACT ADDRESS** Religious Studies Dept, Univ of Colorado, Boulder, Boulder, CO 80309. **EMAIL** Ira.Chernus@Colorado.edu

CHESNUTT, RANDALL D.

PERSONAL Born 07/30/1951, m, 1973, 2 children **DISCIPLINE** NEW TESTAMENT AND CHRISTIAN ORIGINS **EDUCATION** Alabama Christian Col, BA, 73; Harding Univ, MTh, 76, MA, 80; Duke Divinity Sch, ThM, 80; Duke Univ, PhD, 86. **CAREER** Res asst, Duke Univ, 81-83; tchg asst, Duke Univ, 80-84; vis instr, Abilene Christian Univ, 81-83; instr, asst prof, Seaver Col, Pepperdine Univ, 84-88; assoc prof, 88-94 ch, Soc Bibl Lit, 94; prof, 94-. **HONORS AND AWARDS** Edu tech grant, Pepperdine Univ, 94 **MEMBERSHIPS** Mem, ed b Sheffield Acad Press; Cath Bibl Assn, 92-93. **SELECTED PUBLICATIONS** Auth, Prayer from Alexander to Constantine: A Critical Anthology, Routledge, 96; From Death to Life: Conversion in Joseph and Aseneth, Journal for the Study of the Pseudepigrapha Supplement Series 16, Sheffield Acad Press, 95; From Text to Context: The Social Matrix of Joseph and Aseneth,, Society of Biblical Literature 96, Scholars Press, 96; co-auth, Prayer from Alexander to Constantine: A Critical Anthology, Routledge, 96; Prayers in the Old Testament Apocrypha and Pseudepigrapha, Prayer of a Convert to Judaism: Joseph and Aseneth 12-13, Apologetics and Missionary Propaganda in Alexandrian Judaism: Tcherikover Revisited, Proselytism in Early Judaism, Approaches to Ancient Judaism 7. Scholars Press/Brown Judaic Studies, 96; Jewish Women in the Greco-Roman Era, Essays on Women in Earliest Christianity, vol 1, Col Press, 93. **CONTACT ADDRESS** Dept of Relig, Pepperdine Univ, 24255 Pacific Coast Hwy, Malibu, CA 90263. **EMAIL** chesnutt@pepperdine.edu

CHESTER, RONALD
PERSONAL Born 09/20/1944, Jacksonville, IL, m, 1993, 3 children **DISCIPLINE** LAW **EDUCATION** Harvard Univ, BA, 66; Columbia Univ, JD, 70; MA, 70; Cambridge Univ, Dipl in Criminol, 71. **CAREER** Asst prof to prof, New Eng Sch of Law, 73-; vis prof, Ind Univ, 79-80; vis prof, S Methodist Sch of Law, 86-87; vis prof, Univ Calif Law Sch, 88-89; adj prof, Suffolk Univ, 93-95; adj prof, Boston Col Law Sch, 98-99; parsons vis, Univ Sydney Law Sch, 00. **HONORS AND AWARDS** Ford Found Fel, Cambridge Univ, 70-71; NEH Fel, Harvard Law Sch, 75-76; Radcliffe Res Grant, 82; Outstanding Acad Book, Choice Magazine, 83. **RESEARCH** Trust modification; Social and legal implications of human cloning. **SELECTED PUBLICATIONS** Co-auth, "Functionalizing First-Year Legal Education," UC Davis L Rev, 91; auth, "Freezing the Heir Apparent: A Dialogue on Postmortem Conception, Parental Responsibility and Inheritance," Houston L Rev, 96; auth, "Inheritance I American Legal Thought," in Inheritance and Wealth in America, Plenum, 97; auth, "To Be, Be, Be.Not Just to Be: Legal and Social Implications of Cloning for Human Reproduction," Fla L Rev, 97; auth, "Disinheritance and the American Child: An Alternative from British Columbia," Ut L J, 98; auth, "Property: Legal Aspects of Intergenerational Transmission," in Intl Encyclopedia of the Social and Beh Sci, Oxford, 01. **CONTACT ADDRESS** New England Sch of Law, 154 Stuart St, Boston, MA 02116. **EMAIL** rchester@fac.nesl.edu

CHETHIMATTAM, JOHN BRITTO
PERSONAL Born 10/26/1922, Thottakad, India **DISCIPLINE** PHILOSOPHY, COMPARATIVE RELIGION **EDUCATION** Pontif Gregorian Univ, Rome, Lic, 53, MA, 54, ThD, 56; Fordham Univ, PhD(philos), 68. **CAREER** Lectr theol, Dharmaram Col, Bangalore, 56-62, prof philos & theol, 62-65; vis scholar, Harvard Univ, 66-67; from instr to asst prof, 67-70, assoc prof, 70-79, Prof Philos, Fordham Univ, 79-, Rector, Dharmaram Col, Bangalore, 72-75; dir, Dharmanivas Res, Ctr, NJ. **MEMBERSHIPS** Indian Philos Cong; Am Orient Soc; Asn Asian Studies. **RESEARCH** Comparative ethics. **SELECTED PUBLICATIONS** Auth, Consciousness and Reality: An Indian Approach to Metaphysics, Dharmaram Col, Bangalore, 67, Chapman, London & Orbis, NYC, 71; Dialogue in Indian Tradition, Dharmaram Col, 69, Reedited as, Patterns of Indian Thought, Chapman, London & Orbis, NYC, 71; coauth, A Philosophy in Song Poems, 72 & ed, Unique and Universal: Introduction to An Indian Theology, 73, Dharmaram Col; Images of Man, Bangalore, 74; Glimpses of Reality, Dharmanivas, 80. **CONTACT ADDRESS** 89 Warrington Pl, East Orange, NJ 07017.

CHILDRESS, JAMES FRANKLIN
PERSONAL Born 10/04/1940, Mt Airy, NC, m, 1958, 2 children **DISCIPLINE** RELIGIOUS, ETHICS **EDUCATION** Guilford Col, BM, 62; Yale Univ, BD, 65, MA, 67, PhD(Christian ethics), 68. **CAREER** From asst prof to prof relig studies, Univ Va, 68-75, chmn dept, 72-75; J P Kennedy Sr prof Christian ethics, Kennedy Inst, Georgetown Univ, 75-79; prof relig studies, 79-81, Prof Relig Studies & Med Educ, Univ VA, 81-, Fel, Am Coun Learned Soc & Harvard Law Sch, 72-73; vis prof, Univ Chicago Div Sch, 77 & Princeton Univ, 78; co-ed, J of Relig Ethics, 78. **MEMBERSHIPS** Am Soc Christian Ethics; Am Acad Relig; Soc for Values Higher Educ; Am Soc Social & Polit Philos; fel Inst Soc, Ethics & Life Sci. **RESEARCH** Biomedical ethics; political ethics, including just war theory and laws of war; history of Christian ethics. **SELECTED PUBLICATIONS** Auth, Nonviolent Resistance, Trust and Risk-Taking 25 Years Later, Jour Rel Ethics, Vol 0025, 97. **CONTACT ADDRESS** Dept Relig Studies, Univ of Virginia, 1 Cocke Hall, Charlottesville, VA 22903-3248.

CHILDS, BREVARD SPRINGS
PERSONAL Born 09/02/1923, Columbia, SC, m, 1954, 2 children **DISCIPLINE** THEOLOGY **EDUCATION** Univ MI, AB, 47, MA, 48; Princeton Univ, BD, 50; Univ Basel, ThD, 55. **CAREER** Prof exegesis & Old Testament, Mission House Sem, 54-58; from asst prof to assoc prof, 58-66, Prof Old Testament, Divinity Sch, Yale Univ, 66-, Guggenheim fel, Hebrew Univ, 63-64; Am Coun Learned Soc res fel, Cambridge Univ, 70-71; Nat Endowment Hum res grant, 77-78; Fulbright fel, 81. **HONORS AND AWARDS** DD, Univ Aberdeen, 81. **MEMBERSHIPS** Soc Bibl Lit; Soc Old Testament Studies; Am Acad ARts & Sci, 95. **RESEARCH** Old Testament theol; comp relig; New Testament theol. **SELECTED PUBLICATIONS** Auth, Myth and Reality in the Old Testament, 60, Memory and Tradition in Israel, 62 & Isaiah and the Assyrian Crisis, 67, SCM Press, London; Biblical Theology in Crisis, 70, The Book of Exodus, 74, & Old Testament Books for Pastor and Teacher, 77, Westminster; Introduction to the Old Testament as Scripture, Fortress, 79; Biblical Theology of the Old and New Testaments, Fortress, 92. **CONTACT ADDRESS** Divinity Sch, Yale Univ, 409 Prospect St, New Haven, CT 06511.

CHILDS, JAMES M., JR.
DISCIPLINE ETHICS; CHURCH AND SOCIETY **EDUCATION** Concordia Sr Col, BA, 61; Concordia Sem, MDiv, 65; Union Theol Sem, STM, 66; Lutheran Sch Theol, PhD, 74. **CAREER** Assoc prof, ch, Div Theol, Concordia Sr Col, 68-76; lectr, Purdue Univ, 70, 71, 76; assoc prof, Valparaiso Univ, 76-78; assoc prof, 78-87; prof, 87-; dean Acad Aff, 80-00; interim pres, 89-90; adj prof, Grad Sch Bus Admin, Capital Univ, 93-; Joseph A. Sittler prof, 97-; dir, Academic Dev, 00-. **MEMBERSHIPS** Am Acad Rel; Soc Christian Ethics; Coun for Ethics in Economics. **SELECTED PUBLICATIONS** Auth, Ethics and the Promise of God: Moral Authority and the Church's Witness, The Promise of Lutheran Ethics, Fortress, 98; Anna, Ambiguity, and the Promise: A Lutheran Theologian Reflects on Assisted Death, Must We Suffer Our Way To Death?, SMU, 96; Ethics in Business: Faith at Work, Fortress, 95; Faith, Formation and Decision: Ethics in the Community of Promise, Fortress, 92; auth, Greed: Economics and Ethics in Conflict, Fortress, 00; auth, Preaching Justice: The Ethical Vocation of Word and Sacrament Ministry, Trinity Press International, 00. **CONTACT ADDRESS** Hist, Theol, Soc Dept, Trinity Lutheran Sem, 2199 E Main St, Columbus, OH 43209-2334. **EMAIL** jchilds@trinity.capital.edu

CHILDS, WINSTON
PERSONAL Born 02/14/1931, Savannah, GA, s **DISCIPLINE** LAW **EDUCATION** Am Univ, AB 57, JD 59. **CAREER** Booker T Washington Found, special counsel; Minority Consult & Urbanologists, natl assn; GEOC, CIO Labor Union, pres; stock broker; private law pratice; DC Republican Central Committee, gen counsel; Natl Business League, gen counsel; Graham Building Associates Real Estate Development Company, pres; Amer Univ Law School, adjunct prof; MSI Services Inc, a systems engineering and mgmt consulting firm, Washington DC, founder, chairman, CEO, 76-. **MEMBERSHIPS** DC Bar Assn; Amer Management Assn; Armed Forces Communication and Electronics Assn; Republican Senatorial Inner Circle; DC Metropolitan Boys/Girls Club; bd mem, Georgetown Symphony Orchestra; John Sherman Myers Society. **CONTACT ADDRESS** MSI Services, Inc, One Farragut Sq S, Ste 610, Washington, DC 20006.

CHILES, ROBERT EUGENE
PERSONAL Born 03/01/1923, Convoy, OH, m, 1945, 1 child **DISCIPLINE** THEOLOGY **EDUCATION** Kent State Univ, AB, 44; Northwestern Univ, MA, 47; Garrett Theol Sem, BD, 47; Columbia Univ, PhD, 64. **CAREER** Clergyman, Concord Methodist Church, Dayton, 50-60; coordr adult educ prog, Hunter Col, 60-64, asst dean gen studies, 64-67; exec asst to pres, 67-68, assoc prof philos & dean students, 68-72, Prof Relig Studies, 72-88, Prof Emer, 88- , Col Staten Island, 64- . **RESEARCH** Wesleyan and American Methodist theology. **SELECTED PUBLICATIONS** Coauth, A Compend of Wesley's Theology, Abingdon, 54; auth, Methodist apostasy: From free grace to free will, Relig in Life, 58; A glossary of Tillich terms, Theol Today, 60; Theological Transition in American Methodism, 1790-1930, Abingdon, 65; The rights of patients, New England J Med, 67; Grace & Freewill, In: World Dict Methodism, Abingdon, 74; Scriptural Christianity, Francis Asbury Press, 84; The Philosophy they Bring to Class, Tchg Philos, 97. **CONTACT ADDRESS** Dept of Philos, Col of Staten Island, CUNY, Staten Island, NY 10314.

CHILTON, BRUCE
PERSONAL Born 09/27/1949, Roslyn, NY, m, 1982, 2 children **DISCIPLINE** RELIGION **EDUCATION** Bard Col, BA, 71; General Theol Seminary, MDiv, 74; Cambridge Univ, PhD, 76. **CAREER** Tutor, General Theol Seminary, 74; Supvr Studies, St. John's Col, Univ Cambridge, 74-76; Lectr, Sheffield Univ, 76-85; Burghley Preacher, St. John's Col, 77-78; Franz Delitzsch Lectr, Inst Judaicum Delitzschianum, 81; Vis Prof, Union Theol Seminary, 83; Assoc Prof, 85-87, Lillian Claus Assoc Prof New Testament, Yale Univ, 86-87; Prof Relig & Chaplain, 87-, Bernard Iddings Bell Prof Relig & Philos, Bard Col, 89-; Exec Dir, Inst of Advanced Theol, 99-. **HONORS AND AWARDS** Fel, Episcopal Church Found, 74-76; Res & Travel Grants, Sheffield Univ; Heinrich Hertz Stiftung, Bundesrepublik Deutschland, 81; A. Whitney Griswold Res Fund, Yale Univ, 86; Theol Development Grant, Episcopal Church, 87; Asher Edelman Fel, Bard Col, 92; Bishop Henry Martin Memorial Lectr, Univ Col Emmanuel & St. Chad, 96; Igor Kaplan Lectr Jewish Studies, Sch Theol, Univ Toronto, 97; Fel, Pew Charitable Trusts' Evangelical Schol Prog, 97-98. **MEMBERSHIPS** Akademie der Wissenschaften; British Asn Jewish Studies; British New Testament Conf; Europ Asn Jewish Studies; Inst Bibl Res; Nat Conf Christians & Jews; Oriental Club; Soc Bibl Lit; Studiorum Novi Testamenti Soc; The Tyndale House Gospels Res Project; Jesus Seminar; Inst Advanced Theol (founder). **SELECTED PUBLICATIONS** Auth, The Five Gospels. The Search for the Authentic Words of Jesus, HarperSanFranciso, 93; A Feast of Meanings. Eucharistic Theologies from Jesus through Johannine Circles: Supplements to Novum Testamentum 72, Brill, 94; coauth, The Body of Faith. Israel and the Church: Chritianity and Judaism -- The Formative Categories 2, Trinity Press Int, 96; Forging a Common Future. Catholic, Judaic, and Protestant Relations for a New Millenium, Pilgrim, 97; The Acts of Jesus. The Search for the Authentic Deeds of Jesus, HarperSanFrancisco, 98; auth, Rabbi Jesus, Doubleday, 00. **CONTACT ADDRESS** Bard Col, Annandale, NY 12504.

CHINCHAR, GERALD T.
PERSONAL Born 10/09/1943, Cleveland, OH **DISCIPLINE** LITURGICAL STUDIES **EDUCATION** St John's Univ, MA, 73; Univ Notre Dame du Lac, MA, 77; United Theolog Sem, DMin, 92. **CAREER** Dir, Christian Initiation Processes; prof, Univ Dayton. **MEMBERSHIPS** North Amer Acad Liturgy. **RESEARCH** Liturgy and Initiation in the Catholic Tradition. **SELECTED PUBLICATIONS** Auth, Journal Keeping in the Inquiry Period, Catechumenate Mag, 92; Sunday Word, Catechumenate Magazine 15:1, 93; Liturgy of the Hours: Pastoral Perspective, Liturgical Ministry 2, 93; rev, A Promise of Presence, Liturgical Ministry 3, 94; Liturgy With Style and Grace, 97. **CONTACT ADDRESS** Campus Ministry, Univ of Dayton, 300 College Park, 211 Liberty Hall, Dayton, OH 45469-1408. **EMAIL** chinchar@udayton.edu

CHING, JULIA
PERSONAL Born Shanghai, China, m, 1981, 3 children **DISCIPLINE** RELIGION **EDUCATION** Col New Rochelle, BA, 58; Catholic Univ Am, MA, 60; Australian Nat Univ, PhD, 71. **CAREER** Lectr, Australian Nat Univ, 69-74; vis assoc prof, Columbia Univ, 74-75; assoc prof, Yale Univ, 75-79; assoc prof to Lee Chair prof, Univ Toronto, 79-. **HONORS AND AWARDS** Fel, Royal Soc of Canada, 90; LHD, St. Andrew's NC, 97; DD, Queen's Univ, 97, Lee Chair prof, 98. **RESEARCH** East Asian religion and philosophy, Comparative philosophy and religion, East Asian intel history. **SELECTED PUBLICATIONS** Auth, The Religious Thought of Chu His, Oxford Univ Press, 00; auth, The Butterfly Healing, Orbis: New York, 98; auth, Myshinism and Kingship in China, Cambridge Univ Press, 97. **CONTACT ADDRESS** Dept of Relig, Univ of Toronto, Toronto, ON, Canada M5S 1K7. **EMAIL** jching@chass.utoronto.ca

CHINNICI, JOSEPH PATRICK
PERSONAL Born 03/16/1945, Altadena, CA **DISCIPLINE** HISTORY THEOLOGY **EDUCATION** San Luis Rey Col, BA, 68; Grad Theol Union, MA, 71; Franciscan Sch Theol, MDiv, 72; Oxford Univ, DPhil(hist, theol), 76. **CAREER** Asst prof church hist, Franciscan Sch Theol, 75-; asst prof, Grad Theol Union, 75-. **HONORS AND AWARDS** Univ Notre Dame travel grant, 78. **MEMBERSHIPS** AHA; Am Cath Hist Asn; US Cath Hist Soc. **RESEARCH** Church and the Enlightenment; American Catholicism; American religious history. **SELECTED PUBLICATIONS** Auth, Living Stones, The History and Sturcture of Catholic Spiritual Life in the United States, Orbis Books, 96; coauth, Prayer and Practice in the Am Catholic Community, 1785-1979, Orbis Books, 00. **CONTACT ADDRESS** Franciscan Sch of Theol, 1712 Euclid Ave, Berkeley, CA 94709-1294. **EMAIL** jpchinnici@aol.com

CHISMAR, DOUGLAS
PERSONAL Born 06/27/1952, Pittsburgh, PA, m, 1973, 1 child **DISCIPLINE** PHILOSOPHY, ETHICS **EDUCATION** Am Univ, BA; Ashland Theol Sem, MDiv, 76; Ohio State Univ, PhD, 83. **CAREER** Asst prof to assoc prof to chair philos, Ashland Univ, 80-97; Dir, Chowan Col Ctr for Ethics, Assoc Prof, Philos, Chowan Col, 98-. **HONORS AND AWARDS** Mentor Awd, Ashland Univ, 93, 89; Outstanding Fac Member, Ashland Univ, 87; Sears-Roebuck Fnd Awd for Teach Excel, Campus Ldrshp, Ashland Univ, 90. **MEMBERSHIPS** Am Philos Asn; NC Philos Asn; Soc Christian Philos; Asn Practical & Prof Ethics; Asn Moral Educ. **RESEARCH** Empathy and moral decision-making; mystery in science, religion and aesthetics; technology and human nature. **SELECTED PUBLICATIONS** Auth, "Lipps and Scheler on Aesthetic Empathy," Jour of Comp Lit and Aesthetics, 17, 94; rev of Stan Van Hooft, The Ethics of Caring, Ethics107, 96; rev of Ellen Singer More, Maureen Milligan, The Empathic Practitioner, Ethics 106, 96. **CONTACT ADDRESS** Center for Ethics, Chowan Col, Box 1848, Murfreesboro, NC 27855. **EMAIL** Chismd@chowan.edu

CHIU, HUNGDAH
PERSONAL Born 03/23/1936, Shanghai, China, m, 1966, 1 child **DISCIPLINE** INTERNATIONAL LAW & RELATIONS **EDUCATION** National Taiwan Univ, LLB, 58; Long Island Univ, MA, 62; Harvard Univ, LLM, 62, SJD(int law), 65. **CAREER** Assoc res, Chinese law, EAsian Res Ctr, Harvard Univ, 64-65, res assoc, Law Sch, 66-70 & 72-74; assoc prof int law, Col Law, Nat Taiwan Univ, 65-66; prof, Nat Chengchi Univ & Nat Taiwan Univ, 70-72; assoc prof, 74-77, prof Int Law, Univ Md Law Sch, 77-, Reviewer, Nat Endowments for Humanities, 79-; fel, Inst Sino-Soviet Studies, George Washington Univ, 77-79; reviewer, NSF, 81-; vis prof, Dept Govt & Foreign Affairs, Univ Va, 80-81. **HONORS AND AWARDS** Cert Merit, Am Soc Int Law, 76; Inst Chinese Cult ann award, 80; Toulmin Medal, Soc Am Military Engrs, 82; 1st Class Merit Svc Medal, Republic of China (Taiwan), 94. **MEMBERSHIPS** Am Soc Int Law; Asn Asian Studies; Am Asn Chinese Studies; Int Law Asn (London). **RESEARCH** Chinese law and politics; Sino-American relations. **SELECTED PUBLICATIONS** Auth, The Capacity of International Organizations to Conclude Treaties, Martinus Nijhoff, The Hague, 66; The People's Republic of China and the Law of Treaties, Harvard Univ Press, 72; co-ed & contrib, Law in Chinese Foreign Policy, Oceana, 72; ed & contrib, China and the Taiwan Question: Documents and Analysis, Praeger, 73; coauth, People's China and Interna-

tional Law: A Documentary Study (2 vols), Princeton Univ Press, 74; ed & contrib, China and the Taiwan Issue, 79 & auth, Agreements of the People's Republic of China, 1966-1980, A Calandar, 81, Praeger; co-ed & auth, Multisystem Nations and International Law, Occas Papers & Reprint Ser Contemp Asian Studies, No 8, 81; coauth, International Law of the Sea: Cases, Documents and Readings, Elsevier, 81; co-ed & contrib, The Future of Hong Kong: Toward 1997 and Beyond, Greenwood, 87; coauth, Criminal Justice in Post-Mao China: Analysis and Documents, State Univ Press of NY, 85; auth, International Law (China); 94. **CONTACT ADDRESS** Law School, Univ of Maryland, Baltimore, 500 W Baltimore St, Baltimore, MD 21201-1786. **EMAIL** estasia@law.umaryland.edu

CHO, KAH-KYUNG
PERSONAL Born 06/07/1927, Seoul, Korea, 1 child **DISCIPLINE** PHILOSOPHY **EDUCATION** Seoul Nat Univ, BA, 52; Univ Heidelberg, PhD(philos), 57. **CAREER** Prof philos, Seoul Nat Univ, 57-70; prof philos, State Univ NY, Buffalo, 70-, Vis Fulbright prof, Yale Univ, 61-62; vis Asian prof, Fulbright Prof in conjunction with Univs Buffalo, RI, Western Mich & Cent Mich, 62-63; vis res prof, Husserl Arch, Univ Cologne, 63; Humboldt vis prof, Frankfurt, 76; vis prof, Univ Tex, Austin, 77; vis prof Univ Bochum, 83; vis prof, Osaka, 90; vis prof, Soon Sil Univ, 91. **HONORS AND AWARDS** SUNY Chancellor's Awd for Excellence, 90; Fel of Japan Soc for Promotion of Science, 91; SUNY Dist Teaching Prof, 94; SOWU Book prize , 96. **MEMBERSHIPS** Ed Board, Philosophy and Phenomenological Res, 75-90; Husserl Studies, 83-; General Ed, Orbis Phenomenologicus, 93-; Ed Board, Phaenomenologie-Texte und Kontexte, 98-. **RESEARCH** Contemporary European philosophy; phenomenology. **SELECTED PUBLICATIONS** Auth, Philosphy of Existence, Pak Yong-Sa, 61, 11th ed, 95; auth, Anschauung und Abstraktion, In: Kongressbericht IX Dusseldorf, Anto Hain, 71: auth, Mediation and Immediacy for Husserl, In Phenomenology and Natural Existence, State Unv NY, 73; auth, Leben und Wirken Marvin Farbers fru die Phanomenologie in US, In: Phanomenologische forschungun, Alber, Freiburg, 82; auth, Bewusstsein und Natursein, Alber, Freiburg, 87; auth, Philosophy and Science in Phenomenological Perspective, Dordrecht, 84; transl, Ishiki-to Shizen (japanese translation), Tokyo, 94; auth, Phanomenologie der Natur, Freiburg, 99; Phanomenologie in Korea, Freiburg, 00. **CONTACT ADDRESS** Dept of Philosophy, SUNY, Buffalo, 125 Park Hall, PO Box 604150, Buffalo, NY 14260-4150. **EMAIL** KCHO@ACSU.Buffalo.edu

CHOPER, JESSE H.
PERSONAL Born 08/19/1935, Wilkes-Barre, PA, m, 1961, 1 child **DISCIPLINE** LAW **EDUCATION** Wilkes Col, BS, 57, LHD, 67; Univ Pa, LLB, 60. **CAREER** Instr accounting, Univ Pa, 57-60; law clerk, 60-61; from asst prof to assoc prof law, Univ Minn, 61-65; Prof, 65-82, Dean Law Sch, Univ Calif, Berkeley, 82-, Vis prof law, Harvard Univ, 70-71; vis scholar, Syracuse Univ CoL Law, 79. **HONORS AND AWARDS** DHL, Wilkes Col, 67. **RESEARCH** Constitutional law; corporation law; separation of church-state. **SELECTED PUBLICATIONS** **CONTACT ADDRESS** Law Sch, Univ of California, Berkeley, 220 Boalt Hall, Berkeley, CA 94720-7201.

CHOPP, REBECA S.
PERSONAL Born 04/24/1952, KS, m, 1995, 1 child **DISCIPLINE** THEOLOGY **EDUCATION** Kans Wesleyan Univ, BA, 74; St. Paul Sch of Theol, M Div, 77; Univ Chicago Divinity Sch, PhD, 83 **CAREER** Provost and exec vpres, Emory Univ; dean of fac and acad affairs, Emory Univ, Candler Sch of Theol, 93-97; Prof of Syst Theol, 82- . **HONORS AND AWARDS** Alumna of the Year, Univ Chicago, 97; Luce fel, Emory Univ, 90; Charles Howard Candler Chair of Theol, 96 **MEMBERSHIPS** Am Acad of Relig. **RESEARCH** Feminist and liberation theologies **SELECTED PUBLICATIONS** auth, Christian Moral Imagination, A Feminist Practical Theology and the Future of Theological Education, Int Jour of Practical Theol, 97; auth, Bearing Witness: Traditional Faith in Contemporary Expression, Quart Rev, 97; auth, American Feminist Theology, The Modern Theologians, 97; auth, Theorizing Feminist Theology, Horizons in Feminist Theology, 97; ed with Sheila Davaney, Differing Horizons: Feminist Theory and Theology, 97. **CONTACT ADDRESS** Emory Univ, 404 Administration Building, Atlanta, GA 30322. **EMAIL** rchopp@emory.edu

CHORNENKI, GENEVIEVE A.
DISCIPLINE LAW **EDUCATION** Osgoode Hall Law Sch, LLB, 78. **CAREER** Instr; Founded, Mediated Solutions Incorporated **MEMBERSHIPS** Can Bar Asn. **SELECTED PUBLICATIONS** Auth, pubs on monographs about ADR. **CONTACT ADDRESS** Fac of Law, Univ of Toronto, 78 Queen's Park, Toronto, ON, Canada M5S 1A1.

CHRISTENSEN, MICHAEL
PERSONAL 2 children **DISCIPLINE** THEOLOGY; RELIGIOUS STUDIES; HISTORICAL THEOLOGY **EDUCATION** Point Loma Col, BA, 77; Yale Univ Divinity School, MA, 81; M.Phil, 95, PhD, 97, Drew Univ. **CAREER** Asst Prof, 97-, Dir of Doctor of Ministry Program, 95-, Drew Univ. **HONORS AND AWARDS** John Wesley Fel, 93-97; Will Herberg Merit Scholarship, Drew Univ, 93-96; Crossroads Scholar Program (research stipend for writing public policy monograph on nuclear issues in former Soviet Union), 94-96; Research Fel, Newark Project, 94-95; Recipient of the Helen Le Page and William Hale Chamberlain Prize awarded for the PhD Dissertation that is singularly distinguished by creative thought and excellent prose style, 97; Recipient of the Martin Luther King Jr. and Abraham Joshua Heschel Humanitarian Awd for Spirituality and Social Justice, 98; Research Fel, Senior Research Scholar for Russia, The Princeton Project on Youth, Globalization and the Church, 98-01. **MEMBERSHIPS** Amer Acad of Religion; Phi Delta Lamba Honor Soc; The Patristic Soc, Center for Millenial Studies, Boston Univ. **RESEARCH** Theology and Culture; Russian Eschatology; Spirituality **SELECTED PUBLICATIONS** Auto, The Samaritan's Imperative: Compassionate Ministry to People Living With Aids, Abingdon, 91; auth, Aids Ministry and the Article of Death: A Westleyan Pastoral Theological Perspective, Catalyst, 95; " Evangelical-Orthodox Dialogue in Russia" The Journal of Ecumenical Studies, 96; auth, " The Russian Idea of Apocalypse: Nikolai Berdyaev's Theory of Russian Cultural Apocalyptic" , The Journal of Millennial Studies, 98; auth, " Believers Without Borders: Bringing Hope to Kosovo Refugees, The Covenant Companion, 99; auth, " The Chernobyl Prophecy in Russian Apocalyptic Eschatology" The Living Pulpit, vol 8, no 1, 99; auth, " The psychosocial Impact of Chernobyl: Thirteen Years After" The Journal of Intergroup Relations, Vol XXVI, no 1, 99; auth, " Millennial Moments" in forthcoming Encyclopedia of Millenialism and Millennial Movements, Routledge/Berkshire Reference Works, 00; assoc ed, Routledge Encyclopedia of Millennialism and Millennial Movements, Routledge, 00; gen ed, TheNextChurch Series, Three volume series in practical theology, forthcoming , Abingdon: vol 1: Equipping the Saints: Mobilizing Laity for Ministry, 00. **CONTACT ADDRESS** Drew Univ, 12 Campus Dr., Madison, NJ 07940. **EMAIL** mchriste@drew.edu

CHRISTIAN, AMY
PERSONAL Born 12/25/1965, St Louis, MO, s **DISCIPLINE** LAW **EDUCATION** Georgetown Univ, BA, 88; BS, 88; Harvard Law Sch, JD, 91. **CAREER** From assoc prof to prof, Mich State Univ Detroit Col of Law, 94-. **HONORS AND AWARDS** Teacher of the Year, Detroit Col of Law, 96. **MEMBERSHIPS** D.C. Bar; Calif Bar; ABA. **RESEARCH** Tax and Society, Tax and Gender. **SELECTED PUBLICATIONS** Auth, "Designing a Carbon Tax: The Introduction of the Carbon-Burned Tax (CBT)," UCLA J of Environmental Law & Policy (92): 221-281; auth, "The Joint Return Rate Structure: Identifying and Addressing the Gendered Nature of Tax Law," J of Law & Polit (97): 241-376; auth, "Joint and Several Liability and the Joint Return: Its Implications for Women," Univ Cincinnati Law Rev (98): 535-617; auth, "Joint Versus Separate Filing: Joint Return Rates and Federal Complicity in Directing Economic Resources from Women to Men," Calif Rev of Law & Women's Studies (98): 443-469; auth, "Legislative Approaches to Marriage Penalty Relief: The Unintended Effects of Change on the Married Couple's Choice of Filing Status," NY Law Sch J of Human Rights (99): 303-357. **CONTACT ADDRESS** Detroit Col of Law, Michigan State Univ, 364 Law Col Bldg, East Lansing, MI 48824-1300.

CHRISTIAN, OLLIE
PERSONAL Born 09/22/1946, Ocala, FL, m, 1971, 2 children **DISCIPLINE** PHILOSOPHY **CAREER** Asst prof, La State Univ, 84-86; clinical soc work supvr, Xavier Univ, 87-88; asst prof, Xavier Univ, 88-94; from assoc prof to prof, Southern Univ, 94-. **HONORS AND AWARDS** Student govt Asn Dept Awd for contributed services, Xavier Univ; Certificate of Appreciation, Xavier Univ; Awds plaque for contributions made to Soc Sci; Outstanding Service Awd, La State Police Comn; Certificate of Recognition, Southern Univ Dept of Sociol; Appreciation Plaque for Teaching and Service, Southern Univ Departmental Seniors; listed in Who's Who in America, Who's Who in the South and Southwest, and International Who's Who. **MEMBERSHIPS** Am Sociol Asn, Mid-South Sociol Asn, Int Sociol Honor Soc, La State Univ Alumni Asn, Phi Lambda Pi; Int Soc Sci Honor Soc, Am Asn of Black Sociologists, Southwest Soc on Aging. **RESEARCH** Social Gerentology, Political Sociology, Race Relations, Mental Health and Community Organizations. **SELECTED PUBLICATIONS** Coauth, "Socioeconomic Predictors of Alienation Among the Elderly," Int J of Aging and Human Development 3.3 (90):205-207; coauth, "Alienation Among Rural Elderly," J of Soc and Behav Sci 37.2 (92); contribur, "Women in Management," Proceedings of the Int J of Business Disciplines vol 2, 93; coauth, "Just in Time Philosophy," proceedings of the Int J of Business Disciplines vol 1, 93; coauth, "Gender Discrimination: Implications for Workforce 2000," Proceedings of the Int Asn of Business Disciplines vol 2 (93); coauth, "Human Services 2000: Reinventing the System of Care in America," Proceedings of the Southern Sociol Soc (96); auth, "Social Demography in Slave Plantations: 1790-1860," Proceedings of the Southern Sociol Soc (96); auth, "Social Demography of Plantation Slavery," in Plantation Society and Race Relations: The Origins of Inequality, eds. Thomas Durant and David Knottnerus (Praeger Press, 99). **CONTACT ADDRESS** Dept Sociol, So Univ and A&M Col, PO Box 22528, Baton Rouge, LA 70894.

CHRISTIE, DREW
DISCIPLINE PHILOSOPHY **EDUCATION** MIT Univ, PhD, 83. **CAREER** Assoc prof. **RESEARCH** Environmental philosophy; political philosophy; pragmatism; philosophy of law; logic. **SELECTED PUBLICATIONS** Auth, Judging in Good Faith (rev); The Human Prospect (rev). **CONTACT ADDRESS** Philosophy Dept, Univ of New Hampshire, Durham, Hamilton Smith Hall, Durham, NH 03824. **EMAIL** drewc@christa.unh.edu

CHRISTOL, CARL QUIMBY
PERSONAL Born 06/28/1914, Gallup, SD, m, 1949, 2 children **DISCIPLINE** INTERNATIONAL LAW, POLITICAL SCIENCE **EDUCATION** Univ SDak, AB, 34; Fletcher Sch Law & Diplomacy, AM, 36; Inst Univ Hautes Etudes Int, Geneva, cert int law, 38; Univ Chicago, PhD(polit sci), 41; Yale Univ, LLB, 47. **CAREER** Atty, Guthrie, Darling & Shattuck, 48-49; assoc prof, 49-56, Prof Int Law & Polit Sci, Univ Southern Calif, 56-, Atty, Fizzolio, Fizzolio & McLeod, 49-; Rockefeller fel int law & jurisp, 58-59; Stockton chair int law, US Naval War Col, 62-63; mem, Comn Study Organ Peace, 68-78; adv panel int law, US Dept State, 70-74. **HONORS AND AWARDS** Assoc Awd for Excellence in Teaching, Univ Southern Calif, 77; Outstanding Prof & Raubenheimer Fac Awd, Univ Southern Calif, 82; lld, univ sdak, 77. **MEMBERSHIPS** Am Br Int Inst Space Law (vpres, 71-72, pres, 73-74); Am Soc Int Law; Am Bar Asn; Am Inst Aeronaut & Astronaut; Am Polit Sci Asn. **RESEARCH** The international law of outer space; international environmental law; international and national civil and political rights and liberties. **SELECTED PUBLICATIONS** Auth, Cases and Materials on International Law, Univ Southern Calif; coauth, Introduction to Political Science, McGraw, 57, 4th ed, 82; Maritime Quarantine, Am J Int Law, 63; auth, The International Law of Outer Space, Govt Printing Off, 66; The International Legal and Institutional Aspects of the Stratosphere Ozone Problem, Govt Printing Off, 75; Satellite Power System, International Agreements, DOE/NASA, 78; International Liability for Damage Caused by Space Objects, Am J Int Law, 80. **CONTACT ADDRESS** Dept of Polit Sci, Univ of So California, Los Angeles, CA 90007.

CHRISTOPHER, RUSSELL L.
PERSONAL Born 08/07/1961, Goshen, NY, s **DISCIPLINE** PHILOSOPHY **EDUCATION** Hamilton Col, AB, 83; Univ Mich, Sch of Law, JD, 88. **CAREER** Res assoc, Columbia Univ Sch of Law, 4/94-8/96; judicial clerkship and atty, Judge John T. Noonan, Jr., US Ct of Appeals, Ninth Circuit, 8/96-8/97; res scholar, fac of law, Columbia Univ Sch of Law, 9/97-. **HONORS AND AWARDS** Robert Leet Patterson prize, philos, 81-83. **MEMBERSHIPS** NY State Bar; Ctr for Law and Philos; Columbia Univ Sch of Law. **RESEARCH** Substantive and theoretical criminal law. **SELECTED PUBLICATIONS** Auth, Self-Defense and Defense of Others, 27, Philos & Pub Affairs, 123, no 2, Spring, 98; auth, Self-Defense and Objectivity: A Reply to Judith Jarvis Thomson, 1, Buffalo Criminal Law Rev, 537, 98; auth, Unknowing Justification and the Logical Necessity of the Dadson Principle in Private Defense, 15, Oxford Jour of Legal Studies, 229, 95; auth, Mistake of Fact in the Objective Theory of Justification: Do Two Rights Make Two Wrongs Make Two Rights..?, 85, Jour of Criminal Law & Criminol, 295, 94; auth, Control and Desert: A Comment on Moore's View of Attempts, 5, Jour of Contemp Legal Issues, 111, 94. **CONTACT ADDRESS** Law Sch, Columbia Univ, 435 W. 116th St., New York, NY 10027. **EMAIL** rchris@law.columbia.edu

CHRISTOPHER, THOMAS WELDON
PERSONAL Born 10/08/1917, Duncan, SC, m, 1950, 1 child **DISCIPLINE** LAW **EDUCATION** Washington & Lee Univ, BA, 39; Univ Ala, LLB, 48; NYork Univ, LLM, 50, JSD, 57. **CAREER** Prin, Cross Keys Sch, Union, SC, 39-41 & Lorton Sch, Va, 41-42; mem fac, Law Sch, Emory Univ, 50-61, assoc dean, 54-61; prof law, Law Sch, Univ NC, 61-65; prof & dean sch law, Univ NMex, 65-71; prof law & dean sch law, 71-81, Sims Prof, Law Sch, Univ Ala, 81-, Mem exec comt, Asn Am Law Schs, 58; atty legal dept, Corn Prod Co, New York, 60-61. **MEMBERSHIPS** Am Bar Asn. **RESEARCH** Food and drug law; constitutional and property laws. **SELECTED PUBLICATIONS** Auth, Untitled--Comment, Natural Resources Jour, Vol 0036, 96. **CONTACT ADDRESS** Sch Law, Univ of New Mexico, Albuquerque, Albuquerque, NM 87131.

CHRYSSAVGIS, JOHN
PERSONAL Born 04/01/1958, Sydney, Australia, m, 1984, 2 children **DISCIPLINE** THEOLOGY **EDUCATION** Greek Conserv Music, Dipl Byz Mus, 79; Univ Oxford, DPhil, 83; Univ Athens, Lic Th, 80. **CAREER** Lectr, 86-95, Univ Sydney; sub-dean, 85-95, St Andrew's Theol Col, Sydney; acting dean, 97-98, Hellenic Col, Holy Cross; prof, 95-, Holy Cross Sch Theol. **MEMBERSHIPS** N Amer Patristics Soc; Int Relig & Sci Comm. **RESEARCH** Spirituality; environ; ascetic theol. **SELECTED PUBLICATIONS** Auth, Fire and Light, 87; auth, Ascent to Heaven, 89; auth, Repentance and Confession, 90; auth, The Desert is Alive, 91; auth, Love, Sexuality, Marriage, 95; auth, The Way of the Fathers, 98; auth, Beyond the Shattered Image, 99; auth, Soul Mending: the art of spiritual disectiion, 00. **CONTACT ADDRESS** 50 Goddard Ave, Brookline, MA 02445. **EMAIL** JChryisavg@aol.com

CHUANG, RUEYLING
DISCIPLINE WORLD RELIGIONS **EDUCATION** Tamkang Univ, BA, 87; CA State Univ , MA, 92; OH Univ, PhD, 92. **CAREER** Tchg Asst, CA State Univ; Grad Tchg Assoc, OH Univ; Asst prof, St John's Univ,95-. **HONORS AND AWARDS** MacPherson Grant, Service Learning Grant; Fac Develop Grant; Barry Spiker Awd; John Houk Res Grant; Ohio Univ Sch Interpersonal Comm Int Res Grant; John Houk Memorial Grant; Tish & Ray Wagner Int Stud Sch; Int Lion's Club Fel; I-Lan County Government Outstanding Student Awd. **MEMBERSHIPS** Asn for Chinese Comm Studies; Chinese Comm Asn; Central States Comm Asn; Eastern Comm Asn; Int Comm Asn; Interpersonal Network Personal Relationships; Speech Comm Asn; Western States Comm Asn. **SELECTED PUBLICATIONS** Coauth, Die Partei und Wahl, Central Books, 87; Das Theater, Central Books, 87; Gender and ethnicity influences on student attitudes toward speech restrictions, political correctness, and educational models, Southern Ill Univ Press, 96; Auth, Economic prosperity or environmental protection comes first?: An examination of Taiwanese (anti)environmental rhetoric, World Col Journalism & Comm Jour Hum; Coauth, Global versus local advertising in Taiwan, Gazette, 97. **CONTACT ADDRESS** St. John's Univ, Collegeville, MN 56321-7155. **EMAIL** rchuang@csbsju.edu

CHUNG, BONGKIL
PERSONAL Born 05/20/1936, Korea, m, 1975, 2 children **DISCIPLINE** PHILOSOPHY **EDUCATION** Mich State Univ, PhD, 79. **CAREER** Visiting asst prof, Fla Intl Univ, 79-80; lectr, Towson State Univ, 80-81; asst prof, Fla Intl Univ, 81-86; assoc prof, Fla Intl Univ, 86-; prof, Fla Intl Univ, 99-. **MEMBERSHIPS** Amer Philos Asn; Intl Soc for Chinese Philos; Intl Soc for Asian and Comparative Philos. **RESEARCH** Buddhist philosophy; Metaphysics. **SELECTED PUBLICATIONS** Auth, Benefiance as the Moral Found in Won Buddhism, Jour of Chinese Philos, vol. 23, no. 2; auth, "The Relevance of Confucian Ethics," Jour of Chinese Philosophy, vol. 18, no. 2; auth, "Appearance and Reality in Chinese Mahayana Buddhist Metaphysics," Jour, Chinese Philosophy vol. 20, no. 1; auth, "Ultimate Reality and Meaning in Sot'aesan's Inwonism," Ultimate Reality and Meaning vol. 15, no. 1; auth, An Introduction to Won Buddhism, Iksan: Won'gwang Pr, 9; auth, The Dharma Words of Master Chongsan, Iksan: Won'gwang Pr, 00; auth, The Scriptures of Won Buddhism, Univ of Hawaii Pr, 02. **CONTACT ADDRESS** Philosophy Dept., Florida Intl Univ, Miami, FL 33199. **EMAIL** chungb@fiu.edu

CHUNG, CHAI-SIK
PERSONAL Born 07/14/1930, Wonju, Korea, m, 1962, 2 children **DISCIPLINE** SOCIAL ETHICS **EDUCATION** Yonsei Univ, M Th, 57; Harvard Univ, BD, 59; Boston Univ, PhD, 64. **CAREER** Waler G Muelder prof Social Ethics, Boston Univ, 90-; Koret vis prof, Univ Calif Berkeley, 76-78; vis scholar, Univ Calif Berkeley, 74; prof Sociol, Yonsei Univ, 83-87; prof & chair Sociol, Heidelberg Col, 72-80; assoc prof Sociol, Heidelberg Col, 69-72; asst prof, Boston Univ, 66-69; asst prof, Bethany Col, 64-66; instr, Emory Univ, 62-63. **MEMBERSHIPS** Amer Acad Relig; Assoc Asian Studies; Soc Christian Ethics. **RESEARCH** Ethics and Modernization and Globalization in East Asia and Korea. **SELECTED PUBLICATIONS** Auth, Religion and Social Change, Yonsei Univ, 82; coauth, Modern Science and Ethics, Minumsa, 88; auth, Consciousness and History: Korean Cultural Tradition and Social Change, Ilchogak, 91; auth, A Korean Confucian Encounter with the Modern World: Yi Hang-no and the West, Univ of Calif, Berkeley, 95; auth, Korea: The Encounter Between the Gospel and Neo-Confucian Culture, World Council of Churches, 97. **CONTACT ADDRESS** School of Theology, Boston Univ, 19 Brook St, Sherborn, MA 01770. **EMAIL** Sikchung@yahoo.com

CHURCH, JENNIFER
DISCIPLINE PHILOSOPHY **EDUCATION** Macalester Col, BA, 76; Oxford Univ, BPhil, 77; Univ Mich, MA, 77; PhD, 82. **CAREER** Asst prof to prof, Vassar Col, 82-. **HONORS AND AWARDS** Rackham Fel, Univ of Mich, 81; Fel, Sloan Prog, Univ of Chicago, 82; Mellon Grant, 90; NEH Fel, 91-92; Fel, Rockefeller Ctr, Italy, 92. **MEMBERSHIPS** Am Philos Assoc; European Soc for Philos and Psychol; Soc for Women in Philos. **SELECTED PUBLICATIONS** Auth, "Reasonable Irrationality", Mind 96.3 (87): 354-366; auth, "Judgment, Self-Consciousness, and Object Independence", Am Philos Quarterly 27.1, (90): 51-61; auth, "L'emotion et l'interiorisation des actions", in Raisons Pratiques 6: La Coleur des pensees, eds P. Paperman and R. Ogien (Editions de l"ecole des Hautes Etiudes en Sci Soc, (Paris, 95): 219-236; auth, "Ownership and the Body", in Feminist Rethink the Self, ed Diana Meyers, Westview Pr, (97): 85-104; auth, "Two Sorts of Consciousness?", Commun and Cognition 31.1 (98): 57-72; rev, of "Ethics and the Discovery of the Unconscious" by John Riker, Ethics, 99; rev, "Consciousness in Action" by Susan Hurley, Philos Rev, (forthcoming); coauth, "Opening the Gap on Depression: From Monotony to Meaning", Psychoanalytic Rev (forthcoming); auth "The Subjective Side of Negation" Nous, (forthcoming). **CONTACT ADDRESS** Dept Philos, Vassar Col, Box 419, Poughkeepsie, NY 12604. **EMAIL** church@vassar.edu

CHURCHILL, JOHN HUGH
PERSONAL Born 04/01/1949, Hector, AR, m, 1972, 3 children **DISCIPLINE** PHILOSOPHY OF RELIGION **EDUCATION** Southwestern at Memphis, BA, 71; Oxford Univ, BA, 73, MA, 80; Yale Univ, MA, 75, MPhil, 76, PhD(relig studies), 78. **CAREER** Asst Am secy, Rhodes Scholar Trust, 74-77; asst prof, 77-82, Assoc Prof Philos & Chmn, Dept of Philos, Hendrix Col, 82-84; VPres, Academic Affairs, Dean, Prof Philos, Hendrix Col, 84-. **HONORS AND AWARDS** Rhodes Scholarship **MEMBERSHIPS** Soc Philos, Relig; Am Asn Rhodes Scholars. **RESEARCH** Wittgenstein and philosophy of religion; the logic of ethical argument. **SELECTED PUBLICATIONS** Auth, many articles on Wittgenstein, philosophy of religion, and liberal arts. **CONTACT ADDRESS** Office of the Dean, Hendrix Col, 1600 Washington Ave, Conway, AR 72032-3080. **EMAIL** churchill@hendrix.edu

CHURCHILL, MARY
DISCIPLINE RELIGIOUS STUDIES **EDUCATION** Univ Calif Santa Barbara, PhD. **CAREER** Asst prof. **RESEARCH** Native American religious traditions; women and religion; cultural studies. **SELECTED PUBLICATIONS** Auth, Balance and Synthesis: Toward a Dialogical Interpretation of Cherokee Women's Literature. **CONTACT ADDRESS** Religious Studies Dept, Univ of Colorado, Boulder, Boulder, CO 80309. **EMAIL** Mary.Churchill@Colorado.edu

CHURCHLAND, PAUL M.
DISCIPLINE PHILOSOPHY **EDUCATION** Univ Pittsburgh, PhD, 69. **CAREER** Instr, Univ Toronto; Univ Manitoba; Inst Adv Stud, Princeton; Prof, Philos, Univ Calif, San Diego. **RESEARCH** Artificial intelligence and cognitive neurobiology, epistemology, and perception. **SELECTED PUBLICATIONS** Auth, "A Feedforward Network for Fast Stereo Vision with Movable Fusion Plane," Android Epistemology: Human and Machine Cognition, AAAI Press/MIT Press, 94; The Engine of Reason, The Seat of the Soul: A Philosophical Journey into the Brain, MIT Press, 95; "The Neural Representation of Social Reality," Mind and Morals, The MIT Press, 95. **CONTACT ADDRESS** Dept of Philos, Univ of California, San Diego, 9500 Gilman Dr, La Jolla, CA 92093.

CHYET, STANLEY F.
PERSONAL Born Boston, MA, m, 1956, 2 children **DISCIPLINE** AMERICAN JEWISH HISTORY **EDUCATION** Brandeis, BA, 52 Univ; Hebrew Union Col, PhD, 60. **CAREER** Prof; ordained, Rabbi, HUC-JIR, Cincinnati, 57; fac, HUC-JIR, Cincinnati, 60-; fac, HUC-JIR, Los Angeles, 76-. **RESEARCH** Contemp. Hist./Lit. **SELECTED PUBLICATIONS** Pub(s), Amer Jewish biographies, history and literature/translations of 20th Century Israeli Poetry. **CONTACT ADDRESS** Hebrew Union College-Jewish Institute Of Religion, Univ of So California, 3077 University Ave., Los Angeles, CA 90007. **EMAIL** gernbear@aol.com

CIMBALA, STEPHEN J.
PERSONAL m, 2 children **DISCIPLINE** POLITICAL SCIENCE **EDUCATION** Penn State Univ, BA, 65; Univ Wisconsin, MA, 67; PhD, 69. **CAREER** Asst prof, SUNY, Stony Brook, 69-73; assoc prof, Penn State Univ, 73-86; prof, 86-. **HONORS AND AWARDS** Milton S Eisenhower Dist Teach Awd; ACDA Consult; US Dept St, Arms Control, Consult; Omicron Delta Kappa; Incl, 2000 Outstand Schls. **RESEARCH** International politics and foreign policy; defense and security studies; arms control; peace operations; conflict termination and information warfare. **SELECTED PUBLICATIONS** Ed, Mysteries of the Cold War, Ashgate Pub (Aldershot, Eng), 99; auth, Collective Insecurity: U.S. Defense Policy and the New World Disorder, Greenwood Press (Westport, CT), 95; auth, The Politics of Warfare: The Great Powers in the Twentieth Century, Penn State Press (Univ Park, PA), 97; auth, Coercive Military Strategy, Tex AM Univ Press (College Stn, TX), 98; auth, The Past and Future of Nuclear Deterrence, Praeger Pub (Westport, CT), 98; auth, "Information Warfare and Nuclear Conflict Termination," Euro Secur 7 (98): 69-90; auth, "Small Wars and Operations Other Than War: Russia in Search of Doctrine," Low Intensity Conflict Law Enforc 7 (98): 69-95; auth, "Nuclear Deterrence in the Information Age," NATIV: J Polit Arts 11 (98): 33-43; auth, The Cuban Missile Crisis," J Manage Hist 5 (99): 199-222; auth, "Nuclear Weapons Policies," Encycl Violence Peace and Conflict V2 (NY: Academic Press, 99): 591-605; auth, "Accidental/Inadvertent Nuclear War and Information Warfare," Armed Forces Soc 25 (99): 653-675; auth, "Nuclear Crisis Management and Information Warfare," Parameters: U.S. Army War Coll Ouart (99): 117-128. **CONTACT ADDRESS** Dept Political Science, Pennsylvania State Univ, Delaware County, 118 Vairo Library, Media, PA 19063. **EMAIL** SJC@PSU.EDU

CIOFFI-REVILLA, CLAUDIO
PERSONAL Born 05/07/1951, La Habana, Cuba, m, 1973 **DISCIPLINE** POLITICAL SCIENCE **EDUCATION** Inst Patria, Mex, BS, 69; SUNY, PhD, 79. **SELECTED PUBLICATIONS** Auth, Politics and Uncertainty, Cambridge Univ Press, 98. **CONTACT ADDRESS** Dep Polit Sci, Univ of Colorado, Boulder, Dept Polit Sci, CB 333, Boulder, CO 80309-0333. **EMAIL** Cioffi@colorado.edu

CIORRA, ANTHONY J.
PERSONAL Born 10/11/1946, Elizabeth, NJ, s **DISCIPLINE** RELIGIOUS STUDIES **EDUCATION** Seton Hall, MA, 78, Mdiv, 95; St Bonanenture, MA, 84; Fordham, PhD, 91. **CAREER** Assoc prof of theology, dir, Ctr for Theology and Spiritual Development. **HONORS AND AWARDS** Pro Ecclesia et Pontifice, 98. **MEMBERSHIPS** Catholic Theological Society of Amer; Amer Acad of Relig. **RESEARCH** History of theology; relationships of theology and psychology. **SELECTED PUBLICATIONS** Auth, Everyday Mysticism, Crossroad, 95; auth, Moral Formation in the parish, 98. **CONTACT ADDRESS** Col of Saint Elizabeth, 2 Convent Rd, Morristown, NJ 07960. **EMAIL** azambar@aol.com

CITRON, HENRY
PERSONAL Born 01/15/1937, Philadelphia, PA, m, 1963, 2 children **DISCIPLINE** HISTORY, POLITICAL SCIENCE **EDUCATION** Temple Univ, BA, 60, MA, 61, NYork Univ, PhD, 76. **CAREER** Substitute teacher, Philadelphia Pub Sch, 60-61; instr hist, Moravian Col, Bethlehem, Pa, 61-63; teacher social studies, Glen Cove High Sch, Glen Cove, NY, 63-65; dean students & group leader hist dept, Pa State Univ, Monaca, 65-68; prof hist & chemn dept Hist & Polit Sci, County Col Morris, 68-; asst presiding partner, Oglethorpe Group Holdings. **MEMBERSHIPS** AHA, Community Col Social Sci Asn: Eastern Community Col Social Sci Asn. **RESEARCH** Study of the arguments of interest groups which opposed federal aid to education from 1949-1965. **SELECTED PUBLICATIONS** Auth: Some recent discoveries at the Ohioview Archaeological Site, Ohio Archaeologist, 2/66; The Discovery of the Bakery at Old Economy, Pa Hist Comn, 68; Technology and New Teaching Techniques, Community Col Social Sci Conf, Dallas, 11/74; The End of History, Eastern Community Col Social Sci Conf, Princeton, 75; Search for the Czar: Russian Oral History, Kentucky Hist Comn, Frankfort, 3/76; "The American Reaction to the Boxer Rebellion," Community College Social Science Review, winter 76. **CONTACT ADDRESS** County Col of Morris, 214 Center Grove Rd, Randolph, NJ 07869-2086. **EMAIL** hcitron@ccm.edu

CIULLA, JOANNE B.
PERSONAL Born 06/16/1952, Rochester, NY, m, 1990 **DISCIPLINE** PHILOSOPHY **EDUCATION** Univ Maryland, BA, 73; Univ Delaware, MA, 75; Temple Univ, PhD, 85. **CAREER** Harvard Post-Doctoral fel Bus & Ethics, Harvard Univ Grad School Bus Admin, 84-86; vis scholar, Oxford Univ, 89; sr fel, Wharton School Univ Penn, 86-91; prof, Coston Family Chr Leadership & Ethics, Jepson School Leadership Studies, Univ Richmond, 91-; UNESCO ch in Leadership Stud, UN Univ, 99-00. **MEMBERSHIPS** Acad Mgt; Am Philos Asn; Asn Practical & Prof Ethics; Int Soc Bus, Econ & Ethics; Europ Bus Ethics Network; Soc Bus Ethics. **RESEARCH** Leadership studies; business ethics; philosophy of work. **SELECTED PUBLICATIONS** Auth, Casuistry and the Case for Business Ethics, Bus Ethics and Hum, Oxford Univ Press, 94; Leadership Ethics: Mapping the Territory, & Leadership Ethics: A Starter Kit and Annotated Bibliography, The Bus Ethics Quart, 95; Ethics nd Critical Thinking in Leadership Education, The Jour of Leadership Studies, 96; Business Leadership and Moral Imagination in the Twenty-First Century, Moral Values: The Challenge of the Twenty-First Century, Univ Texas Press, 96; Ethics, Chaos and the Demand for Good Leaders, Teaching Leadership: Essays in Theory and Practice, Peter Lang Publ, 96; Meaningful Work, Blackwell Encyclo Bus Ethics, Oxford, 97; Fantasy, Wishful Thinking and Truth, The Bus Ethics Quart, 98; Information, Trust, and the Ethics of Business Leaders, Int Bus Ethics: Challenges and Approaches, Univ Notre Dame & Hong Kong Univ Press, 98; ed, Ethics, The Heart of Leadership, Quorum Books, 98; auth, "The Importance of Leadership in Shaping Business Values," The Journal of Long Range Planning, 99; co-ed, "The Companion to Busienss Ethics," ed. W. Frederick & E. Petry, Basil Blackwell, 99; auth, "Getting to the Futre First," 10th The Business Ethics Quarterly," 00; auth, "The Working Life: The Promise and Betrayal of Modern Work, Times Books, 00; auth, "The Ethics of Leadership," Harcourt Brace, 01. **CONTACT ADDRESS** Jepson School of Leadership Studies, Univ of Richmond, Richmond, VA 23173. **EMAIL** jciulla@richmond.edu

CLADER, LINDA
PERSONAL Born 02/11/1946, Evanston, IL, m, 1991 **DISCIPLINE** CLASSICAL PHILOLOGY; HOMILETICS **EDUCATION** Carleton Col, AB, 68; Harvard Univ, AM, 70, PhD, 73; Church Divinity School of Pacific, M Div, 88. **CAREER** Instr to full prof Classical languages, Carleton Col, 72-90; asst to prof, homiletics, Church Divinity School Pacific, 91-. **HONORS AND AWARDS** Phi Beta Kappa, 68. **MEMBERSHIPS** AAR/SBL; Acad Homiletics; Am Philol Asn. **RESEARCH** Liturgical preaching; Myth; Homer; Metaphor. **SELECTED PUBLICATIONS** Auth, Helen: Evolution from Divine to Heroic in Greek Epic Tradition, Brill, 76; auth, Preaching the Liturgical Narratives: The Easter Vigil and the Language of Myth, Worship, 98. **CONTACT ADDRESS** Church Divinity Sch of the Pacific, 2451 Ridge Rd, Berkeley, CA 94709. **EMAIL** Lclader@cdsp.edu

CLADIS, MARK
PERSONAL Born 05/20/1958, Palo Alto, CA **DISCIPLINE** RELIGION **EDUCATION** Univ of California at Santa Barbara, BA, 80; Princeton Theological Seminary, MDiv, 83; Princeton Univ, MA, 85; PhD, 88. **CAREER** Assoc Prof and Chair, Vassar College, 95-; Asst Prof, Vassar College, 90-95, Visiting Asst Prof, Stanford Univ, 88-90. **HONORS AND AWARDS** Rockefeller Foundation, Bellagio Study Center; Fulbright Senior Research Awd, National Endowments for the Humanities Summer Stipend. **MEMBERSHIPS** American Academy of Religion; Assoc for the Sociology of Religion; Cladis-Kane Center for Speculative Inquiry. **RESEARCH** Philosophy of religion, social theory, environmental studies. **SELECTED PUBLICATIONS** Auth, Politics of the Heart: Rousseau, Religion, and the Relation between the Public and Private Life (New York: Oxford Univ Press) (forthcoming); auth, A Communitarian Defense of Liberalism: Durkheim and Contemporary Social Theory (Stanford: Univ Press, 1992, paperback edition, 94); auth, Emile Durkheim's "The Elementary Forms of the Religious Life", (Oxford: Oxford Univ Press, World's Classics Series, forthcoming); auth, "Durkheim and Foucault: Perspectives on Education and Punishment", (Oxford: Durkheim Press, 99); auth, "Love in Eighteenth Century French Moral Philosophy", Journal of Religious Ethics (forthcoming); auth, "Lessons from the Garden: Rousseau's Solitaires and the Limits of Liberalism," Interpretation 24 (97): 183-200; auth, "What Can We Hope for? Rousseau an Durkheim on Human Nature," Journal of the History of the Behavioral Sciences 32 (96): 456-472; auth, "Rousseau's Soteriology: Deliverance at the Crossroads," Religious Studies (Cambridge Univ Press) 32 (96):79-91; auth, "Tragedy and Theodicy: A Meditation on Rousseau and Moral Evil," Journal of Religion 75 (95): 181-99; auth, "Education, Virtue, and Democracy," Journal of Moral Education 24 (95): 37-52; auth, "Wittgenstein, Rawls, and conservatism," Philosophy Social Criticism 20 (94): 13-37; auth, "Rousseau and Durkheim: The Relation between the Public and the Private," Journal of Religious Ethics 21 (93): 1-25; auth, "Mild-Mannered Pragmatism and Religious Truth," Journal of the American Academy of Religion 60 (92): 19-33; auth, "Durkheim's Individual in Society: A Sacred Marriage?", Journal of the History of Ideas 53 (92): 71-90; auth, "Durkheim's Commnitarian Defense of Liberalism, " Soundings 72 (89): 275-95. **CONTACT ADDRESS** Dept Religion, Vassar Col, 124 Raymont Ave, P O Box 228, Poughkeepsie, NY 12604-0001. **EMAIL** macladis@vassar.edu

CLAPPER, GREG
PERSONAL Born 10/03/1951, Chicago, IL, m, 1973, 2 children **DISCIPLINE** RELIGION **EDUCATION** Carthage Col, BA; Univ Wis, MA; Garrett Evangel Theol Sem, MDiv; Emory Univ, PhD. **CAREER** Asst Prof to Assoc Prof, Westmar Col, 85-91; Sr Pastor, Trinity United Methodist Church, 91-94; Assoc Prof, Huntingdon Col, 94-98; Assoc Prof, Univ Indianapolis, 98-. **HONORS AND AWARDS** John Wesley Fel; Service of Excellence Awd, Westmar Col. **MEMBERSHIPS** Am Acad of Relig, Soc of John Wesley Fellows. **RESEARCH** Wesley Studies; Christian Spirituality. **SELECTED PUBLICATIONS** Auth, When the World Breaks Your Heart: Spiritual Ways of Living with Tragedy, Upper Room Books, 99; auth, As If the heart Mattered: A Wesleyan Spirituality, Upper room Books, 97; auth, John Wesley on Religious affections, Scarecrow Press, 89. **CONTACT ADDRESS** Dept Relig & Philos, Univ of Indianapolis, 1400 E Hanna Ave, Indianapolis, IN 46227-3630. **EMAIL** gclapper@vindy.edu

CLARK, AUSTEN
DISCIPLINE PHILOSOPHY **EDUCATION** Wesleyan Univ, BA, 75; Oxford Univ, PhD, 77. **CAREER** Res asst prof, Dartmouth Med Sch, 78-82; asst prof, Univ Tulsa, 83-86; assoc prof, Univ Tulsa, 87-94; prof, Univ of Conn, 94-. **HONORS AND AWARDS** Postdoc fel, Univ NC, 82-83. **MEMBERSHIPS** Mem, Amer Philos Assn; Philos of Sci Assn; Soc Philos Psychol. **RESEARCH** Sensory qualities, sensory representation, color vision, qualia. **SELECTED PUBLICATIONS** Auth, Psychological Models and Neural Mechanism: An Examination of Reductionism in Psychology, Oxford Univ Press, 80; auth, "Mice, Shrews, and Misrepresentation," Journal of Philosophy, 490 (6), (93): 290-310; auth, Sensory Qualities, Oxford Univ Press, 93; rev, of Martha Farah's Visual Agnosia, Philosophical Psychology, 7(1), (94): 126-29; auth, "Beliefs and Desires Incorporated," Journal of Philosophy, 91 (8), (94): 404-25; auth, "Contemporary Problems in the Philosophy of Perception," American Journal of Psychology, 107(4), (94): 613-22; auth, "True Theories, False Colors," Philosophy of Science, PSA Supplemental Issue, 63 (3), (96): 143-150; rev, of Robert Schwartz, Vision: variations on Some Berkeleian Themes, Philosophical Psychology, 9 (1), (96): 147-51; auth, "Three varieties of visual field," Philosophical Psychology, 9(4), (96): 477-96; auth, A Theory of Sentience, Oxford Univ Press, (forthcoming). **CONTACT ADDRESS** Dept of Philos, Univ of Connecticut, Storrs, 1266 Storrs Rd, Manchester Hall, Unit 2054, Storrs, CT 06269. **EMAIL** austen.clark@uconn.edu

CLARK, DAVID
PERSONAL Born 08/07/1943, Long Beach, CA, m, 1969, 1 child **DISCIPLINE** NEW TESTAMENT **EDUCATION** Univ Notre Dame, PhD. **CAREER** Prof; dir, Grad Stud Prog; leads workshops on the life & writings of C S Lewis; Ed of the Lamp Post, journal of the So Calif, C.S. Lewis Soc; Prof of New Testament & Greek. **MEMBERSHIPS** Soc of Biblical Lit; Catholic Biblical Soc; Evangelical Theological Soc; New York & So Calif CS Lewis Societies. **RESEARCH** Biblical Prophecy; life of Jesus; C.S. Lewis. **CONTACT ADDRESS** Dept of Relig, So California Col, 55 Fair Dr., Costa Mesa, CA 92626. **EMAIL** dclark@vanguard.edu

CLARK, DAVID S.
PERSONAL Born 11/24/1944, San Diego, CA, m, 1970, 5 children **DISCIPLINE** LAW **EDUCATION** Stanford Univ, AB, 66; JD, 69; JSM, 72. **CAREER** Asst Director, Studies in Law, Stanford Univ, 73-76; Asst Prof, La State Univ, 76-78; Assoc Prof to Prof, Univ Tulsa, 78-; Vis Prof, S Ill Univ, 87; vis Prof, Univ Colo, 89; Chair Intl and comparative Law, Loyola Univ, 96; Vis Prof, Univ Houston, 99. **HONORS AND AWARDS** Max Planck Gesellschoft Res Fel, 00, 94, 92; Fulbright Sen Scholar, 99; Alexander von Humboldt Sen Res Fel, 84-87; NEH Summer Humanities Scholar, 81. **MEMBERSHIPS** Am Coun of Learned Soc, Am Soc of Comparative Law, Am Journal of comparative Law, Intl Acad of comparative Law, am Soc for Legal Hist. **RESEARCH** Law and society; Comparative law; Legal History. **SELECTED PUBLICATIONS** Auth, The civil Law Tradition: Europe, Latin America, and East Asia, 94; auth, Introduction to the Law of the United States, 92; auth, comparative and Private International Law, 90; auth, Law and Social Change in Mediterranean Europe and Latin America, 79. **CONTACT ADDRESS** Col of Law, Univ of Tulsa, 3120 E 4th Place, Tulsa, OK 74104-2418. **EMAIL** david-clark@utulsa.edu

CLARK, DON
DISCIPLINE LAW **EDUCATION** Univ London, LLB, 62; Cambride Univ, LLM, 65. **CAREER** Prof, 62-00; retired. **RESEARCH** Ontractual remedies; judicial review. **SELECTED PUBLICATIONS** Auth, "Rethinking the Role of Specific Relief in the Contractual Setting," in Remedies: Issues and Perspectives, ed. Berryman (91); auth, "Recent Developments in the Law of Contracts," in 14 Advocate's Quarterly (93); auth, "Contingency Agreements," in Contracts: Cases and Materials 5th ed, ed. Boyle and Percy (94); coed, Self-Determination: International Perspectives, Macmillan, 96. **CONTACT ADDRESS** Col of Law, Univ of Saskatchewan, 15 Campus Dr, Saskatoon, SK, Canada S7N 5A6.

CLARK, GERARD J.
DISCIPLINE LAW **EDUCATION** Seton Hall Univ, BA, 66; Columbia Univ, JD; 69. **CAREER** Prof. **RESEARCH** Constitutional law; federal courts; professional responsibility. **SELECTED PUBLICATIONS** Auth, Kronman's the Lost Lawyer: A Celebration of the Oligopoly of the Elite Lawyer, 96; The Product of the General Court in 1993: Summary and Critique, 95. **CONTACT ADDRESS** Law School, Suffolk Univ, Beacon Hill, Boston, MA 02114. **EMAIL** gclark@acad.suffolk.edu

CLARK, J. MICHAEL
PERSONAL Born 09/02/1953, Morristown, TN **DISCIPLINE** RELIGIOUS STUDIES **EDUCATION** Emory & Henry Col, Emory, VA, BA, 75; Candler School of Theol, Emory Univ, Atlanta, M Div, 78; Graduate Inst of Liberal Arts, Emory Univ, Atlanta, PhD, 83. **CAREER** Instr, Science Talent Enrichment Prog, Emory Univ, summers 91-93; adjunct asst prof, Human and Natural Ecology Prog, Emory univ, 93-96, vis asst prof, 96; asst prof, Dept of Relig Studies, Agnes Scott Col, Decatur, GA, 97-; vis scholar, Iliff School of Theol, Univ of Denver, CO, 97; instr, Dept of English, GA State Univ, Atlanta, 84-, instr, Program in Relig Studies, 98-. **HONORS AND AWARDS** Am Academy of Relig res assistance grant, 87-88; Keynote speaker, Am Men's Studies Asn Annual Meeting, 97; Vis Scholar Appointment, Iliff School of Theology, 97. **MEMBERSHIPS** Am Academy of Relig, (87-; prog unit book series co-ed, 89-96; prog unit co-chair, 87-93); Soc of Christian Ethics (97-); Sheffield Academic Press (ed bd, 96-98); Journal of Men's Studies (assoc ed, 92-, special issue co-ed, 95-96). **RESEARCH** Ecology; sexual ethics; gender studies. **SELECTED PUBLICATIONS** Auth, A Place to Start: Toward an Unapologetic Gay Liberation Theology, Monument Press, 89; A Defiant Celebration: Theological Ethics and Gay Sexuality, Tangelwuld Press, 90; Masculine Socialization and Gay Liberation: A Conversation on the Work of James Nelson and Other Wise Friends, with Bob McNeir, The Liberal Press, 92; Beyond Our Ghettos: Gay Theology in Ecological Perspective, Pilgrim Press, 93; An Unbroken Circle: Ecotheology, Theodicy, and Ethics, Monument Press, 96; Defying the Darkness: Gay Theology in the Shadows, Pilgrim Press, 97; Doing the Work of Love: I Men's Studies at the Margins, J of Men's Studies 5 4, May 97; Doing the Work of Love: II An Extended Case Study, with Bob McNeir, J of Men's Studies 5 4, May 97; A Gay Man's Wish-List for the Future of Men's Studies in Religion, J of Men's Studies 7 2, winter 99; numerous other articles in refereed journals and series. **CONTACT ADDRESS** 585 Glenwood Pl SE, Atlanta, GA 30316. **EMAIL** jmclark@agnesscott.edu

CLARK, JACK LOWELL
PERSONAL Born 01/15/1929, Albert Lea, MN, m, 1954 **DISCIPLINE** RELIGION **EDUCATION** Gustavus Adolphus Col, AB, 52; Northwestern Lutheran Theol Sem, BD, 55; Univ Minn, MA, 57; Yale Univ, AM, 59; PhD(New Testament), 62. **CAREER** Asst Bible, Northwestern Lutheran Theol Sem, 55-57; from asst prof to assoc prof relig, 62-70, Prof Relig & Classics, Gustavus Adolphus Col, 70-, Assoc ed, Dialogue, 68-69. **MEMBERSHIPS** Am Acad Relig; Soc Bibl Lit; Soc Sci Studies Relig. **RESEARCH** Historical methodology in the study of primary religious documents; the concept of religious authority; the correlation between personality and religious stance. **CONTACT ADDRESS** Dept of Religion, Gustavus Adolphus Col, 800 W College Ave, Saint Peter, MN 56082-1498.

CLARK, KELLY JAMES
PERSONAL Born 03/03/1956, Muncie, IN, m, 1978, 3 children **DISCIPLINE** PHILOSOPHY **EDUCATION** Mich State Univ, BA, 78; Western KY Univ, MA, 80; Univ Notre Dame, MA, 82; PhD, 85. **CAREER** Asst prof, Gordon Col, 85-89; prof, Calvin Col, 89-. **MEMBERSHIPS** Am Philos Asn, Soc of Christian Philosophers, (Secretary-Tresurer). **RESEARCH** Philosophy of Religion, Social Philosophy, Ethics. **SELECTED PUBLICATIONS** Auth, Return to Reason, Eeardmans Publ Co., 90; ed, Our Knowledge of God: Essays on Natural and Philosophical Theology, Kluwer Acad Publ, 92; ed, Philosophers Who Believe, InterVarsity Press, 93; auth, When Faith Is Not Enough, Eeardmans Publ Co., 97; coauth, Five Views on Apologetics, Zondervan Publ Co., 00; auth, Reader in Philosophy of Religion, Broadview Press, 00; auth, Human Nature, Human Morality, Human Fulfillment. **CONTACT ADDRESS** Dept Philos, Calvin Col, 3201 Burton St SE, Grand Rapids, MI 49546-4301. **EMAIL** kclark@calvin.edu

CLARK, LEROY D.
PERSONAL Born 04/27/1934, New York, NY, m, 1993, 2 children **DISCIPLINE** LEGAL STUDIES **EDUCATION** City Col NY, BA, 56; Columbia Univ, Sc Law, LLB, 61. **CAREER** Staff Coun (Civil Rights Div) Atty Gen's Office State of NY, 61-62; Asst Coun, NAACP Legal Defense and Educ Fund Inc, 62-68; Arbitrator, Am Arbit Asn, Fed Mediation and Conciliation Serv, Permanent Panel: Gen Elec Co and Int Union of Electrical Radio and Machine Workers, 74-; Gen Coun, Equal Emply Opportunity Comn, 78-81; Prof, Cath Univ Law Sch, 81-; Consult to NYork State Judicial Comn on Minorities, 89-90; Personnel Appeals Board of the Gen Accounting Office, 92-97; Public Employees Relations Bd - DC, 97-. **HONORS AND AWARDS** Phi Beta Kappa, 56; Fel for Grad Study in Clinical Psychology, 56-58; ABA Cert of Merit for Distinguished Contribution to Public Understanding of Am Law, 75. **MEMBERSHIPS** Am Arbit Asn, Am Bar Asn, Soc of Am Law Teachers. **SELECTED PUBLICATIONS** Auth, The Grand Jury: The Use and Abuse of Political Power, Quadrangle Press NY Times, 75; auth, "Advice to Minority Students," in Looking at Law School, ed. Stephen Gillers (New Am Libr, 77); auth, "Reducing Firearms Availability: Constitutional Impediments to Effective Legislation and an Agenda for Research," in Firearms and Violence - Issues of Public Policy, ed. Kates and Kaplan (Ballinger Publ Co, 84); auth, "Drug Abuse in the Workplace: Arbitration in the Context of a National Solution of Decriminalization," in Arbitration 1987 - The Academy at Forty (BNA, 88); auth, "Ensuring Equal Opportunities in Employment Through Law," in Rethinking Employment Policy (Urban Inst Press, Wash DC, 89), chap 7; auth, "Review of 'The Law and Economics of Racial Discrimination in Employment' by David A. Strauss, " Georgetown Law J 79- 6 (91): 1695; auth, "Employment Discrimination Testing: Theories of Standing and a Reply to Professor Yelonsky, " Univ of Mich J of Law reform 28 -1 (94):1; auth, "A Critique of Professor Derrick A. Bell's Thesis of the Permanence of Racism and His Strategy of Confrontation," Denver Univ Law Rev 73-1 (95): 23; auth, "All Defendants, Rich and Poor, Should Get Appointed Counsel in Criminal Cases: The Route to True Equal Justice," 81 Marquette Univ Law Rev 47 (97); coauth, Employment Discrimination Law -- Cases and Materials, Michie Co, 4th ed, 97, 5th ed forthcoming. **CONTACT ADDRESS** Sch of Law, Catholic Univ of America, 620 Michigan Ave NE, Washington, DC 20064-0001. **EMAIL** clark@law.cua.edu

CLARK, MARY T.
PERSONAL Born Philadelphia, PA **DISCIPLINE** PHILOSOPHY **EDUCATION** Manhattanville Col, BA; Fordham Univ, PhD, 55. **CAREER** Prof, chr, Philos Dept, Manhattanville Col, 51-84; prof emer Manhattanville Col, 86-. **HONORS AND AWARDS** Interacial Justice Awd, 67; LHD, Villanova Univ, 77; LHD, Manhattanville Col, 84; NEH Fel, 84-85; Aquinas Medal, Am Cath Philos Asn, 88; Dist Alumna Awd, Manhattanville Col, 99. **MEMBERSHIPS** Am Philos Asn; Am Cath Philos Asn; Metaphysical Soc; Soc Medieval Renaissance Philos. **RESEARCH** Augustine of Hippo; freedom; person. **SELECTED PUBLICATIONS** Auth, Augustine, Philosopher of Freedom, 59; auth, Augustine, 94; ed, An Aquinas Reader, 88, rev, 00. **CONTACT ADDRESS** Philos Dept, Manhattanville Col, Purchase, NY 10577. **EMAIL** clarkm@mville.edu

CLARK, W. ROYCE
DISCIPLINE CONTEMPORARY RELIGIOUS THOUGHT **EDUCATION** Abilene Christian Univ, BA, 60, MA, 61; Univ Iowa, PhD, 73; Pepperdine Univ, JD, 85. **CAREER** Instr, Columbia Christian Col, 61-67; prof, 70-; vis prof, Pepperdine's

London prog, 89-90; assoc, Seaver Col, 90-92; vis prof, Pepperdine's Japan prog, 92. **HONORS AND AWARDS** Res grant, 86; spec serv award, Comm of Credentials, Calif, 93; Irvine fel, 93; awarded, 95-96; Tyler outstanding tchr yr, Seaver Col, 95-96. **MEMBERSHIPS** Mem, Am Acad Rel; N Am Paul Tillich Soc; Soc Bibl Lit; Soc Buddhist-Christian Studies. **SELECTED PUBLICATIONS** Auth, The Supreme Court and the Legal Status of Religious Studies in Public Higher Education, Beyond the Classics: Essays in Religious Studies and Liberal Education, Scholars Press, 90; The Fourth Gospel and Christology in Modern Dogmatic and Systematic Theology, Johannine Studies: Essays in honor of Frank Pack, Pepperdine UP, 89. **CONTACT ADDRESS** Dept of Relig, Pepperdine Univ, 24255 Pacific Coast Hwy, Malibu, CA 90263. **EMAIL** rclark@pepperdine.edu

CLARKE, ANNE-MARIE
PERSONAL Born St. Louis, MO, m, 1979 **DISCIPLINE** LAW **EDUCATION** Forest Park Comm Coll, 1967-68; Northwest MO State Univ, BA, 1970; St Louis Univ School of Law, JD, 1973. **CAREER** Arthur D Little Inc, researcher, 74-94; Northeast Utilities, asst corp sec, 74-77; Bi-State Develop Agency, staff counsel, 77-79; Self Employed, private practice of law, 80-92; City of St Louis, hearing officer, family court, 86-. **HONORS AND AWARDS** Natl Council of Negro Women Bertha Black Rhoda Section, Achievement Awd, 1990; Natl Organization of Blacks in Law Enforcement (NOBLE), Achievement Awd, 1993; MO Legislative Black Caucus, Jordan-McNeal Awd, 1994. **MEMBERSHIPS** The MO Bar, bd of governors, 1986-90, 1991-95; Mound City Bar Assn, pris, 1981-83; Confluence St Louis, chair, prevention of juvenile crime task force, 1993; Delta Sigma Theta Sorority, Inc; The Bar Plan Mutual Insurance Co., director, 1986-. **SELECTED PUBLICATIONS** The History of the Black Bar, St Louis bar Journal, Spring 1984. **CONTACT ADDRESS** Bd of Police Commissioners, St Louis Police Dept, 1200 Clark, Saint Louis, MO 63103.

CLARKE, BOWMAN LAFAYETTE
PERSONAL Born 09/19/1927, Meridian, MS **DISCIPLINE** PHILOSOPHY **EDUCATION** Millsaps Col, AB, 48; Emory Univ, BD, 51, MA, 52, PhD, 61; Univ Miss, MA, 57. **CAREER** Instr philos, Univ the South, 59-60; res assoc applied logic, Emory Univ, 60-61; from asst prof to assoc prof, 61-67, head dept philos & relig, 72-79, Prof Philos, Univ GA, 67-, Danforth Found grant, 57-58; E L Cabot Trust Fund grant, 60-61; ed, Int J Philos Relig. **MEMBERSHIPS** Southern Soc Philos & Psychol; Soc Philos Relig (pres, 73-74); Am Philos Asn; Am Acad Relig; Metaphys Soc Am. **RESEARCH** Logic and metaphysics. **SELECTED PUBLICATIONS** Auth, 2 Process Views of God, Intl Jour Philos Rel, Vol 0038, 95. **CONTACT ADDRESS** Dept of Philos, Univ of Georgia, Athens, GA 30605.

CLARKE, JAMES W.
PERSONAL Born 02/16/1937, Elizabeth, PA, m, 1983, 2 children **DISCIPLINE** POLITICAL SCIENCE **EDUCATION** Washington and Jefferson Col, BA, 62; Pennsylvania State Univ, MA, 64, PhD, 68. **CAREER** Asst and assoc prof, Florida State Univ, 67-71; prof, Univ Arizona, 71- . **HONORS AND AWARDS** Burlington Northern Found Award for Excellence in Tchg, 87; Fulbright scholar, 99; Univ Distinguished Prof, 00. **MEMBERSHIPS** Am Polit Sci Asn. **RESEARCH** Race and public policy; violent crime and political order. **SELECTED PUBLICATIONS** Auth, American Assassins: The Darker Side of Politics, Princeton, 82; auth, Last Rampage: The Escape of Gary Tison, Houghton Mifflin, 88, updated ed, Univ Arizona, 99; auth, On Being Mad or Merely Angry: John W. Hinckley, Jr. and Other Dangerous People, Princeton, 90; auth, The Lineaments of Wrath: Race, Violent Crime, and American Culture, Transaction, 98, paperback, 01. **CONTACT ADDRESS** Univ of Arizona, 313 Social Sciences Bldg, Tucson, AZ 85721. **EMAIL** jclarke@u.arizona.edu

CLARKE, MURRAY
DISCIPLINE PHILOSOPHY **EDUCATION** W Ontario Univ, PhD. **CAREER** Prof, Concordia Univ; ch. **RESEARCH** Cognitive science and philosophy of science; implications of evolutionary psychology, empirrical psychology, and evolutionary theory for issues in naturalized epistemology and naturalized phiosophy of science. **SELECTED PUBLICATIONS** Auth, Doxastic Voluntarism and Forced Belief, Philos Stud Volume 50, 86; Epistemic Norms and Evolutionary Success, Synthese, Volume 85, 86; Natural Selection and Indexical Representation, Logic and Philosophy of Science in Quebec, Volume II, Boston Stud in the Philos of Sci, 96; "Darwinian Algorithms and Indexical Representation," Philos of Sci, Volume 63, Number 1, 96. **CONTACT ADDRESS** Dept of Philos, Concordia Univ, Montreal, 1455 de Maisonneuve W, Montreal, QC, Canada H3G 1M8. **EMAIL** murc@vax2.concordia.ca

CLARKE, WILLIAM NORRIS
PERSONAL Born 06/01/1915, New York, NY **DISCIPLINE** PHILOSOPHY **EDUCATION** Col St Louis, England, PhL, 39; Fordham Univ, MA, 40; Woodstock Col, STL, 46; Cath Univ Louvain, Belg, PhD, 49. **CAREER** From instr to asst prof philos, Woodstock Col, 49-52; asst prof, Bellarmine Col, 52-55; from asst prof to assoc prof, 55-67, Prof Philos, Fordham Univ, 67-85, Prof Emeritus, 85-; Ed, Int Philos Quart, 61-85. **HONORS AND AWARDS** Aquinas Medal, Amer Cath Philos Asn, 80; H. Morary Dr of Laws, Villanova Univ, 82; Dr Hum, Wheeling Jesuit Col, 93; lhd, villanova univ, 82. **MEMBERSHIPS** Am Philos Asn; Metaphys Soc Am (pres, 67-68); Am Cath Philos Asn (pres, 68-69). **RESEARCH** Metaphysics, especially mediaeval; St Thomas Aquinas; Plotinus. **SELECTED PUBLICATIONS** Auth, Person and Being, Marquette Univ Press, 93; auth, Explorations in Metaphysics, Univ of Notre Dame Press, 94; auth, The One and the Many: A Contempary Thomistic Metaphisics, Univ of Notre Dame Press, 00. **CONTACT ADDRESS** Fordham Univ, Loyola Hall, Bronx, NY 10458.

CLAUDE, RICHARD P.
PERSONAL Born 05/20/1934, St. Paul, MN, 3 children **DISCIPLINE** POLITICAL SCIENCE,CONSTITUTIONAL LAW **EDUCATION** Univ of St. Thomas, BA, 56; Fla State Univ, BS,Govt, 60; Univ of Va, PhD, Polit Sci, 65. **CAREER** Instr, Vassar Col, Polit Sci, 62-64; vis asst prof, govt, William and Mary Col 64-65; asst prof, Univ of Md, 65-68; assoc prof, Univ of Md, 68-78; prof, Univ of Md, 78-93; Prof Emer, Univ of MD, 93-. **HONORS AND AWARDS** Pulitzer Prize Nomination, 71; Best Acad Book, 90. **RESEARCH** Human rights education **SELECTED PUBLICATIONS** auth, The Supreme Court and the Electoral Process, Johns Hopkins Univ Pr, 70; prin auth & ed, "Comparative Human Rights," Johns Hopkins Univ Pr, 78; coauth, Health Professionals and Human Rights in the philippines, Am Asn for the Advan of Sci, 87; co-ed, Human Rights in the World Community: Issues and Action, Univ Of Penn Pr, 89; co-ed, Human Rights and Statistics, Getting the Record Straight, Univ of Penn Pr, 91; auth, Human Rights Education in the Philippines, Kalikasan Pr, 92; coauth, "Medicine Under Siege: Violations of Medical Neutrality in the Former Yugoslavia, 1991-1995," Physicians for Human Rights, 96; auth, Educating for Human Rights: The Philippines and Beyond, Univ of Philippines Pr, 96; co-ed, Human Rights for the 21st Century, Univ of Pa Pr, 97; auth, The Bells of Freedom, with Resource Materials for Facilitators of Non-Formal Education and 24 Human Rights Echo Sessions, Action Prof Asn, 95. **CONTACT ADDRESS** Dept of Govt and Polit, Univ of Maryland, Col Park, College Park, MD 20742. **EMAIL** profclaude@aol.com

CLAYTON, JAMES L.
PERSONAL Born 07/28/1931, Salt Lake City, UT, m, 1957, 3 children **DISCIPLINE** ECONOMIC & LEGAL HISTORY **EDUCATION** Univ Utah, BA, 58; Cornell Univ, PhD(Econ Hist), 64. **CAREER** Case officer, Cent Intel Agency, 57-58; instr Hist, Hamilton Col, 62-63; from instr to assoc prof, 63-71, dir honors prog, 67-70, prof Hist, Univ Utah, 71-, dean, grad school, 78-86; provost, 86-90; vis asst prof, Dartmouth Col, 66-67; mem, Coun Grad Schs, US, 78-84. **HONORS AND AWARDS** Distinguished Teaching Awd, Univ Utah, 66; Minn Hist Soc Solon J Buck Prize, 67; Distinguished Hon Prof, Univ Utah, 77; Univ Prof, 77-78; Phi Kappa Phi; Phi Beta Kappa; Vis Fel, Cambridge Univ, 02. **MEMBERSHIPS** Western Asn Grad Schs (pres, 82); GRE Board, 82-87. **RESEARCH** Economic and social impact of war since 1945; Economic Consequence of Debt; Bear Markets in G7 Natcous; American economic history; legal history. **SELECTED PUBLICATIONS** Coauth, American Civilization: A Documentary History, W C Brown, 66; auth, The growth and economic significance of the American fur trade, Minn Hist, Winter 66; ed, The Economic Impact of the Cold War, In: Forces in Am Growth series, Harcourt, 70; auth, The fiscal cost of the Cold War to the United States: the first 25 years, 1947-1971, Western Polit Quart, 9/72; The fiscal limits of the warfare-welfare state, Western Polit Quart, 76; A comparison of defense and welfare spending in the US and the UK, J Biol & Social Welfare, 77; A Farewell to the Welfare State, Univ Utah Press, 76; Does Defense Beggar Welfare?, Nat Strategy Info Ctr, 79; auth, The Global Debt Boub, M.E. Sharpe, 00. **CONTACT ADDRESS** Univ of Utah, 217 Carlson Hall, Salt Lake City, UT 84112-0311. **EMAIL** Jclayton@lec.hum.utah.edu

CLAYTON, MARCUS
PERSONAL Born 06/14/1931, Atlanta, GA, m, 1956, 4 children **DISCIPLINE** PHILOSOPHY **EDUCATION** Emory Univ, AB, 55, LLB, 56, PhD(philos), 67. **CAREER** From asst prof to assoc prof philos, 59-71, Prof Philos, Paine Col, 71- **MEMBERSHIPS** Metaphys Soc Am; Soc Ancient Greek Philos; Hegel Soc Am; Am Philos Asn. **RESEARCH** Contemporary epistemology and metaphysics; ancient philosophy; early modern philosophy. **SELECTED PUBLICATIONS** Contribr, A defense of individuals, Paine Col J, 71; auth, "Blanchard's Theory of Universals," contribr, Philosophy of Brand Blanchard; Library of Living Philosophers Series. **CONTACT ADDRESS** Dept of Philosophy, Paine Col, 1235 15th St, Augusta, GA 30901-3182.

CLAYTON, PHILIP
PERSONAL Born 04/03/1956, Berkeley, CA, m, 1981, 2 children **DISCIPLINE** PHILOSOPHICAL THEOLOGY; RELIGION & SCIENCE; MODERN RELIGIOUS THOUGHT **EDUCATION** Westmont Col, BA, 78; Fuller Theolog Sem, MA, 80; Ludwig-Maximilians-Universitat, Munich, MA, 81-83; Yale Univ, MA, 84; Yale Univ, M.Phil, 85; Yale Univ, PhD, 86. **CAREER** Sonoma St Univ, 91-; Williams Col, 86-91; vis asst prof, Haverford Col, 86 **HONORS AND AWARDS** CSU Grant, 97; Templeton Grant, 97; Univ Merit Awd, 96; Univ Best Prof, 95; Alexander von Humboldt Prof, Ludwig-Maximilians-Universitat, 94-95; Fulbright Senior Res Fel, Univ Munich, 90-91. **MEMBERSHIPS** Amer Acad Relig; Amer Philos Assoc; Center for Theolog & Natural Sci; Pacific Coast Theolog Soc; Leibniz Soc N Amer; Metaphysical Soc Amer; Soc Study of Process Philos. **SELECTED PUBLICATIONS** Beyond Apologetics: Integrating Scientific Results and Religious Explanations, Fortress Pr, forthcoming; Das Gottesproblem. Moderne Losungsversuche, forthcoming; auth, God and Contemporary Science, Edinburgh Univ Press, 97; auth, Infinite and Perfect? The Problem of God in Modern Thought, Eerdmans Publ, 00. **CONTACT ADDRESS** Dept of Philosophy, Sonoma State Univ, Rohnert Park, CA 94928. **EMAIL** claytonp@sonoma.edu

CLEARY, JOHN J.
PERSONAL Born 06/18/1949, County Mayo, Ireland, m, 1973 **DISCIPLINE** PHILOSOPHY **EDUCATION** Univ Col Dublin, BA, 72, MA, 75; Boston Univ, PhD, 82. **CAREER** Boston Col, Asst prof, assoc prof, prof, 81-; sr lectr, NUI Maynooth, 96-. **HONORS AND AWARDS** Elected Member Royal Irish Acad, NEH fel, Alexander von Humbolt fel. **MEMBERSHIPS** APA, BACAP, IHV; RIA. **RESEARCH** Ancient philosophy; Plato, Aristotle, Proclus; hist and philosophy of science; ancient and modern political theory. **SELECTED PUBLICATIONS** Ed, On the terminology of 'Abstraction' in Aristotle', Phronesis 30, (85); "Science, Universals and Reality," Ancient Philosophy 7, (87); auth, Aristotle on the many Senses of Priority, Carbondale: S IL Univ Press, 88; auth, Working Through Puzzles with Aristotle, Jour Neoplatonic Stud, 93; ed, "Phainomena in Aristotle's Methodology," International Journal of Philosophical Studies 2, (94); ed, The Perennial Tradition of Neoplatonism, Louvain, 97; ed, "Powers that be": The Concept of Potency in Plato and Aristotle," Methexis 11, (98); ed, Traditions of Platonism, London, 99; auth, The Role of Theology in Plato's Laws, Plato's Laws and its Historical Significance, Sankt Augustin, (00); auth, Zurueck zu den Texten selbst, Hermeneutisch Wege, Tuebingen, (00); auth, Proclus's Philosophy of Mathematics, La Philosophie des Mathematique de l'Antiquite tardive, Fribourg, (00); auth, Mathematical Methods in Proclus Theology, Proclus et la Theologie Platonicienne, Leuven, (00); ed, "El papel de las matematicas en la teologia de Proclo," Annuario Filosofico 33, (00). **CONTACT ADDRESS** Dept of Philosophy, Boston Col, Chestnut Hill, Chestnut Hill, MA 02467. **EMAIL** john.cleary@may.ie

CLEGG, JERRY STEPHEN
PERSONAL Born 09/29/1933, Heber City, UT, m, 1960, 3 children **DISCIPLINE** PHILOSOPHY **EDUCATION** Univ Wash, PhD, 62. **CAREER** From instr to assoc prof, 62-76, prof Philos, Mills Col, 76-. **RESEARCH** Aesthetics; epistemology; history of philosophy. **SELECTED PUBLICATIONS** Auth, The Structure of Plato's Philosophy, Bucknell Univ, 77; On Genius: Affirmation and Denial from Schopenhauaz to Wittgenstein, Peter Lang, 94. **CONTACT ADDRESS** Dept of Philosophy, Mills Col, 5000 MacArthur Blvd, Oakland, CA 94613-1000. **EMAIL** cleggj@mills.edu

CLEGG, LEGRAND H., II
PERSONAL Born 06/29/1944, Los Angeles, CA **DISCIPLINE** LAW **EDUCATION** UCLA, BA 1966; Howard Univ Sch Law, JD 1969. **CAREER** City of Compton CA, deputy city atty; Compton Community Coll, instructor; Robert Edelen Law Offices, atty 1975-; LA, legal aid found 1972-74; Compton CA, admin asst 1970-72; Dept Justice Washington, legal intern 1968-69. **HONORS AND AWARDS** Guest lecturer Vassar Coll/NY U/UCLA/U of So CA 1978-79. **MEMBERSHIPS** Mem LA Bar Assn; CA Lawyers Criminal Justice; Langston Law Club; Nat Conf Black Lawyers; Compton Cultural Commn; Assn Black Psychol; Pilgrim Missionary Bapt Ch. **SELECTED PUBLICATIONS** Pub in LA Times 1974; current bibliography on African Affairs 1969, 1972. **CONTACT ADDRESS** Compton City Hall, Compton, CA 90224.

CLELAND, CAROL
PERSONAL Born 12/21/1948, Pittsburgh, PA, d, 1 child **DISCIPLINE** PHILOSOPHY **EDUCATION** Univ Calif, BA, 73; Brown Univ, PhD, 81. **CAREER** Vis Instr and Asst Prof, Wheaton Col, 79-84; Postdoc Fel, CSLI Stanford Univ, 85-86; Asst Prof to Assoc Prof, Univ Colo, 86-. **HONORS AND AWARDS** Fel, Brown Univ,; Fel, Stanford Univ. **RESEARCH** Metaphysics (causation, space & time, events, change, supervenience); Philosophy of Logic (computation theory); Philosophy of Science (scientific methodology, astrobiology, nature of life). **SELECTED PUBLICATIONS** Auth, "The Difference Between Real Change and Mere Cambridge Change," Philosophical Studies, (90): 257-280; auth, "On the Individuation of Events," Synthese, (91): 229-254; auth, "Is the Church-Turing Thesis true?," Minds & Machines, (93): 283-312; auth, "Effectie Procedures and computable Functions," Minds and Machines, (95): 9-23; auth, "Recipes, Agorithms, and Programs," Minds & Machines, in press; auth, "Methodological and Epistemic Differences between Historical Science and Experimental Science," forthcoming. **CONTACT ADDRESS** Dept Philos, Univ of Colorado, Boulder, Campus Box 232, Boulder, CO 80309-0232. **EMAIL** Cleland@colorado.edu

CLEMENT, GRACE
DISCIPLINE PHILOSOPHY **EDUCATION** PhD. **CAREER** Salisbury State Univ **SELECTED PUBLICATIONS** Auth, Care, Autonomy, and Justice: Feminism and the Ethic of Care. **CONTACT ADDRESS** Dept of Philos, Salisbury State Univ, Salisbury, MD 21801-6862. **EMAIL** GACLEMENT@salisbury.edu

CLEMENTS, TAD S.
PERSONAL Born 08/13/1922, Buffalo, NY, m, 7 children **DISCIPLINE** PHILOSOPHY **EDUCATION** Univ Buffalo, BS, 48; PhD, 62; Univ N Mex, MS, 54. **CAREER** Cur, live exhibs, 50-54, Buffalo Mus Sci; jr sci, 60, Rosewell Prk Mem Just; inst 60-61, Univ N Dakota; asst prof, 61-64, Univ Akron; asst prof, 64-65, Univ Idaho; prof, 65-85, SUNY Col Brockport. **MEMBERSHIPS** Center for Inquiry. **RESEARCH** Phil of sci; phil of relig, crotical studies of paranormal claims. **SELECTED PUBLICATIONS** Auth, Science and Man, The Philosophy of Scientific Humanism, 68; auth, Ethics and Human Nature, Building a World Community, Prometheus Bks, 89; co-ed, Religion and Human Purpose, Stud in Phil & Relig Ser, Martinus Nijhoff, 87; auth, art, Religion Versus Science, Encycl of Unbelief, Prometheus Bks, 85; auth, Science vs Religion, Prometheus Bks, 91. **CONTACT ADDRESS** Dept of Philosophy, SUNY, Col at Brockport, Brockport, NY 14420.

CLERMONT, KEVIN MICHAEL
PERSONAL Born 10/25/1945, New York, NY, s, 1 child **DISCIPLINE** LAW, CIVIL PROCEDURE **EDUCATION** Princeton Univ, AB, 67; Harvard Univ, JD, 71. **CAREER** Law clerk to Judge Murray Gurfein, 71-72; assoc, Cleary, Gottlieb, Steen & Hamilton, 72-74; from asst prof to prof, 74-89, Flanagan Prof Law, Law Sch, Cornell Univ, 89-; Fulbright scholar, Univ Nancy, France, 67-68. **HONORS AND AWARDS** Phi Beta Kappa; Sigma Xi; Order of the Coif. **RESEARCH** Federal courts. **SELECTED PUBLICATIONS** Coauth, Materials for a Basic Course in Civil Procedure, Found Press, 7th ed, 97; Law: Its Nature, Functions, and Limits, West Publ Co, 3rd ed, 86; auth, Civil Procedure, West Publ Co, 5th ed, 99; auth, Civil Procedure: Territorial Jurisdiction and Venue, 99. **CONTACT ADDRESS** Law Sch, Cornell Univ, Myron Taylor Hall, Ithaca, NY 14853-4901. **EMAIL** kmc12@cornell.edu

CLIFFORD, RICHARD J.
PERSONAL Born 05/27/1934, Lewiston, ME, s **DISCIPLINE** BIBLICAL STUDIES **EDUCATION** Boston Col, AB, 59; Weston Jesuit Sch Theology, STL, 67; Harvard Univ, PhD, 70. **CAREER** Weston Jesuit Sch Theo, Dean, 83-87; Asst prof to prof, 70-98. **HONORS AND AWARDS** Gen ed, Cath Bib Quart; Pres, Cath Bib Asn; Sabbatical Res Gnts. **MEMBERSHIPS** CBA; Soc Bib Lit. **RESEARCH** Wisdom lit; biblical poetry; psalms. **SELECTED PUBLICATIONS** Proverbs: A commentary, Old Test Lib, Louisville, Westminster John Knox, 99; The Origin and Early Development Themes of Apocalyptic, in: the Encyclopedia of Apocalypticism, ed, J J Collins, NY, Continuum, 98; The Rocky Road to the New Lectionary, America, 97; The Wisdom Literature, Interpreting the Biblical Text, Nashville, Abingdon, 98; numerous book reviews. **CONTACT ADDRESS** Weston Jesuit Sch of Theol, 3 Phillips Place, Cambridge, MA 02138. **EMAIL** rclifford@wjst.edu

CLIFTON, ROBERT K.
DISCIPLINE PHILOSOPHY **EDUCATION** Univ Waterloo, BS, 86; Univ Cambridge, PhD, 91. **CAREER** Assoc Prof, Univ Pittsburgh. **RESEARCH** Conceptual foundations of modern physics, particularly quantum theory. **SELECTED PUBLICATIONS** Ed, Perspectives on Quantum Reality, Kluwer Acad Pub, 96; co-auth, "Losing Your Marbles in Wavefunction Collapse Theories," The British Journal for Philosophy of Science, (99): 697-717; co-auth, "Bipartite Mixed States of Infinite-Dimensional Systems are Generically Nonseparable," Physical Review, (99); co-auth, "Changing the Subject: Redei on Causal Dependence in Algebraic Quantum Field Theory," Philosophy of Science, (99): 156-169; auth, "Beables in Algebraic Quantum Theory," in From Physics to Philosophy, (Cambridge Univ Press, 99); auth, "Maximal Beable subalgebras of Quantum-Mechanical Observables," The International Journal for Theoretical Physics, (99): 2441-2484; auth, "Generic Bell Correlation Between Arbitrary Local Algebras in Quantum Field Theory," Journal of Mathematical Physics, (00): 1711-1717; co-auth, "Non-local Correlations are Generic in Infinite-dimensional Bipartite Systems," Physical Review, (00); co-auth, "Revised Proof for the Uniqueness Theorem for 'No Collapse' Interpretations of Quantum Mechanics," Studies in History and Philosophy of Modern Physics, (00): 95-98; co-auth, "Counting Marbles with 'Accessible' Mass Density: A Reply to Bassi and Ghirardi," The British Journal for Philosophy of Science, 00. **CONTACT ADDRESS** Dept Philos, Univ of Pittsburgh, 1001 Cathedral of Learning, Pittsburgh, PA 15260-6299. **EMAIL** rclifton@pitt.edu

CLINTON, RICHARD LEE
PERSONAL Born 09/20/1938, Cookeville, TN, m, 1986, 2 children **DISCIPLINE** POLITICAL SCIENCE **EDUCATION** Vanderbilt Univ, BA, 60, double MA, 64; Univ of NC at Chapel Hill, PhD, 71. **CAREER** Asst prof, Univ of NC at Chapel Hill, 71-76; assoc prof to prof, Ore State Univ, 76-00. **HONORS AND AWARDS** Fulbright sr lectureship, Lima, Peru, 82-83, & 97; A.J. Hanna Distinguished Visiting Prof, Rollins Col, 90, 93, 94, & 95; master teacher, Col of Liberal Arts, Ore State Univ, 95-97. **MEMBERSHIPS** Latin Am Studies Asn. **RESEARCH** Population & development policies. **SELECTED PUBLICATIONS** auth, Poblacion y Desarrollo en el Peru, Universidad de Lima, 85; auth, The Demographic Erosion of Development Efforts in Latin America: 1960-2000, Population Growth in Latin Am and U.S. Nat Security, Allen & Unwin Inc, 86; auth, Grassroots Development Where No Grass Grows: Small-scale Development Efforts on the Peruvian Coast, Studies in Comparative Int Development, 91; auth, Does Ecological Risk Assessment Fit into Democracy?, Human and Ecological Risk Assessment, 95. **CONTACT ADDRESS** Dept of Political Sci, Oregon State Univ, Corvallis, OR 97331-6246. **EMAIL** richard.clinton@orst.edu

CLINTON, ROBERT N.
PERSONAL Born 08/01/1946, Detroit, MI, m, 1970, 3 children **DISCIPLINE** LAW **EDUCATION** Univ Mich, BA, 68; Univ Chicago, JD, 71. **CAREER** Vis Prof, Univ of San Diego Law Sch, 78; Vis Prof, Cornell Law Sch, 80-81; Asst Prof, Univ of Iowa Col of Law, 76-79; Prof of Law, Univ of Iowa Col of Law, 79-89; Affiliated Fac, Am Indian and Native Studies Program, Col of Liberal Arts, Univ of Iowa, 96; Wiley B. Rutledge Prof of Law, Univ of Iowa Col of Law, 89; Vis Prof, Univ of Mich Law Sch, 00; Vis Prof, Arizona State Univ Col of Law, 01; Barry Goldwater Chair of Am Institutions, Arizona State Univ, 01-02. **MEMBERSHIPS** Am Bar Asn; Am Asn Law Schs. **RESEARCH** Native American, constitutional and federal jurisdiction law. **SELECTED PUBLICATIONS** Auth, Lone-Wolf V Hitchcock--Treaty-Rights and Indian-Law at the End of the 19th-Century, Jour Amer Ethnic Hist, Vol 0016, 97. **CONTACT ADDRESS** College of Law, Arizona State Univ, Armstrong Hall, McAllister & Orange Sts, PO Box 877906, Tempe, AZ 85287-7906. **EMAIL** rclinton@robert-clinton.com

CLOSIUS, PHILLIP J.
DISCIPLINE LAW **EDUCATION** Univ Notre Dame, BA; Columbia University, JD. **CAREER** Prof. **SELECTED PUBLICATIONS** Auth, Rejecting the Fruits of Action, Univ Notre Dame, 95; Social Justice and the Myth of Fairness, Univ Nebraska, 95. **CONTACT ADDRESS** Col Law, Univ of Toledo, Toledo, OH 43606. **EMAIL** pclosiu@utnet.utoledo.edu

CLOTHEY, FREDERICK WILSON
PERSONAL Born 02/29/1936, Madras, India, m, 1962, 4 children **DISCIPLINE** HISTORY OF RELIGIONS **EDUCATION** Aurora Col, BA & BTh, 57; Evangel Theol Sem, BD, 59; Univ Chicago, MA, 65, PhD(hist relig), 68. **CAREER** Dir youth work, Advent Christian Gen Conf, 59-62; from instr to asst prof relig Boston Univ, 67-77; Assoc Prof, Prof Hist Relig, Univ Pittsburgh, 77-, Chmn Dept Relig Studies, 78-88; 95-98, Resident coordr, Great Lakes Cols Asn Year in India Prog, 71-72; producer & dir films, Yakam: A Fire Ritual in South India, spring 73, Skanda-Sasti: A Festival of Conquest, fall 73 & Pankuni Uttiram: A Festival of Marriage, spring 74. **HONORS AND AWARDS** Fulbright fel, 78, 82, 91, 98; AIIS Fellow 66-67, 81, 85, 91, 94. **MEMBERSHIPS** Am Acad Relig; Soc Indian Studies; Conf So Indian Relig; Soc Sci Study Relig; Asn Asian Studies. **RESEARCH** Religion in South India; nature of myth, symbol, ritual; ethnic religion in America; South Indians Abroad. **SELECTED PUBLICATIONS** Auth, The many faces of Murukan: The history and meaning of a South Indian God, Mouton, The Hague, 78; contribr, Chronometry, cosmology and the festival calendar of the Murukan Cultus, In: Interludes: Festivals of South India and Sri Lanka, Manohar Bks, 82; "Sasta-Aiyanar-Aiyappan: The God as prism of social History," Images of Man: Relgion and Historical Process in South Asia, 82; The construction of a temple in an American city & The acculturation process, In: Rythm & Intent: Ritual Studies from South India, Blackie & Son, 82; auth, Quiscence and passion: The vision of Arunakiri, Tamil Mystic Austin and Winfield, 1996; Rhythm & intent: Ritual studies from South India, Blackie & Son, 82; ed, Experiencing Siva: Encounters with a Hindu Deity, Manohar Bks, 82; Images of man: Religion and historical process, New Era Publ, 82; auth, Tale of Four Cities: Religin, Indentity and Tamil Expatriates, forthcoming, Co-Founder, coed, Journal of Ritual Studies, 86-98; auth, Tamil Religion in Encyclopedia of Religion, 87; auth, . **CONTACT ADDRESS** Dept of Relig Studies, Univ of Pittsburgh, 2604 Cathedral/Learn, Pittsburgh, PA 15260-0001. **EMAIL** clothey+@pitt.edu

CLOUD, FRED
PERSONAL Born 04/06/1925, Dallas, TX, m, 1969, 3 children **DISCIPLINE** RELIGIOUS STUDIES **EDUCATION** Vanderbilt Univ, BA, 44; Vanderbilt Divinity Sch, Mdiv, 47; Scarritt Col, MA, 61; Vanderbilt Divinity Sch, DMin, 90 **CAREER** Dir, Nashville Human Rels Commission, 67-90; Assoc Prof, Am Baptist Col, 90-. **HONORS AND AWARDS** Individual Human Rights Worker Awd; Freedom Found Awd, 60; Human Rels Awd, NCCJ, 91. **MEMBERSHIPS** Nat Assoc of Human Rights Workers. **RESEARCH** Mental health, human rights, race relations. **SELECTED PUBLICATIONS** Ed, Methodist Church Col Publ, 53-67; auth, In Step with Time, 60; auth, God's Hand in our Lives, 64; ed, J of Intergroup Rels, 90, 91, 00. **CONTACT ADDRESS** Dept Humanities, American Baptist Col of American Baptist Theol Sem, 1800 Baptist World Center, Nashville, TN 37207. **EMAIL** fredcloud@dellnet.com

CLOUD, W. ERIC
PERSONAL Born 02/26/1946, Cleveland, OH, m **DISCIPLINE** LAW **EDUCATION** Morris Brown Col, BA (cum laude) 73; Dag Hammarskjold Col, fellowship (highest honors) 74; Antioch Sch of Law, JD 77; George Washington Law Sch, LLM Intl & Comparative Law 1980. **CAREER** Pvt Practice Intl Law, atty; US Dept of Treasury, consult 79-80; US Dept of Labor, spl asst to intl tax counsel 76-78; Cloud, Henderson & Cloud, Attorney, 82-; Washington Afro-American Newspaper, correspondent, 88-; Morris Brown College, lectr, 90-95. **HONORS AND AWARDS** Good Samaritan of the Year Mayor Carl Stokes 68; fel Dag Hammarskjold Coll Dag Hammarskjold Found 73; Four Walls/Eight Window, 90; Awd for Best Article of 90; Alumni of the Year, Morris Brown Col, 95. **MEMBERSHIPS** Mem, Am Bar Asn, 77; mem, Nat Bar Asn; mem, Morris Brown Col Alumni Asn, 88-. **SELECTED PUBLICATIONS** Article in George Washington Law Review "Tax Treaties: The Need for the US to Extend its Treaty Network to Developing Countries in Light of the New International Economic and Political Realities" **CONTACT ADDRESS** Cloud Law Firm, 10605 Woodlawn Blvd, Largo, MD 20772. **EMAIL** cloudlaw@aol.com

CLOUGH, SHARON
PERSONAL Born 05/14/1965, Prince George, BC, Canada, s **DISCIPLINE** PHILOSOPHY **EDUCATION** Univ Calgary, BA, 87; MA, 89; Simon Fraser Univ, PhD, 97. **CAREER** Asst prof, Rowan Univ, 98-. **MEMBERSHIPS** Am Philos Asn, Can Philos Asn, Soc for Women in Philos, Can Soc for Women in Philos, Can Soc for the Hist and Philos of Sci, Intl Asn of Women Philos. **RESEARCH** Philosophy of Science, Epistemology, Contemporary Pragmatism, Feminist Theory. **SELECTED PUBLICATIONS** Auth, "A Hasty Retreat from Evidence: The Recalcitrance of Relativism in Feminist Critiques of Science," Hypatia: A Journal of Feminist Philosophy 13 (98). **CONTACT ADDRESS** Dept Philos & Relig, Rowan Univ, 210 Mullica Hill Rd, Glassboro, NJ 08028-1700.

CLOUSER, KARL DANNER
PERSONAL Born 04/26/1930, Marion, OH, m, 1952, 2 children **DISCIPLINE** PHILOSOPHY **EDUCATION** Gettysburg Col, AB, 52; Lutheran Theol Sem, BD, 55; Harvard Univ, MA, 58, PhD, 61. **CAREER** Instr philos, Dartmouth Col, 61-64; asst prof, Carleton Col, 64-68; assoc prof, 68-76, prof humanities 76-90, univ prof humanities, 91-96; univ prof emer, 97-, Col Med PA State Univ, 76-; bd dirs, Lutheran Theol Sem, 70-81; assoc ed, Encycl Bioethics, 73-78; dir, Hastings Ctr Workshops Med Ethics, 74-81; **HONORS AND AWARDS** Humane Lett Thomas Jefferson Univ, 81; Dr Humane Lett, Gettysburg Col, 83; Henry Beecher Awd, 96; Inst Med, 97. **MEMBERSHIPS** Fel Hastings Ctr. **RESEARCH** Medical ethics; philosophy of medicine. **SELECTED PUBLICATIONS** Auth, The sanctity of life: An analysis of a concept, Ann Internal Med, 1/73; What is medical ethics?, Ann Internal Med, 5/74; Medical ethics: Uses, abuses and limitations, New England J Med, 8/75; Biomedical ethics: Some reflections and exhortations, Monist, 1/77; Allowing or causing: Another look, Ann Internal Med, 11/77; Bioethics, In: Encycl Bioethic, Macmillan & Free Press, 78; Teaching Bioethics: Strategies, Problems, and Resources, Hastings Ctr, 80; coauth, A Critique of Principlism. Jour Med and Philos, 90; coauth, Morality vs Principlism, Prin Am Hea Care Ethics, Wiley & Sons, 94; coauth, Morality and The New Genetics, Jones & Bartlett, 96; Biomedical Ethics, Encycl Philos Suppl, Simon & Schuster, 96; coauth, Bioethics: A Return to Fundamentals. Oxford Univ Press, 97; coauth, Malady What is Disease, Humana Press, 97. **CONTACT ADDRESS** Hershey, PA 17033-0850.

CLOUSER, ROY A.
PERSONAL Born 12/20/1937, Philadelphia, PA, m, 5 children **DISCIPLINE** PHILOSOPHY **EDUCATION** Gordon Col, BA; Reformed Episcopal Sem, BD; Univ of Penn, MA, PhD. **CAREER** Instr, La Salle Univ; Instr, Rutgers Univ; Prof, Coll of New Jersey. **HONORS AND AWARDS** Templeton Course Awd. **MEMBERSHIPS** APA, SCP, CPJ, ASA. **RESEARCH** Philosophy of Religion, metaphysics. **SELECTED PUBLICATIONS** Auth, The Myth of Religious Neutrality, An Essay on the Hidden Pole of Religious Beliefs in Theories, Univ Notre Dame Press, 91; Knowing with the Heart, Religious Experience and Belief in God, InterVarsity Press, 99; auth, Is God Eternal? in: The Rationality of Theism, ed A G Sienra, Rodopi Pub Amsterdam, forthcoming; A Critique of Historicism, in: Critica, 97; On the General Relation of Religion, Metaphysics and Science, in: Facets of Faith and Science, ed J Van der Meer, Univ press of Amer, 96; The Uniqueness of Dooyeweerd's Program for Philosophy and Science, Whence the Difference?, in: Christian Philo at the Close of the 20th Century, ed Griffeon & Balk, Kampen Kok Netherlands, 95. **CONTACT ADDRESS** 204 Bradley Ave, Haddonfield, NJ 08033-2904. **EMAIL** royclouser@aol.com

CLUCHEY, DAVID P.
DISCIPLINE LAW **EDUCATION** Yale Univ, AB; SUNY at Albany, MA; Harvard Univ, JD. **CAREER** Prof; Fulbright lectr to Russ, 94; past consult to, US AID Rule of Law prog to Russ; past co-spe coun, Maine Atty Gen; past consult, several com-t(s), Maine Supreme Judicial Ct; fac, Louisiana Tech Univ, 79-;

past prac atty, Maine, 6 yrs; assoc dean law sch, Louisiana Tech Univ, 87-91; **MEMBERSHIPS** Treas, Maine Bar Found; past-ch, Sect on NAmer Coop, Asn Amer Law Sch. **RESEARCH** International trade and business relations. **SELECTED PUBLICATIONS** Coauth, 3-vol bk, Maine Criminal Practice; publ on, int trade regulation; antitrust and health care law. **CONTACT ADDRESS** School of Law, Univ of So Maine, 96 Falmouth St, PO Box 9300, Portland, ME 04104-9300.

COAKLEY, JOHN
PERSONAL Born 04/05/1949, Washington, DC **DISCIPLINE** CHURCH HISTORY **EDUCATION** Wesleyan Univ, AB, 71; Harvard Divinity Sch, Mdiv, 74; ThD, 80. **CAREER** Fac, New Brunswick Theol Sem, 84-. **HONORS AND AWARDS** NEH Fel, 97-98. **MEMBERSHIPS** Am Soc of church Hist, Am Hist Asn, Medieval Acad of Am, Am Acad of Relig. **RESEARCH** History of Christianity (especially Medieval). **SELECTED PUBLICATIONS** Auth, "Gender, Friars and Sanctity: Mendicant Encounters with Saints, 1250-1325," in Medieval Masculinities, ed. Clare Lees (MN: Univ Minn Pr, 94), 91-110; auth, "Devotion, literature de," and "Direction spirituelle," in Dictionnaire encyclopedique du moyen age chretienne, ed. Andre Vauchez (Paris: Editions du Cerf, 97), 458-459, 468; auth, "A Marriage and Its Observer: Christine of Stommeln, the Heavenly Bridegroom, and Friar Peter of Dacia," in Gendered Voices: Medieval Saints and Their Interpreters, ed. Catherine Mooney (PA: Univ Penn Pr, 99), 99-117; co-ed, Patterns and Portraits: Women in the History of the Reformed Church in America, Eerdmans, 99. **CONTACT ADDRESS** Dept Church Hist, New Brunswick Theol Sem, 17 Seminary Place, New Brunswick, NJ 08901-1107. **EMAIL** jwc@nbts.edu

COATES, ROBERT CRAWFORD
PERSONAL Born 01/31/1937, Torrance, CA, d, 2 children **DISCIPLINE** LAW **EDUCATION** San Diego St Univ, BS, 59; Natl Univ, MB, 59; Calif Western Sch Law, JD, 70. **CAREER** Jr civil engg, 59-61, Engg dept, admin analyst, 61-63, city mngrs staff, 61-63, City of San Diego; atty, 71-82, Partner, Coates & Miller; Law Forum dir, 84-87, adj prof, 81-95, Univ San Diego Law Sch; judge, Municipal Superior Cts, 82-, San Diego Judicial Dist. **HONORS AND AWARDS** One of Ten San Diego Citizens of the Yr, City Club, 91; Dist Svc Rotary, 91; Warren Williams Awd of Am & Calif Psychiatric Asns, 91; Paul Harris Fel, Rotary Intl, 95; Awd of Excel, Consumer Atty of San Diego, 97; God and Country Awd, BSA, 98. **MEMBERSHIPS** Am Asn of Mining Engg; Am Geol Inst; Anza-Borrego Hist Soc; The Baja Group, Calif Mining Asn; San Diego Asn of Geol, San Diego Nat Hist Mus; Sierra Club, St Stephens Church of God in Christ; Theodore Roosevelt Asn, Torrey Pines Asn; Yosemite Asn; E Clampus Vitus, Mission Valley East Rotary Club. **RESEARCH** Mental health law, natural resources law, judicial ethics. **SELECTED PUBLICATIONS** Auth, A Street is Not a Home: Solving America's Homeless Dilemma, 90; auth, The Guys Who Can't Cook's Cookbook, 84; auth, Asserting Mineral Rights Against the US Government in Federal Court, 20 Cal WL Rev 377, 84. **CONTACT ADDRESS** 220 W Broadway, (S-45), San Diego, CA 92101.

COBB, JOHN BOSWELL
PERSONAL Born 02/09/1925, Kobe, Japan, m, 1947, 4 children **DISCIPLINE** CONSTRUCTIVE THEOLOGY **EDUCATION** Canadian Academy, Kobe, Japan, 39; Newnan High School, Ga, 39-41; Emory-at-Oxford, Ga, 41-43, Univ Mich, 43; Univ Chicago, MA, 49, PhD, 52. **CAREER** Instr, Young Harris Col, 50-53; instr, Candler School of Theol, Emory Univ, 53-58; Ingrahan Prof, Claremont School of Theol, 58-90; Avery prof, CGS, 60-90; Fulbright prof, Univ of Mainz, 65-66; vis prof, Rikkyo Univ, Tokyo, 78; vis prof, Chicago Divinity School, 80; vis prof, Harvard Divinity School, 87; vis prof, Iliff School of Theology, 91; vis prof, Vanderbilt Divinity School, 93; CO-Dir, Center for Process Studies, Co-Founder, Mobilization for the Human Family, Prof Emeritus, Claremont School of Theology & Claremont Grad School, 90. **HONORS AND AWARDS** Honorary degrees from the Univ Mainz, Emory Univ, Linfield Col, DePauw Univ, and Univ Victoria; Fulbright Prof, Univ Mainz; Fel, Woodrow Wilson Int Center for Scholars; Alumus of the Year, Chicago Divinity School; Distinguished Alumnus Awd, Univ Chicago. **MEMBERSHIPS** Am Acad of Religion; Metaphysical Soc; Center for Process Studies. **RESEARCH** Inter-religious dialogue; process philosophy; theology & economics. **SELECTED PUBLICATIONS** Auth, Becoming a Thinking Christian, 93; Lay Theology, 94; Sustaining the Common Good, 94; Grace and Responsibility, 95; Reclaiming the Church, 97; coauth, The Green National Product: A Proposed Index of Sustainable Economic Welfare, 94. **CONTACT ADDRESS** Sch of Theol, Claremont Graduate Sch, 1401 N College Ave., Claremont, CA 91711. **EMAIL** cobbj@atscgu.edu

COBB, JOHN HUNTER, JR.
PERSONAL Born 05/05/1953, Rocky Mount, NC, m **DISCIPLINE** LAW **EDUCATION** Hampton Univ, BA 1975; Howard Univ, JD 1979. **CAREER** Michie Company, senior editor, 79-85; Robinson Buchanan & Johnson, assoc, 85-88; Virginia Union Univ, Business Law Prof, 85-86; Solo Practicioner, 88-. **HONORS AND AWARDS** Litigation Section VA State Bar 1985-. **MEMBERSHIPS** Mem Old Dominion Bar Assoc 1979-; Young Lawyers Conf VA State Bar 1979-; legal advisor Time Investment Corp 1985-; mem VA Trial Lawyers Assoc 1985-; comm mem Guardian Ad Litem Seminar 1987. **CONTACT ADDRESS** 2025 E Main St, Richmond, VA 23223.

COBB, KELTON
PERSONAL Born 10/08/1958, CA, m, 1990 **DISCIPLINE** RELIGION **EDUCATION** George Fox Col, BA, 81; Princeton Sem, MDiv, 85; Univ Iowa, PhD, 94. **CAREER** Hartford Sem, prof, 95-. **MEMBERSHIPS** AAR, SCE, NAPTS **RESEARCH** Theol and Cult theory; theol ethics; comp relig ethics. **SELECTED PUBLICATIONS** Auth, Ernst Troeltech and Vaclav Havel on the Ethical Promise of Historical Failures, Jour Relig Ethics, 94; Reconsidering the Status of Popular Culture in Tillich's Theology of Culture, Jour Amer Acad Relig, 95. **CONTACT ADDRESS** Dept of Theology, Hartford Sem, 77 Sherman St, Hartford, CT 06105. **EMAIL** kcobb@hartsem.edu

COBURN, ROBERT C.
PERSONAL Born 01/25/1930, Minneapolis, MN, m, 1974 **DISCIPLINE** PHILOSOPHY **EDUCATION** Yale Univ BA, 51; Univ of Chicago, Div School, BD, 54; Harvard Univ, MA, 58, PhD, 58. **CAREER** Ohio State Univ, inst, 58-59; Dartmouth Col, inst, 59-60; Univ of Chicago, asst prof, assoc prof, prof, 60-71; Univ Of Washington, prof, 71-. **HONORS AND AWARDS** Elected Phi Beta Kappa, 51; Elected Kent Fel, 58; Andrew Mellon Postdoctoral Fel, in Philosophy, University of Pittsburgh, 61-62; National Science Found Grant GS-2064, June, 68-October, 69; National Endowment for the Humanities Grant for Summer Seminar for College Teachers, 83; University of Washington Graduate School Release-Time Awd, Spring, 85. **MEMBERSHIPS** APA, AAUP; OBK. **RESEARCH** Metaphysics; Ethics; Social philo. **SELECTED PUBLICATIONS** Auth, Identity and Spatio-temporal Continuity, in: Identity and Individuation, NY Univ Press, 71; auth, The Strangeness of the Ordinary: Issues and Problems in Contemporary Metaphysics, Rowman & Littlefield Pub, 90; auth, "The Idea of Transcendence," Philosophical Investigations, 13, (90), 322-337; auth, "Evolution and Skepticism," Pacific Philosophy Quarterly, 71, (90), 1-14; auth, "A Defense of Ethical Noncognitivism," Philosophical Studies, 62, (91), 67-80; Personal Identity Revisited, in: Personal Identity, Dartmouth Pub Co, 95; auth, "God, Revelation, and Religious Truth: Some Themes and Problems in the Theology of Paul Tillich," Faith and Philosophy, 13, (96), 3-33. **CONTACT ADDRESS** Dept of Philosophy, Univ of Washington, PO Box 353350, Seattle, WA 98195-3350. **EMAIL** coburn@u.washington.edu

COBURN, THOMAS BOWEN
PERSONAL Born 02/08/1944, New York, NY, m, 1998, 2 children **DISCIPLINE** HISTORY OF RELIGION **EDUCATION** Princeton Univ, AB, 65; Harvard Univ, MTS, 69, PhD(comp relig), 77. **CAREER** Teaching fel relig, Phillips Acad, 65-66; instr math & physics, Am Community Sch, Lebanon, 66-67; from Instr to Prof, 74-90, Charles A. Dana Prof Rel Studies, St Lawrence Univ, 90-, Vice Pres St Lawrence Univ and Dean of Acad Affairs, 96-. **HONORS AND AWARDS** Sr res fel, Am Inst Indian Studies, 81-82; Nat Endowment for Humanities fel, 82. **MEMBERSHIPS** Am Acad Relig; Asn Asian Studies; Network liberal arts education. **RESEARCH** South Asian religion, especially the literature and mythology of popular religion in India; goddesses; methods in comparative study. **SELECTED PUBLICATIONS** Auth, The Conceptualization of Religious Change and the Worship of the Great Goddess, St Lawrence Univ, 80; auth, Consort of none, Sakti of all: The vision of the Devi-Mahatmya, In: The Divine Consort: Radha and the Goddesses of India, Berkeley Res Publ, 1982, rev ed, 95; Devi-Mahatmya: The Crystallization of the Goddess Tradition: Motilal Banarsidass, New Delhi, 84; Scripture in India, IN, Rethinking Scripture, SUNY Press, repr 89; Encountering the Goddess: A Trans. of the Devi-Mahatmya and a Study of Its Interpretation, State Univ of NY Press, 91; guest ed, Education About Asia, 2/97; author of numerous other journal articles; auth, Climbing The Mountain of God, Inl. Am Acad. Of Rel., Spring 95; auth, Three-Fold Vision of The Devi-Mahatmya, In Devi: The Great Goddess, Smithsonian Institution, 99; auth, Asia and The Undergraduate Curriculum, In Asia in The Undergraduate Curriculum, M.E. Sharpe, 00. **CONTACT ADDRESS** Vice Pres and Dean of Acad Affairs, St. Lawrence Univ, Canton, NY 13617-1499. **EMAIL** tcoburn@stlawu.edu

COCCHIARELLA, NINO BARNABAS
DISCIPLINE PHILOSOPHY, MATHEMATICAL LOGIC **EDUCATION** Columbia Univ, BS, 58; Univ Calif, Los Angeles, MA & PhD, 66. **CAREER** Instr, Exten, UCLA, 63-64; asst prof philos, San Francisco State Col, 64-68; vis assoc prof, Wayne State Univ, 68; Prof Philos, Ind Univ, Bloomington, 68. **HONORS AND AWARDS** Nat Sci Found grants, 71-74; Nat Endowment for Hum grant, 77-78, 88-89. **MEMBERSHIPS** Central Div Am Philos Asn; Asn Symbolic Logic; Asn Philos Sci; Royal Inst Philos; Soc of Exact Philos; . **RESEARCH** Formal philos; philos linguistics; general metaphysics; cognitive science. **SELECTED PUBLICATIONS** Auth, Logical Investigations of Predication Theory and the problem of Universals, Biblopolis Press, Naples, 86; auth, Logical Studies in early Analytic Philosophy, Ohio State Univ Press, 87; auth, Conceptual Realism versus Quine on Classes and Higher-Order Logic, Synthese, 92; Knowledge Representation in Conceptual Realism, Int J Human-Computer Studies, 95; Conceptual Realism as a Formal Ontology, In: Formal Ontology, Kluwer, 96; auth, "Formally Oriented Work in the Philosophy of Language," in Routledge Hist of philosophy, London, 97; auth, "Reference in Conceptual Realism," Synthese, vol 114, 98; auth of numerous other articles and publ. **CONTACT ADDRESS** Dept. of Philosophy, Indiana Univ, Bloomington, Sycamore 026, Bloomington, IN 47405. **EMAIL** cocchiar@indiana.edu

COCHRAN, AUGUSTUS B.
PERSONAL Born 08/26/1946, Athens, GA, d, 2 children **DISCIPLINE** POLITICAL SCIENCE **EDUCATION** Davidson Col, BA, 68; Ind Univ, MA, 69; Univ NC, PhD, 72; Ga State Univ, JD, 94. **CAREER** Prof, Agnes Scott Col, 73-. **HONORS AND AWARDS** Vulcan Materials Teachings Awd, 00; Woodrow Wilson Fel, 68; Phi Beta Kappa, 68. **MEMBERSHIPS** Am Polit Sci Asn; S Polit Sci Asn; Ga Bar Asn. **RESEARCH** Democratic theory; Labor and Employment Law. **SELECTED PUBLICATIONS** Co-auth, "Class, State, and Popular Organizations in Mozambique and Nicaragua," Latin Am Perspectives, 92; auth, "Georgia's Limited Liability Company act," Ga State Univ law Rev, (93): 79-90; auth, "We Participate, They Decide: The Real Stakes in Revising Section (a) (2) of the Nation Labor Relations Act," Berkeley J of Employment and Labor Law, (95): 458-519; auth, Democracy Heading South: National Politics in the Shadow of Dixie, Univ Press of Kans, 01. **CONTACT ADDRESS** Dept of Polit Sci, Agnes Scott Col, 141 E College Ave, Decatur, GA 30030. **EMAIL** gcochran@agnesscott.edu

COCHRAN, CHARLES LEO
PERSONAL Born 05/03/1940, Salisbury, MD, m, 1966, 4 children **DISCIPLINE** POLITICAL SCIENCE **EDUCATION** Mount St Mary's Coll, BS; Niagara Univ, MA; Tufts Univ, PhD. **CAREER** Asst prof, US Naval Academy, 70; assoc prof, US Navel Acad, 70-75; ch, US Naval Acad, 86-90; Adj Prof, Johns Hopkins Univ, 84-. **RESEARCH** Public policy; political economy. **SELECTED PUBLICATIONS** Coauth, Public Policy: Perspectives & Choices, McGraw-Hill, 95, 99. **CONTACT ADDRESS** Dept Polit Sci, United States Naval Acad, Annapolis, MD 21402. **EMAIL** ccochran@gwmail.usna.edu

COCHRAN, JOHN K.
PERSONAL Born 03/04/1958, Washington, DC, m, 1981 **DISCIPLINE** CRIMINOLOGY **EDUCATION** Univ Fla, BA, 80; MA, 82; PhD, 87. **CAREER** Asst prof, Wichita State Univ, 86-89; asst to assoc prof, Univ of Okla, 89-94; assoc prof, Univ of S Fla, 94-. **HONORS AND AWARDS** Fel, Univ of Fla, 80-81; Margin of Excellence Awd, Wichita State Univ; Sociol Spectrum Outstanding Paper Awd, Mid-South Sociol Assoc, 94; Teaching Incentive Program Awd, Univ of S Fla. **MEMBERSHIPS** Am Soc Criminol; Acad Crim Justice Sci. **RESEARCH** Capital Punishment, Criminological Theory. **SELECTED PUBLICATIONS** Coauth, "Is the Religiosity-Delinquency Relationship Spurious?: A Test of Arousal and Social Control Theories", J of Res in Crime and Delinquency 31.1 (94): 92-103; coauth, "Deterrence or Brutalization?: A Impact Assessment of Oklahoma's Return to Capital Punishment", Criminol 31.1 (94): 107-134; coauth, "Racial Differences in Perceived Sanction Threat" Static and Dynamic Hypotheses", J of Res in Crime and Delinquency, 31.2 (94): 210-224; coauth, "The Sanctuary Movement and the Smuggling of Undocumented Central Americans into the United States: Crime, Deviance, or Defiance?", Sociol Spectrum 14.2 (94): 110-128; coauth, "Assessing Messner and Rosenfeld's Institutional Anomie Theory: A Partial Test", Criminol 33.3 (95): 411-429; coauth, "Social Altruism and Crime", Criminol 35.2 (97): 301-325; coauth, "Nonsocial Reinforcement and Habitual Criminal Conduct: An Extension of Learning Theory", Criminol 35.2 (97): 335-366; coauth, "Causality, Economic Conditions, and Burglary", Criminol, 36.2 (98): 425-440; coauth, "Unemployment and Property Crime: A Consideration of Alternative Measures", J of Quantitative Criminol, (forthcoming). **CONTACT ADDRESS** Dept Dept Criminol, Univ of So Florida, 4202 Fowler Ave, Soc 107, Tampa, FL 33620-8100.

COCHRAN, ROBERT F., JR.
DISCIPLINE FAMILY LAW **EDUCATION** Carson-Newman Col, BA, 73; Univ VA, JD, 76. **CAREER** Law clk, US Court Appeals Fourth Circuit, 76-77; assoc, Boyle and Bain, 78-83; vis prof, Univ Richmond, 87-88; vis prof, Wake Forest Univ, 94; prof, 94-. **HONORS AND AWARDS** Rick J Caruso res fel, 94-95. **SELECTED PUBLICATIONS** Co-auth, Lawyers, Clients, and Moral Responsibility, W Publ Co, 94; Cases and Materials on the Rules of the Legal Profession, W Publ Co, 96. **CONTACT ADDRESS** Sch of Law, Pepperdine Univ, 24255 Pacific Coast Hwy, Malibu, CA 90263.

CODE, MICHAEL
DISCIPLINE LAW **EDUCATION** Univ Toronto, BA, 72, LLB, 76, LLM, 91. **CAREER** Lawyer, Ruby and Edwardh, 81-91; Lawyer, Sack Goldblatt Mitchell, 96-; Asst Deputy Minister, Criminal Law, Ministry of the Attorney General for Ontario; Private practice with the firm of Sack Goldblatt Mitchell **HONORS AND AWARDS** Ed, Can Rights Reporter. **SE-**

LECTED PUBLICATIONS Auth, pubs on criminal and constitutional litigation. CONTACT ADDRESS Fac of Law, Univ of Toronto, 78 Queen's Park, Toronto, ON, Canada M5S 1A1.

CODLING, JIM
PERSONAL Born 11/28/1949, Lloydminster, SK, Canada, m, 1982, 2 children **DISCIPLINE** HISTORY, PHILOSOPHY, **EDUCATION EDUCATION** Univ Saskatchewan, B Ed, 72; Knox Col, M Div, 76; Convent Sem, Th M, 81; Mississippi State Univ, M Ed, 89; Concordia, St Louis, Th D, 90. **CAREER** Prof, Mary Holmes Col, 91-. **HONORS AND AWARDS** Concordia Res Fel; Fisher Prize, Knox Coll; Fac Mem of the Year, 94; Res, 94; Teach, 95. **MEMBERSHIPS** Convent Presbytery. **RESEARCH** Ethics; Reformation History; Local Histories. **SELECTED PUBLICATIONS** Auth, 'The New Deal in Public Policy," 97; auth, Cross Cultural Missions, Coast to Coast (92); auth, Why So Many Churches, Coast to Coast (94). **CONTACT ADDRESS** Dept Soc Science, Education, Mary Holmes Col, PO Box 1257, West Point, MS 39773-1257.

CODY, AELRED
PERSONAL Born 02/03/1932, Oklahoma City, OK **DISCIPLINE** THEOLOGY **EDUCATION** St Meinrad Col, BA, 56; Univ Ottawa, STL, 58, STD, 60; Pontifical Bibl Inst, SSL, 62; Pontifical Bibl Comn, Rome, SSD, 68; Royal Col of Music, ARCM, 74; Royal Col of Organists, ARCO, 75. **CAREER** Prof, Old Testament and ancient Near East hist, Pontifical Atheneum of Sant'Anselmo and Pontifical Bibl Inst, 68-78; organist, Abbazia Primaziale, 68-76; master of novices & jrs, St Meinrad Archabbey, 78-92; assoc ed, 87-92 and ed, 93-, Cath Bibl Q; mem, Official Oriental Orthodox-Roman Cath Consultation in the USA, 81- ; trustee, 84-87, and mem, exec bd, 93-; Cath Bibl Asn of Am. **HONORS AND AWARDS** Christian Res Found Prize, Harvard Univ, 60. **MEMBERSHIPS** Int Asn for Coptic Stud; Am Oriental Soc; Cath Bibl Asn of Am; Soc of Bibl Lit. **RESEARCH** Hebrew language and literature; history of the ancient and Christian Near East; eastern Christian liturgy. **SELECTED PUBLICATIONS** Auth, Heavenly Sanctuary and Liturgy in the Epistle to the Hebrews, Grail, 60; auth, A History of Old Testament Priesthood, Pontifical Biblical Institute, 68; auth, Ezekiel, Michael Glazier, 84; contribur, The New Jerome Biblical Commentary, Prentice Hall, 90; contribur, The Coptic Encyclopedia, Macmillan, 91; contribur, The Oxford Companion to the Bible, Oxford University, 93; auth, High Priest, in McBrien, ed, The Harper-Collins Encyclopedia of Catholicism, Harper San Francisco, 95; contribur, Oriental Orthodox-Roman Catholic Interchurch Marriages and Other Pastoral Relationships, National Conference of Catholic Bishops, 95. **CONTACT ADDRESS** Saint Meinrad Sch of Theol, Saint Meinrad, IN 47557-1010.

COE, WILLIAM JEROME
PERSONAL Born 11/15/1935, Malone, NY, m, 1977, 3 children **DISCIPLINE** PHILOSOPHY **EDUCATION** Dartmouth Col, AB, 57; Vanderbilt Univ, MA, 59; PA State Univ, PhD, 67. **CAREER** Vis lectr philos, Baldwin-Wallace Col, 61-62; from instr to asst prof, Southeast MO State Col, 62-67; asst prof, Northern IL Univ, 67-71; assoc prof Philos, 71-81, Prof Philos, Fr Lewis Col, 82-. **MEMBERSHIPS** Western Div Am Philos Asn; Soc Phenomenol & Existential Philos. **RESEARCH** Metaphilosophy; metaphysics; conceptual analysis. **SELECTED PUBLICATIONS** Conceptsof Leisure in Western Thought, with B. Dare and G. Welton, Kendall Hunt Pub Co, 87, 2nd ed, 98. **CONTACT ADDRESS** Dept of Philos, Fort Lewis Col, 1000 Rim Dr, Durango, CO 81301-3999. **EMAIL** coe_w@fortlewis.edu

COFFEY, DAVID MICHAEL
PERSONAL Born 05/06/1934, Lismore, New South Wales, Australia, s **DISCIPLINE** THEOLOGY **EDUCATION** Catholic Inst Sydney, STB, 56; STL, 58; STD, 60. **CAREER** Prof, Cath Inst of Sydney, 62-95; previs prof, Univ St Louis Aquinas Inst, 91; presidential chair of Catholic Systematic Theol, Marquette Univ, 95-97; William J. Kelly S. J. Chair in Catholic Theol, Marquette Univ, 98. **HONORS AND AWARDS** Vis Fel, Univ Sydney Sancha Sophia Cols, 90. **MEMBERSHIPS** Catholic Theol Soc of Am, Australian Catholic Theol Asn. **RESEARCH** Christology, Pneumatology, Theology of the Trinity, Ecclesiology. **SELECTED PUBLICATIONS** Auth, Grace: The Gift of the Holy Spirit, Faith and Culture, 79; auth, Deus Trinitas: The Doctrine of the Triune God, Oxford Univ Pr (New York), 99. **CONTACT ADDRESS** Dept Theol, Marquette Univ, PO Box 1881, Milwaukee, WI 53201-1881. **EMAIL** david.coffey@marquette.edu

COGDILL, JAMES
PERSONAL Born 04/27/1955, Marion, IL, m, 1974 **DISCIPLINE** THEOLOGY **EDUCATION** Shawnee Community Col, AA, AS, 79; SE Miss State Univ, BA, 82; BS Ed, 82; S Baptist Theol Sem, M Div, 86; PhD, 90. **CAREER** Prof, SE Baptist Theol Sem, 89-; Dean, 97-. **MEMBERSHIPS** Evangel Theol Soc; Acad for Evangel in Theol Educ. **CONTACT ADDRESS** Academic Affairs, Midwestern Baptist Theol Sem, 5001 N Oak Trafficway, Kansas City, MO 64118-4620. **EMAIL** jimcogdill@email.com

COGGINS, GEORGE CAMERON
PERSONAL Born 01/27/1941, Pontiac, MI, m, 1968, 1 child **DISCIPLINE** LAW **EDUCATION** Cent Mich Univ, AB, 63; Univ Mich, JD, 66. **CAREER** Assoc atty, McCutchen, Doyle, Brown & Enersen, San Francisco, 66-70; assoc prof law, 70-73, Prof Law, Univ Kans, 73-, Vis prof law, Law Sch, Univ NC, Chapel Hill, 81 & Northwestern Law Sch, Lewis & Clark Col, 83. **RESEARCH** Environmental law; civil proceudre. **SELECTED PUBLICATIONS** Auth, Concessions Law and Policy in the National-Park System, Denver Univ Law Rev, Vol 0074, 97. **CONTACT ADDRESS** Law Sch, Univ of Kansas, Lawrence, Green Hall, Lawrence, KS 66045-0001.

COGLEY, RICHARD W.
PERSONAL Born 08/04/1950, Gettysburg, PA, s **DISCIPLINE** RELIGIOUS STUDIES **EDUCATION** Franklin & Marshall Col, BA, 72; Yale Univ, M Div, 76; Princeton Univ, PhD, 83. **CAREER** Vis instr, North Carolina State Univ, 81-82; vis asst prof, Loyola Marymount Univ, 82-83; vis asst prof, North Carolina state Univ, 84-85; vis asst prof, reed Col, 85-87; asst prof, Southern Methodist Univ, 87-93; assoc prof, 93-. **HONORS AND AWARDS** Godbey Bk Awd, SMU, 00. **MEMBERSHIPS** ASCH; NEHA; SEA. **RESEARCH** English and American Puritanism. **SELECTED PUBLICATIONS** Auth, John Eliot's Mission to the Indians (Cambridge, MA: Harvard Univ Press, 99). **CONTACT ADDRESS** Dept Religious Studies, So Methodist Univ, PO Box 750001, Dallas, TX 75275-0202. **EMAIL** rcogley@mail.smu.edu

COGLEY, TIMOTHY W.
PERSONAL Born 02/28/1958, Chicago, IL, m, 1987 **DISCIPLINE** ECONOMICS **EDUCATION** Univ Calif Berkeley, AB, 80; PhD, 88. **CAREER** Asst Prof, Univ Wash, 88-92; Vis Asst Prof, Univ Calif Berkeley, 91-92; Sen Econ, Fed Res Bank of San Francisco, 92-99; Assoc Prof, Ariz State Univ, 99-. **MEMBERSHIPS** Am Econ Asn **RESEARCH** Macroeconomics; Business cycles; Inflation; Trends; Equity premium. **SELECTED PUBLICATIONS** Auth, "International Evidence on the Size of the Random Walk in Output," J of Polit Econ, 90; auth, "Empirical Evidence on Nominal Wage and Price Flexibility," Quart J of Econ, 93; co-auth, "Effects of the Hodrick-Prescott Filter on Trend and Difference Stationary Time Series," J of Econ Dynamics and Control, 95; co-auth, "Output dynamics in Real Business Cycle Models," Am Econ Rev, 95; auth, "A Frequency Decomposition of Approximation Errors in Stochastic Discount Factor Models," Intl Econ Rev, 01; auth, "Idiosyncratic Risk and the Equity Premium," J of Monetary Econ, 01. **CONTACT ADDRESS** Dept Econ, Arizona State Univ, PO Box 873806, Tempe, AZ 85287. **EMAIL** timothy.cogley@asu.edu

COHEN, AMY B.
PERSONAL Born 08/05/1952, Bronx, NY, m, 1976, 2 children **DISCIPLINE** LAW **EDUCATION** Conn Col, BA, 74; Harvard Univ, JD, 78. **CAREER** Prof, W New Eng Col Sch of Law, 82-. **HONORS AND AWARDS** Phi Beta Kappa; Winthrop Scholar. **MEMBERSHIPS** Am Bar Asn **RESEARCH** Copyright and trademark law; Contract law. **SELECTED PUBLICATIONS** Auth, "Copyright Law and the Myth of Objectivity: The Idea/Expression Dichotomy and the Inevitability of Artistic Value Judgments," Ind Law J, 90; auth, "'Arising Under' Jurisdiction and the Copyright Laws," Hastings Law J, 93; auth, "Reviving Jacob and Youngs v. Kent: Material Breach Doctrine Reconsidered," Vill Law Rev, 97; auth, "When Does a Work Infringe the Derivative Works Right of a Copyright Owner?" Cardozo Arts & Ent Law J, 99. **CONTACT ADDRESS** Sch of Law, Western New England Col, 1215 Wilbraham Rd, Springfield, MA 01119. **EMAIL** acohen@law.wnec.edu

COHEN, ANDREW I.
DISCIPLINE PHILOSOPHY **EDUCATION** SUNY at Binghamton, BA, 88; Univ NC, Chapel Hill, MA, 90, PhD, 94. **CAREER** Asst prof; Univ Wis-SP, 97-. **RESEARCH** Hobbesian political theory and contemporary social philosophy. **SELECTED PUBLICATIONS** Auth, Virtues, Opportunities, and the Right to do Wrong, J Soc Philos, Vol 28, 97; auth, "Retained Liberties and Absolute Hobbesian Authorization," Hobbes Studies, XI, 98. **CONTACT ADDRESS** Dept of Philosophy, Univ of Oklahoma, 455 W Lindsey, Norman, OK 73019-2006. **EMAIL** aicohen@ou.edu

COHEN, ARNOLD B.
PERSONAL Born 04/01/1939, Philadelphia, PA, m, 1964, 3 children **DISCIPLINE** BANKRUPTCY; SECURED LENDING; E-COMMERCE; BUSINESS ACQUISITIONS **EDUCATION** Brown Univ, AB; Univ Pa Sch Law, LLB. **CAREER** Prof, Villanova Univ; past clerk, US Dist Ct Judge; past associn-Law, Univ Calif Sch Law Berkeley. **MEMBERSHIPS** Order of the Coif; Amer and Philadelphia Bar Asn; Amer Bankruptcy Inst; Eastern Dist Pa Bankruptcy Conf; bd dir, Consumer Bankruptcy Asst Proj. **RESEARCH** Bankruptcy and secured transactions. **SELECTED PUBLICATIONS** Auth, Bankruptcy and Secured Transactions, 3d ed, Lexis-Nexis, 97; Guide to Secured Lending Transactions, Warren, Gorham & Lamont, 88; Bankruptcy, Secured Transactions and Other Debtor-Creditor Matters, Bobbs-Merrill, 81; coauth, Bankruptcy, Article 9 and Creditors' Remedies, 2d ed, Michie Co, 89; Debtors' and Creditors' Rights, Michie Co, 84 & Debtor-Creditor Relations Under the Bankruptcy Act of 1978, Bobbs-Merrill; Consumer Bankruptcy Manual, 2d ed, Warren, Gorham & Lamont, 91, suppl through 97. **CONTACT ADDRESS** Law School, Villanova Univ, 229 N Spring Mill Rd, Villanova, PA 19085. **EMAIL** cohen@law.villanova.edu

COHEN, BURTON I.
PERSONAL Born 05/02/1931, Chicago, IL, m, 1954, 3 children **DISCIPLINE** RELIGIOUS EDUCATION **EDUCATION** Univ Chicago, MA, PhD; Roosevelt Univ, BA. **CAREER** Dir, Camp Ramah, 59-89; assoc prof, 57-. **HONORS AND AWARDS** JTSA Nat Comn Service Awd; JEA Behrman House Lifetime Achievement Awd. **MEMBERSHIPS** United Synagogue Comn Jewish Educ; Nat Exec Comt Jewish Educr Assembly. **SELECTED PUBLICATIONS** Auth, Case Studies in Jewish School Management, Behrman House, 92; ed, Women and Ritual: An Anthology, Nat Ramah, 86; co-ed, Studies in Jewish Education and Judaica in Honor of Louis Newman, Ktav, 84. **CONTACT ADDRESS** Dept of Jewish Educ, Jewish Theol Sem of America, 3080 Broadway, New York, NY 10027. **EMAIL** bucohen@jtsa.edu

COHEN, DAVID
DISCIPLINE LAW **EDUCATION** McGill Univ, BS, 71; Univ Toronto, LLB, 75; Yale Univ, LLM, 79. **CAREER** Vis prof, Osgoode Hall Law Sch; prof, 80-. **HONORS AND AWARDS** Pres, Consumers' Asn Can. **MEMBERSHIPS** Legal Services Soc British Columbia; Can Standards Asn; W Coast Environ Law Asn. **RESEARCH** Law and regulatory policy; commercial law and planning; contract law; law and economics. **SELECTED PUBLICATIONS** Auth, pubs on contract theory, governmental liability, product safety regulation, dispute resolution, and environmental policy and regulation. **CONTACT ADDRESS** Fac of Law, Univ of Victoria, PO Box 2400, Victoria, BC, Canada V8W 3H7. **EMAIL** lawdean@uvic.ca

COHEN, DEBRA R.
DISCIPLINE ADVANCED BUSINESS ORGANIZATIONS, CIVIL PROCEDURE **EDUCATION** Brown Univ, AB, 85; Emory Univ Sch Law, JD, 88. **CAREER** Assoc, Sullivan & Cromwell; assoc couns, Scholastic Inc, 92; vis asst prof, Emory Univ, 93; assoc prof, 95-. **HONORS AND AWARDS** JD with hon(s), 88. **MEMBERSHIPS** Order of the Coif. **SELECTED PUBLICATIONS** Ed, Emory Law Jour. **CONTACT ADDRESS** Law Sch, West Virginia Univ, Morgantown, PO Box 6009, Morgantown, WV 26506-6009.

COHEN, ELLIOT
PERSONAL 2 children **DISCIPLINE** PHILOSOPHY **EDUCATION** Brown Univ, PhD, Philo, 77; AM Philo, 76; Farleigh Dickinson Univ, BA, Philo, 74. **CAREER** Ed In Chief and Founder, The International Journal of Applied Philosophy, 82-; Asst Prof, Assoc Prof to Prof, Philo, 80-, Indian River Comm Coll; Adjunct Prof of Philo, 86-92, Barry Univ; Instr, Dept of Behavioral Stud, 78-79, Univ of Florida; Lect, Philo of Law, 74-77, Providence Coll; Tech Asst, 76-77, Brown Univ. **HONORS AND AWARDS** Pres Amer Assoc for Philo, Counsellor and Psychotherapy; Co-Founder and Executive Board Member, Amer Assoc Philo, Couns and Psychotherapy; Pews Florida Philo Assoc; Lilly Post-Doctoral Awd Hum; Scholarship Brown Univ; Phi Beta Kappa. **RESEARCH** Applied and Professional Ethics, law and medicine, journalism, Critical Thinking, Philosophy of Psychotherapy. **SELECTED PUBLICATIONS** Co-auth, Journalistic Ethics, ABC-CLIO Publishing Co, 97; AIDS, Crisis in Professional Ethics, Temple University Press, 94; auth, Caution, Faulty Thinking Can Be Harmful to Your Happiness, Self-Help, ed, Trace Wilco, 92; Philosophical Issues in Journalism, Oxford University Press, 92; ed, Philosophers at Work, An Introduction to the Issues and Practical Uses of Philosophy, Holt, Rinehart and Winston, 89; Making Value Judgments: Principles of Sound Reasoning, Robert E Krieger, Inc, 85; Belief-Scan 3.1, Artificial Intelligence for Detecting and Diagnosing Faulty Thinking, US Patent No 5,503,561, w/ Operating Manual. **CONTACT ADDRESS** Dept Philosophy, Indian River Comm Col, 3209 Virginia Ave, Fort Pierce, FL 34981-5599. **EMAIL** cohene@mail.firn.edu

COHEN, GEORGE M.
PERSONAL Born 11/22/1960, Brooklyn, NY, m, 1987, 3 children **DISCIPLINE** LAW **EDUCATION** Yale Univ, BA, 82; Univ of Pennsylvania, JD, 86, PhD, 92. **CAREER** Law clerk, U.S. court of appeals for the third circuit, 87-88; asst prof, Univ of Pittsburg Sch of Law, 88-93; visiting asst prof, Univ of Virginia Sch of Law, 92-93, assoc prof of law, 93-95, prof of law, 95-present, research prof, july 97-july 2000. **MEMBERSHIPS** Assn of Amer Law Sch (AALS); Amer Law & Economics Assn (ALEA); Amer Bar Assn (ABA); NY Bar; NJ Bar. **RESEARCH** Law and Economics, contract law, legal ethics, agency law **SELECTED PUBLICATIONS** Auth, The Negligence-Opportunism Tradeoff in Contract Law, 20 Hofstra Law Review 941, 92; The Fault Lines in Contract Damages, 80 Virginia Law Review 1225, 94; Under Cloak of Settlement, 82 Virginia Law Review 1051, 96; Legal Malpractice Insurance and Loss Prevention: A comparative Analysis of Economic Institutions,

4 Connecticut Insurance Law Journal 305, 97; Interpretation and Implied Terms in Contract Law, Encyclopedia of Law and Economics, forthcoming fall 98; When Law and Economics Met Professional Responsibility, forthcoming Fordham Law Review, fall 98. **CONTACT ADDRESS** School of Law, Univ of Virginia, 580 Massie Rd, Charlottesville, VA 22903. **EMAIL** gmc3y@virginia.edu

COHEN, JEREMY
PERSONAL Born New York, NY, m, 1977, 1 child **DISCIPLINE** JEWISH AND MEDIEVAL HISTORY **EDUCATION** Columbia Univ, AB, 74; Jewish Theol Sem Am, BHL, 74; Cornell Univ, MA, 76, PhD(hist), 78. **CAREER** Instr Jewish hist, Cornell Univ, 77-78, asst prof, 78-81 & coordr prog Jewish studies, 78-81; Melton Chair Jewish Hist, Ohio State Univ, 82-, Fac fel, Soc for Humanities, Cornell Univ, 80-81. **HONORS AND AWARDS** Nat Jewish Bk Awd, 82, 89, 99. **MEMBERSHIPS** AHA; Medieval Acad Am; Asn Jewish Studies. **RESEARCH** Judaism and Christianity: comparative cultural history; anti-semitism; history of western religious traditions. **SELECTED PUBLICATIONS** Auth, Refertile and Increase, Fill the Earth and Master It, Cornell Univ Press, 89; auth, Kentucky, Amer Jewish Arch, Vol 0046, 94; Political Liberalism, Mich Law Rev, Vol 0092, 94; Alfonsi,Petrus and His Medieval Readers, Amer Hist Rev, Vol 0100, 95; auth, Living Letters of the Law, Univ of Calif Press, 99. **CONTACT ADDRESS** Dept Jewish Hist, Tel Aviv Univ, 69978 Tel Aviv, Israel. **EMAIL** jecohen@pgt.tau.ac.il

COHEN, JOHATHAN
PERSONAL Born 07/18/1958, Philadelphia, PA, m, 1988, 4 children **DISCIPLINE** PHILOSOPHY **EDUCATION** Harvard Univ, AB, 80; John Hopkins Univ, MA, 84; Jewish Theol Sem, MA, 88; Univ Penn, PhD, 91. **CAREER** Vis asst prof, Swarthmore Col, 91-92; asst prof to assoc prof, Univ Maine, 92-. **MEMBERSHIPS** As Philos Asn, N Am Nietzsche Soc, F Nietzsche Soc (UK), Soc for Phenomenology & Existential Philos, Soc for Anc Greek philos, Maine Philos Inst. **RESEARCH** Nietzsche, Ancient philosophy, Jewish philosophy. **SELECTED PUBLICATIONS** auth, "Nietzsche's fling with Positivism," in Nietzsche, Epistemology, and Philosophy of Science, Dorrecht, 99; auth, "Born to Affirm the Eternal Recurrence: Nietzsche, Buber, and Springsteen," Philosophy in the contemporary World, (96): 1-12; auth, "What's Bad About Death is What's Good About Life," the Maine Scholar, (96): 217-225; auth, "Nietzsche's Elitism and the Cultural Division of Labor," in Rending and Renewing the Social Order, (96): 389-400; auth, "The Roots of Perspectivism," International Studies in Philosophy, (96): 59-75; auth, "Rex Ust Lex," Apeiron, (96): 145-161; auth, "No sour Grapes for Nietzsche," International Studies in Philosophy, (93): 145-149; auth, If Rabbi Akiba Were Alive Today©or the Authenticity Argument," Judaism, (88): 136-142. **CONTACT ADDRESS** Dept Humanities, Univ of Maine, Farmington, 86 Main St, Farmington, ME 04938-1911. **EMAIL** jcohen@maine.edu

COHEN, LLOYD R.
PERSONAL Born 02/12/1947, New York, NY, m, 1982, 3 children **DISCIPLINE** LEGAL STUDIES **EDUCATION** Harpur Col, BA, 68; State Univ NYork, Binghamton, MA, 73; PhD, 76; Emory Univ Sch Law, JD, 83. **CAREER** Assoc prof, Calif Western Sch of Law, San Diego, 85-90; assoc prof, Chicago-Kent Col of Law, 90-94; prof, George Mason Univ Sch of Law, Arlington, Va, 94-. **HONORS AND AWARDS** John M. Olin Fel in Law & Economics, Emory Univ, 80-83; Lon Fuller Prize in Jurisprudence, Inst for Humane Studies, 86; John M. Olin Res Fel in Law & Economics, Univ Chicago Law Sch, 88-89, 89-90; Endowed Chair in Int Capital Market Law, Int Ctr for Comparative Law and Politics, Grad Sch of Law and Politics, Univ Tokyo, summer 97; Int Centre for Economic Res, Fel, Torino, Italy, May-July 98; Who's Who in Am Law; Who's Who in Emerging Leaders in Am, Who's Who in the Midwest. **RESEARCH** Law and economics. **SELECTED PUBLICATIONS** Auth, Increasing the Supply of Transplant Organs: The Virtues Of An Options Market, R.G. Landes (95); auth, "Marriage as Contract," "Holdouts," and "Tender Offers," in The New Palgrave Dictionary of Economics and the Law, Peter Newman, ed, Stockton (98): 618, 236, 580; auth, "The Puzzling Phenomena of Interest Rate Discounts On Auto Loans," J of Legal Studies, 27:2 (98): 483; auth, "Increasing Supply, Improving Allocation, and Furthering Justice and Decency In Organ Acquisition and Allocation: The Many Virtues of Markets," 1:3 Graft (July/Aug 98): 122; auth, "The Human Genome Project and the Economics of Insurance: How Increased Knowledge May Decrease Human Welfare, and What Not To Do About It," Annual Rev of Law and Ethics, 7 (99): 219; auth, "Multi-Jurisdiction Regulation of Germline Intervention: A Policy With Neither Virtue Nor Prospect of Success," in Engineering the Human Germline, Gregory Stock and John Campbell, eds, Oxford Univ Press (99, forthcoming); auth, "Fixing the Race: Re-Engineering The Human Germline," Annual Rev of Law and Ethics, 9 (2000, forthcoming). **CONTACT ADDRESS** Sch of Law, George Mason Univ, Arlington, 3401 Fairfax Dr, Arlington, VA 22201-4411. **EMAIL** LCohen2@aol.com

COHEN, MARJORIE G.
PERSONAL Born 02/17/1944, Franklin, NJ **DISCIPLINE** POLITICAL SCIENCE, WOMEN'S STUDIES **EDUCATION** Iowa Wesleyan Col, BA, 65; NY Univ, MA, 69; York Univ, PhD 85. **CAREER** Lectr, 71-82, prof, York Univ, 84-86; prof, Ont Inst Stud Educ, 86-91; Ruth Wynn Woodward Endowed Prof, 89-90; Chair, Women's Stud & Prof Political Science & Women's Stud, Simon Fraser Univ, 91-. **HONORS AND AWARDS** Marion Porter Prize Feminist Res, 85; York Univ Fac Grad Stud Dissertation Prize, 85; Laura Jamieson Bk Prize, 89. **MEMBERSHIPS** Ed bd, Can Forum, 77-85; ed bd, Labour/Le Travail, 91-94; Nat Action Comt Status Women. **SELECTED PUBLICATIONS** Auth, Free Trade and the Future of Women's Work: Manufacturing and Service Industries, 87; auth, Women's Work, Markets and Economic Development in Nineteenth Century Ontario, 88; coauth, Canadian Women's Issues, Vol I, Strong Voices 93, Vol II, Bold Visions, 95. **CONTACT ADDRESS** Dept of Women's Stud, Simon Fraser Univ, Burnaby, BC, Canada V5A 1S6. **EMAIL** marjorie_cohen@sfu.ca

COHEN, MARTIN AARON
PERSONAL Born 02/10/1928, Philadelphia, PA, m, 1953 **DISCIPLINE** JEWISH HISTORY AND THEOLOGY **EDUCATION** Univ Pa, BA, 46, MA, 49; Hebrew Union Col, Ohio, BHL, 55, MAHL, 57, PhD(Jewish hist), 60. **CAREER** Asst instr Roman lang, Univ Pa, 46-48, instr, 48-50; instr, Rutgers Univ, New Brunswick, 50-51; instr Jewish hist, Jewish Inst Relig, Hebrew Union Col, Ohio, 60-62; from asst prof to assoc prof, 62-69, prof Jewish Hist, Jewish Inst Relig, Hebrew Union Col, NY, 69-, Nat chaplain, Am Vets World War II & Korea, 61-62; vis lectr, Antioch Col, 61-62; vis prof, Temple Univ, 63-65 & Hunter Col, 73-74; chmn, Nat Comt Jewish-Cath Rels Anti-Defamation League, B'rith, 76-. **HONORS AND AWARDS** Chadabee Awd for Outstanding Achievement, Nat Fedn Temple Brotherhoods, 76. **MEMBERSHIPS** Am Jewish Hist Soc; Cent Conf Am Rabbis; Soc Bibl Lit; Am Acad Relig; Am Soc Sephardic Studies (pres, 76-66). **RESEARCH** General Jewish history; Sephardic history; Jewish theology. **CONTACT ADDRESS** Jewish Inst of Relig, Hebrew Union Col-Jewish Inst of Religion, New York, 40 W 68th St, New York, NY 10023. **EMAIL** mcohen@huc.edu

COHEN, SHELDON M.
DISCIPLINE PHILOSOPHY **EDUCATION** Northwestern Univ, PhD, 70. **CAREER** Prof, Philos, Univ Tenn. **HONORS AND AWARDS** Dean's Awd for Dist Tchg in the Stokely Inst, 92; Col of Liv Arts Dist Svc Awd, 93. **RESEARCH** Ancient philosophy; medieval philosophy; war and morality. **SELECTED PUBLICATIONS** Auth, Arms and Judgement: Law Morality, and the Conduct of War in the Twentieth Century, Westview, 89; auth, "Luck and Happiness in the Nicomachean Ethics," Soundings (90); auth, "New Evidence for the Dating of Aristotle's Meteorology, 1-3," Class Philol (90); auth, "Defining a Higher Education: the Curriculum Question," in Points of View on Higher Education, vol 3, ed, Stephen Barnes (Edwin Mellen Pr, 90); auth, "Moral Philosophy, International Law, and the Deaths of Innocents," in Just War, Nonviolence, and Nuvlear Deterrence, ed Richard Werner (Longwood, 91); auth, "Aristotle and a Star Hidden by Jupiter," Sky & Telescope (92); auth, "Aristotle on Elemental Motion," Phronesis (94); auth, Aristotle on Nature and incomplete Substance, Cambirdge Univ Pr, 96. **CONTACT ADDRESS** Dept of Philos, Univ of Tennessee, Knoxville, 801 McClung Tower, Knoxville, TN 37996-0480. **EMAIL** scohen@utk.edu

COHEN, STEPHEN MARSHALL
PERSONAL Born 09/27/1929, New York, NY, m, 1964, 2 children **DISCIPLINE** PHILOSOPHY **EDUCATION** Dartmouth Col, BA, 51; Harvard Univ, MA, 53; Oxford Univ, MA, 77. **CAREER** Asst prof philos, Harvard Univ, 58-62; asst prof and assoc prof, Univ Chicago, 62-67; assoc prof Rockefeller Univ, 67-70; prof philos CUNY, 70-83, exec officer prog in philos Grad Ctr, 75-83; prof philos and law, 83-97, dean div hum, 83-94, interim dean Col Lett Arts & Sci, 93-94, Univ S Calif, now Prof Emer Philos & Law/University Prof Emer and Dean Emer Col of Lett, Arts & Sci. **HONORS AND AWARDS** Vis fel All Souls Col, Oxford, 76-77; mem Inst for Advanced Study, Princeton, 81-82. **RESEARCH** Moral, legal and political philosophy; aesthetics. **SELECTED PUBLICATIONS** Ed, The Philosophy of John Stuart Mill, 61; ed, Philosophy and Public Affairs, 70-99 ; ed, Philosophy and Society series, 77-83; ed, Ethical, Legal and Political Philosophy series, 83-99 ; co-ed, Film Theory and Criticism, 74, 79, 85, 92, 98; co-ed, War and Moral Responsibility, 74; co-ed, The Rights and Wrongs of Abortion, 74; co-ed, Equality and Preferential Treatment, 77. **CONTACT ADDRESS** Law School, Univ of So California, Los Angeles, CA 90089-0071. **EMAIL** mcohen@law.usc.edu

COHEN, STEPHEN P.
DISCIPLINE POLITICAL SCIENCE **EDUCATION** Univ Chicago, BA, MA, Univ Wisconsin, PhD. **CAREER** Sr fel, Foreign Policy Studies, Brookings Inst; prof hist and polit sci, & dir of Program in Arms Control, Disarmament and Int Security, Univ Illinois, Urbana; Public Policy Planning staff, US Dept of State. **HONORS AND AWARDS** Scholar in residence, Ford Found, New Delhi. **RESEARCH** India; Pakistan; South Asian security and proliferation issues. **SELECTED PUBLICATIONS** Ed, Nuclear Proliferation in South Asia, 90; ed, South Asia after the Cold War: International Perspectives, 93; auth, Brasstacks and Beyond: Perception and Management of Crisis in South Asia, 95; auth, The Pakistan Army, 2d ed, 98; auth, India: Emerging Power, forthcoming. **CONTACT ADDRESS** Brookings Inst, 1775 Massachusetts Ave NW, Washington, DC 20036. **EMAIL** scohen@brook.edu

COHEN, TED
PERSONAL Born 12/13/1939, Danville, IL, m, 1994, 2 children **DISCIPLINE** PHILOSOPHY **EDUCATION** Univ Chicago, AB, 62; Harvard Univ, MA, 65, PhD(philos), 72. **CAREER** From asst prof to assoc prof, 67-79, Prof Philos, Univ Chicago, 79-, Chmn Dept, 74-79, mem Comt on the Visual Arts and Comt on General Studies in the Humanities; William R. Kenan Jr Distinguished Prof in the Humanities, Col William and Mary, 86-87. **HONORS AND AWARDS** ACLS travel grants, 80, 85; Ill Philos Asn Keynote Address, 80; Quantrell Awd for Excellence in Undergraduate Teaching, 83; Pushcart XVI prize, 91; Phi betta Kappa vis scholar, 00-01. **MEMBERSHIPS** Am Philos Asn; Am Soc Aesthetics (pres, 97-99). **RESEARCH** Philosophy of art; 18th century aesthetics; philosophy of language. **SELECTED PUBLICATIONS** Co-ed and contribr, Essays in Kant's Aesthetics, Univ Chicago Press, 82; auth, Jokes, In: Pleasure, Preference, and Value: Studies in Philosophical Aesthetics, Cambridge Univ Press, 83; Sports and Art: Beginning Questions, In: Human Agency, Stanford univ Press, 88; Representation: Pictorial and Photographic, In: International Encyclopedia of Communications, Oxford Univ Press, 89; co-ed and contribr, Pursuits of Reason: Essays in Honor of Stanley Cavell, Texas Tech Univ Press, 93; auth, The Relation of Pleasure to Judgement in Kant's Aesthetics, In: Kant and Critique: New Essays in Honor of W.H. Werkmeister, Kluwer Acad Publ, 93; Partial Enchantments of the Quixote Story in Hume's Essay on Taste, In: Institutions of Art: Reconsiderations of George Dickie's Philosophy, Penn State Univ Press, 94; On Consistency in One's Personal Aesthetics, In: Aesthetics and Ethics: Essays at the Intersection, Cambridge Univ Press, 98; auth, Jokes, Univ Chicago Pr, 99; author of numerous journal articles. **CONTACT ADDRESS** Dept of Philos, Univ of Chicago, 1050 E 59th St, Chicago, IL 60637-1512. **EMAIL** tedcohen@midway.uchicago.edu

COHN, HENRY S.
PERSONAL Born 11/24/1945, Hartford, CT, m, 1971, 3 children **DISCIPLINE** LAW **EDUCATION** Johns Hopkins, BA, 67. **CAREER** Asst state attorney general, Conn; Superior Court Judge, Hartford, Conn. **MEMBERSHIPS** Conn Bar Asn. **RESEARCH** Court history. **SELECTED PUBLICATIONS** Auth, Great Hartford Circus Fire, Yale, 91. **CONTACT ADDRESS** Superior Court, 75 Elm St., Hartford, CT 06106. **EMAIL** 132main@house.com

COHN, SHERMAN LOUIS
PERSONAL Born 07/21/1932, Erie, PA, m, 1998, 5 children **DISCIPLINE** LAW **EDUCATION** Georgetown Univ, BSFS, 54, JD, 57, LLM, 60. **CAREER** Law clerk, US Circuit Court of Appeals, DC, 57-58; staff atty, Appellate sect, civil div, US Dept Justice, 58-62, asst chief, 62-65; Prof Law, Georgetown Univ, 65-, Staff dir, Found Fed Bar Asn, 58-61; nat chmn comt younger lawyers, Fed Bar Asn, 62-63, comt uniform rules fed appellate procedure, 63-70, nat coun, 63-66, 68-70 & 72-74, chmn comt fed rules & pract, 64-66 & 68-69, coun fed courts, 68-69; assoc mem, Inst World Policy, Georgetown Univ, 62-80, co-dir, Inst Law, Human Rights & Social Values, 66-73; chmn, Coun Community Affairs, 64-66; mem standing comt civil legal aid, Judicial Conf, 64-68, mem conf, 65-73; secy spec comt on adv comt rules & practice, Judicial Coun DC Circuit, 66-67; Washington dir, Practicing Law Inst, 66-68; mem civil rules comt, DC Judicial Conf, 68-73, DC Superior Court, 71-73; vis prof, Am Univ Law Sch, 69-78, 92-93, 94-95. **HONORS AND AWARDS** Younger Fed Lawyer Awd, 64; 1978 Presidential Citation, 1980 John Carroll Awd, 1984 Univ Recognition Awd for Outstanding Fac, Georgetown Univ Alumni Asn; Honorary Diplomat, Am Bd Trial Advocates, 90; Hon M Ac, Traditional Acupuncture Inst, 93; Civil Justice Awd, Am Bd Trial Advocates, 93. **MEMBERSHIPS** Am Law Inst; Am Bar Asn; Fed Bar Asn; Chair, Accreditation Commission for Ocupuncture & Oriental Medicine, 83-94; Am Inns of Court Found (pres 85-96); Nat Pres, Am Laws of Court, 85-96; Nat Acad of Acupuncture & Oriental Med; Nat Acupuncture Found; Tai Hsuan Found; Chair, Bd of Trustees; Traditional Acupuncture Inst; Pres, Jewish Law Asn, 98-. **RESEARCH** Am legal prof; civil procedure; conflicts. **SELECTED PUBLICATIONS** Auth, Overview of Acupuncture in America, 1971-1993: A Historical Perspective, In: The Oriental Medicine Resources Guide, 93; monthly article on federal practice and procedure, Fed Practice Digest, Barclays Legal Publ, 93-96; Privilege or Coverup?, Nat Law J, 3/97; A Perspective on Progress, Washington Lawyer, 4/97; Professionalism & the Trial Advocate, Voir Dire, Spring 96; The Organizational Client: Attorney-Client Privilege and the No-Contact Rule, Georgetown J of Legal Ethics 10, 97; author of numerous other articles, books, and reviews. **CONTACT ADDRESS** Law Ctr, Georgetown Univ, 600 New Jersey N W, Washington, DC 20001-2022. **EMAIL** cohn@law.georgetown.edu

COHN, STUART R.
DISCIPLINE LAW **EDUCATION** Univ Ill, BA; Oxford Univ, BA; Yale Univ, LLB. **CAREER** Prof, Univ Fla, 77-. **MEMBERSHIPS** Amer Bar Asn Fed Regulation Securities Comm, 80-; Drafting comm for revisions to Fla corporate laws securities laws; Ill Bar; Phi Beta Kappa; Phi Kappa Phi. **RESEARCH** Corporate & securities law, jurisprudence. **CONTACT ADDRESS** School of Law, Univ of Florida, PO Box 117625, Gainesville, FL 32611-7625. **EMAIL** cohn@law.ufl.edu

COHON, RACHEL
DISCIPLINE PHILOSOPHY **EDUCATION** UCLA, PhD. **CAREER** Assoc prof, Univ Albany, State Univ NY. **HONORS AND AWARDS** Stanford Humanities Cnetr Internal Fel, 92-3; NEH Summer Stipend, 93. **RESEARCH** Ethics, philosophy of action, history of ethics, hume. **SELECTED PUBLICATIONS** Auth, "Are External Reasons Impossible?" Ethics 96, 86; auth, "Hume and Humeanism in Ethics," Pacific Philosophical Quarterly 69, no. 2, 88; rev, of Francis Snare, Morals, Motivation, and Convention, In the Philosophical Reviw, vol. 103, no. 3, 93; auth, "On an Unorthodox Version of Hume's Moral Psychology,"" Hume Studies, 2, 94; auth, "Is Hume a Noncognitivist ni the Motivation Argument?", Phiolsophical Studies 85, 97; auth, "Hume's Difficulty with the Virtue of Honesty," Hume Studies XXIII, 1, 97; auth, "Hume on Representation, Reason, and Motivation," with David Owen, Manuscrito, special edition on Hume ed. John Biro, 97; auth, The Common Point of View in Hume's Ethics, Philos and Phenomenological Res, 97; Internalism about Reasons for Action, Pacific Philos Quart, 93; auth, "The Roots of Reasons," The Philosophical Review, 00; ed, Hume: Moral and Political philosophy, Dartmouth/Ashgate Press, 01. **CONTACT ADDRESS** Dept of Philosophy, SUNY, Albany, Albany, NY 12222. **EMAIL** rcohon@albany.edu

COLE, BASIL
PERSONAL Born 03/14/1937, San Francisco, CA, s **DISCIPLINE** THEOLOGY **EDUCATION** Le Sulchoir, Paris, STL, 68; Angelicam Univ, , STD, 91. **CAREER** Pontifica Universita San Tommaso, Rome, Italy, 85-87. **HONORS AND AWARDS** Fel, Cath Scholars. **RESEARCH** Moral theology, esthetics. **SELECTED PUBLICATIONS** Auth, The Moral and Psychological Effects of Music: A Theological Appraisal, 92: auth, Music and Morals: A Theological Appraisal of the Moral and Psychological Effects of Music, Alba House Publ (Staten Island, NY), 93; coauth, A New Catechism of the Consecrated Life: Help for Perplexed Postulants and Novices of the Third Millenium, Asia Trading Corp (Bangalore, India), 97; coauth, Christian Totality: Theology of Consecrated Life, 3rd Ed, Alba House Publ (Staten Island, NY), 97. **CONTACT ADDRESS** Dept Theol, Dominican House of Studies, 487 Mich Ave NE, Washington, DC 20017-1584. **EMAIL** 110167.1021@compuserve.com

COLE, EVE BROWNING
DISCIPLINE ANCIENT GREEK PHILOSOPHY, FEMINIST THEORY, ETHICS, CLASSICAL STUDIES **EDUCATION** Univ Fla, BA, 73; Univ Calif, San Diego, PhD; 79. **CAREER** Instr, Univ Denver; instr, Ohio State Univ; assoc prof, 84-, ch, Environ Stud adv bd, Univ Minn, Duluth. **RESEARCH** Ancient Greek philosophy; ethics. **SELECTED PUBLICATIONS** Auth, Philosophy and Feminist Criticism, Paragon, 93; coed, Explorations in Feminist Ethics: Theory and Practice, Ind UP, 88. **CONTACT ADDRESS** Univ of Minnesota, Duluth, Duluth, MN 55812-2496.

COLE, KENNETH
DISCIPLINE LAW **EDUCATION** Osgoode Hall Law Sch, LLB, 74. **CAREER** Partner, Epstein, Cole **MEMBERSHIPS** Law Soc Upper Can. **SELECTED PUBLICATIONS** Auth, pubs on family law, enforcement of support orders, and procedural issues. **CONTACT ADDRESS** Fac of Law, Univ of Toronto, 78 Queen's Park, Toronto, ON, Canada M5S 1A1.

COLE, RICHARD
PERSONAL Born 10/28/1929, Evanston, IL, m, 1958, 3 children **DISCIPLINE** PHILOSOPHY **EDUCATION** Univ TX, BA, 58; Univ Chicago, PhD, 62. **CAREER** Instr philos, CO Col, 61-62; asst prof, Grinnell Col, 62-65; assoc prof, 65-69, Prof Philos, Univ KS, 69, Res Grants, Univ KS, 74, 75, 76, 77 & 78; referee, NOUS, 77- **MEMBERSHIPS** Philos Sci Asn; Am Philos Asn; Mind Asn; Southwestern Philos Soc(pres, 77-78); Metaphys Soc Am. **RESEARCH** Philos of physical sci; philos of mathematics; logic. **SELECTED PUBLICATIONS** Auth, Ptolemy and Copernicus, Philos Rev, 10/62; Falsifiability, Mind, 1/68; Appearnance, reality and falsification, Int Philos Quart, 6/68; coauth, Concept of Order, Univ Wash, 68; Hard and soft intensionalism, 70 & auth, Causality and sufficient reason, 74, Rev Metaphysics; Causes and explanations, NOUS, 77; Possibility matrices, Theoria, 78. **CONTACT ADDRESS** Dept of Philos, Univ of Kansas, Lawrence, Lawrence, KS 66045-0001. **EMAIL** nobledog@aol.com

COLEMAN, ARTHUR H.
PERSONAL Born 02/18/1920, Philadelphia, PA, m, 1987, 4 children **DISCIPLINE** LAW **EDUCATION** Pa State Univ, BS, 41; Howard Univ, MD, 44; Golden Gate Col, LlB, 56; JD, 68. **CAREER** Medicine, pvt practice 48-; San Francisco Med Assoc, pres. **HONORS AND AWARDS** Bay Area Howard Univ Alumni Awd 66; SF Bay Area Council Certificate 65-67; SF bd of supres Certificate of Awd 68; SF Dept of Health Commendation 76; Omega Psi Phi Awd for Distingushed Serv 73; Distinguished Alumnus, Pa State Univ, 77. **MEMBERSHIPS** Bd dir Sec Drew Inv Corp 1952; pres co-founder Amer Health Care Plan 1973; bd dir Fidelity Savings & Loan Assn 1966; cofounder pres SF Med Assn Inc; exec dir Hunters Point Baypoint Comm Health Serv 1968-72; chmn SF Econ Opportunity Council 1964-67; pres chmn of bd Trans-Bay Fed Savings & Loan Assn 1964-66; guest lectr Golden Gate Coll of Law 1958-60; lectr Univ CA 1968; mem Pathway Comm for Family Med Univ CA Med Ctr 1970; internship Homer G Phillips Hosp 1945; mem AMA 1948; mem CA Med Assn 1948; mem SF Med Soc 1948-; pres Natl Med Assn 1976-77; pres John Hale Med Soc 1970-71; fellow Amer Acad of Forensic Sci 1958; fellow bd of govs Amer Coll of Legal Med 1961; pres Northern California Med Dental Pharm Assn 1964; pres bd Dir Golden State Med Assn 1970-74; memWorld Med Assn 1971-; mem Acad of Med 1971; coord com SF Alliance for Health Care; vice pres Amer Cancer Soc 1969-71; bd of dir SF Hunters Point Boys Club; bd dir adv council SF Planning & Ren Assn 1969-75; pres Amer Coll of Legal Medicine 1983-84; vice pres bd of dir Drew Medical Univ 1987; pres Port of San Francisco 1984-87. **CONTACT ADDRESS** San Francisco Medical Assn, 6301 Third St, San Francisco, CA 94124.

COLEMAN, JOHN ALOYSIUS
PERSONAL Born 03/27/1937, San Francisco, CA **DISCIPLINE** SOCIOLOGY OF RELIGION **EDUCATION** St Louis Univ, BA, 60, MA, 61; Univ Santa Clara, STM, 68; Univ Calif, Berkeley, PhD(sociol), 74. **CAREER** Asst prof relig & soc, Jesuit Sch Theol & Grad Theol Union, Berkeley, 74-77; res fel, Woodstock Ctr, Georgetown Univ, 77-78; Asst Prof Relig & Soc, Jesuit Sch Theol & Grad Theol Union, Berkeley, 78-, Fel social ethics, Univ Chicago Divinity Sch, 73-74. **MEMBERSHIPS** Cath Theol Soc Am; Am Acad Relig; Am Soc Christian Ethics. **RESEARCH** Sociology of comparative Catholicism; history of social Catholicism; human rights. **SELECTED PUBLICATIONS** Auth, On Being the Church in the United-States--Contemporary Theological Critiques of Liberalism, Theol Stud, Vol 0057, 96; Religion and Politics in Latin-America--Liberation-Theology and Christian Democracy, Jour Rel, Vol 0073, 93; Pious Passion--The Emergence of Modern Fundamentalism in the United-States And Iran--Comparative-Studies in Religion and Society, Theol Stud, Vol 0055, 94; Sociology and Social-Justice--The Case-Study of Fichter, Joseph Sj Research, Sociol Rel, Vol 0057, 96. **CONTACT ADDRESS** Graduate Theol Union, 2465 Le Compte Ave, Berkeley, CA 94709.

COLLIER, CHARLES W.
DISCIPLINE LAW **EDUCATION** Reed Col, BA; Yale Univ, MA, MPhil, PhD; Stanford Univ, JD. **CAREER** Prof, aff prof, Univ Fla, 86-. **MEMBERSHIPS** Law and Soc Asn; Amer Philos Asn. **RESEARCH** Constitutional law, jurisprudence, legal theory. **CONTACT ADDRESS** School of Law, Univ of Florida, PO Box 117625, Gainesville, FL 32611-7625. **EMAIL** collier@law.ufl.edu

COLLINGE, WILLIAM JOSEPH
PERSONAL Born 07/14/1947, Erie, PA, m, 1972, 3 children **DISCIPLINE** RELIGION **EDUCATION** Georgetown Univ, AB, 69; Yale Univ, MPhil, 71, PhD(Philos), 74. **CAREER** Asst prof Philos, Loyola Marymount Univ, 74-80; assoc prof Theol & chmn dept, Mt St Marys Col (MD), 80-89; actg chmn Philos Dept, Loyola Marymount Univ, 78-79; prof of Theology and Philosophy, Mt St Mary's Col, MD, 89-97; Forker Prof of Catholic Soc Teaching, Mt St Mary's Col, 97-. **MEMBERSHIPS** Am Philos Asn; Col Theol Soc; Cath Theol Soc Am; Am Acad of Relig. **RESEARCH** Philosophy of religion; ancient and medieval Christian thought; Catholic Social Teaching. **SELECTED PUBLICATIONS** Auth, "Augustine and Theological Falsification," Augustinian Studies, 82; auth, "Metanoia De Trinitate and the understanding of religious language," Augustinian Studies, 87; auth, "The Relation of Religious Community Life to Rationality in Augustine," Faith and Philos, 88; auth, "John Dunne's Journey of The Mind, Heart, and Soul," Horizons, 89; coauth, Saint Augustine, Four Anti-Pelagian Writings, Catholic University of America Press, 92; auth, Historical Dictionary of Catholicism, Scarecrow, 97. **CONTACT ADDRESS** Dept Theol, Mount Saint Mary's Col and Sem, 16300 Old Emmitsburg Rd, Emmitsburg, MD 21727-7700. **EMAIL** collinge@msmary.edu

COLLINS, ARDIS B.
DISCIPLINE PHILOSOPHY **EDUCATION** Univ Toronto, PhD, 68; **CAREER** Assoc prof, Loyola Univ Chicago, 68-; dir, undergrad majors & graduate Philos; philos rep, Acad Coun Col Arts & Sci(s); PhD coun rep, Graduate Stud Coord Bd; 4 terms dir, 2 counr, VP, organizer 92 conf & treas, Exec Coun Hegel Soc Am; fac, St. Mary's Col, Notre Dame, Ind, 66-68; ed consult, Hist Philos Quart; ed in chief, Owl of Minerva, jour the Hegel Soc Am, 96. **RESEARCH** Medieval and renaissance philosophy; modern philosophy, especially Kant and Hegel; metaphysics. **SELECTED PUBLICATIONS** Auth, The Secular Is Sacred: Platonism and Thomism in Marsilio Ficino's Platonic Theology, Martinus Nijhoff, 74; Ed, Hegel on the Modern World, SUNY Press, 95; articles in, J Hist Philos, Method and Speculation in Hegel's Phenomenology-Humanities Press, 82, Hegel and His Critics-SUNY Press, 89, Cardozo Law Rev, Am Catholic Philos Quart. **CONTACT ADDRESS** Dept of Philosophy, Loyola Univ, Chicago, 820 N. Michigan Ave., Chicago, IL 60611.

COLLINS, ELIZABETH F.
PERSONAL Born 08/23/1942, d, 3 children **DISCIPLINE** POLITICAL THEORY **EDUCATION** Univ Calif, Berkeley, PhD, 91. **CAREER** Assoc prof, philos and Southeast Asian stud, Ohio Univ. **CONTACT ADDRESS** Dept of Philosophy, Ohio Univ, 51 Fairview Dr, Athens, OH 45701. **EMAIL** collinse@ohiou.edu

COLLINS, JOHN J.
PERSONAL Born 02/02/1966, Ireland, m, 1973, 3 children **DISCIPLINE** BIBLICAL STUDIES **EDUCATION** Harvard, PhD, 72. **CAREER** Assoc Prof, Munde Lein Sem, 76-78; Assoc Prof, Prof, DePaul, 78-86; Prof, Notre Dame, 86-91; Prof, Univ Chi, 91-. **HONORS AND AWARDS** NEH Fel, 87-88; Exec Com, Soc of Bibl Lit, 89-94; Pres, Cath Bibl Assn, 97. **MEMBERSHIPS** Soc of Bibl Lit; Catholic Bibl Asn **RESEARCH** Apocalypticism; wisdom; dead sea scrolls. **SELECTED PUBLICATIONS** Auth, The Scepter and the Star. The Messiahs of the Dead Sea Scrolls and Other Ancient Literature, Dbl Day, 95; auth, Isaia, Brescia:Q, 95; coauth, Qumran Cave 4.XVII. Parabliblical Tests, Part 3, 96; coauth, Families in Ancient Israel, Westmin, 97; Apolcalypticism in the Dead Sea Scrolls, Routledge, 97; auth, Seers, Sibyls and Sages in Hellenistic-Roman Judaism, Brill, 97; auth, Jewish Wisdom in the Hellenistic Age, Old Test Lib, Westmin, 97; auth, The Apocalyptic Imagination, Eerdmans, 98; co-ed, The Encyclopedia of Apocalypticism, Cont, 98. **CONTACT ADDRESS** 1019 Brassie, Flossmoor, IL 60422. **EMAIL** jj.collins@uchicago.edu

COLLINS, KENNETH J.
DISCIPLINE THEOLOGY **EDUCATION** SUNY Buffalo, BA, 74; Asbury Theol Sem, MDiv, 79; Princeton Theol Sem, ThM, 80; Drew Univ, MPhil, 82; PhD, 84. **CAREER** Chaplain, Methodist Col, 84-86; asst prof to prof, Methodist Col, 86-95; prof, Asbury Theol Sem, 95-. **HONORS AND AWARDS** Regents Scholar; Alpha Kappa Delta; Theta Phi; Goethe Inst Scholar; Teaching Fel Drew Univ; Black Student Movement Awd for Excellence in Relig Educ, Methodist Col, 86; Samuel J and Norma C Womack Endowed Chair in Philos and Relig, 94; Excemplary Teaching Awd, United Methodist Schools, 94. **MEMBERSHIPS** Am Acad of Relig; Oxford Inst; Soc for the Study of Christian Spirituality; Wesleyan Theol Soc; Wesley Hist Soc. **RESEARCH** Wesley Theology/History, Spirituality. **SELECTED PUBLICATIONS** Auth, A Faithful Witness: John Wesley's Homiletical Theology, Wesley Heritage Pr, (Wilmore, KY), 93; auth, Soul Care: Deliverance and Renewal Through the Christian Life, Bridgepoint Books, (Wheaton, IL), 95; auth, The Scripture Way of Salvation: The Heart of John Wesley's Theology, Abingdon Pr, (Nashville), 97; auth, "A Reconfiguration of Power: The Basic Trajectory of John Wesley's Practical Theology", Wesleyan Theol J 33.1 (98): 164-184; auth, "Spirituality and Critical Thinking: Are They Really So Different?", Evangel J 16.1 (98): 30-44; auth, "John Wesley's Topography of the Heart: Dispositions, Tempers and Affections: Methodist Hist 36.3, (98): 162-175; auth, A Real Christian: The Life of John Wesley, Abingdon Pr, (Nashville), 99; auth, "Why the Holiness Movement is Dead", Asbury Theol J 54.2, (99): 27-36; auth, Exploring Christian Spirituality: An Ecumenical Reader, Baker Book House, (Grand Rapids, MI), 00. **CONTACT ADDRESS** Dept Theol, Asbury Theol Sem, 204 N Lexington Ave, Wilmore, KY 40390-1129. **EMAIL** ken_collins@asburyseminary.edu

COLLINS, KENNETH L.
PERSONAL Born 08/23/1933, El Centro, CA, m **DISCIPLINE** LAW **EDUCATION** UCLA, BA 1959; UCLA, JD 1971. **CAREER** LA Co, probation ofcr 1957-68; San Fernando Valley Juvenile Hall, acting dir; Fed Pub Defenders Office, pub defender 1972-75. **HONORS AND AWARDS** UCLA Chancelors Awd 1971. **MEMBERSHIPS** Mem Langston Law Club; CA Attys for Criminal Justice; CA State Bar; chmn bd dir Black Law Journal; past pres Kappa Alpha Psi Upsion 1957-58; cofounderBlack Law Journal; distinguished serv. **CONTACT ADDRESS** 3701 Wilshire Blvd, Ste 700, Los Angeles, CA 90010.

COLLINS, MARY
PERSONAL Born 09/16/1935, Chicago, IL **DISCIPLINE** RELIGIOUS STUDIES **EDUCATION** Mt St Scholastica Col, AB, 57; Cath Univ Am, PhD(relig studies), 67. **CAREER** Asst prof Relig & chmn dept, Mt St Scholastica Col, 67-70, assoc prof, 70-77; vis prof, Kans Sch Relig, Univ Kans, 69-72, vis lectr, 72-73, assoc prof, 73-78; prof Relig, Cath Univ Am, 78-,

chmn dept Relig Studies, Benedictine Col, 71-72; mem, Kans Comt Humanities, 72-75; mem, Am Benedictine Acad. **HONORS AND AWARDS** Berakah Awd, North Am Acad of Liturgy; Michael Mathis Awd, Notre Dame Center for Pastoral Liturgy. **MEMBERSHIPS** Col Theol Soc; Am Acad Relig; NAm Acad Liturgy; Catholic Theological Society of America. **RESEARCH** Worship and ritual; contemporary religious thought; ritual and society. **SELECTED PUBLICATIONS** Auth, Eucharistic proclamation of God's presence, Worship, 11/67; Local liturgical legislation: United States, Concilium, 2/72; Taking peace education seriously, Living Light, Summer 73; Liturgy in America: The Scottsdale conference, 2/74, Liturgical methodology and the cultural evolution of worship in the United States, 2/75 & Ritual symbols and the ritual process: the work of Victor Turner, 7/76, Worship; Response to Charles David's religion and the Sense of the Sacred, Pro Cath Theol Soc Am, 12/76; contribr, Climb Along the Cutting Edge: The Renewal of Religious Life, Paulist, 77. **CONTACT ADDRESS** Dept of Relig/Relig Educ, Catholic Univ of America, 620 Michigan Ave NE, Washington, DC 20064-0002. **EMAIL** collinsm@cua.edu

COLLINS, ROBERT H.
PERSONAL Born 07/10/1934, Chicago, IL **DISCIPLINE** THEOLOGY **EDUCATION** Wilson Jr Clg Chicago IL, AA 1954; Michael Resse Sch of Med Tech, MT 1955; Roosevelt Univ Chicago IL, BS 1957; Concordia Theology Smnry Springfield, IL,BD 1964, MDiv 1965; Concordia Smnry St Louis, Master of Sacred Theology 1974. **CAREER** Univ of IL R&E Hospital, medical tech, 55-56; Northwestern Univ, research chemist, 56; Lab of Vit Tech, chem quality control, 57-59; Concordia Seminary, Springfield IL, 59-63; Bethlehem Lutheran Church, Col GA, pastor, 63-73; St James Lutheran Church, Bakersfield CA, pastor, 73-77; Northern IL Dist LC-MS, missionary-at-large; Corcordia Theological Seminary, Ft Wayne IN, prof of prctl theology counseling, 77-85. **HONORS AND AWARDS** Meritorious Serv City of Col GA 1971, 72-73; Cert of Aprctn Pres Nixon GA State Advsr Com on Edc 1972; Cert of Aprctn TB Assc, Legal Aid Soc, Sr Citizens; mem Bd of Dir 1972-73. **MEMBERSHIPS** Mem Scan 1982-; vacancy pstr Shepherd of the City Luth Ft Wayne 1983-; mem Resolve; vol chpln Parkview Meml Hosp Ft Wayne, IN; part-time chpln Cnty Jail; vacancy pastor Mount Calvary Luth Church; consultant cross-cultural ministry Trinity Luth Church. **CONTACT ADDRESS** Counseling/Evng, Concordia Theol Sem, 6600 N Clinton, Fort Wayne, IN 46825.

COLOMBO, JOHN D.
DISCIPLINE LAW **EDUCATION** Univ Ill, AB; JD. **CAREER** Law clerk, Judge Phyllis Kravitch, US Court Appeals; prof, Univ Ill Urbana Champaign; assoc dean of the Col of Law, 95-. **HONORS AND AWARDS** Ed, Univ Ill Law Rev. **RESEARCH** Tax issues relating to tax-exempt organizations. **SELECTED PUBLICATIONS** Co-auth, The Charitable Tax Exemption, Westview, 95. **CONTACT ADDRESS** Law Dept, Univ of Illinois, Urbana-Champaign, 52 E Gregory Dr, Champaign, IL 61820. **EMAIL** jcolombo@law.uiuc.edu

COLSON, DARREL D.
DISCIPLINE PHILOSOPHY **EDUCATION** Louisiana State Univ, BA, 77; Vanderbilt Univ, MA, 82, PhD, 87. **CAREER** Instr, Western Carolina Univ, 82-87; assoc prof, Louisiana Scholars Col at Northwestern State Univ, 87-96; Fletcher Jones prof of Great Books, Pepperdine Univ, 96-. **MEMBERSHIPS** APA; Southern Soc for Philos and Psych; Soc for Ancient Greek Philos; Hume Soc; Asn for Core Texts and Courses. **RESEARCH** Plato's Socratic Dialogues. **SELECTED PUBLICATIONS** Auth, Crito 51A-C: To What Does Socrates Owe Obedience? Phronesis, 89; auth, rev of Pangle, ed, The Rebirth of Political Rationalism: An Introduction to the Thought of Leo Strauss: Essays and Lectures by Leo Strauss, Ancient Philos, 91; auth, rev of Arieti, Interpreting Plato: The Dialogues as Drama, Tchg Philos, 93; co-ed, Senior Thesis Bulletin: Abstracts and Selected Excerpts from Honors Theses, 1990-1993, Northwestern State, 96. **CONTACT ADDRESS** Humanities and Teacher Education Div, Pepperdine Univ, 24255 Pacific Coast Hwy, Malibu, CA 90263-4225. **EMAIL** dcolson@pepperdine.edu

COLVIN, CHRISTOPHER
PERSONAL Born 05/26/1954, Salzburg, Austria, m, 1995 **DISCIPLINE** PHILOSOPHY **EDUCATION** Yale Univ, BA, 76; Northwestern Univ, MA, 80, MA, 81; Univ Texas-Austin, PhD, 87. **CAREER** Vis asst prof, Bowdoin Col, 87-88; vis asst prof, Univ Dallas, 88-91; instr, Univ Texas-Austin, 91-92 & 93-94; vis asst prof, Southwestern Univ, 92-93; vis instr, Vytautes Maguus Univ (Lithuania), 94-95; instr, hist and math, St. Stephen's Episcopal Sch. **RESEARCH** Plato; Idealist metaphysics; Greek mathematics. **SELECTED PUBLICATIONS** Transl Fichte Schlegel und der Infinitismus in der Platondeutuns, Grad Jour Philos. **CONTACT ADDRESS** St. Stephens Episcopal Sch, PO Box 1868, Austin, TX 78767. **EMAIL** ccolvin@sss.austin.tx.us

COLWELL, CHAUNCEY
PERSONAL Born 10/28/1954, Bryn Mawr, PA, s **DISCIPLINE** PHILOSOPHY **EDUCATION** Lebanon Valley Col, BS, 78; Villanova Univ, MA, 82; Temple Univ, PhD, 92. **CAREER** Adj prof Philosophy, 88-96, vis asst prof, 96-, Villanova Univ, 88-. **MEMBERSHIPS** Amer Philos Asn; Soc Phenomenol & Existential Philos; Int Asn Philos & Lit. **RESEARCH** 20th Century Continental Philosophy; Philosophy of the Bio-Sciences; Social/Political Philosophy. **SELECTED PUBLICATIONS** Auth, Signs of War: Myth, Media and the Selling of Desert Storm, Jour Peace & Justice Studies, 93; The Retreat of the Subject in the Late Foucault, Philos Today, 94; Typology, Racism and The Bell Curve, Jour Peace & Justice Studies, 95; Postmodernism and Medicine: Discourse and the Limits of Practice, Conttinental and Postmodern Perspectives in the Philosophy of Science, Avebury Press, 95; Discourses of Liberation and Discourses of Transformation, Liberalism, Oppression and Empowerment, Edwin Mellen Press, 95; Deleuze, Sense and the Event of AIDS, Postmodern Culture, 96; The Virtual Body of Medicine, International Studies in Philosophy, 96; Discipline and Control: Butler and Deleuze on Individuality and Dividuality, Philosophy Today, 96; Deleuze and Foucault: Series, Event, Genealogy, Theory and Event, 97; Deleuze and the Prepersonal, Philosophy Today, 97. **CONTACT ADDRESS** Philosophy Dept, Villanova Univ, Villanova, PA 19085. **EMAIL** ccolwell@email.vill.edu

COLYER, ELMER M.
PERSONAL Born 04/07/1950, Ludington, MI, m, 1980, 3 children **DISCIPLINE** THEOLOGY **EDUCATION** Univ Wisc, Platteville, BS, 81; Univ Dubuque Theol Sem, MDiv, 85; Boston Col, Andover Newton, PhD, 92. **CAREER** Min, New Hope/Retreat UM Churches, Desoto, Wisc, 81-88; tchg asst, Boston Col, 90-91; scholar in residence, Carter UM Church, Needham, Mass, 88-92; assoc prof of Historical Theology, Stanley Prof of Wesley Stud, Univ Dubuque Theol Sem, 93- . **HONORS AND AWARDS** Loetscher traveling fel, 84; John Wesley fel, 88-92; Bradley fel, 91-92; CHARIS Awd, Univ Dubuque, 96, 98; Lilly Small Grant 00-01. **RESEARCH** Modern theology; Wesleyan theology; theological method. **SELECTED PUBLICATIONS** Auth, Thomas F Torrance, in Musser, ed, A New Handbook of Christian Theologians, Abingdon, 96; auth, A Theology of Word and Spirit: Donald Bloesch's Theological Method, J for Chr Theol Res, 96; auth, rev of Luther's Theology of the Cross, by Alister, Relig Stud Rev, 96; auth, rev of God the Almighty, by Bloesch, Reformation & Revival J, 97; auth, rev of The Christian Doctrine of God, by Torrance, Relig Stud Rev, 97; auth, rev of The Christian Doctrine of God, by Torrance, Scottish J of Theol, 97; auth, rev of Reasoning and Rhetoric in Religion, by Murphy, Tchg Theol and Relig; auth, rev of Worship, Community & the Triune God, by Torrance, Relig Stud Rev; auth, rev of The Cambridge Companion to Christian Doctrine, ed, Gunton, Chr Today; auth, Evangelical Theology in Transition: Theologians in Dialog with Donal Bloesch, InterVarsity, 99. **CONTACT ADDRESS** Theol Sem, Univ of Dubuque, 2000 Univ Ave, Dubuque, IA 52001. **EMAIL** ecolyer@dbq.edu

COMBES, RICHARD E.
PERSONAL Born 04/15/1954, Pittsfield, MA, m, 1992, 3 children **DISCIPLINE** PHILOSOPHY **EDUCATION** Eisenhower Col, BA, 76; Univ Iowa, PhD, 85. **CAREER** Vis asst prof, Iowa State Univ, 86-91; asst prof, 91-94, assoc prof, 94- , Univ South Carolina, Spartansburg. **HONORS AND AWARDS** Nations Bank Excellence in Tchg and Advising Awd, 97. **MEMBERSHIPS** APA; South Carolina Soc for Philos. **RESEARCH** Philosophy of mind; history of modern philosophy; ethics; philosophy of technology. **SELECTED PUBLICATIONS** Auth, "Ockhamite Reductionism," Internaional Philosophical, Quarterly, Vol XXVIII (88): 325-336; auth, "Disembodying' Bodily' Sensations," Journal of Speculative Philosophy, Vol v (91): 107-131. **CONTACT ADDRESS** 168 Timberlake Dr, Inman, SC 29349. **EMAIL** rcombes@gw.uscs.edu

COMER, JOHN
PERSONAL Born 12/07/1946, Memphis, TN, m, 1969, 4 children **DISCIPLINE** SOCIOLOGY, THEOLOGY, PHILOSOPHY **EDUCATION** Auburn Univ, BS, 68, MBA, 69; Univ of the South, MDiv, 75. **CAREER** Pastoral theology, 75-00; university chaplain, 79-85; chaplain, Marion Military Inst, 98-00. **HONORS AND AWARDS** Algeron Sidney Sullivan Awd, Auburn Univ, 68; Paul Harris Fel, Rotary Int, 92; Who's Who in South and Southwest; Who's Who in Religion in Am; Who's Who in Teaching in Am. **MEMBERSHIPS** Omicron Delta Kappa, Omicron Delta Epsilon, Delta Sigma Rho, Tau Kappa Alpha, Scabbord and Blade. **RESEARCH** Psychology, sociology, statistics. **CONTACT ADDRESS** Dept Hist & Soc Sci, Marion Military Inst, 1101 Washington St, Marion, AL 36756-3213.

COMFORT, PHILIP W.
PERSONAL Born 10/28/1950, Pittsburgh, PA, m, 1971, 3 children **DISCIPLINE** NEW TESTAMENT **EDUCATION** Ohio State Univ, MA, 78; Fairfax, PhD, 89; Univ South Africa, DPhil, 97. **CAREER** Adj prof, NT & Greek, Wheaton College and presently, Trinity Seminary; Sr Editor, Bible ref, 16 yrs, Tyndale House Pub. **MEMBERSHIPS** SBL **RESEARCH** New Testament Manuscripts and English translations. **SELECTED PUBLICATIONS** Auth, Essential Guide to Bible Versions, Tyndale, 00; auth, One Year Book of Poetry, Tyndale, 99; auth, editor of New Testament for New Living Translation; auth, Early Manuscripts and Modern Translations of the New Testament, Tyndale, 91, 2nd edition, Baker, 96; The Complete Text of the Earliest New Testaments Manuscripts, Baker, 99; The Complete Guide to Bible Versions, Tyndale, 92, 2nd edition 97; I am The Way, Baker, 94; coauth, Opening the Gospel of John, Tyndale, 94; The Quest for the Original Text of the New Testament, Baker, 92. **CONTACT ADDRESS** 307 Hagley Rd, Pawleys Island, SC 29585. **EMAIL** pc@tyndale.com

COMPIER, DON H.
DISCIPLINE THEOLOGY **EDUCATION** Univ Pacific, BA; Park Col, MA; Emory Univ, PhD. **CAREER** Assoc prof, Church Divinity Sch Pacific. **SELECTED PUBLICATIONS** Auth, Theological Themes, Lectionary Homiletics, 97; The Holocaust, Postmodernism, and Public Theology, History of European Ideas: Proc 1996 ISSEI Conf, MIT Press, 97; Hooker on the Authority of Scripture in Matters of Morality, The Interpreted Establishment: Richard Hooker and the Construction of Christian Community, Medieval and Renaissance Texts and Stud, 97; Problematizing Diakonia, Theol, Vol 3: Revisioning the Church, Graceland/Park Col Press, 95; The Incomplete Recovery of Rhetorical Theology, Dialog, 95; The Eucharist and World Hunger, Anglican Theol Rev, 91. **CONTACT ADDRESS** Church Divinity Sch of the Pacific, 2451 Ridge Rd, Berkeley, CA 94709-1217.

COMPTON, JOHN J.
PERSONAL Born 05/17/1928, Chicago, IL, m, 1950, 3 children **DISCIPLINE** PHILOSOPHY **EDUCATION** College of Wooster, BA, 49; Yale Univ, MA, 51, PhD, 53. **CAREER** Asst prof, 52-55, assoc prof, 55-68, prof, philos, 68-98, prof emer, 98- , chemn, 67-73, 94-95, Vanderbilt Univ; vis prof philos, Colorado Col, 77; vis prof philos, Wesleyan Univ, 84. **HONORS AND AWARDS** Phi Beta Kappa; Kent fel, 51; Belgian Am Educ Fund fel, 56-57; Danforth Found award for distinguished tchg, 66; vis fel, Princeton Univ, 68; sr fel NEH, 74-75; assoc fel, Ctr for Hum, Wesleyan Univ, 74-75; Distinguished Alumni Awd, Wooster Col, 79; Alumni Prof Awd of Vanderbilt Alumni Asn, 82; Distinguished Alumnus Awd, Asheville Sch, 84; Distinguished Tchg Awd, Peabody Col, 90. **MEMBERSHIPS** APA; AAAS; AAUP; Metaphysical Soc of Am; Soc for Phenomenology and Existential Philos; Philos of Sci Asn; Soc for Values in Higher Educ; Soc of Christian Philos. **RESEARCH** Metaphysics; philosophy of science; phenomenology; philosophy of mind; philosophy of nature. **SELECTED PUBLICATIONS** Auth, Science and God's Action in Nature, in Barbour, ed, Earth Might Be Fair: Essays in Religion, Ethics, and Ecology, Prentice-Hall, 72; auth, Death and the Philosophical Tradition, Soundings, 78; auth, Science, Anti-Science, and Human Values, Key Reporter, 78-79; auth, Reinventing the Philosophy of Nature, Rev of Metaphysics, 79; auth, Sartre, Merleau-Ponty, and Human Freedom, J of Philos, 82; auth, Phenomenology and the Philosophy of Nature, Man and World, 88; auth, Some Contributions of Existential Phenomenology to the Philosophy of Natural Science, Am Philos Q, 88; auth, Merleau-Ponty's Thesis of the Primacy of Perception and the Meaning of Scientific Objectivity, in Pietersma, ed, Merleau-Ponty: Critical Essays, Univ Press of America, 90. **CONTACT ADDRESS** 3708 Whitland Ave, Nashville, TN 37205. **EMAIL** jjcompton@aol.com

CONARD, ALFRED FLETCHER
PERSONAL Born 11/30/1911, Grinnell, IA, m, 1939, 2 children **DISCIPLINE** LAW **EDUCATION** Grinnell Col, AB, 32; LLD, 71; Univ Pa, LLB, 36; Columbia Univ, LLM, 39, JD, 42. **CAREER** Asst prof law, Univ Kans City, 39-42, acting dean law sch, 41-42; atty, Off Price Admin, 42-43 & Off Alien Property Custodian, 45-46; from assoc prof to prof law, Univ Ill, 46-54; Prof Law, Univ Mich, Ann Arbor, 54-, Vis prof, Univ Mo, 38, Univ Calif, 47, Univ Tex, 52, Univ Colo, 57, Istanbul, Turkey, 58-59, Luxembourg, 58-59 & Mex, 63; mem assembly behav & soc sci, Nat Res Coun, 73- **RESEARCH** Enterprise organization; European company law; automobile accident compensation. **SELECTED PUBLICATIONS** Coauth, American Enterprise in the European Common Market, 61 & Automobile Accident Costs and Payments: Studies in the Economics of Injury Reparation, 64, Univ Mich; auth, Macrojustice: A systematic approach to conflict resolution, Ga Law Rev, 71; A behavioral analysis of directors' liability for negligence, Duke Law J, 72; Fundamental Changes in Marketable Share Companies, J C B Mohr, Mouton, The Hague & Oceana, 72; auth, Corporations in Perspective, 76 & co-ed, Enterprise Organization, 72, 2nd ed, 77 & Found Press, 3rd ed, 82. **CONTACT ADDRESS** Sch of Law, Univ of Michigan, Ann Arbor, Ann Arbor, MI 48104.

CONCANNON, JAMES M.
PERSONAL Born 10/02/1947, Columbus, GA, m, 1988 **DISCIPLINE** APPELLATE PRACTICE, CIVIL PROCEDURE, AND EVIDENCE **EDUCATION** Univ KS, BS, 68, JD, 71. **CAREER** Res Atty, Kans Suprofeme Court; Vis prof, WA Univ Sch Law. **HONORS AND AWARDS** Dean,Law Sch; Prof. **MEMBERSHIPS** Natl Conf of Commisioners on Uniform State Laws **SELECTED PUBLICATIONS** Sr contrib ed, Evidence in Am: The Federal Rules in the States. **CONTACT ADDRESS** Washburn Univ of Topeka, 1700 SW College, Topeka, KS 66621.

CONCES, RORY
PERSONAL Born 08/08/1954, East Chicago, IN, m, 1977, 3 children **DISCIPLINE** PHILOSOPHY **EDUCATION** Creighton Univ, BA, 76; DePaul Univ, MA, 80; Univ Mo Columbia, PhD, 91. **CAREER** Adj instr, Columbia Col, 85; adj instr, Moberly Area Jr Col, 90; vis asst prof & lectr, Univ Nebr, 92-; lectr, Creighton Univ, 94-. **HONORS AND AWARDS** Who's Who Among Am Teachers, 98, 99. **MEMBERSHIPS** Am Philos Asn, Phi Beta Delta, Central States Philos Asn, Soc for Soc and Polit Philos. **RESEARCH** Ethics, Applied Philosophy, Social and Political Philosophy, Third World Studies. **SELECTED PUBLICATIONS** Auth, "The Semblance of Ideologies and Scientific Theories and the Constitution of Facts," Rev J of Philos and Soc Sci (96); rev, of "The Price of a Dream: The Story of the Grameen Bank and the Idea That Is Helping the Poor to Change Their Lives," by David Borstein, Int Third World Studies J and Rev (96); coauth, "Ethics and Sovereignty," Int Third World Studies J and Rev (96); auth, "A Participatory Approach to the Teaching of Critical Reasoning," The Socratic Tradition: Essays on Teaching Philosophy, ed. Tziporah Kasachkoff (MD: Rowman & Littlefield, 97); auth, "Contract, Trust, and Resistance in the 'Second Treatise'," The Locke Newsletter (97); auth, Blurred Visions: Philosophy, Science, and Ideology in a Troubled World, Peter Lang (New York), 97; rev, of "The Decolonization of Imagination: Culture. Knowledge and Power," by Jan Nederveen Pieterse and Bhikhu Parekh, Int Third World Studies J and Rev (97); auth, "Consensual Foundations and Resistance in Locke's 'Second Treatise'," Theoria (98); rev, of "Chechnya: Tombstone of Russian Power," by Anatol Lieven, Int Third World Studies J and Rev (98/99); rev, of "To End a War," by Richard Holbrooke, Int Third World Studies J and Rev (98/99). **CONTACT ADDRESS** Dept Philos, Creighton Univ, 2500 California Plaza, Omaha, NE 68178-0001. **EMAIL** rconces@unomaha.edu

CONDIT, RICHARD E.
DISCIPLINE ENVIRONMENTAL LAW **EDUCATION** NJ Inst Technol, BS, 80; Antioch Sch Law, JD, 86. **CAREER** Adja prof; past staff mem, US Env Protection Agency; past staff atty, Govt Accountability Proj, GAP & co-dir, GAP's EPA Watch Prog. **SELECTED PUBLICATIONS** Coauth, Citizens' Handbook on Env Rights. **CONTACT ADDRESS** School of Law, Univ of District of Columbia, 4200 Connecticut Ave Northwest, Washington, DC 20008.

CONE, JAMES H.
PERSONAL Born 08/05/1938, Fordyce, AR, s, 4 children **DISCIPLINE** RELIGION **EDUCATION** Philander Smith Col, BA, 58; Garrett Theol Sem, BD, 61; Northwestern Univ, MA, 63; PhD, 65. **CAREER** Asst Prof, Philander Smith Col, 64-66; Asst Prof, Adrian Col, 66-69; Asst Prof to Prof, Union Theol Sem, 69-. **HONORS AND AWARDS** Am Black Achievement Awd, 92; Theol Scholarship & Res Awd, 94. **MEMBERSHIPS** Soc for the Study of Black Relig; Am Acad of Relig; Ecumenical Asn of Third World Theologians. **RESEARCH** Martin Luther King Jr; Malcolm X; Black Liberation Theology; Third World Liberation Theology; African American History & Culture. **SELECTED PUBLICATIONS** Auth, A Black Theology of Liberation, New York, Lippincott, 70, New York, Orbis Books, 90; auth, The Spirituals and the Blues: An Interpretation, Orbis Books, 91; auth, God of the Oppressed, Orbis Books, 97; ed, Black Theology: A Documentary History, 1966-1979, Orbis Books, 93; auth, My Soul Looks Back, Orbis Books, 82; auth, For My People, Orbis Books, 84; auth, Speaking the Truth: Ecumenism, Liberation, and Black Theology, Eerdmans Pub Co, 86; auth, Martin & Malcolm & America: A Dream or a Nightmare, Orbis Books, 91; auth, Black Theology: A Documentary History, Vol II, 1980-1992, Orbis Books, 93; auth, Risks of Faith: The Emergence of a Black Theology of Liberation, 1968-1998, Beacon Press, 99. **CONTACT ADDRESS** Dept Theol, Union Theol Sem, New York, 3041 Broadway, New York, NY 10027-5710. **EMAIL** conevf@aol.com

CONGDON, HOWARD KREBS
PERSONAL Born 12/13/1941, Syracuse, NY, m, 1973, 1 child **DISCIPLINE** PHILOSOPHY **EDUCATION** Syracuse Univ, AB, 63; Wesley Theol Sem, MDiv, 66; Purdue Univ, West Lafayette, MA, 68, PhD, 70. **CAREER** Minister, St George Island United Methodist Churches, 67-68; instr philos, Purdue Univ, 69-70; asst prof, 70-73, Assoc Prof Philos, Lock Haven State Col, 73-75; prof, 75-; Commonwealth teaching fel, 79-80. **HONORS AND AWARDS** Pa Cert Excellence in Teaching, 80. **MEMBERSHIPS** Am Philos Asn; AAUP. **RESEARCH** Philosophy of mind; significance of altered states of consciousness; philosophy of religion; philosophy of death. **SELECTED PUBLICATIONS** Auth, Drugs and religion, Lock Haven Rev, 72; Salzburg as a setting for academic studies, Acad Notes Intercult Affairs & Foreign Study, 72; The Pursuit of Death, Abingdon, 77; Abortion and the law, Philos Res & Anal, spring 78; auth, Problems in Philosophy, McGraw-Hill, 95. **CONTACT ADDRESS** Dept of Philos, Lock Haven Univ of Pennsylvania, 401 N Fairview St, Lock Haven, PA 17745-2390. **EMAIL** hcongdon@lhup.edu

CONGELTON, ANN
PERSONAL Born 08/26/1936, Dayton, OH, m, 1972, 2 children **DISCIPLINE** PHILOSOPHY **EDUCATION** Wellesley Col, BA (philos), 58; Yale Univ, PhD (philos), 62. **CAREER** Member of the Mechanical Translation Group of the Research Lab of Electronics, MIT, 62-64; asst prof to Prof, Dept of Philos, Wellesley Col, 64-. **MEMBERSHIPS** Amer Philos Assoc; Soc for Women in Philos. **RESEARCH** Plato; feminist theory. **CONTACT ADDRESS** Dept of Philos, Wellesley Col, Wellesley, MA 02481.

CONISON, JAY
PERSONAL Born 10/21/1953, Cincinnati, OH, m, 1980, 2 children **DISCIPLINE** LAW **EDUCATION** Yale Col, BA, 75; Univ Minn, MA, 78; JD, 81. **CAREER** Asst prof to prof, Okla City Univ, 90-98; dean, Valparaiso Univ, Sch of Law, 98-. **MEMBERSHIPS** Order of the Coif; Am Bar Assoc; Ind Bar Found. **RESEARCH** Employee Benefit Plans, Legal Philosophy. **SELECTED PUBLICATIONS** Coauth, "State of Illinois", ABA Antitrust Law Section, State Antitrust Practice and Statutes, 90; auth, Employee Benefit Plans in a Nutshell, West, 93; auth, "The Impact of ERISA on Secured Lending", Secured Transactions Under the Uniform Commercial Code", Matthew Bender, 94; auth, "What Does Due Process Have To Do With Jurisdiction?", 46 Rutgers L Rev 1071 (94); auth, "ERISA and the Language of Preemption", 72 Wash ULQ 619 (94); auth, "The Pragmatics of Promise", 10 Can JL & Jurisp 273 (97): auth, "Assurance, Reliance and Expectation", 6 S Cal Interdisc LJ 335 (98). **CONTACT ADDRESS** Dean of Law, Valparaiso Univ, 651 College Ave, Valparaiso, IN 46383-6461. **EMAIL** jay.conison@valpo.edu

CONKLE, DANIEL O.
PERSONAL Born 11/10/1953, Marion, OH, m, 1975, 2 children **DISCIPLINE** POLITICAL SCIENCE, LAW **EDUCATION** Ohio State Univ, BA, 76, JD, 79. **CAREER** Law Clerk for Judge Edward Allen Tamm of the United States Court of Appeals for the District of Columbia Circuit, Washington, DC, 79-80; assoc lawyer for Taft, Stettinius & Hollister, Cincinnati, Ohio, 80-83; asst prof law, Ind Univ Sch of Law, 83-86, assoc prof, 86-89, prof, 89-, Robert H. McKinney Prof of Law, 99-; Nelson Poynter Sr Scholar and Dir of Religious Liberty Project, Ind Univ Poynter Center for the Study of Ethics and Am Institutions, 96-; adjunct prof, Ind Univ Dept of Religious Studies, 97-. **HONORS AND AWARDS** 1986 Gavel Awd, 86; Ira C. Batman Fac Fel, 89-90, 94-95; Leon H. Wallace Teaching Awd, 91-92; Louis F. Niezer Fac Fel, 92-93; Charles L. Whistler Fac Fel, 93-94; co-recipient, 1995 Gavel Awd, 95; Harry T. Ice Fac Fel, 95-96, 98-99; Teaching Excellence Recognition Awd for Sustained Excellence in Teaching, 96-97; Robert H. McKinney Prof, 99-. **MEMBERSHIPS** Order of the Coif, Am Bar Asn. **RESEARCH** Constitutional law; First Amendment; religious liberty; role of religion in politics and public life. **SELECTED PUBLICATIONS** Auth, "The Religious Freedom Restoration Act: The Constitutional Significance of an Unconstitutional Statute," 56 Montana Law Rev, (95): 39-93; auth, "Secular Fundamentalism, Religious Fundamentalism, and the Search for Truth in Contemporary America," 12 J of Law and Religion (95-96): 337-70; auth, "Religiously Devout Judges: Issues of Personal Integrity and Public Benefit," 81 Marquette Law Rev (98): 523-32; auth, "Congressional Alternatives in the Wake of City of Boerne v Flores: The (Limited) Role of Congress in Protecting Religious Freedom from State and Local Infringement," 20 Univ of Ark at Little Rock Law J (98): 633-88; auth, "Professing Professionals: Christian Pilots on the River of Law," 38 Catholic Lawyer (98): 151-83, republished in Religion, Morality and the Professions in America, at 9-34, Ind Univ Poynter Center Monograph Series (99); auth, "Free Exercise, Federalism, and the States as Laboratories," 21 Cardozo Law Rev (99): 493-99; auth, "The Path of American Religious Liberty: From the Original Theology to Formal Neutrality and an Uncertain Future," 75 Ind Law J (2000): 1-36. **CONTACT ADDRESS** Sch of Law, Indiana Univ, Bloomington, 211 S Indiana Ave, Bloomington, IN 47405-7001. **EMAIL** conkle@indiana.edu

CONKLIN, JOHN E.
PERSONAL Born 10/02/1943, Oswego, NY, m, 1982, 4 children **DISCIPLINE** SOCIOLOGY, CRIMINOLOGY **EDUCATION** Cornell Univ, AB, 65; Harvard Univ, PhD, 69. **CAREER** Res assoc, Center for Criminal Justice, Harvard Law Sch, 69-70; asst prof to prof, Tufts Univ, 70-, chair, Dept Sociol and Anthropol, 81-86, 90-91. **HONORS AND AWARDS** Phi Beta Kappa, 65; Bobbs-Merill Awd for outstanding grad student, 67; AB, cum laude, 65; Nat Defense Ed Act Title IV Fel, 65-68. **MEMBERSHIPS** Am Sociol Asn, Am Soc Criminol. **RESEARCH** Criminal behavior, art theft. **SELECTED PUBLICATIONS** Sr auth with Dermot Meagher, "The Percentage Deposit Bail System: An Alternative to the Professional Bondsman," J of Criminal Justice, 1, 299-317 (winter 73); auth, The Impact of Crime, NY: Macmillan Pub Co (75); auth, "Robbery, Elderly, and Fear: An Urban Problem in Search of a Solution," in Jack and Sharon S. Goldsmith, eds, Crime and the Elderly, Lexington, MA: D. C. Heath and Co, 99-110 (76); auth, Illegal but Not Criminal: Business Crime in America, Englewood Cliffs, NJ: Prentice-Hall, Inc (77); auth, Sociology: An Introduction, 2nd ed, NY: Macmillan (87, also, 1st ed, 84); auth, "Crime and Punishment," in The United States of America: A Handbook , Oxford, England: Facts on File, Inc (92); auth, Art Crime, Westport, CT: Praeger (94); ed, New Perspectives in Criminology, Boston: Allyn & Bacon (96); auth, "Art Theft," in Encyclopedia of Crime and Deviant Behavior, Volume 2: Crime and Juvenile Delinquency, Philadelphia: Taylor and Francis (2000); auth, Criminology, 7th ed, Boston: Allyn & Bacon (2001). **CONTACT ADDRESS** Dept Sociol & Anthropol, Tufts Univ, Medford, 520 Boston Ave, Medford, MA 02155. **EMAIL** jconklin@emerald.tufts.edu

CONKLIN, WILLIAM E.
DISCIPLINE JURISPRUDENCE; PHENOMENOLOGY; SEMIOTICS; CONSTITUTIONAL THEORY; POLITICAL PHILOSOPHY; ETHICS AND CIVIL LIBERTIES **EDUCATION** Univ Toronto, BA; London, MSc; Univ Toronto, LLB; Columbia, LLM; York, PhD. **CAREER** Prof; Osgoode Hall, Barrister-at-Law. **SELECTED PUBLICATIONS** Auth, In Defense of Fundamental Rights and Images of a Constitution, U of Toronto P, 93. **CONTACT ADDRESS** Col of Business Administration, Educ and Law, Univ of Windsor, 401 Sunset Ave, Windsor, ON, Canada N9B 3P4. **EMAIL** wconkli@uwindsor.ca

CONLEY, CHARLES S.
PERSONAL Born 12/08/1921, Montgomery, AL, m, 1987 **DISCIPLINE** LAW **EDUCATION** Ala State Univ, BS, 1942; Univ of MI, AM, educ, 1947, AM, histroy, 1948; NYork Univ, JD, 1955. **CAREER** FL A&M College of Law, prof, 56-60; AL State U, 62-64; Dr Martin Luther King SCLC, counsel; Recorder's CT, judge 1968-73; Macon County CT Common Pleas, 72-, Macon County Attorney, 86; Alabama District Court, judge, 77. **MEMBERSHIPS** Am Nat AL Bar Assns. **CONTACT ADDRESS** 315 S Bainbridge St, Montgomery, AL 36104.

CONLEY, JOHN A.
PERSONAL Born 03/10/1928, Springfield, IL, m **DISCIPLINE** LAW **EDUCATION** Univ of Pgh, BS 1952, JD 1955, MSW 1961. **CAREER** Univ of Pittsburgh, prof 1969-; housing developer. **MEMBERSHIPS** Mem Hill House Assn 1955-69; Neighborhood Ctrs Assn 1963-65; Allegheny Co, PA Bar Assns; bd dirs Pgh Public Schs; Freedom House Enterprise Inc; chmn bd Neighborhood Rehab Inc **CONTACT ADDRESS** Dept of Social Work, Univ of Pittsburgh, 2201 C1, Pittsburgh, PA 15260.

CONLEY, JOHN J.
PERSONAL Born 11/25/1951, Philadelphia, PA, s **DISCIPLINE** PHILOSOPHY **EDUCATION** Univ Pa, BA, 73; Fordham Univ, MA, 77; Centre Sevres-Paris, LTh, 83; Univ Catholique de Louvain, PhD, 88. **CAREER** Instr, Wheeling Col, 75-77; Assoc Prof, Fordham Univ, 88-. **HONORS AND AWARDS** Phi Beta Kappa; Alpha Sigma Nu; Folgers Inst Grant, 98; Malta Human Serv Grant, 98; Authors' Guild Grant, 99. **MEMBERSHIPS** APA, ACPA. **RESEARCH** French philosophy, ethics, aesthetics. **SELECTED PUBLICATIONS** Auth, "Problems of Cooperation in an Abortive Culture," Life and Learning VI, Georgetown Publ (97): 103-116; auth, "Narrative, Act, Structure: John Paul II's Method of Moral Analysis," Choosing Life, A Dialogue on Evangelium Vitae, Georgetown Publ (97): 3-20; auth, "At the Origins of the Persons," Homiletic and Pastoral Rev, vol XCVII, no 2 (97): 16-22; auth, "Natural Theology in an Anthropological Key," Josephinum J of Theol, vol 5, no 1 (98): 77-83; auth, "Bernardin's Consistent Ethic: A Critical Evaluation," Life and Learning VII, Georgetown Publ (98): 39-53; auth, "Dialogue and its Counterfeit," Homiletic and Pastoral Rev, vol XCIX, no 6 (99): 17-25; auth, "Hitchcock and McNally: Abortion as Metaphor," Life and Learning VIII, Georgetown Publ (99): 297-304, co-ed, Prophecy and Diplomacy: The Moral Teaching of John Paul II, Fordham UP (New York, NY), 99. **CONTACT ADDRESS** Dept Philos, Fordham Univ, 441 E Fordham Rd, Bronx, NY 10458-5149. **EMAIL** jconley@fordham.edu

CONLEY, PATRICK THOMAS
PERSONAL Born 06/22/1938, New Haven, CT, m, 1962, 6 children **DISCIPLINE** AMERICAN HISTORY, CONSTITUTIONAL LAW **EDUCATION** Providence Col, AB, 59; Univ Notre Dame, MA, 61, PhD(hist), 70; Suffolk Univ, JD, 73. **CAREER** Prof Hist, Providence Col, 63-93, Spec asst to Congressman Robert O Tiernan, RI, 67-74; secy, RI Constitutional Convention, 73; chmn, RI Bicentennial Comn/Found, 74-; chairman U.S. Constitution Council, 88-91. **HONORS AND AWARDS** Elected to Rhode Island Heritage Hall of Fame, 95. **MEMBERSHIPS** AHA; Orgn Am Historians; RI Historical Soc (life member of each). **RESEARCH** Rhode Island history; American ethnic history; constitutional history. **SELECTED PUBLICATIONS** Auth, Proceedings of the Rhode Island Constitutional Convention of 1973, Providence: Oxford Press, 73; auth, Democracy in Decline: Rhode Island's Constitutional Development, 1776-1841, Providence: Rhode Island Historical Society, 77; coauth, Providence: A Pictorial History, with Paul R. Campbell, Norfolk: The Donning Company, 82; auth, Rhode Island Profile, Providence: Rhode Island Publications Society, 82; auth, The Irish in Rhode Island: A Historical Appreciation, Providence: Rhode Island Heritage Commission, 86; auth, An Album of Rhode Island History, 1636-1986, Norfolk: Donning Company, 86; auth, First in War, Last in Peace: Rhode Island and the Constitution, 1786-1790, Providence: Rhode Island Bi-

centennial Foundation, 87; coauth, The Bill of Rights and the States: The Colonial and Revolutionary Origins of American Liberties, with John P. Kaminski, Madison, Wis: Madison House Publishers, 92; auth, Liberty and Justice: A History of Law and Lawyers in Rhode Island, 1636-1998, Providence: Rhode Island Publications Society, 98; auth, Neither Separate Nor Equal: Legislature and Executive in Rhode Island Constitutional History, Providence: Rhode Island Publications Society, 99. **CONTACT ADDRESS** 1 Bristol Point Rd, Bristol, RI 02809.

CONLON, JAMES J.
PERSONAL Born 09/30/1946, NJ, m, 1969, 2 children **DISCIPLINE** PHILOSOPHY **EDUCATION** Marquette, PhD, 75. **CAREER** Mount Mary Col, prof, 74-. **SELECTED PUBLICATIONS** Auth, Why Lovers Can't Be Friends, in: Philosophical Perspectives on Love and Sex, ed R. Stewart, Oxford Univ Press, 95; Silencing the Lambs and Educating Women, in: Post Script: Essays in Film and the Humanities, 92; Kansas, Oz and the Function of Art, Jour of Aesthetic Education, 90; Making Love, Not War: The Solder Male in Top Gun and Coming Home, Jour of Pop Film & TV, 90; The Place of Passion: Reflections on Fatal Attraction, Jour of Pop Film and TV, 89; Stanley Cavell and the Predicament of Philosophy, Proceedings of the American Catholic Philosophical Association, 83. **CONTACT ADDRESS** Dept of philosophy, Mount Mary Col, 2900 N Menomonee River Pkwy, Milwaukee, WI 53222. **EMAIL** conlonj@mtmary.edu

CONN, CHRISTOPHER
PERSONAL Born 08/18/1965, Livonia, MI, m, 1989, 2 children **DISCIPLINE** PHILOSOPHY **EDUCATION** Syracuse Univ, PhD, 96 **CAREER** Asst Prof, Univ of the South, present **RESEARCH** Metaphysics; epistemology; modern philosophy **CONTACT ADDRESS** Dept of Philosophy, Univ of the South, 735 University Ave., Sewanne, TN 37383. **EMAIL** cconn@sewanee.edu

CONN, MARIE A.
PERSONAL Born 01/09/1944, Rockville Center, NY, s **DISCIPLINE** RELIGIOUS STUDIES **EDUCATION** Univ Notre Dame, PhD 93, MA 90; Mary Wood Univ, MS 86, BA 66; Villanova Univ, MA 75. **CAREER** Chestnut Hill Col, assoc prof, 92-; Mary Wood Col, asst prof, 86-90; Various HS, 66-86. **HONORS AND AWARDS** John Templeton Foun Prize; ASA Lect Gnt. **MEMBERSHIPS** NAAL; CTS; CTSA; SL. **RESEARCH** Women in Western Christianity; Health Care Reform; Women in Scripture. **SELECTED PUBLICATIONS** Auth, Noble Daughters: Unheralded Women In Western Christianity, 13th to 18th Centuries, Westport, Greenwood Press, forthcoming; auth, The Anderson Pontifical: An Edition and Study, London, Henry Bradshaw Soc, forthcoming; auth, The Pontifical of Dunstun: An Edition and Study, London, Bradshaw Soc, forthcoming; auth, Rites of King-Making in 10th Century England, Proceedings, Groningen Nthlnds 98; Cracking Open Symbols: An Interdisciplinary Experience In Art and Religion, coauth, Arts, 97; Wisdom Born of Pain, Sisters Today, 97; auth, Health-Care Reform: A Human Rights Issue, Proceedings, 97; contrib, RP McBrien, ed, Encycl of Catholicism, Harper Collins, San Francisco, 95. **CONTACT ADDRESS** 50 S Penn St # 405, Hatboro, PA 19040-3238. **EMAIL** mconn@chc.edu

CONN, WALTER EUGENE
PERSONAL Born 07/11/1940, Providence, RI, m, 1972 **DISCIPLINE** RELIGIOUS STUDIES, THEOLOGICAL ETHICS **EDUCATION** Providence Col, AB, 62; Boston Col, MA, 66; Weston Col, Phl, 66; Columbia Univ, PhD(relig), 73. **CAREER** Instr philos, Boston Col, 66-69; from asst prof to assoc prof Christian ethics, St Patrick's Sem, 73-78; Prof Relig Studies, Villanova Univ, 78-, Bk rev ed, Horizons, 78-80, ed, 80- **HONORS AND AWARDS** Col Theol Soc, best article, 78, best bk, 82. **MEMBERSHIPS** Am Acad Relig; Cath Theol Soc Am; Col Theol Soc; Soc Christian Ethics. **RESEARCH** Foundational theological ethics; moral-religious development; conversion. **SELECTED PUBLICATIONS** Auth, Conscience: Development and Self-Transcedence, 81; auth, Christian Conversion, 86; auth, The Desiring Self, 98. **CONTACT ADDRESS** Theol and Relig Studies Dept, Villanova Univ, 845 E Lancaster Ave, Villanova, PA 19085. **EMAIL** walter.com@villanova.edu

CONNOLLY, JOHN M.
PERSONAL Born 09/20/1943, New York, NY, m, 1969, 2 children **DISCIPLINE** PHILOSOPHY **EDUCATION** Fordham Coll, BA, 65; Oxford Univ, MA, 67; Harvard Univ, PhD, 71. **CAREER** Asst prof, Smith Coll, 73-81; assoc prof, 81-88; prof, 88-; fac dean, 94-; provost, 98-. **HONORS AND AWARDS** Danforth Fel, 65-71; Humboldt Fel, 78-82; NEA Democ Ed Awd, 2000.c **MEMBERSHIPS** APA; Sigma Xi. **RESEARCH** Medieval philosophy; contemporary philosophy. **SELECTED PUBLICATIONS** Auth, "Praxis and Intention," Inquiry 22 (79; auth, "Apel and the Transcendental Pragmatics of Human Action," Inquiry 24 (81); rev, "Transformation in Philosophy," KO Apel, in Mind 90, (81); auth, "Frege, Sense, and Privacy," in Philosophy of Mind, Philosophy of Psychology, eds. R Chisholm, JC Marek, JT Blackmore, A Huebner (Vienna, 85); auth, "Gadamer and the Author's Authority," J Aesthetics Art Crit (86); auth, "The Will as Impression," Hume Studies (87), 276-305; co-trans, Absicht, Alber Verlag (Freiburg, 86); auth, "Whither Action Theory: Artificial Intelligence or Aristotle?" J Philos Res (91); auth, "Anomaly and the Folk Psychology," Inquiry 36 (93); auth, "The Academy's Freedom -- The Academy's Burden," in Professional Passions, ed. P Rose (Northampton, MA, 98). **CONTACT ADDRESS** Dept Philos, Smith Col, 98 Green St, Northampton, MA 01063-1000. **EMAIL** jconnolly@smith.edu

CONSER, WALTER H., JR.
PERSONAL Born 04/04/1949, Riverside, CA, m, 1986, 3 children **DISCIPLINE** AMERICAN RELIGIOUS HISTORY **EDUCATION** Univ Calif Irvine, BA, 71; Brown Univ, MA, 74, PhD, hist, 81. **CAREER** James A. Gray fel in relig, Univ NC Chapel Hill, 82-84; adjunct facul, Univ San Francisco, 85; vis asst prof to asst prof, 85-89, assoc prof, 89-94, chmn, 92-98, prof relig, 94-, Univ NC Wilmington; fel, Albert Einstein Inst for Nonviolent Alternatives, 84-87; vis prof, JF Kennedy Inst for North Amer Studies, Free Univ Berlin, 90; prof, hist, Univ NC Wilmington, 95-. **HONORS AND AWARDS** German Academic Exchange Service Fellowship 77; North Carolina Humanities Grant 87, 98. **MEMBERSHIPS** Amer Acad of Relig; Amer Hist Asn. **SELECTED PUBLICATIONS** Auth, Religious Diversity and American Religious History, Univ Ga Press, 97; auth, God and the Natural World: Religion and Science in Antebellum America, Univ SC Press, 93; co-ed, Experience of the Sacred: Readings in the Phenomenology of Religion, Brown Univ Press, 92; auth, James Marsh and the Germans, New Eng Quart, 86; auth, Church and Confession: Conservative Theologians in Germany, England and America, 1815-1866, Mercer Univ Press; auth, Conservative Critique of Church and State, Jour of Church and State, 83; auth, John Ross and the Cherokee Resistance Campaign, Jour of Southern Hist, 78; co-auth, Cherokee Reponses to the Debate Over Indian Origins, Amer Quart, 89; co-auth, Cherokees in Transition, Jour of Amer Hist, 77. **CONTACT ADDRESS** Dept. of Philosophy and Religion, Univ of No Carolina, Wilmington, 601 S. College Rd., Wilmington, NC 28403.

CONVER, LEIGH E.
DISCIPLINE RELIGION **EDUCATION** E Baptist Col, BA; S Baptist Theol Sem, MDiv, ThM, PhD; Med Col Va, dipl; addn stud, Wash Sch Psychiatry, Shalem Inst for Spiritual Formation. **CAREER** Pastoral Counselor, Smoke Rise Bap Ch; dir training, Georgia Bap Med Ctr; Lawrence and Charlotte Hoover Professor, S Baptist Theol Sem, 91. **HONORS AND AWARDS** Fel, Amer Assn Pastoral Counselors. **MEMBERSHIPS** Soc Pastoral Theol; Assn Clinical Pastoral Edu; Amer Assn of Marriage and Family Therapy; Am Gp Psychotherapy Assn; Am Asn of Pastoral Counselors; Christian Asn for Psychological studies; Am Asn of Christian Counselors. **SELECTED PUBLICATIONS** Ed, Jour Family Ministry; co-auth, Self-Defeating Lifestyles. **CONTACT ADDRESS** School of Theology, So Baptist Theol Sem, 2825 Lexington Rd, Louisville, KY 40280. **EMAIL** lconver@sbts.edu

CONVERSE, HYLA STUNTZ
PERSONAL Born 10/31/1920, Lahore, Pakistan, m, 1951, 2 children **DISCIPLINE** HISTORY OF RELIGIONS, SOUTH ASIAN LITERATURE **EDUCATION** Smith Col, BA, 43; Union Theol Sem, BD, 49; Columbia Univ, PhD(hist of relig), 71. **CAREER** Relief & rehab worker, Eglise Reforme France, 45-48; dir student work, Judson Mem Church, New York, 52-55; dir lit & study, Nat Student Christian Fed, 57-63; asst prof Asian relig & humanities, 68-78, chmn humanities fac, 73-78, assoc prof, 78-80, Prof Asian Relig & Humanities, Okla State Univ, 80-, Fulbright res fel, India, 74-75; Am Inst Pakistan Studies fel, 78-79. **MEMBERSHIPS** Am Orient Soc; Bhandarkar Oriental Res Inst. **RESEARCH** Religions of South Asia; literature of South Asia; arts of South Asia. **SELECTED PUBLICATIONS** Auth, An Ancient Sudra Account of the Origins of Castes, Jour Amer Oriental Soc, Vol 0114, 94. **CONTACT ADDRESS** Dept Relig Studies, Oklahoma State Univ, Stillwater, Stillwater, OK 74074.

CONWAY, GERTRUDE D.
PERSONAL Born 08/12/1950, New York City, NY, m, 1977, 2 children **DISCIPLINE** CONTEMPORARY PHILOSOPHY **EDUCATION** Col New Rochelle, BA; Fordham Univ, MA, PhD. **CAREER** Taught 2 yrs, Shiraz Univ, Iran; fac, Mt Saint Mary's Col, 79-; assoc dean, Undergrad Stud at Mt Saint Mary's Col, 87-91. **HONORS AND AWARDS** Delaplaine Distinguished teaching prof Humanities, 97-00. **RESEARCH** Issue of cross-cultural understanding from a Wittgensteinian perspective; Hermemeutics. **SELECTED PUBLICATIONS** Auth, Wittgenstein on Foundations. **CONTACT ADDRESS** Dept of Philosophy, Mount Saint Mary's Col and Sem, 16300 Old Emmitsburg Rd, Emmitsburg, MD 21727-7799. **EMAIL** conway@msmary.edu

CONWILL, GILES
PERSONAL Born 12/17/1944, Louisville, KY, s **DISCIPLINE** PHILOSOPHY **EDUCATION** University of San Diego, BA, philosophy, 1967; Emory University, PhD, cultural studies, 1986; Athenaeum of OH, MDiv, 1973. **CAREER** Barona & Santa Ysabel Missions, religious education instructor, 65-67; Miramar Naval Air Station, chaplain's assistant, 66-67; St Henry's School, elementary school teacher, 67-68; Verona Fathers Seminary, choir director, assistant organist, 68-69; St Rita's Church, associate pastor, 73-76; San Diego Religious Vocations Office, diocesan coordinator, pre-marriage instructor, 75; National Office of Black Catholics, Department of Church Vocations, director, 76-80; St Anthony's Church, Atlanta, associate pastor, 80-85; St Joseph's Cathedral, San Diego, associate pastor, 85-86; Morehouse College, Department of History, asso professor, 87-; Inst for Black Catholic Studies, Xavier Univ, New Orleans, assoc prof, 90. **HONORS AND AWARDS** City of Selma, Alabama, Key to the City, first city-wide Black Catholic revival; Upper Room Publishing Co., interdenominational sermon contest winner; numerous other awards. **MEMBERSHIPS** Southeast San Diego Interdenominational Ministerial Alliance, vp, 1975; Black Catholic Clergy Caucus, 1975; Assn for the Study of African American Life & History, 1987-; Southern Conference of African Amer Studies, Inc, 1987-; Ass of Southern Historians, 1992-; Georgia Assn of Historians, 1992; Amer Anthropological Assn, 1994; Black Catholic Theological Symposium, 1990. **SELECTED PUBLICATIONS** Author, "The Word Becomes Black Flesh: A Program for Reaching the American Black," What Christians Can Learn from One Another, Tyndale House Publishers, 1988; workshop presenter: "Understanding Transitions: How to Relate to Candidates from Various Backgrounds," Seventh Annual Formation Workshops, Bergamo Center, July 8-10, 1988; African-American history lecture, Shrine of Immaculate Conception, Jan 1991; "Blackology vs Ecology," Leadership Council of the Laity Conference, Feb 1991; Liturgical Sensitivity to the Black Aesthetic, in The Critic, Summer, 1986; Tell It Like It Is: A Black Catholic Perspective on Christian Educ, Natl Black Sisters Conference, 1983; Black Music: The Spirit Will Not Descend Without Song, Pastoral Life, Vol XXXII, June 1983; Blackology vs Ecology, Leadership Council of the Laity. **CONTACT ADDRESS** Professor, Department of History, Morehouse Col, 830 Westview Dr SW, Brawley Hall, Ste 204, Atlanta, GA 30314.

CONYERS, A. J.
PERSONAL Born 05/29/1944, San Bernardino, CA, m, 1964, 2 children **DISCIPLINE** SYSTEMATIC THEOLOGY **EDUCATION** Univ Ga, BA, 66; So Baptist Sem, MDiv, 71; So Baptist Theol Sem, M.Div., 79. **CAREER** Prof of Bible, Central Missouri State Univ, 79-87; chemn, Dept Relig, Charleston So Univ, 87-94; prof theol, G.W. Truett Sem, Baylor Univ, 94-. **HONORS AND AWARDS** Staley Distinguished Scholar; Ed Bd, Review and Expositor. **MEMBERSHIPS** Am Acad Relig; Evangelical Theolog Soc; William Gilmore Simms Soc. **RESEARCH** Christianity and culture. **SELECTED PUBLICATIONS** Auth, God, Hope, and History: Jurgen Moltmann's Christian Concept of History, Mercer, 88; auth, The Eclipse of Heaven, InterVarsity, 92; auth, The End: What the Gospels Say About the Last Things, InterVarsity, 95; auth, A Basic Christian Theology, Broadman & Holman, 95; auth, The Long Truce; How Toleration Made the World Safe for Power and Profit, Dallas: Spence, 01. **CONTACT ADDRESS** 500 N Park Ave, Waco, TX 76708. **EMAIL** Chip_Conyers@baylor.edu

COOEY, PAULA M.
PERSONAL Born Hays, KS, m, 1 child **DISCIPLINE** RELIGION, THEOLOGY AND SOCIAL THEORY **EDUCATION** Univ Ga, BA, philos, 68; Harvard Divinity Sch, MTS, 74; Harvard Univ, grad sch of arts & sci, PhD, 81. **CAREER** Visiting instr, Conn Col, 9/79-9/80; instr part-time, relig, Univ Mass, Harbor Campus, 9/80-1/81; asst prof, relig, Trinity Univ, 9/81-7/87; assoc prof, relig, Trinity Univ, 8/87-8/93; prof, relig, Trinity Univ, 8/93-99; Margaret W. Harmon Prof of Christian Theol and Culture, Macalester College, 9/99- . **HONORS AND AWARDS** Co-dir, Southwest Regional Amer Acad of Relig workshop on teaching for jr facul, 94-96; Sears-Roebuck Found award for excellence in teaching & campus leadership, 91; Trinity Univ nom for CASE award, 88. **MEMBERSHIPS** Amer Acad of Relig; Soc for Buddhist-Christian Studies; Soc for the Sci Study of Relig; Amer Asn of Univ Prof. **RESEARCH** Death and dying from a feminist perspective. **SELECTED PUBLICATIONS** Auth, Family, Freedom, and Faith: Building Community Today, Westminster John Knox Press, ix-131, 96; auth, Religious Imagination and the Body: A Feminist Analysis, Oxford Univ Press, vii-184, 94; auth, After Patriarchy: Feminist Reconstructions of The World Religions, Orbis Press, ix-169, 91; article, Bad Women: The Limitations of Theory and Theology, Horizons in Feminist Theology, Fortress, 97; article, Kenosis, Popular Religiosity, Religious Pluralism, Dict of Feminist Theol, John Knox Westminster Press, 96; article, Re-Membering the Body: A Theological Resource for Resisting Domestic Violence, Theol & Sexuality, 3, 27-47, 95; article, Mapping the Body through Religious Symbolism: The Life and Work of Frida Kahlo as Case Study, Imagining Faith: Essays in Honor of Richard R. Niebuhr, Scholars Press, 105-125, 95; article, Backlash, Jour of Feminist Studies, 10, 1, 109-111, 94. **CONTACT ADDRESS** Dept. of Religious Studies, Macalester Col, 1600 Grand Ave., Saint Paul, MN 55105. **EMAIL** cooey@macalester.edu

COOGAN, MICHAEL
PERSONAL Born 07/30/1942, Madison, WI, m, 1982, 3 children **DISCIPLINE** RELIGION **EDUCATION** Fordham Univ, BA, 66; Harvard Univ, PhD, 71. **CAREER** Adj Asst Prof, Wilfred Laurier Univ, 71-74; Asst Prof, St Jerome's Col, 72-74; Prof, W.F. Albright Inst of Archaeol Res, 75-76; Visiting Prof, Wellesley Col, 86-89; Assoc Prof to Prof, Stonehill Col, 85-. **HONORS AND AWARDS** NEH Fel, 92-93. **MEMBERSHIPS** Catholic Biblical Asn; Soc of Biblical Literature; Archaeol Inst of Am; Am Sch or Oriental Res; Israel Exploration Soc. **RESEARCH** Hebrew Bible; Biblical History and Archaeology. **SELECTED PUBLICATIONS** Co-auth, "Archaeology and Biblical Studies: The Book of Joshua," in The Hebrew Bible and Its Interpreters, (Eisenbrauns, 90), 19-32; auth, "The Great Gulf Between Scholars and the Pew," Bible Review, (94): 44-48, 55; auth, "Ten Great Finds," Biblical Archaeology Review, (95): 36-47; auth, "In the Beginning: The Earliest History," in The Oxford History of the Biblical World, (Oxford Univ Press, 98), 3-31; auth, "The Ten Commandments on the Wall," Bible Review, (99): 2. **CONTACT ADDRESS** Dept Relig Studies, Stonehill Col, 320 Washington Street, Easton, MA 02357-7800. **EMAIL** mdcoogan@aol.com

COOK, DANIEL JOSEPH
PERSONAL Born 06/27/1938, Philadelphia, PA, m, 1977 **DISCIPLINE** GERMAN AND SOCIAL PHILOSOPHY **EDUCATION** Haverford Col, BA, 60; Columbia Univ, MA, 63, PhD(philos), 68; Hebrew Union Col, BHebrew Lit, 64. **CAREER** From instr to asst prof philos, Herbert H Lehman Col, 67-71; res assoc, Univ Bonn, 71-72; Assoc Prof Philos, Dept Philos, Brooklyn Col, 72-. **MEMBERSHIPS** Am Philos Asn; Soc Asian Comp Philos; Hegel Soc Am. **RESEARCH** Hegel; Marx; Leibniz. **SELECTED PUBLICATIONS** Auth, Language and consciousness in Hegel's Jena writings, J Hist Philos, 4/72; Language in the Philosophy of Hegel, Mouton, 73; contribr, Leibniz and Hegel on Language, In: Hegel and the History of Philosophy, Nijhoff, 74; coauth, Discourse on the Natural Theology of the Chinese, Univ Hawaii, 77; James' Ether Mysticism and Hegel, J Hist Philos, 7/77; Metaphysics, politics & ecumenism: Leibniz' discourse on the natural theology of the Chinese, Studia Leibnitiana, 81. **CONTACT ADDRESS** Dept Philos, Brooklyn Col, CUNY, 2901 Bedford Ave, Brooklyn, NY 11210-2813.

COOK, E. DAVID
PERSONAL Born Newcastle, UK, M, 1970, 2 children **DISCIPLINE** CHRISTIAN ETHICS **EDUCATION** Arizona State Univ, BA; Edinburgh Univ, MA; Oxford Univ, MA; New Col, Edinburgh Univ, PhD. **CAREER** Clinical ethicist, John Radcliffe Hospital; fellow, Oxford Univ; prof, S Baptist Theol Sem. **HONORS AND AWARDS** Listed, Who's Who in the World; Oxford Univ Dictionary of Experts; Hon D. Belt Gordon College, Werham MS. **RESEARCH** Christian perspective on such issues as euthanasia, medical ethics, genetics, AIDS, homosexuality, and pornography. **SELECTED PUBLICATIONS** Auth, The Moral Maze; Blind Alley Beliefs; Dilemmas of Life; Medical Ethics Today: Its Practice and Philosophy; Christianity Confronts. **CONTACT ADDRESS** Dept Christian Ethics, So Baptist Theol Sem, 2825 Lexington Rd, Louisville, KY 40280. **EMAIL** admin@atswhitefield.mildram.co.uk

COOK, J. THOMAS
PERSONAL Born 08/07/1951, SC, m, 1989 **DISCIPLINE** PHILOSOPHY **EDUCATION** Johns Hopkins, BA, 72; Vanderbilt, Ma, 78, PhD, 81. **CAREER** Vis lectr, Stetson Univ, 79-80; vis asst prof, Williams Col, 80-92; prof, Rollins Col, 92-; NEH Summer Sem; tchg awards. **MEMBERSHIPS** Am Philos Asn; N Am Spinoza Soc; Spinoza Gesselschaft; Soc Philos & Psychol. **RESEARCH** Spinoza; Enlightenment; Philosophy of mind. **SELECTED PUBLICATIONS** Auth, "Deciding to Believe Without Self-Deception," J of Philos, 86; auth Do Persons Follow from Spinoza's God, The Personalist Forum, 92; Did Spinoza Lie to His Landlady?, Studia Spinozana, 95. **CONTACT ADDRESS** Dept of Philosophy, Rollins Col, 1000 Holt Ave, Box 2659, Winter Park, FL 32789. **EMAIL** tcook@rollins.edu

COOK, JONATHAN A.
DISCIPLINE PHILOSOPHY **EDUCATION** Harvard Univ, BA; Columbia Univ, MA, 88, MPhil, 91, PhD, 93. **CAREER** IND SCHOLAR **MEMBERSHIPS** AM Antiquarian Soc **SELECTED PUBLICATIONS** Auth, Satirical Apocalypse: An Anatomy of Melville's "The Confidence Man," 96. **CONTACT ADDRESS** 4405 SE Alder St, Portland, OR 97215.

COOK, JULIAN ABELE, JR.
PERSONAL Born 06/22/1930, Washington, DC, m **DISCIPLINE** LAW **EDUCATION** PA State Univ, BA, 1952; Georgetown Univ, JD, 1957; Univ of Virginia, LLM, 1988. **CAREER** Judge Arthur E Moore, law clerk, 57-58; private practice, attorney, 58-78; State of MI, special asst, attorney general, 68-78; Univ of Detroit-Mercy, adjunct prof of law, 70-74; East Dist of MI, US Courthouse, Detroit, US Dist Judge, 78-, chief judge, 89-96, Sr Judge, 96-; Trial Advocacy Workship, Harvard Univ, Instructor, 88-. **HONORS AND AWARDS** Distinguished Citizen of the Year, NAACP, Oakland Co, MI, 1970; Citation of Merit, Pontiac, MI Area Urban League, 1971; chmn, Civil Rights Commn, achieved resolution, State of MI, House of Representatives, 1971; Boss of the Year, Legal Secretary Assn, 1973-74; Pathfinders Awd, Oakland Univ, 1977; Serv Awd, Todd-Phillips Home Inc, 1978; Focus & Impact Awd Oakland Univ, 1985; Distinguished Alumnus Awd, Pennsylvania State Univ, 1985; Distinguished Alumnus Awd, John Carroll Awd, Georgetown Univ, 1989; Augustus Straker Awd, 1988; Absalom Jones Awd, Union of Black Episcopalians, Detroit Chapter, 1988; Bench-Bar Awd, Wolverine, Detroit Bar Assn, 1987; Presidential Awd, North Oakland Co, NAACP, 1987; Honor Soc, Univ of Detroit School of Law, 1981; B'nai B'rith Barrister, 1980; Federal Bar Assn, 1978; MI Lawyers Weekly, voted 1 of 25 Most Respected Judges in MI, 1990, 1991; Detroit Monthly, voted 1 of the best Judges in the Metro Detroit area, 1991; Georgetown University, Doctor of Law, Honoris Causa, 1992; Jewish Law Veterans of the US, Brotherhood Awd, 1994; MI State Bar, Champion of Justice Awd, 1994; Univ of Detroit-Mercy, Doctor of Laws, Honoris Causa, 1996; Wayne State Univ, Doctor of Laws, Honoris Causa, 1997; Georgetown Univ, Paul R Dean Awd, 1997; Pontiac, MI, City Wide Choir Union, Humanitarian Awd. **MEMBERSHIPS** Amer & Natl Bar Assns; Am Bar Found; co-chmn, Prof, Devel Task Force, MI Bar Assn; MI Assn of Black Judges; Fed Bar Assn; Oakland Univ Proj Twenty Comm, chmn, bd of dirs, 1966-68; Pontiac Area Urban League, pres, 1967-68; MI Civil Rights Comm, chair, 1968-71; Todd Phillips Children's Home, bd of dirs, 1968-78; Amer Civil Liberties Union, bd of dirs, 1976-78; Amer Inn of Court, pres, master of the bench, chap XI, 1994-96; Cont Legal Educ Comm, Oakland County Bar Assn, 1968-69, judicial liaison, Dist Court Comm, vice chair, 1977; Cont Legal Educ Comm, 1977; Unauthorized Practice of Law, 1977; MI Supreme Court Defense Serv Comm, 1977; exec bd of dir, past pres, Child & Family Serv of MI; chmn, Sixth Circuit Comm on Standard Jury Instruction; bd of dirs, Amer Heart Assn of MI; Amer Bar Assn, fellow, 1981-; Detroit Urban League, bd of dirs, 1983-85; Brighton Health Svcs Corp, 1985-92; Georgetown Univ Alumni Assn; Judicial Conference of the US, chmn, 1990-93; Harvard Univ, trial advocacy workshop, instructor, 1988-; life mem, NAACP; PA State Univ, Alumni Assn, alumni coun, 1986-92; Hutzel Hosp, bd of dirs, 1984-95; Georgetown Univ, bd of visitors, 1991-; NY Univ Root Tilden Snow Scholarship Prog, screening panel, 1991-99; Mediation Tribunal Assn; Third Judicial Circuit of MI, bd of dirs, 1992-; Amer Law Inst, 1996-; Judicial Coun of the Sixth Circuit, sr judge personnel comm, 1996-97; MI Bar Foundation, fellow, 1987-, chair, 1993-. **SELECTED PUBLICATIONS** Published: Jurisprudence of Original Intention, co-author, 1986; A Quest for Justice, 1983; Some Current Problems of Human Administration, co-author, 1971; The Changing Role of the Probation Officer in the Federal Court, article, Federal Sentencing Reporter, vol 4, no 2, p 112, 1991; An Overview of the US District Court for the Eastern District of Michigan, article, Inter Alia, vol 28, no 1, winter 1990; Rule 11: A Judicial Approach to an Effective Administration of Justice in the US Courts, 15 Ohio N U L 397, 1988; ADR in the United States District Court for Eastern District of Michigan, Michigan Pleading and Practice ADR, Section 62A-405-62A-415, 1994; Thurgood Marshall and Clarence Thomas: A Glance at Their Philosophies, Michigan Bar Journal, March 1994, Vol 73, No 3, p298; George A Googasian-58th President of the State Bar of Michigan, Michigan Bar Journal, Oct 1992, Vol 71, No 10; "Family Responsibility, Federal Sentencing Reporter," 1995; Federal Civil Procedure Before Trial: Sixth Circuit, 1996; "Dream Makers: Black Judges on Justice," Univ of MI Law Review, 1996; "Death Penalty," co-author Cooley Law Review, 1996; "Closing Their Eyes to the Constitution: The Declining Role of the Supreme Court in the Protection of Civil Rights," co-author, Detroit Coll of Law, 1996. **CONTACT ADDRESS** Eastern District of Michigan, 231 W Lafayette, 718 Theodore Levin United State Courthouse, Detroit, MI 48226.

COOK, MICHAEL J.
PERSONAL Born 01/15/1942, Altoona, PA, m, 1984, 5 children **DISCIPLINE** NEW TESTAMENT **EDUCATION** Haverford Col, BA, 64; Hebrew Un Col, PhD, 74 **CAREER** Asst Prof, 73-77; Assoc Prof, 77-81; Prof, 81-91; Prof, 92-pres **HONORS AND AWARDS** Phi Beta Kappa, Haverford Col; Exc in Tch Awd **MEMBERSHIPS** Soc of Bibl Lit **RESEARCH** New Testament; Christian-Jewish Relations **SELECTED PUBLICATIONS** Auth, Mark's Treatment of the Jewish Leaders (Leiden: Brill, 78); auth, Rabbinic Judaism & Early Christianity, Review & Expositor, 87; auth, "The Mission to the Jews in Acts--Unraveling Luke's 'Myth of the Myriads'," in Luke-Acts and the Jewish People: Eight Critical Perspectives (Minneapolis 1988), 102-23; 152-58; auth, "Christian Appropriation of Passover: Jewish Responses Then and Now," Occasional Papers in Jewish History and Thought 5, Robert M. Seltzer, ed. (Hunter College, 99), 49-63; auth, Images of Jesus in the Arts, Proceedings of the Center for Jewish-Christian Learning 10, 96, 46-56; auth, "The Death of Jesus: A Catholic-Jewish Dialogue (opposite Raymond Brown)," Nostra Aetate Dialogue Proceedings (New York: Fordham, 98): 56-100; auth, "Jewish Reflections on Jesus: Some Abiding Trends," The Historical Jesus Through Catholic and Jewish Eyes, B.F. LeBeau, L. Greenspoon, & D. Hamm, eds. (Harrisburg: Trinity Press International, 00), 95-113; auth, "Destabilizing the Tale of Judas Iscariot: A Vehicle for Enhancing Christian-Jewish Understanding" An American Rabbinate--A Festschrift for Walter Jacob (Pittsburgh: Rodef Shalom Press, 01), pp. 114-47; auth, "Evolving Jewish Views of Jesus," Jesus Through Jewish Eyes, B. Bruteau, ed. (Maryknoll, NY: Orbis, 01). **CONTACT ADDRESS** Hebrew Union Col-Jewish Inst of Religion, Ohio, 3101 Clifton Ave, Cincinnati, OH 45220. **EMAIL** cookmj@aol.com

COOK, MICHAEL L.
PERSONAL Born 02/26/1936, Wolf Point, MT, s **DISCIPLINE** SYSTEMATIC THEOLOGY, CHRISTOLOGY **EDUCATION** Gonzaga Univ, AB, 59; MA, 60; Santa Clara Univ, STM, 67; Alma Col, STL, 67; Grad Theol Union, ThD, 74. **CAREER** Asst prof, Jesuit Sch of Theol, 71-82; vis prof of Theol, La Pontificia Univ Catolica, 87-88; prof, Gonzaga Univ, 82-86 & 89-. **HONORS AND AWARDS** Grant, ATS, 80-81; Bonus Awd for Distinguished Contributions, Gonzaga Univ, 90-91; Fel, Boston Col, 00-01. **MEMBERSHIPS** Catholic Theol Soc of Am. **RESEARCH** Christology, especially liberation and justice issues in Lation America and elsewhere, Jewish-Christian relations, especially as centering around Jesus and the biblical notion of justice. **SELECTED PUBLICATIONS** Auth, The Jesus of Faith, Paulist Press, 81; auth, The Historical Jesus, Thomas More Press, 86; auth, Responses to 101 Questions About Jesus, Paulist Press, 93; auth, Christology as Narrative Quest, Liturgical Press, 97. **CONTACT ADDRESS** Dept Relig Studies, Gonzaga Univ, 502 E Boone Ave, Spokane, WA 99258-1774.

COOK, S. D. NOAM
DISCIPLINE PHILOSOPHY **EDUCATION** San Fran State Univ, BA, MA; MIT, PhD. **CAREER** Assoc prof of Philos, San Jose State Univ; consult res; Xerox, Palo Alto Res Ctr. **RESEARCH** Knowledge, know-how and technological change in social contexts. **CONTACT ADDRESS** Dept of Philosophy, San Jose State Univ, San Jose, CA 95192-0096.

COOK, STEPHEN L.
PERSONAL Born 07/21/1962, CT, m, 1988 **DISCIPLINE** HEBREW BIBLE AND OLD TESTAMENT **EDUCATION** Yale Univ, PhD, 92. **CAREER** Asst prof, old testament, Union Theol Sem, 92-96; asst prof, old testament, Va Theol Sem, 96-99; assoc prof, 99-. **HONORS AND AWARDS** The Two Brothers fel, Yale Univ, 87; Phi Beta Kappa, 84. **MEMBERSHIPS** Soc of Bibl Lit; Amer Acad of Relig; Amer Sch of Orient Res; Cath Bibl Asn. **RESEARCH** Apocalypticism and post exile Israelite religion; The social roots of biblical Yahwism. **SELECTED PUBLICATIONS** Rev, The Ladies and the Cities: Transformation and Apocalyptic Identity in Joseph and Aseneth, 4 Ezra, the Apocalypse and the Shepherd of Hermas, co-ed, "On the Way to Nineveh: Studies in Honor of George M. Landes," The American Schools of Oriental Research, 99; Jour of Bibl Lit, 117, 2, 375-377, 98; rev, Prophets of Old and the Day of the End: Zechariah, the Book of Watchers and Apocalyptic, Cath Bibl Quart, 59, 757-758, 97; rev, The Five Fragments of the Apocryphon of Ezekiel: A Critical Study, Jour of Bibl Lit, 115, 3, 532-534, 96; rev, Psalms and the Transformation of Stress: Poetic-Communal Interpretation and the Family, Jour of Relig and Health, 35, 3, 263-264, 96; auth, Reflections on Apocalypticism at the Approach of the Year 2000, Union Sem Quart Rev, 49, 1-2, 3-16, 95; guest ed, Countdown to 2000: Essays on Apocalypticism, Union Sem Quart Rev, vol 49, no 1-2, 95; rev, Second Zechariah and the Deuteronomic School, Cath Bibl Quart, 57, 4, 780-781, 95; auth, Innerbiblical Interpretation in Ezekiel 44 and the History of Israel's Priesthood, Jour of Bibl Lit, 114, 2, 193-208, 95; auth, Prophecy and Apocalypticism: The Postexilic Social Setting, Fortress Press, 95; auth, The Text and Philology of 1 Samuel xiii 20-1, Vetus Testamentum, 44, 2, 250-254, 94; auth, The Metamorphosis of a Shepherd: The Tradition History of Zechariah 11:17 + 13:7-9, Cath Bibl Quart, 55, 3, 453-466, 93; auth, Apocalypticism and the Psalter, Zeitschrift fur die alttestamentliche Wissenschaft, 104, 1, 82-99, 92. **CONTACT ADDRESS** 3737 Seminary Rd., Alexandria, VA 22304. **EMAIL** scook@vts.edu

COOK, WILLIAM ROBERT
PERSONAL Born 12/27/1943, Indianapolis, IN, s, 3 children **DISCIPLINE** MEDIEVAL HISTORY, HISTORY OF CHRISTIANITY **EDUCATION** Wabash Col, AB, 66; Cornell Univ, MA, 70, PhD(medieval hist), 71. **CAREER** Asst prof hist, 70-77, Assoc Prof Hist, State Univ NY Col Geneseo, 77-82; Prof, 82-84; Distinguished Teaching Prof, 84-; Nat Endowment for Humanities fel in residence, Harvard Univ, 76-77; adj prof lit, Attica Correctional Facil, 80 & 81; adj prof relig studies, Siena Col, NY, 81. **HONORS AND AWARDS** Phi Beta Kappa; CASE Prof of the Year for NY, 92. **MEMBERSHIPS** AHA; Mediaeval Acad Am; Am Soc Church Hist; Am Friends Bodley; Dante Soc Am. **RESEARCH** Medieval Franciscanism; Monasticism; Siena, Italy. **SELECTED PUBLICATIONS** Coauth, The Medieval World View, Oxford, UP, 83; auth, Frances: The Way of Poverty and Humility, Liturgical Press, 89; auth, St. Francis in America, Franciscan Press, 98; auth, Images of St. Francis in Painting, Stone and from the Earlect Image to ca. 1320 in: A Catalogue. **CONTACT ADDRESS** Dept of Hist, SUNY, Col at Geneseo, 1 College Cir, Geneseo, NY 14454-1401. **EMAIL** cookb@geneseo.edu

COOLEY, JAMES F.
PERSONAL Born 01/11/1926, Rowland, NC, m **DISCIPLINE** THEOLOGY **EDUCATION** Johnson C Smith Univ,

AB Soc Sci 1953, BD Theol 1956; Interdenom Theol Center, DM 1973; World Univ Tucson, AZ, PhD Soc Sci 1982; Life Science Coll, DD 1972; St John Univ NE, MA Sociology 1972; Law Enforcement Official, certified; Law Enforcement Instructor of Jail Opers and Jail Admin, certified. **CAREER** Grant Chapel Presb Ch, minister, 56-57; St Andrews Presb Ch, minister, 57-69; Forrest City Spec Sch Dist #7, 57-69; St Francis Co, juv prob ofcr, 59-68, assoc juv judge, 63-64; Shorter Coll, polit sci dir/minister of svc/dean of men/acad dean, 69-73; State Rep Art Givens Jr, chf legisl on comm affairs; 5th Div Circ Ct for Judge Jack Lessenberg, prob ofcr; Tucker Prison, first black chaplain in AR, 71; Attorney Genl's Office, agent consumer protection; Pulaski County, deputy registrar; County Contact Comm Inc, founder/exec dir. **MEMBERSHIPS** Police commr Wrightsville PD 1984; chaplain Pulaski Co Sheriff Dept 1985; AR Cncl on Human Rel; Natl Hist Soc; Urban League; Early Amer Soc; Natl Conf of Christians and Jews Inc; Postal Commem Soc; Natl Black Veterans Organ Inc; major genl Natl Chaplains Assn; foot distrib for the poor AR Food Bank Network; Amer Legion, Natl Sheriff's Assn; sr warden, comm mem 33rd Degree Mason; Boy Scouts of Amer; bd of dirs AA AWARE Drug and Alcohol Prevention Prog; Worshipful Master, Welcome Lodge #457 masonic 1987-; life member, Disabled American Veteran; life member, Veteran of Foreign Wars. **CONTACT ADDRESS** County Contact Comm Inc, PO Box 17225, North Little Rock, AR 72117.

COOMBS, ROBERT STEPHEN
PERSONAL Born 02/10/1952, Hampton, VA, m, 1979, 2 children **DISCIPLINE** PSYCHOLOGY, MINISTRIES **EDUCATION** Carson-Newman Col, BA, 74; Southern Baptists Theol Sem, MD, 77; PhD Ministry, 88; PhD Philos, Univ Tenn, 94. **CAREER** Assoc Pastor, W Hills Baptist Church Knoxville, 79-90; Dir of Clinical Prog, Knox Area Rescue Ministries Knoxville, 90-92; Adj Prof, Univ of Tenn Knoxville, 93-97; Adj Prof, Carson-Newman Col Jefferson City Tenn, 95-97; Minister, Norris Religious Fel, 94-97; Adj Prof, Univ of Tenn Chattanooga Tenn, 97-98; Adj Prof, Southern Adventist Univ Coldale Tenn, 97-; Therapist, Hiwassee Mental health Cleveland Tenn, 99-. **HONORS AND AWARDS** Phi Sigma Tau, Kappa Omicron Nu, Alpha Phi Omega, Distinguished Teacher Awd, Univ of Tenn Knoxville, 96. **MEMBERSHIPS** Boys' Work Committee, Knox Co Asn of Baptists, 81-83; UNICEF Knox Co, 81-83; Detoxification Rehabil Inst, 81-84; Homeless Coalition Knoxville, 91-92; Inter-Agency Coun on the Homeless, 91-92; Norris Ministerial Asn, 95-97; Int Counc OF Community Churches Editorial 95-97; YMCA, 96-97; Nat Coun on Family Relations, 94-00. **SELECTED PUBLICATIONS** Auth, "The Breakfast Club, "in Group Mag (Group Publ, Loveland, CO), 85; auth, Of Such is the Kingdom, Baker Book House (Grand Rapids, MI), 87; auth, Concise Object Sermons for Children, Baker Book House (Grand Rapids, MI), 89; auth, Enlightening Object Sermons for Children, Baker Book House (Grand Rapids, MI), 92; auth, Building an Effective Youth Program, Community Church Press (Chicago, IL), 95; auth, "I Can See Clearly Now, in Group Mag (Group Publ, Loveland, CO), 96; co-ed, The Inclusive Pulpit Vol I and Vol II, Community Church Press (Chicago, IL), 96,96; auth, "Family Works Column," Cleveland Daily Banner (99). **CONTACT ADDRESS** Dept Educ and Psychology, Southern Adventist Univ, PO Box 370, Collegedale, TN 37315. **EMAIL** DrRCoombs@aol.com

COONEY, BRIAN PATRICK
PERSONAL Born 09/04/1943, Montreal, PQ, Canada, m, 1968, 2 children **DISCIPLINE** PHILOSOPHY **EDUCATION** St Louis Univ, BA, 65; McGill Univ, MA, 69, PhD, 72. **CAREER** Asst prof philos, Univ Notre Dame, 71-72; asst prof, Univ Tex, Austin, 72-80; from Asst Prof to Assoc Prof, 80-91, Prof Philos, Centre Col, 91-. **HONORS AND AWARDS** Am Coun Learned Soc fel, 76-77. **MEMBERSHIPS** Am Philos Asn. **RESEARCH** History of modern philosophy; philosophy of mind. **SELECTED PUBLICATIONS** Auth, John Sergeant's Criticism of Locke's Theory of Ideas, Mod Schoolman, 1/73; Descartes and the external darkness, New Scholasticism, summer 75; Arnold Geulincx: A Cartesian idealist, J Hist Philos, 78; The biological basis of mind, Int Philos Quart, 12/78; The neural basis of self-consciousness, Nature and System, 3/79; A Hylomorphic Theory of Mind, Peter Lang Publ, 91; Dennett's Fictional Selves, SW Philos Rev, 1/94; ed, The Place of Mind, Wadsworth Publ, 99. **CONTACT ADDRESS** Dept of Philos, Centre Col, 600 W Walnut St, Danville, KY 40422-1394. **EMAIL** cooneyb@centre.edu

COONEY, WILLIAM
PERSONAL Born 11/18/1952, Rockford, IL, m, 1975, 3 children **DISCIPLINE** PHILOSOPHY **EDUCATION** Marquette Univ, PhD. **CAREER** Prof, Briar Cliff Col. **HONORS AND AWARDS** Burlington No Fac Excel, 92; Dist Alumni, Marquette Univ, 93. **MEMBERSHIPS** Am Philos Asn. **RESEARCH** Aesthetics; philos and psychology. **SELECTED PUBLICATIONS** Contrib ed, The Human Person and the Human Community, Ginn Press, 88; ed, Reflections on Gabriel Marcel: A Collection of Essays, Edwin Mellon Press, 89; coauth, Ten Great Thinkers: An Integrative Study in Philosophy and Psychology, Univ Press Am, 90; auth, A Fallacy in Person-Denying Arguments for Abortion, J of Applied Philos, Oct 91; coauth, From Plato to Piaget: The Greatest Educational Theorists From Across the Centuries and Around the World, Univ Press Am, 6th print, 93; auth, Affirmative Action Revisited: A Response to Professor Jordan, The Doctrine of Double Effect: Philosophers Debate a Controversial Moral Principle, Univ Notre Dame Press, 96; rev article, on Seymour Cain's Gabriel Marcel's Theory of Religious Experience, Int Stud in Philos, 97; auth, Rights Theory, Encycl of Applied Ethics, Ctr for Professional Ethics, Univ Cent Lancashire, UK, Acad Press, 97; auth, The Death Poetry of Emily Dickinson: A Philosophical Exploration, Omega, the Nat J of Death and Dying, 98; auth, The Quest for Meaning: An Exploration into the Human Journey as Revealed in Philosophy and the Arts, Rowman & Littlefield, forthcoming. **CONTACT ADDRESS** Briar Cliff Col, 3303 Rebecca, Sioux City, IA 51104. **EMAIL** cooney@briarcliff.edu

COOP, JACK
DISCIPLINE LAW **EDUCATION** Univ Manitoba, BA, 78; Osgoode Hall Law Sch, LLB, 83. **CAREER** Senior counsel, Ontario Ministry of the Attorney General; adj prof, Univ of Toronto. **HONORS AND AWARDS** Seconded, Legal Services Branch, Ontario Ministry Environ Energy. **MEMBERSHIPS** Law Soc. **RESEARCH** Environmental law. **SELECTED PUBLICATIONS** Auth, pubs on environmental regulation and environmental assessment law. **CONTACT ADDRESS** Fac of Law, Univ of Toronto, 78 Queen's Park, Toronto, ON, Canada M5S 2C5.

COOPER, ALLAN D.
PERSONAL Born 04/13/1952, Oklahoma City, OK, d, 1980, 2 children **DISCIPLINE** POLITICAL SCIENCE **EDUCATION** Univ Okla, BA, 74; Univ Wis, MA, 76; Atlanta Univ, PhD, 81. **CAREER** From asst prof to assoc prof to chemn, 81-93, St Augustines Col; from assoc prof to prof to chemn, 93-, Otterbein Col. **HONORS AND AWARDS** Fulbright-Hays Res Awd, 00; Am Counc Learned Societies, res grant, 94; Fulbright-Hays Res Awd, 92; NEH Stud Awds, 84, 87, 91, 93; Am Polit Science Asn, Res Awd, 89. **MEMBERSHIPS** Am Polit Science Asn; African Stud Asn; Asn Concerned Africa Scholars; Asn Third World Stud. **RESEARCH** Politics of Namibia and Southern Africa. **SELECTED PUBLICATIONS** Auth, US Economic Power and Political Influence in Namibia, 1700-1982, 82; ed, Allies in Apartheid: Western Capitalism in Occupied Namibia, 88; auth, The Occupation of Namibia: Afrikanerdom's Attack on The British Empire, 91; auth, art, Namibia in Joel Krieger, 93; auth, art, State Sponsorship of Women's Rights and Implications for Patriarchism, 97. **CONTACT ADDRESS** Dept of History and Political Science, Otterbein Col, One Otterbein, Westerville, OH 43081. **EMAIL** acooper@otterbein.edu

COOPER, ALMETA E.
PERSONAL Born 12/27/1950, Durham, NC, m, 1984 **DISCIPLINE** LAW **EDUCATION** Wells Coll, BA 1972; Northwestern Univ Sch of Law, JD 1975. **CAREER** Vedder Price Kaufman & Kammholz, assoc 1975-77; Amer Med Assn, asst dir of health law div 1977-82; Tuggle Hasbrouck & Robinson, partner 1980-82; Meharry Medical Coll, corporate secretary & general counsel, 82-88; St Thomas Hospital, Nashville, TN, general counsel, 88-; College of St Francis, Nashville, TN, adjunct faculty, 89-. **HONORS AND AWARDS** Chicago Urban League; Alumnae Assns of Wells & Spelman Colleges; Outstanding Alumna Spelman Coll; Outstanding Volunteer Chicago Urban League; Natl Finalist White House Fellowship 1982; publications have appeared in Journal of the Amer Med Assn and in St Louis Univ Law Journal. **MEMBERSHIPS** Lecturer Joint Comm on Accreditation of Hospitals; lecturer Amer College of Hospital Administrators; lecturer New England Hosp Assembly; mem Amer Soc of Hospital Attorneys; bd of dir Minority Legal Educ Resources; alternate mem Hines Veterans Admin Cooperative Studies Prog Human Rights Comm; pres bd of dir IL Family Planning Council; mem Renaissance Women; appointed mem Nashville Private Industry Council; fin comm League of Women Voters Nashville; mem Leadership Nashville 1986-87, Music City Chap of the Links, TN Bar Assn, Napier-Looby Bar Assn, Amer Acad of Hospital Attorneys. **CONTACT ADDRESS** Office of Legal Affairs, St. Thomas Hospital, 4220 Harding Rd, Nashville, TN 37205.

COOPER, BURTON
PERSONAL Born 06/13/1932, New York, NY, m, 1955, 4 children **DISCIPLINE** THEOLOGY, PHILOSOPHY OF RELIGION **EDUCATION** Columbia Univ, BA, 54; Union Theol Sem, PhD(syst theol), 68. **CAREER** Instr relig, Wooster Col, 65-68; asst prof, Mary Washington Col, 68-70; Prof Philos Theol, Louisville Presby Theol Sem, 70-. **RESEARCH** Process theology; liberation theology. **SELECTED PUBLICATIONS** Auth, A Scandalous Providence--The Jesus Story of the Compassion of God, Theol Today, Vol 0053, 96. **CONTACT ADDRESS** Louisville Presbyterian Theol Sem, 1044 Alta Vista Rd, Louisville, KY 40205-1758.

COOPER, CLARENCE
PERSONAL Born 05/05/1942, Decatur, GA, m **DISCIPLINE** LAW **EDUCATION** Clark Coll, BA 1960-64; Emory Univ Sch Law, JD 1965-67; MIT Comm Flws Prgm, flwsp 1977; Harvard Univ John F Kennedy Sch Govt Pub Admin, 1977-78. **CAREER** Atlanta Legal Serv Prog, atty 1967-68; Fulton Co GA, asst dist atty 1968-76; Atlant Muncpl Ct, assoc judge 1976; Fulton County Superior Ct, judge; US District Court, judge. **HONORS AND AWARDS** Schlrsp Clark Coll 1960-64. **MEMBERSHIPS** Mem Natl Bar Assn, Gate City Bar Assn, Natl Conf Black Lawyers, State Bar GA, Atlanta Bar Assn; mem exec bd Atlanta Br NAACP; mem Natl Urban League; bd dir Amistrad Prod, EOA's Drug Prog; past mem Atlanta Judicial Comm. **SELECTED PUBLICATIONS** "The Judiciary & Its Budget: An Administrative Hassle". **CONTACT ADDRESS** US District Court, Northern District of GA, 75 Spring St, SW, Atlanta, GA 30303.

COOPER, CLEMENT THEODORE
PERSONAL Born 10/26/1930, Miami, FL, m, 5 children **DISCIPLINE** LAW **EDUCATION** Lincoln Univ, AB 1952; Boston Univ, attended 1954-55; Howard Univ Sch of Law, JD 1958; CO State Christian Coll, Hon PhD 1973; Hastings Coll of Law Univ of CA, first natl coll of advocacy 1971. **CAREER** Private Practice, attorney-at-law 1960-. **MEMBERSHIPS** Mem MI State Bar 1960; mem DC Bar 1960; mem US Sup Ct Bar, US Ct Appeals, DC & Tenth Cir CO, US Ct Mil Appeals, Third Cir Phila, US Ct of Claims, US Second Circuit Ct of Appeals, US Fourth Circuit Ct of Appeals, US Sixth Circuit Ct of Appeals, US Ct of Appeals for Federal Circuit; mem Natl Bar Assn; Amer Bar Assn; Amer Trial Lawyers Assn; mem Amer Judicature Soc; Amer Civil Liberties Union; Pub Welfare Adv Council 1966-68; mem Ch of the Ascension & St Agnes Wash DC; life mem Alpha Phi Alpha; arbitrator, Natl Assoc of Securities Dealers. **SELECTED PUBLICATIONS** Auth, "Sealed Verdict" 1964; auth, "Location of Unpatented Mining Claims" CA Mining Journal Jan-May 1975 Vol 44; contrib ed, Natural Resources Section Amer Bar Assn "Significant Adminis Legislative & State Court Decisions Affecting the Petrol Ind in States East of the Mississippi River" 1979-80. **CONTACT ADDRESS** Law Offices of Clement T Cooper, PO Box 76135, Washington, DC 20013-6135.

COOPER, CORINNE
DISCIPLINE LAW **EDUCATION** Univ Ariz, BA, JD. **CAREER** Prof **RESEARCH** Banking law; contracts; commercial transactions; sales; secured transactions; negotiation; lawyering skills. **SELECTED PUBLICATIONS** Auth, Getting Graphic (TM): Visual Tools for Teaching and Learning Commercial Law; Getting Graphic 2 (TM): Visual Tools for Teaching and Learning Law; ed, The Portable UCC; co-ed, A Drafter's Guide to an Alternative Dispute Resolution. **CONTACT ADDRESS** Law Dept, Univ of Missouri, Kansas City, 5100 Rockhill Rd, Kansas City, MO 64110-2499. **EMAIL** cooperc@umkc.edu

COOPER, JOSEPH
PERSONAL Born 12/20/1937, Hemingway, SC, s, 1 child **DISCIPLINE** LAW **EDUCATION** Univ of Utah, Sacramento City Coll, AA, 65; University of the Pacific, McGeorge Law School, JD (honors), 69. **CAREER** Pres, First Capital Real Estate, Inc.; pres, Joseph Cooper Law Corp, 70-; founder, Success Inst of Am, Inc.; assoc dean of Academic Affairs, Northwestern Calif Univ, School of Law, Sacramento; chairman, Citizens on Police Practice; former pres, Sacramento Urban League; former founder and board mem, Sacramento Commerce and Trade Org; former mem of the Board of Governors of the Calif Trial Lawyers Asn; former mem, Sacramento Trial Lawyers Asn, Board of Directors; former chairman, Tort and Insurance Section of the Sacramento County Bar. **HONORS AND AWARDS** Resolution from the Calif Legislature for Outstanding Community Service; City of Sacramento, Distinguished Service Awd for Outstanding Workers; **MEMBERSHIPS** Am Trial Lawyers Asn; Consumer Attorneys Asn of Calif. **CONTACT ADDRESS** Joseph Cooper Law Corporation, 1310 H St, Sacramento, CA 95814. **EMAIL** jcooperlaw@aol.com

COOPER, M. WAYNE
DISCIPLINE PHILOSOPHY **EDUCATION** UTMB, MA, 69; Texas Tech, MA, phil, 89; MA, History, Lamar University. **CAREER** Assoc prof, 78-89, Texas Tech Univ; prof, 79-91, Mich St Univ; prof, 91-95, Univ Texas Health Ctr, Tyler. **HONORS AND AWARDS** OKO; AEO **MEMBERSHIPS** Amer Col Cardiology; Amer Col Physicians; APS. **RESEARCH** Medical ethics. **CONTACT ADDRESS** 115 W 5th St, Tyler, TX 75701. **EMAIL** mwaylooy@flashnet.com

COOPER-LEWTER, NICHOLAS CHARLES
PERSONAL Born 06/25/1948, Washington, DC **DISCIPLINE** RELIGIOUS STUDIES, PSYCHOTHERAPY, SOCIAL WORK, PSYCHOLOGY **EDUCATION** Ashland Coll, BA 1970; Ecumenical Ctr, African-American church studies, adv studies, DMin prog 1978; Univ of MN, MSW 1978; CA Coast Univ, PhD 1988. **CAREER** Univ of MN, Ctr for Youth Devel Rsrch, rsrch specialist, 72-73; teaching asst, 74-75; City of St Paul Human Rights Dept, field investigator, 74; consultant, various Christian churches, 76-; Cooper Lewter Hypnosis Ctr NB, dir owner 1978-83; New Garden of Gethsemane, senior pastor, 85-90; CRAVE Christ Ministries Inc, founder, psychotherapist, author; Bethel Col and Seminary, professor of social work, visiting instructor of cross cultural counseling, 90-95; Cooper-Lewter Rites of Passage, founder, 95-; McKnight Multi Cultural Grant, coordinator, 91-95; Metropolitan State Univ. Psychology and Social Work Faculty, 97-. **HONORS AND**

AWARDS University of MN School of Social Work, Deans Grad Fellowship, 1974; Teamer School of Religion, Honorary LHD, 1978; Bethel College and Seminary, Distinguished Faculty Service Awd, 1992; St Paul Urban League, SE Hall Community Service Awd, 1992; Society of Medical Hypnoanalysts, Outstanding Contributor to the Field of Medical Hypnoanalysis, 1983; Los Angeles Olympic Committee, Judgeship, 1984. **MEMBERSHIPS** Founder, 1st basileus, Xi Theta Chap, Omega Psi Phi, 1966-70; bd dir, American Academy of Med Hypnoanalysis, 1977-; NASW; BPD; CSWE; NUL; NAACP; AAMH; ACSW; former board member, Adoptive Families of America Inc; TURN Leadership Foundation: Salvation Army. **SELECTED PUBLICATIONS** Author, works include: "Concerns of Working Youth," People Human Svs MN, 1974, "Working Youth: Selected Findings from Exploratory Study," Jrnl Youth & Adolescence, 1974, "Sports Hypnotherapy: Contenderosis & Self Hate," Jrnl of Med Hypnoanalysts, 1980; "The Initial Environmental Experience: A Powerful Took for Psychotherapy & Hypnotherapy," Journal of Medical Hypnoanalysts, 1981; "Keep On Rollin' Along: The Temptations and Soul Therapy," The Journal of Black Sacred Music, vol 6, num 1, Spring 1992; "My Jesus was Jim Crowed!" Colors Magazine Vol 3 Issue 3 May/June 1994. co-author: Soul Theology: The Heart of American Black Culture, Harper and Row, 1986, re-published, Abingdon Press, 1991; Black Grief and Soul Therapy, Univ of Richmond, Tubman Press, 1998; consultant: various Olympic Team members, 1980-; US Junior Olympic Team NRA, 1983-; California State Fullerton Football Program, 1983-84; UCLA Basketball Program, 1984-85; lecturer: Bishop College; LK Williams Institute, 1985; SMU Perkins School of Theology, 1986. **CONTACT ADDRESS** Cooper-Lewter Rites of Passage, 253 E 4th St, Ste 201, Saint Paul, MN 55101. **EMAIL** ncooper-lewter@uswest.net

COPELAND, M. SHAWN

PERSONAL Born 08/24/1947, Detroit, MI, s **DISCIPLINE** SYSTEMATIC THEOLOGY **EDUCATION** Boston Col, PhD, 91 **CAREER** Inst, 83-87, St. Norbert Col; Lect, Assoc Prof, 89-94, Yale Univ Div Sch; Assoc Prof, 94-pres, Marquette Univ **HONORS AND AWARDS** Sojourner Truth Awd, 74; Sabbatical Grant, 96; Fac Res Awd, 90; Congar Awd for Excellence in Theology, 00. **MEMBERSHIPS** Am Acad of Relig; Cath Theol Soc of Am; Black Catholic Theological Symposium, Soc for the Study of Black Relig; Soc for Values in Higher Education. **RESEARCH** Political Theology; African Am Religious Experience. **SELECTED PUBLICATIONS** Auth, Concilium Violence Against Women, 94; Auth, Editorial Reflections, 94; "Difference as a Category in Critical Theologies for the Liberation of Women," in Concilium: Feminist Theologies in Different Context, 96; auth, "The New Anthropological Subject at the Heart of the Mystical Body of Christ," CTSA Proceedings, vol 53, 98; auth, "Tradition and the Traditions of African Am Catholicism," in Theological Studies, 00; ed, "Body, Representation, and Black Religious Discourse," in Postcolonialism, Feminism, and Religious Discourse, ed. By Laura Donaldson and Kwok Pui-lan, Routledge, 01. **CONTACT ADDRESS** Dept of Theol, Marquette Univ, Coughlin Hall 100, PO Box 1881, Milwaukee, WI 53201-1881. **EMAIL** shawn.copeland@marquette.edu

COPELAND, WARREN R.

PERSONAL Born 09/20/1943, Davenport, IA, m, 1965, 2 children **DISCIPLINE** ETHICS AND SOCIETY, DIVINITY SCHOOL **EDUCATION** MacMurray Col, AB, 65; Christian Theol Sem, Mdiv, 68; Univ of Chicago, AM, 71, PhD, 73. **CAREER** Illinois Conf of Churches, 73-77; Wittenberg Univ, 77-. **HONORS AND AWARDS** Dist Alumnus, MacMurray Coll. **MEMBERSHIPS** Amer Acad Rel; Soc of Christian Ethics; Soc Ethics Seminar. **RESEARCH** Economic Policy; Poverty and Welfare Policy; Urban Government. **SELECTED PUBLICATIONS** Auth, Issues of Justice, Mercer Univ Press, 88; Economic Justice, Abingdon Press, 88; And the Poor Get Welfare, Abingdon Press, 93. **CONTACT ADDRESS** Wittenberg Univ, Box 720, Springfield, OH 45501. **EMAIL** wcopeland@wittenberg.edu

COPENHAVER, JOHN

PERSONAL Born 03/04/1949, Roanoke, VA, m, 1979, 1 child **DISCIPLINE** RELIGION **EDUCATION** Washington & Lee Univ, BA, 71; Fuller Theol Sem, MDiv, 76; Catholic Univ of Am, PhD, 86 **CAREER** Chaplain, Asst to Full Prof and Dept Chair, Shenandoah Univ, 87-. **HONORS AND AWARDS** Exemplary Teaching Awd, Shenandoah Univ, 92; Theta Alpha Kappa Honor Soc for Relig Studies. **MEMBERSHIPS** Am Acad of Relig, Soc for the Study of Christian Spirituality. **RESEARCH** Christian spirituality, Theological anthropology. **SELECTED PUBLICATIONS** Auth, "Forerunners of God's Reign," Disciplines 1997, Upper Room, 97; auth, "Scholars Seek to Help Public Understanding of Religion," Winchester Star, Dec 95; auth, "Speaking Spiritual Truth" The Virginia Advocate, Feb 95; auth, "Faithfulness in Difficult Times," The Virginia Advocate, Feb 95; auth, "Shalom: God's Desire for Healing, Wholeness and Holiness," The Virginia Advocate, Oct 94; rev, of "Spirituality, Diversion and Decadence: The Contemporary Predicament," by Peter Van Ness, Christian Spirituality Bulletin, 94; auth, Prayerful Responsibility: Prayer and Social Responsibility in the Religious Thought of Douglas Steer, Univ Press of Am, 92. **CONTACT ADDRESS** Dept Humanities, Shenandoah Univ, 1460 Univ Dr, Winchester, VA 22601-5100. **EMAIL** jcopenha@su.edu

COQUILLETTE, DANIEL R.

PERSONAL Born 05/23/1944, Boston, MA, m, 1969, 3 children **DISCIPLINE** LAW **EDUCATION** Williams Col, BA, 66; Oxford Univ, BA, 69; MA, 80; Harvard Law School, JD, 71. **CAREER** Vis prof, Cornell Univ, 77-78; 83-84; dean, Boston Col, 85-93; prof, Boston Col, 97-. **HONORS AND AWARDS** Founders Medal, Boston; St. Tomas More Awd; Ful Scho, 66-69; Francis Session Hutchins Sch. **MEMBERSHIPS** Am Law Inst, Am Soc for Legal Hist. **RESEARCH** Francis Bacon, English legal history, Professional ethics, History Harvard Law School. **SELECTED PUBLICATIONS** Auth, Anglo-American Legal Heritage, Carolina, 99; auth, Lex Mercatoria, Harvard, 99; auth, Lawyers Fundamental Moral Responsibility, 95; auth, Francis Bacon, 92. **CONTACT ADDRESS** School of Law, Boston Col, Newton Ctr, 885 Centre St, Newton, MA 02459-1148. **EMAIL** coquill@bc.edu

CORATTI, JOHN EDWARD

PERSONAL Born 11/17/1930, Jersey City, NJ, m, 1997, 3 children **DISCIPLINE** CRIMINAL JUSTICE **EDUCATION** Rutgers, New Brunswick, BA, 73; Seton Hall, MA, 81; Univ Dayton, Sch Law, JD,. 88; New York Univ, ABD. **CAREER** Dir of Criminal Justice, Lamar Univ, Orange, Tex. **HONORS AND AWARDS** Am Jur. Awd. **MEMBERSHIPS** MLA, Am Bar Asn. **RESEARCH** Law, criminal justice, philosophy and medieval studies. **CONTACT ADDRESS** Dir Criminal Justice, Lamar Univ, Orange, Orange, TX 77630.

CORCORAN, JOHN

PERSONAL Born 03/20/1937, Baltimore, MD **DISCIPLINE** PHILOSOPHY **EDUCATION** John Hopkins Univ, BES, 59, MA, 62, PhD(philos), 63. **CAREER** Mem res staff ling, res lab, Int Bus Mach Corp, Yorktown, NY 63-64; vis lectr philos, Univ Calif, Berkeley, 64-65; asst prof ling, Univ Pa, 65-69; assoc prof philos, 69-73, dir, Grad Studies, 71-74, prof philos, State Univ NY Buffalo, 73-, vis assoc prof philos, Univ Mich, Ann Arbor, 69-70; vis prof, Univ Santiago de Compostela, Spain, 95. **MEMBERSHIPS** Am Philos Asn; Asn Symbolic Logic. **RESEARCH** Logic; linguistics; mathematics. **SELECTED PUBLICATIONS** Coauth, Variable Binding Term Operators, Zeit f Math Logik u Grundlagen, 72; auth, Conceptual Structure of Classical Logic, Philos & Phenomenol Res, 72; Completeness of an Ancient Logic, J Symbolic Logic, 72; Aristotle's Syllogistic, Arch fur Geschichte der Philos, 73; ed, Ancient Logic and Its Modern Interpretations, Reidel Holland, 74; coauth, String Theory, J Symbolic Logic, 74; Ockham's Theory of Supposition, Franciscan Studies, 78; Categoricity, Hist & Philos Logic, 80; ed, Alfred Tarski's Logic, Semantics, Metamathematics, Hackett Publ Co, 83. **CONTACT ADDRESS** Dept of Philos, SUNY, Buffalo, 135 Park Hall, Buffalo, NY 14260-4150. **EMAIL** corcoran@acsu.buffalo.edu

CORCORAN, KEVIN J.

PERSONAL Born 05/30/1964, Annapolis, MD, m, 2 children **DISCIPLINE** PHILOSOPHY **EDUCATION** Univ Maryland, BA, 88; Yale Univ, MA, 91; Purdue Univ, PhD, 97. **CAREER** Asst prof of philos, Calvin Col, 97- . **HONORS AND AWARDS** Vis grad fel, Univ Notre Dame Center for Philos of Relig, 96-97; Paul Holmer scholar of philos theol, Yale Univ, 89-91. **MEMBERSHIPS** APA; Soc of Christian Philo. **RESEARCH** Metaphysics; philosophy of mind; philosophy of religion. **SELECTED PUBLICATIONS** Auth, Persons, Bodies and the Constitution Relation, Southern J of Philos; auth, Persons and Bodies, Faith and Philos; auth, Is Theistic Experience Phenomenologically Possible? Relig Stud; auth, Experiencing God, Sophia; auth, Pluralism, Secularism and Tolerance, Rhetoric and Public Affairs. **CONTACT ADDRESS** Dept of Philosophy, Calvin Col, 3201 Burton St SE, Grand Rapids, MI 49546-4301. **EMAIL** kcorcora@calvin.edu

CORDELL, LADORIS HAZZARD

PERSONAL Born 11/19/1949, Bryn Mawr, PA, d, 2 children **DISCIPLINE** LAW **EDUCATION** Antioch Coll, BA 1971; Stanford Law School, JD 1974. **CAREER** NAACP Legal Defense & Educ Fund, staff attorney 74-75; attorney private practice 75-82; Stanford Law School, asst dean 78-82; State Court of Appeal Sixth Dist, justice pro tem 86-87; Municipal Ct Santa Clara Co, judge 82-88; Superior Ct Santa Clara Co, judge 88-. **HONORS AND AWARDS** Black History Awd Tulip Jones Womens Club 1977; nominated for Black Enterprise Magazine Annual Achievement Awd in under 30 category 1977, 1978; Comm Involvement Awd East Palo Alto Chamber of Comm 1982, 1983; Public Serv Awd Delta Sigma Theta 1982; Public Serv Awds Natl Council of Negro Women 1982; Outstanding Mid-Peninsula Black Woman Awd Mid-Peninsula YWCA 1983; Political Achievement Awd CA Black Women's Coalition & the Black Concerns Assn 1982; Featured in Ebony Magazine 1980, 1984; Implemented a minority recruitment program at Stanford Law School as asst dean; First Black Woman Judge in Northern CA; elected presiding judge of the Municipal Court 1985-86 term; Achievement Awd, Western Center on Domestic Violence 1986; Santa Clara County Woman of Achievement Awd 1985; Recipient of first Juliette Gordon Lowe Awd for Community Serv 1987; first black woman on Superior Court in Northern California 1988-; Distinguished Citizen Awd, Exchange Club 1989; Don Peters Outstanding Volunteer Awd, United Way of Santa Clara County, 1991; Baha'i Community Service Awd, 1992; Special Recognition Awd, Human Relations Commission of Santa Clara County, 1994; Youth Service Awd, Legal Advocates for Children & Youth, 1996; Unsung Heroes Awd, Minority Access Committee, Santa Clara County Bar Assoc, 1996; Social Justice award, San Fran Women's Center, 1996; Legal Impact Awd, Asian Law Alliance, 1996, Advocate for Justice Awd, Legal Aid Society of Santa Clara County, 1996. **MEMBERSHIPS** Mem Natl Bar Assn; mem American Bar Assn; mem NAACP; mem CA Judges Assn; mem CA Women Lawyers; chairperson bd of dirs Manhattan Playhouse East Palo Alto 1980; bd of dirs & steering comm Natl Conf on Women and the Law 1980, 1984-85; policy bd Center for Rsch on Women Stanford Univ 1980-82; chairperson bd of dirs East Palo Alto Comm Law Project 1984-87; bd of trustees, United Way of Santa Clara County 1987-98; bd of dir, Police Activities League (PAL), San Jose Chapter 1987-89, Natl Conf of Christians & Jews Inc, Santa Clara County 1988-; bd of trustees, Mills College, Oakland, CA, 1996-; bd of dir, Lucik Packard Fndtn for Children, Stanford, CA, 1997-99; mem Silicon Valley Forum Council, Commonwealth Club of CA 1997-; bd of dir, Asian Law Alliance, San Jose, CA, 1997-2000, mem Advisory bd, Healthy Alternatives for African American Babies, San Jose, CA, 1994-; mem American Law Institute, 1996-. **SELECTED PUBLICATIONS** Auth, "Before Brown v Bd of Educ--Was It All Worth It?" Howard Law Journal Vol 23 No 1 1980; co-auth, "The Appearance of Justice: Judges' Verbal and Nonverbal Behavior in Criminal Jury Trials" Stanford Law Review Vol 38, No 1, 1985; "Black Immigration, Disavowing the Stereotype of the Shiftless Negro" Judges' Journal Spring 1986; Co-author, "Musings of a Trial Court Judge," Indiana Law Journal, vol 68, No 4, 1993. **CONTACT ADDRESS** Superior Court, 191 N First St, San Jose, CA 95113.

CORDERO, ALBERTO

PERSONAL Born 01/29/1948, Lima, Peru, s **DISCIPLINE** PHILOSOPHY **EDUCATION** Universidad Nacional de Ingenieria, BSc; Univ Oxford, MSc; Univ Cambridge, MPhil; Univ Md, PhD. **CAREER** Lecturer to Assoc. Prof, Universidad Peruana Cayetano, 71-87; Prof, Universidad de Lima, 81-83; Visiting Assoc Prof, Univ Md, 83-87; Prof, CUNY, 87-. **HONORS AND AWARDS** FIPSE Awd, Queens Col, 96; Res Foundation Awd, CUNY, 95-97; FIPSE Awd, Queens Col, 95; Guggenheim Fel, 93-94; Nat Sci Foundation Awd, CUNY, 93-95. **MEMBERSHIPS** Acad Intl do Philos Sci; Inst de Hautes Sci Theor; **RESEARCH** Philosophy of Science; Philosophy of Physics; Philosophical History of Science. **SELECTED PUBLICATIONS** Co-ed, Philosophy and the Origin and Evolution of the Universe, Synthese Library, 91; auth, "Intelligibility in Quantum Physics," in Intelligibility in Science, (Amsterdam, 92), 175-215; auth, "Science, Objectivity and Moral Values," in Science & Education, (Boston & Dordrecht, 92), 49-70; auth, "Practical Reasoning in the Foundations of Quantum Theory," Synthese Library, (94): 439-452; auth, "On Science and Hypothesis," in Selected Papers from the Henri Poincare Sesquicentennial Conference, (France, 96), 105-126; auth, "Can a Body Act Where it is Not?: The Debate Then and Now," in Actuality of Greek Philosophy, (Univ Crete Press, 97), 233-246; auth, "Two Bad Arguments Against Naturalism," in Current Issues in the Philosophy of Biology, (Spain, 98(, 265-290; auth, "Educacion Superior y Desarrollo: Reflecciones en Torno al Nuevo Siglo," Peru Siglo 21: Propuestas para una Vision Compartida, Lima, 96; auth, "Are GRW Tails as Bad as They Say?," Philosophy of Science , (99): S59-S71. **CONTACT ADDRESS** Dept Philos, Queens Col, CUNY, 6530 Kissena Blvd, Flushing, NY 11367-1575.

CORDERO, RONALD ANTHONY

PERSONAL Born 06/22/1940, Manila, Philippines, m, 1961, 1 child **DISCIPLINE** PHILOSOPHY **EDUCATION** Univ Pa, BA, 62; Univ Ill, MA, 64, PhD(philos), 69. **CAREER** From instr to prof, 67-, prof philos, Univ Wis-Oshkosh, 77-. **RESEARCH** Ethics and Social Philosophy. **SELECTED PUBLICATIONS** Auth, Law, Morality and La Reconquista, Pub Affairs Quart, 10/90; Classics, Culture, and Curricula, Core and Canon: The Great Debat, ed L Robert Stevens, Univ North Tex Press, 93; Unwitting Discrimination, J Social Philosophy, Spring, 96; Aristotle and Fair Admissions, Pub Affairs Quart, January, 97; The demise of morality, J Value Inquiry, fall 74; Having it both ways with ought, Southern J Philos, winter 75; Ethical theory and the teaching of values, Educ Forum 1/76; Ought, Midwestern J Philos, spring 77. **CONTACT ADDRESS** Dept of Philosophy, Univ of Wisconsin, Oshkosh, 800 Algoma Blvd, Oshkosh, WI 54901-8601. **EMAIL** cordero@uwosh

CORDERY, SIMON

PERSONAL Born 07/08/1960, London, England, m, 1992, 1 child **DISCIPLINE** LEGAL AND SOCIAL HISTORY **EDUCATION** Northern Ill Univ, Ba, 82; Univ of York, MA, 84; Univ of Tex at Austin, PhD, 95. **CAREER** Res asst, Am Hist Asn, 85-88; instr, Louisburg Col, 92-94; instr, Monmouth Col, 94-; instr, Knox Col, 00. **HONORS AND AWARDS** NEH summer stipend, 98. **MEMBERSHIPS** AHA; NACBS; RLHS; LHS. **RESEARCH** Modern British labor and social history; the history of mutualism. **SELECTED PUBLICATIONS** Auth,

Joshua Hobson 1810-1876, Dictionary of Labour Bio, Macmillan, 87; Joshua Hobson and the Business of Radicalism, Bio: An Interdisciplinary Quart, 88; Friendly Societies and the Discourse of Respectability in Britain 1825-1875, J of British Studies, 95; Friendly Societies and the British Labour Movement Before 1914, J of the Asn of Historians in NC, 95; Mutual Benefit Societies in the United States: A Quest for Protection and Identity, Social Security Mutualism: The Comparative Hist of Mutual Benefit Societies, Peter Lang, 96. **CONTACT ADDRESS** Hist Dept, Monmouth Col, 700 E Broadway, Monmouth, IL 61462. **EMAIL** simon@monm.edu

CORDUAN, WINFRIED
PERSONAL Born 08/17/1949, Hamburg, Germany, m, 1971, 2 children **DISCIPLINE** THEOLOGY, PHILOSOPHY **EDUCATION** Univ MD, BS, 70; Trinity Evangel Divinity Sch, MA, 73; Rice Univ, PhD, 77. **CAREER** Asst prof, 77-80, assoc prof 80-87, prof relig & philos, Taylor Univ, 87. **HONORS AND AWARDS** Distinguished Prof of Year, 85, 98 **MEMBERSHIPS** Evangel Theol Soc; Evangel Philos Soc; Am Philos Asn; Soc Christian Philos **RESEARCH** Philosophical theology, world relig(s), logic. **SELECTED PUBLICATIONS** Auth, Handmaid to Theology: An Essay in Philosophical Prolegomena, Baker, 81; co-auth, Philosophy of Religion, 2nd ed, Baker, 88; auth, Mysticism: An Evangelical Option?, Zondervan, 91; auth, Reasonable Faith, Broadman & Holman, 93; ed, I & II Chronicles Shepherd's Notes, Broadman & Holman, 98; auth, Neighboring Faiths, InterVarsity, 98. **CONTACT ADDRESS** Taylor Univ, Upland, 236 W Reade Ave, Upland, IN 46989-1001. **EMAIL** wncorduan@tayloru.edu

CORLETT, J. ANGELO
PERSONAL Born 08/27/1958, Pomona, CA **DISCIPLINE** PHILOSOPHY **EDUCATION** Azusa Pacific Univ, BA, 79; Univ Louisville, MA, 85; Univ Calif, Santa Barbara, MA, 88; Univ Arizona, MA, 90, PhD, 92. **CAREER** Assoc prof philos, San Diego State Univ. **MEMBERSHIPS** APA; Am Soc for Polit and Legal Philos; AAUP; Calif Fac Asn; Calif Tchrs Asn; Natl Educ Asn; Soc for Ethics. **RESEARCH** Ethics; legal, moral, social and political philosophy; theory of knowledge. **SELECTED PUBLICATIONS** Auth, Analyzing Social Knowledge, Lanham: Rowman & Littlefield, Publishers, 96; auth, "The Morality and Constitutionality of Secession," Journal of Social Philosophy, XXIX (98): 120-28; auth, "Latino Identity," Public Affairs Quarterly, 13 (99): 273-95; auth, Responsibility and Punishment, Dordrecht: Kluwer Academic Publishers, 00; auth, "Analyzing the Moral Duty to Die," Biomedical Ethics Review, Humana Pr, 00; auth, "Surviving Evil: Jewish, African, and Native-Americans," Journal of Social Philosophy, XXXI, 01; auth, "Secession and Native Americans," Peace Review 12, 01; auth, "Latino Identity and Affirmative Action," in Jorge J.L. Gracia and Pablo DeGrieff, Hispanics/Latinos in the United States: Ethnicity, Race, and Rights, Routledge, 00; auth, "Reparations to Native Americans?" in Alexander Jokic, ed, War Crimes and Collective Wrongdoing, Blackwell, 00. **CONTACT ADDRESS** Dept of Philosophy, San Diego State Univ, San Diego, CA 92182. **EMAIL** corlett@rohan.sdsu.edu

CORLISS, RICHARD LEE
PERSONAL Born 10/17/1931, Chicago, IL, m, 1953, 2 children **DISCIPLINE** PHILOSOPHY **EDUCATION** Taylor Univ, BA, 54; Northern Baptist Theol Sem, BD, 57; Univ Ill, Urbana, MA, 59, PhD(philos), 68. **CAREER** From asst prof to assoc prof, 66-75, Prof Philos, St Cloud State Univ, 75- **MEMBERSHIPS** Am Philos Asn. **RESEARCH** Philosophy of language; philosophy of religion and ethics. **SELECTED PUBLICATIONS** Auth, Schleiermacher Hermeneutic and its Critics, Rel Stud, Vol 0029, 93. **CONTACT ADDRESS** 1729 13th Ave S St, Cloud, MN 56301.

CORMIER, MICHEAL J.
DISCIPLINE LAW **EDUCATION** Univ Waterloo, BA, 76; Windsor Univ, LLB, 81; Osgoode Hall Law Sch, 94. **CAREER** Prof, Community Legal Services and the Faculty's Clinical Legal Education Programs **RESEARCH** Civil procedure; contracts; advocacy; practice skills. **SELECTED PUBLICATIONS** Auth, pubs on legal process and the manner in which law affects the poor. **CONTACT ADDRESS** Fac of Law, Univ of Western Ontario, London, ON, Canada N6A 3K7. **EMAIL** mcormier@julian.uwo.ca

CORNWALL, ROBERT D.
PERSONAL Born 03/03/1958, Los Angeles, CA, m, 1983, 1 child **DISCIPLINE** HISTORICAL THEOLOGY **EDUCATION** Northwest Christian Col, BS, 80; Fuller Theol Sem, M Div, 85, PhD, 91. **CAREER** Dir of the Lib, 92-94, William Carey Int Univ; vis asst prof of Church Hist, 94-95, Fuller Theol Sem; assoc prof Theol, 95-97, Manhattan Christian Col; pastor, First Christian Church, Santa Barbara, CA, 98-. **HONORS AND AWARDS** Winner, Land O' Lakes Essay Competition, Shaw Hist Library, 91. **MEMBERSHIPS** North Am Conf of Brit Stud; Am Acad of Relig; Am Soc of Church Hist. **RESEARCH** Anglicanism 17th & 18th century; church-state issues; Nonjurors; Jacobites; Sacramental Theol. **SELECTED PUBLICATIONS** Auth, Visible and Apostolic: The Constitution of the Church in High Church Anglican and Non-Juror Thought 1688-1745, Univ DE Press, 93; auth, The Later Non-Jurors and the Theological Basis of the Usages Controversy, Anglican Theol Rev, 75, 93; auth, The Church and Salvation: An Early Eighteenth-Century High Church Anglican Perspective, Anglican and Episcopal History, 62, 93; auth, Advocacy of the Independence of the Church from the State in Eighteenth Century England: A Comparison of a Nonjuror and a Nonconformist View, Enlightenment and Dissent, 12, 93; auth, The Crisis in Disciples of Christ Ecclesiology: The Search for Identity, Encounter 55, 94; auth, Unity, Restoration, and Ecclesiology: Why the Stone-Campbell Movement Divided, J of Relig Stud, 19, 95; auth, The Ministry of Reconciliation: Toward a Balanced Understanding of the Global Mission of the Christian Church (Disciples of Christ), Lexington Theol Sem Quart, 30, 95; auth, Education for Ministry in the Augustan Age: A Comparison of the Views of Gilbert Burnet and George Bull and Their Implications for the Modern Church, Anglican Theol Rev, 78, 96; auth, The Scandal of the Cross: Self-Sacrifice, Obedience, and Modern Culture, Encounter 58, 97; ed, Gilbert Burnet, Discourse of the Pastoral Care, Edwin Mellon Press, 97; auth, The Agricultural Revolution: An Interpretive Essay, in Events that Changed the World in the Eighteenth Century, Greenwood Press, 98. **CONTACT ADDRESS** First Christian Church, 1905 Chapala St, Santa Barbara, CA 93101. **EMAIL** bobcornwall@juno.com

CORR, CHARLES A.
PERSONAL Born 10/11/1937, Montreal, QC, Canada, m, 1962, 3 children **DISCIPLINE** PHILOSOPHY **EDUCATION** John Carroll Univ, BS, 59; St Louis Univ, AM, 62, PhD(philos), 66. **CAREER** From instr to assoc prof, 65-78, PROF PHILOS, SOUTHERN IL UNIV, EDWARDSVILLE, 78-. **HONORS AND AWARDS** Charles A. Corr Awd for Lifetime Achievement (literature), from Children's Hospice Int; for Death Education, from Asn for Death Education and Counseling. **MEMBERSHIPS** Am Philos Asn; AAUP; Asn for Death Ed and Counseling; Int Work Group on Death, Dying, and Bereavement. **RESEARCH** Classical Modern Philosophy, Especially 17th and 18th centuries; Death and Dying. **SELECTED PUBLICATIONS** Coauth, Handbook of Childhood Death and Bereavement, Springer, NYC, 96; Handbook of Adolescent Death and Bereavement, Springer, NYC, 96; Death and Dying, Life and Living, 2nd ed, Brooks/Cole, Pacific Grove, CA, 97. **CONTACT ADDRESS** Dept of Philos Studies, So Illinois Univ, Edwardsville, Box 1433, Edwardsville, IL 62026-1433. **EMAIL** ccorr@siue.edu

CORRADO, MICHAEL L.
PERSONAL Born 02/12/1940, Altoona, PA, m, 1966, 2 children **DISCIPLINE** LAW **EDUCATION** Penn State, BA, 65; BS, 66; Brown Univ, AM, 68; PhD, 70; Univ Chicago, JD, 84. **CAREER** Asst to Full Prof, Ohio Univ, 70-81; Assoc to Full Prof, Univ NC, 88-. **HONORS AND AWARDS** NEH Postdoctoral Fel, Mich, 78-79. **MEMBERSHIPS** Am Bar Asn, Am Philos Asn, Am Soc for Polit and Legal Philos. **RESEARCH** Philosophy of Law, Action Theory, Criminal Responsibility, Punishment. **SELECTED PUBLICATIONS** Auth, Analytic Tradition in Philosophy, 75; auth, Justification and Excuse in the Criminal law, 95; auth, Addiction and Responsibility, 99; auth, economics, Equality and Responsibility, 99. **CONTACT ADDRESS** School of Law, Univ of No Carolina, Chapel Hill, Chapel Hill, NC 27599. **EMAIL** corrado@unc.edu

CORRIGAN, JOHN
DISCIPLINE RELIGION; AMERICAN STUDIES **EDUCATION** Univ of Chicago, PhD; 82 **CAREER** Asst prof, rel stud, Univ Va; current, PROF, AM STUD, ARIZ STATE UNIV **MEMBERSHIPS** Am Antiquarian Soc **RESEARCH** 18th century religion **SELECTED PUBLICATIONS** Auth, The Hidden Balance: Religion and the Social Theories of Charles Chauncy and Jonathan Mayhew, 87; auth, The Prism of Piety: Catholic Congregational Clergy at the Beginning of the Enlightenment, 91; auth, "Habits from the Heart: The American Enlightenment and Religious Ideas about Emotion and Habit," Jour of Rel 73, 93; Jews, Christians, Muslims, 97; coauth, Religion in America, 98. **CONTACT ADDRESS** 15236 N 6th Cir, Phoenix, AZ 85023. **EMAIL** john.corrigan@asu.edu

CORRIGAN, KEVIN
PERSONAL Born 08/04/1948, United Kingdom, m, 1976, 4 children **DISCIPLINE** PHILOSOPHY; CLASSICS **EDUCATION** Lancaster, BA, 75; MA, 77, PhD, 80, Dalhousie **CAREER** Asst Prof, Col of Notre Dame, Saskatchewan, 82-86; Asst Prof, Assoc Prof, Full Prof, 86-, Dean, 91-, St. Thomas More Col, Univ of Saskatchewan. **RESEARCH** Philosophy; Classics; Ancient/Medieval Plato; Aristotle; Plotinus **SELECTED PUBLICATIONS** Auth, Plotinus Theory of Matter-Evil and the Question of Substance:Plato, Aristotle, and Alexander of Aphrodisias, 96. **CONTACT ADDRESS** 1437 College Dr., Saskatoon, SK, Canada S7N 0W6. **EMAIL** k.corrigan@usask.ca

CORT, JOHN E.
DISCIPLINE RELIGION **EDUCATION** Univ Wi, BA, 74; MA, 82; Harvard Univ, AM, 84; PhD, 89. **CAREER** Lectr, 89-92, Harvard Univ; vis prof, 94-95, Columbia Univ; asst prof to assoc prof, 92-, Denison Univ. **HONORS AND AWARDS** Asian Cultural Counc Grant, 95-96; Getty Sr Grant, 96-98; Am Institute of Indian Stud Sr Short-Term Grant, 99-00. **MEMBERSHIPS** Am Coun of S Asian Art; Asn of Asian Stud; Am Acad of Relig; Conf on Relig in S India. **RESEARCH** Jainism; relig; culture; soc in S Asia. **SELECTED PUBLICATIONS** Auth, Defining Jainism: Reform in the Jain Tradition, Univ Toronto, 95; auth, Absences and Presences: Ganesh in the Shvetambar Jain Tradition, Marg Publ, 95; art, Religion, and Material Culture: Some Reflections on Method, J Amer Acad of Relig, 96; art, Recent Fieldwork Studies of the Contemporary Jains, Relig Stud Rev, 97; ed, Open Boundaries, Alabny: SUNY, 98; auth, Jains in the World, NY: OUP, 00. **CONTACT ADDRESS** Dept of Relig, Denison Univ, Granville, OH 43023. **EMAIL** cort@denison.edu

CORVINO, JOHN F.
DISCIPLINE PHILOSOPHY **EDUCATION** St John's Univ, BA, 90; Univ Tex, Austin, PhD, 98. **CAREER** Asst inst, Univ Tex, Austin, 95-97; LECTR, WAYNE STATE UNIV, 98-. **CONTACT ADDRESS** Dept Philosophy, Wayne State Univ, 51 W Warren Ave, Rm 3001, Detroit, MI 48201. **EMAIL** j.corvino@wayne.edu

COSCULLUELA, VICTOR
PERSONAL Born 02/20/1966, San Juan, Puerto Rico, s **DISCIPLINE** PHILOSOPHY **EDUCATION** Univ of Miami, PhD, 93. **CAREER** Teaching Philosophy courses in Florida, Connecticut and NY since 89. **HONORS AND AWARDS** Full tuition Acad Scholarship, Univ of Miami. **MEMBERSHIPS** APA. **RESEARCH** Philosophy of Religion, Ethics. **SELECTED PUBLICATIONS** Auth, The Ethics of Suicide, 95. **CONTACT ADDRESS** 400 Amalfi Ave, Coral Gables, FL 33146. **EMAIL** Dustyouare@hotmail.com

COSTA, MICHAEL J.
PERSONAL Born 07/21/1945, Cincinnati, OH, m, 1968, 1 child **DISCIPLINE** PHILOSOPHY **EDUCATION** Princeton Univ, AB, 67; Univ Kent, MA, 77; Ohio State Univ, PhD, 81. **CAREER** Oberlin Coll, vis asst prof, 81-83; asst prof, 83-89; Assoc Prof, Univ SC, 89-. **HONORS AND AWARDS** Nat Merit Scholar, 63067; Haggin Fel Univ Kent, 76-77; Univ Fel Ohio State Univ, 77-78; Willaim H Fink Awd, Ohio State Univ, 80; NEH Summer Stipend, Ind Univ, 84; Philos Dept and Coll of Humanities Stipend Computers Programs for Tchg Logic, 87. **MEMBERSHIPS** Am Philos Asn; southern Soc for Philos and Psychol; Hume Soc; SC Soc for Philos. **RESEARCH** Philosophy of David Hume. **SELECTED PUBLICATIONS** Auth, Hume and Justified belief, David Hume: Critical Assessments, 95; Why Be Just?: Hume's Response in the Inquiry, David Hume: Critical Assessments, 95; Hume and Belief in the Existence of an External World, David Hume: Critical Assessments, 95; rev, A New Justification of the Moral Rules, 95; auth, "Hume on the Very Idea of a Relation," 98; rev., "Hume's Religious Naturalism," 99 **CONTACT ADDRESS** Dept of Philosophy, Univ of So Carolina, Columbia, Columbia, SC 29208. **EMAIL** mjcosta@sc.edu

COSTANZA, STEPHEN E.
PERSONAL Born 12/03/1969, Chalmette, LA, s **DISCIPLINE** CRIMINAL JUSTICE, SOCIOLOGY **EDUCATION** Louisiana State Univ, PhD, 98. **CAREER** Asst prof, Southeastern La Univ, 98-. **HONORS AND AWARDS** ICPSR Stipend, 96; LA Dept Forest Grant, 99; SLU Grant, 99. **MEMBERSHIPS** MSSA; SSI; ACJA. **RESEARCH** Quantitive sociology; crime history. **SELECTED PUBLICATIONS** Auth, "History of Organized Crime In America," Encycl Crime Dev Behavior (00). **CONTACT ADDRESS** Dept Sociology, Southeastern Louisiana Univ, 500 Western Ave, Hammond, LA 70402.

COSTEN, MELVA WILSON
PERSONAL Born 05/29/1933, Due West, SC, m, 1953 **DISCIPLINE** THEOLOGY **EDUCATION** Harbison Jr Coll, Irmo SC, 1947-50; Johnson C Smith Univ, Charlotte NC, AB Educ 1950-52; Univ of North Carolina, Chapel Hill NC MAT Music 1961-64; Georgia State Univ, Atlanta GA, PhD Curriculm and Instruction/Music 1973-78. **CAREER** Mecklenburg County School, Charlotte NC, elementary teacher, 52-55; Edgecombe County, Rocky Mount Nashville NC, elementay teacher, 56-57; Nash County, Nashville NC, elementary and music teacher 1959-65; Atlanta Public Schools Atlanta GA, intinerant music teacher 1965-73; Interdenominational Theological, Atlanta GA, Helmar Emil Nielsen Professor of Worship and Music, 73-. **HONORS AND AWARDS** Conducted 500-voice elementary chorus, Music Educators Natl Conference 1970; Teacher of the Year, Slater School, Atlanta Ga, 1973; Teacher of the Year, Interdenominational Theological Center, 1975; Golden Dove Awd, Kappa Omega Chapter, Alpha Kappa Alpha Sorority 1981; conducted 800-voice adult choir, Reuniting Assembly of Presbyterian Church 1983; Two Doctor of Humane Letters, Erskine Coll, Due West SC, 1987 and Wilson College, Chambersburg PA; chairperson, Presbyterian Hymnal Committee, 1985-90. **MEMBERSHIPS** Regional director, Natl Assn of Negro Musicians 1973-75; co-chair, choral div, District V Georgia Music Educators Assoc 1981-82; mem of bd Presbyterian Assn of Musicians 1982-86; chairperson, Presbyterian Church Hymnal Committee 1984-1990; mem of bd Liturgical Conference

1985-91; mem of bd Mid-Atlanta Unit, Cancer Society of America, 1985-87; artistic dir, Atlanta Olympics, 1996-99; Atlanta University Ctr Choruses, 1996. **SELECTED PUBLICATIONS** Published book African-American Christian Worship, Nashville, Abingdon press, 1993. **CONTACT ADDRESS** Music/Worship Office, Interdenominational Theol Ctr, 700 Martin Luther King Jr Dr, SW, Atlanta, GA 30311.

COSTIGAN, RICHARD F.
PERSONAL Born 03/22/1931, Ottawa, KS **DISCIPLINE** THEOLOGY **EDUCATION** St Louis Univ, AB, 57; Yale Univ, MA, 69; Univ Ottawa (Canada), PhD, 72. **CAREER** Asst prof of theology, 75; assoc prof, 81, Loyola Univ. **MEMBERSHIPS** Am Acad of Relig; Cath Theol Soc of Am. **RESEARCH** Hist of ecclesiology; papacy. **SELECTED PUBLICATIONS** Auth, Rohrbacher and the Ecclesiology of Ultramontanism, Gregorian Univ, 80; auth, Bossuet and the Consensus of the Church, Theological Studies, 95; auth, Behind the Walls: A Theologian Examines our Relationship with the Vatican, Loyola Magazine, 96; auth, Papal Supremacy: From Theory to Practice, The Vital Nexus, 96. **CONTACT ADDRESS** Loyola Univ, Chicago, 6525 N Sheridan Rd, Chicago, IL 60626. **EMAIL** rcostig@luc.edu

COSWAY, RICHARD
PERSONAL Born 10/20/1917, Neward, OH **DISCIPLINE** LAW **EDUCATION** Denison Univ, AB, 39; Univ Cincinnati, JD, 42. **CAREER** Prof law, Univ Cincinnati; Prof Law, Univ Wash, 58-, Comnr, Uniform State Laws for Wash, 65-; vis prof law, Southern Methodist Univ, 66-67 & Hastings Col Law, 81-82. **SELECTED PUBLICATIONS** Coauth, Washington Practice, West Publ, Vols VII & VIII, 67. **CONTACT ADDRESS** Col of Law, Univ of Washington, Seattle, WA 98105.

COTMAN, JOHN W.
PERSONAL Born 03/02/1954, Springfield, MA, d, 1 child **DISCIPLINE** POLITICAL SCIENCE **EDUCATION** Univ Colo, BA, 77; Boston Univ, MA, 87, PhD, 92. **CAREER** Inst, Howard Univ, 90-91; Vis Schol, Am Univ, 94-95; Asst Prof, Polit Sci, 91-96, Assoc Prof, 96-, Howard Univ. **HONORS AND AWARDS** Ford Found Postdoctoral Fellow, 94-95, Doctoral Fellow, 87-88; Ctr for Adv Stud in Behavioral Sci, Fellow nomination, 94; Howard Univ, travel Grant, 94, Fac Res Grants, 92/93, 93/94, 95/96, 96/97, 97/98; Boston Univ Grad Dissertation Fellow, 90; Fulbright Grant for PhD Res, 88-89; Dr. Martin Luther King, Jr Fellow, 84-87; Phi Beta Kappa. **MEMBERSHIPS** AM Polit Sci Asn; Latin Am Stud Asn. **RESEARCH** Political science. **SELECTED PUBLICATIONS** Auth, The Gorrion Tree: Cuba & the Grenada Revolution, Peter Lang Pub, 93; auth, Cuba and Caribbean Integration, Govt & Polit, 1:3, 8-10, 93; auth, Cuba and the Caribbean: The Last Decade, Cuba: New Ties to a New World, Rienner Pubs, 93; auth, Hand Carry Important Documents, Mistakes that Social Scientists Make, St Martin's Press, 100, 96; auth, A Tale of Two Exhibits: Hiroshima, the Enola Gay, and Official History, Govt & Polit, 2:1, 14-21, 98; auth, Grenada: The New JEWEL Revolution, Encycl of Polit Revolutions, Congressional Quart Books, 98; auth, Caribbean Convergence: Cuba and CARICOM Relations Through 1995, Global Development Studies 1:3-4 Winter 98/Spring 99: 197-222; auth, Eloise Linger and John Cotman, eds., Special Issue: Cuban Transitions at the Millenium, Global Development Studies 1:3-4 Winter 98/Spring 99. **CONTACT ADDRESS** Dept of Polit Sci, Howard Univ, 2419 Sixth St. NW Room 144, PO Box 849, Washington, DC 20001-2345. **EMAIL** jcotman@fac.howard.edu

COTTER, JAMES FINN
PERSONAL Born 07/05/1929, Boston, MA, m, 1960, 3 children **DISCIPLINE** ENGLISH LITERATURE, PHILOSOPHY **EDUCATION** Boston Col, AB, 54, MA, 55; Fordham Univ, MA, 58, PhD(English), 63. **CAREER** From instr to asst prof English, Fordham Univ, 60-63; assoc prof, 63-68, prof English, Mt St Mary Col, NY, 68-; Fulbright-Hays lectr, Univ Oran, 70-71. **MEMBERSHIPS** MLA; Conf Christianity & Lit; Dante Soc. **RESEARCH** Dante; Renaissance poetry; Sir Philip Sidney; Gerard Manley Hopkins. **SELECTED PUBLICATIONS** Auth, Visions of Christ in Dante's Divine Comedy, Nemla Studies, 83-84; Hopkins: The Wreck of the Deutschland, 28, The Explicator, 85; Apocalyptic Imagery in Hopkins That Nature is a Heraclitean Fire and of the Comfort of the Resurrections, Victorian Poetry, 86; Look at it loom there! The Image of the Wave in Hopkins' The Wreck of the Deutschland, The Hopkins Quart, 87; Dante and Christ: The Pilgrim as Beatus Vir, The Italian Quart, 88; The Book Within the Book in Medieval Illumination, Florilegium 12, 93; The Song of Songs in The Wreck of the Deutschland in GM Hopkins and Critical Discourse, AMS Press, 94; Augustine's Confessions and The Wreck of the Deutschland in Saving Beauty: Further Studies in Hopkins, Garland, 95; The Divine Comedy and the First Psalm in Dante: Summa Medievalis, Stony Brook: Forum Italicum, 95; auth, Hopkins and Job, Victorian Poetry, 95; auth, Hopkins and Augustine, Victorian Poetry, 01. **CONTACT ADDRESS** 330 Powell Ave, Newburgh, NY 12550-3412. **EMAIL** cotter@msmc.edu

COTTER, THOMAS F.
DISCIPLINE LAW **EDUCATION** Univ Wis-Madison, BS, MS, JD. **CAREER** Asst prof, Univ Fla, 94-; former assoc, Jenner Block, Chicago, and Cravath, Swaine Moore, NY; clerk, Judge Lawrence W. Pierce, US Ct Appeals, 2nd Circuit; sr articles ed, Wis Law Rev. **HONORS AND AWARDS** Ladas mem awd, 96. **MEMBERSHIPS** Amer Law and Econ Asn; Soc for the Advancement of Socioeconomics; Ill Bar; Order of the Coif. **RESEARCH** Civil procedure, evidence, intellectual property, law and economics. **CONTACT ADDRESS** School of Law, Univ of Florida, PO Box 117625, Gainesville, FL 32611-7625. **EMAIL** cotter@law.ufl.edu

COTTON, ROGER D.
PERSONAL Born 07/11/1952, Harvey, IL, m, 1973, 2 children **DISCIPLINE** BIBLICAL STUDIES **EDUCATION** Central Bible Col, BA, 76; Assemblies of God Theol Sem, MDiv, 78; Concordia Sem, STM; PhD, 83. **CAREER** Asst Pastor/Minister of Christian Educ, Repub Assembly of God Repub, Mo, 76-78; Assoc Pastor, West Co Assembly of God, 83-87; Prof, Assemblies of God Theol Sem, 87-. **MEMBERSHIPS** Soc of Bibl Lit, Inst of Bibl Res, Evangel Theol Soc. **RESEARCH** Pentateuch, law collections of the Pentateuch, Leviticus, holiness, Old Testament theology. **SELECTED PUBLICATIONS** Auth, "Commentary on Leviticus," in The Complete Biblical Library: Old Testament Study Bible Vol 3 Lev-Num, ed. Thoral F. Gilbrant and Gregory Lint (World Lib Press, 95); auth, "Wonderful-Gods' Name," in Signs and Wonders in Ministry Today, ed. Benny Calen and Gary McJu (Springfield, MO: Gospel Publ House, 96). **CONTACT ADDRESS** Dept Bible and Theol, Assemblies of God Theol Sem, 1435 N Glenstone Ave, Springfield, MO 65802. **EMAIL** rcotton@agseminary.edu

COTTRELL, JACK WARREN
PERSONAL Born 04/30/1938, Scott County, KY, m, 1958, 3 children **DISCIPLINE** HISTORY OF DOCTRINE **EDUCATION** Cincinnati Bible Coll, AB, 59, ThB, 60; Univ Cincinnati, AB, Philos, 62; Westminster Theol Sem, MDiv, 65; Princeton Theol Sem, PhD, 71. **CAREER** Stud instr, Cincinnati Bible Coll, 59-62; Prof, Theol, Cincinnati Bible Sem, 67-. **MEMBERSHIPS** Evan Theol Sem **SELECTED PUBLICATIONS** Auth, Feminism and the Bible: An Introduction to Feminism for Christians, Coll Press, 92; auth, Gender Roles and the Bible: Creation, the Fall, and Redemption. A Critique of Feminist Biblical Interpretation, Coll Press, 94; Faith's Fundamentals: Seven Essentials of Christian Belief, Standard Publ, 95; TheCollege Press NIV Commentary: Romans, Volume 1, Coll Press, 96; auth, The College Press NIV Commentary: Romans, Volume 2, Coll Press, 98. **CONTACT ADDRESS** Cincinnati Bible Col and Sem, 2700 Glenway Ave, Cincinnati, OH 45204. **EMAIL** Jack.Cottrell@cincybible.edu

COTTROL, ROBERT JAMES
PERSONAL Born 01/18/1949, New York, NY, m, 1987 **DISCIPLINE** LAW **EDUCATION** Yale Univ, BA 71, PhD 78; Georgetown Univ Law Ctr, JD 84. **CAREER** CT Coll, instructor 74-77; Emory Univ, asst prof, 77-79; Georgetown Univ, lecturer, 79-84; Boston Coll Law School, asst prof of law, 84-87, assoc prof of law, 87-90; Rutgers School of Law, Camden, NJ, assoc prof, 90-. **MEMBERSHIPS** Consult GA Commn on the Humanities 78-79; mem Amer Historical Assoc 74-, Amer Soc for Legal History 82-, Amer Bar Assoc 85-; mem Law and Society Assoc 85-. **SELECTED PUBLICATIONS** Auth, The Afro Yankees, Providence's Black Community in the Antebellum Era, Greenwood Press 82. **CONTACT ADDRESS** Rutgers, The State Univ of New Jersey, Newark, Fifth and Penn Sts, Camden, NJ 08102.

COUNTRYMAN, L. WM
PERSONAL Born 10/21/1941, Oklahoma City, OK, 1 child **DISCIPLINE** CLASSICS, NEW TESTAMENT **EDUCATION** Univ of Chicago, BA, 62, MA, 74, PhD, 77; General Theol Sem, STB, 65 **CAREER** Lect, 74-76, Univ of Chicago; Asst Prof, 76-79, SW Mission St Univ; Asst Prof, 79-83 TX Christ Univ; Prof, 83-pres, Church Div Sch of the Pac **HONORS AND AWARDS** Phi Beta Kappa **MEMBERSHIPS** Soc of Bibl Lit; Assoc of Anglican Bibl Schols; Soc for Study of Christian Spirituality **RESEARCH** Spirituality; Sexual Orientation **SELECTED PUBLICATIONS** Auth, The Rich Christian in the Church of the Early Empire, Edwin Mellen Press, 80; Auth, The Mystical Way in the Fourth Gospel, Crossing Over into God, Fortress Press, 87; Living on the Border of the Holy: The Priesthood of Humanity and the Priesthoods of the Church, Morehouse Publ, 99; Forgiven and Forgiving, Morehouse Publ, 98 **CONTACT ADDRESS** Church Divinity Sch of the Pacific, 2451 Ridge, Berkeley, CA 94709. **EMAIL** bcountryman@cdsp.edu

COUNTS, M. REID
PERSONAL Born 09/12/1970, Columbia, SC **DISCIPLINE** SOCIOLOGY, CRIMINOLOGY **EDUCATION** Univ SC, BS, 92; MCJ, 94; PhD, 99. **CAREER** Lect, Univ Nebr, 97-99; Asst Prof, Univ Nebr, 99-00; Asst Prof, Univ SC, 00-. **MEMBERSHIPS** Acad of Criminal Justice Sci. **RESEARCH** School violence, ritualistic crime, juvenile justice. **SELECTED PUBLICATIONS** Coauth, The Evolution of School Disturbance in America, Praeger, 98. **CONTACT ADDRESS** Dept Sociol, Univ of Nebraska, Kearney, 905 W 25th St, Kearney, NE 68847. **EMAIL** countsm@uncwil.edu

COURTNEY, CHARLES
PERSONAL Born 11/02/1935, Elkhart, KS, m, 1958, 2 children **DISCIPLINE** THEOLOGY **EDUCATION** Monmouth Col, BA, 57; Harvard Univ, MDiv, 60; Northwestern Univ, MA, 62; PhD, 65. **CAREER** Prof, Drew Univ, 64-. **HONORS AND AWARDS** Danforth Grad Fel; Rockefeller Bros Theol Fel; Fulbright Scholar; Presbyterian Grad Fel. **MEMBERSHIPS** Am Philos Asn; Soc for Phenomenology and Existential Philos. **RESEARCH** Philosophy of Religion; Philosophy of Human Rights. **CONTACT ADDRESS** Dept Theol, Drew Univ, 35 Madison Ave, Madison, NJ 07940-1434. **EMAIL** ccourtne@drew.edu

COUTURE, PAMELA D.
DISCIPLINE RELIGION **EDUCATION** Ashland College, BA, 72, Garrett-Evangelical Theological Sem, Mdiv, 82, Univ Chicago, PhD, 90. **CAREER** Colgate Rochester Divinity Sch, assoc prof 98-; Assoc of Theological Sch, dir 97-98; Chandler Sch of Theol, asst prof 89-97, dir 91-93; Samaritan Inst, past coun 83-89; N IL Conf BD of Ordained Ministry, 84-92; United Meth Ch, ordained 81; Arlington Hts and Roselle IL, past staff, assoc past 78-83. **MEMBERSHIPS** IAPT; AAPC; SPT; OIMTS; AAR **SELECTED PUBLICATIONS** Auth, Blessed Are The Poor?, Women's Povert, Family Policy, and Practical Theology, Nashville: Abingdon Press, 91; ed, Essays in Honor of Charles V Gerkin, Nashville: Abingdon Press, 95; coauth, From Culture Wars to Consensus: Religion and the American Family Debate, Knoxville: Westminster/John Knox Press, 97; ed, Globalization and Difference:Practical Theology in a World context, Cardiff: Cardiff Academic Press, 99; auth, Seeing Children, Seeing God: A Practical Theology of Children and Poverty, Nashville: Abingdon Press, 00. **CONTACT ADDRESS** Dept of Theology, Colgate Rochester Divinity Sch/Bexley Hall/Crozer Theol Sem, 1100 S. Goodman St, Rochester, NY 14620-2589. **EMAIL** pcouture@crds.edu

COVELL, RALPH
PERSONAL Born 12/23/1922, Redondo Beach, CA, m, 1950, 3 children **DISCIPLINE** MISSIONS **EDUCATION** E Baptist Col, BA; E Baptist Theol Sem, BD, BT; Fuller Theol Sem, ThM; Denver Sem, Ddiv, PhD. **CAREER** Sr prof, Denver Sem. **HONORS AND AWARDS** Edition Missiology, 82-88; bd ch, chinese childen adoption intl; mem, cbfms (now cbint), chian, taiwan; transl consult, bible soc(s) taiwan. **MEMBERSHIPS** Am Society of Missiology, 82-88. **RESEARCH** The history of The Christian Faith in China **SELECTED PUBLICATIONS** Transl, New Testament Into the Language of the Sediq, a Malayo-Polynesian People Living in the Mountains of Taiwan; auth, Confucius, the Buddha, and Christ; Liberating Gospel in China; Mission Impossible: The Unreached Nosuon China's Frontier; auth, W.A.P. Martin Pioneers of Progress in China; auth, Pentecost of the Hills in Taiwan The Christian Faith Among the Original Inhabitants. **CONTACT ADDRESS** Denver Conservative Baptist Sem, PO Box 100000, Denver, CO 80250. **EMAIL** rcovell@aol.com

COVER, JAN
PERSONAL Born 06/26/1958, Modesto, CA, m, 1993, 1 child **DISCIPLINE** EARLY MODERN PHILOSOPHY, METAPHYSICS **EDUCATION** Univ of CA, BS, Syracuse Univ, BA, Syracuse Univ, MA, Syracuse Univ, PhD. **CAREER** Prof of Philosophy, Purdue Univ. **HONORS AND AWARDS** Univ Faculty Scholar, Purdue Univ, National Academy of Sciences Grant. **MEMBERSHIPS** Philosophy of Science Asn, Am Philosophical Asn, Leibniz Society of North Am, Indiana Philosophical Asn, Society of Christian Philosophers, G.-W.-Leibniz Gesellschaft e. V. **RESEARCH** History of Early Modern, Metaphysics, Philosophy of Science. **SELECTED PUBLICATIONS** Auth, Central Themes in Early Modern Philosophy, Hackett Publishing Company, 90; auth, Theories of Knowledge and Reality, McGraw-Hill Publishing Company, 90; 2nd ed. 94; auth, "Framing the Thisness Issue," with J.O'Leary-Hawthorne, Australasian Journal of Philosophy 75 (97): 102-08; auth, Philosophy of Science: The Central Issues, W.W. Norton & Company, 98; auth, "A World of Universals," with J.O'Leary-Hawthorne, Philosophical Studies 91 (98): 205-219; auth, "Miracles and Christian Theism," in M. Murray, ed. Reasons for the Hope Within Us, Eerdmans, (98): 345-74; auth, Substance and Individuation in Leibniz, Cambirdge Univ Press, 99; auth, "A significantly revised version of this paper appears as "Miracles and (Chirstian) Theism," in Eleonore Stump & Michael Murray, eds., Philosophy of Religiion: The Big Questions, Blackwell, (99): 334-352; auth, "Spinoza's Extended Substance: Cartesian and Leibnizian Reflections," in C. Huenemann and R. Genarro, eds., New Essays on the Rationalists, Oxford (99): 105-133; auth, "Leibniz's Modal Metaphysics," The Stanford Encyclopedia of Philosophy, 00. **CONTACT ADDRESS** Dept of Philos, Purdue Univ, West Lafayette, 1360 LAEB, West Lafayette, IN 47907-1360. **EMAIL** jacover@purdue.edu

COVERT, HENRY
PERSONAL Born 03/14/1942, Philadelphia, PA, m, 1989 **DISCIPLINE** ADMINISTRATION OF JUSTICE **EDUCA-**

TION United Wesleyan Col, BS, 84; Ind Univ, MA, 87; Pittsburgh Theol Sem, D.min, 92. **CAREER** Policeman; Park Ranger; Minister; State Prison Chaplain; Adj Prof, Pa State Univ; Vis Prof, Taylor Univ. **HONORS AND AWARDS** Hon Soc, Am Bibl Col Assoc; Hon Soc, United Wesleyan Col; Who's Who Among Students in Am Univ. **RESEARCH** Prison ministry, inmate stressors. **SELECTED PUBLICATIONS** Ministry to the Incarcerated, Loyola Univ Pr, 95. **CONTACT ADDRESS** Dept Admin of Justice, Pennsylvania State Univ, Univ Park, 918 Oswald Tower, University Park, PA 16802.

COVIN, DAVID LEROY
PERSONAL Born 10/03/1940, Chicago, IL, m, 1965, 2 children **DISCIPLINE** POLITICAL SCIENCE **EDUCATION** Univ Illinois, Urbana-Champaign, 62; Colorado Univ, MA, 66; Washington State Univ, PhD, 70. **CAREER** Asst prof, 70-75, assoc dean, general studies, 72-74, assoc prof, 75-79, prof govt and Pan African Studies, 79-, acting dir, 79-81, dir, 86-, Pan African Studies, prof govt and ethnic studies, Calif State Univ-Sacramento, 86-. **HONORS AND AWARDS** Cooper-Woodson Coll Medal 98; John C. Livingston Annual Distinguished Faculty Lecturer, 92; Meritorious Performance Awd, CSU Sacramento, 88. **MEMBERSHIPS** Natl Conf Black Polit Sci; Natl Coun Black Studies; Western Polit Sci Assn. **RESEARCH** Black politics in U.S.; social movements; Afro-Brazilian politics. **SELECTED PUBLICATIONS** Auth, Afrocentricity in the MNU," Journal of Black Studies, 90; auth, : The Future as Paradox," Impuruzu, 90; auth, " Ten Years of the MNU: 1978-1988," Journal of Black Studies, 90; auth, " Social Movement Theory in the Examination of Mobilization in a Black Community: the" 91; auth, " Black Conscious View in the White Media: The Case of Brazil," Western Journal of Black Studies, vol 15, n02, 92; auth, " Reflections on Dilemmas in Black Politics," Dilemmas of Black Politics, Harper Collins, 93; auth, " Political Conciousness as a Congregant of Black Conciousness in Brazil," Explanations in Ethics Studies, vol 18, no 1, 95; auth, " Narrative, Free Spaces, and Communities, of Memory in the Brazilian Black Conciousness Movement," Western Journal of Black Studies, vol 21, no 4, 97; auth, " Wither Goeth Black Nationalism: The Case of the MNU in Bahia," National Political Science Review, 98. **CONTACT ADDRESS** Pan African Studies, California State Univ, Sacramento, 6000 J St, Sacramento, CA 95819-6013. **EMAIL** covindl@csus.edu

COVINGTON, ROBERT N.
DISCIPLINE LAW **EDUCATION** Yale Univ, BA, 58; Vanderbilt Univ, JD, 61. **CAREER** Vanderbilt Law School, 61-. **MEMBERSHIPS** Order of the Coif; Am Bar Assoc; Int Soc for Labour Law and Soc Security. **RESEARCH** Labor and Employment Law. **SELECTED PUBLICATIONS** Coauth, Individual Employee Rights in a Nutshell, 95. **CONTACT ADDRESS** School of Law, Vanderbilt Univ, 131 - 21st Ave S, Nashville, TN 37215. **EMAIL** robert.covington@law.vanderbilt.edu

COWAN, RICHARD O.
PERSONAL Born 01/24/1934, Los Angeles, CA, m, 1958, 6 children **DISCIPLINE** CHURCH HISTORY **EDUCATION** Occidental Col, BA, 58; Stanford Univ, MA, 59, PhD, 61. **CAREER** Asst prof relig instr, 61-65, assoc prof hist relig, 65-71, prof of church hist, Brigham Young Univ, 71-; Danforth Fel, 58. **HONORS AND AWARDS** Phi Beta Kappa, 57. **MEMBERSHIPS** Mormom Hist Asn; Utah Hist Soc. **RESEARCH** Latter-day Saint history and theology. **SELECTED PUBLICATIONS** Coauth, Mormonism in the Twentieth Century 64, auth, The Doctrine and Covenants: Our Modern Scripture, 67, Temple Building Ancient and Modern, 71 & coauth, The Living Church, 74, Brigham Young Univ, Doctrine and Covenants: Our Modern Scripture, 84; Church in the Twentieth Century, 85; Temples to Dot the Earth, 89; Joseph Smith and the Doctrine and Covenants, 92; California Saints, 96; auth, Answers to Your Questions About the Doctrine and Covenants, 96; auth, The Latter-day Saint Century, 99; coauth, Encyclopedia of Latter-day Saint History, 00. **CONTACT ADDRESS** Brigham Young Univ, 270L Joseph Smith Bldg, Provo, UT 84602. **EMAIL** richard_cowan@byu.edu

COWAN, S. B.
PERSONAL Born 04/06/1962, Hattiesburg, MS, m, 1986 **DISCIPLINE** PHILOSOPHY **EDUCATION** Southern Miss, BA, 87; Southwestern Bapt Theol Sem, M. Div, 91; Univ Ark, MA, 93; PhD, 96. **CAREER** Adj prof, christ ethics and New Testament, Southern Bapt Theol Sem, 97; adj prof, philos, Univ Ark, 97-98; adj prof, philos of relig, Midwestern Bapt Theol Sem, 98-00; adj prof of philos, Ouachita Baptist Univ, 96-00; adj prof of phios, Birmingham Theol Sem, 01-; adj prof of philos, Southeastern Bible Col, 01-. **MEMBERSHIPS** Evang Theol Soc; Evang Philos Soc; Soc of Christ Philos. **RESEARCH** Philosophical theology; Free will and determinism; Reformed theology. **SELECTED PUBLICATIONS** Auth, Review of Richard Swinburne's The Christian God in Philosophia Christi, vol 19, no 2, Fall, 96; A Reductio ad Absurdum of Divine Temporality, Relig Studies, vol 32, no 4, Sep, 96; On the Epistemological Justification of Miracle Claims, Philos Christi, vol 18, no 1, Spr, 95; Common Misconceptions of Evangelicals Regarding Calvinism, Jour of the Evang Theol Soc, vol 33, no 2, Jun, 90; ed, Five View on Apologetics, Zondervan, 00. **CONTACT ADDRESS** 3563 Valley Cir, Birmingham, AL 35243. **EMAIL** sbcowan@juno.com

COWARD, HAROLD G.
PERSONAL Born 12/13/1936, Calgary, AB, Canada **DISCIPLINE** RELIGION, HISTORY **EDUCATION** Univ Alta, BA, 58, BD, 67, MA, 69; McMaster Univ, PhD, 73. **CAREER** Prof, Univ Calgary, 73-92, head relig stud, 76, 79-83, assoc dean hum, 77, dir, univ press, 81-83; dir, Calgary Inst Hum, 80-92; Dir, Centre for studies in Relig and Soc & prof Hist, Univ Victoria, 92-. **HONORS AND AWARDS** Fel, Royal Soc Can **MEMBERSHIPS** Pres, Can Soc Stud Relig, 84-86; pres, Shastri Indo-Can Inst, 86-88; pres, Can Corp Stud Relig, 87-90; pres, Can Fedn Hum, 90-91. **RESEARCH** Eastern religions; Hindu thought & religion; religious pluralism. **SELECTED PUBLICATIONS** Auth, Hindu Ethics: Purity, Euthanasia and Abortion, 88; auth, Derrida and Indian Philosophy, 90; auth, Philosophy of the Grammarians, 90; ed, Mantra: Hearing the Divine in India, 91; auth, Aging and Dying: Legal, Scientific and Religious Challenges, 93; auth, Anger in Our City: Youth Seeking Meaning, 94; auth, Population, Consumption and the Environment, 95; auth, Life After Death in World Religions, 97; auth, Traditional and Modern Approaches to the Environment on the Pacific Rim: Tensions and Values, 98; auth, Religious Conscience, the State and the Law, 98. **CONTACT ADDRESS** Ctr for Stud in Relig & Society, Univ of Victoria, Victoria, BC, Canada V8W 3P4. **EMAIL** csrs@uvic.ca

COX, ARCHIBALD
PERSONAL Born 05/17/1912, Plainfield, NJ, 3 children **DISCIPLINE** LAW **EDUCATION** Harvard Univ, AB, 34, LLB, 37. **CAREER** Atty, Ropes, Gray, Best, Coolidge & Rugg, Boston, 38-41; atty, Off Solicitor Gen, US Dept Justice, 41-43; assoc solicitor, Dept Labor, 43-45; lectr law, 45-46, prof, 46-61, mem, Bd Overseers, 62-65, Williston Prof law, 65-76, Carl M Loeb Univ Prof, Harvard Law Sch, 76-, Chmn, Wage Stabilization Bd, 52; co-chmn, Construction Indust Stabilization Comt, 51-52; Solicitor Gen, US Dept Justics, 61-65, spec prosecutor, Watergate Hearings, 73; vis Pitt Prof Am hist & insts & lectr, Cambridge Univ, Eng, 73. **HONORS AND AWARDS** LLD, Loyola Univ, Chicago, 64, Univ Cincinnati, 67, Rutgers Univ, 74, Univ Denver, 74, Amherst Col, 74, Harvard Univ, 75, Univ MI, 76, Wheaton Col, 77, Northeastern, 78, Clark Univ, 80; LHD, Hahnemann Med Col, 80, Univ MA, 81. **MEMBERSHIPS** Am Bar Asm; Am Acad Arts & Sci; Am Philos Soc. **SELECTED PUBLICATIONS** Auth, Cases in Labor Law, 48; coauth, Law and the National Labor Policy, 60; auth, Civil Rights, The Constitution and the Courts, 67; The Warren Court: Constitutional Decision as an Instrument of Reform, 68; The Role of the Supreme Court in American Government, 76; Freedom of Expression, 81. **CONTACT ADDRESS** Law Sch, Harvard Univ, 1563 Massachusetts Ave, LILC 308, Cambridge, MA 02138.

COX, CHANA BERNIKER
PERSONAL Born 10/28/1941, Detroit, MI, m, 1967, 5 children **DISCIPLINE** PHILOSOPHY **EDUCATION** Columbia Univ, PhD, 71. **CAREER** St Lectr Humanities, Lewis & Clark Col. **CONTACT ADDRESS** Lewis and Clark Col, 0615 SW Palatine Hill, Box 83, Portland, OR 97219. **EMAIL** cox@lclark.edu

COX, CLAUDE E.
PERSONAL Born 09/23/1947, Meaford, ON, Canada, m, 1989, 3 children **DISCIPLINE** RELIGION **EDUCATION** Abilene Christian Univ, BA, 69; Knox Col, MDiv, 72; Union Theol Sem-VA, ThM, 73; Univ Toronto, MA, 74, PhD, 79. **CAREER** Asst prof Dept Near E Stud, Univ Toronto, 79-80; asst prof Dept of Relig, 80-84, Chr, 82-84; adj assoc prof of Old Testament & Hebrew, McMaster Divinity Col, 94-; Can Coun Doctoral fel, 75-79; Can-USSR Exch fel, 77-78. **HONORS AND AWARDS** Canada-USSR Exchange Fel, 77-78; Canada Council Doctoral Fel, 75-79; Open Fel, Univ of Toronto, 73-75; Jones Fel, Union Theological Sem in Virginia, 72-73. **MEMBERSHIPS** Int Orgn Septuagint and Cognate Stud; Soc Bibl Lit; Can Soc Bibl Stud; Soc Armenian Stud; Asn Int des Etudes Armeniennes; Ont Chaplains Asn. **RESEARCH** Old Testament; Septuagint studies; Armenian Bible. **SELECTED PUBLICATIONS** Auth, "The Order of Worship at the Church of Christ, Meaford, Ontario," Restoration Quarterly 32 (90): 209-226; auth, "Vocabulary for Wrongdoing and Forgiveness in the Greek Translations of Job," Textus 15, (90): 119-130; auth, "Bible, Armenian," Modern Encyclopedia of Religions in the Russia and the Soviet Union, ed, Paul D. Steeves (Gulf Breeze, FL: Academic International Press, Vol 4, (92): 71-75; auth, "The Vocabulary for Good and Evil in the Armenian Translation of the New Testament," in Text and Contex: Studies in the Armenian New Testament, ed, Shahe Ajamian and Michael E. Stone (UPATS 13; Atlanta: Scholars 95): 49-57; auth, "The Importance of Lifestory in Pastroal Care," Restoration Quarterly 38 (96): 109-120; auth, "Recent Books and Articles Relating to Gender and Christian Service," Leaven 4/2 (Srping 96): 51-54; auth, "Travelling in Armenai with Aquila, Symmachus and Theodotion," in Origen's Hexapla and Fragments, ed, Alison Salvesen (Text und Studien zum Antiken Judentum 58; Tubingen: Mohr Siebeck, 98): 302-316; auth, "The Reading of the Personal Letter as the Background for the Reading of the Scriptures in the Early Church," in The Early Church in Context: Essays in Honor of Everett Ferguson, ed, A.J. Malherbe, F.W. Norris, J.W Thompson (NTSUP 90; Leiden/Boxton/Koln: Brill 98): 74-91. **CONTACT ADDRESS** McMaster Univ, 18 Roslyn Rd, Hamilton, ON, Canada L8S 4K1. **EMAIL** c.cox@sympatico.ca

COX, HOWARD A.
PERSONAL Born 10/10/1958, Jacksonville, TX, m, 1988, 2 children **DISCIPLINE** THEOLOGY **EDUCATION** Stephen F Austin State Univ, BA, 81; Abilene Christian Univ, MA, 83; Theolog Univ of Am, DRE, 94. **CAREER** Instr, Lamar Univ, 90-92; instr 88-90, asst prof, 94-, Magnolia Bible Col. **HONORS AND AWARDS** Who's Who in Am Educ; Miss Asn of Cols Outstanding Faculty Member; Sigma Tau Delta Writer's Key Awd; phi delta kappa; alpha chi; sigma tau delta; phi iota. **MEMBERSHIPS** MLA; MLA; CCCC; Evangelical Theological Asn. **RESEARCH** 20th Century Am Lit; Post WWI Expatriates; assesment & evolution **SELECTED PUBLICATIONS** Auth, Imitating Christ's Forgiveness, 95; auth, Magnolia Bible College Conducts Research on Student's Knowledge of Safety and Security, 95; auth, A New Reading of the Feeding of the Five Thousand, 96; auth, The Christian's Response to Suicide, 97. **CONTACT ADDRESS** PO Box 1109, Kosciusko, MS 39090.

COX, JAMES D.
DISCIPLINE LAW **EDUCATION** Ariz State Univ, BS, 66; Univ Calif, JD, 69; Harvard law School, LLM, 71. **CAREER** Teaching Fel, Boston Univ, 70-71; Asst Prof, Univ San Francisco, 71-74; Vesting Assoc Prof, Stanford Law School, 76-77; Assoc Prof to Prof, Univ Calif, 74-79; Vis Prof to Prof, Duke Univ, 79-. **HONORS AND AWARDS** Most Valuable Prof, Awd, Univ San Francisco, 73-74; John B Hurlbut Awd, Stanford Law School, 77; Most Valuable prof Awd, Univ Calif, 75-76; Mordecai Soc Awd, Duke Univ, 83; duke Bar Asn Teach Awd, 87, 95, Sen Fulbright Fel, Univ Sydney, 89; Order of the Coif, Phi Kappa Phi, ET Bost Res Professorship, 80, 97, Nat Book Awd, Asn of Am Pub, 95. **MEMBERSHIPS** Asn of Am Law Schools, NC Bar Asn. **SELECTED PUBLICATIONS** Auth, Corporations, Little Brown and Co, 95; auth, Securities Regulations: Cases and Materials, Ed Aspen Law and Business, 97; auth, corporations, Aspen law and Business, 97; auth, Financial Information, Accounting and the Law, Little Brown and Co, 80; auth, "Just Desserts for Accountants and attorneys After Dank of Denver", Ariz Law Review, 96; auth, Piercing the corporate Veil in Limited Liability Companies, Liability Co, 97; auth, "addressing Fraudulent Practices Within the Modern Framework of the United States Securities Laws," in essays on Insider Trading and Securities Regulation, 97; auth, "Equal Treatment for shareholders: An essay," Cardozo Law Review, 97; auth, "Making Securi9ties Fraud class Actions Virtuous," Arizona Law Review, 97. **CONTACT ADDRESS** School of Law, Duke Univ, PO Box 90362, Durham, NC 27708-0362.

COX, STEVEN L.
PERSONAL Born 07/16/1956, Greenville, SC, m, 1975, 2 children **DISCIPLINE** NEW TESTAMENT, GREEK **EDUCATION** Anderson Col, AA, 79; Southern Wesleyan Univ, BS, 82; Erspine Theol Sem, MDiv, 86; The Southern Baptist Theol Sem, PhD, 91. **CAREER** Adjunct, Southeastern Baptist Theol Sem, 94-95; Mid-America Baptist Theol Sem, 95-. **MEMBERSHIPS** Soc of Biblical Lit, Tyndale Fel, Inst of Biblical Res, Evangelical Theol Soc. **RESEARCH** Greek language--textual criticism, rhetoric, historiography. **SELECTED PUBLICATIONS** Auth, "Tychicus: A Profile," The Biblical Illustrator (summer 95); auth, Essentials of the New Testament Greek: A Student's Guide, Nashville, Tn: Broadman/Holman (95, revised 99); auth, "Three Millennial Views," SBC Sunday School Bd, Life and Works Series (spring 96); auth, "An Anecdote to Violence: 1 Corinthians 13," The Rev and Expositor (fall 96); auth, "The Jewish Concept of Ghosts in Light of Matthew 14:26," The Biblical Illustrator (winter 97); auth, "The Parable of the Sower in Luke 10:25-37: What Does Love Look Like?," The Mid-America Theol JH (June 97); auth, "Outreach Through Small Groups in New Zealand," Strategies for Today's Leader (July 99); auth, "Angels," a unit intro and two lessons for Life and Works series of Lifeway Christian Resources of the SBC (fall 99). **CONTACT ADDRESS** Dept Bible Studies, Mid-America Baptist Theol Sem, PO Box 381528, Germantown, TN 38183-1528. **EMAIL** scox@mabts.edu

COYLE, J. KEVIN
PERSONAL Born 04/25/1943, Iroquois Falls, ON, Canada, s **DISCIPLINE** EARLY CHRISTIAN HISTORY **EDUCATION** Univ of Ottawa, BA, BPh, 63; Catholic Univ of Amer, BTh, LTh, 65 and 67; Univ de Fribourg en Suisse, DTh, 79. **CAREER** Lectr, 76-79, Asst Prof, 79-84, Assoc Prof, 84-87, Full Prof, 87-, Universite Saint-Paul, Ottawa. **MEMBERSHIPS** Canadian Soc of Patristic Studies; North Amer Patristic Soc; Intl Assoc for Patristic Studies; Intl Assoc of Manichaean Studies; Societe quebecoise pour l etude de las religion; Soc of Biblical Lit. **RESEARCH** History of early Christianity; Latin Palaeography; Development of Christian Thought; Manichaeism **SELECTED PUBLICATIONS** Auth, De moribus ecclesiae catholicae: Augustin chretien a Rome, De moribus ecclesiae catholicae et de moribus Manichaeorum: De quantitate animae, 91; Mary Magdalene in Manichaeism, Le Museon, 91; Augustine's Millenialism Reconsidered, Charisteria Augustiniana Iosepho Oroz Reta dicata, 93; Recent Reviews on the Origins of Clerical Celibacy, Logos, 93; Hands and the Impositions of Hands in Manichaesim, Pegrina Curiositas: Eine Reise durch den orbis antiquus. Zu Ehren von Dirk van Damme, 94; Early Monks, Prayer and the Devil, Prayer and Spirituality in the Early Church, 98. **CONTACT ADDRESS** Saint Paul Univ,

223 Main St., Ottawa, ON, Canada K1S 1C4. **EMAIL** jkcoyle@ustpaul.uottawa.ca

COYNE, ANTHONY M.
PERSONAL Born 09/16/1949, Richmond, VA, m, 1975, 2 children **DISCIPLINE** PHILOSOPHY **EDUCATION** Univ NC Chapel Hill, PhD, 74; Wash and Lee Univ, BS, summa cum laude 70, BA, summa cum laude 70. **CAREER** Assoc Dean, 97-, Univ S Carolina; Prof, 78-97, Univ N Carolina; Asst Prof, 76-78, Elon College; vis Asst Prof, 75, Univ NC Chapel Hill. **HONORS AND AWARDS** Phi Beta Kappa; John Motley Morehead Fel. **MEMBERSHIPS** APA; AIL; HS; NAHE; AAPT. **RESEARCH** History of Philosophy; Logic. **SELECTED PUBLICATIONS** Auth, Introduction to Inductive Reasoning, UPA, 84; auth, Paul and the Value of Philosophy, Explorations, 87; Philosophy and the Modern Mind: A Criticism, S J of Philo, 78; revs in Zentralblatt fur Mathematik: Keith Devlin, Sets Functions and Logic: An Introduction to Abstract Mathematics; Raymond Smullyan, Godel's Incompleteness Theorems; Mary Tiles, Mathematics and the Image of Reason; Anthony Galton, Logic for Information Technology; Wesley C Salmon, Logik; Paul Teller, A Modern Formal Logic Primer, vol 1 and vol 2. **CONTACT ADDRESS** Univ of So Carolina, Sumter, Sumter, SC 29150. **EMAIL** acoyne@uscsumter.edu

CRABTREE, ARTHUR BAMFORD
PERSONAL Born 05/05/1910, Stalybridge, England, m, 1938, 1 child **DISCIPLINE** THEOLOGY **EDUCATION** Univ Manchester, BA, 33, BD, 35; Univ Zurich, Dr(theol), 46. **CAREER** Prof theol, Baptist Theol Sem, Switz, 49-57 & Eastern Baptist theol Sem, Pa, 57-68; assoc prof, Villanova Univ, 68-76, Prof Theol, 76-80; Retired. **MEMBERSHIPS** N Am Acad Ecumenists; Col Theol Soc. **RESEARCH** Ecumenical and Protestant theology. **SELECTED PUBLICATIONS** Auth, Jonathan Edwards' view of man, Relig Educ, 47; The Restored Relationship, Judson, 63. **CONTACT ADDRESS** Dept of Theol, Villanova Univ, Villanova, PA 19085.

CRADDOCK, JERRY RUSSELL
PERSONAL Born 05/19/1935, Pueblo, CO, m, 1961 **DISCIPLINE** ROMANCE PHILOLOGY, MEDIEVAL HISPANIC LITERATURE **EDUCATION** Tex Western Col, BA, 58; Univ Calif, Berkeley, PhD, 67. **CAREER** Asst prof Span, Univ Calif, Davis, 65-68, from asst prof to assoc prof Span & Romance philol, 68-76, Prof Span, Univ Calif, Berkeley, 76-. **MEMBERSHIPS** Ling Soc Am; MLA; Mediaeval Acad Am. **RESEARCH** Linguistics. **SELECTED PUBLICATIONS** **CONTACT ADDRESS** Dept of Span & Port, Univ of California, Berkeley, 4319 Dwinelle Hall, Berkeley, CA 94720-2591.

CRAIG, WILLIAM LANE
PERSONAL Born 08/23/1949, Peoria, IL, m, 1972, 2 children **DISCIPLINE** PHILOSOPHY, THEOLOGY **EDUCATION** Univ Birmingham UK, PhD, 77; Univ Munchen, DTh, 84. **CAREER** Asst Prof, 80-86, Trinity Evang Div Sch; Assoc Prof, 86-87, Westmont College; indep res 87-94, Katoiike Univ Belgium; Res Prof 94-, Talbot Sch Theol. **HONORS AND AWARDS** Humboldt Fel. **MEMBERSHIPS** APA; AAR; SBL; SCP; ASA; SRF; PTS; ETS; EPS. **RESEARCH** Theism and Cosmology; Omniscience; Philosophy of Time; Resurrection. **SELECTED PUBLICATIONS** Auth, On Hasker's Defense of Anti-Molinism, Faith and Philo, 98; Creation and Conservation Once More, Religious Stud, 98; McTaggart's Paradox and the Problem of Temporary Intrinsics, Analysis, 98; Divine Timelessness and Personhood, Intl J for Philo of Religion, 98; coauth, Will the Real Jesus Please Stand Up? ed Paul Copan, Grand Rapids MI, Baker Bookhouse, 98; auth, John Dominic on the Resurrection of Jesus, in: The Resurrection, ed S Davis, D Kendall, G O Collins, Oxford, Oxford Univ Press, 97; On the Argument for Divine Timelessness from the Incompleteness of Temporal Life, Heythrop J, 97; Adams on Actualism and Presentism, Philosophia, 97; In Defense of the Kalam Cosmology Argument, Faith and Philo, 97; A Critique of Grdem's Formulation and Defense of the Doctrine of Eternity, Philosophica Christi, 96; The New B-Theory's Tu Quoque Argument, Synthese, 96; A response to Grunbaum on Creation and Big Bang Cosmology, Philosophia Naturalis, 94; Should Peter go to the Mission Field? Faith and Philo, 93; Talbot's Universalism Once More, Religious Stud, 93; Divine Foreknowledge and Human Freedom: The Coherence of Theism: Omniscience, Studies in Intellectual History, Leiden, EJ Brill, 90. **CONTACT ADDRESS** 1805 Danforth Dr, Marietta, GA 30062.

CRAIG-TAYLOR, PHYLISS
DISCIPLINE LAW **EDUCATION** Univ Ala, BS, JD; Columbia Univ, LLM. **CAREER** Assoc prof, Univ Fla, 95-. **MEMBERSHIPS** Ala Bar; NC Bar. **RESEARCH** Law, bankruptcy, poverty law, and public benefits, capital accumulation and property. **CONTACT ADDRESS** School of Law, Univ of Florida, PO Box 117625, Gainesville, FL 32611-7625. **EMAIL** c-taylor@law.ufl.edu

CRAIGHEAD, HOUSTON ARCHER
PERSONAL Born 01/24/1941, San Antonio, TX, m, 1964, 2 children **DISCIPLINE** PHILOSOPHY **EDUCATION** Baylor Univ, BA, 62, MA, 64; Univ Tex, Austin, PhD(philos), 70. **CAREER** Asst prof philos, ECarolina Univ, 66-70; assoc prof, 70-80, Prof Philos, Winthrop Col, 80- **MEMBERSHIPS** Am Philos Asn; Metaphys Soc Am; Southwestern Philos Soc; Soc Studies Process Philos; Soc Philos Relig. **RESEARCH** Metaphysics, primarily in the concept of non-being; philosophy of religion; existentialism. **SELECTED PUBLICATIONS** Auth, Non-being and Hartshorne's concept of God, Process Studies, spring 71; Reply to Chas Hartshorne's Twelve Elements of my Philosophy, Southwestern J Philos, spring 74; Paul Tillich's arguments for God's reality, Thomist, 4/75; The cosmological argument: Assessment of a reassessment, Int J Philos Relig, summer 75; Edwards, Cox and cosmological composition, New Scholasticism, winter 76; John Hick's Lives After Life, Thomist (in press); Robert Audi's critique of John Hick: An evaluation, Int J Philos Relig (in press). **CONTACT ADDRESS** Dept of Philos, Winthrop Univ, Rock Hill, SC 29730.

CRAMTON, ROGER C.
PERSONAL Born 05/18/1929, Pittsfield, MA, m, 1952, 4 children **DISCIPLINE** LAW **EDUCATION** Harvard Univ, BA, 50; Iniv Chicago, JD, 55; Oxford Univ, LLD, 88. **CAREER** Univ Chicago, 57-61; Univ Mich, 61-73; CORNELL UNIV, 73-. **HONORS AND AWARDS** Guggenheim Fel, 88-89; Am Bar Found, Res Awd, 00. **MEMBERSHIPS** Am Acad Arts & Sci; Am Law Inst Coun **RESEARCH** Legal ethics; Legal profession. **SELECTED PUBLICATIONS** Conflict of Laws: Cases, Comments, Questions, West Publ Co, 93; The Law and Ethics of Lawyering, Found Press, 99. **CONTACT ADDRESS** Cornell Law Sch, Cornell Univ, Ithaca, NY 14853-4901. **EMAIL** rcc10@cornell.edu

CRANFORD, LORIN L.
PERSONAL Born 11/03/1941, Perrin, TX, m, 1993, 5 children **DISCIPLINE** RELIGIOUS STUDIES **EDUCATION** Wayland Baptist Univ, BA; Southwestern Baptist Theol Seminary, Mdiv; ThD. **CAREER** Prof, Southwestern Baptist Theol Seminary 74-98; prof, Gardner-Webb Univ, 98-. **MEMBERSHIPS** Soc Bibl Lit; Nat Assn of Baptist Profs of Rel. **RESEARCH** New Testament; Ancient History. **SELECTED PUBLICATIONS** Auth, Revelation, Garland; auth, Inspiration, Garland; auth, "Lost and Found," Decision Magazine. **CONTACT ADDRESS** Dept of Religious Studies and Philosophy, Gardner-Webb Univ, 105 Twin Lake Dr., Shelby, NC 28152. **EMAIL** lcranford@gardner-webb.edu

CRANOR, CARL F.
DISCIPLINE PHILOSOPHY **EDUCATION** Univ CO, BA, 66; UCLA, PhD, 71; Yale, MSL Law, 81. **CAREER** Prof, Assoc Dean, Human and Soc Sci, Univ Calif, Riverside. **HONORS AND AWARDS** Phi Beta Kappa, 66; Fel, Am Counc of Learned Societies, 80-81; Fel, Master of Studies in Lasw, Yale Law Sch, 80-81; Congressional Fel, Am Philos Asn, 85-86; Fel and Convenor, Univ of Calif, Humanities Res Inst, 91; NSF Scholars Award, 96-98; Distinguished Humanist Achievement Lect, UC Riverside, 97; Elected fel, Am Asn for the Advancement of Sci, 98 **RESEARCH** Legal and Moral Philosophy; Philosophy of Regulatory Law and Science; Philosophy Risk Assessment; Philosophy of Toxic Tort Law. **SELECTED PUBLICATIONS** Auth, "Some Moral Issues in Risk Assessment," Ethics Vol 101, 90; "Science Courts, Evidentiary Procedures, and Mixed Science Policy Decisions," Risk: Issues in Health and Safety, Vol 4, 93; Regulating Toxic Substances: A Philosophy of Science and the Law, Oxford Univ Press, 93; Are Genes Us?, The Social Consequences of the New Genetics, Rutgers Univ Press, 94; "Toxic Substances and Agenda 21: Ethics and Policy Issues in the Science and its Implementation," Sustainable Development: Science, Ethics, and Policy, Kluwer, 95; "The Social Benefits of Expedited Risk Assessment," Risk Analysis, 95; "Improving the Regulation of Carcinogens by Expediting Cancer Potency Estimation," Risk Analysis, 95; "Learning from the Law for Regulatory Science," Law and Philos, 95; "Judicial Boundary-Drawing and the Need for Context-Sensitive Science in Toxic Torts after Daubert v. Merrell-Dow Pharmaceutical," The Va Environ Law Jour, 96; "The Normative Nature of Risk Assessment: Features and Possibilities," Risk: Health, Safety, and Enrivon, 97; "A Philosophy of Risk Assessment and the Law: A Case Study of the Role of Philosophy in Public Policy," Philos Stud, 97; "Eggshell Skulls and Loss of Hair from Fright: Some Moral and Legal Principles which Protect Susceptible Subpopulations," Environ Toxicology and Pharmacology, 98; auth, "Risk Assessment, Susceptible Subpopulations and Environmental Equity," in The Law of Environmental Justice, (99); auth, "Asymmetric Information, the Precautionary Principle and Burdens of Proof in Environmental Health Protections," in Protecting Public Health and the Environment: Implementing the Precautionary Principle, (99); auth, "Empirically and Institutionally Rich Legal and Moral Philosophy" in Midwest Studies in Philosophy. **CONTACT ADDRESS** Dept of Philos, Univ of California, Riverside, Riverside, CA 92521. **EMAIL** carl.cranor@ucr.edu

CRAWFORD, CLAN, JR.
PERSONAL Born 01/25/1927, Cleveland, OH, m, 1949, 3 children **DISCIPLINE** LAW **EDUCATION** Oberlin Col, AB, 48; Univ of Mich, JD, 52. **CAREER** Assoc, Roscoe O. Bonisteel, Ann Arbor, Mich, 53-57; Ann Arbor city councilman, 57-58; pvt practice, Ann Arbor, Mich, 57- ; of counsel, Schlussel, Lifton, Simon, Rands, Galvin & Jackier, 89-90, Ellis, Talcott & Ohlgren, P. C., Ann Arbor, 90- ; lectr in field. **MEMBERSHIPS** Mich Soc Planning Officials; ABA; Mich Bar Asn, Washtenaw County Bar Asn. **RESEARCH** Land use and zoning, incl. planning. **SELECTED PUBLICATIONS** Michigan Zoning and Planning, 65, 3rd ed, 88; Strategy & Tactics in Municipal Zoning, 69, 2nd ed, 79; Handbook of Zoning and Land Use Ordinances with Forms, 74. **CONTACT ADDRESS** 1215 Brooklyn Ave, Ann Arbor, MI 48104. **EMAIL** clan@ix.netcom.com

CRAWFORD, COLIN
PERSONAL Born 11/17/1958, Denver, CO, s **DISCIPLINE** LAW **EDUCATION** Columbia Univ, 80; Cambridge Univ, BA, 82; Harvard Law Sch, 88. **CAREER** Asst prof & instr, Brooklyn Law Sch, 92-97; Thomas jefferson Sch of Law, 97-. **HONORS AND AWARDS** Law & Soc Summer Inst Fel, 99; Macdowell Colony resident, 98; Ledig House Writer's Colony, 96 & 97; Thomas Jefferson Golden Apple for Teaching, 98-99 & 99-00. **MEMBERSHIPS** Law & Soc Asn, Soc of Environmental Journalists, Tom Homann Law Asn. **RESEARCH** Local government, land use, and environmental law. **SELECTED PUBLICATIONS** Auth, Uproar at Dancing Rabbit Creek: Battling Over Race, Class and the Environment, Addison-Wesley, 96; auth, "Chapter 3: Other Civil Rights Titles," The Law of Environmental Justice, Am Bar Asn, 99; auth, "Bankless East Palo Alto Finds a Way to Lure Branch," Wall St J (99); auth, "San Diego Farming Finds it Can Thrive Without Beachfront," Wall St J (00); auth, "Low-Tech Waste Plan Wins Fans--and Raises a Stink," Wall St J (00). **CONTACT ADDRESS** Thomas Jefferson Sch of Law, 2121 San Diego Ave, San Diego, CA 92110-2928.

CRAWFORD, DAN
PERSONAL Born 10/30/1941, m, 3 children **DISCIPLINE** EPISTEMOLOGY, COGNITIVE SCIENCE, AND PHILOSOPHY OF RELIGION **EDUCATION** Univ Pittsburgh, PhD, 72. **CAREER** Sr Lect, Univ Nebr, Lincoln. **SELECTED PUBLICATIONS** Published in the areas of knowledge and perception, Augustine, W. Sellars, Science and Religion. **CONTACT ADDRESS** Univ of Nebraska, Lincoln, Lincoln, NE 68588-0321. **EMAIL** dcrawford1@unl.edu

CRAWFORD, DAVID R.
DISCIPLINE PHILOSOPHY **EDUCATION** Eastern Col, BA; Penn State Univ, MA; DePaul Univ, PhD. **CAREER** Assoc prof, ch, Univ Detroit Mercy, 70-. **HONORS AND AWARDS** NEH grant. **RESEARCH** 19th and 20th century Continental Philosophy. **CONTACT ADDRESS** Dept of Philosophy, Univ of Detroit Mercy, 4001 W McNichols Rd, PO Box 19900, Detroit, MI 48219-0900. **EMAIL** CRAWFODR@udmercy.edu

CRAWFORD, TIMOTHY G.
PERSONAL Born 11/19/1957, Huntsville, AL, m, 1982, 2 children **DISCIPLINE** RELIGION **EDUCATION** Southern Sem, Louisville, KY, PhD, 90; Southwestern Sem, Ft. Worth, TX, Mdiv, 84; Sanford Univ, Birmingham, AL, BA, 80. **CAREER** Assoc Prof, Chr of Hum Div, 90-, Bluefield Coll; Instr of Old Testament Hist and Interp, 88-90, Southern Sem; Chair of Christian Studies Div. **HONORS AND AWARDS** Outstanding Faculty Awd. **MEMBERSHIPS** Soc Biblical Lit; Natl Assoc of Prof of Hebrew; Natl Assoc of Baptist Prof of Rel. **RESEARCH** Masorah; Intertextuality. **SELECTED PUBLICATIONS** Auth, The Masorah of Biblia Hebraica Stuttgartensia, coauth, Eerdmans, 98; co-auth, Handbook to Biblical Hebrew Grammar, Eerdmans, 94; auth, Taking the Promised Land, Leaving the Promised Land: Luke's Use of Joshua for a Christian Foundation Story, Review and Expositor, 98; Blessing and Curse in Syro-Palestinian Inscriptions of the Iron Age, Peter Lang, Pub, 92; co-auth, Mercer Dictionary of the Bible, Seven articles. **CONTACT ADDRESS** Bluefield Col, 3000 College Dr, Box 16, Bluefield, VA 24605. **EMAIL** tcrawford@mail.bluefield.edu

CRAWFORD, WILLIAM EDWARD
PERSONAL Born 12/15/1927, Key West, FL, m, 1962, 3 children **DISCIPLINE** LAW **EDUCATION** La State Univ, BA, 51, JD, 55. **CAREER** Atty at law, Chaffe, McCall, Phillips, Burke & Hopkins, 55-65; assoc prof, 66-71, asst dean sch, 66-69, prof law, Law Sch, La State Univ, Baton Rouge, 71-; dir, La State Law Inst, 78-. **RESEARCH** Trial practice; torts; legal profession. **SELECTED PUBLICATIONS** Auth, Trial and Appellate Advocacy, La State Univ, 72; Faculty symposium, The Work of the Louisiana Appellate Courts for the 1970-1971 Term, Civil Procedure, 72, Faculty symposium, The Work of the Louisana Appellate Courts or the 1971-1972 Term, Torts, 73 & Executory Process and Collateral Mortgages--Authentic Evidence of the Hand Note?, summer 73, La Law Rev; Torts, Louisiana Cases and Materials, La State Univ, 73; coauth, New Code of Civil Procedure in France: Bk I (English transl), Oceana, 78; Louisana Code of Civil Procedure, 1982 ed, Crawford-West's Publ Co, 81. **CONTACT ADDRESS** Law Sch, Louisiana State Univ and A&M Col, Baton Rouge, LA 70803-0001. **EMAIL** wcrawford@lsu.edu

CREAMER, DAVID G.
PERSONAL Born 08/20/1946, Saint John, NB, Canada **DISCIPLINE** MORAL EDUCATION **EDUCATION** St Mary's Univ, BS (Chem), 68; Mem Univ, BEd, 72; Regic Coll, Toronto School of Theol, 77; Med (moral edu), Univ Toronto, 78; EdD (moral edu), 82. **CAREER** Teacher, High School, St John's, 71-74; dir, St Paul's High School, 82-88; asst and assoc prof, Univ Manitoba, 89-. **MEMBERSHIPS** Asn of Moral Edu; Nat Cath Edu Asn; Relig Edu Asn. **RESEARCH** Moral and Religious education; Psychology of Religion. **SELECTED PUBLICATIONS** Auth, rev Caths at the Gathering Place: Historical Essays on the Archdiocese of Tornoto, Can J of Urban Res, 93; Guides for the Journey, John MacMurray, Bernard Lonergan, James Fowler, 96; rev The Jesuit Mystique, Can Cath Rev, 96; rev, The Politics of Spirituality: A Study of a Renewal Process in an English Diocese, Can J of Urban Res, 97; Bernard J F Lonergan: The Possibilty of Ethics, Life Ethics in World Religs, 98; The Jesus Wars, Jesuit Centre for Cath Studies, 98. **CONTACT ADDRESS** Jesuit Ctr, Saint Paul Univ, 70 Dysart Rd, Winnipeg, MB, Canada R3T 2M6. **EMAIL** creamer@ms.umanitoba.ca

CREASE, ROBERT P.
PERSONAL Born 10/22/1953, Philadelphia, PA, m, 1994, 2 children **DISCIPLINE** PHILOSOPHY **EDUCATION** Amherst Col, BA, 76; Columbia Univ, PhD, 87. **CAREER** Vis prof, asst prof, assoc prof, prof, dir, grad prog, SUNY Stony Brook, 87- . **HONORS AND AWARDS** Fulbright-Hayes fel, 79-80. **MEMBERSHIPS** APA; AAAS; APS. **RESEARCH** Philosophy and history of science. **SELECTED PUBLICATIONS** Co-auth, The Second Creation: Makers of the Revolution in Twentieth Century Physics; auth, The Play of Nature: Experimentation as Performance, Indiana, 93; ed, Hermeneutics and the Natural Sciences, Kluwer, 97; auth, Making Physics: A Biography of Brookhaven National Laboratory, Chicago, 99; auth, "Columnist, Physics World". **CONTACT ADDRESS** Dept of Philosophy, SUNY, Stony Brook, 213 Harriman Hall, Stony Brook, NY 11794. **EMAIL** rcrease@notes.cc.sunysb.edu

CREED, BRADLEY
PERSONAL Born 04/20/1957, Jacksonville, TX, m, 1980, 3 children **DISCIPLINE** RELIGION **EDUCATION** Baylor Univ, BA, 79; MDiv, 82, PhD, 86, Southwestern Baptist Theological Seminary. **CAREER** Pastor, 80-93; Assoc Dean, 93-96, Truett Seminary; Dean and Prof of Christian History, 96-, George W. Truett Theological Seminary, Baylor Univ. **HONORS AND AWARDS** President's Merit Scholar in School of Theology, SWBTS, 83-85; Recipient of the Albert Venting Awd, SWBTS, 82; Recipient of the Mayor's Achievement Awd for the City of Natchitoches, LA, 92. **MEMBERSHIPS** Natl Assoc of Baptist Profs of Religion; North Amer Patristics Soc; Amer Acad of Religion; Conference on Faith and History; Amer Soc of Church History; Texas Baptist Historical Soc. **RESEARCH** History of Christianity; free church studies; ministry studies **SELECTED PUBLICATIONS** Auth, Church Leadership in the Southern Baptist Convention, Has Our Theology Changed? Southern Baptist Thought since 1845, 94; The Servant People of God, Proclaiming the Baptist Vision: The Church, 96. **CONTACT ADDRESS** George W. Truett Theological Seminary, Baylor Univ, Waco, Waco, TX 76798-7126. **EMAIL** bradley_creed@baylor.edu

CREEVEY, LUCY
PERSONAL Born 07/02/1940, Cambridge, NY, d **DISCIPLINE** POLITICAL SCIENCE **EDUCATION** Smith Col, BA, 62; Boston Univ, MA, 63; PhD, 67. **CAREER** Assoc prof to prof, Univ of Pa, 74-87; prof, Univ of Conn, 87-. **MEMBERSHIPS** AAUP; AAUW; AICP; ASA; APA; APSA. **SELECTED PUBLICATIONS** Auth, Muslim Brotherhoods and Politics in Senegal, Harvard Univ Pr, (Cambridge), 70; auth, "Supporting Small-Scale Enterprises for Women Farmers in Sahel", J of Int Develop 3.4, (91): 355-386; auth, "The Impact of Islam on Women in Senegal", J of Develop Areas 25.3 (91): 347-368; coauth, The Heritage of Islam: Women, Religion and Politics in West Africa, Lynne Rienner Pub, (Boulder), 94; auth, Changing Women's Lives and Work: An Analysis of Eight Microenterprise Projects, IT Pub, (London), 96; coauth, "Reaction to Devaluation in Senegal", J of Mod African Studies 33.4 (95): 669-683; coauth, "Quasi Democracy in Senegal", Political Reform in Francophone Africa, ed John Clark and David Gardienr, Westview Pr, (Boulder, 97); auth, "Islam, Women and the Role of the State in Senegal", J of Relig in Africa, XXVI.3, (96); coauth, "Evaluation on the Impacts of Grassroots Management Training on Women in India", Can J of Develop Studies XVIII, (97); auth, "Structural Adjustment and the Empowerment or Disempowerment of Women in Niger and Senegal", Rethinking Empowerment, ed Rekha Datta and Judy Kornberg, Lynne rienner Pub, (forthcoming). **CONTACT ADDRESS** Dept Polit Sci, Univ of Connecticut, Storrs, 341 Mansfield Rd U24, Storrs, CT 06269-1024.

CRENSHAW, JAMES L.
PERSONAL Born 12/19/1934, Sunset, SC, m, 1956, 2 children **DISCIPLINE** RELIGION **EDUCATION** Furman Univ, BA, 56; S Baptist Theol Sem, BD, 60; Vanderbilt Univ, PhD, 64. **CAREER** Prof Old Testament, Atlantic Christian Col, 64-65; Mercer Univ, 65-69; Vanderbilt Univ Divinity Sch, 70-87; Duke Univ Divinity Sch, 87- . **HONORS AND AWARDS** Phi Beta Kappa; Soc for Relig in Higher Ed fel, 72-73; AATS fel, 78-79, 90-91; Guggenheim Fel, 84-85; NEH fel, 90-91; hon doctorate, Furman univ, 93; univ wide distinguished prof, 93-; PEW Evangelical scholar, 96-97; ed, Soc of Bibl Lit monograph series. **MEMBERSHIPS** Soc Bibl Lit; Catholic Bibl Asn; Int Org for the Study of the Old Testament; Soc for Old Testament Study; Colloquium for Bibl Res. **RESEARCH** Hebrew Bible, language and literature. **SELECTED PUBLICATIONS** Auth, Trembling at the Threshold of a Biblical Text, Eerdmans, 94; auth, Joel, Doubleday, 95; auth, Urgent Advice and Probing Questions, Mercer, 96; auth, Sirach, Abingdon, 97; auth, Education in Ancient Israel, Doubleday, 98; auth, Old Testament Wisdom, rev ed, Westminster, 98. **CONTACT ADDRESS** Duke Univ, PO Box 90967, Durham, NC 27708. **EMAIL** jlcren@mail.duke.edu

CRENSHAW, RONALD WILLIS
PERSONAL Born 01/04/1940, St. Louis, MO, m **DISCIPLINE** LAW **EDUCATION** Fist U, BA 1962; Univ of SD Sch of Med, grad; Univ of SD Coll of Law, JD 1971. **CAREER** Ronald W Crenshaw & Asso PC, atty 1976-; State of MI, spl asst atty gen 1974-; Elliard Crenshaw & Strong, partner 1973-76; Zechman & Crenshaw, partner 1972-73; US Atty's Ofc, law clrk 1971; Fredrikson Byron & Colborn Law Ofcs, legal intern 1970; Univ of SD Sch of Med, resrch asst 1968; Dept of Aero-Space Med Mcdonnell Aircraft Corp, asso physiologist 1964-67; Dept of Biochemistry Cntrl Resrch Div Monsanto Co, resrch biochemist 1964; Dept of Radiophysics Sch of Med Wash Univ St Louis, resrch asst 1962-64. **HONORS AND AWARDS** Fellow awd Univ of SD 1967; contestant Moot Ct 1969; Am Jurisprudence Awd Univ of SD 1970; gunderson seminar awd Univ of SD 1971. **MEMBERSHIPS** Mem State Bar of MI; mem Wolverine Bar Assn; mem Fed Bar Assn; mem Am Bar Assn; mem num other Bar Assn; mem public adv com on jud cands Detroit Bar Assn; chmn of adm com Detroit Bar Assn 1978-79; vice pres bd of dirs Don Bosco Hall Juvenile Home; chmn Kappa Alpha Psi Frat; found & chmn Martin Luther King Jr Meml Scholar Found Univ of SD 1968-71; chmn Martin Luther King Jr Meml Day Activities 1968-70; mem Hon Code Rev Com Univ of SD 1969; memConstl Rules Com 1969-70; pres Vermillion Chap Phi Delta Phi Legal Frat; licensed State Cts of MI; Fed Dist Ct for the E Dist of MI; US Ct of Appeals 6th Cir. **SELECTED PUBLICATIONS** "The Vagrancy Statute: To Be or Not To Be", "The Purposeful Inclusion of Am Indians". **CONTACT ADDRESS** 405 Riverd, Ste 100, Detroit, MI 48207.

CRESS, DONALD ALAN
PERSONAL Born 12/20/1945, Los Angeles, CA **DISCIPLINE** MEDIEVAL PHILOSOPHY, CARTESIANISM **EDUCATION** St John's Col, BA, 67; Marquette Univ, MA, 69, PhD(philos), 72. **CAREER** Instr philos, Carroll Col, 71-73; asst prof, 73-79, Assoc Prof Philos, Northern Ill Univ, 79-94, prof, 94-98, Chmn Dept, 81-85, 86-88; assoc dean, Col of Liberal Arts and Scis, N Ill Univ, dean, Col of Arts and Scis, Univ Wisc - Parkside **HONORS AND AWARDS** Andrew Mellon Post-Doc fel, ACE fel, NEH res fel, Fulbright Inst, Woodrow Wilson Doctoral fel, Grant, Northern Ill Univ Grad Sch, 75, 77, 78 & 81 **MEMBERSHIPS** Leibniz Soc; Soc Medieval & Renaissance Philos; Soc Study Hist Philos; Int Soc Neo-Platonic Studies; Am Philos Asn. **RESEARCH** Medieval philosophy, renaissance Aristotelianism, Cartesianism **SELECTED PUBLICATIONS** Auth, Truth, Error, and the Order of Reasons: Descartes' Puzzling Synopsis of the Fourth Meditation, Reason, Will and Sensation: Studies in Cartesian Metaphysics, 94; auth, Descartes' Doctrine of Volitional Infinity, S Jou of Phil, 89; auth, A Defense of Augustine's Privation Account of Evil, Augustinian Stu, 89. **CONTACT ADDRESS** Col of Arts and Scis, Univ of Wisconsin, Parkside, PO Box 2000, Kenosha, WI 53141. **EMAIL** cress@uwp.edu

CRESSON, BRUCE COLLINS
PERSONAL Born 10/27/1930, Lenoir, NC, m, 1955, 2 children **DISCIPLINE** RELIGION, ARCHEOLOGY **EDUCATION** Wake Forest Col, BA, 52; Southeastern Baptist Theol Sem, BD, 55, ThM, 56; Duke Univ, PhD(relig), 64. **CAREER** Instr Hebrew, Southeastern Baptist Theol Sem, 62-63; instr relig, Duke Univ, 63-66; assoc prof, 66-77, Prof Relig, Baylor Univ, 77-00, prof emer, 00-; Mem, excavation staff, Aphek-Antipatris, 74-76, Wardeh, 77; dir, excavation to Tel Dalit, 78-80; Tel Ira, 80-81; Horvat Uza, 82-88; Horvat Radarn 89; Tel Malhata, 90-00. **MEMBERSHIPS** Am Sch Org Res; Soc Bibl Lit. **RESEARCH** Edom; history of Old Testament and intertestamental period in its world setting; Biblical archaeology. **SELECTED PUBLICATIONS** Auth, Isaiah and the restoration community, Rev & Exposito, fall 68; auth, Obadiah, In: Broadman Commentary, Broadman, 72; The condemnation of Edom in post-exilic Judaism, In: Use of the Old Testament in the New and or Other Essays, Duke Univ, 72; coauth, Introduction to the Bible, Ronald, 73; auth, Ammon, Moab and Edom--Early States-Nations of Jordan in the Biblical Period, Biblical Archaeol, Vol 0059, 96; contrib, Excovation at Tel Dalit, 96; contrib, Tel Ira, 99. **CONTACT ADDRESS** 212 Harrington, Waco, TX 76706. **EMAIL** bruce_cresson@baylor.edu

CRIBBET, JOHN E.
DISCIPLINE LAW **EDUCATION** Ill Wesleyan Univ, AB, LLD; Univ Ill, JD. **CAREER** Dean emer, Univ Ill Urbana Champaign. **RESEARCH** Concentrated most of his teaching and research efforts on the law of property. **SELECTED PUBLICATIONS** Co-auth, Cases and Materials on Property; Principles of the Law of Property. **CONTACT ADDRESS** Law Dept, Univ of Illinois, Urbana-Champaign, 52 E Gregory Dr, Champaign, IL 61820. **EMAIL** jcribbet@law.uiuc.edu

CRITES, STEPHEN DECATUR
PERSONAL Born 07/27/1931, Elida, OH, m, 1955, 4 children **DISCIPLINE** PHILOSOPHY OF RELIGION **EDUCATION** OH Wesleyan Univ, BA, 53; Yale Univ, BD, 56, MA, 59, PhD(philos theol), 61. **CAREER** Instr philos & relig, Colgate Univ, 60-61; from asst prof to assoc prof relig, Prof Relig & PROF PHILOS, WESLEYAN UNIV, 69-; Managing ed, Christian Scholar, 63-65; ed, Studies Relig, 71-. **MEMBERSHIPS** Soc Relig Higher Educ; Am Philos Asn; Am Acad Relig. **RESEARCH** Hegel; post-Hegelian developments in 19th century philosophy and theology; philosophy of religion in modern existentialism. **SELECTED PUBLICATIONS** Transl, Crisis in the Life of an Actress and Other Essays on Drama, Collins & Harper Torch, 67; auth, In the twilight of Christendom: Hegel vs Kierkegaard on faith and history, Studies Relig, 72; Pseudonymous Authorship as Art and as Act, In: Kierkegaard: A Collection of Critical Essays, Doublday Anchor, 72; Continuities, Soundings, fall 73; Angels We Have Heard, In: Religion as Story, Harper & Row, 76; Dialectic and Gospel in the Development of Hegel's Thinking, PA State Univ Press, 98. **CONTACT ADDRESS** Dept of Philos, Wesleyan Univ, Middletown, CT 06457. **EMAIL** scrites@wesleyan.edu

CRITTENDEN, CHARLES
PERSONAL Born 11/11/1933, Durham, NC, d, 3 children **DISCIPLINE** PHILOSOPHY **EDUCATION** Univ NC-Chapel Hill, BA, 54, MA, 57; Cornell Univ, PhD, 64. **CAREER** Instr, Univ Fla, 60-65; asst prof, Fla State Univ, 65-70; prof, 76-, Cal State Univ-Northridge, 70-; Phi Eta Sigma; Phi Beta Kappa. **MEMBERSHIPS** Am Philos Asn. **RESEARCH** Philosophy of language; Philosophy of mind; Philosophy of religion; Social and political philosophy. **SELECTED PUBLICATIONS** auth Unreality: The Metaphysics of Fictional Objects, Cornell Univ Press, 92; In Support of Paganism: Polytheism as Earth-based Religion, Midwest Stud Philos, 97. **CONTACT ADDRESS** Dept of Philosophy, California State Univ, Northridge, 18111 Nordhoff St., Northridge, CA 91330-8253. **EMAIL** charles.crittenden@csun.edu

CROCKETT, WILLIAM
PERSONAL Born 09/05/1946, Tisdale, SK, Canada, m, 1970, 2 children **DISCIPLINE** NEW TESTAMENT **EDUCATION** Univ Winnipeg, BA; Princeton Seminary, MDiv; Univ Glasgow (Scotland), PhD. **CAREER** Prof New Testament; Alliance Theol Seminary, 80-. **MEMBERSHIPS** SBL **SELECTED PUBLICATIONS** Through No Fault of Their Own?, 91; ed, Four Views on Hell, 92. **CONTACT ADDRESS** Alliance Theol Sem, 350 N. Highland Ave., Nyack, NY 10960.

CROKE, PRUDENCE MARY
PERSONAL Born Woonsocket, RI **DISCIPLINE** THEOLOGY, SCRIPTURE **EDUCATION** Salve Regina Col, BA, 56; Cath Univ Am, MA, 68; Boston Univ, PhD, 75. **CAREER** Tchr gen educ, St Mary's Sch, 47-56; tchr Eng & relig, St Catherine Acad, 56-59; missionary & tchr, Inst Maria Regina, 59, tchr relig, St Xavier's Acad, 61-68; instr Theol & Scripture, Salve Regina Univ, 68-71; teacher theol & scripture, St Mary's-Bay View, 75-77; from Asst Prof to Assoc Prof, 77-00, Prof Theol & Scripture, Salve Regina Univ, 82-; Prof diocesan, Inst Lay Ministry. **MEMBERSHIPS** Cath Theol Soc Am ; Col Theol Soc; Mercy Higher Educ Colloquium; Mercy Asn Scripture & Theol. **RESEARCH** Systematic theology; sacramental theology; New Testament. **SELECTED PUBLICATIONS** Auth, Roman Cath Concepts of the Eucharist and Spiritual Growth in Interrelation with Erikson's Theory of Development in the Life Span, Univ Micro, 75; Eucharistic Devotions Throughout History, Salve Regina Univ, 92; Worship, Sacraments, Salve Regina Univ, 93. **CONTACT ADDRESS** Salve Regina Univ, Newport Univ, 100 Ochre Point Ave, Newport, RI 02840-4192. **EMAIL** croke@salve.edu

CROMWELL, WILLIAM C.
DISCIPLINE INTERNATIONAL RELATIONS OF WESTERN EUROPE **EDUCATION** Emory Univ; BA; Am Univ, MA, PhD. **CAREER** Prof Emeritus, Am Univ. **RESEARCH** Foreign policy of major powers. **SELECTED PUBLICATIONS** Auth, The United States and the European Pillar, St. Martin's Press, 92. **CONTACT ADDRESS** American Univ, 4400 Massachusetts Ave, Washington, DC 20016.

CRONCE, PHILIP
PERSONAL Born 06/20/1965, St Cloud, MN, s **DISCIPLINE** PHILOSOPHY **EDUCATION** St. John's Univ Collegeville, Minn, BA; DePaul Univ Chicago Ill, MA; ABD. **CAREER** Instr, Chicago State Univ, 97-. **MEMBERSHIPS** Am Philos Asn, Soc for Philos and Existential Philos, Int Max Scheler Ges-

sellschaft, Am Mac Scheler Soc. **RESEARCH** Value Theory, Applied Ethics, Continental Philosophy. **CONTACT ADDRESS** Chicago State Univ, 5624 N Artesian Ave, Chicago, IL 60659. **EMAIL** pcronce@hotmail.com

CRONK, GEORGE
PERSONAL Born 12/24/1948, Haledon, NJ **DISCIPLINE** LAW; PHILOSOPHY; RELIGION **EDUCATION** Paterson State College, BA, 63; Rutgers Univ, MA, 65; S IL Univ, PhD, 71; Rutgers Univ, JD, 84. **CAREER** Attorney solo practice 91-, George Cronk, JD PhD, Attorney at Law; Asst Prof, Assoc Prof, Prof, 72-, Bergen Comm College; Asst Prof 70-72, College Misericordia; teach Asst 68-69, S IL Univ; instr 66-68, Union College NJ; teach Asst, Rutgers Univ, 64-65. **HONORS AND AWARDS** NJ Dept Higher Edu Fel; Princeton Grad Fel; SIU Phi Kappa Pi; SIU Univ Fel; Ntl Defen Grad Fel, Rutgers Univ; Kappa Delta Pi; Kappa Delta Pi Acad Schlshp. **MEMBERSHIPS** APA; CLS; SAAP; NJRPA; CCHA; NJSB; SCP; CCGEA. **RESEARCH** History of Philosophy; Philosophical Theology and Anthropology; Epistemology; Traditional and Modern Logic; Comparative Religions; Biblical Studies. **SELECTED PUBLICATIONS** Auth, The Philosophical Anthropology of George Herbert Mead, NY, Peter Lang, 87; The Message of the Bible: An Orthodox Christian Perspective, Crestwood NY, St Vladimir's Seminary Press, 82; translated, Eight Philo Classics: Intro Readings from, Plato, Aristotle, Anselm of Canterbury, Thomas Aquinas, Rene Descartes, David Hume, Immanuel Kant, Jean-Paul Sarte, Orlando FL, Harcourt Brace, 98; Six Classics of Eastern Philosophy: Selections from Confucius, Lao Tzu, Nagarjuna, Vasubandhu, Shamkara, Ramanuja, Orlando FL, Harcourt Brace, 98; The Gospel of John, Orthodox Study Bible: New Testament and Psalms, Nashville, Thomas Nelson Pub, 93; ed, Readings in Philosophy: Eastern & Western Sources, Plymouth MI, Hayden-McNeil, 01. **CONTACT ADDRESS** Dept of Philos and Relig, Bergen Comm Col, Paramus, NJ 07652. **EMAIL** george9252@msn.com

CROOMS, LISA A.
DISCIPLINE CONTRACTS, CRITICAL RACE THEORY, AND GENDER AND LAW **EDUCATION** Howard Univ, BA, 84; Univ Mich, JD, 91. **CAREER** Assoc prof. **MEMBERSHIPS** Adv bd, Women's Rights Proj of Human Rights Watch. **RESEARCH** US obligations under the International Convention for the Elimination of All Forms of Racial Discrimination. **SELECTED PUBLICATIONS** Auth, Indivisible Rights and Intersectional Indentities or, What Do Women's Human Rights Have to Do with the Race Convention, 40 Howard Law J, 97; Speaking Partial Truths and Preserving Power: Deconstructing White Supremacy, Patriarchy, and the Rape Corroboration Rule in the Interest of Black Liberation, 40 Howard Law J, 97; Stepping into the Projects: Lawmaking, Storytelling, and Practicing the Politics of Identification, 1 Mich J Race & Law 1, 96; An Age of [Im]Possibility: Rhetoric, Welfare Reform, and Poverty, 94 Mich Law Rev 1953, 96; Don't believe the hype: black women, patriarchy and the new welfarism, 38 Howard Law J 611, 95; Single Motherhood, the Rhetoric of Poverty and Welfare Reform: A Case of Gender Discrimination in the United States, in From Basic Needs to Basic Rights: Shaping the Women's Rights Agenda for the 90s and Beyond, Inst for Women, Law & Develop, 95; Women, Work, and Family: The National Welfare Reform Debate, Black Political Agenda, 3rd Quart, 94 & Legal Medicine for Sexual Harassment of Health Care Workers, 10:7 Healthspan 12, 93. **CONTACT ADDRESS** Dept of Law, Howard Univ, 2400 Sixth St NW, Washington, DC 20059.

CROSBY, DONALD A.
PERSONAL Born 04/07/1932, Mansfield, OH, m, 1999, 2 children **DISCIPLINE** PHILOSOPHY, RELIGION **EDUCATION** Davidson Col, BA, 53; Princeton Theol Sem, BD, 56; ThM, 59; Columbia Univ, PhD, 63. **CAREER** Asst prof, Centre Col of Ky, 62-65; from asst prof to prof, philos, Colo State Univ, 65- . **HONORS AND AWARDS** Honors prof, 81; Burlington Northern award for grad tchg and res, 89; John N. Stern distinguished fac award, 94. **MEMBERSHIPS** APA; Am Acad Relig; Highlands Inst for Am Relig and Philos Thought; Soc for Advancement of Am Philos; Soc for the Study of Process Philos. **RESEARCH** Philosophy of nature; pragmatism; Process philosophy. **SELECTED PUBLICATIONS** Auth, Horace Bushnell's Theory of Language, in the Context of Other Nineteenth-Century Philosophies of Language, Mouton, 75; auth, Interpretive Theories of Religion, Mouton, 81; auth, The Specter of the Absurd: Sources and Criticisms of Modern Nihilism, SUNY, 88; co-ed, Religious Experience and Ecological Responsibility, Peter Lang, 96; co-ed, Pragmatism, Neo-Pragmatism, and Religion: Conversations with Richard Rorty, Peter Lang, 97; coed, Religion in a Pluralistic Age: Proceedings of the Third International Conference on Philosophical Theology, Peter Lang, 01. **CONTACT ADDRESS** 5151 Boardwalk Dr, Unit K2, Fort Collins, CO 80525. **EMAIL** donaldcrosby@compuserve.com

CROSSLEY, JOHN P.
PERSONAL Born 12/27/1929, Oakland, CA, m, 1984, 2 children **DISCIPLINE** THEOLOGY, ETHICS **EDUCATION** Pepperdine Univ, AB, 51; Princeton Theol Sem, BD, 54; San Francisco Theol Sem, ThD, 62. **CAREER** Prof, Hastings Col, 62-70; prof, Univ of S Calif, 70-. **HONORS AND AWARDS** Ravbenheimer Awd for Excellence in Teaching and Res, Univ of S Calif, 42; Dart Awd for Academic Innovation, Univ of S Calif, 75. **MEMBERSHIPS** Pacific Coast Theol Soc, Soc of Christian Ethics, Soc for Values in Higher Educ, Am Acad of Relig. **RESEARCH** Nineteenth and twentieth century theological ethics. **SELECTED PUBLICATIONS** Auth, "The Relevance of Schleiermacher's Ethics Today," New Athenaeum IV (94); auth, "Christ's Consciousness and the Christian's Consciousness of Christ in the Ethics of Schleiermacher," Understanding Schleiermacher, Edwin Mellen Press (New York), 98; auth, "Schleiermacher's Christian Ethics in Relation to His Philosphical Ethics," The Annual of the Soc of Christian Ethics, 98. **CONTACT ADDRESS** Sch of Relig, Univ of So California, 3501 Trousdale Pkwy, Los Angeles, CA 90089-0355. **EMAIL** crossley@usc.edu

CROSSON, FREDERICK J.
PERSONAL Born 04/27/1926, NJ, m, 1953, 5 children **DISCIPLINE** PHILOSOPHY **EDUCATION** Cath Univ Am, BA, 49, MA, 50; Univ Notre Dame, PhD, 56 **CAREER** Inst, Asst Prof, Assoc Prof, Prof, 53-67, Dean, 68-75, Prof of Philos, 76-84, Prof of Humanities, 84-, Univ Notre Dame **HONORS AND AWARDS** Knights of Columbus Fel, 49-50; Fr Govt Fel, 51-52 **MEMBERSHIPS** Phi Beta Kappa; Am Philos Asn. **RESEARCH** Phenomenology, Philos of Relig **SELECTED PUBLICATIONS** Auth, The Narrative of Conversion: Newman and Augustine, Tradition and Renewal, Louvain, 93; auth, Augustine's Confessions in The Augustinian Tradition. **CONTACT ADDRESS** Dept of Philos, Univ of Notre Dame, Notre Dame, IN 46556. **EMAIL** crosson.1@nd.edu

CROSTHWAITE, JANE FREEMAN
PERSONAL Born 11/07/1936, Salisbury, NC, m, 1964 **DISCIPLINE** AMERICAN RELIGIOUS HISTORY **EDUCATION** Wake Forest Univ, BA, 59; Duke Univ, MA, 62, PhD(relig), 72. **CAREER** Asst dean women & instr philos, Wake Forest Univ, 62-64; head corp rec, Harvard Bus Sch Libr, 64-65q instr English, Queens Col, NC, 69-72, registr, 72-74, assoc prof relig, 74-76; lectr philos & relig, Univ NC, Charlotte, 76-79; Asst Prof Relig, Mount Holyoke Col, 79- **MEMBERSHIPS** Am Acad Relig; MLA; Church Hist Soc. **RESEARCH** American religious history; Emily Dickinson; women in American religion. **SELECTED PUBLICATIONS** Auth, Spiritual Spectacles--Vision and Image in Mid-19th-Century Shakerism, Jour Interdisciplinary Hist, Vol 0026, 95; The Carmelite Adventure--Dickinson, Clare,Joseph Journal of the Trip To America and Other Documents, Church Hist, Vol 0063, 94. **CONTACT ADDRESS** Dept of Relig, Mount Holyoke Col, 50 College St, South Hadley, MA 01075-1461.

CROUCH, MARGARET
DISCIPLINE PHILOSOPHY **EDUCATION** Colo State Univ, BA, 78; Univ Minn, PhD, 85. **CAREER** Prof, Eastern Michigan Univ. **HONORS AND AWARDS** Distinguished tchg awd, 94. **RESEARCH** Feminist philosophy, philosophy of language. **SELECTED PUBLICATIONS** Auth, A 'Limited' Defense of the Genetic Fallacy; Feminist Philosophy and the Genetic Fallacy; The Social Etymology of Sexual Harassmen; Thinking About Sexual Harrassment: A Guide for the Perplexed. **CONTACT ADDRESS** Dept of History and Philosophy, Eastern Michigan Univ, 701 Pray-Harrold, Ypsilanti, MI 48197. **EMAIL** phi_crouch@online.emich.edu

CROUTER, RICHARD E.
PERSONAL Born 11/02/1937, Washington, DC, m, 1960, 2 children **DISCIPLINE** HISTORY OF THEOLOGY **EDUCATION** Occidental Col, AB, 60; Union Theol Sem, BD, 63, ThD, 68. **CAREER** From instr to asst prof 67-73, assoc prof, 73-79, prof relig, Carleton Col, 79-, John M. and Elizabeth Musser Prof of Religious Studies, 97-, Univ Toronto, 72-73; Am Coun Learned Soc fel, 76-77; sr Fulbright scholar, Univ Marburg, 76-77, 91-92; David and Marian Adams Bryn-Jones Distinguished Teaching Prof of Humanities, 93-96, DAAD (German Academic Exchange Service) Fellowship, Univ Munich, 01. **MEMBERSHIPS** Am Soc Church Hist; Am Acad Relig; Hegel Soc Am. **RESEARCH** History of Christian thought; Schleiermacher, Hegel, Kierkegaard. **SELECTED PUBLICATIONS** Auth, Schleiermacher and the Theology of Bourgeois Society: A Critique of the Critics, 86; coauth,Traveling with Luther and Marx: On and Off the Luther Trail in the GDR, 84; auth, Ambrose, Bishop of Milan, 87; transl, Friedrich Schleiermacher, on Religion: Spelcher to its Cultural Despisers, 88, 96; auth, A Historical Demurral,88; auth, Revolution and the Religious Imagination in Kierkegaard's Two Ages, 91; auth, Friedrich Schleiermacher Between Enlightenment and Romanticism, 03. **CONTACT ADDRESS** Dept of Relig, Carleton Col, 1 N College St, Northfield, MN 55057-4044. **EMAIL** rcrouter@carleton.edu

CROWE, FREDERICK E.
PERSONAL Born 07/05/1915, Jeffries Corner, NB, Canada **DISCIPLINE** THEOLOGY **EDUCATION** Univ NB, BS, 34; Loyola Col, Univ Montreal, BA, 43; Gregorian Univ (Rome), STD, 53; Col de l'Immaculee-Conception (Montreal), LPhil, 62; DLitt(hon), St Mary's Univ, 71; DD(hon), Trinity Col, Univ Toronto, 77; LLD(hon), St Thomas Univ, 82; DD(hon), Univ St Michael's Col, 86. **CAREER** Tchr, St Mary's Col (Halifax), 43-46; ordained priest, 49; tchr theol, 53-75, res prof, 75-80, Prof Emer, Regis Col (Toronto), 80-, dir, Lonergan Res Inst, 85-91, dir emer, 91-; vis prof, Gregorian Univ (Rome), 64, 84. **HONORS AND AWARDS** John Courtney Murray Awd, 77. **MEMBERSHIPS** Can Theol Soc; Cath Theol Soc Am; Jesuit Philos Asn. **SELECTED PUBLICATIONS** Auth, A Time of Change, 68; auth, Escatologia e missione terrena in Gesu di Nazareth, 76; auth, Theology of the Christian Word: A Study in History, 78; auth, The Lonergan Enterprise, 80; auth, Old Things and New: A Strategy for Education, 85; coed, Collection, 88; auth, Appropriating the Lonergan Idea, 89; coed, Insight: A Study into Human Understanding, 92; coed, Philosophical and Theological Papers, 1958-64, 96; coed, Verbum: Word and Idea in Aquinas, 97; coed, Grace and Freedom: Operative Grace in the Thought of St. Thomas Aquinas, 00. **CONTACT ADDRESS** Lonergan Research Inst, Univ of Toronto, 10 St. Mary St, Suite 500, Toronto, ON, Canada M4Y 1P9.

CROWELL, STEVEN G.
PERSONAL Born 06/02/1953, San Diego, CA, m, 1992 **DISCIPLINE** PHILOSOPHY **EDUCATION** Univ Calif, Santa Cruz, BA, 74; Northern Ill Univ, MA, 76; Yale Univ, PhD, 81. **CAREER** Vis asst prof, Fordham Univ, 82-83; asst prof, 83-87, assoc prof, 88-97, prof, 98-, Rice Univ. **HONORS AND AWARDS** DAAD; NEH. **MEMBERSHIPS** APA; Soc for Phenomenology and Existential Philos; Husserl Cir; N Am Kant Soc; N Am Nietzsche Soc; Heidegger Conf. **RESEARCH** Phenomenology; European philosophy since Kant; aesthetics; philosophy of history. **SELECTED PUBLICATIONS** Auth, Making Logic Philosophical Again, (1912-1916), in Kisiel, ed, Reading Heidegger from the Start, SUNY Albany, 94; auth, Solipsism, Modalities of the Strange, in Crowell, ed, The Prism of the Self, Kluwer, 95; auth, Heidegger's Phenomenological Decade, Man and World, 95; ed, The Prism of the Self: Philosophical Essays in Honor of Maurice Natanson, Kluwer, 95; auth, Being Truthful, in Drummond, ed, The Truthful and the Good: Essays in Honor of Robert Sokolowski, Kluwer, 96; auth, The Mythical and the Meaningless: Husserl and The Two Faces of Nature, in Nenon, ed, Issues in Husserl's Ideas II, Kluwer, 96; auth, The Cunning of Modernity: Ibanez-Noe, Heidegger, and Nietzsche, Int Stud in Philos, 96; auth, Husserl, Derrida, and the Phenomenology of Expression, Philos Today, 96; auth, Emil Lask: Aletheiology as Ontology, Kant-Studien 87, 96; auth, Dogmatic Anti-Foundationalism, Semiotica, 96; auth, Ontology and Transcendental Phenomenology Between Husserl and Heidegger, in Hopkins, ed, Husserl in Contemprary Context, Kluwer, 97; auth, Philosophy As A Vocation: Heidegger and University Reform in The Early Interwar Years, Hist of Philos Q, 97; auth, Neighbors in Death, Res in Phenomenology XXVII, 97; auth, Neo-Kantianism, in Critchley, ed, A Companion to Continental Philosophy, Blackwell, 98; auth, Mixed Messages: The Heterogeneity of Historical Discourse, Hist and Theory, 98. **CONTACT ADDRESS** Dept of Philosophy, Rice Univ, MS-14, Houston, TX 77005-1892. **EMAIL** crowell@rice.edu

CROWLEY, SUE MITCHELL
PERSONAL Born 10/31/1933, Columbus, OH, m, 1954, 2 children **DISCIPLINE** RELIGION AND LITERATURE **EDUCATION** St Mary's College Notre Dame, BA, cum laude 55; Ohio State Univ, MA, 68; Univ Iowa, course work for PhD. **CAREER** Instr, lectr, Asst Dir, 72 to 02, Univ Missouri; Instr, 82-84, Stephens College; lectr, Instr, 68-79, Univ Iowa; teacher, 67, Ursuline Acad. **HONORS AND AWARDS** Honors Teacher of the Year. **MEMBERSHIPS** AAR; MLA; Cen MO Colloquium on the Study of Religion. **RESEARCH** John Updike; Walker Percy; Robert Lowell; Toni Morrison. **CONTACT ADDRESS** 409 South Greenwood, Columbia, MO 65203.

CROWNFIELD, DAVID R.
PERSONAL Born 06/24/1930, Quincy, MA, d, 3 children **DISCIPLINE** RELIGION, PHILOSOPHY **EDUCATION** Harvard Univ, AB, 51, ThM, 58, ThD, 64; Yale Univ, BD, 54. **CAREER** Instr Relig, Middlebury Col, 61-62; asst prof Philos & Relig, Alma Col, Mich, 62-64; from asst prof to assoc prof, 64-71, prof Philos & Relig, Univ Northern Iowa, 71-98; prof Emeritus, 98-. **HONORS AND AWARDS** Iowa Regents Awd for Excellence, 93. **MEMBERSHIPS** Soc Phenomenol & Existential Philos; Am Theol Soc; Am Acad Relig; Am Philos Asn; NAm Heideger Conf. **RESEARCH** Phenomemology of religious experience; hermeneutics; Heidegger; God. **SELECTED PUBLICATIONS** Auth, Karl Barth: 1886-1968, N Am Rev, Spring 69; Tradition, domination, and resurrection, McCormick Quart, 3/70; The curse of Abel: An essay in biblical ecology, N Am Rev, Summer 73; Religion in the cartography of the unconscious, Summer 75 & The self beyond itself: Hermeneutics and transpersonal experience, Summer 79, J Am Acad Relig; Postmodern perspectives in theology and philosophy of religion, contemporary philos, 89; God among the signifiers, Man and World, 93; The question of God: Thinking after Heidegger, Philosophy Today, 96; auth, "The Last God," in Companion to Heidegger's Contriburtions to Philosophy (Indiana Univ Pr, 01). **CONTACT ADDRESS** Dept of Philosophy & Religion, Univ of No Iowa, Cedar Falls, IA 50614-0501. **EMAIL** david.crownfield@uni.edu

CROY, MARVIN J.
DISCIPLINE PHILOSOPHY OF SCIENCE, PHILSOPHY OF EDUCATION, PHILOSOPHY OF TECHNOLOGY **EDUCATION** FL State Univ, BA, 69, PhD, 79. **CAREER** Assoc prof, Univ NC, Charlotte. **HONORS AND AWARDS** NEH grant, summer sem, Univ MD, College Park, 83; Nat Sci Found grant, 90, 91, 97; NEH, summer inst, 94. **RESEARCH** Educ applications of computer tech, espec using computers to teach logic. **SELECTED PUBLICATIONS** Auth, Collingridge and the Control of Educational Computer Technology, Soc for Philos and Technol Electronic Quart J, 1(4), 1-15, 96; An Incrementalist View of Proposed Uses of Information Technology in Higher Education, Philosophy in the Contemporary World, 4, 1-9, 97; coauth, Assessing the Impact of a Proposed Expert System via Simulation, J of Educ Comput Res, 13, 1-15, 95. **CONTACT ADDRESS** Univ of No Carolina, Charlotte, Charlotte, NC 28223-0001. **EMAIL** mjcroy@email.uncc.edu

CRUISE, WARREN MICHAEL
PERSONAL Born 06/03/1939, Baltimore, MD, d **DISCIPLINE** LAW **EDUCATION** Morgan St U, AB 1963; Howard Univ Law Sch, JD 1970. **CAREER** Nat Ed Assn, legal cnsl 1985; Nghbrhd Legal Srv Prg, staff atty. **HONORS AND AWARDS** MJ Naylor Meml Awd; high acad achvmt in field of Philosophy. **MEMBERSHIPS** Vp, bd of dir NEA Credit Union; mem Retirement Bd, NEA Kappa Alpha Psi Frat; Phi Alpha; Delta Law Frat; NAACP; Nat Bar Assn; Conf of Black-Lwyrs; Am Bar Assn. **CONTACT ADDRESS** 1201 16th St NW, Washington, DC 20036.

CRUMBLEY, DEIDRE H.
PERSONAL Born 12/12/1947, Philadelphia, PA, s **DISCIPLINE** ANTHROPOLOGY, RELIGION & CULTURE **EDUCATION** Temple Univ, BA, 70; North Western, MA, 84, PhD, 89; Harvard, MTS. **CAREER** Jr res fel, 82-84, African Studies Dept; Univ of Ibadan Nigeria West Africa, 82-86; jr lectr, 84-86, Arecheology & Anthropology; Rollins Col, 88-91, Anthropology; Univ FL, Anthropology, 91-98; asst prof, 98, NC State Univ, Africana Studies, Multidisciplinary Studies Div. **HONORS AND AWARDS** Lilly Fel, 79; Fubright Hays, 85; Ford Post doc fel, 91. **MEMBERSHIPS** Amer Anthropological Assn; Amer Acad Religion; **RESEARCH** Religion and change in Africa and the African disapora **SELECTED PUBLICATIONS** Auth, West African Journal of Archeology & Anthropology, vol 16, Ibadan, Nigeria, 88; Impurity and Power: Women in Aladura churches, Africa, 92; Even a Woman: Sex Roles and Mobility in an Aldura Hierarchy, Sept 14, 1988; "Also Chosen: Jews in the Imagination of a Black Storefront Church" IN: Anthropology and Humanism (apublication of the American Anthropological Association) vol 25, issue #1, April 00, pp 6-23; "On Being First: Dogma, Disease and Domination in the Rise of an African Church" In: Religion (an international journal on religion, culture, and society based in London and Berkeley) Volume 30 issue #2-April pp 169-184. **CONTACT ADDRESS** Africana Studies/Div of Multidisciplinary Studies, No Carolina State Univ, Raleigh, NC 27695-7107. **EMAIL** deidre_crumbley@ncsu.edu

CRUMP, ARTHEL EUGENE
PERSONAL Born 10/19/1947, New York, NY, m, 1970 **DISCIPLINE** LAW **EDUCATION** Nebraska Wesleyan Univ, 1965-67; Univ of Nebraska at Lincoln, BA, sociology, 1973; Univ of Nebraska College of Law, JD 1976. **CAREER** Legal Service of Southeast Nebraska, Attorney, 76-82; Nebraska Gov Robert Kerrey, legal counsel, 83-85; Nebraska Dept of Justice, deputy atty general, 85-91, general counsel, chief deputy tax commissioner, 91; Nebraska Wesleyan University, Criminal Justice Department, visiting instructor, 92, 95, 98; Central Interstate Low-Level Radioactive Waste Commission, general counsel, executive director, 91-. **HONORS AND AWARDS** Nebraska Law College, scholarship; Kelso Morgan Scholarship; Council on Legal Educ Opportunity Stipend; Alumni Achievement Awd, Nebraska Wesleyan University; Silver Key Awd, Law Student Division, American Bar Assn; Community Leaders of America; Univ of Nebraska-Lincoln, Maurice Kremer lecturer. **MEMBERSHIPS** Nebraska State Bar Assn House of Delegates; Natl Assn of Atty Generals; Natl Gov's Assn; Educ Comm of the States; board of directors, Univ of NE Gymnastic Booster Club; board of directors, Family Serv Assn of Lincoln; board of directors, United Way of Lincoln & Lancaster Cos; board of directors, Theater Arts for Youth; board of directors, Malone Comm Ctr; board of directors, Lincoln Comm Playhouse, board of directors, Malone Headstart Program; panel mem Nebraska Arts Council; Touring Artists' Progs; Minority Arts Adv Comm; NAACP; Nebraska Civil Liberties Union; Coalition of Black Men; Univ of Nebraska Booster Club Womens' Athletics; bd of trustees, Nebraska Wesleyan Univ; advs comm, Lincoln Public Schools Gifted Children; advs committee, Lancaster Co Child Care; advs committee, NE Leg Sub-Comm Revision of Licensing Regulations for Child Care Insts; advs committee, Lincoln Public Schools Multi-Cultural Educ; reorganization of cofare advs comms, Lancaster Co Ad Hoc Comm; Malone Area Citizens Council; Lincoln Public Schools Evaluation of Student Health Educ Project; State Dept of Public Welfare Comm to Review Daycare Center Licensing Standards; board of directors, Pinewood Bowl Assn; board of directors, Leadership Lincoln; Nebraska State Bar Assn Ways, Means and Planning Comm, board of directors; Nebraska Supreme Court Judicial Nomination Commission; Lincoln Bar Assn; Midwest Bar Assn; Natl Low-Level (Radioactive) Waste Forum Commission Rep; Lincoln Interfaith Council; Cornhusker Council BSA, board of directors; Crucible Club; Troop 49 Boy Scouts of America, Arborland Dist; Nebraska Urban League; NAACP; Foundation for Educational Funding, board of directors; First Natl Bank/Lincoln, board of directors; Nebraska Wesleyan Univ, board of directors; Newman United Methodist Church; Board of Higher Educ & Campus Ministry, Nebraska United Methodist Church. **CONTACT ADDRESS** Central Interstate Low-Level Radioactive Waste Commission, 1033 "O" St, Ste 530, Lincoln, NE 68508. **EMAIL** acrump@cillrwcc.org

CRUMP, DAVID
PERSONAL Born 02/26/1956, Los Angeles, CA, m, 1976, 3 children **DISCIPLINE** NEW TESTAMENT STUDIES **EDUCATION** Univ Aberdeen, Scotland, PhD, 88. **CAREER** Minister, Christian Reformed Church, 88-97; assoc prof, Calvin Col, 97-. **MEMBERSHIPS** Soc of Bibl Lit. **RESEARCH** New Testament Theology; First Century Judaism. **SELECTED PUBLICATIONS** Auth, "The Virgin Birth in New Testament Theology," 89; "The Preaching of George Whitefield and His Use of Matthew Henry's 'Commentary,'" 89; "Jesus, the Victorious Scribal-Intercessor in Luke's Gospel," 92; "Truth," 92; Jesus the Intercessor: Prayer and Christology in Luke-Acts, 92; "Applying the Sermon on the Mount: Once You Have Read It, What Do You Do With It?," 92; "Gone to Hog Heaven," 99. **CONTACT ADDRESS** Dept of Religion & Theology, Calvin Col, 3201 Burton St SE, Grand Rapids, MI 49546. **EMAIL** dcrump@calvin.edu

CRUSTO, MITCHELL F.
PERSONAL Born 04/22/1953, New Orleans, LA, s, 2 children **DISCIPLINE** LAW **EDUCATION** Yale Col, BA, 75; Oxford Univ, BA, 80; MA, 85; PhD; Yale Law Sch, JD, 81. **CAREER** Lectr, Webster Univ, 86; Wash Univ Bus Sch, 85-89; President Bush's Initiative on Historically Black Col, 89-91; Environ Law Inst, 93; assoc prof, Loyola Univ Sch of Law, 95-. **HONORS AND AWARDS** United Way Leadership Participant, 91-; British-Am Project for the Successor Generation, 87-; Who's Who Among Am Lawyers, 91-. **MEMBERSHIPS** La Bar Assoc; Mo Bar Assoc; IL Bar Assoc; Am Bar Assoc; Federal Bar Assoc; US Court of Appeals; Fifth Circuit; US District Court; US Tax Court; Chartered Inst of Arbitration, England; Honorable Soc of the Middle Temple, Britain. **SELECTED PUBLICATIONS** Ed, Business Law, Web Pub, 88-97; auth, "Reflections on Insider Trading", Sloan Management Rev, Fall 87; auth, "Federalism and Civil Rights, The Meredith Case", Nat Black Law J, (Summer 89); auth, "Business Roundtable on Environmental Management", Corporal Legal Times, 93; auth, "Environmental risk Management Programs Expand into the Banking Community", IL Banker, July 93; auth, "The Supreme Court's New Federalism: An Anti-Rights Agenda?", Ga State Univ Law Rev, 99; auth, "All That Glitters Is Not Gold: A Congressionally-Driven Global Environmental Policy, Georgetown Int Environ Law Rev, June 99. **CONTACT ADDRESS** Sch of Law, Loyola Univ, New Orleans, 6363 St Charles Ave, New Orleans, LA 70118-6143.

CRUZ, DAVID B.
DISCIPLINE CONSTITUTIONAL LAW **EDUCATION** Univ Calif, Irvine, BS , BA 88; Stanford Univ, MS,91; NYork Univ, JD,94. **CAREER** Assoc prof,Univ Southern Calif, clerked for, Honorable Edward R. Becker, Circuit Judge US Ct Appeals 3rd Circuit; bristow fel to, Off Solicitor Gen Wash, DC. **RESEARCH** Civil rights & constitutional law. **SELECTED PUBLICATIONS** Auth, Piety & Prejudice: Free Exercise Exemption from Laws Prohibiting Sexual Orientation Discrimination. **CONTACT ADDRESS** School of Law, Univ of So California, University Park Campus, Los Angeles, CA 90089.

CRUZ, VIRGIL
PERSONAL Born 12/21/1929, New York, NY, m **DISCIPLINE** THEOLOGY **EDUCATION** Houghton Coll, BA Greek major 53; Pittsburgh Seminary, MDiv 56; Vrije Universiteit Amsterdam, Neth, PhD 73. **CAREER** Hebron United Presb Ch, 56-60; Univ of Dubuque Seminary, prof of New Testament 66-82; Western Theol Seminary, prof of Biblical studies, 82-86; Louisville Presbyterian Theological Seminary, professor, 86-. **HONORS AND AWARDS** Purdy Scholarship Pittsburgh Seminary 54; Lee Church Hist Awd Pittsburgh Seminary 56; Foreign Student Scholarship Vrije Univ 60; Grant from German Govt for language study 68; Higgins Fellowship (2 times); Presb Grad Fellowship 72; Houghton College, LHD, 91; Westminster College, DD, 92. **MEMBERSHIPS** Moderator Albany Presbtery 59-60; chair Natl Comm for Ordination Examin 79-80; mem Gen Assembly Cncl of Presby Ch 84-; mem The Soc of Biblical Literature 68-; mem The Soc for the Study of Black Religion 75-; dir Presbyterians United for Biblical Concerns 85-; dir Found for Educ & Rsch 85-. **SELECTED PUBLICATIONS** Auth, The Mark of the Beast, A Study of Charagma in the Apocalypse, Amsterdam Acad Press, 73. **CONTACT ADDRESS** New Testament, Louisville Presbyterian Theol Sem, 1004 Alta Vista Rd, Louisville, KY 40205.

CRYSDALE, CYNTHIA S. W.
PERSONAL Born 09/08/1953, Pittsburgh, PA, m, 1976, 2 children **DISCIPLINE** THEOLOGY AND ETHICS; MORAL DEVELOPMENT **EDUCATION** Univ St Michaels Col, Toronto, PhD, 87. **CAREER** Asst to assoc prof, Cath Univ Amer, Wash DC, 89-; **HONORS AND AWARDS** Christian Faith & Life Sabbatical grant Louisville Inst, 98. **MEMBERSHIPS** Soc Christian Ethics; Col Theol Soc; Can Theol Soc; Cath Theol Soc Am. **RESEARCH** Feminist ethics; Theology of suffering; Women in church & society; Ethics & genetics. **SELECTED PUBLICATIONS** Auth, Reason, Faith, and Authentic Religion, The Struggle Over the Past: Religious Fundamentalism in the Modern World, Univ Press Amer, 93; auth, Gilligan and the Ethics of Care: An Update, Relig Studies Rev, 94; auth, Women and the Social Construction of Self-Appropriation, Lonergan & Feminism, 94; auth, Lonergans Philosophy and the Religious Phenomenon: A Commentary, Method: Jour of Longergan Studies, 94; auth, Horizons that Differ: Women and Men and the Flight From Understanding, Cross Currents, 94; auth, Religious Education and Adult Life Stages, Evangelical Outlook, 94; ed, Lonergan and Feminism, Univ Toronto Press, 94; auth, Revisioning Natural Law: From the Classicist Paradigm to Emergent Probability, Theol Studies, 95; auth, Christian Marriage and Homosexual Monogamy, Our Selves, Our Souls and Bodies, Cowley Press, 96; auth, Feminist Theology: Ideology, Authenticity, and the Cross, Eglise et Theologie, 97. **CONTACT ADDRESS** Dept of Religion & Religious Education, Catholic Univ of America, Washington, DC 20064. **EMAIL** crysdale@cua.edu

CRYSTAL, NATHAN M.
PERSONAL Born 03/30/1946, Macon, GA, m, 1974, 2 children **DISCIPLINE** CONTRACTS, PROFESSIONAL RESPONSIBILITY, AND INCOME TAX **EDUCATION** Univ PA, BS, 68; Emory Univ, JD, 71; Harvard Univ, LLM, 76. **CAREER** Prof, 69. **HONORS AND AWARDS** COIF. **SELECTED PUBLICATIONS** Coauth, Problems on Contract Law; auth, An Introduction to Professional Responsibility, 98; auth, Professional Responsibility: Problems of Practice and the Profession, 2nd editon, 00. **CONTACT ADDRESS** School of Law, Univ of So Carolina, Columbia, Law Center, Columbia, SC 29208. **EMAIL** Nathan@law.law.sc.edu

CSIKSZENTMIHALYI, MARK
DISCIPLINE RELIGION **EDUCATION** Harvard, AB, 87; Stanford Univ, PhD, 94. **CAREER** Asst prof, Davidson Col, asst prof, Univ Wis Madison. **HONORS AND AWARDS** Fel Nat Hum Ctr, Res Triangle Pk NC, 97-98. **RESEARCH** China's Han Dynasty (202 BCE-220 CE). **SELECTED PUBLICATIONS** Auth, Fivefold Virtue: Reformulating Mencian Moral Psychology in Han Dynasty China, Religion; coed, Essays on Religious and Philosophical Aspects of the Laozi. **CONTACT ADDRESS** East Asian Lang and Lit, Univ of Wisconsin, Madison, 1220 Linden Dr, Madison, WI 53706. **EMAIL** macsikszentm@facstaff.wisc.edu

CUA, ANTONIO S.
PERSONAL Born 07/23/1932, Manila, Philippines, m, 1956, 1 child **DISCIPLINE** PHILOSOPHY **EDUCATION** Far Eastern Univ Manila, BA, 52; Univ of Cal Berkeley, MA, 54, PhD, 58. **CAREER** Teach Asst, 55-58, Univ of Cal, Berkeley; Instr, Asst Prof, 58-62, Ohio Univ; Prof, dept Chmn Philo, 62-69, SUNY Coll at Oswego; vis Prof Philo, 68-69, Catholic Univ Amer; vis Prof Philo, 74-75, Univ Missouri; vis Prof Philo, 75, George Mason Univ; vis Prof Philo, 76-77, Univ Hawaii; external examiner, 87-89, Presby School Christ Edu; external examiner, 84-85, Chin Univ Hong Kong, 87-88, Macquarie Univ, 91-, Academia Sinica; consultant, 91-00, NSC Taiwan; vis pro Lectr, 95, Nat Tsing Hua Univ Hsin Chu Taiwan; Prof Philo, 69-95, Emeritus Prof, 96-, Cath Univ Amer. **HONORS AND AWARDS** SUNY res fel; Woodrow Wilson fel; Chiang Ching-Kuo Foundation res scholar. **MEMBERSHIPS** APA, SACP, Intl Soc Chinese Philo. **RESEARCH** Chinese ethics, moral philosophy, history of ethics. **SELECTED PUBLICATIONS** Auth, Reason and Virtue, A Study in the Ethics of Richard Price, Athens Ohio Univ Press, 66; Dimensions of Moral Creativity, Paradigms Principles and Ideas, Univ Park, Penn State Univ Press, 78; The Unity of Knowledge and Action, A Study in Wang Yang-ming's Moral Psychology, Honolulu, Univ Hawaii Press, 82; Ethical Argumentation, A Study in Hsun Tzu's Moral Epistemology, Honolulu Univ Hawaii Press, 85; Moral Vision and Tradition, Essays in Chinese Ethics, Wash Cath Univ Press, 98; Between Commitment and Realization, Wang Yang-ming's Vision of the Universe as a Moral Community, in: Philo East & West, 93; A Confucian Perspective on Self-Deception, in: Self and Deception, eds, R Ames and W Dissanayake, Albany, SUNY Press, 96; Reason and Principle in Chinese Philosophy, in: A Companion to World Philosophy, eds, E Deutsch and R Bontekoe Oxford Blackwell, 97; Confucian Philosophy, Chinese, in: Routledge Encyclopedia of Philosophy, London Routledge 98. **CONTACT ADDRESS** School of Philosophy, Catholic Univ of America, Washington, DC 20064. **EMAIL** cua@cua.edu

CUBIE, DAVID LIVINGSTON
PERSONAL Born 02/12/1928, Perth, Scotland, m, 1952, 4 children **DISCIPLINE** RELIGION **EDUCATION** Eastern

Nazarene Col, AB, 51; Nazarene Theol Sem, BD, 54; Boston Univ, PhD, 65. **CAREER** Pastor, Church of the Nazarene, 54-57 & Congregational Christian Churches, 57-66; asst prof Bible & theol, 66-71, assoc prof then prof, relig, 69-71, Eastern Nazarene Col; Chmn Div Philos & Relig, Mt Vernon Nazarene Col, 71-93. **HONORS AND AWARDS** Co teach of the yr, Eastern Nazarene Coll, 69; teach of the yr, Mount Vernon Nazarene Coll, 79, 91; Distinguished Fac Lect, Mount Vernon Nazarene Coll, 82; Gould Lect, Eastern Nazarene Coll, 82. **MEMBERSHIPS** North American Academy of Ecunemilists; Relig Educ Assn; Wesleyan Theol Soc. **RESEARCH** The theology of John Wesley and its origins; contemporary church history. **SELECTED PUBLICATIONS** Art, A Wesleyan Perspective on Christian Unity, Wesleyan Theological Journal, 97-98. **CONTACT ADDRESS** Div of Philos & Relig, Mount Vernon Nazarene Col, 800 Martinsburg Rd, Mount Vernon, OH 43050-9500. **EMAIL** dcubie@mvnc.edu

CUBIE, MICHAEL
PERSONAL Born 11/02/1948, San Francisco, CA, d, 1 child **DISCIPLINE** PHILOSOPHY, PSYCHOLOGY **EDUCATION** San Jose State Univ, BA, 79; MS, 84; Wright Inst, PhD, 88. **CAREER** Counselor, Seven Step Found, 76-78; Counselor, Meadows Boys Home, 80-83; therapist, Bill Wilson Crisis Center, 84-89; counselor, County Health Dept, 87-89; Dir, STEPS Alcohol Prog, 89-90, clinical psychologist, Agnews Develop Center, 90-93, instr, Masters Inst, 93-00, instr, W Valley Col, 93-00. **MEMBERSHIPS** Nat Assoc of Black Psychol; Bay Area Assoc of Black Psychol; Nat Caucus and Center on Black Aged; Nat Black Child Develop Inst. **RESEARCH** Racism and societal institutions, cross cultural psychology, cultural-historical approaches in definitions of psychological functioning, impact of brain lesion on psychological and behavioral functioning. **SELECTED PUBLICATIONS** Auth, The Relationship of Employment and Education to the Role of the Black Father; auth, The Missing Link In the Afro-Centric Perspective. **CONTACT ADDRESS** Dept Counseling, West Valley Col, 14000 Fruitvale Ave, Saratoga, CA 95070-5640. **EMAIL** michael_cubie@wymccd.cc.ca.us

CUDD, ANN E.
DISCIPLINE PHILOSOPHY **EDUCATION** Swarthmore Col, BA, 82; MA Philosophy, 84, MA, Economics, 86, PhD, 88, Univ Pittsburgh **CAREER** Asst Prof, 91-93, Occidental Col; Asst Prof, 88-94, Assoc Prof, 94-, Prof, Univ Kansas, 00-; Dir of Women's Studies, 01-. **RESEARCH** Philos of social science, decision theory, feminist theory, social and political philos. **CONTACT ADDRESS** Dept of Philos, Univ of Kansas, Lawrence, Lawrence, KS 66045. **EMAIL** acudd@ku.edu

CUFFEY, KENNETH H.
PERSONAL Born 04/21/1956, Bloomington, IN, m, 1980, 4 children **DISCIPLINE** BIBLICAL STUDIES, OLD TESTAMENT **EDUCATION** Drew Univ, PhD, 87. **CAREER** Coll pastor, Ind, 81-83; adj fac, Trinity Divinity School, 87-94; Alliance Theol Sem, 87-94; Drew Univ, 87-94; pastor, Wyckoff NJ, 88-94; Scholar, Dir, Christian Studies Center, Ill, 94-. **MEMBERSHIPS** Soc of Bibl Lit; Inst for Bibl Res. **RESEARCH** Coherence in Old Testament/Hebrew Bible Books; Hebrew Prophets & Wisdom Literature. **CONTACT ADDRESS** 314 E. Daniel, Champaign, IL 61820. **EMAIL** klcuffey80@aol.com

CULBERTSON, DIANA
PERSONAL Born 09/18/1930, Atlanta, GA **DISCIPLINE** COMPARATIVE LITERATURE, RELIGION **EDUCATION** Siena Heights Col, BA, 52: John Carroll Univ, MA, 58; Univ NC, Chapel Hill, PhD(comp lit), 71; Aquinas Inst Theol, Iowa, MA, 80. **CAREER** Lectr world lit, St John Col Cleveland, 63-65; instr English, Univ NC, Chapel Hill, 70-71; asst prof, 71-76, Assoc Prof Comp Lit, Kent State Univ, 76-, Danforth Found fel, 76. **MEMBERSHIPS** MLA; Am Acad Relig; Am Comp Lit Asn; Cath Theol Soc Am. **RESEARCH** Comparative literature; religion; theology. **SELECTED PUBLICATIONS** Auth, Aint-Nobody-Clean, the Liturgy of Violence in Glory--Self-Sacrificing Racial Violence in Zwick, Edward Film, Rel and Lit, Vol 0025, 93; Inscribing the Other, So Hum Rev, Vol 0028, 94; The Jews Body, So Hum Rev, Vol 0028, 94. **CONTACT ADDRESS** Dept of English, Kent State Univ, PO Box 5190, Kent, OH 44242-0001.

CULBERTSON, ROBERT G.
PERSONAL Born 05/12/1940, Eldora, IA, m, 1968, 2 children **DISCIPLINE** CRIMINAL JUSTICE **EDUCATION** Webster City Junior Col, AA, 60; Univ Iowa, BA, 62; MA, 64; Univ Cincinnati, PhD, 74. **CAREER** Lecturer, NDEA Summer Inst, Univ Dayton, 67; Instr, Univ Dayton, 66-68; Teaching Fel, Univ Cincinnati, 69-70; Asst Prof, Indiana State Univ, 68-74; Assoc Prof, Grand Valley State Col, 74-76; Prof and Consultant, Univ Wisc, 96-. **HONORS AND AWARDS** Distinguished Service Awd, Maryville Area Chamber of Commerce, 93; Phi Mu Alpha Sinfonia, 90; Founder's Awd, Acad of Criminal Justice Sciences, 84; Distinguished Service Awd, Ill State Univ, 82; Charles P. Taft Fel, Univ Cincinnati, 70-71; Honor Society, Iowa Junior Col, 58-60. **MEMBERSHIPS** Acad of Criminal Justice Sci, Am Asn for Higher Educ, Am Soc of Criminol, Am Soc for Quality Control, Am Sociol Asn, Nat Council on Crime and Delinquency, Nat Org for Victim Assistance, Southern Poverty Law Center. **RESEARCH** Convicted but innocent. **SELECTED PUBLICATIONS** Co-ed, Order Under Law, Readings in Criminal Justice Fifth Ed, Prospect Heights, 97; auth, "Restructuring Academic and Administrative Structures in a Comprehensive University; A Case Study in Politics and Process," in 1996: A Collection of Papers on Self-Study and Institutional Improvement, North Central Asn of Colleges and Schools, 96; auth, "Institutional and Organizational Antecedents of Role Stress, Work Alienation, and Anomie among Police Executives," in criminal Justice and Behavior, (95): 152-171; co-ed, Juvenile Delinquency: A Justice Perspective third Ed, Waveland Press, 95; co-ed, Order Under Law, Readings in Criminal Justice, Fourth Ed, Waveland Press, 92; auth, "Using Composite Measures in Police Cynicism Research: An Application of Canonical Factor Regression," Journal of Quantitative Criminology, (91): 41-58; auth, "Managing the Curriculum: Faculty Governance vs. Administrative Budget Control," in A Collection of Papers on Self-Study and Institutional Improvement, North Central Asn of Colleges and Schools, (91): 79-82; auth, "Career Stage and Cynicism Among Police Chiefs," Justice Quarterly, (90): 593-614; co-ed, Juvenile Delinquency: A Justice Perspective Second Ed, Waveland Press, 90; auth, "Police Cynicism, Job Satisfaction, and Work Relations of Police Chiefs: An Assessment of the Influence of Department Size," Sociological Focus, (89): 161-171. **CONTACT ADDRESS** Dept Criminal Justice, Univ of Wisconsin, Madison, 1 Univ Plaza, Platteville, WI 53818. **EMAIL** culbertR@uwplatt.edu

CULHANE, MARIANNE B.
PERSONAL Born 07/12/1946, Baltimore, MD, m, 1977, 4 children **DISCIPLINE** SECURED TRANSACTIONS, BANKRUPTCY **EDUCATION** Carleton Col, BA, 68; Univ Iowa Col Law, JD, 74. **CAREER** Law Clerk, 74-76; assoc, Eisenstatt, Higgins, Kinnamon, 76-77; Creighton Law School, 77-. **HONORS AND AWARDS** Phi Beta Kappa; Order of the Coif, 74; Kelley Awd for Excellence in Res, 98. **MEMBERSHIPS** ABA, Nebr State Bar Assoc, Am Bankruptcy Inst. **RESEARCH** Consumer Bankruptcy Empirical Studies. **SELECTED PUBLICATIONS** Coauth, "Debt After Discharge: An Empirical Study of Reaffirmation", 73 Am Bankruptcy Law Jour 709-74, (99); coauth, "Taking the New Consumer Bankruptcy Model for a Test Drive: Means Testing Real Chapter 7 Debtors," 7 Am Bankruptcy Inst Law Rev 27-77, (99). **CONTACT ADDRESS** Sch of Law, Creighton Univ, 2500 California Plz, Omaha, NE 68178. **EMAIL** mculhane@creighton.edu

CULLINAN, ALICE R.
PERSONAL Born 05/21/1939, s **DISCIPLINE** RELIGIOUS STUDIES **EDUCATION** Carson-Newman Col, BA; Southwestern Baptist Theol Seminary, PhD. **CAREER** Prof. **HONORS AND AWARDS** Teaching of the Year Awd, 90; Outstanding Advisor of the Year, 99. **MEMBERSHIPS** N.C. Baptist Professors of Relig. **SELECTED PUBLICATIONS** Auth, Time for a Checkup: Assessing Our Progress in Spiritual Growth, Christian Lit Crusade, 94; pubs on spiritual growth in various Christian periodicals; auth, "Sorting it Out: Understanding God's Call to Ministry," Judson Press, 00. **CONTACT ADDRESS** Dept of Religious Studies and Philosophy, Gardner-Webb Univ, PO Box 7286, Boiling Springs, NC 28017. **EMAIL** drac@shelby.net

CULP, SYLVIA
DISCIPLINE PHILOSOPHY **EDUCATION** Univ Calif, PhD; Univ Va, PhD. **CAREER** From asst prof to assoc prof, Philos, W Mich Univ; dir, grad asst. **SELECTED PUBLICATIONS** Auth, "Defending Robustness: The Bacterial Mesosome as a Test Case," PSA Vol 1, 94; auth, "Objectivity in Experimental Inquiry: Breaking Data-Technique Circles;" auth, "Establishing Genotype/Phenotype Relationships: Gene Targeting as an Experimental Approach." **CONTACT ADDRESS** Philos Dept, Western Michigan Univ, 320 Moore Hall, 1903 W Michigan Ave, Kalamazoo, MI 49008-5328. **EMAIL** sylvia.culp@wmich.edu

CULPEPPER, R. ALAN
PERSONAL Born 03/02/1946, Little Rock, AR, m, 1967, 2 children **DISCIPLINE** THEOLOGY **EDUCATION** Baylor Univ, BA, 67, MDiv 70, Southern Baptist Theological Seminary; attended Goethe Institute, 70; Duke Univ, PhD, 74; Sabbaticals: Cambridge Univ, 80-81; Louisville Kentucky, 87-88. **CAREER** Pastor, Macedonia Baptist Church, 68-70; part-time instr, Duke Univ, 71; research asst for W.D. Davies, 71-73; asst prof of New Testament Interpretation, 74-80, assoc prof of New Testament Interpretation, 80-85, assoc dean, sch of theology, 84-87, 88-91, James Buchanan Harrison prof of New Testament Interpretation, 85-91, Southern Baptist Theological Seminary; vis prof, 83, Vanderbilt Divinity Sch; vis prof, 91-92, prof of relig 92-95, Baylor Univ; dean, 95- , McAfee Sch of Theology, Mercer Univ. **MEMBERSHIPS** Westar Institute; Studiorum Novi Testamenti Societas; Society of Biblical Lit, Literary Aspects of the Gospels Group, chairperson 86-91, Semeia, editorial board, 91-; Natl Assn of Baptist Professors of Religion, president, 99. **SELECTED PUBLICATIONS** Auth, John, the Son of Zebedee: The Life of a Legend, 94, received 1995 Choice Outstanding Academic Book Award; auth, The Gospel of Luke, The New Interpreter's Bible, 95; coed, Exploring the Gospel of John, 96; ed, Critical Readings of John 6, 97; The Gospel and Letters of John, 98. **CONTACT ADDRESS** McAfee Sch of Theol, Mercer Univ, Cecil B. Day, 3001 Mercer Univ Dr, Atlanta, GA 30341-4115. **EMAIL** culpepper_ra@mercer.edu

CUMING, RON
DISCIPLINE LAW **EDUCATION** Univ Saskatchewan, BA, 62, LLB, 63; Univ Columbia, LLM, 67. **CAREER** Vis prof, Univ of British Columbia, 72-74; asst dean, Univ of British Columbia, 74-76; chairperson of the Saskatchewan Law Reform Commission, 78-82. **HONORS AND AWARDS** Tchg Excellence Awd, 93, Distinguished Res Awd, 98. **MEMBERSHIPS** Member, Law Soc of Saskatchewan. **RESEARCH** Nat and international secured financing law; debtor-creditor law and bankruptcy. **SELECTED PUBLICATIONS** Auth, Alberta Personal Property Security Act Handbook, Carswell, 96; Alberta Personal Property Security Act Handbook, Carswell, 97; coauth, Saskatchewan and Manitoba Personal Property Security Handbook, Carswell, 95; Commercial and Consumer Transactions; Cases, Text and Materials, 95. **CONTACT ADDRESS** Col of Law, Univ of Saskatchewan, 15 Campus Dr, Saskatoon, SK, Canada S7N 5A6. **EMAIL** Cuming@law.usask.ca

CUMINGS, BRUCE
PERSONAL Born 09/05/1943, Rochester, NY, m, 3 children **DISCIPLINE** POLITICAL SCIENCE **EDUCATION** Columbia Univ, PhD, 75. **CAREER** Asst prof, Swarthmore Col, 75-77; Assoc prof, prof, int stud, Univ Washington, 77-87; prof, Univ Chicago, 87-94; John Evans Prof Int Hist and Polit, Northwestern Univ, 94-97; Norman and Edna Freehling Prof, Univ Chicago, 97-. **HONORS AND AWARDS** John Fairbank Bk Awd, Am Hist Asn, 83; Quincy Wright Bk Awd, Int Stud Asn, 92; Elected to Am Acad of Arts & Sciences, 99; principal hist consult, thames television/pbs documentary, korea: the unknown war. **MEMBERSHIPS** Asn for Asian Stud; Am Hist Asn; Am Polit Sci Asn. **RESEARCH** Modern Korean history; United States - East Asian relations; international political economy; American foreign relations. **SELECTED PUBLICATIONS** Auth, Origins of the Korean War, Princeton, 81, 90; auth, War and Television, Verso, 92; auth, Korea's Place in the Sun: A Modern History, Norton, 97; auth, Parallax Visions: American-East Asian Relations at Century's End, Duke, 99. **CONTACT ADDRESS** Dept of Hist, Univ of Chicago, 1126 E 59th St, Chicago, IL 60637. **EMAIL** Bcumings@midway.uchicago.edu

CUMMINGS, RICHARD M.
PERSONAL Born 03/23/1938, New York, NY, m, 1965, 2 children **DISCIPLINE** POLITICAL SCIENCE **EDUCATION** Princeton Univ, BA 59; Columbia Univ, JD, 62; Cambridge Univ, MLitt, 65, PhD, 89. **CAREER** Prof, Pace Univ School of Law, 87-95; prof, John Marshall Law Sch, 95-98. **HONORS AND AWARDS** Buchanan Prize, polit, Princeton Univ. **MEMBERSHIPS** PEN Am Ctr; Natl Asn Scholars. **RESEARCH** Political sciences; history. **SELECTED PUBLICATIONS** Auth, Proposition Fourteen: A Secessionist Remedy, Grove, 81; auth, The Pied Piper: Allard K. Lowenstein and the Liberal Dream, Grove, 85; ed and intro, Nine Scorpions in a Bottle: Great Judges and Cases of the Supreme Court by Max Lerner, Arcade, 95. **CONTACT ADDRESS** PO Box 349, Bridgehampton, NY 11932. **EMAIL** cummings01@earthlink.net

CUMMINS, W. JOSEPH
DISCIPLINE PHILOSOPHY; CLASSICS **EDUCATION** Xavier Univ, AB, 70; Emory Univ, MA, 71, PhD, 75; Univ Cincinnati, MA, 76, PhD, 89. **CAREER** Asst prof, Old Dominion Univ, 76-80; from asst prof to assoc prof, 84-, Grinnell Col. **RESEARCH** Greek and Roman philosophy; intellectual history **CONTACT ADDRESS** Dept of Philosophy, Grinnell Col, Grinnell, IA 50112. **EMAIL** cummins@grinnell.edu

CUNNINGHAM, JACK R.
DISCIPLINE CHRISTIAN EDUCATION **EDUCATION** Cent Baptist Col BA; Mid-Am Sem, MA; SW Baptist Theol Sem, PhD. **CAREER** Adj instr, Cent Baptist Col; instr, Inst Christian Stud Southwestern Sem; admin distance edu, Sem Extension of the S Baptist Convention; J.M. Frost assoc prof, S Baptist Theol Sem; vis prof on sabbatical summer 00. **RESEARCH** Areas of experiential learning assessment, distance education and adult education. **SELECTED PUBLICATIONS** Auth, ed, ten teachers' and study guides on the subjects of Old Testament, New Testament and teaching; pub(s), on non-traditional education methodology. **CONTACT ADDRESS** Sch Christian Edu and Leadership, So Baptist Theol Sem, 2825 Lexington Rd, Louisville, KY 40280. **EMAIL** jcunningham@sbts.edu

CUNNINGHAM, L. A.
PERSONAL Born 07/10/1962, Wilmington, DE, m, 1999 **DISCIPLINE** LAW **EDUCATION** Univ Delaware, BA 85; Benjamin N Cardozo Sch Law, JD 88. **CAREER** Benjamin N. Cardozo Sch Law, asst prof, assoc prof, prof, 92 to Present-; Samuel and Ronnie Heyman Cen, dir, since 97; Geo. Wash U. Law Sch., vis. Prof. 96-97; Cravath Swaine Moore, assoc, 88-92, 92-94; Skadden Arps Slate Meagher Flom, assoc, 87. **HON-**

ORS AND AWARDS Phi Alpha Theta; NY Bar Assoc Leg Ethics Prize; Samuel Belkin Awd; Who's Who Amer Law. **MEMBERSHIPS** ABA; NYSBA; ABCNY; **RESEARCH** Corporate Governance; Finance; Accounting; Contracts; Markets; Ethics. **SELECTED PUBLICATIONS** Auth, The Essays of Warren Buffet: Lessons for Corporate America, Cunningham, 98; Introductory Accounting and Finance for Lawyers, west 2d ed, 99; Corporate Finance and Governance: Cases, Materials and Problems, with Lawrence E. Mitchell and Lewis D. Solomon, Carolina 96; Corporations Law and Policy, 5th ed West, with E. Weiss and J. Barman; Corbin on Contracts, Annual Supplements, with Arthur J. Jacobson, West 96; auth; The Modern Sensibility of New York's New Business Corporation Law, Aspen Law Bus, 98; Preventive Corporate Lawyering: Averting Accounting Scandals, Cardozo Life, 97; Game Theory and Non-Rundable Retainers: A Response to Professors Croson and Mnookin, with Lester Brickman, Harv Neg Law Rev, 97. **CONTACT ADDRESS** Benjamin N. Cardozo Sch of Law, Yeshiva Univ, 55 Fifth Av, New York, NY 10003. **EMAIL** cunning@ymail.yu.edu

CUNNINGHAM, SARAH B.
PERSONAL Born 04/15/1967, Pittsfield, MA **DISCIPLINE** PHILOSOPHY **EDUCATION** Kenyon Coll, BA, 89; Vanderbilt Univ, MA, 97; PhD candidate, 98. **CAREER** Instr, Belmont Univ, 96-97; asst prof, Univ Maine, 97-98; dir of develop, Verde Valley School, 98-99. **HONORS AND AWARDS** Burke Tchg Fel, Vanderbilt Univ. **MEMBERSHIPS** Am Philos Asn; German Studies Asn. **RESEARCH** Eighteen Century Aesthetics (Kant, Rousseau); Continental Philosophy; Social and Political Thought. **CONTACT ADDRESS** Univ of Maine, 5776, Orono, ME 04469. **EMAIL** developuus@sedena.net

CUNNINGHAM, SARAH GARDNER
PERSONAL Born 12/30/1956, Rochester, MN, 2 children **DISCIPLINE** HISTORY AND RELIGION **EDUCATION** Princeton Univ, BA, 79; Union Theol Sem, MDiv, 89, PhD, 84. **CAREER** Macmillan Lib Ref, Simon and Schuster Acad Ref, 94-98; Marymont Sch, Upper Sch History, 98-. **MEMBERSHIPS** AAR; AHA; ASCH. **RESEARCH** US Religious History; Hist of Christianity; Gender Studies. **CONTACT ADDRESS** 1735 York Ave, #6C, New York, NY 10128. **EMAIL** sgcunningham@atsearthlink.net

CUNNINGHAM, SUZANNE M.
PERSONAL Born Albany, NY, m, 1977 **DISCIPLINE** PHILOSOPHY **EDUCATION** Fla State Univ, PhD, 72. **CAREER** Prof emer, Loyola Univ, Chicago, 98. **HONORS AND AWARDS** Res fel, Inst for Adv Studies in the Humanities, Univ Edinburgh, Scotland, fall, 85; honors teacher of the yr, Loyola Univ, 83-84; Danforth assoc, 76-81; Marion Hay Dissertation award, Fla State Univ, 73; Woodrow Wilson Dissertation fel, 71-72; Univ fel, Fla State Univ, 68-69. **MEMBERSHIPS** Amer Philos Asn; Philos of Sci Asn; Soc for Women in Philos; Soc for Adv of Amer Philos. **RESEARCH** Mind/brain; Evolution and 20th century philosophy. **SELECTED PUBLICATIONS** Article, Two Faces of Intentionality, Philos of Sci, 64, 445-460, Sept, 97; auth, Darwinism and Ethics, Blackwell's Dict of Bus Ethics, Oxford, Blackwell, 97; auth, Ordinary Language Philosophy and Phenomenology, Encycl of Phenomenol, Dordrecht, Kluwer, 97; auth, Classical Modern Philosophy and Husserl's Phenomenology, Encycl of Phenomenol, Dordrecht, Kluwer, 97; auth, Philosophy and the Darwinian Legacy, Univ Rochester Press, 96; article, Dewey on Emotions: Recent Experimental Evidence, Transactions of the C. S. Peirce Society: A Quarterly Journal in American Philosophy, 31, 4, 865-874, Fall, 95; article, Herbert Spencer, Bertrand Russell, and the Shape of Early Analytic Philosophy, Russell, Jour of the Bertrand Russell Archiv, 14, 1, 7-29, Summer, 94; auth, What is a Mind? An Integrative Introduction to Philosophy of Mind, Hackett, 00. **CONTACT ADDRESS** Dept. of Philosophy, Loyola Univ, Chicago, Chicago, IL 60626. **EMAIL** scunnin@orion.it.luc.edu

CURD, MARTIN VINCENT
PERSONAL Born 04/25/1951 **DISCIPLINE** PHILOSOPHY OF SCIENCE, EPISTEMOLOGY **EDUCATION** Univ Cambridge, BA, 72; Univ Pittsburgh, MA, 74, PhD, 78. **CAREER** Instr hist & philos sci, Univ Pittsburgh, 75-77; Mellon instr humanities & philos, Vanderbilt Univ, 77-78; Asst Prof, 78-84, Assoc Prof Philos, Purdue Univ, 84-. **MEMBERSHIPS** Am Philos Asn; Philos Sci Asn. **RESEARCH** The logic of discovery; the Copernican revolution; the direction of time; incongruent counterparts. **SELECTED PUBLICATIONS** Auth, The Logic of Discovery: An Analysis of Three Approaches, in Scientific Discovery, Logic and Rationality: Proceedings of the First Leonard Conf, D Reidel, Dordrecht, Holland, 80; The Rationality of the Copernican Revolution, PSA, 82; coauth, Professional Responsibility For Harm, Kendall/Hunt Publ Co, 84; Principles of Reasoning, St. Martin's Press, 89; auth, Argument and Analysis: An Introduction to Philosophy, West, 92; coauth, Philosophy of Science: The Central Issues, W.W. Norton, 98. **CONTACT ADDRESS** Dept of Philos, Purdue Univ, West Lafayette, LAEB 1360, West Lafayette, IN 47907-1360. **EMAIL** curd@purdue.edu

CURD, PATRICIA
DISCIPLINE ANCIENT PHILOSOPHY, ETHICS **EDUCATION** Pittsburgh, PhD. **CAREER** Assoc prof, Purdue Univ. **SELECTED PUBLICATIONS** Published papers on the Presocratics and on the development of Plato's metaphysics. **CONTACT ADDRESS** Dept of Philos, Purdue Univ, West Lafayette, 1080 Schleman Hall, West Lafayette, IN 47907-1080.

CURRAN, VIVIAN
PERSONAL Born 10/30/1955, Philadelphia, PA, m, 1990, 2 children **DISCIPLINE** LAW **EDUCATION** Univ of Penn, BA, 75; Columbia Univ, MA, 77, MPh, 79, PhD, 80, JD, 83. **CAREER** Univ of Pittsburgh School of Law, instr, 89-95, vis asst prof, 95-96, asst prof, 99- . **MEMBERSHIPS** Am Soc Comp. Law, Int Assoc of Legal Semiotics; Int Assoc of Legal Methodology; East-Central Soc for Eighteenth Century Stud; APA; European Community Stud Assoc. **RESEARCH** Law and society, law and language; legal methodology; comparative law. **SELECTED PUBLICATIONS** Auth, Developing and Teaching F Foreign-Language Course for Law Students, J of Legal Educ, 93; auth, Deconstruction, Structuralism, Antisemitism and the Law, Boston Col Law Rev, 94; auth, Cour d'Appel de Grenoble: Ytong v Lasaosa, le 16 juin, 1993, Law and Commerce, 95; auth, Learning French Through the Law: A French/English Comparative Treatment of Terms in a Legal Context, Columbia Univ, 96; auth, Metaphor Is the Mother of All Law, in Kevelson, ed, Law and the Conflict of Ideologies, Lang, 96; auth, Interpretive Decisions Applying CISG: Translation of Claude Witz's The First Decision of France's Court of Cassation Applying the UN Convention on Contracts for the International Sale of Goods, J Law and Commerce, 97; auth, What Should One Think of Judicial Ritual in Law? in Lindgren, ed, Ritual and Semiotics, 97; auth, Vichy France: A Crisis in Legality, Legitimacy and Identity, in European Memory at the Millennium, MIT, 97, (CD ROM); auth, Cultural Immersion, Difference and Categories in US Comparative Law, J Comp Law, 98; auth, Herder and the Holocaust: A Debate about Difference and Determinism in the Context of Comparative Law, in De Coste, ed, The Holocaust: Art, Politics, Law, Education, forthcoming; auth, Dealing in Difference: Comparative Law's Potential for Broadening Legal Perspectives, Am J Comp Law, forthcoming. **CONTACT ADDRESS** Univ of Pittsburgh, 3900 Forbes Ave, Pittsburgh, PA 15260. **EMAIL** curran@law.pitt.edu

CURREN, RANDALL R.
PERSONAL Born 09/19/1955, New Orleans, LA, m, 1987, 3 children **DISCIPLINE** PHILOSOPHY **EDUCATION** Univ New Orleans, BA, philos, 77; Univ Pittsburgh, MA, 81, PhD, 85. **CAREER** Andrew Mellon instr, philos, Calif Inst of Tech, 85-87; instr, philos, Calif Inst of Tech, 87-88; asst prof, 88-95, assoc prof, 95-, Univ Rochester. **HONORS AND AWARDS** Andrew Mellon fel, 77-78; Charlotte Neucombe fel, 83-84; NEH summer stipend, 91; Spencer fel, 91-92; Spencer found grant, 93-94; NEH grant, 97-98. **MEMBERSHIPS** Asn for Philos of Educ; Philos of Educ Soc; Amer Philos Asn; Amer Educ Res Asn; AMINTAPHIL; Amer Soc for Polit and Legal Philos; Soc for Ancient Greek Philos. **RESEARCH** Political philosophy; Philosophy of education; Philosophy of law; Ethics; Ancient philosophy. **SELECTED PUBLICATIONS** Article, The Contribution of Nicomchean Ethics iii 5 to Aristotle's Theory of Responsibility," History of Philosophy Quarterly 6, no. 3, pp. 261-77, July 89; article, Justice, Instruction, and the Good: The Case For Public Education in Aristotle and Plato's Laws, Part III: Why Education Should Be Public And The Same For All, Studies in Philos and Educ, 13, no 1, 1-31, 94; article, Coercion and the Ethics of Grading and Testing, Educ Theory, 45, no 4, 425-441, fall 95; article, "Punishment and Inclusion," Canadian Journal of Law and Jurisprudence 8, no. 2, pp. 259-74, July 95; The Presuppositions of Corrective Justice in Aristotle and What They Imply, The Can Jour of Law and Jurisprudence, 8, no 2, 259-274, jul, 95; article, Justice and the Threshold of Educational Equality, Philos of Educ 1994, 239-248, 95; auth, Aristotle on the Necessity of Public Education, 00; coauth, Ethical Standards of the American Educational Research Association: Cases and Cementary, 01, ed, Philosophy of Education 99, 00; ed, The Blackwell Companion to Philosophy of Education, 02; articles, "Education, History of Philosophy of" and "Education, Philosophy of" in the Routledge Encyclopedia of Philosophy, 98, vol. 3, pp 222-240; articles, "Moral Education and Juvenile Crime," in Nomos XLIII: Moral and Political Education, 01; **CONTACT ADDRESS** Dept. of Philosophy, Univ of Rochester, Rochester, NY 14627. **EMAIL** rcrn@troi.cc.rochester.edu

CURRIE, DAVID P.
PERSONAL Born 05/29/1936, Macon, GA, m, 1959, 2 children **DISCIPLINE** LAW **EDUCATION** Univ Chicago, AB, 57; Harvard Univ, LLB, 60. **CAREER** From asst prof to prof law, Univ Chicago, 62-; chmn, Ill Pollution Control Bd, 70-72. **RESEARCH** Federal jurisdiction; conflict of laws; constitutional law. **SELECTED PUBLICATIONS** Auth, The Constitution in the Supreme Court, 2 vols, Chicago, 85, 90; auth, The Constitution of the Federal Republic of Germany, Chicago, 94; auth, The Constitution in Congress; auth, The Federal Period, 1789-1801, Chicago, 97. **CONTACT ADDRESS** Sch of Law, Univ of Chicago, 1111 E 60th St, Chicago, IL 60637-2702. **EMAIL** david_currie@law.uchicago.edu

CURRIE, JANET
PERSONAL Born, Canada, m, 2 children **DISCIPLINE** ECONOMICS **EDUCATION** Univ Toronto, BA, MA; Princeton Univ, PhD. **CAREER** Asst Prof, UCLA, 88-91; Asst Prof to Assoc Prof, Mass Inst of Technol, 91-93; Assoc Prof to Full Prof, UCLA, 93-. **HONORS AND AWARDS** Lorne T. Morgan Gold Medal in Econ, Univ Toronto, 82; Alfred P. Sloan Found Doc Diss Fel, 87-88; Mass Penti J.K. Kouri Career Dev Chair in Econ, 91-93; Nat Bureau of Econ Res Olin Fel, 92-93; Fel, Can Inst for Adv Res, 97-99. **MEMBERSHIPS** Econometric Soc; Am Econ Asn; Nat Bur of Econ Res. **RESEARCH** Investments in Children. **SELECTED PUBLICATIONS** Auth, Welfare and the Well-Being of Children, Fundamentals of Pure and Applied Economics #59, Harwood Acad Pub, 95; auth, "Does Head Start Make a Difference?" Am Econ Rev, 95; auth, "Health Insurance Eligibility, Utilization of Medical Care, and Child Health," The Quart Journal of Econ, 96; auth, "Saving Babies: The Efficacy and Cost of Recent Expansions of Medicaid Eligibility for Pregnant Women," J of Polit Econ, 96; auth, "The Effect of Welfare on Child Outcomes: What We Know and What We Need to Know," in Welfare the Family and Reproductive Behavior: Research Perspectives, Nat Acad Press, 98; auth, "Health, Health Insurance and the Labor Market," in The Handbook of Labor Economics, Amsterdam, 99; auth, "Child Health in Developed Countries," in The Handbook of Health Economics, Amsterdam, 00; auth, "Early Childhood Intervention Programs: What Do We Know," Journal of Econ Perspectives, 01. **CONTACT ADDRESS** Dept Econ, Univ of California, Los Angeles, 8283 Bunche, PO Box 951477, Los Angeles, CA 90095-1477.

CURRIE, JOHN H.
DISCIPLINE LAW **EDUCATION** Univ Toronto, BA of Science, 87; Univ of Ottawa, BA of Law, 90; Univ of Cambridge, 93. **CAREER** Asst prof, Univ of Ottawa, 97-. **MEMBERSHIPS** Law Soc of Upper Canada; Canadian Asn of Law Teachers; Canadian Coun on International Law; Canadian Lawyers Asn for International Human Rights; Lawyers for Social Responsibility. **RESEARCH** International law; prosecution of crimes against humanity. **SELECTED PUBLICATIONS** Coauth, "Projecting Beyond the Boundaries: A Canadian Perspective on the Double-Edge Swod of Extra-Territorial Acts," in Trilateral Perspectives on Internation Legal Issues: Relevance of Domestic Law and Policy, (Transnational Publishers, 96); auth, Supreme Court of Canada Manual: Practice and Advocacy, Canada Law Book, (96): 425; coauth, Injunctions, Carswell, (96): 237; contrib ed, Settlement Procedure and Precedents in Ontario, Butterworths, (98): 199; auth, "NATO's Humanitarian Intervention in Kosovo: Making or Breaking International Law?" 1998, 36 Canadian Yearbook of Internationl Law xx, (in press); coauth, The Law of riminal Attempt, 2nd ed., Carswell, (forthcoming). **CONTACT ADDRESS** Fac Common Law, Univ of Ottawa, PO Box 450, Ottawa, ON, Canada K1N 6N5. **EMAIL** jhcurrie@uottawa.ca

CURRY, ALLEN
PERSONAL Born Pennsylvania, PA, m, 1965, 2 children **DISCIPLINE** CHRISTIAN EDUCATION **EDUCATION** Temple Univ, Ed.D. **CAREER** VP/AA; Hugh and Sally Reaves prof. **HONORS AND AWARDS** Dir, Edu Svc(s), cord, Production, Great Commn Publ. **SELECTED PUBLICATIONS** Auth, The God We Love and Serve. **CONTACT ADDRESS** Dept of Christian Education, Reformed Theol Sem, Mississippi, 5422 Clinton Blvd, Jackson, MS 39209-3099. **EMAIL** acurr@rts.edu

CURTIN, JOHN C.
PERSONAL Born 11/27/1932, Fulton, NY, m, 1996, 2 children **DISCIPLINE** CRIMINAL JUSTICE **EDUCATION** San Francisco State Col, BA, 56; MA, 63; Univ Calif, PhD, 70. **CAREER** Prof, San Francisco State Col, 67-; director, Criminal Justice Prog, San Francisco State Univ, 83-. **HONORS AND AWARDS** Distinguished Teaching Awd, San Francisco, 69. **RESEARCH** Criminal law/criminal justice, policing, corrections, political economy. **SELECTED PUBLICATIONS** Auth, Justice Demands, 96; auth, Class Justice, 95; auth, Equity and the Underclass, 98; ed, Crime and Wealth, 98. **CONTACT ADDRESS** Dept Criminal Justice Program, San Francisco State Univ, 1600 Holloway Ave, San Francisco, CA 94132. **EMAIL** crimjust@sfsu.edu

CURTIS-HOWE, E. MARGARET
PERSONAL Born Essex, England **DISCIPLINE** RELIGION **EDUCATION** Univ Sheffield, BA, 60; Univ London, cert educ, 61; Univ Manchester, PhD(New Testament & contempt lit), 64. **CAREER** Teacher relig & hist, Withington Girls' Sch, 64-69; asst prof, 72-81, Prof Middle Eastern Stud, Western KY Univ, 81-, Lectr, Ky Humanities Coun, 81-82. **HONORS AND AWARDS** Fulbright scholar, 96-97, Yemen. **MEMBERSHIPS** Soc Bibl Lit; Inst Bibl Res; North Am Patristic Soc; Bibl Archaeol Soc; Am Schs of Oriental Res; TESOL; Midwest Asn Latin Am Stud. **RESEARCH** New Testament; Dead Sea Scrolls; patristics. **SELECTED PUBLICATIONS** A reappraisal of factors influencing the Easter faith of the early Christian community, J Evangelical Theol Soc, summer 75; The place of feeling in religious experience, Collage, fall 75; Women and church leadership, Evangelical Quart, 4-6/79; The

Positive Case for the Ordination of Women, In: Perspectives on Evangelical Theology, Baker, 79; Interpretations of Paul in the Acts of Paul and Thecla, In: Pauline Studies, Paternoster, UK, 80, Eerdmans, 80; Women and Church Leadership, Zondervan, 82; Commentary on the Greek Text of I Corinthians, Word Publ (in prep). **CONTACT ADDRESS** Dept of Relig and Philos, Western Kentucky Univ, 1 Big Red Way St., Bowling Green, KY 42101-5730. **EMAIL** margaret.curtis@wku.edu

CURTLER, HUGH
PERSONAL Born 12/31/1937, Charlottesville, VA, m, 1962 **DISCIPLINE** PHILOSOPHY **EDUCATION** St. John's Col, BA, 59; Northwestern Univ, MA, 62; PhD, 64. **CAREER** Asst Prof, Univ of Rhode Island, 64-66; Asst Prof, Midwestern College, 66-68; Asst Prof-Professor, Southwest State Univ, 68-. **HONORS AND AWARDS** Northwestern Univ Fellowship, 61-64; Younger Humanist Fellowship (N.E.H.), 71-72. **RESEARCH** Axiology; Philosophy of Culture. **SELECTED PUBLICATIONS** Auth, "Ethical Argument (Paragon House); auth, "Rediscovering Values, M.E. Sharpe, Inc.; auth, "Recalling Educator, I.S.I. Press. **CONTACT ADDRESS** Dept Philosophy, Southwest State Univ, 1501 State St., Marshall, MN 56258-3306. **EMAIL** curtler@ssu.southwest.msus.edu

CURZER, HOWARD J.
DISCIPLINE PHILOSOPHY **EDUCATION** Wesleyan Univ, BA, 74, MA, 75; Univ TX, Austin, PhD, 85. **CAREER** Instr, Univ Houston; assoc prof, TX Tech Univ, 85-. **RESEARCH** Ancient philos; ethics. **SELECTED PUBLICATIONS** His work has appeared in The Can J of Philos, Class Quart, Apeiron, Australasian J of Philos, J of Med and Philos, and Hypatia. **CONTACT ADDRESS** Texas Tech Univ, Lubbock, TX 79409-5015. **EMAIL** AUCUR@ttacs.ttu.edu

CUSSINS, ADRIAN
DISCIPLINE PHILOSOPHY **EDUCATION** Oxford Univ, PhD. **CAREER** Asst prof, Univ Ill Urban Champaign. **RESEARCH** Meaning; reference, representation; information, content, experience, philosophy of mind and language, metaphysics, epistemology, philosophy of science. **SELECTED PUBLICATIONS** Auth, "Subjectivity, Objectivity and Frames of Reference in Evans's Theory of Thought," Electronic Journal of Analytic Phgilosophy; auth, "Content, Embodiment and Objectivity," Mind 101, (92), 651-688. **CONTACT ADDRESS** Philosophy Dept, Univ of Illinois, Urbana-Champaign, 810 S Wright, 105F Gregory Hall, Mail Code 468, Urbana, IL 61801. **EMAIL** acussins@uiuc.edu

CUST, KENNETH F. T.
PERSONAL Born 01/29/1953, Edmonton, AB, Canada, m, 1992, 1 child **DISCIPLINE** PHILOSOPHY **EDUCATION** Bowling Green St Univ, PhD, 93. **CAREER** Assoc prof, phil, 95-, found dir, Ctr for Appl & Prof Ethics, Cent Mo St Univ. **HONORS AND AWARDS** Fac Achieve Awd, 95. **MEMBERSHIPS** Amer Soc Phil; Counseling & Psychotherapy; Tenn Phil Assn. **RESEARCH** Phil coun & consult; phil in a prof pvt pract; soc, moral, pol phil; appl phil. **SELECTED PUBLICATIONS** Art, Assault: Just Part of the Job?, Canadian Nurse, 86; art, Hypothetical Contractarianism and the Disclosure Requirement Problem in Informed Consent, J Med Hum 12:3, 91; art, Medicine, Morality, and Concept Reduction, J Med Hum 13:1, 92; authart Contractarianism and Rational Choice, Australian J Pol Phil 27:1, 93; art, Justice and Rights to Health Care, Reason Papers 18, 93; auth, A Just Minimum of Health Care, Univ Press Amer, 97. **CONTACT ADDRESS** Ctr for Applied & Professional Ethics, Central Missouri State Univ, Warrensburg, MO 64093. **EMAIL** kencust@sprintmail.com

CUSTER, JOHN S.
PERSONAL Born 07/17/1958, Jersey City, NJ **DISCIPLINE** SACRED SCRIPTURE, THEOLOGY, CLASSICS **EDUCATION** Seton Hall Univ, BA (Classics), 79; Pontificia Universita Gregoriana, Rome, STB (Theol), 82; Pontificio Istituto Biblico, Rome, SSL (Sacred Scripture), 85; Pontificia Universita Gregoriana, Rome, STD (Sacred Scripture), 87. **CAREER** Instr, Marymount Int School, Rome, 83-86; adjunct prof, Western CT State Univ, Danbury, 88-89; adjunct prof, St Charles Borromeo Sem, Relig Studies Div, Wynnewood, PA, 90-; asst prof, Pontifical Col Josephinum, Col of Liberal Arts, Columbus, OH, 93-96, dean, 93-94, Dir of Pastoral Formation, 93-94, coord of Pastoral Formation, 94-95, dir of recruitment, 94-96, chmn, Dept of Relig Studies, 94-96; instr of Old Testament, Permanent Diaconate Prog, Eparchy of Newton, St Gregory the Theologian Sem, Newton, MA, 95-; prof of Scripture, Byzantine Cath Sem, Pittsburgh, PA, 96-, dean, 96-. **MEMBERSHIPS** Cath Biblical Soc; Soc for Biblical Lit; North Am Patristic Soc. **RESEARCH** Biblical studies; Byzantine Christian studies; Patristics. **SELECTED PUBLICATIONS** Auth, An Ironic Scriptural Wordplay in Byzantine Hymnography, St Vladimir's Theological Quart 37, 93; Byzantine Rite Slavs in Philadelphia: 1886-1916, Record of the Am Cath Hist Soc 104, 93; Qohelet and the Canon: The Dissenting Voice in Dialogue, The Josephinum J of Theol, 1, 94; The Harp, the Psaltery and the Fathers: A Biblical Image and Its Interpreters, The Downside Review, no 394, 96; The Old Testament: A Byzantine Perspective, God With Us Pubs, 96; Why a Hymn? Form and Content in St Ephrem's Hymn 31 on Virginity, St Vladimir's Theol Quart, 40, 96; Uzhorod, Balamand and Beyond: A Uniate Looks to the Millennium, J of Ecumenical Studies, 97; several other publications. **CONTACT ADDRESS** Byzantine Catholic Sem, 3605 Perrysville Ave, Pittsburgh, PA 15124. **EMAIL** Jackcus@aol.com

CUTNEY, BARBARA
PERSONAL Born 08/28/1941, New York, NY, s, 1 child **DISCIPLINE** PHILOSOPHY **EDUCATION** Queens Col, BA, 63; Boston Univ, MA; 70; NY Univ, PhD, 74. **CAREER** Adj to instr, SICC, 71-72; adj, CCNY, 71-72; adj prof, Montclair State, 94; vis assoc prof, NYork Univ, 77-84; assoc prof, Col of New Rochelle, 66-; chair, 99-. **HONORS AND AWARDS** Phi Beta Kappa, 63; NDEA Fel, Western Res, 64; E.S. Brightman Fel, Boston Univ, 65-66; Walter A. Anderson Fel, NY Univ, 71-73; NEH Res Grants, 87, 89, 96; Univ Sem Publ Grant, Columbia Univ, 97. **MEMBERSHIPS** Am Philos Assoc; Soc for Women in Philos; Am Soc for Philos, Counseling and Psychotherapy; Am Philos Practitioners Assoc; Soc for Philos and Pub Affairs. **RESEARCH** Ethics, philosophical practice, mind/body issues, dance. **SELECTED PUBLICATIONS** Coath, "Bertram Ross", Dance Pages, 87; auth, "From the Ground Up", Dance Teacher, 99; auth, Challenges and Pleasures: Living Ethically in a Competitive World. **CONTACT ADDRESS** Dept Relig and Philos, Col of New Rochelle, 29 Castle Pl, New Rochelle, NY 10805. **EMAIL** bcutney@prodigy.net

CUTROFELLO, ANDREW
DISCIPLINE PHILOSOPHY **EDUCATION** Northwestern Univ, PhD, 89. **CAREER** Assoc prof, Loyola Univ, 94-; fac, St. Mary's Col Ind, 89-94. **RESEARCH** Contemporary French philosophy; contemporary European philosophy; psychoanalysis, Hume, Kant, Hegel, Nietzsche. **SELECTED PUBLICATIONS** Auth, Imagining Otherwise: Metapsychology and the Analytic A Posteriori, Northwestern UP, 97; The Owl at Dawn: A Sequel to Hegel's Phenomenology of Spirit, State Univ NY Press, 95; Discipline and Critique: Kant, Poststructuralism, and the Problem of Resistance, State Univ NY Press, 94. **CONTACT ADDRESS** Dept of Philosophy, Loyola Univ, Chicago, 820 N. Michigan Ave., Chicago, IL 60611.

CUTTER, WILLIAM
PERSONAL Born 02/09/1937, St. Louis, MO, m, 1970, 1 child **DISCIPLINE** MODERN HEBREW LITERATURE, EDUCATION **EDUCATION** Yale Univ, AB, 59; Hebrew Union Col, Ohio, MA, 65; Univ Calif, Los Angeles, PhD(Near Eastern lit), 71. **CAREER** From instr to asst prof Hebrew lit, 65-71, asst dean col, 65-69, dir sch educ, sch Judaic studies, 69-76, assoc prof, 71-76, Prof Hebrew Lit Educ, Hebrew Union Col, Calif, 76-. **MEMBERSHIPS** Cent Conf Am Rabbis; AAUP; Asn Jewish Studies; Nat Asn Temple Educr; Nat Comn Jewish Educ. **RESEARCH** Hebrew literature between 1880 and 1940; contemporary Jewish religious education; American Jewish fiction. **SELECTED PUBLICATIONS** Auth, numerous articles and essays. **CONTACT ADDRESS** Sch of Educ, Hebrew Union Col-Jewish Inst of Religion, California, Los Angeles, CA 90007. **EMAIL** cutter@usc.edu

D

D'AGOSTINO, PETER R.
PERSONAL Born 12/22/1962, New York, NY, s **DISCIPLINE** RELIGIOUS STUDIES; HISTORY **EDUCATION** Brown Univ, BA, 80-84; Univ Chicago, MA, 86-87; Univ Chicago, PhD, 87-93 **CAREER** Visiting asst prof, Univ Ill, 94-95; asst prof Relig Studies & History, Stonehill Col, 95 **HONORS AND AWARDS** PEW Grant for Relig in Amer History, 98-99; Fulbright Jr Fac Res Fel, 96; Jr Fel, Univ Chic, 91-92; Giovanni Agnelli Found Italian Amer Studies Fel, 90-91; John T. McNeil Fel, 88-89 **MEMBERSHIPS** Orgn Amer Historians; Immigration History Soc; Amer Italian Historical Assoc; Amer Cath Historical Assoc; Amer Soc Church History; Amer Acad Relig **RESEARCH** U.S. Immigration History; U.S. Religious History; U.S. Society, 1877-1945; Modern Italy **SELECTED PUBLICATIONS** "The Sacraments of Whiteness: Racial Ambiguity and Religious Discipline Among Italians in Urban America," Religion and the City, forthcoming; "Urban Restructuring and the Religious Adaptation: Cardinal Joseph Bernardin of Chicago (1982-1995)," Public Religion and Urban Transformation, NY Univ Pr, forthcoming; "The Crisis of Authority in American Catholicism: Urban Schools and Cultural Conflict," Records of the American Catholic Historical Association of Philadelphia, forthcoming **CONTACT ADDRESS** 22 Bradbury St, Allston, MA 02134. **EMAIL** pdagostino@stonehill.edu

D'AMICO, ROBERT
PERSONAL Born 01/15/1947, Buffalo, NY, m, 2 children **DISCIPLINE** PHILOSOPHY **EDUCATION** SUNY Buffalo, BA, 69, PhD, 74. **CAREER** Asst prof, 74-79, assoc prof, fall 79, actg ch, 79-80, ch, 98-, prof, 00-, Dept of Philos, Univ Fla. **MEMBERSHIPS** APA. **RESEARCH** Philosophy of social science. **SELECTED PUBLICATIONS** Auth, Historicism and Knowledge, 88; Contemporary Continental Philosophy, 98. **CONTACT ADDRESS** Dept of Philosophy, Univ of Florida, 330 Griffin-Floyd Hall, Gainesville, FL 32611-8545. **EMAIL** rdamico@phil.ufl.edu

D'AOUST, JEAN-JACQUES
PERSONAL Born 01/03/1924, Alfred, ON, Canada, m, 1987, 5 children **DISCIPLINE** PSYCHOLOGY OF DEVELOPMENT, WORLD RELIGIONS **EDUCATION** Univ Ottawa, BA, B Ph, 46; St Vincent Sem, MA, 60; Yale Univ, MA, 65; M Ph, 66; PhD, 68; Slippery Rock Univ, MA, 87. **CAREER** Coord, Unied Rel Init; adj prof, Marshall Univ, Ashland Com Coll; assoc prof, Ashland Com Col, ret. **HONORS AND AWARDS** Can Coun Arts Fel; Kent Fel; Yale Univ Fel. **MEMBERSHIPS** ACR; APS; SVHE. **RESEARCH** Psychology of development; world religions; Biblical research; Jesus seminars. **CONTACT ADDRESS** Dept Social Science, Ashland Comm Col, 1400 College Rd, Ashland, KY 41101.

DABNEY, DEAN A.
PERSONAL Born 04/23/1968, Pittsburgh, PA, s **DISCIPLINE** CRIMINOLOGY **EDUCATION** Ind Univ Penn, BA, 90; MA, 93; Univ Fla, PhD, 97. **CAREER** Instr, Univ Fla, 95-97; asst prof, GA State Univ, 97-. **MEMBERSHIPS** Am Soc of Criminol, Acad of Crim Justice Sci. **RESEARCH** Organizational Crime and deviance, Retail Security, Medical Crime, Drug Abuse. **SELECTED PUBLICATIONS** Auth, "Incompetent Jail and Prison Doctors," Prison Journal (forthcoming); auth, "The Relationship Between Crime and Private Security at U.S. Shopping Center," American Journal of Criminal Justice, (99): 601-621; auth, "Motor Vehicle Theft at the Shopping Center: An Application of the routine Activities Approach," Security Journal 12, (99): 63-78; auth, "Illicit Prescription Drug Use Among Pharmacists: Evidence of a Paradox of Familiarity," Work and Occupations 26, (99): 78-108; auth, "Crime in Shopping Centers," Reducing Crime Through Real Estate Development and Management, (98): 91-103; auth, "An Examination of Cases of Prescription Fraud Prosecuted by Fraud Control Units Throughout the United States," Journal of Drug Issues, (97): 807-820; auth, "The Pharmacy Profession's Reaction to Substance Abuse Among Pharmacists: The Process and Consequences of Medicalization," Journal of Drug Issues, (96): 859-874; auth, "Neutralization and Deviance in the Workplace: Theft of Supplies and Medicines by Hospital Nurses," Deviant Behavior, (95): 313-331; auth, "Workplace Deviance Among Nurses: The Influence of Work Group Norms on Drug Diversion and/or Use," Journal of Nursing Administration, (95): 48-55; auth, "Reducing Shrinkage in the Retail Store: It's Not Just a Job for the Loss Prevention Department," Security Journal, (94): 2-10; auth, "Perceptions of Drug and Supply Diversion Among Nurses," Free Inquiry in Creative Sociology, (94): 13-22. **CONTACT ADDRESS** Dept Criminal Justice, Georgia State Univ, 33 Gilmer St, SE, Atlanta, GA 30303. **EMAIL** ddabney@gsu.edu

DAGGER, RICHARD K.
PERSONAL Born 10/23/1948, Cape Girardeau, MO, m, 1971, 2 children **DISCIPLINE** POLITICAL SCIENCE **EDUCATION** Univ Mo, BA, 70; Univ Minn, PhD, 76. **CAREER** Asst Prof to Prof, Ariz State Univ, 76-. **HONORS AND AWARDS** Hubert H. Humphrey Fel, 92-93; Elaine and David Spitz Prize, 99; Outstanding Teaching Awd, Golden Key Honor Soc, 88; Distinguished Teaching Awd, Ariz State Univ, 84; Distinguished Alumnus Awd, Univ Mo, 98. **MEMBERSHIPS** Am Polit Sci Asn; Am Soc for Polit and Legal Philos; Conf for the Study of Polit Thought. **RESEARCH** Political, legal and moral philosophy. **SELECTED PUBLICATIONS** Auth, "Playing Fair with Punishment," Ethics, 93; auth, Civic Virtues: Rights, Citizenship, and Republican Liberalism, Oxford Univ Press, 97; auth, "The Sandelian Republic and the Encumbered Self," The Rev of Polit, 99; auth, "Membership, Fair Play, and Political Obligation," Polit Studies, 00; auth, "Republicanism and the Politics of Place," Philos Explorations, 01; co-auth, Political Ideologies and the Democratic Ideal, Longman Press, in press. **CONTACT ADDRESS** Dept Polit Sci, Arizona State Univ, 615 E Concorda Dr, Tempe, AZ 85282. **EMAIL** rdagger@asu.edu

DAHL, NORMAN
PERSONAL Born 12/07/1939 **DISCIPLINE** PHILOSOPHY **EDUCATION** Univ Calif Berkeley, PhD. **RESEARCH** Ancient Greek philosophy; ethics. **SELECTED PUBLICATIONS** Auth, Plato's Defense of Justice, Philos Phenomenol Res, 91; On the Moral Status of Weakness of the Will, Logos, 89; Morality and the Meaning of Life: Some First Thoughts, Can J Philos, 87; Obligation and Moral Worth: Reflections on Prichard and Kant, Philos Studies, 86; Practical Reason, Aristotle, and Weakness of the Will, Univ Minn, 84; Paternalism and Rational Desire, Univ Minn, 83; auth, "Morality, Moral Dilemmas, and Moral Requirements," Moral Dilemas and Moral Theory, Oxford Univ Press, 96; auth, "Two Kinds of Essence in Aristotle: A Pale Mn is Not the Same as his Essence," Philosophical Review, 97; auth, "On Substance Being the Same as its Essnece in Metaphysicis Z 6: The Pale Man Argument," Journal of the Hist of Philosophy, 99. **CONTACT ADDRESS** Philosophy Dept, Univ of Minnesota, Twin Cities, 831 Walter Heller Hall, 271-19th Ave S, Minneapolis, MN 55455-0310. **EMAIL** dahlx005@maroon.tc.umn.edu

DAISE, BENJAMIN
PERSONAL Born 05/21/1942, SC, S **DISCIPLINE** PHILOSOPHY **EDUCATION** Morehouse Col, BS, 65; Univ Tex Austin, PhD, 73. **CAREER** Instructor to Prof, Hobart and William Smith Col, 70-. **HONORS AND AWARDS** Merrill Foreign Study Grant; Danish George Marshall Grant. **MEMBERSHIPS** Kierkegaard Soc. **RESEARCH** The Idea of Self; The Ethics of Persuasion; Kierkegaard. **SELECTED PUBLICATIONS** Auth, "The Will to Truth in Kierkegaard's 'Philosophical Fragments'," Journal of Philosophy of Religion, 92; auth, Kierkegaard's Socratic art, Mercer Univ Press, 99. **CONTACT ADDRESS** Dept Philos, Hobart and William Smith Cols, 300 Pulteney St, Geneva, NY 14456-3304. **EMAIL** Daise@hws.edu

DALE, WALTER R.
PERSONAL Born 12/23/1944, Chicago, IL, d **DISCIPLINE** LAW **EDUCATION** University of Illinois, BS, finance, 1966; Governors State University, MBA, 1981; IIT Chicago Kent Law School, JD, 1985; John Marshall Law School, LLM, tax, 1988. **CAREER** Small Business Administration, loan servicing officer, 71-72; Chicago City Bank & Trust Co, commercial loan officer, 72-75; Jackson Park Hospital, internal auditor and patient accounts manager, 80-81; Chicago State University, professor of accounting and finance, 87-; United States Department of the Treasury, Internal Revenue Service, revenue agent, field auditor, tax law researcher, 81-85; Caldwell & Hubbard, tax attorney, 85-86; Brown & Porter, entertainment, tax and corporate lawyer, currently. **MEMBERSHIPS** Alpha Phi Alpha; Chicago Black Attorneys in Sports & Entertainment, president; Black Entertainment & Sports Lawyers Association; National Academy of Recording Arts & Sciences. **SELECTED PUBLICATIONS** "A New Approach to Federal Taxation," Midwest Accounting Society, March 1993. **CONTACT ADDRESS** Brown & Porter, 1130 S Wabash, Ste 501, Chicago, IL 60605.

DALEY, BRIAN EDWARD
PERSONAL Born 01/18/1940, Orange, NJ **DISCIPLINE** HISTORICAL THEOLOGY, CHURCH HISTORY **EDUCATION** Fordham Univ, BA, 61; Oxford Univ, BA, 64, MA, 67, DPhil(theol), 79; Loyola Sem, PhL, 66; Hochschule Sankt Georgen, Frankfurt, Lic theol, 72. **CAREER** Instr classics, Fordham Univ, 66-67; Asst Prof Hist Theol, Weston Sch Theol, 78-, Ed, Traditio, 78-; trustee, Le Moyne Col, 79- **MEMBERSHIPS** Asn Int Etudes Patristiques; Am Soc Church Hist; Soc Values Higher Educ; Am Asn Rhodes Scholars. **RESEARCH** Greek patristic theology; history of spirituality; Neoplatonism. **SELECTED PUBLICATIONS** Auth, Position and Patronage in the Early-Church--Distinguishing Between Personal or Moral Authority and Canonical or Structural Jurisdiction in the Early-Christian Community and Civil-Society--The Original Meaning of Primacy-Of-Honor, Jour Theol; Regnum-Caelorum--Patterns of Future Hope in Early Christianity, Jour Theol Stud, Vol 0045, 94; Apollo as a Chalcedonian--Tracing the Trajectory of a Christian Oracle and Christological Apologia--A New Fragment of a Controversial Work From Early 6th-Century Constantinople, Traditio-Stud Ancient and Medieval Hist Thought and Rel. **CONTACT ADDRESS** Dept of Hist Theol, Weston Jesuit Sch of Theol, Cambridge, MA 02138.

DALLEN, JAMES
PERSONAL Born 04/16/1943, Concordia, KS **DISCIPLINE** THEOLOGY, RELIGIOUS STUDIES **EDUCATION** St Mary's Col, KY, BA, 65; Cath Univ Am, STB, 68, MA, 69, STD, 76. **CAREER** Instr theol, Rosemont Col, 75-76, asst prof, 76-82; asst prof, 82-84, assoc prof, 84-94, prof theol, Gonzaga Univ, 94-. **MEMBERSHIPS** N Am Acad Liturgy; Cath Theol Soc Am; Col Theol Soc; Am Acad Relig. **RESEARCH** Sacrament of Penance; Eucharistic prayer, Cultural adaptation of liturgy. **SELECTED PUBLICATIONS** Auth, Liturgical Celebration: Patterns (4 vols), NAm Liturgy Resources, 71-75; The Mass Today, NAm Liturgy Resources, 76; The Reconciling Community, Liturgical Press, 86; Removing the Barriers, Liturgy Training Pubs, 91; Dilemma of Priestless Sundays, Liturgy Training Pubs, 94. **CONTACT ADDRESS** Dept of Religious Studies, Gonzaga Univ, 502 E Boone Ave, Spokane, WA 99258-0001. **EMAIL** dallen@gonzaga.edu

DALLEY, GEORGE ALBERT
PERSONAL Born 08/25/1941, Havana, Cuba, m, 1970 **DISCIPLINE** LAW **EDUCATION** Columbus Coll, AB 1963; Columbia Univ School of Law, JD 1966; Columbia Univ Grad School & Business, MBA 1966. **CAREER** Metropolitan Appl Res Cntr, assis to the pres 1962-69; Stroock & Stroock & Lavan, assoc cousnel 1970-71; US House of Representatives Comm on the Judiciary, assist counsel 1971-72; Congressman Charles Rangel, admin asst 1973-76; US Dept of State, deputy asst sec of state 1977-79; US Civil Aero Bd, mem 1980-82; Mondale for Pres, deputy camp mgr 1983-84; Cong Charles Rangel, coun and staff dir 1985-1989; senior vice pres Neill and Company Inc, 89-93; Neill and Shaw, partner, 89-93; Holland & Knight, partner, 93-; Adjunct prof Am Univ Schl of Law 1981-; **MEMBERSHIPS** Avat human rights Am Bar Assoc; Intl law comm Nat'l Bar Assoc Fed Bar Assoc 1976-; mem Transafrica, NAACP, Urban League 1974-; Crestwood Comm Assn 1986-; mem bd of dir Africare, Transafrica DC Support Group; consultant, United Nations Devel Program 1989-; American Bar Association; American Bar Foundation; DC Judicial Nominating Commission. **SELECTED PUBLICATIONS** Article, Federal Drug Abuse Enforcement; speeches Dem Corp Select Process 1976; various mag articles. **CONTACT ADDRESS** Holland & Knight, 2100 Pennsylvania Ave, NW, Ste 400, Washington, DC 20036.

DALLMAYR, FRED REINHARD
PERSONAL Born 10/18/1928, Ulm, Germany, m, 1957, 2 children **DISCIPLINE** POLITICAL PHILOSOPHY **EDUCATION** Univ Munich, Dr of Law, 55; S Ill Univ, MA, 56; Duke Univ, PhD Polit Sci, 60. **CAREER** Asst Prof, Milwaukee Downer Col, 61-63; from asst prof to prof, Purdue Univ, 63-71; prof, Univ Georgia, 71-73; Prof & Dept Head, 73-78; Packey Dee Prof, Univ Notre Dame, 78-. **HONORS AND AWARDS** Phi Beta Kappa, 60; NEH Fel, 78-79; Fulbright Res Grant, 91. **MEMBERSHIPS** Amer Polit Sci Assn; Int Polit Sci Assn; Soc for Asian and Comparative Philos; Soc for Phenomenon & Existential Philos. **RESEARCH** Modern and contemporary social and polit philos; comparative philos; cross-cultural studies; critical theory. **SELECTED PUBLICATIONS** Auth, Language and Politics: Why Does Language Matter to political philsophy?, Univ of Notre Dame Pr, 84; auth, Polis and Praxis: Exercises in Contemporary Political Theory, MIT Pr (Cambridge, MA), 84; auth, Critical Encounters: Between Philosphy and Politics, Univ of Notre Dame Pr, 87; auth, margins of Political Discourse, SUNY Pr (Albany, NY), 89; auth, Life-World, Modernity and Critique: Paths between Heidegger and the Frankfurt School, Polity Pr/Blackwell, 91; auth, Between Freiburg and Frankfurt: Toward a Critical Ontology, Univ of Mass Pr, 91; auth, G W F hegel: Modernity and Politics, SAGE Pubs, 93; auth, The Other Heidegger, Cornell univ Pr, 93; auth, Beyond Orientalism: Essays on Cross-Cultural Encounter, SUNY Pr, 96; auth, Alternative Visions: Paths in the Global Village, Rowman & Littlefield, 98; auth, Achieving Multiple Countries: Variations on Self-Other Themes, in prep. **CONTACT ADDRESS** Dept of Govt & Int Studies, Univ of Notre Dame, Notre Dame, IN 46556-0368. **EMAIL** Fred.R.Dallmayr.1@nd.edu

DALMAN, RODGER
PERSONAL Born 07/14/1948, Holland, MI, m, 1976, 3 children **DISCIPLINE** BIBLICAL STUDIES **EDUCATION** Northwestern Col, BA, 70; Biblical Sem, MDiv, 79; Concordia Sem, ThD, 90. **CAREER** Adjunct prof, Trinity Col and Sem, current. **MEMBERSHIPS** Evangelical Theol Soc; Soc of Bibl Lit. **RESEARCH** Old Testament; Archaeology; Ancient Near Eastern history; Literature; Mythology; Geology. **SELECTED PUBLICATIONS** Auth, Research Guide for the Study of Basic Old Testament Theology; Research Guide for Understanding the Egyptian Influence on the Old Testament and the Polemics of Israel's Sea Crossing. **CONTACT ADDRESS** 9441 Bass Creek Cir, New Hope, MN 55428. **EMAIL** rodgerdlaman@cs.com

DALTON, PETER C.
DISCIPLINE PHILOSOPHY **EDUCATION** Northwestern Univ, BA, 68; Univ Rochester, MA, 71, PhD, 73. **CAREER** Tchg asst, 69-70; instr, Univ Rochester, 72; asst prof, 72-77; assoc prof, Fla State Univ, 77-. **HONORS AND AWARDS** Tchg Incentive Prog Awd, 94. **MEMBERSHIPS** Am Philos Asn; Asn of Jour Editors; Fla Philos Asn. **RESEARCH** Modern philosophy; 19th century philosophy; metaphysics. **SELECTED PUBLICATIONS** Auth, A Theological Escape from the Cartesian Circle?, Int Jour Philos Relig, 97; Extended Acts, Philos, 95; The Examined Life, Metaphilos, 92. **CONTACT ADDRESS** Dept of Philosophy, Florida State Univ, 211 Wescott Bldg, Tallahassee, FL 32306. **EMAIL** pdalton@mailer.fsu.edu

DALTON, STUART
PERSONAL Born 04/18/1964, Provo, UT, m, 1986, 2 children **DISCIPLINE** PHILOSOPHY **EDUCATION** Villanova Univ, MA, 92; Emory Univ, PhD, 97. **CAREER** Instr, Georgia State Univ, 94-97; Dean's Teaching Fel, Emory Univ, 96-97; Asst Prof, Univ Hartford, 97-. **HONORS AND AWARDS** Robert Russell Graduate Fel, Villanova Univ, 90-92; Graduate Fel and Teaching Assistantship, Emory Univ, 92-96; Phi Betta Kappa, Emory Univ, 95; Dean's Teaching Fel, Emory Univ, 96-97; NEH Summer Stipend Nominee, Univ Hartford, 97. **MEMBERSHIPS** Amer Assoc of Univ Professors; Amer Phil Assoc. **RESEARCH** 19th and 20th century continental philosophy; 17th and 18th century modern philosophy; social, political and moral philosophy; aesthetics **SELECTED PUBLICATIONS** Auth, Lyotard's Peregrination: Three (and a half) Responses to the Call of Justice, Philosophy Today, 94; Foucalt on Freedom and the Space of Transgression, PoMo2.1, 96; The General Will and the Legislator in Rousseau's On the Social Contract, Southwest Philosophy Review, 96; Heidegger's Return to the Greeks: Three Stories about Origins, Existentia; Beginnings and Endings in Nietzsche's Beyond Good and Evil, The Journal of Nietzsche Studies. **CONTACT ADDRESS** Humanities Dept, Univ of Hartford, West Hartford, CT 06117. **EMAIL** dalton@mail.hartford.edu

DALY, MARKATE
PERSONAL 3 children **DISCIPLINE** PHILOSOPHY **EDUCATION** Univ Wisc, Madison, PhD, 84. **CAREER** Dir Ctr for Public Philos. **MEMBERSHIPS** Soc for Philos and Psychol; Int Soc for Social Philos. **RESEARCH** Philosophy of mind/person; ethics; social philosophy. **SELECTED PUBLICATIONS** Auth, Communitarianism: A New Public Ethic, Wadsworth, 94. **CONTACT ADDRESS** 2730 Parker St, Berkeley, CA 94704. **EMAIL** mkdaly@mindspring.com

DAM, KENNETH W.
PERSONAL Born 08/10/1932, Marysville, KS, m, 1962, 2 children **DISCIPLINE** LAW **EDUCATION** Univ KS, BS, 54; Univ Chicago, JD, 57. **CAREER** Law clerk, Mr Justice Whittaker, US Supreme Court, 57-58; vis asst prof, 60-61, from assoc prof to prof, 61-76, Harold J. & Marion F. Green Prof Law, 76-, Max Pam Prof Am and Foreign Law, Univ Chicago, 92-, Provost, 80-82; Asst dir, US Off Mgt & Budget, 71-73; exec dir, US Coun Econ Policy, 73; Deputy Secy of State, 82-85; vpres, IBM Corp, 85-92; Max Pam Prof of Am and Foreign Law, Univ Chicago, 92-. **MEMBERSHIPS** Am Law Inst; Am Acad Arts & Sci; Am Acad Diplomacy. **RESEARCH** International economic law; trade regulation. **SELECTED PUBLICATIONS** Auth, Law and International Economic Policy--the Gatt, 70 & Oil Resources--Who Gets What How?, 76, Univ Chicago; coauth, Economic Policy Beyond the Headlines, W.W. Norton, 78, 2nd ed, 98; auth, The Rules of the Game: Reform and Evolution in the International Monetary System, 82. **CONTACT ADDRESS** Law Sch, Univ of Chicago, 1111 E 60th St, Chicago, IL 60637-2702. **EMAIL** Kenneth_dam@law.uchicago.edu

DANAHER, JAMES
PERSONAL Born 12/24/1947, Jersey City, NJ, m, 1981, 2 children **DISCIPLINE** PHILOSOPHY **EDUCATION** Ramapo Col of NJers, BA, 75; Montclair State Univ, MA, 76; The New Sch for Soc Res, MA, 83; CUNY, Mphil, 89, PhD, 90. **CAREER** Head, Dept of Philosophy, Prof of Philosophy, Nyack College, Nyack, NY, 90-; Chairman, Dept of Arts and Sciences, Berkley College, White Plains, NY, 80-; Philosopher in Residence at Whitehall (the Rhode Island home (1729-1731) of the Irish philosopher George Berkeley), 93. **MEMBERSHIPS** Am Philos Asn, Evangelical Philos Soc, Int Berkeley Soc. **RESEARCH** 17th and 18th Century British Empiricism, Philosophy of Love, Postmodern Christianity. **SELECTED PUBLICATIONS** Auth, "Is Your Christianity Real or Fake?", Fellowship Today, 29 (91): 2-3; auth, What Locke Should Have Believed About Real Essences.", Locke Newsletter, (92): 83-103; auth, "Submit Therefore to God", Fellowship Today, 31 (93): 10-12; auth, "On Loving and Liking", Philosophia Christi, (95): 18:2, 9-13; auth, "Socrates and Homosexuality", Philosophia Christi, (96): 19:2, 1-6; auth, "Toward an Understanding Love: Human and Divine", Encounter 58 (97): 401-12; auth, "On Faith and Knowledge", The Covenant Quarterly, LVI (98): 3-10; auth, "Why Wives Shouldn't Love Their Husbands", The Preacher's Magazine, 75 (99): 57-60; auth "The Ring of Gyges and the Imagination: Platonic and Christian Perspectives", Theology Today (00), (forthcoming); rev, "Is There a Place for Berkeley's Ideas?, Southwest Philosophy Review (00), (forthcoming). **CONTACT ADDRESS** Dept Phiosophy, Nyack Col, 1 S Blvd, Nyack, NY 10960. **EMAIL** danaherj@nyack.edu

DANIEL, E. RANDOLPH
PERSONAL Born 04/15/1935, Richmond, VA, m, 1960, 3 children **DISCIPLINE** THEOLOGY **EDUCATION** Davidson Col, BA, 58; Union Theol Seminary, BD, 61; Harvard Univ, ThM, 64; Univ Virginia, PhD, 66. **CAREER** Asst Prof, 66-72, Assoc Prof, 72-83, Prof, 83-, Chr, 84-88, Univ Kentucky **HONORS AND AWARDS** NDEA Fel, 63-66. **MEMBERSHIPS** Amer Historical Assoc; Medieval Acad of Amer. **RESEARCH** Apocalypticism and religious orders in the middle ages **SELECTED PUBLICATIONS** Auth, The Franciscan Concept of Mission in the High Middle ages, reprinted, 92; auth, Joachimism and John Calvin: New Approaches, Storia e figure dell 'Apocalisse fra '500 e '600, 96; auth, Reformist Apocalypticism and the Friars Minor, That Others may Know and Love: Essays in Honor of Zachary Hayes OFM, 97. **CONTACT ADDRESS** Dept of History, Univ of Kentucky, Lexington, KY 40506. **EMAIL** erdani01@pop.uky.edu

DANIEL, WILEY YOUNG
PERSONAL Born 09/10/1946, Louisville, KY, m **DISCIPLINE** LAW **EDUCATION** Howard Univ, BA 1968; Howard Univ Sch of Law, JD 1971. **CAREER** Volunteer legal work; Dickinson Wright McKean Cudlip & Moon, Attorney 1971-77; Gorsuch Kirgis Campbell Walker & Grover, Attorney 1977-88; Popham, Haik, Schnobrich & Kaufman, partner, 88-95; US District Court, judge, 95-. **HONORS AND AWARDS** 1986 Disting Serv Awd Sam Cary Bar Assoc, Colorado Assoc of Black Attorneys; Fellow, American Bar Foundation; Fellow, Colorado Bar Foundation; USA Speaker Aboard, Nigeria, 1995. **MEMBERSHIPS** Mem Natl Bar Assn; pres-elect, 1991-92, pres, 1992-93, CO Bar Assn; trustee, Denver Bar Assn, 1990-93; Amer Bar Assn; Managing Ed Howard LLJ; mem Delta Theta Phi Law Frat, Alpha Phi Alpha Social Frat; Law Journal 1970-71; mem Detroit Coll of Law part-time faculty 1974-77; Univ of CO School of Law 1978-81; mem Iliff Sch of Theology; mem, Colorado State Bd of Agriculture, 1989-95. **CONTACT ADDRESS** US District Court, District of Colorado, 1929 Stout St, Denver, CO 80294.

DANIELS, CHARLES B.
DISCIPLINE PHILOSOPHY OF MIND **EDUCATION** Univ Chicago, AB; Univ Oxon, PhD. **CAREER** Instr, Yale Univ; Ind Univ; prof, 71-. **RESEARCH** Ethics; aesthetics; logic; philosophy of religion and ontology. **SELECTED PUBLICATIONS** Auth, The Evaluation of Ethical Theories; Toward an Ontology of Number; Mind; Sign; What Really Goes On In Sophocles' Theban Plays; pub(s), articles in Philos Stud; Jour Philos Logic. **CONTACT ADDRESS** Dept of Philosophy, Univ of Victoria, PO Box 3045, Victoria, BC, Canada V8W 3P4. **EMAIL** cbd@uvic.ca

DANIELS, NORMAN
PERSONAL Born 06/30/1942, New York, NY, m, 1 child **DISCIPLINE** PHILOSOPHY **EDUCATION** Wesleyan Univ, AB, 64; Balliol Col, MA, 66; Harvard Univ, PhD, 70. **CAREER** Teaching Fel, Harvard Univ, 68-69; Lect, Harvard Sch of Public Health, 79; Vis Prof, Brown Univ, 79; From Lect to Prof, Tufts Univ, 79-. **HONORS AND AWARDS** Woodrow Wilson Career Develop Awd, 80; Fel, Hastings Ctr Inst, 86-; Nat Endowment for the Humanities, 88; Ethics Fel, Harvard Univ, 92-93; Robert Wood Johnson Investr Awd, 98-01; Conley Awd, Am Col of Healthcare Exec, 99; Distinguished Alumnus, Wesleyan Univ, 99. **MEMBERSHIPS** APA, Am Assoc for the Advancement of Sci, Am Assoc for Univ Profs, Soc for Legal and Polit Philos, Am Soc for Law and Med, Nat Acad of Soc Insurance. **RESEARCH** Political philosophy, ethics, distributive justice, fairness, health policy, health care reform, health care for the elderly, race and social justice, international work on health reform and equity, social determinants of health and justice. **SELECTED PUBLICATIONS** Auth, Seeking Fair Treatment: From the AIDS Epidemic to National Health Care Reform, Oxford Univ Pr (New York, NY), 95; auth, "Justice and Access to High-Tech Home Care," in Bringing the Hospital Home: Ethical and Social Implications of High-Tech Home care, (Baltimore: Johns Hopkins Univ Pr, 95), 235-251; auth, "Mental Disabilities, Equal Opportunity and the ADA," in Ment Disorder, Work Disability and the Law (Chicago: Univ Chicago Pr, 96), 282-297; coauth, Benchmarks of Fairness for Health Care Reform, Oxford Univ Pr (New York, NY), 96; auth, Justice and Justification: Reflective Equilibrium in Theory and Practice, Cambridge Univ Pr (New York, NY), 96; coauth, "Lessons for U S Managed Care from the British National Health Service II: Setting Priorities," Psychiat Servs 48 (97): 469-470; auth, "Rationing Medical Care: A Philosopher's Perspective on Outcomes and Process," Econom nd Philos 14 (98): 27-50; auth, "Justice and Prudential Deliberation in Long-Term Care," in Public and Private Responsibilities in Long-Term Care (Baltimore: Johns Hopkins Univ Pr, 98), 93-111;coauth, "Closure, Fair Procedures and Setting Limits Within Managed Care Organizations," J of the Am Geriatrics Soc 46 (98): 351-354; coauth, From Chance to Choice: Genes and Social Justice, Cambridge Univ Pr (New York, NY), forthcoming. **CONTACT ADDRESS** Dept Philos, Tufts Univ, Medford, Medford, MA 02155. **EMAIL** ndaniels@emerald.tufts.edu

DANKER, FREDERICK W.
PERSONAL Born 07/12/1920, Frankenmuth, MI, m, 1948, 2 children **DISCIPLINE** NEW TESTAMENT THEOLOGY, LINGUISTICS **EDUCATION** Concordia Sem, BA, 42, BD, 50; Univ Chicago, PhD, 63. **CAREER** From asst prof to prof New Testament exec theol, 54-74; Prof New Testament Exec Theol, Christ Sem-Seminex, 74-. **MEMBERSHIPS** Am Philol Asn; Soc Bibl Lit; Am Soc Papyrologists; Societas Novi Testamenti Studiorum; Cath Bibl Asn. **RESEARCH** Greek tragedy; Greek and Latin Epigraphy; Greek Lexicography. **SELECTED PUBLICATIONS CONTACT ADDRESS** 6928 Plateau Ave, Saint Louis, MO 63139.

DANLEY, JOHN ROBERT
PERSONAL Born 01/12/1948, Kansas City, MO, m, 1969, 1 child **DISCIPLINE** ETHICAL THEORY, SOCIAL-POLITICAL PHILOSOPHY **EDUCATION** Kalamazoo Co, BA, 70; Union Theol Sem, NYork, MDiv, 73; Univ Rochester, MA, 76, PhD, 77. **CAREER** Instr, 76-77, asst prof, 77-80, assoc prof philos, Southern Ill Univ, Edwardsville, 80-93; prof, 93-. **MEMBERSHIPS** Am Philos Assn; Am Acad Mgt; Southwestern Philos Assn; Soc Bus Ethics; Intl Assoc for Bus Soc. **RESEARCH** Contractarianism; corporate responsibility. **SELECTED PUBLICATIONS** Auth, The Modern Corporation and Its Role in a Free Society, University of Notre Dame Press, 94; art, HR's View of Ethics in the Workplace: Are the Barbarians at the Gate?, The Journal of Business Ethics, 96; art, Robert Nozick, Classical and Managerial Business Ideologies, The Blackwell Encyclopedic Dictionary of Business Ethics, London: Basil Blackwell, 97. **CONTACT ADDRESS** Dept of Philos Studies, So Illinois Univ, Edwardsville, 6 Hairpin Dr, Edwardsville, IL 62026-0001. **EMAIL** jdanley@siue.edu

DANNER, DAN GORDON
PERSONAL Born 07/05/1939, Salt Lake City, UT, m, 1961, 2 children **DISCIPLINE** RELIGION, HISTORY OF CHRISTIAN THOUGHT **EDUCATION** Abilene Christian Col, 61, MA, 63; Univ Iowa, PhD(relig), 69. **CAREER** Dir, Church Christ Bible Chair Bibl Lit, Tyler Jr Col, 62-66; asst prof, 69-73, assoc prof, 73-81, Prof theol, Univ Portland 81- **MEMBERSHIPS** Am Acad Refig; Am Soc Reformation Res; Am Soc Church Hist. **RESEARCH** Reformation; Reformation in England; Puritanism and the Geneva exiles, 1555-1560. **SELECTED PUBLICATIONS** Auth, Revelation 20: 1-10 in a history of interpretation of the Restoration movement, Restoration Quart, 63; Anthony Gilby: Puritan in exile--a bibliographical approach, Church Hist, 71; Women's lib or Adam's rib--the problem of women and the church, 72 & Not peace but a sword--an essay on war and peace, fall 76, Univ Portland Rev; Christopher Goodman and the English Protestant tradition of civil disobedience, Sixteenth Century J, 77; The contributions of the Geneva Bible of 1560 to the English Protestant tradition, Sixteenth Century J, 81; Resistance and the ungodly magistrate in the sixteenth century: The Marian Exiles, J Am Acad Relig, 81; auth, Pilgrimage to Puritanism: History and Theology of the Manan Exiles at Geneva, 1555 to 1560, Peter Lang, 98. **CONTACT ADDRESS** Dept of Theol, Univ of Portland, 5000 N Willamette, Portland, OR 97203-5798.

DARBY, DERRICK
DISCIPLINE PHILOSOPHY **EDUCATION** Pittsburgh, PhD. **CAREER** Asst prof, Northwestern Univ. **RESEARCH** Moral and political philosophy; ethics; political philosophy; philosophy of law; and metaphysics. **SELECTED PUBLICATIONS** Auth, "Are Worlds Without Natural Rights Morally Improverished?" The Southern Journal of Philosophy, 99. **CONTACT ADDRESS** Dept of Philosophy, Northwestern Univ, 1818 Hinman, Evanston, IL 60208. **EMAIL** ddarby@norhtwestern.edu

DARDEN, CHRISTOPHER A.
PERSONAL Born 04/08/1956, Martinez, CA, s **DISCIPLINE** LAW **EDUCATION** San Jose State Univ, BA, administrative justice, 1977; Univ of California-Hastings College of Law, JD, 1980. **CAREER** National Labor Relations Board, attorney, 80-81; Los Angeles County, asst head deputy, Special Investigations Division, begin 81; Los Angeles County District Attorney's Office, deputy district attorney; Southwestern Univ School of Law, Prof, 95-. **HONORS AND AWARDS** San Jose State Univ, Dept of Admin Justice, Alumnus of the Year Awd, 1995. **MEMBERSHIPS** California Bar, Criminal Law Section, exec comm, 1994-97; National Black Prosecutors Assn, board member, 1989; Loved Ones of Homicide Victims, past pres, bd of dirs, 1987-; Los Angeles County Assn of Deputy District Attorneys, board member, 1986-87; John M Langston Bar Assn, 1995. The People vs Orenthal James Simpson, BA097211, part of prosecuting team; appeared in television movie. **SELECTED PUBLICATIONS** Co-author, In Contempt, 1996. **CONTACT ADDRESS** Southwestern Univ Sch of Law, 625 S West Moreland Ave, Los Angeles, CA 90005-3905.

DARDEN, GEORGE HARRY
PERSONAL Born 03/14/1934, Cadiz, KY, m **DISCIPLINE** LAW **EDUCATION** KY State Univ, BS 1955; Salmon P Chase College of Law, JD 1964. **CAREER** Hamilton Cnty, OH, asst cnty prosecutor 1964-66; Cincinnati, OH, Hopkinsville, KY, priv pract 1964-69; Legal Serv Proj Ctr OH, chief attny 1967-68; Lincoln Hts, OH, city solicitor 1967-68; EEOC, Washington, DC, staff attny 1969-71, supervisory 1973, chief legal consel div 1973-75; Equal Employment Opportunity Commission, regional Attorney, Atlanta, GA, 75-. **HONORS AND AWARDS** Citations EEOC Houston Hearings 1972-73, Chief Judge, Cincinnati Muncpl Ct 1968, WCIN Radio Station 1968; Cincinnati Herald Paper 1968. **MEMBERSHIPS** Pres Double Dollar Co 1965-68; chrmn, legal comm Hopkinsville, KY, NAACP 1968-69; chrmn, legal redress comm Denver, CO 1984-. **CONTACT ADDRESS** Atlanta Division, US Equal Employment Opportunity Commission, 75 Piedmont Ave, NE, Ste 1100, Atlanta, GA 30335.

DARDEN, LINDLEY
PERSONAL Born 12/17/1945, New Albany, MS **DISCIPLINE** PHILOSOPHY AND HISTORY OF SCIENCE **EDUCATION** Rhodes College, BA, 68; Univ Chicago, AM, 69, SM, 72, PhD, 74. **CAREER** Asst prof, 74-78, Assoc Prof Philos and Hist, Univ MD, College Park, 78-92, prof of phil, 92-; NSF grant, 78-80, 99-01; Am Coun Learned Soc fel, 82. **HONORS AND AWARDS** Fel, AAAS, 95. **MEMBERSHIPS** ISHPSSB, Philos Sci Asn; Hist Sci Soc; AAAS. **RESEARCH** Theory construction in science; discovering mechanisms. **SELECTED PUBLICATIONS** Auth, Theory Change in Science, Oxford Univ Press, 91; coauth, " Thinking About Mechanisms," Phil Sci 67, 1-25, 00. **CONTACT ADDRESS** Dept of Philos, Univ of Maryland, Col Park, College Park, MD 20742. **EMAIL** darden@carnap.umd.edu

DARWALL, STEPHEN L.
PERSONAL Born 09/09/1946, Richmond, VA, m, 1980, 2 children **DISCIPLINE** PHILOSOPHY **EDUCATION** Yale Univ, BA, 68; Univ of Pittsburgh, PhD, 72. **CAREER** Univ of NC Chapel Hill, 72-84; Univ of Mich, 84-. **HONORS AND AWARDS** NEH Fel; Phi Beta Kappa. **MEMBERSHIPS** Am Philos Assoc; David Hume Soc. **RESEARCH** Moral Philosophy, History of Ethics. **SELECTED PUBLICATIONS** Auth, Impartial Reason, 83; auth, The British Moralists and the Internal 'Ought'; auth, Philosophical Ethics, 98. **CONTACT ADDRESS** Dept Philos, Univ of Michigan, Ann Arbor, 435 S State St, Ann Arbor, MI 48109-1003. **EMAIL** sdarwall@umich.edu

DAU-SCHMIDT, KENNETH G.
PERSONAL Born 10/12/1956, Des Moines, IA, m, 1980, 3 children **DISCIPLINE** LAW **EDUCATION** Univ Wis, BA, 78; Univ Mich, MA, 81; JD, 81; PhD, 84 **CAREER** Prof Law, Univ Cincinnati; Prof Law, Univ Wisconsin, 94-97; Willard and Margaret Carr Prof of Labor and Employment Law, Ind Univ, 91-. **HONORS AND AWARDS** Teaching Excellence Recognition Awd, Indiana Univ, 98; John S. Hastings Fac Fel, Indiana Univ, 93-; Leonard D. Fromm Pub Interest Fac Awd, Indiana Univ, 97 **MEMBERSHIPS** AAUP; AEA; L&SA; ALEA; IRRA; Ind Bar Asn; Am Bar Asn; Wis Bar Asn. **RESEARCH** Labor and Employment Law; Law and Economics. **SELECTED PUBLICATIONS** "The First Century of Department of Justice Antitrust Enforcement," Rev Indust Org; "The Execution of Sir William Wallace: Toward a Richer Economic Theory of Punishment," Graven Images; "Preference Shaping by the Law," New Palgrave Dictionary Econ Law, 98. **CONTACT ADDRESS** School of Law, Indiana Univ, Bloomington, 211 S Ind Ave, Bloomington, IN 47405. **EMAIL** kdauschm@indiana.edu

DAUBE, DAVID
PERSONAL Born 02/08/1909, Freiburg im Breisgau, Germany, d, 3 children **DISCIPLINE** ROMAN LAW, BIBLICAL STUDIES **EDUCATION** Univ Gottingen, DrJur, 32; Cambridge Univ, PhD, 35; Oxford Univ, MA & DCL, 55. **CAREER** Fel, Caius Col, Cambridge, 38-46, lectr law, univ, 46-51; prof jurisp, Univ Aberdeen, 51-55; Regius prof civil law, Oxford Univ & fel, All Souls Col, 55-70; Prof Law & Dir Robbins Collection, Univ Calif, Berkeley, 70-, Rockefeller award, 61-62; sr fel, Yale Univ, 62; Gifford lectr, Edinburgh, 62 & 63; Ford rotating prof polit sci, Univ Calif, Berkeley, 64; Gray lectr, Cambridge Univ, 66; hon prof law, Uiv Knostanz, 66-; Lionel Cohen lectr, Jerusalem, 70; Messenger lectr, Cornell Univ, 71; hon fel, Oxford Univ Centre Postgrad Hebrew Studies, 73- & Caius Col, 74- **HONORS AND AWARDS** Gerard lectr, Univ Calif, Irvine, 81; lld, univ edinburgh, 60, univ leicester, 64, cambridge univ, 81; dr, univ paris, 63; chl, hebrew union col, 71; drjur, univ munich, 72. **MEMBERSHIPS** Fel Am Acad Arts & Sci; fel Brit Acad; corresp fel Acad Sci, Gottingen & Bavarian Acad Acad Sci; hon fel Royal Irish Acad; Soc Hist Ancient Law, France (pres, 57-58). **RESEARCH** Hebrew law; Old and New Testament. **SELECTED PUBLICATIONS** Auth, Judas, Calif Law Rev, Vol 0082, 94. **CONTACT ADDRESS** Sch of Law, Univ of California, Berkeley, Boalt Hall, Berkeley, CA 94720.

DAUER, FRANCIS W.
PERSONAL Born 08/17/1939, Leipzig, Germany, m, 1995, 2 children **DISCIPLINE** PHILOSOPHY **EDUCATION** Dartmouth Coll, AB, 60; Harvard Univ, MA, 64; PhD, 70. **CAREER** Lectr, Univ Calif Santa Barbara, 69; asst prof 69-75; assoc prof, 75-82; vis prof, Int Christian Univ, japan, 87-90; guest prof, Osaka Univ Ja Japan, 90; prof, Univ Calif Santa Barbara 82-. **MEMBERSHIPS** Am Philos Asn; Hume Soc; Am Asoc for Aesthetics. **RESEARCH** Philosophy: Hume, Epistemology, Emotions. **SELECTED PUBLICATIONS** Auth, Between Belief and Fantasy: A Study of the Imagination, Pursuits of Reason,93; The Nature of Fictional Characters and the Referential Fallacy, J of Aesthetics and Art Criticism, 95; Hume Skepticism with Regard to Reason: A Reconsideration, Hume Studies, 96. **CONTACT ADDRESS** Dept of Philosophy, Univ of California, Santa Barbara, Santa Barbara, CA 93106. **EMAIL** dauer@humanitas.ucsb.edu

DAURIO, JANICE
PERSONAL Born 06/26/1946, Brooklyn, NY, m, 1985 **DISCIPLINE** PHILOSOPHY **EDUCATION** Hunter Col City Univ NYork, AB, 68; Claremont Grad School, MA Philos, 73; Mount St Mary's Coll Calif, 88; Claremont Grad School, PhD Philos, 94. **CAREER** Marymount High School, 78-89; Mount St Mary's Coll, 78-84; Loyola Marymount Univ, 84-89; St John's Coll, 90-91; W Coast Univ, 95; Ventura Coll, 93; prof, Moorpark Coll, 94-. **HONORS AND AWARDS** Phi Sigma Tau. **MEMBERSHIPS** Ventura Co Fedn of Coll Teachers; Am Philos Asn; Soc for Anal Feminism; Am Cath Philos Asn; Soc of Christian Philos. **RESEARCH** Philosophy; Ethics. **SELECTED PUBLICATIONS** Auth, The Downside Review, 88; book revs, New Oxford Rev, 90-04; Sidgwick's Method of Ethics and Common Sense Morality, History of Philos Quart, 97; book rev, Faith and Philosophy, 97; rev, Philosopher's Annual, 97. **CONTACT ADDRESS** Moorpark Col, 7075 Campus Rd, Moorpark, CA 93021. **EMAIL** jdairop@aol.com

DAVENPORT, CHARLES
PERSONAL Born 01/24/1933, Laredo, MO, m, 1962, 4 children **DISCIPLINE** LAW **EDUCATION** Chico State Col, AB, 54; Harvard Univ, JD, 57. **CAREER** Atty, Brobeck, Phleger & Harrison, 60-67; prof taxation, Univ Calif, Davis, 69-75; asst dir, Cong Budget Off, Washington, 75-79; Prof Taxation, Rutgers Univ, 79-; Atty, Tax Legis Coun, Dept Treas, 67-69; vis prof, Law Ctr, Georgetown Univ, 73-74; dir, Internal Revenue Serv Proj Conf US, 74-75; tax consult, Structure of Agr Proj, Dept Agr, 79-81; Special Reports Ed, 85-90; ed in chief, 90-96; consult ed, tax Analysts, 96-. **RESEARCH** Federal taxation; legislative process; tax policy. **SELECTED PUBLICATIONS** Auth, A bountiful tax harvest, 48 Tex Law Rev 1, 69; ed & auth,

Report on Administrative Procedures of the Internal Revenue Services, Govt Printing Off, Sen Doc 94-266, 75; coauth, Collection of delinquent federal taxes, 28 USC Tax Inst 589, 76; auth, The role of taxation in the regulation of energy consumption and production, 78 & The impact of the congressional budget process on tax legislation, 79, The effects of federal tax policy on American agriculture, Govt Printing Off, 82; Taxes and the family farm, Acad Polit Sci, 82; Nat Tax J; The Farm Income Tax Manual, Lexis Law Publishing, 00. **CONTACT ADDRESS** Law School, Rutgers, The State Univ of New Jersey, Newark, 123 Washington St, Newark, NJ 07102-3192. **EMAIL** cDavenport@Kinoy.Rutgersedu

DAVENPORT, CHRISTIAN A.
PERSONAL Born 06/04/1965, New York, NY, s **DISCIPLINE** POLITICAL SCIENCE **EDUCATION** SUNY Binghamton, MA, 1989, PhD, 1991. **CAREER** University of Houston, assistant professor, 92-96; Univ of Colorado-Boulder, Assoc Prof, 96-. **HONORS AND AWARDS** National Science Foundation, Research Development Grant for Minority Scientists & Engineers, 1997; Ebony Magazine, 50 Young Leaders of Tomorrow, 1996; Malcolm X Loves Network, Keeper of the Flame Awd, 1995; National Association of African-American Honors Program, Scholarly Contributions and Leadership, 1996. **MEMBERSHIPS** American Journal of Political Science, editorial board member, 1994-; National Coalition of Blacks for Reparations in America, 1993-; Midwest Political Science Association, 1991-; American Political Science Association, 1991-; National Black Political Science Association, 1992-; Shape Cultural Ctr, instructor, 1993-95; West Dallas Detention Ctr, instructor, 1995; National Popular Culture Association, 1993-; Comparative Politics Center at Univ of Co. **SELECTED PUBLICATIONS** "Understanding Rhetoric Under The Gun," The Black Panther Party Reconsidered, 1997; "The Political and Social Relency of Malcolm X," The Journal of Politics, 1997; "Constitutional Promises and Repressive Reality," The Journal of Politics, 1996; "The Weight of the Past," Political Research Quarterly, 1996; "Multidimensional Threat Perception & State Repression," The American Journal of Political Science, 1995. **CONTACT ADDRESS** Univ of Colorado, Boulder, Ketchum Hall, Rm 106, Boulder, CO 80309-0333. **EMAIL** christian.davenport@colorado.edu

DAVENPORT, GENE LOONEY
PERSONAL Born 10/09/1935, Sylacauga, AL, d, 2 children **DISCIPLINE** PSYCHOLOGY, RELIGION, OLD TESTAMENT, BIBLICAL THEORY **EDUCATION** Birmingham-Southern Col, BA(psychol), 57; Vanderbilt Divinity School, BD, 60; Vanderbilt Univ, PhD(religion:Old Testament, Biblical theol), 68. **CAREER** Prof of Relig, Lambuth Univ, 63-. **MEMBERSHIPS** Soc of Biblical Lit. **RESEARCH** Apocrypha and pseudepigrapha; theol of culture; Sermon on the Mount; the Book of Revelation. **SELECTED PUBLICATIONS** Auth, The Eschatology of the Book of Jubilees, E J Brill, 71; The Anointed of the Lord in Psalms of Solomon 17, Ideal Figures in Ancient Israel, Scholars Press; Into the Darkness: Discipleship in the Sermon on the Mount, Abingdon Press, 88. **CONTACT ADDRESS** Dept of Relig and Philos, Lambuth Univ, Jackson, TN 38301. **EMAIL** davenpor@lambuth.edu

DAVENPORT, HARBERT WILLIAM
PERSONAL Born 07/09/1940, Dallas, TX, m, 1998, 3 children **DISCIPLINE** PHILOSOPHY **EDUCATION** Univ Houston, BA, 63; Univ Ill, Urbana, MA, 69, PhD(philos), 77. **CAREER** Asst prof philos, Cent Mo State Col, 70-72; instr, Purdue Univ, Lafayette, 72-73; Assoc Prof Philos, Western Ill Univ, 74-, Contrib ed, Peirce Ed Proj, Ind Univ-Purdue Univ, Indianapolis, 76-. **HONORS AND AWARDS** Nat Endowment for Humanities summer sem fel, 78; Am Coun Learned Soc travel grant, 79. **MEMBERSHIPS** Am Philos Asn; Charles S Peirce Soc; Soc Advan Am Philos. **RESEARCH** American philosophy; history of philosophy; history and philosophy of science. **SELECTED PUBLICATIONS** Auth, Peirce's evolutionism and his logic: Two connections, In: Proceedings of the C S Peirce Bicentennial International Congress, Tex Tech Univ, 81; Peirce on Evolution, In: Frontiers in American Philosophy, vol 2, Texas A&M Univ, 95. **CONTACT ADDRESS** Dept of Philos & Relig Studies, Western Illinois Univ, 1 University Cir, Macomb, IL 61455-1390. **EMAIL** Bill_Davenport@ccmail.wiu.edu

DAVENPORT, MANUEL M.
PERSONAL Born 06/14/1929, Colorado Springs, CO, d, 1950, 6 children **DISCIPLINE** PHILOSOPHY **EDUCATION** Southern Nazarene Univ, BA, 50; Colorado Col, MA, 54; Univ of Illinois, PhD, 57. **CAREER** Prof, Texas A & M Univ, 67-80, 81-94, 95-; Head, 67-76; Graduate Program Dir, 90-94; US Air Force Academy; Distinguished Visiting Professor, 80-81, 94-95. **HONORS AND AWARDS** Teaching Awds, 59, 60, 78, 82, 89; Univ Faculty Lecturer, 77-78. **MEMBERSHIPS** Southwestern Philosophical Society; Amer Philosophical Assoc; Amer Society for Aesthetics; Joint Services Conference on Professional Ethics. **RESEARCH** Military Ethics; Aesthetics. **SELECTED PUBLICATIONS** Auth, "The Aesthetically Good vs The Morally Good," Southwest Philosophy Review, 13, 1997: 205-210; auth, "Moral Constraints on the Conduct of War," Perspectives, 16, Spring, 97: 4-5; auth, "War Crimes Trials," Ethics and Justice 2, April, 99: 43-50; auth, "The Mystery of Moralty," Journal of Power and Ethics, 2, 99: 161-168. **CONTACT ADDRESS** Dept Philosophy & Humanities, Texas A&M Univ, Col Station, College Station, TX 77843-0001. **EMAIL** m_davenport@tamu.edu

DAVEY, WILLIAM J.
DISCIPLINE LAW **EDUCATION** Univ Mich, BA; JD, 74. **CAREER** Law clerk, Justice Potter Stewart, US Supreme Court, prof, Univ Ill Urbana Champaign. **MEMBERSHIPS** Mich Law Rev. **RESEARCH** Teaches international trade policy **SELECTED PUBLICATIONS** Coauth, Hand of WTO/GATT Dispute Settlement, 91-98; coauth, European Community Law, 93; coauth, Legal Problems of International Economic Relations, 95; auth, Pine & Swine: Canada-United States Trade Dispute Settlement, 96. **CONTACT ADDRESS** Law Dept, Univ of Illinois, Urbana-Champaign, 504 E Pennsylvania, 125 Law, Mail Code 594, Champaign, IL 61820. **EMAIL** wdavey@law.uiuc.edu

DAVID, GERALD
PERSONAL Born 08/05/1941, Brooklyn, NY, m, 1967, 6 children **DISCIPLINE** PHD-CLINICAL PSYCHOLOGY, DHL-MODERN PHILOSOPHY **EDUCATION** Dr. of Hebrew Literature, 75, Bernard Reval Graduated School, Yeshiva Univ, Professional License, 72, New York State Department of Educ Specialization, PhD, 71, Ferkauf Graduate School, Yeshiva Univ, Professional Diploma, 68, New York State Dept of Educ, Ordination(Semicha), 66, Rabbi Isaac Elechanan Theol Seminary, Yeshiva Univ, Master of Sci in Educ, 66, City Univ of New York, Naster of Sci in Educ, 65, Ferkauf Graduate School, Yeshiva Univ, BA, 63, Yeshiva College. **CAREER** Admin Supvr and Clin Psychol positions, 66-present, New York City Bd of Educ, Supv, Diry and Psychol positions at Ohel Family Serv, 79-present. **HONORS AND AWARDS** Hon Pres-Jewish Community Council at Rockaways, Hon Chm-JASH Senior Center, Hon Chm-Jewish Services Co-ulitius. **MEMBERSHIPS** Amer Psychological Associates. **RESEARCH** Pshchol, Philos, Rel. **SELECTED PUBLICATIONS** Man's Search for Immortality: A Positivist Approach, Yeshiva Univ Press, 78, "Preschool Intellectual Assessment with the Ammons Quick Test",in Psychology in the Schools, 75, 12, 430-431, "The Effects of Special Class Placement on Multiple Disabled Children", in Reading Improvement, 75, 14, 138-143, " The Russians: A New Community in Our Midst", in Proceedings of the Association of Orthodox Jewish Scientists, 82, " A Study of the Needs of Russian Immmigrant Youth", 80, Research Study Monograph sponsored by Ahudath Israel of Amer, funded by the New York City Youth Bd. **CONTACT ADDRESS** 861 East 27th St., Brooklyn, NY 11216.

DAVID, KEITH R.
PERSONAL Born 08/20/1929, Arkansas City, KS, m, 1949, 4 children **DISCIPLINE** SOCIOLOGY AND PHILOSOPHY **EDUCATION** Okla Baptist Univ, BA; Wichita State Univ, MA; Southern Ill Univ, PhD. **CAREER** Detail engr, Boeing Airplane Co, 48-51; Baptist minister, 51-69; lectr, philos, 60-61, dept of eng res, eng grade 3, 54-60, Wichita State Univ; doctoral asst, 62-64, lectr, philos, 64-69, Southern Ill Univ; asst prof to assoc prof to full prof, philos, William Jewell Col, 69-98. **HONORS AND AWARDS** Outstanding Facul Mem, William Jewell Col, 84; Profile in Excellence, Okla Baptist Univ, alumni office, 91; Prof emer, William Jewell Col, 94. **MEMBERSHIPS** Amer Philos Asn; Baptist Philos Teachers Asn. **RESEARCH** American philosophy; Philosophy of religion; Medical ethics. **SELECTED PUBLICATIONS** Auth, Historical Note: The Paul Carus Collection, The Monist, 75; auth, Percept and Concept in William James, The Philos of William James, Felix Meiner Verlag, 76; eng res publ, Aerodynamics, dept of defense, 55-58, Wichita State Univ, dept of eng res. **CONTACT ADDRESS** 1029 Broadmore Ln., Liberty, MO 64068.

DAVID, MARCELLA
PERSONAL Born 09/13/1964, New York, NY, s **DISCIPLINE** LAW **EDUCATION** Rensselaer Polytech Inst, BS, 86; Univ Mich Law Sch, JD, 89. **CAREER** Law Clerk, U.S. Dist Court of Pa, 89-90; Vis Asst Prof, Univ Chicago Law Sch, 90-91; Ford Found Fel, Harvard Law Sch, 91-92; Litigation Assoc, New York, 92-95; Prof, Univ Iowa Col of Law, 95-. **HONORS AND AWARDS** Clarence Darrow Fel, 86-89; Ford Found Fel, Harvard Law Sch, 91-92. **MEMBERSHIPS** NY Bar; Am Bar Asn; Nat Bar Asn; Am Soc of Intl Law. **RESEARCH** Public International Law. **SELECTED PUBLICATIONS** Co-auth, "Shaw v. Reno: A Mirage of Good Intentions with Devastating Racial Consequences," Fordham Law Rev, (94): 1-64; auth, "United States Human Rights Procedures," J of Intergroup Relations, 97; auth, "Commentary: Learning from the Past: Schoolroom Tales, Life Lessons," J of Gender, Race & Justice, 98; auth, "Grotius Repudiated: The American Objections to the International Criminal Court and the Commitment to International Law," Mich J of Intl Law, 99; auth, "Passport Justice: Internationalizing the Political Question Doctrine for Application in the World Court," Harvard Intl Law J, 99. **CONTACT ADDRESS** Col of Law, Univ Iowa, Melrose and Bylington, Iowa City, IA 52242. **EMAIL** marcella-david@uiowa.edu

DAVID, MARIAN
PERSONAL Born 10/03/1959, Austria **DISCIPLINE** PHILOSOPHY **EDUCATION** Univ of Graz, Mag. Phil. 85; Univ Ariz, MA, 89, PhD, 90. **CAREER** Assoc prof; co-ed of Grazer Philosophische Studien. **RESEARCH** Philosophy of language; epistemology. **SELECTED PUBLICATIONS** Auth, Correspondence and Disquotation: An Essay on the Nature of Truth, 94; Analyticity, Carnap, Quine, and Truth, Philos Perspectives, 96; Two Conceptions of the Synthetic A Priori, 97; Kim's Functionalism, 97; auth, Kim's Functionalism, Philos Perspectives, 97; auth, Truth as the Epistemic Goal, 01; aauth, Theories of Truth, Handbook of Epistemology, 01; auth, Truth: Correspondence and Identity, The Nature of Truth, 01; auth, Minimalism and the Facts about Truth, 01. **CONTACT ADDRESS** Philosophy Dept, Univ of Notre Dame, 336/7 O'Shaughnessy, Notre Dame, IN 46556. **EMAIL** david.1@nd.edu

DAVIDSON, DONALD
PERSONAL Born 03/06/1917, Springfield, MA, m, 1984, 1 child **DISCIPLINE** PHILOSOPHY **EDUCATION** Harvard, BA, 39, PhD, 49. **CAREER** Asst in Philos, 41-42, 46, Harvard; instr, 47-51, Queens Coll; asst prof, 51-56, assoc prof, 56-60, prof, 60-67, Stanford Univ; prof, 67-70, Princeton Univ; prof, 70-76, The Rockefeller Univ; lectr with rank of prof, 70-75, Princeton; univ prof, 76-81, The Univ Chicago; prof, 81-86, The Univ CA, Berkeley; appointed Willis S. and Marion Slusser prof of philos, 86-. **HONORS AND AWARDS** Amer Council of Learned Soc Fel, 58-59; Natl Science Found Sr Research Fel 63-64; Fel, Ctr for Advanced Study in the Behavioral Sci, 69-70; Guggenheim Memorial Fel, 73-74; fel, Bellagio Study and Conf Ctr, 91; Hegel Prize, awarded by the City of Stuttgart, 91; honorary degree, doctor of letters, Univ of Oxford, 95. **MEMBERSHIPS** Amer Philos Assn; Council for Philos Studies; Amer Acad of Arts and Sciences; Institute Intl de Philosophie; Guggenheim Found Edu Adv Brd; Correspond Fel British Academy; Fel Amer Assoc Advancement Science; Comite d'honneur; Norwegian Acad of Sci and Letters, elected 87; Life Fel of the Acad of Philos at Lake Sevan, elected 91. **RESEARCH** Philos of Language, mind, epistemology **SELECTED PUBLICATIONS** Auth, Esaays on Actions and Events, 80, various reprint 82, 85, 86, 89; A Coherence Theory of Truth and Knowledge, orig 83, various reprint 85, 86, 88, 91, 92, 95, 97; Inquiries into Truth and Interpretation, 84, various reprint 90, 91, 93, 94; Knowing One's Own Mind, Proceedings and Addresses of the American Philosophical Association, 87, various reprint 92, 94, 95, 96; Readings in the Philosophy of Social Science, 94; The Philosophy of Action, 97; Readings in the Philosophy of Language, 97; Meaning, Truth, Method: Introduction to Analytical Philosophy I, 97. **CONTACT ADDRESS** Philos Dept, Univ of California, Berkeley, 410 Moses Hall, Berkeley, CA 94720-2390. **EMAIL** davidson@socrates.berkeley.edu

DAVIDSON, ROGER HARRY
PERSONAL Born 07/31/1936, Washington, DC, m, 1961, 2 children **DISCIPLINE** POLITICAL SCIENCE **EDUCATION** Univ Colo, BA, 58; Columbia Univ, PhD, 63. **CAREER** Asst prof, Govt, Dartmouth Coll, 62-68; assoc prof, Polit Sci, Univ Calif-Santa Barbara, 68-82; sr spec, Cong Res Serv, Libr Cong, 80-88; Prof, Govt & Polit, Univ MD, 87-. **MEMBERSHIPS** Am Polit Sci Asn; South Polit Sci Asn; Midwest Polit Sci Asn; West Polit Sci Asn; Nat Capitol Area Pol Sci Asn **RESEARCH** US government, policies & legislature; Executive politics; National policy making. **SELECTED PUBLICATIONS** Remaking Congress, 95; Understanding the Presidency, 96; Congress and Its Members, 98. **CONTACT ADDRESS** Univ of Maryland, Col Park, 1140B Tydings Hall, College Park, MD 20742. **EMAIL** rdavidso@bss2.umd.edu

DAVIES, ALAN T.
PERSONAL Born 06/24/1933, Westmount, PQ, Canada **DISCIPLINE** RELIGION **EDUCATION** McGill Univ, BA, 54, BD, 57; Union Theol Sem (NY), STM, 60, PhD, 66. **CAREER** Ordained min, United Church Can, 57; min, NW Interlake Pastoral Charge, Man, 57-59; min, Wesley United Church, Toronto, 64-67; J. Clarence & Corale B. Workman postdoctoral fel, Hebrew Union Col Cincinnati, 67-68; lectr to assoc prof, 69-89, Prof Religion, Victoria Col, Univ Toronto, 89-. **SELECTED PUBLICATIONS** Auth, Anti-Semitism and the Christian Mind, 69; auth, Infected Christianity: A Study of Modern Racism, 88; coauth, How Silent Were the Churches?: Canadian Protestantism and the Jewish Plight During the Nazi Era, 97; ed, Antisemitism and the Foundations of Christianity, 79; ed, Antisemitism in Canada: History and Interpretation, 92. **CONTACT ADDRESS** Victoria Col, Univ of Toronto, 73 Queen's Park Crescent, Toronto, ON, Canada M5S 1K7.

DAVIES, BRIAN
DISCIPLINE PHILOSOPHY OF RELEGION **EDUCATION** Univ London, PhD. **CAREER** Prof, Fordham Univ. **HONORS AND AWARDS** Bk rev ed, Intl Philos Quart. **SELECTED PUBLICATIONS** Auth, An Introduction to the Philosophy of Religion, Oxford UP, 82; Thinking About God, Chapman, 85; The Thought of Thomas Aquinas, Oxford UP, 92. **CONTACT ADDRESS** Dept of Philos, Fordham Univ, 113 W 60th St, New York, NY 10023.

DAVIES, DAVID
DISCIPLINE PHILOSOPHY **EDUCATION** Oxford Univ, BA, 70; Univ Manitoba, MA, 79; Univ Western Ontario, PhD, 87. **CAREER** Prof, McGill Univ. **RESEARCH** Metaphysics; philosophies of language, mind, psychology, art, lit; aesthetics. **SELECTED PUBLICATIONS** Auth, How Not To OutSmart the Anti-Realist, Analysis, 47, (87): 1-8; auth, Horwich on Semantic and Metaphysical Realism, Philosophy of Science, 54, (87): 539-557; auth, Works, Texts, and Contexts: Goodman on the Literary Artwork, Canadian Journal of Philosophy, (91): 331-346; auth, Perspectives on Intentional Realism, Mind and Language, 7, (92): 264-285; auth, Putnam's Brain-Teaser, Canadian Journal of Philosophy, 25, (95): 203-228; auth, Dennett's Stance on Tntentional Ralism, Southern Journal of Philosophy, 33, (95): 299-312; auth, Fictional Truth and Fictional Authors, British Journal of Aesthetics, 36, (96): 43-55. **CONTACT ADDRESS** Philosophy Dept, McGill Univ, 845 Sherbrooke St, Montreal, QC, Canada H3A 2T5. **EMAIL** davidd@philo.mcgill.ca

DAVIES, GORDON F.
PERSONAL Born 07/25/1954, Kenora, ON, Canada **DISCIPLINE** OLD TESTAMENT STUDIES **EDUCATION** Univ Toronto, BA, 76; Ottawa Univ, BTh, 81; Saint Paul Univ, STB, 81; Biblicum, SSL, 87; Gregorian, STD, 92. **CAREER** Dean of stud, 90-96, asst prof, 90-95, spiritual dir, 90-, assoc prof, 95-, sr acad dean, 97-, St. Augustine's Sem; lectr, Ontario Ministry of Ed, relig ed, 95-. **HONORS AND AWARDS** Gov Gen Gold Medal, 76; Summa Cum Laude, 90; jr fel, Can Bibl Assoc, 96. **MEMBERSHIPS** Soc Bibl Lit; Catholic Bibl Assoc; Catholic Bibl Assoc of Can; Can Soc of Bibl Stud; Qahal; Soc for Interpreting the Old Testament as Scripture. **RESEARCH** Narrative Criticism, Rhetorical Criticism, Exodus, Exra-Nehemiah. **SELECTED PUBLICATIONS** Auth, Israel in Egypt: Reading Exod 1-2, JSOT, Sheffield, 92; Auth, Creed and Criticism: The Complementarity of Faith and Exegesis, The New Jerusalem, Food for the Journey, Taking God Seriously, Can Catholic Rev, 95; auth, How to Believe, The Easter Vigil, Paschaltide, Faith and Gratitude, The Last Things, Can Catholic Rev, 96; auth, Disobedience, Covenants, Seeing Stars, Three Short Questions, Massaccio's Peter, On Asking Stupid Questions, Can Catholic Rev, 97; auth, The Parish, The Bible and Everything Else: Scripture and Our Common Quest to Make Sense, New Blackfriars, 98; auth, Ezra-Nehemiah, Liturgical, forthcoming. **CONTACT ADDRESS** St. Augustine's Sem, 2661 Kingston Rd, Scarborough, ON, Canada M1M 1M3. **EMAIL** info@staugustines.on.ca

DAVIES, HORTON
PERSONAL Born 03/10/1916, Cwmavon, Wales, m, 1940, 3 children **DISCIPLINE** RELIGION **EDUCATION** Univ Edinburgh, MA, 37, BD, 40; Oxford Univ, DPhil(ecclesiastical hist), 43; Univ SAfrica, DD(church hist), 51. **CAREER** Prof divinity, Rhodes Univ, SAfrica, 46-53, dean fac of divinity, 51-53; head joint dept church hist, Mansfield & Regent's Park Cols, Oxford Univ, 53-56; prof, 56-60, Putnam Prof Relig, Princeton Univ, 60-, Old St Andrew's Mem lectr, Emmanuel Col, Victoria Univ; Carnegie traveling fel, 52; Guggenheim fels, 59 & 64; consult, Int Missionary Coun & World Coun Churches, 56-; ed adv, Studia Liturgica, 62-; assoc ed, Worship, 67-; lectr, Union Theol Sem, Va, spring 68 & 69 & Drew Univ, 69; Scott lectr, Christian Theol Sem, fall 77. **HONORS AND AWARDS** Gunning Divinity Prize, Univ Edinburgh, 40; littd, la salle col, 66; dlitt, oxford univ, 70. **MEMBERSHIPS** Am Soc Church Hist; Am Theol Soc. **RESEARCH** English church history; medieval pilgrimages; doctrine of providence in the 17th century in England and New England. **SELECTED PUBLICATIONS** Auth, Christian Plain Style--The Evolution of a Spiritual Ideal, Church Hist, Vol 0065, 96; The English Bible and the 17th-Century Revolution, Amer Hist Rev, Vol 0100, 95.

DAVIES, JULIAN A.
PERSONAL Born 01/25/1933, Utica, NY, s **DISCIPLINE** PHILOSOPHY, THEOLOGY **EDUCATION** St. Bonaventure Univ, BA, 56; Fordham Univ, MA, 67; PhD, 70. **CAREER** Prof, Siena Col, 84-. **MEMBERSHIPS** Am Cath Philos Asn. **RESEARCH** Medieval Philosophy, Ockham. **SELECTED PUBLICATIONS** Transl, Ockham on Aristotle's Physics, of Brevis Summa Libri Physicorum (St. Bonaventure, NY: Franciscan Inst, 89); transl, A Compendium of Ockham's Teachings, of Tractatus de Principiis Theologiae (St. Bonaventure, NY: Franciscan Inst, 98); **CONTACT ADDRESS** Dept Philos, Siena Col, 515 Loundonville Rd, Albany, NY 12211-1459. **EMAIL** davies@siena.edu

DAVIS, BENJAMIN G.
PERSONAL Born 07/06/1941, Honesdale, PA, m, 1980, 2 children **DISCIPLINE** THEOLOGY, ECONOMICS **EDUCATION** Univ Mich, AB, 67; AM, 69; Univ Nottingham, MTh, 82; St. Mary's Sem and Univ, DMin, 85. **CAREER** Regional Dir, World Relief, 81-86; Wash Office Dir, Evangelicals for Soc Action, 87-88; Assoc Dean and Prof, Baltimore Int Col, 88-95; Exec Dir, The Relig Coalition, 96-98; Ecumenical Inst Prof, St. Mary's Sem and Univ, 86-; Acad Dean, Potomac Col, 98-. **HONORS AND AWARDS** Rockard's Fel in Theol, Univ of Nottingham; Governor's Citation for Distinguished Serv, State of Md; Omicron Delta Epsilon Econ Hon. **MEMBERSHIPS** Am Asn of Univ Admin, Asn of Overseas Educators. **RESEARCH** Relationship between economics and justice, relationship between theology and science. **SELECTED PUBLICATIONS** Auth, Necessary Manpower Adjustments in the United States Economy during the 1970s, UN (NY), 71; auth, Forty Famous Black Americans, Media Materials Inc (Baltimore), 87; auth, Famous Documents: New Perspectives in History, , Media Materials Inc (Baltimore), 88; auth, "On Religion," weekly column in Gazette; auth, "Teaching the Adult Learner," Classroom Companion (Spring 92); auth, Economics: An Integrated Approach, Prentice Hal (Upper Saddle River, NJ), 97; auth, A Survey of World Cultures: the United States and Canada, 2nd ed, AGS Publ (Circle Pines, MN, 00). **CONTACT ADDRESS** Dept Theol, St. Mary's Sem and Univ, 5400 Roland Ave, Baltimore, MD 21210-1929. **EMAIL** bdavis@potomac.edu

DAVIS, CARL L.
PERSONAL Born 08/27/1934, Bartlesville, OK, m, 1967, 2 children **DISCIPLINE** HISTORY, POLITICAL SCIENCE **EDUCATION** Okla State Univ, AB, 58, MA, 59, PhD(hist), 71. **CAREER** Instr hist & polit sci, 61-64, from asst prof to assoc prof hist, 74-77, Prof Hist, Stephen F Austin State Univ, 77-. **MEMBERSHIPS** AHA; Orgn Am Historians; Southern Hist Asn; Southwestern Soc Sci Asn. **RESEARCH** United States military-industrial; modern United States (since 1945) social attitudes. **SELECTED PUBLICATIONS** Auth, Study Guide to American History to 1865, 71 & Study Guide to American History, 1865-Present, 71, Okla State Univ; contribr, The Mexican War, In: Fighting Men, Kendall, 71; coauth, Dragoons in Indian territory, Chronicles Okla, spring 72; auth, Arming the Union, Kennikat, 74; coauth (with A P McDonald), The War with Mexico, Forum Press, 79; auth, James W Ripley, George D Ramsay & Alexander B Dyer, In: Dict Union Biog, 82. **CONTACT ADDRESS** Dept of Hist, Stephen F. Austin State Univ, Box 3013, Nacogdoches, TX 75962.

DAVIS, CASEY W.
PERSONAL Born 06/05/1958, Springfield, OH, m, 1980, 2 children **DISCIPLINE** NEW TESTAMENT **EDUCATION** Un Theol Sem, PhD, 96; Asbury Theol Sem, MDiv, 85; Miami Univ, BS **CAREER** Chaplain, 98, Roberts Wesleyan Col; Prof of Relig, 97-98, Cent Col; Adj Facul, 97, Youngstown St Univ; Lect, 94, Hampden Sydney Col **MEMBERSHIPS** Am Acad of Relig; Inst for Bibl Res; Soc of Bibl Lit; Wesleyan Theolog Soc; Evangel Theolog Soc **RESEARCH** New Testament; Orality; Rhetoric; Pauline Studies **SELECTED PUBLICATIONS** Oral Biblical Criticism: The Influence of the Principles of Orality on the Literary Structure of Paul's Epistle to the Philippians, Sheffield Acad Pr, 99. **CONTACT ADDRESS** 47 W Forest Dr, Rochester, NY 24624. **EMAIL** davisc@roberts.edu

DAVIS, CHRISTOPHER A.
PERSONAL Born 11/08/1958, Kansas City, MS, m, 1980 **DISCIPLINE** BIBLICAL STUDIES **EDUCATION** Johnson Bibl Col, BA, BTh, 81; Union theol Sem, DMin, 85; ThM, 86; PhD, 92. **CAREER** Prof, Minn Bibl Col, 92-; Vice President Acad, Min Bibl Col, 96-. **HONORS AND AWARDS** Who's Who Among Am Teachers, 98, 00. **MEMBERSHIPS** Soc of Bibl Lit; Cath Bibl Assoc; Am Assoc of Col Registr and Admis Off. **RESEARCH** Pauline Theology, New Testament Theology. **SELECTED PUBLICATIONS** Auth, The Structure of Paul's Theology: The Truth Which is the Gospel, (Lewiston/Lampeter/Queenston: Mellen Bibl Pr, 95); auth, The College Press NIV Commentary: Revelation (Joplin, MO: Col Pr) forthcoming. **CONTACT ADDRESS** Academics, Minnesota Bible Col, 920 Mayowood Rd SW, Rochester, MN 55902-2382. **EMAIL** academic@mnbc.edu

DAVIS, DANIEL CLAIR
DISCIPLINE CHURCH HISTORY **EDUCATION** Wheaton Col, AB, 53, MA, 57; Westminster Theol Sem, BD, 56; Georg-August Univ, Guttingen, ThD, 60. **CAREER** Asst prof, Olivet Col, 60-63; vis prof, asst prof, Wheaton Col, Grad Sch Theol, 63-66; prof, Westminster Theol Sem, 66-. **SELECTED PUBLICATIONS** Contrib, John Calvin: His Influence in the Western World; Challenges to Inerrancy; Inerrancy and the Church; Pressing Toward the Mark; Theonomy: A Reformed Critique. **CONTACT ADDRESS** Westminster Theol Sem, Pennsylvania, PO Box 27009, Philadelphia, PA 19118. **EMAIL** cdavis@wts.edu

DAVIS, DEREK H.
PERSONAL Born 07/14/1949, Laredo, TX, m, 1970, 2 children **DISCIPLINE** LAW **CAREER** Nat Coun of Churches RLC, mem 95-; Intl Acad Freedom of Relig and Belief, fel 95-; Jour of Church and State, editor 93-; Baylor Univ JM Dawson Inst, dir 95-; Dawson, Sodd, Davis, Moe, TX, partner 75-90. **HONORS AND AWARDS** Pew Ch Trsts; Lilly Foun Gnt; Baylor L Rev Ed; Harris Honor Soc; Omicron Delta Kappa; Fel, Salzberg Sem, 95-. **MEMBERSHIPS** Waco, State of Tex, Am Bar Asn, Am, Political Sci Asn, Am Acad of Relig. **SELECTED PUBLICATIONS** Auth, Original Intent: Chief Justice Rehnquist and the Course of American Church-State Relations, 91; co-ed, Legal Deskbook for Administrators of Independent Colleges and Univ's, 94; auth, The Separation of Church and State Defended: Selected Writings of James E Wood Jr, 95; co-ed, Welfare Reform and Faith-based Organizations, 99; auth, Religion and the Continental Congress 1774-1789: Contr to Orig Intent, 00; coauth, Perspectives on Religion in the Twenty-first Century by a Progressive Jew and an Mainline Christian, 00. **CONTACT ADDRESS** JM Dawson Inst Church State Studies, Baylor Univ, PO Box 97311, Waco, TX 76798-7311. **EMAIL** derek.davis@baylor.edu

DAVIS, ELLEN F.
DISCIPLINE OLD TESTAMENT LANGUAGES AND LITERATURE **EDUCATION** Univ Calif, AB, 71; Oxford Univ, Cert Theol, 82; Church Divinity Sch Pacific, MDiv, 83; Yale Univ, PhD, 87. **CAREER** Asst prof, Union Theol Sem, 87-89; asst prof, Yale Divinity Sch, 89-91; assoc prof, Yale Divinity Sch, 91-96; assoc prof, Va Theol Sem, 96-99, Prof, 99-. **SELECTED PUBLICATIONS** Co-auth, And Pharaoh Will Change His Mind (Ezek. 32:31): Dismantling Mythical Discourse, Theol Exegesis Essays in Conversation, Eerdmans, 97; auth, Imagination Shaped: Old Testament Preaching in the Anglican Tradition, Trinity Press Intl, 95. **CONTACT ADDRESS** Virginia Theol Sem, 3737 Seminary Rd, Alexandria, VA 22304. **EMAIL** EDavis@vts.edu

DAVIS, GORDON B.
PERSONAL Born 09/09/1930, Idaho Falls, ID, m, 1954, 4 children **DISCIPLINE** BUSINESS ADMINISTRATION; INFORMATION SYSTEMS **EDUCATION** Idaho State Univ, BA, BS; Stanford Univ, MBA, PhD. **CAREER** Honeywell Prof of MIS, Grad School of Mgmt, 61-, Univ of Minn; Pres, 98, AIS; vis Prof at: NYU, Euro Institute of Adv Stud in Mgmt, Nat Univ Singapore & Nanyang Univ Singapore. **HONORS AND AWARDS** Honorary doctorates: Universite Jean Moulin (Lyon, France), Univ of Zurich (Switzerland), Stockholm Sch of Economics (Sweden); LEO Awd for lifetime distinguished service; AIS; Fel of ACM; Fel of AIS; initiated first mis grad program and established the mgmt info sys research center at univ minn. **MEMBERSHIPS** ACM, ACPA; IEEE Computer Soc; AICPA; Informs; AAA. **RESEARCH** MIS Systems & development, information technology to improve productivity, information requirements determination. **SELECTED PUBLICATIONS** Co-auth, Management Information Systems, Conceptual Foundations, Structure and Development, 2nd ed, McGraw-Hill Book Comp, 85; co-auth, Personal Productivity with Information Technology, McGraw-Hill, 97; coauth, Writing the Doctoral Dissertation, 2nd ed, Barrons Educational Series, 97. **CONTACT ADDRESS** Carlson School of Management, Univ of Minnesota, Twin Cities, 321 19th Ave S, Minneapolis, MN 55455. **EMAIL** gdavis@csom.umn.edu

DAVIS, JEFFREY
DISCIPLINE LAW **EDUCATION** Univ Calif, Los Angeles, BS; Loyola Univ, Los Angeles, JD; Univ Mich, LLM. **CAREER** Prof, Univ Fla, 81-. **MEMBERSHIPS** Exec Coun, Fla Bar Bus Law Sect, 91-; Amer Bar Asn Comt on Consumer Financial Serv, 79-; Calif Bar; Fla Bar; past ch, Fla Bar Bankruptcy/Uniform Commercial Code Comt. **RESEARCH** Contracts, bankruptcy. **CONTACT ADDRESS** School of Law, Univ of Florida, PO Box 117625, Gainesville, FL 32611-7625. **EMAIL** davis@law.ufl.edu

DAVIS, JOHN JEFFERSON
PERSONAL m, 5 children **DISCIPLINE** SYSTEMATIC THEOLOGY, CHRISTIAN ETHICS **EDUCATION** Duke Univ, BS, PhD; Gordon-Conwell Theol Sem, MA. **CAREER** Prof, Gordon-Conwell Theol Sem, 75-. **HONORS AND AWARDS** Danforth Grad Fel; Phi Beta Kappa grad, Duke Univ; ch, bd dir(s) mass citizens for life; founding mem, bd dir(s) birthright of greater beverly; pres, evangel philos soc; bd dir(s), value of life comm; adv bd, presbyterians for democracy and religious freedom; delegate to the white house conf on families. **SELECTED PUBLICATIONS** Ed, The Necessity of Systematic Theology; auth, Theology Primer; Foundations of Evangelical Theology; Abortion and the Christian; Your Wealth in God's World; Handbook of Basic Bible Texts; Evangelical Ethics; The Christian's Guide to Pregnancy and Childbirth; Christ's Victorious Kingdom: Postmillennialism Reconsidered. **CONTACT ADDRESS** Gordon-Conwell Theol Sem, 130 Essex St, South Hamilton, MA 01982.

DAVIS, JOHN WESLEY
PERSONAL Born 11/01/1943, Detroit, MI, m, 1966 **DISCIPLINE** LAW **EDUCATION** Wabash Coll, AB, 1964; Univ of Denver, JD, 1971. **CAREER** Int Assn Human Rights, EEO Program, dir, 75-76; Natl Bar Assn, EEO Program, exec dir, 76-78; Howard Univ, Reggie Program, exec dir, 80-84, law professor, 78-85; Self Employed, Attorney, 85-. **HONORS AND AWARDS** NAACP, Awd of Merit, 1975, Certificate of Appreciation, 1980; Natl Bar Assn, Equal Justice Awd, 1977. **MEMBERSHIPS** DC Neighborhood Legal Services, bd mem, 1992-; Natl Bar Assn, life mem, NBA journal editorial board; NAACP, life mem, 1979-, cooperating Attorney, 1977-. **SELECTED PUBLICATIONS** Employment Discrimination Litigation Manual, 1977; Law Review Article, NCCU Law Journal, The Supreme Court Rationale for Racism, 1976. **CONTACT ADDRESS** 601 Indiana Ave NW, Ste 1000, Washington, DC 20004.

DAVIS, KENNETH G.
PERSONAL Born 09/16/1957, Louisville, KY **DISCIPLINE** PASTORAL THEOLOGY, CROSS-CULTURAL COMMUNICATION **EDUCATION** St. Louis Univ, BA, cum laude, 80; Washington Theol Union, MA, 85; Pacific Sch of Theol, DMin, 91. **CAREER** Deaconate in Honduras, 85-86; found dir, Hispanic ministry, 86-88; assoc pastor, St. Paul the Apostle Church, San Pablo, CA, 88-91; staff, intl office RENEW, 91-94; found dir, DMin, Oblate Sch Theol, 94-97; asst prof, Mundelein Sem, 97- . **MEMBERSHIPS** ACHTUS; Amer Acad Rel; Asn DMin Eduuc; CORHIM; Inst de Litugia Hispana; Nat Org Catechesis for Hispanics; Nalt Catholic Coun Hispanic Ministry. **RESEARCH** Religious faith of US Hispanics. **SELECTED PUBLICATIONS** Auth, Child Abuse in the Hispanic Community: A Christian Perspective, Apuntes, 12(3), Fall, 92, 127-136; Auth, Cuando El Tomar Ya No Es Gozar, LA, Franciscan Comm Press, 93; What's New in Hispanic Ministry, Overheard, Fall 93; auth, Primero Dios, Susquehanna UP, 94; Following the Yellow Brick Road: Rahner Reasons Through Petitionary Prayer, Living Light, 30(4), Summer, 94, 25-30; The Hispanic Shift: Continuity Rather than Conversion, in An Enduring Flame: Studies on Latino Popular Religiosity, NY, Bildner Ctr W Hemispheric Studs, 94, 205-210; The Hispanic Shift: Continuity Rather Than Conversion, Jour Hispanic/Latino Theol, 1(3), May 94, 68-79; Preaching in Spanish as a Second Language, in Perspectivas, Kansas City, Sheed and Ward, 95; Presiding in Spanish as a Second Language, AIM, Wint 95, 22-24; Encuentros, in New Catholic Encycl, vol 19, Wash DC, Catholic UP, 95; Afterward, in Discovering Latino Religion, NY, The Bildner Ctr W Hemispheric Studs, 95; Selected Pastoral Resources, in Perspectivas, Kansas City, Sheed and Ward, 95; Las Bodas de Plata de Una Lluvia de Oro, Revista Latinoamericana de Teologia, 12(37), April, 96, 79-91; coauth, The Attraction and Retention of Hispanics to Doctor of Ministry Programs, Theol Ed, 33(1), Autumn, 96, 75-82; Presiding in Spanish as a Second Language, in Misa, Mesa y Musa, Schiller Park, IL, J.S. Paluch Co, 97; Misa, Mesa y Musa, Schiller Park, IL, J. S. Paluch, 97; From Anecdote to Analysis: A Case for Applied Research in the Ministry, Pastoral Phychol, 46(2), 97, 99-106; La Catequesis ante la Experiencia Rligiosa, Catequetica, 1, 97, 3-8; Introduction, Listening: Jour of Rel and Cult 32(3), Fall, 97, 147-151; Challenges to the Pastoral Care of Central Americans in the United States, Apuntes 17(2), Summer 97, 45-56; A New Catholic Reformation? Chicago Studs, 36(3), Dec 97, 216-223; Petitionary Prayer: What the Masters Have to Say, Spiritual Life, Summer 97, 91-99; A Survey of Contemporary US Hispanic Catholic Theology, Theol Dig, 44(3), fall 97, 203-212; co-ed, Listening: Journal of Religion and Culture, vol 32, no 3, Fall, 97; co-ed, Chicago Studies, vol 36, no 3, Dec, 97; co-ed, Theol Today, vol 54, no 4, Jan, 98; Visions and Dreams, Theol Today, 54(4), Jan 98, 451-452. **CONTACT ADDRESS** Dept of Theology, Saint Meinrad Sch of Theol, 1 Hill Dr, Saint Meinrad, IN 47577. **EMAIL** kdavis@saintmeinrad.edu

DAVIS, LANCE E.
PERSONAL Born 11/03/1928, Seattle, WA, m, 1977, 1 child **DISCIPLINE** ECONOMICS **EDUCATION** Univ Wash, BA, Magna Cum Laude, 50; John Hopkins Univ, PhD, Dist, 56. **CAREER** Prof, Cal Inst Tech, 68-80; vis fel, Australian Nat Univ, 96; prof, Mary Stillman Harkness, Cal Inst Tech, 80-. **HONORS AND AWARDS** Phi Beta Kappa; Ford Diss Fel, 56; Ford Fac Fel, 59-60; Arthur Cole Prize, 96; Alice Hanson Jones Prize, 97-98; Sanwa Monograph Prize, 94; Clio Can Awd, Cliometrics Soc, 94. **MEMBERSHIPS** Trus Cliometric Soc, 93-96; Rev Bd, NSF Econ Panel, 91-92; Fel, Am Acad Arts Sci, 91-. **RESEARCH** The impact of imperialism on the economic growth and welfare with particular reference to the British Empire, 1860-1912. **SELECTED PUBLICATIONS** Auth, "The Economy of Colonial North America: Miles Traveled, Miles to Go," The William and Mary Qtly (99); coauth, "Micro Rules and Macro Outcomes: The Impact of the Structure of organizational Rules on the Efficiency of Security Exchanges: London, New York, and Paris 1800-1914," Am Econ Rev (98) vol 87, no 2; coauth, "International Capital Movements, Domestic Capital Markets and American Growth, 1820-1914," in Cambridge Economic History of the United States, eds. S Engerman, R Gallman (New York and Cambridge, UK, Cambridge Univ Press, 99) vol 2; auth, "The Late Nineteenth Century British Imperialist: Specification, Quantification, and Controlled Conjectures," in Gentlemanly Capitalism and the New World Order: The New Debate on Imperialism, ed. Ray Dumefi (London: Addison Wesley Longman, 99); auth, "Lessons from the Past: Capital Imports and the Evolution of Domestic Capital Markets, 1870-1914," in Victorian Perspectives on Capital Mobility and Financial Fragility in the 1990s, ed. Charles Calormiris (Washington DC: Am Ent Inst, 99); auth, "Whaling" in Encyclopedia of the United States in the Nineteenth Century, ed. Paul Finkelman (New York: Charles Scribners Sons, 99). **CONTACT ADDRESS** Dept Social Sci, California Inst of Tech, 1201 E California, MC 228-77, Pasadena, CA 91125.

DAVIS, LAWRENCE H.
PERSONAL Born 08/21/1943, Chicago, IL, m, 1970, 3 children **DISCIPLINE** PHILOSOPHY **EDUCATION** Columbia Univ, AB, 64; Univ Mich, Ann Arbor, PhD(philos), 69. **CAREER** Asst prof philos, Johns Hopkins Univ, 68-75; from asst prof to assoc prof philos, Univ Mo-St Louis, 76-; chemn dept, Univ Mo-St Louis, 88-94. **HONORS AND AWARDS** Nat Endowment for Humanities younger humanist fel, 72-73; vis fel, Cornell Univ Prog on Sci, Technol & Soc, 75-76; univ res board grant, 95-96. **MEMBERSHIPS** Am Philos Asn; Soc Philos & Psychol. **RESEARCH** Philos of mind; theory of action; philosophy of religion. **SELECTED PUBLICATIONS** Auth, They deserve to suffer, Analysis, 3/72; The intelligibility of rule-utilitarianism, Philos Studies, 10/73; Disembodied brains, Australasian J Philos, 8/74; Prisoners, paradox and rationality, Am Philos Quart, 10/77; Theory of Action, Prentice-Hall, 79; Functionalism and absent qualia, Philos Studies, 3/82; Cerebral Hemispheres, Philos Studies, 9/97; auth, "Functionalism and personal identity," Philos and Phenom Res 12 (98). **CONTACT ADDRESS** Dept of Philosophy, Univ of Missouri, St. Louis, 8001 Natural Bridge, Saint Louis, MO 63121-4499. **EMAIL** lhdavis_philos@umsl.edu

DAVIS, MICHAEL
PERSONAL Born 02/06/1943, Canton, OH, m, 1975, 1 child **DISCIPLINE** PHILOSOPHY **EDUCATION** Western Reserve Univ, BA, 65; Univ Mich, MA, 65; PhD, 72. **CAREER** Vis asst prof, Case-Western Reserve Univ, 72-75; asst prof, IL State Univ, 77-84; vis asst prof, Univ of IL Chicago, 85-86; prof, IL Inst of Tech, 86-. **HONORS AND AWARDS** NEH Awds, 74, 84-85, 90; Hitachi Found, 88-90; Nat Sci Found Grants, 91-85; 95-96, 97-99, Ctr for Innovation in Learning Grant, 94-95. **MEMBERSHIPS** AAUP; Am Soc for Polit and Legal Philos; Am Philos Assoc; Assoc for Prof and Practical Ethics; Soc for the Soc Studies of Sci; Soc for Business Ethics; Midwest Philos of Educ Soc. **RESEARCH** Practical Ethics, philosophy of law, political philosophy and moral theory. **SELECTED PUBLICATIONS** Coed, Ethics and the Legal Profession, Prometheus Books (Buffalo, NY), 86; auth, To Make the Punishment Fit the Crime, Westview Pr, (Boulder, CO), 92; coed, AIDS: Crisis in Professional Ethics, Temple Univ Pr, (Philadelphia, PA,), 94; auth, "Justice in the Shadow of Death: Rethinking Capital and Lesser Punishments, Rowman & Littlefield (Lanham, MD); 96; auth, "Preventive Detention, Corrado and Me", Criminal Justice Ethics 15 (96): 13-24; auth, "Is There a Profession of Engineering?", Sci and Eng Ethics 3, (97): 407-428; auth, "Punishment Theory: Making Sense of What We Know About Punishment", Law Studies 22 (98): 3-10; auth, "Sidgwick's Impractical Ethics", Int J of Applied Philos 12 (98): 153-159; auth, Thinking Like and Engineer: Essays in the Ethics of a Profession, Oxford Univ Pr, (NY), 98; auth, Ethics and the University, Routledge (London), 99. **CONTACT ADDRESS** Dept Humanities, Illinois Inst of Tech, 3300 S Federal St, Chicago, IL 60616-3795. **EMAIL** davism@iit.edu

DAVIS, MICHAEL PETER
PERSONAL Born 12/19/1947, Albany, NY, m, 1969, 2 children **DISCIPLINE** PHILOSOPHY **EDUCATION** Cornell Univ, AB, 69; Penn State Univ, MA, 73, PhD, 74. **CAREER** Vis asst prof Philos, Dickinson Col, 74-75; vis asst prof Philos, Wesleyan Univ, 75-76; asst prof Philos, Alfred Univ, 76-77; prof Philos, Sarah Lawrence Col, 77-; adj prof Philos, New Sch Soc Res, 81-88; vis prof Polit Philos, Dept Polit Sci, Fordham Univ, 95-. **MEMBERSHIPS** Am Philos Asn; APSA; Soc Greek Polit Thought. **RESEARCH** Ancient philosophy; political philosophy; philos and lit. **SELECTED PUBLICATIONS** Auth, Aristotle's Poetics: The Poetry of Philosophy, 92; auth, The Politics of Philosophy: A Commentary on Aristotle's Politics, 96; auth, Euripides Among the Athenians, St, John's Rev, 98; auth, The Autobiography of Philosophy: Rousseau's The Reveries of the Solitary Walker, 99; ed, The Argument of the Action: Essays in Greek Poetry and Philosophy by Seth Benardete, 00. **CONTACT ADDRESS** Dept of Philosophy, Sarah Lawrence Col, Bronxville, NY 10708. **EMAIL** mdavis@mail.slc.edu

DAVIS, MORRIS E.
PERSONAL Born 08/09/1945, Wilmington, NC **DISCIPLINE** LAW **EDUCATION** NC A&T State U, BS 1967; Univ IA Coll of Law, JD 1970; Univ CA Sch Pub Health, MPH 1973. **CAREER** Dept Housing & Urban Devel San Francisco, atty-adv, 70-72; Univ of Calif Berkeley, Inst of Industrial Relations, Labor Occupational Health Prog, executive director, 74-80; Journal of Black Health Perspectives, managing editor 73-74; US Merit Systems Protection Board, administrative judge, 80-85, abritrator and mediator, 86-. **MEMBERSHIPS** CA Bar Assn; IA Bar Assn; The Am Arbtrtn Assn; Am Pub Health Assn; fellow Univ CA (San Fran) Schl of Med 1974; fellow Univ CA (Berkeley) Schl Pub Hlth 1972-73. **CONTACT ADDRESS** American Arbitration Association, 417 Montgomery St, 5th Fl, San Francisco, CA 94104-1113.

DAVIS, NATHANIEL
PERSONAL Born 04/12/1925, Boston, MA, m, 1956, 4 children **DISCIPLINE** POLITICAL SCIENCE **EDUCATION** Brown Univ, BA, 44; Fletcher School of Law and Diplomacy, MA, 47, PhD, 60. **CAREER** Third secy, Prague, 47-49; vice consul, Florence, 49-52; second secy, Rome, Moscow, 52-56; Dept of State, USSR Affairs, 56-60; first secy, Caracas, 60-62; positions within the Peace Corp, 62-65; US Min Bulgaria, 65-66; Nat Security Coun, 66-68; Vice Secy Ambassador, Guatemala, 68-71; US Ambassador Chile, 71-73; Dir General US Foreign Service, 73-75; asst Secy of State for African affairs, 75; US Ambassador Switzerland, 75-77; State Dept Adv to Naval War Col, 77-83; Howard Univ, 62-68; Chester W Nimitz Chair of Nat Security and Foreign Affairs, US Naval War Col, 77-83; Alexander and Adelaide Hixon Chair, Harvey Mudd Col & fac Claremont Grad School, 83- . **HONORS AND AWARDS** Phi Beta Kappa; hon LLD, Brown Univ, 70; US Navy Distinguished Public Service Awd, 83. **MEMBERSHIPS** Am Acad Diplomacy; Am Asn for Advanc of Slavic Stud; Am For Serv Asn; Coun on For Rel; Int Stud Asn. **RESEARCH** Religion in Russia. **SELECTED PUBLICATIONS** Contribur, Ronning, ed, Ambassadors in Foreign Policy, Praeger, 87; auth, The Last Two Years of Salvador Allende, Cornell, 85; auth, A Long Walk to Church: A Contemporary History of Russian Orthodoxy, Westview, 95. **CONTACT ADDRESS** Harvey Mudd Col, Claremont, CA 91711.

DAVIS, PETER L.
DISCIPLINE LAW **EDUCATION** Harvard Univ, BA, 69; NYork Univ, JD, 72. **CAREER** Clin instr, New York University School of Law; trial atty, Criminal Defense Div of the Legal Aid Soc, NYC; assoc prof Law, Touro Col. **HONORS AND AWARDS** Root-Tilden scholar, NY Univ. **MEMBERSHIPS** Chp, bd dir, Andrew Glover Youth Prog, NYC. **SELECTED PUBLICATIONS** Ed, Legal Systems and Institutions: The Criminal Justice System as Paradigm; coed, N.Y.U. Criminal Law Clinic: Materials and Forms, 80, 81. **CONTACT ADDRESS** Touro Col, New York, Brooklyn, NY 11230. **EMAIL** peterd@tourolaw.edu

DAVIS, RALPH
DISCIPLINE OLD TESTAMENT **EDUCATION** S Baptist Theol Sem, PhD. **CAREER** Carl W. McMurray prof. **HONORS AND AWARDS** Pastor, Westminster Reformed Presbyterian Church; sr pastor, Aisquith Presbyterian Church. **SELECTED PUBLICATIONS** Auth, Such A Great Salvation; No Falling Words; Looking on the Heart. **CONTACT ADDRESS** Dept of Philosophy, Albion Col, 611 E Porte St, Albion, MI 49224. **EMAIL** rdavis@albion.edu

DAVIS, RICHARD
PERSONAL Born 10/14/1951, Parkersburg, WV, m, 1978, 1 child **DISCIPLINE** RELIGIOUS STUDIES **EDUCATION** Univ Chicago, BA, 73; Univ Toronto, MA, 78; Univ Chicago, PhD, 86. **CAREER** Instr, Univ Chicago, 87; vis lectr, School of thr Art Inst Chicago, 86-87; asst, assoc prof, Yale Univ, 87-97; Assoc Prof, Bard Coll, 97-. **HONORS AND AWARDS** Univ Toronto Open Fel, 76-78; Univ Chicago Humanities Fel, 78-79; NDEA Title VI Lang Fel, 79-81; AIIS Lang Fel, 81-82; Fulrbight-Hays Lr Res Fel, 83-84; Comm on southern Asian Studies Grant, Univ Chicago, 85; Mrs Giles Whiting Found Fel, 85-86; Paul Moore Fund for Undergraduate Instruction, Yale Univ, 88; A Whitney Griswold Faculty Res Grant, Yale Univ, 89; AIIS Short-term Res Grant, 90; Morse Fel in the Humanities, Yale Univ, 90-91; Whitney Humanities Center Fel, Yale Univ, 93-94; Nat Endowment for the he Humanities Fel for Univ Tchrs, 94. **MEMBERSHIPS** Asn for Asian Studies; Am Acad of Rel; Coll Art Asn; Am Oriental Soc; Am Comm for Sputhern Asian Art. **SELECTED PUBLICATIONS** Auth, Three Styles in Looting India, Hist and Anthropol, 94; Trophies of War: The Case of the Calukya Intruder, Perceptions of South Asia's Visual Past, 94; Carr-Gregg et al (1997) Brief History of Religion in India; The Rebuilding of a Hindu Temple; The Origin of Linga Worship, Rel of India in Practice, 95; The Iconography of Ram's Chariot, Contesting the Nat: Rel, Community and the Politics of Democracy in India, 96; Lives of Indian Images, 97; The Story of the Dissapearing Jains: Retelling the Saiva-Jain Encounter in Medieval South India, Open Boundaries: Jain Communities and Cultures in Indian Hist, 98; ed, Images, Miracles, and Authority in Asian Religious Traditions, 98. **CONTACT ADDRESS** 926 Ridge Rd, Hamden, CT 06517. **EMAIL** rdavis@bard.edu

DAVIS, ROBERT N.
PERSONAL Born 09/20/1953, Kewanee, IL, m, 1979 **DISCIPLINE** LAW **EDUCATION** University of Hartford, BA, 1975; Georgetown University Law School, JD, 1978. **CAREER** US Department of Education, attorney; United State Attorney, special assistant; CFTC, attorney; University of MS School of Law, professor, currently. **HONORS AND AWARDS** Teacher of the Year, 1990; Department of Defense Reserve Officers Foreign Exchange Program, 1996; Scholar in Residence, Office of General Counsel, US Olympic Committee, 1996. **MEMBERSHIPS** American Arbitration Association, mediator/arbitrator. **SELECTED PUBLICATIONS** Founder of Journal of National Security Law. **CONTACT ADDRESS** Professor, Univ of Mississippi, University, MS 38677. **EMAIL** rdavis@olemiss.edu

DAVIS, RONALD E.
PERSONAL Born 11/05/1963, Key West, FL, m, 1989, 3 children **DISCIPLINE** BIBLICAL STUDIES **EDUCATION** Howard Payne Univ, BA 85; Southern Baptist Theol Sem, MDiv 89, PhD 94. **CAREER** Minister of Education, 95-; Prof, Sem ext 97-. **MEMBERSHIPS** SBL **RESEARCH** Rhetorical Critical Analysis of Biblical Texts; Themes Canonical Interpretations. **CONTACT ADDRESS** 7165 McClellan Rd., Mechanicsville, VA 23111-6240. **EMAIL** davisfive@juno.com

DAVIS, WAYNE
PERSONAL Born 12/10/1951, Detroit, MI, m, 1977, 1 child **DISCIPLINE** PHILOSOPHY **EDUCATION** Univ Michigan, BA, 73; Princeton Univ, PhD, 77. **CAREER** Instr, UCLA, 76; asst prof, Rice Univ, 77-78; asst prof to prof, 79-, dept chemn 90-, Georgetown Univ. **HONORS AND AWARDS** Charlotte Elizabeth Proctor Fel; Geotown Univ Acad res Gnt. **MEMBERSHIPS** APA. **RESEARCH** Philosophy of mind; philosophy of language; philosophy of logic. **SELECTED PUBLICATIONS** Auth, An Introduction to Logic, Prentice Hall, 86; auth, Implicature: Intention, Convention, and Principle in the Failure of Gricean Theory, Cambridge Univ Press (Cambridge), 98; auth, Meaning, Expression, and Thought, Cambridge Univ Press (Cambridge), forthcoming; auth, "The Varieties of Fear," Philo Stud 51 (87): 287-310; coauth, "Fundamental Troubles with Coherence," in The Current State of the Coherence Theory, ed. JW Bender (Kluwer Acad Pub, 89); coauth, "Technical Flaws in the Coherence Theory," Synthese 79 (89): 257-78; auth, "Speaker Meaning," Ling Philo 15 (92): 223-253; auth, "Communication, Telling, and Informing," Philo Inq 21 (99): 21-43. **CONTACT ADDRESS** Dept Philosophy, Georgetown Univ, PO Box 571133, Washington, DC 20057-1133. **EMAIL** davisw@gunet.georgetown.edu

DAVIS, WILLIAM V.
PERSONAL Born 05/26/1940, Canton, OH, m, 1971, 1 child **DISCIPLINE** ENGLISH, RELIGION **EDUCATION** Ohio Univ, AB, 62, MA, 65, PhD(English), 67; Pittsburgh Theol Sem, MDiv, 65. **CAREER** Teaching Fel, Ohio Univ, 65-67, Asst prof, 67-68; Asst Prof, Central Connecticut State Univ, 68-72; Asst prof, Univ of Ill, 72-77; Assoc prof, Baylor Univ, 78-79; Guest prof, Univ of Vienna, 79-80; Vis Scholar/Guest prof, Univ of Wales, Swansea, 83; Writer-in-Residence, Univ of Montana, 83; Guest prof, Univ of Copenhagen, 84; Guest prof, Univ of Vienna, 89-90; Adj MFA Fac, Southwest Tex State Univ, 90-98; Adj Mem of the Grad Fac, Tex Christian Univ, 92-96; Consult to the Creative Writing Prog, Ohio Univ, 92-98; Guest prof, Univ of Vienna, 97; Prof of English and Writer-in-Residence, Baylor Univ, 79-. **HONORS AND AWARDS** Scholar in Poetry, Bread Loaf Writers' Conf, 70; Grad Fac Fel in Creative Writing, Univ of Ill, 74; Lilly Found Grant, 79-80; Yale Series of Younger Poets Awd for One Way to Reconstruct the Scene, 79; Winner of the Calliope Press Chapbook Prize. **MEMBERSHIPS** MLA; Poetry Soc Am; Assoc Writing Prog; Acad of Am Poets; IAUPE; PEN; Phi Kappa Phi; Tau Kappa Alpha; Tex Asn of Creative Writing Teachers; Tex Inst of Letters. **RESEARCH** Twentieth century English and American literature; creative writing; contemporary American poetry. **SELECTED PUBLICATIONS** Ed, George Whitefield's Journals, 1737-1741, ed, Scholar's Facsimiles & Reprints, 69; contrib ed, Theodore Roethke: A Bibliography, Kent State Univ Press, 73; auth, One Way to Reconstruct the Scene, Yale Univ Press, 80; auth, The Dark Hours, Calliope Press, 84; auth, Understanding Robert Bly, Univ of South Carolina Press, 88; auth, Winter Light, Univ of North Tex Press, 90. **CONTACT ADDRESS** Dept of English, Baylor Univ, Waco, Waco, TX 76798. **EMAIL** William_Davis@baylor.edu

DAVIS, WILLIE J.
PERSONAL Born 09/29/1935, Fort Valley, GA, m **DISCIPLINE** LAW **EDUCATION** Morehouse Coll, BA 1956; New England School of Law, JD 1963. **CAREER** MA Commiss Against Discrimination, field rep 1963; Commonwealth of MA, asst attny gen 1964-69; Dist of MA, asst US attny 1969-71, former US magistrate; Private practice, attny, currently. **HONORS AND AWARDS** Ten Outstanding Young Men Awd Boston Jr C of C 1971; Hon Deg JD New England School of Law 1972; Hon Deg DSc Lowell Tech Inst 1973; inducted into the Southern Intercollegiate Athletic Conference Hall of Fame, 1998. **MEMBERSHIPS** Mem Amer Bar Assoc, Amer Judicature Soc, Alpha Phi Alpha; Sigma Phi Fraternity; Natl Assn of Guardsmen; pres emeritus, Morehouse College Natl Alumni Assn; vice chairman, Morehouse College Board of Trustees; bd mem, Committee for Public Counsel Services, Commonwealth of Massachusetts; board of directors, Massachusetts Bay Transportation Authority. **CONTACT ADDRESS** Northeastern Univ, 15 Court Sq, Boston, MS 02108.

DAVIS, WINSTON
PERSONAL Born 11/05/1939, Jamestown, NY, m, 1974, 2 children **DISCIPLINE** HISTORY OF RELIGION **EDUCATION** Univ Chicago, PhD, 73. **CAREER** Wash and Lee Univ, 92-; Southwestern Univ, 83-92; Kwansei Gakuin Japan, 79-83; Stanford Univ, 73-79. **HONORS AND AWARDS** Phi Beta Kappa; NEH Fel; Dist Lectr, Univ Lectr, U of AZ. **MEMBERSHIPS** AAAR; ASSR. **RESEARCH** Max Weiber; The Ethics of Responsibility. **SELECTED PUBLICATIONS** Auth, DoJo: Magil and Exorcism in Modern Japan; Japanese Religion and Society; The Moral and Political Naturalism of Baron Kate Hiroyuki. **CONTACT ADDRESS** Dept of Religion, Washington and Lee Univ, Lexington, VA 24450. **EMAIL** davis.w@wlu.edu

DAWE, DONALD GILBERT
PERSONAL Born 07/12/1926, Detroit, MI, m, 1957, 2 children **DISCIPLINE** RELIGION **EDUCATION** Wayne State Univ, BS, 49; Union Theol Sem, BD, 52, ThD(hist theol), 60. **CAREER** Asst dean students & asst prof theol, Union Theol Sem, 58-61; from asst prof to assoc prof relig, Macalester Col, 61-69; Prof Theol, Union Theol Sem, VA, 69-, Eli Lilly Endowment fel, Univ Tubingen, 64-65; Inst Int Educ fel, Harvard Ctr Studies World Relig, 68-69; consult, Asian Med & Social Studies Group, Med Col Va, Va Commonwealth Univ, 73. **MEMBERSHIPS** Fel Soc Relig Higher Educ; Soc Sci Studies Relig; Am Teilhard Soc; AAUP. **RESEARCH** Systematic theology; modern developments of Hinduism and Buddhism; phenomonology of religion. **SELECTED PUBLICATIONS** Auth, A Fresh Look at the Kenotic Christologies, Scottish J Theol, 12/62; The Form of a Servant, 64 & No Orthodoxy but the Truth, 69, Westminster; The Historian, The Guru and the Christ, J Relig Studies, fall 69; Christology in Contemporary Systematic Theology, Interpretation, 7/72; Paul for the Indian Mind, Punjabi Univ, 73. **CONTACT ADDRESS** Dept of Theol, Union Theol Sem, Virginia, Richmond, VA 23227.

DAWES, ROBYN M.
PERSONAL Born 07/23/1936, Pittsburgh, PA, m, 1999, 2 children **DISCIPLINE** PHILOSOPHY, PSYCHOLOGY **EDUCATION** Harvard Univ, BA, 58; Univ Mich, MA, 60; PhD, 63. **CAREER** Prof, Carnegie Mellon Univ, 90-; Acting Head, Dept of Soc and Decision Sci, Carnegie Mellon Univ, 95-96; The Olof Palme Vis Prof, Univ of Stockholm and Goteborg, 99; The Charles J. Queenan Jr Univ Prof, Carnegie Mellon Univ, 97-. **HONORS AND AWARDS** James McKean Sabbatical fel, 78-79; Fel, Ctr for Advanced Study in Behav Sci, 80-81; Outstanding Empirical Paper Awd, Second Int Conf on Socio-Economics, Wash DC, 90; William James Book Awd, APA, 90; Fel, Ctr for rationality and Interactive Decision Making, Univ of Jerusalem, 94; Honorary Degree of Doctor of Philos, Goteborg Univ, Fac of Soc Sci, 99. **RESEARCH** Behavioral decision making, social choice and irrationality. **SELECTED PUBLICATIONS** Auth, "Qualitative consistency masquerading as quantitative fit," in Structures and Norms in Science, ed. M.L. Dalla Chiara et all (The Netherlands: Kluwer Acad Publ, 97), 387-390; auth, "Standards for psychotherapy, in Encyclopedia of Mental Health Vol 3 (98): 589-597; coauth, "Anticipated versus actual reactions to HIV test results," Am J of Psychology 112 (99): 297-311; auth, "A message from psychologists to economists. Mere predictability doesn't matter like it should (without a good story appended to it), " J of Econ Behav and Orgn 39-1 (99): 29-40; auth, "Two methods for studying the incremental validity of Rorschach variable, " Psychol Assessment 11-3 (Sep 99): 297-302; auth, "A theory of irrationality as a 'reasonable' response to an incomplete specification," Synthese (in press); auth, "Clinical versus actuarial prediction," in International Encyclopedia of Social and Behavioral Science (in press); auth, "Problems of probabilistic thinking, " in International Encyclopedia of Social and Behavioral Science (in press); coauth, Rational Choice in an Uncertain World: 2nd ed, forthcoming; auth, Irrationality in Everyday Life, Professional Arrogance, and Outright Lunacy, forthcoming. **CONTACT ADDRESS** Dept Decision Sciences, Carnegie Mellon Univ, 500 Forbes Ave, Pittsburgh, PA 15213. **EMAIL** rd1b@andrew.cmu.edu

DAWN, MARVA J.
PERSONAL Born 08/26/1948, Napoleon, OH, m, 1989 **DISCIPLINE** THEOLOGY **EDUCATION** Univ Notre Dame, MA 86, PhD 92; Pacific Lutheran Theol Sem, ThM 83; Western Evange Sem, MDiv 78; Univ Idaho, MA 72; Concordia Tchrs Col, BA 70. **CAREER** Regent Col BC, adj prof 98-2002; CEM, theol, auth, educ, 79-; Univ Notre Dame, grad/teach asst, 84-86; Good Shep Lutheran Church, dir spec min, 76-79; Concordia Lutheran Church Campus Minister, dir yth/edu, 72-75; Univ Idaho, teacher/stud guide/auth, 70-72. **MEMBERSHIPS** SBL; AAR; PJRS; LPF. **SELECTED PUBLICATIONS** Auth, I'm Lonely Lord- How Long?: The Psalms for Today, 83, 2nd edition, Eerdmans, 98; auth, Truly the Community: Romans 12 and How to Be the Church, Eerdmans, 92, reissued, 97; auth, Is It a Lost Cause? Having the Heart of God for the Church's Children, Eerdmans, 97; auth, To Walk and not Faint: A Month of Meditations from Isaiah 40, 2nd ed, Eerdmans, 97; auth, Reaching Out Without Dumbing Down: A Theology of Worship for the Turn-of -the -Century Cultur, Eerdmans, 95; auth, Joy in Our Weakness: A Gift of Hope from the Book of Revelations, Concordia, 94; auth, Pop Spirituality or Genuine Story? Word and World, 98; auth, How does Contemporary Culture Yearn for God?, Welcome to Christ: A Lutheran Intro to the Catechumenate, Minneapolis, Augsburg Fortress, 97; auth, Worship that Develops Strong Community, Reformed Worship, 97; auth, Beyond the Worship Wars, Christian Century, 97; auth, Practical Theology for a Post-Modern Society, Oslo Norway, Ung Teologi, 96; auth, Are Christianity and Homosexuality Incompatible?, Caught in the Crossfire, Abingdon, 94. **CONTACT ADDRESS** Dept of Theology, Christians Equipped for Ministry, 304 Fredericksburg Way, Vancouver, WA 98664-2147.

DAY, J. NORFLEETE
PERSONAL Born 09/14/1945, Birmingham, AL, s **DISCIPLINE** BIBLICAL STUDIES **EDUCATION** Samford Univ, BA, 67; Univ Alabama, MLS, 75; Beeson Div Sch, MDiv, 93; Baylor Univ, PhD, 99. **CAREER** Assoc dir, Birmingham Public Libr, 75-93; adj fac, Beeson Div Sch, 92-96; from instr to asst prof, Beeson Div Sch, 96-. **MEMBERSHIPS** NABPR; SBL; IBR. **RESEARCH** New Testament Gospels and Acts; inter-testamental period; Gospel in art and literature. **CONTACT ADDRESS** Beeson Divinity School, Samford Univ, 800 Lakeshore Dr, Birmingham, AL 35229. **EMAIL** jnday@samford.edu

DAY, KATE N.
DISCIPLINE LAW **EDUCATION** Univ Ca, JD, 80. **CAREER** Prof, 93-. **RESEARCH** Civil procedure; constitutional law and race; constitutional law; constitutional theory; gender and the law. **SELECTED PUBLICATIONS** Auth, Lost Innocence and the Moral Foundation of Law, Am Univ Jour Gender and Law, 93; The Report of Task force on Technology and Justice of the Chief Justice's Commission on the Future of The Courts, 92. **CONTACT ADDRESS** Law School, Suffolk Univ, Beacon Hill, Boston, MA 02114. **EMAIL** kday@acad.suffolk.edu

DAY, LOUIS A.
DISCIPLINE MEDIA LAW AND ETHICS **EDUCATION** Ohio Univ, PhD, 73. **CAREER** Prof, La State Univ. **SELECTED PUBLICATIONS** Auth, Broadcaster Liability for Access Denial, in Jour Quart, 83; In Search of a Scholar's Privilege, Commun and the Law, 83; Media Access To Juvenile Courts, in Jour Quart, 84; Media Access to Military Courts, in Commun and the Law, 86; The Pro Athlete's Right of Publicity in Live Sports Telecasts, in Jour Quart, 88; Ethics in Media Communications: Cases and Controversies, Wadsworth Publ Co, 96. **CONTACT ADDRESS** The Manship Sch of Mass Commun, Louisiana State Univ and A&M Col, 3030 Congress Blvd, Apt 164, Baton Rouge, LA 70803-3163. **EMAIL** lday@lsu.edu

DAY, PEGGY
PERSONAL Born Winnipeg, MB, Canada **DISCIPLINE** RELIGIOUS STUDIES **EDUCATION** Univ BC, BA, 75, MA, 77; Harvard Divinity Sch, MTS, 79, PhD, 86. **CAREER** Tchr fel, Harvard Univ, 81-86; instr Biblical Hebrew, Harvard Divinity Sch, 83-86; asst prof, Trinity Col, Univ Toronto, 86-89; Assoc Prof & Chair Religious Studs, Univ Winnipeg 89-. **MEMBERSHIPS** SBL; Hebrew Scriptures & Cognate Lit. **SELECTED PUBLICATIONS** Auth, An Adversary in Heaven: Satan in the Hebrew Bible, 88; auth, Gender and Difference in Ancient Israel, 89; auth, The Bible and the Politics of Exegesis, 91. **CONTACT ADDRESS** Dept of Religious Studies, Univ of Winnipeg, Winnipeg, MB, Canada R3B 2E9. **EMAIL** peggy.day@uwinnipeg.ca

DAY, RICHARD B.
PERSONAL Born 07/22/1942, Toronto, ON, Canada **DISCIPLINE** POLITICAL SCIENCE, HISTORY **EDUCATION** Univ Toronto, BA, 65, MA, 67, Dip REES, 67; Univ London, PhD, 70. **CAREER** Asst to assoc prof, 70-79, PROF POLITICAL SCIENCE, ERINDALE COL, UNIV TORONTO, 79-. **HONORS AND AWARDS** Killam sr res fel, 78, 79. **MEMBERSHIPS** Int Soc Study Europ Ideas; Asn Can Slavists; Can Polit Sci Asn. **SELECTED PUBLICATIONS** Auth, Leon Trotsky and the Economics of Political Isolation, 73; auth, The 'Crisis' and the 'Crash' - Soviet Studies of the West (1917-1939), 81; auth, Cold War Capitalism: The View from Moscow (1945-1975), 95; ed/transl, Selected Writings on the State and the Transition to Socialism (N.I. Bukharin); ed/transl, The Decline of Capitalism (E.A. Preobrazhensky), 85; co-ed, Democratic Theory and Technological Society, 88. **CONTACT ADDRESS** Dept o Political Sci, Univ of Toronto, 100 St George St, Rm 3018, Mississauga, ON, Canada M5S 3G3. **EMAIL** rbday@credit.erin.utoronto.ca

DAY, RICHARD E.
DISCIPLINE REMEDIES, CONSUMER PROTECTION, AND INTELLECTUAL PROPERTY **EDUCATION** Univ PA, BS, 51; Univ MI, JD, 57. **CAREER** John William Thurmond ch, prof, Univ of SC. **RESEARCH** Antitrust. **SELECTED PUBLICATIONS** Publ on, antitrust law. **CONTACT ADDRESS** School of Law, Univ of So Carolina, Columbia, Law Center, Columbia, SC 29208. **EMAIL** law0135@univscvm.csd.scarolina.edu

DAY, TERENCE PATRICK
PERSONAL Born 02/02/1930, London, England, m, 1969, 3 children **DISCIPLINE** HISTORY OF RELIGIONS, BUDDHISM **EDUCATION** London Col Divinity, ALCD, 59; Univ London, BD Hons, 60; King's Col, MTh, 63, PhD(hist of relig), 66. **CAREER** Lectr philos, St John's Col, Univ Agra, India, 66-71; lectr hist of relig, Univ Nairobi, Kenya, 71-73; Asst Prof Hist/Relig, Univ Manitoba, 74-. **MEMBERSHIPS** Can Soc Study Relig, Am Acad Relig, Int Asn of Buddhist Studies, Am Oriental Soc, Can Asian Studies Assoc. **RESEARCH** Iconography of Religion, Folk Religion, Modern Movements in Religion. **SELECTED PUBLICATIONS** Auth, Great Tradition and Little Tradition in Theravada Buddhsit Studies (Studies in Asian Thought and Religion, Vol 7), 88. **CONTACT ADDRESS** Dept of Relig, Univ of Manitoba, 327 Fletcher Argue Bldg, Winnipeg, MB, Canada R3T 5V5. **EMAIL** day@ms.umanitoba.ca

DAYE, CHARLES EDWARD
PERSONAL Born 05/14/1944, Durham, NC, m, 1976, 2 children **DISCIPLINE** LAW **EDUCATION** NC Central Univ, BA high honors 1966; Columbia Univ, JD honors 1969. **CAREER** Law clerk, Hon Harry Phillips 6th Cir, 69-70; assoc, Covington & Burlington, 70-72; prof, UNC Chapel Hill School of Law, 72-81; vis prof, NCCU School of Law, 80-81; dean & prof, NCCU Sch of Law, 81-85; prof, UNC Chapel Hill School of Law, 85-; Henry P Brandis Dist Professor, UNC Chapel Hill Sch of Law, 91-. **HONORS AND AWARDS** Lawyer of the Year NC Assn Black Lawyers, 80; Civic Awd, Durham Community on the Affairs of Black People, 81; Honorary Order of the Coif; LLD (Doctor of Laws, Hon), Suffolk Univ, 99. **MEMBERSHIPS** NC Asn of Black Lawyers; mem bars of, US Supreme Ct, NY, DC, NC; chemn Triangle Housing Devel Corp, 1979-91, mem, 1977-; bd dir United Way of Greater Durham 1984-88; president Law School Admission Council 1991-93; mem Amer Bar Assn, NC State Bar, NC Bar Assn. **RESEARCH** Civil rights; fair housing; housing; administrative law; constitutional law; torts. **SELECTED PUBLICATIONS** Coauth, Casebook Housing & Comm Devel, 3rd ed, 99 ; coauth, NC Law of Torts, 2nd ed, 99. **CONTACT ADDRESS** Sch Law, Univ of No Carolina, Chapel Hill, CB#3380, Chapel Hill, NC 27599-3380. **EMAIL** cday@email.unc.edu

DAYTON, DONALD WILBER
PERSONAL Born 07/25/1942, Chicago, IL, m, 1969 **DISCIPLINE** THEOLOGY, AMERICAN RELIGIOUS HISTORY **EDUCATION** Houghton Col, BA, 63; Yale Univ, BD, 69; Univ Ky, MS, 69; Univ Chicago, PhD, 83. **CAREER** From asst to asst prof theol, Asbury Theol Sem, 69-72, acquisitions librn, B L Fisher Libr, 69-72; asst prof theol, North Park Theol Sem, 72-77, assoc prof, 77-80, dir, Mellander Libr, 72-80; Prof Theol, Northern Baptist Theol Sem, 80-97; prof, Drew Univ, 97-. **MEMBERSHIPS** Karl Barth Soc NAm; Wesleyan Theol Soc; Am Theol Libr Asn; Am Soc Church Hist; Am Acad Relig. **RESEARCH** Theology and ethics of Karl Barth; 19th century American religious thought; holiness and Pentecostal churches. **SELECTED PUBLICATIONS** Auth, Creationism in 20th-Century America--A 10-Volume Anthology of Documents, 1903-1961, Zygon, Vol 0032, 97. **CONTACT ADDRESS** Drew Univ, 36 Madison Ave, Madison, NJ 07940.

DE BOLT, DARIAN C.
PERSONAL Born 10/11/1946, Marshalltown, IA, m, 1967 **DISCIPLINE** PHILOSOPHY **EDUCATION** Univ Okla, BA, 68, MA, 85, PhD, 93. **CAREER** Adj prof, Univ Central Okla, Edmond, 93-94; vis asst prof, Univ Okla, Norman, 94-95; adj prof, Univ Central Okla, Edmond, 95-00; spec mem grad fac, Univ Okla, Norman, 94-01. **HONORS AND AWARDS** Phi Kappa Phi; Phi ETA Sigma. **MEMBERSHIPS** APA; Southwestern Philos Soc; Central States Philos Asn; Australasian Asn of Philos. **RESEARCH** Ethics; social and political philosophy; Byzantine philosophy. **SELECTED PUBLICATIONS** Auth, Kant and Clint: Dirty Harry Meets the Categorical Imperative, Southwest Philos Rev, 97; auth, George Gemistos Plethon on God: Heterodoxy in Defense of Orthodoxy, Proc of the Twentieth World Cong of Philos, 99. **CONTACT ADDRESS** Dept of Philosophy, Univ of Oklahoma, 1518 Lindale Circle, Norman, OK 73069. **EMAIL** dcdeboltphil@worldnet.att.net

DE GRAZIA, EDWARD
DISCIPLINE INTERNATIONAL TRANSACTIONS, COMMUNICATIONS LAW **EDUCATION** Univ Chicago, BA, 48; JD 51. **CAREER** Prof; **HONORS AND AWARDS** Dir, Georgetown Univ Prog Pretrial Diversion Accused Offenders to Community Mental Health Treatment Prog; Asso fel, Inst Policy Studies. **MEMBERSHIPS** Office Dir Gen UNESCO, 56-59; U.S. Dept State; U.S. Agency Int Devel; PEN Am Ctr. **RESEARCH** International transations; community law; first admenment legislation. **SELECTED PUBLICATIONS** Coauth, Censorship Landmarks and Banned Films: Movies, Censors; First Amendment; auth, Girls Lean Back Everywhere: The Law of Obscenity and the Assault on Genius, Random House, 92. **CONTACT ADDRESS** Yeshiva Univ, 55 Fifth Ave, New York, NY 10003-4301.

DE KONINCK, THOMAS
PERSONAL Born 05/26/1934, Louvain, Belgium, m, 1960, 3 children **DISCIPLINE** PHILOSOPHY, THEOLOGY **EDUCATION** Laval Univ, BA & BPh, 54, LPh, 56, PhD, 70, Oxford Univ, MA, 63. **CAREER** From instr to asst prof, 60-64, auxiliary prof, 64-70, assoc prof, 70-77, Alexander von Humboldt Stiftung scholar, 72-73, dean philos, 74-78, Prof Philos, Laval Univ, 77-. **RESEARCH** Greek philosophy, metaphysics, ethics. **SELECTED PUBLICATIONS** Coauth, Urgence De LA Philosophie: Actes Du Colloque Du Cinquantenaire De LA Faculte, Univ Laval, Lucien Morin, 85; auth, De la dignitae humaine. **CONTACT ADDRESS** Faculte de Philosophie, Univ Laval, Pavillon Felix-Antoine-Savard, local 622, Quebec, QC, Canada G1K 7P4. **EMAIL** thomas.dekoninck@fp.ulaval.ca

DE LAURENTIIS, ALLEGRA
PERSONAL Born 04/01/1952, Roma, Italy, m, 2 children **DISCIPLINE** PHILOSOPHY **EDUCATION** W V Goethe-Univ Frankfurt Ger, MA, 78; PhD, 82. **CAREER** Asst prof, Villanova Univ, 87-90; Asst prof, Miami Univ Ohio, 91-94; Sr Res Assoc, Dept Philos, SUNY Stonybrook, 94- . **MEMBERSHIPS** APA, SWIP, Hepel Soc Am, Long Island Philosophic Soc. **RESEARCH** HeGel studies, Aristotle, 19th Century interpretations of Greek antiquity. **SELECTED PUBLICATIONS** Auth, A Prophet Turned Backwards: Materialism and Mysticism in W Benjamins Notion of History, Rethinking Marxism, 94; And Yet It Moves: Hegel on Zeno's Arrow, Jour Speculative Philos, 95; Logic and History of Consciousness, Introduction to Hegels Encyclopedia; SW Philos Rev, 98; auth, "Aristotle in the Nineteenth Century: the Case of Goethe's Study of Life," Idealistic Studies, vol 30, 00; auth, "Kant's Shameful Proposition. A Hegel-Inspired Criticsim of Kant's Theory of Domestic Right," International Philosophical Quarterly, 00. **CONTACT ADDRESS** Philosophy Dept, SUNY, Stony Brook, Harriman Hall, Stony Brook, NY 11794. **EMAIL** DELAURENTIIS@CCMAIL.SUNYSB.EDU

DE MARNEFFE, PETER L.
PERSONAL Born 05/28/1957, Boston, MA, m, 1997, 2 children **DISCIPLINE** PHILOSOPHY **EDUCATION** Univ Mass, BA, 81; Harvard Univ, PhD, 89. **CAREER** Teach fel, Harvard Univ, 84-88; vis fel, Princeton Univ, 93-94; vis fel, Stanford Univ, 95; asst prof, assoc prof, Ariz State Univ, 89-; fel ethics, Harvard Univ, 97-98. **HONORS AND AWARDS** Harvard Fel, 84-88, 97-98; Princeton fel, 93-94. **MEMBERSHIPS** APA; ASPLP. **RESEARCH** Individual rights and liberty; government paternalism; morals; legislation; liberalism. **SELECTED PUBLICATIONS** Auth, "Liberalism, Liberty and Neutrality," Philo Pub Aff (90); auth, "Contractualism, Liberty and Democracy," Ethics (94); auth, "Rawls's Idea of Public Reason," Pac Philo Qtly (94); auth, "Rights, Reasons, and Freedom of Association," Freedom Of Assoc (Princeton UP, 98); auth, "Liberalism and Perfectionism," Am J Juris (98). **CONTACT ADDRESS** Dept of Philo, Arizona State Univ, Tempe, AZ 85287-2004. **EMAIL** demarneffe@asu.edu

DE S. CAMERON, NIGEL M.
DISCIPLINE MEDICAL ETHICS **EDUCATION** Univ Cambridge, BA, MA; Univ Edinburgh, BD, PhD. **CAREER** Philos, Trinity Int Univ. **HONORS AND AWARDS** Found ed, Eu Jour Theol. **SELECTED PUBLICATIONS** Auth, The New Medicine: Life and Death after Hippocrates; Ed, Universalism and the Doctrine of Hell; Dictionary of Scottish Church History and Theology. **CONTACT ADDRESS** Col of Arts and Sciences, Trinity Intl Univ, Col of Arts and Sciences, 2065 Half Day Road, Deerfield, IL 60015.

DE SOUSA, RONALD B.
PERSONAL Born 02/25/1940, Lausanne, Switzerland **DISCIPLINE** PHILOSOPHY **CAREER** Assoc prof, Univ of Toronto, 71-82; vis prof, Univ of British Columbia, 83-84; vis prof, Dartmouth Col, 89; vis res scholar, Univ of Amsterdam, 96; pro, Univ of Toronto, 82-. **HONORS AND AWARDS** Canada Coun Res Grant, 71; Canada Coun Leave Fel, 77-78; Social Sciences and Humanities Res Counc of Canada Lave Fel, 81-82; Social Sciences and Humanities Res Coun of Canada Leave Fel, 86. **MEMBERSHIPS** Can Philos Asn; Am Philos Asn; Int Soc Res Emotions. **RESEARCH** Philos of Emotions, Philos of Mind, Philos of Biology; Plato, Psychoanalysis, Epistemology, Philosophy of Sex. **SELECTED PUBLICATIONS** Auth, The Rationality of Emotion, (87): 373; auth, Style, Will, and Individuality: Some na¤ve reflections on Nietzsche," International Studies in Philosophy, 28/3, (96): 121-132; auth, "What can't we do with economics,"" J of Phil Res, 22, (97): 197-209; auth, "Desire and Serendipity," Midwest Studies in Philosophy, 22; auth, "Individual Natures, Philosophia: Philosophical Quarterly of Israel, 26, (98): 3-21; auth, "A qui appartiennent les emotions? De la cladistique au politique," Critique, (France) numero special: Penser les Emotions, (99): 486-498; auth, "Morl Emotions," in Societas Ethica Jahresbericht, (99): 71-85; auth, "Groupies: a review article on E. Sober and D. Wilson, Unto Others: in Semiotic Review of Books; auth, "Prefrontal Kant: Critical study of Damasio, Descartes Error," Emotion and Cognition, 10:329-333; auth, "Meaning and Propensity: a critical discussion of Joelle Proust, Commentl' esprit vient aux betes," in Dialectica, (Switzerland, 00). **CONTACT ADDRESS** Dept of Philosophy, Univ of Toronto, 215 Huron St, Toronto, ON, Canada M5S 1A1. **EMAIL** sousa@chass.utoronto.ca

DE VRIES, JAN
PERSONAL Born 11/14/1943, Netherlands, m, 1968, 2 children **DISCIPLINE** HISTORY, ECONOMICS **EDUCATION** Yale, PhD, 70; Columbia Univ, BA, 65. **CAREER** Univ Calif, Berkeley, Prof, 77-, Assoc Prof 73-77; MI State Univ, asst Prof, 70-73. **HONORS AND AWARDS** Gugganheim fel, vis fel, All Souls Col, Oxford; fel, British Academy; fel, Am Academy of Arts & Sciences; fel, Royal Netherlands Academy of Sciences; Heineken Prize in History, 00. **MEMBERSHIPS** Ec Hist Asn; Am Ec Asn; Soc Sci Hist Asn. **RESEARCH** European Economic Hist; Demographic Hist. **SELECTED PUBLICATIONS** The Dutch Economy in the Golden Age, 1500-1700, New Haven, Yale Univ Press, 74; The Economy of Europe in an Age of Crisis, 1600-1750, Cambridge, Cambridge Univ press, 76, Span trans, 79, Port trans, 83, Catalan trans, 93; Barges and Capitalism: Passenger Transportation in the Dutch Economy, 1632-1839, A A G Bijdragen no 21, Wageningen, The Neth, 78, reissued, Utrecht, Hes Pub 81; European Urbanization, 1500-1800, London, Methuen and Co, Cambridge MA, Harvard Univ Press 84, Span trans 87; with A M van der Woude, The First Modern Economy: Success, Failure and Perseverance of the Dutch Economy, 1500-1815, Cambridge, Cambridge Univ Press, 97, Dutch ed, Nederland, 1500-1815: De eerste ronde van modern economisch groei, Amsterdam, Uitgeverij Balans, 95; ed, with Ad van der Woude and Akira Hyami, Urbanization in History, Oxford, Oxford Univ Press, 90; with David Freedberg, Art in History, History in Art: Studies in 17th Century Dutch Culture, Chicago, Univ Chicago Press, 91. **CONTACT ADDRESS** Univ of California, Berkeley, Dept History, Berkeley, CA 94720-2550. **EMAIL** devries@socrates.berkeley.edu

DE VRIES, WILLEM A.
PERSONAL Born 09/16/1950, New York, NY, m, 1982, 2 children **DISCIPLINE** PHILOSOPHY **EDUCATION** Haverford Coll, BA, 72; Univ of Pittsburgh, MA, 75, PhD, 81. **CAREER** Asst Prof, 71-85, Amherst Coll; Vis Prof, 87-88, Tufts; from asst prof to prof, 88-, Chr, 95-2000, Univ Of New Hampshire. **HONORS AND AWARDS** Fulbright Doctoral Fellow; Fulbright Sr Res Fellow; NEH Fellow; Mellow Postdoc; Faculty Scholar Fellow. **MEMBERSHIPS** APA; North Amer Soc; Soc for Philos and Psychol. **RESEARCH** Philosophy of Mind; German Idealism; Metaphysical and Epistemology. **SELECTED PUBLICATIONS** Auth, Hegel's Theory of Mental Activity, Ithaca, NY, Cornell Univ Press, 88; Reality, Knowledge and the Good Life: An Historical Introduction to Philosophy, NY, St Martin's Press, 91; Hegel's Logic and Philosophy of Mind, Routledge History of Philosophy, vol VI: The Age of German Idealism, 98; Who sees with equal eye, Atoms or systems into ruin hurled: Comment on Brian McLaughlin, Philosophica Studies, vol 71, 93; Experience and the Swamp Creature, Philosophical Studies, 96. **CONTACT ADDRESS** Dept of Philosophy, Univ of New Hampshire, Durham, Durham, NH 03824. **EMAIL** Willem.devries@unh.edu

DE YOUNG, JAMES B.
PERSONAL Born 04/09/1941, Elkhorn, WI, m, 1965, 4 children **DISCIPLINE** BIBLICAL STUDIES **EDUCATION** Moody Bible Inst, diploma; E Tex Baptist Univ, BA; Talbot Theol Sem, BD; ThM; Dallas Theol Sem, ThD. **CAREER** Prof, Multhomah Bible Col, 71-75; prof, Western Sem, 75-. **MEMBERSHIPS** Soc of Biblical Lit, Evangelical Theol Soc, Int Orgn for Septuagint and Cognate Studies. **RESEARCH** Hermeneutics, Exegisis--New Testament Interpretation, Use of Old Testament in New Testament, Ethics. **SELECTED PUBLICATIONS** Coauth, Beyond the Obvious: Discover the Deeper meaning of Scripture; auth, Homosexuality: Contemporary Claims Examined in the Light of the Bible and Other Ancient Literature and Law. **CONTACT ADDRESS** Dept Bible Studies, Western Sem, 5511 Southeast Hawthorne Blvd, Portland, OR 97215-3367. **EMAIL** JDeY7@aol.com

DEAN, WILLIAM D.
PERSONAL Born 07/12/1937, South Bend, IN, m, 1960, 2 children **DISCIPLINE** THEOLOGY **EDUCATION** Carleton Col, BA, 59; Divinity Sch, Univ Chicago, MA, 64, PhD, 67. **CAREER** Asst prof Philos & Relig, Northland Col, 66-68; prof Relig, Florence & Raymond Sponberg Ch Ethics, Gustavus Adolphus Col, 68-96; prof Constructive Theol, Iliff Sch Theol, 96-. **HONORS AND AWARDS** Lilly Fac Fel; Edgar A. Carlson Awd Distinguished Tchg; John Templeton Found; Sci Relig Course Competition; AAR Awd Excellence Study Relig. **MEMBERSHIPS** Am Acad Relig; Highlands Inst Am Relig & Philos Thought. **RESEARCH** American religious thought; religious historicism; religious pragmatism. **SELECTED PUBLICATIONS** Auth, 5 books, 1 edited book, 40 articles, insluding; auth, The Religious Critic in American Culture, 94; auth, Historical Process Theology: A Field in a Map of Thought, Process Studies, Fall-Winter, 99. **CONTACT ADDRESS** Dept of Theology, Iliff Sch of Theol, 2201 S University Ave., Denver, CO 80210. **EMAIL** wdean@du.edu

DEARMAN, JOHN ANDREW
PERSONAL Born 12/06/1951, Columbia, SC, m, 3 children **DISCIPLINE** BIBLICAL STUDIES **EDUCATION** Univ NC, Chapel Hill, BA, 74; Princeton Theol Sem, MDiv, 77; Emory Univ, PhD, 81. **CAREER** Instr Jeremiah, Candler Sch Theol, 79; instr New Testament & Old Testament, La State Univ, 81, asst prof Bible introd Western archeol relig, 81-82; Prof Old Testament Introd, Austin Theol Sem, 82-, Acad Dean, 98-; Vis Schol, Univ Erlangen-Nurnberg, 89-90, Univ Stellenbosch, SAfrica, 95. **HONORS AND AWARDS** Recipient of numerous honors and grants **MEMBERSHIPS** Soc Bibl Lit; Am Schs Orient Res; Bibl Archaeol Soc. **RESEARCH** The impact of ancient civilization on Israelite foreign relations; Moab in the Iron Age. **SELECTED PUBLICATIONS** Auth, Some observations on early Hebrew works and teachers in America 1726-1823, Hebrew Studies, No 20, 79 & No 21, 80; Religion and Culture in Ancient Israel; Studies in the Mesha Inscription and Moab; author numerous papers, reviews, and entries in Harper's Dictionary of the Bible. **CONTACT ADDRESS** Dept of Old Testament, Austin Presbyterian Theol Sem, 100 E 27th, Austin, TX 78705-5711. **EMAIL** adearman@mail.austinseminary.edu

DEASLEY, ALEX R. G.
PERSONAL Born 05/10/1935, Dundee, Scotland, m, 1958, 3 children **DISCIPLINE** BIBLICAL STUDIES **EDUCATION** Univ Cambridge, BA, 58; MA, 62; Univ Manchester, PhD, 72. **CAREER** Lectr, Nazarene Theol Col, Manchester, Eng, 59-69; Dean, Nazarene Theol Col, 66-69; Prof, Chair of Dept of Relig, Can Nazarene Col, Winnipeg, Manitoba, 72-77; Adj Prof, Univ of Manitoba, Winnipeg, 75-77; Prof, Nazarene Theol Sem, Kansas City, Mo, 77-. **HONORS AND AWARDS** Distinguished Serv Awd, Nazarene Theol Col, Manchester, 85. **MEMBERSHIPS** Soc of Bibl Lit, Inst for Bibl Res, Wesleyan Theol Soc. **RESEARCH** Gumran, Epistle of the Romans, Pavline Theology. **SELECTED PUBLICATIONS** Ed, Contribur, The Spirit and the New Age (Wesleyan Theol Perspectives Vol 5), Warner Press (Andesron, IN, 86); auth, Marriage and Divorce in the Bible and the Church, Beacon Hill Press of Kansas City, 00. **CONTACT ADDRESS** Dept Relig, Nazarene Theol Sem, 1700 E Meyer Blvd, Kansas City, MO 64131-1246. **EMAIL** ardeasley@nts.edu

DEBONA, GUERRIC
PERSONAL Born 01/30/1955 **DISCIPLINE** RELIGION **CAREER** Asst Prof of English, St. Meinrad Col, 86-98; Asst Prof of Homiletics, St. Meinrad Theology, 98-. **MEMBERSHIPS** AAR. **RESEARCH** Film; Cultural Studies; Preaching; Church & Media. **SELECTED PUBLICATIONS** Auth, "Into Africa: Orson Welles an d"Heart of Darkness," Cinema Journal 33(3): 16-34, Spring , 94; auth, "The Canon and Cultural Studies: Culture and Anarchy in Gotham City," Journal of Film & Video 49, (1-2) Spring-Summer 97: 52-65; auth, "On the Feast of Mary the Mother of God--Ideas and Illustrations," Homily Service, January 99, 32(1): 9-12; auth, "The Second Sunday of Lent--Ideas and Illustrations," Homily Service, Feb 99, 32(2):64-68; auth, "Trinity Sunday--Ideas and Illustrations," Homily Service, May 99, 32(5): 65-67; auth, "The Fourth Sunday of Ordinary Time, B-Ideas and Ilustrations," Homily Service, Jan 00, 32(10): 64-66; auth, "Easter 2000 Ideas and Illustrations," Homily Service, April 00, 33(1):80-82; auth, "Dickens, the Depression and MGM's David Copperfield," in Film Adaptation, ed. James Naremore, New Brunswick: Rutger UP, 00: 106-128; auth, "Jesus Christ in the Age of Mechanical Reproduction," Forthcoming, May, New Theology Review; auth, "Preaching for the Plot," Forthcoming, February, New Theology Review. **CONTACT ADDRESS** Dept Religion, Saint Meinrad Sch of Theol, 1 Arcabbey, Saint Meinrad, IN 47577-1000. **EMAIL** gdebona@saintmeinrad.edu

DEBRACY, WARREN
PERSONAL Born 03/28/1942, Chicago, IL, m **DISCIPLINE** LAW **EDUCATION** Loyola Univ Chicago, BS Soc Sci 1964; Rutgers Univ New Brunswick, NJ, MA Pol Sci 1966; Cornell Univ Ithaca, NYork, JD Law 1971. **CAREER** Rutgers Univ NJ, asst inst, 66; Loyola Univ Law Sch New Orleans, asst prof, 71-72; Univ of Detroit Law Sch, asst prof, 72-73; Univ of Toledo Law Sch, assoc prof, 73-79; Loyola Univ, New Orleans, LA, visiting prof, 86; Valparaiso Univ, Valparoiso, IN, visiting prof, 88-89. **HONORS AND AWARDS** 1st yr moot court champion Cornell Law Sch 1969; best affimative debator Gennett Newpaper Tournament Rochester 1962. **MEMBERSHIPS** Mem MI Democratic State Central Comm 1985-89; treas 2nd Cong Dist Dem Comm MI 1983-85, vice-chair 1979-81; mem, Rules Comm, Democratic Natl Convention, 1988; delegate, 1980 Democratic Natl Convention. **SELECTED PUBLICATIONS** Legality of Affirmative Action, Journal of Urban Law, 1974-75. **CONTACT ADDRESS** Sch of Law, No Carolina Central Univ, Durham, NC 27707.

DECEW, JUDITH WAGNER
PERSONAL Born 11/19/1948, Oberlin, OH, m, 1969, 3 children **DISCIPLINE** PHILOSOPHY **EDUCATION** Univ of Rochester, BA, 70; Univ Mass, Amherst, MA, 76; PhD, 78. **CAREER** Asst prof, Mass Inst of Technol, 78-87; from asst prof to prof, 87-, assoc dean, 99-, Clark Univ; vis prof, Harvard Univ, summers 90, 91. **HONORS AND AWARDS** Bausch and Lomb Prize, 66; Am Asn of Univ Women Fel, 77-78; Liberal Arts Fel, Harvard Law Sch, 80-81; Res Fel, Am Coun of Learned Socs, 84-85; Res Fel, Bunting Inst, Radcliffe Col/ Harvard Univ, 88-89; Alice Coonley Higgins Fac Fel, Clark Univ, 89-90; Fac Development Fund Awd, Clark Univ, 90-91; Higgins Sch of Humanities Fel, Clark Univ, 90-91; Res Fel, NEH, 93-94; Clark Hayden Fac Fel, 93-94; Exceptional Merit Awds, Clark Univ, 94-95, 96-97; Higgins Sch of Humanities Fels, Clark Univ, 94-99. **MEMBERSHIPS** Am Philos Asn, Am Soc for Political and Legal Philos. **RESEARCH** Ethics, philosophy of law, social and political theory. **SELECTED PUBLICATIONS** Co-ed with Ian Shapiro, Theory and Practice, Nomos XXXVII, New York Univ Press (95, paperback, 96); auth, In Pursuit of Privacy: Law, Ethics, and the Rise of Technology, Cornell Univ Press (97); auth, "Discretion: Its Role in Judicial Decision-Making," The Philosophy of Law: An Encyclopedia, Christopher Berry Gray, ed, Garland Pub Inc (99): 214-216; auth, "Alternatives for Protecting Privacy While Respecting Patient Care and Public Health Needs," Ethics and Information Technology, 1, 4 (2000): 1-7; auth, "The Priority of Privacy for Medical Information," Soc Philos and Policy, 17, 2 (2000); auth, Unionization in the Academy: The Vision and the Reality, Rowan and Littlefield Pubs, Inc, to appear in the series entitled "Issues in Academic Ethics," Steven Cahn, gen ed (in progress). **CONTACT ADDRESS** Dept Philos, Clark Univ, 950 Main St, Worcester, MA 01610. **EMAIL** jdecew@clarku.edu

DECHANT, DELL
PERSONAL Born 07/06/1954, St. Petersburg, FL, m, 1981 **DISCIPLINE** RELIGION **EDUCATION** Univ S Fla, MA, 84. **CAREER** From adj instr to vis prof to instr & undergrad dir, Univ S Fla, 84-. **HONORS AND AWARDS** Outstanding undergrad adv award, 98; Outstanding undergrad teaching award, 00. **MEMBERSHIPS** Am Acad Relig; Col Theol Soc; Soc Study Metaphysical Relig. **RESEARCH** New religious movements; ethics; methodology; religion and popular culture. **SELECTED PUBLICATIONS** Auth, Charles and Myrtle Fillmore, Nona Brooks, Ernest Holmes, Am Nat Biog, 98; auth, Hermeneutics for Allegorical Exegesis in Postmodern Idealistic Religious Systems: Comments and Guidelines, Study of Metaphysical Relig, Spring, 98; auth, Reflections on a Peculiar Religious Culture and Its Emerging Academic Community, Jour Soc Study Metaphysical Relig, Spring, 96; auth, Response to Robert Ellwood's 'Why Are Mythologists Political Reactionaries?', Relig & Soc Order, 95; auth, The Allegorical Trajectory, Int New Thought Quart, Fall, 94; auth, Myrtle Fillmore and Her Daughters, Women's Leadership in Marginal Relig, 93. **CONTACT ADDRESS** Dept of Religious Studies, Univ of So Florida, CPR 305, U.S.F., Tampa, FL 33620-5550. **EMAIL** ddechant@luna.cas.usf.edu

DECHERT, CHARLES RICHARD
PERSONAL Born 03/16/1927, Philadelphia, PA, w, 1957, 1 child **DISCIPLINE** SOCIAL AND POLITICAL PHILOSOPHY **EDUCATION** Cath Univ Am, AB, 49, MA, 50, PhD, 52. **CAREER** Vis prof comp econ & soc policy, Int Univ Soc Studies, Rome, 57-59; assoc prof govt, Purdue Univ, West Lafayette, 59-65, prof polit sci, 65-67; Prof Polit, Cath Univ AM, 67-, Instr, Our Lady of the Lake Col, 53-54; consult, Ist L'Addestramento nell'Industria, Milan, 57-59, Ministero di Grazia e Giustizia, Rome, 57-59, Grad Sch Bus, Columbia Univ, 59, Inst Defense Anal, 60, Joint Econ Comt, US Cong, 61 & Comt House Admin, US House Rep, 70; Fulbright-Hays award, Italy, 65-66 & 82. **HONORS AND AWARDS** Harmon Prize, Am Cath Philos Asn, 64. **MEMBERSHIPS** Am Polit Sci Asn; Am Cath Philos Asn; Soc Gen Syst Res; corresp mem Ist Luigi Sturzo, Rome; Intl Studies Asn; Am Soc Cybernetics; Fellowship of Cath Scholars; Intl Maritian Soc; Natl Cap Area Pol Sci Asn, Pres, 75-76. **RESEARCH** Soc-polit syst; philos of sci; sociology of knowledge. **SELECTED PUBLICATIONS** Auth, Ente nazionale idcoauthocarburi: Profile of a state corporation, Brill, Leiden, 63; Cybernetics and the human person, Int Philos Quart, 65; ed & contribr, The Social Impact of Cybernetics, Univ Notre Dame, 66, Simon & Schuster, 67; coauth, Congress: The First Branch of Government, Am Enterprise Inst, 66, Doubleday, 67; Positive Feedback, Pergamon, 68 & Systems in Society, Soc Gen Syst Res, 73; ed, Sistemi, paradigmi e societa (Systems Paradigm), Angeli, Milano, 78; El Nuevo Mundo de la Filosofia y la Tecnologia, 90; Recovering the Sacred Cath Faith, Worship, Practice, 90; Church and State in Am, 92; Freedom and Choice in a Democracy, 93; Religion in Public Life, 94; Christian Humanism, 95; Civil Society and Social Reconstruction, 96; Civil Society-Who belongs?, 97; Democracy Culture and Values, 91-92; Freedom and Choice in a Democracy, 92-93. **CONTACT ADDRESS** Dept Polit, Catholic Univ of America, 620 Michigan Ave N E, Washington, DC 20064-0002. **EMAIL** dechert@cua.edu

DECK, ALLAN F.
PERSONAL Born 04/19/1945, Los Angeles, CA, s **DISCIPLINE** THEOLOGY; LATIN AMERICAN STUDIES **EDUCATION** St Louis Univ, BA, 69, PhD, 74; Jesuit Sch of Theol at Berkeley, MDiv, 76; Gregorian Univ, STD, 88. **CAREER** Admin, Our Lady of Guadalupe Church, 76-79; Dir, Hispanic Ministry, Diocese of Orange, 79-85; Asst Prof of Theology, Jesuit Sch of Theol, 87-92; Assoc Prof of Theol, Loyola Marymt Univ, 92-96; Exec Dir, Loyola Inst for Spirituality, 97-. **HONORS AND AWARDS** Catholic Press Asn 1st Place Awd Pro Book Category, 89. **MEMBERSHIPS** Acad of Catholic Hispanic Theol of the US, (co-founder & 1st pres); Nat Catholic Counc for Hisp Ministry, (co-founder & 1st pres). **RESEARCH** Hispanic religious expressions & spirituality, faith and culture. **SELECTED PUBLICATIONS** Auth, Francisco Javier Alegre: A Study in Mexican Literary Criticism, Historical Inst of the Soc of Jesus, 76; auth, The Second Wave, Paulist Press, 89; auth, Perspectivas: Hispanic Ministry, Sheed & Ward, 95; Hispanic Catholic Culture in the US, Univ Notre Dame Press, 94. **CONTACT ADDRESS** 480 S Batavia St, Orange, CA 92868. **EMAIL** deck8@juno.com

DECKER, JOHN F.
DISCIPLINE CRIMINAL JUSTICE **EDUCATION** Loras Col, BA, 66; Univ Iowa, BA, 67; Creighton Univ, JD, 70; NY Univ, LLM 71; JSD, 79. **CAREER** Prof, DePaul Univ, 71-; vis prof, Univ of San Francisco, 80. **HONORS AND AWARDS** Res Fel, NYU, 70-73; Staff Ed, Creighton Law Rev, 69-70; Fac Achievement Awd, DePaul Col of Law, 84, 95; Outstanding Teaching Awd, DePaul Col of Law, 85; University Excellence in Teaching Awd, DePaul Univ, 99. **MEMBERSHIPS** Am Bar Assoc; IL State Bar Assoc, State Bar of CA; Assoc of Trial Lawyers of Am. **RESEARCH** Criminal Law, Criminal Procedure, Evidence. **SELECTED PUBLICATIONS** Auth, Prostitution: Regulation and Control, 79; auth, Revolution to the Right, 92; auth, The Investigation and Prosecution of Arson, 99; Auth, Illinois Criminal Law, 3rd Ed, 00. **CONTACT ADDRESS** Col Law, DePaul Univ, 25 E Jackson Blvd, Chicago, IL 60604-2289. **EMAIL** jdecker1@wppost.depaul.edu

DEERING, RONALD F.
PERSONAL Born 10/06/1929, Ford County, IL, m, 1966, 2 children **DISCIPLINE** HISTORY; NEW TESTAMENT; LIBRARY SCIENCE **EDUCATION** Georgetown Col, BA, 51; MDiv, 55, PhD, 61, Southern Baptist Theological Seminary; Columbia Univ, MSLS, 67. **CAREER** Instr, 58-61, Research Librarian, 61-67; Assoc Librarian, 67-71, Seminary Librarian, 71-95, Assoc VP for Academic Resources, Southern Baptist Theological Seminary. **HONORS AND AWARDS** Lilly Endowment Scholarship in Theological Librarianship **MEMBERSHIPS** Amer Theological Library Assoc; Amer Library Assoc; Kentucky Library Assoc; Soc of Biblical Lit; Southeastern Library Assoc; Church and Synagogue Library Assoc. **RESEARCH** Theological librarianship **CONTACT ADDRESS** So Baptist Theol Sem, 2825 Lexington Rd., Louisville, KY 40280. **EMAIL** rdeering@compuserve.com

DEETER, ALLEN C.
PERSONAL Born 03/08/1931, Dayton, OH, m, 1952, 3 children **DISCIPLINE** RELIGION, HISTORY **EDUCATION** Manchester Col, BA, 53; Bethany Theol Sem, BD, 56; Princeton Univ, MA, 58, PhD(hist Christianity), 63. **CAREER** Instr relig, 59-60, from asst prof to assoc prof, 60-72, dir, Peace Studies Inst & Prog Conflict Resolution, 67-80, assoc acad dean, 69-80, Prof Relig & Philos, Manchester Col, 72-; Adminr, Brethren Cols Abroad, 75-, Vchmn bd gov, John F Kennedy Am Haus, Marburg, 65-66; dir Brethren Cols Abroad, Univ Marburg & Univ Strasburg, 65-66; Soc Relig Higher Educ grant, 68-69; lectr, Punjabi Univ & Dibrugarh Univ, India, spring 69; exec secy, Consortium Peace Res, Educ & Develop, 71-72; consult on world order studies, various cols, univs & consortia, 71-; ed, Bull, Peace Studies Inst, Manchester Col, 71-80; spring inaugural lectr, Christian Theol Sem, Indianapolis, 72. **HONORS AND AWARDS** Hon Doctorate, Bridgewater Col. **MEMBERSHIPS** Int Studies Asn; Am Soc Church Hist; Am Acad Relig. **RESEARCH** The origins of modern radical religious and political thought; mysticism and pietism East and West, especially as related to social ethics; Tolstoyan and Gandhian political, social and religious tactics of transformation. **SELECTED PUBLICATIONS** Coauth, In His Hand, Brethren Press, 64; auth, Pietist views of the Church, Brethren Life & Thought, winter 64; Western mysticism and social concern, J Inst Traditional Cult, spring 69; Religion as a social and political force in America, Bull Ramakrishna Inst, fall 69; Toyohiko Kagawa: Mystic and Social Activist, Punjabi Univ, 70; Heirs of a Promise, Brethern Press, 72; auth, The Paradoxical Necessity of Realism and Idealism, Bull of Peace Stu Inst, 98. **CONTACT ADDRESS** Dept of Relig, Manchester Col, 601 E College Ave, North Manchester, IN 46962-1226.

DEGEORGE, RICHARD
PERSONAL Born 01/29/1933, New York, NY, m, 1957, 3 children **DISCIPLINE** PHILOSOPHY **EDUCATION** Universite de Louvain, PhD, 55; Fordham Univ, AB, 54, Yale Univ, PhD, 59; Yale Univ, MA, 58. **CAREER** Assist Prof, Univ of Kansas, 59-62; Assoc Prof, 62-64; Prof, 64-72; Prof, Univ Distinguished, 72-. **HONORS AND AWARDS** Doctor Honoris Causa, Nijenrode Univ, 96; Balfour Jeffrey Research Achievement Awd, Univ of Kansas, 86; Rockefeller Humanities Fel, 77-78; NEH Fel, 69-70; Hope Teaching Awd, Univ of Kansas, 65. **MEMBERSHIPS** Former Pres: American Philosophical Assn.; Metaphysical Society of America; Society for Business Ethics; President; International Society of Business; Economics and Ethics; Former Vice Pres; International Federation of Philosophical Societies. **RESEARCH** Ethics; Business Ethics; Marxism; Political and Social Philosophy. **SELECTED PUBLICATIONS** Auth, "Business Ethics, 5th ed., 99; auth, Academic Freedom and Tenure", 97; auth, "Competing with Integrity in International Business", 93; coauth, "Uncompromising Integrity, 98. **CONTACT ADDRESS** Dept Philosophy, Univ of Kansas, Lawrence, Lawrence, KS 66045-2145. **EMAIL** degeorge@ukans.edu

DEGRAW, DARREL
PERSONAL Born 07/12/1944, Mitchell, NE, s **DISCIPLINE** CRIMINAL JUSTICE **EDUCATION** Univ Nebr, BS, 76, MA, 67, MBA, 78; Am Tech Univ, MS, 88; Univ Dayton, MS, 82; Univ Central Tex, MS, 89; Univ Ala, MS, 93; Central Mo State Univ, MA, 95; Univ Central Tex, MS, 94; Univ Nebr-Lincoln, EdS, 74; Univ Nebr-Lincoln, PhD, 84; Am Col Metaphysical Theol, PhD, 99; numerous other degrees. **CAREER** Assoc prof, Bemidji State Univ, MN, 90-93; Dir, Criminal Justice Prog, Univ Central Tex, 86-93; Dir, Criminal Justice Prog, Mo Valley C Col, 93-96; Dir, Grad Criminal Justice Prog, Delta State Univ, 96-. **HONORS AND AWARDS** Phi Theta Kappa, Pi Gamma Mu, Alpha Phi Sigma, Alpha Kappa Delta, Kappa Delta Pi, Delta Psi Omega, Psi Beta, Psi Chi. **MEMBERSHIPS** Am Police Hall of Fame, AL-MS Soc Asn, etc. **RESEARCH** Domestic violence, substance abuse, capital punishment,

women in law enforcement, corrections, victimology. **SELECTED PUBLICATIONS** Auth, The Utilization of Prison Labor in the Recycling of Solid Waste Materials, ACJS (92); auth, A Comparison of the MBTI of Women in Law Enforcement Compared to that of Women in Educ, ACJS (94); auth, The Issue of Closure and its Relationship to Capital Punishment, ACJS (98). **CONTACT ADDRESS** Dept Soc Sci, Delta State Univ, 1003 W Sunflower Rd, Cleveland, MS 38733. **EMAIL** ddegraw@dsu.deltast.edu

DEHART, PAUL
PERSONAL Born 12/10/1964, Memphis, TN, s **DISCIPLINE** SYSTEMATIC THEOLOGY **EDUCATION** Univ Chicago, AB, 87; The Divinity School, MAR, 90; Univ Chicago, PhD, 97. **CAREER** Asst Prof, Theology, Vanderbilt Univ, 97-. **HONORS AND AWARDS** Phi Beta Kappa; Century fel, Chicago, 90-94; Harper Dissertation grant, 96-97. **MEMBERSHIPS** Am Acad Relig. **RESEARCH** Nineteenth and twentieth century theology; philos and theol doctrines of God; Christian theological method and the university. **SELECTED PUBLICATIONS** Auth, Eberhard Jungel on the Structure of Theology, Theol Studies 57, 96; Divine Simplicity: Theistic Reconstruction in Eberhard Jungel's Trinitarian Glaubenslehre (dissertation), 97; auth, Beyond the Necessary God, AAR/Oxford Univ Press, 00. **CONTACT ADDRESS** The Divinity School, Vanderbilt Univ, Nashville, TN 37240-2701. **EMAIL** paul.jdehart@vanderbilt.edu

DEIBLER, TIMOTHY
DISCIPLINE THEOLOGY; PHILOSOPHY **EDUCATION** Dallas Baptist Univ, BA, 73; Dallas Theological Sem, ThM, 77; MA, 87, PhD, 89, Rice Univ. **CAREER** Interim Asst Prof, Huntington Col, 89-90; Interim Asst Prof, Northwestern Col, 90-91; Asst Prof, Liberty Univ, 91-93; Dialectic and Rhetoric Faculty, New Covenant Schools, 93-. **MEMBERSHIPS** Amer Phil Assoc; Amer Scientific Affil; Soc of Christian Philosophers. **RESEARCH** Philosophy of Religion and Science; Philosophical Theories of Metaphor; Hermeneutics; Theology. **SELECTED PUBLICATIONS** Several journal articles and reviews. **CONTACT ADDRESS** New Covenant Schools, 1350 Liggates Rd., Lynchburg, VA 24502. **EMAIL** cdeibler@ncric.com

DEIGH, JOHN
DISCIPLINE PHILOSOPHY **EDUCATION** UCLA, PhD. **CAREER** Assoc prof, Northwestern Univ. **RESEARCH** Moral and political philosophy. **SELECTED PUBLICATIONS** Auth, The Sources of Moral Agency: Essays in Moral Psychology and Freudian Theory; ed, Ethics and Personality. **CONTACT ADDRESS** Dept of Philosophy, Northwestern Univ, 1801 Hinman, Evanston, IL 60208.

DEIGNAN, KATHLEEN P., CND
PERSONAL Born 12/17/1947, London, England **DISCIPLINE** HISTORICAL THEOLOGY; HISTORY OF CHRISTIAN SPIRITUALITY **EDUCATION** Fordham Univ, PhD, 86. **CAREER** Assoc prof Relig Studies, Iona Col, 81-01; dir, Iona Spirituality Inst, Iona Col. **HONORS AND AWARDS** McCabe Awd Soc Studies, 82; Iona Women of Achievement, 96; Kate Connelly-Weinert Awd AAR, 97. **MEMBERSHIPS** Amer Acad Relig; Cath Theolog Soc Amer; Soc for Study Christian Spirituality. **RESEARCH** Classical and Contemporary Spirituality, legacy of Thomas Merton, teaching spirituality studies. **SELECTED PUBLICATIONS** Road to Rapture: Thomas Merton's Itinerarium mentis in Deum, Franciscan Studies; Christ Spirit: The Eschatology of Shaker Christianity, Scarecrow Pr, 92; composer, six original sacred songs. **CONTACT ADDRESS** Dept of Theology, Iona Col, New Rochelle, NY 10801. **EMAIL** kpdeignan@aol.com; http://www.scholaministries.org

DEJNOZKA, JAN
PERSONAL Born 12/20/1951, Saratoga Springs, NY, m, 1992, 2 children **DISCIPLINE** PHILOSOPHY **EDUCATION** Syracuse Univ, BA, 73; Univ of Iowa, MA, PhD, 76, 79; Univ of Michigan, School of Law, JD, 96. **CAREER** Univ of Iowa, tchg asst, 74-79; US Naval Acad, asst prof, 85-88; Univ of Michigan Ann Arbor, vis scholar, 91-94, 96-00; Union Col, res assoc, 80-00; Hon J. W. Callahan, Law clerk, 97-98; Third Judicial Circuit of Michigan, Domestic Relations Specialist, 98-00. **HONORS AND AWARDS** Navy Expeditionary Medal; Sea Service Deployment Ribbon. **MEMBERSHIPS** American Philosophical Assoc; Bar of Michigan; Bar of Maryland. **RESEARCH** Ontology; Metaphysics; Epistemology; Analytic Philosophy; History of Modern Philosophy; Philosophy of Language; Logic; Mathematics; Science; Religion; Ethics; Law. **SELECTED PUBLICATIONS** Auth, Frege: Existence and Indentity, Ann Arbor MI: University Microfilms Intl, 79; "Zeno's Paradoxes and the Cosmological Argument," International Journal for Philosophy of Religion, 25, (89): 65-81; "The Ontological Foundation of Russell's Theory of Modality," Erkenntnis, 32 (90): 383-418; "Russell's Seventeen Private Language Arguments," Russell n.s. 11/1, (91): 11-35; "Origins of the Private Language Argument," Dialogos, 66, (95): 59-78; "Quine: Whither Empirical Equivalance?," South African Journal of Philosophy 14/4, (95): 175-82; The Ontology of the Analytic Tradition and Its Origins: Realism and Identity in Frege, Russell, Wittgenstein, and Quine, xxvi, Littlefield Adams, (Lanham, MD), 96; Bertrand Russell on Modality and Logical Relevance, ix, Ashgate Publishing Ltd, (Aldershot, England), 99; "Butchvarov: Phenomenology, Ontology, Universals, and Goodness," Philosophia, 00; "Russell and MacColl: A Reply to Grattan-Guiness, Wolenski, and Read," Nordic Journal of Philosophical Logic 6/1, (01) . **CONTACT ADDRESS** 2877 Burlington St., Ann Arbor, MI 48105-1434. **EMAIL** dejonzka@juno.com

DEKAR, PAUL R.
PERSONAL Born 02/08/1944, San Francisco, CA, m, 1967, 2 children **DISCIPLINE** POLITICAL SCIENCE HISTORY, THEOLOGY **EDUCATION** Univ Calif Berkeley, Polit Sci, AB, 65; Colgate Rochester Divinity School, MDiv, 71; Univ Chicago, AM, 73; PhD, 78. **CAREER** US Dept of the State Postings Wash, DC and Cameroon, 67-70; asst to the Chaplan, Univ Rochester, 70-71; asst to ed, Church Hist, 73-75; inst, Central Mich Univ, 75-76; asst prof, McMaster Divinity Coll, 76-79; assoc prof, McMaster Divinity Coll, 79-86; prof, McMaster Divinity Coll, 86-91; acting dir, Center for Peace Studies, McMaster Univ, 91; fac, McMaster Univ, 88-94; centenary prof, McMaster Divinity Coll, 91-94; prof, Memphis Theol Sem, 95-. **HONORS AND AWARDS** Polit Sci Scholar Univ Calif, 61-65; Doctoral Fel Univ Chicago, 73-75; Res Leave, Israel, Palestine, 82-83; Arts Res Bd grant, McMaster Univ, 84-85; Pres Can Soc of Church His, 87; Arts Res Bd grant, McMaster Univ,88-89; Res Leave Oxford Eng, 90-91; Hamilton World Citizen of the Year, 94; Delivered Rattan Lectres, Univ Melbourne Australia, 98. **RESEARCH** Political Science; Theology. **SELECTED PUBLICATIONS** Auth, The Renewal We Seek, 82; Crossing Barriers in World Mission, 83; For the Healing of the Nations, 93; co-ed, In the Great Tradition, Essays in Honor of Winthrop S Hudson, 82; Celebrating the Canadian Baptist Heritage; The McMaster Conference, 85; auth, Holy Boldness. Practices of An Evangelistic Life, 00 (forthcoming). **CONTACT ADDRESS** Memphis Theol Sem, 168 E Pkwy S, Memphis, TN 38104-4395. **EMAIL** pdekar@mtscampus.edu

DEL CARMEN, ALEX
PERSONAL Born 11/09/1967, Nicaragua, m, 1993, 2 children **DISCIPLINE** CRIMINOLOGY AND CRIMINAL JUSTICE **EDUCATION** FL State Univ, PhD. **CAREER** Asst prof, Univ of Texas at Arlington. **RESEARCH** Theoretical criminology, penology; crime prevention; juvenile delinquency. **SELECTED PUBLICATIONS** Auth, Campus Crime: An Environmental Assessment, J Security Admin, 97; rev, The Ecology of Aggression, J Social Pathology, 96; Prisons in Crisis, J Soc Pathology, 95; auth Corrections, 00. **CONTACT ADDRESS** Criminology and Criminal Justice Prog, Univ of Texas, Arlington, 303 Univ Hall, PO Box 19595, Arlington, TX 76019-0595. **EMAIL** adelcarmen@uta.edu

DEL COLLE, RALPH
PERSONAL Born 10/03/1954, New York, NY, m, 1985, 2 children **DISCIPLINE** THEOLOGY **EDUCATION** New York Univ, BA, 76; Union Theol Sem, MDiv, 81, MPhil, 86, PhD, 91. **CAREER** Adj instr, Fordham Univ, 85; adj lectr, Dutchess Community Col, 88; instr, St. Anselm Col, 88-91; from asst to assoc prof, Barry Univ, 91-95; asst prof, Marquette Univ, 95-. **HONORS AND AWARDS** Mellon Grant for Summer Inst, Israel, 97; Union Theol Sem Fel, 81-85; Roothbert Fel, 78-81. **MEMBERSHIPS** Am Acad of Relig; Soc for Pentecostal Studies; Cath Theol Soc of Am; Col Theol Soc; Karl Barth Soc of North Am; Karl Rahner Soc. **RESEARCH** Systematic theology; Trinity; Christology; Holy Spirit; Doctrine of Grace. **SELECTED PUBLICATIONS** Auth, Christ and the Spirit: Spirit-Christology in Trinitarian Perspective, 94; "Trinity and Temporality: A Pentecostal/Charismatic Perspective," 95; "The Two-Handed God: Communion, Community and Contours for Dialogue," 96; "Ecumenism and the Holy Spirit: The Pneumatological Center of Ut Unum Sint," 97; "Reflections on the Filioque," 97; "Oneness and Trinity: A Preliminary Proposal for Dialogue with Oneness Pentecostalism," 97. **CONTACT ADDRESS** Dept of Theology, Marquette Univ, Coughlin 100, Box 1881, Milwaukee, WI 53201-1881. **EMAIL** Ralph.DelColle@marquette.edu

DELACRE, GEORGES
PERSONAL Born 11/09/1922, Buenos Aires, Argentina, m, 1953, 3 children **DISCIPLINE** PHILOSOPHY OF SCIENCE **EDUCATION** Univ Buenos Aires, MA, 50; Univ Paris Sorbonne, PhD, 61. **CAREER** Prof, eng, logic & psychol, Colegio Nacional Gral. Roca, Argentina, 50-55; instr/asst prof, span, humanities, Univ Puerto Rico Mayag & R. Piedras, 55-59; asst prof, humanities, dir, general educ prog, Univ Puerto Rico, 61-67; full prof, philos, assoc dean of studies, Rio Piedras Campus, Univ Puerto Rico, 67-81; prof, philos, chair, grad sch of humanities, Rio Piedras, Univ Puerto Rico, 81-85. **HONORS AND AWARDS** Visiting fel, Princeton Univ, fall, 75; Chevalier de l'Ordre des Palmes Academiques, 77-. **MEMBERSHIPS** Asn Argentina de Filosofia, 77; Amer Philos Asn, 82-. **RESEARCH** Philosophy of science. **SELECTED PUBLICATIONS** Auth, El Tiempo en Perspectiva, Introduccion a Una Filosofia del Tiempo, UPR ed; auth, La Teoria Causal del Tiempo: Recapitulacion, Escritos de Filosofia, Buenos Aires; auth, Los Niveles Temporales Segun J.T. Fraser y el Orden Subyacente Segun D. Bohm, Revista Latinoamericana de Filosofia. **CONTACT ADDRESS** 2151 Jamieson Ave., No. 504, Alexandria, VA 22314.

DELANEY, CORNELIUS F.
DISCIPLINE PHILOSOPHY **EDUCATION** St. Thomas Sem, AA, 58; St. John's Sem, BA, 61; Boston Col, MA, 62; St Louis Univ, PhD. **CAREER** Prof. **RESEARCH** Pragmatism; political philosophy; history of modern philosophy. **SELECTED PUBLICATIONS** Auth, Science, Knowledge and Mind: A Study in the Philosophy of C.S. Peirce, 93; ed, Liberty and Community Values: The Liberalism-Communitarianism Debate, 93; Peirce on the Conditions of the Possibility of Science, 93. **CONTACT ADDRESS** Philosophy Dept, Univ of Notre Dame, 336/7 O'Shaughnessy, Notre Dame, IN 46556. **EMAIL** delaney.1@nd.edu

DELANEY, DAVID K.
PERSONAL Born 10/05/1957, York, PA, m, 1980, 2 children **DISCIPLINE** EARLY CHRISTIANITY **EDUCATION** Univ Va, PhD, 96. **CAREER** Lutheran pastor, St. John Lutheran Church, Roanoke VA. **MEMBERSHIPS** AAR; SBL; N Amer Patristics Soc; Amer Soc of Church Hist. **RESEARCH** History of Biblical interpretation. **CONTACT ADDRESS** St. John Lutheran Church, 4608 Brambleton Ave SW, Roanoke, VA 24018. **EMAIL** dkd7s@ix.netcom.com

DELEEUW, PATRICIA ALLWIN
PERSONAL Born 04/29/1950, Frankfurt, Germany, m, 1971 **DISCIPLINE** CHURCH AND MEDIEVAL HISTORY **EDUCATION** Univ Detroit, BA, 71, PhD(medieval studies), 79; Univ Toronto, MA, 72; Pontifical Inst Medieval Studies, MSL, 75. **CAREER** Asst Prof Theol, Boston Col, 79-. **MEMBERSHIPS** Mediaeval Acad Am; Am Soc Church Hist. **RESEARCH** Religious social history; early medieval Germany; history of pastoral care. **SELECTED PUBLICATIONS** Auth, The changing face of the village parish I: The parish in the early middle ages, In: Pathways to Medieval Peasants, Pontifical Inst Medieval Studies, Toronto, 81. **CONTACT ADDRESS** Dept of Theol, Boston Col, Chestnut Hill, Chestnut Hill, MA 02167.

DELIO, ILIA
PERSONAL Born 08/20/1955, Newark, NJ, s **DISCIPLINE** CHURCH HISTORY **EDUCATION** Univ Mon, PhD, 83; Fordham Univ, MA, 92; PhD, 96. **CAREER** Vis asst prof, Trinity Coll, 96; asst prof, Washington Theo Univ, 97-. **HONORS AND AWARDS** Pres Schlp, 92. **MEMBERSHIPS** AAR; SSCS; MAA. **RESEARCH** Franciscan theology; religion and science. **SELECTED PUBLICATIONS** Auth, Crucified Love: Bonaventure's Mysticism of the Crucified Christ Quincy, Franciscan Press (IL), 98; auth, "The Humility of God in a Scientific World." New Theo Rev 11 (98): 36-49; auth, "The Dangerous Memory of Francis." The Cord 48 (98): 218-23; auth, "Mirrors and Footprints: Metaphors of Relationships in Clare of AssisiÛs Writings," in Resource Study for the Study of Franciscan Christology (Wash, D.C.: Franc Fed, 98); auth, "Bonaventure and Bernard: On Human Image and Mystical Union." Cister Stud 34 (99): 251-63; auth, "The Renaissance of Franciscan Theology: Retrieving the Tradition of the Good." Spirit and Life: A J Contem Franc 8 (99): 21-41; auth, "Bonaventure's Metaphysics of the Good," Theol Stud 60 (1999): 228-46; auth, "Francis of Assisi and Global Consciousness." The Cord 49.6 (99): 273 - 88. **CONTACT ADDRESS** Dept Church History, Washington Theol Union, 6896 Laurel St, Washington, DC 20012. **EMAIL** delio@wtu.edu

DELL'AGOSTINO, DAVID
PERSONAL Born 12/24/1968, Sacramento, CA, m, 1993 **DISCIPLINE** PHILOSOPHY **EDUCATION** SFSU, MA, 95; UCSB PhD student, 97-. **CAREER** Web producer (Instr; var community coll in SF Bay area; De Anza Coll). **HONORS AND AWARDS** Outstanding Grad Student, SFSU, 95. **MEMBERSHIPS** Am Philos Asn. **RESEARCH** Metaethics, Metaphysics. **CONTACT ADDRESS** 1204 36th Ave, San Francisco, CA 94122-1505. **EMAIL** dellagostino@yahoo.com

DELLAPENNA, JOSEPH W.
PERSONAL Born 12/28/1942, MI, m, 1979, 5 children **DISCIPLINE** LAW **EDUCATION** Univ Mich, BBA, 65; Detroit Col of Law, JD, 68; George Wash Univ, LLM, 69; Columbia Univ, LLM, 74. **CAREER** From Instr to Prof, Villanova Univ Sch of Law, 76-. **HONORS AND AWARDS** Phi Kappa Phi. **MEMBERSHIPS** Bar of the Supreme Ct of the U S, ABA, NLA, AAIRVSC, ASCE. **RESEARCH** International comparative law; water management. **SELECTED PUBLICATIONS** Auth, "The Historical Case Against Roe V Wade," NLA Rev (98): 11-13; auth, "'The Phoenix Phillies v the Philadelphia Phillies': A Recent Discovered Opinion on 'Baseball' and the 'Antitrust' Exemption," Villanova Sports and Entertainment (98): 233-257; auth, "Adapting the Law of Water Management to Global Climate Change and Other Hydropolitical Stresses," JAWRA (99): 1301-1326; auth, "Custom-Built Solutions for International Disputes," UNESCO Courier (99): 33-36; auth, "Middle East Water: The Potential and Limits of Law," volume in series, Water: The Mid E Imperative (00). **CONTACT ADDRESS** Dept Law, Villanova Univ, 299 N Spring Mill Rd, Villanova, PA 19085-1515. **EMAIL** dellapen@law.villanova.edu

DELLUMS, LEOLA M. ROSCOE
PERSONAL Born 12/12/1941, Berkeley, CA, d, 1962, 3 children **DISCIPLINE** LAW **EDUCATION** San Francisco State University, BA, 1966; California State Teaching Credential, adult education, 1967; Georgetown University Law Center, JD, 1982. **CAREER** Institute for Services to Education, consultant, 76; American Civil Liberties Union, development director/ publicist, 76-1978; Zuko Interior Designs, Public Relations, advertising mgr, 78-79; Congressman Mickey Leilone, special assistant, 83; Superior Court of District of Columbia, judicial law clerk, 84-85; Assembly California Legislature, principal consultant, Assembly Office of Research, Washington, District of Columbia, rep, 85-92; Washington & Christian, Attorney at law, 93-96; US Dept of Commerce, 96-97; Sole Practioner, Attorney at law, 97-. **HONORS AND AWARDS** The Ella Hill Hutch Awd, Black Women Organized for Political Action, 1992; Inductee Berkeley High School Hall of Fame; The Sojourner Truth Meritorious Service Awd, National Association of Negro Business and Professional Women's Club Inc, 1991; AT&T Volunteer Activist Awd of Washington DC, Area, 1985; Congressional recognition for efforts in attaining passage of HR 1580. **MEMBERSHIPS** National Bar Association; Pennsylvania Bar; California State Society; American Bar Association; The Rainbow Fund; Potomac Links Inc; Alpha Kappa Alpha Sorority; Committee of 21 Human Rights Caucus; Congressional Club; American Society of Composers, Authors and Publishers; San Francisco State Univ Alumni Assn; Berkeley High School Alumni Association; US Supreme Court Bar; District Of Columbia Court of Appeals Bar; US District Court for the District of Columbia Bar; Center to Prevent Handgun Violence, Sasha Bruce Youth Work; Rap Inc Drug Prevention; Minority Breast Cancer Resource Ctr. **SELECTED PUBLICATIONS** Songs published under RREPCO Publishing Company; poetry published in "The Sheet"; prescriptive diagnostic research paper, "Teaching English as a Second Language to Native Born"; hosted "Cloth-A-Thon"; co-hosted "The Place;" hosted local Emmy award-winning television show "Cloth-A-Thon," WGLA; co-hosted local Emmy award-winning television show, "The Place," WRC. **CONTACT ADDRESS** 5423 28th St NW, Washington, DC 20015. **EMAIL** estherleo@aol.com

DELOGU, ORLANDO E.
PERSONAL Born 02/04/1937, New York, NY, m, 1960 **DISCIPLINE** LAW **EDUCATION** Univ Utah, BS; Univ Wisc, MS, JD. **CAREER** Prof; past city councilor, Portland; law sch career, 66-; asst, Thai govt on env, 91. **HONORS AND AWARDS** Mem, Portland Planning Bd. **MEMBERSHIPS** Past ch, Env Law Sect, Asn Amer Law Sch; Maine's Bd Env Protection, 5 yrs. **RESEARCH** Environmental issues; land use law. **SELECTED PUBLICATIONS** Auth, bk on Maine Land Use Law; coauth, 2-vol, Federal Environmental Regulation. **CONTACT ADDRESS** School of Law, Univ of Maine, 246 Deering Ave, PO Box 9300, Portland, ME 04102. **EMAIL** delogu@usm.maine.edu

DEMARAY, DONALD E.
PERSONAL Born 12/06/1926, Adrian, MI, m, 1948, 3 children **DISCIPLINE** THEOLOGY **EDUCATION** L A Pac Col, BA, 46; Dlitt, 60; Asbury Theol Sem, BD, 47; Edinburgh Univ, PhD, 52. **CAREER** Asst Prof, Seattle Pac Col, 52-66; From Assoc Prof to Prof, Asbury Theol Sem, 66-. **HONORS AND AWARDS** Alpha Kappa Sigma; Who's Who in the World; Who's Who in Relig; Int Authors and Writers Who's Who. **MEMBERSHIPS** Contemp Authors, Leaders in Educ. **RESEARCH** Christian healing, devotional classics, gospel communication. **SELECTED PUBLICATIONS** Auth, The Practice of the Presence of God, 2nd Ed, Alba Pr, 97; auth, The Hunger of Your Heart, Partnership Pr, 98; auth, Prayers and Devotions of John Wesley, Russian Pr, 98; auth, Wesley's Daily Prayers, Bristol House, 98; auth, Experiencing Healing and Wholeness: A Journey in Faith, Light and Life Pr, 99. **CONTACT ADDRESS** Dept Theol, Asbury Theol Sem, 204 N Lexington Ave, Wilmore, KY 40390-1129. **EMAIL** don_demaray@asburyseminary.edu

DEMARCO, DON
DISCIPLINE RELIGIOUS STUDIES **EDUCATION** Stonehill Col, BS, 59; AB, 61; Gregroian Univ, Studies Only, 61-62; St. John's Univ, MA, 65; PhD, 69. **CAREER** Instructor, St John's Univ, 66-69; asst prof, St John Univ, 66-70; asst prof, Univ of St. Jerome's, 70-75; assoc prof, Univ of St. Jerome's, 75-97; vis scholar, Holy Apostles Col, 86-87, 88, 90; fac of St. Joseph's Col, Univ of Alberta, 83-84, 87-88; fac of Mater Ecclesia, Wakefield, Rhode Island, 95; assoc prof, Univ of St Jerome's Col, 97. **SELECTED PUBLICATIONS** Auth, Abortion in Perspective: The Rose Palace or the Fiery Dragon?; auth, Biotechnology and the Assault on Parenthood; auth, Chambers of the Heart; auth, Character in a Time of Crisis; auth, Hope for a World without Hope; auth, How to Survive as a Catholic in a Parochical World; auth, In My Mother's Womb: The Church'e Defense of Naturla Life; auth, Sex and the Illusion of Freedom; auth, The Anesthetic Society; auth, The Heart of Virtue: Lessons from Life and Literature Illustrating the Beauty. **CONTACT ADDRESS** Dept of Philos, St. Jerome's Univ, Waterloo, ON, Canada N2L 3G3.

DEMAREST, BRUCE
PERSONAL Born 05/29/1935, New York, NY, m, 1963, 3 children **DISCIPLINE** THEOLOGY; SPIRITUAL FORMATION **EDUCATION** Wheaton Col, BA; Adelphi Univ, MS; Trinity Evangel Divinity Sch, MA; Univ Manchester, Eng, PhD. **CAREER** Prof, Denver Sem, 75-. **HONORS AND AWARDS** Wheaton Col, Scholastic Honor Soc; Bk of the Year Awd. **MEMBERSHIPS** Evangel Christian Publishes Asn, 83; Foreward Mag, 99. **RESEARCH** Area of spiritual formation and direction. **SELECTED PUBLICATIONS** Auth, A History of Interpretation of Hebrews 7:10 From the Reformation to the Present, Who is Jesus?; General Revelation: Historical Views and Contemporary Issues; co-auth, Integrative Theology, 3rds; co-ed, Challenges to Inerrancy: A Theological Response; auth, Satisfy Your Soul: Restoring the Heart of Christian Sprituality. **CONTACT ADDRESS** Denver Conservative Baptist Sem, PO Box 10000, Denver, CO 80250. **EMAIL** bdemarest@aol.com

DEMBO, RICHARD
PERSONAL Born 01/04/1940, New York, NY, m, 1967, 2 children **DISCIPLINE** SOCIOLOGY, CRIMINOLOGY **EDUCATION** NY Univ, BA, 61; Columbia Univ, MA, 65; NY Univ, PhD, 70. **CAREER** Assoc Prof, Clarkson Col, 76-78; Sen Res Assoc, Univ Denver, 79-81; Assoc Prof, Univ Denver, 80-81; Prof, Univ S Fla, 81-00. **HONORS AND AWARDS** Who's Who in Sci and Engineering, 96-97; Int Dir of Distinguished Leadership, 97; Who's Who in the World, 98. **MEMBERSHIPS** Am Soc of Criminology, ASA, Acad of Criminal Justice Sci. **RESEARCH** Develop and test juvenile interventions, alcohol and drug use, research methodology and statistics. **SELECTED PUBLICATIONS** Coauth, "Gender Differences in Service Needs Among Youths Entering a Juvenile Assessment Center: A Replication Study," J of Correctional Health Care, 2 (95): 191-216; coauth, "Juvenile Health Service Centers: An Exciting Opportunity to Intervene with Drug Involved and Other High Risk Youth," in Intervening with Drug Involved Youth, (Newbury Park, CA: Sage, 96); coauth, "A Family Empowerment Intervention for Families of Juvenile Offenders," Aggression and Violent Behavior: A Rev J, 1 (96): 205-216; coauth, "Drug Use and the Delinquent Behavior Among High Risk Youths," J of Child and Adolescent Substance Abuse, 6 (97): 1-25; coauth, "The Relationships Between Youths' Identified Substance Use, Mental Health or Other Problems at a Juvenile Assessment Center and Their Referrals to Needed Services," J of Child and Adolescent Substance Abuse, 6 (97): 23-54; coauth, "The Hillsborough County, Florida Juvenile Assessment Center: A Prototype," The Prison J, 78 (98): 439-450; coauth, "A Longitudinal Study of the Impact of a Family Empowerment Intervention on Juvenile Offender Psychosocial Functioning: A First Assessment," J of Child and Adolescent Substance Abuse, 8 (98): 15-54; coauth, "Predictors of Recidivism to a Juvenile Assessment Center: A Three Year Study," J of Child and Adolescent Substance Abuse, 7 (98): 57-77; coauth, "Engaging High Risk families in Community Based Intervention Services," Aggression and Violence: A Rev J, 4 (99): 41-58; coauth, "Criminal Justice Responses to Adolescent Substance Abuse," in Prevention and Societal Impact of Drug and Alcohol Abuse, (Mahwah, NJ: Lawrence Erlbaum Assoc, 99); **CONTACT ADDRESS** Dept Sociol, Univ of So Florida, 4202 E Fowler Ave, Tampa, FL 33620. **EMAIL** jac@gate.net

DEMECS, DESIDERIO D.
PERSONAL Born 11/08/1923, s **DISCIPLINE** PHILOSOPHY **EDUCATION** Univ degli studi de Bologna, Bologna, Italy, PhD, econ & commerce, 55; State Univ NYork Buffalo, PhD, philos, 65. **CAREER** Teaching fel, State Univ NY Buffalo, 62-65; assoc prof and head, dept philos, Uinv Dubuque, 65-66; prof, humanities & philos, Univ Ark Pine Bluff, 67-94; prof emer, philos & res, Univ Ark, 94-. **HONORS AND AWARDS** NEH grant; Am Asn of State Col and Univ delegate, 78; conference dir, Ark Endow for the Humanities, 76, 80, 85, Ark Humanities Coun, 92; outstanding svc award, Pan-Hellenic Coun, Univ Ark Pine Bluff, 84; contr-dir and princ investigator, US Army Community Support Rev, 87; dir, Hungarian Exposition, Univ Ark Pine Bluff, 88; community svc award, Leadership Pine Bluff Alumni & Greater Pine Bluff Chamber of Commerce, 88. **MEMBERSHIPS** Am Philos Asn; Ark Philos Asn; Soc of Christ Philos. **SELECTED PUBLICATIONS** Auth, Fixing Environment, Human Rights, Rational Laws, Free Market Economy and Democracy Globally Especially in South-Southeast-East Asia's Conditions, UAPB Res Forum, 98; auth, The Failure of the Wicked Communist Don Quixote/Sancho Panza in Central and Eastern Europe and the Problems of the Integration of the Region Into the EU and NATO, UAPB Res Forum, 97, 96; auth, Haiti: A Struggle for Democracy, Human Rights and Law, UAPB Res Forum, 95; auth, The Communist Don Quixote in Cuba, UAPB Res Forum, 95; auth, "Sound Mind In a sound Body Up To the Global Level," 99; auth, "Critical Notes On Authoritarianism IN Rusian Literature During the Tsarist, Soviet and Post-Soviet Periods In the Second Millenium, presented at the UAPB Res Forum, 00. **CONTACT ADDRESS** Univ of Arkansas, Pine Bluff, PO Box 4811, Pine Bluff, AR 71601.

DEMENCHONOK, EDWARD V.
PERSONAL Born 01/01/1942, Vitebsk, Belarus, m, 1993, 2 children **DISCIPLINE** PHILOSOPHY, SPANISH **EDUCATION** Musical Col, Minsk, BA, 61; Moscow State Univ, MA, 69; Inst of Philos of the Russ Acad Sci, PhD, 77. **CAREER** Res, then sr res, Inst of Philos of the Russ Acad Sci, 70-95; assoc prof, Moscow State Univ, 82-84; vis prof, Univ Colombia, 88-90; prof Moscow State Pedag Univ, 91-92; prof, Acad Slavic Cult, Moscow, 91-92; vis prof Univ Georgia, 92-93; assoc prof, Brewton Parker Col, 94-95; assoc prof, Fort Valley State Univ, 95- . **HONORS AND AWARDS** Listed, Who's Who in the South and Southwest, Who's Who in America; Who's Who in the World, 98. **MEMBERSHIPS** APA; MLA; Int Soc for Universal Dialogue; Latin Am Stud Asn; Soc for Iberian and Latin Am Thought; Southeastern Council on Latin Am Stud; Russian Philos Soc. **RESEARCH** Philosophy of culture; social philosophy; ethics; Latin American philosophy and literature. **SELECTED PUBLICATIONS** Auth, Contemporary Technocratic Thought in the USA, Moscow: Nauka, 84; auth, Filosofia Latinoamericana: Problemas y Tendencias, Bogota: El Buho, 90; auth, America Latina en la Epoca de la Revolucion Cientifico-technica, Bogota: COLCIENCIAS, 90; auth, Filosofia en el Mundo Contemporaneo, Bogota: UNINCCA, 90; auth, Discovering the Other and Finding Ourself, Fur Enrique Dussel: Aus Anlas Seines 60 Geburstages, Augustinus-Buchhandlung, 95; auth, Latin American Philosophy in Russia, Concordia, 96; auth, Latin American Philosophy and Multiculturalism, Secolas, 99; auth, The Poetics of Dostoevsky and Borges, For Borges, 99; auth, Th controversies of Globalization and Latin American Thought, SELA, 00. **CONTACT ADDRESS** Fort Valley State Univ, Fort Valley, GA 31030. **EMAIL** demenche@usa.net

DEMING, WILL H.
PERSONAL Born 04/05/1956, Washington, DC, m, 1992, 2 children **DISCIPLINE** THEOLOGY **EDUCATION** Col William and Mary, BA, 78; Univ Chicago, MA, 79; Univ Chicago, PhD, 91. **CAREER** Writing Tutor for the Col, Univ of Chicago, 82-83; Lecturer in Theology, Loyola Univ of Chicago, 87-89; Instr in Religion, Rhodes Coll; 89-91; Asst Prof of Sociology, Univ of Memphis, 91; Asst Prof of Theology, Univ of Portland, 92-98; Assoc Prof of Theology, Univ of Portland, 98-. **HONORS AND AWARDS** National French Honor Society, William and Mary, 77; National Economics Honor Society, William and Mary, 78; Milo P. Jewett Prize for Biblical Interpretation, first place, Univ of Chicago, 81, 82, 88; Outstanding Scholarship Prize, Univ of Portland, 96. **MEMBERSHIPS** Society of Biblical Literature; Classical Association of the Pacific Northwest. **RESEARCH** New Testament Studies; Early Christian Literature; Hellenistic and Roman Philosophy; Greco-Roman World. **SELECTED PUBLICATIONS** Auth, "Mark 9.42-10.12, Matt 5.27-32, and b. Nid. 13b: A First Century Discussion of Male Sexuality," New Testament Studies, Cambridge, 90: 130-41; auth, "Paul on Marriage and Celibacy: The Hellenistic Background of 1 Corinthians 7, Cambridge: Cambridge Univ Press, 95; auth, "A Diatribe Pattern in 1 Cor. 7:21-22: A New Perspective on Paul's Directions to Slaves," Novum Testamentum, Leiden, 95: 130-37; auth, "The Unity of 1 Corinthians 5-6," Journal of Biblical Literature, 115: 291-315 **CONTACT ADDRESS** Dept Theology, Univ of Portland, 5000 N Willamette Blvd, Portland, OR 97203-5798. **EMAIL** deming@up.edu

DEMKOVICH, MICHAEL
PERSONAL Born 01/30/1954, Berwyn, IL **DISCIPLINE** THEOLOGY **EDUCATION** Catholic Univ of Louvain Belgium, PhD, STD, 91. **CAREER** Aquinas Col Grand Rapids, lectr, 81-86; Dominican Studium St Louis, asst prof, 91-96; Univ NM, adj prof, 96-, Blackfriar Oxford Univ, adj prof, 97-, Dominican Ecclesial Inst, founding dir, 96-. **MEMBERSHIPS** AAR, SBL, CTSA. **RESEARCH** Spirituality **SELECTED PUBLICATIONS** Auth, Beyond Subjectivity: Opening the Ego, Listening, 94; auth, Work as Worth: Money or Meaning, Connections Between Spirit and Work, ed., Bloch & Richmond, Danes-Black, 97. **CONTACT ADDRESS** 1815 Las Lomas NE, Albuquerque, NM 87106. **EMAIL** lumen@sprynet.com

DEMOPOULOS, WILLIAM G.
PERSONAL Born 02/21/1943, m, 1964, 2 children **DISCIPLINE** PHILOSOPHY, PHILOSOPHY OF SCIENCE **EDUCATION** Univ Minn, BA, 64; Univ Western Ont, PhD(philos), 74. **CAREER** Assoc Prof Philos, Univ Western Ont, 72-, Lectr philos, Univ NB, 70-73, asst prof, 73-75; consult, NSF & Soc Sci & Humanities Res Coun. **MEMBERSHIPS** Philos of Sci Asn; Soc for Philos & Psychol. **RESEARCH** Philosophy of science, especially physics and cognitive science; philosophy of logic and language. **CONTACT ADDRESS** Dept of Philos, Univ of Western Ontario, Talbot Col 316, London, ON, Canada N6A 3K7. **EMAIL** wgdemo@julian.uwo.ca

DEMOTT, DEBORAH A.
PERSONAL Born 07/21/1948, Collingswood, NJ **DISCIPLINE** LAW **EDUCATION** Swarthmore Col, BA, 70; NYork Univ, JD, 73. **CAREER** Law clerk, Southern Dist of NY, 73; assoc, Simpson, Thacher & Bartlett, 74-75; asst prof, 75-77, assoc prof, 78-80, Eugene T Bost res prof law, 81, Prof Law, Duke Univ, 81-, Vis asst prof law, Sch of Law, Univ Tex, 77-78. **MEMBERSHIPS** Am Law Inst. **RESEARCH** Corporate law. **SELECTED PUBLICATIONS** **CONTACT ADDRESS** Sch of Law, Duke Univ, Durham, NC 27706.

DEMPSEY, CAROL J.
PERSONAL Born 04/16/1955, Ridgewood, NJ **DISCIPLINE** THEOLOGY **EDUCATION** Caldwell Col, BA, 78; St. Louis Univ, MA, 86; Catholic Univ Am, PhD, 94. **CAREER** Tchr, Sacred Ht Grade Sch, 73-75; tchr, St Thomas More Grade Sch, 75-76; Tchr, Essex Cty Corr Ctr, 76-78; tchr, Mt St Dominic Grade Sch, 78-79; tchr, Lacordaire Acad, Upper Montclair NJ, 79-86; instr, bibl stud, Albertus Magnus Col, 86-89; asst prof of bibl stud and theology, Univ Portland, 94-00, assoc prof, 00- . **HONORS AND AWARDS** Cum laude, 78; NEH grant, 80; Natl Catholic Ed Asn Awd, 93; Soc of Bibl Lit Regional Scholar Awd, 96; Natl Regional Scholar, 97-98; Arthur Butine Awd, 97, 98, 99, 00. **MEMBERSHIPS** Catholic Bibl Asn; Am Acad of Relig; Soc of Bibl Lit; Col Theol Soc; Nat Asn of Hebrew Profs; MLA. **RESEARCH** Hebrew Bible/Old Testament; Pentateuch; Prophets; Wisdom; biblical narrative and poetry; biblical theology and spirituality; biblical ethics; literature of the New Testament; exegesis; hermeneutics; biblical languages. **SELECTED PUBLICATIONS** Auth, Listen, O Peoples, All of You: Justice and Economic Issues in Micah 1-3, in Bible Today, 94; auth, Will and Testament, Tribes, Plagues,Nations, Exodus, in Pastoral Dictionary of Biblical Theology, Liturgical, 96; auth, Abraham and Sarah: Called, Uprooted, and Graced, in Vocations and Prayer, 97; auth, Ask the Animals, and They Will Teach You: the Gift of Wisdom and the Natural World, in Bible Today, 97; auth, Compassion: The Embrace of Life, in Mast, 97; auth, Moses: Wonderfully Surprised, in Vocations and Prayer, 97; auth, Samuel: Called from Slumber to Prophecy, in Vocations and Prayer, 97; auth, Jeremiah: Called from the Womb, in Vocations and Prayer, 98; auth, Metaphorical Language and the Expression of Love in the Song of Songs, in Bible Today, 98; The Whore of Ezekiel 16: The Impact and Ramifications of Gender-Specific Metaphors in Light of Biblical Law and Divine Judgment, in Gender and Law in the Hebrew Bible and Ancient Near East, Sheffield Academic, 98; contrib, Eerdmans Dictionary of the Bible, Eerdmans, 99; auth, The Prophets: A Liberation Critical Reading, Fortress, 99; auth, All Creation Is Groaning, Liturgical, 99. **CONTACT ADDRESS** Dept of Theology, Univ of Portland, 5000 N Willamette Blvd, Portland, OR 97203-5798. **EMAIL** dempsey@up.edu

DEMPSEY, JOSEPH P.
PERSONAL Born 03/08/1930, Nashville, NC, m, 1958 **DISCIPLINE** THEOLOGY **EDUCATION** Fayetteville State Univ, BS 1958; Shaw Div Sch, BD 1964; NC Cen Univ, MA 1971; Shaw Div Sch, MDiv 1972; Jacksonville Theological Seminary, Florida, DTh, 1982; Faith Evangelical Lutheran Seminary, Tacoma WA, DMin 1988. **CAREER** Pastor various locations since 1961; NC Cen Univ, Instructor 1971-, Assoc Dir 1988-; Pine Grove Baptist Church, Creedmoor NC, pastor 1986-87; Elementary & High School, instructor; Worthdale United Baptist Church Raleigh, NC, pastor; NCCU Counseling Ctr, assoc dir, currently; NCCU, Grad School of Education, Adjunct Asst Prof, 91-. **HONORS AND AWARDS** Teacher of t e Yr 1967; Raleigh, NC Christian Family of the Yr 1972; Outstanding Serv Awd NC Central Univ 1973-74. **MEMBERSHIPS** Mem Min Bd Wake Baptist Assn 1964; NC Personnel & Guid Assn; Am Personnel & Guid Assn; Exec Com, Wake Co Dem Party; bd dir NC General Baptist Con, bd dir YMCA 1967-; bd dir Comm Day Carde Center; mem Goals for Raleigh Educ Outreach; mem The Raleigh-Wake Martin Luther King Celebration Comm 1989. **CONTACT ADDRESS** Grad Sch of Education, No Carolina Central Univ, PO Box 19688, Durham, NC 27707.

DEMY, TIMOTHY J.
PERSONAL Born 12/06/1954, Brownsville, TX, m, 1978 **DISCIPLINE** THEOLOGY & HISTORY **EDUCATION** Tex Christian Univ, BA, 77; Dallas Theol Sem, Th M, 81, ThD, 90; Salve Regina Univ, MA, 90; Univ Tex at Arlington, MA, 94; Noval War Col, MA, 99; Ph.D, 99. **CAREER** Military chaplain, 81-; adj instr, Naval War Col, 96-. **HONORS AND AWARDS** Phi Alpha Theta; Outstanding Young Men in Amer; Who's Who in the South and Southwest; Who's Who in America; numerous military awards. **MEMBERSHIPS** Evang Theol Soc; Soc of Bibl Lit; Orgn of Amer Hist; Ctr for Bioethics and Human Dignity. **RESEARCH** Bioethics; The crusades; Evangelical theology; Church history. **SELECTED PUBLICATIONS** Coed, Genetic Engineering: A Christian Response, Kregel Pub. 99; coed, Politics and Public Policy: A Christian Response, Kregel Pub, 00; co-auth, Basic Questions on Suicide and Euthanasia, Basic Questions on End of Life Decisions, Basic Questions on Sexuality and Reproductive Technology, Basic Questions on Alternative Medicine, Kregel Publ, 98; coed, Suicide: A Christian Response, Kregel Publ, 98; co-auth, Winning the Marriage Marathon, Kregel Publ, 98; co-auth, Prophecy Watch, Harvest House, 98; auth, Onward Christian Soldiers? Christian Perspectives on War, The Voice, 98; auth, Suicide and the Christian Worldview, Conservative Theol Jour, 97; auth, Chaplain Walter Colton and the California Gold Rush, Navy Chaplain, 97; co-auth, The Coming Cashless Society, Harvest House, 96; auth, A Dictionary of Premillennial Theology, Kregel Books, 96; co-ed, When the Trumpet Sounds!, Harvest House, 95; auth, Blackwell's Dictionary of Evangelical Biography, Blackwells, 95; co-auth, The Rapture and an Early Medieval Citation, Bibliotheca Sacra, 95. **CONTACT ADDRESS** 7 Ellen Rd., Middletown, RI 02842. **EMAIL** tdemy@efortress.com

DEN OUDEN, BERNARD
DISCIPLINE PHILOSOPHY **EDUCATION** Calvin Col, BA; Hartford Col, MA, PhD. **CAREER** Prof, Univ of Hartford. **HONORS AND AWARDS** Harry Jack Gray Distinguished Professor **RESEARCH** 19th century philos; philos of lang; nature philos of creativity; Third World develop. **SELECTED PUBLICATIONS** Auth, The Fusion of Naturalism and Humanism Language and Creativity Reason; Will, Creativity, and Time. **CONTACT ADDRESS** Philos Dept, Univ of Hartford, 200 Bloomfield Ave, West Hartford, CT 06117. **EMAIL** denOuden@whavax.edu

DENBY, DAVID A.
PERSONAL Born 12/24/1963, Cheltenham, United Kingdom, m, 1994 **DISCIPLINE** PHILOSOPHY **EDUCATION** Univ Coll, London Univ, BA, 86; Univ Oxford, B Philos, 88; Univ Mass, PhD, 97. **CAREER** Instr, Univ Mass, 90-94; instr, Randolph-Macon Woman's Coll, 95; instr, Dartmouth Coll, 95; Suffolk Univ, Boston, 96-; Tufts Univ Medford, 96-. **HONORS AND AWARDS** British Acad Fel, 86-88; Univ Fel, Univ Mass, 91-92. **MEMBERSHIPS** Am Philos Asn. **RESEARCH** Metaphysics; Philosophy of language; Logic. **SELECTED PUBLICATIONS** Auth, Determinable Nominalism, Philosophical Studies, (forthcoming). **CONTACT ADDRESS** 31 West Avenue, Salem, MA 01970-5452. **EMAIL** David.Denby2@gte.net

DENG, FRANCIS M.
DISCIPLINE FOREIGN RELATIONS **EDUCATION** Khartoum Univ, LLB, 62; Yale Law Sch, LLM, 65, JSD, 67. **CAREER** Sr Fel, Foreign Policy Stud, Brookings Inst; Minister of State for For Aff of the Sudan; ambassador to US, Scandinavia, and Canada; human rights officer, Div of Human Rights, UN Secretariat; res assoc Woodrow Wilson Ctr. **HONORS AND AWARDS** Dist fel, Rockefeller Bros Found; Jennings Randolph Distinguished Fel, US Inst of Peace; UN Secy Gen special rep on internally displaced persons. **RESEARCH** Africa; conflict management/resolution; human rights; regional conflicts; the Sudan; internally displaced persons. **SELECTED PUBLICATIONS** Auth, War of Visions: Conflicting Identities in the Sudan, 95; coauth, Sovereignty as Responsibility; Conflict Management in Africa, 96; auth, Ethnicity: An African Predicament, Brookings Rev, 97; coauth, Masses in Flight: The Global Cirsis of Internal Displacement, 98; coauth, African Reckoning: A Quest for Good Governance, 98; coauth, The Forsaken People: Case Studies of the Internally Displaced, 98. **CONTACT ADDRESS** Brookings Inst, 1775 Massachusetts Ave NW, Washington, DC 20036.

DENICOLA, ROBERT C.
PERSONAL Born 10/15/1949, Union City, NJ, m, 1987, 2 children **DISCIPLINE** LAW **EDUCATION** Princeton Univ, BSE, 71; Harvard Univ, JD, 74, LLB, 76. **CAREER** Law, Univ Nebr-Lincoln, 76- **HONORS AND AWARDS** Distinguished Prof prize, Univ Nebr Found, 80; Ladas Prize, Int Trademark Asn, 84; ALI Reporter, for: Restatement of Unfair Competition. **MEMBERSHIPS** Copyright Soc US; Am Law Inst. **RESEARCH** Copyright law; trademark law. **SELECTED PUBLICATIONS** Coauth, Restatement of Unfair Competition, ALI, 95; Cases on Copyright, Unfair Competition and Related Topics, Found Press, 98. **CONTACT ADDRESS** Col of Law, Univ of Nebraska, Lincoln, Lincoln, NE 68583-0902. **EMAIL** rdenicola1@unl.edu

DENNETT, DANIEL C.
DISCIPLINE PHILOSOPHY **EDUCATION** Harvard Univ, BA, 63; Oxford, D Phil, 65. **CAREER** Lectr, Oxford Col Tech, 64-65; asst prof, 65-70, assoc prof, 70-71, Univ Calif, Irvine; vis asst prof, 68, assoc prof, 71-75, Prof, 75-, chair, dept philos, 76-82, co-dir, curricular software studio, 85-89, Dist Prof Arts, Scis, 85-, Dir Ctr Cognitive Studs, 85-, Tufts Univ; vis assoc prof, Harvard Univ, 73; vis prof, Univ Pittsburgh, 75; vis lectr, Oxford Univ, 79. **MEMBERSHIPS** Acad Scientiarum et Artum Europaea; Am Acad ARtr, Scis; Am Asn Artificial Intelligence; Am Asn Univ Profs; Am Philos Asn; Cognitive Sci Soc; Counc Philos Studs; Memory Disorder Soc; Soc for Philos, Psychol. **SELECTED PUBLICATIONS** Auth, Elbow Room: The Varieties of Free Will Worth Wanting, MIT Press, Oxford Univ Press, 84, German ed, 86, Span ed, 92; auth, The Intentional Stance, MIT Press/A Bradford Book, 87, Fr ed, 90, Span ed, 91; auth, Consciousness Explained, Little Brown, 91, Penguin, 92, Dutch, It, Fr, Ger, Gr eds, 93; auth, Darwin's Dangerous Idea, Simon & Schuster, 95; auth, Kinds of Minds, Basic Books, 96. **CONTACT ADDRESS** Ctr Cognitive Studies, Tufts Univ, Medford, 11 Miner Hall, Medford, MA 02155. **EMAIL** ddennett@tufts.edu

DENNY, FRED
DISCIPLINE RELIGIOUS STUDIES **EDUCATION** Univ Chicago, PhD. **CAREER** Prof. **RESEARCH** Qur'anic studies; comparative ritual; Islamic education in Malaysia and Indonesia; Islam and Muslim communities in North America. **SELECTED PUBLICATIONS** Auth, An Introduction to Islam; Islamic Theology in the New World: Some Issues and Prospects; Islam in the Americas; Qur'anic Recitation. **CONTACT ADDRESS** Religious Studies Dept, Univ of Colorado, Boulder, Boulder, CO 80309. **EMAIL** Frederick.Denny@Colorado.edu

DENSON, FRED L.
PERSONAL Born 07/19/1937, New Brighton, PA, m **DISCIPLINE** LAW **EDUCATION** Rehsselaer Poly Inst, BChemE 1959; Georgetown U, JD 1966. **CAREER** WOKR-TV ABC, host black dimensions 1972-; Urban League of Rochester, exec dir 1970-71; Eastman Kodak Co, atty 1967-70. **HONORS AND AWARDS** Rochester Comm Serv Awd 1974-76. **MEMBERSHIPS** Bd mem NYS Pub Employ Relat Bd; exec dir Nat Patent Law Assn; dir Armarco Mktg; pres Genessee Region Home Care Assn; chmn adv counc NYS Div of Human Rights Am Bar Assn; Nat Bar Assn; Monroe Co Bar Assn; Nat Patent Law Assn; Am Arbitraton Assn **SELECTED PUBLICATIONS** Author, Know Your Town Justice Court; Minority Involvement in the US Patent System. **CONTACT ADDRESS** 14 E Main St, Webster, NY 14580.

DENZEY, NICOLA
DISCIPLINE RELIGION **EDUCATION** Princeton Univ, PhD, 98. **CAREER** Vis Asst prof, Bowdoin Col, 97-98; vis asst prof, Skidmore Col, 98-99; Andrew Mellon postdoctoral fel, Northwestern Univ, 99-2001; asst prof, Skidmore Col, 99-. **HONORS AND AWARDS** Lilly fel, Wabash Ctr for Teaching and Lrng, 98-2001; Andrew Mellon postdoctoral fel, Northwestern Univ, 99-2001. **MEMBERSHIPS** AAR/SBL; AAUW; Can Soc for Patristic Stud; Can Soc for Bibl Stud; Can Soc for Stud in Relig. **RESEARCH** Early heterodox forms of Christianity; social history of early Christianity; religions in the Greco-Roman world. **SELECTED PUBLICATIONS** Auth, "New Testament Scholarship and the Jesus Seminar," Teaching Theology & Religion 4/1 (01): 23-26; auth, "The Limits of Ethnicity, in A Handbook of Early Christianity and the Social Sciences, ed. By Jean Duhaine and Anthony Blasi," (Alta Mira Press, 01); auth, Genesis Exegetical Traditions in the Trimorphic Protennoia, Vigiliae Christianae, (forthcoming). **CONTACT ADDRESS** Ladd Hall, Skidmore Col, Saratoga Springs, NY 12966. **EMAIL** ndenzey@skidmore.edu

DEPASCUALE, JUAN E.
PERSONAL Born 08/13/1950, Rio Cuarto, Argentina, m, 1989, 4 children **DISCIPLINE** PHILOSOPHY **EDUCATION** Queens Col, BA, 73; Brown Univ, MA, 80, PhD, 87; Louvain Univ, Belgium, LPhil, 81. **CAREER** Tchg fel, Brown Univ, 78-80; instr, Notre Dame Univ, 80-84; assoc prof, Kenyon Col, 84- . **HONORS AND AWARDS** Alum awd disting tchg, Kenyon, 94; Amer Philos asn awd for excellence in tchg Philos, 95; Telluride found tchg grant, 97. **MEMBERSHIPS** Amer Philos Asn. **RESEARCH** Contemporary Continental Philosophy; Philosophy of art; Philosophy of Religion. **CONTACT ADDRESS** Dept of Philosophy, Kenyon Col, Gambier, OH 43022. **EMAIL** depascuale@kenyon.edu

DEPAUL, MICHAEL R.
DISCIPLINE PHILOSOPHY **EDUCATION** Univ Notre Dame, BA, 76; Ohio St Univ, MA, 79; Brown Univ, PhD, 83. **CAREER** Assoc prof. **RESEARCH** Ethics; epistemology. **SELECTED PUBLICATIONS** Auth, Two Conceptions of Coherence Methods in Ethics, Mind, 87; The Problem of the Criterion and Coherence Methods in Ethics, Can J Philos, 88; Naivete and Corruption in Moral Inquiry, Philos Phenomenological Res, 88; Argument and Perception: The Role of Literature in Moral Inquiry, J Philos, 88; Moral Statuses, Australasian J Philos, 88; The Highest Moral Knowledge and the Truth Behind Moral Internalism, S J Philos, 90; Balance and Refinement: Beyond Coherentism in Moral Inquiry, 93. **CONTACT ADDRESS** Philosophy Dept, Univ of Notre Dame, 336/7 O'Shaughnessy, Notre Dame, IN 46556. **EMAIL** depaul.1@nd.edu

DEPPE, DEAN B.
PERSONAL Born 05/16/1951, Grand Rapids, MI, m, 1974, 4 children **DISCIPLINE** THEOLOGY **EDUCATION** Calvin Col, MA, 74; MDiv, 78; M Theol, 79; Vrije Univ Amsterdam, PhD, 89. **CAREER** Minister, Christ's Community Christian Reformed Church, Grand Rapids, 78-81; Oakdak Park Christian Reformed Church, 84-86; Community Christian Reformed Church Toledo Ohio, 86-92; Unity Christian Reformed Church, Prinsbury Minn, 92-98; Calvin Theol Sem, 98-. **MEMBERSHIPS** Inst of Bibl Res, Soc of Bibl Res, Evangel Theol Asn. **RESEARCH** The Sayings of Jesus, The Gospel of Mark. **CONTACT ADDRESS** Dept Theol, Calvin Theol Sem, 3233 Burton St SE, Grand Rapids, MI 49546-4301. **EMAIL** ddeppe@calvin.edu

DER OTTER, SANDRA
DISCIPLINE PHILOSOPHY **EDUCATION** Oxford Univ, DPhil, 90. **CAREER** Dept Philos, Queen's Univ **RESEARCH** Intellectual, cultural, gender and imperial history of late 18th and 19th century Britain. **SELECTED PUBLICATIONS** Auth, The British Idealists, Oxford, 96. **CONTACT ADDRESS** Philosophy Dept, Queen's Univ at Kingston, Watson Hall, Rm 212, Kingston, ON, Canada K7L 3N6. **EMAIL** denotter@post.queensu.ca

DERBY, DANIEL H.
DISCIPLINE LAW **EDUCATION** Univ IL, BA, 74; DePaul Univ, JD, 78; Columbia Univ, 80, LLM. **CAREER** Judicial

Law Clk, IL Appellate Ct; lectr, DePaul Univ; asst prof, Univ Akron; prof Law, Touro Col. **MEMBERSHIPS** Int Asn Penal Law; Am Soc of Inter Law and Am Bar Assoc. **SELECTED PUBLICATIONS** Author of articles on international criminal law and conflicts of law. **CONTACT ADDRESS** Touro Col, New York, Brooklyn, NY 11230. **EMAIL** DanD@tourolaw.edu

DERDAK, THOMAS J.
DISCIPLINE PHILOSOPHY **EDUCATION** Butler Univ Indianapolis, BA; Univ Chicago, MA, PhD. **CAREER** Adj prof, Loyola Univ, 79-; exec dir, Global Alliance for Africa. **RESEARCH** Philosophy of religion; aesthetics; ethics; epistemology. **SELECTED PUBLICATIONS** Publ articles on res interest. **CONTACT ADDRESS** Dept of Philosophy, Loyola Univ, Chicago, 820 N. Michigan Ave., Chicago, IL 60611.

DERNBACH, JOHN C.
PERSONAL Born 05/29/1953, LaRochelle, France, m, 1982, 2 children **DISCIPLINE** LAW **EDUCATION** Univ Wisc, BS, 75; Univ Mich, JD, 78. **CAREER** Instructor, Wayne State Univ, 78-79; Visiting lecturer, Univ Nairobi, 96; Visiting lecturer, Macquarie Univ, 99; Assoc Prof, Widener Univ, 93-. **MEMBERSHIPS** Intl Soc for Ecol Economics; Am Soc of Intl Law; PA Res Coun; Member, Am Bar Asn; Member, PA Bar Asn; Member, MI Bar Asn. **RESEARCH** Environmental law; Sustainable development; International environmental law. **SELECTED PUBLICATIONS** Auth, "Industrial Waste: Saving the Worst for Last?," Environmental Law Review, 90; auth, "The Unfocused Regulation of Toxic and Hazardous Pollutants," Harvard Environmental Law Review, 97; auth, "U.S. Adherence to its Agenda 21 Commitments: A Five-Year Review," Environmental Law Inst, 97; auth, "Reflections on Comparative law, Environmental Law, and Sustainability," Widener L. Symp Journal, 98; auth, "Sustainable Development as a Framework for National Governance," Case W Res Law Review, 98; auth, "Taking the Pennsylvania Constitution Seriously When it Protects the Environment: Part I--An Interpretative Framework for Article I, Sect 27," Law Review, 99; auth, "Taking the Pennsylvania Constitution Seriously When it Protects the Environment: Part II--Environmental Rights and Public Trust I, Sect 27," Law Review, 99; **CONTACT ADDRESS** Sch of Law, Widener Univ, Pennsylvania, PO Box 69382, Harrisburg, PA 17106-9382. **EMAIL** john.c.dernbach@law.widener.edu

DERR, THOMAS S.
PERSONAL Born 06/18/1931, Boston, MA, m, 1986, 5 children **DISCIPLINE** RELIGION **EDUCATION** Harvard, AB, 53; Union Theological Seminary, M.Div, 56; Columbia, Phd, 72. **CAREER** Prof of Religion and Ethics, Smith College, 63; Consultant, Dept on Church and Society and Commission on Faith and Order, World Council of Churches; Editorial Advisory Board; First Things. **HONORS AND AWARDS** Fellow, Institute for the Advanced Study of Religion, University of Chicago, 81; Danforth Foundation grants, 60 & 64. **MEMBERSHIPS** Society for Christian Ethics. **RESEARCH** Environmental Ethics; Bioethics. **SELECTED PUBLICATIONS** Auth, "Ecology and Human Liberation," Geneva: World Council of Churches, 73; auth, "Ecology and Human Need," revised edition of Ecology and Human Liberation, Philadelphia: Westminster, 75; coauth, "Taxes: Fair or Foul? An Ethical Overview of Taxation in Massachusetts, 78; coauth, "Church, State, and Politics, 78; auth, "Barriers to Ecumenism: The Holy See and the World Council of Churches on Social Question," Orbis Books, 83; coauth, "Believable Futures for American Protestantism, Eerdmans, 88; coauth, "Creation at Risk? Religion, Science, and Environmentalism, Eerdmans 95; auth, "Environmental Ethics and Christian Humanism," Abingdon, 96; coauth, "Caring for Creation," Baker Books, 98. **CONTACT ADDRESS** Dept Religion, Smith Col, 98 Green Street, Northampton, MA 01063-1000. **EMAIL** tderr@smith.edu

DERSHOWITZ, ALAN MORTON
PERSONAL Born 09/01/1938, Brooklyn, NY, m, 1986, 2 children **DISCIPLINE** LAW **EDUCATION** Brooklyn Col, BA, 59; Yale Univ, LLB, 62. **CAREER** Asst prof criminal law, 64-67, Prof Law, Law Sch, Harvard Univ, 67-, Consult human rights and media, Ford Found, 77-78; mem adv panel sentencing and parole, Deputy Mayor for Criminal Justice, NY, 77-78; Guggenheim Found fel, 78-79. **RESEARCH** Criminal law; international human rights; prediction and prevention of crime. **SELECTED PUBLICATIONS** Auth, Inadmissible Lies, Aba J, Vol 81, 95; Court Tv--Its Commercialism Hides its Potential, Aba J, Vol 80, 94. **CONTACT ADDRESS** Harvard Univ, 1575 Massachusetts Ave., Cambridge, MA 02138-2903. **EMAIL** alder@law.harvard.edu

DESAUTELS, PEGGY
PERSONAL Born 12/01/1955, Traverse City, MI, m, 1997, 2 children **DISCIPLINE** PHILOSOPHY **EDUCATION** Principia Col, BA, 77; Wash Univ, MS, 88, MA, 93, PhD, 95. **CAREER** Asst prof, Principia Col, 81-89, 94-95; teaching fel, Wash Univ, 90-94; teaching fel, 95-96, asst prof, 96-; asst dir of Ethics Center, 97-. **HONORS AND AWARDS** Olin Fel for Women, Wash Univ, 90-94; Frances Elvidge Post-Doctoral Fel, Univ of South Fl, 95-96. **MEMBERSHIPS** Am Philos Asn; Southern Soc for Philos and Psychol **RESEARCH** Biomedical ethics; cognitive science; ethical theory. **SELECTED PUBLICATIONS** Co-auth, Praying for a Cure: When Medical and Religious Practices Conflict, 99; auth, "Christian Science, Rational Choice, and Alternative World Views," 98; "Religious Women, Medical Settings, and Moral Risk," 99; "Gestalt Shifts in Moral Perception," 96; "Two Types of Theories: The Impact on Churchland's 'Perceptual Plasticity'," 95; "Psychologies of Moral Perceivers," 98. **CONTACT ADDRESS** Dept of Philosophy, Univ of So Florida, 4202 E Fowler Ave, FAO 226, Tampa, FL 33620. **EMAIL** pdesautel@chuma1.cas.usf.edu

DESCHNER, JOHN
PERSONAL Born 10/23/1923, Stillwater, MN, m, 1949, 3 children **DISCIPLINE** THEOLOGY **EDUCATION** Univ Tex, BA, 44; Yale Univ, BD, 47; Univ Basel, DTheol, 60. **CAREER** From asst prof to assoc prof, 56-62, Prof Theol and Grad Prog Relig Studies, Perkins Sch Theol, Southern Methodist Univ, 62-, Vchmn, World Univ Serv, 52-53; vchmn, World Student Christian Fedn, 52-56; Am Asn Theol Schs fel, Heidelberg, 62-63; deleg gen conf, United Methodist Church, 68 and 70; Deleg, IV and V Assemblies and Mem, Comn Faith and Order, World Coun Churches, 68-, chmn theol comn consult church union, 73-75; vmoderator, Comn Faith Order, 76-. **HONORS AND AWARDS** DD, Southwestern Univ, 68. **MEMBERSHIPS** Am Theol Soc; fel Soc Relig Higher Educ; Am Acad Relig. **RESEARCH** Systematic theology; history of doctrine; ecumenics. **SELECTED PUBLICATIONS** Auth, What Could Santiago Accomplish, Ecumenical Rev, Vol 45, 93. **CONTACT ADDRESS** Perkins Sch of Theol, So Methodist Univ, Dallas, TX 75275.

DESLAURIERS, MARGUERITE
DISCIPLINE PHILOSOPHY **EDUCATION** McGill Univ, BA, 77; Univ Toronto, MA, 79; Univ Toronto, PhD, 87. **RESEARCH** Ancient philos; feminist theory. **SELECTED PUBLICATIONS** Auth, "Character and Explanation in Aristotle's Ethics and Poetics," Dialogue 24, no 1, (90), 79-93; auth, "Aristotles's Four Types of Definition," Apeiron 23, (90), 1-26; auth, "Plato and Aristotle on Division and Definition," Ancient Phil 10, (91), 203-219; auth, "Principles and Premises: Interpreting Aristotle's Posterior Analytics," rev of the Origins of Aristotelian Sci, Can J of Phil, 23, no 4, (93); auth, "Social and civic implications of Aristotle's Notion of Authority," in Law and society in the Ancient Mediterranean, Halpern and Hobson ed(s), Sheffield Univ Press, 93; auth, "Sex Difference and Essence in aristotle's Metaphysics and Biology," in re-reading the Canon, ed Cynthia Freeland, Pennsylvania State Univ Press, (98). **CONTACT ADDRESS** Philosophy Dept, McGill Univ, 855 Sherbrooke St, Montreal, QC, Canada H3A 2T5. **EMAIL** deslaur@philo.mcgill.ca

DESMANGLES, LESLIE GERALD
PERSONAL Born 09/28/1941, Port-au-Prince, Haiti, m, 1968, 3 children **DISCIPLINE** ANTHROPOLOGY OF RELIGION **EDUCATION** Eastern Col, BA, 64; Eastern Baptist Theol Sem, MDiv, 67; Temple Univ, PhD(anthop relig), 75. **CAREER** Instr, Eastern Col, 69-70; instr, Ohio Wesleyan Univ, 70-75 & asst prof, 75-76; asst prof, DePaul Univ, 76-78; assoc prof Relig, Trinity Col, 78-, instr, Ohio Univ, 75-76; consult, Miami Univ of Ohio, 73-74 & Hispanic Health Coun of Hartford, 81-; Nat Endowment for Humanities & Trinity Col res grant, 80; dir, Prog Intercult Studies, Trinity Col, 81-. **HONORS AND AWARDS** United States Embassy Awd in Port-au-Prince for valuable contribution in promoting mutual understanding between Haiti and the United States; Haitian-Am Alliance Awd; 2000 Teacher of the Year. **MEMBERSHIPS** Asn Sociol Relig; Am Acad Relig; Caribbean Studies Asn; Pres, Haitian Studies Asn. **RESEARCH** African traditional religions; Caribbean religions. **SELECTED PUBLICATIONS** Auth, African interpretations of the Christian cross in Haitian Vodun, Sociol Analysis, 76; Rites baptismaux: Symbiose du Vodou et du Catholicisme a Haiti, Concilium, 77; The way of Vodun death, J Relig Thought, 80; Vodun baptismal rites, J Inter-Denominational Theol Ctr, 81; The Faces of the Gods: Vodou and Roman Catholicism in Haiti, Univ of NC Press, 93. **CONTACT ADDRESS** Dept Relig & Intercult, Trinity Col, Connecticut, 300 Summit St, Hartford, CT 06106-3186. **EMAIL** leslie.desmangles@mail.trincoll.edu

DESPLAND, MICHEL
PERSONAL Born 07/25/1936, Lausanne, Switzerland **DISCIPLINE** RELIGION **EDUCATION** Univ Lausanne, LTheol, 58; Harvard Univ, ThD, 66. **CAREER** Prof Religion, Concordia Univ, 74-. **HONORS AND AWARDS** Royal Soc Can, 97. **MEMBERSHIPS** Am Acad of rel, Can Soc for the study of Rel **SELECTED PUBLICATIONS** Auth, "La tradition francaise en sciences religieuses," Pages d'histoire, Quebec, Les Cahiers de recherche en sciences de la religion, vol 11, (91), 176; auth, "the heterosexual bosy as metaphor in Plato's religious city," in Relegion 21, (91), 31-50; auth, "Avec gerard Vallee, Religion in histiory," The Word, the, Idea, the reality/La religion dans l'histoire, Le mot, l'idee, la realite, Waterloo. Ont., Wilfred laurier Univ Press, (92), 252; coauth, "On not solving riddles alone," in Derrida and Negative theology, With a Conclusion by Jacques Derrida, ed by Harold Coward and Toby Foshay, Buffalo, N.Y. St Univ of New York Press, (92), 143-166; auth, "Philosophie de la religion et sciences des religions," dans La philosphie des religions a la fin du Xxeme siecle, Carefour 15-1, Ottawa, (93), 103-113; auth, "Le beau moderne: analogue ou rival du religieux?" dans dixieme Colloque de l'Associaiton Paul Tillich, (94), 24-32; auth, "Pour le choix raisonne d'un concept de religion," religionlogiques 9, (94), 217-235; auth, Reading an Erased Code, French Lit Aesthetics and Romantic Rel, Univ of Toronto Press, 94; auth, Les hierarchies sont ebranlees, Politiques et theolgies au XIXe siecle, Montreal, Fides, 98; auth, L'emergences des sciences de la religion, La Monaarchie de Juillet: un moment fondateur, Paris, L'Harmattan, 99. **CONTACT ADDRESS** Dept of Religion, Concordia Univ, Montreal, 1455 Boul de Maisonneuve O, Montreal, QC, Canada H3G 1M8. **EMAIL** desplan@vax2.concordia.ca

DETERDING, PAUL E.
PERSONAL Born 02/19/1953, Jacksonville, IL, m, 1989, 3 children **DISCIPLINE** EXEGETICAL THEOLOGY **EDUCATION** Concordia Seminary, Th D, 81. **CAREER** Pastor, Our Savior Lutheran Church, Satellite Beach Fla, 81-94; pastor, Christ Lutheran Church, Jackson Miss, 94-. **MEMBERSHIPS** Soc Bibl Lit **RESEARCH** Bible; New Testament **SELECTED PUBLICATIONS** Daniel: Encouragement for Faith, God's Word for Today, Concordia Pub, 96; bk revs, Concordia Theological Quarterly, 93, 94, 95; The New Testament View of Time and History, Concordia jour, 95. **CONTACT ADDRESS** 4423 I-55 North, Jackson, MS 39206.

DETLEFSEN, MICHAEL
PERSONAL Born 10/20/1948, Scottsbluff, NE, m, 1969, 2 children **DISCIPLINE** PHILOSOPHY **EDUCATION** Wheaton Col, AB, 71; Johns Hopkins Univ, PhD, 75. **CAREER** Prof. **RESEARCH** Logic; philosophy of mathematics. **SELECTED PUBLICATIONS** Auth, Hilbert's Program, 86; Proof, Logic, Formalization, 91; Proof and Knowledge in Mathematics, 91; Wright on the Non-mechanizability of Intuitionist Reasoning, Philos Mathematica, 95; Philosophy of Mathematics in the 20th Century, Philos Sci, 96. **CONTACT ADDRESS** Philosophy Dept, Univ of Notre Dame, 336/7 O'Shaughnessy, Notre Dame, IN 46556. **EMAIL** detlefsen.1@nd.edu

DETMER, DAVID J.
PERSONAL Born 07/13/1958, Cheverly, MD, m, 1985, 1 child **DISCIPLINE** PHILOSOPHY **EDUCATION** Boston Univ, BA, 80; Northwestern Univ, MA, 82; PhD, 86. **CAREER** Instr, Valparaiso Univ, 85-86; asst prof, Bradley Univ, 86-87; asst prof, Valparaiso Univ, 87-89; asst prof to assoc prof, Purcue Univ Calument, 89-. **HONORS AND AWARDS** Phi Beta Kappa; Choice's "Outstanding Academic Book" Awd, 90. **MEMBERSHIPS** Am Philos Assoc; N Am Sartre Soc; Soc for Phenomendogy and Existential Philos. **RESEARCH** Phenomenology, Existentialism, Ethics, Art, Mass Media News, Animal Rights, Epistemology, Objectivity and Relativism. **SELECTED PUBLICATIONS** Auth, "Freedom at a Value: A Critique of the Ethical Theory of Jean-Paul Sartre; auth, "Husseris Critique of Relativism", Phenomenology and Skepticism, ed Brice Washterhauser; auth, "Sudamer's Critique of the Enlightenment", The Philosophy of Hans Sears Sudamer, ed Lewis Hahn; auth, "Covering Up Iran", The U.S. Media and the Middle East, ed Yahya Kamsipour, auth, "Rivers on Atheism", The Philosophy of Paul Rivers, ed Lewis Hahn. **CONTACT ADDRESS** Dept English Philos, Purdue Univ, Calumet, 2233 - 172st St, Hammond, IN 46323. **EMAIL** detmer@calumet.purdue.edu

DEUTSCH, CELIA
DISCIPLINE RELIGION **EDUCATION** Univ Toronto, MA, PhD. **CAREER** Adj assoc prof, Columbia Univ. **RESEARCH** Early Judaism; early Christianity. **SELECTED PUBLICATIONS** Auth, Hidden Wisdom and the Easy Yoke and Lady Wisdom, Jesus and the Sages. **CONTACT ADDRESS** Dept of Religion, Columbia Univ, 617 Kent Hall, 1140 Amsterdam Ave, MC 3949, New York, NY 10027-6902. **EMAIL** cd142@columbia.edu

DEUTSCH, ELIOT
PERSONAL Born 01/08/1931, 1 child **DISCIPLINE** PHILOSOPHY **EDUCATION** Univ Wisc, BS, 52; Univ Chicago, 52; Harvard Univ, 52-53; Columbia Univ, PhD, 60. **CAREER** Prof, Rensselaer Polytechnic Inst, 60-67; vis prof, Univ Chicago, 66; vis prof, Harvard Univ, 85; Dir, 6th East-West Philosopher's Conf, 87-89; Ed, Philos East & West, 67-87; Chmn, Dept Philos, Univ Hawaii, 86-87, 94, grad chmn,90-, Philos, 91-96; prof, philos, Univ Hawaii, 86- **HONORS AND AWARDS** Faculty Fel, Am Inst of Indian Stud, 63-64; NY St Faculty Schol, 65-67; NEH Sr Fel, 73-74; vis fel, Clarke Col, Cambridge, 98. **MEMBERSHIPS** Soc for Asian and Comparative Philos; Amer Philos Assn; Amer Soc for Aesthetics; Assn for Asian Studies; Metaphysical Soc of Amer; Brit Soc for Aesthetics; Int Metaphysical Soc. **SELECTED PUBLICATIONS** Auth, Bhagavad Gita: An English Translation from the Sanskrit with Introductory Essays and Philosophical Analyses, Gita, Holt, Rinehart & Winston, 68; auth, Advaita Vedanta: A Philosophical Reconstruction, East-West Ctr, 69; auth, Humanity and Divinity: An Essay in Comparative Metaphysics, Univ Hawaii, 70; coauth, A Sourcebook of Advaita Vedanta, Univ Hawaii, 71; auth, Studies in Comparative Aesthetics, Univ Hawaii,

75; auth, On Truth: An Ontological Theory, Univ Hawaii, 79; auth, Personhood, Creativity and Freedom, Univ Hawaii, 82; coed, Interpreting Across Boundaries: New Essays in Comparative Philosophy, Princeton Univ, 88; ed, Culture and Modernity, Univ Hawaii, 91; auth, Creative Being: The Crafting of Person and World, Univ Hawaii, 92; auth, Religion and Spirituality, St Univ NY, 95; auth, Essays on the Nature of Art, St Univ NY, 96; Introduction to World Philosophies, Prentice-Hall, 96; auth, Companion to World Philosophies, Blackwell, 97; auth, Time and History: East and West, Radhakrishna Centenary Vol, 90; auth, Community as Ritual Participation, On Community, 91; auth, Concept of the Body, Self as Body in Asian Thought & Practice, St Univ NY, 92; auth, On the Comparative Study of the Self, Selves, People and Persons, Notre Dame Univ, 92; auth, The Person as Knower and Known, J of Indian Coun of Philos Res, 93; auth, Truth and Mythology, Myths & Fictions, EJ Brill, 93; auth, Creative Friendship, The Changing Face of Friendship, Univ Notre Dame, 94; auth, Self-Deception: A Comparative Study, Self & Deception, St Univ NY, 96; auth, Foreword to Alexander Eliot, The Timeless Myths, Continuum, 96; auth, Seyyed Hossein Nasr's Philosophy of Art, Libr of Living Philosophers, 00. **CONTACT ADDRESS** 1245 Aloha Oe Dr., Kailua, HI 96734.

DEUTSCH, KENNETH L.
PERSONAL Born 03/22/1945, Bronx, NY, s **DISCIPLINE** PHILOSOPHY **EDUCATION** St. Johns Univ, BA, 66; Univ Mass, MA, 68; Univ Mass, PhD, 71. **CAREER** Instr, St Francis Col, 70-71; Asst Prof, Pa State Univ, 71-73; Prof, SUNY Geneseo, 73-. **HONORS AND AWARDS** SUNY Res Awds; NEH Grants; Fulbright Senior Lect, India. **MEMBERSHIPS** Am Pol Sci Asn. **RESEARCH** Political philosophy, constitutional rights and liberties. **SELECTED PUBLICATIONS** Auth, Political Obligation and Civil Disobedience, 73; Auth, Constitutional Rights, 79; Auth, Modern Indian Political Thought, 83; Auth, The Crisis of Liberal Democracy: A Straussian Approach, 87; Auth, Leo Strauss: Political Philosopher and Jewish Thinker, 94. **CONTACT ADDRESS** Dept Philos, SUNY, Col at Geneseo, 1 College Cir, Geneseo, NY 14454-1401.

DEVENISH, PHILIP EDWARD
PERSONAL Born 02/09/1946, Bridgeport, CT, m, 1968, 1 child **DISCIPLINE** CHRISTIAN THEOLOGY **EDUCATION** Hamilton Col, AB, 67; Southern Methodist Univ, PhD (relig), 77. **CAREER** Asst Prof Theol, Univ Notre Dame, 77-, Nat Endowment for the Humanities fel, 79; travel fel, Zahm Found, Notre Dame, 81. **SELECTED PUBLICATIONS** Auth, Christianity confronts modernity, 80, Mind, brain and dualism, 81 & Divinity and dipolarity: Thomas Erskine and Charles Hartshorne on what makes God God, 82, J Relig; Can a Roman Catholic be an historian?, J Ecumenical Studies, winter 82; Postliberal process theology: A rejoinder to Burrell, Theoll Studies, 9/82; The so-called resurrection of Jesus and explicit Christian faith, J Am Acad Relig (in prep). **CONTACT ADDRESS** 1726 N Sherman, South Bend, IN 46616.

DEVIDI, DAVE
DISCIPLINE PHILOSOPHY **EDUCATION** Univ Western Ontario, PhD, 94. **RESEARCH** Mathematical and philosophical logic; philosophy of mathematics; philosophy of language and metaphysics; history of analytic philosophy; philosophy of science. **SELECTED PUBLICATIONS** Auth, pub(s) on relationship between ontological and logical principles, and relationship between non-classical logics and anti-realism. **CONTACT ADDRESS** Dept of Philosophy, Univ of Waterloo, 200 University Ave W, Waterloo, ON, Canada N2L 3G1. **EMAIL** ddevidi@uwaterloo.ca

DEVINE, DONALD J.
PERSONAL Born 04/14/1937, Bronxville, NY, m, 1959, 4 children **DISCIPLINE** POLITICAL SCIENCE **EDUCATION** PhD, Syracuse Univ, 67. **CAREER** Assoc Prof, Univ MD 67-80; Dir, US Office of Personnel Mgt, 81-85; Adjunct Scholar, The Heritage Foundation, Columnist Washington Times, 92-. **HONORS AND AWARDS** A Symposium, New Perspective on John Locke, Univ MD, Univ Coll, Nov 76; General Res Board Faculty Res Awd, 72; Dept of Government and Politics Faculty Research Support, 68; General Res Awd, 68; Univ MD, Natl Sci Foundation, Doctoral Dissertation Res Awd, 67; Fellowship to Maxwell School Syracus; Amer Assoc of Public Opinion Rs; Amer Political Sci Assoc; Amer Soc for Public Admin. **SELECTED PUBLICATIONS** The Attentive Public: Polyarchial Democracy, Chicago Rand McNally, 70; The Political Culture of the United States: The Mass Influence On Regime Maintenance, Little, Brown and Company, 72; Does Freedom Work? Liberty and Justice in America, Caroline House, 78; Reagan Electionomics, 1976-1984: How Reagan Ambushed the Pollster, Green Hill Publ, 91; Testoring the Tenth Amendment: The New American Federalist Agenda, Vytis, 96; Reagan's Terrible Swift Sword: Reforming and Controlling the Federa Bureaucracy, Jameson Books, 91. **CONTACT ADDRESS** 4805 Idlewilde Rd., Shady Side, MD 20764.

DEVINE, PHILIP E.
PERSONAL Born 12/18/1944, Evanston, IL, m, 1986 **DISCIPLINE** PHILOSOPHY **EDUCATION** Yale Univ, BA, 66; Univ Calif, Berkeley, PhD, 71. **CAREER** Prof, Providence Col, 90-. **HONORS AND AWARDS** Listed in Who's Who in the East, 26tgh ed; Fel in Law and Philos, Harvard Law Sch, 80-81; NEH Summer Res at Brown Univ, Wellesley Col, Univ of Nebr-Lincoln, Univ of Notre Dame, and Tufts Univ. **MEMBERSHIPS** Am Philos Asn, Am Cath Philos Asn, Soc of Christian Philos, RI Humanities Forum. **RESEARCH** Ethics, metaphysics, social and political philosophy. **SELECTED PUBLICATIONS** Auth, The Ethics of Homicide, Ithca: Cornell Univ Press (78), reprinted with new Preface, Notre Dame: Notre Dame Univ Press (90); auth, Human Diversity and the Culture Wars, Westport, Ct: Praeger (96); auth, "Of God and Country," Responsive Community, 7, no 2 (spring 97): 92-93; auth, "Taking Diversity Seriously Enough," Providence: Studies in Western Civilization, 4, no 1 (fall 98); auth, "Homicide: Criminal Versus Justifiable" and "Publish-or-Perish Syndrome," Encyclopedia of Applied Ethics, ed Ruth Chadwick, San Diego: Academic Press (98): vol 2, 587-595, and vol 3, 755-757; co-ed with Celia Wolf-Devine, Sex and Gender: A Spectrum of Views, Belmont, Calif: Wadsworth (forthcoming); auth, Natural Law Ethics, Westport, Ct: Greenwood Press (forthcoming). **CONTACT ADDRESS** Dept Philos, Providence Col, 549 River Ave, Providence, RI 02918-0001. **EMAIL** pdevine@providence.edu

DEVITT, MICHAEL
PERSONAL Born 09/29/1938, Kuala Lumpur, Malaysia, m, 2 children **DISCIPLINE** PHILOSOPHY **EDUCATION** Univ Sydney, BA, 66; Harvard Univ, MA, 70, PhD, 72. **CAREER** Lect, assoc prof, 71-87, Univ of Sydney; prof, Univ of Maryland, 88-99; . **HONORS AND AWARDS** Fel of Australian Academy of Humanities; distinguished Prof, Graduate Ctr, Univ of New York, 99-. **MEMBERSHIPS** APA; Australasian Asn of Phil **RESEARCH** Philosophy of language, philosophy of mind/psychology, metaphysics. **SELECTED PUBLICATIONS** Auth, Designation, New York: Columbia Univ Pr, 81; auth, "Meanings Just Ain't in the Head," Method, Reason and Language: Essays in honour of Hilary Putnum, ed George Boolos, Cambridge: Cambridge Univ Pr (90): 79-104; auth, Coming to Our Senses: A Naturalistic Program for Semantic Localism, New York: Cambridge Univ Pr, 96; auth, Realism and Truth, 2nd ed revised "with a new afterword," Princeton: Princeton Univ Pr, 97; auth, "Responses to the Maribor Papers," In the Maribor Papers in Naturalized Semantics, ed Dunja Jutronic, Maribor: Pedagoska fakulteta Maribor (97): 353-411; auth, "Naturalism and the A Priori," Philosophical Studies 92 (98): 45-65; auth, Language and Realtiy: An Introduction to the Philosophy of Language, 2nd ed, Cambridge, MA: MIT Pr, 99; auth, "A Naturalistic Defense of a Realism," In Metaphysics: Contemporary Readings, ed Steven D. Hales, Belmont, CA: Wadsworth Publishing Co (99): 90-103; auth, "A Shocking Idea about Meaning," Revue Internationale de Philosophie, a special issue devoted to Hilary Putnam, 01; auth, "The Metaphysics of Truth," In The Nature of Truth, ed Michael Lynch , Cambridge, MA: MIT Pr, 01. **CONTACT ADDRESS** Philosophy Program, Graduate Sch and Univ Ctr, CUNY, 365 Fifth Ave, New York, NY 10016. **EMAIL** mdevitt@gc.cuny.edu

DEVOS, JEAN
PERSONAL Born Paris, France, m, 1990, 1 child **DISCIPLINE** PHILOSOPHY **EDUCATION** Univ Paris, MA, 86, DEA, 88, Agregation, 90. **CAREER** Prof, Lycee Bayen, 90-91; Lycee Delamare-Deboutteville, 91-93; French Intl School, 93-. **HONORS AND AWARDS** Vis res, Georgetown Univ, 93-99. **MEMBERSHIPS** Am Philos Asn; Can Philos Asn; Int Asn for Philos and Lit; Metaphysical Soc of Am; MLA; North-Am Sartre Soc; World Phenomenol Inst; Merleau-Ponty Circle; Societe Americaine de Philosophie de Laurn Francoise; World Phenomenol Inst. **RESEARCH** Philosophy; Metaphysics; Ethics. **CONTACT ADDRESS** French Intl Sch, 9600 Forest Rd., Bethesda, MD 20814. **EMAIL** devos@rochambesu.org

DEVRIES, DAWN A.
PERSONAL Born 06/11/1961, Hammond, IN, m, 1990, 1 child **DISCIPLINE** THEOLOGY **EDUCATION** Univ Chicago, BA, 83, MA, 84, PhD, 94. **CAREER** Asst prof, San Francisco Theol Sem, 88-90; asst and assoc prof, McCormick Theol Sem, 90-95; assoc prof, Union Theol Sem, Richmond, VA, 95-97; prof, Union Theol Sem, Richmond, VA, 97-98; John Newton Thomas Prof of Systematic Theology, 99-. **HONORS AND AWARDS** Charlotte W Newcombe fel, 88-89; Deutscher Akademische Austauschdienst, 88-89; Henry W Luce, III, fel, 97-98. **MEMBERSHIPS** Am Academy of Relig; Am Soc Church Hist; Schleirmacher Gesellschaft. **RESEARCH** History of Christian thought, especially Continental Reformation-modern systematic theology; reformed tradition; history of preaching; women's studies. **SELECTED PUBLICATIONS** Trans and ed, Servant of the Word: Selected Sermons of Friedrich Schleiermacher, Fortress Press, 87; auth, Jesus Christ in the Preaching of Calvin and Schleiermacher, Westminster John Knox, 96. **CONTACT ADDRESS** Union Theol Sem, Virginia, 3401 Brook Rd, Richmond, VA 23227. **EMAIL** ddevries@union-psce.edu

DEVRIES, PAUL
PERSONAL Born 10/08/1945, MI, m, 1970, 2 children **DISCIPLINE** RELIGION **EDUCATION** Calvin Col, BA, 67; Univ Va, MA, 76, PhD, 78. **CAREER** Pres, NY Evangel Sem Fund, 97-; interim dean, N Baptist Theol Sem, 96; center dean & prof, Sem East, 94-96; prof & ch, King's Col, 89-94; from asst prof to assoc prof to dir and coord, Wheaton Col, 79-89; asst prof, Lenore-Rhine Col, 78-79; instr, Univ Va, 75-78; instr, Piedmont Va Comm Col, 75-78. **HONORS AND AWARDS** Mellon Found grant; Henry Lucce Found grant; Pew Charitable Trust grant. **MEMBERSHIPS** Am Asn Advan Slavic Studies; Am Philos Asn; Baptist Ministers' Conf Greater NY & Vicinity; Hastings Ethics Ctr; Leadership Excellence, Inc.; NY Christian Higher Educ Consortium; Soc Bus Ethics; Soc Christian Philos. **RESEARCH** Applied ethics; philosophical Hermeneutics; ethics theory; social crisis and change; Hermeneutics of Ethics. **SELECTED PUBLICATIONS** Auth, Business Ethics Applied, 00; auth, Ethics Applied, 99; ed, New York Christian Higher Education Directory, 94, 95, 98; contribur, Religion in New York City, 99. **CONTACT ADDRESS** 236 W. 72nd St., New York, NY 10023. **EMAIL** NYESfund@aol.com

DEWART, LESLIE
PERSONAL Born 12/12/1922, Madrid, Spain **DISCIPLINE** RELIGION, PHILOSOPHY **EDUCATION** Univ Toronto, BA, 51, MA, 52, PhD, 54, LLB 79. **CAREER** Prof philos of relig, St Michael's Col, Univ Toronto, 56-88; Prof Emer Religion, Univ Toronto, 88-; Sr Res Assoc, Trinity Col, 95-. **SELECTED PUBLICATIONS** Auth, Evolution and Consciousness: The Role of Speech in the Origin and Development of Human Nature, 89. **CONTACT ADDRESS** Trinity Col, Univ of Toronto, Toronto, ON, Canada M5S 1K7. **EMAIL** ldewart@chass.utoronto.ca

DEWITT, FRANKLIN ROOSEVELT
PERSONAL Born 05/25/1936, Conway, SC, m, 1960, 2 children **DISCIPLINE** LAW **EDUCATION** SCar State Univ, BS Bus Admin 1962, JD 1964; Ga State Univ, Cert Housing Mgt 1973. **CAREER** US Justice Dept, summer law clerk 1963; US Civil Serv Comm Wash DC, trial atty 1965-67; Atlantic Beach SCar, town atty; Pvt pract, atty; Nat Football League Players Asn, contract advisor. **HONORS AND AWARDS** Usher of the Year Cherry Hill Baptist Church 1978; Exec of the Year, 1998. **MEMBERSHIPS** Municipal consult Glenarden MD 1965-67; mem Conway SCar City Coun 1969-84; delegate Nat Dem Party Conv in Miami Beach FL 1972; appt by gov of SCar Spec Study Comt on Home Rule 1972; mem US Court of Appeals for Fourth Circuit, Wash DC Bar, US Supreme Court, mem SCar State Bar Assoc, Am Bar Assoc, Fed Bar Assoc; chmn, bd dir Horry-Georgetown Ment Health Clinic; life mem NAACP; contract advisor, Nat Football League Player Asn; Nat Dem Party Conv, delegate, 1980; Nat Bar Asn, life mem; Kappa Alpha Psi, life mem. **SELECTED PUBLICATIONS** Auth, Super Redskins Pay Bills in Full, 1992; Washington Just Super, Super Bowl, 1988; History of a Family from Slavery to Freedom, 1985. **CONTACT ADDRESS** 510 Highway 378, Conway, SC 29526.

DI FILIPPO, TERRY
PERSONAL Born Bronx, NY, s **DISCIPLINE** PHILOSOPHY, LAW **EDUCATION** Dartmouth Col, AB, 68; SUNY Buffalo, JD, 74, PhD, 87. **CAREER** Practicing Attorney, 75-; vis asst prof, SUNY Binghamton, 87-88. **RESEARCH** History of Modern Philosophy; Philosophy of Law **SELECTED PUBLICATIONS** Auth, Mitchell Franklin and Roman Law, Telos, 86-87; auth, Pragmatism, Interest Theory & Legal Philosophy, Transactions of CS Pierce Soc, 88. **CONTACT ADDRESS** 434 Himrod St, Brooklyn, NY 11237. **EMAIL** terence@mindspring.com

DI NORCIA, VINCENT
DISCIPLINE PHILOSOPHY **EDUCATION** Univ Toronto, PhD. **SELECTED PUBLICATIONS** Auth, Ethics, Technology Development and Innovation, Bus Ethics Quarterly, 94; auth, Sciences economiques et nouvelles Ethiques, 93; art, Communication, Power and Time: An Innisian Perspective, Can Jour Polit Sci, 90; art, An Enterprise/Organization Ethic, Bus Prof Ethics Jour, 89; art, The Leverage of Foreigners: Multinationals in South Africa, Jour Bus Ethics, 89. **CONTACT ADDRESS** Philosophy Dept, Laurentian Univ, 935 Ramsey Lake Rd, Sudbury, ON, Canada P3E 2C6. **EMAIL** vdinorci@nickel.laurentian.ca

DICENSO, JAMES
PERSONAL Born 09/13/1957, Montreal, PQ, Canada **DISCIPLINE** RELIGION **EDUCATION** Syracuse Univ, PhD, 87. **CAREER** Assoc Prof, Univ Toronto. **MEMBERSHIPS** Am Acad Rel. **RESEARCH** Modern religious thoughts. **SELECTED PUBLICATIONS** Auth, Symbolism and Subjectivity: A Lacanian Approach to religion, J of Rel, 94; Contemporary Approaches to Psychoanalysis and Religion: Julia Kristeva'a Black Sun, Studies in Re/Sci Rel, 95; The Displaced Origin: Masuzawa's Analysis of Freud, Method and Theory in the Study of Rel, 96; Totem and Taboo and the Constitutive Function of Symbolic Forms, J of Am Acad of Rel, 96; The Other Freud, Religion, Culture, and Psychoanalysis, 99; The Psychoanalytic Movement, The Routledge Encycl of Postmodernism, forthcoming; Sigmund Freud, The Routledge Encycl of Postmodernism, forthcoming; religion and the Psycho-Cultural Formation of Ideals, What is Rel? Origins, Explanations, and Defi-

nitions, forthcoming. **CONTACT ADDRESS** Dept of Religious Studies, Univ of Toronto, Toronto, ON, Canada M5S 1H8. **EMAIL** James.Dicenso@utoronto.ca

DICICCO, MARIO
PERSONAL Born 01/15/1933, Memphis, TN, s **DISCIPLINE** THEOLOGY **EDUCATION** Quincy Univ, BA 56; Univ Chicago, MA 64; Case Western Reserve, PhD 70; Loyola Univ, MA psychol, 74; Cath Theol Union, MA theol, 82; Lutheran Sch Theol, ThD 93. **CAREER** Quincy Univ, asst prof; Hales Franciscan HS, Principal; Cath Theol Union, adj prof; Lutheran Sch Theol, adj prof; Franciscan Sch Theol, adj prof. **MEMBERSHIPS** SBL; CBA. **RESEARCH** New Testament World, exegesis, introduction; Rhetoric. **CONTACT ADDRESS** Franciscan Sch of Theol, 1712 Euclid Ave, Berkeley, CA 94709. **EMAIL** MarioD@aol.com

DICK, MICHAEL B.
DISCIPLINE RELIGIOUS STUDIES **EDUCATION** Cath Univ Am, BA, 66, MA, 66; Gregorian Univ, Rome, STB & STL, 70; Johns Hopkins Univ, MA, 77, PhD, 77. **CAREER** Post-doctoral work, Johns Hopkins Univ, 77-78; worked, W Semitic res Inst, 97. **SELECTED PUBLICATIONS** Auth, Job XXVIII 4: A New Translation, Vetus Testamentum 29, 79; The Legal Metaphor in Job 31, Catholic Bibl Quart 41, 79; Job 31, The Oath of Innocence, and the Sage, Zeitschrift fur alttestamentliche Wissenschaft 95, 83; Prophetic Poiesis and the Verbal Icon, Catholic Bibl Quart 46, 84; Conversion in the Bible, in Conversion and the Catechumenate, Paulist Press, 84; Elisha and Holy War, Voices, 83; A Syntactic study of the Book of Obadiah, Semitics 9, 84; Conversion in the Old Testament, New Catholic World 229, 86; An Inductive Reading of the Hebrew Bible, Prentice-Hall, 88; The Ethics of the Old Greek Book of Proverbs in Studia Philonica, 91; coauth, Born in Heaven Made on Earth: The Making of the Cult Image. **CONTACT ADDRESS** Dept of Relig Studies, Siena Col, 515 Loudon Rd., Loudonville, NY 12211-1462. **EMAIL** dick@siena.edu

DICKER, GEORGES
PERSONAL Born 11/08/1942, Geneva, Switzerland, d, 1 child **DISCIPLINE** PHILOSOPHY **EDUCATION** San Francisco State Col, BA, 65; Univ Wis-Madison, PhD, 69. **CAREER** Instr, philos and relig, Colgate Univ, 69-70; asst prof, philos, assoc prof, prof of philos, then prof and chair, SUNY Brockport, 70- . **HONORS AND AWARDS** NEH fel in residence for col tchrs, 75-76; council for philos stud summer inst, 72, 80; NEH summer sem, 81, 84. **MEMBERSHIPS** APA; Hume Soc; Int Berkeley Soc; Creighton Club. **RESEARCH** History of modern philosophy; epistemology. **SELECTED PUBLICATIONS** Auth, Dewey's Theory of Knowing, Philos Monographs, 76; auth, Perceptual Knowledge: An Analytical and Historical Study, Reidel, 80; auth, The Concept of Immediate Perception in Berkeley's Immaterialism, in Turbayne, ed, Berkeley: Critical and Interpretive Essays, Univ Minn, 82; auth, Leibniz on Necessary and Contingent Propositions, Studia Leibnitiana, 82; auth, An Idea Can Be Like Nothing But An Idea, Hist of Philos Q, 85; auth, A Refutation of Rowe's Critique of Anselm's Ontological Argument, Faith and Philos, 88; auth, The Limits of Cartesian Dualism, in Hare, ed, Doing Philosophy Historically, Prometheus, 88; auth, Hume's Fork Revisited, His of Philos Q, 91; auth, Berkeley on the Immediate Perception of Objects, in Cummins, ed, Minds, Ideas, and Objects: Essays in the Theory of Representation in Modern Philosophy, Ridgeview, 92; auth, Descartes: An Analytical and Historical Introduction, Oxford, 93; auth, Epistemology Reburied, Trans of the Charles S. Peirce Soc, 95; auth, Hume's Epistemology and Metaphysics: An Introduction, Routledge, 98. **CONTACT ADDRESS** Dept of Philosophy, SUNY, Col at Brockport, 350 New Campus Dr, Brockport, NY 14420. **EMAIL** gdicker@brockport.edu

DICKERSON, DENNIS CLARK
PERSONAL Born 08/12/1949, McKeesport, PA, m, 1977, 4 children **DISCIPLINE** THEOLOGY **EDUCATION** Lincoln Univ, BA 71; Washington Univ, MA 74, PhD 78; Hartford Seminary, additional study; Morris Brown Coll, LHD, 90. **CAREER** Forest Park Comm Coll, part-time instructor 74; PA State Univ, Ogontz Campus, part-time instructor 75-76; Williams Col, asst prof history 76-83, assoc prof history 1983-85; Rhodes Col, assoc prof history 85-87; Carter Woodson Inst Univ of VA, visiting scholar 87-88; Williams Col, assoc prof to prof of history, 87-; Stanfield professor of history, 92-99; chair, Dept of History, 98-99; Prof of History, Vanderbilt Univ, 99-; African Methodist Episcopal Church, historiographer, 88-; Payne Theological Seminary, visiting professor, 92, 96, 98; Yale Divinity School, visiting prof of amer religious history, Spring 95. **HONORS AND AWARDS** Fellowship Natl Endowment for the Humanities 1982; Moody Grant Lyndon B Johnson Found 1983; Grant-in-aid Amer Council of Learned Soc 1983-84; Fellowship Rockefeller Found 1983-84; articles in New Jersey History, Church History, Pennsylvania Heritage, New York State Journal of Medicine, Methodist History, Western PA Historical Magazine, AME Church Review; Journal of Presbyterian History; contributing author: Encyclopedia of Amer Business History and Biography: Iron and Steel in the 20th Century, Bruccoli Clark Layman Boo, 1994, Historical Dictionary of Methodism, Scarecrow Press, 1996; Blackwell Dictionary of Evangelical Biography, Blackwell Publishers, 1995; Black Apostles at Home and Abroad, GK Hall 1982; Biographical Dictionary of Amer Labor Leaders, Greenwood Press 1984; Encyclopedia of Southern Culture, University of North Carolina Press, 1989; Biographical Dictionary of Amer Social Welfare, Greenwood Press 1986; Life and Labor, SUNY Press 1986. **MEMBERSHIPS** Pastor, Payne AME Church Chatham NY 80-85; mem, IBPOEW; Alpha Phi Alpha Fraternity; mem, NAACP; pastor, St Mark AME Church Munford TN 85-87; board of corporators, Williamstown Savings Bank, 92-99; board of trustees, 92-95; North Adams State College; GRE History Committee Educational Testing Service, 90-96; American Society of Church History; Organization of American Historians; American Historical Association; Southern Historical Association; World Methodist Historical Society; Wesley Historical Society; American Bible Study Society, board of trustees, 96-. **SELECTED PUBLICATIONS** Author "Out of the Crucible, Black Steelworkers in Western Pennsylvania 1875-1980," Alb State Univ of NY Press 1986; author, Religion, Race and Region: Research Notes on AME Church History, Nashville AME Sunday School Union, 1995; Militant Mediator: Whitney M Young, Jr, Univ Press of Kentucky, 1998. **CONTACT ADDRESS** Dept of History, Vanderbilt Univ, PO Box 22031, Nashville, TN 37202-2031. **EMAIL** dennis.c.dickerson@vanderbilt.edu

DICKEY, WALTER J.
PERSONAL Born 11/11/1946, Bronx, NY, m, 1970, 2 children **DISCIPLINE** LAW **EDUCATION** Univ Wis, BA, 68, JD, 71. **CAREER** Fel, Int Legal Ctr, 71-73; asst prof criminal law, 76-80, Assoc Prof Criminal Law, Univ Wis Law Sch, 80-, Dir, Legal Assistance to Instnl Persons Prof, Univ Wis Law Sch, 75-. **RESEARCH** Criminal law; corrections; criminal justice. **SELECTED PUBLICATIONS** Coauth, Legal assistance for the institutionalized, Southern Ill Law Rev, 76; auth, The lawyer and the quality of service to the poor, DePaul Law Rev, 78; The lawyer and the accuracy of the presentence report, Fed Probation, 79; Incompetency and the nondangerous mentally ill client, Criminal Law Bull, 80; coauth, Law, trial judges and the psychiatric witness, Int J Law & Psychol, 81; auth, Wisconsin Administrative Code Corrections, State of Wis, 79-82; coauth, Criminal Justice Administration, Michie Co, rev ed, 82. **CONTACT ADDRESS** Law Sch, Univ of Wisconsin, Madison, 975 Bascom Mall, Madison, WI 53706-1301. **EMAIL** 1hicks@gacstaff.wisc.edu

DICKIE, GEORGE T.
PERSONAL Born 08/12/1926, Palmetto, FL, m, 1977, 2 children **DISCIPLINE** PHILOSOPHY **EDUCATION** Florida State Univ, BA 49; Univ Cal Los Angeles, PhD 59. **CAREER** Univ Illinois, prof emer 95-, prof 67-95, assoc prof 65-67; Univ Houston, assoc prof 64-65; Washington State Univ, inst, assoc prof 56-64. **HONORS AND AWARDS** Univ Ill Hum Inst Fel; NEH; NEH Sr Fel; Guggenheim Fel. **MEMBERSHIPS** ASA; APA; IPA **RESEARCH** Aesthetics **SELECTED PUBLICATIONS** Auth, Introduction to Aesthetics: An Analytical Approach, Oxford UP, 97, revised version of Aesthetics: An Introduction, Pegasus Press 71; The Century of Taste: The Philosophical Odyssey of Taste in the Eighteenth Century, Oxford UP, 96; Evaluating Art, Temple Univ Press, 88; The Art Circle: A Theory of Art, Haven, 84. **CONTACT ADDRESS** Dept of Philosophy, Univ of Illinois, Chicago, Apt 9A, Chicago, IL 60660. **EMAIL** gtdickie@aol.com

DICKINSON, CHARLES C.
PERSONAL Born 05/13/1936, Charleston, WV, m, 3 children **DISCIPLINE** THEOLOGY **EDUCATION** Dartmouth Col, BA, 58; Pittsburgh Theol Sem, BD, 65; Univ Pittsburgh, PhD, 73. **CAREER** Vis Prof, union Theol Sem, 74-75; Asst Prof, Morris Harvey Col, 75-79; Prof, Univ Charleston, 80-81; Prof, Hebei Teachers Univ, 83-84. **HONORS AND AWARDS** Entrance Fel, Chicago Theol Sem. **MEMBERSHIPS** Royal Soc of Arts, Am Acad of Relig, Soc for Bibl Lit, Am Theol Soc, Midwest Theol Soc, Am Philos Asn, Am Assoc for the Advancement of Sci, Asn for Humanistic Psychol, Karl Barth Soc of N Am. **RESEARCH** Theology, religion, philosophy, foreign languages and literature. **SELECTED PUBLICATIONS** Auth, One Thing Necessary: The Word of god in Preaching, 88. **CONTACT ADDRESS** Dept Theol, 21 Chestnut St, Boston, MA 02108-3601.

DICKSON, DAVID FRANKLIN
PERSONAL Born 01/20/1933, St. Louis, MO, m **DISCIPLINE** CONSTITUTIONAL LAW, POLITICAL SCIENCE **EDUCATION** Princeton Univ, AB, 54; Yale Univ, LLB, 59; Fla State Univ, MS, 64, PhD(govt), 66. **CAREER** Assoc, Watts, Oakes & VanderVoort, NY, 61-63; res assoc Polit Sci, inst Govt Res, 65-66, from asst prof to assoc prof Law, 66-73, asst dean, 71-72, prof Law, Col Law, Fla State Univ, 73-, VDean Col, 72-, Mem, Fla Law Revision Comn, 67-70. **RESEARCH** Public law; state constitutional revision. **SELECTED PUBLICATIONS** Auth, Proposed amendments to the Florida Constitution of 1885, 66 & Comments on the Drafting of a New Constitution for Florida, 66, Fla State Univ. **CONTACT ADDRESS** Col of Law, Florida State Univ, 425 W Jefferson St, Tallahassee, FL 32306.

DICKSON, W. MICHAEL
PERSONAL Born 05/27/1968, Pensacola, FL **DISCIPLINE** PHILOSOPHY, PHILOSOPHY OF SCIENCE **EDUCATION** Univ SCar, BA, BS, 90; Univ Notre Dame, PhD, 95. **CAREER** Adj instr, Univ SCar, fall 94; vis scholar, Univ Cambridge, spring 95; from asst prof to assoc prof, Ind Univ, 96-. **HONORS AND AWARDS** Ruth N. Halls Post-Doctoral Fel in the Humanities, Dept Hist and Philos of Sci, Ind Univ, 95-96; Indiana Univ Tara Teaching Awd; Ind Univ Dean's Fel; Ind Univ Outstanding Jr Fac Awd; Am Coun of Learned Socs Travel Grant; Ind Univ Int Progs Travel Grant; Ind Univ Summer Fac Fel; Mellon Found Fel; Javitz Found Fel; Univ Notre Dame Presidential Fel; Univ Notre Dame Outstanding PhD in the Humanities. **MEMBERSHIPS** APA, PSA, Brit Soc for Philos of Sci. **RESEARCH** Interpretations of Quantum Theory, Ancient Philosophy. **SELECTED PUBLICATIONS** Auth, "Antidote or Theory? The Undivided Universe and The Quantum Theory of Motion," Studies in Hist and Philos of Modern Physics, 27 (96): 229-238; auth, "Is The Bohm Theory Local?" in Bohemian Mechanics and Quantum Theory: An Appraisal, J. Cushing, A. Fine, and S. Goldstein, eds (96): 321-330; auth, "Determinism and Locality in Quantum Systems," Synthese 107 (96): 52-82; auth, "The Quantum-Classical Connection in the Bohn Theory: Aspects of the Classical Limit," in Quantum-Classical Correspondence, D. H. Feng and B. L. Hu, eds (97): 127-132; coauth with Rob Clifton, "Lorentz-Invariance in the Modal Interpretation," in The Modal Interpretation of Quantum Mechanics, D. Dieks and P. Vermaas, eds (98): 9-47; auth, "On the Plurality of Dynamics," Minn Studies in Philos of Sci, vol XVII, R. Healey and G. Hellman, eds (98): 160-182; auth, Quantum Chance and Nonlocality, Cambridge Univ Press (98); coauth with Guido Bacciagaluppi, "Dynamics for Modal Interpretations," Foundations of Physics, 29 (99): 1165-1201; auth, "The Light at the End of the Tunneling: Observation and Underdetermination," Philos of Sci, 66, Supp (99): 47-58; coauth with Rob Clifton, Structuring Reality: Foundational Issues in Quantum Theory, Oxford Univ Press (forthcoming). **CONTACT ADDRESS** Dept Hist & Philos of Sci, Indiana Univ, Bloomington, 130 Goodbody Hall, Bloomington, IN 47405-2401. **EMAIL** midickso@indiana.edu

DIENER, PAUL W.
DISCIPLINE RELIGION AND ETHICS **EDUCATION** Lebanon Valley Col, BA; Temple Univ, PhD. **SELECTED PUBLICATIONS** Auth, Religion and Morality: An Introduction, Westminster John Knox. **CONTACT ADDRESS** York Col, Pennsylvania, 441 Country Club Road, York, PA 17403.

DIENES, C. THOMAS
PERSONAL Born 01/09/1940, Chicago, IL, m, 1965 **DISCIPLINE** LAW **EDUCATION** Loyola Univ, BS, 61; Northwestern Univ, JD, 64, PhD (polit sci), 68. **CAREER** Asst prof law and polit sci, Col Law, Univ Houston, 69-70; assoc prof law and govt, Am Univ, 70-73, prof law, 73-80; Prof Law, Nat Law Ctr, George Washington Univ, 80-, Lectr constitutional law, Bar Rev Inc, Del and Md, 71-; hearing examr, Off Educ Title I Audit Hearing Bd, 73-78; vis prof law, Cornell Univ, 78-79 and George Washington Nat Law Ctr, 79-80. **HONORS AND AWARDS** Russell Sage Fel in Law and the Social Sciences. **MEMBERSHIPS** Am Polit Sci Asn; Law and Soc Asn; Am Acad Polit and Soc Sci. **RESEARCH** Law and the social sciences; constitutional law. **SELECTED PUBLICATIONS** Auth, Implied Libel, Defamatory Meaning, and State of Mind--The Promise of New York Times, Iowa Law Rev, Vol 78, 93; coauth, Newsgathering and the Law, 97. **CONTACT ADDRESS** College of Law, American Univ, Massachusetts and Nebraska Ave NW, Washington, DC 20016. **EMAIL** tdienes@main.nlc.gwu.edu

DIGIOVANNI, GEORGE
DISCIPLINE PHILOSOPHY **EDUCATION** Univ Toronto, BA, 59; MA, 60; PhD, 70. **RESEARCH** German idealism; nineteenth century philosophy; phenomenology; conceptual realism. **SELECTED PUBLICATIONS** Auth, The First Twenty Years of Critique: The Spinoza Connection, The Cambridge Companion to Kant, ed. Paul Guyer, Cambridge: Univ Press, (92): 417-448; auth, Friedrich Heinrich Jacobi: The Main Philosophical Writings and the Novel Allwill translated with an Introductory Study, Notes, and Bibliography, Kingston and Montreal: McGill-Queen's Press, (94): 1-167; auth, Hegel, Jacobi, and Crypto-Catholicism, or, Hegel in Dialogue with the Enlightenment Hegel on the Modern World, ed. Ardis Collins, Albany: SUNY, (95): 53-72; auth, Fichte's Rhetoric of Deception: Reflection on the Early Fichte in the Spirit of Jacobi Revue internationale de philosophie, XL, (95): 59-78; auth, The Moral Individual: Kant's Reply to Rehberg and Reinhold Proceedings of the Eight International Kant Congress, II.1, ed. Hoke Robinson, Milwaukee: Marquete, (95): 49-60; auth, Hegel's Phenomenology and the Critique of the Enlightenment: An Essay in Interpretation Laval tehologique et philosophique, (95): 251-270; auth, Immanuel Kant: Religion and Rational Theology vol. VI of The Cambridge Edition of the Works of Immanuel Kant, translated and edited by Allen W. Wood and George di Giovanni, New York: Cambridge Univ Press, (96): xxiv-518. **CONTACT ADDRESS** Philosophy Dept, McGill Univ, 855 Sherbrooke St W, Montreal, QC, Canada H3A 2T7. **EMAIL** gdigio@po-box.mcgill.ca

DILLER, MATTHEW
DISCIPLINE CIVIL PROCEDURE, SOCIAL WELFARE LAW **EDUCATION** Harvard Col, AB, 81; Harvard Univ, JD, 85. **CAREER** Law clk, US Court of Appeals, 85-86; staff atty, The Legal Aid Soc, 86-93; adj asst, prof, NY Univ Sch Law, 89, 93; assoc prof, 93. **SELECTED PUBLICATIONS** Rev, Poverty Lawyering in the Golden Age, Mich Law Rev 1401, 95; auth, Introductory Remarks: Is the Issue Welfare or Poverty? 22 Fordham Urban Law Jour 875, 95; Entitlement and Exclusion: The Role of Disability in the Social Welfare System, 44 UCLA Law Rev 361, 96; Dissonant Disability Policies: The Tensions Between the Americans with Disabilities Act and Federal Disability Benefit Programs, 76 Tex Law Rev 1003, 98; Working without a Job: The Shifting Social Messages of the New Workfare, 9 Stanford Law & Policy Rev 19, 98. **CONTACT ADDRESS** Law Sch, Fordham Univ, 113 W 60th St, New York, NY 10023. **EMAIL** mdiller@mail.lawnet.fordham.edu

DILLEY, FRANK B.
PERSONAL Born 11/17/1931, Athens, OH, m, 1953, 3 children **DISCIPLINE** PHILOSOPHY **EDUCATION** Ohio Univ, AB, 52, MA, 53; Union Theol Sem, MDiv, 55; Columbia Univ, PhD (philos of relig), 61. **CAREER** Tutor, Union Theol Sem, 55-57; instr, Sarah Lawrence Col, 56-57; from instr to asst prof relig, Smith Col, 57-61; assoc prof philos and chmn dept, Millikin Univ, 61-65 and 66-67; Am Coun Educ fel acad admin, Univ Denver, 65-66; prof and dept Chair Philos, 67-70, assoc provost, 70-74, Prof and dept Chair, Univ Del, 74-94; Prof, Univ of Delaware, 94-00. **MEMBERSHIPS** Am Philos Asn; Am Acad Relig; Parapsychology Asn. **RESEARCH** Philosophy of Mind, Philosophy of Religion. **SELECTED PUBLICATIONS** Auth, Metaphysics and Religious Language, NY: Columbia Univ Pres, 64; auth, "Telepathy and Mind-Brain Dualism," JSPR [Journal of the Society for Psychical Research], 90; auth, "The Free Will Defence and Worlds Without Moral Evil," IJPR, 90; auth, Philosophical Interactions with Parapsychology: The Major Writings of H.H. Price on Parapsychology and Survival, London: Macmillan, 96; auth, Reincarnation--A Critical Examination, Intl J Philos Rel, Vol 42, 97; The Non Reality of Free Will, Intl J Philos Rel, Vol 34, 93; "A Finite God Reconsidered," IJPR, 00. **CONTACT ADDRESS** Dept of Philosophy, Univ of Delaware, Newark, DE 19711. **EMAIL** fdilley@udel.edu

DILLEY, PATRICIA E.
DISCIPLINE LAW **EDUCATION** Swarthmore Col, BA; Univ Pa, MA; Georgetown Univ, JD; Boston Univ, LLM. **CAREER** Assoc prof, 98-, Univ Fla; asst and assoc prof, Seattle Univ Sch Law, 93-98; fmr assoc, Arnold Porter, Wash, DC & Downs, Rachlin Martin, Burlington Vermont. **MEMBERSHIPS** US House Ways and Means Comt, 81-87; staff dir & ch coun, Soc Security Subcomt, 85-87; past ch, Asn Amer Law Schools Sect on Employee Benefits; Amer Bar Asn Employee Benefits Comt; Nat Acad Soc Insurance. **RESEARCH** Deferred compensation, individual income taxation, corporate taxation, international taxation, advanced employee benefit law and retirement income policy. **CONTACT ADDRESS** School of Law, Univ of Florida, PO Box 117625, Gainesville, FL 32611-7625. **EMAIL** dilley@law.ufl.edu

DILLON, CLARISSA F.
PERSONAL Born 07/24/1933, Chicago, IL, d, 1 child **DISCIPLINE** POLITICAL SCIENCE; AMERICAN HISTORY; HISTORY **EDUCATION** Bryn Mawr Col, AB, 55; Univ Chicago, MA, 60; Bryn Mawr Col, PhD, 86. **CAREER** Classrom teacher, The Latin School of Chicago, grades 1, 2, 5, 6, 7, 8, 11-12; Ithan Elementary, Radnor, PA, grades 1, 4, 5, 6 (public school certification through Immaculata Col); consultant and free-lance Living History demonstrator at Historic Sites and Museums, 73-. **MEMBERSHIPS** Radnor Twp Ed Asn; PA State Ed Asn; NEA; Nat Coalition of Independent Scholars; Asn for Living History, Farms, and Agricultural Museums (ALHFAM). **RESEARCH** 18th century women's work/lives among the English in southeastern PA (demonstration/interpretation of processes based on research findings). **SELECTED PUBLICATIONS** Auth, A Most Comfortable Dinner-18th Century Foods "to subsist a great Number of Persons at a small Expense," printed for the author, 94; "To Make the Face Faire and Smooth," ALHFAM Proceedings for Annual Conference, 95; Beef--It's What's for Dinner, ALHFAM Bul, spring, 96; Barbecues, with Sandra Oliver, Food History News, spring 96; Lewd, Enormous, and Disorderly Practices: Prostitution in 18th-Century Philadelphia and Its English Background, ALHFAM Proceedings for Annual Conference, 96; Margaret Morris Burlington-NJ 1804 Gardening Memorandum, with Nancy V Webster, No 6 in Am Horticultural Series, The AM Botanist, Booksellers, Chillicothe, IL, 96; This is the Way We Wash Our Clothes, Past Masters, Newsletter, winter 98; "Under the Shadow of My Wing," ALHFAM Proceedings for Annual Conference, 98; 18th-Century Dyeng in Pennsylvania, Past Masters Newsletter, summer 98; auth, "So Serve It Up: Eighteenth-Century English Foodstuffs in Eastern Pennsylvania," printed for the author, 99. **CONTACT ADDRESS** 768 Buck Ln, Haverford, PA 19041-1202.

DILLON, M. C.
PERSONAL Born 12/07/1938, Los Angeles, CA, m, 1985, 3 children **DISCIPLINE** PHILOSOPHY **EDUCATION** Univ Virginia, BA, 60; Univ Calif, Berkeley, MA, 64; Yale Univ, MPhil, 68, PhD, 70. **CAREER** Instr, philos, Washington and Lee Univ, 65-66; instr, 68-70, from asst prof, philos, to prof, 70-93, dir, Undergrad Stud, Philos, 78-90, distinguished tchg prof, 93- , Binghamton Univ; instr, Corporate Prof Educ, IBM, Inc., 86-93. **HONORS AND AWARDS** Woodrow Wilson fel, 63-64; Yale Univ fel, 66-67, 67-68; SUNY Chancellor's Awd for Excellence in Tchg, 74; SUNY Fac Res Grant, 71, 73, 78, 80. **MEMBERSHIPS** Merleau-Ponty Circle; Int Asn for Philos and Lit; Int Husserl and Phenomenological Res Soc; APA; Soc for Phenomenology and Existential Philos; NY State Philos Asn; Soc for the Philos of Sex and Love; Human Sci Res Conf; Can Soc for Hermeneutics and Postmodern Thought. **RESEARCH** Contemporary continental philosophy, philosophical psychology, philosophy and literature, history of philosophy. **SELECTED PUBLICATIONS** Auth, Merleau-Ponty's Ontology, Indiana, 88, 2d ed, Northwestern, 97; ed, Merleau-Ponty Vivant, SUNY Press, 91; auth, Semiological Reductionism: A Critique of the Deconstructionist Movement in Postmodern Thought, SUNY Press, 95; ed, Ecart & Differance: Merleau-Ponty and Derrida on Seeing and Writing, Humanities, 97; auth, Beyond Romance, SUNY Press, 01. **CONTACT ADDRESS** Dept of Philosophy, SUNY, Binghamton, Binghamton, NY 13902-6000. **EMAIL** mdillon355@aol.com

DILWORTH, JOHN
DISCIPLINE PHILOSOPHY **EDUCATION** Bristol Univ, PhD. **CAREER** Assoc prof, Philos, W Mich Univ. **RESEARCH** Aesthetics, cognitive science. **CONTACT ADDRESS** Philos Dept, Western Michigan Univ, 320 Moore Hall, 1903 W Michigan Ave, Kalamazoo, MI 49008-5328. **EMAIL** john.dilworth@wmich.edu

DINGES, WILLIAM
PERSONAL Born 07/22/1946, Hays, KS, m, 1966, 3 children **DISCIPLINE** RELIGIOUS STATE **EDUCATION** Fort Hays State Univ, BA, 69; Emporia State Univ, MA, 74; Univ Kan, PhD, 83. **CAREER** Asst prof, Ithaca Col, 82-83; assoc prof, Catholic Univ, 88-. **MEMBERSHIPS** Soc for Sci Study of Relig, Relig Res Asn, Asn for Sociol of Relig. **RESEARCH** Religion in America, Roman Catholic Studies, Religion and Social Change, Religion and Ecology. **SELECTED PUBLICATIONS** Auth, Young Adult Catholics: Religion in the Culture of Choice, Notre Dame, (forthcoming); auth, "Social and Behavioral Science Perspectives on Conversion/Recruitment to New Religious Movements: Theories and Assessments," in Re-Inventing New Religious Movements, (90): 45-64; auth, "Young Adult Catholics: Conservative? Alienated? Suspicious?," America 10, (99): 9-13; auth, " A Faith Loosely Held: The Institutional Allegiance of Young Catholics," Commonweal, (98): 13-18; auth, "The Next Generation of Catholics: Need, Opportunities, and Risks," The Living Light 33, (97): 6-12; auth, "Postmodernism and Religious Institutions," The Way: A Review of Christian Spirituality 36, (96): 215-224; auth, "The Traditionalist Movement," The Encyclopedia of American Catholic History, (97): 1394-1396; auth, "'We Are What You Were': Catholic Traditionalism in the Wake of Schism," Conservative Catholics in America, (96): 241-269; auth, "Roman Catholic Traditionalists," America's Alternative Religions, (95): 101-107. **CONTACT ADDRESS** Dept Relig Ed, Catholic Univ of America, 620 Mich Ave NE, Washington, DC 20064-0001. **EMAIL** dinges@cua.edu

DINGILIAN, DER STEPANOS
PERSONAL Born 12/19/1954, Alexandria, Egypt, m, 1990, 2 children **DISCIPLINE** THEOLOGY **EDUCATION** Sch of Theol, Claremont, PhD, 96. **CAREER** Pastor, 91-96, relig educr, 96- , Armenian Apostolic Church. **MEMBERSHIPS** AAR; SBL. **RESEARCH** Theology and psychology of hope; spirituality in relationships. **SELECTED PUBLICATIONS** Auth, A Spiritual Journey Through the Holy Badarak; auth, The Last Frontier: Hope for the Family. **CONTACT ADDRESS** 1330 E Foothill Blvd #64, Glendora, CA 91741. **EMAIL** drstepanos@aol.com

DINKINS, DAVID N.
PERSONAL Born 07/10/1927, Trenton, NJ, m **DISCIPLINE** LAW **EDUCATION** Howard Univ, BS 1950; Brooklyn Law School, JD, 1956. **CAREER** Dyett, Alexander, Dinkins, Patterson, Michael, Dinkins, Jones, attorney-partner 1956-1975; NY State Democratic Party, district leader 1967-; NY State Assembly, state assemblyman 1966; City of New York, pres bd of elections 1972-73, city clerk 1975-85, Manhattan borough pres 1986-90, mayor, 90-93; Columbia Univ, prof, 93-. **HONORS AND AWARDS** Pioneer of Excellence, World Inst of Black Communications, 1986; Righteous Man Awd, NY Board of Rabbis, 1986; Man of the Year Awd, Corrections Guardians Assn, 1986; Distinguished Service Awd, Federation of Negro Civil Service Org , 1986; Man of the Year Awd, Assn of Negro Bus and Prof Women's Clubs; Father of the Year Awd, Metropolitan Chapter, Jack and Jill of America Inc, 1989; first black mayor of New York City. **MEMBERSHIPS** NY State Amer for Democratic Action, bd of dir; Urban League, mem; 100 Black Men, bd of dir; March of Dimes, bd of dir; Assn for a Better NY, bd of dir; Manhattan Women's Political Caucus, first male mem; NAACP, life mem; Black-Jewish Coalition, mem; Vera Institute of Justice, mem; Nova Anorca & NY State Urban Development Corp; Malcolm King Harlem Coll, bd of trustees; Marymount Manhattan Coll, pres advisory council; Assn of the Bar of the City of NY, exec committee. **CONTACT ADDRESS** Prof, Sch of Intl and Public Affairs, Columbia Univ, 420 W 118th St, 14th Fl, New York, NY 10027.

DIONNE, E. J.
DISCIPLINE GOVERNMENT **EDUCATION** Harvard Univ, BA, 73; Oxford Univ, PhD, 82. **CAREER** Sr Fel, Govt Stud, Brookings Inst; columnist, editorial writer, reporter, Washington Post; reporter, NY Times; former corresp in Paris, Rome & Beirut. **HONORS AND AWARDS** Guest scholar, Woodrow Wilson Int Ctr. **RESEARCH** Elections; public opinion; conservative and liberal ideology; civil society; journalism. **SELECTED PUBLICATIONS** Auth, They Only Look Dead: Why Progressives Will Dominate the Next Political Era, Simon & Schuster, 96; auth, Why Civil Society? Why Now, Brookings Rev, 97; ed, Community Works: The Revival of Civil Society in America, 98. **CONTACT ADDRESS** Brookings Inst, 1775 Massachusetts Ave NW, Washington, DC 20036.

DIPUCCIO, WILLIAM
PERSONAL Born 12/26/1958, Cleveland, OH, m, 1992, 2 children **DISCIPLINE** THEOLOGY **EDUCATION** Marquette Univ, PhD 94. **CAREER** Mount Union Col, adj prof of relig, 94-97. **HONORS AND AWARDS** Arthur J. Schmitt Found Fel. **MEMBERSHIPS** AAR/SBL, ETS, ASCH, NAPS **RESEARCH** Systematic theology; philosophy; early church; hermeneutics; science and faith; 19th cen amer relig. **SELECTED PUBLICATIONS** Auth, The Interior Sense of Scripture: The Sacred Hermeneutics of John W. Nevin, Mercer Press, 98. **CONTACT ADDRESS** 291 Berwin Place, Munroe Falls, OH 44262. **EMAIL** bdipuccio@stratus.net

DISCHER, MARK
PERSONAL Born 03/10/1964, Park Ridge, IL, s **DISCIPLINE** RELIGION, PHILOSOPHY **EDUCATION** Wheaton Col, BA, 86; Fuller Theol Sem, Mdiv, 91; Yale Univ, STM, 93; Oxford Univ, Dphil, 97. **CAREER** Asst prof, chair, Dept of Religion and Philos, Ottawa Univ, 97-. **MEMBERSHIPS** AAR/SBL; SCE; EPS; APA; CPA. **RESEARCH** Ethics/human rights, philosophy of religion. **SELECTED PUBLICATIONS** Auth, "Jonah as a Paradigm for the Universality of Divine Care," The Allen Rev, Michaelmas (95); auth, "Does Fennis Get Natural Rights for Everyone?," New Blackfriars (Jan. 99); auth, "Tolerance and Truth," Am Baptist Evangelicals J (June 99); auth, "A New Natural Law Theory as a Ground for Human Rights," The Kans J of Law and Public Policy (winter 99). **CONTACT ADDRESS** Dept Humanities, Ottawa Univ, 1000 S. Cedar, Ottawa, KS 66067. **EMAIL** discher@ottawa.edu

DITTES, JAMES EDWARD
PERSONAL Born 12/26/1926, Cleveland, OH, m, 1948, 4 children **DISCIPLINE** PSYCHOLOGY OF RELIGION **EDUCATION** Oberlin Col, BA, 49; Yale Univ, BD, 54, MS, 55, PhD(psychol), 58. **CAREER** Instr sci, Am Sch, Turkey, 50-52; from instr to assoc prof relig, 55-67, prof psychol relig, Yale Univ, 67-, chm dept relig studies, 75-82; ed, J Sci Studies Relig, 66-71. **HONORS AND AWARDS** Guggenheim fel, 65-66; Fulbright res fel, Rome, 65-66; Nat Endowment for Humanities sr fel, 72-73. **MEMBERSHIPS** Soc Sci Studies Relig (pres, 72-73); Am Acad Relig. **RESEARCH** Motivation and vocational dilemmas of clergymen; development and decay of self-transcending commitments; continuity between biography and theology of major religious figures. **SELECTED PUBLICATIONS** Coauth, Psychological Studies of Clergymen, Nelson, 65; auth, The Church in the Way, Scribners, 67; Psychology of Religion, In: Handbook of Social Psychology, Addison-Wesley, 69; Minister on the Spot, United Church, 70; Bias and the Pious, Augsburg, 73; Beyond William James, In: Beyond the Classics, Harper, 73; The Investigator as an Instrument of Investigation, In: Encounter With Erikson, Scholars, 77; When People Say No, Harper, 79; The Male Predicament, Harper, 85; Driven by Hope, Westminster John Knox, 96; Men At Work, Westminster John Knox, 96; Pastoral Counseling, Westminster John Knox, 99; auth, Re-Calling Ministry, Choice, 99. **CONTACT ADDRESS** Dept of Religious Studies, Yale Univ, PO Box 208287, New Haven, CT 06520-8287. **EMAIL** james.dittes@yale.edu

DMOCHOWSKI, HENRY W.
PERSONAL Born 11/16/1942, Jersey City, NJ, s **DISCIPLINE** PHILOSOPHY **EDUCATION** Seton Hall Univ, AB, 64; Villanova Univ, MA, 67; New York Univ, PhD, 74. **CAREER** Adj Tchr, Gwynedd Mercy Col, 66-68; St Josephs Univ, 68-73; Voc Coord, Therapeutic Center at Fox Chase, 75-77; Coord of Voc Rehab Svc, Eagleville Hosp, 77-83; Adj Tchr, Lincoln Univ, 79-81; Rowan Univ, 85-89; Temple Univ, 90-95; LaSalle Univ, 95-. **RESEARCH** History of Philosophy, Ethics. **CONTACT ADDRESS** 116 Buckingham Dr, Rosemont, PA 19010.

DOBBS, DAN BYRON
PERSONAL Born 11/08/1932, Ft Smith, AR, m, 1953, 4 children **DISCIPLINE** LAW **EDUCATION** Univ Ark, Ba, 56, LLB, 56; Univ Ill, Urbana, LLM, 61. JSD, 66. **CAREER** Partner, Dobbs, Pryor & Dobbs, Ft Smith, 56-60; from Asst prof to prof law, Univ NC, Chapel Hill, 61-78; Mem Fac, Law Col, Univ Ariz,78-Law clerk, US Dist Judge John E Miller, 57-59; consult, NC Courts Comn, 63-64; vis prof law, Univ Minn, 66-67, Cornell Univ Law Sch, 68-69 & Univ Va Law Sch, 74. **RESEARCH** Remedies; torts. **SELECTED PUBLICATIONS** Auth, Beyond bootstrap, Minn Law Rev, 1/67; The validation of void judgments, Va Law Rev, part 1, 6/67, part 2, 10/67; Contempt of court, Cornell Law Rev, 1/71; Et al Remedies, West, 73; Law of Remedies, (2d ed 3 vols), 93; Torts and Compensation, (with Paul Hayden, (3d ed 97); Prosser and Keeton on Torts (5th ed with Page Keeton, Robert Keeton and David Owen, 84). **CONTACT ADDRESS** Law Col, Univ of Arizona, 1 University of Az, Tucson, AZ 85721-0001. **EMAIL** Dobbs@nt.law.arizona.edu

DOBBYN, JOHN FRANCIS
PERSONAL Born 08/31/1937, Boston, MA, m, 1969, 1 child **DISCIPLINE** LAW **EDUCATION** Harvard Univ, AB, 59, LLM, 69; Boston Col, JD, 65. **CAREER** Law clerk, Fed Dist Ct, Dist Mass, 65-57; atty, Burns & Levinson, Boston, 67-68; Prof Law, Law Sch, Villanova Univ, 69-. **RESEARCH** Corporation law; insurance law; equitable remedies; constitutional rights of the accused. **SELECTED PUBLICATIONS** Auth, Injunctions in a Nutshell, 74 & So You Want to Go to Law School, 75, West Publ; Insurance Law in a Nutshell, West Publ, 81; auth, Handling Property and Casualty Claims, 85; auth, Handling Fidelity and Surety Claims, 85. **CONTACT ADDRESS** Law School, Villanova Univ, 299 N Spring Mill Rd, Villanova, PA 19085-1597. **EMAIL** dobbyn@law.villanova.edu

DOBSEVAGE, ALVIN P.
PERSONAL Born 11/29/1922, New York, NY, m, 1976, 4 children **DISCIPLINE** PHILOSOPHY, FRENCH, LATIN **EDUCATION** City Col New York, BA, 42; Harvard Univ, MA, 48; Columbia Univ, MPhilos, 52; Cent Conn State Univ, MA, 82. **CAREER** Instr philos, Brooklyn Col, 51-53; vconsul info off, US Info Serv, Salisbury, Rhodesia, 55-58; teacher Latin, Wilton High Sch, Conn, 58-65; asst prof, 65-82, Assoc Prof French, Latin and Ling, Western Conn State Col, 82-, Chmn Dept Mod Lang, 81-, Adj asst prof Latin, Saturday Sch Lang, NY Univ, 60-68; adj asst prof philos, Danbury State Col, 60-; lectr, Univ Conn, Stamford Br, 63-64; ed, Hermes Americanus, 90-95; Nat Endowment for Humanities grant, Am Acad Rome, 82. **HONORS AND AWARDS** Letter of Commendation from Off Personnel, Dept of Army for Work as Mem Haines Bd Study Group, 40, regarding civil affairs, Psychol Oper, 67. **MEMBERSHIPS** Am Philos Asn; Am Philol Asn; Mediaeval Acad Am; Class Asn New England; MLA. **RESEARCH** Gaston Bachelard's theory of imagination; aesthetics and metaphysics; teaching French and Latin. **SELECTED PUBLICATIONS** Auth, The Metamorphoses of Apuleius--On Making an Ass of Oneself, Class W, Vol 89, 96. **CONTACT ADDRESS** 45 Dodgingtown Rd, Bethel, CT 06801.

DOCKERY, DAVID S.
PERSONAL Born 10/28/1952, Tuscaloosa, AL, m, 1975, 3 children **DISCIPLINE** HISTORY; RELIGION **EDUCATION** Texas Christian Univ, MA, 86; Univ TX, PhD, 88. **CAREER** Dean & Acad VP, S Baptist Theol Sem, 88-96; pres, Union Univ, 96-. **HONORS AND AWARDS** Who's Who Relig; Who's Who Bibl Studies **MEMBERSHIPS** Soc Bibl Lit; Inst Bibl Res; Amer Acad Relig; Evangelical Theol Soc **RESEARCH** New Testament Studies; Hermeneutics; Baptist Theology. **SELECTED PUBLICATIONS** Auth, New Dimensions in Evangelical Thought, Intervarsity; Our Blessed Hope, LifeWay; Christian Scripture, Broadman & Holman; Biblical Interpretation Then and Now, Baker; auth, Ephesians, Convention; Holman Bible Handbook, Holman. **CONTACT ADDRESS** 1050 Union Univ Dr., Jackson, TN 38305. **EMAIL** ddockery@uu.edu

DODD, VICTORIA J.
DISCIPLINE LAW **EDUCATION** Harvard Univ, BA, 70; Univ Southern Ca, JD, 78. **CAREER** Prof. **SELECTED PUBLICATIONS** Auth, Becoming Gentlemen, Mass Law Jour, 97; Contributor, Analysis of the Code of Civil Procedure Governing the Courts of Estonia for the Republic of Estonia, 95; Introduction to Symposium on Law and Education, 94. **CONTACT ADDRESS** Law School, Suffolk Univ, Beacon Hill, Boston, MA 02114. **EMAIL** vdodd@acad.suffolk.edu

DODGE, MARY J.
PERSONAL Born 02/05/1960, Colorado Springs, CO, s **DISCIPLINE** CRIMINOLOGY **EDUCATION** Univ Colo, BA, 89; MA, 92; Univ Calif, PhD, 97. **CAREER** Asst Prof, Calif State Univ, 97-98; Asst Prof, Univ Colo, 98-. **MEMBERSHIPS** Am Soc of Criminol, Acad of Criminal Justice Sci. **RESEARCH** White-Collar Crime, Medical Fraud, Courts, Policing, Juvenile Justice. **SELECTED PUBLICATIONS** Auth, "A Walk on Balls: Jury Nullification and Three Strikes Cases," Courts and Justice, (00): 354-363; auth, "Fertile Frontiers in medical Fraud: A Case Study of Egg and Embryo Theft," in Contemporary Issues in Crime and Criminal Justice: Essays in Honor of Gilbert Geis, 00; ed, Lessons of Criminology, Anderson Pub, forthcoming; auth, "Racism, Sexism and Marginalization: Reflections of African American Women on Their Careers in Urban Policing," in African American Women: The Law and Justice System, forthcoming; auth, "The Influence of Prior Record Evidence on Jury Decision Making," Law and Human Behavior; auth, "Juror and Expert Conceptions of Battered Women," Violence and Victims, (91): 271-282. **CONTACT ADDRESS** Dept Pub Affairs, Univ of Colorado, Denver, PO Box 173364, Denver, CO 80217.

DODSON, JUALYNNE
DISCIPLINE RELIGIOUS STUDIES **EDUCATION** Univ Calif Berkeley, PhD. **CAREER** Assoc prof. **HONORS AND AWARDS** Ed, J Am Acad Relig. **RESEARCH** African religions in the America. **SELECTED PUBLICATIONS** Auth, Protestant and African Derived Religious Traditions of Cuba, Women Ministries and the AME Tradition; U.S. African American Denominations in Cuba; There's Nothing Like Church Food. **CONTACT ADDRESS** Religious Studies Dept, Univ of Colorado, Boulder, Boulder, CO 80309. **EMAIL** Jualynne.Dodson@Colorado.edu

DOEPKE, FREDERICK C.
PERSONAL Born 10/30/1946, St Louis, MO, m, 1998, 2 children **DISCIPLINE** PHILOSOPHY **EDUCATION** Univ Calif at Berkeley, PhD, 78. **CAREER** Prof, The Metropolitan State Col of Denver, 81-. **RESEARCH** Analytic Metaphysics, Ethics, Metaphilosophy. **SELECTED PUBLICATIONS** Auth, The Kinds of Things: A Theory of Personal Identity Based on Transcendental Argument, Open Court, 96. **CONTACT ADDRESS** Dept Philos, Metropolitan State Col of Denver, PO Box 173362, Denver, CO 80217-3362. **EMAIL** doepkef@mscd.edu

DOEPKE, MATTHIAS
PERSONAL Born 06/30/1971, Gottingen, Germany, s **DISCIPLINE** ECONOMICS **EDUCATION** Humboldt-Universitat Berline, Diploma, 95; Univ Chicago, PhD, 00. **CAREER** Asst prof, UCLA, 00. **HONORS AND AWARDS** Frank H. Knight Fel, 96-00; Fel, Univ Chicago, 96-00; Fulbright Scholar, 95-96. **MEMBERSHIPS** Am Econ Asn; Econometric Soc; Soc for Econ Dynamics. **RESEARCH** Macroeconomics; Population Dynamics and Economic Growth; Monetary Economics; Mechanism Design. **SELECTED PUBLICATIONS** Auth, Fertility, Income Distribution, and Growth, Univ Chicago, 00. **CONTACT ADDRESS** Dept Econ, Univ of California, Los Angeles, 8283 Bunche, PO Box 951477, Los Angeles, CA 90095-1477. **EMAIL** doepke@econ.ucla.edu

DOERMANN, RALPH W.
PERSONAL Born 06/25/1930, Kodaikanal, India, m, 1953, 4 children **DISCIPLINE** RELIGION, OLD TESTAMENT **EDUCATION** Capital Univ, AB, 52; Lutheran Theol Sem, BD, 58; Duke Univ, PhD(Old Testament), 62. **CAREER** Pastor, Trinity Lutheran Church, Albert Lea, Minn, 61-63; from instr to assoc prof Hebrew & Old Testament, 63-72, Prof Hebrew & Old Testament, Trinity Lutheran Sem, 72-, Land of the Bible workshop fel, NY Univ, 66; James A Montgomery fel, Am Sch Orient Res, 69-70; mem staff, Joint Archaeol Exped, Tell el-Hesi, Israel, 70-; field supvr, Idalion, Cyprus, 72-74; ann prof, Albright Inst Archaeol Res, Jerusalem, 76-77, 84-85. **MEMBERSHIPS** Soc Bibl Lit; Am Schs Orient Res; Am Inst Archaeol. **RESEARCH** Biblical archaeology; Old Testament theology; heremeneutics in the intertestamental period. **SELECTED PUBLICATIONS** Auth, Luther's principles of Biblical interpretation, In: Interpreting Luther's Legacy, Augsburg, 69; Biblical Concern for the Poor, Comn Church & Soc, Am Lutheran Church, 72; Idalion 1972: the east Acropolis, Suppl Bull Am Schs Orient Res, 73; God's Hand Stretched Out: A Study of the Bood of Isiah, Am Lutheran Church Women, 76; Salvation in the Hebrew Scriptures: A Christian Perspective, Tantur Yrbk, 76-77; Salvation: Our Common Gift, In: These Things We Hold in Common, Augsburg, 81. **CONTACT ADDRESS** Dept of Old Testament, Trinity Lutheran Sem, 2199 E Main St, Columbus, OH 43209-2334. **EMAIL** rdoerman@trinity.capital.edu

DOHERTY, BARBARA
PERSONAL Born 12/02/1931, Chicago, IL **DISCIPLINE** THEOLOGY, HISTORY OF RELIGIONS **EDUCATION** St Mary-of-the-Woods Col, BA, 53; St Mary's Col, MA, 63; Fordham Univ, PhD (theol), 79. **CAREER** Assoc prof theol, St Mary-of-the-Woods Col, 63-75; Prov Super, Sisters of Providence, 75-, Chairperson, Leadership Conf Women Relig, Region 8, 79-82. **RESEARCH** Eastern and western spirituality. **SELECTED PUBLICATIONS** Auth, Contemplation, New Cath Encycl, Vol 17, 78; I Am What I Do, Thomas More Asn, 81. **CONTACT ADDRESS** 215 Ridge Terrace Park, Ridge, IL 60068.

DOHERTY, JOHN F.
PERSONAL Born 07/02/1947, New York, NY, m, 1975, 2 children **DISCIPLINE** CRIMINAL JUSTICE **EDUCATION** Marist Col, BA, 69; Marist Col, MPA, 88; Walden Univ, PhD, 96. **CAREER** Police Officer, Captain of Detectives, City of Poughkeepsie, NY, 70-90; Asst Prof, Marist Col, 90-. **MEMBERSHIPS** Acad of Criminal Justice Sci, Am Correction Asn, Am Soc of Criminology, Am Soc of Public Admin, Int Asn of Chiefs of Police, Fraternal Order of Police. **CONTACT ADDRESS** Dept of Criminal Justice, Marist Col, 290 North Rd, Poughkeepsie, NY 12601.

DOLAN, FREDERICK M.
PERSONAL Born 03/17/1955, CA, m, 1985, 2 children **DISCIPLINE** POLITICAL PHILOSOPHY **EDUCATION** Univ Calif at Irvine, BA, 77; MFA, 79; Princeton Univ, MA, 82; PhD, 87. **CAREER** From asst prof to assoc prof, Univ Calif at Berkeley, 88-. **HONORS AND AWARDS** Fac Res Fel, 88-; Humanities Res Fel, 93-94; Townsend Humanities Fel, 89-90. **MEMBERSHIPS** Am Polit Sci Asn, MLA. **RESEARCH** Continental Philosophy, Political Philosophy, Modernity & Modernism, Theories of Interpretation, Aesthetics, America. **SELECTED PUBLICATIONS** Auth, Allegories of America: Narratives, Metaphysics, Politics, Cornell Univ Pr, 94. **CONTACT ADDRESS** Dept Rhetoric, Univ of California, Berkeley, 2125 Dwinelle Hall, Berkeley, CA 94720-2670. **EMAIL** fmdolan@socrates.berkeley.edu

DOLAN, JAY P.
DISCIPLINE AMERICAN RELIGIOUS HISTORY **EDUCATION** Gregorian Univ, Italy, STL, 62; Univ Chicago, PhD, 70. **CAREER** Asst prof, Univ San Francisco, 70-71; asst prof, 71-77, dir, Ctr for Stud of Am Cath, 77-93, assoc prof, 77-86, prof, Univ Notre Dame, 86-; Fulbright prof, Univ Col, Ireland, 86; vis instr, Boston Col, 91; chemn, publ ser, Notre Dame Stud in Am Cath, Univ Notre Dame Press, 77-93; publ comt, Immigration Hist Soc, 77-80; ed bd, J of Am Ethnic Hist, 80-; ed bd, Church Hist, 82-86; ed bd, Hebrew Un Co-Jewish Inst of Relig, 84-89; ed bd, Sources of Am Spirituality, publ ser, Paulist Press, 86-90; ed bd, Statue of Liberty-Ellis Island Centennial publ ser, Univ Ill Press, 86-; assoc ed, Am Nat Biogr Mid-America, 88-; assoc ed, Am Nat Biogr, 89-; ed bd, Rel and Am Cult: J of Interp, 89-; ed bd, Church Hist, 94-. **HONORS AND AWARDS** Rockefeller fel, Univ Chicago, 69-70; O'Brien Fund grant, Univ Notre Dame, 72; fac res grant, Univ Notre Dame, 73; fel, Princeton Univ, 73-74; John Gilmary Shea Awd, Am Cath Hist Asn, 75; res grant, Word of God Inst, 76; Frank O'Malley Awd, Univ Notre Dame, 77; fel, Am Coun of Learned Soc, 78-79; fac develop grant, Univ Notre Dame, 80; Alumnus of the Yr, Univ Chicago, 87; Emily Schossberger Awd, Univ Notre Dame Press, 88; res grant Lilly Endowment, 81, 81-87, 83-84, 86-88, 90-93, 91-92. **MEMBERSHIPS** Pres, Am Soc of Church Hist, 87; pres, Am Cath Hist Asn, 95; Immigration Hist Soc; Am Acad of Relig. **RESEARCH** Am Religious History, Immigratin History. **SELECTED PUBLICATIONS** Auth, Patterns of Leadership in the Congregation, in James P Wind and James W Lewis, eds, American Congregations, vol 2: New Perspectives in the Study of Congregations, Univ Chicago Press, 94; Conclusion, in Jay P Dolan and Allan Figueroa Deck, SJ, eds, Hispanic Catholic Culture in the U.S., Univ Notre Dame Press, 94; The People As Well As The Prelates: A Social History of a Denomination, in R Mullin and R Richey, eds, Reimagining Denominationalism: Interpretive Essays, Oxford UP, 94; coed, Mexican Americans and the Catholic Church. 1900-1965, Univ Notre Dame Press, 94; Puerto Rican and Cuban Catholics in the U.S. 1900-1965, Univ Notre Dame Press, 94; Hispanic Catholic Culture in the U.S.: Issues and Concerns, Univ Notre Dame Press, 94. **CONTACT ADDRESS** Dept of Hist, Univ of Notre Dame, Notre Dame, IN 46556.

DOLAN, JOHN M.
DISCIPLINE PHILOSOPHY **EDUCATION** Stanford Univ, PhD. **RESEARCH** Philosophy of language; moral philosophy; medical ethics. **SELECTED PUBLICATIONS** Auth, Is Physician-Assisted Suicide Possible?, Duquesne Law Rev, 96; Inference and Imagination, Archimedean Point, 94; Brain Injury Controversies, J Head Trauma Rehabilitation, 94; Counterfactual Reasoning, Reciprocity, and the Logic of Euthanasia, UFL, 94; Death by Deliberate Dehydration and Starvation: Silent Echoes of the Hungerhauser, Issues Law Medicine, 91. **CONTACT ADDRESS** Philosophy Dept, Univ of Minnesota, Twin Cities, 355 Ford Hall, 224 Church St SE, Minneapolis, MN 55455. **EMAIL** dolan001@maroon.tc.umn.edu

DOLL, MARY A.
PERSONAL Born 06/04/1940, New York, NY, d, 1 child **DISCIPLINE** RELIGION, LITERATURE **EDUCATION** Conn Col, BA, 62; Johns Hopkins Univ, MA, 70; Syracuse Univ, PhD, 80. **CAREER** Lectr, Comm Col Baltimore, 70-71; lectr English, SUNY-Oswego, 76-81; asst prof English, SUNY, 82-84; lecrt English, Univ Redlands, 85-88; Supervisor English ed stud, Calif State Univ, 86-88; lectr Eng, Calif State Univ, 86-88; vis asst prof Eng, Tulane Univ, 88-89; asst prof, Loyola Univ, 88-89; asst prof, Our Lady Holy Cross Col, 89-91; assoc prof Eng, Our Lady Holy Cross Col, 91-95; prof Eng, Our Lady Holy Cross Col, 95- ; ch, Eng Dept, 89- ; Chr, Hon Convocation Comm, 90- . **HONORS AND AWARDS** SUNY Summer Res Grant, 82; Directory of Amer Scholars, Amer Biographical Inst, 82; Hon Mention, Amer Poetry Assn Contest, 86; acad excellence awd tchg, Univ Redlands, 86; In the Shadow of the Giant,

selected as one of Choice mag 89-90 Outstanding academic bks; Sears-Roebuck tchg excellence and campus leadership awd, Our Lady of Holy Cross Col, 91; Nominated for La Humanist of the Yr Awd, 91; Who's Who in Amer Educ, 89-94; Contemporary Authors, 90; Who's Who in Rel, 91; Who's Who in the South and Southwest, 91-94; ed comm for College writing skills, 95-97; Reader for NEH: The Correspondence of Samuel Beckett, 95; Mem, Kappa Delta Pi, Sigma Pi Chapter, Intl hon soc in educa, 97; Mem, Kappa Gamma Pi, Natl Cath Col grad hon soc, 97- . **MEMBERSHIPS** Amer Acad Rel; Modern Lang Asn; S Atlantic Modern Lang Asn; Thomas Wolfe Soc, VP, 97- ; Samuel Beckett Soc; Natl Coun Tchrs Eng. **RESEARCH** The intersection of literature; education; cultural studies; and women's studies. **SELECTED PUBLICATIONS** Auth, Beyond the Window: Dreams and Learning, Jour of Curriculum Theorizing, 4, 1, Winter 82, 35-39; Love Song to Rocks, poem, Escarpments, 4, 1, Spring 83; Hearing Images, Jour Mental Imagery, 7, 1, 83, 135-142; Lewis Turco, Dictionary of Literary Biography Yearbook, 84, 331-338; Doris Lessing, DLBY, 85, 284-292; Joan Didion, Dictionary of Literary Biography Yearbook, 86, 247-252; The Monster in Children's Dreams: Night Alchemies, Jour Mental Imagery, 10, 2, 86, 53-60; Measures of Despair: The Demeter Myth in Beckett, Jour of Beckett Stud, II, Fall 86, 109-122; The Temple Symbol in Scripture, Soundings, LXX, 1-2, Spring/Summer, 87, 145-154; Rites of Story: The Old Man at Play, in Myth and Ritual in the Plays of Samuel Beckett, Katherine H. Burkman, ed, New Jersey, Fairleigh Dickenson UP, 87, 73-85; In the Shadow of the Giant: Thomas Wolfe, ed, Athens, OH, Ohio UP, 88; Beckett and Myth: An Archetypal Approach, New York, Syracuse UP, 88; Walking and Rocking, Make Sense Who may: Selected Essays in Honor of Samuel Beckett's 80th Birthday, Robin J. Davis and Lance St. John Butler, eds, New York, Barnes and Nobles, 89; The Monster in Children's Dreams: Its Metaphoric Awe, The Jour Curriculum Theorizing, 8, 4, Spring 90, 89-99; The Power of Wilderness: Joseph Campbell and the Ecological Imperative, in Uses of Comparative Mythology: Essays on the Work of Joseph Campbell, Kenneth L. Golden, ed, New York, Garland Press, 92, 223-234; Tom Stoppard's Theatre of Unknowing, in British Drama Since 1960, London, Macmillan Press, 94, 117-129; Ghosts of Themselves: The Demeter Women in Beckett, in Images of Persephone, Elizabeth Hayes, ed, UP of Florida, 94, 121-135; Ashborn, poem, and To Larry, With Love, poem, in Taboo, 1, 4, spring 96, 73-74; To the Lighthouse and Back: Writings on Teaching and Living, New York: peter Lang Publ, 95; Winging It, Jour Curriculum Theorizing, 13, 1, Spring 97, 41-44; Winging It, in Reading Curriculum Identity: Shared Readings, Paula Salvio and Dennis Sumara, eds, NY, Tchrs, Col Press, 97; Queering the Gaze, in Studies in Curriculum Theory, William F. Pinar, ed, New Jersey, Lawrence Erlbaum Assoc, 98; Why I Teach, L'Image, Fall 97; The Is-ness of Teaching, English Education, Dec, 97; co-ed, How we Work, New York, Peter Lang, 99; auth, Like Letters in Running Water: A Mythopoetics of Curriculum, Lawrence Erlbaum Press, 00. **CONTACT ADDRESS** Dept of English, Our Lady of Holy Cross Col, 4154 State St Dr, New Orleans, LA 70125. **EMAIL** mdoll4444@aol.com

DOLLING, LISA M.
PERSONAL Born 05/03/1962, m, 1990, 1 child **DISCIPLINE** PHILOSOPHY **EDUCATION** Manhattanville Col, BA, 84; Fordham Univ, MA, 88; City Univ NYork, PhD, 95. **CAREER** Asst prof Philos, St. John's Univ. **MEMBERSHIPS** Am Philos Asn; Philos Sci Asn; ACPA. **RESEARCH** Philosophy of science; aesthetics; women Philosophers. **SELECTED PUBLICATIONS** Auth, Tests of Time: Readings in The History of Scientific Development. **CONTACT ADDRESS** Dept of Philosophy, St. John's Univ, 8000 Utopia Parkway, Jamaica, NY 11439. **EMAIL** muccio.NJ@worldnet.net

DOMBROWSKI, DANIEL A.
PERSONAL Born 08/08/1953, Philadelphia, PA, m, 1977, 2 children **DISCIPLINE** PHILOSOPHY **EDUCATION** Univ Maine, BA, 74; St Louis Univ, PhD, 78. **CAREER** Asst prof, St Joseph Univ, 78-82; assoc prof, Creighton Univ, 82-88; prof, Seattle Univ, 88- . **MEMBERSHIPS** Am Philos Award. **RESEARCH** History of philosophy, Process philosophy, Applied ethics. **SELECTED PUBLICATIONS** Auth, Analytic Theism, Hartshorne, and the Concept of God, State Univ NY Press, (96); auth, Babies and Beasts: The Argument from Marginal Cases, Univ Ill Press, (97); auth, Kazantzakis and God, State Univ NY Press, (97); auth, A Brief, Liberal, Catholic Defense of Abortion, Univ Ill Press, (00); auth, Not Even a Sparrow Falls: The Philosophy of Stephen R.L. Clark, Mich State Univ Press, (00). **CONTACT ADDRESS** Dept Philos, Seattle Univ, 901 12 Ave, Seattle, WA 98122-4411. **EMAIL** ddombrow@seattleu.edu

DOMINGUEZ, JORGE IGNACIO
PERSONAL Born 06/02/1945, Cuba, m, 1967, 2 children **DISCIPLINE** POLITICAL SCIENCE **EDUCATION** Yale Univ, AB 67; Harvard Univ, AM 68, PhD 72. **CAREER** Harvard Univ, asst prof 72-77, assoc prof 77-79, prof 79-, Clarence Dillon Prof of Intl Aff and Dir of the Weatherhead Cen for Intl Aff at Harvard. **HONORS AND AWARDS** Harvard Coll Prof Awd; Dist Fulbright vis prof **MEMBERSHIPS** LASA; NECLAS; ICS; APSA **RESEARCH** Latin American politics, domestic and intl **SELECTED PUBLICATIONS** Democratic Politics in Latin America and the Caribbean, John Hopkins Univ Press, 98; International Security and Democracy: Latin America and the Caribbean in the Post Cold War Era, Pitts PA, Univ Pitts Press 98; From Pirates to Drug Lords: The Post Cold War Caribbean Environment, co-ed, Albany, State Univ NY Press 98; Technopols: Freeing Politics and Markets in Latin America in the 1900s, Univ Pk, Penn State Press, 97; Democratic Transitions in Central America, with M. Lindenberg, Gainesville, Univ Press FL, 97; Constructing Democratic Governance: Latin America and the Caribbean in the 1900s, with A. Lowenthal, Baltimore, John Hop Univ Press, 96. **CONTACT ADDRESS** Weatherhead Cen for Intl Affairs, Harvard Univ, 1737 Cambridge St, Cambridge, MA 02138. **EMAIL** jorge_dominguez@harvard.edu

DOMINO, BRIAN
DISCIPLINE PHILOSOPHY **EDUCATION** Univ of Ariz, BA, 88; Pa State Univ, MA, 90; PhD, 93. **CAREER** Lectr, Pa State Univ, 93; vis asst prof, Siena Col, 94-95; vis asst prof, Miami Univ, 95-96; asst prof, Eastern Mich Univ, 96-99; asst prof, Miami Univ, 99-. **HONORS AND AWARDS** Provost's New Fac Res Awd, 96-97; Provost's Teaching Initiative Grant, 98-99; Phi Beta Kappa. **MEMBERSHIPS** Am Philos Assoc; N Am Nietzsche Soc; Friedrich Nietzsche Soc of GB; Soc for Phenomenology and Existential Philos; The (Other) Nietzshe Soc. **RESEARCH** History of Philosophy, History of Medicine, Philosophy of History. **SELECTED PUBLICATIONS** Auth, "Vincenzo's Portrayal of Nietzsche's Socrates", Philos and Rhetoric 26.1 (93): 39-47; auth, "Two Models of Abductive Inquiry", Philos and Rhetoric 27.1, (94): 63-65; auth, "Bibliography of the Writings of Daivd R Lachterman", St Johns Rev 42.2 (94): 137-141; auth, "The Electronic Agora: Using A Mainframe Computer in Introductory Courses", Teaching Philos 18.2, (95): 115-123; auth, "A Concordance to the Will to Power", J of Nietzsche Studies 9/10, (95): 148-173; auth, "A Revised Concordance to The Will to Power", J of Nietzsche Studies 14, (97): 98-111; auth, "History and Forgetting in Plato's Republic", Memory, History and Critique: European Identity at the Millennium, eds Frank Brinkuis and Sascha Talmor, MIT Pr, 98; auth, "Stendhal's Ecstatic Embrace of History as the Antidote for Decadence", Nietzsche's Futures, ed John Lippitt, Macmillan, (99): 48-61; auth, "Optimism and Pessimism from a Historical Perspective", Optimism and Pessimism, ed Edward Chang, Am Psychol Assoc, (forthcoming); auth, "Nietzsche and the Little Things", J of Nietzsche Studies (forthcoming); "Polyp Man", Nietzsche's Animals, eds R Ralph and Christa Davis Acampora (forthcoming). **CONTACT ADDRESS** Dept Philos, Miami Univ, 4200 E University Blvd, Middletown, OH 45042-3497. **EMAIL** dominob@muohio.edu

DONAGHY, JOHN A.
PERSONAL Born 11/01/1947, Philadelphia, PA, s **DISCIPLINE** PHILOSOPHY **EDUCATION** Univ of Scranton, AB, 70; New Schl for Soc Res, MA, Grad Fac, 72; Boston Col, PhD, 90. **CAREER** Campus Minister, St Thomas Aquinas Church and Cath Stud Center, 83-. **MEMBERSHIPS** APA; AAR; Amer Cath Phil Assoc **RESEARCH** Ethics and population/consumption; war/peace; liberation theology; religious ethics; El Salvador. **SELECTED PUBLICATIONS** Art, The Ideology of Arms Control, in: Philos and Soc Critic, 84; art, Pacifism and Revolution, in: The Interest of Peace :a Spectrum of Philos Views, 90; art, Justice as Participation: An Emerging Understanding, First Intl Conf on Soc Values: Proceedings, 91. **CONTACT ADDRESS** 2321 Baker St, Ames, IA 50014. **EMAIL** jdonaghy@igc.apc.org

DONAHUE, JOHN J.
PERSONAL Born 01/30/1953, Alexandria, VA, m, 1995, 2 children **DISCIPLINE** LAW **EDUCATION** Hamilton Col, BA, 74; Harvard Law School, JD, 77; Yale Univ, MA, 82; MPhil, 84; PhD, 86. **CAREER** Res Fel, Am Bar Found, 86-95; asst prof to prof, Northwestern Univ, 86-95; vis prof, Univ of Va, 90; vis prof, Univ of Chicago, 92; lectr Toin Univ, Japan, 96; prof, Renmin Univ, Beijing, 98; prof, Stanford Law School, 95-. **HONORS AND AWARDS** Phi Beta Kappa **MEMBERSHIPS** Am Bar Assoc; Am Econ Assoc; Law & Soc Assoc; Am Law and Econ Assoc; Nat Bureau of Econ Res. **RESEARCH** Corporate Finance, Anti-Discrimination Laws, Regulation, Crime. **SELECTED PUBLICATIONS** Auth, "Some Thoughts on Affirmative Action", 75 Wash Univ Law Quarterly, 1590, 97; auth, "Did Miranda Diminish Police Effectiveness?", 50 Stanford Law Rev 1147, 98; coauth, "Guns, Violence, and the Efficiency of Illegal Markets", 88 Am Econ Rev 463, 98; coauth, "Allocating Resources Among Prisons and Social Programs in the Battle Against Crime", 27 J of Legal Studies 1, 98; auth, "Some thoughts on Law and Economics and the Theory of the Second Best", 73 Chicago Kent Law Rev 257, 98; auth, "The Legal Response to Discrimination: Does Law Matter?", How Does Law Matter?, eds Bryant Garth, Austin Sarat, Northwestern Univ Pr, (98): 45-75; auth, "Discrimination in Employment", the New Palgrave Dict of Law and Econ, 98; auth, "Understanding the Time Path of Crime", 88 J of Criminal Law and Criminol 1423, 98; auth, "Why We Should Discount the Views of Those Who Discount Discounting", 108 Yale Law J 1901, 99; auth, "Nondiscretionary Concealed Weapons Law: A Case Study of Statistics, Standards of Proof, and Public Policy", 1 Am Law and Econ Rev 436, 99. **CONTACT ADDRESS** School of Law, Stanford Univ, Stanford, CA 94305. **EMAIL** jjd@stanford.edu

DONAKOWSKI, CONRAD L.
PERSONAL Born 03/13/1936, Detroit, MI, m, 1961, 2 children **DISCIPLINE** RELIGION, HISTORY, MUSIC **EDUCATION** Xavier Univ, BA, 58, MA, 59; Columbia Univ, PhD, 69. **CAREER** Instr humanities, Mich State Univ, 66-69; coordr, James Madison Col, Mich State Univ, 67-72; from asst to assoc prof humanities, 69-78, prof, 78-81, prof music hist, Mich State Univ, 81-, asst dean arts & lett, 79-, Am Coun Learned Soc grant, 73. **HONORS AND AWARDS** American Revolutionary Bicentennial Article Prize, Ohio Hist Comt, 76; Rockefeller Found grants, 76 & 77; DAAD, 88, 95. **MEMBERSHIPS** AHA; Am Soc Eighteenth Century Studies; Am Soc Church Hist; Soc Fr Hist Studies. **RESEARCH** Romanticism; enlightenment; popular culture; ritual and liturgy; music. **SELECTED PUBLICATIONS** Auth, A Muse for the Masses: Ritual and Music in an Age of Democratic Revolution, Univ Chicago, 77. **CONTACT ADDRESS** School of Music, Michigan State Univ, East Lansing, MI 48824-1043. **EMAIL** donakows@msu.edu

DONALDSON, DANIEL J.
PERSONAL Born 09/01/1941, Connersville, IN, m, 1961, 3 children **DISCIPLINE** RELIGION **EDUCATION** Johnson Bible Col, BA, 63; Lincoln Christian Col, MA, 68; Univ MO, EdD, 81. **CAREER** Min, 63-73, prof, 67-69, Registr, 73-80, St. Louis Christian Col; acad dean, San Jose Christian Col, 80-81; registr, 82-89, min, Fla Christian Col, 90-97; acad dean, Nebr Christian Col, 97-. **MEMBERSHIPS** Accrediting Asn Bible Cols. **RESEARCH** Higher education admin; leadership; moral education **SELECTED PUBLICATIONS** Auth, art, Effecting Moral Development in Preprofessional College Students, 79; auth, art, Every Scripture Profitable, 84; auth, art, Making Disciples at Home, Pt I-III, 90; auth, Nebraska Christian College Style Sheet, 97. **CONTACT ADDRESS** Nebraska Christian Col, 1800 Syracuse Ave, Norfolk, NE 68701. **EMAIL** ddonaldson@nechristian.edu

DONEGAN, CHARLES EDWARD
PERSONAL Born 04/10/1933, Chicago, IL, m, 1 child **DISCIPLINE** LAW **EDUCATION** Wilson Jr Coll, AA 1953; Roosevelt, BSC 1954; Loyola, MSIR 1959; Howard, JD 1967; Columbia, LLM 1970. **CAREER** US Commisson on Civil Rights, legal intern 1966; Poor Peoples Campaign, legal counsel 1968; F B McKissick Enterprises, staff counsel, 69; SUNY at Buffalo, first asst prof of law 1970-73; Howard Univ, assoc prof of law 1973-77; OH State Univ, visiting assoc prof 1977-78; First US EPA, asst reg counsel 1978-80; So Univ, prof of law 1980-84, visiting professor of law 1992; CE Donegan & Assoc, atty at law; LA State Univ Law Sch, visiting prof 1981; North Carolina Central Univ Law School, visiting prof 1988-89. **HONORS AND AWARDS** Most outstanding Prof So Univ Law Sch 1982; Ford Fellow Columbia Univ Law Sch 1972-73; NEH Fellow Afro Am Studies Yale Univ 1972-73; Speaker & Participant at National & Regional Conferences; named one of top 45, 42, 56, 61 Lawyers in Washington, DC Area; Washington African-American Newspaper, 1993-96. **MEMBERSHIPS** Labor arbitrator Steel Inds Postal AAA 1971-; consultant US Dept of Ag 1972; asst counsel NAACP Legal Defense Fund Inc 1967-69; hrng officer Various Govtl Agy 1975-; officer mem Am Natl Dist of Columbia Chicago Bar Assn 1968-; mem NAACP Urban League; Alpha Phi Alpha; Phi Alpha Delta; Phi Alpha Kappa; labor arbitrator FMCS 1985; counsultant Dist of Columbia Govt Dept of Public Works; mem, District of Columbia Consumer Claims Arbitration Bd 1987-; chmn, legal educ committee, Washington Bar Assn, 1984-91; mem, District of Columbia Attorney-Client Arbitration Board, 1990-91; mem, advisory committee, District of Columbia of Education, Ward 4, 1991; moot court judge, Georgetown, Howard, Balsa, 1987-; vp, Columbia Law Alumni Assn, Washington DC, 1994-; pres, vp, mem, Society of Labor Relations Professionals (SFLRP), 1987-; Natl Bar Assn, Arbitration Section, chair; Natl Assn of Securities Dealers, arbitrator, 1994-; Natl Futures Assn, arbitrator, 1994-; New York Stock Exchange, arbitrator, 1996-; Natl Conference of Black Lawyers, founding mem; Washington Bar Assn; Industrial Relations Research Association; Society of Professionals in Dispute Resolution. **SELECTED PUBLICATIONS** Articles in professional journals; contrib, Dictionary of Am Negro Bio, 1982; Washington Afro-American Newspaper, 1993, 1994, 1995. **CONTACT ADDRESS** 601 Pennsylvania Ave NW, Ste 900, S Bldg, Washington, DC 20004.

DONELAN, JAMES
PERSONAL Born 09/08/1961, Springfield, MA, m, 1983, 2 children **DISCIPLINE** PHILOSOPHY **EDUCATION** SUNY Stony Brook, PhD, 95. **CAREER** Adjunct asst prof, Hofstra Univ, 96; lctr, New England Col, 96-98; lctr, Franklin Pierce Col, 97-. **MEMBERSHIPS** Amer Philos Assoc **RESEARCH** Political Theory **CONTACT ADDRESS** Dept of Philosophy, 35 Blueberry Ln, Peterborough, NH 03458. **EMAIL** jed@monad.net

DONEY, WILLIS
PERSONAL Born 08/19/1925, Pittsburgh, PA **DISCIPLINE** PHILOSOPHY **EDUCATION** Princeton Univ, BA, 46, MA & PhD, 49; Dartmouth Col, AM, 67. **CAREER** Instr philos, Cornell Univ, 49-52; asst prof Ohio State Univ, 53-57; assoc prof, 58-66, prof philos, Dartmouth Col, 66-; vis lectr, Univ Mich,

53; vis lectr, Harvard Univ, 63; Santayana fel, 56; Ford-Dartmouth fel, 70; mem, Inst Advan Studies, 72-73; Camargo Found fel, 78-79; Edinburgh Univ fel, 80. **MEMBERSHIPS** Am Philos Asn; Aristotelian Soc; AAUP; Societe Francaise de Philosophie; Comite de Patronage Studia & Analecta Cartesiana. **RESEARCH** Theory of knowledge; history of philosophy, especially 17th and 18th century. **SELECTED PUBLICATIONS** Eternal Truths and the Cartesian Circle, Garland, 87; Berkeley's Argument Against Abstract/Pleas; Midwest Studies in Philosophy, 83; LaReponse De Deseartes a Caterus, Descartes: Objecter ET Repondre, PUF, 94. **CONTACT ADDRESS** Dept of Philosophy, Dartmouth Col, Hanover, NH 03755. **EMAIL** D2980@aol.com

DONFRIED, KARL P.
PERSONAL Born 04/06/1940, New York, NY, m, 1960, 3 children **DISCIPLINE** RELIGION, BIBLICAL LITERATURE **EDUCATION** Columbia Univ, BA, 60; Harvard Div Sch, BD, 63; Union Theol Sem, STM, 65; Univ Heidelberg, DTheol, 68. **CAREER** Elizabeth A. Woodson Prof of Relig & Bibl Lit, Smith Col, 68- . **HONORS AND AWARDS** Guest Chaplain, US House of Reps, 99; off rep, Evangelical Lutheran Church in Am, signing of 'The Joint Declaration on Justification,' Augsberg, Germany, 99. **MEMBERSHIPS** Am Acad of Relig; Am Schs of Oriental Res; Soc of Bibl Lit; Studioum Novi Testamenti Societas. **SELECTED PUBLICATIONS** Co-ed & co-auth, Peter in the New Testament, Augsburg Pub House (Minneapolis), 73, Paulist Pr (New York), 73; auth, The Setting of Second Clement in Early Christianity, Brill (Leiden), 74; ed & contrib, The Romans Debate, Augsburg Publishing House (Minneapolis), 77; co-ed & co-auth, Mary in the New Testament, Fortress Pr (Philadelphia), 78, Paulist Pr (New York), 78; auth, The Dynamic Word: New Testament Insights for Contemporary Christians, Harper & Ros (New York & San Francisco), 81); auth, The Romans Debate: Expanded and Revised Edition, Hendreickson (Peabody, MA), 91; co-auth, The Theology of the Shorter Pauline Letters, Cambridge Univ Pr, 93; co-auth, Judaism and Christianity in Rome in the First Century, Eerdmans (Grand Rapids, MI), 98; co-auth, The Thessalonians Debate: Methodological Discord or Methodological Synthesis?, Eerdmans (Grand Rapids, MI), 00. **CONTACT ADDRESS** Dept of Relig & Bibl Lit, Smith Col, Northampton, MA 01063. **EMAIL** kdonfrie@smith.edu

DONKEL, DOUGLAS L.
PERSONAL Born 01/20/1959, Portland, OR, m, 1991 **DISCIPLINE** PHILOSOPHY **EDUCATION** Univ Oregon, PhD, 90. **CAREER** Adj asst prof, phil, 92-, Univ of Portland. **MEMBERSHIPS** APA; Soc for Phenomenology and Existential Phil. **RESEARCH** Continental phil; classical Amer phil; metaphysics; phil of religion; phil of technology; applied phil; theory of difference. **SELECTED PUBLICATIONS** Auth, The Understanding of Difference in Heidegger and Derrida, Amer Univ Studies, Series V, Phil Vol 143, Peter Lang Pub, 93; art, Formal Contamination: A Reading of Derrida's Argument, Phil Today 40(2), 96. **CONTACT ADDRESS** 4423 S. E. Lexington St, Portland, OR 97206. **EMAIL** donkel@up.edu

DONNELLY, JOHN
PERSONAL Born 03/30/1941, Worcester, MA, d, 1967, 2 children **DISCIPLINE** PHILOSOPHY **EDUCATION** Holy Cross Col, BSc, 63; Boston Col, MA, 65; Brown Univ, MA, 67, PhD(philos), 69. **CAREER** Asst prof philos, Univ Notre Dame, 69-70; asst prof, Fordham Univ, 70-75, dir grad studies, 70-72; vis prof, State Univ NY, Fredonia, 75-76; assoc prof, 76-81, prof philos & chp, Univ San Diego, 81-, univ prof 00-, Nat Endowment for Humanities grant, 80; coordr, Catholic Studies Minor, Univ San Diego, 98-. **HONORS AND AWARDS** Pres, Soren Kierkegaard Soc, 88-89. **MEMBERSHIPS** Am Philos Asn. **RESEARCH** Thamatology, metaphysics; ethics; philosophical theology. **SELECTED PUBLICATIONS** Auth, Some Remarks on Geach's Predicative and Attributive Adjectives, Notre Dame J Formal Logic, 71; contribr & ed, Logical Analysis and Contemporary Theism, Fordham Univ, 72; contribr & co-ed, Conscience, Alba House, 73; auth, Conscience and Religious Morality, Relig Studies, 73; contribr, Analysis and Metaphysics, D Reidel, 75; contribr, Infanticide and the Value of Life, Prometheus Bks, 78; contribr & ed, Language, Metaphysics and Death, Fordham Univ, 78, 2nd ed, 94; contribr, Kierkegaard's Fear and Trembling: Critical Appraisals, Univ Ala, 81; auth, Thinking Clearly about Death, Philosophia, 86; Self-Knowledge and the Mirror of the Ward, In: International Kierkegaard Commentary: The Sickness Unto Death, Mercer Univ, 87; contribr and ed, Reflective Wisdom: Richard Taylor on Issues that Matter, Prometheus, 89; contribr and ed, Suicide, Right or Wrong, Prometheus, 2nd ed, 98. **CONTACT ADDRESS** Dept of Philos, Univ of San Diego, 5998 Alcala Park, San Diego, CA 92110-2492. **EMAIL** john7@acusd.edu

DONOHO, DOUGLAS L.
PERSONAL Born 04/12/1955, MI, m, 2 children **DISCIPLINE** LAW **EDUCATION** Kalamazoo Col, BA, 77; Rutgers Univ, JD, 81; Harvard Law Sch, LLM, 89. **CAREER** Instr, Univ Ore, 81-82; Law Clerk, U S 6th Circuit Ct of Appeals, 82-83; Assoc Atty, Cadwalader Wilkergham & Taft, 83-88; Prof, Nova Southeastern Univ, 89-00; Vis Prof, Univ Denver, 00-. **MEMBERSHIPS** ABA, Calif Bar Asn, NY Bar Asn. **RESEARCH** International human rights. **SELECTED PUBLICATIONS** Auth, Relativism Versus Universalism in Human Rights: The Search for Meaningful Standards," Stanford J of Int Law 345; auth, The Role of Human Rights in Global Security Issues," Mich J of Int Law 827; auth, Evolution or Expediency: The U N Response to the Disruption of Democracy," Cornell J of Int Law 329. **CONTACT ADDRESS** Dept Law, Nova Southeastern Univ, Davie, 3305 College Ave, Davie, FL 33314-7721. **EMAIL** donohod@nsu.law.nova.edu

DONOHOO, LAWRENCE
PERSONAL Born 05/03/1955, Madison, WI, s **DISCIPLINE** THEOLOGY **EDUCATION** Catholic Univ America, BA, 77; MA, 79; Dominican House Studies, MDiv, 84; STB, 84; STL, 88; Univ Munich, PhD. **CAREER** Ordained Priest, 85; instr of Philosophy, Providence Col, 86-90; Asst Pastor, Archdiocese of Munich, 91-95; instr in Dogmatic Theology, Dominican House of Studies, 95-. **RESEARCH** Fundamental Theology, Fundamental Moral Theology, Psychology and Theology, St Thomas Aquinas. **SELECTED PUBLICATIONS** Auth, "Platonism," In The New Dictionary of Theology, ed. Joseph A. Komonchak et al (Wilmington: Michael Glazier, 87); auth, "On a Mother's November Birthday," The University Bookman 28 (88): 17; auth, "Magnificent," In The Best Poems of the 90's (Owings Mills, MD: The National Library of Poetry, 96); auth, "Apples," In Spirit of the Age (Owings Mills, MD: The National Library of Poetry, 96); auth, "The Nature and Grace of Sacra Doctrina in St Thomas's Super Boetium de Trinitate," The Thomist (99): 343-401. **CONTACT ADDRESS** Dept Theology, Dominican House of Studies, 487 Michigan Ave NE, Washington, DC 20017-1584. **EMAIL** jdonohoo@juno.com

DONOHUE, JOHN WALDRON
PERSONAL Born 09/17/1917, New York, NY **DISCIPLINE** HISTORY & PHILOSOPHY OF EDUCATION **EDUCATION** Fordham Univ, AB, 39; St Louis Univ, MA, 44; Woodstock Col, STL, 51; Yale Univ, PhD, 55. **CAREER** Teacher high sch, NY, 44-47; from assoc prof to prof hist & philos of educ, Sch Educ, Fordham Univ, 55-70, adj prof, 77-80; Assoc Ed, America, 72- . **HONORS AND AWARDS** Mem, Society of Jesus, 39- ; ordained Roman Catholic priest, 50; Trustee, Fordham Univ, 69-77, 78-87, St Peter's Col, 80- ; St Louis Univ, 67-81. **MEMBERSHIPS** Philos Educ Soc; Nat Cath Ed Asn. **RESEARCH** Theory of Christian education; contemporary problems concerning religion and education. **SELECTED PUBLICATIONS** Auth, Work and Education, Loyola Univ, 59; Jesuit Education: An Essay on the Foundations of Its Idea, Fordham Univ, 63; St Thomas Aquinas and Education, Random, 68; Catholicism and Education, Harper, 73. **CONTACT ADDRESS** America 106 W 56th St, New York, NY 10019.

DONOVAN, JOHN F.
DISCIPLINE LATE MODERN GERMAN PHILOSOPHY AND THE PHILOSOPHY OF RELIGION **EDUCATION** Fordham Univ, MA; Georgetown Univ, PhD. **CAREER** Taught, Georgetown Univ, 4 yrs; Mt Saint Mary's Col, 89-. **RESEARCH** The German Enlightenment and the Origins of Religious Studies. **SELECTED PUBLICATIONS** Auth, Doing and Don'ting: A Workbook in Moral Identity. **CONTACT ADDRESS** Dept of Philosophy, Mount Saint Mary's Col and Sem, 16300 Old Emmitsburg Rd, Emmitsburg, MD 21727-7799. **EMAIL** donovan@msmary.edu

DONOVAN, MARY ANN
PERSONAL Born Cincinnati, OH **DISCIPLINE** HISTORICAL THEOLOGY **EDUCATION** St Michaels, Toronto, 77 **CAREER** Prof, 94-pres, Jesuit Sch of Theol, Assoc Prof, 81-94, Assist Prof, 77-81 **HONORS AND AWARDS** Col Theology Bk Awd, 98; Elizabeth Seton Medal, Distinguished Woman Theologian **MEMBERSHIPS** Cath Theol Soc of Am; Col Theology Soc; N Amer Patristics Soc; Soc for Study of Christian Spirituality **RESEARCH** History, Spirituality; Early Christianity; Women's Issues **SELECTED PUBLICATIONS** Auth, One Right Reading? A Guide to Irenaeus, Liturgical Press, 97; Auth, Sisterhood as Power, The Past and Passion of Ecclesial Women, Crossroad, 89 **CONTACT ADDRESS** Jesuit Sch of Theol, Berkeley, 1735 LeRoy Ave, Berkeley, CA 94709. **EMAIL** mdonovan@jstb.edu

DOODY, JOHN A.
PERSONAL Born 11/07/1943, Darby, PA, m, 1 child **DISCIPLINE** PHILOSOPHY **EDUCATION** La Salle Col, BA, 65; Univ Notre Dame, PhD, 74. **CAREER** Prof, asst dean, Villanova Univ. **HONORS AND AWARDS** Lindback Distinguished Teaching Awd, 84; Gauen Distinguished Faculty Awd, 94. **MEMBERSHIPS** Critical Theory; Communitarianism. **SELECTED PUBLICATIONS** Auth, Radical Hermeneutics, Critical Theory and the Political, Int Philos Quart, 91; MacIntyre and Habermas on Practical Reason, Amer Cath Philos Quart, 91 and Communitarianism, Liberalism, and Social Responsibility, Edwin Mellen Press, Lewiston, NY, 91; The Right Way to Think about the Rights of the Bill of Rights, in Studies in Social and Political Theory: Social Philosophy Today, The Edwin Mellen Press, Lewiston, NY, 93. **CONTACT ADDRESS** Dept of Philosophy, Villanova Univ, 800 Lancaster Ave, Villanova, PA 19085-1692. **EMAIL** john.doody@villanova.edu

DOOHAN, HELEN
DISCIPLINE NURSING, RELIGIOUS STUDIES, EDUCATIONAL LEADERSHIP **EDUCATION** Adelphi Univ, BA, 71; Gonzaga Univ, MA, 76, PhD, 83. **CAREER** PROF REL STUD, GONZAGA UNIV, 76-. **CONTACT ADDRESS** 6126 E Willow Springs Rd, Spokane, WA 99223. **EMAIL** hdoohan@gonzaga.edu

DOOLEY, PATRICIA
DISCIPLINE MASS COMMUNICATION, AND MEDIA ETHICS AND LAW **EDUCATION** Univ Minn, MA, PhD. **CAREER** Writer, Minn Hist Soc; asst prof, Univ Maine; dir, Kans Scholastic Press Assn District Four; asst prof. **RESEARCH** History of mass communication; media ethics and law. **SELECTED PUBLICATIONS** Auth, book on the history of journalism as an occupational group. **CONTACT ADDRESS** Dept of Commun, Wichita State Univ, 1845 Fairmont, Wichita, KS 67260-0062. **EMAIL** dooley@elliott.es.twsu.edu

DOOLEY, PATRICK KIARAN
PERSONAL Born 06/23/1942, Fargo, ND, m, 1969 **DISCIPLINE** PHILOSOPHY **EDUCATION** St Paul Sem, Minn, BA, 64; Univ Notre Dame, MA, 67, PhD (philos), 69. **CAREER** From asst prof to assoc prof, 69-77, Prof Philos, St Bonaventure Univ, 77-, Researcher, Finger Lakes Col Consortium, 71-72; mem, Coun Philos Studies, Calvin Col, 73; Nat Endowment for Humanities grant, Duke University, 75 and vis scholar, 77; Nat Endowment for Humanities grant, Univ Kansas, 78; fac res grant, St Bonaventure Univ, 78; Nat Endowment for Humanities grant, Univ Ill, 81. **MEMBERSHIPS** Am Philos Asn; Am Cath Philos Asn. **RESEARCH** American philosophy; William James; philosophy and psychology. **SELECTED PUBLICATIONS** Auth, Thoreau on civil disobedience, J Thought, 78; Nineteenth century business ethics and The Rise of Silas Lapham, Am Studies, 80; Emerson on civil disobedience: The Question of an immoral law, J Thought, 80; Promises, trial marriage and self-fulfilling prophecies, Delta Epsilon Sigma Bull, 80 & Relig Humanism, rev ed; Genteel poverty: Hepzibah in The House of the Seven Gables, Markham Rev, 80; A philosophical defense of the closed Puritan society, Delta Epsilon Sigma Bull, 81; Conscience and immoral laws: Emerson and Thoreau, J Thought, 81; Kuhn and psychology: The Rogers-Skinner, Day-Giorgi debates, J Theory Social Behav (in prep). **CONTACT ADDRESS** Dept of Philos, St. Bonaventure Univ, Saint Bonaventure, NY 14778.

DOORLEY, MARK J.
PERSONAL Born 08/03/1961, Lima, OH, m, 1998 **DISCIPLINE** PHILOSOPHY **EDUCATION** St Alphonsus Col, BA, 84; Washington Theol Union, M Div, 88; Boston Col, PhD, 94. **CAREER** Adj fac, 94-96, St John's Univ; adj fac, 96-97, vis asst prof, 97-, Villanova Univ. **MEMBERSHIPS** APA; Am Cath Philos Asn; The Lonergan Philos Asn; The Soc for Philos in the Contemp World. **RESEARCH** Ethical theory; the thought of Bernard Lonergan, S J. **SELECTED PUBLICATIONS** Auth, The Place of the Heart in Lonergan's Ethics: The Role of Feelings in the Ethical Intentionality of Bernard Lonergan, Univ Press Am, 96; auth, Resting in Reality: Reflections on Crowe's Complacency and Concern, Lonergan Workshop: The Structure and Rhythms of Love: In Honor of Frederick Crowe, SJ, vol 13, Boston Col, 97; auth, The Teaching of Ethics, J of Philos in Contemp World, vol 3, no 1, 96; auth, To Thine Own Self Be True: Self-Appropriation and Human Authenticity, Philos & Everyday Life: A Narrative Intro, Univ KS Press, forthcoming; auth, "Service Learning and Ethics: An Invitation to Authenticity," Academic Exchange Qtly, vol 4, issue 1 (00); auth, "Nonviolence, Creation, Healing," Method: Jrnl of Lonergan Stud, vol 17/2; auth, "Limit and Possibility: An Augustinian Counsel to Authority," in Augustine and Liberal Education, ed by Kevin Hugher and Kim Paffenroth, Ashgate Press, 00. **CONTACT ADDRESS** Ethics Prog, Villanova Univ, 800 Lancaster Ave, Villanova, PA 19085. **EMAIL** mark.doorley@villanova.edu

DOPPELT, GERALD D.
DISCIPLINE PHILOSOPHY OF SCIENCE **EDUCATION** Johns Hopkins Univ, PhD, 69. **CAREER** Instr, Univ Pa, 66-73; vis lectr, Univ Calif-Berkeley; Univ Ill; Prof, Philos, Univ Calif, San Diego. **RESEARCH** Political theory; Philos of Science. **SELECTED PUBLICATIONS** Auth, "Dretske's Conception of Perception and Knowledge," Philos of Sci, 73; "Walzer's Theory of Morality in International Relations," Philos and Public Aff, 78; "Kuhn's Epistemological Relativism: An Interpretation and Defense," Inquiry, 78; "Incorrigibility and the Mental," Australasian Jour Philos, 78; "Rawls's System of Justice: A Critique from the Left," Nous, 81; "Rawls's Kantian Ideal and the Viability of Modern Liberalism," Inquiry, 88; "The Philosophical Requirements for an Adequate Conception of Scientific Rationality," Philos of Sci, 88; "Is Rawls's Kantian Liberalism Coherent and Defensible?," Ethics, 89. **CONTACT ADDRESS** Dept of Philos, Univ of California, San Diego, 9500 Gilman Dr, La Jolla, CA 92093.

DORE, LAURIE KRATKY
PERSONAL Born 11/08/1958, Carmel, CA, m, 1986, 3 children **DISCIPLINE** LAW **EDUCATION** Creighton Univ, BA, 81; S Methodist Univ, JD, 84. **CAREER** Law clerk, U.S. Court

of Appeals, 84-85; atty, private practise, 85-92; prof, Drake Univ, 92-. **HONORS AND AWARDS** Leland F. Forrest Law Prof of the Year, 00. **MEMBERSHIPS** Am Bar Asn; Tex Bar Asn; Iowa Bar Asn. **RESEARCH** Secret Justice and Secrecy in the Courts. **SELECTED PUBLICATIONS** Auth, "Downward Adjustment and the Slippery Slope: The Use of Duress in Defense of Battered Offenders," Ohio State L J, 95; auth, "Secrecy by Consent: The Use and Limits of Confidentiality in the Pursuit of Settlement," Notre Dame L Rev, 99. **CONTACT ADDRESS** Sch of Law, Drake Univ, 2507 University Ave, Des Moines, IA 50311-4505. **EMAIL** laurie.dore@drake.edu

DORN, LOUIS
PERSONAL Born 07/01/1928, Detroit, MI, m, 1953, 4 children **DISCIPLINE** OLD TESTAMENT THEOLOGY **EDUCATION** Lutheran Schl Theol, Chicago, PhD, 80. **CAREER** Ed, Helps for Translators, 78-, United Bible Soc. **MEMBERSHIPS** Soc of Biblical Lit **RESEARCH** Translation theory; studies in Hosea and Joel. **SELECTED PUBLICATIONS** Auth, The unexpected as a speech device: Shifts of thematic expectancy in Jeremiah, The Bible Translator, 37, (86): 215-222; auth, Review of Paul J Achtemeire, The Bible Translator, 98 (87): 145-146; auth, Struggling with the prophets in translation, The Bible Translator, 38, (87): 418-423; auth, Translating for " Reading Someone Else's Mail," Bulletin: UBS, 148/149, (87): 114-122; auth, Review of James D Newsome Jr, A synoptic harmony of Samuel, Kings and Chronicles: with related passages from Psalms, Isaiah , Jeremiah and Ezra, The Bible Translator 39, (88): 342-343; auth, Review of Murray J Harris, Colossians and Philemon, (Exegetical Guide to the Greek New Testament), The Bible Translator 43, (92): 153-154; auth, Philippine poetry and translation: a general survey, The Bible Translator 45, (94): 301-315; auth, Learning how to use a Handbook, The Bible Translator 46, (95): 428-432; auth, "Going down" and "Going up," The Bible Translator 49, (98): 239-245; auth, Untranslatable features in the David and Bathsheva story (2 Samuel 11-12), The Bible Translator 50, (99): 406-411. **CONTACT ADDRESS** 32 Larch Ave, Dumont, NJ 07628-1223. **EMAIL** louis-dorn@compuserve.com

DORNISH, MARGARET HAMMOND
PERSONAL Born 07/25/1934, St. Marys, PA **DISCIPLINE** HISTORY OF RELIGIONS **EDUCATION** Smith Col, AB, 56; Claremont Grad Sch, MA, 67, PhD(relig), 69. **CAREER** Teacher English, Orme Sch, 60-65; asst prof relig, 69-74, assoc prof, 74-92, prof relig & chair, relig studies, Pomona Col, 93-. **MEMBERSHIPS** Am Acad Relig; Pac Coast Theol Soc; Asn Asian Studies; Int Asn Buddhist Studies. **RESEARCH** Buddhist studies. **SELECTED PUBLICATIONS** Auth, D T Suzuki's early interpretation of Buddhism and Zen, Eastern Buddhist, 70. **CONTACT ADDRESS** Dept of Religious Studies, Pomona Col, 551 N College Ave., Claremont, CA 91711-6319. **EMAIL** mdornish@pomona.edu

DORON, PINCHAS
PERSONAL Born 07/05/1933, Poland, m, 1969, 5 children **DISCIPLINE** HEBREW LANGUAGE, BIBLE **EDUCATION** Hebrew Univ, Jerusalem, BA, 62, MA, 64; NYork Univ, PhD (Hebrew studies), 75. **CAREER** Instr Hebrew and Talmud, Jewish Theol Sem, 64-65; lectr Hebrew, Hunter Col, 65-66; Asst Prof Hebrew, Queens Col, 66-, Instr, The Ulpan Ctr, 69-70. **MEMBERSHIPS** Asn Jewish Studies; Nat Asn Professors Hebrew. **RESEARCH** Biblical research; Hebrew language and literature; medieval Hebrew literature. **SELECTED PUBLICATIONS CONTACT ADDRESS** 730 E 7th St, Brooklyn, NY 11218.

DORRIEN, GARY J.
PERSONAL Born 03/21/1952, w, 1 child **DISCIPLINE** RELIGION **EDUCATION** Alma Col, BA (summa cum laude), 74; Union Theological Seminary, MDiv, 78; Princeton Theological Seminary, MA, 79, ThM, 79; Union Grad School, PhD, 89. **CAREER** Teacher, Parsons Center School (for emotionally disturbed students), 79-82; chaplian and rel dept chair, the Doane Stuart School, 82-87; assoc pastor, St Andrew's Episcopal Church, 82-87; ASST/ASSOC/FULL PROF OF RELIGION & DEAN OF STETSON CHAPEL, KALAMAZOO COL, 87-. **HONORS AND AWARDS** Harold Baker Honors Scholar, Alma Col, 70-74; Omicron Delta Kappa honor Soc, 73; Harvard Divinity School Honors Scholar, 74-76; Mrs T. Outstanding Teacher Awd, Univ of Chicago Prog on Secondary School Teaching, 87; Florence J. Lucasse Awd for Outstanding Scholar, Kalamazoo Col, 94; Phi Beta Kappa, 99. **MEMBERSHIPS** Am Acad of Religion; Amnesty Int; Asn for Religion and Intellectual Life; Col Theology Soc; Episcopal Diocese of Kalamazoo; Episcopal Peace Fel; Fel of Reconciliation; Greenpeace; NAACP; Nat Asn of Col and Univ Chaplains; Nat Org of Men Against Sexism; Soc of Christian Ethics. **SELECTED PUBLICATIONS** Auth, Reconstructing the Common Good, Orbis Books, 92; auth, The Neoconservative Mind, Temple Univ Press, 93; auth, Soul in Society: The Making and Renewal of Social Christianity, Fortress Press, 95; auth, The Word as True Myth: Interpreting Modern Theology, Westminster John Knox Press, 97; auth, The Remaking of Evangelical Theology, Westminster John Knox Press, 98; auth, Norman Thomas, The Am Radical, Routledge, 94; auth, Review of Sins of Omission: A Primer on Moral Indifference by S. Dennis Ford, Critical Rev of Books in Relig 1993 Vol 4, 94; auth, Beyond State and Market: Christianity and the Future of Economic Democracy, Cross Currents, 95; auth, Spirit in the World: Christianity and the Clash of Interests, Word & World, 95; auth, Neoliberal, not Neoconservative, Cross Currents, winter 95-96; auth, Beyond the Twilight of Socialism: Rethinking Economic Democracy, Harvard Divinity Bull, 96; auth, The Postmodern Barth?: The Word of God as True Myth, The Christian Century, 97; auth, Communitarianism, Christian Realism, and the Crisis of Progressive Christianity, Cross Currents, 97; auth, Inventing an American Conservatism: The Neoconservative Episode, Unraveling the Right: The New Conservatism in Am Thought and Politics, Westview Pubs, 98; auth, The Barthian Revolt in Modern Theology: Theology Without Weapons, Westminster Joh Knox Press, 00; auth, The Making of American Liberal Theology, 3 vols, Westminster John Knox Press, forthcoming. **CONTACT ADDRESS** Dept of Religion, Kalamazoo Col, 1200 Academy St, Midland, WI 49006. **EMAIL** dorrien@kzoo.edu

DORSEN, NORMAN
PERSONAL Born 09/04/1930, New York, NY, m, 3 children **DISCIPLINE** CONSTITUTIONAL LAW, CIVIL LIBERTIES **EDUCATION** Columbia Univ, BA, 50; Harvard Univ, LLB, 53. **CAREER** Stokes Prof Law, NY Univ, 61-; dir, Arthur Garfield Hays Civil Lib Mem Prog, 61-, vis prof law, London Sch Econ, 68, Univ Calif, Berkeley, 74-75 & Harvard Univ, 80, 83 & 84; exec dir, Spec Comt Courtroom Conduct, New York Bar Asn, 70-73; chmn, Health, Educ & Welfare Rev Panel new drug regulation in US, 75-77; chmn, Treasury Citizen's Panel on Good O'Boy Roundup, 95-96; consult, US Violence Comn, Random House, Nat Educ TV & Brit Broadcasting Corp; trustee, Am Friends London Sch Econ; chmn, Lawyers Comt for Human Rights, 96-00. **HONORS AND AWARDS** Recipient of numerous awards and 2 honorary degrees; Fel of the Am Acad of Arts and Sci; lld, ripon col, 81; founding dir and fac chair of nyu's global law program; founding pres, soc of am law teachers (1973). **MEMBERSHIPS** Am Law Inst; Soc Am Law Teachers (past pres); Coun of For Relations. **RESEARCH** Antitrust law; criminal law; legal process. **SELECTED PUBLICATIONS** Coauth, Political and Civil Rights in the United States, 67 & 76; Frontiers of Civil Liberties, 68; ed, The Rights of Americans, 71; coauth, Disorder in the Court, 73; ed & coauth, None of Your Business: Government Secrecy in America, 74; auth, coauth, and/or ed of numerous other articles and books. **CONTACT ADDRESS** 40 Washington Sq S, New York, NY 10012-1005. **EMAIL** norman.dorsen@nyu.law

DORSEY, ELBERT
PERSONAL Born 10/04/1941, St. Louis, MO, m **DISCIPLINE** LAW **EDUCATION** Harris-Stowe State Coll, BA 1966; St Louis Univ School of Law, JD 1973. **CAREER** St Louis Comm Coll Dist, asst librarian 1965-66; St Louis Bd of Educ, teacher 1966-70; St Louis Legal Aid Soc, law clerk 1971-72; Small Business Admin, loan officer/Attorney 1973-74; Collier, Dorsey, & Williams, Attorney. **HONORS AND AWARDS** Ford Fellowship World Conf of Peace 1973; Humanitarian Awd St Louis Alumni Chptr Kappa Alpha Psi 1985; Dedication Awd Mound City Bar Assn of St Louis 1983. **MEMBERSHIPS** Historian Mound City Bar Assc; mem Judicial Conf Advy Com for the Eighth Circuit Ct of Appeals; chmn/bd of dir Yeatman/Union-Sarah Jnt Commn on Health; Polemarch St Louis Alumni Chptr Kappa Alpha Psi Frat; chmn/advsry bd St Louis Comprehensive Hlth Cntr Home Hlth Bd. **CONTACT ADDRESS** Law Office of Collier, Dorsey & Williams, 625 N Euclid, Ste 402, Saint Louis, MO 63108.

DORTER, KENNETH
PERSONAL Born 07/30/1940, New York, NY, m, 1964, 2 children **DISCIPLINE** PHILOSOPHY **EDUCATION** Queens Col, NY, BA, 62; Pa State Univ, MA, 64, PhD (philos), 67. **CAREER** From instr to asst prof, 66-72, assoc prof, 72-82, prof philos, Univ Guelph, 82-. **MEMBERSHIPS** Can Philos Asn; Hegel Soc Am; Soc Ancient Philos; North Am Nietzche Soc. **RESEARCH** Philosophy of art; history of philosophy; metaphysics. **SELECTED PUBLICATIONS** Auth, Plato's Phaedo: An Interpretation, Univ of Toronto Press, 82; auth, "Conceptual Truth and Aesthetic Truth", J of Aesthetics and Art Criticism, vol. 48, no.1, (90): 37-51; auth, Form and Good in Plato's Eleatic Dialogues: the Parmenides, Theaetetus, Sophist, and Statesman, Univ of Calif Press (Berkeley, CA), 94; auth, "Three Disappearing Ladders in Plato," Philos and Rhet (96): 279-299; auth, "Wisdom, Virtue, and Knowledge," Rev of Metaphysics (97). **CONTACT ADDRESS** Dept of Philosophy, Univ of Guelph, Guelph, ON, Canada N1G 2W1. **EMAIL** kdorter@arts.uoguelph.ca

DOSS, BARNEY J.
DISCIPLINE PHILOSOPHY **EDUCATION** Univ Oklahoma, PhD, 94. **CAREER** Instr, 95-, Southeast Arkansas Col **CONTACT ADDRESS** 210 N Catalpa, Pine Bluff, AR 71603. **EMAIL** baldeag@seark.net

DOSTAL, ROBERT J.
PERSONAL Born 06/12/1947, Fort Benton, MT, m, 1971, 3 children **DISCIPLINE** PHILOSOPHY **EDUCATION** Pennsylvania St Univ, PhD, 77. **CAREER** Asst Prof, 76-80, Memphis St Univ; Prof, 80-98, Provost, 94-00, Bryn Mawr Col. **HONORS AND AWARDS** Humboldt Fel, 82-82, 87, 89. **RESEARCH** Metaphysics; ethics political theory; hermenuetics; Kant & Post-Kantian German Philosophy; Phenomenology. **SELECTED PUBLICATIONS** Das Ubersetzen Kants ins Englische Ubersetzen verstehen Brucken bauen Gottinger Beitraege zur Internationalen Ubersetzungsforschung, Berlin, 93; Eros Freundschaft und Politik Heideggers Versagen Athenaeum, Budapest, 94; The Public and the People Heideggers Illiberal Politics, Rev of Metaphysics, 94; The Experience of Truth for Gadamer and Heidegger Taking Time and Sudden Lightning, Hermeneutics and Truth, Northwestern Press, 94; Gadamers Continuous Challenge Heideggers Plato Interpretation, The Philos of Hans-Georg Gadamer the library of Living Philos, 97; The End of Metaphysics and the Possibility of non Hagelian Speculative Thought, Hegel Hist and Interp, 97; Gadamer Hans-Georg, Ency of Phenomenolgy, 97. **CONTACT ADDRESS** Bryn Mawr Col, Dept of Philos, Bryn Mawr, PA 19010. **EMAIL** rdostal@brynmawr.edu

DOTY, RALPH
PERSONAL Born 05/22/1945, Sapulpa, OK, m, 1983 **DISCIPLINE** PHILOSOPHY **EDUCATION** Univ Okla, BA, 67; Columbia Univ, MA, 69, PhD, 73. **CAREER** Instr, E Los Angeles Col, 77-79; Instr, Rose State Col, 80-82; Asst prof, 83-91, assoc prof, 91-, Univ Oklahoma, 83-. **HONORS AND AWARDS** Baldwin Award Study Prize Super Tchg, 89; Who's Who among Amer Teachers, 94. **MEMBERSHIPS** Amer Philol Asn; Class Asn Mid W & S **RESEARCH** Xenophon; Classical philology, Greek manuscripts, pedagogy. **SELECTED PUBLICATIONS** Auth, How High is the Sky?, Class Bull, 91; The Criterion of Truth, Peter Lang Publ, 92; Xenophons Gynaikologia: The Training of a Greek Housewife, Class Asn New Eng, 94; Xenophone: Oeconomicus VII-XIII, Bristol Class Press, 94; Attitude Change and Right Brain Thinking, Jour of Thought, 96; auth, Xenophon's Cynegeticus, Edwin Mellen Press, 01; auth, Teaching Greek Mythology to Judaeo-Christian Students," Classical Journal, 01; auth, "Romans and Rabbits: Saliens Per Tramitem Cuniculorum," The Classical Outlook, 01. **CONTACT ADDRESS** Dept of Classics, Univ of Oklahoma, 780 Van Vleet Oval, Rm 101, Norman, OK 73019. **EMAIL** rdoty@ou.edu

DOUBLES, MALCOLM CARROLL
PERSONAL Born 08/14/1932, Richmond, VA, m, 1956, 3 children **DISCIPLINE** RELIGION, PHILOLOGY **EDUCATION** Davidson Col, BA, 53; Union Theol Sem, Va, BD, 57; Univ St Andrews, PhD, 62. **CAREER** Pastor, Lebanon & Castlewood Presby Churches, VA, 60-65; asst prof Old Testament, St Andrews Presby Col, 65-69, mem Christianity & cult team, 65-74, chmn freshman Christianity & cult team, 67-71, assoc prof relig, 69-76, dean students, 74-76; prof Relig & Dean Col, 76-97, Distinguished Prof Intl Studies, Coker Col, 97-; Fulbright fel, Pakistan, 84, P R China, 88; NEH younger humanist fel, 71-72; managing ed, St Andrews Rev, 72-76; managing ed, Prog for Comput & Publ Targumic Lit, 74-. **MEMBERSHIPS** Soc Bibl Lit; Int Orgn for Study Old Testament; Asn Targumic Studies 2E **RESEARCH** Aramaic language and literature, with particular reference to Targumic studies; linguistics, with particular reference to Hebrew and Greek; New Testament background, with particular reference to Jewish history. **SELECTED PUBLICATIONS** Auth, Toward the publication of the Palestinian Targum(s), Vetus Testamentum, Vol XV, No 1; Indications of antiquity in the Fragment Targum, in In Memoriam Paul Kahle, Topelmann, 68; contribr, The History of the Jews in the Time of Christ, T&T Clark & Sons, 73. **CONTACT ADDRESS** Coker Col, 300 E College Ave, Hartsville, SC 29550-3797. **EMAIL** mdoubles@aol.com

DOUGHERTY, JAMES E.
PERSONAL Born 05/04/1923, Philadelphia, PA, m, 1950, 4 children **DISCIPLINE** POLITICAL SCIENCE; POLITICAL PHILOSOPHY; INTERNATIONAL RELATIONS **EDUCATION** St. Joseph's Col, BS, 50; Fordham Univ, MA, 54; Univ Pa, PhD, 60. **CAREER** Inst/asst/assoc prof, St. Joseph's Univ, 51-63; prof, 63-92; prof emeritus, 92- ; visiting prof, Nat War Col, 64-65; res assoc, For Policy Res Inst, 55-76; sr res assoc, Inst For Policy Anal, 76-89; US Rep, Un Advisory Bd on Disarmament, 81-90. **HONORS AND AWARDS** Lindback Teaching Awd, 63. **MEMBERSHIPS** Am Polit Sci Asoc (ret); Int Studies Asoc (ret); Int Inst for Stragic Studies, London (ret). **RESEARCH** Arms control; US-Soviet Cold War relations; disarmament; international relations theories; US foreign policy; Europoean Monetary Union and the single currency. **SELECTED PUBLICATIONS** Auth, The Bishops and Nuclear Weapons, 84; auth, American Foregin Policy: FDR to Reagan, 86; auth, Communism, The New Dictionary of Social Thought, 94; auth, The Politics of European Monetary Union, Current Hist, 97; auth with Robert L. Pfaltzgraff, Jr., Contending Theories of International Relations, 97. **CONTACT ADDRESS** Saint Joseph's Univ, 374 Freedom Blvd, West Brandywine, PA 19320.

DOUGHERTY, JUDE PATRICK
PERSONAL Born 07/21/1930, Chicago, IL, m, 1957, 4 children **DISCIPLINE** PHILOSOPHY **EDUCATION** Cath Univ Am, AB, 54; MA, 55; PhD, 60. **CAREER** Instr philos, Marquette Univ, 57-58; from instr to assoc prof, Bellarmine Col,

Ky, 58-66; assoc prof, 66-76, Prof Philos, Cath Univ Am, 76-99, Dean, Sch Philos, 67-, Ed, Rev Metaphys, 71-99; vis prof philos, Univ Louvain, 74-75. **HONORS AND AWARDS** William T Miles Awd, Bellarmine Col, 64; Cardinal Wright Awd, fel of Cath Schol, 94; LHD Thomas More College, 95; LHD, Catholic Univ of Hublin, 00; Knight of St. Gregory, 99; Cardinal Gibbons Medal, Catholic Univ Alumni Assoc, 00. **MEMBERSHIPS** Am Philos Asn; Am Cath Philos Asn (treas, 66-71, pres, 74-75); Metaphys Soc Am (pres, 83-84); Soc Philos Relig (pres, 78-79); Pontifical Acad of St. Thomas Aquinas; European Acad of Scis and Arts. **RESEARCH** Philosophy of religion; ethics; metaphysics. **SELECTED PUBLICATIONS** Auth, Recent American Naturalism, Cath Univ Am, 60; John H Randall's Notion of Substance, Proc Am Cath Philos Asn, 62; coauth, Approaches to Morality, Harcourt, Brace & World, 66; auth, Nagel's concept of science, Philos Today, 66; Lessons from the history of science and technology, Studies Philos and Hist of Philos, 69; Randall's Interpretation of Religion, 74; Finding of law, Proc Am Cath Philos Asn, 75; Dewey on the value of religion, New Scholasticism, 77; ed, The Good Life and Its Pursuit, Paragon, 84; ed, Studies in Philosophy and the History of Philosophy, 74-; auth, Western Creed: Western Identity, CUA Press, 00. **CONTACT ADDRESS** Sch of Philos, Catholic Univ of America, 620 Michigan Ave N E, Washington, DC 20064-0002. **EMAIL** dougherj@cua.edu

DOUGHERTY, RAY CORDELL
PERSONAL Born 09/18/1940, Brooklyn, NY, m, 1982, 3 children **DISCIPLINE** LINGUISTICS, PHILOSOPHY OF LANGUAGE **EDUCATION** Dartmouth Col, BA, 62, MS, 64; Mass Inst Technol, PhD, 68. **CAREER** Res assoc ling, Mass Inst Technol, 68-69; asst prof, 69-72, Assoc Pr of Ling, NY Univ, 72-; Fulbright prof ling, Univ Salzburg, Austria, 76-77. **MEMBERSHIPS** Ling Soc Am; Philos Sci Asn. **RESEARCH** Grammar; Computational Linguistics; history of science. **SELECTED PUBLICATIONS** Auth, A grammar of coordination: I,II, Language, 12/70; coauth, Appositive NP constructions, 1/72 & auth, A survey of linguistic methods, 11/73, Found Lang. **CONTACT ADDRESS** Dept of Ling, New York Univ, 719 Broadway, New York, NY 10003-6806. **EMAIL** doughert@acfz.nyu.edu

DOUGLAS, JAMES MATTHEW
PERSONAL Born 02/11/1944, Onalaska, TX, m, 1996, 2 children **DISCIPLINE** LAW **EDUCATION** TX Southern Univ, BA Math 1966, JD Law 1970; Stanford Univ, JSM Law 1971. **CAREER** Singer Simulation Co, computer analyst 66-72; TX Southern Univ Sch of Law, asst Prof 71-72; Cleveland State Univ Sch of Law, asst Prof 72-75; Syracuse Univ Sch of Law, assoc dean assoc prof 75-80; Northeastern Univ Sch of Law, prof of law 80-81; TX Southern Univ Sch of Law, dean & prof 81-95, interim provost and vp academic affairs, 95; pres 95-99; prof law 99-. **MEMBERSHIPS** State Bar of TX; Houston Jr Bar Assc; Amer Bar Assc Chrmn of Educ Comm of Sci & Tech Section; bd dir Hiscock Legal Soc; fac adv to Natl Bd of Black Amer Law Students; bd of dirs Gulf Coast Legal Foundation; mem Natl Bar Assoc Comm on Legal Educ; mem editorial bd The Texas Lawyer; life mem Houston Chamber of Commerce; bd of dirs, Law School Admission Council; chmn, Minority Affairs Committee, Law Shool Admission Council. **SELECTED PUBLICATIONS** "Some Ideas on the Computer and Law" TX Southern Univ Law Review 20 1971; "Cases & Materials on Contracts". **CONTACT ADDRESS** Texas So Univ, 3100 Cleburne Ave, Houston, TX 77004. **EMAIL** jdouglas@tsulaw.edu

DOUGLAS, WALTER
PERSONAL Born 02/02/1935, Grenada, WI, m, 1963, 3 children **DISCIPLINE** THEOLOGY **CAREER** Prof, Andrews Univ Theol Sem, 70-. **HONORS AND AWARDS** Andrews Medallion Scholar. **MEMBERSHIPS** AAR; DBL; Can Soc for Relig Studies; Adventist Soc for Relig Studies. **CONTACT ADDRESS** Andrews Univ, Berrien Springs, MI 49103.

DOURLEY, JOHN PATRICK
PERSONAL Born 02/20/1936, Ottawa, ON, Canada **DISCIPLINE** RELIGION **EDUCATION** St Patrick's Col, BA, 57; Univ Ottawa, LPh, 60, STL and MTh, 64; St Michael's Col, Univ Toronto, MA, 66; Fordham Univ, PhD (theol), 71; C G Jung Inst, Switz, dipl Jungian psychol, 80. **CAREER** Asst prof, 71-75, Assoc Prof Relig, Carleton Univ, 75-. **MEMBERSHIPS** Am Acad Relig; Am Teilhard de Chardin Asn; Can Theol Soc (treas, 72-74); Can Soc Sci Study Relig. **RESEARCH** Paul Tillich's relation to early Franciscan theology, especially Bonaventure's; Tillich; C G Jung. **SELECTED PUBLICATIONS** Auth, The Implications of Jung, Carl, Gustav Critique of the Symbol of Trinity, Stud Religion Sci Religieuses, Vol 23, 94; Boehme, Jacob and Tillich, Paul on Trinity and God--Similarities and Differences, Religious Stud, Vol 31, 95. **CONTACT ADDRESS** Dept of Relig St Patrick's Col, Carleton Univ, 1125 Colonel By Dr, 2121 Dunton Tower, Ottawa, ON, Canada K1S 5B6. **EMAIL** john_dourley@carleton.ca

DOWD, NANCY E.
DISCIPLINE LAW **EDUCATION** Univ Conn, BA; Univ Ill, MA; Loyola Univ Chicago, JD. **CAREER** Prof, Univ Fla, 89-; instr, Suffolk Univ, 84-89, vis prof, Univ Auckland, New Zealand; Univ Western Australia; Murdoch Univ, Australia; past assoc, Choate, Hall Stewart, Boston; clerk, Judge Robert A. Sprecher, US Ct Appeals, 7th Circuit; pract law in Boston. **HONORS AND AWARDS** Rockefeller Found grant; teacher Yr, 90-91. **MEMBERSHIPS** Law and Soc Asn; Mass Bar; Phi Beta Kappa; Phi Kappa Phi; Alpha Lambda Delta; Mortar bd. **RESEARCH** Contracts, family law, employ discrimination, women and the law **SELECTED PUBLICATIONS** Auth, Defense of Single-Parent Families. **CONTACT ADDRESS** School of Law, Univ of Florida, PO Box 117625, Gainesville, FL 32611-7625. **EMAIL** dowd@law.ufl.edu

DOWD, SHARYN
PERSONAL Born 02/14/1947, Atlanta, GA, s **DISCIPLINE** NEW TESTAMENT **EDUCATION** Wake Forest Univ, BA, 69; Southeastern Baptist Theolog Seminary, Mdiv, 80; Emory Univ, PhD, 86 **CAREER** Instr, Wake Forest Univ, 84-87; assoc prof, Lexington Theolog Seminary, 87-92; prof, Lexington Theolog Seminary, 92- **HONORS AND AWARDS** President, NABPR, 91 **MEMBERSHIPS** Soc Bibl Lit; Ntl Assoc Baptist Professors Relig; Baptist Women in Ministry **RESEARCH** New Testament Theology; Gospel of Mark; Pauline Studies **SELECTED PUBLICATIONS** "Galatians," IVP Women's Bible Commentary, Intervarsity Pr, forthcoming; "Review Essay: The Gospel and the Sacred: Poetics of Violence in Mark by Robert G. Hammerton-Kelly," Lexington Theolog Quart; ed, "Inspiration and Authority According to 2 Timothy," Common Ground, 98 **CONTACT ADDRESS** Lexington Theol Sem, 631 S Lime, Lexington, KY 40508. **EMAIL** sdowd@lextheo.edu

DOWNES, STEPHEN M.
PERSONAL Born 12/21/1960, United Kingdom **DISCIPLINE** PHILOSOPHY **EDUCATION** Manchester Univ, BA; Warwick Univ, MA; Virginia Polytechnic & State Univ, PhD. **CAREER** Vis asst prof, philos, Univ of Cincinnati, 90-91; post-doctoral fel, Northwestern Univ, 91-92; asst prof, 92-98, assoc prof, philos, 98- , University of Utah. **MEMBERSHIPS** APA; Philos of Sci Asn. **RESEARCH** Philosophy of biology; human nature; genome project; cloning. **SELECTED PUBLICATIONS** Auth, The Importance of Models in Theorizing: A Deflationary Semantic Approach, in Hull, ed, Proceedings of the Philosophy of Science Association, vol 1, 92; auth, Modelling Scientific Practice: Paul Thagard's Computational Approach, New Ideas in Psych, 93; auth, Socializing Naturalized Philosophy of Science, Philos of Sci, 93; auth, Science, and, Logical Positivism, and, Logical Empiricism, in Garrett, ed, The Encyclopedia of Empiricism, Greenwood, 97; auth, Constructivism, in Craig, ed, Routledge Encyclopedia of Philosophy, Routledge, 98; auth, Ontogeny, Phylogeny and Scientific Development, in Hardcastle, ed, Biology Meets Psychology: Constraints, Conjectures, Connections, MIT, forthcoming. **CONTACT ADDRESS** Dept of Philosophy, Univ of Utah, Salt Lake City, UT 84112. **EMAIL** s.downes@m.cc.utah.edu

DOWNEY, JAMES PATRICK
PERSONAL Born Waynesboro, VA **DISCIPLINE** PHILOSOPHY, RELIGION, ETHICS **EDUCATION** Univ VA, PhD. **CAREER** Instr, Hollins Col. **SELECTED PUBLICATIONS** Auth, A Primordial Reply to Modern Gaunilos, Relig Stud, 86; On Omniscience, Faith and Philos, 93. **CONTACT ADDRESS** Hollins Col, Roanoke, VA 24020.

DOWNEY, JOHN
DISCIPLINE RELIGIOUS STUDIES **EDUCATION** Marquette Univ, AB, 71; MA, 75; PhD, 83. **CAREER** Instr, Mount Mary Col, 76-80; Vis Lectr, Univ of Ill Urbana, 81-82; Prof, Gonzaga Univ-. **HONORS AND AWARDS** Coolidge Fel, 91; NEH Human Rights, 99; Phi Betta Kappa. **MEMBERSHIPS** Col Theol Soc, Cath Theol Soc of Am, Am Acad of Rel, Asn for Rel and Intellectual Life, Bonhoeffer Soc, Lonergan Philos Soc. **RESEARCH** Religion and society, political theology, language, postmodernity. **SELECTED PUBLICATIONS** Auth, Beginning at the Beginning, 89; auth, "Postmodernity and Pedagogy," Horizons (98); transl, of "In the Pluralism of Religious and Cultural Worlds," by J.B. Metz, Crosscurrents; auth, "Resisting and Yielding to Small Groups," Nat Teaching and Learning Forum; ed, Love's Strategy, 99. **CONTACT ADDRESS** Dept Relig Studies, Gonzaga Univ, 502 E Boone Ave, Spokane, WA 99258-1774.

DOWNS, ANTHONY
PERSONAL Born 11/21/1930, Evanston, IL, m, 1999, 5 children **DISCIPLINE** ECONOMICS **EDUCATION** Carleton Coll, BA, 52; Stanford Univ, MA; PhD, 56. **CAREER** Chemn, Real Estate Res Corp; Econ Anal, Rand Corp; Sr Fel, Brookings Inst; asst prof, Univ Chicago. **HONORS AND AWARDS** Nat Acad of Public Admin; Amer Acad of Arts and Sciences. **MEMBERSHIPS** Am Econ Asn; Am Real Estate and Urban Econ Asn; Counrs of Real Estate, Urban Land Inst. **RESEARCH** Urban affairs; real estate; housing; demographics. **SELECTED PUBLICATIONS** Auth, Stuck in Traffic, 92; New Visions for Metropolitan America, 94; A Reevaluation of Resident Rent Controls, 96; Political Theory and Public Choice: The Selected Essays of Anthony Downs, Volume One, 98; Urban Affairs and Urban Policy: The Selected Essays of Anthony Downs, Volume Two, 98. **CONTACT ADDRESS** Brookings Inst, 1775 Massachusetts Ave, Washington, DC 20036. **EMAIL** anthonydowns@csi.com

DOWTY, ALAN K.
PERSONAL Born 01/15/1940, Greenville, OH, m, 1973, 6 children **DISCIPLINE** INTERNATIONAL RELATIONS **EDUCATION** Shimer Col, BA, 59; Univ Chicago, MA, 60; PhD, 63. **CAREER** Prof Govt & Intl Studies, Univ Notre Dame, 78-; assoc prof Govt & Intl Studies, Univ Notre Dame, 75-78; senior lctr, Hebrew Univ, 72-75; lctr, Hebrew Univ, 65-72; instr, Hebrew Univ, 64-65. **HONORS AND AWARDS** Amer Council of Learned Societies Travel Grant, 94; Twentieth Cent Fund Grant, 83-85; Quincy Wright Awd, Intl Studies Assoc, 85; Res Grant, Ford Found, 77; Res Grant, Intl Crisis Behavior Res Project, 77; Res Grant, Leonard Davis Inst Intl Relations, 73-75; Resident Fel, Adlai Stevenson Inst Intl Affairs, 71-72; vis Res Fel, Univ Chi, 70-71. **MEMBERSHIPS** Amer Polit Sci Assoc; Assoc Jewish Studies; Intl Inst Strategic Studies; Intl Polit Sci Assoc; Intl Studies Assoc; Assoc Israel Studies; World Union Jewish Studies. **RESEARCH** Israel; Arab-Israeli Issues **SELECTED PUBLICATIONS** Auth, The Jewish State: A Century Later, Univ Calif Pr, 98; coauth, The Role of Domestic Politics in Isreali Peacemaking, Leonard Davis Inst for Intl Relations, 97; auth, Closed Borders: The Contemporary Assault on Freedom of Movement, Yale Univ Pr, 87; auth, Zionism's Greatest Conceit, Israel Studies, 98; auth, Israel's First Fifty Years, Current History, 97. **CONTACT ADDRESS** Dept of Government and International Studies, Univ of Notre Dame, 0313 Hesburgh Center, Notre Dame, IN 46556. **EMAIL** dowty.1@nd.edu

DOYLE, DENNIS M.
PERSONAL Born 04/02/1952, PA, m, 1981, 4 children **DISCIPLINE** RELIGIOUS STUDIES **EDUCATION** Cath Univ Am, PhD. **CAREER** Prof, Univ Dayton, 84-. **MEMBERSHIPS** Am Academy of Religion; Catholic Theological Society of America; College Theology Society. **RESEARCH** Ecclesiology, Catholic thought, systematics & religious education. **SELECTED PUBLICATIONS** Auth, The Church Emerging from Vatican II. **CONTACT ADDRESS** Dept of Religious Studies, Univ of Dayton, 300 College Park, Dayton, OH 45469-1530. **EMAIL** dennis.doyle@notes.udayton.edu

DOYLE, JAMES F.
PERSONAL Born 05/16/1927, AK, m, 1954, 4 children **DISCIPLINE** PHILOSOPHY **EDUCATION** Louisiana State Univ, BS, 49; Yale Univ, MA, 57; PhD, 64. **CAREER** Instr, philos, Carleton Col, 58-60; asst prof, philos, Claremont Men's Col, 60-66; assoc prof, prof, philos, Univ Missouri, 66-98. **HONORS AND AWARDS** NEH grant, 85-86. **MEMBERSHIPS** APA; Int Asn for Philos of Law and Social Philos; Am Soc for Polit and Legal Philos. **SELECTED PUBLICATIONS** Auth, Police Discretion, Legality, and Morality, in Police Ethics,, ed, Hefferman, John Jay, 85; auth, Democratic Autonomy: Fulfilling Revolutionary Promises, Archiv fur Rechts- und Sozialphilosophie, 90; auth, Empowering and Restraining the Police: How to Accomplish Both, Criminal Justice Ethics, 92; auth, A Radical Critique of Criminal Punishment, in Griffin, ed, Radical Critiques of the Law, Univ Press of Kansas, 97; auth, Legal Accommodation of Social Diversity, Rechtstheorie, 98. **CONTACT ADDRESS** 6334 Pershing Ave, Saint Louis, MO 63130-4703. **EMAIL** sjfdoyl@umslvma.umsl.edu

DOZIER, ROBERT R.
PERSONAL Born 04/07/1932, New Orleans, LA, m, 1954, 4 children **DISCIPLINE** HISTORY, POLITICAL SCIENCE **EDUCATION** Univ Calif, PhD, 69. **CAREER** Prof, Univ Mont, 82-89; Prof Emer, Univ Mont, 89-. **HONORS AND AWARDS** Teacher of the Year, 77; Outstanding Educr, 82. **RESEARCH** Military history. **SELECTED PUBLICATIONS** Auth, For King, Constitution and Country, Univ KY Pr, 83. **CONTACT ADDRESS** Dept Hist, Univ of Montana, Missoula, MT 59812. **EMAIL** rrdozier@aol.com

DRAGE-HALE, ROSEMARY
DISCIPLINE RELIGION **EDUCATION** Kent State Univ, BA, 66; Eastern Mich Univ, MA, 76; Harvard Univ, MTS, 87; Univ Harvard, PhD, 91. **CAREER** House Tutor, Harvard Univ, 89-91; Instr, Harvard Univ, 90-92; assoc prof, Concordia Univ, 92-; assoc dean, School of Graduate Studies, 97-00. **HONORS AND AWARDS** Harvard Univ Graduate School of Arts & Sciences Merit Fel, 90-91; Mellon Dissertation Fel, 91; Concordia Univ Fac Res and Dev Grant, 92-94; Innovative Teaching Grant for The Use of Audio-Visual Materials in the Teaching of Relig, 93-95; Lilly Foundation Teaching Grant, 93-94; Fonds pour la Formation de Chercheurs et l'Aide a la Recherche, 94-97; co-ch, hist of christianity section, amer acad of rel; ed bd, harvard theol rev and mystics quart. **MEMBERSHIPS** Member of Am Academy of Relig, The Am Soc of Church Hist, Societe canadienne des Medievistes, Canadian Soc for the Study of Relig, Medieval Academy of Am; The Univ Art Asn of Canada. **RESEARCH** History of Christianity in the European Middle Ages and early modern period. **SELECTED PUBLICATIONS** Auth, Imitatio Mariae: Motherhood Motifs in Late Meideval German Piety, Ph.D Thesis, Committee on the Study of Religion, Harvard Univ, Sping 92; auth, Joseph as Mother: Adaptation and Appropriation of Marian Imagery, Medieval Mothering, Feminae Medievalia 4, Univ Toronto Press, 96; Taste and See, for God is Sweet: Sensory Perception and Memory in Medieval Christian Mystical Experience, Vox Mystica: Essays in

Honor of Valerie Lagorio, Boydell and Brewer, 95; co-ed, Models of Holiness: Paradigms of Virtue in Medieval Sermons, Intl Fed of Inst Medieval Stud, Brepols, 96; ed, An Illustrated Guide to World Religions, ed. by Michael Coogan, Duncan Baird, distributed by Oxford Univ Press, 98; auth, Cloistered Women: Fourteenth-Century Convent Literature, Boydell and Brewer, 99; ed, "Taste and See, for God Is Sweet: Sensory Perception and Memory in Medieval Christian Mystical Experience," in Vox Mystica: Essays in Honor of Valerie Lagorio, ed. by Anne Clarke Bartlett, Boydell and Brewer, (95): 23-38; auth, "Joseph as Mother: Adaption and Appropriation in the Construction of Male Virtue," in Medieval Mothering, ed. by John Parsons and Bonnie Wheeler, Garland Press, (96): 100-118; auth, The Silent Virgin: Marian Imagery in the Sermons of Meister Eckhart and Johannes Tauler," in De Ore Domini: Preacher and Word in the Middle Ages, Vol. II, R. Hale and D. Stoudt, eds., Federation Internationale des Instituts d'Etudes Medievales, Louvain-la-Neuve, (98): 76-94; auth, "Rocking the Cradle: Margaretha Ebner (Be) Holds the Divine," in The Performance and Transformation: New Approaches to Medieval Spirituality, ed. By Joanna Ziegler and Mary Suydam, St. Martin's Press, (99): 210-241; auth, "Catherine of Siena," in Encyclopedia of the Renaissance, ed. By Paul F. Grendler, Charles Scribner's Sons, 99; auth, "Margaretha Ebner," "Adelheid Langmann," Caesarius of Heisterbach," "Sermons and Preaching," and "Legends," in The Encyclopedia of Medieval German Literature, ed. by John Jeep, Birll, 00. **CONTACT ADDRESS** Dept of Rel, Concordia Univ, Montreal, 1455 de Maisonneuve W, School of Graduate Studies, Montreal, QC, Canada H3G 1M8. **EMAIL** hale@vax2.concordia.ca

DRANGE, THEODORE MICHAEL
PERSONAL Born 03/14/1934, New York, NY, m, 1959, 2 children **DISCIPLINE** PHILOSOPHY **EDUCATION** Brooklyn Col, BA, 55; Cornell Univ, PhD(philos), 63. **CAREER** Lectr Philos, Brooklyn Col, 60-62; from instr to asst prof, Univ Ore, 62-65; asst prof, Idaho State Univ, 65-66; from asst prof to assoc prof, 66-74, prof Philos, West Va Univ, 74-. **MEMBERSHIPS** Eastern Div Am Philos Asn. **RESEARCH** Philosophy of language, theory of knowledge; philosophy of science; philosophy of religion. **SELECTED PUBLICATIONS** Auth, Type Crossings, Mouton, The Hague, 66; Reply to Martin on type crossings, Philos & Phenomenol Res, 69; Paradox regained, Philos Studies, 69; Harrison and Odegard on type crossings, Mind, 69; Truth and necessary truth, J WVa Philos Soc, 73; A critical review of E Erwin's The Concept of Meaninglessness, J Critical Analysis, 75; Liar Syllogisms, Analysis, 90; The Argument from Nonbelief, Religious Studies, 93; Nonbelief and Evil, Prometheus Books, 98. **CONTACT ADDRESS** Dept of Philosophy, West Virginia Univ, Morgantown, PO Box 6312, Morgantown, WV 26506-6312. **EMAIL** tdrange@wvi.edu

DRAPER, DAVID E.
DISCIPLINE THEOLOGY **EDUCATION** Frostburg State Univ, BS, 71; Winebrenner Sem, MDiv, 79; Bowling Green State Univ, MEd, 85, PhD, 88. **CAREER** Dir develop, 82-85; VP inst advancement, 85-88; pres, dir, Churches of God, General Conf, 92-94; pres, Wiinebrenner Theol Sem, 88-. **HONORS AND AWARDS** Outstanding Young Man Am, 86; assoc ministry, churches of god, gen conf; ed, church advocate; chaplain, cgya workshop. **MEMBERSHIPS** Mem, Impact Admin Comm; bd mem, Great Commn Ministries; mem, Fel Evangel Sem Pres(s). **SELECTED PUBLICATIONS** Ed, Youth Advance mag; Reach 'n Rejoice; pub(s), Church Advocate; The Gem; co-auth, co-author, Bound But Free, Churches of God. **CONTACT ADDRESS** Winebrenner Theol Sem, 701 E Melrose Ave, PO Box 478, Findlay, OH 45839.

DRAY, WILLIAM HERBERT
PERSONAL Born 06/23/1921, Montreal, PQ, Canada, m, 1943, 2 children **DISCIPLINE** PHILOSOPHY **EDUCATION** Univ Toronto, BA, 49, Oxford Univ, BA, 51, MA, 55 DPhil-(philos), 56. **CAREER** Lectr Philos, Univ Toronto, 53-55, from Asst Prof to Prof, 56-68; Prof and Chmn Dept, Trent Univ, 68-73; Prof, Duke Univ, 73-74 and Trent Univ, 74-76; Prof Philos, Univ Ottawa, 76-, Am Coun Learned Soc Fel, 60-61; Can Coun Fel, 71-72 and 78-79,78-79; Killam Fel, 80-81. **MEMBERSHIPS** Am Philos Asn, Can Philos Asn, Royal Soc Can, Can Hist Asn, Societi de Philosophic du Quebec. **RESEARCH** Analytic Philosophy, Philosophy of History, Philosophy of Mind. **SELECTED PUBLICATIONS** Auth, Perspectives on History; ed, Philosophical Analysis and History; auth, Laws and Explanation in History, 79; auth, Perspectives Sur L'Histoire (Collection, Philosophica, No 33) 87; auth, Philosophy of History, 98; auth, On History and Philosophers of History (Philosophy of History and Culture, Vol 2), 97; auth, History As Re-Enactment: R.G. Collingwood's Idea of History, 99. **CONTACT ADDRESS** Dept Philos, Univ of Ottawa, 70 Laurier Ave, Ottawa, ON, Canada K1N 6N5.

DREFCINSKI, SHANE
PERSONAL m, 3 children **DISCIPLINE** PHILOSOPHY **EDUCATION** Univ Minn, MA, 92, PhD, 96. **CAREER** Asst prof. **RESEARCH** Ancient Greek & Roman philosophy; medieval philosophy; early modern philosophy; philosophy of education; ethics. **SELECTED PUBLICATIONS** Auth, pubs on Aristotle's ethical theory. **CONTACT ADDRESS** Dept of Philosophy, Univ of Wisconsin, Platteville, 1 University Plaza, Platteville, WI 53818-3099. **EMAIL** drefcinski@uwplatt.edu

DREHER, JOHN PAUL
PERSONAL Born 08/28/1934, Jersey City, NJ, m, 1959, 3 children **DISCIPLINE** PHILOSOPHY **EDUCATION** St Peter's Col, AB, 55; Fordham Univ, MA, 59; Univ Chicago, PhD, 61. **CAREER** Asst prof philos, Univ NC, 61-63; asst prof, 63-68, assoc prof & chmn dept philos, 68-69, prof, 89-, Lawrence Univ. **HONORS AND AWARDS** Outstanding Teacher Awd, 89 **MEMBERSHIPS** Am Philos Assn. **RESEARCH** History of philosophy; applied ethics; pragmatism. **SELECTED PUBLICATIONS** Art, Moral Objectivity, Southern J Philos, 66; art, The Driving Ration in Plato's Divided Line, Ancient Philosophy, 90. **CONTACT ADDRESS** Dept of Philosophy, Lawrence Univ, PO Box 599, Appleton, WI 54912-0599. **EMAIL** john.p.dreher@lawrence.edu

DREIER, JAMES
PERSONAL Born 04/05/1960, New York, NY, m, 1989, 3 children **DISCIPLINE** PHILOSOPHY **EDUCATION** Harvard Univ, AB, 82; Princeton, PhD, 88. **CAREER** Sr vis lectr, Monash Univ, 93-94; Asst Prof of Philos, 88-95, Assoc Prof of Philos, Brown Univ, 95-. **MEMBERSHIPS** Am Philos Asn. **RESEARCH** Meta-ethics; rationality; decision theory. **SELECTED PUBLICATIONS** Auth, Internalism and Speaker Relativisim, Ethics; The Supervenience Argument against Moral Realism, Southern J of Philos; Expressivist Embeddings and Minimalist Truth, Philos Studies; Rational Preference: Decision Theory as a Theory of Practical Rationality, Theory and Decision; Accepting Agent Centered Norms, Australasian J of Philso; Humean Doubts, Ethics and Practical Reason, Oxford Univ Press, 97. **CONTACT ADDRESS** Dept of Philos, Brown Univ, Box 1918, Providence, RI 02912. **EMAIL** james_dreier@brown.edu

DREISBACH, DONALD FRED
PERSONAL Born 06/25/1941, Allentown, PA, d **DISCIPLINE** PHILOSOPHY & HISTORY OF RELIGION **EDUCATION** MA Inst Technol, BS, 63; Northwestern Univ, MA, 69, PhD, 70. **CAREER** Assoc prof, 69- 80, Prof Philos, Northern MI Univ, 80. **MEMBERSHIPS** AAUP; Am Acad Relig; Am Philos Asn; NAm Paul Tillich Soc. **RESEARCH** Philosophical theology; Paul Tillich. **SELECTED PUBLICATIONS** Auth, Paul Tillich's Herrmeneutic, J Am Acad Relig, Vol XLIII, No 1; Paul Tillich's Doctrine of Religious Symbols, Encounter, Vol 37, No 4; On the love of God, Anglican Theol Rev, Vol LIX, No 1; Circularity and consistency in Descartes, Can J Philos, Vol VIII, No 1; Agreement and obligation in the Crito, New Scholasticism, Vol LII, No 2; The unity of Paul Tillich's existential analysis, Encounter, Vol 41, No 4; On the hermeneutic of symbols: The Buri-Hardwick debate, Theologische Zeitschrift, 9-10/79; Essence, existence and the fall: Paul Tillich's analysis of existence, Harvard Theol Rev, Vol 73, No 1-2; Symbols and Salvation, Univ Press Am, 93. **CONTACT ADDRESS** Dept of Philos, No Michigan Univ, 1401 Presque Isle Av, Marquette, MI 49855-5301. **EMAIL** ddreisba@nmu.edu

DREYFUS, HUBERT LEDERER
PERSONAL Born 10/15/1929, Terre Haute, IN, m, 1974, 2 children **DISCIPLINE** PHILOSOPHY **EDUCATION** Harvard Univ, BA, 51, MA, 52, PhD, 64. **CAREER** Instr philos, Brandeis Univ, 57-59; from instr to assoc prof, Mass Inst Technol, 60-68; assoc prof, 68-72, Prof Philos, Univ Calif, Berkeley, 72-94, Prof Emer, 94-; French Govt grant, 64-65; res assoc computer sci, NSF grant, Harvard Univ, 68; Am Coun Learned Soc grant, 68-69; consult NEH, Nat Bd Consult, 76- **HONORS AND AWARDS** Guggenheim, 85; ACLS grant, 1968-1969;Yrjo Reenpaa medal, Finnish Cultural Foundaition, 91; Phi Beta Kappa lectr, 92-93; Doctorate Honors Causa, Erasmus Univ Roherdauer, the Netherlands, 98 **MEMBERSHIPS** Am Philos Asn; Soc Phenomenol & Existential Philos. **RESEARCH** Phenomenology and existential philosophy; artifical intelligence and computer simulation of cognitive processes; philosophy in literature and film. **SELECTED PUBLICATIONS** Auth, " Husserl's Epiphenomenology," Perspectives on Mind, D Reidel, 88; coauth, " From Depth Psychology to Breadth Psychology: A Phenomenological Approach to Psychopathology," Psychotherapy, and Psychopathology, Rutgers Univ Press, 88; auth, " On the Ordering of Things: Being and Power In Heidegger and Foucault," Le Seuil, Paris, 89; coauth, " Action and the First Person," John Searle and His Critics, Basil Blackwell, 90; auth, " Defending the Difference: The Geistes/Naturwissenschaften Distinction Revisited," Walter De Gruyter, 91; coauth, " Kierkegaard on the Nihilism of the Present Age: The Case of Commitment as Addiction" Syntheses, Kluwer, 94; coauth, " Two Kinds of Antiessentialism and Their Consequences," Critical Inquiry, 22, 96; auth, "Education on the Internet: Anonymity vs Commitment," The Internet and Higher Education, vol 1, no 2, JAI Press, 98; coauth, " The Challenge of Merleau Ponty's Phenomenology of Embodiment for Cognitive Science," Perspective on Embodiment: The Intersections of Nature and Culture, Routledge, 99; coauth, " Coping with Things in Themselves: A Practice-Based Phenomenological Basis of Robust Realism," Inquiry, 42, 49-78, 99; auth, " Kierkegaard and the Internet," Subjektivitaet und Oeffentichkeit, Grundprobleme virtueller Welten," Germany: Leske und Budrich, 00. **CONTACT ADDRESS** Dept of Philosophy, Univ of California, Berkeley, 314 Moses Hall, Berkeley, CA 94720-2391. **EMAIL** dreyfus@cogsci.berkeley.edu

DRIESEN, DAVID
PERSONAL Born 05/07/1953, New York, NY, m, 1994, 3 children **DISCIPLINE** LAW **EDUCATION** Oberlin Univ, Bmus, 80; Yale Sch Music, Mmus, 83; Yale Law Sch, JD, 89. **CAREER** Law Clerk, Justice Robert Utter, Wash State Supreme Ct, 89-90; Asst Atty Gen, Wash State Atty Gen Off, 90-91; Proj Atty, Nat Resources Defense Coun, 92-94; Sen Proj Atty, Nat Resources Defense Coun, 94-95; Asst Prof, Syracuse Univ, 95-99; Assoc Prof, Syracuse Univ, 99-. **HONORS AND AWARDS** Olin Fel; Ed, Int Law Jour. **MEMBERSHIPS** Am Bar Asn **RESEARCH** Environmental law (domestic and international), international trade law, constitutional law, Brazilian law. **SELECTED PUBLICATIONS** Auth, "Brazil's Transition to Democracy: Agrarian Reform and the New Constitution," 8 Wis Int'l LJ 150 (90); auth, "The Congressional Role in International Environmental Law and its Implications for Statutory Interpretation," 19 BC Envtl Aff L Rev 287 (91); auth, "Air Pollution Control," in Powell, Treatise on Property (94); auth, "Five Lessons From Clean Air Act Implementation," 14 Pace Envt'l L Rev 51 (96); auth, "The Societal Cost of Environmental Regulation: Beyond Administrative Cost-Benefit Analysis," 29 Land Use & Environment L Rev 369 (98); auth, "Should Congress Direct the EPA to Allow Serious Harms to Public Health to Continue?: Cost-Benefit Tests and NAAQS Under the Clean Air Act," 11 Tulane Envt'l LJ 217 (98); auth, "Is Emissions Trading an Economic Incentive Program?: Replacing the Command and Control/Economic Incentive Dichotomy," 55 Wash & Lee L Rev 289 (98); auth, "Free Lunch or a Cheap Fix": The Emissions Trading Idea and the Climate Change convention," 26 BC Envtl Aff L Rev 1 (98); auth, "Choosing Environmental Instruments in Transnational Lefal Context," 27 Ecol LQ (00) forthcoming; auth, What is Free Trade? The Real Issue Lurking Behind the Trade and Environment Debate (forthcoming). **CONTACT ADDRESS** Dept Law, Syracuse Univ, Syracuse, NY 13244-1030. **EMAIL** ddriesen@law.syr.edu

DRINAN, ROBERT FREDERICK
PERSONAL Born 11/15/1920, Boston, MA **DISCIPLINE** LAW **EDUCATION** Boston Col, BA, 42, MA, 47; Georgetown Univ, LLB, 49, LLM, 50; Gregorian Univ, Rome, STD, 54. **CAREER** Ordained Jesuit priest, 53; contrib ed, Am Mag, 58-70; dean & prof law, Law Sch, Boston Col, 59-70; chemn, Adv Comt Mass, US Comn Civil Rights, 62-70; vis prof, Law Sch, Univ Tex, Austin, 66-67; vis lectr, Andover-Newton Theol Sem, 66-68; ed, Family Law Quart, 67-70; US Rep, Mass, 71-81; prof law, Law Ctr, Georgetown Univ, 81-; mem, Exec Comt, House Democratic Study Group, 77-78 & New England Congressional Caucus, 79-81; columnist, Nat Cath Reporter, 80-. **HONORS AND AWARDS** Mass Bar Asn Gold Medal recipient, 67; Honorary degrees from Southeaster Mass Univ, 63; Worcester Stat Col, 70; Long Island Univ, 70; Rhode Island Col, 71; St. Joseph's Univ, Penn, 75; Syracuse Univ, 77; Villanova Univ, 77; Framingham State Col, 78; Univ Santa Clara, 80; Gonzaga Univ, 81; Univ Bridgeport, 81; Univ Lowell, 81; Loyola Univ, Chicago, 81; Kenyon Col, 81; Curry Ciol, 82; Hebrew Col, 84; DePaul Univ, 84; Univ San Diego, 84; Mount St. Mary Col, 85; Notre Dame Col, New Hampshire, 89; Walsh Col, 94; Georgetown Univ, 91; Trinity Col, 97. **RESEARCH** Nuclear arms control; international human rights; civil rights and liberties. **SELECTED PUBLICATIONS** Auth, Religion, The Courts, and Public Policy, McGraw-Hill, 63; auth, Democracy, Dissent and Disorder, Seabury, 69; auth, Vietnam and Armageddon, Sheed & Ward, 70; auth, Honor the Promise: America's Commitment to Irael, Doubleday, 77; auth, Beyond the Nuclear Freeze, Seabury, 83; auth, God and Caesar on the Potomac: A Pilgrimage of Conscience, Micael Glazier, 85; auth, Cry of the Oppressed -- The History and Hope of the Human Rights Revolution, Harper & Row, 87; auth, Stories from the Am Soul, Loyola Univ Pr, 90; auth, The Fractured Dream 00 America's Divisive Moral Choices, Crossroad, 91. **CONTACT ADDRESS** Law Ctr, Georgetown Univ, 600 New Jersey NW, Washington, DC 20001-2022. **EMAIL** drinan@law.geocites.edu

DRINKARD, JOEL F., JR.
DISCIPLINE OLD TESTAMENT **EDUCATION** Univ NC, BA; Southeastern Baptist Theol Sem, MDiv, ThM; S Baptist Theoll Sem, PhD; additional stud, Regent's Park Col, Johns Hopkins Univ, Univ Chicago. **CAREER** Prof, S Baptist Theol Sem, 83-. **HONORS AND AWARDS** Curator, Joseph A. Callaway Museum. **RESEARCH** Biblical archaeology. **SELECTED PUBLICATIONS** Assoc ed, contrib auth, Mercer Bible Dictionary; co-auth, Word Biblical Commentary on Jeremiah 1-25. **CONTACT ADDRESS** Old Testament Dept, So Baptist Theol Sem, 2825 Lexington Rd, Louisville, KY 40280. **EMAIL** jdrinkard@sbts.edu

DRISKILL, JOSEPH D.
PERSONAL Born 01/07/1946, Peoria, IL, m, 1985 **DISCIPLINE** RELIGION **EDUCATION** Culver-Stockton Col, BA, 68; Vanderbilt Divinity Sch, MDiv, 71; Univ Regina, MA, 76;

Grad Theol Union, PhD, 96. **CAREER** Minister, 65-75; Lectr, Huron Col, 82-88; Dir, Lloyd Pastoral Coun Ctr, 91-; From Asst Prof to Assoc Prof, Pac Sch of Relig, 93-. **HONORS AND AWARDS** Res Awd, Am Asn Pastoral Counrs, 96. **MEMBERSHIPS** AAR, CAPPE, Soc for the Study of Christian Spirituality, AAPC. **RESEARCH** Protestant spirituality, spirituality and health, spiritual direction and pastoral counseling. **SELECTED PUBLICATIONS** Auth, "The Significance of Ritual in the Case of Joanne: Insights from Depth Psychology," in Relig and Soc Ritual: Interdisciplinary Explorations (Albany, NY: St UP of NY, 96); auth, "Child and Interviewer Behaviors in Drawing and Computer Assisted Interviews," in Relig and Soc Ritual: Interdisciplinary Explorations (Soc for Res in Child Develop Pr, vol 61, nos 4-5, 96); auth, Protestant Spiritual Exercises: Theology, History and Practice, Morehouse (Harrisburg, PA), 99; auth, "Spiritual Guidance in a Mainline Protestant Context," Presence: The J of Spiritual Dir Int, vol 6 (00): 21-32; coauth, Ethics and Spiritual Care, Abingdon Pr, forthcoming; auth, "Spiritual Direction with Persons Who Have Been Traumatized," in Spiritual Direction in the 21st-Century (Morehouse, forthcoming). **CONTACT ADDRESS** Dept Relig, Pacific Sch of Religion, 1798 Scenic Ave, Berkeley, CA 94709-1323. **EMAIL** jdriskill@psr.edu

DRIVER, TOM FAW
PERSONAL Born 05/31/1925, Johnson City, TN, m, 1952, 3 children **DISCIPLINE** THEOLOGY, LITERATURE **EDUCATION** Duke Univ, AB, 50; Union Theol Sem, NYork, MDiv, 53; Columbia Univ, PhD, 57. **CAREER** Instr drama, 56-58, from asst prof to assoc prof theol, 58- 67, prof theol & lit, 67-73, Paul J Tillich Prof Theol & Cult, 73-93, emeritus, 93-, Union Theol Sem; Kent fel, 53-56; Mars lectr, Northwestern Univ, 61; Earl lect, Pac Sch Relig, 62; vis assoc prof, Columbia Univ, 64-65; vis prof, Univ Otago, NZ, 76, Vassar Col, 78 & Montclair State Col, 81. **HONORS AND AWARDS** Guggenheim fel, 62; ODK, 49; Phi Beta Kappa, 49; dlitt, dennison univ, 70. **MEMBERSHIPS** Soc Values Higher Educ; Am Acad Relig; New Haven Theol Discussion Gp; Witness for Peace; United Methodist Church; Presbyterian Church USA; United Church of Christ. **RESEARCH** Classical and modern drama; contemporary theology; ritual studies. **SELECTED PUBLICATIONS** Auth, The Sense of History in Greek and Shakespearean Drama, Columbia Univ, 60; co-ed, Poems of Belief and Doubt, Macmillan, 64; auth, The Shakespearian Clock, Shakespeare Quart, fall 64; Jean Genet, Columbia Univ, 66; History of the Modern Theatre, Delta, 71; The Twilight of Drama: From Ego to Myth, In: Humanities, Religion and the Arts, 72; Patterns of Grace: Human Experience as Word of God, Harper & Row, 77; Christ in a Changing World, Crossroad, 81; auth, The Magic of Ritual, Harper San Francisco, 91; auth, Liberating Rites: Understanding the Transformative Power of Ritual, Westview, 97. **CONTACT ADDRESS** 501 W 123rd St, #14G, New York, NY 10027. **EMAIL** tfd3@columbia.edu

DROST, MARK P.
DISCIPLINE PHILOSOPHY **EDUCATION** Univ Rochester, PhD, 90. **CAREER** Asst prof, Mankato State Univ, 93-94; asst prof, Bloomsburg Univ, 95; adj assoc prof, Monroe Commun Col, current. **RESEARCH** Philosophy of mind; phenomenology; aesthetics. **CONTACT ADDRESS** 5584 Canadice Lake Rd, Springwater, NY 14560. **EMAIL** csophia@prodigy.net

DRUART, THERESE-ANNE
PERSONAL Born 12/23/1945, Brussels, Belgium **DISCIPLINE** PHILOSOPHY **EDUCATION** Universite Catholique de Louvain, BA, 67, MA, 68, MA 71, PhD, 73; Univ de Tunis, certificate of third level of Arabic, summer course, 69; Univ of Oxford, BPhil, 75. **CAREER** Research fel, 75-76, Harvard Univ; researcher exchanged between the Belgian Scientific Research and the British Acad, 76-77; researcher exchanged between the Universite Catholique de Louvain and the Universita Cattolic del Sacro cuore, 77-78; asst prof, 78-83, assoc prof, 83-87, Georgetown Univ; assoc prof, 87-97, prof, 97- , The Catholic Univ of Amer; vis prof, 93, Universidad de Navarra. **HONORS AND AWARDS** Teacher of the Month **MEMBERSHIPS** APA; Amer Catholic Philosophy Assn; Soc for Medieval and Renaissance philosophy. **RESEARCH** Medieval Arabic philosophy; Greek philosophy. **SELECTED PUBLICATIONS** Ed, Arabic Philosophy, East and West: Continuity and Interaction, 88; auth, There is no god but God.., New Catholic World, 88; auth, Al-farabi, Ethics and First Intelligibles, Documentie Studi sulla tradizione filosofica medievale, 97; auth, Medieval Islamic Philosophy and Theology Bibliographical Guide, Bulletin de Philosophie medievale, 97; auth, Le Sommaire du Livre des Lois de Platon par Abu Nasr al-Farabi, Bulletin d'Etudes Orietnales, 98. **CONTACT ADDRESS** Sch of Philosophy, Catholic Univ of America, Washington, DC 20064-0001. **EMAIL** druart@cua.edu

DRUMMOND, JOHN J.
DISCIPLINE CONTEMPORARY EUROPEAN PHILOSOPHY **EDUCATION** Georgetown Univ, BA. PhD, 75. **CAREER** Taught at, Coe Col in Cedar Rapids, Iowa, 12 yrs; vis prof, Georgetown Univ, 1 yr; fac, Mt Saint Mary's Col, 88-; past dept ch & recently app, Distinguished prof Philos. **RESEARCH** Husserl's account of moral intentionality, the moral good, and community. **SELECTED PUBLICATIONS** Auth, a bk on Husserl's theory of intentionality & ed, 2 collections of essays on the work of Husserl and special ed jour Amer Cath Philos Quart devoted to Husserl's philos; gen ed, bk ser Contrib to Phenomenol publ by Kluwer Acad Publ in the N. **CONTACT ADDRESS** Dept of Philosophy, Mount Saint Mary's Col and Sem, 16300 Old Emmitsburg Rd, Emmitsburg, MD 21727-7799. **EMAIL** drummond@msmary.edu

DRURY, KEITH
PERSONAL Born Warren, PA **DISCIPLINE** RELIGIOUS STUDIES **EDUCATION** United Wesleyan Col, BS, 69; Princeton Theol Seminary, MRE, 71; Wesley Biblical Seminary, DD, 89; Ind Wesleyan Univ, LhD, 96. **CAREER** Prof. **SELECTED PUBLICATIONS** Auth, Holiness for Ordinary People; Spiritual Disciplines for Ordinary People, Money; Sex, & Spiritual Power; So, What Do You Think?. **CONTACT ADDRESS** Dept of Religion and Philosophy, Indiana Wesleyan Univ, 4201 S Wash St, Marion, IN 46953.

DUBAY, THOMAS E.
PERSONAL Born 12/30/1921, Minneapolis, MN **DISCIPLINE** PHILOSOPHY **EDUCATION** Cath Univ Am, MA, 51, PhD, 57. **CAREER** Instr theol, Notre Dame Sem, 52-54 & Marist Col, DC, 54-56; instr philos, Notre Dame Sem, 56-67; prof, Marycrest Col, 67-68; researcher, Russell Col, 68-70; lectr theol, Chestnut Hill Col, 70-73; PVT LECTR, 73-, Lectr, Cath Univ Am, 56. **MEMBERSHIPS** Cath Theol Soc Am; Fel Cath Scholars. **RESEARCH** Philosophy of state; life and regimen of religious orders and their members. **SELECTED PUBLICATIONS** Auth, Ecclesial Women, Alba, 70; God Dwells Within Us, 72, Can Religious Life Survive?, 73 & Caring: Biblical Theology of Community, 73, Dimension Bks; Pilgrims Pray, Alba, 74; Authenticity, Dimension, 77; What Is Religious Life?, 79 & Happy Are You Poor, 81, Dimension Bks; Faith and Certitude, Ignatius Press, 85; Fire Within, Ignatius Press, 89; Seeking Spiritual Direction, Servant Pub, 93; auth, Essential Power of Beauty, Ignatius Press, 99. **CONTACT ADDRESS** 4408 8th St NE, Washington, DC 20017.

DUBOFF, LEONARD DAVID
PERSONAL Born 10/03/1941, Brooklyn, NY, m, 1967, 2 children **DISCIPLINE** ART LAW, BUSINESS LAW **EDUCATION** Hofstra Univ, BES, 68; Brooklyn Law Sch, JD, 71. **CAREER** Teaching fel legal res and writing, Stanford Law Sch, 71-72; asst prof, 72-75, assoc prof, 75-77, Prof Bus Law and Art Law, Lewis and Clark Law Sch, 77-, comnr, Ore Comn Blind, 79-; bd mem, Ore Comt Humanities, 81 **MEMBERSHIPS** Am Soc Int Law. **CONTACT ADDRESS** 12440 SW Iron Mountain Blvd, Portland, OR 97219.

DUBOIS, JAMES M.
PERSONAL Born 09/21/1967, Springfield, MA, m, 1988, 5 children **DISCIPLINE** PHILOSOPHY **EDUCATION** Int Acad Philos, Liechtenstein, PhD, 92; Univ Vienna, DSc, 97. **CAREER** Asst prof, Feanciscan Univ, Austria, 92-94; asst prof, Int Acad Philos, Liechtenstein, 94-97; asst prof, 97-00, assoc prof, 00-, St Louis Univ. **MEMBERSHIPS** APA; Asn for Moral Educ; Am Soc for Bioethics and Hum. **RESEARCH** Health care ethics; descriptive ethics; moral development and education. **SELECTED PUBLICATIONS** Ed, "Judgment and Sachverhalt," Kluwer, 95; ed, "Moral Issues in Psychology," UPA, 97. **CONTACT ADDRESS** Cntr for Health Care Ethics, Saint Louis Univ, Saint Louis, MO 63104. **EMAIL** duboisjm@slu.edu

DUBOIS, SYLVIE
DISCIPLINE SOCIOLINGUISTICS, CAJUN **EDUCATION** Univ Laval, PhD, 93. **CAREER** Asst prof, 94-96, assoc prof, 97-, La State Univ; dir, LSU Cajun French Project. **HONORS AND AWARDS** Res grant, 95, SSHRCC; res grant, 96, Nat Sci Found. **SELECTED PUBLICATIONS** Coauth, Le discours direct au quotidien, editions Nuit blache (Quebec), 96; auth, Cajun is Dead: Long Live Cajun, J of Sociolinguistics 1.1 (96); auth, "Attitudes envers l'enseignement et l'apprentissage du francais cadien en Louisiane," Revue des sciences de l'education 23.3 (97): 699-715; auth, "Let's tink about dat: Interdental Fricatives in Cajun English," Language Variation and Change 10.3 (98): 245-261; auth, "From Accent to Marker in Cajun English: A Study of Dialect Formation in Progress, "English World Wide 19.2 (98): 161-188; auth, "When the Music Changes, You Change Too: Gender and Language Change in Cajun English," Language Variation and Change (in press); auth, "Creole is, Creole Ain't: Diachronic and Synchronic Attitudes Toward Creole Identity in South Louisiana," Language in Society (in press). **CONTACT ADDRESS** Dept of Fr Grad Stud, Louisiana State Univ and A&M Col, Baton Rouge, LA 70803. **EMAIL** sdubois@ix.netcom.com

DUCHARME, HOWARD M.
PERSONAL Born 06/04/1950, Saginaw, MI, m, 1975, 2 children **DISCIPLINE** PHILOSOPHY **EDUCATION** Hope Col, BA, 72; Trinity Divinity Sch, MA, 80; Oxford Univ, DPhil, 84. **CAREER** Asst prof, 84-85, Univ Tenn; visiting asst prof, 86, Univ Fla; from asst to assoc prof of philos, 86-, Univ Akron; prof and chr of philos, 00, Univ Akron. **HONORS AND AWARDS** Who's Who of Professionals; Who's Who in the World; Who's Who in Am; Who's Who in Am Educ; Who's Who in Am Tchrs; Who's Who in the Midwest; Strathmore's Who's Who; Men of Achievement; Int Who's Who of Contemporary Achievement; Post Doctorate Awd for Stds at Inst for Advanced Std Seminar on Christianity and Religious Pluralism; who's who among am tchrs; publ in professional philos, medical and bioethics jour. **MEMBERSHIPS** Am Philos Asn; Kennedy Inst Ethics; Hastings Ctr; Am Asn Bioethics; Int Asn Bioethics; Society for Health and Human Values. **RESEARCH** The nature of persons; bioethics; history of ethics. **SELECTED PUBLICATIONS** Auth, The Metaphysics of Defining Death, 90; coauth, Physician Participation in Assisted Suicide, 90; auth, The Vatican's Dilemma: On the Morality of IVF and the Incarnation, 91; auth, Can a Person Be Happily Wicked, 93; coauth, Withholding Therapy, 93; auth, Thrift-Euthanasia, 00. **CONTACT ADDRESS** Dept of Philosophy, Univ of Akron, 302 Olin Hall, Akron, OH 44325-1903. **EMAIL** ducharme@uakron.edu

DUCLOW, DONALD F.
PERSONAL Born 01/11/1946, Chicago, IL, m, 1970 **DISCIPLINE** ENGLISH, PHILSOSOPHY, MEDIEVAL STUDIES **EDUCATION** DePaul Univ, BA, English, philosophy, 68, MA, philosophy, 69; Bryn Mawr Coll, MA, medieval studies, 72, PhD, philosophy, 74, Divinity School, Unv. Of Chicago, 98. **CAREER** Visiting prof, philosophy, Fordham Univ, 78; asst prof of philosophy, 74-79, assoc prof of philosophy, 79-89, prof of philosophy, 89-, Gwynedd-Mercy Coll. **HONORS AND AWARDS** Mellon Fellow in the Humanities, Univ Pa, 80-81; NEH summer seminars, 87, 93; Senior Fellow, Institute for the Advanced Study of Religion, Divinity School, University of Chicago, Spring, 98; Inst for the Advan Study of Relig Sen Fel. **MEMBERSHIPS** Amer Acad Religion; Medieval Acad Am; sec, Amer Cusanus Soc; Amer Assn Univ Profs; pres, Gwynedd-Mercy Coll Chap, 96-97; Exec Committee, Pennsylvania AAUP, 00. **RESEARCH** Medieval philosophy and religion. **SELECTED PUBLICATIONS** Auth, "Divine Nothingness and Self-Creation in John Scotus Eriugena," The Journ of Religion, vol 57, 77; "'My Suffering Is God': Meister Eckhart's Book of Divine Consolation," Theological Studies, vol 44, 83, reprinted in Classical and Medieval Literature Criticism, 93; "Into the Whirlwind of Suffering: Resistance and Transformation," Second Opinion, Nov 88; "Nicholas of Cusa," in Medieval Philosophers, vol 15, Dictionary of Literary Biography, 92; "Isaiah Meets the Seraph: Breaking Ranks in Dionysius and Eriugena?" in Eriugena: East and West, 94. **CONTACT ADDRESS** Gwynedd-Mercy Col, Gwynedd Valley, PA 19437-0901. **EMAIL** duclow.d@gmc.edu

DUDE, CARL K.
PERSONAL Born 12/11/1938, Brooklyn, NY **DISCIPLINE** RELIGION **EDUCATION** Trinity Hall Col and Sem CO, Dr Div 94, Dr Hum 96; NYork Academy of Science and Amer Assoc Adv Science, Post doctoral fellow; Polytech Univ NYork and Univ RI, undergrad: engineering, science, admin. **CAREER** Am Fellowship Church, Ordained Bishop, 98-; American Ministerial Assoc, Pastor; NY Academy of Science, active mem. **HONORS AND AWARDS** NYS Conspicuous Ser Medal; President's National Medal Patriotism; Who's Who in the World; post doctoral fel; bishop. **MEMBERSHIPS** ACS; ACA; ACC; NA; IIE; AMP; APS; NAS. **RESEARCH** Theology; psychology; sociology; engineering and science **SELECTED PUBLICATIONS** Auth, Century Walk, Engraved Brick, My Honor, Univ RI. **CONTACT ADDRESS** American Fellowship Church, 80-08 45th Av, Elmhurst, NY 11373.

DUDZIAK, MARY L.
PERSONAL Born 06/15/1956, Oakland, CA, d, 1 child **DISCIPLINE** LAW, LEGAL HISTORY **EDUCATION** Univ Calif, Berkeley, AB, 78; Yale, JD, 84, MA, 86, MPhil, 86, PhD, 92. **CAREER** Assoc prof, Univ Iowa, 86-90, prof, 90-98; vis prof, Univ Southern Calif, 97-98, prof, 98-. **HONORS AND AWARDS** Charlotte W. Newcombe Fel/Woodrow Wilson Fel, 86-89; Scholars Development Awd, Nancy S. Truman Library Inst, 92; travel grant, Eisenhower World Affairs Inst, 93; Theodore C. Sorenson Fel, Kennedy Library Found, 97; Moody grant, Johnson Library, 98; OAH-JAAS Fel for Short-term travel to Japan, 2000. **MEMBERSHIPS** Org of Am Hists, Am Studies Asn, Am Hist Asn, Am Soc for Legal Hist, Law & Soc Asn, Soc for Hists of Am Foreign Relations, Soc Sci Hist Asn. **RESEARCH** Impact of foreign affairs on U.S. civil rights policy during the cold war; role of U.S. Constitutionalism overseas during the 20th century. **SELECTED PUBLICATIONS** Auth, Cold War Civil Rights: Race and the Image of American Democracy, Princeton Univ Press (forthcoming 2000); articles in J of Am Hist, Stanford Law Rev, Southern Calif Law Rev, etc. **CONTACT ADDRESS** Sch of Law, Univ of So California, 699 Exposition Blvd, Los Angeles, CA 90089-0040.

DUERLINGER, JAMES
PERSONAL Born 02/08/1938, Milwaukee, WI, m, 1987, 5 children **DISCIPLINE** PHILOSOPHY **EDUCATION** Univ Wis, BA, 61; PhD, 66; Univ Wash, MA, 63. **CAREER** Asst prof, 66-71, Univ Wis, Madison; assoc prof, 71-88, prof, 88-, Univ Iowa. **HONORS AND AWARDS** Sr Fulbright Fel, India, 93. **MEMBERSHIPS** Am Philos Asn. **RESEARCH** Indian phil, Buddhism, Greek phil, phil of relig, comparative phil. **SE-**

LECTED PUBLICATIONS Auth, "Aristotle's Conception of the Syllogism," Mind 77 (68): 480-499; auth, "Predication and Inherence in Aristotle's Categories," Phronesis 15 (70): 179-202; auth, "The Verbal Dispute in Hume's Dialogues," Archiv Fur Geschichte Der Philosophie 53 (71): 22-34; auth, "Unspoken Connections in the Design Argument," Philos and Phenomenol Res 42 (82): 519-529; ed, Ultimate Reality and Spiritual Discipline, Paragon House, 84; auth, "Candrakirti's Denial of Self," Philos E and W 34 (84): 261-272; auth, "The Ontology of Plato's Sophist: the Problems of Falsehood, Non-Being, and Being, and their Solutions," The Mod Schoolman 65 (88): 151-184; auth, "A Translation of Vasubandhu's 'Refutation of the Theory of Selfhood: A Resolution of Questions about Persons,'" J of Indian Philos 17 (89): 137-187; auth, "Reductionist and Nonreductionist Theories of Persons in Indian Buddhist Philosophy," J of Indian Philos 21 (93): 79-101; auth, "Vasubandhu's Philosophical Critique of the Vatsiputriyas' Theory of Persons (I), (II), and (III)," J of Indian Philos 28 (00): 1-46. **CONTACT ADDRESS** Philosophy Dept, Univ of Iowa, Iowa City, IA 52242. **EMAIL** james-duerlinger@uiowa.edu

DUFFY, STEPHEN JOSEPH
PERSONAL Born 10/14/1930, Philadelphia, PA **DISCIPLINE** RELIGION, PHILOSOPHY **EDUCATION** Marist Col, BA, 51; Pontif Gregorian Univ, STL, 58; Cath Univ Am, STD(theol), 69. **CAREER** Lectr patristics, Marist Col, 56; lectr theol, Notre Dame Sem, 61-85; prof relig studies, Loyola Univ, La, 70-. **HONORS AND AWARDS** Jesuit Coun Theol Reflection res grant, 75; La Comm Humanities lectureship grant, 77-78. **MEMBERSHIPS** Am Acad Relig; Cath Theol Soc Am; Col Theoll Soc; AAUP. **RESEARCH** Systematic theology; historical theology. **SELECTED PUBLICATIONS** Auth, The Graced Horizon; auth, Dynamics of Grace. **CONTACT ADDRESS** Loyola Univ, New Orleans, 6363 St Charles Ave, New Orleans, LA 70118-6195. **EMAIL** sjduffy@loyno.edu

DUFOUR, JOHN H.
PERSONAL s, 3 children **DISCIPLINE** PHILOSOPHY **EDUCATION** Rutgers Univ, BA, 90; Yale Univ, MA, 93, M.Phil, 93. **CAREER** Instr, 95-, TVI Community Col, Albuquerque. **MEMBERSHIPS** APA; Amer Indian Phil Assn. **RESEARCH** Epistemology; ethics; phil of religion; Native Amer phil. **CONTACT ADDRESS** Dept of Arts and Sciences, TVI Comm Col, 525 Buena Vista S.E., Albuquerque, NM 87106. **EMAIL** john.havens-dufour@yale.edu

DUKE, STEVEN BARRY
PERSONAL Born 07/31/1934, Mesa, AZ, s, 6 children **DISCIPLINE** CRIMINAL LAW & PROCEDURE **EDUCATION** Ariz State Univ, BS, 56; Univ Ariz, JD, 59; Yale Univ, LLM, 61. **CAREER** Law clerk, US Supreme Court, 59-60; fel law, Yale Univ, 60-61, from asst prof to assoc prof, 61-65; vis prof, Univ Calif, Berkeley, 65-66; prof law, Yale Univ, 66-, Dir, New Haven Legal Assistance, Inc, 67-71; mem, Conn Comn on Medico-Legal Investigations, 77-. **MEMBERSHIPS** Nat Asn Criminal Defense Coun; ACLU. **RESEARCH** Criminal law and drug policy. **SELECTED PUBLICATIONS** Auth, The Right to Appointed Counsel, Am Criminal Law Rev, 3/75; Bail Reform for the Eighties: A Reply to Senator Kennedy, Fordham Law Rev, 6/81; America's Longest War: Rethinking Our Tragic Crusade Against Drugs, 94; Drug Prohibition: An Unnatural Disaster, 27 Conn Law Rev, 95. **CONTACT ADDRESS** Law Sch, Yale Univ, PO Box 208215, New Haven, CT 06520-8215. **EMAIL** steven.duke@yale.edu

DUKEMINIER, JESSE
PERSONAL Born 08/12/1925, West Point, MS **DISCIPLINE** LAW **EDUCATION** Harvard Univ, AB, 48; Yale Univ, LLB, 51. **CAREER** Atty at law, New York, 51-53; asst prof law, Univ Minn, 54-55; from assoc prof to prof, Univ Ky, 55-63; Prof Law Univ Calif, Los Angeles, 63-. **HONORS AND AWARDS** Distinguished Teaching Awd, Univ Calif, Los Angeles, 76. **MEMBERSHIPS** Am Bar Asn. **RESEARCH** Property; estate planning; land planning and development. **SELECTED PUBLICATIONS** Auth, Property, Aspen Publ, 4th ed, 98; auth, Wills, Trusts, and Estates, Aspen Publ, 6th ed, 00. **CONTACT ADDRESS** Law School, Univ of California, Los Angeles, Los Angeles, CA 90024.

DUMAIN, HAROLD
PERSONAL Born 03/03/1927, Utica, NY, m, 1965, 2 children **DISCIPLINE** PHILOSOPHY **EDUCATION** SUNY at Buffalo, BA, 50, MSW, 52. **CAREER** Gowanda Psychiatric Center, Dir of Soc Serv, 71-83. **HONORS AND AWARDS** US Victory Medal, WW II, US Army, Occupation Medal. **RESEARCH** Psychiatry; schizophrenia **SELECTED PUBLICATIONS** Auth, A Synthesis of Philosophy, Philo Lib, NY, 75; Professional Problems Contingent to Theory, Jour of Psychiatric Soc Work, 54; Jour of Hospital and Community Psychiatry, coauth, 71. **CONTACT ADDRESS** 4628 Pinecrest Terrace, Eden, NY 14057.

DUMAIS, MONIQUE
PERSONAL Born 09/08/1939, Rimouski, PQ, Canada, s **DISCIPLINE** THEOLOGY; ETHICS **EDUCATION** Universite du Quebec a Rimouski, BA, 70; Harvard Univ, ThM, 73; Union Theol Seminary, PhD, 77. **CAREER** Prof, 70-, Dept Head, 85-89, Universite du Quebec a Rimouski **HONORS AND AWARDS** Bourse de recherche libe du CRSH du Canada **MEMBERSHIPS** Societe canadienne de theologie; Soc canadienne des sciences religieuses; Soc quebecoise des sciences religieuses; Amer Acad of Religion; Assoc des theologiens pour l etude de la morale **RESEARCH** Women and religion; women and the catholic church; ethics in feminist discourses; ethics and women **SELECTED PUBLICATIONS** Auth, Os direitos da mulher, 93; Los derechos de la mujer, 93; Diversite des utilisations feministes de concept experiences des femmes en sciences religieuses, 93; L'autre Parole, lieu de convergence d'une militance et d'une recherche feministes, L'autre Parole no 69, 96; Preoccupations ecologiques et ethique feministe, Religiologiques 13, 96; Ethique feministe de relation et perspectives sur le corps, Laval theologique et philosophique 53, 97; Une ethique de relation soutenue par une dynamique feministe dans las sphere pedagogique, Ethica, 97; Christa et la reconnaissance des femmes, L'autre Parole, 98; Traversees ethiques dans les langages de femmes, Reseaux, 98; Femmes et Pauvrete, 98; avec Marie Beaulieu, Mener sa barque a bonport. Cathier de reflexion ethique sur les interventions aupres des femmes en situation de pauvrete, 98. **CONTACT ADDRESS** Dept de sciences religieuses et ethique, Univ of Quebec, Rimouski, Rimouski, QC, Canada G5L 3A1. **EMAIL** monique_dumais@uqar.qc.ca

DUMONT, LLOYD F.
PERSONAL Born 04/29/1951, Philadelphia, PA, m, 1984, 4 children **DISCIPLINE** SOCIOLOGY, CRIMINAL JUSTICE **EDUCATION** Gloucester County Col, AA, 73; Glassboro State Col, BA, 92; St Joseph's Univ, MS, 95. **CAREER** Police Off, Wash Twp Police, 74-76; County Detective, Gloucester County, 76-89; Spec Agent, Pa State Bureau, 89-90; Lieutenant, Wash Twp Police, 90-99; Adj Prof, Gloucester County Col, 92-; Adj Prof, Rowan Univ, 95-98; Adj Prof, Fairleigh Dickinson Univ, 00-; Adj Prof, Gloucester County Police Acad, 00-. **MEMBERSHIPS** Intl Asn of Chiefs of Police; NJ Narcotics Officers Asn; Intl Narcotics Officers Asn; VIDOCQ Soc; Am Soc of Law Enforcement Trainers. **SELECTED PUBLICATIONS** Auth, "Recognizing Post Shooting Trauma," Law and Order Magazine, 99; auth, "Minimizing Undercover Violence," Law and Order Magazine, 00. **CONTACT ADDRESS** Dept Sociol/Criminal Justice, Fairleigh Dickinson Univ, 1400 Tanyard Rd, Sewell, NJ 08080. **EMAIL** ldumont@gccnj.edu

DUNAWAY, BAXTER
DISCIPLINE REAL ESTATE FINANCE AND TRANSACTIONS **EDUCATION** Auburn Univ, BS, 50; G Wash Univ, JD, 60. **CAREER** Chem engr, 50-56; US Patent off examr, 56-60; patent atty, Petro-Tex Chemical Corporation, 60-63; Patent Attorney, Ethyl Corporation, 64; Counsel, Petro-Tex Chem Corp, 65-73; regist patent atty, US Patent Off. **HONORS AND AWARDS** JD with hon(s). **MEMBERSHIPS** Mem, State Bar TX; Am Bar Assn, Conejo Bd of Realtors. **SELECTED PUBLICATIONS** Auth, Law of Distressed Real Estate, 85-92; FIRREA: Law and Practice, 92; co-ed, Distressed Business and Real Estate Newsletter. **CONTACT ADDRESS** Sch of Law, Pepperdine Univ, 24255 Pacific Coast Hwy, Malibu, CA 90263.

DUNCAN, ELMER H.
PERSONAL Born 05/26/1933, Fullerton, KY, m, 1956 **DISCIPLINE** PHILOSOPHY **EDUCATION** Univ Cincinnati, BA, 58, MA, 60, PhD (philos), 62. **CAREER** From asst prof to assoc prof, 62-71, Prof Philos, Baylor Univ, 71-, Am Coun Learned Soc travel grant, 8th Int Cong Aesthetics, Darmstadt, Ger, 76. **MEMBERSHIPS** Western Div Am Philos Asn; Am Soc Aesthet; Southwestern Philos Soc(pres, 74-). **SELECTED PUBLICATIONS** Auth, Twenty-Year Cumulative Index to the Journal of Aesthetics and Art Criticism, AMS Reprint Co, 64; Rules and exceptions in ethics and aesthetics, Philos & Phenomenol Res, 12/66; Aruguments used in ethics and aesthetics: Two differences, J Aesthet & Art Criticism, summer 67; 18th Century Scottish philosophy: Its impact on the American West, Southwestern J Philos, winter 75; Makers of the Modern Theological Mind: Soren Kierkegaard, Word Bks, 76; coauth, Thomas Reid's criticisms of Adam Smith's Theory of Moral Sentiments, J Hist Ideas, 7-9/77. **CONTACT ADDRESS** Dept of Philos Col Arts and Sci, Baylor Univ, Waco, Waco, TX 76703.

DUNCAN, JOHN C., JR.
PERSONAL Born 06/05/1942, Philadelphia, PA, m, 1989 **DISCIPLINE** LAW **EDUCATION** DePauw Univ, BA 1964; Univ of MI, MS, MA 1965-66; Stanford Univ, PhD 1971; Yale Law Schl, JD 1976; Southeastern Univ, MBPA 1985. **CAREER** Iraklion AS, Crete, Greece, Staff Judge Advocate 1978-79; Tactical Air Command, Chief Civil Law 1979-81; Hurlburt Field, FL, Staff Judge Advocate 1981-82; AF JAG Career Mgmnt, Chief Military Manpower & Analysis (JAG) 1982-84; Legal Advisor to the Asst to the Secretary of Defense (Intelligence Oversight); Deputy Judge Advocate, United Nations Command, US Forces in Korea, Deputy Staff Judge Advocate, HQ Tactical Ser Command, Langley AFB, VA. **HONORS AND AWARDS** Rector Scholar, DePauw Univ 1960-64; Graduate w/distinction DePauw Univ, Leopold Schepp Found Schlrshp 1965-66; Schlrshp Stanford Univ 1967; Flwshp Richardson Dilworth Fellow Yale 1974-76; Outstanding New Teacher Awd, Southeastern Univ 1985. **MEMBERSHIPS** Life mem Alpha Phi Alpha 1968; prof various Univer 1976-; cnslr Marriage Family & Child 1976-; ODO 1976, Amer Assoc of Marriage & Family Therapists 1976; Inter Amer Bar Assoc 1983; ABA, FBA, NBA. **CONTACT ADDRESS** Headquarters Tactical Air Command, Hampton, VA 23665.

DUNDON, STANISLAUS
PERSONAL Born 07/18/1935, Milwaukee, WI, m, 1990, 9 children **DISCIPLINE** PHILOSOPHY **EDUCATION** PhD **CAREER** Cal Poly San Luis Obispo; Univ Calif Davis; Calif State Univ Sacramento, nat coordr, Sould of Agr Proj, 99-; Cong Sci fel; Rockafeller Found grant; NSF fel; Joyce Found. **MEMBERSHIPS** APA; Agr, Food, & Hum Values Soc. **RESEARCH** Agricultural ethics. **SELECTED PUBLICATIONS** Auth Sources of Eikst Principles for an Agricultural Ethic. **CONTACT ADDRESS** PO Box 72084, Davis, CA 95617. **EMAIL** sjdundon@davis.com

DUNLAP, ELDEN DALE
PERSONAL Born 11/01/1921, Rose Hill, KS, m, 1944, 3 children **DISCIPLINE** THEOLOGY **EDUCATION** Southwestern Col, AB, 43; Garrett Theol Sem, BD, 45; Northwestern Univ, MA, 47; Yale Univ, PhD (contemp theol), 56 **CAREER** From instr to east prof relig, Southwestern Col, 51-55, assoc prof and dean col, 55-59; assoc prof theol, 59-64, actg pres, 72-73, Prof Theol, Saint Paul Sch Theol, 64-, Dean, 70-, Mem, Bd Higher Educ and Ministry, United Methodist Church, 80-, chmn, Ministry Study Comt, 80-84. **HONORS AND AWARDS** DD, Southwestern Col. Kans, 71. **MEMBERSHIPS** Am Theol Soc; Am Soc Church Hist; Am Acad Relig; NAm Acad Ecumenists. **RESEARCH** Development of Methodist theology; ecumenical movement. **SELECTED PUBLICATIONS** Coauth, The ministry and the sacraments, In: We Believe, Abingdon, 62; auth, The Methodist ministry-a response, Christian Advocate, 4/63; coauth, Stewardship and vocation, In: All God's People, Bd Laity, 69; auth, United Methodist System of Itinerant Ministry, Occasional Papers, 1/80. **CONTACT ADDRESS** Saint Paul Sch of Theol, Truman Rd and Van Brunt Blvd, Kansas City, MO 64127.

DUNLOP, CHARLES
DISCIPLINE PHILOSOPHY **EDUCATION** Stanford Univ, BA, 65; Wright State Univ, MS, 87; Duke Univ, MA, 69, PhD, 73. **CAREER** Prof & ch dept philos, Univ Mich Flint **RESEARCH** Cognitive science; philosophy of mind; social aspects of computing. **SELECTED PUBLICATIONS** Auth, Philosophical Essays on Dreaming, Cornell UP, 77 & Computer Ethics, Encycl of Comput Sci, 4th ed, 98; coauth, Glossary of Cognitive Science, Paragon House, 93 & Computerization and Controversy: Value Conflicts and Social Choices, Acad Press, 91; rev, William Calvin's How Brains Think, in Minds and Machines, 98. **CONTACT ADDRESS** Dept of Philosophy, Univ of Michigan, Flint, Flint, MI 48502-2186.

DUNN, JOE PENDER
PERSONAL Born 09/21/1945, Cape Girardeau, MO, m, 1972, 1 child **DISCIPLINE** AMERICAN HISTORY, INTERNATIONAL RELATIONS **EDUCATION** Southeast Mo State Col, BS, 67; Univ Mo-Columbia, MA, 68, PhD (hist), 73. **CAREER** Asst prof hist and polit sci, Univ Md, Europe Div, 73-77; asst prof, 77-81, Assoc Prof Hist 81-88, Prof & Department Chair, 88-; Converse Col. **RESEARCH** Recent American political and social history; national security; the Vietnam war. **SELECTED PUBLICATIONS** Auth, "Teaching The Vietnam War," Center for the Study of Armament and Disarmament, 90; auth, "The Future South," University of Illinois Press, 91; auth, "Desk Warrior: Memoirs of a Combat REMF," Pearson Publishing, 99. **CONTACT ADDRESS** Dept of History, Converse Col, Spartanburg, SC 29301. **EMAIL** joe.dunn@converse.edu

DUNN, JON MICHAEL
PERSONAL Born 06/19/1941, St. Wayne, IN, m, 1964, 2 children **DISCIPLINE** PHILOSOPHY LOGIC **EDUCATION** Oberlin Col, AB, 63; Univ Pittsburg, PhD (philos), 66. **CAREER** Asst prof philos, Wayne State Univ, 66-69; assoc prof, 69-76, oscar Ewing prof of philosophy, 89-; Prof Philos, Ind Univ, Bloomington, 76-, Oscar Ewing Prof of Philos, 89-; CHMN, 80-84; 94-97; Prof computer sci 89-, Exec Assoc Dean Col of Arts and Sci(s), 88-93; Dean Sch of Informatics, 99-; Vis asst prof, Yale Univ, 68-69; Fulbright-Hays sr res scholar, Australian-Am Educ Found, 75-76; vis fel, Inst Advan Studies, Australian Nat Univ, 75-76; sr vis, Math Inst, Oxford Univ, 78; ed, J Symbolic Logic, 82-. **MEMBERSHIPS** Asn Symbolic Logic; Am Philos Asn; AAAS; Philos of Sci Asn; Soc Exact Philos. **RESEARCH** Algebraic logic; propositional calculi information-based logics. **SELECTED PUBLICATIONS** Auth, Gaggle theory: An abstraction of Galois connections and residuation, with applications to negation, implication, and various logical operators, in Logics in Al, ed. J. van Eijck, Springer Verlag, 31-51, 90; auth, Entailment: The Logic of Relevance and Necessity, Vol. 2 with A.R. Anderson and N.D. Belnap Princeton, NJ: Princeton University Press, 92; auth, A Comparative Study of Various Semantical Treatments of Negation: A History of Formal Negation, in What is Negation, eds. D. Gabbay and H. Wansing, Kluwer Academic Publishers, 23-61, 99. **CONTACT ADDRESS** Sch of Informatics, Indiana Univ, Bloomington, Bloomington, IN 47405. **EMAIL** dunn@indiana.edu

DUNNAVANT, ANTHONY L.
PERSONAL Born 06/23/1954, Hagerstown, MD, m, 2000, 4 children **DISCIPLINE** RELIGION **EDUCATION** Fairmont State, BA, 74; West VA Univ, MA, 76; Vanderbilt, MDiv, 79, MA, 81, PhD, 84. **CAREER** Cent Mich Univ, asst prof, 86-87; Lexington Theo Sem, asst prof, 87-88, assoc. prof, 88-93, prof, 93-, dean 98-. **MEMBERSHIPS** AAR, AAUP, ASCH, ASR, RRA **RESEARCH** Christianity in Appalachia; congreg studies; Christ primitivism of Stone-Campbell trad. **SELECTED PUBLICATIONS** Auth, Backgrounds for Congregational Portraits: Ideas and Resources for Local Church Historians in the Stone-Campbell tradition, foreword by James M. Seale, Nash, TN, Disciples of Christ Hist Soc, 94; Restructure: Four Historical Ideals in the Campbell-Stone Movement and the Development of the Polity of the Christian Church, Theol and Rel, NY, Peter Lang, 93; ed Christian Faith Seeking Historical Understanding: Essays in Honor of H. Jack Forstman Mercer Univ. Press, 97; Explorations in the Stone-Campbell Traditions: Essays in Honor of Herman A. Norton, Disciples Divinity House at Vanderbilt, 95; art, History and Ecclesiology in Recent Disciples Literature, in: Mid-Stream, 93; Evangelization and Eschatology: Lost Link in the Disciples Tradition?, Lexington Theol Quart, 93. **CONTACT ADDRESS** Lexington Theol Sem, 631 South Limestone, Lexington, KY 40508. **EMAIL** tdunnavant@lextheo.edu

DUNNE, JOHN SCRIBNER
PERSONAL Born 12/03/1929, Waco, TX **DISCIPLINE** PHILOSOPHY, THEOLOGY **EDUCATION** Univ Notre Dame, AB, 51; Gregorian Univ, Rome, STL, 54, STD, 58. **CAREER** From instr to assoc prof, 57-69, Prof Theol, Univ Notre Dame, 69-, Rockefeller res and writing grant, 60-61; vis prof, Divinity Sch, Univ Chicago, 68; Thomas More lectr, Yale Univ, 71, lectr relig studies, 72-73; adv ed, Rev Politics; Sarum lectr, Oxford Univ, 76-77. **HONORS AND AWARDS** Harbison Distinguished Teaching Awd, 69. **MEMBERSHIPS** Am Aced Relig. **RESEARCH** Mysticism; autobiography; death and myth. **SELECTED PUBLICATIONS** Auth, Myth and Culture in Theology and Literature, A Conversation With Dunne, John, S., Reli Lit, Vol 25, 93; auth, The City of the Gods, auth, A Search for God in Time & Memory, auth, The Weay of all the Earth, auth, Time & Myth, auth, The Reasons of the Heart, auth, The Church of the Poor David, auth, The House of Wisdom, auth, The Homing Spirit, auth, The Peace of the Present, Auth, Love's Mind, auth, The Music of Time, auth, the Mystic Road of Love, auth, Reading the Gospel. **CONTACT ADDRESS** Univ of Notre Dame, 327 Oshaugnessy Hall, PO Box L, Notre Dame, IN 46556. **EMAIL** dunne.1@md.edu

DUNNE, TAD
PERSONAL Born 12/19/1938, Detroit, MI, m **DISCIPLINE** THEOLOGY, MEDICAL ETHICS **EDUCATION** BA; MA; MA; PhD; M Div. **MEMBERSHIPS** CTSA; CTS. **RESEARCH** Theology and philosophy of aesthetics, spirituality, psychology; thought of Bernard Lonergan. **SELECTED PUBLICATIONS** Auth, Lonergan and Spirituality, Loyola Press (Chicago, 85); auth, "What Do I Do When I Paint?" Method: J Lonergan Stud 16 (98): 103-132. **CONTACT ADDRESS** Dept Letters, Marygrove Col, 8425 West McNichols Rd, Detroit, MI 48221-2546.

DUNNING, STEPHEN NORTHROP
PERSONAL Born 06/17/1941, Philadelphia, PA, m, 1974, 3 children **DISCIPLINE** MODERN WESTERN RELIGIOUS THOUGHT **EDUCATION** Goddard Col, BA, 64; Harvard Univ, MDiv, 69, PhD, 77. **CAREER** Instr, 77-78, asst prof Mod Western Relig Thought, Univ Pa, 78-84; chair, grad prog in rel studies, 87-94 and 95-96; assoc prof and dept chair, 96-. **HONORS AND AWARDS** Kent Fel for Grad Study (Danforth Found), 71-74; Deutscher Akademischer Austauschdienst (DAAD) Fel, 74-76; Nat Endowment for Humanities fel, 82-83; Lindback Awd for Distinguished Teaching, 93; Templeton Sci and Relig Course Awd, 96-97. **MEMBERSHIPS** Hegel Soc Am; Soren KierbeKaard Society; Am Acad Relig; Philos of Relig Group, Greater Philadelphia Philos Consortium; Soc of Christian Philosophers. **RESEARCH** Philosophy of history; religious language; hermeneutics; dialectical types of thinking. **SELECTED PUBLICATIONS** Auth, The Tongues of Men: Hegel and Hamann on Religious Language and History, Am Acad Relig Dissertation Ser, No 27, Scholars Press, 79; auth, "History and Phenomenology: Dialectical Structure in Ricoeur's The Symbolism of Evil," (Harvard Theological Review, 83), 343-363; Kierkegaard's Dialectic of Inwardness: A structural Analysis of the Theory of Stages, Princeton, 85; auth, " Particularity Not Scandalous: Hegel's Contribution to Philosophy of Religion," In Hegel's Philosophy of Religion: Proceedings of the 1990 Meeting of the Hegel Society of America," ed David Kolb (Albany: SUNY Press, 92), 143-158; auth, "Who Sets the Task? Kierkegaard on Authority," in Foundations of Kierkegaard's Vision of Community: Religion, Ethics, and Politics in Kierkegaard, ed by C. Stephen Evans and George Connell (NJ: Humanities Press, 92), 18-32; auth, "Paradoxes in Interpretation: Kierkegaard and Gadamer," in Kierkegaard in Post/Modernity, ed by Martin J Matusik and Merold Westphal (Bloomington: Indiana Univ Press, 95), 125-141; Dialetical Readings: Three Type of Interpretation, Penn State Press, 97. **CONTACT ADDRESS** Dept of Relig Studies, Univ of Pennsylvania, Logan Hall, 249 S 86th St, Philadelphia, PA 19104-6304. **EMAIL** sdunning@ccat.sas.upenn.edu

DUPRE, ANNE P.
DISCIPLINE LAW **EDUCATION** Univ RI, BA; Univ Ga, JD. **CAREER** Teacher, West Palm Beach, 80-85; Judicial Law Clerk, Washington DC, 89-90; Assoc, Shaw, Pittman, Potts & Trowbridge, Washington DC, 90-94; Asst Prof to Assoc Prof, Univ Ga, 94-. **HONORS AND AWARDS** Lilly Teaching Fel; Fac Book Awd; O'Byrne Awd; Intl Fel. **MEMBERSHIPS** Am Asn of Law Sch; Educ Law Asn. **RESEARCH** Law and Education. **SELECTED PUBLICATIONS** Auth, "Foreign Duty," Business Law Today, 92; auth, "Export Controls," 9 Technology Law Notes, 92; auth, "New Family and Medical Leave Act Guarantees Unpaid Leave," The Changing Workplace, 93; auth, "DuPont Ordered to Disband Joint Labor-Management Committees," The Workplace Health and Safety Monitor, 94; auth, "Should Students Have Constitutional Rights? Keeping Order in the Public Schools," George Washington Law Review, (96): 49-105; auth, "Equal Protection of the Laws: Recent Judicial Decisions and Their Implications for Public Educational Institutions," Educ Law Rep, (97): 1-19; auth, "Disability and the Public Schools: The Case Against Inclusion," Washington Law Review, (97): 775-858; auth, "Disability, Deference, and the Integrity of the Academic Enterprise, GA Law Review, (98): 393-473; auth, "A Study in Double Standards, Discipline and the Disable Student," Washington Law Review, (00): 1-96. **CONTACT ADDRESS** Sch of Law, Univ of Georgia, 0 GA Univ, Athens, GA 30602-0002. **EMAIL** adupre@uga.edu

DUPRIEST, TRAVIS TALMADGE, JR.
PERSONAL Born 08/15/1944, Richmond, VA, m, 2000, 2 children **DISCIPLINE** ENGLISH LITERATURE; LITERATURE; SPIRITUALITY; AND CREATIVE NON-FICTION **EDUCATION** Richmond Univ, BA; Harvard Divinity Sch, MTS; Univ Ky, PhD. **CAREER** English, Carthage Col. **HONORS AND AWARDS** Grants: Nat Endowment Hum; Univ Chicago Midwest Fac Seminar; danforth fel, pres nat huguenot soc; fel huguenot, fel ctr renaissance & reformation studies; vis/occas fel univ chicago, cambridge univ. **MEMBERSHIPS** MLA; Conference Christianity & Literature; former dir Honors Prog Carthage. **SELECTED PUBLICATIONS** Auth, Noon at Smyrna; Summer Storm; Soapstone Wall; auth, Jeremy Taylor's Discourse on Friendship, Scholars Facsimiles; Katherine Philips' Poems, scholars Facsimiles. **CONTACT ADDRESS** Carthage Col, 2001 Alford Dr., Kenosha, WI 53140. **EMAIL** dekoven.center@juno.com

DUQUETTE, DAVID A.
PERSONAL Born 05/22/1949, Nashua, NH **DISCIPLINE** PHILOSOPHY **EDUCATION** Univ NH, BA, 71; Rensselear Polytech Inst, MS, 76; Univ Kans, PhD, 85. **CAREER** Instr, Rensselear Polytech Inst, 75; Assoc Prof, St Norbert Col, 85-. **MEMBERSHIPS** Am Philos Asn, AMINTAPHIL, Hegel Soc of Am. **RESEARCH** Hegel, Marx, Philosophy of Human Rights; History of Political Thought. **SELECTED PUBLICATIONS** Auth, "The Political Significance of Hegel's concept of Recognition in the Phenomenology," International Library of Critical Essays in the History of Philosophy, 98; auth, "The Political Significance of Hegel's Concept of Recognition," in Hegel's Phenomenology of Spirit: A Reappraisal, 97; auth, "A Social and Political Critique of Capitalism," in Rending and Renewing the Social Order Vol 12 in Social Philosophy Today, (96): 219-231; auth, "Philosophy, Anthropology, and Universal Human Rights," in The Social Power of Ideas Vol 11 in Social Philosophy Today, (95): 139-153; auth, "A Critique of the Technological Interpretation of Marx's Historical Materialism," Philosophy of the Social Science, (92): 157-186; auth, "The Basis for Recognition of Human Rights," Southwest Philosophy Review, (92): 49-56; auth, "Kant, Hegel, and the Possibility of a Speculative Logic," in Essays on Hegel's Logic, SUNY Press, 90; auth, "Civic and Political Freedom in Hegel," Southwest Philosophical Review, (90): 37-44; auth, "Marx's Idealist Critique of Hegel's Theory of Politics and Society," Review of Politics, (89): 218-240; auth, "From Disciple to Antagonist: Feuerbach's Critique of Hegel," Philosophy and Theology: Marquette University Quarterly, (88): 183-199. **CONTACT ADDRESS** St. Norbert Col, 100 Grant St, De Pere, WI 54115-2002. **EMAIL** duquda@mail.snc.edu

DURAM, JAMES C.
PERSONAL d, 2 children **DISCIPLINE** US CONSTITUTIONAL, LEGAL, POLITICAL, FAMILY HISTORY AND HISTORIOGRAPHY **EDUCATION** W Michigan Univ, Ba, MA; Wayne State Univ, PhD. **CAREER** Dept prelaw adv; prof-. **HONORS AND AWARDS** Fulbright fel, Intl Inst Soc Hist, Amsterdam. **RESEARCH** Uses and dynamics of constitutional argumentation. **SELECTED PUBLICATIONS** Auth, books on Norman Thomas, US Supreme Court Justice; William O. Douglas, President Dwight D Eisenhower's role in the School Segregation Cases; Biography of a Civil War Chaplain. **CONTACT ADDRESS** Dept of Hist, Wichita State Univ, 1845 Fairmont, Wichita, KS 67260-0062. **EMAIL** duram@twsuvm.uc.twsu.edu

DURHAM, KEN R.
PERSONAL Born 03/21/1948, m, 1973, 2 children **DISCIPLINE** RELIGION AND COMMUNICATION **EDUCATION** David Lipscomb Col, BA, 70; La State Univ, MA, 72, PhD, 74; post doc grad work Austin Presbyterian theol sem, Abilene Christian Univ. **CAREER** Instr, Inst Christian Studies, 77-78; vis fac, 88; lectr, Okla Christian Univ, 91; David Lipscomb Univ, 89; adjunct fac, Harding Univ Grad Sch Rel, 89; contrib ed, 21st Century Christian, 93-; vis fac, 97-. **SELECTED PUBLICATIONS** Auth, Speaking From the Heart: Richer Relationships Through Communication, Sweet Publ, 86; Jesus, Our Mentor and Model, Baker Bk House, 87; co-auth, Becoming Persons of Integrity, Baker Bk House, 88; Anchors For the Asking, Baker Bk House, 89. **CONTACT ADDRESS** Dept of Relig, Pepperdine Univ, 24255 Pacific Coast Hwy, Malibu, CA 90263. **EMAIL** kdurham@pepperdine.edu

DURLAND, WILLIAM
PERSONAL Born 03/28/1931, New York, NY, m, 1977, 4 children **DISCIPLINE** LAW, PHILOSOPHY **EDUCATION** Buchnell Univ, BA, 53; Georgetown Law School, JD, 59; Univ Notre Dame, MA, 75; Union Graduate Sch, PhD, 77. **CAREER** Chair, Philos Dept, Purdue Univ, 74; chair, Pendle Hill Quaker Study Center, 88; Div chair, Soc Sci & Humanities, 99-2000; pres, Facultiys, 92-93. **HONORS AND AWARDS** Who's Who Among Am Teachers, 96; Colo State Humanitarian Awd, 99. **MEMBERSHIPS** Member Bar, Supreme Court of the United States. **RESEARCH** Biblical theology, Constitutional Law and History **SELECTED PUBLICATIONS** Auth, No King But Calser, 75; auth, Ethical Issues, 75; auth, People Pay for Peace, 80; auth, Conscience and Lee Law, 81; auth, The Illegality of War, 82; auth, The Apocalyptic Witness, 88; auth, God or Nations, 89; auth, the 21st Century Crisis in American Federalism, 2000. **CONTACT ADDRESS** Dept Soc Sci & Humanities, Trinidad State Junior Col, 600 Prospect St, Trinidad, CO 81082-2356. **EMAIL** dryland@RIA.net

DURNBAUGH, DONALD F.
PERSONAL Born 11/16/1927, Detroit, MI, m, 1952, 3 children **DISCIPLINE** CHURCH HISTORY, MODERN EUROPEAN HISTORY **EDUCATION** Manchester Col, BA, 49; Univ Mich, MA, 53; Univ Pa, PhD (hist), 60. **CAREER** Dir, Brethren Serv Comn, Austria, 53-56; lectr Brethren hist, Bethany Theol Sem, 58; from instr to asst prof hist, Juniata Col, 58-62; assoc prof, 62-70, Prof Church Hist, Bethany Theol Sem, 70-, Alternate serv, Brethren Serv Comn, Austria and Ger, 49-51 and 53-56; dir in Europe, Brethren Cols Abroad, 64-65; adj prof church hist, Northern Baptist Theol Sem, 68-71; assoc, Ctr Reformation and Free Church Studies, Chicago Theol Sem, 68-; Nat Endowment for Humanities res fel, 76-77. **MEMBERSHIPS** Am Soc Church Hist; Orgn Am Historians; NAm Acad Ecumenists; AHA; Am Soc Reformation Res. **RESEARCH** Modern European church history; German sectarian movements in America; Communitarian societies. **SELECTED PUBLICATIONS** Auth, Spiritual Life in Anabaptism, Church Hist, Vol 66, 97; The German Peasant War and Anabaptist Community of Goods, Church Hist, Vol 63, 94; Mennonite Entrepreneurs, Church Hist, Vol 66, 97; The German Peasant War and Anabaptist Community of Goods, Church Hist, Vol 63, 94; Spiritual Life in Anabaptism, Church Hist, Vol 66, 97; Mennonite Entrepreneurs, Church Hist, Vol 66, 97; The Writings of Philips, Dirk, J Church State, Vol 35, 93. **CONTACT ADDRESS** Bethany Theol Sem, Oak Brook, IL 60521.

DUSEK, RUDOLPH VALENTINE
PERSONAL Born 09/20/1941, Toronto, ON, Canada, m, 1993, 1 child **DISCIPLINE** PHILOSOPHY **EDUCATION** Yale Univ, BA, 63; Univ Tex, Austin, PhD(philos), 72. **CAREER** Instr, 66-70, asst prof, 70-81, prof Philos, Univ NH, 81-. **MEMBERSHIPS** Philos Sci Asn; hist sci so, Soc Lit & Sci; AAUP; Am Philos Assn; ISHPSSB, HOPOS, Radical Phil Assn. **RESEARCH** Evolutionary psychology; the science wars. **SELECTED PUBLICATIONS** Auth, contribr, Geodesy and the earth sciences in the philosophy of C S Peirce, In: Bicentennial Conference on History of Geology, New Eng Univ, 78; co-ed, Sociobiology: The debate evolves, 82 & coauth, Sociobiology: The unnatural selection of a new paradigm, 82, Philos Forum; Philos of Math and Physics in the Sokal Affair, Social Text, 97; Brecht and Lukaes as Teachers of Feyerabend and Lakotos, Hist of Hum Scis, 98; auth, The Holistic Inspirations of Physics, Rutgers, 99; auth, "Science Wars". **CONTACT ADDRESS** Philosophy Dept, Univ of New Hampshire, Durham, 125 Technology Dr, Durham, NH 03824-4724. **EMAIL** valdusek@aol.com

DUSKA, RONALD F.
PERSONAL Born 03/01/1937, Erie, PA, m, 7 children **DISCIPLINE** PHILOSOPHY **EDUCATION** St Mary's Col, BA, 58; St John's Univ, MA, 61; Northwestern Univ, PhD, 70. **CAREER** St. John's Univ, tchr fel, inst, 61-63; Rosemount Col, inst, asst prof, assoc prof, prof, 63-96; Villanova Univ, adj prof, 80-; St Joseph's Univ, adj prof, 85-; Penn State Univ, adj prof, 93-95; Univ Pennsylvania, adj prof, 94-96; The Am Col, Charles Lamont Post Ch of Ethics and the Professions, 96-. **MEMBERSHIPS** SBE, APA, Acad of Mgmt, IASB, ACPA, SASE, Amantifil **RESEARCH** Business ethics; ethical theory; moral development; ethics of finance and insurance. **SELECTED PUBLICATIONS** Auth, Ethics and Corporate Responsibility: Theory, Cases and Dilemmas, NY: Amer Heritage Custom Pub Group, 95; auth, Business Ethics, Princeton, Prentice-Hall, 90; auth, Education, Leadership and Business Ethics: Essays on the Work of Clarence Walton, Dordrecht, Kluwer

Acad Publ, 98; auth, To Disclose or Not to Disclose? That is the Question, Jour of the Am Society of CLU & ChFC, 97; auth, Whistleblowing, in: Encycl Dict of Bus Ethics, ed. P. Werhane & R.E. Freeman, Blackwell, 97; auth, Ethics and Compliance, Jour Am Society of CLU & ChFC, 98; auth, Employee Rights, Anthology of Bus ethics, ed. B. Frederick, Blackwell, 98. **CONTACT ADDRESS** American Col, 270 S Bryn Mawr Ave, Bryn Mawr, PA 19010. **EMAIL** ronaldd@amercoll.edu

DUTCHER-WALLS, PATRICIA
PERSONAL Born 03/17/1952, Glen Ridge, NJ, m, 1983, 2 children **DISCIPLINE** BIBLICAL STUDIES **EDUCATION** Col of Wooster, BA, 74; Harvard Div Sch, MDiv, 78; Graduate Theol Union, ThD, 94. **CAREER** Adj asst prof, Old Testament, United Theol Sem, 94-95; asst prof Old Testament & Hebrew Bible, Knox Col, 95- . **HONORS AND AWARDS** BA with honors; MDiv with honors; ThD with honors. **MEMBERSHIPS** AAR/SBL; Can Soc of Bibl Stud. **RESEARCH** Deuteronomistic history; feminist hermeneutics; sociological method. **SELECTED PUBLICATIONS** Auth, Political Correctness, The Reformed Tradition, and Pluralism: Implications for Theological Education, Theol Educ, 92; auth, Incarnation: Interaction as a Means of Grace in Carter, ed, Of Human Bondage and Divine Grace: A Global Testimony, Open Court, 92; auth, Narrative Art, Political Rhetoric: The Case of Athaliah and Joash, Sheffield Academic, 96; auth, The Social Location of the Deuteronomists: A Sociological Study of Factional Politics in Late Pre-Exilic Judah, in Chalcraft, ed, Social-Scientific Old Testament Criticism, Sheffield Academic, 97; auth, Sociological Directions in Feminist Biblical Studies, Social Compass, 99. **CONTACT ADDRESS** Knox Col, Ontario, 59 St George St, Toronto, ON, Canada M5S 2E6. **EMAIL** p.dutcher.walls@utoronto.ca

DWORKIN, GERALD
DISCIPLINE PHILOSOPHY **EDUCATION** Univ CA Berkeley, MA, PhD. **CAREER** Prof, Univ IL at Chicago. **RESEARCH** Ethics; polit philos; philos of law. **SELECTED PUBLICATIONS** Auth, The Serpent Beguiled Me and I did Eat: Entrapment and the Creation of Crime, Law and Philos, 85; The Theory and Practice of Autonomy, Cambridge, 88; Equal Respect and the Enforcement of Morality, Soc Philos Policy, 90. **CONTACT ADDRESS** Philos Dept, Univ of Illinois, Chicago, S Halsted St, PO Box 705, Chicago, IL 60607. **EMAIL** gdworkin@ucdavis.edu

DWORKIN, ROGER BARNETT
PERSONAL Born 01/19/1943, Cincinnati, OH, m, 1964, 2 children **DISCIPLINE** LAW TORTS **EDUCATION** Princeton Univ, AB, 63; Stanford Univ, JD, 66. **CAREER** Asst prof, 68-71, assoc prof, 71-74, Prof to Robert A. Lucas Prof of Law, Ind Univ, Bloomington, 74-, Vis prof, Sch of Med, Univ Washington, summers, 74-79, prof biomed hist, 80-82; vis prof law, Sch of Law, Univ Va, 78-79. **MEMBERSHIPS** Soc Health and Human Values; Inst Soc Ethics and Life Sci; AAAS. **RESEARCH** Law and biology; law and medicine. **CONTACT ADDRESS** School of Law, Indiana Univ, Bloomington, 211 S Ind Ave, Bloomington, IN 47405. **EMAIL** dworkin@indiana.edu

DWYER, JAMES G.
PERSONAL Born 09/27/1961, Albany, NY, m, 1992, 2 children **DISCIPLINE** LAW **EDUCATION** Boston Col, BA, 84; Yale Law School, JD, 87; Stanford Univ, PhD, 95. **CAREER** Chicago - Kent Col Law, v asst prof, 96-98; Univ WY Col Law, asst prof, 98-00; Asst Prof, Wm & Mary School of Law, 00-. **HONORS AND AWARDS** Cornell Univ, Young Scholar Award, 98. **MEMBERSHIPS** ABA **RESEARCH** Children and the law; religion and the law. **SELECTED PUBLICATIONS** Auth, Parent's Religion and Children's Welfare: Debunking the Doctrine of Parents' Rights, Calif Law Rev, 94; The Children We Abandon: Religious Exemptions to Child Welfare and Education Laws as Denials of Equal Protection to Children of Religious Objectors, N C Law Rev, 96; Religious Schools v. Children's Rights, Cornell Press, 96. **CONTACT ADDRESS** Sch of Law, Col of William and Mary, S Henry St, Williamsburg, VA 23187. **EMAIL** jgdwye@wm.edu

DWYER, SUSAN
DISCIPLINE PHILOSOPHY **EDUCATION** Adelaide Univ, BA; MIT, PhD. **RESEARCH** Theoretical and applied ethics. **SELECTED PUBLICATIONS** Ed, The Problem of Pornography, Wadsworth, 95; co-ed, The Problem of Abortion, Wadsworth, 97. **CONTACT ADDRESS** Philosophy Dept, McGill Univ, 845 Sherbrooke St, Montreal, QC, Canada H3A 2T5.

DYBOWSKI, BRIAN
PERSONAL Born 09/20/1938, Austin, TX, s **DISCIPLINE** PHILOSOPHY, PSYCHOLOGY **EDUCATION** Col Santa Fe (then St Michael's Col), BS, 61; Aquinas Inst, MA, 68; PhD, 70; Ohio State Univ, PhD, 73; St Mary's Univ, MA, 92; Univ St Thomas, Spirituality diploma, 92. **HONORS AND AWARDS** Manuel Lujan Awd for Excellence in Teaching; Fairfax Awd for Outstanding Teaching. **MEMBERSHIPS** Catholic Philos Asn, Fel of Catholic Scholars. **RESEARCH** Learning, Epistemology, Cognitive Psychology. **CONTACT ADDRESS** Dept Soc Sci, Col of Santa Fe, 1600 Saint Michaels Dr, Santa Fe, NM 87505-7615. **EMAIL** bdybowski@csf.edu

DYCH, WILLIAM V.
PERSONAL Born 06/25/1932, Philadelphia, PA, s **DISCIPLINE** THEOLOGY **EDUCATION** St Louis Univ, BA, 56; MA, 57; Univ of Munster Ger, PhD, 71. **CAREER** Instr, Georgetown Univ, 59-60; Assoc Prof, Woodstok Col, 71-78; Assoc Prof, Fordham Univ, 81-. **MEMBERSHIPS** Am Acad of Relig, Cath Theol Soc of Am. **SELECTED PUBLICATIONS** Auth, The Anthropological Structure of Faith: A Study of the Catholic Theology of faith between Vatican I and II," Univ of Munster, 71; transl, Foundations of Christian Faith (Grundkurs des Glaubens), by Karl Rahner (NY: Seabury, 78); ed, "Faith and Imagination," spec issue of Thought LVII-224 (Mar 82); auth, "A Theology of Peace," Blueprint for Soc Justice XXXVIII-1 (Sep 84): 1-7; ed, "The Local Church," spec issue of Thought, LXVI-263 (Dec 91); auth, Karl Rahner, Outstanding Christian Thinkers Series, Geoffrey Chapman (London), Glazier (Collegeville), 92; auth, The Mystery of Faith, Glazier (Collegeville), 94; transl, Spirit in the World (Geist in Welt), by Karl Rahner, Herder and Herder (NY), 67, Continuum, 94; auth, The Kingdom Come: Jesus and the Reign of God, Crossroad/Herder, 99; auth, Anthony DeMello, Modern Spiritual Masters Series, Orbis Books (Maryknoll, NY), 99. **CONTACT ADDRESS** Dept Theol, Fordham Univ, 441 E Fordham Rd., Bronx, NY 10458-5149. **EMAIL** dych@murreny.fordham.edu

DYCK, ARTHUR JAMES
PERSONAL Born 04/27/1932, Saskatoon, SK, Canada, m, 1952, 2 children **DISCIPLINE** ETHICS, PSYCHOLOGY **EDUCATION** Tabor Col, Bs, 53; Univ Kans, MA, 58 and 59; Harvard Univ, PhD (relig ethics), 66. **CAREER** Res asst psychol, Univ Kans, 57-60; spec lectr philos, Univ Sask, 64-65; asst prof social ethics, 65-69, Mary B Saltonstall Prof Population Ethics, Sch Pub Health, Harvard Univ, 69-, Mem Fac, Divinity Sch, 69-, Co-dir, Joseph P Kennedy, Jr Found interfac prog med ethics, Harvard, 71-. **MEMBERSHIPS** Am Soc Christian Ethics; Am Pub Health Asn. **RESEARCH** Ethical theory; ethical analysis of population policy; topics in medical ethics. **SELECTED PUBLICATIONS** Auth, "On Human Care: An Introduction To Ethics," Abingdon, 77; auth, "Rethinking Rights and Responsibilities," Pilgrim, 94; Rethinking Rights, Preserving Community , J Rel Ethics, Vol 25, 97. **CONTACT ADDRESS** Harvard Divinity Sch, Harvard Univ, 45 Francis Ave, Cambridge, MA 02138-1994.

DYCK, CORNELIUS JOHN
PERSONAL Born 08/20/1921, Russia, m, 1952, 3 children **DISCIPLINE** HISTORY, HISTORICAL THEOLOGY **EDUCATION** BA, Bethel Col, N Newton KS, 53; MA Wichita State Univ, 55; BD Divinity School Univ Chicago, 59, PhD, 62. **CAREER** Prof Assoc Mennonite Seminaries, 59-89; Dir Inst of Mennonite Studies, 58-79; Exec Sec, Mennonite World Conf, 61-73. **MEMBERSHIPS** Mennonite Hist Soc, Goshen IN; Mennonitischer Geschichtsverein, Weierhof Germany; Doopsgezind Historische Kring, Amsterdam; Doc for Reformation Res; NA Soc Of Church Hist. **RESEARCH** 16th century Dutch Anabaptism. **SELECTED PUBLICATIONS** Mennonite Encyclopedia vol V ed, 90; Introduction to Mennonite History, 3rd ed, 93; Spiritual Life in Anabaptism, 95. **CONTACT ADDRESS** Associated Mennonite Biblical Sem, 3003 Benham Ave, Elkhart, IN 46514. **EMAIL** ejwdyck@juno.com

DYE, JAMES WAYNE
PERSONAL Born 12/22/1934, Appalachia, VA, m, 1985, 1 child **DISCIPLINE** PHILOSOPHY, HISTORY OF PHILOSOPHY **EDUCATION** Carson-Newman Col, AB, 55; New Orleans Baptist Theol Sem, BD, 58; Tulane Univ, PhD, 60. **CAREER** Teaching asst philos, Tulane Univ, 58-59; from instr to asst prof, Washington Univ, 60-66; assoc prof, 66-76, dir, Philos Inst, 67-70, prof philos, Northern Ill Univ, 76-, assoc ed, The Philos Forum, 67-70. **MEMBERSHIPS** Am Philos Asn; Soc Ancient Greek Philos; Hume Soc; S Soc Philos Psy Psychol, Pres, 94-95. **RESEARCH** Ancient Greek philosophy; philosophy of religion and culture; German idealism; Hume. **SELECTED PUBLICATIONS** Coauth, Religions of the World, Appleton, 67, Irvington, 75; auth, Denton J Snider's interpretation of Hegel, Mod Schoolman, 1/70; Unspoken philosophy: The presuppositions and applications of thought, Studium Gererale, 71; Kant as ethical naturalist, J Value Inquiry, 78; Plato's concept of causal explanation, Tulane Stud Philos, 78; Aristotle's matter as a sensible principle, Int Studies Philos, 78; Nikolai Bendyaev and his ideas on ultimate reality, J Ultimate Reality & Meaning, 79; The sensibility of intelligible matter, Int Studies Philos, 82; In Search of the Philosopher-King, Archeol News, 82; The Poetization of Science, Studies in Sci and Cult II, 86; Hume on Curing Superstition, Hume Stud, 86; Superhuman Voices and Biological Books, Hist Philos Quart, 88; A Word on Behalf of Demea, Hume Stud, 89; Demea's Departure, Hume Stud, 93. **CONTACT ADDRESS** Dept of Philosophy, No Illinois Univ, 1425 W Lincoln Hwy, De Kalb, IL 60115-2825. **EMAIL** jdye@niu.edu

DYE, THOMAS R.
DISCIPLINE POLITICAL SCIENCE **EDUCATION** Pa State Univ, BS, 57, MA, 59; Univ of Pa, PhD, 61. **CAREER** Teacher, Univ of Pa; teacher, Univ of Wis; teacher, Univ of Ga; vis scholar, Bar-Ilan Univ; vis scholar, Brookings Inst; McKenzie prof of Gov, Fla State Univ; Pres, Lincoln Center for Public Service. **HONORS AND AWARDS** Harold Lasswell Awd; Donald C. Stone Awd; listed in Who's Who in Am. **MEMBERSHIPS** James Madison Inst; Phi Beta Kappa; Omicron Delta Kappa; Phi Kappa Phi. **SELECTED PUBLICATIONS** Auth, Politics in Florida, Prentice Hall/Simon & Schuster, 98; auth, The Irony of Democracy; Politics in States and Communities; Understanding Public Policy; Who's Running America?; American Politics in the Media Age; Power in Society; American Federalism: Competition Among Governments; Politics Economics and The Public; Politics in America, Prentice Hall/ Simon & Schuster, 99; auth, Top Down Policymaking, Chatham House, 00. **CONTACT ADDRESS** Lincoln Ctr for Public Service, 1801 S Federal Hwy, Suite 224, Delray Beach, FL 33483. **EMAIL** tomrdye@aol.com

DYER, JAMES MARK
DISCIPLINE THEOLOGY **EDUCATION** St Anselm Col, BA, 59; Univ Ottawa, MTh, STL, 65; Episcopal Sem Southwest, DD, 89; Muhlenberg Col, DD, 90. **CAREER** Rector, Christ Church of Hamilton and Wenham, 78-82; prof, Va Theol Sem, 96-; dir, Spiritual Formation. **HONORS AND AWARDS** Bishop, Diocese of Bethlehem, 82-95; ed, Lambeth Conf, 98. **SELECTED PUBLICATIONS** Auth, The Anglican, Lambeth Conf, 98; Doing Theology Together, Forward Movement Publ, 94. **CONTACT ADDRESS** Virginia Theol Sem, 3737 Seminary Rd, Alexandria, VA 22304. **EMAIL** MDyer@vts.edu

DYKEMAN, KING JOHN
PERSONAL Born 06/01/1934, Seattle, WA, m, 1997, 4 children **DISCIPLINE** PHILOSOPHY **EDUCATION** Creighton Univ, AB, 57; Univ Chicago, MA, 66, PhD, 69. **CAREER** Lectr lib arts, Univ Chicago, 64-67, asst dir lib arts prog adults, 66-67; from instr to asst prof, 67-73, Assoc Prof Philos, Fairfield Univ 73-; ed consult, Choice, 69-; assoc adv mem for US, Centre Superiore de Logica e Scienza Comparate, 72-; Danforth Found fel, 75-; pres bd dir, Greater Bridgeport Area Coun Alcoholism, 77-79. **MEMBERSHIPS** Am Philos Asn; Charles S Peirce Soc; Soc Advan Am Philos. **RESEARCH** Concord school of philos; Am philos; Frances Wright, George Herbert Palmer, and Hartlery Burr Alexander. **SELECTED PUBLICATIONS** Auth, Croce, Creativity and Contemporary Philosophy, Rivista Studi Crociani, 7-12/72; The J S Mill-W Whewell feud: Categories and Their Consequences, Proc 4th Int Cong Logic, Methodology & Philosophy of Sci, Bucharest, 72; coauth, Science, Technology and Man in the Philosophy of Spirit, 73 & auth, Charles Sanders Peirce: The Minute Logic, 73, Proc IVth World Cong Philos, Varna; History of Science and Technology, Choice, 2/74; The Unity and Diversity of Science, Ethics and Aesthetics, Akten des 4 Int Kant-Long, Ger, 74; The Discovery of Significance, Proc World Cong Humanities, GA, 12/74; The principles of induction: J S Mill and C S Pierce, 5th Int Cong Logic, Methodl & Philos of Sci, CAN, 75; American Women Philosophers, Mellon Press, 93. **CONTACT ADDRESS** Dept of Philos, Fairfield Univ, 1073 N Benson Rd, Fairfield, CT 06430-5195. **EMAIL** Dykeman@Fair1.fairfield.edu

DYKSTRA, WAYNE A.
PERSONAL Born 06/24/1944, Lebanon, OR, m, 1966, 2 children **DISCIPLINE** RELIGION **EDUCATION** Puget Sound Christian Col, BA, 87; Pacific Christian Col, MA, 91; Emmanual Sch of Rel, Mdiv, 94; Abilene Christian Univ, Dmin; 99. **CAREER** Assoc min, First Christian Church; assoc prof, Nebraska Christian Col; minister, Prineville Christian Church. **HONORS AND AWARDS** Validictorian, Puget Sound Christian Col. **MEMBERSHIPS** Fel of Professors **RESEARCH** 19th century reformation of the church. **SELECTED PUBLICATIONS** Auth, A New Venture in Christian Higher Education: A History of Puget, 94; auth, Leadership Development in Christian Churches and Churches of Christ in Northeast Nebraska, 99. **CONTACT ADDRESS** Prineville Christian Church, 1685 SE Lynn Blvd, Prineville, OR 97754.

DYMALE, HERBERT RICHARD
PERSONAL Born 07/23/1925, Murke, Poland, m, 1951, 3 children **DISCIPLINE** RELIGION **EDUCATION** United Theol Sem, MDN, 51; Princeton Theol Sem, ThM, 53; Univ Iowa, PhD(hist theol), 66. **CAREER** Asst prof hist & relig, Cascade Col, 64-67; assoc prof, 67-73, Prof Theol, Malone Col, 73- **MEMBERSHIPS** Evangel Theol Soc; Conf Faith & Hist; Wesleyan Theol Soc. **SELECTED PUBLICATIONS** Auth, What kind of hope is adequate, Christianity Today, 6/71; Paul Tillich's dialectical humanism, Christian Scholar's Rev, 11/73; contribr, Baker's Dictionary of Christian Ethics, Baker Bk, 73. **CONTACT ADDRESS** Dept of Relig & Philos, Malone Col, 515 25th St N W, Canton, OH 44709-3897. **EMAIL** hdymale@malone.edu

DYZENHAUS, DAVID
PERSONAL m, 1987, 2 children **DISCIPLINE** PHILOSOPHY, LAW **EDUCATION** Univ Witwatersrand, BA, 77; LLB, 79; Oxford Univ, DPhil, 88. **CAREER** Lectr, Univ Witwatersrand, 81-83; asst prof, Queen's Univ, 88-90; prof, Univ Toronto, 90-. **HONORS AND AWARDS** Humboldt Fel; Connaught Res Fel; Fel, Royal Soc of Can. **RESEARCH** Philosophy of law; Political philosophy; Administrative law. **SELECTED**

PUBLICATIONS Auth, Hard Cases in Wicked Legal Systems: South African Law in the Perspective of Legal Philosophy, Oxford Univ Press, 91; auth, Legality and Legitimacy: Carl Schmitt, Hans Kelsen and Hermann Heller in Weimar, Oxford Univ Press, 97; auth, Judging the Judges, Judging Ourselves: Truth, Reconciliation and the Apartheid Legal Order, Hart Pub, 97. **CONTACT ADDRESS** Dept Philos, Univ of Toronto, 215 Huron St, Toronto, ON, Canada M5S 1A1. **EMAIL** david.dyzenhaus@utoronto.ca

E

EAGAN, JENNIFER
PERSONAL Born 11/09/1969, Arlington, VA, m, 1995 **DISCIPLINE** PHILOSOPHY **EDUCATION** Mary Washington Col, BA, 91; Duquesne Univ, PhD, 99. **CAREER** Adjunct instr, Laroche Col, fall 96- spring 97; adjunct instr, Point Park Col, spring 95; adjunct instr, Carlow Col, fall 94- spring 97; grad instr, Duquesne Univ, fall 93-94; adjunct instr, Erie County Community Col, fall 98; adjunct instr, Buffalo State Col and Canisius Col, fall 97-98; asst prof, Calif State Univ-Hayward, 99-. **HONORS AND AWARDS** Phi Beta Kappa; Mortar Board. **MEMBERSHIPS** Am Philos Asn; Intl Asn for Philos and Lit; North Amer Kant Soc; Soc for Phenomenological and Existential Philos; Soc of Women in Philos; Radical Philos Asn; Public Admin Theory Network; **RESEARCH** Ethics; Human Rights and Social Justice; Gender and Feminist Theory; Critical Theory; Postmodernism; Kant/Lyotard/Irigaray/Adorno; Public Administration. **SELECTED PUBLICATIONS** Auth, Philosophers and the Holocaust: Mediating Public Disputes, Intl Studies in Philo, XXIX, 1, winter, 97. **CONTACT ADDRESS** Dept of Philos, California State Univ, Hayward, 25800 Carlos Bee Blvd., Hayward, CA 94542-3007. **EMAIL** jeagan@csuhayward.edu

EAGLESON, IAN
PERSONAL Born 06/24/1959, Philadelphia, PA, d **DISCIPLINE** PHILOSOPHY **EDUCATION** UC San Diego, Phd, expected, 99. **CAREER** Vis asst prof Univ Cincinnati. **MEMBERSHIPS** APA. **RESEARCH** Kant; Epistemology. **CONTACT ADDRESS** 3240 Biship St, #5, Cincinnati, OH 45220. **EMAIL** eaglesi@email.uc.edu

EAKIN, FRANK EDWIN
PERSONAL Born 09/04/1936, Roanoke, VA, m, 1958 **DISCIPLINE** BIBLICAL STUDIES **EDUCATION** Univ Richmond, BA 58; Southern Baptist Theological Seminary, BD 61; Duke Univ, PhD, 64. **CAREER** Wake Forest Univ, vis asst prof 64-65; Duke Univ, instr 65-66; Univ Richmond, asst prof 66-69, assoc prof 69-75, prof 75. **HONORS AND AWARDS** Phi Beta Kappa; Omicron Delta Kappa; Gurney Harris Kearns Fell; Humanities Scholar; Amer Coun Fell; Weinstein-Rosenthal Prof. **MEMBERSHIPS** Soc Bibl Lit **RESEARCH** Jewish-Christian rel; Bibl theol. **SELECTED PUBLICATIONS** What Price Prejudice? Christian Anti-semitism in America, Paulist Press 98; We Believe in One God: Creed and Scripture, Wyndam Hall Press, 85; The Bible and Anti-semitism, in: Biblical v Secular Ethics: The Conflict, Prometheus Books, 88. **CONTACT ADDRESS** Dept of Relig, Univ of Richmond, Richmond, VA 23173. **EMAIL** feakin@richmond.edu

EAMES, ELIZABETH R.
PERSONAL Born 02/18/1921, Toronto, ON, Canada, w, 1952, 2 children **DISCIPLINE** PHILOSOPHY **EDUCATION** Univ Toronto, BA, 43, MA, 44; Bryn Mawr Col, PhD, 51. **CAREER** Instr, asst prof, 48-52, Univ Mo; lectr, Wash Univ, 52-63; from lectr to assoc prof to prof, 63-90, chair, 85-88, Southern Ill Univ, Carbondale. **HONORS AND AWARDS** Grad Fel Bryn Mawr, 44-46; Carnegie Fel, 47-48, Britain; Awds for res, SIU, Am Philos Soc, NEH. **MEMBERSHIPS** Am Philos Asn; Mo Philos Asn; Ill Philos Asn; Soc for Women in Philos. **RESEARCH** Analytic philosphy; Bertrand Russell; American philosophy and feminism. **SELECTED PUBLICATIONS** Auth, Bertrand Russell's Theory of Knowledge; ed, auth, Russell's 1913 Manuscript on Theory of Knowledge; coauth, Lectures in the Far East; coauth, Logical Methods; auth, Bertrand Russell's Dialogue with His Contemporaries, Southern Univ Pr, 89. **CONTACT ADDRESS** 512 Orchard Dr, Carbondale, IL 62901. **EMAIL** eames@siu.edu

EARHART, HARRY BYRON
PERSONAL Born 01/07/1935, Aledo, IL, m, 1956, 3 children **DISCIPLINE** HISTORY OF RELIGIOUS, ASIAN STUDIES **EDUCATION** Univ Chicago, BD and MA, 60, PhD, 65. **CAREER** Asst prof relig, Vanderbilt Univ, 65-66; from asst prof to assoc prof, 66-69, prof Relig, Western Mich Univ, 75-, Fac res fels, 68 and 73; Fulbright res grant and prof relig, Int Summer Sch Asian Studies, Ewha Womans Univ, Korea, 73; adv Far Eastern relig, Encycl Britannica; ed, Relig Studies Rev, 75-80. **HONORS AND AWARDS** Distinguished Fac Scholar Award, 81; Distniguished Fac Award (from the Michigan asn of Governing Bd), 82; Philo T. Farnsworth Award for his videotape "Fuji: Sacred Mountain of Japan." **MEMBERSHIPS** Am Acad Relig; Asn Asian Studies; Am Soc Study Relig. **RESEARCH** Hist of Japanese relig; Japanese new religions; new religious movements. **SELECTED PUBLICATIONS** Auth, A Religious Study of the Mount Haguro Sect of Shugendo, 70; auth, The New Religions of Japan: A Bibliography of Western-language Material, 2nd ed, 83; auth, Gedatsu-kai and Reilgion in Contemporary Japan, 89; auth, Japanese Religion: Unity an ddiversity, 82; auth, Religious Traditions of the World, 92. **CONTACT ADDRESS** Dept of Relig, Western Michigan Univ, Kalamazoo, MI 49008. **EMAIL** earhart@wmich.edu

EASLEY, RAY
PERSONAL Born 07/09/1951, Altus, OK, m, 3 children **DISCIPLINE** THEOLOGY **EDUCATION** Covenant Found Col, ThB, 73; Anderson Univ, M Div, 79; Univ Arkansas, EdD, 87. **CAREER** Acad dean, 9 yrs, Covenant Found Col; vice pres, enrollment & stud affairs, 2 yrs, vice pres, acad affairs, 11 yrs, Wesley Biblical Sem. **CONTACT ADDRESS** PO Box 9938, Jackson, MS 39286. **EMAIL** rayeasley@aol.com

EASTON, LOYD D.
PERSONAL Born 07/29/1915, Rockford, IL, m, 1963, 5 children **DISCIPLINE** PHILOSOPHY **EDUCATION** DePauw Univ, AB, 37; Boston Univ, MA, 39, PhD, 42. **CAREER** From instr to assoc prof philos, 46-55, chmn dept, 52-76, prof, 55-80, emer and part-time prof philos, Ohio Wesleyan Univ, 80-; prof, philos of relig, Methodist Theol Sch, Ohio, 60-61; Am Counc Learned Soc grant, 61-62; Am Asn State & Local Hist grant, 63; consult philos terms, Webster's New World Dictionary, 66-98; Nat Endowment for Humanities fel, 76. **HONORS AND AWARDS** Phi Beta Kappa, 37; fel, Natl Coun on Religion in Higher Educ, 40; Commendation Medal, HQ US Army European Theater of Operations, 46; hon Dr of Humane Lett, Ohio Wesleyan Univ, 90. **MEMBERSHIPS** Am Philos Asn; Hegel Soc Am; Soc Philos Studies Marxism; Soc for Advanc of Am Philos. **RESEARCH** Social philosophy; history of 19th century thought; American philosophy. **SELECTED PUBLICATIONS** Auth, Alienation and Empiricism in Marx's Thought, Social Res, fall 70; ed, Philosophical Analysis and Human Welfare: Selected Essays and Chapters from Six Decades by D S Miller, Reidel, 75; auth, Marx and Individual Freedom, Philos Forum, spring 81 & winter-spring 81-82; contribur, American National Biography, 99. **CONTACT ADDRESS** 998 Braumiller Rd, Delaware, OH 43015-3114.

EASTON, PATRICIA ANN
PERSONAL Born 05/31/1964, Penetang, Canada, m, 1 child **DISCIPLINE** PHILOSOPHY **EDUCATION** Univ Western Ontario, PhD, 92. **CAREER** Vis prof, 93-95, post-doctoral fel, 93-94, Univ Toronto; post-doctoral fel, Univ of Western Ontario, 92-93; asst prof of philos, Claremont Graduate Univ, 95-. **HONORS AND AWARDS** Soc Sci and Hum Res Council of Canada, doctoral fel, 88-92, post-doctoral fel, 92-94. **MEMBERSHIPS** APA; Canadian Philos Asn. **RESEARCH** History of early modern philosophy; Descartes. **SELECTED PUBLICATIONS** Coauth, The Cartesian Empiricism of Francois Bayle, Garland, 92; coauth, Bibliographia Malebranchiana: An Annotated Bibliography of the Malebranche Literature into 1989, So Illinois, 92; auth, Rorty's History-of- philosophy-as-story-of-progress, Etudes Maritainiennes/Maritainian Stud, 95; auth, Logic and the Workings of the Mind: The Logic of Ideas and Faculty Psychology in Early Modern Philosophy, in Easton, ed, North American Kant Society Studies in Philosophy Series, Ridgeview, 97; auth, Robert Desgabets, and, Antoine LeGrand, in Craig, ed, Routledge Encyclopedia of Philosophy, Routledge, 98; auth, Jacques Rohault, and Samuel Sorbiere, in Ayers, ed, Biographical Appendix in, The Cambridge History of Seventeenth Century Philosophy, Cambridge, 98. **CONTACT ADDRESS** Dept of Philosophy, Claremont Graduate Sch, 736 N College St, Claremont, CA 91711. **EMAIL** patricia.easton@cgu.edu

EATON, JONATHAN
PERSONAL Born 05/27/1950, Los Angeles, CA, m, 1983, 2 children **DISCIPLINE** ECONOMICS **EDUCATION** Harvard Univ, AB, 72; Yale Univ, MA, 73; MPhil, 74; PhD, 76 **CAREER** Asst prof, Princeton Univ, 76-81; assoc prof, Yale Univ, 81-84; prof, Univ Va, 84-90; prof, Boston Univ, 90-. **HONORS AND AWARDS** Hoover Fel, 87-88; Fel, Econometric Soc, 95. **MEMBERSHIPS** Am Econ Asn; Econometric Soc. **RESEARCH** International trade; International capital markets; Technology and the global economy. **SELECTED PUBLICATIONS** Co-auth, "Intertemporal Price Competition," Econometrica, (90:637-659; auth, "The Pure Theory of Country Risk," in International Volatility and Economic Growth: The First Ten Years of the International Seminar on Macroeconomics, Amsterdam, 91; co-auth, "Sanctions," J of Polit Econ, (92): 899-928; co-auth, "Optimal Trade and Industrial Policy under Oligopoly," in Imperfect Competition and International Trade, MIT Press, 92; co-auth, "Trade in Ideas: Patenting and Productivity in the OECD," J of Intl Econ, (96): 1-28; co-auth, "Cities and Growth: Theory and Evidence from France and Japan," Reg Sci and Urban Econ, (97): 443-474; co-auth, "International Technology Diffusion: Theory and Measurement," Intl Econ Rev, (99): 537-570. **CONTACT ADDRESS** Dept Econ, Boston Univ, 270 Bay State Rd, Boston, MA 02215. **EMAIL** jeaton@bu.edu

EATON, KENT A.
PERSONAL Born 12/08/1957, Abilene, TX, m, 1980, 3 children **DISCIPLINE** RELIGION **EDUCATION** Dallas Theol Sem, ThM, 84; Univ Barcelona, 86; Univ Wales, PhD, 98. **CAREER** Prof Church Hist, Facultad Protestante de Teologica, 86-97; dir, lectr, Bethel Sem, 97-. **MEMBERSHIPS** Am Acad Relig; Evangel Theol Soc. **RESEARCH** Mission history; church history. **SELECTED PUBLICATIONS** Auth, Beware the Trumpet of Judgment: John N. Darby and the Nineteenth Century Brethren, The Coming Deliverer, 97; auth, Los Hermanos de Plymouth en el contexto del no-conformismo britanico, Agenda Teologica, Jan, 97; auth, The Work of the Brethren in Spain, Brethren Archs and Hists Network Rev, Autumn, 97. **CONTACT ADDRESS** Dept of Theology, Bethel Sem, San Diego, 6116 Arosa St., San Diego, CA 92115-3902. **EMAIL** k-eaton@bethel.edu

EATON, MARCIA M.
PERSONAL Born 10/05/1938, Galesburg, IL, m, 1964, 1 child **DISCIPLINE** PHILOSOPHY **CAREER** Acting Instructor, Stanford Univ, 62-63; Instructor, Iowa State Univ, 64-65; Visiting Asst Prof, Univ of Illinois, Chicago Circle, 66-69; Asst Prof, Univ of Illinois, Univ of Illinois, Chicago Circle, 69-71; Undervisningassistant, Univ of Copenhagen, 71-72; Asst Prof, Univ of Minnesota, 72-74; Assoc Prof, Univ of Minnesota, 74-81; Full Professor, Univ of Minnesota, 81-; Visiting Prof, Univ of Munich, Spring 90; Visiting Fellow, Univ of Warwick, Winter 92; Visiting Prof, Univ of Amsterdam, Spring 1996. **HONORS AND AWARDS** Rockefeller Bellagio Scholar, 92; Alumni Achievement Awd, Knox College, 97; Univ of Minnesota Graduate School Summer ; Research Fellowships, 73-83; Univ of Minnesota Graduate School Grant in Aid of Research, 80; Minnesota Humanities Commission Grant, 83-84; Bush Foundation Sabbatical Fellowship, 84-85; Minnesota Women's Yearbook, 84-; Travel Grant, Univ of Minnesota China Center, 87; Univ of Minnesota Single Quarter Leave, Spring 88; Minnesota Humanities Commission Grant, 88; University of Minnesota Graduate School Research Grant, Research Asst, 89-91; University of Minnesota Sabbatical, 91-91; Rockefeller Foundation, Scholar-in-Residence, Bellagio Center, Spring 92; Advisory Committee, The Getty Education Institute for the Arts, 95-99; President, American Society for Aesthetics, 95-97; Alumni Achievement Awd, Knox College, 97; Univ of Minnesota Sabbatical, 98-99. **MEMBERSHIPS** American Society for Aesthetics, President, 95-97; American Philosophical Assn. **RESEARCH** Aesthotics. **SELECTED PUBLICATIONS** Auth, "The Intrinsic, Non-Supervenient Nature of Aesthetic Properties," Journal of Aestthetics and Art Criticism, Fall 94, pp. 383-397; auth, Philosophica Aesthetics: A Way of Knowing and Its Limits," for special issue on "Aesthetics for Young People" of Journal of Aesthetic Education, edited by Ronald Moore, Fall 94, pp. 19-31; auth "The Social Construction of Aesthetic Response," British Journal Aesthetics, April 95, pp. 95-107; auth, "Reply to Symposiasts," in conjunction with "Symposium on Marcia Eaton's Philosphy of Art," by Susan L. Feagin, Gary Iseminger, and Ronald Moore, Journal of Aesthetic Education, Summer 1995, pp 29-32; auth"What About Beauty? A Chronicle of a Lecture Series, Sponsored by the Univ of Minnesota Art Department, Minneapolis: Univ of Minnesota Press, 98; auth "Intention, Supervenience, and Aesthetic Realism," Brittish Journal of Aesthetics, July 98, pp 279-293; auth, "Kantian and Contextual Beauty," Journal of Aesthetics and Art Criticism, Winter 99, pp 11-15; edited by Margaret Brand, Indiana Univ Press, forthcoming, 00; auth, "A Sustainable Definition of 'Art'," in What Is Art?, edited by Noel Carroll, Madison: Univ of Wisconsin Press, forthcoming, 00; auth, "The Role of Art in Sustainable Communities," in Community, edited by Philip Alperson, to be published by Blackwell, 00; Rev, "Aesthetics, for Journal of Aesthetics and Art Criticism," by Harold Osborne, Fall 73; rev, Contestable Concepts of Criticism, by Arthur Moore, for Centrum, 73. **CONTACT ADDRESS** Philosophy, Univ of Minnesota, Twin Cities, 271 19th Ave S, Philosophy-831 Heller Hall, Minneapolis, MN 554455-0430. **EMAIL** eaton001@tc.umn.edu

EBBS, GARY
DISCIPLINE PHILOSOPHY **EDUCATION** Univ Mich, PhD, 88. **CAREER** Asst prof, Univ Ill Urban Champaign. **RESEARCH** Philosophy of language and mind; skepticism; self-knowledge; history of analytic philosophy. **SELECTED PUBLICATIONS** Auth, Rule-Following and Realism, Harvard, 97; Skepticism, Objectivity and Brains in Vats; Realism and Rational Inquiry; Can We Take Our Words at Face Value?. **CONTACT ADDRESS** Philosophy Dept, Univ of Illinois, Urbana-Champaign, 52 E Gregory Dr, Champaign, IL 61820. **EMAIL** garyebbs@staff.uiuc.edu

EBEL, ROLAND H.
PERSONAL Born 10/11/1928, Oak Park, IL, m, 1955, 2 children **DISCIPLINE** POLITICAL SCIENCE **EDUCATION** Wheaton Col, BA, 50; Northwestern Univ, MA, 52; Mich St Univ, PhD, 60. **CAREER** Asst prof, 60-64, Western Mich Univ; assoc prof, 64-93, assoc prof emer, 93- Tulane Univ. **HONORS AND AWARDS** Soc Sci res Coun Grant, 65-66; Natl Sci Found Grant, 73-75; Sturgis-Leavitt prize, Best Article on Latin Amer, 90. **MEMBERSHIPS** SE Coun of Latin Amer Stud. **RESEARCH** Latin Amer politics **SELECTED PUBLICATIONS** Auth, Guatemala: The Politics of Unstable Stabili-

ty, Latin Amer Pol & Dev, Westview Press, 96; auth, Guillermo Ungo, Carlos Castillo Armas, Miguel Ydigoras Fuentes, Carlos Arana Osorio, Vinicio Cerezo, Francisco Villagran Kramer, Fidel Sanchez Hernandez, Carlos Humberto Romero, Oscar Osorio, Mario Mendez Montenegro, Julio Cesar Mendez Montenegro, Jose Maria Lemus, Enrique Peralta Azurdia, Juan Jose Arevalo, & Jacobo Arbenz Guzman", Encycl of Latin Amer Hist & Cult, Scribner's Sons, 98; auth, Misunderstood Caudillo: Miguel Ydigoras Fuentes and the Failure of Guatemalan Democracy, Univ Press of Amer, 98. **CONTACT ADDRESS** Dept of Political Science, Tulane Univ, New Orleans, LA 70118. **EMAIL** Tanglewild@juno.edu

EBERLE, ROLF A.
PERSONAL Born 02/07/1931, Aarau, Switzerland, m, 1958, 3 children **DISCIPLINE** PHILOSOPHY **EDUCATION** Univ Calif Los Angeles, PhD, 65. **CAREER** Asst prof, Kans State Univ, 65-67; asst prof, Univ Rochester, 67-69; assoc prof, 69-75; prof, 75-91; prof emer, 91-. **HONORS AND AWARDS** Woodrow Wilson Nat Fel, 60-61. **MEMBERSHIPS** Amer Philos Asn. **RESEARCH** Logic; Metaphysics. **SELECTED PUBLICATIONS** Auth, Logic and Proof Techniques, 96; "Semantic Analysis Without Reference to Abstract Entities," 97; "Goodman on Likeness and Differences of Meaning," 97. **CONTACT ADDRESS** 5167 Canadice Hill Rd, Hemlock, NY 14466-9628. **EMAIL** hie7rae@aol.com

EBERTS, MARY
PERSONAL Born, Canada **DISCIPLINE** LAW **EDUCATION** Univ Western Ontario, BA, 68; LLB, 71; Harvard Univ, LLM, 72. **CAREER** From asst to assoc prof, Univ of Toronto, 74-80; partner, Tory Tory Des Lauriers & Binnington, 80-94; partner Eberts Symes St & Corbett, 94-; adj prof, Univ of Toronto, 87-. **HONORS AND AWARDS** Governor General Person's Awd, 96; founder, women's legal edu action fund. **SELECTED PUBLICATIONS** Contrib and Coed, Equality Rights under the Canadian Charter of Rights and Freedoms, Carswells (Toronto), 85. **CONTACT ADDRESS** Fac of Law, Univ of Toronto, 78 Queen's Park, Toronto, ON, Canada M5S 2C5.

ECHELBARGER, CHARLES G.
PERSONAL Born 06/20/1942, Fostoria, OH, m, 1968, 1 child **DISCIPLINE** PHILOSOPHY **EDUCATION** Ohio State Univ, PhD, 69. **CAREER** Prof of Philos, Suny at Oswego, 70-. **MEMBERSHIPS** Amer Philos Assoc; Hume Soc. **RESEARCH** Hume; philos of mind; hist of modern European philos. **CONTACT ADDRESS** Dept of Philos, SUNY, Oswego, Oswego, NY 13126. **EMAIL** echel@oswego.oswego.edu

ECHOLS, JAMES KENNETH
PERSONAL m, 2 children **DISCIPLINE** AMERICAN CHURCH HISTORY **EDUCATION** Temple Univ, BA, 73; Lutheran Theol Sem at Phil, MDiv, 77 Yale Univ, MA, 79, MPhil, 84, PhD, 89. **CAREER** Dean, Lutheran Theol Sem at Phil; pres-. **HONORS AND AWARDS** Daniel Alexander Payne awd for Ecumenical srv, African Methodist Episcopal Church, 96; bd mem, elca div for ministry; black lutheran commn develop corporation. **MEMBERSHIPS** Mem, ELCA Delegation to Natl Coun of Churches of Christ. **SELECTED PUBLICATIONS** Pub(s), in the areas of church history, theology and Black American Lutheranism. **CONTACT ADDRESS** Dept of American Church History, Lutheran Sch of Theol at Chicago, 1100 E 55th St, Chicago, IL 60615.

ECHOLS, MARSHA A.
DISCIPLINE INTERNATIONAL LAW AND INTERNATIONAL BUSINESS TRANSACTIONS **EDUCATION** Howard Univ, BA, 65; Georgetown Univ Law Ctr, JD, 68; Free Univ Brussels, LLM, 73; Columbia Univ Law Sch, LLM, 96. **CAREER** Prof; Howard Univ, 86-; dir, Master Compe Jurisp MCJ prog; taught at, Univ Va Sch Law & George Washington Univ Nat Law Ctr; J.S.D. Columbia Law School, 01; dir, Project on International Knowledge, Creativity and Dev, Howard Law School. **MEMBERSHIPS** Ch, Task Force on Reg Econ Integration of the ABA & mem, Coun For Relations; Secretary of State's Advisory Committee on Private International Law. **RESEARCH** Nontariff barriers for international trade in foods and agriculture. **SELECTED PUBLICATIONS** Auth, The International Tower of Babel: The Small Business Pespective, 51 Food & Drug Law J 175, 96 & Sanitary and Phytosanitary Measures, in The World Trade Organization, 96; contrib chap, WTO agreement on Sanitary and Phyto sanitary measures to an ABA bk on the WTO int trade agreement & article on int food labeling to the Food and Drug Law J. **CONTACT ADDRESS** Sch of Law, Howard Univ, 2900 Van Ness St NW, Washington, DC 20008. **EMAIL** mechols@law.howard.edu

ECKARDT, ALICE LYONS
PERSONAL Born 04/27/1923, Brooklyn, NY, m, 1944, 2 children **DISCIPLINE** HISTORY OF RELIGIONS, CHRISTIAN-JEWISH RELATIONS **EDUCATION** Oberlin Col, BA, 44; Lehigh Univ, MA, 66; DHL, Leigh Univ, 92. **CAREER** Asst Prof, Lehigh Univ, 76-85; Assoc Prof, 85-87; Adjunct Prof, Cedar Crest Col, 81, 82; Spec Advisor, Educ Comm, U S Holocaust Meml Coun, 81-86; Co-Founder and Co-Dir Leigh Univ, 76-85; Prof Emer, 87; **HONORS AND AWARDS** DHL, Lehigh Univ, 92 **MEMBERSHIPS** Am Acad Relig; Nat Inst Holocaust; Am Professors Peace Mid East.; Christian Scholars Group on Judiasm and the Jewish People, 73; Institute for Jewis-Christian Understanding, Steering Comm, 95-00; Exec Comm 87-88; Journal of Ecumenical Studies, Executive Editorial Review Bd, Advisory Bd, 87-; Berman Center for Jewish Studies, 85-89; United Church of Christ Jewish-Christain Dialogue Project, 88-95. **RESEARCH** History and theology of Jewish-Christian relations; the Holocaust, and post-Holocaust theology; sexism and world religions. **SELECTED PUBLICATIONS** Coauth, Encounter with Israel, 70; coauth, Long Night's Journey Into Day, 82, revised 88; auth, Jerusalem: City of the Ages, 87; auth, " The Refromation and the Jews , " Interwoven Destinies: Jews and Christians Through the Ages, 93; auth, ed, Burinig Memory: Times of Testing and Reckoning, 93; ed, Collecting Myself: A Writer's Perspective, 93; auth, " Suffering, Theology, and the Shoah," The Holocaust Now, , 96; auth, "Creating Christian Yom HaShoah Gutman, 96; auth, " The Shoah Road to a Revised-Revived Christianity," From the Unthinkable to the Unavoidable, 97; auth, " Leiden: Herausforderung des Glaubens - Herausforderung Gottes," Kultur allein inst nicht genug, 98. **CONTACT ADDRESS** Beverly Hill Rd, Box 619A, Coopersburg, PA 18036. **EMAIL** AliceEck@aol.com

ECKENWILER, LISA A.
DISCIPLINE PHILOSOPHY, BIOETHICS **EDUCATION** Univ Wis, BA, 89; Univ Tenn, MA, 91, PhD, 97. **CAREER** Tchr, St. Mary's Med Ctr, Tenn, 93; tchr, Univ Tenn Med Ctr, Tenn, 94; Dept Philos, Univ Tenn-Knoxville, 91-94; Med Human Prog, Stritch Sch Med, Loyola Univ, 96; Grad Prog Pub Hea, Eastern Va Med Sch, 98; Dept Philos, Old Dominion Univ, 97- . **MEMBERSHIPS** Am Philos Assn; Amer Soc Bioethics Human; Intl Assn Bioethics; Network Feminist Approaches to Bioethics; SE Va Bioethics Network. **RESEARCH** Specialization in moral philosophy; biomedical ethics; Competence in feminist philosophy; history of philosophy. **SELECTED PUBLICATIONS** Co-ed, Institutional Policy in Paediatric Practice: Documenting Canadian Experience, Toronto, The Hospital for Sick Children Dept Bioethics, 94; Women and Communities in Clinical Research: Questioning the Influence of Communitarian Ideals, in Soc Philos Today, vol 13, ed, Yeager Hudson, Lewiston, NY, Edwin Mellen Press, 98. **CONTACT ADDRESS** Dept of Philosophy, Old Dominion Univ, 4100 Powhatan Ave, Norfolk, VA 23529.

ECKLEBARGER, KERMIT A.
PERSONAL Born 12/10/1935, Chicago, IL, m, 1956, 2 children **DISCIPLINE** NEW TESTAMENT AND EARLY CHRISTIAN LITERATURE **EDUCATION** Wheaton Col, BA, 58, MA, 61; Univ Chicago, PhD, 87. **CAREER** New Testament prof, London Col of Bible and Missions, 60-68; New Testament prof, Ont Bible Col, 68-72; assoc prof New Testament, 72-, Vpres & Acad Dean, 93-, Denver Sem. **HONORS AND AWARDS** ATS grant curric develp, 77-78. **MEMBERSHIPS** Evangelical Theol Soc; Soc Bibl Lit; Inst Bibl Res. **RESEARCH** Hermenentics; Greek grammar and exegesis. **SELECTED PUBLICATIONS** Auth Growing Towards Spiritual Maturity, 88; Nelson's Illustrated Bible Dictionary, 86; Computer Bible Study, Word, 93; Introduction to Biblical Interpretation, Word, 93. **CONTACT ADDRESS** Box 100000, Denver, CO 80250. **EMAIL** kermit@densem.edu

ECKLEY, RICHARD K.
PERSONAL Born 04/26/1956, Allentown, PA, m, 1977, 2 children **DISCIPLINE** THEOLOGY **EDUCATION** United Wesleyan Col, BS; Asbury Theol Sem, MDiv; Princeton Theol Sem, ThM; Duquesne Univ, PhD. **CAREER** Asst Prof, United Wesleyan Col, 88-90; Assoc Prof, Houghton Col, 90-. **HONORS AND AWARDS** Ichthus New Testament Awd, 83. **MEMBERSHIPS** Soc of Biblical Literature, am Acad of Relig, Catholic Theol Soc of Am, Wesleyan Theol Soc. **RESEARCH** Contemporary Theology, Spirituality. **CONTACT ADDRESS** Dept Relig & Philos, Houghton Col, PO Box 128, Houghton, NY 14744-0128. **EMAIL** reckley@houghton.edu

ECKSTEIN, JEROME
PERSONAL Born 06/25/1928, 3 children **DISCIPLINE** PHILOSOPHY **EDUCATION** Brooklyn Col, BA, 49; Columbia Univ, PhD (philos), 61. **CAREER** Lectr philos, Brooklyn Col and City Col NY, 55-60; isntr philos and contemporary civilization, Columbia Univ, 60-63; from asst prof to assoc prof philos, Dowling Col, 63-66; prof philos educ, 66-70, chmn dept, 70-74, Prof Judaic Studies, State Univ NY Albany, 70-, State Univ NY fac res fel, classification and anal of Babylonian Talmud, 68-72; Am Coun Learned Soc fel, 72-73. **MEMBERSHIPS** Soc Advan Am Philos. **RESEARCH** Religion; Plato; epistemology. **SELECTED PUBLICATIONS** Auth, Biographical Misunderstandings, Tradition J Orthodox Jewish Thought, Vol 30, 96. **CONTACT ADDRESS** Dept of Judaic Studies, SUNY, Albany, 1400 Washington Ave, Albany, NY 12222-1000.

ECONOMOU, ELLY HELEN
PERSONAL Born Thessaloniki, Greece **DISCIPLINE** ECUMENICAL STUDIES **EDUCATION** Pac Union Col, BA, 66; Andrews Univ, MA, 67; Univ Strasbourg, France, PhD, 75. **CAREER** Instr French, 67-70, instr French & Greek, 70-72, Prof Bibl Lang & Relig, Andrews Univ, 72-77. **MEMBERSHIPS** Soc Bibl Lit; MLA; Int Platform Asn; Am Class League. **RESEARCH** Ecumenical studies; religion, the Greek Orthodox church, patristic lit; papyrology. **SELECTED PUBLICATIONS** Auth, Beloved Enemy, Pac Press Publ Asn, 68; numerous articles in Youth's Beakon & Children's Friend, 51-72. **CONTACT ADDRESS** Dept of Relig, Andrews Univ, 100 US Hwy 31, Berrien Springs, MI 49104-0001.

EDDY, PAUL R.
PERSONAL Born 04/04/1959, Minneapolis, MN, m, 1988, 1 child **DISCIPLINE** SYSTEMATIC THEOLOGY **EDUCATION** Bethel Col, BA, 83; Bethel Theol Sem, MATS, 91; Marquette Univ, PLD, 99. **CAREER** Asst prof, Bethel Col, 97-. **MEMBERSHIPS** SBL; EPS; ETS; CTRF. **RESEARCH** Religious diversity; theology of religion; historical Jesus. **SELECTED PUBLICATIONS** Co-ed, Divine Foreknowledge and Human Freedom: Four Views (Intervarsity, forthcoming). **CONTACT ADDRESS** Dept Bible Studies, Bethel Col, Minnesota, 3900 Bethel Dr, Saint Paul, MN 55112-6902. **EMAIL** eddpau@bethel.edu

EDELBERG, WALTER
PERSONAL Born 10/14/1951, Fairborn, OH, m, 1995 **DISCIPLINE** PHILOSOPHY **EDUCATION** Univ Pittsburgh, PhD. **CAREER** Assoc prof, Univ IL at Chicago. **RESEARCH** Philosophical logic; metaphysics; philosophy of language; history of early modern philosophy. **SELECTED PUBLICATIONS** Auth, The Fifth Meditation, Philos Rev, 90; Intentional Identity and the Attitudes, Ling Philos,92; Propositions, Circumstances, Objects, Jour Philo Logic, 94. **CONTACT ADDRESS** Dept of Philos, Univ of Illinois, Chicago, MC 267, Chicago, IL 60607. **EMAIL** edelberg@uic.edu

EDELMAN, DIANA V.
DISCIPLINE BIBLICAL STUDIES; ANCIENT SYNO-PALESTINIAN HISTORY & ARCHAEOLOGY **EDUCATION** Smith Col, AB, 75; Univ Chicago, MA, 78, PhD, 86. **CAREER** Lectr, St Xavier Univ, 90-91; assoc prof, James Madison Univ, 93-00; lectr, Univ Sheffield, 00-; staff mem, Tel Rehov Excavations, Israel. **HONORS AND AWARDS** Grant-in-aid Am Coun Learned Studies, 88; vis prof Ecole biblique et archeol Jerusalem, 96. **MEMBERSHIPS** Soc Bibl Lit; Am Schools of Orient Res; Cath Bibl Asn. **RESEARCH** Ancient Syno-Palestinian history & archaelology; Deuteronomistic history; Ancient Israelite religion; 2nd temple Judaism. **SELECTED PUBLICATIONS** Auth, King Saul in the Historiography of Judah, Journal for the Study of the Old Testament Supplement Series, 91; ed, The Fabric of History: Text, Artifact, & Israels Past, Journal for the Study of the Old Testament Supplement Series, 91; auth, You Shall Not Abhor an Edomite for He is Your Brother: Edom and Seir in History and Tradition, Archaeology and Biblical Studies, 95; The Triumph of Elohim: From Yahuisms to Judaisms, Biblical Exegesis and Theology, 95. **CONTACT ADDRESS** Western Bank, Univ of Sheffield, Sheffield S10 2TN. **EMAIL** d.edelman@sheffield.ac.uk

EDELMAN, DIANE PENNEYS
DISCIPLINE LEGAL WRITING **EDUCATION** Princeton Univ, AB, 79; Brooklyn Law Sch, JD, 83. **CAREER** Prof, Villanova Univ Sch Law, 93-. **HONORS AND AWARDS** Brooklyn J Int Law, 81-83; Ed-in-Ch, 82-83; Philip C. Jessup Int Law Moot Ct Team,82; Best Oralist, Eastern Region; First Runner-Up Team, Eastern Region; Alexander Mehr Mem prize; Oceana Publ prize; Moot Ct Honor Soc; Honorable Mention, Best Brief awd, 81. **MEMBERSHIPS** Amer Soc Int Law; co-founder and Vice Ch, Tchg Int Law Interest Gp Ch, 96-; bd ed, Legal Writing: The Journal of the Legal Writing Institute, 98-; Philadelphia and Amer Bar Asn; Princeton Univ, Alumni Schools Comt; bd dir, Trinity Nursery and Kindergarten, 94-; Wayne Art Ctr, 94-98; Philadelphia Volunteer Lawyers for the Arts & Philadelphia Area Repertory Theatre, 89-95. **RESEARCH** Teaching international law moot court as an alternative to traditional legal writing instruction. **SELECTED PUBLICATIONS** Auth, How They Write:Our Students' Reflections on Writing, 6:1 Perspectives 24, 97; Opening Our Doors to the World:Introducing International Law in Legal Writing and Legal Research Courses,5:1 Perspectives 1, 96; Coauth, Overcoming Language and Legal Differences in the Global Classroom:Teaching Legal Research and Legal Writing to International Law Graduates and International Law Students, 96 Proceedings Issue,3 Legal Writing: J Legal Writing Inst 127, 97; From Product to Process:Evolution of a Legal Writing Program, 58 Pittsburgh Law Rev 719, 97. **CONTACT ADDRESS** Law School, Villanova Univ, 299 N. Spring Mill Rd, Villanova, PA 19085. **EMAIL** edelman@law.villanova.edu

EDGAR, TIMOTHY W.
DISCIPLINE LAW **EDUCATION** Univ Western Ontario, BA, 82, LLB, 85; Osgoode Hall Law Sch, LLM, 88. **CAREER** Prof, 89-. **SELECTED PUBLICATIONS** Co-ed, Materials on Canadian Income Tax. **CONTACT ADDRESS** Fac of Law, Univ of Western Ontario, London, ON, Canada N6A 3K7. **EMAIL** tedgar@julian.uwo.ca

EDGAR, WILLIAM
PERSONAL Born 10/11/1944, Wilmington, NC, m, 1968, 2 children **DISCIPLINE** APOLOGETICS **EDUCATION** Harvard Univ, BA, 66; Westminster Theol Sem, MDiv, 69; Columbia Univ, grad stud; Univ de Geneve, D Th, 93. **CAREER** Fac, Brunswick Sch, 70-78; prof, Faculte Libre de Theologie Reformee, Aix-en-Provence, France, 79-89; prof, Westminster Theol Sem, 89-. **MEMBERSHIPS** Am Musicological soc; soc for Ethnomusicology; Evangelical theological Soc; Am Soc of church His; Columbia Black Music res; Societe de 1"Histoire du Prodtestantisme Francais" **RESEARCH** Sociology of Religion; Historical Theology; Afro-Am Hist; Aesthetics. **SELECTED PUBLICATIONS** Auth, Sur le Rock; Auth, Bibliographie D'ouvrages Apologetique; Auth, Reasons of the Heart, 96; Auth, L'Apologetica di Cornelius Van Til, Studi di teologia VII/1, 95; Auth, No News is Good News: Modernity, the Postmodern, and Apologetics, Westminster Theol Jour 57, 95; Auth, Un' Accomppaniata Insolita: Jazz e Vangelo, Studi di Teologia 15, VIII/1, 96; Auth, La Carte Protestante, 97; auth, The Face of Truth, 01. **CONTACT ADDRESS** Westminster Theol Sem, Pennsylvania, PO Box 27009, Philadelphia, PA 19118. **EMAIL** wedgar@wts.edu

EDGAR, WILLIAM JOHN
PERSONAL Born 01/20/1933, Charlottesville, VA, m, 1962, 4 children **DISCIPLINE** PHILOSOPHY **EDUCATION** Cornell Univ, BA, 59; Syracuse Univ, MA, 66, PhD(philos), 72. **CAREER** Syst analyst, Advan Elec Ctr, Gen Elec Co, 59-62 & Elec Lab, 62-65; instr Philos, Syracuse Univ, 68-69; asst prof, 69-74, assoc prof, 74-79, Distinguished Teaching Prof Philos, State Univ NY, Geneseo, 79-, chairperson Dept, 78-. **HONORS AND AWARDS** Chancellor's Awd for Excellence in Teaching, State Univ NY, 74 & 76. **MEMBERSHIPS** Am Philos Asn; Mind Asn. **RESEARCH** Theory of knowledge; foundations of mathematics and science; philosophy of mind. **SELECTED PUBLICATIONS** Auth, Professor Gotesky and the law of non-contradiction, Philos & Phenomenol Res, 12/71; Is modesty a virtue?, J Value Inquiry, Winter, 72; Is intuitionism the epistemically serious foundation for mathematics?, Philosophia Mathematica, Winter 73; Continuity and the individuation of modes in Spinoza's physics, In: Spinoza's Metaphysics, Van Gorcum, 76; Locations, Can J Philos, 79; Evidence, Univ Am Press, 80; The Problem Solver's Guide to Logic, Univ Am Press, 83; The Elements of Logic, Sci Res Assoc, 89d. **CONTACT ADDRESS** Dept of Philosophy, SUNY, Col at Geneseo, 1 College Cir, Geneseo, NY 14454-1401. **EMAIL** edgarb@geneseo.edu

EDGE, HOYT LITTLETON
PERSONAL Born 02/23/1944, Louisville, KY, d **DISCIPLINE** PHILOSOPHY OF MIND, PARASYCHOLOGY **EDUCATION** Stetson Univ, BA, 66; Vanderbilt Univ, MA, 68, PhD(Philos), 70. **CAREER** Asst prof, 70-74, assoc prof, 74-81, prof Philos, Rollins Col ,81-. **HONORS AND AWARDS** McKean Prof of Philosophy, 97. **MEMBERSHIPS** Am Soc Psychical Res; Soc Psychial Res; Southern Soc Philos & Psychol; Parapsychological Asn. **RESEARCH** Creativity and altered states of consciousness; experiments in ESP, PK and paranormal healing; philosophical implications of parapsychology; cross-cultural concepts of self. **SELECTED PUBLICATIONS** Auth, Rorty on Identity, J Value Inquiry, Fall 74; co-ed, Philosophical Dimensions of Parapsychology, Charles Thomas, 76; auth, Do Spirits Matter: Survival and Disembodied Spirits, J Am Soc Psychical Res 7 (76); The Place of Paradigms in Parapsychology, In: The Philosophy of parapsychology, Parapsychology Found, 77; auth, A Philosophical Justification for the Conformation Behavior Model, J Am Soc Psychical Res 7 (78); coauth, Foundations of Parapsychology, Routledge, 86; auth, A Constructive Postmodern Perspective on Self and Community, 94; Spirituality in the Natural and Social Worlds, Revision, 95; Possession in Two Balinese Trance Ceremonies, Anthropology of Consciousness, 96. **CONTACT ADDRESS** Dept of Philosophy, Rollins Col, 1000 Holt Ave, Winter Park, FL 32789-4499. **EMAIL** edge@rollins.edu

EDINGER, ELIZABETH
DISCIPLINE LAW **EDUCATION** Univ British Columbia, BA, 64; LLB, 67; Oxford Univ, BCL, 77. **CAREER** Asst prof, 78-87; assoc prof, 87-88; assoc dean, 88-92; prof, 92-97; assoc dean, 97-. **RESEARCH** Constitutional Law; conflicts; creditor debtor law. **SELECTED PUBLICATIONS** Auth, pubs about conflict of laws, constitutional law, and creditors' remedies. **CONTACT ADDRESS** Fac of Law, Univ of British Columbia, 1822 East Mall, Vancouver, BC, Canada V6T 1Z1. **EMAIL** edinger@law.ubc.ca

EDLER, FRANK H. W.
PERSONAL Born 09/02/1947, Amorbach, West Germany, m, 1985, 2 children **DISCIPLINE** PHILOSOPHY **EDUCATION** Univ Rhode Island, BA, 71; NYork Univ, MA, 74; Univ Toronto, PhD, 92. **CAREER** Education. **HONORS AND AWARDS** Twice alternate for Fulbright. **MEMBERSHIPS** Am Philos Asn; Heidegger Conf N Am. **RESEARCH** Heidegger; Hermeneutics; Phenomenology; Technology, Classical Philology; Literature. **SELECTED PUBLICATIONS** Auth Philosophy, Language, and Politics; Heideggers Attempt to Steal the Language of the Revolution in 1933-34, Soc Res, 90; Retreat from Radicality: Poggeler on Heideggers Politics, Grad Fac Philos J, 91; trans, Selected Letters from the Heidegger-Blochmann Correspondence, Grad Fac Philos Jour, 91; auth Heideggers Interpretation of the German Revolution, Res in Phenomenol, 93; rev, The Finitude of Being, Int Studies in Philos, 93; rev, Heideggers Crisis: Philosophy and Politics in Nazi Germany, Jour Hist Philos, 95; auth Heidegger and Werner Jaeger on the Eve of 1933: A Possible Rapprochement?, Res In Phenomenol, 97; auth, Alfred Baeumler on Hoelderlin and the Greeks: Reflections on the Heidegger-Baeumler Relationship, Part I, II, III, Janus Head, 99, 99, 00. **CONTACT ADDRESS** 908 Elmwood Ave, Lincoln, NE 68510-3320. **EMAIL** fedler@metropo.mccneb.edu

EDWARDS, ABIYAH, JR.
PERSONAL Born 12/23/1927, Princeton, KY, s, 19 children **DISCIPLINE** RELIGION **EDUCATION** Institute of Divine Metaphysical Research Inc, DD, 1971. **CAREER** UAW Local 600-Ford, CIO, 49-65; Ford Motor Co, Dearborn, MI, 65-92; Kaiser Jeep; Enjoy Restaurant/Palace, creative consultant/mgr, 88-89; Third Baptist Church, assoc pastor; Inst of Divine Metaphysical Research Inc, recruiter, lecturer; Universal School of Spiritual Awareness, Dean, currently. **HONORS AND AWARDS** Project Head Start, Volunteer Service Awd, 1992. **SELECTED PUBLICATIONS** Author, The Beauty of it All, 1995. **CONTACT ADDRESS** Universal School of Spiritual Awareness, 5300 Newport Ave, Detroit, MI 48213.

EDWARDS, CLIFFORD WALTER
PERSONAL Born 07/02/1932, Southampton, NY, m, 1956, 3 children **DISCIPLINE** RELIGION **EDUCATION** Drew Univ, BA, 54; Garrett Theol Sem, BD, 58; Northwestern Univ, PhD(Bibl study & world relig), 64. **CAREER** Prof relig, Wesleyan Col, Ga, 63-68; prof & chmn dept, Randolph-Macon Col, 68-75; Assoc Prof Relig, VA Commonwealth Univ, 75-; Ed, Wesleyan Quart Rev, 65-68. **MEMBERSHIPS** Am Acad Relig; Soc Bibl Lit **RESEARCH** World Religions; religion and culture; biblical studies. **SELECTED PUBLICATIONS** Auth, Christian Being and Doing: A Study-commentary of James and I Peter, Ed Missions, Methodist Church, 65; ed, Methodism in Cuba, 66 & Japanese Contributions to the Study of John Wesley, 67; auth, VanGogh and God: A Creative Spiritual Quest. **CONTACT ADDRESS** Dept of Philos & Relig Studies, Virginia Commonwealth Univ, Box 2025, Richmond, VA 23284-2025. **EMAIL** cedwards@saturn.vcu.edu

EDWARDS, DOUGLAS R.
PERSONAL Born 01/09/1950, Superior, NE, m, 3 children **DISCIPLINE** NEW TESTAMENT AND CHRISTIAN ORIGINS **EDUCATION** Boston Univ, MDiv, 78; Boston Univ Grad School Arts & Sci, PhD, 87. **CAREER** Vis instr, Univ Vermont, 84-85; instr, Col of Holy Cross, 85-87; from asst prof to full of Religion, Univ Puget Sound, 87-99-. **HONORS AND AWARDS** NEH fel, 91-92; sr fel Albright Inst Archaeol Res Jerusalem, 92; Deans Tchg Awd, 96; Soc Bibl Res grant, 98-00; NWACC grant, 98, 99; vis fel, Wolfson Col Oxford, 98. **MEMBERSHIPS** Am Acad Relig; Am Schools Oriental Res; Archael Inst Am; Cath Bibl Asn; Class Soc Am Acad Rome; Soc Bibl Lit. **RESEARCH** Old World archaeology with an emphasis on Israel, the Crimea, and Asia Minor from the Hellenistic through the Byzantine periods; the Gospel of Luke and Acts; Ancient romances religion and power in antiquity. **SELECTED PUBLICATIONS** Auth Yodefat, 1992, Israel Explor Jour, 95; The 1994 Black Sea Project Excavations at Chersonesus: A Preliminary Report, Ukrainian Acad Arts & Sci, 95; The 1995 Black Sea Project Excavations at Chersonesus: A Preliminary Report, Ukrainian Acad Arts & Sci, 96; Religion and Power: Pagans, Jews, and Christians in the Greek East, Oxford Univ Press, 96; Archaeology and the Galilee: Texts and Contexts in the Greco-Roman and Byzantine Periods, Scholars Press, 97; The 1996 Black Sea Project Excavations at Chersonesus: A Preliminary Report, Ukrainian Acad Arts and Sci, 97; Cappadocia, Jotapata, Miletus, Oxford Encycl Archael in the Near East, Oxford Univ Press, 97; The Ancient Road of Sepphoris: A Cultural and Historical Study, Archaeology and the Galilee: Texts and Contexts in the Graeco-Roman and Byzantine Periods, 97; Pleasurable Reading or Symbols of Power: Religious Themes and Social Context in Chariton, Ancient Fiction and Early Christian Narrative, Scholars Press, 98. **CONTACT ADDRESS** Relig Dept, Univ of Puget Sound, 1500 N Warner, Tacoma, WA 98416. **EMAIL** dedwards@ups.edu

EDWARDS, GEORGE CHARLES, III
PERSONAL Born 12/25/1946, Rochester, NY, 4 children **DISCIPLINE** POLITICAL SCIENCE **EDUCATION** Yale, 83, PhD. **CAREER** Assoc Prof, Rensselaer Polytechnic Institute, 18 years. **HONORS AND AWARDS** Woodrow Wilson Fell; Intl Studies; Assoc Sprout Awd in Intl Ecology. **MEMBERSHIPS** Am Pol Sci; Soc for Soc Studies of Sci. **RESEARCH** Wiser Steeing of Tech. **SELECTED PUBLICATIONS** The Polic-Making Process, 3rd ed, Englewood Cliffs Prentice Hall, 93; When Expert Advice Works and When it Does Not, IEEE Technology and Society Magazine, pp23-29, 97; Science, Government and the Politics of Knowledge, in Handbook of Science and Technology Sutdies, Sage, pp533-553, 95; Can Science Be More Useful In Politics? The Case of Ecological Risk Assessment, Human and Ecological Risk Assessment vol 1,pp395-406, 95; Incrementalism, Intelligent Trial-and -Error and the Future of Ploitical Decision Theory, in H. Redner ed, An Heretical Heir of the Enlightenment Westview, 93. **CONTACT ADDRESS** Rensselaer Polytech Inst, Troy, NY 12180-3590. **EMAIL** GEDWARDS@TAMU.EDU

EDWARDS, HARRY T.
PERSONAL Born 11/03/1940, New York, NY, m, 2000, 2 children **DISCIPLINE** LAW **EDUCATION** Cornell Univ, BS 1962; Univ of Michigan Law School, JD, 1965. **CAREER** Seyfarth, Shaw Fairweather & Geraldson, Chicago, attorney, 65-70; Univ of Michigan Law School, professor, 70-75, 77-80; Harvard Univ Law School, prof 1975-77; Amtrak, bd dir, 77-80, chmn bd 1979-80; US Ct of Appeals, Washington, DC, judge 1980-94, chief judge, 94-. **HONORS AND AWARDS** Honorary Doctor of Law degress from Williams Coll, Univ of Detroit, Georgetown University, Brooklyn College, State University of New York, John Jay College of Criminal Justice, Lewis & Clark College, St Lawrence Univ, New York Law School, Univ Conn; Society of Am Law Teachers Awd for distinguished contributions to teaching and public service, 82; Whitney North Seymour Medal, Amer Arbitration Assn, 88; Awd for "contributions to legal education," District of Columbia Law Sch, 91; Awd for "outstanding contributions to the field of Dispute Resolution," Soc of Professionals in Dispute Resolution, 92; Louis A. Smith Distiniguished Jurist Awd, Thomas M. Cooley Law Sch, 93; Awd of Excellence, Florida Bar Labor and Employment Law Section, 93; Hon Fel of the Col, The Col of Labor and Employment Lawyers, Inc., 97. **MEMBERSHIPS** Amer Law Institute; Amer Bar Assn; Amer Academy of Arts & Sciences; Amer Judicature Society; Unique Learning Center, mentor, instructor, bd of directors. **SELECTED PUBLICATIONS** Co-author, Labor Relations Law in the Pub Sector, 85, The Lawyer as a Negotiator, 77, Collective Bargaining & Labor Arbitration, 79, Higher Educ & the Law, 80; author of more than 75 scholarly articles. **CONTACT ADDRESS** US Court of Appeals - DC Circuit, 333 Constitution Ave NW, Washington, DC 20001-2866.

EDWARDS, JAMES
PERSONAL Born 10/28/1945, Colorado Springs, CO, m, 1968, 2 children **DISCIPLINE** BIBLICAL STUDIES **EDUCATION** Whitworth Col, BA, 67; Princeton Theol Sem, MDiv, 70; Fuller Theol Sem, PhD, 78. **CAREER** Assoc minister, Colo, 71-78; prof, Jamestown Coll, 78-97; prof, Whitworth Coll, 97-. **HONORS AND AWARDS** NDHC Speakers Bureau; Prof of the Year, Jamestown Coll; Sears Roebuck Found Teach Excell Awd; Ger Acad Exchange Ser Awd; Templeton Grant; Teach Excell Awd, Whitworth Coll; Pew Gordon Res Grant. **MEMBERSHIPS** SBL. **RESEARCH** New Testament; Synoptic Gospels. **SELECTED PUBLICATIONS** Auth, The Divine Intruder: When God Breaks into Your Life, New Press, 00; auth, "Romans," in New Intl Bible Commentary, Hendrickson, 92; auth, The Gospel of Mark, Pillar New Test Commentary Series, Erdmans, forthcoming; auth, "Romans," in New Interpreter's Study Bible, Abingdon Press, forthcoming. **CONTACT ADDRESS** Dept Religion, Philosophy, Whitworth Col, 300 West Hawthorne Rd, Spokane, WA 99251-2515. **EMAIL** jedwards@whitworth.edu

EDWARDS, REM B.
PERSONAL Born 10/02/1934, Washington, GA, m, 1962, 2 children **DISCIPLINE** PHILOSOPHY **EDUCATION** Emory Univ, AB, 56; Yale Univ, BD, 59; Emory Univ, PhD, 62. **CAREER** Asst prof Philos, Jacksonville Univ, 62-66; assoc prof Philos, Univ Tenn, 66-70; prof Philos, Univ Tenn, 70-97. **HONORS AND AWARDS** Phi Beta Kappa; Danforth Grad Fel; Chancellor's Res Scholar; Distinguished Emory-at Oxford Alumnus; Lindsay Young prof. **MEMBERSHIPS** Tenn Philos Assoc Pres, 73-74; Soc for Philos Relig Pres, 81-82; S Soc Philos & Psychol Pres, 84-85; RS Hartman Value Inst, 89-. **RESEARCH** Ethics; Medical Ethics; Philos Relig; Ethics and Animals; Axiology; Cosmology. **SELECTED PUBLICATIONS** Auth, "How Process Theology Can Affirm creation Ex Nihelo, "Process Studies, 00; Co-ed, Bioethics for Medical Education, JAI Pr, 98; Values, Ethics, and Alcoholism, JAI Pr, 97. **CONTACT ADDRESS** Dept of Philosophy, Univ of Tennessee, Knoxville, 8709 Longmeade Dr, Knoxville, TN 37923. **EMAIL** redwards@utkux.utcc.utk.edu

EDWARDS, RICHARD ALAN
PERSONAL Born 12/31/1934, West Mahanoy Twp, PA, d, 1958, 3 children **DISCIPLINE** NEW TESTAMENT **EDUCATION** Princeton Univ, BA, 56; Univ Chicago, MA, 62, PhD, 68. **CAREER** Instr relig, Bethany Col, Kans, 62-63; instr, Susquehanna Univ, 63-66; assoc prof, Thiel Col, 68-72; assoc prof, Va Polytech Inst & State Univ, 72-78; assoc prof New Testament, Marquette Univ, 78-; Lutheran Church Am res & creativity grant, 69-70. **MEMBERSHIPS** Soc Bibi Lit; Studiorum Novi Testamenti Societas; Cath Bibl Asn. **RESEARCH** Synoptic Gospels and Acts; theology of Matthew. **SELECTED PUBLICATIONS** Coauth, The Sentences of Sextus, Scholars Press, 81; auth, Matthew's Story of Jesus, Fortress, 85; auth, Matthew's Portrait of Disciples: How the Text-Connoted Reader is Informed, Trinity International, 97. **CONTACT ADDRESS** Theol Dept, Marquette Univ, P.O. Box 1881, Milwaukee, WI 53201. **EMAIL** edwardsr@marquette.edu

EDWARDS, RICHARD W.
PERSONAL Born 06/02/1935, Columbus, OH, m, 1958, 2 children **DISCIPLINE** LAW **EDUCATION** Cornell Univ, BA, JD. **CAREER** Prof. **SELECTED PUBLICATIONS** Auth, International Monetary Collaboration, Transnational, 85; International Monetary Policy: The Next 25 Years, Vanderbilt J Transnational Law, 92; Reservations to Treaties, Mich J Int Law, 89. **CONTACT ADDRESS** Col Law, Univ of Toledo, Toledo, OH 43606. **EMAIL** redwards@questinternet.net

EDWARDS, RUTH MCCALLA
PERSONAL Born 04/23/1949, Cleveland, OH, m **DISCIPLINE** LAW **EDUCATION** Hiram Coll, BA 1971; Univ of Cincinnati Coll of Law, JD 1974. **CAREER** Legal Aid Soc of Cincinnati, atty & office mgr 1974-77; Private Law Practice, atty 1977-79; Hamilton County Public Defender Comm, atty 1979; Univ of Cincinnati, atty, prog coord, paralegal prog 1979-. **HONORS AND AWARDS** Hon Degree of Tech Letters Cincinnati Tech Coll 1985; YMCA Black Achievers Awd 1985. **MEMBERSHIPS** Admitted OH State Bar 1974; admitted Fed Bar So Dist of OH 1974; mem bd trustees Cincinnati Tech Coll 1977-; mem Amer, Cincinnati Bar Assns; mem & past pres Black Lawyers Assn of Cincinnati; past bd mem Legal Aid Soc of Cincinnati; bd mem & officer Winton Hills Med & Halth Ctr; bd mem & past officer Comprehensive Comm Child Care; bd mem Cincinnati Tech Coll; mem Alpha Kappa Alpha Sor; arbitrator Better Business Bureau Arbitration Prog; mem Assn of Comm Coll Trustees; sec Central Region Minority Affairs Assembly of the Assn of Comm Coll Trustees; mem Amer Assn for Paralegal Education Inc; chairperson bd trustees Cincinnati Tech Coll 1983-84; past bd mem, officer Winton Hills Med & Health Ctr; arbitrator Amer Arbitration Assoc; chair Central Region Minority Affairs Comm of the Assoc of Conity Coll Trustees. **CONTACT ADDRESS** Paralegal Program, Univ of Cincinnati, Cincinnati, OH 45221.

EDWARDS, SANDRA S.
PERSONAL Born 04/30/1944, Washington, DC **DISCIPLINE** MEDIEVAL PHILOSOPHY **EDUCATION** Univ Pa, PhD. **CAREER** Philos, Univ Ark **RESEARCH** Meister Eckhart and Mysticism. **SELECTED PUBLICATIONS** Transl, St. Thomas Aquinas's Quaestiones Quodlibetales I & II, Pontifical Inst Medieval Studies, 83. **CONTACT ADDRESS** Philosophy Dept, Univ of Arkansas, Fayetteville, Main 318, Fayetteville, AR 72701. **EMAIL** sandrae@comp.uark.edu

EELLS, ELLERY T.
PERSONAL Born 03/26/1953, Lynwood, CA, m, 1981, 2 children **DISCIPLINE** PHILOSOPHY **EDUCATION** Univ CA, Santa Barbara, BA, 75, Berkeley, MA, 78, PhD(philos), 80. **CAREER** Vis asst prof, NC State Univ, Raleigh, 80-81; asst prof, 81-83, assoc prof, 84-87, prof philos, Univ WI-Madison, 87-. **HONORS AND AWARDS** Guggenheim; ACLS; NSF. **MEMBERSHIPS** Am Philos Asn; Philos of Science Asn. **RESEARCH** Philosophical foundations of probability theory; theory of rational decision; philosophy of science; logic, inductive logic; probabilistic causality and the question of transitivits. **SELECTED PUBLICATIONS** Auth, Causality, Utility and Decision, Synthese, 8/81; Rational Decision and Causality, Cambridge Univ Press, 9/82; Probalistic Causality, Cambridge, 91. **CONTACT ADDRESS** Dept Philos, Univ of Wisconsin, Madison, 600 North Park St, Madison, WI 53706-1403. **EMAIL** eteells@facstaff.wisc.edu

EGAN, HARVEY DANIEL
PERSONAL Born 11/06/1937, CT **DISCIPLINE** THEOLOGY **EDUCATION** Worcester Polytech Inst, BS, 59; Boston Col, MA, 65; Woodstock Col, MA, 69; Univ Munster, ThD, 73. **CAREER** Res engr, Boeing Airplane Co, 59-60; lectr philos, Holy Cross Col, 65-66; asst prof theol, Santa Clara Univ, 73-75; asst prof, 75-80, Assoc Prof Theol, Boston Col, 80-, Jesuit priest, R C Priesthood, Soc Jesus, New Eng, 60-. **MEMBERSHIPS** Cath Theol Soc Am; Col Theol Soc; Am Acad Relig. **RESEARCH** Christian mysticism; theology of Karl Rahner; systematic theology. **SELECTED PUBLICATIONS** Auth, The Spiritual Exercises and the Ignatian Mystical Horizon, Inst Jesuit Sources, 76; Christian apophatic and kataphatic mysticisms, Theol Studies, 78; contribr, Rahner Festschrift, Herder, Freiburg, spring 79; Ralmer's mystical theology, In: Theology and Discovery, Essays in Honor of Karl Rahner, Marquette Univ Press, 80; The cloud of unknowing and pseudo-contemplation, Thought, 6/79; The Christian mystics and today's theological horizon, Listening, 82; Selected Reflections of the Christocentrism of St Teresa of Avila, Word & Spirit, 82; What Are They Saying About Mysticism, Paulist Press, 82. **CONTACT ADDRESS** Theol Dept, Boston Col, Chestnut Hill, 140 Commonwealth Ave, Chestnut Hill, MA 02167-3800.

EGLESTON, DON
DISCIPLINE LAW **EDUCATION** Saskatchewan, BA, 66; LLB, 67. **CAREER** Law, Univ of BC **HONORS AND AWARDS** Co-ed, Can Criminal Law Practice. **RESEARCH** Criminal law; criminal procedure; clinical law; advanced criminal law; trial advocacy. **SELECTED PUBLICATIONS** Auth, pubs about criminal law. **CONTACT ADDRESS** Fac of Law, Univ of British Columbia, 1822 East Mall, Vancouver, BC, Canada V6T 1Z1. **EMAIL** egleston@law.ubc.ca

EHRENREICH, N.
PERSONAL Born 05/16/1952, Topeka, KS, s, 1 child **DISCIPLINE** LAW SCIENCE **EDUCATION** Yale Univ, BA 74; Univ Virginia, JD 79, LLM 82. **CAREER** Col Law, Denver Univ **MEMBERSHIPS** SALT; NLG. **RESEARCH** Feminist legal theory. **SELECTED PUBLICATIONS** Auth, Conceptualism by Any Other Name, Univ Denver L Rev, 97; The Progressive Potential in Privatization, U of Denver L Rev, 96; O.J. Simpson and the Myth of Gender/Race Conflict, U of Colorado L Rev, 96; auth, The Colonization of the Womb, Duke L Jour, 93; auth, Surrogacy as Resistance: The Misplaced Focus on Choice in the Surrogacy and Abortion Funding Contexts, DePaul L Rev, 92; auth, Wombs for Hire, Birth Power: The Case for Surrogacy, Shalev, rev, TIKKUN, 91; auth, Pluralist Myths and Powerless Men: The Ideology of Reasonableness in Sexual Harassment Law, Yale L Jour, 90; auth, "Confessions of a White Salsa Dancer: Appropriation, Identity, & the Latin Music Craze," U Denver L Rev, LatCrit V Symposium, (forthcoming, 01); coauth, Putting Theory into Practice: A Battered Women's Clemency Clinic, Clinical L. Rev., (forthcoming, 01). **CONTACT ADDRESS** College of Law, Univ of Denver, 1900 Olive St, Denver, CO 80220. **EMAIL** nehrenre@mail.law.du.edu

EICHELBERGER, WILLIAM L.
PERSONAL Born 02/07/1922, Salisbury, NC, m **DISCIPLINE** THEOLOGY **EDUCATION** Lincoln U, AB 1959; Princeton Theol Sem, MDiv 1962, MTheol 1963; NYork Theol Sem, MST 1968. **CAREER** Christian Soc Ethics, Louisville Presby Theological Seminary, assoc prof; Rutgers Univ & Newark Coll of Engineering, Protestant chaplain 67-72; NY Theological Seminary, visiting lecturer Theology & Ethics 68-70; Newark Coll of Engineering, educ consultant 68-69, instructor Contemp Literature & Expostry Writing 68-72; Univ Coll, instructor Political Science dept 71-72; Laconia Comm Presbytery Church, pastor 65-67; Southern Univ Baton Rouge, campus pastor 63-65; various positions as chaplain & instructional seminars; soc Ethics & Theology, lecturer; consultant in comm devel & soc change. **HONORS AND AWARDS** Dist alumni awd Lincoln U; elec to roll of hon Ministries to Blacks in Hghr Edn. **MEMBERSHIPS** Mem KY Commn on Hum Rights 1975; mem Soc for Study of Blk Rel; Assn for Study of Afro-Am Life & Hist; Am Civ Lib Union; NAACP; Urban Leag; PUSH;pres bd dir Louisville Oppor Indstrlztn Ctrs Inc 0a05 1943-46, 48-58. **SELECTED PUBLICATIONS** Auth, Reality in Black & White; contrib various periodicals. **CONTACT ADDRESS** Camden Metro Ministries, 3513 Merriel Ave, Camden, NJ 08105.

EICHORN, LISA
DISCIPLINE CIVIL PROCEDURE AND LEGAL RESEARCH & WRITING **EDUCATION** Princeton Univ; BA, 87; Duke Law Sch, JD, 90. **CAREER** Litigation assoc, Bingham, Dana & Gould; prof, 92; lectr, dir, Acad Support Prog. **HONORS AND AWARDS** BA with hon(s), 87; JD with hon(s). **RESEARCH** Disability law, employment law. **SELECTED PUBLICATIONS** Style ed, Law & Contemp Problems, an interdisciplinary law jour. **CONTACT ADDRESS** Law Sch, West Virginia Univ, Morgantown, PO Box 6009, Morgantown, WV 26506-6009.

EIESLAND, NANCY L.
DISCIPLINE THEOLOGY **EDUCATION** Central Bible Coll, BA, 86; Emory Univ, MDiv, 91, PhD, 95. **CAREER** Instr, Emory Univ, 92-94; ASST PROF, SOCIOL RELIG, CANDLER SCH THEOLOGY, GRAD DIV REL, EMORY UNIV, 95-. **MEMBERSHIPS** Am Acad Rel; Asn Sociol Relig; Am Sociol Asn; Relig Res Asn; Soc Disability Stud; Soc Scient Stud Relig. **RESEARCH** Sociol relig; gender; sociol culture; orgs; qualitative res methods; soc theory; disability stud in relig; Am relig soc hist. **SELECTED PUBLICATIONS** Co-ed, Human disability and the Service of God: Reassessing Religious PRactice, Abingdon Press, 98; co-ed, Contemporary American Religion: An Ethnographic Reader, AltaMira Press, 97; auth, The Disabled God: Toward a Liberatory Theology of Disability, Abingdon Press, 94; auth, Irreconcilable Differences: Conflict, Schism, and Religious Restructuring in a United Methodist Church, in Pentecostal Currents in American Protestantism, Univ Ill Press, forthcoming; co-auth, Ecology: Seeing the Congregation in Context, in Studying Congregations, Abingdon Press, 98; auth, Mapping Faith: Choice and Change in Local Religious Organizational Environments, in Re-Forming the Center: American Protestantism, 1960 to the Present, Eerdmans Publishers, 98; auth, Barriers and Bridges: RElating the Disability Rights Movement and REligious Organizations, in Human Disability and the Service of God: REassessing Religious Practice, Abingdon Press, 98; auth, Things Not Seen: Women with Disabilities, Oppression, and Practical Theology, in Liberating Faith Practices: Feminist Practical Theologies in Context, Peeters, 98; auth, Contending with a Giant: The Impact of a Megachurch on Exurban Religious Institutions, in Contemporary American Religion: An Ethnographic Reader, AltaMira Press, 97; auth, congregational profile in Congregation and Community: Stability and Change in American Religioun, Rutgers Univ Press, 97; auth, A Strange Road Home: Adult Women Converts to Classical Pentecostalism, in Mixed Blessings: Gender and Religious Fundamentalism Cross Culturally, Routledge, 97; co-auth, Mainline Protestantism in Atlanta, in Religions of Atlanta: Religious Diversity in the Centennial Olympic City, Scholars Press, 96; co- auth, Physical Ability as a Diffuse Status Characteristic: Implications for Small Group Interaction, in Advances in Group Processes, JAI Press, 96. **CONTACT ADDRESS** Candler Sch Theol, Emory Univ, 6 Bishops Hall, Atlanta, GA 30322. **EMAIL** neiesla@emory.edu

EIGO, FRANCIS AUGUSTINE
PERSONAL Born 12/10/1925, Smithville, NJ **DISCIPLINE** THEOLOGY **EDUCATION** LaSalle Coll, BA, 48; Cath Univ Am, STL, 64, MA, 65, STD, 69. **CAREER** From instr to asst prof, 66-73, dir admissions, 66-68, chmn relig studies dept, 72-77, Assoc Prof Theol, Villanova Univ, 73-, Dir Theol Inst, 73-, Chmn Relig Studies Dept, 80-90. **MEMBERSHIPS** NAm Acad Ecumenists; Am Acad Relig; Cath Theol Soc Am; Col Theol Soc; Soc Sci Studies Relig. **RESEARCH** Sacramental theol; French stylistics, poetic imagery; liturgy. **SELECTED PUBLICATIONS** Auth, The Images of Unfulfillment in the Poetry of Andre Chenier, 64 & The Easter Vigil: An Historical, Theological, Pastoral Study, 69, Cath Univ Am; contribr, Liturgy: shaped by and the shaper of the ongoing Christian community, Proc Villanove Univ Theol Inst, 70; ed, The Sacraments: Gods Love and Mercy Actualized, 79, Who Do People Say I Am?, 80, Whither Creativity, Freedom, Suffering?: Humanity, Cosmos, God, 81, Dimensions of Contemporary Spirituality, 82, Villanova Univ Press; Contemporary Spirituality: Responding to the Divine Initiative, 83; Modern Biblical Scholarship: Its Impact on Theology and Proclamation, 84; Called to Love: Towards a Contemporary Christian Ethic, 85; The Professions in Ethical Context: Vocations to Justice and Love, 86; The Human Experience of Conversion: Persons and Structures in Transformation, 87; A Discipleship of Equals: Towards a Christian Feminist Spirituality, 88; The Spirit Moving the Church in the United States, 89; Suffering and Healing in Our Day, 90; Imaging Christ: Politics, Art, Spirituality, 91; The Works of Mercy: New Perspectives on Ministry, 92; Rethinking the Spiritual Works of Mercy, 93; All Generations Shall Call Me Blessed, 94; New Perspectives in Beatitudes, 95; Teach Us to Pray, 96: Prayer the Global Experience, 97; At the Threshold of the Third Millenium, 98, Villanova Univ Pr; Religious Values at the Threshold of the Third Millennium, 99; Ethical Dilemmas in the New Millennium (I), Villanova Univ Pr, 00. **CONTACT ADDRESS** Dept of Theol & Relig Studies, Villanova Univ, 800 E Lancaster Ave, Villanova, PA 19085.

EISELE, THOMAS DAVID
PERSONAL Born 08/26/1948, Madison, WI, m, 1972 **DISCIPLINE** PHILOSOPHY, LAW **EDUCATION** Univ Wis, BA, 70; Harvard Univ, JD, 73. **CAREER** Atty, Isham, Lincoln and Beale, 73-76; dep dir, Lake Mich Fedn, 76-78; Bigelow teaching fel, Univ Chicago Law Sch, 78-79. **SELECTED PUBLICATIONS** Auth, The legal imagination and language: A philosophical criticism, Univ Colo Law Rev, spring 76; The apocalypse of Beckett's Endgame, Cross Currents, spring 76; Simone Weil's witness, Anglican Theol Rev, fall 78; The eagle has landed: Symbol of savagery, symbol of serenity, Mich Quart Rev, summer 79. **CONTACT ADDRESS** 5898 N Globe Ave, Westland, MI 48185.

EISENBAUM, PAMELA
PERSONAL Born 02/24/1961, Washington, DC, m, 1999 **DISCIPLINE** RELIGION; BIBLICAL STUDIES **EDUCATION** Harv Univ Divinity Sch, MTS, 86; Columbia Univ, PhD, 95 **CAREER** Asst Prof, 95-pres, Sch of Theol; Assoc Prof at Iliff, Sch of Theol, 20-. **HONORS AND AWARDS** Pres Fel, 87; Mrs. Giles Whiting Fel 94 **MEMBERSHIPS** Am Acad of Relig; Soc of Bibl Lit **RESEARCH** Jewish Background of the New Testament; Letters of Paul and Hebrews. **SELECTED PUBLICATIONS** Auth, "The Jewish Heroes of Christian History: Hebrews 11 in Literary Context," Scholars Press, 97; Coauth, "Heroes and History in Hebrews 11," in Early Christian Interpretation of the Scriptures of Israel, JSOT Press, 97 **CONTACT ADDRESS** Iliff Sch of Theol, 2201 S University, Denver, CO 80210. **EMAIL** peisenbaum@iliff.edu

EISENBERG, MELVIN ARON
PERSONAL Born 12/03/1934, New York, NY, 2 children **DISCIPLINE** LAW **EDUCATION** Columbia Col, AB, 56; Harvard Univ, LLB, 59. **CAREER** Vis prof law, Harvard Law Sch, 69-70; Prof, Sch Law, Univ Calif, Berkeley, 66-, Asst coun, President's Comn on Assassination of President Kennedy, 64; asst corp coun, City NY, 66; Reporter, Am Law Inst, 81-. **RESEARCH** Contracts; corporations; the legal process. **SELECTED PUBLICATIONS** Auth, The Divergence of Standards of Conduct and Standards of Review in Corporate Law, Fordham Law Rev, Vol 62, 93; An Overview of the Principles of Corporate Governance, Bus Lawyer, Vol 48, 93; 73rd Party Beneficiaries Columbia Law Review, Vol 1992, Pg 1376, 1992 Columbia Law Rev, Vol 92, 92; The Limits of Cognition and the Limits of Contract, Stanford Law Rev, Vol 47, 95; Expression Rules in Contract Law and Problems of Offer and Acceptance, Calif Law Rev, Vol 82, 94; The World of Contract and the World of Gift, Calif Law Rev, Vol 85, 97. **CONTACT ADDRESS** Sch of Law, Univ of California, Berkeley, 220 Boalt Hall, Berkeley, CA 94720-7201.

EISENBERG, PAUL D.
PERSONAL Born 07/07/1939, Worcester, MA, m, 1978, 1 child **DISCIPLINE** PHILOSOPHY **EDUCATION** Clark Univ, BA, 61; Harvard Univ, MA, 65, PhD, 67. **CAREER** Harvard Univ, tchg fel, 63-66; MIT, Inst, 64; Indiana Univ, Asst Prof, 66-70; Univ of ILL (Champaign-Urbana) Vis Asst Prof, 70; Indiana Univ, Assoc Prof, 70-78; Chmn, Dept of Phil, 74-80; Indiana Univ, Prof, 78-; Univ of MA, Vis Adj Prof, 80; Indiana Univ, Adj Prof, 89, Chmn, Dept of Phil, 89-94, Pres, Bloomington Fac Coun, 93-95, Co-Sec Univ Fac Coun, 93-95. **HONORS AND AWARDS** Scholar, Clark Univ, 57-61; Harvard Fel, 61-64; Indiana Univ Course Devel Grant, 86; IU Multi-disciplinary Seminar Grant, 88; Bloomington Campus Distinquished Svc Awd, 97; Pinnell Awd, 98; pres, phi beta kappa, 92-93; univ of indiana panel chmn, hobbes tercentenary con, 79; vpres, 68-69, 78-79, pres, 69-70, 79-80, indiana phil assoc; ed bd, nigerian phil jour, 80-84; exec bd mem, amer assoc tchrs of phil, 91-; harvard fel, 61-64. **MEMBERSHIPS** Phi Beta Kappa; APA; Fac Prof Assoc; Indiana Phil Assoc; Soc for Ancient Greek Phil; Hegel Soc of Amer; North Amer Nietzsch Soc; Amer Assoc Tchrs of Phil **RESEARCH** History of Ethics; Spinoza; Nineteenth-Century Continental Philosophy; especially Nietzsche. **CONTACT ADDRESS** Professor, Indiana Univ, Bloomington, Philosophy Sycamore Hall 026, Bloomington, IN 47405. **EMAIL** eisenber@indiana.edu

EISENSTAT, STEVEN M.
DISCIPLINE LAW **EDUCATION** Univ Ca, BA, 72, MEd, 74; Northeastern Univ, JD, 80. **CAREER** Prof, 93-. **RESEARCH** AIDS and the law; civil procedure; legal practice skills; torts. **SELECTED PUBLICATIONS** Auth, Capping Health Insurance Benefits for AIDS: An Analysis of Disability-Based Distinctions Under the Americans with Disabilities Act, Va Jour Law Polit, 94; The HIV Infected Health Care Worker: the New AIDS Scapegoat, Rutgers, 92; An Analysis of the Rationality of Mandatory Testing for the HIV Antibody; Balancing the Governmental Public Health Interests with the Individuals' Privacy Interest, Univ Pittsburgh Law Rev, 91. **CONTACT ADDRESS** Sch of Law, Suffolk Univ, 120 Tremont St., Boston, MA 02108-4977. **EMAIL** seisenst@acad.suffolk.edu

EISLER, BETH A.
DISCIPLINE LAW **EDUCATION** Univ Wash, BA, JD. **CAREER** Prof. **SELECTED PUBLICATIONS** Auth, pubs on contracts, commercial law, and wills and estates. **CONTACT ADDRESS** Col Law, Univ of Toledo, Toledo, OH 43606. **EMAIL** beisler@utnet.utoledo.edu

EITEL, KEITH E.
PERSONAL Born 10/13/1954, Dallas, TX, m, 1973, 2 children **DISCIPLINE** MISSIOLOGY **EDUCATION** Dallas Baptist Univ, BA, 76; Baylor Univ, MA, 77; Trinity Evangel Divinity School, D Miss, 85; Univ S Africa, D Theol. **CAREER** Prof, Cameroon Baptist Theol Sem, 77-85; prof, Criswell Col, 85-92; prof, Southeastern Baptist Theol Sem, 92-. **MEMBERSHIPS** Am Soc of Missiology; Evangel Missiological Soc; Evangel Theol Soc. **RESEARCH** Historical Missiology. **SELECTED PUBLICATIONS** Auth, "To Be or Not to Be?: The Indigenous Church Question", in Missiology: An Introduction to the Foundations, History, and Strategies of World Missions, ed John Mark Terry, Ebbie Smith and Justice Anderson, Broadman Pr (Nashville, 98), 301-317; auth, "Traditional Religions: Primal Religiosity and Mission Dynamics", in Missiology: An Introduction to the Foundations, History, and Strategies of World Missions, ed John Mark Terry, Ebbie Smith and Justice Anderson, Broadman Pr (Nashville, 98), 347-362; auth, "Paradigm Wars: The Southern Baptist International Board Faces the Third Millenium, Regnum/Paternoster (Carlisle, UK) (forthcoming). **CONTACT ADDRESS** Southeastern Baptist Theol Sem, PO Box 1889, Wake Forest, NC 27588-1889. **EMAIL** keitheitel@bigfoot.com

EKEH, PETER
PERSONAL Born 08/08/1937, Okpara, Nigeria, m, 1965, 5 children **DISCIPLINE** POLITICAL SCIENCE **EDUCATION** Univ Ibadan, BSc, 64; Stanford Univ, MA, 67; Univ Calif, PhD, 70. **CAREER** Asst Prof, Univ Calif, 70-73; Res Fel, Ahmadu Bello Univ, 73-74; Lecturer to Prof, Univ Ibadan, 74-89; Prof, Univ at Buffalo, 89-. **HONORS AND AWARDS** Cadbury Visiting Fel, Univ Binghamton, 78; Fel, Woodrow Wilson Ctr, 88-89. **MEMBERSHIPS** Asn of African Studies, Asn of African Scholars for Dialogue. **RESEARCH** African History, Political sociology of Africa. **CONTACT ADDRESS** Dept Afro-Am Studies, SUNY, Buffalo, PO Box 604680, Buffalo, NY 14260-0001.

EKEYA, BETTE JAN
PERSONAL Born, Kenya, s, 2 children **DISCIPLINE** BIBLICAL THEOLOGY & AFRICAN RELIGION **EDUCATION** MA; PhD, 86. **CAREER** Univ Nairobi Kenya, lectr; Egerton, Univ dept head; OLGS Seminary Scranton, tchr; OLGS, Denton, NE, prof. **RESEARCH** OT; Prophetic movement; sacrifice and holiness. **SELECTED PUBLICATIONS** Auth, In New Eyes for Seeing: Feminist Theology from the Third World. **CONTACT ADDRESS** RR6, PO Box 6496-u, Moscow, PA 18444.

EKLUND, EMMET ELVIN
PERSONAL Born 05/01/1917, Smolan, KS, m, 1945, 2 children **DISCIPLINE** RELIGION **EDUCATION** Bethany Col, Kans, BA, 41; Augustana Theol Sem, Bd, 45; Univ Chicago, MA, 58; Boston Univ, PhD (Am church hist), 64. **CAREER** Assoc prof relig and philos and vpres, Bethany Col, 45-47; assoc prof and chmn dept, 64-70, Prof Relig, Pac Lutheran Univ, 70-, Regency prof, Pac Lutheran Univ, 78-79. **MEMBERSHIPS** Am Acad Relig; Am Soc Church Hist. **RESEARCH** Modern church history; American church history in relation to 19th century Swedish immigration. **SELECTED PUBLICATIONS CONTACT ADDRESS** Dept of Relig, Pacific Lutheran Univ, Tacoma, WA 98447.

ELBOW, GARY S.
PERSONAL Born 11/15/1938, San Francisco, CA, m, 1967 **DISCIPLINE** GEOGRAPHY, ECONOMICS **EDUCATION** Ore State Col, BS, 60; Univ Ore, MA, 64; Univ Pittsburgh, PhD, 72. **CAREER** Asst to prof, Tex Tech Univ, Lubbock, 70-; vis prof, Pontifical Cath Univ of Ecuador, 90, 92, 93; vis prof, Pan Am Inst for Res and Ed, Quito, Ecuador, 88, 90, 92, 93; contributing ed, Handbook of Latin Am Studies, Library of Congress, 76-2001. **HONORS AND AWARDS** Fulbright Scholar, 83, 90, 92; academic specialist, US Information Agency, Quito, Ecudor, 90, 92; Who's Who Among Am Teachers, 96, 97; President's Academic Acheivement Awd, Tex Tech Univ, 98. **MEMBERSHIPS** Asn Am Geog, Latin Am Studies Asn, Nat Coun for Geog Ed. **RESEARCH** Settlements, urban geography, geography education, Latin America. **SELECTED PUBLICATIONS** Auth, "Creating an Atmosphere: Depiction of Climate in the Works of Gabriel Garcia Marquez," in J. Perez and W. Aycock, eds, Climate and Literature: Reflections of Environment, Lubbock, TX: Tex Tech Univ Press (95); auth, "Marketing in Latin America: A Photo Essay," J of Cultural Geog, vol 15, no 2, 55-77 (summer/fall 95); auth, "Territorial Loss and National Image: The Case of Ecuador," Yearbk, Conf of Latin Am Geog, vol 22, 93-107 (96); coauth with Tom L. Martinson, "Geography, Middle America," in Dolores M. Martin, ed, Handbook of Latin Am Studies, Austin,TX: Univ Tex Press (97); auth, "Economic Integration in the Caribbean: The Association of Caribbean States," J of Geograohy, vol 96, no 1, 29-38 (Jan-Feb 97); auth, "Coming Out of the Country: Population Growth, Migration, and Urbanization," in Alfonzo Gonzalez and Jim Norwine, The New Third World, Boulder, Colo: Westview (98); auth, "Scale and Regional Identity in the Caribbean," in David Kaplan and Guntram Herb, eds, Nested Identities: Nationalism, Territory, and Scale,Totowa, NJ: Rowman & Littlefield (99). **CONTACT ADDRESS** Dept Econ & Geog, Texas Tech Univ, Lubbock, TX 79409-1014. **EMAIL** adgse@ttacs.ttu.edu

ELDRIDGE, MICHAEL
PERSONAL Born 10/13/1941, Oklahoma City, OK, m, 2 children **DISCIPLINE** PHILOSOPHY **EDUCATION** Yale Univ, BD; Columbia Univ, MA; Univ FL, PhD. **CAREER** Instr, ch, dept Philos and Relig, Queens Col; asst prof at Queens Col and Spring Hill; instr, Spring Hill Col, Univ Fla; instr, UNC, Charlotte. **HONORS AND AWARDS** Democracy and Educ Fel of the Ctr for Dewey Studies. **MEMBERSHIPS** Soc for the Advancement of Am Phil; Am Phil Assoc; Exec Committee of the Soc for the Advancement of Am Phil. **RESEARCH** Critical thinking and soc reform; John Dewey and Am Phil. **SELECTED PUBLICATIONS** Auth, Transforming Experience: John Dewey's Cultural Instrumentalism, Vanderbilt UP, 98. **CONTACT ADDRESS** Univ of No Carolina, Charlotte, Charlotte, NC 28223-0001. **EMAIL** mleldrid@email.uncc.edu

ELFSTROM, GERARD
PERSONAL Born 02/26/1945, Rockford, IL **DISCIPLINE** PHILOSOPHY **EDUCATION** Cornell Col, BA, 67; Emory Univ, MA, 69, PhD, 75. **CAREER** Prof, Auburn Univ, 97-. **MEMBERSHIPS** Am Philos Asn **RESEARCH** Ethics; Social and Political Philosophy **CONTACT ADDRESS** Auburn Univ, 6080 Haley Ctr, Auburn, AL 36849-5210.

ELHARD, LELAND E.
DISCIPLINE PASTORAL THEOLOGY **EDUCATION** Capital Univ, BA, 53; Evangel Lutheran Theol Sem, BD, 57; Univ Chicago, MA, 63, PhD, 65. **CAREER** Instr, ELTS, 65-68; assoc prof, ELTS, 68-78; assoc prof, 78-81; prof, Trinity Lutheran Sem, 81-. **SELECTED PUBLICATIONS** Auth, The Faithful Person Leads: Self-differentiation and Pastoral Leadership, Trinity Sem Rev, 97; A Dane With The Danes, Case Studies, Assn for CASE Tchg, 96; Law and Order, Case Studies, Assn for CASE Tchg, 95; Narcissism and the Relation Between Pastor and Congregation, Trinity Sem Rev, 92; Special Review on Current Pastoral Care Literature, Trinity Sem Rev, 91. **CONTACT ADDRESS** Hist, Theol, Soc Dept, Trinity Lutheran Sem, 2199 E Main St, Columbus, OH 43209-2334. **EMAIL** lelhard@trinity.capital.edu

ELIAS, JAMAL J.
DISCIPLINE RELIGIOUS STUDIES **EDUCATION** Yale Univ, PhD, 91. **CAREER** Asst prof, Amherst Coll, 89-96; assoc prof, Amherst Coll, 96-. **SELECTED PUBLICATIONS** The Throne-Carrier of God, 95; Death before Dying, 98; Islam, 99. **CONTACT ADDRESS** Dept of Religion, Amherst Col, Amherst, MA 01002. **EMAIL** jjelias@amherst.edu

ELKAYAM, MOSHE
PERSONAL Born 11/09/1941, Mogador, m, 1973, 1 child **DISCIPLINE** BIBLICAL STUDIES **EDUCATION** Univ Paris VIII, PhD, 92. **CAREER** Paris, 85-92; Dir of Jewish Studies, Coll Hillel, Ville Saint-Laurent, 93-96; Scholar in Residence, Temple Emam-Eb, Montreal, 92-. **HONORS AND AWARDS** Highest Honor for PhD Thesis; Eric and Esther Exton Educ Awd. **MEMBERSHIPS** AAR; SBL; AJS; JESNA; NATE; EDA; TU. **RESEARCH** Biblical Studies; Old Testament; Dead Sea Scrolls and Ancient Near Eastern regions and cultures. **SELECTED PUBLICATIONS** Auth, poetry and prose in Hebrew; pubs in folklore and tradition; pubs on Jewish Studies. **CONTACT ADDRESS** 6525 Cote St Luc, Box 506, Montreal, QC, Canada H4V 1G5.

ELKINS, JAMES R.
DISCIPLINE LAW **EDUCATION** Univ Ky, BA, JD; Yale Univ, LLM. **CAREER** Trial atty, Econ Stabilization Sect; asst US atty, US Atty's Office; asst prof, DePaul Univ; vis asst prof, Univ Ky; vis fel, Health Law Inst; vis prof, Wash and Lee Univ; vis adj prof, Univ Mass; prof, 77-; Benedum distinguished scholar, 95. **HONORS AND AWARDS** Order of the Coif; ed bd, jour of legal edu. **SELECTED PUBLICATIONS** Ed, Legal Stud Forum; Legal Ethics and the Legal Profession; Law and Psychiat; Psychol for Lawyers, Practical Moral Philos for Lawyers; Environmental Justice; Author, Legal Interviewing and Counseling in a Nutshell; Lawyers and Lit. **CONTACT ADDRESS** Law Sch, West Virginia Univ, Morgantown, PO Box 6009, Morgantown, WV 26506-6009.

ELLENS, JAY HAROLD
PERSONAL Born 07/16/1932, McBain, MI, m, 1954, 7 children **DISCIPLINE** PSYCHOLOGY; RELIGION **EDUCATION** Calvin Coll, BA, 53; Calvin Theol Sem, MDiv, 56; Princeton Theol Sem, ThM. 65; Wayne State Univ, PhD, 70; Univ Mich, PhD. **CAREER** Univ tchg, 65-85; clin psychol, 70-; Presby Theol, Pastor, Pastoral Counr, 56- ; US Army Chaplain (COL), 55-92; Princeton tchg fel; Finch lectr, Fuller; Wheaton Distinguished lectr; Stob lectr ethics and religion; distinguished lectr, Austin Theol Sem. **HONORS AND AWARDS** Meritorious Serv Medals (4), Legion Merit, numerous for serv, unit, merit citations, medals, ribbons (16), US Army. **MEMBERSHIPS** CAPS; SBL; AAR; AIA; ROA; MOWW; AL. **RESEARCH** Psychology of human development; Christians origins and their roots in ancient Judaism. **SELECTED PUBLICATIONS** auth Models of Religious Broadcasting, 74; God's Grace and Human Health, 82; Turning Points in Pastoral Care, 89; Christian Perspectives on Human Development, 90; coauth, Interpretation of Bible, 97. **CONTACT ADDRESS** 26707 Farmington Road, Farmington Hills, MI 48334-4329. **EMAIL** jharoldellens@Juno.com

ELLER, DAVID B.
PERSONAL Born 04/30/1945, Roanoke, VA, m, 1979, 3 children **DISCIPLINE** HISTORY, RELIGION **EDUCATION** La Verne Col, Calif, BA, 67; Bethany Theol Sem, MA, 71; Miami Univ, Oxford, Oh, PhD, 76. **CAREER** Lectr, Dir of Pub Studies, Rosemont Col, Pa, 96-97; Dir of the Young Center and prof of Hist and Relig, Elizabethtown Col, Pa, 97-. **HONORS AND AWARDS** Phi Alpha Theta, 74; Summer Res Fe3l, Miami Univ, 73, 74; NEH Summer Sem for Col Teachers, Indiana Univ, 83; Smithsonian Inst, Short-Term Vis Awd, 84; Newberry Library, Short-Term Vis Fel, 84. **MEMBERSHIPS** Am Acad of Relig, Communal Studies Asn, Conf on Faith and Hist, Soc for Scholarly Pub. **RESEARCH** Anabaptism, Pietism, communal societies. **SELECTED PUBLICATIONS** Auth, "George Wolfe III and the 'Church of California'," Messenger, 146 (May 97): 12-16; auth, "The Dissent of the Congregational Brethren," Brethren Life and Thought, 42 (summer and fall 97): 158-179; auth, "Tending the Garden: Memories of My Father," in Going For It: Perspectives on Living, ed, Carol S. Lawson, West Chester, Pa: Chrysalis Books (97); ed, From Age to Age: Historians and the Modern Church. A Festschrift for Donald F. Durnbaugh, vol 42, (summer and fall 97) in Brethren Life and Thought (fall 98); auth, Illuminating the World of Spirit. A Sesquicentennial Record of the Swedenborg Foundation, 1850-2000, West Chester, Pa: Swedenborg Found (99). **CONTACT ADDRESS** Dir of the Young Center, Elizabethtown Col, 1 Alpha Dr, Elizabethtown, PA 17022-2298.

ELLICKSON, ROBERT CHESTER
PERSONAL Born 08/04/1941, Washington, DC, m, 1971, 2 children **DISCIPLINE** LAW **EDUCATION** Oberlin Col, AB, 63; Yale Univ, LLB, 66. **CAREER** Asst Prof, USC Law Center, 70-72, Assoc prof, 72-75, Prof, 75-81; Prof, Stanford, 81-85; Robert E. Paradise Prof of Natural Resources Law, 85-88; Meyer prof, Yale, 88-; Deputy Dean, 91-92. **RESEARCH** Property; land use; real estate transactions; torts. **SELECTED PUBLICATIONS** Auth, A Decent Home: The Report of the President's Committee on Urvan Housing (Parts 2, 4, 5, 7, 8, 11, 12), 69; coauth, Cases and Materials on Land-Use Controls, 81; coauth, Order without Law: How Neighbors Settle Disputes, 91; coauth, Prespectives on Property Law, 95. **CONTACT ADDRESS** Yale Univ, 127 Wall St., New Haven, CT 06511. **EMAIL** robert.ellickson@yale.edu

ELLIN, JOSEPH S.
PERSONAL Born 10/31/1936, Brooklyn, NY, m, 1962, 2 children **DISCIPLINE** PHILOSOPHY **EDUCATION** Columbia Univ, BA, 57; Yale Univ, MA, 59; PhD, 62. **CAREER** From instr to asst prof, 62-67, chmn dept, 69-75 & 77-78, assoc prof, 67-79, Prof Philos, Western Mich Univ, 79- **MEMBERSHIPS** Am Philos Asn; Soc Values Higher Educ; Am Soc Polit & Legal Philos; Soc Bus & Prof Ethics. **RESEARCH** Political philosophy; philosophy of law; medical and professional ethics. **SELECTED PUBLICATIONS** Auth, Fidelity to law, Soundings, winter 68; Sterilization, privacy and the value of reproduction, Contemp Issues Bioethics, 79; Consent in political philosophy, Archiv fur Rechts-und Sozialphilosophic, No 12, 79; Collective responsibility in the professions, Dayton Rev, winter 81; Lying and deception: The solution to a dilemma in medical ethics, Westminster Rev, 5/81; Special professional morality and the duty of veracity, Bus & Prof Ethics J, Vol 1; Again: Hume on Miracles, Hume Studies, 4/93; Morality and the Meaning of Life, Harcourt Brace, 95; Assisted Suicide in Michigan, Bioethics, 1/96; Liberalism, Radicalism, Middlism, In: Radical Critiques of Law, Kansas, 97. **CONTACT ADDRESS** Dept of Philosophy, Western Michigan Univ, 1201 Oliver St, Kalamazoo, MI 49008-3805. **EMAIL** joseph.ellin@wmich.edu

ELLINGSEN, MARK
PERSONAL Born 06/18/1949, Brooklyn, NY, m, 1973, 3 children **DISCIPLINE** RELIGION, PHILOSOPHY **EDUCATION** Gettysburg Col, BA, 71; Yale Univ, M.Div, 74; Yale Univ, MA, 75; Yale Univ, M. Philos, 76; Yale Univ, PhD, 80. **CAREER** Assoc prof, Interdenominational Theology Center, 93-; instr, Randolf Community Col, 92-93; assoc prof, Institute Ecumenical Res, 82-88; asst prof, Luther-Northwestern Lutheran Seminaries, 79-82; pastor, Evangelical Lutheran Church in America, ordained, 76 **HONORS AND AWARDS** Phi Beta Kappa; Yale Univ Day Fel; AAL Fel; Undergraduate Departmental Honors in Relig and Philos. **MEMBERSHIPS** Amer Acad Relig; Amer Soc Church Hist. **RESEARCH** History of Christian Thought and Ethics; Reformation Studies; Ecumenics; Hermeneutics; Religion and Science. **SELECTED PUBLICATIONS** auth, Reclaiming Our Roots: An Inclusive Introduction to Church History, Trinity; auth, A Word That Sets Free, C.S.S.; auth, Making Black Ecumenism Happen: A History of the Interdenominational Theological Center As a Paradigm for Christian Unity, ITC; auth, A Common Sense Theology: The Bible, Faith, and American Society, Mercer Univ; auth, The Cutting Edge: How Churches Speak on Social Issues, World Coun of Churches; auth, Preparation and Manifestation: Reflections on Lent and Easter, C.S.S.; auth, The Integrity of Biblical Narrative: Story in Theology and Proclamation, Fortress; auth, The Evangelical Movement: Growth, Impact, Controversy, Dialog; auth, Doctrine and Word, John Knox. **CONTACT ADDRESS** Interdenominational Theol Ctr, 700 Martin Luther King Jr. Dr., Atlanta, GA 30314.

ELLINGTON, JOHN
PERSONAL Born 12/09/1963, Moultrie, GA, m, 1963, 4 children **DISCIPLINE** BIBLICAL LITERATURE **EDUCATION** Emory Univ, BA, 59; Columbia Theological Seminary, ThM, 64; Univ of Wisconsin, PhD, 77. **CAREER** Pastor, 62-63, First Presbyterian Church, Manchester, GA; Missionary, 64-83, Presbyterian Church, US,; Bible Trans Consult, United Bible Societies, Kinshesa, Zaire, Dakar, Dengal, Bouake, Cote d'Ivoire, 75-. **MEMBERSHIPS** SBL **RESEARCH** Common Language Translatuion; Bantu Languages of Rep Dem du Congo. **SELECTED PUBLICATIONS** Auth, A Handbook of Kinshasa Lingala, Kinshasa, Zaire, 74; English-Lingala Dictionary, Kinshasa, Zaire, 82; Basic Lingala, Montreat, NC, 83; coed, A Translator's Handbook on Leviticus, NY, United Bible Societies, 90; A Handbook on Daniel, NY, United Bible Societies, 93; A Handbook on Paul's Second Letter to the Corinthians, NY, United Bible Societies, 93. **CONTACT ADDRESS** Box 1018, Montreat, NC 28757. **EMAIL** johne@buncombe.main.nc.us

ELLIOT, ROBIN
DISCIPLINE LAW **EDUCATION** Univ British Columbia, BS, 69; LLB, 73; London Univ, LLM, 75. **CAREER** Asst prof, 76-83; assoc prof, 83-91; prof, 91-; assoc dean, Univ of British Columbia, 91-93. **HONORS AND AWARDS** Off, Supreme Court Can. **RESEARCH** Constitutional law and theory; human rights legislation. **SELECTED PUBLICATIONS** Auth, pubs about charter and Canadian federalism. **CONTACT ADDRESS** Fac of Law, Univ of British Columbia, 1822 East Mall, Vancouver, BC, Canada V6T 1Z1. **EMAIL** elliot@law.ubc.ca

ELLIOTT, CARL
PERSONAL Born 07/25/1961, Gastonia, NC, m, 1990, 2 children **DISCIPLINE** PHILOSOPHY **EDUCATION** Glasgow Univ, PhD; Med Univ of SC, MD. **CAREER** Chicago, 89-90; Otago, 90-91; Natal, 92; McGill Univ, 93-97; Minnesota, 97-. **RESEARCH** Moral philosophy; bioethics; Wittgenistein. **SELECTED PUBLICATIONS** Auth, The Rules of Insanity: Moral Responsibility and Mental Illness, State Univ NY, 96; auth, A Philosophical Disease: Bioethics, Culture and Identity, Routledge, 98; auth, The Last Physician, Duke, 99; auth, Slow Cures and Bad Philosophers, Duke, 01. **CONTACT ADDRESS** Center for Bioethics, Univ of Minnesota, Twin Cities, 410 Church St SE, N504 Boynton, Minneapolis, MN 55455-0346. **EMAIL** ellio023@tc.umn.edu

ELLIOTT, CAROLYN S.
PERSONAL Born 02/20/1947, Glen Ridge, NJ, m, 1970, 2 children **DISCIPLINE** RELIGION AND CULTURE; HISTORY **EDUCATION** Syracuse Univ, BA, 70, MA, 73; SUNY, MLIS, 94. **CAREER** From dir to adj fac to full-time fac, 72-, Keystone Col. **HONORS AND AWARDS** Theta Chi Beta; Beta Phi Mu. **MEMBERSHIPS** Am Libr Asn; Asn Col & Res Librs; Pa Libr Asn. **RESEARCH** Religion and culture of Asia; library computing options. **SELECTED PUBLICATIONS** Auth, art, NREN Update, 1993: Washington Policy, 94. **CONTACT ADDRESS** Miller Library, Keystone Col, One College Green, La Plume, PA 18440-0200. **EMAIL** celliott@kstone.edu

ELLIOTT, DENI
PERSONAL Born 11/16/1953, Nanticoke, PA, d **DISCIPLINE** PHILOSOPHY **EDUCATION** Univ Maryland, BA, 74; Wayne State Univ, MSTC, 78, MA, 82; Harvard Univ, PhD, 84. **CAREER** Harvard Univ, tchg fel, 82-84; Wayne State Univ, p-t inst, 80-84; Utah State Univ, asst prof, assoc prof, 85-88; Dartmouth Col, adj asst prof, res asst prof, adj assoc prof, res assoc prof, 88-92; Prof Of Philosophy, Univ of Montana, 92- ; Mansfield Prof of Ethics & Public Affairs, 92-96; Dir, Practical Ethics Center, 96- . **HONORS AND AWARDS** Marion and Jasper Whiting Foundation fel, Rockefeller Fel, Outstanding Young Woman in Am Awd, Bronze Plaque Awd, Silver Apple Awd, Who's Who listings: in the East, Authors and Writers, World of Women, in the World, in the West, Am Women and Among Am Tchrs; dartmouth col, ethics inst, dir, 88-92; univ montana practical ethics ctr, dir, 96-. **MEMBERSHIPS** APPE, APA, AEJMC, SPJ, IMH, Citizen Review Board. **SELECTED PUBLICATIONS** Coauth, Contemporary Ethical Issues: Journalism, ABC-CLIO, 98; coauth, The Ethics of Scientific Research: A Guidebook for Course Development, Hanover NH: Univ Press of New Eng, 97; coauth, The Ethics of Asking: Dilemmas in Higher Education Fund Raising, ed, John Hopkins Univ Press, 95; coauth, The Burden of Knowledge: Moral Dilemmas in Prenatal Testing, writer and coproducer, Distrib :Direct Cinema Ltd, 94; coauth, Responsible Journalism, ed, SAGE 86. **CONTACT ADDRESS** Practical Ethics Ctr, Univ of Montana, Missoula, MT 59812. **EMAIL** deni@selway.umt.edu

ELLIOTT, JOHN HALL
PERSONAL Born 10/23/1935, New York, NY, m, 1962, 2 children **DISCIPLINE** THEOLOGY **EDUCATION** Concordia Sem, MO, BA, 57, BD, 60; Univ Munster, Dr Theol, 63. **CAREER** Asst prof theol, Concordia Sem, MO, 63-67; from asst prof to assoc prof, 68-75, prof theol & relig studies, Univ San Francisco, 75-; vis prof, Webster Col, 65-67 & Pontif Bibl Inst, Rome, 78; guest prof, Honore F Zabala Chair of Theol, Univ San Francisco, 67-68; adj prof exegetical theol, Grad Theol Union, Berkeley, Calif, 77-; resident res scholar, Disciples' Inst zur Erforschung des Urchristentums, Tubingen, WGer, 77; vis prof, Pontif Bibl Inst, Cath Bibl Asn Am, Rome, 78 & Univ Notre Dame, 81; Am Coun Learned Soc grant, 81. **HONORS AND AWARDS** Am Coun Learned Soc Travel grant, 81; USF Distinguished Res Award, 82; NEH Summer stipend, 92; USF Distinguished Teaching Award, 92. **MEMBERSHIPS** Soc of New Testament Scholars; Franz Delitzsch Ges; Soc Bibl Lit; Cath Bibl Asn Am; AAUP; Context Group. **RESEARCH** Exegesis; historical sociology; history. **SELECTED PUBLICATIONS** Auth, The Elect and the Holy, Brill, 66; The Christ Life: Jesus Christ the Sacrament and Sacramental Living, Walther League, 68; Man and the Son of Man in the Gospel According to Mark, In: Humane Gesellschaft (H D Wendland Festschrift), Zwingli, 70; Pentecost 3, Fortress, 76; Peter: Estrangement and Community, Franciscan Herald Press, 79; A Home for the Homeless: A Sociological Exegesis of 1 Peter, Its Situation and Strategy, Fortress, 81, 2nd ed, 90; 1 and 2 Peter and Jude, Augsburg Commentary on the New Testament, Augsburg, 82; ed, Social-Scientific criticism of the New Testament and Its Social World, Semeia 35, Scholars Press, 86; auth; Temple vs Household in Luke-Acts: A Contrast in Social Institutions, in The Social World of Luke-Acts, Hendrickson, 91; Matthew 20: 1-15: A Parable of Invidious Comparison and Evil Eye Accusation, Bibl Theol Bull, 92; Peter, First Epistle of, Second Epistle of, Anchor Bible Dictionary, vol 5, Doubleday, 92; What is Social-Scientific Criticism?, Fortress, 93; The Epistle of James in Rhetorical and Social Scientific Perspective: Holiness-Wholeness and Patterns of Replication, Bibl Theol Bull, 93; Sorcery and Magic in the Revelation of John, Listening, J of Relig and Culture, 93; The Evil Eye and the Sermon on the Mount: Contours of a Pervasive Belief in Social Scientific Perspective, Biblical Interpretation, 94; Disgraced Yet Graced: The Gospel According to 1 Peter in the Key on Honor and Shame, Bibl Theol Bull, 95; The Jewish Messianic Movement: From Faction to Sect, in Modeling Early Christianity: Social-Scientific Studies of the New Testament in its Context, Routledge, 95. **CONTACT ADDRESS** Dept of Theol & Relig Studies, Univ of San Francisco, 2130 Fulton St, San Francisco, CA 94117-1080. **EMAIL** elliottj@usfca.edu

ELLIOTT, SUSAN ELLI
PERSONAL Born 10/27/1952, Evanston, IL **DISCIPLINE** NEW TESTAMENT, EARLY CHRISTIANITY **EDUCATION** Jesuit Sch of Theol-Chicago, MDiv, summa cum laude, 78; Loyola Univ, PhD, 97. **CAREER** Pastor, Douglas Park Church, Chicago, 87-90; dir, Justice and Peace Network, 90-92; Lectr, tchg fel, 93-97, vis asst prof, Loyola Univ, 97; Pastor, Zion United Church of Christ, Sterling, Colo, 97- . **HONORS AND AWARDS** Arthur J. Schmitt diss fel, Loyola Univ, 95-96; Loyola Univ tchg fel, 94-95; student paper competition prize, Midwest soc Bibl lit, 93. **MEMBERSHIPS** Soc Bibl Lit; N Amer Patristics Soc; Chicago Soc Bibl Res; Westar Inst fel; Catholic Bibl Asn. **RESEARCH** Greco-Roman mystery cults; Slavery and family in Greco-Roman Antiquity; Pauline Letts. **SELECTED PUBLICATIONS** Auth, John 15:15-Not Slaves but Friends: Slavery and Friendship Imagery and the Clarification of the Disciples' Relationship to Jesus in the Johannine Farewell Discourse, in Proceedings of the Eastern Great Lakes and Midwest Society of Bibl Lit, Toronto, vol 13, 93, 31-46; Who is Addressed in Revelation 18:6-7, Bibl Res, vol 40, 95, 98-113; Paul's Gentile Audiences: Mystery Cults, Anatolian Popular Religiosity, and Paul's Claim of Divine Authority in Galatians, in Listening: A Jour of Rel and Cult, 31, 96, 117-136; rev, Cybele, Attis, and Related Cults: Essays in Memory of M.J. Vermaseren, Rels in the Greco-Roman World, Leiden: E.J. Brill, 96; auth, "Choose Your Mother, Choose Your Master: Galatians 4:21-5:1 in the Shadow of the Antolian Mother of the Gods," Journal of Biblical Literature 118, (99): 661-683. **CONTACT ADDRESS** Zion United Church of Christ, 414 Elm St, Sterling, CO 80751. **EMAIL** ellielliott@msn.com

ELLIOTT, WARD EDWARD YANDELL
PERSONAL Born 08/96/1937, Cambridge, MA, m, 1969, 2 children **DISCIPLINE** POLITICAL SCIENCE **EDUCATION** Univ Va, LlB, 64; Harvard Univ, AB, 59, AM, PhD, 68. **CAREER** Prof of Gov, 68-, Burnet C. Wohlford Prof of Am Politic Inst, Claremont McKenna Col, 95-. **HONORS AND AWARDS** Phi Beta Kappa; Harvard Nat Scholar; NEH Fel; Distinguished Civilian Service Medal; Roy C. Crocker Prize; honorary member of CMC Class of 74. **MEMBERSHIPS** AAAS; Shakespeare Authorship Roundtable. **RESEARCH** Voting rights; transportation; population; smog policy; Shakespeare authorship. **SELECTED PUBLICATIONS** Auth, The Rise of Guardian Democracy; Greenbacks Uber Gridlock; Federal Law and Population Policy; And Then There Were None: Winnowing the Shakespeare Claimants. **CONTACT ADDRESS** Dept of Political Sci, Claremont McKenna Col, 850 N Columbia Ave, Claremont, CA 91711.

ELLIS, ANTHONY JOHN
PERSONAL Born 06/15/1945, England, m, 1978, 3 children **DISCIPLINE** THEOLOGY; PHILOSOPHY **EDUCATION** King's Col, London, BA, 67; MA, 68. **CAREER** Dir, Inst for Ethics & Pub Policy, Virginia Commonwealth Univ, 94-; prof Philos, Virginia Commonwealth Univ, 90-; Univ Fel, Univ of Wollongong, 89; vis prof Philos, Virginia Commonwealth Univ, 87-88; Sr lctr, Univ St Andrews, 87-90; ch Dept Moral Philos, Univ St Andrews, 85-90; lctr Dept Moral Philos, Univ St Andrews, 71-87. **HONORS AND AWARDS** Univ London Fac of Arts Tutorial Studentship, 70; Shelford Prize, 67; McCaul Prize, 67; Univ Fel in Univ of Wollongong, 89; Vis Fel in Australian Ntl Univ in Canberra, 87; Univ Fel in Univ Wollongong, 87; Fulbright Travel Awd, 87. **MEMBERSHIPS** Amer Philos Assoc; Royal Inst of Philos **RESEARCH** Philosophy of Law **SELECTED PUBLICATIONS** Criminal Attempts," in Jour of Applied Philos, forthcoming; Punishment and the Principle of Fair Play, Utilitas, 97; Morality and Scripture, Tchng Philos, 96; Censorship and the Media, in Media Ethics, Routledge, 98. **CONTACT ADDRESS** Dept of Philosophy, Virginia Commonwealth Univ, PO Box 842025, Richmond, VA 23284-2025. **EMAIL** aellis@saturn.vcu.edu

ELLIS, EDWARD EARLE
PERSONAL Born 03/18/1926, Ft Lauderdale, FL **DISCIPLINE** THEOLOGY, HISTORY **EDUCATION** Univ Va, BS, 50; Wheaton Col, Ill, MA and BD, 53; Univ Edinburgh, PhD (Bibl studies), 55. **CAREER** Asst prof Bible and philos, Aurora Col, 56-58; asst prof New Testament interpretation, Southern Baptist Theol Sem, 58-60; from vis prof to prof Bibl Studies, 62-77, Res Prof New Testament, New Brunswick Theol Sem, 77-, Am Asn Theol Schs fel, 68-69; von Humbolt scholar, 68-69 and 75-76; lectr, Princeton Theol Sem, 74, 76, 78; Guggenheim fel, 75-76; lectr, Drew Univ, 67-68 and Univ Tubingen, 75-76; vis distinguished prof Evangel Christianity, Juniata Col, 78-79; Bye fel, Robinson Col, Cambridge Univ, 82-83; exec Comt, Soc Studies New Testament, 67-69. **HONORS AND AWARDS** DD, Wheaton Col, Ill, 82. **MEMBERSHIPS** Soc Bibl Lit (treas, 67-68); Soc Studies New Testament; Inst Biblical Res. **RESEARCH** Early Christian history and thought; Biblical studies. **SELECTED PUBLICATIONS** Auth, Paul's Use of the Old Testament, Oliver & Boyd, London & Eerdmans, 57 & Baker, 81; Paul and His Recent Interpreters, Eerdmans, 61; The World of St John Lutterworth, London & Abingdon, Nashville, 65; The Gospel of Luke, Olifants, London, 66, 2nd ed, 74 & Eerdmans, 81; Eschatology in Luke, Fortress, 73; Prophecy and Hermeneutic in Early Christianity, Mohr, Tubingen & Eerdmans, 78; Dating the New Testament, New Testament Studies, Vol 26: 487-502. **CONTACT ADDRESS** Dept

of Bibl Studies, New Brunswick Theol Sem, New Brunswick, NJ 08901.

ELLIS, RANDALL P.
DISCIPLINE ECONOMICS **EDUCATION** Yale Univ, BA, 76; London Sch Econ and Polit Sci, MS; Mass Inst Technol, PhD, 81. **CAREER** Instr, MIT, 79-81; asst prof to prof, Boston Univ, 81-. **HONORS AND AWARDS** Admin Citation, 88; New Investigator Res Awd, Nat Inst of Mental Health, 87-89; William H. Massee Awd, 76. **MEMBERSHIPS** Am Econ Asn; Am Public Health Asn; Intl Health Econ Asn; Health Econ Res Org. **RESEARCH** Health Economics; Industrial Organization. **SELECTED PUBLICATIONS** Co-auth, "Hospital Response to Prospective Payment: Selection and Moral Hazard Effects," J of Health Econ, (96): 257-279; co-auth, "Bundling Post-Acute Care (PAC) with Medicare DRG Payments: An Exploration of the Distributional and Risk Consequences," Inquiry, (96): 283-291; auth, "Creaming, Skimping, and Dumping: Provider Competition on the Intensive and Extensive Margins," J of Health Econ, (98): 537-555; co-auth, "Health Insurance in India: Prognosis and Prospectus," Econ and Polit Weekly, (00): 207-217; co-auth, "Demand Side Analysis of Health Care Financing and Delivery in Niger," Health Policy and Planning, (00): 76-84; co-auth, "Decision model and cost-effectiveness analysis of colorectal cancer screening and surveillance guidelines for average-risk adults," Intl J of Technol Assessment in Health Care, (00): 799-810; co-auth, "using Diagnoses to Describe Populations and Predict Costs," Health Care Financing Rev, (00): 7-28; co-auth, "Principal Inpatient Diagnostic Cost Group Models for Medicare Risk Adjustment," Health Care Financing Rev, (00): 93-118; co-auth, "Risk Adjustment in Competitive Health Plan Markets," in Handbook in Health Economics, (North Holland, 00), 755-845; co-auth, "Risk selection in the Massachusetts state employee health insurance program," Health Care Management Sci, 01. **CONTACT ADDRESS** Dept Econ, Boston Univ, 270 Bay State Rd, Boston, MA 02215. **EMAIL** ellisrp@bu.edu

ELLIS, ROBERT
PERSONAL Born 07/08/1955, Fort Worth, TX, m, 1989, 2 children **DISCIPLINE** OLD TESTAMENT AND BIBLICAL HEBREW **EDUCATION** Hardin Simmons Univ, BS, 77; Southwest Baptist Theol Sem, MDiv, 81; PhD, 88. **CAREER** Instr, Hardin-Simmons Univ, 84-86; assoc prof, Southwest Baptist Theol Sem, 86-96; prof, Hardin-Simmons Univ, 96-. **HONORS AND AWARDS** Distinguished Alumnus of Logsdon School of Theol. **MEMBERSHIPS** Nat Asn of baptist Porf of Rel; Soc of Bibl Lit. **RESEARCH** Old Testament Prophets and Wisdom Literature; Biblical Hebrew. **SELECTED PUBLICATIONS** Auth, Divine Gift and Human Response: An Old Testament Model for Stewardship, Southwestern J of Theol, 95; Are There Any Cows of Bashan on Seminary Hill?, Southwestern J of Theol, 95; articles in New Int Dictionary of Old Testament Theol and Exegesis, 97; The Theological Boundaries of Inclusion and Exclusion in the Book of Joshua, Rev and Expositor, 98. **CONTACT ADDRESS** Box 16235, Abilene, TX 79698-6235. **EMAIL** rellis@hsutx.edu

ELLSWORTH, RANDALL
DISCIPLINE LAW **EDUCATION** McGill Univ, BA, 84; Osgoode Hall Law Sch, LLB, 87. **CAREER** Law clerk, Ontario Supreme Court; assoc prof. **MEMBERSHIPS** St Health Comun Nursing Found; Metropolitan Toronto Soc Planning Coun. **SELECTED PUBLICATIONS** Auth, pubs on maintenance programs and government consultations and law reform; ed, Poverty Law in Ontario: The Year in Review, Jour Law Soc Policy. **CONTACT ADDRESS** Fac of Law, Univ of Toronto, 78 Queen's Park, Toronto, ON, Canada M5S 1A1.

ELLWOOD, GRACIA F.
PERSONAL Born 07/17/1938, Lynden, WA, m, 1965, 2 children **DISCIPLINE** PHILOSOPHY OF RELIGION **EDUCATION** Claremont Grad Univ, PhD, 98. **CAREER** Private scholar. **HONORS AND AWARDS** Univ Chicago Scholar, 61-64. **MEMBERSHIPS** Amer Soc for Psychical Res; Parapsychol Asn; Intl Asn for Near-Death Studies. **RESEARCH** Near-death studies. **SELECTED PUBLICATIONS** Auth, The Uttermost Deep: The Challenge of Painful Near-Death Experiences, BoobLight, 01; Distressing Near-Death Experiences as Photographic Negatives, Jour of Near-Death Studies, 96; co-auth, In a Faraway Galaxy: A Literary Analysis of Star Wars, Extequer Press, 84; auth, Psychic Visits to the Past, New Amer Libr, 71; auth, Good News from Tolkein's Middle Earth, Eerdmans, 70; auth, The Cheltenham Haunting: An Interpretation, Jour Amer Soc for Psychical Res, 69; auth, The Soal-Cooper-Davis Communal I, Intl Jour of Parapsychol, 68. **CONTACT ADDRESS** 997 Athens St., Altadena, CA 91001. **EMAIL** graciafay@hotmail.com

ELLWOOD, ROBERT S.
DISCIPLINE RELIGION **EDUCATION** Univ Chicago, PhD, 67. **CAREER** Prof, Univ Southern Calif. **RESEARCH** Religions of East Asia; Zen Buddhism; Shintoism. **SELECTED PUBLICATIONS** Auth, The Sixties Spiritual Awakening; Islands of the Dawn: The Story of Alternative Spirituality in New Zealand; Japanese Religion: A Cultural Perspective. **CONTACT ADDRESS** East Asian Studies Center, Univ of So California, University Park Campus, Los Angeles, CA 90089.

ELROD, LINDA DIANE HENRY
PERSONAL Born 03/06/1947, Topeka, KS, 2 children **DISCIPLINE** LAW **EDUCATION** Washburn Univ, BA, 69; JD, 71. **CAREER** Res asst, Kans Judicial Coun, 72-74; asst prof, 74-78, assoc prof, 78-82, distinguished prof law, Washburn Univ, 82-, distinguished, 92-; Consult, Kans Judicial Coun, 75, 76 & 79; mem, Kans Govt Ethics Comn, 78-; ed, The Circuit Rider, Washburn Law Sch Assn, 78-; vchmn, Kans Pub Disclosure Comn, 81-85. **HONORS AND AWARDS** Distinguished Svc Awd, Wasburn Law Sch Assoc, 86; Outstanding Svc Awd, Kansas Bar Assoc, 87; Phi Beta Delta, Hon Soc for Int Scholars; one of Best Lawyers in America in Family Law, 97-98; YWCA Woman of Distinction Awd, 97; NONOSO, Woman's Hon; Phi Kappa Phi. **RESEARCH** Family law; comparative law. **SELECTED PUBLICATIONS** Auth, "Practicing Law in a Unified Kansas Court System," Washburn Law J (77); auth, "Land Transactions: A Survey of Basic Property Principles Relating to the Sale of Real Estate," Washburn Univ Sch of Law (79); auth, "Housing Alternatives for the Elderly," J of Family Law (80); auth, "Vanishing Farmlands And Decaying Downtowns--The Case For Growth Management," Kans Bar Assn J (82); auth, Child Custody Practice and Procedure, 93; auth, Kansas Law and Practice Series: Kansas Family Law, 99; coauth, Principles of Family Law, 98, 00 supplement. **CONTACT ADDRESS** Sch of Law, Washburn Univ of Topeka, 1700 SW College Ave, Topeka, KS 66621-0001.

ELROD, LINDA HENRY
DISCIPLINE FAMILY LAW, COMPARATIVE LAW AND REAL PROPERTY **EDUCATION** Washburn Univ, BA, 69, JD, 71. **CAREER** Vis prof, WA Univ; Vis prof, Univ San Diego Inst; Ed, Family Law Quart. **MEMBERSHIPS** Secy-Treas, KS Bar Asn; Chair,Family Law Section; Profes Topeka Bar Asn. **SELECTED PUBLICATIONS** Areas: family law issues. **CONTACT ADDRESS** Washburn Univ of Topeka, 1700 SW College, Topeka, KS 66621. **EMAIL** zzelro@acc.wuacc.edus

ELSAMAHI, MOHAMED
PERSONAL Born 04/11/1949, Egypt, m, 1993 **DISCIPLINE** PHILOSOPHY OF SCIENCE **EDUCATION** Coll Med Cairo Univ, MD, 71; Univ Calgary Philos PhD, 96. **CAREER** Asst prof, Cairo Univ, 77-90; instr, Univ Calgary, 95-96; instr, SW Mo State Univ, 96-98. **MEMBERSHIPS** Egyptian Med Asn; Can Philos Asn; Am Philos Asn; Am Philos of Sci Asn. **RESEARCH** Philosophy of Science; Epistemology. **SELECTED PUBLICATIONS** Auth, Could Theoretical Entities Save Realism?, 94. **CONTACT ADDRESS** 11314 McFarland Ln, Carbondale, IL 62901. **EMAIL** meesamahi@mciworld.com

ELSBERND, MARY
PERSONAL Born 07/09/1946, Decoral, IA **DISCIPLINE** CATHOLIC SOCIAL TEACHINGS, SOCIAL ETHICS; WOMEN'S STUDIES; GOSPEL OF JOHN **EDUCATION** Briar Cliff Col, BA, 68; St. John's Univ, MA, 77; Katholieke Univ Leuven, Belgium, Sacrae Theologiae Baccalauraum, 82, Sacrae Theologiae Licentiatam, 83, BA, 81, MA, 82, PhD, 85, Sacrae Theologiae Doctor, 86. **CAREER** Asst prof, 92-96, assoc prof Pastoral Stud in Social Ehtics, 96- , Grad Dir Master Div prof, 95, Loyola Univ; asst prof Theology, 85-89, assoc prof, 89-92, Briar Cliff Col; Instr Theol, Briar Cliff Col, 79-80; Rel tchr in Wahlert and Aquin Catholic High Schools, 68-79; French Tchr Aquin Cath High Sch, 68-73; vis guest prof, Katholieke Univ Leuven, fac Moral Theol and Women's Stud, 97; Vrij asst for the Moral Theol Dept, Katholieke Univ, 84; res asst with Ctr of Concern, Wash DC, summer 90; fac mem in the Sioux City Diocesan Church Ministries Prog, 88-92; dir, Briar Cliff Peace Stud Prog, 87-92; **HONORS AND AWARDS** Study leave, Loyola Univ, Chicago, Fall 97; Loyola Univ Scholar Recipient to Faith and the Intellectual Collegium, Summer 95; Res Support Grant, Summer 94, Loyola Univ, for Young Adult Volunteer Proj; Briar Cliff Col nominee to NEH, summer grant, 92; Briar Cliff nominee for Kellogg Natl Fel Prog for the development fo "effective and broad leadership skills and abilities: 89; Briar Cliff Col finalist for Burlington Northern Outstand Tchr, 87; Vrij Asst for the Moral Theol Dept, Katholieke Univ Leuven, 84; Acad Scholar Katholieke Univ Leuven, 81-85. **MEMBERSHIPS** Cath Theol Soc Am; AAR; Soc Christian Ethics; Cath Comm on Intell Cultural Affairs. **RESEARCH** Justice and John; Women's Leadership. **SELECTED PUBLICATIONS** Auth, Papal Statements on Rights, A Historical Contextual study of Encyclical Teaching from Pius VI to oPius XI (1791-1939), Ann Arbor, MI: Univ Microfilms, Inc., 85; auth, "Rights Statements, A Hermeneutical Key to Continuing Development in Magisterial Teaching, in Ephemerides Theologicae Lovanienses LXII, (86): 308-332; co-auth, "What's at Stake? American Women Religious Naming Ourselves Women," in Claiming Our Truth, Reflections on Identity by Am Women Religious, (Washington, DC: LCWR, 88); auth, A Theology of Peacemaking, A Vision, A Road, A Task, Lanham, MD: Univ Press of Am, 88; coauth, When Love is not Enough, The Practice of Justice, Collegeville: The Liturgical Press, (forthcoming); coauth, Integrating Catholic Heritage, Catholic Teacher Supplement to The World Around Us, New York: Macmillan/McGraw-Hill, 91; auth, "Work and Workers," in Louvain Studies 19, (94): 212-234; auth, "And Whatever Happened to Octogesima adveniens, 4?" in Theological Studies 56, (95): 39-60; auth, "The Reinterpretation of Gaudium et spes in Vertatis Splendor," in Bibiotheca Ephemeridum Theooogicarum Lovaniensium, (forthcoming); auth, "Theorectical Foundations of Interactive leadership in Catholic Social Teachings". **CONTACT ADDRESS** Institute of Pastoral Studies, Loyola Univ, Chicago, 6525 N Sheridan Rd, Chicago, IL 60626. **EMAIL** melsber@luc.edu

ELSTON, JULIE A.
PERSONAL Born 10/11/1959, Washington, DC, m, 1 child **DISCIPLINE** ECONOMICS **EDUCATION** Univ Wash, BA, 82; PhD, 92; Baruch Col, City Univ NYork, MS, 85. **CAREER** Res Fel, Wissenschaftszentrum Berlin, Germany, 92-96; vis instr, Calif Inst of Technol, Pasadena, 96-97; vis scholar, Univ Washington, 97-98; co-dir, Berlin Inst for Economic Studies, 97-; asst prof, Univ Central Fl, 98-. **HONORS AND AWARDS** Appointed book review editor of Small Business Economics. **MEMBERSHIPS** AEA, EARIE, WEA. **RESEARCH** Financial economics and industrial organization. **SELECTED PUBLICATIONS** Auth, US Tax Reform and Investment: Reality and Rhetoric in the 1980's, Ashgate Pub, London, England (95); coauth with BoB Chirinko, "Banking Relationships in Germany: Empirical Results and Policy Implications," Res Working Paper for the Federal Reserve Bank of Kansas City 96-05 and in Rethinking Bank Regulation: What Should Regulators Do? (96): 239-255; coauth with David B, Audretch, "Le Financement de la Mittelstand Allemande," Revue Internationale: Petite et Moyenne Enterprise (PME),vol 8, no 3-4 (96): 121-147; auth, "Dividend Policy and Investment: Theory and Evidence from US Panel Data," Managerial and Decision Economics (MDE), vol 17 (96): 1-9; coauth with David B. Audretsch, "Financing the German Mittelstand," Small Business Economics, vol 9 (97): 97-110; rev of "Firms, Contracts and Financial Structure," by Oliver Hart, in J of the Japanese and International Economics, vol 11 (97): 260-261; auth, "Investment, Liquidity Constraints and Bank Relationships: Evidence from German Manufacturing Firms," in Competition and Convergence in Financial Markets: The German and Anglo-Saxon Models, Advances in Finance, Investment, and Banking and Finance series, vol 5 Elsevier Sci Pubs (98); coauth with Stephen Bond, Jacques Marirresse, and Benoit Mulkay, working paper Nat Bureau of Economic Res, No 5900 (98); coauth with James Hastie and Dale Squires, "Market Linkages Between the US and Japan: An Application to the Fishieries Industry," Japan and the World Economy, vol 11 (99): 517-530; coauth with David B. Audretsch, "Does Firm Size Matter? Evidence on the Impacts of Liquidity Constraints on Firm Investment Behavior in Germany," Int J of Industrial Org (2000). **CONTACT ADDRESS** Dept Economics, Univ of Central Florida, PO Box 161400, Orlando, FL 32816. **EMAIL** Julie.Elston@bus.ucf.edu

ELWELL, WALTER ALEXANDER
PERSONAL Born 04/29/1937, Miami, FL, m, 1959, 2 children **DISCIPLINE** NEW TESTAMENT, THEOLOGY **EDUCATION** Wheaton Col, BA, 59; Wheaton Grad Sch, MA, 61; Univ Edinburgh, PhD(New Testament), 70. **CAREER** Instr Greek, Wheaton Col, 59-61; instr, North Park Col, 62-63; assoc prof Bible and Greek, Belhaven Col, 71-75; chmn dept theol studies, 76-81, Prof New Testament, Wheaton Grad Sch, 75-, Bk ed, Christianity Today.; Dean, Wheaton Col Grad Sch, 81-86. **HONORS AND AWARDS** Outstanding Prof of the Year, Belhaven Col, 64. **MEMBERSHIPS** Soc Bibl Lit; Inst Bibl Res; Marketplace Ministries; Evangelical Theol Soc. **SELECTED PUBLICATIONS** Contribr, Current Issues in Biblical & Patristic Interpretation, Eerdmans, 75; Zondervan Pictorial Encycl of the Bible, Zondervan, 76; auth, The Living Bible Study Reference Ed, 76; ed, Evangelical Dictionary of Theology, Baker, 84; ed, Baker Encyclopedia of the Bible, Baker, 88; ed, Evangelical Commentary on the Bible, Baker, 89; ed, Topical Analysis of the Bible, Baker, 91; ed, Handbook of Evangelical Theologians, Baker, 93; ed, Evangelical Dictionary of Biblical Theology, Baker, 96; coauth, Encountering the New Testament, Baker, 97. **CONTACT ADDRESS** 501 College Ave, Wheaton, IL 60187. **EMAIL** walter.elwell@wheaton.edu

EMERY, SARAH W.
PERSONAL Born 08/08/1911, Pleasant City, OH, w, 1948, 2 children **DISCIPLINE** PHILOSOPHY, ENGLISH **EDUCATION** Emory Univ, AB, 33; Ohio State Univ, MA, 38; PhD, 42. **CAREER** Tchg asst, Ohio State Univ, 38-42; tchg asst, Univ Ill, 42-43; instr, Packer Collegiate Inst, 43-46; instr, Syracuse Univ, 46-47; asst prof, Hollins Coll, 47-48; asst prof, Duke Univ, 51-52. **MEMBERSHIPS** Am Philos Asn; Phi Beta Kappa, The Poetry Soc of Tex. **SELECTED PUBLICATIONS** Auth, Blood on the Old Well, 63; auth (pseudonym, J.A. Cheadle), A Donkey's Life, A Story for Children, 79; They Walked into the Rose Garden and Other Poems, 92; Plato's Euthyphro, Apology and Crito, Arranged for Dramatic Presentation from the Jowett Translation with Chornses, 96; auth, J.F.K. and Other Poems, 99. **CONTACT ADDRESS** Box 683, Denton, TX 76202-0683.

EMINHIZER, EARL EUGENE
PERSONAL Born 05/22/1926, Greenville, SC, m, 1955 **DISCIPLINE** RELIGION **EDUCATION** Furman Univ, BA, 48; Youngstown Col, BS, 51; Crozer Theol Sem, BD, 55, ThM, 56; Southern Calif Sch Theol, ThD (hist), 68. **CAREER** Instr relig, Denison Univ, 56-58; instr, 58-77, ASSOC PROF PHILOS

AND RELIG, YOUNGSTOWN STATE UNIV, 77-, Minister, Brookfield Christian Church, Ohio; instruct improv grant, 82-83. **MEMBERSHIPS** AHA; Am Soc Church Hist; Am Philos Asn; Soc Bibl Lit; Am Acad Relig. **RESEARCH** American Baptist history, 1800-1865; Disciples of Christ history, 1800-1864. **SELECTED PUBLICATIONS** Auth, A Case Studyo of Mainstream Protestantism--The Disciples Relation to American Culture, 1880-1989, Church Hist, Vol 62, 93; Victorian America and the Civil War, Church Hist, Vol 63, 94; Victorian America and the Civil War, Church Hist, Vol 63, 94. **CONTACT ADDRESS** 1125 Trumbull Ave, Warren, OH 44484.

EMLER, DONALD
PERSONAL Born 06/01/1939, Kansas City, MO, m, 1968, 2 children **DISCIPLINE** RELIGIOUS STUDIES **EDUCATION** Univ Kansas City, Missouri, BA 60; Garrett-Evang Theol Sem, M.Div, 63; Indiana Univ, Ed.D, M.Ed, 73. **CAREER** Dean, Wimberly School of Relig, Okla City Univ, 89-; Site Coordinator, Okla Grad Theol Studies Prog, Perkins School Theol, 98-; prof Religious Educ, Centenary Col La, 76-89; lctr, Univ Missouri, 74-76; Chaplain & instr, Central Meth Col, 66-68, 73. **HONORS AND AWARDS** Omicron Delta Kappa Member; Outstanding Young Men of Amer, 72; Who's Who in South & Southwest, 84, 90; Who's Who in Relig, 85, 92; Who's Who in Educ, 91; Who Who in Amer, 98; Centenary Col Fac Study Grant, 86. **MEMBERSHIPS** Assoc of Prof & Res of Relig Educ; United Meth Assoc of Scholars of Christian Educ; Relig Educ Assoc; Christian Educ Fel; Amer Acad Relig/ Soc Bibl Lit; Okla Conference of United Meth Church. **SELECTED PUBLICATIONS** Lectr, Adult Learning and Development, 4 video lectures for OCU PLUS Program, 86; auth, The Gospel of Matthew: Using the International Lesson Series, OCU-TV, 95; auth, Content and Models: The Dialogue of Theology and Religious Education, Okla City Univ, 97; auth, History of World Religions: Teacher's Guide, Okla Pub Schools, 98; auth, The Bible as/in Literature: Tchrs Guide, Okla Pub Schools, 98. **CONTACT ADDRESS** Wimberly School of Religion, Oklahoma City Univ, Oklahoma City, OK 73106. **EMAIL** dgemler@okcu.edu

EMPEREUR, JAMES L.
PERSONAL Born 12/21/1933, Tigerton, WI, s **DISCIPLINE** LITURGICAL THEOLOGY **EDUCATION** St Louis Univ, BA, 58, PhL, 59; Woodstock Col, STL, 66; Grad Theol Union, Berkley, PhD, 72. **CAREER** Ed chief, Modern Liturgy Mag, 73-83; prof liturgical and systematic theology, Jesuit School Theology Berkeley, 69-93; founder Inst Spirituality and Worship, 73-93; Parochial Vicar & Liturgist, San Fernando Cathedral; Lectr, Religious studies, Our Lady of the Lake Univ. **HONORS AND AWARDS** Catholic Press Awd **MEMBERSHIPS** Am Acad Relig; Cath Theol Soc; NA Acad Liturgy; Soc Liturgica; Soc for the Study of Christian Spirituality. **RESEARCH** Inculturation of liturgy and sacraments; Liturgy and Hispanic popular religion; Relationship between art and spirituality; Spirituality and psychological growth; Spirituality of homosexuality. **SELECTED PUBLICATIONS** Auth, Prophetic Anointing: God's Call to the Sick, Elderly, and Dying, Michael Glazier, 82; Worship: Exploring the Sacred, Pastoral Press, 87; Models of Liturgical Theology, Grove Books, 87; The Liturgy That Does Justice, Michael Glazier, 90; Starvation in the Midst of Plenty, Liturgical Ministry, 94; Hispanic Celebrations: Popular Religion in Action, Christian Life Communities, 95; Is Liturgy an Art Form?, Liturgical Ministry, 96; The Enneagram and Spiritual Guidance: Nine Paths to Spiritual Guidance, Continuum, 97; Popular Religion and the Liturgy: The State of the Question, Liturgical Ministry, 98. **CONTACT ADDRESS** San Fernando Cathedral, 115 Main Plaza, San Antonio, TX 78205. **EMAIL** jakeempereur@prodigy.net

ENC, BERENT
PERSONAL Born 05/24/1938, Istanbul, Turkey **DISCIPLINE** PHILOSOPHY **EDUCATION** Princeton Univ, MSE, 62; Oxford Univ, Dipl hist & philos of sci, 64, DPhil, 67. **CAREER** Instr elec eng, Bucknell Univ, 61-62; vis lectr philos, 67-69, Assoc Prof, 71-76, Prof Philos, Univ Wis-Madison, 76-. **MEMBERSHIPS** Philos Sci Asn; Am Philos Soc. **RESEARCH** Philosophy of science, metaphysics, philosophy of mind, action theory, history of philosophy, Empiricism. **SELECTED PUBLICATIONS** Auth, Numerical identity and objecthood, Mind, 1/75; Necessary properties and Linnaean essentialism, Can J Philos, 9/75; On the theory of action, J Theory Social Behav, 75; Spiral dependence between theories and taxonomy, Inquiry, 75; Reference of theoretical terms, Nous, 76; Identity statements and microreductions, J Philos, 76; author numerous other articles. **CONTACT ADDRESS** Dept of Philos, Univ of Wisconsin, Madison, 600 North Park St, Madison, WI 53706-1403. **EMAIL** benc@facstaff.wisc.edu

ENDELMAN, TODD MICHAEL
PERSONAL Born 11/10/1946, Fresno, CA, m, 1968, 2 children **DISCIPLINE** JEWISH HISTORY, EUROPEAN HISTORY **EDUCATION** Univ Calif, Berkeley, BA, 68; Hebrew Union Col-Jewish Inst Relig, Calif, BHL, 72; Harvard Univ, Am, 72, PhD (hist), 76. **CAREER** Asst prof Jewish hist, Yeshiva Univ, 76-79; asst prof hist, 79-81, Assoc Prof Hist, Ind Univ, 81-85, Lectr hist, Hebrew Union Col-Jewish Inst Relig, NY, 79; William Haber Prof of Mod Jewish Hist, Univ of Mich, 85-. **HONORS AND AWARDS** Frank and Ethel S Cohen Awd, Jewish Bd Coun, Nat Jewish Welfare Bd, 80; A S Diamond Mem Prize, Jewish Hist Soc England, 80. **MEMBERSHIPS** AHA; Jewish Hist Soc England; Leo Baeck Inst; Asn Jewish Studies. **RESEARCH** Anglo-Jewish history; social history of Western European Jewry; the entry of the Jews into European society, 1700-1880. **SELECTED PUBLICATIONS** Auth, The Jews of Georgian England, 1714-1830: Tradition and Change in a Liberal Society, 79; ed, Jewish Apostasy in the Modern World, 87; auth, Radical Assimilation in Anglo-Jewish History, 1656-1945, 90; ed, Comparing Jewish Societies, 97; auth, The Jews of Modern Britain, forthcoming. **CONTACT ADDRESS** Dept of Hist, Univ of Michigan, Ann Arbor, 555 S State St, 1029 Tisch Hall, Ann Arbor, MI 48109-1003. **EMAIL** endelman@umich.edu

ENGEL, J. RONALD
PERSONAL Born 03/17/1936, Baltimore, MD, m, 1957, 2 children **DISCIPLINE** RELIGIOUS & ENVIRONMENTAL STUDIES **EDUCATION** Johns Hopkins Univ, BA, 58; Meadville Theol Sch Lombard Col, BD, 64; Univ Chicago, MA, 71, Phd, 77. **CAREER** Res Prof of Environmental and Social Ethics, Meadville Theol Sch Lombard Col, 00-, Lectr, Divinity Sch, Univ Chicago, 77-; Environmental Stud Faculty, Col of the Univ of Chicago. **MEMBERSHIPS** Am Acad Relig; Am Soc Environ Hist; Soc Christian Ethics; Int Soc Environmental Ethics. **RESEARCH** Environmental ethics; civil relig; Am philos and theol. **SELECTED PUBLICATIONS** Auth, Sacred Sands: the Struggle for Community in the Indiana Dunes, Wesleyan Univ Press, 83; The Democratic Faith, Am Jour Theolog & Philos, 5 & 9/85; co-ed, the Ethics of Environment and Development: Global Challenge, International Response, Belhaven Press and Ariz Univ Press, 90; Liberal Democracy and the Fate of the Earth, In: Spirit and Nature: Why the Environment is a Religious Issue - An Interfaith Dialogue, Beacon Press, 92; Co-auth, Ecology, Justice, and Christian Faith: A Critical Guide to the Literature, Greenwood Press, 95; Religion and Environment and Sustainable Development, In: The Encyclopedia of Bioethics, rev ed, Macmillan Publ Co, 95; The Religious Authority of Democracy: James Luther Adams's Agenda for Empirical Theology, Am Jour Theolog & Philos, 1/96; auth, "The Faith of Democratic Ecological Citizenship," Special Supplement, Hastings Center Report, 98. **CONTACT ADDRESS** Meadville/Lombard Theol Sch, 5701 S Woodlawn Ave, Chicago, IL 60637-1602. **EMAIL** jronengel@home.com

ENGELHARDT, HUGO TRISTRAM, JR.
PERSONAL Born 04/27/1941, New Orleans, LA, m, 1965, 3 children **DISCIPLINE** PHILOSOPHY **EDUCATION** Univ Texas, Austin, PhD, 69; Tulane Schl Med, MD, 72. **CAREER** Asst prof, Inst for Med Hum, Univ Texas, 72-75; assoc prof, prev med & commun health, Univ Texas Med, 75-77; from prof to Rosemary Kennedy Prof, phil of med, 77-82, Georgetown Univ; prof phil, Rice Univ, 83-, Rice Univ; prof, med & commun med, Baylor Col of Med, 83-; prof, med ethics, obstetrics & gynecology, Baylor Col of Med, 90-; mem, Ctr for Med Ethics & Health Policy, Baylor Col of Med, Houston TX, affil with Rice Univ, 83-. **HONORS AND AWARDS** Natl Defense Ed Act Fel, 66-69; Fulbright Grad Fel, 69-70; sr res fel, Kennedy Inst of Ethics, Ctr for Bioethics, 77-82; Woodrow Wilson Vis Fel, Westminster Col, 88; Fel Inst for Advan Stud, Berlin W Germany, 88-89. **MEMBERSHIPS** Amer Assn for Advan of Science; Amer Assn for History of Med; APA; European Soc for Phil of Med & Health Care; Hegel Soc of Amer; History of Science Soc; Intl Soc for Advan of Hum Stud in Gynecology; Metaphysical Soc of Am; SW Phil Soc, Sigma XI; Am Soc for Bioethics and Humanities. **RESEARCH** Ethics; bioethics; phil of med. **SELECTED PUBLICATIONS** Auth, Sanctity of Life and Menschenwurde: Can these Concepts Help Direct the Use of Resources in Critical Care? Sanctity of Life & Hum Dignity, Kluwer, 96; coauth, From Pagan Greece to Post-Modern Europe, European Phil of Med & Health Care 4, 96; auth, Manners in the Ruins of Community, Gentility Recalled, Soc Affairs Unit, 96; coauth, Ethical Self-Reflections in the Humanities an Social Sciences, The Responsible Scholar, Watson, 96; auth, Germ-Line Genetic Engg & Moral Diversity: Moral Controversies in a Post-Christian World, Soc Phil & Policy 13, 96; art, Suffering, Meaning, and Bioethics, Christian Bioethics 2, 96; art, Unavoidable Pluralism: Rethinking Secular Morality and Community at the End of the 20th Century, Dialektik, 96; art, Bioethics Reconsidered: Theory and Method in a Post-Christian Post-Modern Age, Kennedy Inst of Ethics J, 96; art, Equality in Health Care: Christian Engagement with a Secular Obsession, Christian Bioethics 2, 96; auth, The Foundations of Bioethics, 2nd ed, Oxford, 96; auth, An Orthodox Approach to Bioethics, Living Orthodoxy in the Modern World, London, Soc for Promoting Christian Knowledge, 96; auth, Japanese and Western Bioethics: Studies in Moral Diversity, Japanese & Western Bioethics, Kluwer, 97; auth, Moral Puzzles Concerning the Human Genome: Western Taboos, Intuitions, and Beliefs at the End of the Christian Era, Japanese & Western Bioethics, Kluwer, 97; art, The Crisis of Virtue: Arming for the Cultural Wars and Pellegrino at the Limes, Theoretical Med 18, 97; auth, The Foundations of Bioethics and Secular Humanism: Why is There No Canonical Moral Content?, Reading Engelhardt, Kluwer, 97; auth, Bioetica come termine plurale: di fronte alla diversita morale della fine del secondo millenio, Bioetica: la ragioni della vita e della scienza, Prometheus Intl, 22, 97; auth, II Camp Seccolare Della Bioetica, Bioetica, Editrice Elle Di Ci 97; art, Holiness, Virtue, and Social Justice: Contrasting Understandings of the Moral Life, Christian Bioethics 3, 97; art, Freedom and Moral Diversity: The Moral Failures of Health Care in the Welfare State, Soc Phil & Policy 14, 97; auth, Bioethics and the Philosophy of Medicine Reconsidered, Phil of Med & Bioethics, Kluwer, 97; auth, Sins, Voluntary and Involuntary: Recognizing the Limits of Double Effect, Christian Bioethics 3, 97; auth, Respect for Life and the Foundations of Bioethics, The Ethics of Life, Unesco Pub, 97; auth, The Foundations of Bioethics: Liberty and Life with Moral Diversity, Reason Papers 22, 97; auth, Human Nature Genetically Re-engineered: Moral Responsibilities to Future Generations, Germ-Line Intervention & our Responsibilities to Future Generations, Kluwer, 98; coauth, Emergency Patients: Serious Moral Choices, with Limited Time, Information, and Patient Participation, Ethics in Surgery, Oxford Univ Press, 98; auth, Solidaritat: Postmoderne Perspektiven, Solidaritat, Suhrkamp, Frankfurt, 98; coauth, Medicine, Philosophy of, Encycl of Phil, Routledge, 98; art, Physician-Assisted Death: Doctrinal Development vs Christian Tradition, Christian Bioethics 4, 98; art, Physician-Assisted Suicide Reconsidered: Dying as a Christian in a Post-Christian Age, Christian Bioethics 4, 98; auth, The Foundations of Christian Bioethics, Swets & Zeitlinger, 00. **CONTACT ADDRESS** Ctr for Medical Ethics, Baylor Col of Med, One Baylor Plaza, Houston, TX 77030.

ENGERMAN, STANLEY LEWIS
PERSONAL Born 03/14/1936, New York, NY, m, 1963, 3 children **DISCIPLINE** ECONOMICS, HISTORY **EDUCATION** NYork Univ, BS, 56, MBA, 58; Johns Hopkins Univ, PhD(econ), 62. **CAREER** Asst prof econ, Yale Univ, 62-63; from asst prof to assoc prof, 63-71, prof hist & econ, Univ Rochester, 71-, Nat Sci Found sci fac fel, 69-70; Nat Endowment for Humanities sr fel, 74-75; John Simon Guggenheim mem fel, 80-81. **MEMBERSHIPS** Am Econ Asn; Econ Hist Asn; AHA. **RESEARCH** Slavery; American social and economic history. **SELECTED PUBLICATIONS** Co-ed, The Reinterpretation of American Economic History, Harper, 71; coauth, Time on the Cross: The Economics of American Negro Slavery, Little, Brown, 74; co-ed, Race and Slavery in the Western Hemisphere: Quantitative Studies, Princeton Univ, 75. **CONTACT ADDRESS** Dept of Econ, Univ of Rochester, 500 Joseph C Wilson, Rochester, NY 14627-9000. **EMAIL** enge@troi.cc.rochester.edu

ENGLE, JAMES R.
PERSONAL m, 1990, 7 children **DISCIPLINE** THEOLOGY **EDUCATION** Messiah Col, BA, 62; Mennonite Biblical Sem, BD, 67; Univ Pittsburgh, Pittsburgh Theol Sem, PhD, 79. **CAREER** Freeman Jr Col & Academy, 79-84; Eastern Mennonite Sem, 84-. **MEMBERSHIPS** Soc of Biblical Lit, Am Schs of Oriental Res. **RESEARCH** Hebrew Bible, archaeology. **CONTACT ADDRESS** Eastern Mennonite Sem, Eastern Mennonite Univ, 1200 Park Rd, Harrisonburg, VA 22802-2404. **EMAIL** engle@emu.edu

ENGLER, RUSSELL
PERSONAL Born 01/29/1957, Ridgewood, NJ, m, 1987, 2 children **DISCIPLINE** LAW, LEGAL EDUCATION **EDUCATION** Yale Col, BA, 79; Harvard Law Sch, JD, 83. **CAREER** Clerk, U.S. Circuit Court of Appeals, 83-84; staff atty, Brooklyn Legal Serv, 84-93; asst prof to prof and dir, New Eng Sch of Law, 93-; lectr, Harvard Law Sch, 99-00. **MEMBERSHIPS** Bar Member in Mass, NY and Md; Boston Bar Asn; Mass Bar Asn; Asn of Am Law Sch; Clinical Legal Educ Asn. **RESEARCH** Poverty Law; Public Interest Law; Legal Ethics. **SELECTED PUBLICATIONS** Auth, "Out of sight and Out of Line: The Need for Regulation of Lawyers' Negotiations with Unrepresented Poor Persons," Calif L Rev, 97; auth, "And Justice For All--Including the Unrepresented Poor: Revisiting the Roles of the Judges, Mediators, and Clerks," Ford L Rev, 99. **CONTACT ADDRESS** New England Sch of Law, 154 Stuart St, Boston, MA 02116.

ENNIS, ROBERT H.
PERSONAL Born 11/01/1927, New York, NY, s, 2 children **DISCIPLINE** PHILOSOPHY AND PHILOSOPHY OF EDUCATION **EDUCATION** Univ Wisc, BA, 50; NYork Univ, MA, 51; Univ Ill, PhD, 58. **CAREER** Asst to assoc to full prof, Cornell Univ, 58-70; prof, Univ Ill, 70-94. **HONORS AND AWARDS** Ctr for Advan Study in the Behavioral Sci, 83-84. **MEMBERSHIPS** Amer Philos Asn; Philos of Educ Soc; Philos of Sci Asn; Asn for Informal Logic and Critical Thinking; Amer Asn of Philos Teachers. **RESEARCH** Critical thinking; Causality; Philosophy of language. **SELECTED PUBLICATIONS** Auth, Critical thinking, Prentice-Hall, 96; auth, Is critical thinking culturally biased?, Teaching Philos, 98; auth, Incorporating critical thinking in the curriculum: An introduction to some basic issues, Inquiry, 97; co-auth, Gender bias in critical thinking: continuing the dialogue, Educ Theory, 95; auth, Critical thinking assessment, Theory in Practice, 93; auth, Critical thinking: What is it?, Philos of educ 1992, Philos of Educ Soc, 93. **CONTACT ADDRESS** 495 E. Lake Rd., Sanibel, FL 33957. **EMAIL** rhennis@uiuc.edu

ENO, ROBERT BRYAN
PERSONAL Born 11/12/1936, Hartford, CT **DISCIPLINE** PATRISTICS, CHURCH HISTORY **EDUCATION** Cath Univ Am, BA, 58, MA, 59; Inst Cath de Paris, STD, 69. **CAREER** Asst prof, St Mary's Sem, Baltimore, 68-70; ASST PROF, 70-79, ASSOC PROF PATRISTICS, CATH UNIV AM, 79-, CHMN, DEPT CHURCH HIST, AND ASSOC CHMN, DEPT THEOL, 80-, Ed, Corpus Instrumentorum, 66-70; mem, NAT LUTHERAN-ROMAN CATH DIALOGUE, 76-; vis lectr, Princeton Theol Sem, spring, 77 and 80. **MEMBERSHIPS** NAm Patristic Soc; Asn Int des Etudes Patristiques; Am Soc Church Hist; Cath Hist Asn. **RESEARCH** Latin fathers, especially Augustine; ecclesiology; eschatology. **SELECTED PUBLICATIONS** Auth, Church, Book and Bishop--Conflict and Authority in Early Latin Christianity, Cath Hist Rev, Vol 83, 97; Historical Awareness in Augustine--Ontological, Anthropological and Historical Elements of an Augustinian Theory of History, Cath Hist Rev, Vol 80, 94; A Translation of Jerome Chronicon with Historical Commentary, Cath Hist Rev, Vol 83, 97; Desire and Delight--A New Reading of Augustine Confessions, Cath Hist Rev, Vol 79, 93; After the Apostles--Christianity in the 2nd Century, Church History, Vol 64, 95; Augustine, Arianism and Other Heresies, Cath Hist Rev, Vol 83, 97; Novitas Christiana - the Idea of Progress in the Old Church Before Eusebius, Cath Hist Rev, Vol 81, 95; Sacred and Secular--Studies on Augustine and Latin Christianity, Cath Hist Rev, Vol 83, 97; Augustine, Cath Hist Rev, Vol 83, 97; Augustine and the Catechumenate, Cath Hist Rev, Vol 83, 97; The Collection Sources Chretiennes--Editing the Fathers of the Church in the Xxth Century, Cath Hist Rev, Vol 83, 97; Chiliasm and the Myth of the Antichrist--Early Christian Controversy Regarding the Holy Land, Cath Hist Rev, Vol 80, 94; The Early Church--An Annotated Bibliography in English, Cath Hist Rev, Vol 80, 94; The Significance of the Lists of Roman Bishops in the Anti Donatist Polemic, Vigiliae Christianae, Vol 47, 93; Divine Grace and Human Agency--A Study of the Semi Pelagian Controversy, Theol Stud, Vol 57, 96; Reading the Apostolic Fathers--An Introduction, Cath Hist Rev, Vol 83, 97; After the Apostles--Christianity in the 2nd Century, Church Hist, Vol 64, 95. **CONTACT ADDRESS** Catholic Univ of America, 401 Michigan Ave NE, Washington, DC 20017.

ENOS, V. PUALANI
PERSONAL Born 07/17/1970, Los Angeles, CA, m, 1999 **DISCIPLINE** LAW **EDUCATION** Skidmore Col, BA, 92; George Wash Nat Law Center, JD, 95. **CAREER** Clin Teaching Fel to Asst Prof, Northeastern Univ, 95-. **HONORS AND AWARDS** West's Excellence in Family Law Awd, 95. **MEMBERSHIPS** Mass Women's Bar Asn; Boston Bar Asn; Mass Domestic Violence Coun; Same Sex Domestic Violence Coalition; Dorchester Community Roundtable; Am Asn of Law Sch; Clin Legal Educ Asn. **RESEARCH** Legal/Medical Collaborations; Intimate partner violence prevalence; Prevention; Institutional response. **SELECTED PUBLICATIONS** Auth, "Prosecuting Battered Mothers: State Laws' Failure to Protect Battered Women and Abused Children," Harvard Women's Law J, 96; auth, "Counter-response to the Editor," Harvard Women's Law J, 98. **CONTACT ADDRESS** Sch of Law, Northeastern Univ, 716 Columbus Ave, Ste 212, Roxbury, MA 02151. **EMAIL** p.enos@neu.edu

EPHRAIM, CHARLESWORTH W.
DISCIPLINE PHILOSOPHY **EDUCATION** USAF Tech Sch, radio operations honors 1964; USAF Instr Training Sch, 1964; State Univ of NYork, BA honors purchase valedictorian 1973; Yale U, MA, MPhil, PhD 1979; Nat Fellow Ford Found, 1973-78. **CAREER** US Air Force, tech instructor, sgt, radio op US & overseas 64-68; Bankers Trust Co NY, supr 68-73; State Univ of NY Coll at Purchase, Yale U, instructor; SUNY Empire State Coll, faculty; Mercy Coll, Dept of Philosophy, associate professor, philosophy, currently. **HONORS AND AWARDS** Completed USAF morse-code course in half time; first person in USAF hist to receive 24 GPM while in training, Keesler AFB MS 1964; grad coll in 2 1/2 yrs; rsch being done in Philosophy of the Black Experience; Awded, Summer Rsch Grant, NY African Amer Inst to study. **MEMBERSHIPS** Mem Com for Vets Affairs; mem NY Metropolitan Assoc for Developmental Education; mem Amer Philosophical Assn; mem NAACP; mem Urban League; founder Free Community School of Mt Vernon 1980. **SELECTED PUBLICATIONS** The Logic of Black Protest, 1988. **CONTACT ADDRESS** Mercy Col, 555 B'way, Dobbs Ferry, NY 10522.

EPP, ELDON JAY
PERSONAL Born 11/01/1930, Mountain Lake, MN, m, 1951 **DISCIPLINE** CHRISTIAN ORIGINS, MANUSCRIPT STUDIES **EDUCATION** Wheaton Col, Ill, AB, 52; Fuller Theol Sem, BD, 55; Harvard Univ, STM, 56, PhD (hist, philos relig), 61. **CAREER** Spec res asst, Princeton Theol Sem, 61-62; from asst prof to assoc prof relig, Grad Sch Relig, Univ Southern Calif, 62-67, assoc prof classics, 66-68; from assoc prof to profrelig, 68-71, Fel Claremont Grad Sch, 66-68; AM EXEC COMT, INT GREEK NEW TESTAMENT PROJ, 68-; ASSOC ED, J BIBL LIT, 71-; Guggenheim fel, 74-75. **MEMBERSHIPS** Soc Bibl Lit; Am Acad Relig; Soc Study New Testament; Cath Bibl Asn; Soc Mithraic Studies. **RESEARCH** New Testament textual criticism; Greek and Latin manuscript studies; Greco-Roman religions. **SELECTED PUBLICATIONS** Auth, The International Greek New Testament--Project Motivation Hist, Novum Testamentum, Vol 39, 97. **CONTACT ADDRESS** Off of the Dean Case, Case Western Reserve Univ, 10900 Euclid Ave, Cleveland, OH 44106-4901.

EPPS, GARRETT
PERSONAL Born 04/06/1950, Richmond, VA, m, 1977, 2 children **DISCIPLINE** LAW **EDUCATION** Harvard Univ, BA, 72; Hollins Univ, MA, 75; Duke Law Sch, JD, 91; LLM, 94. **CAREER** Staff Writer, Wash Post, 78-81; Asst Prof to Assoc Prof, Univ Ore, 92-; Vis Assoc Prof, Boston Col, 99-00; Vis Assoc Prof, Duke Law Sch, 01-02. **HONORS AND AWARDS** Fel, Nat Endowment for the Arts/Creative Writing, 78; Lillian Smith Awd, 78. **MEMBERSHIPS** PEN USA W **RESEARCH** Religious freedom; Constitutional history; Political theory as it affects American constitutional law. **SELECTED PUBLICATIONS** Auth, To an Unknown God: Religious Freedom on Trial, St Martins Press, 01. **CONTACT ADDRESS** Sch of Law, Univ of Oregon, 1221 Univ of Ore, Eugene, OR 97403. **EMAIL** gepps@law.uoregon.edu

EPPS, VALERIE C.
PERSONAL Born 03/06/1943, U.K., m, 1969, 2 children **DISCIPLINE** LAW **EDUCATION** Univ Birmingham, BA, 65; Boston Univ, JD, 72; Harvard, LL.M, 78. **CAREER** Prof. **RESEARCH** International law; immigration law; constitutional law. **SELECTED PUBLICATIONS** Auth, International Law for Undergraduates: Documentary Supplement, 98; The New Dynamics of Self-Determination, 97; Treaties - U.S. - U.K. Extradition Treaties - Rule of Expanded Political Offense - type Exception: In Re Requested Extradition of Smyth, Am Jour Int Law, 96; Towards Global Government: Reality or Oxymoron?, Jour Int Comp Law, 96; Elizabeth F. Defeis International Law Video Course, 96; Enforcing Human Rights, 94. **CONTACT ADDRESS** Sch of Law, Suffolk Univ, 120 Tremont St., Boston, MA 02108-4977. **EMAIL** vepps@acad.suffolk.edu

EPSTEIN, EDWIN M.
DISCIPLINE POLITICAL SCIENCE, LAW **EDUCATION** Univ Pa, BA, 58; Yale Univ, LLB Law, 61; Univ Calif Berkeley, MA Polit Sci, 66. **CAREER** Instr, Univ Pa, 62-64; Lectr, 64-67; asst prof, 67-69; assoc prof, 69-73; prof, 73-91; prof Emeritus, Univ Calif Berkeley, 91-; adj prof, grad Theol Union Calif, 76-; Dean and prof St Mary's Coll Calif, 94-. **HONORS AND AWARDS** Fel, Univ Reading UKI, 71; Fellow Woodrow Wilson Int Center for Scholars Wash, 77-78; Inau gural Jayes/ Quantas Vis Lectr Univ Newcastle Aus, 81; Elected Honorary Mem, Golden Key Nat Honor Soc, 87; Outstanding Fac Mem Awd, Polit Economy Students Asn, 87; Elected Honorary Mem, Phi Beta Kappa, 88; Japan Soc for the Promotion of Sci Fel, 89; Howard Chase Book Awd, 89; Summer Marcus Distinguished Awd, Acad of Mgt, 89; The Berkeley Citation, 91. **MEMBERSHIPS** Acad of Mgt; Acad of Legal Studies in Bus; Am Bar Asn; Am Polit Sci Asn; Bars of Calif, PA ans Supreme Ct of the US; Int Asn for Bus and Soc; Int Soc of Bus, Economics and Ethics; Soc for Bus Ethics. **RESEARCH** Political Science; Law. **SELECTED PUBLICATIONS** Auth, We've Come a Long Way ..From ABLA to ALBS - A Thirty Year Personal Reflection, The J of Legal Studies Educ, 96; Bus Ethics and Corporate Social Policy: reflections on an Intellectual Journey, 1964-1996, and beyond, Bus and Soc, 98. **CONTACT ADDRESS** 875 Creston Rd., Berkeley, CA 94618.

EPSTEIN, LEE
PERSONAL Born 03/17/1958, New York, NY, m, 1980 **DISCIPLINE** POLITICAL SCIENCE **EDUCATION** Emory Univ, BA, 80; MA, 82; PhD, 83. **CAREER** Assoc prof to prof and dept chair, Wash Univ, 91-. **HONORS AND AWARDS** Spec Recognition, Am Polit Sci Asn; Outstanding Acad Book Award, CHOICE, 94; Honorable Mention Award, Asn of Am Pub, 94; C. Herman Pritchett Award, Am Polit Sci Asn, 98; Prof of the Year Award, Wash Univ, 00; Fac of the Year Award, Wash Univ, 00; Rotunda Teaching Award, SMU, 87-88, 90-91; Margareta Deschner Teaching Award, SMU, 88. **MEMBERSHIPS** Am Polit Sci Asn; Midwest Polit Sci Asn; Law and Soc Asn; Am Judicature Soc. **RESEARCH** Law; Courts; Judicial process; Constitutional law. **SELECTED PUBLICATIONS** Co-auth, The Supreme Court and Legal Change: Abortion and the Death Penalty, Univ NC Press, 92; co-auth, The Supreme Court Compendium: Data, Decisions, and Developments, Wash DC, 94; co-auth, "Measuring Political Preferences," Am J of Polit Sci, (96): 260-294; co-auth, "On the Struggle for Judicial Supremacy," L and Soc Rev, (96): 87-130; co-auth, "The Norm of Stare Decisis," Am J of Polit Sci, (96): 1018-1035; co-auth, "The Claim of Issue Creation on the U.S. Supreme Court," Am Polit Sci Rev, (96): 845-852; co-auth, The Choices Justices Make, Congressional Quart Press, 98; co-auth, "Measuring Issue Salience," Am J of Polit Sci, (00): 66-83; co-auth, "Field Essay: Toward a Strategic Revolution in Judicial Politics: A Look Back, A Look Ahead," Polit Res Quart, (00): 625-661; co-auth, "The Norm of Consensus on the U.S. Supreme Court," Am J of Polit Sci, (01): 362-377. **CONTACT ADDRESS** Dept Polit Sci, Washington Univ, One Brookings Dr, CB 1063, Saint Louis, MO 63130. **EMAIL** epstein@artsci.wustl.edu

EPSTEIN, RICHARD ALLEN
PERSONAL Born 04/17/1943, New York, NY, m, 1972 **DISCIPLINE** LAW **EDUCATION** Columbia Univ, AB, 64; Oxford Univ, BA, 66; Yale Univ, LLB, 68. **CAREER** From asst prof to assoc prof, Univ Southern Calif, 68-73; PROF LAW, UNIV CHICAGO, 73-, Vis assoc prof, Univ Chicago, 72-73; fel, Ctr Advan Studies Behav Sci, 77-78. **MEMBERSHIPS** Am Soc Polit and Legal Philos. **RESEARCH** Torts, taxation. **SELECTED PUBLICATIONS** Auth, Cases and Materials on the Law of Torts; A Theory of Strict Liability, J Legal Studies, 74. **CONTACT ADDRESS** Law Sch, Univ of Chicago, 1111 E 60th St, Chicago, IL 60637-2702.

ERDEL, TIMOTHY PAUL
PERSONAL Born 08/07/1951, Decatur, IN, m, 1977, 3 children **DISCIPLINE** PHILOSOPHY; HISTORY; THEOLOGICAL LIBRARIANSHIP **EDUCATION** Fort Wayne Bible Col, BA, 73; Trinity Evangel Divinity School, M Div, 76; ThM, 81; Univ Chicago, AM, 78; Univ Ill, MA, 86; PhD, 00. **CAREER** Pastoral ministry, Chicago, 73-77; asst dir, Jesuit-Krauss-McCormick Libr, 77-78; ref librn, Trinity Evangel Divinity School, 78-82; vis lectr, Trinity Col, 82; lectr Hist & Philos Theol, Jamaica Theol Seminary & Carribean Grad School of Theol, 87-93; lectr, Jamaica Theol Sem, 87-93; librn, Zenas Gerig Libr, 87-93; teaching asst Philos & Relig Studies, Univ Ill, 82-87; vis lectr, Instituto Biblico-Teologico, I.E.M., 99; vis lectr, Seminario Bautista Bereana, 99; asst prof Relig & Philos and Archivist & Theol Librn, Bethel Col, 94-. **HONORS AND AWARDS** Jamaica Theol Sem Teacher of Year, 92-93. **MEMBERSHIPS** Am Acad Relig; Am Philos Asn; Am Soc Church Hist; Am Theol Libr Asn; Anabaptist/Mennonite Theol Librn; Conference on Faith & History; Evangel Missiological Soc; Evangel Missiological Soc; Evangelical Theolog Soc; Ill Mennonite Historical & Genealogical Soc; Mennonite Historical Soc; Methodist Librn Fel; Soc Bibl Lit; Soc Am Archivists; Soc Christian Philos; Soc Ind Archivists; Wesleyan Theol Soc. **RESEARCH** History of Missionary Church; History of Ecuador; Faith and Reason; Theological Librarianship. **SELECTED PUBLICATIONS** From the Colonial Christ and Babylonian Captivity to Dread Jesus, 00; From Egly Amish to Global Mission: The Missionary Church Association, 98; The Missionary Church: From Radical Outcast to the Wild Child of Anabaptism, 97; compiler, Guide to the Preparation of Theses, Carribean Grad School of Theol, 89; coauth, Religions of the World, St Martin's Pr, 88. **CONTACT ADDRESS** Dept of Relig and Philos, Bethel Col, Indiana, 1001 W McKinley Ave, Mishawaka, IN 46545-5509. **EMAIL** erdelt@bethel-in.edu

ERICKSON, MILLARD J.
PERSONAL Born 06/24/1932, Stauchfield, MN, m, 1955, 3 children **DISCIPLINE** THEOLOGY **EDUCATION** Univ Minn, BA, 53; Northern Baptist Theol Sem, BD, 56; MPhil, 58, Univ Chicago; PhD, 63, Northwestern Univ. **CAREER** Instr, bibl & apologetics, 64-69, Wheaton Col; asst, assoc prof, chmn, bibl & phil, 69-92, Bethel Theol Sem; assoc prof, prof, theol, dean, vp, exec vp, 92-96, Southwester Baptist Theol Sem; res prof, dist prof, theol, 96-, Truett Sem of Baylor Col. **HONORS AND AWARDS** Phi Beta Kappa. **MEMBERSHIPS** Amer Theol Soc; APA; Soc of Christian Ethics; Evangel Theol Soc; Evangel Phil Soc. **RESEARCH** Systematic theology; contemporary theology. **SELECTED PUBLICATIONS** Auth, Where Is Theology Going? Issues and Perspectives on the Future of Theology, Baker Bks, 94; auth, Does It Matter How I Live? Applying Biblical Beliefs to Your Daily Life, Baker Bks, 94; auth, God in Three Persons: A Contemporary Understanding of the Trinity, Baker Bks, 95; auth, How Shall They Be Saved? The Destiny of Those Who Do Not Hear of Jesus, Baker Bks, 96; auth, Does It Matter If God Exists? Understanding Who God Is and What He Does For Us, Baker Bks, 96; auth, Does It Matter That I'm Saved? What the Bible Teaches About Salvation, Baker Bks, 96; coauth, Old Wine in New Wine Skins: Doctrinal Preaching in A Changing World, Baker Bks, 97; auth, The Evangelical Left: Encountering Postconservative Evangelical Theology, Baker Bks, 97; auth, Christian Theology, Baker Bks, 98; auth, A Basic Guide to Eschatology: Making Sense of the Millennium, Baker Bks, 98; auth, God the Father Almighty: A Contemporary Exploration of the Divine Attributes, Baker Bks, 98; auth, Postmodernizing the Faith: Evangelical Responses to the Challenge of Postmodernism, Baker Bks, 98. **CONTACT ADDRESS** 2677 Lake Court Cir, Mounds View, MN 55112-4101.

ERICKSON, STEPHEN ANTHONY
PERSONAL Born 09/01/1940, Fairmont, MN, m, 1986, 2 children **DISCIPLINE** PHILOSOPHY **EDUCATION** St Olaf Col, BA, 61; Yale Univ, MA, 63, PhD (philos), 64. **CAREER** From instr to assoc prof, 64-73, PROF PHILOS, POMONA COL AND CLAREMONT GRAD SCH, 73-; E. Wilson Lyon Professor of Humanities, Pomona College, 90-. **HONORS AND AWARDS** Phi Beta Kappa; Summa Cum Laude; Graves Awd; Wig Awd; ACLU Travel Grant; Earhart Foundation Grant. **MEMBERSHIPS** Am Philos Asn; K. Jaspers Soc. Of N. Am. **RESEARCH** The intersection of Phil of Culture and Phil of Religion within Am and Continental Thought. **SELECTED PUBLICATIONS** Auth, "Language and Being: An Analytic Phenomenology," Yale Univ Press, 70; auth, "Human Presence: At the Boundaries of Meaning," Mercer Univ Press, 84; auth, "The Coming Age of Thresholding, Kluwer Acad Pub-

lish, 99; Over 75 articles and book reviews in journals such as Review of Metaphysics; Man and World; Philosophy Today, IPQ. J Am Acad Rel. **CONTACT ADDRESS** Dept of Philos, Pomona Col, Claremont, CA 91711. **EMAIL** sperickson@atsaol.com

ERICSON, NORMAN R.
PERSONAL Born 07/21/1932, Loomis, NE, m, 1954, 4 children **DISCIPLINE** NEW TESTAMENT **EDUCATION** Univ Nebr, BA; Trinity Ev Div School, BD; Univ Chicago, PhD. **CAREER** Assoc prof, 62-74, Trinity Intl Univ; prof, 74-77, Trinity Ev Divinity School; prof, 77-00, Wheaton Col. **MEMBERSHIPS** SBL; IBR; ETS; Chicago Soc Bib Lit. **RESEARCH** General Epistles; synoptic gospels. **SELECTED PUBLICATIONS** Auth, Implications from the New Testament for Contextualization, Theology and Mission, Baker, 78; auth, Interpreting I Peter, II Peter and Jude, Lit and Meaning of Scripture, Baker, 81; coauth, John: A New Look at the Fourth Gospel, Tyndale, 81; rev, J.R. Michaels, I Peter, Themelios; rev, Perkins, First and Second Peter, James and Jude, Trinity Jour; gen rev, Letters and Revelation in The Bible: New Living Translation, Tydale, 96. **CONTACT ADDRESS** ON 651 Herrick Dr, Wheaton, IL 60187. **EMAIL** nericson@earthlink.net

ERICSON, RICHARD
DISCIPLINE LAW **EDUCATION** Guelph Univ, BA, 69; Univ Toronto, MA, 71; Cambridge Univ, PhD, 74; DLitt, 91. **CAREER** Prof, 93; prof of soc; principal of Green Col at UBC. **HONORS AND AWARDS** Canada Coun Killam Res Fel; co-ed, can jour soc, 75-. **RESEARCH** Criminal justice; law and communication; law reform; policing and regulation. **SELECTED PUBLICATIONS** Co ed, "The Canadian Journal of Sociology," 75-. **CONTACT ADDRESS** Fac of Law, Univ of British Columbia, 1822 East Mall, Vancouver, BC, Canada V6T 1Z1. **EMAIL** ericson@interchange.ubc.ca

ERNST, CARL W.
PERSONAL Born 09/08/1950, Los Angeles, CA, m, 1974, 2 children **DISCIPLINE** RELIGIOUS STUDIES **EDUCATION** Stanford Univ, AB, 73; Harvard Univ, PhD, 81. **CAREER** Asst prof, 81-87, assoc prof, 87-92, ch, 91-92, Pomona Col; prof, 92- , ch 95- , Univ NC at Chapel Hill; distinguish term prof, Zachary Smith, 00-. **HONORS AND AWARDS** Natl Endowment Hum, dir summer sem Col tchrs, summer res grant, 93, Transl grant, Arabic, 89-90; Fulbright res fel, Pakistan, 90, 86, India, 78-79; res grant, Amer inst Pakistan stud (s), 98; Elect to Amer soc stud Rel, 96; Amer res inst Turkey Travel grant, 90; Amer Coun of learned soc, Ger, 89; sr res fel, Amer inst Indian stud (s), 81; Lang fel, Persian, 76-78 NDFL, 79-80 FLAS; Harvard Grad Sch Arts and Sci merit awd, 79. **MEMBERSHIPS** Amer Acad Rel; Middle East stud (s) asn; soc Iranian stud (s); Amer inst Pakistan stud (s); Amer soc stud (s) Rel, Carolina-Duke-Emory inst for the stud of Islam (co-founder.) **RESEARCH** Islamic Studies; Religion in South Asia. **SELECTED PUBLICATIONS** Auth, Works of Ecstasy in Surfism, SUNY Series in Islam, SUNY Press, 85; From Hagiography to Martyrology: Conflicting Testimonies to a Sufi Martyr of the Delhi Sultanate, History of Religions, XXIV, May 85, 308-327; Controversy Over Ibn Arabi's Fusus: The Faith of Pharaoh, Islamic Culture LIX, 85, 259-266; The Symbolism of Birds and Flight in the Writings of Ruzbihan Baqli, in The Legacy of Mediaeval Persian Sufism, ed Leonard Lewisohn, London, Khaniqahi Nimatullahi, 92, 353-366, also in Sufi, 11, Autumn 91, 5-12; The Spirit of Islamic Calligraphy: Baba Shah Isfahani's Adab al-Mashq, Jour Amer Oriental Soc, 112, 92, 279-286; Mystical Language and the Teaching Context in the early Sufi Lexicons, in Mysticism and Language, ed Steven T. Katz, Oxford UP, 92, 181-201; Eternal Garden: Mysticism, History, and Politics at a South Asian Sufi Center, SUNY Series in Muslim Spirituality in South Asia, SUNY Press, 92; The Man Without Attributes: Ibn Arabi's Interpretation of Abu Yazid al-Bistami, Jour Muhyiddin Ibn Arabi Soc, XIII, 93, 1-18; assoc ed, Manifestations of Sainthood in islam, Istanbul, The Isis Press, 93, also auth, Introduction, xi-xxviii, and An Indo-Persian Guide to Sufi Shrine Pilgrimage, 43-67; The Stages of Love in Persian Sufism, from Rabi'a to Ruzbihan, in Classical Persian Sufism from its Origins to Rumi, ed Leonard Lewisohn, London, Khaniqahi Nimatullahi, 94, 435-455; Ruzbihan Baqli on Love as Essential Desire, in God is Beautiful and He Loves Beauty: Festschrift fur Annemarie Schimmel, ed Alma Giese and J. Christoph Burgel, Bern, Peter Lang, 94, 181-189; The Interpretation of the Classical Sufi Tradition in India: The Shama'il al-atqiya of Rukn al-Din Kashani, Sufi, 22, 94, 5-10; Trans for Religions of India in Practice, ed Donald S. Lopez, jr., Princeton Readings in Religions, 1, Princeton UP, 95: Lives of Sufi Saints, 495-512, Conversations of Sufi Saints, 513-517, and India as a Sacred Islamic Land, 556-64; Sufism and Yoga According to Muhammad Ghawth, Sufi, 29, Spring, 96, 9-13; Ruzbihan Baqli: Mysticism and the Rhetoric of Sainthood in Persian Sufism, Curzon Sufi Series, 4, London, Curzon Press, 96; Local Cultural Nationalism as Anti-Fundamentalist Strategy in Pakistan, Comparative Studies of South Asia, Africa, and the Middle East, 16, 96, 68-76; The Shambhala Guide to Sufism, Boston, Shambhala Pub (s), 97; Ruzbihan Baqli, The Unveiling of Secrets: Diary of a Sufi Master, transl from Arabic, Chapel Hill, NC, Parvardigar Press, 97; Persecution and Circumspection in the Shattari Sufi Order, in Islamic Mysticism Contested: Thirteen Centuries of Debate and Conflict, ed Fred De Jong and Berndt Radtke, Islamic History and Civilization, Leiden, E.J. Brill, 98; Admiring the Works of the Ancients: The Ellora Temples as Viewed by Indo-Muslim Authors, in Beyond Turk and Hindu: Rethinking Religious Identity in Premodern South Asia, ed David Gilmartin and Bruce B. Lawrence, State U of Florida P, 99; auth, Teachings of Sufism, Boston: Shambhala Pub, 99; auth, Chishti Mediation Practices of the Later Mughal Period, The Heritage of Sufism, vol 3: Late Classical Persanate Sufism (1501-1750): The Safavid and Mughal Period, Oxford: OneWorld, 99, 344-57; transl, The Shambhala Guide to Sufism, Oniro, 99; transl, Mondadori, 00; transl, Ruzbihan Baqli: Mysticism and the Rhetoric of Sainthood in Persian Sufism, Nashr-I Markaz, 99. **CONTACT ADDRESS** Dept of Religion, Univ of No Carolina, Chapel Hill, Chapel Hill, NC 27599-3225. **EMAIL** cernst@email.unc.edu

ERWIN, JAMES OTIS
PERSONAL Born 04/28/1922, Marion, NC, m **DISCIPLINE** THEOLOGY **EDUCATION** Johnson C Smith U, BA 1943; Garrett Theol Sem, MDiv 1946; Iliff Sch Theology, MRE 1953, STM 1979; Rust Coll, LLD 1971; WV Wesleyan U, LLD 1972. **CAREER** United Methodist Church, ordained to ministry 46; Morristown Coll TN, chaplain, instructor 46-48; Wiley Coll TX, pres 70-72, chmn dept religion, philosophy, chaplain 48-53; Lincoln Univ MO, asst prof 53-66; Wesley Found Univ of IA, founder 66-67; Philander Smith Coll AR, dean of students, chaplain 67-70; Wesley United Methodist Church, pastor 68-70; St James United Methodist Church Chicago, pastor 72-76. **MEMBERSHIPS** Mem Douglas-Cherokee Ofc Econ Opportunity 1970-72; dist supt The United Meth Ch; mem Cherokee Guidance Center Morristown 1970-72; vice-chmn Little Rock BSA 1968-70; mem Intl Platform Assn; Alpha Phi Omega; Phi Beta Sigma. **SELECTED PUBLICATIONS** Contrib articles to professional jours. **CONTACT ADDRESS** 77 W Washington St, Ste 1806, Chicago, IL 60602.

ERWIN, PAMELA
DISCIPLINE YOUTH AND FAMILY MINISTRIES **EDUCATION** Univ NC, BS; Denver Sem, MA; Univ Colo, PhD. **CAREER** Prof, Denver Sem. **RESEARCH** Educational leadership and innovation. **SELECTED PUBLICATIONS** Coauth, Youth and Family Ministry, New Directions for Youth Ministry; auth, Principles of Mentoring, Youth Ministry Mentoring Manual; ed, Community-Based Family Ministry. **CONTACT ADDRESS** Denver Conservative Baptist Sem, PO Box 10000, Denver, CO 80250.

ESAU, ALVIN
DISCIPLINE LAW **EDUCATION** Univ Alberta, BA, 73, LLB, 76; Harvard Univ, LLM, 77. **CAREER** Asst prof, 77-81; assoc prof, 81-85; prof, Univ of Manitoba, 85-, **RESEARCH** Legal systems; criminal law; professional responsibility; jurisprudence; computer applications. **SELECTED PUBLICATIONS** Ed, Radon and the Law, 90; The Winnipeg General Strike Trials: Research Source, 90; ed, Lawyers and Legal Education, 90; ed, Dimensions of Childhood, 91; ed, Manitoba Law Annul 5, 95; auth, "Competition, Cooperation, or Cartel: A National Law School Accreditation Process for Canada?" Dalhousie Law Journal 23 (00); auth, "Island's of Exclusivity" Religious Organizations and Employment Discrimination 33, U. B.C. Law Review (00). **CONTACT ADDRESS** Fac of Law, Univ of Manitoba, Robson Hall, Winnipeg, MB, Canada R3T 2N2. **EMAIL** esau@cc.umanitoba.ca

ESCHELBACH, MICHAEL A.
PERSONAL Born 10/11/1957, Ann Arbor, MI, m, 1983, 5 children **DISCIPLINE** THEOLOGY **EDUCATION** E Mich Univ, BS, 79; Concordia Theo Sem, MDiv, 85; Westminster Theo Sem, PhD, 98. **CAREER** VP, 74-81, Ann Arbor Craftsmen Inc; Pastor, 85-88, Mount Olive Luth Church; Pastor, 88-, Peace Luth Church. **MEMBERSHIPS** ETS, SBL. **RESEARCH** New Testament studies **CONTACT ADDRESS** 78 Flynn, Sandusky, MI 48471.

ESKILDSEN, STEPHEN E.
PERSONAL Born 02/20/1963, Tokyo, Japan, s **DISCIPLINE** RELIGIOUS STUDIES **EDUCATION** Int Christian Univ, BA, 86, Univ Brit Columbia, MA, 89; PhD, 94. **CAREER** Asst prof, Univ of Sask, 94-95; Postdoctoral fel, Chinese Univ of Hong Kong, 97-98; asst prof, Univ Tenn at Chattanooga, 98-. **MEMBERSHIPS** Am Acad of Relig; Soc for the Study of chinese Relig. **RESEARCH** Taoist Religion, Medieval Taoism, Quanzhen Taoism, Internal Alchemy. **SELECTED PUBLICATIONS** Auth, Asceticism in Early Taoist Religion, SUNY Pr (Albany), 98. **CONTACT ADDRESS** Dept Relig Philos, Univ of Tennessee, Chattanooga, 615 McCallie Ave, Chattanooga, TN 37403-2504. **EMAIL** stephen-eskildsen@utc.edu

ESKRIDGE, CHRIS W.
PERSONAL Born 07/20/1952, Berkeley, CA, m, 1975, 2 children **DISCIPLINE** CRIMINOLOGY; CRIMINAL SCIENCE **EDUCATION** BYU, BS 75; Ohio State Univ, MA 77, PhD 78. **CAREER** Univ Nebraska, prof, 78-; Univ Canterbury NZ, fel, 92; Lincoln Foundation, asst to Pres, 83; US Air Force, res assoc, 81; Utah Attorney General Office, Investigator, 75-; Utah Cnt Attorney's Office, crim investigator, 75-76; Dir, Am Soc of Criminology, 99-. **HONORS AND AWARDS** Herbert Bloch Awd; ASC various teaching Awds; Silliman Univ Philippines, Fulbright/Vist. Prof of Law, 00; **MEMBERSHIPS** ACJS; ASC; IASOC; WSC. **RESEARCH** Organized Crime; Intl Crime. **SELECTED PUBLICATIONS** Auth, Criminal Justice: Concepts and Issues, contrib ed, 3rd ed, LA, Roxbury Press, 99; Liberty v Order: The Ultimate Confrontation, Dubuque IA, Kendall/Hunt, 93; Hist and Devel of Modern Correctional Practices in NZ, co-ed, in: Richter Moore, Charles Fields, eds, Comparative Crim Justice, IL, Waveland, 96; Justice and The Amer Justice Network, in: Crim Justice: Concepts and Issues, LA, Roxbury Press, 96; The Mexican Cartels: A Challenge for the 21st Century, coauth, Crim Organizations, 98; Crime and Justice in Post Cold War Hungary, Fed Probation, 96; The Great Transition: Post War Corrections in Poland, coauth, Jour of Offender Rehab, 96; Crime and Justice in NZ, coauth, Intl, 94; Penal Innovation in NZ: He Ara Hou, coauth, Jour of Offender Rehab, 94. **CONTACT ADDRESS** Dept of Criminal Justice, Univ of Nebraska, Lincoln, Lincoln, NE 68588-0630. **EMAIL** ceskridge@unl.edu

ESKRIDGE, JOHN CLARENCE
PERSONAL Born 06/06/1943, Pittsburgh, PA, s **DISCIPLINE** PHILOSOPHY **EDUCATION** Duquesne Univ Pittsburgh, BA, 66; MA, 71; Pacific So Univ CA, PhD Philosophy, 78. **CAREER** Comm Col, prof philosophy 78-; Carlow Col, dir turial instructor 73-74; Comm Col Allegheny County, philosophy faculty 69-; "Le Sacre Corps" Dance Co, artistic dir 69-79; Pittsburgh Child Guidance Clinic, program dir, creative recreational arts program 69-70; Comm Col Allegheny County Campus, dir black studies 69-71, Col speakers bureau 78-88; First Baptist Church Pittsburgh, bd of deacons 70-73; Pittsburgh High School of Creative & Performing Arts, adv bd 79-90; Community Col Allegheny County, department chairman, 83-; Hot Lix Concert Jazz Band, leader/producer, 78-89; Orpheo Concert Latin Band, leader/producer, 89-. **HONORS AND AWARDS** NDEA study fellowship Duquesne Univ, 67-70; faculty spl serv award Comm Coll Allegheny Co Student Union, 78; College Blue Ribbon Faculty Awd, Community College Allegheny County, 81-82. **MEMBERSHIPS** Mem Soc for Phenomenology & Existential Philosophy, 67-80; mem Am Philos Assn, 69-80; founding chmn Hermeneutic Circle, 77-80; bd dirs Inst For Collective Behavior & Memory, 80-87; vice pres, African American Federation of the Americas, 83-89; member, Pittsburgh Musicians Society, 67-. **CONTACT ADDRESS** Dept Phil & For Lang, Comm Col of Allegheny County, Allegheny, 808 Ridge Ave, Pittsburgh, PA 15212.

ESS, CHARLES
PERSONAL Born 10/08/1951, Tulsa, OK, m, 1975, 2 children **DISCIPLINE** PHILOSOPHY **EDUCATION** PA State Univ, PhD. **CAREER** Prof, Drury Col. **HONORS AND AWARDS** Joe Wyatt Challenge Awd 91; Outstanding Teaching; Scholarship Awds. **MEMBERSHIPS** Am Philosophical Asn; Asn of Internet Researchers. **RESEARCH** Hist of philos; ethics; logic; feminist philos; world relig(s); computer mediated commun. **SELECTED PUBLICATIONS** Auth, Philosophical Perspectives in Computer-Mediated Communication, Suny, 96; Is There Hope for Democracy in Cyberspace, Center Technol Cult, 97; Prophetic Communities On-line?, Presbyterian Church, 97; Values Analysis: an Experiment in Interdisciplinary Ethics, Am Philos Asn Newsletter on Tchg, 97; auth, Cosmopolitan Ideal or Cybercentrism, Comput and Philos, 98; auth, Culture, Technology, Communication, Suny, 01. **CONTACT ADDRESS** Relig and Philos Dept, Drury Col, N Benton, PO Box 900, Springfield, MO 65802. **EMAIL** cmess@nrury.edu

ESTEP, MYRNA LYNNE
PERSONAL Born 01/07/1944, Whitesville, WV, m, 1971, 1 child **DISCIPLINE** PHILOSOPHY; EPISTEMOLOGY **EDUCATION** Ind Univ, PhD 75, MA 71, BA 70. **CAREER** Univ of Incarnate Word, adj fac, 96-98; Our Lady of Lake Univ, adj fac, 98; Univ Zimbabwe, grad fac, 87-89; Acad Hea Sciences, sys analyst, edu spec, 81-84; San Antonio Col, instr, 78-81; Univ Texas SA, asst prof, 75-78; Ind Univ, assoc instr, 72-75. **HONORS AND AWARDS** Who's Who in: Amer, South and SW, Media and Comm, World of Women; Directory of: Am Scholars, Women Hist Of Science; Dictionary of Int Biography; 2 Commendation Letters from Peter Rowe USMC Colonel Commander The Basic School USMCCDC and from David Osborn Captain USN Commanding Officer USNTEC; Best Paper Awd Designing and Systems Vienna Aust; Phi Kappa Phi; Int Affil OSK Univ Vienna; NY Acad of Science Mem. **MEMBERSHIPS** AAAS; MAA; OSK; ISGSR; APA; IUAA. **RESEARCH** Philosophy; mathematics; philosophy of science; logic; philosophy of mathematics; computer science; systems design and development; information theory; epistemology; cognitive science; behavioral research in education. **SELECTED PUBLICATIONS** Auth, Canned Hunts: Women Students at the Univ of Texas, The Shatter the Glass Ceiling, GCCC, Greenville SC, 98; Canned Hunts: Women at the Univ of Texas, Online Jour of Feminist Construction, San Francisco CA, 98; rev, Common Threads: Women Mathematics and Work, by Mary Harris, Initiatives, Washington DC, 98; auth, Fear and Loathing: The History of Affirmative Action in Texas, Feminista, Online Jour of Feminist Reconstruction, 98; auth, What Godel said : On the Non-algorithmic Nature of the Second Theorem, Systems Res, EMCSR, 98; auth, Teaching the Logical

Paradoxes: On Mathematical Insight or Is There a Non-algorithmic Element in Godel's Second Theorem? Abstracts, Am Math Soc, 99; auth, A Theory of Immediate Awareness and Knowing How, Jour of Consciousness Stud, Imprint Acad, UK, 96, and Times Higher Educ Sup, Essex UK, 96. **CONTACT ADDRESS** Dept of Philosophy, Incarnate Word Univ, 16022 Oak Grove, San Antonio, TX 78255. **EMAIL** informus@stic.net

ESTLUND, DAVID
PERSONAL Born 02/20/1958, Clintonville, WI, m, 1986, 3 children **DISCIPLINE** PHILOSOPHY, POLITICS **EDUCATION** Univ of Wis, PhD, 86. **CAREER** Univ of Calif at Irvine, 86-91; Brown Univ, 91-. **HONORS AND AWARDS** Fel, Am Coun of Learned Soc, 89-90; fel, prog in ethics & the professions, Harvard Univ, 93-94; NEH fel, 98. **MEMBERSHIPS** Am Philos Asn. **RESEARCH** Polit & moral philos. **SELECTED PUBLICATIONS** Auth, Opinion Leaders, Independence, and Condorcet's Jury Theorem, Theory and Decision, 94; Beyond Fairness and Deliberation: The Epistemic Dimension of Democratic Authority, Deliberative Democracy, MIT Press, 97; The Visit & The Video: Publication and the Line Between Sex and Speech, Sex, Preference, and Family, Oxford Univ Press, 97; The Insularity of the Reasonable: Why political Liberalism Must Admit the Truth, ETHICS, 98; Political Quality, Soc Philos and Policy; auth, "Liberalism, Equality and Fraternity in Cohen's Egalitarian Critique of Rawls," The Journal of Political Philosophy, vol. 6, number 8, 98; auth, Democracy, edited with introduction, Blackwell, (forthcoming, 01); auth, Deliberation Down and Dirty: Must Political Expressiono Be Civil, "in The Boundaries of Freedom of Expression and Order in Ameriacn Democracy, (Kent State Univ Press, forthcoming, 01); auth, Harsanyi Fellow at Research School of Social Sciences, Australian Nat Univ, 01-02. **CONTACT ADDRESS** 88 Hudson St, Providence, RI 02909. **EMAIL** David_Estlund@brown.edu

ESTRICH, SUSAN
PERSONAL Born 12/16/1952, m **DISCIPLINE** LAW **EDUCATION** Wellesley Col, BA, 74; Harvard Law Sch, JD, 77. **CAREER** Prof, Harvard Law Sch, 81-90; Prof, Univ S Calif, 91-. **SELECTED PUBLICATIONS** Auth, Making the Case for Yourself: A Diet Book for Smart Women, Riverhead Publ, 98; auth, Getting Away with Murder, Harvard UP, 98; auth, Who Needs Feminism? Forthcoming. **CONTACT ADDRESS** Dept Law, Univ of So California, 699 Exposition Blvd, Los Angeles, CA 90089-0040.

ETZKORN, GIRARD J.
PERSONAL Born 09/18/1927, Kirkwood, MO **DISCIPLINE** PHILOSOPHY, FRENCH **EDUCATION** Quincy Col, BA, 53; St Joseph Sem, Ill, STB, 57; Cath Univ Louvain, PhD (philos), 61. **CAREER** From instr to assoc prof philosophy, Quincy Col, 61-71; assoc prof, Southern Ill Univ, CArbondale, 71-72; RES PROF CRITICAL ED OF WILLIAM OCKHAM, FRANCISCAN INST, 73-, Am Philos Soc grant, 65-66. **MEMBERSHIPS** Int Soc Study Medieval Philos; Am Philos Asn; AAUP. **RESEARCH** Critical editions of medieval manuscripts; French and German phenomenology and existentialism; translating of French philosopher Michel Henry. **SELECTED PUBLICATIONS** Auth, William De La Mare, Scriptum in Secundum Librum Sententiarum, Speculum J Medieval Stud, Vol 72, 97; Bonaventure Sermons de Diversis, Speculum J Medieval Stud, Vol 70, 95. **CONTACT ADDRESS** Franciscan Inst, Saint Bonaventure, NY 14778.

EULA, MICHAEL JAMES
PERSONAL Born 05/18/1957, Passaic, NJ, m, 1993, 2 children **DISCIPLINE** HISTORY, LAW **EDUCATION** Rutgers Univ, BA (cum laude), 80; Calif State Univ, MA, 83; Univ of Calif at Irvine, MA, 84, PhD, 87; Newport Univ School of Law, JD, 98. **CAREER** Admin Law Judge, Riverside County, CA, 99-; Vis Lecturer in History and Criminal Justice, Champman Univ, 93-; Teaching asst/assoc, visiting asst prof of hist, Univ of Calif at Irvine, 91; lectr in hist, Calf State Univ, 89; PROF OF HIS, EL CAMINO COL, 89-. **HONORS AND AWARDS** Nat Endowment for the Humanities Fel, 90 & 95; New Jersey Hist Comn Fel, 92; Fac Res Fel, UCLA, 93; Phi Alpha Theta Iota Kappa, Rutgers Univ, 79. **MEMBERSHIPS** Am Hist Asn; Am Italian Hist Asn. **RESEARCH** Italian Americans; social history of ideas; legal history. **SELECTED PUBLICATIONS** Auth, Cultural Identity, Foodways, and the Failure of American Food Reformers Among Ital Immigrants in New York City 1891-1897, Ital Americana, 00; auth, The Politics of Ethnicity and Newark's Italian Tribune, 1934-1980, Ital Americana, forthcoming; Langage, Time, and the Formation of Self Among Italian-American Workers in New Jersey and New York 1880-1940, Ital Americana, 97; auth, Between Peasant and Urban Villager: Italian Americans of New Jersey and New York 1880-1980. The Structures of Counter Discourse, Peter Lang, 93; auth, Cultural Continuity and Cultural Hegemony: Italian Catholics in New Jersey and New York 1880-1940, Relig, 92; auth, Thinking Historically: Using Theory in the Introductory History Classroom, The Hist Teacher, 93. **CONTACT ADDRESS** Dept of History, El Camino Col, Torrance, CA 90506.

EUSTICE, JAMES S.
PERSONAL Born 06/09/1932, Chicago, IL, m, 1995, 2 children **DISCIPLINE** LEGAL STUDIES **EDUCATION** Univ Ill, BS, 54, LLB, 56; New York Univ, LLM, Taxation, 58. **CAREER** Assoc, White & Case, 58-60; New York Univ Sch of Law, Grad Tax Prof, 60-; counsel, Kronish Lieb Weiner & Hellman LLP, 70-. **HONORS AND AWARDS** The Gerald L. Wallace Prof of Taxation, New York Univ. **MEMBERSHIPS** ABA Tax Section; New York State Bar, Tax Section; Am Col of Tax Counsel. **RESEARCH** Corporate taxation. **SELECTED PUBLICATIONS** Auth, The Tax Reform Act of 1984; coauth with Kuntz, Lewis, & Deering, The Tax Reform Act of 1986; coauth with Bittker, Federal Income Taxation of Corporations and Shareholder, 6th ed (94, 7th ed forthcoming), and Supplements (three per year); coauth with Kuntz, Federal Income Taxation of S Corporations, 3rd ed (4th ed in revision); articles (easily findable by electronic search, key word Eustice). **CONTACT ADDRESS** Sch of Law, New York Univ, 40 Washington Sq S, New York, NY 10012-1005.

EVANGELIOU, CHRISTOS C.
PERSONAL Born 12/23/1946, Kyrtoni, Greece, m, 1979 **DISCIPLINE** PHILOSOPHY **EDUCATION** Univ Athens, BA, 69; Emory Univ, MA, 76; PhD, 79. **CAREER** Visiting Prof, Miss State Univ, 80-81; Adj Asst Prof, Emory Univ, 81-84; Visiting Prof, Appalachian State Univ, 84-85; Visiting Scholar, Villanova Univ, 85-86; Asst Prof, Towson Univ, 86-90; Visiting Prof, Cent Conn State Univ, 90-91; Visiting Scholar, NY Univ, 93-94; Full Prof, Towson Univ, 96-. **HONORS AND AWARDS** Ansley-Miller Scholarship, Emory Univ, 78-79; Othon-Athena Stathatos Scholarship, 74-76. **MEMBERSHIPS** Am Philos Asn; am Philol Asn; soc for Ancient Greek Philos; Intl Soc for Metaphysics; Intl Asn of Greek Philos; Intl Soc for Neoplatonic Studies; Intl Center for Philos and Interdisciplinary Res; S African Soc for Greek Philos. **RESEARCH** Ancient Greek Philosophy; History of Philosophy; Metaphysics; Ethics; Classics; Hellenic Literature. **SELECTED PUBLICATIONS** Auth, Aristotle's Categories and Porphyry, 2nd ed, E.J. Brill, 94; auth, When Greece Met Africa: The Genesis of Hellenic Philosophy, SUNY Press, 94; auth, The Hellenic Philosophy: Between Europe, Asia and Africa, SUNY Press, 97; auth, "Pletho's Critique of Aristotle and Averroes and the Revival of Platonism in Renaissance," Skepsis, (97): 146-170; auth, "The Lost Spirit of Hellenic Philosophy," Alexandria, (97): 289-305; auth, "Aristotle's Critique of Communism," TU Lecture Series, (97): 1-11; auth, "Platonic Paideia and European Philosophy," in Plato's Philosophy of Education and Its Relevance to the Contemporary Society, (98): 71-91; auth, "Plotinus' Defense of the Cosmos and Its Demiruge," Phronimon, forthcoming; auth, The Passion of Hellenic Philosophy, IGCS, forthcoming; auth, Porphyry the Philosopher, E.J. Brill, forthcoming. **CONTACT ADDRESS** Dept Relig & Philos, Towson State Univ, 8000 York Rd, Baltimore, MD 21252-0001. **EMAIL** cevangeliou@towson.edu

EVANS, C. STEPHEN
PERSONAL Born 05/26/1948, Atlanta, GA, m, 1969, 3 children **DISCIPLINE** PHILOSOPHY **EDUCATION** Yale Univ, Mphil 71, PhD 74; Wheaton Col, BA high hon 69. **CAREER** Calvin College, prof 94-, dean res and sch 97-00, Wm Spoelhof Teacher-Scholar 94-96; St Olaf Col , Howard and Edna Hong Kierkegaard Lib, prof curator 86-94, assoc prof 84-86; Wheaton Col, asst prof, assoc prof, prof, 74-82; Trinity Cole, asst prof 72-74; Western Kentucky Univ, vis assoc prof 80-81; Regent Col BC, vis prof 90, 92, 95; Northern Baptist Sem, adj prof 82-84; Trinity Evangel Div Sch, vis lectr 76. **HONORS AND AWARDS** Co-Winner Best Christian Sch Bk Awd; Wm Spoelhof Teach-Sch; Pew Evangel Sr Sch; NEH Fel (twice); George C Marshall Fel; Cen Faith Devel Fel; Danforth Fel; pres SCP, 98-01. **MEMBERSHIPS** APA; KS; SCP; AAR. **RESEARCH** Philosophy of Kierkegaard; religion; human sciences; phenomenology and existentialism; philosophical psychology. **SELECTED PUBLICATIONS** Auth, Faith Beyond Reason, Edinburgh, Edinburgh Univ Press, 98, and Grand Rapids MI, Wm B. Eerdmans, 98; The Historical Christ and the Jesus of Faith: The Incarnational Narrative as History, Oxford, Oxford Univ Press, 96; Why Believe: Reason and Mystery as Pointers to God, revised InterVarsity Press 86, Grand Rapids, Wm Eerdmans, 96, Christian Perspectives on Religious Knowledge, co-ed, Wm Eerdmans, 93; Do Robots Have Free Will?, in: Books and Cultures, 98; Soren Kierkegaard's Fear and Trembling, in: Invitation to the Classics, eds Louise Cowan, Os Guinness, Grand Rapids MI, Baker Books, 98; The Concept of Authority in Kierkegaard's Works of Love, in: The Kierkegaard Studies Yearbook 1997, Berlin and NY, Walter de Gruyter, 97; Who is the Other in The Sickness Unto Death?, God and Human Relations in the Constitution of the Self, in: The Kierkegaard Studies Yearbook 1996, Berlin and NY, Walter de Gruyter, 96. **CONTACT ADDRESS** Dept of Philosophy, Calvin Col, 3201 Burton St SE, Grand Rapids, MI 49546. **EMAIL** sevans@calvin.edu

EVANS, DALE WILT
PERSONAL Born 09/27/1939, Philadelphia, PA **DISCIPLINE** PHILOSOPHY, CLASSICS **EDUCATION** Pa State Univ, BA, 65, MA, 66, PhD (Philos), 73. **CAREER** Instr philos, Univ Wyo, 69-72; programmer, Sperry Univac, 74-75; ASST PROF PHILOS, PA STATE UNIV, 75-, Fulbright fel, 70-71. **MEMBERSHIPS** Am Philos Soc. **RESEARCH** Contemporary philosophy; contemporary man. **SELECTED PUBLICATIONS** Auth, Prisoners of objective thinking, 81 & The heterogeneous symmetry of nature, 82, Contemp Philos. **CONTACT ADDRESS** Dept of Philos, Pennsylvania State Univ, DuBois, Du Bois, PA 15801.

EVANS, DONALD D.
PERSONAL Born 09/21/1927, Thunder Bay, ON, Canada **DISCIPLINE** RELIGION, PHILOSOPHY **EDUCATION** Univ Toronto, BA, 50; Oxford Univ, BPhil, 53, DPhil, 62; McGill Univ, BD, 55; Laurentian Univ, DD, 82. **CAREER** Ordained United Church Can, 55; Pastor, Grand Forks, BC, 55-58; asst prof divinity, McGill Univ, 60-64; assoc prof to prof, 64-93, Prof Emer Philosophy, Univ Toronto, 93-. **HONORS AND AWARDS** Killam sr res scholar, 75-77. **SELECTED PUBLICATIONS** Auth, The Logic of Self-Involvement, 63; auth, Communist Faith and Christian Faith, 64; auth, Struggle and Fulfillment, 80; auth, Faith, Authenticity and Morality, 80; auth, Spirituality and Human Nature, 92; coauth, Analytic Philosophy in Canada, 82; ed & coauth, Peace Power and Protest, 67; ed, Against the Psychologist's Act, 78. **CONTACT ADDRESS** Victoria Col, Univ of Toronto, Toronto, ON, Canada M5S 1K7.

EVANS, JOHN WHITNEY
PERSONAL Born 08/06/1931, Kansas City, MO **DISCIPLINE** UNITED STATES CHURCH HISTORY **EDUCATION** St Paul Sem, Minn, MA, 57; Cath Univ Am, MA, 58; Univ Minn, PhD (hist, philos educl, 70. **CAREER** Instr social probs, Cathedral High Sch, Minn, 58-62; chaplain and lectr psychol and educ, Univ Minn, Duluth, 66-69; coord res campus ministry, Ctr Applied Res in Apostolate, Washington, DC, 69-71; dir, Nat Ctr Campus Ministry, Mass, 71-73; CHAPLAIN AND ASST PROF HIST AND RELIG STUDIES, COL ST SCHOLASTICA, 73-, Mem comn campus ministry, Nat Cath Educ Asn, 69-73; Underwood fel, 72-73. **HONORS AND AWARDS** Cath Campus Ministry Asn Serv Awd, 73. **MEMBERSHIPS** Nat Cath Educ Asn; Soc Sci Study Relig; AHA; Am Cath Hist Asn; Relig Educ Asn. **RESEARCH** History and religion in American higher education; philosophy of education; student movements. **SELECTED PUBLICATIONS** Coauth & co-ed, Perspectives for campus ministers, US Cath Conf, 72; coauth, Worship in the university environment, Living Worship, 4/72; auth, Exemplary presence as campus ministry, Counseling & Values, spring 73; The Newman Movement: Roman Catholicism in American Higher Education, 1883-1971, 80. **CONTACT ADDRESS** Off of Chaplain, Col of St. Scholastica, 1200 Kenwood Ave, Duluth, MN 55811-4199.

EVANS, ROD L.
DISCIPLINE ETHICS AND POLITICAL PHILOSOPHY **EDUCATION** Old Dominion Univ, BA, 78; Univ Va, PhD, 87. **CAREER** Adjunct Asst Prof, Old Dominion Univ. **RESEARCH** Bioethics, business ethics, political philos. **SELECTED PUBLICATIONS** Ed, Fundamentalism: Hazards and Heartbreaks; Drug Legalization: For and Against; The Right Words; The Quotable Conservative. **CONTACT ADDRESS** Dept Philos, Old Dominion Univ, Batten Arts and Letters, Rm 401, Norfolk, VA 23529-0083.

EVANS, WARREN CLEAGE
PERSONAL Born 12/30/1948, Detroit, MI, d **DISCIPLINE** LAW **EDUCATION** Madonna College, Livonia, MI, BA, 1975; University of Detroit, Detroit, MI, MA, 1980; Detroit College of Law, Detroit, MI, JD, 1986. **CAREER** Wayne County Sheriffs Dept, Detroit, MI, undersheriff, 70-90; Wayne County Board of Commissioners, Detroit, MI, dir of administration, 90-91; Office of County Executive, director of community corrections, 91-. **HONORS AND AWARDS** Distinguished Corrections Service Awd, 1988; Spirit of Detroit Awd, Detroit City Council, 1987. **MEMBERSHIPS** Vice pres, Detroit Board of Water Commissioners, 1989-; parlamentarian, nati; advisory board, Criminal Justice Comm, WCCC, 1990-; advisory board, Criminal Justice Comm, U of D, 1988-; advisory board, BCN Law Center, 1986-. **CONTACT ADDRESS** Director of Community Corrections, Office of County Executive, 640 Temple St, Ste 210, Detroit, MI 48215.

EVANS, WILLIAM
PERSONAL Born 11/18/1951, Memphis, TN, m, 1977, 2 children **DISCIPLINE** RELIGIOUS STUDIES **EDUCATION** Univ of Memphis, BS, 79; Harding Grad School, MD, 89; Hebrew Union Coll Jewish Inst Rel, MA, 96; Univ of S Africa, PhD, (candidate). **HONORS AND AWARDS** Minister, Church of Christ and Baptist Church; Greek Awd; Who's Who in Colleges and Am Univ. **MEMBERSHIPS** SBL. **RESEARCH** Christian Origins, Dead Sea Scrolls. **CONTACT ADDRESS** 10251 Pendery Dr, Cincinnati, OH 45242-5345. **EMAIL** bevans@cinci.rr.com

EVERETT, RALPH B.
PERSONAL Born 06/23/1951, Orangeburg, SC, m, 1974 **DISCIPLINE** LAW **EDUCATION** Morehouse Coll, BA 1973; Duke Univ Law School, JD 1976. **CAREER** NC Dept of Justice, assoc Attorney general 1976; NC Dept of Labor, admin

asst for legal affairs 1976-77; Senator Fritz Hollings, spec asst 1977-78, legislative asst 1978-83; US Senate Comm on Commerce, Sci & Transportation, attny, democratic chief counsel and staff dir 1983-86; US Senate comm on Commerce, sci & transportation, chief counsel and staff dir 1987-89; Paul Hastings, Janofsky and Walker, LLP partner, 89-. **HONORS AND AWARDS** Phi Beta Kappa; Phi Alpha Theta Intl Hon Soc in History; Earl Warren Legal Scholar. **MEMBERSHIPS** Mem NC & DC Bars; admitted to US Dist Court for DC; US Court of Appeals for DC Court; US Tax Court; US Court of Claims; US Supreme Court; mem Amer Bar Assoc, Alpha Phi Alpha; mem, Alumni Board of Visitors, Duke Univ Law School; former trustee, Natl Urban League; bd of dir, Ctr for Natl Policy; Ambassador, 1998 Intl Telecommunication Union's Plenipotentiary Conference, Head of United States Delegation to the Intl Telecommunication Union's second World Telecommunication Development Conference, 1998. **SELECTED PUBLICATIONS** various **CONTACT ADDRESS** Paul, Hastings, Janofsky and Walker LLP, 1299 Pennsylvania Avenue, NW, Washington, DC 20004-2400. **EMAIL** ralpheverett@paulhastings.com

EVERETT, WILLIAM J.
PERSONAL Born 11/11/1940, Washington, DC, m, 1982, 3 children **DISCIPLINE** RELIGION **EDUCATION** Wesleyan U, BA, 62; Yale Div Schl, BD, 65; Harvard U Grad Schl Arts & Sciences, Phd, 70. **CAREER** Prof Theology and Soc Sci, St. Francis Seminary, 69-84; Prof Ethics and Ecclesiology, Emory Univ, Candler Schl of Theology, 85-95; Prof Christian Social Ethics, Andover Newton Theol Schl, Herbert Gezork, 95-. **MEMBERSHIPS** Society of Christian Ethics; Am Acad Religion; Soc Business Ethics; Soc Scientific Study of Religion. **RESEARCH** Religion and Society; Christian Ethics and Ecclesiology; Ecology Ethics; Theology and Law. **SELECTED PUBLICATIONS** Auth, "Blessed Be the Bond: Christian Perspectives on Marriage and Family, Fortress Press, 85: 130, Reprinted in 90 by University Press of America; auth, "God's Federal Republic: Reconstructing Our Governing Symbol," Paulist Press, 88: 204; auth, "Religion, Fderalism, and the Struggle for Public Life: Cases from Germany, India, and America," Oxford University Press, 97: 200; auth, "The Politics of Worship: Reforming the Language and Symbols of Liturgy," Cleveland: United Church Press, 99: 128; auth, "Couples at Work: A Study in Patterns of Work, Family and Faith," with Sylvia Johnson Everett, in Work, Family, and Religion in Contemporary Society, ed. Nancy Tatom Ammerman and Wade Clark Roof, New York: Routledge, 305-329; auth, "Human Rights in the Church," Religious Human Rights in Global Perspective: Religious Perspectives, eds. John Witte, Jr. and Johann van der Vyver, Dordrecht, London, Boston: Martinus Nijhoff, 121-142; auth, "Ecclesial Freedom and Federal Order: Reflection on the Pacific Homes Case," Journal of Law and Religion, 12:2, 95-96, 371-398; auth, "Constitutional Order in United Methodism and American Culture," with Thomas E. Frank, in Connectionalism: Ecclesiology, Mission, and Identity, Russell E. Richey and Dennis Campbell, eds, Nashville: Abingdon Press, 41-73. **CONTACT ADDRESS** Andover Newton Theol Sch, 210 Herrick Road, Newton, MA 02459-2248. **EMAIL** weverett@auts.edu

EVERSLEY, WALTER V. L.
DISCIPLINE THEOLOGY **EDUCATION** Moravian Col, BA, 69; Harvard Univ, MA, 74, PhD, 76; Columbia Univ, JD, 81. **CAREER** Dir, Interchurch Youth Org; British Civil Svc; admin, personnel dir, Ministry of Home Aff, 58-66; instr, Harvard Divinity Sch, 73-75; adj prof, New Brunswick Theol Sem, 75-86; adj prof, Col New Rochelle, 75-86; prof, NY Theol Sem, 75-86; assoc prof, 88-91; prof, Va Theol Sem, 91-. **HONORS AND AWARDS** Asst pastor, South Church, 69-72; assoc pastor, Church of All Nations, 72-75; pastor, John Hus Moravian Church, 75-85; org pastor, Grace Moravian Church, 77-80; org pastor, Brooklyn Moravian Fel, 85; org pastor, Faith Moravian Church of Nation's Capital, 85-88; priest assoc, St. Mary's Episcopal Church, 89-. **SELECTED PUBLICATIONS** Auth, The Willing Heart: A Theology of Evangelism for the Mainline Church; The Heart of the Priesthood, An Ordination Sermon, Va Sem Jour, 92; auth, "The Pastor as Revivalist" In Edwards in Our Time," 99; auth, "Jesus and Culture," In The Truth About Jesus, 98; auth, "John Donne," In SPCK Handbook of Anglican Theologians, 90; auth, "Sam Vel Taylor Coleridge," In SPCK Handbook---Priest Assoc St. Mary's Episcopal Church, Arlington VA, 89-98; auth, "Priest in Charge Trinity," Episcopal Church, Wash DC, 90; auth, "Heaven Hungry Hearts," Sermon VA, Sem Jour, 97. **CONTACT ADDRESS** Virginia Theol Sem, 3737 Seminary Rd, Alexandria, VA 22304. **EMAIL** WEversley@vts.edu

EVNINE, SIMON
PERSONAL Born 12/06/1959, London, England **DISCIPLINE** PHILOSOPHY **EDUCATION** Univ Calif Los Angeles, PhD, 96. **CAREER** Asst prof, Calif Poly, 96-. **MEMBERSHIPS** APA. **RESEARCH** Epistemology; Philosophy of logic; Philosophy of mind. **SELECTED PUBLICATIONS** Auth, Learning from One's Mistakes, Pacyic Philosophical Qu; auth, Believing Conjunctions, Synthese, 99; auth, Entry on Davidson, Companion to the Philosophers, Blackwell, 98; auth, Hume, Conjectural History, and the Uniformity of Human Nature, Jour of the Hist of Philos, 93; auth, Donald Davidson, Stanford Univ Press and Polity Press, 91; auth, Understanding Madness?, 89; auth, Freud's Ambiguous Concepts, Jour of Speculative Philos, 89; auth, Innate Principles and Radical Interpretation, The Locke Newsletter, 87. **CONTACT ADDRESS** Dept. of Philosophy, California Polytech State Univ, San Luis Obispo, San Luis Obispo, CA 93407. **EMAIL** sevnine@calpoly.edu

EYER, RICHARD
PERSONAL Born 08/03/1939, Newark, NJ, m, 1967, 2 children **DISCIPLINE** PHILOSOPHY **EDUCATION** Concordia Sem, MDiv, 65; Trinity Int Univ, DMin, 98. **CAREER** Asst Prof, Concordia Univ, 98-. **RESEARCH** Bioethics. **SELECTED PUBLICATIONS** Auth, Pastoral Care Under the Cross, God in the Midst of Suffering, Concordia Publ House (St Louis, MO), 95; auth, Holy People Holy Lives: Law and Gospel in Bioethics, Concordia Publ House (St Louis, MO), 00. **CONTACT ADDRESS** Dept Philos, Concordia Univ, Wisconsin, 12800 N Lake Shore, Mequon, WI 53097. **EMAIL** richard.eyer@cow.edu

F

FABBRO, AMATA
PERSONAL Born 08/20/1928, Grand Rapids, MI **DISCIPLINE** THEOLOGY **EDUCATION** Aquinas Col, BA, 61; St Mary's Col, Ind, MA, 65, PhD(sacred scriptures & theol), 67. **CAREER** From instr to asst prof, 67-72, assoc prof scripture, Aquinas Col, 72-87, prof and dept head, 88-, head dept scriptures, Diocese of Grand Rapids Permanent Deaconate Prog, 71-80. **MEMBERSHIPS** Cath Bibl Soc Am; Cath Theol Soc Am; Col Theology Soc; Interfaith Dialogue Asn. **RESEARCH** Charismatic renewal in the Catholic Church; Old Testament typology. **SELECTED PUBLICATIONS** Co-auth with E. O'Connor a chapter in Perspectives on the Charismatic Renewal, 74; auth, paper on Women in the Ministerial Priesthood, presented for Scholar in Residence Weekend at Ahavis Israel Synagogue, Grand Rapids, Mi, 85; book review on Contemplation and the Charismatic Renewal by Paul Hennebusch, Spirituality for Today, 88; contrib to The Catholic Vision; several feature articles for The Catholic Connector. **CONTACT ADDRESS** Dept of Theology, Aquinas Col, Michigan, 1607 Robinson Rd S E, Grand Rapids, MI 49506-1799. **EMAIL** FABBRAMA@aquinas.edu

FACKRE, GABRIEL JOSEPH
PERSONAL Born 01/25/1926, Jersey City, NJ, m, 1945, 5 children **DISCIPLINE** THEOLOGY **EDUCATION** Univ Chicago, BD, 48, PhD, 62. **CAREER** Pastor, Duquesne-West Mifflin, Pa, 51-60; from asst prof to assoc prof hist theol & Christian ethics, 61-66, prof theol & cult, 66-71, Lancaster Theol Sem; prof theol, 71-80, Abbot Prof Christian Theol, 80-96, emeritus, 96-, Andover Newton Theol Sch; Am Asn Theol Schs sr res fel, Mansfield Col, Oxford Univ, 67-68; vis prof relig, Univ Hawaii, 70; vis scholar, Westminster-Cheshent Col, Cambridge Univ, 74-75; vis prof theol, Claremont Sch Theol, 76 & 80, Univ Theological Sem Va, 78; vis prof, Vancouver Sch Theol, 82, 87, 91; vis prof, Pittsburgh Theol Sem, 97; Abbott Prof of Theol Emer, Andover-Newton Theol Sem; res schlr, Ctr of Theol Inquiry, Princeton, NJ. **MEMBERSHIPS** Am Theol Soc (pres, 90-91). **RESEARCH** Systematic theology; mission of the church; Christology. **SELECTED PUBLICATIONS** Auth, The Religious Right and Christian Faith, Eerdmans, 82; auth, The Christian Story, v.2, Eerdmans, 87; auth, Christian Basics, Eerdmans, 91, 94, 98; auth, The Doctrine of Revelation, Edinburgh, 97; auth, Discovering the Center, Intervarsity, 98; coauth, Affirmation and Admonition, Eerdmans, 98; ed, Judgement Day at the White House, 99; auth, The Day After, 00. **CONTACT ADDRESS** Ctr of Theol Inquiry, 50 Stockton St, Princeton, NJ 08540. **EMAIL** fackre@juno.com

FACTOR, RALPH LANCE
PERSONAL Born 08/23/1944, Zanesville, OH, 2 children **DISCIPLINE** PHILOSOPHY **EDUCATION** Ohio State Univ, BA, 65; Univ Ga, MA, 67, PhD, 70. **CAREER** From Asst Prof to Assoc Prof, 69-85, Prof Philos, Knox Col, 85-; director of religious studies; Danforth assoc, 73-79; assoc ed, Int J Philos of Relig, 73-85 & J Critical Anal, 77-80. **HONORS AND AWARDS** Habitat for Humanity Partner Volunteer Awd, 96; Philip Green Wright-Lombrd Col Prize for Distinguished Teaching, 73; Phi beta Kappa, 65; Phi kappa Phi, 67; Danforth Teaching Assoc, 73. **MEMBERSHIPS** Central Div Am Philos Asn; Soc Christian Philosophers. **RESEARCH** Symbolic logic; philosophy of science; philosophy of religion. **SELECTED PUBLICATIONS** Auth, A Note on the Analysis of Mass Terms, Southern J Philos, 76; auth, Newcomb's Paradox and Omniscience, Int J Philos of Relig, 77; auth, Self Deception and the Functionalist Theory of Mental Processes, Personalist, 77; auth, Value Presuppositions in Science Textbooks, 80; auth, Principle of Singular Difference, Southern J Philos, 82; auth, What is the Logic in Buddhist Logic?, Philos East & West, 82; auth, Poetry and Logic of Abduction, 86; auth, Points, Regions and Boundaries, 92; auth, Mercator Decoded, 95; auth, A Peircean Theory of Metaphor, Peirce's Doctrine of Signs, 95. **CONTACT ADDRESS** Dept of Philos, Knox Col, Illinois, 2 E. South St., Galesburg, IL 61401-4999. **EMAIL** lfactor@knox.edu

FADNER, DONALD E.
PERSONAL Born Oshkosh, WI, m, 4 children **DISCIPLINE** RELIGIOUS STUDIES **EDUCATION** Univ Chicago, PhD, 74. **CAREER** Prof; Univ Wis-SP, 74-. **SELECTED PUBLICATIONS** Auth, The Responsible God: A Study of the Christian Philosophy of H. Richard Niebuhr, Chico, Calif: Scholars Press for the Amer Acad Rel Dissertation Ser, 75. **CONTACT ADDRESS** Dept of Philosophy, Univ of Wisconsin, Stevens Point, Stevens Point, WI 54481. **EMAIL** dfadner@uwsp.edu

FAGAN, EILEEN M.
PERSONAL Born 04/20/1942, New York, NY, s **DISCIPLINE** SYSTEMATIC THEOLOGY **EDUCATION** Col Mount St. Vincent, BA, 70; Fordham Univ, MA, 89; PhD, 97. **CAREER** Relig and math teacher, Archbishop Stepinac High Sch, 80-88; adj asst prof, Marymount Col, 88-98; adj instr, St. John's Univ, 97; adj instr, Fairfield Univ, 98. **HONORS AND AWARDS** Outstanding Part-Time Teacher Awd, Marymount Col, 92. **MEMBERSHIPS** Am Acad of Relig/Soc of Bibl Lit; Cath Bibl Asoc; Cath Theol Soc of Amer; Col Theol Soc. **RESEARCH** Liberation theology; Christology; ecclesiology; Catholic Social Teaching. **SELECTED PUBLICATIONS** An Interpretation of Evangelization: Jon Sobrino's Christoloyg and Ecclesiology in Dialogue, 98; Foreword to Pillars of Catholic Social Teaching: A Brief Social Catechism, 99. **CONTACT ADDRESS** 170 Truman Ave., Yonkers, NY 10703-1022. **EMAIL** emfagan@msn.com

FAGER, JEFF
PERSONAL Born 11/04/1952, Redkey, IN, m, 1975 **DISCIPLINE** HEBREW BIBLE **EDUCATION** Univ Evansville, BA, 75; So Methodist Univ, MTh, 79; Vanderbilt Univ, PhD, 87. **CAREER** Prof relig and philos, Kentucky Wesleyan Col, 86- . **MEMBERSHIPS** Soc of Bibl Lit; Am Acad of Relig. **RESEARCH** Ethics of the Hebrew Bible. **SELECTED PUBLICATIONS** Auth, Land Tenure in the Biblical Jubilee: A Moral World View, Hebrew Annual Rev, 88; auth, Back to the Past: Two Instances of Mentoring in the Hebrew Bible, Int J of Mentoring, 88; auth, Land Tenure and the Biblical Jubilee: Discovering a Moral World View through the Sociology of Knowledge, Sheffield Academic, 93; auth, Chaos and the Deborah Tradition, Q Rev, 93; auth, Miriam and Deborah: Legends of women in Power in an Ancient Patriarchal Society, Bible Tod, 94; auth, rev of Janzen, Old Testament Ethics: A Paradigmatic Approach, Princeton Sem Bull, 95; auth, book note on Habel, The Land is Mine: Six Biblican Land Ideologies, Theol Today, 96. **CONTACT ADDRESS** Kentucky Wesleyan Col, PO Box 1039, Owensboro, KY 42302-1039. **EMAIL** jeffreyf@kwc.edu

FAIN, HASKELL
PERSONAL Born 07/01/1926, New York, NY, m, 1949 **DISCIPLINE** PHILOSOPHY **EDUCATION** Univ Ill, BS, 48, MA, 49; Univ Calif, MA, 51, PhD (philos), 56. **CAREER** Assoc prof, 56-57, chmn dept, 68-70 and 72-73, PROF PHILOS, UNIV WIS-MADISON, 67-, Fulbright lectr, Univ Bergen, 61-62; vis assoc prof, Univ BC, 63-64; prof, Fla State Univ, 70-71; vis fel, Linacre Col, Oxford Univ, 66-67, vis lectr, 67; consult, Empire State Col, 72-73; Nat Endowment for Humanities fel, 75-. **HONORS AND AWARDS** Vis fel, Linacre Col, Oxford Univ, 66-7; vis fel, Kerle Col, 75; Who's Who in Am, 70-90. **MEMBERSHIPS** Am Philos Asn. **RESEARCH** Social and political philosophy; philosophy of the social sciences; philosophy of history. **SELECTED PUBLICATIONS** Auth, Some Problems of Causal Explanation, Mind, 63; auth, The Very Thought of Grue, Philosophical Review, LCCVI, 67; auth, Prediction and Constraint, Mind 67, 58; auth, Between Philosophy and History, Princeton Univ Press, 70; auth, Some Moral Infirmities of Justice, in Invidual and Collective Responsibility, Schenkman, 72; On Falsely Believing That One Didn't know, with A Phillips Griffiths, Amercan Philosophical Quarterly, Monograph 6, Studies in the Philosophy of Mind, 72; auth, Normative Politics and the Community of Nations, Temple Univ Press, 87; auth, The Use of Narrative in the Writing of History, New Literary History, v.21, 89-90; auth, Geoffrey Hawthorn's Plausible Worlds, History and Theory, v. 32, No. 1, 93. **CONTACT ADDRESS** Dept of Philos, Univ of Wisconsin, Madison, Madison, WI 53706. **EMAIL** hfain2306@prodigy.net

FAINSTEIN, LISA
DISCIPLINE LAW **EDUCATION** Univ Manitoba, BA, 76; LLB, 79. **CAREER** Asst prof, 81-. **RESEARCH** Legal methods, property law, family law. **SELECTED PUBLICATIONS** Co-ed, Manitoba Queen's Bench Act and Rules, Annotated, 89; Introduction to Motions Court, 89; Equality Issues in Family Law: Considerations for Test Case Litigation. **CONTACT ADDRESS** Fac of Law, Univ of Manitoba, Robson Hall, Winnipeg, MB, Canada R3T 2N2. **EMAIL** lfainst@cc.umanitoba.ca

FAIR, BRYAN K.
DISCIPLINE LAW **EDUCATION** Duke Univ, BA, 82; UCLA, JD,85. **CAREER** Prof, Univ Ala, 91-. **RESEARCH** Constitutional law, civil rights, and women and the law. **SELECTED PUBLICATIONS** Auth, Notes of a Racial Caste Baby: Color Blindness and the End of Affirmative Action, NYU Press, 96. **CONTACT ADDRESS** Law Dept, Univ of Alabama, Tuscaloosa, Box 870000, Tuscaloosa, AL 35487-0383. **EMAIL** bfair@law.ua.edu

FAIR, FRANK KENNETH
PERSONAL Born 06/19/1944, Tallahassee, FL, m, 1967, 2 children **DISCIPLINE** PHILOSOPHY **EDUCATION** Xavier Univ, AB, 66; Boston Col, MA, 68; Univ Ga, PhD(philos), 71. **CAREER** From Asst Prof to Assoc Prof, 71-87, Prof Philos, prog coord, Sam Houston State Univ, 87-. **MEMBERSHIPS** Am Philos Asn; Philos Sci Asn; Southern Soc Philos &, Psychol; Southwestern Philos Soc; AAAS. **RESEARCH** Philosophy of science; contemporary moral problems. **SELECTED PUBLICATIONS** Auth, The fallacy of many questions: Or, How to stop beating your wife, Southwestern J Philos, spring 74; J J Katz' logic of questions: New departure or dead end?, Philos Studies, 4/75; Two problems with Chisholm's Perceiving, Philos & Phenomenol Res, 6/76; On interpreting a philosophy of science: A response to Gareth Nelson, Syst Zool, 3/77; coauth, Morality on the Line: The Role of Ethics in Police Decision Making, Am J of Police, Vol X, No 2, 91. **CONTACT ADDRESS** Dept of Psychol & Philos, Sam Houston State Univ, P O Box 2447, Huntsville, TX 77341-2447. **EMAIL** psy_fkf@shsu.edu

FAIRCHILD, MARK
PERSONAL Born 07/23/1954, Corry, PA, m, 1978, 4 children **DISCIPLINE** RELIGION **EDUCATION** Pa State Univ, BS, 76; Toccoa Falls Col, BA, 80; Asbury Theol Sem, MDiv, 82; Drew Univ, MPhil, 85; PhD, 89. **CAREER** Prof, Huntington Col, 86-. **HONORS AND AWARDS** NEH, 94; Prof of the Year, Huntington Col, 98. **MEMBERSHIPS** Soc of Biblical Literature, Evangelical Theol Soc, Catholic Biblical Asn. **RESEARCH** Gospels; New Testament backgrounds; Pauline Research; Intertestamental History. **SELECTED PUBLICATIONS** Auth, "Paul's Pre-Christian Zealot Associations: A Reexamination of Gal 1:14 and Acts 22:3," New Testament Studies, (99), 514-532; auth, "Review of The Gospel of John: a Theological Commentary," in J of the Evangelcal theol. Soc, vol. 42, (99), 509-511; auth, "Review of Jesus the Messianic Herald of Salvation: The Lost Gospel Q: The Original Sayings of Jesus," in Christian Scholars Review 28, (99), 622-624. **CONTACT ADDRESS** Dept Humanities, Huntington Col, 2303 College Ave, Huntington, IN 46750. **EMAIL** mfairchild@huntington.edu

FAKHRID-DEEN, NASHID ABDULLAH
PERSONAL Born 02/24/1949, Monticello, AR, m **DISCIPLINE** THEOLOGY **EDUCATION** Grand Valley State Univ, BA 1978; Western MI Univ, grad work 1978-79; Univ of Baltimore, School of Law, JD 1984-88. **CAREER** Nation of Islam, minister 1975-79; Grand Valley State Univ, asst dir of talent search 1980-83, asst dir of admissions 1979-83; Bowie State Univ, coordinator of recruitment, assoc dir of admissions 1988-90; Kentucky State University, Frankfort, KY, exec asst to the pres 1990-91; Kentucky State Univ, exec asst to the pres, 90-91; Ohio Univ, coordinator minority student affairs, 92-94; Univ of Kentucky Commun Coll System, coordinator minority affairs community college system, 94-. **HONORS AND AWARDS** Outstanding Community Service World Community of Islam 1981, 1982; Grand Valley St Univ, Outstanding Service Talent Search Prgm 1983; Office of Admissions, Outstanding Service Awd 1983; Outstanding Community Service, 1980-82; Charles Hamilton Houston Awd, Univ of Baltimore Black Law Students Assn 1988; Freedom Fighter Awd, NAACP, Bowie State University Chapter, 1991. Ohio Univ, Asante Awd, 1993, Romeo Awd, 1993; Hopeville Community Coll, Significant Contribution Awd to Project PARADE, 1995. **MEMBERSHIPS** General business mgr Nation of Islam 1972-76; mem bd dirs Climbing Tree School 1977-78; mem bd dirs Family Services Outreach 1982-83; mem Mid-America Assn of Educ Oppor Program Personnel; Exec Council Black Law Students, Univ of Baltimore; Admissions/Retention Committee; Moot Court Board, 1986-88; Developer/presentator of CARE (motivational workshop), Baltimore/Washington Metro Area; pres, Black Law Students Assn, Univ of Baltimore School of Law 1987-88. **CONTACT ADDRESS** Executive to the President, Kentucky State Univ, Hume Hall, Lexington, KY 40514.

FALERO, FRANK
PERSONAL Born 12/22/1937, New York, NY, m, 1990, 4 children **DISCIPLINE** ECONOMICS **EDUCATION** St. Petersburg Jr Col, Fla, AA, 62; Univ South Fla, Tampa, BA, 64; Fla State Univ, Tallahassee, MS, 65; Fla State Univ, Tallahassee, PhD, 67. **CAREER** Prof, econ and finance, Calif State Univ, Bakersfield, Sept 74-; bd of dir, Ctr for Econ Educ and Res, Calif State Univ, Bakersfield, 79-; vis prof, econ and finance, Nat Sch of Finance and Mgt, Fairfield, CT, summer, 86; vis prof, Econ Inst, Univ Colo, summer, 74; dir, Ctr for Econ Educ, Calif State Univ, Bakersfield, Sep 73-Dec 79; assoc prof of econ, Calif State Univ, Bakerfield, Sep 72-Sep 74; cons, US Dept of State, Agency for Intl Develop, The Mission to Ethiopia, Jan 70-Jan 72; asst prof of econ, Va Polytechnic Inst and State Univ, Mar 67-Aug 72; Fulbright vis prof, Univ del Pacifico, Lima, Peru, Jul 68- Mar 69; res econ, Fed Reserve Bank of Richmond, Jul 67-Sep 67. **HONORS AND AWARDS** Fel, Amer Col of Forensic Exam, 97; Who's Who Worldwide, 96; arbit, Nat Futures Asn, 96; dipl, Amer Bd of Forensic Exam, 94; reg forensic econ, Amer Rehabil Econ Asn, 94; Best News Commentary, 1985, Assoc Press TV Radio Asn, Mar 85; Golden Miek, 1984, Radio-TV Newn Asn of Southern Calif, Jan 85; Best News Commentary, 1983, Calif Assoc Press TV Radio Asn, Mar 84; Dict of Intl Bio, 75; Outstanding Educ of Amer, 75; Who's Who in the US, 75; Who's Who in the West, 75; exec comt mem, N Amer Econ Studies Asn, 74-79; trustee, Calif Coun for Econ Educ, 74-79; Kazanjian Found award for the tchg of econ, 1971, hon mention, Joint Coun for Econ Educ; Alpha Kappa Psi, 68; Beta Gamma Sigma, 71; Phi Kappa Phi, 65; Delta Tau Kappa, 65; Omicron Delta Epsilon, 65; NDEA Title IV Fel, 64-67. **MEMBERSHIPS** Nat Asn of Forensic Econ, 88; Amer Acad of Econ and Financial Experts, 90; Amer Arbit Asn, 64; fel, Royal Econ Soc, 64; Amer Econ Asn, 65; Southern Econ Asn, 65; Reg Sci Asn, 65; Amer Asn for the Advan of Sci, 65. **RESEARCH** T-Bill Futures: Prediction or Reaction?; Commodity Markets: Efficient or Inefficient?; Collaborative, Competitive, and Cooperative Tele-Teaching via Teleconferencing and the Internet. **SELECTED PUBLICATIONS** Auth, Wage Loss in Wrongful Death - An Historical Analysis, Jour of Legal Econ, vol 6, no 1, spring/summer, 96; mongr, Economics 395 Interactive Study Guide, Ctr for Econ Educ and Res, Calif State Univ, Bakersfield, 97; Economics 100 Interactive Study Guide, Ctr for Econ Educ and Res, Calif State Univ, Bakersfield, 92, 94, 95, 97; Economics 201 Interactive Study Guide, Ctr for Econ Educ and Res, Calif State Univ, Bakersfield, 91, 92, 95, 97; Economics 309 Interactive Study Guide, Ctr for Econ Educ and Res, Calif State Univ, Bakersfield, 93, 94, 97; res papers, Wage Loss in Wrongful Death - A Historical Analysis, Amer Acad of Econ and Financial Experts, Law Vegas, April, 96; **CONTACT ADDRESS** Spring Valley Ranch, 40144 Balch Park Rd., PO Box 950, Springville, CA 93265. **EMAIL** ffalero@ocsnet.net

FALES, EVAN MICHAEL
PERSONAL Born 12/10/1943, Bryn Mawr, PA, 2 children **DISCIPLINE** PHILOSOPHY **EDUCATION** Haverford Col, BA, 64; Temple Univ, MA, 71, PhD, 74. **CAREER** Asst prof, 74-79, Assoc Prof Philos, Univ Iowa, 79- **MEMBERSHIPS** Am Philos Asn; Philos Sci Asn. **RESEARCH** Philosophy of science; metaphysics; epistemology; philosophy of religion. **SELECTED PUBLICATIONS** Auth, Truth, tradition and rationality, 6/76 & The ontology of social roles, 6/77, Philos Social Sci; Essentialism and the Elementary Constituents of Matter, MidWest Studies in Philos XI, 86; Causation and Universals, 90; Divine Freedom and the Choice of a World, Int J Philos of Relig 35, 94; A Defense of the Given, 96; Plantinga's Case Against Naturalistic Epistemology, Philos Sci 63, 96; Scientific Explanations of Mystical Experience, Parts I & II, Relig Studies 32, 96. **CONTACT ADDRESS** Dept of Philos, Univ of Iowa, 269 English Phil Bld, Iowa City, IA 52242-1408.

FALK, ARTHUR
PERSONAL Born 05/28/1938, New York, NY, m, 1967, 2 children **DISCIPLINE** PHILOSOPHY **EDUCATION** Fordham Univ, AB, 60; Yale Univ, MA, 62, PhD, 65. **CAREER** From instr to assoc prof, 64-77, Prof Philos, Western Mich Univ, 77- **HONORS AND AWARDS** Fulbright vis lectr to India, 84 **MEMBERSHIPS** APA. **RESEARCH** Evolutionary semiotics. **SELECTED PUBLICATIONS** Auth, Ifs and Newcombs, in: the Philo's Annual, 87; Wisdom Updates, Philo of Science, 95, Essays on Natures Semeiosis, Jour Philo Research, 95; Gaia = Maya, Hist and Philo of Life Sciences, 95; William's Domains and Reductionism, in: Quart Rev of Bio, 97; The Judger in Russell's Theories of Judgement, Russell: the Jour of the Bertrand Russell Archives, 97-98. **CONTACT ADDRESS** Philos Dept, Western Michigan Univ, 320 Moore Hall, 1903 W Michigan Ave, Kalamazoo, MI 49008-5328. **EMAIL** arthur.falk@wmich.edu

FALK, CANDACE
PERSONAL Born New York, NY **DISCIPLINE** HISTORY; POLITICAL THEORY **EDUCATION** Univ Chicago, BA, 69; MA, 71; Univ Calif Santa Cruz, PhD, 84. **CAREER** Intermittent fac positions, Univ Calif Berkeley, Univ Calif Santa Cruz, Stockton State Col; dir/ed, The Emma Goldman Papers, 80- . **HONORS AND AWARDS** Guggenheim fel, 98-99. **MEMBERSHIPS** Asoc Documentary Eds; Orgn of Am Historians; Am Hist Asoc. **RESEARCH** History; women's studies; labor and left social movements; intellectual and cultural history; biography. **SELECTED PUBLICATIONS** auth, Love, Anarchy, and Emma Goldman, 84, 90, 99; auth, Emma Goldman Papers: A Comprehensive Microfilm Edition, 91; auth with S. Cole and S. Thomas, Emma Goldman: A Guide to her Life and Documentary Sources, 95; Selected Papers of Emma Goldman, forthcoming. **CONTACT ADDRESS** Emma Goldman Papers, Univ of California, Berkeley, 2372 Ellsworth St., Berkeley, CA 94720-6030. **EMAIL** cfalk@socrates.berkeley.edu

FALK, NANCY ELLEN
PERSONAL Born 09/03/1938, Bethlehem, PA, m, 1967, 2 children **DISCIPLINE** HISTORY OF RELIGIONS **EDUCATION** Cedar Crest Col, AB, 60; Univ Chicago, AM, 63, PhD(hist of relig), 72. **CAREER** Asst prof, 66-71, assoc prof, 71-79, chmn dept, 72-75, Prof Relig, Western Mich Univ, 79-. **HONORS AND AWARDS** Fulbright, India, 84-85; AIIS sr fel, 91-92. **MEMBERSHIPS** Am Acad Relig. **RESEARCH** South Asian religion; women in religion. **SELECTED PUBLICATIONS** Co-ed (with Rita M Gross), Unspoken worlds: Women's Religious Lives, 80,89,00; auth, Women in Religion: An Annotated Bibliography of Sources in English, 1975-1992, 94. **CONTACT ADDRESS** Dept of Comp Relig, Western Michigan Univ, 1903 W Michigan, Kalamazoo, MI 49008-3805. **EMAIL** nancy.falk@wmich.edu

FALKENSTEIN, LORNE
DISCIPLINE PHILOSOPHY **EDUCATION** Univ Toronto, PhD. **RESEARCH** History of 18th century philosophy. **SELECTED PUBLICATIONS** Auth, Kant's Intuitionism, Toronto, 95; Intuition and Construction in Berkeley's Account of Visual Space, Jour Hist Philos, 94; Was Kant a Nativist?, Jour Hist Philos, 90; Hume on Manners of Disposition and the Ideas of Space and Time, 77; Naturalism, Normativity, and Scepticism in Hume's Account of Belief, Hume Stud, 77. **CONTACT ADDRESS** Dept of Philosophy, Univ of Western Ontario, London, ON, Canada N6A 5B8. **EMAIL** lfalkens@julian.uwo.ca

FALLDING, HAROLD J.
PERSONAL Born 05/03/1923, Cessnock, Australia **DISCIPLINE** SOCIOLOGY, RELIGION **EDUCATION** Univ Sydney, BS, 50, BA, 51, Dip Ed, 52, MA, 55; Australian Nat Univ, PhD, 57. **CAREER** High sch tchr, Australia, 52-53; sr res fel, Univ Sydney, 56-58; sr lectr, Univ NSW, 59-62; vis assoc prof, grad sch Rutgers, State Univ NJ, 63-65; prof sociol, 65-88, DISTINGUISHED PROF EMER, UNIV WATERLOO, 89-. **MEMBERSHIPS** Clare Hall, Cambridge Univ; Stratford Shakespearean Found Can; Am Sociol Asn; Can Soc Sociol Anthrop; Asn Sociol Relig; Int Sociol Asn; Int Conf Sociol Relig; Can Inst Int Affairs. **SELECTED PUBLICATIONS** Auth, The Sociological Task, 68; auth, The Sociology of Religion: An Explanation of the Unity and Diversity in Religion, 74; auth, Drinking, Community and Civilization: The Account of a New Jersey Interview Study, 74; auth, The Social Process Revisited: Achieving Human Interests through Alliance and Opposition, 90; auth, Collected Poetry, 97. **CONTACT ADDRESS** 40 Arbordale Walk, Guelph, ON, Canada N1G 4X7.

FALLER, THOMPSON MASON
PERSONAL Born 04/26/1938, Louisville, KY, m, 1969, 1 child **DISCIPLINE** PHILOSOPHY **EDUCATION** St Mary's Col, Ky, BA, 62; Xavier Univ, Ohio, MA, 64; Univ Salzburg, PhD, 69. **CAREER** From instr to asst prof, 64-73, assoc prof, 73-80, prof philos, Univ Portland, 80-, Danforth assoc, 76; Fulbright fel. **HONORS AND AWARDS** Outstanding Educr Am; Clifford Campbell Awd; Culligan Awd; Knight Holy Sepulchre; Pilgrim Shell. **MEMBERSHIPS** Am Philos Asn (pres, 75-76); Am Cath Philos Asn; AAUP. **RESEARCH** Justice; love; phenomenology of Franz Brentano. **SELECTED PUBLICATIONS** Auth, Augustin: Ein Philosoph, Salzburg Jahrbuch fuer Philos, 69; Challenges for today's philosophers, Univ Portland Rev, fall 77; Educating the Magnanimous Person, Univ Portland Rev; The Proper Limits of Reason as a Natural Law, Vera Lex; Ownership of our Schools, NEA Notes; Goals 200 and the School Board, Vera Lex. **CONTACT ADDRESS** Dept of Philos, Univ of Portland, 5000 N Willamette, Portland, OR 97203-5798. **EMAIL** faller@up.edu

FALLON, RICHARD H.
PERSONAL Born 01/04/1952, Augusta, ME, m, 1982, 2 children **DISCIPLINE** LAW **EDUCATION** Yale Univ, BA, 75; Oxford Univ, BA, 77; Yale Law Sch, JD, 80. **CAREER** Asst prof to prof, Harvard Law Sch, 82-. **HONORS AND AWARDS** Albert M. Sacks-Paul A. Freund Award, Harvard Law Sch, 00. **MEMBERSHIPS** Mass Bar Asn; Am Law Inst. **RESEARCH** Constitutional law; Constitutional theory; Federal jurisdiction. **SELECTED PUBLICATIONS** Auth, Implementing the Constitution, 01. **CONTACT ADDRESS** Sch of Law, Harvard Univ, 1525 Massachusetts Ave, Griswold 406, Cambridge, MA 02138. **EMAIL** rfallon@law.harvard.edu

FALTYN, TIM
PERSONAL Born 10/25/1970, Albuquerque, New Mexico, m, 1998 **DISCIPLINE** POLITICAL SCIENCE **EDUCATION** Univ Central OK, BA, 94; MED, 95; OK State Univ, EdD, 99. **CAREER** Asst Dir, Governor's Commission for Service, 93-95; Dir, Care for the Children Inc., 95-97; Adjunct Prof, Redlands Community Col, 95-97; Dept Head Social Services, Oklahoma State Univ, 97-. **HONORS AND AWARDS** U.S. Prof of the Year, Carnegie Foundation, 99, Who's Who Among America's Teachers, 00. **MEMBERSHIPS** ODLA, PGA, APA, OPSL, USGA. **RESEARCH** Public Service: (Exec. Branch), Golf: (Instructor). **SELECTED PUBLICATIONS** Auth, Golf Is Like Life, Pressly Press, 95; auth, Oklahoma State Politics, Kendall Hunt, 98; auth, The Oldest Golf Course in Oklahoma, Oklahoma Heritage, (00): 14-20; auth, Oklahoma State Politics 2nd ed, Kendall Hunt, 00; auth, Theodore Roosevelt An Active-Positive President, UMI Journal 67: 334-502; auth, An Analysis of Character, Oklahoma Journal of Political Science; auth, Straight Lines To Better Golf, McGraw Hill. **CONTACT ADDRESS** Dept Social Science, Oklahoma State Univ, Oklahoma City, 900 N Portland, Oklahoma City, OK 73107. **EMAIL** faltyn@osuouc.edu

FARAH, CAESAR E.
PERSONAL Born 03/13/1929, Portland, OR, m, 1987, 7 children **DISCIPLINE** HISTORY, RELIGION **EDUCATION** Stanford Univ, BA, 52; Princeton Univ, MA, 55; PhD, 57. **CA-**

REER Pub aff asst & educ exchange attache, US Info Serv, Delhi & Karachi, 57-59; asst prof hist & Near E lang, Portland State Univ, 59-63; consult US Army 62-63; asst prof hist, Los Angeles State Univ, 63-64; vis prof Harvard Univ 64-65; assoc prof Near Eastern lang & lit, Ind Univ, Bloomington, 64-69; prof Middle Eastern Studies, Univ Minn, Minneapolis, 69-, Consult, spec oper res off, Am Univ, 60; cult attache's comt, Arab Embassies in Washington, DC, 61; consult, col bks div, Am Libr Asn, 64-; Ford Found grant, 66-67; guest lectr Arabic Ottoman rels, Lebanese Univ, 66 & Univ Baghdad, 67; Fulbright award, Turkey, 67-68; Am Philos Soc res grant, 70-71; guest lectr For Min Spain, Iraq, Lebanon, Iran; Min Higher Educ Saudi Arabia, Yemen, Kuwait, Qatar, Tunisia, Morocco; Syrian Acad Sci, Acad Scis Beijing; vis scholar Cambridge Univ 74; rsrc person on Middle East svc gp MN, 77; bd dir chemn Upper Midwest Consortium for Middle East Outreach, 80-; vis prof Sanaa Univ, Yemen, 84, Karl-Franzens Univ, Austria, 90, Ludwig_Maximilian Univ, Munich, 92-93; exec secy ed Am Inst Yemeni Stud 82-86; secy-gen exec bd dir Int Comt for Pre-Ottoman & Ottoman Studies, 88-; fel Res Ctr Islamic Hist, Istanbul, 93; Ctr Lebanese Stydues & St Anthony Col, Oxford, Eng, 94; vis Fulbright-Hays scholar Univ Damascus, 94; Vice pres, CIEPO Gov Bd, 00-; Exec Dir and Gov Bd Mem, Upper Midwest Consortium. **HONORS AND AWARDS** Cert of Merit Syrian Min Higher Educ, 66-67; Stanford Univ Alumni Asn Ldr Recognition Awd; Fel, Am Res Cntr Egypt, 66-67. **MEMBERSHIPS** Am Orient Soc; Am Asn Arabic Studies; AHA; Royal Asiatic Soc; MidE Studies Asn NAm; Asn Tchr Arabic; Turkish Studies Asn; Pi Sigma Alpha; Phi Alpha Theta; Upper Midwest Consortium, exec dir and govern brd mem. **RESEARCH** Modern Arab world, sociopolitical changes; Islamic religion and mysticism; the West and the Arab world in the 19th century. **SELECTED PUBLICATIONS** Auth, ISLAM Beliefs and Observances, 1st ed, 67, 6th ed, 00; auth, Necib Pasa and the British in Syria, Archivum Ottomanicum, Budapest & Leiden, 72; Islam and revitalization, Quartet, London, 80; The quadruple alliance and proposed Ottoman reforms in Syria, 1839-41, Int J Turkish Studies II, 81; Tarikh Baghdad Ii-Ibn-al-Najjar, 80-83, 3 vols 2 edit 86; Al-Ghazali on Abstinence in Islam, 92; Decision Making in the Ottoman Empire, 92; The Road to Intervention: Fiscal Policies in Ottoman Mount Lebanon, 92; The Politics of Interventionism in Ottoman Lebanon, 2 vols, 97; ISLAM Beliefs and Observances, 1st ed. 67, 6th ed 00; auth, The Politics of Interventionism in Ottoman Lebanon 1831-1861, 00. **CONTACT ADDRESS** Univ of Minnesota, Twin Cities, 267 19th Ave S., 839 Soc Sci, Minneapolis, MN 55455. **EMAIL** farah001@maroon.tc.umn.edu

FARBER, DANIEL ALAN
PERSONAL Born 07/16/1950, Chicago, IL, m, 1971, 3 children **DISCIPLINE** LAW **EDUCATION** Univ Ill, BA, 71, MA, 72, JD, 75. **CAREER** Asst prof, Univ Ill, 78-81; assoc prof to prof Law, Univ Minn, 81-95; prof, Univ Minn, 96-. **MEMBERSHIPS** Am Asn Arts and Sciences, Am Law Inst. **RESEARCH** Law and economics; constitutional law; environmental law. **SELECTED PUBLICATIONS** Auth, The First Amendment, Found Press, 98; Eco-Pragmatism: Making Sensible Environmental Decision in an Uncertain World, 99. **CONTACT ADDRESS** Law Sch, Univ of Minnesota, Twin Cities, 229 19th Ave S, Minneapolis, MN 55455-0401. **EMAIL** farbe001@tc.umn.edu

FARLEY, BENJAMIN WIRT
PERSONAL Born 08/06/1935, Manila, Philippines, m, 1962, 2 children **DISCIPLINE** HISTORICAL THEOLOGY, PHILOSOPHY **EDUCATION** Davidson Col, AB, 58; Union Theol Sem, Va, BD, 63, ThM, 64, ThD, 76. **CAREER** Pastor, Franklin Presby Church, 64-68 & Cove & Rockfish Presby Churches, 68-71; instr relig, Lees-McRae Col, 73-74; assoc prof to Younts Prof Bible, Religion, and Philos, Erskine Col, 74-. **HONORS AND AWARDS** Excellence in Teaching Awd, Erskine Col, 77, 89, 00. **MEMBERSHIPS** Am Acad Refig; pres 97-99, Calvin Studies Soc. **RESEARCH** Reformation studies; philosophy of religion; literature and religion. **SELECTED PUBLICATIONS** Auth, Erskine Caldwell: Preacher's son and Southern prophet, fall 78 & George W Cable: Presbyterian Romancer, Reformer Bible Teacher, summer 80, J Presby Hist; John Calvin's Sermons on the Ten Commandments, 81 & Calvin's Treatises Against the Anabaptists and the Libertines, 82, Baker Book House; The Hero of St Lo and Other Stories, Attic Press, 82; The Providence of God, Baker Book House, 88; Calvin's Ecclesiastical Advice, Westminster/John Knox Press, 91; In Praise of Virtue, Eerdmans, 95; Mercy Road, Cherokee Publishing Co, 86; Corbin's Rubi-Yacht, Sandlapper Press, 92; auth, Son of the Morning Sky, Univ Press of Am, 99. **CONTACT ADDRESS** 1000 Woodleaf Ct., PO Box 595, Columbia, SC 29212. **EMAIL** aag@infoave.net

FARLEY, MARGARET ANN
PERSONAL Born 04/15/1935, St. Cloud, MN **DISCIPLINE** ETHICS **EDUCATION** Univ Detroit, AB, 57, MA, 60; Yale Univ, MPhil, 70, PhD (relig studies), 73. **CAREER** Asst prof philos, Mercy Col Detroit, 62-67; ASSOC PROF ETHICS, YALE UNIV, 71-; Pres, Soc of Christian Ethics, 93; Pres, Cath Theol Soc Am, 99-00; Prof Ethics. **HONORS AND AWARDS** John C. Murray Awd, 92; Luce fel, 96-97. **MEMBERSHIPS** Am Acad Relig; Soc Christian Ethics; Cath Theol Soc Am. **RESEARCH** Medical ethics; history of theological ethics; women's studies; sexual ethics. **SELECTED PUBLICATIONS** Auth, Personal Commitments, 86; auth, A Feminist Version of Respect for Persons, J Feminist Stud Rel, Vol 9, 93. **CONTACT ADDRESS** Divinity Sch, Yale Univ, 409 Prospect St, New Haven, CT 06511.

FARMER, CRAIG S.
PERSONAL Born 10/02/1961, Urbana, IL, m, 1982, 2 children **DISCIPLINE** HISTORY OF CHRISTIANITY **EDUCATION** Haverford Col, BA, 83; Univ Chicago, MA, 84; Duke Univ, PhD, 92. **CAREER** Asst prof of history and humanities, 93-98; assoc prof of hist and humanities, 98-present, Milligan Col. **MEMBERSHIPS** Amer Soc of Church Hist; Amer Acad of Relig; Medieval Acad of Amer; Sixteenth Century Studies Conf. **RESEARCH** Reformation theology; hist of biblical interpretation. **SELECTED PUBLICATIONS** Auth, Changing Images of the Samaritan Woman in Early Reformed Commentaries on John, Church History, 96; Eucharistic Exhibition and Sacramental Presence in the New Testament Commentiries of Wolfgang Musculus, Wolfgang Musculus, 97; The Gospel of John in the Sixteenth Century: The Johannine Exegesis of Wolfgang Musculus, The Oxford Studies in Historical Theology, Oxford University Press, 97; auth, "Revelation in the History of Exegesis, Leaven 8/1, (00). **CONTACT ADDRESS** Milligan Col, PO Box 500, Milligan College, TN 37682-0500. **EMAIL** csfarmer@milligan.edu

FARMER, DAVID
PERSONAL Born 07/01/1935, Barnstable, England, m, 1978, 4 children **DISCIPLINE** POLITICAL SCIENCE, PUBLIC ADMINISTRATION **EDUCATION** London Sch Econ and Political Sci, Univ London, BS, PhD, 84; Univ Toronto, MA, 64; Univ Va, MA, 86; PhD, 89. **CAREER** Prof Political Sci and Publ Admin, Va Commonwealth Univ. **MEMBERSHIPS** Pub Admin Theory Network; Amer Soc Pub Admin; Am Political Sci Asn. **RESEARCH** Political Philosophy; Public Administration; Philosophy of Social Science; Postmodernism. **SELECTED PUBLICATIONS** Auth, "Adam Smith's Legacy," in Handbook of Organization Theory and Management, ed. Thomas D. Lynch (Marcel Dekker, New York, 97), 141-164; auth, "Postmodernism and the End of Public Administration," in Business Research Yearbook: Global Business Perspectives, ed. Abbass F. Alkhataji and Jerry Bieberman (Univ Press Am, Larham, Md, 96), 628-632; auth, Introduction: Listening to Other Voices," Publ Voices, 3, 1 (July 97): 1-8; auth, "Public Administration Discourse as Play with a Purpose," Publ Voices, 3, 1 (July 97): 33-51; auth, "Leopards in the Temple: Bureaucracy and the Limits of the In-Between," Administration and Soc, 29, 5 (Nov 97): 507-528; ed, Papers on the Art of Anti-Administration, Chatelaine Press (Burke, VA), 98; auth, "Schopenhauer's Porcupines: Hegemonic Change in Context," Admin Theory and Praxis 20.4 (98): 422-433; auth, "Briefly Noted: Leo Gorcey's Bowery Boys Salute the New Millenium," Admin Theory and Praxis 21.4 (99): 537-537; auth, "The Discourse Movement: A Centrist View of the Sea Change," Int Review of Public Admin 4.1 (99): 3-10; auth, "The Ladder of Organization-Think: Beyond Flatbed," Admin Theory and Praxis 22.1 (00): 66-88. **CONTACT ADDRESS** Dept of Political Science and Public Administration, Virginia Commonwealth Univ, 1110 West Ave, Richmond, VA 23220. **EMAIL** dfarmer@vcu.edu

FARNSWORTH, E. ALLAN
PERSONAL Born 06/30/1928, Providence, RI, d, 1952, 4 children **DISCIPLINE** LAW **EDUCATION** Univ Mich, BS, 48; Yale Univ, MA, 49; Columbia Univ, JDB, 52. **CAREER** From asst prof to prof, 54-70, ALFRED MCCORMACK PROF LAW, LAW SCH, COLUMBIA UNIV, 70-, Vis prof, Univ Istanbul, 60; Ford fel, France, 61; vis prof, Univ Chicago, 63; consult, Ford Found, Dakar, Senegal, 63-64; dir orientation prog Am law, Asn Am Law Schs, 65-67; US rep, Comt Int Inst Unificatio Pvt Law, Rome, 67-98; chmn comt foreign and comp law, Asn Bar City New York, 67-70; vis prof Law Sch, Harvard Univ, 70-71; US deleg, UN Comn Int Trade Law, 70-80; reporter, Restatement (Second) of Contracts, 71-80; vis prof, Univ Paris, 74-75; US deleg dipt confs, on Int Agency, Bucharest, 79; International Contracts for Sale of Goods, Vienna, 80. **HONORS AND AWARDS** docteur honoris causa Univ of Paris II. Docteur honoris causa Catholic Univ fo Louvain; LL D hon, Dickinson Law School, Pennsylvania State Univ. **MEMBERSHIPS** Am Bar Asn; Am Law Inst. **RESEARCH** Commercial law; contracts. **SELECTED PUBLICATIONS** Auth, Farnsworth on Contracts, 2nd ed, 98; coauth, Cases and Materials on Contracts, 5th ed, 95; auth, The Law of Regretted Decisions, 98; auth, Introduction to the Legal System of the United States, 3rd, 96. **CONTACT ADDRESS** Law Sch Bldg, Columbia Univ, 435 W 116th St, New York, NY 10027-7201.

FARQUHAR, KEITH
DISCIPLINE LAW **EDUCATION** Wellington Univ, LLB, 64; LLM, 67; Univ Mich, LLM, 68. **CAREER** Assoc prof, 76-90; prof, 90-. **HONORS AND AWARDS** Ed, Can Jour Family Law. **RESEARCH** Family law; matrimonial property; trusts and estates; private international law. **SELECTED PUBLICATIONS** Auth, pubs about family law and trusts. **CONTACT ADDRESS** Fac of Law, Univ of British Columbia, 1822 East Mall, Vancouver, BC, Canada V6T 1Z1. **EMAIL** farquhar@law.ubc.ca

FARRELL, FRANK
DISCIPLINE CHURCH HISTORY **EDUCATION** Edinburgh Univ, PhD. **CAREER** Instr, Alliance Theol Sem; vis prof, Reformed Theol Sem. **HONORS AND AWARDS** Founding ed, Christianity Today. **RESEARCH** Puritans. **SELECTED PUBLICATIONS** Ed-in-Chief, World Vision mag. **CONTACT ADDRESS** Dept of Church History, Reformed Theol Sem, Florida, 1231 Reformation Dr, Oviedo, FL 32765. **EMAIL** ffarrell@rts.edu

FARRELL, HOBERT K.
PERSONAL Born 02/15/1939, Charleston, WV, m, 1962, 2 children **DISCIPLINE** BIBLICAL STUDIES **EDUCATION** Wheaton Col, BA, 61, MA, 64; Gordon-Conwell Theol Sem, BD, 64; Union Theol Sem, ThM, 66; Boston Univ, PhD, 72. **CAREER** Instr Greek, Boston Univ, 67-71; prof Bibl Studies, John Wesley Col, 71-78; prof Bibl Studies, Le Tourneau Univ, 78-. **MEMBERSHIPS** Soc Bibl Lit; Inst Bibl Res; Evangel Theol Soc. **RESEARCH** Luke; Acts. **SELECTED PUBLICATIONS** Auth, The Structure and Theology of Lake's Central Section, Trin Jour, 86. **CONTACT ADDRESS** Dept of Biblical Studies, LeTourneau Univ, PO Box 7001, Longview, TX 75607. **EMAIL** farrellh@letu.edu

FARRELL, WARREN THOMAS
PERSONAL Born 06/26/1943, New York, NY, d, 1977, 0 child **DISCIPLINE** POLITICAL SCIENCE **EDUCATION** Montclair St, BA, 65; Univ Calif Los Angeles, MA, 66; NYork Univ, PhD, 74. **CAREER** Lectr, 70, Fordham Univ; instr, 70, NJ St Col; instr, 71-73, Rutgers Univ; instr, 73-74, Amer Univ; instr, 73-75, Georgetown Univ, Schl of Lib Stud; adj asst prof, CUNY; prof, 78-79, Calif Schl of Prof Psychol; prof, 79-80, San Diego St Univ; prof, 86-88, Univ Calif, Schl of Med; Vis Scholar, Fordham Univ, 00-01. **HONORS AND AWARDS** Who's Who in Am, 00-; Who's Who in the World, 00-; World's Thought Leader, Financial Times; Who's Who in West, 27th ed, 00-01; White House Conf on Ed, 65; Awd Outstanding Contribution, Calif Assn of Marriage & Family Therapists, 88; Hon Dr, Humane Letters, Prof Schl of Psychol, San Diego CA, 85; Who's Who Among Students in Amer Col & Univ, 65; Oxford Companion to Phil, Oxford Univ Press, 95; Who's Who in America, 00-; Who's Who in the World, 00-; Financial Times' 1 of 50 of World's Thought Leaders; International Biographic Center, London, Outstanding People of 20th Century; 2000 Oustanding Scholars, 20th Century. **MEMBERSHIPS** Natl Org for Women; Children's Rights Coun; Natl Cong of Fathers & Children; Amer Coalition for Fathers & Children; Amer Bd of Sexology; Coastal Comm Found; Fathers' Rights & Equality Exchange; Board of Directors Advisers. **RESEARCH** Politics & psychology of men & women; the women's & men's movement. **SELECTED PUBLICATIONS** Auth, The Liberated Man: Beyond Masculinity, Random House, 75, Bantam, 75, Putnam-Berkley, 93; auth, The Myth of Male Power, Simon & Schuster, 93, Putnam-Berkley, 94; auth, Why Men Are The Way They Are, McGraw-Hill, 86, Putnam-Berkley, 88; auth, Women Can't Hear What Men Don't Say, Tarcher/Putnam, 99; auth, Father & Child Reunion, Tarcher/Putnam, 01. **CONTACT ADDRESS** 103 N Hwy 101, Box 220, Encinitas, CA 92024. **EMAIL** wfarrell@home.com

FARTHING, JOHN L.
DISCIPLINE RELIGION AND CLASSICAL LANGUAGES **EDUCATION** Univ Tulsa, BA, 69; Duke Univ, MDiv, 74, PhD, 78. **CAREER** Prof Relig and Clas Lang, 78, ch, dept Relig, Hendrix Col. **RESEARCH** Medieval, Reformation, and Renaissance theology. **SELECTED PUBLICATIONS** Auth, Thomas Aquinas and Gabriel Biel; transl, Jean-Claude Margolin, auth, Humanism in Europe at the Time of the Renaissance. **CONTACT ADDRESS** Hendrix Col, Conway, AR 72032.

FASANARO, CHARLES N.
PERSONAL Born 10/25/1943, New York, NY **DISCIPLINE** PHILOSOPHY **EDUCATION** Manhattan Col, BS, 65; Iliff Sch of Theol, MAR, 80; Univ Denver, PhD, 83. **CAREER** Philos dept, 80-85, writing prog and asst to dir, 85-91, Univ of Colo, Boulder; prof, Center for Study of Philos and Relig, 83; prof, St. John's Col, 91-. **HONORS AND AWARDS** Univ Colo tchg award; Alumni of the Year, Iliff Sch of Theol; R. L. Stearns Awd for outstanding fac achievement. **MEMBERSHIPS** APA; AAR. **RESEARCH** Philosophy of religion; comparative philosophy; ethics; theology and science. **SELECTED PUBLICATIONS** Auth, Velocities of Rage, Cadmus, 83; auth, Fellowship of Reconciliation, Music and the Vietnam War, Buddhists, in Tucker, ed, The Vietnam War: An Encyclopedia, Garland, 95; auth, Hunting with the Moon, Pinon Hill, 97. **CONTACT ADDRESS** PO Box 8242, Santa Fe, NM 87504-8242. **EMAIL** cnfasanaro@aol.com

FASCHING, DARRELL
PERSONAL Born 04/13/1944, Green Cove Springs, FL, m, 1974 **DISCIPLINE** RELIGION **EDUCATION** Univ Minn, BA, 68; Syracuse Univ, MA, 71; PhD, 78. **CAREER** Asst Dean, Syracuse Univ, 75-80; Ass Prof, LeMoyne Col, 80-82; Asst Prof to Prof and Chair, Univ S Fla, 82-. **HONORS AND AWARDS** USF/SUS Prof Excellence Awd, 98; USF Outstanding Teaching Awd, 96. **SELECTED PUBLICATIONS** Auth,

comparative Religious Ethics: A Narrative Approach, Blackwells, forthcoming; auth, A Teachers Manual for Comparative Religious Ethics, Blackwells, 00; co-auth, World Religions Today, Oxford Univ Press, 00; auth, The Coming of the Millennium: Good News for the Whole Human Race, Trinity Intl Press, 96; auth, Vreemdeling na Auschwitz: Een nieuwe narratieve inzet in de christelijke ethiek, De Horstink, 95; auth, The Ethical Challenge of Auschwitz and Hiroshima: Apocalypse or Utopia?, SUNY Press, 93; auth, Narrative Theology After Auschwitz: From alienation to Ethics, fortress Press, 92; auth, the Thought of Jacques Ellul, Edwin Mellen Press, 81. **CONTACT ADDRESS** Dept Relig, Univ of So Florida, 4202 E Fowler Ave, Tampa, FL 33620-9951. **EMAIL** fasching@chumal.cas.usf.edu

FASOL, AL
PERSONAL Born 06/06/1937, Chicago, IL, m, 1960, 3 children **DISCIPLINE** HOMILETICS **EDUCATION** Southern Ill Univ, BA, 63; SW Baptist Theol Sem, MDiv, 66; DTh, 75. **CAREER** Newscaster/assignments ed, KXAS-TV, 69-75; prof preaching, SW Baptist Theol Sem, 73- . **HONORS AND AWARDS** Who's Who in Am Col & Univ. **MEMBERSHIPS** Int Commun Asn. **RESEARCH** Mass media. **SELECTED PUBLICATIONS** Auth, Steps to the Sermon; auth, A Complete Guide to Sermon Delivery; auth, With a Bible in Their Hands. **CONTACT ADDRESS** Dept Pastoral Min, Southwestern Baptist Theol Sem, PO Box 22218, Ft Worth, TX 76122-0218.

FAULCONER, JAMES E.
PERSONAL Born 09/27/1947, Warrensburg, MO, m, 1970, 4 children **DISCIPLINE** PHILOSOPHY **EDUCATION** Brigham Young Univ, BA, 72; Pa St Univ, MA, 75; PhD, 77. **CAREER** From Instr to Prof, Brigham Young Univ, 75-. **HONORS AND AWARDS** Prof of the Month, 80; Hon Prof of the Year, Brigham Young Univ, 88; Outstanding Teacher Awd, Brigham Young Univ, 97. **MEMBERSHIPS** IPS, SAPEP, APA. **RESEARCH** Contemporary Continental philosophy. **SELECTED PUBLICATIONS** Auth, "Newton, Science and Causation," J of Mind and Behav 16.1 (95): 77-86; auth, "The Uncanny Interruption of Ethics: Gift, Interruption, or. . .," The Grad Fac Philos J, vol 20, no 2 and vol 21, no 1 (98): 233-247; coauth, "Religion and Mental Health: A Hermeneutic Reconsideration," in Relig, Ment Health and the Latter-Day Saints (Provo, UT: Brigham Young UP, 99), 281-302; auth, Tools for Scripture Study, FARMS (Provo, UT), 99; auth, Romans 1: Notes and Reflections, FARMS (Provo, UT), 99; auth, Appropriating Heidegger, Cambridge UP (Cambridge), forthcoming; auth, "Scripture as Incarnation," Historicity and the Latter-Day Saint Scriptures, Brigham Young UP (forthcoming). **CONTACT ADDRESS** Dept Philos, Brigham Young Univ, PO Box 26279, Provo, UT 84602-6279. **EMAIL** james_faulconer@byu.edu

FAULKNER, RONNIE
PERSONAL Born 09/15/1952, Erwin, NC, s **DISCIPLINE** HISTORY, GOVERNMENT **EDUCATION** Campbell Col, BS, 74; Univ NC, MS, 78; East Carolina Univ, MA, 76; Univ SC, PhD, 83. **CAREER** Instr, TTU, 79-81; Asst Prof, TTU, 81-84; Asst Prof, Glenville State Col, 84-89; Asst Prof to Prof, Campbell Univ, 89-. **HONORS AND AWARDS** Gardner Soc Sci Awd, Campbell Col, 74; Weinefeld Hist Ward, Univ SC, 76; Southeast Libr Asn Wilson Awd, 84; Phi Alpha Theta; Phi Kappa Phi. **MEMBERSHIPS** NC Lit & Hist Asn, Southern Hist Asn, Southeast Libr Asn, NC Libr Asn. **RESEARCH** Southern history and politics, library science, North Carolina history. **SELECTED PUBLICATIONS** Auth, "North Carolina Democrats and Silver Fusion Politics 1892-1896," NC Hist Rev (82); auth, "Taking J C Calhoun to the UN," Polity (83); auth, "UN Ambassador Daniel Patrick Moynihan and the Calhounian Connection," Teaching Polit Sci (85-86); auth, "American Reaction to Hindenburg of the Weimar Republic," The Historian (89); auth, "Jesse Helms and the Legacy of Nathaniel Macon (98). **CONTACT ADDRESS** Dept Hist & Govt, Campbell Univ, Library, PO Box 98, Buies Creek, NC 27506-0098. **EMAIL** faulkner@camel.campbell.edu

FAUPEL, WILLIAM
PERSONAL Born 05/28/1944, Cass City, MI, m, 1992, 2 children **DISCIPLINE** THEOLOGY **EDUCATION** Univ of Birmingham England, PhD, 89. **CAREER** Exec Dir library ser, 78-, Dir Wes/Holiness Stud Cent, 92-, Asbury Theo Sem; Exec Sec, 96-, Soc for Pent Stud. **MEMBERSHIPS** AAR, WTS, ATSPS, KLA, LAWMHS, EPTA. **RESEARCH** Pentecostalism, Anglican theology of history, Methodist theology and history. **SELECTED PUBLICATIONS** Auth, The Everlasting Gospel, The Significance of Eschatology in the Development of Pentecostal Thought, Sheffield ENG, Sheffield Academic Press, 96; advisory ed, The Higher Christian Life, Sources for the Study of the Holiness Movement, A Biographical Essay Pentecostal and Keswick Movements, NY Garland Publishing Co, 85; auth, Resources for Research, A Guide to Selected Bibliographic and Reference Tools, Wilmore KY, Asbury Sem Press, 71; Glossolalia as Foreign Language, Investigation of the Early Twentieth-Century Pentecostal Claim, in: Wesleyan Theo J, 96. **CONTACT ADDRESS** 3291 Nantucket Dr, Lexington, KY 40390. **EMAIL** bill_faupel@asbury.seminary.edu

FAVAZZA, JOSEPH A.
PERSONAL Born 05/25/1954, Memphis, TN, m, 1991, 3 children **DISCIPLINE** RELIGIOUS STUDIES **EDUCATION** Cath Univ Louvain, Belgium MA/STB, 79; Cath Univ Louvain, Belgium, PhD, 87. **CAREER** Asst prof Religious Studies, Rhodes Col. **MEMBERSHIPS** Cath Theolog Soc Amer; Amer Acad Relig; N Amer Patristics Soc; N Amer Acad Liturgy. **RESEARCH** Institutional Life in early Christian Literature; Roman Catholic Theology; Social Reconciliation Rituals & Symbols; Roman Catholic Studies. **SELECTED PUBLICATIONS** Auth, The Efficacy of Ritual Resistance: The Case of Catholic Sacramental Reconciliation, Worship, 98; auth, A Reconciliation Sourcebook, Liturgy Training Publ, 97; auth, Can Reconciliation Be Postmodern? New Theolog Rev, 97; auth, The Order of Penitents: Historical Roots and Pastoral Future. **CONTACT ADDRESS** Dept of Religious Studies, Rhodes Col, Memphis, TN 38112-1690. **EMAIL** favazza@rhodes.edu

FAWKES, DON
PERSONAL Born 02/20/1946, Kansas City, MO, m, 1976, 1 child **DISCIPLINE** PHILOSOPHY **EDUCATION** Univ Ariz, BS, 71; MA, 76; PhD, 93. **CAREER** Assoc Prof, James Madison Univ, 97-; asst prof, Fayetteville St Univ, 94-97; adjunct asst prof, Fayetteville St Univ, 91-94; adjunct prof, Fayetteville St Univ, 89-91; asst prof, US Air Force Acad, 79-81; instr, US Air Force Acad, 76-78. **HONORS AND AWARDS** Scholarship of Josephson Inst of Ethics, 98; Marquis Who's Who in World; NEH Member; Marquis Who's Who in Sci & Engineering; Excellence in Teaching Awd, Fayetteville St Univ, 94; US Air Force Scholarship in Philos, 74-76; Beta Gamma Sigma; Phi Kappa Phi; NEH Fel, Univ Ariz, 92-93. **MEMBERSHIPS** Philos Sci Assoc; Amer Philos Assoc; Intl Soc for Performance Improvement; Amer Assoc Advancement of Sci; Southwestern Philos Soc; Smithsonian Inst; Libr of Congress Assoc; Phi Kappa Phi. **RESEARCH** Philosophy of Science; Epistemology; Metaphysics; Critical Thinking & Logic; Tchg Methodologies & Philosophy of Education; Analytical Philosophy; Ethics; Philosophy of Law; Asian Studies; Philosophy and Humanities; American Philosophers; Theology & Comparative Religions. **SELECTED PUBLICATIONS** Of Tolerance, Analytic Teaching, 98; The Values of Science and the Value of Science, James Madison Univ Annl Arts & Sci Symposium, 98; Critical Thinking and Its Courses, Inquiry, 96; "On Teaching Premise/Conclusion Distinctions, Inquiry, 96. **CONTACT ADDRESS** Dept of Philosophy, James Madison Univ, 492 C Longview Dr, Harrisburg, VA 22802.

FEAGIN, GLYNDLE M.
PERSONAL Born 10/12/1948, McKinney, TX, m, 1972, 1 child **DISCIPLINE** RELIGION **EDUCATION** Baylor Univ, BA, 71; SW Baptist Theol Sem, M Div, 75; Phillips Grad Sem, D Min, 85; S Baptist Theol Sem, PhD, 93. **CAREER** Adj prof, S Baptist Theol Sem, 91-92; from asst prof to assoc prof, Wayland Baptist Univ, 92-. **HONORS AND AWARDS** Outstanding Scholar Awd, Wayland Baptist Univ, 94. **MEMBERSHIPS** Baptist Prof of Rel. **SELECTED PUBLICATIONS** Auth, Irony and the Kingdom in Mark: A Literary-Critical Study, Mellen Biblical Press, 97. **CONTACT ADDRESS** Dept Rel & Philos, Wayland Baptist Univ, 1900 W 7th St, Plainview, TX 79072-6900. **EMAIL** gfeagin@wbui.edu

FEAGIN, SUSAN LOUISE
PERSONAL Born 07/11/1948, New York, NY, m, 1977 **DISCIPLINE** PHILOSOPHY **EDUCATION** Fla State Univ, BA, 69; Univ Wis-Madison, MA, 73, PhD (philos), 75. **CAREER** Vis asst prof philos, Bowling Green State Univ, 76-77; ASST PROF PHILOS, UNIV MO, KANSAS CITY, 77-. **MEMBERSHIPS** Am Philos Asn; Am Soc Aesthet. **RESEARCH** Aesthetics; epistemology. **SELECTED PUBLICATIONS** Auth, Showing Pictures--Aesthetics and the Art Gallery, J Aestet Educ, Vol 27, 93; Philosophy and Art Education, J Aesthet Educ, Vol 29, 95. **CONTACT ADDRESS** Dept of Phillos, Univ of Missouri, Kansas City, 5100 Rockhill Rd, Kansas City, MO 64110-2499.

FEASTER, BRUCE SULLIVAN
PERSONAL Born 07/13/1961, Flint, MI, m, 1993 **DISCIPLINE** LAW **EDUCATION** MI State Univ, BA, 1983; Univ of TX Law School, JD, 1986. **CAREER** WCNLS Children's Ctr for Justice and Peace, dir, currently. **HONORS AND AWARDS** National Mens Scholar. **MEMBERSHIPS** Alpha Phi Alpha; Metro Detroit Optimist. **CONTACT ADDRESS** WCNLS Children's Ctr for Justice & Peace, 3400 Cadillac Towers, Detroit, MI 48226.

FEE, ELIZABETH
PERSONAL Born 12/11/1946, Belfast, Northern Ireland **DISCIPLINE** HISTORY AND PHILOSOPHY OF SCIENCE **EDUCATION** Cambridge Univ, BA, 68, MA, 75; Princeton Univ, MA, 71, PhD (hist and philos sci), 78. **CAREER** Teaching asst hist med, Princeton Univ, 71-72; instr hist sci, State Univ NY Binghamton, 72-74; archivist, 74-78, asst prof, Sch Health Serv, 74-78, Asst Prof Hist Publ Health, Sch Hyg Publ Health, Johns Hopkins Univ, 78-, Ed consult, Int J Health Serv, 79-; consult, Col Allied Health Sci, Thomas Jefferson Univ, 79-80. **MEMBERSHIPS** Am Asn Hist Med; Hist Sci Soc; AHA; Berkshire Conf Women's Hist; Am Publ Health Asn. **RESEARCH** History of public health research and practice; history of Johns Hopkins School of Hygiene and Public Health; women and science and women and health. **SELECTED PUBLICATIONS** Auth, The sexual politics of Victorian social anthropology, Feminist Studies, 1: 23-29 & In: Clio's Consciousness Raised: New Perspectives on the History of Women, Harper & Row, 74; Science and the woman problem: Historical perspectives, In: Sex Differences: Social and Biological Perspectives, Doubleday-Anchor, 76; Women and health care: A comparison of theories, Int J Health Serv, 5: 397-415, Nursing Digest, 4: 74-78 & In: Health and Medical Care in the United States: A Critical Analysis, Baywood, 77; Psychology, sexuality and social control in Victorian England, Soc Sci Quart, 58: 632-646; Nineteenth century craniology: The study of the female skull, Bull Hist Med, 53: 415-433; coauth (with Michael Wallace), The history and politics of birth control: A review essay, Feminist Studies, 5: 201-215; auth, Is feminismm a threat to scientific objectivity?, J Col Sci Teaching, Vol 9, No 2; ed, Women and Health, Baywood Publ Co, 82. **CONTACT ADDRESS** Sch of Hygiene and Publ Health, Johns Hopkins Univ, Baltimore, 3400 N Charles St, Baltimore, MD 21205.

FEELEY, MALCOLM M.
PERSONAL Born 11/28/1942, No Conway, NH, d, 1969, 3 children **DISCIPLINE** POLITICAL SCIENCE **EDUCATION** Austin Col, BA, 64; Univ Minn, MA, 67; PhD, 69. **CAREER** Asst prof, NY Univ, 68-72; lectr, Yale Univ, 72-77; from assoc prof to prof, Univ Wis, 77-84; prof, Univ Calif at Berkeley, 84-96; Claire Sanders Clements Chair, Univ Calif at Berkeley Sch of Law, 96-. **HONORS AND AWARDS** Hubert Humphrey Award, 67-68; Russell Sage Found Fel, 72-74; Silver Gavel Best Book Award, Am Bar Asn, 80. **MEMBERSHIPS** Am Polit Sci Asn, Law & Soc Asn, Legal Hist Asn. **RESEARCH** Judicial Process, Criminal Justice, Women & Crime, Criminal Justice History, American Politics. **SELECTED PUBLICATIONS** Auth, Affirmative School Integration, 69; auth, The Impact of Supreme Court Decisions, 73; auth, The Process is the Punishment, 79; auth, Neighborhood Justice, 82; auth, Court Reform on Trial, 83; auth, American Constitutional Law, 85 & 91; auth, Judicial Policy Making and the Modern State, 98. **CONTACT ADDRESS** Sch of Law, Univ of California, Berkeley, 220 Boalt Hall, Berkeley, CA 94720-0001. **EMAIL** mmf@uclink4.berkeley.edu

FEERICK, JOHN DAVID
PERSONAL Born 07/12/1936, New York, NY, m, 1962, 6 children **DISCIPLINE** LAW **EDUCATION** Fordham Col, BS, 58; Fordham Univ, LLB, 61. **CAREER** Assoc adj prof labor law, 76-82, dean, Sch Law, Fordham Univ, 82-; assoc, Skadden, Arps, Slate, Meagher & Flom, 61, partner, 68-82. **SELECTED PUBLICATIONS** Auth, From Failing Hands: The Story of Presidential Succession, Fordham Univ Press, 65; coauth, The Vice Presidents of the United States, Franklin Watts, Inc, 74; coauth, NLRB Representation Elections-Law, Practice and Procedure, Harcourt Brace Jovanovich, 80; auth, The Twenty-Fifth Amendment, Fordham Univ Press, 92. **CONTACT ADDRESS** Sch of Law Lincoln Ctr, Fordham Univ, 140 W 62nd St, New York, NY 10023-7407.

FEINBERG, BARBARA JANE
PERSONAL Born 06/01/1938, NY, w, 1968, 2 children **DISCIPLINE** POLITICAL SCIENCE **EDUCATION** Wellesley Col, BA, 59; Yale Univ, MA, 60, PhD, 63. **CAREER** City Col NY, lectr instr, 63-67; Brooklyn Col, vis lectr, 67-68; Seton Hall Univ, asst prof, 68-70; Hunta Col, adj asst prof, 70-73; Author of nonfiction books for children, 80-. **HONORS AND AWARDS** Wellesley Col, Durant Schl, Woodrow Wilson Prize, Phi Beta Kappa; Yale, Fellowshp. **RESEARCH** Am Hist, Biography. **SELECTED PUBLICATIONS** General Douglas MacArthur: An American Hero, Danbury Ct, Children's Press, 99; Edith Kermit Caron Roosevelt and Elizabeth Wallace Truman, Danbury CT, Children's Press, in preparation; Patricia Ryan Nixon Danbury CT Children's Press, 98; America's First Ladies, Danbury CT Children's Press, 98; Next in Line: The American Vice Presidency, Danbury Ct Children's Press, 96; many more pub books. **CONTACT ADDRESS** 535 East 86th St, New York, NY 10028-7533.

FEINBERG, WALTER
PERSONAL Born 08/22/1937, Boston, MA, m, 1964, 2 children **DISCIPLINE** PHILOSOPHY, PHILOSOPHY OF EDUCATION **EDUCATION** Boston Univ, AB, 60, AM, 62, PhD, 66. **CAREER** Asst prof philos educ, Oakland Univ, 65-67; from asst prof to assoc prof, 67-75, Prof Philos Educ, Univ IL, Urbana, 75-, Assoc ed, Educ Theory, 67-; mem, Bur Educ Res, Univ IL, 77. **HONORS AND AWARDS** Assoc, Univ IL Center for Advan Study, 88, 98; Spencer Grant, 94-95, 96-97; Univ Chicago Benton Scholar, 95-96. **MEMBERSHIPS** Philos Educ Soc (pres, 88-89); Am Philos Asn; Philos Sci Asn; Am Educ Studies Asn (pres, 77-); Soc Advan Am Philos. **RESEARCH** Am educ philos; racial and ethnic considerations in Am educ; principles regarding the distribution of knowledge. **SELECTED PUBLICATIONS** Auth, Reason and Rhetoric, John Wiley, 75; co-ed, Work, Technology and Education, Univ Ill, 75; Understanding Education, Cambridge, 83; Japan & The Pursuit of a New American Identity, Routledge, 93; On Higher

Ground: Education & The Case for Affirmative Action, Teachers Col Press, 97; Common Schools, Uncommon Identities: Cultural Differences/National Unity, Yale, 98. **CONTACT ADDRESS** 1310 S 6th St, Champaign, IL 61820-6925. **EMAIL** wfeinber@uiuc.edu

FEINGOLD, HENRY L.
PERSONAL Born 02/06/1931, Germany, m, 1954, 2 children **DISCIPLINE** UNITED STATES DIPLOMACY & AMERICAN JEWISH HISTORY **EDUCATION** Brooklyn Col, BA, 53, MA, 54; NYork Univ, PhD, 66. **CAREER** Tchr hist, Sec Schs, NY, 53-65; lectr, City Univ NY, 67-68; from instr to assoc prof hist, 68-76, grad ctr, 75, prof hist, Baruch Col, City Univ NY, 76-, Prof Emeritus, 98-, Dir, Jewish Resource Center, Baruch Col, CUNY; Lectr exten prog in Ger, Univ MD, 55-56; adj prof, Stern Col, Yeshiva Univ, 71-73; adj lectr, Inst Advan Study Hum Jewish Theol Inst Am, 73-76. **HONORS AND AWARDS** Leon Jolson Awd for best bk on Holocaust, 77; Presidential Awd for Excellence in Scholarship, Baruch Col, May 86; Lee Friedman Awd in Am Jewish Hist, 94; Morim Awd, Jewish Tchr(s) Asn, 95. **MEMBERSHIPS** Labor Zionist Alliance (pres, 89-92); Jewish Community Relations Coun (board of dir); World Zionist Org (gen coun); Jewish Agency for Israel (gen assembly); Am Zionist Movement (cabinet); dir, Jewish Resource Ctr, Baruch Col. **RESEARCH** Holocaust. **SELECTED PUBLICATIONS** Auth, The Politics of Rescue: The Roosevelt Administration and the Holocaust, 1938-1945, Rutgers Univ Press, 70; Zion in America: The Jewish Experience from Colonial Times to the Present, Twayne, 74; A Midrash on the History of American Jewry, NY State Univ Press, 82; A Time for Searching: Entering the Mainstream, 1920-1945, Johns Hopkins Univ Press, 92; Bearing Witness: How American and its Jews Responded to the Holocaust, Univ Syracuse Press, 95; Lest Memory Cease, Finding Meaning in the American Jewish Past, Univ Syracuse Press, 96. **CONTACT ADDRESS** Baruch Col, CUNY, 17 Lexington Ave, New York, NY 10010-5518. **EMAIL** jrc@baruch.cuny.edu

FEINMAN, JAY M.
PERSONAL Born 01/22/1951, Easton, PA, m, 2 children **DISCIPLINE** LAW **EDUCATION** American Univ, BA, 72; Univ Chicago, JD, 75. **CAREER** Instr, Univ Miami School of Law, 75-76; assoc, Dechert Price and Rhoads, Philadelphia, PA, 76-77; vis prof of law, Northwestern Univ School of Law, Chicago, IL, fall 90; vis prof of law, Karl Franzens Univ, Graz, Austria, spring 95; asst and assoc prof of law, 77-88, prof of law, 88-96, distinguished prof of Law, Rutgers State Univ of NJ, School of Law, 96-, assoc dean, Curriculum Development and Lawering progs, 92-95, acting dean, 97-98. **HONORS AND AWARDS** Grants: Rutgers Committee for the Improvement of Teaching, 82-83, 87-88; NJ State Bar Found, proj dir, Rutgers Elderlaw Clinic, 93-95; US Dept of Ed, proj dir, Rutgers Elderlaw Clinic, 94-95; various res grant s from Rutgers Res Coun and law school; Provost's Teaching Awd, 99. **MEMBERSHIPS** Am bar Asn; NJ State Bar Asn; Camden County Bar Asn; Conference on Critical Legal Studies. **SELECTED PUBLICATIONS** Auth, Economic Negligence: Liability of Professionals and Businesses to Third Parties for Economic Loss, Little, Brown & Co, 95; Economic Negligence in Construction Litigation, 15, The Construction Lawyer 34, 95; Simulations: An Introduction, 45, J of Legal Ed 469, 95; Attorney Liability to Nonclients, 31 Tort and Insurance Law J 735, 96; Economic Negligence Actions: A Remedy for Third Parties, Trial, June 96; Doctrinal Classification and Economic Negligence, 33 San Diego Law Rev 137, 96; Economic Negligence in Residential Real Estate Transactions, 25 Real Estate Law J 110, 96; Implied Warranty, Products Liability, and the Boundaries Between Contract and Tort, 75 Washington Univ Law Quart 469, 97; Law School Grading, 65 UMKC Law Rev 647, 97; The Future History of Legal Education, 29 Rutgers Law J 475, 98; auth, Professional Liability to Third Parties, Am Bar Assoc, 00; auth, Law 101: Everything You Need to Know About the Am Legal System, Oxford Univ Pr, 00. **CONTACT ADDRESS** School of Law, Rutgers, The State Univ of New Jersey, Newark, 217 N Fifth St, Camden, NJ 08102-1203. **EMAIL** feinman@camden.rutgers.edu

FEISS, HUGH
PERSONAL Born 05/08/1939, Lakeview, OR, s **DISCIPLINE** THEOLOGY **EDUCATION** Mount Angel Seminary, BA, 62, MA, 66, Mdiv, 66; The Catholic Univ, PhL, 73, STL, 67; Anselmianum, Rome, STD, 80; Univ of Iowa, MLS, 87. **CAREER** Prof of Philo, 67-72, Prof of Theo and Hum, 74-96, Mt Angel Seminary. **HONORS AND AWARDS** NEH Summer Seminars. **MEMBERSHIPS** CTS, SBL, AAR, CPA, SSSR, ABA. **RESEARCH** 12th Century Theology. **SELECTED PUBLICATIONS** Hildegard of Bingen, Explanation of the Rule of St Benedict, ed, H Feiss, Toronto, Peregrina, 90; A Poet Abbess from Notre Dame de Saintes, Magistra, 95; The Christology of Greet Groote's Getijdenboek, Amer Benedictine Review, 97; auth, Essential Monastic Wisdom, HarperCollins, 99; coauth, The Lives of Saint Winefride, Toronto, Peregrina, 00. **CONTACT ADDRESS** Ascension Priory, 541 E 100 S, Jerome, ID 83338-5655. **EMAIL** hughf@magiclink.com

FEIT, NEIL
PERSONAL Born 06/17/1966, New York, NY **DISCIPLINE** PHILOSOPHY **EDUCATION** Columbia Col , BA, 88; Univ Mass, PhD, 96. **CAREER** Asst prof, Western Wash Univ, 97-. **MEMBERSHIPS** Am Philos Asn. **RESEARCH** Philosophy of Mind and Language; Metaphysics. **SELECTED PUBLICATIONS** Auth, On a Famous Counterexample to Leibniz's Law, Proceedings of the Aristotelian Soc, 96; More on Brute Facts, Australasian J of Philos, forthcoming; Self-Ascription and Belief De Re, Philos Studies, forthcoming. **CONTACT ADDRESS** Dept of Philosophy, Western Washington Univ, Bellingham, WA 98225-9054. **EMAIL** nfeit@cc.wwu.edu

FELD, ALAN L.
PERSONAL Born 02/05/1940, New York, NY, m, 1962, 3 children **DISCIPLINE** FEDERAL TAX LAW **EDUCATION** Columbia Col, AB, 60; Harvard Law Sch, LLB, 63. **CAREER** Assoc prof, 71-75, PROF LAW, BOSTON UNIV, 75-, Assoc, Paul, Weiss, Rifkind, Wharton and Garrison, 64-67 and Barrett, Knapp, Smith and Schapiro, 67-71; vis prof, Law Sch, Univ Pa, 77-78. **MEMBERSHIPS** Am Law Inst. **RESEARCH** Federal taxation, the Congress, Law and the Arts. **SELECTED PUBLICATIONS** Auth, Legal Differences Without Economic Distinctions--Points, Penalties, and the Market for Mortgages, Boston Univ Law Rev, Vol 77, 97. **CONTACT ADDRESS** Law Sch, Boston Univ, 765 Commonwealth Ave, Boston, MA 02215-1401.

FELDER, CAIN HOPE
PERSONAL Born 06/09/1943, Aiken, SC, d, 1973 **DISCIPLINE** THEOLOGY **EDUCATION** Howard University, Washington, DC, BA, 1966; Oxford University, Oxford, England, dip theol, 1968; Union Theological Seminary, New York, NYork, MDiv, 1969; Columbia University, New York, NYork, MPhil, 1978, PhD, 1982. **CAREER** Black Methodists for Church Renewal, Atlanta, GA, national executive director, 69-72; Morgan State University, Baltimore, MD, director of federal relations/associate professor of philosophy, 72-74; Grace United Methodist Church, New York, NY, pastor, 75-78; Princeton Theological Seminary, Princeton, NJ, instructor, 78-81; Howard University School of Divinity, professor, 81-. **HONORS AND AWARDS** Fellowships awarded by the National Fellowship Fund, The Crusade Fellowship, Union Theological Seminary Graduate Fellowship and Minority Fund, The Rockefeller Brothers Fund-Protestant and Doctoral Fellowships, Columbia University Faculty Fellowship; has received numerous scholarships; Outstanding Leadership Citation, Black Methodists for Church Renewal, The Black Caucus of the Methodist Church, 1973; Martin Luther King, Jr., Scholar-Service Awd, Providence and Vicinity Council of Churches; Progressive Natl Baptist Convention, Martin Luther King Jr Freedom Awd; AME, 2nd Episcopal Dist, Excellence in Scholarship Awd, 1995; public speaker at institutions of higher learning. **MEMBERSHIPS** Mem, Society of Biblical Literature; mem, Society for the Study of Black Religion; mem, Amer Academy of Religion; mem, Middle East Studies Assn; mem, bd of dirs, 1978-, exec committee, 1984-86, chair, 1985, 1986, Natl Convocation Planning Committee, Black Theology Project; bd mem, Interreligious Foundation for Comm Organization, 1970-72; founder, Enterprises Now, Inc; founder, Narco House (drug rehabilitation center), Atlanta, GA; mem, 1985-98, Coun of Univ Senate, Howard Univ; chair, Theology Search Comm, Howard Univ School of Divinity, 1987; founder, chair, the Biblical Inst for Social Change, Washington, DC. **SELECTED PUBLICATIONS** editor and author, Stony the Road We Trod: African American Biblical Interpretation, Fortress Press, 1990; author, Troubling Biblical Waters: Race, Class, and Family, Orbis Books, 1989; author, "Cost of Freedom in Urban Black Churches," Vision of Hope, 1989; author, "The Bible and Re-contextualization," African-AmericanReligious Studies: Anthology, 1989; author, "The Holy Spirit in Jesus' Formative Years," Pacific Theological Review, 1988; author, The Season of Lent,, 1993; general editor, The Original African Heritage Study Bible, Winston Derek Publishing Co, 1993; editor, Journal of Religious Thought; author of numerous other articles and book reviews. **CONTACT ADDRESS** Professor of Biblical Studies, Howard Univ, 1400 Shepherd St, NE, Washington, VT 20017.

FELDER, DAVID W.
PERSONAL Born 04/25/1945, Providence, RI, m, 1977 **DISCIPLINE** PHILOSOPHY **EDUCATION** Boston Univ, BA, 67; Wayne State Univ, MA, 69; Florida State Univ, PhD, 78. **CAREER** Prof, Florida A & M Univ, 76-. **HONORS AND AWARDS** NEH Fel, African Thought Systems at NYU, 77, Enlightenment at Boston Univ, 91, German Social Thought Univ Chicago, 96. **MEMBERSHIPS** Amer Phil Assoc; Florida Phil Assoc. **RESEARCH** Social theory **SELECTED PUBLICATIONS** Auth, Kids Conflicts, Teenage Conflicts, Family Conflicts, Relationships and Ethics, Marital Conflicts, Divorce Conflicts, Institutional Conflicts, and Courtroom Conflicts, 95; auth, Key to High Scores on Standardized Tests: Based on the Logic Used in Test Development, 98; coauth, Freedom and Culture in German Social Theory, 99. **CONTACT ADDRESS** 9601-30 Miccosukee Rd., Tallahassee, FL 32308. **EMAIL** felderdave@aol.com

FELDMAN, RICHARD HAROLD
PERSONAL Born 06/20/1948, Maplewood, NJ, m, 1974, 1 child **DISCIPLINE** PHILOSOPHY **EDUCATION** Cornell Univ, BA, 70; Univ Mass, MA & PhD, 75. **CAREER** Instr philos, Franklin & Marshall Col, 74-75, asst prof, 75-81, Assoc Prof Philos, Univ Rochester, 81-97, prof, Univ Rochester, 91. **MEMBERSHIPS** Am Philos Asn. **RESEARCH** Epistemology; philos of mind; metaphysics. **SELECTED PUBLICATIONS** Auth, An Alleged Defect in Getter Counterexamples, Australasian J Philos, 5/75; Co auth, Evidentialism, Philosophical Studies, 85; Reliability and Justification, 85, Proper Functionalsim, 93; Reason and Argument, Prentice Hall, 99; The Ethics of Belief, Philosophy and Phenomenological Research, 00; Skepticism and Contexualism, Philosophical Perspectives, 99. **CONTACT ADDRESS** Dept of Philos, Univ of Rochester, 500 Joseph C Wilson, Rochester, NY 14627-9000. **EMAIL** feldman@philosophy.rochester.edu

FELDMAN, YAEL S.
PERSONAL Born, Israel, m **DISCIPLINE** HEBREW AND JUDAIC STUDIES **EDUCATION** Tel Aviv Univ, BA, 67; Hebrew Col, Brookline, Mass, MA, 76; Columbia Univ, MPhil, 80, PhD, 81. **CAREER** Asst prof, 81-88, assoc prof, Middle East Langs and Cultures, Columbia Univ, 88-89; vis prof, Yale Univ, winter 93; vis prof, Princeton Univ, winter 96; assoc prof, Skirball Dept of Hebrew and Judaic Studies, New York Univ, 89-. **HONORS AND AWARDS** The Koerner Fel at the Postgraduate Centre for Hebrew Studies, Oxford, England, 96; Littauer Found Travelling Grant, 97; NYU Res Challenge Awd (RCF), 97-98. **SELECTED PUBLICATIONS** Auth, "Ruhama's Daughter: From Hysteria to HerStory in Ruth Almog's Shorshei Avir," Festschrift for Baruch Levin, eds, R. Chazan, W. Hallo, and L. Schiffman, Winona Lake, Ind (98): 509-521; auth, "Postcolonial Memory and/or Postmodern Intersexuality: Anton Shammas's Arabesques Revisited," PMLA 114 (May 99): 373-389; auth, "Otherness and Difference: The Perspective of Gender Theory," Demonizing The Other: Antisemitism, Racism and Xenophobia, ed Robert Wistrich, Harwood Academic Press, England (99): 168-182; auth, "Returning the Gaze: Traces of Simone de Beauvoir in Hebrew Literary Feminism," Re'eh, Paris (99): 25-33; auth, "Making Room for Virginia Woolf in Israeli Culture," Virginia Woolf Miscellany (fall 99): 5-6; auth, "Hebrew 'Gender' and Zionist Ideology: The Palmach Trilogy of Netiva Ben Yehunda," Prooftexts 21:1 (Jan 2000): 139-157; auth, No Room of Their Own: Gender and Nation in Isaeli Women's Fiction, a finalist in the Jewish Book Awards, Columbia Univ Press (99); auth, Shrinking Zionism: The Psychopolitical Narrative in Israeli Culture (forthcoming). **CONTACT ADDRESS** Dept Hebrew & Judaic Studies, New York Univ, 51 Washington Sq S, New York, NY 10012-1018. **EMAIL** yfl@is.nyu.edu

FELDTHUSEN, BRUCE P.
DISCIPLINE LAW **EDUCATION** Queen's Univ, BA, 72; Univ Western Ontario, LLB, 76; Univ Mich, LLM, 77, SJD, 79. **CAREER** Prof. **RESEARCH** Administrative law; human rights; debtor-creditor rights; remedies; regulated industries; legal theory. **SELECTED PUBLICATIONS** Auth, Economic Negligence; co-auth, Cases and Materials on the Law of Torts. **CONTACT ADDRESS** Fac of Law, Univ of Western Ontario, London, ON, Canada N6A 3K7. **EMAIL** bfeldthu@julian.uwo.ca

FELIX, ROBERT E.
DISCIPLINE CONFLICT OF LAWS, LAW & LITERATURE, PRODUCTS LIABILITY, & TORTS **EDUCATION** Univ Cincinnati, AB, 56, LLB, 59, AB, 59; Univ Brit Columbia, MA, 62; Harvard Univ, LLM, 67. **CAREER** James P Mozingo III prof, Legal Res. **SELECTED PUBLICATIONS** Coauth, treatise & casebk on, conflict of laws & a treatise on the SC Law of Torts. **CONTACT ADDRESS** School of Law, Univ of So Carolina, Columbia, Columbia, SC 29208. **EMAIL** Felix@law.law.sc.edu

FELL, ALBERT PRIOR
PERSONAL Born 10/01/1929, Toronto, ON, Canada, m, 1965, 2 children **DISCIPLINE** PHILOSOPHY **EDUCATION** Univ Toronto, BA, 52; St Andrews Univ, BPhil, 56; Columbia Univ, AM, 54, PhD (philos), 63. **CAREER** Teaching fel, 56-58, from lectr to assoc prof, 58-71, assoc dean students, 69-72, prof to prof emer, Queen's Univ, 71-. **MEMBERSHIPS** Can Philos Asn; Am Soc Aesthe; NAm Nietzsche Soc. **RESEARCH** Philosophy of history and art. **CONTACT ADDRESS** Dept of Philos, Queen's Univ at Kingston, Kingston, ON, Canada K7L 3N6.

FELL, JOSEPH PHINEAS
PERSONAL Born 05/22/1931, Troy, NY, w, 1958, 2 children **DISCIPLINE** PHILOSOPHY **EDUCATION** Williams Col, BA, 53; Columbia Univ, MA, 60, PhD(philos), 63. **CAREER** Instr philos, PA State Univ, 62-63; from asst prof to assoc prof, 63-71, Prof Philos, Bucknell Univ, 71-83, John Howard Harris Prof, 83-93, Presidential Prof, 87-93, Head Dept, 77-83, 85-90, Bucknell Univ fac fel, 65, 67 & 73; Nat Endowment for Hum fel, 69-70, Emer pro, 93. **HONORS AND AWARDS** Clarke F Ansley Awd, Columbia Univ, 63; Lindback Awd, 69. **MEMBERSHIPS** Soc Phenomenol & Existential Philos; Am Philos

Asn. **RESEARCH** Existentialism and phenomenology; philo psych; philo of hist. **SELECTED PUBLICATIONS** Auth, Emotion in the Thought of Sartre, Columbia Univ, 65; Sartre's words: an existential self-analysis, Psychoanalytic Rev, Vol LV, No 3; Sartre's theory of motivation, J Brit Soc Phenomenol, 5/70; Heidegger's notion of two beginnings, Rev Metaphys, 12/71; Was Freud a follower of Kant?, In: Der Idealismus und seine Gegenwart, Felix Meiner, 76; coauth, Emotion, Brooks/Cole, 77; Heidegger and Sartre, Columbia Univ, 79; Battle of the giants over being, In: The Philosophy of Jean-Paul Sartre, Open Court, 81; ed, The Philosophy of John William Miller, Bucknell Univ, 90; The Familiar and the Strange, in reading Heidegger Blackwell, 92; Seeing a Thig in a Hidden Whole, Heidegger Studies, Vol X, 94. **CONTACT ADDRESS** Dept of Philosophy, Bucknell Univ, Lewisburg, PA 17837.

FELLER, DAVID EDWARD
PERSONAL Born 11/19/1916, New York, NY, m, 1947, 4 children **DISCIPLINE** LABOR LAW **EDUCATION** Harvard Univ, AB, 38, LLB, 41. **CAREER** Lectr law and econ, Law Sch, Univ Chicago, 41-42; law clerk, US Supreme Ct, 48-49; assoc gen counsel, United Steelworkers Am and Cong Indust Orgns, 49-61; gen counsel, United Steelworkers Am, 61-65 and Ind Union Dept, AFL-CIO, 61-66; PROF Emeritus, LAW, UNIV CALIF, BERKEY, Pres, National Academy of Arbitrators, 91-92. **HONORS AND AWARDS** Berkeley Citation **MEMBERSHIPS** Nat Acat Arbitrators; Indust Rel Res Assoc. **SELECTED PUBLICATIONS** Auth, End of the Trilogy--The Declining State of Labor Arbitration, Arbitration J, Vol 48, 93. **CONTACT ADDRESS** Sch of Law, Univ of California, Berkeley, Berkeley, CA 94720.

FELSENFELD, CARL
DISCIPLINE BANKING LAW **EDUCATION** Dartmouth, AB, 48; Columbia, MS, 50, JD, 54. **CAREER** Prof, 83, Fordham Univ. **HONORS AND AWARDS** Rep, UN Comm Intl Trade Law; adv, Nat Conf of Commnr on Uniform State Laws. **SELECTED PUBLICATIONS** Auth, Holder in Due Course, Under Proposed Article 3, 3 NY State Banking Jour 18, 95; Banking Regulation in the United States; 96; Bankruptcy Law, 96; A Comment About Separate Bankruptcy System, 64 Fordham Law Rev 2521, 96. **CONTACT ADDRESS** Law Sch, Fordham Univ, 113 W 60th St, New York, NY 10023.

FELSON, MARCUS
PERSONAL Born 09/15/1947, Cincinnati, OH, m, 1976 **DISCIPLINE** CRIMINAL JUSTICE **EDUCATION** Univ Chicago, BA, 69; Univ Mich, PhD, 73. **CAREER** Asst/Assoc Prov, Univ IL, 72-84; Prof and Assoc Prof, Univ Southern CA, 84-94; Prof, Rutgers Univ, 95-. **RESEARCH** Routine activities and crime, crime trends, and cycles. **SELECTED PUBLICATIONS** Auth, Crime and Everyday Life, Pine Forge Press (Thousand Oaks), 97. **CONTACT ADDRESS** Dept Criminal Justice, Rutgers, The State Univ of New Jersey, Newark, 180 Univ Ave, Newark, NJ 07102. **EMAIL** felson@andromeda.rutgers.edu

FELSTINER, JOHN
PERSONAL Born 07/05/1936, Mt. Vernon, NY, m, 1966, 2 children **DISCIPLINE** LITERARY TRANSLATION, MODERN POETRY; JEWISH LITERATURE **EDUCATION** Harvard Col, AB, 58--Magna Cum Laude and Class Odist, PhD, 65. **RESEARCH** Poetry; Art; Music from The Holocaust; Poetry and the Environment. **SELECTED PUBLICATIONS** Auth, Celan, Paul--Holograms of Darkness, Compar Lit, Vol 45, 93; Translation as Reversion--Celan, Paul Jerusalem Poems, Judaism, Vol 43, 94. **CONTACT ADDRESS** Dept of English, Stanford Univ, 660 Salvatierra St, Stanford, CA 94305-2087. **EMAIL** felstiner@stanford.edu

FELT, JAMES WRIGHT
PERSONAL Born 01/04/1926, Dallas, TX **DISCIPLINE** PHILOSOPHY **EDUCATION** Gonzaga Univ, BA, 49, MA, 50; Alma Col, Calif, STL, 57; St Louis Univ, MS, 61, PhD, 65. **CAREER** Instr math, Loyola Univ, Calif, 50-52; instr, St Ignatius High Sch, San Francisco, 52-53; asst prof, 65-70, chmn dept, 74-80; assoc prof, Santa Clara Univ, 70-. **MEMBERSHIPS** Metaphys Soc Am, vice pres, 00-01, pres, 00-02; Am Philos Assn; Am Cath Philos Assn. **RESEARCH** Process philosophy; metaphysics. **SELECTED PUBLICATIONS** Art, Fatalism and Truth about the Future, The Thomist, 2/92; auth, Making Sense of Your Freedom, Ccornell U Pr, 94; art, Why Possible Worlds Aren't, Rev Met 96; auth, Coming to Be: Toward a Thomistic-Whiteheadian Metaphysics of Becoming, SUNY Press, 00. **CONTACT ADDRESS** Dept of Philosophy, Santa Clara Univ, 500 El Camino Real, Santa Clara, CA 95053-0001. **EMAIL** jfelt@scu.edu

FENNER, G. MICHAEL
DISCIPLINE CONSTITUTIONAL LAW **EDUCATION** Kansas Univ, BA, 65; Univ Missouri-Kans City, JD, 69. **CAREER** Prof; Creighton Univ, 72-; trial atty, Honors Law Grad Prog US Dept Justice, 69-72; reporter, Nebr Supreme Ct Comt on Practice and Procedure. **HONORS AND AWARDS** US Dept Justice Spec Achievement awd, 70; Nebr State Bar Found-(s) Shining Light awd, 92. **MEMBERSHIPS** Nebr Supreme Ct Comt on Practice and Procedure; House Deleg, Nebr Bar Asn; past chp Evidence sec, Asn Amer Law Sch. **SELECTED PUBLICATIONS** Publ in, Creighton Law Rev; Harvard Civil Rights-Civil Liberties Law Rev; Notre Dame Law Rev; Nebr Law Rev; Wash Univ Law Quart; Univ Mo- Kans City Law Rev and Trial. **CONTACT ADDRESS** Sch of Law, Creighton Univ, 2500 California Plaza , Omaha, NE 68178. **EMAIL** fenner@culaw.Creighton.edu

FERBER, PAUL H.
PERSONAL Born 06/15/1950, Montclair, NJ **DISCIPLINE** POLITICAL SCIENCE **EDUCATION** Am Univ, BA, 72; George Wash Univ, PhD, 86. **CAREER** From Lect to Assoc Prof, Rochester Inst of Technol, 81-. **MEMBERSHIPS** Am Polit Sci Asn, The Lexington Group. **SELECTED PUBLICATIONS** Coauth, "Television Interview Shows," J of Broadcasting (77); coauth, "Measuring Legislator-Constituent Congruency: Liquor Legislators and Linkage," J of Polit (80). **CONTACT ADDRESS** Dept Soc Sci, Rochester Inst of Tech, 1 Lomb Memorial Dr, Rochester, NY 14623-5603. **EMAIL** phfgss@rit.edu

FEREJOHN, JOHN
DISCIPLINE LAW **EDUCATION** Stanford Univ, PhD. **CAREER** Vis prof. **RESEARCH** American governmental institutions and practices; British electoral politics; federalism; interrelations of law and politics. **SELECTED PUBLICATIONS** Auth, pubs on social choice theory and the application of game theory to political and legal institutions. **CONTACT ADDRESS** Dept of Political Sci, Stanford Univ, 1 Stanford Univ, Bldg 160, Stanford, CA, Canada 94305-1926.

FEREJOHN, MICHAEL T.
DISCIPLINE PHILOSOPHY **EDUCATION** Univ CA Irvine, PhD, 76. **CAREER** Prof, Duke Univ. **RESEARCH** Ancient philos; metaphysics; epistemology; philosophical logic. **SELECTED PUBLICATIONS** Auth, The Origins of Aristotelian Science, Yale Univ, 91. **CONTACT ADDRESS** Philos Dept, Duke Univ, West Duke Bldg, Durham, NC 27706. **EMAIL** mtf@acpub.duke.edu

FERGUSON, EVERETT
PERSONAL Born 02/18/1933, Montgomery, TX, m, 1956, 3 children **DISCIPLINE** HISTORY, PHILOSOPHY OF RELIGION **EDUCATION** Abilene Christ Univ, BA, 53, MA, 54; Harvard Univ, STB, 56, PhD, 60. **CAREER** Dean, Northeast Christ Jr Coll, 59-62; Prof, Abilene Christ Univ, 62-98. **HONORS AND AWARDS** Leiden, Brill, 98. **MEMBERSHIPS** North Am Patristics Soc; Am Soc Church Hist; Soc Biblical Lit; Ecclesiastical Hist Soc; Asn Int d'Etudes Patristiques; Inst Biblical Res **RESEARCH** Backgrounds Early Christianity; Early church history **SELECTED PUBLICATIONS** Auth, "Backgrounds of Early Christianity," 2nd ed., Grand Rapids, Eerdmans, 93; ed., "Encyclopedia of Early Christianity, 2nd ed., New York, Garland, 97; Auth, "Early Christians Speak," 3rd ed., Abilene, ACU Press, 99 . **CONTACT ADDRESS** Abilene Christian Univ, 609 E N 16th St, Abilene, TX 79601. **EMAIL** Ferguson@bible.acu.edu

FERGUSON, GERRY
DISCIPLINE LAW **EDUCATION** St. Patrick's Univ, BA, 68; Ottawa Univ, LLB, 71; Univ NY, LLM, 72. **CAREER** Asst prof, 73-76; assoc prof, 76-81; prof, 81-; assoc dean, 80-82. **MEMBERSHIPS** Nat Advis Coun Law Comn Can; Int Centre Criminal Law Reform and Criminal Justice policy; Int Soc Reform Criminal Law; Can Bar Asn; Continuing Legal Edu Soc. **RESEARCH** Criminal law; criminal procedure; sentencing; and mental health law. **SELECTED PUBLICATIONS** Coauth, Canadian Criminal Jury Instructions. **CONTACT ADDRESS** Fac of Law, Univ of Victoria, PO Box 2400, Victoria, BC, Canada V8W 3H7. **EMAIL** gferguso@uvic.ca

FERGUSON, KATHY E.
PERSONAL Born 11/16/1950, Anderson, IN, m, 1986, 2 children **DISCIPLINE** POLITICAL SCIENCE **EDUCATION** Purdue Univ, BA, 72; Univ Minn, PhD, 76. **CAREER** Prof, Siena Col, 76-85; Dir, Women & Minority Studies, Siena Col, 84-85; prof, Univ Haw, 85-, chair, Dept of Political Sci, 94-97. **HONORS AND AWARDS** Chair, Dept of Political Sci, Univ Haw, 94-97; Distinguished Alumna of the Year, Political Sci, Univ Haw, 94; Fulbright grant to Israel, 99. **MEMBERSHIPS** APSA, NWSA, WPSA. **RESEARCH** Feminist theory, political philosophy. **SELECTED PUBLICATIONS** Auth, The Man Question: Visions of Subjectivity in Feminist Theory, Univ Calif Press (93); auth, Kibbutz Journal: Reflections on Gender, Race & Militarism in Israel, Trilogy Books (95); coauth with Phyllis Turnbull, Oh, Say, Can You See? The Semiotics of the Military in Hawaii, Univ Minn Press (99). **CONTACT ADDRESS** Dept Political Sci, Univ of Hawaii, Honolulu Comm Col, 640 Soc Scis Bldg, Honolulu, HI 96822. **EMAIL** kferguson@hawaii.edu

FERGUSON, KENNETH D.
DISCIPLINE LAW **EDUCATION** Drake Univ, BA; Coburn Sch Law, JD. **CAREER** Law clerk, US Bankruptcy Court; asst prof **RESEARCH** Bankruptcy; corporate law. **SELECTED PUBLICATIONS** Auth, Repose or Not? Informal Objections To Claims of Exemptions After Taylor v. Freeland, Okla Law Rev, 97; Does Payment by Check Constitute a Transfer upon Delivery of Payment?, Am Bank Law J, 90; Discourse and Discharge: Linguistic Analysis and Abuse of the 'Exemption Declaration' Process in Bankruptcy, Am Bank Law J, 96. **CONTACT ADDRESS** Law Dept, Univ of Missouri, Kansas City, 5100 Rockhill Rd, Kansas City, MO 64110-2499. **EMAIL** fergusonk@umkc.edu

FERGUSON, KENNETH G.
PERSONAL Born 10/05/1948, Beckley, WV, s **DISCIPLINE** PHILOSOPHY **EDUCATION** Univ Rochester, PhD, philos, 85. **CAREER** Visiting asst prof, Ariz State Univ, 86-87; visiting lectr, Appalachian State Univ, 87-88; visiting asst prof, East Carolina Univ, 88-93, 95-98. **HONORS AND AWARDS** Dissertation Essay Award, 85. **MEMBERSHIPS** Amer Philos Asn. **RESEARCH** Philosophical logic; Evolutionary, and Business ethics. **SELECTED PUBLICATIONS** Abstracts, Proceedings and Addresses of the American Philosophical Association, 85, 87, 89, 92; auth, Truth Conditions for Might Counterfactuals, The Review of Metaphysics, 40, 483-94, 87; rev, History and Philosophy of Logic; article, An Intervention into the Flew/Fogelin Debate, Hume Studies, 18, 105-12, 92; article, Existing by Convention, Relig Studies, 28, 185-194, 92; article, Equivocation in the Surprise Exam Paradox, The Southern Jour of Philos, 29, 291-302, 91; auth, "Semantic and Structural problems in Evolutionary Ethics, Biology and Philosophy, (01), 69-84; auth, "Caller ID--Whose Privacy Is It, Anyway?," Journal of Business ethics, (01), 227-237. **CONTACT ADDRESS** Philosophy Dept., East Carolina Univ, Greenville, NC 27858. **EMAIL** fergusonk@mail.ecu.edu

FERGUSON, MARIANNE
PERSONAL Born 12/25/1932, Rochester, NY **DISCIPLINE** RELIGIOUS STUDIES, THEOLOGY **EDUCATION** State Univ NYork Buffalo, BSEd, 53; St Bonaventure Univ, MA, 68; State Univ NYork Buffalo, MS, 74; McMaster Univ, PhD(relig), 80. **CAREER** Teacher elem schs, Dioceses Buffalo & Brooklyn, 55-61; teacher relig & hist, De Sales Cath Hish Sch, 61-64; instr relig, Damon Col, 68-74; asst prof to assoc prof Relig Studies, State Univ NY Col Buffalo, 75-, lectr adult educ, Diocese Buffalo, 68-; coordr relig educ, Newman Ctr, State Univ NY Col Buffalo, 68-; adj prof psychol educ, Christ King Sem, 68-79; lectr, Head Start teacher training workshops, 75-76. **MEMBERSHIPS** Col Theol Soc (secy, 69-70); Soc Sci Study Relig; Relig Educ Asn; Cath Campus Ministries. **RESEARCH** Attitude of college students toward religion; staying power of religious denominations; women in religion. **SELECTED PUBLICATIONS** Auth, Must Religious Flee the World, Cord Mag, 3/66; Influence of Religious Education on Religious Commitment, Catechist Mag, 11-12/81; Influence of Private Schools on Religious Committment, Private Sch Quart, spring 82; auth, Religious Education "What Eastern Religions Teach Us About Religious Education", auth, "Catholic Attitudes Toward Sexuality" in Human Sexuality, Garland Press, 94; auth, Women and Religion, Prentice Hall, 95; Encyclopedia references, Sage Publ; auth, Woman and Religion, Prentiss Hall, 95; auth,"Network in Women's Interests Groups, Salem Press, 95; auth, "Liberation Theology" in Encyclopedia of Multiculturalism, Salem Press, 95; auth, "An Approach to Ethics Utilizing the Experience of Women", 96; auth, Standing on the Primises, "Biblical Interpretations that Influence promise Keepers", Pilgrims Press, 97; auth, "Women Church" and Women in Judaism" in Women Issues, Salem Press, 97; auth, "Catholicism and Families" In Family Life, Salem Press, 97; auth, Christianity an Introduction, Waveland Press, 00. **CONTACT ADDRESS** Dept of Philos & Relig Studies, SUNY, Col at Buffalo, 1300 Elmwood Ave, Buffalo, NY 14222-1095. **EMAIL** fergusmc@bscmail.buffalostate.edu

FERGUSON, PAUL
PERSONAL Born 06/20/1938, Elgin, IL, m, 1958, 8 children **DISCIPLINE** THEOLOGY **EDUCATION** Univ Tulsa, BS, 62; Wheaton Col, MA, 65, MDiv, 70; Chicago Theolog Sem, PhD, 88; Hebrew Univ, Post doc, 88-94, post doc, Univ of Chicago, 94-00. **CAREER** Prof, Christian Life Col, 84-; prof, SIM Cols, 96-98; prof, ICI Univ, 96-. **MEMBERSHIPS** Nat Educ Asn; Chicago Society Biblical Res; Society Int Missionaries. **RESEARCH** Minor prophets; Elijah-Elisha; comparitive semitics; Jonah; Pentateuch; Daniel. **SELECTED PUBLICATIONS** Auth, Baker's Encyclopedia of Biblical Theology, 95; auth, Biblical Hebrew with Jonah-Stroke by Stroke, 95; auth, Biblical Languages for Fun and Profit, 97; auth, The OT: What's in it For Me, 98; auth, art, Nebuchadnezzar, Gilgamesh and the Babylonian Job, 98. **CONTACT ADDRESS** 577 Glenwood Ave, Elgin, IL 60120.

FERGUSON, WILLIAM DEAN
PERSONAL Born 07/31/1928, Shinglehouse, PA, m, 1955, 2 children **DISCIPLINE** LAW **EDUCATION** Lebanon Valley Col, AB, 49; Cornell Univ, LLB, 55; Univ Va, SJD(law), 75. **CAREER** Assoc, Bliss & Bouch, Albany, NY, 57-62; asst prof law, Univ SDak, 62-63; from asst prof to prof, 63-68, Prof Law, 68-98, Prof Emer, Emory Univ, 98-. **HONORS AND AWARDS** Emory Williams Distinguished Teacher Awd,

Emory Univ. **MEMBERSHIPS** Nat Acad Arbitrators **RESEARCH** Procedure **SELECTED PUBLICATIONS** Auth, Pendent personal jurisdiction in federal courts, Villanova Law Rev, 65; The Statutes of Limitation Savings Statutes, Michie Co, 78. **CONTACT ADDRESS** Sch Law, Emory Univ, 1364 Clifton Rd N E, Atlanta, GA 30322-0001. **EMAIL** lawwdf@law.emory.edu

FERM, DEANE WILLIAM
PERSONAL Born 05/22/1927, Lebanon, PA, m, 1949, 4 children **DISCIPLINE** RELIGION **EDUCATION** Col Wooster, BA, 49; Yale Univ, BD, 52, MA, 53, MDiv, 53, PhD, 54. **CAREER** Dir sch relig, Mont State Univ, 54-59; Dean, Col Chapel, Mt Holyoke Col, 59-, Asst dir, Danforth Found, spring, 58; guest preacher & lectr, cols & univs; vis lectr, Smtih Col, 60-61, 62-63; Danforth Found campus ministry grant, 65-66; Poulson fel, Am Scand Found, 65-66. **MEMBERSHIPS** Nat Asn Col & Univ Chaplains. **RESEARCH** Religion in higher education; contemporary theology. **SELECTED PUBLICATIONS** Auth, Responsible Sexuality Now, Seabury, 71; William James: Moralism, the will to believe and theism, Relig in Life, autumn 72; Honest to Jesus, 3/72 & Taking God seriously, 5/73, Christian Century; Reflections of a college chaplain, Theol Today, 4/76; Protestant liberalism reaffirmed, Christian Century, 5/76; The women's movement and the teaching of religion, Theol Today, 1/78. **CONTACT ADDRESS** Dean of Col Chapel, Mount Holyoke Col, South Hadley, MA 01075.

FERM, ROBERT L.
PERSONAL Born Wooster, OH, m, 1952, 2 children **DISCIPLINE** RELIGION **EDUCATION** Col Wooster, BA, 52; Uale Univ, BD, 55, MA, 56, PhD 58. **CAREER** From instr to asst prof relig, Pomona Col, 58-63, from John Knox McLean assoc prof to John Knox McLean prof, 63-69, chmn dept, 60-69; prof relig & chmn dept, 69-, Tillinghast Prof of Rel, 88, Middlebury Col; Haynes Found fel, 61; assoc prof, 63-67, prof, 67-69, Claremont Grad Sch; vis assoc prof, Midddlebury Col, 64-65; Am Coun Learned Soc grant-in-aid, 77-78; Emer, Tillinghnst Prof, Middlebury Col, 00. **HONORS AND AWARDS** ACLS/Ford Fel, 83; Dew Endowment Fel, 98-99. **MEMBERSHIPS** Am Soc Church Hist; Am Studies Assn; Am Acad Relig. **RESEARCH** American and historical theology. **SELECTED PUBLICATIONS** Ed, Issues in American Protestantism: A Documentary History, Anchor Book, 59; auth, Readings in the History of Christian Thought, Holt Rinehart Winston, 64; auth, Jonathan Edwards the Younger: 1745-1801, A Colonial Pastor, Eerdmans, 76; auth, Piety Purity Plenty: Images of Protestantism in American, Fortress, 91; **CONTACT ADDRESS** Dept of Relig, Middlebury Col, Middlebury, VT 05753-6001.

FERNANDEZ, EDUARDO
PERSONAL Born 04/28/1958, El Paso, TX, s **DISCIPLINE** RELIGION **EDUCATION** Loyola Univ of the South, BA, 80; Jesuit Sch Theol Berk, MDiv, 91; Univ Tex Austin, MA, 86; Gregorian Pontifical Univ, Rome, STD. **CAREER** RC Jesuit Priest, 92; Jesuit School of Theo, asst prof, 98-. **HONORS AND AWARDS** ASN, 80; PKP, 85; Hispanic Theol Inst, Postdoc res Grant, 97 **MEMBERSHIPS** ACH TUS; ILH; AAR; JHMC. **RESEARCH** Hist art and cult Mex/Southwest; missiology; ecumenism; dialogue between culture and religion **SELECTED PUBLICATIONS** Auth, La Cosecha: Harvesting Contemporary US Hispanic Theology, 00; Celebrating Sacraments in a Hispanic Context, coauth; Reading the Bible in Spanish, 94; US Hispanic Catholics: Trends and Works, in: Rev Relig, 94; Reflexiones Sobre la Realidid de los Hispanos en los Estados Unidos: Sombras y Luces, in : Reflex Catequ: Encuentro de San Antonio TX, 95; Seven Tips on the Pastorial CARE of Catholics of Mexican Decent in the United States, in: Chicago Stud, 97; Educating for Inculturation: Why the Arts Cannot Be Ignored, in: Future Arts Wor and Relig Edu, ed Doug Adams and Michael E, Moynahan. **CONTACT ADDRESS** Jesuit Sch of Theol, Berkeley, 1735 LeRoy Ave, Berkeley, CA 94709. **EMAIL** efernand@jstb.edu

FERRAIOLO, WILLIAM D.
PERSONAL Born 02/12/1969, Lyndhurst, NJ, s **DISCIPLINE** PHILOSOPHY **EDUCATION** Univ Okla, PhD, 97. **CAREER** Instr, philos, San Joaquin Delta Community Col, 97-. **HONORS AND AWARDS** Kenneth R. Merrill Teaching award, Univ Okla, 96-97. **MEMBERSHIPS** Amer Philos Asn; Central States Philos Asn. **RESEARCH** Realism & relativism; Abortion; Problem of evil. **SELECTED PUBLICATIONS** Auth, Black's Twin-Globe Counterexample, Southwestern Philos Rev, 97; auth, Individualism and Descartes, Teorema, 96; auth, "The Heaven Problem," Southwest Philos Rev, 99; auth, "Death: A Propitious Misfortune," Bridges, 00; auth, "Metaphysical Realism," Dialogos (forthcoming). **CONTACT ADDRESS** 8724 Lianna Ct, Apt. #3, Stockton, CA 95209-1851. **EMAIL** bferraiolo@sjdccd.cc.ca.us

FERRARA, LOUIS F.
PERSONAL Born 01/27/1933, Brooklyn, NY, s **DISCIPLINE** THEOLOGY **EDUCATION** Wagner College, BA 54; Yale Divinity School Berkeley, STM 57. **CAREER** George Mercer Jr Memorial Sch of Theology, Diocese of Long Island, Episcopal Priest and Teacher, 40 Years. **HONORS AND AWARDS** Res Fell Yale Div Sch. **MEMBERSHIPS** AAR; SBL. **RESEARCH** Biblical Studies; Hebrew Bible. **SELECTED PUBLICATIONS** Auth, Various Diocesan and Parish Publications. **CONTACT ADDRESS** Memorial Sch of Theology, 65 4th St., Garden City, NY 11530.

FERRARIN, ALFREDO
PERSONAL Born 10/07/1960, Thiene, Italy, m, 1996, 2 children **DISCIPLINE** PHILOSOPHY **EDUCATION** Scuola Normale Superiore, Pisa Italy, PhD, 90 **CAREER** Asst Prof, 95-pres, Boston Univ **RESEARCH** Aristotle; Kant; Hegel **SELECTED PUBLICATIONS** Auth, Hegel interprete di Aristotele, Pisa, ETS, 90; auth, Hegel and Aristotle, Cambridge Univ Pr, 00; auth, Artificio, Desiderio, Considerazione Di Se, Pisa, Ets. 01. **CONTACT ADDRESS** Dept of Philos, Boston Univ, 745 Commonwealth Ave, Boston, MA 02215. **EMAIL** ferrarin@bu.edu

FERST, BARRY JOEL
PERSONAL Born 01/13/1946, Chicago, IL, m, 1979, 1 child **DISCIPLINE** PHILOSOPHY OF SCIENCE & RELIGION **EDUCATION** Univ IL, BA, 68; Univ KS, MA, 69; Tulane Univ, PhD(philos), 76. **CAREER** Asst prof Philos, 80-94, PROF, CARROLL COL, 95-. **MEMBERSHIPS** Am Philos Asn. **RESEARCH** Roman science and religion. **CONTACT ADDRESS** Philos Dept, Carroll Col, Montana, 1601 N Benton Ave, Helena, MT 59625-0002. **EMAIL** bferst@carrol.edu

FESMIRE, STEVEN A.
PERSONAL Born 11/06/1967, Memphis, TN **DISCIPLINE** PHILOSOPHY **EDUCATION** So Ill Univ, Carbondale, PhD, 94. **CAREER** Adj prof, 93-94; asst prof, E Tenn St Univ, 95-99; visiting scholar, Dartmouth Col, 00; visiting asst prof, Siena Col, 00-01. **HONORS AND AWARDS** Ford Found Fel, Millsapps Col, 89-90; Summa cum laude, Millsapps Col, 90; Phi Beta Kappa; Hon mention for Douglas Greenlee Prize, Soc for Advancement of Am Philos, 92; Doctoral fel, 92-93, Diss res fel, So Ill Univ, Carbondale, 93-94. **MEMBERSHIPS** APA; Soc for the Advancement of Am Philos. **RESEARCH** Am philos, especially pragmatism; ethics; theory of metaphor. **SELECTED PUBLICATIONS** Auth, Embodied Reason, Kinesis, vol 20, no 1, 93; auth, Aerating the Mind: The Metaphor of Mental Functioning as Bodily Functioning, Metaphor and Symbolic Activity, vol 9, no 1, 94; auth, What is Cognitive About Cognitive Linguistics?, Metaphor and Symbolic Activity, vol 9, no 2, 94; auth, Educating the Moral Artist: Dramatic Rehearsal in Moral Education, Stud in Philos & Ed, vol 13, no 3-4, 94 Ed & the New Scholarship on Dewey, Kluwer Press, 94/95; auth, Dramatic Rehearsal and the Moral Artist: A Deweyan Theory of Moral Understanding, Transactions of the Charles S. Pierce Soc, vol 31, no 3, 95; auth, The Social Basis of Character: An Ecological Humanist Approach, in Practical Ethics, Blackwell Press, 96; auth, "Morality As Art: Dewey, Metaphor, and Moral Imagination," Transactions of the Charles S. Peirce Soc, Vol. 35, No. 3, 99; auth, "Philosophy Disrobed: Lakoff and Johnson's Critique of Western Philosophy," in The Journal of Speculative Philosophy, 01; auth, "Ecological Humanism: A Moral Image for Our Emotive Culture," The Humanist, 01. **CONTACT ADDRESS** Dept of Philosophy, Siena Col, Loudonville, NY 12211-1462. **EMAIL** sfesmire@siena.edu

FETZER, JAMES HENRY
PERSONAL Born 12/06/1940, Pasadena, CA, m, 1977, 4 children **DISCIPLINE** HISTORY AND PHILOSOPHY OF SCIENCE **EDUCATION** Princeton Univ, AB, 62; Ind Univ, MA, 68; Ind Univ, PhD, 70. **CAREER** Asst prof, Univ Ky, 70-77; vis assoc prof, Univ Va, 77-78; vis assoc prof, Univ Cincinnati, 78-79; vis NSF res prof, Univ Cincinnati, 79-80; vis lectr, Univ NC at Chapel Hill, 80-81; vis assoc prof, New Col, Univ South Fla, 81-83; MacArthur vis distinguished prof, New Col, Univ South Fla, 83-84; adjunct prof, Univ South Fla, Fall, 84-85; vis prof, Univ Va, Spring, 84-85; prof, Univ Minn, Duluth, 87-96; dept chair, Univ Minn, Duluth, 88-92; dir, Master of Liberal Studies Program, Univ Minn, Duluth, 96-; distinguished McKnight univ prof, Univ Minn, 96-. **HONORS AND AWARDS** McKnight Endowment Fel, Univ Minn; Summer Faculty Res Fel, Univ Minn; Outstanding Res Awd, Univ Minn; Lansdowne Lectr, Univ Victoria; Pres, Minn Philosophical Society; Vice-pres, Minn Philosophical Society; Medal of the Univ of Helsinki; Summer Fac Res Fel, Univ Minn; Postdoctoral Fel in Computer Sci, Wright State Univ; Postdoctoral Res Fel, Nat Sci Found; Distinguished Teaching Awd, Univ Ky; Summer Fac Res Fellow, 72; Graduate Res Asst, Ind Univ; Fel of the Fac, Colombia Univ; NDEA Title IV Fel, Ind Univ; The Dickinson Prize, Princeton Univ; Magna Cum Laude, Princeton; res scholar, New Col, Univ South Fla, 85-86. **MEMBERSHIPS** Philos of Sci Asn; Am Philosophical Asn; Asn for Computing Machinery; Human Behavior and Evolution Society; Int Society for Human Ethnology; Am Asn of Univ Profs; Society for Machines and Mentality; Am Asn for the Advanc of Sci. **RESEARCH** Philosophy of science; computer science; artificial intelligence; cognitive science. **SELECTED PUBLICATIONS** Auth, Philosophy of Science, Paragon House Publ, 93; coauth, Glossary of Epistemology/Philosophy of Science, Paragon House Publ, 93; coauth, Glossary of Cognitive Science, Paragon House Publ, 93; ed, Foundations of Philosophy of Science, Paragon House Publ, 93; co-ed, Program Verification Fundamental Issues in Computer Science, Kluwer Academic Publ, 93; auth, Philosophy and Cognitive Science, Paragon House Publ, 96; coauth, Assassination Science: Experts Speak Out on the Death of JFK, Catfeet Press, 98, co-ed, The New Theory of Reference: Kripke, Marcusk, and Its Origins, Kluwer Academic Publ, 98. **CONTACT ADDRESS** Dept of Philosophy, Univ of Minnesota, Duluth, Duluth, MN 55812. **EMAIL** jfetzer@d.umn.edu

FEUERHAHN, RONALD R.
PERSONAL Born 12/01/1937, Cape Girardeau, MO, m, 1963, 3 children **DISCIPLINE** HISTORICAL THEOLOGY **EDUCATION** Concordia Sr Col, BA, 59; Concordia Sem, MDiv, 63; Univ Cambridge, England, MPhil, 80; PhD, 92. **CAREER** Pastor, St. David's, Cardiff, Wales, 64-70; pastor, Resurrection, Cambridge, Eng, 70-77; preceptor, Westfield House, Cambridge, England, 77-86; asst prof, 86-95, assoc prof hist theol, 95- , asst chaplain and coord musical and cultural activities, 90-92, acting dean of chapel, 98, Concordia Sem; contributing ed, Logia, 92-; assoc ed, Concordia Hist Inst Quarterly, 96-; vis prof, Urals State Univ, Dept of Arts and Culture, Yekaterinbury, Russia, 98-99; vis prof, Russian Acad of the State Service for the Pres of the Russian Federation, The Urals Acad of the State Service, Dept of Sociology and Psychology of the State Service, Yekaterinburg, Russia, 99; ELCA, LCMS Discussion Panel, 99-00; archivist, Concordia Seminary, St. Louis, MO, 99-. **MEMBERSHIPS** Cambridge Theol Soc; Soc for Liturgial Stud (Gr Britain); Societas Liturgica; Luther Acad; Lutheran Missiology Soc; Am Soc of Church Hist; Luthern Hist Conf; Governing Board, Lutheran Quarterly, 96-; Commission on Worship, LCMS; Liturgy Comm of the Lutheran Hymnal Project, Commission on Music, LCMS (chairman, 98-); Seminary Relations Standing Committee of the Int Lutheran Council (chairman, 00-). **RESEARCH** Liturgy and worship; ecumenical movement; law and Gospel; Hermann Sasse; movements of thought (Pietism, Rationalism. **SELECTED PUBLICATIONS** Co-ed, Scripture and the Church: Selected Essays of Hermann Sasse, Concordia Seminary, 95; auth, A Bibliography of Dr. Hermann Sasse, Scarecrow, 95; auth, "Ne Desperamus," in Logia, Reformation, 95; auth, Hermann Sasse and North American Lutheranism," in Logia, (Reformation, 95); auth, Hermann Sasse: Confessional Ecumenist, Lutherische Theologie und Kirche, 95; auth, Hermann Sasse-Gesetz und Evangelium in der Geshcichte, in Diestelemann, ed, Eintrachtig Lehren: Festrschrift fuer Bischof Dr. Jobst Schone, Heinrich Harms, 97; contrib, Hymnal Supplement, 98, St. Louis: Concordia, 98; contrib, Hymnal Supplement 98, Handbook, St. Louis: Concorida, 98. **CONTACT ADDRESS** Concordia Sem, 801 DeMun Ave, Saint Louis, MO 63105. **EMAIL** feuerhahnr@csl.edu

FEWER, COLIN D.
PERSONAL Born 08/26/1969, Montreal, PQ, Canada **DISCIPLINE** ENGLISH, PHILOSOPHY **EDUCATION** Univ Manitoba, BA, 91; Penn State Univ, MA, 94; PhD, 01. **CAREER** Lectr, Penn State Univ, 99-00; asst prof, Purdue Univ Calumet, 00-. **MEMBERSHIPS** MLA; MAA. **RESEARCH** Chaucer; 15th-century English literature. **SELECTED PUBLICATIONS** Auth, "The 'fygure' of the Market: The N-Town Cycle and East Anglian Lay Piety," Philo Qtly (98). **CONTACT ADDRESS** Eng Dept, Purdue Univ, Calumet, 2200 169th Street, Hammond, IN 46323-2094. **EMAIL** fewer@calumet.edu

FIDELER, PAUL ARTHUR
PERSONAL Born 05/16/1936, Passaic, NJ, m, 1963, 2 children **DISCIPLINE** BRITISH AND EUROPEAN HISTORY, WESTERN POLITICAL THOUGHT, WORLD PHILOSOPHIES **EDUCATION** St Lawrence Univ, BA, 58; Brandeis Univ, MA, 62, PhD(hist), 71. **CAREER** Instr, Framingham State Col, 64-68; asst prof to prof hist, 69-91, prof hist and humanities, Lesley Col, 73-; adv ed, Brit Studies Monitor. **HONORS AND AWARDS** Fel in NEH Summer Seminars and Inst, 74, 76, 77, 84, 89; Res Fel, The Folger Shakespeare Library, spring 90; Am Coun of Learned Soc Fel in Humanities Curriculum Development and Vis Schol, Harvard Univ, 92-93. **MEMBERSHIPS** AAUP; AHA; New Eng Hist Asn (pres 87-88); Am Philos Asn; Conf for the Study of Political Thought; N Am Conf on Brit Studies; NE Conf on Brit Studies (pres 91-93). **RESEARCH** Poor relief policy and political theory in early modern England; historiography and humanities methodologies; character, values, ethics, and justice in the curriculum, K-16. **SELECTED PUBLICATIONS** Auth, Christian Humanism and Poor Law Reform in Early Tudor England, Societas, fall 74; Have Historians Lost Their Perspective on the Past?, Change, Jan/Feb 84; coed, Political Thought and the Tudor Commonwealth London and New York: Routledge, 92; Toward a Curriculum of Hope: The Essential Role of Humanities Scholarship in Public School Teaching, Am Coun of Learned Soc, Occasional Paper, No. 23, 94; Rescuing Youth Culture: Cultivating Children's Natural Abilities as Philosophers, Lesley Mag, winter 94; coauth, Autobiography in the Classroom: A Triptych, Teaching the Humanities, spring 95; auth, Societas, Civitas and Early Elizabethan Poverty Relief, In: State, Sovereigns and Society: Essays in Early Modern English History, St. Martins, 98. **CONTACT ADDRESS** Humanities Faculty, Lesley Col, 29 Everett St, Cambridge, MA 02138-2790. **EMAIL** pfideler@lesley.edu

FIELD, A. J.
PERSONAL Born 04/17/1949, Boston, MA, m, 1982, 2 children **DISCIPLINE** ECONOMICS **EDUCATION** Harvard Univ, BA 70; London Sch Econ, MSc 71; Univ Calif Berk, PhD 74. **CAREER** Stanford Univ, asst prof 74-82; Santa Clara Univ, assoc prof, prof, 82-88, Michel and Mary Orradre Prof 92-, actg acad vpres 86-87, actg dean 96-97. **HONORS AND AWARDS** Allen Nevins Prize; NSF Gnt; Inst Adv Stud. **MEMBERSHIPS** AEA; EHA; Phi Beta Kappa; Beta Gamma Sigma; Cliometrics Soc. **RESEARCH** Economics of technological and institutional change; macro economic history and policy; micro economics and rationality. **SELECTED PUBLICATIONS** Auth, French Optical Telegraphy 1793-1855: Hardware Software Administration, Tech and Culture, 94; auth, Douglas North, entry in: Handbook on Institutional and Evolutionary Economics, Edward Elgar, 94; auth, The Relative Productivity of American Distribution, 1869-1992, Research In Econ Hist, JAI Press, 96; Auth, The Telegraphic Transmission of Financial Asset Prices and Orders to Trade: Implications for Economics Growth Trading Volume and Securities Market Regulation, Research in Econ Hist, JAI Press, 98; auth, Sunk Costs Water Over the Dam and Other Liquid Parables, K. Dennis, ed, Rationality in Economics: Alternative Perspectives, Boston Kluwer-Nijhoff, 98; auth, Alturistically Inclined? Evolutionary Theory, the Behavioral Sciences and the Origin of Complex Social Organization, Ann Arbor, Univ Mich Pr, 01. **CONTACT ADDRESS** Dept of Economics, Santa Clara Univ, 500 El Camino Real, Santa Clara, CA 95053-0385. **EMAIL** afield@scu.edu

FIELD, HARTRY
PERSONAL Born 11/30/1946, Boston, MA, 1 child **DISCIPLINE** PHILOSOPHY **EDUCATION** Univ Wis, BA, 67; Harvard Univ, MA, 68; PhD, 72. **CAREER** Asst prof, Princeton Univ, 70-76; assoc prof, Univ Southern Calif, 76-81; full prof, 81-91; prof, City Univ NY, 91-97; prof, 97-. **HONORS AND AWARDS** Fel from the Nat Sci Found; NEH; guggenheim fel. **MEMBERSHIPS** Am Philos Asn; Philos of Sci Asn. **RESEARCH** Epistemology; Metaphysics; Philosophy of mathematics; theory of truth, objectivity, a priori knowledge, causation. **SELECTED PUBLICATIONS** Auth, Science Without Numbers, 80; auth, Mathematics and Modality, 89; ed, "Which Undecidable Mathematical Sentences Have Determinate Truth Values?, in H. Garth Dales and Gianluigi Oliveri, Truth in Mathematics, Oxford Univ Press, 98; auth, "Mathematical Objectivity and Mathematical Objects," in S. Laurence and C. Macdonald, ed., Comtempoary Readings in the Foundations of Megaphysics, Basil Blackwell, (98): 387-403; auth, "Some Thoughts of Radical Indeterminacy," The Monist, vol. 81, (98): 253-73; auth, "Epistemological Nonfactualism and the A Prioricity of Logic," Philosophical Studies, vol. 92, (98): 1-24; auth, "Deflating the Conservativeness Argument," The Journal of Philosophy, (99): 533-40; ed, "A Prioricity as an Evaluative Notion," to appear in P. Boghossian and C. Peacocke, eds., New Essays on the A Priori, Oxford Univ Press, 00; auth, "Indeterminacy, Degree of Belief, and Excluded Middle," Nous (00): 1-30; auth, Truth and the Absence of Fact, Oxford 01. **CONTACT ADDRESS** Fac of Arts & Sci, New York Univ, Main, 100 Wash Sq E, New York, NY 10003. **EMAIL** hf18@nyu.edu

FIELD, RICHARD
DISCIPLINE PHILOSOPHY **EDUCATION** SUNY Plattsburgh, BA, 79; Mich State Univ, MA, 81; Southern IL Univ, PhD, 87. **CAREER** Instr, Southern IL Univ, 89-90; vis asst prof, Univ of Minn, 90-91; vis asst prof to adj prof, Western Ky Univ, 91-93; asst prof, Northwest Miss State Univ, 93-. **HONORS AND AWARDS** Phi Kappa Phi, 81; Diss Res Awd, Southern IL Univ, 84-85; StudyWeb Acad Excellence Awd, 99. **RESEARCH** Early modern philosophy, American philosophy, value theory. **SELECTED PUBLICATIONS** Auth, "Descartes Proof of the Existence of Matter", Mind 93, (85): 244-49; auth, "Descartes on the Material Falsity of Ideas", Philos Rev 102, (93): 309-33; auth, "St Louis Hegelians" and "John Dewey", Internet Encyclopedia of Philos, 96; auth, "Sigmund Freud" and "Franz Kafka", Encyclopedia of Modern East Europe, 1815-1989, (forthcoming); auth, "Common Values", The World in Perspective: Essays in Honor of Lewis Hahn, (forthcoming); auth, "Textual Commentaries with the Use of Layers", APA Newsletter on Philos and Computers 99, (forthcoming). **CONTACT ADDRESS** Dept Humanities, Northwest Missouri State Univ, 800 University Dr, Maryville, MO 64468-6015. **EMAIL** rfield@mail.nwmissouri.edu

FIELD, THOMAS G., JR.
PERSONAL Born 06/08/1942, Morgantown, WV, m, 1964, 2 children **DISCIPLINE** LAW **EDUCATION** WVU, AB, 64; JD, 69; NYU, LLM, 70. **CAREER** Asst Prof, Ohio N Univ, 70-72; Vis Prof, W New Eng Sch of Law, 74; Assoc Prof to Prof, Franklin Pierce Law Center, 73-. **HONORS AND AWARDS** Food and Drug Law Fel, NYU, 69-70; Von Humboldt Fel, Max Planck Inst, 81. **MEMBERSHIPS** Am Asn Adv of Sci; Consumers Union. **RESEARCH** Intellectual property; Risk regulation. **SELECTED PUBLICATIONS** Auth, "Pharmaceuticals and Intellectual Property," IDEA, 90; auth, "Arbitration Exercises," Cntr Computer-Asst Legal Instn, 90; auth, "Intellectual Property--some Practical and Legal Fundamentals," IDEA, 94; ed, Which Scientist Do You Believe?, RISK, 95; auth, "Pursuing Transparency through Science Courts," RISK, 00; auth, "Making the Most of Commercial Global Domains," IDEA, 01. **CONTACT ADDRESS** Dept Law, Franklin Pierce Law Ctr, 2 White St, Concord, NH 03301. **EMAIL** tfield@fplc.edu

FIELDER, JOHN H.
DISCIPLINE PHILOSOPHY **EDUCATION** Tulane Univ, BS; Univ Tex-Austin, PhD, 70. **CAREER** Prof, Villanova Univ. **HONORS AND AWARDS** Consultant grant from the Nat Endowment for the Humanities, through grants from, Asn Amer Col, Exxon Educ Found; Villanova Fac Summer Res grants, 91; shared grant, Asn for Continuing Higher Educ Res grant; Sears-Roebuck Found Tchg Excellence and Campus Leadership awd, 90; adj sr fel, Leonard Davis Inst Health Econ, Univ Pa; develop and taught courses in, prof ethics for engineers, health care prof, and bus managers; develop, ethical decision making component of the grad course, admin decision making. **MEMBERSHIPS** Amer Philos Assoc; Soc for Philos and Technol, Newsl Ed, 89-93; bd dir, Airline Safety Adv Panel, Airline Passengers Assoc N Am, 90-92; assoc ed, Consulting Medtronic, Inc. **RESEARCH** Professional ethics, case studies in technology and society, and ethical decision making. **SELECTED PUBLICATIONS** Auth, Abusive Peer Review and Health Care Reform, Health Care Crisis: The Search for Answers, Frederick, MD: Univ Publ Gp, 95; The Shiley Heart Valve - Continued, Engineering in Med and Biology, Vol 13, 94; Discarding Doctors, Engineering in Med and Biology, Vol 14, 95; How well do Medical Devices Work, Engineering in Med and Biology, Vol 13, 94 & Ethical Experts and Dr. Ethics, Engineering in Medicine and Biology, Vol 12, 94; coauth, The Ford Pinto Case: A Study in Applied Ethics, Technology, and Society, Albany, NY: SUNY Press, 94; Analyzing Ethical Problems in Medical Products: The Role of Conflicting Ethical Theories, Clinical Res and Regulatory Aff, Vol 11, 94; But Doctor, It's My Hip!: The Fate of Failed Medical Devices, Kennedy Inst Ethics J Vol 5, 95; The Ethics and Politics of Auto Regulation, in The Ford Pinto Case: A Study in Applied Ethics, Technology, and Society, Albany, NY: SUNY Press, 94. **CONTACT ADDRESS** Dept of Philosophy, Villanova Univ, 800 Lancaster Ave, Villanova, PA 19085-1692.

FIELDS, STEPHEN M.
PERSONAL Born 06/19/1952, Baltimore, MD **DISCIPLINE** THEOLOGY **EDUCATION** Loyola Col, BA, 74; Oxford Univ, BA, 77; MA 83; Fordham Univ, MA, 81; Weston Jesuit Sch Theol, M Div, 86; STL, 87; Yale Univ, PhD, 93. **CAREER** Vis instr, St Josephs Univ, 81-83; asst prof, Georgetown Univ, 93-00; assoc prof, 00-. **HONORS AND AWARDS** Mem Soc Jesus; Ord Deacon, 85; Priest, 86; Vis Prof, Bannan Found, 96-97; Fulbright Awdee, 91-92. **MEMBERSHIPS** AAR; CTSA. **RESEARCH** Philosophy of religion; philosophical theory. **SELECTED PUBLICATIONS** Rev of, "Journey up the River" by A Burleigh, Homiletic and Pastoral Rev (96): 11-12; auth, "Doctrine as Symbol: Johann Adam Mohler in Dialogue with Kant and Hegel," in Legacy of the Tobingen School: The Relevance of Nineteenth-C for the Twenty-First Century, eds. Donald J Dietrich, Michael j Himes (NY Crossroad, 97): 130-44; auth, "Blondel's L'Action (1893) and Neo-Thomism's Metaphysics of Symbol," Philos Theol 8 (93): 25-40; auth, "Chartres, Platonism, and Christian Love," Modern Age: Quart rev (94): 46-53; auth "Image and Truth in Newman's Moral Argument for God," Louvain Stud (99): 191-210; auth, "Karl Raliner's Metaphysics of Language." Philos Theol (forthcoming). **CONTACT ADDRESS** Dept Theology, Georgetown Univ, PO Box 571135, Washington, DC 20057-1135. **EMAIL** fieldss@gunet.georgetown.edu

FIENSY, DAVID A.
PERSONAL Born McCleansboro, IL, m, 1971, 2 children **DISCIPLINE** RELIGION; NEW TESTAMENT **EDUCATION** Duke Univ, PhD, 80. **CAREER** Assoc prof, Ky Christ Col, 80-87; Inst Scholar, Inst zur Erforschung des Urchristentums, Ger, 87-89; Pastor, Church of Christ, Jamestown, OH, 89-95; prof, Ky Christian Col, 95- . **HONORS AND AWARDS** Appalachian Col Asn summer fel, 98. **MEMBERSHIPS** Soc Biblical Lit; Context; Evangelical Theol Soc. **RESEARCH** Historical Jesus; Social Scientific Criticism of New Testament; Second Temple; Judaism. **SELECTED PUBLICATIONS** Auth, Prayers Alleged to be Jewish: An Examination of the Constitutiones Apostolorum, Scholars Press, Chico, CA, 85; The Social History of Palestine in the Herodian Period: The Land is Mind, Edwin Mellen Press, Lampeter, Lewiston, Queenston, 91; The Hellenistic Synagogal Prayers, in Anchor Bible Dictionary, Doubleday, 93; Craftsmen as Brokers, Proceedings of the Eastern Great Lakes Biblical Soc, 94; New Testament Introduction, College Press, Jopin, MO, 94; Faith in Practice: Studies in the Book of Acts, co-ed, EES, Atlanta, GA, 95; The Composition of the Jerusalem Church, in Acts in Its Palestinian Setting, Eerdmans, 95; Poverty and Wealth in the Gospels and Acts, in Faith in Practice: Studies in the Book of Acts, EES, D.A. Fiensy and W. Howden, eds, 95; The Message and Ministry of Jesus: An Introduction Textbook, UP of America, Lanham, MD, 96; Jesus' Socio-Economic Background in Hillel and Jesus, eds, J.H. Charlesworth and L. Johns, Fortress, 97. **CONTACT ADDRESS** Dept of Religion, Kentucky Christian Col, 100 Academic Pkwy, Grayson, KY 41143. **EMAIL** dfiensy@email.kcc.edu

FIKE, LAWRENCE UDELL, JR.
PERSONAL Born 03/01/1961, Los Angeles, CA, s, 1 child **DISCIPLINE** PHILOSOPHY **EDUCATION** UCLA, BA, 86; Columbia Univ, MA, 89; MPhil, 90. **CAREER** Instructor, Columbia Univ, 90-91; UY Inst of Tech, 90-93; CUNY, 91-93; Saddleback Col, 95-98; Mt St. Mary's Col, 96; Fullerton Col, 97; Calif State Fullerton, 97-98; Cypress Col, 98-99; Yakima Valley Cmty Col, 99-. **HONORS AND AWARDS** Acad Scholarship, Univ CA, 83-84; Am Legion Awd; CA Scholarship Fed Lifetime Member; Golden Key Nat Honor Soc; John Dewey Fel, Columbia Univ; Pres Fel, Columbia Univ, 88-89. **MEMBERSHIPS** Am Philos Asn; Am Soc Philos, Counseling, and Psychotherapy; Concerned Philos for Peace; Hume Soc. **RESEARCH** Aesthetics; Ancient Philosophy; Consciousness; Critical Thinking; Feminism; Medical ethics. **SELECTED PUBLICATIONS** Auth, "Deconstructing the Myth of Power," Essay Magazine, (92): 1-2; auth, "David O. Brink's Moral Realism and the Foundations of Ethics," Philosophia: Philosophical Quarterly of Israel, (93): 435-439; auth, "Trains Passed & Holiday Pie," Quarto, (94): 18, 78; auth, Obstinate Air: Poems on Beating the Wind, Plowman Press, 96; auth, "Abuse-prevention campaign takes wrong tack," Orange Coty Register, (97): 6; auth, Uheard Tick of Time: poems in the healing mode, 99; auth, "Who's to blame? is not the question," Orange County Register, (99): 4; auth, "Technology, Posture, and Practice: Value as Maker's Knowledge in Education, Rhetoric, and Work-Play," in Twentieth Century Values, (Univ Press, forthcoming). **CONTACT ADDRESS** Dept Philos, Yakima Valley Comm Col, 16th Ave & Nob Hill Blvd, Yakima, WA 98908. **EMAIL** fike@aol.com

FILLINGIM, DAVID
DISCIPLINE PHILOSOPHY **EDUCATION** Mercer Univ, Macon, BA, 82; Southeastern Baptist Theol Sem, Mdiv, 85; clin Pastoral educ, 9 units: Baptist Med Ctr, Columbia, 86-87; Ga Reg Hosp at Augusta, 85-86; John Umstead Hosp, Butner, 84; Southern Baptist Theol Sem, PhD, 96. **CAREER** Asst prof; past dir, Independent Stud: Feminist Theol and Ethics; VP, Fac Forum, 97-98; ch, Comt on Stud Internet Access; Alpha Chi Hon Soc Comt; Fac Develop Comt; Admissions Comt; SACS Comt on Tchr Improvement Prog; Ad Hoc Comt to Draft Ethics Prog Proposal; Registration Comt for Presidential Inauguration; acad adv, Relig and Undecided majors; min trng ldr, Christian Stud Un; reg church leadership trng fac, NC Baptist Conv; adj prof, Shaw Univ Ctr for Alternative Prog in Educ, CAPE, 97; vis instr, Theol Dept, Bellarmine Col, Louisville, 96; instr, Southern Baptist Theol Sem, Louisville, 94-96; instr, Philos Dept, Jefferson Commun Col, Downtown Campus, Louisville, 94 & 95; instr, Philos Dept, Georgetown Col, 94-95; instr, Jefferson Commun Col, LaGrange, 94-95; Pastor, Pleasant Plain Baptist Church, Kershaw, 88-91; gp therapist, Baptist Med Ctr, Columbia, 87-88; Struct Gp Ldr, Lexington-Richland Alcohol and Drug Abuse Coun, Columbia, 87-88; Chaplain Resident, Baptist Med Ctr, Columbia, 86-87; Clin Cha. **MEMBERSHIPS** Exec coun, Popular Cult Asn in the S & Am Cult Asn in the South, 95-97; Am Acad Rel; Soc Christian Ethics; Nat Asn Baptist Prof Rel; Southern Humanities Coun; Baptist Asn Philos Tchr(s); Asn for Practical and Prof Ethics. **CONTACT ADDRESS** Dept of Relig and Philos, Chowan Col, Murfreesboro, NC 27855.

FILONOWICZ, JOSEPH
DISCIPLINE HISTORY OF ETHICS, SOCIAL AND POLITICAL PHILOSOPHY **EDUCATION** Hope Col, BA; Columbia Univ, MA, MPhil, PhD. **CAREER** Assoc prof, Long Island Univ. **MEMBERSHIPS** Ch, Long Island Philos Soc. **RESEARCH** History of the ideas of the British sentimental moralists, moral philosophy, psychology of ethics, American philosophy. **SELECTED PUBLICATIONS** Wrote on ethical sentimentalism for the History of Philos Quart; auth, "Black American Philosophy as American Philosophy," Am Phil Assoc newsletter on Philos and the Black Experience. **CONTACT ADDRESS** Long Island Univ, Brooklyn, Brooklyn, NY 11201-8423. **EMAIL** joseph.filonowicz@liu.edu

FINE, ARTHUR
PERSONAL Born 11/11/1937, m, 1980, 2 children **DISCIPLINE** PHILOSOPHY **EDUCATION** Chichago Univ, PhD. **CAREER** John Evans prof, Northwestern Univ. **HONORS AND AWARDS** NSF grant, 68, 73, 78, 80, 89; sr fel, NEH, 74-75; Guggenheim fel, 82-83; fel Ctr Advanced Study in Behavioral Scis, Stanford, 85-86; vis fel, Dibner Inst, MIT, 96. **MEMBERSHIPS** Philos of Sci Asn; Am Philos Asn. **RESEARCH** Philosophy of physics, philosophy of natural and social science. **SELECTED PUBLICATIONS** Auth, The Shaky Game: Einstein, Realism and Quantum Theory; Science Made Up: Constructivist Sociology of Scientific Knowledge, The Disunity of Science: Boundaries, Contexts and Power, 95; auth, Indeterminism and the Freedom of the Will, Philosophical Problems of the Internal and External Worlds, 93; auth, Causes of Variation: Disentangling Nature and Nurture, Midwest Studies in Philosophy, 90; co-ed, Bohmian Mechanics and Quantum Theory: An Appraisal. **CONTACT ADDRESS** Dept of Philosophy, Northwestern Univ, 1801 Hinman, Evanston, IL 60208.

FINE, KIT
PERSONAL Born 03/26/1946, United Kingdom, s, 2 children **DISCIPLINE** PHILOSOPHY **CAREER** Prof, NYU. **RESEARCH** Metaphysics, Logic, philosophy. **CONTACT ADDRESS** 100 Washington Square E, Philo Main, New York, NY 10003-6688. **EMAIL** kf14@.s4.nyu.edu

FINEGAN, EDWARD J.
PERSONAL Born 06/25/1940, New York City, NY **DISCIPLINE** LINGUISTICS LAW **EDUCATION** Iona Col, BS; Ohio Univ, MA; Ohio Univ, PhD. **CAREER** Prof; post-doc, Univ Southern Calif; Ohio State Univ, Ling Inst & Harvard Law Sch. **HONORS AND AWARDS** Liberal Arts fel, Harvard Law Sch. **MEMBERSHIPS** Past dir, Amer Lang Inst/Nat Iranian Radio and Tv, past chair, linguistics dept, USC. **RESEARCH** Legal writing, register variation. **SELECTED PUBLICATIONS** Auth, Language: Its Structure and Use; coauth, Looking at Languages; coed, Sociolinguistic Perspectives on Register. **CONTACT ADDRESS** School of Law, Univ of So California, Los Angeles, CA 90089. **EMAIL** finegan@usc.edu

FINGER, THOMAS
PERSONAL Born 05/12/1942, Chicago, IL, m, 1969, 2 children **DISCIPLINE** PHILOSOPHY **EDUCATION** Wheaton Col, AB, 65; Gordon Divinity School, MA & BD, 68; Claremont Grad School, PhD, 75. **CAREER** Asst to assoc prof of Philosophy, E Mennonite Col, 73-76; instr Sem Consortium Urban Pastoral Educ, 76-78; asst to assoc to full prof Systematic Theol, N Baptist Sem, 76-86; prof, systematic & spiritual theol, E Mennonite Sem, 89-; int pastor, Circle Evangelical Free Church, 78; fel, Inst Advanced Study Relig, Univ Chicago Divinity School, 80; pastor, N Bronx Mennonite Church, 87-89. **MEMBERSHIPS** Christian Environ Coun Evangelical Environ Network, 94; Soc Study E Orthodoxy and Evangelicalism. **RESEARCH** Systematic, Contemporary, and Historical Theology; Spiritual Theology; Environmental Theology. **SELECTED PUBLICATIONS** Auth, Modern Alienation and Trinitarian Creation, Evangelical Rev Theol, 93; Konrad Raisers View of a New Ecumenical Paradigm, Ecumenical Trends, 93; Modernity, Postmodernity--what in the world are they?, Transformation, 93; Anabaptism and Eastern Orthodoxy: some unexpected similarites?, Jour Ecumenical Studies, 94; In Praise of Sophia, Christianity Today, 94; auth, Trinity, Ecology, and Panentheism, Christians Scholars Rev, 97; Self, Earth and Society, InterVarsity, 97; A Mennonite Theology for Interfaith Relations, Grounds for Understanding, 98. **CONTACT ADDRESS** Eastern Mennonite Univ, Harrisonburg, VA 22802. **EMAIL** fingert@cmu.edu

FINIFTER, ADA WEINTRAUB
PERSONAL Born 06/06/1938, New York, NY, d **DISCIPLINE** POLITICAL SCIENCE **EDUCATION** Univ Wis, PhD, 67. **CAREER** Prof, Dept of Political Science, MI State Univ, 81-; ed, Am Political Science Rev, 95-2001; **HONORS AND AWARDS** Abraham and Rebecca Sive Memorial Prize, Brooklyn Col, 59; Univ fel, Univ MI, 59-60; summer fel, Nat Science Found fellowships for graduate teaching assts, 66; grad fel, Nat Sci Found, 66-67; Nat Sci Found travel grant, 73; Am Political Science Asn Congressional fel, 73-74; vis fel, Dept of Political Science, Res School of Social Services, Australian Nat Univ, April-Dec 78; Sr scholar, Fulbright prog in Australia, Aug-Oct 78; Am Sociol Asn grant, 81; Women in Development Fac Scholar Awd, 83; Excellence in Online Ed Awd of Merit, Higher Ed Div, Dialog Information System, 88; Fac Development Awd for Further Internationalizing MSU, 90; All-University Res Initiation grant, MI State Univ, 90-91; Phi Kappa Phi, 96. **MEMBERSHIPS** Am Political Science Asn; Intl Political Sci Assoc; Southern Political Science Asn; Midwest Political Science Asn. **RESEARCH** Public opinion; political behavior; survey research methods. **SELECTED PUBLICATIONS** Auth, Dimensions of Poitical Alienation, Am Political Science Rev, 64, 2, June 70; The Friendship Group as a Protective Environment for Political Deviants, Am Political Science Rev, 68, 2, June 74; with Bernard M Finifter, Part Identificetion and Political Adaptation of American Settlers in Australia, J of Politics, 51, 3, Aug 89; with Ellen Mickiewitz, Redefining the Political System of the USSR: Mass Support for Political Change, Am Political Science Rev, 86, 4, Dec 92; ed, Political Science: The State of the Discipline II, Am Political Science Asn, 93; auth with Bernard M Finifter, Pledging Allegiance to a New Flag: Citizenship Change and its Psychological Aftermath Among American Migrants in Australia, Can Rev of Studies in Nationalism, 22, 1-2, Sept 95; Attitudes Toward Individual Responsibility and Poltitical Reform in the Former Soviet Union, Am Political Science Rev, 90, 1, March 96; numerous other publications. **CONTACT ADDRESS** Dept of Political Science, Michigan State Univ, 303 South Kedzie Hall, East Lansing, MI 48824. **EMAIL** Finifter@msu.edu

FINK, BEATRICE
PERSONAL Born 09/13/1933, Vienna, Austria, w, 3 children **DISCIPLINE** FRENCH LITERATURE, HISTORY OF IDEAS **EDUCATION** Bryn Mawr Col, BA, 53; Yale Univ, MA, 56; Univ Pittsburgh, PhD (French), 66. **CAREER** From instr to asst prof French, 64-72; assoc prof, 72-91, prof french, U MD Col Par, 91-99, emer, 99. **HONORS AND AWARDS** Sec General, Int Soc 18th Cont Studies, 79-87. **MEMBERSHIPS** Am Soc 18th Century Studies; Soc Fr Etude XVIIIe Siecle; Asn Benjamin Constant; East-Central Am Soc 18th Century Studies (past pres.); Soc Diderot; Soc Etudes Staeliennes. **RESEARCH** Benjamin Constant; aulinary history/discourse in Enlightenment. **SELECTED PUBLICATIONS** Auth, Les Liaisons savoureuses, 95; coed, Etre materialisle a l'age des Lumieres, 99. **CONTACT ADDRESS** 629 Constitution Ave, NE, No. 305, Washington, DC 20002. **EMAIL** bf5@umail.umd.edu

FINKELSTEIN, RONA G.
PERSONAL Born 11/07/1927, Rochester, NY, w, 1950, 2 children **DISCIPLINE** ART; PHILOSOPHY **EDUCATION** Connecticut Col, BA, 49; MA, 61, PhD, 64, Univ Rochester. **CAREER** Delaware State Col, 64-70, chairperson, 66-70; Univ Delaware, Col Parallel Program, 70-72; Exec Dir, Delaware Humanities Forum, 72-81. **MEMBERSHIPS** APA **RESEARCH** Mind-Body **CONTACT ADDRESS** 115 Sorrel Dr., Surrey Pk., Wilmington, DE 19803. **EMAIL** rfinkel850@aol.com

FINKEN, BRYAN W.
PERSONAL Born 03/23/1961, Denver, CO, s **DISCIPLINE** PHILOSOPHY **EDUCATION** Metropolitan State Col, Denver, BA; Univ Illinois, Urbana Champaign, PhD, 93. **CAREER** Vis asst prof, Univ Arkansas, 92-93; vis lectr, Univ Witwatersrand, Johannesburg, 93-95; temp asst prof, Auburn Univ, 96-97; instr, Metropolitan State Col, 97-98. **HONORS AND AWARDS** Named six times to The Incomplete List of Teachers Ranked as Excellent by their Students, at Univ Ill. **MEMBERSHIPS** APA; N Am Nietzsche Soc; S Af Philos Asn. **RESEARCH** Theory of illusion; sciolism in the twentieth century; postmodernism as a hate movement; moral psychology; political theory; degradation of standards in the humanities; Nietzsche's metaphysics. **CONTACT ADDRESS** Dept of Philos, Metropolitan State Col of Denver, PO Box 173362, Campus Box 049, Denver, CO 80217. **EMAIL** finkenb@mscd.edu

FINKIN, MATTHEW W.
DISCIPLINE LAW **EDUCATION** Ohio Wesleyan Univ, AB; Univ NYork, LL.B; Yale Univ, LL.M. **CAREER** Gen Editorship, Comparative Labor Law & Policy Journal, Prof, Univ Ill Urbana Champaign. **HONORS AND AWARDS** Humboldt Foundation's Res Awd, Fulbright Rep, Munster Univ, German Marshall Fund Rep, Konstanz Univ. **MEMBERSHIPS** Am Asn Univ Prof, 76-78. **RESEARCH** Labor law; labor law II; higher education law; individual employee relations. **SELECTED PUBLICATIONS** Auth, pubs on labor and employment law, higher education law, and comparative law; ed, Privacy in Employment Law, BNA, 95; The Case for Tenure, Cornell, 96; co-ed, Labor Law, Foundation, 96; Introduction to German Law, Kluwer, 96. **CONTACT ADDRESS** Law Dept, Univ of Illinois, Urbana-Champaign, 504 E Pensylvania, Champaign, IL 61820. **EMAIL** mfinkin@law.uiuc.edu

FINLAYSON, ARNOLD ROBERT
PERSONAL Born 06/30/1963, Washington, DC, s **DISCIPLINE** LAW **EDUCATION** Bowie State Coll, BS, 1985; Howard University School of Law, JD, 1989. **CAREER** US Dept of State, procurement analyst, 87-90; Hon George W Mitchell, assoc judge, DC Superior Court; judicial law clerk; 1990-92; Shaw, Pittman, Potts & Trowbridge, govt contracts associate, 92-. **HONORS AND AWARDS** Howard University School of Law, Wiley A Branton Leadership Awd, 1989, American Jurisprudence Awd, Professional Responsibility, 1989, American Jurisprudence Awd, Natl Moot Court, 1989. **MEMBERSHIPS** District of Columbia Bar, 1992; Bar of the Commonwealth of Pennsylvania, 1989; US Court of Appeals for the Federal Circuit, 1993; Amer Bar Assn, 1989; Kappa Alpha Psi Fraternity, Inc, 1983. **SELECTED PUBLICATIONS** Co-Author, Financing Govt Contracts, 1993. **CONTACT ADDRESS** Shaw, Pittman, Potts & Trowbridge, 2300 N St NW, 6th Floor, Washington, DC 20037.

FINLEY, THOMAS JOHN
PERSONAL Born 10/29/1945, Jacksonville, FL, m, 1995, 2 children **DISCIPLINE** OLD TESTAMENT, ANCIENT SEMITIC LANGUAGES **EDUCATION** Biola Col, BA, 67, MDiv, 71; Univ Calif, Los Angeles, MA, 74, PhD, 79. **CAREER** Prof Old Testament & Semitics, Talbot Sch Theol, Biola Univ, 77-. **MEMBERSHIPS** Soc Bibl Lit; Evangel Theol Soc. **RESEARCH** Old Testament biblical Hebrew, Aramaic & Akkadian languages; Studies on Joel, Amos and Obadiah. **SELECTED PUBLICATIONS** Auth, Joel, Amos, Obadiah, Wycliffe Exegetical Commentary, Moody, 90; Auth, Joel, Obadiah, and Micah, Everymen Bible Commentary; Moody, 95; auth, A Bilingual Concordance to the Targum of the Prophets: Ezekiel, Brill, 99. **CONTACT ADDRESS** Talbot Theol Sem, Biola Univ, 13800 Biola Ave, La Mirada, CA 90639-0002. **EMAIL** tom.finley@truth.biola.edu

FINN, DANIEL R.
PERSONAL Born 04/30/1947, Rochester, NY, m, 1978, 2 children **DISCIPLINE** RELIGIOUS SOCIAL ETHICS; ECONOMICS **EDUCATION** St John Fisher Col, BS, 68; Univ Chicago, MA, 75, PhD, 77. **CAREER** Asst prof, 77-84, assoc prof, 84-91, prof, 91- , chair, dept of economics and theology, 82-84, dean, sch of theology, 84-89, St John's Univ. **HONORS AND AWARDS** Clemens Chair in Economics and the Liberal Arts, St John's Univ, 89- . **MEMBERSHIPS** Soc of Christian Ethics; Assn for Social Economics; Midwest Assn of Theological Schs; Amer Economics Assn; Assn for Evolutionary Economics; Catholic Theological Soc of Amer; History of Economics Soc; Midwest Economics Soc; MN Economics Assn. **SELECTED PUBLICATIONS** Coauth,Toward a Christian Economic Ethic: Stewardship and Social Power, Winston, 85; auth, Self-Interest, Markets and the Four Problems of Economics Life, Annual of the Society of Chritian Ethics, 89; auth, Employment in the US: Public Discourse and Longterm Trends, Forum for Social Economics, 94; auth, Three Cheers for the Gas Tax, The Christian Century, 96; auth, Just Trading: On the Ethics and Economics of International Trade, Abingdon, 96. **CONTACT ADDRESS** Dept. of Economics, St. John's Univ, Collegeville, MN 56321. **EMAIL** dfinn@csbsju.edu

FINN, THOMAS M.
PERSONAL Born 03/18/1927, New York, NY, m, 1968, 1 child **DISCIPLINE** PATRISTICS **EDUCATION** St. Paul's Col, AB, 56, MA, 58; Cath Univ Am, STL, 61, STD, 65. **CAREER** Chancellor Prof Relig. Col William and Mary, 73-. **HONORS AND AWARDS** Melone Fel, Coun on U.S. Arab Relations, 90; Res Fel, Inst Ecumenical and Cultural Res, 95. **MEMBERSHIPS** Am Acad Relig; Cath Bibl Asn; NAm Patristic Soc; Int Patristic Soc. **RESEARCH** Ritual in Greco-Roman antiquity, paganism, Judaism, and Christianity. **SELECTED PUBLICATIONS** Auth, Early Christian Baptism and the Catechumenate: Italy, North Africa and Egypt, Litturgical Press, 92; Early Christian Baptism and the Catechumenate: West and East Syria, Litturgical Press, 92; From Death to Rebirth: Conversion in Antiquity, Paulist Press, 97; Quodvultdeus: The Preacher and the Audience: The Homilies on the Creed, Studia Patristica 31, 97; Ritual and Conversion: The Case of Augustine, Nova & Vetera: Patristic Studies in Honor of Thomas Patrick Halton, Cath Univ Am Press, 98. **CONTACT ADDRESS** Religion Dept, Col of William and Mary, 310 Wren Building, Williamsburg, VA 23187-8795. **EMAIL** tmfinn@wm.edu

FINNEY, PAUL CORBY
DISCIPLINE HISTORY, ART & ARCHAEOLOGY, RELIGION **EDUCATION** Yale Univ, AB, 62; Maximilians Univ, Germany, 62-63; Harvard Univ, MA, PhD, 73. **CAREER** ASST PROF, ASSOC PROF, PROF, UNIV MO, ST LOUIS, 73-; area supervisor, Am Schs Oriental Res excavation Cathage, Tunisia, 75- 77; sen lectr, Hebrew Univ, Jerusalem, 79; vis lectr, Princeton Theol Sem, 83; sen assoc, Am Sch Class Stud, Athens, 87; assoc archaeologist, Gr Ministry Antiquities, 87; vis fel, Princeton Univ, 92, 95, 98, 99. **CONTACT ADDRESS** Dept of History, Univ of Missouri, St. Louis, 8001 Natural Bridge Rd, Saint Louis, MO 63121. **EMAIL** spcfinn@umslvma.umsl.edu

FINOCCHIARO, MAURICE A.
PERSONAL Born 06/13/1942, Florida, Italy, m, 1966 **DISCIPLINE** PHILOSOPHY **EDUCATION** MIT, BS, 64; Univ Calif, Berkeley, PhD, 69. **CAREER** From asst to assoc prof, 70-77, prof 77- , Distinguished Prof 91- , philos, Univ Nev, Las Vegas; vis scholar, hist sci, Harvard Univ, 98-99. **HONORS AND AWARDS** NSF res grant 76-77; NEH fel 83-84; ACLS fel 91-92; NEH res grant 92-95; Nevada State Bd of Regents Res 93; Guggenheim fel 98-99; NSF res grant, 98-01. **MEMBERSHIPS** APA; Philos Sci Asn; Hist Sci Soc; Asn Informal Logic and Critical Thinking; Am Asn It Stud. **RESEARCH** Philosophy of science; informal logic; Galileo; Antonio Gramsci; Benedetto Croce; Gaetano Mosca. **SELECTED PUBLICATIONS** Auth, History of Science as Explanation, Wayne State Univ, 73; auth, Galileo and the Art of Reasoning, Kluwer-Reidel, 80; auth, Gramsci and The History of Dialectical Thought, Cambridge, 88; auth, Gramsci Critico e la Critica, Armando, 88; transl and ed, The Galileo Affair, Univ Calif, 89; trans and ed, Galileo on the World Systems, Univ Calif, 97; auth, Beyond Right and Left: Democratic Elitism in Mosca and Gramsci, Yale, 99. **CONTACT ADDRESS** Dept of Philosophy, Univ of Nevada, Las Vegas, Las Vegas, NV 89154-5028. **EMAIL** mauricef@nevada.edu

FIORE, ROBIN N.
DISCIPLINE PHILOSOPHY **EDUCATION** Georgetown Univ, PhD, 97. **CAREER** Frances Elridge Post doct res fel, ethics, 97-98, Ethics Ctr, St Petersburg, FL; asst prof, ethics, 98-, Fla Atlantic Univ **HONORS AND AWARDS** Andrew Mellon Dist Fel, 96. **MEMBERSHIPS** APA; Fla Bioethics Network; Soc for Women in Phil. **RESEARCH** Bioethics; managed care; aging. **SELECTED PUBLICATIONS** Auth, Realizing Liberalism: Toward a Feminist Theory of Equality, 97; auth, Caring for Ourselves: Peer Care in Autonomous Aging, Mother Time: Women, Aging, and Ethics, Rowman & Littlefield, 99. **CONTACT ADDRESS** Florida Atlantic Univ, PO Box 3091, Boca Raton, FL 33431. **EMAIL** rfione@fau.edu

FIORENZA, ELIZABETH SCHUSSLER
PERSONAL Born, Germany **DISCIPLINE** NEW TESTAMENT STUDIES **EDUCATION** Univ Munster, Dr theol, 70; Univ Wurzburg, Lic theol, 63, MDiv, 62. **CAREER** Instr theol,

Univ Munster, 65-66; asst prof, 70-75, assoc prof, 75-80, PROF THEOL, UNIV NOTRE DAME, 80-, Vis prof theol, Union Theol Sem, NY, 74-75; scripture coordr clergy educ, Notre Dame Inst Clergy Educ, 76-77; distinguished vis scholar, Col Wooster, 82. **MEMBERSHIPS** Cath Bibl Asn; Soc Bibl Lit; Studiorum Novi Testamenti Soc; Am Acad Relig; Col Theol Soc. **RESEARCH** New Testament studies and early Christianity; women's studies in religion; pastoral theology. **SELECTED PUBLICATIONS** Auth, Speaking Out, J Fem Stud Rel, Vol 12, 96; Feminist Issues Regarding Family Values and the Famil, J Feminist Stud Rel, Vol 12, 96. **CONTACT ADDRESS** Dept of Theol, Univ of Notre Dame, Notre Dame, IN 46556.

FIRMAGE, EDWIN BROWN
PERSONAL Born 10/01/1935, Provo, UT, m, 1955, 7 children **DISCIPLINE** LAW **EDUCATION** Brigham Young Unv, BS, 60, MS, 62; Univ Chicago, JD, 63, LLM & SJD, 64. **CAREER** Asst prof law, Univ Mo, 64-65; White House fel, Vpres Humphrey's Staff, DC, 65-66; from Asst Prof to Prof Law, 66-90, Samuel D. Thurman Prof Law, Univ Utah, 90-; UN vis scholar, 70-71; Int rel fel at arms control negotiations, Geneva, Switz, Coun Foreign Relat, 70-71; fel law & humanities, Harvard Law Sch, 74-75, Univ Tex Law Sch, summer, 79; vis prof, Univ London, 92; Kellogg Lectr, Episcopal Divinity Sch, Cambridge, MA, 93; presently working with the Dalai Lama of Tibet, in exile. **HONORS AND AWARDS** Univ Distinguished Tchg Awd, Univ UT, 77; Reynolds Lectr, Univ UT, 87; Charles Rodd Prize in Humanities, 88; First Place Prize, Alpha Sigma Nu, for "Zion in the Courts..", 89; McDougall Lectr, 89; Governor's Awd in the Humanities, 89; Turner-Fairbanks Awd for contributions to Peace & Justice, 91; Rosenblatt Prize for Excellence, 91. **MEMBERSHIPS** Am Bar Asn; Am Soc Int Law; Am Judicature Soc; Order of the Coif; Coun For Rel. **RESEARCH** International Law; torts; comp law. **SELECTED PUBLICATIONS** Auth, Removal of the President: Resignation and the procedural law of impeachment, Duke Law J, 75; The Utah Supreme Court and the rule of law: Phillips and the Bill of Rights in Utah 1975, Utah Law Rev, 76; Law and the Indo-China War: a retrospective view, In: The Vietnam War and International Law, Princeton Univ, 76; Vladivostok and beyond: An analysis of Salt II, Columbia J Trans Law, 76; The war powers and the political question doctrine, Univ Colo Law Rev, 78; MX: National Security and the Destruction of Society's Values, That Awesome Space, 81; Allegiance & Stewardship, Christianity and Cirsis, 3/82; Zion in the Courts, Ill Press, 88; coauth, The War Powers in History & Law, Ill Press, 89; auth, Religion and Law: Islamic, Jewish, and Christian Perspectives, Eisenbraun's, 90; The International Legal Systems, Foundation Press, 95. **CONTACT ADDRESS** Col of Law, Univ of Utah, Salt Lake City, UT 84112-1107.

FISCELLA, JOAN B.
PERSONAL Born 12/24/1939, Chicago, IL **DISCIPLINE** PHILOSOPHY; LIBRARY SCIENCE **EDUCATION** St. Mary's Col, S Bend, Ind, BA, 63; Univ Notre Dame, PhD, 77; Univ Mich, AMLS, 83. **CAREER** Asst prof, Mary Manse Col, Toledo, Oh, 73-75; vis asst prof, Univ Il, 80-81; asst prof, Wayne St Univ, Detroit, Mich, 75-82; head, Auraria Library, 84-86, 88-90; dept head, Univ Houston Libr, 87; bibliographer, asst prof to assoc prof, Univ Il Chicago, 90- . **HONORS AND AWARDS** Beta Phi Mu, Libr Sci Honor Soc, 83 **MEMBERSHIPS** Amer Libr Assoc; Amer Soc Infor Sci; Assoc Integ Studies. **RESEARCH** Characteristics of interdisciplinary lit & its implications for scholarly commun **SELECTED PUBLICATIONS** Coauth, Independent Office Collections and the Evolving Role of Academic Librarians, Libr Resources & Tech Svc, 94; An Approach to Assessing Faculty Use of Locally Loaded Databases, Col & Res Libr, 95; Collection Development, in Managing Business Collections in Libraries, Greenwood Press, 96; auth, Bibliography as an Interdisciplinary Service, Libr Trends, 96; Interdisciplinary Education: A Guide to Resources, New York, The Col Bd, 99. **CONTACT ADDRESS** Collections Develop Dept, Univ of Illinois, Chicago, PO Box 8198 M/C 234, Chicago, IL 60680. **EMAIL** jbf@uic.edu

FISCH, THOMAS
PERSONAL Born 02/05/1946, Minneapolis, MN, m, 3 children **DISCIPLINE** SACRAMENTAL THEOLOGY, LITURGICAL STUDIES **EDUCATION** St Paul Sem, BA, 68; Col St Thom, MA, 70; Univ Min, MA, 77; St John Univ, MA, 81; Univ Not Dam, MA, 85; PhD, 88. **CAREER** Vis prof, 89, 92, 97, St Johns Univ; assoc prof, St Paul Sem, 81-. **MEMBERSHIPS** NAAL; Soc Liturgica. **RESEARCH** Liturgical Theology; problems in early history of Liturgy. **SELECTED PUBLICATIONS** Coauth, "Echoes of the Early Roman Nuptial Blessing," Ecclesia Oran (94): 225-244; ed, Liturgy and Tradition: Theological Reflections of Alexander Schmeinann (NY: St Vladimir's, 90). **CONTACT ADDRESS** Dept Religion, St Paul Sem School of Divinity, 2260 Summit Ave, Saint Paul, MN 55105-1010.

FISCHEL, DANIEL R.
PERSONAL Born 12/10/1950, New York, NY, 1 child **DISCIPLINE** CORPORATION LAW **EDUCATION** Cornell Univ, BA, 72; Brown Univ, MA, 74; Sch of Law, Univ Chicago, JD, 77. **CAREER** Law clerk, Judge Thomas E Fairchild, Chief Judge, Seventh Circuit Court of Appeals, 77-78 and Assoc Justice Potter Stewart, US Supreme Court, 78-79; atty, Levy and Erens, 79-80; PROF LAW, NORTHWESTERN UNIV, 80-, Consult, Lexecon, Inc, 81-; vis prof law, Sch of Law, Univ Chicago, 82-83. **SELECTED PUBLICATIONS** Auth, Corporate Crime, J Legal Stud, Vol 25, 96; Clustering and Competition in Asset Markets, J Law Economics, Vol 40, 97; Contract and Fiduciary Duty, J Law Economics, Vol 36, 93. **CONTACT ADDRESS** Sch of Law, Northwestern Univ, Chicago, IL 60611.

FISCHER, DAVID ARNOLD
PERSONAL Born 05/10/1943, St. Louis, MO, m, 1969, 1 child **DISCIPLINE** LAW **EDUCATION** Lincoln Col, AA, 63; Univ Mo-Columbia, AB, 65, JD, 68. **CAREER** From asst prof to assoc prof, 72-78, PROF LAW, UNIV MO-COLUMBIA, 78-. **MEMBERSHIPS** Am Bar Asn, **RESEARCH** Products liability. **SELECTED PUBLICATIONS** Auth, Proportional Liability--Statistical Evidence and the Probability Paradox, Vanderbilt Law Rev, Vol 46, 93. **CONTACT ADDRESS** Sch of Law, Univ of Missouri, Columbia, 310 Watson Pl, Columbia, MO 65211-0001.

FISCHER, JOHN
PERSONAL Born 05/27/1946, Budapest, Hungary, m, 1972, 2 children **DISCIPLINE** BIBLICAL STUDIES, JUDAIC STUDIES **EDUCATION** Philadelphia Col Bible, BS, 70; Temple Univ, MS, 70; Trinity Evangel Div Sch, MA, 72; Spertus Col Judaica, BJS, 78; Univ S Fla, PhD, 87; Calif Grad Sch Theol, ThD, 89. **CAREER** Prof, St Petersburg Theol Sem, 85-; dean, 89-. **MEMBERSHIPS** Union of Messianic Jewish Congregations; Lederer Messianic Ministries, Assoc of Messianic Believers; Am Assoc of Messianic Jewish Believers; Int Messianic Jewish Alliance in the Americas. **SELECTED PUBLICATIONS** Auth, "Messianic Services for Festivals and Holy Days", Menorah Ministries, 92; auth, "Foundations of Messianic Theology", Mishkan 1, (95); auth, "The Lifestyle and Teachings of Jesus", Interpreter, (96); auth, "Making Messianic Worship Meaningful", Mishkan (97); auth, "Why is This Night Different?", Messianic Times, (97); auth, "Yeshua and Halacha: Which Direction?", Kesher (97); auth, "Messianic Conversion: It is Viable", Kesher, (97); auth, "Witnesses for the Reliability of the Older Testament", Messianic Jewish Life, (99); auth, "The Resurrection of Yeshua: Myth or Fact?", Messianic Jewish Life, (99); auth, The Enduring Paradox: Jesus and Judaism, Lederer, (forthcoming). **CONTACT ADDRESS** Dept Relig and Philos, St Petersburg Theol Sem, 10830 Navajo Dr, Saint Petersburg, FL 33708-3116.

FISCHER, JOHN MARTIN
DISCIPLINE PHILOSOPHY **EDUCATION** Cornell Univ, PhD. **CAREER** Dir, Honors Prog, Prof, Univ Calif, Riverside. **HONORS AND AWARDS** NEH, Fel for Univ Teachers, 83-4; 94; Nat Humanities Ctr Residential Fel, 90-91, 93-4; Awarded Australian Nat Univ Rs Centre Residential Fel, 94; Center for Ideas and Soc Residential Fel, UC Riverside, 91. **RESEARCH** Metaphysics; Moral philosophy; Philosophy of mind; Philosophy of religion. **SELECTED PUBLICATIONS** Ed, Moral Responsibility, Cornell Univ Press, 86; God, Foreknowledge and Freedom, Stanford Univ Press, 89; The Metaphysics of Death, Stanford Univ Press, 93; co-ed, Ethics: Problems and Principles, Harcourt Brace Jovanovich, 91; Perspectives on Moral Responsibility, Cornell Univ Press, 93; coauth, Responsibility and Control: A Theory of Moral Responsibility, Cambridge Univ Press, 97; auth, The Metaphysics of Free Will: An Essay on Control, Blackwell, 94. **CONTACT ADDRESS** Dept of Philos, Univ of California, Riverside, 1156 Hinderaker Hall, Riverside, CA 92521-0209. **EMAIL** fischer@ucrac1.ucr.edu

FISCHER, MARILYN R.
DISCIPLINE SOCIAL PHILOSOPHY, ETHICS **EDUCATION** Boston Univ, Phd, 78. **CAREER** Dept Philos, Univ Dayton **RESEARCH** Philosophy of music. **SELECTED PUBLICATIONS** Auth, The Orchestral Workplace, Jour Soc Philos, 94; Philanthropy and Injustice in Mill and Addams, Nonprofit and Voluntary Sector Quart, 95; Rawls, Assns and the Political Conception of Justice, Jour Soc Philos, 97. **CONTACT ADDRESS** Dept of Philos, Univ of Dayton, 300 Col Park, Dayton, OH 75062. **EMAIL** fischer@checkov.hm.udayton.edu

FISCHER, MARK F.
PERSONAL Born 05/28/1951, Bethesda, MD, m, 1978, 3 children **DISCIPLINE** THEOLOGY **EDUCATION** Univ Calif at Berkeley, BA; Grad Theol Union, MA; PhD. **CAREER** Dir, Offic of the Diocesan pastoral Counc of the Diocese of Oakland, 84-90; assoc prof, St John's Sem, 90-00. **HONORS AND AWARDS** Outstanding Leadership Awd, Confr for Pastoral Planning & Coun Development. **MEMBERSHIPS** Catholic Theol Soc of Am; Confr for Pastoral Planning & Coun Development. **RESEARCH** Parish Pastoral Councils, Karl Rhaner's "Foundations of Christian Faith." **SELECTED PUBLICATIONS** Auth, "What Was Vatican II's Intent Regarding Parish Councils?" Studia Canonica 33 (99): 5-25. **CONTACT ADDRESS** Dept Relig, St. John's Sem, 5012 Seminary Rd, Camarillo, CA 93012-2500. **EMAIL** fischer@west.net

FISCHER, NORMAN ARTHUF
PERSONAL Born 02/12/1943, Norway, MI, m, 1987, 3 children **DISCIPLINE** PHILOSOPHY **EDUCATION** Univ Wis-Madison, BA, 65; Univ Wash, MA, 68, Phd(philos), 75. **CAREER** Instr, 74-75, asst prof philos, 75-01, prof philo, 01-, Kent State Univ. **MEMBERSHIPS** Am Philos Asn; Am Soc for Aesthetics, Amintaphil, Radical Philo Asn. **RESEARCH** Marxism;Frankfort School, Social philosophy; Philosophy of Art, Film, Law, Environment. **SELECTED PUBLICATIONS** Auth; Economy and Self, Greenwood, 79; Marx's Early Concept of Democrat and the Ethical Bases of Socialism, Cambridge, 81; Hegelian Marxism and Ethics, Canadian Journal of Political and Social Theory, 84; Lucien Goldmann and Tragic Marxist Ethics, Philosophy and Social Criticism, 87; From Aesthetic Education to Environmental Aesthetics, CLIO, 96; Jurgen Habermas' Recent Philosophy of Law and the Optimum Point Between Universalism and Communitarianism, Kansas, 97; Frankfort School Marxism and Ethical Analysis of Art, Communication Theory, 97; auth, Hans-Jurgen Syberberg's Parsifal: Visual Transformatiob and philosophical Reconstruction, Film and Philosophy, III (96): 145-153; auth, Marxist Philosophy of Law, Philosophy of Law: An encyclopedia (NY: Garland, 99), 539-541; auth, Civic Republican Political/Legal Ethics and Echoes, Special Symposium Pynchon and Law, OK City Univ Law Rev 4.3 (99), 557-588. **CONTACT ADDRESS** Dept of Philos, Kent State Univ, PO Box 5190, Kent, OH 44242-0001. **EMAIL** parsquix@aol.com

FISCHER, ROBERT HARLEY
PERSONAL Born 04/26/1918, Williamsport, PA, m, 1942, 1 child **DISCIPLINE** CHURCH HISTORY **EDUCATION** Gettysburg Col, AB, 39; Lutheran Theol Sem, Gettysburg, BD, 42; Yale Univ, PhD, 47. **CAREER** Minister, Hartland Community Parish, VT, 44-45; asst pastor, Zion Lutheran Church, Sunbury, Pa, 47-49; PROF HIST THEOL, LUTHERAN SCH THEOL, CHICAGO, 49-86, Kirchliche Hochschule, Berlin, 73 and Lutheran Sem, Tokyo, 80; tutor, Mansfield Col, Oxford Univ, 57-58; Am Asn Theol Schs fel, Tubingen, 64-65; assoc ed, Lutheran Quart, 66-72. **HONORS AND AWARDS** Phi Beta Kappa, Sterling Research Fellowship, Yale. **MEMBERSHIPS** Am Theol Soc Midwest Div; Am Soc Reformation Res (pres, 54); NAm Acad Ecumenists; Am Soc Church Hist; Lutheran Hist Conf (vpres, 72-76). **RESEARCH** Reformation history, especially theology of Luther; 19th century American Lutheranism; ecumenics. **SELECTED PUBLICATIONS** Ed, Luther's Large Catechism in Tappert, ed Book of Concord, 59; ed, Luther's Works V. 37 (Lord'sSupper Writings), 61; ed, Franklin Clark Fry, 72; ed, A Tribute to Arthur Voobus, 77; auth, Luther, 1966: A Servant of All People (W.A. Passerant), 97. **CONTACT ADDRESS** 5324 Central Ave, Western Springs, IL 60558.

FISCHER, THOMAS C.
PERSONAL Born 05/02/1938, Cincinnati, OH, m, 1972 **DISCIPLINE** LEGAL STUDIES **EDUCATION** Univ Cincinnati, AB, 60; Georgetown Univ Law Center, JD, 66. **CAREER** Asst Dean, Georgetown, 66-72; Asst Exec Dir, American Bar Foundation, 74; Assoc Dean & Prof of Law, Univ Dayton L.S., 76-78; Dean, 78-81. **HONORS AND AWARDS** Fellow, Wolfson College, Cambridge U (UK); Inss of Court Fellow (Lincoln's) London; Cincinnati's Society. **RESEARCH** European Union Law; Trade Globalization. **SELECTED PUBLICATIONS** Auth, "Introduction to Law and Legal Reasoning," 76; auth, "Legal Education, Law Practice, and the Economy," 89; auth, "The Europeanization of America," 96; auth, "Sum & Substance of Conflict of Laws," 2nd ed., 97; auth, "Allies or Adversaries?" The United States, the European Union, and the Globalization of World Trade," 00. **CONTACT ADDRESS** New England Sch of Law, 154 Stuart St, Boston, MA 02116-5616.

FISH, ARTHUR
DISCIPLINE LAW **EDUCATION** Univ Toronto, BA, 80; Osgoode Hall Law Sch, LLB, 82; Oxford Univ, BCL, 86; Univ Toronto, SJD, 94. **CAREER** Chair, Ontario Mental Health Foundation **RESEARCH** Health law; estates and trusts. **SELECTED PUBLICATIONS** Auth, pubs on mental competency assessment, health-care and bioethics; co-auth, When the Mind Fails, Univ Toronto, 94. **CONTACT ADDRESS** Dept of Psychiat, Univ of Toronto, 33 Russell St., Toronto, ON, Canada M5S 2S5.

FISH, STANLEY E.
PERSONAL Born 04/19/1938, Providence, RI, 1 child **DISCIPLINE** ENGLISH, LAW **EDUCATION** Univ of Pa, BA, 59; Yale Univ, MA, 60; PhD, 62. **CAREER** Chair, Johns Hopkins Univ, 83-84; chair, prof, Duke Univ, 86-98; dean, Yale Univ, 99-. **HONORS AND AWARDS** Guggenheim Fel, 69-70; PEN/Spielvogel-Diamonstein Awd, 94; Honored Scholar, Milton Soc of Am; Hanford Book Awd, 98. **RESEARCH** Milton, First Amendment Issues, Affirmative Action, Holocaust Denial. **SELECTED PUBLICATIONS** Auth, Surprised by Sin: The Reader in Paradise Lost, MacMillan, 69; auth, Self-Consuming Artifacts: The Experience of Seventeenth Century Literature, Berkeley, 72; auth, Is There a Text in This Class? The Authority of Interpretive Communities, Harvard, 80; auth, Doing What comes Naturally: Change, Rhetoric, and the Practice of Theory in Literary and Legal Studies, Duke, 89; auth, There's No Such

Thing as Free Speech, and It's A Good Thing Too, Oxford, 94; auth, Professional Correctness: Literary Studies and Political Change, Oxford, 95; auth, the Trouble with Principle, Harvard, 99; auth, How Milton Works, Harvard, 01. **CONTACT ADDRESS** Col of Lib Arts and Sci, Univ of Illinois, Chicago, 601 S Morgan St, Rm 425 UH, Chicago, IL 60607. **EMAIL** sfish@uic.edu

FISHBACK, PRICE VANMETER
PERSONAL Born 07/08/1955, Louisville, KY, m, 1989 **DISCIPLINE** ECONOMICS **EDUCATION** Butler Univ, BA, 77; Univ of Wash, MA, 79; PhD, 83. **CAREER** Teaching asst, Univ of Wash, 77-82; economic res and forecasting, Weyerhaeuser Co, 79-80; temp asst prof, 82-83, asst prof, 83-87, assoc prof, 87-91, Univ of Ga; vis, Univ of Tx, Austin, 87-89; ed board, J of Econ Hist, 91-94; res economist, 93-94; res assoc, 94-; nat bureau of econ res; assoc prof, 90-93; prof, 93-, Univ of Ariz; ed board, explorations in econ hist, 98-; trustee, 94-97; confr coord, 96-, cliometrics soc. **HONORS AND AWARDS** Phi Kappa Phi; Phi Eta Sigma; Col Prize from Econ Asn, 96-97; Swift Teaching Awd, Univ of Ga, 84; Honors Day Recognition for Outstanding Teaching, Univ of Ga, 83, 84, & 86; Univ of Ariz Weekend MBA Fac of the Year Awd 99; Univ of Ariz MBA Fac of the Year Awd, 00; Paul Smauelson Awd Cert from TIAA-CREF Inst, 00. **MEMBERSHIPS** Am Econ Asn; Econ Hist Asn; Western Econ Asn; Cliometrics Soc; Economic Hist Soc; Nat Bureau of Econ Res. **RESEARCH** Economic history; labor economics; law and economics; applied microeconomics. **SELECTED PUBLICATIONS** Auth, Soft Coal, Hard Choices: The Economic Welfare of Bituminous Coal Miners 1890 to 1930, Oxford Univ Pres, 92; coauth, Institutional Change, Compensating Differentials and Accident Risk in American Railroading 1892-1945, J of Economic Hist, 93; coauth, Did Workers Gain from the Passage of Workers' Compensation Laws?, Quart J of Economics, 95; auth, The Durable Experiment: State Insureance of Workers' Compensation Risk in the Early Twentieth Centruy, J of Economic Hist, 96; coauth, Precautionary Saving, Insurance, and the Origins of Workers' Compensation, J of Political Economy, 96; coauth, The Adoption of Workers' Compensation in the United States 1890-1930, J of Law and Economics, 98; auth, Operations of Unfettered Labor Markets: Exit and Voice in American Labor Markets at the Turn of the Century, J of Economic Lit, 98; coauth, Prelude to the Welfare State: The Origins of Workers' Compensation, Univ of Chicago Press, 00. **CONTACT ADDRESS** Dept of Economics, Univ of Arizona, Tucson, AZ 85718. **EMAIL** pfishback@bpa.arizona.edu

FISHBURN, JANET FORSYTHE
PERSONAL Born 01/18/1937, Wilkinsburg, PA, m, 1958, 3 children **DISCIPLINE** AMERICAN CHURCH AND CULTURAL HISTORY **EDUCATION** Monmouth Col, BA, 58; Pa State Univ, PhD, 78. **CAREER** Dir Christian educ, 1st United Presby Church, Cleveland Heights, Ohio, 58-60; Instr humanities and Am studies, Pa State Univ, 77-78; Prof, Teaching Ministry and Church Hist, Theol Sch, Drew Univ, 78-95; Prof and Researchers Relig Educ, 95-. **MEMBERSHIPS** Am Acad Relig; Am Soc of Church Hist; ASC. **RESEARCH** American church history and contemporary Christian ministry; family studies and intergenerational education; theological; Reformed Tradition and Matrerial Culture in US; Social Gospel in the US. **SELECTED PUBLICATIONS** Auth, The Fatherhood of God and the Victorian Family: A Study of the Soicial Gospel in America, Fortress, 82; auth, Confronting the Idolatry of Family: A New Vision For the Household of God, Abingdon, 91; auth, Cultural Diversity and Seminary Teaching, Rel Educ, Vol 90, 95; Tennent, Gilbert, Established Dissenter, Church Hist, Vol 63.95; Preacher, Sunday, Billy and Big Time American Evangelism, Am Presbyterians J Presbyterian Hist, Vol 74, 96. **CONTACT ADDRESS** 74 Barnsdale Rd, Madison, NJ 07940. **EMAIL** jfishbur@drew.edu

FISHER, DAVID HICKMAN
PERSONAL Born 08/28/1943, San Bernardino, CA, m, 1966, 3 children **DISCIPLINE** RELIGION, PHILOSOPHY **EDUCATION** Carleton Col, BA, 65; Columbia Univ and Union Theol Sem, MA, 67; Vanderbilt Univ, MA, 73, PhD (relig), 76. **CAREER** Instr theol, Sch Theol, Univ of the South, 74-76; resident clin pastoral educ, Iowa Methodist Med Ctr, Des Moines, 76-77; asst prof relig, Kalamazoo Col, 77-78; asst prof relig and philos, Blackburn Col, 78-80; ASST PROF RELIG AND PHILOS, GEORGE WILLIAMS COL, 80-, Priest-in-charge, St John's Episcopal Church, Ionia, Mich, 77-78 and Holy Cross Episcopal Church, Fairview Heights, Ill, 79-80; LECTR, C G JUNG CTR, EVANSTON, 80-. **MEMBERSHIPS** Am Acad Relig; Col Theol Soc; Conf Anglican Theologians; Int Asn Philos and Lit. **RESEARCH** Religion and culture (psychology and religion, relation between myth story and belief); post structuralism and theology; process philosophy and theology. **CONTACT ADDRESS** Philos Dept, No Central Col, PO Box 3063, Naperville, IL 60566-7063. **EMAIL** dhf@noctrl.edu

FISHER, ELI D.
PERSONAL Born 11/11/1953, Warren, OH, m, 1990, 3 children **DISCIPLINE** RELIGION (OLD TESTAMENT) **EDUCATION** Vanderbilt Univ, PhD, 98. **CAREER** Author **MEMBERSHIPS** Soc of Bibl Lit **CONTACT ADDRESS** 9265 S Douglas Ave, Nashville, TN 37204. **EMAIL** efisher@gbod.org

FISHER, EUGENE J.
PERSONAL Born 09/10/1943, m, 1 child **DISCIPLINE** RELIGION **EDUCATION** Sacred Heart Seminary, BA, 65; Univ Detroit, MA, 68; NYork Univ, PhD, 76. **CAREER** Adj Prof, Univ Detroit. 69-77; Adj Prof, St. John's Seminary, 73-75; Lectr, St. Francis Sch Christian Educ, 69-71; Dir Catechist Formation, Office Relig Educ, Archdiocese Detroit, 71-77; Exec Dir, Secretariat for Cath-Jewish Relations, Nat Conf Cath Bishops, 77-90; Assoc Dir, Secretariat for Ecumenical & Interreligious Affairs, Nat Conf Cath Bishops, 90-. **HONORS AND AWARDS** Valedictorian, Austin Cath Preparatory Sch, 61; Kittay Fel, NY Univ, 70-71; Morris L. Kirsch Awd for Excellence in Hebrew Studies, 70; Sh. Y. Agnon Awd for Excellence in Hebrew Studies, 71; Walter A. Romig Distinguished Alumnus Awd, Sacred Heart Col, 81; Edith Stein Guild Awd for Extraordinary Contributions to Catholic-Jewish Relations, 83; Nat Workshop - Christian-Jewish Relations Special Awd, 87; Raoul Wallenberg Tribute Awd for Contributions to Christian-Jewish Relations, 95; Lamp of Understanding Awd, Shalom Ctr for Understanding Between Christians, 95; 1995 Nat Jewish Bk Coun Awd for best book in the Jewish-Christian Category, for: John Paul II, Spiritual Pilgrimage: Texts on Jews and Judaism 1970-1995; Nat Jewish Chautaqua Awd, October 98; Doctor of Divinity Honoris Causa, St. Mary's Univ and Seminary, May 99; Matanenbaum Awd for the Advancement of Interreligious Understanding, May 00. **MEMBERSHIPS** Soc Bibl Lit; Cath Bibl Asn; Nat Asn Prof Hebrew; Bibl Archaeol Soc; Service Int de Documentation Judeo-Chretienne; Am Acad Relig; Fel Reconciliation; Christian Study Group Judaism & Jewish People; Nat Inst Holocaust; Ctr Holocaust Studies; Churches' Ctr Theol & Public Policy; Vatican Comn Relig Relations Jewish People; Nat Asn Ecumenical Officers. **SELECTED PUBLICATIONS** Auth, The New Catechism, Catholics and Jews: Cardinal Ratzinger in Jerusalem, Nat Cath Register, 10/94; Jesus and His Fellow Jews, Cath Standard, 1/95; coauth, John Paul II, Spiritual Pilgrimage: Texts on Jews and Judaism 1970-1995, Crossroad Publ, 95; auth, Catholic-Jewish Relations, 1996 Catholic Almanac, Our Sunday Visitor, 96; The Church and Anti-Semitism: Rome is Due to Pronounce, Nat Cath Register, 7/96; The Rochester Agreement in Its Historical Context, The Rochester Agreement, Anti-Defamation League, 97; The Start of the Healing Process, Brotherhood 12, 98; author of numerous other articles, books, and publications. **CONTACT ADDRESS** 3211 Fourth St. NE, Washington, DC 20017-1194.

FISHER, JAMES T.
DISCIPLINE US RELIGIOUS HISTORY **EDUCATION** Rutgers Univ, PhD. **CAREER** Hist Dept, St Edward's Euniv **HONORS AND AWARDS** Managing ed, Jour Policy Hist. **SELECTED PUBLICATIONS** Auth, The Catholic Counterculture in America, 1933-1962; Dr. America: The Lives of Thomas A. Dooley. **CONTACT ADDRESS** St. Edward's Univ, 3001 S Congress Ave, Austin, TX 78704-6489.

FISHER, LOUIS
PERSONAL Born 08/17/1934, Norfolk, VA, 2 children **DISCIPLINE** POLITICAL SCIENCE **EDUCATION** New School for Soc Res PhD 67. **CAREER** Sr Spec in Separation of Power, Compressional Res Service, the Library of Congress, 70; Asst Prof Queens College NY, 67-70. **HONORS AND AWARDS** Louis Brownlow Book Awd, National Academy of Public Admin (twice for Pres Spending Power in 75 and Constitutional Dialogues in 88. **MEMBERSHIPS** American Political Sci Assoc, Natl Academy of Public Admin, Amer Soc of Public Admin. **RESEARCH** Constitutional law, presidency, Congress, war powers, budget policy. **SELECTED PUBLICATIONS** President and Congress, The Free Press, 1972; Presidential Spending Power, Princeton Univ Press, 1975; Constitutional Conflicts between Congress and the President 4th ed Univ Press of KS, 87; Constitutional Dialogues, Princeton Univ Press, 88; encyclopedia of the Am Presidency (with Leonard W. Levy), Simon R. Schuster, 1994; Presidential War Power, Univ Press of KS, 95; Political Dynamics of Constitutional Law 3rd ed West Publishers, 96; The Politics of Shared Power, 4th ed, TX A&M Univ Press, 98; Amer Constitutional Law, 3rd ed, Caroline Academic Press, 99. **CONTACT ADDRESS** Library of Congress, Washington, DC 20540. **EMAIL** lfisher@crs.loc.gov

FISHER, ROBERT THADDEUS
PERSONAL Born 03/08/1926, Detroit, MI, m, 1947, 2 children **DISCIPLINE** PHILOSOPHY **EDUCATION** Wayne State Univ, BS, 48, MEd, 50, JD, 66; Mich State Univ, EdD, 59. **CAREER** Prof philos, Calif State Col, Pa, 61-66; a8st prof, 66-80, ASSOC PROF BUS LAW AND FINANCE, SAN DIEGO STATE UNIV, 80-. **MEMBERSHIPS** Am Psychol Asn. **RESEARCH** Existential analysis; philosophy of law and education. **SELECTED PUBLICATIONS** Auth, Swimming with the Current, Russ Hist Histoire Russe, Vol 21, 94; Hazard, John, N. 1909-1995--In Memoriam, Slavic Rev, Vol 54, 95; War, Revolution, and Peace in Russia--The Passages of Golder, Frank, 1914-1927 - Emmons, T, Patenaude, B, Russ Rev, Vol 52, 93; The Russian Syndrome--1000 Years of Political Murder, Russ Revi Vol 53, 94. **CONTACT ADDRESS** Dept of Bus Law and Finance, San Diego State Univ, San Diego, CA 92115.

FISHER, ROGER
PERSONAL Born 05/28/1922, IL, m, 1948, 2 children **DISCIPLINE** LAW **EDUCATION** Harvard, LLB, 48. **CAREER** Lecturer, 58-60, Prof, Harvard Law School, 60-76, Samuel Williston Prof Law, 76-92; Iran Hostage Crisis, works with White House and Iranian leadership re: Algerian Mediation, 79; Dir Harv Neg Proj, 80-; Fndr Sr Consul, Conflict Mgmt Grp, 84-; Sr Princ, Conflict Mgmt, 84-; South Africa, works with NPA, ANC, Inkatha Freedom Party, 91; Samuel Williston Prof Law Emer, Harvard Law Sch, 92-; Ecuador Peru, leads joint session to gen options re: boundary war, 95; Georgia-Ossetia Conflict, help resolve conflict with invit by Pres Shevardnadze, 95-. **HONORS AND AWARDS** Guggenheim Fel, Vis Prof, Dept Intl Rela, London Sch Econo, 65-66; Szilard Peace Prize, 81; Cen for Pub Resources Pract Ach Awd, 93; LHD, CT Col, 94; orig and exec ed,the advocates, pub tv, 69-70; co-orig and exec ed, tv series arabs and israelis, 74-75. **MEMBERSHIPS** Board Memberships, Council for a Viable World, Conflict Management, Conflict Management Group Inc, Hudson Inst Trustee Emer, Program On Neg, Council on Foreign Relations. **SELECTED PUBLICATIONS** Getting It Done: How to Lead When You Are not in Charge, Roger Fisher and Alan Sharp with John Richardson, Harper Business, 98; Coping With International Conflict: A Systematic Approach to Influence in International Negotiation, with Andrea Kupfer Schneider, Eliz Borgwardt, Brian Ganson, Prentice Hall, 97; Getting Ready to Negotiate: The Getting to Yes Workbook, with Danny Ertle, Penguin Books, 95; Beyond Machiavelli: Tools for Coping With Conflict, with Eliz Kopelman, Andrea Kupfer Schneider, Harvard Univ Press, 94; Getting to Yes: Negotiating Agreement Without Giving In, second ed, Roger Fisher, William Ury, Bruce Patton, Penguin Books, 91. **CONTACT ADDRESS** Law Sch, Harvard Univ, Pound Hall 500, Cambridge, MA 02138.

FISHER, SAUL
DISCIPLINE PHILOSOPHY **EDUCATION** Grad Sch and Univ Ctr, City Univ of NYork, PhD, 97. **CAREER** Prog assoc, Andrew W. Mellon Found, 98-; Assoc Prog Office, The Andrew W. Mellon Foundation, New York, NY, 98-. **HONORS AND AWARDS** Fulbright for study in Fr, 94-95. **MEMBERSHIPS** Amer Philos Asn; Philos of Sci Asn; Hist of Sci Soc; Hist of Philos of Sci Working Grp. **RESEARCH** History and philosophy of science (HOPOS) Working Group-; Aesthetics of architecture; Steering Committee, 00-03. **SELECTED PUBLICATIONS** Rev, Gassendi's Ethics, Brit Jour for the Hist of Sci, 98; rev, "Lisa Sarasohn's Gassendi's Ethics," British Journal for the History of Science, 98; auth, Architectural Aesthetics in the Analytic Tradition: a New Curriculum, Journal of Architectural Education, 00; auth, Architectural Notation and Computer Aided Design, Journal of Aesthetics and Art Criticism, 00; Pierre Gassendi's Philosophy and Science, Brill Studies in Intellectual History, Leiden: Brill, 01. **CONTACT ADDRESS** 140 E 62nd St, New York, NY 10021. **EMAIL** sf@mellon.org

FISHMAN, DAVID E.
PERSONAL Born, NY **DISCIPLINE** JEWISH HISTORY **EDUCATION** Yeshiva Univ, BA; Harvard Univ, MA, PhD. **CAREER** Instr, Brandeis Univ; instr, Russ State Univ, Moscow; fel, Hebrew Univ Inst Adv Studies; assoc prof and chr, Dept Jewish Hist, Jewish Theol Sem Am; sr resh assoc, YIVO Inst Jewish Res. **HONORS AND AWARDS** Dir Project Judaica, JTS and YIVO with the Russ State Univ for the Hum; ed, Yivo-Bletter. **SELECTED PUBLICATIONS** Auth, Russia's First Modern Jews, NY Univ Press; Embers Plucked from the Fire: The Rescue of Jewish Cultural Treasures in Vilna,YIVO; numerous articles on the history and culture of East European Jewry. **CONTACT ADDRESS** Jewish Theol Sem of America, 3080 Broadway, New York, NY 10027. **EMAIL** dafishman@jtsa.edu

FISS, OWEN M.
PERSONAL Born 02/24/1938, m, 1959, 3 children **DISCIPLINE** LAW **EDUCATION** Dartmouth Col, BA, 59; Oxford Univ, BPhil, 61; Harvard Univ, LLB, 64. **CAREER** Law Clerk to Judge Thurgood Marshall, Court of Appeals, 64-65 & to Justice William J Brennan, US Supreme Court, 65-66; spec asst to John Doar, Asst Atty Gen, Civil Rights Div, Dept Justice, 66-68; from assoc prof to prof law, Univ Chicago, 68-74; Vis prof, Law Sch, Stanford Univ, 73-74; Prof Law, 74-82, Alexander M. Bickel Prof Public Law, 82-92, Sterling Prof Law, Yale Univ, 92-. **HONORS AND AWARDS** Summa Cum Laude, Valedictory Standing, Phi Beta Kappa, Rufus Choate Schol & Reynolds Fel, Dartmouth Col; Fulbright Schol, Oxford Univ; Magna Cum Laude, Prize Schol, and Law Rev, Harvard Law Sch. **RESEARCH** History of the Supreme Court-Holmes devise. **SELECTED PUBLICATIONS** Auth, Affirmative Action as a Strategy of Justice, Philos & Pub Policy 37, 97; op ed, Beyond Diversity, Washington Post, 5/7/97; Speech and Power Symposium, Is First Amendment Absolutism Obsolete?, The Nation, 7/21/97; Libertad de Expresion y Estructura Social, Fontamera, 97; Discipline and Passion, In: Rechstheorie, Zeitschrift fur Logik, Methodenlehre, Kybernetik und Sozologie des Rechts, Duncker & Humblot, 98; Money and Politics, Columbia Law Rev 2470, 98; Hong Kong Democracy, Columbia J Transnational Law 493; 98; Globalization and Its Consequences for Democracy: The Case of the World Bank (in press); Political Violence and Freedom of Speech (in press); Abortion Protest and

the Limits of Free Speech (in press); author of numerous other articles and publications. **CONTACT ADDRESS** Law Sch, Yale Univ, PO Box 208215, New Haven, CT 06520-8215. **EMAIL** owen.fiss@yale.edu

FITTIPALDI, SILVIO EDWARD
PERSONAL Born 11/09/1937, Philadelphia, PA **DISCIPLINE** RELIGION, PSYCHOLOGY **EDUCATION** Villanova Univ, AB, 60; Augustinian Col, MA, 64; Temple Univ, PhD (relig), 76. **CAREER** Instr relig, Villanova Univ, 72-76, asst prof, 76-82, chmn dept, 77-80. **MEMBERSHIPS** Col Theol Soc; Cath Theol Soc Am; Friends Conf Relig and Psychol; Asn Humanistic Psychol. **RESEARCH** The encounter of world religions; religion and psychology; mysticism. **SELECTED PUBLICATIONS** Auth, Freedom in Roman Catholicism and Zen Buddhism, In: Liberation, Revolution and Freedom, Seabury, 75; co-ed, From Alienation to At-One-Ness, Villanova Univ, 78; auth, How to Pray Always Without Always Praying, Fides/Claretian, 78; Buddhist Sutras and Enlightenment in Contemporary Zen, Horizons, fall 78; The Zen of Ethics, In: Essays in Morality and Ethics, Paulist Press, 80; Human Consciousness and the Christian Mystic: Teresa of Avila, In: The Metaphors of Consciousness, Plenum, 81; Teaching religion as a spiritual process, In: The Journey of Western Spirituality, Scholars Press, 81; Zen Mind, Christian Mind, Empty Mind, J Ecumenical Studies, 82. **CONTACT ADDRESS** 1325 S Broad St, Philadelphia, PA 19147.

FITTS, LEROY
PERSONAL Born 07/06/1944, Norlina, NC, m, 1963 **DISCIPLINE** THEOLOGY **EDUCATION** Shaw Univ, BA 1967; Southeastern Bapt Theo Sem, M Div 1970; VA Sem, D Div 1975, DHL, 1990; Princeton Univ, (NEH Inst) 1984; Baltimore Hebrew University, MA 1985. **CAREER** First Bapt Ch of Jacksonville, NC, pastor 68-72; First Bapt Church, Baltimore, MD, pastor 72-; Comm Coll of Baltimore, adjunct prof 78-80; VA Sem & Coll, pres 81; ad; prof, Black Church History, St Mary's Seminary & University, Baltimore, MD. **MEMBERSHIPS** Editor Loft Carey Baptist Convention 1975-90; brd of mgrs VA Sem & Coll 1980; mem NAACP, Assoc for the Study of Negro Hist 1978-; bd of mgrs, St. Marys Seminary & University. **SELECTED PUBLICATIONS** Author, Lott Carey First Black Msnry to Africa 1978, A History of Black Baptists 1985; article "The Church in the South & Social Issues", Faith & Mission vol II, No I, Fall 1984. **CONTACT ADDRESS** First Baptist Church, 525 N Caroline St, Baltimore, MD 21205.

FITZ, HOPE K.
DISCIPLINE PHILOSOPHY **EDUCATION** Claremom Grad School **CAREER** CT St Univ, prof, phil, 10 yrs. **HONORS AND AWARDS** NEH grant, 86; fac grant, Mount St. Mary's Col, 86; fac sum develop funds, Eastern CT St Univ, 90; Ct St Univ travel grant, 93. **MEMBERSHIPS** APA; Soc for Asian & Comparative Phil, **RESEARCH** South Asian Phil; esp Hinduism; Gandhi's ethical, religious, political thought. **SELECTED PUBLICATIONS** Art, The Mystical Experience From a Heideggerian Perspective, Jour of Relig Stud, 90; auth, The Importance of Overcoming the False Self in the Process of Self-Development, Miami Univ OH, 90; art, The Role of Self-Discipline in the Process of Self-Realization, Jour of Rel Stud, Vol XIX, 91; art, The Nature and Significance of Intuition in Patanjali's Yoga Sutra and in the Philosophical Writings of Radhakrishnan, AAS, 93; art, The Nature and Significance of Intuition in Patanjali's Yoga Sutra and in the Philosophical Writings of Radhakrishnan, Jour of Relig Stud, Vol XXVI, 95; auth, Intuition and Revelation as They Relate to Transcendence, 95; art, Gandhi's Ethical/Religious Tradition, Jour of Relig Stud, Vol XXVII, 96. **CONTACT ADDRESS** Eastern Connecticut State Univ, Classroom Bldg 356, Willimantic, CT 06226. **EMAIL** fitzh@ecsu.ctstateu.edu

FITZGERALD, DESMOND J.
PERSONAL Born 01/18/1924, Toronto, ON, Canada, m, 1947, 2 children **DISCIPLINE** PHILOSOPHY **EDUCATION** Univ Toronto, BA, 46, MA, 47; Univ CA, Berkeley, MA, 50, PhD, 54. **CAREER** Instr philos, St Louis Univ, 47; from instr to prof emeritus, Univ San Francisco, 48-; vis prof polit sci, Dominican Col, 57; commentator Can Affairs, World Press educ TV prog, KQED, San Francisco, 69-78. **HONORS AND AWARDS** Mercier Gold Medal, 46; res fel, Inst Philos Res, 58-61; Fulbright res fel, Italy, 66-67. **MEMBERSHIPS** Am Philos Asn; Am Cath Philos Asn (pres, 75-76); Renaissance Soc Am; Hist Sci Soc. **RESEARCH** Hist of philos; philos and science; metaphysics and epistemology. **SELECTED PUBLICATIONS** Auth, Descartes--Defender of the Faith, Thought, autumn 58; Problem of the Projectile Again, 64, Is There an Unchanging Human Nature?, 69 & Liberty Versus Equality, 76, Proc Am Cath Philos Asn. **CONTACT ADDRESS** Dept of Philos, Univ of San Francisco, 2130 Fulton St, San Francisco, CA 94117-1050. **EMAIL** fitzgeraldd@usfca.edu

FITZGERALD, J. PATRICK
PERSONAL Born 04/05/1950, Evansville, IN, m, 1970, 2 children **DISCIPLINE** PHILOSOPHY, AESTHETICS **EDUCATION** Univ Southern Ind, BA, 74; Southern Ill Univ at Carbondale, MA, 76; PhD, 86. **CAREER** Instr, Southern Ill Univ at Carbondale, 77-79; chemn of Humanities, John A. Logan Col, 79-87; prof, Seminole Community Col, 88-. **HONORS AND AWARDS** Listed in Who's Who Among Am Teachers, 96. **MEMBERSHIPS** Am Philos Asn. **RESEARCH** Philosophy in the media. **SELECTED PUBLICATIONS** Auth, A Parliament of Minds, State Univ NY Pr, 99; auth, A Parliament of Minds (national PBS television series--18 episodes), 00. **CONTACT ADDRESS** Dept Humanities & Fine Arts, Seminole Comm Col, 100 Weldon Blvd, Sanford, FL 32773-6132. **EMAIL** patfitz@webtv.net

FITZGERALD, JOHN JOSEPH
PERSONAL Born 10/17/1928, North Adams, MA, m, 1954, 6 children **DISCIPLINE** PHILOSOPHY **EDUCATION** Univ Notre Dame, BA, 49; St Louis Univ, MA, 53; Tulane Univ, PhD(philos), 62. **CAREER** From instr to asst prof philos, Univ Notre Dame, 58-66; assoc prof, 66-71, Prof Philos, 71-94, prof emeritus, Univ Mass, Dartmouth. **MEMBERSHIPS** Am Cath Philos Asn; Am Philos Asn; Am Fedn Teachers (1st vpres, 71-72, pres, 73-76). **RESEARCH** Classical realism; American philosophy. **SELECTED PUBLICATIONS** Auth, Peirce's How to Make our Ideas Clear, New Scholasticism, 65; Peirce's Theory of Signs as Foundation for Pragmatism, Mouton, The Hague, 66; Peirce's theory of inquiry, Trans C S Peirce Soc, 68; Peirce's argument for thirdness, New Scholasticism, summer 71; Ambiguity in Peirce's Theory of Signs, Trans C S Peirce Soc, 76; auth, Peirce's Doctrine of Symbol, in Colapietro, ed, Peirce's Doctrine of Signs, de Gruyter, 96. **CONTACT ADDRESS** 14 Sugarmill Dr, Okatie, SC 29910.

FITZGERALD, JOHN THOMAS, JR.
PERSONAL Born 10/02/1948, Birmingham, AL, m, 1970, 2 children **DISCIPLINE** RELIGIOUS STUDIES; NEW TESTAMENT **EDUCATION** Yale Univ, PhD, 84. **CAREER** Instr, Univ Miami, 81-84; asst prof, Univ Miami, 84-88; assoc prof, Univ Miami, 88-; visiting assoc prof, Brown Univ, spring, 92; visiting assoc prof, Yale Divinity Sch, 98-99. **HONORS AND AWARDS** Soc of Bibl Lit res grant, 97-00; Max Orovitz summer res award, 85, 87, 94-95, 98. **MEMBERSHIPS** Asn of Ancient Hist; Soc of Bibl Lit; Studiorum Novi Testamenti Soc. **RESEARCH** New Testament/Early Christianity; Hellenistic philosophy & literature. **SELECTED PUBLICATIONS** article, The Ancient Lives of Aristotle and the Modern Debate about the Genre of the Gospels, Restoration Quart, 36, 209-21, 94; article, The Problem of Perjury in Greek Context: Prolegomena to an Exegesis of Matthew 5:33, 1 Timothy 1:10, and Didache 2.3, The Social World of the First Christians: Essays in Honor of Wayne A. Meeks, Fortress Press, 156-77, 95; article, Introduction, Friendship, Flattery and Frankness of Speech, E. J. Brill, 1-4, 96; article, Philippians in the Light of Some Ancient Discussions of Friendship, Friendship, Flattery and Frankness of Speech, E. J. Brill, 141-60, 96; article, The Catalogue in Ancient Greek Literature, The Rhetorical Analysis of Scripture: Essays from the 1995; London Conference, Sheffield Acad Press, 275-93, 97; article, Friendship, Encycl of Early Christianity, Garland Publ, 1, 439-42, 97; article, Introduction, Greco-Roman Perspectives on Friendship, Scholars Press, 1-11, 97; article, Friendship in the Greek World Prior to Aristotle, Greco-Roman Perspectives on Friendship, Scholars Press, 13-34, 97; Article, Eusebius and The Little Labyrinth, The Early Church in its Context: Essays in Honor of Everett Ferguson, E. J. Brill, 120-46, 98; Article, Concordances, NT, Dictionary of Biblical Interpretation, Abingdon, 1, 212-15, 99; article, Eid [inkl. Meineid]: NT, Religion in Geschichte und Gegenwart, Mohr, 2, 1125-26, 99; article, Lexicons, NT, Dictornary of Biblical Interpretation, Abingdon, 2, 62-66. **CONTACT ADDRESS** Dept. of Religious Studies, Univ of Miami, PO Box 248264, Coral Gables, FL 33124-4672. **EMAIL** jtfitz@umiami.ir.miami.edu

FITZGERALD, PATRICK
PERSONAL Born 05/26/1966, Marysville, OH, s **DISCIPLINE** PHILOSOPHY, ETHICS **EDUCATION** Miami Univ, BA, 88; Univ Arizona, MA, 91, PhD, 96; Oxford Univ, M.Phil, Politics, 93. **CAREER** Grad tchng asst, 88-91 & 93-94, Univ of Ariz; asst prof of Phil, 95-, Louisana St Univ. **HONORS AND AWARDS** NEH Sum Sem Fel, Brown Univ, 96; John M. Olin Fel, 91-93; Claude Lambe Fel, 89-91; Humane Studies Residential Fel, 91; Reisen Prize, 90; Hall Prize, 87 & 88. **MEMBERSHIPS** APA **RESEARCH** Ethical theory, political phil, bioethics. **SELECTED PUBLICATIONS** Coauth, Secrecy, Human Radiation Experiments and Intentional Releases, The Human Radiation Experiments: Final Report of the Pres Adv Comm, Oxford Univ Press, 96; coauth, Atomic Veterans: Human Experimentation in Connection with Atomic Tests, The Human Radiation Experiments: Final Report of the Pres Adv Comm, Oxford Univ Press, 96; art, Service-Learning and the Socially Responsible Ethics Class, Tchng Phil 20:3, 97. **CONTACT ADDRESS** Dept of Philosophy, Louisiana State Univ and A&M Col, Baton Rouge, LA 70803. **EMAIL** pfitzge@lsu.edu

FITZMYER, JOSEPH A.
PERSONAL Born 11/04/1920, Philadelphia, PA, s **DISCIPLINE** RELIGION **EDUCATION** Loyola Univ, AB, 43; MA, 45; Johns Hopkins Univ, PhD, 56; St Albert de Louvain Belgium, STL, 52; Pontificio Istituto Biblico Rome, SSL, 57. **CAREER** Instructor, Gonzaga Col HS, 45-48; Asst to Full Prof, Woodstock Col, 58-69; Prof, Univ Chicago, 69-71; Prof, Fordham Univ, 71-74; Prof, Weston Jesuit Sch of Theol, 74-76; Prof to Prof Emeritus, Catholic Univ, 76-. **HONORS AND AWARDS** Burkitt Medal, British Royal Acad, 84; Patronal Medal, Catholic Univ, 85; Johannes Quasten Awd, Catholic Univ, 93. **MEMBERSHIPS** Soc of Biblical Lit; Catholic Biblical Asn of Am; Studiorum Novi Testamenti Soc **RESEARCH** Aramaic and Semitic background of the New Testament; Dead Sea Scrolls. **SELECTED PUBLICATIONS** Auth, Romans: A New Translation with Introduction and Commentary, Doubleday, 93; auth, Scripture, the Soul of Theology, Paulist, 94; auth, The Biblical Commission's Document 'The Interpretation of the Bible in the Church': Text and Commentary, Biblical Institute, 95; auth, The Aramaic Inscriptions of Sefire: Revised Edition, Biblical Inst, 95; auth, Spiritual Exercises Based on Paul's Epistle to the Romans, Paulist, 95; auth, "Tobit", Qumran Cave 4: XIV, Parabiblical Texts, Part 2, Clarendon, 95; auth, The Semitic Background of the New Testament: Combined Edition of Essays on the Semitic Background of the New Testament and A Wandering Aramean: Collected Aramaic Essays, Dove Booksellers, 97; auth, To Advance the Gospel: New Testament Studies: Second Ed, Dove Booksellers, 98; auth, The Acts of the Apostles: A New Translation with Introduction and Commentary, Doubleday, 98; auth, The Dead Sea Scrolls and Christian Origins, Eerdmans, 00. **CONTACT ADDRESS** Dept Biblical Studies, Catholic Univ of America, 620 Michigan Ave NE, Washington, DC 20064-0001. **EMAIL** fitzmyja@gusun.georgetown.edu

FITZPATRICK, WILLIAM J.
PERSONAL Born 07/03/1964, Syracuse, NY, m, 1989 **DISCIPLINE** PHILOSOPHY **EDUCATION** Princeton Univ, BA, 86; Univ Calif, Los Angeles, MA, 88, PhD, 95. **CAREER** Lectr, Yale Univ, 96- . **MEMBERSHIPS** APA. **RESEARCH** Metaethics; normative ethics; philosophy of biology. **CONTACT ADDRESS** Virginia Polytech Inst and State Univ, 531 Major Williams Hall, 100 Virginia Tech, Blacksburg, VA 24061-0002. **EMAIL** Billjfitz@aol.com

FLANAGAN, JAMES F.
DISCIPLINE CIVIL PROCEDURE, EVIDENCE, FEDERAL PRACTICE & ALTERNATE DISPUTE RESOLUTION **EDUCATION** Univ Notre Dame, AB, 64; Univ PA, LLB, 67. **CAREER** Prof, Univ of SC **RESEARCH** Procedural aspects of litigation. **SELECTED PUBLICATIONS** Coauth, treatise on SC civil procedure; publ on, civil procedure. **CONTACT ADDRESS** School of Law, Univ of So Carolina, Columbia, Law Center, Columbia, SC 29208. **EMAIL** Jimf@law.law.sc.edu

FLANAGAN, KATHLEEN
DISCIPLINE RELIGIOUS STUDIES **EDUCATION** Col St Elizabeth, BA; St John's Univ, MA; Union Theol Sem, MPhil, PhD. **CAREER** Relig, Col St. Elizabeth **RESEARCH** Church hist; Sacraments; Christology; Elizabeth Seton. **SELECTED PUBLICATIONS** Auth, Some Aspects of Elizabeth Seton's Spiritual-Theological World in Vincention Heritage XIV, 93. **CONTACT ADDRESS** Dept of Relig Studies, Col of Saint Elizabeth, 2 Convent Rd., Morristown, NJ 07960. **EMAIL** flanagan@liza.st-elizabeth.edu

FLANAGAN, OWEN
DISCIPLINE PHILOSOPHY **EDUCATION** Boston Univ, PhD, 77. **CAREER** Prof philos, Wellesley Col, 85-86; adj prof, chair dept, Duke Univ, 93-. **HONORS AND AWARDS** Pres, Soc Philos Psychol, 94-95. **MEMBERSHIPS** Soc Philos Psychol. **RESEARCH** Philos of mind; philos of psych; philos of soc sci; ethics; contemp ethical theory; moral psych. **SELECTED PUBLICATIONS** Auth, Varieties of Moral Personality: Ethics and Psychological Realism, Harvard Univ, 91; Consciousness Reconsidered, MIT, 92; Self Expressions: Mind, Morals, and the Meaning of Life, Oxford Univ, 96; ed, The Science of the Mind, MIT, 91; Identity, Character, and Morality: Essays in Moral Psychology, MIT, 90. **CONTACT ADDRESS** Philos Dept, Duke Univ, West Duke Bldg, Durham, NC 27706. **EMAIL** ojf@acpub.duke.edu

FLANNERY, MICHAEL T.
DISCIPLINE LEGAL WRITING AND APPELLATE ADVOCACY **EDUCATION** Univ Del, BA, 87; Cath Univ Am Columbus Sch Law, JD, 91. **CAREER** Prof,Villanova Univ Sch Law, 96-; worked in, Wolf, Block, Schorr and Solis-Cohen; assoc, Gold-Bikin, Clifford and Young, 94; asst city solicitor, Philadelphia, 91-94. **CONTACT ADDRESS** Law School, Villanova Univ, 800 Lancaster Ave, Villanova, PA 19085-1692. **EMAIL** flannery@law.vill.edu

FLANNIGAN, ROB
DISCIPLINE LAW **EDUCATION** Univ Alberta, BS, 76, LLB, 80; Univ Toronto, LLM, 82, SJD, 88. **CAREER** Prof, 85-. **RESEARCH** Contract law; business organizations; trust law. **SELECTED PUBLICATIONS** Auth, The Economic Structure of the Firm, 95; The Legal Construction of Rights of First Refusal, Can Bar Rev, 97. **CONTACT ADDRESS** Col of Law, Univ of Saskatchewan, 15 Campus Dr, Saskatoon, SK, Canada S7N 5A6. **EMAIL** flannigan@law.usask.ca

FLECHTNER, HARRY M.
PERSONAL Born 04/08/1951, Fostoria, OH, m, 1978, 2 children **DISCIPLINE** LAW **EDUCATION** Harvard Col, AB, 73; Harvard Univ, MA, 75; Harvard Law Sch, JD, 81. **CAREER** From Asst Prof to Prof, Univ Pittsburgh, 84-. **HONORS AND AWARDS** Phi Bet Kappa; Excellence in Teaching Awd, Student Bar Asn, 89, 95, 97; Chancellor's Awd for Excellence in Teaching, Univ Pittsburgh, 97. **MEMBERSHIPS** ABIL, Bar Asn. **RESEARCH** International and domestic commercial law, sales law. **SELECTED PUBLICATIONS** Auth, "Enforcing Manufacturers' Warranties, 'Pass Through' Warranties and the Like: Can the Buyer Get a Refund?" Rutgers L Rev 397 (98); auth, "The Several Texts of the CISG in a Decentralized System: Observations on the Uniformity Principle in Article 7(1) of the U N Sales Convention," J L & Com 187 (98); auth, "Breach of Remote Sellers' Warranties-Revocation, Refund and Remedy, Uniform Commercial Code Law J 131 (98); auth, Sales, Leases and Electronic Commerce: Problems and Materials on National and International Transactions, West Group, 00. **CONTACT ADDRESS** Dept Law, Univ of Pittsburgh, 513 Law Bldg, Pittsburgh, PA 15260-7102. **EMAIL** flechtner@law.pitt.edu

FLEER, JACK DAVID
PERSONAL Born 09/21/1937, Washington, MO, m, 1963, 3 children **DISCIPLINE** POLITICAL SCIENCE **EDUCATION** Okla Baptist Univ, AB, 59; Flor St Univ, MS, 61; Univ N Carolina, Chapel Hill, PhD, 65. **CAREER** Res asst, 59-60, inst for govern res, FL St Univ; res asst, 60-61, inst for res in soc science, part-time inst, dept of political science, 61-64, res asst, institute of govern, sum 62 & sum 63, Univ NC; asst prof, 64-69, chmn dept of politics, 69-77, assoc prof, 69-79, prof, 79-, chmn dept of politics, 85-97, Wake Forest Univ. **MEMBERSHIPS** Amer Political Science Asn; Southern Political Science Asn. **RESEARCH** North Carolina govern & politics; southern politics. **SELECTED PUBLICATIONS** Auth, North Carolina: Interest Groups in a State in Transition, Interest Group Politics in the Southern States, Univ AL Press, 92; auth, North Carolina Government and Politics, Univ Nebraska Press, 94; auth, Interest Groups in North Carolina, NC Focus 2nd ed, NC Center for Public Policy Res, 97; coauth, "North Carolina: Between Helms and Hunt No Majority Emerges," in Southern Politics in the 1990s, ed A. Lamis (Louisiana State Univ Pr, 99), 81-106. **CONTACT ADDRESS** Wake Forest Univ, Reynolds Station, PO Box 7568, Winston-Salem, NC 27109. **EMAIL** fleerj@wfu.edu

FLEISCHACKER, SAM
PERSONAL Born 04/22/1961, London, England, m, 1998, 2 children **DISCIPLINE** MORAL, POLITICAL PHILOSOPHY **EDUCATION** Yale Col, BA, summa cum laude, 81; Yale Univ, MA, 84, MPhil, 84; PhD, 89. **CAREER** Vis asst prof, Haverford and Bryn Mawr Col (s), 88-90; fel, Univ Ctr Human Values, Princeton Fellow, Inst Adv Stud Human, Edinburgh, 94-95; assoc prof Philos, Williams Col, 91-99; assoc prof Philos, Univ Ill Chicago, 99- . **HONORS AND AWARDS** Gaudino Memorial Scholar at Williams, 97-99; Amer Philos assn fel, IASH, Edinburgh, 95; Laurance S. Rockefeller fel, UCHV, Princeton, 94-95; John M. Olin fel in Hist and Political Theory, 94-95; ACLS Recent Recipient of the PhD fel, 90-91; Charlotte W. Newcombe fel, 87-88; prize tchg fel, 86-87; various Yale fel, 82-85; Mary Cady Tew prize, 83; Phi Beta Kappa, 81; Gulf Scholar, 78-81. **RESEARCH** Scottish Enlightenment Philosophy; Nineteenth Century Philosophy, esp Hegel and Kierkegaard; Aesthetics; Philosophy of Religion; Wittgenstein. **SELECTED PUBLICATIONS** Auth, Religious Questions: Kafka and Wittgenstein on Giving grounds, Sophia, Ap 82; A Fifth Antinomy, Philosophia, May 89; On the Enforcement of Morality: Aquinas and Narcotics Prohibition, Pub Affairs Quart, Spring 90; Philosophy in Moral Practice: Kant and Adam smith, Kant-Studien, 82, 3, 91; Kant's Theory of Punishment, Kant-studien, 79,4,88, reprinted in Howard Williams, ed, Essays on Kant's Political Philosophy, U of Chicago P, 92; Integrity and Moral Relativism, Leiden, E.J. Brill, 92; The Ethics of Culture, Ithaca: Cornell Univ Press, 94; Frustrated Contracts, Poetry, and Truth, Raritan, Spring, 94, reprinted in Richard Eldridge, ed, Beyond Representation: Philosophy and Poetic Imagination, Cambridge Univ Press, 96; Multiculturalism as a Western Tradition, Academe, Spring 96; Values Behind the Market: Kant's Response to the Wealth of Nations, History of Political Thought, Fall 96; Free Speech and the Education of Governments, The Responsive Community, Winter 97; bk rev, Ethics and the Arts, Ethics, Jan 98; Insignificant Communities, in Amy Gutmann, ed, Freedom of Association, Princeton Univ Press, 98; A Third Concept of Liberty: Judgment and Freedom in Kant and Adam Smith, Princeton Univ Press, 99; **CONTACT ADDRESS** Dept of Philosophy, M/C 267, Univ of Illinois, Chicago, 600 S. Morgan, Chicago, IL 60202-1852. **EMAIL** sfleisch@vic.edu

FLEISCHER, MANFRED PAUL
PERSONAL Born 06/26/1928, Nieder Peilau-Schloessel, Germany, m, 1962, 3 children **DISCIPLINE** EUROPEAN HISTORY, HISTORY OF RELIGION **EDUCATION** Wagner Col, BA, 55; Philadelphia Lutheran Theol Sem, MDiv, 59; Univ Pa, MA, 61; Univ Erlangen, PhD (hist ideas and relig), 65. **CAREER** Lectr philos, Wagner Col, 55-56; pastor, Lutheran Church, NY, 59-61; lectr philos and relig, Wagner Col, 61; assoc, 63, from acting instr to assoc prof, 64-77, prof Hist, Univ Calif, Davis, 77-91, Fulbright res scholar, Univ Strabourg, 67-68; prof emer, 91-. **MEMBERSHIPS** Am Soc Church Hist. **RESEARCH** Interrelationships between humanism, Reformation, and counter-Reformation in central Europe. **SELECTED PUBLICATIONS** Ed, The Harvest of Humanism in Central Europe, St. Louis, Concordia, 92; auth, Der schlesische Spaethumanismus, in Quellenbuch zur Geschichte der Evangelischen Kirche in Schlesien, Munich, Oldenbourg, 92; Screech, M. A--Some Renaissance Studies, Church Hist, Vol 64, 95; auth, The Oxford Encyclopedia of Reformation, 96. **CONTACT ADDRESS** Dept of Hist, Univ of California, Davis, Davis, CA 95616. **EMAIL** mpfleischer@vcdavis.edu

FLEMING, JAMES E.
PERSONAL Born 11/06/1954, Nevada, MO, m, 1992, 2 children **DISCIPLINE** LAW **MEMBERSHIPS** Am Soc for Political & Legal Philos, Am Political Sci Asn, Comn on the Political Economics of the Good Soc, AALS, ABA. **RESEARCH** Constitutional Law, Constitutional Theory, Jurisprudence, Political Philosophy. **SELECTED PUBLICATIONS** Coauth, American Constitutional Interpretation 2nd ed, Foundation Press, 95; auth, "Securing Deliberative Autonomy," Stanford Law Rev vol 48: 1-71; auth, "Constructing the Substantive Constitution," Tex Law rev vol 72: 211-304. **CONTACT ADDRESS** Sch of Law, Fordham Univ, 140 W 62nd St, New York, NY 10023-7485. **EMAIL** jfleming@mail.lawnet.fordham.edu

FLEMING, JOHN G.
PERSONAL Born 07/06/1919, m, 1946, 4 children **DISCIPLINE** LAW **EDUCATION** Oxford Univ, MA, 39, DPhil, 48, DCL, 59. **CAREER** Lectr law, King's Col, Univ London, Eng, 46-48; sr lectr, Australian Nat Univ, 49-55, Robert Garran prof and dean, 55-60; vis prof, 57-58, prof, 60-74, SHANNON CECIL TURNER PROF LAW, UNIV CALIF, BERKELEY, 74-, Mem, Eng Bar, 47; Carnegie Corp traveling grant, 54-55; ed-in-chief, Am J Comp Law, 71-. **MEMBERSHIPS** Am Law Inst; Int Acad Comp Law; Int Asn Legal Soc. **SELECTED PUBLICATIONS** Auth, Mass Torts, Am J Compar Law, Vol 42, 94. **CONTACT ADDRESS** Law Sch, Univ of California, Berkeley, Berkeley, CA 94720.

FLETCHER, ANTHONY Q.
DISCIPLINE POLITICAL SCIENCE **EDUCATION** Columbia Col, AB, 92; Harvard Law Sch, JD, 95. **CAREER** Adj Asst Prof, CUNY, 97-. **HONORS AND AWARDS** Presidential Scholar, Columbia Col, 92; Black Bar Asn Awd, 94; Fel, City Col NY, 98-. **MEMBERSHIPS** ABA, BBA. **RESEARCH** Ethnic and racial politics in the United States, the civil rights movement, race and the American legal system, Malcolm X, introduction to the legal process. **SELECTED PUBLICATIONS** Auth, "Curing Crib Death: Emerging Growth Companies, Nuisance Suits and Congressional Proposals for Securities Litigation Reform," Harvard J on Legis, 32 (96): 493; auth, "A Risky Facelift for Social Security?" Daily Rocket Investment Monitor (97); auth, "Pill Popping on Wall Street," Daily Rocket Investment Monitor (97). **CONTACT ADDRESS** Dept Polit Sci, City Col, CUNY, City University NY, New York, NY 10031. **EMAIL** aqfletch@aol.com

FLETCHER, DAVID B.
PERSONAL Born 08/10/1951, Chicago, IL, m, 1976, 1 child **DISCIPLINE** PHILOSOPHY **EDUCATION** Trinity Col, BA, 73; Loyola Univ, MA, 79; Univ Ill, PhD, 81. **CAREER** Vis Scholar, Univ Of Oxford, 91; Vis Prof, Trinity Evangelical Divinity School, 94-; Assoc Prof to Chair, Wheaton Col, 81-. **HONORS AND AWARDS** Fel, Center for Bioethics and Human Dignity, 97; Aldeen Fund Awd, Wheaton Col alumni, 91. **MEMBERSHIPS** Am Philos Asn, Ill Philos Asn, Center for Bioethics and Human Dignity, Christian Medical and Dental Soc, Chicago Center for Clinical Ethics, Soc of Christian Philos, Inst of Soc, Ethics, and the Life Sciences. **SELECTED PUBLICATIONS** auth, "Particular Divine commands," in Christina and Moral Philosophy, Mercer Univ Press, 99; auth, "Social and Political Perspectives in the eh Thought of Soren Kierkegaard, Univ Press of Am, 81; auth, "Can Christian Ethics be Philosophical?," in Festschrift for Harold O.J. Brown, Crossway Books, forthcoming; auth, "How a Christian Thinks about Medical Ethical Issues," in New Issues in Medical Ethics, 97; auth, "Professional Ethics," "population Policy," "Dehumanization," "Professional Ethics," "Karl Marx," "Alienation," "Reproductive Technology," "Sterilization," "Birth Control," "medical Malpractice," "Martin Luther King Jr," and "Surrogate Mothers," in New Dictionary of Christian ethics and Pastoral Theology, Intervarsity Press, 95; auth, "Abortion and American Christianity," and "Protestant Personal Ethics," in dictionary of Christianity in America, Intervarsity Press, 90; auth, "Utilitarianism," "Polytheism," "Philosophy of Religion," "Unbelief," "Metaphysics," "monism," "Understanding," and "Voluntarism" in Evangelical Dictionary of Theology, Baker Pub, 84; auth, "Is There a Right to Health Care?," Wheaton Col, 91; auth, "A Call to Courage," Wheaton Magazine, 99; auth, "Response to Nigel de s. Cameron's Bioethics and the Challenge of a Postconsensus society," Ethics and Medicine, 95. **CONTACT ADDRESS** Dept Philos, Wheaton Col, Illinois, 501 Col Ave, Wheaton, IL 60187-5501. **EMAIL** david.b.fletcher@wheaton.edu

FLETCHER, GEORGE PHILIP
PERSONAL Born 03/05/1939, Chicago, IL, m, 1962, 2 children **DISCIPLINE** LAW, PHILOSOPHY **EDUCATION** Univ Calif, BA, 60; Univ Chicago, JD, 64, MCompL, 65. **CAREER** Asst prof Law, Univ Fla, 65-66; asst prof, Univ Wash, 66-69; acting assoc prof, 69-72, Prof Law, Calif, Los Angeles 72-83; prof, Columbia Law, 83-. **HONORS AND AWARDS** Order of Coif award, 80; ABA Silver Gavel award, 89. **RESEARCH** Comparative law; criminal and tort theory; legal philosophy. **SELECTED PUBLICATIONS** Auth, Rethinking Criminal Law, 78; A Crime of Self-Defense: Bernard Goetz and the Law on Trial, 88; Loyalty: An Essay on the Morality of Relationships, 93; With Justice for Some: Victims' Rights in Criminal Trials, 95; Basic Concepts of Legal Thought, 96; Basic Concepts of Criminal Law, 98. **CONTACT ADDRESS** Columbia Univ, 616 Jerome Greene Hall, mail code 4013, Box A-12, New York, NY 10027-6900. **EMAIL** gpfl@columbia.edu

FLETCHER, ROBERT E.
PERSONAL Born 12/12/1938, Detroit, MI, m **DISCIPLINE** LAW, FILM **EDUCATION** Fisk Univ, attended 1956-59; Wayne State Univ, BA 1961; Natl Educ TV Film Training Sch, attended 1970; Comm Film Workshop Council TV News Cinematography Prog 1971; Natl Acad of TV Arts & Sci/Third World Cinema Prod Inc 1976-77; New York University School of Law, JD, 1990. **CAREER** No Student Movement Harlem, field organizer 63-64; SNCC Jackson MS, Selma AL Atlanta GA, photographer field coord editorial & air dir 64-68; freelance photographer journalist & film maker 68-; Brooklyn Coll, adj prof dept of film studies 75-76; "Vote for Your Life", prod/dir 77; "Weatherization, What's It all About?"; Video & TV Prod, summer 77; WPIX-TV, bi-weekly talk show; "A Nation in View", co-producer; Cravath, Swaine & Moore, attorney, 91-. **HONORS AND AWARDS** Cinematographer dir "A Luta Continva" 1971; documentary film on liberation struggle in Mozambique "O Povo Organizado" 1975; panelist "Voices of the Civil Rights Movement" Smithsonian Inst 1980. **MEMBERSHIPS** Mem Intl Photographers of the Motion Picture Indus; chmn bd dir Rod Rodgers Dance Co 1973-; photographs pub in Ebony, Essence, Black Enterprises, Tuesday, Life, Redbook, NY Mag; author of publ in MS. **CONTACT ADDRESS** Cravath, Swaine & Moore, 825 Eighth Ave, New York, NY 10019-7415.

FLINT, THOMAS P.
PERSONAL Born 12/14/1954, Cleveland, OH, m, 1983, 1 child **DISCIPLINE** PHILOSOPHY **EDUCATION** St Ambrose Col, BA, 75; Univ Notre Dame, PhD, 80. **CAREER** Harper instr, Univ Chicago, 80-82; asst prof, 82-88, Assoc Prof, Univ Notre Dame, 88-. **MEMBERSHIPS** Soc of Christian Philos; Amer Philos Assoc; Amer Cath Philos Assoc. **RESEARCH** Philos theology; metaphysics. **SELECTED PUBLICATIONS** Co-ed and co-auth of intro with Eleonore Stump, Hermes and Athena: Biblical Exegesis and Philosophical Theology, Univ Notre Dame Press, 93; auth, Providence and Predestination, in Philip L. Quinn and Charles Taliaferro, eds, A Companion to the Philosophy of Religion, Oxford: Blackwell Pubs, 97; Praying for Things to Have Happened, Midwest Studies in Philosophy 21, 97; Divine Providence: The Molinist Account, Ithaca, NY: Cornell Univ Press, 98. **CONTACT ADDRESS** Philos Dept, Univ of Notre Dame, 336 O'Shaughnessy Hall, Notre Dame, IN 46556-5639. **EMAIL** flint.1@nd.edu

FLIPPEN, DOUGLAS
PERSONAL Born 01/08/1945, Washington, DC, m, 1975, 3 children **DISCIPLINE** PHILOSOPHY **EDUCATION** Univ Toronto, MA; Licentiate, Pontifical Inst, 75; Univ Toronto, PhD, 76. **CAREER** Asst Prof, Univ of St Thomas, 76-82; Asst Prof, Carroll Col, 82-85; Asst Prof to Assoc prof, Christendom Col, 89-. **RESEARCH** Epistemology/Metaphysics/Natural Law. **CONTACT ADDRESS** Christendom Col, 134 Christendom Dr, Front Royal, VA 22630-6534. **EMAIL** eap@rma.edu

FLORIDA, ROBERT E.
PERSONAL Born 09/16/1939, St. Louis, MO, m, 1963, 2 children **DISCIPLINE** RELIGION **EDUCATION** Univ Cincinnati, 62; Tufts Univ, BD, 65; McMaster Univ, MA, 69, PhD, 73. **CAREER** Prof, Dept Rel, 69-, rel dept chair, 74-75, 78-82, 84-86, 91, Dean Fac Arts, 93-, Brandon Univ. **MEMBERSHIPS** Am Acad Rel; Can Soc Stud of Rel; Int Asn Buddhist Hist. **RESEARCH** Buddhist ethics, health care ethics. **SELECTED PUBLICATIONS** Auth, "Buddhist Ethics" in Religious Humanism, 94; "Buddhism and the Four Principles," in Principles of Health Care Ethics, 94; "Introduction" and "Bioethics in the Lotus Sutra" J Buddhist Ethics, 98. **CONTACT ADDRESS** Dept of Mod and Class Lang, Brandon Univ, PO Box 270, Brandon, MB, Canada R7A 6A9. **EMAIL** Florida@BrandonU.ca

FLOURNOY, ALYSON CRAIG
DISCIPLINE LAW **EDUCATION** Princeton Univ, BA; Harvard Univ, JD. **CAREER** Prof, Univ Fla, 88-. **MEMBERSHIPS** DC Bar. **RESEARCH** Administrative law, environmental law, property. **CONTACT ADDRESS** School of Law, Univ of Florida, PO Box 117625, Gainesville, FL 32611-7625. **EMAIL** flournoy@law.ufl.edu

FLOWERS, RONALD BRUCE
PERSONAL Born 01/11/1935, Tulsa, OK, m, 1959, 3 children **DISCIPLINE** RELIGION, AMERICAN CHURCH HISTORY **EDUCATION** Tex Christian Univ, BA, 57; Vanderbilt Univ, BD, 60, STM, 61; Univ Iowa, PhD(relig, Am church hist), 67. **CAREER** Asst prof, 66-72, assoc prof relig, Tex Christian Univ, 72-83, prof 84-. **HONORS AND AWARDS** Danforth assoc, 71-; Weatherly Prof of Religion, 98. **MEMBERSHIPS** Disciples of Christ Hist Soc; Am Acad of Relig. **RESEARCH** The history of religion in America; church and state relationships in America. **SELECTED PUBLICATIONS** Auth, An Introduction to Church-State Relationships, Encounter, summer 71; Piety in Public Places, Christianity & Crisis, 11/71; A Selected Bibliography on Religion and Public Education, J Church & State, autumn 72; The Supreme Court's Three Tests of the Establishment Clause, Religion in Life, spring 76; coauth, Toward Benevolent Neutrality: Church, State, and the Supreme Court, Baylor Univ, 77, rev ed, 82, 5th rev ed, 94; Freedom of Religion Versus Civil Authority in Matters of Health, Ann Am Acad Pol Soc Sci, 11/79; The Supreme Court's Interpretation of the Free Exercise Clause, Relig Life, fall 80; The 1960's: A Decisive Decade in American Church-State Relationships, Encounter, summer 82;auth, Religion in Strange Times: The 1960's and 1970's, 84; co-auth, The Naturalization of Rosika Schwimmer, Journal of Church and State, spring 90; auth, In Praise of Conscience: Marie Averil Bland, Angelican and Episcopal History, March 93; Government Accomodation of Religious-Based Conscientious Objection, Seton Hall Law Rev, 93; That Godless Court?: Supreme Court Decisions on Church-State relationships, 94. **CONTACT ADDRESS** Dept of Relig, Texas Christian Univ, Box 298100, Fort Worth, TX 76129-0002. **EMAIL** r.flowers@tcu.edu

FLOWERS, WILLIAM HAROLD, JR.
PERSONAL Born 03/22/1946, Chicago, IL, m **DISCIPLINE** LAW **EDUCATION** Univ of CO, BA 1967, Law School JD 1971. **CAREER** Adams County, deputy district Attorney; Private Practice, 79-; Holland & Hart, Denver CO, partner, 89-97; Hurth Yeager & Sisk LLP, 97-. **HONORS AND AWARDS** Outstanding Alumnus, Univ of CO Black Students Alliance, 1990; Awd in Business-Community Action, Boulder County, CO, 1990; Presidential Awd, Natl Bar Assn, 1987. **MEMBERSHIPS** Bd of dirs KGNU Radio Station 1981-84; bd of dirs CO Criminal Defense Bar 1982-83; regional dir Natl Bar Assoc 1984-85, vice pres, 1990-91, bd of governors 1985-95; exec bd Boy Scouts of Amer 1983-; pres elect 1986, pres 1987 Sam Cary Bar Assoc; mem Comm Corrections Bd 1984-90; bd of governors, Colo Trial Lawyers Assn, beg 1988, pres, 99-00; Judicial Nominating Comm 1988-94; bd of dir, CO ACLU, 1990. **CONTACT ADDRESS** Hurth Yeager & Sisk, 4860 Riverbend Rd, Boulder, CO 80308. **EMAIL** whf@hurth.com

FLOYD, JULIET
PERSONAL Born 03/12/1960, Boston, MA, m, 1995 **DISCIPLINE** PHILOSOPHY **EDUCATION** Wellesley Col, BA, 82; Harvard Univ, MA, PhD, 90. **CAREER** Asst prof, City Col NY, 90-95, Boston Univ, 95-. **HONORS AND AWARDS** NEH Summr fel, 91; ACLS Senior fel, 98-99; Dibnet Inst MIT fel, 98-99; acls senior fel, 98-99; dibnet inst mit fel, 98-99. **MEMBERSHIPS** Am Philos Asn, Am Asn of Univ Women, Assoc Symbolic Logic. **RESEARCH** Philosphy. **SELECTED PUBLICATIONS** Auth, "The Uncaptive Eye: Solipsism in Tractatus," 98; auth, "Frege, Semantics and the Double-Definition Stroke," 97; auth, "Heautonomy and the Critique of Sound Judgment: Kant on Reflective Judgment and Systematicity," 98; auth, "On Saying What You Really Want to Say: Wittgenstein, Godel and the Trisection of the Angle," 95. **CONTACT ADDRESS** Dept of Philosphy, Boston Univ, 745 Commonwealth Ave, Boston, MA 02215.

FLOYD, MICHAEL H.
PERSONAL Born 08/05/1946, Kingstree, SC, m, 1975, 3 children **DISCIPLINE** OLD TESTAMENT STUDIES **EDUCATION** Trinity Col, BA, 69; Episcopal Theol Sch, BD, 71; Claremont Grad Sch, MA, 76, PhD, 80. **CAREER** Asst prof rel, Tex Wesleyan Col, 79-82; assoc prof Old Testament, 82-85, full prof, Episcopal Theol Sem SW, 85- . **MEMBERSHIPS** Soc Bibl Lit; Anglican Asn Bibl Scholars. **RESEARCH** Prophecy and Psalms; form criticism. **SELECTED PUBLICATIONS** Auth, How Can We Sing the Lord's Song?, Reformed Liturgy and Mus 20, 86, 95-101; Obadiah, in Harper's Bible Commentary, Harper, 88, 726-727; Falling Flat on Our Ars Poetica, Or Some Problems in Recent Studies of Hebrew Poetry, in the Psalms and Other Studies on the Old Testament, Festschrift, Cincinnati, Forward Movement Publ, 90, 118-131; Sex and the Bible, Anglican Theol Rev, 72, 90, 95-103; Prophetic Complaints about the Fulfillment of Oracles in Habakkuk 1:2-17 and Jeremiah 15:10-18, Jour Bibl Lit 110, 91, 397-418; Psalm LXXXIX: A Prophetic Complaint about the Fulfillment of the Oracle, Vetus Testamentum 42, 92, 442-257; Prophecy and Writing in Habakkuk 2:1-5, Zeitschrift fur die Alttestamentliche Wissenschaft 105, 93, 462-481; Are the Scriptures Still Sufficient? The Concept of Biblical Authority in the Thirty-Nine Articles, In Our Heritage and Common Life, UP of America, 94, 47-64; The Chimerical Acrostic in Nahum 1:2-10, Jour Bibl Lit, 113, 94, 421-437; The Nature of the Narrative and the Evidence of Redaction in Haggai, Vetus Testamentum 45, 95, 470-490; The Evil in the Ephah: Reading Zechariah 5:1-5 in Its Literary Context, Catholic Bibl Quart 58, 96, 51-68; Cosmos and History in Zechariah's View of the Restoration (Zech 1:7-6:15), in Problems in Biblical Theology, Grand Rapids, Eerdmans, 97, 125-144; auth, "Zechariah and Changing Views of Second Temple Judaism in Recent Commentaries," Religious Studies Review 25 (99): 257-263; auth, Minor Prophets: Part 2, Forms of the Old Testament Literature 22, Grand Rapids, Eerdmans, 00. **CONTACT ADDRESS** Episcopal Theol Sem of the Southwest, PO Box 2247, Austin, TX 78768-2247. **EMAIL** mfloyd@etss.edu

FLYNN, THOMAS R.
PERSONAL Born 06/02/1936, Spokane, WA, s **DISCIPLINE** PHILOSOPHY **EDUCATION** Columbia Univ, PhD, 70. **CAREER** Asst prof, Cath Univ, 71-75; asst, assoc, prof and Samuel Candler Dobbs Prof, Emory Univ, 78- . **HONORS AND AWARDS** Fel, Nat Hum Ctr, N Carolina, 91-92; mem, Inst for Advanced Study, Princeton, 98-99. **MEMBERSHIPS** APA; ACPA; SPEP. **RESEARCH** Contemporary continental, especially French, philosophy. **SELECTED PUBLICATIONS** Auth, Sartre and Marxist Existentialism: The Test Case of Collective Responsibility, Univ Chicago, 84; co-ed and contribur, Dialectic and Narrative, SUNY, 93; auth, Sartre, Foucault, and Historical Reason, v.1: Toward an Existentialist Theory of History, Univ Chicago, 97; auth, Phenomenology of Ethics, Sartrean, in Embree, ed, The Encyclopedia of Phenomenology, Kluwer, 97; auth, Sartre (1905-1980) in Critchley, ed, A Companion to Continental Philosophy, Blackwell, 98; **CONTACT ADDRESS** Dept of Philosophy, Emory Univ, Atlanta, GA 30322. **EMAIL** tflynn@emory.edu

FOARD, JAMES HARLAN
PERSONAL Born 07/09/1948, Washington, DC, m, 1970, 1 child **DISCIPLINE** RELIGIOUS STUDIES **EDUCATION** Col of Wooster, BA, 70; MA, 72, PhD, 77, Stanford Univ. **CAREER** Asst Prof, 77-83, Assoc Prof, 83-97, Prof, 97-, Arizona State Univ. **MEMBERSHIPS** Amer Acad of Religion; Assoc of Asian Studies **RESEARCH** Japanese Religion **SELECTED PUBLICATIONS** Auth, Prefiguration and Narrative in Medieval Hagiography: the Ippen Hijiri E, Flowing Traces: Buddhism in the Literary and Visual Arts of Japan, 92; The Universal and the Particular in the Rites of Hiroshima, Communities in Question: Religion and Authority in Southeast and East Asia, 94; Text, Place and Memory in Hiroshima, Senri Ethnological Studies 95; Ritual in the Buddhist Temples of Japan, Object as Insight: Japanese Buddhist Art and Ritual, 95; Ippen and Pure Land Buddhist Wayfarers in Medieval Japan, The Pure Land Tradition: History and Development, 96; Imagining Nuclear Weapons: Hiroshima, Armageddon, and the Annihilation of the Students of Ichijo School, Journal of the American Academy of Religion, 97; What One Kamakura Story Does: Practice, Place and Text in the Account of Ippen at Kumano, Revisioning Kamakura Buddhism, 98; Pure Land Belief and Popular Practice: The Odori Nembutsu of Ippen Shonin, Engaged Pure Land Buddhism: Studies in Honor of Professor Alfred Bloom, 98. **CONTACT ADDRESS** Religious Studies Dept, Arizona State Univ, Tempe, AZ 85287-3104. **EMAIL** james.foard@asu.edu

FOERST, ANNE
PERSONAL Born 03/24/1966, Germany, m **DISCIPLINE** THEOLOGY; COMPUTERSCIENCE; RELIGION & SCIENCE **EDUCATION** Univ Bonn, BA, 90; Church in Rhineland, M.Div, 92; Univ Bochum, PhD, 96. **CAREER** Res Ass, Harvard Divinity School, 95; Research Scientist, MIT, 95; dir, God & Computers Project, 97-. **HONORS AND AWARDS** Templeton Course Awd, 97. **MEMBERSHIPS** AAR; IRAS **RESEARCH** Religion & Science; Technology; Myths & Christian Theology **CONTACT ADDRESS** 545 Technology Sq NE 43-812, Cambridge, MA 02139. **EMAIL** annef@a1.mit.edu

FOGELMAN, MARTIN
PERSONAL Born 03/16/1928, New York, NY, m, 1952, 2 children **DISCIPLINE** LAW **EDUCATION** Syracuse Univ, BA, 48, JD, 50. **CAREER** Confidential law clerk, chief judge, NY Court of Appeals, 50-54; from asst prof to assoc prof, 56-64, prof law, Sch Law, Fordham Univ, 64-86, McGivney Prof of Law, 86-; Assoc, Saxe, Bacon, O'Shea & Bryan, 54-59; consult, NY State Law Revision Comn, 66-, proj dir, 75-; hearing off, Assoc Hosp Serv, 70-. **MEMBERSHIPS** Am Bar Asn. **RESEARCH** Business corporations; not for profit corporations; mortgages. **SELECTED PUBLICATIONS** Coauth, Cases on Mortgages, Corydon M Johnston, 63; auth, Wests McKinneys Forms and Text-Business Corporation Law, West, 65 & ann suppl; The Deed Absolute as a Mortgage, Fordham Law Rev, 64; Insurance, Syracuse Law Rev, 65 & 66; Wests McKinneys Forms--Not for Profit Corporation Law, West, 72 & ann suppl. **CONTACT ADDRESS** Sch of Law, Fordham Univ, 140 W 62nd St, New York, NY 10023-7407. **EMAIL** McGivney@aol.com

FOLEY, W. TRENT
DISCIPLINE RELIGION **EDUCATION** Kalamazoo Col, BA; McCormick Theol Sem, MDiv; Univ Chicago, AM and PhD. **CAREER** Fac, 84-; Prof, Davidson Col. **HONORS AND AWARDS** Vice-Pres, Am Acad Relig SW region. **MEMBERSHIPS** Am Soc Church Hist; N Am Patristics Soc'; Am Acad Relig. **RESEARCH** Christianity in early Anglo-Saxon England, Early Medieval Biblical Interpretation. **SELECTED PUBLICATIONS** Auth, Images of Sanctity in Eddius Stephanus' Life of Bishop Wilfrid, Edwin Mellen, 92; auth, Bede: A Biblical Miscellany, Liverpool UP, 99. **CONTACT ADDRESS** Dept of Relig, Davidson Col, PO Box 1719, Davidson, NC 28036. **EMAIL** trfoley@davidson.edu

FOLLICK, EDWIN D.
PERSONAL Born 02/04/1935, Glendale, CA, m, 1986 **DISCIPLINE** SOCIOLOGY, RELIGION **EDUCATION** Calif State Univ Los Angeles, BA, 56, MA, 61; Pepperdine Univ, MA, 57, MPA, 77; St Andrews Theol Col, PhD, 58, DTheol, 58; Univ S Calif, MS, 63, MEd, 64, AdvMEd, 69; Blackstone Law, LLB, 66, JD, 67; Cleveland Chiropractic Col, Los Angeles, DC, 72; Academia Theatina, PhD, 78; Antioch Univ, Los Angeles, MA, 90. **CAREER** Instr, Libr Admin, Los Angeles City Sch, 57-68; law libr, Glendale Univ Col of Law, 68-69; col librn, 69-74, dir of educ & admis, 74-84, prof of jurisprudence, 75-, dean student aff, 76-92, dean of educ, 89-, Cleveland Chiropractic Col Los Angeles Campus; assoc prof, Newport Univ, 82; extern prof theology, St Andrews Theol Col, London, 61; Chapalin, Cleveland Los Angeles Campus, 85-; Chaplain of Cleveland Col Multicampus System, 00-. **HONORS AND AWARDS** Undergraduate honors in educ & svc & leadership; three sabbatical leaves which included grants to visit the Soviet Union & China twice; Who's Who in America, 99. **MEMBERSHIPS** ALA; NEA; Amer Assoc Law Librns; Amer Chiropractic Assoc; Int Chiropractors Assoc; Int Platform Assoc; Phi Delta Kappa, Sigma Chi Psi; Delta Tau Alpha. **RESEARCH** Sociological & religious implications of health. **SELECTED PUBLICATIONS** Auth, The Law and Chiropractic: Administrative Discretion-A Concluding Summary, Part 7, Chiropractic Education: A Management Analysis of Professional Study for the 1990s, Part 1-4, Digest of Chiropractic Economics, 80-92. **CONTACT ADDRESS** 6435 Jumilla Ave, Woodland Hills, CA 91367. **EMAIL** follicke@cleveland.edu

FOLLIS, ELAINE R.
PERSONAL Born 01/28/1944, Quincy, MA, s **DISCIPLINE** BIBLICAL STUDIES **EDUCATION** Tufts Univ, AB, 65; BD, 68; Boston Univ, PhD, 76 **CAREER** Prof, 74-pres, Principia Col; Assoc Dean of Fac, 97-, Principia **HONORS AND AWARDS** Phi Beta Kappa, 64 **MEMBERSHIPS** Soc of Bibl Lit **RESEARCH** Holocaust Studies; Cultural History of Israel **SELECTED PUBLICATIONS** Auth, Directions in Biblical Hebrew Poetry, 87 **CONTACT ADDRESS** Principia Col, Elsah, IL 62028. **EMAIL** erf@prin.edu

FOLSE, HENRY J., JR.
PERSONAL Born 05/02/1945, New Orleans, LA, m, 1972, 2 children **DISCIPLINE** PHILOSOPHY **EDUCATION** Harvard Col, BA, 67; Tulane Univ, MA, 70, PhD, 72. **CAREER** Assoc prof, 75-80, Col of Charleston; assoc prof, 80-85, prof, 85-, Loyola Univ New Orleans. **HONORS AND AWARDS** NEH Fel; "Excellence in Teaching Awd" Loyola UNIv, 00. **MEMBERSHIPS** APA; Phil of Sci Assn; So Soc for Phil & Psychol; Metaphysical Soc of Amer. **RESEARCH** Quantum revolution; phil of physics; scientific rationality. **SELECTED PUBLICATIONS** Auth, The Philosophy of Niels Bohr: The Framework of Complementarity, N Holland Physics Pub, 85; art, The Environment and the Epistemological Lesson of Complementarity, Environ Ethics 15, 93; art, Bohr's Framework of Complementarity and the Realism Debate, Niels Bohr & Contemporary Phil: Boston Stud in Phil of Sci 153, Kluwer Acad Pub, 94; coauth, "Introduction" to Niels Bohr and Contemporary Philosophy: Boston Studies in the Philosophy of Science 153, 94; coauth, Bearers of Properties in the Quantum Mechanical Description of Nature, Intl Stud in Phil of Sci 8, 94; co-ed, Niels Bohr and Contemporary Philosophy: Boston Studies in the Philosophy of Science 153, Kluwer Acad Pub, 94; auth, The Bohr-Einstein Debate and the Philosophers' Debate over Realism versus Anti-Realism, Realism & Anti Realism in Phil of Sci; Beijing Intl Conf, 1992, Kluwer, 96; coed, Causality and Complementarity: Philosophical Writings of Niels Bohr: Supplementary Papers, Ox Bow Press, 98; auth, "Ontological Constraints and Understanding Quantim Phenomena:" Dialectics 50 (96): 121-136. **CONTACT ADDRESS** Dept of Philosophy, Loyola Univ, New Orleans, New Orleans, LA 70118. **EMAIL** folse@loyno.edu

FOLTZ, BRUCE
DISCIPLINE PHILOSOPHY **EDUCATION** Pa State Univ, PhD. **CAREER** Assoc prof. **RESEARCH** History of philosophy; recent European methodologies; philosophy of religion. **SELECTED PUBLICATIONS** Auth, Inhabiting the Earth: Heidegger; Environmental Ethics; Metaphysics of Nature; pubs on Heidegger and the the philosophy of the natural environment. **CONTACT ADDRESS** Dept of Philosophy, Eckerd Col, 54th Ave S, PO Box 4200, Saint Petersburg, FL 33711.

FOLTZ, HOWARD L.
DISCIPLINE DIVINITY; GLOBAL EVANGELIZATION **EDUCATION** Southwestern Assemblies of God Col, BS; Assemblies of God Grad Sch; Denver Theol Sem, DMin. **CAREER** Prof, 85. **SELECTED PUBLICATIONS** Auth, Triumph: Missions Renewal in the Local Church, 94; How to Put

Your Church on the Cutting Edge of World Missions, Ministries Today, 94; Building the Home-Base for Global Outreach, Intl Jour of Frontier Missions, 94; Sharpening Your Church's Mission Commitment, Mission Today, 95; Do Miracles Still Happen?, Decision Mag, Messenger Press, 96; How To Have A Healthy Church In A Sick World, Messenger Press, 97. **CONTACT ADDRESS** Dept of Divinity, Regent Univ, 1000 Regent Univ Dr, Virginia Beach, VA 23464-9831.

FONTAINE, CAROLE R.
PERSONAL Born 04/11/1950, Lima, OH, m, 1972 **DISCIPLINE** OLD TESTAMENT **EDUCATION** FL State Univ, BA, 72; Yale Univ, MAR, 76; Duke Univ, PhD, 79. **CAREER** Tchg asst, Duke Univ, 76-79; Prof Hebrew Scriptures, Andover Newton Theol Sch, 79-, Instr wisdom lit, Duke Univ, 79; instr Old Testament, Univ NC, Greensboro, 79; bk rev ed, Andover Newton Quart, 79-81; joint grad fac, Boston Col & Andover Newton Theol Sch, 82-85. **HONORS AND AWARDS** Zion Found Scholarship; Gurney Harris Kearns fel; Artist-in-Residence, ANTS. **MEMBERSHIPS** Cath Bibl Asn; Soc Bibl Lit. **RESEARCH** Hebrew Bible wisdom; structural anthrop; women's studies. **SELECTED PUBLICATIONS** Auth, A modern look at ancient wisdom: The instruction of Ptahhotep, revisited, Bibl Archaeol, 44: 155-60; Traditional sayings in the Old Testament: A contextual study, Bible & Lit, Almond Press, Sheffield, England, 85; Proverbs, Ecclesiastes, In: Womens Bible Commentary (Carol Newsom & Sharon Ringe, ed), Westminster/John Knox, 92; A Feminist Companion to Reading the Bible: Approaches, Methods, Strategies (Athalya Brennere and Carole Fontaine, ed), Sheffield Acad Press, U K, 97; coauth, A Feminist Companion to Wisdom and Psalms, Sheffield Acad Press, 98; coauth, A Feminist Companion to the Song of songs, Sheffield Acad Press, 00. **CONTACT ADDRESS** Andover Newton Theol Sch, 210 Herrick Rd, Newton, MA 02459-2236. **EMAIL** cfontaine@ants.edu

FONTINELL, EUGENE
PERSONAL Born 05/22/1924, Scranton, PA **DISCIPLINE** PHILOSOPHY **EDUCATION** Univ Scranton, BA, 48; Fordham Univ, MA, 50, PhD (philos), 57. **CAREER** Instr philos, Iona Col, 51-54; asst prof, Col New Rochelle, 54-58, assoc prof and chmn dept, 58-61; from asst prof to assoc prof, 61-70, chmn dept, 66-72, Prof Philos, Queens Col, NY, 70-. **MEMBERSHIPS** Am Philos Asn; Am Cath Philos Asn. **RESEARCH** American philosophy; philosophy of religion; philosophy of history. **SELECTED PUBLICATIONS** Auth, Faith and metaphysics, winter 66 & Religious truth in a relational world, summer 67, Cross Currents; Toward Reconstruction of Religion: A Philosophical Probe, Doubleday, 70, reissued, Cross Currents, 79; Immortality: Hope or Hindrance?, summer 81 & Immortality: A Pragmatic-Processive Model, spring 82, Cross Currents. **CONTACT ADDRESS** Dept of Philos, Queens Col, CUNY, Flushing, NY 11367.

FORBES, A. DEAN
PERSONAL Born 03/02/1941, Pomona, CA, m, 1971 **DISCIPLINE** PHYSICS, OLD TESTAMENT **EDUCATION** Harvard Col, AB, 62; Pacific School of Rel, MDiv, 69. **CAREER** Biomed consultant and Biblical researcher; Mem of Technical Staff, Hewlett-Packard Co, 70-90; Proj mgr, Medical Dept, 90-93; Principal Medical Dept Scientist, 93-99 ; Editorial bd, 84-93, Algorithms ed, 93-97, Jour of Clinical Monitoring; Algorithms editor, Jour of Clinical Monitoring & Computing, 98- ; vis scholar, Stanford Univ, 86-89; vis scholar, UCSD, 99-; ad prof, Jewish stud, Penn St, 98-; eight patents. **HONORS AND AWARDS** Who's Who in America, 53rd ed. **MEMBERSHIPS** Soc Bib Lit; senior mem, Inst of Electrical and Electronic Engineers. **RESEARCH** Noninvasive measurements; pattern recognition; statistics/stochastic processes; statistical-linguistic analyses of the orthography and syntax of Biblical Hebrew. **SELECTED PUBLICATIONS** Auth, A Synoptic Concordance to Hosea, Amos, Micah, Volume VI of the Computer Bible, Wooster, Bibl Res Assoc, 74; Eight Minor Prophets: A Linguistic Concordance, Volume X of the Computer Bible, Wooster; Bibl Res Assoc, 76; A Linguistic Concordance of Ruth and Jonah: Hebrew Vocabulary and Idiom, Volume XI of the Computer Bible, Wooster, Bibl Res Assoc, 76; A Linguistic Concordance of Jeremiah: Hebrew Vocabulary and Idiom, Volume XIV of the Computer Bible, Wooster, Bibl Res Assoc, 78; Prose Particle Counts of the Hebrew Bible, in The Word of the Lord Shall Go Forth: Essays in Honor of David Noel Freedman in Celebration of His Sixtieth Birthday, Winona Lake, Eisenbrauns and American Schools for Oriental Res, 83, 165-183; Orthography and Text Transmission, TEXT 2, 85, 25-53; Problems in Taxonomy and Lemmatization, in Proceedings of the First International Colloquium: Bible and the Computer-the Text, Paris-Geneva, Champion-Slatkine, 86, 37-50; Further Studies in Hebrew Spelling, Conference on the History of Hebrew Spelling, Univ Calif San Diego, April 86; Spelling in the Hebrew Bible, Rome, The Pontifical Biblical Inst Press, 86; Syntactic Sequences in the Hebrew Bible, in E.G. Newing and E. W. Conrad, eds, Perspectives on Language and Text: Essays and Poems in Honor of Francis Ian Andersen on His Sixtieth Birthday, Winona Lake, Eisenbrauns, 87, 59-70; Methods and Tools for the Study of Old Testament Syntax, in Proceedings of the Second International Colloquium: Bible and the Computer-Methods, Tools, Results, Paris-Geneva, Champion-Slatkine, 89, 61-72; The Vocabulary of the Old Testament, Rome, The Pontifical Bibl Inst Press, 89, 2nd printing 92; A Key-Word-in-Context Concordance to Psalms, Job, and Proverbs, Volume XXXIV of the Computer Bible, Wooster, Bibl Res Assoc, 92; Statistical Research on the Bible, in David Noel Freedman, ed, The Anchor Dictionary of the Bible, Garden City, NY, Doubleday, 92, VI, 185-206; On Marking Clause Boundaries, in Proceedings of the Third International Colloquium: Bible and the Computer-Methods, Tools, Results, Paris-Geneva, Champion-Slatkine, 92, 181-202; A Critique of Statistical Approaches to the Isaiah Authorship Problem, in Proceedings of the Third Intl Colloquium: Bible and the Computer-Methods, Tools, Results, Paris-Geneva, Champion-Slatkine, 92, 531-545; Studies in Hebrew and Aramaic Orthography, vol 2 of Biblical and Judaic Studies from the Univ Calif, San Diego, ed William Henry Propp, Winona Lake, Eisenbrauns, 92; A Key-Word-in-Context Concordance to the Pentateuch, Volume XXXVa/b of the Computer Bible, Lewiston, NY, Mellen Bibl Press, 95; Opportune Parsing: Clause Analysis of Deuteronomy 8, in Proceedings of the Fourth International Colloquium: Bible and the Computer-Desk & Discipline, Paris, Editions Honore Champion, 95, 49-75; Syntactic Ambiguity in the Hebrew Bible, in Proceedings of the Fourth International Colloquium: Bible and the Computer-Desk & Discipline, Paris, Editions Honore Champion, 95, 356-367; Shards, Strophes, and Stats, in A. Beck, ed, Fortunate the Eyes that See: Essays in Honor of David Noel Freedman in Celebration of His Seventieth Birthday, Grand Rapids, Academie Publ Co, 95, 310-321; Towards a Clause-Type Concordance of TNK, in Proceedings of the Fifth International Colloquium: Bible and the Computer-Translation, Paris, Editions Honore Champion, 98, 41-70; Approximate Graph-Matching as an Enabler of Example-Based Translation, in Proceedings of the Fifth International Colloquium: Bible and the Computer-Translation, Paris, Editions Honore Champion, 98, 285-314. **CONTACT ADDRESS** 820 Loma Verde Ave, Palo Alto, CA 94303. **EMAIL** adforbes@icee.org

FORBES, GRAEME
DISCIPLINE PHILOSOPHY **EDUCATION** Oxford Univ, DPhil, 80. **CAREER** Prof, Tulane Univ; Celia Scott Weatherhead distinguished ch. **SELECTED PUBLICATIONS** Auth, The Metaphysics of Modality, Oxford; Modern Logic, Oxford; pub(s) in, Philos Rev; Nous; J Philos; Ling and Philos. **CONTACT ADDRESS** Dept of Philosophy, Tulane Univ, 105 Newcomb Hall, New Orleans, LA 70118-5698. **EMAIL** forbes@mailhost.tcs.tulane.edu

FORD, JAMES L.
PERSONAL Born 03/21/1957, Richmond, VA, m **DISCIPLINE** EAST ASIAN RELIGION **EDUCATION** Priceton Univ, PhD, 98. **CAREER** Ast prof, Wake Forest Univ, 98-; Exec Secretary. **MEMBERSHIPS** AAR; AAS; Soc for the Study of Japanese Relig Steering Committee Mem, Japanese Religs Group. **RESEARCH** Medieval Japanese Buddhism. **CONTACT ADDRESS** Dept of Religion, Wake Forest Univ, 107 Wingate Hall, Winston-Salem, NC 27109. **EMAIL** fordj@wfu.edu

FORD, JOHN T.
PERSONAL Born 11/21/1932, Dallas, TX, s **DISCIPLINE** THEOLOGY **EDUCATION** Univ Notre Dame, AB; Holy Cross Col, MA; Gregorian Univ, STL; STD. **CAREER** Univ Notre Dame, 62; Holy Cross Col, 62-68; Catholic Univ Am, 68-. **MEMBERSHIPS** AAUP; AAR; CTSA; CHA; NAAE. **RESEARCH** Nineteenth century theology (Newman Vatican I); twentieth century Ecumenism; Hispanic/Latino theology. **SELECTED PUBLICATIONS** Auth, "Differences about infallibility too significant to be brushed aside as inconsequential," in Church and Theology: Essays in Memory of Carl J Peter, ed. Peter C Phan (Washington, DC: Catholic Univ of Am Press, 95), 111-160; auth, "Newman's View of Education: The Oxford Background," in The Literary and Educational Effects of the Thought of John Henry Newman, eds. Michael Sundermeier, Robert Churchill, Roman Catholic Studies 7 (Lewiston/Queenston/Lampeter: Edwin Mellen Press, 95): 27-48; coeditor, Twelve Tales Untold: A Study Guide for Ecumenical Reception, William B. Eerdmans (Grand Rapids, Michigan), 93. **CONTACT ADDRESS** Dept Theology, Catholic Univ of America, 620 Michigan Ave NE, Washington, DC 20064-0001. **EMAIL** ford@cua.edu

FORD, JUDITH DONNA
PERSONAL Born 08/30/1935, Eureka, CA, d, 2 children **DISCIPLINE** LAW **EDUCATION** Univ of CA at Berkeley, BS 1957; University of California-Berkeley, JD 1974. **CAREER** Petty Andrews Tufts & Jackson, assoc atty 74-79; Consumer Fraud Crime Div SF Dist Atty's Office, dir 77-79; Fed Trade Comm, dir 80-82; Oakland-Piedmont-Emeryville Jud Dist, judge 83-92; Alameda Co Superior Ct, 98-. **HONORS AND AWARDS** Women Laywers Alameda County Career Achievement Awd; mem, Judicial Counsel, 87-90; mem, Court Tech Advisory Committee to Judicial Counsel, 91-, chair, 98-; mem, COSCA/NACM Joint Tech Committee, 99-; mem, Global Court Tech Think Tank, 99-. **MEMBERSHIPS** CA Judges Assn; Alameda Co Trauma Review Comm; US Magistrate Merit Selection Comm; San Francisco Bar Assn Lawyer Referral Serv Comm 1976; NSF SoftwareAuditing Wkshp 1976; Comm for Admin of Justice 1976-79; delegate from San Fran Bar Assn Lawyer Refrl Serv Comm 1976; chair E Oakland Planned Prnthd Adv Comm 1977-80; spkr Bank Admin Inst 1977; spkr EDP Audit Cntrls Wkshp 1977; spkr CPA Soc 1977; various TV & Radio appearances; spoke to comm groupson consult fraud 1977-79; spkr Joint meeting of IIA and EDPA 1978; dir Planned Prnthd 1978-80; chair Blk Women Lawyers, N CA Finance Comm 1979-80; San Fran Lawyers Comm Urban Affairs 1979-80; chair SF Bar Assn Comm Legal Ed Comm 1979-80; bd mem Consumer Union 1979-82; ref St Bar Ct 1979-82; cnclr Law CntrBd of Cnclrs 1979-83; radio & TV spkr on FTrade Comm 1980-82; SF Bar Assoc Judiciary Comm 1981-82; Chas Houston Bar Assoc 1974-; CA Assoc of Black Lawyers 1978-; bd mem Peralta Serv Corp 1983-, judicial council, 1991-94; chair, CTC Privacy & Access Subcommittee, 1995-96; Judicial Council Court Technology, advisory comm, 1995-98; trustee, Alameda County Law Library; board member, California Judges Association, 1996-98. **SELECTED PUBLICATIONS** California Criminal Law Procedure & Practice, (CEB 1994, 2nd Ed), co-author, chapters 4 & 6. **CONTACT ADDRESS** Oakland-Piedmont Emeryville Judicial Dist, 661 Washington St, Oakland, CA 94607.

FORD, LEWIS S.
PERSONAL Born 11/18/1933, Leonia, NJ, m, 1957, 2 children **DISCIPLINE** PHILOSOPHY **EDUCATION** Yale Univ, AB, 55, AM, 59, PhD, 63. **CAREER** Asst prof philos and relig, MacMurray Col, 60-62; from asst prof to assoc prof, Raymond Col, Univ of the Pac, 63-70; assoc prof philos, Pa State Univ, University Park, 70-73; Nat Endowment Humanities sr fel, 73-74; PROF PHILOS, OLD DOMINION UNIV, 74-, Soc Relig Higher Educ cross-disciplinary studies fel, 68-69; ed, Process Studies, 71-. **MEMBERSHIPS** Am Philos Asn; Am Acad Relig; Soc Relig Higher Educ; Metaphys Soc Am. **RESEARCH** Process philosophy; philosophical theology; Biblical studies. **SELECTED PUBLICATIONS CONTACT ADDRESS** Dept of Philos, Old Dominion Univ, Norfolk, VA 23508.

FORD, PAUL F.
PERSONAL Born 04/08/1947, Springfield, MA, m, 1985 **DISCIPLINE** THEOLOGY, LITURGY **EDUCATION** St. John's Sem Col, BA, 69; MA, 74; Fuller Theol Sem, PhD, 87. **CAREER** Prof, St. John's Sem, 88-. **HONORS AND AWARDS** Mythopoeic Soc Awd, 82; Laudatus Awd, 95. **MEMBERSHIPS** Archdiocese of Los Angeles Theol Comm; Catholic Theol Soc; Col Theol Soc; Mariological Soc of Am; Nat Assoc of Pastoral Musicians; NY C.S. Lewis Soc; Soc for Catholic Liturgy; Soc for the Study of Christian Spirituality, S Calif C.S. Lewis Soc. **RESEARCH** Systematic Theology, especially ecclesiology, sacramentology, eschatology, and mariology, Liturgy, especially liturgical music, chant, C.S. Lewis: life, writings, circle of friends, influences, influence, Christian spirituality, especially lay spirituality and liturgical spirituality. **SELECTED PUBLICATIONS** Auth, Companion to Narnia, Harper Collins, 94; auth, By Flowing Waters: Chant for the Liturgy, Liturgical Pr, (Collegeville, MN), 99. **CONTACT ADDRESS** St. John's Sem, 5012 Seminary Rd, Camarillo, CA 93012-2500. **EMAIL** paulfford@sjs-sc.org

FORDE, GERHARD OLAF
PERSONAL Born 09/10/1927, Starbuck, MN, 3 children **DISCIPLINE** CHURCH HISTORY, SYSTEMATIC THEOLOGY **EDUCATION** Luther Col, BA, 50; Luther Theol Sem, BTh, 55; Harvard Divinity Sch, ThD, 67; Oxford Univ, MA, 68. **CAREER** Instr relig, St Olaf Col, 55-56; lectr church hist, Luther Theol Sem, 59-61; asst prof relig, Luther Col, 61-63; assoc prof church hist, 64-71, Prof Syst Theol, Luther Theol Sem, 74-, Lutheran World Fed lectr, Mansfield Col, Oxford Univ, 68-70; Frederick A Schiotz fel, 72-73. **MEMBERSHIPS** Am Acad Relig. **RESEARCH** Theology of Martin Luther; 19th century theology. **SELECTED PUBLICATIONS** Auth, The Law-Gospel Debate, 69, Where God Meets Man, 72 & coauth, Free To Be, 75, Augsburg; Justification By Faith: A Matter of Death & Life, 82; Theology is for Proclamation, 90; On Being a Theologian of the Cross, 97. **CONTACT ADDRESS** Luther Sem, 2481 Como Ave, Saint Paul, MN 55108-1445. **EMAIL** gforde@luthersem.edu

FORELL, CAROLINE
PERSONAL Born 11/09/1950, NJ, m, 2 children **DISCIPLINE** LAW **EDUCATION** Univ Iowa, BA, 73, JD, 78. **CAREER** Instr, Asst dean, Asst Prof, Assoc Prof, Prof, 78 to 94-, Univ Oregon. **HONORS AND AWARDS** Phi Beta Kappa, Order of the Coif. **MEMBERSHIPS** OSBA **RESEARCH** Women and the Law; Civil Liability. **SELECTED PUBLICATIONS** Auth, What's Wrong With Faculty-Student Sex? The Law School Context, J Legal Edu, 97; Essentialism Empathy and the Reasonable Women, 1994 IL L Rev, 94; Attorney-Client Sex: Ethical and Liability Issues in Oregon, Willamette L Rev, 93; The Reasonable Women standard of Care, Univ Tasmania L, 92; Lawyers Clients and Sex: Breaking the Silence on the Ethical and Liability Issues, Golden Gate L Rev, 92; coauth, A Law of Her Own: The Reasonable Woman as a Measure of Man, NYU Press, 00; auth, "Statutory Torts, Statutory Duty Actions, and Negligence Per Se: What's the Difference?, 77 Or.L. Rev497 (98). **CONTACT ADDRESS** School of Law, Univ of Oregon, Eugene, OR 97403. **EMAIL** cforell@law.uoregon.edu

FORELL, GEORGE WOLFGANG
PERSONAL Born 09/19/1919, Breslau, Germany, m, 1945, 2 children **DISCIPLINE** THEOLOGY **EDUCATION** Lutheran Theol Sem, Philadelphia, BD, 42; Princeton Theol Sem, ThM, 43; Union Theol Sem, NYork, ThD, 49. **CAREER** From asst prof to assoc prof philos, Gustavus Adolphus Col, 47-54; from asst prof to assoc prof relig, State Univ Iowa, 54-58; prof theol, Chicago Lutheran Sem, 58-61; dir sch: 66-71, prof theol, 61-73, CARVER DISTINGUISHED PROF, SCH RELIG, UNIV IOWA, 73-, Vis prof, Univ Hamburg, 57-58, Japan Lutheran Theol Col, 68, Gurukul Theol Res Inst, Madras, India, 78. **HONORS AND AWARDS** DD, Wartburg Theol Sem; LHD, Gustavus Adolphus Col, 74. **MEMBERSHIPS** Fel Soc Relig Higher Educ; Am Soc Reformation Res (pres, 59); Am Soc Church Hist; Am Philos Asn; Int Cong Luther Res. **RESEARCH** Reformation history; Zinzendorf and the Moravian Missions among the American Indians; history of Christian ethics. **SELECTED PUBLICATIONS** Auth, Luther, Theologians of The Church, Luther Sem, 94; auth, Luther Theology in its Historical Development and its Context, 16th Century J, Vol 28, 97; Spalding, James, Colwell, 1921-1996, 16th Century J, Vol 27, 96; Luther, Martin, his Life and Thought, 16th Century J, Vol 28, 97; Christian Ethics--A Historical Introduction, Church Hist, Vol 65, 96; Christian Ethics--A Historical Introduction, Church Hist, Vol 65, 96. **CONTACT ADDRESS** Sch of Relig, Univ of Iowa, Iowa City, IA 52242. **EMAIL** ctroutl@aol.com

FOREMAN, PEGGY E.
PERSONAL Born 02/18/1958, Houston, TX, s **DISCIPLINE** LAW **EDUCATION** Univ of Pennsylvania, 1976-78; Univ of Houston, BBA, 1981; TSU, Thurgood Marshall School of Law, JD, 1985. **CAREER** Peggy Foreman, Attorney, 85-89; Burney and Foreman, partner, 90-. **HONORS AND AWARDS** Houston Business and Professional Men's Club, Special Recognition; Iota Phi Lambda Sorority Inc, Beta Delta Chapter, Woman of the Year. **MEMBERSHIPS** American Bar Assn; National Bar Assn; State Bar of Texas; Texas Young Lawyers Assn; Harris County Young Assn; Houston Lawyers Assn, Houston Bar Assn, Young Lawyers Assn; National Assn of Bond Lawyers; Texas Trial Lawyers Assn; Gulf Coast Black Women Lawyers Assn; Phi Delta Phi Legal Fraternity Alumni Chap; Thurgood Marshall School of Law Alumni Assn. **SELECTED PUBLICATIONS** Author/Speaker, "Effective Rainmaking", Women in the Law Section Institute, State Bar of Texas, April 1993; Author/Speaker, Wills and Trusts in Texas, Harris County Young Lawyers Assn and Texas Lawyers Assn, May 1989; Author/Speaker, Client Satisfaction, How to Thrive, Not Just Survive in a Solo/Small Firm Practice, State Bar of Texas, December 1993; numerous others. **CONTACT ADDRESS** Burney & Foreman, 5445 Almeda, Ste 400, Houston, TX 77004.

FOREMAN, TERRY HANCOCK
PERSONAL Born 03/12/1943, Long Beach, CA, d, 2 children **DISCIPLINE** RELIGIOUS STUDIES, PHILOSOPHY **EDUCATION** Stanford Univ, AB, 64; Pa State Univ, MA, 68; Yale Univ, PhD(relig studies), 75. **CAREER** Asst prof philos, Earlham Col, 72-73; acting asst prof, Univ Calif, San Diego, 74-75; asst prof & coordr relig studies, 75-78, asst prof, 78-81, assoc prof philos & relig studies, Murray State Univ, 81-, Chmn Dept of Philos & Relig Studies, 78-96. **MEMBERSHIPS** Am Acad Relig. **RESEARCH** Role of scientific ideas in shaping concepts of religion in 18th and 19th centuries; varieties of the Bildung view of personal development in post-Enlightenment Germany. **SELECTED PUBLICATIONS** Auth, "Schleiermacher's Natural History of Religion: Science and the Interpretation of Culture in the Speeches," J Relig (4/78); auth, "Difference and Reconciliation: G. E. Lessing as Partner in Ecumenical Conversation," in Christian Faith Seeking Understanding: Essays in Honor of H. Jack Forstman, ed. James O. Duke and Tony A. Dunnavant (Mercer Univ Press, 97); auth, "Lessing's Quest for Truth 200 Years On: His Role in the Current Anglophone Culture-War," The Lessing Yearbook, XXXII; auth, Henry E. Allison, "Kant's Doctrine of Freedom," the Lessing Yearbook, XXVII, 96; auth, Herder's Copernican Revolution in Philosophy and the Study of Religion, Max Muller, Founder Mytheme for Comparative Religion, forthcoming. **CONTACT ADDRESS** Dept of English & Philos Studies, Murray State Univ, 7C Faculty Hall, Murray, KY 42071. **EMAIL** terry.foreman@murraystate.edu

FORGUSON, LYND W.
PERSONAL Born 01/15/1938, Paducah, KY **DISCIPLINE** PHILOSOPHY **EDUCATION** Baldwin-Wallace Col, BA, 60; Northwestern Univ, MA, 61, PhD, 64. **CAREER** Fulbright-Hayes fel, Oxford Univ, 63-64; asst prof, State Univ NY, 64-67; NEH fel, Oxford Univ, 67-68; prof Philos, Univ Toronto, 68-, prin, Univ Col, 89-97. **MEMBERSHIPS** Can Asn Univ Tchrs; Can Philos Asn; Soc Philos Psychol. **RESEARCH** Philos of mind, philos of lang, metaphysics, 20th century British philos. **SELECTED PUBLICATIONS** Auth, Comon Sense, 89; auth, "The Ontology of Commoon Sense," with A. Gopnik, in Developing Theories of Mind, 88; auth, Reference, Representation and Communication," in Understanding 1984, 84. **CONTACT ADDRESS** Dept of Philosophy, Univ of Toronto, 15 King's College Cir, Toronto, ON, Canada M5S 1A1. **EMAIL** lynd.forguson@utoronto.ca

FORMAN, JONATHAN BARRY
PERSONAL Born 05/19/1952, Cleveland, OH **DISCIPLINE** LAW **EDUCATION** Northwestern Univ, BA 73; Univ Iowa, MA 75; Univ Michigan Law, JD magna cum laude, 78; George Washington Univ, MA 83. **CAREER** Univ Oklahoma Law, prof 97-; OK City Univ Law, adj prof, 95, 96; Brigham Young Univ Law, vis prof 91; Univ Colorado Law, vis prof 87; Univ San Diego Law, vis prof 85; Tax Notes, ed staff 85; Sen D. P. Moynihan NY, tax coun 83,84; US Dept Justice, trial att, tax div 79-83; Antioch Sch Law, adj prof 81-85; Hon R.J. Yock, US Court Clms, jud clk 78-79. **HONORS AND AWARDS** Nat Summit Del; ATPI Trustee; Halliburton Fac Awd; NALJF Fel; US Supreme Court Judicial Fel finalist. **MEMBERSHIPS** Dist Columbia Bar Assoc; ABA; NTA; ACTC; ATPI; AEA; EBRI; World bank. **SELECTED PUBLICATIONS** Auth, The Once and Future Social Security Tax Expenditure, Benefits Quart, 97; auth, What Can Be Done About Marriage Penalties?, Fam Law Quart, 96; auth, Poverty Levels and Federal Tax Thresholds: 1996, Tax Notes, 96; Simplification for Low Income taxpayers: Some Options, OH State Law Jour, 96; auth, How to Reduce the Compliance Burden of the Earned Income Tax Credit on Low Income Workers and on the Internal Rev Service, OK Law Rev, 95; auth, Reconsidering the Income Tax Treatment of the Elderly: It's Time for the Elderly to Pay Their Fair Share, Univ Pitt Law Rev, 95; auth, Improving the Delivery of Benefits to the Working Poor: Proposals to Reform the Earned Income Credit Program, coauth, Amer Jour of Tax Policy. **CONTACT ADDRESS** College of Law, Univ of Oklahoma, 300 Timberdell Rd, Norman, OK 73019. **EMAIL** jforeman@ou.edu

FORMAN, ROBERT
DISCIPLINE RELIGION - SPIRITUAL AND MYSTICAL EXPERIENCE **EDUCATION** Columbia Univ, PhD, 88. **CAREER** Vassar Col, 88-90; Hunter Col, CUNY, 90- ; ed, J Consciousness Studies. **HONORS AND AWARDS** Numerous grants; Fetzer; New World Found; CUNY. **MEMBERSHIPS** AAR; Forge Inst. **RESEARCH** Spiritual experience; spirituality in America; mysticism. **SELECTED PUBLICATIONS** Auth, Problem of Pure Consciousness; auth, Mysticism; auth, Mind Consciousness; auth, Innate Capacity. **CONTACT ADDRESS** 383 Broadway, Hastings on Hudson, NY 10706. **EMAIL** rforman383@aol.com

FORRESTER, WILLIAM RAY
PERSONAL Born 01/14/1911, Little Rock, AR, m, 1942, 4 children **DISCIPLINE** LAW **EDUCATION** Univ AR, AB, 33; Univ Chicago, JD, 35. **CAREER** Atty, Defrees, Buckingham, Jones & Hoffman, Chicago, IL, 35-41; prof law, Tulane Univ, 41-49; prof & dean, law sch, Vanderbilt Univ, 49-52; Irby prof & dean, Tulane Univ, 52-63; Stevens prof, law sch, Cornell Univ, 63-78, dean sch, 63-73; Prof Law, Univ CA, Hastings Col Law, 78-; vis prof, Univ London, Queen Mary Col, 74; Labor arbitrator; Board of Gov, Nat Academy of Arbitrators; L.A. member, Comm on Uniform State Laws; public member, admin conferences of the U. S., 75-78. **HONORS AND AWARDS** LLD, Univ AR, 63; LLD, Tulane Univ, 95. **RESEARCH** Federal jurisdiction and procedure; constitutional law. **SELECTED PUBLICATIONS** Auth, Constitutional Law, 59, cases & materials suppl 61 & 63, coauth, Federal Jurisdiction and Procedure, 70 & suppl to Federal Jurisdiction and Procedure, 73, 3rd ed, 77, West Publ, suppl, 81. **CONTACT ADDRESS** Dept of Law, Univ of California, San Francisco, 200 McAllister St, San Francisco, CA 94102-4907.

FORSBERG, RALPH P.
PERSONAL Born 08/28/1948, Chicago, IL, m, 1970, 1 child **DISCIPLINE** PHILOSOPHY **EDUCATION** Bradley Univ, BS, 70; Roosevelt Univ, MA, 73; Loyola Univ, PhD, 87. **CAREER** Lectr, adj prof, Loyola Univ, 74-87; lectr, adj prof, Harper Coll, 74-87; cis asst prof, Ripon Coll, 88-89; Assoc Prof, Delta Coll, 89-. **HONORS AND AWARDS** Mem Sigma Alpha Nu Honor Soc; Loyola Univ Grant-In-Aid; Roosevelt Univ Grad Scholar. **MEMBERSHIPS** Am Philos Asn; Am Asn of Philos Tchrs; Am Asn of Univ Profs; Comt on Employee Responsibilities and Rights; Int Soc of Bus, Economics, and Ethics; Med Ethics Resources Network Of Mich; Marketing Mgt Asn: Ethics Section; Midwest Acad of Legal Studies in Bus; Soc for Bus Ethics. **RESEARCH** Environmental Ethics and Ecology; Applied Ethics, Medical and Business; Native Am Philos. **SELECTED PUBLICATIONS** Auth, Ethics on the Job: Cases and Strategies, 93; random Selection and the Allocation of Scarce Medical Resources, J of Philos and Med, 94; R L Ewin, Thomas Hobbes's Theory of Morality, Int J of Philos, 94; Richard Flathman, Thomas Hobbes: Skepticism, Individuality and Chastened Politics, Int J of Philos, 95; Seth Allcorn, Anger in the Workplace: A Review, Employee Responsibilities and Rights J. **CONTACT ADDRESS** Dept of Philosophy, Delta Col, University Center, MI 48710. **EMAIL** rpforsbe@alpha.delta.edu

FORSHEY, HAROLD ODES
PERSONAL Born 07/27/1934, Cambridge, OH, m, 1966, 2 children **DISCIPLINE** RELIGION **EDUCATION** Abilene Christian Col, BA, 56, MA, 61; Harvard Univ, STB, 62, ThD, 73. **CAREER** From instr to asst prof, 66-77, assoc prof, 77-82, prof Relig, Miami Univ, 82-, chmn dept, 79-84, 95-; Staff, Lahav Res Proj, 77-87; Staff, Tell Safut Archoeological project, 85; act associate dean, Coll of Arts and Science, 90-91; assoc dean, Col of Arts and Science, 91-94. **MEMBERSHIPS** Cath Bibl Asn; Soc Bibl Lit; Am Sch Orient Res; Archaeol Inst Am; Am Oriental Soc. **RESEARCH** Religion of ancient Israel; ancient Near Eastern languages and literature; archaeology of Near East. **SELECTED PUBLICATIONS** Auth, Circumcision: an initiatory rite in ancient Israel?, Restoration Quart, 73-74; Segullah and Nachalah as designations of the covenant community, Hebrew Abstr, 74; The construct chain nahalat YHWHV/'elohim, Bull Am Schs Orient Res, 75-76; The Bronze Age Settlements at Tell Halif: Phase II Excavations, 83-87, with Joe D Seger, Paul Jacobs, and others, Bulletin of the American Schools of Oriental Research, Supplement 26, 90. **CONTACT ADDRESS** Dept of Corporate Relig, Miami Univ, 500 E High St, Oxford, OH 45056-1602. **EMAIL** forsheho@muohio.edu

FORTNA, ROBERT TOMSON
PERSONAL Born 05/05/1930, Lincoln, NE, m, 1960, 3 children **DISCIPLINE** RELIGION, NEW TESTAMENT **EDUCATION** Yale Univ, BA, 52; Cambridge Univ, BA, 54, MA, 59; Church Divinity Sch Pac, BD, 55; Union Theol Sem, NYork, ThD(New Testament), 65. **CAREER** Tutor theol and instr Greek, Church Divinity Sch Pac, 55-56; lectr New Testament, 56-58; dir exten, 58-60; tutor New Testament, Union Theol Sem, NY, 60-62, lectr, 62-63; from instr to assoc prof relig, 63-74, fac fel, 67-68, dean freshman, 69, chmn dept, 69-71, 74-77 and 80-81, PROF RELIG, VASSAR COL, 74-, William F Albright fel, Am Sch Orient Res, Jerusalem, 67-68; Am Coun Learned Soc fel, 67-68; resident scholar, Ecumenical Inst Advan Theol Studies, Jerusalem, 72 and 78; prof, Albright Inst, Jerusalem, 79. **MEMBERSHIPS** Am Schs Orient Res; Soc New Testament Studies; Cath Bibl Asn Am; Soc Bibl Lit. **RESEARCH** Fourth Gospel. **SELECTED PUBLICATIONS** Auth, The Gospel of Signs: Reconstruction of the Narrative Source Underlying the Fourth Gospel, Cambridge Univ, 70; Source and Redaction in the Fourth Gospel's Portrayal of Jesus' Signs, J Bibl Lit, 6/70; From Christology to Soteriology: A Redaction-Critical Study of Salvation in the Fourth Gospel, Interpretation, 1/73; Theological Use of Locale in the Fourth Gospel, Anglican Theol Rev, Suppl, 3/74; Christology in the Fourth Gospel: Redaction-Critical Perspectives, New Testament Studies, 6/75; Redaction Criticism, New Testament, In: Interpreter's Dict of the Bible, 76. **CONTACT ADDRESS** Dept of Relig, Vassar Col, Poughkeepsie, NY 12601.

FORTNER, JOHN D.
PERSONAL Born 01/13/1949, Greencastle, IN, m, 1971, 1 child **DISCIPLINE** HEBREW BIBLE, LANGUAGES, CULTURES, & RELIGIONS OF THE ANCIENT NEAR EAST **EDUCATION** Hebrew Union Col-Jewish Inst Relig, PhD, 97. **CAREER** Asst prof Bible, Lubbock Christian Col, 78-82; Pulpit ministries in Ohio & Tenn, Church of Christ, 82-90; assoc prof Hebrew Bible & The Ane, Harding Univ Asn, 90-. **MEMBERSHIPS** Soc Bibl Lit; Am Orient Soc; Am Schools Orient Res. **RESEARCH** Biblical & ANE Law, Biblical exegesis & theology, hermeneutics **SELECTED PUBLICATIONS** Contrib, New Eerdmans Dictionary of Bible, 98; in progress, NIV Bible Commentary on Exodus, College Press; Contrib, Eerdmans Dictionary of the Bible, 00. **CONTACT ADDRESS** Harding Univ, 900 E Center St, Box 12280, Searcy, AR 72149-0001. **EMAIL** jdfortner@harding.edu

FOSL, PETER S.
PERSONAL Born 03/15/1963, Bethlehem, PA **DISCIPLINE** PHILOSOPHY **EDUCATION** Bucknell Univ, BA (Philosophy) and BA (Economics), 85; Emory Univ, MA, 90; PhD, 92. **CAREER** Instr, GA State Univ; Instr, Emory Univ; Asst & Assoc Prof, Hollins College; Assoc Prof, Transylvania Univ, 92-. **HONORS AND AWARDS** Fulbright, 90; BinhHam Awd, 98. **MEMBERSHIPS** APA; Hume Soc; ASECS; ECSSS; ACA; AAPT; AAUP. **RESEARCH** Skepticism; Modern philosophy (esp. Hume); History of philosophy. **SELECTED PUBLICATIONS** Coauth, "Stanley Cavell: A Bibliography, 1958-1994," in Philos Passages: Wittgenstein, Emerson, Austin, Derrida (Basil Blackwell Ltd, Oxford, 95), 187-197; auth, "Stanley Cavell: A Bibliography, 1951-1995," in The Cavell Reader (Basil Blackwell Ltd, Oxford, 96), 390-414; auth, "The Moral Imperative to Rebel Against God," Cognito 11.3 (97): 141-150; auth, "The Bibliographic Bases of Hume's Understanding of Sextus Empiricus and Pyrrhonism," J of the Hist of Philos 16.2 (98): 93-109; auth, "Hume, Skepticism, and Early American Deism," Hume Studies 25, 1&2, (99): 171-192; auth, "Animality and Common Life in Hume," 1650-1850: Ideas, Aesthetics, and Inquiries in the Early Modern Era 4 (99): 93-120; auth, "The Moral Imperative to Rebel Against God," in Philosophy in Action (Gradiva Publishers, Lisbon, 00); auth, Makers of Western Culture 1800-1914: A Biographical Dictionary of Literary Influences, Greenwood Pr (Westport, CT), 00; co-ed, "David Hume," in British Philosophers, 1500-1899, vol 2xx for the Dictionary of Literary Biography, Gale Research, Inc. (Detroit & London), 00. **CONTACT ADDRESS** Dept of Philos, Transylvania Univ, 300 N Broadway, Lexington, KY 40508-1797. **EMAIL** pfosl@transy.edu

FOSS, JEFFREY E.
DISCIPLINE PHILOSOPHY **EDUCATION** Univ Alberta, BA; Univ W Ontario, MA, PhD. **CAREER** Instr, Univ Saskatchewan; Univ Alberta; Univ Regina; Univ Winnipeg; Univ Manitoba; assoc prof, 84. **RESEARCH** Philosophy of mind; philosophy of science; and philosophical psychology. **SELECTED PUBLICATIONS** Auth, Can Jour Philos; Philos Sci; Transactions of the Charles Peirce Soc; Amer Philos Quart. **CONTACT ADDRESS** Dept of Philosophy, Univ of Victoria, PO Box 3045, Victoria, BC, Canada V8W 3P4. **EMAIL** jefffoss@uvic.ca

FOSTER, DOUGLAS A.
PERSONAL Born 08/30/1952, Sheffield, AL, m, 1979, 2 children **DISCIPLINE** CHURCH HISTORY **EDUCATION** David Lipscomb Univ, BA, 74; Harding Grad Sch of Religion, 76; Scarritt Col, MA, 80; Vanderbilt Univ, PhD, 86. **CAREER** Assoc Min, Jackson Park Church of Christ, 74-83; Arch, Gospel Adv Co, 88-91; Retention, Inst, Asst Prof, David Lipscomb Univ, 85-91; Asst Prof, Assoc Prof, Abilene Christian Univ, 91-. **HONORS AND AWARDS** Outstanding Tchr Awd, College of Bibl Stud, ACU 94, 99; Outstanding Tchr Awd, DLU, 89; Mayhew Fel Vanderbilt Univ, 83-83. **MEMBERSHIPS** Amer Soc of Church History, Amer Acad of Religion, Conf on Faith and History, disciples of Christ Hist Soc, Rel Res Assn, Southern Baptist Hist Soc, Southwest Archivists, TN Archivists. **RESEARCH** Stone-Campbell History: American Church History; Ecumenism. **SELECTED PUBLICATIONS** Holding Back the Tide: T.B. Larimore and the Disciples of Christ and Churches of Christ, Discipliana, 93; Will the Cycle Be Unbroken: Churches of Christ Face the Twenty-First Century, ACU Press, 94; The Many Faces of Christian Unity: Disciples Ecumenism and Schism, 1875-1900, Nashville Disciples for Christ Hist Soc, 95; Millennial Harbinger, Pop Rel Mag of the USA, 95; Rethinking the History of Churches of Christ: Responses to Richard Hughes, Rest Quart, 96; Reflections on the Writing of Will the Cycle Be Unbroken: Churches of Christ Face the Twenty-First Century, Discipliana, 97. **CONTACT ADDRESS** Abilene Christian Univ, PO Box ACU 29429, Abilene, TX 79699-9429. **EMAIL** foster@bible.acu.edu

FOSTER, HAMAR
DISCIPLINE LAW **EDUCATION** Queen's Univ, BA, 70; Sussex Univ, MA, 71; Univ British Columbia, LLB, 74; Auckland Univ, MJ, 89. **CAREER** Law clerk, Chief Justice British Columbia, 74-75; asst prof, 78-93; prof, Univ of Victoria, 93-. **HONORS AND AWARDS** Commonwealth Scholar; Honourary Woodrow Wilson Fel, 70-71. **MEMBERSHIPS** Can Law Soc Asn; British Columbia Civil Liberties Asn. **RESEARCH** Legal process; criminal law; the law of evidence; legal history; aboriginal law. **SELECTED PUBLICATIONS** Auth, pubs on comparative criminal law, fur trade and colonial legal history, and aboriginal history and law; co-ed, Law for the Elephant, Law for the Beaver: Essays in the Legal History of the North American West and Essays in the History of Canadian Law. **CONTACT ADDRESS** Fac of Law, Univ of Victoria, PO Box 2400, Victoria, BC, Canada V8W 3H7. **EMAIL** hamarf@uvic.ca

FOSTER, JAMES HADLEI
PERSONAL Born 04/29/1938, Valdosta, GA, m, 1982 **DISCIPLINE** RELIGION **EDUCATION** Morris Brown Coll, Atlanta GA, BA, 1960; Pittsburgh (PA) Theological Sem, 1969-70; United Theological Sem, Dayton OH, MDIV, 1973; Vanderbilt Univ, NashvilleTN, DMIN, 1981. **CAREER** Massachusetts Council of Churches, Boston MA, dept pastoral serv, 62-63; Albany State Col, Albany GA, dean of the chapel/instr, 62-66; Alcorn State Univ, Lorman MS, chaplain/asst prof, 66-68; Christian Assoc of Metro Erie, Erie PA, assoc dir, 70-73; Wilberforce Univ, Wilberforce OH, chaplain/assoc prof, 73-80; Dartmouth Coll, Hanover NH, assoc chaplain/lecturer, 80-84; A Better Chance, Boston MA, Northern New England regional dir, 80-82; Mercy Coll, Dobbs Ferry NY, prof of religion, 84-; St Marks AME Church, East Orange, NJ, assoc pastor, 85-. **HONORS AND AWARDS** Union Coll, LHD, 1971. **MEMBERSHIPS** Mem, Optimist Club, 1975-; assoc pastor, St Mark's AME Church, East Orange NJ, 1985-; mem, Community Relations Commission, NJ Council of Churches, 1985-88; mem, Special Task Force, E Orange Bd of Education, 1985-86; pres, Jersey Chapter, Morris Brown Coll Alumni Assn, 1988-. **CONTACT ADDRESS** Dept of Religion, Mercy Col, 555 Broadway, Dobbs Ferry, NY 10522.

FOSTER, JOHN
DISCIPLINE LAW **EDUCATION** Univ Saskatchewan, BA, 62; Univ Toronto, MA, 63, PhD, 77. **CAREER** Prof. **SELECTED PUBLICATIONS** Auth, Strengthening Civil Society in Mexico: From Clientalism to Citizenship, Can For Policy, 97; co-auth, U.N. Futures, U.N. Reforms and the Social Agenda, 97. **CONTACT ADDRESS** Col of Law, Univ of Saskatchewan, 15 Campus Dr, Saskatoon, SK, Canada S7N 5A6.

FOSTER, LAWRENCE
PERSONAL Born 07/08/1939, Jersey City, NJ, m, 1964 **DISCIPLINE** PHILOSOPHY **EDUCATION** Univ Pa, BA, 61, PhD (philos), 66. **CAREER** From instr to assoc prof, Univ Mass, Amherst, 65-75, assoc dir law and justice prog, 75-76, ASSOC PROF PHILOS, UNIV MASS, BOSTON, 75-, DIR LAW AND JUSTICE PROG, 76-, CONSULT, NAT ENDOWMENT FOR HUMANITIES, 77-. **RESEARCH** Ethics; induction; legal and political philosophy. **SELECTED PUBLICATIONS** Auth, Differential and projectible predictates, Critica, 1/69; Feyerabend's solution to the Goodman Paradox, Brit J Philos Sci, 5/69; co-ed, Experience and Theory, Univ Mass, 70 & Duckworth, London, 71; auth, Inductive and ethical validity, Am Philos Quart, 71; Hempel, Scheffler and the ravens, J Philos, 71; Ethical naturalism revisited, 71 & Confirmation and extra information, 77, Critica. **CONTACT ADDRESS** Prof of Law and Justice Harbor Campus, Univ of Massachusetts, Amherst, 100 Morrissey Blvd, Boston, MA 02125-3300.

FOSTER, MATTHEW
DISCIPLINE RELIGIOUS STUDIES **EDUCATION** Earlham Col, BA, 74; Univ Chicago Divinity Sch, MA, 77; PhD, 87. **CAREER** Asst prof, Molloy Col, 92-. **MEMBERSHIPS** Am Acad of Relig, Soc of Buddhist-Christian Studies. **RESEARCH** Inter-religious dialogue, environmental ethics, religion and science. **SELECTED PUBLICATIONS** Auth, Gadamer and Practical Philosophy: The Hermeneuter of Moral Confidence, Scholar Press, 91. **CONTACT ADDRESS** Dept Theol and Relig Studies, Molloy Col, PO Box 5002, Rockville Centre, NY 11571-5002. **EMAIL** mfoster@molloy.edu

FOTI, VERONIQUE M.
PERSONAL Born 09/05/1938, Miskele, Hungary, d, 4 children **DISCIPLINE** PHILOSOPHY **EDUCATION** Oglethorpe Univ, BA, 62; Simmons Col, MLS, 74; Boston Col, PhD, 79. **CAREER** Teaching Fel, Boston Col, 74-78; Asst Prof, Univ Ky, 78=80; Asst Prof, Col of the Holy Cross, 80-81; Asst Prof, New Sch of Soc Res, 81-85; Asst Prof to Assoc Prof, Penn State Univ, 85-. **HONORS AND AWARDS** Woodrow Wilson Fel; Fulbright Fel; NEH Inst grant. **MEMBERSHIPS** Am Philos Asn; Soc for Existential Philos and Phenomenol; Intl Asn for Philos and Lit; Heidegger Conf; Merleau-Ponty Soc; Soc for Ancient Greek Philos. **RESEARCH** Contemporary European Philosophy; History of Philosophy; Philosophy of Art and Literature. **SELECTED PUBLICATIONS** Auth, "Heidegger and the Poets: Poiesis/Sophia/Techne," in Philosophy and Literary Theory Vol II, (Humanities Press, 92); auth, "Aletheia and Oblivion's Field: On Heidegger's Parmenides Lectures," in Ethics and Danger: Essays on Heidegger and Continental Thought, (SUNY Press, 92), 71-82; ed, Merleau-Ponty: Difference, Materiality, Painting, (Humanities Press, 96); auth, "Heidegger, Holderlin, and Sophoclean Tragedy," in Heidegger's Parmenides Lectures," in Heidegger Toward the Turn: Essays on the Work of the 1930's, (SUNY Press, 99), 163-186; auth, "Merleau-Ponty's 'Vertical Genesis' and the Aristotelian Powers of the Soul," in Phenomenology: Japanese and American, (The Hague, 98), 39-58; auth, "The Tragic Thought of Empedocles: Holderlin, Heidegger, Nietzsche," in The Presocratics After Heidegger, (SUNY Press, 99), 277-294; auth, "Descartes's Corporeal and Intellectual Memories," in Descartes's Natural Philosophy, (Routledge, 00), 582-603; auth, "Holderlin, Johann Christian Friedrich," in Eidenburgh Encyclopedia of Literary Theory and Criticism, forthcoming. **CONTACT ADDRESS** Dept Philos, Pennsylvania State Univ, Univ Park, 240 Sparks Bldg, University Park, PA 16802-5201. **EMAIL** viuf3@psu.edu

FOTION, NICHOLAS
DISCIPLINE MORAL PHILOSOPHY **EDUCATION** Univ NC, PhD, 57. **CAREER** Prof & Dir/Undergrad Studies, Philos, Emory Univ. **HONORS AND AWARDS** Fulbright Prof, Yonsei Univ. **RESEARCH** Moral philosophy, philosophy of language **SELECTED PUBLICATIONS** Auth, Moral Situations and Military Ethics: Looking Toward the Future; Coauth, Military Ethics and Toleration; Coed, Hare and Critics: Essays on Moral Thinking. **CONTACT ADDRESS** Emory Univ, Atlanta, GA 30322-1950. **EMAIL** philnf@emory.edu

FOTTLER, MYRON D.
PERSONAL Born 09/05/1939, Boston, MA, m, 1972 **DISCIPLINE** BUSINESS **EDUCATION** Northeastern Univ, BS, 62; Boston Univ, MBA, 63; Columbia Univ, PhD, 70. **CAREER** Asst Prof, State Univ NY-Buffalo, 70-75; Assoc Prof, Univ Iowa, 75-76; Assoc Prof to Prof, Univ Ala, 76-83; Prof and Dir PhD Prog in Admin - Health Services, Univ Ala-Birmingham, 83-; ed of book series, Prof and Dir of Health Services Programs, Univ of Fl; Advances in Health Care Management, JAI Press; Chair pf Editorial Review Board, Health Administration Press. **HONORS AND AWARDS** Edgar Hayhow Awd for Best Paper in Hospital and Health Services Administration. **MEMBERSHIPS** Acad Mgt; Southern Mgt Asn; AUPHA. **RESEARCH** Health care management. **SELECTED PUBLICATIONS** Co-ed, Strategic Management of Human Resources in Health Services Organizations, Delmar Publ, 2nd ed, 94; coauth, Medical Groups Face the Uncertain Future: Challenges, Opportunities, and Strategies, Ctr for Res in Ambulatory Care Admin, 95; Applications in Human Resources Management, SWestern Publ Co, 3rd ed, 96; co-ed, Essentials of Human Resources Management in Health Services Organizations, Delmar Publ, 98; coauth, Strategic Leadership for Medical Groups: Navigating Your Strategic Web, Jossey-Bass, 98; author of numerous other publications and journal articles; Advances in Health Care Management, IAI Press, 00. **CONTACT ADDRESS** Dept of Health Profesionels, Univ of Central Florida, Orlando, FL 32816-2205. **EMAIL** fottler@mail.ucf.edu

FOUKE, DANIEL C.
DISCIPLINE MODERN PHLIOSOPHY, PHILOSOPHY OF RELIGION **EDUCATION** Univ Chicago, PhD, 86. **CAREER** Dept Philos, Univ Dayton **RESEARCH** History of science and technology. **SELECTED PUBLICATIONS** Auth, Mechanical and Organical Models in Seventeenth-Century Explanations of Biological Reproduction, Sci in Context, 89; Emanation and the Perfections of Being: Divine Causation and the Autonomy of Nature, Leibniz, Archiv fur Geschichte der Philos, 94; The Enthusiastical Concerns of Dr. Henry More: Religious Meaning and the Pyschology of Delusion, Brill, 97. **CONTACT ADDRESS** Dept of Philos, Univ of Dayton, 300 Col Park, Dayton, OH 75062. **EMAIL** fouke@checkov.hm.udayton.edu

FOULK, GARY J.
DISCIPLINE PHILOSOPHY **EDUCATION** Portland State Univ, BS, 57; Univ of Oregon, MA, 62, PhD, 66. **CAREER** Instr, philos, Univ Oregon, 63-64; instr, philos, Portland State Univ, 64-66; asst prof, assoc prof, prof, chemn, philos, Indiana State Univ, 66-95. **HONORS AND AWARDS** Outstanding undergraduate tchg, Portland State Univ, 66. **MEMBERSHIPS** APA. **RESEARCH** Ethics; ethics and animals; medical ethics. **SELECTED PUBLICATIONS** Coauth, The Moral Foundation of Nursing: Yarling and McElmurry and Their Critics, Anthology on Caring, National League for Nursing, 91; auth, Ethics and Technology Education: Fact, Possibility, and Value, in Proceedings, Technology Education Symposium XIII, Indiana, 91; coauth, Rationality and Principles: A Criticism of the Ethic of Care, Int J of Applied Philos, 92; auth, Three Reviews of Illiberal Education, Public Affairs Q, 92; coauth, The Perception of Ethical Dilemmas in Clinical Practice: Empirical Diagnosis and Philosophical Therapy, Int J of Applied Philos, 98. **CONTACT ADDRESS** 1511 SW Park Ave, Apt 419, Portland, OR 97201.

FOWLER, VIVIA
PERSONAL Born 08/20/1954, Allendale, SC, m, 1976, 2 children **DISCIPLINE** RELIGIOUS STUDIES **EDUCATION** Columbia Col, BA, 76; Lutheran Theol S Sem, MA, 80; Univ SC, PhD, 94. **CAREER** Assoc prof of Religion & assoc dean undergraduate studies & asst dir honors, Columbia Col, 86-, dir of gen edu, 00-. **HONORS AND AWARDS** Outstanding Fac Mem, 96; ODK Fac Mem Yr, 95. **MEMBERSHIPS** AAR; SC Acad Relig; REA **RESEARCH** Women in religion; Women in Bible; Religious attitudes; Instruction. **CONTACT ADDRESS** Columbia Col, So Carolina, 1301 Columbia Col Dr, Columbia, SC 29203. **EMAIL** vfowler@columbiacollegesc.edu

FOX, CHARLES W.
PERSONAL Born 12/30/1936, Steubenville, OH, d, 4 children **DISCIPLINE** RELIGION **EDUCATION** Baylor Univ, BA, 58; Harvard Univ, PhD, 78. **CAREER** Asst prof religion, Wiliams Col, 65-70; lectr philos, State Univ NY, 70-74; mentor hum, State Univ NY/Empire State Col, 74-. **HONORS AND AWARDS** S Regional Fel, 59-62; Woodrow Wilson Fel, 58-59; Rockefeller Doctoral Fel, 62-63. **MEMBERSHIPS** Am Acad Relig. **RESEARCH** Christian Thought; Origins of Christianity; Meso-American Indian Religions. **CONTACT ADDRESS** Dept of Humanities, SUNY, Empire State Col, 2 Union Ave, Saratoga Springs, NY 12866. **EMAIL** cfox@sescva.esc.edu

FOX, CHRISTOPHER B.
DISCIPLINE PHILOSOPHY OF SCIENCE **EDUCATION** Cleveland State Univ, BA, 71; SUNY-Binghamton, MA, 74, PhD, 78. **CAREER** Asst prof, Wilkes Univ, 78, 84, Assoc prof, 84-86; Assoc prof, Univ of Notre Dame, 86-91, Chairperson, 92-97, Prof, 93-; Reilly Ctr for the Hist and Philos of Sci, Fel, 88-; Keough Inst For Irish Studies, Univ of Notre Dame, cofounder, 93, Assoc Dean for Fac and Res, 97-99, Dir of The Inst For Scholarship in the Liberal Arts, 97-99, Actg Dean, Col of Art and Letters, Univ of Notre Dame, 99-00. **HONORS AND AWARDS** The Distinguished Dissertation in the Humanities and Fine Arts Prize, SUNY-Binghamton, 78; NEH Summer Independent Res Stipend, for work at Oxford Univ, 82; Honorable Mention, James L. Clifford Prize, Am Soc for Eighteenth-Century Studies for the article of the year on an eighteenth-century topic, 83; The Carpenter Awd for Teacher of the Year, Wilkes Univ, 84; NEH Travel to Collections for work at Wellcome Inst for the Hist of Med-London, England, 88; NEH Travel to Collections, for work at Col of Physicians, 92; Mellon Found for a Medieval Fel Prog at the Univ of Notre Dame, 98-99; NEH Challenge Grant, for Building Medieval and Irish Studies at the Univ of Notre Dame, 98-00; NEH Summer Sem for Col and Univ Teachers for Anglo-Irish Identities, 1600-1800, Dir, 01. **RESEARCH** Interactions between literature and medicine; psychology and science during the 18th century. **SELECTED PUBLICATIONS** Ed, Psychology and Literature in the Eighteenth Century, AMS Studies (New York), In The Eighteenth Century, 87; auth, Locke and the Scriblerians: Identity and Consciousness in Early Eighteenth-Century Britain, Univ of California Press (Berkeley, Los Angeles and London) 88; ed, Teaching Eighteenth-Century Poetry, AMS Studies in

the Eighteenth Century (New York), 90; ed, Gulliver's Travels: Text and Case Studies In Contemporary Criticism, Bedford Books of St. Martin's Press (New York), 95; ed, Walking Naboth's Vineyard: New Studies of Swift, Notre Dame, Univ of Notre Dame Press (Indiana and London), 95; ed, Inventing Human Science: Eighteenth-Century Domains, Univ of California Press (Berkeley, Los Angeles and London), 95; auth, "Jonathan Swift and Irish Studies," with Brenda Tooley, In Walking Naboth's Vineyard, New Studies of Swift (95): 1-16; auth, "How To Prepare a Noble Savage: The Spectacle of Human Science," In Inventing Human Science, Los Angeles and London: Univ of California Press, (95): 1-30; auth, "Pope's Ruling Passion," Critical Essays on Alexander Pope, eds. Wallace Jackson and Paul Yoder, New York: Oxford Univ Press (96): 28-33; auth, "Swift and The Spectacle of Human Science," In Proceedings of the Third International Munster Symposium on Johnathan Swift, ed. Herman J. Real, Munchen: Wilhelm Fink Verlag (98): 199-212. **CONTACT ADDRESS** Inst for Scholarship in the Liberal Arts, Univ of Notre Dame, 102B O'Shaughnessy Hall, Notre Dame, IN 46556. **EMAIL** cfox@nd.edu

FOX, DOUGLAS A.
PERSONAL Born 03/20/1927, Mullumbimby, Australia, m, 1958, 2 children **DISCIPLINE** THEOLOGY, HISTORY OF RELIGIONS **EDUCATION** Univ Sydney, BA, 54; Univ Chicago, MA, 57; Pac Sch Relig, STM, 58, ThD, 63. **CAREER** From asst prof to assoc prof, 63-74, Prof Relig, Colo Col, 74-. **HONORS AND AWARDS** Carnegie found "Colorado prof of the year," 95. **MEMBERSHIPS** Am Acad Relig. **RESEARCH** Mahayana Buddhism; philosophy of religion; philosophical theology. **SELECTED PUBLICATIONS** Auth, Buddhism, Christianity, and the Future of Man, Westminster Press, 72; auth, The Heart of Buddhist Wisdom, Edwin Mellen Press, 85; auth, Meditation and Reality: A Critical View, John Knox Press, 86; auth, Dispelling Illusion: Gaudapada's Alatasanti, SUNY, 93; auth, Direct Awareness of the Self: A Translation of the Aparoksanubhuti by Sankara, Edwin Mellin, 95. **CONTACT ADDRESS** Dept of Relig, Colorado Col, Colorado Springs, CO 80903. **EMAIL** dfox@coloradocollege.edu

FOX, ELEANOR M.
PERSONAL Born 01/18/1936, Trenton, NJ, d **DISCIPLINE** LAW **EDUCATION** Vassar Col, AB, 56; NYork Univ Law Sch, LLB, 61. **CAREER** Assoc prof, 76-78, Prof Law, NY Univ Sch Law, 78-, Assoc, Simpson Thacher & Bartlett, 62-70, partner, 70-76; comnr, Nat Comn Rev Antitrust Laws & Procedure, 78-79; Law Review Editor. **HONORS AND AWARDS** Great Tchr Awd, NYU Alum Asn. **MEMBERSHIPS** Am Law Inst; Am Bar Found; Int Compet Policy Advis Comt, 97-00; TriNat NAFTA Task Force; Cnl on For Rels. **RESEARCH** Competition and trade, United States and the world; industry organization; political economy. **SELECTED PUBLICATIONS** Coauth, Corporate Acquisitions and Mergers, Vol I, 68, Vol II, 70 & Vol III, 71, Matthew Bender & Co; co-ed & contribr, Industrial Concentration and the Market System: Legal, Economic, Social & Political Perspectives, Am Bar Asn, 79; auth, Reign of Reason (poem), Corporate Coun Ann, 79; The modernization of antitrust: A new equilibrium, Cornell Law Rev, 66: 1140; co-ed, A Visit with Whitney North Seymour, 84; co-ed, Industrial Concentration and the Market System, 79; coed, Antitrust Policy in Transition: The Convergence of Law and Economics, ABA, 84; co-ed, Collaborations Among Competitors: Antitrust Policy and Economics, ABA, 92; co-auth, Corporate Acquisitions and Mergers, Matthew Bender, 98; coauth, Antitrust: Cases and Materials, West, 89; co-ed, Revitalizing Antitrust in its Second Century, Quorum, 91; coauth, The Competition Dimension of NAFTA, ABA, 94; coauth, Competition Policy and the Transformation of Central Europe, Ctr for Econ Policy Res, 96; coauth, European Community Law: Cases and Materials, West, 93, 98, supp; auth, Toward World Antitrust and Market Access, 91, Am J. Int l 1, 97; auth, National Law Global Markets, and Hartford: Eyes Wide Shut, 68 Antitrust L.J. 73, 00. **CONTACT ADDRESS** 40 Washington Sq S, New York, NY 10012-1005. **EMAIL** foxe@turing.law.nyu.edu

FOX, JAMES WALKER
PERSONAL Born 10/14/1929, Kearney, NE, d, 2 children **DISCIPLINE** CRIMINAL JUSTICE, CRIMINOLOGY **EDUCATION** Ind Univ, Bloomington, BA, 57, MS, 59, EdD, 61; Univ Va, PhD (sociol), 74. **CAREER** Instr interdisciplinary soc sci, Univ Akron, 61-64; prof higher educ, Kent State Univ, 64-67; prof educ and dean student serv and educ develop, Madison Col, Va, 67-73; dir, Ctr Criminal Justice, 73-76, PROF CORRECTIONAL SERV, EASTERN KY UNIV, 73-, Part-time prof sociol and criminol, Southern Sem, 72-73; dir criminal victimization study, Univ Va, 72-74; dir, Ky Parole Recidivism Study, 78-79; consult, juvenile justice agenciens and various state parole/probation agencies, 78-; PRES, J WALKER FOX CRIMINAL JUSTICT CONSULTS, INC, 81-. **MEMBERSHIPS** Am Asn Higher Educ; Am Polit Sci Asn; Am Soc Criminol; Am Correctional Asn; Acad Criminal Justice Sci. **RESEARCH** Criminal justice system; Juvenile Justice System; Political sociology; victimization. **SELECTED PUBLICATIONS** Auth, The Structure, Stability, and Social Antecedents of Reported Paranormal Experiences, Sociological Analysis, Vol 53, 92. **CONTACT ADDRESS** Dept of Correctional Serv, Univ of Kentucky, Stratton Bldg Room 101 Eastern, Richmond, KY 40475. **EMAIL** jwfox@ekucolonels.com

FOX, LAWRENCE J.
PERSONAL Born 07/17/1943, Philadelphia, PA, m, 1998, 2 children **DISCIPLINE** LAW **EDUCATION** Univ Penn, BA, 65, LLB, 68. **CAREER** Clerk, Justice Samuel Roberts, Penn Supreme Court, 68-69; Reginald Hever Smith Commun Lawyer Fel, Commun Action for Legal Serv, NY, 69-72; assoc, 72-76, partner, 76- , mng partner, 89-91, 93-97, Drinker Biddle & Reath LLP. **MEMBERSHIPS** ABA; Am Law Inst; Am Col of Trial Lawyers; Penn Bar Asn; Philadelphia Bar Asn; Authors Guild. **RESEARCH** Legal ethics and professional responsibility; death penalty jurisprudence. **SELECTED PUBLICATIONS** Auth, Cowboy Ethics on the Main Line, Litigation, 93; auth, Can This Marriage be Saved? Natl Law J, 93; auth, Marketing or Mayhem? The Firm is Mythical; the Nightmare is Real, Business Law Today, 94; auth, Lawyers Can't Serve Two Masters Honestly, Natl Law J, 94; auth, Reap As You Sow, Business Law Today, 95; auth, Firing the Client, Litigation, 95; auth, Leave Your Clients at the Door, Litigation, 95; auth, Politics is Threatening the Federal Judiciary, Natl Law J, 96; auth, Advocates for the System; Advocates for Ourselves, Litigation Docket, 96; auth, Money Didn't Buy Happiness, Dickinson Law Rev, 96; auth, Why Does Gift Limit Single out Bond Lawyers? Natl Law J, 97; auth, It's OK To Discuss Billing, Solo, 97; auth, Litigating Conflicts: Is it Time to Revive the Appearance of Impropriety? Professional Lawyer, 98. **CONTACT ADDRESS** Philadelphia National Bank Bldg, 1345 Chestnut St, Philadelphia, PA 19107-3496. **EMAIL** foxlj@dbr.com

FOX, MICHAEL
PERSONAL Born 12/12/1940, Detroit, MI, m, 1961, 2 children **DISCIPLINE** BIBLE STUDIES; ANCIENT NEAR EASTERN STUDIES **EDUCATION** Univ Mich, BA, 62; MA, 63; Hebrew Union Col, Rabbinical ordination, 68; Hebrew Univ Jerusalem, PhD, 72. **CAREER** Lectr, Haifa Univ, 71-74; lectr, Hebrew Univ Jerusalem, 75-77; asst prof to prof, Univ Wis-Madison, 77- . **HONORS AND AWARDS** Nat Endowment for the Humanities, Fel, 92-93; Honorary Doctorate of Hebrew Letters, Hebrew Union Col, 93; Rabbi Joseph L. Baron Faculty Achievement Award, 96; Jay C. and Ruth Halls-Bascom Prof in hebrew Studies, 99; Nat Center for the Humanities, Fel, 99; Nat Center for the Humanities, Fel, 99; Soc for Biblical Lit, Pres, 99-00; Nat Assoc of Prof of Hebrew, Vice-Pres, 99-; Kellett Mid-career Award, 00; Am Acad of Jewish Res, Fel, 00-. **MEMBERSHIPS** Soc for Bibl Lit; Nat Asoc of Profs of Hebrew. **RESEARCH** Biblical literature; ancient Egyptian literature. **SELECTED PUBLICATIONS** Auth, Ideas of Wisdom in Proverbs 1-9, JBL, 97; auth, Words for Folly, ZAH, 97; auth, What the Book of Proverbs is About, VTSup, 97; auth, Qohelet's Catalogue of Times, JNSL, 98; auth, Tearing Down and Building Up: A Rereading of Ecclesiastes, forthcoming. **CONTACT ADDRESS** Univ of Wisconsin, Madison, 1220 Linden Dr., Rm. 1346, Madison, WI 53706. **EMAIL** mfox@lss.wisc.edu

FOX, MICHAEL ALLEN
DISCIPLINE PHILOSOPHY **EDUCATION** Univ Toronto, PhD. **CAREER** Dept Philos, Queen's Univ **RESEARCH** Environmental ethics; ethics and animals; nineteenth-century continental philosophy; existentialism; philosophy of peace. **SELECTED PUBLICATIONS** Auth, "Nuclear Weapons and the Ultimate Environmental Crisis," Environmental Ethics, 9 87: 159-179; auth, "Animal Experimentation: A Philosopher's Changing Views," Between the Species, 3, 87: 55-60, 75, 80, 82; auth, "Peace," Darshana International, 31, 91: 48-56; auth, "Planet for the Apes," Etica & Animali, 96: 44-49; auth, "On the Necessary Suffering of Nonhuman Animals," Animal Law, 3, 97: 23-27; ed, contri, "Schopenhauer: His Philosophical Achievement, Harvester Press/Barnes & Noble, 80; coed, "Nuclear War: Philosophical Perspectives," Peter Lang, 85; auth, "The Case for Animal Experimentation: An Evolutionary and Ethical Perspective, University of California Press, 86; auth, "Deep Vegetarianism," Temple University Press, 99; auth, Deep Vegetarianism, Temple University Press, 99 **CONTACT ADDRESS** Philos Dept, Queen's Univ at Kingston, Kingston, ON, Canada K7L 3N6. **EMAIL** maf@post.queensu.ca

FOX, RICHARD MILAN
PERSONAL Born 06/15/1931, Cleveland, OH, m, 1955, 3 children **DISCIPLINE** PHILOSOPHY **EDUCATION** Ohio Univ, BA, 55; Georgetown Univ, MA, 63; Univ Waterloo, PhD, 67. **CAREER** Asst prof Am civilization, Am lang ctr, Am Univ, 57-61; asst prof, Am lang inst, Georgetown Univ, 61-62; instr philos, Notre Dame Col, Ohio, 62-65; lectr, St Jerome's Col, Univ Waterloo, 65-67; asst prof, Cleveland State Univ, 67-71, assoc prof, Philos, Cleveland State Univ, 71-87; dept chair, 76-78, 83-90; ed, Philos in Context, 78-86; prof 87-. **HONORS AND AWARDS** Woodrow Wilson Fel, 55 **RESEARCH** Ethics; metaethics; metaphysics. **SELECTED PUBLICATIONS** Auth, "Plato's Use of Sport Analogies in The Lesser Hippias," Journal of Sport Hist, (82); auth, "The So-Called Unreality of Sport, Quest," (82); co-auth, "Philosophy and International issues," Phil, in Context, (85); co-ed, New Directions in Ethics, Routledge and Kegan Paul, 86; coauth, "Putting Pressure on Promises," Southern Journal of Phil, (92); coauth, "The Immorality of Promising," Journ of Value Inquiry, (93); coauth, "Toward An Adequate Theory of Applied Ethics," International Journal of Applied Philos, (96); coauth, "On Making and Keeping Promises," Journ of Applied Philos; coauth, The Immorality of Promising, Humanity Books, 01 **CONTACT ADDRESS** Dept of Philos, Cleveland State Univ, 1983 E 24th St, Cleveland, OH 44115-2440.

FOX, SAMUEL
PERSONAL Born 02/25/1919, Cleveland, OH, m, 1942, 1 child **DISCIPLINE** PHILOSOPHY, RELIGION **EDUCATION** Yeshiva Univ, BA, 40; Butler Univ, MA, 44; Harvard Univ, PhD (semitics), 59. **CAREER** Asst prof, 68-80, ASSOC PROF RELIG STUDIES, MERRIMACK COL, 80-, Chaplain, Brigham Women's Hosp, 76. **MEMBERSHIPS** Asn Jewish Studies; AAUP; Am Acad Relig; Col Theol Soc; Rabbinical Coun Am. **RESEARCH** Jewish customs and ceremonies; Jewish philosophy; ancient religion. **SELECTED PUBLICATIONS** Auth, By the Sweat of the Brow, Literature and Labor in Antebellum America, Am Lit, Vol 66, 94; Evans, Chris Could Always be Relied on to Pull a Fast One, Smithsonian, Vol 26, 95; Raising General Awareness of Language Learning Strategies--A Little Bit Goes a Long Way, Hisp J Devoted Teaching Span Port, Vol 78, 95; An Illustrated Glossary of Early Southern Architecture and Landscape, J Southern Hist, Vol 61, 95; Raising General Awareness of Language Learning Strategies--A Little Bit Goes A Long Way, Hisp J Devoted Teaching Span Port, Vol 78, 95; Dugout to Deco--Building in West Texas, 1880-1930, J Southern Hist, Vol 61, 95; Inside Texas--Culture, Identity, and Houses, 1878-1920, J Southern Hist, Vol 59, 93; The Life and Death of Stubbe, Peter, Lit Rev, Vol 40, 97; Sacred Pedestrians, J Southwest, Vol 36, 94; The Making of Virginia Architecture, J Southern Hist, Vol 60, 94. **CONTACT ADDRESS** 145 Lynn Shore Dr, Lynn, MA 01902.

FOX, SANFORD J.
PERSONAL Born 09/28/1929, New York, NY, m, 1954, 3 children **DISCIPLINE** LAW, JUVENILE DELINQUENCY **EDUCATION** Univ Ill, AB, 50; Harvard Univ, LLB, 53. **CAREER** Teaching fel law, Harvard Univ, 57-58; asst dir, Proj Effective Justice, Columbia Univ, 58-59; Prof Law, Law Sch, Boston Col, 59- Nat Inst Mental Health fel psychiat aspects of delinquency, 60-61; Ford Found law fac fels, law and sci, 61-62, 63-64; Off Juvenile Delinquency and Youth Develop, Dept Health Educ and Welfare grant to direct Boston Col juvenile Delinquency training prog, 66-68; sr fel, Nat Endowment for Humanities, 71-72; chief counsel, Maine Criminal Law Rev Comn, 72-75 and Vt Criminal Code Rev Comn, 73-75; reporter for sentencing and corrections, Am Law Inst Proj to Revise Model Penal Code Comments, 76-78; CONSULT CHILD ABUSE AND NEGLECT, US DEPT HEALTH, EDUC AND WELFARE, 76-. **RESEARCH** Juvenile delinquency; law and science; criminal law. **SELECTED PUBLICATIONS** Auth, Beyond the American Legal System for the Protection of Childrens Rights, Family Law Quart, Vol 31, 97. **CONTACT ADDRESS** 44 Summer Rd, Brookline, MA 02146.

FRAADE, STEVEN D.
PERSONAL Born 03/30/1949, New York, NY, m, 1979, 3 children **DISCIPLINE** RELIGIOUS STUDIES **EDUCATION** Brown Univ, 70; Univ Pa, PhD, 80. **CAREER** Acting instr, Yale Univ, 79-80, asst prof, 80-84, assoc prof, 84-89, Mark Taper Prof of the Hist of Judaism, 89-. **HONORS AND AWARDS** Nat Endowment of the Humanities, summer res stipend, 82; Morse Fel, Yale Univ, 83-84; Am Philos Soc Res grant, 84; sr fel, W. F. Albright Inst for Archaeol Res, 84; John Simon Guggenheim Mem Found Fel, 88; Memorial Found for the Jewish Culture Fel, 88; fel, The Inst for Advanced Studies, The Hebrew Univ of Jerusalem, 88-89, 93; Nat Jewish Book Awd, for "From Tradition to Commentary," 92. **MEMBERSHIPS** Am Acad of Relig, Am Oriental Soc, Am Schs of Oriental Res, Asn for Jewish-Am Studies, Hist Soc of Israel, Israel Exploration Soc, Jewish Law Asn, Soc of Biblical Lit, World Union of Jewish Studies. **RESEARCH** History and literature of ancient Judaism in Hellenistic times and Roman late antiquity. **SELECTED PUBLICATIONS** Auth, "Interpreting Midrash 1: Midrash and the History of Judaism," Prooftexts, 7.2 (May 87): 179-94; auth, "Interpreting Midrash 2: Midrash and its Literary Contexts," Prooftexts, 7.2 (Sept 87): 284-300 (with corrigenda in 7.4 [Jan 88: 159-60]); auth, From Tradition to Commentary: Torah and its Interpretation in the Midrash Sifre to Deuteronomy, Jewish Hermeneutics, Mysticism, and Religion Series, Albany: State Univ New York Press (91); auth, "Palestinian Judaism," Anchor Bible Dictionary, ed David Noel Friedman, vol 3, Garden City, NY: Doubleday (92); auth, "Rabbinic Views on the Practice of Targum, and Multilingualism in the Jewish Galilee of the Third-Sixth Centuries," in The Galilee in Late Antiquity, ed Lee I. Levine, New York and Jerusalem: The Jewish Theol Sem of Am (92); auth, "Interpretive Authority in the Studying Community at Qumran," J of Jewish Studies, 44.1 (spring 93): 46-69; auth, "Navigating the Anomalous: Non-Jews at the Intersection of Early Rabbinic Law and Narrative," in The Other in Jewish Thought and History: Constructions of Jewish Culture and Identity, ed Laurence J. Silberstein and Robert L. Cohn, New York: New York Univ Press (94); auth, "Looking for Legal Midrash at Qumran," in Biblical Perspectives: Early Use and Interpretation of the Orion Center for the Study of the Dead Sea Scrolls and Associated Literature, 12-14 May, 1996, ed Michael E. Stone and Esther G. Chazon, Studies on the Texts of the Desert of Judah 28, Leiden: E. J. Brill (98); auth, "Scripture, Targum, and Talmud as Instruction:A Complex Textual Story from the Sifra," in Hesed ve-

Emet: Studies in Honor of Ernest S. Freichs, ed Jodi Magness and Seymour Gitin, Brown Judaic Studies 320, Atlanta: Scholars Press (98); auth, "Enosh and His Generation revisited," in Biblical Figures Outside the Bible, ed Michael E. Stone and Theodore A. Bergren, Harrisburg, Pa: Trinity Press Int (98); auth, "Shifting from Priestly to Non-Priestly Legal Authority: A Comparison of the Damascus Document and the Midrash Sifra," Dead Sea Discoveries, 6.2 (July 99); 109-125. **CONTACT ADDRESS** Dept Relig Studies, Yale Univ, PO Box 208287, New Haven, CT 06520-8287. **EMAIL** steven.fraade@yale.edu

FRANCK, THOMAS M.

PERSONAL Born 07/14/1931, Berlin, Germany **DISCIPLINE** LAW **EDUCATION** Univ BC, BA, 52, LLB, 53; Harvard Univ, LLM, 54, SJD, 59; Univ BC, Hon LLD, 95. **CAREER** Asst prof, Univ Nebr Law Sch, 54-56; assoc prof, 60-62, dir ctr Int Studies, 65-, prof law, Law Sch, NY Univ, 62-, vis lects, US Naval War Col, 60; Can deleg, Conf Rule of Law in Africa, 61; vis prof, Stanford Univ Sch Law, 63; Can deleg, Conf African Customary Law, 64; mem, Comn Legal Educ, Sierra Leone, 64; vis lectr, Col Law, Univ EAfrica, 63-66; consult, US Agency Int Develop, 70-72; consult to Fla Int Univ on starting a Ctr Int Studies, Miami, 72; vis prof law, Osgoode Hall Law Sch, York Univ, 72-76, prof, 74-76; Guggenheim Found res grant, 73-74 & 82-83; dir Int Law prog, Carnegie Endowment Peace, 73-79; vis prof. Woodrow Wilson School, Princeton Univ, 79; mem adv coun procedural aspects, Int Law Inst; mem adv coun, US Inst Human Rights; dir res, UN Inst Training & Res, 80-82; lectr, Hague Acad of Int Law, 93; vis Fellow, Trinity Col, Cambridge, England, 96-97. **HONORS AND AWARDS** Guggenheim Fellowship, 73-74, 82-83; Christopher Medal, for Resignation in Protest, 76; Cert of Merit, awarded by the Am Soc of Int Law, in recognition of United States Foreign Relations Law: Documents and Sources, 81; Cert of Merit, Am Soc Int Law, in recognition of Nation Against Nation: What Happened to the U.N. Dream and What the U.S. Can Do About It, 86; Elected member, Institut de Droit Int, 93-; Cert of Merit, Am Soc Int Law, in recognition of Political Questions/Judicial Answers: Does the Rule of Law Apply to Foreign Affairs?, 94; John E. Read Medal, awarded by the Can Council on Int Law, 94; Cert of Merit, Am Soc Int Law, in recognition of Fairness in International Law and Institutions, 96. **MEMBERSHIPS** Am Soc Int Law(member, exec council, 79-94, pres, April, 98-00); Int League Rights of Man; Am Bar Asn; African Law Asn Am (dir, 70-73); Int Law Asn (secy-treas Am branch, 68-69, vpres, 73-94, hon vpres, 94-); Council on Foreign Relations, 78-; The Century Asn of New York, 79-; Advisory Bd, Int Human Rights Law Group; board of dir, Friends of the Hague Academy of Int Law, Inc, 80-; NYU Soc of Fellows, 84-; Admin Council, The Jacob Blaustein Inst for the Advancement of Human Rights, 88-; bd mem, Africa Watch, 89-; board of dir, Int Peace Acad, 91-; Ger Soc Int Law; Societe francaise de doit international; Can Council on Int Law; U.S. Member, Comm on Int Human Rights Law and Practice, Int Law Asn, 95. **RESEARCH** Resources of the seabed; control of terrorism; international and constitutional law. **SELECTED PUBLICATIONS** Auth, The Structure of Impartiality, Macmillan, 68; Comparative Constitutional Process, Sweet & Maxwell, London, 68, Praeger, 68; coauth, Word Politics: Verbal Strategy Among the Superpowers, 71 & Secrecy and Foreign Policy, Oxford Univ, 73; Resignation in Protest, Viking, 75; Foreign Policy by Congress, Oxford, 79; Foreign Relations Law, Oceana, 80; auth, The Tethered Presidency, NY Univ Press, 81; coauth, Human Rights in the Third World Perspective, vols I-III, Oeana pubs, 84; coauth, United States Foreign Relations Law: Documents and Sources, vols IV-V, Oceana pubs, 84; auth, Nation Against Nation: What Happened to the U.N. Dream and What the U.S. Can Do About It, Oxford Univ Press, 85; Judging the World Court, NY: The Twentieth Century Fund, 86; coauth, Foreign Relations and National Security Law, St. Paul: West Pub Co, 87, 2nd ed, 93; auth, The Power of Legitamacy Among Nations, Oxford Univ Press, 90; Political Questions/Judicial Answers: Does the Rule of Law Apply to Foreign Affairs?, Princeton Univ Press, 92; Fairness in the International Legal and Institutional System, The Hague: Acad of Int Law, Recueil des cours, vol 240, 93-III; auth, Foreign Relations and Nat Security Law, 2nd ed, West Publ Company, 93; auth, Fairness in Int law and Institutions, Oxford Univ Pr, 95; co-ed, International Law Decisions in National Courts, Transnational Pubs, 96; auth, The Empowered Self: Law and Soc in the Age of Individualism, Oxford Univ Pr, 99. **CONTACT ADDRESS** Ctr for Int Studies, New York Law Sch, 40 Washington Sq S, New York, NY 10012-1005.

FRANCO, ABEL B.

PERSONAL Born 05/26/1969, Salamanca, Spain **DISCIPLINE** PHILOSOPHY **EDUCATION** Universidad de Salamanca Spain, LD, 92, LD, 97, PhD, 99; CUNY, MA, 98; Univ of Pitt, MA, 00. **CAREER** Adjunct Lectr at: CUNY, 96; Manhattan Comm Col, 97; Lehman Col, 97-98; John Jay Col, 98; Univ Pitt, tchg asst, 98-. **HONORS AND AWARDS** Erasmus fel, CAJA de Madrid Found res fel; Univ Pitt full tuition scholar. **MEMBERSHIPS** RSA, APA, HSSA. **RESEARCH** 17th century: science, philosophy, and art, 19th-20th century: continental philosophy. **SELECTED PUBLICATIONS** Auth, The Mathematization of Space Before Galileo: The Double Birth of Modern Pictorial Perspective and the Scientific Revolution, ALDEEU, eds., R. Corbalan, G. Pina, N. Toscan, vol XIII, NY, 97, pp 83-101, vol XV, 1 99, pp 109-132; auth, God and His/Her Act of Creation: Leibniz and the Why-Not-Sooner Argument, in Sorties, ed CSI (Madrid, Spain), forthcoming. **CONTACT ADDRESS** Dept of History, Univ of Pittsburgh, 4041 Bigelow Blvd Apt 311, Pittsburgh, PA 15213-1229. **EMAIL** abfst6@pitt.edu

FRANK, DANIEL H.

PERSONAL Born 08/16/1950, San Francisco, CA, m, 4 children **DISCIPLINE** PHILOSOPHY **EDUCATION** Univ of Cal at Berk, BA 73; Cambridge Univ, BA, 75, MA, 82; Univ Pittsburgh, PhD, 82. **CAREER** UCLA, vis assoc prof of philo, 88-89; Univ of Kentucky, asst prof, 81-86, assoc prof, 86-97, prof of philo, 97-, Dir of JSP, 96-. **HONORS AND AWARDS** Brit Acad, Res Fel, 94; Univ of Judaism, Finkelstein Res Fel, 87-89, UCLA Medieval and Renais Stud, Res Fel, 86 **MEMBERSHIPS** APA, AJP, AJS, SAGP, SMRP **RESEARCH** Greek philo; medi Islamic and Jewish philo **SELECTED PUBLICATIONS** Auth, The Cambridge Companion to Medieval Jewish Thought, Cambridge Univ Press, forthcoming; The Jewish Philosophy Reader, Routledge Press, forthcoming; Pride, Humility and Anger: Aristotle and Maimonides on Virtue and the Self, SUNY Press, forthcoming; History of Jewish Philosophy, Routledge Press, 97; Maimonides: Guide of the Perplexed, rev ed, Hackett, 95; Commandment and Community : New Essays in Jewish Legal and Political Philosophy, SUNY Press, 95; art, Ibn Gabirol, Joseph Albo, and Political Philosophy in Islam, in: The Routledge Encyclopedia of Philosophy, Routledge, 98; What is Jewish Philosophy? in: History of Jewish Philosophy, Routledge, 97; Teaching for a Fee: Pedagogy and Friendship in Socrates and Maimonides, in: Friendship East and West, Curzon, 96; Ethics, in: History of Islamic Philosophy, Routledge, 96. **CONTACT ADDRESS** Dept of Philosophy, Univ of Kentucky, Lexington, KY 40506-0027. **EMAIL** dfrank@ukcc.uky.edu

FRANK, SALLY

PERSONAL Born 02/24/1959, Jersey City, NJ, s **DISCIPLINE** LAW **EDUCATION** Princeton Univ, AB, 80; NY Univ, JD, 83; Antioch Univ, MAT, 88. **CAREER** Law clerk, Civil Court, 84-85; clin fel, Antioch Univ, 85-88; clin assoc prof, NY Law Sch, 88-90; asst prof to prof, Drake Univ, 90-. **HONORS AND AWARDS** Alumni Coun Awd for Serv, Princeton, 90; Hardees Hometown Hero Awd for Human Rights, 91; Equality in Legal Educ Awd, Drake Law Women, 92; Cert of Recognition, Amnesty Intl, 92; Key to the City, Bayonne NJ, 93; Order of the Coif, Drake Univ, 98; Honoree, Friends of the Princeton Women's Center, 00. **MEMBERSHIPS** Nat Lawyers Guild; Am Asn of Law Sch; Clin Legal Educ Asn; Joint Commission on Soc Action of the Union of Am Hebrew Congregations and the Central Conf of Am Rabbis. **RESEARCH** Women's rights; The intersection of women in Judaism and law. **SELECTED PUBLICATIONS** Auth, "Tenants' Rights and the District of Columbia Master Meter Act: A Violation of Due Process," DC Law Rev, 93; auth, "The Key to Unlocking the Clubhouse Door: The Application of Anti-Discrimination Laws to Quasi-Private Clubs," Mich J of Gender & Law, 94; auth, "Eve was Right to Eat the Apple: The Importance of Narrative to the Art of Lawyering," Yale J Law & Feminism, 96; auth, "A City Council Examines Pornography: A Roleplay for a Law School Class," Rutgers Women's L Rptr, 00. **CONTACT ADDRESS** Sch of Law, Drake Univ, 2400 University Ave, Des Moines, IA 50311-4505. **EMAIL** sally.frank@drake.edu

FRANK, WILLIAM A.

PERSONAL Born 10/17/1949, M, 5 children **DISCIPLINE** PHILOSOPHY **EDUCATION** Hampton Inst, BA; Cath Univ Am, MA, PhD. **CAREER** Dept Philos, Univ Dallas **MEMBERSHIPS** Metaphysical Society of America; American Catholic Philsophical Assoc; Soc of Medieval & Renaissance Philosoph. **RESEARCH** Philosophy of Education, Medieval Philosophy, Duns Scotus. **SELECTED PUBLICATIONS** "Duns Scotus' Concepts of Willing Freely: What Divine Freedom Beyond Choice Teaches Us," Franciscan Studies, 42 (82): 68-89; Co-ed, Essays Honoring Allan B. Wolter, Franciscan Institute Publications Theology Series No 10, Franciscan Institute, (St. Bonaventure, NY), 85; ed, Duns Scotus on the Will and Morality , The Catholic Univ of America Pr, (Washington, DC), 86; "Authority as Nurse of Freedom and the Common Good," Faith and Reason, 4 (90): 371-86; "Sine Proprio: On Libety and Christ -- A Juxtaposition of Bernard of Clairvaux and John Duns Scotus," Citeaux. Commerntarii Cistercenses, 42 (91), (92): 461-78; "The Right Form of Reason? Controversy in the Philosopher's Academy," Moden Age, 34 (92): 155-64; "Communal Action," In Saints, Soverigns, and Scholars: Studies in Honor of Frederick D. Wilhelmsen, Peter Lang, (NY), 93; Co-auth, Duns Scotus, Metaphysician, Series in the Hist Philos, Purdue Univ Press, 95; The Catholic Mind: Culture, Philosophy, and Responsibility in Higher Education," Catholic Education: A Journal of Inquiry and Practice 4 (00); "Starting Points for Philosophy: History and Metaphysics in Fides et Ratio," Fellowship of Catholic Scholars Quarterly, 23 (00): 15-22. **CONTACT ADDRESS** Dept of Philos, Univ of Dallas, 1845 E Northgate Dr, Irving, TX 75062. **EMAIL** wfrank@acad.udallas.edu

FRANKEL, TAMAR

PERSONAL Born 07/04/1925, Israel, m, 1991, 2 children **DISCIPLINE** LAW **EDUCATION** Jerusalem Law Classes, 48; Harvard Law Sch, LLM, 64; SJD, 72. **CAREER** Lectr to prof, Boston Univ, 68-; vis prof, Harvard Law Sch, 79-80; vis prof, Univ Calif Law Sch, 82-83; vis prof, Univ Tokyo, 97. **HONORS AND AWARDS** Fel, St Catherine's Col, 99; Vis Fel, Wolfson Col, 99; Fel, Berkman Ctr for the Internet and Soc, 98; Guest Scholar, Brookings Inst, 87. **MEMBERSHIPS** Am Law Inst; Mass Bar Asn; Am Bar Asn; Law and Econ Asn. **RESEARCH** Fiduciary law; Trust relationships in law, among individuals and in society; Corporate governance; The financial system (securities, markets, mutual funds, insurance companies, banking and securitization); The Internet infrastructure; Informal law enforcement. **SELECTED PUBLICATIONS** Auth, Securitization, Structured Financing, Financial Assets Pools, and Asset-Backed Securities, 91; auth, "The Legal Infrastructure of Markets: The Role of Contract and Property Law," B.U.L. Rev, 93; auth, "Fiduciary Duties as Default Rules," Ore L Rev, 95; auth, "Fiduciary Duties," in The New Palgrave Dictionary of Economics and the Law, 98; auth, "Cross-Border Securitization: Without Law, But Not Lawlessness," Duke J of Comparative and Intl Law, 98; auth, "Securitization: The Conflict Between Personal and market Law (Contract and Property)," 18 Annual Rev of Banking Law, 99; auth, "The Internet, Securities Regulation and Theory of Law, Symposium on the Internet and Legal Theory," Chi-Kent L Rev, 99; co-auth, The Regulation of Money Managers (Mutual Funds and Investment Advisors), Aspen Law & Business, 01. **CONTACT ADDRESS** Sch of Law, Boston Univ, 765 Commonwealth Ave, Boston, MA 02215. **EMAIL** tfrankel@bu.edu

FRANKFORTER, ALBERTUS DANIEL

PERSONAL Born 05/17/1939, Waynesboro, PA, m, 1972 **DISCIPLINE** MEDIEVAL HISTORY, HISTORY OF RELIGION **EDUCATION** Franklin and Marshall Col, Artium Baccalaeurie, 61; Drew Univ, MDiv, 65; Pa State Univ, MA, 69, PhD (medieval hist), 71. **CAREER** Actg chaplain, Williams Col, 63-64; asst prof, 70-80, Assoc Prof Ancient and Medieval Hist, Behrend Col, PA State Univ, 80-88; prof, Penn State Erie, 80-. **MEMBERSHIPS** Mediaeval Acad Am; Am Soc Church Hist; AHA. **RESEARCH** Medieval English Episcopal registers; medieval female authors. **SELECTED PUBLICATIONS** Auth, A History of the Christian Movement: An Essay on the Development of Christian Institutions (Chicago), Nelson-Hall, 78; auth, Civilization and Survival, vol I (Landham, MD), University Press of Am, 88; co-auth, The Equality of the Two Sexes by Poullain de la Barre: Introduction and Translation (Lewiston, NY), The Edwin Mellen Press, 89; auth, Conversations in Clio's Classroom, Perspectives, 94; co-auth, The Shakespeare Name Dictionary (NY) Garland, 95; auth, Amalsuntha, Procopius, and a Woman's Place, The Journal of Women's History, 96; auth, The Shakespeare Name and Place Dictionary (London), Fitzroy-Dearborn, 99; co-auth, The Western Heritage (NY), Prentice, 96, 2nd edition, 99, 3rd edition, in press; auth, The Medieval Millenium: An Introduction (Upper Saddle River, NJ), Prentice Hall, 99; auth, Stones for Bread: A Critique of Contemporary Worship (Lexington, KY), Westminster/John Knox, in press. **CONTACT ADDRESS** Dept of Hist, Pennsylvania State Univ, Erie, The Behrend Col, Station Rd, Erie, PA 16510. **EMAIL** ADP1@psu.edu

FRANKFURTER, DAVID

PERSONAL Born 02/24/1961, New York, NY, m, 1988, 2 children **DISCIPLINE** RELIGION **EDUCATION** Princeton Univ, PhD 90, MA 88; Harvard Univ, MTS 86; Wesleyan Univ, BA 83. **CAREER** Univ New Hampshire, asst to assoc prof, 95 to 98-; Col of Charleston, asst prof, 90-95. **HONORS AND AWARDS** Fairchild fel, instr advanced study, NEH. **MEMBERSHIPS** AARSBL; EES; IACS **RESEARCH** Apocalyptic lit; magic and ritual; roman Egypt; Christianization; popular religion. **SELECTED PUBLICATIONS** Auth, Religion in Roman Egypt: Assimilation and Resistance, Prin, Prin Univ Press, 98; Elijah in Upper Egypt: The Coptic Apocalypse of Elijah and Early Egyptian Christianity, studies in antiquity and Christianity, Minneapolis, Fortress Press, 93; Pilgrimage and Holy Space in Late Antique Egypt, ed, Leiden, E. J. Brill, 98; Early Christian Apocalypticism: literature and Social world, in: Encycl Apocaly, Jewish and Christian Origins of Apocalypticism, ed John J. Collins, NY, Continuum, 98; Apocalypses Real and Alleged in the Mani Codex, Numen 44, 97; The Legacy of the Jewish Apocalypse in Early Christian Communities: Two Regional Trajectories, in: The Jewish Apocal Hert in Early Christ, ed James C. VanderKam and William Adler, Minneapolis, Fortress Press, 96; Narrating Powert: The Theory and Practice of the Magical Historiola in Ritual Spells, in: Ancient Magic and Ritual Power, ed Marvin Meyer and Paul Mirecki, Leiden, Brill, 95; The Magic of Writing and the Magic of Writing: The Power of the Word in Egyptian and Greek Traditions, Helios, 94. **CONTACT ADDRESS** Dept of History, Univ of New Hampshire, Durham, Durham, NH 03824-3586. **EMAIL** davidtf@hopper.unh.edu

FRANKLAND, ERICH

PERSONAL Born 03/13/1968, Iowa City, IA, m, 1994, 2 children **DISCIPLINE** POLITICAL SCIENCE **EDUCATION** Earlham Col, BA, 90; Univ Okla, MA, 94. **CAREER** Instr, Univ of Okla, 92-96; Assoc Fac, Northland Pioneer Col, 97-98;

Adj Fac, Univ Wyo, 99; Fac, Casper Col, 98-. **HONORS AND AWARDS** Academic Merit Awd, Univ Okla, 96, 95, 94; Centennial Res Fel, Univ Okla, 90-94; John H Leek Memorial Awd, Univ of Okla, Phi Beta Kappa, 90; Dept Honors, Earlham, 90. **MEMBERSHIPS** am Polit Sci Asn, Intl studies Asn, N Am Asn for the study of Welsh Culture and Hist, NE Polit Sci Asn, SW Soc Sci Asn, W Reg Sci Asn, Southern Polit Sci Asn, Grad Asn of Polit Sci, Okla Polit Sci Asn. **RESEARCH** Nationalism; European politics (West and East); Political violence; New World order politics; Environmental politics; Green parties; Democratization; Post-Soviet politics. **SELECTED PUBLICATIONS** auth, "East and Central Green Movements and parties," in International Environmental Encyclopedia, Routledge Pub, 00; auth, "Wales/Plaid Cymru," in International Environment Encyclopedia, Routledge Pub, 00; auth, "The Wise Use Movement," in international Environmental Encyclopedia, Routledge Press, 00; rev, of "Notions of Nationalism," ed by Sukumar Periwal, nationalism and Ethnic Politics, (97): 166-167; auth, "New Nationalism for a New World Order?: The Kurds," in small wars and Insurgencies, (95): 183-208; auth, "The Wastewater Treatment Construction Grants Program: The Impact of New Federalism," Oklahoma Politics, (95): 43-64. **CONTACT ADDRESS** Dept Soc & Beh Sci, Casper Col, 125 College Dr, Casper, WY 82601-4612. **EMAIL** franklan@acad.cc.whecn.edu

FRANKLIN, ALLAN DAVID
PERSONAL Born 08/01/1938, Brooklyn, NY, m, 1994 **DISCIPLINE** HISTORY & PHILOSOPHY OF SCIENCE **EDUCATION** Columbia Col, AB, 59; Cornell Univ, PhD(physics), 65. **CAREER** Res assoc physics, Princeton Univ, 65-66, instr, 66-67; asst prof, 67-73, asoc prof physics, Univ Co, 73-82, prof, 82-. **HONORS AND AWARDS** Ch elect, Forum on History of Physics, Am Phys Soc; Exec Bd, Phil of Sci Asn.; Centennial speaker, Am Physical Soc. **MEMBERSHIPS** Fellow of Am Physical Soc; Hist Sci Soc; Phil of Sci Asn. **RESEARCH** The role of experiment in physics. **SELECTED PUBLICATIONS** Auth, The Principle of Inertia in the Middle Ages, CO Assoc Univ, 76; The Discovery and Nondiscovery of Partly Nonconservation, Studies in Hist & Philos of Sci, 10/79; The Neglect of Experiment, Cambridge Univ Press, 1986; Experiment, Right or Wrong, Cambridge Univ Press, 1990; The Rise and Fall of the Fifth Force, Am Institute of Physics, 1993; The Appearance and Disappearance of the 17-keV Neutrino, Rev. Modern Physics, 1995. **CONTACT ADDRESS** Dept of Physics & Astrophysics, Univ of Colorado, Boulder, Box 390, Boulder, CO 80309-0390. **EMAIL** Allau.Franklin@Colorado.edu

FRANKLIN, CARL M.
PERSONAL Born 02/27/1911, Spokane, WA, w, 1944, 4 children **DISCIPLINE** LAW **EDUCATION** Univ Wash, AB,31; Stanford Univ, MA,39; Columbia Univ, MA,40; Harvard Univ, MBA,48; Univ Va, JD,56; Yale Univ, JSD,56. **CAREER** Prof & VP Emer, Univ Southern Calif; past VP, Financial Aff; past VP, Legal Aff, USC; hon ch, Int Law; past lect & consult, Naval War Col. **HONORS AND AWARDS** Presidential Medallion, USC, 96, for outstanding service. **SELECTED PUBLICATIONS** Auth, Law of the Sea; auth, To Carolyn with Love, 96; auth, Inside Alma Mater, 00. **CONTACT ADDRESS** School of Law, Univ of So California, University Park Campus, Los Angeles, CA 90089.

FRANKLIN, FLOYD
PERSONAL Born 12/26/1929, Hot Springs, m **DISCIPLINE** LAW **EDUCATION** KY State Coll, BA 1953; CA State Coll, MA 1957; San Fernando Vly Coll, JD 1969. **CAREER** CA Community Coll, instructor in law. **HONORS AND AWARDS** Man yr Omega Psi Phi 1966; supporter yr Urban League & YMCA. **MEMBERSHIPS** ABA; CA State Bar Assoc; Langston Law Club; CA Parole Assoc NAACP; bd of dir Legal Aid Found; mem Omega Psi Phi Frat; cosmo Golf Club; pres KY State Club LA Chap 1965-71. **CONTACT ADDRESS** 5140 Crenshaw Blvd, Los Angeles, CA 90043.

FRANKLIN, NAOMI P.
PERSONAL Born 11/22/1946, New York, NY, d **DISCIPLINE** RELIGIOUS STUDIES **EDUCATION** Community Col NYork, BA, 70; Brandeis Univ, MA, 71; Union Theol Sem, MDiv, 81; Duke Univ, PhD, 90. **CAREER** Adjunct asst prof, Nassau Community Col; asst prof, Touro Col. **MEMBERSHIPS** Soc of Bibl Lit. **RESEARCH** Women in Biblical times; Jews of the Caribbean; Native American history and culture. **SELECTED PUBLICATIONS** Auth, Women and Development in Third World Countries; How To Do Historical Research. **CONTACT ADDRESS** School of Gen Studies, Touro Col, New York, 27-33 W 23rd St, New York, NY 10010.

FRANKLIN, ROBERT MICHAEL
PERSONAL Born 02/22/1954, Chicago, IL, m, 3 children **DISCIPLINE** THEOLOGY, AFRICAN-AMERICAN STUDIES **EDUCATION** Morehouse College, BA, 75; University of Durham, England, attended 76; Harvard University Divinity School, MDiv 1978; University of Chicago, PhD 1985. **CAREER** St Paul Church of God In Christ, asst pastor 78-84; St Bernard's Hosp, prot chaplain 79-81; Prairie St College, instr in psych 81; University of Chicago, instr in rel & psych, field ed dir 81-83; Harvard Univ, Divinity Sch, assoc dir of ministerial studies, 84-85, visiting lecturer in ministry and Afro-American religion, 86-88; Colgate Rochester Divinity School, dean/prof of Black Church Studies, 85-89; Emory Univ, Candler Sch of Theology, asst prof, 89-91, Dir of Black Church Studies, 89-, Assoc Prof of Ethics and Soc, 91-; Ford Foundation, Rights and Social Justice, Prog Dir, 95-; Interdenominational Theological Center, Pres, currently. **HONORS AND AWARDS** American Acad of Religion; Soc for the Scientific Study of Rel; Assn for the Sociology of Rel; Soc for the Study of Black Rel; Black Doctoral Fellowship FTE 1978-80; BE Mays Fellowship FTE 1975-78; Phi Beta Kappa, Morehouse Coll 1975; Publications, Union Seminary Qtrly Review 1986, The Iliff Review 1985, Criterion 1984; Liberating Visions: Human Fulfillment and Social Justice in African-American Thought, Augsburg Fortress Press, 1990. **SELECTED PUBLICATIONS** Auth, AnotherDays Journey: Black Churche Confronting the American Crisis, 96. **CONTACT ADDRESS** Interdenominational Theol Ctr, 700 Martin Luther King Jr. Dr., Atlanta, GA 30314. **EMAIL** bevjones@its.edu

FRANSON, ROBERT T.
DISCIPLINE LAW **EDUCATION** Cornell Univ, BEP, 62; Univ Calif, JD. **CAREER** Asst prof, 69-73; assoc prof, 73-90; assoc prof emer 90-. **HONORS AND AWARDS** Dir, IBM-UBC Cooperative Project Law Comput. **MEMBERSHIPS** Dir, IBM-UBC Cooperative Project in Law and Computers, 86-89; Consultant, Law Reform Commission of Canada, 76-77 **SELECTED PUBLICATIONS** Auth, pubs about administrative law; environmental law; computers and law. **CONTACT ADDRESS** Fac of Law, Univ of British Columbia, 1822 East Mall, Vancouver, BC, Canada V6T 1Z1. **EMAIL** franson@law.ubc.ca

FRASE, RICHARD S.
PERSONAL Born 06/19/1945, Washington, DC, m, 1969, 2 children **DISCIPLINE** LAW **EDUCATION** Haverford Col, BA, 67; Univ Chicago, JD, 70. **CAREER** Law clerk, U.S. Court of Appeals, 70; counselor, Chicago, 70-72; assoc atty, Chicago, 72-74; res, Univ Chicago L Sch, 74-77; assoc prof to prof, Univ Minn, 77-91; vis prof, Univ Jean Moulin, 82, 86, 90, 97; vis prof, Christian Albrecht Univ, 90; prof, Univ Minn, 91-. **HONORS AND AWARDS** Phi Beta Kappa, 67. **MEMBERSHIPS** Minn Bar Asn; Am Bar Asn; Minn and Hennepin County Bar Asn; Intl Asn of Penal Law; Am Soc of Criminol. **RESEARCH** Sentencing: Minnesota sentencing guidelines, other state guidelines systems, sentencing purposes and alternatives, comparative sentencing law and practice (within the U.S. and in foreign countries); comparative criminal procedure, especially Germany and France; Criminal justice systems within the U.S. and foreign countries; Minnesota criminal procedure. **SELECTED PUBLICATIONS** Auth, "Comparative Criminal Justice as a Guide to American Law Reform: How Do the French Do It, How Can We Find Out, and Why Should We Care?" Calif L Rev, (90): 539-683; auth, "Implementing Commission-based Sentencing Guidelines: The Lessons of the First Ten Years in Minnesota," Cornell J of L and Public Policy, (93): 279-337; co-auth, "German Criminal Justice as a Guide to American Law Reform: Similar Problems, Better Solutions?" Boston Col Intl and Compar L Rev, (95): 317-360; auth, "Sentencing Principles in Theory and Practice," Crime and Justice: A Review of Research, (97): 363-433; auth, "France," in Criminal Procedure: A Worldwide Study, (Carolina Acad Press, 99), 143-185; co-auth, Minnesota Misdemeanors and Moving Traffic Violations, 3rd ed, Lexis L Pub, 99; auth, "Sentencing Guidelines in Minnesota, Other States, and the Federal Courts: A twenty-year Retrospective," Fed Sentencing Reporter, (00): 69-82; co-ed, Sentencing and Sanctions in Western Countries, Oxford Univ Press, 01. **CONTACT ADDRESS** Sch of Law, Univ of Minnesota, Twin Cities, 229 19th Ave S, Minneapolis, MN 55455. **EMAIL** frase001@tc.umn.edu

FRATIANNI, MICHELE
PERSONAL Born 03/07/1941, Firenze, Italy, m, 3 children **DISCIPLINE** ECONOMICS, MONETARY ECONOMICS **EDUCATION** Ohio State Univ, BA, 67; Ohio State Univ, MA, 67; Ohio State Univ, PhD, 71 **CAREER** W. George Pinnell prof Bus Econ, Indiana Univ, 98-; chair, Bus Econ, Indiana Univ, 97-; visiting prof econ. Latholieke Universiteit te Leuven, Belgium 73-; Allis-Chalmers Distinguished prof Intl Econ, Marquette Univ, 95; Bundesbank prof Intl Monetary Econ, Free Univ, Berlin, 95; prof Bus Econ, Indiana Univ, 79-93 **HONORS AND AWARDS** AMOCO Fel, 93-98; IGIER Visiting Fel, 94; Brit Acad Visiting Prof, 94; Univ Calif, Center for German & European Studies Grant, 91-92; Mont Pelerin Soc, 92-; St. Vincent Prize Econ, 92- **MEMBERSHIPS** Amer Econ Assoc; Intl Trade Finance Assoc **RESEARCH** Monetary Theory and Policy; International Monetary Economics; Political Economy **SELECTED PUBLICATIONS** Auth, "Maxi versus Mini EMU: The Political Economy of Stage III," Columbia Jrnl Europ Law, 98; auth, "Bank Deposit Insurance: The Italian Case," Rev Econ Conditions in Italy, 96; coauth, "Central Banking as a Political Principal-Agent Problem," Econ Inquiry, 97 **CONTACT ADDRESS** Business Economics & Public Policy, Indiana Univ, Bloomington, Kelley School of Business, Rm. 451, Bloomington, IN 47405. **EMAIL** fratiann@indiana.edu

FRAZEE, CHARLES AARON
PERSONAL Born 07/04/1929, Rushville, IN, m, 1971, 2 children **DISCIPLINE** BYZANTINE AND CHURCH HISTORY **EDUCATION** St Meinrad Col, AB, 51; Cath Univ Am, MA, 54; Ind Univ, PhD (hist), 65, cert, Russ and Europ Inst, 65. **CAREER** Assoc prof hist, Marian Col, Ind, 56-70; assoc prof, 70-80, Prof Hist, Calif State Univ, Fullerton, 80-. **MEMBERSHIPS** Cath Hist Soc; Am Asn Slavic Studies; Mod Greek Studies Asn; Am Soc Church Hist. **RESEARCH** Christian communities in Eastern Europe and the Middle East. **SELECTED PUBLICATIONS** Auth, " The Orthodox and Eastern Chruches," The Religious Heritage of Southern Calfornia, Los Angeles CA, (76): 43-61; auth, " Church and State in Greece: Greece in Transition, London, (77): 128-152; auth, " The Orthodox Church of Greece: The Last Fifteen Years," Hellenic Perspectives, Lantham, MD, (80): 145-180; auth, Catholics and Sultans: The Church and the Ottoman Empire, 1453-1923, Cambridge Univ Press, 83; auth, " The Religious of Cyprus" Greece and Cyprus in History, Amsterdam, (85): 13-28; coauth, Princess of the Greek Islands: The Dukes of the Archipelago, 1207-1566, 88; auth, " Between East and West: The Balkan Churches in the First Christian Centuries" Following the Star from the East: essays in honour of Archimandrite Boniface Luykx, Ottawa, (92): 254-268; auth, " Using Vatican Archives in the Study of Eastern Christianity" Seeking God: The Recovery of Religious Identity in Orthodox Russia, Ukraine, and Georgian De Kalb, IL, (93): 164-282; auth, World History- the Easy Way 2 vols Barron's Educaitonal Series, 97; auth, World History: Original an Secondary Source Readings, 2 vols, Greenhaven Press, 99. **CONTACT ADDRESS** Episcopal Theological School at Claremont, 1325 No College Ave, Claremont, CA 91711-3199. **EMAIL** kfrazee@fullerton.edu

FRAZER, WILLIAM JOHNSON
PERSONAL Born 10/15/1924, Greenville, AL, d, 1949, 1 child **DISCIPLINE** ECONOMICS **EDUCATION** Huntingdon Col, BA, 50; Columbia Univ, MA, Econ, 53; Harvard, Fac Fel, math, 59-60; Univ Pa, Fac Fel, statist, 64-65; Columbia Univ, PhD, 68. **CAREER** Tchg fel, Econ, univ Tex, 51; student asst, Wage Stabilization Bd, 52; instr, Econ, Pratt Inst, 53-54; instr, Econ, Rensselaer Polytechnic Inst, 54-56; asst prof, Univ Fla, 57-65; assoc prof, Univ Fla, 64-68; prof, Univ Fla, 68-95; prof, London Sch Econ, 94; prof, FSUs London Center, 89-90, 92; sr. Econ, Fed Reserve Bank Chi, 66-67; vis assoc prof, Univ Ky, 67-68; econ, Prof, Univ Fla, 95-. **RESEARCH** Central banking, Business conditions, Global economy **SELECTED PUBLICATIONS** The Central Banks: Analysis, and International and European Dimensions, Praeger Publ, 94; The Legacy of Keynes and Friedman: Economic Analysis, Money, and Ideology, Praeger Publ, 94; coauth, The Florida Land Boom: Speculation, Money and the Banks, Quorum Bks, 95; The Friedman System: An Economic Analysis of Time Series, Praeger Publ, 97; auth, Central Banking, Crises, and Global Economy, Praeger Publ, 00. **CONTACT ADDRESS** Dept Econ, Univ of Florida, PO Box 117140, Gainesville, FL 32611-7140. **EMAIL** padgetdj@notes.cba.ufl.edu

FREDDOSO, ALFRED J.
DISCIPLINE PHILOSOPHY **EDUCATION** St John Vianney Sem, BA, 68; Univ Notre Dame, PhD, 76. **CAREER** Prof. **RESEARCH** Metaphysics; medieval philosophy; philosophy of religion. **SELECTED PUBLICATIONS** Auth, Francisco Suarez, On Efficient Causality: Metaphysical Disputations 17-19, 94; God's General Concurrence with Secondary Causes: Pitfalls and Prospects, 94; The Openness of God: A Reply to Hasker, 98; Ockham on Faith and Reason, 98; ed, The Existence and Nature of God, 83. **CONTACT ADDRESS** Philosophy Dept, Univ of Notre Dame, 336/7 O'Shaughnessy, Notre Dame, IN 46556. **EMAIL** freddoso.1@nd.edu

FREDERICK, G. MARCILLE
PERSONAL Born 09/30/1960, Freeport, IL, m, 1998 **DISCIPLINE** THEOLOGY **EDUCATION** Beloit Col, BA, 82; Univ Wisc - Madison, MLS, 91, MA, 93; Inst Christian Stud, M Phil F, 92. **CAREER** Dir, libr & info svc, 93-98, Inst for Christian Stud; dir, libr svc, 98-, King's Univ Col, Edmonton, AB. **RESEARCH** Historiography, Philosophical bibliography **CONTACT ADDRESS** 9125 - 50 Street, Edmonton, AB, Canada T6B 2H3. **EMAIL** mfrederick@kingsu.ab.ca

FREDRICKSON, DAVID
DISCIPLINE NEW TESTAMENT **EDUCATION** Carleton Col, BA, 75; Luther Sem, MDiv, 80; Yale Univ, MA, 85, MPhil, 87, PhD, 90. **CAREER** Instr, 87; assoc prof, 92-. **HONORS AND AWARDS** Assoc pastor, St John Lutheran Church, Janesville, Wis. **MEMBERSHIPS** Mem, Soc of Bibl Lit. **SELECTED PUBLICATIONS** Auth, Human Sexuality and the Christian Faith, Resource, Augsburg Fortress, 93; Three Objections to Hamerton-Kelly's Interpretation of the Pauline Epistles, 93; Free Speech in Pauline Political Theology, Word and World, 92; Reading the New Testament, Augsburg Home Bible Study Series, 92; Pentecost: Paul the Pastor in 2 Corinthians, Word & World, 91. **CONTACT ADDRESS** Dept of New Testament, Luther Sem, 2481 Como Ave, Saint Paul, MN 55108. **EMAIL** dfredric@luthersem.edu

FREDRIKSEN, P.
PERSONAL Born 01/06/1951, RI, m, 2000, 3 children **DISCIPLINE** RELIGION & HISTORY **EDUCATION** Wellesley, BA, 73; Oxford, Dipl Theol, 74; Princeton, PhD, 79. **CAREER** Asst prof, History Dept, Univ Calif Berkeley, 81-86; assoc prof, Religious Studies, Univ Pitts, 86-89; aurelio prof, scripture, Boston Univ, 90-. **HONORS AND AWARDS** Lady Davis vis prof Jerusalem, 94; NEH Univ res grant, 92-93; Naitonal Jewish Book Awd, 99. **MEMBERSHIPS** Amer Acad Relig; Soc Bibl Lit; Nat Asn Patristic Studies **RESEARCH** Historical Jesus; Jews & Gentiles in antiquity; Augustine. **SELECTED PUBLICATIONS** Auth, Augustine on Romans, Sholars Press, 82; auth, From Jesus to Christ, Yale 88, 2nd ed 00; auth, "What You See is What You Get: Context and Content in Current Research on the Historical Jesus,' Theology Today 52.1(95), 75-97; auth, " Did Jesus Oppose Purity Laws?" Bible Review XI.3 (95), 18-25, 42-47; auth, " Excaecati Occulta Iustitia Dei: Augustine on Jews and Judaism," Journal of Early Christian Studies 3 (95), 299-324; auth, " Secundum Carnem: History nd Israel in the Theology of St Augustine," the Limits of Ancient Christianity, Essays on Late Antique Thought and Culture in Honor of R A Markus, Ann Arbor, Univ of Michigan, (99), 26-41; auth, Jesus of Nazareth, King of the Jews, Knopf, 99; auth, "The Human Condition in Formative Christianity: The Redemption of the Body," The Human Condtion: A Study of the Comparison of Religious Ideas, SUNY Press, (00); 133-156; auth, " Ultimate Reality in Ancient Christianity: Christ, Blood Sacrifice and Redemption," Ultimate Realities: A Study of the Comparison of Religious Ideas, SUNY Press, (00): 61-73. **CONTACT ADDRESS** Dept of Relig, Boston Univ, Boston, MA 02215. **EMAIL** augfred@bu.edu

FREED, BRUCE
DISCIPLINE PHILOSOPHY **EDUCATION** Kenyon Col, BA, 59; Oxford Univ, MA, 61; Univ Calif Berkeley, PhD, 65. **CAREER** Asst prof, Univ of Wis, 65-70; assoc prof, UWO, 70-. **HONORS AND AWARDS** Fulbright, 59-60. **RESEARCH** Philosophies of language and mind; epistemology; American pragmatism. **SELECTED PUBLICATIONS** Co-ed, Contemporary Research in Philosophical Logic and Linguistic, Reidel, 75; co-ed, Forms of Representation, North Holland, 75; auth, Education and the Limits of Authority, (76): 200; auth, "Critical Notice: Alvin I. Goldman, Epistemology and Cognition," for Canadian Journal of Philosophy, vol. 18, No. 1, (88): 125-146; auth, "Reliability, Reasons, and Belief Contexts," Canadian Journal of Philosophy, vol. 18, no. 4, (88): 681-697. **CONTACT ADDRESS** Dept of Philosophy, Univ of Western Ontario, London, ON, Canada N6A 5B8. **EMAIL** bfreed@julian.uwo.ca

FREEMAN, DONALD DALE
PERSONAL Born 02/24/1937, De Smet, SD, m, 1956, 3 children **DISCIPLINE** PHILOSOPHY, RELIGION **EDUCATION** Huron Col, BS, 57; Oberlin Col, AM, 59, BD, 61; Drew Univ, PhD, 69. **CAREER** Asst prof philos, Union Col, 65-68; asst prof to assoc prof, 68-72, chmn dept, 69-72, Point Park Col; pastor, Christ United Church of Christ, Latrobe, Pa, 72-77; assoc prof, 77-80, prof Theol & Ministry 80-97, prof Congregational Life, 97-, Lancaster Theol Sem, 80-97; pres, Alternative Learning Lab, Inc, Pittsburgh, 72-77; coordr, Partners Educ Ministries, 74-. **HONORS AND AWARDS** Pearl Jones Awd, Commision on Rel in Appalachia, 97; Mitch Snyder Awd, First Church Shelter, Cambridge, Mass, 98. **MEMBERSHIPS** Am Philos Assn; Assn for D Min Edu **RESEARCH** Kant, especially his philosophy of religion; ecclesiology, especially ministry congregational studies of laity and clergy; faith development. **SELECTED PUBLICATIONS** Coauth, Logic and the Forms of Thought, Experimental Ed, Point Park Col, 71. **CONTACT ADDRESS** 555 W James St, Lancaster, PA 17603-2830. **EMAIL** dfreeman@lts.org

FREEMAN, EDWARD C.
PERSONAL Born Beta, NC, w **DISCIPLINE** LAW **EDUCATION** Knoxville Coll, AB; TX So Univ Sch of Law, LLB JD; Howard Univ Sch of Law, attnd legal sem; Univ of MI Sch of Law; Univ of TN Law Sch; Harvard Univ Sch of Law. **CAREER** Pvt Prac, atty couns 1951-; social worker 18 yrs; TN Valley Auth, mail clerk. **MEMBERSHIPS** Dir Nat Yth & Adm; dir Social Welfare for Mil Manhattan Dist; mem Nat Bar Assn; mem TN & TX Bar; licensed to prac before all State Cts Fed Ct & Supreme Ct of US; v chmn Knox Co Tax Equal Bd; Knox Co Dem Primary Bd; deL Dem Nat Conv 1976; mem steering com election of Jimmy Carter; mem TN Voters Coun; charter mem Soc Workers of Am; charter mem Magnolia Fed Savings & Loan Assn; former scout master; mem Sect of Am Bar Assn on Continuing Legal Edn; mem Am Bar Assn; Knoxville Bar & TN Bar Assn; exec bd NAACP; Omega Psi Phi Frat; Elks & Mason; exec com Dem Party; Mount Zion BaptCh; hon trst Juvenile Ct for Knox Co TN. **CONTACT ADDRESS** 2528 McCalla Ave, Knoxville, TN 37914.

FREEMAN, JAMES B.
PERSONAL Born 03/27/1947, Paerson, NJ, s **DISCIPLINE** PHILOSOPHY **EDUCATION** Drew Univ, BA, 68; Indiana Univ, AM, 71, PhD, 73. **CAREER** Lectr, 73 & 74, Indiana Univ; adj lectr, Butler Univ, 74, Bloomfield Col, 74-75; res assoc, Univ Victoria, 75-78; adj asst prof, 78-80, asst prof, 80-84, assc prof, 85-92, prof, 93-, Hunter Col CUNY. **HONORS AND AWARDS** Summa cum laude Drew Univ. **MEMBERSHIPS** Amer Philos Asn; Asn Informal Logic Critical Thinking; Soc Christian Philos **RESEARCH** Informal logic; Argumentation theory; Epistemology; Philosophy of religion. **SELECTED PUBLICATIONS** Auth, Thinking Logically: Basic Concepts for Reasoning, Prentice Hall, 88 & 93; auth, Dialectics and the Macrostructing of Anaumonts: A Theory of Anaumont Structure, Ford's Pub, 91; The Place of Informal Logic in Logic, New Essays in Informal Logic, Informal Logic, 94; The Appeal to Popularity and Presumption by Common Knowledge, Fallacies: Classical and Contemporary Readings, PA State Univ Press, 95 Premise Acceptability, Deontology, Internalism, Justification, Informal Logic, 95; Epistemic Justification and Premise Acceptability, Argumentation 10, 96; Consider the Source One Step in Assessing Premise Acceptability, Argumentation 10, 96. **CONTACT ADDRESS** Dept of Philosophy, Hunter Col, CUNY, 695 Park Ave, New York, NY 10021. **EMAIL** james.freeman@hunter.cuny.edu

FREEMAN, JODY L.
PERSONAL Born 01/02/1964, Vancouver, BC, Canada **DISCIPLINE** LAW **EDUCATION** Stanford Univ, BA, 85; Univ Toronto, LLB, 89; Harvard Univ, LLM, 91; SJD, 95. **CAREER** Acting Prof to Prof, UCLA, 95-. **HONORS AND AWARDS** Fel, Soc Sci and Humanities Res Coun of Can, 90-94; Frank Knox Memorial Fel, 90-94; Laidlaw Fel, 90-92; Fel, Am Asn of Univ Women, 90-91; Chancellor's Career Develop Awd, 98; Dean's Key, Univ Toronto, 89; Class of 1967 Prize, 89. **MEMBERSHIPS** Am Bar Asn; Intl Asn of Law and Soc. **RESEARCH** Administrative law; Environmental law; Privatization; Governance; Dispute Resolution. **SELECTED PUBLICATIONS** Auth, "Collaborative Governance in the Administrative State,' UCLA Law Rev, 97; auth, "Private Parties, Public Functions and the New Administrative Law," in Recrafting the Rule of Law, Hart Pub, 99; auth, "The Private Role in Public Governance," NYU Law Rev, 00; co-co-auth, "Regulatory Negotiation and the Legitimacy Benefit," NYU Env Law J, 00; auth, "The Contracting State," Fla Law Rev, 01. **CONTACT ADDRESS** Sch of Law, Univ of California, Los Angeles, Box 951476, Los Angeles, CA 90095-1476. **EMAIL** Freeman@law.ucla.edu

FREIDAY, DEAN
PERSONAL Born 06/20/1915, Irvington, NJ, m, 1946, 2 children **DISCIPLINE** THEOLOGY, ECUMENISM **EDUCATION** Univ Rochester, BA, 36. **CAREER** CO-ED, QUAKER RELIG THOUGHT, THEOL J, 80-, MEM, CHRISTIAN AND INTERFAITH RELATIONS COMT, FRIENDS GEN CONF, 58-, chmn, 66-72, Co-Opted, 72-; delegate, 4th World Conf Faith and Order of the World Coun of Churches, 63; observer and consult, 3rd World Cong of the Lay Apostolate Vatican City, 67; mem exec comt, US Conf for the World Coun of Churches, 67-72; SPONSOR, CATH AND QUAKER STUDIES, 71-; delegate, 6th Gen Assembly World Coun of Churches, 83. **MEMBERSHIPS** Quaker Theol Discussion Group. **RESEARCH** The theology of 17th century England, especially Quakers; scriptural exegesis and hermeneutics; Roman Cath theology. **SELECTED PUBLICATIONS** Auth, Quakers, Ecumenism and the World Council of Churches Wcc, Ecumenical Rev, Vol 46, 94. **CONTACT ADDRESS** 1110 Wildwood Ave, Manasquan, NJ 08736.

FREIN, BRIGID CURTIN
PERSONAL Born 01/19/1957, St. Paul, MN, m, 1979, 4 children **DISCIPLINE** THEOLOGY **EDUCATION** Gonzaga Univ, BA, 79; St. Louis Univ, PhD, 89. **CAREER** From asst prof to assoc prof to chemn, 88-, Univ Scranton; Assoc. Dean, College of Arts and Sciences, 00. **MEMBERSHIPS** Catholic Biblical Assoc; Society Biblical Literature. **RESEARCH** New Testament; Gospel of Luke. **SELECTED PUBLICATIONS** Auth, art, Fundamentalism and Narrative Criticism of the Gospels, 92; auth, art, The Literary and Theological Significance of Misunderstanding in the Gospel of Luke, 93; auth, art, Old Testament Prophecies, Narrative Predictions, and Luke's Sense of Fulfillment, 94; auth, art, Scripture in the Life of the Church, 97. **CONTACT ADDRESS** Dept of Theology/Religious Studies, Univ of Scranton, Scranton, PA 18510. **EMAIL** freinb1@uofs.edu

FRENCH, HENRY P., JR
PERSONAL Born 11/21/1934, Rochester, NY, m, 1959, 4 children **DISCIPLINE** HISTORY, POLITICAL SCIENCE **EDUCATION** Univ Del, AB, 60; Univ Rochester, AM, 61; AMed, 62; EdD, 68. **CAREER** Chemn, Hist and Polit Sci Dept, SUNY Monroe Community Col, 79-85; Pres, Friends of the Rochester Public Libr, 88-91; Trustee Reynolds Libr Found, 91-; from Vice Pres to Pres, Rochester Public Libr, 96-00; Rochester Regional Libr Coun, 98-; Trustee, Rundel Libr Found, 99-; From Asst Prof to Prof, SUNY Monroe Community Col, 67-; **HONORS AND AWARDS** SUNY Bd of Trustees, Chancellor's Medal for Philanthropy Awd, 99. **MEMBERSHIPS** Asn for Asian Studies, Int Rochester Chapter, Int Asn of Historians of Asian. **RESEARCH** Chinese and Japanese Cultural History since 1800s. **SELECTED PUBLICATIONS** Coauth, China and Rochester, Easter 1990 and Beyond, Episcopal Diocese of Rochester (Rochester, NY), 91. **CONTACT ADDRESS** Dept Hist and Govt, Monroe Comm Col, 1000 E Henrietta Rd, Rochester, NY 14623-5701. **EMAIL** hfrench@monroe.edu

FRENCH, LOUISE
PERSONAL Born 06/23/1918, Indianapolis, IN **DISCIPLINE** PHILOSOPHY **EDUCATION** Mundelein Col, AB, 40; Marquette Univ, AM, 48; St Louis Univ, PhD (philos), 61. **CAREER** Assoc prof philos and chmn dept, Clarke Col, 56-68; PROF PHILOS AND CHMN DEPT, MUNDELEIN COL, 68-; prof, Loyola Univ, Chicago; prof emerita, 92 **MEMBERSHIPS** Metaphys Soc Am; Cath Philos Asn; Am Philos Asn. **RESEARCH** Metaphysics; existentialism; ancient philosophy, medieval philosophy. **SELECTED PUBLICATIONS** Auth, Approaches to Teaching Mann Death in Venice and Other Short Fiction, Ger Quart, Vol 68, 95; Mereaubrentano, Sophie. Freedom, Love, Femininity--Tricolor of Social and Individual Self Determination Ca.1800, Ger Quart, Vol 69, 96; The Experience of Other Countries--Papers Presented at Wiepersdorf Colloquium on Arnim, Achim, Von and Arnim, Bettina, Von, Ger Quart, Vol 69, 96; Merrill, Helen-In Memoriam, Tci, Vol 31, 97. **CONTACT ADDRESS** Dept of Philos, Loyola Univ, Chicago, 6625 Sheridan Rd, Chicago, IL 60626. **EMAIL** lfrench@luc.edu

FRENCH, PETER A.
PERSONAL Born 03/19/1942, Newburgh, NY, m, 1961, 2 children **DISCIPLINE** PHILOSOPHY **EDUCATION** Gettysburg Col, BA, 63; Univ Southern Calif, MA, 64; Univ of Miami, PhD, 71. **CAREER** Instr, 65-66; asst prof, Ariz State Col/Northern Ariz Univ, 66-68; asst prof, Miami-Dade Col, 68-71; vis prof, Dalhousie Univ, 76; from asst prof to prof, Univ Minn, 71-81; coord of philos, Univ Minn, 72-73 & 77-78; Exxon Distinguished Res Prof, Center for the Study of Values, Univ Delaware, 80-81; Lennox Distinguished Prof Hum and Prof Philos, Trinity Univ, 81-94; chmn dept philos, Trinity Univ, 82-88; Dir, Ctr for Undergraduate Philos Res, Trinity Univ, 86-91; prof philos,Univ S Fla, 94-00; ch ethics, 94-00; Dir, ethics ctr, 95-00; ch, dept philos, 97-00; Chair, Arizona State Univ, 00. **MEMBERSHIPS** APA, Soc for Philos and Pub Aff; Soc for Bus Ethics; Soc of Philos J Eds;N Am Soc for Soc Philos; Inst for Criminal Justice Ethics. **RESEARCH** Ethics; ethical theory. **SELECTED PUBLICATIONS** Auth, The Spectrum of Responsibility, St Martin's Pr, 91; coauth, Corporations in the Moral Community, Harcourt Brace, 92; auth, Responsibility Matters, Univ Pr Kansas, 92; auth, Corporate Ethics, Harcourt Brace, 95; auth,Cowboy Metaphysics: Ethics and Death in Westerns, Rowman and Littlefield, 97; auth, Why did Wittgenstein Read Tagore to the Vienna Circle?, in Proto Soziologie, 93; auth, Responsibility and the Moral Role of Corporate Entities, in Business as a Humanity, 94; auth, The Practical and Ethical Costs of Corp Reengineering, in Business and Prof Ethics J, winter, 94; auth, Action Theory, Ration-Choice Theory, and Ethics, in Business Ethics Qtly, Summer, 95; auth, Corp Moral Agency, in the Blackwell Encyclopedic Dict of Bus Ethics, 96; auth Normativity and Private Persons: 1. Responsibility, 2. Status: Individual and Group Membership, in the Philos of Law: an Encyclopedia, 96; auth, the Compensatory Opportunities of Re-engineering, in Perspectives on the Professions, Spring, 96; auth, Rationality and Ethics, in Proto Soziologie, 96; auth, Integrity, Intentions, and Corporations, in American Business Law J, 96; auth, Spatial and Temporal Ethics, in Frontiers in Amer Philos, 96; auth, Moral Principles, Rules, and Policies, in Ethical Policy Making in Local Schools, 97; auth, Forward to Collective Responsibility, in Collective Responsibility, 98; auth, Unchosen Evil and War Crimes, in War Crimes Revisited, forthcoming; auth, The Virtues of Vengeance, Univ Pr Kansas, 00. **CONTACT ADDRESS** Dept of Philosophy, Arizona State Univ, MC 2004, Tempe, AZ 85287.

FRENCH, STANLEY G.
PERSONAL Born 12/24/1933, Hamilton, ON, Canada **DISCIPLINE** PHILOSOPHY **EDUCATION** Carleton Univ, BA, 55; Univ Rochester, MA, 57; Univ Va, PhD, 59; Oxford Univ, 61; Universite de Nice, Institut d'Etudes et de Recherches; Interethniques et Interculturelles, 75-76; McGill Univ, Royal Victoria Hospital, 87-88; The Hastings Center, 92. **CAREER** Asst prof, Univ of Western Ontario, 59-65; assoc prof, Univ of Western Ontario, 65-68; prof of philos, Sir George Williams Univ, 68-74; ch, Sir George Williams Univ, 68-71; prof of philos and dean of Graduate Studies, Sir George williams Univ and Concordia Univ, 71-86; prof of philos, Concordia Univ, 74-. **HONORS AND AWARDS** SSHRC Project Assessor, 89; Editorial Consultant, Biomedical Ethics Project, 90-92; Political and Constitutional Advisor, William H. Donner Foundation, 91-; Editorial Board, 91-; British Council Visitorship, 92; International Visiting Scholar, The Hasting Center, 92; Keynote Speaker, Zonta International Summit on Violence Against Women, 95; Canagian Federation for the Humanities, 95; SSHRC Project Assessor, 97. **MEMBERSHIPS** Can Philos Asn; Can Bioethics Soc; Am Philos Asn; Mind Asn; Am Soc for Political and Legal Philosophy; La Soc de Philosophie du Quebec; La Societe de Philosophie de Montreal; Montreal Conference for Political and Social Thought. **SELECTED PUBLICATIONS** Auth, The Northwest Staging Route, Ottawa: The Queen's Printer, 57; auth, Philosophers Look at Canadian Confederation, 79; auth, Interpersonal Violence, Health and Gender Politics, Dubuque: Brown & Benchmark, 93; auth, Interperson-

al Violence, Health and Gender Politics, 2nd ed, Dubuque: Brown & Benchmark, 94; auth, La violence interpersonnelle, la sante et le pouvoir masculin, Victoriaville: College Victoriaville, 95; auth, Interpersonal Violence, Health and Gender Politics, 3rd ed, Toronto: McGraw-Hill Ryerson, 98; co-ed, Violence Against Women: Philosophical Perspectives, with Laura M. Purdy & Wanda Teays, Ithaca, NY: Cornell Univ Press, 98; auth, "Interpersonal Violence: Power Relationships and their Effects on Health," Interpersonal Violence, Health and Gender Politics, Dubuque: Brown & Benchamrk, (93): 3-27; auth, "Interpersonal Violence: Power Relationships and their Effects on Health," Interpersonal Violence, Health and Gender Politics, 2nd ed, Dubuque: Brown & Benchmark, (94): 3-26; auth, "Interpersonal Violence: Power Relatinoships and their Effects on Health," Interpersonal Violence, Health and Gender Politics, 3rd ed, Toronto: McGraw-Hill Ryerson, (98): 3-25. **CONTACT ADDRESS** Dept of Philos, Concordia Univ, Montreal, Le Mas, 585 Newaygo Rd., Montfort, QB, Canada J0T 1Y0. **EMAIL** frenchs@ietc.ca

FRENCH, WILLIAM
PERSONAL Born 03/24/1951, Washington, DC, m **DISCIPLINE** THEOLOGY **EDUCATION** Dickinson Coll, BA, 73; Harvard Univ, MDiv, 77; Univ of Chicago, PhD, 85. **CAREER** Special edu teach, 73-74, National Children's Center Wash DC; teach, dept head, 78-79, Willibrord Catholic High School; summer Instr, 80, 81, Prairie State Coll Chicago; Asst Prof, Assoc Prof, 85-, Loyola Univ Chicago, Dir 94-, Peace Stud Prog. **MEMBERSHIPS** AAR, SCE, Peace Studies Assoc. **RESEARCH** Religious & environmental ethics, war & peace issues. **SELECTED PUBLICATIONS** Auth, Character and Cruelty in Huckleberry Finn, Why the Ending Works, in: Soundings 81, 98; Knowing Where You Are, in: Peace Review, A Transnational Qtly, 96; Against Biosherical Egalitarianism, in: J of Environmental Ethics, 95; Chaos and Creation, in: The Bible Today, 95; God and Biospheres as Superpowers, in: Peace Review, A Transnational Qtly, 94; Soil And Salvation, Theological Anthropology Ecologically Informed, in: The Whole and Divided Self, ed J McCarthy, New York Crossroad, 97; The World as God's Body, Theological Ethics and Pantheism, in: Broken and Whole, Essays on Religion and the Body, eds, M A Tilly & S A Ross, Lanham Univ Press of Amer, 95. **CONTACT ADDRESS** Dept of Theology, Loyola Univ, Chicago, 6525 N Sheridan, Chicago, IL 60626. **EMAIL** wfrench@luc.edu

FRERICHS, ERNEST S.
PERSONAL Born 04/30/1925, Staten Island, NY, m, 1949, 3 children **DISCIPLINE** RELIGIOUS STUDIES, BIBLICAL STUDIES **EDUCATION** Brown Univ, AB, 48; Harvard Univ, AM, 49; Boston Univ, STB, 52, PhD, 57. **CAREER** Chmn, Dept of Religious Studies, 64-70, prof, Religious Studies and Judaic Studies, 66-95, Dean, graduate school, Pres, PBK Alpha of Rhode Island, 75-77; Brown Univ, 76-82, dir, Prog in Judaic Studies, 82-95, prof Emeritus, 96-; Pres, Albright Inst of Archaeological Research, Jerusalem, 76-82; Vice-pres, Am Schools of Oriental research, 95-97; exec dir, Dorot Found, 95-. **HONORS AND AWARDS** Lilly Post-doctoral fel; Distinguished Alumnus Awd, Boston Univ, 94. **MEMBERSHIPS** Soc of Biblical Lit; Am Academy of Relig; Am Schools of Oriental Res. **RESEARCH** History of Biblical interpretation; history of Biblical translation. **SELECTED PUBLICATIONS** Ed, Bible and Bibles in America, Scholars Press, 88; Joint ed, with Leonard Lesko, Exodus, The Egyptological Evidence, Eisenbraun's, 97. **CONTACT ADDRESS** Dorot Found, 439 Benefit St, Providence, RI 02903. **EMAIL** ErnieF@Dorot.org

FRETHEIM, TERENCE E.
DISCIPLINE OLD TESTAMENT **EDUCATION** Luther Col,BA, 56; Luther Sem, MDiv, 60; Princeton Sem, ThD, 67. **CAREER** Instr, Augsburg Col and Sem, 61-63; asst prof, Augsburg Col, 67-68; vis prof, lectr, Univ Chicago Divinity Sch; asst prof, 68; dean of acad aff, 78-88; act ch, Old Testament dept, 77-78; ch, curriculum comm, 76-77; prof, 78-. **HONORS AND AWARDS** Phi Beta Kappa, 95; Fulbright scholar; grad scholar, Lutheran Brotherhood Sem; Martin Luther scholar; Fredrik A. Schiotz fel award; ATS scholar; co-ch, theol consult for the evangel lutheran church in am; pres, minn consortium of theol sch(s); bk ed, jour bibl lit; pastor, dennison lutheran church, 68-71. **MEMBERSHIPS** Mem, Cath Bibl Assn; Soc of Bibl Lit. **SELECTED PUBLICATIONS** Auth, Genesis, New Interpreter's Bible, 94; Exodus, Interpretation Series, John Knox, 91; Deuteronomy-II Kings, Search Units 9 and 10, 85; The Suffering of God: An Old Testament Perspective, 84; Deuteronomic History, 83; The Message of Jonah: A Theological Commentary, 77; Our Old Testament Heritage, 70-71; Creation, Fall and Flood, Stud (s) in Genesis 1-11, 69. **CONTACT ADDRESS** Dept of Old Testament, Luther Sem, 2481 Como Ave, Saint Paul, MN 55108. **EMAIL** tfrethei@luthersem.edu

FREUND, NORM
PERSONAL Born 07/21/1953, Davenport, IA, m, 1975, 2 children **DISCIPLINE** PHILOSOPHY **EDUCATION** St. Ambrose Col, BA, philos, BS, bio, 75; Southern Ill Univ, MA, philos, 77, PhD, philos, 80. **CAREER** Asst prof, philos, Luther Col, 80-81; asst prof, 81-85, assoc prof, 86-88, full prof, 89-, philos, Clarke Col. **HONORS AND AWARDS** Title III grants for Computer Hypertext Res, 95, 96; Meneve Dunham award for excellence in teaching, 88. **MEMBERSHIPS** Amer Philos Asn; Amer Asn of Philos Teachers; Concerned Philos for Peace. **RESEARCH** History of philosophy and applied ethics; Philosophy of peace and war. **SELECTED PUBLICATIONS** Rev, A Strategy of Nonviolent Defense, A Gandhian Approach, Civilian-Based Defense, Mar, 96; auth, If It's Tuesday This Must Be Bentham, Teaching Philos, Dec, 93; rev, What is Justice?, Contemporary and Classical Readings, Teaching Philos, Sept, 92; rev, The Ethics of War and Peace, Warism to Pacifism: A Moral Continuum, Teaching Philos, Dec, 91; auth, The Just War Theory: Historical Development and Contemporary Analysis, Gandhi Marg, 12, Jul-Sept, 90; rev, Toynbee's Philosophy of World History and Politics, Jour of Social Philos, 19, Fall, 88; auth, Peace: A Myriad of Meanings, The Personalist Forum 4, Spring, 88; auth, A Humanistic Sexual Ethic, Contemporary Philos, 12, Apr, 88; auth, Nonviolent National Defense: A Philosophical Inquiry into Applied Nonviolence, Univ Press of Amer, 87. **CONTACT ADDRESS** 1550 Clarke Dr., Dubuque, IA 52001. **EMAIL** nfreund@keller.clarke.edu

FREUND, RICHARD A.
PERSONAL m, 2 children **DISCIPLINE** PHILOSOPHY AND RELIGION **EDUCATION** Jewish Theol Sem of Am, MA, PhD. **CAREER** Isaacson Prof Relig, ch, dept Philos & Relig, dir, Bethsaida Excavations Proj, Univ Nebr, Omaha; ch ed, Spotlight on Tchg, Am Acad of Relig. **HONORS AND AWARDS** Lilly Endowment tchg fel, 91, Univ-wide res award, 92, tchg award, 95, Univ Nebr, Omaha; founder, bethsaida excavations proj, univ nebr, omaha. **MEMBERSHIPS** Nat secy, Soc of Bibl Lit. **SELECTED PUBLICATIONS** Auth, 1st two Vols of Bethsaida: A City by the North Shore of the Sea of Galilee. **CONTACT ADDRESS** Univ of Nebraska, Omaha, Omaha, NE 68182.

FREYER, TONY ALLAN
PERSONAL Born 12/28/1947, Indianapolis, IN, m, 1976, 1 child **DISCIPLINE** HISTORY; LAW **EDUCATION** San Diego State Univ, AB, 70; Ind Univ, MA, 72, PhD, 75. **CAREER** Univ of Arkansas at Little Rock, 76-81; Univ Res Prof of History and Law, Univ of Ala, 81-. **HONORS AND AWARDS** University of Alabama's Burnum Distinguished fac awd, 92; sr Fulbright awd, Australia, 93; Abe Fellowship, Soc Sci Res Coun to Japan, 95-06; Harvard-Newcomer Postdoctoral Business History Fellow, Harvard Business School, 75-76; Research fellow, Charles Warren Center, Harvard Univ, 81-82; Sr. Fulbright Awd, United Kingdom, 1986; Fulbright Distinguished Chair, American Studies, Poland **RESEARCH** Legal history; Business History; History of Globalization. **SELECTED PUBLICATIONS** Auth, Forums of Order, 79; Harmony and Dissonance: The Swift and Erie Cases in American Federalism, 81; The Little Rock Crisis, 84; Justice Hugo L. Black and the Dilemma of American Liberalism, 90; Hugo L. Black and Modern America, 90; Regulating Big Business: Antitrust in Great Britain and America, 1880-1990, 92; Producers versus Capitalists: Constitutional Conflict in Antebellum America, 94; coauth, for Democracy and Judicial Independence, 95; auth, Defending Constitutional Rights: Frank M. Johnson, 01; auth, Rights Defied: Copper v. Aaron, the Little Rock Crisis, and America's Civil Rights Struggle, 04. **CONTACT ADDRESS** Law Dept, Univ of Alabama, Tuscaloosa, Box 870000, Tuscaloosa, AL 35487-0383. **EMAIL** tfreyer@law.ua.edu

FREYFOGLE, ERIC T.
DISCIPLINE LAW **EDUCATION** Lehigh Univ, BA; Univ Mich, JD. **CAREER** Prof, Univ Ill Urbana Champaign. **HONORS AND AWARDS** Ed, Mich Law Rev; dir, Ill Environ Council. **RESEARCH** Property; environmental law & policy; natural resources; land use planning; modern environmental theory; and wildlife law. **SELECTED PUBLICATIONS** Auth, Justice and the Earth and Bounded People, Boundless Lands. **CONTACT ADDRESS** Law Dept, Univ of Illinois, Urbana-Champaign, 52 E Gregory Dr, Champaign, IL 61820. **EMAIL** efreyfog@law.uiuc.edu

FRICK, FRANK SMITH
PERSONAL Born 04/02/1938, Ponca City, OK, m, 1961, 2 children **DISCIPLINE** RELIGION **EDUCATION** Phillips Univ, AB, 60, BD, 63; Princeton Univ, PhD (relig), 70. **CAREER** Campus minister, United Ministries Higher Educ, Okla State Univ, 64-66; asst prof, 69-77, ASSOC PROF RELIG STUDIES, ALBION COL, 77-, EDUC CONSULT, WMICH CONF, UNITED METHODIST CHURCH, 69-; resident dir, Gt Lakes Cols Asn Mid East prog, Israel, 73-74; vis prof relig, Hebrew Univ Jerusalem, 73-74; mem staff, Archaeol Excavations at Tel Dan, Israel, 77-78; Nat Endowment for Humanities grant, 82. **MEMBERSHIPS** Am Schs Orient Res; Soc Bibl Lit; Cath Bibl Soc. **RESEARCH** Sociology of biblical religion; comparative study of religion; Palestinian archaeology. **SELECTED PUBLICATIONS** Auth, The Rechabites reconsidered, J Bibl Lit, 10/71; The City in Ancient Israel, Scholars, 77; Religion and social political structure in Early Israel, SBL Sem Papers, 79. **CONTACT ADDRESS** Dept of Relig Studies, Albion Col, 611 E Porter St, Albion, MI 49224-1831.

FRIED, CHARLES
PERSONAL Born 04/15/1935, Czechoslovakia, m, 1959, 2 children **DISCIPLINE** LAW, LEGAL PHILOSOPHY **EDUCATION** Princeton Univ, AB, 56; Oxford Univ, BA, 58; Columbia Univ, LLB, 60. **CAREER** Law clerk, Justice Harlan, US Supreme Court, 60-61; asst prof, 61-65, prof law, Law Sch, Harvard Univ, 65-, consult, US Treas & Internal Revenue Serv, 61-62; assoc reporter, Model Code Pre-Arraignment Procedure, Am Law Inst, 64; vis prof, Mass Inst Technol, 68-69; dir, Nat Court Crime & Delinquency; consult, Dept Transp, White House, 81-; Solicitor General of the U.S., 85-89; Assoc Justice, Supreme Judicial Court of Mass, 95-99. **MEMBERSHIPS** AAAS; IOM. **SELECTED PUBLICATIONS** Auth, The Value of Life, Harvard Law Rev, 69; auth, "Perfect Freedom, Perfect Justice, BU Law Rev., 98; An Anatomy of Values, Harvard Univ, 70; contribr, Ethical Issues in Human Genetics, Plenum 73; Ethics of AID and Embryo Transfer, Ciba, 73; Markets and Morals, Hemisphere Publ, 77; auth, The University as Church and as Part, Bull Am Acad Arts St Sci, 12/77; Right and Wrong, Harvard Univ, 78; Contract as Promise, A Theory of Contractual Obligation, Harvard Univ, 81; Law and Order, Simon and Schuster, 91. **CONTACT ADDRESS** Dept of Law, Harvard Univ, Cambridge, MA 02138. **EMAIL** fried@law.harvard.edu

FRIEDLAND, JULIAN
PERSONAL Born 06/07/1968, Chicago, IL, m, 1995 **DISCIPLINE** PHILOSOPHY **EDUCATION** Col Univ-Boulder, BA, 91; San Fran State Univ, MA, 94; Univ Paris-Sorbonne, PhD, 00. **CAREER** Adj prof, Mentrop State Col of Denver. **MEMBERSHIPS** APA; AAUP. **RESEARCH** Wittgenstein, Ethics, Aesthetics, Philosophy of mind and language, Theory of knowledge, Artificial intelligence, Intellectual property. **SELECTED PUBLICATIONS** Auth, "Compassion as a Means to Freedom", Humanist, (99). **CONTACT ADDRESS** Dept Philos, Metropolitan State Col of Denver, PO Box 173362, Denver, CO 80217-3362. **EMAIL** friedlan@mscd.edu

FRIEDLANDER, WALTER J.
PERSONAL Born 06/06/1919, Los Angeles, CA, m, 1976, 3 children **DISCIPLINE** MEDICAL ETHICS AND HISTORY **EDUCATION** Univ Calif, Berkeley, AB, 41; Univ Calif, San Francisco, MD, 45. **CAREER** Asst prof med, Sch Med, Stanford Univ, 54-56; asst prof neurol, Col Med, Boston Univ, 56-61; from assoc to prof neurol, Albany Med Col, 61-66; dir, Ctr Humanities and Med, 75-80, PROF NEUROL, COL MED, UNIV NEBR, 66-, Prof and Chmn Dept Med Humanities, 80-, Regional humanist, Nebr Comt for Humanities, 76-; consult, Nat Libr Med, 79-. **MEMBERSHIPS** Fel Am Col Physicians; Acad Aphasia. **RESEARCH** Medical history; applied medical ethics; medical sociology. **SELECTED PUBLICATIONS** Auth, The Evolution of Informed Consent in American Medicine, Perspectives Biol Med, Vol 38, 95. **CONTACT ADDRESS** Col of Med, Univ of Nebraska, Omaha, Omaha, NE 68105.

FRIEDMAN, EDWARD
PERSONAL Born 12/12/1937, New York, NY, m, 1969, 2 children **DISCIPLINE** POLITICAL SCIENCE, EAST ASIA **EDUCATION** Brandeis Univ, BA (Political Sci), 59; Harvard Univ, MA (East Asia), 61; PhD (Political Sci), 68. **CAREER** To prof, Dept of Political Science, Univ Wis, 67-; res fel, Univ Mich, spring 68; teaching, Harvard Univ, summers 68, 69, 71; res fel, MUCIA, Hong Kong, 70; res fel, Center for Advanced Study, Univ Ill, 71; fac, NYU, SUNY-Purchase, CUNY-Brooklyn, 71-72; SSRC, res grant, 73; consult, China Trade Services, fall 80; staff, US House of Representatives, Committee on Foreign Affairs, Jan 81-July 83; advisor, United Nations Develoment prog, Aug 83; lect, USAI: Australia, South Korea, Hong Kong, Burma, France, summer 84; Wang Found Res fel, 85; Guggenheim fel, 86-87; seminar, China and the Pacific Rim, Univ CA, La Jolla, summer 87; NEH fac seminar leader, summer 90; US AID, Albania, summer 92; US Dept of the Defense, consult, 93-94; US Naval Postgraduate School, Monterey, summer week, 93; US Naval Postgraduate School, summer sem, 94. **HONORS AND AWARDS** Phi Beta Kappa; Fels from Woodrow Wilson, Ford, Fulbright-Hays, Guggenheim; Book titled Chinese Village, Socialist State named best book on modern China for 1991 by AAS. **MEMBERSHIPS** AAS; APSA; AI. **RESEARCH** Democratization; International political economy; Leninist transitions; Revolution; US-Asian relations; Chinese politics. **SELECTED PUBLICATIONS** Auth, America's Asia, Pantheon; auth, Backward Toward Revolution, California; auth, Chinese Village, Socialist State China, Yale Univ Press, 91; auth, National Identity and Democratic Prospects in Socialist China, Sharpe; auth, The Politics of Democratization, ed, Westview; auth, What if China Doesn't Democratize? Implications for War and Peace, Routledge; auth, Revolution, Resistance, and Reform in Village China, fothcoming. **CONTACT ADDRESS** Dept of Political Science, Univ of Wisconsin, Madison, North Hall, Madison, WI 53706-1389. **EMAIL** friedman@polisci.wisc.edu

FRIEDMAN, HARVEY MARTIN
PERSONAL Born 09/23/1948, m, 1973 **DISCIPLINE** LOGIC, FOUNDATIONS OF MATHEMATICS **EDUCATION** Mass Inst Technol, PhD (math), 67. **CAREER** Asst prof

philos, Stnaford Univ, 67-69, assoc prof, 69-73; vis prof math, State Univ NY, Buffalo, 72-73, prof, 73-77; PROF MATH, OHIO STATE UNIV, 77-, Vis assoc prof math, Univ Wis, Madison, 70-71. **MEMBERSHIPS** Asn Symbolic Logic. **RESEARCH** Philosophy of mathematics; intuitionism. **SELECTED PUBLICATIONS** Auth, Higher set theory and mathematical practice, Ann Math Logic, 71; The consistency of classical set theory relative to a set theory with intuitionistic logic, J Symbolic Logic, 6/73; Some applications of Kleene's methods for intuitionistic systems, In: Lecture Notes in Mathematics, Springer, 73. **CONTACT ADDRESS** Dept of Math, Ohio State Univ, Columbus, 231 W 18th Ave, Columbus, OH 43210-1174.

FRIEDMAN, HOWARD M.
DISCIPLINE LAW **EDUCATION** Ohio State Univ, BA; Harvard Univ, JD; Georgetown Univ, LLM. **CAREER** Prof. **SELECTED PUBLICATIONS** Auth, Securities Regulation In Cyberspace, Bowne, 97; Ohio Securities Law & Practice, Anderson, 96; Securities and Commodities Enforcement, Lexington Bk, 81. **CONTACT ADDRESS** Col Law, Univ of Toledo, Toledo, OH 43606.

FRIEDMAN, LAWRENCE M.
PERSONAL Born 04/02/1930, Chicago, IL, m, 1955, 2 children **DISCIPLINE** LAW **EDUCATION** Univ Chicago, AB, 48, JD, 51, LLM, 53; 5honorary degrees. **CAREER** From asst prof to assoc prof law, St Louis Univ, 57-61; from assoc prof to prof, Univ Wis, 61-68; Prof Law, Stanford Univ, 68-. **HONORS AND AWARDS** Triennial Coif Awd, Asn Am Law Schs, 76; lld, univ puget sound, 77. **MEMBERSHIPS** Law and Soc Asn (past pres); Am Soc Legal Hist (past pres.) Am Acad Arts and Sci; Soc of Am Historians. **RESEARCH** American legal history; sociology of law and social welfare legislation; property and succession. **SELECTED PUBLICATIONS** Auth, A History of American Law, 2d ed, 85; auth, Crime and Punishment in American Society, 93; auth, The Horizontal society, 99; over 150 journals articles. **CONTACT ADDRESS** Sch of Law, Stanford Univ, Stanford, CA 94305-1926. **EMAIL** lmf@leland.stanford.edu

FRIEDMAN, LESLEY
PERSONAL Born 06/13/1965, New York, NY, m, 1994 **DISCIPLINE** PHILOSOPHY **EDUCATION** Union Col, BA; Univ Albany, MA; Univ Buffalo, PhD, SUNY. **CAREER** Assoc Prof, Lynchburg Col, 7 yrs. **HONORS AND AWARDS** William T Parry Prize for Outstanding Scholarship in Philos, 92; Res Grant, Lynchburg Col, 95, 97. **MEMBERSHIPS** APA; Soc for the Advancement of Amer Philos; Hume Soc; Intl Berkeley Soc; Charles S. Peirce Soc **RESEARCH** Amer Philos; Charles S. Pierce; Modern European Philos. **SELECTED PUBLICATIONS** Remembrance of of Darkness Past A Rejoinder to Flage, Hume Stud, 93; Another Look at Flages Hume, Hume Stud, 93; C.S. Pierces Reality & Berkeleys Blunders, Jour of the Hist of Philos, 97; Contrib, Pragmatism An Annotated Bibliography 1898-1940 Value Inquiry Book Ser, 98; auth, "Doubt and Inquiry: Peirce and Descartes Revisited," Transactions of the Charles S. Pierce Society XXXV (99): 724-746. **CONTACT ADDRESS** Philosophy Dept, Lynchburg Col, 1501 Lakes, Lynchburg, VA 24501-3199. **EMAIL** friedman_l@mail.lynchburg.edu

FRIEDMAN, MARILYN A.
DISCIPLINE PHILOSOPHY **EDUCATION** Univ Western Ontario, PhD, 74. **CAREER** Assoc Prof, Wash Univ 91-. **HONORS AND AWARDS** Nat Endowment for the Humanities Fel, 88-89. **MEMBERSHIPS** Am Philos Asn; soc for Women in Philos. **RESEARCH** Ethics; Feminist Theory; Social and Political Philosophy. **SELECTED PUBLICATIONS** Auth, What are Friends For?: Feminist Perspective on Personal Relationship and Moral Theory, 93; coauth; Political Correctness: For and Against, 95; co-ed, Feminism and Community, 95; Mind and Morals: Essays on Ethics and Cognitive Science, 95. **CONTACT ADDRESS** Dept Of Philosophy, Washington Univ, Box 1073, Saint Louis, MO 63130. **EMAIL** friedman@artsci.wustl.edu

FRIEDMAN, MAURICE STANLEY
PERSONAL Born 12/29/1921, Tulsa, OK, 2 children **DISCIPLINE** PHILOSOPHY **EDUCATION** Educ. Harvard Univ, BS, 42; Ohio State Univ, AM, 47; Univ Chicago, PhD, 50; Int Col Am,MA, 83. **CAREER** Res asst & statistician, Harvard Univ, 42; asst English, Ohio State Univ, 46-47; teaching asst humanities, Univ Chicago, 48-49; instr basic col prog, Washington Univ, 49-50; instr philos, Ohio State Univ, 50-51; mem fac philos & lit, Sarah Lawrence Col, 51-55, prof philos, 55-64; prof, Manhattanville Col, 66-67; prof relig, Temple Univ, 67-73, grant, 71-72; prof, 73-91, PROF EMERITUS REL STUDIES, PHILOS, COMP LIT, 91-, SAN DIEGO STATE UNIV; Lectr, New Sch Soc Res, 54-66; vis prof, Hebrew Union Col, 56-57; mem fac, Wash Sch Psychiat, 57-59; guest lectr, William Alanson White Inst Psychol, Psychoanal & Psychiat, 58-60; Lucius N Littaeur Found res grant, Israel & Europe, 59-60; treas & mem exec comt, Conf Jewish Philos, 63-69; mem fac, Pendle Hill-Quaker Ctr for Studies & Dialogue, 64-65, 67-73 & I Meier Segals Ctr for Advan Judaism, Can, 65-72; Gustav N Wurzweiler Found grants work on Buber biog, Israel & America, 65-67; vis prof, Union Theol Sem, 65 & 67; vis lectr, Vassar Col, 67; Am Philos Asn fel, 69; vis distinguished prof, Calif State Univ, San Diego, 72; vis fel, Ctr Studies Person, La Jolla, Calif, 72; mem core fac, Calif Sch Prof Psychol, San Diego, 73-75; field fac, Union Grad Sch West, 75-; guild tutors, Int Col, 76-86; res adv, Fielding Inst, 77-80; vis prof rel, Univ Hawaii, 75; vis prof, Gandhi Nat Ctr Arts, New Delhi, 92. **HONORS AND AWARDS** LLD, Univ Vt, 61; Nat Jewish Book Awd for Biography, 85; DHL, Sch Psychol Stud, Sand Diego, 86; DHL, Hebrew Union Col Jewish Inst of Rel, 98; lld, univ vt, 61. **MEMBERSHIPS** Am Philos Asn; Metaphys Soc Am; Relig Educ Asn; Am Asn Existential Psychol & Psychiat; Asn Humanistic Psychol. **RESEARCH** Religious and dialogical existentialism; the image of man in the great religions and in modern literature; the inter-relations of philosophical anthropology, ethics, and psychology. **SELECTED PUBLICATIONS** Auth, The Modern Promethean: A Dialogue with Today's Youth, Pendle Hill, 70; Touchstones of Reality: Existential Trust and the Community of Peace, Dutton, 72, 74; coauth, Searching in the Syntax of Things: Experiments in Religion, Fortress, 72; auth, The Worlds of Existentialism: A Critical Reader, Univ Chicago & Phoenix Bks, 73; The Hidden Human Image, Delacorte & Delta Bks, 74; Martin Buber's Life and Work: The Early Years-1878-1923, Dutton & Search, 82; The human way: A dialogical approach to religion and human experience, Anima, 82; Martin Buber's Life and Work: The Middle Years-1923-1945, Dutton 83, and The Later Years-1945-1965, Dutton, 84; auth, Martin Buber and the Eternal, Human Science, 86; auth, Abraham Joshua Heschel and Elie Wiesel: You Are My Witnesses, Farrar, Straus, Giroux, 87; auth, A Dialogue with Hasidic Tales: Hallowing the Everyday, Human Science, 88; auth, Encounter on the Narrow Ridge: A Life of Martin Buber, Paragon House, 91, paperback, Span ed, 93, Jap trans, 99, Ger trans, 99; auth, Dialogue and the Human Image: Beyond Humanistic Psychology, Sage, 92; auth, Religion and Psychology: A Dialogical Approach, Paragon House, 92; auth, A Heart of Wisdom: Religion and Human Wholeness, State Univ NY Press, 92; auth, Intercultural Dialogue and the Human Image: Maurice Friedman at the Indira Gandhi Centre for the Arts, New Delhi, India, 95; ed-in-chief, Martin Buber and the Human Sciences, State Univ NY Press, 96; auth, The Affirming Flame: A Poetics of Meaning, Prometheus Books, 99. **CONTACT ADDRESS** 421 Hilmen Pl, Solana Beach, CA 92075. **EMAIL** friedma3@mail.sdsu.edu

FRIEDMAN, MICHAEL
DISCIPLINE PHILOSOPHY **EDUCATION** Queens Col, BA, 69; Priceton Univ, PhD, 73. **CAREER** Prof, Ind Univ. **HONORS AND AWARDS** Franklin J. Matchette Prize, 85; Lakatos Awd, 87; 3 NSF fels; NEH fel; ACLS fel; Guggenheim fel. **MEMBERSHIPS** Am Acad of Arts and Sci; Philos of Sci Asn; Am Philos Asn. **RESEARCH** Relationship between the history of science and the history of philosophy in the period from Kant to Carnap; history and philosophy of the exact sciences. **SELECTED PUBLICATIONS** Auth, Foundations of Space-Time Theories: Relativistic Physics and Philosophy of Science, 85; Geometry, Convention, and the Relativized A Priori, Univ Pittsburgh, 94; Poincare's Conventionalism and the Logical Positivists, 95; Overcoming Metaphysics: Carnap and Heidegger, Univ Minn, 96. **CONTACT ADDRESS** Dept of Hist and Philos of Sci, Indiana Univ, Bloomington, 1033 E Third St, Sycamore Hall 026, Bloomington, IN 47405. **EMAIL** mlfriedm@indiana.edu

FRIEDMAN, MURRAY
DISCIPLINE AMERICAN JEWISH HISTORY, AMERICAN SOCIAL AND POLITICAL HISTORY **EDUCATION** Georgetown Univ, PhD. **CAREER** Prof, dir, Myer and Rosaline Feinstein Ctr Am Jewish Hist, Temple Univ; lectr, US Infor Agency, African and India, 74; vice-ch, US Civil Rights Comn, DC, 86-89. **MEMBERSHIPS** Mid Atlantic States dir, Am Jewish Comt. **RESEARCH** Am Jewish Hist; Am Social and Political Hist. **SELECTED PUBLICATIONS** Auth, Overcoming Middle Class Rage, The Westminster Press, 71; Jewish Life in Philadelphia, 1830-1940, ISHI Publ, 83; The Utopian Dilemma: American Judaism in Public Policy, Ethics and Pub Policy Ctr, 85; Philadelphia Jewish Life: 1940 to 1985, Seth Press, 86; When Philadelphia Was the Capital of Jewish America, Assoc UP, 93; What Went Wrong: The Creation and Collapse of the Black-Jewish Alliance, the Free Press, 95. **CONTACT ADDRESS** Temple Univ, Philadelphia, PA 19122.

FRIEDMAN, PHILIP ALLAN
PERSONAL Born 07/19/1927, Brooklyn, NY **DISCIPLINE** ENGLISH LITERATURE, AMERICAN PHILOSOPHY **EDUCATION** NYork Univ, BA, 48; Columbia Univ, MA, 49; Univ Heidelberg, cert ling and philol, 55. **CAREER** Reporter and bk reviewer, Jewish Examiner, 48-49; prof asst, Toby Press, New York, 50-51; asst ed, Random House, Inc, New York, 51-52; instr English compos and contemp lit, Wayne State Univ, 53-54, 55-58; from asst prof to assoc prof Am Lit and studies, Calif State Univ, Los Angeles, 59-77, prof, 77-80., Consult, State Dept Comt For Visitors, Mich, 53-54, 55-58; consult and mem bd, Jewish Community Libr, Jewish Fed Coun Greater Los Angeles, 72; consult drama, Henry Street Settlement Children's Theater, 77-; referee and consult history, Hist, 78-. **MEMBERSHIPS** AAUP. **RESEARCH** Am Lit and culture; philosophy of science. **SELECTED PUBLICATIONS** Auth, Slapping Back, Aba J, Vol 82, 96. **CONTACT ADDRESS** 100 N Detroit Los, Los Angeles, CA 90036.

FRIEDMAN, RICHARD ELLIOTT
DISCIPLINE BIBLE, NEAR EASTERN LANGUAGES AND CIVILIZATIONS **EDUCATION** Harvard Univ, ThD, 78. **CAREER** Prof Hebrew and Comp Lit, Katzin Prof of Jewish Civilization, Univ Calif, San Diego, 76-. **HONORS AND AWARDS** Fel, Am Coun of Learned Soc, 82; Outstanding Fac Awd, Revelle Col, Univ Calif, San Diego, 92; Pres Res Fel in the Humanities, Univ Calif, 97; Sr Fel, Am Schools of Orient Res, 97; Res Awds, Univ Calif, 78, 79, 84, 88, 97. **RESEARCH** Literary and historical research in Bible. **SELECTED PUBLICATIONS** Auth, The Exile and Biblical Narrative, 81; ed, The Creation of Sacred Literature, 81; ed, The Poet and the Historian, 83; ed, The Future of Biblical Studies: The Hebrew Scriptures, 87; auth, Who Wrote the Bible?, 87; The Disappearance of God, 95; auth, The Hidden Face of God, 97; auth, The Hidden Book in the Bible, 98; auth, Commentary on the Torah, 00. **CONTACT ADDRESS** Dept of Lit, Univ of California, San Diego, 9500 Gilman Dr, La Jolla, CA 92093-0410. **EMAIL** refriedm@ucsd.edu

FRIEDMAN, WILLIAM HILLEL
PERSONAL Born 03/21/1937, Philadelphia, PA, m, 1968, 2 children **DISCIPLINE** PHILOSOPHY **EDUCATION** Gratz Col, Bhl, 58; Univ Pa, 60, MA, 62; Univ Va, PhD (philos), 70. **CAREER** Instr math, Philadelphia Pub Schs, 61-66; instr philos, Pa State Univ, 63-66; asst prof, Mary Washington Col, 66-67; asst instr, Univ Va, 67-69; asst prof, Va Commonwealth Univ, 69-75; ASST PROF PHILOS, VA STATE COL, 77-, Evaluator, Project Opportunity, 68. **MEMBERSHIPS** Am Philos Asn: Southern Soc Philos and Psychol. **RESEARCH** Logic; philosophy of science; contemporary philosophy. **SELECTED PUBLICATIONS** Auth, The Nlrb Suffers Institutional Amnesia--The Paramax Decision, Labor Law J, Vol 44, 93. **CONTACT ADDRESS** 5613 Indigo Rd, Richmond, VA 23230.

FRIEDRICHS, DAVID
PERSONAL Born 10/31/1944, White Plains, NY, m, 1976, 2 children **DISCIPLINE** CRIMINAL JUSTICE **EDUCATION** NYU, AB, 66; MA, 70; ABD. **CAREER** Lecturer to Asst Prof, CUNY, 69-77; Visiting Lecturer, Univ S Africa, 88; Visiting Lecturer, Oh Univ, 91; Asst Prof to Prof, Univ Scranton, 77-. **HONORS AND AWARDS** Fac Res Grant, CUNY, 72. **MEMBERSHIPS** Asn for Humanist Soc; Acad Criminal Justice Sci; Soc for the Study of Social Problems; Am Legal Studies Asn; Law and Soc Asn; **SELECTED PUBLICATIONS** Auth, Trusted Criminals - White Collar Crime in Contemporary Society, Belmont, CA, 96; auth, "Law as a Story in Our Lives: A Personal Account," in Private Sociology: Unsparing Reflections, Uncommon Gains, (General Hall Inc, 96), 180-188; co-auth, "Organized Crime: Crime Syndicates and Corporate Crime," in Contemporary Criminology, (Wadsworth Pub Co, 96), 383-394; auth, "The Downsizing of America: A Neglected Dimension of the White Collar Crime Problem," Crime, Law and Social Change 26 (96-97): 351-366; auth, "Responding to the Challenge of White Collar Crime as a Social Problem," Caribbean Journal of Criminology and Social Psychology 2 (97): 84-99; co-auth, "The Most Cited Works and Scholars in Critical Criminology," Journal of Criminal Justice Education 9 (98): 211-232; ed, State Crime, Vol I: Defining, Delineating and Explaining State Crime, Ashgate, 98; ed, State Crime, Vol II: Exposing, Sanctioning and Preventing State Crime, Ashgate, 98; auth, "New Directions in Critical Criminology and White Collar Crime," in Cutting the Edge: Current Perspectives in Radical and Critical Criminology, (Praeger, 98), 77-91; auth, "Can Students Benefit from an Intense Engagement with Postmodern Criminology? No", in Controversial Issues in Criminology, (Boston: Allyn & Bacon, 98), 156-164. **CONTACT ADDRESS** Dept Sociol, Univ of Scranton, 800 Linden St, Scranton, PA 18510.

FRIEL, JAMES P.
PERSONAL Born Bronx, NY, m, 1976 **DISCIPLINE** PHILOSOPHY, LITERATURE **EDUCATION** Marist Col, BA, 56; Fordham Univ, MA, 65. **CAREER** Teacher English, Marist Bro Schs, 56-63 & Cent Sch Dist, Syosset, 63-68; prof philos, Marist Col & Col of Mt St Vincent, 68-69; Prof English & Philos, State Univ NY Farmingdale, 70-, Ed, Aitia Mag, 72-; State Univ NY grant, 73; Matchette Found grant & dir study group, 76-80; chmn two-yr teaching comt, Am Philos Asn, 77-82. **MEMBERSHIPS** Am Philos Asn; Nat Workshop Conf; Nat Info & Resource Ctr Teaching Philos. **RESEARCH** Metaphysics; humor; citizenship. **SELECTED PUBLICATIONS** Ed, Philosophy of Religion, State Univ NY, 73; auth, Citizen apprenticeship, Aitia Mag, 74-75; ed, Philosophy, Law, Modern Citizen, State Univ NY Farmingdale, 75; auth, Report on National Workship Conference, Aitia Mag, 76; Paying through the nose to lift those Sunday blues, Newday, 10/76; The mall the merrier, or is it?, NY Times, 11/76; ed, Nineteenth Century American Literature, State Univ NY, (in press). **CONTACT ADDRESS** SUNY, Col of Tech at Farmingdale, 1250 Melville Rd, Farmingdale, NY 11735-1389. **EMAIL** frieljp@suny.farmingdale.edu

FRIEL, MICHAEL K.
DISCIPLINE LAW **EDUCATION** Harvard Univ, BA, JD; NYork Univ, LLM. **CAREER** Assoc dean, prof; Univ Fla, 86-, assoc dean, 90 and dir, Grad Tax Prog, 88-; instr, Willamette

Univ, 83-87; NY Univ, 82-83; pvt pract, Salem, Oregon 76-81; Oregon Govt Ethics Comt; past dir, Marion-Polk Legal Aid Serv, Salem; VISTA Volunteer Lawyer, Oregon 69-71. **MEMBERSHIPS** Oregon Bar. **RESEARCH** Taxation. **SELECTED PUBLICATIONS** Coauth, Taxation of Individual Income. **CONTACT ADDRESS** School of Law, Univ of Florida, PO Box 117625, Gainesville, FL 32611-7625. **EMAIL** friel@law.ufl.edu

FRIESEN, DUANE K.
PERSONAL Born 04/27/1940, Newton, KS, m, 1962, 2 children **DISCIPLINE** SOCIAL ETHICS **EDUCATION** Bethel Col, BA, 62; Mennonite Bibl Sem, BD, 65; Harvard Divinity Sch, Harvard Univ, ThD, 72. **CAREER** Prof, bibl & relig, Bethel Col, 70-. **HONORS AND AWARDS** Ralph B. Schrag, Distinguished Teaching Award, 89; David H. Richert Award for Distinguished Scholar, 86; summer stipend for younger humanists, Nat Endow for the Humanities, 73. **MEMBERSHIPS** Soc of Christ Ethics; Amer Acad of Relig; Intl Peace Res Asn. **RESEARCH** Theology and culture; Peace and nonviolence. **SELECTED PUBLICATIONS** Auth, Artist, Citizens, Philosophers: Seeking the Press of the City (Scottdale, PA: Herold Press, 00); Co-auth, Just Peacemaking: Ten Practices for Abolishing War, Cleveland, Oh, Pilgrim Press, 98; co-auth, Overcoming Violence: Local and Global Strategies for Christian Peacemaking, Herald Press, 98; article, Religion and Nonviolent Action, Encycl of Nonviolent Action, Albert Einstein Inst, Cambridge, MA, Garland Publ Inc, 97; auth, Toward a Theology of Culture: A Dialogue with Gordon Kaufman, Mennonite Theology in Face of Modernity Essays in Honor of Gordon D. Kaufman, Bethel Col, 96; auth, Living on the Boundary: Singing God's Song as Citizens and Aliens, A Drink From the Stream II, Bethel Col, 96; auth, A Personal Response to J. L. Burkholder's Autobiographical Reflections, The Limits of Perfections: A Conversation with J. Lawrence Burkholder, Inst of Anabaptist-Mennonite Studies, Conrad Grebel Col, Waterloo, Ontario, Can, 93; auth, Means and Ends: Reflections on Opposing Theologies of History, Nonviolent America: History Through the Eyes of Peace, N. Newton, Kans, Bethel Col, 93; article, Toward a Theology of Culture: A Dialogue with John Howard Yoder and Gordon Kaufman, The Conrad Grebel Rev, 39-64, spring, 98; article, What I Learned from John Howard Yoder, Mennonite Life, mar, 98; article, Towards an Anabaptist Political Philosophy, Transformation: An International Evangelical Dialogue on Mission and Ethics, oct-dec, 97; ed, Mennonite Life, Theology of Gordon Kaufman, mar, 97; article, Singing God's Song as Citizens and Aliens: A Christian Theology of Culture, The Mennonite Quart Rev, apr, 97; article, A People's Movement as a Condition for the Development of a Just Peacemaking Theory, The Merton Annual, 9, 96; article, An Anabaptist Theology of Culture for a New Century, Conrad Grebel Rev, 33-53, winter, 95; auth, Christian Peacemaking and International Conflict: a Realist Pacifist Perspective (Scottdale, PA: Herold Press, 86). **CONTACT ADDRESS** Box 31, North Newton, KS 67117. **EMAIL** dfriesen@bethelks.edu

FRIESEN, LAUREN
PERSONAL Born 01/05/1943, NE, m, 1970, 2 children **DISCIPLINE** THEATRE, RELIGION **EDUCATION** Bethel Col, BA, 67; Pac School Relig, MA, 81; Univ Berkeley, PhD, 85. **CAREER** Freelance writer, 70-75; educ dir, Wash Comm for Humanities, 76-98; prof, Goshen Col, 82-97; dir of playwriting, Univ of Mich, 97-. **HONORS AND AWARDS** Merit Awd for Excellence in Teaching, Mich, 99; Excellence in Univ Theater, 98; Outstanding Achievement in Univ Theatre, IA, 97. **MEMBERSHIPS** The Dramatists Guild, Asn for Theatre in Higher Educ. **RESEARCH** Playwriting, 20th Century Theatre. **SELECTED PUBLICATIONS** Ed, Best Student One-Acts, Dramatic Pub Co, 95; auth, Wildflowers, Aran Press, 99; auth, "Transcendence in Modern and Post Modern Plays, 99; auth, King David, Samuel French, Inc., 89. **CONTACT ADDRESS** Dept Drama & Theatre, Univ of Michigan, Flint, 303 E Kearsley St, Flint, MI 48502-1907. **EMAIL** lfriesen@flint.umich.edu

FRIGGE, S. MARIELLE
DISCIPLINE RELIGIOUS STUDIES **EDUCATION** Mt Marty Col, BA, 67; Wash Theol Union, MA, 79; Boston Col, PhD, 92. **CAREER** Prof. **MEMBERSHIPS** Benedictine Sisters of Sacred Heart Monastery; Theta Alpha Kappa; Cath Bibl Asn & Amer Benedictine Acad. **SELECTED PUBLICATIONS** Auth, Mundane Mysteries: Daily Life as Sacrament, Amer Benedictine Acad, Atchison, KS, 94 & Modern Feminism and Monastic Women: A Dialogue, triennial chap of the Benedictine Fed St Gertrude the Great, Yankton, SD, 90; assoc ed, Amer Benedictine Rev, 95-97. **CONTACT ADDRESS** Dept of Hum, Mount Marty Col, Yankton, 1105 W 8th St, Yankton, SD 57078-3724. **EMAIL** mfrigge@rs6.mtmc.edu

FRIQUEGNON, MARIE
PERSONAL Born 11/11/1943, New York, NY, m, 1974, 2 children **DISCIPLINE** PHILOSOPHY **EDUCATION** Barnard, BA, 65; New York Univ, MA, 67, PhD, 74. **CAREER** 31 years at William Paterson Univ, NJ, full prof. **MEMBERSHIPS** APA. **RESEARCH** Philosophy of childhood, ethics, philosophy of religion, Buddhism. **SELECTED PUBLICATIONS** Coauth with R. Aberlon, The Philosophical Immigration, St Martins (78); coauth with R. Aberlon, Ethics for Modern Life, 5th ed, St Martins Press (95); coauth with R. Aberlon, Clarity and Vision, Randall Hunt (2000); auth, On Shantarakshita, Wadsworth (forthcoming). **CONTACT ADDRESS** Dept Philos, William Paterson Univ of New Jersey, 300 Pompton Rd, Wayne, NJ 07470-2103.

FRISCH, MATHIAS F.
PERSONAL Born 04/07/1964, Munich, Germany, m, 1990 **DISCIPLINE** PHILOSOPHY **EDUCATION** Univ Calif Berkeley, PhD, 98. **CAREER** Asst Prof, Northwest Univ, 98-. **MEMBERSHIPS** Am Philos Asn; Phil of Sci Asn; Gesellrchaft fur Analytische Philosophie. **RESEARCH** Philosophy of Science; role of models in scientific theorizing and scientific explanations. **SELECTED PUBLICATIONS** Auth, "Van Fraassen's Dissolution of Putnam's Model Theoretic Argument," Philosophy of Science, 99; auth, "(Dis-)Solving the Puzzle of the Arrow of Radiation British Journal for the Philosophy of Science, 00. **CONTACT ADDRESS** Northwestern Univ, 1818 Hunman Hall, Evanston, IL 60208. **EMAIL** m-frisch@nwu.edu

FRITSCHE, JOHANNES
DISCIPLINE PHILOSOPHY **EDUCATION** Free Univ Berlin, PhD, 82. **CAREER** Assoc prof, Eugene Lang Col. **RESEARCH** Ancient philos; medieval philos; early Frankfurt School. **SELECTED PUBLICATIONS** Auth, Method and Aim in The First Book of Aristotle's Physics, 86. **CONTACT ADDRESS** Eugene Lang Col, New Sch for Social Research, 66 West 12th St, New York, NY 10011.

FRITZ, RON
DISCIPLINE LAW **EDUCATION** Windsor Univ, LLB, 71; London Univ, LLM, 72. **CAREER** Reseacher for the Family Law Project, Law Reform Commission of Canada, 72-74; asst dean, 82-86; Deputy chairperson of the Federal Electoral Boundaries Commission of Saskatchewan. **MEMBERSHIPS** Member of the Bd of Trustees of the Law School Admissions Council. **SELECTED PUBLICATIONS** Auth, The Saskatchewan Electoral Boundaries Case and Its Implications, 92; Effective Representation Denied: MacKinnon v. Prince Edward Island, 94; Drawing Electoral Boundaries in Compliance with the Charter: The Alberta Experience, 96. **CONTACT ADDRESS** Col of Law, Univ of Saskatchewan, 15 Campus Dr, Saskatoon, SK, Canada S7N 5A6. **EMAIL** Fritz@law.usask.ca

FRIZZELL, LAWRENCE E.
PERSONAL Born 05/28/1938, Calgary, AB, Canada **DISCIPLINE** BIBLICAL STUDIES **EDUCATION** Univ Oxford, PhD, 74; Pontifical Bibl Inst, SSL, 67; Univ Ottawa, STL, 62. **CAREER** Instr, St. Joseph's Sem, 62-64, 67-70; assoc prof, Seton Hall Univ, 75-; dir, Inst Judaeo-Christian Studies, 93-. **HONORS AND AWARDS** Can Coun grant for doctorate studies, 70-73. **MEMBERSHIPS** Soc Bibl Lit; Cath Bibl Asn; Bibl Theol. **RESEARCH** Christian origins; Christian-Jewish relations. **SELECTED PUBLICATIONS** Auth, Temple and Community: Foundations for Johannine Spirituality, Mystics of the Book, 93; auth, Twenty-five Years Since Vatican II on the Jewish People: An Assessment, New Visions: Historical and Theological Perspectives on the Jewish-Christian Dialogue, 93; auth, Paul the Pharisee, Jewish-Christian Relations Throughout History, 94; auth, Spoils from Egypt Between Jews and Gnostics, Hellenization Revisited: Shaping the Christian Response within the Greco-Roman World, 94; auth, Mary and the Biblical Heritage, Marian Studies, 95; auth, Law at the Service of Humankind, Seeds of Reconciliation, 96; auth, The Bible and the Holy Land: Pastoral Letter from Jerusalem, New Blackfriars, 94; Jewish-Christian Relations and the Dialogue with World Religions, SIDIC, 95; auth, Rabbi, Theologische Realenzyklopadie, 96; auth, The Magnifiat: Sources and Themes, Marian Studies, 99; auth, "The Jews' in the Fourth Gospel," Radici dell' Antigiudaismo in Ambiente Cristiano, 00. **CONTACT ADDRESS** Dept of Jewish-Christian Studies, Seton Hall Univ, So Orange, South Orange, NJ 07079. **EMAIL** frizzela@shu.edu

FROEHLICH, CHARLES DONALD
PERSONAL Born 05/07/1927, Goose Creek, TX **DISCIPLINE** THEOLOGY, CLASSICS **EDUCATION** Concordia Sem, BA, 52, BD, 55, STM, 58; Univ Tex, Austin, MA, 52. **CAREER** Instr hist, Greek & Latin, St John's Col, Kans, 50-52; instr, New Testament & Greek, Concordia Sem, 55-57; instr, theol & Latin, Lutheran High Schs, St Louis, 57-62; assoc prof, 62-80, Prof Theol & Class Lang, Concordia Teachers Col, Ill, 80- **MEMBERSHIPS** Class Asn Midwest & S. **RESEARCH** New Testament; medieval Christianity; patristics. **SELECTED PUBLICATIONS** Auth, Logophiles of the world, unite!, Lutheran Educ, 11-12/73. **CONTACT ADDRESS** Dept of Theol, Concordia Univ, Illinois, 7400 Augusta St, River Forest, IL 60305-1402.

FROHLICH, MARY
PERSONAL Born 06/15/1950, Athens, OH **DISCIPLINE** SPIRITUALITY **EDUCATION** Antioch Col, BA, 73; Cath Univ, MA, 82; PhD, 90. **CAREER** Lectr, Trinity Coll, 90-02; lectr, Wheeling Jesuit Coll, 91-92; lectr, Cath Univ Am, 86-88 and 91-92; lectr, Georgetown Univ, 91-92; lectr, St Michael's Coll, 94; asst prof, Cath Theol Univ, 93-. **HONORS AND AWARDS** AAUW Dissertation Fel, 88. **MEMBERSHIPS** Soc for the Study of Christian Spirituality; Am Acad of Rel; Cath Theol Soc of Am; Coll Theol Soc. **RESEARCH** Spiritual Classics; Spirituality and Psychology; Ecospirituality. **SELECTED PUBLICATIONS** Auth, Praying with Scripture, 93; The Intersubjectivity of the Mystic: A Study of Teresa of Avila's Interior Castle, 93; articles on spirituality, 87-01; auth, The Lay Contemplative, 00. **CONTACT ADDRESS** Catholic Theol Union at Chicago, 5401 S Cornell Ave, Chicago, IL 60615. **EMAIL** frohlich@ctu.edu

FROMENT-MEURICE, MARC
PERSONAL Born 10/30/1953, Tokyo, Japan, m, 3 children **DISCIPLINE** FRENCH LITERATURE, PHILOSOPHY **EDUCATION** Univ Paris, Doctorat de 3 Cycle (PhD), 79; Univ Nice-Sophia Antipolis, Doctorat D'Etat, 92. **CAREER** Vis prof, Univ of Washington, 89-91; vis prof, Univ de Montreal, 92; vis prof, Univ Calif, Irvine, 93; vis prof, La State Univ, 95-96; full prof, Vanderbilt Univ, 96-. **HONORS AND AWARDS** Fel, Centre National Du Livre, Paris, France, 93-94. **MEMBERSHIPS** MLA, Colleoe International de Philosophie. **RESEARCH** Continental philosophy (Heideguer)- Deconstruction theory; XIXth and XXth century French literature (emphasis on poetry). **SELECTED PUBLICATIONS** Auth, Les Intermittences de la raison, Penser Cage, Entendre Heidegger, Paris: Klincksieck (82); auth, La Disparue, Paris: Gallimard (87); auth, Solitudes, De Rimbaud a Heidegger, Paris: Galilee (89); auth, La Chose Meme, Solitudes II, Paris: Galilee (92); auth, Tombeau de Trakl, Paris: Berlin (92); auth, Solitudes, From Rimbaud to Heidegger, transl by D. Brick & P .Walsh, Albany, NY: SUNY Press (95); auth, That Is To Say. Heidegger's Poetics, transl by Jan Plug, Stanford, CA: Stanford Univ Press (98); auth, Lignes de Fuite, with graphics by Roberto Altmann, La Souterraine: La Main Courante (98); auth, "Personne a/a ce nom," in L'animal autobiographique. Autour du travail de Jacques Derrida, ed Marie-Louise Mallet, Paris: Galilee (99); auth, "In No Way," Po&sie, 90, Paris: Berlin (99); auth, "Aphasia or the Last Word," in Philosophy and Tragedy, ed Miguel de Beistegui and Simon Sparks, London: Routledge (2000). **CONTACT ADDRESS** Dept French & Italian, Vanderbilt Univ, 2201 W End Ave, Nashville, TN 37235-0001. **EMAIL** Mfment@ctrvax.vanderbilt.edu

FROST, JERRY WILLIAM
PERSONAL Born 03/17/1940, Muncie, IN, m, 1963, 1 child **DISCIPLINE** AMERICAN & CHURCH HISTORY **EDUCATION** DePauw Univ, BA, 62; Univ Wis, MA, 65, PhD, 68. **CAREER** Asst prof Am hist, Vassar Col, 67-73; assoc prof & dir relig, Friends Hist Libr, 73-79, prof, 79, Jenkins prof Quaker hist & res, Swarthmore Col, 80-, Fel, John Carter Brown Libr, 70; USIP Fel, 85, Philadelphia Inst for Early Am Studies Fel, 80, Lang Fel, 81, 97; ed, Pa Mag Hist & Biog, 81-86. **HONORS AND AWARDS** Brit Friends Hist Asn, pres, 98. **MEMBERSHIPS** Friends Hist Soc; Am Soc Church Hist. **RESEARCH** Quakers; Am family; peace research. **SELECTED PUBLICATIONS** Auth, Quaker Family in Colonial America, St Martins, 73; Connecticut Education in the Revolutionary Era, Pequot, 74; Origins of the Quaker crusade against slavery: A review of recent literature, spring 78, Quaker Hist; ed, The Keithian Controversy in Early Pennsylvania, 80 & Quaker Origins of Antislavery, 81, Norwood; Years of crisis and separation: Philadelphia yearly meeting, 1790-1860, In: Friends in the Delaware Valley, 81; Seeking the Light, Essays in Quaker History, Pendle Hill, 87; co-auth, The Quakers, Greenwood, 88; auth, A Perfect Freedom: Religious Liberty in Pennsylvania, Cambridge, 90; Our deeds carry our message: The early history of the American Friends Service Committee, Quaker Hist, 92; co-auth, Christianity: a Social and Cultural History, Prentice Hall, 98. **CONTACT ADDRESS** Friends Hist Libr, Swarthmore Col, 500 College Ave, Swarthmore, PA 19081-1306.

FRUG, GERALD E.
PERSONAL Born 07/31/1939, Berkeley, CA, w, 2 children **DISCIPLINE** LAW **EDUCATION** Univ Calif, AB, 60; Harvard Law Sch, LLB, 63. **CAREER** Atty, San Francisco, 65-66; asst to the chair, U.S. Equal Employment Opportunity Commission, 66-69; atty, New York City, 69-70; coun and admin, Health Serv Admin New York, 70-74; assoc prof and prof, Univ Pa, 74-81; prof, Harvard Univ, 81-. **RESEARCH** Urban Law. **SELECTED PUBLICATIONS** Auth, "Administrative Democracy," U Tor L J, 90; auth, "Decentering Decentralization," U Chi L Rev, 93; auth, "The Geography of Community," Stan L Rev, 96; auth, "City Services, NYU L Rev, 98; auth, City Making: Building Communities Without Building Walls, Princeton Univ Press, 99; auth, "Euphemism as a Political Strategy," Environ L Reptr, 00; co-auth, Local Government Law, 3rd ed, Wes Pub Co, 01 **CONTACT ADDRESS** Sch of Law, Harvard Univ, 1525 Massachusetts Ave, Cambridge, MA 02138. **EMAIL** frug@law.harvard.edu

FRY, GERALD W.
PERSONAL Born 06/15/1942, Wichita, KS, m, 1970, 1 child **DISCIPLINE** POLITICAL SCIENCE **EDUCATION** Stanford Univ, BA, 64; PhD, 77; Princeton Univ, MPA, 66. **CAREER** Acting assoc prof, Stanford Univ, 80-81; asst prof, Univ of Ore, 81-82; assoc dir to dir, Univ Ore, 83-00; prof, Univ of

Minn, 00-. **HONORS AND AWARDS** Pew Fel, Harvard Univ, 91. **MEMBERSHIPS** Assoc of Asian Studies; Comp and Int Educ Soc. **RESEARCH** Human Resource Development, Educational Reform, Political Economy of Development, Southeast Asia (primarily Thailand, Laos, Cambodia and Vietnam). **SELECTED PUBLICATIONS** Coauth, Systems of Higher Education: Thailand, Int Counc for Educ Develop, (NY), 78; coauth, Vocational-Technical Education and the Thai Labor Market, Int Inst for Educ Planning, (Paris), 80; coauth, Pacific Basin and Oceania, Clio Pr, (Oxford), 87; coauth, The International Education of Development Consultants: Communicating with Peasants and Princes, Pergamon Pr, (Oxford), 89; coauth, Evaluating Primary Education: Qualitative and Quantitative Policy Studies in Thailand, Int Develop Res Centre, (Ottawa), 90; coauth, The International Development Dictionary, ABC-Clio, ()Oxford), 91; auth, "Kamtai Sipadone"and "Chuan Leekpai", Current Leaders of Nations, Gale Research (Detroit), 98; auth, "The Future of the Lao PDR: Relations with Thailand and Alternative Paths to Internationalization", New Laos, New Challenges, ed Jacqueline Butler-Diaz, Ariz State Univ, (98): 147-179; auth, "Cambodia Rising", Register-Guard, Sept 99. **CONTACT ADDRESS** Dept Educ Policy and Admin, Univ of Minnesota, Twin Cities, 330 Wulling Hall, 86 Plesant St Se, Minneapolis, MN 55455-0221. **EMAIL** gwf81@hotmail.com

FRY, MICHAEL G.
PERSONAL Born 11/05/1932, Brierley, England, m, 1957, 3 children **DISCIPLINE** ECONOMICS, HISTORY **EDUCATION** London Sch of Econ, B Sc, 56, PhD, 63. **CAREER** Prof Hist, 66-77, Carleton Univ, Ottawa, Can; dean & prof, 77-80, Grad Sch of Int Stud, Univ Denver; dir & prof, 80-98, Univ So Calif, School of Int Affairs. **HONORS AND AWARDS** NATO fel; vpres Int Stud Asn; fel of the Royal Hist Soc, UK. **MEMBERSHIPS** Royal Hist Asn; SHAFR. **RESEARCH** North Atlantic relations; north Pacific relations; British foreign policy; Middle East. **SELECTED PUBLICATIONS** Auth, Eisenhower, Dulles and the Suez Crisis of 1956, Reexamining the Eisenhower Presidency, Greenwood Press, 93; auth, The Forgotten Crisis of 1957: Gaza and Sharm-el-Sheikh, Int Hist Rev 15, 1, 93, Revue d'Histoire Diplomatique, 93; auth, Epistemic Communities: Intelligence Studies & International Relations, Intel & Nat Security, 8, 3, 93; auth, Epistemic Communities: Intelligence Studies and International Relations, Espionage: Past, Present and Future, Cass, 94; auth, The Pacific Dominion and the Washington Conference, 1921-22, The Wash Conf, 1921-22 and The Road to Pearl Harbor, Cass, 94; auth, The United States, the United Nations and the Lebanon Crisis, 1958: Intelligence and Statecraft, in Intelligence and National Security 10,1, 95; auth, British Revisionism, Ctr for Ger & European Stud, Univ Calif, 95; auth, British Revisionism, in The 1919 Peace Settlement and Germany, Cambridge Univ Press, 96; auth, The North Pacific Triangle at Century's End: Canada, Japan and the United States, 98; ed, The Guide to Modern Politics and Diplomacy, Cassells, London. **CONTACT ADDRESS** School of Int Relations, Univ of So California, VKC 330, Univ Park, Los Angeles, CA 90089-0043.

FRYMER-KENSKY, TIKVA
PERSONAL m, 2 children **DISCIPLINE** BIBLICAL STUDIES, BIBLICAL THEORY **EDUCATION** City Col NYork, AB, 65; Jewish Theol Sem, BHL, 65; Yale Univ, MA, 67; PhD, 77. **CAREER** Asst, Yale Univ, 68-69; lectr, Mt Vernon Col, 69-71; vis asst prof, Univ Michigan, 78-79; asst prof, Wayne State Univ, 71-82; vis assoc prof, Univ Michigan 83, Jew Theol Sem 83, 88, 91-93, McMas Univ 84, Univ Michigan 84-85, 87, Ben Gurion Univ 85-86; dir, Reconstructionist Rabbinical Col, 88-95; vis ch, Hebrew Un Col, 99; prof, Univ Chicago, 95-. **HONORS AND AWARDS** CJS GNT; Annenberg Res Gnt; NEH; WSU Res Gnt; Phi Beta Kappa Sibley Fel; Danforth Fel; Woodrow Wilson Fel. **MEMBERSHIPS** AJR; SBL. **SELECTED PUBLICATIONS** Auth, In the Wake of the Goddesses: Women, Culture and the Biblical Transformation of Pagan Myth, Free Press, Macmillan (92); coauth, Feminist Approaches to the Bible, Hershel Shanks Bib Arch Soc (95); auth, Motherprayer: The Pregnant Woman's Spiritual Companion, Putnam-Riverhead (95); transl, From Jerusalem to the Edge of Heaven: Meditations on the Soul of Israel by An Elon, Jewish Pub Soc (96); co-ed, Gender and Law in the Hebrew Bible and the Ancient Near East, JSOTS, Sheffield Acad Press (98); auth, Victims, Victors and Virgins: Reading the Women of the Bible, Schocken, forthcoming; ed, Christianity Through Jewish Ideas, Westview Press, forthcoming; auth, "Constructing a Theology of Healing," in Healing in Judaism, NCJH (97); auth, "On the Women of the Exodus," Bible Rev (98); auth, "Reviewing our Foundation Myths, Bible Rev (98); auth, "Sanctifying Torah" in The Shabbat Series: Excellence in Education for Jewish Women, ed. Irene Fine (San Diego Wom Inst Cont Jewish Edu, 97); auth, "The Akedah: The View from the Bible" in Beginning Anew: A Woman's Companion to the High Holy Days, eds. Gail Twersky Reimer, Judith A Kates (Touchstone Books, 97); auth, "Reading Rahab" in Tehillah Le-Moshe: Biblical and Judaic Studies in Honor of Moshe Greenberg, eds. Moshe Greenberg, Mordechai Cogan, Barry L Eichler (Eisenbrauns, 97). **CONTACT ADDRESS** Divinity School, Univ of Chicago, 1025 East 58th St, Chicago, IL 60637. **EMAIL** tfrymerk@midway.uchicago.edu

FUERST, WESLEY J.
PERSONAL Born 10/23/1930, Hildreth, NE **DISCIPLINE** OLD TESTAMENT **EDUCATION** Midland Col, BA, 51; Cent Lutheran Theol Sem, BD, 54; Princeton Theol Sem, ThD, 58. **CAREER** Dean of fac; dir of grad stud; prof-. **SELECTED PUBLICATIONS** Auth, Key Bible Words; Cambridge Bible Commentary on The Books of Ruth Esther; Ecclesiastes; The Songs of Songs, Lamentations: The Five Scrolls. **CONTACT ADDRESS** Dept of Old Testament, Lutheran Sch of Theol at Chicago, 1100 E 55th St, Chicago, IL 60615. **EMAIL** wfuerst@lstc.edu

FUKURAI, HIROSHI
PERSONAL Born 10/22/1954, Japan, m, 1992 **DISCIPLINE** SOCIOLOGY, LEGAL STUDIES **EDUCATION** Calif State Univ, BS, 79; Univ Calif at Riverside, MA, 82; PhD, 85. **CAREER** From asst prof to assoc prof, Univ Calif at Santa Cruz, 90-. **MEMBERSHIPS** Am Soc of Criminology, Am Sociol Asn, Am Statistical Asn. **RESEARCH** Law & Society, Statistics, Race Relations, the Pacific Rim. **SELECTED PUBLICATIONS** Coauth, Common Destiny: Japan and the United States in the Global Age, McFarland & Company, Inc. (Jefferson, NC), 90; coauth, Race and Jury: Racial Disenfranchisement and the Search for Justice, Plenum Publ Corp., 93; auth, "Is O. J. Simpson Verdict and Example of Jury Nullification? Jury Verdicts, Legal Concepts, and Jury Performance in a Racially Sensitive Criminal Case," Int J of Applied and Comparative Criminal Justice 22 (98): 185-210; auth, "Social Deconstruction of Race and Affirmative Action in Jury Selection," La Raza Law J (99); auth, "Further affirmative action strategies for racial and ethnic equality in the jury system: The case study of Eugene "Bear" Lincoln trail and the Native American jury," Chican/Latino Law Rev (99); auth, "Rethinking the representative jury requirement: Jury representatives and cross-sectional participation from the beginning to the end of the jury selection process," Int J of Applied and Comparative Criminal Justice (99); auth, "Where did Hispanic jurors go? Computer graphics and statistical analysis of Hispanic participation in grand juries in California," Western Criminology Rev, forthcoming; auth, Anatomy of the McMartin Child Molestation Case: Pretrial Publicity, Jury Selection, Prosecutorial Misconduct, and Future Reforms in Child Sexual Abuse Cases, Harvard Univ Pr, forthcoming; auth, The Racialized Jury Boxes: Affirmative Action in Jury Selection and Racially Mixed Juries, SUNY Univ Pr, forthcoming. **CONTACT ADDRESS** Dept Sociol, Univ of California, Santa Cruz, 1156 High St, Santa Cruz, CA 95064. **EMAIL** hiroshi@cats.ucsc.edu

FULLER, ALFREDIA Y.
PERSONAL Born 06/19/1958, Miami, FL, d **DISCIPLINE** LAW **EDUCATION** University of Maryland, BSBA, 1982; Antioch School of Law, JD, 1986. **CAREER** Skadden, Arps, law clerk, 86-88; Fidelity Mortgage Company, president, 90-91; George Washington University, Washington Saturday College, lecturer, 92-93; Law Offices of Alfredia Y Fuller, Attorney, 88-. **MEMBERSHIPS** National Bar Association, chairman, Bankruptcy Law Section, 1993-95; National Association of Black Women Attorneys, 1995; District of Columbia Superior Court, certified mediator, 1985-; District of Columbia Bar Association, 1989-; Isle of Patmos Baptist Church WDC, trustee, 1989-91; National Bar Association, board of governors, 1993-; Washington Saturday College, board of trustees, 1992-. **SELECTED PUBLICATIONS** Contributing Writer, National Bar Association Magazine, 1994-95. **CONTACT ADDRESS** Law Offices of Alfredia Y. Fuller, 601 Pennsylvania Ave NW, Ste 700, Washington, DC 20004.

FULLER, GEORGE CAIN
DISCIPLINE PRACTICAL THEOLOGY **EDUCATION** Haverford Col, BS, 53; Princeton Theol Sem, MDiv, 56; Westminster Theol Sem, ThM, 62, ThD, 64; Babson Col, MBA, 76. **CAREER** Prof, Northwestern Col, 63-66; assoc prof, Reformed Theol Sem, 71-72; exec dir, Nat Presbyterian and Reformed Fel, 76-83; pastor, Westminster Theol Sem, 78-; pastor, Covenant Presbyterian Church, Cherry Hill, NJ, 92-. **SELECTED PUBLICATIONS** Auth, Play It My Way; ed, A Sourcebook of Mercy for Deacons; auth, Good News for All Seasons; auth, Practical Theology and the Ministry of the Church; auth, The Voice from the Cross; auth, In Search of a National Morality; auth, "Save Time and Invest People," Eternity, 82; auth, "Game of Life," Eternity, 84; auth, "The Life of Jesus, After The Ascension," Westminister Theological Journal, 94. **CONTACT ADDRESS** Westminster Theol Sem, Pennsylvania, PO Box 27009, Philadelphia, PA 19118.

FULLER, REGINALD H.
DISCIPLINE NEW TESTAMENT **EDUCATION** Univ Cambridge, BA, 37, MA, 41; Gen Theol Sem, STD; Philadelphia Divinity Sch, STD; Seabury-Western Theol Sem, DD; Nashota House, DHL; Univ South, DD. **CAREER** Lectr, Queen's Col, 46-50; Birmingham Univ, 46-50; prof, St David's Univ Col, 50-55; Seabury-Western Theol Sem, 55-66; Baldwin prof, Union Theol Sem, 66-72; Molly Laird Downs prof, 72-85; prof emeri, Va Theol Sem, 85-. **SELECTED PUBLICATIONS** Auth, The decalogue in the New Testament, reprinted from Interpretation, Richmond: Union Theol Sem in Va, 89; auth, He that cometh: the birth of Jesus in the New Testament, Harrisburg, PA: Morehouse Pub., 90; auth, The Quest of the Historical Mary, Hopes and Visions: Papers of the Ecumenical Society of the Blessed Virgin Mary in the United States of America, 96; Biblical studies 1955-1990, Anglican Theol Rev, 94; Christ and Christianity: Studies in the Formation of Christology, Trinity Press Intl, 94; Jesus as Prophet, Va Sem Jour, 94. **CONTACT ADDRESS** Virginia Theol Sem, 3737 Seminary Rd, Alexandria, VA 22304.

FULLER, ROBERT CHARLES
PERSONAL Born 05/06/1952, Grand Rapids, MI, m, 1975, 2 children **DISCIPLINE** RELIGION **EDUCATION** Denison Univ, BA, 74; Univ Chicago, PhD, 78. **CAREER** Prof Religious Studies, Bradley Univ, 78- . **RESEARCH** Contemporary American Religion **SELECTED PUBLICATIONS** "Religion and Ritual in American Wine Culture," Jour of Am Culture, 93; Alternative Therapies, The Encycl of Bioethics, Macmillan, 94; "Wine, Symbolic Boundary Setting, and American Religious Communities," Jour Am Acad Relig, 95; Holistic Health Practices, Spirituality and the Secular Quest, Crossroad, 96; Erikson, Psychology, and Religion, Pastoral Psychol, 96; "The Will to Believe: A Centennial Reflection," Jour Am Acad Religion, 96; Religion and Wine, Univ Tenn Press, 96; Naming the Antichrist, Oxford Univ Press, 95. **CONTACT ADDRESS** Dept of Religious Studies, Bradley Univ, Peoria, IL 61625. **EMAIL** rcf@bradley.bradley.edu

FULLER, RUSSELL T.
PERSONAL Born 03/25/1960, Atlanta, GA, m, 3 children **DISCIPLINE** OLD TESTAMENT, HEBREW **EDUCATION** Bob Jones Univ, BS; MA; Dropsie Col, dr stud; Hebrew Union Col, MPhil, PhD. **CAREER** Asst prof, Mid-Continent Col; asst prof, S Baptist Theol Sem, 98-. **RESEARCH** Ancient Near Eastern languages, literature and history. **SELECTED PUBLICATIONS** Contrib auth, Zondervan's The New International Dictionary of Old Testament Theology. **CONTACT ADDRESS** Old Testament Dept, So Baptist Theol Sem, 2825 Lexington Rd, Louisville, KY 40280. **EMAIL** rfuller@sbts.edu

FULOP, TIMOTHY E.
PERSONAL Born 09/02/1960, Yokohama, Japan, m, 1982, 4 children **DISCIPLINE** RELIGION **EDUCATION** Wheaton Col, BA, 82; Princeton Theol Sem, M Div, 87; Princeton Univ, MA, 90, PhD, 92. **CAREER** Instr, Drew Univ, 91-92; lectr, Princeton Univ, 92-93; visiting asst prof, Harvard Univ, 93-95; asst dean of fac, Columbia Theol Sem, 95-98; acad dean and vpres, King Col, 98-. **MEMBERSHIPS** Amer Soc of Church Hist; Conf on Faith & Hist; Amer Acad of Relig. **RESEARCH** African-American religion; New religious movements; American Evangelicalism. **SELECTED PUBLICATIONS** Ed, African-American Religion: Interpretive Essays in History & Culture, Routledge, 97. **CONTACT ADDRESS** King Col, 1350 King College Rd., Bristol, TN 37620. **EMAIL** tefulop@king.edu

FUMERTON, RICHARD
PERSONAL Born 10/07/1949, Toronto, ON, Canada, m, 1973, 2 children **DISCIPLINE** PHILOSOPHY **EDUCATION** Univ of Toronto, BA, 71; Brown Univ, MA, 73; PhD, 74. **CAREER** Asst Prof, Univ of Iowa, 74-79; Assoc Prof, Univ of Iowa, 79-85; Full Prof, Univ of Iowa, 85-; Vis Prof, Univ of Minnesota, Fall, 78. **HONORS AND AWARDS** Woodrow Wilson Fellowship, 71-72; Canada Council Fellowship, 73-74; M.L. Huitt Awd for Excellence in Teaching, Univ of iowa, 94; Regents Awd for Faculty Excellence, 97. **MEMBERSHIPS** APA. **RESEARCH** Epistemology; Metaphysics, Value:Theory. **SELECTED PUBLICATIONS** Auth, "Metaepistemology and Skepticism," Boston: Rowman and Littlefield, 96, 234 pgs; auth, "Reason and Morality: A Defense of the Egocentric Perspective, Ithaca, NY: Cornell Univ Press, 90, 247 pgs, auth, Metaphysical and Epistemological Problems of Perception," Lincoln and London: Univ of Nebraska Press, 85, 211 pgs. **CONTACT ADDRESS** Dept Philosophy, Univ Iowa, 269 English Philosophy Bld, Iowa City, IA 52242-1408. **EMAIL** richard-fumerton@uiowa.edu

FUNK, DAVID A.
PERSONAL Born 04/22/1927, Wooster, OH, m, 1976, 4 children **DISCIPLINE** LAW **EDUCATION** Wooster Col, BA, 49; Western Reserve Univ, JD, 51; Ohio State Univ, MA, 68; Case Western Reserve Univ, LLM, 72; Columbia Univ, LLM, 73. **CAREER** Partner, Funk, Funk & Eberhart, 51-72; assoc prof to prof, 73-97, Prof Emeritus Law, Ind Univ Sch of Law, Indianapolis, 97-; Vis lectr, Col Wooster, 62-63; chairperson, Law & Religion Sect, Asn Am Law Sch, 77-81. **MEMBERSHIPS** Am Soc for Legal Hist. **RESEARCH** Philosophy of law. **SELECTED PUBLICATIONS** Auth, Historische Rechtstatsachenforschung in Theorie und Praxis, In: Rechtsgeschichte und Rechtssoziologie, West Berlin, Duncker & Humblot, 85; Juridical Science Paradigms as Newer Rhetorics in 21st Century Jurisprudence, N KY Law Rev 12, 85; Applications of Political Science to the Analysis and Practice of Law, Ind Law Rev 21, 88; Varieties of Juridical Science Paradigms For 21st Century Legal Philosophy, In: Nuovi moti per la Formazione del Diritto, CEDAM, Padova, Italy, 88; Traditional Orthodox Hindu Jurisprudence: Justifying Dharma and Danda, S.U. Law Rev 15, 88; Traditional Chinese Jurisprudence: Justifying Li and Fa, S.U. Law Rev 17, 90; Traditional Japanese Jurisprudence: Justifying Loyalty and Law, S.U. Law Rev 17, 90; Traditional Islamic Jurisprudence: Justifying Islamic Law and Gov-

ernment, S.U. Law Rev 20, 93; Cotterell's Politics of Jurisprudence, Ratio Juris 6, 93; author of numerous other journal articles. **CONTACT ADDRESS** Law Sch, Indiana Univ-Purdue Univ, Indianapolis, 6208 N Delaware St, Indianapolis, IN 46220-1824.

FURDELL, ELLZABETH LANE
PERSONAL Born 04/13/1944, Harrisburg, PA, m, 1968 **DISCIPLINE** ENGLISH HISTORY, POLITICAL SCIENCE **EDUCATION** Univ Wash, BA, 66; Kent State Univ, MA, 68, PhD (hist), 73. **CAREER** Asst prof, 71-74, Assoc Prof Hist, Col Great Falls, 74-, Contribr, Hist Abstr, 73-78. **MEMBERSHIPS** AHA; Am Polit Sci Asn; Sixteenth Century Study Conf; Rocky Mountain Soc Sci Asn. **RESEARCH** London history; 16th century historiography; urban politics. **CONTACT ADDRESS** Dept of Soc Sci, Univ of Great Falls, Great Falls, MT 59405.

FURMAN, PATRICK
PERSONAL Born 09/07/1955, Oklahoma City, OK **DISCIPLINE** LAW **EDUCATION** Univ Colo, BA, 76; JD, 80. **CAREER** Dep State Pub Defender, Colo, 80-87; Atty at Law, Colo, 87-88; Prof, Univ Colo, 88-. **MEMBERSHIPS** Colo Bar Asn; Boulder Cty Bar Asn; Nat Asn of Criminal Def Lawyers; Am Bar Asn; Colo Criminal Defense. **RESEARCH** Criminal Law; Criminal Procedure; Evidence Law; Trial Advocacy. **SELECTED PUBLICATIONS** Co-auth, "The Colorado Rules of Professional Conduct: Implications for Criminal Lawyers," The Colorado Lawyer, 92; auth, "Peremptory Challenges: Free Strikes No More," The Colorado Lawyer, 93; auth, "The Introduction of Scientific Evidence in Criminal Cases," The Colorado Lawyer, 93; auth, "The Consent Exception to the Warrant Requirement," The Colorado Lawyer, 94; auth, "Avoiding Error in Closing Argument," The Colorado Lawyer, 95; auth, "Self-Defense in Colorado," The Colorado Lawyer, 95; auth, Colorado Evidentiary Foundations, Lexis Law Pub, 97; auth, "The Execution of Search Warrants," The Colorado Lawyer, 98; auth, "Publicity in High Profile Criminal Cases," St Thomas Law Rev, 98; auth, Colorado DUI Benchbook, Continuing Legal Education in Colo, inc, 01. **CONTACT ADDRESS** Sch of Law, Univ of Colorado, Boulder, 404 UCB, Boulder, CO 80301. **EMAIL** furman@colorado.edu

FURNISH, VICTOR PAUL
PERSONAL Born 11/17/1931, Chicago, IL, m, 1963, 2 children **DISCIPLINE** THEOLOGY **EDUCATION** Cornell Col (Iowa), BA, 52; Garrett-Evangelical Theological Seminary, BD, 55; Yale Univ, PhD, 60. **CAREER** Instr, 59-60, Asst Prof, 60-65, Assoc Prof, 65-71, Prof, 71-83, Univ Distinguished Prof, 83-, Perkins School of Theology, Southern Methodist Univ. **HONORS AND AWARDS** Phi Beta Kappa; United Methodist Church Scholar/Teacher Awd, 93-94; SMU Alumni Awd for Faculty Excellence, 94; L.H.D. Cornell Col, 95; Festschrift (ed by E. Lovering and J. Sumney), 96. **MEMBERSHIPS** Soc of Biblical Lit; Studiorum Novi Testamenti Societas **RESEARCH** Pauline studies; Hellenistic ethics; New Testament theology **SELECTED PUBLICATIONS** Auth, Jesus According to Paul. Understanding Jesus Today, 93; On Putting Paul in His Place, Journal of Biblical Literature, 94; The Bible and Homosexuality: Reading the Texts in Context, Homosexuality in the Church: Both Sides of the Debate, 94; Where is the Truth in Paul's Gospel, Pauline Theology: Looking Back Pressing On, 97; The Theology of the First Letter to the Corinthians, 99. **CONTACT ADDRESS** 6806 Robin Rd., Dallas, TX 75209. **EMAIL** vfurnish@mail.smu.edu

FURROW, DWIGHT
PERSONAL Born 02/09/1950, Bangor, ME, m, 1982, 1 child **DISCIPLINE** PHILOSOPHY **EDUCATION** Univ CA, Riverside, PhD, 93. **CAREER** Vis Asst Prof, Col of William and Mary, 96-. **MEMBERSHIPS** Amer Philos Assoc. **RESEARCH** Contemporary European philos; ethics. **SELECTED PUBLICATIONS** Auth, The Discomforts of Home: Nature and Technology in Hand's End, in Research in Philosophy and Technology, fall 95; Review of Richard A. Cohen, Elevations: the Height of the Good in Rosenzweig and Levinas, in Can Philos Rev, June 95; Against Theory: Continental and Analytic Challenges in Moral Philosophy, Routledge, 95; Review of Ronald Bontekoe, Dimensions of the Hermeneutic Circle, in Can Philos Rev, fall 97; Schindler's Compulsion: A Essay on Practical Necessity, in Amer Philos Quart, vol 35, no 3, July, 98; Postmodern Ethics, forthcoming in The Encyclopedia of Ethics, 2nd ed, ed Lawrence C. Becker, Garland Pub. **CONTACT ADDRESS** Dept of Philos, Col of William and Mary, PO Box 8795, Williamsburg, VA 23187-8795. **EMAIL** BQNR32A@Prodigy.com

FUSS, PETER L.
PERSONAL Born 02/11/1932, Berlin, Germany, m, 1961, 2 children **DISCIPLINE** PHILOSOPHY **EDUCATION** Fordham Univ, BS, 54; Harvard Univ, MA, 56, PhD, 62. **CAREER** Lectr philos, Univ Mich, 60-61; lectr, Univ Calif, Riverside, 61-62; from asst prof to assoc prof, 62-69; assoc prof, 69-75, Prof Philos, Univ MO, St Louis, 75-; Vis assoc prof philos, Univ Washington, 66-67. **MEMBERSHIPS** Conf Study Polit Thought; Hegel Soc Am; AAUP. **RESEARCH** Kant, Hegel and history of 19th century philosophy; political and moral philosophy. **SELECTED PUBLICATIONS** Coauth, Five Philosophers, Odyssey, 63; auth, The Moral Philosophy of Josiah Royce, 65 & co-ed & translr, Nietzsche: A Self-Portrait from His Letters, 71, Harvard Univ; auth, Some perplexities in Nietzsche, Dialogues Phenomenol, 75; Theory and practice in Hegel and Marx, Polit Theory & Praxis, 77; Royce's concept of the self, Am Philos, 77; Hannah Arendt's Conception of Political Community, Hannah Arendt, 79; coauth, Spirit as Recollection: Hegel's Theory of the Internalizing of Experience, 81; The Silhouette of Dante in Hegel's Phenomenology, Clio, 82; Hegel: 3 Essays, Notre Dame, 84; Rousseau's engagement with amour-propre, Canadian J Pol and Soc Theory, 86; The Two-in-One, Idealistic Studies, 88; James Madison and the classical Republican tradition, Philos Res Archives, 89; Kant's teleology of nature, European Studies Conf, 91; Passion and the genesis of self-consciousness, Mo Philol Asn, 93. **CONTACT ADDRESS** Dept of Philos, Univ of Missouri, St. Louis, 8001 Natural Bridge, Saint Louis, MO 63121-4499.

FYKES, LEROY MATTHEWS, JR.
PERSONAL Born 10/23/1945, Indianapolis, IN **DISCIPLINE** LAW **EDUCATION** Univ of So CA, BS 1967; Harvard U, MBA 1974; UCLA, JD 1972; NYork Univ, LlM 1976. **CAREER** Seton Hall Univ Law Ctr, asst prof; Pfizer Inc, atty 72-75; Nat Black MBA Assn, dir, bd chmn, bd sec 74-; NYCTI Assn Inc, dir 75-; Am Arbtrn Assn, arbtrn panel. **MEMBERSHIPS** Mem NY Bar Trustee, bd sec Studio Mus in Harlem 1973; mem 100 Black Men Inc of NYC. **CONTACT ADDRESS** 1111 Raymond Blvd, Newark, NJ 07102.

G

GABHART, MITCHELL
PERSONAL Born 07/11/1958, Harrodsburg, KY **DISCIPLINE** PHILOSOPHY **EDUCATION** Univ Ky, BA; MA; PhD, 93. **CAREER** Vis Asst Prof, Auburn Univ, 93-94; Lectr, Univ Ky, 94-97; Instr, Auburn Univ, 97-. **RESEARCH** History of Philosophy, especially early modern. **SELECTED PUBLICATIONS** Auth, "Mitigated Skepticism and the Absurd," Philos Investigations, 94; auth, "Freedom, Understanding and Therapy in Spinoza's Moral Psychology," Intl J of Applied Philos, 94; auth, "Spinoza, Nagel, and the View from Nowhere," S J of Philos, 94; auth, "Spinoza on Self-Preservation and Self-Destruction," J of the Hist of Philos, 99. **CONTACT ADDRESS** Dept Philos, Auburn Univ, 6093 Haley Center, Auburn, AL 36849-5210. **EMAIL** gabhami@auburn.edu

GABRIELE, EDWARD
PERSONAL Born 04/15/1952, Philadelphia, PA, s **DISCIPLINE** INTERDISCIPLINARY THEOLOGY **EDUCATION** Villanova Univ, BA/BS, 75; Catholic Theological Union, Mdiv, 80; Catholic Univ, DMin, 85. **CAREER** Dir, Office of Res Admin, Naval Medical Res Center, Bethesda, MD; Ecumenical Resident Theologian, Christ the Servant Community, Gaithersburg, MD. **MEMBERSHIPS** Am Acad of Religion; Soc of Res Admins; Nat Coun of Univ Res Admins. **RESEARCH** Ritual analysis; contemporary theological critique; theological literacy. **SELECTED PUBLICATIONS** Auth, Acting Justly, Loving Tenderly, Walking Humbly: Prayers for Peace and Justice, St. Mary's Press, 95; auth, From Many, One. Praying Our Rich and Diverse Cultural Heritage, Ave Maria Press, 95; auth, My Soul Magnifies the Lord: Celebrating Mary in Prayer, Ave Maria Press, 96; auth, Cloud Days and Fire Nights: Canticles for a Pilgrimage Out of Exile, St. Mary's Press, 97; auth, Prayer with Searchers and Saints, St. Mary's Press, 98; auth, Choosing Life and Death: Looking in the Lenten Mirror, Communication, 95; auth, Rending the Veil: The God of Theology Made Manifest, Emmanuel, 95; auth, Partaking at the Table of Justice: The Witness of Christians in Contemporary American Political Life, Emmanuel, 96; auth, Hungering for Peace, Thirsting for Justice: Praying as Jesus Taught Us, Emmanuel, 96. **CONTACT ADDRESS** 20460 Afternoon Ln, Germantown, MD 20874. **EMAIL** efg52@erols.com

GAETKE, EUGENE ROGER
PERSONAL Born 09/12/1948, St. Paul, MN, m, 1971, 2 children **DISCIPLINE** LAW **EDUCATION** Univ Minn, Minneapolis, BA, 71, JD, 74. **CAREER** Atty, Swanson and Gaetke, Grand Marias, Minn, 74-75; special asst to atty gen, Off Atty Gen, State Minn, 75-77; hearing examiner, Off Hearing Examiners, State Minn, 77-78; asst prof, 78-82, Assoc Prof Law, Col Law, Univ Ky, Lexington, 78-. **RESEARCH** Public lands; occupational safety and health; legal ethics. **SELECTED PUBLICATIONS** Auth, Government Lawyers and Their Private Clients under the Fair Housing Act, George Washington Law Rev, Vol 0065, 97. **CONTACT ADDRESS** Dept of Law, Univ of Kentucky, Bloomington, IN 47402. **EMAIL** ggaetke@pop.uky.edu

GAFFIN, RICHARD BIRCH, JR.
PERSONAL Born 07/07/1936, Peking, China, m, 1958, 3 children **DISCIPLINE** SYSTEMETIC, THEOLOGY **EDUCATION** Calvin Col, BA, 58; Westminster Theol Sem, BD, 61, ThM, 62, ThD, 69; Georg-August Univ, Goettingen, grad stud, 62-63. **CAREER** Prof, Westminster Theol Sem, 65. **SELECTED PUBLICATIONS** Auth, The Centrality of the Resurrection, (Resurrection and Redemption); Perspectives on Pentecost; The Holy Spirit and Eschatology, Kerux, 89. **CONTACT ADDRESS** Westminster Theol Sem, Pennsylvania, PO Box 27009, Philadelphia, PA 19118. **EMAIL** rgaffin@hslc.org

GAFFNEY, JOHN PATRICK
PERSONAL Born 04/04/1928, New York, NY **DISCIPLINE** THEOLOGY, PHILOSOPHY **EDUCATION** St Louis de Montfort Sem, STB, 54; Pontif Univ St Thomas, Rome, STL, 56, STD, 57. **CAREER** Prof dogmatic theol, St Louis de Montfort Sem, 57-61, rector and prof Mariol, 62-66; lectr theol, Cath Univ PR and Inter-Am Univ PR, 66-67; assoc profand mem bd dirs divinity sch, 69-74, chmn dept, 69-75, PROF THEOL, ST LOUIS UNIV, 74-,Prof theol, Seat of Wisdom Col, 59-61; supvr, Montfort House Studies, St Louis, Mo, 68-75; examr, NCent Asn Cols and Univs, 69-; vchmn theol comn, St Louis Archdiocese, 70-; assoc ed, Horizons, Col Theol Soc, 80; vis lectr, Mt St Mary's Col, Los Angeles, 82. **HONORS AND AWARDS** Nancy McNeir Ring for Best Teacher of Year, St Louis Univ, 72. **MEMBERSHIPS** Col Theol Soc; Am Acad Relig; Mariological Soc Am. **RESEARCH** Christology; Mariology. **SELECTED PUBLICATIONS** Auth, Should theology be a required course?, Liguorian Mag, 7/73; Spiritual Maternity of Mary According to St Louis de Montfort, Montfort, 76; Let theology be theology, Horizons; Marian spirituality of St Louis de Montfort and process thought, In: Marianum, Rome, 78; Introd to The Complete Works of St Louis de Montfort, Montfort Publ, 82. **CONTACT ADDRESS** Dept of Theol Studies, Saint Louis Univ, Saint Louis, MO 63103.

GAFNI, ABRAHAM J.
DISCIPLINE TRIAL PRACTICE **EDUCATION** Yeshiva Univ, BA, BHL, 60; Harvard Law Sch, JD, 63. **CAREER** Prof & dir,Villanova Univ, 94. **HONORS AND AWARDS** Distinguished serv awd, Pa Conf State Trial Judges; Outstanding serv awd, Pa Dist Attorneys Asn; Distinguished serv awd, Philadelphia Bar Asn. **MEMBERSHIPS** Past Justice, Supreme Ct of the World Zionist Orgn; chem resolutions comt, Jewish Agency Assembly; Steering Comt, Pa Futures Comn on Justice in the 21st Century; Medical Ethics Comt, Philadelphia Geriatric Ctr. **RESEARCH** Trial advocacy; dispute resolution. **SELECTED PUBLICATIONS** Publ in, Temple Law Quart & Pa Law Quart. **CONTACT ADDRESS** Law School, Villanova Univ, 800 Lancaster Ave, Villanova, PA 19085-1692. **EMAIL** gafni@law.vill.edu

GAGNON, CAROLLE
DISCIPLINE PHILOSOPHY **EDUCATION** Laval Univ, PhD. **RESEARCH** Logic; linguistics; semiotics; aesthetics. **SELECTED PUBLICATIONS** Coauth, Marcel Barbeau: le regard en fugue, Edition anglaise: Fugato, meme editeur, (90): 243; auth, "Modelisation semiotique de la peinture gestuelle," Recherches semiotiques/Semiotic Inquiry, 12, (92): 239-259; auth, "Le feminisme est-il une ideologie?" Les cahiers du GRAD, Universite Laval, Faculte de philosophie, 7, (93): 9-20; auth, Marie-Helene Allain: la symbolique de la pierre/Marie-Helene Allain: the symbolism of stone, Moncton, NB: Les Editions de l'Acadie, (94): 175; auth, "Acquistion des connaissances et reconnaissance des acquis," Dans L'Evaluation des acquis extrascolaires, (Moncton, NB: Universite de Moncton, 94): 29-43; auth, "Approche semiotique de la representation de la femme dans la peinture du Surrealisme," Semiotica, 106, (95): 273-299; auth, "Phenomenal Reality in a Key Chapter of The Blood of Others," Simone de Beauvoir Studies, 15, (98-99): 96-104; auth, "Le mythe de la caverne de Platon comme metaphore de la matrice: Irigaray a la recherche de nouveaux modeles de societe, Arachne, 6.1, 99; auth, "Il doit quand meme y avoir un pays ou on puisse vivre: les themes de l'espoir et de la responsabilite dans Les mandarins," Simone de Beauvoir Studies, 16, 99-00. **CONTACT ADDRESS** Philosophy Dept, Laurentian Univ, 935 Ramsey Lake Rd, Sudbury, ON, Canada P3E 2C6.

GAINES, ROBERT N.
PERSONAL Born 01/15/1950, Sulphur, OK, m, 1993 **DISCIPLINE** PHILOSOPHY OF COMMUNICATIONS **EDUCATION** Univ Iowa, PhD, 82. **CAREER** Assoc prof; grad dir, Univ MD, 86-. **RESEARCH** Rhetorical theory in ancient times. **SELECTED PUBLICATIONS** Auth, Cicero's Response to the Philosophers in De oratore, Book 1, Rhetoric and Pedagogy: Its History, Philosophy, and Practice. Essays in Honor of James J. Murphy, Lawrence Erlbaum Assoc, Inc, 95; Knowledge and Discourse in Gorgias' On the Non-Existent or On Nature, Philos & Rhet 30, 97. **CONTACT ADDRESS** Dept of Commun, Univ of Maryland, Col Park, 4229 Art-Sociology Building, College Park, MD 20742-1335. **EMAIL** rg1@umail.umd.edu

GAINEY, RANDY R.
PERSONAL Born 05/11/1963, Atlanta, GA, s **DISCIPLINE** SOCIOLOGY, CRIMINAL JUSTICE **EDUCATION** Univ Wash, PhD, 95. **CAREER** Asst Prof, Old Dom Univ, 95-. **MEMBERSHIPS** Am Soc of Criminology, ASA. **RESEARCH** Fear of crime, sentencing, alternative punishments. **SELECTED PUBLICATIONS** Coauth, "Participation in a Parent Training Program for Methadone Clients," Addictive

Behav, 20 (95): 117-125; coauth, "Reducing Parental Risk Factors for Children's Substance Misuse: Preliminary Outcomes with Addicted Parents," Substance Use & Misuse, 32 (97): 699-721; coauth, ""A Meta-Analysis of Patient Factors Associated with Continued Drug Use During and After Treatment for Opiate Addiction," Addiction, 93 (98): 73-92; coauth, "How Monitoring Punishes," J of Offender Monitoring, 12 (99): 23-26; coauth, "Attitudes Towards Electronic Monitoring Among Monitored Offenders and Criminal Justice Students," J of Offender Monitoring, 29 (99): 195-208; coauth, "Electronic Monitoring Directors' Attitudes About Good Time," J of Criminal Justice (forthcoming). **CONTACT ADDRESS** Dept Sociol, Old Dominion Univ, Norfolk, VA 23529.

GAISER, FREDERICK J.

DISCIPLINE OLD TESTAMENT **EDUCATION** Kalamazoo Col, BA, 59; Evangel Lutheran Theol Sem, MDiv, 63; Univ Heidelberg, Ger, ThD, 85. **CAREER** Instr, CENCOAD, Augustana Col, Sioux Falls; act dean of students, 86-88; lectr, 73; registrar, 75-77; dir, Grad Stud (s); prof, 81-. **HONORS AND AWARDS** Res chemist, Upjohn Pharm, 59-60; interim pastor, Emmanuel Lutheran Church, Warren, Ohio, 63; pastor, St. Paul Lutheran Church, 69-74. **MEMBERSHIPS** Mem, Soc Bibl Lit. **SELECTED PUBLICATIONS** Auth, Psalms, Search Bible Stud, Unit 13; contrib, A Handbook on Conversion; A Primer on Christian Prayer; ed, Word & World, 88. **CONTACT ADDRESS** Dept of Old Testament, Luther Sem, 2481 Como Ave, Saint Paul, MN 55108. **EMAIL** fgaiser@luthersem.edu

GALAMBOS, LOUIS PAUL

PERSONAL Born 04/04/1931, Fostoria, OH, m, 1991, 4 children **DISCIPLINE** ECONOMIC HISTORY **EDUCATION** Ind Univ, BA, 55; Yale Univ, MA, 57, PhD, 60. **CAREER** Asst prof Hist, Rice Univ, 60-66 assoc prof Hist, 66-70; prof Hist, Livingston Col Rutgers Univ, 70-71; prof Hist, Johns Hopkins Univ, 71-, vis asst prof, Johns Hopkins Univ, 65-66; ed, Papers of Dwight D Eisenhower, 71-; coed, J Econ Hist, 76-78; Nat Endowment for Humanities sr fel, 78-79; Woodrow Wilson Center fel, 85-86. **HONORS AND AWARDS** Pres, Economic Hist Assn; pres, business hist conf, 91-92. **MEMBERSHIPS** AHA; Econ Hist Asn; Bus Hist Asn; Am Econ Asn; Orgn Am Historians. **RESEARCH** American economic history; business history. **SELECTED PUBLICATIONS** Auth, The Emerging Organizational Synthesis in Modern American History, Bus Hist Rev, Autumn 70; The Public Image of Big Business In America, 1880-1940, John Hopkins Univ, 75; ed, The Papers of Dwight David Eisenhower, Johns Hopkins Univ, Vol VI-IX, 78; co-ed, Studies in Economic History and Policy: The United States in the Twentieth Century, Cambridge Univ Press, 81; The Triumph of Oligopoly, in American Economic Development, Stanford Univ, 93; coauth, "Organizing and Reorganizing the World Bank, 1946-1972," Business History Review, 95; auth, "The Authority and Responsibility of the Chief Executive Officer," Industrial and Corporate change, 95; co-auth, "The McNamara Bank and Its Legacy, 1968-1987, Business and Economic History, 95; coauth, Networks of Innovation, Cambridge Univ Press, 95; co-auth, The Transformation of the Pharmaceutical Industry in the Twentieth Century, Science in the Twentieth Century, Harwood, 97; auth, "State Owned Enterprise in a Hostile Environment," and "Schumpeter Revisited," in The Rise and Fall of State Owned Enterprise, 00. **CONTACT ADDRESS** Dept of History, Johns Hopkins Univ, Baltimore, 3400 N Charles St, Baltimore, MD 21218-2680. **EMAIL** galambos@jhunix.hcf.jhu.edu

GALANTER, MARC

PERSONAL Born 02/18/1931, Philadelphia, PA, m, 1967, 3 children **DISCIPLINE** LAW, SOCIOLOGY OF LAW **EDUCATION** Univ Chicago BA, 50, MA, 54, JD, 56. **CAREER** Instr law, Univ Chicago, 56-57; asst prof, Stanford Univ, 58-59; from vis asst prof to assoc prof soc sci, Univ Chicago, 59-71; prof law, State Univ NY Buffalo, 71-76; vis prof, 76-77, Prof Law & S Asian Studies, Law Sch, Univ Wis, 77-; Centennial Prof Law, London Sch of Economics, 00; ed, Law & Soc Rev, 72-76; mem comt on law & soc sci, Soc Sci Res Coun, 75-84; mem adv panel for law & soc sci prog, NSF, 76-78; consult, Ford Found, New Delhi, 81-84; chmn, Int Union Anthrop Ethnol Sci Comn on Folk Law & Legal Pluralism, 81-83; pres, Law & Soc Asn, 83-85; Dir, disputes processing res prog, 84-; Dir, Inst Legal Studies, 90-98. **HONORS AND AWARDS** Kalven Prize, Law & Soc Asn; Hon prof, Nat Law Sch India; Sr fel, Law & Modernization Prog, Yale Univ, 70-71; Nat Endowment for Humanities, 79-80; fel, Van Leer Jerusalem Found, 80; Guggenheim Found fel, 85-86; fel, Center Advan Studies Behavioral Sci, 97-98. **MEMBERSHIPS** Law & Soc Asn; Am Law Inst; Am Acad Arts & Sci. **RESEARCH** Law and soc change; lawyers, litigation; law and relig. **SELECTED PUBLICATIONS** Auth, Religious freedoms in the United States: A turning point, Wis Law Rev, 66; The abolition of disabilities: Untouchability and the law, In: The Untouchables in Contemporary India, Univ Ariz, 72; auth, Why the haves come out ahead: Speculations on the limits of legal change, 74; Justice in many rooms: Courts, private ordering and indigenous law, J Legal Pluralism, 81; Reading the Landscape of Disputes, UCLA Law Rev, 83; Competing Equalities, Law, and the Backward Classes in India, Univ of Calif Press, 1984; Law and Society in Modern India, Oxford Univ Press, 89; Tournament of lawyers, Univ Chicago Press, 91; News from Nowhere, Denver Law Rev, 92; Real World Torts, Md Law Rev, 96. **CONTACT ADDRESS** Law Sch, Univ of Wisconsin, Madison, 975 Bascom Mall, Madison, WI 53706-1301. **EMAIL** msgalant@facstaff.wisc.edu

GALGAN, GERALD J.

PERSONAL Born 06/12/1942, New York, NY **DISCIPLINE** PHILOSOPHY **EDUCATION** Fordham Univ, PhD, 71. **CAREER** St Francis Col, Brooklyn, prof, ch dept philos, 66-. **MEMBERSHIPS** APA, ACPA, HSA. **RESEARCH** Modern and medieval philosophy. **SELECTED PUBLICATIONS** Auth, The Logic of Modernity, NY univ Press, 82; God and Subjectivity, Lang, 90; auth, Interpreting the Present, Univ Press Amer, 93. **CONTACT ADDRESS** Dept of Philosophy, St. Francis Col, 180 Remsen St., Brooklyn, NY 11201.

GALIS, LEON

PERSONAL Born 05/16/1939, Athens, GA, m, 1968 **DISCIPLINE** PHILOSOPHY **EDUCATION** Univ GA, AB, 61; Univ NC, PhD, 66. **CAREER** From Asst Prof to Assoc Prof, 65-92, Prof Philos, Franklin & Marshall Col, 92. **MEMBERSHIPS** Am Philos Asn. **RESEARCH** Soc philos; ethics. **SELECTED PUBLICATIONS** Auth, Merely Academic Diversity, J Higher Educ, 64; Of Words and Tools Again, Inquiry, 68; co-ed, Knowing: Essays in the Analysis of Knowledge, Random, 70; auth, The Democratic Case Against the Democratic College, J of Higher Educ, 73; The State-Soul Analogy in Plato's Argument that Justice Pays, J Hist of Philos, 74; The Real and Unrefuted Rights Thesis, Philos Rev, 92; Medea's Metamorphosis, Eranos, 92. **CONTACT ADDRESS** Franklin and Marshall Col, PO Box 3003, Lancaster, PA 17604-3003. **EMAIL** LeonGalis@aol.com

GALL, ROBERT

PERSONAL Born 01/13/1958, Los Angeles, CA, s **DISCIPLINE** RELIGION, PHILOSOPHY **EDUCATION** Univ of Pa, BA, 78; Temple Univ, MA, 80; PhD, 84. **CAREER** Lectr, asst prof, Univ of N Iowa, 84-85;asst prof, Blackburn Col, 86-87; asst prof, Sinclair Comm Col, 88-95; asst prof, Park Col, 95-00; adj grad fac, Univ of Miss, 96-. **HONORS AND AWARDS** Who's Who Among America's Teachers, 98, 00; Who's Who in Religion, 92094; NEH Summer Sem, 91, 94; NEH Summer Inst, 90. **MEMBERSHIPS** Am Acad of Relig; Am Philos Assoc; Soc of Phenomenology and Existential Philos; Int Assoc of Philos and Lit. **RESEARCH** Philosophy of Relgion, Contempory Continental Philosophy i.e., Heidegger, Derrida, etc. **SELECTED PUBLICATIONS** Auth, "Mysticism and Ontology: A Heideggerian Critique of Caputo", The S Jour of Philos 24 (86):463-478; auth, Beyond Theism and Atheism: Heidegger's Significance for Religious Thinking, Dordrecht: Martinus Nijhoff, 87; auth, "Tragedy or Religion? A Question of 'Radical Hermeneutics'", Philos Today 32 (88):244-255; auth, "Heidegger, Tragedy, and Ethical Reflection", Int Studies in Philos XXI (89):33-48; auth, "Of/From Theology and Deconstruction", Jour of the Am Acad of Relig (90):413-437; auth, "Toward a Tragic Theology: The Piety of Thought in Heidegger and Tragedy", Jour of Lit and Theol 7 (93):13-32; auth, "Living On (Happily) Ever After: Derrida, Philosophy and the Comic", Philos Today 38 (94):167-180; auth, "Danger: Philosophy of Religion", Philos Today 42 (98):393-401; auth, "Kami and Daimon: A Cross-Cultural Reflection on What is Divine", Philos E and W 49 (99):63-74; auth, "Interrupting Speculation:The Thinking of Heidegger as Re-enactment of Greek Tragedy", Thinking Between Philos and Poetry, NW Univ Pr, 00. **CONTACT ADDRESS** Dept Relig & Philos, Park Col, 7825 NW 86th Terr, Kansas City, MO 64153. **EMAIL** rsgall@planetkc.com

GALLAGHER, DAVID M.

PERSONAL Born 12/19/1956, Binghamton, NY, s **DISCIPLINE** PHILOSOPHY **EDUCATION** Univ Navarra, Spain, BA, 80; Catholic Univ of Am, MA, 84, PhD, 89. **CAREER** Asst prof, 88-94, assoc prof, 94-99 , Catholic Univ of Am. **MEMBERSHIPS** APA; Am Catholic Philos Asn; Societe Int pour la Etude de la Philos Medievale. **RESEARCH** Ethics; Thomas Aquinas. **SELECTED PUBLICATIONS** Ed, Thomas Aquinas and His Legacy, Catholic University of America, 94; auth, Thomas Aquinas, in Roth, ed, Ready Reference: Ethics, Salem, 94; auth, Free Choice and Free Judgement in Thomas Aquinas, Archiv fur Geschichte der Philosophie, 94; auth, Person and Ethics in Thomas Aquinas, Acta Philos, 95; auth, Aquinas, Abelard and the Ethics of Intention, in Lockey, ed, Studies in Thomistic Theology, Univ of Notre Dame, 96; auth, Desire for Beatitude and Love of Friendship in Thomas Aquinas, Mediaeval Stud, 96; auth, Moral Virtue and Contemplation: A Note on the Unity of the Moral Life, Sapientia, 96; auth, The Role of God in the Philosophical Ethics of Thomas Aquinas, in Was ist Philosophie in Mittelalter? Miscellanea Mediaevalia vol 26, Berlin: Walter de Gruyter, 98; Gewirth, Sterba, and the Justification of Mortality, in Gerwith: Critical Essays on Action, Rationality, and Community, Rowan & Littlefield, 99, pp 183-89; auth, Thomas Awuinas on Self-love as the Basis for Love of Others, Acta Philosophica 8, 99; The Will, in Essays on the Ethics of Thomas Aquinas, Wash: Georgetown Univ Pr, 02, forthcoming. **CONTACT ADDRESS** 139 E 34th St, New York, NY 10016. **EMAIL** dgallagher@mhplace.net

GALLAGHER, SHAUN

PERSONAL Born Philadelphia, PA, m, 1983, 2 children **DISCIPLINE** PHILOSOPHY **EDUCATION** Villanova Univ, MA, 76; SUNY, MA, 87; Bryn Mawr Col, PhD, 80. **CAREER** Adj instr, Villanova Univ, 77-81; asst prof, Gwynedd-Mercy Col, 80-81; asst prof, 81-86, assoc prof, 86-93, dir, cognitive science, 96-, prof, philosophy, 93-, Canisius Col, 81-; invited vis sci, Med Res Coun: Cognitive Brain Sci Unit Cambridge Univ, 94. **HONORS AND AWARDS** Whiting Found Fel, 79-80; Lowery Fac Res Fel, 84; Fac Res Fel Canisius Col, 89, 92, 97; Chercheur libre: Inst Sup de Philos KU Louvain, 79-80. **MEMBERSHIPS** Amer Philos Asn; Merleau-Ponty Circle; Soc Phenomenol & Existential Philo; Int Forum on Persons. **RESEARCH** Philosophy of mind; Cognitive science esp personal identity, embodiment; Phenomenology, Hermeneutics; Critical Theory, Philosophy of Time. **SELECTED PUBLICATIONS** Auth, Hermeneutics and Education, SUNY Press, 92; ed, Merleau-Ponty, Hermeneutics, and Postmodernism, SUNY Press, 92; auth, The Place of Phronesis in Postmodern Hermeneutics, Philos Today, 93; The Historikerstreit and the Critique of Nationalism, History of European Ideas, 93; Body Schema and Intentionality,Teh Body and the Self, MIT/Bradford Press, 95; coauth, Body Schema and Body Image in a Deafferented Subject, Jour Mind & Behavior, 95; auth, Some Particular Limitations on Postconventional Universality: Hegel and Habermas, Phenomenology, Interpretation, and Community, SUNY Press, 96; Critique and Extension: A Response to Robert Young, Studies in Philosophy and Education, 96; coauth, The Earliest Sense of Self and Others: Merleau-Ponty and Recent Developmental Studies, Philosophical Psychology, 96; auth, The Moral Significance of Primitive Self-Consciousness, Ethics: an international journal of social, political and legal philosophy, 96; Hermeneutical Approaches to Educational Research, Hermeneutics in Educational Discourse, 97; Hegel, Foucault, and Critical Hermeneutics, Hegel, History, and Interpretation, SUNY Press, 97; Mutual Englightenment: Recent Phenomenology in Cognitive Science, Jour Consciousness Stud, 97; ed, Models of the Self, Jour Consciousness Stud, 97; Hegel, History, and Interpretation, SUNY, 97; The Inordinance of Time, NW Univ Press, 98. **CONTACT ADDRESS** Dept of Philosophy, Canisius Col, 2001 Main St, Buffalo, NY 14208. **EMAIL** gallaghr@canisius.edu

GALLIGAN, THOMAS C. THOMAS C

PERSONAL Born 09/03/1955, Glen Ridge, NJ, m, 1981, 4 children **DISCIPLINE** LAW **EDUCATION** Stanford Univ, AB, 77; Univ at Puget Sound, JD, 81; Columbia, LLM 86. **CAREER** Asst prof to prof, LSU, 86-98; prof, dean, Univ Tenn, 98-. **HONORS AND AWARDS** John Minor Wisdom Awd; Stephen Victory Awd, LSU Outstanding Teacher Awd. **MEMBERSHIPS** ABA, Wash Bar Asn, Tenn Bar Asn. **RESEARCH** Torts, Products liability. **SELECTED PUBLICATIONS** Auth, Louisiana tort Law, Michie, 96; auth, Legislation and Jurisprudence on Maritime Personal Injury Law, Law Publications Inst, 97; auth, "Hill v Lundin & Associates" Revisited: Duty Risked to Death?, LSU law Publications Inst, 93; auth, "The Admiralty Extension Act at Fifty," Maritime Law and Commerce, 98; auth, "Is 2315.4 Unconstitutional?," La Bar J 230, 98; auth, "A Primer on Cigarette Litigation Under The Restatement (Third) of Torts: Products Liability, Sw.L.Rev, 98; auth, "The Legal System: Defective Product or Sign of the times," La.L.Rev. 411, 98; auth, "Choosing a Metaphor for Negligence: Cats or Gardens, Or, Is simplicity Always simpler?," L.Rev.35; 97; auth, "Revisiting the Patterns of Negligence: Some Ramblings Inspired by Robertson," La L.Review, 97; auth, "Burying Caesar: Civil Justice Reform and the Changing Face of Louisiana Tort Law," Tul. L. Rev, 96. **CONTACT ADDRESS** Dean of Law, Univ of Tennessee, Knoxville, 1505 Cumberland Ave, Knoxville, TN 37916-3199. **EMAIL** galligan@libra.law.utk.edu

GALLOWAY, J. DONALD C.

DISCIPLINE LAW **EDUCATION** Edinburgh Univ, LLB, 74; Harvard Univ, LLM, 75. **CAREER** Prof, 90-. **RESEARCH** Administrative law; jurisprudence. **SELECTED PUBLICATIONS** Auth, pubs on criminal law, tort law, and legal theory. **CONTACT ADDRESS** Fac of Law, Univ of Victoria, PO Box 2400, Victoria, BC, Canada V8W 3H7. **EMAIL** galloway@uvvm.uvic.ca

GALSTON, M.

PERSONAL 1 child **DISCIPLINE** JURISPRUDENCE, BANKRUPTCY, CORPORATIONS, NONPROFITS **EDUCATION** Univ Chicago, PhD, 73; Yale Law School, JD, 82. **CAREER** Vis asst prof, Univ TX, Austin, 76; asst prof, Brandeis Univ, 77-79; lawyer, private practice (tax), 82-90; Law prof, George Washington Univ Law School, 90-. **SELECTED PUBLICATIONS** Articles and a book in areas of ancient and medieval philosophy; articles in area of legal and political theory. **CONTACT ADDRESS** Law School, The George Washington Univ, 2000 H Street NW, Washington, DC 20052. **EMAIL** MGalston@main.nlc.gwu.edu

GAMBLE, CHARLES W.

DISCIPLINE LAW **EDUCATION** Jacksonville State Univ, BS, 65; Univ Ala, JD, 68; Harvard Univ, LLM, 71. **CAREER** Prof, Univ Ala, 82-. **MEMBERSHIPS** Order of the Coif. **RE-**

SEARCH Evidence and torts. **SELECTED PUBLICATIONS** Auth, McElroy's Alabama Evidence, 5th ed, 95; Gamble's Alabama Rules of Evidence: A Trial Manual for Making and Responding to Objections, 94; Alabama Law of Damages, 95; Character Evidence: A Comprehensive Approach, A Lawyer's Guide, 87. **CONTACT ADDRESS** Law Dept, Univ of Alabama, Tuscaloosa, Box 870000, Tuscaloosa, AL 35487-0383. **EMAIL** cgamble@law.ua.edu

GAMBLE, RICHARD C.
DISCIPLINE SYSTEMATIC THEOLOGY **EDUCATION** Univ Basel, Switzerland, PhD. **CAREER** Instr, Freie-Evangel Theol Akad, Basel; dir, H. Henry Meeter Ctr for Calvin Stud; prof, Calvin Theol Sem; prof, Reformed Theol Sem. **HONORS AND AWARDS** Fel of Natl Lib, Fed Rep Ger, The Herzog-August Bibliothek, 93. **RESEARCH** Calvinism. **SELECTED PUBLICATIONS** Auth, Augustinus contra Maximinum: An Analysis of Augustine's anti-Arian Writings; ed, encycl Calvin and Calvinism; co-ed, Pressing Toward the Mark. **CONTACT ADDRESS** Dept of Theol and Philos, Reformed Theol Sem, Florida, 1231 Reformation Dr, Oviedo, FL 32765. **EMAIL** rgamble@rts.edu

GANE, A. BARRY
PERSONAL Born 09/15/1950, Australia, m, 1974, 2 children **DISCIPLINE** YOUTH MINISTRY **EDUCATION** Pacific Union Col, BA, 73; Andrews Univ, MA, 84; Fuller Theo Sem, DMin, 92. **CAREER** Pastor, 74-79; teacher, 80, 81, 85; youth director, 81-84, 85-99; prof, 99-. **MEMBERSHIPS** Youth Ministry Educ. **RESEARCH** Values Transmission, Faith Development, Why Youth leave the Church. **SELECTED PUBLICATIONS** Auth, Building Youth Ministry, A Foundation Guide, 96, 00; auth, Youth Ministry and the Transmission of Beliefs and Values, 96. **CONTACT ADDRESS** Dept Youth Ministry, Andrews Univ, 100 US Hwy 31, Berrien Springs, MI 49104-0001. **EMAIL** bgane@andrews.edu

GANGADEAN, ASHOK KUMAR
PERSONAL Born 09/26/1941, Trinidad, West Indies, m, 1960, 2 children **DISCIPLINE** PHILOSOPHY **EDUCATION** City Col New York, BA, 63; Brandeis Univ, PhD(philos), 71. **CAREER** Asst prof, 68-74, assoc prof, 74-80, PROF PHILOS, HAVERFORD COL, 80-, Fel, Am Inst Indian Studies, 71-72; vis lectr, Univ Poona, 71-72. **MEMBERSHIPS** Am Philos Asn; Soc Asian & Comp Philos; Asn Asian Studies; Am Acad Relig; NAm Buddhist Soc. **RESEARCH** Logical theory; metaphysics; Indian philosophy. **SELECTED PUBLICATIONS** Auth, The Quest for the Primal Word, and What is the Origin of Language, Parabola-Myth Tradition and the Search for Meaning, Vol 0020, 95; The Awakening of Primal Knowledge, and How the Traditions Point Beyond the Ego, Parabola-Myth Tradition and the Search for Meaning, Vol 0022, 97. **CONTACT ADDRESS** Dept of Philos, Haverford Col, 370 Lancaster Ave, Haverford, PA 19041-1392.

GANNAGE, MARK
DISCIPLINE LAW **EDUCATION** Queen's Univ, BA; Osgoode Hall Law Sch, LLB, LLM. **CAREER** Lctr **MEMBERSHIPS** Ontario British Columbia Bars. **SELECTED PUBLICATIONS** Auth, pubs on copyright and designs law, criminal law and procedure, and company law. **CONTACT ADDRESS** Fac of Law, Univ of Toronto, 78 Queen's Park, Toronto, ON, Canada M5S 1A1.

GANZ, DAVID L.
PERSONAL Born 07/28/1951, New York, NY, m, 1996, 3 children **DISCIPLINE** LEGAL STUDIES **EDUCATION** Georgetown Univ, BSFS, 73; St John's Univ Law School, JD, 76; Int Law Prog, Temple Univ Law School, Rome, Italy, 75; NYork Univ Law School, LLM Prog, 77-79. **CAREER** Attorney at Law; NY, NJ, DC, before the Supreme Court of the United States, the US Tax Court, federal and state appellate and trial courts; member of Ganz, Hollinger, & Towe, Esqs, and Ganz & Sivin, PA; consultant to the Subcommittee on Historic Preservation & Coinage on the House Committee on Banking, Housing & Urban Affairs, 94th and 95th Congresses; elected to the Borough Council, Fair Lawn, N.J., 98; elected mayor, 99; re-elected 2000; re-elected 2001. **HONORS AND AWARDS** Phi Sigma Alpha; Numismatic Literary Guild Clement F. Bailey Memorial Awd, 91; Order of St Agatha (Commander) by the Republic of San Marino, 94; Glenn Smedley Memorial Awd, Am Numismatic Asn, 95; Medal of Merit, Token & Medal Soc, 97; listed in several Who's Who honorary directories. **MEMBERSHIPS** Token & Medal Soc; Am Numismatic Asn (Vice-pres, 91-93; Pres, 93-95); Bd of Dirs, Georgetown Univ Lib Assoc, 82-; Founding member, Bd of dirs, Industry Council for Tangible Assets, 83-. **SELECTED PUBLICATIONS** Auth, Landlord/Tenant, in MacGraw Hill Real Estate Handbook, 93; auth, Government Regulation of the Coin Industry, 106 The Numismatic 64 et seq, Jan & Feb, 93; auth, Partition ch 111 in NY Real Estate Guide, 5 vols, Matthew Bender, 93; auth, The World of Coins & Coin Collecting, Scribners, 80, 2nd ed, 85, 3rd ed, Bonus Books, 98; auth, The 90 Second Lawyer, with Robert Irwin, John Wiley & Sons, 96; auth, The 90 Second Lawyer's Guide to Buying Real Estate, with Robert Irwin, John Wiley & Sons, 97; auth, How to Obtain an Instant Mortgage, with Robert Irwin, John Wiley & Sons, 97; auth, Planning Your Rare Coin Retirement, Bonus Books, 98; auth, Official Guide to America's State Quarters, Random House, 00. **CONTACT ADDRESS** 1394 3rd Ave, New York, NY 10021. **EMAIL** DavidLGanz@aol.com

GARBER, DANIEL ELLIOT
PERSONAL Born 09/26/1949, Schenectady, NY, 2 children **DISCIPLINE** PHILOSOPHY, HISTORY OF SCIENCE **EDUCATION** Harvard Univ, AB, 71, AM, 74, PhD, 75. **CAREER** From asst prof to Lawrence Kimpton Distinguished Serv prof, Univ Chicago, 75-; vis asst prof philos, Univ Minn, spring 79 & Johns Hopkins Univ, 80-81; vis assoc prof philos, Princeton Univ, 82-83. **HONORS AND AWARDS** Teaching fel philos, Harvard Univ, 73-75 **MEMBERSHIPS** Am Philos Asn; Int Berkeley Soc; Philos Sci Asn; Hist Sci Soc; Leibniz Soc. **RESEARCH** Philosophy of science; 17th century philosophy and science. **SELECTED PUBLICATIONS** Auth, Mind, body and the laws of nature in Descartes and Leibniz, Midwest Studies Philos, Vol 8; Old evidence and logical omniscience in Bayesian conformation theory, Minn Studies Philos Sci, Vol 10; Descartes Metaphysical Physics, Univ Chicago, 92; ed, The Cambridge History of Seventeenth-Century Philosophy, Cambridge Univ, 98; auth, Descartes Embodied, Cambridge Univ, 00. **CONTACT ADDRESS** Dept of Philos, Univ of Chicago, 1010 E 59th St, Chicago, IL 60637-1512. **EMAIL** garb@midway.uchicago.edu

GARBER, MARILYN
PERSONAL Born Brooklyn, NY, 2 children **DISCIPLINE** HISTORY, LAW **EDUCATION** Univ Calif, Los Angeles, BA, 57, MA, 60, PhD, 67; Calif State Univ, 67-80; Southwestern Univ, JD, 77; **CAREER** Prof hist, Calif State Univ, Dominguez Hills, 80-. **MEMBERSHIPS** Calif State Bar. **RESEARCH** Utopia; legal history; labor law; negotiation; conflict resolution **SELECTED PUBLICATIONS** Natural Law Liberalism, 67. **CONTACT ADDRESS** Dept Hist, California State Univ, Dominguez Hills, 1000 E Victoria, Carson, CA 90747-0005. **EMAIL** dhvx20@csudh.edu

GARBER, ZEV WARREN
PERSONAL Born 03/01/1941, Bronx, NY, m, 2 children **DISCIPLINE** JEWISH STUDIES **EDUCATION** CUNY, BA, 62; Univ Judaism, AA, 66; Univ S Calif, MA, 70; PhD, 70. **CAREER** Instructor, Los Angeles Valley Col, 70-. **HONORS AND AWARDS** Hebrew Cultural Awd, Hunter Col, 62; Scholarship, Univ CA, 63; Ford Foundation Grant, Univ CA, 64; Fel, Hebrew Union Col, 69; Fel, Memorial Foundation for Jewish Culture, 71; Fel, B'nai Brith Los Angeles Hillel Culture, 72; Outstanding Fac Awd, Jewish Federation Coun, 75; Fel, Jewish Fed Coun of Greater Los Angeles, 80; Max Richter Foundation Grant, 86. **MEMBERSHIPS** Am Oriental Soc; Soc of Biblical Lit; Am Acad of Relig; Coun of the Study of Relig; Am Sch of Oriental Res; Israel Exploration Soc; Nat Asn of Prof of Hebrew; An for Jewish Studies; World Union of Jewish Studies; Catholic Biblical Asn of Am. **RESEARCH** Holocaust, Biblica, Hebraica, Judaica **SELECTED PUBLICATIONS** Ed, Methodology in the Academic Teaching of Judaism, 86; ed, Methodology in the Academic Teaching of the Holocaust, 88; ed, Teaching Hebrew Language and Literature at the College Level, 91; ed, Perspectives on Zionism, 94; co-ed, What Kind of God? Essays in Honor of Richard L. Rubenstein, 95; ed, Peace Indeed: Essays in Honor of Harry James Cargas, 98; ed, Academic Approaches to Teaching Jewish Studies, 99. **CONTACT ADDRESS** Dept Jewish Studies, Los Angeles Valley Col, 5800 Fulton Ave, Van Nuys, CA 91401. **EMAIL** zevgarber@juno.com

GARCIA, ALBERT L.
PERSONAL Born 05/02/1947, Havana, Cuba, m, 1968, 2 children **DISCIPLINE** THEOLOGY **EDUCATION** FL Atlantic Univ, BA, 69; Concordia Theol Sem, M Div, 74; Lutheran School of Theol, Th M, 78, PhD, 87. **CAREER** Asst prof, Concordia Theol Sem, 79-87; vis prof, Fla Intl Univ, 87-89; assoc prof to full prof, Concordia Univ, Wis, 92-. **HONORS AND AWARDS** Elected to Phi Sigma Tau, 68; Lutheran Brotherhood Fel, 86. **MEMBERSHIPS** AAR; Assn Ed Teologica Hispana. **RESEARCH** Christology; faith and culture, ethics in particular in relationship to US Hispanic theologies and Latin Am. **SELECTED PUBLICATIONS** Co-ed, contrib, Christ and Culture in Dialogue, Concortia Publ House, 98; contrib essay, Christological Reflections on Faith and Culture, Diccionario de Teologos/Terologas, contributor, forthcoming; auth, Hispanic/Latino Theology in the U.S.A., Concordia J, Jan 98; auth, Luther's Theology of Suffering: An Evangelical Catholic Perspective Toward Latinola Anthropology and Spirituality, Apuntes, 98; auth, "Christian Spirituality in Light of U.S. Hispanic Experience," Word & World, 00. **CONTACT ADDRESS** Concordia Univ, Wisconsin, 1200 N Lake Shore Dr, Mequon, WI 53097. **EMAIL** albert.garcia@cuw.edu

GARCIA, LAURA
PERSONAL Born 06/04/1955, Portland, OR, m, 1983, 4 children **DISCIPLINE** PHILOSOPHY **EDUCATION** Westmont Col, BA, 77; Univ Notre Dame, PhD, 83. **CAREER** Instr, Calvin Col, 79-80; instr, Univ St Thomas, 82-84; adjunct prof, Univ Notre Dame, 84-86; vis lctr, Cath Univ Amer, 86-87; vis asst prof, Georgetown Univ, 88-92; lctr, Rutgers Univ, 93-99; adj, asst prof, Boston Col, 99-. **MEMBERSHIPS** Amer Philos Assoc; Amer Cath Philos Assoc; Soc Christian Philos. **RESEARCH** Philosophy of Religion; Metaphysics **SELECTED PUBLICATIONS** Religious Values and Politics, Proceedings of the Theology Institute, Villanova Univ, forthcoming; Pluralism and Natural Theology, Recovering Nature: Essays in Natural Philosophy, Ethics, and Metaphysics in Honor of Ralph McInerny, Cath Univ Pr, forthcomingj; auth, Can the Global Marketplace Serve the Family?, The World and I, (forthcoming); auth, St. John of the Cross on the Necessity of Divine Hiddenness, (forthcoming); coauth, The Primacy of the Person: Logos 1, 97; auth, Religious Values and Politics, Proceedings of the Theology Institute, Villanova Univ, 99; auth, Pluralism and Natural Theology, Recovering Nature: Essays in Natural Philosophy, Ethics, and Metaphysics in Honor of Ralph McInerny, Notre Dame Press, 99. **CONTACT ADDRESS** Dept of Philos, Boston Col, Chestnut Hill, Carney Hall, 140 Commonwealth Ave, Chestnut Hill, MA 02467. **EMAIL** llgarcia@aol.com

GARCIA-GOMEZ, JORGE
PERSONAL Born 01/14/1937, Havana, Cuba, m, 1961, 3 children **DISCIPLINE** PHILOSOPHY, LITERATURE **EDUCATION** Univ Santo Tomas Villanueva, BA, 58; New Sch Social Res, MA, 65, PhD(Philos), 71. **CAREER** Asst prof Philos, Sacred Heart Univ, 66-69; assoc prof, 69-80, prof Philos, Southampton Col, Long Island Univ, 81-. **MEMBERSHIPS** Am Philos Asn; Am Cath Philos Asn; Am Asn Teachers Span & Port; AAUP. **RESEARCH** Metaphysics; phenomenology; aesthetics. **SELECTED PUBLICATIONS** Auth, A meditation of liberty, Abraxas, New York, fall 70; Ciudades, Ed Plenitud, Madrid, 74; ed & transl Aron Gurwitsch, El Campo de la Conciencia, Madrid, 78; Jose Ortega oy Gasset, Encyclopedia et Phenomenolozy, 97; A Bridge to Temporality, St Augustine's Confessions, Analecta Husser-liana, LII, 98 **CONTACT ADDRESS** Humanities Div Southampton Col, Long Island Univ, Southampton Col, 239 Montauk Hwy, Southampton, NY 11968-4198.

GARDINER, DAVID
PERSONAL Born 08/07/1957, Washington, DC, m, 1984, 2 children **DISCIPLINE** RELIGION **EDUCATION** Amherst Col, BA, 80; Univ Virginia, MA, 86; Stanford Univ, PhD, 95. **CAREER** Asst prof, 94-95, Simpson Col; asst prof, 95-97, Hawaii Pacific Univ; asst prof, 97-98, Univ San Diego; asst prof, 98-, Colorado Col. **HONORS AND AWARDS** Japan Found Fel, 00-01. **MEMBERSHIPS** Am Academy of Relig; Asn of Asian Studies. **RESEARCH** Japanese Religion (pre-modern), Buddhism. **SELECTED PUBLICATIONS** Auth, "Mandala, Mandala on the Wall: Variations of Usage in the Shingon School," in Journal of the International Asn of Buddhist Studies, 19:2 (96): 245-79; auth, "Buddhist Spirituality in the Heian and Kamakura Periods," in Buddhist Spirituality: Later China, Korea, Japan, and the Modern World, ed. by Takeuchi Yoshinori, Crossroads Press, 99; auth, "Japan's First Shingon Ceremony," in Religions of Japan in Practice, ed. by George J. Tanabe, Jr., (Princeton: Princeton Univ Press, 99): 153-58; auth, "The Consecration of the Monastic Compound at Mt. Koya by Kukai," in Tantra in Practice, ed. by David G. White, (Princeton: Princeton Univ Press, 00): 119-130. **CONTACT ADDRESS** Dept of Religion, Colorado Col, 14 E. Cache La Poudre, Colorado Springs, CO 80903. **EMAIL** dgardiner@coloradocollege.edu

GARDNER, CATHERINE
PERSONAL Born 03/17/1962, Chesterfield, England, m, 1996 **DISCIPLINE** PHILOSOPHY **EDUCATION** Univ Leicester, BA, 85; Univ Col of Swansea, Wales, MA, 89; Univ Va, PhD, 96. **CAREER** Asst prof, philos, Univ Mich Flint, 96-. **MEMBERSHIPS** Amer Philos Asn; Soc for the Study of Women Philos. **RESEARCH** Feminist ethics; Women moral philosophers from the history of philosophy. **SELECTED PUBLICATIONS** Auth, Catharine Macaulay's Letters on Education: Odd But Equal, Hypatia, vol 13, no 1, 118-137, Winter, 98; auth, Catharine Macaulay's Letters on Education: Odd but Equal, Hypatia, Winter 98, Volume 13, Number1: 118; 137; auth, An Ecofeminist Perspective on the Urban Environment, in The Nature of Cities, University of Arizona Press, 99, 191-212; auth, Rediscovering Women Philosophers: Philosophers: Philosophical Genre and the Boundaries of Philosophy, Westview Press, January 00. **CONTACT ADDRESS** Univ of Michigan, Flint, 544 Crob, Flint, MI 48502-2186. **EMAIL** cagard@umich.edu

GARDNER, RICHARD NEWTON
PERSONAL Born 07/09/1927, New York, NY, m, 1956, 1 child **DISCIPLINE** INTERNATIONAL LAW, ECONOMICS **EDUCATION** Harvard Univ, AB, 48; Yale Univ, LLB, 51; Oxford Univ, PhD(int econ), 54. **CAREER** Atty, Coudert Bros, NY, 54-57; from assoc prof to prof, 57-66, Henry L Moses Prof Law & Int Orgn, Columbia Univ, 66-; Dep asst to Secy State Int Orgn Affairs, 61-65; US Ambassador to Italy, 77-81; US Ambassador to Spain, 93-97; mem, Coun Foreign Rels of Counc Morgan Lewis, LLP, 97-. **MEMBERSHIPS** Am Soc Int Law; Am Acad Arts & Sci; Am Philos Soc. **RESEARCH** International law and organization, especially economic and political organization. **SELECTED PUBLICATIONS** Auth, New Directions in US Foreign Economic Policy, Sterling-Dollar Di-

plomacy, In Pursuit of World Order, Praeger, 64; Blueprint for Peace, McGraw, 66; coauth, The Global Partnership, Praeger, 68; auth, Negotiating Survival, 92. **CONTACT ADDRESS** Sch of Law, Columbia Univ, 435 W 116th St, New York, NY 10027-7201. **EMAIL** rgardn@law.columbia.edu

GARET, RONALD R.
DISCIPLINE CONSTITUTIONAL LAW **EDUCATION** Harvard Univ, BA; Yale Univ, religious stud, MA, MPhil, PhD; Univ Southern Calif, JD. **CAREER** Carolyn Craig Franklin prof Law and Rel, Univ Southern Calif; taught at, Yale Univ. **MEMBERSHIPS** Pats fac adv, Public Interest Law Found. **RESEARCH** Role of interpretation in law, theology, and literature and in the legal and moral rights of social groups. **SELECTED PUBLICATIONS** Auth, Creation and Commitment: Lincoln, Thomas, & the Declaration of Independence; Dancing to Music: an Interpretation of Mutuality; Gnostic Due Process. **CONTACT ADDRESS** School of Law, Univ of So California, University Park Campus, Los Angeles, CA 90089.

GARFINKEL, STEPHEN PAUL
PERSONAL m, 2 children **DISCIPLINE** RELIGIOUS STUDIES **EDUCATION** Univ Pa, BA; Columbia Univ, MA 73; Mphil, PhD, 83. **CAREER** Vis fac, Yale Univ; adj fac, Hunter Col; asst prof; dean, grad schl, Jewish Theol Sem. **HONORS AND AWARDS** JTS Stroock fac fel, Jewish Theol Sem; Dancinger Fellowship; grants, Nat Found Jewish Cult; bd gov and educ comm, solomon schechter day schl essex-union. **MEMBERSHIPS** Asn Jewish Studies; Columbia Univ Hebrew Biblical Sem; Soc Biblical Lit. **RESEARCH** Early popular perceptions about Moses; modes of biblical exegesis. **SELECTED PUBLICATIONS** Auth and/or ed over fifteen books for informal Jewish education use; scholarly pubs, Vetus Testamentum, Conser Judaism, Jour Ancient Near Eastern Soc. **CONTACT ADDRESS** Jewish Theol Sem of America, 3080 Broadway, New York, NY 10027. **EMAIL** stgarfinkle@jtsa.edu

GARLAND, JOHN WILLIAM
PERSONAL Born 10/24/1944, Harlem, NY, m, 1975, 2 children **DISCIPLINE** LAW **EDUCATION** Central State University, BA, 1971; Ohio State University College of Law, JD, 1974. **CAREER** Hayes & White, PC, sr attorney, 83-84; Law Office of John W Garland, attorney, 84-88; Univ of the District of Columbia, general counsel, 88-91; Univ of Virginia, assoc gen counsel, 91-93, exec asst to the pres, 93-96, assoc vp for intellectual property, 96-97; Central State Univ, Pres, 97-. **HONORS AND AWARDS** District of Columbia, Federation of Civic Association, Father of the Year, 78; TransAfrica Awd, 1987. SPA Legal Svcs of the Coastal Plains, founding dir. OSU col of law certificate of. **MEMBERSHIPS** National Association of College & University Attorneys; National Conference of Black Lawyers, bd of dirs; Association of University Technology Managers; Washington Lawyers Committee for Civil Rights Under Law, bd of dirs; National Veterans Legal Svcs Proj, bd of dirs; Journal of College & University Law, editorial bd; US Supreme Ct; Supreme Ct of NC: Supreme Ct of Virginia; Court of Appeals, District of Columbia; US Ct of Military Appeals; LeDroit Park Civic Association, pres, 1974-76. **CONTACT ADDRESS** Central State Univ, 1400 Brush Row Rd, Wilberforce, OH 45384. **EMAIL** jgarland@cesvxa.ces.edu

GARLAND, MICHAEL JOHN
PERSONAL Born 12/11/1936, Denver, CO, m, 1972, 2 children **DISCIPLINE** BIOETHICS, RELIGIOUS STUDIES **EDUCATION** St Louis Univ, BA, 61; Univ Notre Dame, MA, 68; Univ Strasbourg, Dr Sci Relig, 71. **CAREER** Asst prof relig studies, Regis Col, 70-72; lectr bioethics, Sch Med, Univ Calif, San Francisco, 73-77; asst prof med ethics, sch med, Ore Health Sci Univ, 78-; vis asst prof ethics, Pac Sch Relig, Berkeley, 76-77; vis asst prof bioethics, Portland State Univ, 77-78; Prof, 93-. **HONORS AND AWARDS** Teacher of the Year, Regis Col Student Senate, 71. **MEMBERSHIPS** Am Soc Bioethics and Hum; Am Pub Health Assn; Pub Health Assn. **RESEARCH** Social ethics of American health care system; social responsibility and the medical practice; interpersonal medical ethics. **SELECTED PUBLICATIONS** Auth, Oregon's contribution to define adequate health care, Health Care Reform: A Human Rights Approach, 94; coauth, Health Insurance, Encyclopedia of Bioethics, 95; auth, Community Responsibility for Health Policy: Tools, Structure, and Financing, 95; coauth, Consumers want choice and voice, Grading Health Care, 98; coauth, Translating the human genome project into social policy: a model for participatory democracy, Genes and Morality: New Essays, 98. **CONTACT ADDRESS** Dept of Pub Health, Oregon Health Sciences Univ, 3181 SW Sam Jackson, Portland, OR 97201. **EMAIL** garlandm@ohsu.edu

GARLICK, PETER C.
PERSONAL Born 03/07/1923, Sheffield, England, m, 1960, 2 children **DISCIPLINE** ECONOMICS **EDUCATION** Univ Sheffield, UK, BA 49, Diplo edu 50, MA 51; Univ London PhD 62. **CAREER** State Univ NY, New Paltz, prof and ch, econ, emer. **CONTACT ADDRESS** Dept of Economics, SUNY, New Paltz, New Paltz, NY 12561.

GARRETT, DON JAMES
PERSONAL Born 06/05/1953, Salt Lake City, UT, m, 1975, 2 children **DISCIPLINE** PHILOSOPHY **EDUCATION** Univ Utah, BA, 74; Yale Univ, PhD, 79. **CAREER** Asst prof philos, Harvard Univ, 79-82; asst prof to assoc prof, philos, Univ Utah, 82-99; Kenan Distinguished Prof, Univ NC, Chapel Hill, 99-. **MEMBERSHIPS** Am Philos Asn; Hume Soc. **RESEARCH** History of modern philosophy; philosophy of mind; metaphysics. **SELECTED PUBLICATIONS** Auth, Cognition and Commitment in Hume's Philosophy, Oxford, 97; ed, The Cambridge Companion to Spinoza, Cambridge, 96. **CONTACT ADDRESS** Dept of Philos, Univ of No Carolina, Chapel Hill, CB #3125 Caldwell Hall, Chapel, NC 27705. **EMAIL** Don_Garrett@unc.edu

GARRETT, GERALD R.
PERSONAL Born Mt. Vernon, WA **DISCIPLINE** SOCIOLOGY, CRIMINOLOGY, ADDICTIONS **EDUCATION** Whitman Col, AB, 62; Washington State Univ, MA, 66; Washington State Univ, PhD, 71. **CAREER** Vis prof, Univ of Alaska, 78; vis prof, Wash State Univ, 77-78, 94, 96, 99; Asst prof to prof , Univ Mass, Dir, grad prog in Applied Sociology, 81-84, Dir, Alcohol & Substance Abuse Studies, 86-, Dir, Center for Criminal Justice, Univ Mass, 92-98. **HONORS AND AWARDS** Distinguished Leadership, International Coalition of Addiction Studied Education; Outstanding Service, Northeastern Asn of Criminal Justice Sciences. **MEMBERSHIPS** Northeastern Asn of Criminal Justice Sci; Int Coalition of Addictions Studies Ed; Eastern Sociological Soc. **RESEARCH** Alcohol and other drugs; homelessness; alcohol/drug-related crime; deviance. **SELECTED PUBLICATIONS** Coauth, Substance Use and Abuse Among UMASS Boston Students, 98; Crime, Justice, and Society, General-Hall Inc, 96; Responding to the Homeless, Plenum Pub, 92; Manny: A Criminal-Addict's Story, Houghton-Mifflin, 77; Women Alone, Lexington Books, 76; auth, Working with the Homeless, Center for Commun Media, 90. **CONTACT ADDRESS** Dept. of Sociology, Univ of Massachusetts, Boston, 100 Morrissey Blvd., Boston, MA 02125-3393. **EMAIL** skymen@juno.com

GARRETT, JAMES LEO, JR.
PERSONAL Born 11/25/1925, Waco, TX, m, 1948, 3 children **DISCIPLINE** THEOLOGY **EDUCATION** Baylor Univ, BA, 45; Southwestern Baptist Theol Sem, BD, 48; ThD, 54; Princeton Theol Sem, ThM, 49; Harvard Univ, PhD, 66. **CAREER** From Instr to Prof, Southwestern Baptist Theol Sem, 49-73; Dir and Prof, Baylor Univ, 73-79; Prof, Southwestern Baptist Theol Sem, 79-. **HONORS AND AWARDS** Fel, Am Asn of Theol Schs Faculty, 62-63. **MEMBERSHIPS** Am Soc of Church Hist, AmAcad Rel; Conf Faith & Hist; Southern Baptist Hist Soc, Tex Baptist Hist Soc. **RESEARCH** Systematic theology, history of Chistian doctrine, history of Baptist theology, patristic theology, Reformation theology, religious liberty and church-state relations. **SELECTED PUBLICATIONS** Ed, The Concept of the Believers' Church, 70; ed, Baptist Relations with Other Christians, 74; coauth, Are Southern Baptists "Evangelicals?" 83; auth, "Living Stones: The Centennial History of Broadway Baptist Church," Fort Worth, Texas, 1882-1982, 85; auth, "Systematic Theology: Biblical, Historical and Evangelical," 90, 95; ed, We Baptists, 99. **CONTACT ADDRESS** Dept Theol, Southwestern Baptist Theol Sem, 2001 W Seminary Dr, Fort Worth, TX 76115-1153. **EMAIL** jlg@swbts.swbts.edu

GARRETT, ROBERT I.
PERSONAL Born 09/24/1950, Orange, TX, m, 1970, 3 children **DISCIPLINE** MISSIOLOGY **EDUCATION** Baylor Univ, BA, 72; Southern Baptist Seminary, MDiv, 75; PhD, 80. **CAREER** Teaching Fel, Southern Baptist Theol Sem, 78-79; prof, Sem Int Teologico Bavtista, 81-95; prof, Southwestern Baptist Theol Sem, 95-. **HONORS AND AWARDS** Eagle Scout; Baptist Missionary. **MEMBERSHIPS** Am Soc of Missiology, Am Prof of Mission, Soc of Biblical Lit, Evangelical Theol Soc, Evangelical Missiological Soc. **RESEARCH** Missions, Biblical Studies, Early Church. **SELECTED PUBLICATIONS** Ed, Reinar Valera Actualizada, 96; auth, "Jesus and his followers," Missiology: An Introduction, Broadman (Nashville, TN), 99. **CONTACT ADDRESS** Dept of Missions, Southwestern Baptist Theol Sem, 2001 W Seminary Dr, Ft Worth, TX 76115-1153. **EMAIL** bobgarrett@pobox.com

GARRISON, ROMAN
PERSONAL Born 05/09/1953, Cincinnati, OH, m, 1976, 2 children **DISCIPLINE** EARLY CHRISTIANITY **EDUCATION** Westminster Col, BA, 75; Pittsburgh Theological Seminary, MA, 77; Oxford Univ, MLitt, 79; Univ of Toronto, PhD, 89. **CAREER** Instr, asst prof, minister. **MEMBERSHIPS** SBL. **RESEARCH** Early Christianity. **SELECTED PUBLICATIONS** Auth, Redemptive Almsgiving in Early Christianity, Sheffield Acad Press; auth, The Graeco-Roman Context of Early Christian Literature, Sheffield Acad Press; auth, Why are you Silent, Lord?, Sheffield Acad Press. **CONTACT ADDRESS** 221 Beechwood Rd., New Wilmington, PA 16142. **EMAIL** rgarr56717@aol.com

GARRO, A. M.
PERSONAL Born 04/08/1950, LaPlata, Argentina, m, 1977, 1 child **DISCIPLINE** LAW **EDUCATION** Ntl Univ Of LaPlata, JD, 75; LA State Univ, LLM, 79; Columbia Univ, JSD, 90. **CAREER** Lectr, law, 81-94, Columbia Univ; Asst Prof 80-81, LSU; collab sci, 83-85, Swiss Inst Comp Law. **MEMBERSHIPS** ABA; Colegio de Abogados de la Provincia de Buenos Aires, Colegio de Abogados de Madrid. **RESEARCH** Comparative Law; Latin Amer Law; Intl Comm Arbitration. **SELECTED PUBLICATIONS** Auth, Compraventa Intl de Mercaderias, Buenos Aires, 90. **CONTACT ADDRESS** Law School, Columbia Univ, 435 West 116th St, New York, NY 10027. **EMAIL** garro@law.columbia.edu

GARRY, ANN
PERSONAL Born 09/12/1943, Bristol, VA, m, 3 children **DISCIPLINE** PHILOSOPHY **EDUCATION** Monmouth Col, BA, 65; Univ Chicago, MA, 66; Univ MD, College Park, PhD(philos), 70. **CAREER** Asst prof, 69-77, assoc prof, 77-82, prof philos, CA State Univ, Los Angeles, 82-. **HONORS AND AWARDS** ACLS sr fellowship. **MEMBERSHIPS** Am Philos Asn; Soc Women Philos. **RESEARCH** Feminist philosophy; epistemology; philosophical method; applied ethics. **SELECTED PUBLICATIONS** Auth, Mental images, Personalist, 77; Pornography and Respect for Women, Soc Theory & Pract, 78; Why are Love and Sex Philosophically Interesting, Metaphilosophy, 80; Narcissism & Vanity, Soc Theory & Pract, 82; Abortion: Models of Responsibility, Law and Philosophy, 83; A Minimally Decent Philosophical Method? Analytic Philosophy and Feminism, Hypatia, 95; Women, Knowledge, and Reality: Explorations in Feminist Philosophy, 2nd ed, Routledge, 96; auth, analytic Philosophy, Naturalized Epistemology and Feminism, Hiparquia, 97; Sex from Somewhere Liberally Different, Philos Studies, 98; auth, Medicine and Medicalization, Bioethics, 01; auth, Sex, Lies and Pornography, in Ethics in Practice, Blackwell, 01. **CONTACT ADDRESS** Dept Philos, California State Univ, Los Angeles, 5151 Rancho Castillo, Los Angeles, CA 90032-8114. **EMAIL** agarry@calstatela.edu

GARSON, G. DAVID
PERSONAL Born 01/10/1943, Newark, NJ, m, 1968, 5 children **DISCIPLINE** POLITICAL SCIENCE, PUBLIC ADMINISTRATION **EDUCATION** Princeton Univ, BA, 65; Harvard Univ, PhD, 69. **CAREER** Asst prof, Tufts Univ, 69-74; assoc prof, 74-77; prof, dept hd, N Car State Univ, 77-83; asst dean, 83-87; assoc dean, 87-96; vis schl, Mtn View CA, 96-98; prof, N Car State Univ, 77-. **HONORS AND AWARDS** Bst Instruc Software Awd; Donald Campbell Awd; Aaron Wildavsky Awd; Web Bk Awd; Okidata Bst Instruc Web Site Awd. **MEMBERSHIPS** APSA; ASPA; NASGA; NCPSA; URISA; ACM; IRMA. **SELECTED PUBLICATIONS** Auth, "The Role of Technology in Quality Education," Thought Action 15 (99): 105-118; co-ed, Advances in Social Science and Computers, vol 1, Jai Press (Greenwich, CT), 89; auth, Computer Technology and Social Issues, Idea Gp Pub (Harrisburg, PA), 95; co-ed, Advances in Social Science and Computers, vol 2, Jai Press (Greenwich, CT), 91; co-ed, Advances in Social Science and Computers, vol 3, Jai Press (Greenwich, CT), 93; co-ed, Advances in Social Science and Computers, vol 4, Jai Press (Greenwich, CT), 96; auth, Multimedia Guide to American Government, CD ROM, Prentice Hall (Upper Saddle River, NJ), 96; auth, Approaching Democracy Interactive Edition, CD ROM, Simon & Schuster (Upper Saddle River, NJ), 97; auth, Neural Network Analysis for Social Scientist, Sage Pub (London), 98; ed, Information Technology and Computer Applications in Public Administration: Issues and Trends, Idea Gp Pub (Harrisburg, PA), 99; ed, Handbook of Public Information Systems, Marcel Dekker (NY), 00. **CONTACT ADDRESS** Coll of Humanities and Social Sciences, No Carolina State Univ, Box 8102, Raleigh, NC 27695-0001. **EMAIL** david_garson@ncsu.edu

GARTHOFF, RAYMOND L.
PERSONAL Born 03/26/1929, Cairo, Egypt, m, 1950, 1 child **DISCIPLINE** INTERNATIONAL RELATIONS **EDUCATION** Princeton Univ, BA, 48; Yale Univ, MA, 49, PhD, 51. **CAREER** Res mem Soviet affairs, Rand Corp, 50-57; adv, Off Nat Estimates, Cent Intelligence Agency, 57-61; spec asst Soviet bloc polit-mil affairs, US Dept State, 61-68, counsel polit-mil affairs, US Mission to NATO, 68-70, dep dir, Bur Polit-Mil Affairs, 70-73, mem sr sem, 73-74, sr for serv inspector, 74-77; US ambassador to Bulgaria, 77-79; Sr Fel, Brookings Inst, 80-94, Prof lectr, Inst Sino-Soviet Studies, George Washington Univ, 62-64; lectr, Johns Hopkins Univ Sch Advan Int Studies, DC, 64-67. **HONORS AND AWARDS** Arthur S Flemming Awd, 66; Superior Honor Awd & Medal, US Dept State, 65, Distinguished Honor Awd & Gold Medal, 73; Wilbur Lucius Cross Medal, Yale Univ, 92. **MEMBERSHIPS** Coun on Foreign Relations; Int Inst for Strategic Studies; Am Asn for the Advancement of Slavic Studies; Acad of Political Sci; Soc for Historians of Am Foreign Relations; Asn for Diplomatic Studies; Arms Control Asn. **RESEARCH** Modern Russian history; diplomatic history and international relations; Soviet politics, foreign policy and military affairs. **SELECTED PUBLICATIONS** Auth, Soviet Military Policy, 66; ed, Sino-Soviet Military Relations, 66; auth, Perspectives on the Strategic Balance, 83; auth, Intelligence Assessment and Policymaking: A Decision Point in the Kennedy Administration, 84; auth, Policy Versus the Law: The Reinterpretation of the ABM Treaty, 87; auth, Reflections on the Cuban Missile Crisis, 87, rev. ed. 89; auth, Deterrence and the Revolution in Soviet Military Doc-

trine, 90; auth, Assessing the Adversary: Estimates by the Eisenhower Administration of Soviet Intentions and Capabilities, 91; auth, Detente and Confrontation: American-Soviet Relations from Nixon to Reagan, 85, rev. ed. 94; auth, The Great Transition: American-Soviet Relations and the End of the Cold War, 94. **CONTACT ADDRESS** 2128 Bancroft Pl NW, Washington, DC 20008.

GARVER, NEWTON
PERSONAL Born 04/24/1928, Buffalo, NY, m, 1957, 4 children **DISCIPLINE** PHILOSOPHY **EDUCATION** Swarthmore Col, AB, 51; Oxford Univ, BPhil, 54; Cornell Univ, PhD, 65. **CAREER** Prof, 71-91, Distinguished Serv Prof, SUNY-Buffalo, 91- ; vis prof, Mich, Friends World Col, Rochester, NW, & San Diego State Univ; NEH Summer Sem SUNY, 92. **MEMBERSHIPS** Am Philos Asn; Law & Soc Asn; AMINTAPHIL; Austrian Wittgenstein Soc. **RESEARCH** Wittgenstein; Kant; violence; non-violence. **SELECTED PUBLICATIONS** Auth, Jesus, Jefferson and the Task of Friends, Pendle Hill Pamphlet #250, 83; Naturalism and Rationality, Prometheus Books, 86; Justice, Law, and Violence, Temple Univ Press, 91; Derrida and Wittgenstein, Temple Univ Press, 94; This Complicated Form of Life, Open Court, 94; Violence in America, Johnson Lectures, San Diego State Univ, 94; Nonviolence and Community, Pendle Hill Pamphet, 95; **CONTACT ADDRESS** SUNY, Buffalo, 135 Park Hall, Box 604150, Buffalo, NY 14260-4150. **EMAIL** garver@acsu.buffalo.edu

GARVEY, JOHN LEO
PERSONAL Born 03/22/1927, Covington, KY, m, 1952, 2 children **DISCIPLINE** LAW **EDUCATION** Xavier Univ, AB, 45; Cath Univ Am, LLB, 48; Univ MI, SJD, 67. **CAREER** Atty, 48-51; from instr to prof law, Cath Univ Am, 51-00; assoc dean, Sch Law, Cath Univ Am, 63-69; dean, Cath Univ Am, 77-79. **HONORS AND AWARDS** LLD, Xavier Univ, 78. **MEMBERSHIPS** Am Bar Asn; Am Col Probate Coun; Am Law Inst. **RESEARCH** Probate reform; will substitutes. **SELECTED PUBLICATIONS** Auth, Probate Court Practice in the District of Columbia Supplements, West Publ Co, 60; Some aspects of the merger of law and equity, Cath Univ Law Rev, 61; Revocable gifts of legal interests in land, KY Law J, 65; Revocable gifts of personal property, Cath Univ Law Rev, 68; contribr, Comparative Probate Law Studies, Am Law Inst, 76; auth, Drafting Wills and Trusts: Anticipating the Brith and Death of Possible Beneficiaries, Oregan Law Rev, 92. **CONTACT ADDRESS** Columbus Sch of Law Cath, American Univ, 620 Michigan Ave N E, Washington, DC 20064-0002.

GASS, WILLIAM HOWARD
PERSONAL Born 07/30/1924, Fargo, ND, m, 1952, 5 children **DISCIPLINE** PHILOSOPHY **EDUCATION** Kenyon Col, AB, 47; Cornell Univ, PhD, 54. **CAREER** Instr philos, Col Wooster, 51-55; from asst prof to prof, Purdue Univ, 55-69; prof philos, 69-78, Dist Prof Humanities, Washington Univ, 79-, Vis lectr English & philos, Univ Ill, 58-59; Rockefeller Found grant fiction, 66-67; Guggenheim award fiction, 69-70; judge fiction, Nat Bk Awards, 73 & 75; lectr, Salzburg Sem in Am Studies, 73; judge Pen-Faulkner Prize, 81. **HONORS AND AWARDS** DHL, Kenyon Col, 74 & George Washington Univ, 82. **MEMBERSHIPS** Am Philos Asn; PEN; Am Acad Arts & Sci; Am Acad Arts & Lts; Int Parliament Writers. **RESEARCH** Aesthetics; Greek philosophy; fiction. **SELECTED PUBLICATIONS** Auth, Omensetter's Luck (novel), New Am Libr, 66; In the Heart of the Heart of the Country, Harper, 68; Willie Masters' Lonesome Wife, 68 & Fiction and the Figures of Life 71; introd, The Geographical History of America, Random House, 73; On Being Blue, Godine, 76; The World Within The Word, Knopf, 78; auth, Habitations of the Word, 83; auth, The tunnel, Knopf, 95; auth, Finding a Form, Knopf, 96; auth, Cartesian Sonata, Knopf, 98. **CONTACT ADDRESS** Dept of Philosophy, Washington Univ, Saint Louis, MO 63130. **EMAIL** iwc@artsci.wustl.edu

GASTON, LLOYD
PERSONAL Born 12/02/1929, Morgantown, WV, m, 1951, 3 children **DISCIPLINE** NEW TESTAMENT **EDUCATION** Dartmouth Col, BA, 52; Univ Basel, ThD(New Testament), 67. **CAREER** Res asst Old Testament, Princeton Theol Sem, 60-61; pastor, First Presby Church, Hamburg, NJ, 61-63; from instr to assoc prof relig, Macalester Col, 63-73; assoc prof, 73-78; prof, Vancouver Sch Theol, 78-95; prof emer, Vancouver Sch Theol, 95-. **MEMBERSHIPS** Soc Bibl Lit; Studiorum Novi Testamenti Societas; Can Soc Bibl Studies. **RESEARCH** Synoptic gospels; Paul. **SELECTED PUBLICATIONS** Auth, "Paul and the Torah," 91. **CONTACT ADDRESS** Vancouver Sch of Theol, 6000 Iona Dr, Vancouver, BC, Canada V6T 1L4.

GATES, GARY
PERSONAL Born 05/11/1951, Lebanon, PA, m, 1981, 2 children **DISCIPLINE** WORLD RELIGIONS, RELIGIOUS STUDIES, WRITING **EDUCATION** Messiah Col, Temple Univ, BA; Penn State Univ, MA. **CAREER** Adjunct prof, Harrisburg Area Community Col; Adjunct Prof, Harrisburg Area Community College and Penn State Harrisburg. **MEMBERSHIPS** Am Acad of Rel; Central Pa Writer's Org; Soc of Biblical Lit; Capital Area Writing-Project Board. **RESEARCH** The historical Jesus; history of Christianity; comparative religion/spirituality; science & religion. **SELECTED PUBLICATIONS** Several local books on the Pa Dutch. **CONTACT ADDRESS** 419 W. Pine St., Palmyra, PA 17078.

GAUKER, CHRISTOPHER P.
PERSONAL Born Minneapolis, MN, m **DISCIPLINE** PHILOSOPHY **EDUCATION** Univ Chicago, BA, 79; Univ Pittsburgh, PhD, 84. **CAREER** Tchg asst, fel, 79-84, instr, 85, Univ Pittsburgh; vis asst prof, Wesleyan Univ, 85-86; postdoctoral fel, Univ Cincinnati, 86-87; vis asst prof, Univ Wyoming, 87-88; asst prof, 88-93, assoc prof, 93-, Univ Cincinnati; vis assoc prof, Johns Hopkins Univ, 99. **HONORS AND AWARDS** Phi Beta Kappa, 79; Taft Postdoctoral Fel, 86-87; Taft Grants in Aid, 89, 94, 97; Taft Fac Fel, 92; Taft Sabbatical Grant, 95-96. **RESEARCH** Philosophy of language; philosophy of psychology; history of modern philosophy; philosophical logic. **SELECTED PUBLICATIONS** Auth, An Extraterrestrial Perspective on Conceptual Development, Mind and Lang, 93; auth, Thinking Out Loud: An Essay on the Relation between Thought and Language, Princeton, 94; auth, A New Skeptical Solution, Acta Analytica, 95; auth, Domain of Discourse, Mind, 97; auth, Universal Instantiation: A Study of the Role of Context in Logic, Erkenntnis, 97; auth, What is a Context of Utterance? Philos Stud, 98; auth, Social Externalism and Linguistic Communication, in Acero, ed, The European Review of Philosophy, suppl vol, Cambridge, forthcoming. **CONTACT ADDRESS** Dept of Philosophy, Univ of Cincinnati, Cincinnati, OH 45221-0374. **EMAIL** gaukercp@email.uc.edu

GAUSTAD, EDWIN SCOTT
PERSONAL Born 11/14/1923, m, 1946, 3 children **DISCIPLINE** AMERICAN RELIGIOUS HISTORY **EDUCATION** Baylor Univ, AB, 47; Brown Univ, AM, 48, PhD, 51. **CAREER** Instr relig, Brown Univ, 51-52; Am Coun Learned Soc scholar, 52-53; dean and prof relig and philos, Shorter Col, Ga, 53-57; assoc prof humanities, Univ Redlands, 57-65; assoc prof hist, 65-67, Prof Hist to Prof Emer, Univ Calif, Riverside, 67-. **HONORS AND AWARDS** Am Coun Learned Soc grant-in-aid, 63-64 and 72-73. **MEMBERSHIPS** Am Soc Church Hist; Am Studies Asn; Am Acad Relig; AHA; Orgn Am Historians. **SELECTED PUBLICATIONS** Ed, Religious Issues in American History, Harper, 68; co-ed, Religious Issues in Social Studies, Addison-Wesley, Vols I-III, 72-74; auth, Dissent in American Religion, Univ Chicago, 73; Religion in America: Its history and historiography, AHA, 73; ed, Rise of Adventism, Harper, 74; auth, Baptist Piety, Eerdmans, 78; George Berkely in America, Yale, 79; ed, Documentary History of Regligion in America, Vol I, Eerdmans, 82. **CONTACT ADDRESS** Dept of Hist, Univ of California, Riverside, Riverside, CA 92521.

GAUTHIER, CANDACE
DISCIPLINE PHILOSOPHY AND RELIGION **EDUCATION** SUNY, Oswego, BA; SUNY, Potsdam, MS; Univ NC, Chapel Hill, MA, PhD. **CAREER** Assoc prof, Philos and Relig, clin asst prof, Schl Med, Univ NC, Wilmington. **MEMBERSHIPS** Amer Philos Asn; Soc Health & Hum Values **RESEARCH** Ethical theory; ethics, law, and public policy. **SELECTED PUBLICATIONS** Auth, Philosophical Foundations of Respect for Autonomy, Kennedy Inst of Ethics J, 3:1, 93; The Value of Emotionally Expressive Visual Art in Medical Education, J of Med Hum, 17:2, 96; Teaching the Virtues: Justifications and Recommendations, Cambridge Quart of Healthcare Ethics, 6:3, 97. **CONTACT ADDRESS** Dept of Philosophy & Religion, Univ of No Carolina, Wilmington, Bear Hall, Wilmington, NC 28403-3297. **EMAIL** gauthierc@uncwil.edu

GAUTHIER, JEFF
PERSONAL Born 12/24/1957, Plattsburgh, NY, s **DISCIPLINE** PHILOSOPHY **EDUCATION** Wadhams Hall Col, BA, 80; Bowling Green State Univ, MA, 85; Univ Mich, PhD, 92. **CAREER** Adj prof, Univ Mich, 91-92; asst prof, 92-98, assoc prof, 98-, Univ Portland. **MEMBERSHIPS** Amer Philos Asn; Hegel Soc of Amer; Soc for Phenomenol and Existential Philos; Ore Acad of Sci. **RESEARCH** Ethics; Feminism; Hegel; Kant; Political philosophy. **SELECTED PUBLICATIONS** Rev, Signs of Paradox: Irony, Resentment and Other Mimetic Structures, Philos in Rev , 98; auth, The Real Lives of Women and Children, Portland: The Univ of Portland Mag, 98; auth, Schiller's Critique of Kant's Moral Psychology: Reconciling Practical Reason and an Ethics of Virtue, Can Jour of Philos 27, dec, 97; auth, Hegel and Feminist Social Criticism: Justice, Recognition, and the Feminine, State Univ of NY Press, 97; rev, Listening to the Thunder: Advocates Talk About the Battered Women's Movement, Activist Epizine, 96; rev, Merleau-Ponty's Hermeneutics and Postmodernism, Can Philos Rev, 94. **CONTACT ADDRESS** Dept. of Philosophy, Univ of Portland, Portland, OR 97203. **EMAIL** gauthier@up.edu

GAUTHIER, YVON
PERSONAL Born 02/01/1941, Drummondville, PQ, Canada, m, 1964, 2 children **DISCIPLINE** PHILOSOPHY **EDUCATION** Univ Montreal, MA, 62; Univ Heidelberg, Dr Phil (philos), 66. **CAREER** Lectr philos, Sem St Hyacinthe, Que, 62-63; from asst prof to assoc prof, Univ Sudbury, 66-72; assoc prof, Laurentian Univ, 72; vis assoc prof philos, Univ Toronto, 72-73; assoc prof, 73-77, PROF PHILOS, UNIV MONTREAL, 77-, Res fel math, Univ Calif, Berkeley, 72; bd experts, Dialogue, 76- **MEMBERSHIPS** Can Philos Asn; Asn Symbolic Logic. **RESEARCH** Logic; foundations of mathematics; philosophy of science. **SELECTED PUBLICATIONS** Auth, Hilbert and the Internal Logic of Mathematics, Synthese, Vol 0101, 94. **CONTACT ADDRESS** Dept of Philos, Univ of Montreal, Montreal, QC, Canada H3C 3J7. **EMAIL** gauthiyv@philo.umontreal.ca

GAVIL, ANDREW I.
DISCIPLINE CIVIL PROCEDURE **EDUCATION** Queens Col, CUNY, BA, 78; Northwestern Univ Sch Law, JD, 81. **CAREER** Prof; counsel, Chicago law firm of Bell, Boyd & Lloyd, and past consult, Fed Trade Comn; consult, Int Law Inst & IRIS at, Univ Md; ch, Law School's Student Aff & Libr Prog Plan Comt, 97-98; mem, Committees on Admissions, Warren Rosmarin Awd & Understanding. **SELECTED PUBLICATIONS** Auth, An Antitrust Anthology, Anderson, 96. **CONTACT ADDRESS** Sch of Law, Howard Univ, 2900 Van Ness St NW, Washington, DC 20008. **EMAIL** agavil@law.howard.edu

GAVIN, WILLIAM
PERSONAL Born 12/16/1943, New York City, NY, m **DISCIPLINE** PHILOSOPHY **EDUCATION** Fordham Univ, PhD. **CAREER** Prof; taught philos at, USM, for 31 yrs; 3rd recipient, Walter E. Russell Ch in Philos and Educ; teaches the USM Honors Course entitled, Progress, Process, or Permanence: All That is Solid Melts Into Air; ed-in-ch, The Maine Scholar. **RESEARCH** American philosophy; Ancient philosophy; philosophy of science; death and dying. **SELECTED PUBLICATIONS** Auth, William James and the Reinstatement of the Vague, Temple UP, 92; Cuttin' the Body Loose: Historical, Biological and Personal Approaches to Death and Dying, Temple UP, 95. **CONTACT ADDRESS** Dept of Philosophy, Univ of So Maine, 96 Falmouth St, PO Box 9300, Portland, ME 04104-9300. **EMAIL** wgavin1@maine.rr.com

GAY, WILLIAM CARROLL
PERSONAL Born 04/25/1949, Clearwater, FL, m, 1971, 1 child **DISCIPLINE** PHILOSOPHY **EDUCATION** Carson-Newman Col, BA, 71; Boston Col, PhD(philos), 76. **CAREER** Lectr philos, Brandeis Univ, 76-78; vis asst prof philos, Amherst Col, 78-79, Ind-Purdue Univ, 79-80; asst prof philos, Univ NC, 80-86, assoc prof philos, 86-96, prof philos, 96-, asst ed, Cult Hermeneutics, 75-77, assoc ed, Philos & Social Criticism, 78-86, ed Concerned Philos for Peace newsletter, 87-. **HONORS AND AWARDS** Pres, Concerned Philosphers for Peace, 93. **MEMBERSHIPS** Am Philos Asn; Concerned Philosophers for Peace; IPPNO; North Carolina Philos Soc; Radical Philos Asn. **RESEARCH** War and Peace Studies; Social and political Philosophy; Philosophy of Language; 19th- and 20th-Century Continental Philosophy. **SELECTED PUBLICATIONS** Coauth, The Nuclear Arms Race, Amer Lib Assoc, 87; auth, Ricoeur on metaphor and ideology, Darshana Int, 92; From Wittgenstein to applied philosophy, Int J Applied Philos, 94; co-ed, On the Eve of the 21st Century: Perspectives of Russian and American Philosophers, Rowman & Littlefield, 94; Bourdieu and the social conditions of Wittgensteinian language games, Int J Applied Philos, 96; coauth, Capitalism With a Human Face: The Quest for a Middle Road in Russian Politics, Rowman & Littlefield, 96; Nonsexist public discourse and negative peace, The Acorn: J Gandhi-King Soc, 97; Exposing and overcoming linguistic alienation and linguistic violenc, Philos and Soc Criticism, 98. **CONTACT ADDRESS** Dept Philosophy, Univ of No Carolina, Charlotte, 9201 University City, Charlotte, NC 28223-0001. **EMAIL** wcgay@email.uncc.edu

GAZELL, JAMES A.
PERSONAL Born 03/17/1942, Chicago, IL, m, 1970 **DISCIPLINE** GOVERNMENT **EDUCATION** Roosevelt Univ, BA, 63, MA, 66; Southern Ill Univ at Carbondale, PhD, 68. **CAREER** Asst Prof, 68-72, assoc prof, 72-75, prof, School of Public Admin & Urban Studies, San Diego State Univ, 75-. **HONORS AND AWARDS** Meritorious performance & professional promise award, San Diego State Univ, 88 & 89; International Journal of Public Administration; International Journal of Organizational Theory and Administration; Encyclopedia of Public Administration and Pulbic Policy. **MEMBERSHIPS** Am Soc for Public Admin; Nat Center State Courts; Nat Asn for Crt Management. **RESEARCH** Organization theory; judicial administration; research methods. **SELECTED PUBLICATIONS** Auth of five books and 57 articles in professional journals. **CONTACT ADDRESS** School of Public Admin and Urban Studies, San Diego State Univ, San Diego, CA 92115-4505. **EMAIL** jgazell@mail.sdsu.edu

GEAREY, AMELIA J.
DISCIPLINE CHRISTIAN EDUCATION **EDUCATION** State Univ NYork, BS; Fla State Univ, MS, PhD. **CAREER** Asst prof, 90; asst dir, Ctr Ministry of Tchg; assoc ed, Episcopal Children's Curriculum; assoc prof, 92; dir, Ctr Ministry of Tchg; ed, Episcopal Curriculum for Youth; prof, 00. **SELECTED PUBLICATIONS** Auth, Episcopal Children's Curriculum Director's Guide, Morehouse, 98; The Theological Challenge of Writing Curriculum, Engaging the Curriculum, 97; Young Children and the Expression of Faith, NAES, Worship in Episcopal Schools; Teaching Teenagers: The Joy and the Challenge, Youth and Young Adults. **CONTACT ADDRESS** Virginia Theol Sem, 3737 Seminary Rd, Alexandria, VA 22304. **EMAIL** AGearey@vts.edu

GEDDERT, TIM J.
PERSONAL Born 09/05/1952, Saskatoon, SK, Canada, m, 1987, 6 children **DISCIPLINE** THEOLOGY **EDUCATION** Beth Bib Inst, D Bib, 73; Univ Sask, BA, 76; Menn Breth Bib Sem, M Div, 78; Aberdeen Univ, PhD, 86. **CAREER** Pastor, Ft McMur, 78-83; theol edu, Ger, 90-93; asst prof, 86-90, 93-95; assoc prof, 95-, Menn Breth Bib Sem. **RESEARCH** Gospels, especially Mark; theology of Church; Greek; New Testament theology; Biblical interpretation. **SELECTED PUBLICATIONS** Auth, Watchwords, Sheffield Acad Press, 89; auth, Beitrage zu einer tauferischen Theologie; auth, Gott hat ein Zujause, Agape Verlag, 94; auth, Mark, Herald Press, forthcoming. **CONTACT ADDRESS** Dept Theology, Mennonite Brethren Biblical Sem, 438 N Purdue, Fresno, CA 93727. **EMAIL** tgeddert@fresno.edu

GEIGER, MARY VIRGINIA
PERSONAL Born 02/02/1915, Irvington, NJ **DISCIPLINE** PHILOSOPHY, HISTORY **EDUCATION** Col Notre Dame, Md, AB, 37; Cath Univ Am, MA, 41, PhD(hist, philos), 43. **CAREER** Instr hist, 38-56, PROF PHILOS, Col Notre Dame, MD, 56-. **HONORS AND AWARDS** DHL, Col Notre Dame, Md, 76. **MEMBERSHIPS** Am Cath Philos Asn; Am Hist Asn. **SELECTED PUBLICATIONS** Auth, Daniel Carroll II, One Man and His Descendants, 1730-1978, 78; Daniel Carroll, Signer of the Constitution, Cath Univ Am, 43; Genealogy of Charles Carroll of Carrollton, 98; articles in: Catholic Encyclopedia, McGraw, 67; Encyclopedia of American Catholic History, Glazier Shelley Book, Liturgical Press, 97. **CONTACT ADDRESS** Dept of Philosophy, Col of Notre Dame of Maryland, 4701 N Charles St, Baltimore, MD 21210-2404. **EMAIL** VGEIGER@NDM.EDU

GEIMAN, KEVIN
DISCIPLINE PHILOSOPHY **EDUCATION** Xavier Univ, AB, 83; WA, AM, 87; PhD, 88. **CAREER** Prof, Valparaiso Univ. **HONORS AND AWARDS** Univ res prof, Valparaiso Univ, 96-97; NEH Younger Scholars Awd, 95; fac rsch grant, Valparaiso Univ, 91; NEH texts transl grant, 91; NEH Summer Sem, 89. **MEMBERSHIPS** Am Philos Asn; N Am Kant Soc; N Am Soc Pol Legal Philos; Soc Phenom and Exist Philos. **RESEARCH** Soc and polit philos; mod philos; ethics; contemp europ philos; asian philos; environmental philos. **SELECTED PUBLICATIONS** Auth, Enlightened Cosmopolitanism: The Political Perspective of the Kantian 'Sublime', in What is Enlightenment?: Eighteenth Century Answers and Twentieth Century Questions, Univ Calif P, 96; Lyotard's 'Kantian Socialism', Philos and Soc Crit, 90; Habermas' Early Lifeworld Appropriation: A Critical Assessment, Man and World, 90; trans, Karl Leonhard Reinhold, Thoughts on Enlightenment in What is Enlightenment?; Jean-Francois Lyotard, Political Writings, Univ Minn P, 93; Michel Foucault, What is Critique? in What is Enlightenment?; co-trans, Christoph Martin Wieland, A Couple of Gold Nuggets, from the..Wastepaper, or Six Answers to Six Questions in What is Enlightenment?. **CONTACT ADDRESS** Valparaiso Univ, 1500 E Lincoln Way, Valparaiso, IN 46383-6493.

GEISLER, NORMAN LEO
PERSONAL Born 07/21/1932, Warren, MI, m, 1955, 6 children **DISCIPLINE** PHILOSOPHY, THEOLOGY **EDUCATION** William Tyndale Coll, 55, ThB, 64; Univ Detroit, 56-57, grad school, philosophy, 65-66; Wheaton Coll, BA, philos, 58; Wheaton Graduate School, MA, theology, 60; Wayne State Univ Grad School, philosophy, 64; Northwestern Univ, philosophy, 68; Loyola Univ, Chicago, PhD, philosophy, 70. **CAREER** Dir, Northwest Suburban Youth for Christ, Detroit, 52-54; pastor, Dayton Center Church, Silverwood, MI, 55-57, ordained, 56; asst pastor, River Grove Bible Church, IL, 58-59; Grad asst, Bible-Philosophy Dept, Wheaton Coll, 59; part-time instr in Bible, 59-62; full-time asst prof of Bible and apologetics, 63-66, Detroit Bible Coll; pastor, Memorial Baptist Church, Warren, MI, pastor, 60-63; speaker at churches, retreats, pastor's confs, universities, radio, and television, 60-; pres, Alumni of Detroit Bible Coll, 61-62; several interim pastorates in Michigan, Illinois, and Texas, 65-; full-time assoc prof of philos, Trinity Coll, 70-71; visiting prof philos of religion, 69-70, chm, philos of religion, 70-79, Trinity Evangelical Divinity School; prof systematic theology, Dallas Theological Seminary, 79-88; dean liberty, Center Research, Dean of Southern Evangelical Seminary, 82-. **HONORS AND AWARDS** Elected to Wheaton Scholastic Honor Soc, 77; listed in Who's Who in Religion, Writer's Who Who, Men of Achievement; Alumnus of the Year, William Tyndale Coll, 81; When Skeptics Ask (book) nominated for Medallion Awd of the year, missions/evangelism category, 91; Pres, Evangelical Theological Soc, 98; Received Gold Medallion Awd, 98; nominated for Medallion Awd, 00. **MEMBERSHIPS** Evangelical Theological Soc, 64-; Amer Philos Soc, 68-; Evangelical Philso Soc, 76-; Amer Scientific Assn, 80-; Amer Theological Soc, 80; Amer Acad Religion, 82-. **RESEARCH** Apologetics, theology, epistemology. **SELECTED PUBLICATIONS** Auth, Love Is Always Right, 96; auth, Creating God in the Image of Man?, 97; auth, When Cultists Ask, 97; auth, The Counterfeit Gospel of Mormonism, 98; auth, Legislating Morality, 98. **CONTACT ADDRESS** So Evangelical Sem, 4298 McKee Rd., Charlotte, NC 28270.

GEISTFELD, MARK
PERSONAL Born 07/23/1958, KS, m, 1990, 1 child **DISCIPLINE** LEGAL STUDIES, ECONOMICS **EDUCATION** Lewis and Clark Col, BA, 80; Univ Pa, MA, 81; Columbia Univ, JD, 89; PhD, 90. **CAREER** Assoc in Litigation Dept, Dewey, Ballantine, Bushby, Palmer and Wood, NY, 89-90; Law Clerk, Judge Wildfied Feinberg, US Ct of Appeals, 90-91; Vis Scholar, Columbia Univ Sch of Law, 91-92; Assoc in Litigation Dept, Simpson, Thacher and Bartlett, NY, 91-92; from Asst Prof to Prof, NYork Univ Sch of Law, 92-. **HONORS AND AWARDS** Univ Grad Fel, Univ of Pa, 80-81; President's Fel, Columbia Univ, 86-87; Stone Scholar, Columbia Univ, 84-85, 87-88. **MEMBERSHIPS** Am Econ Asn, Am Law and Econ Asn, Am Bar Asn. **RESEARCH** Torts, Insurance, Regulation and compensation of accidental injuries. **SELECTED PUBLICATIONS** Coauth, "The Divergence Between the Social and Private Incentives to Sue," 16 J of Legal Studies 483 (87); auth, "Imperfect Information, The Pricing Mechanism, and Products Liability," 88 Columbia Law Rev (88); auth, "Implementing Enterprise Liability: A Comment on Henderson and Twerski," 67 NY Univ Law Rev 1157 (92); auth, "The Political Economy of Neocontractual Proposals for Products Liability Reform," 72 Tex Law Rev 803 (94); auth, "Manufacturer Moral Hazard and the Tort-Contract Issue in Products Liability," 15 Int Rev of Law and Econ 241 (95); auth, "Placing a Price on Pain and Suffering: A Method for Helping Juries Determine Tort Damages for Nonmonetary Injuries," 83 Calif Law Rev 773 (95); auth, "Inadequate Product Warnings and Causation" 30 Univ of Mich J of Law Reform 309 (97); auth, "Should Enterprise Liability Replace the Rule of Strict Liability for Abnormally Dangerous Activities?," 45 UCLA Law Rev 611 (98); auth, "Products Liability," in The Encyclopedia of Law and Economics, ed. Gerrit De Geest and Boudewijn Bouckaert (Edward Elgar Press, 00); auth, "Economics, Moral Philosophy, and the Positive Analysis of Tort Law," in Philosophy and the U.S. Law of Torts, ed. Gerald Postema (Cambridge Univ Press, forthcoming). **CONTACT ADDRESS** Sch of Law, New York Univ, 40 Washington Sq S, New York, NY 10012-1005.

GELB, JOYCE
PERSONAL Born 06/01/1940, New York, NY, m, 1966, 2 children **DISCIPLINE** POLITICAL SCIENCE **EDUCATION** City Col NYork, Ba, 62; Univ Chicago, MA, 63; NYork Univ, PhD, 69. **CAREER** Vis prof, Yale Univ, polit sci, 97-98; mem, doctoral fac, Dept Polit Sci, CUNY, 80- ; vis prof, Barnard Col, Smith Col, Conn Col, 78-81; prof, Dept Polit Sci, CCNY, 85-. **HONORS AND AWARDS** Rockefeller vis scholar, 85; Fulbright grant, 88-89; NY Times Found grant, 90-91; vis scholar, Australia Nat Univ, 93; Ford Found grant, 96. **MEMBERSHIPS** Am Polit Sci Asn. **RESEARCH** Women and politics; comparative public policy. **SELECTED PUBLICATIONS** Co-ed, Women of Japan and Korea: Continuity or Change, Temple Univ, 94; auth, Women and Public Policies, rev ed, Univ Va, 96; auth, Women and Reproductive Choice: Politics and Policy in Japan, in Githens, ed, Abortion: Rhetoric and Reality: Public Policy in Cross Cultural Perspective, Routledge, 96; auth, Feminist Politics in a Hostile Environment: Obstacles and Opportunities, in McAdam, ed, Do Movements Matter? Univ Minn, 97; auth, The Equal Opportunity Law in Japan: A Decade of Change for Japanese Women, Yale Asian/Pacific Rev, forthcoming; coauth, Political Women in Japan: A Case Study of the Seikatsusha Movement, Social Sci J of Japan, 98; coauth, Feminist Organizational Success: The State of US Women's Movement Organizations in the 1990s, in Women and Politics, 99. **CONTACT ADDRESS** Dept of Poli Sci, City Col, CUNY, Convent Ave, New York, NY 10031. **EMAIL** jgelb@email.gc.cuny.edu

GELLER, DAVID A.
DISCIPLINE LAW **EDUCATION** Boston Univ, BS; New Eng Sch Law, JD. **CAREER** Adj prof Law, Thomas Col, 95-. **SELECTED PUBLICATIONS** Putting the 'Parens' Back into Parens Patriae: Parental Custody of Juveniles as an Alternative to Pretrial Juvenile Detention, 21:2 New Eng J on Criminal and Civil Confinement. **CONTACT ADDRESS** Thomas Col, Maine, Admin Bldg, Waterville, ME 04901-5097. **EMAIL** gellerd@thomas.edu

GELLHORN, GAY
DISCIPLINE CONTRACTS I AND II, ADVANCED CONTRACTS, AND ALTERNATIVE DISPUTE RESOLUTION **EDUCATION** Radcliffe Col, BA, 60; Harvard Univ, MA, 61; Seattle Univ Sch Law, 82. **CAREER** Prof; co-dir, HIV-AIDS/Publ Entitlements Clin; past law clk, Judge James L Oakes, US Ct of Appeals, 2nd Circuit & Justice Thurgood Marshall, US Supreme Ct; assoc, Wilmer, Cutler & Pickering, DC, 84-89. **MEMBERSHIPS** DC Bar. **SELECTED PUBLICATIONS** Publ on, disability and welfare reform, public interest attorney's fees, client interviewing, equal protection. **CONTACT ADDRESS** School of Law, Univ of District of Columbia, 4200 Connecticut Ave Northwest, Washington, DC 20008.

GELWICK, RICHARD
PERSONAL Born 03/09/1931, Briston, OK, m, 1955, 2 children **DISCIPLINE** THEOLOGY, ETHICS **EDUCATION** Southern Methodist Univ, BA, 52; Yale Univ, MDV, 56; Pacific Sch of Religion, ThD, 65 **CAREER** Intern, 54-55, Campus Ministry, Temple Univer; chaplin, asst prof, Washingon at Lee Univ, 56-58; dir of religious activities, Oberlin Coll, 58-60; Danforth Campus Ministry Research Fel, 60-63; United Church of Christ Campus Ministry, Univ of CA, Berkeley, 63-66; Asst prof, 66-67, Chapman Coll; prof and chair, 67-88, Stephens Coll; research assoc, 88-89, Bowdoin Coll; prof and chair, 88-89; prof of medical hum and ethics, med sch, Univ of New Eng, 89-98; research fel, 98-present, Univ of New England. **HONORS AND AWARDS** Rockefeller Doctoral Fel, 61-62; Soc for Relig in Higher Education post- doctoral fel, 73-74; Distinguished Alumnus Awd, Pacific Sch of Relig, 97. **MEMBERSHIPS** Amer Acad of Relig; Amer Assn for Bioethics and Humanities; Maine Bioethics Network; The Polangi Soc **RESEARCH** Michael Polangi Philosophy; Medical Ethics; Theology in Belief and in Action **SELECTED PUBLICATIONS** Auth, The Planyi-Tillich Dialogue of 1963: Polanyi's Search for a Post-Critical Logic In Science and in Theology, Tradition & Discovery, 95-96; The Calling of Being Human, Polanyiana, 96; Patient, Not Physician Assisted Dying, The Dissident, 97; Rationing Maine Medicaid, A Bioethics Case Study, Bulletin of the General Theological Library of Bangor Theological Seminary, 97; Rationing Maine Medicaid, A Bioethics Case Study, Bulletin of the General Theological Library of Bangor Theological Seminary, 97; Faith as the First Principle of Charles McCoy's Theology and Ethics, Tradition & Discovery, 97-98. **CONTACT ADDRESS** RR#5 Box 2440, Brunswick, ME 04011. **EMAIL** rprogel@juno.com

GENDIN, SIDNEY
PERSONAL Born 01/03/1934, New York, NY, m, 1958, 2 children **DISCIPLINE** PHILOSOPHY **EDUCATION** Brooklyn Col, BA, 55; NYork Univ, MA, 60, PhD, 65. **CAREER** Instr philos, NY Univ, 63-65; asst prof, State Univ NY Stony Brook, 65-70; assoc prof, 70-80, prof Philos, Eastern Mich Univ, 80-. **MEMBERSHIPS** Am Philos Asn. **RESEARCH** Ethics; philosophy of law; epistemology. **SELECTED PUBLICATIONS** Co-ed, A plausible theory of retribution, J Value Inquiry, winter 70; Insanity and criminal responsibility, Am Philos Quart, 4/73; Philosophy; A Contemporary Perspective, Wadsworth, 74; auth, A critique of the theory of criminal rehabilitation, in Punishment & Human Rights, Schenkman, 74; auth, Ethical Issues in Scientific Research, Garland Pub Co, 95. **CONTACT ADDRESS** Dept of Philos, Eastern Michigan Univ, 701 Pray Harrold, Ypsilanti, MI 48197-2201. **EMAIL** phi_gendin@online.emich.edu

GENNARO, ROCCO J.
PERSONAL Born 10/13/1963, Brooklyn, NY, m, 1990, 1 child **DISCIPLINE** PHILOSOPHY **EDUCATION** Syracuse Univ, PhD, 91. **CAREER** Adjunct asst prof, LeMoyne Col, 91-95; asst prof, 95-. **MEMBERSHIPS** Am Philos Asn; Soc for Philos and Psych. **RESEARCH** Philosophy of mind/psychology; History of early modern philosophy (including Kant). **SELECTED PUBLICATIONS** Co-ed, New Essays on the Rationalists, 99; auth, Consciousness and Self-Consciousness: A Defense of the Higher-Order Thought Theory of Consciousness, 96; Mind and Brain: A Dialogue on the Mind-Body Problem, 96; "Leibniz on Consciousness and Self-Consciousness," 99; "The Relevance of Intentions in Morality and Euthanasia" in Int Philos Quart, 96. **CONTACT ADDRESS** Dept of Philosophy, Indiana State Univ, Terre Haute, IN 47809. **EMAIL** rocco@cube.indstate.edu

GENOVA, ANTHONY CHARLES
PERSONAL Born 08/02/1929, Chicago, IL, m, 1953, 1 child **DISCIPLINE** PHILOSOPHY **EDUCATION** Univ Chicago, PhB, 57, BA, 58, MA, 58, PhD, 65. **CAREER** Instr philos, Roosevelt Univ, 59-61; lectr liberal arts, Basic Prog Liberal Educ Adults, Univ Chicago, 59-62; instr philos, Ill Inst Technol, 62; prof & chmn dept, Wichita State Univ, 62-72; Prof Philos, Univ Kans, 72-, Chmn Dept, 78-, Mem regional selection comt, Woodrow Wilson Fel Found, 66-72; Coun Philos Study Grant, Southampton Col, 68; dept grant, Wichita State Univ, 70; Wichita State Univ res grants, 68-69, 69-70, 70-71, 71-72; Am Philos Soc grants, 69-70, 71-72; Univ Kans res grant, 73-74, 74-75, 75-76, 76-77, 77-78. **MEMBERSHIPS** AAUP; Am Philos Asn; Metaphys Soc Am; Soc Phenomenol & Existential Philos; Soc Phenomenol Res. **RESEARCH** Metaphysics; philosophy of Kant; contemporary analytic philosophy. **SELECTED PUBLICATIONS** Auth, Institutional facts and Brute values, Ethics, 70; Searle's use of 'ought', Philos Studies, 73; Kant and alternative frameworks and possible worlds, Kongressakten, Int Kant Cong, Mainze, 4/74; On Anscombe's exposition of Hume, Analysis, 74; Kant's epigenesis of pure reason, Kant-Studien, 74; Speech acts and illocutionary opacity, Found Lang, 75; Speech acts and non-extensionality, Rev Metaphysics, 76; Linsky on Quine's way out, Philos & Phenomenol Res, 76; Good Transcendental Arguments, Kant-Studien, 84; Ambiguities About Realism and Utterly Distinct Objects, Erkenntris, 88; Fantastic Realisms and Global Skepticism, Philos Quart, 88; Craig on Davidson, a Thumbnail Refutation, Analysis, 91; Objectivity Without Causality, SW Philos Rev, 97; On the Very Idea of Massive Truth, Libr Living Philos, 99. **CONTACT ADDRESS** Dept of Philos, Univ of Kansas, Lawrence, Lawrence, KS 66045-0001. **EMAIL** acg@falcon.cc.ukans.edu

GENOVESI, VINCENT JOSEPH
PERSONAL Born 10/09/1938, Philadelphia, PA **DISCIPLINE** CHRISTIAN ETHICS, THEOLOGY **EDUCATION** Fordham Univ, AB, 62, MA, 66; Woodstock Col, Md, PhL, 63, MDiv, 69; Emory Univ, PhD, 73. **CAREER** Instr philos, Loyola Col, Md, 63-66; asst prof, 73-78, from assoc prof to prof Theol, 78-87, St Joseph's Univ, Pa. **HONORS AND AWARDS** The Christian R and Mary F Lindback Awd for Disting Teaching, 85; The Catholic Press Assoc Third Place, for In Pursuit of Love: Catholic Morality and Human Sexuality,97. **MEMBERSHIPS** Cath Theol Soc Am. **RESEARCH** Contemporary Christian ethics; sexual ethics, and theology of Christian marriage. **SELECTED PUBLICATIONS** Auth, In Pursuit of Love: Catholic Morality and Human Sexuality, 2nd ed, The Liturgical Press, 96; auth, To Suffer and Die in Christ: Spirituality and Catholic Morality, America, 96; auth, The Touch of God: Marriage as Sacrament, America, 97; auth, Is Jesuit Education Fulfilling Its Mission?, America, 98. **CONTACT ADDRESS** Dept of Theol, Saint Joseph's Univ, 5600 City Ave, Philadelphia, PA 19131-1376. **EMAIL** vgenoves@sju.edu

GENSLER, HARRY J.
PERSONAL Born 05/05/1945, Detroit, MI, s **DISCIPLINE** PHILOSOPHY **EDUCATION** Sacred Heart Sem, BA, 67; Wayne State Univ, MA, 69; Loyola Univ Chic, MDiv, 74; Univ Mich, MA, 76, PhD, 77. **CAREER** Univ Detroit, 69-70; John Carroll Univ, 70-72 & 98-; Gonzaga Univ, 77-81; Loyola Univ Chicago, 81-96; Univ Scranton, 96-98. **MEMBERSHIPS** Amer Philos Asn; Jesuit Philos Asn **RESEARCH** Logic and ethics. **SELECTED PUBLICATIONS** Auth, Godels Theorem Simplified, Univ Press Am, 84; Logic: Analyzing and Appraising Arguments, Prentic Hall, 89; Symbolic Logic: Classical and Advanced Systems, Prentice Hall, 90; Formal Ethics, Routledge, 96; Ethics: A Contemporary Introduction, Routledge, 98. **CONTACT ADDRESS** Philosophy Dept, John Carroll Univ, 20700 N Park Blvd, Cleveland, OH 44118. **EMAIL** gensler@jcu.edu

GENTRY, PETER J.
PERSONAL Born 04/15/1954, Dallas, TX, m, 1979, 2 children **DISCIPLINE** THEOLOGY **EDUCATION** Univ Toronto, BA, 75, 78; MA, 79; PhD, 94. **CAREER** Lectr, Ont Theol Sem, 88-92; prof, Toronto Baptist Sem, 84-97; res assoc, Univ of Toronto, 97-99; assoc prof, Southern Baptist Theol Sem. **HONORS AND AWARDS** William E Staples Scholar/Gold Medal, 78; Ruby M Jolliffe Scholar, 77-78; Univ of Toronto Fel, 82-83, 83-84; T J Meek Prize, 83. **RESEARCH** Classical Hebrew Linguistics and Philology, Hellenistic Greek Linguistics and Philology, Ancient Versions of the Bible, Textual Criticism. **SELECTED PUBLICATIONS** Auth, "Word Processing in Ancient Greek and Hebrew", Revue Informatique et Statistique dans les Sci Humaniens 28, (92): 59-62; auth, "The Asterisked Materials in the Greek Job", Soc of Biblical Lit 38, 95; auth, "The Place of Theodotion-Job in the Textual History of the Septuagint", Origen's Hexapla and Fragments, ed Alison Salvesen, Mohr Siebeck (Tubingen, 98); auth, "The Asterisked Materials in the Greek Job and the Question of the Kaiye Recension", Textus XIX (98): 141-156; auth, "The System of the Finite Verb in Classical Biblical Hebrew", Hebrew Studies 39 (98): 7-39; coauth, "Towards a New Collection of Hexaplaric Material for the Book of Genesis", X Congress of the Int Org for Septuagint and Cognate Studies: Oslo 1998, ed Bernard A Taylor, Scholars Pr, (99). **CONTACT ADDRESS** Dept Theol, So Baptist Theol Sem, 2825 Lexington Rd, Box 8-1804, Louisville, KY 40280-0001. **EMAIL** pgentry@sbts.edu

GEORGE, KATHRYN PAXTON
PERSONAL Born 06/12/1943, Northville, MI, m, 1985, 2 children **DISCIPLINE** GENETICS AND PHILOSOPHY **EDUCATION** Wash State Univ, BA, 80, MA, 82, PhD, 85. **CAREER** Prof, Dept ch, 89-, Univ Idaho; Asst Prof, philo, Asst Prof vet, 87-89, Wash State Univ; vis Asst Prof, 85-87, Univ Idaho. **HONORS AND AWARDS** NSF Fel; AAAUW Fel; editor of internet/online pub, environwest. **MEMBERSHIPS** ATHENA; NOW. **RESEARCH** Bioethics; Feminism and science. **SELECTED PUBLICATIONS** Animal, vegetable or woman? A feminist critique of ethical vegetarianism (Suny, 2000); Coed, Agricultural Ethics: Issues for the 21st Century, Madison WI, Tri-Soc Pub 94; Feminist Critiques of Science, in: John Norbury, ed, Proceedings of Pions and Beyond 1998; Reply to Adams Donovan Gruen and Gaard, Signs: J Women in Cult and Soc, 95; Discrimination and Bias in the Vegan Ideal, J Agri and Enviro Ethics, 94; Use and Abuse Revisited: Response to Pluhar and Varner, J Agri and Enviro Ethics, 94; Values of Residents of Rural America, in: Encyc of Rural America, ed, Gary A Goreham, Santa Barbara CA, ABC-CLIO, 97; **CONTACT ADDRESS** Dept of Philosophy, Univ of Idaho, 407 Morrill Hall, Moscow, ID 83844-3016. **EMAIL** kpgeorge@uidaho.edu

GEORGE, ROBERT P.
PERSONAL Born 07/10/1955, Morgantown, WV, m, 1982, 2 children **DISCIPLINE** POLITICS **EDUCATION** Swarthmore Col, BA, 77; Harvard Univ, MTS, 81; Harvard Univ, JD, 81; Oxford Univ, Dphil, 86. **CAREER** Presidential Appointee, US Comn on Civil Rights, 93-98; Asst, Assoc, Prof, Princeton Univ, 86-. **HONORS AND AWARDS** Vis Fel in Law, New Col of Oxford Univ, 88-89; Judicial Fel, US Supreme Court, 89-90; Justice Tom C. Clark Awd, US Judicial Fels Comn, 90; Silver Gavel Awd, Am Bar Asn, 91; Paul Bator Awd, Federalist Soc for Law & Public Policy, 94. **MEMBERSHIPS** US Judicial Fels Comn, Federalist Soc for Law & Public Policy, Am Bar Asn. **RESEARCH** Legal and political philosophy, constitutional law. **SELECTED PUBLICATIONS** Auth, Natural Law Theory: Contemporary Essays, Oxford Univ Pr, 96; auth, The Autonomy of Law: Essays on Legal Positivism, Oxford Univ Pr, 96; auth, Natural Law, Liberalism & Morality, Oxford Univ Pr, 96; auth, Great Cases in Constitutional Law, Princeton Univ Pr, 00. **CONTACT ADDRESS** Dept Polit, Princeton Univ, 130 Corwin Hall, Princeton, NJ 08544-0001. **EMAIL** rgeorge@princeton.edu

GEORGE, ROLF A.
DISCIPLINE PHILOSOPHY **EDUCATION** Mich State Univ, PhD. **RESEARCH** Theory of knowledge; logic; hist of philos; Kant; Brentano; Bolzano. **SELECTED PUBLICATIONS** Auth, pub(s) on philos of Kant, logic, and philosophical problems in pub policy. **CONTACT ADDRESS** Dept of Philosophy, Univ of Waterloo, 200 University Ave W, Waterloo, ON, Canada N2L 3G1. **EMAIL** rgeorge@uwaterloo.ca

GERAETS, THEODORE F.
PERSONAL Born 03/12/1926, The Hague, Netherlands **DISCIPLINE** PHILOSOPHY **EDUCATION** Heythrop Col, Berchmanianum LPh, 51, Canisianum LTh, 57; Gregorianum, Sorbonne, Paris, PhD, 69. **CAREER** Lectr, Berchmanianum Nijmegen, 57-59; lectr to prof, 66-94, dean & ch philos, 76-80, PROF EMER PHILOSOPHY, UNIV OTTAWA, 94-. **MEMBERSHIPS** Can Philos Asn; Hegel Soc Am; Int Hegel Ver; Int Hegel Ges; Int Ges Dialektische Philos; Soc Phenomenol & Exist Philos; Merleau-Ponty Cir. **SELECTED PUBLICATIONS** Auth, Vers une nouvelle philosophie transcendantale, 71; auth, Lo Spirito Assoluto Come Apertura del Sistema Hegeliano, 85; auth, La Logica di Hegel tra Religione e Storia, 96; co-transl, Hegel: The Encyclopaedia Logic, 91. **CONTACT ADDRESS** Dept of Philosophy, Univ of Ottawa, 70 Laurier E, Ottawa, ON, Canada K1N 6N5. **EMAIL** geraets@uottawa.ca

GERARD, JULES BERNARD
PERSONAL Born 05/20/1929, St. Louis, MO, m, 1953, 3 children **DISCIPLINE** CONSTITUTIONAL LAW **EDUCATION** Washington Univ, St Louis, AB, 57, JD, 58. **CAREER** Asst prof law, Sch Law, Univ Mo, 60-62; from asst prof to assoc prof, 62-80, PROF LAW AND CONSTITUTIONAL LAW, WASHINGTON UNIV, ST LOUIS, 80-, Ford Found fel, Univ Wis, 63. **RESEARCH** Judicial power and authority; amending the constitution; changing standards of civil commitment and of the insanity defense. **SELECTED PUBLICATIONS** Auth, The 1st-Amendment in a Hostile Environment--A Primer on Free Speech and Sexual Harassment, Notre Dame Law Rev, Vol 0068, 93. **CONTACT ADDRESS** Sch Law, Washington Univ, 1 Brookings Dr, Box 1120, Saint Louis, MO 63130-4899.

GERATY, LAWRENCE THOMAS
PERSONAL Born 04/21/1940, St. Helena, CA, m, 1962, 2 children **DISCIPLINE** NEAR EASTERN ARCHEOLOGY, OLD TESTAMENT **EDUCATION** Pac Union Col, AB, 62; Andrews Univ, AM, 63, BD, 65; Harvard Univ, PhD(Near Eastern lang & lit), 72. **CAREER** Asst prof, 72-76, assoc prof, 76-80, PROF ARCHAEOL and HIST ANTIQ, ANDREWS UNIV, 80-, Ed, Andrews Univ Monographs, 72-; res grants, Ctr for Field Res, 76 and Nat Endowment for Humanities, 77; trustee, Am Ctr Orient Res, Amman, Jordon, 76-; cur, Andrews Univ Archaeol Mus, 76-; assoc ed, Andrews Univ Sem Studies, 77-. **MEMBERSHIPS** Am Schs Orient Res; Soc Bibl Lit; Am Inst Archaeol; Nat Asn Prof Hebrew; Asn Adventist Forums (pres, 72-73). **RESEARCH** Palestinian archaeology; semitic inscriptions; Old Testament exegesis. **SELECTED PUBLICATIONS** Auth, A Tribute to Horn, Siegfried, H.--March-17, 1908 November-28, 1993--In-Memoriam, Biblical Archaeol, Vol 0057, 94. **CONTACT ADDRESS** Theol Sem, Andrews Univ, Berrien Springs, MI 49104.

GERBER, JANE SATLOW
PERSONAL Born 06/17/1938, New York, NY, m, 1964, 3 children **DISCIPLINE** JEWISH HISTORY, MIDDLE EASTERN STUDIES **EDUCATION** Wellesley Col, BA, 59; Radcliffe Col, MA, 62; Columbia Univ, PhD, 72. **CAREER** Instr Jewish hist, Stern Col, Yeshiva Univ, 71-72; asst prof, Lehman Col, 72-77; asst prof, 77-81, Assoc Prof Hist, Grad Ctr, City Univ New York, 81-, Bk rev ed, Jewish Social Studies J, 68-; mem off-campus fac, Sephardic Inst, Yeshiva Univ, 73-; Fac Res Found grant, City Univ New York, 74 and 75; ed, Shoah: Rev of Holocaust Studies and Commemorations, 78- **MEMBERSHIPS** Am Acad Jewish Res, Am Jewish Hist Soc, Am Asn Jewish Studies, Israel Hist Soc, Am Soc for Sephardic Studies. **RESEARCH** Jewish history in Muslim lands; Jews in Morocco; Sephardic history. **SELECTED PUBLICATIONS** Auth, The Jews of Spain, Macmillan, The Free Press, 92; auth, "The Jews of North Africa and the Middle East," in The Modern Jewish Expericence, ed J. Wertheimer, 93; auth, Sephardic Studies in the University, Assoc Univ Pr, 94; auth, "Toward and Understanding of the Term 'The Golden Age' as an Historical Reality" in The Culture of Spanish Jewry, ed Aviva Doron, Tel Aviv, 94; auth, Sephardi Entrepreneurs in Eretz-Israel--The Amzalak Family, 1816-1918, Jewish Quart Rev, Vol 0084, 94. **CONTACT ADDRESS** Graduate Sch and Univ Ctr, CUNY, 33 W 42nd St, New York, NY 10018. **EMAIL** gerberjs@aol.com

GERBER, MITCHELL
PERSONAL Born 12/29/1951, New York, NY, m, 1974, 1 child **DISCIPLINE** POLITICAL SCIENCE **EDUCATION** Brooklyn Col, BA, 73; Columbia Univ, MA, 75; New York Univ, PhD, 82. **CAREER** Assoc Prof to Prof, SE Mo. State Univ, 93-. **HONORS AND AWARDS** Nominated for Best Paper Awd, SW Polit Sci Asn, 00; Outstanding Service Awd, Nat Soc Sci Asn, 99; Grant, SE Mo. State Univ, 99-00; Who's Who Among Am Teachers, 00, 98, 96; Who's Who in the World, 00; Who's Who in Am, 00; NEH Fel, 98; Nominated for the Outstanding Scholarship Honors Awd, SE Mo. State Univ, 98-99; Nominated for the Poster Awd, Midwest Polit Sci Asn, 98; Phi Kappa Phi, 98; Who's Who in the Midwest, 98-99; Holocaust Educ Foundation Fel, Northwestern Univ, 97; Exempli Gratia, SE Mo. State Univ, 96-97; Outstanding Scholarship Honors Awd, SE Mo. State Univ, 96-97; C-SPAN Adv Workshop Grant, 96; Grant, SE Mo. State Univ, 94-95; Outstanding Teaching Honors Awd, SE Mo. State Univ, 92-93; NEH Fel, UCSC, 92; C-SPAN Prof Grant, 90; Grant, SE Mo. State Univ, 90-91; NEH Fel, Newberry Library, 89; Res Residency Awd, NY State Library, 88-89; Grant, Hofstra Univ, 88-89; NEH, Rutgers Univ, 87; Fel, William Andrews Clark Memorial Library, 86; NEH Fel, UCLA, 85; Nominated for the James C Healey Awd, NY Univ, 83-84; Penfield Fel, NY Univ, 80-81; Nominated for the Danforth Grad Fel, NY Univ, 80-81; Scholarship, NY Univ, 77-9. **MEMBERSHIPS** Am Polit Sci Asn, Acad Polit Sci, S Polit Sci Asn, Midwest Polit Sci Asn, NE Polit Sci Asn, Conf for the Study of Polit Thought, Soc for the Study of Greek Polit Thought, Nat Soc Sci Asn, N Am Conf on British Studies, Asn for Integrative Studies, Mo. Polit Sci Asn. **RESEARCH** Political Philosophy: conceptual political analysis, normative political philosophy, and historical political analysis. Areas of specialization with conceptual political analysis: the concepts "interest" and "public interest." Areas of specialization within normative political philosophy, and historical political analysis: French resistance during the Holocaust, classical Greek political thought, seventeenth century English political philosophy, the political theory of the Framers and AntiFederalists. US Political Institutions, Processes, and Behavior: American interest group theory, the American executive branch as an articulator of common interests, and the ideological aspects of public opinion. **SELECTED PUBLICATIONS** Auth, "The Multiple Complex Objectives of Interdisciplinarity: The Construction of a Political Philosophy Curriculum," Nation Social Science Journal, forthcoming; auth, "Interdisciplinary Political Philosophy Curriculum," in Techniques of College Teaching, Nat Louis Univ Press; forthcoming; auth, Sources: Notable Selections in American Government, 2nd Ed, McGraw-Hill, 99; auth, Instructor's Manual for Sources: Notable Selections in American Government 2nd Ed, McGraw-Hill, 99; auth, "Levellers Launch an Egalitarian Movement," in Great Events From History: European Series, Revised Edition, Salem Press, 98; auth, "Classical Greek Political Philosophy and the Concepts of Community and Nomos," National Social Science Journal, (99): 33-53; auth, "Teaching the Holocaust: The Argument for an Interdisciplinary Approach with a Political Philosophical Focus," National Social Science Perspectives Journal, (98): 45-60; auth, "The Multiple Complex Objectives of Interdisciplinarity: The Construction of a Political Philosophy Curriculum," National Social Science Perspectives Journal, (97): 8-16; auth, "Civic Virtue and Civil Religion: The Necessary Political Cultural Habits to Sustain Democracy," Tocqueville in the Classroom: An Educator's Resource, C-SPAN, 97; auth, "Diversity of Voluntary Associations and Interest Group Behavior: A Critical Interpretation of Alexis de Tocqueville's Democracy in America," in Tocqueville in the Classroom: An Educator's Resource, C-SPAN, 97. **CONTACT ADDRESS** Dept Polit Sci, Southeast Missouri State Univ, 1 Univ Plaza, Cape Girardeau, MO 63701-4710. **EMAIL** mgerber@semovm.semo.edu

GERHART, MARY
PERSONAL Born 03/04/1935, Stacyville, IA **DISCIPLINE** THEOLOGY, LITERATURE **EDUCATION** Col St Teresa, Minn, BA, 62; Univ Mo, MA, 68; Univ Chicago, MA, 70, PhD(relig, lit), 73. **CAREER** Asst prof, 72-80, Assoc Prof Relig Studies, Hobart & William Smith Cols, 80-, Ed Chair, Relig Studies Rev, 78-, Nat Endowment for Humanities grant, 76 & Fulbright grant, 82-83. **HONORS AND AWARDS** D J Bowden lectr, Ind Univ, 72; Ida Mae Wilson lectr, Vanderbilt Univ, 80. **MEMBERSHIPS** AAUP; Am Acad Relig; Cath Theol Soc Am. **RESEARCH** Hermeneutical theory; Religion and literature in science and religion. **SELECTED PUBLICATIONS** Auth, "The Question of Belief in Literary Criticism: An Introduction to the Hermeneutical Theory of Paul Ricoeur," Stuttgart: Akademischerr Verlag, Hans-Dieter Heinz, 79; auth, "Metaphoric Process: The Creation of Scientific and Religious Understanding," coauthored with Allan M. Russell, Texas Christian University Press, 84; auth, "Genre, Narrativity, and Theology," Semeia 43, 88, issue co-edited with James Williams; auth, "Morphologies of Faith: Essays in Religion and Culture in Honor of Nathan A. Scott, Jr., co-edited with Antho-

ny C. Yu, Scholas Press, 90; auth, "Genre Choices: Gender Questions," University of Oklahoma Press, 92; auth, "Paul Ricoeur's Hermeneutical Theory as Resource for Theological Reflection," Thomist, 37, July, 77, pp. 496-527; auth, "Paul Ricoeur, La Metaphore vive," Religious Studies Review, 2, January, 76, pp. 23-30; auth, "Paul Ricoeur's Notion of Diagnostics:" Toward a Philosophy of the Human," The Journal of Religion, 56, april, 76, pp. 137-156; auth, "Generic Studies: Their Renewed Importance in Religious and Literary Interpretation," Journal of the American Academy of Religion, 45, September, 77, pp. 309-25; auth, "The Ironic ode of Religious Imagination in Heinrich Boll," CTSA Proceedings, 32, 77, pp. 178-94; auth, "The Extent and Limits of Metaphor," Philosophy Today, 21, Winter, 77, pp. 431-36; auth, "Imagination and History in Ricoeur's Interpretation Theory," Philosophy Today, 23, Spring, 79, pp. 51-68. **CONTACT ADDRESS** Dept of Relig Studies, Hobart & William Smith Cols, Scandling Center, Box 4040, Geneva, NY 14456-3382. **EMAIL** gerhart@hws.edu

GERIG, WESLEY LEE
PERSONAL Born 09/17/1930, Ft Wayne, IN, m, 1952, 4 children **DISCIPLINE** RELIGION, HEBREW, THEOLOGY **EDUCATION** Ft Wayne Bible Col, AB, 51; Fuller Theol Sem, M div, 54, ThM, 56; Univ Iowa, PhD(relig), 65. **CAREER** From instr to assoc prof Bible & theol, 57-69, acad dean, 71-73, Prof Bible & Theol, Ft Wayne Bible Col, 69-91, Chmn Dept Bibl Studies, 62-91; Taylor Univ, 92-;Instr Bibl lang & dir admis, prof Bibl & theol; Winona Lake Sch Theol, 64-. **MEMBERSHIPS** Evangel Theol Soc; Am Acad Relig. **RESEARCH** The Hebrew-Gentile relations in the Old Testament; the social ethics of the Apostolic Fathers; Koine Greek. **CONTACT ADDRESS** Div Bibl Studies, Taylor Univ, Fort Wayne, 1025 W Rudisill Blvd, Fort Wayne, IN 46807-2197. **EMAIL** wsgerig@tayloru.edu

GERKEN, HEATHER K.
DISCIPLINE LAW **EDUCATION** Princeton Univ, BA, 91; Univ Mich, JD, 94. **CAREER** Law Clerk, Court of Appeals/Supreme Court, 94-96; Assoc Atty, Jenner & Block, 96-00; Asst Prof, Harvard Law Sch, 00-. **HONORS AND AWARDS** Bates Prize; Darrow Scholar. **MEMBERSHIPS** AALS; ABA. **RESEARCH** Voting rights; Election law; Constitutional theory. **SELECTED PUBLICATIONS** Auth, "Understanding the Right to an Undiluted Vote," Harvard L Rev, 01; auth, "Morgan Kousser's Noble Dream," Mich L Rev, 01; auth, "The Supreme Court's New Equal Protection Jurisprudence," Fla State L Rev, 01. **CONTACT ADDRESS** Sch of Law, Harvard Univ, Griswold 305, Cambridge, MA 02138.

GERKIN, CHARLES VINCENT
PERSONAL Born 07/30/1922, Garrison, KS, m, 1945, 6 children **DISCIPLINE** RELIGION AND PERSONALITY **EDUCATION** Washburn Municipal Univ, BA, 45; Garrett Theol Sem, BD, 47. **CAREER** Assoc pastor, First Methodist Church, 47-49, chaplain, Vet Admin Hosp, 49- 51 and Boys Indust Sch, Topeka, 51-56; dir chaplaincy serv, Grady Mem Hosp, Atlanta, 57-62; exec dir, Ga Asn Pastoral Care, 62-70; PROF PASTORAL PSYCHOL, EMORY UNIV, 70-, Guest prof pastoral care, Columbia Theol Sem, 59-70; sr group therapist, Ga Clinic Alcoholism, 60-71; asst prof preventive med and community health, Sch Med, Emory Univ, 63-70. **HONORS AND AWARDS** DD, Baker Univ, 73. **MEMBERSHIPS** Asn Clin Pastoral Educ (pres, 70-71); Am Asn Pastoral Counr; Am Asn Marriage & Family Ther. **RESEARCH** Contemporary forms of crisis experience; pastoral theology and personality theory; pastoral theology and changing social values. **SELECTED PUBLICATIONS** Auth, Care of Persons, Care of Worlds--A Psychosystems Approach to Pastoral Care and Counseling, Theol Today, Vol 0050, 94. **CONTACT ADDRESS** Candler Sch of Theol, Emory Univ, Atlanta, GA 30322.

GERRISH, BRIAN ALBERT
PERSONAL Born 08/14/1931, London, England, m, 1955, 2 children **DISCIPLINE** RELIGION, HISTORY **EDUCATION** Cambridge Univ, BA, 52, MA, 56; Westminster Col, Eng, cert, 55; Union Theol Sem, STM, 56; Columbia Univ, PhD(philos relig), 58. **CAREER** From instr to assoc prof church hist, McCormick Theol Sem, 58-65; assoc prof hist theol, 65-68, prof hist theol and Reformation hist, 68-72, PROF HIST THEOL, DIVINITY SCH, UNIV CHICAGO, 72-, Am Asn Theol Schs fac fel, 6i-62; John Simon Guggenheim Mem Found fel, 70-72; CO-ED, J RELIG, 72-; Nat Endowment for Humanities fel, 80-81. **MEMBERSHIPS** Am Acad Relig; Am Soc Reformation Res; Am Soc Church Hist (pres, 79). **RESEARCH** Continental Protestant thought in the 16th and 19th centuries. **SELECTED PUBLICATIONS** Auth, Natural Religion and the Nature of Religion--The Legacy of Deism, J Relig, Vol 0073, 93; Religion and the Religions in the English Enlightenment, J Relig, Vol 0073, 93; Atheism from the Reformation to the Enlightenment, J Relig, Vol 0074, 94. **CONTACT ADDRESS** Univ of Chicago, 18541 Klimm Ave, Homewood, IL 60430.

GERT, BERNARD
PERSONAL Born 10/16/1934, Cincinnati, OH, m, 1958, 2 children **DISCIPLINE** PHILOSOPHY **EDUCATION** Univ Cincinnati, BA, 56; Cornell Univ, PhD, 62. **CAREER** From instr to assoc prof philos, 59-70, chemn dept, 71-74, 79-81, & 98-, Prof Philos, Dartmouth Col, 70-, Stone Prof Intellectual & Moral Philos, 81-92, 98-, Eunice and Julian Cohen Prof for the study of Ethics and Human nature, 92-98; vis assoc prof philos, Johns Hopkins Univ, 67- 68; vis prof, Edinburgh Univ, Fall 74; vis prof, Nacional Universidad de la plata, fall, 95; vis prof, Universidad de Buenos Aires, fall 95; adj prof psychiat, Dartmouth Med Sch, 76-. **HONORS AND AWARDS** Nat Endowment for Humanities-Nsf sustained develop award, 80-84; Nat Endowment for Humanities fel, 69-70; Fulbright Awd, Israel, 85-86, Argentina, Fall 95; Grant from Nat Inst of Health, 90-93; Susan Linn Sage Fel in Philos, 58-59; Delegate, USA-USSR Exch Prog in Applied Ethics, 88; consult Comm Med Educ, Group for Adv Psych, 90; Panel on Sci Respon and Conduct Res, (COSEPUP)NAS/NAEIM 90-92; found Inst Study Applied and Prof Ethics, Dartmouth Col; co-chr, 82-85; exec bd, 89-92; consult ed, Encyclopedia Philos, 93-96; consult, Comm Rev Am Anthrop Asn, 95; Ethics Adv Comm, Mary Hitchcock Mem Hosp, 83-; fel, Hastings Ctr; 86-. **MEMBERSHIPS** Am Philos Asn; Am Soc Polit & Legal Philos. **RESEARCH** Ethics; philosophy of psychology; philosophy of medicine. **SELECTED PUBLICATIONS** Ed, Hobbes' Man and Citizen, Doubleday-Anchor, 72; coauth, The Moral Rules: A New Rational Foundation for Morality, Harper, 70, 73 & 75; Philosophy in Medicine: Conceptual and Ethical Issues in Medicine and Psychiatry, Oxford, 82; Hackett, 91; Morality and the New Genetics: A Guide for Students and Health Care Providers, Jones and Bartlett Pubs, 96; Bioethics: A Return to Fundamentals, Oxford Univ Press, 97; auth, Morality: It's Nature and Justification, Oxford Univ Press, 98. **CONTACT ADDRESS** Dept of Philosophy, Dartmouth Col, 6035 Thornton Hall, Hanover, NH 03755-3592. **EMAIL** bernard.gert@dartmouth.edu

GERT, HEATHER
DISCIPLINE PHILOSOPHY **EDUCATION** Brown Univ, PhD, 91. **CAREER** Asst prof, 91-97, assoc prof, 97- , Texas A&M Univ. **MEMBERSHIPS** APA. **RESEARCH** Wittgenstein; philosophy of mind/language; ethics. **SELECTED PUBLICATIONS** Auth, "Alternative Analyses," Southern J of Philos, 95; "Viability," International J of Philos Stud, 95; "Family Resemblances and Criteria," Synthese, 95; "Wittgenstein on Description," Philos Stud, 97; "Anger and Chess," Midwest Stud in Philos, forthcoming. **CONTACT ADDRESS** Dept of Philosophy, Texas A&M Univ, Col Station, College Station, TX 77843-4237. **EMAIL** heather@snaefell.tamu.edu

GETCHES, DAVID H.
PERSONAL Born 08/17/1942, Abington, PA, m, 1964, 3 children **DISCIPLINE** LAW **EDUCATION** Occidental Col, AB, 64; Univ Southern Calif, JD, 67. **CAREER** Instr polit sci, Univ Calif, San Diego, 69-70; Assoc, Luce, Forward, Hamilton & Scripps, 67-69; Atty, Calif Indian Legal Services, 69-70; dir, Native Am Rights Fund, 70-76; PROF LAW, SCH LAW, UNIV COLO, 79-, Vis lectr, Col Law, Univ Denver, 75; adj prof, Ctr Northern Educ Res, Univ Alaska, 75. **MEMBERSHIPS** Asn Am Law Sch; Rocky Mountain Mineral Law Found. **RESEARCH** Indian law; water law; natural resources. **SELECTED PUBLICATIONS** Auth, Cases & Materials on Federal Indian Law with Wilkins and Water Law in a Nutshell; auth, Water Resource Management with Tarlock & Corbridge; auth, Searching Out the Headwaters with Bates, MacDonnell, & Wilkinson; Conquering the Cultural Frontier--the New Subjectivism of the Supreme-Court in Indian Law, Calif Law Rev, Vol 0084, 96; Dedication to Professor Johnson, Ralph, W, Wash Law Rev, Vol 0072, 97. **CONTACT ADDRESS** Sch Law, Univ of Colorado, Boulder, Campus Box 401, Boulder, CO 80309-0401. **EMAIL** getches@colorado.edu

GEYER, ALAN
PERSONAL Born 08/03/1931, Dover, NJ, m, 1985, 6 children **DISCIPLINE** POLITICAL SCIENCE, CHRISTIAN ETHICS **EDUCATION** Oh Wesleyan Univ, BA, 52; Boston Univ, STB, 55, PhD, 61. **CAREER** Pastor, Trinity Methodist Church, NJ, 58-60; asst to assoc prof, polit sci, Mary Baldwin Col, 60-65; Dir Int Rel, United Church of Christ, 65-68; ed, Christian Century, 68-72; Dag Hammarskjold Prof of Peace Stud and Pol Sci, Colgate Univ, 72-77; exec dir, Churches' Ctr for Theol & Public Policy, 77-87; prof polit ethics & ecumenics, Wesley Sem, 87-96; Canon Ecumenist, Wahington Nat Cathedral, 97- 00; Canon Ethicist, 00-. **HONORS AND AWARDS** Phi Beta Kappa; Omicron Delta Kappa; Delta Sigma Rho; Alpha Kappa Delta; Robinson Fel; Kent Fel; Dempster Fel; LittD, hon, Ohio Wesleyan Univ; distinguished alumnus awards; James K Mathews Distinguished Service Awd; Satterwhite Awd in Christian Social Ethics. **MEMBERSHIPS** Am Polit Sci Asn; Soc of Christian Ethics; Arms Control Asn. **RESEARCH** Ethics and foreign policy; religion and politics. **SELECTED PUBLICATIONS** Auth, Piety and Politics, 63; auth, The Idea of Disarmament! Rethinking the Unthinkable, 82; auth, Redeeming the City, 82; auth, Christianity and the Superpowers: Religion, Politics, and History in US-USSR Relations, 90; auth, Lines in the Sand: Justice and the Gulf War, 92; auth, Ideology in America: Challenges to Faith, 97. **CONTACT ADDRESS** 5014 Smallwood Dr, Bethesda, MD 20816. **EMAIL** 75254.2405@compuserve.com

GHILARDUCCI, TERESA
PERSONAL Born 07/22/1957, Roseville, CA, m, 1986, 1 child **DISCIPLINE** ECONOMICS **EDUCATION** Univ of Calif at Berkeley, BA, 78; PhD, 84. **CAREER** Res Asst, Inst of Industrial Relations, Univ of Calif at Berkeley, 79-83; asst prof, 84-91, assoc prof, Dept of Economics, 91-, Univ of Notre Dame; Asst dir of Employee Benefits, Am Fed of Labor, Congress of Industrial Orgs, 94-95. **HONORS AND AWARDS** In residence fel, Mary Ingraham Bunting Inst, Radcliffe Col, 87-88. **MEMBERSHIPS** Am Economics Asn. **RESEARCH** Pensions; social security; labor markets. **SELECTED PUBLICATIONS** Auth, Labor's Capital: The Economics and Politics of Private Pensions, MIT Press, 92; coauth, Pension Practices of Innovative Firms, Pensions, Savings, and Capital Markets, U.S. Gov Printing Office, 96; auth, Pensions in an International Perspective, Rev of Radical Political Economies, 95; auth, The U.S. Social Security Debate and Integenerational Equity, The Role of the State in Pension Provisions: Provider and Regulator, Kluwer Pub, 98; auth, The Progressivity of the Social Security System: A Case Against Means Testing, Topics on Intergenerational Justice, Dushkin Press, 96; auth, Many Faces of American Multiemployer Pension Funds, Supplementary Pensions: Actors, Issues and the Future, Greenwood Press, 95; coauth, Scale Economies in Union Pension Plan Administration: 1981-1993, Industrial Relations Rev, 99; coauth, Labor's Paradoxical Role and the Evolution of Corporate Governance, J of Law and Soc, 97; coauth, Portable Pension Plans for Casual Labor Markets: Lessons from the Operating Engineers Central Pension Fund, Greenwood Press, 95. **CONTACT ADDRESS** Dept of Economics, Univ of Notre Dame, 434 Flanner Hall, Notre Dame, IN 46556. **EMAIL** Ghilarducci.1@nd.edu

GHOSH, SHUBA
PERSONAL Born 12/08/1964, India, m, 1994 **DISCIPLINE** LAW **EDUCATION** Amherst Col, BA, 84; Univ of Mich, MA, 86; PhD, 88; Stanford Law Sch, JD, 94. **CAREER** Asst prof, Univ of Tex, 88-91; asst prof, Okla City Univ, 96-98; assoc prof, Georgia State Univ, 98-. **MEMBERSHIPS** Am Law & Econ Asn; Law & Soc; Am Econ Asn; Soc for Evolutionary Anal of Law. **RESEARCH** Social Science in Law; Game Theory and Law; Law and Economic Development, especially in India and South Asia; Law and Literature, especially its critics. **SELECTED PUBLICATIONS** Auth, An Economic Analysis of the Common Control Exception to Gray Market Exclusion, in 15 Univ of Penn J of Int Bus Law 373, 94; Understanding Immigrant Entrepreneurs, in Reframing the Immigration Debate, 96; Property Rules, Liability Rules, and Termination Rights: A Fresh Look at the Employment at will Debate with Applications to Franchising and Divorce, in 75 Ore. L.Rev. 101, 96; Takings, the Exit Option, and Just Compensation, in 17 Int Rev of Law and Econ 157, 97; An Intellectual Property Optimist Looks at Article 9 and Bankruptcy, in 7 Fordham Intellectual Property, Media & Entertainment L.J., 97; The Legal, Policy, and Economic Implications of Immigrant Entrepreneurs for the Immigration Reform Debate, in 5 UCLA Asian Pacific Law Rev, 98; Methods, Conclusions, and the Search For Scientific Validity in Economics and Other Social Sciences, in Legal Forum, 98. **CONTACT ADDRESS** Col of Law, Georgia State Univ, PO Box 4037, Atlanta, GA 30302-4037. **EMAIL** sghosh@gsu.edu

GIANNELLI, PAUL CLARK
PERSONAL Born 05/21/1945, New York, NY, m, 1970, 2 children **DISCIPLINE** LAW **EDUCATION** Providence Col, BA, 67; Univ VA, JD, 70; George Washington Univ, MS, 73; Univ Va, LLM, 75. **CAREER** Atty criminal law, US Army, 70-75; PROF EVIDENCE AND CRIMINAL LAW, CASE WESTERN RESERVE UNIV, 75-. **RESEARCH** Evidence; criminal procedure; criminal law. **SELECTED PUBLICATIONS** Auth, Junk Science--The Criminal-Cases, J Criminal Law and Criminology, Vol 0084, 93. **CONTACT ADDRESS** 3129 Chadbourne Rd, Shaker Heights, OH 44120.

GIBBARD, ALLAN FLETCHER
PERSONAL Born 04/07/1942, Providence, RI, m, 1972, 1 child **DISCIPLINE** PHILOSOPHY **EDUCATION** Swarthmore Col, BA, 63; Harvard Univ, PhD(Philos), 71. **CAREER** From asst prof to assoc prof Philos, Univ Chicago, 69-74; assoc prof, Univ Pittsburg; prof Philos, Univ Mich, Ann Arbor, 77-. **HONORS AND AWARDS** Phi Beta Kappa; Sigma Xi assoc mem; Blanshard philos essay prize. **RESEARCH** Ethics; social choice theory; foundations of modal logic. **SELECTED PUBLICATIONS** Auth, Utilitarianism--merely an illusory alternative?, Australasian J Philos, 65; Doing no more harm than good, Philos Studies, 73; Manipulation of voting schemes: A general result, Econometrica, 74; Wise Chice, Apt Feelings, Harvard Univ Press, 90. **CONTACT ADDRESS** Dept of Philosophy, Univ of Michigan, Ann Arbor, 435 S State St, Ann Arbor, MI 48109-1003. **EMAIL** gibbard@umich.edu

GIBBS, DAVID N.
PERSONAL Born 06/01/1958, New Brunswick, NJ, m, 1994, 1 child **DISCIPLINE** POLITICAL SCIENCE **EDUCATION** George Washington Univ, BA, 79; Georgetown Univ, MA, 83; MIT, PhD, 89. **CAREER** MacArthur Postdoctoral Fel, Univ of Wis, Madison, 89-90; ASST PROF OF POLITICAL SCI, 90-96, ASSOC PROF OF POLITICAL SCI, UNIV OF ARIZ, 96-.

HONORS AND AWARDS Udall Res Fel, Udall Center for Studies in Public Policy, 98. **MEMBERSHIPS** Center for Middle East Studies, Univ of Ariz; Int Studies Asn. **RESEARCH** International relations; U.S. foreign policy; African politics, Middle Eastern politics. **SELECTED PUBLICATIONS** Auth, The Political Economy of Third World Intervention: Mines, Money, and U.S. Policy in the Congo Crisis, Univ of Chicago Press, 91; auth, Is There Room for the Real World in the Postmodernist Universe?, in Squaring the Circle: Int Studies and Ideological Faultlines of the Am Acad, forthcoming-99; auth, The Military-Industrial Complex, Sectoral Conflict, and the Study of U.S. Foreign Policy, in Business and the State in Int Relations, Westview, 96; auth, International Commercial Rivalries and the Zairian Copper Ntionalization of 1967, Review of African Political Economy, 97; auth, Secrecy and International Relations, Journal of Peace Res, 95; auth, Political Parties and Int Relations: The United States and the Decolonization of Subsaharan Africa, Int Hist Review, Univ of Toronto Press, 95; auth, Taking the State Back Out: Reflections on a Tautology, Contention, Ind Univ Press, 94. **CONTACT ADDRESS** Dept of Political Sci, Univ of Arizona, 315 Social Sciences, Tucson, AZ 85721-0027. **EMAIL** dgibbs@arizona.edu

GIBBS, JACK GILBERT, JR.
PERSONAL Born 08/11/1953, Columbus, OH, m, 1992 **DISCIPLINE** LAW **EDUCATION** MI State Univ, BA, 1975; Capital Univ Law School, JD, 1981. **CAREER** Columbus Public Schools, teacher, 76-78; Ohio Attorney General, legal intern, 80-81; Ben Espy, law clerk, 82; Self Employed, Attorney, 82-. **HONORS AND AWARDS** Ohio House of Representatives, resolution, 1983; Columbus Dispatch, Community Service Awd, 1988; Capital Law School, Service Awd, 1990; Ohio State Univ, Business School, Comm Service Awd, 1989; Hilltop Civic Council Inc, Service Awd, 1994. **MEMBERSHIPS** Hilltop Civic Council Inc, bd mem, pres, 1987-93; Centenary United Methodist Church, Chairman admin bd, 1987-95; Columbus Bar Assn, 1982-; Ohio State Bar Assn, 1982-; American Bar Assn, 1982-; American Inns of Court, 1994-; Capital Law School Black Alumni, pres, 1990-; UNCF Star Panelist, star panelist, 1993-. **SELECTED PUBLICATIONS** Lecture to community groups; Teach one seminar to Attorneys a year; testified as an expert witness on Probate Law; Written serveral articles on Probate Law & Estate Planning. **CONTACT ADDRESS** 233 S High St, Ste 208, Columbus, OH 43215.

GIBBS, JEFFREY A.
PERSONAL Born 03/04/1952, Trenton, NJ, m, 1973, 4 children **DISCIPLINE** THEOLOGY **EDUCATION** Rice Univ, BA, 74; Concordia Theol Sem, MDiv, 79, STM, 88; Union Theol Sem, PhD, 95. **CAREER** Pastor, Calvary, St. Helens, Ore, 79-86; pastor, Grace, Scappoose, Ore, 79-89; asst prof, 92-97, assoc prof, exegetical theol, 97- , asst acad adv, 96- , Concordia Sem. **MEMBERSHIPS** Soc of Bibl Lit; Cath Bibl Asn. **RESEARCH** Gospel of Matthew; New Testament eschatology. **SELECTED PUBLICATIONS** Auth, The Grace of God as the Foundation for Ethics, Concordia Theol Q, 84; auth, Parables of Atonement and Assurance: Matthew 13-44-46, Concordia Theol Q, 87; auth, The Search for the Idiosyncratic Jesus, Concordia J, 94; auth, An Exegetical Case for Closed Communion, Concordia J, 95. **CONTACT ADDRESS** Concordia Sem, 801 DeMun Ave, Saint Louis, MO 63105. **EMAIL** gibbsj@csl.edu

GIBBS, LEE WAYLAND
PERSONAL Born 03/07/1937, Natchitoches, LA, m, 1960, 3 children **DISCIPLINE** RELIGION **EDUCATION** Macalester Col, AB, 59; Harvard Univ, STB, 62, ThD, 68. **CAREER** Asst prof hist Christian thought, Case Western Reserve Univ, 67-71; asst prof, 71-73, assoc prof, 73-82, prof church hist & psychol of Relig, Cleveland State Univ, 82-. **HONORS AND AWARDS** NEH grant, 77-78 **MEMBERSHIPS** Am Acad Relig; Am Soc Church Hist; AAUP. **RESEARCH** History of Christian thought; myth, ritual and symbol; psychology of religion. **SELECTED PUBLICATIONS** Art, Richard Hooker's Via Media Doctrine of Justification, Harvard Theol Rev, 11/81; art, Religion and Science in a High Technology World, Bulletin of Science, Technology & Society, 97. **CONTACT ADDRESS** Dept of Relig Studies, Cleveland State Univ, 1983 E 24th St, Cleveland, OH 44115-2440. **EMAIL** ligibbs@csuohio.edu

GIBBS, PAUL J.
PERSONAL Born 11/20/1966, Boston, MA, m, 1990, 2 children **DISCIPLINE** PHILOSOPHY **EDUCATION** Univ Cincinnati, PhD, 94. **CAREER** Vis asst prof, 96-. **HONORS AND AWARDS** NEH grant, 98. **MEMBERSHIPS** Am Philos Asn; Asn for the Advan of Philos and Psych. **RESEARCH** Philosophy; Psychology. **SELECTED PUBLICATIONS** Auth, "Schizophrenia as Solipsism: A Grounding for Philosophical Counseling" in Contemp Philos, 98; "Ethical Connectionism" in Contemp Philos, 97. **CONTACT ADDRESS** Dept of Philosophy, John Carroll Univ, 20700 N Park Blvd, Cleveland, OH 44118. **EMAIL** PGIBBS@jcuaxa.jdcu.edu

GIBLIN, CHARLES HOMER
PERSONAL Born 01/22/1928, Chicago, IL **DISCIPLINE** SACRED SCRIPTURE **EDUCATION** Loyola Univ, Ill, AB, 50, MA, 52; WBaden Univ, STL, 59; Pontif Bibl Inst, Rome, SSD, 67. **CAREER** Instr New Testament, Hebrew and Bibl Greek, Bellarmine Sch Theol, 59, asst prof New Testament, 64-65; from asst prof to assoc prof theol, New Testament, 67-76, PROF THEOL, NEW TESTAMENT, FORDHAM UNIV, 77-. **MEMBERSHIPS** Cath Bibl Asn Am; Soc Bibl Lit; Soc New Testament Studies. **RESEARCH** Pauline theology; Lucan theology. **SELECTED PUBLICATIONS** Auth, The Threat to Faith: An Exegetical and Theological Reexamination of 2 Thessalonians 2, Pontifical Bibl Inst, Rome, 67; Reflections on the Sign of the Manger, Cath Bibl Quart, 1/67; In Hope of God's Glory: Pauline Theological Perspectives, Herder, 70; The Things of God in the Question Concerning Tribute to Caesar (Luke 20:25, Mark 12:17, Matthew 22:21), Cath Bibl Quart, 4/71; Structural and Thematic Correlations in The Matthean Burial-Resurrection Narrative (Matt 27:57-28:20), New Testament Studies, Vol 21, 74; Three Monotheistic texts in Paul, Cath Bibl Quart, Vol 36, 75; Suggestion, negative response, and positive action in St John's portrayal of Jesus (John 2:1-11, 4: 46-54, 7:2-14, 11:1-44), New Testament Studies, Vol 26, 80. **CONTACT ADDRESS** Dept of Theol, Fordham Univ, 501 E Fordham Rd, Bronx, NY 10458-5191.

GIBLIN, MARIE J.
PERSONAL Born 05/23/1944, Newark, NJ **DISCIPLINE** CHRISTIAN ETHICS **EDUCATION** Union Theol Sem, PhD, 86. **CAREER** Maryknoll Sch of Theol, 86-94; Xavier Univ, 94-. **MEMBERSHIPS** Am Acad of Relig; Col Theol Soc; Soc of Christian Ethics; Catholic Theol Soc of Am. **RESEARCH** Health care ethics. **SELECTED PUBLICATIONS** Auth, World Health Care Financing and the World Bank : An Ethical Reflection, Jour of Theol and Pub Policy, 93; auth, Corporatism, and, Quadragesimo Anno, in Dwyer, ed, The New Dictionary of Catholic Social Thought, Liturgical, 94; auth, Dualism, Empowerment, Hierarchy, in Russell, ed, Dictionary of Feminist Theologies, John Knox, 96; auth, The Prophetic Role of Feminist Bioethics, Horizons, 97; auth, "Illness, Justice, and Spirituality: The Narrative Connection," Quarterly Review: A Journal of Theological Resources for Ministry, 98-99; auth, Catholic Social Teaching and Domestic Violence," Listening: Journal of Religion nd Culture, 99; auth, "Just Dressing," The Way, 99; auth, "Care of the Dying: A Kairros Moment," Second Opinion, 00. **CONTACT ADDRESS** Dept of Theology, Xavier Univ, Ohio, 3800 Victory Pky, Cincinnati, OH 45207-4442. **EMAIL** giblin@xavier.xu.edu

GIBSON, SCOTT M.
PERSONAL Born 04/28/1957, New Castle, PA **DISCIPLINE** MINISTRY, PREACHING **EDUCATION** Penn State Univ, BS; Gordon-Conwell Theol Sem, MDiv; Princeton Theol Sem, ThM; Knox Col, Univ Toronto, MTh; Univ Oxford, DPhil. **CAREER** Sem archivist; assoc prof, Gordon-Conwell Theol Sem, 92-. **HONORS AND AWARDS** Fel, Case Stud inst; Minister, Am Baptist Churches, USA; founder, Am Baptist Evangel; founder, Evangel Homiletics Soc; minister, amer baptist churches, usa; pres, amer baptist evangel. **MEMBERSHIPS** Mem, Acad Homiletics, Evangel Homiletics Soc. **RESEARCH** Contemporary issues in preaching, pastoral ministry concerns, the history of preaching, history of evangelicalism. **SELECTED PUBLICATIONS** Ed, ABE Jour; co-ed, Integrity, Proj Timothy; coed, The Big Idea of Biblical Preaching, Baker, 98; ed, Making a Differnce in Preaching: Hadden Robinson on Biblical Preaching, Baker, 99; auth, A.J. Gordon: American Premillennialist, Univ of Am, 00. **CONTACT ADDRESS** Gordon-Conwell Theol Sem, 130 Essex St, South Hamilton, MA 01982.

GIBSON, WILLIAM M.
PERSONAL Born 09/11/1934, Hackensack, NJ, m, 1989 **DISCIPLINE** CRIMINAL LAW **EDUCATION** Rutgers, BA 1956; Law Review Boston Univ Law, JD 1959; Boston Coll, MSW 1966; Harvard Business School, AMP Certificate 1973; Valordictorian MDiv Virginia Magna Cum Laude 1989. **CAREER** US Dept of Justice, asst US Atty 1961-64; Boston Univ Law, dir law & poverty project 1966-70; Boston Univ School Afro Amer Studies, Assoc Prof 1968-71; Office Economic Opportunity, regional counsel 1970-72; FTC, regional dir 1972-78; Fuller Mental Health Center, supt area dir; Boston, Metro Dist, deputy district manager; St Paul's Baptist Church, minister of educ and singles; Medical College of VA Hospital, Richmond, staff chaplain, 90-91; Saint Stephen's Baptist Church, Pastor, currently; VA Union Univ, Criminology & Criminal Justice Dept, Instructor, 93-; Police Academy, recruit class chaplain, 98. **HONORS AND AWARDS** 10 Outstanding Young Men Awd Boston Jr CC 1968; Boston Univ Law School, Young Lawyers Chair, 1969; Community Serv Awd Roxbury YMCA 1969; Outstanding Performance Awd FTC 1972; Outstanding Govt Serv Awd NAACP Boston 1975; Outstanding Serv Awd Salvation Army 1980; Samuel H James, Sr Theological Awd, VA Union School of Theology, 1989; St Stephens Bapt Church, Man of the Year, 1996. **MEMBERSHIPS** Mem Natl Assoc Social Work 1966; mem Academy Certified Social Worker 1968; mem MA Bar Assoc 1984; Sports Anglers Club, VA; Henrico County Criminal Justice Commission; Richmond Police Citizens Academy Board. **CONTACT ADDRESS** St. Stephen's Baptist Church of Central Point, 1202 West Graham Rd, Richmond, VA 23220.

GIER, NICHOLAS F.
PERSONAL Born 03/17/1944, North Platte, NE, d, 1 child **DISCIPLINE** PHILOSOPHY **EDUCATION** OR State Univ, BA, 66; Claremont Graduate Univ, MA, 69; PhD, 73. **CAREER** Prof, Univ ID. **HONORS AND AWARDS** Alumni Awd, 91; Phi Kappa Phi Distinguished Fac, 98. **RESEARCH** Virtue Ethics, Comparative Philos, Philos of Relig. **SELECTED PUBLICATIONS** Auth, God, Reason and the Evangelicals: The Case Against Evangelical Rationalism, Univ Am, 87; Wittgenstein and Phenomenology: A Comparative Study of the Later Wittgenstein, SUNY, 81; auth, Spiritual Titanism: Indian, Chinese, and Western Perspectives, SUNY Press, 00. **CONTACT ADDRESS** Philos Dept, Univ of Idaho, Morrill Hall, Rm 403, Moscow, ID 83844-3016. **EMAIL** ngier@uidaho.edu

GIERE, RONALD N.
PERSONAL Born 11/29/1938, Cleveland, OH **DISCIPLINE** PHILOSOPHY **EDUCATION** Oberlin Col, AB, 60; Cornell Univ, MS, 63; PhD, 68. **CAREER** Lectr to prof, Ind Univ, 66-87; prof, Univ of Minn, 87-. **HONORS AND AWARDS** Phi Beta Kappa; Sigma Xi; Phi Kappa Phi; Fel, Am Assoc for the Advan of Sci. **MEMBERSHIPS** Philos of Sci Assoc; British Assoc for Philos of Sci; Am Philos Assoc; Am Assoc for the Advan of Sci; Soc for Soc Studies of Sci. **RESEARCH** Modes of representation in science, the Cognitive Basis of science. **SELECTED PUBLICATIONS** Auth, Understanding Scientific Reasoning, Holt, Rinehart & Winston, (NY), 79; auth, Explaining Science: A Cognitive Approach, Univ of Chicago Pr, 88; ed, Cognitive Models of Science, Minn Studies in the Philos of Sci, vol XV, Univ of Minn Pr, 92; coed, Origins of Logical Empiricism, Univ of Minn Pr, 96; auth, Science without Laws, Univ of Chicago Pr, 99. **CONTACT ADDRESS** Dept Philos, Univ of Minnesota, Twin Cities, 271 - 19TH Ave S, Minneapolis, MN 55455-0430. **EMAIL** giere@tc.umn.edu

GIFFIN, PHILLIP E.
PERSONAL Born 05/30/1944, Maryville, TN, m, 1990, 1 child **DISCIPLINE** ECONOMICS; ECONOMIC HISTORY **EDUCATION** Univ Tex-Austin, BA; Tex Tech Univ, MA; Univ Tenn-Knoxville, PhD. **CAREER** Asst prof econ, Valdosta State Col, 72-76; prof econ, Univ Tenn-Chattanooga, 77-00. **HONORS AND AWARDS** Fulbright fel-Poland, 89-90. **MEMBERSHIPS** Asn Evolutionary Econ. **RESEARCH** History of economic thought, Economic history, Industrial economics. **SELECTED PUBLICATIONS** Auth, "Institutional Development in a Transitional Economy: The Case of Poland" Int J Soc Econ, pp 35-55, (94); auth, "The Origins of Capitalist Markets: Transition in Poland", J Econ Issues, pp 585-590, (95). **CONTACT ADDRESS** Dept Econ, Univ of Tennessee, Chattanooga, 615 McCallie Ave, Chattanooga, TN 37403-2504. **EMAIL** phillip-giffin@utc.edu

GIFFORD, DANIEL JOSEPH
PERSONAL Born 01/07/1932, Utica, NY, m, 1960, 3 children **DISCIPLINE** LAW **EDUCATION** Holy Cross Col, AB, 53; Harvard Univ, LLB, 58 **CAREER** Assoc, Cleary, Gottlieb, Steen and Hamilton, 58-62; from asst prof to assoc prof law, Vanderbilt Univ, 62-65; Ford fel, Columbia Univ, 65-66; prof law, State Univ NY, Buffalo, 66-77; PROF LAW, UNIV MINN, 77-, Reporter admin law, Tenn Law Revision Comn, 63-64; consult, Ark Govt Studies Comn, 68 and Admin Conf US, 68-69; vis fel, Univ Warkwick, UK, 73. **MEMBERSHIPS** AAUP. **RESEARCH** Administrative law; antitrust law. **SELECTED PUBLICATIONS** Auth, Communication of legal standards, policy development and effective conduct regulation, Cornell Law Rev, 71; Decisions, decisional referents and administrative justice, Law & Contemporary Problems, 72; Assessing Secondary-Line Injury, 44 George Washington Law Rev 48, 75; Price Discrimination and Labels, 25 Buffalo Law Rev 395, 76; Promotional Price-Cutting, 1976 Wis Law Rev 1045, 76; Primary-Line Injury, 64 Minn Law Rev 1, 79; Administrative Rulemaking and Judicial Review, 65 Minn Law Rev 63, 80; Rulemaking and Rulemaking Review, 32 Ad Law Rev 577, 80. **CONTACT ADDRESS** Law Sch, Univ of Minnesota, Twin Cities, 229 19th Ave S, Minneapolis, MN 55455-0401.

GIGGER, HELEN C.
PERSONAL Born 12/24/1944, Houston, TX, m **DISCIPLINE** LAW **EDUCATION** TX South U, BA Pol Sci 1965; TX So U, JD 1968. **CAREER** State of OK, OK crime comm, legal coun, planner; Dean of Law Sch, res asst; Houston Leg Found, legal intern; Okla City & Co Comm Act Prog Inc, prog analyst. **HONORS AND AWARDS** Grad with Hons in 1961, 1965 & at top of Law Class in 1968; re chrprsn of Reg VI NAACP Conf 1974; Parli; Nat Delta Conv 1973; Delta Cen Reg Parli 1974; mem of Greater Cleves CME Ch; Ch Prog Chrprsn. **MEMBERSHIPS** Mem Am Nat & OK Bar Assns; sec JJ & Bruce Law Soc; mem Amer Judiccature Soc; EEOC off Okla Crime Comm; mem Nat Spa Courts Plan Org; lect Crim Just OK City U; mem YWCA; Urban League; League of Women Voters Georgia Brown's Demo Women's Club; OK Black Pol Cau; past pres Delta Sigma Theta Sor Inc; sec Local & State NAACP; elected Nat Scholarship & Standards Com 4 yr term; policy making com Delta Sigma Theta Inc 1975. **CONTACT ADDRESS** 3033 N Walnut, Oklahoma City, OK 73105.

GIGNAC, FRANCIS THOMAS
PERSONAL Born 02/24/1933, Detroit, MI **DISCIPLINE** PHILOLOGY, THEOLOGY **EDUCATION** Loyola Univ, Ill, AB, 55, MA, 57, MA, 68; Oxford Univ, DPhil(Greek), 64. **CAREER** Instr Greek, Loyola Univ, Ill, 65-67; from asst prof to assoc prof Theol, Fordham Univ, 68-74; assoc prof Bibl Studies & chmn dept, Cath Univ Am, 74-, NSF travel grant, 67. **MEMBERSHIPS** Cath Bibl Asn; Am Philol Asn; Am Soc Papyrologists. **RESEARCH** The language of the non-literary Greek papyri; the language of the Greek New Testament; textual criticism. **SELECTED PUBLICATIONS** Auth, The language of the non-literary Greek papyri, Am Studies Papyrology, 70; The text of Acts in Chrysostom's homilies, Traditio, 70; The pronunciation of Greek stops in the papyri, Trans & Proc Am Philol Asn, 70; An Introductory New Testament Greek Course, Loyola Univ, 73; A Grammar of the Greek Papyri of the Roman and Byzantine Periods (2 vols), Cisalpino-La Goliardica, Milan, 76 & 81. **CONTACT ADDRESS** Dept of Biblical Studies, Catholic Univ of America, 620 Michigan Ave NE, Washington, DC 20064-0002. **EMAIL** gignac@cua.edu

GILBERT, JOSEPH
PERSONAL Born 12/01/1934, New York, NY, m, 1960, 2 children **DISCIPLINE** ETHICS, CONTEMPORARY PHILOSOPHY **EDUCATION** Brooklyn Col, BA, 62; NYork Univ, MA, 63, PhD(philos), 69. **CAREER** Assoc prof, 66-74, prof Philos, State Univ NY Col Brockport, 74-, chairperson, 77-, dir & ed, Proc Ctr Philos Exchange, 75-, dir ctr philos exchange, 78-. **MEMBERSHIPS** Am Philos Asn; Philos Soc Studies Sport. **RESEARCH** Moral philosophy; philosophy of religion. **SELECTED PUBLICATIONS** Auth, Foot-notes, Philos Exchange, Summer 71; Neutrality and universalizability, Personalist, Autumn 72; Moral notions, Folio Humanistica, 74. **CONTACT ADDRESS** Dept of Humanities & Philos, SUNY, Col at Brockport, 350 New Campus Dr, Brockport, NY 14420-2914.

GILBERT, MARGARET
DISCIPLINE PHILOSOPHY **EDUCATION** Cambridge Univ, BA, 65; Oxford Univ, B Phil, 67; PhD, 78. **CAREER** Prof, Connecticut Univ, Storrs, CT. **HONORS AND AWARDS** Fel, IAS, Princeton, 78-79; ACLS Fel, 89-90. **RESEARCH** Philosophical social theory; political philosophy. **SELECTED PUBLICATIONS** Auth, 'On the Question whether Lang has a Social Nature: Some Aspects of Winch and Others on Wittgenstein', Synthese, 83; auth, 'Coordination problems and the evolution of behavior', Behavioral and Brain Sciences, 84; auth, 'Modelling collective belief', Synthese, 87; auth, 'Rationality and Salience', Philosophical Studies, 89; auth, 'Folk psychology takes sociality seriously', Behavioral and Brain Sciences, 89; auth, 'Fusion: sketch of a contractual model', in Perspectives on the Family, Edwin Mellen Press, Lewiston, 90; auth, 'Rationality, Coordination, and Convention, Synthese, 90; auth, 'Walking together: a paradigmatic social phenomenon', MidWest Studies in Philosophy, The Philosophy of the Human Sciences, Univ of Notre Dame Press, Notre Dame, 90; auth, On Social Facts, Routledge, in the series International Library of Philosophy, Reprinted in hardback and paperback, Princeton Univ Press, 92, (89); auth, Living Together: Rationality, Sociality, and Obligation, Rowman and Littlefield, 96. **CONTACT ADDRESS** Dept Philosophy, Univ of Connecticut, Storrs, 103 Manchester Hall, U-54, Storrs, CT 06269-0001. **EMAIL** margaret.gilbert@uconn.edu

GILBERT, ROBERT EMILE
PERSONAL Born 10/20/1939, New York, NY **DISCIPLINE** POLITICAL SCIENCE **EDUCATION** Fordham Univ, BA (political science), 61, MA (political science), 63; Univ MA, Amherst, PhD (political science), 67. **CAREER** Instr, Boston Col, 65-67, asst prof, 67-73; assoc prof, 73-82, prof of Political Science, Northeastern Univ, 82-. **HONORS AND AWARDS** Phi Kappa Phi;Excellence in Teaching Awd, 84; Kennedy Found grantee, 95; Center for Study of Presidency Grantee, 00. **MEMBERSHIPS** Int Soc of Political Psychology; Am Political Science Asn; Center for Study of Presidency. **RESEARCH** Am politics (presidency, mass media). **SELECTED PUBLICATIONS** Auth, Travails of the Chief: Killer Stress Plagues the White House, The Sciences, Feb 93; JFK and Addison's, MD, Nov 93; The Political Effects of Presidential Illness: The Case of Lyndon B Johnson, Political Psychology, Dec 95; The Physical and Psychological Ailments of Lyndon B Johnson: The Years of Ascent, Presidential Studies Quart, summer 96; Presidential Disability: The Case of John F Kennedy, in Papers on Presidential Disability and the Twenty-Fifth Amendment, Kenneth W Thompson, ed, Univ Press of Am, 96; John F Kennedy: Moral leadership in Civil Rights, in Leadership for the Public Service: Power and Policy in Action, Richard A Loverd, ed, Simon & Schuster, 96; Presidential Disability in Law and Politics: Lessons from 1992, Miller Center J, spring 98; The Mortal Presidency: Illness and Anguish in the White House, 2nd ed, Fordham Univ Press, 98; auth, "The Trauma of Death," New England Journal of Hist, fall 98. **CONTACT ADDRESS** Dept of Political Science, Northeastern Univ, Boston, MA 02115. **EMAIL** rgilbert@lynx.neu.edu

GILDRIC, RICHARD P.
PERSONAL Born 04/18/1945, Norfolk, VA, m, 1966, 2 children **DISCIPLINE** HISTORY & PHILOSOPHY **EDUCATION** Eckerd Col, BA, 66; Univ Va, MA, 68, PhD, 71. **CAREER** Prof, Austin Peay State Univ, 70-. **HONORS AND AWARDS** Kenneth S. Lafaurette Prize. **MEMBERSHIPS** OIEAHC; OAH; AHA; AAUP **RESEARCH** Colonial America; early modern Britian. **SELECTED PUBLICATIONS** Auth, The Profane, The Civil & the Godly: The Reformation of Manners in Orthodox New England 1679-1749, 94. **CONTACT ADDRESS** Dept of History & Philosophy, Austin Peay State Univ, Clarksville, TN 37044. **EMAIL** gildrier@apsu01.apsu.edu

GILES, THOMAS RANSOM
PERSONAL Born 04/10/1937 **DISCIPLINE** PHILOSOPHY **CAREER** Research, 94-. **MEMBERSHIPS** APA. **SELECTED PUBLICATIONS** Auth Dictionary of Philosophers and Terms, Univ Press Univ Sao Paulo, 93. **CONTACT ADDRESS** PO Box 16678, Jersey City, NJ 07306.

GILKES, CHERYL TOWNSEND
PERSONAL Born 11/02/1947, Boston, MA, s **DISCIPLINE** THEOLOGY **EDUCATION** Northeastern Univ, BA 1970, MA 1973, PhD 1979. **CAREER** Harvard Univ the Divinity Sch, research assoc, visiting lecturer 1981-82; faculty fellow Bunting Inst, & Radcliffe Coll; Union Baptist Church, assoc minister 1982-; Boston Univ, asst prof of sociology 1978-. **HONORS AND AWARDS** Eastern Sociological Society, I Peter Gellmon awrd 1986. **MEMBERSHIPS** Sec Cambridge Civic Unity Comm 1978-; asst dean Congress of Christian Education United Baptist Convention of MA, RI, NH 1986-; mem Amer Sociological Assoc, Assoc of Black Sociologist, Delta Sigma Theta 1983-. **CONTACT ADDRESS** Boston Univ, 96-100 Cummington St, Boston, MA 02215.

GILL, DAVID W.
PERSONAL Born 02/02/1946, Omaha, NE, m, 1967, 2 children **DISCIPLINE** ETHICS **EDUCATION** Univ Calif, Berkeley, BA, 68; San Francisco State, MA, 71; Univ So Calif, PhD, 79. **CAREER** Asst prof, 79-82, assoc prof, 82-86, prof, 86-90, ethics, New College, Berkeley; prof, applied ethics, North Park Univ, 92- . **HONORS AND AWARDS** Co-dir, Inst for Bus, Tech and Ethics, 97-; Pres, Int Jacques Ellul Soc, 00-. **MEMBERSHIPS** Asn for Practical and Prof Ethics; Conf on Faith and Hist; Natl Asn for Sci, Technol and Soc; Soc of Christian Ethics; Soc of Business Ethics. **RESEARCH** Technology and ethics; virtue ethics. **SELECTED PUBLICATIONS** Auth, The Word of God in the Ethics of Jacques Ellul, 84; auth, Peter the Rock: Extraordinary Insights from an Ordinary Man, 86; auth, The Opening of the Christian Mind, 89; auth, Becoming Good: Building Moral Character, 00; auth, Doing Right: Practicing Ethical Principles, forthcoming. **CONTACT ADDRESS** Dept of Philosophy, No Park Univ, 3225 W Foster Ave, Chicago, IL 60625. **EMAIL** dgill@northpark.edu

GILL, MARY LOUISE
PERSONAL Born 07/31/1950, Alton, IL, m, 1995 **DISCIPLINE** PHILOSOPHY **EDUCATION** Barnard Univ, BA, 72; Columbia Univ, MA, 74; BA, 76; MA, 81; PhD, 81. **CAREER** Instr to prof, Univ Pittsburgh, 79-01; prof, Brown Univ, 01-. **HONORS AND AWARDS** Ethel Wallis Kimball Fel, 85-86; Vis Scholar, Princeton Univ, 89; Fel, Cambridge Univ, 94-; Member, Inst for Adv Study, Princeton, 99-00. **MEMBERSHIPS** Am Philol Assoc, Am Philos Assoc. **RESEARCH** Ancient Greek Philosophy. **SELECTED PUBLICATIONS** Auth, "Matter and Flux in Plato's 'Timaeus,'", Pronesis 32 (87): 34-53; auth, Aristotle on Substance: The Paradox of Unity, Princeton Univ Pr, 89; auth, "Aristotle on Self-Motion," Essays on Aristotle's Physics, ed Lindsay Judson, (Oxford Univ Pr, 91): 243-65; auth, "Individuals and Individuation in Aristotle", Unity, Identity and Explanation in Aristotle's Metaphysics, ed T Scaltsas, D Charles and ML Gill, (Oxford Univ Pr, 94): 55-71; coed, Unity, Identity, and Explanation in Aristotle's Metaphysics, Oxford Univ Pr, 94; coed, Self-Motion: From Aristotle to Newton, Princeton Univ Pr, 94; cotransl, Plato: Parmenides, (Hackett Publ Co, 96); auth, "Material Necessity and Meteorology AV.12," Aristotelische Biologie. Intentionen, Methoden, Ergebnisse, ed Wolfgang Kullman and Sabine Follinger, (Stuttgart: Verlag, 97): 145-61; auth, "Aristotle's Attack on Universals," Oxford Studies in Ancient Philos 19, (01); auth, "Why Does Theatetus' Final Definition of Knowledge Fail?' Ideal and Culture of Knowledge in Plato, ed Wolfgang Detel, (Stuttgart: Verlag, forthcoming). **CONTACT ADDRESS** Dept Philos, Brown Univ, Box 1918, Providence, RI 02912. **EMAIL** mary_louise_bill@brown.edu

GILL, MICHAEL
DISCIPLINE 20TH CENTURY ETHICS, THE HISTORY OF MODERN PHILOSOPHY **EDUCATION** NC Univ, Chapel Hill, PhD. **CAREER** Asst prof, Purdue Univ. **RESEARCH** 17th and 18th Century British ethics. **SELECTED PUBLICATIONS** Published articles on moral justification, and on Hutcheson and Hume. **CONTACT ADDRESS** Dept of Philos, Purdue Univ, West Lafayette, 1080 Schleman Hall, West Lafayette, IN 47907-1080.

GILL, SAM
DISCIPLINE RELIGIOUS STUDIES **EDUCATION** Univ Chicago, PhD. **CAREER** Prof. **RESEARCH** Dance, Dance Theory, Body. **SELECTED PUBLICATIONS** Auth, Storytracking: Texts, Stories; Histories in Central Australia; Mother Earth: An American Story and the Dictionary of Native American Mythology; ed, The Arts of Living. **CONTACT ADDRESS** Religious Studies Dept, Univ of Colorado, Boulder, Boulder, CO 80309. **EMAIL** Sam.Gill@Colorado.edu

GILLAN, GARTH J.
PERSONAL Born 02/14/1939, Washington, DC, m, 1964, 1 child **DISCIPLINE** PHILOSOPHY **EDUCATION** St John's Univ, Minn, AB, 62; Duquesne Univ, MA, 64, PhD(philos), 66. **CAREER** Asst prof philos, Seton Hill Col, 65-66; asst prof, Canisius Col, 66-69; assoc prof, 69-80, Prof Philos, Southern Ill Univ, Carbondale, 80-. **MEMBERSHIPS** Soc Phenomenol & Existential Philos; Am Philos Asn. **RESEARCH** Phenomenology; structuralism; critical theory. **SELECTED PUBLICATIONS** Auth, Language meaning and symbolic presence, Int Philos Quart, 69; The temporality of language and the symbolic, Philos & Rhetoric, 70; The noematics of reason, Philos & Phenomenol Res, 72; ed, Horizons aof the Flesh: Critical Perspectives on the Thought of Merleau-Ponty, Southern Ill Univ, 73; auth, Toward a critical conception of semiotics, 76 & coauth, The new alternative in critical sociology; Foucault's discursive analysis, 77, Cult Hermeneutics; auth, From Sign to Symbol, Harvester Press, 81; coauth, Michel Foucault: Social Theory and Transgression, Columbia Univ Press, 82; Rising from the Ruins: Reason, Being & The Good after Anschwitz, SUNY Press, 98. **CONTACT ADDRESS** Dept of Philosophy, So Illinois Univ, Carbondale, Carbondale, IL 62901-4300. **EMAIL** gjgillan@siu.edu

GILLEN, MARK R.
DISCIPLINE LAW **EDUCATION** Univ Toronto, BC, 81, LLM, 87; York Univ, MBA, 93, LLB, 85. **CAREER** Asst prof, 87-92; assoc prof, 92-. **MEMBERSHIPS** Can Asn Law Tchr. **RESEARCH** Corporate and securities law. **SELECTED PUBLICATIONS** Auth, Securities Regulation in Canada, Carswell; pubs on Malaysian constitutional law; co-auth, Corporations Principles and Policies, Emond Montgomery; Corporations and Partnerships: Canada, Kluwer. **CONTACT ADDRESS** Fac of Law, Univ of Victoria, PO Box 2400, Victoria, BC, Canada V8W 3H7. **EMAIL** mgillen@uvic.ca

GILLETT, CARL
PERSONAL Born 03/13/1967, Oxford, England, s **DISCIPLINE** PHILOSOPHY **EDUCATION** Cambridge Univ, BA, 89; Rutgers, PhD, 97. **CAREER** Asst prof, Illinois Wesleyan Univ, 96-. **RESEARCH** Cosmology; philosophy of science; metaphysics. **CONTACT ADDRESS** Dept of Philosophy, Illinois Wesleyan Univ, PO Box 2900, Bloomington, IL 61702-2900. **EMAIL** cgillett@titan.iwu.edu

GILLIS, CHESTER
PERSONAL Born 07/20/1951, Providence, RI, m, 1986, 1 child **DISCIPLINE** THEOLOGY **EDUCATION** Catholic Univ Louvain, MA, 77, PhL 74, PhB 73; Univ Chicago, PhD, 86. **CAREER** Asst prof, 87-88, Drew Univ; asst prof, 88-94, assoc prof, 94-present, Georgetown Univ **MEMBERSHIPS** Amer Acad Relig **RESEARCH** Interreligious dialogue; catholicism; philosophical theology **SELECTED PUBLICATIONS** Auth, A Question of Final Belief: John Hick's Pluralistic Theory of Salvation, Macmillan, London, St. Martin, NY, 89; Pluralism A New Paradigm for Theology, Lueven Peeters, Grand Rapids, 93; Roman Catholicism in America, Columbia Univ Press, NY, 99. **CONTACT ADDRESS** Dept of Theology, Georgetown Univ, PO Box 571135, Washington, DC 20057-1135. **EMAIL** gillsc@georgetown.edu

GILLMAN, FLORENCE MORGAN
PERSONAL Born 04/27/1947, Utica, NY, m, 1983, 1 child **DISCIPLINE** BIBLICAL STUDIES **EDUCATION** Cath Univ Louvain, Belgium, PhD, STD. **CAREER** Dept Theo, Univ San Diego **HONORS AND AWARDS** Univ of San Diego's Univ Professorship, 99-00. **MEMBERSHIPS** Society of Biblical Literature; Catholic Biblical Assoc; Catholic Theological Society of America. **RESEARCH** New Testament and Early Christianity. **CONTACT ADDRESS** Dept of Theological and Relig Studies, Univ of San Diego, 5998 Alcaka Park, Maher 292, San Diego, CA 92110-2492. **EMAIL** gillman@pwa.acusd.edu

GILLMAN, NEIL
PERSONAL Born Quebec, PQ, Canada **DISCIPLINE** JEWISH PHILOSOPHY **EDUCATION** McGill Univ, BA, 54; Columbia Univ, PhD, 75. **CAREER** Aaron Rabinowitz and Simon H. Rifkind prof and chm dept Jewish phil, Jewish Theol Sem. **SELECTED PUBLICATIONS** Auth, Gabriel Marcel on Religious Knowledge, Univ Press Am, 80. **CONTACT ADDRESS** Jewish Theol Sem of America, 3080 Broadway, New York, NY 10027. **EMAIL** negillman@jtsa.edu

GILMORE, GEORGE BARNES
PERSONAL Born 02/19/1939, New York, NY, m, 1995, 3 children **DISCIPLINE** THEOLOGY, PHILOSOPHY **EDUCATION** Fordham Univ, BA, 62, MA, 64, PhD, 75; Woodstock Col, PhL, 63, BD, 69. **CAREER** Instr classics & chmn dept, Gonzaga Col High Sch, 63-66; adj instr philos, Fordham Univ, 70-72; asst prof, 74-79, assoc prof, 79-83, Prof Humanities, Spring Hill Col, 84-, Chmn Dept Theol, 77-80. **HONORS AND AWARDS** Teacher of the Year, Spring Hill Col, 76, 87 & 93. **MEMBERSHIPS** Am Acad Relig; Col Theol Soc. **RESEARCH** Religious language; Zen; Buddhist/Christian dialogue. **SELECTED PUBLICATIONS** Auth, J A Mohler on Doctrinal Development, Heythrop J, 10/78. **CONTACT ADDRESS** Spring Hill Col, 4000 Dauphin St, Mobile, AL 36608-1791. **EMAIL** ggilmore@shc.edu

GILMORE, ROBERT MCKINLEY, SR.
PERSONAL Born 05/14/1952, Houston, TX **DISCIPLINE** THEOLOGY **EDUCATION** TX Southern Univ, BA 1980, MA 1981, MA 1984; Univ of Houston, EdD 1985; Houston Graduate School of Theology M.D.V. 1989. **CAREER** City of Houston, asst dir 1982-84; Texas Southern Univ, instructor 1981-83; Univ of Houston, grad asst 1982-85; Prairie View A&M Univ, asst prof 1985-89; Houston Graduate School of Theology urban ministry program director; Real Urban Ministry, pres. **HONORS AND AWARDS** PV Choice Awd Prairie View A&M Univ 1989. **MEMBERSHIPS** Asst to pastor Barbers Memorial Bapt Church 1979-89; radio producer and host KTSU and KPVU 1980-85; pres Real Productions 1980-; consultant Baptist Ministers Assoc 1985-95; mem Phi Delta Kappa Univ of Houston 1985-89; Prairie View A&M Univ 1986-89; dir of Drug Training Programs Independent Missionary Baptist Assn; pres Real Educ Alternatives for Leadership & Learning 1989-91; pres One Church/One Child 1988-90; drug educ consultant City of Houston. **SELECTED PUBLICATIONS** Publication "Effective Communication a Drug Education Solution," 1986. **CONTACT ADDRESS** Executive Director, Real Urban Ministry, 3253 Winbern, Houston, TX 77004.

GILMORE, VANESSA D.
PERSONAL Born 10/26/1956, St Albans, NY, s **DISCIPLINE** LAW **CAREER** Foley's Dept Store, fashion buyer, 77-79; Sue Schecter & Assoc, attorney, 85-86; Vickery, Kilbride, Gilmore & Vickery, attorney, 86-94; US Courts, US district Judge, 94-. **HONORS AND AWARDS** Houston Defender Newspaper, Citizen of the Month, 1990; National Black MBA Assn, Distinguished Service Awd, 1994; Holman Street Baptist Church, Community Service Awd, 1994; Human Enrichment of Life, Houston's Young Black Achiever, 1989. **MEMBERSHIPS** Houston Bar Assn; NAACP, chairperson for church committee, 1989-93; YWCA, pres, bd of dirs, 1990-92; Links Inc, chairperson for LEAD, 1990-91; Univ of Houston Alumni Bd, 1993-; Texas Dept of Commerce, chairperson, 1992-94; Texans for NAFTA, chairperson. **RESEARCH** Law. **SELECTED PUBLICATIONS** Auth, Orisakwe v Marriott Retirement Communities, Inc., 871 F.Supp. 296 (S.D.TX, Dec 15, 94) (NO.CIV.A.H-93-0064); auth, Delverne v. Klevenhagen, 888 F.Supp.64 (S.D.TX, May 30, 1995) (NO.CIV.A.H-3338); auth, Rayha v. United Parcel Service, Inc., 940 F.Supp. 1066, 19 A.D.D. 202 (S.D.TX, Oct 11, 1996) (NO.CIV.A.H-95-3867); auth, Elvis Presley Enterprises, Inc. v. Capece, 950 F. Supp. 783 (S.D.TX, Dec 30, 1993) (NO.CIV.A.H-1197); auth, Oliva v. Chrysler Corp., 978 F.Supp. 685 (S.D.TX, Aug 07, 1997) (NO.CIV.A.H-97-1153); auth, Ginsburg v. Memorial Healthcare Systems, Inc. 993 F.Supp. 998, 1998-1 Trade Cases P 72, 049 (S.D.TX, Dec 24, 1997) (NO.CIV.A.H-96-0907); auth, Corporate Health Ins., Inc. v. Texas Dept. of Ins., 12 F. Supp.2d597, 22 Employee Benefits Cas. 1973 (S.D.TX, Sep 18, 1998) (NO.CIV.A.H-97-2072); auth, Universal Computer Systems, Inc. v. Volvo Cars of North American, Inc., 1998 WL 1297399 (S.D.TX, Sep 30, 1998) (NO.CIV.A.H-96-2389); Merrill Lynch Pierce Fenner & Smith Corp. v. Dufour, 1999 WL 1697629 (S.D.TX, Aug 31, 1999) (NO.CIV.A.H-99-2700); auth, Payne v. U.S., 1999 WL 1427756, 85 A.F.T.R.2d 2000-564 (S.D.TX, Dec 13, 1999) (NO.H-93-1738). **CONTACT ADDRESS** Judge, US Courts, 515 Rusk Avenue, Rm 9513, Houston, TX 77002.

GILMOUR, JOHN C.
PERSONAL Born 01/23/1939, Pittsburgh, PA, m, 1976, 2 children **DISCIPLINE** PHILOSOPHY **EDUCATION** Emory Univ, PhD, 66. **CAREER** Inst, Asst Prof, Hofstra Univ, 63-68; Asst Prof, Norwich Univ, 68-70; Prof, Alfred Univ, 70-. **HONORS AND AWARDS** Woodrow Wilson Fel; Alfred Univ Order of Merit. **MEMBERSHIPS** Amer Soc for Aesthetics; APA **RESEARCH** Philosophy of Art, philosophy of Nietzsche, Post Modern theory. **SELECTED PUBLICATIONS** Educating Imaginative Thinkers, the Tchr's Col Record, 94; Genealogy, Interpretation, and Historical Masks, Hist Reflections/Reflexions Historiques, 95; Ed Nietzsch: Voices, Masks, and Histories, Hist Reflections/ Reflexions Historiques, 95; Fire on the Earth: Anselm Kiefer and the Postmodern World, Temple Univ Press, 90. **CONTACT ADDRESS** 29 Glidden St., Newcastle, ME 04553-3401. **EMAIL** Fgilmour@alfred.edu

GILMOUR, PETER
PERSONAL Born 11/25/1942, Chicago, IL **DISCIPLINE** MINISTRY **EDUCATION** Univ of St. Mary of the Lake, PhD. **CAREER** Assoc Prof, Loyola Univ Chicago **MEMBERSHIPS** Religous Education Assoc; Assoc of Prof and Researchers in Religous Education **RESEARCH** Literatue and Religion **SELECTED PUBLICATIONS** coauth, A Companion to Pastoral Care of the Sick, 90; auth, The Wisdom of Memoir: Reading and Writing Life's Sacred Texts, 97; Growing in Courage, 98. **CONTACT ADDRESS** Inst of Pastoral Studies, Loyola Univ, Chicago, 6525 N. Sheridan Rd., Chicago, IL 60626. **EMAIL** pgilmou@wpo.it.luc.edu

GILPIN, W. CLARK
DISCIPLINE RELIGION **EDUCATION** Univ Okla, BA, 67; Lexington Theol Sem, MDiv, 70; Univ Chicago, MA, 70, PhD,74. **CAREER** Assoc prof, Grad Sem, Phillips; current, Dean, Div Sch, Univ Chicago. **MEMBERSHIPS** Am Antiquarian Soc **SELECTED PUBLICATIONS** Auth, The Millenarian Piety of Roger Williams, 79; auth, "The Seminary Ideal in American Protestant Ministerial Education, 1700-1808," Theol Educ 20, 84; auth, A Preface to Theology, Univ Chicago Press, 96; **CONTACT ADDRESS** Div Sch, Univ of Chicago, 1025 E 58th St, Chicago, IL 60637. **EMAIL** wgilpin@midway.uchicago.edu

GILSON, ANNE BATHURST
PERSONAL Born 08/11/1958, Warren, PA, m, 1995 **DISCIPLINE** THEOLOGY; ETHICS **EDUCATION** Chatham Col, BA, 82; Episcopal Divinity School, MDiv, 86; Union Theol Sem, NYork City, MPhil & PhD, 93. **CAREER** Vis scholar, Episcopal Divinity School, 95-96; Consult, Denominational NAT Agencies, 94-; independent scholar; Assoc for Prog, Christ Episcopal Church, Capitol Hill. **HONORS AND AWARDS** Fel, Soc Values Higher Educ. **MEMBERSHIPS** AAR; Soc Values Higher Educ **RESEARCH** Religious right; Economic policy; Christology. **SELECTED PUBLICATIONS** Auth, Eros Breaking Free: Interpreting Sexual Theo-Ethics, Pilgrim, 95; auth, The Battle for America's Families: A Feminist Response to the Religious Right, Pilgrim, 99. **CONTACT ADDRESS** Christ Church Wash Parish, 620 G St SE, Washington, DC 20003. **EMAIL** abgilson@aol.com

GILSON, GREG
PERSONAL Born 09/16/1966, Green Bay, WI, s **DISCIPLINE** PHILOSOPHY **EDUCATION** Univ Wisc-Madison, BS, MA, PhD. **CAREER** Lecturer, Univ Wisc-River Falls. **MEMBERSHIPS** APA **RESEARCH** Metaphysics and epistemology **CONTACT ADDRESS** 1034 Francis St, #A, Stevens Point, WI 54481-5211. **EMAIL** gregory.gilson@vwrf.edu

GIMELLI, LOUIS B.
PERSONAL Born 10/08/1925, Oswego, NY, m, 1951, 2 children **DISCIPLINE** POLITICAL SCIENCE, HISTORY **EDUCATION** State Univ NYork Oswego, BS, 51; NYork Univ, MA, 54, PhD(hist), 64. **CAREER** Teacher elem and high schs, NY, 51-66; from assoc prof to prof hist, 66-76, Prof Hist and Philos, Eastern Mich Univ, 76-. **MEMBERSHIPS** AHA. **RESEARCH** Jacksonian era, especially New York state politics. **SELECTED PUBLICATIONS** Auth, Oswego, from Indian Pathway Through the French and Indian War, Oswego Hist Soc, 55. **CONTACT ADDRESS** Dept of Hist and Philos, Eastern Michigan Univ, Ypsilanti, MI 48197.

GINGERICH, RAY C.
DISCIPLINE THEOLOGY AND ETHICS **EDUCATION** Eastern Mennonite Univ, BA; Goshen Biblical Sem, Mdiv; Vanderbilt Univ, PhD. **CAREER** Theol Dept, Eastern Mennonite Univ **SELECTED PUBLICATIONS** Articles: Festival Quart; Mennonite Weekly Rev; Conrad Grebel Rev. **CONTACT ADDRESS** Eastern Mennonite Univ, 1200 Park Road, Harrisonburg, VA 22802-2462.

GINI, ALFRED
DISCIPLINE PHILOSOPHY **EDUCATION** Northern Ill Univ, BA; Aquinas Inst Philos, MA, PhD. **CAREER** Assoc prof; managing ed, Bus Ethics Quart. **RESEARCH** Business ethics; contemporary moral issues. **SELECTED PUBLICATIONS** Auth, Philosophical Issues in Human Rights, Random House; coauth, Heigh-Ho! Heigh-Ho! Funny, Insightful, Encouraging and Sometimes Painful Quotes About Work, ACTA Publ; It Comes With the Territory: An Inquiry Into the Nature of Work, Random House; co-ed Case Stud in Business Ethics, Prentice-Hall; auth, My Job My Self: work and the Creation of the Modern Individual, Rutldege Pr (Nyork), 00. **CONTACT ADDRESS** Dept of Philosophy, Loyola Univ, Chicago, 820 N. Michigan Ave., Chicago, IL 60611.

GINSBERG, ROBERT
PERSONAL Born 05/18/1934, Brooklyn, NY, m, 1962 **DISCIPLINE** PHILOSOPHY **EDUCATION** Univ Chicago, BA, 55, MA, 58; Univ Pa, PhD, 66. **CAREER** Lecturer, Ind Univ, 59-60; Prof, Intl Lycee France, 62-63; Lecturer, Univ Md Euro Div, 65; Asst Prof, Drexel Inst of Tech, 66-77; Asst Prof to Prof, Pa State Univ, 67-. **HONORS AND AWARDS** Fulbright Fel, 60-62; Fel, Folger Inst; 81, 87, 94; Literary Grant, MD State Arts Coun, 86; Grant, PA Humanities Coun, 93; Grant, Am Philos Asn, 88; Honorable Mention, Phoenix Awd for Editorial Achievement, 92; Travel Grant, Can Soc for Aesthetics, 93, 94; Provost's Awd, PA State Univ, 93, 94; Travel Grant, Tamkang Univ, 95; James Wilbur Awd, 96; Prize and Grant, Ctr for Theol and the Nat Sci, 99-00. **MEMBERSHIPS** Am Philos Asn; Soc for Philos in Am; N Am Soc for Soc Philos; Intl Philos for Peace; Concerned Philos for Peace; Am Soc for Value Inquiry; Am Soc for Aesthetics; Can Soc for Aesthetics. **RESEARCH** Aesthetics; Peace Studies; Value Inquiry; Social and Political Philosophy; Eighteenth Century Thought. **SELECTED PUBLICATIONS** Ed, Criticism and Theory in the Arts, Parnassus Pub, 63; ed, A Casebook on the Declaration of Independence, Thomas Crowell Co, 67; ed, The Critique of War: Contemporary Philosophical Explorations, Henry Regnery Co, 69; auth, Welcome to Philosophy! A Handbook for Students, Freeman, Cooper & Co, 77; auth, Gustav Vigeland: A Case Study in Art and Culture, The Foundations Press, 84; ed, The Philosopher as Writer: The Eighteenth Century, Susquehanna Univ Press, 87; auth, "The Future of Past Injustices," in Horizons of Justice, (Peter Lang Press, 96), 51-63; auth, "The Photograph on My Mind," in Explorations of Value, (Amsterdam, 97), 179-188; auth, "In Favor of Pornography," in New Approaches to Semiotics and the Human Sciences, (Peter Lang Press, 98), 61-94; auth, "On Montaigne's 'Of the Education of Children,'" in Values and Education, (Amsterdam, 98), 203-217. **CONTACT ADDRESS** Dept Philos, Pennsylvania State Univ, Delaware County, 25 Yearsley Mill Rd, Media, PA 19063-5596.

GINSBURG, MARTIN D.
PERSONAL Born 06/10/1932, New York, NY, m, 1954, 2 children **DISCIPLINE** TAX LAW, CORPORATE TAX **EDUCATION** Cornell Univ, AB, 53; Harvard Law Sch, JD, 58. **CAREER** Prof, Columbia Law Sch, 79-80; vis prof, Stanford Univ, 77-78; vis prof, Harvard, 85-86; vis prof, Univ Chicago, 89-90; vis prof, NYork Univ, 92-93; prof, Georgetown Univ, 80-. **HONORS AND AWARDS** Honoree, the Martin D. Ginsburg Ch in Taxation, est GULC, by H Ross Perot, 86; SNYU, Outstand Achiev Awd; Martin Abzug Good Guy Awd; Marshall Whyte Medallion. **MEMBERSHIPS** ALI; ABA; ABF; NYSB; **RESEARCH** Tax law especially corporate law. **SELECTED PUBLICATIONS** Coauth, Mergers, Acquisitions, and Buyouts, Aspen Law Business, 97- (semi annually); coauth, "Maintaining Subchapter S in an Integrated Tax World," Tax Law Rev 47 (93); coauth, "The Subchapter S One Class of Stock Regulation, Tax Notes 69 (95): 233; auth, "The S Corporation Reform Act: Generally a Good Start, Tax Notes 67 (95): 1825; auth, "The Taxpayer Relief Act of 1997: Worse Than You Think, Tax Notes 76 (97): 1790; coauth, "Evaluating Proposals to Tax Intragroup Spin-Offs, Tax Notes (97); auth, "Taxing the Components of Income: A U.S. Perspective, Georgetown Law J, 23 (97); auth, "Some Thoughts on Working, Saving, and Consuming in Nunn-Domenici's Tax World," Nat Tax J 48 (97): 585; repub, Tax Policy in the Real World, Cambridge Univ Press, 99; auth, "Presentation: U.S. Tax Court's Memorial Service for Senior Judge Theodore Tannenwald, Jr.," TC (99); auth, "In Memoriam: Theodore Tannenwald, Jr," Tax Lawyer (99). **CONTACT ADDRESS** School of Law, Georgetown Univ, 600 New Jersey Ave NW, Washington, DC 20001-2022. **EMAIL** ginsburm@law.georgetown.edu

GINTIS, HERBERT
PERSONAL Born 02/11/1940, Philadelphia, PA, m, 1961, 1 child **DISCIPLINE** ECONOMICS **EDUCATION** Univ of Penn, BA, 61; Harvard Univ, MA, 62, PhD, 64. **CAREER** Vis prof, Univ of Siena, 89,93; vis prof, Univ of Paris, 85, 86; vis prof, Harvard Univ, 82, 83; prof of Economics, 76-; assoc prof, Univ of Massachusetts, 74-76; asst prof, Harvard Univ, 73-74; lectr, Harvard Grad Sch, 69-74. **HONORS AND AWARDS** Fac Res Grant, Univ of Massachusetts, 86-88; Mus of Education's Books of the Century award for Schooling in Capitalist America, 00; Who's Who in Economics. **MEMBERSHIPS** Am Math Asn; Am Economic Asn. **RESEARCH** Behavioral theory; crime theory. **SELECTED PUBLICATIONS** Co-auth, Recasting Egalitarianism: New Rules for Markets, States, Communities, Verso, 99; co-auth, "Comments on The Long Shadow of Work," Critical Sociology, Levine and Mintz eds (Humanities Press, 00); auth, "Strong Reciprocity and Human Sociality," Journal of Theoretical Biology 206 (00): 169-179; auth, Game Theory Evolving, Princeton Univ Press, 00; co-auth, "Egalitarianism on its Own," in V. Francicevic and Milica Uvalic, eds, Equality, Participation, Participation (St. Martins, 00); auth, "Group Selection and Human Prosociality," Journal Consciousness Studies 7 (00); auth, "Classical Versus Evolutionary Game Theory," J Consciousness Studies 7 (00); co-auth, "The Intergenerational Transmission of Economic Status: Education, Class, and Genetics," in Marcus Feldman, ed. Genetics, Behavior and Society (Oxford, Elsevier, 01); co-auth, "The Future of Egalitarian Politics," in Power, Employment, and Accumulation, Jim Stanford, Lance Taylor, and Ellen Houston eds (NY: M.E. Sharpe, 01); co-auth, "Incentive-Enhancing Preferences: Personality Behavior and Earnings," American Economic Review 9 (01); co-auth, "Cooperation, Reciprocity and Punishment in Fifteen Small-scale Societies," American Economic Review 91 (01). **CONTACT ADDRESS** Dept of Economics, Univ of Massachusetts, Amherst, Amherst, MA 01003. **EMAIL** hgintis@mediaone.net

GIRARDOT, NORMAN J.
PERSONAL Born 04/19/1943, 2 children **DISCIPLINE** HISTORY OF RELIGIONS **EDUCATION** Col Holy Cross, BS, 65; Univ Chicago, MA, 72, PhD, 74. **CAREER** Ed asst, Hist Relig J, 68-70; asst prof Theol, Notre Dame Univ, 72-79; vis asst prof, Oberlin Col, 79-80; assoc prof & chmn, Relig Studies Dept, Lehigh Univ, 80-; prof, 89; Nat Endowment for Humanities fel, 83, 93-95; Chiang Ching-kuo fel, 93-95; Pacific Cult Found fel, 93-95; exec comt, Soc Study Chinese Relig, 75-78; Univ Distinguished Prof of Relig, 99; reader Univ Chicago Press, Univ Notre Dame Press, Scholars Press & Greenwood Press. **HONORS AND AWARDS** Phi Beta Kappa . **MEMBERSHIPS** Am Soc for the Study of Religion; Am Acad Relig; Asn Asian Scholars; Soc Study Chinese Relig; Amer Folk Art Society; International Assoc of the History of Religions; President, Society for the Study of Chinese Religions. **RESEARCH** Taoism; Chinese religion and myth; Western study of Asian religion; Visionary folkart; polular religion. **SELECTED PUBLICATIONS** Auth, The problem of creation mythology in the study of Chinese religion, Vol 15, 76 & co-ed, Current perspectives in the study of Chinese religions, Vol 17, 78, Hist Relig; auth, Returning to the Beginning and the arts of Mr Huntun in the Chuang Tzu, J Chinese Philos, Vol 5, 78; Chaotic order and benevolent disorder in the Chuang Tau, Philos East & West, Vol 28, 78; Taoism, In: Encycl of Bioethics, 78; co-ed, China and Christianity, Notre Dame Univ Press, 79; Imagination and Meaning: The Scholarly and Literary Worlds of Mircea Eliade, Seabury Press, 82; auth, Myth and Meaning in Early Taoism, Univ Calif Press, 82, rb, 89; trans, I Robinet's Tavist Meditation, SUNY, 93; auth, "Daoism and Ecology," Howard, 00; auth, "The Victorian Translation of China," California, 01. **CONTACT ADDRESS** Relig Studies Dept, Lehigh Univ, 9 W Packer Ave, #5, Bethlehem, PA 18015-3082. **EMAIL** njgo@lehigh.edu

GIRILL, T. R.
PERSONAL Born 10/02/1946, Rochester, NY **DISCIPLINE** PHILOSOPHY OF SCIENCE **EDUCATION** Univ Ky, BS, 68; Univ Calif, Berkeley, MA, 70, PhD, 73. **CAREER** Asst prof, Lawrence Univ, Wisc, 74-76; instr, Univ Calif, Santa Cruz exten, 86-92; sr tech writer, ed, Univ Calif, Lawrence Livermore Nat Lab, 78- ; ed in chief, Jour of Computer Documentation, 95-00 **HONORS AND AWARDS** Phi Beta Kappa; assoc fel, Soc for Tech Commun, 92; assoc, Faxon Inst, 91-92; ed in chief, Jour of Computer Documentation, 95-; assoc ed, Tech Commun, 83-90; Fel, Soc for Tech Commun, 99; Univ of Kentucky Fel, 98. **MEMBERSHIPS** Philos of Sci Asn; British Soc Philos of Sci; Hist of Sci Soc; APA; ASIS; Soc Tech Commun. **RESEARCH** Scientific explanation; online text structure; information access; text usability. **SELECTED PUBLICATIONS** Auth, Among the Professions, Soc for Tech Commun, 91; auth, Extended Subject Access to Hypertext Online Documentation, JASIS, 91; auth, Information Chunking as an Interface Design Issue for Full- text Databases, in Dillon, ed, Interfaces for Information Retrieval, Greenwood, 91; auth, Hierarchical Search Support for Hypertext Online Documentation, Int Jour of Man-Machine Stud, 92; auth, Contributions of the Open-Commentary Journal, Proceeddings of the 1997 IEEE International Professional Communication Conference, IEEE, 97. **CONTACT ADDRESS** Lawrence Livermore National Laboratory, Univ of California, Lawrence Livermore National Laboratory, L-72, PO Box 808, Livermore, CA 94550. **EMAIL** trg@llnl.gov

GIROUX, MICHEL
DISCIPLINE LAW **EDUCATION** Univ Ottawa, BA, LLB. **CAREER** Assoc prof; Laurentian Univ. **RESEARCH** Constitutional law; criminal law. **SELECTED PUBLICATIONS** Auth, "La Charte canadienne des droits et libertes," Revue penitentiaire et de droit penal, 4, (92): 366-406. **CONTACT ADDRESS** Law and Justice Dept, Laurentian Univ, 935 Ramsey Lake Rd, Sudbury, ON, Canada P3E 2C6. **EMAIL** mgiroux@nickel.laurentian.ca

GITELMAN, MORTON
PERSONAL Born 02/07/1933, Chicago, IL, m, 1956, 3 children **DISCIPLINE** LAW **EDUCATION** Roosevelt Univ, cert personnel admin, 53; DePaul Univ, LLB, 59; Univ Ill, LLM, 65. **CAREER** Teaching fel law, Univ Ill, 59-60; res assoc, Duke Univ, 60-61; from asst prof to assoc prof, Univ Denver, 61-65; assoc prof, 65-69, PROF LAW, UNIV ARK, FAYETTEVILLE, 69-, PROF ARCHIT, 78-, Chmn, Ark Adv Comt US Comn Civil Rights and mem planning comn, City Fayetteville, 67-; vis prof, Univ Ill, 70-71. **MEMBERSHIPS** Am Civil Liberties Union. **RESEARCH** Constitutional law; jurisprudence; land use controls. **SELECTED PUBLICATIONS** Auth, The First Chancery Court in Arkansas: An 1855 Creation of The Arkansas General-Assembly, Ark Hist Quart, Vol 0055, 96. **CONTACT ADDRESS** Sch of Law, Univ of Arkansas, Fayetteville, Fayetteville, AR 72701-1202.

GITHIGA, JOHN GATUNGU
PERSONAL Born 07/27/1942, Muranga, Kenya, m, 1968 **DISCIPLINE** RELIGION **EDUCATION** Makerere University, theology diploma, 1974; University of the South, MDiv, 1979; International Bible Institute and Seminary, DREd, 1980; University of the South, DMin, 1981. **CAREER** Diocese of Nakuru, director of St Nicholars Children Center, five years; St Paul's United Theological College, department head, pastoral theology, 80-86; African Association for Pastoral Studies and Counseling, founder, pres, 85-88; St Cyprian Church, vicar, 86-91; Ecumencial Christian Fellowship, founder, pres, 92-; Lakeview Center, telephone crisis counselor, Kairos spiritual director, voluntary, 92-; Extended Arms Outreach Center, field counselor to juvenile offenders & their parents, 92-96; West Texas A&M Univ, Chaplain, 96-; Grambling State Univ, Vicar, Chaplain, currently. **HONORS AND AWARDS** Pensacola Junior College, certificate of appreciation for presentation, 1987; Kiwanis Club of Greater Pensacola, certificate of appreciation for presentation, 1988; Martin Luther King Commemorative Comm, cert of appreciation for planning, 1989; Kiwanis Cert of Appreciation for Spiritual leadership and Service to community, 1989; Initiation & Pastoral Psychology. **MEMBERSHIPS** University of West Florida Select Committee on Minority Affairs, 1987-92; Martin Luther King Jr Celebration Committee, 1989; Ecumenical and Interfaith Committee, 1987-91; Greater Kiwanis of Pensacola, 1988-92; Association of Theological Institutions in Eastern Africa, 1980-85; National Christian Council of Kenya Youth Department, Nakuru, secretary, 1966-68; Diocese of Nakuru Youth Department, secretary, 1968-71; The First Nakuru Company of the Boys Brigade, captain, 1967-68. **SELECTED PUBLICATIONS** Author, Christ & Roots, 1988; The Spirit in the Black Soul, 1984; "The Use of Psychology in Pastoral Counseling in Africa," Theological Journal, 1982; "Family in Transition," Beyond, July 1987; co-author, Ewe Ki Jana (Oh Young Man), 1971. **CONTACT ADDRESS** St. George's Church West, West Texas A&M Univ, 2216 4th Ave, Canyon, TX 79015.

GITTINS, ANTHONY
PERSONAL Born 02/16/1943, Manchester, United Kingdom, s **DISCIPLINE** THEOLOGY, ANTHROPOLOGY **EDUCATION** Edinburgh, Scotland, MA, Soc Anthropol, 72, MA, Linguistics, PhD, Anthropol, 77. **CAREER** Head of Mission Dept, Missionary Inst London, 80-84; assoc prof, Cath Theol Union, Chicago, 84-90, prof, 90-98, Bishop Fx Ford Prof (Chair), 98-. **HONORS AND AWARDS** Frai Fel, Royal Anthropol Inst; Bishop Fx, Ford Prof of Missiology. **MEMBERSHIPS** RAI, ASA, CTSA, AAA, AMS, APS, MWPM. **RESEARCH** Inculturation; theological method; contemporary theology in Africa; theological anthropology. **SELECTED PUBLICATIONS** Auth, Bread for the Journey, Orbis (93); auth, Gifts and Strangers, Paulist (98); auth, Reading the Clouds, Liguori (99); auth, Life and Death Matters, Steyler (2000). **CONTACT ADDRESS** Dept Theol, Catholic Theol Union at Chicago, 5401 S Cornell Ave, Chicago, IL 60615-5664. **EMAIL** tgittins@ctu.edu

GIURLANDA, PAUL
PERSONAL Born 01/14/1946, Detroit, MI, s **DISCIPLINE** THEOLOGY **EDUCATION** Cath Univ, BA, 69; Syracuse Univ, MS, 74; Grad Theol Un, MA, 78, PhD, 85 **CAREER** Fac, 78-pres, St Marys Col of CA **MEMBERSHIPS** Cath Theol Soc of Am; Am Acad of Relig; AAUP; Col Theology Soc **RESEARCH** Foundational Theology; Gender and Religion **SELECTED PUBLICATIONS** Auth, Faith and Knowledge A Critical Inquiry, University Press of America, Lanham Maryland, 87 **CONTACT ADDRESS** 250 Whitmore St, Apt. 401, Oakland, CA 94611. **EMAIL** pgiurlan@stmarys-ca.edu

GIVELBER, DANIEL JAMES
PERSONAL Born Cleveland, OH, m, 1963, 2 children **DISCIPLINE** COMMON LAW SUBJECTS, LAW AND SOCIETY **EDUCATION** Harvard Col, BA, 61, JD, 64. **CAREER** Pvt pract law, Cahill, Gordon, Reindel and Ohl, New York, NY, 64-67; asst US atty, Off US Atty, Dist of Columbia, 67-69; PROF LAW, SCH OF LAW, NORTHEASTERN UNIV, 69-. **RESEARCH** Developments in law protecting emotional well being; developments in law protecting emotional well being; developments in defamation law. **SELECTED PUBLICATIONS** Auth, Learning Through Work--An Empirical-Study of Legal Internship, J Legal Educ, Vol 0045, 95. **CONTACT ADDRESS** Sch of Law, Northeastern Univ, 400 Huntington Ave, Boston, MA 02115-5005.

GLADSON, JERRY A.
PERSONAL Born 04/21/1943, Dalton, GA, m, 1965, 2 children **DISCIPLINE** OLD TESTAMENT **EDUCATION** Southern Adventist Univ, BA, 65; Vanderbilt Univ, MA,73, PhD, 78. **CAREER** Prof, Southern Adventist Univ, 72-87; dean, Psychol Stud Inst, 87-92; sr minister, First Christian Church, Garden Grove, Calif, 93-97; sr minister, First Christian Church, Marietta, GA 97-. **HONORS AND AWARDS** Tchr of the Year, Southern Adventist Univ, 81. **MEMBERSHIPS** Soc of Biblical Lit, Catholic Biblical Asn, Christian Asn for Psychol Stud, Acad of Parish Clergy **RESEARCH** Hebrew Wisdom; Old Testament Theology and Exegesis. **CONTACT ADDRESS** 569 Frasier St., Marietta, GA 30060. **EMAIL** jgladson1@juno.com

GLADWIN, LEE ALLAN
PERSONAL Born Washington, DC **DISCIPLINE** METHODOLOGY, PHILOSOPHY **EDUCATION** Fairmont State Col, BA, 66; Cath Univ, MA, 68; Carnegie-Mellon Univ, DA, 80. **CAREER** Asst prof hist, Shenandoah Col, 68-76; Asst Prof Human Serv, Nat Grad Univ, 82-, Consult, Oakton Res Corp, 81-82. **MEMBERSHIPS** Am Soc Training & Develop; Nat Soc Performance & Instr. **RESEARCH** Artificial intelligence; problem solving. **SELECTED PUBLICATIONS** Auth, Hollywood Propaganda, Isolationism, and Protectors of the Public Mind, 1917-1941, Prologue-Quart of the Nat Arch, Vol 0026, 94; Turing, Alan, Enigma, and the Breaking of German Machine-Ciphers in World-War-II, Prologue-Quart of the Nat Arch, Vol 0029, 97. **CONTACT ADDRESS** Rt 3, Box 225, Winchester, VA 22601.

GLAHE, FRED RUFUS
PERSONAL Born 06/30/1934, Chicago, IL, m, 1961, 1 child **DISCIPLINE** ECONOMICS **EDUCATION** BS, aero eng, 57, MS, econ, 63, PhD, econ, Purdue Univ, 64. **CAREER** Engineer, Allsion Division, General Motors, 57-61; economist, Buttelle Memorial Inst, Columbus, Ohio, 64-65; PROF OF ECONOMICS, UNIV OF COLO, 65-. **MEMBERSHIPS** The Mount Pelerin Soc. **RESEARCH** Macroeconomics; Money; History of Economic Thought; Technology. **SELECTED PUBLICATIONS** Auth, Adam Smith and the Wealth of Nations: A Concordance, 95; auth, The Drama: The Hayek Keynes Debate Over the Business Cycle, 99; coauth, Praxeology and the Development of Human Capital, Cultural Dynamics, 97. **CONTACT ADDRESS** Dept of Economics, Univ of Colorado, Boulder, Campus Box 256, Boulder, CO 80309. **EMAIL** fred.glahe@colorado.edu

GLANNON, JOSEPH WILLIAM
PERSONAL Born 03/22/1946, New York, NY **DISCIPLINE** LAW **EDUCATION** Harvard Univ, BA, 68, MAT, 71, JD, 77. **CAREER** Asst dean, Bates Col, 71-74; law clerk, Massachusetts Appeals Ct, 77-78; asst corp coun, City of Boston, 78-79; from Instr to Assoc Prof, 79-86, Prof Law, Suffolk Univ, 86-, Dir, Legal Practice Skills Prog, 80-87, Chair, Fac Admin Comt, 90-96, Chair, Grading Policy Comt, 96-98, Chair, Fac Appointments Comt, 91-92; Legal consult, City of Boston, 78-80 & 82; exec comt mem, AALS Civil Procedure Section, 95-97. **HONORS AND AWARDS** Phi Beta Kappa; Cornelius J. Moynihan Awd for Excellence in Tchg, 91. **RESEARCH** Civil procedure; local government law. **SELECTED PUBLICATIONS** Auth, Liability for Public Duties under the Tort Claims Act: The Legislature Reconsiders the Public Duty Role, Mass Law Rev, 94; The Law of Torts: Examples and Explanations, Little, Brown & Co, 95; Fireside Civil Procedure (9-hour audiotape series), Little, Brown & Co, 96; Civil Procedure: Examples and Explanations, 3rd ed, 97; coauth, Coordinating Civil Procedure and the Legal Research and Writing Course: A Field Experiment, J Legal Educ, 97; Politics and Personal Jurisdiction: Suing State Sponsors of Terrorism under the 1996 Amendments to the Foreign Sovereign Immunities Act (in prep); auth numerous other articles and publ. **CONTACT ADDRESS** Sch of Law, Suffolk Univ, 41 Temple St, Boston, MA 02114-4241.

GLASSNER, MARTIN
PERSONAL Born 07/07/1932, Plainfield, NJ, m, 1955, 3 children **DISCIPLINE** POLITICAL SCIENCE, GEOGRAPHY **EDUCATION** Syracuse Univ, BA, 53; Cal State Univ, Fullerton, MA, 64; Claremont Grad Sch, PhD, 68. **CAREER** Lectr, Chapman Col, 64-65; asst prof, Cal State Poly Col, 65-67; asst prof, Univ Puget Sound, 67-68; asst prof, S Conn Univ, 68-95; prof, 93-95; prof emer, 95-. **HONORS AND AWARDS** Am Men Women Sci; Dict Intl Bio; Comm Leaders Noteworthy Am; Who's Who - Intl Auth Writers, Am Edu, World, East; Men of Achiev; Fac Schl Awd, 75; NGS, Res Gnt; CSU Res Gnts; Dist Alum Awd. **MEMBERSHIPS** AAG; MGSG; PGSG; Comm on Antarctica; CLAG; ILA; ISA; IGU; ASIL. **SELECTED PUBLICATIONS** Auth, Neptune's Domain; A Political Geography Of The Sea, Unwin Hyman (London), 90; auth, Bibliography On Land-Locked States, Nijhoft (Dordrecht), 91; auth, Political Geography, John Wiley And Sons (NY), 92; auth, Bibliography On Land-Locked States, Nijhoft (Dordrecht), 95; auth, Political Geography, John Wiley And Sons (NY), 96; auth, "Bolivia's Orientation: Toward The Atlantic or the Pacific?" in Geopolitics of the Southern Cone and Antarctica, eds. Philip Kelly, Jack Child (Boulder And London: Rienner, 88), 154-169; auth, "Resolving The Problems Of Land-Lockedness," in Land-Locked States Of Africa And Asia, eds. Dick Hodder, et al (London: Frank Cass, 98), 197-208; auth, "Different Perspectives on the Law of the Sea," Political Geog Quart (91); auth, "The Frontiers of Earth -- and of Political Geography: The Sea, Antarctica and Outer Space," Polit Geog Quart (91); auth, "The Political Geography of the Sea," Canadian Geog (93); auth, "Recent Books on Marine Affairs," Ocean Devel Intl Law (93); auth, "Political Geography in the United Nations," Political Geog (94); auth, "The Tide Flows On," Ocean Yearbook 11 (94); auth, "New Books on Marine Affairs," Ocean and Coastal Manage (97); auth, "Navigating Difficult Waters," Ocean Yearbook 13 (98). **CONTACT ADDRESS** 742 Paradise Ave, Hamden, CT 06514.

GLAZEBROOK, PATRICIA
PERSONAL Born Edinburgh, Scotland **DISCIPLINE** PHILOSOPHY **EDUCATION** Univ Toronto, PhD, 93. **CAREER** Asst prof, Colgate Univ. **HONORS AND AWARDS** Res grant, DAAD, Freiburg, Ger, 92; Auckland Univ, Honorary Res

Fel, 98; Martha Lile Love Teaching Awd, Univ of Toronto, 94. **MEMBERSHIPS** Society for Phenomenology and Existential Philosophy; North Am Heidegger Society; Am Philosophical Assoc; International Assoc of Environmental Philosophy; Ancient Philosophy Society, (founding member); Massey College (fellow) **RESEARCH** Phenomenology; Heidegger; Philosophy of Science; Philosophy of Nature; Aristotle; Feminism. **SELECTED PUBLICATIONS** Auth, Heidegger on the Experiment, Philos Todav, 98; auth, Heidegger's Philosophy of Science, New York: Fordham Univ Press, 00; auth, Heidegger and Ecofeminism Re-Reading the Canon: Feminist Interpetations of Heidegger, edited by Nancy Holland and Patricia Huntington, The Pennsylvania State Univ Press: Univ Park, PA, forthcoming, 00; auth, From physis to nature, techne to technology: Heidegger on Aristotle, Galileo and Newton The Southern J of Philosophy 38:1, (00), 95-118; auth, Zeno Against Mathematical Physics, J of the History of Ideas, forthcoming. **CONTACT ADDRESS** Dept of Philos and Relig, Colgate Univ, 13 Oak Drive, Hamilton, NY 13346. **EMAIL** pglazebrook@mail.colgate.edu

GLAZIER, IRA ALBERT
PERSONAL Born 08/12/1925, New York, NY, m, 1953, 1 child **DISCIPLINE** ECONOMIC HISTORY **EDUCATION** NYork Univ, BA, 48; Univ Chicago, MA, 51; Harvard Univ, PhD(hist & econ), 63. **CAREER** Instr econ hist, Ill Inst Technol, 50-51 and Ctr Int Affairs, Harvard Univ, 58-59; lectr hist, Northwestern Univ, 59-60; from instr to asst prof, Mass Inst Technol, 61-66; assoc prof, Boston Col, 66-67; Prof Econ Hist, Temple Univ, 69-, Old Dominion grant, 64; fac assoc, Columbia Univ, 70-; Fulbright-Hays res scholar, Bocconi Univ, Milan, 71; ed, Journal Europ Econ Hist, 72-; NATO Professorship, Univ Naples, NAtlantic Treaty Orgn, 78-79; Rockefeller grant, 80. **HONORS AND AWARDS** Widener Trust Awd, 81. **MEMBERSHIPS** AHA; Am Econ Asn; Royal Econ Soc; Econ Hist Soc; Econ Hist Asn. **RESEARCH** Foreign trade and industrialization; economic development of modern Europe; Soviet-Italian economic relations. **SELECTED PUBLICATIONS** Auth, The National-Integration of Italian Return Migration, 1870-1929, Am Hist Rev, Vol 0098, 93; Crossings--The Great Transatlantic Migrations, 1870-1914, Am Hist Rev, Vol 0099, 94. **CONTACT ADDRESS** Dept Hist, Temple Univ, 1115 W Berks St, Gladfelter Rm 913, Philadelphia, PA 19122-6006.

GLAZIER, STEPHEN D.
PERSONAL Born 06/10/1949, New London, CT, m, 1975, 1 child **DISCIPLINE** ANTHROPOLOGY, SOCIOLOGY, THEOLOGY **EDUCATION** Eastern Col, AB, 71; Princeton Theol Sem, MDiv, 74; Univ of Ct, PhD, 81. **CAREER** Prof, Grad Studies, Univ of Nebr, Kearney, 94-; vis prof, Univ of Nebr at Lincoln, 2000-. **HONORS AND AWARDS** Teaching Fel, Am Acad of Relig/Lilly Found Workshops, 97-98; Delegate, Consciousness Studies Summer Inst, Univ of Ariz and the Fetzer Inst, 97; Prog ed, Anthropol of Relig Section, 97th Annual Meeting, Am Anthropol Asn, 98; Vice-Pres, Anthropol of Relig Section, Am Anthropol Asn, 98-2000; Secretary, Soc for the Sci Study of Relig, 98-2001. **MEMBERSHIPS** Am Anthropol Asn, Royal Anthropol Inst, Soc for the Anthropol of Relig, Soc for the Sci Study of Relig, Soc des Americanistes de Paris, Caribbean Studies Asn. **RESEARCH** Anthropology (four subfields), religion, race and ethnicity, ethnohistory, Caribbean and Latin America, ethnomusicology, folklore. **SELECTED PUBLICATIONS** Ed, Anthropology of Religion: A Handbook, Westport, CT: Greenwood (97); auth, "Foreword," special issue: Turkic and Siberian Shamanism in the Former USSR, E. J. N. Fridman, guest ed, Anthropol of Consciousness, vol 10, no 4 (99); auth, "William Wallace Fenn," "John Mifflin Brown," and "Benjamin W. Arnett," in American National Biography, J. A. Garraty, gen ed, New York: Oxford Univ Press (99); auth, "Anthropology and Theology: The Legacies of a Link," Explorations in Anthropology and Theology, 2nd ed, F. A. Salome and W. R. Adams, ed, Lanham, Md: Univ Press of Am (99); auth, "Anti Anti-Reductionism: Biological and Cognitive Approaches to the Anthropology of Religion," Guest ed's intro, special issue, Zygon (2000); auth, "After the Falls: Pilgrimage and Healing in Post Colonial Trinidad," Yearbook of Cross-Cultural Medicine and Psychotherapy, vol 10, M. Winkelman and J. Dubisch, guest eds (200); coauth, "Understanding Caribbean Religions," Ch 10 in Understanding Caribbean Culture, T. d'Agostino and R. Hillman, eds, Kingston, Jamaica: Ian Randle, Boulder, Co: Kynn Riener (2000); ed, Anthropology and Contemporary Religions, Westport, Ct: Greenwood (2000); gen ed, Encyclopedia of Religion and Society (Volume V): African and African American Religions, New York and London: Routledge (2001). **CONTACT ADDRESS** Dept Sociol and Anthropol, Univ of Nebraska, Kearney, 905 W 25th St, Kearney, NE 68847. **EMAIL** glaziers@unk.edu

GLAZIER-MCDONALD, BETH
DISCIPLINE RELIGION **EDUCATION** Gorge Washington University; Univ Chicago, M.Div, Ph.D.-residence and guest speaker at Temple Adath Israel in Lexington, as scholar-in-residence at Keneseth Israel Congregation in Allentown, Penn. **CAREER** Asst prof, Penn State Univ; fac, Centre Col, 80-; NEH Assoc Prof Relig, current. **SELECTED PUBLICATIONS** Contrib auth, Eerdman's Dic of Bible; conribu, Atiqot, Jour Roman Archaeol. **CONTACT ADDRESS** Centre Col, 600 W Walnut St, Danville, KY 40422. **EMAIL** glzrmcd@centre.edu

GLENN, JOHN D., JR.
PERSONAL Born 03/08/1942, Wellington, TX, m, 1967, 1 child **DISCIPLINE** PHILOSOPHY **EDUCATION** Univ Tex Austin, BA, 64; Yale Univ, MA, 66; PhD, 68. **CAREER** Asst prof to assoc prof, Tulane Univ, 68-; Chair, 96-99. **HONORS AND AWARDS** Woodrow Wilson Fel, 64, 67; Mortar Board Awd for Outstanding Teaching, 99-00. **MEMBERSHIPS** Soc for Philos of Relig. **RESEARCH** Kant, Kierkergaard, Philosophy of Religion, History of Philosophy. **SELECTED PUBLICATIONS** Auth, "Marcel and Sartre: The Philosophy of Communion and the Philosophy of Alienation", The Philosophy of Gabriel Marcel, eds Paul A. Schilpp and Lewis E. Hahn, Open Court Publ, 84; auth, "The Behaviorism of a Phenomenologist - The Structure of Behavior and The Concept of Mind", Philos Topics, 13.2 (Spring 85); auth, "Hartshornean Panentheism and Kierkegaardian Paradox", Tulane Studies in Philos, XXXIV (86); auth, "The Definition of the Self and the Structure of Kierkegaard's Work" Int Kierkegaard Commentary, Vol 19, ed Robert Perkins, Mercer Univ Pr, (Macon, GA), 87; auth, "Kierkegaard and Anselm", Int Kierkegaard Commentary, Vol 7, ed Robert Perkins, Mercer Univ Pr, (Macon, GA), 94; auth, "A Highest Good . . . An Eternal Happiness: The Human Telos in Kierkegaard's Concluding Unscientific Postscript", Int Kierkegaard Commentary, Vol 12, ed Robert Perkins, Mercer Univ Pr, (Macon, GA), 97. **CONTACT ADDRESS** Dept Philos, Tulane Univ, 6823 St Charles Ave, New Orleans, LA 70118-5665. **EMAIL** glenn@tulane.edu

GLIDDEN, DAVID
PERSONAL Born 01/07/1945, Chicago, IL, m, 1990, 2 children **DISCIPLINE** PHILOSOPHY **EDUCATION** Princeton Univ, PhD. **CAREER** Prof, Univ Calif, Riverside. **HONORS AND AWARDS** Phi Beta Kappa. **MEMBERSHIPS** Nat Book Critics Circle. **RESEARCH** Ancient applied ethics and social philosophy. **SELECTED PUBLICATIONS** Auth, Moral Vision, Orthos Logos, and the Role of the Phronimos, APEIRON Spec Issue, 96; Josiah Royce's Reading of Plato's Theaetetus, Hist of Philos Quart, 96; Requiem for Philosophy, Rel, 97; Augustine's Hermeneutics and the Principle of Charity, Ancient Philos, 97; auth, "Commonplaces" Philosophy and Geography, 98; auth, "Holy Philosophy" Rel., 99. **CONTACT ADDRESS** Dept of Philos, Univ of California, Riverside, 3304 Humanities, Riverside, CA 92521-0201. **EMAIL** david.glidden@ucr.edu

GLIDDEN, JOCK
DISCIPLINE PHILOSOPHY **EDUCATION** Middlebury Col, AB, 58; Univ Edinburgh, MA, 63; Univ Colo, PhD, 69. **CAREER** Assoc prof, Waynesburg Col. **RESEARCH** British empiricism, wittgenstein, environmental philosophy, medical ethics, philosophy of science and aesthetics. **SELECTED PUBLICATIONS** Auth, Can We Treat Nature Morally, Univ Edinburgh, 73; coauth, Teaching by the Group Method in Philosophy 101, Col Tchg, 90. **CONTACT ADDRESS** Dept of Political Science, Waynesburg Col, 51 W College St, Waynesburg, PA 15370. **EMAIL** jglidden@weber.edu

GLOVER, RAYMOND F.
PERSONAL Born 05/23/1928, m, 1957, 3 children **DISCIPLINE** MUSIC IN LITURGY **EDUCATION** Univ Toronto, BM, 52; Union Theol Sem, MSM, 54; **CAREER** Instr, Hartford Sem Found, 63-65; Berkeley Divinity Sch, 64-70; hd mus dept, St Catherine's Sch, 76-80; prof, Va Theol Sem, 91-00. **HONORS AND AWARDS** Va Theol Sem, LHD, 86; Berkeley Divinity Sch at Yale, MusD, 87; gen ed, church hymnal corp, 80-91. **MEMBERSHIPS** Am Guild of Organists; Assoc of Anglican Musicans; The Hymn Soc of the United States and Canada. **SELECTED PUBLICATIONS** Auth, A Commentary on New Hymns, The Church Hymnal Corp, 87; ed, The Hymnal, 82. **CONTACT ADDRESS** 9202 Westmoor Dr., Richmond, VA 23229. **EMAIL** RGlover@vts.edu

GLOWIENKA, EMERINE FRANCES
PERSONAL Born 03/09/1920, Milwaukee, WI **DISCIPLINE** PHILOSOPHY, SOCIOLOGY **EDUCATION** Marquette Univ, BA, 42, MA, 51, PhD(Philos), 73; St Louis Univ, PhD-(Sociol), 56. **CAREER** Elem & sec teacher, Acad Sacred Heart, Ill, 45-53; instr Philos & Sociol, Barat Col, 55-58; assoc prof Sociol & chmn dept, Duchesne Col, 61-62; prof Sociol & Social Welfare, San Francisco Col Women, 62-70, chmn dept, 61-70; asst prof Philos, Univ San Diego, 71-74; prof Philos & Sociol & chairperson Dept, Gallup Br Col, Univ NMEX, 74-, prof Philos, Gallup Diocesan Sem, 74-. **MEMBERSHIPS** Am Philos Asn; Am Cath Philos Asn; Soc Women Philos. **RESEARCH** Ethics; metaphysics; personalization. **SELECTED PUBLICATIONS** Auth, Social philosophy as a synthesis of the social sciences, Am Cath Sociol Rev, Fall 63; Notes on consciousness in matter, New Scholasticism, Fall 69; Why do we teach?, Mod Soc, 1/70; A brighter side of the new genetics, Bioscience, 2/75; The counsel of poverty: Gospels versus acts, Rev Relig, 3/75; On demythologizing philosophy, Southwest Philos Studies, 4/81; Aquinas With the Realists and the Conceptualists, Southwest Philosophical Studies, 18, 96; auth, "Person as 'That Which Is Most Perfect in Nature'," Southwest Philosophical Studes, vol 20 (98): 56-65; auth, Personization: The Moral Norm for Today, Gallup, New Mexico, The Indian Trader Inc Publisher, 99; auth, "On Knowing the Act of Knowing," Southwest Philosophical Studies, vol 22, 00 (forthcoming). **CONTACT ADDRESS** Dept of Philos Gallup Br Col, Univ of New Mexico, Gallup, 200 College Rd, Gallup, NM 87301-5603.

GLUCK, ANDREW L.
PERSONAL Born 03/21/1944, New York, NY, m, 3 children **DISCIPLINE** PHILOSOPHY **EDUCATION** Univ of Fl, BA, 65; Columbia Univ, MA, 73; M.Ed, Columbia University, 77; NYork Univ, MS, 90; Columbia Univ, EdD, 97. **CAREER** Adjunct fac, Bramson ORT Tech Inst, 94-; adjunct fac, Berkeley Col, 97-; adjunct fac, Empire State Col, 98-; Adjunct Faculty, Hofstra University, 98-. **HONORS AND AWARDS** Profiled in Who's Who in America, 00-01; Honored by Mayor of Caucas, Venezuela, 97. **MEMBERSHIPS** Am Philos Asn; Nat Asn of Forensic Econ. **RESEARCH** Consciousness studies; Medieval philosophy; Forensic economics. **SELECTED PUBLICATIONS** Auth, Economic Damages as a Result of Minimal Personality Changes in Head Injury Cases, (abstract) in J of Forensic Econ, 95; "Philosophical Practice in Career and Management Consulting" in Perspectives in Philosophical Practice, 96; "Chaos Theory and Its Application to Vocational Counseling: A Critical Reappraisal" in The J: Counseling and Values, 96; "Karl Popper's Three Worlds and its Implications for the Study of Consciousness" (abstract) n The J of Consciousness Studies, 96; auth, "Regarding the New Worklife Tables" in The J of Forensic Econ, 96; auth "Philosophical Counseling, Rationality and Healing" in Socrates Mag, 98; "The Consciousness Problem and the Human Sciences" (abstract) in J of Consciousness Studies, 98; auth, Reduced Worklife Expectancy: Computing Lifetime Loss of Earnings for Partially Disabled Persons, in Tual Lawyers Quaterly, 99; auth, Open-mindedness vs. Holding Firm Beliefs in J of Educational Philos, 99; auth, "Maimonides' Arguments for Creation Ex Nihilo in the 'Guide of the Perplexed'" in Medieval Philos and Theol, 99; **CONTACT ADDRESS** 392 Central Park W, Apt 8C, New York, NY 10025. **EMAIL** Andy_Gluck@msn.com

GLYMOUR, CLARK
DISCIPLINE PHILOSOPHY **EDUCATION** Ind Univ, PhD, 69. **CAREER** Instr, Princeton; Chicago Univ; Okla Univ; Univ Ill; Univ Pittsburgh; Carnegie Mellon; Prof, Philos, Univ Calif, San Diego. **RESEARCH** History of late nineteenth and early 20th century science. **SELECTED PUBLICATIONS** Auth, Thinking Things Through, MIT Press, 93; co-auth, "Causation, Prediction and Search", Springer Lecture Notes in Statistics, 93. **CONTACT ADDRESS** Dept of Philos, Univ of California, San Diego, 9500 Gilman Dr, La Jolla, CA 92093.

GLYNN, SIMON
PERSONAL Born 07/11/1948, England, d, 2 children **DISCIPLINE** PHILOSOPHY **EDUCATION** Keele Univ, BA, 71; McMaster Univ, MA, 76; Manchester Univ, PhD, 86. **CAREER** Lectr, 83-85, Manchester Univ; Lectr, 85-87, Liverpool Univ; Asst Prof, 87-88, Central Michigan Univ; Visiting Asst Prof, 88-89, Univ Georgia; Asst Prof, 89-91, Assoc Prof, 91-98, Prof, 98-, Florida Atlantic Univ. **MEMBERSHIPS** Amer Phil Assoc; Soc for Phenomenology and Existential Phil; British Soc for Phenomenology **RESEARCH** Contemporary continental philosophy; philosophy of natural Science; philosophy of technology; philosophy of psychology; political philosophy **SELECTED PUBLICATIONS** Auth, Continental and Postmodern Perspectives in the Philosophy of Science, 95; A Reply to Wil Coleman's Simon Glynn on a Unified Epitemology of the Natural and Human Sciences, Journal of the British Society for Phenomenology, 95; World Starvation and our Moral Bankruptcy, The Emergence of the 21st Century Woman, 95; On the Idea of Continental and Postmodern Perspectives in the Philosophy of Science, Ibid, 95; The Deconstruction of Some Paradoxes in Relativity Quantum Theory and Particle Physics, Continental and Postmodern Perspectives in the Philosophy of Science, 95; From Transcendental Logic to a Phenemenology of the Life-World, Analecta Husserliana, 96; Ethical Issues in Environmental Decision Making and the Limitations of Cost Benefit Analysis, Lectures in Environmental Ethics, 96; Understanding Others: The Structure and Dynamics of Interpersonal and Cross Cultural Communication, Proceedings of the 5th Japanese/American Phenomenology Conference, 96; Identity, Perception, Ation and Choice in Contemporary and Traditional No Self Theories, Ibid; Identity, Intersubjectivity and Communicative Communion, Proceedings of the 20th World Congrss of Philosophy, 98. **CONTACT ADDRESS** Dept of Philos, Florida Atlantic Univ, Boca Raton, FL 33431. **EMAIL** glynn@au.jau.edu

GNUSE, ROBERT
PERSONAL Born 12/04/1947, Quincy, IL, m, 1982, 3 children **DISCIPLINE** OLD TESTAMENT, HISTORY OF CHRISTIAN THOUGHT **EDUCATION** Concordia Sem Exile, MDiv, 74, STM, 75; Univ Chicago, STM, 75; Vanderbilt, MA, 78, PhD(Old Testament), 80. **CAREER** Asst prof Old Testament, Univ Va, 78-79; asst prof relig, NC Wesleyan Col, 79-80; ASST PROF OLD TESTAMENT, Assp prof Old Testament, Univ VA, 78-79; Asst Prof relig, NC, Wesleyan Col, 79-80; Asst Prof Old Testament, LOYOLA UNIV, 80-86; Asso Prof 86-90; Full Prof, 90-. **MEMBERSHIPS** Soc Bibl Lit; Cath

Bibl Asn; Col Theol Soc; Am Schs Orient Res. **RESEARCH** World religions. **SELECTED PUBLICATIONS** Auth, You Shall Not Steal, Maryknoll, 85; auth, Authority of the Bible, Ramsy, NJ, 85; auth, Heilsgeschichte as Model for Biblical Theology, Lanhom, 89; auth, The Temple Experience of Jaddus in the 'Antiquities' of Josephus--A Report of Jewish Dream-Incubation, Jewish Quart Rev, Vol 0083, 93; Dreams in the Night--Scholarly Mirage or Theophanic Formula--The Dream-Report as a Motif of the So-Called Elohist Tradition, Biblische Zeitschrift, Vol 0039, 95, auth, Dreams and Deam Reports in the Writings of Josephus, Leidgw, 97; auth, Emergent Monotheism in Israel, Sheffield, Eng, 98. **CONTACT ADDRESS** Loyola Univ, New Orleans, 6363 St Charles Ave, New Orleans, LA 70118. **EMAIL** rkgnuse@loyno.edu

GOAD, CANDACE SHELBY
PERSONAL Born 06/27/1959, Houston, TX, d, 2 children **DISCIPLINE** PHILOSOPHY **CAREER** Instr, San Jacinto Col, 87-91; Instr, Our Lady of the Lake Univ, 90-96; Vis Scholar, Rice Univ, 92; Adj Instr to Vis Asst Prof, Univ of Houston, 87-96; Asst Prof, Univ Colo, 96-. **HONORS AND AWARDS** Teaching Excellence Awd, UCD Col, 98; Piper Teaching Awd, UH-CL, 95-96; Great Communicator Awd, Tex Student Educ Asn, 95-96; Omicron Delta Kappa Nat Leadership Honor Soc, 95; Piper Teaching Awd, UH-CL, 93-95; President's Fund for the Humanities Grant, 99; Rose Community Foundation Grant, 98; NEH Grant, 95. **SELECTED PUBLICATIONS** Auth, "Leibniz's Early views on Matter, Modes, and God," Journal of Philosophical Research, (00): 261-273; rev, of "Truth in Context: An Essay on Pluralism and Objectivity," by Michael Lynch, Journal of speculative Philosophy, 00; rev, of" Care Ethics in Education," Harvard Educational Review, forthcoming; rev, of "An Ethical School Environment," Phi Delta Kappan, forthcoming; rev, of "Care Ethics and Charity of the Wise,". **CONTACT ADDRESS** Dept Philos, Univ of Colorado, Denver, PO Box 173364, Denver, CO 80217-3364.

GODDU, ANDRE
PERSONAL Born 11/06/1945, Holyoke, MA, m, 1980, 1 child **DISCIPLINE** PHILOSOPHY **EDUCATION** San Luis Rey, BA, 68; Calif State Univ, MA, 73; Grad Theol Union, MA, 73; Univ Calif, PhD, 79. **CAREER** Vis asst prof, Dickinson col, 82-83; asst prof, Univ of Notre Dame, 83-90; assoc prof, Stonehill Col, 90-. **HONORS AND AWARDS** Deutscher Akademischer Austauschdienst Fel, Ger, 77-79; Luftbrueckendank Stipendiu, Berlin, 79-80; IREX Res and Travel Grant, Poland, 91. **MEMBERSHIPS** Soc for Medieval and Renaissance Philos; Hist of Science Soc; Soc for the Hist of Tech. **RESEARCH** Late medieval philosophy, early modern science. **SELECTED PUBLICATIONS** Auth, The Physics of William of Ockham, E.J. Brill (Leiden/Cologne), 84; auth, "Connotative Concepts and Mathematics in Ockham's Natural Philosophy", Vivarium 31 (93):106-139; auth, "Music as Art and Science in the Fourteenth Century", Miscellanea Mediaevalia 22 (94): 1023-1045; auth, "William of Ockham: Academic Theology and its Polemical Phase" in The History of Franciscan Theology, ed Kenan Osborne (St. Bonaventure: The Franciscan Inst, 94), 231-310; auth, "Consequences and Conditional Propositions in John of Glogovi's and Michael of Biestrzykowa's Commentaries on Peter of Spain and their Possible Influence on Nicholas Copernicus", Archives d'histoire doctrinale et litteraire du mouen age 62 (95):137-188; auth, "The Logic of Copernicus's Arguments and his Education in Logic at Cracow", Early Science and Medicine 1 (96):28-68; auth, "Music, Philosophy, and Natural Science in the Middle Ages", Studies in Medieval Thought 40 (98):1-18; auth, "Harmony, Part-Whole Relationships, and the Logic of Consequences" in Musik - und die Geschichte der Philosophie und Naturwissenschaften im Mittelalter, ed. Frank hentschel, Studien und Texte zur Geistesgeschichte des Mittelalters, Vol 62 (98):325-338; auth, "The Use of Dialectical Topics in the Sixteenth and Seventeenth Centuries", Medioevo 24 (98)301-335; auth, "Ockham's Philosophy of Nature" in The Cambridge Companion to Ockham, ed Paul V. Spade, (Cambridge Univ, 99) 143-167. **CONTACT ADDRESS** Hist of Science and Philos Prog, Stonehill Col, 320 Washington St, Easton, MA 02357-7800. **EMAIL** agoddu@stonehill.edu

GODFREY, MARY F.
DISCIPLINE MEDIEVAL SERMON LITERATURE, MEDIEVAL DRAMA, PSYCHOANALYTIC CRITICISM **EDUCATION** Princeton, PhD. **CAREER** Asst prof, Fordham Univ. **RESEARCH** Post-conquest literary cult in Engl. **SELECTED PUBLICATIONS** Auth, Beowulf and Judith: Thematizing Decapitation in Old English Poetry, Tex Stud Lit and Lang 35, 93; Sir Gawain and the Green Knight: The Severed Head and the Body Politic, Assays: Critical Approaches to Medieval and Renaissance Texts 8, 95. **CONTACT ADDRESS** Dept of Eng Lang and Lit, Fordham Univ, 113 W 60th St, New York, NY 10023.

GODSEY, JOHN DREW
PERSONAL Born 10/10/1922, Bristol, TN, m, 1995, 4 children **DISCIPLINE** THEOLOGY **EDUCATION** Va Polytech Inst, BS, 47; Drew Univ, BD, 53; Univ Basel, DTheol, 60. **CAREER** From instr to asst prof syst theol and asst to dean, Drew Univ, 56-62, from asst prof to assoc prof hist and syst theol, 62-66, prof syst theol, 66-68; assoc dean, 68-71, PROF SYST THEOL, WESLEY THEOL SEM, 68-, Fulbright res grant, Univ Goettingen, 64-65. **MEMBERSHIPS** Am Theol Soc; Am Acad Relig; Bibl Theologians; Int Bonhoeffer Soc; Karl Barth Soc NAm. **RESEARCH** History of Christian thought; contemporary theology; philosophy. **SELECTED PUBLICATIONS** Auth, The Theology of Dietrich Bonhoeffer, 60; ed, Karl Barth's Talble Talk, 63; auth, Preface to Bonhoeffer, 65; auth, The Promise of H. Richard Niebuhr, 70; co-ed, Ethical Responsibility: Bonhoeffer's Legacy to the Churches, 81; co-ed, Dietrich Bonhoeffer, Discipleship, 00. **CONTACT ADDRESS** 8306 Bryant Dr, Bethesda, MD 20817.

GOEL, MADAN LAL
PERSONAL Born 06/20/1935, India, m, 1 child **DISCIPLINE** POLITICAL SCIENCE **EDUCATION** The Panjab Univ, BA, 56; Univ of Oregon, MA, 59; State Univ of New York, Buffalo, PhD, 69. **CAREER** Res and teaching asst, State Univ of New York, Buffalo, 63-66; instr to asst prof, Niagra Univ, 66-69; ASST PROF, 69-72, ASSOC PROF 72-78, PROF, UNIV OF WEST FL, PENSACOLA, 68-, dir of int studies, 84-. **HONORS AND AWARDS** Booth Fel in Public Service, Univ of Ore, 58; Grad Fel, State Univ of New York, 63-66; Nat Sci Found Awd, Univ of Colo, 70; Distinguished Res and Creative Activities Awd, Univ of West Fla, 79; Summer Col Fac Awd, Nat Endowment of the Humanities, 90; Distinguished Teaching Awd, Univ W Fla, 96; Distinguished Res Awd, Univ W Fla, 97; Teaching Incentive Prog Awd, Univ W Fla, 97; Professional Excellence Prog Awd, Univ W Fla, 97; Fulbright Scholar, 98. **MEMBERSHIPS** Am Political Sci Asn. **RESEARCH** Political participation; comparative politics. **SELECTED PUBLICATIONS** Auth, Political Science Research: A Methods Handbook, Iowa State Univ Press, 88; auth, Political Science Research: A Methods Workbook, Iowa State Univ Press, 88; coauth, Social and Political Science Research Methods, Ajanta Int Pub, 97; coauth, Political Participation, Rand Genally, 77; auth, Pensacola International Directory, Univ of West Fla, 79. **CONTACT ADDRESS** Dept of Govt, Univ of West Florida, Pensacola, FL 32514. **EMAIL** lgoel@uwf.edu

GOERGEN, DONALD J.
PERSONAL Born 08/16/1943, Iowa City, IA, s **DISCIPLINE** THEOLOGY **EDUCATION** Aquinas Inst of Theol, Dubuque, Iowa, PhD, 72. **CAREER** From asst prof to prof, Theol, Aquinas Inst, 71-84, 96-99; Church admin, Chicago, 85-94; Mem, Dominican Ashram, 99-. **MEMBERSHIPS** Am Acad of Rel; Catholic Theol Soc of Am. **RESEARCH** Religious Pluralism; Theology and Culture. **SELECTED PUBLICATIONS** Auth, The Sexual Celibate, Seabury Press (New York, NY), 75; auth, The Power of Love, Thomas More Press (Chicago, IL), 79; auth, A Theology of Jesus, Vol 1: The Mission and Ministry of Jesus, Michael Glazier Inc (Wilmington,DE), 86; auth, A Theology of Jesus, Vol 2: The Death and Resurrection of Jesus, Michael Glazier Inc (Wilmington, DE), 87; auth, "Presence to God, Presence to the World: Spirituality," in The Praxis of Christian Experience, ed. Schreiter and Hilkert (CA: Harper and Row, 89); auth, A Theology of Jesus, Vol 3: The Jesus of Christian History, The Liturgical Press (Collegeville, MN), 92; auth, A Theology of Jesus, Vol 4: Jesus: Son of God, Son of Mary, Immanuel, The Liturgical Press (Collegeville, MN), 94; auth, "Calling Forth a Healthy Chaste Life," Rev for Relig 57 (98): 260-274; auth, "Preaching as Searching for God," Dominican Ashram 17 (00): 12-17; ed, The Theology of Priesthood, The Liturgical Press (Collegeville, MN), 00. **CONTACT ADDRESS** 720 35th St., Kenosha, WI 53140-1934. **EMAIL** goergend@mac.domcentral.org

GOETSCH, JAMES R.
DISCIPLINE PHILOSOPHY **EDUCATION** Emory Univ, PhD. **CAREER** Asst prof. **RESEARCH** Ancient philosophy; eighteenth century philosophy; Buddhist thought. **SELECTED PUBLICATIONS** Auth, Vico's Axioms: The Geometry of the Human World. **CONTACT ADDRESS** Dept of Philosophy, Eckerd Col, 54th Ave S, PO Box 4200, Saint Petersburg, FL 33711. **EMAIL** goetscjr@eckerd.edu

GOETZ, EDWARD G.
PERSONAL Born 09/17/1957, Chicago, IL, m, 3 children **DISCIPLINE** PUBLIC AFFAIRS **EDUCATION** Northwestern Univ, MA, 81; PhD, 83. **CAREER** Assoc Prof, Univ Minn, 89-. **MEMBERSHIPS** Urban Affairs Asn. **RESEARCH** Housing policy; Community development. **SELECTED PUBLICATIONS** Auth, Housing and Community Development Policy, Addison Wesley Longman, forthcoming; auth, Shelter Burden: Local Politics and Progressive Housing Policy, Temple Univ Press, 93; ed, The new localism: comparative urban politics in a global era, Sage Pub, 93, auth, "An American Perspective, in Stakeholder Housing: A Third Way, Pluto Press, 99; auth, "Competition and Cooperation in Economic Development: A Study of the Twin Cities Metropolitan Area," in Approaches to Economic Development, Sage Pub, 98; auth, "The community-based housing movement and progressive local politics," in Urban Neighborhoods: Growth, Decline, and Revitalization, Univ Press of Kans, 96, auth, "Sandtown-Winchester, Baltimore: Housing as community development," in Housing and Urban Development in the US: Learning from failure and success, Sage Pub, 96; auth, "Fair share or status quo? The Twin cities Livable Communities Act," Journal of Planning Education and Research, forthcoming; auth, "The politics of poverty deconcentration and housing demolition," Journal of Urban Affairs, forthcoming; auth, "Local policy subsystems and issues definition: an analysis of community development policy change," Urban Affairs Review, (97): 490-512. **CONTACT ADDRESS** Dept Public Affairs, Univ of Minnesota, Twin Cities, 301 19th Ave S, Minneapolis, MN 55455.

GOFF, EDWIN L.
DISCIPLINE PHILOSOPHY **EDUCATION** Vanderbilt Univ, BA, 67; Boston Col, MA, 68, PhD, 74. **CAREER** Assoc prof & dir, Univ Honors Prog, Villanova Univ,70-. **HONORS AND AWARDS** NEH Summer Sem, Tufts Univ, 75; NEH Summer Sem, Univ Pa, 78. **MEMBERSHIPS** AAUP & pres, Villanova Chap, 85-88; Amer Soc for Political and Legal Philos; Int Asn for Philos of Law and Soc Philos; Soci for the Study of Black Philos; NAm Soc for Soc Philos. **RESEARCH** Social justice and the grounding of a liberal democratic theory of social change. **SELECTED PUBLICATIONS** Auth, Injustice in American Liberal Democracy: Foundations for a Rawlsian Critique, J Value Inquiry, Vol 18, 84; Justice as Fairness: The Practice of Social Science in a Rawlsian Model, Soc Res Vol 50, 83; John Rawls' A Theory of Justice: A Review in Retrospect, Soc and Thought Vol 1, 83 & Affirmative Action, John Rawls, and a Partial Compliance Theory of Justice, Cultural Hermeneutics, Vol 4, 76. **CONTACT ADDRESS** Dept of Philosophy, Villanova Univ, 800 Lancaster Ave, Villanova, PA 19085-1692.

GOFORTH, CAROL R.
PERSONAL Born 10/12/1960, Fayetteville, AR, m, 1992, 4 children **DISCIPLINE** PSYCHOLOGY, LAW **EDUCATION** Univ AR, BA, 81; JD, 84. **CAREER** Assoc attorney, Doerner, Stuart, Saunders, Daniel & Anderson, OK, 84-89; adjunct prof, Col Law, Univ Tulsa, 87-88; instr, Seton Hall Parma prog, Parma, Italy, summer 90; asst prof law, 89-92, assoc prof law, School of Law, Seton Hall Univ, Newark, NJ, 92-93; from vis assoc prof law to Clayton N. Little prof law, Univ Ark School of Law, Fayettsville, 93-. **HONORS AND AWARDS** Selected AR Bar Found Prof, June 98; Clayton N. Little Prof Law, June 00. **MEMBERSHIPS** Am Bar Asn; AR Bar Asn; Am Law Inst. **RESEARCH** Corporate law; securities law; limited liability companied; limited liability partnerships. **SELECTED PUBLICATIONS** Co-auth, with L Beard, The Arkansas Limited Liability Company, M & M Press, 94; auth, Limited Liability Partnerships: Does Arkansas Need Another Form of Business Enterprize?, 1995 AR L Notes 57; The Rise of the Limited Liability Company: Evidence of a Race Between the States, but Heading Where?, 45 Syracuse L Rev, 1193, 95; What is She? How Race Matters, and Why It Shouldn't, 46 DePaul Univ L Rev 1, 96; Limiting the Liability of General Partners in LLPs: An Analysis of Statutory Alternatives, 75 OR L Rev 1139, 97; Continuing Obstacles to Freedom of Choice for Management Structure in LLC's, 1 Lewis & Clark J of Small and Emerging Bus L, 165, 97; Limited Liability Partnerships: The Newest Game in Town, AR L Notes 25, 97; An Update on Arkansas Limited Liability Companies: New Tax Regulations and New State Laws, 1997 AR L Notes 11; Reflections on What Lawyers Should Reflect On, 30 So TX L Rev, 585, 98; co-auth, with Michael L Closen and Gary S Rosin, Agency & Partnership, Problems and Statutes, supp 96 & supp 97; with Michael L Closen and Gary S Rosin, Agency and Partnership, Cases and Materials, supp 96 & supp 97; auth, The Revised Uniform Partnership Act: Ready or Not, Here It Comes, Ark Law Notes 47 (99); with L Beard, Arkansas LLCs. LLPs, LLLPs, M & M Press, forthcoming; auth, Treatment of LLC Membership Interests Under the Arkansas Securities Act, 1998 AR L Notes, 33; Not In My Back Yard! Restrictive Covenants as a Basis for Opposing the Construction of Cellular Towers, 46 Buffalo L Rev, 705; auth, A Bad Call: Preemtion of State and Local Governmental Authority to Regulate Wireless Communication Facilities on the Basis of Radio Frequency Emissions, NYork Law School Law Review (forthcoming); auth, Use of Simulations and Client Based Exercises in the Basic Course, 34 Ga Law Review (forthcoming). **CONTACT ADDRESS** School of Law, Univ of Arkansas, Fayetteville, Fayetteville, AR 72701. **EMAIL** goforth@comp.uark.edu

GOH, DAVID T.
PERSONAL Born 01/27/1959, Calcutta, India, m, 1984, 2 children **DISCIPLINE** NEW TESTAMENT **EDUCATION** Univ of Durham, United Kingdom, PhD, 94. **CAREER** Sr Pastor, Bakersfield Community Church; Adjunct Prof, Fuller Theological Seminary; VP, Harvest Intl School **CONTACT ADDRESS** 2010 O St., Bakersfield, CA 93301. **EMAIL** docgoh@aol.com

GOLANN, DWIGHT
PERSONAL Born 09/01/1947, Rochester, NY, m, 1982, 2 children **DISCIPLINE** LAW **EDUCATION** Amherst Col, BA, 69; Harvard Univ, JD, 73. **CAREER** Instr, State Univ NY, 69-70; Law Clerk, Mass Appeals Court, 73-74; Atty, Snyder, Tepper and Berlin, 74-77; Clin Instr, Harvard Law Sch, 76-85; Asst Atty Gen, Mass, 79-86; Prof, Suffolk Univ Law Sch, 86-; Chief Govt and Trial Bureaus, Mass, 91-92; Distinguished Neutral and Member of Training Fac, CPR Inst of Dispute Resolution, 94-. **HONORS AND AWARDS** Vis Scholar, Harvard

Univ, 98; Outstanding Book, CPR Inst of Dispute Resolution, 96. **MEMBERSHIPS** Am Bar Asn; Boston Bar Asn; Asn for Conflict Resolution. **RESEARCH** Legal Mediation; Alternative Dispute Resolution. **SELECTED PUBLICATIONS** Auth, Mediating Legal Disputes, Little Brown/Aspen, 96; co-auth, "Evaluation in Mediation," ADR J, 97; auth, "Mediators at Work: Breach of Warranty?" Harvard Prog on Negotiation, 99; co-auth, "The Consensus Building Handbook," Sage, 99; auth, "Representing Clients in Mediation," Am Bar Asn, 00; auth, "Variations in Style: How and Why: Legal Mediators Change Style in the Course of a Case," 2000 J Disp Res, 00. **CONTACT ADDRESS** Sch of Law, Suffolk Univ, 120 Tremont St, Boston, MA 02108. **EMAIL** dgolann@acad.suffolk.edu

GOLB, NORMAN
PERSONAL Born 01/15/1928, Chicago, IL, m, 1949, 3 children **DISCIPLINE** JEWISH HISTORY, HEBREW AND JUDEO-ARABIC STUDIES **EDUCATION** Roosevelt Col, BA, 48; Johns Hopkins Univ, PhD, 54. **CAREER** Warburg res fel Judaeo-Arabic studies, Hebrew Univ, Jerusalem, 55-57; vis lectr Semitic lang, Univ Wis, 57-58; from instr to asst prof Mediaeval Jewish studies, Hebrew Union Col, 58-63; from asst prof to prof Hebrew and Judeo-Arabic Studies, Univ Chicago, 63-88, Rosenberger Prof Jewish Hist and Civilization, 88-. **HONORS AND AWARDS** Adler res fel, Dropsie Col, 54-55; Am Philos Soc grants-in-aid, 59, 63 & 67; Am Coun Learned Soc grants-in-aid, 63 & 65; Guggenheim Mem Found fels, 64-65 & 66-67; vis fel, Clare Hall, Cambridge Univ, 70; Nat Endowment for Humanities grant, 70-72; Grand Medal of Honor of the City of Rouen, 85; Docteur Honoris Causa (Histoire), Univ of Rouen, 87; Medal of Haute Normandie, 87. **MEMBERSHIPS** Fel Am Acad Jewish Res; life mem, Clare Hall, Cambridge Univ, 80-; Soc de l'Histoire de France, 87-; Founder and vice-pres, Soc for Judeo-Arabic Studies, 84-. **RESEARCH** Jewish History, Hebrew and Judeo-Arabic Studies; Voting mem, Orient Inst, 61-. **SELECTED PUBLICATIONS** Auth, A Judaeo-Arabic Court Document of Syracuse, AD 1020, J Near Eastern Studies, 73; The Problem of Origin and Identification of the Dead Sea Scrolls, Proc Am Philos Soc, 80; Nature et destination du monument hebraique decouvert a Rouen, Proc Am Acad Jewish Res, 81; coauth (with Omeljan Pritsak), Khazarian Hebrew Documents of the Tenth Century, Cornell Univ Press, 82, trans to Russ, 97; auth, Les Juifs de Rouen au Moyen Age, Presses Univ de Rouen, 85; Who Wrote the Dead Sea Scrolls?, Scribner, 95, translated in Ger, Dutch, Port, Fr, Japanese; The Jews of Medieval Normandy, Cambridge Univ Press, 98; ed, Judeo-Arabic Studies, Harwood Acad Press, 97. **CONTACT ADDRESS** Univ of Chicago, Oriental Inst, 1155 E 58th St, Chicago, IL 60637-1540. **EMAIL** n-golb@uchicago.edu

GOLD, JEFF
DISCIPLINE PHILOSOPHY **EDUCATION** Ohio State Univ, PhD. **CAREER** Prof, E Tenn State Univ. **RESEARCH** Ancient philosophy; philosophy of religion; mysticism. **SELECTED PUBLICATIONS** Auth, Plato in the Light of Yoga, Philos E W, 96; Utilitarianism and Deontological Approaches to Criminal Justice Ethics, Justice Ethics, Anderson, 96; The Heroic Transformation of Bilbo Baggins, ETSU, 92; The Soul's Relation to the Forms: Plato's Account of Knowledge. Caravan Bk, 92; Criminal Justice Ethics: A Survey of Philosophical Theories, Anderson, 92; Is Fukuyama a Liberal?, E T S U, 91; Spiritual Zionism, Dialogue Alliance, 91; co-auth, Peacemaking, Justice, and Ethics, Anderson, 96. **CONTACT ADDRESS** Philosophy Dept, East Tennessee State Univ, Box 70717, Johnson City, TN 37614-0717. **EMAIL** goldj@etsu.edu

GOLD, JONATHAN
PERSONAL Born 04/19/1941, New Rochelle, NY, m, 1975 **DISCIPLINE** PHILOSOPHY **EDUCATION** Queens Col, BA, 70; SUNY Stony Brook, PhD, 81; Philadelphia Theol Sem, MDiv, 82. **CAREER** Prof Philos and Rel, W Liberty State Col; adj prof Philos, Wheeling Jesuit Univ; adj prof, Col of NJ; adj prof, Thomas Jefferson Univ; adj prof, Col of NJers; pastor, Resurrection Life Reformed Church, Wheeling, WVa. **HONORS AND AWARDS** Woodrow Wilson fel, 70-71; Who's Who Among tchrs, 95, 98. **MEMBERSHIPS** Amer Philos Asn. **RESEARCH** Logic; Metaphysics; Philosophy of Religion; Theology; Biblical Studies. **SELECTED PUBLICATIONS** Auth, Logic, Ordinality, and Pomplexity, 81; Modal Metaphysics, 92; Truth, Translations, and Trees, 92. **CONTACT ADDRESS** Dept of Humanities, West Liberty State Col, West Liberty, WV 26074. **EMAIL** goldj@stratusware.net

GOLD, RICHARD E.
DISCIPLINE LAW **EDUCATION** McGill Univ, BS, 84; Univ Toronto, LLB, 88; Univ Michigan, LLM, 92, SJD, 95. **CAREER** Law clerk, Justice Cory, Supreme Court Can; prof. **RESEARCH** Property Law and Technology Law. **SELECTED PUBLICATIONS** Auth, Body Parts: Property Rights and the Ownership of Human Biological Materials, Georgetown. **CONTACT ADDRESS** Fac of Law, Univ of Western Ontario, London, ON, Canada N6A 3K7. **EMAIL** ergold@julian.uwo.ca

GOLD, VICTOR ROLAND
PERSONAL Born 09/18/1924, Garden City, KS, m, 1979, 3 children **DISCIPLINE** OLD TESTAMENT STUDIES **EDUCATION** Wartburg Theol Sem, BD, 46; Johns Hopkins Univ, PhD(ancient Near Eastern studies), 51. **CAREER** Guest lectr Contemp Am Denominations, Lutheran Deaconess Motherhouse, Baltimore, Md, 51; asst prof Old Testament, Hamma Divinity Sch, 52-53; pastor, Trinity Evangel Lutheran Church, Kalamazoo, Mich, 53-56; guest prof, 56, assoc prof, 56-61, prof Old Testament Studies & dean, Grad Studies, Pac Lutheran Theol Sem, 61-, Lutheran World Fed guest prof, Kirchliche Hochsch, Berlin, Ger, 59 & 68; mem fac & bd dirs, Laymen's Sch Relig, Berkeley, Calif, 59-69; mem fac, Grad Theol Union, Berkeley, 59, chmn, Area I, 65-68; hon assoc, Am Schs Orient Res, 62-64; mem, Comn Comprehensive Studies Ministry, Lutheran Church Am, 66-70; dir, Educ Div, Inst Mediter Studies, Berkeley, 67-73, exec dir inst, 69-74; vis prof, Dept Near Eastern Lang, Univ Calif, Berkeley, 68-; mem, Inter-Lutheran Comn Worship, 69-; mem, Am Lutheran Church-Lutheran Church Am Joint Comn Communion Practices, 74-76; mem, Nat Coun Churches US, 81-; ASOR trustee, 81-84; annual prof, Albright inst Arch Res, 86-. **MEMBERSHIPS** Am Schs Orient Res; Soc Bibl Lit; Am Orient Soc; Archaeol Inst Am. **RESEARCH** Near Eastern archaeology, languages and history; Old Testament exegesis and theology; international studies. **SELECTED PUBLICATIONS** Auth, Mosaic map of Medeba, 59 & Gnostic manuscripts of Chenoboskion, Bibl Archaeol; ed, Episkope, Fortress, 68; auth, Notes on Isaiah, Jeremiah, Ezekiel, In: Annotated Bible, Oxford Univ, 73, 91; ed New Testament & Psalms. An Inclusive version, Oxford Univ, 95. **CONTACT ADDRESS** 2770 Marin Ave, Berkeley, CA 94708-1530. **EMAIL** themccgolds@ntr.net

GOLDBERG, HILLEL
PERSONAL Born 01/10/1946, Denver, CO, m, 1969, 4 children **DISCIPLINE** JEWISH ETHICS **EDUCATION** Yeshiva Univ, BA, 69; Brandeis Univ, MA, 72, PhD(near Eastern & Judaic studies), 79. **CAREER** Lectr Talmud, Machseke Torah Inst, 71-72; lectr Jewish ethical thought, Jerusalem Col Women, 73-77; vis asst prof Judaic studies, Emory Univ, 78; lectr, Jewish Ethics & intellectual hist, Hebrew Univ, Jerusalem, 79- ; ed, Intermountain Jewish News. **MEMBERSHIPS** Am Acad Relig; Asn Jewish Studies; Am Hist Asn; Ctr Study Psychol & Judaism; World Union Jewish Studies. **RESEARCH** Rabbinic, medieval and modern Jewish ethics; Jewish intellectual history; Holocaust. **SELECTED PUBLICATIONS** Auth, Homosexuality, A Religious and Political-Analysis, Tradition-J Orthodox Jewish Thought, Vol 0027, 93; Religious Zionism Revisited: Responses to Questions on Fundamental Issues Concerning Religious and Secular Nationalism, and Non-Zionist Orthodoxy in the State of Israel Today--A Symposium, Tradition-J Orthodox Jewish Thought, Vol 0028, 94; Homosexuality, a Religious and Political-Analysis--A Rejoinder to Goldwasser, Hershel, Tradition-J Orthodox Jewish Thought, Vol 0029, 95; Philosophy of Halakha--The Many Worlds of Mikve, Tradition-J Orthodox Jewish Thought, Vol 0030, 96; Responding to 'Rupture and Reconstruction': Soloveitchik, R. Haym Transformation of Contemporary Jewish Orthodoxy, Tradition-J Orthodox Jewish Thought, Vol 0031, 97. **CONTACT ADDRESS** Intermountain Jewish News, 1275 Sherman St, Denver, CO 80203-2299. **EMAIL** hillel@ijn.com

GOLDBERG, SANFORD C.
PERSONAL Born 11/22/1967, Brooklyn, NY, m, 1994, 3 children **DISCIPLINE** PHILOSOPHY **EDUCATION** Rutgers Univ, BA, 89; Columbia Univ, PhD, 95. **CAREER** Asst prof, Grinnell Col, 95-. **MEMBERSHIPS** Amer Philos Asn; Soc Philos Psych; S Soc Philos Psych. **RESEARCH** Philosophy of mind and language; epistemology; metaphysics **SELECTED PUBLICATIONS** Coed, The Twin Earth Chronicles, 96; coauth, Gray Matters: An Introduction to the Philosophy of Mind, 97; auth, art, Self-Ascription, Self-Knowledge, and the Memory Argument, 97; auth, art, The Very Idea of Computer Self-Knowledge and Self-Deception, 97. **CONTACT ADDRESS** Dept of Philosophy, Grinnell Col, Box 805, Grinnell, IA 50112. **EMAIL** goldberg@ac.grin.edu

GOLDEN, EVELYN DAVIS
PERSONAL Born 06/01/1951, Moultrie, GA, m **DISCIPLINE** LAW **EDUCATION** York Coll of the City Univ of NYork, BA1972; Univ of FL, JD 1976. **CAREER** Dept of Legal Affairs, asst atty gen 1980-; Valencia Community Coll Orlando FL, instr prog dir 1977-79; Central FL Legal Serv, legal intern 1976-77; Pub Defender's Office Gainesville FL, legal intern 1974-75; Legal Aid Soc Brooklyn NY, legal asst 1973. **HONORS AND AWARDS** Outstd young women of Am Bd of Dir for Outstd Young Woman of Am 1977. **MEMBERSHIPS** Mem FL Bar 1978-; mem FL Chap of the Nat Bar Assn 1978-; mem FL Assn of Women Lawyers 1979-; v chmn Ch 24 Seminole Co Prog Adv Com 1976-79; parli Delta Sigma Theta Sorority Inc 1979-80; bd of dir Citrus Council of Girl Scouts 1979-. **CONTACT ADDRESS** Dept of Legal Affairs, 125 N Ridgewood Ave, Daytona Beach, FL 32114.

GOLDFARB, JEFFREY C.
DISCIPLINE LIBERAL STUDIES, COMPARATIVE POLITICS **EDUCATION** Univ Chicago, PhD, 77. **CAREER** Prof, Eugene Lang Col. **RESEARCH** Soc of cult; comp polit; phenomenological soc; relationship between cult, polit, and democratic institutions. **SELECTED PUBLICATIONS** Auth, After the Fall: The Pursuit of Democracy in Central Europe, 92; The Cynical Society: The Culture of Politics and the Politics of Culture in American Life, 91; Beyond Glasnost: The Post-Totalitarian Mind, 89; On Cultural Freedom: An Exploration of Public Life in Poland and America, 82; The Persistence of Freedom: The Sociological Implications of Polish Student Theater, 80. **CONTACT ADDRESS** Eugene Lang Col, New Sch for Social Research, 66 West 12th St, New York, NY 10011.

GOLDFARB, RONALD L.
PERSONAL Born 10/16/1933, NJ, m, 1957, 3 children **DISCIPLINE** LAW **EDUCATION** Syracuse Univ, AB, 54, LLB, 56; Yale Law School, LLM, 60, JSD, 62. **CAREER** U.S. Air Force, JAG, 57-60; Dept of Justice, 61-64; speech writer, 64; pres task force to establish the Office of Economic Opportunity; special counsel, U.S. House of Representatives Select Committee, 67; chemn, Special Review Committee, 75-76; LAWYER, RONALD GOLDFARB & ASSOCS, 96-. **MEMBERSHIPS** DC, NY, and Calif Bars; Bar of the U.S. Supreme Court; chemn of the board/dir, Law Sci Coun; pres & general counsel, Main-Street, 84-; bod of dir, Va Center for the Creative Arts, 92-; bd of dis, Alliance for Justice, 97-. **SELECTED PUBLICATIONS** Auth, Perfect Villains, Imperfect Heroes: Robert F. Kennedy's War Against Organized Crime, Random House, 95; auth, TV or NOT TV: Courts, Television and Justice, The Twentieth Century Fund, NY Univ Press, 98; auth, The Encyclopedia of Publishing and the Book Arts, Henry Holt, 95; contribur, The Encyclopedia of Criminology, Macmillan, 94; contrib, The Encyclopedia of the United States Congress, Simon & Schuster, 94; contrib, The Macmillan Encyclopedia, 97; auth, The Comtempt Power; auth, Ransom: A Critique of the American Bail System; coauth, Crime and Publicity; auth, Migrant Farmworkers, A Taste of Despair; auth, Jails: The Ultimate Ghetto; coauth, After Conviction; coauth, The Writer's Lawyer; coauth, Clear Understandings, Guide to Legal Writing. **CONTACT ADDRESS** 1501 M St. NW, Washington, DC 20005. **EMAIL** rglawlit@aol.com

GOLDFIELD, MICHAEL
PERSONAL Born Brooklyn, NY **DISCIPLINE** POLITICAL SCIENCE **EDUCATION** Williams Col, BA, 65; Univ of Chicago, MA, phil, 67, MA, pol science, 78, PhD, 84. **CAREER** Stat prog, 78-79, Natl Opinion Res Center; syst anal/prog, 79-80, Univ Chicago Comp Ctr; prog & fac manage, 80-84, Hines Veterans Admin Hosp; fac fel, 87-88 Soc for Humanities, asst prof, 84-92, Cornell Univ; sr res assoc, 89-93, ctr for labor-manage pol stud, CUNY; asoc prof, CULMA & pol science, adj prof, Africana Stud, 92-98, prof, CULMA & pol science, adj prof, Africana Stud, 98-, Wayne St Univ. **HONORS AND AWARDS** NDEA fel, pol science, Univ Chicago, 68-69; Outstanding Perf Awd, Hines Vet Admin Hosp, 81; NBER/Sloan Found Grant, 84-87; Cornell Jr Fac Sum Res Fel, 85; Cornell/IBM proj EZRA Grant 85-88; DAAD sum res grant, 86; Humanities Fac Res Grant, Cornell Univ, 86-87; Fac Fel, Soc for Humanities, Cornell Univ, 87-88; Jonathan R. Meigs Res Grants, 84-92; Amer Coun of Learned Soc Res Grant, 91-92; NSF Supercomputer Grant, 87-94; German Marshall Fund US Grant, 96; Wayne St Humanities Ctr Fel Grant, 96; Prog in Mediating Theory & Dispute Resolution Grant, 97; CULMA Fac Res Grant, 97. **MEMBERSHIPS** APSA; IRRA; MWPSA; HAIMC. **SELECTED PUBLICATIONS** Auth, The Decline of Organized Labor in the United States, Univ Chicago, 87; art, Race and the CIO, Intl Labor & Working Class History, 45, 93; art, The Failure of Operation Dixie: A Critical Turning Point in American Political Development, Race, Class, & Comm in So Labor History, Univ Alabama Press, 94; art, Race and the CIO Revisited - Reply to Critics, Intl Labor & Working Class History, 94; art, Was There a Golden Age of the CIO: Race, Solidarity, and Union Growth During the 1930s and 1940s, Trade Union Pol: Amer Union & Amer Unions and Econ Change, 1960s-1990s, Humanities Press, 95; art, The Limits of Rational Choice Theory, Natl Pol Science Rev & Rational Choice Marxism, 96; auth, The Color of Politics: Race and the Mainsprings of American Politics, New Press, 97; art, Race and the Reuther Legacy, Against the Current, 97; art, Race and US Labor, Monthly Review, 97; art, Assessing Union Leaderships, Against the Current, 97; art, US Unions, Racial Discrimination, and the Post-World War II Social Contract, Along Ethnic Lines: Multicultural Solidarity in the Labor Movement, Lars Maischak, 97; art, Lipset's Union Democracy After 40 Years, Extensions, 98. **CONTACT ADDRESS** Coll of Urban Labor and Metro Affairs, Wayne State Univ, 3247 Faculty/Admin Bldg, Detroit, MI 48202.

GOLDIN, CLAUDIA
PERSONAL Born New York, NY **DISCIPLINE** ECONOMICS **EDUCATION** Cornell Univ, BA, 67; Univ of Chicago, MA, 69; PhD, 72. **CAREER** Harvard Univ Prof econo; Prog Dir, Del of the Am Econ; Res Assoc, Nat Bur of Econ Res; NBER Program Dir. of Dev of the Am Economy. **HONORS AND AWARDS** Hon doc hum letters, Univ NE, 94; fel, Am Acad Arts Sci, 92-; fel, Econ Soc, 91-; Vis sch, Russell Sage Found, 97-98;Galbraith Teach Awd, 95; Irving Kravis Teach Awd, 89; Guggenheim fel, 87-88; Mem, Inst Adv Stud, 82-83; numerous grants. **MEMBERSHIPS** EHA; AEA **SELECTED**

PUBLICATIONS Auth, Understanding the Gender Gap, Oxford, 90; Defining the Moment: The Great Depression and the American Economy in the Twentieth Century, ed by M Bordo, C Goldin, E White, Chicago, Univ Chicago, 98; The Regulated Economy: A Historical Approach to Political Economy, ed by C Goldin, G Libecap, Chicago, Univ Chicago Press, 94; Labor Markets in the Twentieth Century, in: S Engerman R Gallman, The Cambr Econ Hist of US, Cambridge Univ Press, forthcoming, many numerous articles and papers. **CONTACT ADDRESS** Dept Economics, Harvard Univ, Cambridge, MA 02138. **EMAIL** cgoldin@harvard.edu

GOLDIN, OWEN MICHAEL
PERSONAL Born 06/07/1957, Philadelphia, PA, 2 children **DISCIPLINE** PHILOSOPHY **EDUCATION** St. John's Col, Santa Fe, BA, 79; Univ Chicago, MA, 82; Univ Texas Austin, PhD, 87. **CAREER** Asst prof, 87-94, asoc prof, 94-, Marquette Univ. **MEMBERSHIPS** APA; Metaphysical Soc Am; Soc Ancient Greek Philos; Int Plato Soc; ISEE. **RESEARCH** Ancient philosophy; metaphysics; ethics. **SELECTED PUBLICATIONS** Auth, "Self, Sameness and Soul in Alcibiades I and the Timaeus," Freiburger Zeitschrift fur Philos und Theol, 93; "Parmenides on Possibility and Thought," Apeiron, 93; "Aristotle on Good and Bad Actualities," J of Neoplatonic Stud, 93; Explaining an Eclipse, Univ Mich, 96; Human Life and the Natural World, Broadview, 97; "The Ecology of the Critias and Platonic Metaphysics," The Greeks and the Environment, Rowman and Littlefield, 97; "Plato and the Arrow of Time," Ancient Philos, 98. **CONTACT ADDRESS** Dept of Philosophy, Marquette Univ, PO Box 1881, Milwaukee, WI 53201-1881. **EMAIL** owen.goldin@marquette.edu

GOLDING, MARTIN P.
PERSONAL Born 03/30/1930, New York, NY, m, 1951, 3 children **DISCIPLINE** PHILOSOPHY **EDUCATION** Columbia Univ, PhD, 59. **CAREER** Prof, 76-, Duke Univ. **MEMBERSHIPS** Am Soc Polit Legal Philos. **RESEARCH** Philos of law; ethical problems in bio medl tech. **SELECTED PUBLICATIONS** Auth, Philosophy of Law, Prentice Hall, 75; Legal Reasoning, Knopf, 84; ed, The Nature of Law, Random House, 66; Jewish Law and Legal Theory, NYU, 94. **CONTACT ADDRESS** Philos Dept, Duke Univ, West Duke Bldg, Durham, NC 27708. **EMAIL** golding@law.duke.edu

GOLDINGAY, JOHN
PERSONAL Born 06/20/1942, Birmingham, England, m, 1967, 2 children **DISCIPLINE** THEOLOGY **EDUCATION** Oxford Univ, BA, 64; Notingham Univ, PhD, 83; Lambeth, DD, 97. **CAREER** Lectr, theol, St John's Theol Col, Nottingham UK, 70-97; David Allan Hubbard prof of Old Testament, Fuller Theol Sem, 97- . **MEMBERSHIPS** SOTS; SBL. **CONTACT ADDRESS** 111 S Orange Grove, #108, Pasadena, CA 91105. **EMAIL** johngold@fuller.edu

GOLDMAN, ALAN H.
PERSONAL Born 08/07/1945, New York, NY, m, 1968, 2 children **DISCIPLINE** PHILOSOPHY **EDUCATION** Yale Univ, BA, 67; Columbia Univ, PhD, 72. **CAREER** Asst prof, Ohio Univ, 72-74; asst prof, Univ Idaho, 74-76; from assoc prof to prof 77-, chemn, 88-98, Univ Miami; vis assoc prof, Univ Mich, 80; vis prof, Univ Auckland, 96. **HONORS AND AWARDS** Excellence in Tchg Awd, 97, Univ Miami. **MEMBERSHIPS** Am Philos Asn; Am Soc Aesthetics. **RESEARCH** Ethics, Aesthetics; Epistemology; Philosophy of law. **SELECTED PUBLICATIONS** Auth, Justice and Reverse Discrimination, 79; auth, The Moral Foundations of Professional Ethics, 80; auth, Empirical Knowledge, 88; auth, Moral Knowledge, 88; auth, Aesthetic Value, 95; auth, Practical Rules, When We Need Them and When We Don't, 01. **CONTACT ADDRESS** Dept of Philosophy, Univ of Miami, Coral Gables, FL 33124. **EMAIL** agoldman@miami.edu

GOLDMAN, ALVIN I.
PERSONAL Born 10/01/1938, New York, NY, m, 1969, 2 children **DISCIPLINE** PHILOSOPHY **EDUCATION** Columbia Univ, BA, 60; Princeton Univ, MA, 62, PhD, 65. **CAREER** Asst prof to prof, Univ Mich, 63-80; prof, Univ Illinois at Chicago, 80-83; prof, Univ Arizona, 83-94; regents prof, Univ Ariz, 94-01. **HONORS AND AWARDS** John Simon Guggenheim Fel, 75-76; Fel, Center for Advanced Study in the Behavioral Sciences, 75-76; Fel, Nat Humanities Center, 81-82; Fel, NEH, 00-01; Romanell-Phi Beta Kappa Prof, 00-01; Profiled in Cambridge Dictionary of Philosophy, 2nd ed., 00. **MEMBERSHIPS** Pres, Pacific Div, 92, member, Amer Philos Assn; pres, 88, member, Soc Philos and Psychol; Philos Sci Assn. **RESEARCH** Epistemology; cognitive science; philosophy of mind, political and legal philosophy. **SELECTED PUBLICATIONS** Auth, A Theory of Human Action, Prentice-Hall, 70; auth, Epistemology and Cognition, Harvard UP, 86; auth, Liaisons: Philosophy Meets the Cognitive and Social Sciences, MIT Press, 92; auth, Philosophical Applications of Cognitive Science, Westview Press, 93; auth, "Consciousness, Folk Psychology, and Cognitive Science," Consciousness and Cognition, vol 2, 93; coauth, "Speech, Truth and the Free Market for Ideas," Legal Theory, vol 2, 96; auth, "Science, Publicity, and Consciousness," Philosophy of Science, vol 64, 97; coauth, "Games Lawyers Play: Legal Discovery and Social Epistemology," Legal Theory, vol 4, 98; auth, "Why Citizens Should Vote: A Casual Responsibility Approach," Social Philosophy & Policy, 99; auth, Knowledge in a Social World, Oxford UP, 99. **CONTACT ADDRESS** Dept of Philosophy, Univ of Arizona, Tucson, AZ 85721-0027. **EMAIL** goldman@u.arizona.edu

GOLDMAN, SHELDON
PERSONAL Born 09/18/1939, Bronx, NY, m, 1963, 3 children **DISCIPLINE** POLITICAL SCIENCE **EDUCATION** Harvard Univ, PhD, 65. **CAREER** Prof, political science, 74-, Univ Massachusetts **HONORS AND AWARDS** Phi Beta Kappa; Pi Sigma Alpha Outstanding Tchr Awd; Col Outstanding Tchng Awd. **MEMBERSHIPS** Amer Political Science Asn; Law and Soc Asn; Northeastern Political Science Asn; Amer Judicature Soc. **RESEARCH** Federal judicial selection; constitutional law; law and politics. **SELECTED PUBLICATIONS** Auth, Picking Federal Judges Lower Court Selection from Roosevelt through Reagan, Yale Univ Press, 97; auth, Federal Judicial Recruitment, Amer Courts A Critical Assessment, CQ Press, 91; art, The Bush Imprint on the Judiciary Carrying on a Tradition, Judicature 74, 91; art, Bushs Judicial Legacy the Final Imprint, Judicature 76, 93; coauth, Clintons NonTraditional Judges, Judicature 78, 94; art, Judicial Selection Under Clinton A Midterm Examination, Judicature 78, 95; coAuth, Clintons First Term Judiciary Many Bridges to Cross, Judicature 80, 97; Coauth, Congress and the Courts A Case of Casting, Great Theater The Amer Congress in Action, Cambridge Univ Press, 98; co-auth, Clinton's Second Term Judiciary: Picking Judges Under Fire, Judicature, 82, 99; co-auth, Clinton's Judges: Summing Up the Legacy, Judicature, 84, 01. **CONTACT ADDRESS** Dept of Polit Sci, Univ of Massachusetts, Amherst, 200 Hicks Way, Amherst, MA 01003-9277. **EMAIL** sheldon.goldman@polsci.umass.edu

GOLDSTEIN, ABRAHAM SAMUEL
PERSONAL Born 07/27/1925, New York, NY, m, 1995, 2 children **DISCIPLINE** LAW **EDUCATION** City Col New York, BBA, 46; Yale Univ, LLB, 49, MA, 61. **CAREER** Law clerk, Circuit Judge David L Bazelon, US Court of Appeals, 49-51; partner, Donohue & Kaufmann, 51-56; assoc prof law, 56-61, dean law sch, 70-75, prof law, 61-75, STERLING PROF, LAW SCH, YALE UNIV, 75-, Provost Univ, 78-79; Mem bar, US Dist Court, Washington, DC, 49- & US Supreme Court, 54; mem adv bd community serv, CT Dept Mental Health, 62-66; vis fel, Inst Criminology & fel, Christ's Col, Cambridge Univ, 64-65; Guggenheim fel, 64-65 & 75-76; consult, President's Comn Law Enforcement, 66-67; mem, Comn to Revise Conn Criminal Code, 66-69, CT Bd Parole, 67-69 & CT Planning Comt Criminal Admin, 67-71; vis prof, Hebrew Univ, Jerusalem, 76, Tel Aviv, 86; vpres, CT Bar Found, 76-78. **HONORS AND AWARDS** MA, Cambridge Univ, 64; LLD, New York Law Sch, 79; De Paul, 87. **MEMBERSHIPS** Am Acad Arts & Sci; Am Bar Asn; Am Jewish Cong (sr vpres, 77-84). **RESEARCH** Criminal law; criminal procedure; evidence. **SELECTED PUBLICATIONS** Auth, Conspiracy to Defraud the United States, 59 & The State and the Accused: Balance of Advantage in Criminal Procedure, Yale Law J, 60; The Insanity Defense, Yale Univ, 67; co-ed, Crime, Law and Society, Free, 71; coauth, Criminal Procedure, Little, 74; The Passive Judiciary: Prosecutorial Discretion and the Guilty Plea, LA State Univ Press, 81. **CONTACT ADDRESS** Law Sch, Yale Univ, PO Box 208215, New Haven, CT 06520-8215. **EMAIL** abraham.goldstein@yale.edu

GOLDSTEIN, ANNE B.
PERSONAL Born 03/04/1949, New York, NY, m, 1972 **DISCIPLINE** LAW **EDUCATION** Simon Fraser Univ, BA, 72; Northeastern Univ, JD, 76. **CAREER** Assoc Atty to Partner, Stern & Shapiro, 77-84; Adj Fac, N Eng Law Sch, 83-84; Asst Prof to Prof, W New Eng Col, 84-; Prof, Univ Conn, 95; Vis Prof, Univ Tex, 95. **MEMBERSHIPS** Mass Lesbian and Gay Bar Asn; Am Bar Asn; AALS. **SELECTED PUBLICATIONS** Auth, "Representing Lesbians," Tex J Women and the Law, 92; auth, "The Tragedy of the Interstate Child: A Critical Reexamination of the Uniform Child Custody Jurisdiction Act and the Parental Kidnapping Prevention Act," U.C. Davis L Rev, 92; auth, "Reasoning About Homosexuality: A Commentary on Janet Halley's Reasoning about Sodomy: Act and Identity In and After Bowers v. Hardwick," Va L Rev, 93; auth, "Representing the Lesbian, in Law and Literature," in Representing Women, Duke Univ Press, 94; auth, "Homosexual Identity and Gay Rights," in A Queer World, NYU Press, 97. **CONTACT ADDRESS** Sch of Law, Western New England Col, 1215 Wilbraham Rd, Springfield, MA 01119. **EMAIL** agoldstein@law.wnec.edu

GOLDSTEIN, IRWIN
PERSONAL Born 07/12/1947, Windsor, ON, Canada, d, 2 children **DISCIPLINE** PHILOSOPHY **EDUCATION** Univ Edinburgh, PhD, 79; Univ Bristol, M. Lit, 74; Carleton Univ, BA, 70. **CAREER** Prof, Davidson Col, 98-; asst prof, Davidson Col, 83-87 **HONORS AND AWARDS** Davidson Col Res Grants; Postdoctorate Fel, Univ Edinburgh; Vans Dunlop Scholar, Univ Edinburgh; Carleton Univ Grant. **MEMBERSHIPS** Amer Philos Assoc; Intl Soc Value Inquiry; S Soc Philos Psychol; NC Philos Assoc **RESEARCH** Philosophy of mind, ethics, and philosophy of language. **SELECTED PUBLICATIONS** Ontology, Epistemology, and Private Ostensive Definition, Philos and Phenomenological Res, 96; Identifying Experiences: A Celebrated Working Hypothesis Refuted, Australasian Jour Philos, 94; "Pleasure and Pain: Unconditional Intrinsic Values," Philos and Phenomenological Res, 89 **CONTACT ADDRESS** Dept of Philosophy, Davidson Col, Davidson, NC 28036. **EMAIL** irgoldstein@davidson.edu

GOLDSTEIN, JOSHUA S.
PERSONAL Born Boston, 2 children **DISCIPLINE** INTERNATIONAL MILITARY AND ECONOMIC RELATIONS **EDUCATION** Stanford Univ, BA; Mass Inst Technol, MA, PhD. **CAREER** Prof, Am Univ. **RESEARCH** International relations theory **SELECTED PUBLICATIONS** Auth, International Relations, 4th ed; Addison-Wesley Longman, 01; Auth, Three-Way Street, Chicago IL Press, 90; Auth, Long Cycles, Yale, 88. **CONTACT ADDRESS** American Univ, 4400 Massachusetts Ave, Washington, DC 20016. **EMAIL** JG@joshuagoldstein.com

GOLDSTEIN, LEON J.
PERSONAL Born 02/06/1927, Brooklyn, NY, m, 1964, 2 children **DISCIPLINE** PHILOSOPHY **EDUCATION** Brooklyn Col, AB, 49; Yale Univ, MA, 50, PhD, 54. **CAREER** Instr, Brandeis Univ, 55-57; lectr, Univ of Md Overseas Prog, 58; res staff, Am Jewish Committee, 58-63; lectr, CCNY, 59-63; assoc prof, Harper Col, SUNY, 63-66; prof, SUNY Binghamton, 66-. **HONORS AND AWARDS** Univ Fel, Res Found, SUNY, 70. **MEMBERSHIPS** Am Philos Assoc; Am Anthrop Assoc; R.G. Collingwood Soc. **RESEARCH** Philosophy and history and social science, open concepts and conceptual tension. **SELECTED PUBLICATIONS** Coauth, Politics in a Pluralist Democracy, 63; auth, Historical Knowing, 76; auth, The What and the Why of History, 96; auth, Thinking about Social Science, 99. **CONTACT ADDRESS** Dept Philos, SUNY, Binghamton, PO Box 6000, Binghamton, NY 13902-6000. **EMAIL** ljgolds@binghamton.edu

GOLDSTEIN, PAUL
PERSONAL Born 01/14/1943 **DISCIPLINE** LAW **EDUCATION** Brandeis Univ, BA, 64; Columbia Univ, LLB, 67. **CAREER** Asst prof law, State Univ NY Buffalo, 67-69, assoc prof, 69-71; Prof Law, Stanford Univ, 75-, Via assoc prof law, Stanford Univ, 72-73. **SELECTED PUBLICATIONS** Auth, Information systems and the role of law: Some prospects, Stanford Law Rev, Vol 25, 204; The private consumption of public goods: A commment on Williams & Wilkins Co v United States, Bull Copyright Soc, Vol 21, 204; Kewanee Oil Co v Bicron Corp: Notes on a Closing Circle, 1974 Supreme Ct Rev, 81; Preempted state doctrines, involuntary transfers, and compulsory licenses: Testing the limits of copyright, Univ Calif Los Angeles Law Rev, 78; Changing the American Schoolbook: Law, Politics and Technology, D C Heath & Co, 78; Real Estate Transactions: Cases and Materials on Land Transfer, Development and Finance, 80 & Copyright, Patent, Trademark and Related State Doctrines: Cases and Materials on the Law of Intellectual Property, 2nd ed, 81, Found Press; Adaptation rights and moral rights in the United Kingdom, the United States and the Federal Republic of Germany, IIC, 82. **CONTACT ADDRESS** Sch of Law, Stanford Univ, Stanford, CA 94305-1926.

GOLDTHWAIT, JOHN T.
PERSONAL Born 03/31/1921, Duluth, MN, m, 1948, 1 child **DISCIPLINE** PHILOSOPHY **EDUCATION** USN Res Midship Sch, Ensign, 43, Columbia Univ; Oglethorpe Univ, Atlanta, GA, BA, MA, 44; Northwestern Univ, Phd, 57. **CAREER** Instr, 41-43, Oglethorpe Univ; naval serv, 43-46; instr, 46-50, Oglethorpe Univ; grad tchng asst, 50-52, Northwestern Univ; instr, 52-55, Sacramento St Col; instr, 56-57, asst prof, 58-64, Univ Calif; fac, 62, Pacific Philos Inst; prof, chmn, div of Hum, dean, fac of Hum, 64-65, SUNY. **HONORS AND AWARDS** Fac summer res fel, Univ CA, 58; Plattsburgh Col Found grant, 71 **MEMBERSHIPS** APA; Am Soc for Aesthetics; Nat Coun of Tchrs of Eng; Col Conf on Composition and Commun; Speech Asn of Am; Am Transl Asn; Speech Arts Asn of Northern Calif; Calif div, Am Soc for Aesthetics; Cent Calif Philos Asn; Berkeley Aesthetics Seminar; Asn for Philos of Ed; Philos of Ed Soc; Asn for Process Philos of Ed; FL Philos Asn. **RESEARCH** Aesthetics; theory of value; ethics; process philos. **SELECTED PUBLICATIONS** Transl & ed, Immanuel Kant, Observations on the Feeling of the Beautiful and Sublime, Univ Calif Press, 60, 81; auth, Value, Language, and Life, Prometheus Bks, 85; auth, Ought Never Is: A Response to Oliver A. Johnson, J of Value Inquiry, 92; auth, A General Education Program Seen Fifty Years Later, J of Gen Ed, vol 43, no 1, 94; Values: What They Are and How We Know Them, Prometheus Bks, 96; auth, Values and Education: Helping History Along, The J of Value Inquiry, 96; auth, The Forward Look of Value Judgements, The J of Value Inquiry, 96. **CONTACT ADDRESS** 49 Sandpiper Dr, Saint Augustine Beach, FL 32080. **EMAIL** jtgoldthw8@aol.com

GOLDWORTH, AMNON
PERSONAL Born 07/11/1927, Breast-Litovsk, Poland, m, 1949, 2 children **DISCIPLINE** PHILOSOPHY **EDUCATION** Queens Col, NYork, BA, 50; Stanford Univ, PhD, 60. **CAREER** Univ Washington, ta, 50-51; Stanford Univ, ta, 52, 54;

San Jose State Univ, inst, asst prof, assoc prof, prof, 56-95, Queens Col, lectr, 64; Stanford Univ, School of Med, clin prof pedi, 95-. **HONORS AND AWARDS** Univ Wash, Univ Tchg Fel, 50-51; Stanford Univ, Abraham Rosenberg Fel, 53; Stanford Univ, vis prof, 72; Stanford Univ, Center for Biomedical Ethics, vis scholar, 90-93; Amer Assoc of Tissue Banks, Ethics Comm / Consultant, 94- **MEMBERSHIPS** APA, AATB, AAP, SCCMS, NCTB **RESEARCH** Biomedical ethics in med practice; informal consent in htt; moral and ethical education for med student. **SELECTED PUBLICATIONS** Ed, The collected Works of Jeremy Bantham: Deontology Together with A Table of the Spring of Action and Articles on Utilitarianism, Oxford Univ Press, 83; co-ed, Ethics and Perinatology: Issues and Perspectives, Oxford Univ Press, 95; co-auth, Considerations of the Appropriateness of Intensive CAR e Applications, in: Fetal and Neonatal Brain Injury: Mechanisms, Management and the Risk of Malpractice, B.L. Decker Inc, 89; Standards of Disclosure in Informed Consent, in: Ethics and Perinatology: Issues and Perspectives, Oxford Univ Press, 95; Medical Technology and the Child, in: Birth to death: Biology, Science and Bioethics, Cambridge Univ Press, 96. **CONTACT ADDRESS** School of Medicine, Stanford Univ, 750 Welch Rd, Palo Alto, CA 94304. **EMAIL** amnon@leland.stanford.edu

GOLLUBER, MICHAEL
PERSONAL Born 02/22/1966, Philadelphia, PA, m, 1998 **DISCIPLINE** PHILOSOPHY **EDUCATION** Sarah Lawrence Col, BA, 88; SUNY Stony Brook, MA, 91; Tulane Univ, PhD, 98. **CAREER** Vis instr, Southwestern Univ, 96-98, vis instr, Loyola Univ, 98; adj instr, Xavier Univ, 98; vis instr, Tulane Univ, 98-; asst prof, Xavier Univ, 99-00; tutor, St. John's Col, Santa Fe, 00-. **RESEARCH** Ancient philosophy; history of philosophy. **SELECTED PUBLICATIONS** Auth, Aristotle on Philosophy and the Sense of Touch, J of Philos Res, forthcoming; auth, "Aristotle on 'How One Becomes What One Is,'" Review of Metaphysics, forthcoming. **CONTACT ADDRESS** 2033 Fern St, New Orleans, LA 70118.

GOLPHIN, VINCENT F. A.
PERSONAL Born 08/07/1952, Youngstown, OH, s **DISCIPLINE** THEOLOGY **EDUCATION** Sacred Heart Seminary, Detroit, MI, BA, 74; University of Dayton, MA, 79; Union Graduate School, PhD, 81. **CAREER** New York State Assembly, senior executive asst, 80-82; National Catholic Reporter, writer, 82-87; Charles County Community College, adjunct professor, 86-87; Herald-Journal, Syracuse, NY, editor/columnist, 87-95; Onondaga Community College, Syracuse, NY, adjunct professor, 90-95; Syracuse University, SI School of Public Communications, adjunct professor, 95-; The Writing Co. Inc, president; adjunct prof, African Am Studies, St. John Fisher Col. **HONORS AND AWARDS** NISOD, Teacher Excellence Awd, 1994. **MEMBERSHIPS** Theta Chi Beta, Phi Delta Kappa, Phi Alpha Theta. **CONTACT ADDRESS** St. John Fisher Col, 3690 E Ave, Rochester, NY 14618.

GOMBERG, PAUL
PERSONAL Born 02/11/1943, San Francisco, CA, m, 1965, 1 child **DISCIPLINE** PHILOSOPHY **EDUCATION** Univ of CA, Berkley, BA, 64; Harvard Univ, PhD, 72. **CAREER** Inst, to Asst Prof, Univ of Missouri-St Louis, 71-72, 72-78; Vis Asst Prof , Univ of Illinois, 86-87; Asst Prof, 87-90, Assoc Prof, 90-94, Prof, 94-, Chicago St Univ. **HONORS AND AWARDS** NEH, 92; Fulbright Fel UK, 67-68, Woodrow Wilson Dissertation Fel, 67-68; Harvard Schl, 65-66, 66-67; Woodrow Wilson Fel, 65-66, Dept Citation in Phil, Univ CA, Berkley, 64. **MEMBERSHIPS** APA **RESEARCH** Social and political philosophy; social philosophy of morality; marxism; racism. **SELECTED PUBLICATIONS** Art, Friendship in the Context of a Consequentialist Life, Ethics 102, 92; art, Against Racism, Against Patriotism, APA News, 93; art, Universalism and Optimism, Ethics 104, 94; art, Autonomy and Free Expression, Jour Soc Phil, 94; art, Against Competitive Equal Opportunity, Jour of Soc Phil, 95; art, How Morality Works and Why it Fails: On Political Philosoph and Moral Consensus, Jour of Soc Phil, 97; auth, "Hegel on History and Freedom," in From Kant to Weber, ed. Thomas M. Powers and Paul Kamolnick (FL: Krieger, 99); auth, "Patriotism in Sports & in War," in Values in Sport, ed. Torbjorn Tannsjo and Claudio Tamburaini (London: E & FN SPON, 00). **CONTACT ADDRESS** Chicago State Univ, 9501 S King Dr, History, P, Chicago, IL 60628-1598. **EMAIL** P-Gomberg@csu.edu

GOMEZ, RAUL R.
PERSONAL Born 09/27/1953, Bisbee, AZ, s **DISCIPLINE** LITURGICAL STUDIES **EDUCATION** Univ Ariz, BA, 76; Calif State Univ, MPA, 83; Franciscan Sch Theol, MDiv, 86; Cath Univ Am, PhD, 98. **CAREER** Hispanic Ministry Preparation, Sacred Heart Sch of Theol, 88-. **HONORS AND AWARDS** Sigma Delta Pi; Phi Kappa Phi; Phi Beta Kappa; Vatican II Awd in Liturgy, 91; Diss Grant, Hispanic Theol Initiative, 99-00. **MEMBERSHIPS** Am Acad of Relig; Acad of Cath Hispanic Theol in the US; Nat Inst of Hispanic Liturgy; Nat Assoc of Hispanic Priests. **RESEARCH** Liturgical Theology, the Hispano-Mozarabic rite, Hispanic Popular Religion, Hispanic History and Culture, Ministry Preparation. **SELECTED PUBLICATIONS** Auth, "Advertencia a la tercera edicion en espanol", El Misterio de Fe: Estudio de los Elementos Estructurales del Ordinario de la Misa, ed, Lawrence J Johnson, CCVI/Instituto de Liturgia Hispana, (Washington, DC), 81; coauth, Don y Promesa, Costumbres y Tradiciones en los Ritos Matrimoles Hispanos: Gift and Promise, Customs and Traditions in Hispanic Rites of Marriage, Ore Cath Pr, 97; auth, "Introduccion a la Instruccion General para el uso del Misal roman", Los documentos Liturgicos: Un Rrecurso pastoral, eds Arturo Perez Rodriguez and Mark Francis, Liturgy Training Pub, (Chicago, 97); auth, "Celebrating the Quinceanera as a Symbol of Faith and Culture", Misa, Mesa, y Musa: Liturgy in the US Hispanic Church, ed Kenneth G Davis, JS Paluch, (Schiller Park, 97); coed, El Cuerpo de Cristo: The Hispanic Presence in the US Catholic Church, Crossroad Herber Book, (NY, 98); auth, "Preaching the Ritual Masses Among Latinos", Chicago Studies, (forthcoming); auth, "Mozarabic Liturgy", New Cath Encycl, (forthcoming). **CONTACT ADDRESS** Dept Gen Educ, Sacred Heart Sch of Theol, PO Box 429, Hales Corners, WI 53130-0429. **EMAIL** rgomezsds@compuserve.com

GONZALEZ, CATHERINE GUNSALUS
PERSONAL Born 05/20/1934, Albany, NY, m, 1973 **DISCIPLINE** HISTORICAL AND SYSTEMATIC THEOLOGY **EDUCATION** Beaver Col, BA, 56; Boston Univ, STB, 60, PhD(syst theol, hist doctrine), 65. **CAREER** From asst prof to assoc prof Bible and relig, WVa Wesleyan Col, 65-70, dir student relig life, 65-70; assoc prof hist theol, Louisville Presby Thcol Sem, 70-73; assoc prof church hist, 74-78, PROF CHURCH HIST, COLUMBIA THEOL SEM, 78-, Mem comt on status of women, Gen Assembly, United Presby Church, 67-70, comt on baptism, 70-72; mem, Faith and Order Comn, Nat Coun Churches, 73-. **MEMBERSHIPS** Presby Hist Soc. **RESEARCH** Liturgical theology; women and theology; comparative systematic theology. **SELECTED PUBLICATIONS** Auth, Between Text and Sermon--Isaiah 43, 8-15, Interpretation-J Bible and Theol, Vol 0048, 94. **CONTACT ADDRESS** Dept of Church Hist, Columbia Theol Sem, PO Box 520, Decatur, GA 30031-0520.

GONZALEZ, JUSTO LUIS
PERSONAL Born 08/09/1937, Havana, Cuba, m, 1973, 1 child **DISCIPLINE** HISTORICAL THEOLOGY **EDUCATION** Union Theol Sem, Cuba, STB, 57; Yale Univ, STM, 58, MA, 60, PhD, 61. **CAREER** Prof, 61-68, dean, 68-69, Evangel Sem PR; assoc prof world Christianity, 69-77, Candler Sch Theol, Emory Univ; res & writing, 77-78; Ed, Apuntes; Journal Hispanic Theol, 79-; res fels hist theol, Yale Univ, 68 & 69; consult theol educ, Protestant Episcopal Church, 71-72 & 73-74; mem, Comn Faith & Order, Nat Coun Churches, 73-81; dir, 87-, Hispanic Sum Prog; exec dir, 96-, Hispanic Theol Initiative. **HONORS AND AWARDS** Hon degree, Divinas Letras, Seminario Evangelico de Puerto Rico, 94; Virgilio Elizondo Awd; Acad of Cath Hispanic Theologians in US, 91; Gold Medallion Bk Awd, Evangelical Christian Publ Assn, 93; Orlando Costas Awd, Latino Pastoral Action Ctr, 98. **RESEARCH** Patristics; liberation theology; contemporary Latin American theology. **SELECTED PUBLICATIONS** Auth, Mana: Christian Theology from a Hispanic Perspective, 90; auth, Faith and Wealth, Harper, 90; auth, Out of Every Tribe and Nation: Christian Theology at the Ethnic Roundtable, Abingdon, 92; auth, Santa Biblia: The Bible Through Hispanic Eyes, Abingdon, 96. **CONTACT ADDRESS** PO Box 520, Decatur, GA 30031. **EMAIL** jgonz02@emory.edu

GONZALEZ, LUIS G.
PERSONAL Born 04/28/1969, Ponce, PR, m, 1989 **DISCIPLINE** PHILOSOPHY **EDUCATION** Andrews Univ, BA, 92; Western Mich Univ, MA, 94; Valparaiso Univ, JD, 97. **CAREER** Vis asst prof, Grand Valley State Univ, 96-. **MEMBERSHIPS** Am Bar Asn. **RESEARCH** Philosophy of law; Professional ethics; Latin American philosophy. **SELECTED PUBLICATIONS** Auth, Sereno en Flor, 94. **CONTACT ADDRESS** PO Box 141011, Grand Rapids, MI 49514-1011. **EMAIL** attorneygonzalez@aol.com

GOOCH, PAUL W.
PERSONAL Born 06/24/1941, Toronto, ON, Canada **DISCIPLINE** PHILOSOPHY, RELIGION **EDUCATION** Bishop's Univ, BA, 63; Univ Toronto, MA, 65, PhD, 70. **CAREER** Asst prof, 70, assoc prof, 73, ch div hum, 77-82, prof, 88, dir grad ctr relig stud, 86-88, assoc dean hum, sch grad stud, 88-90, asst dean to dean, sch grad stud, 90-94, Vice-Provost, Univ Toronto, 94-; Commonwealth fel, St John's Col, Cambridge, 82-83. **MEMBERSHIPS** Can Philos Asn; Class Asn Can; Can Soc Stud Relig; Can Soc Bibl Stud; Soc Christian Philos. **RESEARCH** Ancient philos, especially Plato (ethics and moral psychology, Platonic love, irony and other Socratic themes); Philso of Relig (especially the problem of evil and theodicy, ethics, philosophical issues in biblical studies). **SELECTED PUBLICATIONS** Auth, Partial Knowledge: Philosophical Studies in Paul, 87; auth, "Has Plato Changed Socrates Heart in the Pheaedrus?", 92; auth, "Sovereignty, Soft Determinism and Responsibility," 94; auth, "A Mind to Love: Friends and Lovers in Ancient Greek Philosophy": Word and Silence: Studies in Jesus and Socrates, 96. **CONTACT ADDRESS** Simcoe Hall, Univ of Toronto, 27 King's Col Cir, Toronto, ON, Canada M5S 1A1. **EMAIL** paul.gooch@utoronto.ca

GOOD, ROBERT C.
DISCIPLINE ETHICS AND RELIGION IN AMERICA **EDUCATION** Princeton Univ, AB; Univ Wis, MA, PhD. **CAREER** Instr, Rider Univ, 82; prof. **HONORS AND AWARDS** AB with honors; three NEH fel(s); Lindback Awd, 91. **RESEARCH** Philosophy of religion, Imperative logic, tele-evangelism **SELECTED PUBLICATIONS** Nat and intl publ(s), philos rel, imperative logic and tele-evangelism. **CONTACT ADDRESS** Dept Philos, Rider Univ, 2083 Lawrenceville, Lawrenceville, NJ 08648-3099.

GOODE, JAMES EDWARD
PERSONAL Born 11/18/1943, Roanoke, VA **DISCIPLINE** THEOLOGY **EDUCATION** Immaculate Conceptn Coll, BA 1969; Coll of St Rose, MA 1971; St Anthony Theol Sem, MDiv 1972, MTh 1974; PhD; Univ of Louvain Belgium, post-doctoral studies 1980. **CAREER** Our Lady of Charity, Pastor 1974-; City Univ NY, Adj Prof 1975-, Chaplain 1975-; Center for Positive Directn, Dir 1976-; Black Religious Expernc Inst, co-dir; Directions A Jour of Black Ch/Comm Studies, editor; Black Cath Day, founder; Survival & Faith Inst of NY, cons; Juvenile Justice Task Force of Cntrl Brooklyn, cons; Offc for Black Ministry Diocese of Brooklyn, bd dirs; Bldg a Better Brooklyn, bd dirs; lectr, psychlgy & theology. **HONORS AND AWARDS** Dr of Humane Letters VA Theol Sem; Preacher of First Black Cath Revival in US Chicago 1974; Martin Luther King Schlrshp NY Univ 1975-76; Black Cath Leadrshp Awrd; proclmtn declaring Nov 18 1978 Father James E Goode Day New York City 1978; proclmtn declaring Nov 16 1979 Father James E Goode Day Mayor of Brooklyn 1979; Nat Black Cath Clergy Tribute Awd 1979; proclmtn NY State Assembly; lead Nat Protest Prayer Serv Against Budget Cuts in Human Servs. **MEMBERSHIPS** Mem New York City Comm Sch Bd; mem Central Brooklyn Yth & Fmly Svcs; mem Juvenile Prevntv Pgms Brooklyn; mem New York City Comm Plnng Bd; mem Culture & Worship Adv Bd Nat Offc for Black Cath; mem Coalition of Concerned Black Eductrs of NY; mem Black Ministers Cncl; mem Nat Black Cath Clergy; Nat Assn of Black Social Wrkrs; Educ Task Force for Positive Direction of NY Urban Commn. **CONTACT ADDRESS** 1669 Dean St, Brooklyn, NY 11213.

GOODEN, WINSTON EARL
DISCIPLINE THEOLOGY **EDUCATION** Muskingum College, BA; Yale Univ, MDiv, MS, PhD. **CAREER** Two Churches in CT, pastored; Unoja Juvenile Program, co-founder & director; Univ of IL at Chicago, asst prof; Fuller Theological Seminary, asst prof. **HONORS AND AWARDS** Presented papers across the nation. **SELECTED PUBLICATIONS** Published many articles. **CONTACT ADDRESS** Fuller Theol Sem, 135 N Oakland, Pasadena, CA 91101.

GOODING-WILLIAMS, ROBERT
DISCIPLINE PHILOSOPHY **EDUCATION** Yale Univ, PhD. **CAREER** Prof, Northwestern Univ. **RESEARCH** Nietzsche, Du Bois, Nineteenth-Century European philosophy, literary theory and African-American literature, critical race theory. **SELECTED PUBLICATIONS** Auth, The Massachuettes Review, Special Issue on Du Bois, 94; co-ed, The Souls of Black Folk, 97. **CONTACT ADDRESS** Dept of Philosophy, Northwestern Univ, 1818 Hinman, Evanston, IL 60208. **EMAIL** rjgoodingwil@northwestern.edu

GOODMAN, LENN EVAN
PERSONAL Born 03/21/1944, Detroit, MI, m, 1999, 2 children **DISCIPLINE** PHILOSOPHY **EDUCATION** Harvard Univ, BA, 65; Oxford Univ, DPhil(Arabic philos), 68. **CAREER** Asst prof philos and Near Eastern lang, Univ Calif, Los Angeles, 68-69; asst prof, 69-74, assoc prof, 74-81, PROF PHILOS, UNIV HAWAII, MONOA, 81-, Consult, Sch Jewish Studies, Univ Tel Aviv, 74-77 and Hawaiian Humane Soc, 78-79. **HONORS AND AWARDS** Baumgardt Prize, Am Philos Asn, 78; Littman lectr, Oxford Ctr for Postgrad Hebrew Studies, 79. **MEMBERSHIPS** Am Philos Asn; Am Orient Soc; Mid East Studies Asn NAm; Acad Jewish Philos. **RESEARCH** Jewish and Islamic philosophy; metaphysics; ethics. **SELECTED PUBLICATIONS** Auth, "Jewish and Islamic Philosophy: Crosspollinatons in the Classic Age," Edinburgh University Press and Rutgers University Press, 99, 256 pp.; auth, "Judaism, Human Rights and Human Values," Oxford University Press, 98, 202 pp., republished in digital form in O.U.P.'s NetLibrary, 00; auth, "God of Abraham," Oxford University Press, 96, 364 pp., Gratz Prize, Philadelphia, 97; auth, "Avicenna," Routledge, 92, 240 pp., Italian ed., L'Universo di Avicenna, Genoa: ECIG, 95; auth, "On Justice: An Essay in Jewish Philosophy," Yale University Press, 91, 288 pp.; auth, "Saadiah ben Joesph al-Fayyumi's Book of Theodicy, a tenth century Arabic commentary and translation of the book of Job," translated with philosophical introduction and commentary, Yale Judaica Series XXV, Yale University Press, 481 pp.; auth, "Monotheism: A Philosophic Inquiry into the Foundations of Natural Theology and Ethics," Totowa, N.J.: Allanheld Osmun, 81, 119 pp.; auth, "The Case of the Animals vs Man Before the King of the Jinn," translated from the Rasa'il Ikhwan al-Safa' with philosophic introduction and commentary, Twayne Publishers, 78, 271 pp., excerpted in the Penguin Anthology, 00; auth, "Rambam: Readings in the Philosophy of Moses Maimonides," translated with introduction and commentary, New York: Viking, 76, 444 pp.,

paperback, Schocken, 77, Reissued, 86; auth, "Ibn Tuffayl's Hayy Ibn Yaqzan," translated with introduction and commentary, Twayne Publishers, 72, 246 pp., paperback, 84, reprinted, 90, etc., special student edition Cairo: American University, 92, 94, 96, 999. **CONTACT ADDRESS** Dept of Philos, Vanderbilt Univ, Nashville, TN 37240.

GOODMAN, LOUIS
PERSONAL Born 12/06/1942, New York, NY, m, 1965, 2 children **DISCIPLINE** SOCIOLOGY, ECONOMICS **EDUCATION** Dartmouth Col, BA; Northwestern Univ, MA, PhD. **CAREER** Asst Prof, Yale Univ, 69-75; dir, Latin Am & Caribbean Prog, Soc Sci Res Coun, 72-78; lect, Yale Univ, 78-81; dir, Latin Am Prog, Woodrow Wilson Int Ctr Scholars, 81-86; prof, Am Univ, dean Sch Int Service, 86-. **HONORS AND AWARDS** Dir, Latin Am Prog, Woodrow Wilson Int Ctr Scholars; Dir, Latin Am & Caribbean Prog,Soc Sci Res Coun. **RESEARCH** Impact of transnational corporations on National development, Civil-Military Relations, Democracy Building. **SELECTED PUBLICATIONS** Auth, Small Nations, Giant Firms: Capital Allocation Decisions in Transnational Corporations, Holmes and Mier, 87; The Military and Democracy in Latin America, D.C. Heath-Lexington, 90; Lessons from the Venezuelan Experienc, Johns Hopkins, 95. **CONTACT ADDRESS** American Univ, 4400 Massachusetts Ave, Washington, DC 20016.

GOODMAN, MICHAEL F.
PERSONAL Born 03/23/1950, CA, m, 1975, 4 children **DISCIPLINE** PHILOSOPHY **EDUCATION** Mich State Univ, PhD, 86. **CAREER** Humboldt State Univ, prof. **MEMBERSHIPS** APA, MA **RESEARCH** Logic; epistemology; philosophy of science; moral philosophy. **SELECTED PUBLICATIONS** Auth, First Logic, UPA, 97; Contemporary Readings in Epistemology, co-auth w/ R. A. Snyder, Prentice-Hall, 93; What is a Person? Humana Press, 88; Decision and Practice, coauth, Humboldt Jour of Soc Rel, 87; Concept of Person in: Philo of Edu: An Encycl, 96; A Sufficient Condition for Personhood, Personalist Form, 92; What is a Program?, Contemp Philo, 88. **CONTACT ADDRESS** Dept Philos, Humboldt State Univ, 1 Harpst St., Arcata, CA 95521. **EMAIL** mfg1@humboldt.edu

GOODMAN, RUSSELL B.
DISCIPLINE PHILOSOPHY **EDUCATION** Univ Pa, AB, 66; BA, 68; Oxford Univ, MA, 70; Johns Hopkins Univ, PhD, 71. **CAREER** From Asst Prof to Prof, Univ NMex, 71-. **HONORS AND AWARDS** Phi Beta Kappa, 65; Thouron Brit-Am Exchange Fel, Oxford Univ, 66-68; William Montgomerie Prize, Jesus Col, 67; Nat Defense Educ Act Fel, Johns Hopkins Univ, 68-71; Grant, Nat Endowment for Humanities, 89-90; Fulbright Sen Res Awd, 93. **RESEARCH** Am Philos; Wittgenstein; Philos and Lit; Nineteenth and Twentieth Century Philos. **SELECTED PUBLICATIONS** Auth, American Philosophy and the Romantic Tradition, Cambridge: Cambridge Univ Press, 90; auth, Pragmatism: A Contemporary Reader, London and New York: Routledge, 95; auth, "Reconstructing American Philosophy: Emerson and Dewey," Frontiers in American Philosophy, Vol. II, ed. Robert W. Burch and Herman J. Sattkamp, Jr., (College Station: Texas A&M Press, 96): 223-30; auth, "Emerson the European and Heidegger the American," in American and Eurpean National Identities: Faces in the Mirror, (Keele: Keele Univ Press, 96): 111-25; ed, "Emerson's Mystical Empiricism," in The Perennial Tradition of Neoplatonism, Leuven: Leuven Univ Press, (97): 456-78; auth, "Moral Perfectionism and Democracy in Emerson and Nietzche," ESQ: A Journal of the American Renaissnce, vol. 43, vols. 1-4, (97): 159-80; auth, "American Philosophy in the 18th and 19th Centuries," Routledge Encyclopedia of Philosophy, (98): 201-7; auth, "Ralph Waldo Emerson," Routledge Encyclopedia of Philosophy, (98): 269-72; auth, "Wittgenstein and Pragmatism," Parallax 9, (98): 91-105; auth, Stanley Cavell: The Philosopher Responds to His Critics, Nashville, TN: Vanderbilt Univ Press, (forthcoming). **CONTACT ADDRESS** Dept Philos, Univ of New Mexico, Albuquerque, 1 University Campus, Albuquerque, NM 87131-0001. **EMAIL** rgoodman@unm.edu

GOODMAN, SUSANNE R.
DISCIPLINE LAW **EDUCATION** Univ Toronto, BA, 77; Windsor Univ, LLB, 80. **CAREER** Lectr, 89-. **SELECTED PUBLICATIONS** Auth, pubs on family law. **CONTACT ADDRESS** Fac of Law, Univ of Toronto, 78 Queen's Park, Toronto, ON, Canada M5S 1A1.

GOODMAN-DELAHUNTY, JANE
PERSONAL Born 02/17/1952, Johannesburg, South Africa, 1 child **DISCIPLINE** PSYCHOLOGY, LAW **EDUCATION** Univ Witwatersrand, Johannesburg, S Africa, BA, 72, MA, 73; Univ Seattle Sch of Law, JD, 83; Univ Wa Seattle, PhD, 86. **CAREER** Assoc, 83-84, Bricklin & Gendler, Seattle; trial atty, 84-88, US Equal Employ Opportunity Comm, Seattle; litigation atty, 89-92, Frank & Rosen, Seattle; mediator, arbitrator, 94-, Judicial Arbitration & Mediation Svc, Endispute, Calif; admin judge, 92-, US Equal Employ Opportunity Comm; Assoc Prof, Univ of New South Wales, 00. **HONORS AND AWARDS** Conrad Linder Mem Awd, 73; Amer Jurisprudence Awd, 82, 83; PhD Scholar, 83; Grad Res Fel, 85; Dissertation Prize, 87; Special Commendation, 88; Pres, Amer Psychol-Law Soc, 94; Chairman's Innov Awd, 95; Amer Psychol-Law Soc Fel, 96. **MEMBERSHIPS** Amer Bar Assoc; Amer Judicature Soc; Amer Psychol Assoc; Amer Psychol-Law Soc; Amer Psychol Soc; Int Assoc Applied Psychol; Int Cong Law & Mental Health; Law & Soc Assoc; San Diego Psych-Law Soc; Seattle-King Co Bar Assoc; Soc for Psychol Study of Soc Issue; Wa St Bar Assoc. **RESEARCH** Psychol & law; scientific & expert evidence; employ discrimination; sexual harassment; cultural diversity; collective & political violence; dispute resolution; procedural & distributive justice; causal reasoning; decision-making; stereotyping; eyewitness reliability; jury behavior. **SELECTED PUBLICATIONS** Art, Employment Discrimination and Stereotyping, Encyclopedia of psychology, Oxford Univ Press, Amer Psychol Assoc, 99; art, Civil law: Employment and Discrimination, Perspectives on Psychology and Law: The State of the Discipline, Plenum Press, 99; art, Pragmatic Considerations Supporting the Reasonable Victim Standard in Hostile Workplace Sexual Harassment Cases, Psychology, Public Policy & Law, 99, coauth, Juror Decisions About Damages in Employment Discrimination Cases, Behavioral Sci & the Law, 99; art, Same-Sex Harassment: Implications of The Oncale Decision for Forensic Evaluations of Plaintiffs, Behavioral Sci & the Law, 99. **CONTACT ADDRESS** 2407 Calle Madiera, San Clemente, CA 92672. **EMAIL** jg-d@pacbell.net

GOODNIGHT, G. THOMAS
PERSONAL Born 12/02/1948, Houston, TX, m, 1972, 3 children **DISCIPLINE** COMMUNICATION STUDIES; POLITICAL SCIENCE **EDUCATION** Univ of Houston, 71; Univ of Kansas, 77. **CAREER** Prof, Northwestern Univ, 75- ; dir of Forensics, 75-84; dir of grad studies, 83-86; 88-91. **HONORS AND AWARDS** Awd for outstanding scholar, Am Forensic Asn, 74, 80, 82; Charles Wohlbert Res Awd, SCA, 92; Outstanding Prof, Nat Speakers Asn, 94; Golden Monograph Awd, SCA, 95. ORG Nat Commun Asn. **RESEARCH** Public Culture; Rhet; Argumentation; Policy Controversy; Commun Theory & Practice. **SELECTED PUBLICATIONS** Auth, Toward a Social Theory of Argumentation, Argumentation and Advocacy, 89; The Rhetorical Tradition, Modern Communication, and the Rhetoric of Assent, The Rhetoric of Assent, eds Williams and Hazen, 90; Controversy, Proceedings of the 6th Annual Conference on Argumentation, ed D. Parson, 91; Habermas, the Public Sphere, and Controversy, World Jour of Pub Opinion Res, 4, 92; Rhetoric, Legitimation, and the End of the Cold War: Ronald Reagan at the Moscow Summit, 1988, Reagan and Public Discourse in America, eds M. Weiler and B. Pearce, 92; Legitimation Inferences: An Additional Component for the Toulmin Model, Informal Logic, 15, 93; A New Rhetoric for a New Dialectic, Argumentation: An Int Jour on Reasoning, 7, 93; The Park, The Firm, and the University, Quart Jour of Speech, 81, 95; Reagan, Vietnam and Central America: On Public Memory and the Politics of Fragmentation, Rhet and the Presidency, ed M. Medhurst, 96; Hans J. Morgenthau In Defense of the National Interest and the Recovery of the Rhetorical Tradition, The Rhet of Realism, eds Hariman and Beer, 96; coauth, Entanglements of Consumption, Cruelty, Privacy and Fashion, The Social Controversy over Fur, Quart Jour of Speech, fall issue, 94; Studies in the Public Sphere, Quart Jour of Speech, fall isssue, 97. **CONTACT ADDRESS** Dept of Communication Studies, Northwestern Univ, 1809 Chicago Ave, Evanston, IL 60201-4119. **EMAIL** GTQ@NWU.edu

GOODWIN, JAMES OSBY
PERSONAL Born 11/04/1939, Tulsa, OK, m **DISCIPLINE** LAW **EDUCATION** Univ of Notre Dame, BA 1961; Univ of Tulsa, JD 1965. **CAREER** Atty; OK Eagle Newsppr, publisher. **HONORS AND AWARDS** Awd for Serv as mem bd chmn Tulsa Comprehensive Hlth Ctr 1973. **MEMBERSHIPS** Chmn Tulsa Human Srvc Agncy 1978-80; bd chmn Tulsa Comprhnsv Hlth Ctr 1973; mem Tulsa City Co Bd of Hlth; mem OK Bar Assn; Am Trial Lawyers; sec, vice pres OK Trial Lawyers; mem Tulsa Co Bar Assn; Tulsa Co Legal Aid; ACLU Award for Serv as Chmn Tulsa City Co Bd of Hlth 1975. **CONTACT ADDRESS** 122 N Greenwood, Tulsa, OK 74120.

GOODYEAR, RUSSELL
PERSONAL Born 07/26/1941, Pine Bluff, AR, m, 1993, 3 children **DISCIPLINE** SPANISH, FOLKLORE **EDUCATION** Marion Inst, ASc, 61; Henderson State Col, BA, 63; Univ Ark, MA, 70; Univ Ark, PhD, 77. **CAREER** Prof, Sul Ross State Univ, 77-93; Prof, Midland Col, 93-. **HONORS AND AWARDS** Teacher of the Year, Midland Col, 94-95; Teacher of the Year, Midland Col, 97-98. **MEMBERSHIPS** Tex Folklore Soc, W Tex Hist Asn, Tex St Hist Asn. **RESEARCH** Folklore and Hispanic literature. **SELECTED PUBLICATIONS** Auth, A Critical Anthology of Cuban Short Stories in Translation, 77; auth, Republic of Mexico: Decimal Coinage, 92. **CONTACT ADDRESS** Dept Lang & Fine Arts, Midland Col, 3600 N Garfield St, Midland, TX 79705-6329. **EMAIL** rhgoodyear@midland.cc.tx.us

GORANSON, STEPHEN
PERSONAL Born 11/05/1950, Surrey, England **DISCIPLINE** RELIGION AND HISTORY **EDUCATION** Brandeis Univ, BA, 72; Duke Univ, PhD, 90. **CAREER** Wake Forest Univ; Univ NC Wilmington; NC State Univ; vis asst prof/vis scholar, Duke Univ, 98-. **SELECTED PUBLICATIONS** Auth, Essene Polemic in the Apocalypse of John, Legal Texts, Legal Issues, Proceedings of the Second Meeting of International Organization for Qumran Studies, Cambridge 1995: Published in Honour of Joseph M. Baumgarten, Cambridge, England, STJD, 23, Leiden, E. J. Brill, 97; auth, The Text of Revelation 22:14, New Testament Studies, 97; auth, 7 vs. 8--The Battle Over the Holy Day at Dura-Europos, Bible Rev, 96; auth, Inkwell, Ostracon with Maria Graffito, Sepphoris in Galilee: Crosscurrents of Culture, NC Mus of Art, 96; auth, The Exclusion of Ephraim in Rev. 7:4-8 and Essene Polemic Against Pharisees, Dead Sea Discoveries, 95; auth, Posidonius, Strabo, and Marcus Vipsanius Agrippa as Sources on Essenes, Jour of Jewish Studies, 94; auth, Sectarianism, Geography, and the Copper Scroll, Jour of Jewish Studies, 92; auth, Nazarenes and Ebionites, Anchor Bible Dict, 92; auth, Essenes: Etymology from 'asah, Revue de Qumran, 84; auth, Others and Intra-Jewish Polemic as Reflected in Qumran Texts, in: Dead Sea Scrolls After Fifty Years: A Comprehensive Assessment, vol. 2, Leiden: Brill, 99. **CONTACT ADDRESS** 706 Louise Cir., #30-J, Durham, NC 27705. **EMAIL** goranson@duke.edu

GORDON, DANE R.
PERSONAL Born 06/15/1925, London, England, m, 1952 **DISCIPLINE** PHILOSOPHY, THEOLOGY **EDUCATION** Univ of London, BD, 56; Ordained, 58; Univ of Cambridge, MA, 58, BA, 51; Univ of Rochester, MA, 60. **CAREER** Asst prof to assoc prof to prof, Rochester Inst of Tech, 62-76, actg dean, 76-77; asst dean, 77-79, assoc dean, 79-88, prof, 88-00, dept chair, 94-97, emer prof, 00-; Balkan Scholar, Am Univ in Bulgaria, 99. **HONORS AND AWARDS** Danforth Assoc, 67-68; Grant from the Int Res and Exchange Bd of the Nat Endowment of the Humanities, 95; Vis Distinguished Prof, Am Univ in Bulgaria, Provost Fel in Int Partnerships; The Eisenhart Outstanding Teacher Awd, 97; Provost Fel in Int Partnerships, 99; **MEMBERSHIPS** Am Philos Asn; Am Acad of Relig; Christians Associated for Relations with Eastern Europe; Soc for Ancient Greek Philos; Am Asn of Univ Professors; Am Soc of Composers, Authors and Producers; Presbytery of Genesee Valley of the United Presbyterian Church, USA. **RESEARCH** Hellenistic Philos; Political and Soc Philo; Ethics in the Old Testament. **SELECTED PUBLICATIONS** Auth, Rochester Institute of Technology: Industry Development and Educational Innovation in an American City, Edwin Mellen Press (New York, Toronto), 82; auth, Thinking and Reading in Philosophy of Religion, Haven Publications, 94; auth, The Old Testament in its Theological, Cultural, Historical Context, Univ Press of Am (Lanham, MD), 94; auth, Philosophy in Post-Communist Europe, Metaphilosophy, 94; auth, Religious Seriousness: Lessons from Eastern Europe, J of Ecumenical Studies, 95; co-ed, Criticism and Defense of Rationality in Contemporary Philosophy, Rodopi, 98; ed and contrib, Philosophy in Post-Communist Europe, Rodopi, 98; auth, Philosophy and Vision, Rodopi, 98; auth, The Epicurean Option, Philos Now, 99; co-ed, Civil Society in Uncivil Times, Rodopi Press, 01. **CONTACT ADDRESS** Dept of Philos, Rochester Inst of Tech, 1 Lomb Memorial Dr, Rochester, NY 14623-5603. **EMAIL** drggla@rit.edu

GORDON, MICHAEL W.
DISCIPLINE LAW **EDUCATION** Univ Conn, BS, LLB; Trinity Col, MA; Univ Iberoamericana, Mexico, Maestria en Derecho. **CAREER** Chesterfield Smith prof, Univ Fla, 68-. **MEMBERSHIPS** Bd dir, US-Mexico Law Inst; Amer Soc Comp Law; bd ed, UCLA Pacific Basin Law J; adv bd, Syracuse J Int Law Commerce; NAFTA Rev; Amer For Law Asn; Amer Soc Int Law; Brit Inst Int Comp Law; Conn Bar. **RESEARCH** Corporate law, international business transactions, comparative law, international litigation. **SELECTED PUBLICATIONS** Coauth, Intl Trade and Investment in a Nutshell; Intl Business Transactions in a Nutshell. **CONTACT ADDRESS** School of Law, Univ of Florida, PO Box 117625, Gainesville, FL 32611-7625. **EMAIL** gordon@law.ufl.edu

GORDON, ROBERT MORRIS
PERSONAL Born 07/01/1932, New York, NY, m, 1969, 1 child **DISCIPLINE** PHILOSOPHY **EDUCATION** Carleton Col, BA, 54; Columbia Univ, MA, 58, PhD, 65. **CAREER** Instr philos, Univ Fla, 62-64; lectr, 64-65, asst prof, 65-70, Univ Wis Madison; assoc prof philos, Univ Mo St Louis, 70-87, prof, 87-. **HONORS AND AWARDS** Am Coun Learned Soc fel, 74-75; Fel Nat Endow for the Hum Soc, 89-90. **MEMBERSHIPS** Am Philos Assn; Soc Philos & Psychol. **RESEARCH** Philosophy of mind; cognitive science. **SELECTED PUBLICATIONS** Art, The Simulation Theory: Objections and Misconceptions, Folk Psychology: The Theory of Mind Debate, Blackwell, 95; art, Simulation Without Introspection or Inference From Me to You, Mental Simulation: Evaluations and Applications, Blackwell, 95; art, Radical Simulationism, Theories of Theories of Mind, Cambridge University Press, 96; art, Sympathy, Simulation, and the Impartial Spectator, Ethics, Summer, 95; coauth, Autism and the Theory of Mind Debate, Philosophical Psychopathology: A Book of Readings, MIT Press, 94; Arts, Empathy, Emotion; and Simulation Theory, Cambridge Dictionary of Philosophy, 99; art, Simulation Theory, MIT Encyclopedia of Cognitive Science, 99; auth, The Structure of Emotions, Cambridge U. Press, 87; art, "Simulation and the Explanation of Action," Empathy and Agency, Westview Press, 00. **CONTACT ADDRESS** Dept of Philosophy, Univ of Missouri, St. Louis, 8001

Natural Bridge, Saint Louis, MO 63121-4499. **EMAIL** gordon@umsl.edu

GORDON, RUTH E.
DISCIPLINE INTERNATIONAL ENVIRONMENTAL LAW **EDUCATION** NYork Univ, BA, 77; NYork Univ Sch Law, JD, 80; London Sch Econ and Political Sci, LLM, 87. **CAREER** Prof, Villanova Univ; Riesenfeld Fel in Public Int Law, Univ Calif at Berkeley; Revson Fel Scholar, City Col City Univ NY Ctr for Legal Educ & Urban Policy; repr, island nation of Vanuatu in the UN & served as, legal adv to the island's Permanent Mission to the UN. **MEMBERSHIPS** Bd dir, Amer Soc Int Law & Amer Bar Asn Int Law and Practice Section; Amer Bar Asn Standing Comt on World Order Under Law. **RESEARCH** International law and development. **SELECTED PUBLICATIONS** Coauth, United Nations Council for Namibia's Study Addressing Namibia's Violations of UN Decrees and Resolutions; publ on, Roles the UN Plays in Develop Countries, in Cornell Int Law J & Michigan J Int Law. **CONTACT ADDRESS** Law School, Villanova Univ, 800 Lancaster Ave, Villanova, PA 19085-1692. **EMAIL** gordon@law.vill.edu

GORDON, WALTER LEAR, III
PERSONAL Born 03/06/1942, Los Angeles, CA, m, 2 children **DISCIPLINE** LAW **EDUCATION** Ohio State Univ, BA 1963; UCLA, MPA 1965, JD 1973, PhD 1981. **CAREER** UCLA Law School, lecturer 1978-82; private practice, attorney, currently. **MEMBERSHIPS** Bd mem SCLC-West 1980-85; mem Langston Bar Assoc 1986. **SELECTED PUBLICATIONS** Published "The Law and Private Police," Rand 1971, "Crime and Criminal Law," Associated Faculty Press 1981; has also published several articles. **CONTACT ADDRESS** 2822 S Western Ave, Los Angeles, CA 90018.

GORDON, WALTER MARTIN
PERSONAL Born 03/05/1928, San Francisco, CA **DISCIPLINE** ENGLISH, THEOLOGY **EDUCATION** Gonzaga Univ, MA, 53; Col St Albert de Louvain, STL, 60; Univ London, PhD(English), 66. **CAREER** Instr English, Univ Santa Clara, 55-56; asst prof, Loyola Univ, Calif, 67-71; asst prof, 72-79, ASSOC PROF ENGLISH, UNIV GA, 79-. **MEMBERSHIPS** Amici Thomae More; Renaissance Soc Am; SAtlantic Mod Lang Asn; MLA. **RESEARCH** Dramatic form in Thomas More's writings; More's writings on the Eucharist; seriocomic art of More and Erasmus. **SELECTED PUBLICATIONS** Auth, The Complete Works of More, Thomas, Vol 7--The 'Letter to Bugenhagen', the 'Supplication of Souls', the 'Letter Against Frith,' Moreana, Vol 0029, 92; Maiestas in More, Thomas Political-Thought, Moreana, Vol 0034, 97. **CONTACT ADDRESS** Dept of English, Univ of Georgia, 0 Georgia University, Athens, GA 30602-0001.

GORDON, WENDY
DISCIPLINE LAW **EDUCATION** Cornell Univ, BA, 71; Penn Univ, JD, 75. **CAREER** Law clerk, Judge Theodore Newman Jr., Superior Court District Columbia, 75-76; vis prof. **SELECTED PUBLICATIONS** Auth, What's Yours is Ours: Ethics, Economics and Intellectual Property; pubs on intellectual property theory. **CONTACT ADDRESS** Sch of Law, Boston Univ, 765 Commonwealth Ave, Boston, MA, Canada 02215-1401.

GORE, BLINZY L.
PERSONAL Born 06/13/1921, Hinton, WV, m **DISCIPLINE** LAW **EDUCATION** West Virginia State College, Institute, WV, BS, education, 1946; IA Univ, JD 1950; NYork Univ, MA 1958, PhD 1967. **CAREER** South Carolina State College, Orangeburg, SC, law professor, 50-66; private practice of law, 56-; South Carolina State College, Orangeburg, SC, associate professor of social science, 66; Claflin College, Orangeburg, SC, vice president for academic affairs, 67-85. **HONORS AND AWARDS** Founders Day Awd NY Univ 1967; Kappa Man of 1975 Orangeburg Alumni Chap Kappa Alpha Psi 1975; Orangeburg Kappa Achievement Awd, 1994; Claflin Coll Presidential Citation, 1994. **MEMBERSHIPS** Mem IA Bar & SC Bar; Pi Gamma Mu 1974; life mem NAACP; past pres Assn of Coll Deans, Registrars and Admissions Officers; United Methodist Church. **SELECTED PUBLICATIONS** Auth, On A Hilltop High, The Origin & History of Claflin College to 1994. **CONTACT ADDRESS** 1700 Belleville Rd, Orangeburg, SC 29115.

GOREE, WILLIAM K.
PERSONAL Born 07/25/1959, Nashville, TN, m, 1983, 2 children **DISCIPLINE** APPLIED ETHICS **EDUCATION** Harding Univ, BA, 80; Abilene Christian Univ, MA, 82; Univ South Fla, post-grad work. **CAREER** Youth and family ccounselor, Northwest Church of Christ, St Petersburgh, Fla, 83-88; adjunct prof, St Petersburgh Jr Col, 86-88, prof, 88-. **HONORS AND AWARDS** Semifinalist, Fla Prof of the Year Awd, Fla Asn of Community Cols, 97; Winner, Nat Carol Burnett Prize for Advancement of Ethics in Journalism, 99. **MEMBERSHIPS** Fla Asn of Community Cols, Int Asn of Ethics Trainers. **RESEARCH** Applied ethics, ethics education, professional ethics training, law enforcement ethics training. **SELECTED PUBLICATIONS** Auth, "Integrating Ethics into Business Education," Business Ed Forum (Feb 92); auth, Ethics in American Life, Southwestern-ITP (96); auth, "Teaching Moral Development in Media Education," J of Mass Media Ethics (summer 2000); auth, Ethical Issues and Decision Making in Law Enforcement (training manual funded by US Justice Dept); auth, "Ethics Overview," in The Encyclopedia of Business and Finance, MacMillan Pub (2000); contrib auth to Effective Communication for Colleges, South-western, ITP (2000); contrib auth of chapter, "Business and Professional Codes of Ethics," Ethics Applied, Pearson Pub (2000). **CONTACT ADDRESS** Applied Ethics Prog, St. Petersburg Junior Col, 6605 5th Ave N, Saint Petersburg, FL 33710-6801. **EMAIL** goreek@spjc.edu

GORMAN, MICHAEL J.
PERSONAL Born 11/03/1955, MD, m, 1976, 3 children **DISCIPLINE** NEW TESTAMENT, EARLY CHURCH HISTORY AND THEOLOGICAL ETHICS **EDUCATION** BA, Gordon Col, 77; M Div, Princeton Theol Sem, 82; PhD, 89. **CAREER** Tchg fel, 81-85, instr, 86, Princeton Theol Sem; adjunct facul, 91-93, assoc dean, 93, assoc prof, 93-98, acting dean, 94-95, dean, 95-, prof, 98-, Ecumenical Inst of Theol, St Mary's Sem & Univ Baltimore. **MEMBERSHIPS** Soc of Bibl Lit. **RESEARCH** NT/early Christian ethics; Paul; Abortion; Non-violence. **SELECTED PUBLICATIONS** Auth, Texts and Contexts, 89, 97; Abortion and the Early Church, 82; auth, The Elements of Exegesis, 00; auth, Cruciformity: Paul's Narrative Spirituality of the Cross, 00. **CONTACT ADDRESS** Ecumenical Institute of Theology, St. Mary's Sem and Univ, 5400 Roland Av., Baltimore, MD 21210. **EMAIL** mgorman@stmarys.edu

GORMAN, ROSEMARIE E.
PERSONAL Born 08/30/1946, Danbury, CT **DISCIPLINE** THEOLOGY **EDUCATION** Yale Divinity Sch, MAR, 86; Cath Univ of Am, PhD, 96. **CAREER** Lectr, Loyola Col; lectr, Sacred Heart Univ; lectr, Fairfield Univ, 93-. **MEMBERSHIPS** Cath Theol Soc of Am; Soc of Christian Ethics; Am Acad of Relig. **RESEARCH** Moral theology. **CONTACT ADDRESS** 17 Grassy Plain Terr, Bethel, CT 06801.

GOROFF, DAVID B.
DISCIPLINE LAW **EDUCATION** Univ Ill, BA; Columbia Univ, JD. **CAREER** Adj prof, Chicago-Kent Col of Law; Kirkland & Ellis Assoc Attorney, 86; Law Clerk, United States Court of Appeals for the Seventh Circuit, 85-86; Assoc Attorney, Hopkins & Sutter, 87-91; Partner, Hopkins & Sutterk, 92-. **HONORS AND AWARDS** Robert C. Watson Awd; ed, columbia law rev. **MEMBERSHIPS** Am Bar Asn. **SELECTED PUBLICATIONS** Auth, "The First Amendment Side Effects of Curing Pac-Man Fever," 84 Columbia Law Review 744, (84); auth, "Fair Use and Unpublished Works: Harper & Row v. Nation Enterprises," 9 VLA?Columbia Journal of Law and the Arts, 125, (85); co-ed, "The Antitrust Health Care Chronicle," Am Bar Asn, Antitrust Section, 1988-89); auth, "Clayton's Commentaries," Am Bar Asn, Antitrust Section, (95). **CONTACT ADDRESS** Law Dept, Hopkins & Sutter, Three First National Plaza, Chicago, IL 60602-4305.

GORRELL, DONALD KENNETH
PERSONAL Born 01/24/1928, Cleveland, OH, m, 1951, 3 children **DISCIPLINE** CHURCH HISTORY **EDUCATION** Miami Univ, BA, 49; Western Reserve Univ, MA, 51, PhD, 60; Yale Univ, BD, 55. **CAREER** Minister to students, Ohio State Univ, 55-60; asst prof, 60-68; Prof Church Hist, United Theol Sem, Ohio, 68-93; secy, Gen Comn Arch and Hist, United Methodist Church, 68-72, 76-80 and 80-84. **HONORS AND AWARDS** Am Asn Theol Sch fac fel, 65-66; fel, Case-Study inst, Mass, 72. **MEMBERSHIPS** AHA; Am Soc Church Hist; Orgn Am Historians; World Methodist Hist Soc. **RESEARCH** Social Gospel in the Progressive Era, 1900-1920; American church history; United Methodist Church history; Women in church history. **SELECTED PUBLICATIONS** Contribr, Encycl of World Biography, McGraw-Hill, 73 & Encycl of World Methodism, Abingdon, 74; auth, The Methodist Federation for social service and the social creed, 1/75, Methodist Hist; ed, Woman's Rightful Place, United Theol Sem, 80; auth, A New Impulse, In: Women in New Worlds, Abingdon, 81; auth, "Ride A Circuit or Let It Alone," Methodist Hist, (86); auth, The Age of Social Responsibility, Mercer 88; contribr, Dictionary of the Ecumenica Movement, Eerdmans 91; auth, "The Social Creed and Methodism Through Eighty Years, In: Perspectives on American Methodism," (Abingdon, 93); contribr, Historical Dictionary of Methodism, Scarecrow, 96. **CONTACT ADDRESS** United Theol Sem, 1810 Harvard Blvd, Dayton, OH 45406.

GORSUCH, RICHARD L.
PERSONAL Born 05/14/1937, Wayne, MI, m, 1961, 2 children **DISCIPLINE** PSYCHOLOGY, RELIGION **EDUCATION** Tex Christian Univ, AB, 59; Univ Ill, MA, 62, PhD, 65; Vanderbilt Univ, MDiv, 68. **CAREER** Res asst, Univ Ill, 59-61; acting psychol trainee, State Hospital North, Orofino, summer 60; postdoctoral fel, Nat Inst of Mental Health, Public Health Service, 61-63; res assoc, Vanderbilt Univ, 63-65, instr, 65-66; Kennedy Asst prof of psychol, Kennedy Center for Res on Ed & Human Develop, George Peabody Col for Teachers, 68-70, assoc prof, 70-73; assoc prof, Inst of Behav Res, Tex Christian Univ, 73-75; assoc prof to prof, Univ Tex, 75-79; prof psychol, Fuller Theol Sem, 79-. **HONORS AND AWARDS** Diplomate in assessment (Charter mem, ABEP status in development); Fel, Am Psychol Asn, Pres, Div 36, 90-91; Mem, Coun of Representatives, 84-85, 89-90; William James Awd, Am Psychol Asn, 86; pubs in measurement/methodology, personality & soc psychol, psychol of rel and substance abuse. **MEMBERSHIPS** Am Psychol Asn, Soc of Multivariate Experimental Psychol, Soc for the Sci Study of Relig, Relig Res Asn. **RESEARCH** Multivariate statistics and psychology of religion. **SELECTED PUBLICATIONS** Auth, Factor Analysis, Hillsdale, NJ: Lawrence Erlbaum Assoc, Pub (83); coauth with S. McPherson, "Intrinsic/Extrinsic Measurement: I/E-Revised and Single-Item Scales," J for the Sci Study of Relig, 28, 3 (89): 348-354; auth, "Religious aspects of substance abuse and recovery," J of Soc Issues, 51, 2 (95): 65-83; auth, "Exploratory factor analysis: Its role in item analysis," J of Personality Assessment, 68, 3, (97): 532-560; auth, "Toward motivational theories of intrinsic religious commitment," in B. Spilka & D. N. McIntosh, eds, The psychology of religion: Theoretical approaches, Boulder, CO: Westview Press (97); auth, UniMult: for Univariate and Multivariate Data Analysis, (computer prof and guide) Pasadena, CA: Unimult (90-99). **CONTACT ADDRESS** Dept Psychol, Fuller Theol Sem, 180 N Oakland, Pasadena, CA 91001.

GOSS, JAMES
PERSONAL Born 08/21/1939, San Pedro, CA, m, 1961, 3 children **DISCIPLINE** RELIGION & LITERATURE **EDUCATION** Univ Southern Calif, BA, 60; Southern Calif Sch Theol, MTh, 63; Claremont Grad Sch, PhD, 70. **CAREER** Assoc prof & campus minister, Cornell Col, 65-67; asst prof, 69-80, from prof to chemn, Relig Studies, Calif State Univ, Northridge, 80-; exec assoc to the pres, 98-; prof relig studies/assoc to pres. **MEMBERSHIPS** Soc Bibl Lit; Am Acad Relig. **RESEARCH** Religion in literature; New Testament. **SELECTED PUBLICATIONS** Auth, Camus, God and process thought, Process Studies, summer 74; art, O'Connor's redeemed man: Christus et/vel Porcus?, Drew Gateway, winter-spring 74; art, The double action of mercy in The Artificial Nigger, Christianity & Lit, spring 74; art, Eschatology, autonomy, and individuation: The evocative power of the kingdom, Jour Am Acad of Relig, 81. **CONTACT ADDRESS** President's Office, 18111 Nordhoff St, Northridge, CA 91330-8200. **EMAIL** james.goss@csun.edu

GOSSAI, HEMCHAND
PERSONAL Born 04/11/1954, Guyana, m, 3 children **DISCIPLINE** RELIGION **EDUCATION** Concordia Col Moorhead, BA, 79; Luther Sem, MDiv, 83; Univ St. Andrews Scotland, PhD, 86. **CAREER** Luther Sem, lect, 87; Concordia Col, asst prof, 90-91; Culver-Stockton Coll, assoc prof, 92-00; Muhlenberg Coll, assoc prof, 00-. **HONORS AND AWARDS** Helsabeck Awd, Faculty Mentorship Awd, Governor's Awd. **MEMBERSHIPS** SBL, CBA. **RESEARCH** Marginality issue in Genesis; social critique in the prophets. **SELECTED PUBLICATIONS** Auth, Justice, Righteousness and the Social Critique of the Eighth Century Prophets, Peter Lang Pub, 93; auth, Power and Marginality in the Abraham Narrative, Univ Press of Am, 95; auth, Genesis, Augsburg/Fortress Pub House, 93; auth, Power and Marginality in the Hagar Narrative, Ex Scientia, 95; auth, Divine Vulnerability and Human Marginality in the Akedah: Exploring a Tension, in: Horizons in Biblical Theology: An International Dialogue, 97. **CONTACT ADDRESS** Dept of Religion, Muhlenberg Col, 2400 Chew Street, Allentown, PA 18104-5586. **EMAIL** hgossai@culver.edu

GOSSE, RICHARD
DISCIPLINE LAW **EDUCATION** McGill Univ, BA, 47; Univ British Columbia, LLB, 50; Oxford Univ, DPhill, 60. **CAREER** Prof, 60- **SELECTED PUBLICATIONS** Auth, Continuing Poundmaker and Riel's Quest. **CONTACT ADDRESS** Col of Law, Univ of Saskatchewan, 15 Campus Dr, Saskatoon, SK, Canada S7N 5A6. **EMAIL** der@law.usask.ca

GOSTIN, LO
PERSONAL Born 10/19/1949, New York, NY, m, 1977, 2 children **DISCIPLINE** LAW **EDUCATION** Duke Univ, JD 73. **CAREER** Georgetown Univ Law, Prof of Law, 7 years; Am Soc of Law, Med and Ethics, Exec Dir, 6 years; NCCL UK, Gen Sec, 3 years; MIND Ntl assoc Mental Hlth UK, Legal Dir, 5 years. **HONORS AND AWARDS** Rosemary Delbridge Memorial Awd. **RESEARCH** Public Health and the Law. **SELECTED PUBLICATIONS** Auth, Public Health and Human Rights in the HIV Pandemic, coauth, WHO, Oxford U Press, 97; Law Science and Medicine, coauth, U Case Bk Series, Foundation Press, 96; Rights of Persons Who are HIV Positive: The Authoritative Guide to the Rights of People Living with HIV Disease and Aids, coauth, Carbondale IL, S IL U Press, 96; The Americans with Disabilities Act: What it Means for All Americans, co-ed, Brookes Pub Co, 93; Health Legislation and Communicable Diseases: The Role of Law in an Era of Microbial Threats, Intl Digest of Health Legisl, 98; Piercing the Veil of Secrecy in HIV/AIDS and Other Sexually Transmitted Diseases: Theories of Privacy and Disclosure in Partner Notification, coauth, Duke J of Gender L and Policy, 98; The Names Debate: The Case for Ntl HIV Reporting in the United States,

coauth, Albany L Rev, 98; HIV Infection and AIDS in the Public Health and Health Care Systems: The Role of Law and Litigation, coauth, J. A. M. A., 98; The AIDS Litigation Project: HIV/AIDS in the Courts in the 1990s, Part one, AIDS and Pub Policy Jour, 97, Part two, in press; Ntl HIV case Reporting for the United States: A defining Moment in the History of the Epidemic, New Eng Jour Med, 97; Deciding Life and Death in the Court Room: From Quinlan to Cruzan Glucksberg and Vacco-A Brief History and Analysis of Constitutional Protection of the Right to Die, J. A. M. A. , 97; coauth, "The Law and the Public's Health: A Study of Infectious Disease Law in the United States," Columbia L Rev (99); auth, Public Health Law: Power, Duty, Restraint, U Calif Press, 00; auth, "Human Rights of Persons with Mental Disabilities: The European Convention of Human Rights," Intl J Law andPsychiat (00). **CONTACT ADDRESS** Law Center, Georgetown Univ, 600 New Jersey Ave NW, Washington, DC 20001. **EMAIL** gostin@law.georgetown.edu

GOTANDA, JOHN YUKIO
DISCIPLINE INTERNATIONAL COMMERCIAL ARBITRATION **EDUCATION** Univ Hawaii, BA, 84; William S. Richardson Sch Law, Univ Hawaii, JD, 87. **CAREER** Asst prof, 94-96, assoc prof, 96-98, prof, 98-, dir of JD/MBA Prog, Villanova Univ Sch Law. **MEMBERSHIPS** Dist Columbia Bar; Mass Bar; Hawaii State Bar; US Ct Appeals for the Dist of Columbia Circuit Bar; US Dist Ct for the Dist of Columbia Bar; Amer Soc Int Law; London Ct Int Arbitration; Int Law Asn; Amer Bar Asn. **RESEARCH** Damages in private international law, international commercial arbitration. **SELECTED PUBLICATIONS** Auth, Supplement Damages in Private International Law, Kluwer Law Int, 98; awding Costs and Attorneys' Feees in International Commercial Arbitrations, 21 Michigan Jrnl of Intl Law 1 (99); awding Punitive Damages in International Commercial Arbitrations in the Wake of Mastrobuono v. Shearson Lehman Hutton, Inc, 38 Harvard Int Law J 59, 97; awding Interest in International Arbitration, 90 American Journal of International Law 40, Amer Soc Int Law, 96; Glomar Denials Under FOIA: A Problematic Privilege and a Proposal for Alternative Procedures of Review, 56 Univ Pittsburgh Law Rev 165, 94; The Emerging Standards for Issuing Appellate Stays, 45 Baylor Law Rev 810, 93; coauth, The Responsible Corporate Officer: Designated Felon or Legal Fiction, 25 Loyola Univ Chicago Law J 169, 94. **CONTACT ADDRESS** Law School, Villanova Univ, 800 Lancaster Ave, Villanova, PA 19085-1692. **EMAIL** Gotanda@law.villanova.edu

GOTTHELF, ALLAN
PERSONAL Born 12/30/1942, Brooklyn, NY **DISCIPLINE** PHILOSOPHY **EDUCATION** Columbia Univ, PhD, 75. **CAREER** Philos, Col NJ. **HONORS AND AWARDS** Vis tchr, Oxford Univ, Tokyo Metropolitan Univ, Georgetown Univ, Swarthmore Col; mem Inst for Advanced Study, Princeton, 01. **RESEARCH** Aristotle; Ayn Rand. **SELECTED PUBLICATIONS** Auth, Philosophical Issues in Aristotle's Biology, Cambridge Univ Press 87; Aristotle on Nature and Living Things, Bristol Classical Press 85; auth, On Ayn Rand, Wadsworth Publ. Co, 00. **CONTACT ADDRESS** The Col of New Jersey, PO Box 7718, Ewing, NJ 08628-0718. **EMAIL** gotthelf@tcnj.edu

GOTTLIEB, ROGER SAMUEL
PERSONAL Born 10/20/1946, White Plains, NY **DISCIPLINE** PHILOSOPHY, SOCIAL THEORY **EDUCATION** Brandeis Univ, BA, 68, PhD, 75. **CAREER** Vis asst prof philos, Univ CT, Storr, 74-77; asst prof, Tufts Univ, 78-80; Asst Prof Philos, Dept Hum, Worcester Polytech Inst, 80-, Nat Endowment for Hum fel, 80-81. **MEMBERSHIPS** Am Philos Asn; Marxist Activist Philosophers, Am Acad of Religion. **RESEARCH** Marxism; soc theory; existentialism; environment; spirituality. **SELECTED PUBLICATIONS** Auth, A Marxian concept of ideology, 75 & A critique of Kierkegaard's doctrine of subjectivity, 78, Philos Forum; Habermas and critical relfective emancipation, Univ Ottawa, 78; The dialectics of National Identity Zionism and the Arab-Israeli conflict, Socialist Rev, 79; Marxism and the three forms of social primacy, J Philos, 78; Kierkegaard's ethical individualism, Monist, 79; The contemporary theory of Jurgen Habermans, Ethics, 79; Some implications of the Holocaust for ethics and social philosophy, Philos & Social Criticism, 82; History and subjectivity, Temple Univ Press, 87; An anthology of western Marxism, Oxford, 89; Thinking the unthinkable, Paulist Press, 90; Marxism 1844-1990, Routledge, 92; Radical Philosophy, Temple Univ Press, 93; This sacred earth, Routledge, 96; The ecological community, Routledge, 97; A Sprituality of Resistance, Crossroad, 99. **CONTACT ADDRESS** Dept of Hum, Worcester Polytech Inst, 100 Institute Rd, Worcester, MA 01609-2247. **EMAIL** gottlieb@wpi.edu

GOTTLIEB, STEPHEN ELLIOT
PERSONAL Born 06/02/1941, New York, NY, m, 1967, 2 children **DISCIPLINE** CONSTITUTIONAL LAW **EDUCATION** Princeton Univ, BA, 62; Yale Univ, LLB, 65. **CAREER** Assoc, 67-69, Golenback and Barrell; mem staff & managing atty, 69-72, Legal Aid Soc, St Louis; asst gen coun, 73-76, Commun Action for Legal Serv, New York; assoc prof clin tchng & constitutional law, 76-79 Col Law, WVa Univ; assoc prof, 79-82, prof constitutional law & jurisprudence, 82, Albany Law Sch, Union Univ; consult, 74-76, Legal Serv Training Prog. **HONORS AND AWARDS** Suffolk Univ. Law School, Distinguished Visiting Professor of Law, 00; Marquette Univ Law Schl, Robert F Boden Dist Vis Chmn, 97; Cleveland-Marshall Col of Law, Joseph C Hostetler-Baker and Hostetler vis chmn in las, 95-96; res grant division of res prog, NEH, 86-88. **MEMBERSHIPS** Bd dir, New York Civil Liberties Union **RESEARCH** Mass communications law; election and political campaign law; constitutional history, theory and the US Supreme Court. **SELECTED PUBLICATIONS** Morality Imported: The Rehnquist Court and Liberty in Am, New York Univ Press, 00; Ed & contrib, Public Values in Constitutional Law, Univ Mich Press, 93; art, The Paradox of Balancing Significant Interests, 45 Hastings Law J 825, 94; art, Three Justices in Search of A Character: The Moral Agendas of Justices O'Connor, Scalia and Kennedy, 49 Rutgers Law Rev, 96; art, The Philosophical Gulf on the Rehnquist Court, 29 Rutgers Law J, 97. **CONTACT ADDRESS** Albany Law Sch, 80 New Scotland Ave, Albany, NY 12208-3494. **EMAIL** stevegot@alumni.princeton.edu

GOTTSCHALK, ALFRED
PERSONAL Born 03/07/1930, Oberwesel, Germany, m, 1977, 2 children **DISCIPLINE** JEWISH RELIGIOUS THOUGHT **EDUCATION** Brooklyn Col, BA, 52; Hebrew Union Col, MA, 55; Univ Southern Calif, PhD(philos), 65. **CAREER** Asst prof, 59-62, assoc prof, 62-65, Prof Bible & Jewish Relig Thought, Jewish Inst Relig, Hebrew Union Col, 65-, Via prof Near Eastern studies, Univ Calif, Los Angeles, 60- 62, 65, 68 & 70; from pres to Chancellor, Hebrew Union Col, 70-; mem, Pres Johnson Comt, Equal Employ, Pres Carter's Comt, Holocaust, 80-81 & US Holocaust Memorial Coun, 81-; chemn, Academic Com US Holocaust Memorial Coun; pres, Museum of Jewish Heritage, 00. **HONORS AND AWARDS** Smithsonian res grant, 67; Bertha Guggenheimer fel, 67, 69; Am Jewish Comt Human Rel Awd, 71; Tower of David Awd for Cult Contrib, Israel & Am Israel Govt, 72; Gold Medallion Awd, Jewish Nat Fund, 72; fel Hebrew Univ, Jerusalem, 75; Myrtle Wreath Awd, Southern Pac Coast Region of Hadassah, 77; Louis Dembitz Brandeis Awd, Zionist Orgn Am, 77; Nat Brotherhood Awd, Nat Conf Christians & Jews, 79; dlit, dropsie univ, 74; lld, univ southern calif, 76, univ cincinnati, 76 & xavier univ, ohio, 81; dreled, loyola univ, 77. **MEMBERSHIPS** Albright Inst Archeol Res; Am Schs Oriental Res; Am Acad Relig; Israel Exploration Soc; World Union of Jewish Studies. **RESEARCH** Jewish intellectual history; modern Hebrew literature; history and archeology of the Ancient Near East. **SELECTED PUBLICATIONS** Auth, Hesed in the Bible, Hebrew Union Col Press, 6/67; The light of reason and the light of spirit: Spinoza and Ahad Ha-Am, In: Festschrift for President Zalman Shazar, Brit Ivrit Olamit, Jerusalem, fall 70; Ahad Ha-Am as Biblical Critic--A Profile, Studies in Jewish Bibliog Hist & Lit, KTAV Publ House, 71; The use of reason in Maimonides--An evaluation by Ahad Ha-Am, Proc 5th World Cong Jewish Studies, Vol III, Jerusalem, 72; United States of America: Perspectives, In: The Yom Kippur War: Israel and the Jewish People, Arno Press, 74; The image of man in Genesis and in the Ancient Near East, In: Social Psychiatry Vol II, The Range of Normal in Human Behavior, Grune & Stratton Publ, 76; From tradition to modernity: Ahad Ha-Am's quest for a spiritual Zionism, In: Shiv'im: Essays and Studies in Honor of Ira Eisenstein, Ktav Publ House, 76; Ahad Ha-Am and Leopold Zunz: Two perspectives on the Wissenschaft Des Judentums, Judaism, Vol 29, No 3; The German-Jewish Legacy: A Question of Fate, American Jewish Archives, November, 88; Ahad Ha'Am and the Jewish National Spirit, Hebrew, Hassifriya, Haziyonit, 92; At the Crossroads, World Jewry Faces Its Future, Gesher, Janmuary, 96. **CONTACT ADDRESS** 1 Battery Park Plaza, New York, NY 10004-1484.

GOTTSCHALK, PETER
DISCIPLINE HISTORY OF RELIGION **EDUCATION** Col of the Holy Cross, BA, 85; Univ Wis, MA, 89; Univ Chicago, PhD, 97. **CAREER** Asst prof, Southwestern Univ, 97- . **MEMBERSHIPS** AAR; AAS **RESEARCH** Narrative, identity, Hinuism, and Islam in South Asia; Time and space in religion. **CONTACT ADDRESS** Dept of Religions, Southwestern Univ, Box 6318, Georgetown, TX 78756. **EMAIL** gottschp@southwestern.edu

GOTTWALD, NORMAN KAROL
PERSONAL Born 10/27/1926, Chicago, IL **DISCIPLINE** OLD TESTAMENT **EDUCATION** Eastern Baptist Theol Sem, AB & ThB, 49; Union Theol Sem, MDiv, 51; Columbia Univ, PhD(Bibl lit), 53. **CAREER** Assoc relig, Columbia Univ, 53-54, asst prof, 54-55; from assoc prof to prof Old Testament, Andover Newton Theol Sch, 55-62, Lowry prof, 62-65; prof Old Testament and Bibl theol and ethics, Grad Theol Union, 65-80; W W WHITE PROF BIBL STUDIES, NEW YORK THEOL SEM, 80-, Vis asst prof, Princeton Univ, 55; Fulbright res scholar, Jerusalem, 60-61; vis lectr, Brown Univ, 62-63 and Brandeis Univ, 63-65; prof Old Testament, Am Baptist Sem West, 65-73; vis prof, Univ Calif, Santa Cruz, 67; res fel, Hebrew Union Col Bibl and Archaeol Sch, Jerusalem, 68-69; lectr, Ecumenical Inst Advan Theol Studies, Jerusalem, 73-74; vis prof environ ethics, Univ Calif, Berkeley, 74-75, vis prof relig, Univ of the Pac, 75-76, vis prof hist of relig, Bryn Mawr Col, 77-78, vis prof Old Testament, Union Theol Sem, 82-83. **MEMBERSHIPS** Cath Bibl Asn; Am Acad Relig; Soc Bibl Lit. **RESEARCH** Sociology, history and religion of ancient Israel; Biblical theology and the sociology of religion; sociology of the Bible and political theology. **SELECTED PUBLICATIONS** Auth, Lamentations, Cath Biblical Quart, Vol 0055, 93; Social-Class as an Analytic and Hermeneutical Category in Biblical Studies, J Biblical Lit, Vol 0112, 93. **CONTACT ADDRESS** New York Theol Sem, New York, NY 10011.

GOUGH, RUSSELL W.
DISCIPLINE ETHICAL THEORY, MORAL EDUCATION **EDUCATION** David Lipscomb Univ, BA, 84; Vanderbilt Univ, MA, 88, PhD, 90. **CAREER** Univ Vanderbilt Univ Med Ctr, 87-88; vis lectr, 87-89; instr, David Lipscomb Univ, 88-89; assoc prof, 90-. **HONORS AND AWARDS** Freshman Sem Excellence tchg award, Pepperdine Univ, 95; Sports Ethics fel, Univ RI, 94, 95;Irvine Found grant, 93; Graves Found Res award, 92; Sears-Roebuck Asian studies fellow, 90-91. **MEMBERSHIPS** Mem, Am Philos Assn; Philos Soc Study Sport; Soc Christian Philosophers. **SELECTED PUBLICATIONS** Auth, Character Is Destiny: The Value of Personal Ethics in Everyday Life, Prima Pub, 98; Facilitating Self-reflection Concerning Personal Character Development in Physical Education and Sport, Jour Phys Edu, 98; Moral Development Researchers' Quest for Objectivity: On Whether the Judgment-Passing Hurdle Can Be Cleared, in McNamee, M.J. & Parry S.J., Chapman and Hall, 97; Character Is Everything: Promoting Ethical Excellence In Sports, Harcourt Brace Col Publ, 97; On Reaching First Base with a 'Science' of Moral Development in Sport: Problems with Scientific Objectivity and Reductivism, Jour Philos Sport, Vol XXII, 95; NCAA Policy's Strangling Effect on Ethics, Record, Vol 5, 94; Testing, Scoring, and Ranking Athletes' Moral Development: The Hubris of Social Science as Moral Inquiry, Nat Rev Athletics, 94. **CONTACT ADDRESS** Dept of Philos, Pepperdine Univ, 24255 Pacific Coast Hwy, Malibu, CA 90263. **EMAIL** rgough@pepperdine.edu

GOUINLOCK, JAMES
DISCIPLINE PHILOSOPHICAL ANTHROPOLOGY **EDUCATION** Columbia Univ, PhD, 69. **CAREER** Prof emer, Philos, Emory Univ. **SELECTED PUBLICATIONS** Auth, John Dewey's Philosophy of Value; Excellence in Public Discourse; and Rediscovering the Moral Life: Philosophy and Human Practice; Ed, The Moral Writings of John Dewey; Coed, Ethics in the History of Western Philosophy. **CONTACT ADDRESS** Dept of Philos, Emory Univ, Atlanta, GA 30322.

GOULD, JOSIAH B.
PERSONAL Born Cleveland, OH, m, 1980, 3 children **DISCIPLINE** PHILOSOPHY **EDUCATION** Johns Hopkins Univ, PhD, 1962. **CAREER** Dist tchg prof Philos, Univ Albany, SUNY, 69- . **MEMBERSHIPS** Amer Philos Asn, E Div. **RESEARCH** Greek philosophy; history and Philosophy of Logic. **CONTACT ADDRESS** Dept of Philosophy, SUNY, Albany, HU 257, Albany, NY 12222. **EMAIL** gouldaristotle@aol.com

GOULD, WILLIAM BENJAMIN
PERSONAL Born 07/16/1936, Boston, MA, m, 1963, 3 children **DISCIPLINE** LAW **EDUCATION** Univ RI, AB, 58; Cornell Law Sch, LLB, 61. **CAREER** Asst gen coun labor law, United Automobile Workers, 61-62; atty, Nat Labor Rel Bd, Washington, DC, 63-65; assoc, Battle, Fowler, Stokes anf Kheel, 65-68; prof law, Wayne State Univ Law Sch, 68-71; PROF LAW, STANFORD UNIV LAW SCH, 72-, Via prof law, Harvard Law Sch, 71-72; vis scholar, Univ Tokyo Law Fac, 75; fel anf vis scholar, Churchill Col, Cambridge, England, 75; Guggenheim fel anf vis scholar, Univ Tokyo Law Fac, 78; Fulbright-Hays distinguished lectr, Kyoto-Am Studies Summer Sem, 78. **MEMBERSHIPS** Am Bar Asn; Am Arbitration Asn; Nat Acad Arbitrators. **RESEARCH** Labor law with special interest in labor arbitration; comparative labor law and industrial relations with special interest in Japan; employment discrimination law. **SELECTED PUBLICATIONS** Auth, Assessing the Work of the United-Nations War-Crimes Tribunals--Introductory-Remarks, Stanford J Int Law, Vol 0033, 97. **CONTACT ADDRESS** Stanford Law Sch, Stanford Univ, Stanford, CA 94305-1926.

GOULDING, JAMES ALLAN
PERSONAL Born 09/09/1937, Berea, OH, m, 1969, 2 children **DISCIPLINE** RELIGION **EDUCATION** DePauw Univ, BA, 59; Yale Univ, BD, 63, STM, 64; Claremont Grad Sch, PhD, 71. **CAREER** Instr relig, Hamline Univ, 69-70; pastor, Orwell-United Methodist Church, 72-74; asst prof, 74-80, assoc prof philos & relig & chaplain, Macmurray Col, 80-. **MEMBERSHIPS** Am Soc Church Hist; Am Acad Relig; Nat Assn Col & Univ Chaplains. **RESEARCH** Puritanism; American religion; biomedical ethics. **CONTACT ADDRESS** MacMurray Col, 447 E College Ave, Jacksonville, IL 62650-2510. **EMAIL** goulding@mac.edu

GOUREVITCH, VICTOR
PERSONAL Born 07/13/1925, Berlin, Germany, m, 1954, 2 children **DISCIPLINE** PHILOSOPHY **EDUCATION** Univ Wisconsin, BA, 46; Univ Chicago, PhD, 55. **CAREER** Vis

prof, Yale Univ; Hebrew Univ, Jerusalem; Fordham Univ; grad fac of The New Sch for Soc Res; dir, Wesleyan Ctr for Hum, 70-73; William Griffin Prof of Philos, emer, Wesleyan Univ. **HONORS AND AWARDS** Fel, Institut fur Interdisziplinare Forschung, 78-79; fel, Wesleyan Ctr for the Hum, 86-87; fel, Wissenschaftskolleg zu Berlin, 87-88. **MEMBERSHIPS** APA. **RESEARCH** Polit philosophy; Rousseau. **SELECTED PUBLICATIONS** Auth, Philosophy and Politics I-II, Rev of Metaphysics, 68; auth, Rousseau on the Arts and Sciences, Jour of Philos, 72; auth, Jean-Jacques Rousseau: The First and Second Discourses Together with the Replies to Critics and Essay on the Origin of Languages, Harper & Row, 86; auth, The 'First Times' in Rousseau's Essay on the Origin of Languages, Essays in Honor of Richard Kennington, Grad Philos Jour, 86; auth, Rousseau's Pure State of Nature, Interpretation, 88; ed, trans, Leo Strauss, On Tyranny, rev ed, Macmillan, 91, Chicago, 00; auth, The Political Argument of Rousseau's Essay on the Origin of Languages, in Pursuits of Reason: Essays in Honor of Stanley Cavell, Texas Tech, 93; auth, Jean-Jacques Rousseau: The Discourses and Other Early Political Writings, Cambridge, 97; auth, Jean Jacques Rousseau: The Social Contract and Other Later Political Writings, Cambridge, 97; auth, Rousseau on Providence, in The Wisdom of Humility: Essays in Ancient and Literary Imagination in Honor of David Grene, Chicago, 99. **CONTACT ADDRESS** 120 Duane St, New York, NY 10007. **EMAIL** vgoure1127@aol.com

GOURGUES, MICHEL

PERSONAL Born 08/22/1942, St. Michel, PQ, Canada **DISCIPLINE** BIBLICAL STUDIES **EDUCATION** Col Dominicain, MA, 71; Inst Cath, ThD, 76. **CAREER** Prof, Col Dominicain de Philos et de Theol, 76-, dean, 78-87, Pres and Regent, 88- ; vis prof, Ecole Bibl et Archaeol, 96-97. **MEMBERSHIPS** Cath Bibl Asn; Asn Cath des Etudes Bibl au Can; Studiorum Novi Testamenti Soc; Soc of Bibl Lit. **RESEARCH** New Testament Christology; Gospel of John; Parables of the Gospel. **SELECTED PUBLICATIONS** Auth, Le Parabole di Luca. Dalla Sorgente Alla Foce, 98; Les Deux Livres de Luc. Cles de Lecture du Troisieme Evangile et des Actes, 98; Fede, Felicita et Sensor Della Vita. Rileggere Oggi le Beatitudini, 97; Les Paraboles de Luc. D'Amont en Aval, 97; Os Hinos do Novo Testamento, 95; auth, "The Priest, the Levite and the Samaritan Revisited: A Critical Notes on Luke 10:31-35," in J of Bibl Studies, 98; "Sur l'Articulation des Beatitudes Mattheennes (Mt 5.3-12: Une Proposition," in New Testament Studies, 98. **CONTACT ADDRESS** Faculte de Theologie, Col Dominicain de Philosophie et de Theologie, 96, Ave Empress, Ottawa, ON, Canada K1R 7G3. **EMAIL** michel.gourgues@collegedominicain.ca

GOUVIN, ERIC J.

PERSONAL Born 02/15/1961, Westerly, RI, m, 1986, 2 children **DISCIPLINE** LAW **EDUCATION** Cornell Univ, BA, 83; Boston Univ, JD, 86; LLM, 90; Harvard Univ, MPA, 99. **CAREER** Vis prof, Univ of Conn Sch of Law, Hartford, Ct, spring 99; asst prof, Western New England Col Sch of Law, 91-94, assoc prof, 94-96, prof, 96- (sabbatical 98-99). **HONORS AND AWARDS** Bd of eds, Ctr for Computer Assisted Legal Instruction; exec comt, Asn of Am Law Schs; Am Bar Asn, Comt on Banking Law. **MEMBERSHIPS** Center for Computer Assisted Legal Instruction, Asn of Am Law Schs, Am Bar Asn. **RESEARCH** Banking law, corporate law. **SELECTED PUBLICATIONS** Auth," Resolving the Subsidiary Director's Dilemma," in The Best in D&O Duties and Liabilities, Kathryn Schoenbrun, ed, Bowne & Co (97); auth, "Of Hungry Wolves and Horizontal Conflicts: Rethinking the Justification for Bank Holding Company Liability," 1999 Univ Ill Law Rev (99): 949; auth, Cross-Border Bank Branching Under the NAFTA: Public Choice Over Public Policy, 32 Cornell Int Law J 1 (99): 257; auth, "The Massachusetts Law and Moderate Income Housing Act and Rural Communities," Western New England Law Rev (forthcoming); coauth with Philip Blumberg, Kurt Strasser and Nichloas Georgakopoulos of Blumberg on Corporate Groups, 2nd ed (forthcoming). **CONTACT ADDRESS** Sch of Law, Western New England Col, 1215 Wilbraham Rd, Springfield, MA 01119-2612. **EMAIL** egouvin@law.wnec.edu

GOUWENS, DAVID J.

PERSONAL Born 05/06/1948, South Holland, IL, m, 1990 **DISCIPLINE** THEOLOGY **EDUCATION** Hope Col, BA, 70; Mdiv, 73, StM, 74, Yale Divinity School; PhD, 82, Yale Univ. **CAREER** Visiting Lectr, Hope Col, 76; Asst Prof, 83-89, Acting Dir of Doctor of Ministry Studies, 89-90, Interim Asst Dean for Academic Affairs 90-91, Assoc Prof, 89-, Assoc Dean of Academic Affairs, Brite Divinity School, Texas Christian Univ. **HONORS AND AWARDS** Univ Fel, Yale Univ, 74-77 and 79-80; Douglas Clyde MacIntosh Fel, Yale Univ, 77-78; Brite Divinity School nominee for Burlington Northern Teaching Awd 89, 90; The Louise Clark Brittan Endowed Memorial Faculty Exellence Awd, Brite Divinity School, 98; Brite Divinity School nominee for TCU Chancellor's Awd for Distinguished Teaching, 98. **MEMBERSHIPS** Minister of Word and Sacrament, Presbyterian Church; The Soren Kierkegaard Soc; The Karl Barth Soc of North Amer; Amer Acad of Religion **RESEARCH** Kierkegaard; Reformed Theology and Aesthetics; Modern Christian Theology; Systematic Theology **SELECTED PUBLICATIONS** Auth, Heresy, New Handbook of Christian Theology, 92; Understanding, Imagination, and Irony in Kierkegaard's Repetition, International Kierkegaard Commentary: Fear and Trembling and Repetition, 93; Kierkegaard's Either/Or Part 1: Patterns of Interpretation, International Kierkegaard Commentary: Either/Or, Part 1, 95; Kierkegaard as Religious Thinker, 96; Imagination and Introspection, Dictionary of Existentialism, 99. **CONTACT ADDRESS** Brite Divinity School, Texas Christian Univ, PO Box 298130, Fort Worth, TX 76129. **EMAIL** d.gouwens@tcu.edu

GOVAN, REGINALD C.

PERSONAL Born 12/02/1953, New York, NY **DISCIPLINE** LAW **EDUCATION** Carnegie-Mellon University, BA, 1975; University of Pennsylvania Law School, JD, 1978. **CAREER** Squire, Sanders & Dempsey, associate, 78-79; US Court of Appeals, 6th Circuit, Judge Nathaniel R Jones, sr law clerk, 79-81; Manhattan District Attorney, assistant district Attorney, 81-83; sole practitioner, federal civil rights and general litigation, 83-85, 87-89; US Senate, Committee on the Judiciary, counsel, 85-87; US House of Representatives, Education & Labor Committee, counsel, 89-94; Organization Resource Counselors, Inc, sr consultant, 95-. **MEMBERSHIPS** District of Columbia Bar, Attorney-Client Arbitration Board, chairman, 1991-94, Disciplinary Review Committee, 1991-93, Task Force on Continuing Legal Education, 1992-94; National Bar Assn, 1984-; Washington Bar Association, 1990-. **SELECTED PUBLICATIONS** "Employment Law is a Fishbowl: Coping with Less Privilege and Confidentiality," Employee Relations L.J., Vol. 23, No.3 (Winter 1997); "Honorable Compromises and the Moral High Ground: The Conflict Between the Rhetoric and the Content of the Civil Rights Act of 1991," 46 The Rutgers Law Review 7, 1993; "Framing Issues and Acquiring Codes: An Overview of the Legislative Sojourn of the Civil Rights Act of 1991," 41 The DePaul Law Review 1057, 1992; One Nation, Indivisible: The Civil Rights Challenge for the 1990's, Washington, DC, Citizens' Commission on Civil Rights, 1989. **CONTACT ADDRESS** Organization Resource Counselors, 1211 Avenue of Americas, 15th Fl, New York, NY 10036.

GOVIG, STEWART D.

PERSONAL Born 03/30/1927, Walnut Grove, MN, m, 1954, 3 children **DISCIPLINE** RELIGION **EDUCATION** St Olaf Col, BA, 48; Luther Theol Sem, BTh, 52; Princeton Theol Sem, MTh, 54; NYork Univ, PhD(relig educ, philos), 66. **CAREER** Pastor, Am Lutheran Church, Grand Marais, Minn, 54-57; assoc prof relig, 58-76, PROF RELIG, PAC LUTHER UNIV, 76-, Clergyman, Am Lutheran Church, 52-; Martin Luther fel, Nat Lutheran Educ Conf; prof dir grant relig and pub schs, Washington Comn for Humanities, 76. **RESEARCH** Religion and literature; modern church history. **SELECTED PUBLICATIONS** Auth, Religious-Education and Mental-Illness--A Higher-Education Model, Relig Educ, Vol 0091, 96. **CONTACT ADDRESS** Dept of Relig Pac, Pacific Lutheran Univ, 12180 Park Ave S, Tacoma, WA 98447-0014.

GOWAN, DONALD E.

PERSONAL Born 01/31/1929, Cleghorn, IA, m, 1958, 2 children **DISCIPLINE** OLD TESTAMENT **EDUCATION** Univ SDak, BA, 51; Dubuque Theol Sem, BD, 57; Univ Chicago, PhD(Bible), 64. **CAREER** Pastor, Presby Church, Princeton, Iowa, 55-59; asst pastor, Presby Church Roseland, Chicago, Ill, 59-60; head dept Bible, NTex State Univ, 62-65; asst prof Old Testament, 65-69, assoc prof, 69-78, prof Old Testament, Pittsburgh Theol Sem, 78-99. **HONORS AND AWARDS** Phi Beta Kappa. **MEMBERSHIPS** Soc Bibl Lit. **RESEARCH** Old Testament prophets; post-exilic period; intertestamental Judaism; biblical theology. **SELECTED PUBLICATIONS** Auth, When Man Becomes God: Humanism and Hybris in the Old Testament, 75 & Bridge Between the Testaments: A Reappraisal of Judaism from the Exile to the Birth of Christianity, 76, Pickwick; The Triumph of Faith in Habakkuk, John Knox, 76; Reclaiming the Old Testament for the Christian Pulpit, John Knox, 80; Ezekiel, John Knox, 85; Eschatology in the Old Testament, Fortress, 86; From Eden to Babel: Genesis 1-11; Eerdmans, 88; Theology in Exodus, Westminster John Knox, 94; Theology of the Prophetic Books, Westminster John Knox, 98. **CONTACT ADDRESS** Pittsburgh Theol Sem, 616 N Highland Ave, Pittsburgh, PA 15206-2525. **EMAIL** gowandon@msn.com

GOWANS, CHRISTOPHER W.

DISCIPLINE CONTEMPORARY MORAL AND POLITICAL PHILOSOPHY **EDUCATION** Univ Notre Dame, PhD. **CAREER** Dir, grad stud; prof, Fordham Univ. **RESEARCH** French moral philos from the Reformation to the Revolution. **SELECTED PUBLICATIONS** Auth, Moral Dilemmas, Oxford UP, 87; Innocence Lost: An Examination of Inescapable Moral Wrongdoing, Oxford UP, 94; Moral Theory, Moral Dilemmas and Moral Responsibilities, Moral Dilemmas and Moral Theory, Oxford UP, 96; Intimacy, Freedom and Unique Value: A Kantian' Account of the Irreplaceable and Incomparable Value of Persons, Amer Philos Quart, 96. **CONTACT ADDRESS** Dept of Philos, Fordham Univ, 113 W 60th St, New York, NY 10023.

GOWLER, DAVID B.

DISCIPLINE RELIGION **EDUCATION** Univ IL, Champaign, BA, 81; Southern Sem, Louisville, Mdiv, 85; Cambridge Univ, Engl, 87; Southern Sem, Louisville, PhD, 89. Yale Univ NEH Summer Sem, 95. **CAREER** Pierce prof of religion, Oxford Col, Emory Univ; Assoc prof ; asst dean Acad Aff, Chowan Col, 96-; assoc prof, Chowan Col, 90-; asst prof, 90-94; dir, Global Educ Prog, Chowan Col, 97-; dir, Thinking and Writing Across the Curric prog, Chowan Col, 95-; asst prof, Berry Col, Rome, Ga, 89-90; assoc ed, Emory Stud in Early Christianity, Schol Press, 92-; assoc ed, Emory Stud in Early Christianity, Peter Lang Press, 91-93; instr, Southern Sem, Louisville, 88-89; res asst, Dr R Alan Culpepper, Southern Sem, 87; Garrett tchg fel, Southern Sem, 84-87. **SELECTED PUBLICATIONS** Auth, Host, Guest, Enemy and Friend: Portraits of the Pharisees in Luke and Acts, Emory Stud in Early Christianity, vol. 1, NY, Bern, Frankfurt am Main, Paris: Peter Lang Publ, 91; ed, New Boundaries in Old Territory: Form and Social Rhetoric in Mark, Emory Studies in Early Christianity, vol 3, NY, Bern, Frankfurt am Main: Peter Lang Press, 94; co-ed, Recruitment, Conquest and Conflict: Strategies in Judaism, Early Christianity and the Greco-Roman World, Emory Stud in Early Christianity, vol 6, Atlanta: Scholars Press, 98; H. Wayne Merritt, In Word and Deed: Moral Integrity in Paul, Emory Stud in Early Christianity, vol 2, NY, Bern, Frankfurt am Main: Peter Lang Press, 93; Jan Botha, Subject to Whose Authority Multiple Readings of Romans 13, Emory Stud in Early Christianity, vol 4, Atlanta: Scholars Press, 94; Kjell Arne Morland, The Rhetoric of Curse in Galatians: Paul Confronts a Different Gospel, Emory Stud in Early Christianity, vol 5, Atlanta: Scholars Press, 95; auth, What Are They Saying About the Parables?, Paulist Press, 00. **CONTACT ADDRESS** Religion Dept, Emory Univ, Oxford, GA 30054. **EMAIL** dgowler@msn.com

GRABER, DORIS A.

PERSONAL Born 11/11/1923, St. Louis, MO, m, 1941, 5 children **DISCIPLINE** POLITICAL SCIENCE **EDUCATION** Wash Univ, AB, 41, MA, 42; Columbia Univ, 47. **CAREER** Feat writer, St Louis Count Observer, 39-41; civ dir, US Army Ednl Recond Prog, Camp Maxey, 43-45; edr, Commerce Clearing House, 45-56; lectr, Polit Sci, Univ Chicago, 50-51; res assoc, Center for Stud Am For & Mil Pol, 52-71; lectr, Polit Sci, North Park Coll, 52, assoc prof, Univ Ill, 64-69; PROF, POLIT SCI, UNIV ILL, 70-. **HONORS AND AWARDS** Goodnow Awd; Am Poli Sci Assoc, 99. **MEMBERSHIPS** Int Polit Sci Asn; Int Commn Asn; Asn Educ Journalism; Acad Polit Sci; Am Acad Polit & Soc Sci; Int Soc Polit Psychol **RESEARCH** Political communication; information processing; political psychology. **SELECTED PUBLICATIONS** Co-ed, The Politics of News: The News of Politics, 98; rev, Political Psychology, 98-; auth, Mass Media and Am Politics, 98; ed, Media Power in Politics, 00; auth, Processing Politics, 01. **CONTACT ADDRESS** Dept Polit Sci, Univ of Illinois, Chicago, Chicago, IL 60607. **EMAIL** dgraber@uic.edu

GRABER-MILLER, KEITH A.

PERSONAL Born 05/08/1959, Kokomo, IN, m, 1987, 3 children **DISCIPLINE** RELIGION **EDUCATION** Franklin Col, BA 81; Goshen Bibl Sem, Mdiv, 88; Emory Univ, PhD, 94. **CAREER** Ed & Mgr, (Bureau Ch , Kokomo Tribune) Howard County News, IN, 81-83; Int Min, Asst Prof of Comm, Goshen Col, 87-89; Tchg Asst, Emory Univ, 89-93; Prof, Goshen Col, 93-; Vis Fac, Assoc Mennonite Bibl Sem, IN, 97-. **HONORS AND AWARDS** Summa cum laude, Franklin Col, 81; Grad Fel & Tuition Scholar, Emory Univ, 89-93; Schowalter Fnd Grant, 92-93; Res Grant, IN Univ Center on Philanthropy, 92-93; Dissertation fel, Louisville Inst, 93-94; Goshen Col Multicultural Affairs Grant, 94-95, 98-99; Faculty Res Grant, Goshen Col, 97-98, 98-99. **MEMBERSHIPS** Soc for the Scientific Stud of Religion; Amer Acad of Religion; Soc of Christian Ethics; Anabaptist Soc and Anthropology Assoc. **RESEARCH** Religion and Politics; Church-Related Higher Education; Christian Ethics; Human Sexuality; Dynamics of Religious Collectivities; Mennonite History and Theology; Peacemaking. **SELECTED PUBLICATIONS** Auth, Mennonite Lobbyists in Washington, The Annual of the Soc of Christian Ethics, 95; Bumping into the State: Developing a Washington Presence, Mennonite Quart Rev, 96; Wise as Serpents, Innocent as doves: American Mennonites Engage Washington, Univ of TN Press, 96; Teaching the Bible in the Classroom: Vision and Goals, The Word Among Us, PPP, 97; Worshiping with the Early Anabaptists, Gospel Herald 90:34, 97; Mennonite Mutual Aid: A Margin of Difference?, Building Com of Compassion Mennonite Mutual Aid in Theory and Practice, Herald/Pandora Press, 98; CoAuth, Worshipping with the Early Anabaptist, What Mennonites Are Thinking, 98; ed, Teaching to Transform: Perspectives on Mennonite Higher Education, Pinchpenny Press, 00. **CONTACT ADDRESS** Goshen Col, Goshen, IN 46526. **EMAIL** keithgm@goshen.edu

GRACIA, JORGE JESUS EMILIANO

PERSONAL Born 07/18/1942, Camaguey, Cuba, m, 1966, 2 children **DISCIPLINE** PHILOSOPHY **EDUCATION** Wheaton Col, BA, 65; Univ Chicago, MA, 66; Pontif Inst Mediaeval Studies, Toronto, MSL, 70; Univ Toronto, PhD, 71. **CAREER** From asst prof to prof philos & chmn dept, 71-85; State Univ NYork Buffalo; vis prof philos, Univ PR, 72-73; vis prof philos, Fordham Univ, 97; from distinguished prof to Samuel P. Capen chair, State Univ NYork Buffalo, 95-. **HONORS AND AWARDS** Can Coun grant, 71; Nat Endowment for Humanities grant, 82; NY Coun for Hum grant, 87; John N Findlay prize Metaphysical Soc Am, 92. **MEMBERSHIPS** Am Cath

Philos Asn; Am Philos Asn; Can Philos Asn; Medieval Acad Am; Metaphysical Soc Am; Soc for Iberian and Latin Am Thought; Soc for Medieval and Renaissance Philos; Soc de Philos Iberoamericana; Int Federation of Latin Am and Caribbean Stud; Federation Int de Soc de Philos. **RESEARCH** Medieval philosophy; metaphysics; humaneutics; Hispanic philosophy. **SELECTED PUBLICATIONS** Auth, Philosophy and its History: Issues in Philosophical Historiography, 91; ed, Individuation in Scholasticism, 94; co-ed, Individuation and Identity in Early Modern Philosophy, 94; auth, A Theory of Textuality: The Logic and Epistemology, 95; auth, Metaphysics and Its Task: The Search for the Categorial Found of Knowledge, 99; auth, Hispanic/Latino Identity: A Philos Perspective, 00. **CONTACT ADDRESS** Dept of Philosophy, SUNY, Buffalo, PO Box 601010, Buffalo, NY 14260. **EMAIL** gracia@acsu.buffalo.edu

GRAD, FRANK P.
PERSONAL Born 05/02/1924, Vienna, Austria, m, 1946, 2 children **DISCIPLINE** LAW **EDUCATION** Brooklyn Col, AB, 47; Columbia Univ, LLb, 49. **CAREER** Assoc law, 49-50, from asst dir to assoc dir, legis drafting res fund, 53-69, lectr law, 54-65, adj prof legis, 64-69, prof law & dir legis drafting res fund, 69-95, Joseph P Chamberlain Prof Legis, 82-95, emeritus, 95-, Special Lecturer, 95-; Columbia Univ; consult, Depts of Health & State Constitutional Convs, 60-; coun, Nat Munic League, 67-89; mem legal adv comt, US Coun Environ Quality, 70-72; assoc ed, Health & Soc, 72-76. **HONORS AND AWARDS** Magna cum laude, 47; 10th Horace E. Read Mem lectr, Dalhouse Law Sch, 84; **MEMBERSHIPS** Am Bar Asn; fel Am Pub Health Asn; AAUP; Am Law Inst; NY Bar Asn; Am Soc Law and Medicine; World Conservation Union; Human Genome Orgn; Int Coun Environ Law; NY Soc Medical Jurisprudence. **RESEARCH** Legislation; environmental law; public health law. **SELECTED PUBLICATIONS** Auth, Treatise on Environmental Law, Pools, 72-00 (Semiannual Supps); coauth, The Automobile and the Regulation of Its Impact on the Environment, Okla Univ, 75; Physicians License and Discipline, 79; auth, Public Health Law Manual, APHA, 90. **CONTACT ADDRESS** Law Sch, Columbia Univ, 435 W 116th St, New York, NY 10027-7201.

GRAETZ, MICHAEL J.
PERSONAL Born 11/20/1944, Atlanta, GA, m, 5 children **DISCIPLINE** LAW **EDUCATION** Emory Univ, BBA, 66; Univ Va, LLB. **CAREER** Vis prof, Univ Southern Calif, 76-77; vis prof, Calif Inst of Technol, 78; vis prof, Harvard Univ, 78-79; Law prof, Univ Va, 72-79; prof, Univ Southern Calif and Calif Inst of Technol, 79-83; Deputy Asst Secretary, U.S. Dept of the Treasury, 90-91; asst to the Secretary and Special Counsel, U.S. Dept of the Treasury, 92; Justus S. Hotchkiss Prof of Law, Yale Law Sch, 86-, prof since 83-. **HONORS AND AWARDS** Treasury Dept Exceptional Service Awd, 72; selected for the Esqire Register, 88; Guggenheim Fel, 89; Treasury Medal, 92; Honoris causa, LLD, Doctor of Laws, Capital Univ, 93. **MEMBERSHIPS** Va Bar. **SELECTED PUBLICATIONS** Auth, Federal Income Taxation; Principles and Policies, Found Press (2nd ed, 88, 3rd ed, 95); auth, "Distributional Tables, Tax Legislation, and the Illusion of Precision," in David Bradford, ed, Distributional Analysis of Tax Policy, Am Enterprise Inst (95); coauth, "Comprehensive Tax Reform and Fringe Benefits: The Case of Employer-Provided Pensions and Health Insurance," in Dallas L. Salisbury, ed, Tax Reform: Implications for Economic Security and Employee Benefits, (EBRI, 97); auth, The Decline and (Fall?) of the Income Tax, W. W. Norton & Co (97); auth, Framing the Social Security Debate: Values, Politics, and Economics, ed with R. Douglas Arnold and Alicia Munnell, Brookings Inst Press (98); auth, Integration of the U.S. Corporate and Individual Income Taxes: The Treasury Department and American Law Institute Reports, Tax Analysts, with Alvin C. Warren (98); coauth, True Security: Rethinking American Social Insurance, Yale Univ Press (99). **CONTACT ADDRESS** Sch of Law, Yale Univ, PO Box 208215, New Haven, CT 06520-8215. **EMAIL** Michael.graetz@yale.edu

GRAGLIA, L. A.
PERSONAL Born 01/22/1930, Brooklyn, NY, m, 1954, 3 children **DISCIPLINE** LAW **EDUCATION** City Col NYork, BA, 52; Columbia Univ Law Sch, LLB, 54. **CAREER** Atty, Dept Justice, 54-57; private prac, 57-66; teaching, Univ Tex Sch Law, 66- . **RESEARCH** Judicial review, race discrimination. **SELECTED PUBLICATIONS** Auth, Disaster by Decree: The Supreme Court Decisions on Race and the Schools, Cornell Univ, 76. **CONTACT ADDRESS** Sch of Law, Univ of Texas, Austin, 727 E 26th St, Austin, TX 78705. **EMAIL** LGRAGLIA@mail.law.utexas.edu

GRAHAM, DANIEL W.
PERSONAL Born 03/28/1948, Glendale, CA, m, 1973, 2 children **DISCIPLINE** PHILOSOPHY **EDUCATION** Davidson Col, AB, 70, Brigham Young Univ, MA, 75; Univ Tex Austin, 80. **CAREER** Asst prof, Grinnell Col, 80-84; asst prof, Rice Univ, 84-86; assoc prof to de prof, Brigham Young Univ, 86-. **HONORS AND AWARDS** NEH Fel, 83-84, 93-94; Vis Fel, Cambridge, 88-89; Vis Fel, Yale Univ, 95. **RESEARCH** Ancient Greek Philosophy. **SELECTED PUBLICATIONS** Auth, Aristotle's Two Systems, Clarendon Pr, (Oxford), 87; ed, Studies in Green Philosophy by Gregory Vlastos, Princeton Univ Pr, (Princeton, NJ), 95; transl, Aristotle, Physics, Book VIII, Clarendon Pr, (Oxford), 99. **CONTACT ADDRESS** Dept Philosophy, Brigham Young Univ, PO Box 26279, Provo, UT 84602-6279. **EMAIL** daniel_graham@byu.edu

GRAHAM, GEORGE
PERSONAL Born 09/03/1945, Brooklyn, NY, m, 1972, 1 child **DISCIPLINE** PHILOSOPHY **EDUCATION** Brandeis, PhD, 75. **CAREER** Chmn, prof, phil, prof, psychol, 75-, Univ Ala, Birmingham **HONORS AND AWARDS** 3 tchng awards; 4 scholar awards. **MEMBERSHIPS** APA; Soc Phil & Psychol. **RESEARCH** Philosophical psychopathology; phil of mind & cognitive sci. **SELECTED PUBLICATIONS** Coauth, Philosophical Psychopathology, MIT, 94; auth, Philosophy of Mind, Blackwells, 98; coauth, A Companion to Cognitive Science, Blackwells, 98. **CONTACT ADDRESS** Dept of Philosophy, Univ of Alabama, Birmingham, Birmingham, AL 35294. **EMAIL** ggraham@uab.edu

GRAHAM, GEORGE JACKSON
PERSONAL Born 11/12/1938, Dayton, OH, d, 1 child **DISCIPLINE** POLITICAL SCIENCE, POLITICAL PHILOSOPHY **EDUCATION** Wabash Coll, Hist, AB, 60; Ind Univ. PhD, Govt, 65. **CAREER** Instr, Vanderbilt Univ, 63-64; asst prof, Vanderbilt Univ, 65-72; assoc prof, Vanderbilt Univ, 72-77; PROF, VANDERBILT UNIV, 77-. **HONORS AND AWARDS** Guggenghim Fellowship, 73-74; Nat Humanities Institute Fellow, 76-77; John Marshall, Fulbright Foundation, 95-96. **MEMBERSHIPS** Am Polit Sci Asn **RESEARCH** Political philosophy; Ethics & public policy **SELECTED PUBLICATIONS** "Contextualizing Regime Change: Transformation Windows and Systemic Reforms in Eastern Europe," Agenda Formation, Univ Mich Press, 93; "Pluralism, Parliaments, and the Public," Budapest Papers on Democratic Transition, 97. **CONTACT ADDRESS** Dept Polit Sci, Vanderbilt Univ, Nashville, TN 37235. **EMAIL** grahamgj@ctrvax.vanderbilt.edu

GRAHAM, J. MICHELE
PERSONAL Born 06/08/1952, Long Beach, CA, s **DISCIPLINE** THEOLOGY **EDUCATION** Fuller Theol Sem, Pasadena CA, MDiv, 80; Univ Aberdeen, Scotland, PhD, 93. **CAREER** Asst prof, 94-97, Sterling Col, KS; asst prof, 97-, Whitworth Col. **HONORS AND AWARDS** William McCrery Teaching Awd, 96-97; Sterling Col, Sterling, KS. **MEMBERSHIPS** AAR. **RESEARCH** Trinity, atonement, women in ministry issues. **CONTACT ADDRESS** Whitworth Col, 300 W Hawthorne Rd., Spokane, WA 99251. **EMAIL** jmgraham@whitworth.edu

GRAHAM, STEPHEN R.
PERSONAL Born 12/29/1957, m, 1977, 2 children **DISCIPLINE** RELIGIOUS STUDIES **EDUCATION** Wheaton Col, BA, 82; Wheaton Grad School, MA, 84; Univ Chicago, PhD, 89. **CAREER** Vis instr, Governors State Univ, 86; adjunct prof, North Park Theol Sem, 86-87; asst prof, 88-93; assoc prof, 94-97; full prof, 97-. **MEMBERSHIPS** Am Acad of Relig; Am Soc of Church Hist. **RESEARCH** Religious studies. **SELECTED PUBLICATIONS** Auth, Cosmos in the Chaos: Philip Schaff's Interpretation of Nineteenth-Century American Religion, 95; "Looking Forward and Looking Backward: Schaff and Nevin at Mercersburg" in John Williamson Nevin: A Collection of Essays, 96; "Philip Schaff: Organic Development in Christianity" in Broadman Handbook of Church Historians, 95; "Thus Saith the Lord: Biblical Hermeneutics in the Early Pentecostal Movement" in Ex Auditu, 96. **CONTACT ADDRESS** No Park Theol Sem, 3225 W Foster Ave, Chicago, IL 60625. **EMAIL** sgraham@northpark.edu

GRAHAM, W. FRED
PERSONAL Born 10/31/1930, Columbus, OH, m, 1953, 4 children **DISCIPLINE** RELIGION, HISTORY **EDUCATION** Tarkio Col, BA, 52; Pittsburgh Theol Sem, BD, 55; Louisville Presby Sem, ThM, 58; Univ Iowa, PhD(relig), 65. **CAREER** From instr to asst prof relig, 63-65, from asst prof to assoc prof dept relig studies, 66-73, PROF RELIG, MICH STATE UNIV, 73-. **MEMBERSHIPS** Am Soc Church Hist; Calvin Studies Soc; Am Acad Relig; Soc 16th Century Studies. **RESEARCH** Reformation, particularly 16th century Geneva and Calvin; relationship between religion and social, economic and political life and thought; science and religion. **SELECTED PUBLICATIONS** Auth, An Uncounseled King--Charles-I and the Scottish Troubles, 1637-1641, Church Hist, Vol 0062, 93; Calvin, John Preaching, Church Hist, Vol 0063, 94; Where Shall Wisdom Be Found--Calvin Exegesis of Job from Medieval and Modern Perspectives, 16th Century J, Vol 0026, 95; Calvinism in Europe, 1540-1610--A Collection of Documents, Church Hist, Vol 0064, 95; Ecclesia-Reformata--Studies on the Reformation, Vol 2, 16th Century J, Vol 0026, 95; Humanism and Reform--The Church in Europe, England and Scotland, 1400-1643, Church Hist, Vol 0064, 95; Calvin, John Concept of the Law, Church Hist, Vol 0064, 95; Sin and the Calvinists--Morals Control and the Consistory in the Reformed Tradition, Cath Hist Rev, Vol 0082, 96; Politics, Religion, and Diplomacy in Early-Modern Europe--Essays in Honor of Jensen, de, Lamar, Church Hist, Vol 0065, 96; The Uses of Reform--Godly Discipline and Popular Behavior in Scotland and Beyond, 1560-1610, 16th Century J, Vol 0028, 97. **CONTACT ADDRESS** Dept of Relig Studies, Michigan State Univ, East Lansing, MI 48823.

GRAHAM, WILLIAM
PERSONAL Born 08/16/1943, Raleigh, NC, m, 1983, 1 child **DISCIPLINE** HISTORY OF RELIGION, ISLAMIC STUDIES **EDUCATION** Univ NC, BA, 66; Harvard Univ, AM, 70; PhD, 73. **CAREER** Lectr to Prof, Harvard Univ, 73-. **HONORS AND AWARDS** Woodrow Wilson Fel, 66; Danforth Fel, 66-73; Phi Beta Kappa, Univ NC, 64. **MEMBERSHIPS** AOS, AAR, MESA, ASSR, MEM. **RESEARCH** Islamic religion, Qur'an, Hadith. **SELECTED PUBLICATIONS** Auth, "'The Winds to Herald his Mercy': Nature as Token of God's Sovereignty and Grace in the Qur'an," in Faithful Imaging (Atlanta, GA: Scholars Pr, 95), 19-38; auth, "Politics and Religion in Islam in Historical Perspective: Some Reflections," in Future Dimensions (Vienna, Austria: 96), 22-23; auth, "Sahrif," in The Encycl of Islam, New Ed (97), 329-337; coauth, The Heritage of World Civilizations, Prentice Hall, 00; auth, "Basmalah," in Encycl of the Qur'an (Leiden: E J Brill, 00), forthcoming; auth, "Fatihah," in Encycl of the Qur'an (Leiden: E J Brill, 00), forthcoming. **CONTACT ADDRESS** Dept Lang, Harvard Univ, Semetic Museum, Cambridge, MA 02138. **EMAIL** wgraham@fas.harvard.edu

GRAHAM, WILLIAM C.
PERSONAL Born 04/16/1950, Duluth, MN **DISCIPLINE** HISTORICAL THEOLOGY **EDUCATION** Fordham Univ, PhD, 93. **CAREER** Assoc prof, Caldwell Col, NJ; dir, Caldwell Pastoral Ministry Inst. **HONORS AND AWARDS** Asst ed, Listening; columnist for Natl Cath Reporter. **MEMBERSHIPS** Am Acad Relig; Asn of Grad Prog in Ministry; New Jersey Consortium for Grad Prog in Theol; N Am Acad of Liturgy. **SELECTED PUBLICATIONS** Co-ed, Common Good, Uncommon Questions: A Primer in Moral Theology, Liturgical, 95; auth, Half Finished Heaven: The Social Gospel in American Literature, Univ Pr Am, 95; ed, More Urgent Than Usual: The Final Homilies of Mark Hollenhorst, Liturgical, 95; auth, Is There A Case Against St. Therese As Doctor of the Church? Sisters Today, 95; auth, Sadness of the City, in Legalized Gambling, Greenhaven, 98; auth, Up In Smoke: Preparation for Ash Wednesday, Mod Liturgy, 97/98; auth, Television, Resistance and Orthodoxy, Natl Cath Reporter, 98; auth, The Preacher and the Abortion Opponent, Celebration, 98; auth, Sacred Adventure: Beginning Theological Study, (UPA,99). **CONTACT ADDRESS** 5887 S Pike Lake Rd, Duluth, MN 55811. **EMAIL** wcgnycpl@aol.com

GRAMMER, MICHAEL B.
PERSONAL Born 10/26/1961, Wheeling, WV, m, 1994, 4 children **DISCIPLINE** LITURGY **EDUCATION** Wheeling Jesuit Univ, BA, 84; Univ Notre Dame, MA, 94. **CAREER** Instr, relig stud, 81-82, Mont de Chantal Vis Acad; dir, relig ed, 86-90, St Ladislaus & St Mary Churches; assoc pastor, 91-93, Church of St Boniface; tchng asst, 93-94, Cath Univ of Am; bus mngr, 93-94, N Am Forum on the Catechumenate; asst prof, spec fac, 94-96, Notre Dame Ctr for Pastoral Lit, Notre Dame; dir, Off Initiation & Spiritual Formation, 96-99, dir, Office for Worship and Word, 99-, Diocese of Greensburg, PA. **MEMBERSHIPS** Asn for Relig & Intel Life; Natl Cath Ed Asn; Relig Ed Asn; Liturgy Network, NA Forum, NCCL; NCEA; NALM; REACH; CACE; NACARE. **RESEARCH** Liturgical Catechesis; RCIA. **SELECTED PUBLICATIONS** Auth, Ideas and Illustrations, Homily Svc 27, 94; auth, Liturgically Minded People: A History of the Notre Dame Center for Pastoral Liturgy, Assembly 21:2, 95; auth, The Heart of Catechesis, Cath Accent 36:13, 96; auth, Is There Gravity In Heaven?, Cath Accent, 97; auth, Focus on Prayer, Cath Accent, 98; auth, Baptism, Cath Accent, 98. **CONTACT ADDRESS** Office for Worship and Word, Diocese of Greensburg, 723 E Pittsburgh St, Greensburg, PA 15601-2697. **EMAIL** mgrammer@dioceseofgreensburg.org

GRANBERG, STAN
PERSONAL Born 02/09/1956, Seattle, WA, m, 1978, 4 children **DISCIPLINE** BIBLICAL STUDIES **EDUCATION** Harding Univ, BA, 78; Harding Univ Grad Sch Relig, MTh, 83; Fuller Theol Sem, ThM, 95; Open Univ, PhD, 00. **CAREER** Vis fac, Lubbuch Christian Univ, 93-96; assoc prof, Cascade Col, 96-. **MEMBERSHIPS** Soc of Biblical Lit. **RESEARCH** Leadership, African Leaders, Missions. **SELECTED PUBLICATIONS** Auth, "Enter Your Target Culture by Bonding," Evangelical Missions Quart 24 (88): 344-352; auth, "Philemon," in Commentary on the New Testament in Simple English, ed. Van Tate (AR: Cloverdale Church of Christ, 91), 1129-1133; auth, "Stages in the Life of a New Church," Church Planter 2 (92): 1-4; coauth, Reaching Russia, ACU Press (Abilene, TX), 94; **CONTACT ADDRESS** Dept Bible Studies, Cascade Col, 9101 E Burnside St, Portland, OR 97216. **EMAIL** sgranberg@cascade.edu

GRANDY, RICHARD E.
PERSONAL Born 12/06/1942, Pittsburgh, PA, 2 children **DISCIPLINE** PHILOSOPHY **EDUCATION** Univ Pittsburgh, BS,

63; Princeton Univ, PhD, 67. **CAREER** Asst prof philos, Princeton Univ, 67-74; assoc prof philos, 74-79, prof, 79-80, Univ NC, Chapel Hill; prof philos, 80-, Rice Univ; NSF fel, 70-71; Am Coun Learned Soc study fel, 76. **MEMBERSHIPS** Asn Symbolic Logic; Philos Sci Asn; Am Philos Asn. **RESEARCH** Philosophy of science; philosophy of mathematics; logic. **SELECTED PUBLICATIONS** Art, A Definition of Truth for Theories With Intensional Definite Description Operators, J Philos Logic, 72; art, Reference, Meaning and Belief, J Philos, 9/73; ed, Theories and Observation in Science, Prentice-Hall, 73; Advanced Logic for Applications, D Reidel, 77. **CONTACT ADDRESS** Dept of Philosophy, Rice Univ, Houston, TX 77251. **EMAIL** rgrandy@rice.edu

GRANGE, JOSEPH
DISCIPLINE PHILOSOPHY **EDUCATION** Fordham Univ, PhD, 70. **CAREER** Prof; taught at, USM, for over 25 yrs; taught in, Hawaii, Ireland, China, and, Belgium; dir, Soc for the Study of Process Philos. **MEMBERSHIPS** Metaphysical Soc Am. **RESEARCH** Philosophy of the environment; metaphysics; Asian philosophy; American philosophy; philosophy of religion. **SELECTED PUBLICATIONS** Auth, Nature: An Environmental Cosmology, SUNY Press; The City: An Urban Cosmology, SUNY Press. **CONTACT ADDRESS** Dept of Philosophy, Univ of So Maine, 96 Falmouth St, PO Box 9300, Portland, ME 04104-9300. **EMAIL** grange@usm.maine.edu

GRANGER, CHRISTOPHER
DISCIPLINE LAW **EDUCATION** Southern Univ, LLB; Univ Mich, LLM. **CAREER** Prof., 66. **RESEARCH** Contracts, conflicts and criminal procedure. **SELECTED PUBLICATIONS** Auth, Canadian Coroner Law; auth, Canadian Criminal Jury Trials. **CONTACT ADDRESS** Fac Common Law, Univ of Ottawa, 550 Cumberland St, PO Box 450, Ottawa, ON, Canada K1N 6N5. **EMAIL** cgranger@uottawa.ca

GRANGER, HERBERT
PERSONAL Born 10/25/1944, Beaumont, TX, m, 1990, 0 child **DISCIPLINE** PHILOSOPHY **EDUCATION** Trinity Univ, BA, 67; Univ TX, PhD, 77. **CAREER** Assoc to full prof, Wayne State Univ, 91-. **HONORS AND AWARDS** Res and Inquiry Award, Liberal Arts, Wayne State Univ, 98. **MEMBERSHIPS** AAUP, Soc for Ancient Greek Philos. **RESEARCH** Ancient Greek Philosophy: Aristotle, Plato, Presocratics. **SELECTED PUBLICATIONS** Auth, "Aristotle and the Finitude of Natural Kinds," Philosophy 62 (87): 523-526; auth, "Deformed Kinds and the Fixity of Species," Classical Quarterly 37 (87): 110-116; auth, "Aristotle's Natural Kinds," Philosophy 64 (89): 245-247; auth, "Aristotle and the Functionalist Debate," Apeiron 23 (90): 27-49; auth, "Aristotle and the Concept of Supervenience," The Southern Journal of Philosophy 31 (93): 161-177; auth, "Supervenient Dualism," Ratio NS 7 (94): 1-13; auth, "Aristotle on the Subjecthood of Form," Oxford Studies in Ancient Philosophy 13 (95): 135-159; auth, Aristotle's Idea of the Soul, Kluwer (Dordrecht), 96. **CONTACT ADDRESS** Dept Philos, Wayne State Univ, Detroit, MI 48202. **EMAIL** ad4985@wayne.edu

GRANQUIST, MARK
PERSONAL Born 01/29/1957, Waukegau, IL, m, 1982, 2 children **DISCIPLINE** RELIGION **EDUCATION** St. Olaf Col, BA, 79; Yale Univ, MDiv, 84; Univ of Chicago, PhD, 92. **CAREER** Asst prof, St. Olaf Col, 92-. **MEMBERSHIPS** Am Soc of Church Hist; Am Acad of Relig; Soc of Bibl Lit. **RESEARCH** Lutheranism, Scandinavian immigrant religion, religion and ethnicity. **SELECTED PUBLICATIONS** Auth, "The Role of 'Common Sense' in the Hermeneutics of Moses Stuart", Harvard Theol Rev 83.3 (90): 305-19; auth, "A Comparison of Swedish- and Norwegian-American Religious Traditions, 1860-1920", Lutheran Quart 8.3 (94): 299-320; auth, "Conrad Bergendoff and the LCA Merger of 1962", Swedish Am Hist Quart 46.3, (July 95): 256-271; auth, "The Relgious Vision and Academic Quest At St. Olaf", in Models for Christian Higher Educ: Strategies for Success in the Twenty-First Century, ed Richard t. Hughes and William b. Adrian, Wm. B. Eerdmans (Grand Rapids, 97), 82-96; auth, "Lutherans in the United States, 1930-1960 - Searching for the Center", in Reforming the Center: Am Protestantism, 1900 to the Present, ed Douglas Jacobsen and William Vance Trollinger, Jr, Wm B. Eerdmans (Grand Rapids, 98), 234-51; auth, "Five American Lutheran Histories", Lutheran Quart 12.2 (Summer 98): 199-211. **CONTACT ADDRESS** Dept Relig, St. Olaf Col, 1520 Saint Olaf Ave, Northfield, MN 55057-1574. **EMAIL** granquise@stolaf.edu

GRANT, ISABEL
DISCIPLINE LAW **CAREER** Law Clerk, Justice Willard Estey, Supreme Court Can, 86-87; asst prof, 87-92; assoc prof, 92-. **RESEARCH** Criminal law; constitutional law; mental health law. **SELECTED PUBLICATIONS** Auth, The Law of Homicide in Canada; pubs about criminal law and charter and mental health law. **CONTACT ADDRESS** Fac of Law, Univ of British Columbia, 1822 East Mall, Vancouver, BC, Canada V6T 1Z1. **EMAIL** grant@law.ubc.ca

GRANT, J. KIRKLAND
DISCIPLINE LAW **EDUCATION** Univ MI, BBA, 65, JD (Cum Laude), 67. **CAREER** Vis scholar, Harvard Univ, Columbia Univ; acad dean, Touro Univ; dean, prof Law, Del Law Sch; prof Law, Univ SC; asst prof Law, Ga State Univ; asst prof, Univ Toledo; vis prof, Univ Ky; arbitrator, Am Arbit Asn; prof Law, Touro Col. **MEMBERSHIPS** Am Bar Asn; NY State Bar Asn; Am Law Inst; Scribes. **SELECTED PUBLICATIONS** Auth, New York Corporation Law Handbook, Gould Publ; Securities Arbitration, Quorum Bks, 94. **CONTACT ADDRESS** Touro Col, New York, Brooklyn, NY 11230. **EMAIL** KirkG@tourolaw.edu

GRANT, JACQUELYN
PERSONAL Born 12/19/1948, Georgetown, SC, m, 1995 **DISCIPLINE** THEOLOGY **EDUCATION** Bennett Coll, BA 1970; Interdenominational Theol Ctr, MDiv 1973; Union Theol Seminary, MPhil 1980, PhD 1985. **CAREER** Union Theol Seminary, tutor & relief teacher 1975-77; Harvard Divinity School, assoc in rsch 1977-79; Candler School of Emory/Theol Univ, visiting lecturer 1981; Princeton Theol Seminary, visit lectr 1985; Interdenominational Theol Center, prof 1980-. **HONORS AND AWARDS** DuBois Fellowship Harvard Univ 1979-80; Dissertation Fellowship Fund for Theological Educ 1979-80; Amer Black Achievement Awd nominee Johnson Publishing Co 1982; Woman of the Year in Religion nominee Iota Phi Lambda Sorority 1984; Martin Luther King, Jr Ministry Awd, 1986; Colgate/Rochester Theological Seminary, Outstanding Alumni: Turner Theological Seminary at ITC. **MEMBERSHIPS** Assoc minister Allen AME Church 1973-80; itinerant elder African Methodist Episcopal Church 1976; assoc minister Flipper Temple AME Church 1980-93; Victory AME Church, 1993; founder/dir Black Women in Church & Soc 1981; bd of dirs Black Theology Project in the Americas. **RESEARCH** Systematic Theology, Womanist Theology, Black Women and Religion, Black Theology, Femisnist Theology. **SELECTED PUBLICATIONS** Auth, White Women's Christ and Black Women's Jesus: Feminist Theology nd Womist Response, Atlanta, Scholars Press, 89; auth, Recovery of Black Presence: An Interdisciplinary Explanation, Nashville, Abington Press, 95. **CONTACT ADDRESS** Systematic Theology, Interdenominational Theol Ctr, 700 Martin Luther King Jr Dr, Atlanta, GA 30314. **EMAIL** jgrant@itc.edu

GRANT, JOHN W.
PERSONAL Born 06/27/1919, Truro, NS, Canada **DISCIPLINE** RELIGION **EDUCATION** Dalhousie Univ, BA, 38, MA, 41; Princeton Univ, grad stud politics, 38-39; Pine Hill Divinity Hall (NS), Cert Theol, 43; Oxford Univ, DPhil, 48. **CAREER** Ordained, 43; min, West Bay, NS, 43; dir relig infor, Wartime Infor Bd, 43-45; lectr, Pine Hill Divinity Hall, 45-46; Woodward Found Prof Church Hist, Union Col, BC, 49-59; ed-in-chief, The Ryerson Press, 60-63; prof church hist, Emmanuel Col, Univ Toronto, 63-84. **SELECTED PUBLICATIONS** Auth, Free Churchmanship in England 1870-1940, 55; auth, God's People in India, 59; auth, George Pidgeon: A Biography, 62; auth, God Speaks.. We Answer, 65; auth, The Canadian Experience of Church Union, 67; auth, The Church in the Canadian Era, 72; auth, Moon of Wintertime, 84; auth, A Profusion of Spires, 88; ed, Salvation! O the Joyful Sound: the Selected Writings of John Carroll, 67; ed, Die unierten Kirchen, 73; co-ed, The Contribution of Methodism to Atlantic Canada, 92. **CONTACT ADDRESS** 86 Gloucester St, #1002, Toronto, ON, Canada M4Y 2S2. **EMAIL** john.grant@utoronto.ca

GRASSIE, WILLIAM
PERSONAL Born 05/03/1957, Wilmington, DE, m, 1984, 2 children **DISCIPLINE** RELIGION **EDUCATION** Temple Univ, PhD, 94. **CAREER** Asst prof, Intellectual Heritage Prog, Temple Univ, 94-99. **HONORS AND AWARDS** Templeton Science and Religion Course Program, Roothbert fel, AFSC fel. **MEMBERSHIPS** AAR; IRAS. **RESEARCH** Philos of Science and Relig. **SELECTED PUBLICATIONS** Auth, Reinventing Nature: Science Narratives as Myths for an Endangered Planet, doctoral dissertation, Temple Univ, defended May 94; Cyborgs, Tricksters, and Hermes: Donna Haraway's Metatheory of Science and Religion, Zygon: J of Relig and Science, June 96; Powerful Pedagogy in the Science and Religion Classroom, Zygon: J of Relig and Science, Sept 97; Postmodernism: What One Needs to Know, Zygon: J of Relig and Science, March 97; Wired for the Future: Kevin Kelly's Techno-Utopia, Terra Nova: Nature & Culture, 2:4, fall 97. **CONTACT ADDRESS** PO Box 586, Unionville, PA 19375. **EMAIL** grassie@voicenet.com

GRATZ, DELBERT L.
PERSONAL Born 03/05/1920, Allen Co, OH, m, 1943, 4 children **DISCIPLINE** CHURCH HISTORY **EDUCATION** Bluffton Col, AB, 42; Ohio State Univ, MA, 45; Univ Bern, DPhil-(hist), 50; Univ Mich, Ann Arbor, AMLS, 52. **CAREER** Librn, Mennonite Hist Libr and Col Libr and Prof Hist, Bluffton Col 50-, Scholar, Nordrhein-Westfalen Ministry of Educ, Bonn, Ger, 64; fel, Pro Helvetia, Zurich, Switz, 64-65; Ger Acad Exchange Serv fel, Bad Godesberg, 64-65; res scholar, Baptist Theol Sem, Zurich, 64-65 and 71-72; Fulbright travel grant, 71-72. **MEMBERSHIPS** Church Hist Soc; Am Soc Reformation Res; Swiss Am Hist Soc; Mennonite Hist Soc. **RESEARCH** Anabaptist and Mennonite research; genealogical research. **SELECTED PUBLICATIONS** Auth, The Bernese Anabaptists, Herald, 53; Records relating the Mennonite story, World Conf on Records, 69; The Swiss Menonnites of Allen and Putnam Counties, Ohio, Northwest Ohio Quart, 56; Manuscript materials in Europe that concern the Anabaptists, Mennonite Quart Rev, 67; A personal contact with Hans Landis, Mennonite Res J, 69-70. **CONTACT ADDRESS** Mennonite Hist Libr, Bluffton Col, Bluffton, OH 45817.

GRAVEL, PIERRE
PERSONAL Born 03/13/1942, Montreal, PQ, Canada **DISCIPLINE** PHILOSOPHY, LITERATURE **EDUCATION** Univ Montreal, BPaed, 63; Univ Aix-Marseille, MA, 69, DPhil, 71. **CAREER** Asst lectr, Inst Am Univs and Univ Aix-Marseille, 68-71; prof, Col Maisonneuve, 71-73; asst prof, 73-78, ASSOC PROF PHILOS, UNIV MONTREAL, 78-, Consult philos, Rev Philos, 75-; mem, Comite de Lear, Rev Etudes Francaiscs, 78-; dir, Determinations, 82. **MEMBERSHIPS** Can Philos Asn. **RESEARCH** History of philosophy; aesthetics. **SELECTED PUBLICATIONS** Auth, 'Macbeth'--Shakespeare Depiction of the Workings of Power, Laval Theol et Philos, Vol 0051, 95. **CONTACT ADDRESS** 2910 Ed Montpetit, Montreal, QC, Canada H3C 3J7. **EMAIL** gravelpi@philo.umontreal.ca

GRAVELLE, JANE GIBSON
PERSONAL Born 05/22/1947, Sandersville, GA, w, 1969, 1 child **DISCIPLINE** ECONOMICS **EDUCATION** Univ GA, BA, 68, MA, 69; George Washington univ, PhD, 81. **CAREER** Vis Economist, Labor Dept, 77; vis prof, Boston Univ, 88; vis Economist, Treasury Dept, 89-90; Research asst, 69-72; sr specialist in Economic Policy, Economist/Analyst, Congressional Research Service, 72-. **HONORS AND AWARDS** Outstanding Doctoral Dissertation in Public Finance, Nat Tax Asn. **MEMBERSHIPS** Am Economic Asn; Nat Tax Asn. **RESEARCH** Tax policy. **SELECTED PUBLICATIONS** Auth, Effects of the 1981 Depreciation Revisions on the Taxation of Income from Business Capital, Nat Tax J 35, March 82; The Incidence and Efficiency Costs of Corporate Taxation when Corporate and Noncorporate Firms Produce the Same Goods, with Laurence J Kotlikoff, J of Political Economy 97, Aug 89; Differential Taxation of Capital Income: Another Look at thre Tax Reform Act of 1986, Nat Tax J 42, Dec 89; Do Individual Retirement Accounts Increase Savings?, J of Economic Perspectives 5, spring 91; Income, Consumption, and Wage Taxation in a Life-Cycle Model: Separating Efficiency From Redistribution, Am Economic Rev, 81, Sept 91; Equity Effects of the Tax Reform Act of 1986, J of Economic Perspectives 6, winter 92; What Can Private Investment Incentives Accomplish? The Case of the Investment Tax Credit, Nat Tax J 46, Sept 93; Corporate Tax Incidence and Efficiency When Corporate and Noncorporate Goods are Close Substitutes, with Laurence J Kotlikoff, Economic Inquiry 31, Oct 93; Corporate Taxation and the Efficiency Gains of the 1986 Tax Reform Act, with Laurence Kotlikoff, Economic Theory, vol 6, 95; Dynamic tax Models: Why They Do the Things They Do, with Eric Engen and Kent Smetters, Nat Tax J, 42, Sept 97; numerous other articles. **CONTACT ADDRESS** Library of Congress, 101 Independence Ave SE, Washington, DC 20540-7430. **EMAIL** jgravelle@crs.loc.gov

GRAVES, JOHN W.
PERSONAL Born 06/25/1942, Little Rock, AR, s **DISCIPLINE** HISTORY, POLITICAL SCIENCE **EDUCATION** Univ Ark, BA, 64; MA, 67; Univ Va, PhD, 78. **CAREER** Grad teaching asst, Univ Ark, 65-66; instr, Univ Southwestern La, 66-68; grader, Univ Va, 70-72; instr, Southwest Tex State Univ, 72-77; lectr, St Edward's Univ, 77-85; prof, Henderson State Univ, 85-. **HONORS AND AWARDS** Stonewall Jackson memorial Scholar, Ark Hist Comn, 65-66; Grad Teaching Fel, Univ Ark, 65-66; George L. Seay Fel in Hist, Univ Va, 68-69; Fac Res Grant, Henderson State Univ, 86; Best Paper Awd, Ark Asn of Col Hist Teachers, 90; Arkansiana Awd, Ark Libr Asn, 91; State Res Grant, Ark Hist Preservation Prog of the Dept of Ark Heritage, 96. **MEMBERSHIPS** Ark Hist Advisory Coun, Ark Black Hist Advisory Comt, Woodward Lecture Comt, Soc for the Preservation of the Mosaic Templars of America Building, Phi Alpha Theta. **RESEARCH** U.S. Southern and Arkansas History, U.S. Race Relations, U.S. Urban and Black History, Gilded Age America. **SELECTED PUBLICATIONS** Rev, of "Opening Doors: Perspectives on Race Relations in Contemporary America," ed. by H. J. Knopke, Robert J. Norrell, and Ronald W. Rogers, J of Southern Hist (May, 94): 434-435; auth, "President's Report to the Membership," Ark Hist Quart 994): 90-94; rev, of "Carpenter from Conway: George Washington Donaghey as Governor of Arkansas, 1909-1913," by Calvin R. Ledbetter, Jr, Am Rev of Politics (Autumn, 94): 419-421; auth, "President's Report to the membership," Ark Hist Quart (95): 80-84; rev, of "Civil Obedience: An Oral History of School Desegregation in Fayetteville, Arkansas, 1954-1965," by Julianne Lewis Adams and Thomas A. DeBlack, Ark Hist Quart (95), 396-400; rev, of "Race and the City: Work, Community, and Protest in Cincinnati, 1820-1970," by Henry Louis Taylor, Jr, J of Southern Hist (95): 798-799; auth, "President's Report to the Membership," Ark Hist Quart (96): 95-106. **CONTACT ADDRESS** Dept Soc Sci, Henderson State Univ, 1100 Henderson St, PO Box 7793, Arkadelphia, AR 71999-0001.

GRAVES, PHILIP E.
PERSONAL Born 12/20/1945, Hammond, IN, d, 2 children **DISCIPLINE** ECONOMICS **EDUCATION** Ind Univ, AB, 68; Northwestern Univ, MA, 71; PhD, 73. **CAREER** Asst prof, Ariz State Univ, 71-74; part-time fac, Roosevelt Univ, 75-77; res fel to vis asst prof, Univ Chicago, 74-78; fac, Econ Inst, 79-87; vis prof, Pepperdine Univ, 81-82; vis assoc prof, UCLA, 82; assoc prof to prof, Univ Colo, 78-. **HONORS AND AWARDS** Nat Sci Found Trainee, 68-71; Dept Honors and Distinction, Ind Univ; Phi Beta Kappa; Merit Scholar; Little 500 Scholar; distinguished Speaker, 14th Annual Ky Econ Asn; Teacher Recognition Awd; Soc Sci Writing Awd, Univ Colo, 92; Stanford Calderwood Teaching Excellence Awd, 97. **MEMBERSHIPS** Am Econ Asn. **RESEARCH** Environmental valuation; Regional growth and decline; Money demand; Miscellaneous microeconomic topics; Political economy. **SELECTED PUBLICATIONS** Co-auth, "Multimarket amenity Compensation and the Behavior of the Elderly," Am Econ Rev, (91): 1374-1381; co-auth, "Examining the role of Economic Opportunity and Amenities in Explaining Population Redistribution," J of Urban Econ, (95): 1-25. **CONTACT ADDRESS** Dept Econ, Univ of Colorado, Boulder, Campus Box 256, Boulder, CO 80309-0256. **EMAIL** gravesp@spot.Colorado.edu

GRAVLEE, G. SCOTT
PERSONAL Born, CA **DISCIPLINE** PHILOSOPHY **EDUCATION** Univ Wash, BA, 88; Stanford Univ, PhD, 96. **CAREER** Fel, Stanford Univ, 94-95; instru, 95-96; lectr, Christopher Newport Univ, 97-98; vis asst prof, Col of William and Mary, 96-98; asst prof, Mount Union Col, 98-. **HONORS AND AWARDS** Mellon fel, 89-91. **MEMBERSHIPS** Am Philos Asn; Soc for Ancient Greek Philos; Southern Soc for Philos and Psychol; Soc of Christian Philos. **RESEARCH** Aristotelian philosophy; Ancient Greek philosophy; Ethics. **SELECTED PUBLICATIONS** Auth, "The Pluralist University: Christian Graduate Students," 92; rev, of The Christian God, by Richard Swinburne, Ashland Theol Jrnl 29 (97): 172-174; auth, "Aristotle on Hope," Jrnl of the Hist of Philos (00). **CONTACT ADDRESS** Dept of Religion and Philosophy, Mount Union Col, Alliance, OH 44601. **EMAIL** gravlegs@muc.edu

GRAY, BONNIE JEAN
PERSONAL Born 08/19/1947, Alexandria Bay, NY **DISCIPLINE** PHILOSOPHY, ETHICS & VALUE THEORY **EDUCATION** Hope Col, BA, 69; Syracuse Univ, MA, 71, PhD(philos), 73. **CAREER** Asst prof, 74-78, assoc prof philos, Eastern KY Univ, 78-83, full prof, 83-, dir, honors program, 88-. **MEMBERSHIPS** Am Philos Asn; AAUP; Hastings Ctr Inst. **RESEARCH** Hume scholarship; business ethics. **SELECTED PUBLICATIONS** Ed & contribr, Seminar in Post-Watergate Morality, Eastern Ky Univ, 77; coauth, What to Bid? & Promoters, Entertainers and Audience: A Question of Ethics (intercol cases), Clearing House, 77; Criteria for Resolving Ethical Dilemmas in Organizations, Credo; coauth, Are You Ready for Tomorrow's Management Style?, 11-12/79 & What Price Allegiance?, A Case of Managerial Ethics, 1-2/81, Business. **CONTACT ADDRESS** Eastern Kentucky Univ, 521 Lancaster Ave, Richmond, KY 40475-3102. **EMAIL** HONGRAY@acs.eku.edu

GRAY, CHRISTOPHER
DISCIPLINE PHILOSOPHY OF LAW **EDUCATION** Cath Univ Am, PhD; McGill Univ, BCL, LLB. **CAREER** Prof, Dept Philos, Concordia Univ. **SELECTED PUBLICATIONS** Pub(s), in prof and philos jour(s) on philos of law and associated topics; ed, Philosophy of Law: An Encyclopedia, 96. **CONTACT ADDRESS** Dept of Philos, Concordia Univ, Montreal, 1455 de Maisonneuve W, Montreal, QC, Canada H3G 1M8. **EMAIL** graycb@vax2.concordia.ca

GRAY, DONALD P.
PERSONAL Born 03/29/1937, Rochester, NY, m, 1978, 4 children **DISCIPLINE** RELIGIOUS STUDIES **EDUCATION** Univ Toronto, BA, 61; Univ Notre Dame, MA, 63; Fordham Univ, PhD(theol), 68. **CAREER** From instr to assoc prof, 62-78, prof theol, Manhattan Col, 78-. **MEMBERSHIPS** Theol Soc Am; Col Theol Soc; Am Acad Relig; Am Teilhard de Chardin Asn. **RESEARCH** Christology; death and dying; Christian systematics. **SELECTED PUBLICATIONS** Auth, The One and the Many, Herder & Herder, 69; Sacramental consciousness-raising, Worship, 3/72; Was Jesus a convert?, Relig Life, winter 74; The phenomenon of Teilhard, Theol Studies, 3/75; Patience: Human and divine, Cross Currents, winter 75; The Divine and the human in Jesus Christ, Proc Cath Theol Soc Am, 76; Finding God Among Us, St Mary's Col, 77; Jesus, the Way to Freedom, St Mary's Press, 79. **CONTACT ADDRESS** Dept of Relig Studies, Manhattan Col, 4513 Manhattan Coll, Bronx, NY 10471-4004.

GRAY, PATRICK T. R.
PERSONAL Born 10/16/1940, Toronto, ON, Canada, 4 children **DISCIPLINE** THEOLOGY **EDUCATION** Univ Toronto, BA, 62, Trinity Col, STB, 65, ThD, 73; Yale Univ, STM, 66. **CAREER** Divinity tutor, Trinity Col, 67-69; assoc rector, Ch St Simon the Apostle, 69-71; instr & vis asst prof, 72-75, sr tutor, Stong Col, York Univ, 73-76; res assoc, Pontif Inst Medieval Stud, 76-78; asst to assoc prof hist & philos theol, McMaster Divinity Col, 78-84; PROF HUMANITIES, ATKINSON COL, YORK UNIV, 84-. **HONORS AND AWARDS** Killam res scholar, 76-78. **MEMBERSHIPS** Can Fedn Hum (dir 84-87); Can Soc Patristic Stud (pres 77-79); Asn Int Etudes Byzantines. **RESEARCH** Sixth Century C.E. and the transformations that period saw take place. **SELECTED PUBLICATIONS** Auth, The Defense of Chalcedon in the East (451-553), 79. **CONTACT ADDRESS** Atkinson Col, York Univ, 4700 Keele St N, North York, ON, Canada M3J 1P3. **EMAIL** pgray@yorku.ca

GRAY, RONALD A.
PERSONAL Born 12/15/1952, Blackstone, VA, m, 1985 **DISCIPLINE** LAW **EDUCATION** Ohio University, BA, economics, 1975; Case Western Reserve University, College of Law, JD, 1978. **CAREER** Federal Trade Commission, Attorney, 78-81; American Express, Attorney, 81-85, associate counsel, 85-87, counsel, 87-91, senior counsel, 91-95, managing counsel, 95-. **HONORS AND AWARDS** Harlem Black Achieves in Industry Awd, 1998; Ohio University, Gene Chapin Memorial Awd, 1975. **MEMBERSHIPS** American Bar Association, 1978-; City of New York Bar Association, vice chair, Committee on Minorities, 1994-; City Bar Arbitration Committee; South African Legal Services and Legal Assistance Project, board member, 1993-; Childrens Hope Foundation, board member, 1991-94; MFY Legal Services, board member, 1996-; New York State Bar Assoc, Corporate Counsel Executive Committee, 1997-; Committee on Multi-Discipline Practice, 1998-. **SELECTED PUBLICATIONS** Companies Aim for Diversity, New York Law Journal, 1993; Employees at Risk, New York Law Journal, 1994; Chairman, Succeeding in the Business Card Market, Cred Card Institute, Executive Enterprises, 1997. **CONTACT ADDRESS** American Express Co, 200 Vesey St, New York, NY 10285-4911.

GRAY, SHERMAN W., JR.
PERSONAL Born 07/04/1943, Montague, MA, s **DISCIPLINE** NEW TESTAMENT **EDUCATION** Catholic Univ, STL, 70; Pontifical Bib Inst, Rome Italy, SSL, 76; Catholic Univ, PhD, 87. **CAREER** Asst prof, scripture, 76-81, St Joseph Sem Yonkers NY; asst prof, scripture, Mt St Mary's Sem, Emmitsburg MD, 82-85; assoc prof, 87-, St Basil Col, Stamford CT. **MEMBERSHIPS** CBA; SBL. **RESEARCH** Gospel of Matthew, Matt 25:31-46, last judgement pericope. **SELECTED PUBLICATIONS** Auth, The Least of My Brothers, SBLDS 114, Soc of Bibl Lit, 89. **CONTACT ADDRESS** 4 Pulaski St, Stamford, CT 06902. **EMAIL** HNCSWG@aol.com

GRAY, WALLACE
PERSONAL Born 05/03/1927, Palmyra, MO, m, 1948, 2 children **DISCIPLINE** PHILOSOPHY AND RELIGION **EDUCATION** Cent Methodist Col, BA; Southern Methodist Univ, BD; Vanderbilt Univ, PhD. **CAREER** Kirk prof; Southwestern Col, 56-96; chmn, Div Soc Sci, 60-66; vis prof, Friends Univ & Wichita State Univ; asst prof, Southern Methodist Univ; lectr, Univ Tenn & Vanderbilt Univ; vis scholar, Hiroshima Inst Technol, 71-72 & Univ Hawaii, 71 & 69, acad yr in E-W Philos, 63-64; Visiting Prof, Kitakyushu Univ, 97-98. **HONORS AND AWARDS** Citizen Ambassador to China, 93. **MEMBERSHIPS** Mem, E-W Philos Conf, 64, 69 & 84, Unive Hawaii & E-W Ctr; Med Ethics Comt, Newton Mem Hosp, Winfield & Rotary Int; chem, Task Force on Upgrading Human Life, Wesley Med Ctr, Wichita, Kan. **RESEARCH** Global history of philosophy. **SELECTED PUBLICATIONS** Cheng and Tucker: A Comparative Appraisal of Two Important Recent Confucian and Neo-Confucian Studies, J Chinese Philos, Vol. 20, 93; Slavery and Oppression in Japanese History: A Case Study in Scholarly Works on Japan, Proce 14th Int sym on Asian Stud, 92, Hong Kong: Asian Res Serv, 94; Women in Ancient Japanese History, Asian Profile, Vol 22, 94 & Return of the Scarlet Letter: A Literary and Biblical Convergence with Medical Technology," Metanoia, Vol 4, 94; transl, Japanese of Eiji Hattori's Letters from the Silk Roads (Univ Press of America, 00). **CONTACT ADDRESS** Southwestern Col, Kansas, 100 College St, Winfield, KS 67156. **EMAIL** gray@sckans.edu

GRCIC, JOSEPH
PERSONAL Born Olib, Croatia **DISCIPLINE** PHILOSOPHY **EDUCATION** City Col NYork (CUNY), BA, 74; Univ Notre Dame, PhD, 80. **CAREER** Asst Prof, Ind State Univ, 96-99; Assoc Prof, Ind State Univ, 99-. **HONORS AND AWARDS** Fel, Univ Notre Dame. **MEMBERSHIPS** APA. **RESEARCH** Ethics and politics, philosophy. **SELECTED PUBLICATIONS** Auth, Ethics and Political Theory (Moral Choices); co-ed, Perspectives on the Family. **CONTACT ADDRESS** Dept Philos, Indiana State Univ, 210 N 7th St, Root Hall, Terre Haute, IN 47809-0001. **EMAIL** pigrcic@root.indstate.edu

GRECO, JOHN
DISCIPLINE PHILOSOPHY **EDUCATION** Brown Univ, PhD. **CAREER** Assoc prof; interim dir grad stud, Fordham Univ. **RESEARCH** Moral responsibility. **SELECTED PUBLICATIONS** Auth, Modern Ontology and the Problems of Epistemology, Amer Philos Quart, 95; Reid's Critique of Berkeley and Hume: What's the Big Idea?, Philos and Phenomenol Res, 95; A Second Paradox Concerning Responsibility and Luck, Metaphilos, 95; Catholics vs. Calvinists on Religious Knowledge, Amer Cath Philos Quart, 95. **CONTACT ADDRESS** Dept of Philos, Fordham Univ, 113 W 60th St, New York, NY 10023.

GREELEY, ANDREW M.
PERSONAL Born 02/05/1928, Chicago, IL **DISCIPLINE** SOCIOLOGY, ENGLISH LITERATURE, RELIGION **EDUCATION** St Mary Lake Sem, STL, 54; Univ Chicago, MA, Soc, 61, PhD, 62. **CAREER** Sr stud dir, Nat Opinion Res Center, Univ Chicago, 62-68; prog dir, High Educ, univ Chicago, 68-70; lectr, Soc dept, Univ Chicago, 63-72; Prof, Soc, Univ Ariz, 78-; Prof, Soc Sci, Univ Chicago, 91-. **SELECTED PUBLICATIONS** Religion as Poetry, Trans Publ, 95; Sociology and Religion: A Collection of Readings, Harper Collins Coll Publ, 95; coauth, Common Ground, Pilgrim Press, 96; coauth, Forging a Common Future, Pilgrim Press, 1997; I Hope You're listening God, Crossroads Publ, 97. **CONTACT ADDRESS** Nat Opinion Res Center (NORC), Univ of Chicago, 1155 E 60th St, Chicago, IL 60637. **EMAIL** agreel@aol.com

GREEN, BARBARA S.
DISCIPLINE LAW **EDUCATION** Smith Col, BA, 66; Boston Univ, JD, 71, LLM, 80. **CAREER** Asst to ed, Amer Trial Lawyers' Asn, 71-72; pvt prac, Peabody, Mass, 74-80; prof, Creighton Univ. **SELECTED PUBLICATIONS** Pub(s) on taxation, Creighton Law Rev. **CONTACT ADDRESS** Sch of Law, Creighton Univ, 2500 California Plaza , Omaha, NE 68178. **EMAIL** bgreen@culaw.Creighton.edu

GREEN, CLIFFORD JAMES
PERSONAL Born 04/29/1934, Sydney, Australia, m, 1955, 3 children **DISCIPLINE** THEOLOGY, ETHICS **EDUCATION** Univ Sydney, BA, 55; Melbourne Col Divinity, BD, 59; Union Theol Sem, NYork, STM, 64, PhD(theol), 72. **CAREER** From instr to asst prof relig, Wellesley Col, 66-72; from asst prof to assoc prof, Goucher Col, 72-79; vis lectr, Univ Md, College Park, 73-75; lectr relig, Bates Col, 75-76; adj prof, Ecumenical Inst, St Mary's Sem, Baltimore, 77-81; vis assoc prof, Hollins Col, 80; from prof Theol & Dir, Pub Policy Ctr to prof emeritus, Hartford Sem, 81-00; exec dir, Dietrich Bonhoeffer Works Eng Ed, 93-. **HONORS AND AWARDS** Am Coun Learned Soc res grant, 75. **MEMBERSHIPS** Soc of Christian Ethics; Am Acad Relig; NAm Karl Barth Soc; Soc Values Higher Educ; New Haven Theological Discussion Group; Int Bonhoeffer Soc. **RESEARCH** Contemporary theology; Bonhoeffer studies. **SELECTED PUBLICATIONS** Coauth, Critical Issues in Modern Religion, Prentice-Hall, 73, 2nd ed, 90; auth, Liberation theology?, Karl Barth on women and men, Union Sem Quart Rev, spring-summer 74; Bonhoeffer: The Sociality of Christ and Humanity, Scholars, 75, 2nd ed, 99, revised as Bonhoeffer: A Theol of Sociality, 00; contribr, Psychohistory and religion: The case of young man Luther, Fortress, 77; ed, Bonhoeffer, Fiction from prison, Fortress, 81; contribr, A Bonhoeffer Legacy, Eerdmans, 81; coauth, Bonhoeffer Bibliography, Primary Sources and Secondary Literature in English, Am Theol Lib Asn, 92; co-ed, Jugend und Studium, 1918-1927, by Bonhoeffer, Kaiser, 86; ed, contrib auth, Karl Barth: Theologian of Freedom, Collins & Harper, 89, Fortress, 91; ed, contrib auth, Churches, Cities, and Human Community, Urban Ministry in the United States, 1945-1985, Eerdmans, 96; auth, "Bonhoeffer, Dietrich," Int Encyclopedia of the Church, 1 (87): 26-27; coed, Ethik, by Bonhoeffer, 92, 2nd ed, 98; ed, Sanctorum Communio, by Bonhoeffer, Fortress, 98; ed, Fiction from Tegel Prison, by Bonhoeffer, Fortress, 99; contribur, The Cambridge Companion to Dietrich Bonhoeffer, Cambridge, 99; contribur, Reflections on Bonhoeffer, Covenant, 99; **CONTACT ADDRESS** Hartford Sem, 77 Sherman St, Hartford, CT 06105-2279. **EMAIL** green@hartsem.edu

GREEN, GARRETT
PERSONAL Born 06/01/1941, Oakland, CA, m, 1970, 2 children **DISCIPLINE** RELIGIOUS STUDIES **EDUCATION** Stanford Univ, AB, 63; Union Theol Sem, MDiv, 67; Yale Univ, MPhil, 70; PhD, 71 **CAREER** Grad tchng prof, 68-70, vis prof, 89, Yale Univ; asst prof, 70-76, assoc prof, 76-82, chmn, 77-79, prof, 82-, Class of 1943 Prof of Relig Studies, 00-, Chair, Depart of Rel Studies, Conn Col, 77-79, 82-. **HONORS AND AWARDS** Alexander von Humboldt res fel, Univ Tubingen, Ger, 76-77, 79-80; Sr Fulbright Scholar, Fed Rep Ger, 76-77; Student Fulbright Scholar, Univ Munster, Ger, 63-64; Edward Cadbury Lectr, Univ Birmingham, UK, 98. **MEMBERSHIPS** AAR; APA; 19th Century Theol Group; Duodecim Theol Soc; Karl Barth Soc of N Am. **RESEARCH** Hermeneutical issues in relig & theol; the concept of imagination in modern & post modern relig thought; Christian theol & post modern phil; Karl Barth's theory of relig. **SELECTED PUBLICATIONS** Auth, Imagining God: Theology and the Religious Imagination, Harper & Row, 89; auth, Kant as Christian Apologist: The Failure of Accommodationist Theology, Pro Ecclesia 4, 95; auth, The Hermeneutic Imperative: Reading the Bible as Scripture, Nederlands Theol Tijdshrift 50, 96; auth, The Sociology of Dogmatics: Niklas Luhmann's Challenge to Theology, Theol & Sociology: A Reader, Cassell, 96; auth, Who's Afraid of Ludwig Feuerbach? Suspicion and the Religious Imagination, Christian Faith Seeking Hist Understanding: Essays in Hon of H Jack Forstman, Mercer Univ Press, 97; auth, Theolo-

gy, Hermeneutics, and Imagination: The Crisis of Interpretation at the End of Modernity, Cambridge Univ Press, 00. **CONTACT ADDRESS** Connecticut Col, 270 Mohegan Ave, Box 5525, New London, CT 06320-4196. **EMAIL** ggre@conncoll.edu

GREEN, J. PATRICK
DISCIPLINE LAW AND MEDICINE **EDUCATION** Creighton Univ, BA, 63, JD, 65. **CAREER** Prof, Creighton Univ, 71-; pvt prac, Omaha, 65-66, 69-71; in Chicago, 68; Fed Power Comn, Wash, DC, 66-68; judge, Nebr Ct Indust Rel, 75-79, **SELECTED PUBLICATIONS** Pub(s) in, Creighton Law Rev. **CONTACT ADDRESS** School of Law, Creighton Univ, 2500 California Plaza, Omaha, NE 68178.

GREEN, JOEL B.
PERSONAL Born 05/07/1956, Lubbock, TX, m, 1979, 2 children **DISCIPLINE** NEW TESTAMENT STUDIES **EDUCATION** Tex Tech Univ, BS, 78; Perkins Sch of Theol Southern Meth Univ, M Th, 82; Univ Aberdeen, Scotland, PhD, 85. **CAREER** Asst and assoc prof, new testament, New Col Berkeley, 85-92; assoc prof, new testament, Amer Bapt Sem of the West and Grad Theol Union, Berkeley, 92-97; prof, new testament interpretation, Asbury Theol Sem, 97-. **HONORS AND AWARDS** Soc of New Testament Studies. **MEMBERSHIPS** Soc of Bibl Lit; Cath Bibl Asn; Inst for Bibl Res; Tyndale Fel. **RESEARCH** Hermeneutics; New Testament theology and ethics; Luke-Acts. **SELECTED PUBLICATIONS** Auth, Witnesses of his Resurrection: Resurrection, Salvation, Discipleship, and Mission in the Acts of the Apostles in Life in the Face of Death: The Resurrection Message of the New Testament ed. Richard N. Longenecker, McMaster New Testament Studies 3, Grand Rapids, Mich, W. B. Eerdmans, 98; auth, Bodies-That Is, Human Lives: A Re-examination of Human nature in the Bible, in Whatever Happened to the Soul? Scientific and Theological Portraits of Human Nature, ed. Warren S. Brown, Nancey C. Murphy, H. Newton Malony, Theology and the Sciences, Minneapolis, Fortress 98; auth, The Death of Jesus and the Ways of God: Jesus and the Gospels on Messianic Status and Shameful Suffering, Interpretation 52, 98; auth, Salvation to the End of the Earth (Acts 13:47): God as Saviour in the Acts of the Apostles, in The Theolofy of Acts, ed. I. Howard Marshall and David Perterson, Grand Rapids, Mich, W. B. Eerdmans, 98; auth, The Gospel of Luke, New Intl Commentary on the New Testament, Grand Rapids, Mich, W. B. Eerdmans, 97; co-auth, The Death of Jesus in Early Christianity, Peabody, Mass, Hendrickson, 95; auth, Hearing the New Testament: Strategies for Interpretation, Grand Rapids, Mich, W. B. Eerdmans, 95; auth, The Theology of the Gospel of Luke, New Testament Theol 3, Cambridge, Cambridge Univ, 95; co-ed, Jesus of Nazareth: Lord and Christ. **CONTACT ADDRESS** Asbury Theol Sem, 204 N Lexington Ave, Wilmore, KY 40390-1199. **EMAIL** joel_green@asburyseminary.edu

GREEN, JUDITH
DISCIPLINE AMERICAN PHILOSOPHY **EDUCATION** Univ MN, PhD. **CAREER** Asst prof, Fordham Univ. **SELECTED PUBLICATIONS** Co-auth, Notorious Philosopher: the Transformative Life and Work of Angela Davis, Hypatia's Daughters: Fifteen Hundred Years of Women Philosophers, Ind UP, 96. **CONTACT ADDRESS** Dept of Philos, Fordham Univ, 113 W 60th St, New York, NY 10023.

GREEN, MICHAEL
DISCIPLINE PHILOSOPHY **EDUCATION** Univ KS, BA, 73; Univ Chicago, PhD, 79. **CAREER** Lctr, IN Univ NE, 76-79; asst prof, Marquette Univ, 79-81; asst prof, SUNY Col Oneonta, 81-88; to assoc prof, 88-95; to prof, 95-. **MEMBERSHIPS** Am Philos Asn; Am Soc 18th Century Studies; Interdisciplinary 19th Century Studies; N Am Kant Soc; Am Pop Cult Asn; N Am Soc Study of Jean-Jacques Rousseau; Creighten Club, NY State Philos Asn; Dante Soc Interdisciplinary Values Indigenous Cults Net; Southern Mktg Asn. **RESEARCH** Ethics; Philos of Action; Applied Ethics; Issues in: War, Abortion, World Hunger and Racism and Sexism; Polit and Soc Philos; Hist of Philos (Ethics, Plato, Aristotle, Medieval, Rationalists, Hume, Kant, 19th Century Philos); African Philos; Business Ethics; Native Am Philos. **SELECTED PUBLICATIONS** Auth, Images of Justice, Int Jour Semiotics Law, 94; Cultural Identity and the Twenty-first Century Issues in Native American Culture Identity in Center for the Semiotic Study of Law, Politics and Government, Peter Lang, 94; Cultural Themes in European Philosophy, Law, and Economics, Hist Europ Ideas, 94; Images of Native Americans in Advertising, Some Moral Issues, Jour Business Ethics, 93; ed, Center for the Semiotic Study of Law, Politics, and Government, Peter Lang, 94 and 95. **CONTACT ADDRESS** SUNY, Col at Oneonta, Oneonta, NY 13820. **EMAIL** Greenmk@Oneonta.edu

GREEN, MICHAEL J.
PERSONAL Born 12/20/1966, St. Louis, MO, m, 2000 **DISCIPLINE** PHILOSOPHY **EDUCATION** Univ Michigan, Ann Arbor, BA, 89; Univ Calif, Berkeley, PhD, 97. **CAREER** Lectr, philos, McGill Univ, 96-97; lectr, philos, Stanford Univ, 97-99; Asst Prof, Philosophy, Univ of Chicago, 99-. **HONORS AND AWARDS** Phi Beta Kappa, 88; Ralph W. Church Scholarship, 89-90; outstanding grad student instr award. 94; chancellor's fel, 95-96. **RESEARCH** Ethics; political philosophy; history of political philosophy. **SELECTED PUBLICATIONS** Auth, National Identity and Liberal Political Philosophy, Ethics & Int Affairs, 96; auth, Review of Brian Barry: Justice as Impartiality, Ethics & Int Affairs, 97; auth, the Idea of a Momentary Self and Hume's Theory of Personal Identity, British J for the Hist of Philos, forthcoming. **CONTACT ADDRESS** Dept of Philosophy, Univ of Chicago, 1010 E. 59th St, Chicago, IL 60637. **EMAIL** michael.green@stanford.edu

GREEN, MITCHELL S.
PERSONAL Born 06/11/1963, NV, m, 1994, 2 children **DISCIPLINE** PHILOSOPHY **EDUCATION** Univ Calif, BA, 85; Oxford Univ, BPhil, 87; Univ Pittsburgh, PhD, 93. **CAREER** Asst Prof to Assoc Prof, Univ Va, 93-. **HONORS AND AWARDS** ACLS Awd. **MEMBERSHIPS** Am Philos Asn. **RESEARCH** Aesthetics; Philosophy of mind. **SELECTED PUBLICATIONS** Co-auth, "Symmetry Arguments for Cooperation in the Prisoners' Dilemma," in contemporary Action Theory: The Philosophy and Logic of Social Action, (Kluwer, 97), 229-250; auth, "Truthtelling," in The Blackwell Encyclopedia of Business Ethics, 97; auth, "The Logic of Imperatives," in The Routledge Encyclopedia of Philosophy, Routledge, 97; auth, "Direct Reference and Implicature," Philosophical Studies, (98): 61-90; auth, "Illocutions, Implicata, and What a Conversation Requires," Pragmatics & Cognition, (99): 65-92; auth, "Attitude Ascription's Affinity to Measurement," International Journal of Philosophical Studies, (99): 323-348; auth, "Moore's Many Paradoxes," Philosophical Papers, 99; auth, "Illocutionary force and Semantic Content," Linguistics & Philosophy, 00; auth, "The Status of Supposition, Nous, 00. **CONTACT ADDRESS** Dept Philos, Univ of Virginia, 1 Cabell Hall, Charlottesville, VA 22903-3125. **EMAIL** msgreen@virginia.edu

GREEN, O. HARVEY
DISCIPLINE PHILOSOPHY **EDUCATION** Vanderbilt Univ, PhD, 66; Oxford Univ, DPhil, 70. **CAREER** Assoc prof, Tulane Univ. **SELECTED PUBLICATIONS** Auth, The Emotions, Kluwer; pub(s) in, Philos; Amer Philos Quart; Analysis; Mind. **CONTACT ADDRESS** Dept of Philosophy, Tulane Univ, 6823 St Charles Ave, New Orleans, LA 70118.

GREEN, RONALD MICHAEL
PERSONAL Born New York, NY, M, 1965, 2 children **DISCIPLINE** RELIGION, ETHICS **EDUCATION** Brown Univ, AB, 64; Harvard, PhD, 73. **CAREER** Asst prof, 73-79, assoc, 79-84, PROF ETHICS, 84-, COHON PROF FOR STUD ETHICS & HUMAN, DARTMOUTH COL. **HONORS AND AWARDS** Am Academy of Religion, 96-; Society of Christian Ethics, 98-99. **MEMBERSHIPS** Society of Christian Ethics, Am Academy of Religion, Society of Business Ethics. **SELECTED PUBLICATIONS** Auth, Religious Reason, 79; auth, Religion and Moral Reason, 88; auth, Kierkegaard and Kent, 92; auth, The Ethical Manager, 94. **CONTACT ADDRESS** Ethics Inst, 6031 Parker House, Hanover, NH 03755. **EMAIL** ronald.m.green@dartmouth.edu

GREEN, THOMAS ANDREW
PERSONAL Born 03/18/1940, New York, NY, m, 1968 **DISCIPLINE** ANGLO-AMERICAN LEGAL HISTORY **EDUCATION** Columbia Univ, AB, 61; Harvard Univ, PhD(hist), 70, JD, 72. **CAREER** Asst prof hist, Bard Col, 67-69; asst prof law, 72-75, assoc prof, 75-77, Prof Law, Law Sch, Univ Mich, 77-, Prof Hist, Hist Dept, 80-. **HONORS AND AWARDS** NEH fel, Fel, Guggenheim fel **MEMBERSHIPS** AHA; Medieval Acad Am; Am Soc Legal Hist; Royal Hist Soc; Conf Critical Legal Studies. **RESEARCH** History of criminal law; history of legal and social theory; history of law in America, 1870-present. **SELECTED PUBLICATIONS** Auth, Societal concepts of criminal liability, Speculum, 72; The jury and the English law of homicide, Mich Law Rev, 76; co-ed, On the Law and Customs of England: Essays in Honor of S E Thorne, Univ NC Press, 81; auth, Art: Seditious libel, juries and the criminal law, Univ Calif, Los Angeles (in press). **CONTACT ADDRESS** Law Sch, Univ of Michigan, Ann Arbor, 625 S State St, Ann Arbor, MI 48109-1215. **EMAIL** tagreen@umich.edu

GREENAWALT, ROBERT KENT
PERSONAL Born 06/25/1936, New York, NY, m, 1995, 5 children **DISCIPLINE** CONSTITUTIONAL LAW, JURISPRUDENCE **EDUCATION** Swarthmore Col, AB, 58; Oxford Univ, BPhil, 60; Columbia Univ, LLB, 63. **CAREER** Law clerk, US Supreme Court, 63-64; spec asst, AID, 64-65; from asst prof to assoc prof, 65-69, Prof Law, 69-75, cARDOZO pROF OF jURISPRUDENCE, 75-90, uNIV pROF, 90- , Columbia Univ; Chief ed, Columbia Law Rev, 62-63; Am Coun Learned Soc fel & vis fel, Cambridge Univ, 72-73; dep solicitor gen, US Dept Justice; vis fel, All Souls Col, Oxford Univ, 79. **HONORS AND AWARDS** Mem, Am Philos Soc; fel, Am Acad of Arts and Sci. **MEMBERSHIPS** Am Soc Legal & Polit Philos (pres 92-93); ed bd, J of Philos, Ethics, Law and Philos; ed bd, J of Church and State; ed bd, Ratio Juris; ed bd, Criminal Justice Ethics; ed bd, Legal Theory; ed bd, J of Criminal Law and Criminol. **RESEARCH** Free speech; religion and political participation; legal theory; legal obligation; religious liberty. **SELECTED PUBLICATIONS** Auth, Discrimination and Reverse Discrimination, Knopf, 83; auth, Religious Convictions and Political Choice, Oxford, 88; auth, Speech, Crime, and the Uses of Language, Oxford, 89; auth, Law and Objectivity, Oxford, 92; auth, Fighting Words, princeton, 95; auth, Private Consciences and Public Reasons, Oxford, 95; auth, Statutory Interpretations, Twenty Questions, 99. **CONTACT ADDRESS** 435 W 116th St, New York, NY 10027.

GREENBAUM, MICHAEL B.
PERSONAL Born, NJ, m, 4 children **DISCIPLINE** JEWISH EDUCATION AND STUDIES **EDUCATION** Univ Miami, BS; Jewish Theol Sem, MA; Columbia Univ, PhD, 94. **CAREER** Asst prof, vice chancellor, and CEO, Jewish Theol Sem. **HONORS AND AWARDS** Secy, Nat Ramah Comm; secy, Joint Ret Bd Conser Mvmt; secy, Morningside Area Alliance; evaluator, Nat Comm Accrediting; evaluator, Mid States Asn Cols and Schls. **MEMBERSHIPS** E Asn Col and Univ Bus Officers. **RESEARCH** Louis Finkelstein. **SELECTED PUBLICATIONS** Auth, The Finkelstein Years, Tradition Renewed: A History of The Jewish Theological Seminary, 97. **CONTACT ADDRESS** Jewish Theol Sem of America, 3080 Broadway, New York, NY 10027. **EMAIL** migreenbaum@jtsa.edu

GREENBERG, GERSHON
PERSONAL Born 09/05/1940, New York, NY **DISCIPLINE** RELIGION, PHILOSOPHY **EDUCATION** Columbia Univ, PhD(philos relig), 69. **CAREER** Asst prof relig, Dartmouth Col, 68-77; ASSOC PROF PHILOS AND RELIG, AM UNIV, 77-. **RESEARCH** Nineteenth century German-Jewish religious philosophy. **SELECTED PUBLICATIONS CONTACT ADDRESS** Dept Philos and Relig, American Univ, 4400 Mass Ave NW, Washington, DC 20016-8200.

GREENE, MARTHA D.
PERSONAL Born 06/14/1965, Boone, NC, s **DISCIPLINE** ENGLISH, LITERATURE, RELIGION, THEATER **EDUCATION** Wake Forest Univ, BA, 87; MA, 93; Univ NCar Chapel Hill, MA, 96; PhD, 01. **CAREER** Counr, Wake Forest Univ, 87-89; rep, Appalachian State Univ, 89-90; hall dir, Salem Col, 92-93; asst dir to teaching fel, Univ NCar Chapel Hill, 95-01; Lilly fel/lectr, Valparaiso Univ, 01-03. **HONORS AND AWARDS** Lilly Found Fel, 01-03; PEW Found Mentoring Prog, 00-03; Teaching Fel, Univ NCar, 00-01; Rotary Ambassador Scholar, 91-92. **MEMBERSHIPS** MLA; SAMLA; Dorothy L. Sayers Soc; CCL. **RESEARCH** British modernism; drama; theology and literature. **SELECTED PUBLICATIONS** Auth, "H. D.'s Challenge to the Institution in 'The Flowering of the Rod,'" Theol 97 (94): 344-52; auth, "An Interview with Doris Betts," Carolina Quart 52 (00): 59-73; rev, "Literature in Christian Perspective," by Bridgit Nichols, Christianity/Lit 50 (01): 241-3; auth, "Dorothy L. Sayers's Anti-Romantic Comedies," Mod Drama (forthcoming). **CONTACT ADDRESS** Dept Humanities, Valparaiso Univ, Linwood House, Valparaiso, IN 463832. **EMAIL** Martha.Greene@valpo.edu

GREENFIELD, LIAH
PERSONAL Born 08/22/1954, Vladivostock, USSR, m, 1979, 1 child **DISCIPLINE** SOCIOLOGY, POLITICAL SCIENCE **EDUCATION** Hebrew Univ Jerusalem, BA, 76; MA, 78; PhD, 82. **CAREER** Asst to The John L. Loeb Assoc Prof of Sociol and Soc Studies, Harvard Univ, 85-94; vis assoc prof, Dept of Political Sci, MIT, fall 92; univ prof and prof of Sociol and Political Sciences, Boston Univ, 94-; vis prof, Ecole des Hautes Etudes en Sciences Sociales, Paris, spring 97. **HONORS AND AWARDS** Ford Found Grant for Grad Res, 80-81; Mellon Fel, 85-86; John M. Olin Fac Fel, 87-88; Inst for Advanced Study, Princeton, mem, 89-90; Grant from the Nat Coun for Soviet & East European Res, 91-94; United Nations, "expert on mission" to UNRISD and UNDP, invited speaker on ethnic conflict at a preparatory conference for the World Summit on Social Development, Aug 17-19, 94; Nat Intelligence Coun, consult, participant in the workshop "New fundamentals of Global Relations," Sept 21, 94; United Nations, Vienna Office, expert consult, invited speaker on ethnic conflict at the meeting organized by the UNPROFOR in Yugoslavia, Jan 16-17, 95; Woodrow Wilson Int Centre for Scholars, Fel, 97-98; Earhart Found Fel, 97-98. **MEMBERSHIPS** Nat Sci Found, Am Sociol, Israeli Sociol, Critical Rev, Encyclopedia of Nationalism (Academic Press), Am Sociol Asn. **RESEARCH** Nationalism; modern society, politics, and economy; philosophy and methodology of social sciences. **SELECTED PUBLICATIONS** Auth, Nationalism: Five Roads to Modernity, Harvard Univ Press (92); auth, "The Origins and Nature of American Nationalism in Comparative Perspective," Knud Krakau, ed, The American Nation--National Identity--Nationalism, Berlin: JFK Institut fuer Nordamerikastudien, Freie Univ (97): 19-53; auth, "Metodologies en l'esrudi del nacionalisma," transl by Esther Sala Miralles, in Nacionalismes I cienties socials, Editorial Meditterrania (97): 239-248. Auth, "Is Nationalism Legitimate? A Sociological Perspective on a Philosophical Question," Can J of Philos, Supplementary Vol 22 (98): 93-108; auth, Nacionalismo: Cinco Caminhos para a Modernidade (Portuguese), Publicacoes Europa-America, Bibliotec Universitaria (98); auth, "Is Nation Unavoidable? Is Nation Unavoidable Today?," in Hanspeter Kriese, et al, eds, Nation and National Identity: The European Experience in Perspective, Zurich: Verlag Ruegger (99); auth,

Nacionalisme I Modernitat, Catarroja: Editorial Afers, Universitat de Valencia (99); auth, Then Spirit of Capitalism: Nationalism and Economic Growth (completed June 99); auth, National Consciousness, the Intelligentsia, and Political Change in Russia: An Interpretation of a Culture (in progress); auth, "Etymology, Definitions, Types," lead theoretical essay, Encyclopedia of Nationalism, vol 1 (in press). **CONTACT ADDRESS** The University Professors, Boston Univ, 745 Commonwealth Ave, Boston, MA 02215.

GREENFIELD, MICHAEL M.
DISCIPLINE COMMERCIAL & CONSUMER LAW **EDUCATION** Grinnell Col, AB, 66; Univ Tex, Austin, JD, 69. **CAREER** Prof Law, Washington Univ, 69-, Vis prof, Univ Calif, Davis, 74-75. **RESEARCH** Consumer protection. **SELECTED PUBLICATIONS** Art, Coercive Collection Tactics: An Analysis Of The Interests And The Remedies, Washington Univ Law Quart, 72; art, Consumer protection in service transactions: Implied warranties and strict liability in tort, Utah Law Rev, 74; art, A Constitutional limitation on the enforcement of judgments: Due process and exemptions, Washington Univ Law Quart, 75; art, Debtor proceedings, Becker, Savin & Becker, Legal Checklists, Callaghan & Co, 78. **CONTACT ADDRESS** Sch of Law, Washington Univ, Anheuser-Busch Hall, One Brookings Dr, Saint Louis, MO 63130. **EMAIL** greenfim@wulaw.wustl.edu

GREENHAW, DAVID M.
PERSONAL Born Kansas City, MO **DISCIPLINE** THEOLOGY **EDUCATION** Univ Kans, BGS, 76; Eden Theol Sem, MD, 79; Drew Univ, PhD, 87. **CAREER** Asst prof Vanderbilt Univ Divinity School, 86-90; Assoc prof and dean of the Sem Lancaster Theol Sem, 90-97; Pres and prof of preaching and Worship, Eden Theol Sem, 97-. **MEMBERSHIPS** AAL/SBL. **RESEARCH** Hermeneutics; Liturgical Theology. **SELECTED PUBLICATIONS** Auth, Proclamation IV: Pentecost 2: aids for Interpreting the Lessons of the Church Year, 91; As One With Authority: The Status of Concepts, Preaching, Intersections: Preaching and Biblical Interpretation, 94; Theology of Preaching, Encyclopedia of Preaching, 95; Passion Sunday, Seasons of Preaching, 96; David Buttrick and the Formation of Consciousness, World, Gospel, Scripture: Preaching as a Theological Task, 96. **CONTACT ADDRESS** Eden Theol Sem, 475 E Lockwood Ave, Saint Louis, MO 63119-3192. **EMAIL** dgreenhaw@eden.edu

GREENSPAHN, FREDERICK E.
PERSONAL Born 10/07/1946, Los Angeles, CA, m, 1997, 2 children **DISCIPLINE** BIBLICAL STUDIES **EDUCATION** Univ Calif, Santa Cruz, BA, 68; Hebrew Union Col, Jewish Inst of Relig, MA, 73; Brandeis Univ, PhD, 77. **CAREER** Lectr, relig stud, Assumption Col, Worcester MA, 77-79; asst prof, 79-85, assoc prof, 85-93, prof, 93-, Relig and Judaic Stud, Univ Denver. **HONORS AND AWARDS** Phi Beta Kappa, 91; ed, Hebrew Stud, 94-98; Univ Denver United Methodist Church Scholar- Tchr Awd, 95. **MEMBERSHIPS** Soc of Bibl Lit; Assoc for Jewish Stud; Natl Assoc of Prof of Hebrew; Central Conf of Am Rabbis. **RESEARCH** Hebrew Bible; history of Jewish Biblical interpretation; Hebrew language. **SELECTED PUBLICATIONS** Auth, Hapax Legomena in Biblical Hebrew, Scholars, 84; auth, Why Prophecy Ceased, Jour of Bibl Lit, 89; auth, How Modern are Modern Biblical Studies, in Brettler, ed, Minhah le-Nahum, Biblical and Other Studies Presented to Nahum M Sarna in Honour of His 70th Birthday, JSOT, 93; auth, A Mesopotamian Proverb and its Biblical Reverberations, Jour of the Am Oriental Soc, 94; auth, When Brothers Dwell Together: The Preeminence of Younger Siblings in the Hebrew Bible, Oxford, 94; auth, An Introduction to Aramaic, Scholars, 99. **CONTACT ADDRESS** Dept of Religion, Univ of Denver, Denver, CO 80208. **EMAIL** fgreensp@du.edu

GREENSPAN, EDWARD L.
DISCIPLINE LAW **EDUCATION** Univ Toronto, BA, 65; Osgoode Hall Law Sch, LLB, 68. **CAREER** Lectr, 72-. **HONORS AND AWARDS** Ed, Martin's Ann Criminal Code; ed, Martin's Related Criminal Statutes; ed, Martin's Ontario Criminal Practice. **SELECTED PUBLICATIONS** Auth, pubs on criminal law. **CONTACT ADDRESS** Fac of Law, Univ of Toronto, 78 Queen's Park, Toronto, ON, Canada M5S 1A1.

GREENSPOON, LEONARD JAY
PERSONAL Born 12/05/1945, Richmond, VA, m, 1968, 2 children **DISCIPLINE** BIBLICAL STUDIES **EDUCATION** Univ Richmond, BA, 67, MA, 70; Harvard Univ, PhD, 77. **CAREER** Instr, 75-77, Asst Prof Hist, Relig and Latin, Clemson Univ, 77-00; Klutznick Chair in Jewish Civilization, Creighton Univ. **MEMBERSHIPS** Int Orgn Septuagint & Cognate Studies, Asn Jewish Studies, Soc Bibl Lit, Soc Values Higher Educ. **RESEARCH** Greek translations of the Old Testament; Judaism in the Hellenistic period; history of Biblical scholarship. **SELECTED PUBLICATIONS** Auth, The LXX-Version--A Guide to the Translation Technique of the Septuagint, Cath Biblical Quart, Vol 0055, 93. **CONTACT ADDRESS** Creighton Univ, 2500 Calif Plaza, Omaha, NE 68178. **EMAIL** ligm@creighton.edu

GREENSTEIN, HAROLD
PERSONAL Born 11/07/1936, New York, NY, m, 1962 **DISCIPLINE** PHILOSOPHY **EDUCATION** City of New York, BA, 60; NYork Univ, MA, 64, PhD(philos), 68. **CAREER** Asst prof philos, State Univ NY Col Geneseo, 65-68; from asst prof to assoc prof, 68-76, prof philos, State Univ NY Col Brockport, 76-, State Univ NY Res Found rea fel, 69; pres, Senate Fac State Univ NY Col Brockport, 77-78. **MEMBERSHIPS** Am Philos Asn; Mind Asn; Am Acad Polit & Soc Sci. **RESEARCH** Philosophy of history and the behaviorial sciences; philosophical psychology; philosophy of social sciences; philosophy of law; social and political philosophy. **SELECTED PUBLICATIONS** Coauth, Biologists as philosophers, Biosci, 11/66; Intrinsic values and the explanation of behavior, J Value Inquiry, 76; The logic of functional explanations, Philosophia, 73. **CONTACT ADDRESS** Dept of Philos, SUNY, Col at Brockport, 350 New Campus Dr, Brockport, NY 14420-2914. **EMAIL** hgreenst@brockport.edu

GREENWOOD, MICHAEL J.
PERSONAL Born 05/08/1939, Chicago, IL, m, 1964, 4 children **DISCIPLINE** ECONOMICS **EDUCATION** DePaul Univ, BA, 62; Northwestern Univ, MA, 65; PhD, 67. **CAREER** Asst Prof to Assoc Prof, Kans State Univ, 65-73; Policy Fel, U.S. Dept of Commerce, 71-72; Assoc Prof to Prof, Ariz State Univ, 73-80; Prof and Dir, Univ Colo, 80-. **HONORS AND AWARDS** Fel, Brookings Econ Policy, 71-72; Fac Res Fel, Univ Colo, 99-00; Dist Res Prof, Ariz State Univ, 77-78 **MEMBERSHIPS** Am Econ Asn; Am Statist Asn; Soc of Labor Econ; Reg Sci Asn; W Econ Asn; W Reg Sci Asn; Population Asn of Am; N Am Reg Sci Asn. **RESEARCH** International migration; Internal migration. **SELECTED PUBLICATIONS** Co-auth, "Differential Economic Opportunity, Transferability of Skills, and Immigration to the United States and Canada," Rev of Econ and Statist, 91; co-auth, "Migration, Regional Equilibrium, and the Estimation of Compensating Differentials," Am Econ Rev, 91; co-auth, "The Influence of Social Programs in Source Countries on Various Classes of U.S. Immigration," J of the Am Statist Asn, 99; co-auth, "Source-Country Social Programs and the Age Composition of Legal U.S. Immigrants," J of Public Econ, 01. **CONTACT ADDRESS** Dept Econ, Univ of Colorado, Boulder, Campus Box 256, Boulder, CO 80309. **EMAIL** greenwood@colorado.edu

GREGG, ROBERT
DISCIPLINE INTERNATIONAL ORGANIZATION **EDUCATION** Colgate Univ, AB; Cornell Univ, PhD. **CAREER** Prof, Am Univ. **RESEARCH** International organizations and the United Nations. **SELECTED PUBLICATIONS** Auth, About Face? The United States and the United Nations, L. Rienner Publs, 93; International Relations on Film, Lynne Rienner, 97. **CONTACT ADDRESS** American Univ, 4400 Massachusetts Ave, Washington, DC 20016.

GREGORY, DAVID L.
DISCIPLINE LAW **EDUCATION** Catholic Univ Am, BA, 73; Wayne State Univ, Grad Sch of Business, MBA, 77; Univ Detroit Mercy Sch Law, JD, 80; Yale Univ Law Sch, LLM, 82, JSD, 87. **CAREER** Asst prof, 82-84, assoc prof, 84-86, prof, 86- , St. John's Univ School of Law. **HONORS AND AWARDS** Magna cum laude, 80; Kenneth Wang Res Prof, 87-88; Vincentian Ctr for Church and Soc Awd, 98; **MEMBERSHIPS** Who's Who in Am Law; New York State Bar Asn; Michigan Bar Asn; Am Law Inst; Asn of the Bar of the City of NY; ABA; Am Arbitration Asn; Asn of Am Law Sch; Fel of Cath Scholars; Industrial Rel Res Asn; Soc of Policy Scientists; Federal Mediation and Conciliation Service; NY State Public Employment Rel Bd; NY City Office of Collective Bargaining. **SELECTED PUBLICATIONS** Auth, Labor Law, NYU and Dartmouth, 93; bd contrib ed, Handling Employment Disputes in New York, Lawyers Cooperative, 95; auth, Legal Arguments Against The Death Penalty, in Kelly, ed, St John's Univ Vincentian Chair of Social Justice and Center for Church and Society, 95; auth, Labor Law and Religion, in Finkelman, ed, The Encyclopedia of Religion and the Law, Garland, 98; coauth Labor-Management Relations and the law, Foundation, 99; ed, Labor and the Constitution, Garland, 99; auth, Catholic Social Teaching, in Carmlla, ed, Christian Perspective on Law, 99; auth, From Negligence Theory to Negligence in Employment, in Feliu, ed, Negligence in Employment, Bureau of Natl Affairs, 99. **CONTACT ADDRESS** School of Law, St. John's Univ, 8000 Utopia Pky, Jamaica, NY 11439. **EMAIL** dgregory@sjulawfac.stjohns.edu

GREGORY, WANDA TORRES
PERSONAL Born 09/04/1958, San Juan, PR **DISCIPLINE** PHILOSOPHY **EDUCATION** Universidad de Puerto Rico, BA, 83-84; MA, 87, Boston Univ, Ph D, 95. **CAREER** Tchg fel, 87, lectr, 88, Universidad de Puerto Rico; tchg fel, 88-90, lectr, 95, Boston Univ; vis jr fel, Institut fur die Wissenschaften vom Menschen, Vienna, 90, 92; lectr Metropolitan Col, Boston, 91, 93; lectr Univ Mass, Boston, 95-96; lectr Simmons Col, 95-97; master lectr, Suffolk Univ, 92-98; vis asst prof Simmons Col, 97-99; ast prof Simmons Col, 01-. **HONORS AND AWARDS** Highest honors, 83, 87; Hum Scholar Awd, 94; Philos Soc Fac Awd, 96; nom Tchr of the Year, 96. **MEMBERSHIPS** APA. **RESEARCH** Ethics, Heidegger, philosophy of language; Quine. **SELECTED PUBLICATIONS** Auth, Indeterminacy of Translation/Subdeterminacy of Theory: A Critique, Dialogos, 89; auth, Heidegger y Quine: La Posibilidad de un Dialogo, Dialogos, 94; auth, Traditional Language and Technological Language, Jour of Philos Res, 98; auth, Quine and Heidegger on Meaning, Dialogos, 98; auth, Heidegger on Traditional Language and Technological Language, Proceedings, Twentieth World Congress of Philosophy, 99. **CONTACT ADDRESS** Dept of Philosophy, Simmons Col, Boston, MA 02115. **EMAIL** torres@simmons.edu

GREIG, ALEXANDER JOSEF
PERSONAL Born 11/18/1938, Lander, WY, m, 1961 **DISCIPLINE** THEOLOGY **EDUCATION** Union Col, BA, 61; Andrews Univ, MA, 62; Seventh-day Adventist Theol Sem, BD, 63; Edinburgh Univ, PhD(Old Testament), 74. **CAREER** Pastor, Seventh-day Adventist Church, 64-71; Prof Relig, Andrews Univ. **MEMBERSHIPS** Soc Bibl Lit. **RESEARCH** Old Testament theology; Biblical studies. **CONTACT ADDRESS** Andrews Univ, 100 US Hwy 31, Berrien Springs, MI 49104-0001. **EMAIL** greigj@andrews.edu

GREIG, GARY S.
DISCIPLINE OLD TESTAMENT **EDUCATION** Hebrew Univ, BA; Univ Chicago, MA, PhD. **CAREER** Assoc prof, 95. **RESEARCH** Near eastern languages and civilizations. **SELECTED PUBLICATIONS** Auth, The World with Power, Ventura: Regal, 93; Signs and Wonders: Bibl Overview, Third Wave Movement, A Practical Encycl of Evangel and Church Growth, Ventura, Regal, 95; Repenting of the Sins of Our Fathers, Ministries Today, 97. **CONTACT ADDRESS** Wagner Leadership Inst, 11005 Hwy 83 N, Colorado Springs, CO 80921.

GRELLE, BRUCE
PERSONAL Born 04/20/1956, Indianapolis, IN, m, 1974, 1 child **DISCIPLINE** RELIGION **EDUCATION** Univ Chicago, PhD, 93. **CAREER** Instr, Univ Tenn, 86-89; asst prof, 89-95, assoc prof, 95-00, prof, 00-, dir, Relig and Public Educ Resource Ctr, Calif State Univ, Chico, 95- . **MEMBERSHIPS** Am Acad Relig; Soc of Christian Ethics. **RESEARCH** Comparative religious ethics; religion and society; religion and public education. **SELECTED PUBLICATIONS** Auth, Comparative Religious Ethics as a Form of Critical Inquiry, Annual of the Soc of Christian Ethics, 93; auth, Hegemony and the Universalization of Moral Ideas: Gramsci's Significance for Comparative Religious Ethics, Soundings, 95; coauth, Comparative Religious Ethics and Human Rights: A New Venue, Annual of the Soc of Christian Ethics, 95; coauth, Beyond Socialization and Multiculturalism: Rethinking the Task of Citizenship Education in a Pluralistic Society, Social Educ, 96; auth, Scholarship and Citizenship: Comparative Religious Ethicists as Public Intellectuals, in Twiss, ed, Explorations in Global Ethics: Comparative Religious Ethics and Interreligious Dialogue, Westview, 98; co-ed, Explorations in Global Ethics: Comparative Religious Ethics and Interreligious Dialogue, Westview, 98. **CONTACT ADDRESS** Dept of Religious Studies, California State Univ, Chico, Chico, CA 95929-0740. **EMAIL** bgrelle@csuchico.edu

GRENZ, STANLEY J.
PERSONAL Born 01/07/1950, Alpena, MI, m, 1971, 2 children **DISCIPLINE** THEOLOGY **EDUCATION** Univ Colorado, BA, 73; Denver Conservative Baptist Sem, MDiv, 76; Univ Munich, DTheol, 80. **CAREER** Adj prof, Univ Winnipeg and Providence Sem, 80-81; prof theol, North Am Baptist Sem, 81-90; prof, Carey/Regent Col, 90- ; affil prof, Northern Baptist Theolog Sem, 96- . **HONORS AND AWARDS** Phi Beta Kappa, 73; Robert G. Kay Scholastic Awd, 76; Magna Cum Laude, 80; Outstanding Young Men of Am,82; Fulbright Scholar, 87-88; listed, Who's Who in Religion, 92-93, Men of Achievement, 93; Theol Scholar and Res Awd, 93; Intl Man of the Year, 93. **MEMBERSHIPS** Can Evangel Theolog Asn; Am Acad of Relig; Natl Asn of Baptist Prof of Relig. **SELECTED PUBLICATIONS** Auth, Revisioning Evangelical Theology, InterVarsity, 93; auth, Theology for the Community of God, Broadman & Holman, 94; co-auth, Betrayal of Trust: Sexual Misconduct in the Pastorate, InterVarsity, 95; auth, Women and the Church: A Biblical Theology of Women in Ministry, InterVarsity, 95; auth, A Primer on Postmodernism, Eerdmans, 96; auth, Created for Community: Connecting Christian Belief with Christian Living, Baker/BridgePoint, 96; coauth, Who Needs Theology? An Invitation to the Study of God, InterVarsity, 96; auth, Sexual Ethics: An Evangelical Perspective, John Knox, 97; auth, The Moral Quest: Foundations for Christian Ethics, InterVarsity, 97; auth, What Christians Really Believe..and Why, John Knox, 98; coauth, The Fortress Introduction to Contemporary Theology, Fortress, 98; auth, Welcoming But Not Affirming: An Evangelical Response to Homosexuality, John Knox, 98; auth of numerous articles. **CONTACT ADDRESS** 5920 Iona Dr, Vancouver, BC, Canada V6T 1J6. **EMAIL** sgrenz@unixg.ubc.ca

GRESCHNER, DONNA
DISCIPLINE LAW **EDUCATION** Univ Saskatchewan, BC, 79, LLB, 80; Oxford Univ, BCL, 82. **CAREER** Prof, 82- **SELECTED PUBLICATIONS** Auth, pubs on women and the

constitution, Aboriginal peoples, and human rights legislation. **CONTACT ADDRESS** Col of Law, Univ of Saskatchewan, 15 Campus Dr, Saskatoon, SK, Canada S7N 5A6. **EMAIL** Greschne@law.usask.ca

GREY, THOMAS C.
PERSONAL Born 09/01/1941, San Francisco, CA, 1 child **DISCIPLINE** LAW **EDUCATION** Stanford Univ, BA, 63; Oxford Univ, BA, 65; Yale Univ, L1B, 68. **CAREER** Asst prof, 71-74, assoc prof, 74-78, PROF LAW, STANFORD UNIV, 78-. **RESEARCH** Constitutional law; legal philosophy; history of legal thought. **SELECTED PUBLICATIONS CONTACT ADDRESS** Law Sch, Stanford Univ, Stanford, CA 99305.

GRIBBEN, ALAN
PERSONAL Born 11/21/1941, Parsons, KS, m, 1974, 2 children **DISCIPLINE** ENGLISH, PHILOSPHY **EDUCATION** Univ Kans, BA, 64; Univ Ore, MA, 66; Univ Calif, PhD, 74. **CAREER** Res Ed, Univ Calif, 67-74; From Asst Prof to Prof, Univ Tex, 74-91; Prof, Auburn Univ, 91-. **HONORS AND AWARDS** President's Assocs Teaching Excellence Awd, 83; Katherine Ross Richards Centennial Teaching Fel, 88-89; Phi Kappa Phi, 91; Henry Nash Smith Fel, Elmira Col, 97. **MEMBERSHIPS** Mark Twain Circle of Am. **RESEARCH** American literature, American humor, literary biography, library history, travel literature, history of academic administration. **SELECTED PUBLICATIONS** Auth, Mark Twain's Library: A Reconstruction, 2 vols, G K Hall and Co (Boston, MA), 80; ed, Mark Twain's Rybaiyat," Jenkins Publ Co (Austin, TX), 83; auth, "The Importance of Mark Twain," Am Quart 37 (New York: Oxford UP, 97), 24-49; co-ed, Overland with Mark Twain: James B Pond's Photographs and Journal of the North American Lecture Tour of 1895, Elmira Col Pr (Elmira, NY), 92. **CONTACT ADDRESS** Dept English & Philos, Auburn Univ, PO Box 244023, Montgomery, AL 36124-4023. **EMAIL** gribben@edla.aum.edu

GRIENER, GEORGE E.
PERSONAL Born 02/04/1942, Atlanta, GA, s **DISCIPLINE** THEOLOGY **EDUCATION** Spring Hill Col, BS, 67; Regis Col, MDiv, 73; St Michael's Col, MA, 75; Univ Tubingen, ThD, 88. **CAREER** Jesuit School Theol Berkeley, asst prof, assoc prof, acad dean, 89-. **MEMBERSHIPS** AAR, CTSA, USCHS. **RESEARCH** 18th and 19th century theological history. **CONTACT ADDRESS** Jesuit Sch of Theol, Berkeley, 1735 LeRoy Ave, Berkeley, CA 94709. **EMAIL** ggriener@jstb.edu

GRIEVES, FOREST L.
PERSONAL Born 09/19/1938, Beatty, NV, m, 1963, 2 children **DISCIPLINE** POLITICAL SCIENCE **EDUCATION** Stanford, BA, 60; Univ Nev, MA, 64, PhD, 67. **CAREER** Tchr, US Army, Europe, 60-62; Tchng Asst, Univ Ariz, 64-67; Asst Prof, W Ill Univ, 67-69; Asst Prof (69) to Assoc Prof (72) to Prof (76), Dept Polit Sci, Univ Mont; Guest Prof, Universitat des Saarlandes, 78-79, 81 2E **HONORS AND AWARDS** Grant, Univ Ariz, 65; Grant, Univ Mont, 70, 72, 74, 87, 92; Grant, Am Philo Soc, 72; Grant, NEH, 73; Grant, Ger Acad Exchange Service, 78, 87; Fulbright Hayes Sr Lectureship, 78-79; Grant, Alexander von Humboldt Foundation, 79, 81; Univ Montana, Distinguished Teaching Awd, 83-94; Outstanding Advisor Awd, 90; Fulbright, Sr Scholar, 94, 98. **MEMBERSHIPS** Ger Stud Asn. **RESEARCH** International relations; comparative government; American government. **SELECTED PUBLICATIONS** Auth, Supranationalism and International Adjudication, Univ Ill Press, 69; auth, Conflict and Order: An Introduction to International Relations, Houghton Mifflin, 77; ed, Transnationalism in World Politics and Business, Pergamon Press, 79; co-auth, International Environmental Protection at the Regional Level, International Dimensions of the Environmental Crisis, Westview Press, 82;auth, Great events from History II, Human Rights, Salem Press, 92; auth, entries in The African American Encyclopedia, Supplement, Marshall Cavendish Corp, 96. **CONTACT ADDRESS** Dept Polit Sci, Univ of Montana, Missoula, MT 59812. **EMAIL** fgrieves@selway.umt.edu

GRIFFIN, NICHOLAS
PERSONAL Born 10/22/1947, Loughborough, England, m, 1971, 1 child **DISCIPLINE** PHILOSOPHY **EDUCATION** Univ Leicester, BA, 70; Australian Nat Univ, PhD(philos), 75. **CAREER** Asst lectr gen studies, Grimsby Col Technol, 70-71; fel philos, Victoria Univ, Wellington, 75-76; asst prof, 76-82, ASSOC PROF PHILOS, MCMASTER UNIV, 82-. **MEMBERSHIPS** Can Philos Asn. **RESEARCH** Philosophical logic; Bertrand Russell; philosophy of science; Epistemology, 19th and 20th Century. **SELECTED PUBLICATIONS** Auth, Relative Identity (Oxford, Oxford Univeristy Press, 77); auth, 'Russell and the Nature of Logic', Synthese, Vol 45 (81): 117-188; auth, 'What's Wrong With Bradley's Theory of Judgment?', Idealistic Studies, vol 13 (83): 199-225; auth, 'Russell's Multiple Relation Theory of Judgement', Philosophical Studies Vol 47 (85): 213-47; auth, 'Lifeboat USA' (Parts 1 & 2, International Journal of Moral and Social Studies' Vol 3 (88): 217-38 & Vol 4 (89): 17-36; auth, 'Was Russell Shot or Did He Fall?' Dialogue, 30 (91): 549-53; auth, Russell's Idealist Apprenticeship (Oxford: Oxford Univ Press, 1991); auth, The Selected Letters of Bertrand Russell, Vol 1, The Private Years 1884-1914 (London: Allan Lane Press; New York: Houghton Mifflin, 1992); auth, 'Terms, Relations, Complexes' in Irvine &Wedeking, eds. Russell and Analytic Philosophy (Toronto: University of Toronto Press, 1993), 159-92. **CONTACT ADDRESS** Dept Philos, McMaster Univ, 1280 Main St W, Hamilton, ON, Canada L8S 4K1. **EMAIL** ngriffin@mcmaster.ca

GRIFFIN, RICHARD W.
PERSONAL Born 07/01/1945, Austin, TX, m, 1990, 5 children **DISCIPLINE** POLITICAL SCIENCE **EDUCATION** Lamar Univ, BS, 67; Fla State Univ, MS, 69; PhD, 70. **CAREER** Prof, Ferris State Univ. **RESEARCH** Social Movements. **CONTACT ADDRESS** Dept Soc Sci, Ferris State Univ, ASC 2094, Big Rapids, MI 49307. **EMAIL** griffinr@ferris.edu

GRIFFIN, RONALD CHARLES
PERSONAL Born 08/17/1943, Washington, m **DISCIPLINE** LAW **EDUCATION** Hampton Inst, BS 1965; Harvard Univ, attended 1965; Howard Univ, JD 1968; Univ VA, LLM 1974. **CAREER** Office Corp Counsel Dist of Columbia Govt, legal intern 68-69, legal clerk 69-70, asst corp counsel 70; the JAG School AUS, instructor 70-74; Univ of OR, asst prof; Notre Dame Univ, visiting prof 81-82; Washburn Univ, prof of law. **HONORS AND AWARDS** Rockefeller Found Grant; Outstanding Young Men of Amer Awd 1971; Outstanding Educators of Amer Awd 1973; Intl Men of Achievement 1976; Outstanding Young Man of Amer Awd 1979; William O Douglas Awd Outstanding Prof 1985-86. **MEMBERSHIPS** Mem Legal Educ Com Young Lawyers Sect Amer Bar Assn; Young Lawyers Liaison Legal Educ & Admission to Bar Sect Amer Bar Assn; mem Bankruptcy Com Fed Bar Assn; mem OR Consumer League 1974-75; grievance examiner Mid-West Region EEOC 1984-85; mediator NE Kansas Region Consumer Protection Complaints Better Business Bureau 1984-87, pres Central States Law School Assn 1987-88; vice chairperson, Kansas Continuing Legal Education Commission, 1989-90; board member, The Brown Foundation. **CONTACT ADDRESS** Sch of Law, Washburn Univ of Topeka, 17th and MacVicar, Topeka, KS 66621.

GRIFFITH, ELWIN JABEZ
PERSONAL Born 03/02/1938, m **DISCIPLINE** LAW **EDUCATION** Long Island Univ, BA 1960; Brooklyn Law Sch, JD 1963; NYork Univ, LLM 1964. **CAREER** Modern HS, teacher 55-56; Chase Manhattan Bank, asst couns 64-71; Cleveland Marshall Law Sch, asst prof 68; Tchrs Ins & Annuity Assn, asst consl 71-72; Drake Univ, asst dean & asst prof 72-73; Univ of Cincinnati Coll of Law, assoc dean & prof 73-78; DePaul Law School, dean & prof 78-85; FLorida State Univ Coll of Law, prof 86-. **MEMBERSHIPS** Barbados Indp Com 1966; Bedford-Stuyvesant Jr C of C 1970-72; mem Black Exec Exchg Prof 1971; mem NY State Bar Assn; Amer Bar Assn. **SELECTED PUBLICATIONS** Publ "Final Payment & Warranties Under the Uniform Commercial Code" 1973; "Truth-in-Lending & Real Estate Transactions" 1974; "Some Rights & Disabilities of Aliens" 1975; "Deportation of Aliens - Some Aspects" 1975; "The Creditor, Debtor & the Fourteenth Amendment Some Aspects" 1977. **CONTACT ADDRESS** Law Sch, Florida State Univ, Tallahassee, FL 32306.

GRIFFITH, GWENDOLYN
DISCIPLINE ALTERNATIVE DISPUTE RESOLUTION; FAMILY LAW; FEDERAL TAXATION **EDUCATION** Rollins Col, BA, 78; Stanford Univ, JD, 81. **CAREER** Attache de Recherche, Europ Univ Inst, Florence, 81-82; assoc, Akin, Gump, Strauss, Hauer & Feld, Dallas, 82-86; asst prof, Fla State Univ, 86-87; assoc prof, 87-93; prof, 93-. **MEMBERSHIPS** Mem, Stanford Law Rev. **SELECTED PUBLICATIONS** Co-auth, Corporate Taxation, 92; editor-in-ch, Stanford Jour Intl Law. **CONTACT ADDRESS** Sch of Law, Willamette Univ, 900 State St, Salem, OR 97301. **EMAIL** ggriffit@willamette.edu

GRIFFITH, R. MARIE
PERSONAL Born 05/07/1967, TN, m, 1995, 2 children **DISCIPLINE** RELIGION **EDUCATION** Univ Va, BA, 89; Harvard Univ, MA, 92; PhD, 95. **CAREER** Lectr, assoc dir, Princeton Univ. **HONORS AND AWARDS** Phi Beta Kappa; Mellon Fel; Northwestern Univ Writing Fel. **MEMBERSHIPS** Am Acad of Relig; Am Studies Assoc; Org of Am Hist. **RESEARCH** Religion and gender in American culture, Women, the Body. **SELECTED PUBLICATIONS** Auth, God's Daughters: Evangelical Women and the Power of Submission, Univ of Calif Pr, (Berkeley), 97; auth, "The Promised Land of Weight Loss: Law and Gospel in Christian Dieting", Christian Century 114.15, (97): 448-454; auth, "The Affinities Between Feminists and Evangelical Women", Chronicle of Higher Educ 17, (97): B6-7; auth, "Submissive Wives, Wounded Daughters, and Female Soldiers: Prayer and Christian Womanhood in Women's Aglow Fellowship", Lived Religion in America: Toward a History of Practice, ed David D. Hall, Princeton Univ Pr, (97): 160-195; auth, "Revising Our Assessment of Evangelical Women", Tikkun 13.2 (98): 18-19; auth, "Joy Unspeakable and Full of Glory": The Vocabulary of Pious Emotion in the Narratives of American Pentecostal Women, 1910-1945", An Emotional History of the United States, ed Peter Stearns and Jan Lewis, NYU Pr, (NY, 98): 218-240; auth, "Fasting, Dieting, and the Body in American Christianity", Perspectives on American Religion and Culture, ed Peter W. Williams, Basil Blackwell (Malden, MA 99): 216-227; auth, "Apostles of Abstinence: Fasting and Masculinity During the Progressive Era", Am Quart, (forthcoming); auth, Diet, Discipline and Devotion: Christianity and the Body in American Culture, Univ of Calif Pr, (forthcoming). **CONTACT ADDRESS** Dept Relig, Princeton Univ, 1879 Hall, Princeton, NJ 08544. **EMAIL** griffith@princeton.edu

GRIFFITH, STEPHEN R.
PERSONAL Born 07/01/1943, Williamsport, PA, m, 1965, 4 children **DISCIPLINE** PHILOSOPHY **EDUCATION** Cornell Univ, AB, 66; Univ Pittsburgh, MA, 68, PhD, 73. **CAREER** Prof, philos, Lycoming Col, 70-. **HONORS AND AWARDS** Phi Beta Kappa, Cornell; Phi Sigma Tau; Phi Kappa Phi; NDEA Title IV Fel; Andrew Mellon Fel; Woodrow Wilson Dissertation Fel; NEH Summer Seminars. **MEMBERSHIPS** Amer Philos Asn; Soc of Christ Philos. **RESEARCH** Philosophy of religion; Philosophy of science; Ethics; Political philosophy; Philosophy of mind. **SELECTED PUBLICATIONS** Auth, Miracles and the Shroud of Turin, Faith and Philos; vol 13, no 1, jan, 96; auth, Could It Have Been Reasonable For the Disciples to Have Believed That Jesus Had Risen From the Dead?, Jour of Philos Res, vol XXI, 96; auth, Fetal Death, Fetal Pain, and the Morality of Abortion, Pub Affairs Quart, vol 9, no 2, apr, 95; auth, Prayer in Public School, Pub Affairs Quart, vol 1, no 2, 97-109, apr, 87; auth, How Not to Argue About Abortion, Philos Res Archives, vol XI, 347-354, mar, 86; rev, The Actor and the Spectator, Philos Rev, vol 86, 418-421, jul, 77. **CONTACT ADDRESS** 136 Huffman Av., Williamsport, PA 17701. **EMAIL** griffith@uplink.net

GRIFFITH, THOMAS D.
DISCIPLINE TAXATION **EDUCATION** Brown Univ, AB,71; Harvard Univ, MAT,72, JD,82. **CAREER** John B. Milliken prof, Univ Southern Calif; private practice, Boston. **RESEARCH** Contracts, corporate taxation, criminal law &federal income tax. **SELECTED PUBLICATIONS** Auth, Do Three Strikes Make Sense? Habitual Offender Statutes as a Method of Crime Control & Theories of Personal Deductions in the Income Tax; coauth, Fed Income Tax: Examples & Explanation; Social Welfare & the Rate Structure: A New Look at Progressive Taxation. **CONTACT ADDRESS** School of Law, Univ of So California, University Park Campus, Los Angeles, CA 90089.

GRIGG, RICHARD M.
PERSONAL Born 01/10/1955, Cherokee, IA, m, 1975, 2 children **DISCIPLINE** RELIGIOUS STUDIES **EDUCATION** Univ Iowa, BA, 76; Drew Univ, MDiv, 79; Univ Iowa, PhD, 84. **CAREER** From Asst Prof to Prof, Sacred Heart Univ, 85-. **HONORS AND AWARDS** Phi Beta Kappa; Mellon Post-Doctoral Fel, Univ of Rochester. **MEMBERSHIPS** Am Acad of Relig, N Am Paul Tillich Soc. **RESEARCH** Contemporary Western religious thought. **SELECTED PUBLICATIONS** Auth, Symbol and Empowerment: Paul Tillich's Post-Theistic System, Mercer Univ Press (Macon, GA), 85; auth, Theology as a Way of Thinking, Am Acad of Rel and Soc of Bibl Lit Ventures in Relig 1, Scholars Press (Atlanta, GA), 90; auth, When God Becomes Goddess: The Transformation of American Religion, Continuum (NY), 95; auth, Imaginary Christs: The Challenge of Christological Pluralism, SUNY Press (Albany), 00. **CONTACT ADDRESS** Dept Philos and Relig, Sacred Heart Univ, 5151 Park Ave, Fairfield, CT 06432-1023. **EMAIL** griggr@sacredheart.edu

GRIGSBY, MARSHALL C.
PERSONAL Born 08/18/1946, Charlotte, NC, m **DISCIPLINE** THEOLOGY **EDUCATION** Morehouse Coll, BA 1968; Univ of Chicago Div Sch, MTh 1970, DMn 1972. **CAREER** Black Legislative Clearing House, exec dir 1970-72; First Unitarian Church of Chicago, assoc minister 1970-75; S Shore Comm Planning Assn, project dir 1972; Assn of Theology Schools, assoc dir 1973-75; Howard Univ School of Religion, asst dean/assoc professor, 76-85; Benedict College, Columbia, SC, President, 85-. **HONORS AND AWARDS** Fellowship recipient So Fellowships Fund Inc 1968-71; Fellowship recipient Fund for Theol Educ Inc 1969-71; Regional Finalist White House Fellows Program 1978. **MEMBERSHIPS** Ordained minister Unitarian Universalist Ch 1970-; mem Soc for the Study of Black Religion 1973-; consult Assn of Theol Schs 1975-; natl selection panel Fund for Theol Educ Inc 1976; consult Religion Div of the Lilly Endowment 1977-; mem Natl Counc of Negro Women 1979-; member, Columbia City Board of South Carolina National; member, Junior Achievement of Greater Columbia; board of trustees, ETV Endowment of South Carolina. **CONTACT ADDRESS** Benedict Col, Harden & Blanding St, Columbia, SC 29204.

GRILLO, LAURA
PERSONAL Born 08/22/1956, New York, NY, m, 1998 **DISCIPLINE** HISTORY OF RELIGIONS **EDUCATION** Brown Univ, Ab, 78; Union Theol Sem NYork, MDiv, 86; Univ Chica-

go, PhD, 95. **CAREER** Asst prof, Millsaps Coll, 95-97; Sr Fel, Inst for Advanced Study of Rel, Univ Chicago, 97-98; Vis Asst Prof, Coll Wooster, 98-99; Adj Prof, Pacifica Grad Institute, 00; Vis Res Assoc, Univ Calif, Los Angeles, 99-00. **HONORS AND AWARDS** Charles M Ross Trust grants 80-84, 89-90; Joseph M Kitagawa Scholar, Awd in Hist of Rel, 87-88; Jr Fel, Inst for Advanced Study of Rel, 92-93; am Acad of Rel grant, 96; west African Res Asn grant, 97; Nat Endowment for Humanities grant, 97; Inst for Advanced Study of Rel, Univ Chicago Sr Fel, 97-98. **MEMBERSHIPS** Am Acad of Rel; African Studies Asn; West African Res Asn; Int Asn of Hist of Rel; am Asn Univ Prof. **RESEARCH** Method and theory of the Study of Religions; African Religions; Anthropology; Comparative Ethics; Philosophy of religion. **SELECTED PUBLICATIONS** Auth, African Traditional Religions, Encarta Encycl, 97; Divination in Contemporary Urban West Africa, Rel Study News, 98; The Body in African Religions, Purification, The Circle and African Religions, Encycl of Women and World Rel, forthcoming; Dogon: religionsgeschichtlich, Rel in Geschichte und Gegenwart, forthcoming. **CONTACT ADDRESS** 1320 Riviera Dr, Pasadena, CA 91107. **EMAIL** lsgrillo@earthlink.net

GRIM, JOHN A.
PERSONAL Born 10/07/1946, ND, m, 1978 **DISCIPLINE** HISTORY OF RELIGION **EDUCATION** St. John's Univ, BA, 68; Fordham Univ, MA, 75, PhD, 79. **CAREER** Adj lectr, Col of Mt St Vincent, 76-79; adj lectr, St Francis Col, 79; adj lectr, Col of New Rochelle, 79-80; vis prof, Fordham Univ, 79-80; vis prof, Maryknoll Grad Sch of Theol, 80-81; assoc prof, Elizabeth Seton Col, 77-87; Hum Div, Sarah Lawrence Col, 86-89; assoc prof, 89-98, Prof, Chair Relig Dept, Bucknell Univ, 98-; Coord, Forum on Relig and Ecology, 96-. **HONORS AND AWARDS** V.Kann-Rasmussen Awd, 98; Aga Khan Trust for Culture Grant, 98; Sacharuna Found Grant, 97; Laurance Rockefeller Found Grant, 97; Sr Fel, Center for the Study of World Religions, Harvard Univ, Spring 97. **SELECTED PUBLICATIONS** Auth, The Shaman: Patterns of Siberian and Ojibway Healing, Civilization of the Am Indian Series, Univ of Okla Press, 83, 87; Native North and South American Mystical Traditions, An Anthology of Mysticism, Univ of Calif Press, 00; An Awful Feeling of Loneliness: Native North American Mystical Traditions, Doors of Understanding: Conversations on Global Spirituality in Honor of Ewert Cousins, Franciscan Press, 97; A Comparative Study in Native American Philanthropy, Philanthropy and Culture: A Comparative Perspective, Indiana Univ Press, 97; Rituals Among Native Americans, Handbook in Anthrop of Relig, Greenwood Press, 97; co-ed, Worldviews and Ecology: Religion, Philosophy, and the Environment, Bucknell Univ Press, 93, Orbis Press, 94. **CONTACT ADDRESS** Dept of Relig, Bucknell Univ, Lewisburg, PA 17837. **EMAIL** grim@bucknell.edu

GRIM, PATRICK
PERSONAL Born 10/29/1950, Pasadena, CA, m, 1998 **DISCIPLINE** PHILOSOPHY **EDUCATION** Univ Calif, Santa Cruz, AB(philos), 71, AB(anthrop), 71; Univ St Andrews BPhil, 75; Boston Univ, MA and PhD(philos), 76. **CAREER** ASST PROF PHILOS, STATE UNIV NY, STONY BROOK, 78-85; ASSOC PROF, PHILOS, STATE UNIV NY, STONY BROOK, 85-94; FULL PROF PHILOS, STATE UNIV NY, STONY BROOK, 94-. **HONORS AND AWARDS** Fulbright fel, 71-72; Mellon fac fel, 77-78; President's Award for Excellence in Teaching, Stony Brook, 88; Chancellor's Award for Excellence in Teaching, SUNY system, 88; Acad of Teachers/ Scholars, 96. **MEMBERSHIPS** Am Philos Asn; Int Asn Phil of Law. **RESEARCH** Logic; ethics; metaphysics; philosophy of religion; computer modeling. **SELECTED PUBLICATIONS** ed, Founding editor, 23 volumes of The Philosopher's Annual, 76-; ed, Philosophy of Science and the Occult, 82, 91; auth, The Incomplete Universe: Totality, Knowledge, and Truth, MIT Press, 91; auth, Operators in the Paradox of the Knower, Synthese, Vol 0094, 93; auth, Self-Reference and Chaos in Fuzzy Logics, IEEE Transactions Fuzzy Systems, 93; auth, Operators in the Paradox of the Knower, Synthese, 93; auth, Undecidability in the Spatialized Prisoner's Dilemma, Theory and Decision 97; auth, The Philosophical Computer: Exploratory Essays in Philosophical Computer Modeling, with Mar and St. Denis, MIT Press, 98. **CONTACT ADDRESS** Dept Philos, SUNY, Stony Brook, Stony Brook, NY 11794-3750. **EMAIL** pgrim@notes.cc.sunysb.edu

GRIMES, JOHN A.
PERSONAL Born 01/24/1948, Berkeley, CA, m, 1979, 1 child **DISCIPLINE** RELIGIOUS STUDIES **EDUCATION** Univ Calif, BA, 77; Univ Madras, MA, 80; PhD, 85. **CAREER** Prof, Nat Univ Singapore, 93-95; Prof, Mich St Univ, 97-. **MEMBERSHIPS** APA, AAR, AAS, IPA, ISIP, SACP. **RESEARCH** Hinduism, Classical Indian philosophy, ancient Indian education. **SELECTED PUBLICATIONS** Auth, Ganapati: Song of the Self, SUNY Pr (Albany, NY), 95; auth, A Concise Dictionary of Indian Philosophy, Rev Ed, SUNY Pr (Albany, NY), 96; auth, "Hinduism," in South Asian Relig (Routledge, forthcoming); auth, "Dasana," in The Hindu World (Routledge, forthcoming). **CONTACT ADDRESS** Dept Relig, Michigan State Univ, 116 Morrill Hall, East Lansing, MI 48824. **EMAIL** grimesj@pilot.msu.edu

GRIMES, RONALD L.
PERSONAL Born 05/19/1943, San Diego, CA, m, 1984, 2 children **DISCIPLINE** RELIGION **EDUCATION** Ky Wesleyan Col, BA, 61; Emory Univ, MDiv, 64; Columbia Univ & Union Theol Sem, PhD, 70. **CAREER** Asst prof, Lawrence Univ, 70-74; prof Relig & Culture, Wilfrid Laurier Univ, 74-; vis prof, Univ Pittsburgh, 85-86; vis prof, Univ Notre Dame, 87; vis prof, Univ Colo, 92-94. **HONORS AND AWARDS** Westview Press award of excellence, 96. **MEMBERSHIPS** Am Acad Rel; Am Anthro Asn; Can Soc Study Rel; Soc Cult Anthro; Soc for Study Native Am Rel Traditions. **RESEARCH** Ritual studies; relig and the arts, especially biography, autobiography, and performing arts; anthrop of relig, especially Native religions in the southwestern U.S.A; Christianity in North Am, especially involving cultural conflict; new religious movements in North Am, especially their ritual practices; psychology of relig, insofar as it relates to ritual, especially rites of passate and healing rites, and lifestories. **SELECTED PUBLICATIONS** Auth, The Divine Imagination, 72; auth, Symbol and Conquest, 76, 2nd ed, 92; auth, Beginnings in Ritual Studies, 82, 2nd ed, 94; auth, Research in Ritual Studies, 85; auth, Ritual Criticism, 90; auth, Reading, Writing and Ritualizing, 93; auth, Marrying & Burying, 95; auth, Readings in Ritual Studies, 96. **CONTACT ADDRESS** Dept of Relig & Culture, Wilfrid Laurier Univ, 75 Univ Ave W, Waterloo, ON, Canada N2L 3C5. **EMAIL** rgrimes@wlu.ca

GRIMSHAW, JAMES
PERSONAL Born 12/10/1940, Kingsville, TX, m, 1961, 2 children **DISCIPLINE** ENGLISH, PHILOSOPHY **EDUCATION** Tex Tech Univ, BA, 62; MA, 68; La State Univ, PhD, 72. **CAREER** Asst prof to prof, USAF Acad, 72-83; Head, E Tex State Univ, 83-90; prof, Tex A&M Univ, 90. **HONORS AND AWARDS** Flannery O'Connor Vis Prof, Ga Col, 77; Fac Senate Distinguished Fac Awd, E Tex State Univ, 88; Poet Magazine Editor's Choice Awd, 92; Tex Asn of Col Teachers Distinguished Fac Teaching Awd, 93; Honor Prof of the Yeard Awd, 93; Fac Senate Distinguished Fac Awd, 95; Regents Prof, 95; Tex A&m Univ System Regents Prof Serv Awd, 97. **MEMBERSHIPS** Soc for the Study of S Lit; Bibliog Soc of the Univ of Va; SCMLA; Col Teachers of English; Bibliog Soc of Am; Robert Penn Warren Circle; Am Lit Assoc; Assoc of Lit Scholars and Critics; Assoc of Teachers of Technical Writing. **RESEARCH** Southern Literature, Bibliography, Technical Writing, Moral Philosophy. **SELECTED PUBLICATIONS** Ed, Cleanth Brooks at the United States Air Force Academy, USAF Acad, 80; auth, The Flannery O'Connor Companion, Greenwood, (westport, CT), 81; auth, Robert Penn Warren: A Descriptive Bibliography, 1922-1979, Univ Pr of Va, 82; ed, Robert Pen Warren's Brother to Dragons: A Discussion, La State univ Pr, (Baton Rouge), 83; ed, Time's Glory: Original Essays on Robert Penn Warren, Univ of Central Ark Pr, 86; ed, The Paul Wells Barrus Lectures, 1983-1989, E Tex State Univ Pr, 90; ed, Robert Penn Warren/Cleanth Brooks: Friends of Their Youth, King Libr Pr, (Lexington), 93; ed, Cleanth Brooks and Robert Penn Warren: A Literary Correspondence, Univ of Mo Pr, (Columbia), 98; coed, Robert Penn Warren's All the Kings Men: Three Stage Versions, Univ of Ga Pr, (Athens), 00. **CONTACT ADDRESS** Dept Lang and Lit, Texas A&M Univ, Commerce, PO Box 3011, Commerce, TX 75429-3011. **EMAIL** james_grimshaw@tamu-commerce.edu

GRIMSRUD, THEODORE G.
DISCIPLINE THEOLOGY & PHILOSOPHY **EDUCATION** Univ OR, BS, 76; Assoc Mennonite Biblical Sem, MA, 83; Grad Theol Union, PhD, 88. **CAREER** Theol Dept, Eastern Mennonite Univ **SELECTED PUBLICATIONS** Auth, Triumph of the Lamb, Herald Press, 87; Peace Theology and the Justice of God in the Book of Revelation, Inst Mennonite Studies, 88; Mennonite Theology and Historical Consciousness: A Pastoral Perspective, Mennonite Theol Face Modernity, 96. **CONTACT ADDRESS** Eastern Mennonite Univ, 1200 Park Road, Harrisonburg, VA 22802-2462.

GRISEZ, GERMAIN
PERSONAL Born 09/30/1929, University Heights, OH, m, 1951, 4 children **DISCIPLINE** THEOLOGY **EDUCATION** John Carroll Univ, AB, 51; Dominican Col St Thomas Aquinas, River Forest, Ill, MA, 51, PhL, 51; Univ Chicago, PhD, 59. **CAREER** Archbishop Harry J. Flynn Prof of Christian Ethics, Mount St Mary's Col and Sem, Emmitsburg, Md, 79-. **HONORS AND AWARDS** De Rance, Inc: grants in support of research, 80, 81, 82; Fel of Cath Scholars, special Awd in recognition of scholarly work, 81; the Cardinal Wright Awd for service to the Church, 83; Am Cath Philos Asn: exec coun, 68-70, vice-pres, 82-83, pres, 83-84; founding mem, Fel of Cath Scholars. **MEMBERSHIPS** Cath Theol Soc of Am, Am Cath Philos Asn, Fel of Cath Scholars. **RESEARCH** Moral Theology of Priesthood and Religious Life. **SELECTED PUBLICATIONS** Auth, "Legalism, Moral Truth, and Pastoral Practice," Anthropotes, 6 (90): 111-21; coauth with Russell Shaw, Fulfillment in Christ: A Summary of Christian Moral Principles, Notre Dame: Univ of Notre Dame Press (91); auth, "When Do People Begin?," in Abortion: A New Generation of Catholic Responses, ed Stephen J. Heaney, Braintree, Mass: The Pope John Center (92); auth, with the help of Joseph Boyle, Jeanette Grisez, Russell Shaw, and other, The Way of the Lord Jesus, vol 2, Quincy, Ill: Franciscan Press (93); auth, "The Christian Family as Fulfillment of Sacramental Marriage," Studies in Christian Ethics, 9, 1 (spring 96): 23-33; auth with the help of Joseph Boyle, John Finnis, Jeanette Grisez, Russell Shaw, and others, The Way of the Lord Jesus, vol 3, Difficult Moral Questions, Quincy, Ill: Franciscan Press (97). **CONTACT ADDRESS** Flynn Chair in Christian Ethics, Mount St. Mary's Col, 16300 Old Emmitsburg Rd, Emmitsburg, MD 21727-7799. **EMAIL** grisez@msmary.edu

GRITSCH, ERIC W.
PERSONAL Born 04/19/1931, Neuhaus, Austria, m, 1955 **DISCIPLINE** RELIGION, HISTORY **EDUCATION** Yale Univ, STM, 55, MA, 58, PhD(relig), 60; Univ Vienna, BD, 56. **CAREER** Instr Bible, Wellesley Col, 59-61; PROF CHURCH HIST, LUTHERAN THEOL SEM, GETTYSBURG, 61-, DIR INST LUTHER STUDIES, 70-, Asn Am Theol Schs fel, Univ Heidelberg, 67-68; rep scholar, Lutheran-Roman Cath Dialog in USA, 72-. **MEMBERSHIPS** Am Soc Church Hist; Am Soc Reformation Res; AAUP. **RESEARCH** German Reformation to 1900; European history of theology; Thomas Muenzer and Martin Luther. **SELECTED PUBLICATIONS** **CONTACT ADDRESS** Dept of Church History, Gettysburg Col, Gettysburg, PA 17325.

GROARKE, LEO A.
PERSONAL Born 07/18/1953, London, England **DISCIPLINE** PHILOSOPHY **EDUCATION** Univ Calgary, BA, 75, MA, 77; Univ Western Ont, PhD, 82. **CAREER** Fac mem, 83-94, prof Philosophy, Wilfrid Laurier Univ, 94-. **MEMBERSHIPS** Can Philos Asn; Int Soc Stud Argumentation; Concerned Philos Peace. **RESEARCH** History of philosophy, logic, & ethics. **SELECTED PUBLICATIONS** Co-ed, Nuclear War: Philosophical Perspectives, New York: Peter Lang, 85, 2nd printing 87; auth, Greek Scepticism: Anti-Realist Trends in Ancient Thought, Kingston, Montreal: McGill-Queen's Univ Press, 90; auth, "Prakticheckii razum I polemika vokrug pornographii," ("Pratical Reason and Pornography"), in R. Apresyan, ed. Morality and Rationality, (Moscow: Russian Academy of Sciences, 95); auth, Good Reasoning Matters!, Toronto: Oxford Univ Press, 97; co-ed; Argumentation and Advocacy, Special Issue on Visual Argumentation, 97; auth, "Skepticism, Ancient," and "Logic, Informal", articles in the Stanford World Wide Web Encyclopedia of Philosophy; auth, "There's (Virtually) Nothing New Under the Sun," a commentary on the social consequences of virtual reality, (forthcoming in Technology Studies); coauth, "Seven Principles for Better Practical Ethics," (forthcoming in Teaching Philos); auth, "Logic, Art and Argument," (forthcoming in Informal Logic). **CONTACT ADDRESS** Dept of Philosophy, Wilfrid Laurier Univ, Waterloo, ON, Canada N2L 3C5. **EMAIL** lgroarke@wlu.ca

GROFMAN, BERNARD N.
PERSONAL Born 12/02/1944, Houston, TX **DISCIPLINE** POLITICAL SCIENCE, SOCIAL PSYCHOLOGY **EDUCATION** Univ Chicago, BS, mathematics, 66, MA, political sci, 68, PhD, political sci, 72. **CAREER** Instructor, political sci, 70-71, adjunct asst prof, applied mathematics, 75, asst prof, 71-76, SUNY at Stony Brook; visiting lecturer, political sci, Univ Mannheim (Germany), 73; visiting asst prof, School of Social Scis, visiting asst prof, 75-76; Univ Calif, assoc prof of political sci, 76-80; guest scholar, Brookings Institution, Governmental Studies Program, 84; visiting prof, Univ Wash, Seattle, Dept of Political Sci, 85; fellow, Center for Advanced Study in the Behavioral Sciences, 85-86; visiting prof, Univ Mich, 89; scholar-in-residence, Inst for Legal Studies, Kansai Univ, Japan, 90; prof of political sci and social psychol, Univ Calif, Irvine, 80-. **HONORS AND AWARDS** Pi Sigma Alpha Awd, Best Paper, Annual Meeting of the Midwest Political Science Assn, 79; co-chair, American Political Science Assn, Conf Group on Representation and Electoral Systems, 82-85; Carl B. Allendoerfer Awd (corecipient), for mathematical writing for undergraduates, Mathematical Assn of Am, 85; chair, Amer Political Science Assn, Section on Representation and Electoral Systems, 91-93; designation by the Gustavus Myers Center for the Study of Human Rights in North Amer of Controversies in Minority Voting (book) as one of the outstanding books on intolerance published in North America in 1992; Richard Fenno Prize co-recipient, for the best book published in 1994 in the field of legislative studies (Quiet Revolution in the South) , Legislative Studies Section of the Amer Political Science Assn, 95; Lauds and Laurels Awd for Professional Achievement, UCI Alumni Assn, 95; Awd for Teaching Innovation in the School of Social Sciences, UCI Dean for Undergraduate Education, 96. **MEMBERSHIPS** Chair, American Political Science Assn, Section on Representation and Electoral Systems, 91-93; Inst for Math and Behavioral Sci, 90-. **RESEARCH** Mathematical models of group and individual decision making with a focus on electoral behavior and voter choice and issues connected with representation and redistricting; individual and group information processing and decision heuristics; political propaganda, particularly political cartooning and satire; law and social science, particularly in the domain of civil rights; use of computers as a teaching aid. **SELECTED PUBLICATIONS** Ed, Political Gerrymandering and the Courts, 90; co-editor, Controversies in Minority Voting: The Voting Rights Act in Perspective, 92; ed, Information, Participation and Choice: An Economic Theory of Democracy in Perspective, 93; co-editor, Quiet Revolution in the South: The Voting Rights Act, 1965-1990, 94; ed, Legisla-

tive Term Limits: Public Choice Perspectives, 96; ed, Race and Redistricting, 98. **CONTACT ADDRESS** Dept of Political Science, Univ of California, Irvine, 3151 Social Science Plaza, Irvine, CA 92697-5100. **EMAIL** bgrofman@uci.edu

GROMADA, CONRAD T.
PERSONAL Born 01/18/1939, Youngstown, OH, m, 1987 **DISCIPLINE** ROMAN CATHOLIC THEOLOGY; SYSTEMATIC THEOLOGY **EDUCATION** Duquesne Univ, Pittsburgh, PhD, 88. **CAREER** Dean Arts & Sciences, Ursuline Col. **MEMBERSHIPS** Am Acad Relig; Col Theol Soc; Cath Theol Soc Am **RESEARCH** Sacraments; Ecclesiology; Christology. **SELECTED PUBLICATIONS** Auth, Theology of Ministry in the Lima Document: A Roman Catholic Critique, Int Scholars Press, 95. **CONTACT ADDRESS** Ursuline Col, 2550 Lander Rd., Pepper Pike, OH 44124-4398. **EMAIL** cgromada@ursuline.edu

GRONBACHER, GREGORY
PERSONAL Born 05/27/1965, New York, NY, s **DISCIPLINE** PHILOSOPHY **EDUCATION** Milltown Institute of Theology and Philosophy, PhD, 95. **CAREER** Asst prof of theology and philosophy, Mt Aloysius Col, 94-95; Dir of Academic Research, Acton Institute, 95- . **RESEARCH** Philosophy of economics; social theory; Catholic social thought. **CONTACT ADDRESS** 161 Ottawa NW, #301, Grand Rapids, MI 49503. **EMAIL** ggbacher@acton.org

GROOME, THOMAS H.
PERSONAL Born 09/30/1945, Dublin, Ireland, m, 1985, 1 child **DISCIPLINE** RELIGIOUS EDUCATION **EDUCATION** St Patrick's Sem IR, Mdiv (equiv.), 68; Fordham Univ, MA, Rel/Edu, 71; Union Theol SEM, Doc Rel/Edu, 75. **CAREER** Prof Theol, presently, Boston College. **HONORS AND AWARDS** The Emmaus Awd for Catechetical Leadership from NPCD, 99; Leadership in Catechesis award from NCCL, 97. **MEMBERSHIPS** AAR; CTSA; APRRE. **RESEARCH** Interface of Ideology and Contemporary Culture. **SELECTED PUBLICATIONS** Auth, Educating for Life: A Spiritual Vision for Every Teacher and Parent, Allen TX, Thomas Moore Press, 98; auth, Christian Religious Education: Sharing Our Story and Vision, San Francisco: Jossey Bass, 98; Language for a Catholic Church, KA City, Sheed and Ward, 91; primary auth of new revised, Coming to Faith, series, WH Sadlier, 95. **CONTACT ADDRESS** Inst of Religious Education, Boston Col, Chestnut Hill, Chestnut Hill, MA 02167. **EMAIL** groomet@bc.edu

GROOTHUIS, DOUGLAS
PERSONAL m **DISCIPLINE** PHILOSOPHY OF RELIGION AND ETHICS **EDUCATION** Univ Wis-Madison, MA; Univ Ore, PhD. **CAREER** Prof, Denver Sem, 93-. **MEMBERSHIPS** Society of Christian Philosophers, Evangelical Theological Society, Evangelical Philophical Society, Am Philophical Assoc. **SELECTED PUBLICATIONS** Auth, Unmasking the New Age; Confronting the New Age; Christianity That Counts; Deceived by the Light; Jesus in an Age of Controversy and The Soul in Cyberspace; Truth Decay, pub(s), scholarly jour(s), Rel Stud, Sophia, Jour of the Evangel Theol Soc, Trinity Jour; Christianity Today; Moody Magazine; Christian Res Jour; Revealing The New Age Jesus. **CONTACT ADDRESS** Denver Conservative Baptist Sem, PO Box 100000, Denver, CO 80250. **EMAIL** doug@densem.edu

GROS, JEFFREY
PERSONAL Born 01/07/1938, Memphis, TN **DISCIPLINE** THEOLOGY **EDUCATION** Marquette Univ, MA, 65; Forham Univ, PhD, 73. **CAREER** Seminary/Univ teaching, Christian Brothers Univ/Memphis Theol Sem, 72-81; ecumenical administration, Faith and Order, Nat Coun of Churches, 81-91; Ecumenical Affairs, Nat Conf of Cath Bishops, 91-. **HONORS AND AWARDS** Chicago Heart Asn, fel, 60, 61; Cath Diocesean Ecumenical Officers Awd, 84. **MEMBERSHIPS** Cath Theol Soc; Col Theol Soc; Am Academy Relig; Nat Asn of Evangelicals; North Am Academy of Ecumenists; Soc for Pentecostal Studies. **RESEARCH** Ecclesiology: Catholicism, the Reformation Churches, Am Evangelicalism; Sacramental Theol: Eucharist, Ministry, Baptism; Church History: Reformation, US churches, ecumenism. **SELECTED PUBLICATIONS** Ed, The Search for Visible Unity, Pilgrim Press, 84; Building Unity, co-ed with Joseph Burgess, Paulist Press, 89; Growing Consensus, co-ed with Joseph Burgess, Paulist Press, 94; Common Witness to the Gospel, Documents on Anglican-Roman Catholic Relations 1983-1995, co-ed with Rozanne Elder and Elen Wondra, US Catholic Conf, 97; Deepening Communion, co-ed with William G Rusch, US Cath Conf, 98; co-auth, with Ann Riggs, Eamon McManus, Introduction to Ecumenism, Paulist Press, 98; auth, Challenges to Lasallian Leadership in Christian Reconciliation, Lasalliana, 44, May-August 98; A Pilgrimage Together: Ecumenical Decisions before US Churches, Catechetical Leadership, Dec 98; Grace: A Challenge Together for Lutherans and Catholics, Catechetical Leadership, April/May 98; Toward a More Perfect Communion: Ecumenical Agreement and Sacramental Preparation, Catechetical Leadership, summer 98; author of numerous other articles. **CONTACT ADDRESS** Secretariat for Ecumen & Interre, National Conf of Catholic Bishops, 3211 4th St NE, Washington, DC 20017. **EMAIL** seia@uscb.org

GROSS, KAREN
DISCIPLINE LAW **EDUCATION** Smith Col, BA, 74; Temple Univ Sch Law, JD, 77. **CAREER** Prof, NYork Law Sch, 89-. **HONORS AND AWARDS** Otto Walter Fac Writing Awd, 97; Pro Bono Serv Awd, NY Legal Aid Soc, 99; Godfrey Distinguished Lectr, Univ Maine, 00; Fel, ACB, 00. **MEMBERSHIPS** AALS, ABA, ABCNY, AAA, ABI. **SELECTED PUBLICATIONS** Coauth, Collier on Bankruptcy, 15th rev ed, 96; auth, Failure and Forgiveness: Rebalancing the Bankruptcy System, Yale UP, 97; auth, "Perceptions and Misperceptions of Reaffirmation Agreements," 102 Comm L J 339 (97); auth, "On the Merits: A Response to Professors Girth and White," 73 Am Bankr L J 485 (99); rev, "The Ethics of Bankruptcy," by Jukka Kilpi, 26 J of Law and Soc 555 (99); auth, Ladies in Red: Women Debtors from 1800-2000, forthcoming. **CONTACT ADDRESS** Dept Law, New York Law Sch, 57 Worth St, New York, NY 10013-2960. **EMAIL** kgross@nyls.edu

GROSS, NANCY LAMMERS
PERSONAL Born St. Louis, MO, m, 2 children **DISCIPLINE** HOMILETICS **EDUCATION** Willamette Univ, BS; Princeton Theol Sem, MDiv, PhD. **CAREER** Assoc prof, E Baptist Theol Sem. **HONORS AND AWARDS** Parish assoc, First Presbyterian Church of Plainsboro, New Jersey **MEMBERSHIPS** Mem, Acad of Homilectics. **CONTACT ADDRESS** Eastern Baptist Theol Sem, 6 Lancaster Ave, Wynnewood, PA 19096.

GROSS, RITA M.
PERSONAL Born 07/06/1943, Rhinelander, WI **DISCIPLINE** HISTORY OF RELIGIONS **EDUCATION** Univ Wis-Milwaukee, BA, 65; Univ Chicago, MA, 68, PhD(hist relig), 75. **CAREER** Instr theol, Loyola Univ, Chicago, 70-71; instr Indian rel, New Col, Fla, 71-73; instr, 73-75, asst prof, 75-80, ASSOC PROF EASTERN RELIG, UNIV WIS-EAU CLAIRE, 80-, Mem, rev bd relig, Anima; An Experiential J, 73- and Nat Endowment Humanities, 77-. **MEMBERSHIPS** Soc Values Higher Educ; Am Acad Relig; Women's Caucus Am Acad Relig. **RESEARCH** Hindu Theism, especially the Hindu Goddesses; Hindu inconography and mythology. **SELECTED PUBLICATIONS** Auth, Why Me--Methodological-Autobiographical Reflections of a Wisconsin Farm Girl Who Became a Buddhist Theologian when She Grew Up, J Feminist Stud in Relig, Vol 0013, 97; Toward a Buddhist Environmental Ethic: Religious Responses to Problems of Population, Consumption, and Degradation of the Global Environment, J Am Acad of Relig, Vol 0065, 97. **CONTACT ADDRESS** Dept of Philos and Relig Studies, Univ of Wisconsin, Eau Claire, Eau Claire, WI 54701.

GROSSI, ELIZABETH L.
PERSONAL Born Canton, OH **DISCIPLINE** CRIMINOLOGY **EDUCATION** Kent State Univ, AA, 81; Columbia Col, BA, 85; Univ Louisville, MS, 89; Ind Univ Pa, PhD, 92. **CAREER** Assoc Prof, Univ of Louisville. **MEMBERSHIPS** Am Soc of Criminol, Acad of Criminal Justice Sci, Southern Criminal Justice Asn. **RESEARCH** Criminology, Corrections, Domestic Violence. **SELECTED PUBLICATIONS** Coauth, "Stress and job dissatisfaction among correctional officers: An unexpected finding," Int J of Offender Ther and Comp Criminol 35-1 (91): 73-81; coauth, Instructor's manual, Criminology: Theory, research and policy, Wadsworth (Belmont, CA), 94; auth, Criminal Justice: Concepts and Issues, 2nd ed, Intructor's Manual and testing prog for C.W. Eskridge, (Los Angeles, CA: Roxbury), 96, 3rd ed, forthcoming; coauth, "Surviving the 'joint': Mitigating factors of correctional officer stress," J of Crime and Justice 19-2 (96): 103-120; coauth, "Student misconduct: Historical trends in legislative and judicial decision-making in American Universities," The J of Col and Univ Law 23-4 (97): 829-853; coauth, "Assessing education gains of boot camp inmates: A preliminary analysis," J of Crime and Justice 21-1 (98): 103-118; auth, "Hate crime gay men and lesbian women: A routine activity approach for predicting victimization risk," Humanity and Soc 23-2 (99): 125-142; coauth, "Intermediate sanctions and the halfway back program in Kentucky," Criminal Justice Policy Rev 9-4 (99): 431-449. **CONTACT ADDRESS** Dept Admin of Justice, Univ of Louisville, 22301 S 3rd St, Louisville, KY 40292-2001. **EMAIL** elgros01@gwise.louisville.edu

GROSSMAN, GEORGE S.
PERSONAL Born 05/31/1938, Czechoslovakia, m, 1960, 1 child **DISCIPLINE** LAW, LIBRARY SCIENCE **EDUCATION** Univ Chicago, BA, 60; Stanford Law School, LIB, 66; Brigham Young Univ, MSLS, 71. **CAREER** Tech Services Librarian, Univ of Pa, 66-68; prof of law and law librn, Univ of Ut, 68-73; prof of law and law librn, Univ of Minn, 73-79; prof of law and law librn, Northwestern Univ, 79-93. **MEMBERSHIPS** Am Asn of Law Libraries. **RESEARCH** Legal research, American legal history. **SELECTED PUBLICATIONS** Auth, Legal Research: Historical Foundations of the Electronic Age, Oxford, 94; auth, The Spirit of American Law, Westview, 99. **CONTACT ADDRESS** School of Law, Univ of California, Davis, 400 Mrak Dr, Davis, CA 95616. **EMAIL** gsgrossman@ucdavis.edu

GROSSMAN, NEAL
PERSONAL Born 12/09/1941, Boston, MA, d, 2 children **DISCIPLINE** PHILOSOPHY **EDUCATION** Univ IN, PhD. **CAREER** Assoc prof, Univ IL at Chicago. **HONORS AND AWARDS** Silver Circle Tchg Awd. **RESEARCH** Spinoza; paranormal psych; mysticism. **SELECTED PUBLICATIONS** Auth, pubs in Journal of Philosophy; Metaphilosophy; Philosophy of Science; and Synthese. **CONTACT ADDRESS** Dept of Philosophy, M/C 267, Univ of Illinois, Chicago, 601 S Morgan St, Chicago, IL 60607-7114. **EMAIL** nealg@uic.edu

GROTH, ALEXANDER J.
PERSONAL Born 03/07/1932, Warsaw, Poland, m, 1961, 2 children **DISCIPLINE** POLITICAL SCIENCE **EDUCATION** CUNY, BA, 54, MA, 55; Columbia Univ, PhD, 60. **CAREER** Instr of Political Sci, CCNY, 60-61; asst prof of Political Sci, Harpur Col, 61-62; Asst Prof to Prof of Political Sce, 62-93, Prof Emeritus, Univ Calif Davis, 93-. **HONORS AND AWARDS** Phi Beta Kappa, Ward Medal, CCNY. **MEMBERSHIPS** APSA; Western Polit Sci Asn; Policy Studies Org; Western Slavic Studies Asn; Heritage Found. **RESEARCH** Comparative Politics. **SELECTED PUBLICATIONS** Auth, Comparative Politics: A Distributive Approach, Macmillan, 71; Major Ideologies: An Interpretative Survey of Democracy, Socialism and Nationalism, John Wiley, 71, Robert Krieger, 83; People's Poland: Government and Politics, Chandler, 72; Lincoln: Authoritarian Savior, Univ Press of Am, 96; Democracies Against Hitler, Ashgate, 99; ed, Revolution and Political Change, Dartmouth Pub Co, 96; co-ed & contribur, Comparative Resource Allocation, Sage, 84; Public Policy Across Nations: Social Welfare in Industrial Settings, JAI Press, 85. **CONTACT ADDRESS** Dept of Political Sci, Univ of California, Davis, Davis, CA 95616.

GROTH, MILES
PERSONAL Born 12/04/1946, Greensburg, PA **DISCIPLINE** PHILOSOPHY; PSYCHOLOGY **EDUCATION** Franklin and Marshall Col, AB; Fordham Univ, PhD. **CAREER** Asst prof, dept of psychology, Wagner Col; existential psychotherapy & psychoanalysis, private practice. **HONORS AND AWARDS** Outstanding Educators in Amer, 76. **MEMBERSHIPS** Amer Philos Asn; Soc Existential Anal; Amer Heidegger Conf; Asn Study Philos Unconscious; Int Soc Phenomenol & Human Sci. **RESEARCH** Heidegger; Existential analysis **SELECTED PUBLICATIONS** Auth, Preparatory Thinking in Heideggers Teaching, Philos Libr, 87; Newsletter of the Society for Existential Analysis, 96; Existential Therapy on Heideggerian Principles, Jour Soc Existential Anal, 97; Some Precursors of Poppers Evolutionary Theory of Knowledge, Philos Sci, 97; Acknowledgement on the Conferment of the National Hebel Memorial Prize, Delos, 97; The Voice That Thinks: Heidegger Studies, Eadmer Press, 97; Listening with the Mind's Ear, Heidegger's Philosophy of Translation, Prometheus Books, 2000. **CONTACT ADDRESS** Dept of Psychology, Wagner Col, 111 Parker Hall, Staten Island, NY 10301. **EMAIL** mgroth@wagner.edu

GROUNDS, VERNON
PERSONAL m, 1939 **DISCIPLINE** ETHICS AND COUNSELING **EDUCATION** Rutgers Univ, BA; Faith Theol Sem, BD; Gordon Col, LHD; Wheaton Col, DD; Drew Univ, PhD. **CAREER** Sr prof, Denver Sem, 79. **HONORS AND AWARDS** Contrib ed, Christianity Today; intl ed, Themelios. **SELECTED PUBLICATIONS** Auth, The Reason for Our Hope; Evangelicalism and Social Responsibility; Revolution and the Christian Faith; Emotional Problems and the Gospel, Radical Commitment; co-auth, Is God Dead? **CONTACT ADDRESS** Denver Conservative Baptist Sem, PO Box 10000, Denver, CO 80250.

GROVER, DOROTHY
DISCIPLINE PHILOSOPHY **EDUCATION** Univ Pittsburgh, PhD. **CAREER** Prof emer, Univ IL at Chicago . **HONORS AND AWARDS** Mellon Postdoctoral Fel from the Univ of Pittsburgh. **RESEARCH** Philosophical logic; philos of lang; metaphysics; epistemology. **SELECTED PUBLICATIONS** Auth, A Prosentential Theory of Truth, Princeton, 92; Truth and Language-World Connections, Journal Philo, 90; Death and Life, Can Jour Philos, 87. **CONTACT ADDRESS** Philos Dept, Univ of Illinois, Chicago, S Halsted St, PO Box 705, Chicago, IL 60607. **EMAIL** grover@uic.edu

GROVER, ROBINSON ALLEN
PERSONAL Born 02/15/1936, New York, NY **DISCIPLINE** PHILOSOPHY **EDUCATION** Yale Univ, BA, 58; Brown Univ, MA, 62, PhD(philos), 69; Yale Univ Law Sch, MA, 76. **CAREER** Instr philos, Univ CT, Storrs, 64-68; Lectr, Chapman Col, World Campus Afloat Prog, 68-69; asst prof, 69-80, Assoc Prof Philos, Univ CT, Torrington, 80-. **MEMBERSHIPS** AAUP; Am Philos Asn; Soc Legal & Polit Philos. **RESEARCH** Thomas Hobbes; Ethics; Philo of Law; Polit Theory. **SELECTED PUBLICATIONS** Auth, The Ranking Assumption, J Theory & Decision, fall 74; The Legal Origins of Thomas Hobbes's Doctrine of Contract," Spring 80; Thomas Hobbes and International Law, 89; Individualism, Absolutism, and Contract in Thomas Hobbes's Political Theory. **CONTACT ADDRESS** Dept of Philosophy, Univ of Connecticut, Torrington, 855 Univ Dr, Torrington, CT 06790-2635. **EMAIL** grover@uconnvm.uconn.edu

GROVES, HARRY EDWARD
PERSONAL Born 09/04/1921, Manitou Springs, CO, m **DISCIPLINE** LAW **EDUCATION** Univ of CO, BA 1943; Univ of Chicago, JD 1949; Harvard Univ, LLM 1959. **CAREER** TX So Univ, dean/sch of law 1956-60; Univ of Singapore, dean/faculty of law 1960-64; Central State Univ, pres 1965-68; Sch of Law of Cincinnati, prof 1968-70; NC Central Univ Durham, dean/sch of law 1976-81; Univ of NC, prof sch of law 1981-86; Memphis State Univ, Herbert Heff visiting prof of law, 89-90; University of Minnesota, visiting professor of law, 92. US Olympic Committee Ethics Committee Chair, 93. **HONORS AND AWARDS** Phi Beta Kappa; Phi Delta Kappa; Kappa Delta Pi; president, Wake County North Carolina Phi Beta Kappa 1989-90; sire archon, Alpha Tau Chapter of Sigma Pi Phi 1986-88; The Constitution of Malaysia, 4th ed. (with Sheridan) 1979; Malayan Law Journal (PTE.) LTD; Tun Abdul Razak Memorial Lecturer, Kuala Lumpur Malaysia 1983; Judge John J Parker Awd, North Carolina Bar Association, 1986; American Bar Association, Robert L Kutak Awd, 1997. **MEMBERSHIPS** Elected mem City Council Fayetteville NC 1951-52; chmn Gov's Task Force on Sec & Privacy 1979-; bd of dir Mutual Svgs & Loan Assn 1979-80; pres NC Prisoner Legal Serv Inc 1979-81; pres Legal Serv of NC 1983-85; mem Sigma Pi Phi, Alpha Phi Alpha Frat; mem NC, TX, OH Bar Assns; vice pres bd of gov NC Bar Assn 1986-87; board of directors, American Bar Foundation, 1986-; member, American Bar Association Council of the Section on Legal Education and Admission to the Bar, 1989-95, sec, 1998-99; board of directors, Law School Admissions Council, 1980-82. **SELECTED PUBLICATIONS** "Comparative Constitutional Law Cases & Materials" Oceana Publs Inc 1963; "The Constitution of Malaysia" Malaysia Publs Ltd 1964; pub more than 30 other books & articles. **CONTACT ADDRESS** 3050 Military Rd NW, Apt 601, Washington, DC 20015.

GRUBB, FARLEY
PERSONAL Born 09/14/1954, Kennewick, WA, m, 1992 **DISCIPLINE** ECONOMICS **EDUCATION** Univ Washington, BA, 77; Univ Chicago, MA, 81, PhD, 84. **CAREER** Asst Prof; Assoc Prof, Prof, 83-93-, Univ Delaware. **MEMBERSHIPS** AEA; EHA; Cliometrics Soc. **RESEARCH** Economic History; Colonial Amer; Contract Labor. **SELECTED PUBLICATIONS** Auth, Lilliputians and Brobdingnagians Stature in British Colonial America: Evidence from Servants, Convicts and Apprentices, Research in Economic Hist, 99; Withering Heights: Did Indentured Servants Shrink from Their Encounter with Malthus?, Econ Hist Rev, 99; Labor Markets and Opportunity: Indentured Servitude in Early America, A Rejoinder to Salinger, Labor Hist, 98; Penal Slavery, in: Seymour Drescher, Stanley Engerman, eds, A Historical Guide to World Slavery, NY Oxford Univ Press, 98; The End of European Immigrant Servitude in the United States: An economic Analysis of Market Collapse 1772-1835, J Econ Hist, 94; German Immigrant Service Contracts Registered at the Port of Philadelphia 1817-1831, Baltimore, Genealogical Pub Co Inc, 94; The Liverpool Emigrant Servant Trade and the Transition to Slave Labor in the Chesapeake 1697-1707: Market Adjustments to War, coed, Explorations in Econ Hist, 94; The Disappearance of Organized Markets for European Immigrant Servants in the United States: Five Popular Explanations Reexamined, Social Science Hist, 94. **CONTACT ADDRESS** Economic Dept, Univ of Delaware, Newark, DE 19716. **EMAIL** grubbf@be.udel.edu

GRUENDER, CARL DAVID
PERSONAL Born 05/24/1927, Cleveland, OH, m, 1955, 3 children **DISCIPLINE** PHILOSOPHY **EDUCATION** Antioch Col, AB, 51; Univ Chicago, AM, 53; Univ Wis, PhD, 57. **CAREER** From instr to asst prof philos, Kans State Univ, 57-63; asst prof, Case Inst Technol, 63-67; assoc prof, 67-71, chmn dept, 72-78, Prof Philos, Fla State Univ, 71-99, Prof Emer, 99-. **MEMBERSHIPS** AAAS; Western Div Am Philos Asn; Philos Sci Asn; Hist Sci Soc. **RESEARCH** Theory of knowledge; philosophy and history of science; metaphysics. **SELECTED PUBLICATIONS** Auth, Wittgenstein on Explanation and Description, J Philos, 62; auth, On Distinguishing Science from Magic, Proc 10th Int Cong Hist Sci, 64; auth, The Achilles Paradox and Transfinite Numbers, Brit J Philos Sci, 66. **CONTACT ADDRESS** Dept of Philosophy, Florida State Univ, Tallahassee, FL 32306-1500. **EMAIL** gruender@phil.fsu.edu

GRUENLER, ROYCE GORDON
PERSONAL Born 01/10/1930, Laconia, NH, m, 4 children **DISCIPLINE** NEW TESTAMENT **EDUCATION** Williams Col, BA; Philadelphia Theol Sem, BD; Kings Col, Univ Aberdeen, Scotland, PhD. **CAREER** Prof, Gordon-Conwell Theol Sem, 79-. **HONORS AND AWARDS** Fulbright Scholar, Kings Col, Univ Aberdeen; post-grad Fulbright res grant, Univ Heidelberg, Ger; sr pastor, second congregational church. **MEMBERSHIPS** Mem, Phi Beta Kappa; Soc Biblical Lit; Evangel Theol Soc. **RESEARCH** Jesus and the Gospels, Romans, Pauline thought and process theology. **SELECTED PUBLICATIONS** Auth, Jesus, Persons, and the Kingdom of God, 67; New Approaches to Jesus and the Gospels, 82; The Inexhaustible God: Biblical Faith and the Challenge of Process Theism, 83; The Trinity in the Gospel of John: A Thematic Commentary on The Fourth Gospel, 86; contrib auth, Process Theology, Baker Bk House, 87; Baker's Evangelical Commentary on the Bible, Mark and Romans, 89; Meaning and Understanding: The Philosophical Framework for Biblical Interpretation, Zondervan, 91. **CONTACT ADDRESS** Gordon-Conwell Theol Sem, 130 Essex St, South Hamilton, MA 01982.

GRUNBAUM, ADOLF
PERSONAL Born 05/15/1923, Cologne, Germany, m, 1949 **DISCIPLINE** PHILOSOPHY **EDUCATION** Wesleyan Univ, BA 43; Yale Univ, MS, 48, PhD(philos), 51. **CAREER** Physicist, Div War Res, Columbia Univ, 44, 46, consult physicist, Div Govt-Aided Res, 46-48; from instr to prof philos, Lehigh Univ, 50-56, Selfridge prof, 56-60; dir, Ctr Philos Sci, 60-78, MELLON PROF PHILOS, UNIV PITTSBURGH, 60-, Chmn Res Prof Psychiat, 79-, Ford Found fac fel, 54-55; res prof, Ctr Philos Sci, Univ Minn, 55-56; Matchette Lectr, Wesleyan Univ, 66; Louis Clark Vanuxem Lectr, Princeton Univ, 67; Monday lectr, Univ Chicago, 68; Thalheimer lectr, Johns Hopkins Univ, 69; lectr hist sci, Univ London, 76; Einstein Centennial lectr, Inst Advan Study, Princeton, 79-80. **HONORS AND AWARDS** Robinson Awd, Lehigh Univ, 53; J Walker Tomb Prize, Princeton Univ, 58. **MEMBERSHIPS** AAAS; Am Acad Arts & Sci; Philos Sci Asn (pres, 65-70); Eastern Div Am Philos Asn (pres, 82). **RESEARCH** Philosophy of physics; philosophy and methodology of the natural sciences; philosophy of psychiatry. **SELECTED PUBLICATIONS** Auth, Narlikar Creation of the Big-Bang Universe Was a Mere Origination--Discussion, Philos of Sci, Vol 0060, 93; 'Freuds Permanent Revolution': A Response to Nagel, Thomas--An Exchange, NY Rev of Bks, Vol 0041, 94; Empirical Evaluations of Theoretical Explanations of Psychotherapeutic Efficacy--A Reply to Greenwood, John, D, Philos of Sci, Vol 0063, 96. **CONTACT ADDRESS** Ctr for Philos of Sci, Univ of Pittsburgh, 1001 Cathedral/Learn, Pittsburgh, PA 15260-0001.

GRUNDY, KENNETH WILLIAM
PERSONAL Born 08/06/1936, Philadelphia, PA, m, 1960, 3 children **DISCIPLINE** POLITICAL SCIENCE **EDUCATION** Ursinus Col, BA, 58; Penn State, MA, 61, PhD, 63. **CAREER** Asst prof, San Fernando Valley State Col, 63-66; Assoc prof, 66-73, prof, 73-88, M A Hanna Prof of Political Science, Case W Reserve Univ, 66-; Dir, Ctr for Policy Studies, CWRU, 98-00. **MEMBERSHIPS** Int Studies Asn; African Studies Ans; Int Consortium Armed Forces & Soc. **RESEARCH** International Relations; Comparative Politics, Africa. **SELECTED PUBLICATIONS** auth Guerrilla Struggle in Africa, 72; Confirmation & Accommodation in Southern Africa, 73; Soldiers without Politics, 83; The Militarization of South African Politics, 86 & 88, South Africa, 91. **CONTACT ADDRESS** Case Western Reserve Univ, Mather House 223, Cleveland, OH 44106-7109. **EMAIL** kwg@po.cwru.edu

GRUNFELD, JOSEPH
PERSONAL Born 08/13/1924, Berlin, Germany, m, 1955, 2 children **DISCIPLINE** PHILOSOPHY **EDUCATION** Hebrew Univ, BA, 52; Hebrew Univ, MA, 55; Hebrew Univ, PhD, 59. **CAREER** Part time lectr, Hebrew Univ, 57-63; asst prof, 63-66, assoc prof, 66-70, Haile Sellassie I Univ, Addis Ababa, Ethiopia; assoc prof, 70-90, prof, 90-, Drexel Univ, Philadelphia, Penn. **MEMBERSHIPS** Amer Philos Asn; Intl Metaphysical Soc; Inst of Human Values. **RESEARCH** Philosophy of logic; Aesthetics. **SELECTED PUBLICATIONS** Auth, Incomplete Coherence, Sci et Espirit, 98; auth, Fuzzy Logic, Sci et Esprit, 95; auth, Conceptual Relevance, B. R. Gruner, Amsterdam, 89; auth, Changing Rational Standards, A Survey of Modern Philosophy of Science, Univ Press of Amer, 85; auth, Method and Lang, B. R. Gruner, Amsterdam, 82; auth, Science and Values, B. R. Gruner, Amsterdam, 73; auth, Soft Logic, The Epistemic Role of Aesthetic Criteria, Univ Press Amer, 00. **CONTACT ADDRESS** Nesbitt College, Drexel Univ, Philadelphia, PA 19104.

GUALTIERI, ANTONIO ROBERTO
PERSONAL Born 03/08/1931, Toronto, ON, Canada, m, 1955, 4 children **DISCIPLINE** COMPARATIVE RELIGION, PHILOSOPHY OF RELIGION **EDUCATION** McGill Univ, BA, 60, BD, 61, STM, 63, PhD(hist of relig), 69. **CAREER** Minister, United Church of Can, 56-64; instr relig, Vassar Col, 65-66, lectr relig and chaplain, 66-67; asst prof, 67-70, assoc prof, 70-81, adj prof, Carleton Univ, 81-, Can Coun res grant, India study, 72-73. **MEMBERSHIPS** Can Soc Studies Relig; Can Theol Soc; Am Acad Relig. **RESEARCH** Methodology and epistemology in religion; religious indigenization and syncretism; religious ethics. **SELECTED PUBLICATIONS** Auth, Religious Cosmologies as Justifications of Moralities, Stud in Relig-Sci Religieuses, Vol 0022, 93; Founders and Apostates: Radical Contradictions between Soteriological Programs of the Founders of Great Religious Traditions and the Transformative Intentions of Devotees, J Am Acad of Relig, Vol 0061, 93. **CONTACT ADDRESS** Dept of Religion, Carleton Univ, 1125 Colonel By Dr, 2014 Dunton Tower, Ottawa, ON, Canada K1S 5B6.

GUDER, DARRELL L.
PERSONAL Born 11/12/1939, Ventura, CA, m, 1979, 5 children **DISCIPLINE** MISSIOLOGY **EDUCATION** Univ Hamburg, PhD, 65; Jamestown Col, DD. **CAREER** Student pastor, Church Schleswig-Holstein, Ger, 64-67; Min Christian Educ, Hollywood First Presby Church, 67-71; prof, Karlshohe Col, Ludwigsburg, Ger, 71-75; dir Inst Youth Min, Filler Theol Sem, 75-85; VP & Acad Dean, Whitworth Col, 85-91; prof, Mission & Evangel, Louisville Presby Theol Sem, 91-97; prof, Evangel & Church Growth, Columbia Theol Sem, 97-. **MEMBERSHIPS** Am Soc Missiologists, Am Acad Relig, Asn Prof of Mission, Inter Asn Mission Student. **RESEARCH** North America & Europe as Mission Fields, Gospel & Culture. **SELECTED PUBLICATIONS** Auth, Mission Church: A Vision for the Sending of the Church in N. America, 98; coauth, Historical Dictionary of Reformed Churches, 99; auth, The Continuing Conversion of the Church. **CONTACT ADDRESS** Columbia Theol Sem, PO Box 520, Decatur, GA 30031-0520. **EMAIL** Guder@CTSnet.edu

GUDORF, CHRISTINE E.
PERSONAL Born 06/13/1949, Louisville, KY, m, 1968, 3 children **DISCIPLINE** RELIGION **EDUCATION** IN Univ BS 71; Columbia Univ, MA 76, Mphil 78, PhD 79. **CAREER** Xavier Univ, asst prof, assoc prof, prof 78-93; FL Intl Univ, assoc prof, 93-95, prof dept rel stud 95-. **HONORS AND AWARDS** Visiting Professorships, Temple Univ, Pacific Sch of Rel, Seminario San Jose in Peru, Cath Press Awds, Gutavus Meyer Awd. **MEMBERSHIPS** AAR; SCE; CTSA. **RESEARCH** Ethics in world relig soc theory; Women in world relig(s), sexuality, economic develop. **SELECTED PUBLICATIONS** Body, Sex and Pleasure: Reconstructing Christian Sexual Ethics, Pilgrim, 94; Christian Ethics: A Case Method Approach, 2d ed, with R Stivers, R Evans, A Evans, Orbis, 94; Sacrifice and Mutuality In Catholic Spirituality, US Catholic, 97; Probing the Politics of Difference, Journal of Religious Ethics, Fall 1999; Our Increasing Prospects for Reproductive, Union Seminary Quarterly Review, 53: 5-4, 1999; Ethics and World Religions: Crosscultural Case Studies, with Regina Wolfe, Orbis 99. **CONTACT ADDRESS** Dept of Relig Studies, Florida Intl Univ, Miami, FL 33199. **EMAIL** gordorf@fiu.edu

GUERRIERE, DANIEL
PERSONAL Born 03/02/1941, Latrobe, PA, s **DISCIPLINE** PHILOSOPHY **EDUCATION** Duquesne Univ, PhD, 72. **CAREER** Prof, Calif State Univ Long Beach, 69-. **MEMBERSHIPS** SPEP, ACPA, Jaspers Soc. **RESEARCH** Phenomenology, Philosophy of Religion, Philosophy of Politics, Metaphysics. **SELECTED PUBLICATIONS** Ed, Phenomenology of the Truth Proper to Religion. **CONTACT ADDRESS** Dept Philos, California State Univ, Long Beach, 1250 N Bellflower Rd, Mhb 917, Long Beach, CA 90840-0006. **EMAIL** dguerr@csulb.edu

GUIGNON, CHARLES B.
PERSONAL Born 02/01/1944, Amarillo, TX, m, 1998, 2 children **DISCIPLINE** PHILOSOPHY **EDUCATION** Univ Calif, 79. **CAREER** Lect, Princeton Univ, 76-77; Asst Prof, Univ Tex, 77-84; Prof, Univ Vt, 84-. **HONORS AND AWARDS** Fulbright Fel, Germany. **MEMBERSHIPS** APA, Soc for Phenomenology and Existential Philos. **RESEARCH** Hermeneutics, Heidegger, psychotherapy theory. **SELECTED PUBLICATIONS** Auth, Heidegger and the Problem of Knowledge; ed, Cambridge Companion to Heidegger; ed, The Good Life; ed, Re-Envisioning Psychology; ed, Existentialism: Basic Writings. **CONTACT ADDRESS** Dept Philos, Univ of Vermont, 70 S Williams St, Burlington, VT 05401. **EMAIL** cguignon@zoo.uvm.edu

GUILD, SONNY
PERSONAL Born 07/28/1944, Albany, OR, m, 1967, 3 children **DISCIPLINE** BIBLE & MISSIONS **EDUCATION** Harding Univ, BA, 66; ACU, MDiv, 69, Dmin, 96. **CAREER** Missionary-in-Residence, 93-; ACU facult (Bible Missions); Dir of for Missions & Evangelism. **HONORS AND AWARDS** African Mission fel; Dmin Project Thesis Awd. **RESEARCH** Team Building. **SELECTED PUBLICATIONS** Auth, Biblia Inasemaje, 82; Prepping the Mission Team, Gospel Advocate 139, 97. **CONTACT ADDRESS** Dept of Missions, Abilene Christian Univ, P O Box 29439, Abilene, TX 79699-9000. **EMAIL** guild@bible.acu.edu

GUINAN, MICHAEL DAMON
PERSONAL Born 02/16/1939, Cincinnati, OH **DISCIPLINE** SEMITICS, SYRIAC PATRISTICS **EDUCATION** San Luis Rey Col, BA, 61; Old Mission Theol Sem, STB, 65; Cath Univ Am, STL, 67, MA, 70, PhD(Semitics), 72. **CAREER** Prof Bibl Theol & Semitic Lang, Franciscan Sch Theol, Grad Theol Union, 72-. **MEMBERSHIPS** Cath Theol Soc Am; Cath Bibl Asn; Soc Bibl Lit; Soc for Study of Christian Spirituality. **RESEARCH** Old Testament; Syriac patristic theology. **SELECTED PUBLICATIONS** Auth, The Making of Many Images: Scripture Film and Religious Education, Multimedia Int, 73; Convenant in the Old Testament, Franciscan Herald, 75; Where are the dead?, Purgatory and immediate retribution in James of Sarug, Proc Syriac Symp of 1972; Jacob of Sarug, In: New Cath Encycl, Vol XVI; The Creation Story of Genesis: Does It Really Establish Evolution?; Angels: Their Meaning for Today; The Messiah and the Millenium; Christian Spirituality: Many Styles, One Spirit-Catholic Update, 94, 95, 97, 98. **CONTACT ADDRESS** Franciscan Sch of Theol, 1712 Euclid Ave, Berkeley, CA 94709-1294. **EMAIL** mdguinan@aol.com

GUINIER, (CAROL) LANI
PERSONAL m **DISCIPLINE** LAW **EDUCATION** Radcliffe Col, BA, 71; Yale Law School, JD, 74. **CAREER** US District Judge, Damon Keith, clerk, 74-76; Wayne County Juvenile Court, referee, 76-77; US Dept of Justice, Civil Rights Division, 77-81; NAACP Legal Defense Fund, 81-88; Univ of Pennsylvania, law prof, 92-98; prof, Harvard Law Sch, 98-01; Bennett Boskey Prof of Law, Harvard, 01- . **HONORS AND AWARDS** First female African-American prof appointed to Harvard Law Sch, 98. **MEMBERSHIPS** Open Society Institute, trustee, 1996-; Commonplace, Inc, founder/president, 1994; Juvenile Law Ctr, Philadelphia, PA, bd of dirs, 1992-. **RESEARCH** Professional responsibility; voting rights; public interest lawyering; race & gender; racetalks initiatives; criminal process **SELECTED PUBLICATIONS** Auth, The Tyranny of the Majority: Fundamental Fairness in Representative Democracy, Free Press, 94; co-auth, Becoming Gentlemen: Women, Law School and Institutional Change, Beacon Press, 97; auth, "Lessons and Challenges of Becoming Gentlemen" NYork Univ Rev of Law and Social Change 24 (98): 1-16; auth, Lift Every Voice: Turning a Civil Rights Setback into a New Vision of Social Justice, Simon & Schuster (NY), 98; auth, "President Clinton's Doubt; Lani Guinier's Certainty," in Rebels in Law: Voices in History of Black Women Lawyers, ed J.C. Smith, Jr (Ann Arbor: Univ of Mich Pr, 98), 123-127; auth, "Reframing the Affirmative Action Debate," Kentucky Law J 86 (98): 505-525; auth, "Lawyers as Bridge People: Architects of a New Public Space," in Civil Rights Litigation and Attorney Fees Annual Handbook, ed S. Saltzman (St Paul: West Group, 99). **CONTACT ADDRESS** Harvard Law Sch, Harvard Univ, 1525 Massachusetts, Cambridge, MA 02138. **EMAIL** lguinier@law.harvard.edu

GULLEY, ANTHONY D.
PERSONAL Born 04/27/1930, Watervliet, NY **DISCIPLINE** PHILOSOPHY **EDUCATION** St Joseph's Sem, NYork, BA, 52; St Bernardine of Siena Col, MS, 58; Cath Univ Am, PhD, 61. **CAREER** From instr to assoc prof philos, 61-73, Prof Educ, Col St Rose, 73- **MEMBERSHIPS** Am Cath Philos Asn; Nat Cath Educ Asn; NEA. **CONTACT ADDRESS** Col of Saint Rose, Albany, NY 12203-1490.

GUMMS, EMMANUEL GEORGE, SR.
PERSONAL Born 01/16/1928, Opelusas, LA, w **DISCIPLINE** THEOLOGY **EDUCATION** Leland College, AB cum laude 1954; Union Seminary, BD 1955; Inter Baptist Theological, ThD 1974, LLD 1976; Universal Bible Institute, PhD 1978; Straigth Business Coll, exec sec 1960. **CAREER** West NO Baptist Assn, president 1972-76; LA Cristian Training Institute, president 73-75; Christian Bible College of LA, Academic Dean, 76-; First New Testament B C, Pastor 58-. **HONORS AND AWARDS** Outstanding leadership 2nd Congress LBA 1978; communicator West Bank American Muslem 1980; dedicated service ML King Community Center 1981. **MEMBERSHIPS** Supervisor LSU Dental School 1971-77; secretary Jefferson Parish Ministers Union 1973-81; bd chairman Jefferson Parish Voters League 1975-84; general secretary LA Progressive Baptist Assn 1978-; chaplain Veterans of Foreign Wars #2403 1981-. **CONTACT ADDRESS** First New Testament BC, 6112 W Bank Expy, Marrero, LA 70072.

GUNDERSON, KEITH
DISCIPLINE PHILOSOPHY **EDUCATION** Princeton Univ, PhD. **RESEARCH** Philosophy of artifical intelligence; aesthetics. **SELECTED PUBLICATIONS** Auth, Leibniz's Walk-In Machine, Perception, and the Perils of Physicalism, Univ Am, 88; Mentality and Machines, Univ Minn, 85; Purposes and Poetry, Body Mind and Method, 79; A Continual Interest in the Sun and Sea; Inland Missing the Sea, Nodin, 76; ed, Language, Mind and Knowledge, Univ Minn, 75. **CONTACT ADDRESS** Philosophy Dept, Univ of Minnesota, Twin Cities, 355 Ford Hall, 224 Church St SE, Minneapolis, MN 55455. **EMAIL** gunde002@tc.umn.edu

GUNDRY, ROBERT H.
PERSONAL Born 10/15/1932, Los Angeles, CA, m, 1954, 3 children **DISCIPLINE** RELIGION **EDUCATION** Los Angeles Baptist Col & Sem, BA, 54, BD, 57; Univ Manchester, England, PhD, 61. **CAREER** From asst prof to assoc prof Bibl studies, 62-70, chmn dept relig studies, 66-75, 90-96, prof, 70-97, Kathleen Smith Prof Relig Studies, Westmont Col, 97-. **HONORS AND AWARDS** Teacher of Year, 69, 79 & 96. **MEMBERSHIPS** Soc New Testament Studies; Soc Bibl Lit; Inst Bibl Res. **RESEARCH** Biblical studies, higher and textual criticism; theology. **SELECTED PUBLICATIONS** Auth, The Use of the Old Testament in St Matthew's Gospel, Brill, Leiden, 67; A Survey of the New Testament, 70 & The Church and the Tribulation, 73, Zondervan; Soma in Biblical Theology, Cambridge Univ, 76; Matthew: A Commentary on His Literary & Theological Art, Eerdmans, 82; Mark: A Commentary on His Apology for the Cross, Eerdmans, 93. **CONTACT ADDRESS** Dept of Relig Studies & Philos, Westmont Col, 955 La Paz Rd, Santa Barbara, CA 93108-1099. **EMAIL** gundry@westmont.edu

GUNLICKS, ARTHUR B.
PERSONAL Born 07/07/1936, North Platte, NE, m, 1962, 2 children **DISCIPLINE** COMPARATIVE POLITICS **EDUCATION** Univ of Denver, BA, 58; Univ of Freiburg, Germany, 58-59; Univ of Gottingen, Germany, 64-65; Georgetown Univ, PhD, 67. **CAREER** PROF OF POLITICAL SCI, UNIV OF RICHMOND. **HONORS AND AWARDS** Two Fulbright Res Grants; One Fulbright Travel Grant; Two German Acad Exchange Summer Grants. **MEMBERSHIPS** APSA; So Political Sci Asn; German Studies Asn; European Studies Asn; European Community Studies Asn; Confr Group on German Politics; AAUP. **RESEARCH** Western European politics; German politics; German federalism. **SELECTED PUBLICATIONS** Ed, Campaign & Party Finance in North America & Western Europe, Westview Press, 93; auth, Local Government in the German Federal System, Duke Univ Press, 86; auth, Local Government Reform & Reorganization: An International Perspective, 81. **CONTACT ADDRESS** Dept of Political Science, Univ of Richmond, Richmond, VA 23173. **EMAIL** agunlick@richmond.edu

GUNN, J.
PERSONAL Born 08/17/1937, Quebec City, QC, Canada, 2 children **DISCIPLINE** POLITICAL SCIENCE **EDUCATION** Queen's Univ, BA, 59; Univ Toronto, MA, 61; Oxford Univ, PhD, 66. **CAREER** Lectr to prof and dept head, Queen's Univ, 60-. **HONORS AND AWARDS** Fel, Royal Soc of Canada. **RESEARCH** History of Political thought; Britain and France, 16th to 19th Century; Scholarly editing; Disraeli letters and Hume essays; Civil Society; Parliamentary Government. **SELECTED PUBLICATIONS** Auth, Queen of the World: Opinion in the Public Life of France from the Renaissance to the Revolution, Oxford; auth, Benjamin Disraeli, Letters: 1815-1834; auth, "Conscience, Honor and the Failure of Party in Restoration France," Hist of Polit Thought, (00): 449-466. **CONTACT ADDRESS** Dept Polit Sci, Queen's Univ at Kingston, 99 University Ave, Kingston, ON, Canada K7L 3N6. **EMAIL** gunnj@politics.queensu.ca

GUNTER, PETER A. Y.
PERSONAL Born 10/20/1936, Hammond, IN, m, 1969, 1 child **DISCIPLINE** PHILOSOPHY **EDUCATION** Univ Tex, BA, 58; Cambridge Univ, BA, 60, Yale Univ, PhD. **CAREER** Asst prof, Auburn Univ, 62-65; assoc prof, Univ of Tenn at Knoxville, 65-69, prof, Univ of N Tex, 69-, prof, Regents' Univ 90-. **HONORS AND AWARDS** San Antonio Conserv Soc Book Awd, 98; Lone Star Sierra Club Special Service Awd, 96; Univ of N Tex Top Prof, 91; Phi Beta Kappa Scholars Awd, 84; Dallas Public Libr Lit Map of Tex, 76; Marshall Scholar, 58-60. **MEMBERSHIPS** Soc for Process Philos of Educ; Phi Beta Kappa; Sigma Xi, S Soc for Philos and Psych. **RESEARCH** Philosophy of Natural Science; Environmental Ethics; Process Philosophy (Henri Bergson, Sm. James, A.N. Whitehead); Philosophy of Education; History of Western Philosophy. **SELECTED PUBLICATIONS** Auth, Bergson and the Evolution of Physics, Knoxville, 69; auth, Henri Bergson: A Bibliography, 74; auth, The Big Thicket: A Challenge for Conservation, Austin, 92; auth, Bergson and Modern Thought, Gordon Breach, 87; auth, Texas Land Ethics, Austin, 98; auth, Founders of Constructive Postmodernism, Suny, 93. **CONTACT ADDRESS** Dept Relig & Philos, Univ of No Texas, PO Box 310920, Denton, TX 76203-0920. **EMAIL** gunter@po6.cas.unt.edu

GUNTHER, GERALD
PERSONAL Born 05/26/1927, Germany, m, 1949, 2 children **DISCIPLINE** AMERICAN CONSTITUTIONAL LAW AND HISTORY **EDUCATION** Brooklyn Col, AB, 49; Columbia Univ, MA, 50; Harvard Univ, LLB, 53. **CAREER** Law clerk, Judge Learned Hand, 53-54 and Chief Justice Earl Warren, 54-55; from assoc prof to prof law, Sch Law, Columbia Univ, 56-62; prof, 62-72, WILLIAM NELSON CROMWELL PROF LAW, SCH LAW, STANFORD UNIV, 72-, Res dir, Inter-Law Sch Comn Const Simplification, 57-58; Guggenheim fel, 62-63; Fulbright lectr, Ghana, 69; fel, Ctr Advan Studies Behav Sci, 69-70, vis prof const law, Harvard Law Sch, 72-73; Nat Endowment for Humanities fel, 80-81. **HONORS AND AWARDS** Distinguished Alumnus Awd, Brooklyn Col, 61. **MEMBERSHIPS** Fel Am Acad Arts & Sci; Am Philos Soc; AHA; Am Law Inst; Orgn Am Historians. **RESEARCH** Judicial biography. **SELECTED PUBLICATIONS** Auth, Learned Hand--Outstanding Copyright Judge--The 24th Annual Donald-C-Brace-Lecture, J Copyright Soc of USA, Vol 0041, 94; Objectivity and Hagiography in Judicial Biography--Transcript, NY Univ Law Rev, Vol 0070, 95; Contracted Biographies and Other Obstacles to Truth, NY Univ Law Rev, Vol 0070, 95; Members of the Warren-Court in Judicial Biography--Transcript, NY Univ Law Rev, Vol 0070, 95; Judge Hand, Learned: Examining the Life of an American Jurist--The Choices and Satisfactions of a Biographer, Proc of Am Philos Soc, Vol 0140, 96. **CONTACT ADDRESS** Sch of Law, Stanford Univ, Stanford, CA 94305.

GUPTA, ANIL
PERSONAL Born 02/05/1949, Ambala, India, m, 2 children **DISCIPLINE** PHILOSOPHY **EDUCATION** Univ London, BS, 69; Univ Pittsburgh, MA, 73; PhD, 77. **CAREER** From Asst Prof to Assoc Prof, McGill Univ, 75-82; Assoc Prof, Univ Ill, 82-89; Prof, Ind Univ, 89-. **HONORS AND AWARDS** Andrew Mellon Fel, 70-71, 73-74; Fel, Univ Ill, 85-86; NEH Fels, 88-89, 95-96; Fel, Stanford Univ, 98-99. **MEMBERSHIPS** APA, ASL. **RESEARCH** Logic, philosophy of language, metaphysics. **SELECTED PUBLICATIONS** Auth, "Two Theorems Concerning Stability," in Truth or Consequences (Kluwer Acad Pr, 90), 49-60; coauth, The Revision Theory of Truth, MIT Pr (Cambridge), 93; auth, "Minimalism," in Philos Perspectives 7: Lang and Logic (Ridgeview Publ Co, 93), 359-369; auth, "A Critique of Deflationism," Philos Topics 21 (93): 57-81; auth, "Definition and Revision: A Response to McGee and Martin," Philos Issues 8 (97): 419-443; auth, "Meaning and Misconceptions," Lang, Logic and Concepts: Essays in Hon of John Macnamara, MIT Pr (99): 15-41. **CONTACT ADDRESS** Dept Philos, Indiana Univ, Bloomington, 1033 E 3rd St, Bloomington, IN 47405-7005. **EMAIL** agupta@indiana.edu

GUPTA, NEENA
DISCIPLINE LAW **EDUCATION** Queen's Univ, BA, 84; LLB, 87; Univ Toronto, LLM, 94. **CAREER** General civil litigator, Goodman and Carr; adj prof, Univ of Toronto. **MEMBERSHIPS** Can Bar Asn; Law Soc Upper Can; Law Soc Saskatchewan. **RESEARCH** Employment and human rights law. **CONTACT ADDRESS** Fac of Law, Univ of Toronto, 78 Queen's Park, Toronto, ON, Canada M5S 2C5.

GURTLER, GARY M.
PERSONAL Born 02/27/1947, Rochester, NY **DISCIPLINE** PHILOSOPHY **EDUCATION** Fordham Univ, PhD, 78. **CAREER** Asst Prof, 80-91, Assoc Prof, 91-92, Loyola Univ of Chicago; Assoc Prof, Boston Coll, 92-97, 99-; Miller Prof of Classics, John Carrol Univ, 98. **HONORS AND AWARDS** Pres, Jesuit Philo Assoc. **MEMBERSHIPS** APA, APAED, ACPA, ISNS, JPA. **RESEARCH** Plotinus, Plato, Aristotle, ancient and medieval philosophy, Spanish philosophy. **SELECTED PUBLICATIONS** Auth, Plotinus, the Experience of Unity, Bern, Peter Lang Pub Co, 88; auth, "Plotinus and Byzantine Aesthetics," The Mod Schoolman, 89; auth, "Plotinus and the Platonic Parmenides," Intl Philo Qtly, 92; auth, "Plotinus and the Alienation of the Soul," The Perennial Tradition of Noeplatonism, Leuven Univ Press, 97; art, Meeting on Philosophy's Own Ground, Zubiri's Critic of Plato's Dualism, in: Intl Philo Qtly, 98; auth, "La Noetica de Zubiri y Noetica Aristotles,"Analogia Revista de Filosofia, 99. **CONTACT ADDRESS** Dept of Philosophy, Boston Col, Chestnut Hill, Chestnut Hill, MA 02467. **EMAIL** gurtlerg@bc.edu

GUSHEE, DAVID P.
PERSONAL Born 06/17/1962, VA, m, 1984, 4 children **DISCIPLINE** CHRISTIAN ETHICS **EDUCATION** Union Theol Sem, PhD, 93. **CAREER** Graves Professor of Moral Philosophy, 4 yrs, Union Univ TN. **HONORS AND AWARDS** Phi Beta Kappa; 2 Evang Press Assoc Awds; writer of column in jackson sun. **MEMBERSHIPS** SBC **SELECTED PUBLICATIONS** Auth, The Righteous Gentiles of the Holocaust, Fortress Press. **CONTACT ADDRESS** 156 Claiborne Dr, Jackson, TN 38305. **EMAIL** dgushee@uu.edu

GUSTAFSON, DAVID
PERSONAL Born 01/25/1942, Cokate, MN, m, 1964, 2 children **DISCIPLINE** CHURCH HISTORY **EDUCATION** Hamline Univ, BA, 64; M. Div Lutheran School of Theol, 68; Luther Seminary, Th M, 73; Union Inst, PhD, 90. **CAREER** Lutheran Pastor, 68-98, Univ of St Thomas, St Paul, MN, 98-. **HONORS AND AWARDS** Concordia Hist Inst Book Awd, 94. **MEMBERSHIPS** ASCH, LHC, AAR, Sixteenth Century Soc. **RESEARCH** American Religious History. **SELECTED PUBLICATIONS** Lectr, The theme of Lutheran identity at the meeting of the Concordia Academy, St Paul, MN, 91; rev, of George M Marsden, Understanding Fundamentalism and Evangelicalism, The Lutheran Quarterly, 92; auth, Lutherans in Crisis: The Question of Identity in the American Republic, Minneapolis: Fortress Press, 93; rev, of William Lazareth and Peri Rasolondraibe, Lutheran Identity and Mission, Augsburg Fortress Book Newsletter, 94; auth, "A Quiet Week in the ELCa" Forum Letter, 95; auth, "The ELCA: Its Past, Present, and Future" Logia, Eastertide, 96; auth, "The ELCA and Ecumenism: Past, Present, and Future" Lectures in St Louis, MO, 97; auth, "The Church: Community of the Crucified or Community that Crucifies?" Lutheran Forum, 97; rev, of Francis McGrath, John Henry Newman: Universal Revelation, Church History, 98; auth, rev, of Karin Maag, ed, melanchthon in Europe: His Work and Influence Beyond Wittenberg, The Sixteenth Century Journal, 00. **CONTACT ADDRESS** 5220 Oakley St., Duluth, MN 55804. **EMAIL** DAGusto@aol.com

GUSTASON, WILLIAM
DISCIPLINE LOGICAL THEORY, INDUCTIVE LOGIC, EARLY 20TH-CENTURY ANALYSIS **EDUCATION** Univ Mich, PhD. **CAREER** Assoc prof, Purdue Univ. **RESEARCH** Frege and Wittgenstein. **SELECTED PUBLICATIONS** Auth, Reasoning From Evidence: Inductive Logic; coauth, Elementary Symbolic Logic. **CONTACT ADDRESS** Dept of Philos, Purdue Univ, West Lafayette, 1080 Schleman Hall, West Lafayette, IN 47907-1080.

GUTMANN, AMY
PERSONAL Born 11/19/1949, New York, NY, m, 1 child **DISCIPLINE** POLITICAL SCIENCE **EDUCATION** Harvard Univ, BA, 71; London Sch of Econ, MSc, 72; Harvard Univ, PhD, 76. **CAREER** Univ., Prof, politics, Univ Ctr for Human Values, Princeton Univ. **HONORS AND AWARDS** American Academy of Arts and Sciences; National Academy of Education; Ralph Bunche Awd, Am Polit Sci Asn; North Am Soc of Soc Philos award for best book; Tanner lect, Stanford Univ; Gustavus Myers Awd for best book on huamn rights. **MEMBERSHIPS** APSA; APA. **RESEARCH** Moral and political philosophy; education; race, religion, gender and politics; ethics and public policy; ethics and the professions; democratic theory and practice; multiculturalism. **SELECTED PUBLICATIONS** auth, Liberal Equality, 80; Color Conscious: The Political Morality of Race, Princeton Univ Pr, 96; coauth, Democracy and Disagreement, Harvard Univ Pr, 96; ed, Multiculturalism Princeton Univ Pr, 94; ed, The Lives of Animals, Princeton Univ Pr, 99; Democratic Education, Princeton Press, 99. **CONTACT ADDRESS** Univ Center for Human Values, Princeton Univ, 304 Louis Marx Hall, Princeton, NJ 08540. **EMAIL** agutmann@princeton.edu

GUTOWSKI, CAROLYN
PERSONAL Born Pittsburgh, PA **DISCIPLINE** RELIGION, GERONTOLOGY **EDUCATION** LaRoche Col, BA, 69; Duquesne Univ, MAT, 73; Walden Univ, PhD, 90. **CAREER** Adj prof, MaryMount Univ, 94-; teacher, Pittsburgh parochial schs, 61-; founder, dir, Bonaventure Soc Svcs Ctr, 76-80; prof coord, Ctr App Res and the Apostolate, 87-88; prog coord Nat Inst for the Family, 80-87; Exec Dir, Advisory Neighborhood Comm 3-C, 92-98; Dir of Prog, National Institute for the Family. **MEMBERSHIPS** Am Acad Rel; Am Soc Aging; Environ Alliance Senior Involvement; N Am Coalittion Rel & Ecology (NACRE). **RESEARCH** Grandparenting; spirituality and aging. **SELECTED PUBLICATIONS** Auth, Grandparents are Forever, Paulist Press, 94; auth, The Regenerative Role of Grandparents, AARP/Cornell Univ, 91; auth, Grandparents are Forever, Catholic Woman, Sept 94. **CONTACT ADDRESS** 8101 Connecticut Ave, N410, Chevy Chase, MD 20815. **EMAIL** gutgeist@ioip.com

GUTTING, GARY MICHAEL
PERSONAL Born 04/11/1942, St. Louis, MO, m, 1965, 3 children **DISCIPLINE** PHILOSOPHY OF SCIENCE **EDUCATION** St Louis Univ, BA, 64, PhD(philos), 68. **CAREER** Instr philos, St Louis Univ, 67-68; Fulbright fel, Cath Univ Louvain, 68-69; asst prof, 69-75, assoc prof, 75-82, prof philos, Univ Notre Dame, 82-; visiting prof, Free Univ of Amsterdam, 87; chemn, dept philos, Univ Notre Dame, 90-96. **MEMBERSHIPS** Philos Sci Asn; Am Philos Asn. **RESEARCH** Philosophy of science; continental philsophy; of religion. **SELECTED PUBLICATIONS** Auth, Religious Belief and Religious Skepticisim, Univ Notre Dame Press, 82; Michel Foucault's Archaelogy of Scientific Reason, Cambridge Univ Press, 89; Pragmatic Liberalism and the Critique of Modernity, Cambridge Univ Press, 98; Einstein's Discovery of Special Relativity, Philos Sci, 72; contribr, Scientific Realism, In: The Philosophy of Wilfrid Sellars, Reidl, 78; Continental Philosophy of Science, In: Current Research in Philosophy of Science, Philos Sci Asn, 78; auth, Husserl and Scientific Realism, Philos & Phenomenol Res, 78; Science as Discovery, Rev Int de Philos, 80; ed, Paradigms and Revolutions: Applications and Appraisals of Thomas Kuhn's Philosophy of Science, Univ Notre Dame, 80; auth, Religious Belief and Religious Skepticism, Univ Notre Dame, 82; Can Philosophical Beliefs Be Rationally Justified?, Am Philos Quart, 82. **CONTACT ADDRESS** Dept of Philosophy, Univ of Notre Dame, Notre Dame, IN 46556. **EMAIL** Gary.M. Gutting.1@nd.edu

GUTTMAN, EGON
PERSONAL Born 01/27/1927, Neuruppin, Germany, m, 1966, 2 children **DISCIPLINE** SECURITIES & COMMERCIAL LAW **EDUCATION** London Univ, LLB, 50, LLM, 52. **CAREER** Mem law fac, Northwestern Univ, 58-59; mem law fac, Rutgers Univ, 59-60; mem law fac, Univ Atlanta, 60-62; prof law, Sch Law, Howard Univ, 62-68; Prof Law, Com Law & Securities Regulations, WA Col, Am Univ, 68-, Barrister, Mid Temple, 52-; lectr law, Univ Khartoum, Sudan & Fac Law, Univ London, 53-58; lectr, Practicing Law Inst, 66-; adj prof law, Sch Law, Howard Univ, 68-96; spec adv to gen coun, Securities & Exchange Comn, 76-77; spec adv to dir, Enforcement, 78-80; Louis P Levitt Mem Scholar, WA Col Law, 82. **HONORS AND AWARDS** Am Law Institute Leverhulm Scholar, 48-51; Univ of London postgraduate fel, 51-52; Ford Found graduate fel, Northwestern Univ, 58-59; Outstanding Educators of Am, 70, 73; Louis P. Levitt Memorial Scholar, 82. **MEMBERSHIPS** Am Law Inst; Am Bar Asn; Brit Inst Int & Comp Law; Soc Pub Teachers Law; Hardwick Soc Inns of Ct England. **RESEARCH** Securities regulations, transfer of securities; international finance; economic crimes. **SELECTED PUBLICATIONS** Auth, The Comparative Conflict of Laws, with Reference to the Legitimacy and Legitimation of Children, London: Univ of London Press, 52; auth, Crime, Cause and Treatment, Khartoum: Sudan Judiciary, 57; coauth, Cases and Materials on Domestic Relations, Alberta: Univ of Alberta, 62; auth, Cases and Materials on Policy and the Legal Environment, Baltimore: Johns Hopkins Univ, 73; coauth, Problems and Materials on Negotiable Instruments Under the Uniform Commercial Code and the United Nations Convention on International Bills of Exchange and International Promissory Notes, (Commercial Transactions Vol. 3), Cincinnati, OH: Anderson Pub Co, 92; coauth, Problems and Materials on Sales Under the Uniform Commercial Code, and the Convention on International Sale of Goods, (Commercial Transactions Vol. 2), Cincinnati, OH: Anderson Pub Co, 92; auth, Problems and Materials on sales Under the Uniform Commercial Code, and the Convention on International Sale of Goods, (Commercial Transactions Vol. 2), Cincinnati, OH: Anderson Pub Co, 92; auth, Problems and Materials on Sacured Transactions Under the Uniform Commercial Code, (Commercial Transactions, Vol. 1, Cincinnati, OH: Anderson Pub Co, 93; auth, Modern Securities Transfers, Third Ed, Boston: Warren, Gorham & Lamont, 87; auth, Analysis of a Proposal for a Securities Law for the Republic of Macedonia, Am Bar Asn Central and East European Law Initiative, 96; auth, Law of the United States Affecting Trade with Latiin America/El Derecho de los Estados Unidos en Materia de Inversiones y Libre Comerci: U.S. Ssecurities Law, Univ of Arizona Nat Law Center for Inter-American Free Trade, 97. **CONTACT ADDRESS** WA Col of Law, American Univ, 4801 Mass Ave 320, Washington, DC 20016. **EMAIL** guttman@wcl.american.edu

GUY, DANIEL SOWERS
PERSONAL Born 07/12/1928, Columbus, OH, m, 1962, 2 children **DISCIPLINE** LAW **EDUCATION** Ohio Wesleyan Univ, BA, 49, JD, 52; Univ Mich, Ann Arbor, LLM, 56, SJD, 70. **CAREER** Asst atty gen, Ohio, 57-58; from asst prof to prof Law, Ohio Northern Univ, 59-73, asst dean, 64-73; prof, Univ NDak, 73-77; prof Law, Ohio Northern Univ, 77-98, dean, 78-84, atty, Ohio, 52-73; fel, Inst Soc Sci Methods in Legal Educ, Univ Denver, 67. **HONORS AND AWARDS** Phi Beta Kappa. **MEMBERSHIPS** Am Bar Asn; Am Judicature Soc. **RESEARCH** Eminant domain law; condemnation law. **SELECTED PUBLICATIONS** Contribr, State Taxation of Interstate Commerce, Judiciary Comt, US House of Rep, 64; auth, State Highway Condemnation Procedures, Int Continuing Legal Educ, 71; Empirical study of fact-finders, Ohio Northern Univ Law Rev, 73; Comparison of condemnation procedures, 74 & Open meetings and open records in North Dakota, 76, Univ NDak Law Rev. **CONTACT ADDRESS** Col of Law, Ohio No Univ, 525 S Main St, Ada, OH 45810-1555.

GUY, FRED
DISCIPLINE ANCIENT PHILOSOPHY **EDUCATION** Auburn Univ, BA, Univ Ga, MA, PhD. **CAREER** Assoc Prof, Univ Baltimore, 77-; Chairman, dept hist & philos, Univ Baltimore, 77-92; Codir, Hoffberger Ctr Professional Ethics, 91-94; Dir, Hoffberger Ctr Professional Ethics, 91-94. **MEMBERSHIPS** Asn Practical & Professional Ethics; Am Asn Philos Tchrs; Am Philos Asn; Asn Advancement Community Col Tchrs; Soc Values Inquiry; Soc Business Ethics. **SELECTED PUBLICATIONS** Auth, The Role of Praxis Today, Jour Value Inquiry, 91; auth, Ethics in the Workplace: Top to Bottom, Chesapeake Human Resource Asn, 97; auth, Personal, Professional, and Business Ethics, Woods Memorial Presbyterian Church, 97; auth, An Ethical Life in Today's World, Suburban Club Baltimore County, 97. **CONTACT ADDRESS** Univ of Baltimore, 1420 N. Charles Street, Baltimore, MD 21201.

GUY, MARY E.
PERSONAL Born 12/02/1947, Carlinville, IL, d **DISCIPLINE** POLITICAL SCIENCE **EDUCATION** Jacksonville Univ, 69; Univ Fla, Master Rehab Counseling, 70; Univ SC, MA, 76, PhD, 81. **CAREER** Psychologist, SC Dept Mental Health, 73-82; Prof, Univ Ala - Birmingham, 82-97; Pres, Am Soc Public Admin, 97-98; Jerry Collins Prof Public Admin, Fla State Univ, 97-. **HONORS AND AWARDS** Distinguished Res Awd, Am Soc Public Admin, 91; Dimock Awd, Am Soc Public Admin, 94; Fac Mentor Awd, Am Polit Sci Asn, 96. **MEMBERSHIPS** Am Soc Public Admin; Am Polit Sci Asn; Acad Management. **RESEARCH** Public management; American government; gender & workplace issues. **SELECTED PUBLICATIONS** Auth, Professionals in Organizations, 85; From Organizational Decline to Organizational Renewal, 89; Ethical Decision Making in Everyday Work Situations, 90; Women and Men of the States, 92. **CONTACT ADDRESS** Askew Sch Public Admin & Policy, Florida State Univ, Tallahassee, FL 32306-2250.

GUZELDERE, GUVEN
PERSONAL Born 01/23/1963, Ankara, Turkey **DISCIPLINE** PHILOSOPHY, PSYCHOLOGY, COGNITIVE SCIENCE **EDUCATION** Bogazici Univ, BS, 86; Indiana Univ, MS, 89, MA, 89; Stanford Univ, PhD, 97. **CAREER** Asst Prof, 97-, Duke Univ. **HONORS AND AWARDS** National Humanities Center Fellow. **MEMBERSHIPS** APA, CSS, AAAI, APS, Soc for Neuroscience. **RESEARCH** Philosophy of mind, consciousness, foundations of artificial intelligence. **SELECTED PUBLICATIONS** Ed, The Nature of Consciousness, MIT Press, 97. **CONTACT ADDRESS** Dept of Philosophy, Duke Univ, 201 W Duke Bldg, Box 90743, Durham, NC 27708. **EMAIL** guven@acpub.duke.edu

GYATSO, J.
DISCIPLINE BUDDHIST STUDIES **EDUCATION** Univ CA, Berkeley, PhD, 87. **CAREER** Assoc prof, Relig Dept, Amherst Col. **RESEARCH** Tibet; Buddhism; religion; philos; cultural studies. **SELECTED PUBLICATIONS** Ed, In the Mirror of Memory: Reflections on Mindfulness and Remembrance in India and Tibetan Buddhism, Albany: SUNY Press, 89; auth, Apparitions of the Self: The Secret Autobiographies of a Tibetan Visionary, Princeton, 98. **CONTACT ADDRESS** Amherst Col, Amherst, MA 01002. **EMAIL** jbgyatso@amherst.edu

GYUG, RICHARD F.
DISCIPLINE MEDIEVAL LITURGY, RELIGION AND SOCIETY **EDUCATION** Univ Toronto, PhD. **CAREER** Chair; assoc prof, Fordham Univ. **SELECTED PUBLICATIONS** Auth, Missale ragusinum: The Missal of Dubrovnik, 90; The Diocese of Barcelona during the Black Death: The Register 'Notule communium' 15, 94. **CONTACT ADDRESS** Dept of Hist, Fordham Univ, 441 E Fordham Rd, Bronx, NY 10458. **EMAIL** gyug@fordham.edu

H

HAACK, SUSAN
PERSONAL Born 07/23/1945, England **DISCIPLINE** PHILOSOPHY **EDUCATION** Oxford, BA, 66, B Phil, 68; Cambridge, PhD, 72. **CAREER** Fel, 69-71, New Hall, Cambridge UK; lectr, 71-76, Univ of Warnick UK; from reader to prof philos to prof law, Univ Miami, 76-. **HONORS AND AWARDS** Harkness Fellow; Romaness Phi Beta Kappa Prof; Cooper Sr Scholar in Arts and Sci, 98-. **MEMBERSHIPS** APA, Charles S. Peirce Soc; CSICOP. **RESEARCH** Philosophy of logic and language; Epistemology and Philosophy of Science; Metaphysics; Pragmatism; Law and Scientific Evidence. **SELECTED PUBLICATIONS** Auth, Philosophy of Logics, Cambridge Univ Pr, 78; auch, Evidence and Inquiry, Towards Reconstruction in Epistemology, Blackwell, 93; auth, Deviant Logiz, Fuzzy Logic: Beyond the Formalism, Univ Chicago Pr, 96; auth, Manifesto of a Passionate Moderate: Unfashionable Essays, Univ Chicago Pr, 98. **CONTACT ADDRESS** Dept of Philosophy, Univ of Miami, Coral Gables, FL 33124.

HAAKONSSEN, KNUD
PERSONAL Born 07/09/1947, Tingsted, Denmark, w, 1987, 1 child **DISCIPLINE** PHILOSOPHY **EDUCATION** Univ Copenhagen, cand art, 68, mag art, 72; Univ Edinburgh, PhD, 78; Univ Copenhagen, Dr Phil, 96. **CAREER** Tutor in Philos, Krogerup Folk High School, Copenhagen, 68-69; tutor, dept of philos, Univ Copenhagen, 69-70; part-time lect in philos, Folkeuniversitetet, Copenhagen, 70-73; sr tutor, Dept of Philos, Monash Univ, Melbourne, 76-79; lect, School of Political Science, Victoria Univ of Wellington, 79-82; res fel, sr res fel, fel, sr fel, Res School of Social Studies, Inst for Advanced Studies, Australian Nat Univ, 82-94; prof, Dept of Philos, and assoc fac, Dept of Political Science, Boston Univ, 95-; vis fel at the following: Australian Nat Univ, 80-81, 95, 96, 98, Univ Aarhus, 85, Univ Ediburgh, 86, 89, Max-Planck-Institut fur Geschichte, Gottingen, 89, McGill Univ, Montreal, 92-93; fel, Woodrow Wilson Int Center for Scholars, Washington, DC, 88; co-dir, prog on the Bicentenary of the Bill of Rights, Woodrow Wilson Int Center for Scholars, Washington, DC, 89-91; lect, Int Hume Soc, Nat Endowment for the Humanities, Dartmouth Col, 90; Distinguished Vis, Univ Manitoba, Winnipeg, 92; co-ed, Newsletter of the IVR, 87-91; ed bd, Edinburgh Studies in Intellectual History, Edinburgh Univ Press, 92-97; ed adv, British J for the Hist of Philos, 92-; ed bd, Hist of European Ideas, 97-; consul ed, J of the Hist of Ideas, 92-98; ed bd, Reid Studies, 97-; bd of ed, J of the Hist of Ideas, 98-, international consultant, Cites; Japan Soc for the Promotion of Science, 99. **HONORS AND AWARDS** Gold Medal of the Univ of Aarhus, Denmark, 70; fel, Academy of Social Sciences in Australia, 92; foreign member, Royal Danish Academy of Sciences and Letters, 95; Centenary Fellow, Scots Phil, Club, 01. **MEMBERSHIPS** Am Philos Asn; Australian Soc of Legal Philos; Int Asn for Philos of Law and Social Philos; British Soc for the History of Philos; Am Soc for Eighteenth-Century Studies; Australasian & Pacific Soc for Eighteenth-Century Studies; Deutsche Gesellschaft fur die Erforschung des achtzehnten Jahrhunderts; Int Soc for Eighteenth-Century Studies; Int Hume Soc; Eighteenth-Century Scottish Studies Soc; The Conference for the Study of Political Thought, Lessing Akademie, Wolfenbuttel; Int Soc for Intellectual Hist; North Am Kant Soc. **RESEARCH** History of early modern philos; legal and political philos. **SELECTED PUBLICATIONS** Auth, The Science of a Legislator, The Natural Jurisprudence of David Hume and Adam Smith, Cambridge Univ Press, 81, paperback, 89, French trans, Presses Universitaires de France, 98, Japanese trans, Tokyo: Minerva Shobo, forthcoming; ed, Traditions of Liberalism, Essays on John Locke, Adam Smith and John Stuart Mill, CIS, 88; ed, Thomas Reid, Practical Ethics: being Lectures and Papers on Natural Religion, Self-Government, Natural Jurisprudence and the Law of Nations, ed with intro and commentary, Princeton Univ Press, 90; ed, A Culture of Rights: The Bill of Rights in Philosophy Politics and Law-1791 and 1991, ed with M J Lacey, Cambridge Univ Press,

91, paperback ed, 92; ed, David Hume, Political Essays, ed with intro, Cambridge Texts in the History of Political Thought, Cambridge Univ Press, 94; ed, Enlightenment and Religion: Rational Dissent in Eighteenth-Century Britain, Ideas in Context, Cambridge Univ Press, 96; auth, Natural Law and Moral Philosophy, from Grotius to the Scottish Enlightenment, Cambridge Univ Press, 96; ed, Adam Smith, International Library of Critical Essays in the History of Philosophy, Dartmouth Pub Co, 98; auth, Grotius, Pufendorf and Modern Natural Law, Int Library of Critical Essays in the Hist of Phil, Darmouth Pub, Co, 98; gen ed, The Edinburgh Edition of Thomas Reid, Edinburgh Univ Press, 94-; forty scholarly articles; twenty opuscula; three dozen book-reviews; translations into Danish of Kuhn, Magee, Popper, and Russell. **CONTACT ADDRESS** Dept of Philosophy, Boston Univ, 745 Commonwealth Ave, Boston, MA 02215. **EMAIL** haakon@bu.edu

HAAR, CHARLES MONROE
PERSONAL Born 12/03/1920, Antwerp, Belgium, m, 1946, 3 children **DISCIPLINE** LAW **EDUCATION** NYork Univ, AB, 40; Univ Wis, MA, 41; Harvard Univ, LLB, 48. **CAREER** Pvt practice law, New York city, 49-52; from asst prof to prof, Law Sch, Harvard Univ, 52-66; asst secy, Dept Housing and Urban Develop, Washington, DC, 66-69; prof, 69-72, LOUIS D BRANDEIS PROF LAW, HARVARD UNIV, 72-, Chief reporter, Proj Model Code Lang Develop, Am Land Inst, 64-66; chmn, Joint Ctr Urban Studies, Mass Inst Technol-Harvard Univ, 69-; dir, Charles River Assocs, Cambridge, Mass; consult, Agency Int Develop, Housing and Home Finance Agency and US Senate Subcomt Govt Opers; mem, Cambridge Redevelop Authority Metrop Area Planning Coun; chmn, President's Task Forces Suburban Probs, Model Cities and Reservation Natural Beauty; chmn, Mass Home Finance Agency; mem, Mass Gov Management Task Force. **HONORS AND AWARDS** LLD, Lake Erie Univ, 68. **MEMBERSHIPS** Fel AAAS; Am Inst Planners; Brit Town Planning Inst; Am Law Inst. **RESEARCH** Law education. **SELECTED PUBLICATIONS** Auth, Preface, Harvard Environ Law Rev, Vol 0020, 96. **CONTACT ADDRESS** Law Sch, Harvard Univ, FOB 300, Cambridge, MA 02138.

HAAS, PETER J.
PERSONAL Born 11/29/1947, Detroit, MI, m, 1971, 3 children **DISCIPLINE** RELIGIOUS HISTORY, JUDAISM **EDUCATION** Hebrew Union Col, MA, 74; Brown Univ, PhD, 80. **CAREER** Asst prof to assoc prof, Vanderbilt Univ, 80-99; prof, Case Western Reserve Univ, 00-. **MEMBERSHIPS** AAR; SBL; MJSA; CCAR. **RESEARCH** Jewish Moral Discourse, Science and Religion. **SELECTED PUBLICATIONS** Auth, Morality After Auschwitz; auth, Responsa: Literary History of a Rabbinic Genre. **CONTACT ADDRESS** Dept Relig, Case Western Reserve Univ, Cleveland, OH 44106. **EMAIL** pjh7@po.cwru.edu

HABER, JORAM G.
PERSONAL Born 01/03/1955, New York, NY, m, 1981, 3 children **DISCIPLINE** PHILOSOPHY **EDUCATION** Columbia, MA, 80; Pace, JD, 84; CUNY, PhD, 90. **CAREER** Assoc prof of philos, Bergen Community Col, 89-. **HONORS AND AWARDS** Am Soc for Value Inquiry, Pres-elect, 2000. **MEMBERSHIPS** APA, ABA. **RESEARCH** Ethics. **SELECTED PUBLICATIONS** Auth, Ethics for Today and Tomorrow, Wadsworth; auth, 3 entries in Ethics of Philosophy of Law, Garland (99); author of six books and several articles. **CONTACT ADDRESS** Dept Relig & Philos, Bergen Comm Col, 400 Paramus Rd, Paramus, NJ 07652-1508.

HABERMAN, DAVID L.
DISCIPLINE RELIGIOUS STUDIES **EDUCATION** Univ Chicago, PhD, 84. **CAREER** Assoc prof, Ind Univ Bloomington. **RESEARCH** History of South Asian religions; Indian arts and aesthetics; ritual studies; theories of religion; Native American religions; culture of Braj. **SELECTED PUBLICATIONS** Auth, Acting as a Way of Salvation: A Study of Raganuga Bhakti Sadhana, Oxford, 88; Journey through the Twelve Forests, Oxford, 94; transl, The Yoga of Divine Emotions: A Translation of the Bhaktirasamrtasindhu of Rupa Gosvamin, (Indira Gandhi National Centre for the Arts, 99). **CONTACT ADDRESS** Dept of Religious Studies, Indiana Univ, Bloomington, 300 N Jordan Ave, Bloomington, IN 47405. **EMAIL** dhaberma@indiana.edu

HABERMAS, RONALD T.
PERSONAL Born 09/20/1951, Detroit, MI, m, 1973, 3 children **DISCIPLINE** RELIGIOUS EDUCATION, HUMAN DEVELOPMENT **EDUCATION** William Tyndale Col, BA, 73; North Am Baptist Sem, MDiv, 76; Wheaton Grad Sch, MA, 82; Mich State Univ, PhD, 85. **CAREER** Assoc prof, Liberty Univ, 82-87; assoc prof, Columbia Biblical Sem, 87-93; Mc Gree Prof of Biblical Studies, John Brown Univ, 93-. **HONORS AND AWARDS** Richards Awd in Christian Ministry, Wheaton Grad Sch, 82; Fel, Mich State Univ, 83; Mc Gree Prof of Biblical Studies, John Brown Univ, 93-. **MEMBERSHIPS** North Am Profs of Christian Ed. **RESEARCH** Foundations of religious education; human development; education. **SELECTED PUBLICATIONS** Coauth with Klaus Issler, Teaching for Reconciliation: Foundations and Practice of Christian Educational Ministries, Baker Book House (92); coauth with Klaus Issler, How We Learn: A Teacher's Guide to Educational Psychology, Baker Book House (94); coauth with David Olshine, Tag-Team Youth Ministry: 50 Practical Ways to Involve Parents and Other Caring Adults, Standard Pub (95); coauth with David Olshine, Down But Not Out Parenting: 50 Ways to Win With Your Teen, Standard Pub (95); coauth with Joyce Armstrong Carroll, Jesus Didn't Use Worksheets: A 2000 Year Old Model for Good Teaching, Absey & Co (96); coauth with David Olshine, "How to Have a REAL Conversation With Your Teen, Standard Pub (98); auth, Raising Teens While They're Still in Preschool: What Experts Advise for Successful Parenting, Col Press (98). **CONTACT ADDRESS** Bibllical Studies, John Brown Univ, 2000 W Univ St, Siloam Springs, AR 72761-2112. **EMAIL** Rhabermas@acc.jbu.edu

HABERMEHL, LAWRENCE L.
PERSONAL Born 06/13/1937, Joplin, MO, d, 3 children **DISCIPLINE** PHILOSOPHY; PHILOSOPHY OF RELIGION **EDUCATION** Phillips Univ, AB, 59; Union Theol Sem, NYork City, BD, 61; Boston Univ, PhD, 67. **CAREER** Teaching fel, Dept of Philos, Boston Univ, 65-66; instr, asst prof, Assoc Prof, Am Int Col, Springfield, MA, 66-. **MEMBERSHIPS** Amer Philos Assoc; Amer Assoc Univ Profs; Metaphysical Soc Amer. **RESEARCH** Contemporary moral issues; contemporary relig issues; superstitious and pseudoscience in popular culture. **SELECTED PUBLICATIONS** Auth/ed, Morality in the Modern World: Ethical Dimensions of Contemporary Human Problems, 76; auth, The Counterfeit Wisdom of Shallow Minds: A Critique of Some Leading Offenders of the 1980's, 94. **CONTACT ADDRESS** Dept of Philos, American Intl Col, 1000 State St., Springfield, MA 01109. **EMAIL** LawLH@aol.com

HABIBI, DON
PERSONAL Born 07/30/1956, Glendale, CA, m, 1995, 2 children **DISCIPLINE** PHILOSOPHY, RELIGION **EDUCATION** Univ Calif, BA, 78; Cornell Univ, MA, 82; PhD, 85. **CAREER** Lectr, Calif State Univ, 86-87; Asst Prof, Pomona Col, 87-88; Asst Prof, Univ NC, 88-96; Assoc Prof, Univ NC, 96-. **HONORS AND AWARDS** Cahill Res Grant, Univ NC, 93; Best Article, Midwest Law Rev, 96; Chancellor's Teaching Excellence Awd, 99. **MEMBERSHIPS** ASA, Int Soc for Utilitarian Studies, Asn for Philos of Educ. **RESEARCH** Social and political philosophy, philosophy of law, philosophy of education, utilitarianism, liberalism, ethics. **SELECTED PUBLICATIONS** Coauth, "Law, Ethics and the Dilemma of Modern Liberalism," Midwest Law Rev, vol 13 (95): 1-19; auth, "The Positive/Negative Liberty Distinction and J S Mill's Theory of LIberty," Archiv fut Rechtsund Soc Philos. 81:3 (95); 347-368; auth, "J S Mill's Grand, Leading Principle," Iyyun: The Jerusalem Philos Quart, vol 45 (96): 79-104; auth, "'Review of Chaim Gans,' Philos Anarchism and Polit Disobedience," Philos, vol 26:1-2: 271-277; auth, "Mill's Revisionist Utilitarianism," Brit J of the Hist of Philos, 6:1 (98): 89-114; auth, "The Moral Dimensions of J S Mill's Colonialism," J of Soc Philos, 30:1 (99); auth, John Stuart Mill and the Ethic of Human Growth, Kluwer Acad Publ, 99. **CONTACT ADDRESS** Dept Philos & Relig, Univ of No Carolina, Wilmington, 601 S College Rd, Wilmington, NC 28403-3201. **EMAIL** habibid@uncwil.edu

HACKETT, DAVID H.
DISCIPLINE AMERICAN RELIGIOUS HISTORY, SOCIOLOGY OF RELIGION **EDUCATION** Emory Univ, PhD, 86. **CAREER** Assoc prof. **RESEARCH** Gender and American culture, American catholicism. **SELECTED PUBLICATIONS** Auth, Religion and American Culture: A Reader, Routledge, 95; Gender and Religion in American Culture, 1870-1930, Rel and Amer Cult, 95; The Silent Dialogue: Zen Letters to a Trappist Monk, Continuum, 96. **CONTACT ADDRESS** Dept of Relig, Univ of Florida, 226 Tigert Hall, Gainesville, FL 32611. **EMAIL** dhackett@religion.ufl.edu

HACKETT, ELIZABETH
PERSONAL Born 12/19/1961, Detroit, MI **DISCIPLINE** PHILOSOPHY **EDUCATION** Univ Notre Dame, BA, 83; Univ Pa, PhD, 96. **CAREER** Asst Prof, Agnes Scott Col, 99-. **MEMBERSHIPS** Soc for Women in Philos; Am Philos Asn; Nat Women's Studies Asn . **RESEARCH** Feminist theory. **CONTACT ADDRESS** Women's Studies Prog, Agnes Scott Col, 141 E College Ave, Decatur, GA 30030. **EMAIL** ehackett@agnesscott.edu

HACKETT, JEREMIAH M.
PERSONAL Born 02/27/1968, m, 1998, 2 children **DISCIPLINE** PHILOSOPHY **EDUCATION** Univ Toronto, PhD, 83. **CAREER** Asst prof, 82-84, Notre Dame Col, Oh; asst prof, 84-91, assoc prof, 91-99, prof, 99-, grad dir, 96-98, Univ SCar. **RESEARCH** Medieval/Renaissance phil, Roger Bacon, George Berkeley. **CONTACT ADDRESS** Dept of Philos, Univ of So Carolina, Columbia, J. Welsh Humanities Bldg 616, Columbia, SC 29208. **EMAIL** hacke@sc.edu

HACKING, IAN
PERSONAL Born 02/18/1936, Vancouver, BC, Canada, m, 1984, 3 children **DISCIPLINE** PHILOSOPHY **EDUCATION** Univ British Columbia, BA, 56; Cantab, BA, 58, MA; Cambridge Univ, PhD, 62. **CAREER** Prof, Univ Toronto, 83-; Stewart prof, Stanford, 74-82; Cambridge Univ, lectr, 69-74; Univ Brit Col, asst, assoc, prof, 64-69. **HONORS AND AWARDS** Fel, Royal Soc Canada; fel, Am Hd of Arts. **MEMBERSHIPS** Fel British Academy **RESEARCH** Philos **SELECTED PUBLICATIONS** The Social Construction of What?, forthcoming, Harvard Press, 99; Mad Travelers: Reflections on the Reality of Transient Mental Illnesses, VA Univ Press, 98; Rewriting the Soul: Multiple Personality and the Sciences of Memory, Princ, Princ Univ Press, 95; Le Plus pur nominalisme, L'enigme de Goodman: Vleu' et usages de Vleu', Combas, Ed de l'Eclat, 93; The Taming of Chance, Cambridge Univ Press, 90. **CONTACT ADDRESS** Dept Philosophy, Univ of Toronto, 215 Huron St, Room 911, Toronto, ON, Canada M5S 1A1.

HAFFNER, MARLENE ELISABETH
PERSONAL Born 03/22/1941, Cumberland, MD, m, 1963, 2 children **DISCIPLINE** MEDICINE, PUBLIC HEALTH **EDUCATION** Western Reserve Univ, Chem, 58-61; George Washington Univ, Dr of Medicine, 61-65; Johns Hopkins Univ, Master of Public Health, 89-91; Harvard Univ, Program for Sr Mgrs in Govt, 95. **CAREER** Chief, Adult Outpatient Dept, Gallup Indian Mex Center, 71-74; chief, Dept of Internal Med, Gallup Indian Mex Center, 71-74; preceptor, Univ of Calif San Diego, 75, 81; dir, NAIHS Arizona, 74-81; Assoc dir for Health Affairs, Bureau of Med Devices FDA, 81-82; Dir of Health Affairs, Center of Devices and Radiological Health, FDA, 82-87; Asst Prof, F Edward Hebert School of Med, 85, 86, 87; mentor for FDA-sponsored students; clinical asst prof, adj assoc prof, F Edward Hebert School of Med, 95-; FDA rep to the Off of the Surgeon General, 87-; dir, Off of Orphan Products Develop FDA, 87-. **HONORS AND AWARDS** Awd of Recognition, NORD, 88; Nat Hemophilia Found, 92; Outstanding Service to the Public Health Awd NORD 96; Robert Brutsche Awd COA, 96; numerous professional awards by PHS and academic awards; Distinguished Service Medal USPHS. **MEMBERSHIPS** Am Public Health Asn; Am Med Asn; Commissioned Offrs Asn, Anchor and Caduceus Soc; Asn of Mil Surgeons of USA; Nat Nil families Asn; Am Col of Physicians; numerous health professional organizations. **RESEARCH** Public Health. **SELECTED PUBLICATIONS** Auth, Orphan Products - Origins, Progress and Prospects, Annual Rev of Pharmacology and Toxicology, 91; numerous articles, presentations and interviews on public health; coauth, Home Health Care Devices, Encycl of Med Devices and Instrumentations, 88; The Incentives of the Orphan Drug Act and Immunosuppressive Drug Development, Principles of Drug Develop in Transplantation and Autoimmunity, 96. **CONTACT ADDRESS** Office of Orphan Products Development, US FDA, 5600 Fisher Ln, Rockville, MD 20857. **EMAIL** mhaffner@oc.fda.gov

HAGEDORN, RICHARD B.
DISCIPLINE LAW **EDUCATION** Ore State Univ, BS, 70; Willamette Univ, JD, 83. **CAREER** Partner, Weatherford, Thompson, Horton, Brickey & Powers, Albany, 73-77; asst prof, Univ Mo, 77-79; asst prof, Gonzaga Univ, 79-81; assoc prof, Gonzaga Univ, 81-85; vis assoc prof, Univ Ore, 82; prof, 84-. **HONORS AND AWARDS** Comm, Uniform Commercial Code of the Amer Bar Assn, 89-. **MEMBERSHIPS** Mem, Phi Kappa Phi; Amer Law Inst; Wash State Bar Assn, 79-82. **SELECTED PUBLICATIONS** Co-auth, Secured Transactions in a Nutshell, 88; The Law of Debtors and Creditors, 91; auth, Brady on Bank Checks, 92; The Law of Promissory Notes, 92. **CONTACT ADDRESS** Sch of Law, Willamette Univ, 900 State St, Salem, OR 97301. **EMAIL** rhagedor@willamette.edu

HAGEL, THOMAS L.
PERSONAL Born 11/02/1948, Ainsworth, NE, d **DISCIPLINE** LAW **EDUCATION** Univ Nebr, BS, 72; Univ Nebr Col Law, JD, 76; Temple Univ Sch Law, LLM, 82. **CAREER** Deputy public defender, 76-80; law and humanities fel, Temple Univ Sch of Law, 80-82; prof, Univ Dayton Sch of Law, 82-. **HONORS AND AWARDS** Law Rev, Law and Humanities Fel. **RESEARCH** Law of Evidence and Criminal Law, Trial Practice and Procedure. **SELECTED PUBLICATIONS** Auth, "Defending the Mentally Ill," Nebr Law Rev (78): 1-25; auth, "Representing the Mentally Ill: Civil Commitment Actions," Am Jur Trials 26 (80): 97-240; auth, "Representing the Mentally Disabled Criminal Defendant," Am Jur Trials (80): 1-259; auth, "Defending Against Claim of Ineffective Assistance of Counsel," Am Jur Trials 30 (83): 607-710; auth, "Issues Common to All (Justification) Defenses," in Proving Criminal Defenses, 91; auth, "Evidence," in Bar Examination Subject Outline (OH: Supreme Court of Ohio), 68-80; auth, Issues of Credibility and the Proposed Amendments to the Ohio Rules of Evidence, Ohio Judicial Col, 98; auth, Ohio Forms of Pleading and Practice, Matthew Bender Co., forthcoming. **CONTACT ADDRESS** Sch of Law, Univ of Dayton, 300 College Park Ave, Dayton, OH 45469-2772. **EMAIL** hagel@udayton.edu

HAGGARD, THOMAS R.
DISCIPLINE EMPLOYMENT DISCRIMINATION, LABOR LAW, CONTRACTS AND LEGAL DRAFTING **EDUCATION** Univ TX, BA, 64, LLB, 67. **CAREER** David W. Robinson ch prof, Univ of SC. **SELECTED PUBLICATIONS** Publ

on, employment law issues & regular columnist on legal writing. **CONTACT ADDRESS** School of Law, Univ of So Carolina, Columbia, Law Center, Columbia, SC 29208. **EMAIL** Tom@law.law.sc.edu

HAGNER, DONALD A.
PERSONAL Born 07/08/1936, Chicago, IL, m, 1962 **DISCIPLINE** BIBLICAL STUDIES; NEW TESTAMENT **EDUCATION** NW Univ, BA, 58; Fuller Theol Sem, BD, ThM, 66; Univ Manchester, PhD, 69. **CAREER** Asst, assoc prof, Wheaton Col, 69-76; prof New Testament, 76-93, george eldon ladd prof new testament, 93-, Fuller Theol Sem, 76-. **HONORS AND AWARDS** C Davis Weyerhaeuser Awd Excellence. **MEMBERSHIPS** Studiorum Novi Testamenti Soc; Soc Bibl Lit; Tyndale Fel; Inst Bibl Res; Uppsala Exeg Soc. **RESEARCH** Matthew; Paul; Apostolic Fathers; Second Temple Judaism. **SELECTED PUBLICATIONS** Auth, The Use of the Old and New Testaments in Clement of Rome, Supplements to Novum Testamentum, E. J. Brill, 73; The Epistle to the Hebrews, Good News Bible Commentaries, Harper & Row, 83; The Jewish Reclamation of Jesus: An Analysis and Critique of Modern Jewish Study of Jesus, Zondervan, 84; Matthew 1-13, Word Biblical Commentary, 93; coed, Anti-Semitism and Early Christianity: Issues of Polemic and Faith, Fortress, 93; ed, George Eldon Ladd, A Theology of the New Testament, Eerdmans, 93; coedm, New International Greek Testament Commentary, Eerdmans, 94; auth, Matthew 14-28, Word Biblical Commentary, Word, 95; New Testament Exegesis and Research: A Guide for Seminarians, FTS, 98. **CONTACT ADDRESS** Fuller Theol Sem, Pasadena, CA 91182. **EMAIL** dhagner@fuller.edu

HAHM, DAVID EDGAR
PERSONAL Born 09/30/1938, Milwaukee, WI, m, 1964, 4 children **DISCIPLINE** CLASSICAL LANGUAGES, ANCIENT PHILOSOPHY, INTELLECTUAL HISTORY **EDUCATION** Northwestern Col, BA, 60; Univ Wis-Madison, MA, 62, PhD(classics), 66. **CAREER** Asst prof class lang, Univ Mo-Columbia, 66-69; from asst prof to assoc prof class, 69-78, Prof Classics, Ohio State Univ, 78-, Fel, Ctr Hellenic Studies, Wash, DC, 68-69. **MEMBERSHIPS** Am Philol Asn; Am Philos Asn; Hist Sci Soc; Class Asn Midwest & South. **RESEARCH** Ancient philosophy and science, Greek literature. **SELECTED PUBLICATIONS** Auth, The origins of Stoic cosmology, Columbus, 77; auth, "A neglected Stoic argument for human responsibility," Illinois Classical Studies 17, (92): 23-48; auth, "Galen and Chrysippus on the soul: argument and refutation in the 'De placitis, bks. 2-3," Bulletin of the Hist of Medicine 73, (99): 302-3; auth, "Plato, Carneades and Cicero's Philus, (Cicero, Rep. 3.8-31)," Classical Quarterly ns. 49, (99): 167-83. **CONTACT ADDRESS** Dept of Greek & Latin, Ohio State Univ, Columbus, 230 N Oval Mall, Columbus, OH 43210-1335. **EMAIL** hahm.1@osu.edu

HAHN, HARLAN
PERSONAL Born 07/09/1939, Osage, IA **DISCIPLINE** POLITICAL SCIENCE **EDUCATION** BA, magna cum laude, St Olaf Col, 60; PhD, Harvard Univ, 64; MS, Calif State Univ, 82. **CAREER** Asst Prof Res, Assoc, Univ MI, 64-67; Assoc Prof, Prof Univ CA 67-72; Prof, of S CA, 72-98. **HONORS AND AWARDS** Who's Who; Alexander Hamilton; Woodrow Wilson, Robert A Taft, Ed Robets, NIHR Fellowships. **MEMBERSHIPS** Soc of Disability Studies. **RESEARCH** Disability Studies; Discrimination. **SELECTED PUBLICATIONS** Urban-Rural Conflicr: The Polotics of Change, Sage Publ, 71; Health Politics and Policy; Antidiscrimination Laws and Social Research: The Minority Group Perspective; Behavioral Sciences and the Law Vol 14, 96; The Apperance of Physical Differences: A New Agenda for Political Research, Journal of Health and Human Rsources Admin Vol17, 95; Feminist Perspectives, Disability, Sexuality and Law: New Issues and Agendas, Southern California Review of Law and Women's Studies Vol 4 No 1, 94; Civil Rights in Robert P Martinelli and Arthur E Dell Orto eds Encylopedia of Rehabilitation, MacMillan(in press); Embodied Differences: Achieving a Positive Identity, In Motion Vol 6, 96. **CONTACT ADDRESS** Dept Political Sci, Univ of So California, Los Angeles, CA 90089-0044.

HAIGHT, DAVID F.
PERSONAL Born 05/23/1941, Polson, MT, m, 1968, 1 child **DISCIPLINE** PHILOSOPHY **EDUCATION** Stanford, BA, 63; Northwestern, MA, 65; Oxford Univ, 66; Northwestern, PhD, 68. **CAREER** Thirty-five years of teaching experience. **HONORS AND AWARDS** Fulbright Scholar, Oxford Univ. **RESEARCH** Cosmology. **SELECTED PUBLICATIONS** Contribur, Library of Living Philosophers, 90; auth, The Scandal of Reason, 00. **CONTACT ADDRESS** Dept Philos, Plymouth State Col of the Univ System of New Hampshire, 17 High St, Plymouth, NH 03264-1595.

HAILE, GETATCHEW
PERSONAL Born 04/19/1931, Shenkora, Shoa, Ehtiopia, m, 1964, 6 children **DISCIPLINE** LINGUISTICS, RELIGION **EDUCATION** Am Univ Cairo, BA, 57; Coptic Theol Col Cairo, BD, 57; Univ Tubingen, PhD(semitic philol), 62. **CAREER** Lectr, Amharic, Ge'ez and Arabic, HSI Univ, Ethiopia, 62-64, asst prof Amharic, Ge'ez and Arabic and chmn dept Ethiopian lang, 64-69; exchange scholar ling, Univ Calif, Los Angeles, 69-70; vis prof African studies, Okla State Univ, 70-71; assoc prof Amharic, Ge'ez and Arabic, HSI Univ, Ethiopia, 71-75; Cataloguer of Oriental Manuscripts and Regents Prof of Medieval History, Hill Monastic Manuscript Libr, St John's Univ, Minn, 76-, Contrib ed, Northeast African Studies, Mich State Univ. **HONORS AND AWARDS** MacArthur Foundation Awd. **MEMBERSHIPS** Corresponding Fellow of the British Academy. **RESEARCH** Ge'ez literature; Amharic grammar. **SELECTED PUBLICATIONS** Auth, A Catalogue of Ethiopian Manuscripts Micorfilmed for the Ethiopian Manuscript Microfilm Library, addis Ababa and for The Hill Monastic Manuscript Library, Collegeville, 83; auth, The Faith of the Unctionists in the Ethiopian Church, 90; auth, The Epistle of Humanity, 91; auth, The Mariology of Emperor Zar'a Yaeqob of Ethiopia, 92; auth, From Emperor Selassie, Haile to Polotsky, H. J.--An Ethiopian and Semitic Miscellany, J Royal Asiatic Soc, Vol 0006, 96. **CONTACT ADDRESS** Hill Monastic Ms Libr, St. John's Univ, Collegeville, MN 56321. **EMAIL** ghaile@csbsju.edu

HAINES, DIANA
PERSONAL Born 03/04/1955, Brooklyn, NY, s **DISCIPLINE** LAW **EDUCATION** Oberlin College, BA, 1977; George Washington University Law Center, JD, 1980; Antioch University, MA, legal education, 1985. **CAREER** Antioch Law School, clinical law professor, 82-86; Department of Consumer & Regulatory Affiars, chief office of compliance, 86-92; American University Law School, adjunct instructor, 86-; DC Government, Civilian Complaint Review Board, executive director, 92-. **MEMBERSHIPS** My Sister's Place, Shelter for Battered Women, staff attorney, 1990-; DC Bar, Consumer Affairs Section, steering committee, 1992-; Coalition of 100 Black Women, 1986-; Christian Social Action Committee, United Church of Christ, chairperson, 1991-. **CONTACT ADDRESS** Executive Director, Civilian Complaint Review Board, 1010 Massachusetts Ave NW, 4th Fl, Washington, DC 20001.

HAJDIN, MANE
PERSONAL Born 09/30/1959, Belgrade, Serbia, s **DISCIPLINE** PHILOSOPHY **EDUCATION** Univ of Belgrade, BA, 82; McGill Univ, PhD, 88. **CAREER** TA & lectr, McGill Univ, 83-87; lectr, Univ of Papua New Guinea, 87-90; lectr, Univ of Waikato New Zealand, 90-97; res assoc, Univ of Calif-Berkeley, 94-95 & 96-97; lectr, Sonoma State Univ, 97-98; adj lectr, Santa Clara Univ, 97-00; lectr, Dominican Col of San Rafael, 98-00; lectr, San Jose State Univ, 99-00. **MEMBERSHIPS** Am Philos Asn, Can Philos Asn, Int Asn for Philos of Law and Soc Philos, N Am Soc for Soc Philos, Soc for the Philos of Sex and Love, Soc for the Study of Ethics & Animals. **RESEARCH** Ethics, philosophy of law, social/political philosophy. **SELECTED PUBLICATIONS** Auth, "External and Now-For-Then Preferences in Hare's Theory," Dialogue 29 (90): 305-310; auth, "Is There More Speech Acts Than Illocutionary Force and Propositional Content?" Nous 25 (91): 353-357; auth, "External reasons and the Foundations of Morality: Mother Theresa vs. Thrasymachus," J of Value Inquiry 26 (92): 433-441; auth, "Sanctions and the Notion of Morality," Dialogue 32 (93): 757-760; auth, "Sexual Harassment in the Law: The Democratic Problem," J of Soc Philos 25.3 (94): 102-122; auth, "Sexual Harassment and Negligence," J of Soc Philos 28.1 (97): 37-53; auth, The Boundaries of Moral Discourse, Loyola Univ Press (Chicago, IL), 94; coauth, Sexual Harassment: A Debate, Rowman & Littlefield (Lanham, MD), 97; ed, The Notion of Equality, Ashgate/Dartmouth Publ Co (Aldershot, Eng), forthcoming. **CONTACT ADDRESS** Dept Rel & Philos, Dominican Col of San Rafael, 339 Post St #309, San Francisco, CA 94109-6047.

HALAL, WILLIAM E.
PERSONAL Born 06/29/1933, Lebanon, m, 1972, 2 children **DISCIPLINE** BUSINESS & ECONOMICS **EDUCATION** Purdue Univ BSc; Univ CA Berkeley, MBA, PhD. **CAREER** George Washington Univ, prof mgmt 79; Am Univ, assoc prof mgmt 71-79. **HONORS AND AWARDS** Awded Mitchell Prize; George Wash Honor Medal Freedoms Found, Smithsonian Awd; speaker; conference maker; consultant. **MEMBERSHIPS** Acad of Mgt World Future Soc. **RESEARCH** Engineering Technol; The New Management. **SELECTED PUBLICATIONS** Auth, Encyclopedia of the Future, Ed Bd, MacMillan, 96; The IT Generation, Eng Horizons, 93; Internal Markets, 94; Organization for the Year 2000: The New Portable MBA, Wiley, 95; The New Management: Democracy and Enterprise Are Transforming Organizations, San Fran, Berrett-Koehler, 96; auth, The Infinite Resource, Jossey-Bass; 98; auth, 21st Century Economics, 99. **CONTACT ADDRESS** Dept of Management Serv, The George Washington Univ, Washington, DC 20052. **EMAIL** halal@gwu.edu

HALBERSTAM, MALVINA
PERSONAL Born 05/02/1937, Kempno, Poland, d, 2 children **DISCIPLINE** LAW **EDUCATION** Brooklyn Col, BA, 57; Columbia Univ, JD, MIA, 61. **CAREER** Law clerk, to Judge Edmund L. Palmieri, 61-62; res assoc, Columbia Proj on Int Procedure, 62-63; asst district atty, NY county, 63-67; pvt pract, Rifkind and Sterling, Los Angeles, 67-68; sen atty, Nat Legal Prog on Health Problems of the Poor, 69-70; prof, Loyola Univ Sch of Law, 70-76; vis prof, Univ of Southern Calif Gould Law Ctr, 72-73; vis prof, Univ of Tex, 74; vis prof, Univ of Va, 75-76, reporter, Am Law Inst, Mode Penal Code Proj, 77-79; vis prof, Hebrew Univ of Jerusalem, 84-85; coun on Int Law, U.S. Dept of State, Off of the Legal Adviser, 85-86; consult, U.S. Dept of State, Off of the Legal Adviser, 86-92; prof, Yeshiva Univ, 92-. **HONORS AND AWARDS** Biographical listings include Who's Who in Am, Who's Who in Am Law, World's Who's Who of Women, Who's Who of Am Women, Who's Who in Am Educ, Int Dictionary of Biographies, Community Leaders and Noteworthy Americans, Who's Who in World Jewry. **MEMBERSHIPS** AALS; Am Bar Asn; Am Law Inst; Am Soc of Int Law; Asn of the Bar of the City of NY; Columbia Law Sch Alumni Asn; Int Asn of Jewish Lawyers and Jurists; Int Law Asn; Phi Beta Kappa Asn. **RESEARCH** International law; human rights, US foreign relations law. **SELECTED PUBLICATIONS** Auth, The Rationale for Excluding Self-incriminating Statements: U S Law Compared to Ancient Jewish Law, Jewish Law and Current Legal Problems, The Jewish Heritage Society, 84; auth, Model Penal Code and Commentaries, Part 1, Article 1, The American Law Institute, 85; coauth, Legal Rights of Women: International Covenants an Alternative to ERA? Transnational Publishers, 87; auth, Ruth Bader Ginsburg: The First Jewish Woman on the United States Supreme Court, Jewish Women in America: An Historical Encyclopedia, Routledge, 97; auth, Framing the Issues: The Holocaust, Moral and Legal Issues Unresolved Fifty Years Later, 20 Cardozo L Rev 443, 98; auth, The Jerusalem Embassy Act: U S Recognition of Jerusalem ad the Capital of Israel Jerusalem, City of Law and Justice, The Jewish Legal Heritage Society, 98; auth, AALS Panel Discussion on the International Criminal Court, 36 Am, Cr L Rev, 231. 99; auth, The Constitutional Authority of the Federal Government In State Criminal Proceedings That Involve U S Treaty Obligations or Affect U S Foreign Relations, 10 Indiana Int and Comp L Rev 1, 99; auth, Crimes Against International Maritime Navigation and Installations on the High Seas, International Criminal Law, Second Revised Ed, Transnational Publishers, 99; auth, United States Ratification of the Convention on the Elimination of all Forms of Discrimination against Women , Women and International Human Rights Law, vol 2., Transnational Publishers, 00. **CONTACT ADDRESS** Benjamin N. Cardozo Sch of Law, Yeshiva Univ, 55 Fifth Ave, New York, NY 10003.

HALBERSTAM, MICHAEL
DISCIPLINE PHILOSOPHY **EDUCATION** Yale Univ, PhD, 96 **CAREER** Asst prof, 95-, Univ SC. **MEMBERSHIPS** APA **RESEARCH** German philosophy, political philosophy **SELECTED PUBLICATIONS** Auth, Totalitarianism as a Problem for the Modern Conception of Politics, Pol Theory vol 26, 98; auth, The Meaning of Totalitarianism for the Modern Conception of Politics, Yale Univ Press, 99. **CONTACT ADDRESS** Dept of Philos, Univ of So Carolina, Columbia, 1 University of South Carolina, Columbia, SC 29225-0001. **EMAIL** mhalberstam@wesleyan.edu

HALBERT, DEBORA
DISCIPLINE POLITICAL SCIENCE **EDUCATION** Western Washington Univ Political Science, BA, 89; Western Washington Univ Politcal Science, MA, 92; Univ Hawaii, PhD, 96. **CAREER** Asst Prof of Political Science, Otterbein Col, 96-. **RESEARCH** Intellectual Property; Environmental Politics. **SELECTED PUBLICATIONS** Auth, "Intellectual Property in the Information Age: The Politics of Expanding Property Rights," Quorum Press, 99. **CONTACT ADDRESS** Dept History & Government, Otterbein Col, One Otterbein College, Westerville, OH 43081.

HALBERT, TERRY ANN
PERSONAL Born 02/23/1948, Philadelphia, PA, m, 1987, 1 child **DISCIPLINE** LEGAL STUDIES **EDUCATION** Colby Col, BA, 70; Rutgers Univ Sch Law, JD, 81. **CAREER** Assoc prof, Legal Studies, Temple Univ, 81-. **HONORS AND AWARDS** Temple Univ Teacher of the Year Awd, 99. **RESEARCH** Business ethics, employment law. **SELECTED PUBLICATIONS** Auth, "Setting Aside Releases for Personal Injury," The Pa Bar Quart, Vol LIII, No 4 (Oct 82); auth, "Insurers' Bad Faith Refusal to Settle," The Pa Bar Quart, Vol LVII, no 1 (Jan 86); auth, "The Cost of Scruples: Common Law Protection for the Professional Whistleblower," Nova Law J (spring 86); auth, "Free Speech at the Workplace: A Call for Statutory Reform," Seton Hall Law Rev (fall 86); auth, "Coming Up Dirty: Drugtesting at the Workplace," Villanova Law Rev, Vol 32 (87); coauth with Elaine Ingulli, "Ethics & Electronic Monitoring of Employees," Workplace Ethics (summer 98); coauth with Lewis Maltby, "Reference Check Gridlock: A Proposal for Escape," Employee Rights and Employment Policy J, Vol 1, No 2 (Jan 99); auth, "The Fire-Safe Cigarette: The Other Tobacco War," Business and Soc Rev, (Jan 99): 102/103; coauth with Elaine Ingulli, Law and Ethics in the Business Environment, 3rd ed, West Pub Co (2000). **CONTACT ADDRESS** Fox Sch of Business & Management, Temple Univ, 1810 N 13th St, 208 Speakman Hall, Philadelphia, PA 19122. **EMAIL** thalbert@sbm.temple.edu

HALES, STEVEN D.
PERSONAL Born 01/07/1966, Chicago, IL, m, 1993 **DISCIPLINE** PHILOSOPHY **EDUCATION** Southwestern Univ, BA, 87; Brown Univ, MA, 90, PhD, 92. **CAREER** Vis asst prof, Ga State Univ, 92-94; assoc prof, Bloomsburg Univ, 92. **HONORS AND AWARDS** Richard M. Griffith Memorial Awd, Southern Soc for Philos and Psychol, 95; Dean's Salute for Excellence, Bloomsburg Univ, 98. **MEMBERSHIPS** Am Philos Asn, North Am Nietzche Soc. **RESEARCH** Metaphysics, epistemology, Nietzsche. **SELECTED PUBLICATIONS** Auth, "Ockham's Disposable Razor," in The Role of Pragmatics in Contemporary Philosophy: Contributions of the Austrian Ludwig Wittgenstein Society, Paul Weingartner, Gerard Schurz, and George Dorn, eds, Vienna: Holder-Pichler-Tempsky (97); auth, "Reply to Shogenji on Relativism," Mind, vol 106, n0 424:33-52 (97); auth, "An Epistemologist Looks at the Hot Hand in Sports," J of the Philos of Sport, vol 26:79-87 (99); coauth with Rex Welshon, "Nietzsche, Perspectivism, and Mental Health," Philos, Psychiatry, and Psychol, vol 6, no 3: 173-177 (99); ed with prefaces and pedagogical appartatus, Metaphysics: Contemporary Readings, Belmont, CA: Wadsworth Pub Co (99); coauth with Rex Welshon, Nietzsche's Perspectivism, Urbana: Univ Ill Press (2000); auth, "The Problem of Intuition," Am Philos Quart, vol 37, no 2: 135-147 (2000); auth, "Evidence and the Afterlife," Philosophia (forthcoming); ed, with intro, Analytic Philosophy: Classic Readings, Belmont, CA: Wadsworth Pub Co (forthcoming); auth, "Reincarnation Redux: A Reply to Almeder," Philosophia (forthcoming). **CONTACT ADDRESS** Dept Philos, Bloomsburg Univ of Pennsylvania, 400 E 2nd Street, Bloomsburg, PA 17815-1301. **EMAIL** hales@bloomu.edu

HALIVNI, DAVID
DISCIPLINE RELIGION **EDUCATION** Columbia Univ, PhD. **CAREER** Prof. **RESEARCH** Talmud and Rabbinics. **SELECTED PUBLICATIONS** Auth, Peshat and Derash: Plain and Applied Meaning in Rabbinic Exegesis, 91; Revelation Restored: Divine Writ and Critical Responses, 97; The Book and the Sword: A Life of Learning in the Shadow of Destruction. **CONTACT ADDRESS** Dept of Religion, Columbia Col, New York, 2960 Broadway, New York, NY 10027-6902. **EMAIL** dw13@columbia.edu

HALL, BENJAMIN LEWIS, III
PERSONAL Born 03/13/1956, Laurens, SC, m, 1981, 2 children **DISCIPLINE** LAW **EDUCATION** University of South Carolina, BA (cum laude), 77; Duke Divinity School, MDiv, 79; Rheinische Friedrich-Wilheims Universitat, BONN Fed'l Fulbright Rep of Germany Scholar-DAAD, 80-82; Duke University Graduate School, PhD, 85; Harvard Law School, JD, 86. **CAREER** South Texas Col of Law, adjunct professor of law, 91; Vinson & Elkins LLP, trial lawyer, special counsel, 86-92; University of Houston Law Center, adjunct professor of law, 87-91; City of Houston, city attorney, 92-95; O'Quinn and Laminack, attorney, currently. **HONORS AND AWARDS** Rockefellar Scholar, 77-78; Benjamin E Mays Scholar, 78-79; Duke Black Grad Fellow, 79-80; German Research Fellow, Bonn Universitat, 80; James B Duke Grad Fellow, 80-81; DADD Scholar to Germany, 81-82; Black Doctoral Dissertation Fellow, 82-83; Shell Fellow to Lambarene, Gabon, Africa, 82-83; Duke Merit Scholar, 77-79; Merrill Griswold Scholar, 86. **MEMBERSHIPS** Houston Bar Asn; Am Bar Asn; Houston Lawyers Asn; NAACP. **RESEARCH** Franchise litigation; public utility litigation; insurance law. **SELECTED PUBLICATIONS** Auth, Bad Faith Exposure for Insurance Agents, 91; auth,The Duty of Good Faith and Fair Dealing - Can it be Extended to Include Agents, Adjusters, and Brokers, 91; auth, Production of "Tangible Things:" Its Mechanics and Strategies, 91; auth, The ABC's of Reducing Litigation Costs, 93; auth, Governmental Liability, 94; coauth, Governmental Liability: Preparing, Trying, and Settling Auto Collision Cases, State Bar of Tex, 95; auth, Production of Documents and Tangible Things Under the New Rules, 98. **CONTACT ADDRESS** O'Quinn and Laminack, 2300 Lyric Centre Building, 440 Louisiana, Houston, TX 77002.

HALL, BRONWYN H.
PERSONAL Born 03/01/1945, West Point, NY, m, 1966, 2 children **DISCIPLINE** ECONOMICS **EDUCATION** Wellesley Col, BA, 66; Stanford Univ, PhD, 88. **CAREER** Programmer, Lawrence Berkeley Lab, 63-65, 67-70; Programmer, Harvard Univ, 66-67; Sen Programmer, Harvard Inst of Econ Res, 70-77; Partner to CEO and Owner, TSP Intl, 77-; Asst Prof to Prof, Univ Calif Berkeley, 87-; Res Assoc, Inst for Fiscal Studies, 95-; Prof, Oxford Univ, 96-01. **HONORS AND AWARDS** Fel, Sloan Found, 86-87; Fel, Hoover Inst, 92-93; Fel, Rockefeller Found, 98; Sigma Xi. **MEMBERSHIPS** Am Econ Asn; Econ Soc; Am Fin Asn; Intl Joseph Schumpeter Soc; Europ Econ Asn; Royal Econ Soc. **RESEARCH** Economics and econometrics of technical change and innovation; Policy issues surrounding intellectual property rights and open science: R&D; investment; liquidity; and technology strategy at the firm level, including international comparisons; Valuation of intangible corporate assets; Estimation of models using panel data; Mergers, exit and R&D. **SELECTED PUBLICATIONS** Auth, "The Impact of Corporate Restructuring on Industrial Research and Development," Brookings Papers on Economic Activity, (90); 85-136; auth, "R&D Tax Policy During the Eighties: Success or Failure?" Tax Policy and the Economy, (93): 1-36; co-auth, "Exploring the Relationship Between R&D and Productivity in French Manufacturing Firms," J of Econometrics, (95): 263-294; co-auth, "Heart of Darkness: Public-Private Interactions Inside the R&D Black Box," Res Policy, (00): 1165-1183; co-auth, "Market Value and Patent citations: A First Look," NBER Working Paper No 7741, 00; co-auth, "The Determinants of Patenting in the U.S. Semiconductor Industry, 1980-1994," R and J of Econ, forthcoming. **CONTACT ADDRESS** Dept Econ, Univ of California, Berkeley, 549 Evans Hall, Berkeley, CA 94720-3880. **EMAIL** bhhall@econ.berkeley.edu

HALL, DAVID
PERSONAL Born 05/26/1950, Savannah, GA, m, 1990, 3 children **DISCIPLINE** LAW **EDUCATION** Kans State Univ, BA, 72; Univ of Ok, MA, 75, JD, 78; Harvard Law Sch, LLM, 85, SJD, 88. **CAREER** Federal Trade Commission, staff attorney 1978-80; Univ of Mississippi Law School, asst prof of law 1980-83; Univ of Oklahoma Law School, assoc prof of law 1983-85; Northeastern Univ School of Law, assoc professor of law, 85-88, associate dean & professor, 88-98, Provost/Sr Vice Pres, 98-; Sabbatical research, South Africa, beginning 1992. **HONORS AND AWARDS** Professor of the Year, Oxford Miss Branch of NAACP; Floyd Calvert Law Faculty Award, Univ of Oklahoma Law School 1984; Order of the Coif, Univ of Oklahoma Law School Chapter 1984; Robert D Klein, Northeastern Univ; Floyd Calvert Law Faculty, Univ of OK; professor of the year, NAACP, Oxford, MS; MA Black Lawyers Outstanding Contribution to the Legal Profession Award, 93; Outstanding Dean of the Year by the Nat'l Asn of Public Interest Lawyers, 97; Nat Conference of Community and Justice Humanitarian Award, 99. **MEMBERSHIPS** Pres of the Nat Black Wholistic Society; Natl Conference of Black Lawyers 1978-80; Oklahoma Bar Assn 1978-; attorney, Fed Trade Commn, Chicago, IL, 1978-80; Amer Bar Assn. **CONTACT ADDRESS** Northeastern Univ, 360 Huntington Ave, Boston, MA 02115. **EMAIL** d.hall@nunet.neu.edu; c.willis@nunet.neu.edu

HALL, DAVID LYNN
PERSONAL Born Shreveport, LA, 2 children **DISCIPLINE** PHILOSOPHY OF CULTURE ASIAN AND COMPARATIVE, AMERICAN PHILOSOPHY **EDUCATION** Tex Western Col, BA, 61; Chicago Theol Sem, BD, 64; Yale Univ, PhD(philos theol), 67. **CAREER** Asst prof philos, Univ Tulsa, 67-69; assoc prof, 69-75, PROF PHILOS, UNIV TEX, EL PASO, 75-, Nat Endowment for Humanities res grant, 78-. **HONORS AND AWARDS** Am Phil Soc; Phi Kappa Phi; Distginguished Res Awd. **MEMBERSHIPS** Southwestern Philos Soc; Soc Studies Process Philos; Soc Asian & Comp Philos. **RESEARCH** Contemporary philosophy of culture; Asian and comparative philosophy; American Philosophy. **SELECTED PUBLICATIONS** Auth, The Civilization of Experience, Fordham, 73; auth, The Uncertain Phoenix, Fordham, 82; auth, Eros and Irony, SUNY, 82; auth, Thinking Through Confucius, SUNY, 82; auth, The Arimaspian Eye, SUNY, 92; auth, Anticipating China, SUNY, 96; auth, Richard Rorty- Poet and Prophet of New Pragmatism, SUNY, 94; auth, Thinking from the Han, SUNY, 98; auth, The Democracy of the Dead, Open Court, 98. **CONTACT ADDRESS** Dept of Philos, Univ of Texas, El Paso, 500 W University Ave, El Paso, TX 79968-0001. **EMAIL** dhall@utep.edu

HALL, JAMES
PERSONAL Born 10/20/1933, Houston, TX, m, 1977, 3 children **DISCIPLINE** PHILOSOPHY **EDUCATION** John Hopkins Univ, AB, 55; BD, 58, ThM, 60, Southeastern Seminary; UNC-Chapel Hill, PhD, 64. **CAREER** Instr, 60-62, UNC-Chapel Hill; Asst Prof, 63-65, Furman Univ; Assoc Prof, 65-74, Prof, 74-, Univ Richmond. **HONORS AND AWARDS** Thomas Chr in Phil, 82-; Omicron Delta Kappa, 84. **MEMBERSHIPS** Amer Phil Assoc; AAUP **RESEARCH** Philosophy of religion **SELECTED PUBLICATIONS** Auth, Knowledge Belief and Transcendence, 75; coauth, Biblical & Secular Ethics, 88; Auth, Logic Problems, 91. **CONTACT ADDRESS** Philosophy/North Ct., Univ of Richmond, Richmond, VA 23173. **EMAIL** jhall@richmond.edu

HALL, JOHN
PERSONAL Born Washington, DC **DISCIPLINE** PHILOSOPHY **EDUCATION** Vanderbilt Univ, PhD, 70. **CAREER** Asst prof, assoc prof, Randolph-Macon Col, 68-78; assoc prof, prof, Virginia Commonwealth Univ, 79-87; prof, Davidson Col, 87-. **MEMBERSHIPS** Am Phil Asn; Phil of Sci Asn; Soc for Phil and Psych, Southern Soc for Phil and Psych; N Carolina Phil Soc. **RESEARCH** Philosophy of mind; metaphysics; epistemology. **SELECTED PUBLICATIONS** North Am ed, Phil Quart; auth, Logic and Language, Univ Pr of Am, 78; Perception and Cognition, Univ of Calif, 83; Nature of True Minds, Cambridge Univ, 92; First-Order Logic, Jones and Bartlett, 94; Philosophy of Mind, Routledge, 98. **CONTACT ADDRESS** Dept of Philosophy, Davidson Col, Davidson, NC 28036. **EMAIL** joheil@davidson.edu

HALL, P. W.
PERSONAL m, 1 child **DISCIPLINE** ENGLISH, RELIGIOUS STUDIES **EDUCATION** Univ Ore, BS, 87; Northern Ariz Univ, MA, 99. **CAREER** Assoc fac, Coconino Community Col, 99-. **HONORS AND AWARDS** Nat Deans List; Outstanding Col Students of Am; Golden Key Nat Honor Soc; NAU Jr Scholar Awd. **MEMBERSHIPS** Asian Chamber of Commerce. **RESEARCH** Multicultural Issues, Gender and Race Issues. **SELECTED PUBLICATIONS** Articles in Asian American Encyclopedia, Mountain Living, Asian Week, Asian Sun News, Encyclopedia of Multiculturalism Supplement, and Brushstrokes. **CONTACT ADDRESS** Dept Liberal Arts, Coconino County Comm Col, PO Box 80000, Flagstaff, AZ 86003-8000. **EMAIL** hallpw@hotmail.com

HALL, PAMELA M.
DISCIPLINE ETHICS AND MORAL PSYCHOLOGY **EDUCATION** Vanderbilt Univ, PhD, 87. **CAREER** Assco prof of Philos, Emory Univ. **RESEARCH** Ethics and moral psychol, medieval philos, feminist thought, and philos of lit. **SELECTED PUBLICATIONS** Auth, Narrative and the Natural Law: An Interpretation of Thomistic Ethics. **CONTACT ADDRESS** Emory Univ, Atlanta, GA 30322-1950. **EMAIL** philph@emory.edu

HALL, RICHARD JOHN
PERSONAL Born 07/11/1937, Vancouver, BC, Canada, m, 1959, 2 children **DISCIPLINE** PHILOSOPHY **EDUCATION** Oberlin Col, BA, 59; Princeton Univ, PhD, 63. **CAREER** From instr to assoc prof philos, Franklin and Marshall Col, 62-69; assoc prof, 69-80, PROF PHILOS, MICH STATE UNIV, 80-. **MEMBERSHIPS** Am Philos Asn. **RESEARCH** Philos of mind. **SELECTED PUBLICATIONS** Auth, The Evolution of Color-Vision without Colors, Philos of Sci, Vol 0063, 96. **CONTACT ADDRESS** Dept of Philos, Michigan State Univ, 503 S Kedzie Hall, East Lansing, MI 48824. **EMAIL** hallrj@msu.edu

HALL, ROBERT WILLIAM
PERSONAL Born 04/06/1928, Arlington, MA, m, 1958, 6 children **DISCIPLINE** PHILOSOPHY **EDUCATION** Harvard Univ, AB, 49, MA, 51, PhD, 53. **CAREER** Vis asst prof philos, Vanderbilt Univ, 55-57; vis asst prof, 57-63, assoc prof, 63-67, chmn dept, 64-72, Prof Philos & Relig, Univ Vt, 67, Church Soc Col Work fel, 63-64; ed, Apeiron, 67; Shedd fel, relig in higher educ, 68-69. **MEMBERSHIPS** Soc Ancient Greek Philos (secy-treas, 63-73); Brit Studies Group in Greek Polit Thought; Am Soc Polit & Legal Philos. **RESEARCH** Plato and Greek philos; philos of relig; aesthetics. **SELECTED PUBLICATIONS** Auth, Plato and the Individual, Martinus Nijhoff, 63; Gorgias, In: Essays in Ancient and Greek Philosophy, State Univ NY, 71; Plato's just and happy man: Fact or fallacy?, J Hist Philos, 71; Egalitarianism and justice in the Republic, Apeiron, 72; Plato's theory of art: A reassessment, J Aesthet & Art Criticism, 74; Plato's political analogy: Fallacy or analogy, J Hist Philos, 74; Plato, Allen and Unwin, 81; Plato and Totalitariansim, Polis, 88; Art and Morality in Plato, A Reappraisal, Jour Aesthetic Educ, 90; Natural law Revisited, Studies in Political Thought, 92; Hanslick and Musical Expressiveness, Jour Aesthetic Educ, 95; Hanslick with Feeling, Canadian Aesthetics Jour, 98. **CONTACT ADDRESS** Dept of Philos, Univ of Vermont, 70 S Williams St, Burlington, VT 05401-3404.

HALL, RONALD L.
PERSONAL Born 01/02/1945, Moultrie, GA, m, 1965, 2 children **DISCIPLINE** PHILOSOPHY, RELIGION **EDUCATION** Stetson Univ, BA, 67; Duke Univ, MDiv, 70; Univ NC, Chapel Hill, PhD(Philo), 73. **CAREER** Asst prof, 73-80, Assoc Prof, 80-85, Prof, Philos & Relig, Francis Marion Univ, 85-00; Prof, Stetson Univ, 00-. **HONORS AND AWARDS** NEH Summer Seminar, Purdue Univ, 78; NEH Summer Seminar, Harvard Univ, 84. **MEMBERSHIPS** Am Philos Asn; Am Acad Relig; kierkegaard Soc; Polany Soc; Soc Philos Relig. **RESEARCH** Metaphysics and epistemology. **SELECTED PUBLICATIONS** Auth, Responsibility and intention: Reflections on the problem of God's will and human suffering, Perspectives Relig Studies, summer 79; Wittgenstein and Polanyi: The problem of privileged self-knowledge, Philos Today, fall 79; Freedom: Merleau-Ponty's critique of Sartre, Philos Res Arch, winter 80; The ontological context of God's omniscience and man's freedom, Perspectives Relig Studies, spring 81; The origin of alienation: Some Kierkegaardian reflections on Merleau-Ponty's phenomenology of the body, Int J Philos Relig, summer 81; Word and Spirit: A Kierkegaardian Critique of the Modern Age, Indiana Univ Press, 93; auth, The Human Embrace: The Love of Philosophy and the Philosophy of Love, Kierkegaard, Cavell, Nussbaum, Penn State Press, 99. **CONTACT ADDRESS** Dept of Philosophy, Stetson Univ, De Land, DeLand, FL 29501-0547. **EMAIL** ronhall@stetson.edu

HALL, THOR
PERSONAL Born 03/15/1927, Larvik, Norway, m, 1950, 1 child **DISCIPLINE** THEOLOGY **EDUCATION** Scand Methodist Sem, Sweden, BD, 50; Duke Univ, MRE, 59, PhD, 62. **CAREER** Asst minister, Hamar Methodist Church, Norway, 46-47; minister, Odalen Methodist Church, Kongsvinger, 51-53; nat dir Christian educ, Methodist Bd Educ, Norway, 53-57; minister, Ansonville Methodist Church, NC, 58-59; asst to minister, First Presby Church, Durham, DC, 60-62; asst preaching, Divinity Sch, Duke Univ, 61-62, from asst prof to assoc prof

preaching and theol, 62-72; DISTINGUISHED PROF RELIG STUDIES, UNIV TENN, CHATTANOOGA, 72-, Ed, Var Ungdom, 53-57; Am Asn Theol Schs fac fel, Sweden, 68-69; mem, Gen Bd Evangelism, United Methodist Church, 68-72; chmn, Workgroup Scand Theol, Am Acad Relig, 74-81; vis prof, Oslo Univ, spring sem, 77, Sbarnga Sch Theol, Siberia, 80. **HONORS AND AWARDS** James Sprunt lectr, Union Theol Sem Va, 70. **MEMBERSHIPS** Am Acad Relig; Soc Philos Relig; Soc Sci Studies Relig; AAUP. **RESEARCH** Philosophy of religion; theological methodology; systematic theology. **SELECTED PUBLICATIONS** Auth, A Theology of Christian Devotion, Upper Room, 69; A Framework for Faith, Brill, Leyden, 70; The Future Shape of Preaching, Fortress, 71; Whatever Happened to the Gospel, Tidings, 73; coauth, Advent-Christmas, Fortress, 75; ed, A Directory of Systematic Theologians in North America, Coun Study Relig, 77; auth, Anders Nygren, Word, 78; Systematic Theology Today, Univ Press Am, 78; The Evolution of Christology, Abingdon, 82. **CONTACT ADDRESS** Dept of Philos and Relig, Univ of Tennessee, Chattanooga, Chattanooga, TN 37401.

HALLBERG, FRED WILLIAM

PERSONAL Born 08/13/1935, Minneapolis, MN, m, 1985, 5 children **DISCIPLINE** PHILOSOPHY **EDUCATION** Iowa St Univ, MS, 74; Univ Minn, MA, 63, PhD, 69. **CAREER** Instr, Univ Minn, 64-67; assoc prof, Univ N Iowa, 67-98. **MEMBERSHIPS** APA; Am Acad Relig. **RESEARCH** Theory of knowledge; philosophy of religion; philosophy of science. **SELECTED PUBLICATIONS** Auth, "Is Lady Philosophy Being Straight with Boethius," Carmina Philos, 93; "Neo-Kantian Constraints on Legitimate Religious Belief," Am Jrnl of Theol and Phil, 95; rev of Paul Jerome Croce, Science and Religion in the Era of William James, Am Jrnl of Theol and Phil, 96; Demythologization of Eschatological Environmentalism," Proc of 2nd Int Conf on Philos and Theol, 98; "Satisfaction and Power Components of the Pragmatic Definition of Truth," Pragmatism in Am Relig Thought, 98. **CONTACT ADDRESS** 630 Main St., PO Box 323, Janesville, IA 50647. **EMAIL** hallberg@uni.edu

HALLBORG, ROBERT B., JR.

PERSONAL Born 05/24/1947, Newport, RI, m, 1971, 2 children **DISCIPLINE** PHILOSOPHY **EDUCATION** SUNY Buffalo, JD, 80, PhD, 84. **CAREER** Criminal appeals atty, Legal Aid Bureau of Buffalo, 87- . **HONORS AND AWARDS** Boldy Found Fel. **MEMBERSHIPS** Am Philos Asn; NY St Public Defenders Asn; Natl Asn Criminal Def Lawyers. **RESEARCH** Philosophy of Criminal Law justifications; Necessity Defense. **SELECTED PUBLICATIONS** Auth, Comparing Harms: The Lesser Evil Defense and the Trolley Problem, in Legal Theory 3, 97, 291-316. **CONTACT ADDRESS** Dept of Criminal Appeals, Legal Aid Bureau, 237 Main St, Ste 1602, Buffalo, NY 14203-2723. **EMAIL** rhailborg@aol.com

HALLEN, BARRY

PERSONAL Born 04/05/1941, Chicago, IL **DISCIPLINE** PHILOSOPHY **EDUCATION** Carleton Col, BA, 63; Boston Univ, MA, 68, PhD, 70. **CAREER** Lectr, 70-75, Univ of Lagos, Nigera; reader in philosophy, 75-88, Univ of Ife, Nigera; visiting prof, 97-99, Morehouse Col, **HONORS AND AWARDS** Dir, UNESCO Intercultural Project, 88-98; research fel, W.E.B. DuBois Institute for Afro-Amer Research, Harvard Univ, 95-99. **MEMBERSHIPS** ACASA; ASA; APA **RESEARCH** Africana Philosphy; interdisciplinary and intercultural studies. **SELECTED PUBLICATIONS** Auth, What's It Mean?: 'Analytic' African Philosophy, in Quest Philosophical Discussions, 96; auth, African Meanings, Western Words, African Studies Review, The African Studies Association, 97; coauth, Knowledge, Belief, and Witchcraft: Analytic Experiments in African Philosophy, 97; auth, Moral Epistemology: When Propositions Come Out of Mouths, 98; auth, entries on Aesthetics, African and on Yoruba Epistemology for the Encyclopedia of Philosophy, 98; auth, entry on African Aesthetics for the Encyclopedia of Aesthetics, 98. **CONTACT ADDRESS** Morehouse Col, 830 Westview Dr SW, Atlanta, GA 30314-3776. **EMAIL** ablesus@aol.com

HALLER, MARK HUGHLIN

PERSONAL Born 12/22/1928, Washington, DC, s **DISCIPLINE** HISTORY, CRIMINAL JUSTICE **EDUCATION** Wesleyan Univ, BA, 51; Univ of MD, MA, 54; Univ of Wis, PhD, 59. **CAREER** Instr & asst prof of Hist, Univ of Chicago, 59-68; ASSOC PROF & PROF OF HIST & CRIMINAL JUSTICE, 68-, TEMPLE UNIV. **MEMBERSHIPS** Am Hist Assoc, Org of Am Historians; Am Soc of Criminology; Law & Soc Asn. **RESEARCH** Hist of the Am City; Hist of Crime and Criminal Justice. **SELECTED PUBLICATIONS** Auth, Eugenics; Hereditarian Attitudes in American Thought, 63; auth, "Urban Cirme and Cirminal Justice: Th eChicago Case: Journal of American History, 70; auth, "Bootleggers as Businessmen: From City Slums to City Builders," in David Kyvig, ed., Law, Alcohol, an dORder: Perspectives on National Prohibition, 85; auth, "Illegal Enterprise: A Theoretical and Historical Interpretation," Criminology, 90; auth, "Policy Gambling, Entertainment, and the Emergence of Black Politics: Chicago from 1900 to 1940," Journal of Social History, 91. **CONTACT ADDRESS** Dept of History, Temple Univ, Philadelphia, PA 19122. **EMAIL** hallerm@vm.temple.edu

HALLETT, MICHAEL

DISCIPLINE PHILOSOPHY **EDUCATION** Univ London, BS, 72; PhD, 79. **CAREER** Prof, McGill Univ. **RESEARCH** Philos and hist of mathematics; philos of sci; hist of logic; logic and set theory; development of set theory; development of analytic philos. **SELECTED PUBLICATIONS** Auth, Cantorian set theory and limitation of sixe, Oxford: Clarendon Press, Oxford Logic Guides, vol. 10, ed. Dana S. Scott, 88; auth, Physicalism, reductionism and Hilbert in Andrew Irvine, ed.: Physicalism in Mathematics, Dordrecht: D. Reidel Publishing Co., (90): 182-256; auth, Hilbert's axiomatic method and the laws of thought, in A. George, ed., Mathematics and Mind, New York: Oxford Univ Press, (94): 158-200; auth, Putnam and the Skolem paradox, (with Putnam's reply), in Peter Clark and Bob Hale, eds., Reading Putnam, Oxford: Basil Blackwell, (94): 66-97; auth, Logic and mathematical existence, in Lorenz Kruger and Brigitte Flakenburg, ed., Physik, Philosophie und die Einheit der Wissenschaft, Fur Erhard Scheibe, Heidelberg: Spektrum Akademischer Verlag, (95): 33-82; auth, Hilbert and logic, in Mathieu Marion and Robert Cohen, eds., Quebec Studies in the Philosophy of science, Part 1: Logic, Mathematics, Physics and the History of Science, Boston Studies in the Philosophy of Science, Vol. 177, Dordrecht: Kluwer Publishing Co., (95): 135-87. **CONTACT ADDRESS** Philosophy Dept, McGill Univ, 855 Sherbrooke St, Montreal, QC, Canada H3A 2T5. **EMAIL** hallett@philo.mcgill.ca

HALLMAN, JOSEPH MARTIN

PERSONAL Born 10/08/1939, Chicago, IL, m, 1966, 3 children **DISCIPLINE** CONTEMPORARY & PATRISTIC THEOLOGY **EDUCATION** St Francis Sem, BA, 62; Marquette Univ, MA, 65; Fordham Univ, PhD(theol), 70. **CAREER** Instr theol, Webster Col, 64-67; asst prof, Wheeling Col, 70-76, assoc prof, 77-81; Assoc Prof Theol, Col Of St Thomas, 81- **MEMBERSHIPS** Am Acad Relig; Cath Theol Soc Am; Soc for the Philos of Relig. **RESEARCH** Process theology; patristic theology, especially the understanding of the nature of God. **SELECTED PUBLICATIONS** Auth, The Seed of Fire - Divine Suffering in the Christology of Cyril-Of-Alexandria And Nestorius-Of-Constantinople, J Early Christian Studies, Vol 0005, 97; The Seed of Fire - Divine Suffering in the Christology of Cyril-Of-Alexandria and Nestorius-Of-Constantinople, J Early Christian Studies, Vol 0005, 97. **CONTACT ADDRESS** Dept of Theol, Univ of St. Thomas, Minnesota, 2115 Summit Ave, Saint Paul, MN 55105-1096.

HALLMAN, MAX

PERSONAL Born 02/21/1952, Lexington County, SC, 3 children **DISCIPLINE** PHILOSOPHY **EDUCATION** Univ SC, BA, 74, MA, 76; Tulane Univ, PhD, 86. **CAREER** Instr, Loyala Univ, 83-85; prof, coordr, Merced Col, 86-. **HONORS AND AWARDS** Phi Theta Kappa Giles Distinguished Advisor, 94; Phi Theta Kappa Advisor Continued Excellence Awd, 97; Phi Theta Kappa Moselle Scholar, 95; NISOD Tchg Excellence Awd, 93. **MEMBERSHIPS** Am Philos Asn **RESEARCH** Nietzsche; environmental philosophy; native American Philosophy, comparative cultures. **SELECTED PUBLICATIONS** Auth, The Shattered Self: Self-Overcoming and the Transfiguration of Nature in the Philosophy of Nietzsche, 88; auth, art, Nietzsche's Environmental Ethics, 91; auth, art, Becoming Multiculturally Literate, 93; auth, Expanding Philosophical Horizons: A Non-Traditional Philosophy Reader, 95; auth, Traversing Philosophical Boundaries, 98. **CONTACT ADDRESS** Dept of Philosophy, Merced Col, 3600 M St, Merced, CA 95340. **EMAIL** hallmanm@merced.cc.ca.us

HALPER, EDWARD CHARLES

PERSONAL Born 09/28/1951, Barberton, OH, m, 1979, 3 children **DISCIPLINE** PHILOSOPHY **EDUCATION** Univ Chicago, BA, 73; Columbia Univ, MA, 75; Univ Toronto, PhD, 80. **CAREER** Tchng fel, 80, Canisius Col; asst prof, 80-84, Gustavus Adolphus Col; asst prof, 84-87, assoc prof, 87-92, prof, 92-, Univ GA. **HONORS AND AWARDS** Grad fel, 73-74, Columbia Univ; Grad Fel, 76-77. 77-78, 78-79, Univ Toronto; George Paxton Young Mem Fel, 79; NEH Grants, 80-81, 83, 86; Aristotle's Metaphysics and Epistemology, FL ST Univ; Univ GA Res Found Grant, 88, 90, 97; Univ GA Humanities Center Fel, 95-96. **MEMBERSHIPS** APA, Can Phil Asn, Hegel Soc of Am, Intl Asn for Greek Phil, Intl Plato Soc, Metaphysical Soc of Am, Soc for Ancient Greek Phil, Soc for Medieval & Renaissance Phil. **RESEARCH** Ancient phil; medieval phil; 19th century German phil; metaphysics. **SELECTED PUBLICATIONS** Auth, One and Many in Aristotle's Metaphysics: The Central Books, Oh St Univ Press, 89; auth, Form and Reason: Essays in Metaphysics, SUNY Press, 93, art, The Substances of Aristotle's Ethics, Crossroads of Norm & Nature: Essays on Aristotle's Ethics and Metaphysics, 94; art, Virtue and the State, Aristotelian Pol Phil, Vol 2, 95; auth, "Aitia,"" Autarkia,"" Dianoia," "Elenchus," "Nous," " One-Many Problem," "Ousia," "Telos", Cambridge Dict of Phil, Cambridge Univ Press, 95; auth, "The Logic of Hegel's Philosophy of Nature: Nature, Space, and Time," In Essays on Hegel's Philosophy of Nature, by Stephen Houlgate, (Albany: State Univ of New York Press, 98): 29-49; auth, "Judaism and the Liberal State," in On Liberty: Jewish Philos Perspectives, by Daniel Frank, London: Curzon Press, 99; ed, Poetry, History, and Dialectic," in From Puzzles to Problems?: Essays on Aristotle's Dialectic, by May Sim, (Lexington Press, 99): 211-23; auth, "Aristotle on the Unity of Virtue," Oxford Stud in Ancient Philos XVII, (99): 115-43. **CONTACT ADDRESS** Dept of Philosophy, Univ of Georgia, Athens, GA 30602-1627. **EMAIL** ehalper@uga.edu

HALPERIN, DANIEL

PERSONAL Born 01/02/1937, Brooklyn, NY, m, 1962, 3 children **DISCIPLINE** LAW **EDUCATION** Baruch Col, BBA, 57; Harvard Law Sch, JD, 61. **CAREER** Assoc, Kaye, Scholar, Fierman, Hays & Handler New York, 61-67; legislative coun, Off of Tax Legislative Coun, 67-70; prof, Univ Pa Law Sch, 70-77; prof, Georgetown Univ, 81-96; prof, Harvard Law Sch, 96-. **MEMBERSHIPS** Nat Acad Soc Insurance; Am Law Inst; Am Bar Asn. **RESEARCH** Income Tax Policy; Retirement and Social Security; NonProfit Organizations. **SELECTED PUBLICATIONS** Auth, "Valuing Personal Consumption: Cost Versus Value and the Impact of Insurance," Fla Tax Rev, 92; auth, "Special Tax Treatment for Employer Based Retirement Programs: Is It 'Still' Viable as a Means of Increasing Retirement Income?" Tax Law Rev, 93; auth, "Assumption of Contingent Liabilities on Sale of a Business," Fla Tax Rev, 96; auth, "Saving the Income Tax: An Agenda for Research for Research," Northern L Rev, 98; co-auth, "Regulating Tax Qualified Pension Plans in a Hybrid World," in New York Univ 58th Inst on Federal Taxation, 00. **CONTACT ADDRESS** Sch of Law, Harvard Univ, Sch of Law, Cambridge, MA 02138. **EMAIL** Halperin@law.harvard.edu

HALPERIN, STEPHEN H.

DISCIPLINE LAW **EDUCATION** Concordia Univ, BA, 72; McGill Univ, BCL, 75, LLB, 78. **CAREER** Lectr, Univ of Toronto, 92-99. **MEMBERSHIPS** Editorial Board, Corporate Financing Quarterly; Advisory Board, CCH Ontario Corporations Law Guide **SELECTED PUBLICATIONS** Auth, pubs on corporate and securities law matters. **CONTACT ADDRESS** Goodmans LLP, 250 Yonge Street, Suite 2400, Toronto, ON, Canada M5B 2M6. **EMAIL** shalperin@goodmans.ca

HALPERN, BETH

PERSONAL Born 07/28/1962, New York, NY, m, 1994 **DISCIPLINE** PHILOSOPHY **EDUCATION** Binghamton Univ, PhD, 95. **CAREER** Landmark Col, asst prof, 95-. **MEMBERSHIPS** APA **RESEARCH** Ideas of Selfhood and value inquiry; literature and the ethical imagination; eastern representations; Development of overseas program of studies in Tibetan culture and thought in Dharansaya, India. **SELECTED PUBLICATIONS** Auth, Conflicting Values, Fractured Selves, Intl Philo Quart, Fordham Univ Press, 98; books rev, The Self in Social Theory, by CF Alford, 97; The Authentic Self, by R. Ehman, Intl Stud Philos, 97; auth, The Site of Our Lives: The Self and the Subject from Emerson to Foucault, by J. S. Hans, Intl Stud Philos, forthcoming; auth, For Love of Country: Debating the Limits of Patriotism, by MC Nussbaum, Intl Stud Philos, forthcoming. **CONTACT ADDRESS** Landmark Col, RR 1, PO Box 1000, Putney, VT 05346. **EMAIL** Batya222@aol.com

HALSTEAD, THOMAS

PERSONAL Born, CA, m, 1977, 3 children **DISCIPLINE** RELIGION **EDUCATION** CAL St Univ, MS; Talbot Theol Sem, Mdiv; Nova SE Univ, EdD **CAREER** Chair, 14 yrs, The Masters Col **HONORS AND AWARDS** Tchr of yr, 94 **MEMBERSHIPS** Evang Theol Soc **CONTACT ADDRESS** The Masters Col, 21721 Placerita Canyon Rd., Newhall, CA 91321. **EMAIL** thalstead@masters.edu

HALWANI, RAJA

PERSONAL Born 04/22/1967, Beirut, Lebanon, s **DISCIPLINE** PHILOSOPHY **EDUCATION** Am Univ of Beirut, BA, 88; Syracuse Univ, MA, 95, PhD, 96 **CAREER** Visit Asst Prof, 96-97, Rollins Col; Asst Prof, 97-pres, Sch of the Art Inst of Chicago **MEMBERSHIPS** Am Philos Assoc **RESEARCH** Ethics, Sexuality **SELECTED PUBLICATIONS** In Journals of Aesthetic Edu; Social Philos; Homosexuality **CONTACT ADDRESS** Liberal Arts, Sch of the Art Inst of Chicago, 37 S Wabas, Chicago, IL 60613. **EMAIL** rhalwa@artic.edu

HAMBRICK, A. FRED

PERSONAL Born 03/14/1935, Dallas, TX, m, 1963, 4 children **DISCIPLINE** RELIGION **EDUCATION** Okla Baptist Univ, BA, 57; City Univ, MAT, 68; Southwestern Seminary, BD (MDiv), 60; Luther Rice Seminary, DMin, 84. **CAREER** Teacher, Putnam City High School, 65-70; asst principal, Putnam City West High School, 70-72; Pastor, First Baptist Church, 72-73 & 75-83; Pastor, First United Methodist Church, 80-91; Superintendent Headmaster, Moody Christian Acad, 72-75; Principle, Okmulgee High School, 75-80; prof, Redlands Community Col, 90-97; Am Bible Col and Seminary, 98-; Pastor, Franklin Road Baptist Church, 92-. **MEMBERSHIPS** Nat Asn of Sec Sch Prin; Okla Sec Sch Prin Asn. **CONTACT ADDRESS** 200 23rd Ave, NE, Norman, OK 73071. **EMAIL** RNALOL@aol.com

HAMELIN, LEONCE
PERSONAL Born 12/04/1920, St. Narcisse, PQ, Canada **DISCIPLINE** THEOLOGY **EDUCATION** Laval Univ, BA, 45; Franciscan Int Univ, Rome, DTh, 54. **CAREER** Prof theol, Franciscan Sem Theol, 51-52 & 54-67, dean, 57-61; Prof Theol, Univ Montreal, 55-, Mem ed comt, Concilium, 65-; asst Prof, Univ Louvain, 72. **MEMBERSHIPS** Can Soc Theol: Int Soc Medieval Studies; Mediaeval Acad Am. **SELECTED PUBLICATIONS** Auth, In the Belly of the Narrative--Reading Bessette, Voix & Images, Vol 0020, 95. **CONTACT ADDRESS** 5750 Rosemont Blvd, Montreal, QC, Canada H1T 2H2.

HAMILTON, CHARLES VERNON
PERSONAL Born 10/19/1929, Muskogee, OK, m, 1956 **DISCIPLINE** LAW **EDUCATION** Roosevelt University, Chicago, IL, BA, 1951; Loyola University, School of Law, Chicago, IL, JD, 1954; University of Chicago, Chicago, IL, MA, 1957, PhD, 1964. **CAREER** Tuskegee University, Tuskegee, AL, assistant professor, 58-60; Rutgers University, Newark, NJ, assistant professor, 63-64; Lincoln University, Oxford, PA, professor, 64-67; Roosevelt University, Chicago, IL, professor, 67-69; Columbia, University, New York, professor, 69-. **HONORS AND AWARDS** University of Chicago, Alumni Awd, 1970; Roosevelt University Alumni Awd, 1970; Lindback Teaching Awd, Lincoln University, 1965; Van Doren Teaching Ward, Columbia University, 1982; Great Teacher Awd, Columbia University, 1985. **MEMBERSHIPS** Board of trustees, Twentieth Century Foundation, 1973-; board member, NAACP, 1975-; board of editors, Political Science Quarterly, 1975-. **SELECTED PUBLICATIONS** Adam Clayton Powell Jr, 1991. **CONTACT ADDRESS** Professor, Columbia Univ, 420 W 118th St, Room 727, New York, NY 10027.

HAMILTON, EUGENE NOLAN
PERSONAL Born 08/24/1933, Memphis, TN, m, 1956, 9 children **DISCIPLINE** LAW **EDUCATION** Univ of Illinois, BA, 1955, JD, 1959. **CAREER** US Army, judge advocate officer, 59-61; US Dept of Justice, trial attorney, 61-70; Superior Court of DC, Judge, 70-; Harvard Law School, lecturer, 95, Teacher, 85-. **HONORS AND AWARDS** Washington Bar Assn, Ollie Mae Cooper Awd, 1993; National Bar Assn, Wiley A Branton Issues Symposium Awd; Oldender Foundation Generous Heart Awd; Charles Hamilton Houston, Medallion of Merit. **MEMBERSHIPS** American Bar Assn, executive committee, 1970-; Washington Bar Assn, 1970-; Bar Assn of DC, 1990-; DC Bar Assn, 1970-. **RESEARCH** Trial Advocacy and Genetic and Scientific Evidence **CONTACT ADDRESS** Superior Court of DC, 500 Indiana Ave, NW, Washington, DC 20001.

HAMILTON, JOHN DANIEL BURGOYNE
PERSONAL Born 10/19/1939, Los Angeles, CA **DISCIPLINE** CLASSICAL LANGUAGES, GREEK MYTHOLOGY & RELIGION **EDUCATION** St Louis Univ, AB, 63; AM, 64; Weston Col, Cambridge, MS, MDiv, 69; Univ MN, PhD, 73. **CAREER** Instr classics, Univ Santa Clara, 65-66; asst prof, 72-76, assoc prof Classics, 77-, Grad Studies Adv, Classics, Col of the Holy Cross, 89-. **MEMBERSHIPS** Am Philol Asn; Class Asn New England; Class Asn Midwest & South; Soc Promotion Hellenic Studies; Class Asn Gt Brit. **RESEARCH** Greek epic and drama; mythology; Roman satire. **SELECTED PUBLICATIONS** Auth, Justin's Apology 66: A review of scholarship, 72 & The church and the language of mystery, 77, Ephemerides Theol Lovanienses; transl (with B Nagy), L Gernet, The Anthropology of Ancient Greece, Johns Hopkins, 81; Antigone: Kinship, Justice and the Womb, in Myth and the Pelis, Cornell, 91; At Sea with Myth: A Bibliography for Charting a Course, NE Clas J, Dec 89; contrib, articles in The World Book Encyclopedia, 93. **CONTACT ADDRESS** Dept of Calssics, Col of the Holy Cross, 1 College St, Worcester, MA 01610-2395. **EMAIL** jhamilto@holycross.edu

HAMILTON, ROBERT W.
PERSONAL Born 03/04/1931, Syracuse, NY, m, 1953, 3 children **DISCIPLINE** LAW **EDUCATION** Swarthmore Col, BA, 52; Univ Chicago, JD, 55. **CAREER** From assoc prof law to prof, 64-72, Vinson & Elkins prof, 72-81, Benno C Schmidt Prof Bus Law, Univ Tex, Austin, 81-, vis prof, Univ Minn, 66-67; consult, Admin Conf US, 70-; vis prof, Univ Ariz, 71-72; vis prof, Univ Pa, 78; vis prof, Washington Univ, St Louis, 82; Minerva House Drysdale Regents Chair in Law, 87-98; Godfrey Vis Prof, Univ of Maine, 87, 92. **SELECTED PUBLICATIONS** Auth, Fundamentals of Modern Business, Little Brown, 89; 557; auth, Money Management for Lawyers and Clients, Little Brown, 93; auth, Registered Limited Liability Partnerships, Colo L Review, 95; Business Organizations, Aspen, 96; Black Letter Series on Corporations, West, 97; Corporate General Partners of Limited Partnerships, Int Small Bus Law, 97; Limited Liability and the Real World (with Ribstein), Wash and Lee L. Rev, 97; auth, Texas Law and Practice: Business Organizations, (2 vols), 73 & Cases & Materials on Corporations, West Publ, 6th ed, 98; auth, "Business Basics for Law Students: Essential Terms and Concepts with Richard Booth," Aspen Law & Business, (98); auth, "The Law of Corporations in a Nutshell," 5th Ed. West Publishing Co., St. Paul, Minn. 00; **CONTACT ADDRESS** Sch of Law, Univ of Texas, Austin, 727 E 26th St, Austin, TX 78705-3224. **EMAIL** rhamilton@mail.law.utexas.edu

HAMILTON, VICTOR PAUL
PERSONAL Born 09/26/1941, Toronto, ON, Canada, m, 1965, 4 children **DISCIPLINE** OLD TESTAMENT STUDIES, ANCIENT NEAR EASTERN HISTORY **EDUCATION** Houghton Col, BA, 63; Asbury Theol Sem, BD, 66, ThM, 67; Brandeis Univ, MA, 69, PhD, 71. **CAREER** From asst prof to assoc prof, 71-85, prof Old Testament, Asbury Col, 85-. **MEMBERSHIPS** Soc Bibl Lit; Evangelical Theol Soc. **RESEARCH** Old Testament languages. **SELECTED PUBLICATIONS** Auth, The Shepherd Psalm: Psalm 23, Asbury Seminarian, 72; Handbook on the Pentateuch, Baker, 82; Genesis Chapters 1-17, Eerdmans, 92; Genesis, Chapters 18-50, Eerdmans, 95. **CONTACT ADDRESS** 1 Macklem Dr, Wilmore, KY 40390-1198. **EMAIL** victor.hamilton@asbury.edu

HAMLIN, ERNEST LEE
PERSONAL Born 12/09/1943, Sussex County, VA, m, 1978 **DISCIPLINE** RELIGION **EDUCATION** Virginia Union University, BA, 1970, School of Theology, MDiv, 1974; Presbyterian School of Christian Education, 1976; Virginia Commonwealth University, pastoral education, 1976-77. **CAREER** Bethesda Baptist Church, pastor, 81-83; Richmond Virginia Seminary, theology and christian education, professor, 82-89; Ebenezer Baptist Church, supply pastor, 84; Union Hill United Church of Christ, pastor, 86-89; Christian Education Ministries, president, 90-; Emmanuel-St Mark's United Church of Christ, pastor, 90-92; Tubman-King Community Church, senior pastor, 92-. **HONORS AND AWARDS** Emmanuel-St Mark's UCC, Outstanding Leadership Awd, 1992; Richmond Virginia Seminary, Outstanding Service Awd, 1986; United Negro College Fund, Honorary Chairperson, 1983. **MEMBERSHIPS** Habitat for Humanity, board of directors, 1992-; Northeast Ministerial Alliance, executive vice pres, 1991-92; East Side Ecumenical Fellowship, executive secretary, 1990-91, executive vice pres, 1991-92; OIC Metro Saginaw, board of directors, 1990-92; One Church One Child of Michigan, board of directors, 1991-92; SCLC, Virginia State Unit, board of directors, 1982-90, Richmond Chapter, board of directors,1981-85. **SELECTED PUBLICATIONS** "A True Mother and Christ," published poem, 1990 **CONTACT ADDRESS** Senior Pastor, Tubman-King Community Church, 425 N Seneca St, Daytona Beach, FL 32114.

HAMM, MICHAEL DENNIS, S. J.
PERSONAL Born 01/18/1936, Cincinnati, OH, s **DISCIPLINE** NEW TESTAMENT, BIBLE **EDUCATION** Marquette Univ, BA, 58; St Louis Univ, MA, 64, PhD(Theol), 75. **CAREER** Instr English, Creighton Preparatory Sch, 64-65; instr, 65-67, asst prof, 75-81, from assoc prof to prof Theol, Creighton Univ, 81-91, Managing ed, Theol Digest, 70. **MEMBERSHIPS** Soc Bibl Lit; Cath Bibl Asn; Col Theol Soc, 85. **RESEARCH** Gospel of Luke; Acts of the Apostles. **SELECTED PUBLICATIONS** Auth, Preaching Biblical Justice, Church, Spring, 96; Ascension, The Pastoral Dictionary of Biblical Theology, Collegeville, MN: Liturgical Press, 96; Pentecost, The Pastoral Dictionary of Biblical Theology, Collegeville, MN: Liturgical Press, 96; Spirit of God/Holy Spirit--New Testament, The Pastoral Dictionary of Biblical Theology, Collegeville, MN: Liturgical Press, 96; auth, Let The Scriptures Speak, Liturgical Press, 99. Let the Scriptures Speak, Liturgical Press, 99. **CONTACT ADDRESS** Dept of Theology, Creighton Univ, 2500 California Plz, Omaha, NE 68178-0001. **EMAIL** dhamm@creighton.edu

HAMMER, JANE R.
PERSONAL Born 04/09/1916, Charlotte, NC, m, 1937, 3 children **DISCIPLINE** PHILOSOPHY **EDUCATION** Central High Schl, 33; UNC-Chapel Hill, AB, 36, MA, 37; Radcliffe/Harvard, 38-39. **CAREER** Tchr, 48-60, Spelman Col; Adult Citizen Ed tchr, League of Women Voters Ed Fund (Overseas Ed Fund). **HONORS AND AWARDS** Kenan Fel, 36-37, 38-39, UNC-CH; 500 Environ Achiever, Friends of UN Environ Prog, 87; Woman of The Year, ABI & IB Congress 92, 98; Millennium Hall of Fame, 98; World Laureata, 00; ABI Raleigh. **MEMBERSHIPS** Soc List of Wash; Cromwell Assn; US Woman's Natl Dem Club; Fri Morning Music Club; Am Philosophy Asn and Hegel Society. **RESEARCH** Phil & eEthics; governance - dem, constitutions & prac of citizen resp; biography. **SELECTED PUBLICATIONS** Auth, Logic for Living, Lectures of Horace Williams, Phil Lib NY, 52; ed, Origin of Belief by H Williams, UNC-CH Dept Phil, & HWP Soc, 72; auth, Protector: A Life History of Richard Cromwell, Vantage Press, 97. **CONTACT ADDRESS** 521 Holly Rd, Edgewater, MD 21037-3832. **EMAIL** hammerjaner@aol.com

HAMMOND, GUY BOWERS
PERSONAL Born 11/07/1930, Birmingham, AL, m, 1959, 2 children **DISCIPLINE** PHILOSOPHY, RELIGION **EDUCATION** Washington & Lee Univ, BA, 51; Yale Univ, BD, 55; Vanderbilt Univ, PhD, 62. **CAREER** Assoc prof, 62-67, Prof Philos & Relig, VA Polytech Inst & State Univ, 67- **MEMBERSHIPS** AAUP; Am Acad Relig; Paul Tillich Soc NAm. **RESEARCH** Contemporary theology and philosophy of religion; religion and culture. **SELECTED PUBLICATIONS** Auth, A Theology of Power--Being Beyond Domination, J Church State, Vol 0036, 94. **CONTACT ADDRESS** Dept of Philos & Relig, Virginia Polytech Inst and State Univ, Blacksburg, VA 24060.

HAMMOND, PAUL Y.
DISCIPLINE POLITICAL SCIENCE **EDUCATION** Univ Utah, BA, 49; Harvard Univ, MA, 51, PhD, 53. **CAREER** Instr, Govt, Harvard Univ, 53-55; lectr, Publ Law & Govt, Columbia Univ, 56-57; fell, Naval Hist, US Naval Acad, 55-56; asst prof, Polit Sci, Yale Univ, 57-62; res assoc/Rockefeller fell, Wash Ctr For Policy Res, Johns Hopkins Univ, 62-64; sr scientist, Rand Corp, 64-76; Prof, Univ Pittsburgh, 76; Distinguished Prof, 83-. **HONORS AND AWARDS** Distinguished Service Prof, Univ of Pittsburgh, 83-. **RESEARCH** US foreign & security policy; Presidency & foreign relations; Information systems for public organizations; Regional foreign policy; NATO & Asia; Policy formation & policy implementation with respect to foreign relations **SELECTED PUBLICATIONS** "Central Organization in the Transition from Bush to Clinton," Am Defense Annual 1994, Lexington Books, 94; "Towards a Workable European Architecture: Political-Military Problems in the New Europe," The International System after the Collapse of the East-West Order, Martinus Nijhoff, 94; "Security and Morality in a Contingent World," Moral Perspectives on US Security Policy: View from the LDS Community, David M Kennedy Center for International Studies, 95; "Doing Without America?", The Evolving Pacific Power Structure , Inst of Southeast Asian Studies, 97; "On Taking Peacekeeping Seriously," To Sheath the Sword: Civil-MilitaryRElations in the Quest for Democracy, Greenwood Press, 97. **CONTACT ADDRESS** Grad Sch Public & Int Affairs, Univ of Pittsburgh, 3N23 Posvar Hall, Pittsburgh, PA 15260. **EMAIL** PYH@pitt.edu

HAMRE, JAMES S.
PERSONAL Born 10/28/1931, Montevideo, MN, m, 1957, 2 children **DISCIPLINE** RELIGION IN AMERICAN HISTORY **EDUCATION** Augsburg Col, BA, 53; Luther Theol Sem, Minn, BTh, 57; Univ Chicago, MA, 59; Univ Iowa, PhD(-Relig), 67. **CAREER** Prof Religion & Philosophy to prof emeritus, Waldorf Col, Iowa, 67-; visiting lectr, Luther Theo Sem, MN, spring 76; vis lectr, Augsburg Col, MN, spring 81; vis lectr, District College, Volda, Norway, spring 95. **HONORS AND AWARDS** Endowment for Humanities, 74, 87; Regents Outstanding Fac Awd, Waldorf Col, 84; Holmen Fac Achievement Awd, Waldorf Col, 92. **MEMBERSHIPS** Norwegian-American Historical Association. **RESEARCH** Life and thought of Georg Sverdrup; Norwegian immigrant experience; American religious history. **SELECTED PUBLICATIONS** Auth, Georg Sverdrup concerning Luther's principles in America, Concordia Hist Inst Quart, 70; Georg Sverdrup's concept of theological education in the context of a free church, Lutheran Quart, 70; A Thanksgiving Day Address by Georg Sverdrup, Norweg-Am Studies, 70; The Augsburg Triumvirate and the Kvartal-Skrift, Luther Theol Sem Rev, 72; Georg Sverdrup and the Augsburg Plan of Education, Norweg-Am Studies, 74; John O Evjen: Teacher, theologian, biographer, 74 & Georg Sverdrup's Errand into the Wilderness: Building the Free and Living Congregation, 80, Concordia Hist Inst Quart; Norwegian immigrants respond to the common school: A case study of American values and the Lutheran Tradition, Church Hist, 81; auth, Georg Sverdrup: Educator, Theologian, Churchman, 86; The Creationist-Evolutionist Debate and the Public Schools, Journal of Church and State, 91. **CONTACT ADDRESS** Dept of Religion & Philosophy, Waldorf Col, 106 S 6th St, Forest City, IA 50436-1713. **EMAIL** hamrej@Waldorf.edu

HAN, JIN HEE
PERSONAL Born 07/18/1956, Seoul, Korea, m, 3 children **DISCIPLINE** OLD TESTAMENT STUDY **EDUCATION** Princeton Theological Seminary, PhD 88, M Div 83; Sogang Univ, Korea, BA 79. **CAREER** NY Theological Seminary, prof, 91-; Drew Univ, adj prof, 92-; Alliance Theol Seminary, 90-91. **MEMBERSHIPS** SBL. **RESEARCH** Eegesis; Biblical Interpretations; History of Eegesis. **SELECTED PUBLICATIONS** Auth, The Sacrifice of Abraham, Pulpit Digest, 98; The Word that Gives Life, in: The Upper Room Disciplines 88, Nashville Upper Room Books, 97; How Does the Holy Spirit Enter into Preaching:, Living Pulpit, 96; Biblical Understanding of the Year of Jubilee, Korea Daily News, 95; Consultant for the Korean translation of Rule of the Community, in its Intl ed of the Dead Sea Scrolls Project, Princeton Theol Sem. **CONTACT ADDRESS** Dept of Old Testament, New York Theol Sem, 5 W 29th St, New York, NY 10001. **EMAIL** jhan@nyts.edu

HANCHEY, HOWARD
DISCIPLINE PASTORAL THEOLOGY **EDUCATION** Univ NC, BA, 63; Va Theol Sem, MDiv, 67; Union Theol Col, DMin, 75; St George's Col, Jerusalem, 90. **CAREER** Rector, Piedmont Parish, 67-69; asst to rector, missioner to the deaf, St Paul's Episcopal Church, 69-72; assoc rector, E Shore Chapel, 72-76; fac mem, Union Theol Sem; rector, chaplain, St Andrew's Episcopal Church, 76-78; Arthur Lee Kinsolving prof, 78-. **HONORS AND AWARDS** Fel, Col of Chaplains; 1984 Tenure Granted, 84; chaplain supvr, assn for clinical pastoral edu; chaplain supvr, med col va of va commonwealth univ, 69-72; organizer, first episcopal parish based , acpe certified prog of clin pastoral edu, 74-76; presiding priest, founding pastor, st peter's in the wood **MEMBERSHIPS** Assembly of Episcopal Hospital Chaplains. **SELECTED PUBLICATIONS** Auth, From Survival to Celebration, Leadership For the Confident Church, Cowley Publ, 94; Church Growth and the Power of

Evangelism, Ideas that Work, Cowley Publ, 90; Christian Edu Made Easy, Morehouse Publ, 89; Creative Christian Edu, Morehouse Publ, 86. **CONTACT ADDRESS** Virginia Theol Sem, 3737 Seminary Rd, Alexandria, VA 22304. **EMAIL** HHanchey@vts.edu

HAND, MICHAEL
DISCIPLINE PHILOSOPHY **EDUCATION** Univ SC, BS, 75, MA, 83; Fla State Univ, PhD, 85. **CAREER** Instr, Fla A&M Univ, 84-85; instr, Fla State Univ, 85; visiting asst prof, Univ of Okla, 85-87; asst prof, Univ of Okla, 87-89; visiting asst prof, Univ of NC, 88-89; prof, Tex A&M Univ, 97-; assoc prof, Tex A&M Univ, 92-97; asst prof, Tex A&M Univ, 89-92. **HONORS AND AWARDS** Associates' Distinguished Lectr, Univ Okla, 87-88; Univ fel, Fla State Univ, 81-85; Phi Kappa Phi, Fla State Univ, 84; Phi Beta Kappa, Univ SC, 75. **SELECTED PUBLICATIONS** Co-auth, Logic Primer, (Cambridge, MA: MIT Press, 92); rev, "Classical and Intuitionistic Negation," Southwest Philosophy Rev 8, (92): 157-64; auth, "Negations in Conflict," Erkenntnis 38, (93): 115-29; auth, "A Defense of Branching Quantification," Synthese 95, (93): 419-32; auth, "Mathematical Sturcturalism and the Third Man," Canadian Journal of Philosophy 23, (93): 179-92; auth, "More on Pronouns of Address and Truth Conditions," Linguistics 31, (93): 749-51; auth, "Parataxis and Parentheticals," Linguistics and Philosophy 16, (93): 495-507; auth, "Demonstrative Reference and Unintended Demonstrata," Communication and Cognition 26, (93): 37-48; auth, "Informational Variability," Synthese 99, (94): 417-56; auth, "What the Null Set Could Not Be," Australasian Journal of Philosophy 73, (95): 429-31. **CONTACT ADDRESS** Dept of Philosophy, Texas A&M Univ, Col Station, College Station, TX 77843. **EMAIL** mhand@tamu.edu

HANDLER, JOEL F.
PERSONAL Born 10/04/1932, Newark, NJ **DISCIPLINE** LAW **EDUCATION** Princeton Univ, BA, 54; Harvard Law Sch, JD, 57. **CAREER** Asst prof, Vanderbilt Univ, 61-62; asst prof, Univ Ill, 62-64; assoc prof to prof, Univ Wisc, 64-85; vis prof, Stanford Univ, 69-70; prof, Georgetown Univ, 80-82; prof, UCLA 85-. **HONORS AND AWARDS** Guggenheim Fel, 74-75; Fel, German Marshall Fund, 77-78; Travel Grant, German Marshall Fund, 79; Gladys M. Kammerer Award, Am Polit Sci Asn, 97; Reginald Heber Smith Award, Nat Equal Justice Libr, 98; Distinguished Prof Award, ACLU Found, 99. **MEMBERSHIPS** Law and Soc Asn; Nat Acad of Sci. **RESEARCH** Welfare; Poverty; Comparative welfare. **SELECTED PUBLICATIONS** Auth, Law and the Search for Community, Univ Pa Press, 90; co-auth, The Moral Construction of Poverty: Welfare Reform in America, Sage Pub, 91; auth, The Poverty of Welfare Reform, Yale Univ Press, 96; auth, Down from Bureaucracy: The Ambiguity of Privatization and Empowerment, Princeton Univ Press, 96; auth, "Women, Families, Work and Poverty: A Cloudy Future," UCLA Women's L J, (96): 3-75; co-auth, We the Poor People: Work, Poverty, and Welfare Reform, Yale Univ press, 97; auth, "Poverty, Dependency, and Social Welfare: Procedural Justice for the Poor," in Justice and Power in the Study of Law and Society, (Northwestern Univ Press, 98); auth, "Welfare-to-Work: Reform or Rhetoric?" Admin L Rev, (98): 635-658; co-ed, Hard Living: Women and Work in the Post-Welfare Era, M.E. Sharpe, 99; auth, "The Third Way or the Old Way," Univ Kans L Rev, (00): 765-800. **CONTACT ADDRESS** Sch of Law, Univ of California, Los Angeles, PO Box 951476, Los Angeles, CA 90095-1476. **EMAIL** handler@law.ucla.edu

HANDWERK-NORAGON, PATRICIA
PERSONAL Born 12/02/1941, Philadelphia, PA, m, 1969, 2 children **DISCIPLINE** PHILOSOPHY **EDUCATION** Swarthmore Col , 63; Ohio State Univ, PhD, 68. **CAREER** Lectr, Waterloo Lutheran Univ, 67-68; asst prof,68-89; asst prof, Baldwin Wallace Coll, 69-75; adj asst prof, Cleveland State Univ, 75-76; adj asst prof, Kenyon Coll, 88; lectr, 79-97; sr lectr, Ohio State Univ Marion, 98-. **MEMBERSHIPS** Am Philos Asn. **RESEARCH** Teaching Philosophy to Undergraduates. **CONTACT ADDRESS** Col of Education, Ohio Univ, 1465 Mount Vernon Ave, Marion, OH 43302-5695. **EMAIL** noragon1@osu.edu

HANDY, LOWELL
PERSONAL Born 07/18/1949, Fort Dodge, IA, s **DISCIPLINE** BIBLE **EDUCATION** Univ Iowa, BA, 71; MA, 74; Univ Chicago, MA, 80; PhD, 87. **CAREER** Lectr, Loyola Univ, 87-; Indexer Analyst, Am theol Libr Assoc, 88-. **HONORS AND AWARDS** Post-Doctoral Fel, Inst for the Advan Study of Relig, Univ Chicago. **MEMBERSHIPS** Soc of Bibl Lit; Am Schools of Oriental Res; Chicago Soc of Bibl Res. **RESEARCH** Biblical Historiography, Ancient Israelite religion. **SELECTED PUBLICATIONS** Auth, "The Appearance of Pantheon in Judah" in The Triumph of Elohim: From Yahwisms to Judaisms, ed. D.V. Edelman, (Grand Rapids: Eerdmans) (95):27-43; auth, "The Phoenicians in the Tenth Century BCE" in The Age of Solomon: Scholarship at the Turn of the Millennium, ed. L.K. Handy, (Leiden: E.J. Brill, 97), 154-166; auth, "Biblical Bronze Age Memories: The Abraham Cycle as Usable Past", BR 42 (97):43-57; ed, The Age of Solomon: Scholarship at the Turn of the Millennium in Studies in the History and Culture of the Ancient Near East, E.J. Brill (Leiden), 97; auth, The Educated Person's Thumbnail Introduction to the Bible, Chalice Pr (St. Louis), 97; auth, Entertaining Faith: Reading Short Stories in the Bible; Chalice Pr (St. Louis), 00; auth, "A Historical Context for Judah and Israel" in Chalice Introduction to the Old Testament, Chalice Pr (forthcoming). **CONTACT ADDRESS** Dept Theology, Loyola Univ, Chicago, 6525 N Sheridan Rd, Chicago, IL 60626-5344.

HANDY, WILLIAM TALBOT, JR.
PERSONAL Born 03/26/1924, New Orleans, LA, m, 1948 **DISCIPLINE** THEOLOGY **EDUCATION** Attended Tuskegee Institute, 1940-43; Dillard University, New Orleans, BA, 1948; Gammon Theological Seminary, Atlanta, GA, M Div, 1951; Boston Univ School of Theology, Boston, MA, STM, 1982. **CAREER** Newman Methodist Church, Alexandria, LA, pastor, 52-59; St Mark Methodist Church, Baton Rouge, LA, pastor, 59-68; The Methodist Publishing House, Nashville, TN, publishing representative, 68-70; The United Methodist Publishing House, Nashville, TN, vice-president, personnel and public relations, 70-78; Baton Rouge-Lafayette, LA, district superintendent, 78-80; resident bishop, 80-92; Missouri Area, United Methodist Church, bishop; United Methodist Publishing House, chaplain, 96-; Drew University Theological School, Adjunct Dir, Doctor of Ministry Program, 96-. **HONORS AND AWARDS** Honorary DD, Huston-Tillotson College, Austin, TX, 1973; Honorary DD, Wiley College, Marshall, TX, 1973; Honorary DD, Centenary College, Shreveport, LA, 1979; Honorary LLD, Dillard University, New Orleans, LA, 1981; Honorary LHD, Philander Smith College, Little Rock, AR, 1982; Honorary DD, Central Methodist Coll, 1991; Tuskegee University & Dillard University, NAFEO Distinguished Alumnus. **MEMBERSHIPS** General bd of publication, 1988-92, past chmn, bd of trustees, St Paul School of Theology; past chmn, bd of trustees, Interdenominational Theological Center; past chmn, bd of trustees, Gammon Theological Sem; past sec, Southern Methodist Univ, bd of trustees; life and Golden Heritage member, NAACP; Hymnal Revision Committee, United Methodist Church, 1984-88; Bishop's Special Committee on SMU, 1986-87. **CONTACT ADDRESS** United Methodist Church, 201 8th Ave S, Nashville, TN 37202.

HANEY, MARSHA SNULLIGAN
PERSONAL Born St Louis, MO, m, 1981 **DISCIPLINE** PHILOSOPHY **EDUCATION** Johnson C. Smith Univ, BA, 75; Interdonominational Theol Center, MRE, 77; Fuller Theol Sem, ThM, 90; PhD, 94. **CAREER** Adjunct Fac, San Francisco Theol Sem, Southern Branch, Pasadena, Calif, 93-94; asst prof of Missiology and Religions of the World, Interdenominational Theological Center, Atlanta, GA, 94-99, assoc prof, 99-. **HONORS AND AWARDS** Alan Tippett Academic Awd, Fuller Theol Sem, 94; ITC Student Christian League (female) Teaching Awd, 98, 99; ITC Theta Phi Honor Soc Teaching Awd, 99; Who's Who Among Am Teachers, 99, 2000. **MEMBERSHIPS** Am Soc of Missiology, Am Acad of Relig/Soc for the Study of Biblical Lit, Asn for Contextual Urban Theol Educs, Asn of Mission Profs, Asn of Presbyterian Mission Profs, Asn of Presbyterian Evangelism Profs, Soc for the Study of Black Relig, Presbyterian Church, USA (Minister of Word and Sacraments, World Coun of Reformed Churches (Pentacostal and Reformed Dialogue). **RESEARCH** Islamic studies, mission and evangelism, Christian Anthropology, contextualization, religion and culture. **SELECTED PUBLICATIONS** Auth, "Walking with Africans: A Healing Journey," in The J of Church and Soc, Presbyterian Church, USA, Louisville, Ky (spring/summer 95); auth, "What is Worth Living For and Worth Dying For," Presbyterian Church Bull No197924, Presbyterian Pub Corp (Feb 23, 97); auth, "Community Life as an Expression of Holy Living (I Thessalonians 4), African Am Devotional Bible, Congress of Nat Black Churches, Zonderman (97); auth, "Issues of Contextualization: Challenges for African American Christians and Muslims," in the Edinburgh Review of Theology and Religion, Vol 3, Part 2, Orbis, NY (97); guest ed with Darius Swann, Seventh Assembly of the All Africa Conference of Churches, Addis Ababa, Ethiopia, The Journal of the Interdenominational Theological Center, Vol XXVI, No 2, Atlanta (spring 99); auth, Islam and Protestant African American Churches: Responses and Challenges to Religious Pluralism, Univ Press of Am, Lanham, Md (99); auth, "Toward the Development of a New Christian Missiological Identity," in Presbyterian Mission for a New Millenium, 2000, Presbyterian Pub House, Louisville (2000). **CONTACT ADDRESS** Dept Relig, Interdenominational Theol Ctr, 700 MLK Jr Dr SW, Atlanta, GA 30314-4143.

HANEY, MARY-ANN
DISCIPLINE LAW **EDUCATION** Trent Univ, BA, 79; Queens Univ, LLB, 83. **CAREER** Partner, McMillan Binch; adj prof, Univ of Toronto. **SELECTED PUBLICATIONS** Contrib, Canadian Tax Journal. **CONTACT ADDRESS** Fac of Law, Univ of Toronto, 78 Queen's Park, Toronto, ON, Canada M5S 2C5.

HANFORD, JACK
PERSONAL Born 08/30/1932, Jackson, KY, m, 1967, 5 children **DISCIPLINE** RELIGION **EDUCATION** Albion Col, AB, 52; Garrett Theol Sem, MDiv, 59; Northwestern Univ, MA, 61; Iliff Sch Theol Denver Univ, ThD, 74. **CAREER** Pastor & tchr, DePauw Univ, 59-60; pastor & instr, Univ N Iowa, 62-68; prof philos & relig, Ferris State Univ, 70-. **HONORS AND AWARDS** Soc Sci Study Relig Fel, 94; Nat Recognized Fac, Ferris State Univ, 95. **MEMBERSHIPS** Am Philos Asn; Am Acad Relig; Soc Sci Study Relig; Asn Moral Educ; Soc Creative Philos; Hastings Ctr; Kennedy Inst Ethics; Mich Med Ethics Rsrc Network; Soc Bus Ethics; Asn Relig Intellectual Life; Inst Relig Age Sci; Park Ridge Ctr Study Health, Faith, Ethics; Soc Values Higher Educ; Mich Acad Arts Sci; Soc Christian Philos; Soc Health Human Values. **RESEARCH** Biomedical ethics; psychology of religion; moral and faith development. **SELECTED PUBLICATIONS** Auth, Religion, Medical Ethics and Transplants, Jour Med Hum, 93; auth, Is the Faith of Faith Development Christian Faith?, Jour Pastoral Psychol, 93; auth, Advancing Moral Reasoning within a Biomedical Ethics Course, Insider: Ferris Fac and Staff Jour, April, 96. **CONTACT ADDRESS** 17220 Valley Dr., Big Rapids, MI 49307. **EMAIL** jhan1722@tucker-usa.com

HANIGAN, JAMES P.
PERSONAL Born 04/16/1938, New York, NY, m, 1976 **DISCIPLINE** THEOLOGY; ETHICS **EDUCATION** Fordham Univ, MA, 65; Woodstock Col, MDiv, 68; Duke Univ, PhD, 73. **CAREER** Asst Prof, Marquette Univ, 73-75; Asst Prof, Villa Maria Col, 75-79; Asst Prof to Assoc Prof, 79-86, Prof, Duquesne Univ, 86-, Dir Grad Studies, 86-94, Dept Chair, 94-97, 00-. **HONORS AND AWARDS** President's Univ Awd for Excellence in Scholarship, 88. **MEMBERSHIPS** Am Acad Relig; Soc Christian Ethics; Cath Theol Soc Am; Col Theol Soc. **RESEARCH** Sexual ethics; social ethics. **SELECTED PUBLICATIONS** Auth, What Are They Saying About Sexual Morality?, Paulist Press, 82; Martin Luther King, Jr and the Foundations of Nonviolence, Univ Press Am, 84; As I Have Loved You: The Challenge of Christian Ethics, Paulist Press, 86; Homosexuality: The Test-Case for Christian Se Sexual Ethics, Paulist Press, 88; author of numerous articles and book chapters. **CONTACT ADDRESS** Theology Dept, Duquesne Univ, Pittsburgh, PA 15282. **EMAIL** hanigan@duq.edu

HANKS, DONALD
DISCIPLINE PHILOSOPHY OF RELIGION, PHILOSOPHICAL PSYCHOLOGY, SOCIAL AND POLITICAL PHIL **EDUCATION** Univ Denver, BA, 56, MA, 65; Duke Univ, BD, 60; Univ New Orleans, ThD, 67; Tulane Univ, PhD, 70. **CAREER** Assoc prof, Univ New Orleans. **HONORS AND AWARDS** Amoco Found Awd, LSU Syst, 81. **SELECTED PUBLICATIONS** Auth, Statistical Victims and Their Rights, Contemp Philos, Vol XVI, No 5, 94; Pluralism: Truth and World Community, Contemp Philos, Vol XVII, No 5, 95; The Judicial Surcharge: A Violation of Prisoner Rights, Contemp Philos, Vol XVII, No 6, 95; Christ as Criminal: Antinomian Trends for a New Millennium, Edwin Mellen Press, 97. **CONTACT ADDRESS** Univ of New Orleans, New Orleans, LA 70148. **EMAIL** dkhpl@uno.edu

HANNAFORD, R.
PERSONAL Born 09/28/1929, Anderson, IN, m, 1951, 2 children **DISCIPLINE** PHILOSOPHY **EDUCATION** Wabash Col, AB, 50, Columbia Univ, PhD, 55. **CAREER** Ripon Col, 56-00. **HONORS AND AWARDS** ACLU Grant; NEH; Am Philos Asn Fel; Uhrig, Severy and Underkofler Awds, Ripon Col. **MEMBERSHIPS** Am Philos Assoc; Assoc Moral Educ; Phi Beta Kappa. **RESEARCH** Ethical Theory, Moral Development and Moral Education. **SELECTED PUBLICATIONS** Auth, Concept Formation and the Explanation of Behavior; auth, Moral Anatomy and Moral Reason. **CONTACT ADDRESS** Dept Philos, Ripon Col, PO Box 248, Ripon, WI 54971-0248. **EMAIL** hannafrd@vbe.com

HANNAN, BARBARA
DISCIPLINE PHILOSOPHY OF MIND, PHILOSOPHY OF SCIENCE, EARLY ANALYTIC PHILOSOPHY **EDUCATION** Randolph-Macon Woman's Col, BA, 79; Univ Ariz, JD, 82, PhD, 89. **CAREER** Assoc prof, Univ NMex. **SELECTED PUBLICATIONS** Auth, Subjectivity and Reduction, Westview, 94; contribur, Love Analyzed, Westview, 96. **CONTACT ADDRESS** Dept of Philos, Univ of New Mexico, Albuquerque, 513 Humanities Bldg, Albuquerque, NM 87131. **EMAIL** bhannan@unm.edu

HANS, JAMES STUART
PERSONAL Born 05/06/1950, Elgin, IL, m, 1974, 1 child **DISCIPLINE** ENGLISH LITERATURE, PHILOSOPHY **EDUCATION** Southern IL Univ, Edwardsville, BA, 72, MA, 74; Washington Univ, St Louis, PhD(English), 78. **CAREER** Teaching asst English, Southern IL Univ, 72-74; asst prof, Kenyon Col, 78-82; asst to prof English, Wake Forest Univ, 82-; ed consult, Kenyon Rev, 79-82; dir, Kenyon & Exeter Prog, Exeter Univ, England, 80-81. **HONORS AND AWARDS** Listed in Outstanding Scholars of the 21st Century; Listed in Who's Who in the South and Southwest, 96-97; Listed in Men of Achievement, 97. **RESEARCH** Twentieth century lit; literary theory; contemporary philosophy. **SELECTED PUBLICATIONS** Auth, Gaston Bachelard and the Phenomenology of the Reading Consciousness, J Aesthetics & Art Criticism, spring 77; Hans-Georg Gadamer and Hermeneutic Phenomenology, Philos Today, spring 78; Derrida and Freeplay,

Mod Lang Notes, 5/79; Presence and Absence in Modern Poetry, Criticism, fall 80; Hermeneutics, Play, Deconstruction, Philos Today, winter 80; The Play of the World, Univ MA Press, 81; Form and Measure in the Postmodern World, Kenyon Rev; Imitation and the Image of Man, John Benjaminis, 87; The Question of Value: Thinking Through Nietzsche, Heidegger and Freud, SIU Press, 89; The Value(s) of Literature, SUNY Press, 90; The Fate of Desire, SUNY Press, 90; The Origins of the Gods, SUNY Press, 91; Contextual Authority and Aesthetic Truth, SUNY Press, 92; The Mysteries of Attention, SUNY Press, 93; The Golden Mean, SUNY Press, 94; The Site of Our Lives: The Self and the Subject from Emerson to Foucault, SUNY Press, 95; auth, Named Wake Forest Professor of English, 99. **CONTACT ADDRESS** Dept English, Wake Forest Univ, PO Box 7387, Winston-Salem, NC 27109-7387. **EMAIL** hans@wfu.edu

HANSEN, CARL L.
PERSONAL Born 03/15/1938, Denver, CO, m, 1960, 4 children **DISCIPLINE** PHILOSOPHY, THEOLOGY **EDUCATION** Bethany Col, KS, BA, 60; Augustana Theol Sem, BD, 63; Princeton Theol Sem, ThM, 64; Univ CO Boulder, PhD, 76. **CAREER** Pastor, Holy Trinity Lutheran Church, Camden, NJ, 64-66; from instr to assoc prof, Bethany Col, Kans, 66-76, dir continuing educ, 69-76, prof philos & relig, 76-78, Johann Seleen distinguished prof, 78-81; Pres, Midland Lutheran Col, Nebr, 81-99, Consult, US 7th Army Chaplains, Heidelberg, Ger, 76-77. **HONORS AND AWARDS** Johann Seleen Distinguished Professorship, Bethany Col, 78. **RESEARCH** Philos of relig; interpersonal growth; death and dying. **SELECTED PUBLICATIONS** Auth, Ethical issues in death and dying, Lutheran Women, 75; The learning society, Bethany Col Mag, 75; Dear Sara, Lutheran Mag, 76; Roots and wings, Bethany Col Mag, 78. **CONTACT ADDRESS** Lutheran Family Services of Colo, 363 So. Harlan St., Denver, CO 80226. **EMAIL** chansen@lfsco.org

HANSEN, GARY
PERSONAL Born 05/14/1958, Seattle, WA, m, 1994 **DISCIPLINE** ECONOMICS **EDUCATION** Univ Puget Sound, BS, 80; Univ Minn, PhD, 86. **CAREER** Asst prof, Univ Calif Santa Barbara, 85-87; prof, UCLA, 87-. **MEMBERSHIPS** Am Econ Asn; Econometric Soc; Soc for Econ Dynamics. **RESEARCH** Macroeconomics. **SELECTED PUBLICATIONS** Co-auth, "The Role of Unemployment Insurance in an Economy with Liquidity Constraints and Moral Hazard," J of Polit Econ, (92): 118-142; co-auth, "The Labor Market in Real Business Cycle Theory," Fed Res Bank of Minn Quart Rev, (92): 2-12; co-auth, "Tax Distortions in a Neoclassical Monetary Economy," J Econ Theory, (92): 290-316; auth, "The Cyclical and Secular Behavior of the Labor Input: Comparing Efficiency Units and Hours Worked," J of Applied Econometrics, (93): 71-60; co-auth, "Did Technology Shocks Cause the 1990-1991 Recession?" Am Econ Rev, (93): 280-286; co-auth, "Money and the Business Cycle," in Frontiers of Business Cycle Research, Princeton Univ Press, 95; co-auth, "Recursive Methods for Computing Equilibria of Business Cycle Models," in Frontiers of Business Cycle Research, Princeton Univ Press, 95. **CONTACT ADDRESS** Dept Econ, Univ of California, Los Angeles, 8283 Bunche, PO Box 951477, Los Angeles, CA 90095-1477. **EMAIL** ghansen@econ.ucla.edu

HANSON, BRADLEY
PERSONAL Born 08/02/1935, Mankato, MN, m, 1962, 3 children **DISCIPLINE** SYSTEMATIC THEOLOGY **EDUCATION** St. Olaf Col, BA, 57; Luther Theol Sem, BD, 61; Yale Univ, MA, 63; Princeton Theol Sem, PhD, 70. **CAREER** Prof relig, Luther Col, 68-00 ; Dennis M. Jones distinguished tchg prof, Luther Col, 98-00; prof emeritus, Luther Col, 00-. **HONORS AND AWARDS** Phi Beta Kappa; Malone Fel. **MEMBERSHIPS** Am Acad Relig; Soc for the Stud of Christian Spirituality. **RESEARCH** Lutheran spirituality. **SELECTED PUBLICATIONS** Auth, Isms and Issues, Augsburg Fortress, 77; auth, The Call of Silence, Augsburg, 80; auth, Teach Us to Pray, Augsburg, 90; ed, Modern Christian Spirituality, Scholars, 90; auth, Introduction to Christian Theology, Fortress, 97; auth, A Graceful Life, Augsburg, 00. **CONTACT ADDRESS** 810 Ridge Rd, Decorah, IA 52101. **EMAIL** hansonbr@luther.edu

HANSON, BRUCE
PERSONAL Born 03/31/1952, Park Rapids, MN, m, 1982, 1 child **DISCIPLINE** RELIGION; PHILOSOPHY **EDUCATION** Claremont Grad Univ, MA, PhD, 91. **CAREER** Assoc prof, Philosophy & Religious studies. **MEMBERSHIPS** AAR; APA **CONTACT ADDRESS** Fullerton Col, 321 E Chapman Ave, Fullerton, CA 92632. **EMAIL** hanson1ful@aol.com

HANSON, ERIC O.
PERSONAL Born 03/05/1942, San Francisco, CA, m, 1972, 2 children **DISCIPLINE** POLITICAL SCIENCE **EDUCATION** Stanford, PhD, 76. **CAREER** Donahoe Prof of Polit Sci, 92-. **RESEARCH** Religion & politics; Asian politics. **SELECTED PUBLICATIONS** Auth, Catholic Politics in China and Korea, Orliss, 80; auth, The Catholic Church in World Politics, Princeton, 87. **CONTACT ADDRESS** Dept of Polit Sci, Santa Clara Univ, Santa Clara, CA 95053.

HANSON, PAUL DAVID
PERSONAL Born 11/17/1939, Ashland, WI, m, 1966, 3 children **DISCIPLINE** OLD TESTAMENT **EDUCATION** Gustavus Adolphus Col, BA, 61; Yale Univ, BD, 65; Harvard Univ, PhD, 70. **CAREER** Asst prof Old Testament, 70-74, prof, 75-81, Bussey Prof Divinity, Divinity Sch, Harvard Univ, 81-89, Lamont prof, 89-; Fulbright, 61-62; Woodrow Wilson, 65-66; Danforth, 66-70; Thayer fel archaeol, Am Sch Orient Res, 69-70; Von Humboldt, 81-82. **MEMBERSHIPS** Soc Bibl Lit; Am Sch Orient Res; Cath Bibl Asn. **RESEARCH** Late Bibl prophecy, Jewish apocalyptic lit; Bibl theology; ancient Near Eastern lang and civilizations. **SELECTED PUBLICATIONS** Auth, Jewish apocalyptic against its Near Eastern environment, Rev Biblique, 1/71; The Dawn of Apocalyptic, Fortress, 75, 2nd ed, 79; Masculine metaphors for God and sex-discrimination in the Old Testament, Ecumenical Rev, 75; Apocalypticism, In: Interpreters Dict of the Bible, suppl vol, Abingdon, 76; Rebellion in Heaven, Azazel and Euhemeristic heroes in I Enoch 6-11, J Bibl Lit, 77; The theological significance of contradiction within the Book of the Covenant, In: Canon and Authority, 77, Dynamic Transcendence, Fortress, 78; The Diversity of Scripture, 82, Fortress; The People Called, 86, Fortress; Isaiah 40-66, 95. **CONTACT ADDRESS** Divinity Sch, Harvard Univ, 45 Francis Ave, Cambridge, MA 02138-1994. **EMAIL** pdhanson@fas.harvard.edu

HANSON, WILLIAM H.
DISCIPLINE PHILOSOPHY **EDUCATION** Yale Univ, PhD. **RESEARCH** Logic and philosophy of logic. **SELECTED PUBLICATIONS** Auth, Algorithmic Translation in Propositional Logic, Comput Philos, 92; Indicative Conditionals Are Truth-Functional, Mind, 91; Second-Order Logic and Logicism, Mind, 90; Two Kinds of Deviance, Hist Philos Logic, 89; First Degree Entailments and Information, Notre Dame J Formal Logic, 80; co-auth, Validity in Intensional Languages: A New Approach, Notre Dame J Formal Logic, 85; auth,"The concept of logical consequence," The Philosophical Rev 106 (97); auth, "Ray on Tarski on logical consequence," Jrnl of Philosophical Logic 28 (99): 607-618. **CONTACT ADDRESS** Philosophy Dept, Univ of Minnesota, Twin Cities, 271 19th Ave S, 831 Heller Hall, Minneapolis, MN 55455. **EMAIL** whanson@tc.umn.edu

HAPPEL, STEPHEN P.
PERSONAL Born 08/18/1944, Indianapolis, IN, s **DISCIPLINE** RELIGION & THE ARTS; HERMENEUTICS; SACRAMENTS; FOUNDATIONAL THEOLOGY. **EDUCATION** St. Meinrad Col, BA, 66; Ind Univ, MA, 69; Hoger Inst voor Wijsbegeerte, PhB, 74; Katholieke Univ te Leuven, PhD, 77, STD, 79. **CAREER** Instr to Asst Prof, Cath Univ Am, 73-78; Assoc Prof, St. Meinrad Sch Theol, 78-83; Assoc Prof, Cath Univ Am, 83-; Dean School of Religious Studies, 99-; Vis Assoc Prof, Univ Notre Dame, 84, 85; Vis Assoc Prof, Boston Col, 84; Flannery Vis Prof Theol, Gonzaga Univ, 92-93. **HONORS AND AWARDS** All degrees granted "summa cum laude". **MEMBERSHIPS** Mod Lang Asn; Cath Theol Soc Am; Am Acad Relig; Am Soc Aesth; Soc Arts, Relig, & Contemp Cult; Christianity & Lit; Soc Values Higher Educ. **RESEARCH** Religion and the arts; religion and science; hermeneutics; systematic theology. **SELECTED PUBLICATIONS** Auth, Divine Providence and Instrumentality: Metaphors for Time in Self-Organizing Systems and Divine Action, Chaos, Complexity and Self-Organization: Perspectives on Divine Action, Vatican Observatory Publ, 95; coauth, Geography of the Soul: An Intellectual Map, In: Nourishing the Soul: Discovering the Sacred in Everyday Life, HarperSanFrancisco, 95; auth, Double Marginality and the Name of Love: Literary AIDS and the Power of Religion, Marginality and Dissent, Macmillan, 97; Communion with Fast Food: The Spirituality of Work and Sacrament, The Way, 97; God's Journey in Time: Metaphors for Time in Science and Religion, (forthcoming); ed, Artwork as Revelation: Religious Meanings in Works of Imagination, CUA Press (forthcoming). **CONTACT ADDRESS** Office of Dean, Catholic Univ of America, School of Religious Studies, Washington, DC 20064. **EMAIL** Happel@cua.edu

HARBERGER, ARNOLD C.
PERSONAL Born 07/27/1924, Newark, NJ, m, 1958, 2 children **DISCIPLINE** ECONOMICS **EDUCATION** Univ Chicago, MA, 47; PhD, 50. **CAREER** Asst prof, Johns Hopkins Univ, 49-53; assoc prof to prof, Univ of Chicago, 53-; prof, Univ of Calif Los Angles, 84-. **HONORS AND AWARDS** Phi Beta Kappa; Fel, Am Acad of Arts and Sci; Carlos Diaz Alejandre Prize, Latin Am & Caribbean Econ Assoc; Holland Medal; Doctor honoris causa, Catholic Univ of Chile, Nat Univ of Tucuman, Central Am Tech Univ; Gustavus F and Ann M Swift Distinguished Serv Prof, 77-91; **MEMBERSHIPS** Am Econ Assoc, Western Econ Assoc. **RESEARCH** Economic Policy in Developing Countries, The Process of Economic Growth, The Phenomenon and Cause of Inflation. **SELECTED PUBLICATIONS** Ed and contributor, The Demand for Durable Goods, Univ of Chicago Pr, 60; auth, Project Evaluation, Markham, 72; auth, Taxation and Welfare, Little Brown, 74; ed and contributor, World Economic Growth, Int Center for Econ Growth. **CONTACT ADDRESS** Dept Econ, Univ of California, Los Angeles, 8283 Bunche, Box 951477, Los Angeles, CA 90095-1477. **EMAIL** harberger@econ.ucla.edu

HARBIN, MICHAEL A.
PERSONAL Born 05/24/1947, Vincennes, IN, m, 1971, 3 children **DISCIPLINE** BIBLICAL STUDIES, OLD TESTAMENT AND SEMITIC STUDIES, ENGLISH LITERATURE **EDUCATION** US Naval acad, BS, 69; Calif State Univ, MA, 93; Dallas Theol Sem, ThM, 80, ThD, 88. **CAREER** Adj prof of Bible, Le Tourneau Univ, 90-93; adj prof English, El Centro Col, 90-93; assoc prof Biblical Stud (s), Taylor Univ, 93- . **HONORS AND AWARDS** Who's Who in Amer, 98, 00; Who's Who in Rel, 92-93; Who's Who in the Midwest, 95, 96; Phi Kappa Phi, 93. **MEMBERSHIPS** Soc Bibl Lit; Near East Archaeol soc; Inst Bibl res; Evangel Theol Soc. **RESEARCH** Old Testament History. **CONTACT ADDRESS** Dept of Biblical Studies, Taylor Univ, Upland, 236 W Reade Ave, Upland, IN 46989. **EMAIL** mcharbin@tayloru.edu

HARDESTY, NANCY A.
PERSONAL Born 08/22/1941, Lima, OH, s **DISCIPLINE** RELIGION **EDUCATION** Wheaton Col, BA, 63; Northwestern Univ, MSV, 64; Univ Chicago, PhD, 76. **CAREER** Asst Prof, Trinity Col; Asst Prof, Emory Univ; Asst Prof to Prof, 88-. **HONORS AND AWARDS** Lilly Teaching Fel, 00; Am Acad of Religion; Pew Charitable Trusts, United Study of Foreign Missions, 96-98; Kathryn and Calhoun Lemon Summer Res Fel, 96 **MEMBERSHIPS** Am Acad of Relig, Am Soc of Church Hist. **RESEARCH** Women in Am Protestantism; Healing. **SELECTED PUBLICATIONS** Auth, All We're Meant to Be: Biblical Feminism for Today, Word Books, 74; auth, "Your Daughters shall Prophesy: Revivalism and Feminism in the Age of Finney, Carlson Pub, 91; auth, The Memory Book, Presbyterian Pub, 89; auth, Inclusive Language in the church, John Knox Press, 87; auth, Women Called to Witness: Evangelical Feminism in the Nineteenth Century, Abingdon Press, 84; auth, Great Women of Faith, Baker Books, 80. **CONTACT ADDRESS** Dept Relig & Philos, Clemson Univ, 1 Clemson Univ, Clemson, SC 29634-0001. **EMAIL** nhardes@clemson.edu

HARDIMON, MICHAEL O.
DISCIPLINE EUROPEAN PHILOSOPHY **EDUCATION** Univ Chicago, PhD, 85. **CAREER** Prof, Philos, Univ Calif, San Diego. **RESEARCH** Kant philos through the nineteenth century; Ethics; social and polit philos. **SELECTED PUBLICATIONS** Auth, "The Project of Reconciliation," Philos and Public Aff, 92; Hegel's Social Philosophy, Cambridge Univ Press, 94; "Role Obligations," Jour of Philos 91, 94. **CONTACT ADDRESS** Dept of Philos, Univ of California, San Diego, 9500 Gilman Dr, La Jolla, CA 92093.

HARDIN, CLYDE LAURENCE
PERSONAL Born 08/27/1932, Des Moines, IA, m, 1967, 3 children **DISCIPLINE** PHILOSOPHY **EDUCATION** Johns Hopkins Univ, AB, 53; Univ Ill, AM, 54; Princeton Univ, PhD, 58. **CAREER** Instr philos, Univ Tex, 57-59; from instr to asst prof philos, 59-64, Assoc Prof Philos, Syracuse Univ, 64-, Dir Honors Prog, 68-75; prof, Philos, Syracuse Univ, 84-95, Prof Emeritus, 95 **HONORS AND AWARDS** Phi Beta Kappa **MEMBERSHIPS** Am Philos Asn. **RESEARCH** History and philosophy of science; philosophy of mind; color theory **SELECTED PUBLICATIONS** Auth, "Color for Philosophers: Unweaving the Rainbow," Hackett Publishing Company, 88; auth, "Color Categories in Thought and Language," Cambridge University Press, 97; auth, "Basic Color Terms and Basic Color Categories," in Werner G. K. Backhaus, Reinhold Kliegel, and John S. Werner, 97; auth, "Reinverting the Spectrum," in Martin Carrier and Peter Machamer, 97; auth, "Color and Illusion," in William Lycan, Mind and Cognition, Blackwell, 90; auth, "Qualia and Materialism: Closing the Explanatory Gap," Philosophy and Phenomenological Research, 87; auth, "Established Theories," with Fritz Rohrlich, Philosophy of Science 50, 83; auth, "In Defense of Convergent Realism," with Alexander Rosenberg, Philosophy of Science 49, 82; auth, "Spinoza on Immortality and Time," in Shahan and Biro, Spinoza: New Perspectives. Norman: Oklahoma University Press, 78; auth, "Wittgenstein on Private Language," Journal of Philosophy, 59. **CONTACT ADDRESS** Dept of Philosophy, Syracuse Univ, Syracuse, NY 13210. **EMAIL** chardin1@twcny.rr.com

HARDING, DAVID R., JR.
PERSONAL Born 01/27/1962, Alton, IL **DISCIPLINE** POLITICAL SCIENCE **EDUCATION** Univ Mo, BA, 85; Ohio State Univ, PhD, 91. **CAREER** Asst Prof to Assoc Prof and Dir, Ark State Univ, 92-. **MEMBERSHIPS** Am Polit Sci Asn; Soc of Environ Toxicology and Chemistry; Ark Polit Sci Asn. **RESEARCH** Environmental Policy; Gaming Policy; Gun Control and Criminal Justice Policy. **SELECTED PUBLICATIONS** Co-auth, "Arkansas Regionalism and the Indirect Effects of Culture," Midsouth Polit Sci Rev, 97; co-ed, Appearance and Transparence in Attitudes Toward Gun Control: The Changing Politics of Gun Control, 98. **CONTACT ADDRESS** Dept Polit Sci, Arkansas State Univ, Box 1750, AR 72467. **EMAIL** drharding@mail.astate.edu

HARDING, ROBERT E., JR.
PERSONAL Born 05/31/1930, Danville, KY, m, 2 children **DISCIPLINE** LAW **EDUCATION** KY State Univ, BA 1954; Univ KY, JD 1957. **CAREER** USPHS, corr officer 1952-58; Natl Labor Relations Bd, atty 1958-74; EEO consultant 1980-

86; labor arbitrator 1981-; Univ New Mexico, tchr Afro-Amer studies 1974-87. **HONORS AND AWARDS** New Mexico Reg Medical Prog, Certificate of Recognition, 1976; Better Bus Bur of New Mexico, Arbitrator of the Year, 1987; Governor of New Mexico Toney Anaya, Certificate of Appreciation, 1984; Sickle Cell Council of New Mexico, Certificate of Appreciation, 1990; Women United for Youth, Certificate of Recognition, 1993. **MEMBERSHIPS** Mem KY, NM, Natl; New Mexico Black Lawyers Assn; mem US Dist Ct NM; mem US Court of Appeals 10th Circuit; US Ct Appeals DC & US Supreme Ct; mem Phi Alpha Delta Legal Frat; pres, Albuquerque Branch NAACP, 1971; pres, bd dir Albuquerque Child Care Centers 1980-81; mem NM Adv Comm to the US Commiss on Civil Rights 1981-97; Better Business Bureau, Albuquerque, volunteer arbitrator, 1983-. **CONTACT ADDRESS** PO Box 14277, Albuquerque, NM 87191.

HARDMAN, KEITH J.
PERSONAL Born 05/20/1931, Wellsville, NY, m, 1963, 3 children **DISCIPLINE** RELIGION, PHILOSOPHY **EDUCATION** Haverford Col, BA, 54; Princeton Theol Sem, MDiv, 57; Columbia Univ, MA, 62; Univ Pa, PhD, 71. **CAREER** Pastor, SW Presbyterian Church, 57-67; prof, Ursinus Col, 67-. **MEMBERSHIPS** SBL; ASCH; AHA. **RESEARCH** Religion in America, Puritanism. **SELECTED PUBLICATIONS** Auth, Charles G. Finney, 1792-1875, Revivalist and Reformer, Syracuse Univ Pr, 87; auth, Season of Refreshing, 94; auth, Issues in American Christianity, 91. **CONTACT ADDRESS** Dept Relig and Philos, Ursinus Col, 601 E Main St, Collegeville, PA 19426-2562.

HARDWIG, JOHN R.
PERSONAL Born 09/10/1940, Waverly, IA, m, 1997 **DISCIPLINE** PHILOSOPHY **EDUCATION** Univ of TX, PhD, 75. **CAREER** Lect, Wellesley Col, 67-69; Inst, Univ of TN, 69-74 & 78-79; Lect, Humbolt St Univ, 75-78; Inst, Maryville Col, 79-82; Lect, E TN State Univ, 82-?; prof, dept head, Univ Tenn. **HONORS AND AWARDS** NEH Fel. **MEMBERSHIPS** APA. **RESEARCH** Bioethics. **SELECTED PUBLICATIONS** Auth, The Problem of Proxies With Interests of Their Own, UT Law Rev, 92; auth, Toward and Ethics of Expertise, Prof Ethics and Soc Resp, 94; auth, Support and the Invisible Family, Hastings Center Rep, 95; auth, Privacy Self-Knowledge and the Commune Toward an Epistemology of the Family, Fem Refl On Family, 96; auth, Elder Abuse Context and Ethics, JAI Press, 96; auth, "Duty to Die," in Hastings Center Report, 96; auth, Dying at the Right Time-Reflections on Assisted and Unassisted Suicide, Ethics in Prac, 96; auth, Autobiography Biography and Narrative Ethics, Stories and Their Limits Nar Appr to Bioethics, 97; auth, Is There a Duty to Die?, 99; auth, "Spiritual Issues at the End of Life: A Call for Discussion," in Hastings Center Report, 00. **CONTACT ADDRESS** Dept of Philosophy, Univ of Tennessee, Knoxville, 801 McClung Towers and Plaza, Knoxville, TN 37996. **EMAIL** jhardwig@utk.edu

HARDY, MICHAEL A.
PERSONAL Born 07/02/1955, New York, NY, s **DISCIPLINE** LAW **EDUCATION** Carleton College, BA, 1977; New York Law School, JD, 1988. **CAREER** NYC Health and Hospital Corp, analyst, 77-81; NYC Tax Commission, special asst, 81-83; Natl Alliance Newspaper, exec ed, 83-88; Intl Law Institute, Attorney, 88-92; Torres, Martinez, & Hardy, Attorney/partner, 92-. **HONORS AND AWARDS** Somerset Comm Action Program, Distinguish Legal Service, 1989; Natl Action Network, Martin Luther King Service Awd, 1993. **MEMBERSHIPS** Natl Bar Assn, 1988-; Assn Bar City of New York, 1988-; Natl Assn Criminal Defense Lawyers, 1990-; Natl Action Network, board member, 1989-. **SELECTED PUBLICATIONS** Author, Minister Louis Farrakhan, Practice Press, 1986; Narrator, A More Perfect Democracy, Film Documentary, 1988. **CONTACT ADDRESS** Torres, Martinez & Hardy, 11 Park Pl, Rm 916, New York, NY 10007-2801.

HARE, DOUGLAS ROBERT ADAMS
PERSONAL Born 03/22/1929, Simcoe, ON, Canada, m, 1951, 2 children **DISCIPLINE** NEW TESTAMENT **EDUCATION** Univ Toronto, BA, 51, BD, 54; Union Theol Sem, STM, 59, ThD(New Testament), 65. **CAREER** Teaching fel New Testament, 62-63, dir continuing educ, 63-64, from instr to assoc prof, 64-74, Prof New Testament, Pittsburgh Theol Sem, 74-, Am Asn Theol Schs fac fel, Ger, 71; chmn, sem Jewish Christianity, Studiorum Novi Testamenti Soc, 76-80. **MEMBERSHIPS** Studiorum Nori Testamenti Socs; Soc Bibl Lit; Cath Bibl Asn. **RESEARCH** Jewish-Christian relations in first century; Gospel of Matthew; gnosticism. **SELECTED PUBLICATIONS** Auth, The Theme of Jewish Persecution of Christians in the Gospel According to St Matthew, Cambridge, 67; The relationship between Jewish and Gentile persecution of Christians, J Ecumenical Studies, 67; translr, H J Schoeps, Jewish Christianity, Fortress, 69; coauth, Make disciples of all the Gentiles (Matthew 28: 19), Cath Bibl Quart, 7/75. **CONTACT ADDRESS** Pittsburgh Theol Sem, 616 N Highland Ave, Pittsburgh, PA 15206.

HARE, JOHN
PERSONAL m, 2 children **DISCIPLINE** CLASSICAL PHILOSOPHY **EDUCATION** Princeton Univ, PhD, 75 **CAREER** Staff Assoc, House Foreign Affairs Comm, Washington DC, 82-83; Amer Philos Assn Congressional fel, 81-82; vis fel, Hum, Medical Col Penn, 78-81; vis asst prof, Univ Mich, 75; Instr, 74, asst prof, 75-81, assoc prof, 81-87, prof 87, Lehigh Univ; prof, Calvin Col, 89. **HONORS AND AWARDS** Inst Adv Christian Stud (IFACS) Bk prize, 97; Pew Evangelical fel, 91-92; Jr Lindback awd for disting tchg, 81; Elected Hon Mem Phi Beta Kappa, 79. **MEMBERSHIPS** APA; APA Congressional fel selection comm, 83-89; Mem NY Aristotle Group, 75-81; Prog Comm APA Central Div, 96-97. **SELECTED PUBLICATIONS** Auth, The Apology as an Inverted Parody of Rhetoric, Arethusa, 14.2, Fall, 81, 205-216; Ethics and International Affairs, London, MacMillan, 82; Plato's Euthyphro, Bryn Mawr, 81, 2nd ed, 85; The Unfinished Business of the Peace Process in the Middle East, Report of Congressional Study Mission to Europe and the Middle East, Nov 82, House Foreign Affairs Comm, 97th Congress, 2nd Session; The Hospice Movement and the Acceptance of Death, Hospice USA, ed Austin H. Kutscher, New York, Columbia UP, 83, 9-17; Threats and Intentions, Evangelical Perspective on the Catholic Bishops' Pastoral Letter, ed Dean Curry, Grand Rapids, Eerdmans, 84, 139-157; Philosophy in the Legislative Process, Intl Jour Applied Ethics, 2, 2, Fall 84, 81-88; Credibility and Bluff, in Nuclear Weapons and the Future of Humanity, Totowa, Rowman and Allanheld, 86, 191-199; Nuclear Deterrence as Bluff, in Political Realism and International Morality: Ethics in the Nuclear Age, Boulder, Westview Press, 87, 144-152; Aristotelian Justice and the Pull to Consensus, in Intl Jour Applied Ethics, 3,3, Spring 89, 37-49; Commentary on Timothy J. Brennan, Academic Disciplines and Representative Advocacy, Bus and Prof Ethics Jour, 6, 1, 88, 56-62; Il Movemento Hospice e L'accettazione della Morte, Progressi Clinici: Medicina, 3, 3, 88, 137-140; Eleutheriotes in Aristotle's Ethics, in Ancient Philos, Spring, 88, 19-32; The Moral Argument for the Existence of God, and The Claims of Religious Experience, in Evidence for Faith, Richardson, Probe, 90, 231-252, and 253-273; Jackie Kennedy and the Seven Dwarfs, in Dialogue, April/May, 91, 23, 6, 20-31; The Atonement: How Does Christ Bridge the Gap, in The Banner, April 13, 92, 4-6; Government, Ethics in, in Encycl of Ethics, 92, 412-416, rev 97; Puffing up the Capacity, Jour Philos Res, XIX, 94, 75-88; Commercial Contracts and the Moral Contract, in Christian Scholar's Rev, XXIII, 3, 94, 259-266; The Invitation, poem, Dialogue, March/April 95, 8; The Atonement, Perspectives, May 95, 16-18; The History of Christian Ethics, in New Dictionary of Christian Ethics and Pastoral Theology, ed David Kingon, InterVarsity Press, 95, 33-42; The Unhappiest Man, in Kierkegaard's Either/Or, International Kierkegaard Commentary, Mercer Press, 95, 91-108; Kantian Ethics, International Politics and the Enlargement of the Foedus Pacificum, in Sovereignty at the Crossroads, Rowman, 96, 71-92; The Moral Gap, Oxford, Clarendon Press, 96; Atonement, Justification, and Santification, in A Companion to the Philosophy of Religion, Blackwell, 97, 549-555; Augustine, Kant and the Moral Gap, The augustinian Tradition, ed Gareth Matthews, U of California P, 97, 220-230; Why Bertrand Russell was not a Christian, Bk (s) and Cult, May/June, 98, 26-28. **CONTACT ADDRESS** Philosophy Dept, Univ of Notre Dame, Flanner 1112, Notre Dame, IN 46556. **EMAIL** jhare@calvin.edu

HARGIS, JEFFREY W.
PERSONAL Born 10/04/1961, Wichita Falls, TX, m, 1993 **DISCIPLINE** RELIGION **EDUCATION** Temple Univ, PhD, 98. **CAREER** Instr, Western Sem, 98- . **MEMBERSHIPS** Am Acad Relig; Soc of Bibl Lit; Evangelical Theol Soc; N Am Patristic Soc. **RESEARCH** Early church history. **SELECTED PUBLICATIONS** auth, Against the Christians: The Rise of Early Anti-Christian Polemic, Peter Lang, 99. **CONTACT ADDRESS** 8741 Church St, Gilroy, CA 95020. **EMAIL** hindsight2020@compuserv.com

HARLESTON, ROBERT ALONZO
PERSONAL Born 01/28/1936, Hempstead, NY, m, 3 children **DISCIPLINE** CRIMINAL JUSTICE **EDUCATION** Howard University, Washington, DC, BA, 1958; Michigan State University, East Lansing, MI, MS, 1965; Georgetown Law Center, Washington, DC, JD, 1984. **CAREER** Chair, Criminal Justice Dept, Univ of Maryland, Eastern Shore, Chair, currently. **HONORS AND AWARDS** Maryland Classified Employees Association, Martin Luther King Jr Awd, 1996. **MEMBERSHIPS** Govenors Education Coordinating Committee on Correctional Institutions, 1997-; bd of dirs, Eastern Shore Red Cross, 1990-93; bd of dirs, Delmarva Boy Scouts, 1990-93; member, Rotary Club, 1990-93; member, Black Advisory Committee to the Episcopal Bishop, 1990-; sire archon, Gamma Theta Boule, Sigma Pi Phi, 1996; member, Omega Psi Phi, 1953-; Interview Committee, Habitat for Humanity, 1995-. **CONTACT ADDRESS** Criminal Justice Program, Univ of Maryland, Eastern Shore, Princess Anne, MD 21853. **EMAIL** RAHARLESTON@MAIL.UMES.EDU

HARLEY, GAIL M.
PERSONAL Born 07/26/1943, Parris Island, SC, d, 2 children **DISCIPLINE** RELIGION IN NEW MOVEMENTS AND ASIAN RELIGIONS **EDUCATION** Fla State Univ, PhD, relig in interdisciplinary humanities, 91. **CAREER** Adjunct assoc prof, relig and humanities, Univ South Fla, 92-; acting pres, Emma Curtis Hopkins Col, 97. **HONORS AND AWARDS** Deans list, Univ South Fla, 82. **MEMBERSHIPS** Amer Acad of Relig; Soc for the Study of Metaphysical Relig. **RESEARCH** New thought movement; New religious movements; Asian cultural and religious thought; Asian humanities. **SELECTED PUBLICATIONS** Auth, Emma Curtis Hopkins, The Historical Encyclopedia of Chicago Women, vol 2, Univ Ill Press, 98; auth, Why Ramtha is worthy of scholarly study, News Tribune, Tacoma, 97; auth, New Thought and the Harmonial Family, Amer Alternative Relig, State Univ NY Press, 95; auth, Public Library & Priority, St. Petersburg Times, 4 nov, 94; auth, A Reflection of Social Conscience, St. Petersburg Times, 1 oct, 93; auth, Developers Must Be Environmentally Sensitive, St. Petersburg Times, 93; auth, Emma Curtis Hopkins: Forgotten Founder of New Thought, Syracuse Univ Press, forthcoming, 01. **CONTACT ADDRESS** P.O. Box 185, Aripeka, FL 34679. **EMAIL** gharley@atlantic.net

HARLEY, PHILIP A.
PERSONAL Born Philadelphia, PA, m **DISCIPLINE** THEOLOGY **EDUCATION** Morgan State Coll, BA 1945; Temple U; Univ Cincinnati; Capital Univ Sch Theol; Garrett Theol Sem, MDiv 1956. **CAREER** IL, IN, OH, SD, WI, pastor; Garrett Theol Seminary, assoc prof. **MEMBERSHIPS** Chmn Regional Consultative Com Race; Mayors Com Human Relations; dist dir Research & Devel; ministries educ IN, SD; prog leadership devel Prog Council Northern IL Conf; v chmn Leadership Devel Com N Central Jurisdictron; regional vice pres Nat Com Black Churchmen; chmn Chicago Coordinating Com Black Churchmen; v chmn Serv Review Panel Comm Fund; Ch Federation Met Chicago; Chicago Conf Religion & Race; mem bd dir Welfare Council Met Chicago. **CONTACT ADDRESS** Field Education Office, Garrett-Evangelical Theol Sem, 2121 Sheridan Road, Evanston, IL 60201.

HARLOW, DANIEL C.
PERSONAL Born 09/25/1962, Hialeah, FL, m, 1995, 1 child **DISCIPLINE** BIBLICAL STUDIES **EDUCATION** Oral Roberts Univ, BA, 84; Princeton Theol Sem, MDiv, 87; Univ of Notre Dame, MA, 91, PhD, 94. **CAREER** Instr theol, Univ Notre Dame, 92-93; asst prof bibl stud, Calvin Col, 94-96; ed bibl stud, William Eerdmans Publ, 96-; Asst Prof, Calvin Col. **HONORS AND AWARDS** Fulbright fel Israel, 91-92. **MEMBERSHIPS** Soc Bibl Lit. **RESEARCH** History and literature of early Judaism and Christianity, Early Jewsih and Christian apocalypticism, Early Jewish and Christian apocrypha and pseudepigrapha. **SELECTED PUBLICATIONS** Auth, The Greek Apocalypse of Baruch (3 Baruch) in Hellenistic Judaism and Early Christianity, Brill, 96. **CONTACT ADDRESS** Dept of Relig and Theology, Calvin Col, Grand Rapids, MI 49546. **EMAIL** dharlow@calvin.edu

HARMS, PAUL W. F.
DISCIPLINE HOMILETICS **EDUCATION** Concordia Sem, BA, 45, MDiv, 48, STM, 54; Northwestern Univ, MA, 57, PhD, 73; Valparaiso Univ, DA, 95. **CAREER** Assoc prof, Dir Drama and Forensics, Concordia Col, 52-56; prof, resident couns, Dir Drama, Concordia Sr Col, 56-76; prof, dean Community Life, Dir Drama, ELTS, 76-78; dean Community Life, 78-90; prof, 78-94; dir, Trinity Lutheran Sem Theater, 78-; prof emeri, Trinity Lutheran Sem, 94-. **SELECTED PUBLICATIONS** Auth, Seek Good Not Evil, CSS, 85; Presenting the Lessons, Augsburg, 80; ed, Praise of Preaching. CSS, 84. **CONTACT ADDRESS** Ministry Dept, Trinity Lutheran Sem, 2199 E Main St, Columbus, OH 43209-2334. **EMAIL** pharms@trinity.capital.edu

HARMS, WILLIAM F.
PERSONAL Born 11/19/1959, Baton Rouge, LA, m, 1995 **DISCIPLINE** PHILOSOPHY **EDUCATION** Univ Calif, Santa Cruz, BA 90.; Univ of Calif, Irvine, MA, 93; PhD, 96. **CAREER** Bowling Green State Univ, vis prof, 96-98; Univ British Columbia, post doc res, 98-99. **MEMBERSHIPS** APA; PSA. **RESEARCH** Epistemology; Philosophy of Biology; Philosophy of Science; Evolutionary Garme Theory. **SELECTED PUBLICATIONS** Auth, Evolution and Ultimatum Bargaining, Theory and Decision, 97; auth, Discrete Replicator Dynamics for the Ultimatum Game, U of Calif Irvine, Inst Math Behav Sciences, Tech Repot Serv, 95; auth, Cultural Revolution and the Phenotype, Biology and Philos, 96; auth, Reliability and Novelty: Information Gain in Multilevel Selection Systems, Erkenntnis; The Epistemology Use of Information Theory, Philos of Science; rev, Dan Sperber's, Explaining Culture, Economics and Philos, 98. **CONTACT ADDRESS** Centre for Applied Ethics, Univ of British Columbia, 227-6356 Agricultural Rd, Vancouver, BC, Canada V6T 1Z2. **EMAIL** billharms@billharms.com

HARNED, DAVID B.
DISCIPLINE CHRISTIAN THOUGHT AND ETHICS **EDUCATION** Yale Univ, PhD, 63. **CAREER** Prof Emer, La State Univ. **SELECTED PUBLICATIONS** Auth, Faith and Virtue, United Church Press, 76; Creed and Personal Identity, Fortress, 81. **CONTACT ADDRESS** Dept of Philos and Relig Stud, Louisiana State Univ and A&M Col, 106 Coates Hall, Baton Rouge, LA 70803.

HARNSBERGER, R. SCOTT
PERSONAL Born 04/16/1952, Lincoln, NE, d, 1 child **DISCIPLINE** PHILOSOPHY **EDUCATION** Univ Wisc-Madison, PhD, 81. **CAREER** Assoc prof, Newton Gresham Libr, Sam Houston State Univ, 87-. **MEMBERSHIPS** Am Libr Asn; Am Philos Asn; Texas Libr Asn. **RESEARCH** 20th Century American art. **SELECTED PUBLICATIONS** Auth Ten Precisionist Artists: Annotated Bibliographies, Greenwood Press, 92; coed Popular Culture in Libraries, Haworth Press, 96-99. **CONTACT ADDRESS** Sam Houston State Univ, PO Box 2179, Huntsville, TX 77341-2179. **EMAIL** lib_rsh@shsu.edu

HARPER, BILL
DISCIPLINE PHILOSOPHY **EDUCATION** Rensselaer Polytech Inst, BS, 64; Univ Rochester, MA, 70; PhD, 74. **CAREER** Prof **RESEARCH** Newton; testing of general relativity; Kant; decision theory; game theory. **SELECTED PUBLICATIONS** Auth, Reasoning from Phenomena: Newton's Argument for Universal Gravitation and the Practice of Science, Action and Reaction: Proceedings of a Symposium to Commemorate the Tercentenary of Newton's Principia, 93; Kant on Incongruent Counterparts, Kluwer, 91; co-auth, Newton's New Way of Inquiry, Kluwer; Unification and Support: Harmonic Law Ratios Measure the Mass at the Sun, Kluwer, 94; co-ed, Causation, Chance and Credence, Kluwer, 88; Causation in Decision, Belief Change, and Statistics, Kluwer, 88; Kant on Causality, Freedom, and Objectivity, Univ Minn, 84; Ifs, Reidel, 80. **CONTACT ADDRESS** Dept of Philosophy, Univ of Western Ontario, London, ON, Canada N6A 5B8. **EMAIL** wlharp@julian.uwo.ca

HARRELSON, WALTER
PERSONAL Born 11/28/1919, Winnabow, NC, m, 1942, 3 children **DISCIPLINE** THEOLOGY **EDUCATION** Univ NC, AB, 47; Union Theol Sem, BD, 49, ThD, 53. **CAREER** Instr philos, Univ NC, 47; prof Old Testament, Andover Newton Theol Sch, 51-55; assoc prof Old Testament & dean divinity sch, Univ Chicago, 55-60; prof, 60-75, dean, 67-75, distinguished prof, 75-77, Harvie Branscomb distinguished prof, 77-78, Distinguished Prof Old Testament, Vanderbilt Univ, 78-, Mem comt hist relig, Am Coun Learned Soc, 56-62, chmn, 61-62; Fulbright res scholar & Am Asn Theol Schs fac fel, Rome, Italy, 62-63; chmn, Ethiopia Manuscript Microfilm Libr, 71-; rector, Ecumenical Inst Advan Theol Studies, Jerusalem, 77-78 & spring, 79. **HONORS AND AWARDS** DD, Univ of the South, 74; DLitt, Mars Hill Col, 77. **MEMBERSHIPS** Soc Bibl Lit (pres, 71-72); Soc Values Higher Educ; Am Schs Orient Res; Am Soc Study Relig. **RESEARCH** Old Testament; Semitic languages and literatures; Biblical theology. **SELECTED PUBLICATIONS** Auth, The Anchor Bible Dictionary, J Biblical Lit, Vol 0113, 94; The Inferior Religion--A Study of the Attitudes Toward Judaism Within German Old-Testament Scholarship, J Biblical Lit, Vol 0113, 94; The Land Called Holy--Palestine In Christian History and Thought, J Am Acad Relig, Vol 0063, 95. **CONTACT ADDRESS** Divinity Sch, Vanderbilt Univ, Nashville, TN 37240.

HARRIES, KARSTEN
PERSONAL Born 01/25/1937, Jena, Germany, m, 1959, 3 children **DISCIPLINE** PHILOSOPHY **EDUCATION** Yale Univ, BA, 58, PhD, 62. **CAREER** Instr philos, Yale Univ, 61-63; asst prof, Univ Tex, 63-65; from asst prof to assoc prof, 65-70, chmn dept, 73- 78, Prof Philos, Yale Univ, 70-, Guest prof, Univ Bonn, 65-66 & 68-69; Guggenheim fel, 71-72. **MEMBERSHIPS** Am Philos Asn; Soc Phenomenol & Existential Philos; AAUP; Am Soc Aesthet. **RESEARCH** Aesthetics; German philosophy. **SELECTED PUBLICATIONS** Auth, Two conflicting interpretations of language in Wittgenstein's Investigations, Kantstudien, Vol 59, No 4; Das befreite Nichts, In: Durchblicke: Martin Heidegger zum 80 Geburtstag, Klostermann, 70; Hegel on the future of art, Rev Metaphys, 6/74; The infinite sphere: comments on the history of a metaphor, J Hist Philos, 1/75; Language and silence: Heidegger's dialogue with Georg Trakl, Boundary, winter 76; Heidegger as a political thinker, Rev Metaphys, 6/76; Metaphor and transcendence, Critical Inquiry, autumn 78; Meta-criticism and meta-poetry: A critique of theoretical anarchy, Res Phenomenol, 79; The Bavarian Rococo Church: Between Faith and Aestheticism, Yale (in prep). **CONTACT ADDRESS** Dept of Philos, Yale Univ, P O Box 208306, New Haven, CT 06520-8306.

HARRILL, J. ALBERT
PERSONAL Born 07/02/1963, Winston-Salem, NC **DISCIPLINE** RELIGION **EDUCATION** Univ N Carolina, Chapel Hill, BA, 86; Univ Chicago, MA, 89, PhD, 93. **CAREER** Asst prof theol, Creighton Univ, 94-96; asst prof relig stud, DePaul Univ, 96- . **HONORS AND AWARDS** Phi Beta Kappa, 85; Bernard Boyd Mem Fel, 86. **MEMBERSHIPS** Sos of Bibl Lit; North Am Patristic Soc; Soc for the Promotion of Roman Stud; Catholic Bibl Asn. **RESEARCH** Greco-Roman environment of Early Christianity; ancient slavery. **SELECTED PUBLICATIONS** Auth, Ignatius, Ad Polycarp, 4.3 and the Corporate Manumission of Christian Slaves, J of Early Christian Stud, 93; auth, The Manumission of Slaves in Early Christianity, Mohr, 95; auth, The Indentured Labor of the Prodigal Son (Luke 15: 15), J of Bibl Lit, 96; auth, The Vice of Slave Dealers in Greco-Roman Society: The Use of a Topos in 1 Timothy 1:10, J of Bibl Lit, 99; auth, "The Dramatic Function of the Running Slave Rhoda (Acts 12.13-16): A Piece of Greco-Roman Comedy," New Testament Studies, 00; auth, "The Use of the New Testament in the American Slave Controversy," Rel and Am Culture, 00. **CONTACT ADDRESS** Dept of Religious Studies, DePaul Univ, 2320 N Kenmore Ave, Chicago, IL 60614-3298. **EMAIL** jharrill@condor.depaul.edu

HARRINGTON, DANIEL JOSEPH
PERSONAL Born 07/19/1940, Arlington, MA **DISCIPLINE** BIBLICAL STUDIES, JEWISH HISTORY **EDUCATION** Boston Col, BA, 64, MA, 65; Harvard Univ, PhD(Oriental lang), 70; Weston Sch Theol, BD, 71. **CAREER** PROF NEW TESTAMENT, WESTON JESUIT SCH THEOL, 72-; Vis lectr Old Testament, Harvard Divinity Sch, 72-; ed, New Testament Abstracts, 72-; pastoral assoc, St Agnes Church, Mass, 72-; coordr, New Testament Colloquium, Boston, 77-; trustee, Holy Cross Col, Mass, 78- **MEMBERSHIPS** Cath Bibl Asn of Am, pres 85-86; Soc Bibl Lit; Soc New Testament Studies. **SELECTED PUBLICATIONS** Auth, The Gospel According to Matthew, Collegeville: Liturgical, 83; The Gospel According to Mark, NY: Sadlier, 83; The Gospel According to Luke, NY: Sadlier, 83; Pentecost 2, Series B, Philadelphia: Fortress, 85; The New Testament: A Bibliography, Wilmington: Glazier, 85; Targum Jonathan of the Former Prophets, Wilmington: Glazier, 87; The Maccabean Revolt: Anatomy of a Biblical Revolution, Wilmington: Glazier, 88; John's Thought and Theology: An Introduction, Wilmington: Glazier, 90; The Gospel of Matthew, Collegeville: Liturgical, 91; Paul on the Mystery of Israel, Collegeville: Liturgical, 92; How to Read the Gospels, Hyde Park, NY: New City Press, 96; Wisdom Texts from Oumran, London: Routledge, 96; Paul's Prison Letters, Hyde Park, NY: New City Press, 97; Romans. The Good News According to Paul, Hyde Park, NY: New City Press, 98; and author of many other articles in directories, encyclopedias, scholarly journals, and other publications; auth, Who Is Jesus?, Franklin, WI: Sheed & Ward, 99; auth, Invitation to the Apocrypha, Grand Rapids, MI: Erdmans, 99; auth, Why Do We Suffer?, Franklin, WI: Sheed & Ward, 00. **CONTACT ADDRESS** Bibl Studies Dept, Weston Jesuit Sch of Theol, 3 Phillips Place, Cambridge, MA 02138-3495. **EMAIL** dharrington@wjst.edu

HARRINGTON, HENRY R.
PERSONAL Born 12/23/1943, Evanston, IL, m, 1968, 1 child **DISCIPLINE** ENGLISH LITERATURE & THEOLOGY **EDUCATION** Williams Col, AB, 66; Stanford Univ, MA, 68, PhD, 71. **CAREER** Asst prof, 71-80, ASSOC PROF ENGLISH, UNIV MONT, 80- **MEMBERSHIPS** MLA; AAUP; Am Acad Relig. **RESEARCH** Victorian literature; comtemporary theology and literature; novel. **SELECTED PUBLICATIONS** **CONTACT ADDRESS** Dept of English, Univ of Montana, Missoula, MT 59801.

HARRINGTON, MICHAEL LOUIS
PERSONAL Born 07/08/1944, Portland, OR, m, 1976, 2 children **DISCIPLINE** PHILOSOPHY **EDUCATION** Davidson Col, AB, 66; Emory Univ, Ma, 69, PhD(philos), 72. **CAREER** Asst prof, 70-75, Assoc Prof Philos, Univ Miss, 75-98; PROF PHILOS, UNIV MISS, 98-; Consult philos, Nat Endowment Humanities, 76-78; Miss Hum Council, 94-. **MEMBERSHIPS** Am Philos Asn; Metaphys Soc Am. **RESEARCH** Metaphysics; epistemology; philosophical theol. **SELECTED PUBLICATIONS** Auth, Evangelicism and racism in the development of Southern religion, Miss Quart, spring 74; co-auth, Traditions & Changes, 95, 96, 97, 98. **CONTACT ADDRESS** Univ of Mississippi, P.O. Box 1848, University, MS 38677. **EMAIL** prmlh@olemiss.edu

HARRIS, BOND
PERSONAL Born 08/23/1932, Richmond, VA, m, 1956, 2 children **DISCIPLINE** PHILOSOPHY, RELIGION **EDUCATION** Univ Richmond, BA, 55; Southeastern Sem, BD, 58, ThM, 61; Drew Univ, PhD(philos relig), 70. **CAREER** Asst prof philos & relig, Ky Wesleyan Col, 68-73; asst prof, 73-75, assoc prof philos, 75-98, prof philos, Eastern Ky Univ, 98-. **MEMBERSHIPS** AAUP; Am Philos Asn; Metaphys Soc Am; Soc Phenomenol & Existential Res; Mind Soc; Hegel Soc of Am. **RESEARCH** Metaphysics, German idealism; epistemology; philosophy of religion. **CONTACT ADDRESS** Dept Philosophy, Eastern Kentucky Univ, 521 Lancaster Ave, Richmond, KY 40475-3102. **EMAIL** phiharris@acs.eku.edu

HARRIS, CHARLES EDWIN
PERSONAL Born 06/21/1938, Nashville, TN, m, 2 children **DISCIPLINE** ETHICAL THEORY **EDUCATION** Vanderbilt Univ, AB, 60, PhD, 64. **CAREER** Assoc prof, Texas A&M Univ75-. **HONORS AND AWARDS** Danforth assoc, 70. **MEMBERSHIPS** APA; Southwestern Philos Soc. **SELECTED PUBLICATIONS** Auth, Applying Moral Theories, Wadsworth, 86 & Aborting Fetuses: The Parental Perspective, J Applied Philos, 91; couth, Engineering Ethics: Concepts and Cases, Belmont, CA: Wadsworth Publ Co, 94. **CONTACT ADDRESS** Dept of Philosophy, Texas A&M Univ, Col Station, College Station, TX 77843-4237.

HARRIS, CHARLES WESLEY
PERSONAL Born 09/12/1929, Auburn, AL **DISCIPLINE** POLITICAL SCIENCE **EDUCATION** Morehouse Cool, BA, 49; Univ Pa, MA, 50; Univ Wis, PhD, 59. **CAREER** Assoc. Prof, Grambling Col, 59-61; Prof, Coppin State Col, 61-70; Prof, Howard Univ, 71-. **HONORS AND AWARDS** James Fund Feel, Univ Wis, 56; Ford Found Advanced Studies Grant, 68-69; Who's Who in America; Woodrow Wilson Ctr Feel. 92-93; Alpha Phi Alpha. **MEMBERSHIPS** ASPA, Am Polit SCI Asn, Nat Conf Black Polit Scientists. **SELECTED PUBLICATIONS** Auth, Regional Councils of Government and the Central City, 70; auth, Resolving the Legislative Veto Issue, 79; auth, Perspectives of Political Power in D C, 81; auth, Congress and the Governance of the Nation's Capital, 95; auth, **CONTACT ADDRESS** Dept Polit Sci, Howard Univ, 2400 6th St NW, Washington, DC 20059-0002.

HARRIS, DAVID A.
DISCIPLINE LAW **EDUCATION** Northwestern Univ, BA; Yale Univ, JD; Georgetown Univ, LLM. **CAREER** Prof. **SELECTED PUBLICATIONS** Auth, 'Driving While Black' and All Other Traffic Offenses: The Supreme Court and Pretextual Traffic Stops, J Criminal Law Criminology, 97; Superman's X-Ray Vision and the Fourth Amendment: The New Gun Detection Technology, Temple Law Rev, 96; Frisking Every Suspect: The Withering of Terry, Davis Law Rev, 95; Factors For Reasonable Suspicion: When Black and Poor Means Stopped and Frisked, Bloomington, 94. **CONTACT ADDRESS** Col Law, Univ of Toledo, Toledo, OH 43606. **EMAIL** dharris@uoft02.utoledo.edu

HARRIS, ERROL E.
PERSONAL Born 02/19/1908, Kimberley, South Africa, w, 1946, 4 children **DISCIPLINE** PHILOSOPHY **EDUCATION** Rhodes Univ, BA, 27, MA, 29; Oxford Univ, B. Litt, 34; Witwatersrand Univ, D. Litt, 51. **CAREER** Lectr, 30-31, Fort Hare Col; Private Sec, Minister for Mines Southern Rhodesia, 34-35; asst master, 36, Uppingham Schl England; asst master, 37, Charterhouse Schl England; ed officer, Basutoland, 37-40, Zanzibar, 41-42, British Colonial Svc; military svc: S African Army Info Svc, 42-44, chief instr, 44-46, British Army Ed Corps, Middle East Command Ed Col; lectr, phil, 46-49, sr lectr, phil, 50-52, prof, dept head, phil, 53-56, Witwatersrand Univ; vis lectr, 56-57, Yale Univ; prof, 56-62, CT Col; acting head dept, logic and metaphysics, 59-60, Univ Edinburgh (Scotland); Roy Robert Dist Prof, 63-66, Univ KS; prof, 66-76, John Evans Prof, intel and moral phil, 72-80, Northwestern Univ; vis dist prof, 77-78, Marquette Univ; Cowling Prof, 78-, Carlton Col; vis dist prof of Christian phil, 82, Villanova Univ; vis prof phil, 83-84, Emory Univ; hon res fel, 85-, Center for Phil and History of Science, Boston Univ. **HONORS AND AWARDS** Alfred Beit Scholar, Rhodes Univ, 28-29; Queen Victoria Scholar, Oxford Univ, 31-33; Hugh le May Res Fel, Rhodes Univ, 49; Bollingen Fel, 64; Ford Found Fel, 67; Res Fel, Inst for Advanced Stud in Humanities, Univ Edinburgh, 78; Terry Lectr, Yale Univ, 57; Machette Lectr, Old Dominion Univ, 65, Tulane Univ, 75; Werner Lectr, Clark Univ, 74; Aquinas Lectr, Marquette Univ, 77; Suarez Lectr, Fordham Univ, 82; Gilbert Ryle Lectr, Trent Univ, 84; Pres, Metaphysical Soc of Amer, 68; Pres, Hegel Soc of Amer, 77-78; Paul Weiss Medalist, Outstanding contr to Metaphysics, 89. **MEMBERSHIPS** APA; Hegel Soc of Am; Hegel Soc of Great Britain; Metaphysical Soc of Am. **RESEARCH** Hegel, Spinoza, Philos of nature & science, Metaphysics, Political Philos, Intl Politics. **SELECTED PUBLICATIONS** Art, The Obstacle to Global Solutions, Med and Global Survival, 93; art, Science, Mysticism, Belief and Conscience, Conf on Science, Mystique, Poesy and Conscience, Lisbon, 94; art, Being-for-Self in the Greater Logic, Owl of Minerva, 94; art, Dialectica and Lo(?) transcendentale e tempo, Criterio 3, 95; auth, Scepticism and Dialectic, Phenomenology and Skepticism, Northwestern Univ Press, 95/6; art, Reminiscences of Hegelians I have met, Owl of Minerva, Vol 27, 95; auth, The Restitution of Metaphysics, Humanities Press, Atlantic Highlands, 98; ed, Towards Genuine Global Governance: World Federalist Reactions to "Our Global Neighborhood, 99. **CONTACT ADDRESS** 9 Marie Ave, Cambridge, MA 02139.

HARRIS, FRED O.
DISCIPLINE LAW **EDUCATION** Univ Ark, BA; JD. **CAREER** Prof, Univ Ill Urbana Champaign. **RESEARCH** Products liability; toxic torts; environmental law; and insurance law **SELECTED PUBLICATIONS** Auth, Arkansas Wrongful Death Actions; co-auth, Warranty Law in Tort and Contract Action. **CONTACT ADDRESS** Law Dept, Univ of Illinois, Urbana-Champaign, 52 E Gregory Dr, Champaign, IL 61820. **EMAIL** fharris@law.uiuc.edu

HARRIS, HENRY SILTON
PERSONAL Born 04/11/1926, Brighton, England, m, 1952, 4 children **DISCIPLINE** PHILOSOPHY **EDUCATION** Oxford Univ, BA, 49, MA, 52; Univ Ill, PhD(philos), 54. **CAREER** Instr philos, Univ Ill, 53-54; instr, Ohio State Univ, 54-57; from asst prof to assoc prof, Univ Ill, 57-62; assoc prof univ, 62-65, Prof Philos, Glendon Col, York Univ, Ont, 65-, Am Philos Asn res fel, 57-58; Can Coun leave fel, 64-65, 71-72 & 78-79. **MEMBERSHIPS** Am Philos Asn; Can Philos Asn; G Gentile Found Studies Philos; Hegel Soc Am (vpres, 72-74, pres, 78-

80); Charles S Peirce Soc. **RESEARCH** Italian philosophy; German idealism; social theory. **SELECTED PUBLICATIONS** Auth, How Philosophy Instructs the World--The Preface of Hegel 'Philosophy Of Right' in its Relation to the Work Itself, Laval Philos, Vol 0051, 95; Philosophy and Poetry--Verene, Donald, Phillip Studies of Giambattista Vico--The War Renewed, Clio, Vol 0023, 94. **CONTACT ADDRESS** Dept of Philos Glendon Col, York Univ, Toronto, ON, Canada M4N 3M6.

HARRIS, ISHWAR C.
PERSONAL Born 07/13/1943, India, m, 1977, 2 children **DISCIPLINE** RELIGION, ASIAN STUDIES **EDUCATION** Claremont Grad School, PhD, 74. **CAREER** Asst prof Rel, Rutgers Univ, 74-81; asst to assoc prof to Prof, College of Wooster, 81-. **HONORS AND AWARDS** Luce Grant Prof Res; GLCA Japan Travel Grant, 99. **MEMBERSHIPS** Am Acad Rel **RESEARCH** Modern India; Hinduism, Gandhian studies. **SELECTED PUBLICATIONS** Auth, Radhakrishnan: Profile of a Universalist, 82; Gandhians in Contemporary India, 98. **CONTACT ADDRESS** Dept of Religious Stud, The Col of Wooster, Wooster, OH 44691. **EMAIL** iharris@aes.wooster.edu

HARRIS, J. GORDON
PERSONAL Born 11/01/1940, LA, m, 1967, 2 children **DISCIPLINE** GERONTOLOGY, BIBLICAL STUDIES **EDUCATION** Baylor Univ, BA, 62; SW BTS Sem, BD, 65; ThM, 67; S Sem, PhD, 70; Hebrew Col, MA, 81. **CAREER** Prof, BT Sem, Philippines, 70-75; prof, N Am Baptist Sem, 75-; Acad VP, 82-95; Dir, 95-. **HONORS AND AWARDS** Outstanding Young Men in Am; Who's Who in Relig, 77; Distinguished Am in 20th Century; Pres, Lions Club; Pres, NAPH; Pres, Upper Midwest SBL/AAR. **MEMBERSHIPS** NAPH; NABPR; Soc of Bibl Lit; Am Soc of Ageing. **RESEARCH** Hebrew Scriptures, Joshua, prophets, wisdom literature; Gerontology, spirituality and aging, Bible and aging. **SELECTED PUBLICATIONS** Auth, Biblical Perspectives on Aging, Fortress, 87; Auth, Joshua, NI Biblical Commentary, Hendrikson, 00. **CONTACT ADDRESS** Dept Relig, No American Baptist Sem, 1525 S Grange Ave, Sioux Falls, SD 57105-1526. **EMAIL** gharris@nabs.edu

HARRIS, JIMMIE
PERSONAL Born 07/27/1945, Winona, MS **DISCIPLINE** LAW **EDUCATION** Univ of CA Berkeley, JD 1972; Univ of IL Champaign-Urbana, IL, BS Elec Engrng 1967. **CAREER** Vidal Sassoon Inc, counsel; Daylin Inc Asso Irell & Manella, gen counsel. **MEMBERSHIPS** Mem Beverly Hills Bar Assn; LA Co Bar Assn; Langston Law Club. **SELECTED PUBLICATIONS** Pub articles, ed CA Law Review. **CONTACT ADDRESS** 555 W 5th St, 40th Floor, Los Angeles, CA 90013.

HARRIS, JOHN
PERSONAL Born 07/13/1962, Pensacola, FL, m, 1983, 2 children **DISCIPLINE** THEOLOGY **EDUCATION** Central Baptist Col, BA, 84; Southwestern Baptist Theol Sem, MDiv, 88; PhD, 94. **CAREER** Asst/Assoc Prof, E Tex Baptist Univ, 95-. **HONORS AND AWARDS** Who's Who Among Students of Am Univ of Col, 83, 84, 91, 93; Outstanding Scholar ward, 84; Who's Who Am Teachers, 00. **MEMBERSHIPS** Soc of Bibl Lit. **RESEARCH** Hebrew Bible, Archaeology. **SELECTED PUBLICATIONS** Auth, "Thank Offerings," Bibl Illusr (Summer 97): 28-30; auth, "Judges in Ancient Isreal," Bibl Illusr (Spring 00): 34-36. **CONTACT ADDRESS** Dept Relig, East Texas Baptist Univ, 1209 N Grove St, Marshall, TX 75670-1423. **EMAIL** jharris@etbu.edu

HARRIS, MAX R.
PERSONAL Born 03/26/1949, Rotherham, England, m, 1974, 2 children **DISCIPLINE** RELIGIOUS STUDIES **EDUCATION** Cambridge Univ, BA, 70; Univ Calif - Santa Barbara, MA, 72; Covenant Theol Seminary, MDiv, 78; Univ Va, PhD, 89. **CAREER** Pastor, Presbyterian churches in England and the US, 78-; Asst Prof, Dept Relig Studies and Psychiat Med, Univ Va, 91-93, Assoc Dir, Ctr on the Study of Mind and Human Interaction, 91-93; Exec Dir, Wis Humanities Coun, 93-. **HONORS AND AWARDS** Numerous research and travel awards from various organizations. **MEMBERSHIPS** Am Acad Relig; Medieval/Renaissance Drama Soc; Soc Int L'Etude du Theatre Medieval. **RESEARCH** Medieval theater; folk theater; the religious and theatrical aspects of fiestas in Spain and the Americas. **SELECTED PUBLICATIONS** Auth, Theatre and Incarnation, St. Martin's Press, 90; The Dialogical Theatre: Dramatizations of the Conquest of Mexico and the Question of the Other, St. Martin's Press, 93; A Catalan Corpus Christi Play: The Martyrdom of St. Sebastian with the Hobby Horses and the Turks, Comp Drama 31, 97; The Impotence of Dragons: Playing Devil in the Trinidad Carnival, The Drama Rev 42, 98; Fireworks, Turks, and Long-Necked Mules: Pyrotechnic Theater in Germany and Catalonia, Comp Drama 32, 98; auth, Aztecs, Moors, and Christians: Festivals of Reconquest in Mexico and Spain, Univ of Texas Press, 00; author of numerous other articles and chapters. **CONTACT ADDRESS** Exec Dir, Wisconsin Humanities Coun, 802 Regent St., Madison, WI 53715-2610. **EMAIL** mrharri1@facstaff.wisc.edu

HARRIS, NORMAN
DISCIPLINE PHILOSOPHY **EDUCATION** Univ Ind, BA, MA, PhD. **CAREER** Prof. **RESEARCH** African American Studies; creative and technical writing; African philosophy; Egyptian philosophy. **SELECTED PUBLICATIONS** Auth, The Sixties A Black Chronology, 90; African American Social Change; A Philosophical Base, 91; Education or Initiation: Reading the Interior of the Black World Experience, 94; Can the Big Dog Run?, Black Cult J, 93; A Philosophical Basis for Afrocentricity, W J Black Studies, 92; The Sixties: An Analytical Chronology, W J Black Studies, 92; Multicultural Education in A Changing World, 90. **CONTACT ADDRESS** Philosophy Dept, Union Inst, 440 E McMillan St, Cincinnati, OH 45206-1925.

HARRIS, STEPHEN LEROY
PERSONAL Born 02/05/1937, Aberdeen, WA, d, 1965, 2 children **DISCIPLINE** RELIGIOUS STUDIES **EDUCATION** Univ Puget Sound, BA, 59; Cornell Univ, MA, 61, PhD, 64. **CAREER** Actg cur-libr, WA State Hist Soc, 63; asst prof Eng, WA State Univ, 64-65; from asst prof to assoc prof, 65-72, chmn hum dept, 72-76, 92-98; prof hum, CA State Univ, Sacramento, 74. **HONORS AND AWARDS** Woodrow Wilson Fellow, 60-61; Faculty Research Award, CSUS, 81-82. **RESEARCH** Member Soc of Biblical Literature Fellow of Jesus Seminar. **SELECTED PUBLICATIONS** Auth, The Humanist Tradition in World Literature, Merrill, 70; Fire and Ice: The Cascade Volcanoes, Pac Search & the Mountaineers, 76, rev ed, 80, 2nd ed, 83; Understanding the Bible, A reader's Guide and Reference, Mayfield Publ, (5th ed, 00); Five Mountains of the West, Mountain Press, 88, The New Testament: A Students Introduction, Mayfield Publ, 98; Classical mythology: Images and Insights, Mayfield Publ, (3rd ed, 00); Touchstones: Classic Readings in the Humanities, Holt Reinhart Winston, 90; Agents if Chaos, Mountain Press, 90; Restless Earth, National Geographic Books, 97; Wonders of the World, contrib, National Geographics Books, 98. **CONTACT ADDRESS** Dept of Hum and Relig Study, California State Univ, Sacramento, 6000 J St, Sacramento, CA 95819-6083. **EMAIL** sharris2@ix.netcom.com

HARRIS, XAVIER
PERSONAL Born 06/30/1922, Wahoo, NB **DISCIPLINE** RELIGION **EDUCATION** San Luis Rey Col, BA, 45; Franciscan School Theol, STB, 49; Univ San Francisco, MA, 54; Univ Notre Dame, PhD, 62; Univ Ga, Postgrad, 70-72. **CAREER** Principal, St Mary's High School, Phoenix, 49-56; Principal, St Mary's High School, Stockton, 56-60; Prof, San Luis Rey Col, 63-64; Rector, St Anthony's Seminary, 64-74; Instr, Univ San Francisco, 74-75; Prof, Col of Notre Dame, 74-. **HONORS AND AWARDS** Ten Year Awd, Western Asn of Schools and Col; Excellence in Teaching Awd, Col of Notre Dame; Carnegie Fel, Univ of Notre Dame; Who's Who in Religion 2nd ed; Who's Who in California, 7th ed; Who's Who in the West 22nd ed; Who's Who in am Educ, 90-91; 5000 Personalities of the World 3rd ed. **MEMBERSHIPS** Nat Catholic Educ Asn, Western Asn of Schools and Col, Western Catholic Educ Asn. **RESEARCH** Virtues and character, Fourth Gospel as Instant Theater, Sacramental Theology. **SELECTED PUBLICATIONS** Auth, Catholic Schools in Action; auth, Survey of Religious of Outcomes; auth, New Testament Surprises. **CONTACT ADDRESS** Dept Relig Studies, Col of Notre Dame, 1500 Ralston Ave, Belmont, CA 94002-1908. **EMAIL** xharris@cnd.edu

HARRISON, FRANK RUSSELL
PERSONAL Born 11/13/1935, Jacksonville, FL, d, 1 child **DISCIPLINE** PHILOSOPHY **EDUCATION** Undergraduate, Duke Univ, 54; Loyola Univ of the S, 55; Univ of the S. Sewanee, BA, Philos, 57; Graduate, MA, Philos, 59; PhD, Philos, 61, Univ of VA. **CAREER** Graduate Asst, Univ of VA, Charlottesville, 58-61; Inst Philos, Roanoke Coll, 61-62; Asst Prof Philos, 62-66; Assoc Prof Philos, 66-72; Prof of Philos 72-; Graduate Faculty, 66-79, 92-; Vis Prof, Univ NC, Chapel Hill, 63; Vis Prof, Emory Univ, Atlanta GA, 65; GA Inst Tech School of Info and Cmpt Sci, Atlanta GA 65-66. **HONORS AND AWARDS** Hon Program Faculty, 68; Vis Prof, Keele Univ England, 84; Phi Kappa Phi; Phi Beta Delta; Phi Sigma Tau; Outstanding Educ of Amer; Gridiron Secret Soc; The Panhellenic Council Oustanding Faculty Member of the year, 91; Tchg Improvement Program Mentor, 88-90. **MEMBERSHIPS** Phi Kappa Lit Soc; Faculty advisor 90-; Athens Torch Club; Intl Assoc of Torch Clubs, 82-; Rotary Intl 81-; Intercollegiate Studies Inst Faculty Assoc 78-; Exec Comm United Way Campaign. **SELECTED PUBLICATIONS** Truth Trees and Natural Deductions-Tools of the Trade, Intl Government Mgt Info Sci, Ashville NC, 94; Perfect Decisions in an Imperfect World, Allegany Health Group, Tampa FL, 95; Patients Rights and Bottom Line Costs, Allegany Health Group, Tampa FL, 95; Virtue and Vice, Hoffberger Center for Business Ethics, Univ Baltimore MD, 96; Deductive Well, West Publ 94. **CONTACT ADDRESS** Dept Philos, Univ of Georgia, Athens, GA 30602. **EMAIL** harrison@uga.edu

HARRISON, JEFFREY L.
DISCIPLINE LAW **EDUCATION** Univ Fla, BS, MBA, PhD; Univ NC, JD. **CAREER** Stephen C. O'Connell Chair, Univ Florida, 83-; ch, Asn Amer Law Schools Sect Socioeconomics; prof, Univ Houston 78-84; Univ NC Greensboro 70-78; vis prof, Leiden Univ, Neth; Univ NC, Univ Texas, Tufts Univ; staff; Univ NC Law Rev. **HONORS AND AWARDS** Fellow, National Endowment for the Humanities, Tufts University; univ tex; fel, neh. **MEMBERSHIPS** Texas Bar; Order of the Coif; Phi Kappa Phi; Omicron Delta Epsilon. **RESEARCH** Antitrust, contracts. **SELECTED PUBLICATIONS** Auth, Understanding Antitrust and Its Economic Implications and Monopoly: Economic Theory and Antitrust Policy; auth, Law and Economics in a Nutshell. **CONTACT ADDRESS** School of Law, Univ of Florida, PO Box 117625, Gainesville, FL 32611-7625. **EMAIL** harrison.j@law.ufl.edu

HARRISVILLE, ROY A., III
PERSONAL Born 11/26/1954, Mason City, IA, m, 1978, 2 children **DISCIPLINE** BIBLICAL STUDIES **EDUCATION** Concordia Col, BA, 77; Luther Northwestern Sem, MDiv, 81; Union Theol Sem in Va, PhD, 90. **CAREER** Prof to Acadmeic Dean, Trinity Lutheran Col, 94-. **HONORS AND AWARDS** James A. Jones Graduate Fel; Herbert W. Jackson Jr. Fel; Adele Mellen Award for publication; Who's Who Among America's Teachers. **MEMBERSHIPS** Soc of Biblical Lit. **RESEARCH** Hermeneutics, New Testament studies. **SELECTED PUBLICATIONS** Auth, The Figure of Abraham in the Epistles of Saint Paul, Mellen Res Univ Press (San Fransico, CA), 92; auth, Pistis Christou: Witness of the Fathers, Novum Testamentum 36 (94). **CONTACT ADDRESS** Academic Dean, Trinity Lutheran Col, 4221 228th Ave SE, Issaquah, WA 98029-9299. **EMAIL** royh@tlc.com

HARROD, HOWARD L.
PERSONAL Born 06/09/1932, Holdenville, OK, m, 1971, 2 children **DISCIPLINE** SOCIOLOGY OF RELIGION **EDUCATION** Oklahoma Univ, BA, 60; Duke Univ, BD, 60; Yale Univ, STM, 61, MA, 63, PhD, 65. **CAREER** Asst prof, Howard Univ, 64-66; assoc prof, Drake Univ, 66-68; prof, social ethics and sociol, relig, Vanderbilt Univ, 68- . **HONORS AND AWARDS** Rockefeller Doctoral Fel, 62-63; NEH, 67; Am Coun Learned Soc Fel, 81-82; Vanderbilt Univ Fel, 87-88; Rockefeller Fel, 88. **MEMBERSHIPS** Soc for the Sci Study of Relig; Soc for Values in Higher Ed; Am Acad of Relig; Soc for the Sci Study of Relig; Soc of Christian Ethics; Plains Anthrop Soc. **RESEARCH** Religion and culture; Northern Plains religions. **SELECTED PUBLICATIONS** Auth, Mission among the Blackfeet, Univ Okl, 71; auth, The Human Center: Moral Agony in the Social World, Fortress, 81; auth, Renewing the World: Plains Indians Religion and Morality, Univ Ariz Pr, 92; auth, Becoming and Remaining a People: Native American Religions on the North Plains, Univ Ariz Pr, 95; auth, numerous articles and book ch. **CONTACT ADDRESS** Divinity School, Vanderbilt Univ, Nashville, TN 37240. **EMAIL** howard.harrod@vanderbilt.edu

HARROLD, JEFFERY DELAND
PERSONAL Born 10/16/1956, Detroit, MI, m **DISCIPLINE** THEOLOGY **EDUCATION** University of MI, BA Economics 1978; Trinity Evangelical Divinity School, MDiv. **CAREER** ADP Network Services Inc, tech analyst, 83-84; Bethel Ame Church, Asst Pastor, 84-; Trinity Ame Church, Assoc Pastor, 84-; Trinity Coll, Dir of Minority Student Develop, 85-. **HONORS AND AWARDS** Kearney Black Achievement Awd Trinity Evangelical Divinity School 1985. **MEMBERSHIPS** Mem Assoc of Christians in Student Develop 1986-87; student council pres Trinity Evangelical Div Sch 1986-87; mem Omega Psi Phi Frat. **CONTACT ADDRESS** Minority Student Dev, Trinity Christian Col, 2077 Half Day Rd, Deerfield, IL 60015.

HARROP, CLAYTON KEITH
PERSONAL Born 02/18/1924, Berryton, KS, m, 1944, 3 children **DISCIPLINE** RELIGION **EDUCATION** William Jewell Col, AB, 49; Southern Baptist Theol Sem, BD, 52, PhD, 56. **CAREER** From instr to assoc prof to prof New Testament, 55-92; VP Acad Aff, 92-94, Sr prof New Testament, 94-, Golden Gate Baptist Theol Sem, 55-. **MEMBERSHIPS** Soc Bibl Lit; Asn Baptist Professors of Relig. **RESEARCH** Background of New Testament times; development of early Christianity; Greek. **SELECTED PUBLICATIONS** Auth, The Letter of James, Convention Press, 69; History of the New Testament in Plain Language, Word, 84. **CONTACT ADDRESS** Golden Gate Baptist Theol Sem, 201 Seminary Dr, Mill Valley, CA 94941-3197. **EMAIL** ckharrop@aol.com

HART, BILL
DISCIPLINE PHILOSOPHY **EDUCATION** Harvard Univ, PhD, 69. **CAREER** Prof, Univ IL at Chicago . **RESEARCH** Logic; philos of mathematics; metaphysics; epistemology. **SELECTED PUBLICATIONS** Auth, The Engines of the Soul, Cambridge, 88; On Non-Well-Founded Sets, Critica, 92; Motions of the Mind, Blackwell, 92; Hat-tricks and Heaps, Philos Studies, 92. **CONTACT ADDRESS** Philos Dept, Univ of Illinois, Chicago, S Halsted St, PO Box 705, Chicago, IL 60607.

HART, CHRISTOPHER ALVIN
PERSONAL Born 06/18/1947, Denver, CO, d **DISCIPLINE** LAW **EDUCATION** Princeton University, BSE, 1969, MSE 1971; Harvard Law School, JD, 1973. **CAREER** Peabody Riv-

lin & Lambert, assoc 1973-76; Air Transport Assoc, Attorney 1976-77; US Dept of Transportation, deputy asst genl counsel 1977-79; Hart & Chavers, managing partner 1979-90; National Transportation Safety Board, member, 90-93; Natl Hwy Traffic Safety Admin, deputy admin, 93-95; Federal Aviation Administration, asst admin for system safety, 95-. **MEMBERSHIPS** Natl, Amer, Federal, Washington Bar Assns, 1973-; Princeton Engineering Adv & Resource Council, 1975-; dir/pres, Beckman Place Condo Assn, 1979-83; Federal Communications Bar Assn, 1981-; dir, WPFW-FM, 1983-; Lawyer Pilots Bar Assn, 1975-; Aircraft Owners & Pilots Assn, 1973-. **SELECTED PUBLICATIONS** "Antitrust Aspects of Deepwater Ports," Transportation Law Journal 1979; "State Action Antitrust Immunity for Airport Operators," Transportation Law Journal 1981. **CONTACT ADDRESS** Federal Aviation Administration, 800 Independence Ave SW, Rm 1016D, Washington, DC 20591.

HART, DARRYL GLENN
DISCIPLINE CHURCH HISTORY, THEOLOGICAL BIBLIOGRAPHY **EDUCATION** Temple Univ, BA, 79; Westminster Theol Sem, MAR, 81; Harvard Univ, MTS, 83; Johns Hopkins Univ, MA, 85, PhD, 88. **CAREER** Tchg asst, Johns Hopkins Univ, 85-88; post-dr fel, lectr, Divinity Sch, Duke Univ, 88-89; dir, Inst Stud of Amer Evangelicals, Wheaton Cole, 89-93; assoc prof, Westminster Theol Sem, 93-. **HONORS AND AWARDS** Co-ed, Dictionary of the Presbyterian and Reformed Tradition in America, 91-; bk rev ed, Fides et Historia 92-96; ed, Westminster Theol Jour, 96-; **MEMBERSHIPS** Historical Society; Amer Historical Assoc; Organization of Amer Historians; Amer Society of Church History. **RESEARCH** American Presbyterianism; Religion and Higher Education; Secularism. **SELECTED PUBLICATIONS** Auth, J. Gresham Machen and the Crisis of Conservative Protestantism in Modern America; The Troubled Soul of the Academy: American Learning and the Problem of Religious Studies, Rel and Amer Cult, 92; The Legacy of J. Gresham Machen and the Identity of the Orthodox Presbyterian Church, Westminster Theol Jour 53, 92; auth, The University Gets Religion: Religious Studies and American Higher Education, 99. **CONTACT ADDRESS** Westminster Theol Sem, Pennsylvania, PO Box 27009, Philadelphia, PA 19118. **EMAIL** dhart@wts.edu

HART, JAMES G.
DISCIPLINE RELIGIOUS STUDIES **EDUCATION** Univ Chicago, PhD, 72. **CAREER** Prof, Ind Univ, Bloomington. **RESEARCH** Philosophy of religion; philosophical theology; peace and conflict studies. **SELECTED PUBLICATIONS** Auth, A Precise of an Husserlian Philosophical Theology, SUNY, 86; The Person and the Common Life: Studies in a Husserlian Social Ethics, Kluwer, 92; auth, Michel Henry's Phenomenological Theology of Life: A Husserlian Reading of 'C'est Moi, La Verite,' Husserl Studies, 99. **CONTACT ADDRESS** Dept of Religious Studies, Indiana Univ, Bloomington, Sycamore Hall 230, Bloomington, IN 47405. **EMAIL** hart@indiana.edu

HART, JEFFREY ALLEN
PERSONAL Born 12/29/1947, New Kensington, PA, m, 1968, 1 child **DISCIPLINE** POLITICAL SCIENCE **EDUCATION** Swarthmore Col, BA, 69; Univ CA, Berkeley, PhD, 75. **CAREER** Asst prof, 73-80, Princeton Univ; assoc prof, 81-87, prof,87-, Ind Univ. **HONORS AND AWARDS** NDEA Title IV Fel, 69-72; Interuniversity Consortium for World Order Studies, 73l; Paul Henri Spaak Fel in US-European Relations, 82-83; John D. and Catherine T. MacArthur Found, Postdoctoral Fel, Univ CA, Berkeley, 89; Alfred P. Sloan Found, 96-98. **MEMBERSHIPS** Am Polit Sci Asn; Int Stud Asn. **RESEARCH** Int political economy; int competitiveness; high technology industries. **SELECTED PUBLICATIONS** Auth, Rival Capitalists: International Competitiveness in the United States, Japan, and Europe, Cornell Univ Press, 93; co-auth, The Politics of International Economic Relations, 5th ed, St. Martin's Press, 97; co-ed, Globalization and Governance; co-ed, Coping With Globalization, 00; co-ed, Responding to Globalization, 00; auth, Digital Divergence: The Politics of High Definition Television. **CONTACT ADDRESS** Dept of Political Science, Indiana Univ, Bloomington, Bloomington, IN 47405. **EMAIL** hartj@indiana.edu

HART, JOHN
PERSONAL Born 10/05/1943, New York, NY, m, 1975, 2 children **DISCIPLINE** THEOLOGY, ENVIRONMENTAL ETHICS **EDUCATION** Marist Col, BA, 66; Union Theol Sem, STM, 72, MPhil, 76, PhD, 78. **CAREER** Vis asst prof, Howard Univ Sch of Relig, Washington, DC, 78-79; adjunct instr, St Edward's Univ, Austin, Tex, 82-83; assoc prof, Col of Great Falls, Montana, 83-85; vis prof, Northland Col, Ashland, Wisc, fall 92; prof, Carroll Col, Helena, Montana, 85-, Theol Dept Chair, 93-, Founder & Dir of Environmental Studies, 97-; mem of Steering Comt, Columbia River Pastoral Letter Proj of the NW Cath Bishops, 97-. **HONORS AND AWARDS** NEH Summer Grants, 85, 86; Delegate to the United Nations Int Human Rights Comn, Geneva, Switzerland, on behalf of the Int Indian Treaty Coun, 87, 90; Certificate of Appreciation, Montana Comt for the Humanities, 92; John M. Templeton Found Awd, 95, 99-2001; Outstanding Teacher Awd, Carroll Col Fac, 95; Lilly Teaching Scholar, 97-98; 1999 Develop Grant, Center for Theol and the Natural Scis, Berkeley, Ca. **MEMBERSHIPS** Am Acad of relig, Soc of Christian Ethics. **RESEARCH** Christian social ethics, theology and ecology, Native American spirituality. **SELECTED PUBLICATIONS** Auth, The Spirit of the Earth--A Theology of the Land, Ramsey, NJ: Paulist Press (84); auth, "Jubilee and New jubilee: Values and Visions for the Land," in Charles Blatz, ed, Ethics and Agriculture, Moscow, ID: Univ Idaho Press (91); auth, "Para um Jubileu Novo," in Alfredo Ferro Medina, ed, A Teologia se Fez Terra, Sao Leopoldo, Brazil: Editora Sinodal (91); auth, "Caring for Creation: Church Teachings on Environmental Responsibility," The Critic--A J of Am Cath Culture, Vol 50, No 1 (fall 95); auth, Ethics and Technology: Innovation and Transformation in Community Contexts, Cleveland, OH: Pilgrim Press (97); auth, "Native American Religions," and "Black Elk" in the Encyclopedia of Contemporary American Religion, New York: Macmillan Reference (2000). **CONTACT ADDRESS** Dept Theol, Carroll Col, Montana, 1601 N Benton Ave, Helena, MT 59625-0001. **EMAIL** jhart@carroll.edu

HART, RICHARD E.
PERSONAL Born 07/12/1949, Columbus, OH, m, 1972, 2 children **DISCIPLINE** PHILOSOPHY **EDUCATION** Ohio Univ, BGS, 71; SUNY Stony Brook, PhD, 84. **CAREER** Dir cont Ed, Long Island Univ, CW Post campus, 80-86; prof philos, Bloomfield Col, 86- . **HONORS AND AWARDS** Phi Kappa Phi; Alpha Sigma Lamda, hon memb. **MEMBERSHIPS** APA; Soc for Advan of Am Philos; Am Assoc of Philos. **RESEARCH** Philosophy and literature; American philosophy. **SELECTED PUBLICATIONS** Ed, Ethics and the Environment, Univ Press of Am, 92; co-ed Philosophy in Experience: American Philosophy in Transition, Fordham, 97; co-ed, Plato's Dialogues: The Dialogical Approach, Edwin Mellen, 97. **CONTACT ADDRESS** Philosophy/Humanities Dept, Bloomfield Col, Bloomfield, NJ 01003.

HART, W. D.
PERSONAL Born 02/18/1943, Ithaca, NY, m, 1974, 1 child **DISCIPLINE** PHILOSOPHY **EDUCATION** Harvard Col, BA summa cum laude, 64; Harvard Univ, PhD 68. **CAREER** Univ of Michigan, asst prof, 69-74; Univ Col London, lectr, sr lectr, reader, 74-91; Univ New Mexico, assoc prof, prof, 92-93; Univ IL, prof, ch, 93 to 94-. **HONORS AND AWARDS** Detur Awd; John Harvard Scholar; Harvard Col Scholar; Phi Beta Kappa; Woodrow Wilson Fel; Harvard Grad Ntl Fel; Arthur Lehman Scholar. **MEMBERSHIPS** ASL, APA. **RESEARCH** Philos of mathematics, logic, metaphysics. **SELECTED PUBLICATIONS** Auth, Philosophy of Mathematics, ed, intro, Oxford Univ Press, 96; The Engines of the Soul, Cambridge Univ Press, 88; The Syntax of the World, Critica, 96; Meaning and Verification, Routledge Encycl of Philos, ed, E Craig, Graham Forbes, forthcoming; auth, Lowenheim-Skolem Theorems and Non-Standard Models, Routledge Encycl of Philos, ed, E. Craig, M Detlefsen, forthcoming; Dualism Companion to Philo of Mind, ed, S. Guttenplan, Blackwell, forthcoming; Godel and the Soul, Companion to Metaphysics, ed J. Kim, E. Sosa, Blackwell, 94; rev, George Boolos, ed, Meaning and Method, Philos Quart, forthcoming; DH Mellor, Matters of Metaphysics, Philos Books, 93; Long Decimals, forthcoming, in a Festschrift for Burton S. Dreben. **CONTACT ADDRESS** Dept of Philosophy, Univ of Illinois, Chicago, M/C 267, Chicago, IL 60607-7114. **EMAIL** hart@uic.edu

HARTIN, PATRICK
PERSONAL Born 12/07/1944, Johannesburg, S Africa, s **DISCIPLINE** RELIGION **EDUCATION** Univ S Africa, BA, 66; Dth, 81; Dth, 88. **CAREER** Sen Lectr, Univ Witwatersrand, 88-89; Assoc Prof, Univ S Africa, 90-95; From Assoc Prof to Prof, Gonzaga Univ, 95-. **MEMBERSHIPS** Cath Bibl Asn of Am, Cath Theol Soc of Southern Africa, New Testament Soc of Southern Africa, Soc of Bibl Lit, Studiorum Novi Testamenti Societas. **RESEARCH** The Letter of James, the Sayings Source, Thomasine literature. **SELECTED PUBLICATIONS** Auth, "'Call to be Perfect through Suffering' (James 1,2-4): The Concept of Perfection in the Epistle of James and the Sermon on the Mount," Biblica, 77 4 (96): 477-492; auth, "Christian Ethics in a Pluralistic Society: Towards a Theology of Compromise," Relig & Theol, 4 1 (97): 21-34; auth, "The Poor in the Epistle of James and the Gospel of Thomas," Hervormde Teologiese Studies, 53 1&2 (97): 146-162; auth, "'Who is Wise and Understanding Among You' (James 3:13)? An Analysis of Wisdom, Eschatology and Apocalypticism in the Epistle of James," Hervomde Teologiese Studies, 53 4 (97): 969-999; auth, "Disciples as Authorities Within Matthew's Christian-Jewish Community," in The Church, One yet Multifarious -- A Study from Many Perspectives: Essays in Honour of John H. Roberts," Neotestamentica, 32 1 (98): 389-404; auth, "The Search for the True self in the Gospel of Thomas, the Book of Thomas and the Hymn of the Pearl," Hervomde Teologiese Studies (99); auth, A Spirituality of Perfection: Faith in Action in the Letter of James, The Liturgical Pr (Collegeville, MN), 99. **CONTACT ADDRESS** Dept Relig, Gonzaga Univ, 502 E Boone Ave, Spokane, WA 99258-1774. **EMAIL** hartin@gonzaga.edu

HARTLE, ANN
DISCIPLINE THE NATURE OF PHILOSOPHY **EDUCATION** CUNY, PhD, 76. **CAREER** Prof, Philos, Emory Univ. **HONORS AND AWARDS** Nat Endowment Hum fel, 82-83. **RESEARCH** The nature of philosophy, philosophical anthropology **SELECTED PUBLICATIONS** Auth, The Modern Self in Rousseau's Confessions: A Reply to St. Augustine, Death and the Disinterested Spectator: An Inquiry into the Nature of Philosophy, auth, Self Knowledge in the Age of Theory. **CONTACT ADDRESS** Emory Univ, Atlanta, GA 30322-1950. **EMAIL** ahartle@emory.edu

HARTLE, ANTHONY E.
PERSONAL Born 12/28/1942, Wichita, KS, m, 1964, 3 children **DISCIPLINE** PHILOSOPHY, LITERATURE **EDUCATION** US Mil Acad, BS, 64; Duke Univ, MA, 71; Univ of Texas, PhD, 82. **CAREER** Prof, Dep Head, English, USMA. **MEMBERSHIPS** Am Philos Asn, Joint Serv Conf on Prof Ethics. **RESEARCH** Moral philosophy; applied ethics **SELECTED PUBLICATIONS** Auth, Moral Issues in Military Decision Making; Dimensions of Ethical Thought. **CONTACT ADDRESS** Dept of English, United States Military Acad, West Point, NY 10996-1791. **EMAIL** ca5868@usma.edu

HARTLEY, LOYDE HOBART
PERSONAL Born 07/21/1940, Parkersburg, WV, m, 1962, 3 children **DISCIPLINE** SOCIOLOGY OF RELIGION **EDUCATION** Otterbein Col, AB, 62; United Theol Sem, BD, 65; Emory Univ, PhD, 68. **CAREER** Lectr, Emory Univ, 67-68; Assoc Prof and Society, Union College, 68- 71; Prof of Religion and Society, Lancaster Theo Sem, 71-; Dir of Doctoral Studies, 71-74; dir, doctoral studies, 73-75, Dean of the Seminary, 75-82, Lancaster Theol Sem; Dean of the Seminary, LTS, 75-82. **MEMBERSHIPS** Am Sociol Assn; Soc Sci Studies Relig; Relig Res Assn. **RESEARCH** Religious beliefs and attitudes; organization of religious groups; professional characteristics of clergy. **SELECTED PUBLICATIONS** Auth, The Placement And Deployment Of Ministers in the United Church of Christ, Res Ctr Relig & Soc, Pa, 73; auth, Understanding Church Finances, Pilgrim Press, 84; auth, Cities and Churches, Scarecrow Press; 92. **CONTACT ADDRESS** Lancaster Theol Sem, 555 W James St, Lancaster, PA 17603-2830. **EMAIL** lhartley@lts.org

HARTLEY, ROGER
PERSONAL Born 04/26/1969, Charleston, WV, m, 1997 **DISCIPLINE** PUBLIC AFFAIRS **EDUCATION** Ind Univ, BSPA, 91; Univ Ga, MA, 93; PhD, 99. **CAREER** Instr, CUNY, 97-98, asst prof, Roanoke Col, 98-. **HONORS AND AWARDS** Pi Alpha Alpha, Pub Affairs Honorary **MEMBERSHIPS** Am Polit Sci Assoc; S Polit Sci Assoc; Law and Soc Assoc, Am Judicature Soc. **RESEARCH** Trial courts, courts as institutions, institutional change related to courts (ADR). **SELECTED PUBLICATIONS** Coauth, "A Profile of State Appellate Court Decision Making: Rape Shields and Conviction Appeals, State Constitutional Commentaries and Notes (Summer 93) 4:1-15; coauth, "The Increasing Scrutiny of Lower Federal Court Nominees in Senate Confirmations", 80 Judicature (June/July 97); coauth, "Attorney Expertise, Litigant Success, and Judicial Decision Making in the United States Courts of Appeals", Law and Soc Rev (forthcoming). **CONTACT ADDRESS** Dept Pub Affairs, Roanoke Col, 221 College Lane, Salem, VA 24153. **EMAIL** hartley@roanoke.edu

HARTMAN, LAURA PINCUS
PERSONAL Born 10/06/1963, Chicago, IL, m, 1997, 2 children **DISCIPLINE** LAW **EDUCATION** Tufts Univ, BS, 85; Univ Chicago, Doctor of Law, 88. **CAREER** Assoc prof, chmn in Professional Ethics, Dir, assoc prof, DePaul Univ, 90-; visiting prof of Bus Law, Northwestern Univ, 92. **HONORS AND AWARDS** DePaul Univ Excellence in Teaching Awd, 91; Kellogg Grad Sch of Mgt Fac Honor Roll for Excellence in Teaching, 92; Who's Who in Am Law, 92; Best Teaching Awd, 92, 93; Best Paper, Prof Dev, by the UNESCO Dev Inst, 91; Outstanding Presentation, by the UNESCO Dev Inst, 92; Best Res Awd, 92, 93; DePaul Col of Commerce Outstanding Serv Awd, 93; Phi Kappa Honor Soc; Beta Gamma Sigma Honor Soc; Who's Who in Am, 94; Notable am Women, 94; Int Who's Who, 95; **MEMBERSHIPS** Am Bar Asn, Chicago Bar Asn, 88-; Comt on Employee Rights and Responsibilities, Am Bar Asn, 91-; Midwest Acad of Legal Stud in Bus; Soc for Bus Ethics; Soc for Bus Ethnics; memr, Bd of Dir, Eclipse Theatre Co, Chicago, IL, 94-95; mem, Advisory Bd of Dir, I Have A Dream Found, Chicago, 98; . **RESEARCH** Business ethics. **SELECTED PUBLICATIONS** Co-auth, Instructor's Manual for Irwin's Business Law, Irwin, 94; co-auth, Law, Business and Society, 4th, 5th ed, Irwin, 95; auth, legal and ethical briefs for Hornsby, Human Resource Management: A Practical Approach, West, 95; co-auth, Employment Law for Business, Irwin, 97; auth, Property Law, draft, in Taylor, et al, Contemporary Legal Studies in Business, Irwin, 97; co-auth, Legal Environment of Business: Ethical and Public Policy Concerns, Irwin, 97; auth, Perspectives in Business Ethics, Irwin, 98; auth, Ethics and Economics of Workplace Privacy, in 1999 Handbook of Business Strategy, J of Bus Strategy, 99; auth of numerous articles. **CONTACT ADDRESS** Dept of Law, DePaul Univ, One E Jackson, Chicago, IL 60604. **EMAIL** lpincus@wppost.depaul.edu

HARTT, JULIAN NORRIS
PERSONAL Born 06/13/1911, Selby, SD **DISCIPLINE** RELIGION **EDUCATION** Dakota Wesleyan Univ, AB, 32, DLitt, 61; Garrett Bibl Inst, BD, 37; Northwestern Univ, AM, 38; Yale Univ, PhD, 40; Bucknell Univ, DD, 73. **CAREER** Instr philos & relig, Berea Col, 40-43; assoc prof theol, Divinity Sch, Yale Univ, 43-53, Porter prof philos theol, 53-72, chmn dept relig studies, 67-72; William Kenan prof, 72-81, Emer Prof Relig Studies, Univ Va, 81-, Fulbright fel, Italy & Guggenheim fel, 63-64. **MEMBERSHIPS** Am Philos Asn; Am Asn for Advan Sci; Am Polit Sci Asn. **RESEARCH** Philosophical theology; the ontological argument for the existence of God. **SELECTED PUBLICATIONS** Auth, Toward a Theology of Evangelism, Abingdon, 55; The Lost Image of Man, La State Univ, 63; coauth, Humanism vs Theism; auth, Christian Critique of American Culture, The Restless Human Quest, Westminster, 75; Theological Method and Imagination, Seabury, 77. **CONTACT ADDRESS** Dept of Relig Studies, Univ of Virginia, Charlottesville, VA 22903.

HARVEY, CAMERON
PERSONAL Born 07/25/1939, Kitchener, ON **DISCIPLINE** LAW **EDUCATION** Univ Toronto, BA, 61; Osgoode Univ, LLB, 64, LLM, 66. **CAREER** Asst prof, 66-70, assoc prof, 70-74, prof, 74-, assoc dean, 89-, Univ of Manitoba. **RESEARCH** Agency; conflict of laws; wills; property. **SELECTED PUBLICATIONS** Auth, The Law of Habeas Corpus in Canada, 74; Chief Justice Samuel Freedman: A Great Canadian Judge, 83; Legal Wit and Whimsy, 1988, Agency Law Primer, 93; The Law of Dependants Relief in Canada, 99. **CONTACT ADDRESS** Fac of Law, Univ of Manitoba, Robson Hall, Winnipeg, MB, Canada R3T 2N2. **EMAIL** cam_harvey@umanitoba.ca

HARVEY, CHARLES W.
PERSONAL Born 12/21/1954, Springfield, MA, m, 2 children **DISCIPLINE** PHILOSOPHY **EDUCATION** Fla State Univ, BA, 78, PhD, 83. **CAREER** Lectr, Fla State Univ, 84-85; Asst prof to prof, Central Ark Univ, 83-. **HONORS AND AWARDS** Deutscher Akademischer Austausch Dienst grant; NEH grant; UCA grants. **MEMBERSHIPS** Am Philosophical Assoc; Soc for Phemenology and Existential Philos; Soc for Philos in the Contemporary World. **SELECTED PUBLICATIONS** Auth, Husserl's Phenomenology and The Foundations of Natural Science, Ohio Univ Press, 89; auth, Conundrums: A Book of Philosophical Questions, Univ Press Am, 95. **CONTACT ADDRESS** Univ of Central Arkansas, 201 S. Donaghey Ave, Conway, AR 72035-0001. **EMAIL** charlesh@mail.uca.edu

HARVEY, JAMES CARDWELL
PERSONAL Born 07/15/1925, Italy, TX, m, 1974, 2 children **DISCIPLINE** PUBLIC POLICY AND ADMINISTRATION; HUMAN RESOURCES **EDUCATION** SMU, BA, 49; Univ Texas at Austin, MA, 52, PhD, 55; Univ Ariz, MA, 69. **CAREER** Asst prof, Pan Am Col, 54-57; asst prof, Univ Texas El Paso, 57-64; assoc prof Ft Lewis Col, 64-65; assoc prof & chr Social Sciences, W New Mex Univ, 65-68; prof, 70-92, Ret & Adj Prof, Jackson State Univ, 70-; Fulbright schol, 52-53; NASVAA PA fel, 74-75; Pi Alpha Alpha; Phi Alpha Theta, Pi Sigma Alpha, Pi Gamma Mu, Pi Delta Phi. **MEMBERSHIPS** ASPA **RESEARCH** Human Resources **CONTACT ADDRESS** Jackson State Univ, 3825 Ridgewood Rd, Box 18, Jackson, MS 39211.

HARVEY, JOHN D.
PERSONAL Born 03/11/1951, Johnstown, PA, m, 1974, 0 child **DISCIPLINE** NEW TESTAMENT **EDUCATION** Wycliffe Col, Univ Toronto, ThD, 97. **CAREER** Assoc prof, New Testament & Greek, Columbia Bibl Sem, 91- . **MEMBERSHIPS** ETS; IBR; SBL; So Carolina Acad of Relig. **RESEARCH** Paul; Gospels; New Testament theology; New Testament Greek. **SELECTED PUBLICATIONS** Auth, Toward a Degree of Order in Ben Sira's Book, ZAW, 93; auth, Citizenship, & Nature, Natural, in Elwell, ed, Evangelical Dictionary of Biblical Theology, Baker, 96; auth, Mission in Jesus' Teaching, & Mission in Matthew, in Larkin, ed, Mission in the New Testament: An Evangelical Approach, Orbis, 98; auth, Listening to the Text: Oral Patterning in Paul's Letters, Baker, 98; auth, Biblical Criticism and Mission, in Moreau, ed, Evangelical Dictionary of World Missions, Baker, forthcoming; auth, Redemption, in Freedman, ed, Eerdmans Dictionary of the Bible, Eerdmans, forthcoming. **CONTACT ADDRESS** Columbia Intl Univ, PO Box 3122, Columbia, SC 29230-3122. **EMAIL** jharvey@ciu.edu

HARVEY, LOUIS-CHARLES
PERSONAL Born 05/05/1945, Memphis, TN, s, 2 children **DISCIPLINE** THEOLOGY **EDUCATION** LeMoyne-Owen Coll, BS 1967; Colgate Rochester Divinity School, MDiv 1971; Union Theological Seminary, MPhil 1977, PhD 1978. **CAREER** Colgate Rochester-Divinity School, prof, 74-78; Payne Theological Seminary, dean, 78-79, pres, 89-; United Theological Seminary, prof 1979-; Metropolitan AME Church, senior minister, 96-. **HONORS AND AWARDS** Rsch grant Assn of Theological Schools 1984-85; pioneered study of Black Religion in Great Britain, 1985-86. **MEMBERSHIPS** Speaker, preacher, writer, workshop leader African Methodist Episcopal Church 1979-. **SELECTED PUBLICATIONS** Articles published Journal of Religious Thought 1983, 1987; biographer of William Crogman in Something More Than Human Cole, 1987. **CONTACT ADDRESS** Senior Minister, Metropolitan AME Church, 1518 M St NW, Washington, VT 20005.

HARVEY, MARK S.
PERSONAL Born 07/04/1946, Binghamton, NY, m, 1983 **DISCIPLINE** RELIGIOUS STUDIES **EDUCATION** Syracuse Univ, BA, 68; Boston Univ, ThM, 71; PhD, 83. **CAREER** Lectr, 17 yrs, MIT. **HONORS AND AWARDS** NEH Fel; Readers Digest comm Awd; Whiting Foun Fel. **MEMBERSHIPS** AAR; SSAM; ASA; DES; SARCC; ASCAP. **RESEARCH** Music Religion Culture, American Music, Jazz. **SELECTED PUBLICATIONS** Auth, Jazz Time and Our Time, in: This is How We Flow: Rhythm in Black Cultures, ed Angela S Nelson, Columbia SC, U of SC press, 99 forthcoming; Rhythm Ritual and Religion: Postmodern Musical Agonistes, in: Theomusicology: A Special Issue of Black Sacred Music : A J of Theomusicology, 94; New World a' Comin': Religious Perspectives on the Legacy of Duke Ellington, in: Scared Music of the Secular City: From Blues to Rap, J of Theomusicology, 92. **CONTACT ADDRESS** JFK Station, Box 8721, Boston, MA 02114. **EMAIL** mharvey@mit.edu

HARWOOD, ROBIN
DISCIPLINE PHILOSOPHY OF MIND, PHILOSOPHY OF RELIGION, ANCIENT AND MEDIEVAL PHILOSOPHY **EDUCATION** Reading, Eng, PhD, 95. **CAREER** Lectr, Ga State Univ. **SELECTED PUBLICATIONS** Auth, The Survival of the Self. **CONTACT ADDRESS** Georgia State Univ, Atlanta, GA 30303. **EMAIL** phlrrh@panther.gsu.edu

HASKER, WILLIAM
PERSONAL Born 03/06/1935, Washington, DC, m, 1960, 2 children **DISCIPLINE** PHILOSOPHY **EDUCATION** Univ Edinburgh, PhD. **CAREER** Prof, emer of Philos, 01-. **HONORS AND AWARDS** Ctr for Philos Relig, Univ Notre Dame, fel; Pew Evangelical Scholars Fel, 97-98. **MEMBERSHIPS** Am Philos Asn; IN Philos Asn; Soc for Philos of Rel; Soc of Christian Philos. **RESEARCH** Philosophy of Religion, Philosophy of Mind. **SELECTED PUBLICATIONS** Auth, Reason and Religious Belief: An Introduction to the Philosophy of Religion, Oxford UP & God, Time, and Knowledge, Cornell UP; auth, Metaphysics: Constructing a Worldview, InterVarsity Pr; The Emergent Self, Cornell Univ Pr; co-auth, The Openness of God, InterVarsity Pr; ed, Journal of Faith and Philosophy, July 00. **CONTACT ADDRESS** Dept of Philosophy, Huntington Col, Huntington, IN 46750. **EMAIL** whasker@huntington.edu

HASSING, ARNE
PERSONAL Born 04/02/1943, Umtali, Rhodesia, m, 1966, 2 children **DISCIPLINE** RELIGION, HISTORY **EDUCATION** Boston Univ, BA, 64; Garrett-Evangel Theol Sem, MDiv, 68; Northwestern Univ, PhD(relig), 74. **CAREER** Asst Prof Humanities, Northern Ariz Univ, 73 **HONORS AND AWARDS** Jesse Lee Prize, Gen Comn Arch & Hist, United Methodist Church, 77. **MEMBERSHIPS** Am Soc Church Hist; Am Acad Relig; Soc Advan Scand Study; World Methodist Hist Soc. **RESEARCH** History of religion in Scandinavia; religion and modern culture; history of Christianity in the American Southwest. **SELECTED PUBLICATIONS** Auth, Norway's organized response to emigration, Norweg-Am Studies, 72; Methodism in Norway: The social and cultural relation between the Evangelical minority and the state church, Methodist Hist, 74. **CONTACT ADDRESS** Dept of Humanities, No Arizona Univ, Box 6031, Flagstaff, AZ 86011-0001.

HASSING, RICHARD F.
DISCIPLINE HISTORY AND PHILOSOPHY OF SCIENCE **EDUCATION** Cornell Univ, PhD. **CAREER** Philos, Catholic Univ Am. **RESEARCH** Atistotle; hist of physics & philos of nature. **SELECTED PUBLICATIONS** Auth, The Use and Non-Use of Physics in Spinoza's Ethics; The Southwestern Jour Philos 11, 80; Wholes, Parts, and Laws of Motion; Nature and System 6, 84; Thomas Aquinas on Physics VII;1 and the Aristotelian Science of the Physical Continuum, Catholic Univ Press, 91; Animals versus the Laws of Inertia; Rev Metaphysics 46, 92, Introduction, and Modern Natural Science and the Intelligibility of Human Experience, Catholic Univ Press, 97; The Exemplary Career of Newton's Mathematics, The St John's Rev 44, 97. **CONTACT ADDRESS** Catholic Univ of America, 620 Michigan Ave Northeast, Washington, DC 20064. **EMAIL** hassing@cua.edu

HATAB, LAWRENCE J.
PERSONAL Born 06/12/1946, Brooklyn, NY, m, 1995, 1 child **DISCIPLINE** PHILOSOPHY **EDUCATION** Villanova Univ, BA, 68; MA, 71; Fordham Univ, PhD, 76. **CAREER** Prof, Old Dominion Univ, 76-. **HONORS AND AWARDS** Phi Beta Kappa, Tau, NY; Robert L Stern Awd, Outstand Teach. **RESEARCH** Continental philosophy; ancient philosophy; ethics; political philosophy. **SELECTED PUBLICATIONS** Auth, Nietzsche and Eternal Recurrence: The Redemption of Time and Becoming, Univ Press of Am (Lanham, MD), 78; auth, Myth and Philosophy: A Contest of Truths, Open Court (Chicago), 90; auth, A Nietzschean Defense of Democracy: An Experiment in Postmodern Politics, Open Court (Chicago), 95; auth, Ethics and Finitude: Heideggerian Contributions to Moral Philosophy, Rowman Littlefield (Lanham: MD), 00. **CONTACT ADDRESS** Philosophy Dept, Old Dominion Univ, Norfolk, VA 23529. **EMAIL** lhatab@odu.edu

HATCHER, DONALD L.
PERSONAL Born 11/01/1947, Monett, MO, m, 1993, 5 children **DISCIPLINE** PHILOSOPHY **EDUCATION** Univ Kansas, PhD, 83. **CAREER** Prof, philos, Baker Univ, 78- . **HONORS AND AWARDS** Duboc Univ Prof, 92-98. **MEMBERSHIPS** APA; Asn for Informal Logic and Critical Thinking; Simon de Beauvoir Soc; Philos of Educ Soc. **RESEARCH** Critical thinking; feminism. **SELECTED PUBLICATIONS** Auth, Understanding the Second Sex, Peter Lang, 84; auth, Science, Ethics and Technological Assessment, 2d ed, American, 95; auth, Reasoning and Writing, 2d ed, Am Pr, 00. **CONTACT ADDRESS** Baker Univ, PO Box 65, Baldwin City, KS 66006. **EMAIL** dhatcher@idir.net

HATCHER, RICHARD GORDON
PERSONAL Born 07/10/1933, Michigan City, IN, m, 1973, 3 children **DISCIPLINE** LAW **EDUCATION** IN Univ, BS 1956; Valparaiso Univ, JD 1959. **CAREER** Lake Co IN, deputy prosecuting atty 61-63; City of Gary, city councilman 63-67, mayor 67-88; Hatcher and Associates, pres, 88-; Valparaiso Univ, law prof, 92-; Roosevelt University, Harold Washington Prof, political science, currently. **HONORS AND AWARDS** Outstanding Achievement Civil Rights 10 Annual Ovington Awd; life mem & Leadership Awd NAACP; Man of Yr Harlem Lawyers Assn; Disting Serv Awd Capital Press Club; Disting Serv Awd Jaycees; Employment Benefactors Awd Intl Assn Personnel Employment Security; Serv Loyalty & Dedication Awd Black Students Union Prairie State Coll; Outstanding Cit Yr Awd United Viscounts IN; Inspired Leadership IN State Black Caucus; among 100 Most Influential Black Americans Ebony Magazine 1971; among 200 most outstanding young leaders of US, Time Magazine, 1974; Urban Leadership award, IN Assn of Cities and Towns, 1986; Natl League of Cities President's Awd, 1987; Natl Black Caucus of Local Elected Officials Liberty Awd, 1987; Honorary Doctorates, Coppin St College, DuquesneU, Fisk U, Valparaiso U, Clevnd St U. **MEMBERSHIPS** Dem Conf of Mayors 1977; instr IN Univ NW; many publs; chmn Human & Resources Devel 1974; mem Natl League of Cities; past pres, US Conf of Mayors; Natl Conf of Black Mayors; Natl Black Polit Conv; former vice chair, Natl Dem Comm; Mikulski Commn report dem party policy; Natl Urban Coalition; natl chmn bd dir Operation PUSH; mem IN Exec Bd NAACP; mem Natl Dem Comm on Delegate Selection (co-author Com Report); founder Natl Black Caucus of Locally Elected Officials; Natl Black Caucus; IN State Dem Central Com; Assn Councils Arts; chair TransAfrica Inc; Jesse Jackson for Pres Campaign; pres Natl Civil Rights Museum and Hall of Fame; mem bd of dirs Marshall Univ Socof Yeager Scholars; fellow, Kennedy School of Govt, Harvard U; chair, African American Summit, 1989. **RESEARCH** Judicial Reform, Civil Rights, Local Government. **SELECTED PUBLICATIONS** Auth, Towards An Urban Common Market, DePaul Univ Business Journal. **CONTACT ADDRESS** Law Sch, Valparaiso Univ, Valparaiso, IN 46383.

HATCHETT, JOSEPH WOODROW
PERSONAL Born 09/17/1932, Clearwater, FL, s **DISCIPLINE** LAW **EDUCATION** FL A&M Univ, AB 1954; Howard Univ, JD 1959; Naval Justice Sch, Certificate 1973; NYork Univ, Appellate Judge Course 1977; Amer Acad of Jud Educ, Appellate Judge Course 1978; Harvard Law Sch, Prog Instruction for Lawyers 1980, 1990. **CAREER** Private Law Practice, Daytona Beach FL 1959-66; City of Daytona Beach, contract consul 1963-66; US Attorney, asst Jacksonville FL 1966; US Atty for the Middle Dist of FL, first asst 1967-71; Middle Dist of FL, US magistrate 1971-75; Supreme Court of FL, justice 1975-79; US Court of Appeals for the 5th Circuit, US circuit judge 1979-81; US Court of Appeals for the 11th Circuit, US Circuit Judge, 81-. **HONORS AND AWARDS** Stetson Law Sch Dr Laws 1980; FL Memorial Coll Honoris Causa Dr Laws 1976; Howard Univ Post Grad Achievement Awd 1977; High Risk Awd State Action Cncl1977; President's Citation Cook Co Bar Assn 1977; Most Outstanding Citizen Broward Co Natl Bar Assn 1976; Bicentennial Awd FL A&M Univ 1976; Comm SvcsAwd Edward Waters Coll 1976; An Accolate for Juristic Distinction Tampa Urban League 1975; Medallion for Human Relations Bethune Cookman 1975; Man of the YrAwd FL Jax Club 1974; first black person apptd to the highest court of a state since reconstruction; first black personelected to public office in a statewide election in the south; first black person to serve on a federal appellate court in the south; **MEMBERSHIPS** Mem FL Bar, Amer Bar Assn, Natl Bar Assn; bd dir Amer Judicature Soc; mem Jacksonville Bar Assn; mem DW Perkins Bar Assn; mem FL Chap of Natl Bar Assn; mem Psi Phi Delta Phi Legal Frat, Phi Alpha Delta Legal Frat, Omega Psi Phi Frat. **SELECTED PUBLICATIONS** Publs including "Criminal Law Survey-1978" Univ of Miami Law Review; "1978 Devements in FL Law" 1979; "Pre-Trial Discovery in Criminal Cases" Fedl Judicial Ctr Library 1974. **CONTACT ADDRESS** 11th Circuit Ct of Appeals, 110 E Park Ave, Tallahassee, FL 32301-7750.

HATFIELD, GARY C.
PERSONAL Born 11/25/1951, Wichita, KS **DISCIPLINE** PHILOSOPHY **EDUCATION** Wichita State Univ, BA, BFA, 74; Univ Wisc, Madison, PhD, 79. **CAREER** Asst prof, Harvard Univ, 79-81; asst prof, Johns Hopkins, 81-87; assoc prof, 87-91; prof, 91-, Univ of Penn. **HONORS AND AWARDS** Adam Segbert Professor in Moral and Intellectual Philosophy, 99-. **MEMBERSHIPS** APA; Philos of Sci Asn; Hist of Sci Soc. **RESEARCH** History of modern philosophy; philosophy of psychology. **SELECTED PUBLICATIONS** Auth, "Reason, Nature and God in Descartes," in Essays on the Philosophy and Science of Rene Descartes, Oxford, 93; "Remaking the Science of Mind," in Inventing Human Science, Univ of Calif Press, 95; "Was the Scientific Revolution Really A Revolution in Science," in Tradition, Transmission, Transformation, Brill, 96; "The Workings of the Intellect," in Logic and the Workings of the Mind, Ridgeview, 97; ed and trans, Immanuel Kant, Prolegeoma to Any Future Metaphysics, Cambridge, 97; "The Cognitive Faculties," in Cambridge History of Seventeenth Century Philosophy, Cambridge, 98; "Wundt and Psychology as Science," Perspectives on Sci, 97. **CONTACT ADDRESS** Dept of Philosophy, Univ of Pennsylvania, 433 Logan Hall, Philadelphia, PA 19104-6304. **EMAIL** hatfield@phil.upenn.edu

HATTAB, HELEN
PERSONAL Born 03/17/1969, Seoul, Korea, m, 1990 **DISCIPLINE** PHILOSOPHY **EDUCATION** Trenton State Coll, BA, 90; Univ Penn, MA, 94, PhD, 98. **CAREER** Vis Asst Prof, 98-, Virginia Poly Inst & State Univ. **MEMBERSHIPS** APA, HSS **RESEARCH** Renaissance philosophy & intellectual history, 17th century philosophy & history of science, Descartes views on causation in their historical context. **SELECTED PUBLICATIONS** Auth, One Cause or Many? Jesuit Influences on Descartes' Division of Causes, Proceedings of the Societe Intl d'Etudes Medievales, forthcoming; Laws of Nature, in: The Sci Revolution An Encyclopedia, ed, W Applebaum, NY, Garland Pub Inc, forthcoming. **CONTACT ADDRESS** Dept of Philosophy, Virginia Polytech Inst and State Univ, Major Williams Hall 229, Blacksburg, VA 24061-6367. **EMAIL** hhattab@vt.edu

HAUCK, ALLAN
PERSONAL Born 05/19/1925, Springfield, OH, m, 1942, 2 children **DISCIPLINE** PHILOSOPHY, RELIGION **EDUCATION** Kenyon Col, BA, 45; Wittenburg Univ, BD, 47; Hartford Sem Found, ThD, 50. **CAREER** Asst prof philos St Christianity, Roanoke Col, 50-51; prof, Midland Lutheran Col, 58-68; Prof, Carthage Col, 68- **MEMBERSHIPS** Am Soc Church Hist. **SELECTED PUBLICATIONS** Auth, Calendar of Christianity, Asn Press, 61; A type chart of international reply coupons, 61 & A catalogue of Arab Postal Union reply coupons, 62, Soc Reply Coupon Collectors. **CONTACT ADDRESS** Dept of Relig, Carthage Col, Kenosha, WI 53140.

HAUGELAND, JOHN CHRISTIAN
PERSONAL Born 03/13/1945, Harrisburg, IL, m, 1 child **DISCIPLINE** PHILOSOPHY **EDUCATION** Harvey Mudd Col, BS, 66; Univ Calif, Berkeley, PhD, 76. **CAREER** Asst prof 74-81, assoc prof, 81-86, prof philos, Univ Pittsburgh, 86-99; Prof philosophy, Univ of Chicago, 99. **MEMBERSHIPS** Am Philos Asn **RESEARCH** Philos of mind; metaphysics; Heidegger. **SELECTED PUBLICATIONS** Auth, Mind Design, MIT Press, 81; Artificial Intelligence: The Very Idea, MIT Press, 85; Mind Design II, MIT Press, 97; Having Thought, Harvard Univ Press, 98. **CONTACT ADDRESS** Dept of Philosophy, Univ of Chicago, Chicago, IL 60637. **EMAIL** jhaugela@midway.uchicago.edu

HAUSER, ALAN J.
PERSONAL Born 10/15/1945, Chicago, IL, m, 1989, 4 children **DISCIPLINE** BIBLICAL STUDIES **EDUCATION** Concordia Univ, BA, 67; Concordia Sem, MAR, 68; Univ Iowa, PhD, 72. **CAREER** From asst prof to assoc prof to prof, Appalachian State Univ, 72-. **MEMBERSHIPS** Soc Bibl Lit. **RESEARCH** Biblical interpretation; rhetorical criticism; the Book of Judges; early Judaism; Old Testament literature. **SELECTED PUBLICATIONS** Coauth, From Carmel to Horeb: Elijah in Crisis, 90; coauth, Rhetorical Criticism of the Bible: A Comprehensive Bibliography with Notes on History and Method, 94; auth, The Minor Judges: A Re-evaluation, Jour Bibl Lit, June, 75; auth, Israel's Conquest of Palestine: A Peasant's Rebellion?, Jour Study Old Testament, May, 78; auth, Judges 5: Parataxis in Hebrew Poetry, Jour Bibl Lit, March, 80; auth, Genesis 2-3: The Theme of Alienation, Art & Meaning: Rhetoric in Bibl Lit, 82; auth, Jonah: In Pursuit of the Dove, Jour Bibl Lit, March, 85; auth, Two Songs of Victory: A Comparison of Exodus 15 and Judges 5, Directions Bibl Hebrew Poetry, 87; ed, Currents in Research: Biblical Studies, Sheffield Academic Press. **CONTACT ADDRESS** Dept of Philosophy & Religion, Appalachian State Univ, 114 Greer Hall, Boone, NC 28608. **EMAIL** hauseraj@appstate.edu

HAUSER, RICHARD JOSEPH
PERSONAL Born 06/22/1937, Milwaukee, WI **DISCIPLINE** CHRISTIAN SPIRITUALITY **EDUCATION** St Louis Univ, BA, 61, MA & PHL, 64, STL, 69, MA, 69; Cath Univ Am, PhD(relig & relig educ), 73. **CAREER** Asst prof, Creighton Univ, 73-77; Associate prof, 77-87; prof 87-; Dept chair, 78-90 and 96-; Director MA in Theology, in Ministry, and in Chr Spirituality. **HONORS AND AWARDS** Creighton's Distinguished Faculty Administrator Awd, 91. **MEMBERSHIPS** Cath Theol Soc Am; Am Acad Relig. **RESEARCH** Role of Holy Spirit in contemporary spirituality, especially personal prayer and discernment of spirits; spirituality of Thomas Merton; history of Christian spirituality; mysticism; priestly spirituality; suffering. **SELECTED PUBLICATIONS** Auth, In His Spirit: A Guide to Today's Spirituality, Paulist Press, 82; Moving in The Spirit: Becoming A Contemplative in Action, Paulist, 86; Finding God in Troubled Times: The Holy Spirit and Suffering, Paulist, 94. **CONTACT ADDRESS** Theol Dept, Creighton Univ, 2500 California Plz, Omaha, NE 68178-0001. **EMAIL** hausersj@breighton.edu

HAUSER, THOMAS
PERSONAL Born 02/27/1946, New York, NY **DISCIPLINE** LAW **EDUCATION** Columbia Col, BA, 67; Columbia Law Sch, JD, 70. **CAREER** Author **HONORS AND AWARDS** Prix Lafayette; Haviva Reik Awd. **SELECTED PUBLICATIONS** Missing; The Trial of Thomas Shea; For Our Children (with Frank Macchiarola); The Family Legal Companion; The Black Lights: Inside the World of Professional Boxing; Final Warning: The Legacy of Chernobyl, (with Dr Robert Gale); Muhammad Ali: His Life and Times; Arnold Palmer: A Personal Journey; Muhammad Ali: In Perspective; Healing: A Journey of Tolerance and Understanding; Muhammad Ali and Company; Ashworth and Palmer; Agatha's Friends; The Beethoven Conspiracy; Hanneman's War; The Fantasy; The Hawthorne Group; Mark Twain Remembers; Finding the Princess; Martin Bear and Friends; The Four Chords; Dear Hannah; Confronting America's Moral Crisis; Muhammad Ali: Memories. **CONTACT ADDRESS** 11 Riverside Dr, Apt 11-JE, New York, NY 10023.

HAUSMAN, CARL R.
DISCIPLINE PHILOSOPHY **EDUCATION** Northwestern Univ, PhD. **CAREER** Adj prof, Univ Louisville. **RESEARCH** Philosophical approaches to creativity and metaphor theory as applied to the arts. **SELECTED PUBLICATIONS** Auth, Metaphor and Art, Cambridge, 89; The Evolutionary Philosophy of Charles S Peirce, Cambridge, 93; A Discourse on Novelty and Creation, State Univ NY Press, 84; co-ed, bk(s) on the relation between pragmatism and phenomenology and an anthology, The Creativity Question. **CONTACT ADDRESS** Dept of Philos, Univ of Louisville, 2301 S 3rd St, Louisville, KY 40292.

HAUSMAN, DANIEL M.
PERSONAL Born 03/27/1947, Chicago, IL, m, 1980, 2 children **DISCIPLINE** PHILOSOPHY **EDUCATION** Harvard Col, BA, 69; NYork Univ, MAT, 71; Cambridge Univ, BA, 73; MA, 77; Columbia Univ, M Phil, 75; PhD, 78. **CAREER** Teacher, NYC Public Schs, 70-71; preceptor, Columbia Univ, 75-77; asst prof, Univ MD, 78-84; assoc prof, Carnegie-Mellon Univ, 84-88; assoc prof, Univ Wis-Madison, 88-91; prof, 91-; vis prof, London Sch Econ, 94; vis res assoc, Centre du Recherche en Epistemologie Appliquee, 94; vis res assoc, THEMA, Univ Cergy-Pontoise, 94; res fel, London Sch Econ, 96-98. **HONORS AND AWARDS** Bancroft Awd, Columbia Univ, 78. **MEMBERSHIPS** Am Econ Asoc; Am Philos Asoc; Hist of Econ Soc; Int Network for Econ Methodology; Philos of Sci Asoc. **RESEARCH** Philosophy of economics; social and political philosophy; metaphysics (causality). **SELECTED PUBLICATIONS** Co-auth with Michael S. McPherson, Economic Analysis and Moral Philosophy, 96; auth, Problems with Supply-Side Egalitarianism, Polit and Soc, 96; ed with Roger Backhouse, Uskali Maki, and Andrea Salanti, Economic Methodology: Crossing Disciplinary Boundaries, 98; auth, Causal Asymmetries, 98; auth, Philosophy of Economics, Routledge Encyclopedia of Philosophy, 98. **CONTACT ADDRESS** Philosophy Dept, Univ of Wisconsin, Madison, Madison, WI 53706. **EMAIL** dhausman@macc.wisc.edu

HAVAS, RANDALL E.
DISCIPLINE PHILOSOPHY **EDUCATION** Univ Calif, Berkeley, Ba, 79; Harvard Univ, PhD, 86. **CAREER** Asst prof, assoc prof, Yale Univ, 87-97; from asst prof to assoc prof, Willamette Univ, 97- . **MEMBERSHIPS** APA; N Am Nietzsche Soc. **RESEARCH** Nineteenth and twentieth century continental philosophy; psychoanalysis; Buddhism. **SELECTED PUBLICATIONS** Auth, Nietzsche's Genealogy: Nihilism and the Will to Knowledge, Cornell, 95. **CONTACT ADDRESS** 3005 NE 59th Ave, Portland, OR 97213. **EMAIL** rhavas@teleport.com

HAVEMAN, ROBERT H.
PERSONAL Born 07/22/1936, Grand Rapids, MI, m, 1983, 3 children **DISCIPLINE** ECONOMICS, PUBLIC FINANCE **EDUCATION** Calvin Col, AB, 58; Vanderbilt Univ, PhD, econo, 63. **CAREER** John Bascom Prof, Dept Econo La Follette Inst Pub Aff; Res Assoc, Inst Res on Poverty, Univ WI-Madison, 65-; Inst to Prof, Econ, Grinnel Col, 62-70; Brookings Res Prof, 65-66; Sr Econ, Jt Econ Comm, 68-69; Fel, Neth Inst for Advn Study Soc Ser, Human, Wassenaar, The Neth, 75-76, 96-97; Tinbergen Prof, Erasus Univ, Neth, 84-85; Chair, Dept Econ, Univ WI-Madison, 93-; Board of Editors, Am Econ Rev, 91-95, J Econ Lit, 83-87, Public Fin, 83-, Evaluation Quart, 76-80, co ed, Am Econ Rev, 85-91. **MEMBERSHIPS** Pres, Intl Inst of Pub Fin, 97-00; Pres, Midwest Econ Asn,92-93; Mem, Bd Dir, Resources for the Future, 90-; Pres, Midwest Econ Asn, 92-93. **SELECTED PUBLICATIONS** Poverty Policy and Poverty Research: The Great Society and Social Sciences, Univ Wisconsin Press, 87; Starting Even: An Equal Opportunity Program for the Nation's New Poverty, NY, Simon and Schuster, 88; Earnings Inequality" The Influence of Changing Opportunities and Choices, Washington, DC, Urban Inst Press, 94; Succeeding Generations: On the Effects of Investments in Children, with B Wolfe, NY, Russell Sage Found, 94; The Work Alternative, ed and auth with D Nightingale, Washington DC, Urban Inst Press, 94; coauth, "Neighborhood Attributes as Determinants of Children's Outcomes: How Robust are the Relationships?" Journal of Human Resources, 00. **CONTACT ADDRESS** Dept Economics, Univ of Wisconsin, Madison, 3412 Social Science Bldg, Madison, WI 53706. **EMAIL** haveman@lafollette.wisc.edu

HAVERLY, THOMAS
PERSONAL Born 10/22/1953, Chicago, IL, 2 children **DISCIPLINE** RELIGION, LIBRARY STUDIES **EDUCATION** Olivet Nazarene Col, BA, 74; Nazarene Theol Sem, MDiv, 78; Edinburgh Univ, PhD, 83; Syracuse Univ, MLS, 93. **CAREER** Assoc Prof, Eastern Nazarene Col, 83-94; Assoc Librarian, Colgate Rochester Div School, 94-. **MEMBERSHIPS** SBL, ATLA. **RESEARCH** New Testament; Educational Technology and Media. **CONTACT ADDRESS** Ambrose Swasey Library, Colgate Rochester Divinity Sch/Bexley Hall/Crozer Theol Sem, 1100 Goodman St S, Rochester, NY 14620-2530. **EMAIL** thaverly@crds.edu

HAVIGHURST, CLARK C.
PERSONAL Born 05/25/1933, Evanston, IL, m, 1965, 2 children **DISCIPLINE** LAW **EDUCATION** Princeton Univ, AB, 55; Northwestern Univ, JD, 58. **CAREER** Assoc prof, 64-68, Prof Law, Duke Univ, 68-86, William Neal Reynolds Prof of Law, 86-; Ed, Law & Contemporary Problems, 65-70; scholar in residence, Inst Med, Nat Acad Sci, 72-73; res prof, Ctr for Health Policy Res and Educ, Duke Univ, 91; Prof of Community Health Sciences, Duke Univ Medical Ctr, 74-. **HONORS AND AWARDS** World Health Organization Fel, 76; Mem Inst of Med, Nat Acad of Scis, 82; Who's Who in Am; International Who's Who; Mccdonald-Merrill-Ketcham Awd, Indiana Univ, 00. **MEMBERSHIPS** Inst Med- Nat Acad Sci. **RESEARCH** Antitrust; health care; law and policy. **SELECTED PUBLICATIONS** Auth, Deregulating the Health Care Industry: Planning for Competitition, Ballinger Publishing Company, 82; auth, Doctors and Hospitals: An Antitrust Perspective on Traditional Relationships, Duke Law J, 84; auth, Practice Guidelines for Medical: The Policy Rationale, St. Louis University Law J, 90; auth, Prospective Self-Denial: Can Consumers Contract Today to Accept Health Care Rationing Tomorrow?, U. Pa. L. Rev. 92; auth, Private Reform of Tort-law Dogma: Market Opportunities and Legal Obstacles, id., auth, Antitrust Issues in the Joint Purchasing of Health Care, Utah Law Review, 95; auth, Accrediting and the Sherman Act, auth, Health Care Choices: Private Contracts as Instruments of Health Reform, AEI Press, 95; co-auth, Health Care Law and Policy: Readings, Notes, and Questions, The Foundation Press, 98; auth, Vicarious Liability: Relocating Responsibility for the Quality of Care, Am J of Law and Med, 00. **CONTACT ADDRESS** Law Sch, Duke Univ, PO Box 90360, Durham, NC 27708-0360.

HAWK, CHARLES NATHANIEL, III
PERSONAL Born 10/25/1957, Atlanta, GA **DISCIPLINE** LAW **EDUCATION** Morehouse Coll, BA cum laude 1979; Georgetown Univ Law Center JD 1982. **CAREER** Cooper & Weintraub PC, assoc 1982-83; Morehouse Coll, dir office of alumni affairs; Hawk Law Firm, Attorney, currently. **HONORS AND AWARDS** Serv Awd United Negro Coll Fund 1985. **MEMBERSHIPS** Sec Deacon Bd Friendship Baptist Church 1978-; mem Council for Advancement and Support of Educ 1983-; chmn United Way Campaign Morehouse Coll 1983-; mem GA Bar Assn 1983-; of counsel Law Firm Cooper & Assoc 1983-; legal counsel Natl Black Alumni Hall of Fame 1983-; legal counsel Hank Aaron Found Inc 1984-; legal counsel Council of Natl Alumni Assoc Inc 1984-. **SELECTED PUBLICATIONS** Writer and dir of "Balls, Balloons, and Butterflies" presented 1981 Washington DC; artistic achievement Georgetown Univ Church Ensemble 1982; writer & dir "Black Gold" 1982 Washington DC. **CONTACT ADDRESS** Hawk Law Firm, 34 Peachtree St, Ste 1100, Atlanta, GA 30303.

HAWKINS, BENJAMIN SANFORD, JR.
PERSONAL Born 09/26/1936, Miami, FL, s **DISCIPLINE** PHILOSOPHY **EDUCATION** Univ Miami Coral Gables, BA, 62, MA, 64, PhD, 71; advan work, Univ Birmingham, England, 64-66. **CAREER** Instr, Central Michigan Univ, 68-69; Sr tutor, Univ Western Australia, 72-73; asst prof, Calif St Col, Sonoma, 73-77; lectr, Centre for Continuing Ed, Australian Natl Univ, 79-80; lectr, Univ Ilf, Nigeria, 85-86; asst prof, Columbus Col, Georgia, 87. **HONORS AND AWARDS** Grad tchg asst, Univ Miami, 62-64, 66-68. **MEMBERSHIPS** APA; Charles Sanders Peirce Soc. **RESEARCH** History and philosophy of logic; phi-

losophy of language/semiotics; formal ontology; work of C.S. Peirce, Frege, Wittgenstein; philosophy and logic. **SELECTED PUBLICATIONS** Auth, "Peirce and Frege, a Question Unanswered," Mod Logic, 93; "De Morgan, Victorian Syllogistic and Relational Logic," Mod Logic, 95; auth, Peirce and Russell, Peirce and Russell: The History of a Neglected Controversy, and Appendix (on a falsigratics in Bertrand Russell's Principles of Mathematics), Charles S. Peirce, Indiana Univ 97, Charles S. Peirce Sesquicentennial Cong, Harvard Univ, 89, (On a Falsigrafis in Bertrand Russell's Principles of Mathematics), Stud in the Logic of Charles S. Peirce, Indiana Univ, 97. **CONTACT ADDRESS** 935 NE 88 St, Miami, FL 33138-3326.

HAWKINS, EMMA
PERSONAL Born, OK **DISCIPLINE** ENGLISH, RELIGION **EDUCATION** Okla Baptist Univ, BA, 68; SW Baptist Theol Sem, MDiv, 76; Univ N Tex, MA, 90, PhD, 95. **CAREER** Teacher, Univ of N Tex, 90-95; asst prof, Lamar Univ, 95-. **HONORS AND AWARDS** Mary Patchell Awd, Univ of N Tex, 93; Univ Writing Awd, Univ of N Tex, 93; Go the Extra Mile Awd, 97; James Sims Prize, SCCCL Conf, 00. **MEMBERSHIPS** SCMLA; TEMA; CCTE; SCCCL. **RESEARCH** Old English Literature and Language, Ancient, Classical, Medieval Mythology. **SELECTED PUBLICATIONS** Auth, "Hild und Guth, The War Maidens of Beowulf" in Geardagum 15 (94):55-75; auth, "Gender, Power and Language in 'The Dream of the Rood'", Women and Language 18.2 (95):33-36; auth, Topics for Writers in Media-Based, Entry-Level Composition Courses", English in Texas 27.3 (96):40-49; auth, "Chalk Figures and Scouring in Tolkien-land", Extrapolation (forthcoming); auth, "Chronicles" in Companion to Old and Middle English Literature, Greenwood Pr (forthcoming). **CONTACT ADDRESS** Dept English and Lang, Lamar Univ, Beaumont, PO Box 10023, Beaumont, TX 77710-0023.

HAWKINS, MERRILL M.
PERSONAL Born 12/04/1963, Vicksburg, MS, m, 1988, 1 child **DISCIPLINE** RELIGION **EDUCATION** Baylor Univ, BA, 85; PhD; Southwestern Baptist Theol Sem, MDiv. **CAREER** Grad asst, Baylor Univ, 90-94; asst prof, Carson-Newman Col, 95-. **HONORS AND AWARDS** Faculty Awd for Res, 98; Teaching Excellence & Leadership Awd, 99. **MEMBERSHIPS** Am Acad of Relig, Am Soc of Church Hist, Nat Asn of Baptist Professors of Relig. **RESEARCH** American Religion, Religion in the South, Baptist Studies. **SELECTED PUBLICATIONS** Auth, Will Campbell: Radical Prophet of the South, Mercer Univ Press (Macon, GA), 97. **CONTACT ADDRESS** Dept Relig, Carson-Newman Col, 1634 Russell Ave, Jefferson City, TN 37760-2204. **EMAIL** hawkins@cncacc.cn.edu

HAWKINS, RALPH K.
PERSONAL Born 06/24/1969, Yuma, AZ, m, 1990, 1 child **DISCIPLINE** BIBLICAL LANGUAGES **EDUCATION** David Lipscomb Univ, BA, 90, MA, 95; Univ of the South, DMin, 98. **HONORS AND AWARDS** Rabbi Falk Prize in Interfaith Relutrans, 97; Endowment for Archaeological Research, 97 & 98; endow for bibl res, 97. **MEMBERSHIPS** Am Schools of Orient Res; Cath Bib Asn; Soc of Bibl Lit. **RESEARCH** Archaeology; Historiography of ancient Israel. **SELECTED PUBLICATIONS** Auth, A Heritage in Crisis. **CONTACT ADDRESS** 128 Castleridge Dr., New Market, AL 35760. **EMAIL** rhawkins@sewance.edu

HAWLEY, JOHN STRATTON
DISCIPLINE COMPARATIVE RELIGION **EDUCATION** Amherst Col, AB, 63; Union Theol Sem, MDiv, 66; Harvard Univ, PhD, 77; Univ Delhi, 72; Univ Wis, 71; Hebrew Univ, 66-67. **CAREER** Inst, St. George's Sch, Jerusalem, 67-68; asst prof, Bowdoin Col, 77-78; vis assoc prof, Grad Theol Union, 82; from asst to assoc to prof, Asian Langs & Lit, Univ Wash, 78-85; dir, Southern Asian Inst, Columbia Univ, 89-95; dir, Nat Resource Ctr S Asia, Columbia Univ, 89-97; PROF REL, BARNARD COL, COLUMBIA UNIV, PRESENTLY. **SELECTED PUBLICATIONS** Coed, The Divine Consort: Radha and the Goddesses of India Berkeley, Berkeley Religious Studies Series, 82; auth, Krishna, the Butter Thief, Princeton: Princeton Univ Press, 83; auth, Sur Das: Poet, Singer, Saint, Seattle: Univ of Washington Press, Delphi: Oxford Univ Press 84; ed, Saints and Virtues, Berkeley: Univ of Cali Press, 87; cotransl, Songs fo the Saints of India, New York: Oxford Univ Press, 88; ed, Studying the Sikhs: Issues for North America, Albany State Univ Press, NY, 93; ed, Fundamentalism and Gender, New York: Oxford Univ Press, 94; ed, Sati, The Blessing and the Curse: The Burning of Wives in India, NY: Oxford Univ Press, 94; ed, Devi: Goddesses of India, Berkeley: Univ of Cali Press, 96; ed, Indian religions except Buddhism and Islam, Merriam-Webster's Encyclopedia of World Religions, Springfield, MA: Merriam-Webster; 99. **CONTACT ADDRESS** Barnard Col, New York, NY 10027. **EMAIL** jsh3@columbia.edu

HAWORTH, LAWRENCE L.
PERSONAL Born 12/14/1926, Chicago, IL **DISCIPLINE** PHILOSOPHY **EDUCATION** Rollins Col (Fla), BA, 49; Univ Ill, MA, 50, PhD, 52. **CAREER** Prof, 65-96, assoc dean grad stud, 75-81, 84-86, ch philos, 67-70, 88-89, distinguished prof emer, Univ Waterloo, 96-. **MEMBERSHIPS** Can Philos Asn. **RESEARCH** Social and Political Philos. **SELECTED PUBLICATIONS** Auth, The Good City, Indiana, 63; auth, Decadence and Objectivity, Toronto, 77; auth, Autonomy, Yale Univ Press, 86; coauth, Value Assumptions in Risk Assessment, Wilfrid Laurier Univ Press, 91; auth, A textured Life, wilfrid Laurier Press, 99; auth, The Inner Citadel; auth, The Possibility of Aesthetic Experience, Power, Poverty, and Urban Policy; auth, Concepts in Social and Political Philosophy; auth, Dialogue; Philosophy of Science; Ethics; Plan Canada. **CONTACT ADDRESS** Dept of Philosophy, Univ of Waterloo, Waterloo, ON, Canada N2L 3G1. **EMAIL** lhaworth@watarts.uwaterloo.ca

HAWTHORNE, GERALD F.
PERSONAL Born 08/16/1925, Los Angeles, CA, m, 1955, 3 children **DISCIPLINE** CLASSICAL GREEK, NEW TESTAMENT **EDUCATION** Wheaton Col, Ill, BA, 51, MA, 54; Univ Chicago, PhD, 69. **CAREER** From instr to assoc prof, 53-73, Prof Class Greek & New Testament Exegesis, Wheaton Col, Ill, 73-. **MEMBERSHIPS** Am Acad Relig; Soc Bibl Lit; Evangel Theol Soc; Studiorum Novi Testamenti Soc; Inst Bibl Res (treas, 73-). **RESEARCH** Early Christian literature and church history; New Testament studies. **SELECTED PUBLICATIONS** Auth, Chained in Christ--The Experience and Rhetoric of Paul Imprisonments, J Biblical Lit, Vol 0116, 97. **CONTACT ADDRESS** Dept of Bibl and Theol Studies, Archaeol and World Relig, Wheaton Col, Illinois, Wheaton, IL 60187. **EMAIL** gerald.f.hawthorne@wheaton.edu

HAYDEN, JOHN CARLETON
PERSONAL Born 12/30/1933, Bowling Green, KY, m, 2 children **DISCIPLINE** THEOLOGY **EDUCATION** Wayne State, BA 1955; Univ of Detroit, MA 1962; Coll of Emmanuel & St Chad, LTh honors 1963; Howard U, PhD 1972; College of Emmanuel & St Chad, MDiv, 1991. **CAREER** St Mary's School for Indian Girls, teacher, 55; Detroit Public Schools, teacher, 56-59; St Chad's Secondary School, instructor, 62-64; Univ of Regina, Anglican chaplain, 63-67, instructor in history, 65-68; St George's Church, assoc rector, 68-71, 73-82, 86-87, 94-; Church of The Atonement, asst, 71-72; St Monica's Church, priest-in-charge, 72-73; Howard Univ, asst prof of history, 72-78, scholar in church history, 78-79; Morgan State Univ, Depart of History and Geography, chmn, 79-86; Holy Comforter Church, St Andrew's Parish, rector, 82-86; Frostburg State University, prof of history, 86-87; Univ of the South School of Theology, assoc dean, 87-92; Episcopal Office for Black Ministries, consultant, 92-94; St Michael and All Angels Church, Adelphi Parish, priest-in-charge, 92-94; Montgomery Col, adjunct lecturer of history, 92-94; Episcopal/Anglican chaplain, lecturer in church history, Howard Univ, 94-. **HONORS AND AWARDS** Angus Dunn Fellowship, 1973, 1974, 1978, 1989, 1995, 1998; Faculty Research in the Social Sciences Awd, 1973, 1974; Spencer Foundation Awd, 1975; Am Philosophical Soc Awd, 1976; Commn for Black Minsters, Grant, 1976-78; Bd For Theol Education, Fellowship, 1978-79; Robert R Moton Fellowship, 1978-79; Absalom Jones Awd, 1987; Grambling University Awd, Grambling State University, 1990; Kanuga Conference Center Awd, 1991. **MEMBERSHIPS** Ch Historical Soc; asso editor, "Anglican Episcopal History;" board of directors, 1975-85, Assn for Study of Afro-American Life & History; Am Historical Assn; Southern Historical Assn; Union of Black Episcopalians, Parliamentarian; pres, Saskatchewan Assn for Retarded Children, 1966-68; chmn youth conf, Saskatchewan Centennial Corp, 1964-67; Tuxis and Older Boys' Parliament Bd, 1963-68; lieutenant-gen of Saskatchewan, 1967; Royal Canadian Mountain Police, Regina, chaplain's assoc, 63-68; Saskatchewan Correctional Institution, Anglican chaplain, 1963-68; Wascana Student Housing Corp, founding dir, 1965-68; Ranch Ehrlo, founding dir, 1967-68; Saskatchewan Boys' Schl, Protestant chaplain, 1963-68; Com for Community Improvement; pres, Black Episcopal Clergy, Washington Diocese, 1974-76; board of directors, Washington Urban League, 1980-87; board of directors, St Patrick's Episcopal Day School, 1981-87; secretary, board of trustees, St Mary's Episcopal Center, Sewanee, TN., 1988-92; board of advisors, St Andrew's/Sewanee School, 1989-99; Society for the Promotion of Christian Knowledge/USA Board, 1987-92; KANUGA Conference Center, program committee, 1989-93, diversity comm, board of advisors, 1996-; Evangelical Education Society, board of directors, 1992-99; Washington Episcopal School, board of trustees, 1992-. **RESEARCH** History of African Am Religion; History of Afro-Anglicanism; The Episcopal Church; African American History, especially, 1877-1915. **CONTACT ADDRESS** Howard Univ, PO Box 6, Washington, DC 20059. **EMAIL** fathercarl@webtv.net

HAYDOCK, ROGER S.
PERSONAL Born 05/01/1945, Chicago, IL, m, 3 children **DISCIPLINE** LAW **EDUCATION** St. Mary's Univ, AB, 67; DePaul Univ, JD, 69. **CAREER** Instr to Prof and Clinical Dir, , WMCL, 70-; Fac, Minn Judicial Col, 93-98; Vis Prof, Univ San Diego School of Law, 87, 00. **MEMBERSHIPS** Master of the Inns of Court, Delta Theta Phi, Am Bar Asn, Minn Bar Asn, . **RESEARCH** Dispute resolution. **SELECTED PUBLICATIONS** Auth, Civil Rules Annotated, Minnesota Practice; auth, Civil Rules forms, Minnesota Practice; auth, Trial: Advocacy Before Judges, Jurors, and arbitrators, West Group, 99; auth, Discovery Practice, 3rd ed, Aspen , 98; co-auth, Motion Practice, 3rd ed, Aspen, 96; co-auth, Lawyering, West, 96; co-auth, Fundamentals of Pretrial Litigation, West, 96; co-auth, Trialbook, 2nd ed, West, 95; **CONTACT ADDRESS** William Mitchell Col of Law, 875 Summit Ave, Saint Paul, MN 55105-3030. **EMAIL** rhaydock@wmitchell.edu

HAYES, ALAN L.
PERSONAL Born 09/29/1946, Oakland, CA **DISCIPLINE** RELIGION, CHURCH HISTORY **EDUCATION** Pomona Col, BA, 67; Brown Univ; McGill Univ, BD, 71, PhD, 75. **CAREER** Asst to assoc prof, 75-89, registr, 79-94, PROF CHURCH HIST, UNIV TORONTO, 89-, acad dean, 92-94, vice prin, 96-; priest, Anglican Church Can. **HONORS AND AWARDS** Can Coun doctoral fel, 72-75. **SELECTED PUBLICATIONS** Ed & contribur, By Grace Co-workers, 89; ed & contribur, A New Introduction to John Wycliffe, 94; ed & contribur, Church and Society in Documents 100-600 AD, 95; contribur, Dictionary of Canadian Biography. **CONTACT ADDRESS** Univ of Toronto, Toronto, ON, Canada M5S 1H7. **EMAIL** alhayes@chass.utoronto.ca

HAYES, DIANA L.
PERSONAL Born 05/30/1947, Buffalo, NY **DISCIPLINE** THEOLOGY **EDUCATION** SUNY, BA, 69; George Wash Nat Law Ctr, JD, 73; Cath Univ Am, STB, 83, STL, 85; Cath Univ Louvain, STD, 88, PhD, 88. **CAREER** Attorney, 73-85; from asst prof to assoc prof, Georgetown Univ, 88-; adj fac, Xavier Univ Inst Black Cath Studies, 91-. **HONORS AND AWARDS** Ann Ohara Graff Memorial Awd, CTSA, 00; Hon Doctor of Humane Letters, Ursuline Col, 00; Walter and Mary Tvohy Chair in Interreligious Dialogue, John Conoll Univ, 99; Joint Travel Grant, 97; Consortium Univ Wash Coop Grants Fac, 95-96; 11th Madeleva Lectr, St. Mary's Col, 95; Keck Fel Am Studies, 94-95; Bunn Awd Fac Excellence, Georgetown Univ, 94; Off Student Affairs Outstanding Contrib Georgetown Community Awd, 93; Landegger Semester Res Grant, 92; Jr Fac Summer Res Grant, 92, 93; Dr Fel 87-88; Jean Fairfax-Muskiwinni Fel Black Women Relig, 85-88. **MEMBERSHIPS** Cath Theol Soc Am, Nat Ctr Pastoral Leadership, Georgetown Univ Women's Ctr Bd Advocates & Women's Studies Bd Adv, Woodstock Theol Ctr, Am Acad Relig, Col Theol Soc, Soc Study Black Relig; Black Cath Theol Symposium, Nat Ctr Pastoral Leadership, Woodstock Theol Ctr, 92-96, Nat Policy Comm Catholic Ground Initiative Adjunct Faculty, Howard Univ Divinity Sch. **RESEARCH** Liberation & contextual theologies in the U.S.; public religion. **SELECTED PUBLICATIONS** Auth, And Still We Rise: An Introduction to Black Liberation Theology, 96; auth, Trouble Don't Last Always: Soul Prayers, 95; auth, Hagar's Daughter's: Womanist Ways of Being in the World, 95; auth, Through the Eyes of Faith: The Nguzo Saba and the Beatitudes of St. Matthew, J Relig Thought, 98; auth, Different Voices: Black, Womanist and Catholic, The Tablet, 93; auth, To Be Black, Catholic and Female, New Theol Rev, May, 93; auth, My Hope is in the Lord: Transformation and Salvation in the African American Community, Embracing the Spirit: Womanist Perspectives on Hope, Salvation, and Transformation, 97; auth, The Human Face of the Other, Multicultural Experience in U.S. Church & Theol, 95; auth, Feminist Theology/Womanist Theology: A Black Catholic Perspective, Black Theol: A Documentary Hist, 93; auth, Trusting the Voices: Educating Women for the 21st Century, One Vision, One Voice: Lectures Delivered at the Mother Caroline Friess Centenary Celebrations, 93; auth, Bonaventure: Mystical Writing, 99; auth, The Gift of Being, 00. **CONTACT ADDRESS** Dept of Theology, Georgetown Univ, Box 571135, Washington, DC 20057-1135.

HAYES, EDWARD L.
PERSONAL m, 3 children **DISCIPLINE** CHRISTIAN EDUCATION **EDUCATION** Westmont Col, BA; Dallas Theol Sem, ThM; Univ Denver, PhD. **CAREER** Prof, pres Denver Sem, 93. **HONORS AND AWARDS** Baptist minister, First Baptist Church of Montebello, Calif; exec dir, Mount Hermon Assn, 79-92. **RESEARCH** Teaching, preaching, administering and fundraising. **SELECTED PUBLICATIONS** Auth, The Focused Life and Other Devotion; Words to Live By and The Focused Life. **CONTACT ADDRESS** Denver Conservative Baptist Sem, PO Box 10000, Denver, CO 80250.

HAYES, ZACHARY JEROME
PERSONAL Born 09/21/1932, Chicago, IL **DISCIPLINE** HISTORY OF CHRISTIAN THEOLOGY **EDUCATION** Quincy Col, BA, 56; Univ Bonn, Ger, ThD, 64. **CAREER** Lectr syst theol, St Joseph Sem, Ill, 64-68; assoc prof, 68-74, Prof Hist Of Theol, Cath Theol Union, Chicago, 74. **HONORS AND AWARDS** Res grant, Asn of Theol Schs, 77, res scholar, 78, Scholar-in-Residence, 84, 91; J.C. Murray Awd, CTSA, 85; LittD, Quincy Univ, 85; littd, st bonaventure univ, 74. **MEMBERSHIPS** Cath Theol Soc Am; Soc for Sci Study Relig. **RESEARCH** Mediaeval philos and theol; contemp theological developments, particularly in Christology. **SELECTED PUBLICATIONS** Auth, The General Doctrine of Creation in the Thirteenth Century, Schoningh, 64; transl, The Theology of History in St Bonaventure, Franciscan Herald, 71; What Manner of Man? Sermons on Christ by St Bonaventure, Franciscan Herald, 64; The meaning of Convenientia in the metaphysics of St Bonaventure, Franciscan Studies, 74; Incarnation and creation in the theology of St Bonaventure, In: Studies Honoring

Ignatius Brady, Franciscan Inst, 76; Christology and metaphysics, J of Relig, 78; Disputed Questions on the Trinity, Franciscan Inst, 79; The Hidden Center, Paulist, 81; Visions of a Future, Glazier, 89; Disputed Questions on the Knowledge of Christ, Franciscan Inst, 92; Reduction of the Arts to Theology, Franciscan Inst, 96; A Window to the Divine, Franciscan Press, 96; auth, Bonaventure: Mystical Writings, 99; auth, The Gift of Being, 00. **CONTACT ADDRESS** Catholic Theol Union at Chicago, 5401 S Cornell Ave, Chicago, IL 60615-6200. **EMAIL** zach@ctu.edu

HAYNES, WILLIAM J., JR.
PERSONAL Born Memphis, TN **DISCIPLINE** LAW **EDUCATION** Coll of St Thomas, BA 1970; Vanderbilt School of Law, JD 73. **CAREER** TN State Atty Gen Office, asst atty general 73-77; TN State Antitrust & Consumer Protection, dep atty general 78-84, spec dep atty general for special litigation 84; US District Court Middle District of TN, Magistrate Judged, 84-99. **HONORS AND AWARDS** Bennett Douglas Bell Awd Vanderbilt School of Law 73; Federal Exec Assn; Black History Month Awd, 90. **MEMBERSHIPS** Mem Amer Bar Assn 78, 85, 88-91; vice chair, State Enforcement Comm, Antitrust Section; mem 1st vice pres Nashville Bar Assn, 80-84; dist atty gen pro tem Shelby Cty Criminal Court 80; mem Rotary Intl, 80-90; mem bd of dir Cumberland Museum & Sci Ctr 81-87; mem bd of professional responsibility TN Supreme Court 82-84; mem bd of dir Napier Lobby Bar Assn 83-84; chmn antitrust planning comm Natl Assn of Atty General 84; mem, bd of advisors, Corporate Practice Series, Bureau of Natl Affairs, 89,90; Lecturer-in-law Vanderbilt School of Law, 87-94. **SELECTED PUBLICATIONS** Author, "State Antitrust Laws" published by the Bureau of National Affairs, 88; Contributing Author, "The Legal Aspects of Selling & Buying," Shepard's McGraw Hill, 91. **CONTACT ADDRESS** US District Court, 649 US Courthouse, Nashville, TN 37203.

HAYS, DANNY
PERSONAL Born 05/20/1953, San Francisco, CA, m, 1979, 2 children **DISCIPLINE** OLD TESTAMENT **EDUCATION** New Mexico State Univ, BS, 76; Dallas Theol Sem, ThM, 80; Southwestern Baptist Theol Sem, PhD, 92. **CAREER** Assoc Prof Rel, 92-, Ouachita Baptist Univ. **MEMBERSHIPS** ETS, SBL. **RESEARCH** Hermeneutics, Cushites. **SELECTED PUBLICATIONS** Auth, Verb Forms in the Expository Discourse Sections of Ecclesiastes, Journal of Translation and Textlinguistics, 95; The Sushite: A Black Nation in the Bible, Bibliotheca Sacra, 96; Ebedmelech, in: Eerdmans Dictionary of the Bible, Grand Rapids, Eerdmans, forthcoming; From the Land of the Bow: Black Soldiers in the Ancient Near East, Bible Review, 98; co-auth, Grasping the Word of God: A Hands On Approach to Reading, Interpreting and Applying the Bible, Zondervan, forthcoming. **CONTACT ADDRESS** Ouachita Baptist Univ, Box 3677, Arkadelphia, AR 71998-0001. **EMAIL** haysd@alpha.obu.edu

HAYWARD, DOUGLAS
PERSONAL Born 06/24/1940, Midland, ON, Canada, m, 1961, 3 children **DISCIPLINE** CULTURAL STUDIES, ANTHROPOLOGY, MISSIOLOGY **EDUCATION** Westmont Col, BA; Fuller Theol Sem, MA; Univ Calif, Santa Barbara, MA; PhD. **CAREER** Assoc Prof, Biola Univ, 89-. **HONORS AND AWARDS** Who's Who Among Am Teachers, 96, 98, 00; Marquis Who's Who in the World, 17th Ed, 00. **MEMBERSHIPS** ASM, WMS, ASAO. **RESEARCH** Anthropological study of religion, Christianity and culture, socio-religious change. **SELECTED PUBLICATIONS** Auth, Vernacular Christianity Among the Mulia Dani: An Ethnography of Religious Belief Among the Western Dani of Irian Jaya, Indonesia, UP of Am (Lanham, MD), 97; auth, "Selected Bibliography of Pre-Industrial Peoples for Church Workers," J of Frontier Missions, vol 14:4 (97): 199-203; auth, "Sociology of Religion," in Evangelical Dict of World Missions (Grand Rapids, MI: Baker Publ Co, 00); auth, "Satanism, Satanism," in Evangelical Dict of World Missions (Grand Rapids, MI: Baker Publ Co, 00); auth, "Wicca, Wiccan," in Evangelical Dict of World Missions (Grand Rapids, MI: Baker Publ Co, 00); auth, "Neopagan, Neopaganism," in Evangelical Dict of World Missions (Grand Rapids, MI: Baker Publ Co, 00); auth, "Totem and Totemism," in Evangelical Dict of World Missions (Grand Rapids, MI: Baker Publ Co, 00); auth, "Saturday Night in Pasadena: A Case Study of Harvest Rock Church," in The Relig of Generation X. (Routledge Pr, forthcoming). **CONTACT ADDRESS** Dept Cult Studies, Biola Univ, 13800 Biola Ave, La Mirada, CA 90639-0001. **EMAIL** doug_hayward@peter.biola.edu

HAYWOODE, M. DOUGLAS
PERSONAL Born 02/24/1938, Brooklyn, NY, d **DISCIPLINE** LAW **EDUCATION** Brooklyn Coll, BA 1959; Brooklyn Law Schl, JD 1962; LLM 1967; New Sch Social Resrch, MA 1970; PhD. **CAREER** Private Practice Law, 62; City Univ Brooklyn Col, of NY, prof Political Science, 69-90; New York City Branch NAACP, counsel, 62-64; Human Resources Admin NYC, assoc gen counsel, 72-74. **HONORS AND AWARDS** Governor personal Appointee, New York Housing Corp. **MEMBERSHIPS** Mem New York City Bar Assn; Nat Conf Black Lawyers; Am Soc Intl Law; Intl African Centre; Enterprise 9 Investigation Agency, director. **CONTACT ADDRESS** 71 Maple St., Brooklyn, NY 11225-5001. **EMAIL** ahaywoode@cs.com

HAZEN, THOMAS LEE
PERSONAL Born 09/06/1947, New York, NY, m, 1969, 1 child **DISCIPLINE** BUSINESS & TORT LAW **EDUCATION** Columbia Col, Columbia Univ, BA, 69, Law Sch, JD, 72. **CAREER** Asst prof, Col Law, Univ Nebr, 74-77, assoc prof, 77-79, prof, 79-80; Prof Law, Sch Law, Univ NC, 80- **RESEARCH** Securities law; corporate law. **SELECTED PUBLICATIONS** Auth, Defining Illegal Insider Trading--Lessons From the European Community Directive on Insider Trading, Law Contemp Problems, Vol 0055, 92. **CONTACT ADDRESS** Sch of Law, Univ of No Carolina, Chapel Hill, Chapel Hill, NC 27514.

HEAD, IVAN
DISCIPLINE LAW **EDUCATION** Univ Alberta, BA, 51; LLB, 52; Harvard Univ, LLM, 60; Univ Notre Dame, LLD. **CAREER** UBC Chair in South-North Studies; Prof, 63- **RESEARCH** International law; south-north relations. **SELECTED PUBLICATIONS** Auth, pubs about legal scholarship and foreign and developmental policy; co-auth, The Canadian Way. **CONTACT ADDRESS** Fac of Law, Univ of British Columbia, 1822 East Mall, Vancouver, BC, Canada V6T 1Z1. **EMAIL** ihead@interchange.ubc.ca

HEAD, JOHN W.
PERSONAL Born 03/08/1953, Hannibal, MO, m, 1979, 3 children **DISCIPLINE** LAW **EDUCATION** Univ Mo, BA, 75; Oxford Univ, MA, 77; Univ Va, JD, 79. **CAREER** Judicial clerk, DC Court of Appeals, 79-80; assoc atty, Cleary, Gottlieb, Steen and Hamilton, 80-83; counsel, Asian Development Bank, 83-88; legal counselor, Int Monetary Fund, 88-90; prof, Univ Kans, 90- . **MEMBERSHIPS** ABA; Am Soc of Int Lawyers. **RESEARCH** International law, finance and business; comparative law. **CONTACT ADDRESS** Law School - Green Hall, Univ of Kansas, Lawrence, Lawrence, KS 66045.

HEADRICK, THOMAS E.
PERSONAL Born 06/28/1933, East Orange, NJ, m, 1957, 2 children **DISCIPLINE** LAW **EDUCATION** Franklin & Marshall Col, BA, 55; Oxford Univ, BLitt, 58; Yale Univ, LLB, 60; Stanford Univ, PhD(polit sci), 75. **CAREER** Law clerk, Hon Harry Foster, State Supreme Ct, Olympia, Wash, 60-61; atty, Pillsbury, Madison & Sutro, San Francisco, 61-64; mgt consult, Emerson Consult, London, 64-66 & Baxter, McDonald & Co, Berkeley, Calif, 66-67; asst dean, Stanford Law Sch, 67-70; vpres acad affairs, Lawrence Univ, 70-76; Prof Law & Dean Sch Law, State Univ NY Buffalo, 76-, Asst dir, Ansonia Redevelop Agency, Ansonia, Conn, 59-60; mgt consult, Emerson Consult, London, 64-66 & Baxter, McDonald & Co, Berkeley, Calif, 66-67. **MEMBERSHIPS** Am Polit Sci Asn; Law & Soc Asn. **RESEARCH** Medieval property law; political economy of declining regions. **SELECTED PUBLICATIONS CONTACT ADDRESS** Fac of Law & Jurisp, SUNY, Buffalo, J L O Hall, Buffalo, NY 14260-0001.

HEALEY, ROBERT MATHIEU
PERSONAL Born 06/01/1921, New York, NY, m, 1953, 1 child **DISCIPLINE** CHURCH, HISTORY **EDUCATION** Princeton Univ, BA, 42; Yale Univ, MFA, 47, BD, 55, MA, 56, PhD(relig), 59. **CAREER** Instr English, Mercersburg Acad, 42-44 & Rensselaer Polytech Inst, 48-52; assoc prof commun, 56-63, from assoc prof to prof Am church hist, 63-74, chnin div hist & theol, 68-70, interim acad dean, 70-71, Prof Church Hist, Theol Sem, Univ Dubuque, 74-, Mem comt relig & pub educ, Nat Coun Churches, 58-62; consult, Nat Studies Conf Church & State, Ohio, 64; theologian in residence, Am Church in Paris, 65-66; mem bd dirs, Asn Theol Fac Iowa, 67-71 & 76-80; consult Gen Coun, United Presby Church USA, 71-72; resident scholar, Ecumenical Inst Advan Theol Studies, Israel, 73-74; pres, Asn Fac & Theol Educ Prof Theol Sem, Univ Dubuque, 73-77; vis prof, Univ Edinburgh, 80-81; Asn Theol Schs in US & Can basic res grant, 80-81. **MEMBERSHIPS** Am Soc Church Hist; Am Acad Relig; Presby Hist Soc. **RESEARCH** Relationships of church, state and education in the United States and in France; Andrew Melville (1545-1622), and Scottish reformation; Judaism in American religious history. **SELECTED PUBLICATIONS** Auth, The Mainstream Protestant Decline--The Presbyterian Pattern, Church Hist, Vol 0064, 95; The Organizational Revolution--Presbyterian and American Denominationalism, Church Hist, Vol 0064, 95; The Language of Liberty 1660-1832--Political Discourse and Social Dynamics in the Anglo-American World, Church Hist, Vol 0066, 97; John Duns-Scotus, Doctor of the Church, J Ecumenical Studies, Vol 0030, 93; Waiting For Deborah-- John Knox, And 4 Ruling Queens, Sixteenth Century J, Vol 0025, 94. **CONTACT ADDRESS** Dept of Hist & Theol Theol Sem, Univ of Dubuque, Dubuque, IA 52001.

HEATH, EUGENE
PERSONAL Born 04/03/1958, Lakeland, FL **DISCIPLINE** PHILOSOPHY **EDUCATION** Davidson Coll, BA, 80; Yale Univ, MA, 82, PhD, 88. **CAREER** Vis Asst Prof, 88-90, Coll of Wooster; vis Asst Prof, 90-91, Coll of Charleston; vis Asst Prof, 91-92, Kenyon Coll; vis Asst Prof, 92-93, Lyon Coll; Asst Prof, 93-, SUNY New Paltz; Assoc Prof 99-SUNY New Paltz. **HONORS AND AWARDS** Phi Beta Kappa; European Enlightenment Fellowship, Institute for Advanced Studies in Humanities, Univ of Edinburgh. **MEMBERSHIPS** APA, Hume Soc, Adam Smith Soc. **RESEARCH** Social & political philosophy, 18th century British moral philosophy. **SELECTED PUBLICATIONS** Auth, On the Normative Implications of a Theory of Spontaneous Order, in: Time Order Chaos, The Study of Time IX, ed by JT Fraser, MP Soulsby, A Argyros, Madison Conn Intl Univ Press, 98; Mandeville's Bewitching Engine of Praise, in: Hist of Philo Qtly, 98; Two Cheers and a Pint of Worry, An On-Line Course in Political and Social Philosophy, in: Teaching Philo, 97; The Commerce of Sympathy, Adam Smith on the Emergence of Morals, in: J of Hist of Philo, 95; auth, Rules, Function and the Invisible Hand, An In Interpretation of Hayek's Social Theory, in: Philo of Social Sci, 92; How to Understand Liberalism as Gardening, Galeotti on Hayek, in: Political Theory, 89. **CONTACT ADDRESS** Dept of Philosophy, SUNY, New Paltz, 75 S Manheim, New Paltz, NY 12561-2440. **EMAIL** heathe@matrix.newpaltz.edu

HEATH, JOSEPH
PERSONAL Born 10/09/1967, Saskatoon, SK, Canada, m **DISCIPLINE** PHILOSOPHY **EDUCATION** McGill Univ, BA, 90; Northwestern Univ, MA, 94; PhD, 95. **CAREER** Asst prof, Univ Toronto, 96-01; Can res chair, Univ Montreal, 01-. **HONORS AND AWARDS** Olmsted Vis Scholar, Yale Univ, 97-98; Can Res Chair, 01. **MEMBERSHIPS** Can Philos Asn. **RESEARCH** Critical theory; Practical rationality; Decision and game theory; Theories of distributive justice. **SELECTED PUBLICATIONS** Auth, "Rational Choice as Critical Theory," Philos and Soc criticism, (96): 43-62; auth, "Foundationalism and Practical Reason," Mind, (97): 452-473; auth, The Efficient Society, Penguin, 01; auth, communicative Action and Rational Choice, MIT Press, 01. **CONTACT ADDRESS** Dept Philos, Univ of Toronto, 215 Huron St, Toronto, ON, Canada M5S 1A1.

HECHT, NEIL S.
PERSONAL Born 07/29/1934, New York, NY, m, 1960, 3 children **DISCIPLINE** LAW **EDUCATION** Yeshiva Univ, BA, 54; Yale Univ, JD, 59; Columbia Univ, LLM, 64, JSD, 72. **CAREER** Pvt pract law, 59-62; vpres & gen counsel, John Small & Co, 62-63; assoc prof, 64-66, Prof Law, Boston Univ, 66-, Consult, Orgn Social & Tech Innovations, 67-68; bd dirs, Nat Jewish Comn Law & Pub Affairs, 70-; Am rep, Acad Comt, Bar-Ilan Univ, Israel, 71- **MEMBERSHIPS** Am Judicature Soc; Am Bar Asn. **RESEARCH** Long term leases; Jewish law; evidence. **SELECTED PUBLICATIONS CONTACT ADDRESS** Sch of Law, Boston Univ, 765 Commonwealth Ave, Boston, MA 02215-1401.

HECK, RICHARD
PERSONAL Born 03/21/1964, Troy, NY, m, 1998, 1 child **DISCIPLINE** PHILOSOPHY **EDUCATION** Duke Univ, BA, 85; Oxford Univ, BPhil, 87; MIT, PhD, 91. **CAREER** Asst Prof to Assoc Prof, 91-00; prof, 00-, Harvard, Dept of Philos. **HONORS AND AWARDS** Marshall Scholarship, 85. **MEMBERSHIPS** Am Philos Asn; ASL. **RESEARCH** Philosophy of Language; Philosophy of Mind; Philosophy of Math; Philosophy of Logic; Frege. **SELECTED PUBLICATIONS** Auth, "The Sense of Communication," Mind 104 (95):79-106; auth, "Finitude and Hume's Principle," Journal of Philosophical Logic 26 (97): 589-617; auth, "Tarski, Truth, and Semantics," Philosophical Review 106 (97): 533-554; auth, "Grundgesetze der Arithmetik I, 29-32," Notre Dame Journal of Formal Logic 38 (98): 437-474; auth, "Syntactic Reductionism," Philosophia Mathematica 8 (00): 124-149. **CONTACT ADDRESS** Philos Dept, Harvard Univ, 208 Emerson Hall, Cambridge, MA 02138. **EMAIL** HECK@FAS.HARVARD.EDU

HECKMAN, HUGH W.
PERSONAL Born 06/25/1941, Lynchburg, VA, d, 3 children **DISCIPLINE** PHILOSOPHY **EDUCATION** Univ of Tenn, BS, 66; Ashbury Sem, BS, 70; Catholic Univ of Amer, PhD. **CAREER** Andrew Col, adj prof, 82. **HONORS AND AWARDS** USAF Commendation Medal, Morino Assoc Inc, MVE, **MEMBERSHIPS** APA, PADI, NAVI **RESEARCH** Comparative religion; Judaism; Christianity; Islam; Buddhism; Taoism; Hinduism. **CONTACT ADDRESS** RR1, PO Box 115A, Coleman, GA 31736.

HECKMAN, PETER
PERSONAL Born 01/17/1956, NJ, m **DISCIPLINE** PHILOSOPHY **EDUCATION** Grinnell Col, BA, 78; Northwestern Univ, MA, 80; Northwestern Univ, PhD, 88. **CAREER** Neb Wesleyan Univ, asst prof, 93-. **HONORS AND AWARDS** Felshp NTI, 77; Grinnell Col, Hon in Philo, 78; Felshp School of Crit and Theory **RESEARCH** Hist of philo; aesth, bus ethics; 19th and 20th cent continental philo. **SELECTED PUBLICATIONS** Auth, The Role of Music in Nietzsche's Birth of Tragedy, Brit Jour of Aesthetics, 90; Nietzsche's Clever Animal: Metaphor in Truth and Falsity, Philo and Rhet, 91; Business and Games, Jour of Bus Ethics, 92; The Role of Science in Nietzsche's Human-all-too-Human, Man and World, 93; The Indictment of Morality in Daybreak, Intl Stud in Philo, 96. **CONTACT ADDRESS** Dept of Philosophy, Nebraska Wesleyan Univ, Lincoln, NE 68504-2796. **EMAIL** pheckman@NebrWesleyan.edu

HEDRICK, CHARLES W.
PERSONAL Born 04/11/1934, Bogalusa, LA, m, 1955, 3 children **DISCIPLINE** BIBLICAL STUDIES **EDUCATION** Miss Col, BA, 58; Golden Gate Southern Baptist Theol Sem, BD, 62; Univ Southern Calif, MA, 68; Claremont Grad Univ, PhD, 77. **CAREER** Lectr, Claremont Grad Sch, 78-80; asst prof, Wagner Col, 80-83; from asst prof to prof & distinguished scholar, Southwest Mo State Univ, 80-. **HONORS AND AWARDS** Confr Grant, NEH; Fels, Southwest Mo State; Excellence in Res Awds, Southwest Mo State Univ; John G. Grammie Distinguished Scholar Awd; Distinguished Scholar, Southwest Mo State Univ. **MEMBERSHIPS** Soc of Biblical Lit, Int Asn for Coptic Studies, Studiorum Novi Testamenti Societas, Egyptian Exploration Soc, Nat Asn Baptist Professors of Relig, The Jesus Sem. **RESEARCH** New Testament and Christian Origins, NAG Hammadi and Gnosticism, Coptic Studies. **SELECTED PUBLICATIONS** Auth, The Apocalypse of Adam. A Literary and Critical Analysis, 80; co-ed, Nag Hammadi, Gnosticism, and Early Christianity, 86; ed, Nag Hammadi Codices XI, XII, XIII, (90); auth, Parables as Poetic Fictions. The Creative Voice of Jesus, 94; auth, When History and Faith Collide. Studying Jesus, 99; coauth, The Gospel of the Savior. A New Ancient Gospel, 99. **CONTACT ADDRESS** Dept Relig Studies, Southwest Missouri State Univ, Springfield, 901 S National Ave, Springfield, MO 65804-0027. **EMAIL** charleshedrick@mail.smsu.edu

HEELAN, PATRICK AIDAN
PERSONAL Born 03/07/1926, Dublin, Ireland, s **DISCIPLINE** PHILOSOPHY **EDUCATION** Univ Coll, Nat Univ Ireland, BA, MA, 48; St Stanislaus Col, LicPhil, 54; Milltown Inst Theol, Philos, Dublin, STL, 59; St. Louis Univ, PhD(geophsyics), 52; Cath Univ Louvain, Belgium, PhD(philos), 64. **CAREER** Res assoc, Dublin Inst Adv Stud, 53-54, 64-65; vis fel, Fordham Univ, NY & Palmer Lab, Princeton Univ, 60-62; summer fel, Stanford Univ, Univ Colo; lectr Univ Col, Dublin 64-65; asst, assoc prof, Fordham Univ, 65-70; co-dir honors prog, Thomas More Col, Fordham Univ, 69-70; vis prof, physics, Boston Univ, 68-69; PROF PHILOS, 70-92, CHAIR DEPT, 70-74, PROF EMER, 92-, SUNY, STONY BROOK; prof hum, soc scis, Health Scis Ctr, SUNY, Stony Brook, 72-75; vpres lib stud, dean arts scis, 75-79, dean hum & fine arts, 90-92, SUNY, Stony Brook; mem, Ctr Relig Stud, 80-92, act chair, dept relig stud, 85-86, SUNY, Stony Brook; NSF sen fel, sen vis fel, Ctr Philos Sci, Univ Pittsburg, 83; exec VPres, prof philos, 92-95; WILLIAM A GASTON PROF PHILOS, 95-, GEORGETOWN UNIV. **CONTACT ADDRESS** Dept Philosophy, Georgetown Univ, Washington, DC 20057. **EMAIL** leelamp@georgetown.edu

HEER, LARRY G.
PERSONAL Born 09/03/1946, Decatur, IL, m, 1977, 1 child **DISCIPLINE** RELIGION **EDUCATION** Andrews Univ, BA, 70; Harvard Univ, PhD, 77. **CAREER** Seventh-day Adventist Sem, asst prof, assoc prof, 78-84, Can Univ Col, prof, 84-. **HONORS AND AWARDS** Albright Institute, A.P. **MEMBERSHIPS** SBL, PEF, ASOR. **RESEARCH** History, near east arch, Hebrew Bible, NW Semitic Epigraphy. **CONTACT ADDRESS** Dept of Religious Studies, Canadian Univ Col, 235 College Ave, College Heights, AB, Canada T4L 2E5. **EMAIL** iherr@canu.ab.ca

HEFFERNAN, JAMES
PERSONAL Born 08/06/1940 **DISCIPLINE** PHILOSOPHY **EDUCATION** Fordham Univ, BA, 64, MA, 67; Univ Notre Dame, PhD, 76. **CAREER** Asst prof, 72-77; assoc prof, 77-82; prof, 82-, Univ Pacific. **RESEARCH** Philosophy of science; philosophy of mind; environmental ethics. **SELECTED PUBLICATIONS** Auth, The Land Ethic: A Critical Appraisal, 93; Why Wilderness?, 93. **CONTACT ADDRESS** Philos Dept, Univ of the Pacific, Stockton, Pacific Ave, PO Box 3601, Stockton, CA 95211. **EMAIL** jheffernan@uop.edu

HEFFNER, JOHN HOWARD
PERSONAL Born 01/13/1947, Lebanon, PA **DISCIPLINE** PHILOSOPHY **EDUCATION** Lebanon Valley Col, BS, 68, BA, 87; Univ Edinburgh, Cert philos, 70; Boston Univ, AM, 71, PhD, 76; Diploma in Anglican Stud, General Theol Sem, 01. **CAREER** Asst prof, 72-80, Assoc Prof, 80-84, Prof Philos, Lebanon Valley Col, 84-; Nat Sci Found fel psychol, Northwestern Univ, 77-78; postdoctoral fel, Relig Stud, Univ of Penn, 86-91. **HONORS AND AWARDS** John Templeton Found, 97. **MEMBERSHIPS** Metaphys Soc Am; Hegel Soc Am. **RESEARCH** Philosophy of religion; philosophy of science; Hegel. **SELECTED PUBLICATIONS** Auth, Husserl's critique of traditional Empiricism, J Brit Soc Phenomenol, 5/74; Some epistemological aspects of recent work in visual perception, Proc Philos Sci Asn, Vol I, 76; Perception and animal consciousness: The philosophical context, Behav & Brain Sci, 12/78; The causal theory of visual perception: Its scientific basis and philosophical implications, Int Philos Quart, 9/81; Causal relations in visual perception, in Naturalistic Epistemology: A Twenty Year Symposium, Reidel, 87; Contemporary Issues in Philosophy, in The Reader's Adviser, 14th ed, R R Bowker, 1994. **CONTACT ADDRESS** Lebanon Valley Col, 101 N College Ave, Annville, PA 17003-1400. **EMAIL** heffner@lvc.edu

HEFFRON, PAUL THAYER
PERSONAL Born 11/05/1920, Newton, MA, m, 1963 **DISCIPLINE** POLITICAL SCIENCE; AMERICAN HISTORY **EDUCATION** Boston Col, AB, 42, MA, 47; Fordham Univ, PhD, 51. **CAREER** Assoc prof Am govt, Boston Col, 50-66; Historian, Libr of Cong, 66-. **MEMBERSHIPS** AHA; Am Polit Sci Asn; Am Soc for Legal Hist; Orgn Am Historians; Supreme Court Hist Soc. **RESEARCH** American constitutional law; American presidency: twentieth century political history. **SELECTED PUBLICATIONS** Auth, Theodore Roosevelt and the appointment of Mr Justice Moody, Vanderbilt Law Rev, 3/65; Secretary Moody and naval administrative reform, Am Neptune, 1/69; William Moody: Profile of a Public Man, Supreme Court Hist Soc Yearbk, 80. **CONTACT ADDRESS** Manuscript Div Libr of Cong, Washington, DC 20540.

HEFT, JAMES L.
DISCIPLINE RELIGIOUS STUDIES **EDUCATION** Univ Toronto, PhD. **CAREER** Prof; chancellor, Univ Dayton; Past Chair, ACCU. **MEMBERSHIPS** Ch, bd Dir, Asn Cath Colleges and Universities. **RESEARCH** Doctrinal and moral theology. **SELECTED PUBLICATIONS** Auth, John XXII and Papal Teaching Authority, 86; ed, Faith and the Intellectual Life, Notre Dame, 96; Ed, "A Catholic Modernity? Charles Taylor's Marianist Award Lecture," Oxford Univ Press, 99. **CONTACT ADDRESS** Dept of Religious Studies, Univ of Dayton, Univ Prof of Faith and Culture and Chancellor, 300 College Park, 466B Humanities, Dayton, OH 45469-1549. **EMAIL** heft@udayton.edu

HEGGEN, BRUCE A.
PERSONAL Born 06/18/1950, Pelican Rapids, MN **DISCIPLINE** THEOLOGY **EDUCATION** Concordia Coll, BA, 72; Lutheran Sem, MDiv, 82; McGill Univ, PhD, 96. **CAREER** Pastor, Lutheran Campus Ministry, 96-, adj Asst Prof English, 97-, Univ of Delaware. **HONORS AND AWARDS** Del Div of the Arts, Individual Artist Fel. **MEMBERSHIPS** AAR; N Am Paul Tillich Soc; Conf on Christianity Lit. **RESEARCH** Christian theology, American religious life, Religion & Literature. **SELECTED PUBLICATIONS** Auth, Outside Yom Ha'Shoah, in: Plumbline, J of Min in Higher Edu, 98; The Spirit of God in the Life of the Institute, in: Plumbline, J Of Min IN Higher Edu; That Afternoon in Harvest, in: Vermont Woodlands, 97; Dappled Things, Poetry Ecology and the Means of Grace in Joseph Sittler's Theology for Earth, in: Union Sem Qtly Rev, 97; Beggars to God, Masculine Identity in Light of Martin Luther's Spirituality, in: Gender in World Religions, 91; Hammer-Handle Piety and the Care of the Earth, Joseph Sittler on Ecology and Christian Faith, in: ARC, J of Fac of Relig Stud, McGill Univ, 90. **CONTACT ADDRESS** Lutheran Campus Ministry, Univ of Delaware, 247 Haines St, Newark, DE 19711. **EMAIL** heggen@udel.edu

HEIDE, KATHLEEN M.
DISCIPLINE CRIMINAL JUSTICE **EDUCATION** Vassar Col, BA; SUNY Albany, MA; PhD. **CAREER** Asst prof to full prof, Univ S Fla, 82-. **HONORS AND AWARDS** Phi Beta Kappa, Vassar Col; Presidential Awd for a Distinguished Dissertation, SUNY. **MEMBERSHIPS** Am Psychol Asn, Am Soc Criminol, Homicide Res Group, Acad of Crim Justice Sci, Am Mental Health Counselors Asn, Fla Mental Health Counselors Asn. **RESEARCH** Juvenile violence, Child abuse and family violence, Treatment of survivors of trauma. **SELECTED PUBLICATIONS** Auth, "Defining Serial Murder," Serial Killers, (00): 15-21; auth, "Young Homicide: An Integration of Psychological, Sociological, and Biological Approaches," Homicide Studies: A Sourcebook of Social Research, (99): 221-238; auth, Young Killers: The Challenge of Juvenile Homicide, Sage Pub: Thousand Oaks, 99; auth, "Youth Homicide," Issues in the Study and Prevention of Homicide, 99; auth, "Music Preferences as Data in Assessing and Treating Victims and Offenders," Journal of Police and Criminal Psychology, (98): 1-14; auth, "Mental Health Professionals in Forensic Arenas," Journal of Police and Criminal Psychology, (97): 35-41; auth, "Juvenile Homicide in America: How can we stop the killing?," Behavioral Sciences and the Law, (97): 203-220; auth, "Why Kids Keep Killing: The correlates, Causes, and Challenge of Juvenile Homicide," Stanford Law and Policy Review, (96): 43-49; auth, "Dangerously Antisocial Children Who Kill Parents," Journal of Police and criminal Psychology, (95): 10-14; auth, Why Kids Kill Parents: Child Abuse and Adolescent Homicide, Sage Publications, 92. **CONTACT ADDRESS** Dept Criminol & Sociol, Univ of So Florida, 4202 Fowler Ave, Tampa, FL 33620. **EMAIL** kheide@chuma1.cas.usf.edu

HEIDENHEIMER, ARNOLD J.
PERSONAL Born 11/23/1929, Wurzburg, Germany, m, 1990, 2 children **DISCIPLINE** POLITICAL SCIENCE **EDUCATION** Cornell Univ, AB, 50; Am Univ, MA, 52; London Sch of Econ and Polit Sci, PhD, 57. **CAREER** Asst prof, Wayne State Univ, 57-60; assoc prof, Univ Fla, 60-67; prof, Wash Univ St Louis, 67-. **HONORS AND AWARDS** Fulbright Fel; APSA Kammerer Prize. **MEMBERSHIPS** Intl Polit Sci Asn; Conf Group on German Polit. **RESEARCH** Political corruption; Comparative education policy; Comparative welfare states; West European politics. **SELECTED PUBLICATIONS** Coauth, Comparative Public Policy, 3rd ed, St. Martin's Press, 90; auth, Disparate Ladders: Why School and University Policies Differ in Germany, Japan, and Switzerland, Transaction Pub, 97; auth, Political Corruption: Concepts and Contexts, Transaction Pub, 01. **CONTACT ADDRESS** Dept Polit Sci, Washington Univ, One Brookings Dr, CB 1063, Saint Louis, MO 63130. **EMAIL** heidenhe@artsci.wustl.edu

HEIDER, GEORGE C.
PERSONAL Born 06/13/1953, Washington, DC, m, 1979, 2 children **DISCIPLINE** OLD TESTAMENT **EDUCATION** Concordia Sr Col, BA, 75; Concordia Sem, M Div, 79; Yale Univ, PhD, 84. **CAREER** Asst to assoc to full prof, theol, Concordia Col, (NE) 84-95; exec vpres, acad svc, Concordia Col, 87-95; pres, Concordia Univ, (IL) 95-. **HONORS AND AWARDS** Amer Coun on Educ Fel, 94-95. **MEMBERSHIPS** Soc of Bibl Lit; Cath Bibl Asn; Amer Asn of Higher Educ. **RESEARCH** History of divided monarchy in Israel. **SELECTED PUBLICATIONS** Auth, Lahmu, Molech, Tannin, Dict of Deities and Demons in the Bible, Leiden, Brill, 95; auth, Molech, Anchor Bible Dict, 4, 895-898, NY, Doubleday, 92; auth, The Cult of Molek: A Reassessment, Sheffield, England, JSOT Press, 85. **CONTACT ADDRESS** Concordia Univ, Illinois, 7400 Augusta St., River Forest, IL 60305-1499. **EMAIL** heider@curf.edu

HEIDT, SARAH L.
PERSONAL Born 11/15/1968, Roanoke, VA, m, 1 child **DISCIPLINE** PHILOSOPHY **EDUCATION** Yale Univ, BA, 91, PhD, 97. **CAREER** Lectr, Yale Univ, 97-99. **HONORS AND AWARDS** Yale Prize fel, 96-95. **MEMBERSHIPS** Am Philos Asn; North Am Kant Soc. **RESEARCH** Kant; Heidegger. **SELECTED PUBLICATIONS** Auth, "From Bestimmung to Verstimmung: Community in Hegel's Philosophy of Religion," in New Perspectives on Hegel's Philos of Relig, 92. **CONTACT ADDRESS** 306 E 96th St, Apt 16J, New York, NY 10128. **EMAIL** sarah.heidt@yale.edi

HEIL, JOHN P.
PERSONAL Born 10/13/1947, St. Louis, MO **DISCIPLINE** THEOLOGY **EDUCATION** Pontifical Bibl Inst Rome, Italy, SSD, 79. **CAREER** Kenrick Sch of Theol, prof, 79-. **MEMBERSHIPS** SNTS, CBA, SBL. **RESEARCH** Narrative and rhetorical criticism of the New Testament. **CONTACT ADDRESS** Kenrick-Glennon Sem, 5200 Glennon Dr, Saint Louis, MO 63119.

HEIM, JOEL
PERSONAL Born 11/12/1958, Grand Island, NE, m, 1990 **DISCIPLINE** RELIGION, SOCIAL ETHICS **EDUCATION** Univ Nebr, BS, 82; Union Theol Sem, MDiv, 90; Univ Southern Calif, PhD, 00. **CAREER** Assoc pastor, Wilshire Christian Church, 92-95; grad student in residence, The Graduate Sch of The Univ of Southern Calif, 94-95; lectr, Azuza Pacific Univ, 95-96; asst prof, Carroll Col, 96-. **MEMBERSHIPS** Am Acad of Relig, Soc of Christian Ethics. **RESEARCH** War & Peace, International Ethics. **CONTACT ADDRESS** Dept Relig Studies, Carroll Col, Wisconsin, 100 N East Ave, Waukesha, WI 53186-3103. **EMAIL** jheim@cc.edu

HEIM, MICHAEL R.
PERSONAL Born 11/08/1944, Milwaukee, WI, m, 1969, 1 child **DISCIPLINE** PHILOSOPHY **EDUCATION** NIU, MA, 68; Penn State Univ, Phd, 79. **CAREER** Freelance tchr/writer in S Cal. **HONORS AND AWARDS** Great Tchr Awd Digital Media, Art Ctr Col Design, 95. **MEMBERSHIPS** Am Philos Soc. **RESEARCH** Impact of computerization; Designing knowledge interface. **SELECTED PUBLICATIONS** Auth Electric Language, Yale Univ Press, 87; Metaphysics of Virtual Reality, Oxford Univ Press, 93; Virtual Realism, Oxford Univ Press, 98. **CONTACT ADDRESS** 2305 Ruhland Ave, Redondo Beach, CA 90278. **EMAIL** mike@mheim.com

HEIMAN, LAWRENCE FREDERICK
PERSONAL Born 08/24/1917, Decatur, IN **DISCIPLINE** CHURCH MUSIC **EDUCATION** Cath Univ Am, MA, 49; Pontifical Inst Sacred Music, Rome, LCG, 58, MCG, 59, DS Mus, 70. **CAREER** Prof Emeritus Music & Dir Emeritus Rensselaer Prog Church Music & Liturgy, St Joseph's Col, IN, 44. **HONORS AND AWARDS** Papal Gold Medal res for doctoral dissertation, 70; Nat Merit Awd, Nat Cath Music Educr Asn, 72; President's Fel, St Joseph's Col; Doctor of Letters, honoris causa, St. Joseph's Col, 96. **MEMBERSHIPS** Int Consociatio Sacred Music; N Am Acad Liturgy; Nat Asn Pastoral Musicians. **SELECTED PUBLICATIONS** Auth, The Rhythmic Value of the Final Descending Note After a Puncture in Codex 239 of Library of Laon, Etudes Gregoriennes, 72. **CONTACT ADDRESS** Saint Joseph's Col, Indiana, PO Box 815, Rensselaer, IN 47978-0815. **EMAIL** lheiman@saintjoe.net

HEIN, DAVID
PERSONAL Born 10/02/1954, Baltimore, MD, s **DISCIPLINE** RELIGION **EDUCATION** Univ VA, BA, 76; Univ Chicago, MA, 77; Univ VA, PhD, 82. **CAREER** Asst prof, to prof, Hood Coll, 83-; dept chair, Hood Coll, 88-. **HONORS AND AWARDS** Raven Soc; Om Delta Kappa; Fel, Univ

South, 97; Eng Speak Union Schol, Oxford Univ, 75. **MEMBERSHIPS** AAR, ASCH, HSEL. **RESEARCH** 19th and 20th century church history and theology. **SELECTED PUBLICATIONS** Coauth, with Hans J. Morgenthau, Essays on Lincoln's Faith and Politics, 83; ed, A Student's View of the College of St. James on the Eve of the Civil War: The Letters of W. Wilkins Davis, 88; ed, Readings, in Anglican Spirituality, 91; auth, Nobel Powell and the Episcopal Establishment in the Twentieth Century, 01. **CONTACT ADDRESS** Dept Religion Philos, Hood Col, 401 Rosemount Ave, Frederick, MD 8575. **EMAIL** hein@hood.edu

HEIN, NORVIN
PERSONAL Born 08/19/1914, East Canton, OH, m, 1951, 3 children **DISCIPLINE** COMPARATIVE RELIGION **EDUCATION** Col Wooster, BA, 37; Yale Univ, BD, 46, PhD(relig), 51. **CAREER** Instr Eng, Ewing Christian Col, Univ Allahabad, 39-43; from instr to assoc prof, 50-76, Prof Comp Relig, Yale Univ, 76-85, Dir Grad Studies, 78-85, Fulbright res grant, India, 64-65; consult & panelist, Nat Endowment for Hum, 77-Emer Prof, Yale Univ. **MEMBERSHIPS** Am Orient Soc; Asn Asian Studies; Royal Asiatic Soc; Am Soc Study Relig (vpres, 72-75, pres, 75-78); Am Acad Relig. **RESEARCH** Hinduism, hist of relig; Indian hist. **SELECTED PUBLICATIONS** Auth, The Miracle Plays of Mathura, Yale Univ & Oxford Univ, 72; Hinduism, In: Reader's Guide to the Great Religions, Free Press, 65, 2nd rev & enlarged ed, 77; Caitanya's ecstasies and the theology of the name, In: Hinduism: New Essays in the History of Religion, E J Brill, 76; contribr, Die Religion in Geschichte und Gegenwart, Hinduism in Religions of the World, St. Martin's Press, 83, 3rd ed, 93. **CONTACT ADDRESS** 6 Tuttle Rd Bethany, New Haven, CT 06524-3539. **EMAIL** morvin.hein@yale.edu

HEIN, ROLLAND NEAL
PERSONAL Born 09/12/1932, Cedar Rapids, IA, m, 1954, 2 children **DISCIPLINE** ENGLISH, THEOLOGY **EDUCATION** Wheaton Col, BA, 54; Grace Theol Sem, BD, 57; Purdue Univ, PhD, 71. **CAREER** Assoc prof English, Bethel Col, Minn, 62-70; from Assoc Prof to Prof English, 70-97, Fac Emeritus, Wheaton Col, Ill, 97-. **MEMBERSHIPS** MLA. **RESEARCH** Life and writings of George MacDonald, 1824-1905. **SELECTED PUBLICATIONS** Auth, A biblical view of the novel, Christianity Today, 1/73; Lilith: theology through mythopoeia, Christian Scholar's Rev, 74; ed, Life Essential: The Hope of the Gospel, 74, Creation in Christ: The Unspoken sermons of George MacDonald, 76 & George MacDonald's World: An Anthology from the Novels, 78, H Shaw; The Harmony Within 1982; Sunrise, 89; George MacDonald: Victorian Mythmaker, 93; G.K. Chesterton: Myth, Paradox, and the Commonplace, Seven: An Anglo-Am J, 96; Lilith: A Variorum Edition, Johannesen, 97; Christian Mythmakers, Cornerstone, 98. **CONTACT ADDRESS** Dept of English, Wheaton Col, Illinois, 501 College Ave, Wheaton, IL 60187. **EMAIL** RollandNHein@Wheaton.edu

HEINE, STEVEN
PERSONAL Born 01/15/1950, Philadelphia, PA, m, 1981, 2 children **DISCIPLINE** EAST ASIAN RELIGIONS **EDUCATION** Univ PA, BA, 71; Temple Univ, MA, 76, PhD, 80. **CAREER** Asst prof, LaSalle Univ, 87-90; assoc prof, PA State, 91-96; prof, FL Int Univ, 97-. **HONORS AND AWARDS** Fulbright, 81-82; NEH, 96-97; NEH, 00-01. **MEMBERSHIPS** Am Academy of Relig; Asn for Asian Studies; Southern Japan Seminar. **RESEARCH** Medieval Japanese Buddhism. **SELECTED PUBLICATIONS** Auth, Dogen and the Koan Tradition: A Tale of Two Shobogenzo Texts, series in philos and psychotherapy, State Univ New York Press, 94; co-ed, with Charles Wei-hsun Fu, Japan in Traditional and Postmodern Perspectives, State Univ NY Press, 95; ed, Buddhism and Interfaith Dialogue, Zen and Western Thought, Univ HI Press, 95; auth, Putting the 'Fox' Back Into the 'Wild Fox Koan": On the Intersection of Philosophical and Popular Religious Elements in the Ch'an/Zen Koan Tradition, Harvard J of Asiatic Studies 56/2, 96; Philosophical and Rhetorical Modes of Zen Discourse: Contrasting Nishida's Logic and Koan poetry, Buddhist-Christian Studies 11, 97; The Dogen Canon: Dogen's Pre-Shobogenzo Writings and the Question of Change in His Later Works, Japanese J of Religious Studies 24/1-2, 97; Sayonara Can Mean 'Hello': Rethinking the Butterfly Syndrome in Postwar American Films, Post Script 16/3, 97; ed, Zen and Comparative Studies, pt 2 of a two-vol sequel to Zen and Western Thought, Univ HI Press, 97; auth, Motion and Emotion in Medieval Japanese Buddhism, J of Chinese Philos, forthcoming; Verses From the Mountain of Eternal Peace: The Zen Poetry of Dogen, Charles E Tuttle, 97; Shifting Shape, Shaping Text: Putting the 'Fox' Back in the 'Wild Fox Koan', Univ HI Press, 99; auth, The Koan, Oxford Univ Press, 00; numerous other articles, monographs, and reviews. **CONTACT ADDRESS** Dept of Asian Stud, Florida Intl Univ, University Park, Miami, FL 33199. **EMAIL** heines@fiu.edu

HEINZ, JOHN P.
PERSONAL Born 08/06/1936, Carlinville, IL, m, 1967, 2 children **DISCIPLINE** LAW, SOCIOLOGY **EDUCATION** Wash Univ, AB, 58; Yale Univ, LLB, 62. **CAREER** Teaching fel, Wash Univ, 58-59; atty, Off Secy Air Force, 62-65; from asst prof to prof, 65-88, Owen L. Coon Prof Law, Northwestern Univ, 88-, Prof Soc, 87-; dir Russell Sage prog law & soc sci, Northwestern Univ, 68-70, dir res, Sch Law, 73-74; consult, Ill Judicial Conf, 71-73; pres, John Howard Asn, 74-75; mem res adv comt, Am Judicature Soc, 75-77; affiliated scholar, Am Bar Found, 75-; mem, bd trustees, Law & Soc Asn, 78-81; exec dir, Am Bar Found 82-86. **HONORS AND AWARDS** Harry Kalven Prize of the Law and Soc Asn, for distinguished research on law and society, 87; Distinguished Alumni Achievement Awd, Washington Univ, 98; recipient of numerous research grants. **MEMBERSHIPS** Law & Soc Asn; Am Bar Asn. **RESEARCH** Law and the behavioral sciences; the legal profession; criminal law. **SELECTED PUBLICATIONS** Coauth, A theory of Policy Analysis and some Preliminary Applications, In: Policy Analysis of Political Science, Markham, 70; Public Access to Information, Transaction Bks, 79; Chicago Lawyers: The Social Structure of the Bar, Russell Sage Found & Am Bar Found, Basic Book, 82, rev ed, Northwestern Univ Press and Am Bar Found, 94; The Hollow Core: Private Interests in National Policy Making, Harvard Univ Press, 93; The Constituencies of Elite Urban Lawyers, Law & Soc Rev, vol 31, 97; auth or coauth of numerous other journal articles. **CONTACT ADDRESS** Sch of Law, Northwestern Univ, 357 E Chicago Ave, Chicago, IL 60611-3069. **EMAIL** j-heinz@nwu.edu

HEINZE, RUTH-INGE
PERSONAL Born 11/04/1919, Berlin, West Germany **DISCIPLINE** RELIGION, ASIAN FOLKLORE **EDUCATION** Univ Calif, Berkeley, BA, 69, MA, 71, PhD(Asian studies), 74. **CAREER** Ed text bks, Follett Publ Co, Chicago, 55-56; lectr anthrop, Exten Course, Berlin, 63-73; producer, Radio Broadcast Berlin, 63-68; lectr English, Univ Chiang Mai, Thailand, 72; Res Assoc, Ctr South & Southeast Asia Studies, Univ Calif, Berkeley, 73-, Am Inst Indian Studies travel grant, 75; lectr Southeast Asia, Univ San Francisco, 75-76; Fulbright res fel, Inst Southeast Asian Studies, Singapore, 78-79; dir & ed newslett, Asian Folklore Studies Group; nat dir, Independent Scholars Asia, 81- **MEMBERSHIPS** Asn for Asian Studies; Asian Folklore Studies Group; Independent Scholars Asia; Int Asn Study Asian Med. **RESEARCH** Historical and functional analysis of religious practices in South and Southeast Asia; psychological anthropology; translation of foreign texts. **SELECTED PUBLICATIONS** Auth, The Rock Art of Utah, Am Indian Culture Res J, Vol 0019, 95. **CONTACT ADDRESS** Ctr for South & Southeast Asia Studies, Univ of California, Berkeley, 260 Stephens Hall, Berkeley, CA 94720.

HEISE, MICHAEL
PERSONAL Born 03/30/1960, Chicago, IL, m, 1988, 2 children **DISCIPLINE** LAW **EDUCATION** Stanford Univ, AB, 83; Univ Chicago, JD, 87; Northwestern Univ, PhD, 90. **CAREER** Asst prof law, Ind Univ School of Law, 94-. **CONTACT ADDRESS** School of Law, Indiana Univ-Purdue Univ, Indianapolis, 735 West New York St., Indianapolis, IN 46202-5194.

HEITZENRATER, RICHARD
PERSONAL Born 11/09/1939, Dover, NJ, m, 1962, 3 children **DISCIPLINE** CHURCH HISTORY **EDUCATION** Duke Univ, AB; BD; PhD. **CAREER** Assoc prof, Center Col of Ky, 69-77; prof, S Methodist Univ, 77-98; prof, Duke Univ. **HONORS AND AWARDS** Kearns Fel, 67-68; Dempster Fel, 68-69; ACLS Fel, 75-76; Distinguished Teaching Awd, 76; Distinguished Service Awd, 99. **MEMBERSHIPS** Am Soc of Church Hist; Wesley Hist Soc. **RESEARCH** John and Charles Wesley, Early Methodism, History of Books and Printing. **SELECTED PUBLICATIONS** Auth, Wesley and the People Called Methodists; auth, Mirror and Memory: Reflections on Early Methodism; auth, The Elusive Mr. Wesley; auth, Diary of an Oxford Methodist; coed, The Works of John Wesley: Journal and Diaries. **CONTACT ADDRESS** Divinity School, Duke Univ, PO Box 90964, Durham, NC 27708-0964. **EMAIL** rheitz@duke.edu

HELLER, AGNES
PERSONAL Born Budapest, Hungary, 2 children **DISCIPLINE** PHILOSOPHY **EDUCATION** Lorand Eotvos Univ, PhD, 55. **CAREER** Hannah Arendt Prof Philos and Pol Sci. **RESEARCH** Ethics; polit philos; Hegel; Marx; Lukacs; existentialism; postmodernity as a philos attitude within modernity. **SELECTED PUBLICATIONS** Auth, General Ethics, 88; Beyond Justice, 87; The Power of Shame, 86; Radical Philosophy, 84; Everyday Life, 84; A Theory of History, 82; A Theory of Feelings, 79; Renaissance Man, 78; The Theory of Need in Marx, 76; ed, Lukacs Revalued, 83. **CONTACT ADDRESS** Dept of Philosophy, New Sch for Social Research, 65 5th Ave., New York, NY 10003.

HELLERSTEIN, WALTER
PERSONAL Born 06/21/1946, New York, NY, m, 2 children **DISCIPLINE** LAW **EDUCATION** Harvard Col, AB, 67; Univ Chicago Law, JD, 70. **CAREER** Counsel, KPMG, 99-; partner, Sutherland Asbill Brennan, GA, 96-98 ; 86-96, of counsel, Morrison Foerster, CA; Francis Shaekel Ford Prof of Taxation, 98-, 78 to 98-, prof & assoc prof, Univ GA Law; 76 to 78, assist prof, Univ Chicago Law; 73 to 75, assoc, Covington Burling, WA DC. **HONORS AND AWARDS** Phi Beta Kappa; Order of the Coif; Multistate Tax Comm 25th Ann Awd; admitted to the bar, dc 70; il 76; ny 89 **MEMBERSHIPS** ALI, NTA, ABA, NY Bar Assoc; State and Local Tax Advisory Bd. **SELECTED PUBLICATIONS** Coauth, State and Local Taxation, Cases and materials, 6th ed, West Pub 97; auth, State Taxation, 3rd ed, 98; numerous law rev articles in Univ Chicago, Cornell, Mich, Va, and other law revs. **CONTACT ADDRESS** School of Law, Univ of Georgia, Athens, GA 30602-6012.

HELLMAN, ARTHUR D.
PERSONAL Born 12/09/1942, New York, NY, s **DISCIPLINE** LAW **EDUCATION** Harvard Col, BA, 63; Yale Law School, JD, 66. **CAREER** Law clerk, Minn Supreme Court, 66-67; asst prof, William Mitchell Col, 67-70; asst prof, Univ Conn, 70-72; vis asst prof, Univ Ill, 72-73; vis assoc prof, Univ Pa, 75-80; assoc prof to full prof, Univ Pittsburgh, 75-. **MEMBERSHIPS** Am Jedicature Soc, Am Bar Found, Pres Commission on Mental Health, Am Law Inst, Who's Who in Am, Who's Who in Am Law. **RESEARCH** US Supreme Court, US Courts of Appeal. **SELECTED PUBLICATIONS** Auth, "The Unkindest Cut: The White Commission Proposal to Restructure the Ninth Circuit, 00; auth, "Precedent, Predictability, and Federal Appellate Structure," Univ Pittsburgh, 99; auth, "Light on a Darkling Plain: Intercircuit Conflicts in the Perspective of Time and Experience," Supreme Court Review, 99; auth, "The Shrunken docket of the Rehnquist Court, 97; auth, "Dividing the Ninth Circuit: An Idea Whose Time Has Not Yet Come, 96; auth, By Precedent Unbound: The Nature and Extent of Unresolved Intercircuit Conflicts, Univ Pittsburgh Review (95): 693-800; auth, "Breaking the Banc: The Common Law Process in the Large Appellate Court, 91; auth, "Restructuring Justices: The innovations of the Ninth Circuit and the Future of the Federal Courts, 90; auth, "Deciding Who Decides: Understanding the Realities of Judicial Reform,: Law and Social Inquiry, (90): 343-361. **CONTACT ADDRESS** School of Law, Univ of Pittsburgh, 219 Law Bldg, Pittsburgh, PA 15260-7102. **EMAIL** hellman@law.pitt.edu

HELLMAN, GEOFFREY
PERSONAL Born 08/16/1943, m, 1 child **DISCIPLINE** PHILOSOPHY **EDUCATION** Harvard Univ, A.B.; PhD. **HONORS AND AWARDS** NSF Scholars Awd (4 times). **MEMBERSHIPS** Asn for Symbolic Logic; Philos of Sci Asn; Am Philos Asn; AAAS. **RESEARCH** Philosophy of mathematics and logic; philosophy of physics; philosophy of language; aesthetics. **SELECTED PUBLICATIONS** Auth, Logical Truth by Linguistic Convention, 86; auth, Mathematics without Numbers: Towards a Modal-Structural Interpretation, Oxford, 89; auth, Bell-Type Inequalities in the Non-ideal Case: Proof of a Conjecture of Bell, Foundations Physics, 92; auth, Constructive mathematics and Quantum Mathematics, J Philos Logic, 93; auth, Predicative Foundations of Arithmetic, J Philos Logic, 95; auth, Structuralism without Structures, Philosophia Mathematica, 96; auth, Bayes and Beyond, Philos Sci, 97; auth, Mathematical Constructivism in Space-Time, British J Philos Sci, 98; coed, Quantum Measurement: Beyond Paradox, Unic of Minn Press, 98; auth, Three Varieties of Mathematical Structuralism, Philosophia Mathematica, 01. **CONTACT ADDRESS** Philosophy Dept, Univ of Minnesota, Twin Cities, 224 Church St SE, 355 Ford Hall, Minneapolis, MN 55455. **EMAIL** hellm001@tc.umn.edu

HELM, THOMAS EUGENE
PERSONAL Born 01/20/1943, Hammond, IN, m, 1966, 1 child **DISCIPLINE** RELIGION & LITERATURE **EDUCATION** Earlham Col, AB, 65; Havard Univ, STB, 68; Univ Chicago, AM, 72, PhD, 77. **CAREER** Asst prof, 74-80, assoc prof, 80-86, Prof Relig Studies, Western Ill Univ, 86-, dir Univ Honors, 98-, Res Coun grant, Western Ill Univ, 78; jr fel, Inst Med & Renaissance Studies, 79. **MEMBERSHIPS** Am Acad Relig; Midwest Am Acad Relig; Renaissance Soc; Soc Values Higher Educ. **RESEARCH** Renaissance and reformation studies; rhetoric. **SELECTED PUBLICATIONS** Auth, The warp of piety, the woof of politics: American civil religion, Perkins J, spring 78; Enchantment and the banality of evil, Relig Life, spring 80; The Christian Religion, Prentice Hall, 91. **CONTACT ADDRESS** Dept of Philos & Relig Studies, Western Illinois Univ, 1 University Cir, Macomb, IL 61455-1390. **EMAIL** te-helm@wiu.edu

HELMHOLZ, R. H.
PERSONAL Born 07/01/1940, Pasadena, CA **DISCIPLINE** HISTORY, LAW **EDUCATION** Princeton Univ, AB, 61; Harvard Univ, LLB, 65; Univ Calif, Berkeley, MA, 66, PhD(hist), 70; Trinity Col, Dublin, LLD(h.c.), 92. **CAREER** Asst Prof Hist to Prof Law and Hist, Washington Univ, St. Louis, 70-81; Prof Law, 81-84, Ruth Wyatt Rosenson Prof Law, Univ Chicago, 84-; co-ed, Comparative Studies in Continental and Anglo-Am Legal Hist, 97-; assoc ed, New Dictionary of Nat Biography, 98-. **HONORS AND AWARDS** Fulbright Schol, Univ Kent, 68-69; Royal Hist Soc, Fel, 78-; Guggenheim Fel, 86-87; Cambridge Univ, Maitland Lectr and Vis Fel Commoner, Trinity Col, 86-87; Am Acad of Arts and Sci, Fel, 91-; Alexander von Humboldt Found, Res Prize, 92-93; Medieval Acad of Am, Fel, 97-; All Souls Col, Oxford, vis fel, Michaelmas term, 98. **MEMBERSHIPS** Selden Soc; Am Soc Legal Hist; Royal Hist Soc. **RESEARCH** Legal history. **SELECTED PUBLICA-**

TIONS Auth, Canonical Defamation, Vol 15, Am J Legal Hist, 72; Marriage Litigation in Medieval England, Cambridge Univ, 74; Assumpsit and fidei laesio, Law Quart Rev, Vol 91, 75; Writs of prohibition and ecclesiastical sanctions, Minn Law Rev, 76; Support Orders, Church Courts and the Rule of Filius Nullius, Va Law Rev, Vol 63, 77; Early Enforcement of Uses, Columbia Law Rev, Vol 79, 79; Canon Law and English Common Law, London, 83; Select Cases on Defamation to 1600, Seldon Soc, Vol 101, 85; Canon Law and the Law of England, London, 87; Roman Canon Law in Reformation England, Cambridge, 90; coauth, Notaries Public in England since the Reformation, London, 91; ed and contribur, Canon Law in Protestant Lands, Berlin, 92; auth, The Spirit of Classical Canon Law, Athens, Ga, 96; coauth, The Privilege against Self-Incrimination: its Origins and Development, Chicago, 97. **CONTACT ADDRESS** Law Sch, Univ of Chicago, 1111 E 60th St., Chicago, IL 60637-2702. **EMAIL** dick_helmholz@law.uchicago.edu

HELMINIAK, DANIEL A.
PERSONAL Born Pittsburgh, PA **DISCIPLINE** EDUCATIONAL PSYCHOLOGY, SYSTEMIC THEOLOGY **EDUCATION** Boston Coll Andover Newton Theol Sch, PhD, 79; Univ Tex, Austin, PhD, 84. **CAREER** Asst prof, Oblate Sch Theol, 81-85; pastoral couns, 89-95; asst prof, State Univ W Ga, 95-97; psychotherapist, Pittsburgh Pastoral Inst, 97-98; coord educ, Consumer Credit & Counseling Svcs, 98-99; asst prof, State Univ West Georgia, 00-. **HONORS AND AWARDS** Catholic Journalist Book Awds hon mention, 87. **MEMBERSHIPS** Am Acad Rels; Am Asn Pastoral Counrs; Am Psychol Asn Cath Theol Soc Am; Soc Sci Stud Rel; Soc Sci Stud Sexuality. **RESEARCH** Midlife transition; relationship of psychol and theol; spirituality; sexual integration. **SELECTED PUBLICATIONS** Auth, Spiritual Development: An Interdisciplinary Study, Loyola Univ Press, 87; auth, What the Bible Really Says About Homosexuality, Alamo Square Press, 94; auth, The Same Jesus: A Contemporary Christology, Loyola Univ Press, 96; auth, The Human Cove of Spirituality: Mind as Psyche and Spirit, State Univ NY Press, 96; auth, Religion and the Human Sciences: An Approach via Spirituality, State Univ NY; auth, What the Bible Really Says About Homosexuality, revised edition, Alamo Square Pr, 00. **CONTACT ADDRESS** Psychology Dept, State Univ of West Georgia, Carrollton, GA 30118. **EMAIL** dhelmini@westga.edu

HELYER, LARRY R.
PERSONAL Born 11/06/1942, Seattle, WA, m, 1965, 2 children **DISCIPLINE** BIBLICAL STUDIES **EDUCATION** Biola Col, BA, 65; W Conserv Baptist Sem, M.Div, 68; Fuller Theol Sem, PhD, 79. **CAREER** Asst prof, 79-84, assoc prof, 84-89, prof, 89-, Taylor Univ. **HONORS AND AWARDS** Clyde Cook Awd, scholar/athlete, 65, Biola Col; Delta Epislon Chi Natl Honor Soc, 65, Biola Col; St Dept Fel, 68-69, Amer Inst of Holy Land Stud; Dist Prof of Year, 88, Taylor Univ. **MEMBERSHIPS** Soc of Biblical Lit; Inst for Biblical Res; Evangelical Theol Soc; Near East Archaeological Soc. **RESEARCH** Old Testament, Jewish lit of the 2nd temple; New Testament, Biblical archaeology. **SELECTED PUBLICATIONS** Art, Recent Research on Col 1:15020 (1980-1990), Grace Jour, 92; art, Luke and the restoration of Israel, Jour of the Evangel Theol Soc, 93; art, Cosmic Christology and Col 1: 15-20, JETS, 94; auth, Yesterday, Today and Forever: the Continuing Relevance of the Old Testament, Sheffield Pub, 96; art, Old Testament Hero and Heroine Narratives, S Baptist Jour of Theol, 98. **CONTACT ADDRESS** Taylor Univ, Upland, 236 W Reade Ave., Upland, IN 46989-1001. **EMAIL** lrhelyer@tayloru.edu

HEMAND, JOST
PERSONAL Born 04/11/1930, Kassel, Germany, m, 1956 **DISCIPLINE** GERMAN LITERATURE, HISTORY, PHILOSOPHY **EDUCATION** Univ Marburg, Ger, PhD, 55. **CAREER** From Asst Prof to Vilas Res Prof, Univ Wis, 58-. **HONORS AND AWARDS** ACLS Fel, 63; Vilas Res Prof, 67; Mem of Saxon Acad, 85. **RESEARCH** German Culture 1750 to the Present, German-Jewish History, Comparative Arts, Fascism and Exile. **SELECTED PUBLICATIONS** Auth, Judentum und deutsche Kultur, 96; auth, A Hitler Youth to Poland, 97; auth, Deutsche Diditer bunde, 98; auth, Formen des Eses tu der Kunst, 00. **CONTACT ADDRESS** Dept German, Univ of Wisconsin, Madison, 1230 Linden Dr, Van Hise Hall, Madison, WI 53706-1525.

HEMMER, JOSEPH
DISCIPLINE COMMUNICATION LAW **EDUCATION** Bradley Univ, MA; Univ Wisc, PhD, 78. **CAREER** Law, Carroll Col. **HONORS AND AWARDS** Marquette Univ DSR-TKA Outstanding Alumni Awd, 68; Wisc Comm Asn Andrew T. Weaver Awd, 82; chair, comm dept. **SELECTED PUBLICATIONS** Auth, Communication Law: Judicial Interpretation of the First Amendment. **CONTACT ADDRESS** Carroll Col, Wisconsin, 100 N East Ave, Waukesha, WI 53186.

HENDERSON, EDWARD H.
PERSONAL Born 04/21/1939, Atlanta, GA, m, 1973, 4 children **DISCIPLINE** PHILOSOPHY **EDUCATION** Rhodes Col, BA, 61; Tulane Univ, MA, 64, PhD, 67. **CAREER** Asst prof, Westminster Col, 64-66; from asst to full prof, 66- , chemn dept, 79- , Louisiana State Univ. **HONORS AND AWARDS** Phi Beta Kappa; Omicron Delta Kappa; Woodrow Wilson fel, 61-64; Natl Defense Educ Act Fel, 61-64; Distinguished Faculty Awd, 81. **MEMBERSHIPS** Soc for Philos of Relig; Soc of Christian Philos; Scholarly Engagement with Anglican Doctrine. **RESEARCH** Philosophy of religion; philosophical theology; Austin Farrer. **SELECTED PUBLICATIONS** Co-ed, Divine Action: Studies Inspired by the Philosophical Theology of Austin Farrer, T & T Clark, 90; auth, The Divine Playwright, The Personalist Forum, 96; auth, How to be a Christian Philosopher in the Postmodern World, in, Spirituality and Theology, John Knox, 98; auth, The Supremely Free Agent, in McLain, ed, Free-Will and Theology, University Press of America, forthcoming. **CONTACT ADDRESS** Dept of Philosophy and Religious Studies, Louisiana State Univ and A&M Col, Baton Rouge, LA 70803. **EMAIL** ehender@lsu.edu

HENDERSON, HERBERT H.
PERSONAL m **DISCIPLINE** LAW **EDUCATION** WV State Coll, BS 1953; George Wash Univ Coll of Law, JD 1958. **CAREER** Attorney, civil rights & general practice; Marshall Univ, part-time instructor in black history, 67-80; Henderson & Henderson General Practice, Huntington, WV, sr partner, currently. **HONORS AND AWARDS** W Robert Ming Awd, NAACP Bd of Dirs; Justitia Officium Awd, West Virginia Univ Coll of Law, 1989. **MEMBERSHIPS** Mem Cabell Co Bar Assn; bd dir WV Trial Lawyers Assn; WV State Bar; Nat Bar Assn; Am Trial Lawyers Assn; Mountaineer Bar Assn; mem bd dir Region III Assn of Mental Hlth; chmn bd trustees Huntington Dist united Methodist Ch; state United Meth Ch Conf; pres Meth Men's Club; Ebenezer Meth Ch; mem Kappa Alpha Psi Frat; mem, bd of trustees, Morristown Coll; mgr & supvr, WV NAACP Jobs Program, 1978-; state pres WV NAACP, 1966-; mem, natl bd of dirs, NAACP, 1980-. **CONTACT ADDRESS** 317 Ninth St, Huntington, WV 25711.

HENDERSON, JOHN B.
DISCIPLINE HISTORY AND RELIGIONS OF CHINA **EDUCATION** Univ Calif, Berkeley, PhD, 77. **CAREER** Prof Hist and Relig Stud, La State Univ. **SELECTED PUBLICATIONS** Auth, The Development and Decline of Chinese Cosmology, Columbia, 84; Auth, Scripture, Canon, and Commentary: A Comparison of Confucian and Western Exegesis, Princeton, 91; Auth, The Construction of Orthodoxy and Heresy, SUNY, 98. **CONTACT ADDRESS** Dept of History, Louisiana State Univ and A&M Col, Baton Rouge, LA 70803. **EMAIL** jbhende@lsu.edu

HENDLEY, BRIAN
DISCIPLINE PHILOSOPHY **EDUCATION** Yale Univ, PhD, 66. **RESEARCH** Philos of educ; Amer philos. **SELECTED PUBLICATIONS** Auth, Dewey, Russell, Whitehead: Philosophers as Educators, Southern Ill Univ, 86; ed, Plato, Time, and Education: Essays in Honor of Robert S. Brumbaugh, SUNY, 87. **CONTACT ADDRESS** Dept of Philosophy, Univ of Waterloo, 200 University Ave W, Waterloo, ON, Canada N2L 3G1. **EMAIL** bhendley@uwaterloo.ca

HENDLEY, STEVE
PERSONAL Born 12/03/1955, Nashville, TN, m, 1986, 2 children **DISCIPLINE** PHILOSOPHY **EDUCATION** Rhodes Col, BA, 78; Vanderbilt Univ, MA, 80; Duquesne Univ, MA, 81, PhD, 88. **CAREER** Teaching asst, Duquesne Univ, 82; visiting faculty, West Virginia Univ, 88; assoc prof, Birmingham-Southern Col, 88-. **MEMBERSHIPS** Alabama Philosophical Soc, 90-91; APA; The Sartre Soc of North Amer, 99-00 ; Soc for Phenomenology and Existential Philosophy. **RESEARCH** Contemporary continental philosophy; moral and political philosophy. **SELECTED PUBLICATIONS** Auth, From Communicatve Action to the Face of the Other: Habermas and Levinas on the Foundations of Moral Theory, Philosophy Today, 96; auth, Autonomy and Alterity: Sartre and Levinas on the Grounds of Moral Obligation, Journal of the British Society for Phenomenology, Winter 96; auth, Lyotard and the Question of Community, in Phenomenology, Interpretation, and Community: Selected Studies in Phenomenology and Existential Philosophy, 96; auth, Reconsidering the Limits of Democracy with Castoriadis and Lefort, in Reinterpreting the Political: Selected Studies in Phenomenology and Existential Philosophy, 98; auth, From Communicative Action to the Face of the Other: Levinas and Habermas on Language, Obligation + Community, Lexington Books, 00; auth, "Sartre and the Idea of Socialism: Narative Limitations of Collective Autonomy," Philosophy Today, 00. **CONTACT ADDRESS** Birmingham-So Col, 900 Arkadelphia Rd, Birmingham, AL 35254. **EMAIL** shendley@bsc.edu

HENKIN, LOUIS
PERSONAL Born 11/11/1917, Russia, m, 1960, 3 children **DISCIPLINE** LAW; DIPLOMACY **EDUCATION** Yeshiva Univ, AB, 37; Harvard Univ, LLB, 40; Columbia Univ, LLD, 95. **CAREER** Law clerk, Judge Learned Hand, US Court of Appeals, 40-41; foreign affairs officer, Us Dept State, 45-46; law clerk, Justice Frankfurter, US Supreme Court, 46-47; foreign affairs officer, US Dept State, 48-57; prof law, Univ Pa Law Sch, 57-62; prof law & int law & diplomacy, 62-63, Hamilton Fish Prof Int Law & Diplomacy & Prof Law, Columbia Univ, 63-98; Harlan Fiske Stone prof const law, 78-79;Univ Prof, 79-, Mem bar, NY, 41- & US Supreme Court, 47-; consult, UN Legal Dept, 47-48, US Dept State, 58 & 61, US Arms Control & Disarmament Agency, 61-66 & Nat Coun Marine Resources & Engineering Develop, 68-70; assoc dir legis drafting res fund, Columbia Univ, 56-57; US mem, Permanent Court of Arbit, 63-69; pres, US Inst Human Rights, 70-; mem, US Adv Comt Law of Sea, 72-; Am Acad Arts & Sci fel, 74; mem human rights comt, Nat Comn for UNESCO, 77-; dir, Columbia Ctr Human Rights, 78-; co-ed-in-chief, Am J Int Law, 78-; chief reporter, Am Law Inst, 79- **HONORS AND AWARDS** DHL, Yeshia Univ, 63; Columbia Univ, LLD, 95; Bklyn Law School, JD (hon), 97; dhl, yeshiva univ, 63; bklyn law school, jd (hon), 97. **MEMBERSHIPS** Am Soc Int Law; Int Law Asn; Coun Foreign Relat; Am Polit Sci Asn; Am Soc Polit & Legal Philos. **RESEARCH** United States Constitutional law; international law; human rights. **SELECTED PUBLICATIONS** Ed, Arms Control: Issues for the Public, 61; Auth, How Nations Behave: Law and Foreign Policy, Praeger, 68 & Columbia Univ, 2nd ed, 79; Law for the Sea's Mineral Resources, Inst Study Sci in Human Affairs, Columbia Univ, 68; Foreign Affairs and the Constitution, Foundation, 72; ed, World Politics and the Jewish Condition, Quadrangle, 72; co-ed, Transnational Law in a Changing Society, Columbia Univ, 72; auth, The Rights of Man Today, Westview, 78; ed, The International Bill of Rights: The Covenant on Civil and Political Rights, Columbia Univ, 81; co-ed, International Law, Cases and Materials, West, 2nd ed, 80; co-auth Human Rights in Comtemporary China, 86; Right v Might: International Law and the Use of Force, 89; Constitutionalism and Rights: The Influence of the United States Constitution Abroad, 89; Foreign Affairs and the US Constitution, Oxford, 96; The Age of Rights, 90; Constitutionalism, Democracy and Foreign Affairs, 90; International Law: Cases and Materials, 93; International Law: Politics and Values, 95; co-ed, Human Rights Foundation, 99. **CONTACT ADDRESS** Sch of Law, Columbia Univ, 435 West 116th St, New York, NY 10027. **EMAIL** henkin@law.columbia.edu

HENNESSY, ANNE
PERSONAL Born 03/30/1938, San Francisco, CA **DISCIPLINE** RELIGION **EDUCATION** Grad Theol Union, MA, 83, PhD, 88; Calif State Univ, MA, 69; St. Joseph Col, BA, 62. **CAREER** Coordr, Sisters St. Joseph, 69-74; acad dean, Loyola Marymount Univ, 75-80; asst dir, Inst Living Water, Tabgha, Israel, 89-97; prof, Pontifical Gregorian Univ, Rome, Italy, 93-00; dir, St. Joseph Theol Libr, Orange, Calif, 00. **RESEARCH** New Testament; 1st Century Galilee; historical expressions of Christian discipleship. **SELECTED PUBLICATIONS** Auth, The Formation of Adult Disciplines: A Reading of John 20-21, Emmanuel, April, 96; auth, Contemplative Pilgrimage to the Holy Land, Prayer & Serv, Jan-March, 96; auth, The Galilee of Jesus, 94; auth, Holy Land Pilgrims and Ministry to Them, Rev Relig, July-Aug, 94; coauth, The Family of Jesus, The Family: A Cath Perspective, Dec, 95; auth, Galilean Perspectives on Religious Life, Rev Relig, March-April, 93; coauth, Joseph and Mary: Their Vocations and Mission, 92; auth, The Multiplication of Loaves and Fishes: A Formative Experience, Emmanuel, Sept, 92. **CONTACT ADDRESS** 480 S Batavia St., Orange, CA 92868. **EMAIL** annehcsj@earthlink.net

HENRICH, DIETER
PERSONAL Born 01/05/1927, Marburg, Germany, m, 1975 **DISCIPLINE** PHILOSOPHY **EDUCATION** Heidelberg Univ, DPhil, 50, DPhil habil, 56. **CAREER** Asst prof philos, Heidelberg Univ, 56-60; prof, Free Univ Berlin, 60-65 & Heidelberg Univ, 65-81; Prof Philos, Univ Munich, 81-; Vis Prof Philos, Harvard Univ, 73-, Vis prof philos, Columbia Univ, 68-73. **MEMBERSHIPS** Int Hegel Asn (pres, 70-). **SELECTED PUBLICATIONS** Auth, Philosophy of Naturalism, Merkur-Deutsche Zeitschrift Fur Europaisches Denken, Vol 0050, 96. **CONTACT ADDRESS** Dept of Philos, Harvard Univ, Cambridge, MA 02138.

HENRICH, SARAH
DISCIPLINE NEW TESTAMENT **EDUCATION** Muhlenberg Col, BA, 69; Bryn Mawr Univ, MA, 71; Lutheran Theol Sem, MDiv, 79; Yale Univ, PhD, 94. **CAREER** Asst prof, Lutheran Sch Theol, 89; dir, Christian edu, St. Michael's Lutheran Church, New Canaan, 83-88; ch, Bible Div; assoc prof, 92-. **HONORS AND AWARDS** Assoc ed, Word and World; asst pastor, St. Michael's Lutheran Church. **MEMBERSHIPS** Mem, Soc Biblical Lit. **SELECTED PUBLICATIONS** Pub(s) in Augsburg Fortress; auth, Great Personalities of the New Testament; See God's Grace in Action. **CONTACT ADDRESS** Dept of New Testament, Luther Sem, 2481 Como Ave, Saint Paul, MN 55108. **EMAIL** shenrich@luthersem.edu

HENRY, BRENT LEE
PERSONAL Born 10/09/1947, Philadelphia, PA, m, 3 children **DISCIPLINE** LAW **EDUCATION** Princeton Univ, BA 1969; Yale Law Sch, JD 1973; Yale Univ, Master of Urban Studies 1973. **CAREER** New Haven Housing Information Ctr, counsel 1973-74; Yale Univ, lecturer in Afro-Amer studies 1973-74; Jones Day Reavis & Pogue, atty 1974-78; NYCHuman Resources Adminstrn, dept admin 1978-79; Jones Day Reavis & Pogue, atty 1979-82; Greater Southeast Comm Hospital Found, dir of business and govt affairs 1982-84; Howard Univ School

of Business Admin, adjunct prof, 82-94; MedStar Health, sr vice pres/gen counsel 1985-. **HONORS AND AWARDS** Frederick Abramson Awd, DC Bar Association, 1996. **MEMBERSHIPS** Bd of trustees, Princeton Univ 1969-72, 99-; adv council Woodrow Wilson School of Pub & Intl Affairs Princeton Univ 1969-72; ABA; NBA; Ohio Bar Assns; DC Bar Assn; board of directors, Natl Health Lawyers Assn, 1988-96, president, 1994-95; board of directors, Mental Health Law Project 1987-98; bd of dirs, Combined Health Appeal of the Natl Capital Area, 1989-93; Princeton University Alumni Council, executive committee, 1994-, vice chair, 1995-97, chair, 1997-99; Public Welfare Foundation, bod, 1995. **SELECTED PUBLICATIONS** Auth, "The Provision of Indigent Defense Servs in Greater Cleveland" Cleveland Found. **CONTACT ADDRESS** Helix/Medlantic Health Care Group, 100 Irving St NW, Washington, DC 20010.

HENRY, CARL F. H.
PERSONAL Born 01/22/1913, New York, NY, m, 1940, 2 children **DISCIPLINE** RELIGION **EDUCATION** Wheaton Col, BA, 38, MA, 40; North Bap Theol Sem, BD, 41, Thd, 42, Boston Univ, PhD, 49. **CAREER** North Bap Theol Sem, asst prof, prof, 40-47; Fuller Theol Sem, prof, act dean, 47-56; Eastern Bap Sem, prof, 69-74; World Vision Intl, lectr at large, 74-86; Trinity Evan Div School, vis prof, 74-97. **HONORS AND AWARDS** Boston Univ, Distinguished Alumnus, 98; South Bap Conven, 50-years Gold Service Awd, 93; Hillsdale Col, Hon LLD, 89; Gordon-Conwell Theol Sem, Hon DD, 84; Northwestern Col, Hon DD, 79; Relig Herit of Amer, Faith and Freedom Awd, 75 **MEMBERSHIPS** WVI, WCE, PF, RHA **SELECTED PUBLICATIONS** Auth, God, Revelation and Authority; A Plea for Evangelical Demonstration, 71; Aspects of Christian Social Ethics, 64; Remaking the Modern Mind, 48; founding editor of Christianity Today; ed, Contemporary Evangelical Thought, 57; The Bible Expositor, 60; Jesus of Nazareth: Savior and Lord, 73. **CONTACT ADDRESS** 1141 Hus Dr, #20 B, Watertown, WI 53098.

HENRY, DANIEL JOSEPH
PERSONAL Born 01/03/1945, New York, NY, m **DISCIPLINE** LAW **EDUCATION** Columbia Univ School of Law, JD 1967-70. **CAREER** Rubin Wachtel Baum & Levin, assoc 1969-71; Bernard M Baruch Coll, adj lecturer 1971-72; NY State Spec Comm on Attica, asst counsel 1971; NY State Supreme Ct, law sec 1971-73; Carver Dem Club, counsel 1972-76; Montgomery Ward & Co, sr attny 1973-74; Caterpillar Tractor Co, attny 1976-84; Univ of MN, assoc attny. **MEMBERSHIPS** Mem Amer Bar Assoc, Natl Bar Assoc, Intl Law Sec Council, IL State Bar Assoc 1979-80; vchmn Natl Urban Coaltion Salute to Cities Dinner 1980. **CONTACT ADDRESS** Univ of Minnesota, Twin Cities, 100 Church St SE, Minneapolis, MN 55455.

HENRY, GRAY
PERSONAL 2 children **DISCIPLINE** COMPARATIVE RELIGION, ART HISTORY **EDUCATION** Sarah Lawrence, BA, 65; Univ Mich, MA, 80; doctoral work, Univ Kent, Canterbury. **CAREER** Teach, Fordham Univ, Dalton Sch, 66-68; teach, Azhar Acad, Cairo Am Col, 70-78; lect, Cambridge Univ, 88; instr, Bellarmine Col, 91-92; instr, Center Col, 93; Dir, Found Pub House: Islamic Texts Soc, Quinta essentia, Founs Vitae, 80-. **SELECTED PUBLICATIONS** Ed, Merton and Sufism: The Untold Story; narrator, Cairo, 1001 Years of Islamic Art and Architecture; Production, Islam: A Pictorial Essay in Four Parts, video, 86; ed, Islam in Tebet, 97; Production, the Ornaments of Lhasa: Islam in Tabet, 97; **CONTACT ADDRESS** 49 Mockingbird Valley Dr, Louisville, KY 40207. **EMAIL** grayh101@aol.com

HENSHAW, RICHARD A.
PERSONAL Born 11/06/1921, San Francisco, CA, m, 1943, 2 children **DISCIPLINE** RELIGIOUS STUDIES **EDUCATION** Univ Calif Berkeley, BS, 43; Church Divinity Sch of the Pac, BD, 53; Hebrew Union Col, PhD, 63. **CAREER** Vis Prof, Chinese Univ of Hong Kong, 85-98; Prof, Colgate Roch, 94-; **MEMBERSHIPS** Soc for Bibl Lit, Am Oriental Soc, Astron Soc of the Pac. **RESEARCH** Biblical Translation, Ancient Near Eastern Languages. **SELECTED PUBLICATIONS** Auth, Female and Male. The Cultoc Personnel, Pickwick Press, 94. **CONTACT ADDRESS** Dept Religious Studies, Colgate Rochester Divinity Sch/Bexley Hall/Crozer Theol Sem, 1100 Goodman St S, Rochester, NY 14620-2530.

HENSLEE, WILLIAM D.
PERSONAL Born 01/14/1954, TX, m, 2 children **DISCIPLINE** COPYRIGHT LAW, ENTERTAINMENT LAW, SPORTS LAW **EDUCATION** Univ HI, BA, 77; J.D., Pepperdine Univ, JD, 84; Univ CA, MFA, 96. **CAREER** Recruitment coord, 94; admin dir, staff instr, Multistate Legal Studies, Inc, 85-88; dir, Planned Giving, 88-89; nat dir, HBJ Multistate Advantage, 89-90; asst prof; ed, ABA Career Series bk(s), 84-. **HONORS AND AWARDS** Clark Awd for Creative Writing. **MEMBERSHIPS** Mem, AR, CA, Nmex, PA Bar Assn(s). **SELECTED PUBLICATIONS** Auth, Careers in Entertainment Law, Am Bar Assn, 90; How to Survive the First Year of Law School, ABA Law Student Div, 86; co-auth, Non-Legal Careers for Lawyers, Am Bar Assn, 94; nt **CONTACT ADDRESS** Sch of Law, Pepperdine Univ, 24255 Pacific Coast Hwy, Malibu, CA 90263. **EMAIL** william.henslee@pepperdine.edu

HERBENICK, RAYMOND M.
DISCIPLINE CLASSICAL PHILOSOPHY, LOGIC **EDUCATION** Georgetown Univ, Phd, 68. **CAREER** Dept Philos, Univ Dayton **RESEARCH** Applied ethics, history of Slavic philosophy. **SELECTED PUBLICATIONS** Auth, Remarks on Abortion, Abandonment, and Adoption Opportunities, Philosophy and Public Affairs, Princeton Univ Press, 75; Basic Logic: A Systems Approach to the Structures and Principles of Logical Reasoning, Ginn, 85; Carpatho-Rusyn American Index: A Computerized Bibliography Vols1-11 (78-88), Carpatho-Rusyn Res Ctr, 91; Augustine's Moral Thermometer of Human Goodness, Univ Dayton Rev, 94. **CONTACT ADDRESS** Dept of Philos, Univ of Dayton, 300 Col Park, Dayton, OH 75062. **EMAIL** herbenic@flyernet.udayton.edu

HERBERT, GARY B.
PERSONAL Born 12/24/1941, Rockford, IL, m, 1967, 2 children **DISCIPLINE** PHILOSOPHY **EDUCATION** Ill Wesleyan Univ, BA, 65; Am Univ, MA, 67; Pa State Univ, PhD, 72. **CAREER** Prof, Loyola Univ, 72-. **MEMBERSHIPS** APA; ASPLP; ACPA. **RESEARCH** Political philosophy; seventeenth century philosophy; metaphysics; German idealism. **SELECTED PUBLICATIONS** Auth, Thomas Hobbes: The Union of Scientific and Political Wisdom, Univ Brit Colum Press (Vancouver), 89; auth, "Transcendental Consent: The Apriori Sociability of Rights in Kant," SW Philos 12 (96); auth, "Immanuel Kant: Punishment and the Political Preconditions of Moral Existence," Interpretation 23 (95). **CONTACT ADDRESS** Dept Philosophy, Loyola Univ, New Orleans, 6363 St Charles Ave, New Orleans, LA 70118-6143. **EMAIL** gherbert@loyno.edu

HERDT, JENNIFER A.
PERSONAL Born 12/10/1967, New Delhi, India, m, 1995 **DISCIPLINE** THEOLOGY **EDUCATION** Oberlin Col, BA, 89; Princeton Univ, MA, 92, PhD, 94. **CAREER** Asst prof Rel, New Col of the Univ S Fla, 94-99; Postdoc fel, Ctr Philos Rel, Univ Notre Dame, 98-99; Asst Prof Theology, Univ of Notre Dame, 99-. **HONORS AND AWARDS** Whiting fel, 92; Mellon Grad Prize fel, 92; Mellon fel Hum, 89; Phi Beta Kappa, 88. **MEMBERSHIPS** Amer Acad Rel; Amer Philos Asn; Amer Soc 18th c stud (s); Soc Christian Ethics; Hume Soc. **RESEARCH** History of Modern Moral Philosophy; Cambridge Platonists, Modern religious thought. **SELECTED PUBLICATIONS** Auth, Cruelty, Liberalism, and the Quarantine of Irony: Rorty on the Disjunction Between Public and Private, Soundings 75, 92; Opposite Sentiments: Hume's Fear of Faction and the Philosophy of Religion, Amer Jour Theol and Philos, Sept 95; auth, Religion and Faction in Hume's Moral Philosophy, Cambridge UP, 97; auth, Asasdair MacIntyre's Rationality of Traditions and Tradition-Transcendental Standards of Justification, The Journal of Religion 78 (98): 524-46; auth, Free Choice, Self-Referential Arguments, and the New Natural Law, American Catholic Philosophical 72 (98): 581-600; auth, Cudworth, Autonomy, and the Love of God: Transcending Enlgihtenment and Anti-Enlightenment Christian Ethics, The Annual of the Society of Christian Ethics 19 (99): 47-68; auth, Superstition and the Timid Sex, in Feminist Interpretations of David Hume, ed Anne Jaap Jacobse, Penn State Press (00): 283-307. **CONTACT ADDRESS** Dept of Theology, Univ of Notre Dame, 3270 O'Shaughnessy Hall, Notre Dame, IN 46556. **EMAIL** herdt.1@nd.edu

HERMAN, ARTHUR L.
PERSONAL Born 11/16/1930, Minneapolis, MN, m, 1956, 2 children **DISCIPLINE** PHILOSOPHY **EDUCATION** Univ Minn, PhD, 70. **CAREER** Prof; Univ Wis-SP, 65-; fac adv, Philos Club, 84-; ch, Search and Screen Comt for Assoc Dean; fac adv, Col Letters and Sci; Univ Honors Soc, 86-88; dir, Univ Honors Prog, 86-88. **HONORS AND AWARDS** Univ Scholar awd, 93; Acad Letters & Sci awd for Scholarship, 90; Excellence in Tchg awd, 73 and 68. **SELECTED PUBLICATIONS** Auth, The Problem of Evil and Indian Thought, New Delhi, Oxford: 94; The Way of the Lotus:Critical Reflections on the Ethics of the Saddharmapundarika Sutra, Asian Philos, 97. **CONTACT ADDRESS** Dept Religious Studies, Univ of Wisconsin, Stevens Point, Stevens Point, WI 54481.

HERMAN, JONATHAN R.
PERSONAL Born 05/13/1957, Hartford, CT, m, 1992, 1 child **DISCIPLINE** TAOISM, CONFUCIANISM, BUDDHISM, MYSTICISM **EDUCATION** Harvard Univ, PhD, 92. **CAREER** Assoc prof, Ga State Univ. **HONORS AND AWARDS** Cert of Distinction in Tchg, Harvard Univ. **MEMBERSHIPS** Am Acad of Relig; Asn for Asian Studies; Soc for the Study of Chinese Religions. **RESEARCH** Comparative study of mysticism, religion and popular culture, theory, and method in the study of religion. **SELECTED PUBLICATIONS** Auth, I and Tao: Martin Buber's Encounter With Chuang Tzu. **CONTACT ADDRESS** Dept of Philos, Georgia State Univ, Box 4089, Atlanta, GA 30302-4089. **EMAIL** jherman2@gsu.edu

HERMAN, STEWART W.
PERSONAL Born 09/25/1948, m **DISCIPLINE** SOCIAL ETHICS **EDUCATION** Univ Chicago, Divinity Sch, 88. **CAREER** Asst Prof, Concordia Col, Moorhead, Minn, 88-. **MEMBERSHIPS** SCE, AAR, SBE, Assoc of Core Texts and Courses; Acad Mgt. **RESEARCH** Business Ethics. **SELECTED PUBLICATIONS** Auth, Durable Goods: A Covenantal Ethic for Management and Employees, Univ of Notre Dame, 97; Luther, Law and Social Covenants: Cooperative Self-Obligation in the Reconstruction of Lutheran Social Ethics, Journal of Religious Ethics, 97; co-ed, Business Ethics Quarterly 7:2, 97; The Modern Corporation and an Ethics of Trust, Journal of Religious Ethics, 92. **CONTACT ADDRESS** Dept Religion, Concordia Col, Minnesota, Moorhead, MN 56562. **EMAIL** herman@cord.edu

HERMANN, ROBERT M.
PERSONAL Born 07/29/1921, Philadelphia, PA, m, 1992 **DISCIPLINE** PHILOSOPHY **EDUCATION** Univ Pittsburgh, PhD, 62. **CAREER** Indiana Univ Panna, prof, dept ch, 59-87. **MEMBERSHIPS** APA **CONTACT ADDRESS** 155 Wrigden Run Rd., Marion Center, PA 15759-7201.

HERNANDEZ, ARTHUR E.
PERSONAL Born 08/04/1954, San Antonio, TX **DISCIPLINE** PSYCHOLOGY, PHILOSPHY **EDUCATION** St. Mary's Univ, BA, 75; MA, 78; Univ Tex San Antonio, MA, 82; Tex A&M Univ Col Station Tex, PhD, 87. **CAREER** Instruct Specialist, Chemn of English Dept, Edgewood Independent Sch Dist San Antonio Tex, 76-79; Consult, Alamo Are Teacher's Center, San Antonio Tex, 79; Teacher, San Antonio Independent Sch Dist, 79-80; Educ Specialist, Acad of Health Sci, Ft. Sam Houston Tex, 80-82; Teaching Asst, Tex A&M Univ, Col Station Tex, 83; Assoc Sch Psychologist, San Antonio Independent Sch Dist, 84-85; Project Dir, Tex A&M Univ, Col Station Tex, 85-88; Dir of Enrichment Serv, Hisp Asn of Col and Univ, 88-89; Lectr, Our Lady of the Lake Univ, San Antonio Tex, 89; Instr, Incarnate Word Col, San Antonio Tex, 89; Assoc Prof, Univ of Tex San Antonio, 89-; Dir Interdisciplinary Studies Prog, Univ of Tex at San Antonio, 98-. **HONORS AND AWARDS** IWW, Kellags Found Fel, 99-01. **MEMBERSHIPS** Am Educ Res Asn, Nat Asn of Sch Psychologists. **RESEARCH** Measurement, evaluation, multiculturalism. **SELECTED PUBLICATIONS** Auth, "Do Role Models Influence Self Efficacy and Aspiration in Mexican American At-Risk Females," Hisp J of Behav Sci 17-2 (95); coauth, "The Role of Student, Instructor and Administrator Perceptions of Effective Teaching," J of Excellence in Col Teaching 6-3 (96); auth, "Attention Deficit Disorder/Hyperactivity Disorder: A Primer," Prof Med Asst (Nov/Dec 96); coauth, We the People, Houghton Mifflin Elem Soc Studies Ser, 97; auth, "Percentiles: Debunking The Myths," Prof Med Asst (Mar/Apr 97); coauth, "A Pilot Study of the Bienstar Health Program: A Diabetes Risk Factor Prevention," J of Sch Health 68-2 (98): 62-67; auth, "Observational Learning: Modeling and Patient Education," Prof Med Asst (Jan/Feb 98); coauth, "Bienstar: A Diabetes Risk Factor Modification Program," Diabetes 48, suppl 1 (99): A305; auth, Success in the Classroom: Maximizing the Opportunity of American Diversity, Houghton Mifflin Publ Co (Boston), in press; ed, Appleseeds, Cobblestone Publ Co (Peterborough, NH), in press. **CONTACT ADDRESS** Dept Educ, Univ of Texas, San Antonio, 6900 N Loop 1604 W, San Antonio, TX 78249. **EMAIL** aehernandez@utsa.edu

HERR, STANLEY S.
PERSONAL Born 08/07/1945, Newark, NJ, m, 1979, 3 children **DISCIPLINE** LAW **EDUCATION** Yale Univ, BA, 67; Yale Law Sch, JD, 70; Oxford Univ, DPhil, 79. **CAREER** Assoc prof to prof, Univ of Md Law Sch, 83-; vis crossman prof, Univ of Haifz, 99-. **HONORS AND AWARDS** Fulbright Fel, 90-91; White House Kennedy Fel, 93-94; Distinguished Res Fel, U.S. Dept of Educ. **MEMBERSHIPS** Am Asn on Metal Retardation. **RESEARCH** Human rights, disability law. **SELECTED PUBLICATIONS** Auth, Aging, Rights, and Quality of Life: Prospects for Older People with Developmental Disabilities, Brookes Pub, 99. **CONTACT ADDRESS** Sch of Law, Univ of Maryland, Baltimore, 515 W Lombard St, Baltimore, MD 21201-1701.

HERRERA, ENRIQUE
PERSONAL Born 02/22/1965, Peru, m **DISCIPLINE** SPANISH, ECONOMICS **EDUCATION** Pontificia Univ Catolica del Peru, BS; Fla State Univ, MA; PhD. **CAREER** Instr, Luther Col, 92-93; asst prof, Valparaiso Univ, 98-00. **RESEARCH** Golden Age Narrative and Theater, Contemporary Hispanic Narrative. **CONTACT ADDRESS** Dept For Lang, Valparaiso Univ, 651 College Ave, Valparaiso, IN 46383-6461. **EMAIL** enrique.herrera@valpo.edu

HERRERA, ROBERT ANTHONY
PERSONAL Born 10/31/1933, Spring Lake, NJ, m **DISCIPLINE** MEDIEVAL PHILOSOPHY, PHILOSOPHY OF RELIGION **EDUCATION** Col St Thomas, BA, 53; New Sch Soc Res, MA, 65, PhD, 75. **CAREER** Vis asst prof philos, Rutgers Univ, 70-71; assoc prof, 73-79, Prof Philos, Seton Hall Univ, 79-97, Prof Emeritus, 98-; Adj fac, New Sch Soc Res, 68-73, Baruch Col, 70-72 & Immaculate Conception Sem, 70-71; consult, Judeao-Christian Inst, Seton, 76- & Christendom Col, 77. **HONORS AND AWARDS** Seton Hall Univ res grant, 77, 78, 79, 82, 84; Canagie summer grant, 70; NS Hum grant, 82; Wilbur Found grant, 95; Earhart Found grant, 98. **MEMBERSHIPS** Am Philos Asn; Am Cath Philos Asn. **RESEARCH**

Early medieval thought (emphasis on Anselm); the Augustinian tradition; 19th-20th century Span polit thought (emphasis on Donoso Cortes). **SELECTED PUBLICATIONS** Auth, John of the Cross: Introductory studies, Rev Espiritualidad, Madrid, 68; contribr, God in Contemporary Thought Nauwelaerts, Louvain, 77; auth, Anselm's Proslogion, Univ Press, 78; contribr, J Hist Philos, Mod Schoolman, Angus Triniana, Philos Today & Analecta Anselmiana; Lamps of Fire, St Bedes Pub, 79; Donoso Contes: Cassandrs of the Age; Eerdmans, 95; ed, Mystics of the Book, Peter Lang, 93; Saints Scholars and Sovereigns, Peter Lang, 94. **CONTACT ADDRESS** Dept of Philos, Seton Hall Univ, So Orange, 400 S Orange Ave, South Orange, NJ 07079-2697.

HERRUP, CYNTHIA
PERSONAL Born 03/10/1950, Miami Beach, FL **DISCIPLINE** HISTORY, LAW **EDUCATION** Northwestern Univ, PhD, 82. **CAREER** Asst prof, Univ of Mich, 81-84; Asst Prof, 84-88, Assoc Prof, 88-91, Prof of Law, Duke Univ, 91-; vis prof, Birkbeck Col, Univ of London, 98- ; ed, J of Brit Studies, 91-96. **HONORS AND AWARDS** Distinguished vis, Centre for British Studies, Univ of Adelaide, 98; fel, Royal Hist Soc, 86-; Walter D. Love Prize, North Am Confr on British Studies, 86; NEH/Folger Shakespeare Libr Fel, 96-97; John Simon Guggenheim Fel, 89-90; NEH Fel for Univ Teachers, 88-89; ACLS Recent Recipients of the PhD Awd, 84; Fletcher Jones Found Dist Fel, Henry E. Huntington Lib, 00-01. **MEMBERSHIPS** Am Hist Asn; Am Soc for Legal Hist; North Am Confr on British Studies. **RESEARCH** Early modern Britain; legal hist; social hist. **SELECTED PUBLICATIONS** Auth, Crimes Most Dishonorable: Sex, Law, and the 2nd Earl of Castlehaven, Oxford Univ Press, 99; The Common Peace: Participation and the Criminal Law in Seventeenth-Century England, Cambridge Univ Press, 87; The Pluck Bright Honour from the Pale-Fac'd Moon: Gender and Honor in the Castlehaven Story, Transactions of the Royal Hist Soc, 96; The Patriarch at Home. The Trial of the Earl of Castlehaven for Rape and Sodomy, Hist Workshop J, 96; Law and Morality in Seventeenth-Century England, Past & Present, 85; auth, Finding the Bodies, GLQ, 99. **CONTACT ADDRESS** Dept of Hist, Duke Univ, Box 90719, Durham, NC 27708. **EMAIL** cherrup@duke.edu

HERTIG, PAUL
PERSONAL Born 09/06/1955, Minneapolis, MN, m, 1983, 1 child **DISCIPLINE** BIBLICAL THEOLOGY **EDUCATION** Fuller Theol Sem, PhD, 95. **CAREER** Asoc dean, prof missiology, World Mission Univ, 95-98; lectr, New Testament, Azusa Pacific Univ, 95-98; assoc prof, world Christianity, United Theol Sem, 98-. **HONORS AND AWARDS** Theol award, diss, 95; Azuse Pacific Univ mini-grant, 97, 98. **MEMBERSHIPS** Soc of Bibl Lit; Am Soc of Missiology. **RESEARCH** Matthew and mission; Luke-Acts and mission; mission and marginalization. **SELECTED PUBLICATIONS** Auth, The Role of Mission in Church Renewal: Matthean Foundations, Am Baptist Quart, 96; auth, The Galilee Theme in Matthew: Transforming Mission through Marginality, Missiology, 97; auth, Galilean Christianity, in Dictionary of the Later New Testament and Its Developments, InterVarsity, 97; auth, The Multi-Ethnic Journeys of Jesus in Matthew: Margin-Center Dynamics, Missiology, 98; auth, The Jubilee Mission of Jesus in the Gospel of Luke: Reversals of Fortunes, Missiology, 98; auth, Matthew's Narrative Use of Galilee in the Multicultural and Missiological Journeys of Jesus, Mellen Bibl, 98; auth, "Geographical Marginality in the Matthean Journeys of Jesus," SBL 1999 Pr, 99. **CONTACT ADDRESS** 1810 Harvard Blvd., Dayton, OH 45406. **EMAIL** phertig@united.edu

HERTIG, YOUNG LEE
PERSONAL Born 03/02/1954, Seoul, Korea, m, 1983, 1 child **DISCIPLINE** THEOLOGY **EDUCATION** Yonsei Grad Univ, MA, 79; Bethel Theol Sem, MA, 83; Fuller Theol Sem, MA, 87, PhD, 91. **CAREER** Asst prof, 92-95, adj prof, 96-98, cross cultural ministry, Fuller Theol Sem; assoc prof, Vera B Blinn Chair, World Christianity, United Theol Sem, 98- . **HONORS AND AWARDS** Assoc for Theol Sch grant, 93; Global Res Inst grant, 96. **MEMBERSHIPS** Asn of Prof of Mission; Am Acad Relig. **RESEARCH** Reconciliation and peacemaking inside out, from interdisciplinary perspectives. **SELECTED PUBLICATIONS** Auth, Coping as a Minority Female Leader, Theol News and Notes, 93; auth, On Liberating Theology from Sexual, Racial Bias, Los Angeles Times, 94; auth, Expanding and Balancing Our Horizons, Korean Christian J, 96; auth, Asian- American Women in the Workplace and the Church, in Ng, ed, People On the Way: Asian North Americans Discovering Christ, Culture, and Community, Valley Forge, 96; auth, Sugar/Sugary, in Banks, ed, The Complete Book of Everyday Christianity: An A-to-Z Guide to Following Christ in Every Aspect of Life, InterVarsity, 97; auth, The Asian-American Alternative to Feminism: A Yinist Paradigm, Missiology: An Int Rev, 98. **CONTACT ADDRESS** 1443 N Euclid Ave, Dayton, OH 45406. **EMAIL** yhertig@united.edu

HERTZ, RICHARD C.
DISCIPLINE JUDAISM **EDUCATION** Univ Cincinnati, BA; Northwestern Univ, PhD. **CAREER** Ch, Jewish Stud; ordained, Hebrew Union Col in Cincinnati; honorary doct, Hebrew Union College-Jewish Inst Rel and Univ of Detroit Mercy; prof, Univ of Detroit Mercy, 70-. **HONORS AND AWARDS** Temple Beth El as their spirtual leader for the past forty-three years. **RESEARCH** Introduction to Judaism, Bibical courses, history of Judaism and the Jewish people, modern Jewish life and thought, and the Holocaust **CONTACT ADDRESS** Dept of Religious Studies, Univ of Detroit Mercy, 4001 W McNichols Rd, PO Box 19900, Detroit, MI 48219-0900. **EMAIL** HERTZRC@udmercy.edu

HERWITZ, DAVID RICHARD
PERSONAL Born 12/08/1925, Lynn, MA, m, 1960, 2 children **DISCIPLINE** LAW **EDUCATION** Mass Inst Technol, BS, 46; Harvard Univ, LLB, 49. **CAREER** Assoc prof, 54-57, Prof Law, Harvard Univ, 57-, Consult, US Treasury Dept, 60-63. **SELECTED PUBLICATIONS** Auth, Stock redemptions and the accumulated earnings tax, 61, Allocation of stock between services and capital, 62 & Installment repurchase of stock: Surplus limitations, 65, Harvard Law Rev; Business Planning, 66, Corporations Game Plan, 75; Accounting for Lawyers, 2nd ed, 97, with Barrett, Foundation Press. **CONTACT ADDRESS** Dept of Law, Harvard Univ, Cambridge, MA 02138. **EMAIL** herwitz@law.harvard.edu

HERZOG, PETER EMILIUS
PERSONAL Born 12/25/1925, Vienna, Austria, m, 1970, 2 children **DISCIPLINE** LAW **EDUCATION** Hobart Col, BA, 52; Syracuse Univ, JD, 55; Columbia Univ, LLM, 56. **CAREER** From dep asst attorney gen to asst attorney gen, NY State Dept Law, 56-58; from asst prof to assoc prof, 58-66, law librn, 60-67, Prof Law, Col Law, Syracuse Unix, 66-, Legal asst metropolitan areas studies, NY State Joint Legis Comt, 58-60; staff mem, Prof Int Procedure, Columbia Univ Law Sch, 60-64, assoc dir, Proj European Legal Inst, 68; consult, NY State Comt Eminent Domain, 71-72; assoc prof, Univ Paris, 76-77. **MEMBERSHIPS** Am Soc Int Law; Soc Comp Legis, France. **RESEARCH** Conflict of law; comparative law; law of European communities. **SELECTED PUBLICATIONS** Auth, Brussels and Lugano, Should you Race to the Courthouse or Race for a Judgment, Am J Comp Law, Vol 0043, 95. **CONTACT ADDRESS** Col of Law, Syracuse Univ, Syracuse, NY 13210. **EMAIL** herzog@law.syr.edu

HESLEP, ROBERT DURHAM
PERSONAL Born 12/18/1930, Houston, TX, m, 1964, 2 children **DISCIPLINE** PHILOSOPHY OF EDUCATION **EDUCATION** Tex Christian Univ, AB, 55; Univ Chicago, AM, 57, PhD(philos educ), 63. **CAREER** Teacher, Harvard Sch Boys, Chicago, 58-63; instr philos educ, Pestalozzi-Froebel Teachers Col, Chicago, 59-61; assoc prof educ found & philos, Edinboro State Col, 63-65; assoc prof, 65-72, prof philos of educ, Univ GA, 72-, consult, Res for Better Sch, 76-77; adv, Nat Soc for Study Educ, 76-77; mem, Philos of Educ Soc Comn to Analy Am Educ, 74-75. **MEMBERSHIPS** Philos Educ Soc (pres, 76-77); Southeast Philos Educ Soc (pres, 71-72). **RESEARCH** The concept of action; philosophy of mind; political philosophy; moral education. **SELECTED PUBLICATIONS** Auth, Thomas Jefferson & Education, Random, 69; ed, Philosophy of Education, 1971, Philos Educ Soc, 71; co-ed, Social Justice and Preferential Treatment, Univ Ga, 77; auth, The Mental in Education: A Philosophical Study, Univ Ala Press, 81; auth, Education in Democracy, Iowa State Univ Press, 89; auth, Moral Education for Americans, Praeger, 95; auth, Philosophical Thinking in Educational Practice, Praeger, 97. **CONTACT ADDRESS** Col of Educ, Univ of Georgia, 308 River's Crossing, Athens, GA 30602-0001. **EMAIL** rheslep@uga.edu

HESS, RICHARD S.
PERSONAL Born 12/17/1954, Lancaster, PA, m, 1996, 3 children **DISCIPLINE** RELIGION **EDUCATION** Wheaton Col, BA, 76; Trinity Evangel Divinity Sch, MDiv, 79; ThM, 80; Hebrew Union Col, PhD, 84. **CAREER** Prof, Denver Sem, 97-; rd, Reohampton Inst London, 95-97; lectr, Glasgow Bibl Col, 89-95; instr, Univ Sheffield, 88-89; guest lectr, St. George's Col, 86; lectr, Loyola Univ, 84-85; lectr, Xavier Univ, 83-84; tutor, Hebrew Union Col, 81-84. **HONORS AND AWARDS** Nat Endowment Hum Fel for Col Tchrs & Independent Scholars, 96-97; Nat Endowment Hum Summer Travel Grant, 90; Tyndale House Res Fel, 86-89, 90; Fulbright Post-Dr Res Fel, 86; Nat Endowment Hum/Am Sch Oriental Res Fel, 85; David Lefkowicz Interfaith Fel, Hebrew Union Col, 79-82; Isaac & Rachel Berg Found Fel, Hebrew Union Col, 81-82; Erna & Julius Krouch Fund Fel, Hebrew Union Col, 82-84. **MEMBERSHIPS** Am Oriental Soc; Am Sch Oriental Res; British Asn Near Eastern Archaeol; Cath Bibl Asn Am; Inst Bibl Res; Int Orgn Study Old Testament; Israel Exploration Soc; Soc Study Old Testament; Soc Bibl Lit. **RESEARCH** Hebrew Bible; Genesis 1-11; Deuteronomistic history; comparative philology; ancient Near East; West Semitic archives; personal names; Leviticus. **SELECTED PUBLICATIONS** Auth, "Achan and Anchor: Names and Wordplay in Joshua 7," Hebrew Annual Rev (94); auth, Alalakh and the Bible: Obstacle or Contribution?, Scripture & Other Artifacts: Essays Archael & Bibl in Honor of Philip J. King, 94; auth, Fallacies in the Study of Early Israel: An Onomastic Perspective, Tyndale Bull, 94; auth, One Hundred Fifty Years of Comparative Studies on Genesis 1-11: An Overview, I Studies Inscriptions Before the Flood: Ancient Near Eastern Literary & Linguistic Approaches to Genesis 1-11, 94; auth, Asking Historical Questions of Joshua 13-19: Recent Discussion Concerning the Date of the Boundary Lists, Faith, Tradition, Hist: Old Testament Hist in Its Near Eastern Context, 94; auth, "Bringing Alive the Old Testament: Its Role in the Wider Curriculum," in Make the Old Testament Come Live: From Curriculum to Classroom, ed. R.S. Hess and G.J. Wenham (Eerdmans, Grand Rapids, 98), 3-18; auth, "Issues in the Study of Personal Names in the Hebrew Bible," Currents in Biblical Research 6 (98): 169-192; auth, "Joshua 10 and the Sun that Stood Still," Buried History 35.1 (99): 26-33; coed, Zion, City of Our God, Eerdmans (Grand Rapids), 99; ed, Denver Jour: An Online Review of Current Biblical and Theological Studies, www.DenverSeminary.edu. **CONTACT ADDRESS** Dept of Old Testament, Denver Conservative Baptist Sem, PO Box 100,000, Denver, CO 80250-0100. **EMAIL** rick@densem.edu

HESTER, D. MICAH
PERSONAL Born 07/16/1966, Pomona, CA, m, 1993, 1 child **DISCIPLINE** PHILOSOPHY **EDUCATION** Pomona Col, BA, 88; Vanderbilt Univ, MA, 95; PhD, 98. **CAREER** Adj Asst Prof, TN State Univ, 93-96 and 98-99; asst prof, Biomedical ethics, 99-. **MEMBERSHIPS** Soc for the Adv of Amer Philo; Assoc of Pract & Prof Ethics; Amer Soc of Bioethics & Humanities; APA. **RESEARCH** Bioethics; amer philo; computer ethics. **SELECTED PUBLICATIONS** The Place of Community in Medical Encounters, Jour of Med and Phil, 98; Competition or Community: Ethical Concerns in the Residency Matching Process, JAMA, 98. **CONTACT ADDRESS** School of Medicine, Mercer Univ, Macon, 1550 Col St., Macon, GA 31207-0001. **EMAIL** d.hester@columbia.net

HESTER, JAMES D.
PERSONAL Born 02/15/1939, Philadelphia, PA, m, 1961 **DISCIPLINE** RELIGION **EDUCATION** Eastern Baptist Col, BA, 60; Calif Baptist Theol Sem, BD, 63; Univ Basel, DTheol, 66. **CAREER** Asst prof, Univ Redlands, 67-; prof of relig, 67-98; dir, Rhetorical New Testament Project; emer, 98-; res prof, 01-03; Dir, Rhetorical New Testament Project, Inst for Antiquity and Christianity. **HONORS AND AWARDS** Fac Member of the Year, 69-70; Distinguished Teaching Awd, 89; Honorary member, Phi Beta Kappa, 95; Fac Service Awd, 93; Fel, Jesus Seminar. **MEMBERSHIPS** Soc Biblical Lit; Studiorum Novi Testamentum Soc. **RESEARCH** NT Rhetorical Criticism and General Thoeries of Rhetoric. **SELECTED PUBLICATIONS** Auth, The Rhetorical Structure of Galatians 1:11-2:14, 84; The Use and Influence of Rhetoric in Galatians 2:1-14, 86; Placing the Blame: The Presence of Epideictic in Galatians 1 and 2, Sheffield Acad, 91; ed, "Creating the Future: Apocalytic Rheetoric in 1 Thessalonians," Relig and Theol 7, (00); 192-212; ed, Journal for the Study of Rhetorical Criticism of the New Testament. **CONTACT ADDRESS** Dept of Religion, Univ of Redlands, 1200 E Colton Ave, PO Box 3090, Redlands, CA 92373-0999. **EMAIL** hester@uor.edu

HESTER, LEE
PERSONAL Born 06/23/1961, Oklahoma City, OK, m, 1987 **DISCIPLINE** PHILOSOPHY **EDUCATION** Univ Okla, BA, 87; MA, 91; PhD, 99. **CAREER** Adj Prof, Okla City Univ, 94-99; vis asst prof, Lakehead Univ, Ontario, 96; asst prof & dir of Am Indian Studies, Univ of Science and Arts of Okla, 00-; **HONORS AND AWARDS** President's Awd for Excellence for Environ Protection Servs. **MEMBERSHIPS** APA, Am Indian Philos Asn. **RESEARCH** Native American sovereignty, Native American philosophy, environmental ethics. **SELECTED PUBLICATIONS** Auth, Pishukch: One Choctaw's Examination of the Differences in English and Choctaw Lanage Use," Ayaangwaamizin: The Int J of Indigenous Philos, vol 1, no 1 (97); auth, Political Principles and Indian Sovereignty, Garland Publ, forthcoming; auth, "Assimilation Redux: Indigenous Worlds meet Post(?) Modern Evolutionary Ecological Environmental Ethics," Environment Ethics, forthcoming. **CONTACT ADDRESS** Dept Philos & Am Indian Studies, Univ of Science and Arts of Oklahoma, 1353 Dorchester Dr, Norman, OK 73069. **EMAIL** leehester@aol.com

HESTER, MARCUS B.
PERSONAL Born 06/20/1937, Raleigh, NC, m, 1998, 1 child **DISCIPLINE** PHILOSOPHY **EDUCATION** Wake Forest Col, BA, 60; Vanderbilt Univ, PhD, 64. **CAREER** From instr to assoc prof, 63-76, prof philos, 76-, Wake Forest Univ; fel, coop prog humanities, Univ NC, Chapel Hill, 66-67. **MEMBERSHIPS** Southern Soc Philos & Psychol; Am Soc Aesthet. **RESEARCH** Aesthetics; philosophy of mind; contemporary analytical philosophy. **SELECTED PUBLICATIONS** Auth, The Meaning of Poetic Metaphor, Mouton, 67; art, Purpose In Painting And Action, Am Philos Quart, 1/70; art, Are Paintings And Photographs Inherently Interpretative, J Aesthet & Art Criticism, winter 72; art, Sensibility And Visual Acts, Am Philos Quart, 10/75; art, Aristotle on Function of Man in Relation to Eudaimonia, Hist of Phil Quarterly, 91. **CONTACT ADDRESS** Dept of Philosophy, Wake Forest Univ, PO Box 7332, Winston-Salem, NC 27109-7332. **EMAIL** hester@wfu.edu

HESTEVOID, H. SCOTT
PERSONAL Born 03/26/1952, Nashville, TN, m, 1979, 2 children **DISCIPLINE** PHILOSOPHY **EDUCATION** Vanderbilt

Univ, BA, 74; Brown Univ, AM, 78, PhD, 78. **CAREER** Prof, Univ Ala, 78- . **HONORS AND AWARDS** Richard M. Griffith mem awd, 79, Southern Soc Philos and Psych. **MEMBERSHIPS** SSPP; APA. **RESEARCH** Analytic metaphysics; moral psychology. **SELECTED PUBLICATIONS** Auth, Conjoining, Philos and Phenomen Res, XLI, 81, 371-385; Disjunctive Desert, Amer Philos Quart, 20, 83, 357-363; Justice to Mercy, Philos and Phenomen Res, XLVI, 85, 281-291; Passage and the Presence of Experience, Philos and Phenomen Res, L, 90, 537-552, reprinted in The New Theory of Time, ed, Oaklander and Smith, Yale UP, 94; Berkeley's Theory of Time, Hist of Philos Quart, 7, 90, 179-192; The Concept of Religion, Public Affairs Quart, 5, 91, 149-162; The Anselmian Single-Divine-Attribute Doctrine, Relig Stud (s), 29, 93, 63-77; coauth, On Passage and Persistence, Amer Philos Quart, 31, 94, 269-283. **CONTACT ADDRESS** Dept of Philosophy, Univ of Alabama, Tuscaloosa, PO Box 870218, Tuscaloosa, AL 35487. **EMAIL** hhestevo@philos.as.ua.edu

HETZEL, OTTO J.
PERSONAL Born 06/02/1933, New York, NY, m, 1957, 3 children **DISCIPLINE** LAW **EDUCATION** Pa State Univ, BA, 55; Yale Univ, JD, 60; Harvard Univ, LLM, 70. **CAREER** Dept atty gen, State of Calif, 60-64 & 65-67; assoc, Hardy, Carley & Love, Palo Alto, Calif, 64-65; asst gen counsel equal opportunity & labor relat, US Dept Housing & Urban Develop, 67-68, assoc gen counsel model cities & govt relat, 68-69; prof law, Wayne State Univ, 70-75, assoc dir, Ctr Urban Studies, 70-72; vis prof, Univ Man, Inst Sci & Technol, 75-76; Prof Law to prof emer, Wayne State Univ, 76-, Lectr, George Washington Univ, 69-70; consult, US Dept Housing & Urban Develop, 69-72, city of Kansas City, Mo, 72-73 & Urban Inst, Wash, DC, 75-78; ed, Urban Law & Policy, 77-; vis prof, State Univ Utrecht, Holland, 80. **MEMBERSHIPS** Am Bar Asn; Soc Am Law Teachers. **RESEARCH** Urban housing and community development programs; legislative law and process; communications law-cable television. **SELECTED PUBLICATIONS** Auth, Some Historical Lessons for Implementing the Clinton Administrations Empowerment Zones and Enterprise Communities Program--Experiences From the Model-Cities Program, Urban Lawyer, 94. **CONTACT ADDRESS** Sch of Law, Wayne State Univ, Detroit, MI 48202.

HEXHAM, IRVING
PERSONAL Born 04/14/1943, Whitehaven, England **DISCIPLINE** RELIGION **EDUCATION** Univ Lancaster, BA, 70; Univ Bristol, MA, 72, PhD, 75. **CAREER** Asst prof, Bishop Lonsdale Col, 74-77; asst prof, Regent Col, 77-80; asst prof, Univ Man, 80-84; asst to assoc prof, 84-92, PROF RELIGIOUS STUDIES, UNIV CALGARY, 92-. **MEMBERSHIPS** S African Inst Race Relations; Can Soc Stud Relig; Am Acad Relig; Soc Sci Stud Relig; Berlin Missiological Soc; S African Missiological Soc; Royal Anthrop Inst. **SELECTED PUBLICATIONS** Auth, The Irony of Apartheid, 81; coauth, New Religions as Global Cultures: The Sacralization of the Human, 77; coauth, Understanding Cults and New Religions, 86; auth/comp, A Concise Dictionary of Religion, 93; ed, Texts on Zulu Religion, 86; ed, The Scripture of the Amanazaretha of Ekuphakameni, 94; co-ed, Afro-Christian Religion at the Grassroots in Southern Africa, 91; co-ed, Empirical Studies of African Independent-Indigenous Churches, 92; co-ed, The Oral History and Sacred Traditions of the Nazareth Baptist Church: Volume One-The Story of Isaiah Mdliwamafa Shembe, 96. **CONTACT ADDRESS** Dept of Religious Studies, Univ of Calgary, Calgary, AB, Canada T2N 1N4. **EMAIL** hexham@ucalgary.ca

HEYD, THOMAS
DISCIPLINE PHILOSOPHY **EDUCATION** Univ Calgary, BA, MA; Univ W Ontario, PhD. **CAREER** Instr, Univ Calgary; Univ W Ontario; Univ Alberta; sessional lectr. **RESEARCH** Philosophy of science; aesthetics, environmental philosophy; ethics and history of philosophy. **SELECTED PUBLICATIONS** Pub(s), Intl Philos Quart; Brit Jour Aesthet; Environ Ethics; Jour of the Hist of the Behavioral Sci. **CONTACT ADDRESS** Dept of Philosophy, Univ of Victoria, PO Box 3045, Victoria, BC, Canada V8W 3P4.

HICKS, ALEXANDER
PERSONAL Born 07/18/1946, Jersey City, NJ, m, 1970, 1 child **DISCIPLINE** POLITICAL SCIENCE **EDUCATION** Univ Wisc Madison, PhD, 79. **CAREER** Asst prof, Northwestern University, 79-86; assoc prof to prof, Emory Univ, 86-. **HONORS AND AWARDS** Nat Sci Found Fel, 71-72; Nat Opinion Res Fel, 81-82. **MEMBERSHIPS** ASA; APSA; SASE. **RESEARCH** Political Sociology/Economy of Social and Economic Policy. **SELECTED PUBLICATIONS** Coauth, "Civil Disorders, Relief Mobilization, and AFDC Caseloads: Piven and Cloward Reexamined", Am J of Polit Sci, 83; auth, "Elections, Keynes, Bureaucracy and Class: Explaining US Budget Deficits, 1961-1;978", Am Sociol Rev 84; auth, "National Collective Action and Economic Performance", Int Studies Quarterly, 88; auth, "Social Democratic Corporatism and Economic Growth", J of Politics, 88; coauth, "Politics, Institutions and Welfare Policy", Am Polit Sci Rev 92; coed, The Comparative Political Economy of the Welfare State, Cambridge Univ Pr, 94; coauth, "Cooperation and Political Economic Performance in Affluent Capitalist Democracies", Am J of Sociol 98; auth, Social Democracy and Welfare Capitalism: A Century of Income Security Politics, Cornell Univ Pr, 99. **CONTACT ADDRESS** Dept Sociol, Emory Univ, 1364 Clifton Rd NE, Atlanta, GA 30322-0001. **EMAIL** ahicks@emory.edu

HICKS, H. BEECHER, JR.
PERSONAL Born 06/17/1944, Baton Rouge, LA, m **DISCIPLINE** THEOLOGY **EDUCATION** Univ of AR Pine Bluff, BA 1964; Colgate Rochester, MDiv 1967, Dr of Ministry 1975; Richmond Virginia Seminary LLD honorary. **CAREER** Second Baptist Church, intern pastorate 1965-68; Irondequoit United Church of Christ, minister to youth 1967-68; Mt Ararat Baptist Church, sr minister 1968-73; Antioch Baptist Church, minister 1973-77; Metro Baptist Church, Sr Minister 1977-; Colgate Rochester Divinity School and United Theological Seminary, Adj Prof. **MEMBERSHIPS** Chmn Bd of Funeral Dirs 1985; vp, Eastern Reg Natl Black Pastors Conf; admin Natl Black Pastors Conf; bd Council for Court Excellence; asst sec Progressive Natl Baptist Convention, Co-chair American Baptist Ministers Council of D.C., pres Kerygma Assoc, A Religious Consulting Service; pres Martin Luther King Fellows, Inc; co-chair Ministers in Partnership (Pregnancy Prevention); board of trustees, United Theological Seminary, Dayton, OH. **SELECTED PUBLICATIONS** "Give Me This Mountain" Houston TX 1976; "Images of the Black Preacher, The Man Nobody Knows" Valley Forge PA 1977; "The Black Church as a Support System for Black Men on the Simon Syndrome" Howard Univ; Comm Leaders & Noteworthy Amers 1977; Gubernatorial Citation for Serv 1977; Martin Luther King Fellowship in Black Church Studies 1972-75; Preaching Through A Storm Zondervan Press 1987; author, Correspondence with a Cripple from Tarsus, Zondervan Press, 1990. **CONTACT ADDRESS** Metropolitan Baptist Church, 1225 R St NW, Washington, DC 20009.

HICKS, STEPHEN R. C.
PERSONAL Born Toronto, ON, Canada, m, 2000, 1 child **DISCIPLINE** PHILOSOPHY **EDUCATION** Univ Guelph, BA, MA, 85; Ind Univ, PhD, 92. **CAREER** Assoc prof & CHEMN, Rockford Col, 92-. **MEMBERSHIPS** Amer Philos Asn; Soc for Bus Ethics; Ayn Rand Soc. **RESEARCH** Objectivism; Intellectual history; Business ethics Postmodernism. **SELECTED PUBLICATIONS** Auth, Readings for Logical Analysis, WW Norton & Co, 98. **CONTACT ADDRESS** Dept. of Philosophy, Rockford Col, Rockford, IL 61108. **EMAIL** shicks@rockford.edu

HIEBERT, THEODORE
PERSONAL Born 07/24/1946, Paraguay, m, 1979, 2 children **DISCIPLINE** RELIGION **EDUCATION** Fresno Pacific Univ, BA, 68; Princeton Theological Seminary, MDiv, 76; Harvard Univ, PhD, 84. **CAREER** Assoc Prof, Harvard Divinity Sch, 86-95; vis asst prof, Gustarus Adolphus Col, 92-95; asst prof, Louisiana State Univ, 95-96; prof, McCormick Theol Sem, 95-. **MEMBERSHIPS** Society of Biblical Literature. **SELECTED PUBLICATIONS** Auth, God of My Victory, Atlanta: Scholars Press, 86; auth, The Yahuist's Landscape: Nature and Religion in Early Israel, Oxford, 96; co-ed, Realia Dei: Essays in Archaeology and Biblical Interpretation, Atlanta: Scholars Press, 99. **CONTACT ADDRESS** McCormick Theol Sem, 555 South Woodlawn Ave, Chicago, IL 60637-1620. **EMAIL** thiebert@mccormick.edu

HIERONYMI, PAMELA
DISCIPLINE PHILOSOPHY **EDUCATION** Princeton Univ, AB, 92; Harvard Univ, PhD, 00. **CAREER** Asst prof, UCLA, 00-. **HONORS AND AWARDS** Charlotte W. Newcombe Dis Fel, 99-00; Harvard Cen Eth Prof, 98-99; Jacob K. Javits Fel, 94-98. **MEMBERSHIPS** APA; SCP. **RESEARCH** Ethics. **SELECTED PUBLICATIONS** Auth, Articulating an Uncompromising Forgiveness, Philo and Phenom Res (01). **CONTACT ADDRESS** Philosophy Dept, Univ of California, Los Angeles, PO Box 951451, Los Angeles, CA 90095-1451. **EMAIL** hieronym@ucla.edu

HIERS, RICHARD H.
PERSONAL Born 04/08/1932, Philadelphia, PA, m, 1954, 2 children **DISCIPLINE** LAW **EDUCATION** Yale Univ, BA, BD, MA, PhD; Univ Fla, JD. **CAREER** Prof Rel and aff prof Law; Univ Fla, 61-; law clerk, US 5th, Circuit Judge Jerre S. Williams, 87-88. **HONORS AND AWARDS** Phi Beta Kappa, Florida Blue Key Distinguished Faculty Awd, 98, Order of the Coif; Phi Kappa Phi. **MEMBERSHIPS** Fla Bar Public Interest Law Sect; Bar Asn 5th Fed Circuit; US Dist Ct, Western Div Tex; adv commt, J Law and Rel. **RESEARCH** Law, Ethics & Social Policy. **SELECTED PUBLICATIONS** Auth, Southwestern Law Journal; auth, Journal of College and Univ Law; auth, Fith Circuit Reporter; auth, Legal Studies Forum; auth, Cumberland Law Review; auth, Univ of Florida Journal of Law and Public Policy; auth, Journal of Law and Religion; auth, Wayne Law Review. **CONTACT ADDRESS** School of Law, Univ of Florida, PO Box 117625, Gainesville, FL 32611-7625. **EMAIL** hiers@law.ufl.edu

HIGGINS, KATHLEEN MARIE
PERSONAL Born 10/15/1954, Jacksonville, FL, m, 1990 **DISCIPLINE** PHILOSOPHY **EDUCATION** Univ Missouri-Kansas City, music, 77; Yale Univ, MA, 78, MPhil, 79, PhD, philos, 82. **CAREER** Instr, 82-83, asst prof, 83-89, assoc prof, 89-95, prof, 95-, Univ Texas at Austin; visiting asst prof, Univ Calif Riverside, 86-87; visiting sr lecturer, May - June 89, June - July 90, June 91, June 92, visiting prof, June 93, June 94, June 95, May 96, May 98, Univ Auckland, New Zealand. **HONORS AND AWARDS** Univ Res Inst Summer Res Awd, Univ Texas at Austin, 85; resident scholar, Rockefeller Found Bellagio Study and Conf Center, 93; Outstanding Academic Books of 1988-89 (Nietzsche's Zarathustra), Choice; Univ Research Inst Faculty Awd, fall 94; visiting fellow, Australian Natl Univ Philos Dept and Canberra School Music, June-Aug 97. **MEMBERSHIPS** Amer Philos Assn, Comm Status Women, 95-98; Amer Soc Aesthetics; Humanities Tech Assn; North Amer Nietzsche Soc, Exec Comm, 97-; Intl Assn Aesthetics. **RESEARCH** Nineteenth and twentieth century continental philosophy; aesthetics; philosophy of psychology; philosophy of music; ethics; feminism. **SELECTED PUBLICATIONS** Coauth, A Passion for Wisdom, 97; auth, "Death and the Skeleton," in Death and Philosophy, 98; auth, "Nietzsche's Aesthetic: Nietzsche's Literary Style," in Encyclopedia of Aesthetics, 98; coauth, "Emotions: Historical Overview," in The Encyclopedia of Aesthetics, 98; auth, Comic Relief: Nietzche's Frohliche Wissenschaft, 99. **CONTACT ADDRESS** Dept of Philosophy, Univ of Texas, Austin, Austin, TX 78712. **EMAIL** plac645@utxvms.cc.utexas.edu

HIGH, DALLAS MILTON
PERSONAL Born 11/14/1931, Van Wert, OH, m, 1957, 3 children **DISCIPLINE** PHILOSOPHY **EDUCATION** Ohio Wesleyan Univ, BA, 56; Yale Univ, BD, 59; Duke Univ, PhD(-philos relig), 65. **CAREER** From asst prof to assoc prof philos & relig, Hiram Col, 64-69; assoc prof, 69-72, chmn dept, 69-77, Prof Philos, Univ KY, 72-, Danforth assoc 71-; Rockefeller Found res fel, 75-76. **MEMBERSHIPS** Am Philos Asn; Am Acad Relig; Southern Soc Philos & Psychol; Soc Health & Human Values; Soc for Values in Higher Educ. **RESEARCH** Philosophy of religion; health and values; Ludwig Wittgenstein. **SELECTED PUBLICATIONS** Auth, Language, Persons, and Belief, 67 & ed, New Essays on Religious Language, 69, Oxford; contribr, Communication: Ethical and Moral Issues, Gordon & Breach, 72; auth, Death: Its conceptual elusiveness, Soundings, 72; Belief, falsification and Wittgenstein, Int J Philos Relig, 72; co-ed, Medical Treatment of the Dying: The Moral Issues, Schenkman, 78; auth, Is Natural Death an Illusion?, The Hastings Ctr Report, 78; Wittgenstein on doubting and groundless believing, J Am Acad Relig, 81. **CONTACT ADDRESS** Dept of Philos, Univ of Kentucky, 500 S Limestone St, Lexington, KY 40506-0003.

HIGHFIELD, RONALD CURTIS
PERSONAL Born 06/01/1951, m, 2 children **DISCIPLINE** RELIGION **EDUCATION** Harding Univ, BA, 75; Harding Grad Sch Rel, MTh, 79; Rice Univ, MA, PhD, 88. **CAREER** Campus min, Col Church of Christ, 79-80; yputh min, Bering Drive Church of Christ, 81-84; campus min, Univ Houston, 86-88; adjunct instr, Univ St Thomas, 89; assoc prof, 89-. **HONORS AND AWARDS** Post doc fel, Rice Univ, 88; first prize, Ted Ward wrtg award contest, 84; co-coord, restoration theol res fel. **MEMBERSHIPS** Mem, Am Acad Rel; Christian Theol Res Fel. **SELECTED PUBLICATIONS** Auth, Barth and Rahner: Toward an Ecumenical Understanding of Sin and Evil. Peter Lang, 89; The Superstitions of the Modern Mind Examined, Jour Ctr Christianity and Cult, 96; Children's Education and the Kingdom of God in America, Leaven Jour, 95; The Freedom to Say "NO"?, Karl Rahner's Doctrine of Sin, Theol Studies, 95; An Essay on the Christian Mission in Higher Education, Fac Dialogue, 95; Galileo, Scientific Creationism and Biblical Hermeneutics, Studies in Honor of Thomas H. Olbricht on the Occasion of His Sixty-Fifth Birthday , Restoration Quart, 94; rev, A Review of The Second Incarnation: A Theology for the 21st Century Church, by Rubel Shelly and Randall J Harris, Howard Pub Co, 92, Restoration Quart, 94. **CONTACT ADDRESS** Dept of Relig, Pepperdine Univ, 24255 Pacific Coast Hwy, Malibu, CA 90263. **EMAIL** ronald.highfield@pepperdine.edu

HIGHTOWER, ANTHONY
PERSONAL Born Atlanta, GA, s **DISCIPLINE** LAW **EDUCATION** Clark Coll, Atlanta GA, BA, 1983; Univ of Iowa, Iowa City IA, JD, 1986. **CAREER** Self-employed, College Park GA, Attorney, 86-; Clark Coll, Atlanta GA, teacher, 88-; City of College Park, College Park, GA, city councilman, 86-90, mayor pro-tem, 90; Clark Atlanta Univ, Atlanta, GA, adjunct prof, 88-; State of GA, Atlanta, GA, state rep, 91-. **HONORS AND AWARDS** Selected for Membership, Alpha Kappa Mu Honor Soc, 1981, Pi Gamma Mu Intl Honor Soc, 1981; Participated and Completed Inaugural Class of South Fulton Leadership, 1987; Golden Rule Awds Panel, United Way/J C Penny, 1988; Appreciation Awd, Metro Atlanta Private Indus Council, 1988; Political Service Awd, Delta Sigma Theta Sorority Inc, 1988; Leadership Institute for Municipal Elected Officials, Univ of GA, 1989. **MEMBERSHIPS** Mem, NAACP, 1979-, Alpha Phi Alpha Frat, 1980-; bd mem, Clark Coll, 1982-83; natl bd mem, Alpha Phi Alpha Frat Inc, 1982-83; mem, State Bar

of Georgia, 1986-, Natl Bar Assn, 1986-, Amer Bar Assn, 1986-, Natl League of Cities, 1986-, Natl Black Caucus of Local Elected Officials, 1986-, Georgia Municipal Assn, 1986-; bd mem, Fulton County Public Safety Training Center, 1989-. **CONTACT ADDRESS** 1568 Willingham Dr, Suite 212A, College Park, GA 30337.

HILBERT, DAVID
DISCIPLINE PHILOSOPHY **EDUCATION** Stanford Univ, PhD. **CAREER** Assoc prof, Univ IL at Chicago. **RESEARCH** Include philos of mind; philos of perception; color; philos of biology. **SELECTED PUBLICATIONS** Auth, Color and Color Perception, CSLI, 87; What is Color Vision?, Philos Studies, 92. **CONTACT ADDRESS** Philos Dept, Univ of Illinois, Chicago, S Halsted St, PO Box 705, Chicago, IL 60607. **EMAIL** hilbert@uic.edu

HILDEBRAND, DAVID
PERSONAL Born 11/21/1964, New York, NY, m, 1997 **DISCIPLINE** PHILOSOPHY **EDUCATION** Univ Pa, BA, 87; Univ Tex, PhD, 97. **CAREER** Instr, Univ Tex Austin, 95-96; adjunct prof, Univ Tex, 97-00; adjunct prof, Austin Community Col, 97-99; Adj Prof, St Edward's Univ, 97-00; Lectr, Rice Univ, 00-01. **HONORS AND AWARDS** Travel grant, JFK Inst, Berlin. **MEMBERSHIPS** Am Philos Asn, Soc for the Adv of Am Philos, Southwest Philos Soc. **RESEARCH** Figures in American philosophy, metaphysics & epistemology; Pedagogy in college teaching; Pragmatism; Process philosophy; Literary criticism; Philosophy of science. **SELECTED PUBLICATIONS** Auth, "Putnam, Pragmatism and Dewey," Transactions of the Charles S. Peirce Society; auth, "Progress in History: Dewey on Knowledge of the Past," The Review Journal of Philosophy and Social Science; auth, "Philosophy's Relevance and the Pattern of Inquiry," Teaching Philosophy 22:4 (99): 375-387; auth, "Pragmatism and Literary Criticism: The Practical Starting Point," REAL: Yearbook of Research in English and American Literature 15 (Berlin, New York: de Gruyter, 99): 303-322; auth, Genuine Doubt and the Community in Peirce's Theory of Inquiry, Southwest Philos Res, vol 12, no 1, 33-43, 96; auth, Was Kenneth Burke a Pragmatist?, Trans of the Charles S. Peirce Soc, vol 31, no 3, 632-658, 95; auth, Kimball on Whitehead on Perception. Process Studies, vol 22, no 1, 13-20, 93. **CONTACT ADDRESS** 5010 Hazard St, No 3, Apt. D, Houston, TX 77098. **EMAIL** hilde@uts.cc.utexas.edu

HILDRETH, RICHARD GEORGE
PERSONAL Born 10/11/1943, Hollywood Beach, FL **DISCIPLINE** ENVIRONMENTAL & PROPERTY LAW **EDUCATION** Univ Mich, BSE, 65, JD, 68; Oxford Univ, dipl, 69. **CAREER** Atty, Steinhart Law Firm, 69-72; prof, Univ San Diego, 73-78; Prof Law, Univ Ore, 78-, Vis scholar, Harvard Law Sch, 75-76. **MEMBERSHIPS** Coastal Soc. **RESEARCH** Ocean and coastal law. **SELECTED PUBLICATIONS** Auth, The coast: Where energy meets the environment, San Diego Law Rev, 75; Coastal natural hazards management, Ore Law Rev, 80; co-ed, Ocean and Coastal Law, Prentice-Hall, 82. **CONTACT ADDRESS** Sch of Law, Univ of Oregon, Eugene, OR 97403.

HILL, CHARLES
DISCIPLINE NEW TESTAMENT **EDUCATION** Cambridge Univ, PhD. **CAREER** Assoc prof, RTS; Northwestern Col. **SELECTED PUBLICATIONS** Auth, "Paul's Understanding of Christ's Kingdom in I Corinthians 15:20-28," Novum Testamentum XXX, (88): 297-126; auth, "Hades of Hippolytus or Tartarus of Tertullian: The Authorship of the Fragment De universo," Vigiliae Christianae 43, (89): 105-126; auth, "Hippolytus and Hades: The Authorship of the Fragment De universo," in E.A. Livingstone, ed, Studia Partistica XXI, (89): 254-259; auth, Regnum Caelorem: Patterns of Future Hope in Early Christianity, Oxford Early Christian Stud, Oxford UP, 92; The Marriage of Montanism and Millennialism, Studia Patristica XXXI, 92; Study Notes to I and II Thessalonians, The New Geneva Study Bible, Thomas Nelson Publ, 95. **CONTACT ADDRESS** Dept of New Testament, Reformed Theol Sem, Florida, 1231 Reformation Dr, Oviedo, FL 32765.

HILL, CHRISTOPHER
DISCIPLINE PHILOSOPHY OF LANGUAGE **EDUCATION** Harvard Univ, PhD. **CAREER** Philos, Univ Ark **HONORS AND AWARDS** Nat Hum Ctr fel. **SELECTED PUBLICATIONS** Auth, Sensations, Cambridge Univ Press, 91. **CONTACT ADDRESS** Univ of Arkansas, Fayetteville, Fayetteville, AR 72701. **EMAIL** cshill@comp.uark.edu

HILL, HARVEY
PERSONAL Born 09/07/1965, Atlanta, GA, m, 1992, 2 children **DISCIPLINE** RELIGION **EDUCATION** Yale Univ, BA, 87; Candler Sch Theol, MTS, 91; Emory Univ, PhD, 96. **CAREER** Asst prof, Berry Coll, 96-. **HONORS AND AWARDS** Dean Teach Fel, 95-96; Fac Mem of Year Awd, 99-00; Bernadette E Schmitt Gnt, AHA, 95. **MEMBERSHIPS** AAR; SBL; ASCH; HSEC. **RESEARCH** Roman Catholic modernism; Anglican studies. **SELECTED PUBLICATIONS** Auth, "Worship in the Ecclesiology of William White," Anglican Episc Hist 62 (93): 317-342; coauth, "Literary Art in the Moral Theology of Jeremy Taylor," Anglican Theol Rev 76 (94): 27-43; auth, "Sarah Dickey," "Leo the Great," in For All the Saints, ed. Clifton F Guthrie (Akron, OH: Order of Saint Luke Pub, 95); auth, "La science catholique: Alfred Loisy's Program of Historical Theology," Zeitschriftfur neuere Theologiegeschichte, J Hist Mod Theol 3 (96): 39-59; auth, "French Politics and Alfred Loisy's Modernism," Church History: Studies in Christianity and Culture 67 (98): 521-536; auth, "Ferdinand Cartwright Ewer," "Thomas Gallaudet," "Charles Chapman Grafton," "John Stark Ravenscroft," in American National Biography, ed. John A Garaty (Cary, NC: Oxford Univ Press, 99); auth, "The Politics of Moral Education: Alfred Loisy's Modernism in Context," in Catholicism Contending with Modernity: Roman Catholic Modernism and Anti-Modernism, ed. Darrell Jodock (Cambridge Univ Press, 99). **CONTACT ADDRESS** Dept Religion, Berry Col, Mount Berry, GA 30149. **EMAIL** hhill@berry.edu

HILL, JACQUELINE R.
PERSONAL Born 05/23/1940, Topeka, KS, d **DISCIPLINE** LAW **EDUCATION** Univ of CA Berkeley, BA 1957-62; Univ of Southern CA, Teachers Credential 1965-66; Southwestern Univ School of Law, JD (cum laude) 1968-72; California State Univ, Long Beach, Certitificate in Calligraphy 1987-89. **CAREER** Univ of CA Lawrence Radiation Lab, admin exec 1963-66; LA Unified School Dist, math teacher 1966-1973; LA Comm Coll Dist, evening instr 1972-75; Los Angeles County, deputy dist atty, 73-; California State University-Long Beach, instructor, 90-91. **HONORS AND AWARDS** Legal Book Awds Southwestern Univ School of Law 1969-72. **MEMBERSHIPS** CA State Bar; Amer Bar Association; CA State Adv Grp Juvenile Justice and Delinquency Prevention 1983-. **CONTACT ADDRESS** Los Angeles County, 210 W Temple St, Los Angeles, CA 90012.

HILL, JASON D.
PERSONAL Born 06/10/1965, Kingston, Jamaica, s **DISCIPLINE** PHILOSOPHY **EDUCATION** Ga State Univ, BA, 91; Purdue Univ, MA, 95; PhD, 98. **CAREER** Asst Prof, Southern Ill Univ Edwardsville, 98-00; Asst Prof, De Paul Univ, 00. **HONORS AND AWARDS** Outstanding Philos Major, Ga State Univ, 92; Opportunities Fel, Purdue Univ, 93-96; Soc for the Humanities Post Doctoral Fel, Cornell Univ, 99-00. **MEMBERSHIPS** Am Philos Asn. **RESEARCH** Moral Psychology, Ethics. **SELECTED PUBLICATIONS** Auth, Becoming a Cosmpolitan: What It Means to be a Human Being in the New Millennium, Rowrriew and Littlefiled, 00. **CONTACT ADDRESS** Dept Philos Studies, So Illinois Univ, Edwardsville, Po Box 1433, Edwardsville, IL 62026-1433. **EMAIL** jh243@cornell.edu

HILL, RANDOLPH K.
PERSONAL Born 11/13/1960, Palo Alto, CA, d, 2 children **DISCIPLINE** PHILOSOPHY **EDUCATION** Univ Cincinnati, BA, 84; Univ Ill, PhD, 92. **CAREER** Lecturer, Univ Calif, 92-93; Lecturer, Ind Univ, 93-94; Asst Prof, Northwestern Univ, 94-. **HONORS AND AWARDS** Phi Kappa Phi; DAAD Res Grant, 91; Fel, Univ Ill, 89-90. **MEMBERSHIPS** Am Philos Asn. **RESEARCH** Continental Philosophy, Kant, Nineteenth and Twentieth Century Continental Philosophy; Ethics, Political Philosophy; Aesthetics; Philosophy of Mind. **SELECTED PUBLICATIONS** Auth, "Ultimate skepsis," International Studies in Philosophy, 97; auth, "Genealogy," in Routledge Encyclopedia of Philosophy; auth, "Nietzsche," in Companion to Continental Philosophy, Blackwell, forthcoming; rev, of "Nietzsche: A Re-Examination, by Irving M Zeitlin, Nineteenth Century Prose, 96; rev, of "Nietzsche: Ethics of an Immoralist," by Peter Berkowitz, Ethics, 96. **CONTACT ADDRESS** Dept Philos, Northwestern Univ, 1818 Hinman Ave, Evanston, IL 60208-0001. **EMAIL** kevin-hill@nwu.edu

HILL, RENEE AFANAN
DISCIPLINE PHILOSOPHY **EDUCATION** Univ MI, Ann Arbor, BA, 74; Eastern MI Univ, Ypsilanti, MA, 78; Univ VA, Charlottesville, MA, 90, PhD, 95. **CAREER** Asst prof, VA State Univ, 94-& WV State Col Inst, 92-94; tchg asst, Univ VA, Charlottesville, 91; exec dir, Richmond Black Stud Found, 88-89; dir std activ, VA Union Univ, 85-87 & VP, Stud Aff, 86-87; instr, VA Union Univ, 81-85: instr, adj, VA Commonwealth Univ, Richmond, 83- 83; asst dir, Nataki Talibah Sch house, Detroit, 78-81. **HONORS AND AWARDS** Nat Achievement Scholar, 70; Inducted into Phi Beta Kappa, 74; SHEV fel, 87-88, 88-89, 89-90, 90-91 & 91-92 . **MEMBERSHIPS** APA; Southern Soc Philos Psychol; VA Philos Asn; WV Philos Asn. **RESEARCH** Polit philos; philos of mind; non-western philos; philos for children. **SELECTED PUBLICATIONS** Auth, Sins of the Fathers: Compensation Through the Generations, W Va Philos Asn, W Va State Col, 94; Compensation and Serendipitous Events, W Va Philos Asn, W Va Univ, Morgantown, 93; Compensatory Justice Versus Existence: A Comment on Morris, Va Philos Asn, William & Mary Col, 93. **CONTACT ADDRESS** Dept of Hist and Philos, Virginia State Univ, 1 Hayden Dr, Petersburg, VA 23806. **EMAIL** renhill@aol.com

HILL, ROSCOE EARL
PERSONAL Born 07/04/1936, Lincoln, NE, m, 1959, 2 children **DISCIPLINE** PHILOSOPHY **EDUCATION** Carleton Col, BA, 58; Univ Chicago, MA, 63, PhD, 68. **CAREER** Instr Philos, Carleton Col, 61-62; asst prof, Yale Univ, 67-73; asst prof, 73-80, assoc prof Philos, Univ Denver, 80-; dean of Arts, Humanities, Social Sciences, 90-98. **MEMBERSHIPS** Am Philos Asn; Am Soc Legal & Polit Philos; Soc Relig Higher Educ. **RESEARCH** Philosophy of law; ethics; philosophy of mind. **SELECTED PUBLICATIONS** Coauth, Affirmative School Integration, Sage Publ, 69; Legal validity and legal obligation, Yale Law, J, 71; Virtue for its own sake, Personalist, 72. **CONTACT ADDRESS** Dept of Philosophy, Univ of Denver, 2199 S University, Denver, CO 80210-4711. **EMAIL** rhill@du.edu

HILL, THOMAS E.
PERSONAL Born 03/25/1937, Atlanta, GA, m, 1981, 2 children **DISCIPLINE** PHILOSOPHY **EDUCATION** Harvard, BA, 59; Oxford, BPhil, 61; Harvard, MA, 64, PhD, 66. **CAREER** Johns Hopkins Univ, 65-66; Asst Prof, Pomona Col, 66-68; Asst, Assoc, Prof, Univ Calif LA, 68-84; Kenan Prof, Univ NC at Chapel Hill, 84-. **HONORS AND AWARDS** Rhodes Schol, 59-62; Danforth Fellow, 59-65; Tanner Lecturer, Stanford, 94; Dist Tchng Awd for Post-BA Instr, 98. **MEMBERSHIPS** Am Philos Asn; N Am Kant Soc. **RESEARCH** Ethics; political philosophy; Kant. **SELECTED PUBLICATIONS** Auth, Autonomy and Self-Respect, Cambridge Univ Press, 91; Auth, Dignity and Practical Reason in Kant's Moral Theory, Cornell Univ Press, 92; auth, Respect, Pluralism and Justice: Kantian Perspectives, Oxford Univ Press, 00. **CONTACT ADDRESS** Dept of Philos, Univ of No Carolina, Chapel Hill, Chapel Hill, NC 27599-3125. **EMAIL** thill@email.unc.edu

HILLAR, MARIAN
PERSONAL Born 03/22/1938, Poland, m, 1970, 2 children **DISCIPLINE** PHILOSOPHY **EDUCATION** Univ Medical School of Danzig, MD Summa cum laude, 56-72, PhD, 66. **CAREER** Univ Med School of Danzig, Biochemistry, instr to asst prof 58-69; Baylor Col of Med, sr research assoc, adj asst prof, 69-75; Texas Southern Univ, asst prof, assoc prof, prof 71-85, dir lab of molecular biology and biochemistry, 71-85; Universita degli Studi di Camerino, Italy, vis prof, 80; Ponce School of Medicine, PR, prof, dept chemn of biochem, 85-86, prof & dir of center for Philo & Socinian Studies, 86-, Corresponding Ed, Bez Dogmatu, Warsaw, 93-. **HONORS AND AWARDS** Pol Acad of Science, Research Awd, 65; Univ Med School of Danzig, biomed award, listed in: Amer Men & Wom of Science, 75; Who is Who, in: Frontiers of Science, 82, Southwest, 82, Theology and Science, 92 & American Education, 93. **MEMBERSHIPS** BS; The Biochem Soc; AAAS; AHA; PIASA; AF; IRAS; SAAP; APA; AAR; SBL. **RESEARCH** Hist of W and E Philo; hist of relig and relig doctrines; orig of Christianity and doctrine; socinianism **SELECTED PUBLICATIONS** Auth, Biochemical Energetics, NIH & TSU, 77; Energetics and Kinetic Mechanisms of Enzyme Function, TSU, 92; co-edit, Ethics and Humanism: Anthology of Essays, Amer Human Assoc, Houston, 92; Humanism and Social Issues, coedit, AHA, Houston, 93; Contributors to the Philosophy of Humanism: Anthology of Essays, AHA, Houston, 94; The Philosophy of Humanism and the Issues of Today: Anthology of Essays, AHA, Houston, 95; The Case of Michael Servetus (1511-1553)- The Turning Point in the Struggle for Freedom of Conscience, Edwin Mellen Press, 97, articles, The Logos and Its Function in the Writings of Philo of Alexandria: Greek Interpretation of the Hebrew Thought and Foundations of Christianity, Parts I & II, in: A Jour from the Rad Reform, A Testimony to Biblical Unitarianism, vol 7, no 4, 98. **CONTACT ADDRESS** Dept of Philosophy, 9330 Bankside, Houston, TX 77031-1713. **EMAIL** noam@swbell.net

HILLERS, DELBERT ROY
PERSONAL Born 11/07/1932, Chester, SD, m, 1958, 2 children **DISCIPLINE** OLD TESTAMENT, SEMITIC LANGUAGES **CAREER** Instr Hebrew, Concordia Sr Col, 58-60; from asst prof to assoc prof Hebrew & Old Testament, 63-70, Prof Semitic Lang, Johns Hopkins Univ, 70-, Ann prof, Am Sch Orient Res, Jerusalem, 68-69; Am Philos Soc grant, 68-69. **MEMBERSHIPS** Soc Bibl Lit; Am Orient Soc. **RESEARCH** Northwest Semitic languages; Old Testament. **SELECTED PUBLICATIONS** Auth, Treaty-Curses and the Old Testament Prophets, Pontif Bibl Inst, Rome, 64; An alphabetic cuneiform tablet from Taanach, Bull Am Schs Orient Res, 64; Delocutive verbs in Biblical Hebrew, J Bibl Lit, 68; Covenant: The History of a Biblical Idea, Johns Hopkins Univ, 69; Lamentations, Anchor Bible, Doubleday, 72. **CONTACT ADDRESS** Dept of Near Eastern Studies, Johns Hopkins Univ, Baltimore, 3400 N Charles St, Baltimore, MD 21218.

HILLIARD, DAVID C.
PERSONAL Born 06/22/1937, Framingham, MA, m, 1974 **DISCIPLINE** LAW **EDUCATION** Tufts Univ, BS, 59; Univ Chicago, JD, 62. **CAREER** Adjunct prof, Northwestern Univ School of Law, 71-, chmn, Symposium on Intellectual Property & Law, 87-, lectr, Univ of Chicago Law School. **MEMBERSHIPS** Am Bar Asn; Am Col of Trial Lawyers. **RESEARCH** Intellectual law. **SELECTED PUBLICATIONS** Auth, Trademarks and Unfair Competition, Matthew Bender, 4th ed, 00; Trademarks and Unfair Competiton Deskbook, Matthew Bender, 00. **CONTACT ADDRESS** 1320 N State Parkway, Chicago, IL 60610. **EMAIL** dhilliard@pattishall.com

HILLMER, MARK
DISCIPLINE OLD TESTAMENT **EDUCATION** Northwestern Col, BA; 57; Concordia Sem, BD, 62; Univ Wis, MA, 63; Hebrew Union Col, PhD. **CAREER** Vis prof, St. John's Univ, 70-71; vis asst prof, Concordia Tchr(s) Col; asst prof, Thiel Col, 66-67; assoc prof, 67; Louise Grunow prof, 82. **HONORS AND AWARDS** Fulbright scholar, Univ Heidelberg; asst pastor, grace lutheran church, cincinnati, 63-77 **MEMBERSHIPS** Mem, Soc Bibl Lit; Cath Bible Soc; Lutheran Coun, USA Consult on the Holy Spirit, 76-77. **SELECTED PUBLICATIONS** Contrib, Ezekiel notes, New Intl Version Study Bible, 85; Ezekiel, Minor Prophets, Lamentations, and Ecclesiastes, New Intl Version Reference Edition, 83; transl, Ruth, Malachi, and Ecclesiastes, New Intl Version, 78. **CONTACT ADDRESS** Dept of Old Testament, Luther Sem, 2481 Como Ave, Saint Paul, MN 55108. **EMAIL** mhillmer@luthersem.edu

HILTON, RONALD
PERSONAL Born 07/31/1911, Torquay, England, m, 1939, 1 child **DISCIPLINE** INTERNATIONAL RELATIONS **EDUCATION** Oxford Univ, BA, 33, MA, 36, Univ Perugia, Italy, dipl, 36. **CAREER** Dir, Comite Hispano-Ingles Libr, Madrid, 36; Univ of California; asst prof mod lang, Univ BC, 39-41; assoc prof Romanic langs, 42-49, dir Hisp Am & Luso-Brazilian studies, 44-64, Prof Romanic Lang, Stanford Univ, 49-, Pres, World Assoc of Historical Studies, 64-, Ed, Who's Who in Latin Am, 43-; assoc ed, Southern Republic's Who's Who in Am, 43-; ed, Hisp Am Report, 48-64; hon prof, Univ San Marcos, Peru, vis prof, Univ Brazil & lectr, Latin Am Repub, 49; cult dir, KGEI, Univ of Air, 53-56; consult, Stanford Res Inst, 64-70; ed, World Affairs Report, 70-; vis prof, Fr univs, 70 & Acad Sci, USSR, 71; vis fel, Japanese univs, 73; vis prof Brazil, 74; South African, 74; Amer Univ of Paris, 76; Univ of Mexico (UNAM) vis, 80. **MEMBERSHIPS** MLA; Am Asn Teachers Span & Port; Hisp Soc Am. **RESEARCH** East-West relations; Soviet foreign policy; cultural history of the West. **SELECTED PUBLICATIONS** Auth, Commonwealth Fund Dallas at Berkeley, 1937-39; many books and articles on Spain and Latin American. **CONTACT ADDRESS** Stanford Univ, 766 Santa Ynez, Stanford, CA 94305-8441. **EMAIL** hilton@stanford.edu

HIMES, MICHAEL J.
PERSONAL Born 05/12/1947, New York, NY, s **DISCIPLINE** CHRISTIAN THEOLOGY **EDUCATION** Cathedral Col, Brooklyn, NYork, BA, 68; Sem of the Immaculate Conception, Huntington, NYork, Master of Divinity, 72; Univ of Chicago, PhD, 81. **CAREER** Prof, Sem of the Immaculate Conception, 77-87; from asst acad dean to acad dean, Sem of the Immaculate Conception, 77-87; assoc prof, Univ of Notre Dame, 87-93; collegiate dir, Univ of Notre Dame, 91-93; from assoc prof to prof, Boston Col, 93-. **HONORS AND AWARDS** Divinity Sch of the Univ of Chicago Fel, 75, 76, 77; Dr of Letters, honoris causa, conferred by St Joseph's Col, NY, 92; Catholic Press Asn Book Awd in Theol, 94; Notre Dame Social Concerns Awd, Ctr for Soc Concerns of the Univ of Notre Dame, 95; Cath Press Asn Book Awd in Theol, 98; Sophia Awd for Contribs to Cath Theol, Wash Theol Union, 99. **MEMBERSHIPS** Am Acad of Relig; AHA; Am Soc of Church Hist; Cath Hist Soc of Am; Cath Theol Soc of Am. **RESEARCH** History of theology from the seventeenth century to the present; contemporary Catholic theology. **SELECTED PUBLICATIONS** Auth, Holiness and Finitude: Creaturely Spirituality, in PACE 19, 90; Tragedy and the Goodness of Creatureliness, in PACE 19, 90; Incarnational Spirituality and the Terror of Time, in PACE 19, 90; The Trinity and Creaturely Spirituality, in PACE 19, 90; The Intrinsic Sacramentality of Marriage: The Theological Ground for the Inseparability of Validity and Sacramentality in Marriage, in The Jurist 50, 1, 90; Our Amazing Dignity: An Address to the National Federation of Catholic Physicians' Guilds, in The Linacre Quart 58, #3, 91; Catholicism as Integral Humanism: Christian Participation in Pluralistic Moral Education, in The Challenge of Pluralism: Education, Politics, and Values, ed. F. Clark Power and D.K. Lapsley, 92; Historical Theology as Wissenschaft: Johann Sebastian Drey and the Structure of Theology, in Revisioning the Past: Prospects in Hist Theol, ed. M. Potter Engel and W.E. Wyman, 92; The Ecclesiological Significance of Reception of Doctrine, in The Heytrop Journal 33, #2, 92; Doing theTruth in Love: Conversations about God, Relationships and Service, 95; Living Conversation: Higher Education in a Catholic Context, in Conversations 8, 95; 'A Great Theologian of Our Time': Moehler on Schleiermacher, in The Heythrop Journal 37, #1, 96; Talking with Contemporary American Culture: A Catholic Starting Point, in Evangelization, Culture and Catholic Identity, ed. D.M. McCarron and H.B. Bumpus, 96; Divinizing the Church: Strauss and Barth on Moehler's Ecclesiology, in The Legacy of the Tuebingen Sch, ed. D.J. Dietrich and M.J. Himes, 97; Why Do We Need a Church?, in The Furrow 48, 97; Ongoing Incarnation: Johann Adam Moehler and the Beginnings of Modern Ecclesiology, 97. **CONTACT ADDRESS** Dept of Theology, Boston Col, Chestnut Hill, Chestnut Hill, MA 02167-3806.

HIMMELBERG, ROBERT F.
PERSONAL Born 07/16/1934, Kansas City, MO, m, 1958, 3 children **DISCIPLINE** AMERICAN POLITICAL ECONOMIC HISTORY **EDUCATION** Penn State Univ, PhD. **CAREER** Prof of History. **RESEARCH** Study of the Democratic party in Congress during the Republican Era. **SELECTED PUBLICATIONS** Auth, The Great Depression and American Capitalism, D C Heath, 68; Co-auth, Herbert Hoover and the Crisis of American Capitalism, Cambridge, Schenckman, 74; The Origins of the National Recovery Administration: Business, Government and the Trade Association Issue, 1921-1933, Fordham UP, 76, revised, 93; ed, Business and Government in America Since 1870, 94; co-ed, Historians and Race: Autobiography and the Writing of History , 96. **CONTACT ADDRESS** Dept of Hist, Fordham Univ, Bronx, NY 10458. **EMAIL** himmelberg@fordham.edu

HINCHMAN, LEWIS P.
PERSONAL Born 07/07/1946, Detroit, MI, m, 1977, 1 child **DISCIPLINE** PHILOSOPHY **EDUCATION** Princeton Univ, BA, 68; Cornel Univ, MA; PhD, 79. **CAREER** From Asst Prof to Prof, Clarkson Univ, 82-. **HONORS AND AWARDS** NEH Summer Sem, 91; NEH Summer Inst, 95; Summer Fulbright Ger, 99. **RESEARCH** German Philosophy and Political Thought of 19th and 20th Century, Environmentalism and Politics, Autonomy, Individuality, Human Rights. **SELECTED PUBLICATIONS** Auth, Hegel's Critique of the Enlightenment, Univ of Fla Press, 84; auth, "Virtue of Autonomy: Alasdair MacIntyre's Critique of Liberal Individualism," Polity (summer 89); auth, "The Idea of Individuality: Origins, Meaning and Prospects,", J of Polit (fall 90); coauth, "Existentialism Politicized: Hannah Arendt's Debt to Karl Jaspers," the Rev of Polit (summer 91); co-ed, Hannah Arendt: Critical Essays, State Univ of NY Press, 94; auth, "Aldo Leopold's Hermeneutic of Nature," Rev of Polit (spring 95); auth, "Autonomy, Maturity and Individuality," in What is Enlightenment? Eighteenth Century Answers and Twentieth Century Questions, ed. James Schmidt (Univ of Calif Press, 96); coauth, "Nature Preservation in the Global South: A Survey and Assessment," in Law, Values, and the Environment: a Reader and Bibliography, ed. Robert N. Wells Jr (Scarecrow Press, 96); co-ed, Memory, Identity, Community: The Idea of Narrative in the Human Sciences, State Univ NY Press, 97; coauth, "Australia's Judicial Revolution and the Transformation of Liberalism," Polity (fall 98). **CONTACT ADDRESS** Dept Lib Arts, Clarkson Univ, 1 Clarkson Ave, Potsdam, NY 1376-1409. **EMAIL** hinchman@clarkson.edu

HINDERER, WALTER
PERSONAL Born 09/03/1934, Ulm, Germany, m, 1966 **DISCIPLINE** GERMAN LITERATURE, PHILOSOPHY **EDUCATION** Abitur, Kepler Gymnasium, Ulm, 54; Univ Tuebingen, German & Eng Lit, European History & Phil, 54-55; Univ Munich, 55-60, PhD, 60. **CAREER** Dir, Acad Div, 61-66, R. Piper & Co (publ), Munich, 61-66; asst prof, German, 66-69, Penn St Univ; assoc prof, German, 69-71, Univ CO; vis prof, 70-71, Stanford Univ; prof, German, 71-78, Univ MD; prof, German, 78-, Princeton Univ. **HONORS AND AWARDS** Fel, Inst for Res in Humanities, Univ WI, 76-77; DAAD Res Grant, 84; Fel, Inst for Advanced Study Berlin, 85-86; Fel, Franz Rosenzweig Res Center, 95, Hebrew Univ; Order of Merit of the Fed Rep of Germany, 95; Alexander von Humboldt Awd, 98. **MEMBERSHIPS** Intl Vereinigung fuer Germanische Sprac und Lit; Modern Language Asn; AATG; Schiller-Gesellschaft; Buechner-Gesellschaft; Heine-Gesellschaft; Gesellschaft fuer Interkulturelle Germanistik. **RESEARCH** German & European lit of the 18th, 19th, and 20th centuries; concepts and ideas of German drama; political poetry; politics and lit; German soc and cult history; rhetoric and oratory; lit theory; poetics and aesthetics; history of criticism. **SELECTED PUBLICATIONS** Auth, Arbeit an der Gegenwart. Zur deutschen Literatur nach 1945, Wuerzburg: Verlag Koenigshausen und Neumann, 94; ed, Brechts Dramen, Intrepretationen, Verlag Philipp Reclam jun, 95; ed, Kleists Dramen Literaturstudium, Interpretationen, Verlag Philipp Reclam jun, 97; ed, Codierungen von Liebe in der Kunstperiode, Verlag Koenigshausen & Neumann, 97; auth, Von der Idee des Menschen, Ueber Friedrich Schiller, Verlag Konigshausen & Neumann, 98; ed, Kleists Erzahlungen, Literaturstudium, Interpretationen, Reclam Verlag, 98; auth, Die Rhetorik der Parabel. Zu ihrem asthetischen Funktionszuusammenhang und Funktionswechsel bei Friedrich Schiller, Fabel und Parabel Kulturgeschichtliche Prozesse im 18, Jahrhundert. 94; auth, Die Depotenzierung der Vernunft: Kompensationsmuster im praeromantischen und romantischen Diskurs, Romantiches Erzahlen, Verlag Koenigshausen & Neumann, 95; auth, Den Dichtern geht es wie dem Araukaner, Anmerkungen zu Gunter Kunerts Poetik, Kunert Werkstatt, Materialien und Studien zu Gunter Kunerts literarischem Werk, Aisthesis Verlag, 95; auth, Das Roecheln der Mona Lisa. Aspeckt von Ernst Jandyls Lyrik im Kontext der sechziger Jahre, Text & Kriktik. Zeitschrift fur Literatur, 96; auth, Die Entmuendigung der Muendigkeit. Zum Paradigmawechsel eines anthropologischen Konzepts im philosophischen und literarischen Diskurs der Kinstperiode, Lit und Erfahrungswandel 1789-1930, Intl Corvey-Symposiums 9 & 12, 93; auth, Im babylonischen Turm, oder: Steine aus dem Glashaus, Amerikas Kampf um den Kanon und um kulturelle Einheit, Neue Rundschau. Der postkoloniale Blick. Eine neue Weltliteratur?, Jahrgang 96; auth, Das Reich der Schatten In Interpretationen. Gedichte von Friedrich Schiller, Stuttgart Philipp Reclam Verlag, 96; auth, Torquato Tasso, Goethe-Handbuch Vol II, JB Metzler Verlag, 96; auth, Literatur als Anweisung zum Fremdverstehen, Deutsch und fur Asien, IDV-Regionaltagung Asien - Beijing, 94, Intl Cul Pub, 96; ed, Zur Liebesauffassung der Kunstperiode, Codierungen von Liebe in der Kunstperiode, Verlag Konigshausen & Neumann, 97; auth, Liebessemantik als Provokation, Codierunger von Liebe in der Kunstperiode, Verlag Koenigshausen & Neumann, 97; auth, Prinz Friedrich von Homburg. Zweideutige Vorfaelle, Kleists Dramen, Literaturstudium, Interpretationen, Verlag Philipp Reclam jun, 97; auth, Literarisch-Aesthetische Auftakte zur Romantischen Musik, Jahrbuch der deutschen Schillergesellschaft, 1997, Alfred Kroener Verlag, 97; auth, Das Kollektivindividuum Nation im deutschen Kiontext. Zu seinem Bedeutungswandel im vor-und nachrevolutionaren Diskurs, Volk-Nation-Europa. Zur Romantisierung und Entromantisierung politischer Begriffe, Verlag Koenigshausen & Neumann, 98; auth, Die heilige Caecilie oder die Gewalt der Musik, Kleists Erzaehlungen. Literaturstudium, Interpretationen, Reclam Verlag, 98; auth, Erzaehlte Bilder und eingebildete Texte, Bild und Schrittinder Tomantik, Verlag Koenigshausen & Neumann, 99; auth, Diskursueber Judustrialisierung und Natur im deutschen Roman des A9 Jahrhunderts, Erich Schmidt Verlag, 99. **CONTACT ADDRESS** Dept of Germanic Lang and Lit, Princeton Univ, 230 E Pyne, Princeton, NJ 08544-5264. **EMAIL** Hinderer@Princeton.edu

HINDS, LENNOX S.
PERSONAL Born Port of Spain, Trinidad and Tobago, m **DISCIPLINE** LAW **EDUCATION** City Coll, BS; Rutgers School of Law, JD 1972. **CAREER** Natl Conf Of Black Lawyers, natl dir; Prisoner's Rights Organization Defense, dir 1971-72; Heritage Fnd, dir 1969-72; Citgo Corp, rsch sect chief 1964-69; Rutgers State Univ, prof of criminal law, chmn Administration of Justice Program, currently. **HONORS AND AWARDS** J Skelly Wright Civil Rights Awd; Assn of Black Law Students Community Service Awd 1973; Distguished Alumnus Awd Black Amer Law Students 1974. **MEMBERSHIPS** Permanent del UN Non-Govt Organization; Intl Assn of Democratic Lawyers; Intl Bd, Organization of Non-Govt Organizations; NJ Bar Assn; Committee on Courts & Criminal Procedure; Natl Minority Adv Commn for Criminal Justice; Natl Adv Council for Child Abuse; bd mem Society Mobilization Legal Project; past natl secretary Black-American Law Students Assn; past bd mem Law Students Civil Rights Research Council; State Bar of New York, New Jersey. **SELECTED PUBLICATIONS** numerous publications. **CONTACT ADDRESS** Administration of Justice Program, Rutgers, The State Univ of New Jersey, New Brunswick, New Brunswick, NJ 08903.

HINES, MARY E.
DISCIPLINE RELIGIOUS STUDIES **EDUCATION** Emmanuel Col, BA; Univ St. Michael's Col, MA, PhD. **CAREER** Relig, Emmanuel Col. **MEMBERSHIPS** Cath Theol Soc Am; Am Acad Relig; Col Theol Soc; Boston Theol Soc; N Am Acad Ecumenists; Anglican Roman Cath Consultation US. **SELECTED PUBLICATIONS** Auth, The Transformation of Dogma: An Introduction to Karl Rahner on Doctrine. New York: Paulist Press, 89; Rahnerian Spirituality: Implications for Ministry, In Handbook of Spirituality for Ministers, Paulist Press, 95; Community for Liberation: Church. In Freeing Theology: Contemporary Catholic Theology in Feminist Perspective, Harper, 93; Introduction to Ecclesiology, In The Church in the Nineties: Its Legacy, Its Future, Liturgical Press, 93; Mary, In The New Dictionary of Catholic Spirituality, Liturgical Press, 93; What Ever Happened to Mary?, New Theol Rev, 92; Mary and the Prophetic Mission of the Church, Jour Ecumenical Studies, 91; Ministry: The Praxis of the Kingdom of God, The Praxis of Christian Experience: An Introduction to the Thought of Edward Schillebeeckx, Harper & Row, 89; Women Religious in Transition, New Thepol Rev, 88. **CONTACT ADDRESS** Emmanuel Col, Massachusetts, 400 The Fenway, Boston, MA 02115. **EMAIL** hines@emmanuel.edu

HINES, N. WILLIAM
PERSONAL Born 12/17/1936, Chicago, IL, m, 1958, 3 children **DISCIPLINE** LAW **EDUCATION** Baker Univ, AB, 58; Univ Kans, JD, 61. **CAREER** Law clerk, US Court of Appeals, 60-61; teaching fel, Harvard, 61-62; asst prof to prof, Iowa Law School, 62-. **HONORS AND AWARDS** Fel, Harvard Univ, 61-62; Joseph F. Rosenfeld Prof, 73-; LLD, Hancher-Finkbine Fac Medal, 91;Baker Univ, 99. **MEMBERSHIPS** Am Bar, Iowa State Bar, Int Environ Law Inst, Environ Law Inst, Am Law Inst. **RESEARCH** Property Law, Wealth Transfer Law, Environmental Law, Land Use Control Law. **SELECTED PUBLICATIONS** Auth, Public Regulation of Water Quality, State, Interstate and Federal, 66; auth, Real Property joint Tenures, 66; auth, A Decade of Experience under the Iowa Water Permit System, 67; auth, Water Pollution: Control and Abatement, 67; auth, Personal Property Joint Tenures, 70; auth, Improving Water Quality Regulation in Iowa, 71; auth, Public Regulation of Water Quality in the United States, 71; auth, A Decade of Non Regulation Policy in Congress and the Courts, 77. **CONTACT ADDRESS** Col of Law, The Univ of Iowa, Melrose and Bylington, Iowa City, IA 52242. **EMAIL** n-hines@uiowa.edu

HINGLE, NORWOOD N., III
PERSONAL Born 05/18/1963, New Orleans, LA, m, 1989, 3 children **DISCIPLINE** NEW TESTAMENT **EDUCATION**

Univ New Orleans, BS, 85; Gordon-Conwell Theol Sem, M Div, 89; Univ Aberdeen, Scotland, PhD, 95. **CAREER** Ordained elder in full connection, La Conf of United Methodist Church, 97-; Minister, Lake Vista United Methodist Church, 99-. **MEMBERSHIPS** Amer Acad of Relig; Soc of Bibl Lit; Inst for Bibl Res. **RESEARCH** Gospels of Matthew and John; Christology; Second Temple Judaism. **SELECTED PUBLICATIONS** Rev, Evang Quart, 98; rev, Scottish Bull of Evang Theol, 96. **CONTACT ADDRESS** 6645 Spanish Fort Blvd., New Orleans, LA 70124-4323. **EMAIL** nnh3@bellsouth.net

HINSDALE, MARY ANN
PERSONAL Born 04/10/1947, Chicago, IL **DISCIPLINE** THEOLOGY **EDUCATION** Marygrove Col, BA, 70; Cath Univ Am, MA, 71; Regis Col, STL, 83; Univ St Michael's Col, PhD, 84. **CAREER** Asst prof. **HONORS AND AWARDS** Annual Bk Awd, 87. **MEMBERSHIPS** Col Theol Soc; Am Acad Relig; Cath Theol Soc Am. **SELECTED PUBLICATIONS** Auth, Women and Theology, Orbis Bk, 95; auth, It Comes From the People, Temple, 95. **CONTACT ADDRESS** Boston Col, Chestnut Hill, Chestnut Hill, MA 02467. **EMAIL** hinsdale@bc.edu

HINSON, E. GLENN
PERSONAL Born 07/27/1931, St. Louis, MO, m, 1956, 2 children **DISCIPLINE** CHURCH HISTORY **EDUCATION** Washington Univ; BA 54; Southern Baptist Theological Seminary; BD, ThD, 57,62; Oxford Univ; D Phil 74. **CAREER** Southern Baptist Theological Sem; prof, 62-92, prof of spirituality, John Loftis Prof of church hist, 92-99; Wake Forest Univ; prof 82-84. **HONORS AND AWARDS** Johannes Quasten Medal; Cuthbert Allen Awd; 2 ATS Fell; Prof of the Year SBTS. **MEMBERSHIPS** ASCH; AAR; IPS; EIS; NAPS; NABPR; ITMS. **RESEARCH** Early Christianity and Spirituality. **SELECTED PUBLICATIONS** Auth, Love At the Heart of Things: A Biography of Douglas V. Steer, Pendle Hill Pub, 98; The Early Church, Abingdon, 96; The Church Triumphant: A History of Christianity up to 1300, Mercer Univ, 95; A Serious Call to a Contemplative Lifestyles, rev, ed, Smith & Helwys 93. **CONTACT ADDRESS** Dept of Church History, So Baptist Theol Sem, 3400 Brook Rd, Richmond, VA 23227.

HINTIKKA, JAAKKO
PERSONAL Born 01/12/1929, Vantaa, Finland, m, 1987 **DISCIPLINE** PHILOSOPHY **EDUCATION** Univ Helsinki, PhD. **CAREER** Jr fel of the soc of fels, 56-59, Harvard Univ; prof, 59-70, Univ Helsinki; prof, part-time, 65-82, Standford Univ; research prof, 70-81, Acad of Finland; prof, 90-, Boston Univ. **HONORS AND AWARDS** John Locke Lecturship, Oxford Univ, 64; Wihuri Int Prize, 76; Guggenheim Fel, 79-80; Hagerstrom Lecturship, Uppsala Univ, 83; Hon Doctorate, Univ of Liege, 84; Immanuel Kant Lecturship, Stanford Univ, 85; Hon Doctorate, Jagiellonian Univ, 95; Hon Doctorate, Uppsala Univ, 00. **MEMBERSHIPS** Scientific advisor and foreign member of the Internationales Forschungszentrum Salzburg, 66- ; Acad of Science and Letters of FIN, 61- ; Fel of Societas Scientiarum Fennica, 66- ; Council for Philosophical Studies, 82-86; Norwegian Acad of science and letters, 91- ; Russ Acad of Sci. **SELECTED PUBLICATIONS** Auth, Lingua Universalis vs. Calculus Ratiocinator, Kluwer, 96; auth, The Principles of Mathematics Revisited, Cambridge Univ Pr, 96; auth, Language, Truth and Logic in Mathematics, Kluwer, 97; auth, Paradigms for Language Theory and Other Essays in the Foundations of Language, Kluwer, 97; auth, Language, Truth and Logic in Mathematics, Kluwer, 98; Paradigms for Language Theory and Other Essays, Kluwer, 98. **CONTACT ADDRESS** Dept of Philosophy, Boston Univ, Boston, MA 02215. **EMAIL** hintikka@bu.edu

HINTZEN, PERCY CLAUDE
PERSONAL Born 01/26/1947, Georgetown, Guyana, m **DISCIPLINE** PHILOSOPHY **EDUCATION** University of Guyana, Georgetown, Guyana, BS, 1975; Clark University, Worcester, MA, MA, 1976; Yale University, New Haven, CT, MA, 1977; MPhil, 1977, PhD, 1981. **CAREER** Yale University, New Haven, CT, acting instructor, 78-79; University of Guyana, Guyana, lecturer, 77-78; University of California, Berkeley, CA, associate professor, 79-; African Amer Studies, chairperson, 94-; Peace & Conflict Studies, dir, 94-. **MEMBERSHIPS** Member, American Sociological Society, 1979-; member, Caribbean Studies Association, 1979; member, American Political Science Association, 1979-81. **SELECTED PUBLICATIONS** The Costs of Regime Survival, Cambridge University Press, 1989. **CONTACT ADDRESS** Univ of California, Berkeley, 660 Barrows, Berkeley, CA 94720.

HIRSCH, HERBERT
PERSONAL Born 04/29/1941, New York, NY, m, 1998, 4 children **DISCIPLINE** POLITICAL SCIENCE **EDUCATION** Concord Col, BA, 63; Villanova Univ, MA, 65; Univ KY, PhD, 68. **CAREER** Asst prof, Univ TX, Austin, 68-73, assoc prof, 73-80; prof and chair, 81-90, dir, Int studies, 90-91, prof of Political Science, VA Commonwealth Univ, 91-. **HONORS AND AWARDS** Distinguished lect, VA Commonwealth Univ, 89. **MEMBERSHIPS** Int Coun for the Inst of the Holocaust & Genocide; Gouldnet Holocaust Symposium, Oxfordshire, England; Int Network on Holocaust & Genocide, Sydney, Australia; Inst on Holocaust & Genocide, Jerusalem. **RESEARCH** Politics of war; violence and genocide. **SELECTED PUBLICATIONS** Auth, Poverty and Politicization: Political Socialization in an American Sub-Culture, The Free Press, 71; Comparative Legislative Systems: A Reader in Theory and Research, with M Donald Hancock, The Free Press, 71; Violence as Politics: A Series of Original Essays, with David C Perry, Harper & Row, 73; Learning to Be Militant: Ethnic Identity and the Development of Political Militance in a Chicago Community, with Armando Gutierrez, R & E Res Assocs, 77; The Right of the People: An Introduction to American Politics, Univ Press of Am, 80; Persistant Prejudice: Prespectives in Anti-Semitism, with Jack Spiro, George Mason Univ Press, 88; Genocide and the Politics of Memory: Studying Death to Preserve Life, Univ NC Press, April 95; articles in The Am Political Science Rev, Western Political Quart; Social Science Quart, Aztlan, Int J of Group Tensions, Ed Forum, Armenian Rev, Australian J of Jewish Studies. **CONTACT ADDRESS** Dept of Political Science, Virginia Commonwealth Univ, 923 Franklin St, Richmond, VA 23284. **EMAIL** hhirsch@atlas.vcu.edu

HIRSCH, WERNER Z.
PERSONAL Born 06/10/1920, Linz, Germany, M, 1945, 3 children **DISCIPLINE** ECONOMICS **EDUCATION** Univ Cal Berkeley, PhD, 49. **CAREER** Prof, Univ Cal Los Angeles. **HONORS AND AWARDS** Phi Beta Kappa; Sigma Xi. **MEMBERSHIPS** Am Econ Asoc. **RESEARCH** Law and economics. **SELECTED PUBLICATIONS** "Privatisation of Local Government Inputs when Outputs Resist Privatization," Chihou Zaier, No 488, (95), 80-93; "Law and Economics: An Overview and Analysis," in Research in Law and Policy Studies, Jay Press, (Greenwich, Con), (95), 3-37; "Financing Universities Through Non-Traditional Sources: Opportunities and Threats," Challenges Facing Higher Education, Phoenix: American Council of Education/The Oryx Press, (99), 75-84; The University at the Millenium, Glio Colloquim, (Geneva, Switzerland), (98), 1-9, reprinted in The Presidency, fall (98), 27-31; Law and Economics -- an Introductory Analysis, 3rd Ed, Academic Press, (San Diego), 99; Challenges Facing Higher Education at the Millenium, Phoenix: American Council on Education/The Oryx Press, 99; "The Regulation of Immobile Housing Assets Under Divided Ownership," International Review of Law and Economics, 19, No 3, (99), 383-397; "Renting" Encyclopedia of Law and Economics, The Regulations of Contracts, 3, (00), 907-949; "Privatization of Government Services: Pressure Group Resistance and Service Transparency," Journal of Labor Research, 21, 2: (00), 315-326; "Why are Municipal Services Rarely Privatized? Causes and Cures," California Policy Options 2001, UCLA School of Public Policy and Social Research, (01), 147-158. **CONTACT ADDRESS** 11601 Bellagio Rd., Los Angeles, CA 90049. **EMAIL** whirsch@ucla.edu

HIRSTEIN, WILLIAM
DISCIPLINE PHILOSOPHY **EDUCATION** Univ Calif at Davis, PhD, 94. **CAREER** Prof, William Paterson Univ, 97; 2 yrs postdoctoral fel, Univ Calif, San Diego; asst dir, VS Ramachandran's Brain and Perception Lab, 96. **RESEARCH** Bringing current findings in neuroscience to bear on classical philosophical issues; Questions about self, and self-representation; The problem of consciousness; Questions about self-deception and confabulation. **SELECTED PUBLICATIONS** coauth, Capgras Syndrome: A Novel Probe for Understanding the Neural Representation of the Identity and Familiarity of Persons, Proceedings of the Royal Soc of London, 264, 97; Three Laws of Qualia: Clues From Neurology About the Biological Functions of Consciousness and Qualia, J of Consciousness Stud, 4, 97, part of a special issue on, Models of the Self, be publ as bk by the MIT Press. **CONTACT ADDRESS** Dept of Philosophy, William Paterson Col of New Jersey, 300 Pompton Rd., Atrium 267, Wayne, NJ 07470.

HISKES, ANNE L.
DISCIPLINE PHILOSOPHY OF SCIENCE **EDUCATION** Hope Col, BA; Ind Univ, MA, PhD. **CAREER** Dept Philos, Univ Conn **RESEARCH** Philosophy and spacetime theories, theories of scientific explanation. **SELECTED PUBLICATIONS** Coauth, Science, Technology, and Policy Decisions, Westview Press, 86; auth, Theoretical Explanation and Unification, Logic and Philosophy of Science in Uppsala, Kluwer Acad Publ, 94. **CONTACT ADDRESS** Dept of Philos, Univ of Connecticut, Storrs, 344 Mnsfield Rd, Storrs, CT 06269.

HITCHCOCK, DAVID
DISCIPLINE PHILOSOPHY **EDUCATION** B.A. McMaster, Ph.D., Claremont **CAREER** Assoc prof. **RESEARCH** Philos of logic; metaphysics; philos of language. **SELECTED PUBLICATIONS** Auth, "Enthymemeatic Arguments," Informal Logic vol 7, (85): 83-97; auth, "The Good in Plato's Republic," Apeiron vol 19, (85): 65-92; auth, "Some Principles of rational Mutual Inquiry," in Eemeren, (Amsterdam: SICSAT, 91): 236-243 auth, "Relevance," Argumentiation vol 6, (92): 251-270; auth, "Reasoning by Analogy: a General Theory," in Sthephen P Norris, The Genenralizability of Critical Thinking: Multiple Perspectives on an Educ Ideal, (New York: Teachers Co Press, 92): 109-124; auth, "Valididyt in Conductive Arguments," in ralph H Johnson and J Anthony Blair, New Essays in Informal Logic, (Windsor, ON, Informal Logic, 94): 58-66; auth, "Does the traditional treatment of enthymemes rest on a mistake?" Argumentation vol 12, (98): 15-37; auth, "the Origin of Professional Eristic," in te selected proceedings of the Fifth Symposium Platonicum, (98). **CONTACT ADDRESS** Philosophy Dept, McMaster Univ, 1280 Main St W, Hamilton, ON, Canada L8S 4L9. **EMAIL** hitchckd@mcmcmaster.ca

HIZ, HENRY
PERSONAL Born 10/08/1917, Leningrad, Russia, m, 1943 **DISCIPLINE** LINGUISTICS, PHILOSOPHY **EDUCATION** Free Univ Brussels, lic en philos, 46; Harvard Univ, PhD(-philos), 48. **CAREER** Asst philos, Underground Univ Warsaw, 40-44; adj math, Univ Warsaw, 49-50; asst prof, Univ Utah, 52-54 & Pa State Univ, 55-60, assoc prof, 60-64, Prof Ling, Univ Pa, 64-, Vis lectr, Univ Pa, 51, 53, 54 & 58-59; investr, NSF Tranformation & Discourse Analysis Proj, 58-; vis prof philos, NY Univ, 69- 71 & Jagiellonian Univ, 77; vis fel philos, Clare Hall, Cambridge, Eng, 76-77; Guggenheim fel ling, 76-77. **MEMBERSHIPS** Ling Soc Am; Semiotic Sco Am (pres, 75-76); Am Philos Asn. **RESEARCH** Formal grammars; mathematical logic; philosophy of art; ethics. **SELECTED PUBLICATIONS** Auth, Zellig Harris, 23-October-1909 May-22-1992, In-Memoriam, Proceedings Am Philos Soc, Vol 0138, 94; auth, Autobiography, in First Person Singular III, ed E.F.K. Koerner, 98. **CONTACT ADDRESS** Dept of Ling, Univ of Pennsylvania, Philadelphia, PA 19174. **EMAIL** hiz@babel.ling.upenn.edu

HOAG, ROBERT W.
PERSONAL Born 04/16/1954, m **DISCIPLINE** PHILOSOPHY, RELIGION **EDUCATION** Davidson Col, BA, 76; Univ Va, MA, 80; Univ Va, PhD, 83. **CAREER** Vis Instr, Tex A&M Univ, 82-83; From Asst Prof to Prof, Berea Col, 83-. **HONORS AND AWARDS** Omicron Delta Kappa, 76; Phi Beta Kappa, 76; Fel, Davidson Col, 72-76, Dupont Fel, Univ Va, 77-78, 79-82; Newcombe Fel, Woodrow Wilson Nat Fel Found, 82-83; NEH Summer Fel, Univ Ariz, 84; Phi Kappa Phi, 90. **MEMBERSHIPS** Woodrow Wilson Nat Fel Found. **RESEARCH** Social and political philosophy, ethics, philosophy of law, logic, modern philosophy, philosophy of logic and language, ancient philosophy. **SELECTED PUBLICATIONS** Auth, "Mill on Conflicting Moral Obligations," Analysis 43 (83): 49-54; auth, "Happiness and Freedom: Recent Work on J S Mill," Philos and Public Affairs 15 (86): 188-199; auth, "Mill's Conception of Happiness as an Inclusive End," J of the Hist of Phil 25 (87): 417-431; auth, "J S Mill's Language of Pleasures," Utilitas 4 (92): 248-278; rev, Rationality, Rules and Utility: New Essays on the Moral Philosophy of Richard Brandt, Philos Books 36 (95): 203-204; rev, Mill's Principle of Utility: A Defense of John Stuart Mill's Notorious Proof: by Necip Alican, Int Studies in Philos 29 (97): 106-107; rev, Utilitarianism as a Public Philosophy: by Robert Goodin, Philos Books 39 (98): 134-136. **CONTACT ADDRESS** Dept Philos & Relig, Berea Col, 101 Chestnut St, Berea, KY 40404-0001. **EMAIL** bob_hoag@berea.edu

HOAGLUND, JOHN ARTHUR
PERSONAL Born 06/15/1936, Houston, TX, m, 1966, 2 children **DISCIPLINE** PHILOSOPHY **EDUCATION** Free Univ Berlin, PhD, 67. **CAREER** Lectr Am studies, Free Univ Berlin, 67-72; asst prof philos, 72-75, assoc prof, 75-80, chmn dept, 76-79, prof philos, Christopher Newport Univ, 79-, sr Fulbright res fel, Univ Bergen, Norway, 80-81. **HONORS AND AWARDS** Am Coun Learned Soc Travel Awd, 75. **MEMBERSHIPS** AAUP; Am Philos Asn; Am Soc Aesthet; Asn Informal Logic and Critical Thinking, Pres 85-87; Int Soc Study Argumentation. **RESEARCH** Aesthetics; ethics; critical thinking; informal logic. **SELECTED PUBLICATIONS** Auth, The thing in itself in English interpretations of Kant, Am Philos Quart, 73; Originality and aesthetic value, Brit J Aesthet, 76; Music as expressive, Brit J Aesthet, 80; On artistic creativity, Proc 19th Int Cong Aesthet, 80; Some Moral Problems of the Damaged Neonate, Philos in Context, 84; Reasons and Premises in Informal Logic, CT News, 88; Fiction and Belief, Primum Philosophia, 93; Critical Thinking: A Socratic Model, Argumentation, 93; auth, Ennis on the Concept of Critical Thinking, Inquiry, 95; ed Studies in Critical Thinking and Informal Logic, Vale Press; auth, Textbook Critical Thinking, 3rd ed, 99; auth, Reasoning and Giving Reasons, Australas J. of Philos, 00. **CONTACT ADDRESS** Dept Philos, Christopher Newport Univ, 1 University Pl, Newport News, VA 23606-2949. **EMAIL** hoaglund@cnu.edu

HOBBS, TREVOR RAYMOND
PERSONAL Born 01/31/1942, Pontypridd, Wales, m, 1966, 2 children **DISCIPLINE** OLD TESTAMENT **EDUCATION** Univ London, BD, 66, PhD(theol), 73; Baptist Sem, Ruschlikon, MTh, 68. **CAREER** Lectr, 69-70, asst prof Bible studies, 70-74, assoc prof, 74-78, Prof Hebrew & Old Testament Interpretation, McMaster Divinity Col, McMaster Univ, 78- **MEMBERSHIPS** Soc Old Testament Studies, UK; Soc Bibl Lit; Can Soc Bibl Studies. **RESEARCH** Old Testament prophetic literature, theology and hermeneutics; Old Testament historical geography; Historigraphy. **SELECTED PUBLICATIONS** Auth, The End of the Bronze-Age--Changes in Warfare and the Catastrophe C.1200bc, Cath Biblical Quarterly, Vol 0057, 95; The History of Ancient Palestine from the Paleolithic

Period to Alexander Conquest, Cath Biblical Quarterly, Vol 0056, 94. **CONTACT ADDRESS** McMaster Divinity Col, McMaster Univ, 1280 Main St W, Hamilton, ON, Canada L8S 4K1.

HOBGOOD-OSTER, LAURA
PERSONAL Born 09/18/1964, Indiana, m, 1995 **DISCIPLINE** HISTORICAL THEOLOGY **EDUCATION** St Louis Univ, PhD, 97; Vanderbilt Univ, Mdiv, 89; James Madison Univ, BA, 85. **CAREER** Asst Prof of Rel, 98-, Southwestern Univ; Lectr/Instr of Rel Studies, 97-98, Cal State Univ. **HONORS AND AWARDS** Pres Fellow, 94-97, St Louis Univ; Faculty Merit Scholar, 88-89, Vanderbilt Univ. **MEMBERSHIPS** AAR **RESEARCH** Christianity in America, Theology of Nature, Gnostic Christianity, Women and Religion. **SELECTED PUBLICATIONS** Auth, As Heaven and Earth Combine: Perceptions of Nature in American Shakerism, Esoteric Studies, 98; She Glanceth From Earth to Heaven: The Phenomenon of Love Mysticism Among Women in Antebellum Virginia and Maryland, Univ Press of the South, 98; Mary Magdalene, Gnostic Revealer, Koinonia Journal, Princeton Seminary Graduate Forum 96; Sexuality-One of God's Gifts, A Year in the Life, St Louis, Chalice Books, 93; Building Self Esteem, Christian Children's Fellowship Manual, Chalice Books, 92; ed, The Sabbath Journal of Judith Lomax, Scholar Press, Texts and Translations Series, forthcoming; **CONTACT ADDRESS** Southwestern Univ, 1001 E University, Georgetown, TX 78626. **EMAIL** hoboster@southwestern.edu

HOCHBERG, STEPHEN
DISCIPLINE LAW **EDUCATION** NYork Univ, BA, 67; Yale Univ, JD, 70. **CAREER** Asst instr, Yale Univ; US Ct of Appeals for the Third Circuit; gen coun, Lefrak Orgn, NY; asst prof, NY Law Schl; pvt pract, NYC; founding assoc prof Law, Touro Col. **SELECTED PUBLICATIONS** Ed, Cooperative Conversions: A Tenants Survival Guide, 80. **CONTACT ADDRESS** Touro Law Center, Touro Col, New York, 300 Nassau Rd, Huntington, NY 11743.

HOCKENBERY, JENNIFER D.
PERSONAL Born 07/16/1971, London, OH, m, 1996 **DISCIPLINE** PHILOSOPHY **EDUCATION** Bowdoin Col, BA, 93; Boston Univ, MA, 96, PhD, 98. **CAREER** Lectr, Univ Mass, 96-97; asst prof, Mt Mary Col, 97-. **HONORS AND AWARDS** Boston Univ, Pres Fel, Outstanding TA Awd. **MEMBERSHIPS** APA, Phi Beta Kappa **RESEARCH** Augustine; Ancient philo; Christ philo; philo of relig. **CONTACT ADDRESS** Dept of Philosophy, Mount Mary Col, 5001 N. Kent Ave, Milwaukee, WI 53217-5521. **EMAIL** hockenberyj@mtmary.edu

HOCKS, ELAINE
DISCIPLINE PHILOSOPHY, ETHICS **EDUCATION** Mo Univ, PhD, 91. **CAREER** Adj prof; dir, Learning Center's Writing Lab, coordr, Stretch Engl 20; **MEMBERSHIPS** Elected pres, Alpha chap of Phi Beta Kappa, 96-97, still on bd. **RESEARCH** Post-critical theorists and their relationship between Samuel Taylor Coleridge and Michael Polanyi. **CONTACT ADDRESS** Learning Ctr, Univ of Missouri, Columbia, 231 Arts & Science Bldg, Columbia, MO 65211. **EMAIL** HocksE@missouri.edu

HODAPP, PAUL F.
PERSONAL Born 11/04/1943, Kalamazoo, MI, m, 1966, 1 child **DISCIPLINE** PHILOSOPHY **EDUCATION** Western Mich Univ, AB, 65; Wash Univ, PhD, 70; Denver Univ, JD, 80. **CAREER** Prof, Univ N Colo, 72-. **HONORS AND AWARDS** NDEA Fel, 67-69; NEH Summer Fel, 75. **MEMBERSHIPS** Acad of Legal Studies in Bus. **RESEARCH** Abortion, Plato, business ethics, European comparative law. **SELECTED PUBLICATIONS** Auth, Business Ethics and the Law; auth, Ethics in the Business World. **CONTACT ADDRESS** Dept Philos, Univ of No Colorado, 501 20th St, Greeley, CO 80639-0001. **EMAIL** pfhodap@unco.edu

HODDER, ALAN
DISCIPLINE COMPARATIVE RELIGION **EDUCATION** Harvard Col, BA; Harvard Divinity Sch, MTS; Harvard Univ, MA, PhD. **CAREER** Assoc prof, dir, undergrad educ in Comp Stud of Relig, Harvard Univ; assoc prof, Hampshire Col. **SELECTED PUBLICATIONS** Publ include studies of Puritan pulpit rhetoric, orientalism, American transcendentalism, and the Bengal renaissance. **CONTACT ADDRESS** School of HACU, Hampshire Col, Amherst, MA 01002. **EMAIL** ahodder@hampshire.edu

HODES, HAROLD T.
DISCIPLINE PHILOSOPHY **EDUCATION** Columbia Col, BA, 70; Harvard Univ, PhD, 77. **CAREER** Assoc prof, Cornell Univ. **RESEARCH** Philosophy; Logic. **CONTACT ADDRESS** Dept of Philosophy, Cornell Univ, 218 Goldwin Smith Hall, Ithaca, NY 14853.

HODGES, DONALD CLARK
PERSONAL Born 10/22/1923, Fort Worth, TX, m, 1980, 6 children **DISCIPLINE** PHILOSOPHY **EDUCATION** NYork Univ, BA, 47; Columbia Univ, MA, 48, PhD(philos), 54. **CAREER** Instr humanities, Hobart & William Smith Cols, 49-50, instr philos, 50-52; from instr to assoc prof, Univ Mo, 52-63, chmn humanities, 56-61; prof philos, Univ Nebr, 63; prof, Univ SFla, 63-64; chmn dept, 64-69, Prof Philos, Fla State Univ, 64-, Univ Mo res grants, 58, 61, 62; vis prof philos, Univ Hawaii, 65-66; consult ed, Indian Sociol Bull, 65-69; Fla State Univ res grant, 67-68; dir, Fla Ctr Studies Soc Philos, 67-71; assoc ed, Soc Theory & Practice, 69-72, co-ed, 72-; assoc ed, Philos Currents, 72-; assoc mem, Inst Social Philos, Pa State Univ, 72-; mem adv bd, Centro Superiore di Logica e Scienze Comparate, Univ Bologna, 72- **HONORS AND AWARDS** Univ Teaching Award, 00. **MEMBERSHIPS** Am Philos Asn; Soc Philos Studies Dialectical Materialism (secy-treas, 63-73). **RESEARCH** Social and political philosophy; philosophy of the social sciences; philosophy of economics, history, and political science. **SELECTED PUBLICATIONS** Coauth, Revaloracion de la guerilla urbana, El Caballito, Mex, 77; auth, The Legacy of Che Guevara, Thames & Hudson, 77; coauth, El destino de la revolucion mexicana, D.F.: El Caballito (Mexico), 1st ed., 77; 2nd ed., 82; auth, Marxismo y revolucion en el siglo XX, D.F.: El Caballito, (Mexico) 78; coauth, Mexico 1910-1976: Reform or Revolution? Zed Press (London), 79, Enlarged and updated 2nd ed, 83; auth, The Bureaucratization of Socialism, Univ of Massachusetts Press (Amherst), 81; coauth, Todos los revolucionarios van al infierno, D.F.: Costa-Amic (Mexico), 83; auth, Intellectual Foundations of the Nicaraguan Revolution, Univ of Texas Press (Austin and London), 86; auth, Argentina, 1943-1987: The National Revolution and Resistance, Univ of New Mexico Press (Albuquerque), 88; auth, Argentina's Dirty War: An Intellectual Biography, Univ of Texas Press, (Austin), 91; auth, Sandino's Communism: Spiritual Politics for the 21st Century, Univ of Texas Press (Austin), 92; auth, Mexican Anarchism After the Revolution, Univ of Texas Press, (Austin), 95; auth, America's New Economic Order, Sydney, Avebury (Aldershot, Brookfield, USA, Hong Kong, Singapore), 96; auth, The Literate Communist: 150 Years of the Communist Manifesto, Peter Lang (New York, Bern, Berlin, Paris, London Frankfurt), 99; auth, Class Politics in the Information Age: The Political Economy of Expertise, Univ of Ill Press (Champaign, IL), 00; auth, Mexico 2000: The End of the Revolution, Under contract with Praeger (Westport, CT), 00. **CONTACT ADDRESS** Dept of Philos, Florida State Univ, Dodd Hall, Tallahassee, FL 32306-1096.

HODGES, JOHN O.
PERSONAL Born 01/26/1944, Greenwood, MS, m, 1972 **DISCIPLINE** RELIGIOUS STUDIES **EDUCATION** University of Nantes, France, certificate, 1966-67; Morehouse College, Atlanta, GA, BA, 1968; Atlanta University, Atlanta, GA, MA, 1971; University of Chicago, Chicago, IL, MA, 1972, PhD, 1980. **CAREER** Morehouse College, Atlanta, GA, director of language laboratory, 69-70; Barat College, Lake Forest, IL, director of Afro-American studies, 72-75, assistant professor of English, 72-75; University of Chicago, Chicago, IL, assistant dean of university students, 80-82; University of Tennessee, Knoxville, TN, associate professor, 88-, acting head of department rel studies, 89-90. **HONORS AND AWARDS** Merrill Overseas Fellow, Morehouse, 1966-67; Rockefeller Fellow, Rockefeller Foundation, 1970-71; Ford Fellow, Ford Foundation, 1976-78; NEH Fellow, National Endowment for Humanities, 1984. **MEMBERSHIPS** Member, American Academy of Religion, 1982-; member, Modern Language Association, 1981-; member, College Language Association, 1982-; member, South Atlantic Modern Language Assn, 1983; annual dinner committee, Urban League, Langston Hughes Society, 1984-. **CONTACT ADDRESS** Department of Religion, Univ of Tennessee, Knoxville, 501 McClung Tower, Knoxville, TN 37914.

HODGES, LOUIS WENDELL
PERSONAL Born 01/24/1933, Eupora, MS, m, 1954, 2 children **DISCIPLINE** RELIGION & JOURNALISM **EDUCATION** Millsaps Col, BA, 54; Duke Univ, BD, 57, PhD, 60. **CAREER** From asst prof to assoc prof, 60-68, prof relig, 68-97, dir ethics, 74-97, Knight Prof Journalism, 97-, Univ Prog Soc & Professions, Washington & Lee Univ. **RESEARCH** Theology of race relations; theology and ethics, ethics and the press. **SELECTED PUBLICATIONS** Art, Christian Ethics and Non-Violence, Relig in Life, 62; art, The Roots of Prejudice, Christian Advocate, 62; coauth, The Christian and His Decisions, Abingdon, 69. **CONTACT ADDRESS** Dept of Journalism, Washington and Lee Univ, Lexington, VA 24450. **EMAIL** lhodgesl@wlu.edu

HODGES, MICHAEL P.
PERSONAL Born 11/23/1941, Youngstown, OH, m, 1991, 2 children **DISCIPLINE** PHILOSOPHY **EDUCATION** William & Mary, AB, 63; Univ Va, MA, 66, PhD, 67. **CAREER** Asst Prof, Univ Tenn, 67-70; Asst Prof, Vanderbilt Univ, 70-76; Assoc Prof, Vanderbilt Univ, 76-91; Prof, Vanderbilt Univ, 91-; Chair, Vanderbilt, 98- **HONORS AND AWARDS** NEH Fellow, 94. **MEMBERSHIPS** APA; S Soc for Philos & Psychol. **RESEARCH** Wittgenstein; Philosophy of Religion; American Philosophy. **SELECTED PUBLICATIONS** Auth, Transcendence and Wittgenstein's Tractatus, Temple Univ Press, 90; auth, The Ontological Project Considered: The Displacement of Theoretical by Practical Unity, The S J of Philos, Spring 92; auth, The States of Ethical Judgements in the Philosophical Investigations, Philos Investigations; 18:2, 4/95; coauth, Thinking in the Ruins: Two Overlooked Responses to Contingency, Overheard in Seville, no 13, 108, 95; auth, Sensibility, Pragmatism, and Modernity, Bulletin of the Santayana Soc; no 15, 97; auth, Faith: Transcendence and Genealogy, Claremont Stud in the Philos of Relig, forthcoming. **CONTACT ADDRESS** Dept of Philos, Vanderbilt Univ, 111 Furman Hall, Nashville, TN 37240. **EMAIL** hodgesmp@ctrvax.vanderbilt.edu

HODGSON, PETER C.
PERSONAL Born 02/26/1934, Oak Park, IL, m, 1960, 2 children **DISCIPLINE** THEOLOGY **EDUCATION** Princeton Univ, AB, 56; Yale Univ, BD, 59, MA, 60, PhD, 63. **CAREER** Asst prof, Trinity Univ, 63-65; Vanderbilt Univ Divinity Sch, from asst prof to assoc prof, 65-73; prof 73-; ch, grad dept of relig, 75-80 & 90-97; grad fac coun, 75-80 & 90-97; univ res coun, 78-80; grad dean search comt, 83-84; ch, divinity fac, 85-86; fac sen, 85-86; univ comt on promotion and tenure, 87-88; divinity dean search comt, 88-89; ch, divinity acad prog comt, 88-89; grad dept of relig long range planning comt, 90-94; ch, New Testament, Homiletics, and Church Hist Search Comts, 93-96; ch, divinity dean search committee, 99-00. **HONORS AND AWARDS** Phi Beta Kappa, 56; cum laude, 59; Woodrow Wilson Fel, 56-57; Danforth Fel, 56-62; Guggenheim Fel, 74-75; Fulbright Scholar, 81; NEH, 81-87; Vanderbilt Univ Fel, 80-81, 86-87, & 92-93; Lilly Endowment, 98. **MEMBERSHIPS** Soc for Values in Higher Ed; Am Acad Relig; Hegel Soc Am; 19th C. Theology Group; Workgroup on Constructive Christian Theology. **RESEARCH** Modern theology. **SELECTED PUBLICATIONS** Auth, The Formation of Historical Theology: A Study of Ferdinand Christian Baur, Harper & Row, 66; auth, Jesus--Word and Presence: An Essay in Christology, Fortress, 71; auth, Children of Freedom: Black Liberation in Christian Perspective, Fortress, 74; auth, New Birth of Freedom: A Theology of Bondage and Liberation, Fortress, 76; auth, Revisioning the Church: Ecclesial Freedom in the New Paradigm, Fortress, 88; auth, God in History: Shapes of Freedom, Abingdon, 89; auth, Winds of the Spirit: A Constructive Christian Theology, Westminster John Knox, 94; auth of numerous articles and essays; auth, G.W.F. Hegel: Theologian of the Spirit, Fortress, 97; auth, God's Wisdom: Toward a Theology of Education, Westminster John Knox, 99. **CONTACT ADDRESS** Vanderbilt Divinity School, Vanderbilt Univ, Nashville, TN 37240. **EMAIL** peter.c.hodgson@vanderbilt.edu

HOEFER, CARL
DISCIPLINE PHILOSOPHY **EDUCATION** Stanford Univ, PhD. **CAREER** Assoc Prof, Univ Calif, Riverside; Sr Lectr, London Sch Econ, Philos. **RESEARCH** Philosophy of physics, metaphysics, philosophy of science. **SELECTED PUBLICATIONS** Coauth, "Substantivalism and the Hole Argument," Philosophical Problems of the Internal and External Worlds, Univ Pittsburgh Press, 94; "The Metaphysics of Spacetime Substantivalism," The Jour Philos, 96; "On Lewis' Objective Chance: Human Supervenience Debugged," Mind vol 106, 97; auth, Absolute vs. Relational Spacetime: For Better or Worse, the Debate Goes On, Bristish Journal for the Philosophy of Science, 98; auth, Kant's Hands and Earman's Pions: Chirality Arguments for Absolute Space, International Studies in Philosophy of Science, 00; auth, Energy Conservation in GTR Studies in History and Philosophy of Modern Physics, 00. **CONTACT ADDRESS** London Sch of Econs & Polit Sci, Houghton St, London, England WC2A 2AE. **EMAIL** c.hoefer@lse.ac.uk

HOEFER, RICHARD
DISCIPLINE SOCIAL WORK, POLITICAL SCIENCE **EDUCATION** Univ Kans, BSW, 79, MSW, 81; Int Grad Sch, Univ Stockholm, Diploma, 82; Univ Mich, MA, 84, PhD, 89. **CAREER** Lectr, Univ Mich, Ann Arbor, 88-89; res assoc, Center for Governmental Studies, Northern Ill Univ, DeKalb, 89-92; asst prof, Northern Ill Univ, 89-92; assoc dir, Center for Res, Evaluation and Technol, Sch of Soc Work, Univ Tex at Arlington, 94-, asst prof, Univ Tex at Arlington, 92-95, assoc prof, 95-. **HONORS AND AWARDS** Dept of Labor Human Resources Management Training Grant, 80-81; Senator James B. Pearson Overseas Study Fel, 81-82; Swedish Inst Fel, 82; Nat Inst of Mental Health Fel, 82-83; Univ Mich Rackham Predoctoral Grant, 86-87; American-Scandinavian Found Fel, 86-87; Fulbright-Hays Fel, 86-87; Fernando G. Torgerson Awd, Sch of Soc Work, Univ Tex, Arlington, May 98; Soc Worker of the Year, Tarrant Co Unit of the Tex Chapter of the Nat Asn of Soc Workers, March 99. **MEMBERSHIPS** Nat Asn of Soc Workers, Coun for Soc Work Educ, Asn for Community Orgn and Soc Admin, The Soc Welfare Policy and Policy Practice Group, Asn for Res on Nonprofit Orgns and Voluntary Action, Int Soc for Third Sector Res. **RESEARCH** Nonprofit organization management, work and life issues, program evaluation, nonprofit advocacy, American social welfare policy, Swedish social policy. **SELECTED PUBLICATIONS** Auth, "A Conceptual Model for Studying Social Welfare Policy Comparatively, J of Soc Work Educ, 32, 1 (Winter 96): 101-113; coauth, "Private Social Welfare Expenditures: The Mirror Welfare State," Encyclopedia of Social Work (97): 274-281; auth, "The Social Work

and Politics Initiative: A Model for Increasing Political Content in Social Work Education," J of Community Practice, (99): 6, 3; auth, "Protection, Prizes or Patrons? Explaining the Origins and Maintenance of Human Services Interest Groups," J of Sociol and Soc Welfare, 26, 4 (Dec 99): 115-136; auth, "Making a Difference: Human Service Interest Group Influence on Social Welfare Program Regulations," J of Sociol and Soc Welfare (forthcoming); auth, "Human Services Interest Groups in Four States: Lessons for Effective Advocacy," J of Community Practice (forthcoming); coauth, "Reliability and Validity in Qualitative Research," in Bruce Thyer, ed, Handbook of Social Work Research Methods (forthcoming). **CONTACT ADDRESS** Dept Soc Work, Univ of Texas, Arlington, Box 19129, Arlington, TX 76019-0001. **EMAIL** rhoefer@utarlg.uta.edu

HOEFFNER, KENT
PERSONAL Born 08/02/1958, Dallas, TX, m, 1986, 1 child **DISCIPLINE** THEOLOGY **EDUCATION** S Baptist Theol Sem, PhD. **CAREER** Asst prof, Truett-McConnell Col, 96-. **MEMBERSHIPS** AAR/SBL, Baptist Asn Philos Tchr. **RESEARCH** Post-modernism and Christianity; pedagogy and theology. **CONTACT ADDRESS** Dept of Theology, Truett-McConnell Col, 1201 Bishop Farms Pkwy, Watkinsville, GA 30677. **EMAIL** kent@truett.cc.ga.uc

HOEFLICH, MICHAEL H.
PERSONAL Born 01/11/1952, New York, NY, m, 1986 **DISCIPLINE** LAW, HISTORY **EDUCATION** Haverford Col, BA, 73; MA, 73; Cambridge Univ, MA, 76; Yale Law Sch, JD, 79. **CAREER** Res fel, Clare Col at Cambridge Univ, 75-77; tax assoc, Cravath, Swaine & Moore, 79-81; from asst prof to prof, Univ of Ill at Ubana-Champaign, 84-88; dean & prof, Syracuse Univ, 88-94; dean, prof & Courtesy Prof of Hist, Univ of Kans Sch of Law, 94-97; dean, Courtesy Prof of Hist, and John H. & John M. Kane Distinguished Prof of Law, Univ of Kans Sch of Law, 97-. **HONORS AND AWARDS** Fulbright Fel, 73; Sr Studentship, Clare Col at Cambridge, 74; NEH Travel Awd, 85; Surrency Prize, Am Soc for Legal Hist, 85; NEH Summer Stipend, 88; grant, Delmas Found, 95-96; Phillips Fel, Am Philos Soc, 95-96; grant, Kans Bar Found; vis res fel, Univ of Aberdeen, 00. **MEMBERSHIPS** ABA, NYSBA, Kans Bar Asn, Wichita Bar Asn. **RESEARCH** Legal History. **SELECTED PUBLICATIONS** Coauth, Property Law & Legal Education, Univ of Ill Press, 88; ed, The Gladsome Light of Jurisprudence, Learning the Law in England and the United States in the 18th & 19th Centuries, Greenwood Press (Westport, CT), 88; coauth, Cases & Materials on Federal Taxation of Deferred Compensation, Commerce Clearing House (Chicago, IL), 89; coauth, Der Einfluss deutscher Emigranten auf die Rechtsentwicklung in den USA und in Deutschland, JCB Mohr, 93; auth, Roman & Civil Law & the Development of Anglo-American Jurisprudence in the Nineteenth Century, Univ of Ga Press, 97; ed, Lex et Romanitas. Essays in Honor of Alan Watson, Robbins Inst Press, forthcoming. **CONTACT ADDRESS** Sch of Law, Univ of Kansas, Lawrence, 202 Green Hall, Lawrence, KS 66045.

HOEFLIN, RONALD K.
PERSONAL Born 02/23/1944, Richmond Heights, MO, s **DISCIPLINE** PHILOSOPHY **EDUCATION** New Sch for Soc Res, PhD, 87 **CAREER** Self Employed, Test Designer & Editor of various journals **HONORS AND AWARDS** Rockefeller Prize, 88; Who's Who in Amer; Who's Who in World **MEMBERSHIPS** Amer Philos Assoc **RESEARCH** Metaphysics; Categories; Metaphilosophy **CONTACT ADDRESS** PO Box 539, New York, NY 10101.

HOEKEMA, DAVID A.
PERSONAL Born 06/10/1950, Peterson, NJ, m, 1972, 2 children **DISCIPLINE** PHILOSOPHY **EDUCATION** Calvin Col, BA, 72; Princeton Univ, PhD, 81. **CAREER** Asst prof, 77-84, St Olaf Col; exec dir, Amer Phil Asn, & assoc prof, phil, 84-92, Univ Del; dean, Nat Sci & Math, & Contextual Disc, prof, phil, 92-98, dir grad stud, 93-94, actng v pres, Student Life, 98-99, prof philos, 99-, Calvin Col **HONORS AND AWARDS** Calvin Ctr for Christian Scholar grant; Am Coun of Learned Soc grant, 87-88; Danforth Fel, 72; Nat Merit Scholar, 68; Alvin M Bentley Scholar, 68; Who's Who in Am; Who's Who in the World; Dict of Intl Biog. **MEMBERSHIPS** Soc of Christian Phil; Bd of Trustees, Grand Rapids Art Mus; APA; Soc for Values in Higher Ed; Am Asn of Advancement of Sci; Am Coun of Learned Soc; Int Asn for Phil of Law, Soc Phil. **RESEARCH** Political phil; phil of art; hist of phil; phil of relig. **SELECTED PUBLICATIONS** Auth, Rights and Wrongs: Coercion, Punishment, and the State, Susquehanna Univ Press, 86; auth, Handbook for Administrators of Learned Societies, ACLS, NY 90; auth, Campus Life and Moral Community: In Place of In Loco Parentis, Rowman & Littlefield, 94; auth, Liberalism Revisited: Religion, Reason, Diversity, Christian Century 111:29, 94; auth, Conversations for Christian Higher Education: Introduction, Calvin Col, 96; auth, College Life in America: Historical Context and Legal Issues, Contemp Issues in Judicial Affairs, Jossey-Bass, 96; auth, Politics, Religion, and Other Crimes Against Civility, Academe 82:6, 96; co-ed, Christianity and Culture in the Crossfire, Eerdmans, 97. **CONTACT ADDRESS** Calvin Col, Grand Rapids, MI 49546. **EMAIL** dhoekema@calvin.edu

HOESLE, VITTORIO
PERSONAL Born 06/25/1960, Milano, Italy, m, 1997, 2 children **DISCIPLINE** PHILOSOPHY **EDUCATION** Univ Tubingen, Ph, 82; Habilitation, 86. **CAREER** Assoc prof, New Sch for Soc Res, 88; prof, Univ Essen, 93; dir, Res Inst for Philos, 97; Paul-Kimball-Professor for Arts and Letters, Univ Notre Damem 99. **HONORS AND AWARDS** Heisenberg-scholar, 87-93; Fritz-Winter-Price for outstanding achievements, 94. **RESEARCH** History of Philosophy, Metaphysics, Ethics, Political Philosophy. **SELECTED PUBLICATIONS** Auth, Moral und Politik, Munchen, 97; auth, Objective Idealism, Ethics and Politics, Notre Dame, 98; auth, Die Philosophie und die Wissenschaften, Munchen 99. **CONTACT ADDRESS** Dept Ger & Russian Lang, Univ of Notre Dame, 318 O'Shaugnessy Hall, Notre Dame, IN 46556-5639. **EMAIL** vhosle@nd.edu

HOFBECK, JOSEF
PERSONAL Born 05/30/1938, Germany, m, 1964, 4 children **DISCIPLINE** THEOLOGICAL STUDIES, ETHICS **EDUCATION** Sorbonne Univ, CES, 63 & 65; Inst Cath Paris, STL, 64, STD, 67. **CAREER** Asst prof, 67-72, chmn dept theol studies, 72-75, Assoc Prof Theol, Concordia Univ, Loyola Campus, 72- **MEMBERSHIPS** Soc Can Theol; Cath Theol Soc Am; Am Soc Christian Ethics; Prov Asn Teachers Ethics & Relig. **RESEARCH** Fundamental theology; Christian ethics. **SELECTED PUBLICATIONS** Auth, The Irony of Theology and the Nature of Religious Thought, Studies Relig, Vol 0021, 92. **CONTACT ADDRESS** Concordia Univ, Montreal, 7141 Sherbrooke St W, Montreal, QC, Canada H4B 1R6.

HOFF, JOAN WHITMAN
DISCIPLINE PHILOSOPHY **EDUCATION** Roger Williams Col, AS, 73, BA, 74; Univ RI, MA, 77; Am Univ, PhD, 82. **CAREER** Prof, Lock Haven Univ, 90-; Assoc Dir PA Con Studies Consortium. **HONORS AND AWARDS** NEH, summer sem for College Teachers, 83; fac summer fel, Northern Ky Univ, 85; fac summer res grant, Bentley Col, 87; Adele Mellen Prize, Edwin Mellen Press, 86-87; NEH, summer sem for col tchr, 88; summer grant, Bentley Col, 89; Can stud fc res grant, Can Embassy, 89-90; Can stud fac enrichment grant, Can Embassy, 90-91; LHU grants, 90-00; SSHE-PA grants, 95, 99; Con Emb Fac Enrich grant, 00. **SELECTED PUBLICATIONS** Auth, The Texaco Incident, J of Bus Ethics, 87; Theoretical Frameworks for Worker-Management Cooperation, Int Asn of Quality Circles State of The Art Conf Proc, 89; Child Custody, Children's Rights and Education, The Midwest Philos of Educ Soc Proc, 1989; Students, Ethics and the Surveys, A Commentary, J of Bus Ethics, 89; The Exxon Valdez Crisis, in The Corporation, Ethics And The Environment, ed W. Hoffman et al, Quorum Bks, 90; Selected Comments on Crocker's 'Functioning and Capability: The Foundation of Sen's Development Ethic', Montclair State Univ's Inst for Critical Thinking Working Paper ser, 91; coauth, Risky Business, McGraw-Hue, 97; coauth, Philosophies for Living, Prentice Hall, 01. **CONTACT ADDRESS** Dept of Philos, Lock Haven Univ of Pennsylvania, Lock Haven, PA 17745.

HOFF, SAMUEL B.
DISCIPLINE POLITICAL SCIENCE **EDUCATION** Susquehanna Univ, BA, 79; Am Univ, MA, 81; Stony Brook, MA, 83; State Univ NY, PhD, 87. **CAREER** Instr, State Univ NYork Stony Brook, 83-85; adj instr, NYork Inst of Technol, 86; adj asst prof, Wittenberg Univ, 87; vis asst prof, Ohio Wesleyan Univ, 86-87; asst prof, State Univ NYork Col at Geneseo, 88-89; vis asst prof, Wichita State Univ, 88-89; from asst prof to George Washington Distinguished Prof, Del State Univ, 89-. **HONORS AND AWARDS** Professional Development Awd, Del State Univ, 90-99; Merit Pay Awd, Del State Univ, 92 & 94-99; Employee of the Year for Fac Excellence in Teaching, Del State Univ, 96; listed in Who's Who in America, 98; Best Paper Awd, Pa Polit Sci Asn, 99; Alpha Kappa Mu Honor Soc, Del State Univ, 99; Chi Alpha Sigma National Athlete Honor Soc, Del State Univ, 99. **MEMBERSHIPS** Nat Network of State Polls, United Nations Asn of the United States of America-Delaware Div, Ctr for the Study of the Presidency, Acad of Polit Sci, Nat Capitol Area Polit Sci Asn, Northeastern Polit Sci Asn, Nat Soc Sci Asn, Southern Polit Sci Asn, Midwest Polit Sci Asn, Western Polit Sci Asn, Soc Sci Hist Asn, Western Soc Sci Asn, Pa Polit Sci Asn, NY State Polit Sci Asn. **SELECTED PUBLICATIONS** Rev, of "The American Presidency Under Siege," by Gary L. Rose, Soc Sci J (Spring 98): 294-295; auth, "Toward 2000: The CIA's role in American Foreign and Security Policy," in Strategic Challenges to U.S. Foreign Policy in the Post-Cold War, ed. Marco Rimanelli (Saint Leo Press, 98), 73-82; auth, "Presidents and Governing," Congress and the Presidency (98): 199-202; auth, "Reassessing Public Financing of Presidential Campaigns," Nat Soc Sci J (98): 23-26; rev, of "Star-Spangled Men: America's Ten Worst Presidents," by Nathan Miller, Presidential Studies Quart (Winter 99): 215-216; rev, of "All the Presidents' Words: The Bully Pulpit and the Creation of the Virtual Presidency," by Carol Gelderman, Presidential Studies Quart (Winter 99): 213-215; rev, of "The President's Call: Executive Leadership From FDR to George Bush," by Judith Michaels, Soc Sci Quart (June 99): 430-431; auth, "The Separation of Powers Doctrine and its Relation to Presidential Removal Power," The Polit Chronicle (Spring 99): 13-24. **CONTACT ADDRESS** Dept Hist & Polit Sci, Delaware State Univ, Dover, DE 19901.

HOFF, TIMOTHY
PERSONAL Born 02/27/1941, Freeport, IL, m, 1987, 4 children **DISCIPLINE** LAW **EDUCATION** Tulane Univ, AB, 63; Tulane Univ, JD, 66; Harvard Law Sch, LLM, 70. **CAREER** Prof, Univ Ala, 70-. **HONORS AND AWARDS** Student Bar Association's Outstanding fac mem awd, 86. **MEMBERSHIPS** Phi Beta Kappa; Fla Bar; Al Bar. **RESEARCH** Admiralty, civil procedure, conflict of laws, law in literature, federal jurisdiction, and law and religion. **SELECTED PUBLICATIONS** Auth, Alabama Limitations of Actions and Notice Provisions, 2d, 92. **CONTACT ADDRESS** Law Dept, Univ of Alabama, Tuscaloosa, Box 870382, Tuscaloosa, AL 35487-0382. **EMAIL** thoff@law.ua.edu

HOFFECKER, W. ANDREW
DISCIPLINE CHURCH HISTORY **EDUCATION** Dickinson Col, BA; Gordon-Conwell, MDiv; Brown Univ, PhD. **CAREER** Prof, Grove City Col; prof; Reformed Theol Sem. **HONORS AND AWARDS** Captain, US Army. **MEMBERSHIPS** Evangel Theol Soc. **RESEARCH** Princeton Theology; C.S. Lewis; Worldview. **SELECTED PUBLICATIONS** Auth, Piety and the Princeton Theologians; ed, Building a Christian World View. **CONTACT ADDRESS** Dept of Church History, Reformed Theol Sem, Mississippi, 5422 Clinton Blvd, Jackson, MS 39209-3099. **EMAIL** ahoffecker@rts.edu

HOFFHEIMER, MICHAEL H.
PERSONAL Born 12/21/1954, Cincinnati, OH, m, 2 children **DISCIPLINE** LEGAL STUDIES **EDUCATION** The Johns Hopkins Univ, BA, 77; Univ Chicago, MA, PhD, 78, 81; Univ Mich, JD, 84. **CAREER** Assoc, Frost & Jacobs, 84-87; Appointed Public Defender in Criminal Cases, 85-87; Asst Prof of Law, 87-90; Assoc Prof of Law, 90-97; Prof of Law, Univ of Mississippi School of Law, 97-. **HONORS AND AWARDS** Mississippi Defense Lawyers Asn Lecturer at Law; Bencher emeritus William C. Keady Inn of Court; Am Inns of Court. **MEMBERSHIPS** Amer Bar Assoc; Assoc of Trial Lawyers of Amer; Amer Society for Legal History; Legal Society of Amer. **RESEARCH** Law; History; Philosophy; Literature. **SELECTED PUBLICATIONS** Auth, "Justice Holmes and the Natural Law," (New York: Garland Publishing, Inc., 92); auth, "Eduard Gans and the Hegelian Philosophy of Law," International Archives of the History of ideas (Dordrecht: Kluwer Academic Publishers, 95; auth, "Law, Fossils, and the Configuring of Hegel's Philosophy of Nature," Idealistic Studies 25, 95: 155-73; auth, "Hegel's First Philosophy of Law," tennessee Law Review 62, 95: 823-97; auth, "Hegel's Manuscript The Transcendental Idea of God," Clio 24, 95: 419-26; auth, "Mississippi Conflict of Laws," Mississippi Law Journal, 67, 97: 175-321; auth, "Baptism and Law in the Young Hegel," Clio 27, 98: 533-50; auth, "Law and Legal Education as a Hotbed for the Novel: The Case of Goethe," Wayne Law Review 44, 98: 1-27; auth, "Observing Capital Punishment in Arnold Bennett's The Old Wives' Tale," Mississippi Law Journal 69, 99: 441-53; auth, "Entry on Edward Christian in New Dictionary of National Biography," Oxford Univ Press, forthcoming. **CONTACT ADDRESS** School of Law, Univ of Mississippi, General Delivery, University, MS 38677-9999.

HOFFMAN, DANIEL
PERSONAL Born 01/07/1957, Hamilton, OH, m, 1987 **DISCIPLINE** ANCIENT AND CHURCH HISTORY **EDUCATION** Miami Univ, PhD, BS Ed; Trinity Evangelical Divinity School, MA; Moody Bible Inst, BA. **CAREER** Asst Prof of Hist, 94-, Lee Univ of Cleveland; Tchr, Dept Chr, 86-94, Soc Stud, Charlotte Christian School. **HONORS AND AWARDS** John Stephenson Fellowships; Who's Who in Amer Tchr; Lee Univ Faculty Res Grants. **MEMBERSHIPS** NAPS, ASOR, The Conf on Faith and Hist. **RESEARCH** Gnosticism; Women in the Early Church; Karak Region of Jordan during the Roman Era. **SELECTED PUBLICATIONS** Auth, The Status of Women and Gnosticism in Irenaeus and Tertullian, Studies in Women and Religion 36, Lewiston NY, Edwin Mellen, 95; Bathe, Jewish and Prisons in: A Dictionary of Biblical Manners and Customs, eds, RK Harrison, M Wilson, S Carroll & E Yamauchi, Grand Rapids, Zondervan, forthcoming; Walter Bauer, Suetonius, in: Encyclopedia of Historians and Historical Writing, ed, K Boyd, London, Fitzroy Dearborn, 97; Phoenix, The Anchor Bible Dictionary, ed, DN Freedman, NY, Doubleday, 92. **CONTACT ADDRESS** Dept of Behavioral and Social Science, Lee Col, Tennessee, Box 3450, Cleveland, TN 37320-3450. **EMAIL** dhoffman@leeuniversity.edu

HOFFMAN, JOHN C.
PERSONAL Born 12/07/1931, Toronto, ON, Canada **DISCIPLINE** THEOLOGY **EDUCATION** Univ Toronto, BA, 54; McGill Univ, PhD, 57, BD, 59, STM, 60; Union Theol Sem (NY), ThD, 64. **CAREER** Prof relig stud, Univ Windsor, 64-90, prin Iona Col, 64-85, dean students, 87-90; prin, Emmanuel Col, 90-96, Prof to Prof Emer, Emmanuel Col, Univ Toronto, 90-. **SELECTED PUBLICATIONS** Auth, Ethical Confrontation in Counselling, 79; auth, Law, Freedom and Story, 86; auth, Faithfull Stories, 94. **CONTACT ADDRESS** Emmanuel Col, Univ of Toronto, 75 Queen's Park Crescent East, Toronto, ON, Canada M5S 1K7.

HOFFMAN, MARK G.
DISCIPLINE RELIGION **EDUCATION** Univ Ill, BA, 78; Luther Northwestern Theol Sem, MDiv, 83; Yale Univ, MA, 85, MPhil, 87, PhD, 96. **CAREER** Instr Greek and New Testament, Luther Northwestern Theol Sem, 87-88; pastor, Faith Lutheran Church, Spicer, MN, 88-92; pastor, Hope Lutheran Church, Fargo, ND, 92-. **MEMBERSHIPS** Soc Bibl Lit; Cath Bibl Asn. **RESEARCH** New Testament. **CONTACT ADDRESS** Dept of Ministry, Hope Lutheran Church, 3246 Elm St., Fargo, ND 58102-1126. **EMAIL** mgvh@minister.com

HOFFMAN, PAUL
DISCIPLINE HISTORY OF EARLY MODERN PHILOSOPHY **EDUCATION** UCLA, PhD. **CAREER** Assoc Prof, Univ Calif, Riverside. **RESEARCH** Moral psychology; Philosophy of mind. **SELECTED PUBLICATIONS** Coauth, "Alternative Possibilities: A Reply to Lamb," Jour Philos 91, 94; "Responses to Chappell and Watson," Philos Stud 77, 95; "Strength and Freedom of Will: Descartes and Albritton," Philos Stud 77, 95; "The Being of Leibnizian Phenomena," Studia Leibnitiana 28, 96; "Descartes on Misrepresentation," Jour Hist of Philos 34, 96. **CONTACT ADDRESS** Dept of Philos, Univ of California, Riverside, 1156 Hinderaker Hall, Riverside, CA 92521-0209. **EMAIL** phoffman@ucrac1.ucr.edu

HOFFMAN, PETER TOLL
PERSONAL Born 05/05/1946, Schenectady, NY, d, 1 child **DISCIPLINE** LAW **EDUCATION** Mich State Univ, BA, 68; Univ Mich, JD, 71. **CAREER** Instr & dir clinical law prog, Univ Mich Sch Law, 72-73; asst prof to Earl Dunlap Prof of Law, Univ Nebr Col Law, 74-; vis assoc prof, Univ Hawaii Sch Law, 77-78; vis Sr Fel, City Univ of Hong Kong, 92; Assoc Justice, Supreme Court of Palau, 94-96; vis Prof, Univ of San Diego, 99; vis prof, Washington Univ, St. Louis, 00. **RESEARCH** Lawyering skills. **SELECTED PUBLICATIONS** Auth, Trial court responses to claims for relief under the Nebraska Post Conviction Act: A taxonomy, Nebr Law Rev, 57: 355; Clinical course design and the supervisory process, Ariz State Law Rev, 82; Valuation of Cases for Settlement: Theory and Practice, J Dispute Resolution, 91; coauth, The Effective Deposition, 2nd ed, 96; auth, Nebraska Divorce, Practice Manual, 2nd ed, 99. **CONTACT ADDRESS** Col of Law, Univ of Nebraska, Lincoln, East Campus, Lincoln, NE 68583. **EMAIL** phoffman@unl.edu

HOFFMAN, PIOTR
DISCIPLINE HISTORY OF PHILOSOPHY AND CONTINENTAL PHILOSOPHY **EDUCATION** Univ Paris, Sorbonne, PhD, 70. **CAREER** Prof, Univ Nev, Reno. **RESEARCH** Ontological implications of the political philosophies of Hobbes, Locke, and Rousseau. **SELECTED PUBLICATIONS** Auth, The Anatomy of Idealism, Kluwer/Martinus Nijhoff, 82; The Human Self and the Life and Death Struggle, Univ Fla, 83; Doubt, Time, and Violence, Univ Chicago, 86; Violence in Modern Philosophy, Univ Chicago, 89; The Quest for Power: Hobbes, Descartes and the Emergence of Modernity, Hum Press, 96. **CONTACT ADDRESS** Univ of Nevada, Reno, Reno, NV 89557.

HOFFMAN, VALERIE J.
PERSONAL Born 04/27/1954, New York, NY, M, 1998, 3 children **DISCIPLINE** RELIGION **EDUCATION** Univ Chicago **CAREER** Univ IL, vis lectr, asst prof, assoc prof, 83-. **HONORS AND AWARDS** Full Re Grant, 87-88; NEH Fel, 91-92; Univ Ill, Univ Schol, 96 **MEMBERSHIPS** MESANA, AAR, AMEWS, AIMS, ASA, AIYS. **RESEARCH** Islamic thought and pop relig; late med & mod n and e Africa; Islamic gender ideology; woman's relig lives. **SELECTED PUBLICATIONS** Auth, Polemics on the Modesty and Segregation of Women in Contemporary Egypt, Int'l J of ME St, 87; auth, Devotion to the Prophet and His Family in Egyptian Sufism, Int'l J of ME St, 92; auth, Women and Religion: Women's Religious Observance, Encyclopedia of Modern Islam, 95; auth, Eating and Fasting for God in Sufi Tradition, JAAR, 95; auth, Sufism, Mystics and Saints in Modern Egypt, 95; The Role of Visions in Contemporary Egyptian Religious Life, Religion, 97; auth, Annihilation in the Messenger of God, Int'l J of ME St, 99. **CONTACT ADDRESS** Program for the Study of Religion, Univ of Illinois, Urbana-Champaign, 707 S Matthews Ave, Urbana, IL 61801. **EMAIL** vhoffman@uiuc.edu

HOFFMANN, STANLEY
PERSONAL Born 11/27/1928, Vienna, Austria, m, 1963 **DISCIPLINE** GOVERNMENT; POLITICS. **EDUCATION** Institut d'Etudes Politiques, diplome, Paris, 45-48; Institut des Hautes Etudes Internationales, Paris, diplome, 48-50; Law Sch, Univ of Paris, licence 48, doctorate, 53; Harvard Univ, Dept of Govt, MA, 52. **CAREER** Instr, 55-57, Asst prof, 57-59, assoc prof, 59-62, 60-68 chmn, Comt on Degrees in Soc Studies, prof, 63-present, Harvard; vis prof, 75-76, Institut d'Etudes Politiques, vis prof, chair of Am civilization, ecole des Hautes Edtudes en Sciences Sociales, 83-84; presi, Int Inst of Polit Psychology, 84-85; Paul and Catherine Buttenwieser Univ Professorship, 97. **HONORS AND AWARDS** Carnegie Endow for Int Peace, Intl Org Prize, 55; John Simon Guggenheim Mem Found Grant, 65; Rockefeller Found aand Am Coun of Lrnd Societies Grants, 69-70; Chevalier, Fr Legion of Honor, 76; Prix Adolphe Bentinck, 82; Commander, Fr Legion of Honor; Commander's Cross of the Order of Merit of the Fed Republic of Ger; Balzan Prize in Int Relations, 96; Awd for Lifetime achievement in Polit studies assoc, 00. **MEMBERSHIPS** Am Acad of Arts and Sci; Am Polit Sci Assn; Am Soc of Int Law; Coun on Foreign Relations; Fr-Am Found; Fr Historical Studies; Assn Francaise de Sci Politique; Intl Soc of Polit Psychology **SELECTED PUBLICATIONS** Auth, After the Cold War, 93; The European Sisyphus:Essays on Europe, 1964-1994, 95; The Ethics and Problems of Humanitarian Intervention, 97; auth, World Disorders, 98. **CONTACT ADDRESS** Harvard Univ, Cambridge, MA 02138. **EMAIL** shhoffm@fas.harvard.edu

HOFFMASTER, BARRY
DISCIPLINE PHILOSOPHY **EDUCATION** Dartmouth Col, BA, 69; Univ Minn, MA, 78; PhD, 75. **CAREER** Prof **RESEARCH** Methodological approaches to bioethics. **SELECTED PUBLICATIONS** Auth, Hanging Out a Shingle: The Public and Private Services of Professionals, Can Jour Law Jurisprudence, 96; Dragons in the Sunset: The Allure of Assisted Death, 94; The Forms and Limits of Medical Ethics, Social Sci Medicine, 94; Morality and Culture: Putting Ethical Issues in Context, 94; coauth, Bioethics for Clinicians: 7. Truth Telling, Can Medical Asn Jour, 97; A Decision-making Aid for Long-term Care Waiting List Policies: Modelling First-come, First-served vs Needs-based Criteria, 96; co-ed, Deadlines and Diversity: Journalism Ethics in a Changing World, Fernwood, 96; Health Care Ethics in Canada, Harcourt Can, 95. **CONTACT ADDRESS** Dept of Philosophy, Univ of Western Ontario, London, ON, Canada N6A 5B8. **EMAIL** choffmas@julian.uwo.ca

HOFSTADTER, DOUGLAS RICHARD
PERSONAL Born 02/15/1945, New York, NY, w, 1985, 2 children **DISCIPLINE** PHILOSOPHY, PSYCHOLOGY, HISTORY, PHILOSOPHY OF SCIENCE, COMPARATIVE LIT **EDUCATION** Stanford Univ, BS, 65; Univ of Ore, MS, 72; PhD, 75. **CAREER** Visiting Scholar, inst for Math Studies in the Social Sci, Stanford Univ, 75-77; asst prof of computer sci, 77-80, assoc prof of computer sci, 80-83, Ind Univ; visiting scholar, computer sci dept, Stanford Univ, 80-81; columnist, Sci Am, 81-83; visiting sci, Artificial Intelligence Lab, MIT, 83-84; Walgreen Prof for the Study of Human Understanding and prof of psychology and cognitive sci, Univ of Mich, 84-88; visiting scholar, Center for Computer-Assisted Res in the Humanities, Stanford Univ, 97; DIR, CENTER FOR RES ON CONCEPTS AND COGNITION, 88-, ADJUNCT PROF OF PSYCHOLOGY, PHILOS, HIST, PHILOS OF SCI, & COMPARATIVE LIT, 88-, COL PROF OF COGNITIVE SCI AND COMPUTER SCI, 88-, IND UNIV. **HONORS AND AWARDS** Pulitzer Priz, 80; Am Book Awd, 80; Guggenheim Fel, 80-81; Polya Prize, 83; Senior Fel, Mich Soc of Fels, 85; Arts and Sci Alumni Fels Awd, Univ of Ore, 97; Tracy M. Sonneborn Awd, Ind Univ, 98. **RESEARCH** Cognitive science; philosophy of the mind; creativity in translation; the mechanisms underlying discovery and creation in mathematics. **SELECTED PUBLICATIONS** Coauth, Fluid Concepts and Creative Analogies: Computer Models of the Fundamental Mechanisms of Thought, Basic Books, 95; auth, Rhapsody on a Theme by Clement Marot, Grace A. Tanner Center for Human Values, 95; auth, Le Ton beau de Marot: In Praise of the Music of Language, Basic Books, 97; auth, Breaking Out of Egocentrisms and Chauvinisms: The Many-layered Process of Building a Modern Mind, Evolution: Entwicklung und Organisation in der Natur, Rowohlt, 93; auth, Speechstuff and Thoughtstuff: Musings on the Resonances Created by Words and Phrases via the Subliminal Perception of their Buried Parts, Of Thoughts and Words: The Relation between Language and Mind, 95; On Seeing A's and Seeing As, Stanford Humanities Rev, 95; auth, Popular Culture and the Threat to Rational Inquiry, Sci, 98. **CONTACT ADDRESS** Center for Research on Concepts and Cognition, Indiana Univ, Bloomington, 510 N Fess St., Bloomington, IN 47408-3822. **EMAIL** dughof@cogsci.indiana.edu

HOGAN, MELINDA
DISCIPLINE PHILOSOPHY **EDUCATION** Univ Calif, Berkeley, AB, 79; Univ Wis, MA, 85, PhD, 89. **CAREER** Asst prof. **RESEARCH** Philosophy of mind, philosophy. of language, metaphysics. **SELECTED PUBLICATIONS** Auth, What is wrong with an Atomistic Account of Mental Representation?, Synthese, 94; "Natural Kinds and Ecological Niches," Biol and Philos, 92. **CONTACT ADDRESS** Dept of Philos, Dalhousie Univ, 1236 Henry St, Halifax, NS, Canada B3H 3J5. **EMAIL** melinda.hogan@dal.ca

HOGAN, WILBUR C.
PERSONAL Born 12/27/1903, Kansas City, MO, m, 1992, 3 children **DISCIPLINE** PHILOSOPHY, LOGIC, MATH **EDUCATION** US Coast Guard Acad; BS, 28; Purdue Univ, MS, 59. **CAREER** Coast Guard officer, 28-58; commander, Coast Guard Inst, 50-52; Calif Polytech Inst, 59-73. **HONORS AND AWARDS** Number One Student at USCG Acad, 28; Number One Student at Purdue Univ Grad Prog, 59; Emeritus Prof, Calif Polytech Inst, 73. **MEMBERSHIPS** Naval Inst; Am Philos Soc. **RESEARCH** World religions of the ancient world - Sumeria and Mexico. **SELECTED PUBLICATIONS** Auth, articles in The Naval Inst Preceedings, 54-56. **CONTACT ADDRESS** 162 Serrano Heights, San Luis Obispo, CA 93401.

HOGE, DEAN R.
PERSONAL Born 05/27/1937, New Knoxville, OH, m, 1965, 2 children **DISCIPLINE** SOCIOLOGY, RELIGIOUS STUDIES **EDUCATION** Ohio State Univ, BA, 60; Harvard Divinity Sch, BD, 64; Harvard Univ, PhD, 70. **CAREER** Instr/Asst Prof, Princeton Theol Sem, 69-74; Assoc Prof/Prof, Cath Univ of Am, 74-. **HONORS AND AWARDS** Distinguished Book Awd, for "Vanishing Boundaries," Soc for the Sci Study of Relig, 94. **MEMBERSHIPS** Am Sociol Asn, Soc for the Sci Study of Relig, Relig Res Asn. **RESEARCH** Sociology of religion and churches. **SELECTED PUBLICATIONS** Auth, Converts, Dropouts, Returnees: A Study of Religious Change Among Catholics, US Cath Conf, 81; auth, The Future of Catholic Leadership: Responses to Priest Shortage, Sheed and Ward, 87; coauth, Vanishing Boundaries: The Religion of Mainline Protestant Baby Boomers, Westminster/John Knox Press, 94; coauth, Money Matters: Personal Giving in American Churches, Westminster/John Knox Press, 96; coauth, Laity, American and Catholic: Transforming the Church, Sheed and Ward, 96. **CONTACT ADDRESS** Dept Sociol, Catholic Univ of America, 620 Michigan Ave, Washington, DC 20064-0002. **EMAIL** hoge@cua.edu

HOGENSON, GEORGE B.
PERSONAL Born 02/23/1948, Rochester, MN, m, 1987, 2 children **DISCIPLINE** PHILOSOPHY **EDUCATION** St. Olaf Col, BA, 70; Yale Univ, PhD, 79. **CAREER** Asst prof, Yale Univ, 79-86; prog officer, MacArthur Found, 86-89; private practice, Jungian analyst, 89-. **RESEARCH** History and philosophy of psychoanalysis; Evolutionary theories of cognitive development. **SELECTED PUBLICATIONS** Auth, Jung's Struggle with Freud. **CONTACT ADDRESS** 711 S. Dearborn, Apt. 801, Chicago, IL 60605. **EMAIL** hogenson@msn.com

HOGGATT, JERRY CAMERY
PERSONAL Born 04/14/1950, Burbank, CA, m, 1977, 3 children **DISCIPLINE** NEW TESTAMENT **EDUCATION** Boston Univ, PhD. **CAREER** Prof, Vanguard Univ. **SELECTED PUBLICATIONS** Auth, Speaking of God; Irony in the Mark's Gospel: Text and Subtext. **CONTACT ADDRESS** Division of Religion, Vanguard Univ, 55 Fair Dr., Costa Mesa, CA 92626. **EMAIL** jerrych@vanguard.edu

HOITENGA, DEWEY J.
PERSONAL Born 02/05/1931, Hancock, MN, m, 1953, 4 children **DISCIPLINE** PHILOSOPHY OF RELIGION **EDUCATION** Calvin Col, AB, 52; Calvin Theological Seminary, BD, 55; MA, 57, PhD, 59, Harvard Univ. **CAREER** Instr, Worcester Jr Col, 59; Asst Prof, 59-61, Assoc Prof, Chr, 61-65, Chr, Humanities Dept, 62-62, Chr, Committee for guest Lectrs and Performing Artists, 63-65, Juniata Col; Assoc Prof, 65-69, Prof, 69-, Grand Valley State Univ. **HONORS AND AWARDS** Adjunct Fel, Univ Notre Dame, 87-88; Michigan Assoc of Governing Boards of State Univ Distinguished Fac Awd, 92; Henry Stob Lectureship, Calvin Col, 93; Meeter Center Colloqium Series (invited lectureship), 95. **MEMBERSHIPS** Amer Phil Assoc; Soc of Christian Philosphers **RESEARCH** Epitemology; philosophy of mind; philosophy of religion; specialty and reformed epistemology **SELECTED PUBLICATIONS** Auth, Faith and Reason from Plato to Plantinga: An Introduction to Reformed Epitemology, 91; Faith Seeks Understanding: Augustine's Alternative to Nature Theology, Collectanea Augustiniana, 93; Happiness: Goal or Gift? Two Lectures on the Relationships Between Knowledge, Goodness, and Happiness in Plato and Calvin, The Stob Lectures, 94; John Calvin on the Will: Critique and Corrective, 97. **CONTACT ADDRESS** Grand Valley State Univ, 221 Lake Superior Hall, Allendale, MI 49401. **EMAIL** hoitengd@gvsu.edu

HOLDER, ARTHUR G.
DISCIPLINE CHRISTIAN SPIRITUALITY **EDUCATION** Duke Univ, AB, PhD; Gen Theol Sem, MDiv. **CAREER** Prof; dean, Acad Aff, Church Divinity Sch Pacific **SELECTED PUBLICATIONS** Co-auth, Bede: A Biblical Miscellany, Liverpool UP, 98; auth, (Un)Dating Bede's De Arte Metrica, Northumbria's Golden Age, Sutton, 98; Styles of Clerical Address in the Letters of Augustine, Studia Patristica, 97; Bede: On the Tabernacle, Liverpool UP, 94; The Mosaic Tabernacle in Early Christian Exegesis, Studia Patristica, 93; Saint Basil the Great on Secular Education and Christian Virtue, Rel Edu, 92. **CONTACT ADDRESS** Church Divinity Sch of the Pacific, 2451 Ridge Rd, Berkeley, CA 94709-1217.

HOLIFIELD, E. BROOKS
PERSONAL Born 01/05/1942, Little Rock, AR, m, 1963, 2 children **DISCIPLINE** HISTORY, RELIGION **EDUCATION** Hendrix Col, BA, 63; Yale Divinity Sch, BD, 66; Yale Grad Sch, MA, 68, PhD, 70. **CAREER** Asst prof, Candler Sch of Theol and Grad Div of Relig, Emory Univ, 70-75, assoc prof, 75-80, prof, 80-84, chair, Dept Hist Studies, Grad Div, 77-79, Dir, Grad Div of Relig, 79-83, Charles Howard Candler Prof of Am Church Hist and Assoc Member of the Dept of Hist, 84-. **HONORS AND AWARDS** Woodrow Wilson Fel, 63; Danforth Fel, 63-70; Yale Steering Fel, 69; NEH Res Fel, 76-77, 83-84, 91-92; Pew fel, 98-99; Louisville Inst Fel, 98-99. **MEMBERSHIPS** Am Acad of Relig, Am Soc of Church Hist, Am Hist Asn. **RESEARCH** American religious history. **SELECT-**

ED PUBLICATIONS Auth, The Covenant Sealed: The Development of Puritan Sacramental Theology in Old and New England, 1570-1720, New Haven: Yale Univ Press (74); auth, The Gentlemen Theologians: American Theology and Southern Culture, 1795-1860, Durham: Duke Univ Press (78); auth, A History of Pastoral Care in America: From Salvation to Self-Realization, 1570-1970, Nashville: Abingdon Press (83); auth, Health and Medicine in the Methodist Tradition, NY: Crossroad Press (86); auth, Era of Persuasion: American Thought and Culture 1521-1680, Boston: Twayne Pubs (89). **CONTACT ADDRESS** Sch of Theol, Emory Univ, 1364 Clifton Rd NE, Atlanta, GA 30322-1061. **EMAIL** eholifi@emory.edu

HOLLADAY, CARL R.
PERSONAL Born 10/18/1943, Huntingdon, TN, m, 1964, 3 children **DISCIPLINE** THEOLOGY **EDUCATION** Abilene Christian Univ, BA, 65, MDiv, 69; Princeton Theo Sem, MTh, 70; Cambridge Univ, PhD, 75. **CAREER** Asst Prof, 75-78, Assoc Prof, 78-80, Yale Univ Div School; Assoc Prof, 80-90, Prof NT, 90-, Assoc Dean, 83-85, act Dean, 85, Assoc Dean, 86-91, Dean fac & acad affairs, 92-94, Emory Univ Candler School Theo. **HONORS AND AWARDS** Fulbright Senior Scholar, Germany, 94-95; Henry T. Luce III Fel in Theol, 99-00. **MEMBERSHIPS** SBL, SNTS, AAUP. **RESEARCH** New Testament literature & history, Greek speaking Judaism in the Hellenistic-Roman world. **SELECTED PUBLICATIONS** Auth, Fragments from Hellenistic Jewish Authors, SBL, Scholars Press, 83-95; Theios Aner in Hellenistic Judaism, SBL, Scholars Press, 77; co-auth, Biblical Exegesis, A Beginners Handbook, Atlanta John Knox Press, 87; co-auth, Preaching Through the Christian Year, Trinity, 92-92. **CONTACT ADDRESS** 668 Clifton Rd NE, Atlanta, GA 30307-1789. **EMAIL** theocrh@emory.edu

HOLLADAY, WILLIAM LEE
PERSONAL Born 06/23/1926, Dallas, TX, m, 1948, 4 children **DISCIPLINE** RELIGION **EDUCATION** Univ Calif, BA, 48; Pac Sch Relig, BD, 51; State Univ Leiden, THD, 58. **CAREER** Asst prof relig, Elmhurst Col, 60-63; prof Old Testament, Near East Sch Theol, 63-70; prof, 70-71, Lowry Prof Old Testament, Andover Newton Theol Sch, 71- **MEMBERSHIPS** Soc Bibl Lit. **RESEARCH** Jeremiah studies; patterns of pre-exilic Hebrew poetry. **SELECTED PUBLICATIONS** Auth, The Root Subh in the Old Testament, Brill, Leiden, 58; ed, A Concise Hebrew and Aramaic Lexicon of the Old Testament, Brill, Leiden & Eerdmans, Grand Rapids, 71; auth, Jeremiah: Spokesman Out of Time, United Church, 74; The Structure of Jeremiah 1-20, Bucknell Univ, 76; Isaiah: Scroll of a Prophetic Heritage, Eerdmans, 78. **CONTACT ADDRESS** Andover Newton Theol Sch, Newton, MA 02159.

HOLLAND, MARGARET G.
DISCIPLINE PHILOSOPHY **EDUCATION** State Univ NYork Buaaflo, PhD, 91. **CAREER** Assoc prof, current. **MEMBERSHIPS** Am Philos Asn. **RESEARCH** Ethics; Moral psychology. **SELECTED PUBLICATIONS** Auth, "Touching the Weights: Moral Perception and Attention," in Int Philos Quart, 98; "What's Wrong With Telling the Truth: An Analysis of Gossip," in Am Philos Quart, 96. **CONTACT ADDRESS** Dept of Philosophy and Religion, Univ of No Iowa, Cedar Falls, IA 50614. **EMAIL** margaret.holland@uni.edu

HOLLAND, ROBERT A.
PERSONAL Born 11/24/1953, St. Louis, MO, m, 1990 **DISCIPLINE** PHILOSOPHY **EDUCATION** Univ Ill-Chicago, PhD, 89. **CAREER** Assoc Prof, Hofstra Univ, 89-. **MEMBERSHIPS** Am Philos Asn; Philos Sci Asn; Asn Symbolic Logic. **RESEARCH** Philosophy of mathematics & science; Metaphysics; Non-western philosophy. **SELECTED PUBLICATIONS** Auth Kant, Reichenbach, and Aprioricity, Philos Stud, 92; Apriority and Applied Mathematics, Synthese, 92; A Modern Formulation of Anselm's Response to Gaunilo, Tchg Philos, 93; Towards a Resolution of Sankara's Atmavidya and the Buddhist Doctrine of Anatman, Int Philos Quart, 95. **CONTACT ADDRESS** Dept of Philosophy, Hofstra Univ, 104 Heger Hall, Hempstead, NY 11049. **EMAIL** phirah@hofstra.edu

HOLLANDER, RACHELLE D.
PERSONAL Born 07/04/1944, Balto, MD, m, 1969, 2 children **DISCIPLINE** PHILOSOPHY **EDUCATION** Goucher Col, BA, 65; UMCP, PhD, 79. **CAREER** Prog dir, US Natl Science Found, 76-. **HONORS AND AWARDS** Phi Beta Kappa; AAAS Fel. **MEMBERSHIPS** AAAS; Coun of Soc for Social Stud of Science; APA, Soc for Phil and Tech; Asn for Practical and Prof Ethics. **RESEARCH** Ethics and Risk; Engineering Ethics; Research Ethics. **SELECTED PUBLICATIONS** Coed, Acceptable Evidence: Science and Values in Risk Management, Oxford Univ Press, 91. **CONTACT ADDRESS** National Sci Foundation, Rm 995, Arlington, VA 22230. **EMAIL** rholland@nsf.gov

HOLLENBACH, PAUL WILLIAM
PERSONAL Born 05/09/1926, Lawrence, MA, m, 1952, 3 children **DISCIPLINE** RELIGION, BIBLE **EDUCATION** Wheaton Col, BA, 49; Univ Rochester, MA, 52; Union Theol Sem, NYork, BD, 54; Drew Univ, PhD, 65. **CAREER** Asst prof relig, Emory & Henry Col, 59-63; asst prof philos, Cent Col Iowa, 64-67; asst prof, 67-69, Assoc Prof to prof emer, Philos, Iowa State Univ, 69-, Coordr Relig, 73-, Chmn Prog In Relig, 74- **MEMBERSHIPS** Am Acad Relig; Soc Bibl Lit. **RESEARCH** New Testament; life of Jesus. **SELECTED PUBLICATIONS** The Social World of Luke-Acts--Models For Interpretation, Cath Biblical Quarterly, 93. **CONTACT ADDRESS** Dept of Religious Studies, Iowa State Univ of Science and Tech, Ames, IA 50011.

HOLLER, CLYDE
PERSONAL Born 07/05/1948, Washington, PA **DISCIPLINE** PHILOSOPHY OF RELIGION **EDUCATION** Univ Chicago, BA, 70; Episcopal Theol School, MDiv, 73; Boston Univ, PhD, 81. **CAREER** Indiana Purdue Fort Wayne; owner-manager, Buckhead Editorial Service Atlanta, 85-. **HONORS AND AWARDS** Assoc Fac in Philos Dept, 81-85. **MEMBERSHIPS** Am Acad of Rel. **RESEARCH** Black Elk; Kierkegaard; Lakota Religion; Philosophy of Religion. **SELECTED PUBLICATIONS** Auth, Tragedy in the Context of Kierkegaard's Either/Or, in Int Kierkegaard Commentary: Either/Or, 95; Black Elk's Religion: The Sun Dance and Lakota Catholicism, 95; The Black Elk Reader, forthcoming. **CONTACT ADDRESS** Buckhead Editorial Service, 3091 Maple Dr NE, Ste 204, Atlanta, GA 30305. **EMAIL** buckword@mindspring.com

HOLLERAN, JOHN WARREN
PERSONAL Born 04/23/1928, San Francisco, CA **DISCIPLINE** SCRIPTURE, THEOLOGY **EDUCATION** St Patrick's Col, Calif, HA, 49; Univ Calif, Berkeley, MA, 60; Gregorian Univ, Rome, Italy, STL, 53, STD, 73; Univ San Francisco, MA, 77. **CAREER** Asst prof ethics, Holy Names Col, Calif, 55-57; lectr theol, Lone Mt Col, San Francisco, Calif, 57-62; spiritual dir, N Am Col, Rome, 62-68; prof scripture, St Patrick's Sem, Menlo Park, Calif, 68-. **MEMBERSHIPS** Cath Theol Soc Am; Cath Bibl Asn; AAUP. **RESEARCH** Scripture; theology; spirituality. **SELECTED PUBLICATIONS** Auth, The Synoptic Gethsemane, Gregorian Univ, 73; Christ's prayer & Christian prayer, Worship, 3/74. **CONTACT ADDRESS** St. Patrick's Sem, 320 Middlefield Rd., Menlo Park, CA 94025.

HOLLEY, DAVID M.
DISCIPLINE PHILOSOPHY **EDUCATION** Southern Baptist Theol Sem, Louisville, Mdiv; Univ TX at Austin, PhD. **CAREER** Dept Phil, Univ S Miss **RESEARCH** Transformation of the self and strategies for avoiding wrongdoing. **SELECTED PUBLICATIONS** Publ on, studies in philosophy of religion, philosophy and rhetoric, ethics & philosophical psychology. **CONTACT ADDRESS** Dept of Philos and Relig, Univ of So Mississippi, 2701 Hardy St, Hattiesburg, MS 39406. **EMAIL** dmholley@ocean.st.usm.edu

HOLLEY, JIM
PERSONAL Born 12/05/1943, Philadelphia, PA, w, 1 child **DISCIPLINE** THEOLOGY **EDUCATION** Wayne State University, PhD, Higher Education; University of Chicago, Chicago, IL, Master of Divinity. **CAREER** Little Rock Baptist Church, Detroit, MI, Pastor, 72-; Cognos Advertising, Detroit, Pres, CEO, 88-; Ashland Theol Sem, Dean; D.Min, Drew Univ; Sr Pastor; Pres and CEO Cognos Adv; Founder: Pres Detroit Academy of Arts and Sciences, 00. **CONTACT ADDRESS** Little Rock Baptist Church, 9000 Woodward Ave, Detroit, MI 48202.

HOLLIS, SUSAN T.
PERSONAL Born 03/17/1939, Boston, MA, d, 2 children **DISCIPLINE** RELIGION; ANCIENT NEAR EASTERN LANGUAGES & CIVILIZATIONS **EDUCATION** Harvard, PhD, 82 **CAREER** Prof, Union Inst Los Angeles, 91-93; dean & prof, Sierra Nevada Col, 93-95; center dir & assoc dean, Central NY Center, State Univ of NY, Empire State Col, 96-; Assoc Prof, Genesee Valley Century, State University of New York, Empire State Col, 99- **HONORS AND AWARDS** Teaching Excellence, Harvard Col; Who's Who in the West, East, America, World, Women **MEMBERSHIPS** Amer Res Egypt; Amer Acad Relig; Soc Bibl Lit; Int Assoc Egyptologist; Amer Folklore Soc **RESEARCH** Ancient Egypt; Ancient Israel; Egyptian Relations; Folklore; Ancient Women's Studies **SELECTED PUBLICATIONS** auth, The Ancient Egyptian "Tale of Two Brothers": The Oldest Fairy Tale in One World, u. and OK Press, 90; co-ed & contributor, Feminist Theory and the Study of Folklore, Univ Ill, 93; ed, Ancient Egyptian Hymns, Prayers, and Songs. An Anthology of Ancient Egyptian Lyric Poetry, Scholar's Press, 95; contri, Civilizations of the Ancient Near East, "Tales of Magic and Wonder" (Scribner 95); auth, "Otiose Deities and the Ancient Egyptian Pantheon," Jrnl Amer Res Center in Egypt, 98; contri, "Two Brothers"; contri, "Oval Tradition"; contri, The Oxford Encyclopedia and Ancient Egypt, Oxford, 01 **CONTACT ADDRESS** SUNY, Empire State Col, 1475 Winton Rd. N, Rochester, NY 14609. **EMAIL** susan_hollis@esc.edu

HOLLOWAY, ALVIN J.
PERSONAL Born 07/02/1926, Shreveport, LA, s **DISCIPLINE** PHILOSOPHY **EDUCATION** Spring Hill Col, BS, 49; St Louis Univ, STL, 57; Fordham Univ, PhD, 65. **CAREER** Chemn, philos dept, Loyola Univ, 67-98. **MEMBERSHIPS** APA; Am Catholic Philos Asn. **RESEARCH** Medieval philosophy; Augustine; biomedical ethics. **CONTACT ADDRESS** 6363 St Charles Ave, New Orleans, LA 70118. **EMAIL** holloway@loyno.edu

HOLM, TAWNY L.
PERSONAL Born 08/29/1966, WY, s **DISCIPLINE** RELIGION **EDUCATION** John Hopkins Univ, PhD, 97. **CAREER** Vis Lect, 95-96, Central Col; Adj Prof, 97-98, Loyola Col; Adj Prof, 97-98, St Marys Ecumenical Inst; Vis Asst Prof, 98-99, DePauw Univ; asst prof, Ind Univ of Penn, 99- . **MEMBERSHIPS** Soc of Bibl Lit; Catholic Bibl Assoc **RESEARCH** The book of Daniel; Syriac philology; Demotic Egyptian story cycles. **CONTACT ADDRESS** Philos & Religious Studies, Indiana Univ of Pennsylvania, 1011 S Drive, Indiana, PA 15705. **EMAIL** tholm@grove.iup.edu

HOLMAN, CHARLES L.
PERSONAL Born 03/30/1935, Oxnard, CA, m, 1966, 1 child **DISCIPLINE** NEW TESTAMENT **EDUCATION** Westmont Col, BA; Fuller Theol Sem, BD, ThM; Univ Nottingham, Eng, PhD. **CAREER** Instr, Jamaica Theol Sem, 64-69; dean, instr, Trinity Christian Training Inst, 72-78; asst prof, 82-86; assoc prof, 87-93; prof, 93-. **HONORS AND AWARDS** Prof of the Year, 96-97, Regent Univ. **RESEARCH** Biblical hermaneutics. **SELECTED PUBLICATIONS** Auth, A Response to Roger Stronstad's The Biblical Precedent for Historical Precedent, 93; Paul's Preaching Cognitive and Charismatic, Spirit and Renewal: Essays in Honor of J. Rodman Williams, Jour Pentecostal Theol, Supplement Series 5, Sheffield Acad Press, 94; Titus 3:5-6: A Window on World-Wide Pentecost, Jour Pentecostal Theol 8, 96; Till Jesus Comes: Origins of Christian Apocalyptic Expectation, Hendrickson, 96. **CONTACT ADDRESS** Dept of New Testament, Regent Univ, 1000 Regent Univ Dr, Virginia Beach, VA 23464-9831. **EMAIL** charhol@regent.edu

HOLMES, RICHARD H.
DISCIPLINE PHILOSOPHY **EDUCATION** Wash Univ, PhD, 72. **RESEARCH** Contemporary European philos; philos of/in lit. **SELECTED PUBLICATIONS** Auth, The Transcendence of the World, Wilfrid Laurier, 94; ed, Moritz Geiger's The Significance of Art; Husserl Memorial Issue of Eidos. **CONTACT ADDRESS** Dept of Philosophy, Univ of Waterloo, 200 University Ave W, Waterloo, ON, Canada N2L 3G1. **EMAIL** rholmes@watarts.uwaterloo.ca

HOLMES, ROBERT A.
PERSONAL Born 07/13/1943, Shepherdstown, WV, 3 children **DISCIPLINE** POLITICAL SCIENCE; PUBLIC LAW AND GOVERNMENT **EDUCATION** Shepherd Coll, BS, 64; Columbia Univ, MA, 66, PhD, 69. **CAREER** Coordinator, 68, Harvard-Yale-Columbia Intensive Summer Study Program; Assoc prof, 69-70; Southern Univ; Dir, 70-71, Search for Elevation, Education and Knowledge; prof, 71-75, 76-, Atlanta Univ; dir, 89-, Southern Ctr for Studies in Public Policy, Clark Atlanta Univ. **HONORS AND AWARDS** Georgia Environmental Council Legislator of the Year; Shepher Coll Alumni of the Year; Sickle Cell Found of Georgia Torchbearer Award; Concerned Black Clergy Father of the Year. **MEMBERSHIPS** Natl Conf of Black Political Scientists **RESEARCH** Environmental policy; African Amer politics; Urban politics **SELECTED PUBLICATIONS** Coed and auth, Appropriations/Budget, Governmental Affairs and Other Issues, Georgia Legislative Review, 99; ed, The Status of Black Atlanta, 99, ed, The Georgia Legislative Review, 99; auth, A Survey of Members of the National Black Caucus of State Legislators on Alternatives to Single Member District Elections, 00. **CONTACT ADDRESS** Dept of Political Sci, Clark Atlanta Univ, 223 Chesnut St. SW, Atlanta, GA 30314. **EMAIL** bholmes@cau.edu

HOLMES, ROBERT ERNEST
PERSONAL Born 07/24/1943, New York, NY, s **DISCIPLINE** LAW **EDUCATION** NYork Univ, BA 1966; NYork Univ Sch of Law, JD 1969; Manhattan Sch Of Music & Univ of So CA, addl study. **CAREER** Paul Weiss Rifkind Wharton & Garrison, summer assoc 1968, part time atty 1968-69, assoc atty 1969-71; WA Sq Coll of Arts & Sci, guest lectr 1969-70, adj instr Amer Lit 1970-71; NY School of Continuing Educ, adj instr Black Amer 1969-70; Motown Record Corp, sr counsel 1971, legal counsel 1971; Columbia Pictures Music Group, sr vp, gen mgr, pres Columbia Pictures Music Publ Div. **HONORS AND AWARDS** Dean's List Temple Univ & NY Univ Sch of Law; Univ Schlrshp NY U, NY State Schlrshp NY U; Leopold Schepp Fnd Schlrshp NY U; various debate & pub spkng awrds; Am Jurisprudence Prize in Copyright; Military History Awd Temple Univ 1963; recipient Fulbright-Dougherty Travel Grant 1967; Samuel Rubin SchlrshpCarnegie Fnd Schlrshp **MEMBERSHIPS** Bd dir Pacific Psychotherapy Asso CA; bd dir NAACP; bd dir Constl Rights Found CA; bd dir Black Music Assoc; past pres Black Entertainment & Sports Lawyers' Assoc. **SELECTED PUBLICATIONS** numerous publs. **CONTACT ADDRESS** Columbia Pictures and Music Publ, Columbia Plaza E, Rm 231, Burbank, CA 91505.

HOLMES, ROBERT LAWRENCE
PERSONAL Born 12/28/1935, Watertown, NY, m, 1958, 2 children **DISCIPLINE** PHILOSOPHY **EDUCATION** Harvard Univ, AB, 57; Univ MI, MA, 59, PhD, 61. **CAREER** Instr philos, Univ TX, 61-62; from asst prof to assoc prof, 62-71, Prof Philos, Univ Rochester, 71-, Am Coun Learned Soc grant-in-aid, 64; fel, Ctr Advan Studies, Univ IL, 70-71; fel, Nat Hum Inst, Yale Univ, 76-77; Sr fulb lec, moscow univ, 83; Ed, Public Affairs Quarterly, 95-99. **MEMBERSHIPS** Am Philos Asn. **RESEARCH** Ethics; philos of war; soc and polit philos. **SELECTED PUBLICATIONS** Auth, Descriptivism, supervenience and universalizability, J Philos, 3/66; John Dewey's moral philosophy in contemporary perspective, Rev Metaphysics, 9/66; co-auth, Philosophic Inquiry: An Introduction to Philosophy, 2nd ed, Prentice-Hall, 68; auth, Violence and nonviolence, In: Violence, McKay, 71; University neutrality and ROTC, Ethics, 4/73; On pacifism, Monist, 10/73; Is morality a system of hypothetical imperative?, Analysis, 1/74; Nozick on anarchism, Polit Theory, 5/77; auth, "Frankena on Is and Ought," The Monist, (81); auth, "Perspectives on Morality and War in American Society: A Symposium," in While Soldiers; auth, "Fought: War in American Society," (86); auth, "Ethics Before Profits," in Ethics for Modern Life, " 3rd ed., (87); On War and Morality, 89; Ed, Nonviolence in Theory and Practice, 90; Basic Moral Philosophy, 93, 2nd edition, 98. **CONTACT ADDRESS** Dept of Philos, Univ of Rochester, 500 Joseph C Wilson, Box 270078, Rochester, NY 14627-0078. **EMAIL** HLMS@mail.rochester.edu

HOLMSTROM-HINTIKKA, GHITA B. E.
PERSONAL Born 01/12/1936, Helsinki, Finland, m, 1987, 2 children **DISCIPLINE** PHILOSOPHY **EDUCATION** Univ Helsinki, MA, 75; Ph Lic, 85; Uppsala Univ, PhD, 91. **CAREER** Teacher/Lectr, Univ of Helsinki, 71-87; Docent, Dept Syst Theology, Univ of Helsinki, 95-; Vis Prof, Uott, Finland, 97-98; Asst Prof/ Adj Asst Prof/Adj Assoc Prof, Boston Univ, 90-. **MEMBERSHIPS** Am Philos Asn, Finish Philos Asn, Swedish Philos Asn. **RESEARCH** Action Theory, Applied Logic, Theory of Argumentation, Legal Philosophy, Medieval Philosophy (from an analytical point viewpoint), Applied Ethics. **SELECTED PUBLICATIONS** Co-ed, "Action, Logic and Social Theory," Acta Philosophica Vol 38 (Helsinki), 85; auth, "Action, Purpose and Will, A Formal Theory," Acta Philosophica Vol 50 (Helsinki), 91; ed, "Legal Argumentation," Communication and Cognition 28-1 (95); co-ed, "Contemporary Action Theory," in Vol I-II Syntheses Library (Kluwer Acad Publ, Dordrecht, Holland, 97), 266-267; auth, "Reasonable Doubt," in Festschrift fur Aulis Aarnio, ed. Werner Krawietz et al (Duncker & Humboldt GMBH, Berlin, 98); auth, "Expert Witnesses in Model of Interrogation," in Artificial Intelligence and Law, ed. A.A. Martino and Ephraim Nissan (98); ed, "Inadmissible Evidence," in Not Without Cause, Festschrift for Paul Needham, by Lars Lindahl, Jan Odelstad and Rysiek Sliwinski (Uppsala UPS 48, 98); ed, Medieval Philosophy and Modern Times, Kluwer Acad Publ, Dordrecht (Holland and Boston, Mass), 99; auth, "Questions about a Question in Ockham," in Medieval Philosophy and Modern Times, ed. Ghita Holmstrom-Hintikka, Syntheses Library (Dordrecht, Holland and Boston, Mass: Kluwer Acad Publ, 99), 101-119; auth, "Kanger's Actions and Influence," in Stig Kanger's Collected Works, ed. Ghita Holmstrom-Hintikka, Sten Lindstrom and Rysiel Sliwinski, Syntheses Library (Kluwer, 99). **CONTACT ADDRESS** Dept of Philos, Boston Univ, Boston, MA 02215. **EMAIL** Ghita.Holmstrom-Hintikka@helsinki.fi

HOLSTI, OLE R.
PERSONAL Born 08/07/1933, Geneva, Switzerland, m, 1953, 2 children **DISCIPLINE** POLITICAL SCIENCE **EDUCATION** Stanford Univ, BA, 54; Wesleyan Univ, MAT, 56; Stanford Univ, PhD, 62. **CAREER** Instr and asst prof, polit sci, Stanford Univ, 62-65; res coordr and assoc dir, Studies in Int Conflict and Integration, Stanford Univ, 62-67; assoc prof and prof, polit sci, Univ British Columbia, 67-74; George V. Allen Prof, Dept Polit Sci, Duke Univ, 74- ; chemn dept, 78-83; Dir Undergrad Studies, 92- . **HONORS AND AWARDS** Own D. Young Fel, GE Found, 60-61; Canada Coun Res Grant, 69; fel, Ctr for Adv Study in Behavioral Sci, 72-73; Ford Found Fac Fel, 72-73; NSF Res Grant, 75-77, 79-81; Guggenheim Fel, 81-82; Best Published Paper Awd, Int Studies Q, 79-81; NSF Res Grant, 83-85, 88-90; Nevitt Sanford Awd, Int Soc of Polit Psychol, 88; Pew Fac Fel, Harvard Univ, 90; NSF Res Grant, 92-94, 96-98; Alumni Distinguished Undergrad Tchg Awd, 95. **SELECTED PUBLICATIONS** Coauth, Enemies in Politics, Rand McNally, 67; auth, Content Analysis for The Social Sciences and Humanities, Addison-Wesley, 69; auth, Crisis, Escalation, War, McGill-Queen's, 72; auth, Unity and Disintegration in International Alliances: Comparative Studies, Wiley, 73; co-ed, Change in the International System, Westview, 80; coauth, American Leadership in World Affairs: Vietnam and The Breakdown of Consensus, Allen & Unwin, 84; auth, Public Opinion and American Foreign Policy, Michigan, 96; co-ed, Encyclopedia of U.S. Foreign Relations, Oxford, 96. **CONTACT ADDRESS** Dept of Political Science, Duke Univ, 302 Perkins Library, PO Box 90204, Durham, NC 27708. **EMAIL** holsti@acpub.duke.edu

HOLTMAN, SARAH WILLIAMS
DISCIPLINE PHILOSOPHY **EDUCATION** Col of William and Mary, BA, 82; Univ Virginia, JD, 86; UNC-Chapel Hill, PhD, 95. **CAREER** Law Clerk, Massachusetts Superior Ct, 86-87; Law Clerk, New Hampshire Supreme Ct, 87-89; Asst Prof, 95-, Univ Minnesota-Twin Cities. **HONORS AND AWARDS** Phi Beta Kappa; Charlotte W. Newcombe Fel, Woodrow Wilson Fdn, 94-95; NEH Summer Stipend, 00. **MEMBERSHIPS** Amer Phil Assoc; Mass Bar. **RESEARCH** Ethics; political philosophy; philosophy of law; Kant's practical philosophy **SELECTED PUBLICATIONS** Auth, Kant's Formula of Humanity and the Pursuit of Subjective Ends, Proceedings of the 8th International Kant Congress, 95; A Kantian Approach to Prison Reform, Jahrbuch fur Rechtund Ethik, 97; Toward Social Reform: Kant's Penal Theory Reinterpreted, Utilitas, 97; auth, "Kant, Ideal Theory and the Justice of Exclusionary Zoning," Ethics (99). **CONTACT ADDRESS** Dept of Philosophy, Univ of Minnesota, Twin Cities, 271 19th Ave S, 831 Heller Hall, Minneapolis, MN 55455. **EMAIL** holtm001@maroon.tc.umn.edu

HOLTZ, AVRAHAM
PERSONAL Born 05/26/1934, New York, NY, m, 4 children **DISCIPLINE** MODERN HEBREW LITERATURE **EDUCATION** Brooklyn Col, BA, 55; Jewish Theol Sem Am, MHL, 59, DHL, 62. **CAREER** Dean acad develop, 77-80, Prof Mod Hebrew Lit, Jewish Theol Sem Am, 73-. **HONORS AND AWARDS** Nat End of the Hum. **SELECTED PUBLICATIONS** Ed, The Holy City: Jews on Jerusalem, Norton/Viking, 71; auth, Isaac Dov Berkowitz: Voice of the Uprooted, Cornell Univ, 73; auth, B'Olam Hanah shava shel Hazal Marot U-Meqorot: Mahadura; Mueret u-meuyeret shel Hakhnasat Kallah le-Shmuel Yosef Agnon. **CONTACT ADDRESS** Jewish Theol Sem of America, 3080 Broadway, New York, NY 10027-4649.

HOLTZ, BARRY
PERSONAL Born Boston, MA, m, 1985, 2 children **DISCIPLINE** JEWISH EDUCATION AND STUDIES **EDUCATION** Tufts Univ, BA; Brandeis Univ, PhD. **CAREER** Vis prof, Hebrew Univ; co-dir, Melton Res Ctr; assoc prof, Jewish Theol Sem; lect, 92nd Street Y, New York. **SELECTED PUBLICATIONS** Auth, Back to the Sources: Reading the Classic Jewish Texts, Simon and Schuster 84; Finding Our Way: Jewish Texts and the Lives we Lead Today, Schocken, 90; The Schocken Guide to Jewish Books, 92; coauth, Your Word is Fire: The Hasidic Masters on Contemplative Prayer, Jewish Lights Press. **CONTACT ADDRESS** Jewish Theol Sem of America, 3080 Broadway, New York, NY 10027. **EMAIL** baholtz@jtsa.edu

HOMANS, PETER
PERSONAL Born 06/24/1930, New York, NY, m, 1958, 3 children **DISCIPLINE** RELIGIOUS STUDIES, RELIGION & PSYCHOLOGY **EDUCATION** Princeton Univ, AB, 52; Va Theol Sem, BD, 57; Univ Chicago, PhD(relig & psychol), 64. **CAREER** Lectr relig, Trinity Col, Univ Toronto, 62-64; asst prof, Hartford Sem Found, 64-65; asst prof relig & psychol, 65-68, assoc prof, 68-79, prof Psychol and Relig Studies, Univ Chicago, 80-, Soc Values Higher Educ res grant popular cult, 73-74; Asn Theol Sch res grant relig & psychol, 77. **MEMBERSHIPS** Am Psychol Asn; Am Acad Relig. **RESEARCH** Hist of Religions; psychology and culture. **SELECTED PUBLICATIONS** Ed & contribr, The Dialogue Between Theology and Psychology, Univ Chicago, 68; auth, Theology After Freud: An Interpretive Inquiry, Bobbs Merrill & Co, 70; ed & contribr, Childhood and Selfhood: Essays on Tradition, Religion and Modernity in the Psychology of Erik H Erikson, Bucknell Univ, 78; The Ability to Mourn: Disillusionment and the Social Origins of Psychoanalysis, Univ Chicago Press, 89; auth, Jung in Context: Modernity and the Making of a Psychology, Univ of Chicago Press, 95, second editon; ed & contrib, Symbolic Loss: The Amiguity of Mournig and Memory at Century's End, Univ Press of Virginia, 00. **CONTACT ADDRESS** Univ of Chicago, 1025-35 E 58th St, Chicago, IL 60637-1577. **EMAIL** phomans@midway.uchicago.edu

HOMERIN, T. EMIL
PERSONAL Born 05/19/1955, Pekin, IL, m, 1977, 2 children **DISCIPLINE** RELIGION **EDUCATION** Univ Illinois, BA, 77, MA, 78; Univ Chicago, PhD, 87. **CAREER** Lect Rel Stud, DePaul Univ, 82-83; lect Islamic Civ, George Williams Col, 83; asst prof Islamic Stud, Temple Univ, 86-88; asst prof Rel to Assoc Prof, Dept Chair, Univ Rochester, 94-. **HONORS AND AWARDS** Nom, Goergen Awd Dist Ach, Artistry in Teach, 97; Hon men, Golden Key Nat Hon Soc Exemplary Commitment to Higher Educ, 95; G. Granyon & Jane W. Curtis Awd Exc, 93; finalist, Teach Year, 92; Abraham J. Karp Awd Exc, Univ Roch, 91; Am Asn Teachers of Arabic Translation Contest; Michael A. Scherer Awd, Univ Ill, 77; James Scholar, Univ Ill, 75-76; whitehall fnd scholar, 73-77; ill state scholar, 73-77; ndfl/ndea fel, 77-78; ctr arabic stud abroad fel, 79-80; nat defense for lang fel, 80-82; fulbright-hays fel res abroad, 83-84; mrs. giles whiting fel hum, 85-86; neh fel, cairo, (declined), 88- 89; **MEMBERSHIPS** Am Acad Rel; Am Oriental Soc; Am Res Ctr Egypt; Middle East Stud Asn. **RESEARCH** Arabic poetry; Islam; mysticism. **SELECTED PUBLICATIONS** Auth, From Arab Poet to Muslim Saint: Ibn al-Farid, His Verse, and His Shrine, Univ SC Press, 94; auth, "Sufis and their Detractors in Mamluk Egypt: A Survey of Protagonists and Institutional Settings," in Islamic Mysticism Contested, E.J. Brill, (98) 225-46; auth, " Poetry and the Study of the Medieval Middle East," Al. 'Usur Al-Wusta: The Bulletin of the Middle East Medievalists," (99), 4-5, 11; auth, "Reflections on Arabic Poetry in the Mamluk Age," Mamluk Stud Rev 1, 97; auth, "Ibn al-Farid," and Munawi's Literary Hagiography of Ibn al-Farid," in Windows on the House of Islam, Univ Calif Press, 98; auth, "Saving Muslim Souls: the Khanqah and the Sufi Duty in Mamluk Lands," Mamluk Stud Rev, 3, 99; auth, "A Saint, His Shrine, and Poetry's Power," Forthcoming in Islamic Mysticism in Practice," University of Princeton Press; auth, "In the Gardens of az-Zahra: Love Echoes in a Poem by Ibn Zaydun" Forthcoming in The Shaping of an American Islamic Discourse: A Memorial to Fazlur Rahman," Scholars Press, (98), auth, "Arabic Religious Poetry: 1200-1800" Forthcoming in The Cambridge History of Arabic Literature: The Post-Colonial Period, Cambridge University Press. **CONTACT ADDRESS** Dept Religion and Classics, Univ of Rochester, 430 Rush Rhees Library, Rochester, NY 14627. **EMAIL** THEH@mail.rochester.edu

HONEYCUTT, DWIGHT A.
PERSONAL Born 10/17/1937, Bessemer, AL, m, 1960, 3 children **DISCIPLINE** CHURCH HISTORY **EDUCATION** Mercer Univ, BA; Midwestern Baptist Sem, BD; Intl Baptist Theol Sem, Switzerland, ThM; New Orleans Baptist Theol Sem, ThD. **CAREER** Instr, Intl Baptist Theol Sem, Cali, Colombia, 77; vis prof, New Orleans Baptist Theol Sem; Midwestern Baptist Theol Sem, 87-88; prof, 88; William A. Carleton prof, Golden Gate Baptist Theol Sem, 92-. **HONORS AND AWARDS** Assoc secy, missionary personnel, S Baptist For Mission Bd, 72. **MEMBERSHIPS** AAR, Am Soc of Church History. **SELECTED PUBLICATIONS** Pub(s), Theol Educator; Bolotin Teologico de ABITHA; El Heraldo; Dialogo Teologica; Jour Church and State; SBC Quart Rev. **CONTACT ADDRESS** Golden Gate Baptist Theol Sem, 201 Sem Dr, Mill Valley, CA 94941-3197. **EMAIL** dhoneycutt@ggbts.edu

HONG, CHANG-SEONG
PERSONAL Born 09/03/1964, Incheon, Korea, m, 1993 **DISCIPLINE** PHILOSOPHY **EDUCATION** Brown Univ, MA, 95, PhD, 00. **CAREER** Adj prof, RI Col, 97-98; asst prof, St Cloud State Univ, 98-99; Asst Prof, Minn State Univ, Moorhead, 99-. **MEMBERSHIPS** Am Philos Asn; Soc for Philos in the Contemp World. **RESEARCH** Philosophy of mind; metaphysics. **SELECTED PUBLICATIONS** Auth, Natural Kinds and the Identity of Property, Teorema, 98; auth, Kripke's Reference Theory, Philos Forum, 91; auth, Falsifiability and the Growth of Knowledge, Philos Forum, 88. **CONTACT ADDRESS** Dept of Philosophy, Minnesota State Univ, Moorhead, Moorehead, MN 56563. **EMAIL** cshong@mnstate.edu

HONG, HOWARD V.
PERSONAL Born 10/19/1912, Wolford, ND, m, 1938, 8 children **DISCIPLINE** PHILOSOPHY **EDUCATION** St. Olaf Col, BA, 34; Univ Minn, PhD, 38. **CAREER** Prof, philos, St. Olaf Col, 38-78; general ed, Kierkegaard's Writings, Princeton Univ Press, 72-00. **HONORS AND AWARDS** Knight of Danebrog; Latuian Order of Three Stars; D. Hum., Carleton Col; Lt. D., McGill Univ; Th. D., Univ Copenhagen. **MEMBERSHIPS** Amer Philos Asn. **RESEARCH** Kierkegaard; Philosophical anthropology. **SELECTED PUBLICATIONS** Auth, Kierkegaard's Writings, 78-00. **CONTACT ADDRESS** 5174 E. 90 Old Dutch Rd., Northfield, MN 55057.

HOOD, EDWIN T.
DISCIPLINE LAW **EDUCATION** Univ Iowa, JD; Univ NYork, LLM. **CAREER** Prof **HONORS AND AWARDS** Pearson Awd, 93. **RESEARCH** Taxation. **SELECTED PUBLICATIONS** Auth, Closely Held Businesses in Estate Planning, Aspen Law Bus, 98; co-auth, Federal Taxation of Close Corporations, Callaghan. **CONTACT ADDRESS** Law Dept, Univ of Missouri, Kansas City, 5100 Rockhill Rd, Kansas City, MO 64110-2499. **EMAIL** hoode@umkc.edu

HOOKER, PAUL K.
PERSONAL Born 12/17/1953, Wartrace, TN, m, 1990, 2 children **DISCIPLINE** OLD TESTAMENT **EDUCATION** Univ TN, BA, 75; Union Theological Sem, VA, DMin, 79; Emory Univ, PhD, 93. **CAREER** Presbyterian minister, 20 years; Pastor, Rock Spring Presbyterian Church, 93-; Exec Presbyter, Presbytery of St. Augustine. **MEMBERSHIPS** Soc of Biblical Lit **RESEARCH** 1-2 Kings; 1-2 Chronicles; church's use of scripture. **SELECTED PUBLICATIONS** Auth, A New Chronology for the Kings of Israel and Judah, with John H. Hayes. **CONTACT ADDRESS** Presbytery of St. Agustine, PO Box 10207, Jacksonville, FL 32247. **EMAIL** pkhooker@staugpres.org

HOOKS, BENJAMIN LAWSON
PERSONAL Born 01/31/1925, Memphis, TN, m, 1951 **DISCIPLINE** LAW **EDUCATION** LeMoyne College, attended, 1941-43; Howard University, attended, 1943-44; DePaul University, JD, 1948. **CAREER** Attorney, 49-65, 68-72; Mutual Federal Savings & Loan Assn, co-founder, vice pres, director,

chairman, 55-69; Middle Baptist Church, pastor, 56-72; asst public defender, 61-64; Greater New Mt Moriah Baptist Church, pastor, 64-; Shelby County Criminal Court, judge, 65-68; Federal Communications Commission, 72-78; NAACP, executive director, 77-93; Chapman Co, senior vice pres, 93; Fisk Univ, prof of social justice, 93-. **HONORS AND AWARDS** Howard University, honorary LLD, 1975; Wilberforce University, honorary LLD, 1976; Central State University, honorary DHL, 1974, honorary LLD, 1976; Masons, Man of the Year Awd, 1964, Gold Medal Achievement Awd, 1972; Optimist Club of America Awd, 1966; Lincoln League Awd, 1965; Tennessee Regional Baptist Convention Awd; Spingarn Awd, NAACP, 1986; producer/host, Conversations in Black & White; co-producer, Forty Percent Speaks; panelist, What Is Your Faith?. **MEMBERSHIPS** Natl Bar Assn, judicial council; American Bar Assn; Tenessee Bar Assn; bd trustee, LeMoyne-Owen College; bd dir, Southern Christian Leadership Conference, 1968-72; grand chancellor, Knights Pythias; bd trustee, Hampton Institute; Natl Civil Rights Museum, bd member. **CONTACT ADDRESS** Fisk Univ, 1000 17th Ave N, Nashville, TN 37208-3051.

HOOPS, MERLIN HENRY
PERSONAL Born 10/02/1926, Byron, NE, m, 1955, 2 children **DISCIPLINE** THEOLOGY; NEW TESTAMENT **EDUCATION** Capital Univ, AB, 51; Evangel Lutheran Theol Sem, BD, 55; Univ Hamburg, ThD(New Testament), 58. **CAREER** Assoc prof, 60-71, prof, 71-81, Ernest W & Edith S Ogram Prof, 81-94, Ernest W & Edith S Ogram prof emer New Testament studies, Trinity Lutheran Sem, OH, 94-; mem, Lutheran-Orthodox Comn, 66-68 & dept of theol studies, Lutheran Coun. **MEMBERSHIPS** Soc Bibl Lit; Lutheran Acad Scholar (treas, 71-). **RESEARCH** New Testament backgrounds; Gospel of Matthew and John; liberation theology. **SELECTED PUBLICATIONS** Auth, The concept of Liberation, Lutheran Quart, 8/76; Translating the Bible: The Challenge of an Ongoing Process, Trinity Sem Rev, fall 81; auth, "First Peter: A Renewed Appreciation?" Trinity Seminary Review, 83; auth, "First Peter: A Community at Witness," Trinity Seminary Review, 85; auth, "Christ and Mission," Bible and Mission, Wayne Stumme, Ed, Published by Augsburg, 86. **CONTACT ADDRESS** Trinity Lutheran Sem, 2199 E Main St, Columbus, OH 43209-2334.

HOOVER, KENNETH R.
DISCIPLINE POLITICAL SCIENCE **EDUCATION** Beloit Col, Wisconsin, BSc, 62; Univ Wis-Madison, PhD, 70. **CAREER** Asst prof, Univ Wis, Whitewater, 64-70; asst, assoc, Col Wooster, 70-78; assoc, Univ Wis, Parkside, 78-88; prof, Western Wash Univ, 88-. **HONORS AND AWARDS** Acad Vis, London School of Econ, 97; Vis Scholar, Univ Wash, 96; Eugenio Battisti Awd, Utopian Studies, 92; Dist Teach Awd, Univ Wis-Parkside, 84. **MEMBERSHIPS** APSA; IPSA; AAUP. **RESEARCH** Political theory; Identity and ideology. **SELECTED PUBLICATIONS** Auth, A Politics of Identity, Univ of Illinois Press (75); coauth, Conservative Capitalism in Britain and the United States: A Critical Appraisal, Routledge (89); auth, Ideology and Political Life, Harcourt Brace (94); coauth, The Elements of Social Scientific Thinking, St. Martin's (95); auth, The Power of Identity: Politics in a New Key, Chatham House (97); auth, "Identity, Democracy, and the Politics of Human Development," Rev Center for the Study of Soc and Politics (97): 40-49; auth, "The American Political Science Association," Encyclopedia USI, Supplement, Academic International Press (99): 181-184; auth, "Ideologizing Institutions: Hayek, Keynes, Laski and the Creation of 20th C Politics," J of Political Ideologies, Oxford 4 (99): 87-115. **CONTACT ADDRESS** Dept Political Sci, Western Washington Univ, MS 9082, Bellingham, WA 98225. **EMAIL** ken.hoover@wwu.edu

HOOVER, STEWART
DISCIPLINE RELIGIOUS STUDIES **EDUCATION** Univ Pa, PhD. **CAREER** Prof. **RESEARCH** Media and religion; cultural studies; contemporary American religious movements. **SELECTED PUBLICATIONS** Auth, Media and Moral Order in Post-Positivist Media Studie; Religion in the Media; co-ed, Media, Religion and Culture. **CONTACT ADDRESS** Religious Studies Dept, Univ of Colorado, Boulder, Boulder, CO 80309. **EMAIL** Stewart.Hoover@Colorado.edu

HOPKINS, DONALD RAY
PERSONAL Born 11/14/1936, Tulsa, OK, d **DISCIPLINE** LAW **EDUCATION** University of Kansas, BA 1958; Yale University, MA 1959; University of California Berkeley, JD 1965; Harvard Law School, LLM (cum laude) 1969. **CAREER** Univ of California Berkeley, teaching asst 1960-63, asst dean of students 1965-67, asst exec v chancellor 1967-68; NAACP Legal Defense Fund Inc, staff Attorney 1969-70; Pacific Cons, exec vice pres 1970-71; Eighth California Cong Dist, dist admins 1971-; Attorney in Private Practice 1981-. **HONORS AND AWARDS** Various achievement awds; Woodrow Wilson Fellow; Phi Beta Kappa; Pi Sigma Alpha. **MEMBERSHIPS** Estate tax examiner US Treasury Dept 1965; coll teacher Univ of California Laney Coll 1966-68; Acad of Polit Sci; Arbitration Assn Bd of Arbitrators; bd dir ACLU, No California 1969-71; bd dir Univ of California Alumni Assn 1976-79; bd dir African Film Soc; bd dir Travelers Aid Soc; Kansas/Yale/Harvard/Univ of California Alumni Assn; California State, Natl, American, Federal, Alameda Cty Bar Assns; bd dir Chas Houston Bar Assn; Amer Trial Lawyers Assn; Natl Conference of Black Lawyers; Natl Lawyers Guild; California Assn of Black Lawyers; bd dir Volunteer on Parole. **SELECTED PUBLICATIONS** Co-auth "Politics & Change in Berkeley" Nathan & Scott; various articles. **CONTACT ADDRESS** District Administrator, 8th CA Cong Dist, 201-13th St, Ste 105, Oakland, CA 94612.

HOPKINS, DWIGHT N.
PERSONAL Born 02/22/1953, Richmond, VA, m, 2 children **DISCIPLINE** THEOLOGY **EDUCATION** Harvard Univ, BA, 76; Union Theol Seminary, Mdiv, 84, Mphil, 87, PhD, 88; Univ of Cape Town, PhD, 00. **CAREER** Assoc Prof, 88-95, Santa Clara Univ; Assoc of Theol, 96-, Univ Chicago Divinity School; Prof of Theo, Univ Chicago Divinity School, 00-. **MEMBERSHIPS** Amer Acad of Rel; Soc for the study of Black Rel; Ecumenical Assoc of Third World Theol. **RESEARCH** Rel; Polit; culture; Econ. **SELECTED PUBLICATIONS** Auth, Black Theology USA and South Africa, Maryknoll, NY, Orbis Books, 89; We Are One Voice: Essays on Black Theology in South Africa and the USA, Johannesburg, South Africa, Slotaville Press, 89; Cut Loose Your Stammering Tongue: Black Theology in the Slave Narratives, Maryknoll, NY, Orbis Books, 91' Shoes That Fit Our Feet: Sources for a Constructive Black Theology, Maryknoll, NY, Orbis Books, 93; Changing Conversations: Religious Reflection and Cultural Analysis, NY, Routledge, 96; Liberation Theologies, Postmodernity and the Americas, NY, Routledge, 97; Introducing Black Theology of Liberation, Maryknoll, NY, Orbis Books, 99; auth, Down, Up, and Over: Slave Religion and Black Theology, Minneapolis, MN, Fortress Press, 99; auth, Black Faith and Pulic Talk, Maryknoll, NY Orbis Books, 99; auth, Religion and Globalization, Durham, NC, Duke Univ Press, 01. **CONTACT ADDRESS** Div Sch, Univ of Chicago, 1025 E 58th St, Chicago, IL 60637. **EMAIL** Dhopkins@midway.uchicago.EDU

HOPKINS, JASPER
PERSONAL Born 11/08/1936, Atlanta, GA **DISCIPLINE** PHILOSOPHY **EDUCATION** Wheaton Col, BA, 58; Harvard Univ, MA, 59; PhD, 63. **CAREER** Teaching Fel in Humanities, Harvard Univ, 59-63; vis assoc prof, Univ of Ark, 69; assoc prof, Univ of Mass, 69-70; assoc prof, Univ of Minn, 70-74; prof, Univ of Minn, 74. **HONORS AND AWARDS** NEH, 67-68; Am Council of Learned Societies, 73-74; NEH, 79; John Simon Guggenheim Memorial Found, 80-81; Nat Humanities Ctr, 83-8444; Bush Sabbatical Fel, 92-93. **RESEARCH** Ancient, medievval, and Renaissance philosohy; philosophy of religion; existentialism; philosophy of history; nineteenth-century german philosophy; kantian studies; hermeneutics; medical ethics. **SELECTED PUBLICATIONS** Auth, "The Role of Pia Interpretatio in Nicholas of Cusa's Hermeneutical Approach to the Koran," ed. Gregorio Piaia, Concordia discors, (Padua: Editrice Antenore, 93): 251-273; auth, Philosophical Criticism: Essays and Reviews, Minneapolis: Banning Press, 94; auth, Niholas of Cusa on Wisdom and Knowledge, Minneapolis: Banning Press, 96; auth, "Glaube und Vernunft im Denken des Nikolaus von Kues, Prolegomena zu einem Umrib seiner Auffassung, Trier: Paulinus Verlag, (96); auth, "Nicholas of Cusa (1401-64)," Routledge Encyclopedia of Philosophy, Vol, VI, (98): 832-838; auth, "Anselm of Canterbury (1033-1109)," Routledge Encyclopedia of Philosophy, vol. I, (98): 283-297; auth, Nicholas of Cusa: Metaphysical Speculations, vol. 1, Minneapolis: Banning, 98; auth, Nicholas of Cusa: Metaphysical Speculations: Vol. 2, Minneapolis : Banning, 00; transl, Complete Philosophical and Theoligical Treatises of Anselm of Canterbury, by J. Hopkins and Herbert Richardson, (Minneapolis: Banning Press, 00); auth, "Die Tugenden in der Sicht des Nikolaus von Kues. Ihre Veilfalt, ihr Verhaltnis untereinander und ihr Sein, Eerbe und Neuansaatz," Mitteilungen und Foschungsbeitrage der Cusanus-Gesellschaft, 26, (00): 9-37. **CONTACT ADDRESS** Philosophy Dept, Univ of Minnesota, Twin Cities, 355 Ford Hall, 224 Church St SE, Minneapolis, MN 55455. **EMAIL** hopki001@umn.edu

HOPKINS, THOMAS J.
PERSONAL Born 07/28/1930, Champaign, IL, m, 1956, 4 children **DISCIPLINE** HISTORY OF RELIGIONS **EDUCATION** Col William & Mary & Mass Inst Technol, BS, 53; Yale Univ, BS, 58, MA, 59, PhD, 62. **CAREER** From instr to assoc prof, 61-72, Prof Relig, 72-96, EMER PROF RELIG STU, 96-, FRANKLIN & MARSHALL COL, 61- ; Dir India Studies prog, Cent Pa Consortium, 71-75; chmn group Indian philos & relig, Coun Intercult Studies & Prog, 72-77; chr AAR Asian Relig/Hist Relig Sect, 75-80; co-chr AAR Comp Stud Relig Section, 80-87. **MEMBERSHIPS** Asn Asian Studies; Am Orient; Am Soc Study Relig. **RESEARCH** Indian history; phenomenology of religion. **SELECTED PUBLICATIONS** Auth, The social teaching of the Bhagavata Purana, In: Krishna: Myths, Rites and Attitudes, East-West, 66; The Hindu Religious Tradition, Dickenson, 71; Contribr, Six Pillars: Introduction to the Major Works of Sri Avrobindo, Conchocheague Assoc, 74; contrib Hare Krishna, Hare Krishna, Grove Press, 83; Krishna Consciousness in the West, Bucknell Univ Press, 89; Death and Afterlife: Perspectives of World Religions, Greenwood Press, 92. **CONTACT ADDRESS** 323 N West End Ave, Lancaster, PA 17603. **EMAIL** tjhopkins@supernet.com

HOPPE, E. A.
PERSONAL Born 10/14/1963, Seattle, WA, s **DISCIPLINE** PHILOSOPHY **EDUCATION** DePaul Univ, PhD, 99. **CAREER** Part-time instr, DePaul Univ, 95-99. **HONORS AND AWARDS** DePaul Fel. **MEMBERSHIPS** APA; SPEP; Nietzsche Soc. **RESEARCH** Plato; metaphysics. **CONTACT ADDRESS** 4539 N Whipple St, #3W, Chicago, IL 60625. **EMAIL** eahoppe@worldnet.att.net

HOPPE, LESLIE JOHN
PERSONAL Born 09/22/1944, Chicago, IL **DISCIPLINE** HEBREW SCRIPTURES, ANCIENT NEAR EAST RELIGIONS **EDUCATION** St Francis Col, BA, 67; Aquinas Inst Theol, MA, 71; Northwestern Univ, PhD(relig), 78. **CAREER** Asst prof Old Testament, Aquinas Inst Theol, 76-79; assoc prof, St Mary of the Lake Sem, 79-81; prof Old Testament, Cath Theol Union, 81-; vis lectr, North Park Theol Sem, 76; vis prof, Garrett-Evangelical Theol Sem, 80-81; Studium Biblicum Franciscanum, 94, 98. **MEMBERSHIPS** Soc Bibl Lit; Cath Bibl Asn; Am Schs Orient Res **RESEARCH** Deuteronomic literature; post-exilic literature; wisdom literature. **SELECTED PUBLICATIONS** Auth, Joshua-Judges, 82; What Are They Saying About Biblical Archaeology, 84; Being Poor: A Biblical Study, 87; Deuteronomy, 86; A New Heart: The Book of Ezekiel, 91; Churches and Synagogues of Ancient Palestine, 94; auth, The Lands of the Bible, 99. **CONTACT ADDRESS** 5401 S Cornell Ave, Chicago, IL 60615-6200. **EMAIL** lesliejh@ctu.edu

HOPPER, DAVID HENRY
PERSONAL Born 07/31/1927, Cranford, NJ, m, 1967, 3 children **DISCIPLINE** RELIGION **EDUCATION** Yale Univ, BA, 50; Princeton Theol Sem, BD, 53, ThD, 59. **CAREER** From Asst prof to assoc prof, 59-73, Prof Relig, Macalester Col, 73- **MEMBERSHIPS** Am Acad Relig; Int Bonhoeffer Soc, AAUP. **RESEARCH** Systematic theology; Biblical studies; existentialism. **SELECTED PUBLICATIONS** Auth, Tillich: A Theological Portrait, Lippincott, 68; A Dissent on Bonhoeffer, Westminster, 75. **CONTACT ADDRESS** Dept of Relig Studies, Macalester Col, 1600 Grand Ave, Saint Paul, MN 55105-1899. **EMAIL** hopper@macalester.edu

HOPPERTON, ROBERT J.
DISCIPLINE LAW **EDUCATION** Baldwin Wallace Col, BA; Univ Toledo, MA; Ohio State Univ, JD. **CAREER** Prof. **SELECTED PUBLICATIONS** Auth, Majoritarian and Counter-Majoritarian Difficulties: Democracy, Distrust, and Disclosure in American Land-Use Jurisprudence-A Response to Professors Mandelker and Tarlock, Boston Col Environ Affairs Law Rev, 97; Standards of Judicial Review in Supreme Court Land Use Opinions: A Taxonomy, an Analytical Framework, and a Synthesis, Univ Wash J Urban Contemporary Law, 97; The Presumption of Validity in American Land Use Law: A Substitute for Analysis, A Source of Significant Confusion, Boston Col Environ Affairs Law Rev, 96; Teaching Present and Future Interests: A Methodology for Students That Unifies Estates in Land Concepts, Structures, and Principles, Univ Toledo, 95. **CONTACT ADDRESS** Col Law, Univ of Toledo, Toledo, OH 43606. **EMAIL** rhopper@uoft02.utoledo.edu

HORI, G. VICTOR SOGEN
DISCIPLINE RELIGIOUS STUDIES **EDUCATION** Stanford, PhD, 76 **CAREER** Asst Prof, Faculty of Religious Studies, Mcgill Univ. **CONTACT ADDRESS** Faculty of Religious Studies, McGill Univ, 3520 University St., Montreal, QC, Canada H3A 2A7. **EMAIL** czvh@musica.mcgill.ca

HORN, JOHN STEPHEN
PERSONAL Born 05/31/1931, San Juan Bautista, CA, m, 1954, 2 children **DISCIPLINE** POLITICAL SCIENCE, U.S. HISTORY **EDUCATION** Stanford, AB, 53; PhD, 58; Harvard, MPA, 55. **CAREER** Admin asst, U.S. Secretary of Labor James P. Mitchell, 59-60; legislative asst to U.S. Senator Thomas H. Kuchel, 60-66; sr fel, The Brookings Inst, 66-69; Dean of Grad Studies, The Am Univ, Washington, DC, 69-70; Pres, Calif State Univ, 70-88, prof, 71-95, Trustee Prof of Political Sci, 88-95; U.S. Representative, 93-, member of Congress, 103rd, 104th, 105th, 106th. **HONORS AND AWARDS** Stanford, AB with Great Distinction, 58. **RESEARCH** Political theory, public administration, political parties, Constitutional law, 19th and 20th century U. S. history. **SELECTED PUBLICATIONS** Auth, The Cabinet and Congress (selected for White House Library); auth, Unused Power: The Work of the Senate Committee on Appropriations; coauth with Edmund Beard, Congressional Ethics-The View From the House. **CONTACT ADDRESS** U.S. Representative, House of Representatives, 2331 Rayburn, Washington, DC 20515-0538.

HORNE, GERALD CHARLES
PERSONAL Born 01/03/1949, St. Louis, MO, m, 1994 **DISCIPLINE** LAW, AFRICAN-AMERICAN STUDIES **EDUCATION** Princeton Univ, BA, 1970; Univ California-Berkeley, JD, 1973; Columbia Univ , PhD, 1982. **CAREER** Affirmative Action Coord Center, dir counsel 1979-82; Sarah Lawrence Coll, prof, 82-88; Natl Conf of Black Lawyers, exec dir, 85-86; Local 1199 Health and Hospital Workers Union

AFL-CIO, special counsel, 86-88; Univ of California, Santa Barbara, prof; Univ of North Carolina, Prof, currently. **HONORS AND AWARDS** Natl Conf of Black Lawyers, Hope Stevens Awd, 1983; Univ of California, Santa Barbara, Getman Service to Students Awd, 1990; Council on Intl Exchange of Scholars, Fullbright Scholar/Univ of Zimbabwe, 1995; Univ of Virginia, Carter G Woodson Fellow, 1991-92; City Univ of NY, Belle Zeller Visiting Prof, 1993-94. **MEMBERSHIPS** Natl Lawyers Guild, Intl Committee, chair, 1988-92; Natl Conf of Black Lawyers, Intl Committee, chair, 1982-85; Pears and Freedom Party, chair, 1991-92; American Federation of Teachers, Local 2274, sec/treas, 1976-78. **CONTACT ADDRESS** Univ of No Carolina, Chapel Hill, CB5250, Chapel Hill, NC 27599-5250.

HORNE, JAMES R.
DISCIPLINE PHILOSOPHY **EDUCATION** Univ Columbia, PhD, 64. **RESEARCH** Philos of religion; ethics. **SELECTED PUBLICATIONS** Auth, Beyond Mysticism, WLU, 78; The Moral Mystic, WLU, 83; Mysticism and Vocation, WLU, 96. **CONTACT ADDRESS** Dept of Philosophy, Univ of Waterloo, 200 University Ave W, Waterloo, ON, Canada N2L 3G1. **EMAIL** jrhorne@watarts.uwaterloo.ca

HORNE, MARTHA J.
DISCIPLINE NEW TESTAMENT **EDUCATION** Duke Univ, AB, 70; Va Theol Sem, MDiv, 83; Episcopal Divinity Sch, DD, 98. **CAREER** Adj instr, field edu mentor, 83-85; asst to Vicar, St. Andrew's Episcopal Church, 83-85; asst rector, Christ Church, 85-86; asst to the dean, 86-88; assoc dean for admin, 88-94; dean, pres, Va Theol Sem, 94-. **SELECTED PUBLICATIONS** Auth, A Vision for Theological Education in North America, Anglicanism: A Global Communion, Mowbray, 98; Sabbath and Compasssion, The Living Pulpit, 98; rev, Review of Saving Work: Feminist Practices of Theological Education by Rebecca Chapp, In Trust mag, 96. **CONTACT ADDRESS** Virginia Theol Sem, 3737 Seminary Rd, Alexandria, VA 22304. **EMAIL** MHorne@vts.edu

HORNE, MILTON P.
PERSONAL Born 03/19/1956, Antlers, OK, m, 1975, 2 children **DISCIPLINE** RELIGION **EDUCATION** Missouri Univ, Columbia, BA, 79; Midwestern Baptist Seminary, KC, MDiv, 83; Oxford Univ., Oxford, Eng, D.Phil., 90. **CAREER** Inst, Asst, Assoc, and Prof, William Jewell Col, 86-; assoc dean for General Eudcation, 95-. **HONORS AND AWARDS** Wand Keatley Award in Archaeology, NEH Summer Seminar, Tenure at William Jewell Col. **MEMBERSHIPS** SBL; Natl Asn of Baptist Prof of Rel. **RESEARCH** Hebrew-Wisdom Literature; sociology of religion; Academic Teaching of Bible and Religion. **SELECTED PUBLICATIONS** Auth, Rereading the Bible, Prentice-Hall, 00; auth, Proverbs and Ecclesiastes, Smith-Helwys, forthcoming. **CONTACT ADDRESS** Dept of Religion, William Jewell Col, 500 College Hill, Liberty, MO 64068. **EMAIL** hornem@william.jewell.edu

HORNE, RALPH ALBERT
PERSONAL Born 03/10/1929, Haverhill, MA **DISCIPLINE** CHEMISTRY, PHILOSOPHY, LAW **EDUCATION** MIT, SB, 50; Univ Vermont, MS, 52; Boston Univ, MA, 53; Columbia Univ, PhD, 55; Suffolk Univ Law Sch, JD, 79. **CAREER** Tchg asst, Univ Vermont, 50-52; tchg asst, Columbia Univ, 53; res asst, Brookhaven Nat Lab, 53-55; post doc fel, MIT, 55-57; sr sci, Radio Corp Am, 57-58; sr sci, Jos Kaye & Co, 58-60; sci staff, Arthur D Little Inc, 60-69, 72-78; assoc sci, Hole Ocean Inst, 70-71; prin sci, JBF Sci Corp, 71-72; Sr Sci, Energy & Envir Eng Inc, 80-; pres & found, Free Speech Found, 80-. **RESEARCH** Electron-Exchange Reactions, Structure of Liquid Water and Aqueous Solutions, Environmental Chemistry. **SELECTED PUBLICATIONS** Marine Chemistry, Wiley & Sons, 69; edr, Water and Aqueous Solutions, Wiley & Sons, 72; The Chemistry of Our Environment, Wiley & Sons, 78. **CONTACT ADDRESS** 9 Wellington St, Boston, MA 02118.

HORNECKER, RONALD L.
PERSONAL m, 2 children **DISCIPLINE** MINISTRY **EDUCATION** Northwest Mo State Univ, BA; Midwestern Baptist Theol Sem, MDiv, DMin. **CAREER** Assoc, supervised ministry, 85; assoc prof, 87; prof, Golden Gate Baptist Theol Sem, 97. **HONORS AND AWARDS** PACT Church of the Yr award, Noland Road Baptist Church in Independence; pastor, noland road baptist church in independence; founding co-pastor, novato christian fel; supvr, midwestern baptist theol sem's field edu prog. **MEMBERSHIPS** Mem, Assn for Theol Field Edu; S Baptist In-Service Guidance org. **SELECTED PUBLICATIONS** Contrib, Experiencing Ministry Supervision. **CONTACT ADDRESS** Golden Gate Baptist Theol Sem, 201 Sem Dr, Mill Valley, CA 94941-3197. **EMAIL** RonHornecker@ggbts.edu

HOROVITZ, AMIR
PERSONAL Born 02/23/1959, Israel, m, 1995 **DISCIPLINE** PHILOSOPHY **EDUCATION** Tel-Aviv Univ, PhD, 93. **CAREER** Instr, 91-93, Instr Dr, 93-95, Tel-Aviv Univ; sr lectr, Suffolk Univ, 97-. **RESEARCH** Philosophy of mind and cognitive science; Philosophy of languages; Philosophy of science; Epistemalogy; Philosophy of law. **SELECTED PUBLICATIONS** Coauth, "Semantics and the Psyche," Philos and Phenomenological Res 52 (92); auth, Searle's Mind: Physical, irreducible, subjective and noncomputational, Pragmatics & Cognition, 94; A Note on The Intentionality of Fear, Philosophica 53, 94; Content and Sensitivity, Iyyun 44, 95; Mind and Body in the Thought of Yeshayahu Leibowitz, Yeshayahu Leibowitz, His World and Philosophy, Keter, 95; Philosophy of Mind, The Hebrew Encyclo, 95; Putnam, Searle, and Externalism, Philos Studies 81, 96; auth, A Critical Study of Mental Causation, Philosophia, 98; auth, "Is there a Problem in Physicalist Epiphenomenalism?", Philos and Pehnomenological Res 59 (99): 421-434; auth, "Semantic Fetishism and Legal Interpretation," Am Philos Quart, forthcoming; auth, "Contents Just are in the Head," Erkenntnis, forthcoming. **CONTACT ADDRESS** 6 Ashton Pl., Cambridge, MA 02138. **EMAIL** hjacobs@fas.harvard.edu

HOROWITZ, DONALD L.
PERSONAL Born 06/27/1939, New York, NY, m, 1960, 3 children **DISCIPLINE** LAW, POLITICAL SCIENCE **EDUCATION** Syracuse Univ, AB, 59, LLB, 61; Harvard Univ, LLM, 62, MA, 65, PhD(polit sci), 68. **CAREER** Law clerk to Joseph S Lord, US Dist Ct, Philadelphia, 65-66; res assoc, Ctr Int Affairs, Harvard Univ, 67-69; atty, Civil Div, US Dept Justice, 69-71; fel, Am Foreign Relations & Woodrow Wilson Ctr, 71-72; res assoc, Brookings Inst, 72-75; sr fel, Res Inst Immigration & Ethnic Studies, 75-81; Prof Law, Sch Law, Duke Univ, 80-, Consult, Ford Found, 77-82; mem, Coun on the Role Courts, 79-; Guggenheim fel, Guggenheim Found, 80-81; James B. Duke chair, 94-. **HONORS AND AWARDS** Louis Brownlow Prize, Nat Acad Pub Admin, 77; McDonald-Currie lectr, McGill Univ, 80; Bunche Prize; Am Pol Sci Asn, 92; Opsahl Lectr, Queen's Univ Belfast, 00. **MEMBERSHIPS** Am Acad Arts & Scis, 93. **RESEARCH** Ethnic group relations; labor law and labor relations; legal philosophy. **SELECTED PUBLICATIONS** Auth, The Courts and Social Policy; auth, The Jurocracy, 77; auth, Comp Theories and Officers Motives, 80; auth, Ethnic Groups in Conflict, 85; auth, A Democratic South Africa?, 91; auth, The Quran and the Common-Law--Islamic Law Reform and the Theory of Legal Change, Am J Comp Law, Vol 0042, 94; auth, The Deadly Ethnic Riot, 01. **CONTACT ADDRESS** Sch of Law, Duke Univ, Durham, NC 27708-0360.

HORSNELL, MALCOLM J. A.
PERSONAL Born 01/31/1939, London, England, m, 1965, 1 child **DISCIPLINE** BIBLICAL STUDIES **EDUCATION** Toronto Baptist Sem, BD, 67; Wilfred Laurier Univ, BA, 67; Princeton Theol Sem, ThM, 68; Univ Toronto, PhD, 74. **CAREER** Min, St John's Road Baptist Church, 75-78; asst prof, Univ Toronto, New Testament, Univ Toronto, 77-78; asst prof, assoc prof, prof, 78-, assoc dean, 93- , dir, Basic Degree Prog, 98-, McMaster Div Col. **HONORS AND AWARDS** Arts Res Bd, 81-89, McMaster Univ; Social Sci and Hum Res Coun, 86-89. **MEMBERSHIPS** Sos of Bibl Lit; Am Oriental Soc; Can Soc of Bibl Stud; Can Soc for Mesopotamian Stud. **RESEARCH** Hebrew Biblical language; Sumeria. **SELECTED PUBLICATIONS** Auth, Biblical Concepts of Aging, McMaster Jour of Theol, 93; auth, Magic, Mantic, Jewelry/Ornaments, Incision/Cutting, in, The New International Dictionary of Old Testament Theology and Exegesis, Zondervan, 97; auth, A Review and Reference Grammar for Biblical Hebrew, McMaster, 98. **CONTACT ADDRESS** McMaster Divinity Col, McMaster Univ, Hamilton, ON, Canada L8S 4K1. **EMAIL** horsnell@mcmaster.ca

HORST, STEVEN
DISCIPLINE PHILOSOPHY OF MIND **EDUCATION** Boston Univ, BA; Univ Notre Dame, PhD. **CAREER** Asst prof, 90-97; Assoc prof, 97-; Chair, 98-; Wesleyan Univ. **HONORS AND AWARDS** NEH Fel; NEH Summer Inst; Prize Interdisciplinary Studies; Trustee Sch. **MEMBERSHIPS** Am Philos Asn; Soc Philos & Psychol; Phi Beta Kappa. **SELECTED PUBLICATIONS** Auth, Symbols and Computation; Divine Eternity and Special Relativity; Phenomenology and Psychophysics; Evolutionary Explanation and the 'Hard Problem' of Consciousness; Broad Content, Narrow Content, Phenomenological Content; Formalist and Conventionalist Views of Language. **CONTACT ADDRESS** Wesleyan Univ, Middletown, CT 06459. **EMAIL** shorst@mail.wesleyan.edu

HORSTMAN, ALLEN
PERSONAL Born 08/01/1968, Seymour, IN, 2 children **DISCIPLINE** HISTORY, LAW **EDUCATION** Purdue Univ, BS, 65; Harvard Law Sch, LLB, 68; Univ Calif, Berkeley, PhD, 77. **CAREER** Prof hist, Albion Col, 77-. **MEMBERSHIPS** AHA; Am Bar Asn; Conf Brit Studies. **RESEARCH** English legal history; American legal history. **SELECTED PUBLICATIONS** Auth, Victorian Divorce, Croom Helm, London, and St. Martins, NY. **CONTACT ADDRESS** Dept of History, Albion Col, 611 E Porte St, Albion, MI 49224. **EMAIL** ahorstman@albion.edu

HORTY, JOHN F.
DISCIPLINE PHILOSOPHY **EDUCATION** Oberlin Col, BA, 77; Univ Pittsburgh, PhD, 86. **CAREER** Res scientist, Computer Sci Dept, Carnegie Mellon Univ, 86-89; asst prof, 89-94, assoc prof, 94-98, prof, Philos Dept and Inst for Advanced Computer Studies, and affiliate prof, Computer Sci Dept, Univ Md, 99-. **HONORS AND AWARDS** Graduation with highest honors, Oberlin Col, 77; Phi Beta Kappa, Oberlin Col, 77; Florence Frew Prize in Classics, Oberlin Col, 77; Andrew Mellon Fel, Univ Pittsburgh, 80; NEH Fel, 93-94; paper selected for Philosopher's Annual, 95. **RESEARCH** Philosophical logic, artificial intelligence, philosophy of language, philosophy of mathematics, decision theory, philosophy of law, ethics. **SELECTED PUBLICATIONS** Coauth, "A clash of intuitions: the current state of nonmonotonic multiple inheritance systems," in Proceedings of the Tenth Int Joint Conf on Artificial Intelligence (IJCAI-87), Morgan Kaufmann Pubs (87): 476-482; coauth, "A skeptical theory of inheritance in nonmonotonic semantic networks," Artificial Intelligence, vol 42 (90): 311-348; auth, "Moral dilemmas and nonmonotonic logic," J of Philos Logic, vol 23 (94): 35-65; auth, "Some direct theories of nonmonotonic inheritance," in Handbook of Logic in Artificial Intelligence and Logic Programming, Vol 3: Nonmonotonic Reasoning and Uncertain Reasoning, D. Gabbay, C. Hogger, and J. Robinson, eds, Oxford Univ Press (94): 111-187; coauth with N. Belnap, "The deliberative stit: a study of action, omission, ability, and obligation," J of Philos Logic, Vol 24 (95): 583-644; auth, "Agency and obligation," Synthese, Vol 108 (96): 269-307; auth, Agency and Deontic Logic, Oxford Univ Press (2000). **CONTACT ADDRESS** Dept Philos, Univ of Maryland, Col Park, College Park, MD 20742. **EMAIL** horty@umiacs.umd.edu

HORWITZ, HENRY GLUCK
PERSONAL Born 08/02/1938, New York, NY, d, 1 child **DISCIPLINE** EARLY MODERN ENGLISH HISTORY; ENGLISH LEGAL HISTORY **EDUCATION** Haverford Col, BA, 59; Oxford Univ, DPhil(English hist), 63; J.D., Univ of Iowa, 82 **CAREER** From asst prof to assoc prof, 63-68, prof hist, Univ Iowa, 70-. **HONORS AND AWARDS** Nat Endowment for Humanities younger scholar award, 69; Guggenheim fel, 78; NEH Senior Fel, 00. **RESEARCH** Later seventeenth and eighteenth century English political and legal history. **SELECTED PUBLICATIONS** Auth, Revolution Politicks: The Career of Daniel Finch, 2nd Earl of Nottingham, Cambridge Univ, 68; ed, The Parliamentary Diary of Narcissus Luttrell, Clarendon, 72; auth, Parliament, Policy and Politics in the Reign of William III, Manchester Univ, 77; Chancery Equity Records and Proceedings 1600-1800, HMSO, 95; auth, Exchegver Equity Records and Proceedings 1649-1841, PRO, 01. **CONTACT ADDRESS** Dept of Hist, Univ of Iowa, 280 Schaeffer Hall, Iowa City, IA 52242-1409. **EMAIL** henry-horwitz@uiowa.edu

HOSOI, Y. TIM
DISCIPLINE PHILOSOPHY **EDUCATION** Univ Chicago, PhD. **CAREER** Assoc prof, Ore State Univ. **HONORS AND AWARDS** Dir, Prog Ethics, Sci, Environment. **MEMBERSHIPS** Cascade-W Japan Am Soc. **RESEARCH** Japanese Religions. **SELECTED PUBLICATIONS** Contribur The Oxford Companion to World Religions. **CONTACT ADDRESS** Dept Philos, Oregon State Univ, Hovland Hall 102A, Corvallis, OR 97331-3902. **EMAIL** thosoi@orst.edu

HOSPITAL, CLIFFORD G.
PERSONAL Born 03/09/1937, Rockhampton, Australia **DISCIPLINE** RELIGION **EDUCATION** Univ Queensland, BA, 61, BD, 64; Harvard Univ, PhD, 73. **CAREER** Lectr to assoc prof, 71-83, head dept, 83-90, PROF COMPARATIVE RELIGION, QUEEN'S UNIV & QUEEN'S THEOL COL, 83-. **MEMBERSHIPS** Can Soc Stud Relig; Am Acad Relig; Soc Hindu-Christian Stud. **SELECTED PUBLICATIONS** Auth, The Righteous Demon: A Study of Bali, 84; auth, Breakthrough: Insights of the great Religious Discoverers, 85; ed bd, Stud Relig, 83-86. **CONTACT ADDRESS** Dept of Religious Studies, Queen's Univ at Kingston, 99 University Ave, Kingston, ON, Canada K7L 3N6. **EMAIL** cgh1@post.queensu.ca

HOSSEIN, ZIAI
PERSONAL Born 07/06/1944, Mashhad, Iran, m, 1970, 1 child **DISCIPLINE** PHILOSOPHY **EDUCATION** Yale BS, 67, Harvard PhD, 76. **CAREER** UCLA, dir Iranian stud, prof Islamic Iranian stud. **MEMBERSHIPS** CIS, SIP&S **RESEARCH** Post Avicennan Illuminationist; Platonist philo. **SELECTED PUBLICATIONS** Auth, Knowledge and Illumination, Atlanta, 90; auth, Suhrawardi's The Book of Radiance, text, trans, intro & notes, Costa Mesa: Mazda Pub, 98; Entries on Islamic Philosophy, in: Oxford Comp to Philo, ed Ted Honderich, Oxford and London: Oxford UP 95; Shihab al-Din Yahya Suhrawardi, The Illuminationist Tradition, and Sadr al-Din al-Shirazi: 17th c Syncretism in Islamic Philosophy, in: Routledge Hist of Islamic Philo, ed S H Nasr and Oliver Leaman, London Routledge, 95; Shams al-Din Muhammad Shahrazuuri's Sharh Hikmat al-Ishraq, Commentary on the Philosophy of Illumination, crit ed intros notes and indexes, Cult Stud & Research Inst Tehran, 93; auth, The Philosophy of Illumination, Bilingual, with John Walbridge, Provo: BYU Press, 00; auth, The Ball and Polo Stick, with W. M. Thackston, Jr. Costo Mesa: Mazda Publishers, 00. **CONTACT ADDRESS** Dept of Near Eastern Languages and Cultures, Univ of California, Los Angeles, 405 Hilgard Ave, Los Angeles, CA 90095-1511. **EMAIL** ziai@ucla.edu

HOSTETTER, EDWIN C.
DISCIPLINE RELIGIOUS STUDIES **EDUCATION** John Hopkins Univ, PhD 92. **CAREER** Adj prof, John Hopkins Univ, 87-90; St. Mary's Sem and Univ, Ecumenical Inst of Theol, prof, 89-. **HONORS AND AWARDS** Dunning Dist Fac lectr, St. Mary's Sem and Univ. **MEMBERSHIPS** IBR; SBL **RESEARCH** Habakkuk; Hebrew grammar; white collar crime. **SELECTED PUBLICATIONS** Auth, Amir, bikkura, bls, gabia, kad, kos, keli, s'p, abot, pag, perudot, prh, sws, so'ar and te'ena, in: New Intl Dictionary of Old Testament Theology Exegesis, ed Willem A. VanGemeren, Grand Rapids, Zondervan Pub House, 97; Mistranslation in Cant 1:5, Andrews Univ Sem Studies, 96; JUS230 Restorative Justice, coauth, Taylor Univ Fort Wayne, 96; Old Testament Introduction, IBR Bibliog, Grand Rapids, Baker Book House, 95; Nations Mightier and More Numerous: The Biblical View of Palestine's Pre-Israelite Peoples, Fort Worth, Bibla Press, 95; Geographic Distribution of the Pre-Israelite Peoples of Ancient Palestine, Biblische Zeitschrift, 94; Prophetic Attitudes toward Violence in Ancient Israel, Criswell Theol Rev, 94; Is American Justice Color-Blind?, ESA Advo, 93. **CONTACT ADDRESS** Ecumenical Inst of Theol, St. Mary's Sem and Univ, 5400 Roland Ave, Baltimore, MD 21210-1994. **EMAIL** edwin@access.digex.net

HOULGATE, LAURENCE DAVIS
PERSONAL Born 02/19/1938, Pasadena, CA, m, 1970, 1 child **DISCIPLINE** PHILOSOPHY **EDUCATION** Los Angeles State Col, BA, 60; Univ Calif, Los Angeles, MA, 65, PhD (philos), 67. **CAREER** Instr philos, Calif State Col Fullerton, 64-66; lectr, Univ Calif, Santa Barbara, 66-67, asst prof, 67-72; vis assoc prof, Reed Col, 72-73; assoc prof, George Mason Univ, 73-79; Assoc Prof Philos, Calif Polytech State Univ, San Luis Obispo, 79- **MEMBERSHIPS** Am Philos Asn; Am Soc Polit & Legal Philos. **RESEARCH** Philosophy of law; ethics. **SELECTED PUBLICATIONS** Auth, Ignorantia Juris: a plea for justice, Ethics, 10/67; Knowledge and responsibility, Am Philos Quart, 4/68; Virtue is knowledge, Monist, 70; The Child and the State, Johns Hopkins Univ Press, 80. **CONTACT ADDRESS** Dept of Philos, California Polytech State Univ, San Luis Obispo, 1 Grand Ave, San Luis Obispo, CA 93407-0001.

HOUSE, PAUL R.
PERSONAL d, 1 child **DISCIPLINE** OLD TESTAMENT **EDUCATION** Southwest Baptist Univ, BA; Univ Missouri-Columbia, MA; S Baptist Theol Sem, MDiv, PhD; additional stud, Ecumenical Inst Theol Res, Jerusalem; Whitefield Inst, Eng; Oxford Univ. **CAREER** Instr, Taylor Univ, 86-96; dept ch, Biblical Stud, Taylor Univ, 91-96; Martha & Talmage prof, S Baptist Theol Sem, 96-99; prof, Trinity Epis Sch Ministry, 99-. **SELECTED PUBLICATIONS** Ed, S Baptist Jour Theol; auth, Old Testament Theology, Intervarisity Press. **CONTACT ADDRESS** Trinity Episcopal Sch for Ministry, Eleventh St., Ambridge, PA 15003. **EMAIL** PaulHouse@tesm.edu

HOUSER, NATHAN
PERSONAL Born 05/10/1944, IN, m, 1975, 2 children **DISCIPLINE** PHILOSOPHY **EDUCATION** Univ of Waterloo, PhD, 85 **CAREER** Pierce Edition Proj, 80-83, res asst, asst ed, assoc ed, dir, general ed, 80-93, Indiana Univ Purdue Univ Indianapolis, asst prof, assoc prof, prof, 86-. **HONORS AND AWARDS** SSHRC fel, Fulbright-Hayes Awd, NEH Grant. **MEMBERSHIPS** CSPS, APA, SAAP, ADE. **RESEARCH** Charles S. Pierce; Am Philos; philos of mind; textual theory. **SELECTED PUBLICATIONS** Auth, Toward A Piercean Semiotic Theory of Learning, in: Am Jour of Semiotics, 87; Pierce and the Law of Distribution, Perspectives on the History of Mathematical Logic, ed T. L. Drucker, Boston: Birkhauser, 91; auth, Charles Sanders Pierce, in: The Encyclopedia of Philosophy Supplement, Simon & Schuster Macmillan, 96; auth,Writings of Charles S. Pierce: A Chronological Edition, vol 3, 4, & 5, asst/assoc editor, Bloomington: Indiana Univ Press, 86, 89, 93; auth, Essential Pierce: Selected Philosophical Writings, gen ed (Pierce Edition Project), Bloomington: Indiana Univ Press, 98. **CONTACT ADDRESS** Dept of Philosophy, Indiana Univ-Purdue Univ, Indianapolis, 425 University Blvd., Indianapolis, IN 46202-5140. **EMAIL** nhouser@iupui.edu

HOVENKAMP, HERB
PERSONAL Born 08/27/1948, MI, m, 1970, 2 children **DISCIPLINE** LAW **EDUCATION** Calvin Col, BA, 69; Univ Tex, MA, 72; JD, 78. **CAREER** Prof, Univ Iowa, 86-. **HONORS AND AWARDS** Univ Iowa Fac Scholars Awd; Pres Lectr, Rockefeller Found; Am Hist Asn Prize. **RESEARCH** Antitrust; Legal history. **SELECTED PUBLICATIONS** Auth, Enterprise and American Law, 91; auth, Federal Antitrust Policy: the Law of Competition and its Practice, 99; auth, American Property Law, 99; co-auth, Antitrust Law (18 volumes). **CONTACT ADDRESS** Col of Law, Univ Iowa, Melrose and Bylington, Iowa City, IA 52242.

HOWARD, A. E. DICK
PERSONAL Born 07/05/1933, Richmond, VA, m, 1991, 1 child **DISCIPLINE** LAW **EDUCATION** Univ Richmond, BA, 54; Univ Virginia, LLB, 61; Oxford Univ, MA, 65. **CAREER** Associate, Covington and Burling, 61-62; Law Clerk to Justice Hugo L. Black, Supreme Court of the United States, 62-64. **HONORS AND AWARDS** Honorary Degree, James Madison Univ, Univ of Richmond, Campbell Univ, College of William and Mary. **MEMBERSHIPS** Council on Foreign Relations, American Bar Assoc. **RESEARCH** Constitutional law, US Supreme Court, Comparative Constitutionalism. **SELECTED PUBLICATIONS** Auth, The Road from Runnymede: Magna Carta and Constitutionalism in America, 68; auth, Commentaries on the Constitution of Virginia, 75; auth, Democracy's Dawn, 91; auth, Toward the Open Society in Central and Eastern Europe, 94; auth, Constitution-making in Eastern Europe, 93; auth, Magna Carta: Text and Commentary, 98. **CONTACT ADDRESS** Sch of Law, Univ of Virginia, 580 Massie Rd, Charlottesville, VA 22903-1738. **EMAIL** aedh@virginia.edu

HOWARD, DAVID M., JR.
PERSONAL Born 07/21/1952, Billings, MT, m, 1979, 2 children **DISCIPLINE** RELIGION **EDUCATION** Geneva Col, BS, 74; Wheaton Col, MA, 77; Univ Mich, AM, 80, PhD, 86. **CAREER** From instr to asst prof to assoc prof, Bethel Theol Sem, 82-90; from asst to assoc prof, Trinity Evangel Divinity Sch, 90-97; from assoc prof to prof, New Orleans Baptist Theol Sem, 97-00; prof, Bethel Sem, 00-. **MEMBERSHIPS** Soc Bibl Lit; Evangel Theol Sem; Inst Biblical Res. **RESEARCH** Hebrew language; Hebrew poetry; Psalms; Old Testament historical narrative. **SELECTED PUBLICATIONS** Auth, An Introduction to the Old Testament Historical Books, 93; auth, The Structure of Psalms 93-100, 97; auth, Rhetorical Criticism in Old Testament Studies, Bull Bibl Res, 94; auth, Editorial Activity in the Psalter: A State-of-the-Field Survey, The Shape & Shaping Psalter, 93; auth, A Contextual Reading of Psalms 90-94, The Shape & Shaping Psalter, 93; auth, Philistines, Peoples of Old Testament World, 94; auth, All Israel's Response to Joshua: A Note on the Narrative Framework of Joshua 1, Fortunate the Eyes that See, 95. **CONTACT ADDRESS** Bethel Theol Sem, 3949 Bethel Dr, Saint Paul, MN 55112. **EMAIL** d-howard@bethel.edu

HOWARD, DON A.
DISCIPLINE PHILOSOPHY OF SCIENCE **EDUCATION** Mich State Univ, BSc, 71, AM, 73; Boston Univ, PhD, 79. **CAREER** Prof. **RESEARCH** Philosophy of science; foundations of physics; history of philosophy of science. **SELECTED PUBLICATIONS** Auth, Was Einstein Really a Realist?, 93; Einstein, Kant, and the Origins of Logical Empiricism, 94; Relativity, Eindeutigkeit, and Monomorphism: Rudolf Carnap and the Development of the Categoricity Concept in Formal Semantics, 96; A Peek Behind the Veil of Maya: Einstein, Schopenhauer, and the Historical Background of the Conception of Space as a Ground for the Individuation of Physical Systems, 97; co-ed, Einstein and the History of General Relativity, 89; co-ed, The Collected Papers of Albert Einstein, 89. **CONTACT ADDRESS** History and Philosophy of Science Dept, Univ of Notre Dame, Notre Dame, IN 46556. **EMAIL** Don.A.Howard.43@nd.edu

HOWARD, MICHAEL W.
PERSONAL Born 12/28/1952, El Dorado, KS, m, 1995, 1 child **DISCIPLINE** PHILOSOPHY **EDUCATION** Univ Chicago, BA, 74; Boston Univ, PhD, 81. **CAREER** Chemn, 93-98, assoc prof, Univ Maine, 81-. **MEMBERSHIPS** APA; RPA; Intl Inst for Self Mgt. **RESEARCH** Economic democracy; Theories of justice; Marxism. **SELECTED PUBLICATIONS** Auth, Where Do We Go From Here": Another View, Grassroots Econ Organizing Newsletter, 97; auth, Mondragon at 40, Grassroots Econ Organizing Newsletter, 96; auth, Does Generalizing the Mondragon Model Require Revising It?, Social Econ and Social Participation: The Ways of the Basques, Marcial Pons and Gezki, 96; auth, Market Socialism and the International Mobility of Capital, Radical Philos Rev of Books, 95; auth, Self-Management, Ownership, and the Media, Jour of Mass Media Ethics, 94; auth, Ethics Education in the University: Origins and Pitfalls, Focus on Public Policy, 94; auth, Reflections on Cuba, Radical Philos Newsletter, 94; auth, Self-Management and the Crisis of Socialism, Rowman & Littlefield, 00. **CONTACT ADDRESS** Philosophy Dept., Univ of Maine, Orono, ME 04469. **EMAIL** mhoward@maine.edu

HOWE, LAWRENCE W.
PERSONAL Born 09/08/1953, Pensacola, FL, m, 1988 **DISCIPLINE** PHILOSOPHY **EDUCATION** Univ Mo, PhD, 83. **CAREER** Assoc prof, ch, Dept Philos, Univ W Fla. **HONORS AND AWARDS** Tchg Incentive Prog Awd, Univ W Fla, 94. **MEMBERSHIPS** Am Philos Asn, Fla Philos Asn. **RESEARCH** Bergson; environmental ethics; process philosophy. **CONTACT ADDRESS** Dept of Philosophy, Univ of West Florida, Pensacola, FL 32514. **EMAIL** lhowe@uwf.edu

HOWE, LEROY T.
PERSONAL Born 08/22/1936, Coral Gables, FL, m, 1962, 2 children **DISCIPLINE** PHILOSOPHY, RELIGION **EDUCATION** Univ Miami, AB, 58, MA, 60; Yale Univ, BD, 62, MA, 63, PhD(relig studies), 65. **CAREER** Instr philos, Southern Conn State Col, 64-65; asst prof, Fla Southern Col, 65-67; asst prof, Cent Mich Univ, 67-69; assoc dean, 72-78, Prof, Perkins Sch Theol, Southern Methodist Univ, 69-, Ed, Perkins J, 71- **MEMBERSHIPS** Am Acad Relig; Am Cath Philos Asn; Soc Values Higher Educ. **SELECTED PUBLICATIONS CONTACT ADDRESS** Perkins Sch of Theol, So Methodist Univ, Dallas, TX 75275.

HOWE, RUTH-ARLENE W.
PERSONAL Born 11/21/1933, Scotch Plains, NJ, m, 1957 **DISCIPLINE** LAW **EDUCATION** Wellesley Coll, BA 1955; Simmons Coll Sch of Social Work, SM 1957; Boston Coll Law School JD 1974. **CAREER** Cleveland OH Catholic Youth Serv Bureau, casewkr, 57-61; Tufts Delta Health Ctr Mound Bayou MS, housing devel consultant, 69-70; Simmons Coll Sch of Social Work, instr soc pol, 70-78; Law & Child Dev Project DHEW/ACYF Funded B C Law Sch, asst dir, 77-79; Boston Coll Law Sch, asst prof of law, 77-81, assoc prof of law with tenure, 81-97, prof, 98-. **HONORS AND AWARDS** Wellesley scholar Wellesley Coll 1955; Nat'l Inst of Mental Health Fellowship 1956-57; Honored by MA Black Legislative Caucus 1988; Honored by Museum of Afro-American History as one of Sojourner's Daughters; Boston African American Women Who Make A Difference, an exhibition of portraits by photographer Lou Jones, 1991; Mary Ingraham Bunting Inst Radcliffe Coll, Hermon Dunlap Smith Fellow in Law & Social/Public Policy, 1994-95; Honored by Boston College Law School Alumni Association, 1996. **MEMBERSHIPS** Bd mem Boston League of Women Voters 1963-68; clerk Grimes-King Found for the Elderly Inc 1972-; guardian ad litem MA Family and Probate Court 1979-; ABA Tech to NCCUSL Uniform Adoption and Marital Property Acts 1980-83; reviewer CWLA Journal-Child Welfare 1984-91; mem MA Gov St Com on Child Support Enforcement 1985; mem MA Adv Comm on Child Support Guidelines 1986-; mem MA Gov/MBA Commn on the Legal Needs of Children 1986-87; NCCUSL Uniform Putative and Unknown Fathers Act Reporter 1986-88; member, editorial board, Family Advocate, ABA section of Family Law, 1989-95; mem, Massachusetts Supreme Judicial Court Commission to Study Racial & Ethnic Bias in the Courts, 1990-94; US State Department, Study Group on Intercountry Adoption, 1991-. **SELECTED PUBLICATIONS** Co-auth, Katz McGrath Child Neglect Laws in Am ABA Press 1976. **CONTACT ADDRESS** Law Sch, Boston Col, Newton Ctr, 885 Centre St, Newton, MA 02459. **EMAIL** rutharlene.howe.1@bc.edu

HOWELL, JOHN C.
PERSONAL Born 02/24/1924, Miami, FL, m, 1947, 2 children **DISCIPLINE** CHRISTIAN ETHICS **EDUCATION** Stetson Univ, BA, 49; Southwestern Baptist Theol Sem, BD, 52, ThD, 60, PhD(ethics), 75; Univ MO, Kansas City, MA, 72. **CAREER** Pastor, First Baptist Church, Crowley, Tex, 50-56; pastor, West Bradenton Baptist Church, Fla, 56-60; prof Christian Ethics to prof emeritus, Midwestern Baptist Theol Sem, 60-; coun, Midwest Christian Counseling Ctr, 69-75; acad dean, Midwestern Baptist Theol Sem, 75-82. **HONORS AND AWARDS** Am Asn Theol Schs fel, Univ London, 67-68; dd, stetson univ, 79. **MEMBERSHIPS** Am Soc Christian Ethics; Nat Coun Family Rel. **RESEARCH** Family life; sexual educ. **SELECTED PUBLICATIONS** Auth, Teaching About Sex: A Christian Approach, Broadman; Gambling and the family, In: The Gambling Menace, Broadman, 66; contribr, The Cutting Edge, Word, Vol I, 69; Extremism Right and Left, Eerdmans, 72; Growing in Oneness, Convention, 72; Teaching Your Children About Sex, Broadman, 73; auth, Senior Adult Family Life, 79 & Equality and Submission in Marriage, 79, Broadman; auth, Transitions in Mature Marriage, Convention, 99. **CONTACT ADDRESS** Midwestern Baptist Theol Sem, 5001 N Oak, Kansas City, MO 64118-4620. **EMAIL** jhowell@mbts.edu

HOWELL, ROBERT
PERSONAL Born 01/23/1940, Indianapolis, IN, m, 1977, 2 children **DISCIPLINE** PHILOSOPHY **EDUCATION** Kenyon Col, AB, 61; Univ Mich, MA, 63; PhD, 67. **CAREER** Asst Prof, Univ Ill, 66-68; Asst Prof, Stanford Univ, 68-75; Vis Asst Prof, Johns Hopkins Univ, 74; Asst Prof, State Univ NY (SUNY), 75-76; From Assoc Prof to Prof, State Univ NY (SUNY), 76-. **HONORS AND AWARDS** Fulbright Fel, Oxford Univ, 65-66; ACLS Fel, 76-77; **MEMBERSHIPS** Am Philos Assoc, Am Soc for Aesthetics, N Am Kant Soc, **RESEARCH** Kant, early modern philosophy, aesthetics, analytical metaphysics. **SELECTED PUBLICATIONS** Auth, "Intuition, Synthesis, and Individuation in the 'Critique of Pure Reason'," Mous, vol 7 (73): 207-232; auth, "Fictional Objects: How They Are and How They Aren't," Poetics, Vol 8 (79): 129-177; auth, "Kant's First Critique Theory of the Transcendental Object," Dialectica, vol 35 (81): 85-125; auth, "Apperception and the 1787 Transcendental Deduction," Synthese, vol 47 (91): 385-448; auth, Kant's Transcendental Deduction: An Analysis of Main Themes in His Critical Philosophy, Kluwer (Dordrecht), 92; auth, "Fiction, Semantics of," Routledge Encycl of Philos, vol 3 (98): 659-663; auth, "Kant, the I Think and Self-Awareness," in Kant's Lassting Legacy: Essays in Hon of Lewis White Beck, (Rochester, NY: Univ Rochester Pr, forthcoming). **CONTACT ADDRESS** Dept Philos, SUNY, 1400 Washington Ave, Albany, NY 12222-0100.

HOWIE, JOHN
PERSONAL Born 12/03/1929, Jackson, MS, m, 1954, 3 children **DISCIPLINE** PHILOSOPHY **EDUCATION** Vanderbilt Univ, BA, 51; BD, 54; Emory Univ, MA, 55; Boston Univ, PhD, 65. **CAREER** Methodist Minister, Bluffton, South Carolina, 55-57; asst prof, Randolph-Macon Col, 62-64; asst prof, Earlham Col, 65-66; prof of philos, Humanities Inst, Summers, 65 & 66; asst prof, SIUC, 66-71, assoc prof, 71-82; asst dir of

grad studies, Dept of Philos, 72-74; undergraduate advisor, 74, 77, prof, 82-94; acting chairperson, 94-95; chairperson, 95-96; prof, 97 **HONORS AND AWARDS** Vis Scholar, Cambridge Univ, Cambridge, Eng, 72; Staff Mem on NEH proj, Applied Personal and Soc Values, 76-78; Summer teaching Improvement Grant, 79; Mini-sabbatical Leave to attend a Workshop on Bioethics and Public Policy, SIU, Carbondale, 79; Outstanding Teacher Award, Col of Liberal Arts, Southern Ill Univ, 80; Participant in "Philos for Children" workshop, 85 **MEMBERSHIPS** Am Philos Asn; Metaphysical Society of Am; Int Soc for Metaphysics; Am Acad of Relig; Southern Soc for Philos and Psychology; Ill Philos Conf, Soc for the Advan of Am Philos; Am Asn of Univ Profs; N Am Society for Soc Philos; Am Civil Liberties Union; Asn for the Dev of Philos Teaching A.D. O.P.T, Exec Comt, 77-79; Southern Soc for Philos and Psychology. **RESEARCH** The Philosophy of William Ernest Hocking, the Philosophy of Edgar S. Brightman. **SELECTED PUBLICATIONS** Auth, Perspectives for Moral Decisions, Univ Pr of Am (Washington, DC), 81; ed, Ethical Principles for Social Policy, S Il Univ Pr, (Carbondale), 83; ed, Ethical Principles and Practice, S IL Univ Pr, 87; auth, "Joseph Leon Blau" and "Borden Parker Bowne", Am Nat Biography, ed John A. Garraty, Oxford Univ Pr, 94; auth, "Human-centered or Ecocentric Environmental Ethics?", Dialogue and Humanism 4, (93-94): 127-137; auth, "World Hunger and A Moral Right to Subsistence", Contemporary Moral Issues: Diversity and Consensus, ed Lawrence M. Hinman, Prentice Hall, (96): 442-466; auth, "Personalism and A Holistic Environmental Ethics", Relig Experience and Ecological Responsibility, eds Donald A Crosby and Charley D. Hardwick Peter Lang Pub (NY, 96): 225-253. **CONTACT ADDRESS** Dept Philos, So Illinois Univ, Carbondale, Faner Hall 3065, Carbondale, IL 62901. **EMAIL** jbhowie@midamer.net

HOWZE, KAREN AILEEN

PERSONAL Born 12/08/1950, Detroit, MI, s, 3 children **DISCIPLINE** LAW **EDUCATION** Univ of S California, BA 1972 (cum laude); Hastings Coll of Law, JD 1977. **CAREER** Detroit Free Press, reporter 1971; San Francisco Chronicle, reporter 1972-78; Newsday, Long Island, asst editor 1978-79; Gannett Newspapers, Rochester NY, asst managing editor/Sunday features editor 1979-80; USA Today, founding editor 1981, managing editor/systems 1982-86, managing editor/international edition 1986-88; Gannett Co Inc, Corporate News Systems, editor 1988-90; management consultant, 90-; Howze and Associates, Karen Aileen Howze, Esq, Attorney, 90-; Special Master, DC Superior Court, Family Div., 00- ; Howard Univ School of Communications, lecturer, 90-92; Adoption Support Institute, President/Founder, 90-; American University School of Communication, professor, 91-94. **HONORS AND AWARDS** Business Woman of the Year, Spellman Alumni, Washington DC 1986. **MEMBERSHIPS** Mem Nat Assn of Black Journal; past mem Sigma Delta Chi; past mem Women in Commun; mem Alameda Co Comm Hlth Adv Bd; guest lectu local comm coll; mem, Amer Society of Newspaper Editors; vice-chair, Minority Opportunities Comm, Amer Newspaper Publisher's Assn; board of directors, North American CNL on Adoptable Children; board of directors MAAT Institute; board of directors Chelsea School; chairperson Mayor's Committee on Placement of Children in Family Homes; District of Columbia Bar Association & State of Maryland Bar Association, licensed to practice law in District of Columbia and Maryland. **SELECTED PUBLICATIONS** Publications: And Still We Rise, Interviews with 50 Black Americans by Barbara Reynolds, sr editor, 1987; Making Differences Work: Cultural Context in Abuse and Neglect Practice for Judges and Attorneys, 1996. **CONTACT ADDRESS** PO Box 1127, Silver Spring, MD 20910. **EMAIL** kahowze@msn.com

HOXIE, RALPH GORDON

PERSONAL Born 03/18/1919, Waterloo, IA, m, 1997 **DISCIPLINE** HISTORY POLITICAL SCIENCE **EDUCATION** Univ Northern Iowa, BA, 40; Univ Wis, MA, 41; Columbia Univ, PhD, 50. **CAREER** Asst to provost, Columbia Univ, 48-49; asst prof hist, ed studies, Soc Sci Found & asst to chancellor, Univ Denver, 50-53; proj assoc, Bicentennial, Columbia Univ, 53-54; dean col lib arts & sci, Long Island Univ, 54-55, dean, C W Post Col, 55-60, provost, 60-62, pres col, 62-68; pres dep, Mitchel Col, 55-60, vpres univ, 62, chancellor, 64-68; Founder, Pres, Chm Emery, Ctr for Study of Presidency, 69-97: Vis lectr numerous univs & cols; consult col training & develop progs & educ policies; adv mil educ progs, US Air Force, Brig Gen, ret; mem adv coun, Robert A Taft Inst Govt; dir, Greater NY Coun Foreign Studies; secy, Comn Govt Rev Nassau County; co-chmn, Nassau-Suffolk Conf Christians & Jews; pub mem, US State Dept Selection Bd, 69. **HONORS AND AWARDS** Legion of Merit; Distinguished Serv Medal, City New York; Gold Medal, Paderewski Found; Korean Cult Medal; Gold Medal, Univ Northern Iowa, 65; LLD, Chungang Univ, Korea, 65; LHD, Gannon Univ, 88; Wesley Col, 89; Univ N Iowa, 90; Shepherd Col, 92; Teikyo Post Univ, 94; Long Island Univ, 95; Fitchburg State Col, 97; Alumni Achievement Awd, Columbia Univ, 97; lld, chungang univ, korea, 65; littd, d'youville col, 66. **MEMBERSHIPS** Am Soc Pub Admin; AHA; Acad Polit Sci; Am Polit Sci Asn. **RESEARCH** History of education; American presidency; American foreign policy. **SELECTED PUBLICATIONS** Ed, Frontiers for Freedon, 52; ed, Presidential Studies Quart, 1970-1995; The Presidency of the 1970's, 73; contrib, The Coattailless Landslide, Tex Western, 74; Power and the Presidency, Scribner's, 76; auth, Command Decision and the Presidency, Reader's Digest, 77; coauth, Organizing and Staffing the Presidency, 80; Presidency and Information Policy, 81; contribr, The Presidency and National Security Policy, 84; Encycl Britannica, World Book Encycl, Greenwood Encycl of American Institutions. **CONTACT ADDRESS** 208 E 75th St, New York, NY 10021. **EMAIL** rghoxie@aol.com

HOYT, CHRISTOPHER R.

DISCIPLINE LAW **EDUCATION** Northwestern Univ, BA; Univ Wis, MS, JD. **CAREER** Prof **MEMBERSHIPS** Am Bar Asn. **RESEARCH** Federal taxation; business organizations; retirement plans; tax-exempt organizations. **SELECTED PUBLICATIONS** Auth, The Legal Compendium for Community Foundations. **CONTACT ADDRESS** Law Dept, Univ of Missouri, Kansas City, 5100 Rockhill Rd, Kansas City, MO 64110-2499. **EMAIL** hoytc@umkc.edu

HOYT, THOMAS L., JR.

PERSONAL Born 03/14/1941, Fayette, AL, m **DISCIPLINE** THEOLOGY **EDUCATION** Evansville Coll and Lane Coll, BA 1962; Interdenominational Theological Center, MDiv 1965; Union Theological Seminary, STM 1967; Duke Univ, PhD 1975. **CAREER** Jefferson Park Methodist, assoc pastor 1965-67; St Joseph CME, pastor 1967-70; Fawcett Memorial, pastor 1970-72; Interdenominational Theological Center, professor 1972-78; Howard Univ, professor 1978-80; Hartford Seminary, professor 1980-. **HONORS AND AWARDS** Rockefeller Doctoral Fellowship; Assn of Theological Schools Fellowship; worked on Joint Committee, which published an Inclusive Lectionary (year A,B,C,)1983-85; Natl Assn for Equal Opportunity in Higher Education, award; Bilateral Dialogue between Methodist/Roman Catholic Churches, participant; African Methodist Episcopal Zion/Christian Methodist Episcopal Unity Committee. **MEMBERSHIPS** Society of Biblical Literature; American Academy of Religion; Society for the study of Black Religion; Theology Commission of Consultation onChurch Union; CT Bible Society, board of directors; Christian Methodist Church; Alpha Phi Alpha; NAACP; Faith and Order Commission of Natl Council and World Council of Churches; Institute for Ecumenical and Cultural Research, board of directors. **CONTACT ADDRESS** Professor, Hartford Sem, 77 Sherman St, Hartford, CT 06105.

HOYT-O'CONNOR, PAUL E.

PERSONAL Born 04/01/1960, Brooklyn, NY, m, 1987, 1 child **DISCIPLINE** PHILOSOPHY; HISTORY **EDUCATION** Fordham Univ, BA, 92; Boston Col, PhD, 92. **CAREER** Asst prof, 94- , Spalding Univ. **MEMBERSHIPS** APA; Amer Catholic Philos Assn; Kentucky Philos Assn **RESEARCH** Social and political philos; Ethical theory. **SELECTED PUBLICATIONS** Auth, Lonegan and Bellah: Social Science in Public Philosophy, American Catholic Philosophy Quarterly, 95; auth, Progress Without End, International Philosophical Quarterly, 98. **CONTACT ADDRESS** Dept of Philos, Spalding Univ, 851 S 4th St, Louisville, KY 40203.

HSIEH, DINGHWA EVELYN

PERSONAL Born 05/06/1961, Taipei, Taiwan **DISCIPLINE** BUDDHIST STUDIES **EDUCATION** UCLA, PhD, 93. **CAREER** Asst Prof, 98-pres, Tsuman St Univ; Vis Asst Prof, 96-98, Reed Col; Vis Lect, 95-96, Harvard Div Sch; Res Fel, 93-95, UC Berkeley. **HONORS AND AWARDS** Chanc Post Doc Fel; Scholarship from Alpha Asn of Phi Beta Kappa Alumni, Southern Calif, 89; Awd of Academic Achievement and Promise in Graduate Study, Univ of Calif, 89-90; Laffin Dissertation Year Fel, Univ of Calif, 92-93; Chancellor's Postdoctoral Fel, Univ of Calif, 93-95. **MEMBERSHIPS** AAR, Assoc of Asian Stud. **RESEARCH** Zen; Literati Cult; Women and Buddhism. **SELECTED PUBLICATIONS** Auth, "Yuan-wu K'o-ch'in's (1063-1135) Teaching of Ch'an Kung-an Practice: A Transition from the Literary Study of Ch'an Kung-an to the Practical K'an-hua Ch'an," Journal of the International Asn of Buddhist Stud, 17:1, (94): 66-95; auth, Images of Women in Ch'an Buddhist Literatire of the Sung Period, Sung Buddhism, 99; ed, Images of Women in Ch'an Buddhist Literature of the Sung Period," in Buddhism in the Sung, with Peter Gregory and Daniel Getz, the Kuroda Institute's Studies in East Asian Buddhims Series, Honolulu: Univ of Hawai'I Press, (99): 148-187; rev of Buddhist Women Across Cultures: Realizations, with Karma Lekshe Tsomo, in the Journal of the American Academy of Relig, (99): 148-187; auth, "Buddhist Nuns in Sung China (960-1279)," in Journal of Sung-Yaun Studies, 30, (00): 63-96. **CONTACT ADDRESS** Soc Scis, Truman State Univ, Kirksville, MO 63501. **EMAIL** dhsieh@truman.edu

HUANG, SIU CHI

PERSONAL Born 07/07/1913, Fujian, China **DISCIPLINE** PHILOSOPHY **EDUCATION** Fujian Christian Univ, BA, 36; Univ Penn, MA, 39, PhD, 44. **CAREER** Prof Philos and dept ch, 50-85, Emer prof philos, Beaver Col, 96- ; vis prof, Univ Hawaii, 72; vis prof, Xiamen Univ, 80, 84; vis prof, Fudan Univ, 88. **HONORS AND AWARDS** Lindback awd for dist-ing tchg, Beaver Col, 61; Hon dr letts, 95. **MEMBERSHIPS** Amer Philos Asn; Amer Oriental Soc; Soc Philos E and W. **RESEARCH** Neo-Confucianism and Comparative Philosophy. **SELECTED PUBLICATIONS** Auth, Lu Hsiang-Shan A 12th Century Chinese Idealist Philosophy; Zhang Zai and Josiah Royce, in Chinese; Trans Chinese, George Berkeley's Three Dialogues Between Hylas and Philonous, and Sources of Religious Insight; auth, Essentials of Neo-Confricanism, auth, Pholosophers of Song and Ming Periods, 99. **CONTACT ADDRESS** Dept of Philosophy, Beaver Col, Rydal Park, Apt 457, Rydal, PA 19046. **EMAIL** allents@aol.com

HUBBARD, F. PATRICK

DISCIPLINE LAW **EDUCATION** Davidson Col, BA, 66; NYork Univ, JD, 69; Yale Univ, LLM, 73. **CAREER** Ronald L. Motley Tort prof Law, Univ of SC. **RESEARCH** Torts; jurisprudence; evidence; criminal law. **SELECTED PUBLICATIONS** Publ, on torts & criminal law. **CONTACT ADDRESS** School of Law, Univ of So Carolina, Columbia, Main and Greene St., Columbia, SC 29208. **EMAIL** Path@law.law.sc.edu

HUBER, DONALD L.

PERSONAL Born 09/19/1940, Columbus, OH, m, 3 children **DISCIPLINE** CHURCH HISTORY **EDUCATION** Capital Univ, BA, 62; Evangel Lutheran Theol Sem, BD, 66; Duke Univ, PhD, 71; Univ Mich, MALS, 73. **CAREER** Instr, ELTS, 69-72; librarian, ELTS, 73-78; librarian, Trinity Lutheran sem, 78-91; sec fac, 78-80; act dean Acad Aff, 84-85; guest lectr, Luther Sem, Adelaide, Australia, 86-87; prof, Trinity Lutheran Sem, 88-; archiv, Trinity Lutheran Sem, 91-; Acad Dean, Trinity Lutheran Sem, 00-. **MEMBERSHIPS** Am Sic of Church Hist, Lutheran Hist Conf. **SELECTED PUBLICATIONS** Auth, The Rise and Fall of Lane Seminary: An Antislavery Episode, 95; auth, Teddy, Rah! Theodore Roosevelt and German-Americanism, Timeline, Ohio Hist Soc, 96; auth, Red, White, and Black: The Wyandot Mission at Upper Sandusky, Timeline XIII, 96; auth, Luther A. Gottwald, John H. Tietjen, Dictionary of Heresy Trials in Amer Christianity, Greenwood, 97; auth, The Prophet Joseph In Ohio, Timeline, 99; auth, funk and Wagnalls, Timeline, 99; World Lutheranism: a select Bibliography for English Readers, 00. **CONTACT ADDRESS** Hist, Theol, Soc Dept, Trinity Lutheran Sem, 2199 E Main St, Columbus, OH 43209-2334. **EMAIL** dhuber@trinity.capital.edu

HUDDLESTON, MARK

PERSONAL Born 06/12/1947, Indianapolis, IN, m, 1968, 4 children **DISCIPLINE** RELIGION, LINGUISTICS **EDUCATION** Milligan Col, BA, 69; Emmanuel Sch Religion, MDiv, 75, DMin, 99; Emory Univ, 76-78; Univ Tex, MA, 84. **CAREER** Min, Beaver Creek Christian Church, 71-76; min, Christs Church, 76-78; transl, 80-88, vp, 88-92, trning, 92-97, Pioneer Bible Translators; assoc prof, Nebr Christian Col, 97-; prof of missions, Nebr Christian Col. **MEMBERSHIPS** Theta Phi; Eta Beta Rho **RESEARCH** Linguistics; Missiology **SELECTED PUBLICATIONS** Auth, Which Language for Literacy, 80; auth, Language Learning and Cross-Cultural Communication, 87; auth, Equivalent Dynamics: For Whom Do I Translate, 88; auth, Financial Planning and Accountability, 92; ed, Buku Ye Membe Mba K'Akulugu, 83. **CONTACT ADDRESS** 1007 Madison Ave, Norfolk, NE 68701. **EMAIL** mhuddleston@nechristian.edu

HUDDLESTON, TOBIANNA W.

DISCIPLINE PHILOSOPHY **EDUCATION** Simmons Col, BA, 70; NYork Univ Washington Square, NYork City, MA, PhD, 77. **CAREER** Vineyard Fine Arts Crown, Edgartown, Aesthetics Programs Development. **HONORS AND AWARDS** Most Promising Genius, NYU, 77; William Barret Prize. **MEMBERSHIPS** ABP, APA, CPPS **RESEARCH** Logic **SELECTED PUBLICATIONS** Auth, Pure Philosophy Jour. **CONTACT ADDRESS** Eden Place Farm Corp Retreat, PO Box 331, Burgin, KY 40310.

HUDEC, ROBERT EMIL

PERSONAL Born 12/23/1934, Cleveland, OH, m, 1956, 2 children **DISCIPLINE** LAW **EDUCATION** Kenyon Col, BA, 56; Cambridge Univ, BA, 58; Yale Univ, LLB, 61. **CAREER** Law clerk, US Supreme Court, 61-63; asst gen counsel, Off Spec Rep Trade Negotiations, Exec Off pres, 63-65; from asst prof to assoc prof law, Yale Univ, 66-72; prof law, Law Sch, Univ Minn, Minneapolis, 72- **HONORS AND AWARDS** LLD, Kenyon Col, 79. **RESEARCH** International trade; commercial law. **SELECTED PUBLICATIONS** Auth, The Gatt Legal System and World Trade Diplomacy, Praeger, 75, 2nd ed, Butterworths, 90; Developing Countries in the Gatt Legal System, Thames Essay No 50, Gower, Trade Policy Res Ctr, 88; Enforcing International Trade Law: The Evolution of the Modern Gatt Legal System, Butterworths, 93; co-ed, Harmonization and Fair Trade: Prerequisites for Free Trade?, MIT Press, 96; auth, Essays on the Nature of International Trade Law, Cameron, 99. **CONTACT ADDRESS** Law Sch, Univ of Minnesota, Twin Cities, 229 19th Ave S, Minneapolis, MN 55455-0401. **EMAIL** hudec001@tc.umn.edu

HUDELSON, RICHARD HENRY

PERSONAL m, 2 children **DISCIPLINE** PHILOSOPHY **EDUCATION** De Pauw Univ, BA, 68; Univ Mich, MA, 75, PhD(philos), 77. **CAREER** Teaching asst philos, Univ Mich, 72-75;

res asst hist philos, Inst Advan Studies, 76-77; Asst Prof Philos, Univ Minn, Duluth, 77-00; asst prof, Philos, Univ Wis-Superior, 00- . **HONORS AND AWARDS** Nat Endowment for Humanities summer res grant, 82. **MEMBERSHIPS** Am Philos Asn. **RESEARCH** History of social philosophy; history of German philosophy. **SELECTED PUBLICATIONS** Auth, Marxism and Philosophy in the Twentieth Century, Praeger, 90; auth, The Rise and Fall of Communism, Westview, 93. **CONTACT ADDRESS** Dept of Hist, Politics & Society, Univ of Wisconsin, Superior, Sundquist Hall, Rm 208, Belknap & Catlin PO Box 2000, Superior, WI 54880-4500. **EMAIL** rhudelso@staff.uwsuper.edu

HUDNUT-BEUMLER, JAMES

PERSONAL Born 02/21/1958, Detroit, MI, m, 1987, 2 children **DISCIPLINE** RELIGION **EDUCATION** Princeton Univ, PhD, 89. **CAREER** Prof, Dean of Fac, 93-, Columbia Theol Sem; Prod Assoc, 91-93, Lilly Endow Inc; Lectr, 88-91, Princeton Univ. **HONORS AND AWARDS** Phi Beta Kappa; Leopold Scheap Schl. **MEMBERSHIPS** AAR; ASCH; SSSR. **RESEARCH** American Religion History. **SELECTED PUBLICATIONS** Auth, Looking for God in the Suburbs: The Religion of the American Dream and Its Critics, 1945-1965, New Brunswick, Rutgers U Press, 94; auth, Myth's and Realities in the Financing of Amer Religion, in: The Financing of America, Mark Chaves, ed, Walnut Creek CA, Alta Mira Press, 98; Religion and Suburbs, The Encyc of Cities and Their Suburbs, Westport CT, ABC-Clio, forthcoming; auth, Ecclesial Accountability in the Missional Church, The Gospel and Our Culture, 98; auth, Creating a Commonwealth: The History Ethics and Theol of Church Endowments, Congregations, 97; auth, A New Dean Meets a New Day in Theol Education, Theol Edu, 96; auth, The Tithes that Bind? Protestants and Giving, The Cultures of Giving, Dwight Forthcoming; Burlingame, ed, San Fran, Jossey Bass, 95; rev, Money Matters: Personal Giving in American Churches, by Dean Hoge, Charles Zech, Patrick McNamara, Michael J Donahue, Religious Stud Rev, forthcoming; The Fifties Spiritual Marketplace: American Religion in a Decade of Conflict, by RS Ellwood, in: American Presbyterians: The J Presby History, forthcoming; ed, Behind the Stained Glass Window: Money Dynamics in the Church, by John and Sylvia Ronsvalle, in: Theol Today, 98. **CONTACT ADDRESS** Columbia Theol Sem, Box 520, Decatur, GA 30031. **EMAIL** hudnut-beumlerj@ctsnet.edu

HUDSON, DAVIS M.

DISCIPLINE LAW **EDUCATION** Wake Forest Univ, BS; Fla State Univ, JD; Univ Fla, LLM; Univ London, LLM. **CAREER** Prof, Univ Fla, 76-. **MEMBERSHIPS** Fla Bar. **RESEARCH** Taxation, state and local taxation, international tax, immigration law. **SELECTED PUBLICATIONS** Coauth, Black Letter on Federal Income Taxation. **CONTACT ADDRESS** School of Law, Univ of Florida, PO Box 117625, Gainesville, FL 32611-7625. **EMAIL** hudson@law.ufl.edu

HUDSON, JAMES L.

PERSONAL Born 06/27/1944, Washington, DC, m, 1968, 3 children **DISCIPLINE** PHILOSOPHY **EDUCATION** Johns Hopkins Univ, BA, 66; PhD, 72. **CAREER** Asst to assoc prof, N Ill Univ, 70-. **HONORS AND AWARDS** Fel, NDEA; Fel, Woodrow Wilson, NEH Summer Sem. **MEMBERSHIPS** Am Philos Assoc. **RESEARCH** Ethics, metaphysics. **SELECTED PUBLICATIONS** Auth, "The Ethics of Immigration Restriction," Soc Theory and Practice 10, (84): 201-39; auth "Rights and the Further Future," Philos Studies 49, *86): 99-107; auth, "The Philosophy of Immigration," Jour of Libertarian Studies 8, (86): 51-62; auth, "The Diminishing Marginal Value of Happy People," Philos Studies 51, (87): 123-37; auth, "Subjectivization in Ethics," Am Philos Quart 26, (89): 221-29; auth, "Happiness and Community: Charles Murray's Political Philosophy," Critical Rev 8, (94): 175-216; auth, "What Kinds of People Should We Create?" Jour of Appl Philos 17, (00): 131-43; auth, "Against Deontic Egalitarianism," Twentieth Century Values, forthcoming; auth, "The Passionate Opposition to Hereditarianism," Jour of Soc Philos, forthcoming. **CONTACT ADDRESS** Dept Philos, No Illinois Univ, 1425 W Lincoln Hwy, Dekalb, IL 60115-2828. **EMAIL** jhudson@niu.edu

HUDSON, ROBERT

DISCIPLINE HISTORY AND PHILOSOPHY OF SCIENCE AND EPISTEMOLOGY **EDUCATION** W Ontario Univ, PhD. **CAREER** Dept Philos, Concordia Univ **RESEARCH** Contemporary experimental microbiology. **SELECTED PUBLICATIONS** Pub(s), in Synthese; Stud in Hist and Philos of Sci. **CONTACT ADDRESS** Dept of Philos, Concordia Univ, Montreal, 1455 de Maisonneuve W, Montreal, QC, Canada H3G 1M8. **EMAIL** hudsonr@alcor.concordia.ca

HUDSON, YEAGER

PERSONAL Born 08/14/1931, Meridian, MS, m, 1953, 2 children **DISCIPLINE** PHILOSOPHY **EDUCATION** Educ: Millsaps Col, BA, 54; Boston Univ, STB, 58, PhD, 65. **CAREER** From Instr to Prof, 59-94, Charles A. Dana Prof Philos, Colby Col, 94-98; Emer 98; Chmn Dept, 80-88; Fulbright lectr, Poona Univ & Ahmednagar Col, India, 67-68; dir self-study Ahmednagar Col under stipulation of Univ Grants Comn Indian Govt, 67-68. **MEMBERSHIPS** Am Philos Asn; Metaphys Soc Am; Soc Advan Am Philos; Philos Relig. **RESEARCH** Metaphysics; philos of educ; Indian philos. **SELECTED PUBLICATIONS** Auth, Emerson & Tagore: The Poet as Philosopher, Cross Roads Bks, 88; Philosophy of Religion, Mayfield Publ, 91; ed, Philosophy of Religion: Selected Readings, Mayfield Publ, 91; Rending and Renewing the Social Order, Edwin Mellen Press, 96; Technology, Morality, and Social Policy, Edwin Mellen Press, 97; co-ed, The Bill of Rights: Bicentennial Perspectives, Edwin Mellen Press, 93; Freedom, Dharma, and Rights, Edwin Mellen Press, 93; Liberalism, Oppression, and Empowerment, Edwin Mellen Press, 94; The Social Power of Ideas, Edwin Mellen Press, 95. **CONTACT ADDRESS** PO Box 229, Georgetown, ME 04548. **EMAIL** y_hudson@colby.edu

HUENEMANN, CHARLES

DISCIPLINE PHILOSOPHY **EDUCATION** Univ Ill, Chicago, PhD, 94. **CAREER** Assoc prof, philos, Utah State Univ, 94- . **CONTACT ADDRESS** Dept of Languages and Philosophy, Utah State Univ, Logan, UT 84322-0720. **EMAIL** hueneman@cc.usu.edu

HUFF, PETER A.

PERSONAL Born 11/01/1958, Atlanta, GA, m, 1994, 1 child **DISCIPLINE** HISTORICAL THEOLOGY **EDUCATION** Mercer Univ, BA, 80; Southern Baptist Theol Seminary, MDiv, 84; St Louis Univ, PhD, 94. **CAREER** Asst Prof, Univ Puget Sound, 94-95; Asst Prof Theol, St. Anselm Col, 95-; chair, dept of theology, St. Anselm Col, 00-. **HONORS AND AWARDS** Phi Beta Kappa. **MEMBERSHIPS** Am Acad Relig; Am Soc Church Hist; Col Theol Soc. **RESEARCH** Religion in American culture; religion and literature; catholic studies. **SELECTED PUBLICATIONS** Co-ed, Knowledge and Belief in America: Enlightenment Traditions and Modern Religious Thought, Cambridge Univ Press, 95; auth, With the Body of This World: Allen Tate's Quarrel with Modern Gnosticism, Fides et Hist, 95; New Apologists in America's Conservative Catholic Subculture, Horizons, 96; Allen Tate and the Catholic Revival: Trace of the Fugitive Gods, Isaac Hecker Studies in Religion and American Culture, Paulist Press, 96; John Locke and the Prophecy of Quaker Women, Quaker Hist, 97. **CONTACT ADDRESS** Theology Dept, Saint Anselm Col, 100 Saint Anselm Dr., Manchester, NH 03102. **EMAIL** pehuff@anselm.edu

HUFF-CORZINE, LIN

PERSONAL Born 09/23/1949, Macomb, IL, m, 1974, 2 children **DISCIPLINE** CRIMINOLOGY, DEVIANCE, WOMEN'S ISSUES **EDUCATION** Univ Neb, BA, 82; Washington Univ, PhD, 86. **CAREER** Lectr, Univ Neb, Lincoln; 84; vis lectr, Creighton Univ, 85; lectr, Col St Mary, 86; vis asst prof, Univ Neb, Omaha, 86-87; temp asst prof, Kansas State Univ, 87-88; asst prof, 88-94; assoc prof, 94-96; assoc prof, Univ Cen Fla, 96-; intr asst vice pres, 99-. **HONORS AND AWARDS** Alpha Lambda Delta; Phi Eta Sigma; Charles E Towle Schlp; Alpha Kappa Delta; regents Merit Schlps; Phi Beta Kappa; Teach Fel, Univ Fel, WU; Vis Schl Awd; Dist Bk Awd; Sr Fac Fel, UCF. **MEMBERSHIPS** ASC; HRWG; ASA; ACJS; MSSA; SSS; MSS. **RESEARCH** Structural and cultural influences on lethal violence. **SELECTED PUBLICATIONS** Coauth, Currents of Lethal Violence: An Integrated Model of Suicide and Homicide, State Univ NY Press (Albany, NY), 94; coauth, "Clean Up and Go Straight: Effects of Drug Treatment on Recidivism Among Felony Probationers," Am J Crim Just 22 (98): 169-87; coauth, "Strangers in the Night: An Application of the Lifestyle/Routine Activities Approach to Elderly Homicide Victimization," Homicide Stud 2 (98):130-59; coauth, "Return to the Scene of the Punishment: Recidivism of Adult Male Property Offenders on Probation, 1986-1989," J Res Crime Delinq 34 (97): 237-52; coauth, "Rethinking Lynching: Extralegal Executions in Postbellum Louisiana," Deviant Behavior 17 (96):133-158; coauth, Gender and Age Differences in Food Cognition," Appetite 20 (93): 33-52; coauth, "Racial Inequality and Black Homicide: An Analysis of Felony and Non-Felony Rates," J Contemp Crim Just Issues 8 (92):150-165; coauth, "The Violent West Reexamined: A Research Note on Regional Homicide Rates," Criminology 32 (94):149-161; coauth, "Food Preferences in Daily Life: Cognitive, Affective, and Social Predictors," Ecology of Food and Nutrition 33 (95): 215-228. **CONTACT ADDRESS** Dept Sociology, Anthropology, Univ of Central Florida, PO Box 161360, Orland, FL 32816-1360.

HUFFMAN, DOUGLAS S.

PERSONAL Born 01/01/1961, Minneapolis, MN, m, 1985 **DISCIPLINE** THEOLOGY **EDUCATION** Northwest Col, BA, 83; Weaton Col Grad School, MA, 85; Trinity Evangel Divinity School, MA, 89; PhD, 94. **CAREER** Dean of Admission & Records, assoc prof of Bible, Northwest Coll, St Paul MN, 94-. **HONORS AND AWARDS** Outstanding Young man of Am, 86; Trinity Fac Scholar, 89; Who's who among Am Teachers, 96. **MEMBERSHIPS** Evangel Theol Soc; Soc of Bibl Lit; Inst for Bibl Res. **RESEARCH** Luke-Acts; NT Greek; Christian Aplologetics. **SELECTED PUBLICATIONS** Auth, The Historical Jesus of Ancient Unbelief, JETS, 97; rev The Preface to Luke's Gospel: Literary Convention and Social Context in Luke 1:1-4 and Acts 1:1 JETS, 97; rev The Modern Search for the Real Jesus: An Introductory Survey of the Historical Roots of Gospels Criticism, JETS, forthcoming; Assassins, Bernice, Drusilla, Gentile, Yokefellow, Eerdmans Dictionary of the Bible, forthcoming; Acts, 00. **CONTACT ADDRESS** Northwestern Col, Minnesota, 3003 Snelling Ave N, Saint Paul, MN 55113. **EMAIL** dsh@nwc.edu

HUFFMAN, GORDON, JR.

DISCIPLINE CHRISTIAN MISSION **EDUCATION** Capital Univ, BA, 64; Evangel Lutheran Theol Sem, BD, 68; Chinese Univ, Hong Kong, grad stud, 76-77; Univ St Andrews, PhD, 77. **CAREER** Prof, Lutheran Theol Sem, Hong Kong, 77-79; fac, Southeast Asia Grad Sch Theol, 78-79; assoc dean, Lutheran Theol Sem, Hong Kong, 79; vis prof, 79-80; asst prof, 81-83; assoc prof, 83-91; John H. F. Kuder prof, 84-; prof, Trinity Lutheran Sem, 91-. **SELECTED PUBLICATIONS** Auth, Mission is the Heart of the Church, World Encounter, 85; The Shape of Mission, Trinity Sem Rev, 85. **CONTACT ADDRESS** Hist, Theol, Soc Dept, Trinity Lutheran Sem, 2199 E Main St, Columbus, OH 43209-2334. **EMAIL** thuffman@trinity.capital.edu

HUGGETT, NICK

DISCIPLINE PHILOSOPHY **EDUCATION** Rutgers Univ, PhD. **CAREER** Asst prof, Univ IL at Chicago . **RESEARCH** Philos of physics. **SELECTED PUBLICATIONS** Co-auth, Interpretations of Quantum Field Theory, Philos Sci. **CONTACT ADDRESS** Philos Dept, Univ of Illinois, Chicago, S Halsted St, PO Box 705, Chicago, IL 60607. **EMAIL** huggett@uic.edu

HUGHES, GLENN

PERSONAL Born 12/18/1951, Seattle, WA, s **DISCIPLINE** PHILOSOPHY **EDUCATION** Univ Wash, BA, 72; BA, 75; MA, 79; Boston Col, MA, 85; PhD, 89. **CAREER** Asst prof, Simmons Univ, 88-90; from asst prof to assoc prof, St Marys Univ, 90-. **HONORS AND AWARDS** Distinguished Fac Awd, St Mays Univ, 94. **MEMBERSHIPS** Eric Voeglin Soc, Lonergan Philos Soc, Am Polit Sci Asn, Ernest Becker Found. **RESEARCH** Eric Voegelin, Bernard Lonergan, philosophy of religion. **SELECTED PUBLICATIONS** Auth, Mystery and Myth in the Philosophy of Eric Voegelin, Univ of Mo Press, 93; ed, The Politics of Soul: Eric Voegelin on Religious Experience, Rowland and Littlefield, 99. **CONTACT ADDRESS** Dept Philos, St. Mary's Univ of San Antonio, 1 Camino Santa Maria St, San Antonio, TX 78228-5433. **EMAIL** philglen@stmarytx.edu

HUGHES, JOYCE A.

PERSONAL Born 02/07/1940, Gadsden, AL, s **DISCIPLINE** LAW **EDUCATION** Carleton Coll Northfield MN (magna cum laude), BA 1961; Univ Madrid Spain 1961-62; Univ MN Law Sch (cum laude), JD 1965. **CAREER** Northwestern Univ School of Law, prof, 79-, assoc prof, 75-79; Chicago Transit Authority, general counsel, 84-88; Continental Illinois Bank, attorney, 82-84; Univ MN Law Sch, assoc prof, 71-75; Peterson & Holtze Minneapolis, consult, 71-74; Auerbach Corp Philadelphia, consult, 70-71; LeFevere Lefler Hamilton & Peterson Minneapolis, atty, 67-71; Judge Earl R Larson Minneapolis, law clk, 65-67. **HONORS AND AWARDS** Phi Beta Kappa, 1961; Fulbright Scholarship 1961-62; John Hay Whitney Fellowship 1962-63; Achievement Awd Carleton College Alumni 1969; 100 Top Business & Professional Women, Dollars & Sense Magazine, 1986; Superior Public Service Awd, Cook County Bar Assn, 1987. **MEMBERSHIPS** Mem, Amer Bar Assn, Natl Bar Assn, Illinois Bar Assn, Cook County Bar Assn; dir, Chicago Bd of Educ, 1980-82; dir, Federal Home Loan Bank of Chicago, 1980-84; dir, First Plymouth Bank, 1971-82; trustee, Natl Urban League, 1972-78; trustee, Carleton Coll, 1969-94. **CONTACT ADDRESS** School of Law, Northwestern Univ, 357 E Chicago Ave, Chicago, IL 60611.

HUGHES, KEVIN L.

PERSONAL Born 11/12/1969, Baltimore, MD, m, 1995, 1 child **DISCIPLINE** HISTORY OF CHRISTIANITY **EDUCATION** Univ Chicago, PhD, 97. **CAREER** Asst Prof , theology and Religious Studies, Villanova Univ, 00-. **HONORS AND AWARDS** Phi Beta Kappa, 90; Pres Scholar, Villanova Univ, 87-91; Dist Stud Award (Relig Studies), Villanova Univ, 91; summa cum laude, Villanova Univ, 91; Valedictorian, Villanova Univ, 91; Century Fel, Univ Chicago, 91-95; jr fel, Inst for Advanced Stud of Relig, 95-96. **MEMBERSHIPS** Am Soc of Church Hist; AAR; Soc of Bibl Lit. **RESEARCH** Theology, religion, and culture of the Middle Ages; history of biblical exegesis; apocalypticism. **SELECTED PUBLICATIONS** Auth, Visionary Exegesis: Vision, Text and Interparetation in Hildegard's Scivias," Am Benedictine Rev 50:3, 99; coauth, Augustine and Liberal Education, London: Ashgate, 00; auth, The Arts Reputed Liberal: Augusine on the Perils of Liberal Education, " Augustine and Liberal education, London: Ashgate, 00; auth, Faith Handed On: Church History, Chicago: Loyola Univ Press, 2nd ed, (01), 1st print 2000. **CONTACT ADDRESS** Dept of Theology and Reoigius Studies, Villanova Univ, 800 Lancaster Ave, Villanova, PA 19085. **EMAIL** kevin.hughes@villanova.edu

HUGHES, PAMELA S.
DISCIPLINE LAW **EDUCATION** McGill Univ, BA, 74, LLB, 77; Univ Toronto, LLM, 78. **CAREER** Securities law, Blake, Cassels & Graydon **HONORS AND AWARDS** Dir, Capital Markets Int Markets Branch. **SELECTED PUBLICATIONS** Auth, pubs on international securities markets. **CONTACT ADDRESS** Fac of Law, Univ of Toronto, 78 Queen's Park, Toronto, ON, Canada M5S 1A1.

HUGHES, PAUL
PERSONAL Born 03/25/1954, Boston, MA, m, 1992 **DISCIPLINE** PHILOSOPHY **EDUCATION** Univ of Mass Boston, BA, 80; Univ of IL - Chicago, MA, 82; PhD, 87. **CAREER** Vis asst prof, Col of William and Mary, 86-87; asst prof to prof, chair, Univ of Mich Dearborn, 87-. **HONORS AND AWARDS** Charlotte Newcombe Diss Fel, 85. **MEMBERSHIPS** Am Philos Assoc; Central States Philos Assoc. Southern Soc for Philos and Psychol; Am Assoc of Higher Educ. **RESEARCH** Moral psychology, political theory, philosophy of law, gender issues. **SELECTED PUBLICATIONS** Auth, "Moral anger, forgiving, and condoning", J of Soc Philos XXVI.1 (95): 103-118; auth, "Taking ethics seriously: virtue, validity, and the art of moral reasoning", Teaching Philos 19.3, (96): 219-232; auth, "What is involved in forgiving?", Philosophia, 25.1-4, (97): 33-50; auth, "Exploitation, autonomy, and the case for organ sales", Int J of Applied Philos 12.1 (98): 89-97; auth, "Paternalism, battered women, and the law", J of Soc Philos 30.1 (99): 18-30; auth, "Temptation and the manipulation of desire", J of Value Inquiry 33.3 (99): 371-379; auth, "Anger" and "Hatred", Encycl of Ethics, Vol 2 (forthcoming). **CONTACT ADDRESS** Dept Humanities, Univ of Michigan, Dearborn, 4901 Evergreen Rd, Dearborn, MI 48128-2406. **EMAIL** pmhughes@umich.edu

HUGHES, RICHARD ALLAN
PERSONAL Born 07/30/1941, Batavia, NY, m, 1973, 2 children **DISCIPLINE** RELIGIOUS STUDIES **EDUCATION** Univ of Indianapolis, BA, 63; Boston Univ, STB, 66, PhD(theol), 70. **CAREER** Asst prof to prof Relig, Lycoming Col, 70-. **HONORS AND AWARDS** The Szondi Prize, 93; Res Grant, The Louisville Inst, 99. **MEMBERSHIPS** Int Szondi Asn; N Amer Paul Tillich Soc. **RESEARCH** Theology; thanatology; ethics. **SELECTED PUBLICATIONS** Auth, Szondi's Theory of the Cain Complex, fall 79 & On Aggression: The Szondian View, fall 81, Am Imago; Theology and the Cain Complex, Univ Press Am, 82; The Cain Complex and the Apostle Paul, Soundings, spring 82; Bereavement and Pareschatology, Encounter, fall 82; Aggression and Expiation, Univ Press of Am, 87; The Judge and the Faith Healer, Univ Press of Am, 89; Return of the Ancestor, Peter Lang, 92; The Radiant Shock of Death, Peter Lang, 95; auth, "Lament in Christian Theology," Encounter (00). **CONTACT ADDRESS** 700 College Pl, Williamsport, PA 17701-5192. **EMAIL** hughes@lycoming.edu

HUGHES, RICHARD T.
PERSONAL Born 02/21/1943, Lubbock, TX, m, 1963, 1 child **DISCIPLINE** CHRISTIAN HISTORY **EDUCATION** Harding Univ, BA (Bible), 65; Abilene Christian Univ, MA (Christian history), 67; Univ IA, PhD (Christian history), 72. **CAREER** Asst prof, relig div, Pepperdine Univ, 71-76; assoc prof and prof, Dept of Religious Studies, Southwest MO State Univ, 77-82; prof, history dept, Abilene Christian Univ, 83-88; prof, relig div, 88-94, Distinguished Prof, Religion Division, Pepperdine Univ, 94-. **HONORS AND AWARDS** Outstanding Alumnus, Col of Arts and Sciences, Harding Univ, 86; Faculty Person of the Year, Seaver Col, Pepperdine Univ, 92-93; Distinguished Alumnus, Col of Biblical and Family Studies, Abilene Christian Univ, 96. **MEMBERSHIPS** Am Soc Church Hist; Am Academy Relig. **RESEARCH** 19th century Am relig, especially restorationist movements; religion and higher ed in the US. **SELECTED PUBLICATIONS** Co-auth with Leonard Allen, Illusions of Innocence, Chicago, 88; Ed, The Primitive Church in the Modern World, Univ IL Press, 95; auth, Reviving the Ancient Faith: The Story of Churches of Christ in America, Eerdmans, 96; co-ed with Wm. B. Adrian, Models for Christian Higher Education, Eerdmans, 97. **CONTACT ADDRESS** Religion Division, Pepperdine Univ, 24255 Pacific Coast Hwy, Malibu, CA 90263. **EMAIL** rhughes@pepperdine.edu

HUGHES, ROBERT DON
DISCIPLINE RELIGION **EDUCATION** Calif Baptist Col, BA; Golden Gate Baptist Theol Sem, MDiv; S Baptist Theol Sem, PhD. **CAREER** Assoc VP, Acad Prog, dir, Cont Edu and Extension Stud, act dir, Prof Dr Stud, S Baptist Theol Sem. **HONORS AND AWARDS** Mass media consult, Intl Mission Bd. **RESEARCH** Cross cultural missions. **SELECTED PUBLICATIONS** Auth, Satan's Whispers. **CONTACT ADDRESS** Sch Theol, So Baptist Theol Sem, 2825 Lexington Rd, Louisville, KY 40280. **EMAIL** rhughes@sbts.edu

HUGHES, ROBERT G.
DISCIPLINE HOMILETICS **EDUCATION** B.A. Lehigh Univ, 59; MDiv, LTSP, 62; ThM, Princeton Sem, 74; PhD, 81; Pastorates in Pa, 62-71. **CAREER** Prof, 72; pres, 90; ch of the fac-; fac 00. **SELECTED PUBLICATIONS** Coauth, Preaching Doctrine: For the Twenty-first Century, Fortress Press, 97. **CONTACT ADDRESS** Dept of Practical Theol, Lutheran Theol Sem at Philadelphia, 7301 Germantown Ave, Philadelphia, PA 19119-1794. **EMAIL** Mtairy@ltsp.edu

HUGLY, PHILIP
DISCIPLINE LOGIC, THE PHILOSOPHY OF MATHEMATICS **EDUCATION** Univ Calif, Berkeley, PhD, 65. **CAREER** Prof, Univ Nebr, Lincoln. **RESEARCH** Wittgenstein. **SELECTED PUBLICATIONS** Coauth, Theories of Truth and Truth-Value Gaps, Ling and Philos 16, 93; The Disquotational Theory of Truth is False, Philos 22, 93; Quantifying over the Reals, Synthese 101, 94; Intentionality and Truth: An Essay on the Philosophy of Arthur Prior. **CONTACT ADDRESS** Univ of Nebraska, Lincoln, Lincoln, NE 68588-0417.

HULL, DAVID L.
PERSONAL Born 06/15/1935, Burnside, IL **DISCIPLINE** PHILOSOPHY **EDUCATION** Indiana Univ, PhD, 64. **CAREER** Univ Wis, Milwaukee, 64-84; Northwestern Univ, 85-01; emer, 01- . **HONORS AND AWARDS** Guggenheim Fel. **MEMBERSHIPS** Am Acad of Arts and Sci; Philos of Sci Asn; Soc of Syst Biol. **RESEARCH** History and philosophy of biology. **SELECTED PUBLICATIONS** Auth, Die Rezeption von Darwin's Evolutionstheorie bei Britischen Wissenschaftsphilosophen des 19. Jahrhunderts, in Engels, ed, Die Rezeption von Evolutionstheorien im 19. Jahrhundert, Suhrkamp, 95; auth, Rainbows in Retrospect: L.A. Johnson's Contributions to Taxonomic Philosophy, Telopea, 96; auth, A Revolutionary Philosopher of Science, Nature, 96; auth, What's Wrong with Invisible-Hand Explanations? PSA, 97; auth, That Just Don't Sound Right: A Plea for Real Examples, in Earman, ed, The Cosmos of Science, Pittsburgh, 97; auth, Species, Subspecies and Races, Social Research, 98; co-ed, Philosophy of Biology, Oxford, 98. **CONTACT ADDRESS** Dept of Philosophy, Northwestern Univ, Evanston, IL 60208. **EMAIL** d-hull@northwestern.edu

HULL, MICHAEL F.
PERSONAL Born 04/01/1963, Bronx, NY **DISCIPLINE** BIBLICAL STUDIES **EDUCATION** St Joseph's Sem, MA, 93; Pontifical Gregorian Univ, STL, 96, STD (cand), 96-. **CAREER** Ordained Roman Cath Priest of the Archdiocese of New York, 93; graduate studies, Pontifical Gregorian Univ, Rome, 94-98; prof of Sacred Scripture, St Joseph's Seminary, NY, 98-. **MEMBERSHIPS** Cath Biblical Asn; Soc of Biblical Lit; Am Academy of Relig. **RESEARCH** Biblical studies; ancient Near East; theology. **SELECTED PUBLICATIONS** Auth, Prophesy and Revelation 10, 1-11; 11, 1-13: The Creative Use of the Old Testament by a New Testament Prophet, Dunwoodie Rev 16, 93; Jezebel and John: Authority in Thyatira, Dunwoodie Rev 17, 94, auth, "Hermeneutics Begins At Home: On Retrieving The Reader In Biblical Interpretation," Dunwoodie Review 23, (00):77-99. **CONTACT ADDRESS** St. Joseph's Sem, 201 Seminary Ave, Apt 25A, Yonkers, NY 10704-1896. **EMAIL** mfhull@hotmail.com

HULL, N. E. H.
PERSONAL Born 08/27/1949, New York, NY, m, 1970, 2 children **DISCIPLINE** LAW, HISTORY **EDUCATION** Ohio State, Univ, BA, 74; Columbia Univ, PhD, 81; Univ of Georgia, JD, 85. **CAREER** Assoc prof, 87-93, prof, 93-97, distinguish prof of law and hist, 97-present, Rutgers Univ. **HONORS AND AWARDS** Scribes Book Awd for 1998; Erwin Surrency Prize of Amer Soc for Legal Hist, 99. **MEMBERSHIPS** ABA, New Jersey Bar Assn; AHA; ASLA; OAH **RESEARCH** Amer Legal and Jurisprudential Hist **SELECTED PUBLICATIONS** Auth, Vital Schools of Jurisprudence: Roscoe Pound, Wesley Newcomb Hohfeld, and the Promotion of an Academic Jurisprudential Agenda, 1910-1919, Journal of Legal Education, 95; The Romantic Realist: Art, Literature and the Enduring Legacy of Karl Llewellyn's Jurisprudence, 40 American Journal of Legal History, 96; Roscoe Pound & Karl Llewellyn: Searching for an American Jurisprudence, 97; Back to the Future of the Institute: William Draper Lewis's Vision of the ALI's Mission During Its First Twenty-Five Years and The Implications for the Institute's Seventy-Fifth Anniversary, 98. **CONTACT ADDRESS** Sch Law-Camden, Rutgers, The State Univ of New Jersey, Camden, 217 N. Fifth St., Camden, NJ 08102-1203. **EMAIL** nehhul@crab.rutgers.edu

HULL, RICHARD T.
PERSONAL Born 12/29/1939, Oklahoma City, OK, m, 1962, 1 child **DISCIPLINE** PHILOSOPHY **EDUCATION** Austin Col, MA, 63; Ind Univ, PhD, 71. **CAREER** Headmaster, Calasanctius Prep School Buffalo, NY, 83-86; scholar in res, Buffalo Gen Hosp, 95; prof Philos, SUNY-Buffalo, 67-97; Exec Dir Texas Coun Hum, 97-99. **MEMBERSHIPS** Am Philos Asn; Nat Soc Fund Raising Exec. **RESEARCH** Humanities; biomedical ethics; philosophy of mind. **SELECTED PUBLICATIONS** Auth, Ethical Issues in the New Reporductive Technologies, Wadsworth, 90; A Quarter Century of Value Inquiry: Presidential Addresses of the American Society of Value Inquiry, Editions Rodopi, 94; Symposium: Russian Value Theory, The Jour of Value Inquiry, 96; William H. Werkmeister, Martin Heidegger on the Way, Editions Rodopi, 96; Presidential Addresses of The American Philosophical Association, 1901-1910 and Presidential Addresses of The American Philosophical Association, 1911-1920, Kluwer Acad Publ, 99; auth, "Presidential Addresses of the American Philosphical Association 1921-1930," auth, "Presidential Addresses of The American Philosophical Association, 1931-1940," Kluwer Acad Publ, 00. **CONTACT ADDRESS** Texas Council on Humanities, 4845 Spaulding Dr., Clarence, NY 14031-1563. **EMAIL** rthull@swbell.net

HULL, WILLIAM E.
PERSONAL Born 05/28/1930, Birmingham, AL, m, 1952, 2 children **DISCIPLINE** RELIGION **EDUCATION** Samford Univ, BA, 51; S Baptist Theol Sem, MDiv, 54, PhD, 60. **CAREER** Ordained Baptist Minister, 50; S Baptist Theol Sem, fel, inst, asst prof, assoc prof, prof, 54-75; chair, New Testament Dept, The Southern Theol Sem, 58-60, 63-68; Vis prof. at: Baptist Theol Sem, Switzerland, 63; dir, Graduate Studies, School of Theol, The Southern Baptist Theol Sem, 68-70; dean, School of Theol, The Southern Baptist Theol Sem, 69-75; provost, The Southern Baptist Theol Sem, 72-75; Louisiana State Univ Sch of Med, 75-78; S Baptist Theol Sem, 79, 90-92; Nigerian Baptist Theol Sem, 82; provost, Samford Univ, 87-96; Univ prof, Samford Univ, prof, 87-00; prof, Samford Univ, 87-00; acting pres, Samford Univ, 93; reseach prof, Samford Univ, 00-. **HONORS AND AWARDS** Phi Eta Sigma, Nat Scholastic Fraternity, 48; Omicron Delta Kappa, National Leadership Fraternity, 51; Denominational Service Awd, Samford Univ, 74; Phi Kappa Phi, Nat Scholastic Fraternity, 75; Liberty Bell Awd, Shreveport Bar Asn, 84; Brotherhood and Humanitarian Awd, Shreveport and Bossier City Chapter, Nat Conf of Christians and Jews, 87; Phi Alpha Theta, Hist Honor Soc, 88; Pi Gamma Mu, Soc Sci(s) Honor Soc, 88; Lamplighter Awd, Alabama League for Nursing, 97; Charles D. Johnson Outstanding Educator Awd, Asn of Southern Baptist Colleges and Schools, 99. **MEMBERSHIPS** AAPS, AAR, AAHE, AAUP, ASOR, NABPR, SBL **SELECTED PUBLICATIONS** Auth, The Gospel of John, Alpha-Omega Series, Broadman, 64; auth, John, Broadman Bible Commentary, Broadman, 70; auth, The Bible, Covenant, 74; auth, Beyond the Barriers, Broadman, 81; auth, Love in Four Dimensions, Broadman, 82; auth, The Christian Experience of Salvation, Layman's Library of Christian Doctrine, Broadman, 87; auth, Handbook of Contemporary Preaching, Broadman, 93; auth, Proclaiming the Baptist Vision: The Bible, Smith & Helwys, 94; auth, The University Though the Eyes of Faith, Light & Life, 98; contrib, The Ministers Manual: 2000, Jossey-Bass, 99. **CONTACT ADDRESS** Dept of Theology, Samford Univ, 435 Ves Club Way, Birmingham, AL 35216-1357. **EMAIL** wehull@samford.edu

HULLETT, JAMES N.
PERSONAL Born 03/02/1939, Toledo, OH, m, 1981, 1 child **DISCIPLINE** PHILOSOPHY **EDUCATION** Brandeis Univ, PhD, 67. **CAREER** Asst prof, Dartmouth Col, 66-68; asst prof, Boston Univ, 68-75; vis prof, Bennington Col, 83-85; publ, Hackett Pub Co., 76- . **MEMBERSHIPS** APA. **CONTACT ADDRESS** Hackett Pub Co, PO Box 390007, Cambridge, MA 02139.

HULLOT-KENTOR, ROBERT
DISCIPLINE PHILOSOPHY **EDUCATION** Univ of Mass, PhD, 85. **CAREER** Assoc prof, Southampton Col, 97-. **SELECTED PUBLICATIONS** Trans, Kierkegaard, by Adorno, 89; trans Aesthetic Theory, by Adorno, 98. **CONTACT ADDRESS** Dept Humanities, Southampton Col, 239 Montauk Hwy, Southampton, NY 11968-4100. **EMAIL** kentor@southampton.uunet.edu

HULTGREN, ARLAND J.
PERSONAL Born 07/17/1939, Muskegon, MI, m, 1965, 3 children **DISCIPLINE** NEW TESTAMENT STUDIES **EDUCATION** Augustana Col, BA, 61; Univ Mich, MA, 63; Lutheran Sch Theol Chicago, MDiv, 65; Union Theol Sem, ThD, 71. **CAREER** Instr to assoc prof, rel stud, Wagner Col, 69-77; assoc prof to Prof New Testament, Luther Sem, 77-. **HONORS AND AWARDS** Phi Beta Kappa, 61; Outstanding Alumni Achievement Awd, Augustana Col, 96. **MEMBERSHIPS** Soc Bibl Lit; Studiorum Novi Testamenti Societas. **RESEARCH** Gospel of Matthew; Parables of Jesus; Epistle to the Romans. **SELECTED PUBLICATIONS** Auth, Paul's Gospel and Mission, 85; auth, Christ and His Benefits: Christology and Redemption in the New Testament, 87; auth, The Rise of Normative Christianity, 94; co-ed, The Earliest Christian Heretics: Readings from Their Opponents, 96; auth, The Parables of Jesus: A Commentary, 00. **CONTACT ADDRESS** Dept of New Testament, Luther Sem, 2481 Como Ave, Saint Paul, MN 55108. **EMAIL** ahultgre@luthersem.edu

HUMBER, JAMES MICHAEL
PERSONAL Born 11/10/1942, Erie, PA, m, 1980, 2 children **DISCIPLINE** PHILOSOPHY **EDUCATION** Colgate Univ, AB, 64; State Univ NYork Buffalo, MA, 67, PhD, 70. **CAREER** From Asst Prof to Assoc Prof, 69-83, Prof Philos, GA State Univ, 83. **MEMBERSHIPS** Am Philos Asn; Southern Soc Philos & Psychol; Hum Soc. **RESEARCH** Early mod hist of philos; applied ethics. **SELECTED PUBLICATIONS** Co-ed, Biomedical ethics and the Law, Plenum Press, 76, 2nd ed, 79; Biomedical Ethics Reviews: 1983, Humana Press, 83, 84, and to the present; Business Ethics, Promethus Books, 92; auth, Justifying the Foreign Corrupt Practices Act, Business Ethics, rev ed, Promethus Books, 92; Hume's Invisible Self, Am Cath Philos Quart, Summer 95; Maternity, Paternity, and Equality, Biomedical Ethics Reviews: 1995, Humana Press, 95; Hume, The Blackwell Companion to the Philosophers, Blackwell; author of numerous other articles and book reviews. **CONTACT ADDRESS** Dept of Philos, Georgia State Univ, Box 4089, Atlanta, GA 30302-4089. **EMAIL** phljmh@panther.gsu.edu

HUME, WENDELIN M.
PERSONAL Born 02/04/1961, St Louis Park, MN, m, 1980, 3 children **DISCIPLINE** SOCIOLOGY, CRIMINAL JUSTICE **EDUCATION** Black Hills State Col, BS, 87; Sam Houston State Univ, MA, 91; PhD, 00. **CAREER** Teaching Asst, Sam Houston State Univ, 87-88; Asst Prof, Univ ND, 91-. **HONORS AND AWARDS** Outstanding Academic Book Awd, Encycl of Am Prisons; Who's Who Among Am Teachers, 96-98. **MEMBERSHIPS** Midwestern Criminal Justice Assoc, Assoc of Am Indian and Alaska Native Profs, Drug Policy Found. **RESEARCH** Victimization issues, gender equity, native American crime issues, drug laws. **SELECTED PUBLICATIONS** Auth, "1988 Texas Crime Poll Report on Experience with and Performance of the Texas Criminal Justice System," Survey Res Prog (88); auth, "1989 Texas Crime Poll Report," Survey Res Prog (89); coauth, Texas Jails: Law and Practice, Sam Houston Pr (Huntsville, TX), 90; coauth, "Texas Crime Poll Report," Survey Res Prog (91); coauth, Texas Juvenile Law and Practice, Sam Houston Pr (Huntsville, TX), 91; auth, "A Difference in Perceptions: The Final Report of the North Dakota Commission on Gender Fairness in the Courts," North Dakota Law Rev, vol 72, no 4 (96): 1112-1344; auth, "The Reliability of Drug testing," New Frontiers in Drug Policy (91): 317-322; auth, "Change Name for a Better Atmosphere," Grand Forks Herald, p 2b (97); auth, "The Interstate Compact Agreement," The Encycl of Am Prisons, Garland Publ Co, 96. **CONTACT ADDRESS** Dept Sociol, Univ of No Dakota, PO Box 8050, Grand Forks, ND 58202-8050. **EMAIL** whume@badlands.nodak.edu

HUMMEL, BRADFORD SCOTT
PERSONAL Born 02/06/1966, Santa Paula, CA, m, 1990, 2 children **DISCIPLINE** THEOLOGY **EDUCATION** William Corey Col, BA, 87; Hebrew Univ, 88-89; Southwestern Baptist Theol Sem, M.Div, 91, PhD, 96. **CAREER** Adj prof, Southwestern Baptist Theol Sem, 93-94, 98; asst prof, LeTourneau Univ, 98-. **HONORS AND AWARDS** Greek Awd; Hebrew Awd; Jenkins-Chastain Citizenship Awd; President's Scholar; Rotary Int Fel. **MEMBERSHIPS** Soc Biblical Lit; Am Soc Oriental Res; Am Acad Relig; Nat Asn Baptist Profs of Relig. **RESEARCH** Hebrew Bible; Second Temple Period. **CONTACT ADDRESS** 505 Wain Dr, Longview, TX 75604. **EMAIL** hummels@letu.edu

HUMPREYS, FISHER H.
PERSONAL Born 02/05/1939, Columbus, MS, m, 1963, 2 children **DISCIPLINE** THEOLOGY **EDUCATION** Miss Col, MA, 61, New Orleans Baptist Theol Sem, BD, 64; Oxford, Mlitt, 67; Loyola Univ, MA, 77, New Orelans Baptist Theol Sem, ThD, 72. **CAREER** Prof, New Orelans Baptist Theol Sem, 70-90; prof, Samford Univ, 90-. **HONORS AND AWARDS** George Macon Awd for Excellence in Teaching, 98. **MEMBERSHIPS** AAR; NABPR; CTS. **SELECTED PUBLICATIONS** Auth, The Way We Were, 94; Thinking at God, 94. **CONTACT ADDRESS** Beeson Divinity School, Samford Univ, 800 Lakeshore Dr, Birmingham, AL 35229-0001. **EMAIL** fhhumphr@samford.edu

HUNT, JAMES
PERSONAL Born Socorro, NM, m **DISCIPLINE** AMERICAN HISTORY, HISTORICAL, POLITICAL AND INTERNATIONAL STUDIES **EDUCATION** Univ Wash, BA, MA, PhD, 73. **CAREER** Tchg, Univ Wash; Core prog; Cent Amer Stud/Serv prog; prof, Whitworth Col, 73-. **HONORS AND AWARDS** Burlington Northern award for teaching excellence; grants, FIPSE, NEH, Wash Comm for Hum. **RESEARCH** Latin American Colonial History. **SELECTED PUBLICATIONS** Publ, articles on the faith journeys of Frederick Douglass and Jane Addams. **CONTACT ADDRESS** Dept of Hist, Whitworth Col, 300 West Hawthorne Rd, Mail Stop 1103, Spokane, WA 99251. **EMAIL** jhunt@whitworth.edu

HUNT, MARY ELIZABETH
PERSONAL Born 06/01/1951, Syracuse, NY **DISCIPLINE** THEOLOGY **EDUCATION** Marquette Univ, BA (magna cum laude), theology, philos, 72; Harvard Divinity School, master theol studies, 74; Jesuit School of Theology, master divinity, 79; Graduate Theol Union, PhD, philos and systematic theol, 80. **CAREER** Visiting prof theol, frontier internship in mission, ISEDET, 80-82; co-dir, co-founder, Women's Alliance for Theol Ethics and Ritual, 83-; visiting asst prof religion, Colgate Univ, 86-87; adjunct asst prof of Women's Studies, Georgetown Univ, 95-; res fel, Center for the Study of Values in Public Life, Harvard Divinity Sch, Harvard Univ **HONORS AND AWARDS** Isaac Hecker Awd, Paulist Center; Prophetic Figure Awd, Women's Ordination Conf; Crossroads Women's Studies Prize, 90; Mary Rhodes Awd, Loretto Community, 93. **MEMBERSHIPS** Amer Acad Religion, Women and Religion, chair, 92-94; Soc Christian Ethics; Inst Study Christianity and Sexuality, bd dirs; Phi Sigma Tau; Alpha Sigma Nu. **SELECTED PUBLICATIONS** Auth, Fierce Tenderness: A Feminist Theology of Friendship, 91; ed, From Woman-Pain to Woman-Vision: Writings in Feminist Theology, 89; auth, "Variety Is the Spice of Life: Doing It Our Ways," in Our Families, Our Values: Snapshots of Queer Kinship, 97; auth, "Re-Imagining Backlash," in Concilium: Feminist Theology in Different Contexts, 96; ed, "Good Sex: Feminist Perspectives From The World's Religions," Rutgers University Press, 01. **CONTACT ADDRESS** Women's Alliance for Theol, Ethics and Ritual, 8035 13th St, Stes. 1, 3, 5, Silver Spring, MD 20910. **EMAIL** mhunt@hers.com

HUNTER, ALLAN
PERSONAL Born 07/05/1955, United Kingdom, d **DISCIPLINE** PSYCHOLOGY, PHILOSOPHY **EDUCATION** Oxford Univ, St. John's Col, BA, 76; MA, 78; PhD, 83. **CAREER** Prof, Curry Col, 86-. **HONORS AND AWARDS** Surrey Co Scholar; Stratosch Scholar, **MEMBERSHIPS** Asn for Psychological Type. **RESEARCH** Joseph Conrad, Writing for Self Exploration. **SELECTED PUBLICATIONS** Auth, "Some Unpublished Letters by Conrad to Arthur Symons, " Conradiana xviii: 183-198; auth, "Edmund Gosse: Four Unpublished Letters," Notes and Queries xxxiv: 179-184; auth, "Three Letters and a poem by Hardy," Notes and Queries xxxiv: 53-54; auth, "An Unpublished Letter by H.G. Wells," Notes and Queries xxxiv: 54-55; rev, of "A Portrait in Letters: Correspondence to and about Conrad," by ed. J.H. Stape and O.Knowles, Notes and Queries xliv: 137-138; rev, of "The Collected Letters of Joseph Conrad," by J. Conrad, ed. Karl and Davies, Notes and Queries xliv: 418-419; auth, "Writing as a Therapeutic Tool," in A Closer Look, ed. Adelizzi and Goss (Milton: CC Press, 95); auth, Joseph Conrad and the Ethics of Darwinism, Croom Helm (London, NY, Canberra), 83,85; auth, The Therapeutic Uses of Writing, Nova Sci and Kroshka Books (NY), 97, reprinted as Sanity Manual, 99; auth, Life Passage: Writing Exercises for Self-Exploration, Nova Sci and Kroshka Books (NY), forthcoming. **CONTACT ADDRESS** Dept Humanities, Curry Col, 1071 Blue Hill Ave, Milton, MA 02186-2302.

HUNTER, FREDERICK DOUGLAS
PERSONAL Born 01/30/1940, Pittsburgh, PA, m **DISCIPLINE** LAW **EDUCATION** Univ of Pittsburgh, BS 1961, PhD 1967; Univ of Maryland, JD 1974. **CAREER** The Lubrizol Corp, chief patent counsel, associate general counsel; EI Dupont De Nemours & Co, corporate counsel 1972-89; W R Grace & Co, sr rsch chem 1967-72. **MEMBERSHIPS** Amer Bar Assn; Delaware Bar Assn; District of Columbia Bar Assn; AOA Fraternity; AIPLA. **SELECTED PUBLICATIONS** Publ 5 papers various sci jour. **CONTACT ADDRESS** Lubrizol Corp, 29400 Lakeland Blvd, Wickliffe, OH 44092-2298.

HUNTER, JERRY L.
PERSONAL Born 09/01/1942, Mt. Holly, NC, s **DISCIPLINE** LAW **EDUCATION** NC, BS; A&T State U, 1964; Howard Univ Schl of Law, JD 1967. **CAREER** Roundtree Knox Hunter & Parker, Partner Law firm. **HONORS AND AWARDS** Am Jurisprudence Awd for Academic Achievement in Legal Methods & History. **MEMBERSHIPS** Mem US Supreme Court Bar; US Dist Court (MD & DC); US Court of Appeals & DC Court of Appeals; mem Natl Bar Assn; Am Bar Assn; DC Bar Assn; Assn of Plaintiffs Trail Atty; Sigma Delta Tau Legal Frat Alpha Kappa Mu Honor Soc; Kappa Pi Intl Honorary Art Soc **SELECTED PUBLICATIONS** Co-auth, "Current Racial Legal Developments" 12 How-L J 299, Spring 66 No 2. **CONTACT ADDRESS** Roundtree, Knox, Hunter & Parker, 1822 11th St NW, Washington, DC 20001. **EMAIL** jhunteresq@aol.com

HUNTER, JOEL
DISCIPLINE PRACTICAL THEOLOGY **EDUCATION** Ohio Univ, BA; Christian Theol Sem, MDiv, DMin. **CAREER** Vis lectr **SELECTED PUBLICATIONS** Auth, The Journey To Spiritual Maturity; The Challenging Road and Prayer; Politics & Power. **CONTACT ADDRESS** Dept of Practical Theology, Reformed Theol Sem, No Carolina, 2101 Carmel Rd, Charlotte, NC 28226.

HUNTER, RODNEY J.
PERSONAL Born 10/08/1940, Detroit, MI, m, 1970, 1 child **DISCIPLINE** PASTORAL THEOLOGY **EDUCATION** Yale Col, BA, 62; Princeton Theol Sem, BD, 62, PhD, 74. **CAREER** From instr to asst prof and assoc prof to prof of pastoral theol, Candler School of Theol, Emory Univ, 71-. **MEMBERSHIPS** Soc for Pastoral Theol; AAR; Asn for Practical Theol; Asn for Clinical Pastoral Educ. **RESEARCH** Theology of pastoral care and counseling; theology and personality studies; Freud, Jung and religion; psychology and religion; personal commitment. **SELECTED PUBLICATIONS** Auth, Law and Gospel in Pastoral Care, J of Pastoral Care, 76; auth, The Future of Pastoral Theology, Pastoral Psychol, 80; auth, A Perspectival Pastoral Theology, in Aden; ed, Turning Points in Pastoral Care: The Legacy of Anton Boisen and Seward Hiltner, Baker Book House, 90; co-ed/contributor, Dictionary of Pastoral Care and Counseling, Abingdon, 90; auth, Participation in the Life of God: Revisioning Lapsley's Salvation-Health Model, in Childs; ed, The Treasure of Earthen Vessels: Explorations in Theological Anthropology, John Knox, 94; co-ed and contribur, Pastoral Care and Social Conflict: Essays in Honor of Charles V. Gerkin, Abingdon, 95; auth, Religious Caregiving and Pedagogy in a Postmodern Context: Recovering Ecclesia, J of Pastoral Theol, 98; auth, The Power of God for Salvation: Transformative Ecclesia and the Theological Renewal of Pastoral Care and Counseling, J of the Interdenominational Theol Ctr, 98. **CONTACT ADDRESS** Candler School of Theology, Emory Univ, Atlanta, GA 30322. **EMAIL** rhunt02@emory.edu

HURD, HEIDI M.
PERSONAL Born 10/19/1960, Laramie, WY, m, 1987, 2 children **DISCIPLINE** PHILOSOPHY; LAW **EDUCATION** Queens Univ, BA, 82; Dalhousie Univ, MA, 84; Univ Southern Calif, JD, 88, PhD, 92. **CAREER** Asst prof, law, Univ Penn, 89-94; prof, law & philos, Univ Penn, 94-; visiting asst prof, philos, Univ Iowa, 91-92; assoc dean, acad affairs, Univ Penn Law Sch, 94-96; visiting prof, law, Univ Va, 97-98; prof, law, Univ of San Diego, 00-. **MEMBERSHIPS** Univ of San Diego Herzog Award, 02; Bd of ed, Legal Theory, Cambridge Press, 93-; Univ of Penn Teaching Award, 97; comt mem, AALS jurisprudence sect, 92-93, 98-99; Order of the Coif, 88-. **RESEARCH** Philosophy of law; Ethics; Criminal law; Tort law. **SELECTED PUBLICATIONS** Article, Interpreting Authority, Legal Interpretation, Oxford Univ Press, 94; article, What in the World is Wrong?, 5 Jour of Comtemp Legal Issues, (94): 157-216; article, "The Moral Magic of Consent," 2 Legal Theory, (95): 121-146; article, The Deontology of Negligence, 76 B.U. L. Rev, (95): 249-75; article, The Levitation of Liberalism, 105 Yale Law Jour, 795-824, 95; Article, Duties Beyond the Call of Duty, 5 Annual Rev of Law and Ethics, 97; auth, Moral Compat, Cambridge Press, 99; article, "Can It be Wrong to Do Right When Others Do Wrong?", Legal 7, Theory, (01); article, "Why Liberals Should Hate Hate Crime Legislation," J of Law Philosophy, (01); article, "Moral Rights and Legal Rules: A Natural Law Theory," Legal Theory 6 (00): 423-55; article, "Justification and Excuse, Wrong doing and Culpability," Notre Dameh 74, Rev (99): 101-23. **CONTACT ADDRESS** Univ of San Diego, 5998 Alcala Park, San Diego, CA 92110. **EMAIL** hhurd@acusd.edu

HURST, THOMAS R.
DISCIPLINE LAW **EDUCATION** Univ Wis, AB; Harvard Univ, JD. **CAREER** Prof, Univ Florida. **MEMBERSHIPS** Wis Bar. **RESEARCH** Corporate law, contracts, corporate finance. **CONTACT ADDRESS** School of Law, Univ of Florida, PO Box 117625, Gainesville, FL 32611-7625. **EMAIL** hurst@law.ufl.edu

HURWITZ, ILANA
PERSONAL Born 02/23/1962, South Africa, m, 1988, 2 children **DISCIPLINE** LAW **EDUCATION** Univ Witwatersrand, BA, 82; LLB, 84; Harvard Law Sch, LLM, 86; Suffolk Law Sch, JD, 88. **CAREER** Fel, Legal Resources Center Johannesburg, South Africa, 85; law clerk, U.S. District Court Mass, 87-88; assoc, Hill & Barlow, Boston, 89-95; adj prof, Clark Univ, 96-98; vis prof, Boston Univ Sch of Law, 97-; adj prof, Boston Col Law Sch, 97-. **HONORS AND AWARDS** Am Fulbright Scholarship; Fel, Legal Resources Centre. **MEMBERSHIPS** Mass Bar Asn; Mass Coun of Family Mediators. **RESEARCH** Domestic and international implications of dynamic family; Parental and gender roles and identities; Family Law; Probate Law; Human Rights. **SELECTED PUBLICATIONS** Co-auth, "The 'Genius Factor' and Equitable Distribution of Property at Divorce," Boston Bar J, 94; auth, "Collaborative Reproduction: Finding the Child in the Maze of Legal Motherhood," Conn Law Rev, 00. **CONTACT ADDRESS** Sch of Law, Boston Col, Newton Ctr, Stuart House 885 Centre St, Newton, MA 02459. **EMAIL** hurwitzi@bc.edu

HUSAK, DOUGLAS NEIL
PERSONAL Born 06/11/1948, Cleveland, OH **DISCIPLINE** PHILOSOPHY, LAW **EDUCATION** Denison Univ, BA, 70; Ohio State Univ, MA, PhD(Philos) & JD, 76. **CAREER** Vis asst prof Philos, Ind Univ, 76-77; asst prof Philos, Rutgers Univ, New Brunswick, 77-, vis asst prof, Univ Pittsburgh, Summer 80. **HONORS AND AWARDS** Rutgers Parents Asn Outstanding Teacher Awd, 80. **MEMBERSHIPS** Am Philos Asn; Soc Am Social & Legal Philosophers; Soc Business Ethics. **SELECTED PUBLICATIONS** Auth, University practices of preferential hiring and reverse discrimination in favor of Blacks--a moral analysis, Am J Jurisp, 78; Political violence, Nous, 78; Sovereigns and third party beneficiaries, J Value Inquiry, 78 Ronald Dworkin and the right to Paternalism and autonomy, Philosophy and Public Affairs, 80 Obscenity and speech, J Value Inquiry (in prep); The presumption of freedom, Nous (in prep); Philosophy of Crimal Law, Rowman & Littlefield, 87; Drugs and Rights, Cambridge Univ Press, 92. **CONTACT ADDRESS** Dept of Philosophy, Rutgers, The State Univ of New Jersey, New Brunswick, PO Box 270, New Brunswick, NJ 08903-0270. **EMAIL** husak@rci.rutgers.edu

HUSTWIT, RONALD E.
PERSONAL Born 04/02/1942, Pittsburgh, PA, m, 1966, 3 children **DISCIPLINE** PHILOSOPHY **EDUCATION** Westminster Col , BA, 64; Nebraska, MA, 65; Texas, PhD, 70. **CAREER** Prof, Coll Of Wooster. **MEMBERSHIPS** Am Philos Asn. **RESEARCH** Ludwig Wittgenstein; Philosophy of Mind, Religion, Language. **SELECTED PUBLICATIONS** Auth, Something about OK Bouwsma; Wittgenstein Interest in Kiekegaand, Wittgenstein Studies,97. **CONTACT ADDRESS** 806 E Wayne Ave, Wooster, OH 44691. **EMAIL** rhustwit@wooster.edu

HUTCHESON, RICHARD E.
PERSONAL Born 01/20/1928, Washington, DC, w, 1953, 2 children **DISCIPLINE** PHILOSOPHY **EDUCATION** Coll of

William & Mary, BA, 52; Harvard Univ, MA, 54, PhD, 62. **CAREER** Asst prof, Wofford Col, 57-59; Asst prof, Allegheny Coll, 59-67; assoc prof, Kansas State, 67-69; chemn, St. Mary's Notre Dame, 69-71; prof, dean, SUNT Potsdam, 72-90. **HONORS AND AWARDS** Phi Beta Kappa; Omicron Delta Kappa. **MEMBERSHIPS** APA; Metaphysical Soc Am. **RESEARCH** Nineteenth century British metaphysics. **CONTACT ADDRESS** 387 Savage Farm Dr, Ithaca, NY 14850. **EMAIL** rhutche1@tweny.rr.com

HUTCHINSON, DOUGLAS S.
PERSONAL Born 10/13/1955, Dorval, PQ, Canada **DISCIPLINE** PHILOSOPHY **EDUCATION** Queen's Univ, BA, 76; Oxford Univ, BPhil, 78, DPhil, 83. **CAREER** Lectr philos, Balliol Col, 79-80, Corpus Christi Col, Oxon Univ, 80-83; asst prof, 83-87, assoc prof Philos, Univ Toronto, 87-. **HONORS AND AWARDS** Rhodes scholar, 76; res fel, Humboldt Fedn(Ger), 93-94. **RESEARCH** Ancient philso, its hist, its interpretation, and its influence. **SELECTED PUBLICATIONS** Auth, The Virtues of Aristotle, 86; auth, The Epicurus Reader, 94; auth, "Aristotle's Ethics," in The Cambbridge Companion to Aristotle, (95); ; assoc ed, Plato: Complete Works, 97. **CONTACT ADDRESS** Dept of Philosophy, Univ of Toronto, 6 Hoskin Ave, Toronto, ON, Canada M5S 1H8. **EMAIL** dhutchin@chass.utoronto.ca

HUTCHINSON, ROGER CHARLES
PERSONAL Born 11/13/1935, Camrose, AB, Canada, m, 1965, 2 children **DISCIPLINE** RELIGIOUS STUDIES, SOCIAL ETHICS **EDUCATION** Univ Alta, BSc, 58; Queen's Univ, BD, 66; Univ Chicago, MA, 68; Victoria Univ, ThD, 75. **CAREER** Lectr, 69-75, asst prof, 75-78, Assoc Prof Relig Studies, Univ Toronto, 78- **MEMBERSHIPS** Can Soc Study Relig; Soc Christian Ethics. **RESEARCH** Religion and public policy in Canada; Christian socialism in Canada; inter-church coalitions. **SELECTED PUBLICATIONS** Auth, Prophets, Pastors, and Public Choices: Canadian Churches and the Mackenzie Valley Pipeline Debate, ed. P. Airhart, 92; auth, "Christianizing the Social Order: A Founding Vision", ed. Ted Reeve et.al., 96; auth, Action Training in Canada - Reflections on Church-Based Education for Social Transformation, 97; auth, "Social Ethics in a Post Liberal Age", 98. **CONTACT ADDRESS** Dept of Relig Studies Victoria Col, Univ of Toronto, 123 George St, Toronto, ON, Canada M5S 2E8. **EMAIL** r.hutchinson@utoronto.ca

HUTCHISON, HARRY GREENE, IV
PERSONAL Born 04/12/1948, Detroit, MI, m, 1994 **DISCIPLINE** LAW **EDUCATION** Wayne State Univ, BA, 69, MA, 75, JD, 86; Univ Mich, MBA, 77; Univ of Bristol, PGCE, 99; Univ of Oxford, Diploma, 00. **CAREER** Detroit Edison, Detroit, MI, business analyst, 70-74; Ford Motor Co, Troy, MI, financial analyst, 77-80; Lawrence Technol Univ, prof, 81-89; Law Prof, Univ of Detroit Mercy, 89-; Fac Dir, Univ Detroit Mercy London Law Program, 98-00. **MEMBERSHIPS** Senior policy analyst, Mackinac Center, 1987-; board of advisors, Heartland Institute, 1990-. **RESEARCH** Labor and Employment Law, Corporate Law, International Law. **CONTACT ADDRESS** Sch of Law, Univ of Detroit Mercy, 651 E Jefferson, Detroit, MI 48226. **EMAIL** hutchiso@udmercy.edu

HUTCHISON, JOHN A.
PERSONAL Born 03/02/1912, m, 1938, 5 children **DISCIPLINE** PHILOSOPHY **EDUCATION** LaFayette Col, MA; Columbia Univ, PhD. **CAREER** Williams Col, 47-55; Columbia Univ, 55-60; Claremont Grad Sch, 60-77. **HONORS AND AWARDS** Ford fel, 53; Danforth fel, 60, 61. **MEMBERSHIPS** APA; Soc for Relig Stud. **RESEARCH** World religions; philosophy and religion. **SELECTED PUBLICATIONS** Auth, Paths of Faith, 4th ed, 95; auth, Living Options in World Faiths, 77. **CONTACT ADDRESS** 720 Mayflower Rd, Claremont, CA 91711.

HUTSON, CHRISTOPHER R.
PERSONAL Born 01/08/1961, Chattanooga, TN **DISCIPLINE** NEW TESTAMENT STUDIES **EDUCATION** David Lipscomb Col, BA, 83; Univ Cincinnati, MA, 87; Yale Univ, MDiv, 89, PhD, 98. **CAREER** Adj instr, St Xavier Univ, 97-98; asst prof, New Testament, Hood Theol Sem, 98- . **MEMBERSHIPS** Soc of Bibl Lit; Chicago Soc of Bibl Res; Disciples of Christ Hist Soc; Am Institute of Archaeology. **RESEARCH** New Testament and Early Christianity; social history. **SELECTED PUBLICATIONS** Auth, Was Timothy Timid?, On the Rhetoric of Fearlessness, and Cowardice, Bivlical Res, (97): 58-73; auth, Thomas Campbell's Use of Scripture in the Declaration and Address, In the Quest for Christian Unity, Peace, and Purity in Thomas Campbell's Declaration and Address: Text and Studies, ed. by Thomas H. Olbricht and Hans Rollmann, ATLA Monograph Series 46, Scarecrow Press, (00): 211-222. **CONTACT ADDRESS** Hood Theol Sem, 800 W Thomas St, Salisbury, NC 28144. **EMAIL** crhutson@salisbury.net

HUTTER, REINHARD
DISCIPLINE CHRISTIAN ETHICS; THEOLOGY **EDUCATION** Duke Divinity Sch, ThM; Univ Erlangen, ThD; post dr res, Inst for advan stud of Rel, Univ Chicago Divinity Sch. **CAREER** Assoc prof, Lutheran Sch Theology, 90-99; assoc prof, Duke Divinity Sch, 99-. **HONORS AND AWARDS** Ed bd, Currents in Theol and Mission; Henry Luce III Fel; res fel, Ctr of Theological Inquiry, Princeton. **MEMBERSHIPS** Mem, Community Life Comm; Library Adv Comm; Admissions Comm. **RESEARCH** Christian beliefs and practices; European and North American theology. **SELECTED PUBLICATIONS** Coauth, George Lindbeck's The Nature of Doctrine: Religion and Theology in a Post-Liberal Age; The Peaceable Kingdom: A Primer in Christian Ethics; co-ed, Ecumenical Ventures in Ethics: Protestants Engage Pope John Paul II's Moral Encyclicals, Eerdmans, 98; auth, Theologie als kirchliche Praktik, Gutersloher Verlagshaus, 98. **CONTACT ADDRESS** Theological Studies Division, Duke Univ, Durham, NC 27708. **EMAIL** rhutter@lstc.edu

HUTTON, CHANE
PERSONAL Born 11/07/1951, Tulsa, OK, m, 1987, 2 children **DISCIPLINE** RELIGION **EDUCATION** Okla Baptist Univ, BA, 74; Midwestern Baptist Sem, MDiv, 85; Midwestern Baptist Sem, DMin, 88. **CAREER** Pastor, Langsford Rd Baptist Church, 89-. **HONORS AND AWARDS** Who's Who in Am Col and Univ, 84-85; Intl Youth in Achievement, 80; Outstanding Young Men of Am, 76. **SELECTED PUBLICATIONS** Auth, Dynamic Preaching Sermon, Vol X No. 10, 95. **CONTACT ADDRESS** Dept Relig, Central Baptist Theol Sem, 741 N 31st St, Kansas City, KS 66102-3964.

HUTTON, RODNEY R.
DISCIPLINE OLD TESTAMENT **EDUCATION** Dana Col, BA, 70; Evangel Lutheran Theol Sem, MDiv, 74; Univ Heidelberg, grad stud, 74-75; Claremont Grad Sch, PhD, 83. **CAREER** Instr, ELTS, 73-74; assoc, Inst Antiquity and Christianity, 76-77; asst prof, 82-87; assoc prof, 87-93; guest prof, Univ Tubingen, 89-90; prof, Trinity Lutheran Sem, 93-. **MEMBERSHIPS** Soc Biblical Lit; Cath Biblical Soc; E Great Lakes Bible Soc. **SELECTED PUBLICATIONS** Co-auth, Covenants and Care, Augsburg/Fortress, 98; auth, Innocent or Holy? Justification and Sanctification in Old Testament Theology, Word and World 17, 97; Narrative in Leviticus: The Case of the Blaspheming Son , Altorientalische und Biblische Rechtsgeschichte, Harrasowitz, 97; Magic or Street-Theater? The Power of the Prophetic Word, Zeitschrift fur die alttestamentliche Wissenschaft 107, 96; Charisma and Authority in Israelite Society, Augsburg/Fortress, 94; Moses on the Mount of Transfiguration, Hebrew Annual Rev 14, 94. **CONTACT ADDRESS** Bible Dept, Trinity Lutheran Sem, 2199 E Main St, Columbus, OH 43209-2334. **EMAIL** rhutton@trinity.capital.edu

HWANG, TZU-YANG
PERSONAL Born 09/21/1953, Taiwan, m, 1980 **DISCIPLINE** RELIGION **EDUCATION** Tainan Theol Col, MDiv; Princeton Univ Theol Sem, MTh, 86; Chinese for Christ Theol Sem, PhD, 90; Duke Univ Divinity Sch and Harvard Univ Divinity Sch, 91-92. **CAREER** Tchg asst, Tainan Theol Sem; pastor, Good Shepherd Formosa Presbyterian Church; Chemn Chinese for Christian Theol Sem; adj prof Holy Light Theol Sem; pres, prof, Am Chi-Chou Theo-Philos Inst, 95- ; pres, Light Christ Church, 94- ; res assoc, Am Biographical Inst, 94- . **HONORS AND AWARDS** Mil prize, Natl Dfense Dept, Taiwan, 73; Int cultural diploma of honour; Millennium Hall of Fame Medal of Honour; fel, Am Biog Inst; presidential Seal of Honor listed, Five Thousand Personalities of the World, Who's Who in Religion, Who's Who in Am; Key of Success-Achievemet of Res; World Laureate. **MEMBERSHIPS** Int Governors Clubs; Int Order of Ambassadors; Am Acad Relig; Am Acad Relig; Soc Bibl Lit; Sci Stud Relig. **RESEARCH** Fundamental and systematic theology and culture; sixteenth to twentieth century religious thoughts and their relation to religion, philosophy and culture; methods to develop religious cultural philosophy and theology in the east and west. **SELECTED PUBLICATIONS** Auth, Theologies of Christianity and Thoughts of Chinese Culture, diss, 91; auth, Cultural Theologies in Asia, 92; auth, Theology and Piety, 93; auth, Theology and Life, 93; auth, An Impact of Hearts and Spriits Shaking, 93; auth, A Philosophy of Religion and Theology of Christianity, 93; auth, An Approach to History of Ministry Thinking of Dr. Campbell Moody in Taiwan, Chinese, 93; auth, A New Testament Theology for Christians-Elements of New Testament Theology in Themes, 96; auth, Neo-Contemporary Cultural Theologies, 98; auth, Commenting to the Paul Tillich of the Religious Philosopher and Cultural Theological In 20th Century, 99; auth, Commenting On the Grass rooting Cultural Contintual Theological in the Phillippine, 99; auth, From The Bible to Look at Relationship Between Philosophies, Religion Philosophies an Theologies, 00. **CONTACT ADDRESS** 11768 Roseglen St., El Monte, CA 91732.

HYDE, ALAN
PERSONAL Born 05/24/1951, Los Angeles, CA, m, 1976, 2 children **DISCIPLINE** LAW **EDUCATION** Stanford Univ, AB, 72; Yale Univ, JD, 75. **CAREER** Instr, New York Univ, 76-78; asst prof, 78-81, assoc prof, 87-89, Sch Law, prof, 89-, Rutgers Univ, Newark, Sidney Reitman Scholar, 91-, vis prof Michigan, 83-84, Yale, 93-94, YeShiva, 94-95, Columbia, 95-96. **RESEARCH** Labor law; sociology of law; philosophy of law. **SELECTED PUBLICATIONS** Coauth, Cases and Materials on Labor Law, Found Press, 82; auth, Bodies of Law, Princeton Univ Press, 97; auth, Working in Silicon Valley: Economic and Legal Analysis of a High-Velocity Labor Market, M.E. Sharpe, 01. **CONTACT ADDRESS** Sch Law, Rutgers, The State Univ of New Jersey, Newark, 123 Washington St, Newark, NJ 07102-3192. **EMAIL** hyde@andromeda.rutgers.edu

HYERS, M. CONRAD
PERSONAL Born 07/31/1933, Philadelphia, PA, m, 1955, 3 children **DISCIPLINE** COMPARATIVE MYTHOLOGY & HISTORY OF RELIGIONS **EDUCATION** Carson-Newman Col, BA, 54; Eastern Theol Sem, BD, 58; Princeton Theol Sem, ThM, 59, PhD(phenomenol relig), 65. **CAREER** From instr to assoc prof hist relig, Beloit Col, 65-77; assoc prof, 77-81, Prof Hist Relig, Gustavus Adolphus Col, 81-97, Prof Emer, 97-. **HONORS AND AWARDS** Humanities develop grant, 69; Assoc Col Midwest non-Western studies fel, East-West Ctr, 70; Nat Found Humanities fel, 70-71; Fund Studies Great Relig fel, 71; Nat Found Humanities res fel, 75-76. **MEMBERSHIPS** Am Acad Relig **RESEARCH** A phenomenological study of the mythological motifs of Paradise Lost, fall and degeneration; a phenomenological study of the nature and function of comedy and humor in relation to the sacred; interfaith relations. **SELECTED PUBLICATIONS** Auth, Holy Laughter: Essays on Religion in the Comic Perspective, Seabury, 69; The Dialectic of the Sacred and the Comic, Cross Currents, winter 69; The Ancient Ch'an Master as Clown Figure and Comic Midwife, Philos East & West, winter, 69-70; The Comic Perspective in Zen Literature and Art, Eastern Buddhist, 72; Zen and the Comic Spirit, Rider, London, 73; The Chickadees: A Contemporary Zen Fable, Westminster, 74; The Comic Vision and the Christian Faith, Pilgrim, 81; The Meaning of Creation: Genesis and Modern Science, John Knox, 84; And God Created Laughter, The Bible as Divine Comedy, John Knox, 86; Once-Born, Twice-Born Zen, The Soto and Rinzai Schools of Japan, Hollowbrook, 89; The Laughing Buddha, Hollowbrook, 90; The Spirituality of Comedy, Comic Heroism in a Tragic World, Transaction Publ, 96. **CONTACT ADDRESS** 2162 Harbor View Drive, Dunedin, FL 34698.

HYLAND, DREW ALAN
PERSONAL Born 02/09/1939, Wilkes-Barre, PA, m, 1964, 2 children **DISCIPLINE** PHILOSOPHY **EDUCATION** Princeton Univ, BA, 61; Pa State Univ, MA, 63, PhD(philos), 65. **CAREER** From lectr to asst prof philos, Univ Toronto, 64-67; asst prof, 67-74, prof philos, Trinity Col, Conn, 74-; Charles A. Dana Prof of Philos. **HONORS AND AWARDS** Brownell Prize for Excellence in Teaching, 90; Dir, Trinity Center for Collaborative Teaching and Research, 97. **MEMBERSHIPS** Mem Soc Phenomenol & Existential Philos; Heidegger Circle; Hegel Soc Am; Philos Soc for Study of Sport; IAPL; APA. **RESEARCH** Greek philosophy; Continental philosophy; philosophy of sport. **SELECTED PUBLICATIONS** Auth, Why Plato wrote Dialogues, Philos & Rhetoric, 1/68; Eros, Epithumia and Philia in Piston, Phronesis, 68; Self-reflection and knowing in Aristotle, Giornali di Metarisica, 68; Art and the happening of truth: Relections on the end of philosophy, J Aesthet & Art Criticism, 2/71; contribr, Sport and the Body: A Philosophical Symposium, Lea & Febiger, 72; auth, The Origins of Philosophy, Putnam, 73; And that is the best part of us: Human being and play, J Philos of Sport, 77; The Virtue of Philosophy: An Interpretation of Pluto's Charmidis, Ohio Univ Press, 81; The Question of Play, Univ Press of America, 84; The Philosophy of Sport, Paragon, 90; Finitude and Transcendence in the Platonic Dialogues, SUNY Press, 95. **CONTACT ADDRESS** Dept of Philos, Trinity Col, Connecticut, 300 Summit St, Hartford, CT 06106-3186. **EMAIL** Drew.Hyland@Trincoll.edu

HYLTON, MARIA
PERSONAL Born 09/01/1960, Baltimore, MD, m, 1986, 6 children **DISCIPLINE** LAW **EDUCATION** Harvard Univ, AB, 82; Yale Law Sch, JD, 85. **CAREER** Law clerk, US Court of Appeals, 85-86; atty, Hale & Dorr, 86-88; assoc prof, Boston Univ, 88-89; asst to assoc prof, DePaul Univ, 89-95; prof, Boston Univ, 95-. **MEMBERSHIPS** ABA, ALEA, IRRA, Soc of Am Law Teachers, Law & Soc Assoc. **SELECTED PUBLICATIONS** Coauth, Using Civil Remedies for Criminal Behavior: Rational, Case Studies and Constitutional Issues, Nat Inst of Justice, 94; auth, "The Case Against Regulating the Market for Contingent Employment," 52 Wash & Lee Law Rev 849, (95); auth, "Insurance Risk Classification After McGann: Managing Risk Efficiently in the Shadow of the ADA," 47 Baylor L Rev, 59 (95): auth, "Legal and Policy Implications of the Flexible Employment Relationship," 17 Jour of Labor Res 589, (96): auth, "Some Preliminary Thoughts on the Deregulation of Insurance to Advantage the Working Poor," 24 Fordham Urb LJ 687, (97): auth, "Evaluating the Case for Social Security Reform: Elderly Poverty, Paternalism and Private Pensions," 64 Brooklyn L Rev 749, (98); coauth, Cases and Materials on Employee Benefits Law, West Publ, 98; auth, "ERISA in the Larger EEO Context, in Proceedings of the 1999 Annual meeting AALS Section on Employment Discrimination Law: Is There a Disconnect Between EEO Law and the Workplace?" 3 Emp Rights & Emp Pol J 131, (99): auth, 'Y2K ERISA Update: Key Issues and Trends Facing Employers and Plan Participants," Labor Law Jour (00): 96-105. **CONTACT ADDRESS** Sch of Law, Boston Univ, 765 Commonwealth Ave, Boston, MA 02215. **EMAIL** mhylton@bu.edu

HYLTON, PETER
DISCIPLINE PHILOSOPHY **EDUCATION** Harvard Univ, PhD. **CAREER** Prof, Univ IL at Chicago. **RESEARCH** Philos of lang; logic; hist of analytic philos. **SELECTED PUBLICATIONS** Auth, Russell; Idealism; Emergence of Analytic Philosophy, Oxford, 90. **CONTACT ADDRESS** Philos Dept, Univ of Illinois, Chicago, S Halsted St, PO Box 705, Chicago, IL 60607.

HYMAN, JONATHAN MORRIS
PERSONAL Born 01/09/1943, Washington, DC **DISCIPLINE** LAW **EDUCATION** Harvard Univ, AB, 65; Yale Univ, LLB, 68. **CAREER** Co-dir clinical law, Law Sch, Northwestern, 73-75; asst prof, 75-78, ASSOC PROF, 78-89; prof of Law, Rutgers Univ, 89-; Alfred C. Clapp Public Interest Scholar, 01-. **MEMBERSHIPS** Am Arbitration Asn; Asn for Conflict Resolution. **RESEARCH** Negotiation theory; remedies in law; mediation; civil rights. **SELECTED PUBLICATIONS** Auth, Minitrials and Matchmakers--Styles of Conducting Settlement Conferences, Judicature, Vol 0080, 96; coauth, "Negotiation Methods and Litigation Settlement in New Jersey: You Can't Always Get What You Want," Ohio State Journal on dispute resolution 12; auth, "Slip-Sliding into Mediation: Can Lawyers Mediate Their Clients Problems," Clinical Law Review 5. **CONTACT ADDRESS** Law Sch, Rutgers, The State Univ of New Jersey, Newark, 123 Washington St, Newark, NJ 07102-3192. **EMAIL** jhyman@andromeda.rutgers.edu

HYMERS, MICHAEL
DISCIPLINE PHILOSOPHY **EDUCATION** Univ Dalhousie, BS, 85, MA, 88; Univ Alberta, PhD, 93. **CAREER** Asst prof. **RESEARCH** Epistemology, philosophy of language, metaphysics, history of modern philosophy. **SELECTED PUBLICATIONS** Auth, "Bad Faith," Philos, 89; "Wittgenstein on Names and Family Resemblances," Eidos, 90; "Something Less Than Paradise: The Magic of Modal Realism," Australasian Jour of Philos, 91; "The Role of Kant's Refutation of Idealism," S Jour Philos, 91; "Internal Relations and Analyticity: Wittgenstein and Quine," Can Jour Philos, 96; "Truth and Metaphor in Rorty's Liberalism," Intl Stud in Philos, 96; Kant's Private-Clock Argument, Kant-Stud, 97; "Realism and Self-Knowledge," Philos Stud, 97. **CONTACT ADDRESS** Dept of Philos, Dalhousie Univ, Halifax, NS, Canada B3H 3J5. **EMAIL** michael.hymers@dal.ca

HYSON, JOHN M.
DISCIPLINE CIVIL PROCEDURE, ENVIRONMENTAL LAW **EDUCATION** Boston Col, BA, 63; Univ NC, MA, 64; Harvard Law Sch, LLB, 67. **CAREER** Prof, Villanova Univ. **MEMBERSHIPS** Rules Comt, Pa Env Hearing Bd, 84-88. **RESEARCH** Environment law and land use. **SELECTED PUBLICATIONS** Auth, Pennsylvania Exclusionary Zoning Law: A Workable Alternative to Mount Laurel, 36 Land Use Law & Zoning Digest, 84; The Impact of Act 249 of 1978 Upon the Casey Pending Ordinance Doctrine in Pennsylvania Exclusionary Zoning Litigation, 26 Vill. L. Rev 322, 81; The Problem of Relief in Developer-Initiated Exclusionary Zoning Litigation, 12 Urb L. Ann 21, 76; coauth, A Comparative Analysis of the Fed and Pennsylvania Superfund Acts," 1 Vill Env. L.J. 1, 90; co-ed, Environment Litigation, 91. **CONTACT ADDRESS** Law School, Villanova Univ, 800 Lancaster Ave, Villanova, PA 19085-1692. **EMAIL** hyson@law.vill.edu

HYUN, INSOO
PERSONAL Born 06/28/1970, Seoul, South Korea, m, 1997, 1 child **DISCIPLINE** PHILOSOPHY **EDUCATION** Stan Univ, BA, 92; MA, 93; Brown Univ, PhD, 99. **CAREER** Instr, Stonhl Coll, 96; asst prof, West Mich Univ, 98-. **HONORS AND AWARDS** William A Dye Diss Fel. **MEMBERSHIPS** APPE. **RESEARCH** Biomedical ethics; moral theory. **SELECTED PUBLICATIONS** Auth, "When Adolescents 'Mismanage' Their Chronic Medical Conditions: An Ethical Exploration," Kennedy Inst of Ethics J (June 00); auth, "Authentic Values and Individual Autonomy," Jl of Value Inquiry, forthcoming. **CONTACT ADDRESS** Dept Philosophy, Western Michigan Univ, 1201 Oliver St, Kalamazoo, MI 49008-3804. **EMAIL** insoo.hyun@wmich.edu

HYUN, YONG SOO
PERSONAL Born 08/18/1947, Seoul, Korea, m, 1975, 4 children **DISCIPLINE** RELIGION **EDUCATION** Myong-Ji, Univ, BS, 74; Azusa Pacific Univ, MAR, MDiv, 87; Biola Univ, PhD, 09. **CAREER** Prof, Bethesda Christ Univ, 88-; pres, Shema Edu Inst, 95-. **RESEARCH** Orthodox Jewish Education. **SELECTED PUBLICATIONS** Auth, Culture and Religious Education, (Korea), 93; auth, Father Develops IQ, Mother Nurtures EQ, vol 2, Biblical Jewish Edu (Korea), 96, vol 3, 99. **CONTACT ADDRESS** Dept Religion, Bethesda Christian Univ, 730 N Euclid St, Anaheim, CA 92801-4132.

I

IANNONE, A. PABLO
PERSONAL Born 09/18/1940, Buenos Aires, Argentina, m, 1985, 2 children **DISCIPLINE** PHILOSOPHY **EDUCATION** Univ Wisconsin-Madison, PhD, 75; Univ Wisconsic-Madison, MA, 72; UCLA, BA, 69. **CAREER** Prof Philos, Central Conn St Univ, 93-; assoc prof Philos, Central Conn St Univ, 87-93; vis prof Philos, Dalhousie Univ, 87; asst prof Philos, Central Conn St Univ, 83-87; Postdoctoral Tchg Fel, Univ Fla, 82-83; temporary asst prof, Iowa St Univ, 82. **HONORS AND AWARDS** Conn St Univ Res Grant, 85, 87, 89, 91, 94, 95, 96, 97, 98, 00; Central Conn St Univ Res Grant, 83; Central Conn St Univ Minority & Staff Develop Grant, 89; Amoco Found Outstanding Tchg Awd, Univ Tex at Dallas, 76; Kemper K Knapp Grad Teaching Awd, Univ Wisc at Mad, 74; Ford Fel, 73; Phi Beta Kappa, 70. **MEMBERSHIPS** Amer Philos Assoc; Amer Assoc Advancement of Sci; Argentine-N Amer Assoc for Advancement of Sci, Tech, and Culture-New York. **RESEARCH** Ethics and Socio-Political Philosophy; Business Ethics; Ethics of Technology; Environmental Ethics; History and Philosophy of Science and Technology; Philosophy of Culture; Philosophical. **SELECTED PUBLICATIONS** Dictionary of World Philosophy, Routledge Ltd, forthcoming 01; Dealing with Diversity: Cultural Fragmentation, Intercultural Conflicts, and Philosophy, in Crossing Cultural Boundaries: Philosophy and Cultural Diversity, Humanity Books, 99; Cross-Cultural Ecologies: The Expatriate Experience, the Multiculturalism Issue, and Philosophy, In the Company of Others: Perspectives on Community, Family, and Culture, Rowman & Littlefield Pub, 96; Philosophy as Diplomacy: Essays in Ethics and Policy Making, Humanities Pr, 94; auth, Contemporary Moral Controversies in Business, Oxford UP, 89; auth, Contemporary Moral Controversies in Technology, Oxford UP, 87; Contemporary Moral Controversies in Business, Oxford Univ Press, 89; auth, "South," in Paradise Lost or Gained?: The Literature of Hispanic Exile, Arte Publico P, 90. **CONTACT ADDRESS** Dept of Philosophy, Central Connecticut State Univ, 1615 Stanley St, New Britain, CT 06050. **EMAIL** iannone@ctstateu.edu

IANNUZZI, JOHN N.
PERSONAL Born 05/31/1935, New York, NY, m, 1979, 6 children **DISCIPLINE** LAW **EDUCATION** Fordham Col, BS-SS, 56; NYork Law Sch, JD, 1962. **CAREER** Law, Iannuzzi and Iannuzzi, 63-; Adjunct Prof, Fordham Univ, Sch of Law, 88-. **HONORS AND AWARDS** Who's Who in the World, 9th and 11th eds; Who's Who in Am Law, ed 1-8. **SELECTED PUBLICATIONS** What's Happening?, Thomas Yoseloff, 63; Part 35, Richard W. Baron, 70; Sicilian Defense, Richard W Baron, 73; auth, Courthouse, Doubleday, 80; auth, J.T., Berkeley Books, 84; auth, Cross Examination: The Mosaic Art, Prentice Hall, 2nd ed, 84; auth, Trial Strategy and Psychology, Prentice Hall, 92; Disposition by Guilty Plea, Appellate Div of Supreme Court, 1st - 6th ed. **CONTACT ADDRESS** 233 Broadway, New York, NY 10279. **EMAIL** iannuzzi@aol.com

IDE, HARRY
DISCIPLINE ANCIENT, HELLENISTIC, AND MEDIEVAL PHILOSOPHY **EDUCATION** Cornell Univ, PhD, 88. **CAREER** Assoc prof, Univ Nebr, Lincoln. **RESEARCH** Aristotle's views about possibility and necessity. **SELECTED PUBLICATIONS** Auth, Dunamis in Metaphysics 9, Apeiron 35, 92; Aristotle, Metaphysics 6.2-3, and determinism, Ancient Philos 13, 93; Hobbes Contractarian Account of Individual Responsibility for Group Actions, J of Value Inquiry 27, 93. **CONTACT ADDRESS** Univ of Nebraska, Lincoln, Lincoln, NE 68588-0417.

IHDE, DON
PERSONAL Born 01/14/1934, Hope, KS, m, 1985, 4 children **DISCIPLINE** PHILOSOPHY **EDUCATION** Univ Kans, BA, 56; Andover Newton Theol Sch, BD, 59; Boston Univ, PhD(philos), 64. **CAREER** Lectr philos, Boston Univ, 62-64; asst prof, Southern Ill Univ, 64-67; Fulbright res fel, Univ Paris, 67-68; assoc prof, Southern Ill Univ, Carbondale, 68-69; prof philos, 69-96, SUNY Stony Brook, distinguished prof, 97-; Nat Endowment Humanities sr fel, 72. **MEMBERSHIPS** Southern Soc Philos & Psychol; Eastern Div Am Philos Asn; Soc Phenomenol & Existential Philos. **RESEARCH** Recent European philosophy, particulary phenomenology and existentialism; phenomenology of man-machine relations. **SELECTED PUBLICATIONS** Auth, Hermeneutic Phenomenology, Northwestern Univ Press, 71; auth, Sense and Significance, Humanities Press, 73; auth, Listening to the Void, Ohio Univ Press, 76; auth, Existential Technics, SUNY Press, 81; auth, Consequences of Phenomenology, SUNY Press, 86; auth, Technology and the Lifeworld, Indiana Univ Press, 90; auth, Instrumental Realism, Indiana Univ Press, 91; auth, Philosophy of Technology: An Introduction, Paragon House, 93; auth, Postphenomenology: Essays in the Postmodern Context, Northwestern Univ Press, 93; auth, Expanding Hermeneutics: Visualism in Science, Northwestern Univ Press, 98. **CONTACT ADDRESS** Dept of Philos, SUNY, Stony Brook, Stony Brook, NY 11794-3750. **EMAIL** dihde@notes.sunysb.edu

IHLAN, AMY
DISCIPLINE PHILOSOPHY **EDUCATION** Harvard Law School, JD, 84; Univ Minn, PhD, 95. **CAREER** Asst prof philos, Cornell Col, 94- . **HONORS AND AWARDS** Phi Beta Kappa; grad fel, Univ Minn. **MEMBERSHIPS** APA; Soc for Women in Philos; Minnesota Bar Asn. **RESEARCH** Moral particularism; ethical theory; legal reasoning; feminist ethics and jurisprudence. **SELECTED PUBLICATIONS** Auth, Wang Yang-Ming: A Philosopher of Practical Action, J of Chinese Philos, 93; auth, The Dilemma of Difference and Feminist Standpoint Theory, APA Newsl on Feminism and Philos of Law, 95; auth, Burning Crosses, Political Expression, and the First Amendment: The Case of R.A.V. v City of St. Paul, in Kaplan, ed, Philosophical Perspectives on Power and Domination, Rodopi, 97; auth, Feminism and Firearms, in Curtin, ed, Institutional Violence, Rodopi, forthcoming. **CONTACT ADDRESS** Dept of Philosophy, Cornell Col, 600 First St W, Mount Vernon, IA 52314. **EMAIL** aihlan@cornell-iowa.edu

IKE, ALICE DENISE
PERSONAL Born 03/25/1955, Washington, DC, s **DISCIPLINE** LAW **EDUCATION** University of Maryland, Baltimore County, BA, 1977, School of Law, JD, 1981. **CAREER** Morgan State Univ, part-time instructor, 84, 85; Legal Services Institute, legal intern, 80-81; Legal Aid of Maryland Inc, staff attorney, 81-82; City of Baltimore, Office of the State's Attorney, assistant states attorney, 83-85; Univ of Maryland, Baltimore County, part-time instructor, 90-; Department of Health and Mental Hygiene, Office of the Attorney General, assistant attorney general, 85-. **MEMBERSHIPS** DC Bar Assn, 1982-; State of Maryland Bar Assn, 1981-; Alliance of Black Women Attorneys, 1982-; Foster Care Review Bd of Baltimore City, chairperson of the bd, 1986-. **CONTACT ADDRESS** Assistant Attorney General, Office of the Attorney General, Department of Health and Mental Hygiene, 300 W Preston St, Ste 302, Baltimore, MD 21201.

IMMERWAHR, JOHN
PERSONAL Born 09/08/1945, Catonsville, MD, m, 2000, 2 children **DISCIPLINE** PHILOSOPHY **EDUCATION** Princeton Univ, AB, 67; Univ Mich, MA, 68, PhD, 72. **CAREER** Prof & dept ch, Villanova Univ,73-. **HONORS AND AWARDS** Lindback awd Distinguished Tchg, Villanova Univ, 92; Philadelphia Inquirer Mag Story, Ten Top Profs, 86; Silver Medalist in CASE prof Yr awd, 86; Philadelphia Mag, 84 People to Watch in 84; creation of the John Immerwahr prize in Philos, endowed by a former student, Oakland Univ, 74 & Princeton, 67, Phi Beta Kappa, Summa Cum Laude, McCosh prize. **SELECTED PUBLICATIONS** Auth, Preserving the Higher Education Legacy: A Conversation with California Leaders, San Jose: Calif Higher Educ Policy Ctr, 95; The Broken Contract: Connecticut Citizens Look at Public Education, New Haven: Graustein Memorial Fund, 94; The Socratic Classroom: Classroom Communication Strategies, J Mgt Syst 6:1, 94; Hume's Revised Racism, J Hist Ideas 53:3, 92; Hume on Tranquilizing the Passions, Hume Stud 18:2, 92; Asking Questions, Metaphilosophy 22:4, 91 & earlier version publ as, A Taxonomy of Questions, in The Newsl of the Amer Asn Philos Teachers 14:1, 91; Coauth, Race and the Modern Philosophy Course, Tchg Philos 16:1, 93; Assignment Incomplete: The Unfinished Business of Education Reform, NY: Public Agenda Found, 95; Goodwill and Growing Worry: Public Perceptions of American Higher Education, Wash, DC: Amer Coun Educ, 95; The Fragile Coalition: Public Support for Higher Education in the 1990s, Wash, DC: Amer Coun Educ, 95; Teaching Values: What does the Public Really Want, Soc for the Advan Educ, 95; What the Public Thinks of Colleges, in The Chronicle of Higher Educ, 95; First Things First: What Americans Expect from the Public Schools, NY: Public Agenda Found, 94; The Rules of Public Engagement, in Beyond the Beltway:Engaging the Public In For Policy, NY: W.W. Norton, 94 & Second Opinions: Americans' Changing Views on Healthcare Reform, NY: Public Agenda Found, 94. **CONTACT ADDRESS** Dept of Philosophy, Villanova Univ, 800 Lancaster Ave, Villanova, PA 19085-1699. **EMAIL** jimmerwa@email.vill.edu

IMWINKELRIED, EDWARD
PERSONAL Born 09/19/1946, San Francisco, CA, m, 1978, 2 children **DISCIPLINE** LAW **EDUCATION** Univ San Francisco, BA, 67, JD, 69. **CAREER** Captain, US Army Judge Advocate General's Corps, 70-74; prof, law, Univ San Diego, 74-79; prof, law, Wash Univ St. Louis, 79-85; prof, law, Univ Calif Davis, 85-. **HONORS AND AWARDS** Distinguished teacher, Univ of Calif Davis; distinguished teacher, Univ Calif Davis Law Sch; Outstanding teacher, Wash Univ; Distinguished facul, Nat Col of District Atty. **MEMBERSHIPS** Amer Acad of Forensic Sci; Amer Bar Asn. **RESEARCH** Scientific evidence; Uncharged misconduct; Evidentiary priviledges. **SELECTED PUBLICATIONS** Auth, Where There's Smoke, There's Fire: Should the Judge or the Jury Decide the Question of Whether the Accused Committed an Alleged Uncharged Crime Proffered Under Federal Rule of Evidence 404?, 42, St. Louis Univ Law Jour, 813, 98; co-auth, Cyberspace: The Newest Challenge for Traditional Legal Doctrine, 24, Rutgers Computer and Tech Law Jour, 305, 98; auth, Evidentiary Foundations, LEXIS Law Publ, 4th ed, 98; co-auth, North Carolina Evidentiary Foundations, LEXIS Law Publ, 98; auth, Article V Priviledges, Emerging Problems Under the Federal Rules of Evidence, 3rd ed, 98;

auth, Foreword, Symposium: International Perspectives on Scientific Evidence, 30, Univ Calif Davis Law Rev, 941, 97; co-auth, The Supreme Court's Decision to Recognize a Psychotherapist Priviledge in Jaffee v. Redmond, 116 S. Ct. 1923, 96; co-auth, The Meaning of Experience and the Role of Reason Under Federal Rule of Evidence 501, 65, Univ Cincinnati Law Rev, 1019, 97; co-auth, Issues Once Moot: The Other Evidentiary Objections to the Admissibility of Exculpatory Polygraph Examinations, 32, Wake Forest Law Rev, 1045, 97; ed bd, Jefferson's California Evidence Benchbook, chap 35-38, 40, 3rd ed, 97; co-auth, Criminal Evidentiary Foundations, LEXIS Law Publ, 97; auth, The Methods of Attacking Scientific Evidence, Michie Publ Co, 3rd ed, 97; auth, Evidentiary Heresy: Disregarding the Rules of Evidence at Trial!, 41, Trial Lawyer's Guide, 40, 97; auth, The Next Step in Conceptualizing the Presentation of Expert Evidence as Education: The Case for Didactic Trial Procedures, 1, Intl Jour of Evidence and Proof, 128, 97; co-auth, Federal Evidence Tactics, 97; auth, A New Threat to Plaintiff's Discovery Rights?, 33, Trial, 36, 97. **CONTACT ADDRESS** School of Law, Univ of California, Davis, 400 Mrak Hall Dr., Davis, CA 95616-5201. **EMAIL** ejimwinkelried@ucdavis.edu

INADA, KENNETH K.
PERSONAL Born 05/07/1923, Honolulu, HI, m, 1954, 1 child **DISCIPLINE** PHILOSOPHY **EDUCATION** Univ Hawaii, BA, 49; Univ Chicago, MA, 51; Univ Tokyo, Japan, PhD (Buddhist philos), 60. **CAREER** From instr to assoc prof philos, Univ Hawaii, 60-69; assoc prof, 69-71, Prof Philos, State Univ NY Buffalo, 71-, Sr fac fel, Am Inst Indian Studies, 66-67; State Univ NY Res Found grant, 70 & 74. **MEMBERSHIPS** Eastern Div, Am Philos Asn; Am Orient Soc; Asn Asian Studies; Soc Asian & Comp Philos (pres, 72-76); Int Soc Chinese Philos. **RESEARCH** Buddhist philosophy; comparative East-West philosophy. **SELECTED PUBLICATIONS CONTACT ADDRESS** Dept of Philos, SUNY, Buffalo, 680 Baldy Hall, Buffalo, NY 14260-1010.

INBODY, TYRON LEE
PERSONAL Born 03/21/1940, Goshen, IN, m, 1961, 2 children **DISCIPLINE** THEOLOGY **EDUCATION** Univ Indianapolis, BA, 62; United Theol Sem, MDiv, 65; Univ Chicago, MA, 67, PhD, 73. **CAREER** Adrian Col, prof, 69-76; United Theol Sem, prof, 76-. **HONORS AND AWARDS** NEH. **MEMBERSHIPS** AAR, HIARPT. **RESEARCH** American Theology and philosophy. **SELECTED PUBLICATIONS** Auth, The Transforming God: An Interpretation of Suffering And Evil, Westminster John Knox Press, 97; auth, The Constructive Theology of Bernard Meland: Postliberal Empirical Realism, AAR Studies in Religion, Atlanta: Scholars Press, 95; ed. Changing Channels: The Church and the Television Revolution, Dayton OH: Whaleprints, 90; auth, The Power of Prayer and the Mystery of Evil, Anglican Theol Rev, 98; auth, Prayer in the Midst of Suffering, Keeping in Touch, 98; auth, Delwin Brown's Constructive Historicism as a Reconstruction of Empirical Theology, Am Jour Theol and Philos, 97. **CONTACT ADDRESS** Dept of Theology, United Theol Sem, 1810 Harvard Blvd., Dayton, OH 45406. **EMAIL** tyinbody@united.edu

INGLIS, JOHN
DISCIPLINE MEDIEVAL PHILOSOPHY **EDUCATION** Univ Ky, PhD, 93. **CAREER** Dept Philos, Univ Dayton **RESEARCH** Relation between philosophy and theology. **SELECTED PUBLICATIONS** Auth, Philosophical Anatomy and the Historiography of Medieval Philosophy, Brit Jour Hist Philos, 97. **CONTACT ADDRESS** Dept of Philos, Univ of Dayton, 300 Col Park, Dayton, OH 75062. **EMAIL** inglis@checkov.hm.udayton.edu

INGOLFSLAND, DENNIS E.
PERSONAL Born 06/19/1954, Minot, ND, m, 1974, 3 children **DISCIPLINE** BIBLICAL STUDIES **EDUCATION** Calvary Bible Col, BA, 83; Univ Mo at Columbia, MALS, 84; Fuller Theol Sem, MA, 90; Oxford Grad Sch, DPhil, 99. **CAREER** Prof, libr dir, & dean of students, Ariz Col of the bible, 84-91; reference librn, George Fox Col, 91-92; dir libr services, dir of Hower's Prog, & assoc prof, Bryan Col, 92-. **HONORS AND AWARDS** Biblical Languages Awd; Oxford Grail Awd. **MEMBERSHIPS** Evangelical Theol Soc, Asn of Christian Librn. **RESEARCH** Historical Jewish Studies. **SELECTED PUBLICATIONS** Auth, "The 'Teacher of Righteousness' and the Book of Daniel," Archaeol and Biblical Res (89): 69-76; auth, "The Modern Quest for Jesus," Alliance Life (96): 6ff; auth, "A Review of Who Wrote the New Testament?," Bibliotheca Sacra (97): 205-221; auth, "Q, M, L and Other Sources for the Historical Jesus," The Princeton Theol Rev 4.5 (97): 17-22; auth, "The Historical Jesus According to John Meier and N. T. Wright," Bibliotheca Sacra (98): 460-473; auth, "The Third Quest for the Historical Jesus," Christian Libr J (00): 13-14. **CONTACT ADDRESS** Dept Bible Studies, Bryan Col, PO Box 7000, Dayton, TN 37321-7000.

INGRAM, DAVID B.
PERSONAL Born 01/27/1952, Whittier, CA, m **DISCIPLINE** PHILOSOPHY **EDUCATION** Univ Calif San Diego, PhD, 80. **CAREER** Asst to assoc prof, Univ Northern Iowa, 80-87; assoc to full prof, Loyola Univ of Chicago, 87-. **HONORS AND AWARDS** Alpha Sigma Nu prize for best book in philos/theol, 92-95. **MEMBERSHIPS** Amer Philos Asn; Soc for Phenomenol and Existential Philos. **RESEARCH** Social and political philosophy; French; German philosophy. **SELECTED PUBLICATIONS** Auth, Reason: History and Politics, State Univ of NY Press, 95; auth, Critical Theory and Philosophy, Paragon House, 90; Habermas and the Dialectic of Reason, Yale Univ Press, 87; ed, Critical Theory: The Essential Readings, Paragon House, 91; auth, Group Rights: Reconciling Equlity and Difference, Kans Univ Press, 00; ed, The Political: Blackwell Readings in Continental Philosoophy, Blackwell, 01. **CONTACT ADDRESS** Dept. of Philosophy, Loyola Univ, Chicago, Chicago, IL 60626. **EMAIL** dingram@orion.it.luc.edu

INTRILLIGATOR, MICHAEL D.
PERSONAL Born 02/05/1938, New York, NY, m, 1963, 4 children **DISCIPLINE** ECONOMICS **EDUCATION** Mass Inst Technol, SB, 59; Yale Univ, MA, 60; Mass Inst Technol, PhD, 63. **CAREER** Asst prof to prof, Univ Calif, 63-. **HONORS AND AWARDS** Woodrow Wilson Fel; Warren C. Scoville Teaching Awd, UCLA. **MEMBERSHIPS** Econometric Soc; Econ Allied for Arms Reduction; Am Econ Asn. **RESEARCH** Economic theory and mathematical economics, econometrics, health economics, reform of the Russian economy, and strategy and arms control. **SELECTED PUBLICATIONS** Co-auth, Econometric models, Techniques, and Applications, 2nd ed, 96; co-auth, "A New Economic Policy for Russia," in Economic Notes and Economics of Transition, 97. **CONTACT ADDRESS** Dept Econ, Univ of California, Los Angeles, 8283 Bunche, Box 951477, Los Angeles, CA 90095-1477. **EMAIL** intriligator@econ.ucla.edu

INYAMAH, NATHANIEL GINIKANWA N.
PERSONAL Born 01/21/1934, Mbaise, Nigeria, m **DISCIPLINE** THEOLOGY **EDUCATION** Univ Nigeria, Diploma Tehol 1958; STM NW Seminary MN, BD MDiv 1969; Temple, MA 1973f Temple, PhD 1976;1971. **CAREER** Nigeria, tchr, 51-53; Nigeria HS, 54-55; Holy Trinity & Lutheran Nigeria, pastor 59-66; LCA, asst & supply pastor; Camden NJ, teacher; positions in Nigeria Traditional Priest Earth Goddess; Trinity Lutheran Church, pastor & founder. **HONORS AND AWARDS** Crowned chief Okonko Igbo Soc US Lutheran Missionary At Large 1967-71; Aid Assn Lutheran Ins Scholarship 1967; NW Students Assn Scholarship 1968; Lutheran Wmn Missionary & League Scholarship 1969; Elmer O & Ida Preston Educ Trust Awd 1969-71; Temple Univ Grad Sch Awd 1972, 73. **MEMBERSHIPS** Bd dir & vice pres Lutheran Ch; pres Ezinihitte Cultural Union; vice pres Owerri Divisional Union; Owerri Provincial Union; WHO; exec mem Eastern Nigeria Soc Welfare Soc; youth prog dir; Utheran Commn Soc Equality Justice; Educ Com Minority Group; African Studies Assn. **CONTACT ADDRESS** PO Box 9786, Philadelphia, PA 19140.

IORIO, DOMINICK ANTHONY
PERSONAL Born 09/13/1931, Trenton, NJ, m, 1957, 2 children **DISCIPLINE** PHILOSOPHY **EDUCATION** Seton Hall Univ, AB, 55; Fordham Univ, AM, 60, PhD(philos), 66. **CAREER** Instr hist, Trenton Jr Col, 57-61, asst prof philos, 61-65, coordr lib arts, 62-65; asst prof philos, 65-68, asst dean sch lib arts & sci, 71-73, ASSOC PROF PHILOS, RIDER COL, 68-, Dean Sch Lib Arts & SCI, 73-, Consult, Dept Higher Educ, NJ, 77; chmn, Educ Adv Comt, NJ, 82. **HONORS AND AWARDS** Cor ad Cor Loquitor Medal, Nat Newman Fedn, 62; Christian R & Mary Lindback Awd for Distinguished Teaching, Rider Col, 71. **MEMBERSHIPS** Am Philos Asn; Am Cath Philos Asn; Renaissance Soc Am. **RESEARCH** Italian Renaissance philosophy; Cartesianism, with special emphasis on Nicolas Malebranche; social philosophy, with special emphasis on phenomenological and existential methods. **SELECTED PUBLICATIONS** Auth, Chardin and his critics, Kelsey Rev, 11/62; The problem of the soul and the unity of man in Pietro Pomponazzi, New Scholasticism, 7/63; James McCoch: Princeton realist, Kelsey Rev, 11/64; transl & ed, Nicolas Malebranche: Dialogue Between a Christian Philosopher and a Chinese Philosopher on the Existence and Nature of God, Univ Press Am, 80. **CONTACT ADDRESS** Off of Dean, Rider Univ, 2083 Lawrenceville, Lawrenceville, NJ 08648-3099.

IOZZIO, MARY JO
PERSONAL Born 11/25/1956, Paterson, NJ, m, 1994 **DISCIPLINE** THEOLOGY **EDUCATION** Penn State Univ, BA, 77; Providence Col, MA, 86; Fordham Univ, MA, 82, PhD, 94. **CAREER** Assoc prof, Barry Univ, 92- . **HONORS AND AWARDS** Fulbright award, 98-99; professional development award, 95, 96, 97, 98; Barry Univ Honors Students Teaching Awd, 95. **MEMBERSHIPS** Am Acad Relig; Catholic Theol Soc of Am; Soc of Christian Ethics. **RESEARCH** Fundamental moral theology; bioethics; feminist ethics; virtue theory and application. **SELECTED PUBLICATIONS** Auth, Three Perspectives of Virtue Theory, Providence: Stud in Western Civilization, 93; auth, Self-Determination and the Moral Act: A Study of the Contributions of Odon Lottin, OSB, Peeters, 95; auth, Science, Ethics, and Cloning Technologies, Linacre Q, 97; auth, Justice is a Virtue Both in and out of Healthcare, Irish Theol Q, 98; auth, Old Wine, New Skins: A Study of the Catechetical Tradition in Transition, in Allsopp, ed, Christian Ethics and the New Catechism, Scranton, 99 forthcoming; ed and auth, Recovering the Traditions: Religious Perspectives in Medical Ethics, Scranton, 99 (forthcoming); auth, Fides et ratio, the Academic Context, Catholic Education Journal of Inquiry and Practice (forthcoming); auth, From a Consideration of Disability, the Body as Training Ground for Virtue, Jouranl of Religion, Disability & Health, 99. Forthcoming. Auth, Fides et ratoo, the Academic Context, Catholic Education Journal of Inquiry and Practice, forthcoming. **CONTACT ADDRESS** Dept of Theology and Philosophy, Barry Univ, 11300 Northeast 2nd Ave, Miami Shores, FL 33161. **EMAIL** miozzio@mail.barry.edu

IRELAND, RODERICK LOUIS
PERSONAL Born 12/03/1944, Springfield, MA, d **DISCIPLINE** CRIMINAL JUSTICE, LAW **EDUCATION** Lincoln U, BA 1966; Columiba Law Sch, JD 1969; Harvard Law, LLM 1975. **CAREER** Boston Juvenile Ct, judge 1977-90; Bd of Appeal on Motor Vehicle Policies & Bonds, chmn of bd 1977; Sec of Adminstrn & Finance MA, counsel 1975-77; Harvard Law Sch, teaching fellow 1975; Roxbury Defenders Com, dir 1971-74, Massachusetts Appeals Court, judge, begin 1990; MA Supreme Court, Justice, currently; Northeastern University School of Law, Faculty, currently, College of Criminal Justice, Faculty, currently. **HONORS AND AWARDS** Recip 10 Outstndg yng ldrs of Boston award Boston Jaycees 1979; 10 outstndg men of Am award US Jaycees 1980. First African American justice On Massachusetts Supreme Court. **MEMBERSHIPS** Bd of dirs Columbia Law Sch Alumni Assn; mem MA Bar Assn; mem Boston Bar Assn; mem ABA; mem MA Black Lawyers Assn; mem NY Bar Assn Bd Dirs Proj Aim; bd dirs First Inc; bd dirs Roxbury YMCA; bd dirs MA Minority Council on Alcoholism; mem Omega Psi Phi; mem Lincoln Alumni. **CONTACT ADDRESS** Massachusetts Supreme Court, 1500 New Courthouse, Boston, MA 02108.

IRSCHICK, EUGENE FREDERICK
PERSONAL Born 08/15/1934, Kodaikanal, m, 1998, 5 children **DISCIPLINE** HISTORY, ANTHROPOLOGY, PHILOSOPHY **EDUCATION** Gettysburg Col, AB, 55; Univ Pa, AM, 59; Univ Chicago, PhD(hist), 64. **CAREER** Instr Indian civilization & Carnegie Corp teaching internship, Univ Chicago, 60-61; asst prof hist, 63-69, assoc prof, 69-78, Prof Hist, Univ Calif Berkeley, 78-, Am Inst Indian Studies grant, 67-68 & 79; Fulbright res fel, Institute for the International Exchange of Persons, 80. **HONORS AND AWARDS** Walmull Prize, 69. **MEMBERSHIPS** Asn Asian Studies; Am Hist Asn; Am Philosophical Soc, 82; Humanities Institute, 85; Am Institute of Indian Studies, 85-6; Fulbright, Institute for the International Exchange of Persons, 89; Fulbright, Institute for the International Exchange of Persons, 93; Am Institute of Indian Stud, 93; Fulbright-Hays Fel, 96. **RESEARCH** South Asian history; social change; peasant culture and economy; critical stud, postcolonialism. **SELECTED PUBLICATIONS** Auth, "Peasant Survival Stratagies and Rehearsals for Rebellion in Eighteenth Century South India," Peasant Studies, Vol. 9:4, (82): 215-241; auth, "Gandhian non-violent Protest," Economic and Political Weekly, (86): 1276-1285; auth, Tamil Revivalism in the 1930s, Madas: Crea, 86; auth, "Order and Disorder in Colonial South India," Modern Asian Studies, (89): 459-492; auth, Dialogue and History: Constructing South India, 1795-1895, Berkeley: Univ of Calif Press, 94; auth, The Nation and its Fragments--Colonial and Postcolonial Histories, Int Hist Rev, Vol 0017, 95; Gandhi,Mahatma--Nonviolent Power in Action, J Interdisciplinary Hist, Vol 0026, 95; Caste, Nationalism and Communism in South-India, Malabar, 1900-1948, J Interdisciplinary Hist, Vol 0027, 96; Hindu Nationalists in India--The Rise of the Bahratiya-Janata Party, J Church and State, Vol 0038, 96; The Origins of Industrial Capitalism in India--Business Strategies and the Working Classes in Bombay, 1900-1940, J Interdisciplinary Hist, Vol 0027, 97. **CONTACT ADDRESS** Univ of California, Berkeley, 3229 Dwinelle MC2550, Berkeley, CA 94720. **EMAIL** irschick@socrates.berkeley.edu

IRVIN, DALE T.
PERSONAL Born 01/26/1955, OH, m, 1978, 2 children **DISCIPLINE** RELIGION **EDUCATION** Union Theolo Sem, NYork, PhD; Princeton Theol Sem, MDiv; Thomas Edison College, BA. **CAREER** New York Theol Sem, prof 89 to 98-. **SELECTED PUBLICATIONS** Auth, Christian Traditioning, Christian Histories: Rendering Accounts, Orbis 98; The Agitated Mind of God: Theology of Koyama with Akintunde Akuinde, Orbis 96. **CONTACT ADDRESS** New York Theol Sem, 5 W 29th St, New York, NY 10001. **EMAIL** dirvin@drew.edu

IRVINE, STUART
PERSONAL Born 05/11/1954, Los Angeles, CA, m, 1981, 4 children **DISCIPLINE** RELIGION **EDUCATION** Pomona Col, BA, 76; Yale Univ, MDiv, 80; Emory Univ, PhD, 89. **CAREER** Louisiana State Univ, assoc prof 98-. **MEMBERSHIPS** SBL/AAR **RESEARCH** Hebrew; Prophecy **SELECTED PUBLICATIONS** Auth, Isaiah, Ahaz, and the Syro-Ephraimitic Crisis, in Scholars, 90; Isaiah's She'ar-yashub and the Davidic House, in Biblische Zeitschrift NF 36, 93. **CONTACT ADDRESS** Dept of Religious Studies, Louisiana State Univ and A&M Col, 1848 Glendale Ave, Baton Rouge, LA 70808.

IRWIN, JOYCE LOUISE
PERSONAL Born 11/04/1944, Joplin, MO, m, 1980 **DISCIPLINE** REFORMATION & POST-REFORMATION THOUGHT, HISTORY OF CHRISTIANITY **EDUCATION** Wash Univ, AB, 66; Yale Univ, MA, 68, MPhil, 69, PhD(relig studies), 72. **CAREER** Asst prof hist, Univ Ga, 70-77; ASST PROF PHILOS & RELIG, COLGATE UNIV, 77-82. **MEMBERSHIPS** Am Soc Reformation Res; Am Acad Relig; Am Soc Church Hist. **RESEARCH** Theology and music; women in religion. **SELECTED PUBLICATIONS** Auth, Crautwald and Erasmus--A Study in Humanism and Radical Reform in 16th-Century Silesia, Renaissance Quart, Vol 0047, 94; The Radical Reformation, Renaissance Quart, Vol 0047, 94. **CONTACT ADDRESS** Colgate Univ, 13 Oak Dr, Hamilton, NY 13346.

IRWIN, RAYMOND D.
PERSONAL Born 07/12/1966, Marysville, OH, m, 1990, 2 children **DISCIPLINE** HISTORY, RELIGION **EDUCATION** Ohio State Univ, BA, 88; PhD, 96. **CAREER** Res assoc to teaching assoc, 90-96; instr to director, Just Inst, 96-. **HONORS AND AWARDS** Eugene Roseboom Prize, Ohio State Univ; Travel grant, Ohio State Univ, Alumni Res Awd, Ohio State Univ, Tuition Fel, Univ Minn. **RESEARCH** Early American historiography, Religion and government in seventeenth-century America. **SELECTED PUBLICATIONS** Auth, Books on Early American History and Culture: An Annotated Bibliography, 1991-1995, Greenwood Pub: Westport, 00; auth, "A Study in Schism: Sabbatarian Baptists in England and America, 1665-1672," American Baptist Quarterly, (94): 237-248; auth, "Cast Out from the 'City Upon a Hill': Antinomian Exiles in Rhode Island, 1638-1650," Rhode Island History, (94): 3-19; auth, "A Man for All Eras: The Changing Historical Image of Roger Williams, 1636-1993," Fides et Historia (94): 6-23. **CONTACT ADDRESS** 5295 Olentangy River Rd, Columbus, OH 43235. **EMAIL** irwin@just-inst.org

IRWIN, WILLIAM HENERY
PERSONAL Born 10/25/1932, Houston, TX **DISCIPLINE** BIBLE PHILOSOPHY **EDUCATION** Univ Toronto, BA, 56, MA, 58; Pontif Univ St Thomas Aquinas, STL, 61; Pontif Bibl Inst, Rome, SSL, 63, SSD, 74; Ecole Biblique, Jerusalem, Eleve titule, 64. **CAREER** Asst prof, 65-70, asst dir, Toronto Sch Theol, 77-80, Assoc Prof sacred Scripture, St michael's Col, Univ Toronto, 73-, DEAN FAC THEOL, ST MICHAEL'S COL, 80-, Assoc ed, Cath Bibl Quart, 76-79. **MEMBERSHIPS** Cath Bibl Asn; Can Soc Bibl Studies. **RESEARCH** Hebrew poetry; Old Testament; Ugaritic literature. **SELECTED PUBLICATIONS** Auth, Reading Isaiah, Cath Bibl Quart, Vol 0055, 93; The so Called City of Chaos in Isaiah-Xxiv, 10 and the Genitive of Result + The Treatment of the Genitive in Biblical Hebrew Syntax and its Function in Translation and Interpretation, Biblica, Vol 0075, 94; Cyrus in Deutero Isaiah--A Redaction-History of the Origins and Theology of Isaiah-Xl-Lv, Cath Bibl Quart, Vol 0056, 94; The Servant of Yhwh and Cyrus--A Reinterpretation of the Exilic Messianic Program in Isaiah-Xl-Lv, Cath Bibl Quart, Vol 0056, 94; Fear of God, the Analogy of Friendship and Ben-Sira Theodicy + An Examination of the Traditional Concept of Divine Testing From the Book of Sirach, Biblica, Vol 0076, 95; Conflicting Parallelism in Job-V,13, Isaiah-Xxx,28, Isaiah-Xxxii,7 + A Note on a Stylistic Phenomenon in Hebrew Poetic Phrases, Biblica, Vol 0076, 95; Rhetorical Criticism and the Poetry of the 'Book of Job, Cath Bibl Quart, Vol 0058, 96; The Book Called 'Isaiah'--'Deutero-Isaiah's Role in Composition and Redaction, J Bibl Lit, Vol 0116, 97. **CONTACT ADDRESS** Fac of Theol St Michael's Col, Univ of Toronto, 81 St Mary St, Toronto, ON, Canada M5S 1J4. **EMAIL** irwinw@chass.utoronto.ca

IRWIN, WILLIAM T.
PERSONAL Born 04/02/1970, Bronx, NY **DISCIPLINE** PHILOSOPHY **EDUCATION** Fordham Univ, BA, 92; SUNY at Buffalo, PhD, 96. **CAREER** Asst Prof Philos, 96-, King's Col Wilkes-Barre, PA; Tchg Fellow, State Univ of NY, 93-96; Res Asst to Jorge J.E. Gracia, 92. **HONORS AND AWARDS** Phi Beta Kappa, Fordham Univ; Outstanding Russian Lang Stud Awd, Fordham Univ; Phi Sigma Tau, Intl Honor Soc in Philos; Hughes Awd for the Outstanding Stud of Philos at Fordham Univ; Recipient of the King's Col Summer Res Grant; Perry Dissertation Prize. **MEMBERSHIPS** Amer Philos Assoc; Soc Phenomenal and Existential Philos; North Amer Nietzsche Soc; The North Amer Sartre Soc; Amer Catholic Philos Assoc; Assoc Devel of Philos Tchg; Referee for Journal of Value Inquiry. **RESEARCH** 19th and 20th Century Continental Philosophy, Hermeneutics, Phenomenology and Existentialism, Aesthetics. **SELECTED PUBLICATIONS** Auth, "Philosophical Literacy: Are There Things Every Philosopher Needs to Know?," Am Philos Asn Newsletter 98 (98): 128-130; auth, "A Modest Proposal to Students," The Teaching Prof 13 (99): 8; auth, "An Author Construct There Must Be," Dialogos 74 (99): 169-177; auth, Intentionalist Interpretation: A Philosophical Explanation and Defense, Greenwood Press, 99; auth, Seinfeld and Philosophy: A Book about Everything and Nothing, Open Ct Press, 00. **CONTACT ADDRESS** Dept of Philosophy, King's Col, Wilkes-Barre, PA 18711. **EMAIL** wtirwin@rs01.kings.edu

ISAAC, GORDON L.
PERSONAL Born Seattle, WA, m **DISCIPLINE** ADVENT CHRISTIAN STUDIES, CHURCH HISTORY **EDUCATION** Seattle Pacific Univ, BA; Western Evangel Theol Sem, MDiv; Luther Theol Sem, MTh; Marquette Univ, PhD. **CAREER** Berkshire asst prof, Gordon-Conwell Theol Sem, 97-. **HONORS AND AWARDS** Dir, Ctr Advent Christian Stud. **MEMBERSHIPS** Mem, Sixteenth Century Soc; Amer Soc Church Hist. **RESEARCH** Theology of Martin Luther, history of exegesis, Trinitarian theology, the Early Church Fathers. **SELECTED PUBLICATIONS** Assoc ed, Luther Digest. **CONTACT ADDRESS** Gordon-Conwell Theol Sem, 130 Essex St, South Hamilton, MA 01982. **EMAIL** gisaac@gcts.edu

ISADORE, HAROLD W.
PERSONAL Born Alexandria, LA **DISCIPLINE** LAW **EDUCATION** Southern Univ, BS 1967; Southern Univ Schl of Law, JD 1970; SUNY at Buffalo Law Schl, Cert 1978. **CAREER** US Dept of Labor Office of the Solicitor, atty 1970-73; Baton Rouge Legal Aid Scty, atty 1973-74; Public Defender of Baton Rouge, atty 1974-75; Southern Univ School of Law, assoc law libririan 1975-. **HONORS AND AWARDS** Serv Awd Student Bar Assoc, SU Law Sch, 1970; Humanitarian Awd, Louis A Martinet Legal Soc, 94; Southern Univ Law Ctr, Staff Awd, 1980-81, 1985-87, 1990-94. **MEMBERSHIPS** Mem Am Bar Assn, Nat Bar Assn, Delta Theta Phi Law Frat, Am Assn of Law Libraries, Kappa Alpha Psi Frat, Inc. **SELECTED PUBLICATIONS** Hypotext on Security Devices Southern Univ Pblshr 1979; Hypotext on Civil Procedure Vols 1 and 11 S Univ Pblshr 1980-81. **CONTACT ADDRESS** Law Sch, So Univ and A&M Col, Baton Rouge, LA 70813.

ISASI-DIAZ, ADA MARIA
PERSONAL Born 03/22/1943, La Habana, Cuba, s **DISCIPLINE** CHRISTIAN ETHICS **EDUCATION** Union Theological Seminary, PhD, 90. **CAREER** Prof of Christian Ethics and Theology, 91- , Drew Univ. **HONORS AND AWARDS** One of 26 prominent contemporary thinkers in Questions of Faith II and Faces of Faith videos, produced by UMCom and Trinity Parish of New York, 89; Honorary Degree, Doctor of Laws, Lynchberg Col, 93. **SELECTED PUBLICATIONS** auth, En La Lucha-A Hispanic Women's Liberation Theology, 93; auth, Women of God, Women of the People, 95; co-ed and contributor, Hispanic/Latino Theology-Challenge and Promise, 96; auth, Mujerista Theology: A Theology for the 21st Century, 96. **CONTACT ADDRESS** 100 Overlook Terrace, #818, New York, NY 10040. **EMAIL** aisasidi@drew.edu

ISEMINGER, GARY H.
PERSONAL Born 03/03/1937, Middleboro, MA, m, 1965, 2 children **DISCIPLINE** PHILOSOPHY **EDUCATION** Wesleyan Univ, BA, 58; Yale Univ, MA, 60; PhD, 61. **CAREER** Instr, Yale Univ, 61-62; instr to prof, Carleton Col, 62-; vis prof, Univof Minn, 79; Mayo Med School, 86, 87; Lancaster Univ, 94; Trinity Col, Dublin, 00. **HONORS AND AWARDS** Woodrow Wilson Fel, 58; NEH Stipend, 71, 78; Distinguished Alumnus Awd, Wesleyan Univ, 93. **MEMBERSHIPS** Am Philos Assoc; Am Soc for Aesthetics. **RESEARCH** Philosophy of the Arts, Philosophy of Logic. **SELECTED PUBLICATIONS** Auth, "Meaning, Criteria, and P-Predicates", Analysis 24 (63): 11-18; auth, "The Connection Argument", Mind 75 (66): 131-134; auth, An Introduction to Deductive Logic, Appleton Century Crofts, (NY), 68; ed, Logic and Philosophy: Selected Readings, Appleton Century Crofts, (NY), 68; auth, "Aesthetic Judgments and Non-Aesthetic Conditions" Analysis 33, (73): 129-132; auth, "Is Relevance Necessary for Validity?", Mind 89 (80): 196-213; auth, "Aesthetic Appreciation", J of Aesthet and Art Criticism 39, (81): 389-397; auth, "An Intentional Demonstration?", Intention and Interpretation, ed G. Iseminger, Temple Univ Pr, (Philadelphia, 92): 76-96; ed, Intention and Interpretation, Temple Univ Pr, (Philadelphia), 92; auth, "Actual Intentionatism vs. Hypothetical Intentionalism", J of Aesthet and Art Criticism 54, (96): 319-326. **CONTACT ADDRESS** Dept Philos, Carleton Col, 1 N College St, Northfield, MN 55057-4001. **EMAIL** giseming@carleton.edu

ISENBERG, SHELDON ROBERT
PERSONAL Born 10/21/1941, Fall River, MA **DISCIPLINE** HISTORY OF JUDAISM & EARLY CHRISTIANITY **EDUCATION** Columbia Univ, AB, 62; Harvard Univ, MA, 65, PhD (relig), 69. **CAREER** Asst prof relig, Duke Univ, 68-69 & Princeton Univ, 69-73; asst prof relig, 73-76, ASSOC PROF RELIG, CTR JEWISH STUDIES, UNIV FLA, 76-, Assoc Dir Ctr, 73-, Soc Relig Higher Educ cross-disciplinary fel, 72-73. **MEMBERSHIPS** Asn Jewish Studies; Soc Values Higher Educ; Am Acad Relig; Soc Bibl Lit. **RESEARCH** Judaism in Greco-Roman Palestine; Biblical text criticism; historical method from social psychological and social anthropoligical perspectives. **SELECTED PUBLICATIONS** Auth, An anti-Sadducee polemic in the Palestinian Targum tradition, Harvard Theol Rev, 70; On the Jewish-Palestinian origins of the Peshitta to the Pentateuch, J Bibl Lit, 71; Millenarism in Greco-Roman Palestine, Relgion, 74; Temple and Torah in Palestinian Judaism, In: Christianity, Judaism, and Other Grego-Roman Cults, E J Brill, 75; coauth, Bodies, natural and contrived: The work of Mary Douglas, Relig Studies Rev, 77; auth, Some uses and limitations of social scientific methodology in the study of early Christianity, Proc Soc Bibl Lit, 80. **CONTACT ADDRESS** Ctr for Jewish Studies, Univ of Florida, PO Box 118020, Gainesville, FL 32611. **EMAIL** sri@religion.ufl.edu

ISERSON, KENNETH V.
PERSONAL Born 04/08/1949, Washington, DC, m, 1973 **DISCIPLINE** BIOEMEDICAL ETHICS **EDUCATION** Univ Md, College Pk, MD, BS, bio educ, 71; Univ Md Sch of Med, Baltimore MD, 75; Univ Phoenix, Tucson, MBA, 84-86; sr fel, bioethics, Ctr for Clinical Med Ethics, Univ Chicago, Pritzker Sch of Med, 7/90-6/91. **CAREER** Clinical asst prof, dept of emergency med, Col of Osteopathic Med, Ft Worth, 79-82; chair, dept of emergency med, fac, family practice residency, Carswell AFB Regional Hospital, Ft Worth, 78-80; clinical assoc dir, emergency med residency, Darnall Army Hospital, Ft Hood, Tex, 80-81; chair and clinical assoc prof, div of emergency med, Tex A&M Univ Col of Med, Temple, Tex, 80-81; asst prof, sect of emergency med, dept of surgery, Univ Ariz Col of Med, 81-85; residency dir, 82-91, assoc prof, 85-92, prof, 92-, sect of emergency med, dept of surgery, Univ Ariz Col of Med; dir, Ariz Bioethics Prog, Univ Ariz Col of Med, 91-. **HONORS AND AWARDS** Intl Authors and Writers Who's Who, 99; Emergency Med Residents' Teacher of the yr, 97; Who's Who of Medicine and Healthcare, 96; Contemporary Authors, 95; NY Public Libr award, 95; Pew Charitable Trusts Sr fel, Ctr for Clinical Med Ethics, Univ Chicago, 90-91; Intl Who's Who of Professionals, 94; Global Business Leaders, 93; Who's Who of Emerging Leaders in America, 89; Amer Men and Women of Sci, 89; Who's Who in the West, 89; Valedictorian, Univ Phoenix, Tucson, 87; Amer Med Asn Physician Recognition award, 80, 83, 86, 89, 93, 94, 97; fel, Amer Col of Emergency Physicians, 82; diplomat, Amer Bd of Emergency Med, 80, 90. **MEMBERSHIPS** Amer Col of Emergency Physicians; Amer Med Asn; Amer Philos Asn; Amer Soc for Bioethics and Humanities; Europ Soc for Philos of Med & Health Care; Nat Asn of Advisors for Health Professionals; Soc for Acad Emergency Med; Wilderness Med Soc. **RESEARCH** Ethical issues related to emergency medical care, end-of-life issues, and medicine's future. **SELECTED PUBLICATIONS** Auth, Asking the Right Questions--Physician-Assisted Suicide and Emergency Medical Systems, Acad Emergency Med, 847-9, 98; auth, Nonstandard Advance Directives: A Pseudoethical Dilemma, Jour of Trauma, 139-42, 98; auth, Elegant Emergency Medicine, Jour of Emergency Med, 483-4, 98; co-auth, Financial Relationships with Patients, Surgical Ethics, Oxford Univ Press, 322-41, 98; auth, Bioethics, Emergency Medicine: Concepts and Clinical Practice, 4th ed, C. V. Mosby, 212-221, 98; auth, Bioethical Dilemmas in Emergency Medicine and Prehospital Care, Health Care Ethics: Critical Issues for the 21st Century, Aspen Publ, 138-145, 97; auth, Human Subjects in Trauma Research, Emergency Medicine, 2nd ed, Galen Press Ltd, 134-142, 95; auth, Practicing Procedures on the Newly Dead, Ethics in Emergency Medicine, 2nd ed, Galen Press Ltd, 123-129, 95; auth, Ethics of Wilderness Medicine, Wilderness Medicine: Management of Wilderness and Environmental Emergencies, 3rd ed, C. V. Mosby, 1436-1446, 95; auth, Bioethical Dilemmas in Emergency Medicine and Prehospital Care, Health Care Ethics: Critical Issues, Aspen Publ, 146-150, 94; auth, Get Into Medical School! A Guide fro the Perplexed, Galen Press, Ltd, 95; auth, Grave Words: Notifying Survivors About Sudden, Unexpected Deaths, Galen Press, Ltd, 99; auth, Pocket Protocol: Notifying Survivors About Sudden, Unexpected Deaths, Galen Press, Ltd, 99; auth, Getting Into A Residency, Galen Press, Ltd., 5th ed, 00; auth, Death to Dust: What Happens to Dead Bodies, Galen Press, Ltd, 2nd ed., 00. **CONTACT ADDRESS** Arizona Bioethics Program, Univ of Arizona, 1501 N. Campbell Av., Box 245057, Tucson, AZ 85724. **EMAIL** kvi@u.uug.arizona.edu

ISH, DANIEL
DISCIPLINE LAW **EDUCATION** Univ Saskatchewan, BA, 70, LLB, 70; Osgoode Hall Law Sch, LLM, 74. **CAREER** Asst prof, McGill Univ, 72-75; dean, 82-88; acting dean, 96-97. **HONORS AND AWARDS** Fulbright Scholar, Stanford Univ, 95-96. **MEMBERSHIPS** Law Societies of Alberta and Saskatchewan. **SELECTED PUBLICATIONS** Auth, The Law of Canadian Co-operatives, Carswell, 81; Absenteeism Attendance Programs, 95; co-auth, Legal Responsibilities and Duties of Directors in Canadian Co-operatives, 95; Co-operatives in Principle and Practice, 92. **CONTACT ADDRESS** Col of Law, Univ of Saskatchewan, 15 Campus Dr, Saskatoon, SK, Canada S7N 5A6. **EMAIL** Ish@law.usask.ca

ISMAEL, JENANN
PERSONAL Born 01/27/1968, s **DISCIPLINE** PHILOSOPHY **EDUCATION** Reed Col, BA, 90; Princeton Univ, MA, 93; PhD, 96. **CAREER** Vis prof, Stanford; asst prof, Univ Ariz, 96-00. **HONORS AND AWARDS** Phi Beta Kappa, Mellon Post-Doctoral Fel, SSHRC post-Doctoral Fel (declined); honorary fel, Calgary Inst for Humanities, 99-00. **MEMBERSHIPS** Am Philos Asn, Philos of Sci Asn. **RESEARCH** Metaphysics, Epistemology, Philosophy of Physics, Philosophy of Science, Philosophy of Mind, Philosophy of Mathematics & Language. **CONTACT ADDRESS** Dept Philos, Univ of Arizona, PO Box 210027, Tucson, AZ 85721-0027. **EMAIL** jtismael@u.arizona.edu

ISOM, DALLAS W.
DISCIPLINE ANTITRUST, CIVIL PROCEDURE, FEDERAL JURISDICTION, PLEADING **EDUCATION** Univ Utah, JD, 65; Univ of Iowa, BA. **CAREER** Grad fel, Stanford Univ, 65-66; tchg fel, Stanford Univ, 65-66; private practice, King, Miller, Anderson, Nash & Yerke, 66-68; asst prof, 68-70; assoc prof, 70-74; prof, 74; Prof of Law Emer. **MEMBERSHIPS** Mem, Order of the Coif. **SELECTED PUBLICATIONS** Auth, Oregon Civil Pleading and Practice Handbook, 74, 78, 80; ed, note ed, Utah Law Rev. **CONTACT ADDRESS** Sch of Law, Willamette Univ, 900 State St, Salem, OR 97301. **EMAIL** disom@willamette.edu

ISRAEL, JEROLD H.
PERSONAL Born 06/14/1934, Cleveland, OH, m, 1959, 3 children **DISCIPLINE** LAW **EDUCATION** Western Reserve Univ, BBA; Yale Univ, LLB. **CAREER** Ed Rood Eminent scholar, Trial Advocacy and Procedure, Univ Fla, 93-; Stephen C. O'Connell vis prof, 91; Alene and Allen F. Smith prof emer, Univ Mich Law Sch, 61-96. **MEMBERSHIPS** Ohio Bar; Mich Bar; Order of the Coif. **RESEARCH** Criminal procedure, white collar crime. **SELECTED PUBLICATIONS** Coauth, White Collar Crime: Law and Pract; coauth, Criminal procedure Treatise; coauth, Modern Criminal Procedure. **CONTACT ADDRESS** School of Law, Univ of Florida, PO Box 117625, Gainesville, FL 32611-7625. **EMAIL** israel@law.ufl.edu

IVES, CHRISTOPHER
DISCIPLINE RELIGION **EDUCATION** Williams Col, BA, 76; Claremont Grad School, MA, 84; PhD, 88. **CAREER** Assoc Prof to Prof and Dept Chair, Univ Puget Sound, 92-. **HONORS AND AWARDS** NEH Fel, Col Teachers and Independent Scholars, 98; Res Grant, Soc Sci Res Council, 98; Fulbright-Hays Fac Res Abroad Prog grant, 93. **MEMBERSHIPS** Am Acad of Relig, Asn for Asian Studies, Intl Asn of Buddhist Studies. **RESEARCH** Japanese Buddhism and Ethics. **SELECTED PUBLICATIONS** Auth, Zen Awakening and society, Macmillan Press, 92; ed, Divine Emptiness and Historical Fullness: A Buddhist-Jewish-Christian Conversation with Masao Abe, Trinity Press Intl, 95. **CONTACT ADDRESS** Dept Relig, Univ of Puget Sound, 1500 N Warner St, Tacoma, WA 98416-0001. **EMAIL** ives@ups.edu

IYER, NITYA
DISCIPLINE LAW **EDUCATION** Univ Toronto, BA, 83, LLB, 86; Harvard Univ, LLM, 89. **CAREER** Asst prof, 90-94; assoc prof, 94-. **RESEARCH** Feminist theory; race and racism; family law; constitutional law. **SELECTED PUBLICATIONS** Auth, pubs about constitutional and human rights, family law, feminist and anti-racist analyses of law, and reproduction and the law. **CONTACT ADDRESS** Fac of Law, Univ of British Columbia, 1822 East Mall, Vancouver, BC, Canada V6T 1Z1. **EMAIL** iyer@law.ubc.ca

J

JABLONSKI, LEANNE M.
DISCIPLINE RELIGIOUS STUDIES **EDUCATION** McGill Univ, PhD. **CAREER** Post-doc scholar, Ohio State Univ; rel stud adj fac mem and Assoc Dir, Marianist Env Educ Ctr at Mt St John/Bergamo in Dayton. **RESEARCH** Plant Ecology and the impacts of Global Climate Change. **CONTACT ADDRESS** Dept of Religious Studies, Univ of Dayton, 300 College Park, 473 Humanities, Dayton, OH 45469-1679. **EMAIL** jablonsk@checkov.hm.udayton.edu

JACKMAN, BARBARA
DISCIPLINE LAW **EDUCATION** Windsor Univ, BA, 72; Univ Toronto, LLB, 76. **CAREER** Lectr; Practicing Immigration & Refugee Law, Jackman & Associates **MEMBERSHIPS** Can Bas Asn; Law Union Ontario; Can Civil Liberties Asn. **SELECTED PUBLICATIONS** Auth, pubs on immigration and refugee law, administrative law and constitutional law. **CONTACT ADDRESS** Fac of Law, Univ of Toronto, 78 Queen's Park, Toronto, ON, Canada M5S 1A1.

JACKMAN, HENRY
PERSONAL Born 04/04/1965 **DISCIPLINE** PHILOSOPHY **EDUCATION** Columbia Univ, BA; Pittsburgh Univ, MA; PhD. **CAREER** Prof, Univ Toledo; prof, York Univ, Toronto. **RESEARCH** Philosophy of language; American Pragmatism; philosophy of mind; history of analytic philosophy; epistemology; history of modern philosophy; William James; philosophy of science; metaphysics; logic. **SELECTED PUBLICATIONS** Auth, Review of Declerck: Tense In English: Its structure and use in discourse, Language, 93; auth, Radical Interpretation and the Permutation Principle, Erkenntnis; James on Prudential Arguments and the Will to Believe, 97; auth, James' Pragmatic Account of Intentionality and Truth, 98; auth, Individualism and Interpretation, SW Philos Rev, 98; auth, "Moderate Holism and the Instability Thesis," America Philosophical Quarterly 36(4) (99): 361-369; auth, "We Live Forwards but Understand Backwards: Linguistic Practices and Future Behavior," Pacific Philosophical Quarterly 80 (99): 157-177; auth, "Deference and Self-Knowledge," Southwest Philosophy Review 16(1) (00): 171-180; auth, Belief, Rationality, and Psychophysical Laws, in Twentieth World Congress of Philosophy, vol 9: Philosophy of Mind, (forthcoming); auth, Ordinary Language, Conventionalism, and A Priori Knowledge, Dialectica (forthcoming). **CONTACT ADDRESS** Dept of Philos, York Univ, Toronto, Ontario, Canada M3J 1P3. **EMAIL** hjackman@yorku.ca

JACKSON, CAROL E.
DISCIPLINE LAW **EDUCATION** Wellesley College, BA, 1973; Univ of Michigan, JD, 1976. **CAREER** Thompson & Mitchell, attorney, 76-83; Mallinckrodt Inc, counsel, 83-85; US District Court, Eastern District MO, magistrate, 86-92, District Judge, 92-; Washington Univ, Adjunct Prof of Law, 89-92. **MEMBERSHIPS** St Louis Art Museum, trustee, 1987-91; National Assn of Women's Judges; Federal Magistrate Judges Assn; Missouri Bar; St Louis County Bar Assn; Metro St Louis; Mound City Bar Assn; Lawyers Assn of St Louis. **CONTACT ADDRESS** US District Court-Eastern Missouri, 1114 Market St, Saint Louis, MO 63101-2043.

JACKSON, GORDON EDMUND
PERSONAL Born 01/11/1918, Spokane, WA, m, 1939, 2 children **DISCIPLINE** PASTORAL THEOLOGY **EDUCATION** Monmouth Col, AB, 40; Pittsburth-Xenia Theol Sem, BD, 43; Tarkio Col, DD, 53; Univ Chicago, PhD, 54. **CAREER** Minister, Westminster United Presby Church, Olympia, Wash, 44-49; prof philos of relig, 49-70, dean, 55-77, HUGH THOMSON KERR PROF PASTORAL THEOL, PITTSBURGH THEOL SEM, 75-, Mem comn on accrediting, Asn Am Theol Schs, 62-68; adj prof relig studies, Univ Pittsburgh, 69- **MEMBERSHIPS** Soc Sci Studies Relig; Am Acad Relig. **RESEARCH** Concept of the image of God and its implications for Christian education; hostility in man; spiritual formation of the self. **SELECTED PUBLICATIONS** Auth, The Diaconate--A Full and Equal Order--A Comprehensive-Study and Critical Study of the Origin, Development, and Decline of the Diaconate in the Context of the Churchs Total Ministry and the Renewal of the Diaconate Today With Re, J Ecumenical Stud. **CONTACT ADDRESS** Pittsburgh Theol Sem, 616 N Highland Ave, Pittsburgh, PA 15206.

JACKSON, JANICE TUDY
PERSONAL Born 09/30/1945, New York, NY **DISCIPLINE** LAW **EDUCATION** City Coll of New York, BA 1977; Univ of MI Labor/Industrial Relations, Certification 1983; Inst of Applied Mgmt & Law, Certification 1985; Cornell Univ/Baruch Coll NYork, NYork MS-ILR 1989; Columbia University Law School, JD 1992. **CAREER** St Luke's Hosp Sch of Nursing, asst registrar 1970-74; Continental Grain Co, research asst 1975-77, personnel admin 1977-79, EEO officer 1979-80, mgr coll relations 1980-82, regional personnel mgr 1982-84, corp labor relations mgr 1984-86, asst vice pres human resources 1986-88, vice pres labor relations 1988-89; Morgan, Lewis & Bockius, Attorney, 92-. **HONORS AND AWARDS** Natl Selection for Weinberg Natl Labor Mgmt Certificate; Graphic Art/Design Continental Grain Co Annual Employee Statement 1976-81; International Human Rights Fellowship, Kenya, Columbia Law School, 1990; National YWCA Academy of Woman Achievers, National YWCA, 1989; Barbara Aronstein Black Scholarship, Columbia Law School, 1990; Harlan Fiske Stone Scholar; Charles Evans Hughes Fellow; Jane Marks Murphy Prize, Columbia Law School, 1992; Outstanding Woman Law Graduate, National Assn of Women Lawyers, 1992. **MEMBERSHIPS** Speaker/lecturer Cornell Univ, Purdue Univ, Atlanta Univ, Yale Univ, Howard Univ, Univ of IL 1979-; adv bd mem Atlanta Univ Grad Sch of Business 1979-82; panelist Women Business Owners of NY 1982,83; dir Tutorial Prog Manhattan Ctr for Science & Math 1985-; exec bd mem The EDGES Group Inc 1986-; life mem Delta Sigma Theta Inc 1986; aux mem NY City Commn on the Status of Women 1987-; board of trustees, Manhattan Country School, 1990-. **SELECTED PUBLICATIONS** "ET to Denny - Bossism or Crucifixion," The Esplanade News 1983; editorial "Miscarriage of Justice," NY Amsterdam News 1985. **CONTACT ADDRESS** Morgan, Lewis & Bockius, 101 Park Ave, New York, NY 10178.

JACKSON, JARED JUDD
PERSONAL Born 07/26/1930, New Haven, CT, m, 1953, 4 children **DISCIPLINE** OLD TESTAMENT SEMITIC STUDIES **EDUCATION** Harvard Univ, AB, 52; Episcopal Theol Sch, BD, 58; Union Theol Sem NYork, ThD(Old Testament), 62. **CAREER** Asst prof Old Testament, Huron Col Ont & Univ Western Ont, 62-64; vis prof relig, Williams Col, 64-65; from asst prof to prof, 65-97, Prof Emeritus Old Testament, Pittsburgh Theol Sem, 97-; adj prof grad studies relig, Univ Pittsburgh, 69-. **HONORS AND AWARDS** Church Soc Col Work fel, 58-60; Rockefeller Bros Fund fel, 60-62; Am Asn Theol Schs fac fel, 68-69. **MEMBERSHIPS** Soc Bibl Studies; Soc Study Egyptian Antiq; Soc Bibl Lit; Am Schs Orient Res. **RESEARCH** Ugaritic and Egyptian studies in relation to Old Testament. **SELECTED PUBLICATIONS** Contribr to the interpreter's dictionary of the Bible, Abingdon, 62; co-ed, Rhetorical Criticism, 74. **CONTACT ADDRESS** Pittsburgh Theol Sem, 616 N Highland Ave, Pittsburgh, PA 15206-2525. **EMAIL** jjackson@pitt.edu

JACKSON, JEROME E.
PERSONAL Born 11/16/1951, Houston, TX, m, 1976, 3 children **DISCIPLINE** CRIMINOLOGY **EDUCATION** Southern Univ, BA, 74; TX Southern Univ, MPA, 81; Sam Houston State Univ, PhD, 92. **CAREER** Prof, TX Southern Univ, 81-88; prof, Calif State Univ, 90-. **HONORS AND AWARDS** Rosa Parks Awd for Outstanding community service, 98; Prof Achievement Awd, 98; Community Service, 98; Provost's Excellence in Teaching Awd, 98. **MEMBERSHIPS** Am Soc of Criminology, Acad Criminal Justice Sci, Western Soc of Criminologists. **RESEARCH** Non-violent gangs, police and technology, corrections and minorities, law enforcement executives, juvenile delinquency, ethnic and gender issues in criminology/victimology. **SELECTED PUBLICATIONS** Auth, "Policing America: The African American Executive," American Criminal Justice Association Journal, (98): 33-41; auth, "Race and Correctional Oficers' Attitudes Toward Treatment Programs for Inmates," Journal of Criminal Justice, (96): 153-166; auth, "Fraud Masters: Professional Credit Card Criminals and Crime," Criminal Justice Review, (94): 24-55; auth, "Fieldwork and Economic Law-Violators: The Case of the Fraud Master," Journal of Police Science, (94): 275-292; auth, " Computer Crimes and Criminals," American Criminal Justice Association Journal, (96): 32-36. **CONTACT ADDRESS** Dept Criminology, California State Univ, Fresno, 2225 E San Ramon Ave, Fresno, CA 93740-8029. **EMAIL** jeromej@csufresno.edu

JACKSON, JOE C.
PERSONAL Born 04/24/1911, Gene Autrey, OK, 1 child **DISCIPLINE** HISTORY, GOVERNMENT **EDUCATION** Univ Okla, BSEd, 34, EdM, 40, EdD(hist, govt), 50. **CAREER** Instr speech, hist & govt, Sulphur High Sch, 34-37; vprin, Bristow High Sch, 37-40; dean, Bristow Jr Col, 40-44; prin, Bristow Jr High Sch, 44-48; assoc prof hist & govt, 48-51, dean col, 51-59, prof hist & polit sci, 51-76, Emer Prof Hist & Polit Sci, Cent State Univ, 76-, VPres Acad Affairs, 69-. **MEMBERSHIPS** NEA **RESEARCH** History of the Southwest. **SELECTED PUBLICATIONS** Auth, Born to Wander--Autobiography of Ball, John, Oregon Hist Quart, Vol 0096, 95. **CONTACT ADDRESS** Academic Affairs, Central State Univ, Oklahoma, Edmond, OK 73034.

JACKSON, JOSEPH HOLLISTER
PERSONAL Born 10/13/1912, Springfield, VT, m, 1941, 1 child **DISCIPLINE** PHILOSOPHY, PSYCHOLOGY **EDUCATION** Middlebury Col, AB, 35; Brown Univ, MA, 37, PhD(philos), 40. **CAREER** Personnel dir, Columbia Broadcasting Syst, Inc, 44-50; training dir, Am Electric Power Co, 50-54; publ dir, Soc Advan Mgt, 54-55; managing ed, Ronald Press Co, 55-60; consult ed sci, Encycl Americana, 60-64; writer, Sci Fortnightly & Dateline in Sci, Richard Sigerson, 64-65; ed-in-chicf, Investigating the Earth, Houghton, 65-67; instr philos, New Sch Social Res, 66-67; asst prof, Univ Conn, 68-72; Res & Writing, 72-, Nat Sci Found fel, Conn Res Found, 68-69; proj ed, Earth Sci Curriculum Proj, Nat Sci Found, 65-67; WRITER HARVARD PHYSICS PROF, 68-. **MEMBERSHIPS** Am Philos Asn; AAAS. **RESEARCH** Ethics; motivation; developmental and social psychology. **SELECTED PUBLICATIONS** Auth Pictorial guide to the Planets, 65, 3rd ed, 81 & coauth, Pictorial Guide to the Moon, 69, 3rd ed, 73, Crowell; Spaceship Earth-Earth Sciences, Houghton, 73, 2nd ed, 80; contribr, Psychology 73/74, Dushkin, 73; auth, Measurement of ethical values, Perceptual & Motor Skills, 36: 1075-1088; coauth, Investigating Behavior, Harper, 76; Infant Culture, Crowell, 78. **CONTACT ADDRESS** 57 Attawan Ave, Niantic, CT 06357.

JACKSON, RANDOLPH
PERSONAL Born 10/10/1943, Brooklyn, NY **DISCIPLINE** LAW **EDUCATION** NYork Univ, BA 1965; Brooklyn Law Sch, JD 1969. **CAREER** Mudge Rose Guthrie & Alexander, asso atty 1969-70; Private Practice of Law, 71-81; New York City Family Court, hearing examiner 1981; Civil Court, Housing Part, judge 1981-87; Civil Court, judge 1987-88; Supreme Court Brooklyn NY, justice 1988-. **MEMBERSHIPS** Life mem Nat Bar Assn 1971-; mem Brooklyn Bar Assn 1971-; mem Crown Hgts Lions Club 1980-; Sigma Pi Phi; NAACP. **SELECTED PUBLICATIONS** Auth, How to Get a Fair Trial By Jury, 78; auth, Black People in the Bible, 90. **CONTACT ADDRESS** Supreme Court, Kings County, 360 Adams St, Brooklyn, NY 11201.

JACKSON, RICARDO C.
DISCIPLINE LAW **EDUCATION** Va Union Univ, BA, 62; Howard Univ, BL, 65; JD, 69. **CAREER** Adj Prof, Chyney Univ, 92; Adj Lecturer, Temple Univ, 84-. **MEMBERSHIPS** Nat Bar Asn, Am Bar Asn, Penn Bar Asn, Philadelphia Bar An, Penn conf of State Trial Judges, Judicial Coun of the Nat Bar Asn. **SELECTED PUBLICATIONS** Co-auth, "Racial Discrimination in Administration of the Pennsylvania Bar Examination," Temple Law Quarterly, 71; auth, "Handling Death Penalty Case Benchbook," National Judicial Col, 92. **CONTACT ADDRESS** Dept Business Law, Temple Univ, 1810 N 13th St, Philadelphia, PA 19122.

JACKSON, ROGER
PERSONAL Born 06/05/1950, London, England, m, 1979, 1 child **DISCIPLINE** BUDDHISM, RELIGIONS OF SOUTH

ASIA **EDUCATION** Wesleyan, BA; Wisconsin, MA, PhD. **CAREER** Religion, Carleton College; fel, Univ of Mich; religious stud, Fairfield Univ. **MEMBERSHIPS** IABS: AAS: AAR. **RESEARCH** Indian and Tibetan Buddhist philosophy; tantric ritual and meditation; religious poetry of South Asia. **SELECTED PUBLICATIONS** Coauth, The Wheel of Time: Kalachakra in Context, 85; Auth, Is Enlightenment Possible?, 93; Coed, Tibetan Literature: Studies in Genre, 96; co-ed, Buddhist Theology: Critical Reflections by Contemporary Buddhist Scholars, 00. **CONTACT ADDRESS** Carleton Col, 1 N College St., Northfield, MN 55057-4016. **EMAIL** rjackson@carleton.edu

JACKSON, WILLIAM JOSEPH

PERSONAL Born 08/31/1943, Rock Island, IL, m, 1968, 1 child **DISCIPLINE** RELIGION **EDUCATION** Lyndon (VT) St Col, BA, 75; Harvard Univ, PhD, 84. **CAREER** Asst prof, 85-92, assoc prof, 92-, Indiana Univ, Purdue. **HONORS AND AWARDS** Danforth Fel to Grad Schl, 75. **MEMBERSHIPS** AAR. **RESEARCH** S Indian religious music; Hindu singer-saints; fractals in humanities. **SELECTED PUBLICATIONS** Auth, Tyagaraja: Life and Lyrics, Oxford Univ Press, 91; auth, J.L. Mehta on Heidegger, Hermeneutics and Indian Tradition, Netherlands, 92; art, Features of the Kriti: A Song Form Developed by Tyagaraja, Asian Music Jour, Cornell Univ, 93; auth, The Power of the Sacred Name: V Raghavan's Studies on Namasiddhanta and Indian Culture, India Book Center, 94; art, Purandaradasa's Songs on the Holy Name, Jour of Vaisnava Stud, 94; auth, Tyagaraja and the Renewal of Tradition: Translations and Reflections, New Delhi, 95; art, Music as Reflectaphor for Cosmic Order in the Vijayanagara Empire, Jour of Vaisnava Stud, 96; art, Annamacarya's Spiritual Thinking, Jour of Vaisnava Stud, 96; auth, The Songs of Three Great South Indian Saints, Oxford Univ Press, 98; art, Fractals of Love: Self-Similarity in the Bhakti Community, Jour of Vaisnava Stud, 98. **CONTACT ADDRESS** Dept of Religious Studies, Indiana Univ-Purdue Univ, Indianapolis, 425 Univ Blvd, Indianapolis, IN 46202-5140. **EMAIL** wjackson@iupui.edu

JACOB, BRUCE ROBERT

PERSONAL Born 03/26/1935, Chicago, IL, m, 1962, 3 children **DISCIPLINE** LAW **EDUCATION** FL State Univ, BA, 57; Stetson Univ, JD, 59; Northwestern Univ, LLM, 65; Harvard Univ, SJD, 80; Univ FL, LLM(taxation), 95. **CAREER** Asst atty gen, Off of the Atty Gen of Fla, 60-62; assoc, Holland, Bevis & Smith, Attys, 62-64; from asst prof to assoc prof criminal law, Sch Law, Emory Univ, 65-69; res assoc, Ctr Criminal Justice, Harvard Law Sch, 69-70; staff atty, Community Legal Assistance Off, Cambridge, Mass, 70-71; from assoc prof to prof & dir clinical progs, Col Law, Ohio State Univ, 71-78; prof & dean, Sch Law, Mercer Univ, 78-81; Prof, Dean & Vpres, Col Law, Stetson Univ, 81-94; Prof and Dean Emer, 94-, Special officer, conscientious objector cases, US Dept Justice, 65-68; mem, Ga Governor's Comn on Crime & Justice, 67-68. **MEMBERSHIPS** Am Judicature Soc. **RESEARCH** Correctional law; criminal procedure; criminology; administrative law; taxation **SELECTED PUBLICATIONS** Coauth, Sit-in demonstrations: Are they punishable in Florida?, Univ Miami Law Rev, 60-61; auth, Reparation or restitution by the criminal offender to his victim, J Criminal Law, Criminol & Police Sci, 70; Prison discipline and inmate rights, Harvard Civil Rights- Civil Liberties Law Rev, 70; coauth, Justice after trial: Prisoners' need for legal services in the criminal-correctional process, Kans Law Rev, 70; contribr, The Concept of Restitution: An Historical Overview, In: Restitution in Criminal Justice, Lexington Books, 77; coauth, Disciplinary and Punitive Decisions and Due Process Values in the American Correctional System, 12 Stetson L. Rev 1, (82); auth, Developing Lawyering Skills and the Nurturing of Inherent Traits and Abilities, in Symposium on Maximizing the Law School Experience, 12 Stetson L. Rev, 577 (83); auth, Gideon v. Wainwright, 43 American U.L. Rev 1, 33 (93). **CONTACT ADDRESS** Col of Law, Stetson Univ, St. Petersburg, 1401 61st St S, Saint Petersburg, FL 33707-3299. **EMAIL** jacob@law.stetson.edu

JACOBS, DAVID C.

DISCIPLINE PHILOSOPHY **EDUCATION** Ca State Univ, BA; New Sch Soc Res, MA, 90; Vanderbilt Univ, PhD, 93. **CAREER** Instr, Vanderbit Univ, 92; Adj prof, 93-96; asst prof, 96-. **RESEARCH** Contemporary European philosophy; philosophy of the body. **SELECTED PUBLICATIONS** Auth, Introduction: Heidegger, the History of Being, the Presocratics; Parmenides' Ontological Education; Martin Heidegger and the Phenomenon of Natural Science (rev), 95; The Tain of the Mirror, in Auslegung (rev), 90; co-ed, Heidegger and the Political, Graduate Fac Philos Jour, 91. **CONTACT ADDRESS** Dept of Philosophy, 615 McCallie, Chattanooga, TN 37403. **EMAIL** hodos@hotmail.com

JACOBS, ENNIS LEON, JR.

PERSONAL Born 01/19/1954, Tampa, FL, m, 1976 **DISCIPLINE** LAW **EDUCATION** Florida A & M Univ, Magna Cum Laude, BS, technology, 1976; Florida State Univ Coll of Law, JD, 1986. **CAREER** Eastman Kodak Co, systems analyst, 76-80; RCA Corp, systems representatives, 80-82; Florida Public Service Commission, staff Attorney, 86-89; Florida Attorney General, staff Attorney, 89-91; Florida Senate, staff Attorney, 91-93; Florida Legislative House, staff Attorney, 93-. **MEMBERSHIPS** Tallahassee Habitat for Humanity, pres of board; National Bar Assn; Amer Bar Assn; Leon County Guardian Ad Litem. **SELECTED PUBLICATIONS** Author, "State Regulation of Information Services," Barrister, ABA Young Lawyers Division, Spring 1991. **CONTACT ADDRESS** Florida House of Rep-Comm on Insurance, House Office Bldg, Rm 302, The Capitol, Tallahassee, FL 32399-1300.

JACOBS, JO ELLEN

PERSONAL Born 11/21/1952, Flora, IL, m, 1975, 2 children **DISCIPLINE** PHILOSOPHY **EDUCATION** E Ill Univ, BA, 73; Boston Col, MA, 75; Wash Univ, PhD, 77. **CAREER** E Ill Univ, 77-80; Millikin Univ, 81-. **HONORS AND AWARDS** Teacher of the Year Awd, 98; Griswold Distinguished Prof of Philos, 90-92, 95-97. **MEMBERSHIPS** Am Soc for Aesthetics, Int Soc for Aesthetics, Am Philos Asn. **RESEARCH** Harriet Taylor Mill, aesthetics. **SELECTED PUBLICATIONS** Auth, "Identifying Musical Works," J of Aesthetic Educ 24.4 (90): 75-85; rev, of "Rethinking the Forms of Visual Expression," by Robert Sower, J of Aesthetics and Art Criticism (91); rev, of "Art and Engagement," by Arnold Berleant, J of Aesthetics and Art Criticism (92); rev, of "The Psychobiography of a Moralist," by Bertrand Russell, J of Psychohistory 20.3 (92); rev, of "Music Education in Theory and Practice," J of Aesthetic Educ 27.1 (93); auth, "Philosophy on Music and Time," in Encycl of Time, ed. Samuel L. Macy (New York, NY: Garland Publ, 94): 453-455; auth, "'The Lot of Gifted Ladies is Hard': A Study of Harriet Taylor Mill Criticism," Hypatia 9.3 (94): 132-162; auth, The Collected Works of Harriet Taylor Mill, Ind Univ Press, 98; auth, "Harriet Taylor Mill's Collaboration with John Stuart Mill," in Interruptions: The Voices of Women Philosophers, eds. Cecile Tougas and Sara Ebenreck (Philadelphia, PA: Temple UP, 00): 155-166; auth, Harriet Taylor Mill: Portrait of a Victorian Radical (forthcoming). **CONTACT ADDRESS** Dept Philos, Millikin Univ, 1184 W Main St, Decatur, IL 62522-2039. **EMAIL** cxjej@eiu.edu

JACOBS, JONATHAN

PERSONAL Born 11/28/1955, Stamford, CT, m, 1990, 2 children **DISCIPLINE** MORAL PHILOSOPHY, EPISTEMOLOGY, METAPHYSICS **EDUCATION** Univ PA, PhD, 83. **CAREER** Assoc prof, Colgate Univ. **HONORS AND AWARDS** John MacMurray Visting Prof of Philosophy at Univ of Edinburgh, Vis fel at Centre for Philosophy and Public Affairs at Univ of St Andrews, Life Member of Clare Hall at Cambridge Univ, Vis Senior Member at Linacre College Oxford Univ. **MEMBERSHIPS** Am Philosophical Assoc, British Soc for Ethical Theory. **RESEARCH** Moral Psychology, Metaethics, Realism-Antirealism debate. **SELECTED PUBLICATIONS** Auth, Practical Realism and Moral Psychology, 95; Plasticity and Perfection: Maimonides and Aristotle on Character, 97; Why is Virtue Naturally Pleasing, 95; auth, A Philosopher's Compass, 00; auth Metaethics and Teleology, 00; auth, Willing Necessity, 01. **CONTACT ADDRESS** Dept of Philos and Relig, Colgate Univ, 13 Oak Drive, Hamilton, NY 13346. **EMAIL** jjacobs@mail.colgate.edu

JACOBS, MICHELLE S.

DISCIPLINE LAW **EDUCATION** Princeton Univ, AB; Rutgers Univ, JD. **CAREER** Prof, Univ Fla, 93-; past supv atty, Rutgers Univ Urban Legal Clinic; pvt pract, McGee Jacobs, NY, 85-90; prof, Columbia Univ Fair Housing Clinic. **MEMBERSHIPS** NJ Bar; NY Bar. **CONTACT ADDRESS** School of Law, Univ of Florida, PO Box 117625, Gainesville, FL 32611-7625. **EMAIL** jacobsm@nervm.nerdc.ufl.edu

JACOBSON, ARLAND D.

PERSONAL Born 09/25/1941, Mitchell, SD, m, 1964, 2 children **DISCIPLINE** RELIGION **EDUCATION** Augustana Col, BA, 63; Univ Chicago Div Sch, 64-65; Luther Sem, BD, 67; Claremont Grad Univ, PhD, 78. **CAREER** Pastor, Humboldt Lutheran Church, SD, 67-71; and Scranton Lutheran Parish, ND, 74-76; vis asst prof relig stud, Loyola Marymount Univ, 78-79; asst prof relig, 79-83, dir, CHARIS Ecumenical Ctr and Fargo-Moorhead Communiversity, 83- , Concordia College. **HONORS AND AWARDS** Scholar in residence, Inst for Ecumenical and Cultural Res, Collegeville MN, 90; Bush Summer Fel, 92; Who's Who in Relig, 92; scholar in residence, Tantur Ecumenical Inst, Jerusalem, 97; Who's Who in The Midwest, 98; Who's Who in America, 99, 00. **MEMBERSHIPS** Soc of Bibl Lit; Catholic Bibl Asn of Am; Westar Inst; Soc for the Advan of Cont Educ for Ministry. **RESEARCH** The synoptic gospel source Q; anti-family tendencies in the Jesus movement; social context of first-century Galilee; ecumenical shared ministry. **SELECTED PUBLICATIONS** Coauth, Exploring the yearly Lectionary, Fortress, 91; auth, The First Gospel: An Introduction to Q, Polebridge, 92; auth, Apocalyptic and the Sayings Source Q, in Van Segbroeck, ed, The Four Gospels 1992: Festschrift Frans Neirynck, v 1, Leuven Univ, 92; coauth, Ecumenical Shared Ministry: Bringing Congregations Together From Different Denominations, Alban Inst, 93; auth, Which Was the First Gospel? The Fourth R, 93; auth, Q, in Miller, ed, The Complete Gospels, rev ed, Polebridge, 94; auth, The Literary Unity of Q, in Kloppenborg, ed, The Shape of Q: Signal Essays on the Sayings Gospel, Fortress, 94; auth, Divided Families and Christian Origins, in Piper, ed, The Gospel Behind the Gospels, Brill, 95; coauth, Ecumenical Shared Ministry and the United Methodist Church, General Commission on Christian Unity and Interreligious Concerns, 95; auth, "A Journey Into Our Christian Past," 99; auth, "Jesus Against The Family, in From Quest to Q:Festschrift," James M Robinson, 00. **CONTACT ADDRESS** CHARIS Ecumenical Center, Concordia Col, Minnesota, Moorhead, MN 56562. **EMAIL** jacobson@cord.edu

JACOBSON, ARTHUR J.

PERSONAL Born 03/22/1948, New York, NY, m, 1987, 2 children **DISCIPLINE** LAW **EDUCATION** Harvard Col, BA, 69; Harvard GSAS, PhD, 70; Harvard Law Sch, JD, 74. **CAREER** Asst prof to Max Freund prof, Benjamin N Cardoza Sch of Law, 77-; vis prof, Univ Trento, 98. **RESEARCH** Legal history. **SELECTED PUBLICATIONS** Co-ed, State Limited Liability Company and Partnership Laws, Aspen Law & Business (Englewood Cliffs); co-ed, State Limited Partnership Laws, Prentice Hall Law & Business (Englewood Cliffs); coauth, A Jurisprudence of Crisis, Univ Cal Press (Berkeley), 00; auth, Dynamic Jurisprudence: Rights and Revelation in the Modern Age, Univ Cal Press (Berkeley), forthcoming; coauth, Justice and the Legal System: A Coursebook, Anderson Pub (Cincinnati), 92; auth, "The Game of the Laws," Political Theory (99); auth, "Origins of the Game Theory of Law," Cardozo Law Rev (99); rev, "Murphy's Law," J Law and Soc (99); auth, "Prendere la rivelazione sul serio [Taking Revelation Seriously]," 3 Ars Interpretandi 85 (98); auth, "Luhmann, Niklas," in The Philosophy of Law: An Encyclopedia, ed. Christopher B Gray (NY: Garland Pub, 98); auth, "Taking Responsibility: Law's Relation to Justice and D'Amato's Deconstructive Practice," NW Law Rev (96); auth, "Law and Order," Cardozo Law Rev (96). **CONTACT ADDRESS** Sch of Law, Yeshiva Univ, 55 5th Ave, New York, NY 10003-4301. **EMAIL** ajacobsn@ymail.yu.edu

JACOBSON, DIANE L.

DISCIPLINE OLD TESTAMENT **EDUCATION** Connecticut Col, BA, 70; Columbia Univ/Union Theol Sem, MA, 75, MPhil, 82, PhD, 90. **CAREER** Instr, NY Theol Sem, 80-82; tutor, instr, Union Theol Sem, 76-78, 79; asst prof, 82; assoc prof, 90-; ch, Bibl Div, 93. **MEMBERSHIPS** Mem, Soc Bibl Lit. **SELECTED PUBLICATIONS** Coauth, Beginner's Guide to the Bible, 91; auth, Psalms: A Prayer Tutor, 86. **CONTACT ADDRESS** Dept of Old Testament, Luther Sem, 2481 Como Ave, Saint Paul, MN 55108. **EMAIL** djacobso@luthersem.edu

JACOBSON, PAUL KENNETH

PERSONAL Born 06/21/1946, Bayonne, NJ, m, 1968, 2 children **DISCIPLINE** PHILOSOPHY, INTELLECTUAL HISTORY **EDUCATION** Seton Hall Univ, AB, 67; Duquesne Univ, MA, 70, PhD(philos), 75. **CAREER** Instr philos, St Peter's Col, 70-71; asst prof, Marywood Col, 72-77; assoc prof philos, 77-85, prof philos, 85-, dean, col of arts and sci, 87-98, assoc vp acad affairs, 82-87, dir honors prog, 78-79, registrar, St Ambrose Univ, 77-. **HONORS AND AWARDS** NDEA Fel, 68-70. **MEMBERSHIPS** Am Philos Asn; Soc Phenomenol & Existential Philos; Merleau-Ponty Circle US; Consult/evaluator, 91-, team chemn, 95-, accrditation rev coun, 96-00, North Central Asn of Col and Schools. **RESEARCH** Phenomenology; epistemology; philosophical anthropology. **SELECTED PUBLICATIONS** Auth, Plato's theory of Anamnesis, 66 & Longinus's conception of the sublime, 67, Bayley Rev; One more new botched beginning: Review of Merleau-Ponty's La Prose du Monde, 72 & Dirty work: Gurwitsch on the phenomenological theory of science and constitutive phenomenology, 76, Res Phenomen; The return of Alcibiades: An approach to the meaning of sexuality through the works of Freud and Merlear-Ponty, Philos Today, 78. **CONTACT ADDRESS** Dept Philosophy, St. Ambrose Univ, 518 W Locust St, Davenport, IA 52803-2898. **EMAIL** pjacobsn@saunix.sau.edu

JACOBSON, STEPHEN

DISCIPLINE PHILOSOPHY, EPISTEMOLOGY **EDUCATION** Univ Del, BA, 72; MA, 74; Univ Mich, PhD, 89. **CAREER** Vis asst prof, Univ Fla, 89-92; vis asst prof, Kalamazoo Col, 92-93; vis instr, St Michael's Col, 92-93; vis asst prof, Univ Vt, 93-94, Spring 95; vis asst prof, Dartmouth Col, Fall 94, 95-96; instr, Bloomsburg Univ, 96-97; lectr, Ga State Univ, 97- . **RESEARCH** Hist of philos; philos of mind, lang & sci. **SELECTED PUBLICATIONS** Auth, "Alston on Iterative Foundationalism and Cartesian Epistemology," Can J of Philos vol 22, no 1 (March 92): 133-144; auth, "Internalism in Epistemology and the Internalist Regress," Australasian J of Philos vol 70, no 4 (Dec 92): 415-424; auth, "In Defense of Truth and Rationality," Pacific Philos Q vol 73, no 4 (Dec 92): 335-346; auth, "Skepticism, Mitigated Skepticism, and Contextualism," in Knowledge, Teaching and Wisdom, Philosophical Studies Series, vol 67, eds Keith Lehrer et al (Dordrecht: Kluwer Acad Pubs, 96), 195-205; auth, "Externalism and Action-Guiding Epistemic Norms," Synthese vol 110, no 3 (March 97): 381-397. **CONTACT ADDRESS** Dept of Philos, Georgia State Univ, PO Box 4089, Atlanta, GA 30302-4089. **EMAIL** phlsrj@panther.gsu.edu

JACOBUS, LEE ANDRE
PERSONAL Born 08/20/1935, Orange, NJ, m, 1958, 2 children **DISCIPLINE** ENGLISH, PHILOSOPHY **EDUCATION** Brown Univ, AB, 57, AM, 59; Claremont Grad Sch, PhD(English), 68. **CAREER** Instr, Western Conn State Col, 60-68; PROF ENGLISH, UNIV CONN, 68-. **MEMBERSHIPS** MLA; James Joyce Soc; Milton Soc Am; Am Comt Irish Studies. **RESEARCH** Milton; 17th century English authors; modern Irish literature. **SELECTED PUBLICATIONS** Auth, Thaumaturgike in Paradise Lost, Huntington Libr Quart, 70; Self-knowledge in Paradise Lost, Milton Studies III, 71; Imamu Amiri Baraka: The quest for moral order, In: Modern Black Poets, Prentice, 73; John Cleveland: A Critical Study, Twayne, 75; Sudden Apprehension: Aspects of Knowledge in Paradise Lost, Mouton, 76; Humanities through the Arts, McGraw, 2nd ed, 78; ed, The Longman Anthology of Americn Drama, 82; Improving College Reading, Harcourt, 4th ed (in prep). **CONTACT ADDRESS** Dept of English, Univ of Connecticut, Storrs, 337 Mansfield Rd, Storrs, CT 06269. **EMAIL** jacobus@uconnvm.uconn.edu

JACOBY, SANFORD M.
PERSONAL Born 05/13/1953, New York, NY, m, 1984, 2 children **DISCIPLINE** ECONOMICS **EDUCATION** Univ Penna, AB, 74; Univ Calif - Berkeley, PhD, 81. **CAREER** Prof, 80-, UCLA. **RESEARCH** US Labor, economic & bus hist. **CONTACT ADDRESS** Univ of California, Los Angeles, Los Angeles, CA 90095-1481. **EMAIL** sjacoby@agsm.ucla.edu

JAFFA, HARRY VICTOR
PERSONAL Born 10/07/1918, New York, NY, m, 1942, 3 children **DISCIPLINE** POLITICAL SCIENCE **EDUCATION** Yale Univ, BA, 39; New Sch Social Res, PhD(polit sci), 51. **CAREER** Mem fac, Queens Col, NY, 45-48, City Col New York, 48-49, Univ Chicago, 49-51 & Ohio State Univ, 51-64; prof, 64-71, Henry Salvatori Res Prof Polit Philos, Claremont Men's Col & Claremont Grad Sch, 71-, Ford fac fel, 52-53; Rockefeller fel, 56-57 & 59-60; Guggenheim fel, 61-62; Relm Found fel, 64-65. **MEMBERSHIPS** Winston S Churchill Asn (pres, 69). **RESEARCH** Political philosophy; American government. **SELECTED PUBLICATIONS** Auth, Thomism and Aristotelianism, Univ Chicago, 52 & Greenwood, 79; Crisis of the House Divided, Doubleday, 59 & Univ Wash, 73; coauth, Shakespeare's Politics, Basic Bks, 64; auth, Equality and Liberty, Oxford Univ, 65; The Conditions of Freedom, Johns Hopkins Univ, 75; How to Think About the American Revolution: A Bicentennial Cerebration, Carolina Acad Press, 78. **CONTACT ADDRESS** Dept of Polit Sci, Claremont Graduate Sch, Claremont, CA 91711.

JAINI, PADMANABH S.
PERSONAL Born 10/23/1923, Mangalore, India **DISCIPLINE** LINGUISTICS, SOUTH & SOUTHEAST ASIAN RELIGIONS **EDUCATION** HPT Col, India, BA, 47; BJ Inst Res, Ahmedabad, MA, 49; Vidyodaya Pirivena, Ceylon, Tripitakacarya, 51; Univ London, PhD (Sanskrit Lit) 59. **CAREER** Lectr Sanskrit & Pali, Benaras Hindu Univ, 52-56; Pali & Buddhist Sanskrit, Univ London, 56-64, reader, 65-67; vis lectr Buddhism, Univ Mich, Ann Arbor, 64-65, prof Indic Lang, 67-72; prof Buddhism, Univ Calif, Berkeley, 72-94; prof Emeritus, grad school, 94. **RESEARCH** Pali and Buddhist Sanskrit language and literature; Abhidharma studies; comparative study of Indian religions; Jaina studies. **SELECTED PUBLICATIONS** Auth, "Silonmam be Varsh, Gujarat Vidyasabha, Ahmedabad," 52; auth, "Abhidharmadipa with Vibhasaprabha-vrtti," K.P. Jayaswal Research Institute, Patna, 59; reprinted 77; auth, "Milinda-tika, Pali Text Society," London, 61; auth, "Laghutattvasphota by Amrtacandra," Sanskrit text with English translation, L. D. Institute of Indology Series, No. 62, Ahmedabad, 78; auth, "Saratama: A Panjika on the Astasahasrika-Prajnaparamita by Ratnakarasanti," K. P. Jayaswal Research Institute, Patna, 79; auth, "The Jaina Path of Purification," University of California Press, Berkeley, 79, Reprinted by Motilal Banarsidass, Delhi, 97; auth, "Pannasa-Jataka or Zimme Pannasa (in Burmese Recension), vol I Jatakas 1-25, Pali Text Society, London, 81; auth, "Jaina Sampradaya men Moksa, Avatara our Punarjanma," B. J. Institue of Learning and Research, Ahmedabad, 82 (in Hindi); auth, "Pannasa-Jataka or Zimme Pannasa (in Burmese ecension), vol. II (Jatakas 30-50), Pali Text Society, London, 83; auth, "Apocryphal Birth-Stories (translation of the Pannasa-Jataka), vol. I (with I.B. Horner), Pali Text Society, London, 85. **CONTACT ADDRESS** Dept of South and Southeast Asian Lang & Lit, Univ of California, Berkeley, 7303 Dwinelle Hall, Berkeley, CA 94720-0001.

JAMAR, STEVEN D.
PERSONAL Born 05/11/1953, Ishpeming, MI, m, 1979, 2 children **DISCIPLINE** LAW **EDUCATION** Carleton Col, BA, 75; Hamline Law Sch, JD, 79; Georgetown Univ, LLM, 94. **CAREER** Clinic Instr and Adj Prof, Wm Mitchell Col Law, 86-89; Vis Asst Prof, Univ Baltimore Sch of Law, 89-90; Asst Prof to Prof and Dir, Howard Univ, 91-. **HONORS AND AWARDS** Law Libr of Congress, 00-01; Who's Who in Am; Who's Who in the World; Who's Who in am Law; ALWD Citation Manual Contrib Awd. **MEMBERSHIPS** Asn of Legal Writing Dir; Legal Writing Inst; Am Soc of Intl Law; Wash DC Bar Asn; Minn State Bar Asn; Computer Law Asn; am Bar Asn; LegalX-ML. **RESEARCH** International Human Rights; Intellectual Property Ownership in Professional/Public Partnerships. **SELECTED PUBLICATIONS** Auth, "The Protection of Intellectual Property under Islamic Law," Cap U.L. Rev, 92; auth, "The International Human Right to Health," Southern U.L. Rev, 94; auth, "Accommodating Religion at Work: A Principled Approach to Title VII and Religious Freedom," N.Y.L. Sch L Rev, 96; auth, "This Article has no Footnotes: 1 An Essay on RFRA2 and the Limits of Logic in the Law," Stetson L Rev, 97; auth, "ALWD Citation Manual", Aspen Law & Business, 00; auth, "The Human Right of Access to Legal Information: Using Technology to Advance Transparency and the Rule of Law," forthcoming; auth, "Aristotle Teaches Persuasion: The Psychic connection," Scribes, 01; auth, "A Lawyering Approach to Law and Development," in press. **CONTACT ADDRESS** Sch of Law, Howard Univ, 2900 Van Ness St NW, Washington, DC 20008. **EMAIL** sjamar@law.howard.edu

JAMES, ALLIX BLEDSOE
PERSONAL Born 12/17/1922, Marshall, TX, m, 1945, 2 children **DISCIPLINE** THEOLOGY **EDUCATION** VA Union Univ, AB 1944, MDiv 1946; Union Theol Seminary, ThM 1949, ThD 1957. **CAREER** Third Union Baptist Church, former minister; Mount Zion Baptist Church, former minister; Union Zion Baptist Church, former minister; Virginia Union Univ, instr Biblical studies 1947-50, dean of students 1950-56, dean of sch of theology 1956-70, vice pres 1960-70, pres 1970-79, pres emeritus, 79-85, Chancellor, 85-92; prof emer, 92-. **HONORS AND AWARDS** Alpha Phi Alpha, Beta Gamma Lambda Chapter, Outstanding Achievement Award, 1981; Richmond First Club, Good Government Award, 1985; Metropolitan Business League, MF Manuel Community Service Award, 1991; Fullwood Foods Inc, Exemplary Vision Award, 1992; International Ministers' Wives Association, The Shirley A Hart Award for Global Humanitarian Service, 1992; Honorary Degrees: University of Richmond, LLD, 1971; St Paul's College, DD, 1981. The University Chapel was named in his honor, The Allix B. James Chapel, 1992, Virgina Power Strong Men and Women Excellence in Leadership Award, 00. **MEMBERSHIPS** Nat Conference of Communiity and Justice Inc, board of directors, national executive board; Richmond Gold Bowl Sponsors, co-founder, president, board of directors; Nat Council for America's First Freedom, board of directors; Black History Museum and Cultural Center of Virginia Inc, president, board of trustees; Richmond Tommorrow, education task force, chairman; Leadership Roundtable, founder, chairman, board of directors; Virginia Electric and Power Co., board of directors; Consolidated Bank and Trust Co., board of directors; Am Council of Life Insurance, univ advisory council; Beekne Investment Co. Inc, board of directors; Alpha Phi Alpha Fraternity Inc; Sigma Pi Phi Fraternity Inc, Alpha Beta Boule; Moore Street Baptist Church, board of trustees. First African-American to serve as president of Virginia State Board of Education; Asn of Theological Schools in the US; Nat Conference of Christians and Jews, Virginia Region; first African-American chairman, Richmond Planning Commission; Board of trustees, Virginia Union Univ named the restored Univ Chapel in Coburn Hall, The Allix B James Chapel, 1992; guest of the Government of Republic of Taiwan to explore possiblities for educational cooperation, 76; conferences with European theological educators from Germany, Switzerland, Italy, France, and England, 69; study of higher education in USSR, 73. **SELECTED PUBLICATIONS** Contributing editor, The Continuing Quest; author: Calling a Pastor in a Baptist Church; numerous articles, local and national publications and professional journals; auth, Three Score and Ten Plus Pilgrimage of an African American Education. **CONTACT ADDRESS** Virginia Union Univ, 1500 N Lombardy St, Richmond, VA 23220.

JAMES, BERNARD
DISCIPLINE CONSTITUTIONAL LAW **EDUCATION** Univ MI, BGS, 77, JD, 83. **CAREER** Law clk, Mich Court Appeals, 83-84; lectr, Nat Criminal Justice Inst; prof. **HONORS AND AWARDS** Am jurisp awards. **MEMBERSHIPS** Mem, Am Bar Assn; Nat Org Legal Problems Edu; The Am Sch Bd(s) Assn. **SELECTED PUBLICATIONS** Contrib ed, ABA Preview US Supreme Court Jour; contrib columnist, Nat Law Jour; contrib writer, Sch Safety J. **CONTACT ADDRESS** Sch of Law, Pepperdine Univ, 24255 Pacific Coast Hwy, Malibu, CA 90263.

JAMES, FRANK A., III
DISCIPLINE CHURCH HISTORY **EDUCATION** Oxford Univ, PhD. **CAREER** Instr, Ctr for Medieval and Renaissance Stud, affil Keble Col, Oxford Univ; assoc prof, Reformed Theol Sem. **HONORS AND AWARDS** Transl, ch, Ed Comm of the Peter Martyr Lib. **SELECTED PUBLICATIONS** Auth, Peter Martyr Vermigli: Praedestinatio Dei in the Thought of an Italian Reformer; ed/transl, Selected Works of Peter Martyr Vermigli: Theological Treatises; co-ed, Via Augustini: Augustine in the Later Middle Ages, Renaissance and Reformation; gen ed, Peter Martyr Lib; sr ed, Library of Classical Protestant Theology Texts on CD-ROM; consult ed, The Blackwell Encycl of Medieval, Renaissance and Reformation Christian Thought. **CONTACT ADDRESS** Dept of Church Hist, Reformed Theol Sem, Florida, 1231 Reformation Dr, Oviedo, FL 32765. **EMAIL** fjames@rts.edu

JAMES, FRANK SAMUEL, III
PERSONAL Born 08/10/1945, Mobile, AL, m **DISCIPLINE** LAW **EDUCATION** Campbell Coll, BS 1973; Univ of AL, JD 1978; US Army War College, graduate, 1990. **CAREER** Fed Judge Virgil Pittman, law clerk 1978-80; US Dept of Justice, asst us atty 1980-86; Univ of AL School of Law, prof, asst dean 1986-90; Berkowitz, Lefkovits, Isom and Kushner, partner, 90-. **HONORS AND AWARDS** Bench and bar Legal Hon Soc 1978; Distinguished Alumnus, Campbell University, 1987. **MEMBERSHIPS** Mem Amer Bar Assoc 1978-, AL State Bar 1978-, Birmingham Bar Assoc 1980-; bd of mgmt YMCA of Metro Birmingham 1996-; mem of council Synod of the Mid South 1985-86; moderator, mem of council Birmingham Presbytery 1986; pres of bd 1988-90, chmn of bd, 1991-, Alabama Capital Representation Resource Center 1991-; director, Columbia Theological Seminary, 1991-; trustee, Farrah Law Society, 1990-; trustee, The Presbytery of Sheppards and Lapsley, 1990-98. **SELECTED PUBLICATIONS** Auth, Contingent Fees in Domestic Relations Actions 3 Jrnl of the Legal Prof 209 1978; co-auth, Perspectives on the Evidence Law of Alabama: A Decade of Evolution 1977-87, 40 Alabama Law Review 95, 1988; auth, Protecting Final Judgments: A Critical Overview of Provisional Injunctive Relief in Alabama, 20 Cumberland Law Review 227, 1990. **CONTACT ADDRESS** Berkowitz, Lefkovits, Isom & Kushner, 1600 Southtrust Tower, Birmingham, AL 35203.

JAMES, H. RHETT
PERSONAL Born 12/01/1928, Baltimore, MD, m **DISCIPLINE** EDUCATION, THEOLOGY **EDUCATION** VA Union U, AB 1950; Our Lady of the Lake Coll, MEd 1951; VA Union U, MDiv 1957; TX Christian U, MTh 1961; Harvard Univ Inst of Mgt, 1974; Univ ofIN, Memphis Univ Insts on on Mgt-Commun Servs 1974-75; Univ of TX at Arlington, PhD 1974. **CAREER** Urban Affairs & Community Devel Center, asst prof of soc sci, assoc dir of devel, dir; New Careers for the Handicapped Program Bishop Coll TX, dir, 62-; New Hope Baptist Church TX, pastor, 58-; VA Union Univ, instructor, 55-58; San Antonio School System St Phillips Jr Coll, instructor, 50-55. **HONORS AND AWARDS** Goals for Dallas Commun Serv Aw; OIC Commun Serv Aw; Urban Leag Disting Serv Aw; NKOK Radio Sta Commun Serv Aw; Big Bros Commun Serv Aw; Disting Serv Aw Urban Leag; Trail Blazers Aw; Dllas City Counc Serv Aw. **MEMBERSHIPS** Educ com chmn Dallas NAACP 1961; pres Dallas NAACP 1962; bd of dir TX Counc of Chs; del Pres Com on Equal Employ Opportun; fdr, 1st pres Dallas Frontiers Internat; pres Dallas Dem Men; bd mem Family Guid Ctr; bd mem Am Civ Lib Union; ret bd mem Dallas Urban Leag; bd mem TX Assn of Devlpng Colls 1970-74; bd mem City of Dallas; mem Am Mensa Soc; bd mem N Dallas Am Cancer Soc; mem So Histl Assn; mem Am Assn of Univ Profs; bd mem Am Bapt Conv Chs of the S; mem Sigma Pi Phi & Kappa Alpha Psi Frat. **CONTACT ADDRESS** New Hope Baptist Church, 5002 S Central Expressway, Dallas, TX 75215.

JAMES, MARQUITA L.
PERSONAL Born 11/09/1932, Philadelphia, PA **DISCIPLINE** LAW **EDUCATION** Wilberforce Univ Wilberforce OH, BA 1955; Seton Ahll Univ S Orange NJ, MA 1966; Candidacy NYork Univ, PhD 1974. **CAREER** Nassau Comm Coll Garden City, Long Island NY, assoc prof History 1969-; Wyandanch Schools, Wydandanch NY, chmn 1964-68; Freeport NY, Afro-Amer History curr coor 1968-69. **HONORS AND AWARDS** Listed among black edrs in Black Hist Museum Hempstead LI NY; natl def educ award Tchrs Coll Columbia Univ NY UL,; inst intl educ award Univ of Ghana Legon W Africa 1969; m l kingr jr grad fellow award NY Univ 1968-71. **MEMBERSHIPS** Hist & ldr crea of estab of Afro-Am Hist Soc in Freeport & Long Island NY; activist leader in successful fight to deseg sch buses & discrim prac in Freeport Schls 1968-69; mem Assn Univ Prof Assn Afro-Am Edn; Am Hist Assn; Afro-Am Black Heritage Assn; Cong of Racial Equal; Coun on Interracl Books for Child; Alpha Kappa Alpha Sor; Nat Black Feminist Org; pres Nassau-Suffolk Br Assn for Study of Afro-Am Life & Hist.Univ of TN, asst prof & asst librarian 1973-77; Univ of KY, asst prof of law/law librarian; assoc prof of law/law librarian Univ of KY 1977-82; prof of law/law lib 1982-88; Villanova Univ, prof of law/dir of law library, 1988-95, associate dean for information svcs & professor of law, 1995-. **CONTACT ADDRESS** Dept of Hist and Govt, Nassau Comm Col, 1 Education Dr, Garden City, NY 11530-6793.

JAMES, ROBERT N.
PERSONAL Born 03/20/1931, Denver, CO, m, 1971, 2 children **DISCIPLINE** RELIGIOUS STUDIES **EDUCATION** Empire State Col, SUNY, BA, 75; Greenwich Univ, Hawaii, 96, Greenwich Univ, Ph.D., 00. **CAREER** Retired **RESEARCH** Monistic Theology **CONTACT ADDRESS** 28350 Winthrop Cir, Bonita Springs, FL 34134. **EMAIL** robtnuma@gulfcoast.net

JAMES, SCOTT C.
PERSONAL Born 09/28/1955, Palo Alto, CA, m, 1999 **DISCIPLINE** POLITICAL SCIENCE **EDUCATION** Univ Calif Santa Cruz, BA, 85; Univ Calif Los Angeles, PhD, 92. **CAREER** Asst Prof, Univ Calif Davis, 93-95; Asst Prof, UCLA,

95-. **HONORS AND AWARDS** E.E. Schattschneider Awd, 94. **MEMBERSHIPS** Am Polit Sci Asn; W Polit Sci Asn; Soc Sci Hist Asn; Midwestern Polit Sci Asn. **RESEARCH** American political development; American political institutions. **SELECTED PUBLICATIONS** Auth, "Prelude to Progressivism: Party Decay, Populism, and the Doctrine of 'Free and Unrestricted Competition' in American Antitrust Policy, 1890-1897," Studies in Am Polit Develop, 99; co-auth, "The Political Economy of Voting Rights Enforcement in America's Gilded Age: Electoral College Competition, Partisan Commitment, and the Federal Election Law," Am Polit Sci Rev, 99; auth, "Presidents, Parties, and the State: A Party System Perspective on Democratic Regulatory Choice, 1884-1936," Cambridge Univ Press, 00. **CONTACT ADDRESS** Dept Polit Sci, Univ of California, Los Angeles, Dept Polit Sci, Los Angeles, CA 90095-1472. **EMAIL** scjames@ucla.edu

JAMES, WILLIAM
DISCIPLINE LEGAL RESEARCH **EDUCATION** Morehouse Col, BA, 67; Howard Univ Sch Law, JD, 72; Atlanta Univ Sch Libr Sci, MSLS, 73. **CAREER** Prof, Villanova Univ; dir, Law Libr, 88-; assoc dean, Inf serv, 95-. **MEMBERSHIPS** Asn Amer Law Schools Comt on Libr; bd adv, Legal Reference serv Quart; Amer Asn Law Libraries, served on comt for Placement, Educ, Minorities, Scholarship and grants; chem, Minorities Comt, 85-87; past chep, Scholarship and Nomination Comt, Southeastern Asn Law Librarians **RESEARCH** Legal research. **SELECTED PUBLICATIONS** Auth, Law Libraries Which Offer serv to Prisoners, Am Ass'n of Law Libraries Comt on Law Libr serv to Prisoners, 75; Recommended Collections for Prison Law Libraries, 75;"Legal Reference Materials and Law Library servs, Am Ass'n of Law Libraries Comt on Law Libraries serv to Prisoners, 76; Legal Reference Materials and Law Library servs, U Ken Continuing Legal Educ, 76; contrib, Fundaments of Legal Research, 77; co-contrib, Law and Psychiatry, 79 & Natural Resources and Development, 87. **CONTACT ADDRESS** Law School, Villanova Univ, 800 Lancaster Ave, Villanova, PA 19085-1692. **EMAIL** wjames@law.vill.edu

JAMES, WILLIAM CLOSSON
PERSONAL Born 05/20/1943, Sudbury, ON, Canada, m, 1964, 3 children **DISCIPLINE** RELIGION, ENGLISH LITERATURE **EDUCATION** Queen's Univ, Ont, BA, 65, BD, 68; Univ Chicago, MA, 70, PhD(relig & lit), 74. **CAREER** Lectr, 73-75, asst prof, 75-80, chmn undergrad studies relig, 78-81, Assoc Prof Relig & Lit, Queen's Univ, Ont, 80-, Exec bd mem relig, Can Soc for Study Relig, 75-78; mem bd dirs relig, Can Corp for Studies Relig, 78-; book rev ed, Studies in Relig, 79-. **MEMBERSHIPS** Can Soc for Study Relig; Am Acad Relig. **RESEARCH** Religion and literature; modern Canadian fiction; heroism and the quest in literature; religious meaning of contemporary Canadian culture **SELECTED PUBLICATIONS** Auth, Nature and the Sacred in Canada + Role of Geography and Climate in Shaping a Canadian Identity, Stud in Religion Sciences Religieuses, Vol 0021, 92; auth, "The Canoe trip as Religious Quest;" auth, A Fur Trader's Photographs; auth, Locations of the Sacred: Essays on Religion, Literature, and Canadian Culture, Wilfried Laurier University Press, 98. **CONTACT ADDRESS** Dept of Religious Studies, Queen's Univ at Kingston, Theological Hall, Rm. 414, Kingston, ON, Canada K7L 3N6. **EMAIL** jameswc@post.queensu.ca

JAMROS, DANIEL
PERSONAL Born 03/11/1942, Adams, MA **DISCIPLINE** THEOLOGY **EDUCATION** Vanderbilt, PhD, 86. **CAREER** Assoc Prof, 85-, Canisius College. **MEMBERSHIPS** AAR, HSA, CTS of A, **RESEARCH** Hegel, Catholic theology, philosophy of religion. **SELECTED PUBLICATIONS** Auth, The Human Shape of God, Religion in Hegel's Phenomenology of Spirit, NY Paragon House, 94; art, Hegel on the Incarnation, Unique or Universal, in: Theological Studies, 95; The Appearing God' in Hegel's Phenomenology of Spirit, CLIO, 90; Satisfaction for Sin, Aquinas on the Passion of Christ, in: Irish Theo Qtly, 90; rev, of Philip M. Merklinger, "Philosophy, Theology, and Hegel's Berlin Philosophy of Relig, 1821-1827", (Albany: State Univ of New York Press, 93); rev, Thomas Steinherr, Der Begriff Absoluter Geist in der Philosophie G W Hegels, Erzabtei St Ottilien, EOS Verlag, in: Hegel-Studien, 95; auth, "The Owl of Minerva", 29, (97): 71-84. **CONTACT ADDRESS** Canisius Col, 2001 Main St, Buffalo, NY 14208-1098. **EMAIL** jamros@canisius.edu

JAN, GEORGE POKUNG
PERSONAL Born 01/06/1925, China, m, 1946, 3 children **DISCIPLINE** POLITICAL SCIENCE **CAREER** Vis prof, Political Science, Beijing Univ, 88; asst, assoc prof, and prof, Univ SD, 61-68; prof, Political Science, 68-93; prof Emeritus, Univ Toledo, 93-. **HONORS AND AWARDS** Phi Beta Kappa; Pi Sigma Alpha; Pi Gamma Mu; Phi Kappa Phi; Phi Beta Delta; Honorary res fel, Res Inst of Contemporary China, Beijing Univ, 88-. **MEMBERSHIPS** Am Political Science Asn; Asn for Asian Studies; Am Assoc for Chinese Studies. **RESEARCH** Government, politics and international relations in the Asian-Pacific region, with special interest in China. **SELECTED PUBLICATIONS** Auth, Government of Communist China; International Politics of Asia; the Chinese Commune Experiment; How to Do Business With China; Introduction to Political Science and numerous articles published in professional journals. **CONTACT ADDRESS** 3041 Valleyview Dr, Toledo, OH 43615. **EMAIL** AITJE@aol.com

JANACK, MARIANNE
PERSONAL Born 02/04/1964, Syracuse, NY **DISCIPLINE** PHILOSOPHY **EDUCATION** Colgate Univ, BA, 86; Syracuse Univ, MA, 93, PhD, 96. **CAREER** Instr, Colgate Univ, 92-97; asst prof, Worcester Polytechnic Inst, 97-. **HONORS AND AWARDS** Syracuse Univ, Fel, 88-96; Pembroke Ctr Post-Doctoral Fel, Brown Univ, 2000-01. **MEMBERSHIPS** Am Philos Asn, Soc for Women in Philos, Soc for Phenomenology and Existential Philos, Int Soc for the Hist of Rhetoric. **RESEARCH** Feminist theory, epistemology, moral philosophy. **SELECTED PUBLICATIONS** Auth, "Standpoint Epistemology Without the 'Standpoint'?: An Examination of Epistemic Privilege and Epistemic Authority," Hypatia, Vol 12, no 2 (spring 97); auth, "Rorty on Ethnocentrism and Exclusion," J of Speculative Philos, Vol 12, no 3 (98); coauth with John C. Adams, "Feminist Epistemologies, Rhetorical Traditions, and the Ad Hominem," The Changing Tradition: Women in the History of Rhetoric, Calgary: Univ of Calgary Press (99); auth, "Struggling for Common Ground: Identity Politics and the Challenge to Feminist Politics," Soc Theory and Practice, Vol 25, no 2 (summer 99); auth, "Engenderings: Book Review," Soc Epistemology, Special Issue: Feminist Epistemology (forthcoming); auth, "John Dewey" entry in The Encyclopedia of Postmodernism, ed Charles Windquist and Victor Taylor, Routledge: New York (forthcoming); auth, "opacity" entry in The Encyclopedia of Postmodernism,, ed Charles Long and Victor Taylor, Routledge: New York (forthcoming); auth, "Emotion and Conversion," Am Philos Asn Newsletters: Philos and Feminism, Vol 100, no 1 (forthcoming). **CONTACT ADDRESS** Dept Humanities and Arts, Worcester Polytech Inst, 100 Institute Rd, Worcester, MA 01609-2247. **EMAIL** mjanack@wpi.edu

JANZEN, JOHN GERALD
PERSONAL Born 08/09/1932, Meadow Lake, SK, Canada, m, 1959, 2 children **DISCIPLINE** OLD TESTAMENT **EDUCATION** Univ Sask, BA, 58, LTh, 59; Harvard Univ, PhD, 66. **CAREER** Prof Old Testament, Col Emannuel & St Chad, 65-68; MacAllister-Pettigrew prof Old Testament, Christian Theol Sem, 68-00. **MEMBERSHIPS** Soc Bibl Lit. **RESEARCH** Biblical interpretation. **SELECTED PUBLICATIONS** Auth, Studies in the Text of Jeremiah (Harvard Semitic Monographs, Vol 6), Harvard Univ, 73; Commentaries on Job. 85; Genesis 12-50, 93; Exodus, 97; articles in Catholic Biblical Quart, Harvard Theological Review, Journal of Biblical Literature, Journal of Religion, Journal for the Study of the New Testament, Journal for the Study of the Old Testament, Lexington Theological Quart, Religion and Literature, Semeia, Vetus Testamentum. **CONTACT ADDRESS** PO Box 88267, Indianapolis, IN 46208-0267. **EMAIL** jgjanzen@cts.edu

JARDINE, MURRAY D.
PERSONAL Born 10/14/1954, Regina, Sask, Canada **DISCIPLINE** POLITICAL SCIENCE **EDUCATION** Univ Regina, BSc, 77; Tex Tech Univ, BBA, 83; MA, 85; Duke Univ, PhD, 92. **CAREER** Vis Asst Prof, La State Univ, 90-96; Vis Asst Prof, State Univ of W Ga, 96-97; Asst Prof to Assoc Prof, Auburn Univ, 97-. **MEMBERSHIPS** Am Polit Sci Asn; AM Acad of Relig; Rhetoric Soc of Am. **RESEARCH** Political Theory. **SELECTED PUBLICATIONS** Auth, "Eric Voegelin's Interpretation(s) of Modernity," Rev of Polit, 95; auth, "Sight, Sound, and Epistemology," J of the Am Acad of Relig, 96; auth, Speech and Political Practice, SUNY Press, 98. **CONTACT ADDRESS** Dept Polit Sci, Auburn Univ, 2260 E University Dr, Auburn, AL 36830. **EMAIL** jardimu@mail.auburn.edu

JAROW, E. H. RICK
PERSONAL Born 09/26/1952, New York, NY, m, 1993, 2 children **DISCIPLINE** RELIGION **EDUCATION** Columbia Univ, BA, 81, MA, 84, Mphil, 86; PhD, 91; vis asst prof, Vassar Col, 94-00; vis asst prof, Barnard Col, 93-94. **CAREER** Asst Prof, Rel and Asian, Vassar Col, 94-. **HONORS AND AWARDS** Fulbrigh-Hays Res Fel, 87-88; Foreign Lang Area Studies Fel, 82-86; Roothbert Fund Fel, 84-86; Andrew W. Mellon Post-Doctoral Fel in the Humanities, 91-93; Vassar Col Abbey Fund Fel, 97; Mellon Fel in the Humanities. **MEMBERSHIPS** Int Asn of Lang and Philos. **RESEARCH** Religions of South Asia; The Eastern Romance of Jack Kerouac; Indian Languages and Literatures; The Poetics of Religious Experience **SELECTED PUBLICATIONS** Auth, In Search of the Sacred: A Pilgrimage to Holy Places, Theosophical Publishing House, 86; auth, The Place of R_dh_in Caitanya-Vai__avaite Theology, in Vaisnavism: Contemporary Scholars Discourse on the Gaud_ya Tradition, Folk Books, 93; auth, The Semiotics of Separation: Narratives of Absence in the Bh_gavata-Pur__a, Journal of Vai__ava Studies, 94; auth, Who is V_1m_ki? The Generation of the Indian Epic Tradition, Journal of Vai__ava Studies, 94; auth, Asia and the Oversoul, A review of A. Versluis American Transcendentalism and Asian Religion, Journal of the American Oriental Society, 94; auth, A Note on the Multi-Centered Imagination of the Mah_bh_rata, Journal of Vai__ava Studies, 96; auth, Voyage by the Mind through a Sea of Stars: Hanum_n as a Shamanic Figure in the R_m_ya_a of V_1m_ki, Hanuman Foundation, 97; auth, The p_ra-bhakti of the Gop_s, Journal of Vai__ava Studies, vol 6, 99; auth, The Letter of the Law and the Discourse of Power: Kar_a and Controversy the Mah_-bh_rata, Journal of Vai__ava Studies, vol 7, 99; auth, Freedom in Action: Emerging Paradigms of Right Livelihood, Conscious Living Magazine, 00. **CONTACT ADDRESS** Dept Relig, Vassar Col, 124 Raymond Ave, Box 374, Poughkeepsie, NY 12604-0001. **EMAIL** jarow@vassar.edu

JARRETT, JAMES L.
PERSONAL Born 10/07/1917, Little Rock, AR, m, 1956, 7 children **DISCIPLINE** PHILOSOPHY **EDUCATION** Univ Utah, BS, 39, MS, 40; Univ Mich, PhD, 48. **CAREER** Instr English & speech, Murray High Sch, Utah, 39-40; instr sec educ, Univ Utah, 40-41, 42-43, from instr to prof philos, 43-44, 46-55; regional dir, Great Bks Found, 55-57, pres, 58-59; lectr philos, Univ Mich, 57-58; prof philos & pres, Western Wash State Col, 59-64; PROF EDUC, UNIV CALIF, BERKELEY, 64-, Vis assoc prof philos, Columbia Univ, 51-52; mem, Res Adv Coun, 61-64, chmn, 63-64; assoc dir, Univ Calif Studies Ctr UK & Ireland, 72-74. **MEMBERSHIPS** Am Philos Asn. **RESEARCH** Aesthetics; philosophy of literature and education; logic of language. **SELECTED PUBLICATIONS** **CONTACT ADDRESS** Sch of Educ, Univ of California, Berkeley, 1501 Tolman Hall, Berkeley, CA 94720-1671.

JARRETT, JON
DISCIPLINE PHILOSOPHY **EDUCATION** IA State Univ, BS, 75; Cornell Univ, MS, 77; Univ Chicago, PhD, 83. **CAREER** Assoc prof, Univ IL at Chicago. **RESEARCH** Philos of sci; logic; metaphysics; epistemology. **SELECTED PUBLICATIONS** Auth, Bell's Theorem: A Guide to the Implications, Philos Consequences Quantum, 89. **CONTACT ADDRESS** Philos Dept, Univ of Illinois, Chicago, 601 S Morgan St, MC 267, Chicago, IL 60607. **EMAIL** jarrett@uic.edu

JARVIE, IAN CHARLES
PERSONAL Born 07/08/1937, South Shields, England, m, 1962, 2 children **DISCIPLINE** PHILOSOPHY, ANTHROPOLOGY **EDUCATION** Univ London, BS, 58, PhD(philos), 61. **CAREER** Lectr philos, Univ Hong Kong, 62-66; chmn dept, 76-79, PROF PHILOS, YORK UNIV, 67-. **MEMBERSHIPS** Royal Anthrop Inst; Brit Soc Philos Sci; Soc Cinema Studies. **RESEARCH** Philosophy of the social sciences; anthropological theory; movies. **SELECTED PUBLICATIONS** Auth, The Postwar Economic Foreign Policy of the American Film Industry: Europe 1945-1950 in David Ellwood and Rob Kroes eds., Hollywood in Europe, Experiences of Cultural Hegemony, Amsterdam: VU University Press, (1994): pp. 154-75; auth, The Justificationist Roots of Relativism, and "Reply" in Charles M. Lewis, ed., Relativism and Religion, London: Macmillan, (1995): pp. 52-70 and 125-28; auth, Popper, Sir Karl, in Edward Craig, ed., The Routledge Encyclopedia of Philosophy, London: Routledge, Volume 7, (1998), pp. 533-40; auth, Free Trade as Cultural Threat: American film and tv exports in the post-war period, in Geoffrey Nowell-Smith and Steven Ricci, eds., Hollywood and Europe, Economics, Culture, National Identity 1948-95, London: BFI, (1998), PP. 34-46; auth, Creativity, in Michael J. Kelly, ed., Encyclopedia of Aeshetics, New York: Oxford Unviersity Press, Volume I, pp. 456-59; auth, Popper's Contribution to the Social Sciences, in a volume of lectures to be published in Vienna; auth, National Cinema: A Theoretical Assessment, in a volume edited by Matte Hjort and Scott Mackenzie, Cinema and Nation: Interdisciplinary Approaches to Nationalism and Nation Identity, Routledge; auth, Working Rationality and the Reasonable of Dogmatism in David Johnson and Christina Erneling, eds., The Mind as Scienticic Object: Brain and Culture, Oxford University Press. **CONTACT ADDRESS** Dept of Philos, York Univ, 4700 Keele St, S428 Ross Bldg, Toronto, ON, Canada M3J 1P3. **EMAIL** jarvie@yorku.ca

JARVIS, ROBERT M.
PERSONAL Born 10/17/1959, New York, NY, m, 1989 **DISCIPLINE** LAW **EDUCATION** Northwestern Univ, BA, 80; Univ Penn, JD, 83; New York Univ, LLM, 86. **CAREER** Assoc, Haight, Gardner, Poor & Havens, 83-85; assoc, Baker & McKenzie, 85-87; Asst prof, assoc prof, prof, Nova Southeastern Univ, 87-. **MEMBERSHIPS** MLA of US; SALI. **RESEARCH** Admiralty law; art law; international law; legal ethics; sports law; travel and leisure law. **SELECTED PUBLICATIONS** Auth, Sports Law: Cases and Materials, West, 99; auth, Prime Time Law, Carolina Acad Press, 98. **CONTACT ADDRESS** Law Ctr, Nova Southeastern Univ, Fort Lauderdale, 3305 College Ave, Fort Lauderdale, FL 33314-7721. **EMAIL** jarvisb@nsu.law.nova.edu

JASANOFF, SHEILA S.
PERSONAL Born 02/15/1944, Calcutta, India, m, 1968, 2 children **DISCIPLINE** LAW; SCIENCE & TECHNOLOGY POLICY **EDUCATION** Harvard Univ, AB, 64, PhD, 73, JD, 76; Univ Bonn, MA, 66. **CAREER** Assoc, Bracken Selig & Baram, 76-78; res asst to sr res asst, 78-84, assoc prof, 84-89, prof, 90-98, Cornell Univ, 78-98; prof, Harvard Univ, 98-; res scholar, Italy, Rockefeller Found, 96; vis prof, Yale Univ, 90-91; vis scholar, Oxford Univ, Wolfson College, 96; vis prof,

Harvard Univ, Kennedy School, 95; vis prof, Kyoto Univ, Japan 99. **HONORS AND AWARDS** Distinguished Achievement Awd, Soc Risk Anal, 92; Don K Price Book Awd, 98. **MEMBERSHIPS** Mass Bar; Amer Asn Advan Sci; Soc Stud Sci; Sigma XI; Am Political Science Assoc; New York Acad of Sciences. **RESEARCH** Law, science, and technology; Science and public policy; Comparative politics of science and technology. **SELECTED PUBLICATIONS** Coauth, Controlling Chemicals, Cornell Univ Press, 85; auth, Risk Management and Political Culture, Russell Sage Foundation, 86; auth, The Fifth Branch: Science Advisers as Policymakers, Harvard Univ Press, 90; ed, Learning From Disaster: Risk Management After Bhopal, Univ Penn Press, 94; coed, Handbook of Science and Technology Studies, Sage Publ, 95; auth, Science at the Bar: Law, Science, and Technology in America, Harvard Univ Press, 95; ed, Comparative Science and Technology Policy, Cheltenham Gos UK, 97; coauth, Conversations with the Community: AAAS at the Millennium, Science, 97; Written 70 articles and book chapters and more than 2 dozen reviews. **CONTACT ADDRESS** John F Kennedy School of Govt, Harvard Univ, 79 John F. Kennedy St, Cambridge, MA 02138. **EMAIL** sheila_jasanoff@harvard.edu

JAY, STEWART
PERSONAL Born 06/27/1950, Havre, MT **DISCIPLINE** LAW, PHILOSOPHY **EDUCATION** Georgetown Univ, AB, 73; Harvard Univ, JD, 76. **CAREER** Law clerk to Judge George L Hart Jr, US Dist Ct, Washington, DC, 76-77 & Chief Justice Warren Burger, US Supreme Ct, 77-78; asst prof law, Univ NC, 78-80; ASSOC PROF LAW, UNIV WASH, 81-, Vis Prof, Sch Law, Univ Tex, 80. **RESEARCH** Philosophy of law; Federal jurisdiction; civil procedure. **SELECTED PUBLICATIONS** Auth, Minimum contacts as a unified theory of personal jurisdiction, Univ NC Law Rev, 1/81. **CONTACT ADDRESS** Sch of Law, Univ of Washington, 1100 N E Campus Pky, Seattle, WA 98105-617. **EMAIL** smj@u.washington.edu

JEAL, ROY R.
PERSONAL Born 06/28/1952, Vancouver, BC, Canada, m, 1972, 3 children **DISCIPLINE** BIBLICAL STUDIES **EDUCATION** Univ Sheffield, PhD, 90. **CAREER** Assoc prof, William & Catherine Booth Coll, 95-. **MEMBERSHIPS** Can Soc of Bibl Studies; Soc of Bibl Lit. **RESEARCH** New Testament; Paul the Apostle; Critical Method. **SELECTED PUBLICATIONS** Auth, A Strange Style of Expression, Ephesians 1:23, Filologia Neotestamentaria, 97. **CONTACT ADDRESS** William and Catherine Booth Col, 447 Webb Pl, Winnipeg, MB, Canada R3B 2P2. **EMAIL** jeal@mb.sympatico.ca

JEFFERS, CLIFTON R.
PERSONAL Born 02/08/1934, Roxboro, NC, m **DISCIPLINE** LAW **EDUCATION** TN State Univ, AB (magna cum laude) 1956; Hastings Coll Law Univ CA, JD 1964. **CAREER** State of CA, state deputy atty, 64-69; US Dept HUD, reg admin, 69-76; State of CA, chief asst state pub defender, 76-84; James & Jeffers, Sr Partner, currently. **HONORS AND AWARDS** Outstanding Pres Awd NAACP 1967, 1969; Amer Jurisprudence Awd; US Dept HUD Equal Empl Oppt Awd; US Dept HUD Cert of Fair Housing Achvmt; NAACP Meritorious Serv Awds; guest lectr in Criminology Univ of CA Berkeley; Outstanding Performance Awd HUD; commendations San Francisco bd of supervisors; Certificate of Honor San Francisco bd of supervisors; guest lecturer Stanford Univ Law School; guest lecturer, Univ of Southern CA School of Law. **MEMBERSHIPS** Mem Natl, CA, San Francisco Bar Assns; Charles Houston Bar Assn; bd of dir Bar Assn of SF 1984-; bd dirs Lawyers Club of San Francisco 1981-82; mem Amer Judicature Soc; pres SF NAACP 1966-69; bd dir Amer Civil Liberties Union of No CA 1969-73; SF Coun of Chs 1967-72; SF Econ Oppt Coun 1967-68; founding president William Hastie Lawyers Assn; bd dir Frederick Douglas Haynes Gardens; gen counsel 3rd Baptist Ch; bd dir CA Rural Legal Assistance Found; founding mem San Francisco Black Leadership Forum; trustee 3rd Bapt Ch; bd dir NAACP; bd of dir First District Appellate Project; co-founder, State Bar Standing Comm on Legal Services to Criminal Defendants; mem, CA Assn of Black Lawyers; co-founder and dir Third Baptist Gardens, Inc.; mem Afro-Amer Agenda Council. **CONTACT ADDRESS** James & Jeffers, 870 Market St, Ste 1200, San Francisco, CA 94102.

JEFFERSON, M. IVORY
PERSONAL Born 09/10/1924, Logan, WV, w **DISCIPLINE** LAW, THEOLOGY **EDUCATION** Attended, Univ of So CA, Univ of Manila; Emmanus Bible Sch, grad; Robert H Terrell Sch of Law, LLB LLD 1950. **CAREER** Manpower Commn & Housing Div of Newport News Ofc of Human Affrs, consult in field of pastoral counseling; Sixth Mt Zion Baptist Temple, Hampton, VA, pastor, 66-96, pastor emeritus, 96; Richmond Virginia Seminary, professor of systematic theology, 90-. **HONORS AND AWARDS** Authority in fields of pastoral counseling, taxation and domestic relations. **MEMBERSHIPS** Admitted to VA Bar 1951; admitted to US Supreme Ct Bar 1956; licensed & ordained in Gospel Ministry 1961 1963; moderator Tidewater Peninsula Bapt Assn; legal adv Progressive Natl Baptist Conv; mem validating Comm for the Fund of Renewal Amer Bapt Ch Inc; consult Office of Offender Aid & Restoration Newport News; chairman, Riverside Regional Medical Center Clergy Relations, 1990-; board member, Peninsula AIDS Foundation, 1988-; member, Peninsula Crime Line, 1988-; Peninsula Aids Foundation, chairman of bd, 1994-; Peninsula Crime Line, pres, 1995-. **CONTACT ADDRESS** Sixth Mt Zion Baptist Temple, 2003 Kecoughtan Rd, Hampton, VA 23661.

JEFFREY, RICHARD C.
PERSONAL Born 08/05/1926, Boston, MA, m, 1955, 2 children **DISCIPLINE** PHILOSOPHY **EDUCATION** Univ Chicago, MA, 52; Princeton Univ, PhD(philos), 58. **CAREER** Asst prof elec engr, Mass Inst Technol, 59-60; asst prof philos, Stanford Univ, 60-64; Vis mem math, Inst Advan Studies, 63; vis assoc prof philos, Princeton Univ, 64; assoc prof, City Col New York, 64-67; prof, Univ Pa, 67-74; PROF PHILOS, PRINCETON UNIV, 74-. **MEMBERSHIPS** Am Philos Asn; Asn Symbolic Logic; Philos Sci Asn; Am Acad Arts & Scis. **RESEARCH** Decision theory; probability theory; logic. **SELECTED PUBLICATIONS** Auth, The Logic of Decision, 65 & 82 & Formal Logic: Its Scope and Limits, 67, 81, 91, McGraw; co-ed (with Rudolf Carnap), Studies in Inductive Logic and Probability, Vol 1, 71, Vol 2, 80; coauth, Computability and Logic, Cambridge Univ, 74, 80, 89; Probability and the Art of Judgment, 92. **CONTACT ADDRESS** Dept of Philosophy, Princeton Univ, Princeton, NJ 08544. **EMAIL** dickjeff@princeton.edu

JEGSTRUP, ELSEBET
PERSONAL Born 05/17/1937, Copenhagen, Denmark **DISCIPLINE** POLITICAL PHILOSOPHY **EDUCATION** Loyola Univ Chicago, PhD, 92. **CAREER** Assoc prof of Philos, Augusta State Univ, 93-. **MEMBERSHIPS** Am Philos Asn; Soc Phenomenol & Existential Philos; Int Asn Philos & Lit; Kierkegaard Soc. **RESEARCH** Kierkegaard; Political philosophy; Contemporary continental philosophy; Plato. **SELECTED PUBLICATIONS** Auth A Questioning of Justice: Kierkegaard, the Postmodern Critique and Political Theory, Political Theory, 95; Kieregaard on Tragedy: the Aporias of Interpretation, Philos Today, 96; rev Kieregaard in Post/Modernity, Tchg Philos, 98; rev Becoming a Self: A Reading of Kierkegaard's Concluding Unscientific Postscript, Tchg Philos, 98. **CONTACT ADDRESS** Dept of Polit Sci & Philos, Augusta State Univ, Augusta, GA 30904. **EMAIL** jegstrup@aug.edu

JENEMANN, ALBERT HARRY
PERSONAL Born 08/16/1927, Philadelphia, PA **DISCIPLINE** PHILOSOPHY **EDUCATION** Spring Hill Col, AB, 54; Boston Col, STL, 61; Gregorian Univ Rome, PhL, 67, PhD(philos), 69. **CAREER** Instr math, Loyola High Sch, Baltimore, Md, 54-57, instr philos, Loyola Col, Baltimore, Md, 62-63; from instr to asst prof, Wheeling Col, 63-66, from asst prof to assoc prof, 69-74, super, Jesuit Commun, 70-74, chmn dept, 73-74; assoc prof philos, St Joseph's Univ, PA, 74-, chm dept philos, 74-80; ordained Jesuit priest, 60; mem bd trustees, Loyola Col, Md, 72-78 & Wheeling Col, 74-82; Ethics Comm, St Agnes Hosp, Philadelphia, 76-; ed, Jesuit Philos Asn Ann Proc, 77-80; dir Faith-Justice Inst, 80-83; VP Student Life, 85-89. **HONORS AND AWARDS** Alpha Sigma Nu (Honorary), 82; Barbelin Awd, St Joseph's Univ, 86; Greek Advisor of the Year, St Joseph's Univ, 97, 99. **MEMBERSHIPS** Am Cath Philos Asn (pres, Philadelphia Chap, 80-81); Am Philos Asn; Jesuit Philos Asn (secy-treas, 77-80, pres, 93-94). **RESEARCH** Medical ethics; French existentialism; contemporary scholasticism. **SELECTED PUBLICATIONS** Auth, The Political Freedom of John Stuart Mill, Gregorian Univ, 69; ed, An Institutional Profile of Wheeling College (2 vols), Wheeling Col, 71; co-ed, Hunger and the American Conscience, St Joseph's Col, 76; auth, Philosophy and the Right to Food, Int Symp Hunger, 8/76; auth, Medical Decisions: Ethical and Economic Dimensions, Quality Assurance and Utilization Rev, Feb 87; Multiple Pregnancy, Confidentiality, Discontinuing Treatment, etc, Proc JPA, Feb 95; coauth, Application of Medical and Surgical Interventions Near the End of Life, J of Am Col of Cardiology, April 98; auth, "Informed Consent: What It Means to Physicians and Patients," Astro News, 99; auth, "Patient Confidentiality: Rights, Responsibilities," Astro News, 99. **CONTACT ADDRESS** Saint Joseph's Univ, 5600 City Ave, Philadelphia, PA 19131-1395. **EMAIL** ajeneman@sju.edu

JENKINS, JOHN
DISCIPLINE PHILOSOPHY **EDUCATION** Univ Notre Dame, BA; Univ Oxford, DPhil. **CAREER** Assoc prof, Univ Notre Dame, 90- . **HONORS AND AWARDS** Lilly Teaching fel, 93. **RESEARCH** Medieval philosophy. **SELECTED PUBLICATIONS** Auth, Knowledge and Faith in Thomas Aquinas, Cambridge Univ Press. **CONTACT ADDRESS** Dept Philos, Univ of Notre Dame, 124 Corby Hall, Notre Dame, IN 46556.

JENSEN, DEBRA J.
PERSONAL Born 07/29/1953, Wetaskiwin, AB, Canada, 2 children **DISCIPLINE** PHILOSOPHY OF RELIGION **EDUCATION** Univ Calgary, BA, 86, MA, 89; Univ Toronto, PhD, 95. **CAREER** Sessional instr, Relig Stud, Univ Calgary, 93-96; Tenurable Instr, Relig Stud, Mount Royal Col, 96-; Religious Stud Coord, Dept of Humanities, Mt Royal Col, 96-. **HONORS AND AWARDS** Judith Sloman Mem Awd Womens Stud & Eng, Univ Calgary, 84 & 85; Lizzie Arthur Russell Theosophical Scholar, 87-88; Grad Asst Res Univ Calgary, 88-89; Special Entrance fel, 90; Soc Sci & Hum Res Coun Can Doctoral fel, 90-93; Soc Sci & Hum Res Can Post-doctoral fel, 95-96; Teaching Ecellence Awd, Mount Royal Col, 99. **MEMBERSHIPS** Am Acad Relig; Can Soc Stud Relig; Gender Inst-Univ Calgary; Mount Royal Col Fac Asn; Asn Transpersonal Psychol; Soc Phenomenol & Existentialist Philos. **RESEARCH** Nature of religion, especially philosophy and psychology of religion; religious experience, especially mysticism; women and religion. **SELECTED PUBLICATIONS** Auth, "Soteriology From a Christian and Hindu Perspective," Journal of Dharma, Vol. XIV, No. 4, (89): 353-365; auth, "Self, Identity and Gender in the Life and Work of Simone Weil," Grail: An Ecumenical Journal, Vol. 11, Issue 2, 96; auth, "Florence Nightingale's Mystical Vision and Social Action," Scottish Journal of Religious Sutides," Vol. 19, No. 1, (98): 69-81. **CONTACT ADDRESS** Humanities Dept, Mount Royal Col, 4825 Richard Rd SW, Calgary, AB, Canada T3E 6K6. **EMAIL** djensen@mtroyal.ab.ca

JENSEN, GORDON A.
PERSONAL Born 02/09/1956, Camrose, AB, Canada, m, 1979, 2 children **DISCIPLINE** THEOLOGY **EDUCATION** Univ Alberta, BA, 80; Lutheran Theol Sem SK, MDiv, 84; St Michael's Coll Toronto, PhD, 92. **CAREER** Pastor, St Olaf Lutheran Church, Swift Current Can, 84-88; PASTOR, Armene Lutheran Parish, Armena, Can, 92-. **HONORS AND AWARDS** Governor Gold Medal at Univ of St Michael's Coll, 92. **MEMBERSHIPS** AAR; Can Soc for the Study of Rel; Can Theol Soc. **RESEARCH** Luther; Contextual Theologies. **SELECTED PUBLICATIONS** Auth, The Christology of Luther's Theology of the Cross, Consesus: A Can Lutheran J of Theol, 97; A Reluctant Denomination, Practice of Ministry in Can, 98; At a Fork in the Road: Potential Paths for the Church in the 21st Century, Consesus: A Can Lutheran J of Theol, forthcoming; coauth, The Story of Jesus, 93. **CONTACT ADDRESS** Box 7, Armena, AB, Canada T0B 0G0. **EMAIL** alparish@telusplanet.net

JENSEN, RONALD H.
PERSONAL Born 08/02/1939, Oakland, CA, m, 1992 **DISCIPLINE** LAW **EDUCATION** Yale Univ, AB, 61; Harvard Law School, LLB, 64. **CAREER** Lecturer, SUNY, 87-88; Prof, Pace Univ, 88-; Visiting Prof, Washington and Lee School of Law, 00. **HONORS AND AWARDS** Phi Beta Kappa. **MEMBERSHIPS** Am Bar Asn, N Y State Bar Asn, Westchester County Bar Asn. **RESEARCH** Income and Transfer fax issues. **SELECTED PUBLICATIONS** Auth, "The Estate and Gift Tax Effects of Selling a Remainder: Have D'Ambrosio, Wheeler and Magnin changed the Rules?," Fla Tax Review, 99; auth, "Schneer v. Commissioner: continuing confusion Over the Assignment of Income Doctrine and personal Service Income," Fla Tax Review, 93; auth, "Reflections on United States v. Leona Helmsley: Should 'Impossibility' be a Defense to Attempted Income Tax Evasion," Va Tax Review, 93; auth, "Of Form and Substance: Tax-Free Incorporation and Other Transactions Under Section 351," Va Tax Review, 91; co-auth, "The American Bar Association and the Supreme Court - Old Wine in a New Bottle?," Law Review, 70; rev, of "Federal Income Taxation of Estates and Trusts," by M. Carr Ferguson et al, Law Review, 71. **CONTACT ADDRESS** School of Law, Pace Univ, White Plains, 78 N Broadway, White Plains, NY 10603-3710. **EMAIL** rjensen@law.pace.edu

JENSEN, TIM
PERSONAL Born Edmore, MI, m, 2 children **DISCIPLINE** RELIGIONS OF ASIA **EDUCATION** Dana Col, BA, 66;Univ Chicago, MA, 70, PhD, 76. **CAREER** Instr, Mary Washington Col, 72-78; instr, Sturt Col of Advan Educ, Adelaide, S Australia, 78-82; instr, Univ Nebr, Omaha. **HONORS AND AWARDS** Off of Educ grant, 73. **RESEARCH** Christianity. **SELECTED PUBLICATIONS** Published in the areas of Hinduism and Guddhism; published an article on Danish immigration to the U.S. and Canada. **CONTACT ADDRESS** Univ of Nebraska, Omaha, Omaha, NE 68182.

JERIN, ROBERT A.
DISCIPLINE LAW AND JUSTICE **EDUCATION** Univ New Haven, BS; FL State Univ, MS; Sam Houston State Univ, PhD, 87 **CAREER** Fac, N Ga Col, Salem State Col, and Appalachian State Univ; chr Law and Justice Dept, Endicott Col. **RESEARCH** Restorative justice and crime prevention. **SELECTED PUBLICATIONS** Auth, articles in the American Journal of Police and Criminal Justice Policy Review; chapters published in edited volumes on Media and Crime, Crime in the 21st Century, Crime Victims Services and the Juvenile Justice System. **CONTACT ADDRESS** Endicott Col, 376 Hale St, Beverly, MA 01915.

JERVIS, ROBERT
DISCIPLINE INTERNATIONAL AFFAIRS **EDUCATION** Oberlin Col, BA, 62; Univ Calif-Berkeley, PhD, 68. **CAREER** Asst prof, harvard Univ, 68-74; prof, UCLA, Polit Sci, 74-80; PROF, COLUMBIA UNIV, INT AFFAIRS. **SELECTED PUBLICATIONS** The Meaning of Nuclear Revolution, Cornell Univ Press, 89; System Effects: Complexity in Political and Social Life, Princeton Univ Press, 97. **CONTACT ADDRESS** Dept Polit Sci, Columbia Univ, New York, NY 10027.

JESSE, JENNIFER G.
PERSONAL Born 01/19/1959, Akron, OH, m, 1991 **DISCIPLINE** RELIGIOUS STUDIES **EDUCATION** Kent State Univ, BA, 79; Butler Univ, MA, 87; Christian Theol Sem, MDiv, 87; Univ Chicago, PhD, 97. **CAREER** Asst prof of Relig, Truman State Univ, 00. **MEMBERSHIPS** Am Acad of Relig; Highlands Inst for Am Relig and Philos Thought. **RESEARCH** Postliberal theology; William Blake. **SELECTED PUBLICATIONS** Auth, "Radical Empiricism and the Holographic Model of Reality," 97; "Postliberal Theology in the Valley of Dry Bones," in Encounter, 97; "Mythic Logic: Theological Implications of a Melandean Epistemology," 93; "A Process Perspective of Revelation: A Nonfoundational Epistemology," in Encounter, 87. **CONTACT ADDRESS** Social Science, Truman State Univ, 100 East Normal, Kirksville, MO 63501-4221. **EMAIL** jgjesse@truman.edu

JIAO, ALLAN
DISCIPLINE JUSTICE **EDUCATION** Lewis and Clark Col, MA, 91; Rutgers Univ, PhD, 96. **CAREER** Seton Hall Univ, 94; Rowan Univ, 95-. **MEMBERSHIPS** Acad of Criminal Justice Sci. **RESEARCH** Police Studies, Public Policy, Public Ethics, Violence, Evaluation, International/Comparative Studies. **SELECTED PUBLICATIONS** Auth, Police Auditing, Charles C. Thomas, (Springfield, IL), 99. **CONTACT ADDRESS** Dept Law and Justice, Rowan Univ, 201 Mullica Hill Rd, Glassboro, NJ 08028. **EMAIL** jiao@rowan.edu

JICK, LEON ALLEN
PERSONAL Born 10/04/1924, St. Louis, MO, m, 1959, 4 children **DISCIPLINE** JEWISH HISTORY **EDUCATION** Washington Univ, BA, 47; Hebrew Union Col, MA, 54; Columbia Univ, PhD(Am immigration hist), 73. **CAREER** Asst prof, 66-69, dean col, 69-71, dir contemp Jewry, Inst for Jewish Life, 71-73, prof, 69-80, Schneider Prof Am Jewish Studies, Brandeis Univ, 80-, Trustee, Boston Hebrew Col, 72-76. **MEMBERSHIPS** Asn for Jewish Studies (pres, 70-72); Am Jewish Hist Soc; Inst for Contemp Jewry, Jerusalem; Acad Jewish Studies; Boston Hebrew Col. **RESEARCH** American Jewish history, Holocaust **SELECTED PUBLICATIONS** Auth, The Teaching of Judaism in American Universities, 70; The American system of the Synogogue, 74; Uses and Abuse of the Holocaust in the American Jewish Public, Yad Vashbein Annual XIII, 81; The Reformation of Zionism, 97; Method in Madness - An Analysis of for the Nazi Extermination Policy, Modern Jewish Thought, 90; The Transformation of Jewish Social Work, Journal of Jewish Communal Service, Winter, Spring, 98-99; Wise, Isaac, Meyer--Shaping American Judaism, Amer Jewish Arch, Vol 0046, 94; Comments on the Washington Hebrew Congregation Article--Response, Amer Jewish Hist, Vol 0084, 96. **CONTACT ADDRESS** Near Eastern and Judaic Studies, Brandeis Univ, 415 South St, Waltham, MA 02454. **EMAIL** mljick@aol.com

JIH, LUKE
PERSONAL Born 10/08/1955, Taipei, Taiwan, s, 1 child **DISCIPLINE** RELIGION, PHILOSOPHY **EDUCATION** Nat Chengchi Univ, BA, 78, MA, 81; Temple Univ, PhD, 2000. **CAREER** Instr, Univ Fu-shin Gwang, 83-88; instr, Temple Univ, 91-94; instr, Manor Col, 91-2000. **HONORS AND AWARDS** Manor Jr Col: Employee Awd, 97, Best Col Teachers Awd, 98, Presidential Awd, 98. **RESEARCH** Comparative religion & philosophy. **SELECTED PUBLICATIONS** auth, The Tao of Jesus, Penlise Press (98). **CONTACT ADDRESS** Dept Liberal Arts, Manor Junior Col, 700 Fox Chase Rd, Jenkintown, PA 19046-3319. **EMAIL** LukeJih@freei.net

JINDRA, MICHAEL
PERSONAL Born 06/29/1962, Manitowoc, WI, m, 1997, 1 child **DISCIPLINE** ANTHROPOLOGY, SOCIOLOGY, RELIGION **EDUCATION** Univ Wis Madison, ABA, 84; MA, 91; PhD, 97. **CAREER** Prof, Bethany Luterhan Col, 97-; dir, Ylvisakor Center for Personal and Pub Responsibility, 99-. **MEMBERSHIPS** Am Anthrop Assoc. **RESEARCH** Religion and popular culture, Africa, public policy. **SELECTED PUBLICATIONS** Auth, "Star Trek Fandom as a Religious Phenomenon", Sociol of Relig, 55.1 (94): 27-51; auth, "Star Trek to Me is a Way of Life: Fan Expressions Star Trek Philosophy", in Star Trek and Sacred Ground: Essays on Star Trek, Religion and Popular Culture, eds Jennifer Porter and Carcee McLaren, SUNY Pr, 99; auth, "It's About Faith in Our Future: Star Trek Fandom as Cultural Religion", in Religion and Popular Culture in America, eds Jeffrey Mahan and Bruce Forbes, Univ of Calif Pr, 00. **CONTACT ADDRESS** Dept Soc Sci, Bethany Lutheran Col, 700 Luther Dr, Mankato, MN 56001. **EMAIL** mjindra@blc.edu

JOBES, KAREN H.
PERSONAL Born 07/02/1952, Trenton, NJ, m, 1980 **DISCIPLINE** BIBLICAL STUDIES **EDUCATION** Westminster Theol Sem, Philadelphia, PhD, 95. **CAREER** Assoc Prof of New Testament Studies, Westmont Col, 96-. **HONORS AND AWARDS** IOSCS Awd for Outstanding Paper in Septuagint Res, 95. **MEMBERSHIPS** Inst for Biblical Res; Soc of Biblical Lit; Int Org for Septuagint and Cognate Studies; Evangelical Theol Soc. **RESEARCH** Septuagint; New Testament; biblical Greek. **SELECTED PUBLICATIONS** Auth, Distinguishing the Meaning of Greek Verbs in the Semantic Domain for 'Worship' in Biblical Words and their Meaning: An Introduction to Lexical Semantics, by Moises Silva, 2nd ed, Zondervan, 94; A Comparative Syntactic Analysis of the Greek Versions of Daniel: A Test Case for New Methodology, BIOSCS 28, fall 95 (recipient of the 1995 IOSCS Int award); For Such a Time As This: A Defining Moment in Christian Ministry, Faith and Mission 14, fall 96; The Alpha-Text of Esther: Its Character & Relationship to the Masorectic Text, SBLS 153: Atlanta: Scholars Press, 96; How an Assassination Changed the Greek Texts of Esther, ZAW, 98; NIV Application Commentary: Esther, Zondervan, 99; coauth, Invitation to the Septuagint, Bakern in press; auth, First Peter, BECNT, Baker, forthcoming. **CONTACT ADDRESS** Dept of Relig Studies, Westmont Col, 955 La Paz Road, Santa Barbara, CA 93108. **EMAIL** jobes@westmont.edu

JOBLING, DAVID
PERSONAL Born 09/03/1941, England, m, 1981, 2 children **DISCIPLINE** JEWISH BIBLE, OLD TESTAMENT **EDUCATION** First Class in Divinity Tripos Part II, BA, 63; Cambridge Univ, MA, 67; Union Theol Sem, PhD, 72. **CAREER** Asst prof, Louisville Presbyterian Theol Sem, 70-74; assoc prof, Louisville Presbyterian Theol Sem, 74-77; vis ssoc prof, Union Theol Sem, 77-78; prof, St. Andrews Col, 78-; ch, Univ of Saskatchewan, 78-. **HONORS AND AWARDS** Pres, Can Soc of Bibl Stud, 92-93. **MEMBERSHIPS** Soc of Biblical Lit, 71-; Am Academy of Relig, 73-; Canadian Soc for Biblical Studies, 79-; Soc for Old Testament Study, 80-; Steering Comt member, 95-; the Bible and Culture Collective, 90-. **RESEARCH** Idealogical readings of the Bible. **SELECTED PUBLICATIONS** Auth, The Sense of Biblical Narrative: Structural Studies in the Hebrew Bible, Vol I, Sheffield: Sheffield Academic Press, 78; auth, The Sense of Biblical Narrative: structural Studies in the Hebrew Bible, Vol II, Sheffield: Sheffield Acdemic Press, 86; co-ed, "Ruth Finds a Home: Canon, Politics, Method,' The New Literary Criticism and the Hebrew Bible, (ed. J.C. Exum and D.J.A. Clines, Sheffield: Sheffield Academic Press): 125-39; auth, "Hannah's Desire," CSBS Bulletin 53, (93): 19-32; auth, "Transference and Tact in Biblical studies: A Psychological Approach to Gerd Theissens Psychological Aspects of Pauline Theoogy," Studies in Religion 22, (94): 451-62; auth, "Structuralist Criticism: The Text's World of Meaning," Judges and Method, Minneapolis: Frotress, (95): 91-118; coauth, The Bible and Cultrue Collective, The Postmodern Bible, New Haven: Yale Univ Press, 95; coauth, "Reading as a Philistine: The Ancient and Modern History of a Cultural Slur," Ethnicity and the Bible, Leiden: Brill, (96): 381-417; auth, "Experiencing the Many: A Response to Camp, Mack, and Wimbush," Power, Powerlessness, and the Divine, ed. Cynthia Rigby, (Atlanta: Scholars Press, 97): 281-88; auth, 1 Samuel, Collegeville, MN: Liturgical Press, 98. **CONTACT ADDRESS** Dept of Relig Studies, St. Andrew's Col, Saskatoon, 1121 Col Dr, Saskatoon, SK, Canada S7K 2Z4. **EMAIL** jobling@sask.usask.ca

JOHANNES, JOHN R.
PERSONAL Born 12/15/1943, Milwaukee, WI, m, 1967, 3 children **DISCIPLINE** POLITICAL SCIENCE **EDUCATION** Marquette Univ, BS, Math & Polit Sci, 66; Harvard Univ, GOVT, AM, 68, PhD, 70. **CAREER** Instr, Marquette Univ, 70; vis asst prof, Harvard Univ, 72; asst prof, Marquette Univ, 70-75; assoc prof, Marquette Univ, 75-84; ch, Marquette Univ, 80-88; prof, Marquette Univ, Polit Sci, 84-95; dean, Marquette Univ, Coll Arts & Sci, 88-93; VPRES, VILLANOVA UNIV, ACAD AFFAIRS & PROF POLIT SCI, 95-. **HONORS AND AWARDS** NEH Summer fel, 72; Am Philos Soc grant, 78; Dirksen Center grant, 81, 82; Lynde and Harry Bradley Found Res Grant, 94. **MEMBERSHIPS** Am Polit Sci Asn; Midwest Polit Sci Asn; South Polit Sci Asn; West Polit Sci Asn; Wisconsin Polit Sci Asn; Asn Am Coll & Univ; Am Asn High Educ **SELECTED PUBLICATIONS** Auth, Policy Innovation in Congress, General Learning Pr (Morristown, New Jersey), 72; auth, "Congress, The Bureaucracy, and Casework," Administration and Soc 16 (83): 41-70; auth, To Serve the People: Congress and Constituency Service, Univ Nebraska Pr (Lincoln, Nebraska), 84; auth, "Women As Congressional Staffers: Does It Make a Difference?", Women and Politics 4 (84): 69-81; coauth, "The Voter in the 1982 House Elections," Am J of Political Science 28 (84): 778-781; coauth, "Constituency Attentiveness in the House: 1977-1982," J of Politics 47 (88): 1108-1139; coauth, "Determinants of Spending by House Challengers: 1974-1984," Am J of Political Science 31 (87): 457-483; coauth, "Entrepreneur or Agent; Congressmen and the Distribution of Casework, 1977-1984," Western Political Quart 40 (87): 535-554; coauth, "Congressmen, Perquisites, and Elections," J of Politics 50 (May 88): 412-439; co-ed, co-contrib, Money, Elections, and Democracy: Reforming Congressional Campaign Finance, Westview Pr (Boulder, Colorado), 90. **CONTACT ADDRESS** Off Acad Affairs, Villanova Univ, 800 Lancaster Ave, Villanova, PA 19085. **EMAIL** john.johannes@villanova.edu

JOHANSON, HERBERT A.
PERSONAL Born 01/10/1934, Jersey City, NJ, m, 1983, 2 children **DISCIPLINE** CONST LAW, AND LEGAL HISTORY **EDUCATION** Columbia Univ, AB, 55, MA, 61, PhD, 65; NYork Law Sch, LLB, 60. **CAREER** Ernest F. Hollings prof Const Law, Univ of SC. **HONORS AND AWARDS** Am Council of Learned Soc(s) Fel, 74-75; Inst for Humane Studies Fellow, 81-85; Univ of South Carolina Educational Found, Res Awd for Professional Schools, 00. **MEMBERSHIPS** Am Soc for Legal Hist, 74-75, 99-02; Am Historical Assoc, The Historical Soc, Am Law Inst. **RESEARCH** The Supreme Court under John Marshall; History of Criminal Justice; English and American Constitutional Thought, 17th to19th century. **SELECTED PUBLICATIONS** Auth, casebk on Amer legal and const hist & textbk on the hist of criminal justice; auth, Foundations of Power: John Marshall, 1801-15, vol 2, History of the United States Supreme Court, with George L. Haskins, 81; coauth, History of Criminal Justice, 2nd editon, 95; auth, The Chief Justiceship of John Marshall, 98. **CONTACT ADDRESS** School of Law, Univ of So Carolina, Columbia, Law Center, Columbia, SC 29208. **EMAIL** hjohnson@law.law.sc.edu

JOHN, EILEEN
DISCIPLINE PHILOSOPHY **EDUCATION** Yale Univ, BA; Univ MI, PhD. **CAREER** Dept Philos, Univ Louisville **RESEARCH** The role of fiction in prompting moral and conceptual knowledge; aesthetics; philosophy of literature. **SELECTED PUBLICATIONS** Auth, Subtlety and Moral Vision in Fiction, Philos and Lit. **CONTACT ADDRESS** Dept of Philos, Univ of Louisville, 2301 S 3rd St, Louisville, KY 40292. **EMAIL** e0john01@ulkyvm.louisville.edu

JOHN, PM
PERSONAL Born 06/17/1929, Kerala, India, w, 1965, 2 children **DISCIPLINE** RELIGIOUS STUDIES **EDUCATION** Seramapore Col, BD, 59; SMU, STM, 61; Drew Univ, MA, 72, PhD, 73. **CAREER** Instr, 65-70, Lafayett Col; Asst prof and instr, 70-73, Northeastern Univ; Assoc and asst prof, 77-80, Pahlavi Univ; Adjunct, 81-90, Univ of Lowell, Simmons Col; Assoc and asst prof, 90-98, Framingham St Col. **HONORS AND AWARDS** Steering Cmm, NGO Forum Working Group at Habitat II, UN Conf at Istanbul, 96; Institute:Infusing Asian Studies into the Undergrad Curriculum, Univ Hawaii & E/West Ctr, 95; Amer Assoc of State Col and Univ, 91; Lyceum Lecture: I Ching for Timely Decisions: Ancient Chin Phil Revisited, Framingham, 91. **MEMBERSHIPS** Amer Acad of Relig; Hegel Soc of Amer; Amer Philosophy Assn; Third World Scholars Consortium **RESEARCH** Global Thresholds in Philosophy, Education, Business and Goverance Issues in Third World Cultures. **SELECTED PUBLICATIONS** Auth, Teacher as..Hermeneut of Faith, Religion & Soc, Indian Journal of Theology, 70; auth, Issues of Religion in Early Marx, 70; auth, The World of the I Ching, A chapter in Echoes of the Wordless Word, 73; auth, On Interpreting Myths, 75; auth, Marx on Alienation: Elements of a Critique of Capitalism and Communism, 76; auth, Hindu Dharma, 79; auth, Five editorials in TWIST: A Third World Forum, 85-89; auth, Human Rights, 87; auth, Between Two Cultures, 95. **CONTACT ADDRESS** Dept of Philos, Westfield State Col, 577 Western Ave., Westfield, MA 01085-2501. **EMAIL** pmjohn@twist.org

JOHNNSON, THOMAS F.
PERSONAL Born 06/01/1943, Detroit, MI, m, 1965, 3 children **DISCIPLINE** RELIGION **EDUCATION** Wayne St Univ, BPh, 65; Fuller Theo Sem, Mdiv, 68; Princeton Sem, ThM, 69; Duke Univ, PhD, 79. **CAREER** VP Acad Affairs, Sioux Falls Col, 81-83; Prof, N Amer Baptist Sem, 83-88; Pres, Univ of Sioux Falls, 89-97; Int Pres, George Fox Univ, 97-98; VP/Dean George Fox Evangelical Sem, 98-. **MEMBERSHIPS** AAR; Soc of Bibl Lit **RESEARCH** Johannine Studies; Biblical Theology; Christian Mysticism **SELECTED PUBLICATIONS** Auth, 1, 2 and 3 John, New Intl Bibl Comm, Hendrickson Pub, 93. **CONTACT ADDRESS** George Fox Ev Sem, George Fox Univ, 12753 SW 68th St, Portland, OR 97223. **EMAIL** tjohnson@georgefox.edu

JOHNS, LOREN L.
PERSONAL Born 03/08/1955, Goshen, IN, m, 1978, 2 children **DISCIPLINE** THEOLOGY **EDUCATION** Princeton Theol Sem, PhD, 98. **CAREER** Theol book editor, Herald Press, 85-89; Assoc Prof, Religion, Bluffton Col, 93-; chair, 98-99. **HONORS AND AWARDS** Outstanding grad bibl studies, Associated Mennonite Bibl Sem, 84. **MEMBERSHIPS** Soc of Bibl Lit; Mennonite Hist Soc. **RESEARCH** Apocalypse of John, Dead Sea Scrolls. **CONTACT ADDRESS** Bluffton Col, 280 W College Ave, Bluffton, OH 45817. **EMAIL** johnsl@bluffton.edu

JOHNSEN, BREDO C.
PERSONAL Born 06/19/1939, Boston, MA, d, 2 children **DISCIPLINE** PHILOSOPHY **EDUCATION** Wayne State Univ, BA, 62; Harvard Univ, PhD, 72. **CAREER** Asst/Assoc Prof, Univ of Houston, 71-; Chair Philos Dept, Univ of Houston, 74-76, 79-94; Assoc Dean of Fac, Univ of Houston, 76-79. **RESEARCH** Epistemology, Skepticism. **SELECTED PUBLICATIONS** Auth, "Nozick on Scepticism," Philos 16 (86): 65-69; auth, "The Given," Philos and Phenomenol Res 46 (86): 597-613; auth, "The Inverted Spectrum," Australasian J of Philos 64 (86): 471-476; auth, "On Perceiving God," Philos 19 (87): 519-522; auth, "Relevant Alternatives and Demon Scepticism," J of Philos 84 (87): 643-653; auth, "The Intelligibility of Spectrum Inversion," Can J of Philos 23 (93): 629-634; auth, "Mental States as Mental," Philos 23, 1-4 (94): 223-245; auth,

"Dennett on Qualia and Consciousness: A Critique," Can J of Philos 27,1 (97): 47-82; auth, "On Richard Rorty's 'Culs-de-sac'," Philos Forum 30,2 (99): 133-160; auth, "Contextualist Swords, Skeptical Plowshares," Philos and Phenomenol Res (fortchoming 01). **CONTACT ADDRESS** Dept Philos, Univ of Houston, Houston, TX 77204-0001.

JOHNSON, BEN
PERSONAL Born 06/29/1937, m, 1960, 4 children **DISCIPLINE** THEOLOGY **EDUCATION** Gustavus Adolphus College, BA 59; Lutheran Sch Theol, Mdiv 61; Harvard Univ, ThD 66; Oxford Univ, 71-72. **CAREER** Wittenberg Univ Hamma Sch Theo, prof, dean, 65-78; Trinity Lutheran Sem, prof 78-80; Salem Lutheran Church MN, Sr pastor, 80-92; St Cloud State Univ, adj fac, 87-92; Concordia Univ Irvine, adj fac, 94-; Lutheran Bible Inst, VP, prof, 92-96; Concordia Univ, pres since 96, appointed as first Dir of the LBI House of Stud, 98-. **HONORS AND AWARDS** Danforth Fel; Soc Val Higher Edu Fel; ATS Fel; Concordia Bk Awd. **MEMBERSHIPS** SBL **RESEARCH** Unusual Religious Experiences **SELECTED PUBLICATIONS** Auth, The Didache and Christian Ethics, Let Christ Be Christ: Theology Ethics and World Religions in the Two Kingdoms, essays in honor of Charles Manske on the occasion of his sixty-fifth birthday, forth coming; How We Got the Bible, Church and Life, 98; Theology and the Bible, F O C L Point, 94; Built on a Rock, pub and preface, St Cloud MN, 82. **CONTACT ADDRESS** LBI House of Studies, Concordia Univ, California, 5321 University Dr., Suite H, Irvine, CA 92612. **EMAIL** LBIC@aol.com

JOHNSON, CALIPH
PERSONAL Born 10/03/1938, St. Joseph, LA, m **DISCIPLINE** LAW **EDUCATION** Univ of Maryland, BA 1964; San Jose State U, MA 1968; Univ of San Francisco Sch of Law, JD 1972; Georgetown Univ Law Ctr, LlM 1973. **CAREER** Thurgood Marshall School of Law, Southwest Inst for Equal Employment, Thurgood Marshall School of Law TX Southern Univ, dir 1975-78; Office of Gen Counsel Equal Employment Opportunity Commn, appellate atty 1973-75; Inst for Public Interest Represent, atty 1972-73; Oakland Citizens Com for Urban Renewal, exec dir 1970-72; City of Oakland CA, admin analyst 1970-72; Univ of Miaduguri Nigeria, consultant 1978-80; Office of Lawyer Training Legal Serv Corp , advocacy trainer 1978-80; EEOC, hearing examiner 1979-80; Title VII Project Natl Bar Assn Bd of Dir Gulf Coast Legal Found, faculty. **MEMBERSHIPS** Mem commn on law office exon Am Bar Assn; labor law sect Nat Bar Assn; civil litigation com Fed Bar Assn; civil procedure & clin sec assn of Am Law Sch; Grad Fellowship Inst for Pub Int Rep Georgetown Univ Law Ctr 1972-73; a response to crises of enforcing fair employment Houston Lawyer 1975; **SELECTED PUBLICATIONS** Book review Let Them Be Judges Howard Univ Law Jour 1980; course material on fair empl lit TX So Univ 1976; integrated clinical curr module TX So Univ & HEW 1978-80; teamsters v US Impact on Seniority Relief TX SoNBA Law Rev 1979. **CONTACT ADDRESS** 3201 Wheeler, Houston, TX 77004.

JOHNSON, CHAS FLOYD
PERSONAL Born Camden, NJ, m, 1983 **DISCIPLINE** LAW **EDUCATION** Univ of Delaware 1960-61; Howard Univ, BA 1962; Howard Univ Sch of Law, JD 1965. **CAREER** Howard Berg Law Offices, Attorney 1965; US Copyright Office, Attorney 1967-70; Swedish Ministry of Justice Stockholm, Sweden, Attorney 1970; Universal Television, prod coordinator, 71-74, associate prod, 74-76, producer, 76-82, suprvsng prod 1982-, executive producer 1985-. **HONORS AND AWARDS** Emmy Awd, Rockford Files, Best TV Drama; Alumni Achvmnt Awd Stony Brook Coll Prep, 1979; Outstanding Alumnus Howard Univ Alumni Club of So CA, 1982; Outstanding Alumnus Howard Univ, 1985; LA Area Emmy Awd Winner for producing and performing in a KCET/PBS Special "Voices of Our People, A Celebration of Black Poetry" 1981; 3 Emmy Nominations for: Rockford Files, 1978-79, 1979-80, Magnum PI 1982-83, 1983-84; City of LA, Commendations, 1982, 1993; CA State Legislature, Commendation, 1982; CA State Senate, Commendation, 1982; Hawaii State Senate, Commendation, 1988; Hawaii House of Representatives, Commendation, 1988; City of Honolulu, Commendation, 1988. **MEMBERSHIPS** Screen Actors Guild of America; Producers Guild of America, board of directors; Writers Guild of America; National Academy of Television Arts & Sciences; American Film Institute; Omega Psi Phi; Caucus for Producers, Directors and Writers, 1990-; Crossroads Theatre Arts Academy, 1990; board of directors, Kwanza Foundation, 1985; board of directors, American Independent Video Filmmakers, 1985-90; vice chairman, The Media Forum, 1978-82; Assn of Black Motion Picture and Television Producers, 1980-82. **SELECTED PUBLICATIONS** Production credits include: "Rockford Files," producer, 1974-80; "Bret Maverick," producer, 1981-82; "Magnum PI," co-executive producer, 1982-88; "BL Stryker," co-executive producer, 1988-90; "Revealing Evidence," NBC Movie of the Week, executive producer, 1990; "Quantum Leap," co-executive producer, 1992; "Baa Baa Black Sheep," pilot, producer, 1975; "Hellinger's Law," pilot, producer, 1980-81; "Simon and Simon," pilot, producer, 1980; "Silver Fox," pilot, co-creator, executive producer, 1991; "Rockford Files" Movies for TV, 1994-; author: "The Origins of the Stockholm Protocol," US Copyright Society, 1970; co-author: Black Women in Television, 1990. **CONTACT ADDRESS** Universal TV, 846 North Cahuenga Blvd, Los Angeles, CA 90038.

JOHNSON, CURTIS
DISCIPLINE 19TH CENTURY AMERICAN SOCIAL AND RELIGIOUS HISTORY **EDUCATION** Univ Minn, PhD, 85. **CAREER** Dept Hist, Mt. St. Mary's Col **SELECTED PUBLICATIONS** Auth, Redeeming America: Evangelicals and the Road to Civil War. **CONTACT ADDRESS** Dept of History, Mount Saint Mary's Col and Sem, 16300 Old Emmitsburg Rd, Emmitsburg, MD 21727-7799. **EMAIL** johnson@msmary.edu

JOHNSON, DALE
PERSONAL Born 10/10/1954, Lapeer, MI, m, 1983, 1 child **DISCIPLINE** HISTORY, RELIGION **EDUCATION** Cedarville Col, BA, 76; Covenant Theol Sem, MA, 84; Fla Atlantic Univ, MA, 88; Georgia State Univ, PhD, 95. **CAREER** Adj Prof, Erskine Theol Sem; Assoc Prof, Southern Wesleyan Univ, 87-. **HONORS AND AWARDS** Max Beltz Awd, Covenant Theol Sem, 83; English Speaking Union Scholar's Fel, Oxford Univ, 87; SC Governor's Distinguished Prof Awd, 91, 98; Summer Fel, Univ SC, 98. **MEMBERSHIPS** Am Soc of Church Historians, Calvin Studies Soc. **RESEARCH** English and Scottish Reformations, American religious history, second great awakening, Nineteenth-Century revivals. **SELECTED PUBLICATIONS** Auth, "The Sixties in America," in The Encycl of the U S Supreme Ct; auth, "Prophet in Scotland: The Prophetic Self Image of John Knox," The Calvin Theol J, vol 3 (98). **CONTACT ADDRESS** Dept Soc Sci, So Wesleyan Univ, PO Box 1020, Central, SC 29630-1020. **EMAIL** dwjohnson@hotmail.com

JOHNSON, DALE ARTHUR
PERSONAL Born 03/13/1936, Duluth, MN, m, 1958, 3 children **DISCIPLINE** RELIGION **EDUCATION** Colgate Univ, BA, 57; Oxford Univ, BA, 59, MA, 63; Lutheran Sch Theol, BD, 62; Union Theol Sem, NYork, ThD, 67. **CAREER** Asst prof relig, Luther Col, 65-69; exchange prof theol, St. John's Univ, Minn, 68-69; asst prof to prof of Church History, Divinity School, Vanderbilt Univ, 69-; dir continuing educ, 73-77; assoc dean, 85-89. **HONORS AND AWARDS** Phi Beta Kappa, Rhodes Scholarship, Albert C. Outler Prize in Ecumenical Church History, 96. **MEMBERSHIPS** Am Soc Church Hist; Am Acad Relig; Conf Brit Studies; Eccles Hist Soc. **RESEARCH** Reformation and modern European church history; 19th-century English religion; religion in America. **SELECTED PUBLICATIONS** Co-ed, Moral Issues and Christian Response, Holt, 71, rev 6th ed, 98, Harcout, Brace; ; auth, Between Evangelicalism and a Social Gospel: The Case of Joseph Rayner Stephens, Church Hist, 73; Church and Society in Modern History: Beyond Church and State, J Church & State, 77; Pedagogy and Polemic in Modern English Hymns, 79, Hist Mag of Protestant Episcopal Church; The End of the Evidences: A Study in Nonconformist Theological Transition, J United Reformed Church Hist Soc, 79; Popular Apologetics in Late Victorian England: The Work of the Christian Evidence Soc, J Relig Hist, 81; The Methodist Quest for an Educated Ministry, Church Hist, 82; Women in English Religion, 1700-1925, Mellon, 83; auth, "The Oxford Movement and English Nonconformity, Anglican & Epis Hist, 90;" Women and Religion in Britain and Ireland: An Annotated Bibliography from the Reformation to 1993, Scarecrow, 95; auth, "Fissures in Late-Nineteenth Century English Nonconformity: A Case Study in One Congregation," Church Hist 97; The Changing Shape of English Nonconformity, 1825-1925, Oxford, 98. **CONTACT ADDRESS** Divinity Sch, Vanderbilt Univ, Nashville, TN 37240. **EMAIL** dale.johnson@vanderbilt.edu

JOHNSON, DAVID LAWRENCE
PERSONAL Born 01/25/1941, Minneapolis, MN, w, 1963, 1 child **DISCIPLINE** RELIGION AND PHILOSOPHY OF INDIA, ETHICS AND TECHNOLOGY **EDUCATION** Augsburg Col, AB, 66; Univ Iowa, PhD, 72. **CAREER** Asst prof, 70-76, chmn dept, 78-82, assoc prof humanities, Ind State Univ, Terre Haute, 76-, prof Relig, 82-, adj prof humanities, Rose Hulman Inst Technol, 76 & 78. **MEMBERSHIPS** Am Acad Relig; Asn Asian Studies. **RESEARCH** Modern religious thought, India; religion and politics; technology and human condition. **SELECTED PUBLICATIONS** Auth, The task of relevance: Aurobindo's synthesis of religion and politics, Philos East & West, 10/73; Religious Roots of Nationalism: Aurobindo's Early Political Thought, Mukhopadhyay, Calcutta, 74; Technology, Society and Human Development, Davis Publ, 78 & 82; Indian Thought Between Tradition and the Culture of Technology, D.K. Printworld, 95; Reason and Religion in the Traditions of China and India, The Davies Group Publ, 97. **CONTACT ADDRESS** Dept of Humanities, Indiana State Univ, 921 South Fifth St., Terre Haute, IN 47807. **EMAIL** hujohnso@root.indstate.edu

JOHNSON, DONALD ELLIS
PERSONAL Born 04/07/1918, Plaistow, NH, m, 1942, 3 children **DISCIPLINE** HISTORY, INTERNATIONAL RELATIONS **EDUCATION** Mass State Col Fitchburg, BSEd, 40; Clark Univ, AM, 41, PhD(hist & int rels), 53. **CAREER** From instr to assoc prof, 46-66, head dept hist, 68-74, Prof Hist, Worcester Polytech Inst, 66-, Head Dept Humanities, 74-, Vis lectr US dipl hist, Col Holy Cross, 68; abstractor, Hist Abstr. **MEMBERSHIPS** AHA; AAUP **RESEARCH** Local United States Colonial history; Worcester in the war for independence. **SELECTED PUBLICATIONS** Coauth, Pioneer Class, LaVigne, 66. **CONTACT ADDRESS** 16 Lowell Ave, Holden, MA 01520.

JOHNSON, E. ELIZABETH
PERSONAL Born 11/29/1951, Morgantown, WV, m, 1993, 2 children **DISCIPLINE** RELIGIOUS STUDIES **EDUCATION** Ohio Univ, BGS, 73; Princeton Theol Sem, MDiv, 77; Princeton Theol Sem, PhD, 87. **CAREER** Assoc Prof, New Brunkswick Theol Sem, 86-98; Prof, Columbia Theol Sem, 98-. **MEMBERSHIPS** Soc Bibl Lit, Bibl Theologians. **RESEARCH** Pauline letters. **SELECTED PUBLICATIONS** Auth, "The Function of Apocalyptic and Wisdom Traditions in Romans 9-11," SBLDS 109, Scholars Pr (89); auth, "1 and 2 Thessalonions," New Testament LIbr, Westminster Pr (forthcoming). **CONTACT ADDRESS** Dept Relig Studies, Columbia Theol Sem, PO Box 520, Decatur, GA 30031-0520.

JOHNSON, EDWARD
PERSONAL Born 12/26/1950, Lincoln, NE **DISCIPLINE** PHILOSOPHY **EDUCATION** Univ Nebr-Lincoln, BA, 72; Princeton Univ, PhD(philos), 76. **CAREER** Asst prof Philos, Univ New Orleans, 76-83, assoc prof Philos, Univ New Orleans, 83-90, prof Philos, 90-, chmn dept, 82-. **HONORS AND AWARDS** Alumni Awd for Excellence in Teaching, 84, Outstanding Honors Faculty Member, 90. **MEMBERSHIPS** Am Philos Asn. **RESEARCH** Moral theory, environmental ethics, medical ethics, philos of technology, philos of education. **SELECTED PUBLICATIONS** Contribr, Videotheraphy in Mental Health, Charles C Thomas, 81; Ethics and Animals, Humana Press, 83; Earthbound, Random, 84; Animal Rights and Human Obligations, Prentice-Hall, 89; Encyclopedia of Ethics, Garland, 92; Cambridge Dictionary of Philosophy, Cambridge Univ Press, 95; Nagging Questions: Feminist Ethics in Everyday Life, Rowman and Littlefield, 95; Sex, Love, and Friendship, Rodopi, 97; Human Sexuality, Ashgate, 97; Encyclopedia of Applied Ethics, Academic Press, 97; auth, Animal Liberation versus the Land Ethic, Environ Ethics, 81; Ingoring Persons, Tulane Studies in Philos, 82; (E)Quality Education, Forum for Honors, 88; Contratto e Status Morale, Etica & Animali, 89; Inscrutable Desires, Philosophy of the Social Sciences, 90; Singer's Cookbook, 91; & Carruthers on Consciousness and Moral Status, 91; Between the Species: A Journal of Ethics; contribr, Encyclopedia of Greece and the Hellenic Tradition, Fitzroy Dearborn, 00; contribr, Encyclopedia of Postmodernism, Routledge, 00. **CONTACT ADDRESS** Philos Dept, Univ of New Orleans, 2000 Lakeshore Dr, New Orleans, LA 70148-2330. **EMAIL** erjohns1@uno.edu

JOHNSON, ELIZABETH A.
PERSONAL Born 12/06/1941, Brooklyn, NY, s **DISCIPLINE** THEOLOGY **EDUCATION** Brentwood Col, BA, 64; Manhattan Col, MA, 70; Cath Univ of Am, PhD, 81. **CAREER** Asst prof to assoc prof, Cath Univ of Am, 81-91; prof to distinguished prof, Fordham Univ, 91-. **HONORS AND AWARDS** Five honorary doctorates; Grawemeyer award; Univ Medal, Sienna Heights Univ, 99; Teacher of the Year Awd, Fordham Univ, 98; US Catholic Awd for promoting the cause of women in the church; Sacred Universe Awd, 99; Loyola-Mellon Humanities Awd, Loyola Univ, Chicago. **MEMBERSHIPS** Cath Theol Soc of Am, Am Acad of Relig, Col Theol Soc, Am Theol Soc. **RESEARCH** Theology - in dialogue with contemporary faith question, women's experience, science, environmental studies, and world religions. **SELECTED PUBLICATIONS** Auth, Consider Jesus: Waves of renewal in Christology, New York, 90; auth, She Who Is: The Mystery of God in Feminist theological Discourse, New York, 92; auth, Women, Earth, and Creator Spirit, New York: Paulist Press, 93; auth, "Does God Play Dice? Divine Providence and Chance," Theological Studies, (96): 3-18; auth, Friends of God and Prophets: A Feminist theological Reading of the Communion of Saints, New York, 98. **CONTACT ADDRESS** Dept Theol, Fordham Univ, 441 E Fordham Rd, Bronx, NY 10458-5149. **EMAIL** ejohnson@fordham.edu

JOHNSON, ERNEST L.
PERSONAL Born 08/24/1950, Ferriday, LA, m, 1992 **DISCIPLINE** LAW **EDUCATION** Grambling State University, BS, 1973; Southern University School of Law, JD, 1976. **CAREER** Johnson, Taylor & Thomas, sr partner, 80-89; Southern University Law Center, professor; Life Savings Bank, chairman of the board, president, currently. **HONORS AND AWARDS** NAACP, National President Leadership Awd, 1992; Louis A Martinet Legal Society, Leadership Awd, 1991; JK Haynes Education Foundation, The Prestigious Seervice Awd, 1990; Southern University Law Center, Earl Warren Fellowship, 1973-76; Scotlandville Jaycees, Scotlandville Man of the Year Awd, 1990. **MEMBERSHIPS** Louisiana NAACP, exec vp, 1991-; Louisiana State Bar Association, 1976-; Louis A Martinet Legal Society, 1986-; Project Invest in Black, board of directors; Church Point Ministries Feed a Family, board of directors. **CONTACT ADDRESS** President, Life Savings Bank, 7990 Scenic Hwy, 1st Fl, Baton Rouge, LA 70807.

JOHNSON, FREDERICK A.
DISCIPLINE PHILOSOPHY **EDUCATION** Ohio State Univ, PhD, 71. **CAREER** Prof. **SELECTED PUBLICATIONS** Auth, pubs on formal logic and philosophy of mathematics. **CONTACT ADDRESS** Philosophy Dept, Colorado State Univ, Fort Collins, CO 80523.

JOHNSON, GERALDINE ROSS
PERSONAL Born 05/13/1946, Moline, IL, m **DISCIPLINE** LAW **EDUCATION** Augustana Coll, BA 1968; Univ of PA Sch of Social Work, MSW 1974; Univ of IA Coll of Law, JD 1982. **CAREER** Linn Co IA Dept of Soc Svcs, caseworker 1968-69; Children's Serv City of St Louis, intake case worker 1969-70; Get Set Day Care, preschool tchr 1970-72; Franciscan Mental Health Ctr, social worker 1974-78; Davenport Civil Rights Commn, Attorney 1984-86; City of Davenport Legal Dept, atty 1986-. **MEMBERSHIPS** Mem Iowa State Bar Assoc, Scott Co Bar Assoc; mem Sounds of Peace Choral Group 1981-86; mem Davenport Civil Rights Commn 1982-84; bd of dirs Family Resources Inc 1982-; mem Delta Sigma Theta Public Serv Sor Inc 1984-; volunteer United Way 1986; guest speaker Upward Bound, Marycrest Sociology Dept, MeritEmployment Council, Blackhawk Coll Alpha Ctr; mem Tabernacle Baptist Church Moline IL; mem Pulpit Comm 1986. **SELECTED PUBLICATIONS** Survey of sex educ literature on file in the British Library by request 1984. **CONTACT ADDRESS** City of Davenport, City Hall 226 W Fourth St, Davenport, IA 52801.

JOHNSON, GOLDEN ELIZABETH
PERSONAL Born 03/21/1944, Newark, NJ **DISCIPLINE** LAW **EDUCATION** Douglass Coll, AB, 65; Rutgers Newark Sch of Law, JD, 71. **CAREER** Hoffman La Roche Inc, gen atty 1977-; Rutgers Law Sch, prof 1976-; Newark Muncpl Ct, judge 1974-77; Hoffmann-La Roche Inc, atty 1974; Comm Leagl Action Wrkshp, proj dir 1972-74; State of NJ, dep atty & gen 1971-72; US Atty Ofc, intern 1970; W Kinney Jr HS, tchr 1969; Newark Legal Serv, intern 1969; Spec Rsrch Lab, microblgst 1965-68. **HONORS AND AWARDS** Comm serv awd Rutgers Law Sch 1972; comm serv awd Donald Tucker Civic Assn 1974; achvmt awd Essex Co Civic Assn 1975; black woman achvmt awd COM-BIN-NATION 1975; life mem Guild Legal Serv; awd Nat Cncl of Negro Women 1975; achvmt awd No Reg of Fedn of Colored Women's Club 1975; oust achvmt NJFedn of Colored Women's Club 1975; achvmt awd Delta Sigma Theta Inc 1975; comm serv awd Newark Title 1 Ctrl Parents Cncl 1975; achvmt awd Neward Sect Nat Cncl of Negro Women 1975; awd of excell Oper PUSH 1975; comm serv awd Roosevelt Homes Housing Proj 1975; achvmt awd Nat Assn of Negro Bus & Professional Women's Clubs 1975; comm serv awd Essex Co Legal Serv 1975; serv awd Newark Housing Cncl Comm 1976; disgshd serv awd Seton Hall Univ 1976; certof apprctnCtrl Ward Girls Club 1976; Oper PUSH Tidewa Women Achvmt Awd 1976; achvmt awd Dr Martin Luther King Jr Comm Ctr 1976; achiev awd Guyton-Callahan Post 152 1976; outsdng Woman of Yr NJ Jaycee-ETTES 1977; hon life mem Zeta Alpha Iota 1977; Alumni Roster of Superior Merit E Side HS 1977;Outstdg Young Woman of Am 1975, 77; gen Couns to Young Dems of NJ. **MEMBERSHIPS** Mem NJ State Bar Assn; Essex Co Bar Assn; Garden State Bar Assn; present mem bd of Gov & exec comm Nat Bar Assn; past pres bd mem Women's Div Nat Bar Assn; bd of tst NJ State Opera; bd of tst & past chmn Newark-Essex Co Legal Serv & Joint Law Reform; bd of dir Ctrl Ward Girls Club; mem NJ Adv Bd US Commn on Civil Rights 1973-77; bd of dir Leaguers Inc; mem NJ Coll of Med & Denistry's Bd of Concerned Citzs 1972-75; NAACP; life mem Nat Cncl of Negro Women; chtr mem Assn of Black Women Lwyrs; mem liaison City of Newark for Essex Co Fed of Dem Women 1977; 100 Women for Integ in Govt; mem Rutgers Newark Sch of Law Alumni Assn. **CONTACT ADDRESS** 555 Mount Prospect Ave, Newark, NJ 07104.

JOHNSON, HERBERT A.
PERSONAL Born 01/10/1934, Jersey City, NJ, m, 1983, 2 children **DISCIPLINE** AMERICAN LEGAL AND CONSTITUTIONAL HISTORY **EDUCATION** Columbia Univ, AB, 55; MA, 61; PhD, 65; NY Law Sch, LLB, 60. **CAREER** Lectr and asst prof, Hunter Col of CUNY, 64-67; from assoc ed to ed, The Papers of John Marshall, Inst of Early Am Hist and Culture, 67-77; from prof to Ernest F. Hollings Prof, Univ of SC, 77-. **HONORS AND AWARDS** Schiff Fel, Columbia Univ, 63-64; ACLS Fel, 74-75. **MEMBERSHIPS** Am Soc for Legal Hist, Am Hist Asn, Am Law Inst. **RESEARCH** John marshall and the Marshall Court, History of Criminal Justice, Early Air Force History 1907-1918. **SELECTED PUBLICATIONS** Auth, American Legal and Constitutional History: Cases and Materials, Austin & Winfield (San Francisco, CA), 94; coauth, History of Criminal Justice 2nd edition, Anderson Pub Co. (Cincinnati, OH), 95; auth, The Chief Justiceship of John Marshall 1801-35, Univ of SC Press (Columbia, SC), 97 & 98. **CONTACT ADDRESS** Sch of Law, Univ of So Carolina, Columbia, Columbia, SC 29208. **EMAIL** johnsonh@sc.edu

JOHNSON, J. PRESCOTT
PERSONAL Born Tumalo, OR, m, 1943, 3 children **DISCIPLINE** PHILOSOPHY **EDUCATION** Northwestern Univ, PhD, 59. **CAREER** Inst, Kansas City Col & Bible Sch, 43-45; Asc prof, Bethany Nazarene Col, 49-57; ast prof, Univ Okla, 57-62; prof, 62-86 & prof emer, 86-, Monmouth Col. **MEMBERSHIPS** APA. **RESEARCH** Theory of value; philosophy of religion. **SELECTED PUBLICATIONS** Ontological Argument in Plato, Personalist, 63; auth, The auth, The Axiological Theism of Wilbur Marshall Urban, Int. Phil. Quartery, 65; auth, The Fact-Value Question, Journal of Value Inquiry, 67; auth, Human Dignity and the Nature of Society, in Human Dignity, 70; auth, The Idea of Dignit in Classical and Christian Thought, Journal of Thought, 71; Spirituality and Community," Jrnl of Speculative Philos, 97; "Beauty of Holiness," Asbury Theol Jrnl, 97; auth, The Gate of Light: A Story of the American Civil War, 00. **CONTACT ADDRESS** 1040 E. 3rd Ave., Monmouth, IL 61462. **EMAIL** bengtas@misslink.net

JOHNSON, JACOB EDWARDS, III
PERSONAL Born 02/21/1922, Charleston, WV, w, 1944 **DISCIPLINE** CRIMINAL JUSTICE **EDUCATION** West Virginia State College, Institute, ES, 1928; North Carolina Central University, 1940; Kentucky State University, 1940-43; University of Wisconsin Law School, 1949; Howard University Law School, LLB, 1950, JD, 1968; National University Law School, 1952; George Washington University, 1956. **CAREER** US Department of Justice, federal legal liaison, retired; District of Columbia Department of Justice, Corrections, and Parole Board, 35 years; Prof of Law and Criminal Justice, currently. **HONORS AND AWARDS** Kappa Alpha Psi, 50 Year Awd, 1991; IBPO Elks, Past Grand Exalted Ruler, with Honors, 1984. **MEMBERSHIPS** IBPO Elks, past grand exalted ruler(w/ honors), legal liaison officer, 1984-91, W Grand Federal Census, officer, 1989-92, Elks Veterans, national service officer, 1984-91, Civil Liberties Department, Elks grand commissioner, 1992; life member, commander, 1983-84, American Legion Post 5, Washington, DC, 1983-84; life member, vice commander, 1989-91, Veterans of Foreign Wars Post 7456, Fairmount, MD, 1983-91; life member, service officer, 1983-91, Disabled American Veterans Post 7, Camp Springs, MD; life member, NAACP; life member, National Bar Association; numerous others. **CONTACT ADDRESS** Col, Lodge #85, 1846 3rd St NW, Washington, DC 20001.

JOHNSON, JAMES TURNER
PERSONAL Born 11/02/1938, Crockett Mills, TN, m, 1968, 2 children **DISCIPLINE** RELIGION, RELIGIOUS ETHICS **EDUCATION** Brown Univ, AB, 60; Vanderbilt Univ, BD, 63; Princeton Univ, MA, 67, PhD(Relig), 68. **CAREER** Instr Philos & Relig, Newberry Col, 63-65; lectr Relig, Vassar Col, 68-69; asst prof, 69-77, Univ Res Coun fac fel, 72-73, assoc prof & chairperson dept, 77-82, prof Relig, Rutgers Univ, New Brunswick, 82-, Rockefeller Found Humanities fel, 76-77; Nat Endowment for Humanities grant, 76; Guggeuheim Fel, 84. **HONORS AND AWARDS** US Inst of Peace grants, 88-89, 90-91; Nat Endowment for Humanities fel, 92-93; Earhart Found grant, 97. **MEMBERSHIPS** Am Acad Relig; Am Soc Christian Ethics; Coun Relig & Int Affairs; AAUP . **RESEARCH** Limitation of war; history of just war thought; religion and international law; comparative religious ethics. **SELECTED PUBLICATIONS** Auth, A Society Ordained by God: English Puritan Marriage Doctrine, Abingdon, 70; The covenant idea and the Puritan view of marriage, J Hist Ideas, 1-2/71; The meaning of non-combatant immunity in the just war/limited war tradition, J Am Acad Relig, 6/71; Toward reconstructing the Jus ad Bellum, Monist, 10/73; ed, Love and Society: Essays in the Ethics of Paul Ramsey, Scholars Press, 74; auth, Natural law as a language for the ethics of war, J Relig Ethics, Fall 75; Ideology, Reason and the Limitation of War: Secular and Religious Concepts, 1200-1740, 75 & Just War Tradition and the Restraint of War, 81, Princeton Univ; Ethics and Public Policy Center; co-ed, Beyond Confrontation, Univ of Michigan, 95; The Holy War Idea in Western and Islamic Tradition, Penn State, 97. **CONTACT ADDRESS** Dept of Religion, Rutgers, The State Univ of New Jersey, New Brunswick, 140 Loree Hall 70 Lipman Dr, New Brunswick, NJ 08901-8525. **EMAIL** jtj@rci.rutgers.edu

JOHNSON, JOHN M.
PERSONAL Born 06/10/1941, IN, m, 1990, 2 children **DISCIPLINE** CRIMINAL JUSTICE **EDUCATION** Ind Univ, AB, 63; San Diego State Univ, MS, 69; Univ Calif, PhD, 73. **CAREER** Asst Prof, San Diego State Univ, 70-71; Asst to Full Prof, Ariz State Univ, 72-; Visiting Prof, Univ Paris, 93. **HONORS AND AWARDS** Career Achievement Awd, Pacific Sociol Asn, 88; Fac Achievement Awd, AZ State Univ, 95. **MEMBERSHIPS** Soc for the Study of Symbolic Interaction. **RESEARCH** Philosophies and Theories of Justice; Domestic Violence; Qualitative Methods. **CONTACT ADDRESS** Sch of Justice, Arizona State Univ, PO Box 870403, Tempe, AZ 85287.

JOHNSON, JOHN W.
PERSONAL Born 11/06/1934, Summerfield, LA **DISCIPLINE** LAW **EDUCATION** Georgetown Univ Law Center, LlM 1964; Howard Univ Sch of Law, JD 1962; So Univ Baton Rouge, BA 1957. **CAREER** AT & T, atty 1972; NY Law Sch, law prof 1978-; US Dept of Just Wash, trial lawy 1964-68; OH Bell Tel & Co Cleveland Corp ABA, lawy 1968-72. **MEMBERSHIPS** Nat Bar Assn; NY Bar Assn; OH Bar Assn; DC Bar Assn; LA Bar Assn; World Peace thru Law; Adm to Prac before Supreme Ct of US Sigma Delta Tau Legal Frat Part in LA first "sit in" demonstrn 1960 case reviewed by US Sup Ct Garner V LA. **CONTACT ADDRESS** AT&T, 195 Broadway, New York, NY 10007.

JOHNSON, JOHNNIE L., JR.
PERSONAL Born 01/01/1946, Nesbitt, MS, m, 1967, 4 children **DISCIPLINE** LAW **EDUCATION** Morris Brown Coll, BA 67; OH Northern Univ, JD 70. **CAREER** Dept of Justice, asst us atty 70-73; Equal Employment Oppty Commission, asst reg atty 73-75, spec asst to comm 1975-78, dir trial team II 78-81; EEOC, assistant Gen Counsel, 81-83; director, Legal & Special Pol Div, 83-84; Director Special Projects, 84-85; Sr trial Attorney, 85-. **HONORS AND AWARDS** Donnie Delaney Comm Defense Awd 1974; Outstanding Young Man of Amer 1979; participant in "Old Dominion 100 Mile Endurance Run" 1979, Empire State Run Up 1979, 1980, JFK 50 Miler 1980; Marine Corp Marath 1979, 1980 and 1981; Ohio Northern University, College of Law, 16th annual Law Review Symposium, lecturer. **MEMBERSHIPS** Pres, Nat Coun of EEOC Locals No. 216, 98-; pres, AFGE Local No. 2667, 98-; pres, Morris Brown Col Alumni Assoc 85-92, Mediator, DC Mediation Service 89-; bd of dir(s), Ohio Northern Univ Law Alumni Assoc 88-; pres, Mediterranean Villa Cluster Assn 86-99; Mediator, Multi-Door Disput Resolutim Center, 90-; pres, BF Jones Bar Assoc, 70-74; pres, Board of Dir, Memphis & Shelby City, Legal Services Assn 72-74; first vice pres, Memphis Chapter, Federal Bar Assn, 72-74; lecturer, Ohio Northern Univ Col of Law 16th Annual Law Review Symposium. **CONTACT ADDRESS** Equal Employment Opportunity Comm, 1801 L St, NW, Washington, DC 20507. **EMAIL** jljmed@aol.com

JOHNSON, JUSTIN MORRIS
PERSONAL Born 08/19/1933, Wilkinsburg, PA, m, 1960 **DISCIPLINE** LAW **EDUCATION** Univ Chicago, AB, 1954, Law School, JD, 1962; attended Univ of VA, 1982-83. **CAREER** Partner/sole proprietor, Johnson & Johnson, 62-77; Board of Education, School District of Pittsburgh and Pittsburgh-Mt Oliver Intermediate Unit, assistant solicitor, 64-70, solicitor and assistant secretary, 70-78; Berkman Ruslander Pohl Lieber & Engel, partner, 78-80; Superior Court of PA, Judge, 80-; Adjunct Porfessor, Duquesne Univ School of Law. **HONORS AND AWARDS** Bond Medal, Univ Chicago, 1954; Dr Martin Luther King Jr Citizen's Medal, 1973; Top Hat Awd, 1981, for distinguished judicial service; Homer S Brown Service Awd, 1982; Man of the Year, Bethesda Presbyterian Church, 1983; President's Awd, Pennsylvania Trial Lawyers Association, 1983; Awd of Merit, Pittsburgh Young Adult Club, 1983; St Thomas More Awd, 1985; Public Service Awd, Pittsburgh chapter, ASPA, 1986. **MEMBERSHIPS** Active elder Bethesda Presbyterian Church; mem Natl Cong Bar Examiners 1969-83; mem, PA Bd Law Examiners 1969-89, vice chairman 1975-83, chairman 1983-89; bd of trustees Mercy Hospital 1976-93, Southside Hosp 1978-88, United Way of Allegheny Co 1979-90; Carnegie Mellon University, 1988-93, 1995-; Pittsburgh Theological Seminary, 1985-93; Princeton Theological Seminary, 1992-; Urban League of Pittsburgh; hearing comm PA Supreme Court Disciplinary Bd. **CONTACT ADDRESS** Superior Ct of Pennsylvania, 330 Grant St, Pittsburgh, PA 15219.

JOHNSON, KEVIN R.
PERSONAL Born 06/29/1958, Culver City, CA, m, 1987, 3 children **DISCIPLINE** LAW **EDUCATION** Univ Calif, AB, 80, JD, 83. **CAREER** Acting Prof to Prof and Assoc Dean, Univ Calif, 89-. **HONORS AND AWARDS** Phi Beta Kappa, Distinguished Teaching Awd, 93 **MEMBERSHIPS** Am Bar Asn. **RESEARCH** Immigration and refugee law; Civil rights; Civil procedure; Latinos and the Law. **SELECTED PUBLICATIONS** Auth, complex Litigation, Carolina Acad Press, forthcoming; auth, Perspectives on Race and the Law: A Multiracial Approach, Carolina Acad Press, forthcoming; auth, Immigration and citizenship Law and Policy for the twenty-First Century: A Modern Approach, LEXIS Law Pub, forthcoming; auth, How Did You Get to Be Mexican?: a White/Brown Man's Search for Identity, Temple Univ Press, 99; auth, "Legal challenges for Latinos and Latinas in the New Millennium: the Quest for full Membership and Equal Citizenship," in Columbia History of Latinos in the United States, 1960 to the Present, Columbia Univ Press, forthcoming; auth, "The Moral High Ground? The relevance of International Human Rights Law to Racial Discrimination Under US Immigration Law," in Moral Imperialism: A Critical Anthology, NY Univ Press, forthcoming; auth, Race Matters: Immigration Law and Policy Scholarship, Law in the Ivory Tower, and the Legal Indifference of the race Critique, Univ of Ill Law Review, forthcoming; auth, "The Rodrigo Chronicles, Latino/as, and Racial Oppression: a Blueprint for the next Generation," Harvard Latino Law Review, forthcoming; auth, "Race and Immigration Law and Enforcement: a response to "Is There a Plenary Power doctrine?," Georgetown Immigration Law Journal, forthcoming; auth, "discrimination Against Latin/os by Proxy: the Case of Proposition 227 and the Ban on bilingual Education," UC Davis Law Review, forthcoming. **CONTACT ADDRESS** School of Law, Univ of California, Davis, 1 Shields Ave, Davis, CA 95616-5270. **EMAIL** krjohnson@ucdavis.edu

JOHNSON, LUKE TIMOTHY
PERSONAL Born 11/20/1943, Park Falls, WI, m, 1974, 1 child **DISCIPLINE** NEW TESTAMENT STUDIES, THEOLOGY **EDUCATION** Notre Dame Sem, BA, 66; St Meinrad Sch Theol, MDiv, 70; Ind Univ, MA, 70; Yale Univ, PhD(New Testament), 76. **CAREER** Asst prof relig, St Joseph Sem Col, 70-71; asst prof New Testament, Yale Divinity Sch, 76-79, assoc prof, 79-82; ASSOC PROF NEW TESTAMENT, IND UNIV, 82-92; Robert W. Woodruff, Prof of New Testament, Crandler School of Theology, Emory Univ, 92-. **MEMBERSHIPS** Soc Bibl Lit; Cath Bibl Asn; Soc Values Higher Educ; Soc New Testament Studies. **RESEARCH** Christian origins. **SELECTED PUBLICATIONS** Auth, The Literary Function of Possessions in Luke-Acts, Scholars, 76-; The Red Jesus, 96; Living Jesus, 98; Religious Experience in Early Christianity, 98; Writings of the New Testament, 2nd ed, 99. **CONTACT ADDRESS** Candler School of Theology, Emory Univ, Bishops Hall, Atlanta, GA 30322. **EMAIL** ljohno1@emory.edu

JOHNSON, M. GLEN
PERSONAL Born 11/18/1936, Pikeville, KY, m, 1963, 2 children **DISCIPLINE** POLITICAL SCIENCE **EDUCATION** Georgetown College (KY), BA, 58; Univ of NC, Chapel Hill, MA, 61, PhD, 66. **CAREER** Inst of Political Sci, Univ of Ky, 63-64; instr, 64-66, ASST PROF, 66-72, ASSOC PROF, 72-77, PROF OF POLITICAL SCI, 77-, ACTING PRES, 97-98, VASSAR COLL; dir, Am Studies Res Centre, Hyderabad, India, 90-93. **HONORS AND AWARDS** Fulbright Prof, Poena Univ, India, 77-78; Fulbright Prof & Dir, Am Studies Res Centre, Hyderabad, India, 90-93. **MEMBERSHIPS** Amer Political Sci Asn; Int Studies Asn; Asn for Asian Studies. **RESEARCH** U.S. Foreign Policy; International Human Rights; South Asia. **SELECTED PUBLICATIONS** Coauth, The Universal Declaration of Human Rights: 45th Anniversary, 1948-1993, UNESCO, 94 & 98; auth, Structures, Order and Interests: Coping with the End of the Westphalian Era, in Ganging Global Political/Ideological Context and Afro-Asia: Strategies for Development, South Asian Pubs Pvt. Ltd., 96; auth, Some Reflections on Federalism in India and the United States, in Democracy and Federalism, Andhra Pradesh Judicial Acad, 95. **CONTACT ADDRESS** Dept of Political Sci, Vassar Col, 124 Raymond Ave, Poughkeepsie, NY 12604-0376. **EMAIL** johnsong@vassar.edu

JOHNSON, MERWYN S.
PERSONAL Born 10/27/1938, Annapolis, MD, m, 1964, 3 children **DISCIPLINE** THEOLOGY **EDUCATION** Univ Va, BA, 60; Union Theol Sem, BD, 63; Union Theol Sem, ThM, 64; Universitat Basel, DTheol, 76. **CAREER** Prof, Stephens Col, 73-74; Asst Prof, Austin Presbyterian Theol Sem, 74-80; From Assoc Prof to Prof, Erskine Theol Sem, 85-. **HONORS AND AWARDS** Fel, Case Study Inst, 73. **MEMBERSHIPS** Calvin Studies Soc, Karl Barth Soc, Sixteenth-Century Studies Soc, SBL, AAR. **RESEARCH** John Calvin, Karl Barth, current issues in theology, biblical interpretation/hermeneutics, theology of ministry, paradigms in theology, reformed theology. **SELECTED PUBLICATIONS** Auth, Whose Ministry Is It? The Issue of Instrumentality and the Theology of Ministry, Due West, 97; ed, The Theology of ministry: A Collection of Papers, Due West, 97; auth, "Calvin's Ethical Legacy," in Calvin Studies Soc Papers (Grand Rapids, MI: CRC Product Servs, 99); auth, Resource Materials for the Study of Basic Christian Theology. Due West, 99. **CONTACT ADDRESS** Dept Theol, Erskine Theol Sem, PO Box 368, Due West, SC 29639-0368. **EMAIL** johnson@erskine.edu

JOHNSON, PATRICIA ALTENBERND
PERSONAL Born 03/05/1945, Seattle, WA, m, 1968, 1 child **DISCIPLINE** CONTINENTAL PHILOSOPHY **EDUCATION** Eckerd Col, BA, 67; Columbia Univ, MA, 69; Univ Toronto, MA, 74, PhD, 79. **CAREER** Prof philos, Univ Dayton, 79-. **MEMBERSHIPS** Am Philos Asn; Hegel Soc Am; Soc Christian Philosophers; Soc Philos Relig. **RESEARCH** Hermeneutics; Hegel; philosophy of religion. **SELECTED PUBLICATIONS** Co-ed, With Both Eyes Open, Pilgrim Press, 88; auth, Feminist Christian Philosophy?, Faith and Philosophy, 92; Gadamer: Incarnation, Finitude, and the Experience of Divine Infinitude, Faith and Philos, 93; auth, On Wollstonecraft, Wadsworth, 00; auth, On Heidegger, Wadsworth, 00; auth, On Gadamer, Wadsworth, 00. **CONTACT ADDRESS** Dept of Philos, Univ of Dayton, 300 College Park, Dayton, OH 45469-1546. **EMAIL** patricia.johnson@notes.udayton.edu

JOHNSON, PATRICIA L.
PERSONAL Born 01/29/1956, New York, NY, s **DISCIPLINE** LAW **EDUCATION** John Jay Coll of Criminal Justice, BA 1977, MA 1979; Cornell Univ Sch of Law, pre-law prog 1978; Rutgers Sch of Law Newark, JD 1985; Office of Court Admin NYork Frontline Leadership Certificate 1988. **CAREER** Bureau of Alcohol Tobacco & Firearms, student aide 1977; US Rsch Svcs, branch mgr 1979-82; Bronx Family Court, notifications supervisor 1982-83; Bronx Dist Attorney's Office, legal asst 1983-85; Judicial Friends, law intern 1985; Bronx District Attorney's Office, asst dist atty 1985-86; Bronx Public Admin Office, assoc counsel 1986-88; Walter Kaitz Foundation Fellowship finalist 1989; John Jay Coll of Criminal Justice, New York, NY, adjunct prof, 86; Bronx Surrogate's Court, Bronx, NY, deputy chief clerk, 88-. **HONORS AND AWARDS** Outstanding Achievement w/Distinction Rutgers Women's Rights Reporter 1985; Assoc of Black Law Students Serv to Black Comm 1985; moderator Entertainment & Sports Law Forum Black Bar Assoc of Bronx Cty 1987; battling the motion picture assoc of Amer movie rating of "The White Girl" published in NY Law Journal 1988; Walter Kaitz Foundation Fellowship Finalist, 1989. **MEMBERSHIPS** Mem Black Women Attorneys 1981-; mem Natl Bar Assoc 1983-; mem Phi Alpha Delta Law Frat Intl 1983-; mem Professional and Business Women 1985-, NAACP 1985-, Natl Women's Political Caucus 1985-, Black Entertainment and Sports Lawyers Assoc 1986-; recording sec Black Bar Assoc of Bronx County 1986-; corresponding sec/chair program bd Black Bar of Bronx 1987-89; exec dir & founder Black Entertainment & Sports Tribune 1989-; Big Sister, The Big Sisters, Inc, 1989; chairperson, Entertainment & Sports Law Comm for Metropolitan Black Bar Assn, 1989-; exec dir, Black Entertainment & Sports Tribune, 1989-. **CONTACT ADDRESS** Professor, Law & Police Science, John Jay Col of Criminal Justice, CUNY, 899 Tenth Ave, Room 422T, New York, NY 10019.

JOHNSON, RICK L.
PERSONAL Born 03/18/1952, Houston, TX, m, 1976, 2 children **DISCIPLINE** OLD TESTAMENT **EDUCATION** La Col, BA, 74; Southwestern Bapt Theol Sem, M Div, 77; Southwestern Bapt Theol Sem, PhD, 83. **CAREER** Instr, relig, Wayland Bapt Univ, 82-84; asst prof, relig, Wayland Bapt Univ, 84-87; assoc prof, relig, Wayland Bapt Univ, 87-90; prof, relig, Wayland Bapt Univ, 90-92; assoc prof, old testament, Southwestern Bapt Theol Sem, 92-96; prof, old testament, Southwestern Bapt Theol Sem, 96-. **HONORS AND AWARDS** Who's Who Among America's Teachers, 94; Outstanding Facul Awd, Wayland Bapt Univ, 87-88, 92; Broadman Seminarian Awd, Southwestern Bapt Theol Sem, 77. **MEMBERSHIPS** Soc of Bibl Lit; Nat Asn of Bapt Prof of Relig. **RESEARCH** Old Testament theology; Literary criticism of the Bible. **SELECTED PUBLICATIONS** Auth, Introducing 1 Corinthians, Bibl Illus, 23, 13-17, summer, 97; auth, Modern Old Testament Interpretation, Biblical Hermeneutics: A Comprehensive Introduction to Interpreting Scripture, 99-115, Nashville, Broadman & Holman Publ, 96; auth, Prepare to Meet the Lion: The Message of Amos, Southwestern Jour of Theol, 38, 20-28, fall, 95; auth, A Leper's Status in Ancient Israel, Bibl Illus, 21, 76-78, spring, 95; auth, God's Jealousy, Bibl Illus, 20, 40-43, fall, 93; auth, Hosea 4-10: Pictures at an Exhibition, Southwestern Jour of Theol, 36, 20-26, fall, 93; auth, Bar-Kochba, Kidron Valley, Midian, Midianites, and Rechabites, Holman Bibl Dict, Nashville, Holman Bibl Publ, 91; auth, The Old Testament Demand for Faith and Obedience, Southwestern Jour of Theol, 32, 27-35, summer, 90; auth, Heavenly Strength for an Earthly Journey. The System of Hebrews, Religious Writings and Religious Systems. Systemic Analysis of Holy Books in Christianity, Islam, Buddhism, Greco-Roman Religions, Ancient Israel and Judaism, vol 2, 75-87, Brown Studies in Relig, Atlanta, Scholar Press for Brown Judaic Studies, 89. **CONTACT ADDRESS** Southwestern Baptist Theol Sem, PO Box 22246, Fort Worth, TX 76122. **EMAIL** rickljohn@aol.com

JOHNSON, ROGER A.
PERSONAL Born 09/07/1930 **DISCIPLINE** HISTORY, THEOLOGY **EDUCATION** Northwestern Univ, BA, 52; Yale Divinity Sch, BD, 55; Harvard Divinity Sch, ThD, 66. **CAREER** Elisabeth Luce Moore Prof of Christian Studies, Wellesley Col, 59-. **RESEARCH** Philosophical origins of demythologizing; existentialist theology and philosophy; psychoanalysis and theology. **CONTACT ADDRESS** 7 Appleby Rd., Wellesley, MA 02181. **EMAIL** rjohnson@mediaone.net

JOHNSON, RONALD W.
PERSONAL Born 10/06/1949, Newnan, GA, m, 1970, 3 children **DISCIPLINE** THEOLOGY **EDUCATION** West GA Col, BA, 71; So Baptist Theol Sem, M Div, 74, D Min, 85; Univ SAfrica, ThD, 99. **CAREER** Ed, SBC Sunday Sch Bd, 74-79; ed, 79-91, SBC Home Mission Bd; prof, 91-93, So Baptist Sem; dir of Evangel, 93-96, GA Baptist Convention; prof, missions & evangel, 96-., Mcafee Sch Of Theol. **HONORS AND AWARDS** Outstanding Dir of GA Baptist Leaders, 95. **MEMBERSHIPS** Acad for Evangel in Theological Education. **RESEARCH** Missiology and evangelism in postmodernism. **SELECTED PUBLICATIONS** Auth, Doctrine of Salvation, Convention Press; auth, Oikos: A Practical Approach to Family Evangelism, Brodman Press; auth, Evangelism for All God's People, Brodman Press; auth, How Will They Hear If We Don't Listen, Brodman Press. **CONTACT ADDRESS** 3001 Mercer Univ Dr, Atlanta, GA 30341. **EMAIL** Johnson_RW@Mercer.edu

JOHNSON, RONNIE J.
PERSONAL Born 12/09/1956, Springhill, LA, m, 1963 **DISCIPLINE** CHRISTIAN EDUCATION **EDUCATION** Southern Ark Univ, BS, 79; Baptist Missionary Assoc Theol Sem, MDiv, 83; Tex A&M Univ, Commerce, MS, 85; PhD, 94. **CAREER** Prof, Baptist Missionary Assoc Theol Sem, 90-. **MEMBERSHIPS** NAPCE. **RESEARCH** General Education and Ministry with Older Adults. **SELECTED PUBLICATIONS** Auth, "Parade of Love", E Tex Christian Monthly (96): 5; auth, "When to Say I Told You So", E Tex Christian Monthly, (96): 18; auth, "Don't Wear Protective Clothing When Handling God's Word", E Tex Christian Monthly, (96): 7; auth, Facing the Crises of Life Teacher's Guide, Baptist Pub House, (Texarkana), 96; auth, Knowing and Doing God's Will, Baptist Pub House, (Texarkana), 96; auth, Patterns for Prayer, Baptist Pub House, (Texarkana), 97; auth, The Parables of Jesus, Baptist Pub House, (Texarkana), 98; auth, Making Disciples, Baptist Pub House, (Texarkana), 98; auth, Social Issues in the Minor Prophets, Baptist Pub House, (Texarkana), 99; auth, Social Issues in the Minor Prophets Teacher's Guide, Baptist Pub House, (Texarkana), 99. **CONTACT ADDRESS** Dept Theol, Baptist Missionary Association Theol Sem, 1530 E Pine St, Jacksonville, TX 75766-5407.

JOHNSON, STEPHEN M.
PERSONAL Born 06/28/1941, St. Louis, MO, m, 1991, 2 children **DISCIPLINE** RELIGION **EDUCATION** Spring Hill Col, AB, 65; Marquette, MA, 68; Yale, MPhil, 71, PhD, 73. **CAREER** Prof, Montclair St Univ, 71-. **MEMBERSHIPS** Amer Acad of Religion; Soc for Values in Higher Ed; Amer Culture Assn; Popular Culture Asn **RESEARCH** American civil religion; civic affairs and philosophy; american religious history and american studies; religion and psychology. **SELECTED PUBLICATIONS** Popular Culture as Religion: Faiths by Which We Naturally Live, Pop Cul Rev, 94; In Uno Plures: From Civil Religion to Civic Responsibility, Pop Cul Rev, 95; Re-constructing American In(ter)dependence: Feminist Method and American Civic Tradition, Pub Affairs Quart, 96; A Southern Sense of America: From Jackson Square, Gettysburg, and the Vietnam Wall toward Tomorrow, Stud in Pop Cul, 96; Pedagogical and Civic Response-Abilities, Chron of Higher Ed, 97; Pedagogical Responsibility and Professional Self Disclosure: Liberating Classrooms from False Dilemmas, Thinking, 98. **CONTACT ADDRESS** 94 Elmwood Rd, Verona, NJ 07044-2508. **EMAIL** johnson@saturn.montclair.edu

JOHNSON, STEVEN D.
PERSONAL Born 10/12/1958, McDowell, KY, m, 1988 **DISCIPLINE** THEOLOGY, RELIGIOUS STUDIES **EDUCATION** Case Western Univ, BA, 81; Eden Theol Sem, MDiv, 89; Drew Univ, PhD, 95. **CAREER** Adj prof Philos and Ethics, Broome Commun Col, 95-97; Minister, United Church Christ Col, Higher and Theologcial Education, 98-. **HONORS AND AWARDS** Will Herberg Scholar; Niebuhn Scholar; Grad stud fel; Press Prize; Natl merit scholar. **MEMBERSHIPS** AAR **RESEARCH** Jurgen Moltmann, Hermeneutics, Theological Ethics, Theology. **CONTACT ADDRESS** Local Church Ministries, United Church of Christ, 700 Prospect Ave, Cleveland, OH 44115-1100. **EMAIL** johnsons@ucc.org

JOHNSON, WALTER THANIEL, JR.
PERSONAL Born 05/18/1940, Greensboro, NC, m, 1985 **DISCIPLINE** LAW **EDUCATION** A&T State U, BS, 61; Duke Univ Sch of Law, JD, 64; Univ of North Carolina Chapel Hill Govt Executives Inst, 81; Univ of North Carolina Chapel Hill Justice Exec Program, 84. **CAREER** Frye & Johnson, atty; Guilford Co Superior Ct, asst dist atty, 68-69; USAF, judge adv, 65-68; Law Office of Elreta Alexander, assoc, 64-65; Redevel Com Greensboro, relocation adv, 62-63; Public Storage & Warehousing Inc, sec, exec com, 71-76; Barjo Inc, sec, exec com, 73-; Duke Univ Law Sch, adjunct prof of law, 75-; Barbee & Johnson partner, 87-88; Barbee Johnson & Glenn partner, 88-. **HONORS AND AWARDS** Outstdng young men of NC NC Jaycees, 70; Freedom Guard Awd NC Jaycees, 70-71; disting serv award Greensboro Jaycees, 70; Peacemaker Awd Carolina Peacemaker Newspaper; vice pres Assn of Paroling Authorities, 82-85; Citizens Comm on Alternatives to Inceration, 81-83. **MEMBERSHIPS** Mem Greensboro Bd Dirs of NC Nat Bank, 76-; vice pres planning for United Way of Greensboro, 69-71; mem, chmn, Greensboro Cty Bd of Educ, 70-; mem Bd of Govs NC Bar Asn, 75-; chmn NC Inmate Grievance Co Com, 75-; chmn bd trustee Univ NC, 74-; bd mem Eastern Music Festival, 72-76; chmn North Carolina Parole Comm, 81-85; Adjunct prof North Carolina Central School of Law, 85-87; vice chmn Greensboro Vision, 85-; bd mem Greensboro Economic Devel Council, 88-. **CONTACT ADDRESS** Barbee, Johnson & Glenn, 102 N Elm Street, Greensboro, NC 27401.

JOHNSON, WILLARD
PERSONAL Born 05/30/1939, IA, m, 1980 **DISCIPLINE** RELIGION **EDUCATION** Oberlin Col, BA; Univ of Wis, MA, PhD **CAREER** Dir, 71-76, Cal St Univ; Prof, 77-pres, San Diego St Univ **HONORS AND AWARDS** Phi Beta Kappa; Woodrow Wilson Fel **MEMBERSHIPS** Am Acad of Relig **RESEARCH** Shamanism; South & East Asian Religions **SELECTED PUBLICATIONS** Auth, Poetry and Speculation of the Rg Veda, Univ of Cal, 80; Auth, Riding the Ox Home, Beacon, 86; auth, The Buddhist Religion, Wadsworth, 4th Ed. **CONTACT ADDRESS** Dept Relig Studies, San Diego State Univ, 5500 Campanile, San Diego, CA 92182-8143. **EMAIL** wjohnson@mail.sdsu.edu

JOHNSTON, CAROL F.
PERSONAL Born 05/01/1951, Panama, s **DISCIPLINE** THEOLOGY **EDUCATION** Kalamazoo Col, AB, 73; Union

Theol Sem, MDiv, 78; Claremont Grad Sch, PhD, 94. **CAREER** Res Theol, Presby Church, 89-90; consultant, coordinatory, Lilly Endow, 90-96; asst prof, Christian Theol Sem, 96-. **HONORS AND AWARDS** Presby Church Fel, 83-85; Diss Fel, Claremont, 87; Lilly Endowment Res Grant, 96-00. **MEMBERSHIPS** Am Acad of Relig; Theol Educ for Presby Soc Witness. **RESEARCH** Ecotheology, Public Theology, Faith and Wealth. **SELECTED PUBLICATIONS** Rev, of "Community: A Trinity of Models", by Frank Kirkpatrick, J of Process Studies 16.1 (87): auth, "Learning Reformed Theology from the Roman Catholics: The US Pastoral Letter on the Economy", Reformed Faith and Econ, ed Robert L Stivers, Univ Pr of Am, (Lanham, 89); coauth, "Can Capitalism Be Christian?" What's A Christian to Do?, ed David P Polk, Chalice, (St Louis, 91); auth, "Justice and Injustice: Un/Damning the Waters of Life", Encounter 53.4, (92); auth, "Essential Connections: Spirituality and Justice in a Reformed Perspective", Church and Society, (92); auth, "Thinking Theologically About the Election: A Proposal for Churches", Encounter 54.1 (93); auth, The Wealth or Health of Nations: Transforming Capitalism From Within, Pilgrim Pr, (Cleveland), 98; auth, "A Theological Critique of Economics", A Just Asia: The Challenge of A Globalized Economy, ed Viggo Mortensen, Lutheran World Fed Studies, (Geneva), 98; auth, A Biblical Eco-Theology, Pilgrim Pr, (forthcoming); auth, Thinking Theologically About Faith, Wealth, and Community Leadership, Alban Inst, (forthcoming). **CONTACT ADDRESS** Dept Theol, Christian Theol Sem, PO Box 88267, Indianapolis, IN 46208-0267. **EMAIL** johnston@cts.edu

JOHNSTON, R. K.
PERSONAL Born 06/09/1945, CA, m, 2 children **DISCIPLINE** THEOLOGY **EDUCATION** Stanford Univ, AB, 67; Fuller Theol Sem, BD, 70; Duke Univ, PhD, 74. **CAREER** Asst prof to assoc prof, Western Ky Univ, 74-82; vis prof, New Col, Berkeley, 80-81; prof, dean and provost, North Park Theol Sem, 82-93; prof, Fuller Theol Sem, 93-. **HONORS AND AWARDS** Phi Beta Kappa. **MEMBERSHIPS** Am Acad of Relig; am Theol Soc; Bonhoeffer Soc. **RESEARCH** Theology and Culture, Theology and Film, Theology and Contemporary Literature, Evangelical Theology, Old Testament Wisdom Literature. **SELECTED PUBLICATIONS** Auth, Evangelicals at an Impasse, John Knox, 82; auth, Psalms for God's People, Regal Books, 82; auth, The Christian at Play, Eerdmans, 83; ed, The Use of the Bible in Theology: Evangelical Options, John Know, 95; coed, The Variety of American Evangelicalism, Univ of Tenn, 91; coed, Studies in Old Testament Theology, Word, 92; coed, Servant Leadership, Covenant, 93; coed, Grace upon Grace, Abingdon, 99; auth, Reel Spirituality, Baker, 00. **CONTACT ADDRESS** Dept Theol, Fuller Theol Sem, 135 N Oakland Ave, Pasadena, CA 91182-0001. **EMAIL** johnston@fuller.edu

JOKIC, ALEKSANDER
PERSONAL Born 06/19/1960, Belgrade, Yugoslavia, m, 1990, 1 child **DISCIPLINE** PHILOSOPHY **EDUCATION** Belgrade Univ, BA, 84; UC Santa Barbara, PhD, 91. **CAREER** Exec dir Ctr for Philos Educ, Santa Barbara City Col, 97-; asst prof of Philos, W Virg Univ, 98-; October Prize City of Belgrade, 84. **MEMBERSHIPS** Am Philos Asn; Serbian Philos Soc. **RESEARCH** Moral philosophy; Metaphysics; Philosophy of science. **SELECTED PUBLICATIONS** Auth Why Potentiality Cannot Matter, Jour Soc Philos, 93; Consequentialism, Deontological Ethics, and Terrorism, Theoria, 95; Potentiality and Identity, Human Rights, 96; Aspects of Scientific Discovery, Serbian Philos Soc, 97; Kant, Supereerogation, and Praiseworthiness of Actions, Philos Stud, 97. **CONTACT ADDRESS** Dept of Philosophy, West Virginia Univ, Morgantown, 252 Stansbury Hall, PO Box 6312, Morgantown, WV 26505-6312. **EMAIL** ajokic@sbcc.sbceo.kiz.ca.us

JOLLEY, NICHOLAS
DISCIPLINE SEVENTEENTH AND EIGHTEENTH CENTURY PHILOSOPHY **EDUCATION** Cambridge Univ, PhD, 74. **CAREER** Prpf, Philos, Univ Calif, San Diego. **RESEARCH** Polit philos. **SELECTED PUBLICATIONS** Auth, The Reception of Descartes' Philosophy,The Cambridge Companion to Descartes, Cambridge Univ Press, 95; "Leibniz: Truth, Knowledge, and Metaphysics," The Renaissance and 17th Century Rationalism, Routledge Hist of Philos Vol 4, Routledge, 93; "Intellect and Illumination in Malebranche," Jour Hist of Philos 32, 94; ed, The Cambridge Companion to Leibniz, Cambridge Univ Press, 95. **CONTACT ADDRESS** Dept of Philos, Univ of California, San Diego, 9500 Gilman Dr, La Jolla, CA 92093.

JOLLIMORE, TROY
PERSONAL Born 01/03/1971, Liverpool, NS, Canada, m, 1997 **DISCIPLINE** PHILOSOPHY **EDUCATION** Univ of King's Col, BA, 93; Princeton Univ, MA, 96, PhD, 99. **CAREER** Georgetown Univ, vis lectr; asst prof, 98-. **MEMBERSHIPS** APA, CPA **RESEARCH** Ethics; polit; philo. **CONTACT ADDRESS** Dept of Philosophy, California State Univ, Chico, 400 W First St, Chico, CA 95929. **EMAIL** tjollimore@csuchico.edu

JOLLS, C.
DISCIPLINE LAW **EDUCATION** Stanford Univ BA 89; Harvard Law Sch, JD 93; MIT, PhD 95. **CAREER** US CT of App Judge S. Williams, law clerk, 95-96; US Sup CT Judge A. Scalia, law clerk, 96-97; Harvard Law Sch, asst prof, 94-95 and 97-. **HONORS AND AWARDS** PHI Beta Kappa. **MEMBERSHIPS** Nat Bur of Econ Res (Fac Res Fel); Harvard Univ Mind/Brain/Behavior Inter-fac Initiative (Fac Fel) reporter, Restatement of Employ Law; Ed Bd, Am Law Econ Rev. **RESEARCH** Employment law, Intersection of psychology with law and economics. **SELECTED PUBLICATIONS** Auth, A Behavioral Approach to Law and Economics, coauth, Stanford L Rev, 98; auth, Theories and Tropes: A Reply to Posner and Kelman, coauth, Stanford L Rev, 98; auth, Behavioral Economic Analysis of Redistributive Legal Rules, in: Symposium: Behavioral Law and Econ, Vanderbilt L. Rev, 98; auth, Contracts as Bilateral Commitments: A New Perspective on Contract Modification, Jour of Legal Stud, 97; auth, Hands-Tying and the Age Discrimination in Employment Act, in: Symposium: The Changing Workplace, Texas L Rev, 96; Managerial Value Diversion and Shareholder Wealth, with Lucian Bebchuk, 15, Journal of Law, Econ, and Orgn 487, 99. **CONTACT ADDRESS** School of Law, Harvard Univ, Cambridge, MA 02138. **EMAIL** jolls@law.harvard.edu

JONAS, HANS
PERSONAL Born 05/10/1903, Germany, m, 1943, 3 children **DISCIPLINE** PHILOSOPHY **EDUCATION** Univ Marburg, PhD, 28. **CAREER** Lectr ancient hist, 46-48, Brit Coun Sch Higher Studies, Jerusalem; tchng fel, 49-50, McGill Univ; vis prof, 50-51, Carleton Univ; assoc prof, 51-54, prof, 55-66, Alvin Johnson prof, 66-77, Emer Prof Philos, 77-, New Sch Social Res; guest lectr, 38-39 & 46-48, Hebrew Univ, Israel; Lady Davis fel, 49-50; Rockefeller fel, 59-60 & 74-75; vis lectr, 58, 61-62, Princeton Univ; Ingersoll lectr, 61, Harvard Univ; vis prof, 61, 66-67, Columbia Univ; adj prof, 63-64, Hunter Col; fel, Ctr Advan Studies, 64-65, Wesleyan Univ; vis prof, 66-67, Union Theol Sem; comt social thought, Univ Chicago, 68, 69 & 70; NEH grant, 73-74; fel, Am Acad Arts & Sci, 76. **HONORS AND AWARDS** DHL, Hebrew Union Col-Jewish Inst Relig, 62; DLL, New Sch Social Res, 76; DTheol, Philipps Univ, Marburg, 76. **MEMBERSHIPS** Am Philos Assn; Am Soc Studies Relig. **RESEARCH** History of philosophy and religion in late antiquity and early Christianity, especially gnosticism; technology and ethics; philosophy of organism. **SELECTED PUBLICATIONS** Auth, Macht oder Ohnmacht der Subjektivitat, Das Leib-Seele-Problem im Vorfeld des Prinzips Verantwortung, Ibid, Frankfurt, 81; auth, On Faith, Reason, and Responsibility, 81. **CONTACT ADDRESS** 9 Meadow Ln, New Rochelle, NY 10805.

JONAS, W. GLENN, JR.
PERSONAL Born 06/16/1959, Gastonia, NC, m, 1989, 1 child **DISCIPLINE** RELIGION **EDUCATION** Mars Hill Col, BA, 81; SW Baptist Theol Sem, MDiv, 84; Baylor Univ, PhD, 90. **CAREER** Instr, Temple Jr Col, 89-93; oral historian, Instr Oral Hist, Baylor Univ, 93-94; asst prof relig, Campbell Univ, 94-99, assoc prof & chmn dept of Relig and Phil, 99-. **HONORS AND AWARDS** Prof of the Year, Campbell Univ, 97; Grad Student Asn Fel, 89. **MEMBERSHIPS** Am Acad Relig; S Baptist Hist Soc; NC Baptist Hist Soc; Am Soc Church Hist; Tex Baptist Hist Soc; Nat Asn Baptist Prof Relig. **RESEARCH** Baptists; church hist; social Christianity. **SELECTED PUBLICATIONS** Auth, A Critical Evaluation of Albert Henry Newman, Church Historian, 92; auth, Through the Dark Valley: Albert Henry Newman's Experience at the Rochester Theological Seminary, Tex Baptist Hist, 93; auth, He Lives Yet in Baylor University: The Life and Influence of John Stephenson Tanner, Tex Baptist Hist, 95; co-auth, The Baylor List of Effective Preachers, The Christian Ministry, July/Aug, 96; auth, Historical Vignettes, Bibl Recorder, Aug/Sept, 96; auth, Is Unity Really Possible, Bibl Recorder, Dec, 97; auth, The Political Side of B.H. Carroll, Baptist Hist & Heritage, Fall, 98. **CONTACT ADDRESS** Dept of Religion, Campbell Univ, PO Box 143, Buies Creek, NC 27506. **EMAIL** jonas@mailcenter.campbell.edu

JONES, BARNEY LEE
PERSONAL Born 06/11/1920, Raleigh, NC, m, 1944, 5 children **DISCIPLINE** AMERICAN CHURCH HISTORY, BIBLICAL LITERATURE **EDUCATION** Duke Univ, BA, 41, PhD(Am Christiani y), 58; Yale Univ, BD, 44. **CAREER** Instr Bible, Duke Univ, 48-50, chaplain, 53-56, asst dean, Trinity Col, 56-64, assoc prof relig, 64-72, PROF RELIG, 72-80. **MEMBERSHIPS** Soc Relig Higher Educ; Am Soc Church Hist. **RESEARCH** Colonial American church history, particularly New England area; Charles Chauncy, 1707-1782. **SELECTED PUBLICATIONS** Auth, John Caldwell, critic of the Great Awakening in New England, in: A Miscellany of American Christianity, Duke Univ, 63. **CONTACT ADDRESS** 2622 Pickett Rd, Durham, NC 27705.

JONES, BARRY ALAN
DISCIPLINE RELIGION **EDUCATION** Duke Univ, PhD, 94. **CAREER** Pastor, Park View Baptist Church, Durham NC, 94-97; asst prof, Mars Hill Col, 97- 00; asst prof, Campbell Univ Divinity School, 00-. **MEMBERSHIPS** Soc of Bibl Lit. **RESEARCH** Prophetic literature. **SELECTED PUBLICATIONS** Auth, Formation of the Book of the Twelve, Scholars, 95. **CONTACT ADDRESS** Dept of Religion, Mars Hill Col, Mars Hill, NC 28754. **EMAIL** dbjones@mhc.edu

JONES, BONNIE LOUISE
PERSONAL Born 02/03/1952, Philadelphia, PA, s **DISCIPLINE** LAW **EDUCATION** Lincoln Univ, BA 1970; NC Central Univ School of Law, JD 1982. **CAREER** VA Legal Aid Soc, law clerk 1982-83; Newport News Police Dept, permits examiner 1983-85; Hampton Roads Regional Acad of Criminal Justice, training/evaluation specialist 1985-86; Blayton Allen & Assocs, assoc Attorney 1986-88; self-employed atty Hampton VA, 88-; McDermott, Roe & Sons, 92-96; College of William and Mary, School of Law, adj prof, 94-97; Hampton Gen Dit Court, judge, 96-. **HONORS AND AWARDS** Commendation for 5 city talent show from Committee for Educ of Gifted Students Hampton School System 1979; on-air Attorney for WAVY Channel 10 Midday TV program 1990-96; series of lectures to Chinese lawyers, journalists, and economists at Hampton Univ on practicing law as a minority in Amer; on-air atty for WVEC Channel 13, midday, 1987-92. **MEMBERSHIPS** Mem Phi Alpha Delta Law Fraternity 1982-; mem Big Brother/Big Sisters of Peninsula 1985; mem Amer & VA Bar Assocs 1986; mem Assoc of Trial Attorneys of Amer; mem PA Bar Assn 1987-; Hampton Bar Assn 1988-92; council vice pres Intl Training in communication council II 1988-89; Commission in Chancery for the Hampton Circuit Courts; Girls, Inc of The Greater Peninsula, former president board of directors. **CONTACT ADDRESS** Hampton Gen District Court, P.O. Box 70, Hampton, VA 23669. **EMAIL** bljones@courts.state.va.us

JONES, BRUCE WILLIAM
PERSONAL Born 08/28/1935, Palo Alto, CA, d, 3 children **DISCIPLINE** HEBREW BIBLE **EDUCATION** Amherst Col, BA, 56; Grad Theol Union, PhD(Old Testament), 72; Azusa Pac Univ, MA, 80. **CAREER** Prog secy, Student Christian Movement India, 60-62; minister, United Church of Christ, Petersburg, Ill, 62-64; lectr Old Testament, Pac Sch Relig, 68-69; asst prof relig studies, Holy Names Col, 70-73; asst prof, 73-75, ASSOC PROF RELIG STUDIES, CALIF STATE COL, BAKERSFIELD, 76-, Lectr Bible, Mills Col, 69-73; therapist, Bakersfield Family Therapy Group, 81-. **MEMBERSHIPS** Soc Bibl Lit; Am Acad Relig; Am Asn Marriage & Family Therapy. **RESEARCH** Apocalyptic literature; the Book of Esther; computer assisted instruction in Bible and religion. **SELECTED PUBLICATIONS** Auth, The prayer in Daniel 9, Vetus Testamentum, 18: 488; More about the apocalypse as apocalyptic, J Bibl Lit, 87: 325; Religious studies as a test case for computer assisted instruction in the humanities, Proc 4th Conf Comput in Undergrad Curricula, Claremont Col, 73; Computer assisted instruction in religious studies, Bull Coun Study Relig, 74; Two misconceptions about the Book of Esther, Cath Bibl Quart, 39: 171; The so-called appendix to the Book of Esther, Semitics, 6: 36; Antiochus Epiphanes and the persecution of the Jews, in: Scripture in Context: Essays on the Comparative Method, Pickwick Press, 80; Using the computer to teach methods and interpretative skills in the humanities: Implementing a project, Resourses Educ, 82. **CONTACT ADDRESS** Dept of Philosophy & Religious Studies, California State Univ, Bakersfield, 9001 Stockdale Hwy, Bakersfield, CA 93311.

JONES, CHARLES B.
PERSONAL Born 03/24/1957, Durham, NC, m, 1980, 2 children **DISCIPLINE** RELIGIOUS STUDIES **EDUCATION** Univ of Va, PhD, 96. **CAREER** Visiting asst prof, Carleton Col, 95-96; ASST PROF, CATHOLIC UNIV OF AM, 96-. **MEMBERSHIPS** Am Acad of Religion; Asn for Asian Studies; Soc for Buddhist-Christian Studies. **RESEARCH** Chinese pure land Buddhism; interreligious dialogue. **SELECTED PUBLICATIONS** Auth, Buddhism in Taiwan: Religion and the State 1660-1990, Univ of Hawaii Press, 99. **CONTACT ADDRESS** Dept of Religion and Religious Ed, Catholic Univ of America, Washington, DC 20064. **EMAIL** CBJones57@aol.com

JONES, CHRISTOPHER R. A. MORRAY
PERSONAL Born 02/03/1952, Solihull, United Kingdom, m, 1993, 2 children **DISCIPLINE** RELIGIOUS STUDIES **EDUCATION** Univ of Manchester, BA, 80; Cambridge Univ, PhD, 88 **CAREER** Res Fel, 89-92, Gordon Milburn; Visit Sch, 92-94, Stanford Univ; Lect, 94-pres, Univ of CA **MEMBERSHIPS** Am Acad of Relig; Soc of Bibl Lit; Assoc for Jewish Stud **RESEARCH** Jewish Mysticism; Christian Origins; Comparative Mysticism **SELECTED PUBLICATIONS** Auth, The Temple Within-The Embodied Divine Image and its Worship in the Dead Sea Scrolls and Other Jewish and Christian Sources, Scholars Press, 98; Auth, Paradise Revisited-The Jewish Mystical Background of Paul's Apostolate, 93, 265-292 **CONTACT ADDRESS** Dept. of Religious Studies, Univ of California, Berkeley, 325 Campbell Hall, Berkeley, CA 94720. **EMAIL** cmorjon@uclink2.berkeley.edu

JONES, DAVID CLYDE
PERSONAL Born 07/26/1937, Greenville, SC, m, 1962, 2 children **DISCIPLINE** SYSTEMATIC THEOLOGY **EDU-**

CATION Bryan Col, BA, 59; Westminster Theol Sem, BD, 62, ThM, 64; Concordia Sem, St Louis, ThD(syst theol), 70. **CAREER** Prof theol & ethics, Covenant Theol Sem, 68-. **MEMBERSHIPS** Soc Christian Ethics; Evangel Theol Soc. **RESEARCH** Cntr for Bioethics and Human Dignity; Cntr for Public Justice **SELECTED PUBLICATIONS** Auth, Who are the Poor?, Presbyterion, 77.Auth, Biblical Christian Ethics, 94. **CONTACT ADDRESS** 12330 Conway Rd, Saint Louis, MO 63141. **EMAIL** djones@covenantseminary.edu

JONES, DONALD D.
DISCIPLINE THEOLOGY; ETHICS **EDUCATION** Augustana Col, BA, 57; Drew Univ Theological School, Mdiv, 61; Drew Univ, PhD, 69. **CAREER** Instr, 66, Asst Prof, 69, Assoc Prof, 74, Prof, 81-, Drew Univ. **CONTACT ADDRESS** Drew Univ, 36 Madison Ave, Madison, NJ 07940.

JONES, DONALD L.
PERSONAL Born 08/07/1938, Xenia, OH, m, 1961, 3 children **DISCIPLINE** RELIGIOUS STUDIES **EDUCATION** Ohio Wesleyan Univ, BA, 60; Methodist Theol Sch, MDiv, 63; Duke Univ, PhD, 66. **CAREER** Asst prof relig, Earlham Col & Sch Relig, 66-67; from asst prof to assoc prof to prof Relig Studies, grad dir, assoc chair, Univ SCar, 67-. **MEMBERSHIPS** Am Acad Relig; Soc Bibl Lit; SC Acad Relig. **RESEARCH** Luke-Acts; Roman Imperial Cult; New Testament; Christian origins. **SELECTED PUBLICATIONS** Auth, The Title 'Author of Life (Leader)' in the Acts of the Apostles, Soc Bibl Lit Seminar Papers 94, 94; auth, Religion in the 1940s, Am Decades: 1940-1949, 95; auth Emperor, Emperor Cult, HarperCollins Bibl Dict, 96. **CONTACT ADDRESS** Dept of Religious Studies, Univ of So Carolina, Columbia, Columbia, SC 29208. **EMAIL** jonesd@sc.edu

JONES, EILEEN G.
PERSONAL Born Woodbury, NJ **DISCIPLINE** LAW **EDUCATION** Temple Univ, BA, 85; JD, 88. **CAREER** Asst Prof, Southern Univ, 95-. **HONORS AND AWARDS** Teaching Awd, Tulane Univ Col. **MEMBERSHIPS** Am Bar Asn. **RESEARCH** Environmental Law and Policy. **SELECTED PUBLICATIONS** Auth, Inventory of Public Concerns at the US Dept of Energy's Nuclear Weapons Complex, Xavier Univ Press, 95; co-auth, Inventory of Public Concerns at the Fernald Environmental Management Project, Xavier Univ Press, 95; auth, "Environmental Justice and Risk Communication," Proceedings of 1996 Intl Conf on Incineration and Thermal Treatment Tech, Univ CA Press, 96; auth, "Nights at the Roundtable: Public Participation Joins the Battle Against Cold War Waste," Fordham Environmental Law Journal, 97; auth, "Risky Assessments: Scientific Uncertainty and the Human Dimensions of Environmental Decision Making," William and Mary Environmental Law and Policy Law Review, 97; auth, "Postcard from South Africa," The Public Defender, 98; auth, "Gatekeeping Quacks, Magicians, and Soothsayers: Defining Science in the Courtroom," William Mitchell Law Review, 99. **CONTACT ADDRESS** Sch of Law, So Univ and A&M Col, 500 Jesse Stone, Baton Rouge, LA 70813-5000. **EMAIL** ejones@sus.edu

JONES, F. STANLEY
DISCIPLINE RELIGIOUS STUDIES **EDUCATION** Yale Univ, BA, 75; Univ Oxford, BA, 78; Universitat Gottingen, Dr Theol, 87; Vanderbilt Univ, PhD, 89. **CAREER** Full Res Post, Inst, Universitat Gottingen, 84-88; From Asst to Full Prof, Calif State Univ, 88-. **HONORS AND AWARDS** Guest Prof, Ecole Pratique des Hautes Etudes, Sorbonne, Section des Sci Religieuses, Paris, 90, 98. **MEMBERSHIPS** Am Acad of Rel, Asn pour l'etude de la litterature apocryphe chretienne, Inst for Antiquity and Christianity, Int Asn of Manichaean Studies, Soc of Bibl Lit, Studorium Novi Testamenti Societas. **RESEARCH** Jewish Christianity, the Pseudo-Clementines, New Testament Apocrypha. **SELECTED PUBLICATIONS** Auth, "'Freiheit' in den Briefen des Apostels Paulus: Eine historische, exegetische und religionsgeschichtliche Studie," in Gottinger Theologische Arbeiten 34 (Gottingen: Vandenhoeck & Ruprecht, 87); auth, An Ancient Jewish Christian Source on the History of Christianity: Pseudo-Clementine 'Recognitions' 1. 27-71," Texts and Translations 37, Christian Apocrypha Series 2 , Scholars (Atlanta, Ga), 95, 98. **CONTACT ADDRESS** Dept Rel Studies, California State Univ, Long Beach, 1250 N Bellflower Rd, Mhb 820, Long Beach, CA 90840-0006. **EMAIL** fsjones@csulb.edu

JONES, JAMES EDWARD, JR.
PERSONAL Born 06/04/1924, Little Rock, AR, m **DISCIPLINE** LAW **EDUCATION** Lincoln Univ, BA 1950; Univ IL Inst Labor and Indus Relations, MA 1951; University of Wisconsin School of Law, JD 1956; auth, "Twenty-one Years of Affirmative Action: The Maturation of the Administrative Enforcement Process under the Executive Order, 11, 246 -- as amended," 59 Chicago Kent Law Review 67 (82); auth, "Time For a Mid-course Correction?" in The Changing Law of Fair Representation, J. McKelvey, ed, Cornell Univ Pr, 85; auth, "Some Reflection on Title VKK of the Civil Rights Act, 1964 at Twenty, " 36 Mercer Law Review 813 (85); auth, "Genesis & Present Status of Affirmative Action in Employment: Economic, Legal and Political Realities, "Proceedings of the 1984 Annual Meeting of The American Political Science Asn, Sept 2, 1984, 70 Iowa L. Rev (85): 901-44; auth, "Equality and Prohibitions of Discrimination in Employment -- USA, " Bulletin No 14 of Comparative Labour Relations, Ch 14, Institute of Labour Relations -- The Catholic University of Leuven, Kluwer Law & Taxation Publishers, Deventer, The Netherlands, 85; auth, "Past, Present and Future of Affirmative Action," Second Annual Conference on Labor Law, School Law, University of Louisville. Fred B. Rothman & Co. publishers, (85): 295-329; auth, "An Introduction to the Union Duty of Fair Representation", 32 Practical Lawyer no. 2 (86); auth, "Equal Employment and Affirmative Aciton in Local Governments - A Profile" Vol VII, Law and Inequality, Univ of Minn Law School, 90; auth, "Disparate Treatment in Labor Arbitration: **CAREER** US Wage Stabilization Board, industrial relations analyst, 51-53; US Department of Labor, legislative attorney, 56-63, counsel for labor relations, 63-66; Office of Labor Management Policy Development, director, 66-67; associate solicitor, Division of Labor Relations and Civil Rights, 67-69; Univ WI-Madison, vistg prof law and indus relations 1969-70; Inst for Rsch on Poverty, assoc 1970-71; Inst Relations, Rsch Inst, dir 1971-73; Ctr for Equal Employment and Affirmative Action, Indus Relations Rsch Inst, dir 1974-; Univ WI, prof of law 1970-, Bascom prof law 1982-91; Nathan P Feinsinger Professor of Labor Law, 91-93; Prof Emeritus, 93-. **HONORS AND AWARDS** Sec Labor Career Service Awd Dept Labor 1963; John Hay Whitney Fellow; contributor articles, chapters to professional publs; Smongeski Awd, 1988; Alumni Achievement Awd, Lincoln University, 1967; Order of the Coif, 1970; Phi Kappa Phi, 1987; Prof of the Year, UW Leo Students, 1986; Hilldale Awd, Social Sci Div, 1991; Martin Luther King Humanitarian Awd, City of Madison, WI, 1991; C Clyde Ferguson, Jr Memorial Awd, American Assn of Law Schools Minority Group Section, 1993; Distinguished Service Awd, Wisconsin Law Alumni Association, 1995; Distinguished Alumni Awd, University of Illinois, 1996; Society of American Law, Teachers Achievement Awd, 1998. **MEMBERSHIPS** National Bar Assn; member, State Bar of Wisconsin; American Bar Assn, 1985-; public review board member, UAW, 1970; advisory committee, National Research Council National Academy of Sciences, 1971-73; Wisconsin Governor's Task Force on Comparable Worth, 1984-86; Madison School District Affirmative Action Advisory Committee, 1988-91; National Academy of Arbitrators, 1982-. **SELECTED PUBLICATIONS** Auth, "Twenty-one Years of Affirmative Action: The Maturation of the Administrative Enforcement Process under the Executive Order 11, 246 -- as amended, " 59 Chicato Kent Law Review 67 (82); auth, "Time For a Mid-Course Correction?" in The Changing Law of Fair Representation, J. McKelvey, ed, Cornell Univ Pr, 85; auth, "Some Reflections on Title VII of the Civil Rights Act, 1964 at Twenty," 36 Mercer Law Review 813 (85); auth, "Genesis & Present Status of Affirmative Action in Employment: Economic, Legal and Political Realities," Proceedings to the 1984 Annual Meeting of The American Political Asn, Sept. 2, 1984, 70 Iowa L. Rev (85): 901-44; auth, Equality and Prohibitions of Discrimination in Employment--USA," Bulletin No. 14 of Comparative Labour Relations, Ch. 14, Institute of Labour Relations--The Catholic University of Leuven, Kluwer Law & Taxation Publishers, Deventer, The Netherlands, (85); auth, "Past, Present and Future of Affirmative Action," Second Annual Conference on Labor Law, School of Law, University of Lousiville, Fred B. Rothman & Co. publishers (85): 295-329; auth, "An Introduction to the Union Duty of Fair Representation," 32 Practical Lawyer no. 2 (86); auth, "Equal Employment and Affirmative Action in Local Governments - A Profie" vol. VIII, Law and Inequality, Univ of Minn Law School, 90; auth, "Disparate Treatment in Labor Arbitration: An Empirical Analysis" 41 Lab. L.J. 751 (90); auth, "The Rise and Fall of Affirmative Action" Race in America, Univ of Wis Pr (93): 345-369. **CONTACT ADDRESS** Law Sch, Univ of Wisconsin, Madison, Madison, WI 53706.

JONES, JOE FRANK
PERSONAL Born 08/02/1949, Warner Robbins, GA, m, 1983, 1 child **DISCIPLINE** PHILOSOPHY **EDUCATION** Armstrong Col, BA, 75; Univ of Ga, MA, 79; Fla State Univ, MA, 81; Fla State Univ, PhD, 83. **CAREER** Asst prof to assoc prof, relig and philos, Barton Col, 91-. **HONORS AND AWARDS** Univ fel, Univ Ga and Fla State Univ; AAAS fel, Univ Ga; editor, the international journal for philosophy in the contemporary world, 97 **MEMBERSHIPS** Amer Philos Asn; Soc for Philos in the Contemporary World; The NC Relig Studies Asn; Amer Soc for Philos; Counseling and Psychotherapy; Soc for Philos of Relig. **RESEARCH** The realism/constructionism debate; Philosophy of religion; Interpretations of the history of philosophy; Philosophical counseling. **SELECTED PUBLICATIONS** Auth, Moral Growth in Children's Literature: A Primer with Examples, Philosophy in the Contemporary World, vol 1, no 4, 10-19, winter, 94; auth, Religion and Ethics and Altruism, Magill's Ready Ref: Ethics, Pasadena, Calif, Salem Press, 95; auth, Theological Perspectives on Substance Abuse, Faith and Mission, vol IX, no 2, 3-24, spring, 92; auth, Striking Commensurate from the Oxford Translation of An Post A24, Philos Res Archives, vol X, 197-202, 84; auth, Intelligible Matter and Geometry in Aristotle, Apeiron: A Jour for Ancient Philos and Sci, vol XVII, no 2, 94-102, 83; auth, A Blackstone Bibliography, Soc Theory and Practice, vol 5, no 2, 239-242, 79. **CONTACT ADDRESS** Dept of Religion and Philosophy, Barton Col, 1701 Chamberlain Dr. NW, Wilson, NC 27896-1561. **EMAIL** jjones@barton.edu

JONES, JUDITH A.
DISCIPLINE PHILOSOPHY **EDUCATION** Emory Univ, PhD. **CAREER** Asst prof, Fordham Univ. **RESEARCH** Questions of individualism, contemp naturalism. **SELECTED PUBLICATIONS** Auth, The Rhythm of Experience in Whitehead and Dewey, Listening: A Jour Rel and Cult, 94; Teach Us to See It: A Retrieval of Metaphysics in Ethics, Jour of Speculative Philos, 96; Introduction to reprint of Whitehead's Religion in the Making, Fordham UP, 96. **CONTACT ADDRESS** Dept of Philos, Fordham Univ, 113 W 60th St, New York, NY 10023.

JONES, L. GREGORY
PERSONAL Born 12/28/1960, Nashville, TN, m, 1983, 3 children **DISCIPLINE** CHRISTIAN THEOLOGY AND ETHICS **EDUCATION** Univ Denver, BA, 80, MPA, 82; Duke Univ, MDiv, 85, PhD, 88. **CAREER** Res & tchg asst, 84-87, lectr Theol, 87-88, Duke Univ; asst prof Theol, 88-94, dir Ctr for Hum, 92-96, chr Dept of Theol, 96-97, assoc prof Theol 94-97, Loyola Coll; co-ed, Modern Theol, 91-00; dean and prof of Theology, Duke Divinity School, 97-. **HONORS AND AWARDS** Acad Pol Comt, 95- , Mem Exed Bd, 95- ,Ecumenical I nst St Mary's Sen & Univ. N Am Min fel, 83-85; John Wesley fel, 85-88; Andrew Mellon fel, 87-88; Loyola Col Summer Res grants, 89, 91, & 92. **MEMBERSHIPS** Am Acad Relig; Karl Barth Soc N Am; Soc John Wesley Fellows; Soc Christian Ethics. **RESEARCH** Theology and Christian Ethics. **SELECTED PUBLICATIONS** Co-ed, Rethinking Metaphysics, Blackwells, 95; auth Embodying Forgiveness: A Theological Analysis, Wm B. Eerdmans, 95; coed Spirituality and Social Embodiment, Blackwells, 97; coed Blackwell Readings in Modern Theology, 96-99; Forgiveness, Practicing Our Faith: A Way of Life for a Searching People, Jossey-Bass, 97; Spirituality Life: Thomas Moore' Misguided Care of the Soul, The Christian Century, 96; A Thirst for God or Consumer Spirituality? Cultivating Disciplined Practices of Being Engaged by God, Mod Theol, 97; God and The Craft of Forgiveness, The Circuit Rider, 97; Finding the Will to Embrace the Enemy, Christianity Today, 97. **CONTACT ADDRESS** New Divinity, Duke Univ, Box 90968, Durham, NC 27708-0968. **EMAIL** greg.jones@div.duke.edu

JONES, OWEN D.
PERSONAL Born 05/29/1963, Glen Ridge, NJ, m, 1996 **DISCIPLINE** LAW **EDUCATION** Amherst Col, BA; MA, 85; Yale Law School, JD, 91. **CAREER** Judicial Clerk, US District Court Washington, 91-92; Assoc, Covington & Burling, 92-94; Editor, Journal of Law, Science and Technology, 97-98; Assoc Prof to Prof, Ariz State Univ, 94-. **HONORS AND AWARDS** Honorable Mention Awd, Asn of AALS Scholarly Papers Competition, 98; Jewell Prize, 90; Grant, Nat Sci Foundation; Fel, Ctr for the Study of Law, Sci and Technol, Res Fel, Gruter Inst. **MEMBERSHIPS** Soc for Evolutionary Analysis in Law, Penn Bar, Washington D.C. Bar. **RESEARCH** Law and Behavioral Biology. **SELECTED PUBLICATIONS** Auth, Sex, Culture, and the biology of Rape: Toward Explanation and Prevention, Calif Law Review, 99; auth, Evolutionary Analysis in Law: an Introduction and application to Child Abuse, Carolina Law Review, 97; **CONTACT ADDRESS** Col of Law, Arizona State Univ, PO Box 877906, Tempe, AZ 85287-7906.

JONES, PAUL HENRY
PERSONAL Born 06/28/1949, Richmond, VA, m, 1976, 2 children **DISCIPLINE** HISTORICAL THEOLOGY **EDUCATION** Yale Univ, BA, 72; Brite Div Sch, Tex Christian Univ, MDiv, 78; Vanderbilt Univ, MA, 84, PhD, 88. **CAREER** Dean of the Chapel, prof, prog dir Rel, Transylvania Univ, 85- ; tchg asst, Vanderbilt Univ, 81-83. **HONORS AND AWARDS** Alpha Omicron Pi Awd for tchg excellence, 98, Transylvania Univ; Bingham Awd excellence tchg, 97, Transylvania Univ; T.A. Abbott Awd fac excellence, Div higher educ, Christian Church, 97; John H. Smith fel, Vanderbilt Univ; Theta Phi Hon Soc, Fac Bk Awd (s) in New Testament, Hebrew Bible, Rel ed, and Christian Board of Publ Awd (s) for scholastic excellence at Brite Div Sch. **MEMBERSHIPS** AAR, NAAL. **SELECTED PUBLICATIONS** Auth, An Eidetics of the Eucharist, Mid-stream: An Ecumenical Jour, Jan 91; Worship as Identity Formation, Lexington Theol Quart, April 91; Tarry at the Cross: A Christian Response to the Holocaust, Perspectives, March 92; The Meaning of the Eucharist: Its Origins in the New Testament Texts, Encounter, Spring 93; Christ's Eucharistic Presence: A History of the Doctrine, NY, Peter Lang Publ, 94; Making a Differnce is Imperative, The Disciple, Aug 94; We Are How We Worship: Corporate Worship as a Matrix for Christian Identity Formation, Worship, July 95; Worship and Christian Identity, The Disciple, Dec 96; Disciples at Worship: From Ancient Order to Thankful Praise, in Christian Faith Seeking Historical Understanding, Macon, GA, Mercer UP, 97; coauth, 500 Illustrations: Stories from Life for Preaching and Teaching, Nashville, Abingdon Press, 98; auth, "Christian Worship for Secular People," The Christian Ministry (99). **CONTACT ADDRESS** Dept of Religion, Transylvania Univ, 300 N. Broadway, Lexington, KY 40508. **EMAIL** pjones@transy.edu

JONES, PETER D. A.
PERSONAL Born 06/09/1931, Hull, England **DISCIPLINE** ECONOMIC HISTORY **EDUCATION** Univ Manchester, Eng, BA, 52, MA, 53; London Sch Econ, PhD, 63. **CAREER**

Asst lectr Am hist & insts, Dept Am Studies, Univ Manchester, 57-58; vis asst prof econ & hist, Tulane Univ, 59-60; from asst prof to prof hist, Smith Col, 60-68; Prof Hist to Prof Emer, Univ Ill, Chicago, 68-; Am Specialist, US Dept State, 76-, Danforth teaching fel, 63; ed in hist & soc sci, Pegasus, New York, 66-68; mem hist comt, Grad Rec Exam, Educ Testing Serv, Princeton Univ, NJ, 66-70; vis prof US hist, Univ Hawaii, 72, 76; vis prof Am hist, Univ Warsaw, 73-74; mem Am studies comt, Am Coun Learned Soc, 73-; vis prof, Univ Dusseldorf, 74-75. **MEMBERSHIPS** AHA; Econ Hist Asn; Econ Hist Soc; Am Econ Asn; Conf Brit Studies. **RESEARCH** United States social and economic history; comparative history; foreign affairs. **SELECTED PUBLICATIONS** Auth, Economic History of the US since 1783, Routeledge, 56, coauth, The Christian Socialist Revival, 1877-1914: Religion, Class, and Social Conscience in Late-Victorian England, Princeton Univ, 68; The Robber Barons Revisited, Heath, 68; auth, Since Columbus: Pluralism and Poverty in the History of the Americas, Heinemann, London, 75; The USA: A History of its People and Society (2 vols), Dorsey, 76; co-ed, The Ethnic Frontier: Group Survival in Chicago and the Midwest, Eerdmans, 77; Ethnic Chicago, Eerdmans, 81; Biographical Dict of American Mayors, Greenwood Press, 82. **CONTACT ADDRESS** Dept of Hist, Univ of Illinois, Chicago, 1021 Univ Hall, Chicago, IL 60607.

JONES, RICHARD J.
DISCIPLINE MISSION AND WORLD RELIGIONS **EDUCATION** Oberlin Col, BA, 64; Johns Hopkins Univ, MA, 66; Va Theol Sem, MDiv, 72; Univ Toronto, PhD, 88. **CAREER** Tchg Eng as for lang, Phan-chau-Trinh sec sch, DaNang, Univ Hue, Viet-Nam, 66-69; tchg asst, Wycliffe Col, 84-88; prof, Va Theol Sem, 88-. **HONORS AND AWARDS** First coord, Episcopal Church of Ecuador, Diocesan Extension Sem, 72-75. **SELECTED PUBLICATIONS** Auth, How to talk to your Muslim Neighbor, Forward Movement Publ, 96; Wilfred Cantwell Smith and Kenneth Cragg on Islam as a Way of Salvation, Bulletin of Missionary Res XVI, 92; rev, Review of: The Quest for Human Unity: A Religious History by Joseph Mitsuo Kitagawa, Anglican Theol Rev, 92. **CONTACT ADDRESS** Virginia Theol Sem, 3737 Seminary Rd, Alexandria, VA 22304.

JONES, ROBERT ALUN
DISCIPLINE RELIGIOUS STUDIES **EDUCATION** Univ Redlands, BA, 65; Univ Pa, MA, 66; PhD, 69. **CAREER** Prof, Univ Ill Urbana Champaign,72-. **RESEARCH** Emile Durkheim (French philospher and social theorist), methodology of the history of ideas, and scholary use of electronic documents and networked information systems. **SELECTED PUBLICATIONS** Auth, The Ethics of Research in Cyberspace, 94; co-auth, Contextualization, Cognitive Flexibility, and Hypertext: The Convergence of Interpretive Theory, Cognitive Psychology, and Advanced Information Technologies, Blackwell, 95; auth, The Other Durkheim: History and Theory in the Treatment of Classical Sociological Thought, Blackwell, 96, Durkheim, Rousseau, and Realism, J Hist Behavioral Sci, 96; Religion and Science in Les Formes Alimentaires de la vie religieuse; Sociology and Irony, Swiss J Sociology, 97; co-ed, Durkheim's Elementary Forms of the Religious Life, Routledge, 97; Metaphysicians and Ironists: Some Reflections on Sociology and Its History, Blackwell, 98; Emile Durkheim, Blackwell, 98; auth, The Development of Durkheim's Social Realism, 99. **CONTACT ADDRESS** Religious Studies Dept, Univ of Illinois, Urbana-Champaign, 707 S Mathews, 3014 FLB, MC 166, Urbana, IL 61801. **EMAIL** rajones@uiuc.edu

JONES, SHAWN
PERSONAL Born Boise, ID, m, 3 children **DISCIPLINE** MINISTRY **EDUCATION** Columbia Christian Col, BA, 81, BS, 85; Pepperdine Univ, MS, 90; Northwest Grad Sch Ministry, D.Min. **HONORS AND AWARDS** Fac Member of the Year, 98, Student Awd. **MEMBERSHIPS** SBL **CONTACT ADDRESS** 9101 E Burnside, Portland, OR 97216-1515.

JONES, THOMAS CANBY
PERSONAL Born 09/25/1921, Karuizawa, Japan, m, 1945, 1 child **DISCIPLINE** RELIGION, PHILOSOPHY **EDUCATION** Haverford Col, BA, 42; Yale Univ, BD, 52, PhD, 56. **CAREER** From asst prof to assoc prof, 55-65, chmn dept relig & philos, 59-79, chmn div humanities, 72-75, Prof, 65-95, Prof Emeritus Relig & Philos, Wilmington Col, Ohio, 95-; Dir, Thomas R Kelly Relig Ctr, 62- & Actg Dir Peace Studies, 78-, Ed, J Quaker Relig Thought, 63-69; chmn, Quaker Theol Discussion Group, 69-77; asst clerk Am sect, Friends World Comt, 68-; Woodbrooke Col fel, spring, 72; Wistar Brown fel, Haverford Col, 78-79; Founder, Friend's Asn for Higher Educ, 80; co-chair, FAHE, 80-85. **MEMBERSHIPS** Am Soc Church Hist. **RESEARCH** Seventeenth century Puritanism; historical theology. **SELECTED PUBLICATIONS** Auth,The concept of Christ as servant as motivation for Quaker service, Quaker Relig Thought, fall 63; A believing people: Contemporary relevance, In: Conference on Concept of the Believer's Church, Scottsdale, Pa Herald, 70; The message of Quakers, In: The Three M's of Quakerism, Friends United, 71; George Fox's attitude toward war, Acad Fel Annapolis, 72; ed, Quaker Understanding of Christ & Authority, Friends World Comt, 74; auth, Worship as experienced, In: Quaker Religious Thought, Quaker Theol Disc Group, Alburtis, Pa, winter 75; Biblical basis of Peacemaking, In: New Call to Peacemaking, Friends World Comt, 77; Christ the center of holism, In: Essays in Holism: A Quaker Approach, Friends United, 78; ed, The Power of the Lord is Over All: The Pastoral Letters of George Fox, Friends United Press, 89; auth, Subject of Festschrift: Essays in Honor of T. Canby Jones: Practiced in the Presence, Friends United Press, 94. **CONTACT ADDRESS** Wilmington Col, Ohio, 251 Ludovic St, Box 1323, Wilmington, OH 45177-2499.

JONES, WILLIAM A., JR.
PERSONAL Born 02/24/1934, Louisville, KY, m **DISCIPLINE** THEOLOGY **EDUCATION** Univ of KY, BA 1958; Crozer Theol Sem, BD 1961; Benedict Coll, SC, Hon DD 1969; Colgate Rochester-Bexley Hall-Crozer Theol Sem, PhD 1975. **CAREER** 1st Baptist Church Phila, pastor 1959-62; Bethany Baptist Chucrch, Brooklyn, Pastor, 62-. **HONORS AND AWARDS** Editor Missions Outlook 1961-62; cited "Man in the News" NY Times; Man of the Yr Brooklyn Jaycees 1967; Outstanding Brooklynite NY Recorder Poll 1970; Ophelia Devore Achievement Awd 1970; Black Heritage Assn Awd 1971; Capital Formation Comm Leader Awd 1971; Comm Serv Awd Brooklyn Chap Phi Beta Sigma 1972; Frederick Douglass Awd NY Urban League 1972; Natl Assn of Health Serv Exec Awd 1975; Disting Serv Awd Colony Club First AME Zion Ch Brooklyn 1977; Freedom Awd Comm Mus of Brooklyn Inc 1978; listed in 100 Most Influential Black Amers Ebony Magazine 1979; 1 of America's 15 Outstanding Black Preachers Ebony Mag 1984. **MEMBERSHIPS** Preacher at churches, conventions, conferences univs & colls in Amer, England, Israel, India, Australia, W Africa; pres Prog Nat Bapt Conv 1968-70; prof Black Ch Studies Colgate Rochester Bexley Hall Crozer 1972-76; preacher for NBC's "Art of Living" 1977; frequently featured Conf Echoes Family Radio Network; mem Martin Luther King Jr Fellow Inc; mem Genl Council Bapt World Alliance; trustee, vis prof, Colgate Rochester Div Sch; vis prof Princeton Theol Sem; coord Min's Com on Job Oppors for Brooklyn 1963-64; bd chmn Bedford Stuyvesant Youth in Action 1965-67; founder/chmn Greater NY SCLC Operation Breadbasket 1967-72; chmn Natl SCLC Operation Breadbasket 1972-73; vis prof Practical Tehol Union Theol Sem 1975-76; chmncombd Kings Co Hosp Ctr 1970-77; adj prof romiletics Wesley Tehol Semsh DC 1976-77. **SELECTED PUBLICATIONS** Co-author "The Black Ch Looks at the Bicentennial" PNB Pub House Elgin IL 1976; author "Freedom of Conscience, The Black Experience in Amer" Religious Liberty in the Crossfire of Creeds-Ecumenical Press Philadelphia 1978; author "God in th Ghetto" PNB Pub House Elgin IL 1979. **CONTACT ADDRESS** Bethany Baptist Church, 460 Sumner Ave, Brooklyn, NY 11216.

JONES, WILLIAM B.
DISCIPLINE PHILOSOPHY **EDUCATION** Univ Va, PhD(-physics), 70; Vaderbilt Univ, PhD(philos), 75. **CAREER** Chair, dept, 85-91. **SELECTED PUBLICATIONS** Areas: philosophy of science and technology. **CONTACT ADDRESS** Old Dominion Univ, 4100 Powhatan Ave, Norfolk, VA 23058. **EMAIL** WBJones@odu.edu

JONES, WILLIAM K.
PERSONAL Born 09/01/1930, New York, NY, m, 1952, 3 children **DISCIPLINE** LAW **EDUCATION** Columbia Univ, AB, 52; LLB, 54. **CAREER** From assoc prof to prof law, 59-71, JAMES L DOHR PROF LAW, COLUMBIA UNIV, 71-, Res asst, Am Law Inst, 59-60; res dir comt on licenses & authorizations, Admin Conf US, 61-62; consult, President's Task Force on Commun Policy, 67-68, mem, Task Force on Antitrust Policy, 67-68; consult, Ford Found, 67-68. **MEMBERSHIPS** Am Bar Asn. **RESEARCH** Antitrust policy; communications policy; regulated industries. **SELECTED PUBLICATIONS** Auth, Strict Liability for Hazardous Enterprise, Columbia Law Rev, Vol 92, Pg 1744, 92, Columbia Law Rev, Vol 0092, 92. **CONTACT ADDRESS** Sch of Law, Columbia Univ, 435 W 116th St, New York, NY 10027-7201. **EMAIL** jones@law.columbia.edu

JONES, WILLIAM PAUL
PERSONAL Born 02/13/1930, Johnstown, PA, m, 1954, 5 children **DISCIPLINE** RELIGION **EDUCATION** Mt Union Col, BA, 51; Yale Univ, BD, 54; MA, 55, PhD, 60. **CAREER** Part-time instr, Divinity Sch, Yale Univ, 55-56, col, 56-57; from instr to asst prof relig, Princeton Univ, 58-65; assoc prof, 65-72, PROF PHILOS THEOL, ST PAUL SCH THEOL, MO, 72-, Soc Relig Higher Educ Kent fel, 56; Procter-Gamble & Lilly fels, France, 63-64; theol consult, Joint Strategy for Action Comt, 68- **MEMBERSHIPS** Soc Relig Higher Educ; Am Theol Soc. **RESEARCH** Philosophy of religion; religion and the arts; contemporary theology. **SELECTED PUBLICATIONS** Contribr, Masterpieces of World Philosophy, Salem & Harper, 61; auth, The Recovery of Life's Meaning: Understanding Creation and Incarnation, Asn Press, 63; Evil and creativity: Theodicy re-examined, Relig in Life, 63; The Province Beyond the River, Paulist Press, 81. **CONTACT ADDRESS** Saint Paul Sch of Theol, Kansas City, MO 63127.

JONES-CORREA, MICHAEL
DISCIPLINE POLITICAL SCIENCE **EDUCATION** Rice Univ, BA, 87; Princeton Univ, PhD, 94. **CAREER** Asst Prof to Assoc Prof, Harvard Univ, 94-. **HONORS AND AWARDS** Russell Sage Foundation Grant, 97-98; Soc Sci Res Council Post-Doc Res Fel, 97-98; Ford foundation Grant, 97-98; Open Soc Inst Individual project Grant, 97-98; William F Milton Fund, 96-97; Best Book of 1998, Am Political Sci Asn, Andrew W Mellon Fel, 92-93; Lasser Fel, 91; Nat Sci Foundation Minority Fel, 88-91; Res Grant, David Rockefeller Ctr, 96-97, 99-00; Phi Beta Kappa, 87; Nat Merit Scholarship, 83-87. **MEMBERSHIPS** Am Political Sci Asn, Soc Sci History Asn, Latin Am Studies Asn, Am Sociol Asn. **RESEARCH** Inter-ethnic conflict, negotiation and coalition-building in US urban areas; Institutional approaches to urban politics and intergovernmental relations; Immigrant naturalization and political mobilization; Social movements; Racial and ethnic identity in the United States. **SELECTED PUBLICATIONS** Auth, "The Return of the State: Immigration, Transnationalism and Dual Nationality," DRCLAS News, 00; auth, "Gendered Participation in Immigrant Politics," in Gender and Migration, Edward Elgar Pub, 00; auth, "Seeking Shelter: Immigrants and the Divergence of Social Rights and Citizenship in the US," in Reinventing Citizenship: dual Citizenship, Social Rights and Federal Citizenship in Europe and the United States, Berghan press, forthcoming; auth, Between Two Nations: The Political Predicament of Latinos in New York City, Cornell Univ Press, 98; auth, "Different paths: Immigration, Gender, and Political participation," International Migration Review, (98): 326-349; auth, "Why Immigrants Want Dual Citizenship (And We Should Too)," in Immigration and Citizenship in the 21st Century, New York, (98): 193-197; auth, "The Politics of discontent: comments on 'Immigration and Public Opinion," in Crossings: Mexican Immigration in Interdisciplinary Perspective, Harvard Univ Press, (98): 404-412; auth, "Becoming Hispanic: Secondary Pan-Ethnic Identification among Latin American-Origin Populations in the United States," Hispanic Journal of Behavioral Sciences, (96): 214-255; auth, "New Directions for Latinos as an Ethnic Lobby in US Foreign Policy," Harvard Journal of Hispanic Policy, (96): 47-86. **CONTACT ADDRESS** Dept Government, Harvard Univ, 1737 Cambridge St, Cambridge, MA 02138. **EMAIL** correa@fas.harvard.edu

JONTE-PACE, DIANE E.
PERSONAL Born 07/07/1951, Berkeley, CA, m, 1976, 2 children **DISCIPLINE** RELIGIOUS STUDIES **EDUCATION** Univ Calif, BA, 73; Univ Chicago, MA, 75; PhD, 84. **CAREER** From lectr to assoc prof, Santa Clara Univ, 84-. **MEMBERSHIPS** Am Acad of Relig. **RESEARCH** Psychology of Religion, Feminist Theory, Psychoanalysis. **SELECTED PUBLICATIONS** Coed, Mapping Religion and Psychology, Routledge, 00; auth, Speaking the Unspeakable: Religion, Misogyny and the Uncanny Mother in Freud's Cultural Texts, Univ of Calif, forthcoming. **CONTACT ADDRESS** Relig Studies, Santa Clara Univ, 500 El Camino Real, Santa Clara, CA 95053-0001. **EMAIL** djontepace@scu.edu

JOOHARIGIAN, ROBERT B.
DISCIPLINE PHILOSOPHY **EDUCATION** Univ of Wisconsin, PhD, 77. **CAREER** Adj prof, Schoolcraft Comm Col, 81-, adj inst, Macomb Comm Col, 88-, adj inst, Central Mich Univ, 88-; adj inst, Oakland Comm Col, 00-. **MEMBERSHIPS** APA **RESEARCH** Philosophy of religion. **SELECTED PUBLICATIONS** Auth, God and Natural Evil, Wyndham Hall Press, Bristol IN. **CONTACT ADDRESS** PO Box 1485, Royal Oak, MI 48068-1485.

JOOS, ERNEST
PERSONAL Born 01/06/1923, Uraiujfalu, Hungary, m, 1949, 6 children **DISCIPLINE** PHILOSOPHY, LITERATURE **EDUCATION** McGill Univ, MA, 59; Inst d'Etudes Medievales, Montreal, Lic en Phil, 66; Univ Montreal, PhD(medieval philos), 70. **CAREER** Asst prof philos, Loyola Col, Montreal, 67-75; PROF PHILOS, CONCORDIA UNIV, 75-, Vis prof philos, Univ Laval, Quebec, 77-78 & Univ de Montreal, 79-81. **MEMBERSHIPS** Can Philos Asn; Am Cath Philos Asn. **RESEARCH** Intentionality; metaphysics-ontology. **SELECTED PUBLICATIONS** Auth, Dialogue With Heidegger on Values: Ethics for Times of Crisis (American University Studies: Series V, Philosophy, Vol 127, December 92; ed, George Lukacs and His World: a Reassessment (American University Studies, Series XIX: General Literature, Vol 9, April 88; auth, Intentionlity, Source of Intelligibility: The Genesis of Intentionality (American University Studies, V: Philosophy, Vol 69), March 89. **CONTACT ADDRESS** Dept of Philosophy, Concordia Univ, Montreal, 1455 De Maisonneuve Blvd W, Montreal, QC, Canada H3G 1M8.

JORDAN, EDDIE J., JR.
PERSONAL Born 10/06/1952, Fort Campbell, KY, m, 1974 **DISCIPLINE** LAW **EDUCATION** Wesleyan Univ, Middletown, CT, BA, 1970-74; Rutgers Law School, Newark, NJ, JD, 1974-77. **CAREER** Pepper, Hamilton & Scheetz, assoc; Southern Univ Law School, prof, 81; US Attorney's Office, assist US attorney, 84-87; Sessions & Fishman, assoc, 87-90, partner, 90-92; Bryan, Jupiter & Lewis, of counsel, 92-94; US Dept of Justice, US Attorney, 94-. **HONORS AND AWARDS** Louis A Martinet Legal Society, A P Tureaud Awd, 1992; Victims & Citizens Against Crime, Outstanding Prosecutor Awd, 1995; NAACP, New Orleans Chap, David Ellis Byrd Awd, 1997;

Crimefighters Assn of New Orleans, Distinguished Public Svc Awd, 1998. **MEMBERSHIPS** Human Relations Commission, City of N Orleans, advisory comm human relations, 1993; LA State Bar Assn, bd of governors, 1984; Metropolitan Area Comm, bd of dirs, 1990-94; Planned Parenthood of LA, bd of dirs, 1989-94, vice pres, bd of dirs, 1991-93; St Thomas/Irish Channel Consortium, bd of dirs, 1990-94; NAACP, 1993-95; Reducing Alcohol Accessibility to Youth, adv bd; New Orleans chapter of Federal Bar Assn, bd of dirs; Pediatric AIDS Prog, adv bd; New Orleans Community, Teach for America, adv bd; Atty General's Adv Comm, Subcommittee for Controlled Substances/Drug Abuse Prevention, vice chair; Reducing Alcohol Accessibility to Youth, bd of dirs for the New Orleans Chapter of the Federal Bar Assoc, advisory bd for the Pediatric AIDS Program, New Orleans comm advisory bd for Teach for America; vice chair of the Attorney General's advisory comms, subcomm for Controlled Substances/Drug Abuse Prevention; mem, subcommittees for Justice Programs and Organized Crime/ Violent Crime; 1998, two-year term on the Attorney General's, advisory comm. **SELECTED PUBLICATIONS** In Search of the Meaning of RICO, LA State Bar Assn; Changing Carnival's old ways is a progressive step, The Times Picayune; Recent Dev in the Law Manual, LA State Bar Assn, 1985-96; Louisiana Appellate Practice Handbook, Lawyers Cooperative Publishing, contributing author. **CONTACT ADDRESS** US Atty's Office, 501 Magazine St, New Orleans, LA 70130.

JORDAN, EMMA COLEMAN
PERSONAL Born 11/29/1946, Berkeley, CA **DISCIPLINE** LAW **EDUCATION** CA State U, BA 1969; Howard U, JD 1973. **CAREER** Stanford Law School, tching fellow 1973-74; Univ of Santa Clara, asst prof 1974-75; Georgetown Univ Law Center, prof, 87- present. **HONORS AND AWARDS** White House Fellow, 1980-81, Outstdng Acad Achvmt Awd Phi Alpha Delta 1973; grad 1st in class Howard Law Sch 1973; **MEMBERSHIPS** Exec comm, 1988-91, pres-elect, 1991-92, pres, 1992-93; Assoc of Amer Law Schools; mem Nat Conf of Black Lawyers; Nat Bar Assn; Am Soc of Intl Law; pub mem CA State Bd of Dental & Exmnrs; Am Assn of Law Schs Sects on Commercial Law & Contracts, Minority Grps; mem Charles Houston Bar Assn; bd of dir CA Assn of Black Lawyers; pres Soc of Amer Law Teachers 1986-88; chr CA St Bar Financial Inst Comm; chr AALS Financial Inst & Consumer Fin Serv Sect; bd mem Consumer Action; adv comm Natl Consumer Union Northern CA; mem Amer Law Inst; special asst, Attorney General of the US, 1981. **SELECTED PUBLICATIONS** Co-ed, Race, Gender and Power in America, Oxford Univ Press, 95; Lynching: The Dark Metaphor of American Law, Basic Books, spring 99; Litigation without representation; The Need for Intervention to Affirm Affirmative Action, Harvard Civil Liberties Civil Rights Law Rev 1979; "After the Merger of Contribution & Indemnity, What are the Limits of Comparative Loss Allocation" AR St Law Rev 1980; "Problems & Prospects of Participation in Affirmative Action Litigation" UC Davis Law Rev 1980; Limitations of the Intl Lega Mech Namibia 1972; "Ending the Floating Check Game," Hastings Law Review, 1986; "Taking Voting Rights Seriously," Nebraska Law Review, 1986. **CONTACT ADDRESS** Sch of Law, Georgetown Univ, 600 New Jersey Ave, Washington, DC 20001-2075.

JORDAN, MARK
PERSONAL Born 02/15/1953, Cannes, France **DISCIPLINE** RELIGION, PHILOSOPHY, MEDIEVAL STUDIES **EDUCATION** St Johns Col, BA, 73; Univ Tex, MA, 75; PhD, 77. **CAREER** Asst prof, 77-78, 85-87; assoc prof, 87-88; assoc prof MC, 88-95; prof, 95-00, Univ Not Dam; asst prof, assoc prof, Univ Dal, 78-84; vis prof, PIMS, 90; prof, Emory Univ, 99-. **HONORS AND AWARDS** Thomas J Watson Fel; Fulbright-Hays Gnt, Spain; Guggenheim Fel. **MEMBERSHIPS** AAR; APA; MAA; CTSA. **RESEARCH** Homosexuality and Christianity; rhetorical form in theology and philosophy; "Scholastic" theology. **SELECTED PUBLICATIONS** Auth, The Invention of Sodomy in Christian Theology, Univ Chicago Press (Chicago, IL), 97; auth, The Silence of Sodom: Homosexuality in Modern Catholicism, Univ Chicago Press (Chicago, IL), 00; auth, The Ethics of Sex, Basil Blackwell (Oxford), forthcoming. **CONTACT ADDRESS** Dept Religion, Emory Univ, 1364 Clifton Rd NE, Atlanta, GA 30322-1061.

JORDAN, ROBERT WELSH
PERSONAL Born 12/20/1936, Miami Beach, FL, m, 1962, 1 child **DISCIPLINE** PHILOSOPHY, PHILOSOPHY OF HISTORY **EDUCATION** Univ Houston, BS, 57; New Sch Social Res, MA, 70. **CAREER** Asst prof, 70-82, ASSOC PROF PHILOS, CO STATE UNIV, 82-. **MEMBERSHIPS** Husserl Circle; Soc Phenomenol & Existential Philos; Am Soc Value Inquiry. **RESEARCH** Twentieth century Continental philosophy; German philosophy since Kant; philosophy of history and social science. **SELECTED PUBLICATIONS** Auth, Vico and Husserl: History and Historical Science, In: Giambattista Vico's Science of Humanity, John's Hopkins Univ Press, 76; Vico and the Phenomenology of the Moral Sphere, Social Res, Vol 43, 76; Das transzendentale Ich als Seiendes in der Welt, Persperktiven Philos, Vol 5, 79; Das Gesetz, die Anklage und Klc Prozess: Franz Kafka und Franz Brentano, Jahrbuch deutschen Schillerges, Vol 24, 80; auth, intro to & transl of Husserl's Inaugeral Lecture at Freiburg im Breisgau (1917): Pure Phenomenology, its Method and its Field of Investigation, In: Husserl: The Shorter Works, Univ Notre Dame Press, 80; Extended Critical Review of Edmind Husserl's Vorlesungen uper Ethik and Wertlehre, 1908-1914, ed by Ullrich Melle (Husserliana, vol 28), Dordrecht, Boston, London: Kluwer Academic Pubs, 88, in Husserl Studies 8, 92; Phenomenalism, Idealism, and Gurwisch's Account of the Sensory Noema, in To Work at the Foundations, J. C. Evans and R. W. Stufflebeam, eds, Kluwer Academic Pubs, 97; The Part Played by Value in the Modification of Open into Attractive possibilities, Ch 5 oh Phenomenology of Values and Valuing, J. G. Hart and Lester Embree, eds, Kluwer Academic Pubs, 97; Hartmann, Nicolai, in Encyclopedia of Phenomenology, Lester Embree, gen ed, Kluwer Academic Pubs, 97; Value Theory in Encyclopedia of Phenomenology, Lester Embree, gen ed, Kluwer Academic Pubs, 97. **CONTACT ADDRESS** Dept of Philos, Colorado State Univ, Fort Collins, CO 80523-0001. **EMAIL** rjordan@vines.colostate.edu

JORDAN, SANDRA D.
PERSONAL Born 12/03/1951, Philadelphia, PA, m, 1973 **DISCIPLINE** LAW **EDUCATION** Wilberforce University, BS Ed, magna cum laude, 1973; University of Pittsburgh Law School, JD, 1979. **CAREER** US Dept of Justice, asst US attorney, 79-88; US Dept of Independent Counsel, Iran Contra, assoc counsel, 88-91; University of Pittsburgh Law School, prof, 89-. **HONORS AND AWARDS** US Attorney General Special Commendation, 1984; Allegheny County Bar Association, Exceptionally Qualified for Judiciary, 1992. **MEMBERSHIPS** Homer S Brown Law Association, 1979-; National Bar Association, 1979-; Disciplinary Bd, Supreme Court of PA, 1990-94; Pennsylvania Judicial Conduct Bd, vice chair, 1994-. **SELECTED PUBLICATIONS** Published "Classified Information & Conflicts," Columbia Law Review vol 91, No 7, 1991. **CONTACT ADDRESS** Professor, Univ of Pittsburgh, Bradford, 3900 Forbes Ave, Rm 529, Pittsburgh, PA 15260. **EMAIL** jordan@law.pitt.edu

JORGENSEN, DANNY L.
PERSONAL Born 01/23/1951, Sidney, MT **DISCIPLINE** RELIGION **EDUCATION** N Ariz Univ, BS, 72; W Ky Univ, MA, 74; Ohio State Univ, PhD, 79. **CAREER** Prof relig studies, 92- courtesy prof sociol, 97-, undergrad honors prg fac, 96-, Univ S Fla. **HONORS AND AWARDS** Best Article Awd, John Whitmer Hist Asn, 94, 96; Outstanding Undergrad Tchg Awd, Univ S Fla, 91-92. **MEMBERSHIPS** John Whitmer Hist Asn; Mormon Hist Asn. **SELECTED PUBLICATIONS** Auth, Less-Known and Historically Unimportant? Studying the Lives of Reorganized Latter Day Saint Women, Restoration Studies, 98; auth, Religion and Modernization: Secularization or Sacralization?, Relig & Political Order: Politics in Class & Contemporary Christianity, Islam & Judaism, 96; auth, Neo-Paganism in America: How Witchcraft Matters Today, The Relig Factor: Intro to How Relig Matters, 96; auth, The Old Fox: Alpheus Cutler, Differing Visions: Dissenters in Mormon Hist, 94; auth, Cutler's Camp at the Big Grove on Silver Creek: A Mormon Settlement in Iowa, 1847-1853, Nauvoo Jour, Fall, 97; auth, Sisters' Lives, Sisters' Voices: Neglected RLDS Herstories, John Whitmer Hist Asn Jour, 97; auth, Dissent and Schism in the Early Church: Explaining Mormon Fissiparousness, Dialogue: Jour Mormon Thought, Fall, 95; auth, Conflict in the Camps of Israel: The Emergence of the 1853 Cutlerite Schism, Jour Mormon Hist, Spring, 95; auth, The Scattered Saints of Southwestern Iowa: Cutlerite-Josephite Conflict and Rivalry, 1855-1865, John Whitmer Hist Asn Jour, 93. **CONTACT ADDRESS** Dept Religious Studies, Univ of So Florida, 4202 E Fowler Ave. CPR 107, Tampa, FL 33620-5550.

JOSEPH, NORMA BAUMEL
PERSONAL Born 10/12/1944, m, 4 children **DISCIPLINE** JUDAISM, JEWISH LAW AND ETHICS **EDUCATION** Brooklyn Col, BA, 66; CUNY, MA, 68; Concordia Univ, PhD, 95. **CAREER** Visiting prof, SUNY Albany, 81; Adj Asst Prof, 89-90; fac, 90-92; asst prof, Concordia Univ, 92-98; assoc prof, 98; Scholar, Brandeis Univ, 99-00. **HONORS AND AWARDS** Heritage Canada/Chair in Quebec and Canadian Jewish Studies; Faculty Res Dev Grant; The Leo Wasserman Prize for best article published in Am Jewish Hist in 95; Dissertation nominated for Govenor Generals' Gold Medal Awd for Excellence, 95; Audio Visual Resources for the Teaching of Relig; Nominated: Governor General's Persons Awd, 95; Woman of Distinction Awd, 98; Scholar-in-Residence, Brandeis Univ, 99-00; pres, intl coalition for agunah rights (icar); consult, can coalition of jewish women for the get; founder, montreal women's prayer group. **MEMBERSHIPS** Am Academy of Relig, Asn of Jewish Studies, Asn of Canadian Jewish Studies, Canadian Soc for the Study of Relig. **RESEARCH** Women and Judaism, Jewish law and ethnics, and women and relig. **SELECTED PUBLICATIONS** Auth, "Personal Reflections on Jewish Feminism," in M. Weinfeld, B. Shafir and I. Cotler, The Canadian Jewish Mosaic, (Toronto: Wiley & Sons, 81), 205-220; auth, "Response 4," "Response 6," in Oppenheim, M., Mutual Upholding: Fashioning Jewish Philosohpy Through Letters," (New York: Peter Lang, 92), 113-6, 167-71; auth, "Norma Joseph," "Dialogue,", "Trialouge," in Zuckerman, Francine, ed, Half the Kingdom: Seven Jewish Feminists, (Montreal: Vehicule Press, 92), 89-105, 118-144; auth, "The Jew as Other in Feminist Discourse," in Shogun, Debra ed, A Reader in Feminist Ethics, Canadian Scholars; Press, (Canadian Scholars' Press, 92), 217-222; auth, "Mehitza: Halakhic Decisions and Political Consequences," in Grossman, S. and R. Haut, eds, Daughters of the King: Women and the Synagogue, (Philadelphia: The Jewish Publication Soc, 92), 117-134; auth, "The Feminist Challenge to Judaism: Critique and Transformation," in Morny Joy and Eva K. Neumaier-Dargay, ed, Gender, Genre and Religion: Feminist Reflections, (Wilfred Laurier Univ Press, 95); auth, "You don't know me because you can label me: Self-identity of an Orthodox Feminist," Celebrating the Lives of Jewish Women: Patterns in a Feminist Sampler, eds Rachel Siegel and Ellen Cole, (Haworth Press, 97); auth, "A Feminist Scenario of the Jewish Future," Creating the Jewish Future, Centre for Jewish studies York Univ, (Alta Mira Press, 98); auth, "Hair Distractions: Women and Worship in the Responsa of Rabi Moshe Feinstein," Jewish Legal Writings by Women, Micah Halperin and Hannah Safrai, eds, Jerusalem: (Urim Press, 98), 9-22; auth, "Feinstein, Moses," Am Nat Biography, ed, John A. Garrity and Mark C. Carnes, vol 7, (New York: Oxford Univ Press, 99); auth, **CONTACT ADDRESS** Dept of Rel, Concordia Univ, Montreal, 1455 de Maisonneuve W, Montreal, QC, Canada H3G 1M8. **EMAIL** nojo@vax2.concordia.ca

JOSEPH, STEPHEN
PERSONAL Born 11/27/1940, Worcester, MA **DISCIPLINE** PHILOSOPHY **EDUCATION** Brown Univ, BA, 62; Univ Penn, MA, 65, PhD, 79. **CAREER** Philo Dept Ch, 91-, Prof, 82-98, Framingham State College; math Teach, 82, Univ MA; philo Teach, 68-82, Boston State College. **MEMBERSHIPS** APA; MSCA. **RESEARCH** Ethics; Philosophy of Religion. **CONTACT ADDRESS** Dept of Philos, Framingham State Col, 100 State St, Framingham, MA 01701. **EMAIL** sjoseph@fsc.edu

JOSEPH, WEILER H. H.
PERSONAL Born 09/02/1951, Johannesburg, South Africa, 5 children **DISCIPLINE** LEGAL STUDIES, LAW **EDUCATION** Sussex Univ, BA, 76; Hague Acad, Dp Intl Law, 78; Cambridge Univ, LL B, 77, LL M, 82; Univ Euro Inst, PhD, 82. **CAREER** Prof, Euro Univ Inst, 78-85; prof, Univ Mich LS, 85-92; prof, Harvard Law Sch, 92-01; prof, NYU Sch Of Law, 01-. **HONORS AND AWARDS** Dr. Honoris Causa, Univ Col, London, 00; Jean Monnet Chair, Harv Law Sch, 95. **MEMBERSHIPS** ASIL; ECSA; IACL; AAAS. **RESEARCH** European union and European Integration; Int. economic law and justice; intl dispute settlement; WTO and NAFTA; Middle East and Arab-Israeli conflict. **SELECTED PUBLICATIONS** Auth, Der Fall Steinmann, Bettina Wassmann Verlag (Bremen, Munich), 98, 00; auth, The Constitution of Europe--do the new clothes have an emperor? Cambridge Univ Press, 98; auth, The EU, the WTO and the NAFTA, Academy of European Law, European Univ Inst, Florence, and Oxford Univ Press, 00; auth, Integration Through Law--Europe and the American Federal Experience, Walter de Gruyter (Berlin/New York), 85, 88. **CONTACT ADDRESS** Sch of Law, New York Univ, 40 Washington Sq S, New York, NY 10012-1099. **EMAIL** weiler@jeanmonnetprogram.org

JOSEPHSON, SUSAN G.
PERSONAL Born 07/30/1945, Tubingen, Germany, m, 1967, 2 children **DISCIPLINE** PHILOSOPHY **EDUCATION** Ohio State Univ, BA, 68; MA, 72; PhD, 81. **CAREER** Prof, Columbus Coll of Art and Design, 72-; res assoc, Laboratory for Artificial Intelligence Research, Ohio State Univ, 87-. **MEMBERSHIPS** Am Philos Asn; Society for Minos and Machine's. **RESEARCH** Artificial Intelligence; Philosophy of Art; Philosophy of Design; Philosophy of Media; Illustrator. **SELECTED PUBLICATIONS** Auth, Controversies in Artificial Intelligence, The World & I, 95; Remedial Readings on Advertising, AIGA J of Graphic Design, 97; auth, "What advertising does to Us, The World and I", 96; From Idolatry to Advertising: Visual Art and Contemporary Culture, 96; coauth, Architecture of Intelligence: The Problems and Current Approaches to Solutions, Artificial Intelligence and Neural Networks, 94; Abductive Inference, Computations, Philosophy, Technology, 94. **CONTACT ADDRESS** 93 East Riverglen Dr, Worthington, OH 43085. **EMAIL** sjosephson@ccad.edu

JOST, TIMOTHY STOLZFUS
PERSONAL Born 11/25/1948, Reedley, CA, m, 1982, 3 children **DISCIPLINE** LAW **EDUCATION** Univ CA, Santa Cruz, BA, 70; Univ Chicago, JD, 75. **CAREER** Asst Prof Law to Newton D. Baker, Baker & Hostetler Chair of Law and Prof of Col of Medicine and Public Health, Division of Health Services and Management and Policy, OH State Univ, 81-. **HONORS AND AWARDS** OH State Univ Distinguished Scholar Awd, 96; Fulbright Awds, 89, 96. **MEMBERSHIPS** Am Soc of Law, Medicine and Ethics; Am Health Lawyers Asn; Gesellschaft fur Recht und Politik im Gesundheitswesen. **RESEARCH** Law and medicine; property law. **SELECTED PUBLICATIONS** Auth, Health LawTreatise, with Barry Furrow, Thomas Greaney, Sandra Johnson, and Robert Schwartz, West, 95; Health Law Hornbook, with Barry Furrow, Thomas Greaney, Sandra Johnson, and Robert Schwartz, West, 95; Cases, Problems & Materials in Health Law, 3rd ed, with Barry Furrow, Thomas Greaney, Sandra Johnson, and Robert Schwartz, West, 97; Regulation of the health Care Professions,

ed, Health Admin Press, 97; The Law of Medicare and Medicaid Fraud and Abuse, with Sharon Davies, West, 98. **CONTACT ADDRESS** Law Sch, Ohio State Univ, Columbus, 55 W 12th Ave, Columbus, OH 43210-1306. **EMAIL** jost.1@osu.edu

JOY, LYNN S.
DISCIPLINE PHILOSOPHY **EDUCATION** Harvard Univ, PhD, 82. **CAREER** Asst Prof of philos and hist, Vanderbilt Univ, 82-88; fel, Bunting Inst, 88-89; assoc prof of philos Univ Notre Dame, 89-94; prof of philos, and hist, Duke Univ, 95-00; prof of philos, Univ of Notre Dame, 00-. **RESEARCH** Philosophy and History of Science, Ethics, Modern Philosophy. **SELECTED PUBLICATIONS** Auth, Gassendi the Atomist: Advocate of History in an Age of Science, Cambridge Univ, 87. **CONTACT ADDRESS** Dept of Philos, Univ of Notre Dame, 336 O' Shaughnessy Hall, Notre Dame, IN 46556. **EMAIL** ljoy@acpub.duke.edu

JOY, PETER
PERSONAL Born 12/02/1951, Youngstown, OH, s **DISCIPLINE** LAW **EDUCATION** Case Western Reserve Univ Law School, JD, 77. **CAREER** Asst prof and dir, Milton A. Kramer Law Clinic, Case Western Univ School of Law, 84-98; prof and dir, Milton A. Kramer Law Clinic, Case Western Univ School of Law, 98; prof, Washington Univ School of Law, 98-. **MEMBERSHIPS** AALS; CLEA. **RESEARCH** Legal profession; clinical legal educ; trial practice and procedure; criminal law. **SELECTED PUBLICATIONS** Contributor, "Report of the Committee on the Future of the In-House Clinic", in 42 J. Legal Ed 508, 94; auth, "The MacCrate Report: Moving Toward Integrated Learning Experiences", in 1 Clinical L Rev 401, 94; auth, "What We Talk About When We Talk About Professionalism", in 1 Geo J Legal Ethics 987, 94; auth, "A Time to Disrobe to Save Your Honor", in National J, 95; auth, "Losing Titles", in Ohio Law, 96; auth, "Unpublished Opinions Stunt Common Law", in National J, 96; auth, "Clients Are Consumers, Too", in 82 ABAJ 120, 96; auth, "Clinical Scholarship: Improving the Practice of Law", in 2 Clinical L Rev 385. 96; auth, "Amendments to Disciplinary Rules Create New Expectations for Ohio Lawyers", in Law & Fact, 97; auth, "Ethics Perspectives: What Are the Ethical Ramifications of an 'Of Counsel' Affiliation?", in 68 Cleveland B J 20, 97; auth, "Clinical Experience Translates to Client Experience", in 11 NALP Bull, 98; auth, "Submission of the Association of American Law Schools to the Supreme Court's Student Practice Rule", in 4 Clinical L Rev 539, 98; coauth, "Access to Justice, Academic Freedom, and Political Inference: A Clinical Program Under Siege", in 4 Clinical L Rev 531, 98; auth, "Political Interference with Clinical Legal Education: Denying Access to Justice," 74 TUL, L.R. 235, 99; auth, "Insulation Needed for Elected Judges," National J (00). **CONTACT ADDRESS** Sch of Law, Washington Univ, One Brookings Dr., Campus Box 1120, Saint Louis, MO 63130. **EMAIL** joy@wulaw.wustl.edu

JOYNER, IRVING L.
PERSONAL Born 12/11/1944, Brooklyn, NY, d, 3 children **DISCIPLINE** LAW **EDUCATION** Long Island Univ, Brooklyn NYork, BS, 1970; Rutgers Univ School of Law, Newark NJ, JD. **CAREER** United Church of Christ Comm for Racial Justice, New York NY, dir of criminal justice, 68-78; Currie & Joyner, Raleigh NC, attorney at law, 78-80; Natl Prison Project of ACLU, Washington DC, staff attorney, 80-81; Currie, Pugh & Joyner, Raleigh NC, attorney at law, 81-85; NC Central Univ School of Law, Durham NC, assoc dean and prof of law, 85-. **HONORS AND AWARDS** Outstanding Contribution to Racial Justice, Assn of Black Law Students, 1977; Paul Robeson Awd, Black Amer Law Student Assn, 1977; Professor of the Year, NCCU Student Bar Assn, 1985; Living Legacy Awd OA Dupree Scholarship Foundation, 1987; Outstanding Contribution to Civil Rights, Wake Forest Black Law Student Assn 1987; author of The Black Lawyer in NC, article, 1988; Conflicts of Interest, article, 1988; President's Awd by La-Grange, Frink Alumni and Friends Assn, 1991; Lawyers of the Year Awd by North Carolina Assn of Black Lawyers, 1995; Outstanding Teacher's Awd, North Carolina Central University Law School Student Bar Association. **MEMBERSHIPS** Mem/former pres, NC Assn of Black Lawyers, 1977-; mem, NC State Bar, 1977-; mem, Natl Bar Assn, 1977-; mem, NC Academy of Trial Lawyers, 1977-; Federal Bar Advisory Council, 1985-. **SELECTED PUBLICATIONS** Police Misconduct Litigation CLE manuscript and Law Review article, 1991; Preparation and Use of Requests for Jury Instructions, CLE manuscript, 1988; Criminal Procedure in NC, book, 1989; Supplements to Criminal Procedure in North Carolina, 1991-94; The Status of African-American Lawyers in North Carolina, article, 1992; auth, Criminal Procedure in North Carolina, 2nd ed, 99. **CONTACT ADDRESS** Professor of Law, No Carolina Central Univ, 1512 S Alston Ave, Durham, NC 27707.

JUERGENSMEYER, JULIAN C.
DISCIPLINE LAW **EDUCATION** Duke Univ, AB, JD. **CAREER** Fac mem, Ind Univ, Bloomington, 65-68; fac mem, Tulane Univ, 70-72; dir, Cambridge-Warsaw Int Trade Law prog, 73-86; prof, Univ Fla, 69-. **HONORS AND AWARDS** Res fel, Int Legal Ctr. **MEMBERSHIPS** Ohio Bar; Order of the Coif; Phi Beta Kappa; Omicron Delta Kappa. **RESEARCH** Land use planning law, property, intl environmental law, agricultural law. **SELECTED PUBLICATIONS** Coauth, A Practitioner's Guide to Impact Fees; Florida Land Use and Growth Management Law; Urban Planning and Land Development Control Law. **CONTACT ADDRESS** School of Law, Univ of Florida, PO Box 117625, Gainesville, FL 32611-7625. **EMAIL** juergens@law.ufl.edu

JULIANO, ANN CAREY
DISCIPLINE CIVIL PROCEDURE AND EMPLOYMENT DISCRIMINATION **EDUCATION** Univ Pa, BA, 89; Cornell Law Sch, JD, 92. **CAREER** Asst prof, Villanova Univ; law clerk, Honorable Stephanie K. Seymour, US Ct Appeals 10th Circuit and later to, Honorable Raymond J. Pettine, US Dist Ct Dist RI; from trial atty in the Indian Resources Sect to spec asst to asst atty gen Lois J. Schiffer, US Dept Justice; Env and Natural Resources Div; past prof lectr, George Washington Univ Nat Law Ctr. **HONORS AND AWARDS** Special Commendation for Outstanding serv, Dept Justice, 97. **RESEARCH** Employment discrimination. **SELECTED PUBLICATIONS** Auth, Did She Ask For It: The Unwelcome Requirement in Sexual Harassment Cases, 77 Cornell L. Rev 1558, 92. **CONTACT ADDRESS** Law School, Villanova Univ, 800 Lancaster Ave, Villanova, PA 19085-1692. **EMAIL** juliano@law.vill.edu

JUNG, DARRYL
PERSONAL Born 02/24/1962, Montreal, PQ, Canada, m, 1993, 1 child **DISCIPLINE** PHILOSOPHY **EDUCATION** McGill Univ, BA, 85, MA, 90; MIT, PhD, 94. **CAREER** Asst prof. **RESEARCH** Philosophy of mathematics; philosophy of logic; philosophy of language; early analytic philosophy; mathematical logic; set theory. **SELECTED PUBLICATIONS** Auth, A Formalisation of the Logical Theory of Principia Mathematica, Bull Symbolic Logic, 97; Russell's Early Mathematical Philosophy (rev), 97; On Russell's Conception of Logic: The Notion of Formal System in Principia Mathematica, Bull Symbolic Logic, 96; The Vicious-Circle Principle, Bull Symbolic Logic, 95. **CONTACT ADDRESS** Dept of Philosophy, Florida State Univ, 151 Dodd Hall, Tallahassee, FL 32306-1500. **EMAIL** djung@mailer.fsu.edu

JUNG, L. SHANNON
PERSONAL Born 07/23/1943, Baton Rouge, LA, M, 1974, 3 children **DISCIPLINE** ETHICS **EDUCATION** Washington & Lee Univ, BA, 65; Union Theological Seminary, BD, 68; Yale, STM 69; Vanderbilt, PhD, 74. **CAREER** Assoc prof, 79-87, Concordin Col; prof of rural ministry and dir, 87- , Wartburg and the Univ of Dubuque **HONORS AND AWARDS** Outstanding faculty award; NEH grants; Northwestern area, Lilly, Louisville, Pew, other grants. **MEMBERSHIPS** AAR; SCE; Amer Sociological Assn. **RESEARCH** Ecology; the implications of physical constitution of human beings for ethics; Theology of land; Rural congregations. **SELECTED PUBLICATIONS** Auth, We Are Home: A Spirituality of the Environment, Paulist, 93; coauth, Rural Congregational Studies: A Guide for Good Shepherds, Abingon, 97; coauth, Moral Issues and Christian Response, 98; auth, Rural Ministry: The Shape of the Renewal to Come, Abingdon, 98. **CONTACT ADDRESS** 3099 St. Anne Dr., Dubuque, IA 52001. **EMAIL** sjung@wartburgseminary.edu

JUNG, PATRICIA BEATTIE
PERSONAL Born 09/21/1949, Great Falls, MN, m, 1974, 3 children **DISCIPLINE** CHRISTIAN ETHICS **EDUCATION** Unv of Santa Clara, BA, 71; Vanderbilt Univ, MA, 74, PhD, 79. **CAREER** Assoc prof, Loyola Univ Chicago, 95-; Asst prof, Concordia Col, 79-87; adj fac, Lutheran Theol Sem, 93; assoc prof, Wartburt Theol Sem, 88-95. **HONORS AND AWARDS** John and Therese Mulcahy Res Support Grant, 98; John Franklin East vis prof, Lynchburg Col, 98; john and theresa mulcahy res support grant on cath issues, 98; exxon vis fel in ethics and med, baylor col of med, 85. **MEMBERSHIPS** Soc of Christian Ethics; Cath Theol Soc of Am; Am Acad of Relig. **RESEARCH** Sexual and medical ethics; Feminist ethics. **SELECTED PUBLICATIONS** Ed, Sexual Diversity and Catholicism: Toward the Development of Moral Theology; coauth, Just Good Sex; coed, Moral Issues and Christian Response, 6th & 7th ed; coauth, Heterosexism: An Ethical Challenge, 93; coed, Good Sex, 01. **CONTACT ADDRESS** Loyola Univ, Chicago, 6525 N Sheridan Rd, Chicago, IL 60626-5385. **EMAIL** pjung@wpo.it.luc.edu

JURCZAK, PAUL M.
DISCIPLINE PHILOSOPHY **EDUCATION** Univ Florida, PhD, 97; Univ Kansas, MA, 89; Univ Calif, BA, 81. **CAREER** Prof of Philosophy and Humanities, Lansing Community Col, 97-. **MEMBERSHIPS** Society for the Advancement of Amer Philosophy; Jean Diaget Society. **RESEARCH** Philosophy of Education-esp. freedom. **SELECTED PUBLICATIONS** Auth, "The Language and Metaphors of Jean Piaget" Educational Psychology Review, Sept, 97; auth, "A Life for Freedom: The Philosophy of Maxine Greene," International Journal of the Humanities, June 95. **CONTACT ADDRESS** Dept Humanities, Lansing Comm Col, PO Box 40010, Lansing, MI 48901-7210. **EMAIL** pjurczak@lansing.cc.mi.us

JURISSON, CYNTHIA
PERSONAL Born 09/09/1958, Chicago, IL, m, 1990, 3 children **DISCIPLINE** RELIGIOUS STUDIES **EDUCATION** Augustova Col, BA, 80; Luther Northwestern Theol Sem, MDiv, 84; Princeton Theol Sem, PhD, 94. **CAREER** Assoc prof, 88- **MEMBERSHIPS** Am Soc of Church Hist; Am Acad of Relig; Lutheran Hist Conf. **RESEARCH** Women in the history of Christiantiy; Revivalism; History of Christian thought. **SELECTED PUBLICATIONS** Auth, Understanding One Another: A Congregational Resource for the African Methodist Episcopal Church and the Evangelical Lutheran Church in America. **CONTACT ADDRESS** Lutheran Sch of Theol at Chicago, 1100 E 55th St, Chicago, IL 60615. **EMAIL** cjurisson@lstc.edu

JUST, FELIX, S. J.
PERSONAL Born 11/02/1959, Berlin, Germany, s **DISCIPLINE** RELIGIOUS STUDIES, NEW TESTAMENT **EDUCATION** Yale Univ, PhD, 98. **CAREER** Asst prof Theol Stud, Loyola Marymount Univ, 96-. **HONORS AND AWARDS** Phi Beta Kappa **MEMBERSHIPS** Catholic Bibl Asn; Soc Bibl Lit; Cath Theol Soc Am; Col Theol Soc. **RESEARCH** Gospel of John, medicine and miracles in the Greco-Roman world, Book of Revelation. **CONTACT ADDRESS** Dept of Theological Studies, Loyola Marymount Univ, 7900 Loyola Blvd, Los Angeles, CA 90045-8400. **EMAIL** fjust@lmumail.lmu.edu

K

KAC, MICHAEL
DISCIPLINE PHILOSOPHY **EDUCATION** Univ Calif Los Angeles, PhD. **RESEARCH** Syntax and semantics of natural language; philosophical foundation of linguistics. **SELECTED PUBLICATIONS** Auth, What Is Categorial Grammar Really Good For?, John Benjamins, 93; Grammars and Grammaticality, John Benjamins, 92; A Simplified Theory of Boolean Semantic Types, J Semantics, 92; Corepresentation of Grammatical Structure, Univ Minn, 78; co-auth, Theoretical Implications of Disordered Syntactic Processing, Lang Sci, 92; auth, The proper treatment of singular terms in ordinary English, Mind, 97. **CONTACT ADDRESS** Philosophy Dept, Univ of Minnesota, Twin Cities, 355 Ford Hall, 224 Church St SE, Minneapolis, MN 55455. **EMAIL** kac@cs.umn.edu

KADENS, MICHAEL G.
DISCIPLINE LAW **EDUCATION** Univ Mich, BA; Stanford Univ, JD. **CAREER** Prof. **SELECTED PUBLICATIONS** Auth, Practitioner's Guide to Treatment of Seller's Products Liability in Asset Acquisitions, Univ Toledo, 78; Proposed Subchapter S Amendments, Taxes, 80. **CONTACT ADDRESS** Col Law, Univ of Toledo, Toledo, OH 43606. **EMAIL** mkadens@utnet.utoledo.edu

KADISH, MORTIMER R.
PERSONAL Born 12/02/1916, New York, NY, m, 1973, 1 child **DISCIPLINE** PHILOSOPHY **EDUCATION** Columbia Univ, PhD, 50. **CAREER** Asst, assoc, full prof, Western Reserve Univ, Case Western Reserve Univ, 50-84; chairman Dept Philos, Case Western Reserve Univ, 65-67, 72-76; dir ,Western Reserve Univ-case Program of Philos Studies, 64-66; Emeritus Prof, 85-. **HONORS AND AWARDS** Special Rockefeller Fel, 51; Ford Fel, 54-55; John Simon Guggnheim Fel, 54-55; Yadoo App as Resident, 65; Fel Am Coucil of Learned Soc, 67-68. **MEMBERSHIPS** AAUP; Easter Div Am Philos Asn. **RESEARCH** Philosophy of Art and Literature; Ethics; Political and Legal Philosophy. **SELECTED PUBLICATIONS** Auth, Discretion to Disobey, co-author S.H. Kadish, 73; auth, Reason and Controversy in the Arts, 68; with auth, articles on philosophical topics; Toward a Theory of Higher Education, 91; The Ophelia Paradox, 94. **CONTACT ADDRESS** 13906 Larchmere Blvd, Cleveland, OH 44120. **EMAIL** mrk7@atspo.cwru.edu

KADISH, SANFORD H.
PERSONAL Born 09/07/1921, New York, NY, m, 1942, 2 children **DISCIPLINE** LAW **EDUCATION** City Col New York, BSS, 42; Columbia Univ, LLB, 48. **CAREER** Asst prof to prof law, Univ Utah, 51-61; prof of law, Univ Mich, 61-64; prof of law, Univ of Calif Berkeley, 64-91, Morrison Prof, 74-91, Dean 1975-82, Emeritus 1991-; Visiting Prof, U Melbourne 1956; Harvard Law School, 60-61; Columbia Law School, 85; Lewis & Clark School, 85; McGeorge Law School, St Louis Univ, 95; Ariz State Univ, 96; Visiting Fellow, Ctr Advan Studies Behav Sci, Stanford, 67; Cambridge Inst of Crim, 68; All Sould College, Oxford, 83; Reporter, Joint Calif Legis Comt Revise Penal Code, 64-67; consult, Pres, Crime Comm, DC, 66-67. **HONORS AND AWARDS** Juris Dr, Univ Cologne, 83; LLD (hon), City Univ NY, 85; LLD (hon), Southwestern Univ, 93; Fel, British Academy (cor); fel, Amer Acad Arts and Sciences, Amer Bar Found, Res Awd, 99; Clark Kerr Medal Contrib Hghr Ed, 97. **MEMBERSHIPS** Amer Assn Univ Prof, pres 70-72; Amer Assn Law Schools, pres 82; Amer Acad Arts and Sciences, VP, 84-87. **RESEARCH** Criminal law; jurisprudence. **SELECTED PUBLICATIONS** Discretion to Disobey,

Stanford Univ Press, 73; Encyclopedia of Crime and Justice, Free Press, 83; Blame and Punishment, Macmillan, 87; auth, The Criminal Law and the Luck of the Draw--Foreword, J Criminal Law & Criminology, Vol 0084, 94; The Folly of Overfederalization, Hastings Law J, Vol 0046, 95; Reckless Complicity, J Criminal Law & Criminology, Vol 0087, 97; Criminal Law and its Processess, Aspen Law & Bus, 7th ed, 01. **CONTACT ADDRESS** Sch of Law, Univ of California, Berkeley, 225 Boalt Hall, Berkeley, CA 94720. **EMAIL** shk@law.berkeley.edu

KAEBNICK, GREGORY E.
PERSONAL Born 11/29/1963, Gallup, NM, m, 1987, 2 children **DISCIPLINE** PHILOSOPHY **EDUCATION** Univ Minn, PhD, 98. **CAREER** Assoc ed, Hastings Ctr Reports, The Hastings Ctr. **MEMBERSHIPS** Am Soc Bioethics & Hum; Am Philos Asn. **RESEARCH** Moral realism; Particularism. **CONTACT ADDRESS** 2 Larkin Pl, Croton On Hudson, NY 10520-2620. **EMAIL** kaebnick@thehastingscenter.org

KAELIN, EUGENE FRANCIS
PERSONAL Born 10/14/1926, St. Louis, MO, m, 1952, 3 children **DISCIPLINE** PHILOSOPHY **EDUCATION** Univ Mo, AB, 49, MA, 50; Univ Bordeaux, DES, 51; Univ Ill, PhD(philos), 54. **CAREER** Instr philos, Univ Mo, 52-53; from instr to assoc prof, Univ Wis, Madison, 55-65; assoc prof, 65-67, chmn dept, 69-72, Prof Philos, Fla State Univ, 67-, Fel from Univ Ill, Univ Bordeaux, 54-55; assoc ed, Arts in Soc, 58-64; Am Coun Learned Soc fel, Inst Studies Humanities, Univ Wis, 60-61; res scholar, Freiburg, 64-65; mem nat adv bd, Aesthetic Educ Prog, Cent Midwestern Regional Educ Lab, Inc, 68-73; chmn ed comt, Social Theory & Pract, 72-73. **MEMBERSHIPS** Am Philos Asn; Am Soc Aesthet; Soc Phenomenol & Existential Philos; Int Soc Phenomenol & Lit. **RESEARCH** Aesthetics; contemporary phenomenology; philosophy of aesthetic education. **SELECTED PUBLICATIONS** Auth, An Existentialist Aesthetic, Univ Wis, 62; Aesthetic education: A role for aesthetics proper, J Aesthetic Educ, 68; Art and Existence, Bucknell Univ, 70; The social uses of art: A plea for the institution, Arts in Soc, fall-winter 72; coauth, The limits of aesthetic inquiry: A guide to educational research, In: Philosophical Redirection of Educational Research, Nat Soc Study Educ, 72; The Unhappy Consciousness, Vol XIII, Analecia Husserliana, 81. **CONTACT ADDRESS** Dept of Philos, Florida State Univ, Tallahassee, FL 32306.

KAGAN, ROBERT A.
PERSONAL Born 06/13/1938, Newark, NJ, m, 1967, 1 child **DISCIPLINE** POLITICAL SCIENCE **EDUCATION** Harvard, BA, 59; Columbia, LLB, 62; Yale Univ, PhD, 74. **CAREER** Prof of Poli Sci, 74-, Prof of Law, 88-, Dir, Center for the Study of Law & Society, 93-00, Univ of Cal, Berkeley. **HONORS AND AWARDS** AAAS Member **MEMBERSHIPS** APSA, L&SA. **RESEARCH** Sociolegal studies, government regulation of business, comparative legal institutions. **SELECTED PUBLICATIONS** Auth, Regulatory Justice, Implementing a Wage-Price Freeze, Russell Sage Foundation, 78; Going by the Book: The Problem of Regulatory Unreasonablenesss, with Eugene Bardach, Temple Univ Press, 82; Patterns of Port Development, Government Intermodal Transportation and Innovation in the United States, China and Hong Kong, 90; Regulatory Encounters: Multinational Corporations and American Adversarial Legalism, with Lee Axelrad, Univ Calif Press, 00; Adversarial Legalism: The American Way of Law, Harvard Univ Press, 01; Regulatory Enforcement, in: Handbook of Administrative Law and Regulation, eds, D Rosenbloom & R D Schwartz, Marcel Dekker, 94; Should Europe Worry About Adversarial Legalism? Oxford J Legal Studies, 97. **CONTACT ADDRESS** Center for the Study of Law and Society, Univ of California, Berkeley, Berkeley, CA 94720-2150. **EMAIL** rak@uclink4.berkeley.edu

KAHAN, MARCEL
PERSONAL Born Munich, Germany **DISCIPLINE** LAW **EDUCATION** Harvard, JD, 88; MIT Sloan, MS, 88. **CAREER** Prof, NYork Univ Sch of Law **RESEARCH** Corporate law. **SELECTED PUBLICATIONS** Auth, Anti-Dilution Provisions in Convertible Securities, Stanford J of Law Bus Fin, 95; coauth, Path Dependence in Corporate Contracting: Increasing Returns, Herd Behavior and Cognitive Biases, Washington Univ Law Qtly, 96; auth, The Incentive Effects of Settlement Under Joint and Several Liability, Intl Rev Law Econ, 96; coauth, Matsuchita and Beyond: The Role of State Courts in Class Actions Involving Exclusive Federal Claims, Supreme Court Rev, 97; coauth, Lockups and the Market for Corporate Control, Stanford Law Rev, 96; coauth, Corporate Contracting: Standardization, Innovation and the Role of Contracting Agents, VA Law Rev, 97; coauth, The Inadequate search for "Adequacy" In Class Actions: A Critique of Epstein v. MCA, Inc, NY Univ Law Rev, 98; coauth, Investment Opportunities and the Design of Debt Securities, J Law Econ Org, 98; coauth, A New Governance Structure for Corporate Bonds, Stanford Law Rev, 99. **CONTACT ADDRESS** School Law, New York Univ, 40 Washington Sq S, New York, NY 10012-1005.

KAHANE, HOWARD
PERSONAL Born 04/19/1928, Cleveland, OH, d, 1 child **DISCIPLINE** PHILOSOPHY **EDUCATION** Univ Calif, Los Angeles, BA, 54, MA, 58; Univ Pa, PhD, 62. **CAREER** Asst prof philos, Whitman Col, 62-64; from asst prof to assoc prof, Univ Kans, 64-70; from asst prof to assoc prof, Baruch Col, 70-76; Prof Philos, Univ MD, Baltimore County, 76-, Nat Sci Found res grant, 67-68. **MEMBERSHIPS** Western Div Am Philos Asn; Eastern Div Am Philos Asn. **RESEARCH** Theory of knowledge; logic and philosophy of science; ethics. **SELECTED PUBLICATIONS** Auth, A difficulty on conflict and confirmation, Philos Sci, 65; Logic and Philosophy: A Modern Introduction, Wadsworth, 69, 2nd ed, 73, 3rd ed, 78 & 4th ed, 82; coauth, Hard and soft intensionalsim, Rev Metaphys, 70; auth, Logic and Contemporary Rhetoric, Wadsworth, 71, 2nd ed, 76 & 3rd ed, 80; Pathological predicates and projection, Am Philos Quart, 71; Making the World Safe for Reciprocity, in: Reason and Responsibility, Wadsworth, 5th ed, 81; auth, "Sociobiology, Egoism, and Reciprocity," In Moral Philosophy, ed Louis Pojman, Indianapolis: Hackett Publishing Co, (93): 68-84; auth, Contract Ethics: Evolutionary Biology & the Moral Sentiments, Rowman & Littlefield (Lanham, Maryland, 95). **CONTACT ADDRESS** Dept of Philos, Univ of Maryland, Baltimore County, Baltimore, MD 21228.

KAHN, CHARLES H.
PERSONAL Born 05/29/1928, New Iberia, LA, m, 1988, 2 children **DISCIPLINE** HISTORY OF PHILOSOPHY **EDUCATION** Univ Chicago, BA, 46, MA, 49; Columbia Univ, PhD, 58. **CAREER** From instr to assoc prof Greek & Latin, Columbia Univ, 57-65; assoc prof, 65-68, chmn dept, 75-78, PROF PHILOS, UNIV PA, 68-, Univ Chicago exchange fel to Univ Paris, 49-50; Cutting traveling fel, Columbia Univ, 55-56; Am Coun Learned Soc res fel, 63-64; co-ed, Arch Geschichte Philos, 65-79; mem managing comt, Am Sch Class Studies in Athens, 70-99, vis prof, 74-75; Nat Endowment for Humanities fel, 74-75. **HONORS AND AWARDS** Guggenheim Fellow 79-80; ACLS Research Fellow, 85; NEH Research Fellow, 90-91. **MEMBERSHIPS** Am Philos Asn; Soc Ancient Greek Philosophers (pres, 76-78). **RESEARCH** Greek philosophy, especially Presocratics, Plato and Aristotle; political philosophy. **SELECTED PUBLICATIONS** Auth, Anaximander and the Orignis of Greek Cosmology, Columbia Univ Press, 1960, 250 pp. Translation into Modern Gree, 82. Reprinted by Hackett Pub, 94; auth, The Verb "Be in Ancient Greek, Reidel, Dordrecht, 1973 (Vol. 16, Foundations of Language Supplementary Series, ed JWM Verhaar): The Verb "Be" and its Synonyms, part 6, 486 pp.; auth, The Art and Thought of Heraclitus: An edition of the fragments with translation and commentary, Cambridtge Univ Pres, 99 (paperback, 81), 356 pp.; auth, Pitagora e I pitagorici (Instituto della encicolpedia Italiana, 1993). Italian translation of Pythagoras and the Pythagoreans, 100-page monograph; auth, Plato and the Socratic Dialogue, Cambridge Univ Press, (96): 431. **CONTACT ADDRESS** Dept of Philos/CN, Univ of Pennsylvania, 433 Logan Hall, Philadelphia, PA 19104. **EMAIL** chcon@sas.upenn.edu

KAHN, DOUGLAS A.
PERSONAL Born 11/07/1934; Spartanburg, SC, m, 1970, 2 children **DISCIPLINE** LAW **EDUCATION** Univ NC, Chapel Hill, BA, 55; George Wash Univ, JD, 58. **CAREER** Trial atty, Civil Div, Appellate Sect, Dept Justice, 58-60 & Tax Div, Appelate Sect, 60-62; atty-at-law, Sachs & Jacobs, 62-64; from Asst Prof to Prof, 64-84, Paul G, Kauper Prof Law, Sch Law, Univ Mich, Ann Arbor, 84-; Vis prof, Law Sch, Stanford Univ, 73-74; vis prof, Duke Univ, Univ NC, 77; vis prof & George Bacon-Victor Kilkenny chair, Fordham Univ, 80-81; vis prof, Cambridge Univ, 96. **HONORS AND AWARDS** Emil Brown Found Prize, 70. **MEMBERSHIPS** Am Bar Asn; Am Col of Trust and Estate Counsel. **RESEARCH** Taxation; estate planning. **SELECTED PUBLICATIONS** Auth, Mandatory buy-out agreements for stock of closely held corporations, 69, A definition of liabilities in Internal Revenue code sections 357 & 358 (d), 75 & Accelerated depreciation--tax expenditure or proper allowance for measuring net income?, 79, Mich Law Rev; coauth, Corporate Taxation, West Publ Co, 89; Corporate Income Taxation, West Publ Co, 4th ed, 94; Federal Taxation of Gifts, Trusts and Estates, West Publ Co, 3rd ed, 97; auth, Federal Income Tax, Found Press, 4th ed, 99. **CONTACT ADDRESS** Law Sch, Univ of Michigan, Ann Arbor, 625 S State St, Ann Arbor, MI 48109-1215. **EMAIL** dougkahn@umich.edu

KAHN, JEFFREY P.
PERSONAL Born 10/12/1960, Santa Monica, CA, m, 2 children **DISCIPLINE** BIOETHICS **EDUCATION** Univ Calif, Los Angeles, BA, 83; Johns Hopkins Univ Sch of Hygiene and Public Health, MPH, 88; Georgetown Univ, PhD, 89. **CAREER** Dir, grad prog, asst prof, Ctr for the Stud of Bioethics, Med Col Wisc, 92-96; dir, Ctr for Bioethics, assoc prof, Univ of Minn, 96- . **MEMBERSHIPS** APA, Am Pub Hea Asn; Am Soc for Bioethics and Hum. **RESEARCH** Applied ethics; ethics and genetics; ethics and public health; research ethics; ethical theory. **SELECTED PUBLICATIONS** Ed, Kennedy Inst of Ethics J, 96; ed, Accountability in Res, 98; ed, J of Andrology, 98; Policies for Human Subjects Research, University Pub Grp, 98; Beyond Consent, Oxford, 98. **CONTACT ADDRESS** Center for Bioethics, Univ of Minnesota, Twin Cities, 410 Church St SE, Ste N504, Boynton, MN 55455. **EMAIL** kahnx009@tc.umn.edu

KAIN, JOHN FORREST
PERSONAL Born 11/09/1935, Fort Wayne, IN, m, 1957, 2 children **DISCIPLINE** ECONOMICS **EDUCATION** Bowling Green State Univ, AB (Honors in Economics and Political Science), 57; Univ CA, Berkeley, MA, PhD, 61. **CAREER** Grad res asst, 57-61, lect, Business Admin & Economics, Univ CA, Berkeley, 59-61; assoc prof, economics, US Air Force Academy, 62-64; asst prof economics, Harvard Univ, 65-67, prof, 68-90, dir, prog in Regional and Urban Economics, 67-78; Henry Lee prof of Economics and prof of Afro-American Studies, Harvard Univ, 91-97, chmn, dept of economics, 88-91, Emeritus, 97-; The Cecil and Ida Green chair for the Study of Science and Society, prof of Economics and prof of Political Economy, dir, Cecil and Ida Green Center for the Study of Science and Society, Univ TX, Dallas, 97-; vis res assoc, London School of Economics, 64; vis res scholar, dept economics, Univ TX, Arlington, 87-88; vis fel, Korean Devel Inst, 91; vis prof, School of Social Sciences, Univ TX, Dallas, 91-92, 96-97; non-resident fel, WEB DuBois inst for Afro-American res, Harvard Univ, 97-. **HONORS AND AWARDS** Scholarship, Bowling Green State Univ, 54-57; fel, Real Estate Res prog, Univ CA, Berkeley, 59-61; Harvard Univ, AM (honorary), 68; Taussig Res Prof, Dept of Economics, 87-88. **MEMBERSHIPS** Am Economics Asn, 61-; Am Real Estate and Urban Economics Asn, 80-; Asn for Public Policy Analysis and Management, 98-. **RESEARCH** Urban economics; transportation; determinants of student achievement and performance of schools and teachers. **SELECTED PUBLICATIONS** Auth, with William C Apgar Jr, Housing and Neighborhood Dynamics: A Simulation Study, Harvard Univ Press, 85; A Defense of Demand Subsidies--The Cost-Effective Way of Assisting Low Income Households, in Joseph Pechman and Michael S McPherson, eds, Fulfilling America's Promise, Cornell Univ Press, 92; The Use of Strawmen in the Economic Evaluation of Transport Investments, Am Economic Rev, May 92; The Spatial Mismatch Hypothesis: Three Decades Later, Housing Policy Debate, vol 3, issue 2, 92; The Impacts of Congestion Pricing on Transit and Carpool Demand and Supply, in Committee for the Study of Urban Transportation Congestion Pricing, Transportation Res Bd, Nat Res Coun, Curbing Gridlock: Peak-Period Fees to Relieve Traffic Congestion: Vol 2, Commissioned papers, Washington, DC, Nat Academy Press, 94; with Kraig Singleton, Equality of Educational Opportunity Revisited, New England Economic Rev, May/June 96; with Jeffrey Zax, Moving to the Suburbs: Do Relocating Companies Leave Their Black Employees Behind?, J of Labor Economics, July 96; Cost-Effective Alternatives to Atlanta's Costly Rapid Transit System, Transport Economics and Policy, vol XXI, no 1, Jan 97; The Case for Bus Rapid Transit, Nieman Reports, winter 97; numerous other publications. **CONTACT ADDRESS** Dir, The Cecil and Ida Green Center for the Study of Science and Society, Univ of Texas, Dallas, PO Box 830688, Richardson, TX 75083-0688. **EMAIL** jkain@utdallas.edu

KAISER, CHRISTOPHER BARINA
PERSONAL Born 10/16/1941, Greenwich, CT, m, 1970, 3 children **DISCIPLINE** DIVINITY; PHYSICS **EDUCATION** Harvard Univ, AB, 63; Univ Colo, PhD, 68; Univ Edinburgh, PhD, 74. **CAREER** Lectr, Univ Edinburgh, 73-75; from asst to assoc to Prof of Historical-Systematic Theology, W Theol Sem, 76-. **MEMBERSHIPS** Am Soc Church Hist; Am Scientific Affiliation Ctr of Theol Inquiry. **RESEARCH** New Testament Christology; Comparative historical sociology of science. **SELECTED PUBLICATIONS** auth From Biblical Secularity to Modern Secularism: Historical Aspects and Stages, Secularism versus Biblical Secularity, ITEST Faith/Science Press, 94 & 96; "The Integrity of Creation and the Social Nature of God," Scottish Jour Theol, 96; The Laws of Nature and the Nature of God, Facets of Faith and Science, Univ Press Am, 96; Scientific Work and Its Theological Dimensions: Toward a Theology of Natural Science, Facets of Faith and Science, Univ Press Am, 96; Quantum Complementarity and Christological Dialectic, Religion and Science: History, Method, Dialogue, Routledge, 96; Creational Theology and the History of Physical Science: The Creationist Tradition from Basil to Bohr, E J Brill, 97; Extraterrestrial Life and Extraterrestrial Intelligence, Reformed Review, 98; John Calvin Climbing Jacob's Ladder, Perspectives: A Journal of Reformed Thought, 98; The Nature of the Church from a Reformed Perspective, Reformed World, 98. **CONTACT ADDRESS** Western Theol Sem, 101 E 13, Holland, MI 49423. **EMAIL** chrisk@westernsem.org

KAISER, KEVIN ROBERT
PERSONAL Born 03/17/1964, Oakland, CA, s **DISCIPLINE** BIBLICAL STUDIES, NEAR EASTERN ART AND ARCHAEOLOGY **EDUCATION** San Jose State Univ, BA, 87; Grad Theol Union, Berkeley, MA, 90; Univ Calif, Berkeley, C. phil. 98, PhD, expected 01. **CAREER** Mus dir, Bade Inst Bibl Arch, Berkeley CA, 90-98. **HONORS AND AWARDS** Phi Kappa Phi; ASOR summer travel grant; Univ Calif, Berkeley summer fel. **MEMBERSHIPS** ASOR. **RESEARCH** Archaeology; history; Near Eastern languages. **CONTACT ADDRESS** 14328 Cuesta Ct., Sonora, CA 95370. **EMAIL** krkaiser@aol.com

KAISER, WALTER C., JR.
PERSONAL Born 04/11/1933, Folcroft, PA, m, 1957, 4 children **DISCIPLINE** BIBLICAL ARCHAEOLOGY **EDUCATION** Wheaton Col, AB, 55, BD, 58; Brandeis Univ, MA, 62, PhD, 73. **CAREER** Instr, 58-60, asst prof of Bible, 60-64, actg dir of archaeol & Near Eastern stud, 65-55, Wheaton Col; asst prof, 66-70, assoc prof, 70-75, chmn dept of OT, 75-79, sr vice pres, acad dean, 80-92, sr vice pres of Distance Learning, 92-93, Trinity Evangel Divin Schl; Coleman M Mockler Dist Prof of OT, 93-96; pres, 97-, Gordon Conwell Theol Sem. **HONORS AND AWARDS** Danforth Tchr Stud grant. **MEMBERSHIPS** Evangel Theol Soc; Inst of Bibl Res; Near Eastern Archaeol Soc; Soc of Bibl Lit. **RESEARCH** Old Testament Theol; Israel, history and archaeology; ethics. **SELECTED PUBLICATIONS** Auth, The Journey Isn't Over: The Pilgrim Psalms (120-134) for Life's Challenges and Joys, Baker 93; coauth, An Introduction to Biblical Hermeneutics: The Search for Meaning, Zondervan, 94; auth, The Book of Leviticus: Introduction, Commentary and Reflections, New Interpreter's Bible, Abingdon, 94; auth, Proverbs: Wisdom for Everyday Life, Zondervan, 95; auth, Psalms: Heart to Heart with God, Zondervan, 95; auth, The Messiah in the Old Testament, Zondervan, 95; auth, Hard Sayings of the Bible, InterVarsity, 96; auth, A History of Israel, Broadman & Holman, 98; auth, The Christian and the "Old" Testament, US Ctr for World Mission, 98; auth, An Urgent Call For Revival and Renewal in Our Times: Sixteen Revivals in the Old and New Testament with a Study Guide, Broadman & Holman, 99; auth, Are the Old testament Documents Reliable?, InterVarsity, 99. **CONTACT ADDRESS** Gordon-Conwell Theol Sem, 130 Essex St, South Hamilton, MA 01982. **EMAIL** wckaiser@gcts.edu

KAJEVICH, STEVEN N.
PERSONAL Born 07/29/1937, Yugoslavia, d **DISCIPLINE** THEOLOGY **EDUCATION** Prizren, Yugoslavia, BD, 56; Belgrade, MTh, 62; DePaul Univ, MA, 71, PhD, 74. **CAREER** Priest, Scebien Orthodox Church, Paris, 66-78; asst prof philos, ethics, Lewis Univ & DePaul Univ, 85- . **HONORS AND AWARDS** World Council of Churches scholarship. **MEMBERSHIPS** APA; CPA; Writers Club. **RESEARCH** Political and social philosophy; international relations, crime and punishment. **SELECTED PUBLICATIONS** Auth, Un-Created Freedom: Origin of Being and Its Negation, Univ Press of Am, 77. **CONTACT ADDRESS** 5701 N Sheridan Rd, #4-P, Chicago, IL 80660.

KALANTZIS, GEORGE
PERSONAL Born 04/18/1967, Athens, Greece **DISCIPLINE** HISTORY OF CHRISTIANITY **EDUCATION** Univ IL, BS, 90; Northeastern IL Univ, MS, 93; Moody Grad Sch, MABS, 93; Garrett-Evangelical Theol Sem, MTS, 94; Northwestern Univ, PhD, 97. **CAREER** Assoc, pastor, ed, Hellenic Christ Prog, Greek Free Church, 92-; adj fac, Moody Bible Inst, 95-96; asst prof, Garrett-Evangelical Theol Sem, 96-. **HONORS AND AWARDS** Hartman Fel; Ernest W. Saunders End Doct Fel; Ester Y. Armstrong Schl; Teach Gnt, Wabash Cen; Doct Schl, Garrett-Evangelical Theol Sem; Schl, Grad Sch Northwestern Univ; Schl, Hellenic Christian Prog; Schl, Northeastern IL Univ, Schl Moody Bible Inst. **MEMBERSHIPS** NAPS; ASOR; ASCH; SBL; ETS. **RESEARCH** Development of early Christological models, esp Antioch from the fourth to the sixth century by Diodore of Tarsus, Theodore of Mopsuestia, and Nestorius of Constantinople; classical Graeco-Roman and early Christian philosophical understandings of anthropology and biblical hermeneutics as shown in the works of Origen, Tertullian, and the Cappadocians; Byzantine archaeology and architecture in Palestine. **SELECTED PUBLICATIONS** Auth, "Ephesus: A Roman, Jewish, and Christian Metropolis in the First and Second Centuries C.E.," Jian Dao: A J of Bible and Theol 7 (97): 103-119; auth, A translation of the critical text of the Greek New Testament into Modern Greek, 00. **CONTACT ADDRESS** Dept Christianity, Garrett-Evangelical Theol Sem, 2121 Sheridan Rd, Evanston, IL 60201-2926. **EMAIL** george-kalantzis@northwestern.edu

KALIN, EVERETT ROY
DISCIPLINE NEW TESTAMENT **EDUCATION** Concordia Sem, BA, MDiv; Harvard Univ Divinity Sch, ThD. **CAREER** Instr, Concordia Col; assoc prof, Concordia Sem; Prof, Christ Seminary - Seminex: prof, Pacific Lutheran Theol Sem, 83-99; Prof Emer, 99-. **SELECTED PUBLICATIONS** Transl, Suffering by Dorothee Soelle, Fortress Press; Jesus of Nazareth by Herbert Braun, Fortress Press; Christ and Power by Martin Hengel, Fortress Press; Reconciliation, Law, and Righteousness by Peter Stuhlmacher, Fortress Press; transl, The God of Israel and the Nations, by Norbert Lohfink and Erich Zenger (Litergical Press). **CONTACT ADDRESS** Dept of New Testament, Pacific Lutheran Theol Sem, 2770 Marin Ave, Berkeley, CA 94708-1597. **EMAIL** ekalin@sirius.com

KALLENBERG, BRAD J.
PERSONAL Born 04/14/1958, Minneapolis, MN, m, 1980, 3 children **DISCIPLINE** PHILOSOPHICAL THEOLOGY **EDUCATION** Fuller Theo Sem, PhD, 98. **CAREER** Instr, 96-99, Intl School of Theol; adj Asst Prof, 94-99, Fuller Theo Sem; Instr, 98-, Azusa Pacific Univ. **HONORS AND AWARDS** Full Doc Fel, Fuller Theo Sem. **MEMBERSHIPS** APA, AAR. **RESEARCH** Wittgenstein & theology, Anglo-American postmodernism, Christian ethics. **SELECTED PUBLICATIONS** Co-ed, Virtues and Practices in the Christian Tradition, Christian Ethics after MacIntyre, Harrisburg PA Trinity Press Intl, 97; auth, Conversion Converted, A Postmodern Formulation of the Doctrine of Conversion, in: The Evangelical Qtly, 95; On Cultivating Moral Taste, in: Virtues and Practices in the Christian Tradition, Christian Ethics after MacIntyre, eds, N Murphy, M T Nation, Harrisburg PA, Trinity Press Intl, 97; Unstuck from Yale, Theological Method After Lindbeck, in: Scottish J of Theo, 97; The Gospel Truth of Relativism, in: Scottish J of Theo, forthcoming; co-auth, Ludwig Wittgenstein, A Christian in Philosophy, in: Scottish J of Theo, 98; auth, Ethics as Grammar: Changing the Postmodern Subject, Univ of Notre Dame Press, forth. **CONTACT ADDRESS** 3471 N Arrowhead Ave, San Bernardino, CA 92405. **EMAIL** bkallenb@apu.edu

KALVODA, JOSEF
PERSONAL Born 01/15/1923, Czechoslovakia, m, 1956 **DISCIPLINE** HISTORY, POLITICAL SCIENCE **EDUCATION** Hunter Col, BA, 56; Columbia Univ, MA, 57, PhD, 60. **CAREER** From instr to assoc prof polit sci & hist, St Joseph Col, Conn, 57-61; assoc prof, Col for Women, Univ San Diego, 61-64, prof, 64-77; assoc prof govt, La State Univ, 66-68; Prof Polit Sci & Hist, St Joseph Col, Conn, 68-. **MEMBERSHIPS** AAUP; Am Asn Advan Slavic Studies; Am Polit Sci Asn. **RESEARCH** East central Europe; international relations; comparative government. **SELECTED PUBLICATIONS** Auth, Titoism, 58; auth, Czechoslovakia's Role in Soviet Strategy, 78; auth, The Genesis of Czechoslovakia, 86; auth, Z boju o zitrek, Fighting for Tomorrow, vol.I, 95; auth, Z boju o zitrek, Fighting for Tomorrow, vol.II, 96; auth, Genese Ceskoslovenska, The Genesis of Czechoslovakia, 98; auth, Z boju o zitrek, vol.III, Historicke eseje, Fighting for Tomorrow, Historical Essays, 98. **CONTACT ADDRESS** 9 Greenwood Dr, Avon, CT 06001-4115.

KAMBEITZ, TERESITA
PERSONAL Born Richmond, SK, Canada **DISCIPLINE** RELIGIOUS EDUCATION **EDUCATION** St.Angela's Acad, ARTC, 57; tchrs col, 58-59; Univ Sask, BA, 69, BEd, 69; St Paul Univ, Ottawa, Theol, 69-70; St. Michael's Col, MRE, 76; Ont Inst Stud Educ, Univ Toronto, MEd, 86, PhD, 88. **CAREER** Tchr, various schs Sask, 59-64; princ/tchr, St. Patrick, Swift Current, Sask, 64-68; tchr, Holy Cross Sch, Saskatoon, 70-85; Dir Religious Educ, Newman Theol Col, Edmonton, 88-. **HONORS AND AWARDS** Peter Craigie Awd, Alta Tchrs Asn. **MEMBERSHIPS** Newman Theol Col; Alta Tchrs Asn; Asn Profs Res Relig Educ; Relig Educ Asn US & Can; Ursuline Congregation Prelate. **SELECTED PUBLICATIONS** Auth, Death and Dying, 79; auth, Health Hazards of So-Called Low-Radiation, 80; auth, Ursulines Remember, vol 1, 94, vol 2, 95. **CONTACT ADDRESS** Religious Education Program, Newman Theol Col, Edmonton, AB, Canada T5L 4H8.

KAMINSKY, JACK
PERSONAL Born 03/19/1922, New York, NY, m, 1947 **DISCIPLINE** PHILOSOPHY **EDUCATION** Yale, 43-44; US Army, 43-46; City Univ of NYork, BSS, 44; NYork Univ, MA, 47, PhD, 50. **CAREER** Asst Inst, 49-50, NYU; Inst, Univ of Akron, 50-51; Inst, 52-53, City Univ of NY; Chmn, Dept of Philos, 53-65, Asst Prof, 53-57, Assoc Prof, 57-61, Prof, 61-92, Prof Emeritus, 92-, Binghamton Univ. **HONORS AND AWARDS** Assistantship, NYU, 49-50; Fel, ACLU, 51-52, Fel, Binghamton Univ, 63, 66; Distinguished Res Fel, 67; Pres Creighton Philos Club, 61-62; awarded bronze star in wwii, 45. **MEMBERSHIPS** APA **RESEARCH** Language; logic; epistemology; metaphysics. **SELECTED PUBLICATIONS** Logic and Language, Knopf, 56; Language and Ontology, Univ S Illin Press, 69; Logic a Philosophical Introduction, Wesley, 74; Essays in Linguistic Ontology, Univ of S Illin Press, 82; Articles in Jour: Jour of Phil, Phil & Phenomenological Res, Jour of the Hist of Ideas, Philos of Science, Jour of Gen Ed, Revue Intl de Philos, Kant Studies, Indian Jour of Philos, Encyl of Philos; Art and Philos, 96. **CONTACT ADDRESS** PO Box 542, Cortland, NY 13045.

KAMIONKOWSKI, SUSAN T.
PERSONAL Born 07/22/1963, Cleveland, OH **DISCIPLINE** BIBLICAL STUDIES **EDUCATION** Oberlin Col, BA, 85; Harvard Div Sch, MTS, 87; Brandeis Univ, PhD, 00. **CAREER** Lectr, Hebrew Col of Brookline MA, 92-97; Dir of Bibl Civilization, Reconstructionist Rabbinical Col, 96-. **MEMBERSHIPS** Am Orient Soc; Soc of Bibl Lit; Asn for Judaic Stud. **RESEARCH** Biblical literature; Pentateuch and prophecy; ancient Near Eastern literature; gender studies. **CONTACT ADDRESS** Reconstructionist Rabbinical Col, 1299 Church Rd, Wyncote, PA 19047. **EMAIL** tamarkam@aol.com

KAMISAR, YALE
PERSONAL Born 08/29/1929, New York, NY, w, 3 children **DISCIPLINE** LAW **EDUCATION** NYork Univ, AB, 50; Columbia Univ, LLB, 54. **CAREER** Assoc Prof to Prof Law, Univ Minn, 57-65; Prof, 65-79, Henry K. Ransom Prof Law, 79-92, Clarence Darrow Distinguished Univ Prof, Univ Mich, 92-. **HONORS AND AWARDS** Research Awd for outstanding contributions to the law and the legal profession, Am Bar Found Fels, 96. **MEMBERSHIPS** Am Law Inst; Am Acad Arts & Sci. **RESEARCH** Criminal procedure; criminal law. **SELECTED PUBLICATIONS** Coauth, Constitutional Law: Cases, Comments & Questions, 1st ed, 64, 8th ed, 65; Modern Criminal Procedure: Cases, Comments & Questions, 1st ed, 65, 9th ed, 99; auth, On the "Fruits" of Miranda Violations, Coerced Confessions, and Compelled Testimony, Mich Law Rev 93, 95; On the Meaning and Impact of Physician-Assisted Suicide Cases, Minn Law Rev 82, 98; Physician-Assisted Suicide: The Problems Presented by the Compelling Heartwrenching Case, J Criminal Law & Criminol 88, 98. **CONTACT ADDRESS** Univ of Michigan, Ann Arbor, 801 Monroe St, 914 LR, Ann Arbor, MI 48109. **EMAIL** ykamisar@umich.edu

KAMM, FRANCES MYRNA
PERSONAL Born New York, NY **DISCIPLINE** PHILOSOPHY **EDUCATION** Barnard Col, BA, 69; Mass Inst Technol, PhD(philos), 80. **CAREER** Instr, Univ Mass, Boston, 73; instr, NY Univ, 79-80, Prof Philos, NY Univ, 80-, Prof. Medicine (Bioethics), NY Medical Schools, Affiliated fac, NY Univ Law Sch, vis prof philos, UCLA, 97-98. **HONORS AND AWARDS** Amer Coun Learned Soc grant 82-83, fel Ethics, Harvard Univ, 89-90, Guggenheim Fel. **MEMBERSHIPS** Am Philos Asn; Soc Philos & Pub Affairs. **RESEARCH** Ethics; social and political philosophy; bioethics. **SELECTED PUBLICATIONS** Auth, Creation and Abortion, OUP, 92, Morality, Mortality, vols 1 & 2, OUP, 93, 96. **CONTACT ADDRESS** Dept of Philosophy, New York Univ, 100 Washington Sq E, New York, NY 10003-6688. **EMAIL** fmk1@is4.nyu.edu

KAMTEKAR, RACHANA
PERSONAL 1 child **DISCIPLINE** PHILOSOPHY **EDUCATION** Stanford Univ, BA, 87; Univ Chicago, PhD, 95. **CAREER** Asst prof, Williams Col, 95- . **HONORS AND AWARDS** Mellon Fel, 93-94; Ill Inst Tech teaching fel, 94-95; Friedrich Solmsen fel, Univ Wis-Madison, 98-99. **MEMBERSHIPS** Am Philos Asoc; Am Philol Asoc. **RESEARCH** Ancient moral and political philosophy. **CONTACT ADDRESS** 1401 Observatory Dr., Madison, WI 53706. **EMAIL** rkamteka@williams.edu

KANE, FRANCIS
PERSONAL Born 03/06/1944, Wilmington, DE, m, 1970, 5 children **DISCIPLINE** PHILOSOPHY **EDUCATION** PhD. **CAREER** Salisbury State Univ **HONORS AND AWARDS** Outstanding Fac Award. **RESEARCH** Political Philosophy, Medical Ethics. **SELECTED PUBLICATIONS** Areas: assisted suicide, the death and dying movement. **CONTACT ADDRESS** Salisbury State Univ, Salisbury, MD 21801-6862. **EMAIL** fikane@politicsssu.edu

KANE, JOHN
DISCIPLINE RELIGIOUS STUDIES, WOMEN'S ISSUES **EDUCATION** Univ Dayton, BA, 64; Univ Fribourg, Switz, STB, 68; Saint Louis Univ, MA, 70; McMaster Univ, Canada, PhD, 78. **CAREER** Prof Relig Stud, Regis Col, 80-. **MEMBERSHIPS** Am Acad of Relig; Col Theol Soc; Pax Christi, USA. **RESEARCH** Contemporary catholicism; religion and society/politics; Christianity and contemporary culture. **SELECTED PUBLICATIONS** Auth, Of Christ & Culture - Building Faith's Body, in American Catholic Teaching: Resources for Renewal, Sandra Yocum Mize and William Portier, eds, Orbis Bks, 97. **CONTACT ADDRESS** Dept of Relig Stud, Regis Univ, 3333 Regis Blvd, Denver, CO 80221.

KANE, ROBERT H.
PERSONAL Born 12/25/1938, Boston, MA, m, 1965, 2 children **DISCIPLINE** PHILOSOPHY **EDUCATION** Holy Cross Col, AB, 60; Yale Univ, MA, 62; PhD, 64. **HONORS AND AWARDS** Acad Distinguished Teachers, Univ Texas, 95; R.W. Hamilton Fac Book Awd, 97; Friar Soc Centennial Fel; Pres Assoc Teaching Exc Awd. **MEMBERSHIPS** Am Philos Asn; Mid Asn. **RESEARCH** Philosophy of mind and action, Free will, Ethics, Theory of values, Philosophy of religion. **SELECTED PUBLICATIONS** Auth, Free Will and Values, 85; auth, Through the Moral Maze, 94; auth, The Significance of Free Will, 96. **CONTACT ADDRESS** Dept Philos, Univ of Texas, Austin, Austin, TX 78712-1013. **EMAIL** rKane@uts.cc.utexas.edu

KANE, STANLEY G.
PERSONAL Born 04/03/1938, Shanghai, China, m, 1959, 1 child **DISCIPLINE** PHILOSOPHY OF RELIGION, HISTORY OF PHILOSOPHY, ENVIRONMENTAL PHILOSOPHY **EDUCATION** Barrington Col, BA; Brown Univ, AM; Harvard Univ, PhD. **CAREER** Prof, Miami Univ **RESEARCH** Philosophy of religion, Environmental Philosophy. **SELECTED PUBLICATIONS** Publ on, problems of God and evil; nature of God; nature of religious lang; Anselm's theory of free will; Aquinas' doctrine of the soul and personal identity; 17th century mechanism phylos & histl roots of the env crisis. **CONTACT ADDRESS** Dept of Philosophy, Miami Univ, Oxford, OH 45056. **EMAIL** kanegs@muohio.edu

KANE, THOMAS ANTHONY
PERSONAL Born 06/27/1945, Philadelphia, PA, s **DISCIPLINE** RITUAL COMMUNICATION **EDUCATION** Univ Notre Dame, MA, 70; Cath Univ Am, STL, 73; Ohio State Univ, PhD, 82. **CAREER** Lectr relig & the arts, Cath Univ, 75-82; asst prof Pastoral Theol, Weston Jesuit Sch Theol, 83-; lectr, Cath Mission Coun Cult & Liturgy, 79-81; vis prof, Josephinum Pontif Inst, 77-78, DeSales Sch Theol, 81-82 & Washington Theol Union, 82. **HONORS AND AWARDS** Silver Angel Awd for FIESTA! Video, 00. **MEMBERSHIPS** Societas Liturgica; NAm Acad Liturgy. **RESEARCH** Celebration, art and ritual. **SELECTED PUBLICATIONS** Coauth, Textures of the Spirit, 1-2/79 & Psalm Dance 36, 9-10/79, Liturgy Mag; ed, Celebrating 1979, 79 & Celebrating 1980, 80, Winston Press; 1980: The Year of the Spirit, Paulist Press, 80; auth, Environmental Artists, Life Gifts, 81; video documentaries: The Dancing Church of Africa; The Dancing Church of South Pacific; Movements Meditations to the Songs of Taize with Carla De-Sola; FIESTA! Celebrations at San Fernando Cathedral; coauth, Introducing Dance to Christian Worship. **CONTACT ADDRESS** 3 Phillips Place, Cambridge, MA 02138-3495. **EMAIL** TKANECSP@aol.com

KANET, ROGER E.
PERSONAL Born 09/01/1936, Cincinnati, OH, m, 1963, 2 children **DISCIPLINE** POLITICAL SCIENCE **EDUCATION** Berchmanskolleg, Pullach-bei-Munchen, Germany, PhB, 60; Xavier Univ, AB, 61; LeHigh Univ, MA, 63; Princeton Univ, AM, 65, PhD, 66. **CAREER** Asst to Assoc Prof, Univ Kans, 67-74; Dir, Undergrad Stud, 69-70; Assoc Ch, Dept Polit Sci, 70-71; Vis Assoc Prof to Assoc prof to prof, Univ Ill at UC, 73-97; Hd of dept of polit sci, 84-87; assoc V Chan, 89-97; dir, International Programs and Studies, 89-97; mem, Russian & E European Ctr, 74-97; prof emeritus, 97-; prof, dean, Sch of Int Stud, Univ Miami, Coral Gables, 97-. **HONORS AND AWARDS** Joint Sr Fellow, Columbia Univ, 72-73; Fellow, Am Counc of Learned Soc, 72-73, 78; IREX Fellow in Hungary & Poland, 76; NATO Fac Fellow, 77; Assoc, Ctr for Adv Stuf, UIUC, 81-82; Awds for Excellence in Udergrad Tchng, 81; Burlington N Fac Ach Awd, UIUC, 89. **MEMBERSHIPS** Counc on Foreign Relations; Chicago Comt of Chicago Counc on Foreign Relations; Int Commission of the Nat Asn of State Univ & Land Grant Col, 89-97; Bd of Dir, MidW Univ Cons for Int Activities, 89-97; Asn of Int Educ Admin (exec committee, 95-00); Int Polit Sci Asn; Int Comte for Cent & E Eur Stud; Am Polit Sci Asn; Int Stud Asn; Am Asn for the Adv of Slavic Stud. **RESEARCH** Foreign & domestic policies of Russia & other countries of Central & Eastern Europe; democratization in postcommunist states. **SELECTED PUBLICATIONS** Co-ed, Soviet Foreign Policy in Transition, Cambridge Univ Press, 92; Coping with Conflict after the Cold War, Johns Hopkins Univ Press, 96; co-ed, The Foreign Policy of the Russian Federation, St Martin's Press, 97; co-ed, Resolving Regional Conflict, Univ Ill Press, 98; co-ed, The Post-Communist States in the World Community, St Martin's Press, 98. **CONTACT ADDRESS** Sch of Int Stud, Univ of Miami, PO Box 248123, Coral Gables, FL 33124-3010. **EMAIL** rkanet@sis.miami.edu

KANG, WI JO
PERSONAL Born 03/10/1930, Chinju, Korea, m, 1961, 4 children **DISCIPLINE** HISTORY OF RELIGIONS, MISSIONS **EDUCATION** Concordia Sem, BA, 57, 1313, 60; Univ Chicago, MA, 62, PhD, 67. **CAREER** Instr hist of relig, Columbia Univ, 64-66; asst prof, Valparaiso Univ, 66-68; assoc prof, Concordia Sem, 68-74 & Christ Sem-Seminex, 74-78; vis prof, Yonsei Univ, Korea, 78-79; Prof of Mission, Wartburg Sem, 80-98, prof emer, 98-. **MEMBERSHIPS** Am Acad Relig; Am Hist Soc; Int Soc Buddhist Studies; Am Soc Missiology; Am Soc Church Hist. **RESEARCH** History of religions in Asia; history of Christian missions in East Asia; world religions and politics. **SELECTED PUBLICATIONS** Auth, Korean Religions Under the Japanese Government (in Japanese), Seibunsha, Tokyo, 76; In Search of Light (in Korean), 76 & Religion and Politics of Korea Under Japanese Rule (in Korean), 77, Christian Lit Soc Korea, Seoul; The secularization of Korean Buddhism, Actes du XXIXe Cong Int des Orient Paris L'Asiatheque, 77; Religious response to Japanese rule, Ctr for Korean Studies, Kalamazoo, Mich, 77; co-ed, Christian Presence in Japan, Seibunsha, Tokyo, 81; auth, Christianity under the government of Chung Hee Park, Missiology: Int Rev, 81; Christianity in China, Currents in Theol & Mission, 82; auth, Christ and Caesar in Modern Korea: A History of Christianity and Politics, SUNY Press, 97. **CONTACT ADDRESS** 9980 Farthing Dr, Colorado Springs, CO 80906. **EMAIL** wjcjkang@aol.com

KAPLAN, DAVID M.
DISCIPLINE PHILOSOPHY **EDUCATION** Fordham univ, PhD, 98. **CAREER** Adj instr, Fordham Univ, 96-98; adj instr, Hofstra Univ, 97- ; adj instr, Polytechnic Univ, 96- . **HONORS AND AWARDS** Pres scholar, Fordham Univ, 90-94. **MEMBERSHIPS** APA; Soc for Phenomenology and Existential Philos. **RESEARCH** Twentieth century continental philosophy; social/political philosophy. **CONTACT ADDRESS** 617 Manhattan Ave, Brooklyn, NY 11222. **EMAIL** kaplan@murray.fordham.edu

KAPLAN, LAURA DUHAN
DISCIPLINE FEMINIST PHILOSOPHY, PHILOSOPHY OF EDUCATION, PHILOSOPHY OF PEACE, PHENOMEN **EDUCATION** Brandeis Univ, BA, 80; Cambridge Col, MEd, 83; Claremont Grad Sch, MA, 87, PhD, 91. **CAREER** Assoc prof, coord, Women's Stud prog, Univ NC, Charlotte. **RESEARCH** Family life, from the perspective of existential phenomenology. **SELECTED PUBLICATIONS** Auth, Speaking for Myself in Philosophy, Philos and the Contemp World, 1:4, 94; My Mother the Mirror, The Trumpeter, 11:4, 94; Teaching As Applied Philosophy, Tchg Philos , 17:1, 94; Woman as Caretaker: An Archetype That Supports Patriarchal Militarism, Hypatia: A J of Feminist Philos, 9:2, 94; Persons and Mystery: Art, Conflict and Self-Knowledge, in Becoming Persons, ed, Robert N. Fisher, Oxford: App Theol Press, 94; The Parable of the Levite's Concubine, in From the Eye of the Storm: Regional Conflicts and the Philosophy of Peace, eds, Laurence F. Bove and Laura Duhan Kaplan, Rodopi, 95; Physical Education for Domination and Emancipation: A Foucauldian Analysis of Aerobics and Hatha Yoga, in Philosophical Perspectives on Power and Domination: Theories and Practices, eds, Laura Duhan Kaplan and Laurence F. Bove, Rodopi, 96; Devaluing Others to Enhance our Self-Esteem: A Moral Phenomenology of Racism, in Institutional Violence, eds, Robert Litke and Deane Curtin, Rodopi, 96; coauth, Paradigms for the Philosophy of Peace, in From the Eye of the Storm: Regional Conflicts and the Philosophy of Peace, eds, Laurence F. Bove and Laura Duhan Kaplan, Rodopi, 95; coed, From the Eye of the Storm: Regional Conflicts and the Philosophy of Peace, Rodopi, 95; Philosophical Perspectives on Power and Domination: Theories and Practices, Rodopi, 97. **CONTACT ADDRESS** Univ of No Carolina, Charlotte, Charlotte, NC 28223-0001. **EMAIL** ldkaplan@email.uncc.edu

KAPLAN, RICHARD L.
DISCIPLINE LAW **EDUCATION** Univ Ind, BS; Yale Univ, JD. **CAREER** Prof,Univ Ill Urbana Champaign. **HONORS AND AWARDS** Urbana-Champaign Campus Awd, 94. **RESEARCH** Income taxation; taxation of international transactions; elder law; and federal tax policy. **SELECTED PUBLICATIONS** Auth, pubs on income taxation, taxation of international transactions, and elder law. **CONTACT ADDRESS** Law Dept, Univ of Illinois, Urbana-Champaign, 52 E Gregory Dr, Champaign, IL 61820. **EMAIL** rkaplan@law.uiuc.edu

KAPLAN, WILLIAM
DISCIPLINE LAW **EDUCATION** Univ Toronto, BA, MA; Osgoode Hall Law Sch, LLB; Stanford Univ, JSD. **CAREER** Assoc prof. **SELECTED PUBLICATIONS** Auth, Presumed Guilty: Brian Mulroney, the Airbus Affair and the Government of Canada. **CONTACT ADDRESS** Fac Common Law, Univ of Ottawa, Fauteux Hall, 57 Louis Pasteur, Ottawa, ON, Canada K1N 6N5. **EMAIL** wkaplan@sympatico.ca

KAPLOW, LOUIS
PERSONAL Born 06/17/1956, Chicago, IL, m, 2 children **DISCIPLINE** LAW **EDUCATION** Northwestern Univ, BA, 77; Harvard Law School, JD (magna cum laude), 81; Harvard Univ, MA, 81, PhD, 87. **CAREER** Law Clerk to Hon. Henry J. Friendly, United States Court of Appeals for the Second Circuit, 81-82; PROF, HARVARD LAW SCHOOL, 87-. **MEMBERSHIPS** Am Economic Asn; Nat Tax Asn; Am Law and Economics Asn. **RESEARCH** Taxation; antitrust; law & economics. **SELECTED PUBLICATIONS** Coauth, Fairness Versus Welfare, Harvard Univ Pr, forthcoming; auth, Accuracy, Complexity, and the Income Tax, J of Law, Economics and Organization, 98; auth, A note on the Optimal Supply of Public Goods and the Distortionary Cost of Taxation, Nat Tax Journal, 98; auth, Tax Policy and Gifts, Am Economic Asn Papers and Proceedings, 98; auth, Tax and Non-Tax Distortions, J of Public Economics, 98; auth, Accuracy in Adjudication, The New Palgrave Dictionary of Economics and the Law, 98; auth, General Characteristics of Rules, Encycl of Law and Economics, 98; auth, Tax Treatment of Families, Encycl of Taxation and Tax Policy, 98; auth, Comment on Antitrust Issues in the Licensing of Intellectual Property, Brookings Papers on Economic Activity: Microeconomics, 97; auth, Regional Cost-of-Living Adjustments in Tax-Transfer Schemes, Tax Law Review, 96; auth, The Optimal Supply of Public Goods and the Distortionary Cost of Taxation, Nat Tax J, 96; auth, On the Divergence Between Ideal and Conventional Income Tax Treatment of Human Capital, Am Economic Asn Papers and Proceedings, 96; auth, Fiscal Federalism and the Deductibility of State and Local Taxes in a Federal Income Tax, Va Law Review, 96; coauth, Accuracy in the Assessment of Damages, J of Law and Economics, 96; auth, Antitrust Analysis, Aspen Pub, 97. **CONTACT ADDRESS** Dept of Law, Harvard Univ, Cambridge, MA 02138.

KARABAN, ROSLYN A.
PERSONAL Born 06/27/1953, Waterbury, CT, m, 1982, 2 children **DISCIPLINE** RELIGION **EDUCATION** Stonehill Col, BA, 75; Harvard Divinity Sch, MDiv, 78; Grad Theol Union, PhD, 84. **CAREER** Instr, pacific school of Relig, 81; Instr, United Theol Col, Bangalore, 85-87; Instr to Assoc prof, St Bernard's Inst, 87-. **MEMBERSHIPS** Am Asn of Pastoral Counselors, Soc for Pastoral Theol, Certified Death Educator and Grief Therapist, ADEC. **SELECTED PUBLICATIONS** Auth, Guide for Ministering to the Grieving, Resource Pub, 00; auth, Responding to God's Call: A Survival Guide, Resource Pub, 98; ed, Extraordinary Preaching: 0 Homilies by Roman Catholic women, Resource Pub, 96; auth, "Cross-cultural Pastoral counseling: Method or Hermeneutic? A Response," pastoral Psychology, 92; auth, "The Sharing of Cultural Variation," The Journal of Pastoral Care, 91; auth, 'Cross Cultural counseling: Is it Possible?," pastoral psychology, 90; auth, "Jung's Concept of the anima/Animus: enlightening or Frightening?', Bangalore Theological Forum, 87; auth, "Women in the Pulpit," St Joan's International Alliance bulletin, 81; auth, "Choose the Good Portion: Your Way," New women/New Church, 80. **CONTACT ADDRESS** Dept Relig, Saint Bernard's Inst, 1100 Goodman St S, Rochester, NY 14620-2530.

KARAMUSTAFA, AHMET T.
PERSONAL Born 11/15/1956, Turkey, m, 1986, 3 children **DISCIPLINE** HISTORY; RELIGIOUS STUDIES **EDUCATION** Hamilton Col NYork, BA, 78; McGill Univ Can, MA, 81; PhD, 87. **CAREER** Asst prof, Wash Univ, 87-94; acting chair, Wash Univ, 94; dir, Center for the Study of Islamic Socs and civilizations, Wash Univ, 94-97; Assoc Prof, Wash Univ, 94-; dir, Relig Studies Program, 99-. **HONORS AND AWARDS** Phi Beta Kappa, 78; Grad magna cum laude, Hamilton Coll, 78; Dean's List, McGill Univ, 87. **MEMBERSHIPS** Am Acad of Rel; Am Res Inst in Turkey; Middle E Studies Asn; Soc for Iranian Studies; Turkish Studies Asn. **RESEARCH** Premodern Islamic intellectual traditions. **SELECTED PUBLICATIONS** Auth, God's Unruly Friends: Dervish Groups in the Islamic Later Middle Period, 1200-1550, 94; Vahidid's Menakib-I Hvoca-I Cihan ve Nefice-I can: critical Edition and Analysis, 93; asst ed, The History of Cartography, cartography in the Traditional Islamic and South Asian Societies, 92. **CONTACT ADDRESS** Dept of Hist, Washington Univ, CB 1062, One Brookings Dr, Saint Louis, MO 63130. **EMAIL** akaramus@artsci.wustl.edu

KARDONG, TERRENCE G.
PERSONAL Born 10/22/1936, Minneapolis, MN **DISCIPLINE** MONASTIC STUDIES **EDUCATION** Catholic Univ, MA, 68; Licentiate, Theology, Sant Ansolmo, 77. **CAREER** ED, THE AMERICAN BENEDICTINE REV **HONORS AND AWARDS** Honorary doctorate, Belmont Col. **MEMBERSHIPS** Norht Am Patristic Soc. **RESEARCH** Rule of St. Benedict; pre-Benedictine sources. **SELECTED PUBLICATIONS** Auth, Benedicts Rule: Tranlation and Commentary, Liturgical Press, 96. **CONTACT ADDRESS** Assumption Abbey, Richardton, ND 58652. **EMAIL** abredit@popctel.com

KARJALA, DENNIS S.
PERSONAL Born 12/19/1939, New York, NY, m, 1996, 3 children **DISCIPLINE** LAW **EDUCATION** Princeton Univ, BSE, 61; Univ Ill, Ms; PhD, 65; Univ Calif, JD, 72. **CAREER** Prof, Ariz State Univ, 78-; Vis Prof, Hokkaido Univ, 80; Vis Prof, UCLA, 84; Vis Prof, Univ Tokyo, 90; Vis Prof, Wash Univ, 88; Vis Prof, Univ Minn, 97-98. **HONORS AND AWARDS** Fel, Japan Found, 85-86; Fulbright Fel, 80-81, 92-93. **MEMBERSHIPS** ABA; AAAS **RESEARCH** Copyright and intellectual property, especially in application to digital technologies. **SELECTED PUBLICATIONS** Auth, "Copyright and Misappropriatio?" Dayton L J, 92; auth, "Copyright Protection of Computer Software, Reverse Engineering, and Professor Miller," Dayton L J, 94; auth, "Copyright in Electronic Maps," Jurimetrics J, 95; auth, "Federal Preemption of Shrinkwrap and On-Line Licenses," Dayton L Rev, 97; auth, "A Coherent Theory for the copyright Protection of Computer Software and Recent Judicial Interpretations," Cincinnati L Rev, 97; auth, "Copyright Protection of Operating Software, Copyright Misuse, and Antitrust," Cornell J of Law & Pub Policy, 99. **CONTACT ADDRESS** Col of Law, Arizona State Univ, Tempe, AZ 85287-7906. **EMAIL** dennis.karjala@asu.edu

KARKHANIS, SHARAD
PERSONAL Born 03/08/1935, Khopoli, India **DISCIPLINE** POLITICAL SCIENCE, AMERICAN GOVERNMENT **EDUCATION** Bombay Libr Asn, diploma, 56; Univ of Bombay, BA, 58; Rutgers State Univ, MLS, 62; Brooklyn Col, CUNY, MA, 67; NYork Univ, PhD, 78. **CAREER** Librn, U.S. Infor Service Libr, 55-58; librn trainee, Leyton Public Libr, 58-59; librn trainee, Montclair Public Libr, 59-60; librn, East Orange Pub Libr, 60-63; librn, Brooklyn Col Libr, 63-64; prof of Libr & Political Sci, Kingsborough Community Col, CUNY, 64-. **HONORS AND AWARDS** Distinguished Service Awd, Asian/Pacific Am Librn Asn, 89; Taraknath Das Awd, NY Univ Grad School, 77; Certificate of Appreciation by the Libr Asn of the City Univ of NY, 73. **MEMBERSHIPS** Am Libr Asn, 64-; Asian/Pacific Am Libr Asn, 80-. **RESEARCH** Press and politics of India; Judaism in America. **SELECTED PUBLICATIONS** Auth, Jewish Heritage in America: An Annotated Bibliography, Garland Pub, 88; Indian Politics and the Ride of the Press, Vikas Pub, 81. **CONTACT ADDRESS** Kingsborough Comm Col, CUNY, 2001 Oriental Blvd, Brooklyn, NY 11235. **EMAIL** skarkhanis@kbcc.cuny.edu

KARMAN, JAMES
PERSONAL Born 08/12/1947, Moline, IL, m, 1968 **DISCIPLINE** ENGLISH, LITERATURE, ART, RELIGION **EDUCATION** Augustana Col, BA, 69; Univ Iowa, MA, 71; Syracuse Univ, PhD, 76. **CAREER** Postdoctoral fel, Syracuse Univ, 76-77; ast prof, 77-84, asoc prof, 84-87, prof coord, 87-, Calif St Univ, Chico. **HONORS AND AWARDS** Res fel, Nat Endowment Hum, 98-99; Book Club of California grnt, 99. **MEMBERSHIPS** Robinson Jeffers Tor House Found; Robinson Jeffers Asn; MLA; Col Art Asn; Am Acad Relig; Asn for Documentary Editing; Soc for Textua Scholar. **RESEARCH** Art; religion; literature; twentieth century history and culture; life and work of Robinson Jeffers. **SELECTED PUBLICATIONS** Ed, Critical Essays on Robinson Jeffers, GK Hall, 90; auth, Robinson Jeffers: Poet of California, rev., Story Line, 95; ed, Of Una Jeffers, Story Line, 98. **CONTACT ADDRESS** Dept of English, California State Univ, Chico, Chico, CA 95929-0830. **EMAIL** Jkarman@csuchico.edu

KARMEL, ROBERTA S.
PERSONAL Born 05/04/1937, Chicago, IL, m, 1995, 4 children **DISCIPLINE** LAW **EDUCATION** Radcliff Col, BA, 59; New York Univ Schl of Law, LLB, 62. **CAREER** Comm, Securities & Exchange Com, 77-80; Prof, Brooklyn Law Schl, 86-; Partner, 87-94, Counsel, 95-, Kelly Drye & Warren LLP. **HONORS AND AWARDS** Hon doctorate of humanities, Kings Col, Wilkes Barre PA, 98. **MEMBERSHIPS** ABA; Amer Bar Found Fel; Amer Law Inst; Assoc of the Bar of the City of NY; Intl Bar Assoc **RESEARCH** Securities regulation; international financial law. **SELECTED PUBLICATIONS** Auth, National Treatment Harmonization and Mutual Recognition, Capital Mkts Forum Intl Bar Assoc, 93; Securities Law in the European Community Harmony or Cacophony?, Toulane Jour Intl & Comp, 93; Implications of the Stakeholder Model, Geo Wash Law Rev, 93; Barriers to Foreign Issuer Entry Into US Markets, Law & Policy in Intl Bus, 93; The Relationship Between Mandatory Disclosure and Prohibitions Against Insider Trading: Why a Property Rights Theory of Inside Information is Untenable, Brooklyn L Rev, 93; Living with US Regulations Complying with the Rules and Avoiding Litigation, Fordham Intl L Jour, 94; Is the Shingle Theory Dead? Wash & Lee Law Rev, 95; A Report on the Attitudes of Foreign Companies Regarding a US Listing, Stan JL & Bus, 97; auth, Stock Markets and the Globalization of Retirement Savings--Implications of Government Pensions for Securities Regulation, International Lawyer, 99; auth, The Case for a European Securities Commission, Columbia Journal of Transitional Law, 99; auth, The Challenge to Financial Regualtors Posed by Social Security Privatization, Brooklyn Law Review, 98; auth, Creating Law at the Securities and Exchange Commission--The Lawyer as Prosecutor, Law & Contemporary Problems, 98; auth, Outsides Trading on Confidential Information--A French in Search of a Duty, Cardozo Law Review, 98; auth, Transnational Takeover Talk--Regulations Relatin to Tender offers and Insider Trading in one United States, The United Kingdom, Germany and Australia, Univ Cincinnati Law Review, 98. **CONTACT ADDRESS** 250 Joralemon St, Brooklyn, NY 11201. **EMAIL** rkarmel@brooklaw.edu

KARST, KENNETH L.
PERSONAL Born 06/26/1929, Los Angeles, CA, m, 1950, 4 children **DISCIPLINE** CONSTITUTIONAL LAW **EDUCATION** UCLA, AB, 50; Harvard Univ, LLB, 53. **CAREER** Law practice in Los Angeles, 54, 56-57; US Air Force, JAGD, 54-56; Col of Law, Ohio State Univ, 58-65; Sch of Law, UCLA, 65-. **HONORS AND AWARDS** James A. Rawley Awd from Organization of Am Hist, 90. **MEMBERSHIPS** Am Academy of Arts and Sciences. **RESEARCH** U.S. constitutional law. **SELECTED PUBLICATIONS** Auth, Belonging to America: Equal Citizenship and the Constitution, Yale U Press, 89; auth, Law's Promise Law's Expression: Visions of Power in the Politics of Gender, Race, and Religion, Yale U Press, 93; co-ed, Encyclopedia of the Am Constitution, 2nd ed., Macmillan/Gale Group, 00. **CONTACT ADDRESS** Sch of Law, Univ of California, Los Angeles, PO Box 951476, Los Angeles, CA 90095-1476. **EMAIL** karst@law.ucla.edu

KASACHKOFF, TZIPORAH
PERSONAL Born 04/12/1942, Washington, DC **DISCIPLINE** ETHICS, PHILOSOPHY, LAW **EDUCATION** New York Univ, PhD, 72. **CAREER** Lect, 69-72; asst prof, 72-76; assoc prof, 76-81; prof, 81-, Borough Man Comm Col, CUNY; prof, 88-, dep exec off, 99-, Grad Sch Univ Cen, CUNY. **HONORS AND AWARDS** Deans Hon List; Phi Beta Kappa; Matchette Awd; Marvin J Kratter Awd; Nat Def Fel; Founders Day Awd; Hoover Inst Nat Fel; Outstand Young Women; Pres Cet Achiev, 80, 82; NEH Fel; Harvard Hon Fac Appt; Who's Who, Schl; PSC CUNY Awd; PSC CUNY Res Awd; Vis Schl, Inst Crim, England; Schl Incent Awd; Higher Edu Act Gnt. **MEMBERSHIPS** AAUP; APA; NASSP; SPPA; ASPLP; ICJE; SWIP; PPA NY. **RESEARCH** Professional ethics; theoretical ethics; philosophy; law. **SELECTED PUBLICATIONS** Ed, In the Socratic Tradition: Essays on Teaching Philosophy, Rowman & Littlefield Pub (Lanham, Maryland), 98; auth, "Teaching Nursing Ethics" Intl J Law and Med 8 (89): 593-599; auth, "Paternalistic Solicitude and Paternalistic Behavior: Appropriate Contexts and Justifications," in Freedom, Equality and Social Change, eds. Creighton Peden, James Sterba (Lewiston NY: Edwin Mellen Press, 89), 79-93; auth, "Wissenschaft ais Gegenstand 'angewandter Philosophie" ("What Does Ethics Have to Offer Science and Applied Ethics Have to Offer Philosophy?") Ethik in den Wissenschaften: Ariadnefaden im technischen Labyrinth? eds. Klaus Steigleder, Dietmar Mieth (Tubingen: Attempto Verlag, 90), 175-187; auth, "Paternalism and Drug Abuse," Mt Sinai J Med 58 (91): 1-4; auth, "Euthanasia and Religious Belief: The Importance of How We Frame the Questions" Intl J Applied Philo 6 (91): 37-44; auth, "A Capitalist or Socialist Approach to Medicine? A Reply," Pub Health Rev (92); auth, "Some Complaints About and Some Defenses of Applied Philosophy" Intl J Applied Philo 7 (92): 5-9; auth, "Tolerance and Moral Compromise" Synthesis Philo 9 (94): 53-81; auth, "Paternalism: Does Gratitude Make It Okay?" Soc Theory and Practice 20 (94): 1-23; rev, Autonomy & Intervention: Parentalism in the Caring Life, by John Kultgen, forthcoming; rev, Argument Structure: A pragmatic Theory, by Douglas Walton, forthcoming. **CONTACT ADDRESS** Dept Social Sciences, Borough of Manhattan Comm Col, CUNY, 199 Chambers St, New York, NY 100007-1044. **EMAIL** tkasachkoff@gc.cuny.edu

KASELY, TERRY S.
PERSONAL Born 10/06/1958, Rochester, PA, m, 1986, 3 children **DISCIPLINE** PHILOSOPHY **EDUCATION** Duquesne Univ, PhD, 92. **CAREER** Part-time inst, Indiana Univ of PA, Univ of PGH, Duquesne Univ, Penn State Univ, & Butler Comm Coll, 87-. **MEMBERSHIPS** APA **RESEARCH** History of philosophy **SELECTED PUBLICATIONS** The Method of the Geometer: A New Angle on Husserl's Cortesianism, Husserl Studies 13:141-154, 97. **CONTACT ADDRESS** 306 S Pike Road, Sarver, PA 16055.

KASFIR, SIDNEY L.
DISCIPLINE IDOMA MASQUERADE AND SACRED KINGSHIP **EDUCATION** Univ London, PhD, 79. **CAREER** Assoc Prof, Dept of Art History and Faculty Curator of African Art, Michael C. Carlos Museum, Emory Univ **HONORS AND AWARDS** Rockefeller Residency fell, 93-94; Nat Endowment for the Humanities, 89; auth, Am Philosophical Soc Grant, 86 **RESEARCH** Idoma masquerade and sacred kingship; contemporary urban and tourist art; museum representation **SELECTED PUBLICATIONS** Ed and contrib, West African Masks and Cultural Systems, Musee Royal de l'Afrique Centrale, Tervuren, 88, "Masquerading as a Cultural System" and "Celebrating Male Aggression: the Idoma Oglinye Masquerade," auth, "Remembering Ojiji: Portrait of an Idoma Artist," African Arts, XXII (4), 89: 44-51, 86-87; Auth, "African Art and Authenticity: A Text with a Shadow" African Arts, XXV (2), 92, 41-53, 96-97; Auth, "Ivory from Zariba Country to the Land of Zinj," Catalog essay for Elephant: The Animal and its Ivory in African Art, ed. By Doran H. Ross, Los Angeles: Fowler Museum of Cultural History, UCLA, 92; auth, "Taste and Distaste: The Canon of New African Art," Transition 57, vol 2, no 3, 92: 52-70; auth, "Arts of the Lower Benue," Catalog essay and Idoma, Tiv and Afo catalog entries, L'Art du Nigeria, ed. By Ekpo Eyo and Jean Paul Barbier, Paris, 97; "Elephant Women, Furious and Majestic," African Arts, XXXI (3), 98; auth, "Samburu Souvenirs" in Unpacking Culture: Art and Commodity in the Postcolonial World, ed. By Ruth B. Phillips and Christopher Steiner, Berkeley: University of California Press, 99; auth, Contemporary African Art, Thames and Hudson, 99, French edition 00; auth, "Artists' Reputations: Negotiating Power through Distance and Ambiguity," African Arts, 33 (1), spring 00. **CONTACT ADDRESS** Emory Univ, Atlanta, GA 30322-1950. **EMAIL** hartsk@emory.edu

KASSAM, ZAYN
DISCIPLINE HISTORY OF RELIGIONS **EDUCATION** McGill Univ, PhD, 95. **CAREER** Assoc prof, Pomona Col, 95-. **HONORS AND AWARDS** Wig Awd for Distinguished Teaching, 98. **MEMBERSHIPS** Am Acad of Rel; Middle East Studies Asn; Soc for Iranian Studies; North Am Asn for the Study of Rel; Asian Studies Asn. **RESEARCH** Islamic Philosophy, Comparative Studies in Philosophy, Mysticism, Gender in the Islamic World. **CONTACT ADDRESS** Religious Studies, Pomona Col, 551 N College Ave, Claremont, CA 91711. **EMAIL** zkassam@pomona.edu

KASSIM, HUSAIN
PERSONAL Born 03/15/1939, Bombay, India, m, 1977 **DISCIPLINE** PHILOSOPHY **EDUCATION** Univ Kerachi, MA, 68; Univ Bonn, PhD, 68. **CAREER** Asst prof to assoc prof, Univ Central Fla, 70-. **HONORS AND AWARDS** Fulbright, Germany, 88-89; Post-Doctoral Fel, SUNY, 69-70. **MEMBERSHIPS** APA. **RESEARCH** Philosophy and Middle Eastern Studies. **SELECTED PUBLICATIONS** Auth, "Existential Tendencies in Ghazali and Kierkegaard", Islamic Studies (71): 103-128; auth, Phenomenological Encounter with Death, Fla Tech Univ, 73; auth, "Islam in Contemporary World", Ecumenical Studies, (82); auth, "Sarakhsi's Doctrine of Juristic Preference as a Methodological Approach Toward Worldly Affairs", Am Jour of Islamic Soc Sci (88):181-204; auth, Sarakhsi: The Doctrine of Juristic Preference in Islamic Jurisprudence and Concepts of Treaties and Mutual Relations, Austin & Winfield, 95; auth, Aristotle and Aristotelianism in Medieval Muslim, Jewish and Christian Philosophy, Austin & Winfield, 00. **CONTACT ADDRESS** Dept Philos, Univ of Central Florida, PO Box 161352, Orlando, FL 32816-1352. **EMAIL** h.kassim@worldnet.att.net

KATADA, SAORI
DISCIPLINE INTERNATIONAL RELATIONS **EDUCATION** Univ NC at Chapel Hill, PhD, 94. **CAREER** Asst prof, Univ Southern Calif. **RESEARCH** International relations of the Pacific Rim including East Asia and Latin America; Japanese foreign policy; Japanese politics. **SELECTED PUBLICATIONS** Auth, Official Flows to China: Recent Trends and Major Characteristics; grants and Debt Forgiveness to SPA Countries: a Descriptive Analysis. **CONTACT ADDRESS** East Asian Studies Center, Univ of So California, University Park Campus, Los Angeles, CA 90089.

KATER, JOHN L., JR.
DISCIPLINE MINISTRY DEVELOPMENT **EDUCATION** Columbia Col, AB; Gen Theol Sem, MDiv; McGill Univ, PhD. **CAREER** Prof; dir, Ctr for Anglican Lrng and Life, Church Divinity Sch Pacific. **SELECTED PUBLICATIONS** Ed, The Challenges of the Past, of the Future: Essays on Mission in the Light of Five Hundred Years of Evangelization in the Americas, CDSP, 94; auth, Campus Ministry and the Reign of God, Plumbline, 95; A Life of Practical Devotion: The Company of Mission Priests in the Church of England 1940-1993, Anglican and Episcopal Hist, 94; Whose Church Is It Anyway? Anglican Catholicity Reconsidered, Anglican Theol Rev, 94; Finding Our Way: American Christians in Search of the City of God, Cowley, 91. **CONTACT ADDRESS** Church Divinity Sch of the Pacific, 2451 Ridge Rd, Berkeley, CA 94709-1217.

KATES, CAROL A.
PERSONAL Born 11/05/1943, Coral Gables, FL **DISCIPLINE** PHILOSOPHY **EDUCATION** Univ Calif, Berkeley, BA, 65; Tulane Univ, MA, 67, PhD(Philos), 68; Cornell Univ, MILR, 86. **CAREER** Asst prof, 68-71, from assoc prof to prof Philosophy, Ithaca Col, 71-, res assoc ling, Cornell Univ, 73; Am Coun Learned Socs res grant, 76-77; Nat Endowment for Humanities res grant, 73. **MEMBERSHIPS** Am Philos Asn; Southern Soc Philos & Psychol. **RESEARCH** Philosophy of Public Policy; phenomenology; existentialism; philosophy in literature. **SELECTED PUBLICATIONS** Auth, "Heidegfer and the Myth of the Cave," Personalist, 69; auth, "Perception and Temporality in Husserl's Phenomenology," PhilosToday, 70; auth, Psychical distance and temporality, Tulane Studies in Philos, 71; A critique of Chomsky's Theory of Grammatical Competence, 76 & Linguistic relativity and generative Semantic grammar, 77, Forum Ling; The Problem of Universals: An empiricist account of ideal objects, Man and World, Vol XII, 79; An intentional analysis of the law of contradiction, Res in Phenomenology, Vol IX, 79; A pragmatic theory of metaphor, Forum Ling, 12/79; auth, Pragmatics and Semantics, Cornell Univ Press, 80; Art and myth: The authentic image, In: Philos & Archaic Experience, Duquesne Univ Press, 82; auth, "Working Class Feminism and Feminist Unions," Labor Studies Jrnl, 89; "Pay Equity and Wage Justice," Rev of Radical Political Economics, 94; auth, "Pay Equity in Local Government: A case study," Labor Studies Jnrl, 94; "A Labor Perspective on Fair Pay," Employee Responsibilities and Rights Jrnl, 96. **CONTACT ADDRESS** Dept of Philosophy, Ithaca Col, 953 Danby Rd, Ithaca, NY 14850-7002. **EMAIL** kates@ithaca.edu

KATSORIS, CONSTANTINE N.
DISCIPLINE TAX LAW **EDUCATION** Fordham, BS, 53, JD, 57; NYork Univ, LLM, 63. **CAREER** Pvt practice, Cahill, Gordon, Reindel & Ohl, NYC, 58-64; pres, Fordham Law Rev Assn, 63-64; consult, NY Comm on Estates, 64-67; arbitrator, Nat Assn Securities Dealers, 68-; arbitrator, NY Stock Exch, 71-; dir, Fordham Law Alumni Assn, 72-; public mem, Securities Ind Conf on Arbit, 77-; pvt judge, Duke Law Sch Pvt Adjudication Ctr, 89-; arbitrator trainer, Nat Assn Securities Dealers, 94-; arbitrator trainer, NY Stock Exch, 94-; prof, 64-. **SELECTED PUBLICATIONS** Auth, Mastrobuono: Not the Last Word on Punitives, 13 Alternatives 29, 95; Ruder Report is a Delicate Compromise, 14 Alternatives 29, 96; SICA: The First Twenty Years, 23 Fordham Urban Law Jour 483, 96; The Betrayal of McMahon, 24 Fordham Urban Law Jour 221, 97. **CONTACT ADDRESS** Law Sch, Fordham Univ, 113 W 60th St, New York, NY 10023.

KATZ, IRVING
PERSONAL Born 09/24/1932, New York, NY, 2 children **DISCIPLINE** AMERICAN POLITICAL & JEWISH HISTORY **EDUCATION** City Col NYork, BA, 54; NYork Univ, MA, 59, PhD(hist), 64. **CAREER** Res assoc bus hist, Harvard Univ, 61-64; asst prof, 64-68, assoc prof, 68-81, Prof Hist, Ind Univ, Bloomington, 81-. **HONORS AND AWARDS** Am Philos Soc res grant, 68. **MEMBERSHIPS** AHA; Orgn Am Historians; Am Jewish Hist Soc. **RESEARCH** American political history; immigration and labor history; investment banking. **SELECTED PUBLICATIONS** Auth, August Belmont: A Political Biography, Columbia Univ Press, 68; auth, "August Belmont's Cuban Acquistion Scheme," Mid-Am, 68; auth, "Henry Lee Higginson vs Louis Dembitz Brandeis," New England Quart, 68; contrib, Investment Banking in America: A History, Harvard Univ Press, 70. **CONTACT ADDRESS** Dept of Hist, Indiana Univ, Bloomington, Ballantine Rm 742, Bloomington, IN 47405. **EMAIL** ikatz@indiana.edu

KATZ, LEWIS ROBERT
PERSONAL Born 11/15/1938, New York, NY, m, 1964, 1 child **DISCIPLINE** CRIMINAL LAW **EDUCATION** Queens Col, NYork, BA, 59; Ind Univ, Bloomington, JD, 63. **CAREER** Assoc, Snyder, Bunger, Cotner & Harrell, 63-65; instr law, Univ Mich, 65-66; from asst prof to prof, 66-72, John C Huthins Prof Law, Sch Of Law, Case Western Reserve Univ, 72-; Dir Ctr Criminal Justice, 73-; Lectr, US Int Commun Agency, Africa, 81-82. **RESEARCH** Criminal procedure; criminal justice administration. **SELECTED PUBLICATIONS** Auth, Ohio Arrest Search and Seizure, West Annul Publ, 00; coauth, New York Suppression Manual: Arrest, Search and Seizure, Interrogation and Identification, Matthew Bender Annual supplement, 99; auth, Know Your Rights, West, 94; coauth, Ohio Felony Sentencing Law, West Annual Publ, 99; Baldwin's Ohio Practice Criminal Law, Banks Baldwin Law Publ, 96; Ohio Criminal Justice, West Annual Publ, 97. **CONTACT ADDRESS** Sch of Law, Case Western Reserve Univ, 11075 East Blvd, Cleveland, OH 44106-1769. **EMAIL** lrk@po.cwru.edu

KATZ, MILTON
PERSONAL Born 11/29/1907, New York, NY, m, 1933, 3 children **DISCIPLINE** LAW **EDUCATION** Harvard Univ, AB, 27, JD, 31. **CAREER** Solicitor, War Pro Bd, 41-43; Byrne prof admin law, Law Sch, Harvard Univ, 46-48; US spec rep, Europe, 50-51; Stimson prof law & dir int legal studies, Law Sch, Harvard Univ, 54-78, dir int prog taxation, 61-65, res assoc, Prog Technol & Soc, 67-69. Trustee & mem exec comn, Carnegie Endowment Int Peace, 53-78, chmn bd trustees, 71-78; lect, Nat War Col, 53-55 & US Army War Ccl, 54-56; consult, Ford Found, 54-67; lectr, Haverford Col, 55; trustee, Longy Sch Music, 55-67; trustee & mem exec comt, World Peace Found, 55-; trustee & mem exec comt, Citizens Res Found, 59-78, pres, 72-78; mem, Comt Foreign Affairs Personnel, 61-63; chmn comt manpower, White House Conf Int Coop, 65; trustee, Brandeis Univ, 66-; consult, Secy Educ, Dept Health, Educ & Welfare, 67; trustee, Case Western Reserve Univ, 67-79; trustee, Int Legal Ctr, 67-78, chmn bd trustees, 74-78; chmn comt life sci & social policy, Nat Acad Sci-Nat Res Coun, 68-76; mem technol assessment panel, Nat Acad Sci, 68-70; Sherman Fairchild vis scholar, Calif Inst Technol, 74; Chmn Energy Adv Comt, Off Technol Assessment, US Cong, 75-80. **HONORS AND AWARDS** LLD, Brandeis Univ, 72. **MEMBERSHIPS** Am Bar Asn; Am Asn Comp Studies Law; Am Soc Int Law; Am Law Inst; fel Am Acad Arts & Sci (pres, 79-82). **RESEARCH** International legal studies; foreign policy; science, technology and law. **SELECTED PUBLICATIONS** Coauth, Law of International Transactions and Reactions, Foundation Press, 60; auth, The Things that are Caesar's, Knopf, 66; The Relevance of International adjudication, Harvard, 68; contribr, Man's Impact on the Global Environment, Mass Inst Technol, 70; Decision making in the production of power, Sci Am, 70; auth, International Aspects of Education in Law, Cyclopedia Educ, Macmillan & Free Press, 71; contribr, Assessing Biomedical Technologies, Nat Acad Sci, 73; Technology, Trade and the US Economy, Nat Res Coun, 78. **CONTACT ADDRESS** Law Sch, Harvard Univ, Cambridge, MA 02138.

KATZ, NATHAN
PERSONAL Born 08/11/1948, Philadelphia, PA, m, 1982 **DISCIPLINE** BUDDHIST STUDIES, COMPARATIVE RELIGIONS **EDUCATION** Temple Univ, AB, 70, MA, 75, PhD(relig), 78. **CAREER** Instr relig, Rutgers Univ, 75-78; vis prof Buddhism, Naropa Inst, 78-79; Asst Prof Eastern Religs, Williams Col, 79-, Am Coun Learned Soc Travel Grant, Austria, 81, Fulbright-Hays res fel, Sri Lanka, 76-78. **MEMBERSHIPS** Fel, Royal Asiatic Soc; Int Asn Buddhist Studies; Am Acad Relig; Asn Asian Studies; Am Philos Asn. **RESEARCH** Buddhist social philosophy; biography of Indrabhuti (8th century Tantric philosopher); Hermeneutics: Buddhist and contemporary western. **SELECTED PUBLICATIONS** Auth, An appraisal of the Svatantrika-Prasangilca debates, Philos East & West, 76; Anima and mKha' 'gro ma: A comparative study of Jung & Tibeton Buddhism, Tibet J, 77; Indrabhuti's Confession of Errors in the Roots and Branches of the Vajrayana, J Int Asn Buddhist Studies, 79; ed, Buddhist and Western Philosophy, Sterling, New Delhi, 81; Buddhist and Western Psychology, Shambhala, 82; auth, Buddhist Images of Human Perfection, Motilal Banarsidass, Delhi, 82; Tibetan hermeneutics and the Yana controversy, Wiener Studien fur Tibetologie u Buddhismuskunde, 82; Scholarly approaches to Buddhism: A political analysis, Eastern Buddhist, 82. **CONTACT ADDRESS** Dept of Relig, Florida Intl Univ, Miami, FL 33199.

KATZ, SANFORD NOAH
PERSONAL Born 12/23/1933, Holyoke, MA, m, 1958, 2 children **DISCIPLINE** LAW, BEHAVIORAL SCIENCES **EDUCATION** Boston Univ, AB, 55; Univ Chicago, JD, 58. **CAREER** Assoc prof law, Cath Univ Am, 59-64; prof, Univ Fla, 64-68; prof law, Boston Col, 68-, Darald and Juliet Libby Chair, 01-; lectr law & social work, Smith Col, 65-68; ed-in-chief, Family Law Quart, 71-; assoc law, Clare Hall, Cambridge Univ, 73; visiting fel All Souls Col, Oxford, 97. **HONORS AND AWARDS** Ford Found law fac fel, 64-65; Sterling Fel, Yale Law Sch, 63-64; dept Health, Educ & Welfare res grant, 66-78; Field Found res grant, 68-70; **MEMBERSHIPS** Am Bar Asn; Int Soc Family Law. **RESEARCH** Law and social work; family law. **SELECTED PUBLICATIONS** Auth, Judicial and Statutory Trends In The Law Of Adoption, Georgetown Law J, 62; auth, When Parents Fail: The Law's Response to Family Breakdown, Beacon, 71; ed, The Youngest Minority (2 vols), Am Bar Assn, 74; auth, Creativity in Social Work, Temple Univ, 75; coauth, Adoptions Without Agencies, Child Welfare League Am, 78; co-ed, Family Violence, 78; coauth, Marriage and Cohabitation in Contemporary Society, Butterworths, 81; auth, Child Snatching-The Legal Response to the Abduction of Children, Am Bar Assn, 81; auth, Cross Currents, Oxford Univ Press. **CONTACT ADDRESS** Law School, Boston Col, Newton Ctr, 885 Centre St, Stuart House F317, Newton, MA 02459. **EMAIL** sanford.katz.1@bc.edu

KATZ, STANLEY NIDER
PERSONAL Born 04/23/1934, Chicago, IL, m, 1960, 2 children **DISCIPLINE** AMERICAN LEGAL AND CONSTITUTIONAL HISTORY, HISTORY OF PHILANTHROPY **EDUCATION** Harvard Univ, AB, 55, MA, 59, PhD(Am colonial hist), 61. **CAREER** From instr to asst prof hist, Harvard Univ, 61-65, Allston Burr sr tutor, Leverett House, 63-65; from asst prof to assoc prof hist, Univ Wis-Madison, 65-70; prof legal hist, Law Sch, Univ Chicago, 70-78; prof, Princeton Univ, 78-86; President, Am Council of Learned Societies, 86-97; Prof Public adnd International Affairs, 97-, Woodrow Wilson School, 82-, Res fel, Charles Warren Ctr, Harvard Univ, 66-67, fel law and hist, Law Sch, 69-70; Am Bar Asn fel legal hist, 66-67; Am Coun Learned Soc fel, 69-70; Editing on Oliver Wendell Holmes, History of the U.S. Supreme Court, 77-, 77-; Vis Meme, Inst Advan Study, 81-82. **HONORS AND AWARDS** LLD, Stockton State Col, 81, DHL, Univ of Pugit Sound, 94; C.W. Post, LIU, 97, Sacred Heart Univ, 97, Ohio State Univ, 98. **MEMBERSHIPS** VP res, 97-00, AHA Orgn Am Historians; Am Soc Legal Hist (pres, 78-80); Am Studies Asn; Selden Soc. **RESEARCH** Anglo-Am legal and constitutional, history of philanthropy. **SELECTED PUBLICATIONS** Auth, "Influences on Public Policies in the United States," in W. McNeil Lowry, ed., The Arts and Public Policy, Prentice-Hall (84): 23-37; auth, "The Strange Birth and Unlikely History of Constitutional Equality," The Journal of American History, vol 75, no. 3 (88): 747-762; ed, Constitutionalism and Democracy: Transitions in the Contemporary World, Oxford Univ Press, New York, 93; auth, Constitutionalism in East Central Europe: Some Negative Lessons from the American Experience, German Historical Institute, Annual Lecture Series no. 7, Washington, DC, 94; auth, "Do Disciplines Matter? History and the Social Sciences," Social Science Quarterly, vol 76, no. 4 (95): 863-877; auth, "Restructuring for the Twenty-First Century," in Nicholas H. Farnham and Adam Yarmolinsky, eds, Rethinking Liberal Education, Oxford Univ Press, New York (96): 77-90; coauth, with Warren F. Ilchman and Edward L. Queen, II, eds, Philanthropy in the World's Traditions, Indiana Univ Press, 98; auth, Can Liberal Education Cope?, The Journal of Graduate Liberal Studies, vol 4 no 1 fall (98): 1-10. **CONTACT ADDRESS** Woodrow Wilson School, Princeton Univ, Robertson Hall 428, Princeton, NJ 08544. **EMAIL** snkatz@princeton.edu

KATZ, STEVEN T.
DISCIPLINE JUDAIC STUDIES **EDUCATION** Rutgers Col, BA, 66; NY Univ, MA, 67; Cambridge Univ, PhD, 72. **CAREER** Asst prof to prof, Dartmouth Col, 72-84; prof, Cornell Univ, 84-96, prof, Univ of Pa, 89-90 **HONORS AND AWARDS** Hon Doctorate, Gratz Col, 87, Joseph Meyerhoff Prof, Univ of Pa, 89-90; Fel, Annenberg Res Inst, 90; Leopold Lucas Prize, Univ of Tubingen, 99. **SELECTED PUBLICATIONS** Coauth, Jewish Philosophers: A History, Bloch Publ Co, NY, 75; coauth, Jewish Ideas and Concepts, Schoken Pr, 77; ed, Mysticism and Philosophical analysis, Oxford Univ Pr, 78; ed, Mysticism and Religious Traditions, Oxford Univ Pr, 83; auth, Post Holocaust Dialogues: Studies in 20th Century Jewish Thought, NY Univ Pr, 83; ed, Mysticism and Language, Oxford Univ Pr, (NY) 92; auth, Historicism. The Holocaust and Zionism, NY Univ Pr, 92; auth, The Holocaust in Historical Context, Oxford Univ Pr, (NY), 94; ed, Mysticism and Sacred Scripture, Oxford Univ Pr, (NY), 00; ed, Comparative Mysticism: An Anthology, Oxford Univ Pr, forthcoming. **CONTACT ADDRESS** Center for Judaic Studies, Boston Univ, 745 Commonwealth Ave, Rm 540, Boston, MA 02215. **EMAIL** stkatz@bu.edu

KAUCHECK, KEN
PERSONAL Born 10/14/1946, Highland Park, MI **DISCIPLINE** CANON LAW **EDUCATION** St. Mary's Univ, DDiv, 92; Gregorian Univ, Rome, PhD Canon Law, JCD, 94. **CAREER** Roman Catholic Priest, 78-, Archdiocese of Detroit, Sacred Heart Sem, adj prof, Metropolitan Tribunal - Judge: Defender of the Bond, 91-. **HONORS AND AWARDS** Summa Cum Laude **MEMBERSHIPS** CLSA, ATA **RESEARCH** Teaching magisterium of the church. **SELECTED PUBLICATIONS** Auth, Must the Act of Divine and Catholic Faith Be Given to Ordinatio sacerdotalis?: A Study of the Ordinary Universal Magisterium, in Studia canonica Saint Paul Univ Press, 97. **CONTACT ADDRESS** St. Anastasia Catholic Church, 4571 John R. Rd, Troy, MI 48098. **EMAIL** kkaucheck@aol.com

KAUFER, DAVID S.
DISCIPLINE ARGUMENT THEORY **EDUCATION** Univ Wisc, PhD. **CAREER** Lit, Carnegie Mellon Univ. **SELECTED PUBLICATIONS** Area: author-reader interactions across a variety of organizational contexts. **CONTACT ADDRESS** Carnegie Mellon Univ, 5000 Forbes Ave, Pittsburgh, PA 15213.

KAUFMAN, ANDREW L.
PERSONAL Born 02/01/1931, Newark, NJ, m, 1959, 4 children **DISCIPLINE** LAW **EDUCATION** Harvard Univ, AB, 51; LLB, 54. **CAREER** Assoc, Bilder, Bilder & Kaufman, 54-55; Law Clerk, Supreme Court U.S., 55-57; Partner, Kaufman, Kaufman, & Kaufman, 57-65; Lectr to Prof, Harvard Law Sch, 65-66, 86-89. **HONORS AND AWARDS** Michael Franck Awd, 00; Erwin N Griswold Prize; Scribes Book Awd; NY Board of Regents and NY State Archives Week Awd. **MEMBERSHIPS** Mass Bar Asn. **SELECTED PUBLICATIONS** Auth, Cardozo, Harvard Univ Press, 98 **CONTACT ADDRESS** Sch of Law, Harvard Univ, 1545 Massachusetts Ave, Cambridge, MA 02138. **EMAIL** kaufman@law.harvard.edu

KAUFMAN, GEORGE G.
PERSONAL Born 03/06/1933, Germany, s **DISCIPLINE** ECONOMICS, FINANCE **EDUCATION** Oberlin Col, BA, 54; Univ of Mich, MA, 55; Univ of Iowa, PhD, 62. **CAREER** Res Economist, Federal Reserve Bd, Chicago, 59-70; John Rogers Prof of Finance, Univ of Ore, 70-80; John Smith Prof of Finance and Econcomics, Loyola Univ, 81-. **MEMBERSHIPS** Western Finance Asn; Midwest Finance Asn; Am Finance Asn; Am Economic Asn. **RESEARCH** Banking; financial regulation; bond management. **SELECTED PUBLICATIONS** Auth, Designing an Efficient, Incentive Compatible, Government-Provided Deposit Insurance for Developing and Transitional Economies, Review of Pacific Basin Financial Markets and Policies, 98; auth, Preventing Banking Crises in the Future: Lessons From Past Mistakes, Independent Review, 97 and Review of Monetary and Financial Studies, 97; auth, The New Depositor Preference Act: Time Inconsistency in Action, Managerial Finance Vol 23, No 11, 97; auth, Comment on Financial Crises, Payment System Problems and Discount Window Lending, Journal of Money, Credit and Banking, 96; coauth, FDICIA After Five Years, Journal of Economic Perspectives, 97; auth, The Appropriate Role of Bank Regulation, Economic Journal, 96; auth, Managing Interest Rate Risk with Duration Gaps to Achieve Multiple Targets, Journal of Financial Engineering, 96; auth, Is the Banking and Payments System Fragile?, Journal of Financial Services Res, 95. **CONTACT ADDRESS** Col of Business Admin, Loyola Univ, Chicago, 820 N. Michigan Ave, Chicago, IL 60611. **EMAIL** gkaufma@luc.edu

KAUFMAN, GORDON DESTER
PERSONAL Born 06/22/1925, Newton, KS, m, 1947, 4 children **DISCIPLINE** THEOLOGY **EDUCATION** Bethel Col, Kans, AB, 47; Northwestern Univ, MA, 48; Yale Univ, BD, 51; PhD(philos theol), 55. **CAREER** Asst instr philos, Yale Univ, 50-52; from instr to asst prof relig, Pomona Col, 53-58; assoc prof theol, Div Sch, Vanderbilt Univ, 58-63; prof, 63-69, Edward Mallinckrodt Jr Prof Divinity, 69-95, Mallinckrodt Prof Div Emeritus, Harvard Univ Div Sch, 95-; Fulbright res fel, Univ Tubingen, 61-62; Guggenheim fel, Oxford Univ, 69-70; vis prof, United Theol Col, Bangalore, India, 76-77; vis prof, Dashisha Univ, Kyoto, 83; vis prof, Univ S Africa, Pretoria, 84; vis lectr, Oxford Univ, 86; vis prof, Chung Chi Col, Chinese Univ Hong Kong, 91. **HONORS AND AWARDS** LHD, Bethel Col, Kans, 73. **MEMBERSHIPS** Am Theol Soc (pres, 79-80); Am Acad Relig (pres, 81-82). **RESEARCH** Philosophical and systematic theology; philos of rel. **SELECTED PUBLICATIONS** Auth, Relativism, Knowledge and Faith, Univ Chicago, 60; The Context of Decision, Abingdon, 61; Systematic Theology: A Historicist Perspective, Scribners, 68; God the Problem, Harvard Univ, 72, Fr trans, 75; An Essay on Theological Method, Scholar's Press, 75, rev ed, 79, 3d ed, 95, Jap trans, 89; Nonresistance and Responsibility, Faith & Life Press, 79; The Theological Imagination: Constructing the Concept of God, Westminster, 81; auth, Theology for a Nuclear Age, Manchester Univ Press and Westminster Press, 85, It, Jap, Ger trans; auth, In Face of Mystery: A Constructive Theology, Harvard Univ Press, 93; auth, God-Mystery-Diversity: Christian Theology in a Pluralistic World, Fortress Press, 96. **CONTACT ADDRESS** Divinity Sch, Harvard Univ, 45 Francis Ave, Cambridge, MA 02138.

KAUFMAN, STEPHEN ALLAN
PERSONAL Born 09/11/1945, Minneapolis, MN, m, 1972, 2 children **DISCIPLINE** ANCIENT NEAR EASTERN LANGUAGES, OLD TESTAMENT **EDUCATION** Univ Minn, BA, 62; Yale Univ, PhD(Near Eastern lang and lit), 70. **CAREER** Asst prof North-West semitics, Univ Chicago, 71-76; assoc prof, 76-81, Prof Bible and Cognate Lit, Hebrew Union Col, 81-, Vis sr lectr, Haifa Univ, Israel, 74-76; Ed, Soc Bibl Lit, Aramaic Series, 79- **MEMBERSHIPS** Am Oriental Soc; Soc Bibl Lit. **RESEARCH** Aramaic studies; humanities micro computing. **SELECTED PUBLICATIONS** The Causative Stem in Ugartic and the Causative Form in Semitic--A Morphologic-Semantic Analysis of the S-Stem and Disputed Non-Sibilant Causative Stems in Ugartic, J Am Oriental Soc, Vol

113, 93; Old Aramaic Grammar of Texts from 7th-8th Century BC, J Am Oriental Soc, Vol 115, 95; A Scholars; Dictionary of Jewish Palestinian Aramaic--An Article Rev of Sokoloff, Michael Dictionary, J Am Oriental Soc, Vol 114, 94; The Dead Sea Scrolls on Microfiche--A Comprehensive Facsimile Edition of the Texts from the Judean Desert, Vol 3, Inventory List of Photographs, J Am Oriental Soc, Vol 116, 96; The Function of the Niphal in Biblical Hebrew in Relationship to Other Passive-Reflexive Verbal-Systems and to the Pual and Hophal in Particular--Siebesma,Pa, Cath Bibl Quart, Vol 56, 94; Living Waters--Scandinavian orientalistic Studies Presented to Lokkegaard,Frede on His 75th Birthday, January 27th, 1990, J Am Oriental Soc, Vol 113, 93; The Dead-Sea-Scrolls on Microfiche--A Comprehensive Facsimile Edition of the Texts from the Judean Desert, Vol 2, Companion Volume, J Am Oriental Soc, Vol 116, 96; The Dead-Sea-Scrolls Catalog--Documents, Photographs, and Museum Inventory Numbers, J Am Oriental Soc, Vol 116, 96. **CONTACT ADDRESS** Dept Bible and Cognate Lit, Hebrew Union Col-Jewish Inst of Religion, Ohio, Cincinnati, OH 45220.

KAUFMAN, WILLIAM E.
PERSONAL Born 06/20/1938, Philadelphia, PA, m, 1965, 2 children **DISCIPLINE** PHILOSOPHY **EDUCATION** Univ of PA, BA, 59; Jewish Theol Sem of Amer, Rabbi, M of Hebrew Letters, 64; Boston Univ, PhD, 71. **CAREER** Congregational Rabbi for 34 yrs; Rabbi of Temple Bethel, Fall River, MA; Adjunct Prof, Philos, Rhode Island Coll. **HONORS AND AWARDS** Phi Beta Kappa. **MEMBERSHIPS** Amer Philos Assoc; Amer Acad Rel; Assoc for Jewish Stud. **RESEARCH** Modern and Contemporary Jewish Philos; Process Theol. **SELECTED PUBLICATIONS** Auth, Contemporary Jewish Philosophies, Wayne State Univ Press, 92; Journeys, An Introductory Guide to Jewish Mysticism, NY Block Pub Co, 80; The Case for God, St Louis, MO, The Chalice Press, 91; A Question of Faith, Jason A., Northvale, NJ, 94; John Wild: From Realism to Phenomenology, NY, Peter Lang, 96; The Evolving God in Jewish Process Theology, Mellen Press, Lewiston, NY, 97. **CONTACT ADDRESS** 404 Langley St, Fall River, MA 02720.

KAUFMANN, FRANK
PERSONAL Born 12/23/1952, New York, NY, m, 1982, 3 children **DISCIPLINE** CHURCH HISTORY **EDUCATION** Vanderbuilt Univ, PhD 85. **CAREER** adj prof, Pace Univ; adj prof, Univ Theol Sem; founder, dir, The Common-Good Project. **HONORS AND AWARDS** Vanderbilt Univ Schshp; F U Berlin Schshp; Sr Res Fel, Center for Ethics, Relig, and International Relations. **MEMBERSHIPS** AAr **RESEARCH** Religion and society; New religions; Inter religious dialogue. **SELECTED PUBLICATIONS** Auth, Religion and Peace in the Middle East, New Era Books (NYork), 87; auth, The Foundations of Modern Church History, Lang Publ (NYork), 89; ed, Dialogue and Alliance, Quart J; ed, Newsletter of the Interreligious Federation for World Peace, quart; sr ed consul, Today's World, monthly; ed, Christianity in the Americas, Paragon Publ (NYork), 98; auth, ed, Religion and the Future of South African Societies. **CONTACT ADDRESS** Inter Religious Federation, Pace Univ, New York, 4 West 43rd St, New York, NY 10036. **EMAIL** fortl@pipeline.com

KAULBACH, ERNEST NORMAN
PERSONAL Born 01/03/1935, Bridgeport, CT, m, 1970, 2 children **DISCIPLINE** MEDIEVAL STUDIES AND PHILOSOPHY **EDUCATION** St Mary's Univ, AB, 57, STL, 61; Fairfield Univ, MA, 61; Cornell Univ, PhD(medieval studies), 70. **CAREER** Instr English, St Joseph's Col, 61-62; instr English and theol, St Mary's Col, 63-66; vis assoc prof English, classics and philos, 70-73, Assoc Prof English and Classics, Univ Tex, Austin, 73- **MEMBERSHIPS** Mediaeval Acad Am; Dante Soc Am. **RESEARCH** Medieval philosophy, literature and theology. **SELECTED PUBLICATIONS** Auth, Inferno XIX, 45: The Zanca of temporal power, Dante Studies, 68; Piers Plowman B IX, 18, 52: Further refinements of Inwit, In: Festschrift for A A Hill, 73. **CONTACT ADDRESS** Dept of English, Univ of Texas, Austin, 0 Univ of Texas, Austin, TX 78712-1026.

KAVANAGH, AIDAN
PERSONAL Born 04/20/1929, Mexia, TX **DISCIPLINE** RELIGION **EDUCATION** St Meinrad Sem, BA, 56; Univ Ottawa, Ont, STL, 58; Fakultat Trier, Ger, STD, 63. **CAREER** Asst prof theol, St Meinrad Sem, 62-66; from assoc prof to prof theol, Univ Notre Dame, 66-74, dir grad prog liturgical studies, 66-74; actg dir, Yale Inst Sacred Music, 75-77; Prof Liturgics, Yale Divinity Sch, 74-, Dir and vpres, World Ctr Liturgical Studies, 67-68; consult, Nat Cath Off Radio and TV, 67-69 and Int Comt English in Liturgy, 67-69; mem Am Roman Cath Bishop's Subcomt Liturgy, 67-69; assoc ed, Worship, 67-; Vis Prof, Divinity Sch, Yale Univ, 72-73; Assoc Ed, Studia Liturgica, 72- **HONORS AND AWARDS** Berakah Awd, NAm Acad Liturgy, 76; Hale Lectr, Seabury-Western Theol Sch, 82; ma, yale univ, 74. **MEMBERSHIPS** Nat Liturgical Conf; Am Acad Relig; Nat Asn Pastoral Musicians; Roman Cath-Oriental Orthodox Ecumenical Consultation; NAm Acad Liturgy. **RESEARCH** Hist and theory of ritual; social anthropology of symbolic forms; sacramental theology. **SELECTED PUBLICATIONS** Auth, The Concept of Eucharistic Memorial, Abbey Press, 64; Thoughts on the Roman anaphora, Worship, 12/65-1/66; contribr, Liturgy: self-expression of the church, Concilium/Herder, 72; co-ed, Roots of Ritual, Eerdmnn, 73; Life-cycle events, civil ritual and the Christian, Concilium, 78; Christian initiation in Post-Conciliar Roman Catholicism, Studia Liturgica, 78; The Shape of Baptism, 78 & Elements of Rite, 82, Pueblo. **CONTACT ADDRESS** Liturgics Dept, Yale Univ, New Haven, CT 06510.

KAWASHIMA, YASUHIDE
PERSONAL Born 10/22/1931, Nagasaki, Japan **DISCIPLINE** AMERICAN LEGAL & ASIAN HISTORY **EDUCATION** Keio Univ, Japan, LLB, 54, LLM, 56; Univ Calif, Santa Barbara, BA, 61, MA, 63, PhD(hist), 67. **CAREER** From instr to asst prof, 66-73, assoc prof, 73-80, Prof Am Hist, Univ Tex, El Paso, 80-, Colonial Williamsburg Found grant-in-aid, 70; fel, John Carter Brown Libr, Brown Univ, 71; Soc Sci Res Coun res training fel, 71-72; Charles Warren fel, Am legal hist, Harvard Law Sch, 71-72; Am Philos Soc res grant, 73; Huntington Libr fel, 80; Japan Found Professional fel, 81-82. **MEMBERSHIPS** AHA; Orgn Am Historians; Asn Asian Studies; Western Hist Asn; Am Soc Legal Hist. **RESEARCH** Indian-white relations; early Am legal history; history of Am-Japanese legal relations. **SELECTED PUBLICATIONS** Auth, Racial Fault Lines--The Hist Origins of White Supremacy in California, Am Hist Rev, Vol 101, 96; auth, Frontier and Pioneer Settlers--A Study of the Am Westward Movement, J Am Hist, Vol 83, 96; auth, Exemplar of Liberty--Native Am and the Evolution of Democracy, Am Hist Rev, Vol 98, 93; auth, The New-Deal and Am Capitalism--From a ViewpoInt of Popular Movements, J Am Hist, Vol 81, 94; auth, Am Holocaust--The Conquest of the New-World, Western Hist Quart, Vol 25, 94; auth, Essays on English Law and the Am Experience, J Am Hist, Vol 82, 95; auth, Civil-Law in Qing and Republican China, Am J Legal Hist, Vol 40, 96; auth, The New-Deal and Am Democracy--The Political-Process of the Agricultural Policy, J Am Hist, Vol 81, 94; auth, The Fox Wars--The Mesquakie Challenge to New France, Am Hist Rev, Vol 100, 95. **CONTACT ADDRESS** Dept of Hist, Univ of Texas, El Paso, 500 W University Ave, El Paso, TX 79968-0001. **EMAIL** ykawashi@miners.utep.edu

KAY, GERSIL N.
PERSONAL Born Philadelphia, PA, m, 1980 **DISCIPLINE** PHYSICS; BUSINESS ADMINISTRATION **EDUCATION** Univ Pa; Wharton Sch. **CAREER** Adj Prof, Drexel Univ; Pres, Conservation Lighting Int'l; Founder/Chmn, Building Conservation Int'l; adj prf, South Bank Univ, London; co-chair, Charter Sch for Craftsmen in Phila. **HONORS AND AWARDS** Victorian Society Am; Pa Hist and Mus Comn; BOMA; Asn of Gen Contractors Am; 1st Pres of the United States Hist Preserv Awd; 2001 Int Illumination Design Awd. **MEMBERSHIPS** AIA/HRC; IESNA; AIC; SAH; SIA; AASLH; AAM; VSA; ICADS; SPAB. **RESEARCH** Conservation lighting; older building construction techniques. **SELECTED PUBLICATIONS** Auth, Mechanical/Electrical Systems for Historic Buildings, 92; auth, "Mechanical/Electrical Segment for the ICOMOS," in Guidelines on Education, 93; auth, Fiber Opitcs in Architectural Lighting, 98. **CONTACT ADDRESS** 1901 Walnut St., Ste. 902, Philadelphia, PA 19103.

KAY, HERMA HILL
PERSONAL Born 08/18/1934, Orangeburg, SC, m, 1975, 1 child **DISCIPLINE** LAW **EDUCATION** Southern Methodist Univ, BA, 56; Univ Chicago, JD, 59. **CAREER** Law clerk, Calif, Supreme Court Justice Traynor, 59-60; from asst prof to assoc prof, 60-63, prof law, Univ Calif, Berkeley, 63-, fel, Ctr Advan Studies Behav, Sci, 63-64; dir family law proj, Children's Bureau, 64-67; co-reporter, Uniform Marriage & Divorce Act, Nat Conf Comnrs on Uniform State Laws, 68-70; dean, Univ of Cal, Berkeley School of Law, 92-00. **HONORS AND AWARDS** Margaret Brent Women Lawyers of Distinction Awd, 92. **MEMBERSHIPS** Am Law Inst, Council; Am Philo Soc, elected 00. **RESEARCH** Family law; sex-based discrimination; conflict of laws. **SELECTED PUBLICATIONS** Auth, From the Second the Joint Venture: An Overview of Women's Rights and Family Law During the Twentieth Century, 88 California Law Rev 2017, 00; coauth, Text, Cases and Materials on Sex Based Discrimination, 4th ed, 94 and 99 suppl, Westgroup Pub; A Defense of Currie's Governmental Interest Analysis, 215 Receuil Des Cours 12, Martinus Nijhoff Publishers 1989-III. **CONTACT ADDRESS** Sch of Law, Univ of California, Berkeley, 220 Boalt Hall, Berkeley, CA 94720-7201. **EMAIL** kayh@law.berkeley.edu

KAY, JAMES F.
PERSONAL Born 05/18/1948, Kansas City, MO **DISCIPLINE** HOMILETICS; SYSTEMATIC THEOLOGY **EDUCATION** Pasadena Col, BA 69; Harvard Univ M Div 72; Union Theol Sem, M Phil 84, PhD 91. **CAREER** Northern Lakes Presby Parish MN, 74-78; Bemidji State Univ MN, campus pastor 77-79; Presby Hlth Edu Wel Assoc NY, consultant 80-82; Princeton Theological Sem, inst homiletics, asst prof, assoc prof, 88-97, Joe R Engle assoc prof, 97-. **HONORS AND AWARDS** Phi Delta Lambda; BA magna cum laude; Warrack Lectr. **MEMBERSHIPS** AH; AAR; DTS; Karl Barth Soc of N Amer. **RESEARCH** History of Homiletics; Greco-Roman rhetoric; Pauline theology. **SELECTED PUBLICATIONS** Auth, Women Gender and Christian Community, co-ed, Louisville, Westminster John Knox Press, 97; Seasons of Grace: reflections from the Christian Year, Grand Rapids, William B. Eerdmans Pub Co, 94; Christus Praesens: A Reconsideration of Rudolf Bultmann's Christology, Grand Rapids, William B. Eerdmans Pub Co, 94; Preaching at the Turn of the Ages, St Mary's Col Bull, 98; In Whose Name: Feminism and Trinitarian Baptismal Formula, Theology Today, 93. **CONTACT ADDRESS** Dept of Practical Theology, Princeton Theol Sem, PO Box 821, Princeton, NJ 08542. **EMAIL** james.kay@ptsem.edu

KAY, JUDITH WEBB
PERSONAL Born 12/19/1951, m, 1972, 1 child **DISCIPLINE** ETHICS **EDUCATION** Oberlin Col, BA, 73; Pac School of Relig, MA, 78; Grad Theol Union, PhD, 88. **CAREER** Prof of Prof & Med Ethics, Am Col Traditional Chinese Med, 81-88; asst prof Dept Relig, Wake Forest Univ, 88-92; asst prof Dept Relig, 92-93; 00-; actg dean Stud, 93-94, DEAN OF STUDENTS, DIV STUDENT AFFAIRS, UNIV PUGET SOUND, 94-99; Woodrow Wilson Newcombe fel finalist, 87; Woodrow Wilson Womens Stud Prog finalist, 87; Roothbert Fund grad fel excellence in scholar, 75-78. **MEMBERSHIPS** Am Acad Relig; Soc Christian Ethics. **RESEARCH** Moral psychology; Virtue ethics from a liberation perspective; death penalty. **SELECTED PUBLICATIONS** Auth, Politics without Human Nature? Reconstructing a Common Humanity, Hypatia: A Jour of Feminist Philos, 94; Natural Law, Dictionary of Feminist Theol, Westminster John Knox Press, 96; Getting Egypt Out of the People: Aquinas Contributions to Liberation, Aquinas and Empowerment: Classical Ethics for Ordinary Lives, Georgetown Univ Press, 96; rev Gloria Albrecht: The Character of our Communities: Toward an Ethic of Liberation for the Church, Relig Stud Rev, 97; rev Birnab Care: Living With Ones Past: Personal Fates and Moral Pain, Jour of Relig, 98; auth, "In the Shadow of the Execution Chamber: Affirming Wholeness in a Broken Place," in Practice What You Preach: Virtues, Ethics and Power in the Lives of Parish Ministers and their Congregations, ed, James Keenan and Joseph Kotva, Franklin, WI: Sheed and Ward, 99; auth, "Why Procedures Are Important," The Annual: Society of Christian Ethics 19, (99): 383-389. **CONTACT ADDRESS** Univ of Puget Sound, 1500 N Warner, Tacoma, WA 98416. **EMAIL** jkay@ups.edu

KAYE, LAWRENCE J.
PERSONAL Born 02/25/1960, Milwaukee, WI **DISCIPLINE** PHILOSOPHY **EDUCATION** MIT, PhD, 90. **CAREER** Univ Massachusetts, Lectr, 90-. **MEMBERSHIPS** APA **RESEARCH** Philosophy of Mind; Cognitive Science; Philos of Language; Epistemology; Metaphysics. **SELECTED PUBLICATIONS** Auth, Semantic Compositionality: Still The Only Game in Town, Analysis, 93; Are Most of Our Concepts Innate?, Synthese, 95; The Computational Account of Belief, Erkenntnis, 94; The Languages of Thought, Philo of Science, 95; A Scientific Psychologistic Foundation for Theories of Meaning, Minds and Machines, 95; rev, Another Linguistic Turn?, Language Thought and Consciousness: An Essay in Philo Psychol by Peter Carruthers, Psyche, 98. **CONTACT ADDRESS** Philosophy Dept, Univ of Massachusetts, Boston, 100 Morrissey Blvd, Boston, MA 02125-3393. **EMAIL** larry.kaye@umb.edu

KAYLOR, ROBERT DAVID
PERSONAL Born 10/01/1933, New Market, AL, m, 1956, 5 children **DISCIPLINE** RELIGION **EDUCATION** Rhodes Col, AB; Louisville Presbyterian Sem, BD; Duke Univ, PhD. **CAREER** Fac, 64-; James Sprunt Prof Relig, Emer, present. **HONORS AND AWARDS** Thomas Jefferson Awd, Davidson Col, 87. **MEMBERSHIPS** Omicron Delta Kappa, Soc Bibl Lit, Am Acad Relig and Presbytery of Charlotte. **RESEARCH** New Testament studies; Asian religions. **SELECTED PUBLICATIONS** Auth, Paul's Covenant Community: Jew and Gentile in Romans, Westminster John Knox, 88; Jesus the Prophet: His Vision of the Kingdom on Earth, Westminster John Knox, 94. **CONTACT ADDRESS** Dept of Relig, Davidson Col, 102 N Main St, PO Box 1719, Davidson, NC 28036. **EMAIL** dakaylor@davidson.edu

KAZEMZADEH, MASOUD
DISCIPLINE POLITICAL SCIENCE **EDUCATION** Univ Southern California, PhD, 95 **CAREER** Asst Prof, Utah Valley State Coll, 99- . **CONTACT ADDRESS** Dept of Poli Sci & Hist, Utah Valley State Coll, 800 West Univ Pkwy, Orem, UT 84058-5999. **EMAIL** kazemzma@uvsc.edu

KEALY, SEAN P.
PERSONAL Born 03/29/1937, Thurles, Ireland, s **DISCIPLINE** THEOLOGY **EDUCATION** Univ Col Dublin, BA; MA, 62; Gregorian Univ Rome, BD, STL, 62-65; Biblical Inst Rome, BSS, LSS, 65-67. **CAREER** Dean of Theol, St. Thomas Aquinas Seminary, Nairobi; Sen Lecturer, Kenyatta Univ, Nairobi; Rector, Holy Ghost Missionary Col, Dublin; Prof and President, Blackrock Col, Dublin; Prof, Duquesne Univ. **MEMBERSHIPS** Irish Biblical Asn, Catholic Biblical Asn, Catholic Theol Asn. **RESEARCH** History of escegeses, Ireland, Catholic Studies. **SELECTED PUBLICATIONS** Auth, Matthew's Gospel and the History of Biblical Interpretation, Mellen Bibli-

cal Press, 97; auth, Spirituality for Today, Mercier Press, 94; auth, Jesus and Politics, Collegeville, 90; auth, Science and the Bible, Columbia Press, Dublin, 87; auth, The Apocalypse of John, Liturgical Press, Collegeville, 87; auth, The Vision of the Ten Commandments, Carmelite Press, Dublin, 89; auth, Towards a Biblical Spirituality, Carmelite Press, Dublin, 85; auth, Soundings in Irish Spirituality, Carmelite Press, Dublin, 83; auth, A History of Mark's Gospel, Paulist Press, New York, 82; auth, That You May Believe, St. Paul's, London, 78. **CONTACT ADDRESS** Dept Theol, Duquesne Univ, 600 Forbes Ave, Pittsburgh, PA 15282-0001. **EMAIL** kealy@duq3.cc.duq.edu

KEARNEY, RICHARD
PERSONAL Born 12/08/1954, Cork, Ireland, m, 1980, 2 children **DISCIPLINE** PHILOSOPHY **EDUCATION** Univ Col Dublin, BA, 75; McGill Univ, MA, 77; Univ Paris, PhD, 80. **CAREER** Prof, UCD, 81-. **HONORS AND AWARDS** NUI Scholarship, 77-80; Awd, Am Libr Assoc, 88. **MEMBERSHIPS** RIA; Irish Philos Assoc; SPEP; Royal Irish Acad. **RESEARCH** Narrative, Imagination, Hermeuetics, Phenomenology. **SELECTED PUBLICATIONS** Auth, Poetics of Imagining, 89; auth, Angel of Patrick's Hill, 89; auth, Visions of Europe, 92; ed, Les Metamorphoses de la Raison Hermeneutique, 92; ed, Continental Philosophy in the Twentieth Century, 93; auth, Poetics of Modernity, 96; auth, Sam's Fall, 97; ed, Paul Richoeur Festschrift: Philosophy and Social Criticism, 97; auth, States of Mind, 97. **CONTACT ADDRESS** Dept Philos, Boston Col, Chestnut Hill, 140 Commonwealth Ave, Chestnut Hill, MA 02467-3800. **EMAIL** kearneyr@bc.edu

KEARNS, JOHN THOMAS
PERSONAL Born 10/28/1936, Elgin, IL, m, 1963, 4 children **DISCIPLINE** PHILOSOPHY **EDUCATION** Univ Notre Dame, AB, 58; Yale Univ, MA, 60, PhD(philos), 62. **CAREER** Asst prof, 64-69, assoc prof, 69-79, prof Philos, State Univ NY Buffalo, 78-; chmn, 94-. **MEMBERSHIPS** Am Philos Assn; Assoc Symbolic Logic, Linguistics Soc of America. **RESEARCH** Logic; philosophy of language; cognitive science. **SELECTED PUBLICATIONS** Contribr, The logical concept of existence, Notre Dame J Formal Logic, 60; Combinatory logic with discriminators, J Symbolic Logic, 69; contribr, Substance and time, J Philos, 70; Vagueness and failing sentences, Logique et Analyse, 74; auth, Sentences and propositions, In: The Logical Enterprise, Yale Univ, 75; contribr, Denoting and referring, Philos & Phenomenological Res, 76; The logic calculation, Z Math Logik und Grundlagen Math, 77; Reconceiving Experience, a Solution to a Problem Inherited from Descartes, SUNY, 96; contribur, Thinking Machines, Some Fundamental Confusions, Minds and Machines, 97; contribur, Propositional Logic of Supposition and Assertion, Notre Dame J Formal Logic, 97; contribur, Representing, In: Truth in Perspective, Ashgate, 98; auth, "Using Language, The Structures of Speech Arts," SUNY, 84; contribur, "An Illocutionary Logical Explanation of the Surprise Execution," History and Philosophy of Logic, 00. **CONTACT ADDRESS** Dept of Philosophy, SUNY, Buffalo, 135 Park Hall, SUNY Buffalo, Buffalo, NY 14260-4150. **EMAIL** kearns@acsu.buffalo.edu

KEATING, GREGORY C.
PERSONAL Born 10/15/1956, New York, NY, m, 1983, 2 children **DISCIPLINE** LAW **EDUCATION** Amherst Col, BA 79; Harvard Univ JD, 85; Princeton Univ, MA 81, PhD 93. **CAREER** USC Law School, prof 96-, assoc prof 93-96, asst prof 91-93; Palmer and Dodge, MA 87-90; Foley, Hoag and Eliot, assoc 85-87. **HONORS AND AWARDS** Phi Beta Kappa **MEMBERSHIPS** AALS **RESEARCH** Torts Prod Liability; Jurisprudence; Legal Profession. **SELECTED PUBLICATIONS** Auth, Reasonableness and Rationality in Negligence Theory, 96; The Idea of Fairness in Enterprise Liability, 97; Keeton, Sargentich & Keatings, Tort and Accident Law, 98. **CONTACT ADDRESS** School of Law, Univ of So California, University Park, Los Angeles, CA 90089-0071. **EMAIL** gkeating@law.usc.edu

KEATING, JAMES
PERSONAL Born 08/01/1961, New York, NY, m, 1991 **DISCIPLINE** THEOLOGY **EDUCATION** Cath Univ Am, PhD, 98. **CAREER** Asst prof, 96- . **MEMBERSHIPS** AAR. **RESEARCH** Biblical theology; Systems theology. **CONTACT ADDRESS** Dept of Theology, Providence Col, Providence, RI 02918. **EMAIL** keatingjs@aol.com

KEAY, ROBERT
PERSONAL Born 08/16/1959, Brockton, MA **DISCIPLINE** BIBLE **EDUCATION** Bob Jones Univ, BA, 84, MA, 86, PhD, 91; Gordon-Conwell Theol Sem, ThM, 98. **CAREER** Dir of res, New England Inst of Relig Res, Lakeville, MA, 91-94; adjunct instr, 92-94, academic dean & prof of Bible, New England Bible Col, S Portland, ME, 94-. **HONORS AND AWARDS** Phi Alpha Chi. **MEMBERSHIPS** Soc of Biblical Lit; Evangelical Theol Soc; Evangelical Philos Soc. **RESEARCH** Pauline theol; eschatology; new religions. **SELECTED PUBLICATIONS** Auth, A Biblical-Theological Evaluation of Theonomic Ethics, PhD thesis, Bob Jones Univ, Greenville, SC, 91; A Proposal Concerning Paul's Use of Hosea in Romans 9: Canonical-Traditional-Contextual, ThM thesis, Gordon-Conwell Theol Sem, 98; The OT Background of the Firtsborn: A Preliminary Study for Understanding the Firstborn of All Creation in Colossians 1:15, J of Christian Apologetics 1, 98 (online journal- http://www/sesdigiweb.com/journal). **CONTACT ADDRESS** New England Bible Col, 879 Sawyer St, PO Box 2886, South Portland, ME 04116-2886. **EMAIL** nebc@maine.rr.com

KECK, LEANDER E.
PERSONAL Born 03/03/1928, Washburn, ND, m, 1956, 2 children **DISCIPLINE** RELIGION **EDUCATION** Linfield Col, BA, 49; Andover Newton Theol Sch, BD, 53; Yale Univ, PhD, 57. **CAREER** Instr Bibl hist, Wellesley Col, 57-59; from asst prof to prof New Testament, Divinity Sch, Vanderbilt Univ, 59-72; Prof New Testament, Candler Sch Theol and Chmn Div Relig, Grad Sch, Emory Univ, 72-, Am Asn Theol Schs fel, Tubengen, 64-65; researcher, Cambridge Univ, Eng, 71; Ed Monogr Ser, Soc Bibl Lit, 73-; res award, Cambridge Univ, Eng, Asn Theol Schs, 76. **HONORS AND AWARDS** STD, Bethany Col, 75. **MEMBERSHIPS** Am Acad Relig; Soc Bibl Lit. **RESEARCH** Gospels and early traditions about Jesus; New Testament Christology; ethos and ethics en early Christianity. **SELECTED PUBLICATIONS** The Premodern Bible in the Postmodern World, Interpretation-A J Bible Theol, Vol 50, 96; The Gospel According to Mark, J Theol Studies, Vol 45, 94; Rethinking So-Called New-Testament Ethics in A Rhetorical Analysis and Historical Justification of Emergent Christian Ethics from Its Greco-Roman Environment, J Bibl Lit, Vol 115, 96; From Jewish Prophet to Gentile God--The Origins and Development of New-Testament Christology, Interpretation-A J Bible Theol, Vol 47, 93; Paul as Thinker in the Resurrection of the Crucified Jesus as an Eschatological Event in the Theology of the Apostle, INTERPRETATION-A J Bible Theol, Vol 47, 93; Studies on the Epistle to the Romans, J Theol Studies, Vol 44, 93; The Rhetoric of Righteousness in Romans-III, 21-26, J Bibl Lit, Vol 112, 93. **CONTACT ADDRESS** Sch Divin, Yale Univ, New Haven, CT 06520. **EMAIL** lekeck@pantheon.yale.edu

KEE, HOWARD CLARK
PERSONAL Born 07/28/1920, Beverly, NJ, m, 1951, 3 children **DISCIPLINE** RELIGION, HISTORY **EDUCATION** Bryan Col, BA, 40; Dallas Theol Sem, ThM, 44; Yale Univ, PhD(relig), 51. **CAREER** Instr relig thought, Univ Pa, 51-53; from asst prof to prof New Testament, Drew Univ, 53-67; Rufus Jones prof hist relig, Bryn Mawr Col, 68-77; prof New Testament, 77-82, William Goodwin Aurelio Prof Biblical Studies and Dir Grad Div Relig Studies, Sch Theol, Boston Univ, 82-, Vis prof relig, Princeton Univ, 55-56; mem bd managers and chmn transl comt, Am Bible Soc, 58-; Am Asn Theol Schs fel, Marburg, Ger, 59-60; Guggenheim Found fel archaeol, Jerusalem, 66-67; ed, Soc Bibl Lit Dissertation Ser; Bd Adv, Yale Univ Inst Sacred Music, 79- **MEMBERSHIPS** Soc Relig Higher Educ; Soc Bibl Lit; Am Acad Relig; Aaup; Soc New Testament Studies. **RESEARCH** Hist and literature of early Christianity; archaeology of the Hellenistic and early Roman periods; social setting of early Christianity in the Graeco-Roman world. **SELECTED PUBLICATIONS** Auth, Jesus in History, Harcourt, 69, 2nd ed, 77; translr, W G Kummel, The New Testament: The History of the Investigations of its Problems, Abingdon, 71; auth, The Origins of Christianity: Sources and Documents, 72; Community of the New Age: Studies in Mark, Westminister, 77; translr, Introduction to the New Testament, 17th ed, Abingdon, 77; Christianity (Major World Religions ser), Argus, 79; Christian Origins in Sociological Perspective, Westminster, 80; Understanding the New Testament, 4th ed (in press). **CONTACT ADDRESS** Sch of Theol, Boston Univ, Boston, MA 02215.

KEEFE, ALICE ANN
PERSONAL m, 3 children **DISCIPLINE** RELIGIOUS STUDIES **EDUCATION** Syracuse Univ, PhD, 95. **CAREER** Asst prof; Univ Wis-SP, 64-; fac senate, 95-; Women's Stud Comt; adv, Stevens Point Pagan Alliance. **SELECTED PUBLICATIONS** Auth, Rapes of Women/Wars of Men, in Women, War and Metaphor, Lang and Soc in the Study of the Hebrew Bible, Semeia 61, 93; The Female Body, the Social Body and the Land: A Socio-Political Reading of Hosea 1-2, in The Feminist Biblical Commentary: The Prophets, Sheffield Acad Press; Religious Pluralism, Interreligious Dialogue, and the Academic Study of Religion:Christian Perspectives, for Soc for Buddhist-Christian Stud, 96; Men Are Not Our Enemies: 'Us' And 'Them' in Thich Nhat Hanh's Engaged Buddhism and Feminist Spirituality, for Conf on Rel, War and Peace, 96; Interconnectedness in Engaged Buddhism and Feminist Theology, for Soc for Buddhist-Christian Stud Int Conf, 96. **CONTACT ADDRESS** Dept of Religious Studies, Univ of Wisconsin, Stevens Point, Stevens Point, WI 54481. **EMAIL** akeefe@uwsp.edu

KEEFER, DONALD R.
PERSONAL Born 06/05/1955, Baltimore, MD, m, 1993 **DISCIPLINE** PHILOSOPHY **EDUCATION** Univ MD, Baltimore Co, BA, 78; Temple Univ, PhD, 88 **CAREER** Asspc Prof Philos, Rhode Island School of Design, 88-, Chair, Dept of Hist, Philos, Social Science, 97-2000. **HONORS AND AWARDS** NEH Summer fel, 92. **MEMBERSHIPS** Am Soc Aesthetics; Am Philos Asn; RI Philos Soc. **RESEARCH** Pragmatism; theories of culture; cognition and creativity. **SELECTED PUBLICATIONS** Auth, Review of J-J. Nattiez's Music and Discourse, J of Aesthetics and Art Criticism, spring 93; Reports on the Death of the Author, Philos and Lit, vol 19, no 1, April 95; The Rage of Innocents: On Casting the First Stone in a Sea of Cultural Pain, in States of Rage: Emotional Eruption, Violence, and Social Change, Renee Curry and Terry Allison, eds, NY Univ Press, 96; review of Michael O'Toole's The Language of Displayed Art, J of Aesthetics and Art Criticism, vol 54, no 3, summer 96; Message of the Bottle: Design Products on the Shores of Semiotics, in Zed, vol 4; Review of Shusterman, Practicing Philosophy, forthcoming in the J of Metaphilos. **CONTACT ADDRESS** 5 Burr's Lane, Providence, RI 02904. **EMAIL** dkeefer@risd.edu

KEEGAN, JOHN E.
PERSONAL Born 04/29/1943, Spokane, WA, m, 2 children **DISCIPLINE** LAW **EDUCATION** Gonzaga Univ, BA (English, Psychol), 65; Harvard Law School, JD (Law), 68. **CAREER** Partner, Davis Wright Tremaine, Seattle, 86-; previously Deputy Prosecuting Attourney, King County and Office of General Counsel, Dept of Housing and Urban Development, Washington, DC. **MEMBERSHIPS** WA State Bar Asn; Am Bar Asn; Seattle-King Co Bar Asn; Author's Guild. **RESEARCH** Fiction. **SELECTED PUBLICATIONS** Auth, Clearwater Summer, Carroll & Graf, 94; Piper, The Permanent Pr, 01. **CONTACT ADDRESS** Davis Wright Tremaine, 2600 Century Sq, Seattle, WA 98101. **EMAIL** johnkeegan@dwt.com

KEEL, VERNON
DISCIPLINE MEDIA LAW, INTERNATIONAL COMMUNICATION, AND RESEARCH METHODOLOGY **EDUCATION** Univ Minn, PhD. **CAREER** Vis res, Univ Montreal; pres, Assn Sch Journalism and Mass Commun; exec comm; Assn Commun Admin; Nat Accrediting Coun Edu in Journalism and Mass Commun; steering comm, William Randolph Hearst found; founder, dir, prof, Elliott Sch Commun, 89-96. **HONORS AND AWARDS** Vis res, Univ Montreal. **SELECTED PUBLICATIONS** Ed, Communication and Community. **CONTACT ADDRESS** Wichita State Univ, 1845 Fairmont, Wichita, KS 67260-0062. **EMAIL** keel@elliott.es.twsu.edu

KEELING, LYTLE BRYANT
PERSONAL Born 04/01/1934, Jasper, AR, m, 1970, 1 child **DISCIPLINE** ANALYTIC PHILOSOPHY, PHILOSOPHY OF RELIGION **EDUCATION** Okla Northeastern State Col, BA, 56; Southern Methodist Univ, BD, 59; Univ Chicago, MA(theol), 63, MA(philos), 64, PhD(philos theol), 71. **CAREER** From asst prof to assoc prof, 65-77, Prof Philos, Western Ill Univ, 77-99. **MEMBERSHIPS** Am Philos Asn; Am Acad Relig. **RESEARCH** Interpretation of God-language; Wittgenstein's philosophy. **SELECTED PUBLICATIONS** Auth, The pantheism of Charles Hartshorne, In: Philosophy of Religion: Contemporary Perspectives, Macmillan, 74; Feeling as a metaphysical category: Hartshorne from an analytical view, Process Studies, spring 76; coauth, Beyond Wittgensteinian Fideism? A critique of Hick's concept of faith, Int J Philos Relig, winter 77. **CONTACT ADDRESS** Dept of Philosophy, Western Illinois Univ, 1 University Cir, Macomb, IL 61455-1390. **EMAIL** Bryant_Keeling@ccmail.wiu.edu

KEEN, RALPH
PERSONAL Born 12/21/1957, Philadelphia, PA, m, 1987, 1 child **DISCIPLINE** RELIGION **EDUCATION** Columbia Univ, BA, 79; Yale Univ, MA, 80; Univ Chicago, PhD, 90. **CAREER** Asst prof, Alaska Pacific Univ, 91-93; asst prof to assoc prof, Univ of Iowa, 93-. **MEMBERSHIPS** Am Cath Hist Assoc; Am Soc of Church Hist; Medieval Acad of Am. **RESEARCH** Early-modern religious controversy. **SELECTED PUBLICATIONS** Auth, Divine and Human Authority in Reformation Thought, Nieuwkoop, 97. **CONTACT ADDRESS** School Relig, Univ Iowa, 314 Gilmore Hall, Iowa City, IA 52242-1320. **EMAIL** ralph-keen@uiowa.edu

KEENAN, J. F.
PERSONAL Born 02/15/1953, Brooklyn, NY **DISCIPLINE** RELIGION **EDUCATION** Gregorian Univ Rome, STD 88. **CAREER** Fordham Univ, asst prof 87-91; Weston Jesuit Sch Theol, asst prof, assoc prof 91 to 93-. **HONORS AND AWARDS** ATS Gnt; Inst Adv Stud Humanities Edinburgh fel; Cen Theo Inq Princeton fel. **MEMBERSHIPS** CTS; SCE **RESEARCH** Casuistry; Aquinas; Virtues; Bioethics; Puritan; Practical Divinity. **SELECTED PUBLICATIONS** Auth, Virtues for Ordinary Christians, Kansas City, Sheed Ward, 96; The Context of Casuistry, coauth, Wash DC, Georgetown Univ Press, 95; Josef Fuchs and the Question of Moral Objectivity in Roman Catholic Ethical Reasoning, Rel Stud Rev, 98; Are You Growing Up in the Virtues?, Priests and People, 98; Moral Theology Out of Western Europe, Theo Stud, 98; What's New in the Ethical and Religious Directives?, Linacre Quart, 98; Virtue Ethics, Basic Christian Ethics: An Introduction, Bernard Hoose, ed, London, Chapman, 97; Institutional Cooperation and the Ethical and Religious Directives, Linacre Quart, 97. **CONTACT ADDRESS** Dept of Theology, Weston Jesuit Sch of Theol, 3 Phillips Place, Cambridge, MA 02138. **EMAIL** jfkweston@aol.com

KEENAN, JOHN P.
PERSONAL Born 10/13/1940, Philadelphia, PA, m, 1972, 2 children **DISCIPLINE** ASIAN RELIGIONS AND THEOLOGY **EDUCATION** Charles Borromeo Sem, AB; Univ Pa, MA; Univ Wis, PhD. **CAREER** Prof; Middlebury Col, 86-. **HONORS AND AWARDS** Frederick Streng awd. **MEMBERSHIPS** AAR; Society for Buddhist Christian Studies; Intl. Assn/ For Buddhist Studies; Intl. Assn for Shin Buddhist Studies. **RESEARCH** Mahayana philosophy and Christian theology. **SELECTED PUBLICATIONS** Auth, The Gospel of Mark: A Mahayana Reading; How Master Mou Removes our Doubts: A Reader Response Study of the Mou-tzu Li-huo-lun & The Meaning of Christ: A Mahayana Theology auth, Dharmapala's Yogacara Critique of Bhavavieka's Madhyamika Explanation of Emptiness. **CONTACT ADDRESS** Dept of Religion, Middlebury Col, Middlebury, VT 05753. **EMAIL** keenan@middlebury.edu

KEENER, CRAIG S.
PERSONAL Born 07/04/1960, s **DISCIPLINE** NEW TESTAMENT **EDUCATION** Duke Univ, PhD, 91. **CAREER** Hood Theol Seminary, 92-96; Vis Prof Bibl Studies, Eastern Seminary, 96-99; Prof of New Testament Eastern Seminary, 00-. **HONORS AND AWARDS** IVP Bible Background Commentary was highest-ranked biblical work in 1995 Christian Today book awards; Gospel of Matthew (Eerdmans) was in 2000. **MEMBERSHIPS** Soc Bibl Lit; Inst Bibl Res. **RESEARCH** Greco-Roman & Jewish contexts of early Christianity. **SELECTED PUBLICATIONS** Auth, ..And Marries Another: Divorce & Remarriage in the Teaching of the New Testament, Hendrickson Publ, 91; Paul, Women & Wives: Marriage & Women's Ministry in the Letters of Paul, Hendrickson Publ, 92; The IVP Bible Background Commentary: New Testament, InterVarsity Press, 93; The Spirit in the Gospels and Acts: Rebirth and Auth, Black Man's Religion, InterVarsity Press, 96; Prophetic Empowerment, Hendrickson, 97; auth, Matthew, InterVarsity Press, 97; auth, Defending Black Faith, InterVarsity Press, 97; auth, The Gospel According to Matthew, Eerdmans, 99; auth, Revelation, MV Application Commentary, Zondermann, 99. **CONTACT ADDRESS** Eastern Baptist Theol Sem, 6 Lancaster Ave, Wynnewood, PA 19096-3494. **EMAIL** ckeener@ebts.edu

KEENEY, DONALD E.
PERSONAL m **DISCIPLINE** THEOLOGY **EDUCATION** Wheaton Coll, BA, 76, MA, 79; S Baptist Theo Sem, MDiv, 82, PhD, 87; Columbia Univ, MSLS, 92. **CAREER** Assoc Prof, librarian, 97-, Central Baptist Sem. **MEMBERSHIPS** SBL, NABPR, ATLA. **RESEARCH** Theology and bibliography, theology & librarianship. **CONTACT ADDRESS** Central Baptist Theol Sem, 741 N 31st St, Kansas City, KS 66102-3964.

KEETON, MORRIS TEUTON
PERSONAL Born 02/01/1917, Clarksville, TX, w, 3 children **DISCIPLINE** PHILOSOPHY **EDUCATION** Southern Methodist Univ, AB, 35, AM, 36; Harvard Univ, AM, 37, PhD, 38. **CAREER** Dean, 63-67, acad vpres, 67-72, provost & vpres, 72-77; CEO, Coun Advan Experiential Learning, 77-89, Head mission in Ger, Am Friends Serv Comt, 53-55; exam, NCent Asn Cols & Sec Schs, 61-77, mem exec bd, Comn Higher Educ, 73-77; chmn, Carus lectr comt, Am Philos Asn, 64-69; dir, Institute for Res on Adults in Higher Educ, Univ of Md Univ Col, 90-97; sr scholar, Institute for Res on Adults in Higher Educ, Univ of Md Univ Col, 97-. **MEMBERSHIPS** Western Div Am Philos Asn (secy-treas, 59-61); Asn Higher Educ (pres, 72-73); fel Soc Relig Higher Educ; Southwestern Philos Soc (secy-treas, 40-41). **RESEARCH** Epistemology; ethical theory; adult learning. **SELECTED PUBLICATIONS** Auth, The Philosophy of Edmund Montgomery, Southern Methodist Univ, 50; Values Men Live by, Abingdon, 60; coauth, Range of Ethics, Am Bk Co, 66; Struggle and Promise .., McGraw, 69; auth, Shared Authority on Campus, Am Asn Higher Educ, 70; coauth, Ethics for Today, Van Nostrand, 5th ed, 73; Experiential Learning, Jossey-Bass, 77; coauth, Employability in a High Performance Economy, 93; auth, Improving Employee Dev, 97; auth, Efficiency in Adult Higher Education: A Guide for Fostering Learning, (in press). **CONTACT ADDRESS** 10989 Swansfield Rd, Columbia, MD 21044. **EMAIL** mkeeton@polaris.umuc.edu

KEETON, ROBERT ERNEST
PERSONAL Born 12/16/1919, Clarksville, TX, m, 1941, 2 children **DISCIPLINE** LAW **EDUCATION** Univ Tex, BBA, 40, LLB, 41; Harvard Univ, SJD, 56. **CAREER** Assoc prof law, Southern, Methodist Univ, 51-53; Thayer teaching fel, 53-54, from asst prof to prof, 54-73, Langdell Prof Law, Harvard Univ, 73-, Assoc Dean Law Sch, 75-, Mem law fac, Salzburg Sem Am Studies, 61; trustee, Col Retirement Equities Fund, 65-69; Mass Comnr Uniform State Laws, 71-; Mem Fac, Nat Inst Trial Advocacy, 72-, Dir, 73-76, Ed Consult, 76-; Trustee, Flaschner Judicial Inst, 78- **HONORS AND AWARDS** Clarence Arthur Kulp Mem Awd, Am Risk and Insurance Asn, 66. **MEMBERSHIPS** Am Law Inst; Am Bar Asn; Am Risk and Insurance Asn; Am Acad Arts and Sci. **RESEARCH** Torts; insurance; trial practice. **SELECTED PUBLICATIONS** Restating Strict Liability and Nuisance, Vanderbilt Law Rev, Vol 48, 95. **CONTACT ADDRESS** Law Sch, Harvard Univ, Cambridge, MA 02138.

KEGLEY, CHARLES W.
PERSONAL Born 03/05/1944, Evanston, IL, d, 1 child **DISCIPLINE** INTERNATIONAL RELATIONS **EDUCATION** Syracuse Univ, Maxwell School, PhD 71; Am Univ, Sch Intl Ser, BA 66. **CAREER** Univ of SC, prof 70-99, Pearce Prof Intl Rel 84-, Ch 81-85; Rutgers Univ, vis prof 89; Univ TX, vis assoc prof 76; Georgetown univ, asst prof 71-72. **HONORS AND AWARDS** Distg Sch For Pol Analy Awd; Pres ISA; Pew Facul Fell; Dist Alumni Awd. **MEMBERSHIPS** APSA; ISA. **RESEARCH** International rel theory; comparaive foreign policy; peace res; intl ethics; quantitative methodology. **SELECTED PUBLICATIONS** World Politics: Trend and Transformation, 7th ed, NY, St Martins Press, co auth Eugene R Wittkopf, 99; How Nations Make Peace, NY, Macmillan, co auth, Gregory A Raymond, 99; Controversies in International Relations Theory: Realism and the Neoliberal Challenge, NY, St Martins Press, 95; Controlling Economic Competition In the Pacific Rim, USA Today, 98; Placing Global Ecopolitics in Peace Studies, Peace Review, 97; The U S Use of Military Intervention to Promote Democracy : Evaluating the Recoed, Intl Interactions, co auth Margaret G Hermann, 98. **CONTACT ADDRESS** Dept of Govt and International Studies, Univ of So Carolina, Columbia, 350 Gambrell Hall, Columbia, SC 29208. **EMAIL** kegs@sc.edu

KEGLEY, JACQUELYN A.
PERSONAL Born 07/18/1938, Conncaut, OH, w, 1962, 4 children **DISCIPLINE** PHILOSOPHY **EDUCATION** Allegheny Col, BA, 60; Rice Univ, MA, 64; Columbia Univ, PhD, 71. **CAREER** Vis prof, Univ of the Philippines, 66-68; adj lectr to prof, Calif State Univ Bakersfield, 69-. **HONORS AND AWARDS** CSU Outstanding Prof, 88-89; Bakerfield Leadership Awd, CSU, 97-98; Wang Teaching Excellence Awd, 00. **MEMBERSHIPS** Am Philos Assoc; Philos of Sci Assoc. **RESEARCH** Bioethics, especially genetics, Philosophy of Technology. **SELECTED PUBLICATIONS** Auth, "Using Genetic Information: A Radical Problematic for an Individualistic Framework", Med and Law, 15.4, Dec 96; auth, Genuine Individuals and Genuine Communities. A Roycean Public Philosophy, Vanderbilt Univ Pr (Nashville, TN), 97; auth, "Genetic Information and Genetic Essentialism: Will We Betray Science, The Individual and the Community?", in Genetics and Human Values, ed J. Kegley, (NY: Paragon, 88); auth, "Walking in Another's Shoes: Technology and Ethics in Situ", in Teaching Excellence, ed Michael Flachmann, (Long Beach: Calif State Univ Inst, 98); auth, "Community, Autonomy, and Managed Care" in Pragmatic Bioethics, ed G. McGee, (Nashville, TN: Vanderbilt Univ Pr, 98); ed, Genetic Knowledge, Human Values, and Responsibilities, Paragon, (New York, 99); auth, "Confused Legal and Medical Policy: The Misconceptions of Genetic Screening" Jof Med and Law, Apr 00; auth, "The Contextual Human Person: Reflections on the Philosophy of Marjorie Grene" in The Philosophy of Marjorie Grene, ed Lewis E. Hahn, (forthcoming). **CONTACT ADDRESS** Dept Relig and Philos, California State Univ, Bakersfield, 9001 Stockdale Hwy, Bakersfield, CA 93311-1022. **EMAIL** jkegley@csubak.edu

KEIFERT, PATRICK
DISCIPLINE SYSTEMATIC THEOLOGY **EDUCATION** Valparaiso Univ, BA, 73; Christ Sem, MDiv, 77; Divinity Sch, Univ Chicago, PhD, 82; additional stud, Univ Heidelberg; Univ Tubingen, Ger. **CAREER** Tchg asst, Christ Sem-Seminex, 76-77; instr, 80; adj prof, Sch of Law, Hamline Univ, 84; assoc prof, 86-; dir, Lutheran Leadership Inst. **HONORS AND AWARDS** Travel grant, Fulbright-Hays lang grant, Deutscher Akademischer Austauschdienst; post dr fel, Franklin Clark Frye; asst pastor, pilgrim evangel lutheran church, chicago, 78-80; interim pastor, lord of life lutheran church, 82; trinity and hope lutheran churches, 83; galilee lutheran church, 85. **SELECTED PUBLICATIONS** Auth, Welcoming the Stranger: A Public Theology of Worship and Evangelism, 92; Worship and Evangelism: A Pastoral Handbook, 90; People Together, 94. **CONTACT ADDRESS** Luther Sem, 2481 Como Ave, Saint Paul, MN 55108. **EMAIL** pkeifert@luthersem.edu

KEIM, ALBERT N.
DISCIPLINE THEOLOGY **EDUCATION** Eastern Mennonite Univ, BA; Univ VA, MA; OH State Univ, PhDs. **CAREER** Theol Dept, Eastern Mennonite Univ **SELECTED PUBLICATIONS** Articles: Conrad Grebel Rev. **CONTACT ADDRESS** Eastern Mennonite Univ, 1200 Park Road, Harrisonburg, VA 22802-2462.

KEIM-CAMPBELL, JOSEPH
PERSONAL Born 12/08/1958, m, 1991, 1 child **DISCIPLINE** PHILOSOPHY **EDUCATION** Rutgers Univ, BA, 83; Univ Ariz, PhD, 92. **CAREER** Asst prof, Kent State Univ, 91-94; vis asst prof, Boise State Univ, 94-97; ASST PROF, WASH STATE UNIV, 97-. **MEMBERSHIPS** Am Philos Assoc; Pacific Hume Soc. **RESEARCH** Free Will; Hume; Scepticism. **SELECTED PUBLICATIONS** Auth, Hume's Refutation of the Cosmological Argument, International Journal for Philosophy of Religion, 96; auth, A Compatibilist Theory of Alternative Possibilities, Philosophical Studies, 97; auth, Hugh Blair, Encyclopedia of Aesthetics, Oxford Univ Press, 98; auth, Descartes on Spontaneity, Indifference, and Alternative, New Essays on the Rationalists, Oxford Univ Press, 99; ed & intr, Paradoxes of Time Travel: A Philosophical Reader, forthcoming; co-ed, co-auth intro, Contemporary Philosophical Inquiries: Truth and Meaning. **CONTACT ADDRESS** PO Box 645130, Pullman, WA 99164-5130. **EMAIL** josephc@wsu.edu

KEITER, ROBERT B.
PERSONAL Born 07/05/1946, Bethesda, MD, m, 1976, 2 children **DISCIPLINE** LAW; HISTORY **EDUCATION** Northwestern Univ, JD 72; Washington Univ, BA 68. **CAREER** Univ Utah Col Law, Wallace Stegner prof, dir, 93-; Wallace Stegner Cen Land Resource Environ, prof, James I. Farr prof, 93-98, Univ Wyoming College of Law, assoc prof, interim dean, prof, Winston S. Howard dist prof, 78-93; vis prof, Boston Col, 85; Southwestern Univ, assoc prof, 76-78; Idaho Legal Aid, managing att, 75-76; Appalachian Res Def Fund, Reginald Heber Smith Fel, 72-74. **HONORS AND AWARDS** Omicron delta Kappa; Phi Kappa Phi; Sr Fulbright Sch **MEMBERSHIPS** ABA; State Bars of Wyoming, Idaho, West Virginia; RMMLF Trustee; NPCA trustee. **RESEARCH** Nat Resources Law and Policy; Constitutional Law. **SELECTED PUBLICATIONS** Auth, Reclaiming the Native Home of Hope: Community Ecology and the West, ed, Univ Utah Press, 98; Visions of the Grand Staircase-Escalante: Examining Utah's Newest National Monument, co-ed, Wallace Stegner Cen Utah Museum Natural Hist, 98; The Greater Yellowstone Ecosystem: Redefining America's Wilderness Heritage, coed, Yale Univ Press, 91; Ecosystems and the Law: Toward an Integrated Approach, Ecolo Apps, Preserving Nature in the National Parks: Law Policy and Science in a Dynamic Environment, rev, Denver U L, 97; Ecological Policy and the Courts: Of Rights, Processes, and the Judicial Role, Human Ecolo Rev, 97; Greater Yellowstone's Bison: The Unraveling of an Early American Wildlife Conservation Achievement, Jour of Wildlife Mgmt, 97; Law and Large Carnivore Conservation in the Rocky Mountains of the Us and Canada, coauth, Conservation Biology, 96. **CONTACT ADDRESS** College of Law, Univ of Utah, 332 S. 1400 E. Front, Salt Lake City, UT 84112. **EMAIL** keiterb@law.utah.edu

KEITH, HEATHER
DISCIPLINE PHILOSOPHY **EDUCATION** Southern Ill Univ, PhD. **CAREER** Adj prof, E Tenn State Univ. **SELECTED PUBLICATIONS** Auth, An Interview with Martha Nussbaum, Kinesis, 97. **CONTACT ADDRESS** Philosophy Dept, East Tennessee State Univ, Box 70717, Johnson City, TN 37614- 0717. **EMAIL** keith@etsu.edu

KEKES, JOHN
PERSONAL Born 11/22/1936, Budapest, Hungary, m, 1967 **DISCIPLINE** PHILOSOPHY **EDUCATION** Queen's Univ, Ont, Can, BA, 61, MA, 62; Australian Nat Univ, PhD(philos), 67. **CAREER** Asst prof to assoc prof Calif State Univ, Northridge, 65-71; prof, Univ Sask, Regina, Can, 71-74; prof philos & chm dept, State Univ NY Albany, 74-, Rev ed, Metaphilos, 77-80; consult ed, Am Philos Quart, 78-; consult ed, Hist Philos Quart, 84-87; gen ed, Studies in Moral Philos, 87-91; consult ed to ed, Public Affairs Quart, 87-, ed Public Affairs Quarz, 99-. **HONORS AND AWARDS** W. Wilson Fel, 61; Can Coun Fel, 61; Res Scholar, Australian Nat Univ, 62-65; NEH Summer Fel, 71; Can Coun Grant, 73; Rockefeller Found, Humanities Fel, 80-81; Rockefeller Found Bellagio Study Str, 82, 89; Earhart Found Fel, 83, 88, 89, 98; Sen Res Fel, Ctr for Philos Sci Univ, Pittsburgh, 84-85; Visiting Prof, United States Mil Acad West Point, 85-86; Estonian Acad of Sci, 89; Nat Univ of Singapore, 89; Hungarian Acad of Sci, 98. **MEMBERSHIPS** Am Philos Asn; Royal Inst of Philos. **RESEARCH** Moral and political philos; public policy. **SELECTED PUBLICATIONS** Auth, A Justification of Rationality, State Univ NY Albany, 76; The Nature of Philosophy, Oxford, 80; The Examined Life, Assoc Univ Presses, 88; Moral Tradition and Individuality, Princeton Univ Press, 89; Facing Evil, Princeton Univ Press, 93; The Morality of Pluralism, Princeton Univ Press, 93; Moral Wisdom and Good Lives, Cornell Univ Press, 95; Against Liberalism, Cornell Univ Press, 97; Against Liberalism, Cornell Univ Press, 97; A Case for Conservatism, Cornell Univ Press, 98; auth, Pluralism in Philosophy: Changing the Subject, Cornell Univ Press, 00. **CONTACT ADDRESS** Dept of Philos, SUNY, Albany, 1400 Washington Ave, Albany, NY 12222-1000. **EMAIL** johnkekes@aol.com

KELBLEY, CHARLES A.
DISCIPLINE PHILOSOPHY **EDUCATION** Sorbonne, PhD; Fordham Univ, JD. **CAREER** Assoc prof, Fordham Univ. **RESEARCH** Philos issues in the theory of law and justice. **SELECTED PUBLICATIONS** Auth, Hart's Legacy, Newsletter on Philosophy and Law, APA Newsletters, 96; Rawls: From Moral to Political Theory, Intl Philos Quart, 96. **CONTACT ADDRESS** Dept of Philos, Fordham Univ, 113 W 60th St, New York, NY 10023. **EMAIL** ckelb@aol.com

KELLENBERGER, BERTRAM JAMES
PERSONAL Born 05/04/1938, San Francisco, CA, m, 1981, 2 children **DISCIPLINE** PHILOSOPHY **EDUCATION** San Jose Univ, BA, 60; Univ Calif Berkeley, MA, 63; Univ Ore, PhD, 67. **CAREER** Lectr, Cameroon Coll of Arts and Sci, 62-64; asst prof, Calif State Univ Northridge, 67-71; vis prof, Albion Coll, 71-72; assoc prof, Calif State Univ Northridge, 71-75; adj prof, Claremont Grad School, 91; prof Calif State Univ

Northridge, 75-. **MEMBERSHIPS** Am Philos Asn; Soc of Christian Philos. **RESEARCH** Philosophy of Religion; Ethics. **SELECTED PUBLICATIONS** Auth, Religious Discovery: Faith and Knowledge, 72; the Cognitivity of religion: Three Perspectives, 85; God-Relationships With and Without God, 89; Relationship Morality, 95; Kierkegaard and Nietzsche: Faith and Eternal Acceptance, 97; ed, Inter-Religious Models and Criteria, 93. **CONTACT ADDRESS** Dept of Philosophy, California State Univ, Northridge, Northridge, CA 91330-8253. **EMAIL** james.kellenberger@csun.edu

KELLER, CHESTER
PERSONAL Born 09/26/1925, Lenbanon, PA, m, 1952, 3 children **DISCIPLINE** PHILOSOPHY **EDUCATION** Bridgewater Col, AB, 50; Univ S Calif, MA, 53; PhD, 55. **CAREER** Ashand Col, 55-56; Denison Univ, 56-60; Cental Wash Univ, 60-. **HONORS AND AWARDS** Phi Kappa Phi; Central Wash Univ Distinguished Prof, 77-. **MEMBERSHIPS** Am Phil Assoc; Philos of Educ Soc. **RESEARCH** Ecology - Philosophy of Utopian Studies, Mysticism, Philosophy of Education. **CONTACT ADDRESS** Dept Philos, Central Washington Univ, 400 E 8th Ave, Ellensburg, WA 98926-7502.

KELLER, DAVID R.
PERSONAL Born 12/17/1962, Salt Lake City, UT, m **DISCIPLINE** PHILOSOPHY **EDUCATION** Franklin & Marshall Col, BA, 87; Boston Col, MA, 90; Univ of Georgia, Ph.D, 95. **CAREER** Instr philos, Univ Georgia, 93-94; instr philos, Univ Hawaii, 95; asst prof philos, Dept Hum and Philos, 96-, Dir, Center for the Study of Ethics, 99- , asst prof philos, Dept of Integrated Stud, 98- , Utah Valley State Col. **HONORS AND AWARDS** Merit Awd for Religion and Views of Nature, 98; Fac Senate Teacher of the Year, 98-99. **MEMBERSHIPS** Utah Rivers Coun. **RESEARCH** Ethics; environmental philosophy; history of the Western intellectual tradition; literature; aesthetics; philosophy of science; existentialism. **SELECTED PUBLICATIONS** Auth, "Deleuze's Ecological Philosophy of Self," Encyclia, 97; auth, "Review of David Rothenberg's Wild Ideas," Environmental Ethics, 97; auth, "Gleaning Lessons from Deep Ecology," Ethics and the Environment, 97; auth, "Ethics and Values: Basic Readings in Theory and Practice, Simon & Schuster Custom Publishing, 99; auth, " Nietzsche in Yeats," Interdisciplinary Humanities, (forthcoming); auth, The Philosophy of Ecology: From Science to Synthesis, Univ of George Pr, 00. **CONTACT ADDRESS** Dept of Humanities and Philos, Utah Valley State Col, 800 W Univ Parkway, Orem, UT 84058-5999. **EMAIL** kellerda@uvsc.edu

KELLER, JAMES ALBERT
PERSONAL Born 10/20/1939, Pittsburgh, PA, m, 1983, 3 children **DISCIPLINE** PHILOSOPHY **EDUCATION** Mass Inst Technol, BS, 61; Pittsburgh Theol Sem, MDiv, 64; Yale Univ, MPhil, 67, PhD(relig studies), 69. **CAREER** Asst prof philos, MacMurray Col, 67-72; asst prof, 72-74, Assoc Prof Philos, Wofford Col, 74-87, Chmn Dept, 72-; Prof of Philos, Wofford College, 87-. **MEMBERSHIPS** Am Philos Asn; Soc Christian Philos; Ctr Process Studies. **RESEARCH** Philosophy of religion; metaphysics; thought of Alfred North Whitehead. **SELECTED PUBLICATIONS** The Hiddenness of God and the Problem of Evil, Int J Philos Relig, Vol 37, 95; The Power of God and Miracles In-Process Theism, J Am Acad Relig, Vol 63, 95; The Philosophy Of Hartshorne, C, J Relig, Vol 73, 93. **CONTACT ADDRESS** Dept of Philos, Wofford Col, Spartanburg, SC 29303. **EMAIL** kellerja@wofford.edu

KELLER, PIERRE
DISCIPLINE NINETEENTH-CENTURY PHILOSOPHY **EDUCATION** Columbia Univ, PhD. **CAREER** Assoc Prof, Univ Calif, Riverside. **RESEARCH** Kant; Phenomenology; 19th century philos. **SELECTED PUBLICATIONS** Auth, "Personal Identity and Kant's Third Person Perspective," Idealistic Stud, 94; "Heidegger's Destruction of Pragmatism in the History of Philosophy," Jour Hist of Ideas, 95; "Heidegger's Critique of the Vulgar Notion of Time," Intl Jour of Philos Stud, 96; "Hegel on the Nature of the Perceptual Object," Jahrbuch fuer Hegelforschung, 97; coauth, "Heidegger and the Source(s) of Intelligibility," Continental Philos Rev, 98. **CONTACT ADDRESS** Dept of Philos, Univ of California, Riverside, 1156 Hinderaker Hall, Riverside, CA 92521-0209. **EMAIL** pierrek@ucrac1.ucr.edu

KELLER, ROBERT L.
PERSONAL Born 08/17/1945, Denver, CO, m, 1965, 1 child **DISCIPLINE** SOCIOLOGY, CRIMINOLOGY **EDUCATION** Univ Colo, BA, 68; Colo State Univ, MS, 70; Univ Mont, PhD, 76. **CAREER** Instr, Southwest Mo State Col, 70-71; instr, Univ Wis, 71-72; prof, Univ Southern Colo, 74-. **RESEARCH** Criminological Theory, Government Crime, UFO Coverup, Animal Mutilations. **SELECTED PUBLICATIONS** Auth, "From Cons to Counselors," Int J of Offender Therapy 37.1 (93); coauth & co-ed, Prison Crisis, Harrow and Heston, 95. **CONTACT ADDRESS** Dept Sociol & Anthrop, Univ of So Colorado, 2200 Bonforte Blvd, Pueblo, CO 81001. **EMAIL** keller@uscolo.edu

KELLOGG, FREDERIC R.
PERSONAL Born 01/27/1942, Boston, MA, m, 1993 **DISCIPLINE** PHILOSOPHY OF LAW **EDUCATION** Harvard Univ, BA, 64, LLB, 68; George Wash Univ, LLM, 78, SJD, 83. **CAREER** Attorney, 68-94; vis Prof, Fulbright fel, 96, Univ Warsaw; vis Prof, Moscow State Univ. **HONORS AND AWARDS** Dewey Essay Proj Prize; Fulbright Fel. **MEMBERSHIPS** APA; SAAP; CSPS. **RESEARCH** History and theory of law, responsibility. **SELECTED PUBLICATIONS** Auth, The Formative Essays of Justice Holmes: The Making of an American Legal Philosophy, Westport CT, Greenwood Press, 84. **CONTACT ADDRESS** 2027 Que St NW, Washington, DC 20009. **EMAIL** fredkellogg@compuserve.com

KELLY, DAVID F.
PERSONAL Born 12/05/1940, Somerville, MA, s **DISCIPLINE** THEOLOGY **EDUCATION** Col of the Holy Cross, BA English, 62; Cath Univ of Louvain, Belgium, BA Theol, 66; MA Theol, 66; STB 66; Loyola Univ Chicago, M Relig Educ, 71; Univ of St. Michael's Col Toronto, PhD, 78. **CAREER** Instr, The Cleveland State Univ, Ohio, 76; Asst Prof to Assoc Prof, St. Bernard's Sem, Rochester NY, 76-77, 78-8; Vis Assoc Prof, Univ of Rochester, 81; Asst Prof, Assoc Prof, Tenured, Prof, Duquesne Univ, 81-. **HONORS AND AWARDS** Undergraduate Scholar, Holy Cross, 58-62; BA English Magna Cum Laude, 62; BA Theol Summa Cum laude, 64; MA Theol Maga Cum Laude, 66; STB Magna Cum Laude, 66; Delta Epsilon Sigma Honor Soc; Scholar, St. Michael's, 73-74; NEH Grant, Summer Inst in Nursing Ethics, 83; Pa Humanities Coun Commonwealth Speaker, 92-93; Duquesne Univ President's Awd for Excellence in Scholar, 93; Phi Kappa Phi Inductee, Duquesne Univ, 96; Presidential Scholar Grant, Duquesne Univ, 98. **MEMBERSHIPS** Am Acad of Relig, Soc of Christian Ethics, Col Theol Soc, Cath Theol Soc of Am, Hastings Center Inst of Soc, Ethics, and the Life Sci, Soc of Critical Care Med, Bishop's Theol Commission, Diocese of Pittsburgh. **RESEARCH** Medical Ethics/Nursing Ethics, Moral Theology/Religious Ethics. **SELECTED PUBLICATIONS** Auth, The Emergence of Roman Catholic Medical Ethics in North America: An Historical, Methodological, Bibliographical Study, Edwin Mellen Press (NY), 79, 82; auth, A Theological Basis for Health Care and Health Care Ethics, Special Publ of the Nat Asn of Cath Chaplains 1-3 (Nov 85); auth, Critical Care Ethics: Treatment Decisions in American Hospitals, Sheed & Ward (Kansas City, MO), 91; auth, "Ethical Arguments about Physician-Assisted Suicide, " St. Francis J Of Med (96): 18-21; auth, "Karl Rahner and Genetic Engineering: The Use of Theological Principles and Moral Analysis, " Philos and Theol (95/97): 177-200; auth, "Medical Futility and the Ethics of Forgoing Treatment," St. Francis J Of Med (97): 37-44; auth, "Organic Transplantation," in Christian Ethics, ed. Bernard Hoose (London: Cassell, 98): 304-316; auth, "The Ethics of Forgoing Treatment: The Ameican Consensus," St. Francis J Of Med (98): 54-57; auth, "Methodological and Practical Issues in the 'Ethical and Religious Directives for Catholic Health Care Services'," Louvain Studies 23 (98): 312-337; auth, "Ethics of Forgoing Treatment," RT: The J for Respiratory Care Practitoners 12-3 (Apr/May 99): 85-90. **CONTACT ADDRESS** Dept Theol, Duquesne Univ, 600 Forbes Ave., Pittsburgh, PA 15282-0001. **EMAIL** kellyd@duq.edu

KELLY, DOUGLAS
PERSONAL Born 09/23/1943, Lumberton, NC, m, 1973, 5 children **DISCIPLINE** SYSTEMATIC THEOLOGY **EDUCATION** Univ of NC, BA; Univ Lyon, Dipl; Union Theol Sem, BD; Univ Edinburgh, PhD. **CAREER** J. Richard Jordan prof. **HONORS AND AWARDS** Willie Parker Peace Awd for Carolina Scots by the NC Soc of Historians, 99; Vice-Pres Scottish Heritage , USA; The Am Arm of the Nat Trust for Scotland; Trustee of Highland Theoligical Col, Scotland; gen ed, calvin's old testament commentaries. **MEMBERSHIPS** Mem, Calvin Stud Soc; La Societe Internationale pour L'Etude de la Philosophie Medievale. **SELECTED PUBLICATIONS** Transl, of John Calvin's Sermons on II Samuel, Edinburgh, 92; auth, Emergence of Liberty in the Modern World: Five Calvinist Governments from the 16th to 18th centuries, Presbyterian and Reformed, 92; auth, Preachers with Power: Four Stalwarts of the South, Banner of Truth, 92; auth, Creation and Change: Genesis, 1:1-2:4 in the Light of Changing Scientific Paradigms, Christian Focus: Mentor, Scotland, 97; auth, If God Already Know, Why Pray?, Wolgemuth, & Hyatt, 89, Korean edition, 92; Portuguese ed, 96; Spanish and Romanian editions to appear, 98; auth, Carolina Scots: An Historical and Genealogical Study of Over 100 Years of Emigration, with Caroline Switzer Kelly, 1739 Publications, Dillon, SC, 98; auth, The Truine God, Christian Dogmatics, 98; transl, Calvin's Harmony of the Pentateuch, vol 1, Rutherford House, 99; auth, Christin Ministry Today: Studies in II Corinthians, Rutherford House, 98; transl, John Calvin's Commentary on Joshua, Eerdmans, 99. **CONTACT ADDRESS** Dept of Systematic Theology, Reformed Theol Sem, No Carolina, 2101 Carmel Rd, Charlotte, NC 28226. **EMAIL** dkelly@rts.edu

KELLY, JIM KELLY
DISCIPLINE METAPHYSICS, MORAL THEORY, PHILOSOPHY **EDUCATION** SUNY at Oswego, BA; Ohio State Univ, MA, PhD. **CAREER** Assoc prof, Miami Univ **RESEARCH** Intersection of metaphysics, morality, and moral theory. **SELECTED PUBLICATIONS** Auth, Wide and Narrow Interdisciplinarity, in J Gen Educ, 45 2, 96. **CONTACT ADDRESS** Dept of Philosophy, Miami Univ, Oxford, OH 45056. **EMAIL** kellyjs@muohio.edu

KELLY, JOSEPH F.
PERSONAL Born 08/13/1945, New York, NY, m, 1968, 3 children **DISCIPLINE** RELIGIOUS STUDIES **EDUCATION** Boston Col, BA, 67; Fordham Univ, MA, 70; PhD, 73. **CAREER** Instr, Molloy Col, 69-72; asst prof to prof, John Carroll Univ, 72-. **HONORS AND AWARDS** Grant, Medieval Acad of Am, 70; NEH Fel, 84; Distinguished Fac Awd, John Carroll Univ, 97. **MEMBERSHIPS** Am Soc of Church Hist; N Am Patristic Soc. **RESEARCH** History of Christianity in roman era, History of Christmas. **SELECTED PUBLICATIONS** Auth, Why Is There a New Testament?, 86; auth, Dictionary of Early Christianity, 91; auth, World of the Early Christians, 97. **CONTACT ADDRESS** Dept Relig Studies, John Carroll Univ, 20700 N Park Blvd, Cleveland, OH 44118-4520. **EMAIL** kelly@jcu.edu

KELLY, RITA MAE
PERSONAL Born 12/10/1939, Waseca, MN, m, 1962, 2 children **DISCIPLINE** POLITICAL SCIENCE **EDUCATION** Univ Minn, BA, 61; Ind Univ, MA, 64; PhD, 67. **CAREER** Res Scientist, Am Inst for Res, 68-72; Consultant, Rita Mae Kelly & Assoc, 72-75; Prof Dept Chair, Rutgers Univ, 75-82; Prof, Ariz State Univ, 82-96; Prof and Dean, Univ Tex Dallas, 96-. **HONORS AND AWARDS** Policy Studies Org Appreciation Awd, 90; Outstanding Mentor in the Discipline Awd, Women's Caucus of Polit Sci, 91, 96; Fulbright Fel Awd, Brazil, 91; Aaron Wildavsky Awd, Policy Studies Org, 93; Merriam Mills Awd, Policy Studies Org, 95. **MEMBERSHIPS** W Polit Sci Asn; Policy Studies Org; Nat Women's Polit Caucus; NJ Polit Sci Asn; Intl Polit Sci Asn; AZ Foundation for Women; am Biographical Inst. **SELECTED PUBLICATIONS** Auth, The Making of Political Women, Nelson-Hall, 78; auth, Gender and Socialization to Power, Haworth Press, 86; auth, Promoting Productivity in the Public Sector, MacMillan Press, 88; auth, Comparable Worth, Pay Equity, and Public Policy, Greenwood Press, 88; auth, Women and the Arizona Political Process, Univ Press of Am, 88; auth, Gender, Bureaucracy, and Democracy, Greenwood Press, 89; auth, The Gendered Economy: Work, Careers, and Successes, Sage, 91; auth, Advances in Policy Studies since 1950, Transaction press, 92; auth, Gender Power, Leadership and Governance, Univ MI Press, 95. **CONTACT ADDRESS** Dept Soc Sci, Univ of Texas, Dallas, PO Box 830688, Richardson, TX 75083.

KELLY, SEAN D.
PERSONAL Born 06/22/1967, Columbus, OH, s **DISCIPLINE** PHILOSOPHY **EDUCATION** Brown Univ, BS, 89; MS, 89; Univ Cal, Berkeley, PhD, 98. **CAREER** Lectr, Stanford Univ, 98-99; asst prof, Princeton Univ, 99-. **HONORS AND AWARDS** Campbell's Coll Schlp; Bach/Mast Prog Awd; Vice Chan Grant; Howison Fel; Grad Res Grants; Ralph K Church Fel; Stanford Fel; McDonnell Fel. **MEMBERSHIPS** APA; BBSA. **RESEARCH** Philosophy of mind; cognitive science; phenomenology. **SELECTED PUBLICATIONS** Coauth, "Non-representational intentionality in Heidegger and Merleau-Ponty," Elect J Analytic Philo (96); auth, "What makes perceptual content non-conceptual?" Elect J Analytic Philo (98); coauth, "Phenomenology, dynamical neural networks, and brain function," Philo Psychol (00); auth, "Grasping at straws: Motor intentionality and the cognitive science of skillful action," Essays in Honor of Hubert Dreyfus, vol 2, eds. Mark Wrathall, Jeff Malpas, Genevieve Dreyfus (Cambridge: MIT Press, 99); auth, "What do we see (when you do)?" Philo Topics (99); auth, "Merleau-Pony's account of spatial perception," in Companion to Merleau-Pont, ed. Taylor Carmen (Cambridge: Cambridge Univ Press, forthcoming); auth, "Husserl and Phenomenology," in Blackwell Guide to Continental Philosophy, ed. Robert C Solomon (Oxford: Blackwell Pub, forthcoming). **CONTACT ADDRESS** Dept Philosophy, Princeton Univ, 1879 Hall, Princeton, NJ 08544-0001. **EMAIL** skelly@princeton.edu

KELMAN, STEVEN
PERSONAL Born 05/01/1948, New York, NY, m, 1980, 2 children **DISCIPLINE** POLITICAL SCIENCE **EDUCATION** Harvard Col, AB, 70; Harvard Univ, PhD, 78. **CAREER** Asst and assoc prof, 78-86, prof of pub mgt, 86-, Harvard Univ, JFK Sch of Govt. **HONORS AND AWARDS** Nat Achievement Awd, Nat Contract Mgt Asn, 97; Distinguished Pub Svc Awd, Amer Soc of Pub Admin, Wash chap, 96; Gabriel Almond Awd, Outstanding Dissertation in Comparative Polit, Amer Polit Sci Asn, 80; Fulbright scholar, Univ Stockholm, 70-71; Harvard Univ Sheldon Traveling fel, 70-71; Junior Twelve, Phi Beta Kappa, 69; Harvard Nat Scholar, 66-70. **MEMBERSHIPS** Coun for Excellence in Govt; GTSI Inc; Fed Sources Inc; Nat Acad of Pub Admin; Nat Contract Mgt Asn; Jour of Pub Admin Res and Theory; The Amer Prospect; Acad Adv Bd, Volvo Res Found; Intl Adv Grp; Amer Coun on Ger. **RESEARCH** Public management. **SELECTED PUBLICATIONS** Auth, American Democracy and the Public Good, Harcourt Brace, 96; Procurement and Public Management: The Fear of Discretion and the Qualtiy of Public Performance, Amer

Enterprise Inst, 90; Making Public Policy: A Hopeful View of American Government, Basic Books, 87; coauth, with Sidney Verba, Elites and the Idea of Equality, Harvard Univ Press, 87; auth, What Price Incentives? Economists and the Environment, Auburn House, 81; Regulating American, Regulating Sweden: A Comparative Study of Occupational Safety and Health Policy, MIT Press, 81; Improving Doctor Performance: A Study in the Use of Information and Organizational Change, Human Sci Press, 79; Behind the Berlin Wall, Houghton Mifflin, 71; Push Comes to Shove, Houghton Mifflin, 70. **CONTACT ADDRESS** JFK School of Government, Harvard Univ, Cambridge, MA 02138. **EMAIL** steve_kelman@harvard.edu

KELSEY, SEAN
PERSONAL Born 09/24/1970, Neptune, NJ, m, 1992, 4 children **DISCIPLINE** PHILOSOPHY **EDUCATION** Thomas Aquinas Col, BA, 92; Princeton Univ, PhD, 97. **CAREER** Asst prof, Iowa State Univ, 97-98; asst prof, Univ Calif, 98-. **HONORS AND AWARDS** Fel, NEH, 91; Fel, Nat Sci Found, 92-95; Fel, Princeton Univ, 95-97; Summer Stipend, NEH, 00; Jr Fel, Ctr for Hellenic Studies, 01-02; Fel, Pres Res Fel, 01-02. **MEMBERSHIPS** Am Philos Asn; Soc of Christian Philos; Soc for Ancient Greek Philos. **RESEARCH** Aristotle's Natural Philosophy; Aristotle's Metaphysics; Plato's Metaphysics. **SELECTED PUBLICATIONS** Auth, "Recollection in the Phaedo," Proceedings of the Boston Area Colloquium in Ancient Philosophy, (forthcoming). **CONTACT ADDRESS** Dept Philos, Univ of California, Los Angeles, Box 951451, Los Angeles, CA 90095-1451. **EMAIL** kelsey@humnet.ucla.edu

KEMENY, P
PERSONAL Born 12/13/1960, Morristown, NJ, m, 1983, 1 child **DISCIPLINE** AMERICAN RELIGIOUS HISTORY **EDUCATION** Wake Forest, BA, 83; Westminster Sem, MAR, 86, MDiv, 87; Duke Univ, ThM, 88; Princeton Sem, PhD, 95. **CAREER** Vis fel, ctr stud (s) Amer Rel, Princeton Univ, 95-96; asst prof, Rel, Calvin Col, 96- . **HONORS AND AWARDS** Woodrow Wilson awd, 97 **MEMBERSHIPS** AAR; HEQ; AHA; ASOH; Conf Earth Hist. **CONTACT ADDRESS** Dept of Relig and Philos, Grove City Col, 100 Campus Dr, Grove City, PA 16127-2104.

KEMPF, STEPHEN W.
PERSONAL Born 10/23/1948, Chicago, IL, m, 1979, 5 children **DISCIPLINE** THEOLOGY **EDUCATION** Univ Laval, PhD, 96. **CAREER** Bible research; Wycliffe Bible Translators. **MEMBERSHIPS** SBL. **RESEARCH** Pentateuch; Old Testament studies. **SELECTED PUBLICATIONS** Auth, Genesis 3:14-19: Climax of the Discourse? Jour of Transl and Textlinguistics, 93; auth, Introducing the Garden of Eden: The Structure and Function of Genesis, Jour of Transl and Textlinguistics, 96; auth, Translator's Notes on Genesis 11:27-25: 11, Translator's Notes on Genesis, SIL, 98. **CONTACT ADDRESS** 1253 du Bellay, Ste. Foy, QC, Canada G2E 4T8. **EMAIL** stevekempf@compuserve.com

KENDE, MARK
PERSONAL Born New York, NY, s **DISCIPLINE** CONSTITUTIONAL LAW **EDUCATION** Yale Univ, BA, 82; Univ Chicago, JD, 86. **CAREER** Atty, Chicago, 88-93; assoc prof, Thomas Cooley Law Sch, 93-99; assoc prof, Univ of Mont, 99-. **HONORS AND AWARDS** Cert of Excellence in Teaching, 97, 98; Fulbright Sr Scholar, S Africa, 00; Distinguished Vis, Univ Durban-Westville, 00. **MEMBERSHIPS** Fulbright Assoc, ABA, Am Soc of Legal Writers. **RESEARCH** Constitutional Law, Civil Rights, Law and Cyberspace. **SELECTED PUBLICATIONS** Auth, "Deconstructing Constructive Discharge," 71 Notre Dame Law Rev 39, (95); auth, "Michigan's Proposed Prenatal Protection AcT," 5 Am Univ Jour of Gender Law 247, (96); auth, "Lost in Cyberspace," 77 Ore Law Rev 1125, (98); auth, "Gender Stereotypes in South African and American Constitutional Law," S African Law Jour, (00). **CONTACT ADDRESS** Sch of Law, Univ of Montana, 32 Campus Dr, Missoula, MT 59812-0004. **EMAIL** kendem@selway.umt.edu

KENDRICK, JOY A.
PERSONAL Born Burlington, NC, s **DISCIPLINE** LAW **EDUCATION** Univ of North Carolina at Chapel Hill, BA, 1977; State Univ of New York at Buffalo, JD, 1981; Indiana Univ, MBA, 1985. **CAREER** Alamance Technical Col, orientation librarian, 77-78; Cora P Maloney Col, academic coordinator, 80-81; Neighborhood Legal Services Inc, staff attorney, 81-83; law clerk, 79-81; NCR Corporation, business intern, 84; JA Kendrick Business Enterprises Inc, president, 85-; Law Office of Joy Kendrick, managing counsel, 85-. **MEMBERSHIPS** Erie County Bar Association; New York State Bar Association; American Bar Association; Leadership Buffalo, 1988; Chamber of Commerce, board of directors, 1987-90; Buffalo Private Industry Council, board of directors, 1990-; Buffalo Business, contributing writer; Minority Business Council, bd of directors; Housing Assistant Center, bd of directors. **CONTACT ADDRESS** Lawyer/Business Consultant, JA Kendrick Business Enterprise, 107 Delaware Ave, Ste 327, Buffalo, NY 14202.

KENEVAN, PHYLLIS BERDT
PERSONAL Born Minneapolis, MN, d, 2 children **DISCIPLINE** PHILOSOPHY **EDUCATION** Univ Minn, BA, 51; MA, 58; Northwestern Univ, PhD, 69. **CAREER** Teaching asst, Northwestern Univ, 59-61; asst prof to assoc prof, Univ Colo, 61-; prog dir, Study Abroad Prog, 64-65. **HONORS AND AWARDS** Fulbright Fel, Univ Paris, 56-57; Fel, Northwester Univ, 58-59; Nominee, Teacher Recognition Award, 76, 80; Fac Teaching Award, Univ Colo, 82. **RESEARCH** Existentialism; Philosophy of literature; Philosophy and psychology. **SELECTED PUBLICATIONS** Auth, Paths of Individuation in Literature and Film: A Jungian Approach, Lexington Books, 99. **CONTACT ADDRESS** Univ of Colorado, Boulder, Boulder, CO 80309-0001.

KENNEDY, BRUCE
DISCIPLINE LAW **EDUCATION** Univ Mich, BA, AMLS; Univ Minn, JD. **CAREER** Assoc prof. **SELECTED PUBLICATIONS** Auth, Confidentiality of Library Records & Problems, Policies and Laws, Law Lib J, 89; A Draft User Guide to the AALL Universal Case Citation, Law Lib J, 97. **CONTACT ADDRESS** Col Law, Univ of Toledo, Toledo, OH 43606. **EMAIL** bkenned@uoft02.utoledo.edu

KENNEDY, D. ROBERT
PERSONAL Born 08/24/1946, Jamaica, WI, m, 1970, 3 children **DISCIPLINE** THEOLOGY **EDUCATION** West Indies Col, BTh; Andrews Univ, MA; McGill Univ, STM; Columbia Univ, EdD; Greenwich Univ, PhD cand. **CAREER** Religious educator; seven years as prof of theol, relig. **HONORS AND AWARDS** AAR/Lilly tchg fel, 93-94. **MEMBERSHIPS** Soc Relig Stud; Am Acad of Relig; Soc of Bibl Lit. **RESEARCH** Silence in Heaven: a study of Revelation 8:1 with special focus on its socio-cultural understanding, and an understanding of science and spirituality. **SELECTED PUBLICATIONS** Auth, The politics of the Basin: A Study of Lost Washing, Univ Press of Am, 95; auth, The Politics of the Spirit: Understanding the Spirit in the Church, Univ Press of Am, 96. **CONTACT ADDRESS** Dept of Relig, Atlantic Union Col, PO Box 554, South Lancaster, MA 01561. **EMAIL** drkennedy@atlantic.edu

KENNEDY, DAVID
DISCIPLINE LAW **EDUCATION** Brown Univ, BA, 76; Harvard Univ, JD, 80. **CAREER** Vis prof. **SELECTED PUBLICATIONS** Auth, pubs on European community law, evidence, international law, and international trade and legal theory. **CONTACT ADDRESS** Fac of Law, Univ of Toronto, 78 Queen's Park, Toronto, ON, Canada M5S 1A1.

KENNEDY, ROBERT E.
PERSONAL Born 06/20/1933, Brooklyn, NY **DISCIPLINE** SYSTEMATIC THEOLOGY **EDUCATION** Univ of Ottawa, Canada, PhD, 70. **CAREER** Prof, St Peter's Coll, Jersey City, NJ. **HONORS AND AWARDS** Excellent Tchg Awd; Durant Prof. **MEMBERSHIPS** AAR. **RESEARCH** Buddhism, Zen; Buddhist Christian Interfaith Work. **SELECTED PUBLICATIONS** Auth, Zen Spirit, Christian Spirit, Continuum, NY, 95; auth, Zen Gifts to Christians, Continulm, 01. **CONTACT ADDRESS** 50 Glenwood Ave, #908, Jersey City, NJ 07306. **EMAIL** rekennedy@earthlink.net

KENNEDY, ROBIN M.
DISCIPLINE LAW **EDUCATION** Univ Notre Dame, BA; Case Western Reserve Univ, JD. **CAREER** Assoc prof. **SELECTED PUBLICATIONS** Auth, Clinical Law in the Area of Mental Health, Univ Wis, 79; co-auth, Alternative Dispute Resolution, Ohio Jurisprudence, 97; Mediating Status Offender Cases: A Successful Approach, Mediation Quarterly, 96. **CONTACT ADDRESS** Col Law, Univ of Toledo, Toledo, OH 43606. **EMAIL** rkenned@utnet.utoledo.edu

KENNEDY, THOMAS
PERSONAL Born 04/23/1955, Anderson, SC, m, 1976, 2 children **DISCIPLINE** PHILOSOPHY **EDUCATION** Calvin Col, BA, 75; Univ of Virginia, PhD, 86. **CAREER** Austin P State Univ, asst prof, 87-89; Valparaiso Univ, asst prof, assoc prof, 89-. **HONORS AND AWARDS** Valparaiso Univ Alumni, Distinguished Tchg Awd, Res Awd; ed bd, ethics and medicine, 95-; neh younger scholars proj adv, 91 and 93; dir soc christ philos summer conference, valparaiso univ, 91. **MEMBERSHIPS** Am Philos Asn; Soc Christ Philos; Am Soc Aesthetics; 18th-Century Scottish Studies Soc. **RESEARCH** Philos of art; ethics, philos of religion; Eighteenth century Scottish thought. **SELECTED PUBLICATIONS** Coauth, From Christ to the World, Wm. B. Eerdmans, Grand Rapids, 94. **CONTACT ADDRESS** Dept of Philosophy, Valparaiso Univ, Valparalso, IN 46383. **EMAIL** Tom.Kennedy@valpo.edu

KENNEDY-DAY, KIKI
PERSONAL Born Chicago, IL, m, 1988 **DISCIPLINE** NEAR EASTERN LANGUAGES AND LITERATURE-ARABIC (ISLAMIC PHILOSOPHY) **EDUCATION** NYork Univ, PhD, 96. **CAREER** St John's Univ Jamaica; Adj Asst Prof, Hofstra Univ NY, 98-. **MEMBERSHIPS** APA. **RESEARCH** Islamic Philosophy; Ibn Sina. **SELECTED PUBLICATIONS** Auth, articles about Al-Kindi, Aristotelianism in Islamic Philos, Routledge Encycl of Islamic Philos, 98. **CONTACT ADDRESS** Fort Washington Ave, 4A, New York, NY 10033.

KENNESON, PHILIP D.
PERSONAL Born 10/28/1958, Fort Wayne, IN, m, 1983, 5 children **DISCIPLINE** THEOLOGY AND PHILOSOPHY **EDUCATION** Butler Univ, BA, 81; Emmanuel Sch Relig, Johnson City, Mdiv, 86; Duke Univ, Durham, PhD, 91. **CAREER** Intr, Duke Univ, Writing Prog, 87, 88, 90; instr, rel, Duke Univ, 90-91; instr, Duke Div School, 92; asst prof, 92-98, assoc prof, Milligan Col, 98-. **SELECTED PUBLICATIONS** Auth, "Worship Wars and Rumors of Worship Wars," Reviews in Religion and Theology (96): 72-75; auth, "Spirituality American Style," Reviews in Religion and Theology (97): 72-75; coauth, Selling Out the Church: The Dangers of Church Marketing, Abingdon Press, 97; auth, Beyond Sectarianism: Re-Imagining Church and World. Christian Mission and Modern Culture Series, ed. Alan Neely, H. Wayne Pipkin, and Wilbert R. Shenk (Trinity Press Int, 99); auth, "Can the Christian Faith Survive if Belief in Objective Truth is Abandoned?," Stone-Campbell Journal 2.1 (99): 43-56; auth, "The Frog in the Kettle," The Restoration Herald 78.2 (99): 1-6; auth, Life on the Vine: Cultivating the Fruit of the Spirit in Christian Community, InterVaristy Press, 99; auth, "Out of Control: Cultivating Selfless Self-Control," Prism 6.6 (99); 10-13; auth, (To Market)2. (Pro/Con Discussion of Church Marketing)," Vital Ministries (99): 44-49; auth, "Visible Grace: The Church as God's Embodied Presence," in Grace Upon Grace: Essays in Honor of Thomas A. Langford, ed. Robert K. Johnston, L. Gregory Jones, and Jonathan R. Wilson (Abgindon Press, 99), 169-179. **CONTACT ADDRESS** Dept of Theology and Philosophy, Milligan Col, Box 500, Milligan College, TN 37682. **EMAIL** pkenneson@milligan.edu

KENNEY, GARRETT C.
PERSONAL Born 12/31/1950, Spokane, WA, m, 1971, 4 children **DISCIPLINE** RELIGIOUS STUDIES **EDUCATION** Gonzaga Univ, educ leadership, PhD, 94. **CAREER** Adjunct instr, Gonzaga Univ, 89-94; visiting asst prof, Eastern Wash Univ, 94-; Senior lecturer, Eastern Wash Univ, 00-. **MEMBERSHIPS** Amer Acad of Relig; Soc of Bibl Lit. **RESEARCH** New Testament; Johannine studies. **SELECTED PUBLICATIONS** Auth, Lessons in Religion, Kendall/Hunt, 96; auth, Introduction to Religion, Kendall/Hunt, 88; auth, "Lessons & Lectures in Religion," Kendall/Hunt, 00; auth, "Leadership in John: An Analysis of the Situation and Strategy of the Gospel and Epistles of John," University Press of America, 00; auth, "The Relation of Christology to Ethics in the First Epistle of John, University Press of America, 00. **CONTACT ADDRESS** Humanities Program, Eastern Washington Univ, Patterson 250, MS 25, Cheney, WA 99004. **EMAIL** gkenney@ewv.edu

KENNEY, JOHN PETER
PERSONAL Born 05/01/1952, Lawrence, MA, m, 1974, 2 children **DISCIPLINE** RELIGIOUS STUDIES **EDUCATION** Bowdoin Coll, AB, 74; Brown Univ, PhD, 82. **CAREER** Asst prof, 80-85; assoc prof, 86-92; prof, Reed Coll, 92-95; dean, prof, Saint Michael's Coll, 95-. **HONORS AND AWARDS** Phi Beta Kappa, 73; Nat Endowment for the Humanities Res Fel, 84-85, 91-92; Burlington Northern Faculty Achievement Awd, 90. **MEMBERSHIPS** Am Acad of Rel; N Am Patristic Soc. **RESEARCH** Philosophical Theology. **SELECTED PUBLICATIONS** Auth, Mystical Monotheism A Study in Ancient Platonic Theology, 91; St Augustine and the Invention of Mysticism, Studia Patristica, 97; Ed, The School of Moses: Studies in Philo and Hellenistic Religion, 95; Mysticism and Contemplation in the Enneads, Am Cath Philos Quart, 97; auth, The Greek Tradition in Early Christian Philosophy, The Columbai History of Philosophy, 99. **CONTACT ADDRESS** Office of the Dean of the College, Saint Michael's Col, Colchester, VT 05439. **EMAIL** Jkenney@smcvt.edu

KENNICK, WILLIAM ELMER
PERSONAL Born 05/28/1923, Lebanon, IL, m, 1949, 3 children **DISCIPLINE** PHILOSOPHY **EDUCATION** Oberlin Col, BA, 45; Cornell Univ, PhD(philos), 52. **CAREER** Instr philos, Boston Univ, 50-51; instr, Oberlin Col, 47-48, 51-54, asst prof & chemn dept, 54-56; from assoc prof to prof, 56-76, William F Kenan Jr prof, 78-80, G Henry Whitcomb Prof Philos, Amherst Col, 76-, Lectr, Smith Col, 63-64; mem Comn Inst Higher Educ, New England Asn Schs & Cols, 72-75, vchmn, 75, chemn, 76; actg dean fac, Amherst Col, 80. **HONORS AND AWARDS** MA, Amherst Col, 62. **MEMBERSHIPS** Am Philos Asn; Am Soc Aesthet; Medieval Acad Am. **RESEARCH** Aesthetics; metaphysics. **SELECTED PUBLICATIONS** Auth, Does Traditional Aesthetics Rest on a Mistake?, Mind, 58; Art and Philosophy: Readings in Aesthetics, St Martins, 64; coauth, Metaphysics: Readings and Reappraisals, Prentice-Hall, 66; auth, Moore on Existence and Prediction, In: G E Moore: Essays in Retrospect, Allen & Unwin, 70; On Solipsism, In: Psychoanalysis and Philosophy, Int Univ Press, 70; Philosophy as Grammar and the Reality of Universals, In: Ludwig Wittgenstein: Philosophy and Language, Allen & Unwin, 72. **CONTACT ADDRESS** Dept of Philos, Amherst Col, Amherst, MA 01002-5003. **EMAIL** wekennick@amherst.edu

KENNY, ALFREIDA B.
PERSONAL Born 03/12/1950, Richmond, VA **DISCIPLINE** LAW **EDUCATION** Syracuse U, AB 1968-72; Columbia Univ

Sch of Law, JD 1972-75. **CAREER** Federal Reserve Bank of NY, staff atty 1975-76; Harper & Row Publ Inc, asst gen counsel 1976-80; Weil Gotshal & Manges, assoc 1980-84; Cooper & Kenny, partner 1984-. **HONORS AND AWARDS** Charles Evans Hughes Fellowship Columbia Law Sch 1976; Outstanding Young Women of Am US Jaycees 1978; Professional Awd for Outstanding Serv Natl Assn of Negro Business & Professional Women's Club; Columbia Univ Chap Outstanding Alumnus Awd Black Law Students Assn. **MEMBERSHIPS** Mem Phi Delta Phi Legal Frat 1973-; mem Nat Assn of Black Women Atty 1977-; mem Am Bar Assn 1977-; mem Assn of the Bar of the City of NY 1977-; pres Assn of Black Women Atty NY 1978-80; mem Com on Labor & Employ of the assn of the Bar of the City of NY; bd of dir Nat Bar Assn Women's Div 1980-82; treas 1975-80, mem bd of dirs 1975-, vice pres Alumni Assn Columbia Law Sch Class of 1975, 1980-85; vice pres Friends of Syracuse (Black Alumni Assn) 1979-80; admitted to the bar of Dist Ct for Southern Dist of NY, Dist Ct Eastern Dist for the Dist of NY, US Supreme Court 1981, Ct of Appeals for the 6th Circuit; mem Zeta Phi Beta Sor Inc 1980-; mem Paul Robeson Scholarship Comm Columbia Univ Sch of Law 1980-; Civil Court Comm of Assoc of Bar of the City of NY 1986-. **SELECTED PUBLICATIONS** "The Voting Rights Act of 1965 & Minority Access to th Polit Process" Columbia Human Rights Law Review Vol 6 No 1 1974. **CONTACT ADDRESS** Cooper & Kenny, 71 Broadway, New York, NY 10006.

KENT, DAN GENTRY

PERSONAL Born 10/13/1935, Palestine, TX, m, 1957, 3 children **DISCIPLINE** OLD TESTAMENT PROPHECY AND CRITICISM **EDUCATION** Baylor Univ, BA, 57; Southwestern Bapt Theol Sem, BD, 59; Southwestern Bapt Theol Sem, ThD, 65. **CAREER** Assoc prof, relig, Wayland Bapt Univ, 75-80; prof, old testament, Southwestern Bapt Theol Sem, 80-99; adj prof, Truett Theol Sem; Coordr, Cooperative Baptist Fel, 01. **HONORS AND AWARDS** Pastor, Brandon Baptist Church, 60-62; First Baptist Church, De Leon, 62-66; Hampton Rd Baptist Church, 66-71; Calvary Baptist Church of Oak Cliff, 71-75. **MEMBERSHIPS** Soc Biblical Lit; Nat Assn of Baptist Prof Rel; Southern Baptist Hist Soc; Christians for Biblical Equality. **RESEARCH** Women in the Old Testament; Social justice in the Old Testament. **SELECTED PUBLICATIONS** Auth, Joshua, Judges, Ruth (Layman's Bible Book Commentary), Broadman Press, 80; auth, Lamentations (Bible Study Commentary), Zondervan, 83; Hosea: Man, Times, and Material, Southwestern Jour of Theol, fall, 93. **CONTACT ADDRESS** Truett Theol Sem, PO Box 97126, Waco, TX 76798. **EMAIL** dgk@swbts.swbts.edu

KEOHANE, NANNERL O.

DISCIPLINE POLITICAL SCIENCE **EDUCATION** Wellesley College, BA, 61; Oxford Univ, BA/MA, 63; Yale Univ, PhD, 67. **CAREER** Prof, Pres, 93-, Duke Univ; Prof, Pres, 81-93, Wellesley College; Asst Prof, Assoc Prof, Chmn, 73-81, Stanford Univ; Lectr, Asst Prof, 67-73, Swarthmore College; vis Lectr, 70-72, Univ Penn. **HONORS AND AWARDS** Phi Beta Kappa; Marshall Schshp; Woodrow Wilson fel; Gores Awd Excell Teach; CASBS Fel; Wilbur Cross Medal; AAAS Fel; APS Fel; OU St Anne's Hon Fel; Ntl Women's Hall of Fame; AAA Golden Plate Awd; Eleven Honorary Degrees. **MEMBERSHIPS** APSA **RESEARCH** Political Philosophy; Feminism; Education. **SELECTED PUBLICATIONS** Auth, Moral Education in the Modern University, Proceedings of the Amer Philo Soc, 98; The Mission of the Research University, in: DAEDALUS, J the Amer Acad of Arts and Sciences, 93; The Role of the President, in: Strategy and Finance of Higher Education, by WF Massy, Joel W Myerson, Peterson's Guides, Princeton NJ, 92; Women and the Transformation of the World, in: Preparing for the 21st Century: Models for Social Change, AAUW Edu Foun Occasional Paper, 89. **CONTACT ADDRESS** 207 Allen Bldg, Box 90001, Durham, NC 27708-0001. **EMAIL** nkeohane@mail.duke.edu

KEPNES, STEVEN D.

PERSONAL Born 05/21/1952, Boston, MA, m **DISCIPLINE** JEWISH STUDIES **EDUCATION** Hobart and William Smith Colleges, BA, 74; Univ Chicago, Divinity, MA, 76; Univ Chicago, PhD (Modern Jewish thought and relig and psychol studies), 83; study abroad, Hebrew Univ of Jerusalem, 83, 85, 87, 93-95. **CAREER** Assoc prof, Dept of Philos and Relig and Dir of Jewish Studies, Colgate Univ Hamilton, NY, 93-; ed, Judaism section, Religious Studies Rev, 94-; ed, Biblical Hermeneutics, Textural Reasoning, 96-. **HONORS AND AWARDS** Phi Beta Kappa, 74; Sheuer fel in Jewish Studies, Univ Chicago, 79-80; Lakritz grant in Buber Scholarship, 85, 88; Mellon Found fel, 86-88; Memorial Found for Jewish Culture, 86-87; Am Academy of Relig Res grant, 87-88; Colgate Univ Major Res grant, 93-94; Hartman Inst Fel, Jerusalem, 93-95. **MEMBERSHIPS** AJS; AAR. **RESEARCH** German Jewish thought; hermaneutics. **SELECTED PUBLICATIONS** Co-ed with David Tracy, The Challenge of Psychology to Faith, Concilium, vol 156, Seabury, 82(published in eight languages); auth, The Text as Thou: Martin Buber's Dialogical Hermaneutics and Narrative Theology, IN Univ Press, 92; The Dialogic Self, The Endangered Self, Don Capps and Richard Fenn, eds, Princeton Theol Sem, 92; Introduction, Martin Buber, Toward a New German Translation of the Scriptures, trans by Alan Swensen, ed by Steven Kepnes, Post-Critical Biblical Interpretation, Peter Ochs, ed, Fortress Press, 93; Martin Buber's Dialogical Biblical Hermaneutics, Protestans Szemle (Hungarian), 17:2, 92; Budapest, also in Literary Criticism and Biblical Hermeneutics (Hungarian and English), Tibor Fabiny, ed, Szged: Attlia Jozsef Univ Press, 93; Martin Buber's Dialogical Biblical Hermaneutics, Martin Buber and the Human Sciences, Maurice Friedman, ed, SUNY, 96; ed, Interpreting Judaism in a Postmodern Age, NY Univ Press, 96; auth, Postmodern Interpretations of Judaism: Deconstructive Approaches, Interpreting Judaism in a Postmodern Age, Steven Kepnes, ed, NY Univ Press, 96; co-auth with Peter Ochs and Robert Gibbs, Reasoning After Revelation: Dialogues in Postmodern Jewish Philosophy, Westview, 98; auth, Surviving Holocaust Judaism, Modern Judaism, forthcoming. **CONTACT ADDRESS** Dept of Philos and Relig, Colgate Univ, Hamilton, NY 13346-1398. **EMAIL** skepnes@center.colgate.edu

KERCKHOVE, LEE

PERSONAL Born 04/15/1963, Chicago, IL **DISCIPLINE** PHILOSOPHY **EDUCATION** Univ Calif San Diego, BA, 88; Logola Univ Chicago, MA, 91; PhD, 96. **CAREER** Assoc Prof, Palomar Coll, 97-. **HONORS AND AWARDS** Fulbright Scholar, Technische Universitat, Berlin, Germany, 93-94. **MEMBERSHIPS** Am Philos Asn; North Am Nietzsche Soc. **RESEARCH** Social and Political Philosophy; Ethics; Neitzsche. **SELECTED PUBLICATIONS** Auth, Moral Fanaticism and the Holocaust: A Defense of Kant Against Silber, Philos in Contemp World, 94; Re-Thinking Ethical Naturalism: Nietzsche's 'Open Question" Argument, Man and World, 94; Emancipation Social Science and Genealogy: Habermas on Nietzsche, Philos in Contemp World, 95; coauth, Fetal Personhood and the Sorites Paradox, 98. **CONTACT ADDRESS** Dept of Philosophy, Palomar Col, 1140 W Mission Rd, San Marcos, CA 92069. **EMAIL** lkerckhove@palomar.edu

KERLIN, MICHAEL J.

PERSONAL Born 01/13/1936, Philadelphia, PA, m, 1971, 2 children **DISCIPLINE** PHILOSOPHY **EDUCATION** LaSalle Univ, BA, 57, MA, 58, MBA, 89; Gregorian Univ, PhD, 66; Temple Univ, PhD, 74. **CAREER** Asst prof, 66-71, asoc prof, 71-76, prof philos, 76- , LaSalle Univ. **HONORS AND AWARDS** Lendback Awd for Distinguished Tchg, 87. **MEMBERSHIPS** AAR; APA; Am Cath Philos Asn; Soc of Christian Philos. **RESEARCH** Social philosophy; business and society; philosophy of religion; Roman Catholic modernism. **SELECTED PUBLICATIONS** Auth, St. Philip Veri and 16th Century Church Renewal, America, 95; auth, Peter French, Corporate Ethics and the Wizard of Oz, 97; auth, From Kerlin's Pizzeria to MJK Reynolds : A Socratic and Cartesian Approach to Business Ethics, 97. **CONTACT ADDRESS** Dept of Philosophy, La Salle Univ, 1900 W Olney Ave, Philadelphia, PA 19141. **EMAIL** kerlin@lasalle.edu

KERN, GILBERT RICHARD

PERSONAL Born 12/05/1932, Detroit, MI, 6 children **DISCIPLINE** CHURCH & AMERICAN HISTORY **EDUCATION** Findlay Col, AB, 54; Winebrenner Theol Sem, BD, 58; Univ Chicago, MA, 60, PhD, 68. **CAREER** From lectr to prof church hist, Winebrenner Theol Sem, 60-70, pres, 63-70; Prof Relig, 70-75, Prof Hist, 75-98, Professor Emeritus, The Univ of Findlay, 98-; Lectr Hist, Winebrenner Theol Sem, 72-84. **HONORS AND AWARDS** Dist Alumni Awd, Univ Findlay, 89. **MEMBERSHIPS** Am Soc Church Hist; Am Hist Asn. **RESEARCH** Nineteenth century Am church. **SELECTED PUBLICATIONS** Auth, John Winebrenner: 19th Century Reformer, Cent Publ House 74; Findlay College: The first one hundred years, 82. **CONTACT ADDRESS** Dept Hist, Univ of Findlay, 1000 N Main St, Findlay, OH 45840-3695. **EMAIL** kern@lucy.findlay.edu

KERR, GREGORY

PERSONAL Born 12/17/1958, New York, NY, m, 4 children **DISCIPLINE** PHILOSOPHY **EDUCATION** Boston Col, BA, 81; MA, 83; Fordham, PhD, 92. **CAREER** Assoc prof, Allentown Col, 92-. **HONORS AND AWARDS** Phi Kappa Phi. **MEMBERSHIPS** APA, ACLP, Am Philos Asn, am Catholic Philos Asn, Am Maritain Asn. **RESEARCH** Aesthetics, History of Philosophy, Philosophy of God. **SELECTED PUBLICATIONS** Ed, Maritain Notebook, 93-; auth, "Knowing Our Knowings," American Maritain Association, (forthcoming); auth, "On Pope John Paul II's Fides et Ratio," Fellowship of catholic scholars Quarterly, (99); auth, "Art's invaluable Uselessness," American Maritain Association, (forthcoming); auth, "Deconstruction and Artistic creation: Maritain and the Bad Boys of Philosophy," Postmodernism and Christian Philosophy, American Maritain Association; auth, "The elements of Discord: The sine Qua Non of Education," The Common Things: Essays on Thomism and Education, American Maritain Association; auth, "Christ the form of Beauty," Crisis, (96). **CONTACT ADDRESS** Dept Relig & Philos, Allentown Col of St. Francis De Sales, 2755 Station Ave, Center Valley, PA 18034-9565. **EMAIL** gjk@allenol.edu

KERSTEN, FREDERICK IRVING

PERSONAL Born 09/26/1931, Niagara Falls, NY, m, 1994, 2 children **DISCIPLINE** PHILOSOPHY **EDUCATION** Lawrence Univ, BA, 54; New School for Soc Res, MA, 59, PhD, 64. **CAREER** Insr, asst prof, assoc prof, Univ Montana, Missoula, 64-69; assoc prof, prof, Univ Wisconsin, Green Bay, 69-94. **HONORS AND AWARDS** Halle Fel, 60-61; Frankenthal prof, Univ of Wisconsin, Green Bay, 84-94. **MEMBERSHIPS** Ed bd, Human Stud; ed bd, Husserl Stud. **RESEARCH** Husserl's and Husserlian phenomenology; phenomenological philosophy in metaphysics and epistemology; philosophy and art in the Renaissance and Baroque; nineteenth century philosophy. **SELECTED PUBLICATIONS** ed, trans, Alfred Schutz, Collected Papers, Kluwer, 95; auth, "Notes from the Underground," The Prism of the Self, ed by Crowell, Kluwer, 95; Constitutive Phenomenology, Intentionality, Alfred Schutz, Encyclopedia of Phenomenology, ed Embree, Kluwer, 97; "Some Reflections on the Ground for Comparison of Multiple Realities," Alfred Schutz' Sociological Aspect of Literature, ed by Embree, Kluwer, 97; Galileo and the Invention of Opera, Kluwer, 97; Stuffed Cabbage in the Old New School Cafeteria, Hum Stud, 97; "The Purely Possible Political Philosophy of Alfred Schutz," Schutzian Social Science, ed Embree, Kluwer, 98; "Angela Thirkell," UK J of the Angela Thirkell Soc, 98; ed, Reconstruction of Alfred Schutz, Hum Stud, forthcoming. **CONTACT ADDRESS** 2355 Old Plank Rd, De Pere, WI 54115.

KESAN, JAY P.

DISCIPLINE LAW **EDUCATION** Univ Tex Austin, MS; PhD; Georgetown Univ, JD. **CAREER** Law clerk, Judge Patrick E. Higginbotham, US Court Appeals; asst prof,Univ Ill Urbana Champaign. **HONORS AND AWARDS** Assoc ed, Georgetown Law J. **RESEARCH** Intellectual property; law and regulation of cyberspace; and science; technology and the law; Patent law; Law and Regulation of Cyberspace and Theoretical Foundations of Intellectual Property. **SELECTED PUBLICATIONS** Auth, pubs on intellectual property, law and regulation of cyberspace, and science, technology and law. **CONTACT ADDRESS** Law Dept, Univ of Illinois, Urbana-Champaign, 52 E Gregory Dr, Champaign, IL 61820. **EMAIL** kesan@law.uiuc.edu

KESSLER, ANN VERONA

PERSONAL Born 01/28/1928, Aberdeen, SD **DISCIPLINE** MODERN & CHURCH HISTORY **EDUCATION** Mt Marty Col, BA, 53; Creighton Univ, MA, 57; Univ Notre Dame, PhD, 63. **CAREER** Teacher elem schs, 47-49, 57-59 & Mt Marty High Sch, 52-56; from instr to assoc prof, 62-73, acad dean, 63-65, head dept hist, 68-77, Prof Hist, Mt Marty Col, 73-98, Professor Emeritus, 98-; mem, Am Benedictine Acad, 67-98; mem, Fulbright Scholar Selection Comt, 77, 79. **HONORS AND AWARDS** Teaching Excellence and Campus Leadership Awd, Sears-Roebuck Found, 91. **MEMBERSHIPS** Am Acad Polit & Soc Sci; AHA; Am Polit Sci Asn. **RESEARCH** Fate of religious orders in France since the revolution; modern churchstate controversies; monastic history and biography of Benedictines. **SELECTED PUBLICATIONS** Auth, French Benedictines under stress, fall 66 & Political legacy to the religions in France: Laic laws of the Third Republic, 12/69, Am Benedictine Rev; Post-Revolution Restoration of French Monasticism, SDak Soc Sci Asn J, fall 77; Founded on Courage, Inspired with Vision: Mt Marty Col, In: From Idea to Institution, 89; First Catholic Bishop of Dakota: Martin Marty, In: South Dakota Leaders, 89; Benedictine Men and Women of Courage, 96. **CONTACT ADDRESS** Mount Marty Col, Yankton, 1105 W 8th St, Yankton, SD 57078-3724. **EMAIL** akessler@rs6.mtmc.edu

KETCHEN, JIM

DISCIPLINE LAW **EDUCATION** Univ Windsor, BA, MA, LLB. **CAREER** Lectr. **MEMBERSHIPS** Ontario Asn Family Mediation. **RESEARCH** Politics; law. **CONTACT ADDRESS** Law and Justice Dept, Laurentian Univ, 935 Ramsey Lake Rd, Sudbury, ON, Canada P3E 2C6. **EMAIL** jketchen@nickel.laurentian.ca

KETCHUM, RICHARD J.

PERSONAL Born 05/06/1941, Lexington, KY, m **DISCIPLINE** ANCIENT PHILOSOPHY **EDUCATION** Beloit Col, BA; Albert Ludwig's Univ, 61-62; Univ Penn, PhD 71. **CAREER** Vanderbilt Univ, inst, asst prof, 68-73; Univ Rochester, vis lect, 72; Univ Cal SB, asst prof, 73-79; FL INTL Univ, vis prof, 79-80; Univ Texas, vis prof, 80-81; Univ Missouri, vis prof, 81-83; Lindenwood Col, asst prof, 83-85; New Mexico State Univ, asst prof, assoc prof, 85 to 91-. **MEMBERSHIPS** APA; SAGP **RESEARCH** Ancient philosophy **SELECTED PUBLICATIONS** Auth, Philosophy is not a Trivial Pursuit, coauth, Champaign, Stipes Pub, 97; Plato: Parmenides, trans by Mary Louise Gill and Paul Ryan, in: Can Philo Rev, IN, Hackett Pub, 96; Companions to Ancient Thought: Language, ed, Steven Everson, Cambridge, Cambridge Univ Press, 94; in: Ancient Philo, 96; On the Impossibility of Epistemology, Philosophical Studies: Ab Intl Jour for the Analytic Tradition, 97;C. S. Pierce on Naturalism, Philosophia Scientiae: Travaux d' Histoire et de Phil des Sciences, Archives Cen d'Etudes et de Recherche Henri Poine, 96. **CONTACT ADDRESS** Dept of Philosophy, New Mexico State Univ, Las Cruces, NM 88003. **EMAIL** rketchum@nmsu.edu

KETNER, KENNETH LAINE
PERSONAL Born 03/24/1939, Mountain Home, OK, m, 1963, 1 child **DISCIPLINE** PHILOSOPHY, FOLKLORISTICS **EDUCATION** OK State Univ, BA, 61, MA, 67; Univ CA, Los Angeles, MA, 68; Univ CA, Santa Barbara, PhD, 72. **CAREER** Instr philos, OK State Univ, 64-67; res asst folklore, Univ CA, Los Angeles, 67-68; teaching asst philos, Univ CA, Santa Barbara, 69-70; asst prof, 71-75, assoc prof, 75-77, Prof, 77-81, Peirce Prof Philos, TX Tech Univ, 81-, Dir Iinst Studies In Pragmaticism, 72-. **HONORS AND AWARDS** Res Merit Awd, TX Tech Univ, 80; NEH fel. **MEMBERSHIPS** Am Philos Asn; Charles S Pierce Soc. **RESEARCH** Am philos, philosophical anthropology; folkloristic method and theory. **SELECTED PUBLICATIONS** Auth, A Comprehensive Bibliography of the Published Works of Charles S Peirce, KTO Microform, 77; Charles S Peirce: Contributions to the Nation, TX Tech Univ, 78; Proceedings, Peirce Bicentennial Int Congress, TX Tech Univ, 81; The role of Hypotheses in Folkloristics, J Am Folklore, 86: 114-130; auth, Reasoning and the Logic of Things, Harvard Univ Press, 92; auth, A Thief of Peirce: The Letters of Kenneth Laine Ketner and Walker Percy, 95; auth, His Glassy Essence: An Autobiography of Charles Sanders Peirce, 98. **CONTACT ADDRESS** Institute for Studies in Pragmaticism, Texas Tech Univ, Lubbock, TX 79409-0002. **EMAIL** b9oky@ttacs.ttu.edu

KEVELSON, ROBERTA
PERSONAL Born 11/04/1931, Brooklyn, NY, d, 2 children **DISCIPLINE** SEMIOTICS AND PHILOSOPHY **EDUCATION** Brown Univ, PhD, 78; Yale Univ, post doctoral, 79. **CAREER** Asst prof, Pa State Univ, 81; full prof, Pa State Univ, 86; distinguished prof, philos, Pa State Univ, 87; exec dir, Ctr Semiotic Res, 84-98. **HONORS AND AWARDS** Amoco award, outstanding teaching; distinguished prof of philos. **MEMBERSHIPS** APA; Intl Asn Semiotics of Law; IUR; Amintaphic Semiotic Soc of Amer. **RESEARCH** Works of Charles S. Peirce; Philosophy of law; Aesthetics; Semiotics; General theory. **SELECTED PUBLICATIONS** Auth, Peirce's Pragmatism, NY, 98; ed, Hi-Fives: A Trip to Semiotics, NY, 98; auth, Peirce, Science, Signs, NY, 96; auth, Peirce's Esthetics of Freedom, NY, 93; series ed-in-chief, Critic of Institutions, NY; series ed-in-chief, Semiotics & the Human Sciences, NY; series co-ed; Semaphores & Signs, St. Martin's Press, NY. **CONTACT ADDRESS** 104 Woodbine Ct., Williamsburg, VA 23185. **EMAIL** bobbieke@earthlink.net

KEVERN, JOHN
DISCIPLINE CHURCH HISTORY **EDUCATION** Univ Paris-Sorbonne, Dipl Sup, 74; Univ Ill, BA, 75; Gen Theol Sem, MDiv, 80; Univ Chicago Divinity Sch, PhD, 97. **CAREER** Asst prof, Cooke Ch of Hist Theol, Bexley Hall Sem, 92-; dean, Bexley Hall Sem, 96. **SELECTED PUBLICATIONS** Auth, The Future of Anglican Theology, Anglican Theol Rev 75th Anniversary Ed, 94; Form in Tragedy: A Study in the Methodology of Hans Urs von Balthasar, In Communio, 94; The Fullness of Catholic Identity, In The Anglican Cath, 96; The Trinity and the Search for Justice, Anglican Theol Rev, 97. **CONTACT ADDRESS** Hist, Theol, Soc Dept, Trinity Lutheran Sem, 2199 E Main St, Columbus, OH 43209-2334. **EMAIL** jkevern@trinity.capital.edu

KEYT, DAVID
PERSONAL Born 02/22/1930, Indianapolis, IN, m, 1975, 2 children **DISCIPLINE** PHILOSOPHY **EDUCATION** Kenyon Col, AB, 51; Cornell Univ, MA, 53; PhD, 55. **CAREER** United States Army, 55-57; From Instructor to Professor, Univ of Washington, 57-; Visiting Asst Prof, Univ of Calif at Los Angeles, 62-63; Visiting Assoc Prof, Cornell Univ, 68-69; Visiting Prof, Univ of Hong Kong, Fall Term, 87; Visiting Prof, Princeton Univ, Fall Term, 88-89; Visiting Prof, Univ of Calif at Irvine, Fall Quarter; Acting Philosphy Chairman, Univ of Washington, 67-68, 70, Autumn Quarter, 86, Winter and Spring Quarters, 94; Philosophy Chairman, Univ of Washington, 71-78; Participant, Institute in Greek Philosophy and Science, Colo College, 70; Director, NEH Summer Seminar for College Teachers on Aristotle's Ethical and Political Philosophy, Univ of Washington, 79. **HONORS AND AWARDS** Junior Fellow, Institute for Research in the Humanities, Univ of Wisconsin-Madison, 66-67; Junior Fellow, Center for Hellenic Studies, Washington, DC, 74-75; Member, Institute for Advanced Study, Princeton, NJ, 83-84. **MEMBERSHIPS** Member of the Executive Committee, Pacific Division, 74-77; Member of the Program Committee, Pacific Division, 80-83; Member of the Nominating Committee, Pacific Division, 86-87. **RESEARCH** Plato; Aristotle. **SELECTED PUBLICATIONS** Auth, "A Companion to Aristotle's Politics", co-edited with Fred D. Miller, Jr., Oxford: Basil Blackwell, 1991, pp xiv & 407; auth, "Analyzing Plato's Arguments: Plato and Platonism," with S. Marc Cohen, in Methods of Interpreting Plato and His Dialogues, ed. By James C. Klagge and Nicholas D. Smith, Oxford, 92, 173-200; auth, Supplementary Essay," to the reissue of Aristotle's Politics, Book III and IV, translated with a commentary by Richard Robinson Oxford, 95, 125-152; auth, Aristotle and the Ancient Roots of Anarchism," Topoi 15, March, 1996, 129-42; auth, Aristotle Politics Books V and VI, Translation with introduction and commentary, Oxford Univ Press, Clarendon Aristotle Series, 99, pp xvii & 265. **CONTACT ADDRESS** Dept Philosopy, Univ of Washington, PO Box 353350, Seattle, WA 98195-3350. **EMAIL** keyt@u.washington.edu

KHAN, ABRAHIM H.
PERSONAL Born 04/13/1943, Guyana, m, 1969, 3 children **DISCIPLINE** RELIGION **EDUCATION** Howard Univ, BS, 65; Yale Univ, BD, 68; McGill Univ, MA, 71, PhD, 73; **CAREER** Lectr, Mcgill Univ, 73-75; res assoc, McGill, 74-75; lectr, Concordia Univ & Champlain Col, 74-75; asst prof, Univ Manitoba, 75-76; asst prof Univ Toronto, 76-79; asst prof, McGill, 79-81; relig stud, Univ Toronto, 81-82; lectr, Trent Univ, 82-83; asst prof, Trent Univ, 83-84; lectr, Univ Toronto, 83-84; res assoc, Trinity Col, assoc prof, McMaster Univ, 84-85; lectr, hon fel, Univ Toronto, 85-86; lectr, Trinity Col & Univ Toronto, 86-; assoc prof, Concordia Univ, 91-92; lectr, Trinity Coll, Scarborough Coll, 92-; lectr Knox Coll, 95-; sr fel, Harvard univ, 96-97; lectr, Univ Toronto, fel Trinity Coll, 98-. **HONORS AND AWARDS** Intl Conference Travel Grant, Univ Toronto, 90-91; SSHRCC Res Grant, 85-91; sr fel, harvard, 97. **MEMBERSHIPS** AAR; CPA; CSSR; CTS; SKS; AASSC; NAASR **RESEARCH** Kierkegaard studies; cross-cultural philosophy of religion; Islam; Hinduism; Caribbean studies. **SELECTED PUBLICATIONS** Salighed as Happiness, Wilfrid Laurier, 85; "Kierkegaard and the Glory of our Common Humanity," Joyful Wisdom v 3, Thought House, 94; "Melancholy: An Elusive Dimension of Depression," Jrnl Med Hum, 94; "The Center Out There for Early Pre-Islamic Pilgrims: Is the Kab'ah the Original Sacra of Meca," Year Book of Christian Archology Supplement, 95; "Challenge of Information Technol for Literary Studies," Jrnl of Relig & Technol Infor, 96; "Kierkegaard as Firechief in Denmark," Relig Stud, 96; "Identity, Personhood and Religion in Caribbean Context," Harvard Working Papers on Latin Am, 97. **CONTACT ADDRESS** Trinity College, Univ of Toronto, Toronto, ON, Canada M5S 1H8. **EMAIL** khanah@chass.utoronto.ca

KHUSHF, GEORGE
PERSONAL Born 07/13/1961, New York, NY, m, 1986, 3 children **DISCIPLINE** BIOETHICS **EDUCATION** Rice Univ, PhD, 93, MA. 90; Texas A&M Univ, BS, 83. **CAREER** Humanities Dir, 95-, Center for Bioethics; Asst Prof, Dept of Philos, 95-, Univ of South Carolina; Mng Ed, Journal of Med and Philos, 93-95. **MEMBERSHIPS** ASBH, APA. **RESEARCH** Concepts of Health, administrative and organizational ethics, medical epistimology. **SELECTED PUBLICATIONS** Review, Hegel and the Spirit: Philosophy as Pneumatology, by A Olson, in: The Owl of Minerva, 94; auth, Ethics, Politics and Health Care Reform, in: J of Medicine and Philosophy, 94; Grammacentrism and the Transformation of Rhetoric, in: Philosophy and Rhetoric, 95; Nursing Ethics at the Juncture of Two Kinds of Care, in: South Carolina Nurse, 97; Embryo Research: On the Ethical Geography of the Debate, Journal of Medicine and Philosophy, 97; coauth, Understanding, Assessing and Managing Conflicts of Interest, Surgical Ethics, Oxford Univ Press, 98. **CONTACT ADDRESS** 1719 Oriole, Columbia, SC 29204. **EMAIL** khushf@iopa.sc.edu

KIDD, REGGIE MCREYNOLDS
DISCIPLINE NEW TESTAMENT **EDUCATION** Col William & Mary, BA, 73; Westminster Theol Sem, MAR, 75, MDiv, 77; Duke Univ, PhD, 89. **CAREER** Instr, Duke Divinity Sch, 81-86; teaching asst, UNC, 84, 85; Correspondence Course Instr, UNC, 84-90; vist lectr, UNC, 84, 90; assoc prof, Reformed Theol Sem, 90-. **HONORS AND AWARDS** Pastor, Worship, Chapel Hill Bible Church. **MEMBERSHIPS** Soc of Biblical Lit; Evangelical Theol Soc; The Hymn Soc. **RESEARCH** Pauline epistles. **SELECTED PUBLICATIONS** Auth, "Bach, Bubba, & the Blues Brothers: The Singing Savior's Many Voices," in Reformed Quarterly, 99; auth, "Titus as Apologia: Grace for Liars, Beasts, and Bellies," in Horizons in Biblical Theology 21.2, (99): 185-209; auth, Wealth and Beneficence in the Pastoral Epistles: A "Bourgeois" Form of Early Christianity? Soc of Biblical Literature Dissertation Series 122, Atlanta: Scholars Press, 90; Rev, of Yann Redalie, Paul apres Paul: Le temps, le salut, la morale selon les epitres a Timothee et a Tite, in Journal of Biblical Literature 115/4, (96): 768-770; auth, "Colossians" and "Ephesians" in the New Geneva Study Bible, Nelson, 95; Rev, of Clinton Arnold, Ephesians: Power and Magic, The Concept of Power in Ephesians in Light of its Historical Setting, in Westminster Tehological Journal 56, (94): 201-203; Rev, of Helmut Merkel, Die Pastoralbriefe, in Journal of Biblical Literature 112, (93): 733-735. **CONTACT ADDRESS** Dept of New Testament, Reformed Theol Sem, Florida, 1231 Reformation Dr, Oviedo, FL 32765. **EMAIL** rkidd@rts.edu

KIECKHEFER, RICHARD
PERSONAL Born 06/01/1946, Minneapolis, MN, m, 1986, 2 children **DISCIPLINE** RELIGION, HISTORY **EDUCATION** Saint Louis Univ, BA, 68; Univ Tex Austin, MA Philos, 70; PhD Hist, 72. **CAREER** Instr, Univ Tex Austin, 73-74; lectr, 74; asst prof, Philips Univ, 75; asst prof, 75-79; assoc prof, 79-84, Prof, Northwest Univ, 84-. **HONORS AND AWARDS** Tchg citation from Council for Advancement and Support of Education, 82, 83; Nat Endowment for the Humanities Fel, 87-88; Guggenheim Found Fel, 92-93; Fel of Medieval Acad Of Am, 98. **MEMBERSHIPS** Medieval Acad Of Am; Am Soc of Church Hist; An Acad of Rel; Societas Magica. **RESEARCH** Late medieval religious culture-including mystical theology, magic and witchcraft, and church in relation architecture to parish religion. **SELECTED PUBLICATIONS** Auth, The holy and the unholy: sainthood, witchcraft, and magic in late medieval Europe, J of Medieval And Renaissance Studies, 94; The specific rationality of medieval magic, Am Hist Rev, 94; Forbidden Rites: A Necromancer's manual of the fifteenth Century, 98; The office of inquisition and medieval heresy: the transition from personal to institutional jurisdiction, J of Ecclesiastical Hist, 95; Avenging the blood of children: anxiety over child victims and the origins of the European witch trials, the Devil, Heresy and Witchcraft in the Middle Ages: Essays in Honor of Jeffrey B Russel, 98; The Devils' contemplative: the Liber iuratus, the Liber visionum, and Christian appropriation of Jewish occultism, Conjuring Spirits: Texts and Traditions of Medieval Ritual magic, 98; auth, Magic in the Middle Ages, new ed, Cambridge U.PR. 00. **CONTACT ADDRESS** Dept of Religion, Northwestern Univ, 1940 Sheridan Rd, Evanston, IL 60208-4050. **EMAIL** kieckhefer@northwestern.edu

KIELKOPF, CHARLES F.
PERSONAL Born 04/16/1935, St. Paul, MN, m, 1957, 5 children **DISCIPLINE** PHILOSOPHY **EDUCATION** Univ of Minn, BA, 62; PhD, 62. **CAREER** Instr, Univ of Minn, 62-63; assist prof, Ohio State, 63-69; assoc prof, Ohio State, 69-76; prof, Ohio State Univ, 76-; Full Prof, OSU, Ohio State Univ. **MEMBERSHIPS** Am Philos Asn. **RESEARCH** Metaphsics, Kant, Entailment systems. **SELECTED PUBLICATIONS** Auth, Strict Finitism, Mouton, The Hague, 70; Formal Sentential Entailment, Washinton D.C., 77; A Kantian Condemnation of Atheistic Despair, Peter Lang, Bern, 97. **CONTACT ADDRESS** Dept of Philos, Ohio State Univ, Columbus, 230 N Oval Mall, Columbus, OH 43210-1335. **EMAIL** kielkopf.1@osu.edu

KIERSKY, JAMES H.
PERSONAL Born 04/22/1946, Memphis, TN, m, 1988, 2 children **DISCIPLINE** PHILOSOPHY **EDUCATION** Washington & Lee Univ, BA, 68; Emory Univ, MA, 75, PhD, 83. **CAREER** Instr, Atlanta Jr Col, 75-78; instr, Spelman Col, 77-78; instr, lectr, Georgia Inst of Technol, 78-79; vis adj fac Atlanta Metropolitan Col, 95, Kennesay State Col, 95, DeKalb Col, 97; adj prof, Emory Univ, 83, 95-98; asst prof, Georgia State Univ, 78- . **HONORS AND AWARDS** DAAD, 76; Outstanding Teaching Awd, 78. **MEMBERSHIPS** APA; Georgia Philos Soc. **RESEARCH** Ethics; free will and determinism; social/political philosophy; logic and critical thinking; multiculturalism. **SELECTED PUBLICATIONS** Auth, Bhopal: A Case Study & Ethical Complexities Involving Multinational Corporations, in, Snoeyenbos, ed, Business Ethics, Prometheus, 93; coauth, Thinking Critically: Techniques for Logical Reasoning, West, 95; auth, Instructors Manual with Test Bank and Solutions to Accompany Thinking Critically, West, 97; auth, A Multicultural Introduction to Philosophy, West, forthcoming. **CONTACT ADDRESS** Dept of Philosophy, Emory Univ, 214 Bowden Hall, Atlanta, GA 30322. **EMAIL** phljhk@panther.gsu.edu

KIERSTEAD, MELANIE STARKS
PERSONAL Born 03/20/1960, Potsdam, NY, m, 1984, 2 children **DISCIPLINE** RELIGION **EDUCATION** Houghton Col, BA, 82; Bethany Bible Col, Ba, 83; Wesley Biblical Sem, M. Div, 86; Reformed Theolog Sem, Th.M, 87; Drew Univ, M. Phil, 93, PhD, 96 **CAREER** Tchr, Capital City Christian Acad, 87-88; prof, Phillips Junior Col, 88-89; campus pastor 96-97, prof, 89-90, 92-97, Bartlesville Wesleyan Col; asst prof, IN Wesleyan Univ, 97-. **HONORS AND AWARDS** Extraordinary People, 97, Houghton Col. **MEMBERSHIPS** Soc Biblical Lit; Am Acad Rel; Wesleyan Theolog Soc. **RESEARCH** 2nd Century Montanism; Luke-Acts; Pastorals. **SELECTED PUBLICATIONS** Auth, art, God of Comfort, 91; auth, art, The Word Inspires Confession, 95; auth, Calling God's people back to Hope, 95; auth, art, The Letter, 96; auth, art, Remembering the One True God's Faithful Love, 97. **CONTACT ADDRESS** 1723 Beechwood Blvd, Marion, IN 46952. **EMAIL** mkierstead@indwes.edu

KILCOYNE, JOHN R.
DISCIPLINE LAW **EDUCATION** Univ Victoria, LLB, 78, LLM, 84. **CAREER** Asst prof, 84-90; assoc prof, 90-. **RESEARCH** Employment law; legislation and policy; computer technology. **SELECTED PUBLICATIONS** Auth, pubs on labour relations and collective bargaining. **CONTACT ADDRESS** Fac of Law, Univ of Victoria, PO Box 2400, Victoria, BC, Canada V8W 3H7. **EMAIL** jrk@uvvm.uvic.ca

KILLEN, PATRICIA O'CONNELL
PERSONAL Born 11/30/1951, Portland, OR, m, 1975 **DISCIPLINE** RELIGION **EDUCATION** Gonzaga Univ, BA, 70; Stanford Univ, MA, 76, PhD, 87. **CAREER** Instr, 78-85, School of Theo, Univ of the South; vis Asst Prof & Asst Prof, 85-89, Univ of Chicago Loyola; Asst Prof, 89-92, Assoc Prof, 92-99, Prof, 99-, Pacific Lutheran Univ. **HONORS AND AWARDS** Arnold & Lois Graves Awd, Outstanding Humanities Prof; Burlington Northern Fac Achievement Awd; Elizabeth Seton Medal. **MEMBERSHIPS** AAR, ASCH, AHA, Cath

Theo Soc of Am; Am Cath Hist Asn; Can Cath Hist Asn; Can Soc of Church Hist. **RESEARCH** Religion in the American west, Roman Catholicism in the United States. **SELECTED PUBLICATIONS** Auth, The Irish in Washington State, in: The Encyclopedia of the Irish in America, ed, M Glazier, Univ Notre Dame Press, 00, 161-165; Finding Our Voices, Women's Wisdom and Faith, NY Crossroad Pub Co, 97; Geography Denominations and the Human Spirit, A Decade of Studies on Religion the Western United States, in: Religious Stud Rev, 95; co-auth, The Art of Theological Reflection, NY Crossroads Pub, 94; auth, "An Historians Perspective, Then Now and Then?" is in Listening a Journal of Religion and Culture 28, no 1, (93) 14-27; auth, "Graious Play: Discipline, Insight and the Common Good," Teaching Theology and Reglion, vol 4, no 1, (01): 2-8; auth, "The Geography of a Religious Minority: Roman Catholicism in the Pacific Northwest," US Catholic Historian, vol 18, no 3 (00): 51-72; auth, "Writing the Pacific Northwest into Canadian and US Catholic History: Geography, Demographics, and Regional Religion," Canadian Catholic Historical Association, Historical Studies 66 (00): 94-91; co-auth, The Catholic Experience of Small Christian Communities, (NY: Press (00); auth, "Faithless in Seattle? The WTO Protects," Religion in the News, vol 3, no 1 (00), 12-14. **CONTACT ADDRESS** Dept of Religion, Pacific Lutheran Univ, Tacoma, WA 98447. **EMAIL** killenpo@plu.edu

KIM, AI RA
PERSONAL Born 09/01/1938, Korea, s, 2 children **DISCIPLINE** RELIGION **EDUCATION** Drew Univ, PhD, 91. **CAREER** United Meth Church, ordained clergy; United Theological Sem, assoc prof, 99. **MEMBERSHIPS** AAR, RRA **RESEARCH** Women's issues in religion and culture. **SELECTED PUBLICATIONS** Auth, Women Struggling for a New Life: The Role of Religion in the Cultural Passage from Korea to America, SUNY Press, 96; Christianity and the Korean Immigrant Women in the US, in: Korean American Women Living in Two Cultures, ed Young In Song and Aileen Moon, Los Angeles: Baylor Univ Press, 97; br, Bridge Makers and Cross Bearers, (by Juug Ha Kim), in Academia Koreana, Los Angeles: Baylor Univ Press, 98; Article published in Summer, 00; Religion Humanization and World Transformation Quarterly," Review: A Journal of Theological Resources for Ministry the United Methodist Publishing House, Summer 00. **CONTACT ADDRESS** Dept of Religion & Society, United Theol Sem, 1810 Harvard Blvd., Dayton, OH 45406. **EMAIL** airakim@united.edu

KIM, CHAN-HIE
PERSONAL Born 06/07/1935, Hoeryung, Korea, m, 1962, 1 child **DISCIPLINE** BIBLICAL STUDIES; NEW TESTAMENT **EDUCATION** Yonsei Univ, BA, 58; Vanderbilt, BD, 64, PhD, 70. **CAREER** Asst prof, Yonsei Univ, 72-73; prof of new testament & christian ministries, Claremont of Theol, 77-. **MEMBERSHIPS** Soc Bibl Lit; Cal-Pac Annual Conf United Meth Church; National Assoc of Parliamentarians. **RESEARCH** New Testament; Ancient Greek epistolography **SELECTED PUBLICATIONS** Auth, Form and Function of the Greek Letter of Recommendation **CONTACT ADDRESS** 1325 N. College Ave., Claremont, CA 91711. **EMAIL** chkim@cst.edu

KIM, WONIL
PERSONAL Born 03/15/1949, Seoul, Korea, m, 1977 **DISCIPLINE** RELIGION **EDUCATION** Claremont Grad Sch, PhD. **CAREER** Asst prof, Old Testament Studies, Sch Relig, La Sierra Univ, 94-. **MEMBERSHIPS** AAR; SBL. **RESEARCH** Theology; literary theory; ideology criticism. **CONTACT ADDRESS** Dept of Religion, La Sierra Univ, 4700 Pierce St, Riverside, CA 92515-8247. **EMAIL** wkim@lasierra.edu

KIM, YONG CHOON
PERSONAL Born 01/01/1935, Pusan, Korea, m, 1965, 1 child **DISCIPLINE** ORIENTAL PHILOSOPHY & RELIGION **EDUCATION** Belhaven Col, BA, 60; Westminster Theol Sem, BD, 63, ThM, 64; Temple Univ, PhD(comp relig), 69. **CAREER** Asst prof philos & relig, Frederick Col, 66-67; asst prof Asian philos, York Col, Pa, 69-70; asst prof philos & relig, Cleveland State Univ, 70-71; asst prof philos, 71-74, assoc prof, 74-79, Prof Philos, Univ RI, 79- **HONORS AND AWARDS** Outstanding Educr of Am Awd, Outstanding Educr Am Inc, 74, Korea Found Fel, 92. **MEMBERSHIPS** Soc Asian & Comp Philos; Asn Asian Studies; Am Acad Refig. **RESEARCH** Korean philosophies and religions; Oriental thought; Ch'ondogyo thought. **SELECTED PUBLICATIONS** Aut, The Ch'ondogyo concept of the origin of man, Philos East & West, 10/72; Aspects of Ch'ondogyo social ethics, Korea Observer, 10/72; The Ch'ondogyo concept of the nature of man, Int Philos Quart, 6/73; The Ch'ondogyo Concept of Man: An Essence of Korean Thought, Pan Korea Bk Corp, 78; Oriental Thought: An Introduction to the Philosophical and Religious Thought of Asia, Littlefield, Adams & Co, 81. **CONTACT ADDRESS** Dept of Philos, Univ of Rhode Island, Kingston, RI 02881. **EMAIL** yhongkim@uri.edu

KIM, YOUNG HUM
PERSONAL Born 12/19/1920, Korea, m **DISCIPLINE** HISTORY, POLITICAL SCIENCE **EDUCATION** Schinheung Univ, Korea, BA, 53; Bradley Univ, BS, 55; Univ Southern CA, MA, 56, PhD, 60. **CAREER** Instr, Inchon Commerce Inst, Korea, 48-50; res assoc Soviet studies, Sch Int Rel, 60-61; from asst prof to assoc prof, 61-70, prof hist & polit sci, US Int Univ, CA, 70, Asst dir, Soviet-Asian Studies Ctr, Univ Southern CA. **MEMBERSHIPS** AHA; Am Polit Sci Asn; Asn Asian Studies; Am Acad Polit & Social Sci; Coun For Rel. **RESEARCH** US diplomatic hist. **SELECTED PUBLICATIONS** Auth, East Asia's Turbulent Century, Appleton, 66; Patterns of Competitive Coexistence: USA vs USSR, Putnam, 66; Struggle Against History: US Foreign Policy in an Age of Revolution, Simon & Schuster, 68; The Central Intelligence Agency: Problems of Secrecy in a Democracy, Heath, 68; Twenty Years of Crisis: The Cold War Era, Prentice-Hall, 68; American Frontier Activities in Asia: Nelson-Hall, 81; Ideology vs National Interests, USA Today, 85; Centennial History of American Diplomacy in Asia, Shinku Cultural Press, Korea, 88; Women Liberation Issue in Korea, Jeonju Univ Press, Korea, 88; War of No Return: The Korean War, 2 vol, Kwiin Publ, Korea, 88; U S-Asian Relations in the 20th Century, Edwin Mellen Press, 96. **CONTACT ADDRESS** Dept of Hist & Polit Sci, US Int Univ, 10455 Pomerado Rd, San Diego, CA 92131-1717. **EMAIL** ykim1@san.rr.com

KIM, YOUNGLAE
PERSONAL Born 07/25/1961, Korea, m, 1986, 1 child **DISCIPLINE** THEOLOGY; CHRISTIAN EDUCATION **EDUCATION** Yonsei Univ, BA, 95; Drew Univ, MDiv, 90; Yale Univ, STM, 92; Columbia Univ, PhD, 96. **CAREER** Adj Prof, Drew Univ Theol School, 97- . **MEMBERSHIPS** Relig Educ Asn. **RESEARCH** Higher education; theological education; holistic education. **SELECTED PUBLICATIONS** Auth, Broken Knowledge: The Sway of the Scientific and Scholarly Ideal at Union Theological Seminary in New York, 1887-1926, Univ Press Am, 97. **CONTACT ADDRESS** 46 Minton Ave., Chatham, NJ 07928. **EMAIL** Ylaekim@aol.com

KIMBALL, ROBERT
DISCIPLINE PHILOSOPHY **EDUCATION** Yale Univ, PhD. **CAREER** Dept Philos, Univ Louisville **RESEARCH** Intersection of epistemology. **SELECTED PUBLICATIONS** Auth, articles on the connection between thought and lang, on Wittgenstein, and on Whitehead. **CONTACT ADDRESS** Dept of Philos, Univ of Louisville, 2301 S 3rd St, Louisville, KY 40292. **EMAIL** rhkimb01@ulkyvm.louisville.edu

KIMBLE, MELVIN
DISCIPLINE PASTORAL CARE **EDUCATION** Wittenberg Univ, BA, 47; Hamma Sch Theol, MDiv, 50; S Baptist Theol Sem, ThM, 60; Univ Vienna, 60-61; US Intl Univ, PhD, 74. **CAREER** Guest prof, summer grad prog, 68, 74; vis prof, Leonard Davis Sch, Univ S Calif, 91-92; assoc prof, 65, prof, 67-99, dir of intership, 65-74, prof emer, Luther Sem, 99- . **HONORS AND AWARDS** Lutheran World Federation scholar; res award, Amer Col of Health Care Administrators, 86; Edu Found of Am award, 82; post-doctoral fel, Gerontology, Andrus Gerontology Ctr, 81-82; pastor, grace lutheran church, 50-55; calvary lutheran church, 55-58; head chaplain, miss state hospital, 59-60; pastor, amer protestant church, bonn, 61-65. **MEMBERSHIPS** Mem, Amer Soc on Aging; Assn for Hum Psychol; Gerontol Soc Am; Soc for Pastoral Theol; Viktor E. Franklin Inst of Logotherapy. **SELECTED PUBLICATIONS** Auth, Education for Ministry with the Aging, Ministry with the Aging: Designs, Challenges, Foundations, , 81; Aging and Ministry, Primary Pastoral Care, 90; Age and the Search for Meaning, Spiritual Maturity in the Later Years, 90; sr ed, Handbook on Aging, Spirituality and Religion, 95. **CONTACT ADDRESS** Dept of Pastoral Care, Luther Sem, 2481 Como Ave, Saint Paul, MN 55108. **EMAIL** mkimble@luthersem.edu

KIND, AMY L.
PERSONAL Born 01/11/1969, NJ, m, 1999 **DISCIPLINE** PHILOSOPHY **EDUCATION** Amherst Col, AB, 90; Univ Calif at Los Angeles, MA, 93; CPhil, 95; PhD, 97. **CAREER** Asst prof, Claremont McKenna Col, 97-. **HONORS AND AWARDS** Gail Kennedy Prize in Philos, Amherst Col, 90; George A. Plimpton Fel, Amherst Col, 90; Mellon Fel in the Humanities, 90-92; Univ Calif, Los Angeles, Dept of Philos Fel, 92-93; Mellon Dissertation Year Fel, 95; Collegium of Univ Teaching Fel, Univ Calif, Los Angeles, 96-97; Gould Ctr for Humanistic Studies Summer Res Grant, 98; Summer Res Grants, Claremont McKenna Col, 98 & 99. **MEMBERSHIPS** Am Philos Asn, Phi Beta Kappa. **RESEARCH** Philosophy of Mind, Metaphysics, Epistemology, Philosophy of Language, Ethics (theoretical and applied), History of Analytic Philosophy, Logic, Critical Reasoning. **SELECTED PUBLICATIONS** Auth, Instructor's Manual to accompany A Guide to Good Reasoning, McGraw Hill Pub Co. (New York, NY), 99; auth, "Patricia Smith Churchland" and "Jerry Fodor," World Philosophy: Revised Edition, 00; auth, Putting the Image Back in Imagination," Philosophy and Phenomenological Research, forthcoming. **CONTACT ADDRESS** Dept Relig & Philos, Claremont McKenna Col, 500 E 9th St, Claremont, CA 91711-5903. **EMAIL** akind@benson.mckenna.edu

KING, PATRICIA ANN
PERSONAL Born 06/12/1942, Norfolk, VA, m, 1981 **DISCIPLINE** ETHICS, LAW **EDUCATION** Wheaton Coll, BA 1963; Harvard Law School, JD 1969. **CAREER** Dept of State, budget analyst 1964-66; Equal Employment Opportunity Commn, special asst to chmn 1969-71; Dept of Health Educ & Welfare, dept dir office of civil rights 1971-73; Civil Div Dept of Justice, dep asst atty general 1980-81; Georgetown Univ, assoc prof of law 1974-88; Georgetown Univ, Law Center, prof of law, 88-. **HONORS AND AWARDS** Honorary LLD, Wheaton College 1992; Distinguished Serv Awd HEW 1973; Secretary's Special Citation HEW 1973; John Hay Whitney Fellowship John Hay Whitney Found 1968. **MEMBERSHIPS** Adj prof Johns Hopkins Sch of Hygiene and Pub Health; brd, Henry J. Kaiser Family Fnd; brd, Hospice Fnd; Amer Law Institute 1988-; National Academy of Sciences, Institute of Medicine; bd, 1987-; Natl Partnership for Women and Families; chair, brd of trustees, Wheaton Coll, 1989-. **SELECTED PUBLICATIONS** "The Juridicial Status of the Fetus" MI Law Review 1647, 1979; co-author "Law Science and Medicine" 1984. **CONTACT ADDRESS** Law Sch, Georgetown Univ, 600 New Jersey Ave NW, Washington, DC 20001.

KING, ROBERTA R.
PERSONAL Born 07/05/1949, CA, s **DISCIPLINE** MUSIC, MISSIOLOGY, ANTHROPOLOGY, ETHNOMUSICOLOGY **EDUCATION** Univ Calif Santa Barbara, BA, 72; Univ Ore, M Mus, 76, Fuller Theol Sem, MA, 82; PhD, 89. **CAREER** Lectr, Daustar Univ, Kenya, 78-99; ethnomusicologist, CBI Int, 82-99; Fuller Theol Sem, 00-. **HONORS AND AWARDS** David Allen Hubbard Awd, Fuller Sem; Regent Scholar, Univ of Calif. **MEMBERSHIPS** Soc for Ethnomusicology. **RESEARCH** African music, Communication (intercultural), ethnomusicology, Anthropology. **SELECTED PUBLICATIONS** Auth, Pathways in Christian Music Communication, Fuller Theol Sem, (Pasadena, CA), 89; auth, A Time to Sing, Evangel Pub (Nairobi, Kenya), 99. **CONTACT ADDRESS** School of World Mission, Fuller Theol Sem, 135 N Oakland Ave, Pasadena, CA 91182-0001. **EMAIL** rking@fuller.edu

KING, SALLIE B.
PERSONAL Born 03/22/1952, Washington, DC, m, 1977, 2 children **DISCIPLINE** PHILOSOPHY AND RELIGION **EDUCATION** Smith Col, BA, 73; Univ of BC, MA, 75; Temple Univ, PhD, 81. **CAREER** Lectr, State Univ of NY at Buffalo, 79-80; asst prof, Colby Col, 81-82; asst prof, Bates Col, 82-83; from asst prof to assoc prof, Southern Ill Univ at Carbondale, 83-89; dir of undergrad studies, Southern Ill Univ at Carbondale, 85-89; from assoc prof to prof, James Madison Univ, 92-; dept head, 92-97. **HONORS AND AWARDS** Japan Found Professional Fel, 83-84; Nat Endowment for the Hums, 85; Outstanding Teacher in the Col of Liberal Arts, Southern Ill Univ, 89; Edna T. Schaeffer Humanist Awd, James Madison Univ, 97. **MEMBERSHIPS** Am Acad of Relig; Am Philos Asn; Int Asn of Buddhist Studies; Asn for Asian Studies; Phi Beta Kappa; Soc for Buddhist-Christian Studies; Soc for Comp and Asian Philos. **SELECTED PUBLICATIONS** Auth, Two Epistemological Models for the Interpretation of Mysticism, in J of the Am Acad of Relig 56 (2), 88; Toward a Buddhist Model of Inter-Religious Dialogue, in Buddhist-Christian Studies 10, 90; Buddha Nature, 91; Religion as Practice, in Buddhist-Christian Studies 14, 94; On Pleasure, Choice and Authority, in Buddhist-Christian Studies 14, 94; It's a Long Way to a Global Ethic: A Response to Leonard Swidler, in Buddhist-Christian Studies 15, 95; A Buddhist Perspective on a Global Ethic and Human Rights, in J of Dharma 20 (2), 95; Charles Hartshorne: Pioneer Buddhist-Christian Dialogian, in Creative Transformation 6 (2), 97; Transformative Nonviolence: The Social Ethics of George Fox and Thich Nhat Hanh, in Buddhist-Christian Studies 18, 98; Journey in Search of the Way: The Spiritual Autobiography of Satomi Myodo, 98; coauth, Process Metaphysics and Minimalism: Implications for Public Policy, in Environmental Ethics 13, 91; A Buddhist-Christian Contribution to the Earth Charter, in Buddhist-Christian Studies 17, 97; coed, Engaged Buddhism: Buddhist Liberation Movements in Asia, 96; co-ed, The Sound of Liberating Truth: Buddhist-Christian Dialogues in Honor of Frederic J. Streng, 98; rev, Kenosis and Action: A Review Article, in Buddhist-Christian Studies 12, 92. **CONTACT ADDRESS** Dept of Philosophy and Religion, James Madison Univ, MSC 7504, Harrisonburg, VA 22807. **EMAIL** kingsb@jmu.edu

KINGHORN, KENNETH CAIN
PERSONAL Born 06/23/1930, Albany, OK, m, 1955, 4 children **DISCIPLINE** CHURCH HISTORY **EDUCATION** Ball State Univ, BS, 52; Asbury Theol Sem, BD, 62; Emory Univ, PhD, 65. **CAREER** From prof church hist to Dean Sch Theol, Asbury Theol Sem, 65-. **MEMBERSHIPS** Am Soc Church Hist. **RESEARCH** Wesley studies; Protestant Reformation; spiritual formation. **SELECTED PUBLICATIONS** Auth, Dynamic Discipleship, Fleming H Revell, 73; Fresh Wind of the Spirit, 75, Gifts of the Spirit, 76 & Christ Can Make You Fully Human, 79, Abingdon; Discovering Your Spiritual Gifts, 81 & A Celebration of Ministry, 82, Francis Asbury Publ Co; The Gospel of Grace, Abingdon, 92; auth, The Heritage of American Methodism, Abingdon, 99. **CONTACT ADDRESS** Dept of Church Hist, Asbury Theol Sem, 204 N Lexington Ave, Wilmore, KY 40390-1199. **EMAIL** ken_kinghorn@asburyseminary.edu

KINNAMAN, THEODORE J.
PERSONAL Born 02/11/1963, Galena, IL, m, 1995 **DISCIPLINE** PHILOSOPHY, RELIGION **EDUCATION** Carleton Univ, BA, 85; Univ Wis, MA, 88; PhD, 95. **CAREER** Instr Pa St Univ, 95-96; Asst Prof, George Mason Univ, 96-. **MEMBERSHIPS** APA, NAKS. **RESEARCH** History of modern philosophy, Kant. **SELECTED PUBLICATIONS** Auth, "Kant's Transcendental Deduction of the Ideas of Pure Reason," in Proceedings of the VIII Int Kant Cong (Milwaukee: Marquette UP, 95); auth, "'Ein groBer Philosoph hat behauptet': Der EinfluB Berkeleys auf Hamanns Kantkritik," in Theol and Philos (99); auth, "Symbolism and Cognition in General in Kant's 'Critique of Judgement'," in Archiv fut Geschichte der Philos (forthcoming); auth, "What is an Indeterminate Concept?" in Proceedings of the IX Int Kant Cong (forthcoming). **CONTACT ADDRESS** Dept Philos & Relig, George Mason Univ, Fairfax, 4400 University Dr, Fairfax, VA 22030-4422. **EMAIL** tkinnama@gmu.edu

KINNEY, E. D.
PERSONAL Born 01/17/1947, Boston, MA, m, 1983, 1 child **DISCIPLINE** LAW **EDUCATION** Duke Univ, AB, 69; Univ Chicago, MA, 70; Univ N Carolina, MPH, 79; Duke Univ, JD, 73. **CAREER** Prof of Law, 84- , dir, Ctr for Law and Health, 87- , Indiana Univ Sch of Law, Indianapolis. **MEMBERSHIPS** ABA; NC State Bar Asn; Am Asn of Law Schools; Nat Health Lawyers Asn; Am Soc of Law, Medicine and Ethics; Am Pub Health Asn; Indiana Pub Health Asn. **RESEARCH** Health policy; medical malpractice; quality assurance. **SELECTED PUBLICATIONS** Coauth, The Potential Role of Diabetes Guidelines in the Reduction of Medical Malpractice Claims Involving Diabetes, in Diabetes Care, 94; coauth, Bringing the Patient Back in : the Rhetoric of Victimization and Medical Malpractice, in Perspectives on Social Problems, 94; auth, Private Accreditation as a Substitute for Direct Government Regulation in Public Health Insurance Programs: When is it Appropriate?, in Law and Contemporary Problems, 94; coauth, Quality Improvement in Community-Based, Long-Term Care: Theory and Reality, in Am J of Law and Med, 94; auth, Protecting Consumers and Providers under Health Reform :An Overview of the Major Administrative Law Issues, in Health Matrix, 95; auth, Malpractice Reform in the 1990s: Past Disappointments, Future Success?, in J of Health Politics, Policy and Law, 95; coauth, Collaborative Quality Improvement in Community-Based, Long-Term Care: Translating Theory into Practice, in the Joint Commission J on Quality Improvement, 95; auth, Rule and Policy Making under Health Reform, in Admin Law Rev, 95; coauth, The Merits of State Action Antitrust Immunity to Promote Hospital Collaboration: A Good Idea for Indiana?, in Ind Law Rev, 95; auth, Resolving Consumer Grievances in a Managed Care Environment, in Health Matrix, 96; auth, Medicare Managed Care from the Beneficiary's Perspective, in Seton Hall Law Rev, 96; auth, Procedural Protections for Patients in Capitated Health Plans, in Am J of Law and Med, 96; coauth, History and Jurisprudence of the Patient-Physician Relation in Indiana, in Indiana Law Rev, 96; auth, Health Insurance Coverage in Indiana: is there a Problem, in IN-ROADS, 96; auth, Administrative Law Issues in Professional Regulation, in Regulation of the Healthcare Professions, Health Admin Pr, 97; coauth, Automating Assessment for Community-Based, Long-Term Care: Indiana's Experience, in Generations, 97; coauth, Serious Illness and Private Health Coverage: A Unique Problem Calling for Unique Solutions, in J of Law, Med & Ethics, 97; auth, Indiana's Medical Malpractice Reform Revisited: A Limited Constitutional Challenge, in Ind Law Rev, 98; auth, Consumer Grievance and Appeal Procedures in Managed Care Plans, in the Health Lawyer, 98. **CONTACT ADDRESS** 735 W New York St, Indianapolis, IN 46202. **EMAIL** ekinney@iupui.edu

KIRBY, TORRANCE W.
PERSONAL Born 07/04/1955, Red Deer, AB, Canada, m, 1980, 2 children **DISCIPLINE** RENAISSANCE & REFORMATION **EDUCATION** Dalhousie Univ,BA; MA, Oxford Univ, DPhil, 88. **CAREER** Commonwealth Schol, Christ Church, Oxford, 80-84; Fel, King's Col, Nova Scotia, 84-89; Tutor, St. John's Col, 89-96; Mem, Princeton Ctr Theol Inquiry, 96-; Prof Church Hist, Mc McGill Univ, 97-. **HONORS AND AWARDS** Univ Medal in Classics, Dalhousie, 77; Killam Fel, Dalhousie, 77-79. **MEMBERSHIPS** Am Acad Relig; Soc Christian Ethics; Sixteenth Century Studies Conf; Atlantic Theol Conf. **RESEARCH** Richard Hooker, Peter Martyr Vermigli, Reformation and Neoplatonism, Patristic Studies. **SELECTED PUBLICATIONS** Auth, Richard Hooker's Doctrine of the Royal Supremacy, Leiden, New York, Copenhagen and Cologne: E.J. Brill, 90; auth, "Richard Hooker as an Apologist of the Magisterial Reformation in England," Richard Hooker and the Construction of Christian Community, Tempe, AZ: Medieval and Renaissance Texts and Studies, (97); 219-233, auth, "Richard Hooker," The Oxford Dictionary of the Christion Church 3rd ed, Oxford University Press, (97); auth, " Praise as the Soul"s Overcoming of Time in the Confessions of St. Augustine," Pro Ecclesia: A Journal of Catholic and Evangelical Theology vol 6, (97), 333-350; auth, "Richard Hooker's Theory of Natural Law: Magisterial reform and the Question Orthodoxy," Animus vol 3, (98); auth, "the Neoplatonic Logic of Procession and Return," Richard Hooker's Discourse on Law, Animus vol 4, (99). **CONTACT ADDRESS** 3520 University St., Montreal, QC, Canada H3A 2A7. **EMAIL** tkirby@wilson.lan.mcgill.ca

KIRGIS, FREDERIC LEE
PERSONAL Born 12/29/1934, Washington, DC, m, 1997, 2 children **DISCIPLINE** LAW **EDUCATION** Univ of Calif, Berkeley, JD, 60; Yale Univ, BA, 57. **CAREER** Asst prof to prof of law, Univ of Colo, 67-73; prof of law, UCLA, 73-78; PROF OF LAW, WASHINGTON AND LEE UNIV, 78-, dean, school of law, 83-88, law alumni asn prof, 90-. **HONORS AND AWARDS** Order of the Coif, 60; Deak Prize for int law scholar by a young scholar, 74. **MEMBERSHIPS** Amer Soc for Int Law, 94-; Amer Law Inst; Amer Bar Asn. **RESEARCH** International Law. **SELECTED PUBLICATIONS** Auth, International Organizations in Their Legal Setting, 2nd edition, West Pub Co., 93; auth, Prior Consultation in International Law: A Study of State Practice, Univ Press of Va, 83; auth, The Formative Years of the American Society of International Law, Am J. Int, 96; auth, A Mythical State's Attitude Toward the Role of the United Nations in Maintaining and Restoring Peace, Ga J. Int &Comp., 96; auth, The Security Council's First Fifty Years, Am J. Int, 95; auth, Claims Settlement and the United Nations Legal Structure, in The United Nations Compensation Commission 103, 95; chapters on specialized law-making processes, shipping, & aviation, United Nations Legal Order 109, 95; auth, The Degrees of Self-Determination in the United Nations Era, Am J. Int, 94. **CONTACT ADDRESS** School of Law, Washington and Lee Univ, Lexington, VA 24450. **EMAIL** kirgisr@wlu.edu

KIRK-DUGGAN, CHERYL ANN
PERSONAL Born 07/24/1951, Lake Charles, LA, m, 1983 **DISCIPLINE** THEOLOGY, MUSICOLOGY **EDUCATION** University of Southwestern Louisiana, BA 1973; University of Texas at Austin, MM 1977; Austin Presbyterian Theological Seminary, MDiv 1987; Baylor University, PhD, 1992. **CAREER** Univ of Tex at Austin, music of Black Am coach accomp 74-77; Austin Commun Col, music of Black Am 76-77; Prairie View A&M Univ, teacher 77-78; The Actor's Inst, teacher 82-83; Williams Inst CME Church, organist, choir dir 79-83; Self-employed, professional singer, voice teacher, vocal coach 80-85; Christian Methodist Church, ordained minister, deacons orders 84, elders orders 86; Baylor Univ, Inst of Oral Hist, grad asst, 87-89, Dept of Relig, teaching asst, 89-90; Meredith Col, asst prof, 93-96; Ctr For Women & Relig, Dir, Grad Theol Union, Asst Prof, 97-; Assoc Pastor, Phillips Temple CME, Berkeley, 97- ; Ed Bd, Contagion: J of Violence, Mimesis & Cult, 94-; Asn for Black Awareness, Meredith Col, Advisor, 94-96. **HONORS AND AWARDS** University of Southwestern Louisiana, Magna Cum Laude; University of Texas at Austin, University Fellowship, 1975-77; Fund for Theological Education, Fellowship for Doctoral Studies, 1987-88, 1988-89. **MEMBERSHIPS** Pi Kappa Lambda, 1976-; Omicron Delta Kappa, 1977-; associate pastor, Trinity CME Church, 1985-86; president, Racial Ethnic Faith Comm, Austin Seminary, 1986-87; Golden Key Honor Society, 1990; Colloquim On Violence & Religion; Society of Biblical Literature; American Academy of Religion; Center for Black Music Research; Society of Chritian Ethics; American Society for Aesthetics; Sigma Alpha Iota. **SELECTED PUBLICATIONS** Carnegie Hall debut, 81; featured: "Life, Black Tress, Das Goldene Blatte, Bunte," 81, 82; recording: "Third Duke Ellington Sacred Concert," Virgil Thompson's Four Saints in Three Acts, EMI Records, 81-82; author: Lily Teaching Fellow, 95, 96; Collidge Scholar with Asn for Religion & Intellectual Life, 96; "African-American Spirituals: Exorcising Evil Through Song," A Troubling in My Soul: Womanist Perspectives on Evil and Suffering, Orbis Press, 91; "Gender, Violence and Transformation," Curing Violence: The Thought of Rene Girard, Polebridge Press, 91; African-American Special Days: 15 Complete Worship Services, Abingdon Press, 96; It's In the Blood: A Trildgy of Poetry Harvested from a Family Tree, River Vision, 96; Exorcizing Evil: A Womanist Perspective on the Spirituals, Orbis, 97; auth, Refiner's Fire: A Religious Engagement with Violence, Fortress, 00. **CONTACT ADDRESS** Ctr for Women, Religion, 2400 Ridge Rd, Berkeley, CA 94709-5298. **EMAIL** kirkdugg@gtu.edu

KIRKPATRICK, FRANK GLOYD
PERSONAL Born 08/04/1942, Washington, DC, m, 1966, 2 children **DISCIPLINE** PHILOSOPHY OF RELIGION, HISTORICAL THEOLOGY, ETHICS **EDUCATION** Trinity Col, Conn, BA, 64; Columbia Univ, MA, 66; Brown Univ, PhD(relig studies), 70. **CAREER** Teaching asst relig, Brown Univ, 67-68; asst prof, 69-78, dir individualized degree prog, 73-75, assoc prof relig, Trinity Col, Conn, 78-; prof of relig, 86-. **HONORS AND AWARDS** Charles A. Dana Research Professor, 93-95. **MEMBERSHIPS** Am Acad Relig. **RESEARCH** John Macmurray; process thought; social ethics: economics. **SELECTED PUBLICATIONS** Auth, Process of agent: Models for self and God, Thought, spring 73; Subjective becoming: an unwarranted abstraction?, Process Studies, summer 73; coauth, Bellah's beliefless religion: The objectivity of God and moral value, Philos Relig, fall 73; (with R Nolan), Living Issues in Ethics, Wadsworth, 82; Community, Georgetown Univ Press, 86; Together Bound, Oxford Univ Press, 94. **CONTACT ADDRESS** Dept of Relig, Trinity Col, Connecticut, 300 Summit St, Hartford, CT 06106-3186. **EMAIL** fkirkpatrick@mail.trincoll.edu

KIRKPATRICK, W. DAVID
PERSONAL m, 2 children **DISCIPLINE** THEOLOGY **EDUCATION** Baylor Univ, MA, 64; Southwestern Baptist Theol Sem, MDiv, 69, ThD, 74; addn stud, Univ Cambridge, 86. **CAREER** Grad tchg asst, Baylor Univ, 63-64; instr, Dallas Baptist Col, 65-69; Dallas Community Col, 70; assoc prof, Wayland Baptist Col, 71-75; prof, Southwestern Baptist Theol Sem, 80-. **HONORS AND AWARDS** Albert Venting Awd, 68; Kenneth Moore Scholar Grad Stud, 69-74. **MEMBERSHIPS** Soc Biblical Lit; Amer Acad Rel, Southwestern Assoc Baptist Prof Rel; Nat Assn Baptist Prof Rel. **SELECTED PUBLICATIONS** Auth, Creation, Southwestern Jour Theol, 81; Theol Sects and Cults, Word and Way, 78. **CONTACT ADDRESS** Sch Theol, Southwestern Baptist Theol Sem, PO Box 22000, Fort Worth, TX 76122-0418.

KIRSCHNER, TERESA
PERSONAL Born Barcelona, Spain **DISCIPLINE** SPANISH, SPANISH LITERATURE **EDUCATION** Lycee Francis de Barcelone, Baccalaureate Studs; Roosevelt Univ, Chicago, BA, 62; Univ Chicago, MA, 64, PhD, 73. **CAREER** Lectr, Spanish, Ind Univ, 66-67; instr, 67-74, asst prof, 74-81, assoc prof, 81-90, Prof, Simon Fraser Univ, 90-. **HONORS AND AWARDS** Univ Fel, Univ Chicago, 65-66; Prize, best book, Can Asn Hispanists, 81; Excellence in Tchg Awd, Simon Fraser Univ, 87; Killam Res Fel, 95. **MEMBERSHIPS** Can Comn UNESCO; SSHRCC; Can FedN Hum; Can Asn Hispanists; MLA; Can Asn Univ Tchrs; N Am Catalan Soc; Can Asn Latin Am & Caribbean Studs. **SELECTED PUBLICATIONS** Auth, El protagonista colectivo en Fuenteovejuna de Lope de Vega, 79; auth, The Mob in Shakespeare and Lope de Vega, in Parallel Lives: Spanish and English National Drama, 1580-1680, 91; auth, The Staging of the Conquest in a Play by Lope de Vega, in Pacific Coast Philol, 92; auth, Typology of Staging in Lope de Vega's Theatre, in The Golden Age Comedia Text, Theory and Performance, 94. **CONTACT ADDRESS** Hum Prog, Simon Fraser Univ, Burnaby, BC, Canada V5A 1S6. **EMAIL** teresa_kirschner@sfu.ca

KIRSHBAUM, HAL
DISCIPLINE PHILOSOPHY **EDUCATION** Antioch Col, BA; Univ Calif Berkeley, MA, PhD. **CAREER** Prof. **RESEARCH** Philosophy of science; infant mental health; language and anthropology; ericksonian hypnosis; social philosophy; psychology of physical disability; family therapy. **SELECTED PUBLICATIONS** Auth, Disability and Humiliation, J Primary Prevention, 91; The Americans With Disabilities Act: An Opinion, Network, 91; Theories of Infant Development, 89. **CONTACT ADDRESS** Philosophy Dept, Union Inst, 440 E McMillan St, Cincinnati, OH 45206-1925.

KIRTLAND, ROBERT
PERSONAL Born 07/09/1929, Toledo, OH, s **DISCIPLINE** LAW **EDUCATION** St Peter's Col, BA; Univ Mich, MA, PhD. **CAREER** Adj prof. **RESEARCH** Corporation, origins and development. **SELECTED PUBLICATIONS** Auth, George Wythe, Lawyer, Revolutionary, Judge, 85. **CONTACT ADDRESS** Col Law, Univ of Toledo, Toledo, OH 43606. **EMAIL** rkivtla@iopener.net

KIS, MIROSLAV M.
PERSONAL Born 11/06/1942, Miklusevci, Croatia, m, 1971, 2 children **DISCIPLINE** ETHICS **EDUCATION** SAS FRance, BA, 74; Andrews Univ, MDiv, 76; Mcgill Univ, PhD, 83. **CAREER** Asst Prof, 83-86, Assoc Prof, 86-90, Prof, Christian Ethics, 90-, Andrews Univ. **CONTACT ADDRESS** SDA Theol Sem, Andrews Univ, Berrien Springs, MI 49104.

KISIEL, THEODORE JOSEPH
PERSONAL Born 10/30/1930, Brackenridge, PA, m, 1963, 2 children **DISCIPLINE** PHILOSOPHY **EDUCATION** Univ Pittsburgh, BS, 52; Duquesne Univ, MA, 61; PhD(philos), 62. **CAREER** Res metallurgist, Armour Res Found, 52-53; nuclear engr, Westinghouse Atomic Power Div, 53-58; asst prof philos, Canisius Col, 63-69; Prof Philos, Northern Ill Univ, 69-, Alexander von Humboldt Found sr fel philos, 70-71, 74, 81, 82; ed adv, Z fur Allgemeine Wissenschaftstheorie, 71-; vis prof philos, Northwestern Univ, 73-74; vis prof philos, Duquesne Univ, 75; Am Coun Learned Soc res fel philos, 77-78; Ger Acad Exchange Service sr fel philos, 83, 93; Fulbright res fel philos, 84-85, Germany; Fulbright prof, Bochum, Germany, 89; Presidential res prof, NIU, 98-02. **HONORS AND AWARDS** NEH transl grant, 81-83; NEH travel to collections grant, 84, 87; Inter Nationes transl award, 85. **MEMBERSHIPS** AAUP; APA; SPEP; Deutsche Schillergesellschaft. **RESEARCH** Phenomenology; philosophy of science; history of 19th & 20th century continental philosophy. **SELECTED PUBLICATIONS** Coauth, Phenomenology and the Natural Sciences, 70 & cotranslr, Werner Marx, Heidegger and the Tradition, 71, Northwestern Univ; auth, Scientific discovery: Logical, psychological, or hermeneutical?, In: Explorations in Phenomenology, Nijhoff, The Hague, 73; On the dimensions of a phenomenology of science in Husserl and the younger Dr Heidegger, J Brit Soc Phenomenol, 73; Aphasiology, phenomenology of perception, and the shades of structuralism, In: Language & Language Disturbances, Duquesne Univ, 74; New philosophies of science in the USA: A selective survey, Z fur Allgemeine Wissenschafts-

theorie, 74; Heidegger and the new images of science, Res Phenomenol, 77; Habermas' purge of pure theory: Critical theory without ontology?, Human Studies, 4/78; translr, Martin Heidegger, History of the Concept of Time, Ind Univ, 85; auth, The Genesis of Heidegger's Being and Time, Univ Calif, 93; co-ed, Reading Heidegger from the Start, State Univ NY, 94; Why Students of Heidegger Will Have to Read Emil Lask, Man and World, 95; Heidegger's Gesamtausgabe: An International Scandal of Scholarship, Phil Today, 95; A Hermeneutics of the Natural Sciences? The Debate Updated, Mand and World, 97; Die formale Anzeige: Die methodische Geheimwaffe des fruehen Heidegger, In: Heidegger - neu gelesen, Koenigshausen & Neumann, Wuerzburg, 97; auth, "Man and World," 97; auth, "Situating Rhetorical Politics in Heidegger's Protopractical Ontology, Interntl J Philos Studies, 00. **CONTACT ADDRESS** Dept of Philos, No Illinois Univ, 1425 W Lincoln Hwy, De Kalb, IL 60115-2825. **EMAIL** tkisiel@niu.edu

KISSLING, PAUL J.
PERSONAL Born 08/03/1967, Toledo, OH, m, 1999, 2 children **DISCIPLINE** RELIGION **EDUCATION** Great Lake Christian College, THM, Trinity Evangelical Divinity School; Lincoln Christian Seminary, MDiv. **CAREER** Prof of Old Testament and Biblical Language, Great Lakes Christian College, 91-. **MEMBERSHIPS** Society of Biblical Literature; Institute for Biblical Research. **RESEARCH** Hebrew Narrative and Theology. **SELECTED PUBLICATIONS** Auth, "Reliable Characters in the Primary History," Sheffield: Sheffield Academic Press, 96; auth, "A Sketch of Old Testament Theology," Lansing, MJ: GLCC Press, 99. **CONTACT ADDRESS** Dept Religion, Great Lakes Christian Col, 6211 West Willow Highway, Lansing, MI 48917-1231. **EMAIL** pkissling@glcc.edu

KISTEMAKER, SIMON
DISCIPLINE NEW TESTAMENT **EDUCATION** Free Univ Amsterdam, PhD. **CAREER** John and Frances Gwin prof, dept ch, RTS/Jackson; prof emer, Reformed Theol Sem. **HONORS AND AWARDS** Gold Medallion, Evangel Bk of the Yr Awd, New Testament Commentary; past pres, evangel theol soc. **SELECTED PUBLICATIONS** Auth, New Testament Commentary; The Parables of Jesus; The Gospels in Current Study. **CONTACT ADDRESS** Dept of New Testament, Reformed Theol Sem, Florida, 1231 Reformation Dr, Oviedo, FL 32765. **EMAIL** skistemaker@rts.edu

KITCHEL, MARY JEAN
PERSONAL Born New York, NY **DISCIPLINE** PHILOSOPHY, MEDIEVAL STUDIES **EDUCATION** Rice Univ, BA, 64; Pontif Inst Mediaeval Studies, MSL, 68; Univ Toronto, PhD, 74. **CAREER** Asst prof philos, Univ St Thomas, TX, 68-69; asst prof, Emmanuel Col, MA, 69-74; loan asst, Student Financial Aid, Houston Community Col Syst, 76-77; asst prof, 77-79, assoc dean extended educ, 80-82, Assoc Prof Philos, Univ St Thomas, TX, 79-88, Prof Phil, 88-, Dean Acad Serv, 90-93, Dept Ch Phil, 96-, Asst prof church hist, St Mary's Sem, TX, 68-69; res assoc philos & text ed, Pontif Inst Mediaeval Studies, Toronto, 73-75; Nat Endowment for Hum grant, 79. **HONORS AND AWARDS** Piper Professorship, 90; Sears-Roebuck Found Awd, 90 **MEMBERSHIPS** Am Cath Philos Asn. **RESEARCH** Ed and analysis of texts of Walter Burley; philos psychol, philos of hum person; medl ethics. **SELECTED PUBLICATIONS** Auth, The De potentis animae of Walter Burley, 71, Walter Burley's Doctrine of the Soul: Another view, 77 Mediaeval Studies; Walter Burley and radical Aristotelanism, Proc World Cong on Aristotle (in press). **CONTACT ADDRESS** Dept of Philos, Univ of St. Thomas, Texas, 3800 Montrose, Houston, TX 77006-4696. **EMAIL** kitchel@stthom.edu

KITCHENER, RICHARD F.
DISCIPLINE PHILOSOPHY **EDUCATION** Univ Minn, PhD, 70. **CAREER** Prof. **RESEARCH** Philosophy of science. **SELECTED PUBLICATIONS** Ed, New Ideas in Psychology and author of Piaget's Theory of Knowledge, 86; The World View of Contemporary Physics: Does it Need a New Metaphysics?, 88; Psychology and Philosophy, 94. **CONTACT ADDRESS** Philosophy Dept, Colorado State Univ, Fort Collins, CO 80523.

KITCHER, PATRICIA
PERSONAL Born 05/21/1948, New Haven, CT, m, 1971, 2 children **DISCIPLINE** PHILOSOPHY **EDUCATION** Wellesley, BA, 70; Princeton Univ, PhD, 74. **CAREER** Univ Vermont; Univ of Minnesota, Univ Calif, San Diego, Columbia Univ. **RESEARCH** Philosophy of Kant and the philosophy of psychology. **SELECTED PUBLICATIONS** Auth, "Revisiting Kant's Epistemology," Nous, 95; "From Neurophilosophy to Neurocomputation:Searching for the Cognitive Forest," The Churchlands and their Critics. Blackwell's, 95; auth, "Kant on Self Consciousness," Philosophical Review (99); auth, "On Interpreting Kant!" Thinlaw as Wittgenstein!" Philosophy and Phenomenological Research (00). **CONTACT ADDRESS** Dept of Philos, Columbia Univ, Mail code 4971, New York, NY 10027. **EMAIL** pk206@columbia.edu

KITCHER, PHILIP
PERSONAL Born 02/20/1947, London, England, m, 1971, 2 children **DISCIPLINE** PHILOSOPHY OF SCIENCE **EDUCATION** Cambridge, BA, 69; PhD, Princeton, 74. **CAREER** Asst prof, Vassar Coll, 73-74; asst prof, Univ Vt, 74-78; vis asst prof, Univ Mich, 79; assoc prof, Univ Vt, 70-83; prof, Univ Minn, 83-86; dir, Minn Center Philos Sci, 84-86; prof, Univ Calif San Diego, 86-99; presidential prof, 93-; Prof of Philos, Columbia Univ, 00-. **HONORS AND AWARDS** Henry Schuman Prize, 71; ACLS Study Fel, 81-82; Univ Vt Distinguished Scholar in Humanities and Soc Sci. **MEMBERSHIPS** US Comt, Int Union of Logic, Methodology and Philos of Sci; ICSU Working Group for Oxford Univ Press; NIH/DOE Working Group on the Ethical, Legal, and Soc Implications of the Human Genome Proj. **RESEARCH** Ethical Issues in Contemporary Biology; History and Philosophy of Biology; Growth of Scientific Knowledge; Scientific Explanation; Realism; Naturalistic Epistemology; Philosophy of Social Sciences; History and Philosophy of Mathematics. **SELECTED PUBLICATIONS** Auth, Abusing Science: The Case Against Creationism, 82; The Nature of Mathematical Knowledge, 83; Vaulting Ambition: Sociobiology and the Quest for Human Nature, 85; The Advancement of Science, 93; The Lives to Come: The Genetic Revolution and Human Possibilities, 96. **CONTACT ADDRESS** Dept of Philos, Columbia Univ, New York, NY 10027. **EMAIL** psk16@columbia.edu

KITCHING, BENITA
PERSONAL Born 02/10/1944, Springfield, IL **DISCIPLINE** PHILOSOPHY **EDUCATION** Univ Ill, Chicago, PhD, 88. **CAREER** Vis lectr, Southern Ill Univ, Edwardsville, 81; vis lectr, Univ Ill, Springfield, 90. **HONORS AND AWARDS** Phi Beta Kappa; Richter Scholar; Magna Cum Laude. **MEMBERSHIPS** APA. **RESEARCH** Aesthetics; philosophical treatment of the spiritual. **CONTACT ADDRESS** 820 S English Ave, Springfield, IL 62704.

KITTAY, EVA FEDER
PERSONAL Born 08/13/1946, Malmo, Sweden, m, 1967, 2 children **DISCIPLINE** PHILOSOPHY **EDUCATION** Sarah Lawrence Col, BA, 67; CUNY, PhD, 78. **CAREER** Adj lectr, John Jay College of Criminal Justice, CUNY, 85; adj lectr, Lehman Col, CUNY, 74, 75; vis asst prof, Univ Md, College Park, 78-79; asst prof, 79-86, assoc prof, 86-93, prof, 93- , SUNY at Stony Brook; vis prof, Sarah Lawrence Col, 93. **HONORS AND AWARDS** SUNY summer fel, 82; res asst award, 81-82; subvention, Soc for Philos and Public Affairs, 84; Exxon Educ Found, 84-86; tchg commend, 86; AUUP travel grant, 87; NSF grant, 89; ACLS travel grant; Founders Fel AAUW, 89-90; CUNY Alumni Assoc Annual Achievement Awd, 92. **MEMBERSHIPS** Soc for Women in Philos, NY chap & Eastern Div; APA; Philos of Sci Asn; Soc for Philos and Psychol; Soc for Philos and Public Affairs; Soc for Women in Philos; NY Acad of Sci; Soc for Philos for Social Responsibility. **RESEARCH** Feminist theory; philosophy and public policy; philosophy of language. **SELECTED PUBLICATIONS** Auth, Metaphor: Its Linguistic Structure and Its Cognitive Force, Oxford, 87; co-ed, Women and Moral Theory, Rowman and Littlefield, 87; co-ed, Frames, Fields and Contrasts: New Essays in Semantics and Lexical Organization, Lawrence Erlbaum, 92; auth, Social Policy and Feminist Theory, in Jaggar, ed, Blackwell's Companion to Feminist Philosophy, Blackwell, 98; auth, Welfare, Dependency and a Public Ethic of Care, Social Justice, 98; auth, On Dependency and Welfare Justice: The Case for Scholarship and Activism, Feminist Stud, 98; auth, Love's Labor: Essays on Equality and Dependency, Routledge, 99; coauth, Concerning Expressivity and the Ethics of Selective Abortion for Disability: Conversations with My Son, in Haber, ed, Norms and Values: Essays in Honor of Virginia Held, forthcoming; auth, Not My Way, Sesha, Your Way, Slowly: Maternal Thinking in the Raising of a Child with Profound Intellectual Disabilities, in Hanisberg, ed, On Behalf of Mothers: Legal Theorists, Philosophers and Theologians Reflect on Dilemmas of Parenting, Beacon, forthcoming. **CONTACT ADDRESS** Dept of Philosophy, SUNY, Stony Brook, Stony Brook, NY 11794-3750. **EMAIL** ekittay@ccmail.sunysb.edu

KITTELSON, JAMES
DISCIPLINE CHURCH HISTORY **EDUCATION** St. Olaf Col, Phi Beta Kappa grad, 63; Stanford Univ, MA, 64, PhD, 69. **CAREER** Instr, Ohio State Univ, 71; vice-ch, Ohio State Univ, 74-77; ch, grad stud, Ohio State Univ, 89-91; vis grad prof, Luther Northwestern Theol Sem, 92; Concordia Univ. 97; prof, 97-; dir, Lutheran Brotherhood Res Prog. **HONORS AND AWARDS** Pres, bd of the Sixteenth Century Stud (s) Conf; exec comm, Coun Amer Soc for Reformation Res; Soc for Reformation Res; bd of dir(s), Ctr for Reformation Res. **SELECTED PUBLICATIONS** Auth, Luther the Reformer: The Story of the Man and His Career, 86; sr ed, Oxford Encycl of the Reformation, 96. **CONTACT ADDRESS** Dept of Church History, Luther Sem, 2481 Como Ave, Saint Paul, MN 55108. **EMAIL** jkittels@luthersem.edu

KITTS, MARGO
PERSONAL Born Colusa, CA, d, 1 child **DISCIPLINE** RELIGION **EDUCATION** Univ Calif, BA; MA; PhD, 94. **CAREER** Asst Prof, Merrimack Col, 96-. **HONORS AND AWARDS** Fac Development Grant, Merrimack Col, 00. **MEMBERSHIPS** MLA, AHR, CTS. **RESEARCH** Homeric epics; Religion; Sacrifice and violence; Women and religion. **SELECTED PUBLICATIONS** Auth, "The Wide Bosom of the Sea, Maternal and Sacrificial Imagery in Iliad 21," in Literature and Theology, Oxford Univ Press, forthcoming; auth, "Killing, Healing, and the Hidden Motif of Oath-Sacrifice in Iliad 21," Journal of Ritual Studies, (99): 42-56; auth, "Two Expressions for Human Mortality in the Epics of Homer," History of Religions, (94): 132-151; auth, "The Sacrifice of Lykaon, Iliad 21," Metis, (92): 161-176. **CONTACT ADDRESS** Dept Relig Studies, Merrimack Col, 315 Turnpike St, North Andover, MA 01845-5806.

KIVY, PETER NATHAN
PERSONAL Born 10/22/1934, New York, NY **DISCIPLINE** PHILOSOPHY **EDUCATION** Univ Mich, AB, 56, MA, 58; Yale Univ, MA, 60; Columbia Univ, PhD(philos), 66. **CAREER** From asst prof to assoc prof, 67-76, Prof Philos, Rutgers Univ, 76- **HONORS AND AWARDS** Deems Taylor Awd, Am Soc Composers. **MEMBERSHIPS** Am Soc Aesthet; Am Musicol Soc; Am Philos Asn. **RESEARCH** Aesthetics; 18th century philosophy; music aesthetics. **SELECTED PUBLICATIONS** Auth, Hume's standard of taste: Breaking the circle, Brit J Aesthet, 67; Child Mozart as an aesthetic symbol, J Hist Ideas, 67; Aesthetic aspects and aesthetic qualities, J Philos, 68; Speaking of Art, 73 & ed, Francis Hutcheson: Inquiry Concerning Beauty, Order, Harmony, Design, 73, Martinus Nijhoff; The Seventh Sense, B Franklin, 76; The Corded Shell: Reflections on Musical Expression, Princeton Univ Press, 80. **CONTACT ADDRESS** Dept of Philos, Rutgers, The State Univ of New Jersey, New Brunswick, P O Box 270, New Brunswick, NJ 08903-0270.

KLAASSEN, WALTER
PERSONAL Born 05/27/1926, Laird, SK, Canada, m, 1952, 3 children **DISCIPLINE** HISTORY, THEOLOGY **EDUCATION** McMaster Univ, BA, 54; McMaster Divinity Sch, BD, 57; Oxford Univ, DPhil(hist theol), 60. **CAREER** Assoc prof Bible, Bethel Col, Kans, 60-62, chmn dept Bible and relig, 62-64; assoc prof Bible and relig, 64-70, assoc prof hist, 71-73, Prof Hist, Conrad Grebel Col, Univ Waterloo, 73-; Can Coun grants, 70-73 and 78-79. **MEMBERSHIPS** Am Soc Church Hist; Can Soc Church Hist; Mennonitischer Geschichtsverein; NAm Comt for Doc Free Church Origins (secy, 71). **RESEARCH** Just war theory; dissent in the 16th century; unilateral peace initiatives in history. **SELECTED PUBLICATIONS** Jesus, A Crucified Pharisee, J Ecumenical Studies, Vol 0029, 92; Homosexuality in the Church in Both Sides of the Debate, J Ecumenical Studies, Vol 0033, 96. **CONTACT ADDRESS** Conrad Grebel Col, Univ of Waterloo, 200 Westmount Rd, Waterloo, ON, Canada N2L 3G6.

KLAGGE, JAMES C.
PERSONAL Born 10/14/1954, Cleveland, OH, 2 children **DISCIPLINE** PHILOSOPHY **EDUCATION** Col William & Mary, AB, 76; UCLA, PhD, 83. **CAREER** Visiting Asst Prof, UCSD, 83-85; Asst to Assoc Prof, Va Tech Inst, 85-. **CONTACT ADDRESS** Dept Philos, Virginia Polytech Inst and State Univ, Blacksburg, VA 24061-0126. **EMAIL** jklagge@vt.edu

KLARE, KARL E.
PERSONAL Born 01/08/1947, New York, NY **DISCIPLINE** LAW **EDUCATION** Columbia Col, BA, 67; Yale Univ, MA, 68; Harvard Univ, JD, 75. **CAREER** Instr polit sci, Adelphi Univ, 69-72; staff atty, Nat Labor Relations Bd, 75-76; assoc, Segal, Roitman & Coleman, 76-77; assoc prof, 77-80, Prof Law, Northeastern Univ, Mass, 80-. **MEMBERSHIPS** Conf Critical Legal Studies. **RESEARCH** Labor law; law and social theory; legal history. **SELECTED PUBLICATIONS** co-ed, The Unknown Dimension: European Marxism Since Lenin, Basic Bks, 72; auth, Judicial Deradicalization of the Wagner Act, Minn Law Rev, Vol 62, 78; Labor Law as Ideology, Indust Relations Law J, Vol 4, 81. **CONTACT ADDRESS** Sch of Law, Northeastern Univ, 400 Huntington Ave, 48 Cargill Hall, Boston, MA 02115. **EMAIL** k.klare@nunet.neu.edu

KLARE, MICHAEL T.
PERSONAL Born 10/14/1942, New York, NY, 1 child **DISCIPLINE** INTERNATIONAL PEACE & SECURITY STUDIES **EDUCATION** Columbia Col, BA, 63; Columbia Univ, MA, 68; Union Inst, PhD, 76. **CAREER** Dir, Nat Security Proj, Inst for Policy Stud, Wash, DC, 76-84; Five Col Prof of Peace & World Security Stud, Hampshire Col, 85-. **MEMBERSHIPS** Comm on Int Security Stud; Am Acad of Arts & Sci. **RESEARCH** Military strategy; arms control & disarmament. **SELECTED PUBLICATIONS** Auth, War Without End, Knopf, 72; auth, American Arms Supermarket, Univ Tex Press, 84; co-ed, Low Intensity Warfare, Pantheon, 88; auth, Rogue States and Nuclear Outlaws, Hill & Wang, 95; co-ed, Lethal Commerce, Am Acad of Arts & Sci, 95; co-ed, World Security, 3rd ed, St. Martin's Press, 97; coed, Light Weapons and Civil Conflict, Rowman and Littlefield, 99. **CONTACT ADDRESS** Peace & World Security Stud, Hampshire Col, Amherst, MA 01002. **EMAIL** mklare@hampshire.edu

KLASS, DENNIS
DISCIPLINE RELIGION **EDUCATION** Elmhurst Col, BA, 63; Andover Newton Theol Schl, BD, 67; Univ Chicago MA, 70, Phd, 74. **CAREER** Res fel, 68-69, crse asst and clin supvr, Univ Chicago, 69; fac, 71-, adj fac, 75-92, prof, Webster Univ; ed bd, Omega:J of Death & Dying, Death Stud; mng ed, Relig & Educ. **HONORS AND AWARDS** Appreciation Awd, Nat Bd of The Compassionate Friends, 92; Kemper Awd for Outstanding Tchg, 95. **SELECTED PUBLICATIONS** Auth, Solace and Immortality: Bereaved Parents' Continuing Bond with Their Children, in George E. Dickinson, Michael R. Leming, and Alan C. Mermann, eds, Dying, Death, and Bereavement, 2nd ed, Dushkin Publ Gp, 94; Death and Spirituality, in Hannelore Wass and Robert A. Neimeyer, eds, Dying: Facing the Facts, 3rd ed, Taylor and Francis, 95; The Deceased Child in the Psychic and Social Worlds of Bereaved Parents during the Resolution of Grief, In Dennis Klass, Phyllis Silverman, and Steven Nickman, eds, Continuing Bonds: New Understandings of Grief, Taylor & Francis, 95; Continuing Bonds in Japanese Ancestor Worship, in Dennis Klass, Phyllis Silverman, and Steven Nickman, eds, Continuing Bonds: New Understandings of Grief, Taylor & Francis, 95 ; Managing Bonds with the Dead: Japanese Ancestor Worship, The Forum, Nov/Dec, 95; coauth, Grief and the Role of the Inner Representation of the Deceased, Omega 30:4, 94-95; Continuing Bonds: New Understandings of Griefed, Taylor & Francis, 96. **CONTACT ADDRESS** Webster Univ, Saint Louis, MO 63119. **EMAIL** klassde@websteruniv.edu

KLASSEN, WILLIAM
PERSONAL Born 05/18/1930, Halbstadt, MB, Canada, m, 1977, 3 children **DISCIPLINE** RELIGION **EDUCATION** Goshen Col, BA, 52, BD, 54; Princeton Theol Sem, PhD(New Testament), 60. **CAREER** Instr Greek, Goshen Col, 57-58; Instr New Testament, Mennonite Bibl Sem, 58-62, from assoc prof to prof, 62-69; Prof relig, Univ Man, 69-82, Head dept, 71-82; Dir Develop, Simon Fraser Univ, Burnaby, BC, 82-; Menninger Found fel, 61-62; Vis prof, NY Theol Sem, 64-65; Exec dir, Mennonite Ment Health Serv, Inc, 65-66; Asst prof, Univ Notre Dame, 68-69; Instr, Ind Univ, South Bend, 68-69; Can Coun leave fel, 73-74; Fel, Ecumenical Inst Advan Theol Studies, Jerusalem, 73-74. **HONORS AND AWARDS** John F Funk lectr, 63; Menno Simons lectr, 64; Weyerhaueser lectr, McCormick Theol Sem, 67. **MEMBERSHIPS** Am Acad Relig; Soc Studies New Testament; Soc Bibl Lit; Can Soc Studies Relig; Int Asn Hist Relig. **RESEARCH** Stoic ethics; reformation history, especially hermeneutics; women in the early Christian movement. **SELECTED PUBLICATIONS** Auth, Theology, Cath Hist Rev, vol 0080, 94; The Sacred Kiss in the New Testament in An Example of Social Boundary Lines, New Testament Studies, vol 0039, 93; Galilean Upstarts, Jesus 1st Followers According to Q, Rev Bibl, vol 0102, 95. **CONTACT ADDRESS** Dept of Relig, Univ of Manitoba, Winnipeg, MB, Canada R3T 2N2.

KLEBBA, JAMES MARSHALL
PERSONAL Born 09/08/1942, Jefferson City, MO, m, 1968, 1 child **DISCIPLINE** LAW **EDUCATION** St John's Univ, BA, 64; Harvard Univ, JD, 67. **CAREER** Prof Law, Sch Law, 73- , assoc dean, 83-89, 97-99, interim dean, 89-90, Loyola Univ; Vis prof, Kansas Univ, 76, Sch Law, Univ Minn, 81-82 & Sch Law, Univ Mo, 81; consult, Comt Civil Rules, Minn Supreme Ct, 81-82; mem adv comt on code of civil procedure, La Law Inst, 82- **MEMBERSHIPS** Am Bar Asn; Asn Am Law Schs (chemn, Civil Procedure Sect, 78-79). **RESEARCH** Civil procedure; evidence; environmental law; water rights and water resources; comparative judicial systems. **SELECTED PUBLICATIONS** Auth, The fifth circuit and environment: The quest for effective review of agency action, 74 & Fifth circuit symposium: Federal jurisdiction and civil procedure, 77, Loyola Law Rev; Insuring solar access on retrofits: The problem and some solutions, Solar Eng Mag, 1/80; auth, Water REsources for Louisiana, 82; auth, Legal and Institutional Analysis of Louisiana's Water Laws, 83; coauth, Evidence Cases and Problems, 1995; auth, Conflict and Cooperation in the American Judicial System, Univ Budapest Law Rev, 97. **CONTACT ADDRESS** Dept of Law, Loyola Univ, New Orleans, 7214 St Charles Ave, New Orleans, LA 70118-6195. **EMAIL** klebba@loyno.edu

KLECK, GARY
PERSONAL Born 03/02/1951, Elmhurst, IL, m, 1982, 2 children **DISCIPLINE** CRIMINOLOGY **EDUCATION** Univ of Ill, AB, 73, AM, 75, PhD, 79. **CAREER** Instr, 78-79, asst prof, 79-84, assoc prof, 84-91; prof, School of Criminology and Criminal Justice, Fla State Univ, 91-. **HONORS AND AWARDS** Univ of Ill Found Fel; Michael J. Hindelang Awd of the Am Soc of Criminology. **MEMBERSHIPS** Am Soc of Criminology. **RESEARCH** Firearms and violence; crime control. **SELECTED PUBLICATIONS** Auth, Point Blank, 91; Targeting Guns, 97; The Great American Gun Debate, 97. **CONTACT ADDRESS** School of Criminology and Criminal Justice, Florida State Univ, 306 Hecht House, Tallahassee, FL 32306-1127. **EMAIL** gkleck@mailer.fsu.edu

KLEHR, HARVEY
PERSONAL Born 12/25/1945, Newark, NJ, m, 1998, 3 children **DISCIPLINE** POLITICAL SCIENCE **EDUCATION** Franklin and Marshall Col, BA, 67; Univ NC, PhD, 71. **CAREER** Asst prof, assoc prof, prof, Emory Univ, 71-; Samuel Candler Dobbs prof polit, 86-95; Andrew Mellon prof polis and hist, 96-. **HONORS AND AWARDS** Emory Williams tchg award, 83; F&M Alumni medal, 85; scholar/tchr of the year award, 95; Thomas Jefferson Awd, 99. **MEMBERSHIPS** Am Polit Sci Asn; Orgn of Am Hist. **RESEARCH** Am Communism; Soviet espionage. **SELECTED PUBLICATIONS** Auth, the Heyday of American Communism: The Depression Decade, Basic, 84; auth, Far Left of Center: The American Radical Left Today, Transaction, 88; coauth, The American Communist Movement: Storming Heaven Itself, Twayne, 92; coauth, The Secret World of American Communism, Yale, 95; coauth, The American Spy Case: Prelude to McCarthyism, Univ North Carolina, 96; coauth, The Soviet World of American Communism, Yale, 98; auth, Venona: Decoding Soviet Espionage in America, Yale Univ Press, 99. **CONTACT ADDRESS** Political Science Dept, Emory Univ, Atlanta, GA 30322. **EMAIL** polshk@emory.edu

KLEIMAN, LOWELL
DISCIPLINE PHILOSOPHY **EDUCATION** Brooklyn Col, BA, 64; NYork Univ, MA, 66; PhD, 72. **CAREER** Prof of Philos, Suffolk Community Col, 68-, Head, Dept of Philos, 94-. **HONORS AND AWARDS** NEH Fel in Residence for Col Teachers, Richard Rorty, Princeton Univ, 76-77; Mellon Found Fel, 81, 87; NEH Fel, summer 82. **MEMBERSHIPS** Am Philos Asn, Long Island Philos Soc. **SELECTED PUBLICATIONS** Auth, "Morality As The Best Explanation," Am Philos Quart, Vol 26, No 2 (April 89): 161-167; coauth with Stephen Lewis, Philosophy: An Introduction Through Literature, NY: Paragon House Pubs (spring 90, reprinted 92); coauth with Ed Erwin and Sidney Gendin, The Ethics of Scientific Research, NY: Garland Pub, Inc (94); auth, "Ethics and Science," Ethics for Today and Tomorrow, ed by Joram Graf Haber, Boston: Jones and Bartlett Pubs (97): 362-373. **CONTACT ADDRESS** Dept Philos, Suffolk County Comm Col, Ammerman, 533 Col Rd, Selden, NY 11784-2851. **EMAIL** kleimal@sunysuffolk.edu

KLEIN, ANNE
DISCIPLINE RELIGIOUS STUDIES, TIBETAN BUDDHISM, CLASSICAL TIBETAN LANGUAGE **EDUCATION** Univ VA, PhD, 81. **CAREER** Prof, ch, dept Relig Stud, Rice Univ. **HONORS AND AWARDS** Fulbright dissertation res fel, India and Nepal, 80; NEH summer grant, 94; NEH transl grant, 94; adv bd, Women & Religion Prog, Harvard Divinity Sch; Ford Found Fel, 99-01. **MEMBERSHIPS** AAR; Int Asn of Tibetan Scholars. **RESEARCH** Bon & Buddhis Dzogchen philos/epistemology in early Tibetan tradition; issues of gender & embodiment. **SELECTED PUBLICATIONS** Auth, Knowing, Naming, and Negation: A Sourcebook on Tibetan Sautrantika; Knowledge and Liberation; Path to the Middle: Oral Madhyamika Philosophy in Tibet: The Spoken Scholarship of Kensur Yeshey Tupden; Meeting the Great Bliss Queen: Buddhists, Feminists, and the Art of the Self, Beacon Press, 94. **CONTACT ADDRESS** Rice Univ, PO Box 1892, Houston, TX 77251-1892. **EMAIL** klein-A@rice.edu

KLEIN, BENJAMIN
PERSONAL Born 01/29/1943, New York, NY **DISCIPLINE** ECONOMICS **EDUCATION** Brooklyn Col, BA, 64; Univ Chicago, MA, 67; PhD, 70. **CAREER** Asst Prof to Prof, Univ Calif Los Angeles, 68-. **MEMBERSHIPS** Am Econ Asn; Am Law and Econ Asn; Am Bar Asn. **RESEARCH** Law and economics of contractual arrangements; Antitrust regulation. **SELECTED PUBLICATIONS** Auth, "Market Power in Antitrust: Economic Analysis After Kodak," Supreme Court Econ Rev 3, 93; auth, "The Economics of Franchise Contracts," J of Corporate Finance 2, 95; co-auth, "Monopolization by 'Raising Rivals' Costs': The Standard Oil Case," Journal of Law and Econ 39, 96; auth, "Why Hold-Ups Occur: The Self-Enforcing Range of Contractual Relationships," Economic Inquiry 34, 96; auth, "The Microsoft Case: What Can a Dominant Firm Do To Defend its Market Position?" J of Economic Perspectives, 01. **CONTACT ADDRESS** Dept of Econ, Univ of California, Los Angeles, 8283 Bunche, Box 951477, Los Angeles, CA 90095-1477. **EMAIL** bklein@econ.ucla.edu

KLEIN, BERNARD
PERSONAL Born 10/15/1928, Czechoslovakia, m, 1961, 2 children **DISCIPLINE** MODERN & JEWISH HISTORY; THE NAZI HOLOCAUST **EDUCATION** Rabbi, Torah Vodaath Talmudical Sem, 53; Brooklyn Col, BA, magna cum laud, 54; Columbia Univ, MA, 56, PhD, 62. **CAREER** Lectr hist, Brooklyn Col, 58-61 & City Col New York, 64; from instr to assoc prof, 65-69, chmn, Div Behav & Soc Sci, 68-70, chmn, Dept Hist & Polit Sci, 70-71, chmn, Dept Hist & Philos, 72-79, Prof Hist, Kingsborough Community Col, 69-, Chmn Dept Soc Sci, 79-95, Chmn Dept Hist, Philos & Polit Sci, 95-; Lectr, Long Island Univ, 60; consult, Nat Curric Res Inst, Am Asn Jewish Educ, 65-67; mem educ coun, Fed Jewish Philanthropists, pres, 67-69; pres, Jewish Fac Asn, City Univ New York, 79-. **HONORS AND AWARDS** Phi Beta Kappa, 54; Fel, Conf Material Claims Jews against Ger, 57-58, 59-60; Fel, Res Found State Univ NY, 71; Chemn & Coordr of Annual Interdisciplinary Conferences on the Holocaust at the Hebrew Univ, Jerusalem, Israel. **MEMBERSHIPS** AHA **RESEARCH** German international policy during the Nazi Period; the right-radical movements in Hungary during the inter-war period; Jewish history and the Nazi Holocaust. **SELECTED PUBLICATIONS** Auth, Rudolf Kasztner and the Hungarian Rescue Effort, in Perspective, Vol I, 59; The Judenrat, Jewish Social Studies, 1/60; New developments in Jewish school curricula, Am Asn Jewish Educ, 65 & in Jewish Education Register and Directory, 65; The decline of a Sephardic community in Transylvania, Studies in Honor of M J Benardete, 65; Hungarian politics and the Jewish question, 4/66 & Anti-Jewish demonstrations in Hungarian universities, 1932-1936: Their role in the struggle for political power between Istvan, Bethlen, and Gyula Gombos, 82, Jewish Soc Studies, 82; Hungarian politics and the Jewish question, in Hostages of Modernization: Studies on Modern Antisemitism, 1870-1933/39, Walter de Gruyer, 93. **CONTACT ADDRESS** Dept Hist, Philos & Polit Sci, Kingsborough Comm Col, CUNY, 2001 Oriental Blvd, Brooklyn, NY 11235-2333. **EMAIL** bklein@kbcc.cuny.edu

KLEIN, CHRISTINE A.
PERSONAL Born 01/29/1956, St Louis, MO, m **DISCIPLINE** LEGAL STUDIES **EDUCATION** Columbia Univ, School Law, LLM, 94; Univ Colo, School Law, JD, 87; Middleburg Col, BA, 78. **CAREER** Assoc Prof of Law, Michigan State Univ, Detroit Col of Law, 95-; vis Assoc Professor of Law, Univ of Denver Col of Law, fall, 99. **HONORS AND AWARDS** Harlan Fiske Stone Scholar, Columbia Univ; Myna Cum Laude, Middleburg College. **MEMBERSHIPS** Amer Bar Assoc. **RESEARCH** Natural Resources Law; Water Law. **SELECTED PUBLICATIONS** Auth, "Bersani v. EPA The EPA's Authority Under the Clean Water Act to Veto Section 404," Weland-Filling Permits, 19 Environmental Law 389, 88; auth, "The Constitutional Mythology of Western Water Law," 14 Virginia Environmental Law Journal 101, 95; auth, "Treaties of Conquest: Property Rights, Indian Treaties, and the Treaty of Guadalupe Hidalgo," 26 New Mexico Law Review 201, 96; auth, "A Requiem for the Rollover Rule: Capital Gains, Farmland Loss, and The Law of Unintended Consequences," 55 Washington & Lee Law Review 403, 98; auth, "Beating a Dead Mouse: Do IOLTA programs Create on Unconstitutional Taking of Private Property?," Michigan State Univ, Detroit Coll of Law Review, 99; auth, "On Dams and Democracy," Oregon Law Review, 99, auth, "On Dams and Democracy," Oregon Law Review, forthcoming 00. **CONTACT ADDRESS** Dept Law, Detroit Col of Law at Michigan State Univ, 364 Law College Bldg, East Lansing, MI 48824-1300. **EMAIL** kleinch@msu.edu

KLEIN, DENNIS B.
PERSONAL Born 05/28/1948, Cleveland, OH, m, 1979, 3 children **DISCIPLINE** HISTORY, JEWISH HISTORY **EDUCATION** Hobart Col, BA, 70; Univ Rochester, MA, 72, PhD, 78. **CAREER** Dorst Teaching Fel, New York Univ, 81-84; Dir, ADL Holocaust Studies, 84-93; assoc prof and Jewish Studies Dir, Kean Univ, 96-. **HONORS AND AWARDS** Phi Beta Kappa, 70; Hobart Col, BA, cum laude, 70; Fulbright-Hays Diss Fel, Vienna, 74-75; Post-doctoral Fel, Harvard Univ, 79-81; New York State Governor's Awd in Ed, 87; Awds: Nat Endowment for the Humanities, Nat Acad of Ed; listed: Who's Who in the East, Who's Who in Am Cols and Univs, Dict of Int Biog. **MEMBERSHIPS** Am Hist Soc, Asn for Jewish Studies. **RESEARCH** Central European history, Jewish history, history and psychology. **SELECTED PUBLICATIONS** Auth, American Deeds-Jewish Dreams: A Study of the American Jewish Movement, 1916-1955, Waltham, MA: Am Jewish Hist Soc (80); auth, Jewish Origins of the Psychoanalytic Movement, New York: Praeger (81), Univ Chicago Press (85); founding ed, Dimensions: A J of Holocaust Studies, 85-; coauth with J. M. Muffs, The Holocaust in Books and Films: A Selected Annotated List, New York: Hippocrene (86); auth, "The Fate of Holocaust Literature," Handbook of Holocaust Literature, ed Saul Friedman, Westport, CT: Greenwood Press (93); ed, Hidden History of the Kovno Ghetto, in collaboration with the U.S. Holocaust Memorial Museum, Little, Brown (Bulfinch, 97); auth, "Holocaust, " Encyclopedia of Historians and Historical Writing, London and Chicago: Fitzroy Dearborn (99); auth, "Dimensions Magazine: Wrestling with Memory," Encyclopedia of Genocide, Jerusalem: Hebrew Univ Inst on the Holocaust and Genocide (forthcoming); rev, "Thinking About the Holocaust," German Politics and Soc (forthcoming); auth, "Myth of the Hidden Jew," Holocaust and Genocide Studies (forthcoming). **CONTACT ADDRESS** Dept Hist, Kean Col of New Jersey, Union, NJ 07083. **EMAIL** dbklein1@juno.com

KLEIN, ELLEN R.
PERSONAL Born 04/15/1958, s **DISCIPLINE** PHILOSOPHY **EDUCATION** New Col of the Unif of S Fla, BA, 81; Univ of S Fla, MA, 83; Univ of Miami, MA, 87; PhD, 89. **CAREER** Vis Instr, Rollins Col, 88-89; vis asst prof, Wash Col, 89-91; asst prof, Univ of N Fla, 91-95; Johnston Assoc Prof, Whitman Col, 96-97; invited vis lectr, Central Wash Univ, 97-98; asst prof, Flagler Col, 98-. **HONORS AND AWARDS** Fac Enhancement Fund Grant, 90; Academic Computing Comt Software Grant, 90; Fac Enhancement Fund Grant, Wash Col, 90; UNF Division of Sponsored Res Grant, 94; listed in Who's Who Among America's Teachers, 94; UNF Found Account Grant, 94; Whitman Col Presidential Account, 96. **MEMBER-**

SHIPS Am Philos Asn, Asn of Practical and Professional Ethics, Am Asn of Philos Teachers, Fla Philos Asn, Hegel Soc, Phi Sigma Tau, Phi Kappa Phi, Phi Beta Lambda. **SELECTED PUBLICATIONS** Auth, Feminism Under Fire, Prometheus Books, 96; auth, "Professional Philosophers vs. Professionals as Philosophers," Ethically Speaking: The Newsletter of the Association for Practical and Professional Ethics 1, 97; auth, "Can Feminism Be Rational?" J of Interdisciplinary Studies (98): 17-29; auth, "The One Necessary Condition for a Successful Business Ethics Course: That it is Taught by a Philosopher," Business Ethics Quart 3 (98): 561-574; auth, "Gender Images: Voice or Vice," Zeitschrift Fuer Philosophie (99): 26-35; auth, Just Problems, Wadsworth, forthcoming. **CONTACT ADDRESS** Dept Soc Sci, Flagler Col, PO Box 1027, Saint Augustine, FL 32085-1027.

KLEIN, KENNETH
PERSONAL Born 09/29/1930, Springfield, IL, m, 1999, 2 children **DISCIPLINE** PHILOSOPHY **EDUCATION** WA Univ, AB, 52; Univ Chicago, BD, 55; Harvard Univ, PhD, 63. **CAREER** Philos, Valparaiso Univ. **HONORS AND AWARDS** Caterpillar Awd for Excel Tchg, Valparaiso Univ, 95; Rockefeller Fel Relig, Harvard Univ, 60-62; Frank Knox Mem Fel, Harvard Univ, 59-60; fel Mansfield Col, Oxford Univ. **RESEARCH** Philos of reigion; hist and philos of relig. **SELECTED PUBLICATIONS** Auth, Positivism and Christianity, Martinus Nijhoff, 74; co-ed, In the Interest of Peace: A Spectrum of Philosophical Views, Longwood Acad, 90; Issues in War and Peace: Philosophical Inquiries, Longwood Pub, 89. **CONTACT ADDRESS** Valparaiso Univ, 1500 E Lincoln Way, Valparaiso, IN 46383-6493. **EMAIL** kennethklein@home.com

KLEIN, PETER DAVID
PERSONAL Born 09/17/1940, Cincinnati, OH, d, 1 child **DISCIPLINE** PHILOSOHY **EDUCATION** Earlham Col, BA, 62; Yale Univ, MA, 64, PhD, 66. **CAREER** Asst prof philos, Colgate Univ, 66-70; from asst prof to assoc prof, 70-81, Prof, Rutgers Univ, 81-, Chmn, 82-87 and 93-96, vice provost, Undergrad Educ and assoc provost for Hum and Fine Arts, 87-92; Lectr, NEH Summer Inst on Epistemology, 93; Subj ed (with R Foley), epistemology, Encyclopedia of Philosophy, Routledge. **HONORS AND AWARDS** Danforth Grad Fel, 62-66; Ford Found grant, Oxford Univ, 69-70; NJ Comn for Hum, 73-74 & 79-80, Control Data Corp, computer asst instr in elementary logic, 79-80; NEH publ prog grant, Certainty, 81; various Rutgers Res Counc grants. **MEMBERSHIPS** Am Philos Asn. **RESEARCH** Epistemology. **SELECTED PUBLICATIONS** Auth, The Private Language Argument and The Sense-Datum Theory, Australasian Jour Phil, 69; Are Strawson's Persons Immortal? -- A Reply, Philos Studies, 69; A Proposed Definition of Propositional Knowledge, Jour Philos, 71, reprinted, Knowing, Univ Press Am, 84, Knowledge and Justification, Ashgate Publ Co, 94, and On Knowing and the Known, Prometheus Books, 96; Knowledge, Causality and Defeasibility, Jour Philos, 76; Misleading Misleading, Defeators, Jour Philos, 76, reprinted, On Knowing and the Known, Prometheus Books 96; Misleading Evidence and the Restoration of Justification, Philos Studies, 80; Certainty: A Refutation of Skepticism, Univ Minn Press, 81, 2nd printing, 84; Reply to Professor Odegard, Philos Books, 82; Real Knowledge, Synthese, 83; Virtues of Inconsistency, Monist, 85; Radical Interpretation and Global Scepticism, In: Truth and Interpretation (Ernest LePore, ed), Basil Blackwell, 86; Immune Belief Systems, Philos Topics, 86; On Behalf of the Skeptic, The Possibility of Knowledge: Nozick and His Critics (S Luper-Foy, ed), Rowman & Littlefield, 87; Epistemic Compatibilism and Canonical Beliefs, In: Doubting: Contemporary Perspectives on Scepticism (M Roth & G Ross, ed), Kluwer Acad Publ, 90; Certainty, In: A Companion to Epistemology (J Dancy & E Sosa, ed), Basil Blackwell, 92; Contemporary Scepticism, In: A Companion to Epistemology (J Dancy & E Sosa, ed), Basil Blackwell, 92; Scepticism, In: A Companion to Epistemology (J Dancy & E Sosa, ed), Basil Blackwell, 92; Co-auth (with Ted Warfield), What Price Coherence?, Analysis, 7/94; Skepticism and Closure: Why the Evil Genius Argument Fails, Philos Topics, spring 95; Closure, In: The Cambridge Dictionary of Philosophy (R Audi, ed), Cambridge Univ Press, 95; Certainty, In: The Cambridge Dictionary of Philosophy (R Audi, ed), Cambridge Univ Press, 95; Co-auth (with Ted Warfield), No Help for the Coherentist, Analysis, 4/96; Warrant, Proper Function, Reliabilism and Defeasibility, In: Warrant and Contemporary Epistemology (Jonathan Kvanvig, ed), Rowman & Littlefield, 96; Certainty, In: Encyclopedia of Philosophy (E Craig, ed), Routledge, 98; The Concept of Knowledge, In: Encyclopedia of Philosophy (E Craig, ed), Routledge, 98; Epistemology, In: Encyclopedia of Philosophy (E Craig, ed), Routledge, 98; Foundationalism and the Infinite Regress of Reasons, Philosophy and Phenomenological Research, 58.4, 99, 919-925; auth, Human Knowledge and the Infinite Regress of Reasons, Philosophical Perspectives, 13, J. Tomberlin ed., 99, 297-325; auth, Why Not Infinitism? In Epistemology: Proceedings of the Twentieth World Congress in Philosophy, Richard Cobb-Stevens, ed., 00, vol 5, 199-208. **CONTACT ADDRESS** Dept of Philos, Rutgers, The State Univ of New Jersey, New Brunswick, PO Box 270, New Brunswick, NJ 08901-2882. **EMAIL** pdkleincrei@rutgers.edu

KLEIN, RALPH W.
PERSONAL m, 2 children **DISCIPLINE** OLD TESTAMENT **EDUCATION** Concordia Sem; Harvard Univ Divinity Sch, PhD. **CAREER** Dean; Christ Sem-Seminex prof. **HONORS AND AWARDS** Humboldt fel, Univ Gottingen; Humboldt Univ, Berlin; ed, currents in theol and mission, 74-. **SELECTED PUBLICATIONS** Auth, Textual Criticism of the Old Testament, Israel in Exile, 1 Samuel, Word Biblical Commentary 10; Ezekiel: The Prophet and His Message; commentary on Ezra and Nehemiah for the New Interpreter's Bible. **CONTACT ADDRESS** Dept of OldTestament, Lutheran Sch of Theol at Chicago, 1100 E 55th St, Chicago, IL 60615. **EMAIL** rklein@lstc.edu

KLEIN, RICHARD
PERSONAL Born 06/21/1943, New York, NY, m, 1971, 2 children **DISCIPLINE** LAW **EDUCATION** Univ Wis, BA, 64; Columbia Univ, MA, 68, MIA, 69, doctorate, 70, Harvard Univ, JD, 72. **CAREER** Touro Law Sch, prof, 83-; Hofstra prof 82-83; Legal Aid Society, Sr Trial att, 72-82. **HONORS AND AWARDS** Fac Mem of the Yr. **MEMBERSHIPS** ABA; AATL. **RESEARCH** Intl Human Rights; Criminal Law. **SELECTED PUBLICATIONS** Auth, Human Rights in Hong Kong, The Humanist, 97; Law and Racism in an Asian Setting, Hastins Intl Law Rev, The Empire Strikes Back: Britain's Use of Law to Suppress Political Dissent, Boston U Intl L Jour, 97. **CONTACT ADDRESS** Touro Law School, Touro Col, New York, 300 Nassau Rd, Huntington, NY 11743. **EMAIL** klein@lawyer.com

KLEIN, WILLIAM A.
PERSONAL Born 03/03/1931, Chicago, IL, m, 4 children **DISCIPLINE** LAW **EDUCATION** Harvard Univ, AB, 52, JD, 57. **CAREER** Atty, US Dept of Justice, Wash, DC, 57-59; Clerk, US Court of Appeals, District of Columbia, 59; Teaching fel, Harvard Sch, 59-60; Atty, Bingham, Dana & Gould, Boston, 60-61; Asst Prof, Prof, Univ of Wis, 61-71; Staff Asst, Chief Counsel, Internal Revenue Serv, Wash, DC, 66-67; Vis prof, UCLA Sch of Law, 69-70, prof, 71-94; vis prof, Univ of Hawaii Law Sch, Fall 76; vis prof, Yale Law Sch, Winter 82; vis prof, Stanford Law Sch, Fall 88; Maxwell prof of Law Emer, UCLA Sch of Law, 94-. **RESEARCH** Federal income taxation; legal organization of business. **SELECTED PUBLICATIONS** Authm Tailor to the Emperor With No Clothes: The Supreme Court's Tax Rules for Deposits and Advance Payments, 41 UCLA L. Rev. 1685, 94; auth, Business Form, Limited Liability, and Tax Regimes: Lurching Toward a Coherent Outcome, with Eric M. Zolt, 66 U. Colo. L. Rev. 1001, 95; auth, High-Yield Junk, Bonds As Investments and As Financial Tools, 19 Cardozo L. Rev. 505, 97; auth, Investment Alternatives and Tax Vehicles: Accumulations and Payouts Compared, 78, Tax Notes 1707, 98; auth, Federal Income Tax Code and Regulations, Selected Sections, Found Press, 98, 99, 00; auth, Business Associations, Agency, Partnerships, and coporations, Statutes and Rules, Found Press, 00; auth, Business Organization and Finance, Foundation Press, 7th ed. 00; auth, Federal Income Taxation, 12th ed, Shaviro 00; auth, Business Associations, Cases and Materials on Agency, Partnership, and Corporations, 4th ed. 00; auth, Connected Contracts and Economic Organization, with G. Mitu Gulati and Eric M. Zolt, forthcoming April 00 UCLA Law Review. **CONTACT ADDRESS** Univ of California, 1032 Enchanted Way, Pacific Palisades, CA 90272. **EMAIL** klein@law.ucla.edu

KLEIN, WILLIAM W.
PERSONAL Born 02/11/1946, Weehawken, NJ, m, 1968, 2 children **DISCIPLINE** NEW TESTAMENT EXEGESIS **EDUCATION** Univ of Aberdeen, Scotland, PhD, 78 **CAREER** Inst, 77-78, Columbia Internatl Univ; Prof, 78-pres, Denver Sem **HONORS AND AWARDS** Whos Who Among Students; Whos Who in Relig; Outstanding Young Men of Amer; Who's Who in World; Men of Achievement; Who's Who in Bibl Studies & Archaeology **MEMBERSHIPS** Soc of Bibl Lit; Inst for Bibl Res; Evangelical Theolog Soc; Tyndale Fel for Bibl Res **RESEARCH** Hermeneutics; Pauline theology; Sermon on the Mount; Theology of Election **SELECTED PUBLICATIONS** Auth, "Evangelical Hermeneutics," in Initiation into Theology, JL Van Schaik, 98; "Election," in Dictionary of the Later New Testament and Its Developments, Inter Varsity Pr, 97 **CONTACT ADDRESS** Denver Conservative Baptist Sem, PO Box 100000, Denver, CO 80250-0100. **EMAIL** bill.klein@densem.edu

KLEINER, SCOTT ALTER
PERSONAL Born 12/22/1938, Cincinnati, OH, m, 1960, 2 children **DISCIPLINE** PHILOSOPHY, PHILOSOPHY OF SCIENCE **EDUCATION** Williams Col, AB, 60; Univ Chicago, AM, 61, PhD(Philos), 68. **CAREER** From instr to asst prof, 65-69; asst prof, 69-77, from assoc prof to prof Philos, Univ GA, 77-97, Sarah B Moss fel, 73-74. **MEMBERSHIPS** AAAS; Philos Sci Asn; Asn Symbolic Logic. **RESEARCH** History and philosophy of natural science; foundations of physics; philosophy of biology. **SELECTED PUBLICATIONS** Auth, Erotetic logic and the structure of scientific revolution, Brit J Philos Sci, 70; Criteria for Meaning Change in Physics, In: Studies in the Foundations, Methodology and Philosophy of Science, 71; Ontological Commitment and the Methodological Commensurability of Theories, In: Boston Studies in Philosophy of Science, 71; Recent theories of theoretical meaning, Philosophica, 76; The philosophy of biology, Southern J Philos, 76; Referential Divergence in Scientific Theories, 77 & Feyerabend, Galileo and Darwin, 79, In: Studies in History & Philosophy of Science; Problem Solving and Discovery in the Growth of Darwin's Theories of Evolution, Synthese, 81; Logic of Discovery, Kluwer, 93. **CONTACT ADDRESS** Dept of Philosophy & Religion, Univ of Georgia, Athens, GA 30602-0001. **EMAIL** skleiner@arches.uga.edu

KLEINGELD, PAULINE
PERSONAL Born Rotterdam, m, 1 child **DISCIPLINE** PHILOSOPHY **EDUCATION** Leiden Univ, MA, BA, PhD, 94. **CAREER** Asst prof, 93-, Washington Univ of St Louis. **HONORS AND AWARDS** Howard Foundation Fellowship, NEH Summer Stipend; Washington Univ Fac Res Grant; Lilly Endowment Tchng Fel; DAAD Fel. **MEMBERSHIPS** APA; ASECS; NAKS; NASSP; Kant-Gesellschaft. **RESEARCH** History of modern phil, esp Kant. **SELECTED PUBLICATIONS** Auth, The Problematic Status of Gender-Neutral Language in the History of Philosophy: The Case of Kant, Phil Forum, 93; auth, Progress and Reason: Kant's Philosophy of History, Wurzburg Konigshausen und Neumann, 95; art, What Do the Virtuous Hope For?: Re-reading Kant's Doctrine of the Highest Good, Proc of the 8th Intl Kant Congress, Memphis 95, Marquette Univ Press, 95; art, Between Copernican Turn and Grand Narrative: The Relevance of Kant's Philosophy of History, Fischer Verlag, 96; art, Kants Politischer Kosmopolitismus, Jahrbuch fur Recht und Ethik 5, 97; art, The Conative Character of Reason in Kant's Philosophy, Jour of the History of Phil 36, 98; art, Just Love? Marriage and the Question of Justice, Soc Theory and Practice 24, 98; auth, Kant's Cosmopolitan Law: World Citizenship for a Global Order, Kantian Review 2 (98); auth, Kant on the Unity of Theoretical and Practical Reason, Review of Metaphysics, 52 (98); auth, Kant, History, and the Idea of Moral Development, History of Phil Quarterly, 16 (99); auth, Six Varieties of Cosmopolitanism in Late Eighteenth-Century Germany, Jour of the History of Ideas 60 (99). **CONTACT ADDRESS** Dept of Philosophy, Washington Univ, 1 Brookings Dr., Campus Box 1073, Saint Louis, MO 63130-4899. **EMAIL** pkleinge@artsci.wustl.edu

KLEMKE, ELMER DANIEL
PERSONAL Born 07/29/1926, St. Paul, MN **DISCIPLINE** PHILOSOPHY **EDUCATION** Hamline Univ, BA, 50; Northwestern Univ, MA, 58, PhD(philos), 60. **CAREER** Asst prof philos, DePauw Univ, 59-64; prof, Roosevelt Univ, 64-74, chmn dept, 65-74; assoc dean and prof, 74-76, Prof Philos, Iowa State Univ, 76-. **MEMBERSHIPS** Am Philos Asn; Western Div Am Philos Asn (secy-treas, 69-72); AAUP. **RESEARCH** Contemporary Brit and Am philos; philos of logic; metaphysics. **SELECTED PUBLICATIONS** Auth, Reflections and Perspectives: Essays in Philosophy, The Hague, Mouton, 74; (with A Jacobson & F Zabeeh), Readings in Semantics, Univ Ill Press, 74; auth, Studies in the Philosophy of Kierkegaard, Nijhoff, The Hague, 76; Bibliography of G E Moore scholarship, 1903-present, Southwestern J Philos, Vol VII, No 3; coauth, (with Robert Hollinger & A David Kline), Introductory Readings in the Philosophy of Science, Prometheus Bks, 3rd ed., 98; auth, The Meaning of Life, Oxford Univ Press, 2nd ed., 99; coauth, (with Robert Hollinger & A David Kline), Philosophy: The Basic Issues, St Martin's Press, 4th ed. 94; auth, "Contemporary Analytic and Linguistic Philosophies, 2nd ed., 00; auth, A Defense of Philosophical Realism, Humanity Books, fall 00. **CONTACT ADDRESS** Dept of Philosophy, Iowa State Univ of Science and Tech, 402 Catt Hall, Ames, IA 50011-0002.

KLERMAN, DANIEL M.
PERSONAL Born 06/23/1966, New Haven, CT, m **DISCIPLINE** LAW **EDUCATION** Yale, BA, 88; Univ Chicago, JD, 91; PhD, 98. **CAREER** Law Clerk, Judge Richard Posner, 92-93; Law Clerk, Justice John Paul Stevens, 93-94; Asst Prof, Univ Chicago, 95-98; Vis Asst Prof, Stanford Law Sch, 97-98; Assoc Prof, Univ S Calif, 98-. **HONORS AND AWARDS** Fulbright Fel; Law and Soc Sci Grant; Soc Sci Res Coun Fel; Olin Fel. **MEMBERSHIPS** Am Soc for Legal Hist, Am Law and Econ Asn. **RESEARCH** English legal history, law and economics. **SELECTED PUBLICATIONS** Auth, "Settling Multidefendant Lawsuits: The Advantage of Conditional Setoff Rules," J of Legal Studies 25 (96): 445-462; auth, Settlement and the Decline of Private Prosecution in Thirteenth-Century England," Law and Hist Rev, vol 19, no 1 (forthcoming). **CONTACT ADDRESS** Dept Law, Univ of So California, 699 Exposition Blvd, Los Angeles, CA 90089-0071. **EMAIL** dklerman@law.usc.edu

KLIBANSKY, RAYMOND
PERSONAL Born 10/15/1905, Paris, France **DISCIPLINE** PHILOSOPHY **EDUCATION** Univ Heidelberg, PhD, 28; Oxford Univ, MA, 36. **CAREER** Asst philos, Heidelberg Acad, 27-33; Hon lectr, Kings Col, Univ London, 34-36; Lectr, Oriel Col, Oxford, 36-48; Frothinghem prof, 46-75, Emer Prof Logic and Metaphysics, McGill Univ, 75-; Hon Fel, Univ London, 50-; Guest prof, Inst Mediaeval Studies, Univ Montreal, 47-68; Mahlon Powell prof philos, Ind Univ, 50; Gretler Found lectr, Univ Zurich, 50; Guggenheim fel, 53 and 65; Cardinal Mercier

prof philos, Cath Univ Louvain, 56; Found lectr, Univ Rome, 57; Vis prof philos, 61; Prof ordinarius (aD), Ministry Educ Baden-Wurttemberg, 59-75, Emer prof, 75-; Vis prof, Univ Genoa, 64; Mem Coun, Ctr Humanistic Studies, Rome, 49-; Fel, Int Inst Philos, Paris, 53-; Pres, Comn Chroniques Et Travaux Bibliog, 53-; Pres Comn Philos Et Communaute Mondale, 58-; Pres, Inst, 66-69 and Can rep exec comt, Int Fed Philos Socs, 53-; Actg chmn nat comt hist and philos sci, Nat Res Coun Can, 69-69 and Mem Nat Comt Int Coun Sci Unions, 63-; Fel, Acad Athens, 70-; Pres Int Comt, Anselm Studies, 70-; Vis fel, Wolfson Col, Oxford, 76-78; Dir, Can Acad Ctr, Italy, 80; Fel, Wolfson Col, Oxford, 81-. **HONORS AND AWARDS** DPhil, Univ Ottawa, 71. **MEMBERSHIPS** Fel Royal Soc Can; Int Soc Studies Medieval Philos(vpres, 64-69, pres, 69-72, hon pres, 72-); Int Inst Philos (hon pres, 69-), fel Int Acad Hist Sci; Can Soc Hist and Philos Sci (pres, 59-72, emer pres, 72-); Royal Hist Soc. **RESEARCH** Philosophy of history and metaphysics; history of Platonism; Nicholas of Cusa. **SELECTED PUBLICATIONS** Auth, Beyond the Limits of Academic Life in An Interview with Klibansky, Raymond, a Canadian Philosopher, About Cassirer, Ernst and the Wartburg Library, Merkur-Deutsche Zeitschrift fur Europaisches Denken, Vol 0050, 96. **CONTACT ADDRESS** Dept of Philos, McGill Univ, 855 Sherbrooke St, W, Rm 908, Montreal, QC, Canada H3A 2T7. **EMAIL** 103430.1325@compuserve.com

KLIMA, GYULA
PERSONAL Born 10/20/1956 **DISCIPLINE** PHILOSOPHY **EDUCATION** Univ Budapest, MA, 82; PhD, 86. **CAREER** Asst prof, Yale Univ, 92-95; sr res fel, Hungarian Acad, 93-97; assoc prof Univ Notre Dame, 95-. **RESEARCH** Philosophical semantics; ontology; comparative analysis of medieval and modern theories. **SELECTED PUBLICATIONS** Auth, Saint Thomas Aquinas on Being and Essence, 90; Ars Artium, Essays in Philosophical Semantics, Medieval and Modern, 88; The Semantic Principles Underlying Saint Thomas Aquinas's Metaphysics of Being, Medieval Philos Theol, 96; Man=Body+Soul: Aquinas's Arithmetic of Human Nature, Philso Studies Relig, 97; Contemporary 'Essentialism' vs. Aristotelian 'Essentialism', 98; Saint Anselm's Proof: A Problem of Reference, Intentional Identity and Mutual Understanding, Medieval Philos Modern Times, 98. **CONTACT ADDRESS** Philosophy Dept, Univ of Notre Dame, 336/7 O'Shaughnessy, Notre Dame, IN 46556. **EMAIL** klima.1@nd.edu

KLINE, GEORGE LOUIS
PERSONAL Born 03/03/1921, Galesburg, IL, m, 1943, 3 children **DISCIPLINE** PHILOSOPHY **EDUCATION** Columbia Univ, AB, 47, AM, 48, PhD, 50. **CAREER** Instr philos, Columbia Univ, 50-52 and 53-54, asst prof, 54-60; assoc prof philos and Russ, 60-66, chmn dept, 77-82, prof, 66-81; Vis asst prof, Univ Chicago, 52-53; consult, USSR res prog, 52-55; Ford fel, Paris, 54-55; Inter-Univ Comt travel grant, USSR and Czech, 56 and 57; ed philos sect, Am Bibliog Slavic Studies, 57-67; consult, Foreign Area Fel Prog, 59-64; co-ed, J Philos, 59-64, consult ed, 64-78; Rockefeller fel, USSR, Poland, Czech, Hungary and Western Europe, 60; consult ed philos, Current Digest of the Soviet Press, 61-64; Consult Ed, Studies in Soviet Thought (now Studies in E European Thought), 62-; J Value Inquiry, 67-; Process Studies, 70-; J Hist of Ideas, 76-; SLAVIC REV, 77-79; vis prof Soviet Studies in Philos (now Russian Studies in Philos), 87-; vis prof philos, Johns Hopkins Univ, 68-69, Univ Pa, 80-81 and Swarthmore Col, 81-82; Nat Endowment for Humanities sr fel, 70-71, consult, 72-76; Guggenheim fel, 78-79; Fulbright res fel, Paris, 79; Milton C Nahm prof Philos, Bryn Mawr Col, 81-91, prof emer Philos, 91-; Philos Quarterly, 90-93. **HONORS AND AWARDS** Decorated DFC, 44; Awd for Distinguished Contributions to Slavic Studies, Am Asn Adv Slavic Studies, 99. **MEMBERSHIPS** Am Philos, Asn; Am Asn Advan Slavic Studies; Metaphys Soc Am (vp 84-85, pres, 85-87); Hegel Soc Am (vp, 71-73, pres, 84-86). **RESEARCH** Ethics; metaphysics; Russian philosophy, especially ethical and social theory. **SELECTED PUBLICATIONS** Auth, Spinoza in Soviet Philosophy, Routledge & Kegan Paul & Humanities Press, 52, auth rpt, Hyperion, 81; trans, VV Zenovsky, A History of Russian Philosophy, vols I & II, Routledge & Kegan Paul & Columbia Univ Press, 53; ed & auth introd, Alfred North Whitehead: Essays on his Philosophy, Prentice Hall, 63, rpt, Univ Press Am, 89; ed and contrib, European Philosophy Today, Quadrangle, 65; auth, Religious and Anti-Religious Thought in Russian, Univ Chicago, 68; trans, Boris Pasternak, Seven Poems, Univorn, 69, 2nd ed, 72; co-trans & auth introd, Joseph Brodsky, Selected Poems, Penguin & Harper, 73; co-trans, Joseph Brodsky, A Part of Speech, Farrar, Straus & Giroux, Oxford Univ Press, 80; co-ed & contrib, Explorations in Whitehead's Philosophy, Fordham Univ, 83; co-ed, Iosif Brodskii, Ostanovka v pustyne, Pushkinskii Fond, 00. **CONTACT ADDRESS** 632 Valley View Rd, Ardmore, PA 19003.

KLINE, MARLEE
DISCIPLINE LAW **EDUCATION** Simon Fraser Univ, BA, 82; Oxford Univ, BA, 84; Dalhousie Univ, LLB, 85; Osgoode Univ, LLM, 91. **CAREER** Asst prof, 89-94; assoc prof, 94-. **RESEARCH** Child welfare law; social welfare law; feminist legal theory; racism and law; property law. **SELECTED PUBLICATIONS** Auth, pubs about child welfare law, feminist analysis of law and structures of racism within the law. **CONTACT ADDRESS** Fac of Law, Univ of British Columbia, 1822 East Mall, Vancouver, BC, Canada V6T 1Z1. **EMAIL** kline@law.ubc.ca

KLINE, MEREDITH GEORGE
PERSONAL Born 12/15/1922, Coplay, PA, m, 1944, 3 children **DISCIPLINE** RELIGION **EDUCATION** Gordon Col, AB, 44; Westminster Theol Sem, ThB and ThM, 47; Dropsie Col, PhD (Assyriol and Egyptol), 56. **CAREER** Prof Old Testament, Westminster Theol Sem, 48-65; Prof Old Testament, Gordon-Conwell Theol Sem, 65-93; Emeritus 93-; Vis Prof Old Testament, Sch Theol, Claremont, 74-75 and Reformed Theol Sem, 80-; Prof Old Testament, Westminister Theol Sem, Calif, 82-. **HONORS AND AWARDS** Festadirift: Creator, Redeemer, Consummator, 00. **RESEARCH** Old Testament. **SELECTED PUBLICATIONS** Auth, Treaty of the Great King, 63; auth, By Oath Consigned, 68; auth, The Structure of Biblical Authority, 72; auth, Images of the Spirit, 90; auth, Kingdom Prologue, 91, 93; auth, Heaven On Earth in The Social And Political Agendas of Dominion Theology; J Church State, Vol 0036, 94. **CONTACT ADDRESS** Gordon-Conwell Theol Sem, South Hamilton, MA 01982.

KLING, DAVID
PERSONAL Born 04/21/1950, Mora, MN, m, 1985, 4 children **DISCIPLINE** HISTORY OF CHRISTIANITY, RELIGION IN AMERICAN LIFE **EDUCATION** Trinity Col, IL, BA, 72; Northern IL Univ, 76; Univ Chicago, PhD, 85. **CAREER** Asst prof hist, Palm Beach Atlantic Col, 82-86; Univ administration, Univ Miami, 86-93; asst prof of relig studies, 93-95, assoc prof, Univ Miami, 95-. **HONORS AND AWARDS** Kenneth Scott Latourette Prize in Religion and Modern Hist (Best Book Manuscript), 92. **MEMBERSHIPS** Am Academy of Relig; Am Soc of Church Hist. **RESEARCH** Revivalism in Am; biblical texts in hist of Christianity. **SELECTED PUBLICATIONS** Auth, A Field of Divine Wonders: The New Divinity and Village Revivals in Northwestern Connecticut, 1792-1822, PA State Univ Press, 93; For Males Only: The Image of the Infidel and the Construction of Gender in the Second Great Awakening in New England, J of Men's Studies 3, May 95; twenty-five entries in The Blackwell Dictionary of Evangelical Biography, 1730-1860, ed Donald M Lewis, 2 vols, Blackwell Pubs, 95; The New Divinity and Williams College, 1793-1836, Religion and American Culture: A Journal of Interpretation 6, summer 96; By the Light of His Example: New Divinity Schools of the Prophets and Theological Education in New England, 1750-1825, in American Theological Education in the Evangelical Tradition, eds D G Hart and R Albert Mohler, Jr, Baker Books, 96; Smyth, Newman, in Dictionary of Heresy Trials in American Christianity, ed George H Shriver, Greenwood Press, 97; New Divinity Schools of the Prophets, 1750-1825: A Case Study in Ministerial Education, History of Ed Quart 37, summer 97. **CONTACT ADDRESS** Dept of Relig Studies, Univ of Miami, PO Box 248264, Miami, FL 33124. **EMAIL** dkling@miami.edu

KLINGHOFFER, ARTHUR JAY
PERSONAL Born 07/30/1941, New York, NY, m, 1969, 1 child **DISCIPLINE** POLITICS, SOVIET FOREIGN POLICY **EDUCATION** Columbia Univ, PhD, 66 **CAREER** Prof, Rutgers Univ, 70- **HONORS AND AWARDS** Fulbright (2), Nobel **RESEARCH** Russian politics, African politics, politics of oil **SELECTED PUBLICATIONS** Auth, Red Apocalypse, 96; auth, The International Dimension of Genocide in Rwanda, 98. **CONTACT ADDRESS** Dept Political Sci, Rutgers, The State Univ of New Jersey, Camden, Camden, NJ 08102. **EMAIL** klinghof@crab.rutgers.edu

KLONOSKI, RICHARD
PERSONAL Born 06/10/1952, Scranton, PA, m, 1974, 3 children **DISCIPLINE** PHILOSOPHY **EDUCATION** Univ Scranton, BA, 74; Kent State Univ, MA, 76; Duquesne Univ, PhD, 83. **CAREER** Prof, Univ Scranton, 81-. **HONORS AND AWARDS** Award for Excellence in Teaching, Alpha Sigma Nu, 86; Fac Senate Awd for Excellence in Teaching, 98. **MEMBERSHIPS** Soc for Ancient Greek Philos, Int Hobbes Asn, Int Soc for Neoplatonic Studies. **RESEARCH** Greek Philosophy, Political Philosophy, Philosophy of Evolution. **SELECTED PUBLICATIONS** Auth, "Being and Time Said All At Once: An Analysis of Section 42," Tulane Studies in Philos: The Thought of Martin Heidegger 32 (84): 61-68; auth, "The Portico of the Archon Basileus: On the Significance of the Setting of Plato's Euthyphro," The Classical J 81.2 (86): 130-137; coauth, Business Ethics, Prentice-Hall, Inc. (Englewood Cliffs, NJ), 86 & Osnovy Publ, 97; auth, "Foundational Considerations in the Corporate Social Responsibility Debate," Business Horizons 34.4 (91): 9-18; auth, "The Preservation of Homeric Tradition: Heroic R-Performance in the Republic and the Odyssey," CLIO: A J of Lit, Hist and the Philos of Hist 22.3 (93): 251-271; auth, "On Friendship as Our Own Most Salvation," The McNeese Rev 34.1 & 2 (95-96): 91-102; auth, "Homonoia in Aristotle's Ethics and Politics," Hist of Polit Thought 17.2 (96): 1-13. **CONTACT ADDRESS** Dept Philos, Univ of Scranton, 800 Linden St, Scranton, PA 18510-2429.

KLOSTERMAIER, KLAUS KONRAD
PERSONAL Born 06/14/1933, Munich, Germany, m, 1971, 3 children **DISCIPLINE** COMPARATIVE RELIGION **EDUCATION** Pontif Gregorian Univ Rome, B Phil, 54, Lic Phil, 55, Dr Phil, 61; Univ Bombay, PhD(ancient Indian hist and cult), 69. **CAREER** Res guide philos, Inst Orient Philos, Agra Univ, 62-64; vis prof Indian Anthrop, Tata Inst Soc Sci, Bombay-Chembur, 64-65; dir, Inst Indian Cult, Bombay Bandra, 65-70; from asst prof to assoc prof World relig, 70-73, Prof World Relig, Univ Man, 73-; S L Swamikannu Pillai lectr, Univ Madras, 68-69; mem bd dirs, Shastri Indo-Can Inst, Montreal-New Delhi, 72-75. **MEMBERSHIPS** Asn Asian Studies; Am Orient Soc; Can Soc Studies Relig; Int Soc Psychol Relig; Ger Soc Missions Sci. **RESEARCH** Interreligious dialogue; Indian philosophies and religions; Judian art. **SELECTED PUBLICATIONS** Transl, The Infancy of Krsna in Critical Edition of the Harivamsa Couture, J Am Orient Soc, Vol 0113, 93; Buddhism Reevaluated by Prominent 20th-Century Hindus, J Dharma, Vol 0020, 95; Studying the Sikhs in Issues for North America, Studies Relig-Scis Religieuses, Vol 0024, 95; The Hermeneutic Center in An Investigation of Interpretive Methodologies in The Study of Theology Through Dialogue and a Transcultural Understanding of Religion, J Ecumenical Studies, Vol 0034, 97; Religious Studies as World Theology J Ecumenical Studies, Vol 0034, 97; Interreligious Dialogue Between Tradition and Modernity, J Ecumenical Studies, Vol 0034, 97. **CONTACT ADDRESS** Dept of Relig, Univ of Manitoba, Winnipeg, MB, Canada R3T 2N2.

KLUDZE, A. KODZO PAAKU
DISCIPLINE LEGAL STUDIES **EDUCATION** Univ Ghana, BA, 63, LLB, 65; Univ London,UK, PhD, 69. **CAREER** Sr lect, fac of law, Univ Ghana, 65-79; prof & dean, Univ of Calaban, Nigeria, 86-88; prof, Rutgers Univ, 79-91, Distinguished Prof of Law, 91-. **MEMBERSHIPS** Ghana Bar, 65; New York State Bar, 84. **RESEARCH** Property; wills and trusts; equity; African law; international law. **SELECTED PUBLICATIONS** Auth, "Problems of interstate succession in Ghana," U. G. L. J., 9 (72): 89; auth, Ewe Law of Property, Sweet & Maxwell, London (73); auth, Modern Principles of Equity, Foris Pubs, Dortrecht, Holland (88); auth, Modern Law of Succession in Ghana, Foris Pubs, Dorecht, Holland (88); auth, Ghana Law of Landlord and Tenant, Lephany Academic Pub, New York (93). **CONTACT ADDRESS** Sch of Law, Rutgers, The State Univ of New Jersey, Camden, 217 N 5th St, Camden, NJ 08102-1226. **EMAIL** kludze@crab.rutgers.edu

KLUGE, EIKE-HENNER W.
DISCIPLINE BIOMEDICAL ETHICS **EDUCATION** Univ Calgary, BA; Univ Mich, AM, PhD. **CAREER** Instr, Univ Calif; prof, 71; dept ch. **RESEARCH** History of philosophy and theory of perception. **SELECTED PUBLICATIONS** Auth, bk(s) and articles in medical ethics, hist philos. **CONTACT ADDRESS** Dept of Philosophy, Univ of Victoria, PO Box 3045, Victoria, BC, Canada V8W 3P4. **EMAIL** ekluge@uvic.ca

KMIEC, DOUGLAS WILLIAM
PERSONAL Born 09/24/1951, Chicago, IL, m, 1973, 2 children **DISCIPLINE** PROPERTY AND LAND USE LAW **EDUCATION** Northwestern Univ, BA, 73; Univ Southern Calif, JD, 76. **CAREER** Atty, Vedder, Price, Kaufman and Kammholz, 76-78; asst prof property and land use, Valparaiso Univ, 78-80; adj prof environ law, Ind Univ, 80; Assoc Prof Property, Land Use, State and Local Govt, Notre Dame Univ, 80-99; Constitutional legal council to Pres Reagan, 85-89; prof, Pepperdine Univ, 99-. **HONORS AND AWARDS** Fel, Inst for Humane Studies, 81 and Law and Econ Inst, 82; special asst to the President of the US and White House fel, 82-83; Edmund J. Randolph Award, 88; Fullbright Distinguished Scholar. **MEMBERSHIPS** Am Asn Law Sch; Am Bar Asn; Intercollegiate Studies Inst. **RESEARCH** The philosophy of property; federalism and the limits of government; natural law and jurisprudence. **SELECTED PUBLICATIONS** Auth, The 91 Civil-Rights Act in A Constitutional, Statutory, and Philosophical Enigma, Notre Dame Law Rev, Vol 0068, 93; Clarifying the Supreme Courts Taking Cases in An Irreverent But Otherwise Unassumable Draft Opinion in Dolan V City of Tigard, Denver Univ Law Rev, Vol 0071, 94; Mere Creatures of The State in Education, Religion, and The Courts, a View From The Courtroomm, Notre Dame Law Rev, Vol 0070, 95; At Last, the Supreme-Court Solves the Takings Puzzle, Harvard J Law Pub Policy, Vol 0019, 95; Prof Murphy,Edward, Notre Dame Law Rev, Vol 0071, 95; co-author, The American Constitutional Order, Individual Rights and the American Constitution, The History, Structure and Philosophy of the American Constitution; auth, The Attorney General's Lawer; auth, Cease-Fire on the Family. **CONTACT ADDRESS** School of Law, Pepperdine Univ, 24255 Pacific Coast Highway, Malibu, CA 90263. **EMAIL** Douglas.Kmiec@pepperdine.edu

KNELLER, JANE E.
DISCIPLINE PHILOSOPHY **EDUCATION** Univ Rochester, PhD, 84. **CAREER** Assoc prof. **HONORS AND AWARDS** Past VP, NAm Kant Soc; editorial bd, Kantian Rev; Hist of Philos Quarterly. **MEMBERSHIPS** Soc Women Philos; Am Soc Aesthet. **RESEARCH** Kant; aesthetics; faminist theory; early

german romanticism. **SELECTED PUBLICATIONS** Auth, pubs on history of modern philosophy, aesthetics, and feminist social and ethical theory; Autonomy and Community: Readings in Contemporary Kantian Social Philosophy, SUNY, 98; Klaus Reich's The Completeness of Kant's Table of Judgments, Stanford. **CONTACT ADDRESS** Philos Dept, Colorado State Univ, Fort Collins, CO 80523. **EMAIL** kneller@lamar.colostate.edu

KNIGHT, CAROLY ANN
PERSONAL Born Denver, CO, s **DISCIPLINE** THEOLOGY **EDUCATION** Bishop Coll, Dallas, TX, BA, 1977; Union Theological Seminary, New York City, MDiv, 1980; United Theoligical Seminary, Dayton, OH, DMin, 1995. **CAREER** Canaan Bapt Ch, NYC, asst pastor, 78-87; Philadelphia Bapt Ch, NYC, pastor, 88-93; Union Theological Seminary, NYC, asst prof, 89-93; ITC, Atlanta, Asst Prof, 95-. **HONORS AND AWARDS** Ebony Magazine, 15 Greatest Black Women Preachers, 1997; Morehouse Coll, Coll of Preachers, 1996; United Negro Coll Fund, Alumni Awd, 1993; Natl Coun of Negro Women, Bethune Awd, 1991; Negro Professional Women Comm Svc, Laurelton Chap, 1987. **MEMBERSHIPS** Delta Sigma Theta, golden life mem, 1982-; NAACP, 1980-. **SELECTED PUBLICATIONS** "If The Worst Should Come!," sermon, 1997; "When You Talk to Yourself!," sermon, 1997; "How To Deal With Failure," Sister to Sister, devotional, 1993. **CONTACT ADDRESS** Interdenominational Theol Ctr, 700 Martin Luther King Jr Dr, SW Rm 207, Atlanta, GA 30314-4143.

KNIGHT, DEBORAH
DISCIPLINE PHILOSOPHY **EDUCATION** Univ Carleton, BA; MA; Univ Toronto, PhD. **CAREER** Adj prof. **HONORS AND AWARDS** Assoc ed, Film Philos. **RESEARCH** Philosophy of mind; philosophy of language; philosophy of art. **SELECTED PUBLICATIONS** Auth, "Making Sense of Genre," Film and Philosophy, 2, 96: 58-73; auth, "Aristotelians on Speed: Paradoxes of Genre in the Context of Cinema," Film Theory and Philosophy, Murray Smith and Richard Allen, Oxford: Oxford University Press, 97; auth, "Naturalism, Narration, and Critical Perspective: Ken Loach and the Experimental Method," Agent of Challenge and Defiance: The Film of Ken Loach, ed. George McKnight, Westport: Praeger, 97; auth, "Back to Basics: Film/Theory/Aestthetics" Journal of Aesthetic Education 31 no. 2, 97: 37-44; coauth, "The Case of the Disappearing Enigma," Philosophy and Literature 21, no.1, 97: 123-138; auth, "A Poetics of Psychological Explanation," Metaphilosophy 28, no. 1-2, 97: 63-80; auth, "Not an Actual Demonstration," Journal of Aesthetics and Art Criticism, forthcoming **CONTACT ADDRESS** Philos Dept, Queen's Univ at Kingston, Kingston, ON, Canada K7L 3N6. **EMAIL** knightd@post.queensu.ca

KNIGHT, GARY
PERSONAL Born 12/08/1939, St. Joseph, MO, m, 1962, 3 children **DISCIPLINE** LAW **EDUCATION** Stanford Univ, AB, 61; Southern Methodist Univ, JD, 64. **CAREER** Assoc, Nossaman, Waters, Scott, Krueger and Riordan, Los Angeles, Calif, 64-68; from asst prof to assoc prof law, 68-75, Prof Law, Law Ctr, LA State Univ, Baton Rouge, 75-; Campanile Prof Marine Recources Law, 71-; Mem Adv Comt Law of Sea, US Govt Inter-Agency Law of Sea Task Force, 72-; Assoc Ed, Ocean Develop and Int Law J, 72-; mem exec bd, Law of Sea Inst, 75-80; consult, US Dept State, 74-75; consult, Cent Intel Agency, 77-; chmn Sci and Statist Comt, Gulf of Mex Fishery Mgt Coun, 77-78; Pres, Jonathan Publ Co, 81-. **MEMBERSHIPS** Am Bar Asn; Am Soc Int Law. **RESEARCH** Law of the sea; ocean resources. **SELECTED PUBLICATIONS** Auth, An Inventory of the Supreme Court of the Holy-Roman-Empire from the Hauptstaatsarchiv-Stuttgart A-D, J Soc Archivists, Vol 0015, 94; Swedish Archive Bibliographies 1980-1989 J Soc Archivists, Vol 0015, 94. **CONTACT ADDRESS** Law Ctr, Louisiana State Univ and A&M Col, Baton Rouge, LA 70803.

KNIGHT, HENRY H., III
PERSONAL Born 02/14/1948, Atlanta, GA, m, 1979, 1 child **DISCIPLINE** EVANGELISM, WESLEY STUDIES, SYSTEMATIC THEOLOGY **EDUCATION** Emory Univ, BA, 70; PhD, 87; Candler Sch Theol, MDiv, 77. **CAREER** Adj lectr, Candler Sch Theol, 86-93; asst prof, St Paul Sch Theol, 93-99; assoc prof, 99-. **MEMBERSHIPS** AAR; AETE; WTS; SPS. **RESEARCH** Theology of John Wesley; theology and practice of Evangelism; contemporary Evangelical theory. **SELECTED PUBLICATIONS** Auth, The Presence of God in the Christian Life: John Wesley and the Means of Grace, 92; auth, A Future for Truth: Evangelical Theology in a Post modern World, 97; coauth, The Conversation Matters: Why United Methodists Should Talk With One Another, 99. **CONTACT ADDRESS** Dept Theology, Saint Paul Sch of Theology, 5123 E Truman Rd, Kansas City, MO 64127-2440. **EMAIL** halk@spst.edu

KNIGHT, W. H.
PERSONAL Born Beckley, CA, m **DISCIPLINE** LEGAL STUDIES **EDUCATION** UNC-C.H., BA; Columbia Univ, JD. **CAREER** Vice Provost, Univ of Iowa 97-; Assoc Dean, Univ of Iowa, 91-93; Prof of Law, Univ of Iowa, 88; Assoc Prof of Law, Univ of Iowa; 83-88. **HONORS AND AWARDS** Woodrow Wilson Administrative Internship Recipient; Univ of Iowa Old Gold Fellowship. **MEMBERSHIPS** Amer Bar Assn; Nat Bar Assn; Society of Amer Law Teachers; Amer Law Institute. **RESEARCH** Banking; Financial institutions; Commercial Law; Contracts; & Critical Race Theory. **SELECTED PUBLICATIONS** Auth, Commercial Transactions Under the Uniform Commercial Code, by Mathew Bender, 97. **CONTACT ADDRESS** Dept Law, Univ Iowa, 1 Boyd Law Bldg, Iowa City, IA 52242-1113. **EMAIL** w-knight@uiowa.edu

KNIKER, CHARLES R.
PERSONAL Born 08/20/1936, Austin, TX, m, 1962, 2 children **DISCIPLINE** RELIGION AND EDUCATION **EDUCATION** Elmhurst College, BA, 58; Eden Sem, BD 62; San Francisco Sem, MA 66; Columbia U Teach College, EdD 69. **CAREER** Assoc Dir acad affs, 98-, Iowa Bd of Regents; vis Prof, 97-, Texas A&M College of Ed; pres and Prof rel and edu, 93-96, Prof, 69-93, Iowa State Univ. **HONORS AND AWARDS** ISU Outstanding Teacher; Chautaged Cert Merit; ISU Fac Citation; 3 Lilly Endows; US Dept Edu Gnt; Global Perspectives Inc Gnt. **MEMBERSHIPS** AERA; AESA; NCR; ASCD; HES. **RESEARCH** Religion and Education. **SELECTED PUBLICATIONS** Auth, Seminary Inertia, Christian Century, 98; ch 1 & 2, Religion and Schooling in Contemporary America: Confronting our Culturalism Pluralism, NY, Garland Pub, 97; Should the Bible be Taught in Public Schools: Yes!, Bible Rev, 95, reprinted, New Conversations, 95; Religion in the Secondary Schools: A Necessary Fact of Life for Today's Adolescents, Fam Perspective, 92; Accommodating the Religious Diversity of Public School Students: Putting the CARTS Before the Horse, Rel and Pub Edu, 88; Reflections on the Continuing Crusade for Common Schools: in: Religious Schooling in America: Hist Insights and Contemporary Concerns, ed, James C Carper, Thomas Hunt, Birmingham AL, Religious Educ Press, 84; coauth, Teaching Today and Tomorrwo, Merrill, 81; Coed, Myth and Reality, 2nd edition, Boston, Allyn and Bacon, 75; Teaching About Religion in the Public Schools, Bloomington IN, Phi Delta Kappa Educ Foun, 85; The Values of Athletics in Schools: A Continuing Debate, Phi Delta Kappa, 74. **CONTACT ADDRESS** Board of Depts, 100 Ct Ave, Ste 203, Des Moines, IA 50319. **EMAIL** ckniker@iastate.edu

KNIPE, DAVID MACLAY
PERSONAL Born 11/25/1932, Johnstown, PA, m, 3 children **DISCIPLINE** HISTORY OF RELIGION, SOUTH ASIAN STUDIES **EDUCATION** Cornell Univ, AB, 55; Union Theol Sem, MA, 58; Univ Chicago, MA, 65, PhD(hist relig), 71. **CAREER** Lectr, 67-69, from instr to asst prof, 69-73, assoc prof, 73-79, Prof South Asian Studies, Univ Wis-Madison, 79-; Sr res fel, Am Inst Indian Studies, 71-72, and 80. **MEMBERSHIPS** Am Acad Relig; Asn Asian Studies; Am Soc Study Relig. **RESEARCH** Vedic religion; Hinduism Jainism; methodology and religion. **SELECTED PUBLICATIONS** Auth, The heroic theft: Myths from Rgveda IV and the Ancient- Near East, 5/67 & One fire, three fires, five fires: Vedic symbols in transition, 8/72, Hist Relig; In the image of fire: Vedic experiences of heat, Motilal Banarsidass, Delhi, 75; Religious encounters with death: Essays in the history and anthropology of religion, Pa State Univ, 77; Exploring the religions of South Asia, A series of fifteen color video productions, WHA-TV, 74 & 75; Vedas, Vedic Hinduism, Sacrifice and 26 other articles, In: The Abingdon Dict of Living Religions, Abingdon, 81; coauth, Focus on Hinduism: Audio-visual resources for teaching religion, Chambersburg, Anima, 2nd ed 81. **CONTACT ADDRESS** Dept of S Asian Studies, Univ of Wisconsin, Madison, 1220 Linden Drive, Madison, WI 53706-1557.

KNITTER, PAUL FRANCIS
PERSONAL Born 02/25/1939, Chicago, IL, m, 1982, 2 children **DISCIPLINE** SYSTEMATIC THEOLOGY, COMPARATIVE RELIGIONS **EDUCATION** Divine Word Sem, Ill, BA, 62; Pontif Gregorian Univ, BA, 64, Licentiate, 66; Philipps Univ, WGer, PhD (theol), 72. **CAREER** Asst prof theol, Cath Theol Union, Chicago, 72-75; assoc prof, 75-78, Prof Theol, Xavier Univ, Ohio, 78-. **MEMBERSHIPS** Am Acad Relig; Cath Theol Soc Am; Col Theol Soc; Am Soc Missiology. **RESEARCH** Dialogue among World religions; eastern religions; Christology. **SELECTED PUBLICATIONS** Auth, One Earth, Many Religions, 95; auth, Jesus and Other Names, 96. **CONTACT ADDRESS** Dept of Relig, Xavier Univ, Ohio, 3800 Victory Pky, Cincinnati, OH 45207-4442. **EMAIL** knitter@xu.edu

KNOLL, MICHAEL S.
PERSONAL Born 04/23/1957, New York, NY, m, 1999 **DISCIPLINE** LAW **EDUCATION** Univ Chicago, AB, 77; AM, 80; PhD, 83; JD, 84. **CAREER** Prof, Univ S Calif Law School, 90-00; Prof, Univ Penn Law School, 00-. **RESEARCH** Application of financial theory to tax. **CONTACT ADDRESS** School of Law, Univ of So California, 699 Exposition Blvd, Los Angeles, CA 90089-0040.

KNOX, GEORGE F.
PERSONAL Born 10/17/1943, Cleveland, TN, m, 1985 **DISCIPLINE** LAW **EDUCATION** MI State Univ, BS Zoology 1966; Univ of Miami School of Law, JD 1973. **CAREER** Univ of Miami School of Business Admin, lecturer 1973-74; City of Miami, FL, asst city Attorney 1974-75; Univ of AR Fayetteville, asst prof of law 1975-76; Univ of Miami School of Law, lecturer 1978-80; Nova Univ Center for the Study of Law, lecturer 1980-82; City of Miami, FL, city Attorney and dir of law dept 1976-82; Paul, Landy Beiley & Harper PA, partner 1982-84; Long & Knox, partner 1984-; Kubicki Draper Gallagher, Miami, FL, Attorney 1990-. **HONORS AND AWARDS** Jaycees Outstanding Young Men of Amer 1976; Miami-Dade Chamber of Commerce Awd of Outstanding Contribution to Social and Economic Development 1977; Black Lawyers' Assn Virgil Hawkins Achievement Awd 1977; Alpha Phi Alpha Fraternity Achievement Awd 1977; participant "Law and Justice in Today's Society" seminar sponsored by Natl Endowment for the Humanities Harvard Univ 1978; FL Jr Coll at Jacksonville Community Awareness Awd; Beta Beta Lambda Chap Alpha Phi Alpha Fraternity Community Service Awd 1981; NAACP Appreciation Awd 1981; Northwest Council of Jacksonville Chamber of Commerce Jacksonville Achiever Awd 1986. **MEMBERSHIPS** Mem FL, Natl, Amer, DC Bar Assns; mem, Natl Inst of Municipal Law Officers; mem Assn of Amer Law Schools, Black Lawyers Assn, FL League of Cities, Assn of Amer Trial Lawyers, Acad of FL Trial Lawyers; mem US Dist Court Southern Dist of FL, US Court of Appeals for Fifth Circuit, United States Supreme Court; mem NAACP; bd dirs Miami-Dade Community College Foundation Inc; mem Greater Miami Chamber of Commerce; mem FL Memorial College Ctr of Excellence; bd dirs YMCA of Greater Miami; Member Dade County Blue Ribbon Committee; member of board of trustees, Florida Memorial College; board of directors, United Way; member, The Miami Coalition for a Drug-Free Community. **SELECTED PUBLICATIONS** Numerous publications. **CONTACT ADDRESS** Kubicki, Draper, Gallagher & McGrane, 25 W Flagler St, Miami, FL 33130.

KOBACH, KRIS W.
DISCIPLINE LAW **EDUCATION** Harvard Univ, BA; Oxford Univ, MPhil, PhD; Yale Sch Law, JD. **CAREER** Law clerk, Judge Deanell Reece Tacha, US Court Appeals; assoc prof **HONORS AND AWARDS** Ed, Yale Law J. **RESEARCH** Constitutional law and theory; American legal history; Legislation **SELECTED PUBLICATIONS** Auth, Political Capital: The Motives, Tactics, and Goals of Politicized Businesses in South Africa, Univ Am, 90;The Referendum: Direct Democracy in Switzerland, Dartmouth, 94; pubs on political science, constitutional law, and legal history; Kris W. Kobach, The Origins of Regulatory Takings: Setting the Record Straight, 1996 UTAH L. REV. 1211 97; auth, Kris W. Kobach, Contingency Fees May Be Hazardous to Your Health A Constitutional Analysis of Congressional Interference with Tobacco Litigation Contracts, 49 S.C. L. REV. 215 (1998); Kris W. Kobach, May "We the People" Speak? The Forgotten Role of Constituent Instructions in Amending the Constitution, 33 U. CAL DAVIS L. REV. 1, 99. **CONTACT ADDRESS** Law Dept, Univ of Missouri, Kansas City, 5100 Rockhill Rd, Kansas City, MO 64110-2499. **EMAIL** kobachk@umkc.edu

KOCH, GLENN A.
DISCIPLINE NEW TESTAMENT STUDIES **EDUCATION** Marshall Univ, BA; E Baptist Theol Sem, BD, ThM; Univ Pa, MA, PhD. **CAREER** Prof, E Baptist Theol Sem. **MEMBERSHIPS** Mem, Soc of Biblical Lit; Philadelphia Sem on Christian Origins; Nat Assn of Baptist Prof(s) of Rel. **SELECTED PUBLICATIONS** Co-auth, Learning to Read New Testament Greek. **CONTACT ADDRESS** Eastern Baptist Theol Sem, 6 Lancaster Ave, Wynnewood, PA 19096.

KOCH, MICHAEL
DISCIPLINE PHILOSOPHY **EDUCATION** Bard Col, BA; SUNY Albany, DA; Univ IL, PhD. **CAREER** Adj lctr, Univ Albany, 94; adj lctr, SUNY Oneonta, 93-. **RESEARCH** Hist of philos: pragmatism, citical theory; continental philos: hermeneutics, phenomenology; 20th century soc and polit philos; philos of soc sci(s), tech; aesthetics. **SELECTED PUBLICATIONS** Auth, Marco's Letters: The EZLN and the Rhetoric of Nationalism in the age of Global Capitalism; The Manikin and Its Masks: The Negative Hermeneutics of Henry Adams; Aristotle's Posterior Analytics: Reconstructive Rationality for Social Scientific Inquiry. **CONTACT ADDRESS** SUNY, Col at Oneonta, Oneonta, NY 13820.

KOCHANEK, STANLEY ANTHONY
PERSONAL Born 05/10/1934, Bayonne, NJ, w, 1984, 2 children **DISCIPLINE** POLITICAL SCIENCE **EDUCATION** Univ Pennsylvania, PhD, 63; Rutgers Univ, MA, 57; Rutgers Univ, BA, 56 **CAREER** Prof Polit Sci, Pennsylvania State Univ, 73-; assoc prof Polit Sci, Pennsylvania State Univ, 67-73; assist prof Polit Sci, Pennsylvania State Univ, 63-67; Prof Emer, Pa State Univ. **HONORS AND AWARDS** Research Fel, Amer Inst Pakistan Studies, 96-97; Fulbright South Asia Regional Research Fel, 93-94; Faculty Research Fel, Amer Inst of Bangladesh Studies, 90-91 **MEMBERSHIPS** Amer Polit Sci Assoc; Assoc Asian Studies; Amer Pakistan Research Orgn **RESEARCH** India, Pakistan and Bangladesh **SELECTED PUBLICATIONS** CoauthIndia: Government and Politics in a Developing Nation, Harcourt Brace, 6th ed, 00; Patron Client Politics and Business in Bangladesh, Sage, 93; "Ethnic Conflict

and the Politicization of Pakistan Business." Pakistan 1995, Westview, 95 **CONTACT ADDRESS** 4601 N Park Ave, No 108-H, Chevy Chase, MD 20815.

KODDERMANN, ACHIM D.
PERSONAL Born 01/07/1961, Wiesbaden, Germany **DISCIPLINE** PHILOSOPHY **EDUCATION** Johannes-Gutenberg-Univ; MA, 88; PhD, 91. **CAREER** Vis prof, Univ Denver, 89-90; counsellor/corp planner/pers asst to CEO, Nat Ger Pub Broadcasting, 90-93; asst instr, Univ ME, 90-93; asst prof, SUNY Oneonta, 93-96; vis prof, Sripatum Univ, 96; assoc prof, SUNY Oneonta, 96-. **HONORS AND AWARDS** Richard Siegfried Fac Prize Acad Excellence, SUNY Oneonta, 95; fellow, NEH summer inst PA State Univ, 94; rep hum, Ctr Environ Studies, 89-93. **MEMBERSHIPS** APA; Deutsche Kant Gesellschaft ev.; Int Kant Soc; Dante Soc, Ger Sec;, DAIMON, Int Soc Neoplatonic Studies; Int Soc Study Europ Ideas; Soc Ancient Gr Philos. **RESEARCH** Ethics: applied ethics, environmental ethics, professional and business ethics, media ethics; continental philos: hermeneutics, Ger idealism, romanticism, phenomenology, mod French philos; philos of law; sci, tech and soc studies. **SELECTED PUBLICATIONS** Auth, Why the Medieval Idea of a Community-Oriented University is Still Modern, Educ Change, 95; World Debt and the Human Condition Structural Adjustment and the Right to Development (rev) in Studies in Human Rights, Greenwood, 94, and Denver Jour Int Law & Policy, 95; Television as a Moral Medium and as a Factor in an Information Society in The Image of Technology, Soc Interdisciplinary Study Soc Imagery, 94; Jere P Surber--Language and German Idealism, Fichte's Linguististic Philosophy Daimon, Revista de Filosofea, 94. **CONTACT ADDRESS** SUNY, Col at Oneonta, Oneonta, NY 13820. **EMAIL** Koeddea@Oneonta.edu

KOEGEL, LYNNE
PERSONAL Born 10/04/1942, St Charles, IL, m, 3 children **DISCIPLINE** THEOLOGY **EDUCATION** Univ Calif at Los Angeles, BA, 66; Wayne State Univ, MA, 74; McCormick Theol Sem, M Div, 91; D Min, 97. **CAREER** Fac, Macomb Col, 83-89; Pres, Lynco Inc, Southfield Mich, 86-; Pres, RTK Enterprises Inc, Mich, 92-; Asst Prof, Ecumenical Theol Sem, 92-; Dir of Sem Life, 97-99. **HONORS AND AWARDS** 3 Awds, Gross Pointe Pub Schools; 2 Awds, Girls Scouts US; Who's Who of Am Women. **MEMBERSHIPS** Am Acad of Rel, Soc of Bibl Lit, Presbytery of Detroit, Ancient Bibl Manuscript Center, Scholar's Trialog, Greater Detroit Interfaith Round Table. **RESEARCH** Dead Sea Scrolls, Pseudoepigraphia. **SELECTED PUBLICATIONS** Contribur, Eerdmann's Biblical Dictionary. **CONTACT ADDRESS** Ecumenical Theol Sem, 2930 Woodward St, Detroit, MI 48201.

KOEGLER, HANS-HERBERT
PERSONAL Born 01/13/1960, Darmstadt, Germany **DISCIPLINE** PHILOSOPHY **EDUCATION** Goethe Univ Ger, PhD. **CAREER** Asst prof, Univ Ill, 91-97; vis scholar, Boston Univ, 97; asst prof, 97, assoc prof, 99, Univ N Fla. **HONORS AND AWARDS** Honorary Fac Mem, Univ Catamarca Arg; Fel of the Ger Nat Fel Orgn. **MEMBERSHIPS** Int Soc Theory Consortium. **RESEARCH** Recent European Philosophy, Philosophy of Language, Interpretive Theory/Hermeneutics, Social and Political Philosophy. **SELECTED PUBLICATIONS** Auth, Michel Foucault: Ein anti-humanistischer Aufklarer, 94; The Power of Dialogue: Critical Hermeneutics after Gadamer and Foucault, 96; co-ed, Empathy and Agency: The Problem of Understanding in the Human Sciences,99; auth, Empathy and Agency: The Problem of Understanding in the Human Sciences, 00. **CONTACT ADDRESS** Dept of Philos, Univ of No Florida, 4567 St Johns Bluff Rd, Jacksonville, FL 32224. **EMAIL** hkoegler@gw.unf.edu

KOENIG, THOMAS ROY
PERSONAL Born 04/07/1934, Detroit, MI, m, 1971, 4 children **DISCIPLINE** PHILOSOPHY, THEOLOGY **EDUCATION** Villanova Univ, BA, 57; Colegium Int Augustinianum, Rome, 61; DePaul Univ, MA, 65; Cath Univ Louvain, PhD(philos), 67. **CAREER** Teacher math & Latin, Mendel Cath High Sch, Chicago, 61-64; asst prof philos, Tolentine Col, 65-70; asst prof, 70-74, Assoc Prof Philos, Purdue Univ, Calumet Campus, 74-, Nat Found for Humanities fel philos, 70; Purdue Res Found fel, 71; participant, Ind Comt for Humanities & humanists, Midwest Ctr, 73-74; Nat Found for Humanities grant, 77-79; Fulbright fel, Belgium, 65-67. **MEMBERSHIPS** AAUP; Am Philos Asn; Am Catholic Philols Asn; Southern Soc Philos and Psychol. **RESEARCH** Problem of maturity in existential philosophy and psychology; Paul Ricoeur's interpretation of Freud; problems of leisure in a contemporary world. **SELECTED PUBLICATIONS** Auth, The Philosophy of Georges Bastide, Martinus Nijhoff, The Hague, 71; An Introduction to Ethics, MSS, 74. **CONTACT ADDRESS** Dept of Philos, Purdue Univ, Calumet, 2233 171st St, Hammond, IN 46323-2094.

KOERTGE, NORETTA
PERSONAL Born 10/07/1935, Olney, IL **DISCIPLINE** PHILOSOPHY OF SCIENCE, HISTORY OF SCIENCE **EDUCATION** Univ Ill, BS, 55, MS, 56; London Univ, PhD(philos of sci), 69. **CAREER** Instr chem, Elmhurst Col, 60-63; head chem sect, Am Col for Girls, Instanbul, Turkey, 63-64; lectr philos of sci, Ont Inst for Studies Educ, 68-69; asst prof, 70-73, assoc prof, 74-81, Prof Hist and Philos of Sci, Ind Univ, Bloomington, 81-; Editor-in-Chief, Phil of Sci, 99-. **HONORS AND AWARDS** Fellow of Amer Assoc Adv Sci. **MEMBERSHIPS** Philos Sci Asn. **RESEARCH** Theories of scientific method; historical development of philosophy of science; Poppers philosophy of science. **SELECTED PUBLICATIONS** Auth, A House Built on Sand, professing Feminism, Philosophy and Homosexuality. **CONTACT ADDRESS** Indiana Univ, Bloomington, 130 Goodbody Hall, Bloomington, IN 47401. **EMAIL** koertge@indiana.edu

KOESTENBAUM, PETER
PERSONAL Born 04/06/1928, Berlin, Germany, m, 4 children **DISCIPLINE** PHILOSOPHY **EDUCATION** Stanford Univ, BA, 49; Harvard Univ, MA, 51; Boston Univ, PhD, 58. **CAREER** Prof, phil, 54-88, San Jose St Univ, CA **HONORS AND AWARDS** Outstanding Prof CA St Col & Univ System, 69 **MEMBERSHIPS** APA **RESEARCH** Philos; business **SELECTED PUBLICATIONS** Auth, Leadership: The Inner Side of Greatness, Jossey Bass. **CONTACT ADDRESS** 3927 Fairbreeze Circle, Westlake Village, CA 91361. **EMAIL** pkipeter@ix.netcom.com

KOESTER, CRAIG R.
PERSONAL Born 08/25/1953, Northfield, MN, m, 1979, 2 children **DISCIPLINE** THEOLOGY **EDUCATION** Union Theolog Sem, PhD, 86; Luther Theolog Sem, M.Div, 80; St Olaf Col, BA, 76. **CAREER** Asst pastor, Immanuel Luth Church, Princeton, MN, 80-83; interim Pastor, Trinity Luth Church, NY City, 85-86; asst prof New Testament, Luther Theolog Sem, 86-91; from assoc prof to prof, New Testament, Luther Theolog Sem, 91-. **HONORS AND AWARDS** Who's Who in Relig; Associated Church Pr Awd for Bibl Exposition, 91; Who's Who in Bibl Studies & Archaeology; Bruce Prize for New Testament Study, Luther Theolog Sem, 80 **MEMBERSHIPS** Center of Theolog Inquiry Member; Studiorum Novi Testamenti Societas. **SELECTED PUBLICATIONS** Symbolism in the Fourth Gospel: Meaning, Mystery, Community, Fortress Pr, 95; forthcoming: Hebrews, Anchor Bible, Doubleday, forthcoming; Revelation and the End of All Things, Eerdmans, forthcoming. **CONTACT ADDRESS** Dept of Theology, Luther Sem, 2481 Como Ave, Saint Paul, MN 55108.

KOESTER, HELMUT
PERSONAL Born 12/18/1926, Hamburg, Germany, m, 1953, 4 children **DISCIPLINE** NEW TESTAMENT STUDIES **EDUCATION** Univ Marburg, Ger, D Theol, 54. **CAREER** From instr to asst prof, Univ Heidelberg, Ger, 54-58; prof of New Testament Studies and Ecclesiastical Hist, Harvard Univ, 58-98. **HONORS AND AWARDS** Dr Theol, hon, Univ Geneva, Switzerland, 84. **MEMBERSHIPS** Soc of Biblical Lit; Societas Novi Testamenti Studiorum; Am Academy of Arts and Sciences. **RESEARCH** Early-Christian lit; archaeology. **SELECTED PUBLICATIONS** Auth, Athens A and Isthmia in Helmut Koester and Ann Graham Brock, eds, Archaeological Resources for New Testament Studies, vol 1 and 2, Trinity Press Int, 94; Archaologie und Paulus in Thessalonike, in Lukas Bormann, et al, eds, Religious Propaganda and Missionary Competition in the New Testament World: Essays Honoring Dieter Georgi, Brill, 94; History, Culture, and Religion of the Hellenistic Age, Introduction to the New Testament, vol 1, 2nd ed, De Gruyter, 95; Jesus' Presence in the Early Church, Cristianesimo nella Storia 15, 94; The Red Hall in Pergamon, in Michael White and O Larry Yarbrough, The Social World of the Early Christians: Essays in Honor of Wayne A Meeks, Fortress, 95; Ephesos in Early Christian Literature, in Ephesos: Metropolis of Asia, Harvard Theol Studies 41, Trinity Press Int, 95; The Sayings of Q and Their Image of Jesus, in William L Peterson et al, eds, Sayings of Jesus: Canonical and Non-Canonical: Essays in Honor of Tjitze Baarda, Brill, 97; Philippi at the Time of Paul and After His Death, with Charalambos Bakitzis, Trinity Press Int, 98; auth, Hist and Lit of Early Christianity, Introduction to the New Testament, vol. 2, 2nd ed, De Grugteo, 00; several other publications. **CONTACT ADDRESS** 45 Francis Ave, Cambridge, MA 02138.

KOHL, MARVIN
PERSONAL Born 05/19/1932, New York, NY, m, 1955, 4 children **DISCIPLINE** PHILOSOPHY **EDUCATION** City Col New York, BA, 54; NYork Univ, MA, 58, PhD(philos), 66. **CAREER** Instr philos, Long Island Univ, 61-65; from asst profto assoc prof, 65-73, Prof Philos, State Univ NY Col Fredonia, 73-; NIH Fel, Mass Inst Tech, 70-71; Contrib Ed, Free Inquiry, 80-. **RESEARCH** Ethical theory and medical ethics. **SELECTED PUBLICATIONS** Auth, Enforcing a Vision of Community in the Role of the Test Oath in Missouri Reconstruction, Civil War History, Vol 0040, 94. **CONTACT ADDRESS** Dept of Philos State, SUNY, Col at Fredonia, Fredonia, NY 14063.

KOHN, LIVIA
PERSONAL Born 03/14/1956, Hofheim, Germany, d **DISCIPLINE** RELIGION **EDUCATION** Univ Calif Berkeley, BA, 77; Bonn Univ, PhD, 81; Goettingen Univ, Dr. Habil, 91. **CAREER** asst prof to prof, Boston Univ, 88-. **HONORS AND AWARDS** Fel, Japan Soc for the Promotion of Sci, 81-83; Fel, Univ Mich, 86-87; Fel, Japan Soc for the Promotion of Sci, 91-93; NEH Res Fel, 01. **MEMBERSHIPS** Am Acad of Relig; Asn for Asian Studies; Soc for the Study of Chinese Relig; Japan Soc for the Study of Daoism. **RESEARCH** Daoism; Chinese religion; Meditation. **SELECTED PUBLICATIONS** Auth, Taoist Mystical Philosophy: The Scripture of Western Ascension, SUNY Press, 91; auth, Early Chinese Mysticism: Philosophy and Soteriology in the Taoist Tradition, Princeton Univ Press, 92; auth, Laughing at the Tao: Debates Among Buddhists and Taoists in medieval China, Princeton Univ Press, 95; co-ed, Lao-tzu and the Tao-te-ching, SUNY Press, 98; auth, God of the Dao: Lord Lao in History and Myth, Univ Mich, 98; ed, Daoism Handbook, Leiden, 00; auth, Daoism and Chinese Culture, Three Pines Press, 01. **CONTACT ADDRESS** Dept Relig, Boston Univ, 745 Commonwealth Ave, Boston, MA 02215. **EMAIL** lkohn@bu.edu

KOHN, RICHARD
PERSONAL Born 07/20/1948, New York, NY, m, 1 child **DISCIPLINE** BUDDHIST STUDIES **EDUCATION** Univ Wisc, BA, MA, PhD, 98. **CAREER** Lectr, 90, Univ Calif; adj assoc cur, 90-91, Asian Art Museum of SF; vis asst prof, 92, Indiana Univ; res assoc, 93-, Ctr for South Asian Stud, lectr, 99-Univ Calif, Berkeley. **HONORS AND AWARDS** Phi Beta Kappa; Soc Sci Res Coun; Diss, abroad fel; Fulbright-Hays Fel; Red Ribbon, Amer Film Fest. **MEMBERSHIPS** AAR. **RESEARCH** Himalayan art; Tibetan relig & cult; Buddhist ritual. **SELECTED PUBLICATIONS** Art, Trance Dancers and Aeroplanes: Montage and Metaphor in Ethnographic Film, 1942-1992, 50 Years after Balinese Character. Yearbk Visual Anthropology, IUAES, vol 1, Firenze: Angelo Pontecorboli Editore, 93; coauth, Paramsukha-Chakrasamvara and Vajravarahi, Seated Vairocana with Attendants, Asian Art Mus: Selected Works, Univ Wash Press, 94; art, The Ritual Preparation of a Tibetan Mandala, Mandala & Landscape, Printworld, 97; art, A Rite of Empowerment, An Offering of Torma, A Prayer to the God of the Plain, Relig of Tibet in Pract, Princeton Univ Press, 97; art, Himalayan Buddhism, Encycl of Women & World Relig, Macmillan, 98. **CONTACT ADDRESS** 454 Beloit Ave, Kensington, CA 94708-1114. **EMAIL** rjkohn1@socrates.berkeley.edu

KOLAK, DANIEL
PERSONAL Born 06/30/1955, Zagreb, Croatia, m, 2 children **DISCIPLINE** PHILOSOPHY **EDUCATION** Univ Md, BA; MA, 81; PhD, 86. **CAREER** Asst prof, Touson State Univ, 86-87; asst prof, Univ of Wisconsin, 87-89; dir, Cognitive Sci Lab, William Poterson Univ, 95-; Chairman Philos dept, Prof, Wilaim Poterson Univ, 95-. **MEMBERSHIPS** APA. **RESEARCH** Philosophy of Mind; Philosophy of Science; Cognitive Science; Mathematics and Logic, Philosophy of Language; Philosophy of Art. **SELECTED PUBLICATIONS** Auth, In Search of God: The Language and Logic of Belief, 94; Lovers of Wisdom, 97; In Search of Myself: Life, Death, and Personal Identity, 98; From the Presocratics to the Present: a Personal Odyssey, 98; Wittgenstein Tractatus, 98; coauth, Wisdom Without Answers, 98; ed, From Palto to Wittgenstein, 94; The Mayfield Anthology of Western Philosophy, 98; Philosophical Bridges, 99; co-ed, The Experience of Philosophy; auth, I Am You: The Metaphysical Foundations for Global Ethics, kluwer, 00. **CONTACT ADDRESS** 38 White Birch Dr, Pomona, NY 10970. **EMAIL** kolardan@msn.com

KOLASNY, JUDETTE M.
PERSONAL Born 10/15/1938, Tiffini, OH, s **DISCIPLINE** THEOLOGY **EDUCATION** Marquette Univ, PhD, 85. **MEMBERSHIPS** CBA, CTSA, SBL. **RESEARCH** Gospel of John **CONTACT ADDRESS** 1007 N Marshall St #314, Milwaukee, WI 53202-3225. **EMAIL** kolasnyj@juno.com

KOLB, DAVID ALAN
PERSONAL Born 04/15/1939, Brooklyn, NY **DISCIPLINE** PHILOSOPHY **EDUCATION** Fordham Univ, AB, 63, MA, 65; Woodstock Col, PhL, 64; Yale Univ, MPhil, 70, PhD, 72. **CAREER** Instr philos, Fordham Univ, 64-67, asst prof, Univ Chicago, 72-77; assoc prof Philos & chmn dept, 77-88, Charles A. Dana Professor of Philosophy, Bates Col, 89-. **HONORS AND AWARDS** Fulbright Fellowship; NEH Fellowship. **MEMBERSHIPS** Am Philos Asn; Hegel Soc Am; Heidegger Conference Asn for Computing Machinery. **RESEARCH** Hist of philos; philos of art, hypertext; German philos. **SELECTED PUBLICATIONS** Critique of Pure Modernity, Univ of Chicago Press; Postmodern Sophistications, Univ of Chicago Press; Socrates in the Labyrinth, Eastgate Systems. **CONTACT ADDRESS** Dept of Philos, Bates Col, 75 Campus Ave, Lewiston, ME 04240-6018. **EMAIL** dkolb@bates.edu

KOLDEN, MARC
PERSONAL Born 01/15/1940, Bemidji, MN, m, 1962, 1 child **DISCIPLINE** SYSTEMATIC THEOLOGY **EDUCATION** Univ Harvard, BA, 62; Luther Theol Sem, 66; Univ Chicago, MA, PhD, 69, 76. **CAREER** Instr, Hamma Sch Theol, Luther Sem, 71-73; asst prof, 73-78; , assoc prof, 81; prof, 89-; acad dean, 96. **HONORS AND AWARDS** Assoc pastor, Our Redeemer Lutheran Church; dir, Northern Rockies Inst of Theol, 78-81. **SELECTED PUBLICATIONS** Auth, Christ Our Sure

Foundation: Sermons for Pentecost, 95; Living the Faith, 92; coauth, co-ed, Called and Ordained: Lutheran Perspectives on the Office of Ministry, 90. **CONTACT ADDRESS** Dept of Systematic Theology, Luther Sem, 2481 Como Ave, Saint Paul, MN 55108. **EMAIL** mkolden@luthersem.edu

KOLLAR, NATHAN RUDOLPH
PERSONAL Born 07/20/1938, Braddock, PA, m, 1972, 2 children **DISCIPLINE** RELIGIOUS STUDIES, HISTORY **EDUCATION** St Bonaventure Univ, BA, 60; Cath Univ Am, STL, 64, STD, 67; Univ Notre Dame, MA, 68. **CAREER** Instr theol, Whitefriars Hall, 64-67; asst prof, Washington Theol Coalition, 68-71; asst prof relig studies, St Thomas Univ, 71-74; assoc prof, 74-82, Prof Relig Studies, St John Fisher Col, 82-; Chmn Dept, 79-; prof, St Bernards Institute, 86-; sr lectr, grad school of ed, Univ of Rochester, 89-; assoc ed, Explorations, 84-. **HONORS AND AWARDS** Trustees Awd, St John Fishe, 91; Lilly Grant, 96-97; Louisville Inst Research Grant, 98. **MEMBERSHIPS** Am Acad Relig; Col Theol Soc; Soc Sci Study Relig; Can Soc Study Relig; Forum for Death Educ and Coun. **RESEARCH** "Values, Leadership and Religion." **SELECTED PUBLICATIONS** Auth, "The Death of National Symbols: Roman Catholism in Quebec," Ethinicity, Nationality, and Religious Experience, Lanham, MD: Univ Press of America, 95; auth, "Doing It Together: Changing Pedagogies," Teaching Theology nad Religion , 99. **CONTACT ADDRESS** St. John Fisher Col, Rochester, NY 14618. **EMAIL** kollar@sjfc.edu

KOMONCHAK, JOSEPH ANDREW
PERSONAL Born 03/13/1939, Nyack, NY **DISCIPLINE** THEOLOGY **EDUCATION** St Josephs Sem, NYork, AB, 60, Pontif Gregorian Univ, Rome, STL, 64; Union Theol Sem, NYork, PhD(theol), 76. **CAREER** Assoc prof theol, St Josephs Sem, NY, 67-77; assoc prof theol, Cath Univ Am, 77-80. Mem, bd dirs, Cath Theol Soc Am, 73-75. **MEMBERSHIPS** Cath Theol Soc Am; Am Acad Relig. **RESEARCH** Thought of John Henry Newman; ecclesiology and ministry; theology of social mission of the Church. **SELECTED PUBLICATIONS** Auth, Ordinary Papal magisterium and religious assent, In: Contraception: Authority and Dissent, Herder & Herder, 69; Redemptive justice: An interpretation of the Cur Deus Homo, Dunwoodie Rev, 72; Theological reflections on teaching authority in the Church, Concilium, 76; Humanae Vitae and its reception: ecclesiological reflections, Theol Studies, 78. **CONTACT ADDRESS** 3711 Kennedy St, Hyattsville, MD 20783.

KONDITI, JANE
PERSONAL Born 01/14/1957, Kenya, m, 1972, 5 children **DISCIPLINE** LIBERAL ARTS, EDUCATION, ACCOUNTING **EDUCATION** Tex Wesleyan Univ, BBA; Tex Woman's Univ, MBA; Univ North Tex, PhD. **CAREER** Chairman, Accounting Dept; Academic Dean. **HONORS AND AWARDS** Started an accounting prog at Northwood Univ; Fac Excellence Awd; Elizabeth Armstrong Scholarship Awd; Who's who of Professionals; Professor of the Year, Northwood Univ. **MEMBERSHIPS** Nat Soc of Accountants. **RESEARCH** Women issues, education, children issues. **CONTACT ADDRESS** Chief Academic Dean, Northwood Univ, Texas, 1114 W Fm 1382, Cedar Hill, TX 75104. **EMAIL** konditi@northwood.edu

KONIG, DAVID THOMAS
PERSONAL Born 01/22/1947, Baltimore, MD, 2 children **DISCIPLINE** EARLY AMERICAN AND LEGAL HISTORY **EDUCATION** NYork Univ, AB, 68; Harvard Univ, AM, 69, PhD(hist), 73. **CAREER** From asst prof to prof hist, Washington Univ, 73-; dir, Nat Endowment for Humanities summer sem, 80; Fulbright sr lectr, Italy, 81-82. **RESEARCH** American legal development; colonial through Jacksonian America; science and witchcraft. **SELECTED PUBLICATIONS** Auth, Law and Soc in Puritan Mass, 79; auth, A Summary View of the Law of British America, William Mary Quart, Vol 0050, 93; Devising Liberty, 95. **CONTACT ADDRESS** Dept of Hist, Washington Univ, 1 Brookings Dr, Saint Louis, MO 63130-4899.

KONVITZ, MILTON R.
PERSONAL Born 03/12/1908, Israel, m, 1942, 1 child **DISCIPLINE** CONSTITUTIONAL LAW **EDUCATION** NYork Univ, JD, 1930; Cornell, PhD, 1933. **CAREER** Private practice, Newark, NJ, 33-46; Newark Housing Authority, gen counsel, 38-43; NJ State Housing Authority, gen counsel, 43-45; NYU Law Sch, lectr, 38-46; NAACP Legal Def Fund, asst gen counsel, 43-46. **HONORS AND AWARDS** Honorary degrees from Syracuse Univ, Rutgers Univ, Yeshiva Univ, Jewish Thelo Sem, Hebrew Union Col; awards from NYU, Hebrew Univ. **MEMBERSHIPS** Amer Academy of Arts and Sciences, Fel. **RESEARCH** Constitutional law **SELECTED PUBLICATIONS** Auth, Constitution and Civil Rights, Expanding Liberties, Immigration and Civil Rights, Alien and Asiatic in American Law, Judaism and the American Idea, Torah and Constitution. **CONTACT ADDRESS** 150 Norwood Ave, Oakhurst, NJ 07755-1604.

KOONS, ROBERT C.
PERSONAL Born 02/22/1957, St Paul, MN, m, 1979, 3 children **DISCIPLINE** PHILOSOPHY **EDUCATION** Mich State Univ, BA, 79; Oxford Univ, BA, 81; Univ Calif, PhD, 87. **CAREER** From Asst Prof to Prof, Univ Tex, 87-. **HONORS AND AWARDS** Gustave O Arlt Awd Humanities, 92; Weaver Fel; Danforth Fel. **MEMBERSHIPS** Asn for Symbolic Logic, Soc of Christian Philosophers, European Asn for logic, lang and Infor. **RESEARCH** Metaphysics and epistemology, causation and teleology. **SELECTED PUBLICATIONS** Auth, Paradoxes of Belief and Strategic Rationality, Cambridge Univ Pr, 92; auth, Realism Regained: An Exact Theory of Causation, Teleology and the Mind, Oxford Univ Pr, 00. **CONTACT ADDRESS** Dept Philos, Univ of Texas, Austin, Austin, TX 78712-1013. **EMAIL** rkoons@mail.utexas.edu

KOPACZYNSKI, GERMAIN
PERSONAL Born 04/24/1946, Chelsea, MA **DISCIPLINE** PHILOSOPHY, THEOLOGY **EDUCATION** St Hyacinth Col, BA, 69; Seraphicum, Rome, STL, 75; Boston Col, PhD, 77; Alphonsianum, Rome, STD , 92. **CAREER** Asst Prof Philos, St Hyacinth Col Sem, 76-; pres, St. Hyacinth Col; dir, Education, NCBC. **HONORS AND AWARDS** Fr Adam Zajdel fel, St Hyacinth Clg and Sem. **MEMBERSHIPS** Am Philos Asn; Am Cath Philos Asn. **RESEARCH** Philos of God; Medieval philos; linguistic philos; feminism; biomedical ethics. **SELECTED PUBLICATIONS** Auth, Van Buren e le frontiers del linguaggio, Citta di Vita, 75; Some Franciscans on St Thomas' Essence-Existence Doctrine, Franciscan Studies 38, Ann XVI, 78; Linguistic Ramifications of the Essence-Existence Debate, Univ Press Am, 79; The essence-existence question in a linguistic key, Miscellanea Francescana 80, 80; ed, St Bonaventure: Sermon I on the Annunciation, 3/81 & St Bonaventure: Sermon II on the Assumption, 7-8/81, The Cord; auth, Review of Joseph Donceel's The Searching Mind: An Introduction to a Philosophy of God, Miscellanea Francescana 81, 81; Abstract of Linguistic Ramifications of the Essence-Existence Debate,The Monist 65, 82; Abortion's Mother: Early Works of Simone de Beauvoir, Faith and Reason, winter 94; No Higher Court: Contemporary Feminism and the Right to Abortion, Univ Scranton Press, 95; A Fight for the Work of God, Homiletic and Pastoral Rev, 7/95; auth, Review of Brad Stetson, The Silent Subject: Reflections on the Unborn in American Culture, Ethics, 4/97. **CONTACT ADDRESS** 159 Washington St, Boston, MA 02135-4325. **EMAIL** frgermai@ncbcenter.org

KOPAS, JANE
PERSONAL Born Garfield, NJ **DISCIPLINE** PHILOSOPHY OF RELIGION **EDUCATION** St Bonaventure Univ, BS, 66, MA, 71; Grad Theol Union, PhD(theol), 76. **CAREER** Asst prof relig, Col Wooster, 75-78; Asst Prof Theol and Relig Studies, Univ Scranton, 78-. **MEMBERSHIPS** Am Acad Relig; Cath Theol Soc Am. **SELECTED PUBLICATIONS** **CONTACT ADDRESS** Dept of Theol and Relig Studies, Univ of Scranton, 800 Linden St, Scranton, PA 18510-4501.

KOPELMAN, LORETTA M.
PERSONAL Born 09/05/1938, New York, NY, m, 2 children **DISCIPLINE** PHILOSOPHY, MEDICINE **EDUCATION** Syracuse Univ, BA, 60, MA, 62; Univ Rochester, NYork, PhD, 66. **CAREER** Asst lect, 65-66, Univ Rochester; lect, 67-68, Univ Tenn; lect, 68-69, New Haven Col; lect, 71, Univ MD; assoc lect, 71-73 instr, 74-76, asst prof, 76-78,, Sch of Med, Jr Humanist Award, 73-74, fel, Nat Endowment for the Hum, 74-76, Univ Rochester; dir, 78-84, Hum Prog, Sch of Med; assoc prof, 78-85, chmn, 84-, prof, 85- Dept of Med Hum, Sch of Med, E Carolina Univ. **HONORS AND AWARDS** Founder, Dept of Med Hum, E Carolina Univ Sch of Med, 78; Pres, Soc for Health and Human Values, 97-98; founding Pres, Am Soc for Bioethics & Humanities, 97-98; ed bds: J of Med & Philos, The Encycl of Bioethics (2nd ed), mem, exec coun, Am Asn for the Advancement of Philos & Psychiatry, & founding editorial bd, medical humanities bd mem, Am Soc for Bioethics and Humanities; Research Awd , Brody School of Medicine. **MEMBERSHIPS** Phi Beta Kappa; Am Soc for Bioethics and Humanities; Asn for the Advancement of Philos and Psychiatry; APA; Am Asn of Univ Profs; Phi Kappa Phi; Hastings Ctr; Kennedy Inst of Ethics; The European Soc for Philos of Med & Health Care; Soc for Law, Med & Ethics; Am Asn of Bioethics; the Int Asn of Bioethics. **RESEARCH** Publications reflect interests in the rights and welfare of patients in research subjects including children and vulnerable populations, death and dying, moral problems in psychiatry, research ethics and other issues in philosophy of medicine and bioethics, as well as cross-cultural issues such as female genital cutting and duties to be truthful. **SELECTED PUBLICATIONS** Auth, Female Circumcism and Genital Mutilation, Encycl of Applied Ethics, 3, 97; coauth, The US Health Delivery System: Inefficient and Unfair to Children, Am J of Law & Med, XXIII: 2-3, 97; auth, The Best-Interests Standard as Threshold, Ideal, and Standard of Reasonableness, The J of Med & Philos, 22:3, 97; auth, Children and Bioethics: Uses and Abuses of the Best-Interest Standard, Intro, The J of Med & Philos, 22:3, 97; auth, Bioethics and Humanities: What Makes Us One Field?, J of Med & Phiolos, 23:4, 98; coauth, Moral and Social Issues Regarding Pregnant Women Who Use and Abuse Drugs, Obstetrics and Gynecology Clinics of North Am, 98; coauth, Preventing and Managing Unwarranted Biases Against Patients, Surgical Ethics, Oxford Univ Press, 98; auth, Help from Hume Reconciling professionalism and Managed Care, J of Med and Philos 24:4, 99; ed, Building Bioethics, Kluwer, 99; auth, Values and Virtues: How Should they Be Taught?, Acad med 74:12, 99; coed, Physician-Assisted Suicide: What are the Issues, Kluwer, 00. **CONTACT ADDRESS** Dept of Medical Humanities, East Carolina Univ, Brody 2S-17, Greenville, NC 27858. **EMAIL** kopelman@brody.med.ecu.edu

KOPERSKI, JEFFREY
PERSONAL Born 02/25/1965, Dayton, OH, m, 1988, 2 children **DISCIPLINE** PHILOSOPHY **EDUCATION** Univ Dayton, BEE, 87; Liberty Univ, MA, 91; Ohio State Univ, MA, 94; PhD, 97. **CAREER** Asst Prof of Philosophy, Saginaw Valley State Univ, 97-. **HONORS AND AWARDS** Phi Kappa Phi, Tau Beta Pi, Eta Kappa Nu. **MEMBERSHIPS** Philosophy of Science Assoc, Society of Christian Philosophers, National Institute for Engineering Ethics. **RESEARCH** Philosophy of Science, Philosophy of Religion. **SELECTED PUBLICATIONS** Auth, "God, Chaos, and the Quantum Dice," Zygon, 00; auth, "Models, Confirmation, and Chaos," Philosophy of Science, 98. **CONTACT ADDRESS** Dept Philosophy, Saginaw Valley State Univ, 7400 Bay Rd, University Center, MI 48710-0001. **EMAIL** koperski@svsu.edu

KOPERSKI, VERONICA
PERSONAL Born 08/07/1940, Detroit, MI, s **DISCIPLINE** THEOLOGY **EDUCATION** Cath Univ Louvain Belgium, PhD 91, STD 92. **CAREER** SS Cyril Methodius Sem, asst prof, 92-93; from asst prof to prof, Barry Univ, 93-. **HONORS AND AWARDS** Who's Who Among Amer Tchrs; KUL Doctoral Fel. **MEMBERSHIPS** SBL; CBA; IBR; FCCS. **RESEARCH** New Testament and Letters of Paul. **SELECTED PUBLICATIONS** Auth, Scriptural Reflections, Jour of Liturgical Conf, 98; The Scriptures: Eastertime, Liturgy: From Ashes to Fire, Jour of Liturgical Conf; Serving the Word, in Homily service, Liturgical Conf, 95; rev, Gordon D. Fee's, Paul's Letter to the Philippians, NICNT, 95, Louvain Studies, 96; Knowledge of Christ and Knowledge of God in the Corinthian Correspondence, The Corinthian Correspondence, ed, Reimund Bieringer, Leuven, Peeters, 96; The Knowledge of Christ Jesus My Lord, The High Christology of Philippians 3:7-11, Biblical Theol and Exegesis, Kampen, Kok Pharos, 96. **CONTACT ADDRESS** Dept of Theology and Philosophy, Barry Univ, 11300 N E Second Ave, Miami, FL 33027. **EMAIL** vkoperski@mail.barry.edu

KOPPEL, GLENN
PERSONAL Born 04/21/1947, New York, NY, s, 1 child **DISCIPLINE** LEGAL STUDIES **EDUCATION** City Col New York, BA, 67; Harvard Law School, JD, 70. **CAREER** Assoc, Donovan Leisure Newton & Irvine, 70-77; Attorney, Gen'l Counsel's Office, AT&T, 77-79; Law Prof, Western State Univ Col of Law, 82-. **MEMBERSHIPS** Amer Bar Assoc; Orange County Bar Assn. **RESEARCH** Court Admin. **SELECTED PUBLICATIONS** Auth, "Populism, Politics, and Procedure: The Saga of Summary Judgment and the Rulemaking process in Calif," 24 Pepperdine Law Review 455, 97; auth, "When Push Comes to Shove Between Court Rule and Statute: The Role of Judicial Interpretation in Court Admin Stration," 40 Santa Clara Law Review 103, 99; Auth, "A Tale of Two Countries: Divergent responses in Los Angeles and Orange County Superior Courts to the Ban on Electronic Recording in California Court Reporters Assn v Judicial Council," 37 San Diego Law Reviews 47, 00. **CONTACT ADDRESS** Dept Law, Western State Univ Col of Law, Orange County, 1111 N State College Blvd, Fullerton, CA 92831-3014. **EMAIL** glennk@wsuedu.law

KOPTAK, PAUL E.
PERSONAL Born 04/01/1955, Denville, NJ, m, 1983 **DISCIPLINE** COMMUNICATION, OLD TESTAMENT **EDUCATION** Rutgers Univ, BA, Psychology, with honors, 77; N Park Theol Seminary, Master of Divinity, highest honors, 86; Garrett-Evangelical Theol Seminary/Northwestern Univ, PhD, Philosophy, 90. **CAREER** Part time instr in biblical and commun studs, N Park Col, 88-93; visiting lecturer, Carib Grad Sch of Theol, Kingston, Jam, 89-90; part-time instr in biblical studs, N Park Theol Seminary, 89-93; Interim Dean of studs, N Park Theol Seminary, 93-94; Assoc prof of Commun & Biblical interpretation, Paul & Bernice Brandel Chr in Preaching, N Park Theol Seminary, 93-. **MEMBERSHIPS** Acad of Homeletics; Assoc for Commun in Theol Educ; Chicago Soc of Biblical Res; Evangelical Homelitic Soc; Inst for Biblical Res; Kenneth Burke Soc; Relig Speech and Commun Assoc; Soc of Biblical Lit; Nat Commun Assoc. **SELECTED PUBLICATIONS** auth, Rhetorical Identification in Paul's Autobiographical Narrative: Galatians 1:13-2:14, Journal for the Study of the New Testament, vol 40, 97-115, 90; auth, What's New in Interpreting Genesis? A Survey of Recent Commentaries and Books, Covenant Quarterly, vol 53 no 1, 3-16, 2/95; auth, Preaching Lawfully, Litany on Law and Liberty: A Response to Psalm 119, Ex Audita, vol 11, 145-152, 95; auth, The Temple, the Scribe, and the Widow, Preaching On-Line, 3/96; Rhetorical Criticism of the Bible: A Resource for Preaching, Covenant Quarterly, vol 54 no 3, 26-36, 7/96; On Namings and New Years, Preaching, 43-46, 11/96; co-ed, To Hear and Obey: Essays in Honor of Frederick Carlson Holmgren, Covenant Pubs, 84-94, 97; Rhetorical Identification in Preaching, Preaching, 11/98. **CONTACT ADDRESS** No Park Theol Sem, 3225 W Foster Ave, #14, Chicago, IL 60625-4895. **EMAIL** pkoptak@northpark.edu

KORCZ, KEITH
DISCIPLINE PHILOSOPHY **EDUCATION** Ohio State Univ, PhD, 96; Arizona State Univ, BA, 87. **CAREER** Instr, Univ of Louisiana at Lafayette, 98-; Lecturer, California State Univ, Fresno, 97-98; Instr, Winona State Univ, Winona, MN, 96-97. **MEMBERSHIPS** Amer Philosophical Assoc **RESEARCH** Theory of Knowledge; Selected issues in applied ethics. **SELECTED PUBLICATIONS** Auth, "The Casual-Doxastic Theory of the Basing Relation," The Canadian Journal of Philosophy, (forthcoming); auth, "Recent Work on the Basing Relation," American Philosophical Quarterly, vol. 34, No. 2, April 97. **CONTACT ADDRESS** Dept Philosophy, Univ of Louisiana, Lafayette, 200 Hebrard Boulevard, Lafayette, LA 70504-8400. **EMAIL** keithk@louisiana.edu

KORN, HAROLD LEON
PERSONAL Born 06/25/1929, Bronx, NY **DISCIPLINE** LAW **EDUCATION** Cornell Univ, AB, 51; Columbia Univ, LLB, 54. **CAREER** Law clerk to Judge Stanley H Fuld, Court Appeals State NY, 54-56; dir res, NY State Adv Comm Practice & Procedure, 56-60; assoc dir legis drafting res fund, Columbia Univ, 61-63, lectr law, Law Sch, 62-63, adj assoc prof, 63-65; prof, State Univ NY Buffalo, 65-68; prof, Sch Law, NY Univ, 68-71; Prof Law, Columbia Univ, 71-, Spec consult criminal conspiracy, Am Law Inst Model Penal Code, 60; civil practice revision, NY State Senate, 60-62. **RESEARCH** Civil procedure; Conflict of Laws; jurisdiction of federal courts. **SELECTED PUBLICATIONS** Coauth, Comments on procedural reform-preliminary motions in New York: A critique, 4/57; The treatment of inchoate crimes in the model penal code of the American Law Institute: Attempt, Solicitation and conspiracy, part 1, 4/61, part 2, 6/61; Catastrophic accidents in government Programs, Nat Security Indust Asn, 63 & New York civil practice (8 vols), Matthew Bender, 63-64; Chief draftsman, Model city charter, Nat Munic League, 6th ed, 64; auth, Law, fact and science, Columbia Law Rev, 6/66; The Choice of Law Revolution: A Critique, 83 Columbia Law Rev; The Development of Internal Jurisdiction in the United States: Point One, Brooklyn Law Rev, 00. **CONTACT ADDRESS** Sch of Law, Columbia Univ, 435 W 116th St, New York, NY 10027-7201.

KORNBLATT, JUDITH DEUTSCH
PERSONAL Born 10/26/1955, Chicago, IL, m, 1985, 2 children **DISCIPLINE** PHILOSOPHY, RUSSIAN, LITERATURE; LANGUAGE **EDUCATION** Williams Col, BA, 77; Columbia Univ, MA, 80; MPhil, 82; PhD, 85. **CAREER** Instr, Dalhousie Univ, 81; precept, Columbia Univ, 82-85; vis lectr, Williams Col, 84; adj vis asst prof, Columbia Univ, 86; vis asst prof, Ind Univ, 86-87; vis scholar, Hebrew Univ, 98; vis asst prof to assoc prof to prof to chmn to assoc dean, Univ Wis Madison, 87-. **HONORS AND AWARDS** H. I. Romnes Fel, 97; IREX Grant, 97; NEH, 93, 91-92; ACLS/SSRC Fel, 92-94; Postdoc Fel, 85-86. **MEMBERSHIPS** AAASS; AATSEEL; MLA; ACTR; AAR; AAUW; Phi Beta Kappa. **RESEARCH** Russian religious philosophy; Jews in Russia; 19th and 20th-century Russian literature. **SELECTED PUBLICATIONS** Auth, The Cossack Hero in Russian Literature: A Study in Cultural Mythology, Univ Wis Pr (Madison): 92; co-ed, Russian Religious Thought, Univ Wis Pr (Madison), 96; auth, "Gogol and the Muses of Mirgorod," Slavic Rev 50 (91): 309-316; auth, "Solov'ev's Androgynous Sophia and the Jewish Kabbalah," Slavic Rev 50 (91): 486-496; auth, "The Transfiguration of Plato in the Erotic Philosophy of Vladimir Solov'ev," Relig/Lit 24 (92): 35-50; auth, "Vladimir Solov'ev on Spiritual Nationhood, Russia, and the Jews," Russian Rev 56 (97): 157-77; auth, "On Laughter and Vladimir Solov'ev's 'Three Encounters,'" Slavic Rev 57 (98): 563-84; auth, "Why a Ladies' Tailor: Ladies' Tailor and the End of Soviet Jewry," Jewish Soc Studies 5 (99): 180-195; co-auth, "Vladimir Solov'ev: Confronting Dostoevsky on the Jewish and Christian Questions," J Am Acad Relig 68 (00): 69-98; auth, "When Fiction Meets Philosophy: Solov'ev's Three Conversations and Tolstoy's Resurrection," SEED 45 (01); auth, Doubly Chosen: The Question of Jews in the Post-Stalinist Russian Orthodox Church, (forthcoming). **CONTACT ADDRESS** Dept Slavic Lang, Univ of Wisconsin, Madison, 1220 Linden Dr, Madison, WI 53706-1525. **EMAIL** jkornbla@falstaff.wisc.edu

KORNBLITH, HILARY
PERSONAL Born 11/03/1954, New York, NY, m, 1980, 2 children **DISCIPLINE** PHILOSOPHY **EDUCATION** Cornell Univ, PhD, 80. **CAREER** Prof of Philos, Univ Vt, 91-. **HONORS AND AWARDS** NEH Fellowship for Col Teachers, 84-85. **MEMBERSHIPS** Am Philos Asn; Soc for Philos and Psychol; Philos of Sci Asn. **RESEARCH** Epistomology; philosophy of psychology. **SELECTED PUBLICATIONS** Auth, Inductive Inference and Its Natural Ground, MIT Press, 93; ed, Naturalizing Epistomology, MIT Press, 85, 2nd ed, 94; auth, Naturalistic Epistomology and Its Critics, Philos Topics, 23, 237-255, 95; auth, The Role of Intuition in Philosophical Inquiry, Rethinking Intuition, Rowman & Littlefield, 98; auth, Distrusting Reason, Midwest Stud in Philos, XXII, 98. **CONTACT ADDRESS** Dept Philos, Univ of Vermont, 70 S Williams St, Burlington, VT 05401. **EMAIL** hkornbli@zoo.uvm.edu

KORP, MAUREEN
PERSONAL Born 05/18/1945, NJ, d, 1 child **DISCIPLINE** RELIGIOUS STUDIES **EDUCATION** Rutgers Univ, AB Philos, 66; MA Art Hist, 76; Univ Ottawa, MA Rel Studies, 87; PhD, 91. **CAREER** Atlantic Community Coll, 73-74; Mercer County Community Coll, 73-74; Rutgers Univ, 75-76; Thomas Edison State Coll, 76-80; Ottawa Public School Bd, 81; Univ Ottawa, 86-95, 96-98; Pacifica Grad Inst Calif, 94-98; Univ Bucharest Romania, 95-96; McGill Univ, 97-98. **HONORS AND AWARDS** Breadloaf Writers Conference Scholar, Middlebury Coll, 65, 68; Rutgers Univ, tchg assistantship, 74-76; Consulting Scholar in Humanities, the State Library of New Jersey, 78-79; Univ Ottawa res assistantship, 86-91; Univ Ottawa Merit Grad Res Scholar, 86-88; Univ Ottawa Res Excellence Scholar, 88-91; Doctoral Fel, 88-89; Margaret Denton Wagner Aluma Fel, Rutgers Univ, 89; Post-doctoral Fel, Soc Sci and Humanities Res Council Can, 91-92; can Museum of Civilization Res Assoc, 91-96; AAR/Lilly Tchg Fel, 93-94; Fulbright, 94-95; Civic Educ Project, Univ Bucharest, 95-96; Invited speaker UNESCO Conference Paris, 98. **MEMBERSHIPS** Am Acad Rel. **RESEARCH** Sacred Sites; Indigenous beliefs; Interrelationship of artistic and religious experiences and society. **SELECTED PUBLICATIONS** Auth, Problems of Prejudice in the Thwaites edition of the Jesuit Relations, Hist Reflections, 95; Teaching from the Headlines: Myth and the Media Coverage of Diana's Death, Rel Studies News, 97; Sacred Art of the earth: Ancient and Contemporary Earthworks, 97; Images of Bucharest, Do uglass, 98; Craft: Microhistorical Traditions: Encycl of Women and World Rel, 98; The Eye of the Artist, 98; Queuing, Douglass, forthcoming. **CONTACT ADDRESS** 703 B King Edward Ave, Ottawa, ON, Canada K1N 7N9. **EMAIL** mkorp@aix1.uottawa.ca

KORSGAARD, CHRISTINE M.
PERSONAL Born 04/09/1952, Chicago, IL, d **DISCIPLINE** PHILOSOPHY **EDUCATION** Univ IL at Urbana, BA, 74; Harvard Univ, PhD, 81. **CAREER** Asst prof of philos, 80-83, Univ CA at Santa Barbara; prof of philos and general studies in the humanities, 83-91, Univ Chicago; prof of philos, 91- Havard Univ. **HONORS AND AWARDS** Fel of the Ctr for Human Values, 95-96; Phi Beta Kappa **MEMBERSHIPS** APA; int Kant Soc; Hume Soc; Soc for Political and Legal Philosophy. **RESEARCH** Ethics; hist of ethic. **SELECTED PUBLICATIONS** Auth, From Duty and for the Sake of the Noble: Kant and Aristotle on Morally Good Action, Aristotle, Kant, and the Stoics: Rethinking Happiness and Duty, 96; auth, Creating the Kingdom of Ends, 96; coauth, The Sources of Normativity, 96; auth, Taking the Law into Our Own Hands: Kant on the Right to Revolution, Reclaiming the History of Ethics: Essays for John Rawls, 97; auth, The Normativity of Instrumental Reason, Ethics and Practical Reason, 97, auth, Self-Constituion in the Ethics of Plato and Kant, The Journal of Ethics, 99. **CONTACT ADDRESS** Philosophy Dept, Harvard Univ, 208 Emerson Hall, Cambridge, MA 02138. **EMAIL** korsgaar@fas.harvard.edu

KORSMEYER, CAROLYN
DISCIPLINE PHILOSOPHY **EDUCATION** Brown Univ, PhD, 72. **CAREER** Prof Philos, SUNY-Buffalo, 96-. **MEMBERSHIPS** APA; ASA; SWIP. **RESEARCH** Aesthetics; Philosophy of mind; Feminism. **SELECTED PUBLICATIONS** Auth Taste as Sense and as Sensibility, Philos Topics, 97; Aesthetics in Feminist Perspective, Ind Univ Press, 93; coauth Feminism and Tradition in Aesthetics, Penn State Press, 95; Aesthetics: The Big Questions, Basil Blackwell, 98. **CONTACT ADDRESS** Philosophy Dept, SUNY, Buffalo, Baldy Hall, Buffalo, NY 14260. **EMAIL** ckors@acsu.buffalo.edu

KORT, WESLEY A.
PERSONAL Born 06/08/1935, Hoboken, NJ, m, 1960, 3 children **DISCIPLINE** RELIGION **EDUCATION** Calvin Col, BA, 56; Calvin Theol Sem, BD, 59; Univ Chicago, MA, 61, PhD, 65. **CAREER** Instr, relig, Princeton Univ, 63-65; asst prof, relig, 65-70, assoc prof, 70-77, prof, 77- , Duke Univ. **HONORS AND AWARDS** Fel, Soc for the Arts, Relig and Contemp Culture; fel, Ctr Theol Inquiry, Princeton Univ; outstanding prof award, Duke Univ. **MEMBERSHIPS** Am Acad Relig; Conf on Christianity and Lit. **RESEARCH** Religion in modern and postmodern culture; narrative and belief. **SELECTED PUBLICATIONS** Auth, Modern Fiction and Human Time: A Study in Narrative and Belief, Univ S Fla, 85; auth, Story, Text, and Scripture: Literary Interests in Biblical Narrative, Penn State, 88; auth, Bound to Differ: The Dynamics of Theological Discourses, Penn State, 92; auth, Take, Read: Scripture, Textuality and Cultural Practice, Penn State, 96. **CONTACT ADDRESS** Dept of Religion, Duke Univ, PO Box 90964, Durham, NC 27708-0964. **EMAIL** wkort@acpub.duke.edu

KORWAR, ARATI
DISCIPLINE MEDIA LAW, FREEDOM OF EXPRESSION, MASS COMMUNICATION AND SOCIETY, VISUAL CO **EDUCATION** Univ NC, Chapel Hill, PhD, 97. **CAREER** Asst prof, La State Univ, 97-. **HONORS AND AWARDS** Freedom Forum J Scholar, 95-96; Shirley and Whitney Awd, AEJMC Law Div, 97; Outstanding Graduating Ph.D. Student, UNC Sch of J and Mass Commun, 97. **SELECTED PUBLICATIONS** Auth, Daily Life, in Amherst Through the Years, Munchkin Press, 79; War of Words: Speech Codes at Colleges and Universities in the United States, 1995, Freedom Forum First Amendment Ctr, 95; coauth, Choice of Law in Multistate Media Law Cases: Have the 'Quaking Quagmires' Been Quelled?, in Jour and Mass Commun Monogr 153, 95. **CONTACT ADDRESS** The Manship Sch of Mass Commun, Louisiana State Univ and A&M Col, 206 Journalism Building, Baton Rouge, LA 70803. **EMAIL** akorwar@unix1.sncc.lsu.edu

KOSROVANI, EMILIO M.
DISCIPLINE PHILOSOPHY **EDUCATION** Univ Washington, PhD, 89; JD, 00. **CAREER** Lectr, Humboldt State Univ, 88-90. **MEMBERSHIPS** APA. **RESEARCH** Philosophy of action. **CONTACT ADDRESS** PO Box 45165, Seattle, WA 98145. **EMAIL** philosop@nwlink.com

KOSS, DAVID H.
PERSONAL Born 11/24/1935, Elgin, IL, s **DISCIPLINE** RELIGION **EDUCATION** N Cent Col, BA, 56; Evangelical Theol Sem, BD, 59; Princeton Theol Sem, ThM, 61; Northwestern Univ, PhD, 72. **CAREER** Prof, Ill Col, 72-. **HONORS AND AWARDS** Dunbough Awd, IL Col. **MEMBERSHIPS** Am Soc of Church Hist; Renaissance Soc Am; 18th Cent Soc. **RESEARCH** German Reformation; American Sects and Cults. **SELECTED PUBLICATIONS** Ed, Bush-Meeting Dutch (quarterly), 83. **CONTACT ADDRESS** Dept Relig, Illinois Col, Jacksonville, IL 62650. **EMAIL** koss@hilltop.ic.edu

KOSTENBERGER, ANDREAS J.
PERSONAL Born 11/02/1957, Vienna, Austria, m, 1989, 3 children **DISCIPLINE** NEW TESTAMENT AND BIBLICAL STUDIES **EDUCATION** Columbia Biblical Ssem, MDiv, 88; Trinity Evan Div Sch, PhD, 93. **CAREER** Assoc Prof, Southern Baptist Theol Sem; Dir of Ph D / Th M Studies; Ed, Journal of the Evangelical Theological Soc. **HONORS AND AWARDS** Scholarly Productivity Awd, Trinity Evang, 96. **MEMBERSHIPS** SBL; ETS; EMS; IBR **RESEARCH** Biblical Studies; Hermeneutics, New Testament Theology. **SELECTED PUBLICATIONS** Ed, Women in the Church, Baker, 95; trans, Adolf Schlatter, New Testament Theology, Baker, 97-98; auth, The Mission of Jesus and the Disciples According to the Fourth Gospel, Eerdmans, 98; auth, Encountering John, Baker, 99; coauth, Salvations to the Ends of the Earth, 01; auth, Studies in John and Genders, Peter Lang, 01; **CONTACT ADDRESS** Southeastern Baptist Theol Sem, 222 N Wingate St, Wake Forest, NC 27588. **EMAIL** Akostenber@aol.com

KOTERSKI, JOSEPH
PERSONAL Born 11/28/1953, Cleveland, OH, s **DISCIPLINE** PHSILOSOPHY, THEOLOGY **EDUCATION** Xavier Univ, HAB, 76; St Louis Univ, PhD, 82; Weston Sch of Theol, STL, 93. **CAREER** Assoc Prof, Fordham Univ, 92-. **HONORS AND AWARDS** Danforth Fel, 76; Phi Beta Kappa, 82. **MEMBERSHIPS** Am Philos Asn, Am Cath Philos Asn. **RESEARCH** Religion and culture. **SELECTED PUBLICATIONS** Auth, Prophecy and Diplomacy: The Social Thought of Pope John Paul II, Fordham Univ Press, 99. **CONTACT ADDRESS** Dept Philos, Fordham Univ, 441 E Fordham Rd, Bronx, NY 10458-5149. **EMAIL** koterski@fordham.edu

KOTLER, NEIL G.
PERSONAL Born 04/17/1941, Chicago, IL, m, 1971, 1 child **DISCIPLINE** POLITICAL SCIENCE **EDUCATION** Branders Univ, AB, 62; Univ Wisconsin, MS, 63; Univ Chicago, PhD, 74. **CAREER** Smithsonian Inst, 86-; Georgetown Univ, 81; Legislative Aide US House of Repr, 75-84; Univ TX, Austin, 74-75; Dartmouth Col, 71-74; de Paul univ, 69-71. **HONORS AND AWARDS** Phi Beta Kappa **RESEARCH** Popular Image and Perception Politics; the experiences visitors have in museums. **SELECTED PUBLICATIONS** Museum Strategy and Marketing; Designing Missions; Building Audiences; Generating revenue and Resources, Jossey-Bass Inc, 98. **CONTACT ADDRESS** Office of the Provost, Smithsonian Inst, Washington, DC 20560. **EMAIL** nkotler@si.edu

KOTZ, SAMUEL
PERSONAL Born 08/28/1930, Harbin, China, m, 1963, 3 children **DISCIPLINE** MATHEMATICAL STATISTICS **EDUCATION** Cornell Univ, PhD, 60. **CAREER** Assoc prof, Univ Toronto, 63-67; prof, Temple Univ, 67-79; Univ Md, 79-97; Visiting Scholar, George Wash Univ, 97- . **HONORS AND AWARDS** Honorary Doctorates from Harbin Inst Technol; Univ Athens, Greece; Bowling Green State Univ. **MEMBERSHIPS** Royal Statist Soc; Inst Math Statist; Int Stat Inst. **RESEARCH** Statistical sciences; probability theory; quality control. **SELECTED PUBLICATIONS** ed, Encyclopedia of Statistical Sciences. **CONTACT ADDRESS** Dept of Eng Management, The George Washington Univ, Washington, DC 20052. **EMAIL** kotz@seas.gwu.edu

KOTZIN, RHODA HADASSAH
PERSONAL Born 05/05/1933, Chicago, IL **DISCIPLINE** PHILOSOPHY **EDUCATION** Brandeis Univ, BA, 54; Yale Univ, MA, 56, PhD(philos), 60. **CAREER** Instr Philos, La

State Univ, 61 & Western Mich Univ, 61-62; from asst prof to assoc prof, 62-70, Prof Philos, Mich State Univ, 70- **HONORS AND AWARDS** Distinguished Fac Awd, Mich State Univ, 81. **MEMBERSHIPS** Am Philos Asn; N Am Kant Soc; Kantgesellschaft Leibniz Soc; Soc Women Philos. **RESEARCH** History of philosophy; feminist philosophy; phenomenology; metaphysics/epistemology. **CONTACT ADDRESS** Dept of Philos, Michigan State Univ, 503 S Kedzie Hall, East Lansing, MI 48824-1032. **EMAIL** kotzin@pilot.msu.edu

KOVALEFF, THEODORE PHILIP
PERSONAL Born 02/08/1943, New York, NY, m, 1977, 2 children **DISCIPLINE** MODERN AMERICAN AND LEGAL AND ECONOMIC HISTORY **EDUCATION** Columbia Univ, BA, 64, MA, 66; NYork Univ, PhD, 72. **CAREER** From instr to asst prof hist, St John's Univ, NY, 69-75; lectr hist, 75-77, Barnard Col; dir admis, sch law, 77-80, asst dean, Sch Law, Columbia Univ, 77-92, hist adv, Westinghouse Broadcasting Co, 72-80; moderator & producer, Nighttalk, WOR radio, New York City; adv bd, The Antitrust Bull, 88-; ed bd, Presidential Stud Q, 91-; anal, small banks/thrifts, national securities, 96-. **HONORS AND AWARDS** NY Univ Founder's Day Awd, 73; Borough Pres Certificate of Service, 77; Borough Pres Citation for Service to the Commun, 83; City of NY Certification of Appreciation, 87; Ted Kovaleff Day proclaimed by Borough Pres Ruth Messinger, Jan 18, 1996, in recognition of service to Manhattan. **MEMBERSHIPS** AHA; Orgn Am Historians; AAUP; Bus Hist Conf. **RESEARCH** Diplomatic history; antitrust. **SELECTED PUBLICATIONS** Coauth, Poland and the Coming of World War II, Ohio, 77; auth, Business and Government During the Eisenhower Administration, Ohio, 80; auth, The Antitrust Impulse, Sharpe, 94; ed, J of Reprints for Antitrust Law and Econ, 94; ed, The Antitrust Bull, 94; auth, Interview with Anne Bingaman, The Antitrust Bull, 94. **CONTACT ADDRESS** 454 Riverside Dr, New York, NY 10027. **EMAIL** kovaleff@dirksco.com

KOZAR, JOSEPH F.
PERSONAL Born 19/17/1946, Pittsburgh, PA **DISCIPLINE** BIBLICAL STUDIES **EDUCATION** Univ St Michael's Col, Toronto, MDiv, PhD. **CAREER** Prof, Univ Dayton. **MEMBERSHIPS** Soc of Biblical Lit, Eastern Great Lakes Region of the Society of Biblical Lit. **RESEARCH** Hebrew bible, christian testament, first century of the common era, social location of early jewish and christian communiteis. **SELECTED PUBLICATIONS** Pub(s), Catechist; Toronto J Theol; Proceedings Eastern Great Lakes Midwest Bible Soc. **CONTACT ADDRESS** Dept of Religious Studies, Univ of Dayton, Humanities Bldg 345, Dayton, OH 455469-1530. **EMAIL** kozar@checkov.hm.udayton.edu

KOZYRIS, PHAEDON JOHN
PERSONAL Born 01/02/1932, Thessaloniki, Greece, m, 1956, 2 children **DISCIPLINE** LAW **EDUCATION** Univ Thessaloniki, Dipl law, 54; Univ Chicago, MCL, 55; Int Univ Comp Law, Luxembourg, Dipl droit compare, 58; Cornell Univ, JD, 60. **CAREER** Assoc atty, Cahill, Gordon, Sonnett, Reindel and Ohl, New York and Paris, 60-69; Prof to Prof Emer Law, Oh State Univ, 69-; Vis prof, Duke Univ, 71-72, Univ Tex, 78 and Univ Thessaloniki, Greece, 80. **MEMBERSHIPS** Am Soc Int Law; AAUP; Am Asn Law Schs. **RESEARCH** Corporate law; law of international transactions; conflict of laws. **SELECTED PUBLICATIONS** Auth, Reflections on the Impact of Membership in the European Communities on Greek Legal Culture, J Mod Greek Studies, Vol 0011, 93; Denying Human Rights and Ethnic Identity in The Greeks of Turkey, J Mod Greek Studies, Vol 0012, 94; The Conflicts Provisions of the Alis Complex Litigation Project in A Glass Half Full, La Law Rev, Vol 0054, 94; The Conflict of Laws Aspects of the New American Business Entity in The Limited Liability Company, Am J Comp Law, Vol 0043, 95; The Limited Liability Company, Does It Exist Out of State in What Law Governs It, Univ Cincinnati Law Rev, Vol 0064, 96; The Macedonians of Greece in Denying Ethnic Identity, J Mod Greek Studies, Vol 0014, 96. **CONTACT ADDRESS** School of Law, Ohio State Univ, Columbus, 55 W 12th Ave, 302 Drinko Hall, Columbus, OH 43210.

KRAABEL, ALF THOMAS
PERSONAL Born 11/04/1934, Portland, OR, m, 1956, 3 children **DISCIPLINE** RELIGIOUS STUDIES, CLASSICS **EDUCATION** Luther Col, BA, 56; Univ Iowa, MA, 58; Luther Theol Sem, BD, 61; Harvard Univ, ThD, 68. **CAREER** Asst prof classics and relig studies, 67-70, assoc prof classics and chmn relig studies, 70-76, Prof Classics and Relig Studies, Univ Minn, Minneapolis, 76-; Chmn Dept and Dir Grad Study, 80-; Assoc dir, Joint expedition to Khirbet Shema, Israel, 69-73; Sabbatical fel, Am Coun Learned Soc, 77-78. **MEMBERSHIPS** Soc Bibl Lit; Am Acad Relig; Am Soc Study Relig; Soc Values Higher Educ. **RESEARCH** Greco-Roman religions; archaeology. **SELECTED PUBLICATIONS** Auth, Jewish Communities in Asia-Minor, Cath Bibl Quart, Vol 0055, 93; Ancient Jewish Epitaphs in An Introductory Survey of a Millennium of Jewish Funerary Epigraphy Cath Bibl Quart, Vol 0055, 93; From Synagogue to Church in Public Services and offices in the Earliest Christian Communities Interpretation-A, J Bible Theol, Vol 0048, 94; Mission and Conversion in Proselytizing in the Religious History of the Roman Empire, J Early Christian Studies, Vol 0004, 96; Early Christian Epitaphs from Anatolia, Cath Bibl Quart, Vol 0058, 96. **CONTACT ADDRESS** Dept of Classics, Univ of Minnesota, Twin Cities, 310A Folwell Hall, Minneapolis, MN 55455.

KRAEMER, DAVID
PERSONAL Born 10/23/1955, Newark, NJ, m, 1977, 2 children **DISCIPLINE** THEOLOGY **EDUCATION** Brandeis Univ, BA 77; Jewish Theol Sem, MA, PhD, 84. **CAREER** Prof, Jewish Theol Sem. **HONORS AND AWARDS** Consultant, Jewish Museum. **MEMBERSHIPS** CLAL, Nat Jewish CCtr Lrng and Ldrshp; Soc of Biblical Lit; Asn of Jewish Studies. **RESEARCH** Literary analysis of rabbinic literature, particularly the Talmud, and the social and religious history of Jews in late antiquity. **SELECTED PUBLICATIONS** Auth, The Mind of the Talmud: An Intellectual History of the Bavli, Oxford, 90; Reading the Rabbis: Literature and Religion in Talmudic Babylonia, Oxford U Press, 96; Responses to Suffering in Classical Rabbinic Literature, Oxford U Press, 95; Evil and Suffering, Judaic Doctrines of, in: The Millennial Encycl of Judaism, The Religion, WS Green et al eds, forthcoming; Rabbinic Sources for Historical Study, in: Judaism in Late Antiquity, Issues and Debates, J. Neusner, Alan J. Avery-Peck, eds, Leiden, EJ Brill, 98; The Spirit of the Rabbinic Sabbath, Conservative Judaism, 97; Child and Family Life in Judaism, in: Religious Dimensions of Child and Family life, Harold Coward, Phillip Cook eds, Victoria, Univ of Vict, 96; When God is Wrong, Sh'ma: A Jour of Jewish Responsibility, 95; auth, The Meanings of Death in Rabbinic Judaism, Routledge, 00. **CONTACT ADDRESS** Jewish Theol Sem of America, 3080 Broadway, New York, NY 10027. **EMAIL** dakraemer@jtsa.edu

KRAFT, ROBERT ALAN
PERSONAL Born 03/18/1934, Waterbury, CT, m, 1955, 4 children **DISCIPLINE** HISTORY OF WESTERN RELIGION **EDUCATION** Wheaton Col, IL, BA, 55, MA, 57; Harvard Univ, PhD, 61. **CAREER** Asst lectr New Testament studies, Univ Manchester, 61-63; from asst prof to assoc prof relig thought, 63-76, acting chmn dept, 72-73, 92, Prof Relig Studies, Univ PA, 76-, Chmn Grad Studies, 73-84, 96-, Chmn Dept, 77-84; Vis lectr, Lutheran Theol Sem, Philadelphia, 65-66; ed, Monogr ser, Soc Bibl Lit, 67-72 & Pseudepigrapha ser, 73-78; task force on scholarly publ, Coun Studies Relig, 71-72. **HONORS AND AWARDS** Fels, Guggenheim, 69-70 & Am Coun Learned Soc, 75-76. **MEMBERSHIPS** Soc Bibl Lit; Int Orgn Septuagint & Cognate Studies; NAm Patristic Soc; Studiorum Nov Testamenti Societas; Am Soc Papyrologists. **RESEARCH** Judaism in the Hellenistic era, especially Greek-speaking Judaism; Christianity to the time of Constantine, espec the second century; computers and Ancient lit. **SELECTED PUBLICATIONS** Auth, Was There a Messiah-Joshua Tradition at the Turn of the Era?, RKMESSIA ARTICLE on the IOUDAIOS Electronic Discussion Group, 6/10/92; Philo's Text of Genesis 2.18 (I will make a helper), on the IOUDAIOS Electronic Discussion Group, 6/10/93; The Pseudepigrapha in Christianity, In: Tracing the Threads: Studies in the Vitality of Jewish Pseudepigrapha, SBL Early Judaism and Its Literature 6, Scholars, 94; coauth, Jerome's Translation of Origen's Homily on Jeremiah 2.21-22 (Greek Homily 2; Latin 13), Revue Be/ne/dictine 104, 94; auth, The Use of Computers in New Testament Textual Criticism, In: The Text of the NT in Contemporary Research, Studies and Documents 46, 95; Scripture and Canon in Jewish Apocrypha and Pseudepigrapha, In: Hebrew Bible/Old Testament: The History of its Interpretation, I: From Beginnings to the Middle Ages (Until 1300), 1: Antiquity, Vandenhoeck & Ruprecht, 96; author of numerous other articles. **CONTACT ADDRESS** Relig Studies, Univ of Pennsylvania, Logan Hall, Philadelphia, PA 19104-6304. **EMAIL** kraft@ccat.sas.upenn.edu

KRAHMER, SHAWN MADISON
DISCIPLINE THEOLOGY **EDUCATION** Univ Illinois, BS, summa, cum laude, 81; Garrett-Evangelical Theol Sem, MDiv, summa, cum laude, 84; Univ Chicago, MA, 87, PhD, honors, 95. **CAREER** Asst Prof, 95-, St Joseph's Univ; Research Asst 92-94, 89-91, Data Base mgr 88-95, Univ Chicago. **HONORS AND AWARDS** Phi Beta Kappa. **MEMBERSHIPS** AAR; SSCS; Del Valley Medieval Assoc. **RESEARCH** Christian Monastic Theol; Spirituality, Christian Mysticism, Ancient and Medieval Historical Theol, Feminist Theol. **SELECTED PUBLICATIONS** Auth, "Interpreting the Letters of Bernard of Clairvaux to Ermengarde, Countess of Brittany: The Twelfth-Century Context and the Language of Friendship," Cistercian Studies Quart 27 (92): 217-50; auth, "Friend and Lover as Metaphors of Right Relation in Bernard of Clairvaux," Cistercian Studies Quart 30 (95): 15-26; auth, "The Friend as 'Second Self' and the Theme of Substitution in the Letters of Bernard of Clairvaux," Cistercian Studies Quart 81 (96): 21-33; auth, "The Bride as Friend in Bernard of Clairvaux's 'Sermones Super Cantica,'" Am Benedictine Rev 48 (97): 69-87; auth, "Loving 'in God:' An Examination of the Hierarchical Aspects of the 'Ordo Caritatis' in Bernard of Clairvaux and Aelred of Rievaulx," Am Benedictine Rev 50 (99): 74-93; auth, "Aelred of Rievaulx and the Feminine in the Marian Sermons on the Feasts of the Assumption and the Purification," Cistercian Studies Quart (forthcoming); auth, "The Virile Bride of Bernard of Clairvaux," Church Hist (forthcoming). **CONTACT ADDRESS** Dept of Theology, Saint Joseph's Univ, 5600 City Ave, Philadelphia, PA 19131. **EMAIL** skrahm@sju.edu

KRAKAUER, ERIC
PERSONAL Born Cincinnati, OH **DISCIPLINE** PHILOSOPHY MEDICAL ETHICS AND INTERNAL MEDICINE **EDUCATION** Yale Univ, Grad Schl, PhD, 91; Yale Univ, Med Schl, 92. **CAREER** Inst, Harvard Medical Schl, 97-. **HONORS AND AWARDS** Fulbright Fel. **MEMBERSHIPS** APA; Modern Language Assoc; Amer Soc for Bioethics and Humanities; AMA **RESEARCH** Ethical and cultural issues in end-of-life care. **CONTACT ADDRESS** Palliative Care Service, Massachusetts General Hospital, 55 Fruit S, Boston, MA 02114.

KRAMER, PHYLLIS S.
PERSONAL Born New York, NY, 4 children **DISCIPLINE** JEWISH STUDIES **EDUCATION** Hunter Col , BA, 61; Syracuse Univ, MA, 63; McGill Univ Montreal, PhD, 94. **CAREER** Chaplain, Marianopolis Coll Montreal, 78-96; vis prof, Univ Haifa, Israel, 95 & 98; vis prof, Tel Aviv Univ, 97-98. **HONORS AND AWARDS** Jewish Studies Shloime Wiseman Book Prize, McGill Univ, 90. **MEMBERSHIPS** AAR; SBL. **RESEARCH** Women in Hebrew Scripture. **SELECTED PUBLICATIONS** Auth, Biblical Women That Come in Pairs: The Use of Pairs as a Literary Device in the Hebrew Bible, Genesis; A Feminist Companion to 2nd Series the Bible; The Dismissal of Hager in Five Art Work of the 16th and 17th Centuries; Jephthah's Daughter: A Thematic Approach to the Narrative as Seen in Selected Rabbinic Exegesis and in Artwork, in Judges, A Feminist Companion to the Bible, 2nd Series. **CONTACT ADDRESS** 6848 Palmetto Circle South, Apt #1215, Boca Raton, FL 33433. **EMAIL** drpcsk@aol.com

KRAMER, ROBERT
PERSONAL Born 08/17/1913, Davenport, IA **DISCIPLINE** LAW **EDUCATION** Harvard Univ, AB, 35, LLB, 38. **CAREER** From assoc prof to prof law, Duke Univ, 47-59; asst atty gen of US Dept Justice, 59-61; prof, 61-79, Emer Prof Law and Dean, Law Sch, George Washington Univ 80-; Ed, Law and Contemporary Probs, 47-56 and J Legal Educ, 48-56. **MEMBERSHIPS** Am Law Inst. **SELECTED PUBLICATIONS** Auth, Against Recycling and Schubert, Heine, Song Cycles, Nineteenth Century Mus, Vol 0020, 96; Spirit at Work in Discovering the Spirituality in Leadership, J Relig Health, Vol 0036, 97. **CONTACT ADDRESS** Sch of Law, The George Washington Univ, Washington, DC 20006.

KRAMER-MILLS, HARTMUT
PERSONAL Born 12/14/1962, Jena, Germany, m, 1988, 2 children **DISCIPLINE** PROTESTANT THEOLOGY **EDUCATION** McCormick Theol Sem Chicago, MD, 88; Marburg Univ Germany, Ecclesiastical Exam, 90; Greifswald Univ Germany, Dr Theol, 97. **CAREER** Vicar, Ev Kirche der Kirchenprovinz Sachsen Germany, 91; tchg asst, Kirchliche Hochschule Naumburg Germany, 92-93; lectr, Pedagogische Hochschule Erfurt Germany, 93-98. **HONORS AND AWARDS** World Alliance of Reformed Churches/McCormick Theol Sem: full scholar, 86-87. **MEMBERSHIPS** Am Soc of Church Hist. **RESEARCH** Christianity in Europe during the 19th century until 1945; History of the English Reformation. **SELECTED PUBLICATIONS** Auth, Von Arnoldshain und Sagorsk nach bad Urach. Anmerkungen zum gegenwartigen Dialog Zwischen der Evangelischen Kirche in Deutschland und der Russischen Orthodoxen Kirche, Die Zeichen der Zeit, 96; Wilhelminische Moderne und das fremde Christentum. Untersuchumngen zu Friedrich Naumanns "Briefe uber Religion", 97; Die Gemeinde der Heiligen. Erinnerungen an die Zukunft der Kirche. Hartmut Kramer-Mills uber Manfred Josuttis, Die Zeichen der Zeit, 98. **CONTACT ADDRESS** 123 Buckelew Ave, Jamesburg, NJ 08831.

KRANTZ, ARTHUR A.
PERSONAL Born 09/14/1938, Edmonton, AB, Canada, m, 1965, 2 children **DISCIPLINE** PHILOSOPHY **EDUCATION** Concordia Sr Col, BA, 62; Concordia Sem, MDiv, 65; Univ Tor, MA, 67; Univ Waterloo, PhD, 72. **CAREER** Wilfred Lauier Univ, sess lecrt, lectr, 67-71; Univ Regina, Luther Col, asst prof, prof, acad dean, 71-. **MEMBERSHIPS** CPA, CSHPT, AAR, SKS, CSCP, AI, CCLA **RESEARCH** Plato; Kierkegaard; Heidegger; Nietzsche; Sartre; Gadamer. **CONTACT ADDRESS** Dept of Philosophy, Luther Col, 700 College Dr, Regina, SK, Canada S4S 0A2. **EMAIL** Arthur.Krentz@uregina.ca

KRASSEN, MILES
DISCIPLINE JUDAIC STUDIES **EDUCATION** St. John Col, BA, 67; Ind Univ, MA, 83; Univ Pa, MA, 85, PhD, 90. **CAREER** Asst prof. **RESEARCH** Jewish mysticism, hasidism, Kabbalah texts. **SELECTED PUBLICATIONS** Au, Isaiah Horowitz: Generations of Adam. **CONTACT ADDRESS** Dept of Relig, Oberlin Col, Oberlin, OH 44074.

KRATTENMAKER, THOMAS GEORGE
PERSONAL Born 01/15/1943, Camden, NJ, m, 1965, 2 children **DISCIPLINE** LAW **EDUCATION** Swarthmore Col, BA, 65; Columbia Univ, JD, 68. **CAREER** Asst prof, Sch Law, Univ Conn, 68-72; Prof Law, Georgetown Univ Law Ctr, 72-94; Law clerk, US Supreme Ct, 70-71; asst dir, Bur Consumer Protection, Fed Trade Comn, 71-72; secy, DC Law Revision

Comm, 76-78; co-dir, Network Inquiry Staff, Fed Common Comn, 78-80; Dean and Professor of Law at the William and Mary School of Law, 94-97; Special Counsel for Policy and Regulatory Affairs, Antitrust Division of the U.S. Department of Justice 97-98; Director of Research, Office of Plans and Policy of the Federal Communications Commission FCC; Senior Counsel, Mintz Levin, Cohn Ferris, Glovsky and Popeo PC. **RESEARCH** Constitutional law; antitrust law; communications law. **SELECTED PUBLICATIONS** Auth, "Telecommunications Law and Policy" **CONTACT ADDRESS** Law Ctr, Mintz, Levin, Cohn, Ferris, Glovsky and Popeo PC, 701 Pennsylvania Ave., NW, Washington, DC 200004-2608. **EMAIL** tkrattenmaker@mintz.com

KRAUSE, JOAN H.
PERSONAL Born 12/01/1965, Boston, MA, m **DISCIPLINE** LEGAL STUDIES **EDUCATION** Yale Univ, BA, 87; Stanford Law School, J.D., 92. **CAREER** Asst Prof, Institute for Health Law, Loyola Univ Chicago, School of Law 97-; Assoc, Hogan & Hartson LLP, 93-97; Clerk, Hon. Dorothy W. Nelson, US Court of Appeals for the Ninth Circuit 92-93. **HONORS AND AWARDS** BA Summa cum laude; Phi Beta Kappa; J.D. with Distinction; Order of the Coif; Hilmer Oehlmann, Jr. Awd for Legal Research & Writing, Fall 89. **MEMBERSHIPS** State Bar of California; District of Columbia Bar; Amer Health Lawyers Assoc; Amer Society of Law, Medicine & Ethics; Illinois Assoc of Health Care Attorneys. **RESEARCH** Health Law; Criminal Law; Women and the Law. **SELECTED PUBLICATIONS** Auth, "Accutane: Has Drug Regulation in the United States Reached Its Limits? 6 J.L. & Health 1, 91-92; auth, "Of Merciful Justice and Justified Mercy: Commuting the Sentences of Battered Women Who Kill, 46 Fla. L. rev. 699, 94; auth "The Brief Life of the Gag Clause: Why Anti-Gag Clause Legislation Isn't Enough, 67 Tenn. L. Rev. (Forthcoming)99; auth, "Reconceptualizing Informed Consent in an Era of Health Care Cost Containment, 85 Iowa L. Rev. 261, 91; auth, "The Role of the States in Combating Managed Care Fraud and Abuse, 8 Annals Health L. 179, 99; auth, "Kickbacks, Courtesies, or Cost-Effectiveness?: Application of the Medicare Antikickback Law to the Marketing and Promotional Practices of Drug and Medical Device Manufacturers, 54 Food & Drug L.J. 279, 99, with Thomas N. Bulleit, Jr. **CONTACT ADDRESS** School of Law, Loyola Univ, Chicago, 1 Eastt Pearson St, Chicago, IL 60611-2055. **EMAIL** jkraus@luc.edu

KRAUSZ, MICHAEL
PERSONAL Born 09/13/1942, Geneva, Switzerland, m, 1976 **DISCIPLINE** PHILOSOPHY **EDUCATION** Rutgers Univ, BA, 65; Indiana Univ, MA, 67; Univ Toronto, PhD, 69. **CAREER** Asst prof, Univ Toronto, Victoria Coll, 69-70; instr, Trent Univ, 69-70; from asst prof to Milton C. Nahm prof philos, 70-. **HONORS AND AWARDS** Bryn Mawr Col Fac Res Grant, 98; George Washington Univ Elton Lect, 98; Univ Ulm, Germany, Hans-Kupczyk Gastprofessur Lect and Awd, 97; David Norton Memorial Lect, Univ Del, 97; Tata Enery Res Inst Honorary Fel, New Delhi, India; Alice Hardenberg Clark Res Grant, 89; NEH Summer Inst participant; Oxford Univ Senior Mem; Res Grant Oxford Univ; Alfred Sloan Found Grant, 86; Res Grant to Kenya, 85; Ossabaw Found Res Fel, 78, 80; Andrew W Mellon Fel, 77-78; Madge Miller Res Grant, 76, 85; Bryn Mawr Col Fac Res Grant. **MEMBERSHIPS** Amer Philos Assoc; Amer Soc Aesthetics; Intl Development Ethics Assoc; Collingwood Soc; Royal Soc of Arts; Soc of Intercultural Philos. **RESEARCH** Epistemology; Aesthetics; Philosophy of History; Culture and Interpretation. **SELECTED PUBLICATIONS** Co-ed, The Concept of Creativity in Science and Art, Marinus Nijhoff Publ (The Hague), 81; co-ed, Relativism: Cognitive and Moral, Notre Dame Univ Pr (Notre Dame), 82; co-ed, Rationality, Relativism and the Human Sciences, Martinus Nijhoff Pub (The Hague), 86; ed, Relativism: Interpretation and Confrontation, Notre Dame Univ Pr (Notre Dame), 89; auth, Rightness and Reasons: Interpretation in Cultural Practices, Cornell Univ Pr, 93; co-ed, Jewish Identity, Temple Univ Pr (Philadelphia), 93; ed, The Interpretation of Music: Philosophical Essays, Clarendon Pr (Oxford), 93; coauth, Varieties of Relativism, Basil Blackwell Pub, 95; co-ed, Interpretation, Relativism and the Metaphysics of Culture, Humanity Pr, 99; auth, Limits of Rightness, Rowman and Littlefield Publ (Lantham, Maryland), 00. **CONTACT ADDRESS** Dept of Philosophy, Bryn Mawr Col, Bryn Mawr, PA 19010. **EMAIL** mkrausz@brynmawr.edu

KRAUT, BENNY
PERSONAL Born 12/24/1947, Munich, Germany, m, 1972, 3 children **DISCIPLINE** MODERN JEWISH HISTORY, MODERN JUDAISM **EDUCATION** Yeshiva Univ, BA, 68; Brandeis Univ, MA, 70, PhD(Jewish hist), 75. **CAREER** Vis asst prof Judaica, Vassar Col, 75-76; Assoc Prof Judaica, Univ Cincinnati, 76-. **MEMBERSHIPS** Orgn Am Historians; Asn Jewish Studies; World Union Jewish Studies. **RESEARCH** Development of American Judaism; religious and theological responses to the Holocaust; Jewish-Christian relations in American history. **SELECTED PUBLICATIONS** Auth, The approach to Jewish law of Martin Buber and Franz Rosenzweig, Tradition, Vol XII, 72; Perspectives on the drug issue, In: Judaism and Drugs, Hermon Press, 73; A unique American apostate, Columbia Libr Columns, 5/78; From Reform Judaism to Ethical Culture: The Religious Evolution of Felix Adler, Hebrew Union Col Press, 79; Francis E Abbott: Perceptions of a 19th century religious radical on Jews and Judaism, Studies Am Jewish Experience, spring 81; The role of the Jewish academic in Jewish affairs, Occasional Papers, 81; Faith and the Holocaust, Judaism, spring 82; Judaism triumphant: Isaac Mayer Wise on unitarianism and liberal Christianity, Asn Jewish Studies Rev, 82. **CONTACT ADDRESS** Judaic Studies, Univ of Cincinnati, P O Box 210169, Cincinnati, OH 45221-0169.

KRAUT, RICHARD
PERSONAL Born 10/27/1944, Brooklyn, NY **DISCIPLINE** PHILOSOPHY **EDUCATION** Univ Mich, BA, 65; Princeton Univ, PhD, 69. **CAREER** Asst prof, Philosophy, 69-76, assoc prof, Philosophy, 76-83, prof, Philosophy, 83-95, chr, Dept Philos, 88-91, res prof, Humanities, 89-95, Univ Ill Chicago, 69-95; vis prof, Univ Chicago, 97; prof philosophy, 95-, prof, classics, 97-, chr, dept philos, 97-, Northwestern Univ, 95-. **HONORS AND AWARDS** Pres, APA, 93-94; NEH, Am Council of Learned Soc, Center for Hellenic Studies. **MEMBERSHIPS** Amer Philos Asn. **RESEARCH** Moral and political philosophy, particulary in Socrates, Plato, and Aristotle. **SELECTED PUBLICATIONS** Auth, Socrates and the State, Princeton Univ Press, 84; Aristotle on the Human Good, Princeton Univ Press, 89; ed, The Cambridge Companion to Plato, Cambridge Univ Press, 92; ed, Critical Essays on Plato's Republic, Rowman & Littlefield, 97; auth, Aristotle Politics Books VII and VIII, Clarendon Press, 97. **CONTACT ADDRESS** Dept of Philosophy, Northwestern Univ, 1818 Hinman Ave, Evanston, IL 60208-1315. **EMAIL** rkraut1@northwestern.edu

KRAWCHUK, ANDRII
DISCIPLINE THEOLOGY **EDUCATION** McGill Univ, BA, 76, BTh, 79; Accademia Alfonsiana, Rome, LThM, 81; Univ Ottawa, PhD, 90; St Paul Univ, DTh, 90. **CAREER** Acad Prog Coordr, Harvard Ukrainian Res Inst, 90; res fel, 90-91, proj dir, 92-93, Central State Hist Archiv L'viv; ed, publ div, Greek Cath Archeparchy of L'viv, 91-92; postdoct fel, 93-94 & ed, Logos, A J of Eastern Christian Stud, lectr, St Paul Univ, 94-95; res assoc, Can Inst of Ukrainian Stud, 95-97; prof, Christian ethics, L'viv Theol Acad, 97-98. **HONORS AND AWARDS** Postdoctoral fel, Univ Alberta, 89; postdoctoral fel, Harvard Univ, 90; Can-USSR exchange fel, 90-91; Cenko Prize in Bibliog, 91; tchg and res fel, Can Inst Ukrainian Stud, 93-94; Reform through Knowledge Program, Asn of Univ and Col of Can, 96-97; Can Ethnic Studies Awd, 97. **MEMBERSHIPS** Shevchenko Sci Soc Can; Can Asn of E Christian Stud; Christians Assoc for Relations with E Europe; AAR; Can Asn of Slavists; Soc of Christian Ethics. **RESEARCH** History of Christian ethics, East and West. **SELECTED PUBLICATIONS** Ed, Moral'ne Bohoslovia, by Jean-Marie Aubert, Catholic Archeparchy of L'viv, 93; comp, The Bohdan Bociurkiw Collection on Religion and Church-State Relations in the Soviet and Post-Soviet Republics: A Preliminary Inventory of Its Principal Sections, Ottawa: CIUS Reports, 94; ed, Zaklyk do pokaiannia, by Andrei Sheptytsky, Rare Books Library Series, L'viv: Svichado, 94; transl, Paps'ka Rada v Spravakh Sim'yi, L'viv: Svichado, 97; ed, Moral'ne Bohoslovia, 2d ed, L'viv: Strim, 97; auth, Christian Social Ethics in Ukraine: The Legacy of Andrei Sheptytsky, Can Inst of Ukrainian Stud, 97; ed, Andrei Sheptytsky: His Life and Works, v.2: Christian Social and Political Ethics, L'viv: Central State Historical Archives, 98; auth, A Systematic Bibliography of Ukrainian-Language Religious and Theological Periodical Literature, 1871-1939, L'viv Theolog Acad, 99. **CONTACT ADDRESS** Sheptytsky Inst, Saint Paul Univ, 223 Main St, Ottawa, ON, Canada K1S 1C4. **EMAIL** akrawchuk@ustpaul.uottawa.ca

KRAWIEC, KIMBERLY D.
DISCIPLINE LAW **EDUCATION** NCar State Univ, BA, 87; Georgetown Univ, JD, 92. **CAREER** Lobbyist/Fund Raiser, NCar, 88-89; Staff Dir, NCar Council on the Homeless, 89; Asst Prof, Univ Tulsa, 95-97; Assoc Prof, Univ Ore, 97-; Visiting Assoc Prof, NW Univ, 99-00; Visiting Assoc Prof, Univ Calif, 00; Visiting Assoc Prof, Univ Penn, 01. **HONORS AND AWARDS** Best Corporate and Securities Law Articles, 99; Robert Childres Memorial Awd, NW Univ, 99-00. **MEMBERSHIPS** Am Bar Asn; Am Law and Economics Asn; State Bar of NY. **SELECTED PUBLICATIONS** Auth, "Electronic Surveillance," Geo Crime Proc Project 678 91; auth, "Gustafson v. Alloyd Co.: The Wrong Decision, But it is Still Business As Usual in the Securities Markets," Tulsa Law Journal, 96; auth, "Corporate Debt Restructurings in Mexico: For Foreign Creditors, Insolvency Law Is Only Half the Story, NYL Sch J Intl, 97; auth, Fiduciaries, Misappropriators and the Murky Outlines of the Den of Thieves: A Conceptual Continuum for Analyzing United States v O'Hagan", Tulsa Law Journal, 97; auth, "More Than Just New Financial Bingo: A Risk-based Approach to Understanding Derivatives," Journal Corporate Law, 97; auth, "Don't Ask, Just Tell: Insider Trading After United States v. O'Hagan, VA Law Review, 98; auth, "Derivatives, Corporate Hedging and Shareholder Wealth: Modigliani-Miller Forty Years Later," Univ ILL Law Review, 99; auth, "Building the Basic Course Around Intra-Firm Relations," GA Law Review, forthcoming; auth, "Accounting for Greed: Norms, Psychology and the Rogue Trader," OR Law Review, forthcoming; auth, "Insider Trading, Economics & Critical Theory: Deconstructing the Coin of the Realm in the Information Age," NW Univ Law Review, forthcoming. **CONTACT ADDRESS** School of Law, Univ of Oregon, 1101 Kincaid St, Eugene, OR 97401-3720.

KREBS, VICTOR J.
PERSONAL Born 01/26/1957, Lima, Peru **DISCIPLINE** PHILOSOPHY **EDUCATION** Vanderbilt Univ, BA, 81; Univ Notre Dame, MA, 84, PhD, 92. **CAREER** Asst prof, 93-94, assoc prof, philos, 94- , dir grad stud in philos, 96- , Univ Simon Bolivar, Venezuela. **HONORS AND AWARDS** Phi Beta Kappa; Konrad Adenauer res fel; Inst of Int Educ scholar; Pew Teaching Leadership Awd; Outstanding Young Men of Am Awd. **MEMBERSHIPS** APA; North Am Kant Soc; Sociedad Venezuelana Filosofia. **RESEARCH** Wittgenstein; philosophy of psychology; aesthetics; philosophy of language and mind; Kant; archetypal psychology and psychoanalysis. **SELECTED PUBLICATIONS** Auth, El Silencio de Wittgenstein, Criterion 8, 94; auth, La Transfiguracion de la Filosofia: Wittgenstein y la Recuperacion del Sentido, Proceedings IV Congreso Nacional de Filosofia, 94; auth, El Naturalismo Trascendental de Wittgenstein, Ideas y Valores, 96; auth, Locura y Memoria del Arte, in Arte y Locura serie Conversaciones en el Museo, 98; auth, Espiritus Sobre las Ruinas: Wittgenstein y el Pensamiento Estetico, Arete X, 98; auth, La Labor Olvidada del Pensar, Argos, 98; auth, Lenguaje Mente, y Alma en Wittgenstein, Proceedings, Primer Congreso Iberamericano de Filosofia, 98; auth, Pensando con el alma y el Tonto Prejuicio Cientifico de Nuestro Tiempo, Filosofia, Merida-Venezuela, 98; auth, Lo Bueno, lo Malo, y lo Bello, La Belleza en Todas partes, Museo de Bellas Artes de Caracas, forthcoming. **CONTACT ADDRESS** CCS 90170, PO Box 025323, Miami, FL 33102-5323. **EMAIL** vkrebs@usb.ve

KREMER, MICHAEL
PERSONAL Born 12/24/1957, New Haven, CT, m, 1989, 3 children **DISCIPLINE** PHILOSOPHY **EDUCATION** Univ Toronto, BA, 80; Univ Pittsburgh, MA, 83, PhD, 86. **CAREER** Instr, 86-87, asst prof, 87-93, assoc prof, 93-, Univ Notre Dame. **HONORS AND AWARDS** Nat Endow Hum, Fel Univ tchrs, ALTERNATE, 98-99. **MEMBERSHIPS** Amer Philos Asn; Asn Symbolic Logic. **RESEARCH** History of Analytic Philosophy; Philosophy of Language; Logic; Philosophy of Mathematics. **SELECTED PUBLICATIONS** Auth, Logic and Meaning: The Philosophical Significance of the Sequent Calculus, Mind 97, 88, 50-72; Kripke and the Logic of Truth, Jour Philos Logic 17, 88, 225-278; Set-Theoretic Realism and Arithmetic, Philos Stud (s) 64, 91, 253-271; The Multiplicity of General Propositions, Nous 26, 92, 409-426; The Argument of On Denoting, Philos rev 103, 94, 249-297; Auth, "Contextualism and Holism in the Early Wittgenstein: From Prototactaus to Tractatus," Philosophical Topics, 97, 87-120; Auth, "Wilson on Kripke's Wittgenstien," Philosophy and Phenomenological Research (60), 00, 571-584; Auth, "The Purpose of Tractarian Nonsense," forthcoming; Auth, "Nous Sense and Meaning: The Origins and Developmet of the Distinction," forthcoming in the Cambridge Companion to Frege. **CONTACT ADDRESS** Dept of Philosophy, Univ of Notre Dame, 336 O'Shaughnessy Hall, Notre Dame, IN 46556-5639. **EMAIL** Kremer.2@nd.edu

KRENTZ, EDGAR
DISCIPLINE NEW TESTAMENT **EDUCATION** Concordia Sem, MDiv; Wash Univ, MA, PhD; additional stud, Univ Chicago; Amer Sch of Class Stud at Athens, Greece. **CAREER** Christ Sem-Seminex prof. **HONORS AND AWARDS** Assoc dir, Joint Expedition to Caesarea Maritima in Israel. **RESEARCH** Pauline studies in relation to the Greco-Roman world. **SELECTED PUBLICATIONS** Auth, The Historical-Critical Method; Augsburg New Testament Commentary on Galatians; Hymnody as Epideictic Literature. **CONTACT ADDRESS** Dept of New Testament, Lutheran Sch of Theol at Chicago, 1100 E 55th St, Chicago, IL 60615. **EMAIL** ekrentz@lstc.edu

KRESS, ROBERT LEE
PERSONAL Born 09/22/1932, Jasper, IN **DISCIPLINE** THEOLOGY, PHILOSOPHY **EDUCATION** St Meinrad Col, BA, 54; Univ Innsbruck, STB, 56, STL, 58; Univ Notre Dame, MA, 64; Univ St Thomas Aquinas, Rome, STD, 68. **CAREER** Supt, Washington Cath High Sch, 59-64; lectr philos and relig, Univ Evansville, 68-70; asst prof theol, St Louis Univ, 71-73; assoc prof philos and relig, Univ Evansville, 73-74, prof, 78-79; Assoc Prof, Dept Theol, Cath Univ Am, 79-; Vis fel theol, Princeton Theol Sem, 70-71; vis prof, Lutheran Theol Sem, 80, Princeton Theol Sem, 81 and Toronto Sch Theol, 82; fel, Ctr Libertarian Studies, 82. **HONORS AND AWARDS** Outstanding Bk of Year, Col Theol Soc, 76. **MEMBERSHIPS** Col Theol Soc; Int Soc Metaphysics; Cath Theol Soc Am; Am Acad Relig. **RESEARCH** Religion and culture; gnosticism; Christian philosophy. **SELECTED PUBLICATIONS** Auth, Femininity, Castration and the Phallus, Lit Psychol, Vol 0042, 96. **CONTACT ADDRESS** Dept of Theol, Catholic Univ of America, Washington, DC 20064.

KREY, PHILIP D. W.
DISCIPLINE EARLY; MEDIEVAL CHURCH HISTORY **EDUCATION** Univ Mass/Boston, BA, 72; Lutheran Theol Sem at Gettysburg, MDiv, 76; Cath Univ Am, MA, 85; Univ Chicago, PhD, 90. **CAREER** Dean; prof-. **HONORS AND AWARDS** Fulbright fel, Univ Munich, 89; co-founder, soc stud of the bible in the middle ages. **SELECTED PUBLICATIONS** Auth, transl, medieval Franciscan's Revelation Com-

mentary - Nicholas of Lyra; co-ed, Sources of Medieval Christian Thought, Cath UP. **CONTACT ADDRESS** Dept of History and Systematic Theology, Lutheran Theol Sem at Gettysburg, 7301 Germantown Ave, Philadelphia, PA 19119 1794. **EMAIL** Pkrey@ltsp.edu

KRIEG, ROBERT A.

PERSONAL Born 02/08/1946, Hackensack, NJ, s **DISCIPLINE** THEOLOGY **EDUCATION** Stonehill Col, BA, 69; Univ of Notre Dame, PhD, 76. **CAREER** Asst prof, King's Col, 75-77; Prof, Univ Notre Dame, 77-. **MEMBERSHIPS** Catholic Theological Soc of Am; Col Theology Soc. **RESEARCH** Christology; 19th and 20th Century Theology in Germany; Jewish-Catholic dialogue. **SELECTED PUBLICATIONS** Auth, Romano Guardini: Precursor of Vatican II, Univ of Notre Dame Press, 97; ed & contrib. Romano Guardini: Proclaiming Sacred in a Modern World, Liturgy Training Pub, 95; assoc ed & coauth, Encyclopedia of Catholicism, Harper Collins, 95; Die Rezeption Roman Guardinis in Nordamerika, Theologie und Glaube, 98; Introduction in the 1997 Edition, The Spirit of Catholicism, Crossroad, 97; Peyton, Patrick J., New Catholic Encyclopedia, Writers' Guild Inc with McGraw-Hill Book Co, 96. **CONTACT ADDRESS** Dept of Theology, Univ of Notre Dame, 327 O'Shaughnessy Hall, Notre Dame, IN 46556-5639. **EMAIL** krieg.1@ND.EDU

KRIER, JAMES EDWARD

PERSONAL Born 10/19/1939, Milwaukee, WI, m, 1974, 2 children **DISCIPLINE** LAW **EDUCATION** Univ Wis- Madison, BS, 61, JD, 66. **CAREER** Law clerk, Supreme Court Calif, 66-67; assoc, Arnold and Porter, DC, 67-69; from actg prof to prof law, Univ Calif, Los Angeles, 69-78; prof law, Stanford Law Sch, 78-80; Prof Law, Law Sch, Univ Calif, Los Angeles, 80-; Consult, Environ Quality Lab, Calif Inst Technol, 71-; vis fel, Wolfson Col, Oxford Univ, 76. **MEMBERSHIPS** AAAS **RESEARCH** Environmental law; law and economics; property law. **SELECTED PUBLICATIONS** Auth, "The Cathedral at Twenty-Five: Citations and Impressions," with Stewart J. Schwab, 106 Yale Law Journal 2121-39, May 97; auth, "Property" with J. Dukeminier, 4th ed., Aspen, 98; auth, "Risk Assessment." The New Palgrave Dictionary of Economics and Law, McMillan, 98; auth, "Making Something Out of Nothing: The Law of Takings and Phillips v. Washington Legal Foundation" with Michael A. Heller, 7 Supreme Court Economic Review 285-301, 99; auth, "Deterrence and Distribution in the Law of Takings," with Michael A. Heller, 112 Harvard Law Review 997-1025, 99, an excerpt appeared as "Uncoupling the Law of Takings," 43.1 Law Quadrangle Notes 97-104 **CONTACT ADDRESS** Law Sch, Univ of Michigan, Ann Arbor, 971-A Legal Research 1210, Ann Arbor, MI 48109. **EMAIL** jkrier@j.imap.itd.umich.edu

KRIMERMAN, LEONARD I.

DISCIPLINE PHILOSOPHY OF WORK **EDUCATION** Cornell Univ, BA, 55; PhD, 64. **CAREER** Dept Philos, Univ Conn **RESEARCH** Theory and prospects of democracy, recent political philosophy. **SELECTED PUBLICATIONS** Co-auth, When Workers Decide, New Soc Publ, 91; From the Ground Up, S End Press, 92; Education for Democratic Community and Work, Critical Education for Work: Multidisciplinary Approaches, 94; From the Kitchen to the World: Three Decades of Cooperative Development in Japan, GEO, 94; auth, Contours of Collaboration--A New State of Organizing?, GEO, 94. **CONTACT ADDRESS** Dept of Philos, Univ of Connecticut, Storrs, 344 Mansfield Rd, Storrs, CT 06269.

KRIMM, HANS HEINZ

PERSONAL Born 01/08/1933, Tallinn, Estonia, m, 1955, 2 children **DISCIPLINE** PHILOSOPHY **EDUCATION** Johns Hopkins Univ, AB, 55, PhD(philos), 60. **CAREER** Asst, John Hopkins Univ, 57-60; from instr to asst prof philos, Utica Col, Syracuse Univ, 60-63; from asst prof to assoc prof, 63-78, prof philos, 78-98, prof emeritus, CO Col, 98-; steering comt, prog sci, technol & humanism, Aspen Inst Humanistic Studies, 74-77; open space adv comt, Colo Springs, 76. **RESEARCH** Common sense conceptions of causality; philosophy of science and logic; the value-structure of science and technology; environmental ethics. **CONTACT ADDRESS** Dept Philos, Colorado Col, 14 E Cache La Poudre, Colorado Springs, CO 80903-3294.

KRIMSKY, SHELDON

PERSONAL Born 06/26/1941, New York, NY, m, 1970, 2 children **DISCIPLINE** PHILOSOPHY, HISTORY OF SCIENCE **EDUCATION** Brooklyn Col, BS, 63; Purdue Univ, MS, 65; Boston Univ, PhD(philos), 70. **CAREER** Urban & environ policy: prof, 90-; assoc prof, 83-90; assit prof, 80-82; Prog Urban, Social & Env Policy, acting dir, 78-80; assoc dir, 75-78; res assoc, Boston Univ, 73-75; assit prof, Univ of South Fla, 70-73. **HONORS AND AWARDS** NDEA Fel; Distinguished Alumnus, Boston Univ fel; Am Asn for the Advancement of Sci; Fel, Hastings Center. **MEMBERSHIPS** AAAS. **RESEARCH** Biotechnology; science and society; bioethics; chemicals and health; environmental ethics; environmental policy; risk management. **SELECTED PUBLICATIONS** Auth, Regulating Recombinant DNA Research in Controversy: Politics of Technical Decisions, Sage, 78; auth, The Role of the Citizen Court in the Recombinant DNA Debate, Bull Atomic Scientists, 10/78; coauth, Recombinant DNA research: The Scope and lLimits of Regulation, The Am J Pub Health, 12/79; auth, Genetic Alchemy: The Social History of the Recombinant DNA Debate, MIT Press, 82; auth, Patents for Life Forms sui generis: Some New Questions for Science Law and Society, Recombinant DNA Tech Bull, 4/81; coauth, Environmental Hazards, Auburn House Publ Co, 88; auth, Social Theories of Risk, Praeger, 92; auth, Biotechnics and Society, Praeger, 92; coauth, Agricultural Biotechnology and the Environment, Univ Ill Press, 96; auth, The Profit of Scientific Discovery and its Normative Implications, Chicago Kent Law Review 75 (99): 15-39; auth, Hormonal Choas, John Hopkins Univ Press, 00. **CONTACT ADDRESS** Dept of Urban Environ Policy, Tufts Univ, Medford, 97 Talbot Ave, Medford, MA 02155-5555. **EMAIL** sheldon.krimsky@tufts.edu

KRISHNA, VERN

DISCIPLINE LAW **EDUCATION** Alta Univ, LLB; Harvard Univ, LLM. **CAREER** Prof, 81-. **HONORS AND AWARDS** Pres, Certified General Accountants Asn. **MEMBERSHIPS** Law Soc Upper Can. **SELECTED PUBLICATIONS** Auth, The Fundamentals of Canadian Income Tax; The Essentials of Income Tax Law. **CONTACT ADDRESS** Fac Common Law, Univ of Ottawa, Fauteux Hall, 57 Louis Pasteur, Ottawa, ON, Canada K1N 6N5. **EMAIL** vkrishna@uottawa.ca

KRISLOV, JOSEPH

PERSONAL Born 08/14/1927, Cleveland, OH, m, 1956, 1 child **DISCIPLINE** ECONOMICS **EDUCATION** Ohio Univ, BS Ed., 49; Western Reserve Univ, MA, 50; Attended Ohio State Univ, 50-51; Univ of Wisconsin, PhD, 54. **CAREER** Asst prof, Baldwin-Wallace and Western Reserve, 53-54; Exec Sec, Ohio Councils, AFSCME, AFL-CIO, 54-57; lectr, Ohio State Univ, 54-55; res and educ dir, Kentucky State AFL-CIO, 57-58; supervisory res analyst, soc security, 58-64; lectr, Johns Hopkins Univ, 60-64; Fulbright prof, Trinity Col, Ireland, 70-71; prof, Tel-Aviv U., Israel, 77-78; volunteer speaker, US Infor Agency, Ger, Italy, and Portugal, 77-78; res fel, Indo-American Found, Tata Instit, India, 81; vol speaker, US Infor Agency, India, Parkistan, Nepal, Finland, 81; sr teaching fel, Natl Univ of Singapoe, 83-84; vol speaker, United States Info Serv, Indonesia, New Zealand, Papua New Guinea, Australia, 83-84; fulbright prof, Catholic Univ of Rio de Janeiro and Univ of Sao Paulo, Brazil, 89; volunteer speaker, US Infor Serv, Brazil, Argentina, Venezuela, 89; fulbright prof, Univ of Sao Paulo, Brazil, 90; prof, Univ of Kentucky, 64-99. **HONORS AND AWARDS** Sum fel, Kentucky res found, 65; Grievance arbitration in educ units sum fel, Kentucky res found, 66; AFT res found, 68; Kentucky res found, 69-70; Soc security admin, 72; Swedish and Finnish pension reinsurance Finnish ministry of educ, 72; Kentucky res found, 73; Israel insti for bus res, 77; Ctr for labor educ and res, Univ of Kentucky, 80; Indo-Am found, 81-82; Ctr for labor educ and res, Univ of Kentucky, 82-83; Ctr for labor educ and res, Univ of Kentucky, 84-85; US/Japan int mgt instit, 88. **MEMBERSHIPS** Nat Acad of Arbitrators. **RESEARCH** Labor organizations; arbitration. **SELECTED PUBLICATIONS** Auth, "Representation Elections in the Railroad and Airline Industries, 1955-1984," Labor Law Journal, April 88; auth, "Disciplining Arbitral Behavior," Labor Law Journal, July 90; auth, With R. Gift, "Are There Classics in Economics?" Journal of Economic Education, Winter 90; auth, "The AFL-CIO Internal Disputes Plan," Labor Studies Journal, Summer, 91; auth, "Entry and Advancement in the Arbitration Profession," in National Academy of Arbitrators, The Profession and Practice of Labor Arbitration in America, 92; auth, "Labor Organizations," in Encyclopedia of Kentucky, 92; rev, "Fishback, Soft Coal, Hard Choices: The Economic Welfare of Bituminous Coal Miners, 1890-1930 in Growth and Change, Summer 93; rev, "Boulding, The Structure of a Modern Economy: The United states 1929-89 in Growth and Change," Winter 94; auth, "The Ethics of the Consent Award in Grievance Arbitration" Proceedings, Ninth Annual University of Louisville Labor Law Conference, 94; auth, "The Consent Award in Labor Arbitration: Where and Why?" Labor Law Journal, November, 95; auth, "Disclosure Problems of the Academic Labor Arbitrator," Dispute Resolution Journal, October, 97. **CONTACT ADDRESS** Dept of Econ, Univ of Kentucky, Gatton Col of Business & Economics, Lexington, KY 40506-0034.

KRISPIN, GERALD

DISCIPLINE SYSTEMATIC THEOLOGY **EDUCATION** Univ Alberta, BA, 81; Lutheran Theol Sem, Saskatoon, Mdiv, 83; Concordia Sem, St Louis, STM, ThD, 91. **CAREER** Assoc prof, Concordia Univ, 87-. **SELECTED PUBLICATIONS** Auth, True Lutheran Confessions, Can Lutheran, XI:1, 96; auth, Paul Gerhardt: Confessional Subscription and the Lord's Supper, Logia: A J Lutheran Theol IV:3, 95; auth, Spirituality and Spiritual Formation in the Hymnody of Paul Gerhardt, Lutheran Theol Rev VI:1, 93, Christ, the Way, Can Lutheran, 92; auth, Odo Cassel and the Kultmysterium: A Study in Liturgical Synergism, Confessional Lutheran Res Soc Newsl, 91; coauth, The Christian Faith: A Biblical Introduction, Edmonton: Pioneer Press, 96, 2nd Rev and Expanded Ed, 98. **CONTACT ADDRESS** Dept of Religious Studies, Concordia Univ Col of Alberta, 7128 Ada Blvd, Edmonton, AB, Canada T5B 4E4. **EMAIL** gkrispin@concordia.ab.ca

KRISTELLER, PAUL OSKAR

PERSONAL Born 05/22/1905, Berlin, Germany, m, 1940 **DISCIPLINE** PHILOSOPHY **EDUCATION** Univ Heidelberg, PhD, 28; Univ Pisa, PhD, 37. **CAREER** Lectr Ger, Inst Super Magistero, Florence, Italy, 34-35; Univ Pisa, 35-38; lectr Philos, Yale Univ, 39; assoc, 39-48, from assoc prof to prof, 48-68, F J E Woodbridge prof, 68-73, emer F J E Woodbridge prof philos, Columbia Univ, 73-. **HONORS AND AWARDS** Serena Medal, Brit Acad, 58; Premio, Int Forte dei marmi, 68; Fulbright vis prof, Univ Pisa, 52; mem, Inst Advan Studies, Princeton, 54-55, 61 and 68-69; Guggenheim fel, 58 and 68-69; phd, univ padua, 62, middlebury col, 72, columbia univ, 74, cath univ am, 76, univ rochester, 77, duke univ, 79, washington univ, 82, state univ ny, binghamton, 82. **MEMBERSHIPS** Am Philos Asn; fel Mediaeval Acad Am; Am Soc Church Hist; Asn Teachers Ital; Renaissance Soc Am. **RESEARCH** Renaissance philosophy; ancient and medieval philosophy; intellectual history. **SELECTED PUBLICATIONS** Auth, Musica Scientia in Musical Scholarship in the Italian Renaissance, Am Hist Rev, 93; Gordan, Phyllis, Goodhart In-Memoriam, Renaissance Quart, 94; Iter Kristellerianum and Honoring the Career of Kristeller, Paul, Oskar, Renaissance Scholar in The European Journey 1905-1939, Renaissance Quart, 94; Humanist Jurisprudence in Studies in the Field of Jurisprudence Under the Influence of Humanism, Renaissance Quart, 95; Comment on Black Athena, J Hist Ideas, 95; Ferrariis, Antonio, De, Called Il-Galateo, De Educatione 1505, Renaissance Quart, 96. **CONTACT ADDRESS** 1161 Amsterdam Ave, New York, NY 10027.

KRODEL, GOTTFRIED G.

PERSONAL Born 07/14/1931, Redwitz, Germany, m, 1956, 1 child **DISCIPLINE** CHURCH HISTORY **EDUCATION** Univ Erlangen, ThD, 55. **CAREER** Instr church hist, Univ Chicago, 56-59; from asst prof to assoc prof relig, Concordia Col, Moorhead, Minn, 59-65; assoc prof hist and church hist, 65-71, Prof Hist and Church Hist, Valparaiso Univ, 71-. **MEMBERSHIPS** Am Soc Church Hist; Am Soc Reformation Res; AHA; Renaissance Soc Am; Lutber Ges. **RESEARCH** History of Christian thought; Renaissance and humanism; constitutional history of 16th century Germany. **SELECTED PUBLICATIONS** **CONTACT ADDRESS** Dept of Hist, Valparaiso Univ, Valparaiso, IN 46383.

KROME, FREDERIC

PERSONAL Born 11/23/1962, Berlin, Germany, m, 1994, 2 children **DISCIPLINE** JUDAIC STUDIES **EDUCATION** Wilkes Col, BA, 84; Bowling Green State Univ, MA, 86; Univ Cincinnati, PhD, 92. **CAREER** Adj Prof, Northern Ky Univ, 92-94; Adj Lecturer, Raymond Walters Col, 91, 92-96; Adj Lecturer, Univ Cincinnati, 92-96; Lecturer, Northern Ky Univ, 95-98; Adj Prof, to Adj Asst Prof, Univ Cincinnati, 92-. **HONORS AND AWARDS** Bernard and Audre Rapoport Fel, Jacob Rader Marcus Ctr, 96-97; NEH Summer Seminar Grant, 93; Rockefeller archive Ctr and foundation Grant, 92; Charles Phelps Taft Dissertation Fel, 90-91; 91-92; Lenore McGrance Scholarship, Univ Cincinnati, 91; Res Fel, Univ Cincinnati, 90; Univ Res Coun Grant, Univ Cincinnati, 90. **MEMBERSHIPS** Asn for Jewish Studies, Ohio Acad of Hist. **RESEARCH** Anglo-Jewish History; History of Anti-Semitism; Film and History. **SELECTED PUBLICATIONS** Auth, "The True Glory and the Failure of Anglo-American Film Propaganda," The Journal of contemporary History, (98): 21-34; auth, "Tunisian victory and Anglo-American Film Propaganda in World War II," the Historian 58, (96): 517-529; auth, "Mobilization for War in early Elizabethan England: The Newhaven expedition of 1562," Perspectives in History XI, (1995-1996): 13-26; auth, "From Liberal Philosophy to Conservative ideology? Walter Lippmann's Opposition to the New Deal," Journal of American Studies, (87): 57-64. **CONTACT ADDRESS** Dept Judaic Studies, Univ of Cincinnati, PO Box 210169, Cincinnati, OH 45221-0169. **EMAIL** fkrome@cn.huc.edu

KRONDORFER, BJOERN

PERSONAL Born 03/29/1959, Frankfurt, Germany, m, 1991, 2 children **DISCIPLINE** RELIGIOUS STUDIES **EDUCATION** Goethe Univ, BA (equivalent), 81; Temple Univ, MA, 84, PhD, 90. **CAREER** Adj Asst Prof, Lehigh Univ, 90; Instr, Temple Univ, 90-91; Vis Asst Prof, 92-96, Assoc Prof Religious Studies, St. Mary's Col Md, 96-. **HONORS AND AWARDS** DAAD Stipend, Ger Acad Exchange Service, 83; Luther Stipend, 84; Fel Coolidge Res Colloquium, 86; Dissertation Fel, Temple Univ, 89; Post-Doctoral Fel, Temple Univ, 90-91; Selected Schol for Speakers Bureau Md Humanities Coun, 96-99. **MEMBERSHIPS** Am Acad Relig; Soc Values Higher Educ; Am Men's Studies Asn; Bibliodrama Gesellschaft/Germany. **RESEARCH** Religion and culture; religion and gender; holocaust studies; religion, bible, arts. **SELECTED PUBLICATIONS** Ed, Body and Bible: Interpreting and Experiencing Biblical Narratives, Trinity Press Int, 92; auth, Remembrance and Reconciliation: Encounters Between Young Jews and Germans, Yale Univ Press, 95; ed, Men's Bodies, Men's Gods: Male Identities in a (Post-) Christian Culture, NY Univ Press, 96; auth, The Non-Absent Body: Confessions of an African Bishop and a Jewish Ghetto Policeman, In: Revealing Male Bodies (in progress); ed, My Father's Testament: Memoir of a Jewish Teenager, 1938-1945, Temple Univ Pr, 00. **CONTACT ADDRESS** Dept of Religious Studies, St. Mary's Col of Maryland, Saint Mary's City, MD 20686. **EMAIL** bhkrondorfer@osprey.smcm.edu

KRUG, BARBARA C.
PERSONAL Born 02/08/1940, Newark, NJ, s **DISCIPLINE** THEOLOGY **EDUCATION** Caldwell Col, BA, 64; Providence Col, MA, 69; Fordham Univ, MA, 96; Drew Univ, Doctor Ministry, 00. **CAREER** Dir, Saint Cassian Parrish, 82-85; dir, adj, coun, Caldwell Col, 85-91; dev, Sisters St Dominic, 91-92; asst prof, Caldwell Col, 92-. **MEMBERSHIPS** Theta Alpha Kappa; Am Weil Soc; Montclair Hist Soc; Cath Theol Soc Amer; Coll Theol Soc; Fordham Theol Assoc; Women Grad Students Theol Fordham Univ; AAR; Bd Trustees, Lacordaire Acad. **RESEARCH** Theology; deep ecology. **SELECTED PUBLICATIONS** Trans, "Adoro Te Devote" copyright, 00; auth, Raising Cosmic Consciousness and Conscience, pending. **CONTACT ADDRESS** Dept Religion Philos, Caldwell Col, 9 Ryerson Ave, Caldwell, NJ 07006-6109. **EMAIL** sbkrug@caldwell.edu

KRYCH, MARGARET A.
PERSONAL Born 04/04/1942, Perth, Western Australia, m, 1971, 2 children **DISCIPLINE** RELIGION **EDUCATION** Princeton Theol Sem, PhD, 85. **CAREER** Prof, Lutheran Theol Sem, 77-. **HONORS AND AWARDS** ATS Teaching and Learning Grant, 99. **MEMBERSHIPS** SRCD, APRRE, REA, AAR/SBL. **RESEARCH** Cognitive development. **SELECTED PUBLICATIONS** Auth, Teaching About Lutheranism, Augsburg Fortress (Minneapolis, MN), 93; auth, "The Bible and Those Difficult Topics," Parish Teacher, vol 19:4 (95): 2-3; auth, "The Gospel Calls Us," in Lifelong Learning (Minneapolis: Augsburg Fortress, 97), 12-32; auth, "Children and Worship,' in Sundays and Seasons 2000 (Minneapolis: Augsburg Fortress, 99), 11-15. **CONTACT ADDRESS** Dept Relig, Lutheran Theol Sem, 7301 Germantown Ave, Philadelphia, PA 19119-1726. **EMAIL** mkrych@ltsp.edu

KUBICKI, JUDITH M.
PERSONAL Born 08/21/1946, Buffalo, NY **DISCIPLINE** RELIGION **EDUCATION** Catholic Univ of Amer, PhD, 97. **CAREER** Dir of Music, 86-93, acad dean, 97-, Christ the King Sem. **RESEARCH** Liturgy, liturgical music, symbol, semiotics ritual. **CONTACT ADDRESS** 711 Knox Rd, East Aurora, NY 14502. **EMAIL** jkubicki@pcom.net

KUCHEMAN, CLARK ARTHUR
PERSONAL Born 02/07/1931, Akron, OH, m, 1961 **DISCIPLINE** PHILOSOPHY, RELIGION **EDUCATION** Univ Akron, BA, 52; Meadville Theol Sch of Lombard Col, BD, 55; Univ Chicgo, MA, (Economics) 59, PhD(Relig & Ethics), 65. **CAREER** From instr to asst prof Social Ethics, Univ Chicago, 61-67; prof Relig & Philos, 67-80, Arthur V Stoughton Prof Christian Ethics, Claremont McKenna Col & Claremont Grad Univ, 80-, Nat Endowment for Humanities, fel, 70. **MEMBERSHIPS** Am Acad Relig; North Amer Soc for Social Philosophy; Hegel Society of America. **RESEARCH** Ethics, especially philosophical and religious; philosophy of economic science. **SELECTED PUBLICATIONS** Auth, Professor Tillich: Justice and the economic order, J Relig; Toward a theory of normative economics, In: Social Ethics: Issues in Ethics and Society, Harper, 68; Religion, culture and religious socialism, J Relig, 7/72; Morality versus economic science in religious socialism, In: Belief and Ethics, Ctr Sci Study Relig, 78; Rationality and moral obligation, In: The Life of Choice, Beacon Press. **CONTACT ADDRESS** 850 Columbia Ave, Claremont, CA 91711-6420. **EMAIL** clark_kucheman@mckenna.edu

KUEHN, MANFRED
DISCIPLINE THE HISTORY OF EARLY MODERN PHILOSOPHY **EDUCATION** McGill Univ, PhD. **CAREER** Prof, Purdue Univ. **RESEARCH** 18th century philosophy; Immanuel Kant, Hume, Reid. **SELECTED PUBLICATIONS** Auth, Scottish Common Sense in Germany, 1768-1800. **CONTACT ADDRESS** Dept of Philos, Purdue Univ, West Lafayette, 1080 Schleman Hall, West Lafayette, IN 47907-1080.

KUHN, STEVEN THOMAS
PERSONAL Born 03/01/1949, Baltimore, MD, m, 1970, 1 child **DISCIPLINE** PHILOSOPHY **EDUCATION** Johns Hopkins Univ, BA, 70; Stanford Univ, PhD, 76. **CAREER** Asst Prof, Univ Michigan, 76-77; Fel comput sci, Univ Pa, 77-78; Prpf Philos, Georgetown Univ, 78- **HONORS AND AWARDS** Humboldt Fel, 83; Fel, Inst for Advanced Study in the Humanities Edinburgh, 87. **MEMBERSHIPS** Am Philos Soc; Asn Symbolic Logic; Soc Exact Philos; Asn Comput Mach. **RESEARCH** Logic; philosophy of science; philosophy of language. **SELECTED PUBLICATIONS** Auth, Many Sorted Modal Logics, Uppsala Studies Philos, 77; The Pragmatics of Tense, Vol 40, Synthese; Quantifiers as modal operators, Vol 39, Studia Logica; coauth (with A K Joshi), Centered logic, Proc 1979 Int Joint Conf Artificial Intel, 79; auth, Logical expressions, constants and operation logic, Vol 78, J Philos; auth, The Domino Relation, J Phil Logic 18l coauth, Numbers without Ones, The Fibbonacci Qrt vol 30; auth, Minimal Non-Contingency Logic, Notre Dame J of Formal Logic, vol 36; auth, "Agreement Keeping and Indirect Moral Theory," Journal Philos, volume 93; auth, "Embedded Definite Descriptions," Mind 109 (00): 443-454.; **CONTACT ADDRESS** Dept of Philos, Georgetown Univ, 1421 37th St N W, Washington, DC 20057-0001.

KUHNS, RICHARD
PERSONAL Born 05/03/1924, Chicago, IL, m, 1 child **DISCIPLINE** PHILOSOPHY **EDUCATION** Dartmouth, BA, 47; Columbia Univ, PhD, 55 **CAREER** Prof, 50-95 Columbia Univ **CONTACT ADDRESS** 420 Riverside Dr, New York, NY 10025. **EMAIL** rfk2@columbia.edu

KUJAWA, SHERYL A.
PERSONAL Born 05/30/1956, Milwaukee, WI **DISCIPLINE** RELIGIOUS STUDIES **EDUCATION** Marquette Univ, BA, 77; Sarah Lawrence Col, MA, 79; Harvard Divinity Sch, MTS, 81; Episcopal Divinity Sch, Mdiv, 83; Boston Col, PhD, 93. **CAREER** Adjunct fac, Episcopal Divinity Sch, 86-88; adjunct fac, Union Theol Sem, 92-95; assoc prof of Pastoral Theol, Episcopal Divinity Sch, 98-. **HONORS AND AWARDS** Ford Found fel, 78-79; Hist fel, Boston Col, 81-84. **MEMBERSHIPS** Asn of Prof and Res in Relig Educ; Asn of Theol Field Educ. **RESEARCH** Religious studies. **SELECTED PUBLICATIONS** Auth, "Youth Ministry: Evangelization, Conscientization, and Liberation," 98; auth, Disorganized Religion: The Evangelization of Youth and Young Adults, 98; co-auth, God-Works: Youth and Young Adult Ministry Models..Evangelism at Work With Young People. **CONTACT ADDRESS** 99 Brattle St, Cambridge, MA 02138. **EMAIL** Skujawa@episdivschool.org

KUKLA, REBECCA
DISCIPLINE HISTORY OF MODERN PHILOSOPHY, SOCIAL PHILOSOPHY, GENDER THEORY **EDUCATION** Univ Toronto, BA, 90; Univ Pittsburgh, PhD, 95. **CAREER** Asst prof, Univ NMex. **RESEARCH** The writing of Jean-Jacques Rousseau. **SELECTED PUBLICATIONS** Published in The Brit J for Psihol of Sci, Metaphilosophy, J of Speculative Philos, J of Brit Soc for Phenomenol, Poznan Stud, Eidos, and Anal, as well as contributing chapters to volumes on Rousseau, Feminist Theory, and Popular Cult. **CONTACT ADDRESS** Univ of New Mexico, Albuquerque, Albuquerque, NM 87131. **EMAIL** rkukla@ccs.carleton.ca

KULSTAD, MARK ALAN
PERSONAL Born 01/08/1947, Minneapolis, MN, m, 1984 **DISCIPLINE** PHILOSOPHY **EDUCATION** Macalester Col, BA, 69; Univ Mich, PhD(philos), 75. **CAREER** Asst prof, 75-81, Assoc Prof Philos, Rice Univ, 81-96; Chair of Philosophy Dept, 88-90, 91-92; Prof of Philosophy, 96-. **HONORS AND AWARDS** Alexander von Humboldt Found res fel, Hanover, WGer, 79-80. **MEMBERSHIPS** Am Philos Asn; Am Leibniz Soc (pres, 81 -). **SELECTED PUBLICATIONS** Auth, "Leibniz on Apperception Consciousness, and Reflection," Philosophia Verlag: Munich, 91. **CONTACT ADDRESS** Dept of Philos, Rice Univ, Houston, TX 77005.

KULTGEN, JOHN
PERSONAL Born 10/16/1925, Dallas, TX, m, 1980, 5 children **DISCIPLINE** PHILOSOPHY **EDUCATION** Univ Texas, Austin, BA, 46; Univ Chicago, MA, 48; PhD, 52. **CAREER** Asst prof philos, Ore State Univ, 52-56; assoc prof and prof, philos, Southern Methodist Univ, 56-67; prof philos, Univ Mo, Columbia, 67-. **HONORS AND AWARDS** Peace Stud Prof of the Year, 96; Byler Dist Prof, 98. **MEMBERSHIPS** APA; Southwest Philos Soc; Concerned Philos for Peace. **RESEARCH** Epistemology; ethics; war and peace; professional ethics. **SELECTED PUBLICATIONS** Coauth, The Nature of Man, William Brown, 67; auth, Ethics and Professionalism, Pennsylvania, 88; auth, Parentalism and the Caring Life, Oxford, 95; auth, In the Valley of the Shadow, Peter Lang, 99; coed, Problems for Democracy, Rodopi (forthcoming). **CONTACT ADDRESS** Dept of Philos, Univ of Missouri, Columbia, Columbia, MO 65211. **EMAIL** kultgenj@missouri.edu

KUMAR, RAHUL
PERSONAL Born 11/08/1967, Canada, s **DISCIPLINE** PHILOSOPHY **EDUCATION** Queens Univ, Canada, BA; Univ of Oxford, MA, 92; PhD, 95. **CAREER** Asst prof philos, Univ of Pa. **HONORS AND AWARDS** SSHRC Post-Dr Fel, 95-97; Post-Dr Fel, Harvard Univ, 95-97. **MEMBERSHIPS** APA **RESEARCH** Ethical Theory and Psychology. **CONTACT ADDRESS** Dr, Univ of Pennsylvania, Logan Hall # 466, Philadelphia, PA 19104-6304. **EMAIL** rakumar@phil.upenn.edu

KUMFER, EARL T.
DISCIPLINE THEOLOGY **EDUCATION** Cath Univ Am, AB, 62, MA, 63; Southern Ill Univ, Carbondale, 82. **CAREER** CHAIR, PROF PHILOS & THEOL, UNIV ST FRANCIS, 65-. **CONTACT ADDRESS** Dept of Relig and Philos, Univ St. Francis, Fort Wayne, 2701 Spring St, Fort Wayne, IN 46808-3994. **EMAIL** ekumfer@sfc.edu

KUNKEL, JOSEPH C.
DISCIPLINE ETHICS **EDUCATION** St Bonaventure Univ, PhD, 64. **CAREER** Dept Philos, Univ Dayton **RESEARCH** Philosophy of peace. **SELECTED PUBLICATIONS** Co-ed, In the Interest of Peace: A Spectrum of Philosophical Views, Longwood Acad, 90; auth, Power Politics, Human Nature, and Morality, On the Eve of the 21st Century: Perspectives of Russian and American Philosophers, Rowman and Littlefield, 94; The Rich Get Richer and the Poor Starve: Is There an Ethical Alternative?, Philosophical Perspectives on Power and Domination: Theories and Practices, Editions Rodopi, 97. **CONTACT ADDRESS** Dept of Philos, Univ of Dayton, 300 Col Park, Dayton, OH 75062. **EMAIL** kunkel@checkov.hm.udayton.edu

KUNREUTHER, HOWARD
PERSONAL Born 11/14/1938, New York, NY, m, 1990, 4 children **DISCIPLINE** DECISION SCIENCES, ECONOMICS **EDUCATION** Bates Col , AB (magna cum laude), economics, 59; MIT, PhD, economics, 65. **CAREER** Fulbright Scholar, Econometric Inst , Netherlands School of Econ, 63-64; econ, Inst Defense Analyses, Econ Political Studies Div, 64-66; asst prof, Univ Chicago, Graduate Sch Bus, 66-72; res adv, Pakistan Inst Development Econ (under Ford Found-Yale Univ Pakistan Project), 70-71; assoc prof, decision sciences, 72-75, chm, Decision Sciences Dept, 77-80, sr fellow, Wharton Financial Institutions Center, currently, co-dir, Wharton Risk Mgt Decision Processes Center, currently, Cecelia Yen Koo Professor Decision Sci Public Policy, currently, Univ Pa; task leader, Risk Group, Intl Inst Applied Analysis, 80-82; prog mgr, Decision Risk and Mgt Sci Program, Natl Sci Found, 88-89. **HONORS AND AWARDS** Fellowships and grants received: "Socioeconomic Impacts of Sitting High Level Radioactive Waste Repository," State of Nevada, 87-; with other faculty, EPA cooperative agreement on "Implementing the Clean Air Act," 93-; with Financial Institutions Center, "Managing Catastrophic Risks," 97-; Natl Sci Found, "role of Insurance and Other Policy Instruments in Managing Catastrophic Risks," 98-. **MEMBERSHIPS** Natl Sci Found Mentoring Program Natural Hazards, 96-98; Building Seismic Safety Comn, Natl Res Coun, 93-; Phi Beta Kappa; Amer Econ Assn;. **RESEARCH** Catastrophic risk management. **SELECTED PUBLICATIONS** Co-ed, Paying the Price: The Status and Role of Insurance Against Natural Disasters in the United States, 68; assoc ed, Risk Analysis, 84-; assoc ed, Journ of Risk and Uncertainty, 87-; assoc ed, Journ of Regulatory Econ, 88-; co-editor, "Challenges in Risk Assessment and Management," Annals of Amer Acad Polit Social Sci, May 96; co-auth, "Energy, Environment and the Economy: Asian Perspectives, 96; auth, "Managing Catastrophic Risks Through Insurance and Mitigation," Proceedings of the 5th Alexander Howden Conf on Financial Risk Mgt for Natural Catastrophes, 97; co-auth, Managing Environmental Risk Through Insurance, 97; co-auth, "Utilizing Third Party Inspections for Preventing Major Chemical Accidents," Risk Analysis, Apr 98. **CONTACT ADDRESS** Dept of Operations and Information Management, Univ of Pennsylvania, The Wharton School, Philadelphia, PA 19104-6366. **EMAIL** kunreuther@wharton.upenn.edu

KUNTZ, J. KENNETH
PERSONAL Born 01/20/1934, St Louis, MO, m, 1962, 2 children **DISCIPLINE** RELIGION **EDUCATION** Grinnell Col, BA, 56; Yale Univ, BD, 59; Theol Sem NYC, PhD, 63. **CAREER** Instructor to Asst Prof, Wellesley Col, 63-67; Asst Prof to Prof, Univ Iowa, 67-. **HONORS AND AWARDS** Dozentenstipendium, Alexander von Humboldt Foundation, 71-72, 73, 79; NEH Grant, 71, 84. **MEMBERSHIPS** Catholic Biblical Asn, Soc for Old Testament Study, Soc of Biblical Literature, Chicago Soc of Biblical Res. **RESEARCH** Biblical poetry; Book of Psalms; Biblical role of women; Rhetorical criticism of Biblical texts. **SELECTED PUBLICATIONS** Auth, "Grounds for Praise: The Nature and Function of the Motive Clause in the Hymns of the Hebrew Psalter," in Worship and the Hebrew Bible: Essays in Honour of John T. Willis, Sheffield Acad Press, 99; auth, "Contextualizing the Text: Assessing a Social-Scientific Approach to Understanding the Hebrew Bible," Proceedings of the Central States, Society of Biblical Literature and American Schools of Oriental Research, (98): 14-20; auth, "Biblical Hebrew Poetry in Recent Research," Currents in Research: Biblical Studies, Sheffield Acad Press, 98; auth, "The Form, Location, and Function of Rhetorical Questions in Deutero-Isaiah," in Writing and Reading the Scroll of Isaiah: Studies in an Interpretive Tradition, Vetus Testamentum Supplement, 97; auth, "Engaging the Psalms: Gains and Trends in Recent Research," Currents in Research: Biblical Studies, Sheffield Acad Press, 94; auth, "The Bible and Related Literature," The Reader's Adviser, (94): 792-838; auth, "recent Perspectives on Biblical Poetry," Religious Studies review, (93): 321-327; auth, The People of Ancient Israel: An Introduction to Old Testament Literature, History, and Thought, Harper & row, 74; auth, The Self-revelation of God, Westminster Press, 67. **CONTACT ADDRESS** School of Relig, Univ Iowa, 314 Gilmore Hall, Iowa City, IA 52242-1320. **EMAIL** ken-kuntz@uiowa.edu

KUO, LENORE
PERSONAL Born New York, NY **DISCIPLINE** METAPHYSICS, ETHICS AND THE HISTORY OF PHILOSOPHY

EDUCATION Univ Wis, Madison, BA, MA, PhD. **CAREER** Assoc prof Philos and Women's Stud, Univ Nebr, Omaha, 85-. **RESEARCH** Social policy analysis. **SELECTED PUBLICATIONS** Published on topics as diverse as surrogate mothering, corruption in bureaucracy and recent U.S. attempts to require women to use Norplant (a form of birth control) as a condition of probation. **CONTACT ADDRESS** Univ of Nebraska, Omaha, Omaha, NE 68182.

KUPPERMAN, JOEL J.
PERSONAL Born 05/18/1936, Chicago, IL, m, 1964, 2 children **DISCIPLINE** PHILOSOPHY **EDUCATION** Univ Chicago, AB, 54; SB, 55; MA, 56; Cambridge Univ, PhD, 63. **CAREER** Univ Conn, 60-; prof, 72-; vis fel, Corpus Christi Coll, 85; vis fel, Clare Hall, Cambridge, 88. **MEMBERSHIPS** APA. **RESEARCH** Ethics; Asian and comparative philosophy. **SELECTED PUBLICATIONS** Auth, Ethical Knowledge, Geo Allen & Unwin, Muirhead Library of Philo (London), 70; auth, The Foundations of Morality, Geo Allen & Unwin (London and Boston), 83; auth, Character, Oxford Univ Press (NY), 91; auth, Value.. And What Follows, Oxford Univ Press (NY), 99; auth, Learning from Asian Philosophy, Oxford Univ Press (NY), 99; auth, "Xunzi : Morality as Psychological Constraint," in Virtue, Nature and Moral Agency in the Xunzi, eds. TC Kline III, Philip J Ivanhoe (Indianapolis: Hackett Books, 00); auth, "How Values Congeal Into Facts," Ratio (00); auth, Classic Asian Philosophy: A Guide to the Essential Texts, Oxford Univ Press (NY), 00. **CONTACT ADDRESS** Dept Philosophy, Univ of Connecticut, Storrs, 344 Mansfield Rd, U-54, Storrs, CT 06269-0001. **EMAIL** jkupper@uconnvm.uconn.edu

KURLAND, ADAM H.
DISCIPLINE LAW **EDUCATION** Univ Calif, Los Angeles, BA, 78, JD, 81. **CAREER** Prof. **MEMBERSHIPS** Amer Bar Asn; participated, Cent Eastern and Europ Law Initiative Workshop in Alma-Ata Kazakhstan; active mem, ABA White Collar Crime Subcomt & Criminal Justice Sect Bk Publ Comt. **RESEARCH** Negotiating immunity and plea agreements in the state and federal criminal justice systems. **SELECTED PUBLICATIONS** Auth, Providing a Federal Criminal Defendant with a Unilateral Right to a Bench Trial: A Renewed Call to Amend Federal Rule of Criminal Procedure 23 (a), 26 UC Davis L Rev 309, 93 & First Principles of American Federalism and the Nature of Federal Criminal Jurisdiction, Emory Law J 1, 96. **CONTACT ADDRESS** Sch of Law, Howard Univ, 2900 Van Ness St NW, Washington, DC 20008. **EMAIL** akurland@law.howard.edu

KURTZ, PAUL
PERSONAL Born 12/21/1925, Newark, NJ, m, 1960, 4 children **DISCIPLINE** PHILOSOPHY **EDUCATION** NYork Univ, BA, 48; Columbia Univ, MA, 49, PhD, 52. **CAREER** Instr, Queens Col, 50-52; instr to assoc prof, Trinity Col, 52-59; vis lectr New Sch of Soc Res, 60-65; assoc prof, Vassar Col, 60; prof Philos Union Col, 61-65; prof emer philos SUNY Buffalo, 65- ; pres, Prometheus Books, 70- ; chmn, com for the Sci Investigation of Claims of the Paranormal, 76- ; ed-in-chief, Free Inquiry Mag, 80- . **HONORS AND AWARDS** Fel, AAAS; John Dewey fel; Bertrand Russell Soc Awd; John Dewey Fel; International Humanist Awd **MEMBERSHIPS** AAAS; Am Philos Asn; Int Acad of Numanism; Int Humanist and Ethical Union. **RESEARCH** Value theory; social philosophy; science and the paranormal; Humanism **SELECTED PUBLICATIONS** Auth, The New Skepticism: Inquiry and Reliable Knowledge, Prometheus, 92; auth, Living without Religion: Eupraxophy, Prometheus, 94; auth, Toward a New Enlightenment: The Philosophy of Paul Kurtz, Transaction, 94; auth, The Courage to Become: The Virtues of Humanism, Praeger, 97; The Transcendental Temptation, Prometheus, 86; Forbidden Fruit, Prometheus, 88; Humanist Manifesto, 00; Prometheus, 99; Embracing The Power of Humanism, Rowman & Littlefield, 00; Skepticism and Humanism: The New Paradigm, Transactio, 00. **CONTACT ADDRESS** PO Box 664, Amherst, NY 14226. **EMAIL** pksksh@aol.com

KURZ, WILLIAM STEPHEN
PERSONAL Born 11/09/1939, Detroit, MI **DISCIPLINE** NEW TESTAMENT, CHRISTIAN ORIGINS **EDUCATION** St Louis Univ, BA, 63, MA, 64, PhL, 64, MA, 70, STL, 71; Yale Univ, PhD(New Testament), 76. **CAREER** Instr philos, Creighton Univ, 64-65; teacher Greek and Latin, Creighton Prep Sch, 65-67; Asst Prof New Testament, Marquette Univ, 75-. **MEMBERSHIPS** Soc Bibl Lit; Cath Bibl Asn. **RESEARCH** Gospel of Luke-Book of Acts; the Greek Bible and Hellenistic Judaism; intertestamental and New Testament reinterpretation of earlier scriptures. **SELECTED PUBLICATIONS** Auth, The Function of Christological Proof from Prophecy for Luke and Justin, Yale Univ, 12/76; Acts 3:19-26 as a Test of the Role of Eschatology in Lukan Christology, Soc Bibl Lit, Sem Papers, 10/77; Inspiration and the Origins of the New Testament, In: Scripture and Charismatic Renewal, Servant Bks, 79; An Example of Typology: Manna, Trust and Our Daily Bread, Cath Charismatic, 10/79; Hellenistic Rhetoric in the Christological Proof of Luke-Acts, Cath Bibl Quart, 4/80; Luke-Acts and Historiography in the Greek Bible, Soc Bibl Lit & Sem Papers, 80; Test Every Prophecy: Ignatian Helps for Pauline Discernment, Rev for Relig, 9/81; Acts of the Apostles, New Reaading Guide to the New Testament, Liturgical Press, 82. **CONTACT ADDRESS** Dept of Theol, Marquette Univ, Milwaukee, WI 53233.

KUSHNER, JAMES ALAN
PERSONAL Born 04/14/1945, Philadelphia, PA, m, 1970, 3 children **DISCIPLINE** LAW, CONSTITUTIONAL HISTORY, URBAN PLANNING **EDUCATION** Univ Miami, BBA, 67; Univ Md, LLB & JD, 68. **CAREER** Adj prof housing law, Univ Mo-Kansas City, 73; vis lectr, Univ Calif, Berkeley, 74-75; assoc prof, 75-78, Prof Law, Southwestern Univ, Calif, 78-; Consult, Am Bar Asn, 74-76; vis lectr, Univ Va, 81; vis prof, UCLA, 83 & 93. **HONORS AND AWARDS** Irving D. and Florence Rosenberg Prof, 00. **MEMBERSHIPS** Am Asn Law Schs. **RESEARCH** Race and Law; urban housing and planning. **SELECTED PUBLICATIONS** Auth, Apartheid in America, Carrollton Press, 80; Urban Transportation Planning, Urban Law & Policy, Vol 4, 81; Housing & Community Development (with Mandelker et al), Michie/Bobbs-Merrill, 81, 2nd ed, 89, 3rd ed, 99; The Reagan Urban Policy: Centrifugal Force in the Empire, UCLA J Environ Law & Policy, 82; Non-Owner Rights in Real Property and the Impact on Property Taxes, Urban Law & Policy, 85; Government Discrimination, West, 88; DMS: The Development Monitoring System is the Latest Technique for Subdivision Review and Growth Management, Zoning and Planning Law Report, 88; Unfinished Agenda: The Federal Fair Housing Enforcement Effort, Yale Law & Pol Review, 88; Substantive Equal Protection: The Rehnquist Court and the Fourth Tier of Judicial Review, Mo Law Rev, 88; The Fair Housing Amendments Act of 1988: The Second Generation of Fair Housing, Vanderbilt Law Rev, 89; Subdivision Law and Growth Management, West, 91; Property and Mysticism: The Legality of Exactions as a Condition for Public Development Approval in the Time of the Rehnquist Court, J Land Use & Environ Law, 92; Vested Development Rights, in 1992 Zoning and Planning Law Handbook, 92; A Tale of Three Cities: Land Development and Planning for Growth in Stockholm, Berlin, and Los Angeles, Urban Lawyer, 93; Growth Management and the City, Yale Law & Pol Rev, 94; Fair Housing: Discrimination in Real Estate, Community Development and Revitalization, 2nd ed, West, 95; Growth for the Twenty-First Century: Tales from Bavaria and the Vienna Woods -- Comparative Images of Urban Planning in Munich, Salzburg, Vienna, and the United States, Southern Calif Interdisciplinary Law J, 97; co-auth, Land Use Regulation: Cases and Materials, Aspen Law and Business, 99; co-auth, Housing and Community Development: Cases and Materials, 3rd ed, Carolina Acad Press, 99. **CONTACT ADDRESS** Southwestern Univ Sch of Law, 675 S Westmoreland Ave, Los Angeles, CA 90005-3905. **EMAIL** jkushner@swlaw.edu

KUZMINSKI, ADRIAN
PERSONAL Born 02/21/1944, Washington, PA, m, 1966, 2 children **DISCIPLINE** HISTORY, PHILOSOPHY **EDUCATION** Amherst Col, BA, 66; Univ of Rochester, PhD, 73. **CAREER** Prof of Hist, 71-80, Univ of Hawaii; Res Scholar in Philos, 96-, Hartwick Coll. **HONORS AND AWARDS** Fulbright and Wilson Fellow. **MEMBERSHIPS** APA **RESEARCH** Consciousness, political economy. **SELECTED PUBLICATIONS** The Soul, Peter Lang Pub, NY, 94. **CONTACT ADDRESS** RD #1, Box 68, Fly Creek, NY 13337. **EMAIL** adrian@clarityconnect.com

KWON, KYEONG-SEOG
PERSONAL Born 03/18/1962, Seoul, Korea, m, 1987, 2 children **DISCIPLINE** RELIGION **EDUCATION** Yale Univ, STM, 91; Claremont Grad Univ, PhD, 98. **CAREER** Adj prof, KPCA Presbyterian Theol Sem, Whittier, Calif, 95-; vis scholar, Harvard Univ, 98; adj. Prof. San Francisco Theological Seminary, Southern California, 98-. **HONORS AND AWARDS** Grad student paper competition award, Am Acad of Relig, western div, 95. **MEMBERSHIPS** Am Acad Relig; APA; CTS College Theology Society. **RESEARCH** World religions; systematic theology; Christian thought; philosophy of religion; Asian religion and thought. **CONTACT ADDRESS** 913 La Salle Cir, Corona, CA 92879. **EMAIL** kskwon@earthlink.net

KYMLICKA, WILL
DISCIPLINE PHILOSOPHY **EDUCATION** Queen's Univ, BA, 84; Univ Oxford, BPhil, 86, PhD, 87. **CAREER** Lectr, Queen's Univ, 86-87; Princeton Univ, 87-88; Univ Toronto, 88-89; asst prof, Univ Toronto, 89-90; sr policy analyst, Royal Commission on New Reproductive Tech, 90-91; visiting prof, Univ Ottawa, 91-93; visiting prof, 94-98; res dir, Univ Ottawa, 94-98; visiting fel, Europ Forum, Europ Univ Inst, 96-; vis prof, Inst for Adv Stud, Vienna, 97-; Queen's Nat scholar, Queen's Univ, 98-; visiting prof, Univ Pompeau Fabra, Barcelona, 98-; Nationalism Stud Prog, Cent Europ Univ, Budapest, 98-; adj res prof, Carleton Univ. **HONORS AND AWARDS** Commonwealth scholar, 84-86; doc fel, SSHRC, 86-87; postdoc fel, SSHRC, 87-89; Can res fel, SSHRC, 89-92; Strategic Grants award, SSHRC, 94-97; Ralph J Bunche award, Amer Polit Sci Assn, 96; Macpherson prize, Can Polit Sci Assn, 96; Strategic Grants award, SSHRC, 98. **SELECTED PUBLICATIONS** Auth, Liberalism, Community, and Culture, Oxford UP, 89; Contemp Polit Philos, Oxford UP, 90; Multicultural Citizenship, Oxford UP, 95; Finding Our Way: Rethinking Ethnocultural Relations in Canada, Oxford UP, 98; ed, Justice in Political Philosophy, Elgar, 92; The Rights of Minority Cultures, Oxford, 95; Ethnicity and Group Rights, NYU, 97. **CONTACT ADDRESS** Dept of Philos, Carleton Univ, 1125 Colonel By Dr, 2123 Dunton Tower, Ottawa, ON, Canada K1S 5B6.

L

LABYS, WALTER CARL
PERSONAL Born 07/25/1937, Latrobe, PA, w, 1967, 2 children **DISCIPLINE** ECONOMICS **EDUCATION** Carnegie Mellon Univ, SB, 59; Duquesne Univ, MBA, 62; Harvard Univ, MA, 65; Nottingham Univ, PhD, 68. **CAREER** Visiting prof, Grad Inst of Int Studies, Univ of Geneva, 69-75; res assoc, Nat Bureau of Economic Res, 77-81; visiting scholar, Energy Lab, MIT, 81-82; chemn, Dept of Mineral and Energy Resource Economics, 84-87; res assoc, Minerals Trade Project, Inst for Applied Systems Analysis, 83-84; res fel, Inst for Int Economic Studies, Univ of Stockholm, 83-85; visiting prof, Inst Superieure de Petrochemie et de Synthese Organique Industrielle, Univ d' Aix-Marseille, 87; Gunnar Myrdal Scholar in Residence, United Nations Economic Comn for Europe, 90-91; visiting prof, Centre d;Econometrie pour L'enterprise, Univ de Montpellier and the Res Center on World Commodity Markets, Conservatoire des Arts et Metiers de Paris, 90-91; PROF OF RESOURCE ECONOMICS, ADJUNCT PROF OF ECONOMIS, FAC RES ASSOC-REGIONAL RES INST, & BENEDUM DISTINGUISHED SCHOLAR, WEST VA UNIV; RES ASSOC, GREQAM, & VISITING PROF, FACULTE D'ECONOMIE APPLIQUEE, UNIV D'AIX-MARSEILLE; VISITING PROF, LAMETA, UNIV DE MONTPELLIER; VISITING PROF, APPLIED ECONOMICS DEPT, INST FOR ADVANCED STUDIES; RES FEL, RES GROUP ON INT COMMODITY MARKETS, FACULTE DES SCIS ECONOMIQUES, UNIVERSITE PIERRE-MENDES FRANCE; LECTR, INTER-UNIVERSITY CONSORTIUM FOR POLITICAL AND SOC SCI RES, UNIV OF MICH. **HONORS AND AWARDS** Alumnus of Distinction, St. Vincent Col, 97; Outstanding Researcher, Col of Agriculture and Forestry, West Va Univ, 97; Master Knight, Order of the Vine, Sacramento Chapter, 94; Claude Worthington Benedum Distinguished Scholar, Wes Va Univ, 90; Gunnar Myrdal Scholar, United Nations Economic Comn for Europe, 90; visiting scholar, MIT, 81-82; honorary member, Societe d'Honneur Francaise, 81. **MEMBERSHIPS** Am Economics Asn; Mineral Economics and Management Soc. **RESEARCH** International commodity market modeling and forecasting; time series analysis; resources, environment, trade, & development; mineral, energy, & agricultural market analyses. **SELECTED PUBLICATIONS** Coauth, Industrial Development and Environmental Degradation, Edward Elgar (London), 98; auth, Modeling Mineral and Energy Markets, Kluwer Academic Publishers (Doston), 99; auth, "Commodity Market and Models: The Range of Experience," in The Economics of Commodity Markets, D. Greenaway and W. Morgan, eds, Edward Elgar (London), 99; coauth, Fractional Dynamics in International Commodity Prices, J of Futures Markets, 97; coauth, Long Term Memory In Commodity Futures Prices, Financial Rev, 97; coauth, Spatial Price Equilibrium as the Core to Spatial Commodity Modeling, Regional Sci Papers, 96; coauth, Uncertainty, Carbon Dioxide Concentrations and Fossil Fuel Use, Int J of Environment and Pollution, 96; coauth, CO2 Emissions and Concentration Coefficients Revisited, Int J of Global Energy Issues, 94; coauth, Divergences in Manufacturing Energy Consumption between the North and the South, Energy Policy, 94; coauth, Wavelet Analysis of Commodity Price Behavior, Advances in Computational Economics, Chapman Hall Pub Co, 97; coauth, An Econometric Approach to CO2 Concentration Modeling, Measuring and Accounting Environmental Nuisances and Benefits: Essays in Environmetrics, 97; coauth, Le Chatelier's principle and the allocation sensitivity of spatial commodity models, Recent advances in spatial equilibrium modeling: Methodology and application (essays in honor of Takashama Takayama, 96; coauth, Modeling of the petroleum spot market: A vector autoregressive appraoch, Models for Energy Policy, Routledge Pub Co, 96. **CONTACT ADDRESS** Resource Economics, West Virginia Univ, Morgantown, PO Box 6108, Morgantown, WV 26506-6108. **EMAIL** wlabys@wvu.edu

LACHS, JOHN
PERSONAL Born 07/17/1934, Budapest, HUN, m, 1967, 2 children **DISCIPLINE** PHILOSOPHY **EDUCATION** McGill Univ, BA, 56; MA, 57; Yale Univ, PhD, 61. **CAREER** Asst prof to prof, Col of William & Mary, 59-67; prof to centennial prof, Vanderbilt Univ, 67-. **HONORS AND AWARDS** Awd for the Advancement of Scholar, Phi Beta Kappa, 62; Chancellor's Cup, 69; Alumni Educ Awd, 91; Outstanding Commitment to Teaching Freshmen Awd, 99. **MEMBERSHIPS** Am Philos Asn, Soc for the Advancement of Am Philos, Metaphysical Soc of Am. **RESEARCH** American philosophy, ethics, German idealism, medical ethics, human nature. **SELECTED PUBLICATIONS** Auth, Intermediate Man, Hackett, 81; auth, Mind and Philosophers, Vanderbilt Univ Press, 87; auth, The Relevance of Philosophy to Live, Vanderbilt Univ Press, 95; auth, In Love with Life, Vanderbilt Univ Press, 98; coauth,

Thinking in the Ruins, 99. **CONTACT ADDRESS** Dept Philos, Vanderbilt Univ, 2201 West End Ave, Nashville, TN 37235-0001. **EMAIL** john.lachs@vanderbilt.edu

LACKEY, DOUGLAS PAUL
PERSONAL Born 08/27/1945, New York, NY **DISCIPLINE** PHILOSOPHY **EDUCATION** Mich State Univ, BA, 66; Yale Univ, PhD(philos), 70. **CAREER** Ass prof philos, NY Univ, 70; asst prof, 72-76, assoc, 76-82, prof philos, Bernard Baruch Col, 82-, Nat Endowment for Humanities fel, 81. **RESEARCH** Hist of Bertrand Russell's philosoph; ethics. **SELECTED PUBLICATIONS** Auth, Tense and special relativity, Nous, 7 1; ed, B Russell's Essays in Analysis, Allen & Unwin, Braziller & Longanesi, 73; auth, Moral Principles and Nuclear Weapons, Rowman and Allenheld, 84; auth, God, Immortality, and Ethics, Wadsworth, 90; auth, The Ethics of War and Peace, Prentice-Hall, 90; auth, Ethics and Strategic Defense, Wadsworth, 91. **CONTACT ADDRESS** Dept of Philosophy, Baruch Col, CUNY, 17 Lexington Ave, New York, NY 10010-5518. **EMAIL** dlackey@email.gc.cuny.edu

LACY, ALLEN
PERSONAL Born 01/07/1935, Dallas, TX, m, 1958, 2 children **DISCIPLINE** PHILOSOPHY **EDUCATION** Duke Univ, AB, 56, PhD, 62. **CAREER** Ed asst, Duke Univ Press, 58-60; instr English, Clemson Col, 61-62; from asst prof to assoc prof philos, Madison Col, Va, 62-66; asst prof humanities, Mich State Univ, 66-68; assoc prof philos, Kirkland Col, 68-71; assoc prof, 71-74, actg dean soc and behav sci, 72-73, Prof Philos, Stockton State Col, 74-, Prof Relig, 80-, Nat Endowment for Humanities fel, 70. **RESEARCH** Religion and culture; philosophical ideas in literature; social ethics; existentialism. **SELECTED PUBLICATIONS** Auth, The uselessness of art, Christian Scholar, spring 66; coauth, Censorship and Como se Hace una Novela, Hisp Rev, 66; auth, Miguel de Unamuno: the Rhetoric of Existence, Mouton, the Hague, 67; Marshall McLuhan, playful prophet, in: the Religious Situation, Beacon, 68; ed, Selected Works of Miguel de Unamuno in English, Vol I, Princeton Univ (in press). **CONTACT ADDRESS** 1511 Shore Rd, Linwood, NJ 08221.

LACY, HUGH GALE
PERSONAL Born 03/23/1948, Huntsville, AL, m, 1977 **DISCIPLINE** LAW **EDUCATION** Alabama A&M University, BA, 1972, MEd, 1974; Miles Law School, JD, 1989. **CAREER** Huntsville City Board of Education, teacher corps intern, 72-74; US Army Ballistic Missle Defense Systems Command, supply management assistant, 74-75; US Army Ordnance Missile & Munitions Center & School, education specialist, 75-92; Hugh G Lacy, PC, attorney, 90-; US Army Corps of Engineers, education specialist, 92-. **HONORS AND AWARDS** 4-H Club Leadership Awd, 1974; US Army Ordnance Missile & Munition Center & School, Performance, 1985-92, Letters of Appreciation, 1982, 1988-91; US Army Missile Command, Equal Employment Opportunity Counselor Appreciation Certificate, 1992; Alpha Phi Alpha Fraternity, Inc, Brother of the Year, State of Alabama, 1990, Brother of the Year, Delta Theta Lambda, 1991. **MEMBERSHIPS** St Bartley P B Church, building & education committees, 1986-; Alpha Phi Alpha Fraternity, Inc, area director, 1982-, associated editor to Sphinx, 1990-; Alabama Lawyers Association, 1989-; Alabama Trial Lawyers Association, 1990-; American Bar Association, 1990-; National Bar Association, 1990-; NAACP, 1972-; Special Education Action Committee, counselor, 1989-; Huntsville/ Madison County Bar Association, legislative committee, 1990-. **CONTACT ADDRESS** Attorney, PO Box 18341, 300 E Clinton Ave, Ste 2, Huntsville, AL 35804.

LACY, PHILIP T.
DISCIPLINE CONTRACTS AND COMMERCIAL LAW **EDUCATION** Duke Univ, BA, 69; Univ VA, LLB, 72. **CAREER** Assoc dean & prof, Univ SC. **RESEARCH** Bankruptcy law. **SELECTED PUBLICATIONS** Coauth, a treatise on commercial law; publ on, bankruptcy and commercial law. **CONTACT ADDRESS** School of Law, Univ of So Carolina, Columbia, Law Center, Columbia, SC 29208. **EMAIL** Phil@law.law.sc.edu

LACY, WILLIAM LARRY
DISCIPLINE PHILOSOPHY **EDUCATION** Rhodes Col, BA, 59; Univ Virginia, PhD, 63. **CAREER** Chr, Dept of Philosophy, Rhodes Col. **CONTACT ADDRESS** Dept of Philos, Rhodes Col, 2000 N. Parkway, Memphis, TN 38112. **EMAIL** lacy@rhodes.edu

LADD, ROSALIND EKMAN
PERSONAL Born 10/13/1933, Manchester, NH, m, 1963, 2 children **DISCIPLINE** PHILOSOPHY **EDUCATION** Wheaton Col, Mass, BA, 55; Brown Univ, MA, 56, PhD, 62. **CAREER** From instr to asst prof Philos, Smith Col, 59-67; assoc prof, 67-73, prof Philos, Wheaton Col, MA, 73-, vis prof, Biomed Ethics, Brown Univ, 80 & 82. **MEMBERSHIPS** Am Philos. **RESEARCH** Ethics; medical ethics; children's rights. **SELECTED PUBLICATIONS** Ed, Readings in the Problems of Ethics, Scribner, 65; auth, The paradoxes of formalism, Brit J Aesthet, 70; coauth, Ethical Dilemmas in Pediatrics, Springer, 91; ed, Children's Rights Re-Visioned, Wadsworth, 96. **CONTACT ADDRESS** Dept of Philosophy, Wheaton Col, Massachusetts, 26 E Main St, Norton, MA 02766-2322. **EMAIL** rladd@wheatonma.edu

LADEN, ANTHONY
DISCIPLINE PHILOSOPHY **EDUCATION** Harvard Univ, PhD, 96. **CAREER** Asst prof, Univ IL at Chicago. **RESEARCH** Moral and polit philos; liberalism; feminism; hist of moral and polit thought. **SELECTED PUBLICATIONS** Auth, Games, Fairness and Rawls's A Theory of Justice, 91. **CONTACT ADDRESS** Philos Dept, Univ of Illinois, Chicago, S Halsted St, PO Box 705, Chicago, IL 60607.

LADENSON, ROBERT
PERSONAL Born 08/03/1943, Chicago, IL, m, 1982, 2 children **DISCIPLINE** PHILOSOPHY, LAW **EDUCATION** Univ of Wis, BA, 65; John Hopkins Univ, PhD, 70; DePaul Univ, JD, 80. **CAREER** From asst prof to prof, Ill Inst of Technol, 69-, **HONORS AND AWARDS** Booz-Allen Hamilton Awd for Excellence in Teaching and Service; Grantee, NEH, Nat Science Found. **MEMBERSHIPS** Am Philos Asn, Asn for Practical and Prof Ethics. **RESEARCH** Ethics, political philosophy, philosophy of law. **SELECTED PUBLICATIONS** Auth, A Philosophy of Free Expression, Rowman and Littlefield (Toyata Town, NJ), 83; coauth, Values and Ethics in Organization and Human Systems Development, Jossey Bass (San Francisco, CA), 90; auth, Ethics in the American Workplace: Policies and Decisions, LRP Publ (Horsham, PA), 95; auth, "Journalism Ethics: Judicial Decisions," in Contemporary Ethical Issues: Journalism Ethics (Santa Barbara, CA: ABC-CLIO, 98): 123-137; auth, "Judging Responsibly," Am Philos Asn Newsletter on Philos of Law 93(1) (94); auth, "Ethics in the American Workplace," Bus and Prof Ethics 14(1) (95); auth, "What is a Disability?" Int J of Applied Philos 11(1) (96); auth, "Is the Right of Free Speech Special?" Social Theory and Practice 23(2), (97); coauth, "On the Scope of Legitimate Authority," J of Soc Philos 29(3) (98); auth, "The Role of Reason in Ethics," Understanding Computer Ethics (99). **CONTACT ADDRESS** Dept Humanities, Illinois Inst of Tech, 3300 S Federal St, Chicago, IL 60616-3795. **EMAIL** ladenson@iit.edu

LAFAVE, WAYNE R.
DISCIPLINE LAW **EDUCATION** Univ Wis, BS; LLB; JD. **CAREER** Prof, Univ Ill Urbana Champaign, Law Prof, emeritus. **HONORS AND AWARDS** Ed, Wis Law Rev. **RESEARCH** Criminal procedure, the Fourth Amendment. **SELECTED PUBLICATIONS** Auth, pubs: Criminal Procedure; auth, pubs: Search and Seizure. **CONTACT ADDRESS** Law Dept, Univ of Illinois, Urbana-Champaign, 52 E Gregory Dr, Champaign, IL 61820. **EMAIL** w-lafave@law.uiuc.edu

LAFFEY, ALICE L.
PERSONAL Born 12/01/1944, Pittsburgh, PA, s **DISCIPLINE** RELIGION **EDUCATION** Pontifical Biblical Institute, Doctorate Sacred Scripture, 81, Licentcate in Sacred Scripture, 76, Bachelor Sacred Scripture, 74; Carlow Col, Bachelor Arts, 67. **CAREER** Assoc Prof, Col of The Holy Cross, 81-; Vis Prof at Episcopal Divinity School; Hartford Seminary, Boston Col; St. Michael's Col; Assumption Col; St. Vincent's Seminary, and others. **HONORS AND AWARDS** SSL and SSD with honor; elected for 2 year term to Executive Committee of the Catholic Biblical Assoc; elected for 4 year term to Executive Board of The College Theology Society; Bachelor Ford Fel, 84; and two Fac research Fel, 91 & 98. **MEMBERSHIPS** Society of Biblical Literature; College Theology Society; Catholic Theological Society of America. **RESEARCH** Hebrew Bible/ Old Testament; Feminist. **SELECTED PUBLICATIONS** Auth, "First Kings, Second Kings," Collegeville Bible Commentary, 9, The Liturgical Press, 85; auth, "First Chronicles, Second Chronicle," Collegeville Bible Commentary, 10, The Liturgical Press, 85; auth, "A Liberation Perspective: Patriarchy, Monarchy and Economics in the Deuteronomistic History," in Paul F. Knitter, ed. Pluralism and Oppression: Theology in World Perspective, 88: 221-35; auth, "An Introduction to the Old Testament: A Feminist Perspective, Fortress, 88; auth, "Appreciating God's Creation Through Scripture," Paulist, 97; auth, "The Pentateuch: A Liberation-Critical Reading," Augsburg Fortress, 98. **CONTACT ADDRESS** Dept Religious Studies, Col of the Holy Cross, 1 College Street, Worcester, MA 01610-2322. **EMAIL** alaffey@holycross.edu

LAFOLLETTE, HUGH
DISCIPLINE PHILOSOPHY **EDUCATION** Belmont Univ, BA, 70, MA, 75, 77, Vanderbilt Univ, PhD. **CAREER** Vis Instr, Univ of Ala at Birmingham, 76-77; Asst Prof, 77-83; Assoc prof, 83-89; Prof, East Tennessee State Univ, 89-. **HONORS AND AWARDS** NEH Summer Sem, 79; Norwegian Res Coun and Univ of Oslo grant, 01; Vis Res Scholar, Univ of Stirling, 96-97; Tennent Caledonian Fel, Univ of St. Andrews, 86-87; NEH Summer Sem, 84. **RESEARCH** Ethics; political philosophy; philosophy of law. **SELECTED PUBLICATIONS** Co-ed, World Hunger and Moral Obligation, Prentice-Hall, 77; co-ed, Whose Child? Rowman & Allenheld, 80; co-ed, Person to Person, Temple Univ Press, 89; co-ed, World Hunger and Morality, Prentice-Hall, 96; auth, Personal Relationships: Love, Identity, and Morality, Blackwell, 96; co-auth, Brute Science: The Dilemmas of Animal Experimentation, Routledge, 97; ed, Blackwell Guide to Ethical Theory, Blackwell, 00; auth, "Gun Control," Ethics, (00): 263-81; ed, Ethics in Practice: An Anthology 2nd edition, Blackwell, 01; auth, "Controlling Gun," Criminal Justice Ethics, (01). **CONTACT ADDRESS** Philos Dept, East Tennessee State Univ, Box 70717, Johnson City, TN 37614- 0234. **EMAIL** Hugh.Lafollette@att.net

LAFONT, CRISTINA
DISCIPLINE PHILOSOPHY **EDUCATION** Frankfurt, PhD. **CAREER** Asst prof,Northwestern Univ. **RESEARCH** Philosophy of language, theories of rationality, phenomenology, hermeneutics, critical theory. **SELECTED PUBLICATIONS** Auth, The Linguistic Turn in Hermeneutic Philosophy, MIT Press, 99; auth, Heidegger, Language, and World-disclosure, Cambridge Univ Press, 00. **CONTACT ADDRESS** Dept of Philosophy, Northwestern Univ, 1818 Hinman, Evanston, IL 60208. **EMAIL** clafont@northwestern.edu

LAFRANCE, YVON
PERSONAL Born 12/01/1930, Montreal, PQ, Canada, m **DISCIPLINE** PHILOSOPHY **EDUCATION** Univ Montreal, BA, 51; Univ Sao Paulo, Brazil, LPh, 59; Univ Louvain, Beig, DPh, 67. **CAREER** Prof philos, Univ Sao Paulo, 62-64, Univ Sherbrook, 67-68 and Univ Que, 68-71; Prof Philos, Univ Ottawa, 71-, Can Coun res grant, 77-78 and 80-82. **HONORS AND AWARDS** Doctorat d'Etat en philos, Paris-Nanterre, 82. **MEMBERSHIPS** Asn Guillaume Bude; Can Asn Philos; Int Soc Neoplatonic Studies; Soc Promotion Hellenic Studies London. **RESEARCH** Greek philosophy; Plato and Aristotle. **SELECTED PUBLICATIONS** Auth, La thaeorie platonicienne de la doxa; auth, Maethode et exaegaese en histoire de la philosophie. **CONTACT ADDRESS** Dept of Philos, Univ of Ottawa, Arts Bldg, 70 Laurier, Ottawa, ON, Canada K1N 6N5. **EMAIL** ylafranc@uottawa.ca

LAHEY, STEPHEN
PERSONAL Born 12/02/1960, PA, m, 1994 **DISCIPLINE** PHILOSOPHY **EDUCATION** West Chester Univ, BA, 86; Univ Kans, MA, 90; Univ Conn, Doctor Philos, 96. **CAREER** Asst prof, Le Moyne Col, 99-. **MEMBERSHIPS** The Lollard Soc, Medieval Acad, Am Philos Asn. **RESEARCH** Medieval philosophy and theology. **SELECTED PUBLICATIONS** Auth, Metaphysics and Politics in the Thought of John Wyclif, Cambridge Univ Press (forthcoming). **CONTACT ADDRESS** Dept Philos, Le Moyne Col, 1419 Salt Springs Rd, Syracuse, NY 13214-1302. **EMAIL** laheyse@maple.lemoyne.edu

LAIDLAW, ELIZABETH SANTANA
DISCIPLINE PHILOSOPHY **EDUCATION** Univ of Rochester, PhD, 90. **CAREER** Prof, Monroe Comm Col, 93-. **HONORS AND AWARDS** Teaching **MEMBERSHIPS** APA **CONTACT ADDRESS** Dept of English/Philos, Monroe Comm Col, 1000 E Henrietta Rd, Rochester, NY 14623. **EMAIL** elaidlaw@Monroecc.edu

LAINE, JAMES W.
PERSONAL Born 05/08/1952, Midland, TX, m, 1983, 4 children **DISCIPLINE** RELIGION **EDUCATION** TX Tech, BA, 74; Harvard, MTS, 77, ThD, 84. **CAREER** Asst prof , 83-85 CT Col; asst prof, 85-91, acad dean, 92-95, assoc prof, 95-97, prof, 98-, Macalester Col. **MEMBERSHIPS** AAR; Asn of Asian Studies. **SELECTED PUBLICATIONS** Auth, Visions of God, 89; auth, Epic of Shivaji, 99. **CONTACT ADDRESS** Relig Stud Dept, Macalester Col, 1600 Grand Ave, Saint Paul, MN 55105-1899. **EMAIL** laine@Macalester.edu

LAITOS, JAN GORDON
PERSONAL Born 05/06/1946, Colorado Springs, CO **DISCIPLINE** LAW, AMERICAN LEGAL HISTORY **EDUCATION** Yale Univ, BA, 68; Law Sch, Univ Colo, JD, 71; Law Sch, Univ Wis, SJD, 74. **CAREER** Law clerk, Colo Supreme Ct, 71-72; atty, Off Legal Coun, US Dept of Justice, 74-76; Prof Law, Law Sch, Univ Denver, 76-, Sr legal adv, Solar Energy Res Inst, 78-81; consult, Colo State Dept of Natural Resources, 79-80, US Dept of Interior, 79-80 and US Dept of Energy, 80-81. **MEMBERSHIPS** Natural resources law; energy law. **RESEARCH** Auth, Causation and the Unconstitutional Conditions Doctrine--Why the City of Tigards Exaction Was a Taking, Denver Univ Law Rev, Vol 0072, 95; National Parks and the Recreation Resource, Denver Univ Law Rev, Vol 0074, 97. **CONTACT ADDRESS** Law Sch, Univ of Denver, Denver, CO 80208.

LAMARCHE, PIERRE
PERSONAL Born 04/20/1965, Quebec City, QC, Canada, s **DISCIPLINE** PHILOSOPHY **EDUCATION** Univ Toronto, BA, 89; Univ Tex at Austin, MA, 92; PhD, 99. **MEMBERSHIPS** Am Philos Asn, Radical Philos Asn, Soc for Phenomenology and Existential Philos, Int Asn for the Philos of Lit. **RESEARCH** Critical Theory, Phenomenology, Existentialism, Post-Structuralism, Marxism, Scepticism. **SELECTED PUBLICATIONS** Auth, "The Langourod Scepticism: Reflections on Burnyeat, on Pyrrhonian Subjectivity," Southwest Philos Rev (96); auth, "Schemata of Ideology in Camera Obscura and

Specters of Marx," in Enigmas: Essays on Sarah Kofman, eds. P. Deutscher and K. Oliver (NY: Corneel Univ Pr, 99); auth, "The Boredom of the Work: Blanchot Not Reading Prouts," in Feeling The Differences, eds. J. Cutting-Gray and J. Swearingen (IL: Northwestern Univ Pr, 00). **CONTACT ADDRESS** Dept Humanities, Austin Comm Col, 1020 Grove Blvd, Austin, TX 78741-3337. **EMAIL** slamarch@austin.cc.tx.us

LAMB, CHARLES M.
PERSONAL Born 03/01/1945, Murfreesboro, TN, s **DISCIPLINE** POLITICAL SCIENCE **EDUCATION** Middle Tenn State Univ, BA, 67; Univ of Ala, MA, 70, PhD, 74. **CAREER** Res sci, George Washington Univ, 73-75; equal opportunity specialist, U.S. Comn on Civil Rights, 75-77; Asst prof of Pol Sci, 77-84, asst prof of Pol Sci, SUNY Buffalo, 84-. **HONORS AND AWARDS** Choice Outstanding Book Awd, 83; listed in Who's Who in the East; Who's Who in Emerging Leaders in Am; Who's Who in Am Ed; Contemporary Authors. **MEMBERSHIPS** Am Political Sci Asn. **RESEARCH** Civil rights; civil liberties; constitutional law; constitutional history; judicial behavior. **SELECTED PUBLICATIONS** Auth, Supreme Court Activism and Restraint, 82; Implementation of Civil Rights Policy, 84; Judicial Conflict and Consensus, 86; The Burger Court, 91; Presidential Influence and Fair Housing Policy, forthcoming. **CONTACT ADDRESS** Dept of Political Sci, SUNY, Buffalo, 520 Hall Park, Buffalo, NY 14260.

LAMB, RAMDAS
PERSONAL m, 1978, 2 children **DISCIPLINE** RELIGIOUS STUDIES **EDUCATION** Univ of California, Santa Barbara, PhD, 91. **CAREER** Assoc Prof, 91-, Dept of Rel, Univ of Hawaii. **MEMBERSHIPS** AAS; AAR; ASR. **RESEARCH** South Asian Religion; Medieval & Contemporary Hinduism; Religion & Contemporary Soc. **SELECTED PUBLICATIONS** Auth, Rapt in the Name: The Ramnam is Ramnam and the Ram Bhakti Tradition, Albany, NY, SUNY Press, forthcoming, 99; Consulting Ed, Corsini Dictionary of Psychology, Washington, DC, Taylor and Francis, 98; Religion, Atlas of Hawaii, 3rd ed, Honolulu, Univ of Hawaii Press, 98; Asceticism and Devotion: The Many Faces of Ram Bhakti in the Ramananda Sampraday, Journal of Vaisnava Studies, vol 2, #4, 94. **CONTACT ADDRESS** Dept of Religion, Univ of Hawaii, Manoa, 2530 Dole St., Honolulu, HI 96822. **EMAIL** RAMDAS@HAWAII.EDU

LAMBERT, BENJAMIN FRANKLIN
PERSONAL Born 03/06/1933, Lowell, MA, s **DISCIPLINE** LAW **EDUCATION** Boston Univ, BA 1955; Brandeis Univ, MA 1959; Seton Hall Univ Sch of Law, JD 1968. **CAREER** Ciba Phar Co Inc, rsch chem 1957-66; Ciba Ltd, rsch asst 1962-63; Merck & Co Inc, atty 1966-70; Fitzpatrick, Cella, Harper & Scinto, atty 1970-72; Johnson & Johnson, patent atty 1973-. **HONORS AND AWARDS** Delta Hon Soc; Scarlet Key Hon Soc; Student Fac Asmbl; Augustus Howe Buck Schlr; Tchng Fellow Brandeis Univ. **MEMBERSHIPS** Mem NJ Bar Assn; Reg US Patent Ofc 1968, NJ Bar, 1969; NY Bar 1972; US Ct of Customs & Patent Appeals 1977; US Dist Ct Dist of NJ 1969; Dist Ct So Dist NY 1972; Dist Ct Eastern Dist NY 1972; NJ Patent Law Assn; Amer Patent Law Assn; NAACP 1977. **SELECTED PUBLICATIONS** numerous **CONTACT ADDRESS** Johnson & Johnson, One Johnson & Johnson Plaza, New Brunswick, NJ 08933.

LAMBERT, BYRON C.
PERSONAL Born 04/19/1923, Delta, OH, m, 1949, 1 child **DISCIPLINE** CHRISTIAN DOCTRINE; HISTORY OF CULTURE **EDUCATION** Univ Buffalo, BA, 45, MA, 46; Butler Univ sch Rel, BD, 50; Univ Chicago, PhD, 57. **CAREER** Assoc prof English, Milligan Col, 57-60; dean, assoc prof English, Simpson Col, 60-62; dean, 62-65, campus dean, 65-71, assoc prof Hum, 71-75, assoc dean, Col ed, 71-75, Fairleigh Dickinson Univ; Prof Philos, 75-85, actg dean, Arts and Sci, 82-83, acting Provost, Madison Campus, 81. **HONORS AND AWARDS** Fairleigh Dickinson Univ, Campus Achieve Awd, 74; Pres James A. Garfield Awd, Emmanuel Sch Rel, Tenn, 98. **MEMBERSHIPS** Amer Philos Asn; Soc Christian Philso; Disciples of Christ Hist Soc. **RESEARCH** C.S. Lewis; Paul Elmer More; Christian theology, sacraments, Holy Spirit. **SELECTED PUBLICATIONS** Auth, The Essential Paul Elmer More, 72; The Rise of the Anti-Mission Baptist, 80; The Recovery of Reality, 80; The Restoration of the Lord's Supper and the Sacramental Principle, 92; Experience-Different Semantic Worlds, Wasleyan Theol Jour, Spring 95; Shifting Frontiers and the Invisible Hand, Discipliana, Fall 95; The Middle Way of Frederick Doyle Kershner, 98; The Regrettable Silence of Paul Elmer More, Modern Age, Fall 98; C.S. Lewis and the Moral Law, Stone-Campbell Jour, Fall 98. **CONTACT ADDRESS** 300 North Perry St, Hagerstown, IN 47346. **EMAIL** phybylam@infocom.com

LAMBERT, J. KAREL
PERSONAL Born 04/10/1928, Chicago, IL, m, 1949, 3 children **DISCIPLINE** LOGIC, PHILOSOPHY OF SCIENCE **EDUCATION** Willamette Univ, BA, 50; Univ Oregon, MS, 52; Mich St Univ, PhD, 56. **CAREER** Asst prof, 56-60, assoc prof, 60-63, Univ of Alberta; prof & chmn Dept of Phil, 63-67, West Virginia Univ; Prof, 67-, Above Scale, 90-, res prof of logic, philos of sciences, Univ Calif, 94-; honor prof, Univ of Salzburg, Austria, 84-. **HONORS AND AWARDS** Fulbright Hayes Scholar, 3 times; NEH Fel, 3 times; Univ of Calif Pres Fel; Medal of Col of France, 80. **MEMBERSHIPS** Amer Phil Asn; Amer Psych Asn; Asn for Symbolic Logic. **RESEARCH** Logic; philosophy of science; experimental psychology. **SELECTED PUBLICATIONS** Art, A Theory about Logical Theories of Expressions of the Form The So and So Where The is in the Singular, Erkenntnis, 91; coauth, Logic Bivalence and Denotation, 2nd ed, Ridgeview, 91; ed, Philosophical Applications of Free Logic, Oxford NY & London, 91; coauth, An Introduction to the Philosophy of Science, 4th ed, Ridgeview, 92; art, Russells Version of the Theory of Definite Descriptions, Phil Stud, 92; Coauth, Outline of a Theory of Scientific Understanding, Synthese, 94; coauth, Characterizing and Classifiying Explicating a Biological Distinction, Monist, 94; art, On the Reduction of Two Paradoxes and the Philosophical Significance Thereof, Physik Philosophie und die Einheit der Wiessenschaften,Spektrum, 95; coauth, Resiliency and Laws in the Web of Belief, Laws of Nature, 95; Auth, Free Logics Their Foundations Character and Some Applications Thereof, Akademia Verlag Sankt Augustin bei Bonn, 97; art, Nonextensionality, Das weite Spektrum der Analytischen Philosophie, 97; coauth, Definitions in nonstrict positive free logic, Modern Logic, 97; auth, A Theory of Definite Descriptions, in Definite Descriptions, A Reader, 98; auth, Free logic and Definite Descriptions, New Directions in Free Logic Essays in Honor of Karel Lambert, forthcoming. . **CONTACT ADDRESS** 480 Enterprise St, Hammond, OR 97121. **EMAIL** jlambert@uct.edu

LAMBERT, JEAN CHRISTINE
PERSONAL Born 06/21/1940, Berwyn, IL **DISCIPLINE** CHRISTIAN THEOLOGY **EDUCATION** North Park Col, Chicago, BA, 62; Columbia Univ, MA, 67, MPhil, 74, PhD(-relig), 81. **CAREER** Asst prof, 76-82, Assoc Prof Theol, St Paul Sch Theol, Kansas City, 82-, Mem task force relig, Kansas City Metrop Regional Comn Status Women, 79-; mem, Bk of Worship Revision Comt, Evangel Covenant Church, 75-82, bd publ, 76-81. **MEMBERSHIPS** Am Acad Relig. **RESEARCH** Feminist theology; Whiteheadian and Hartshornian process philosophy. **SELECTED PUBLICATIONS** Auth, Daniel Day Williams: a bibliography, Union Sem Quart Rev, 75; Response to Penelope Washbourn's paper the Dynamics of Female Experience ..., in: Feminism and Process Thought Conference Papers, Harvard Divinity Sch, 77; Becoming human: a Whiteheadian exploration of issues underlying the discussion of abortion, in: Feminism and Process Thought, Mellin Press, 81; Response to David Cassell, Narthex, 82. **CONTACT ADDRESS** Dept of Theol, Saint Paul Sch of Theol, Kansas City, MO 64127.

LAMBERT, RICHARD THOMAS
PERSONAL Born 03/28/1943, Rochester, NY, m, 1978, 3 children **DISCIPLINE** HISTORY OF PHILOSOPHY, LOGIC, ETHICS **EDUCATION** St Bernard's Col, BA, 65; Univ Notre Dame, PhD, 71. **CAREER** Asst prof, 70-80, philos dept chmn, 77-82, assoc prof 80-, prof philos, Carrol Col, Mont, Dir, Summer, 81-82, Dir, Continuing Educ, 81-85, Exchange prof philos, Loras Col, 76-77. **HONORS AND AWARDS** NY State Regents Scholar, 61-65; NDEA Grad Fel, 66-70; Exec Comt, Delta Epsilon Sigma, 90-94, vpres & pres, 94-98. **MEMBERSHIPS** Int Berkeley Soc; Am Cath Philos Asn; Am Philos Asn; Delta Epsilon Sigma. **RESEARCH** Berkeley; Aquinas; Camus. **SELECTED PUBLICATIONS** Auth, Berkeley's use of the relativity argument, Idealistic Studies, 10: 107-121; Albert Camus and the paradoxes of expressing a relativism, Thought, 56: 185-198; A textual study of Aquinas' comparison of the intellect to prime matter, New Scholasticism, Vol 56; Berkeley's commitment to relativism, Berkeley: Critical and Interpretive Essays, Univ Minn Press, 82; Habitual knowledge of the soul in St Thomas Aquinas, Mod Schoolman, 40: 1-19; The literal intent of Berkeley's Dialogues, Philos & Lit, 6: 165-171; Nonintentional experience of oneself in Thomas Aquinas, New Scholasticism, 59: 253-275; Teaching Camus's The Plague in an introductory philosophy course, Approaches to Teaching Camus's The Plague, MLA, 85; transl, Thomas Aquinas, Disputed Question on the Soul's Knowledge of Itself, Clearinghouse for Medieval Philos Transl, 87; Conferring honors in a democratic society, Delta Epsilon Sigma Jour, 33: 59-60; President's report to the membership, Delta Epsilon Sigma Jour, 43: 77-78; Ethics column, Helena Independent Record, 90. **CONTACT ADDRESS** Carroll Col, Montana, 1601 N Benton Ave, Fac Box 49, Helena, MT 59625-0002. **EMAIL** rlambert@carroll.edu

LAMIRANDE, EMILIEN
PERSONAL Born 05/22/1926, St-Georges de Windsor, Canada **DISCIPLINE** HISTORY OF CHRISTIANITY **EDUCATION** Univ Ottawa, BA, 49, LPh, 50, MA, 51, LTh, 55; Univ Innsbruck, DTh, 60; Union Theol Sem, NY, STM, 65;. **CAREER** Assoc prof theol, Univ Ottawa, 60-65; prof, St Paul Univ, Ont, 65-70, dean fac theol, 67-69; chmn dept, 72-74, Prof Relig Studies, Univ Ottawa, 70-. **MEMBERSHIPS** Am Acad Relig; Can Cath Hist Asn; Can Theol Soc (vpres, 67-70); Asn Can d'Estudes Patristiques (vpres, 79-). **RESEARCH** Early Christianity; North African Church; ecclesiology. **SELECTED PUBLICATIONS** Auth, Sulpician Priests in Canada--Major Figures in Their History, Stud in Rel-Sciences Religieuses, Vol 0022, 93; Body of the Church, Body of Christ--Sources for the Ecclesiology of the Communion, Stud in Rel-Sciences Religieuses, Vol 0022, 93; Writings of the Reformation Fathers, Stud in Rel-Sciences Religieuses, Vol 0025, 96; The Aggiornamento and Its Eclipse--Free Thinking in the Church and in the Faithful, Stud in Rel-Sciences Religieuses, Vol 0025, 96. **CONTACT ADDRESS** Dept of Relig Studies, Univ of Ottawa, Ottawa, ON, Canada K1H 8M5.

LAMM, ALAN K.
PERSONAL Born 03/01/1959, Wilson, NC, m **DISCIPLINE** HISTORY, RELIGION **EDUCATION** Univ NC at Greensboro, BA, 81; Duke Univ, Masters Divinity, 87; MTh, 88; Univ SC, PhD, 95. **CAREER** Chaplain asst, U.S. Army, 81-84; adj prof, Mount Olive Col, 88-90; Chaplain & Army Historian, U.S. Army Reserve, 89-97; adj instr, Wayne Community Col, 89-90; adj instr, Midlands Technical Col, 90-93; instr, Orangeburg-Calhoun Technical Col, 93-95; U.S. Army Historian, U.S. Army Reserve Command, 96; instr, Trident Technical Col, 96-97; assoc prof, Mount Olive Col, 97-. **MEMBERSHIPS** Orgn of Am Historians, Soc for Military Hist, NC Literary and Hist Asn, Coun on Am Military Past, Army Hist Found. **RESEARCH** Nineteenth- and Twentieth-Century American History, Religious History, Military History, African American History. **SELECTED PUBLICATIONS** Rev, of "The Unwept: Black American Soldiers and the Spanish-American War," by John W. Bailey, NC Hist Rev (April 99); auth, Five Black Preachers in Army Blue, 1884-1901: The Buffalo Soldier Chaplains, Edwin Mellen Press (Lewiston, NY), 98; auth, "Buffalo Soldier Chaplians of the Old West," The J of America's Military Past Vol XXVI (99): 25-40; rev, of "The Life and Works of General Charles King, 1844-1933: Martial Spirit," by John W. Baily, The J of America's Military Past (forthcoming); auth, "General Wesley Merritt" and "Black Army Chaplains in the Civil War," Encyclopedia of the American Civil War, ABC-Clio Pub, forthcoming; rev, of "Southern Unionist Pamphlets and the Civil War," edited by Jon L. Waklyn, The J of Military Hist (forthcoming). **CONTACT ADDRESS** Dept Soc Sci, Mount Olive Col, 634 Henderson St, Mount Olive, NC 28365-1263. **EMAIL** lamm1084@aol.com

LAMM, JULIA A.
PERSONAL Born 06/06/1961, Cincinnati, OH **DISCIPLINE** THEOLOGY **EDUCATION** Col St. Catherine, BA, 83; Univ Chicago, AM, 84, PhD, 91. **CAREER** Asst prof, 89-95, Assoc Prof, Georgetown Univ, 95-. **HONORS AND AWARDS** Alexander von Humboldt Fel, 96-97. **MEMBERSHIPS** Am Acad of Religion. **RESEARCH** Historical theology; F.D.E. Schleiermacher; Doctrine of God. **SELECTED PUBLICATIONS** Auth, The Living God: Schleiermacher's Theological Appropriation of Spinoza, Pa State Univ Press, 96; Scleiermacher as Plato Scholar, J of Religion, 00; The Early Philosophical Roots of Schleiermacher's Notion of Gefuhl 1788-1794, Harvard Theological Rev, 94; Schleiermacher's Post-Kantian Spinozism: The Essays on Spinoza 1793-94, J of Religion, 94; Catholic Substance Revisited: Reversals of Expectations in Tillich's Doctrine of God, Paul Tillich: A New Catholic Assessment, Liturgical Press, 94; Tensions in a Catholic Theology of the Body, Choosing Life: A Dialogue on Evangelium Vitae, Georgetown Univ Press, 97; A Hermeneutics of Revulsion, Papers of the North Am Paul Tillich Soc, 95; Schleiermacher as a Resource for Feminist Theology, Harvard Divinity Bulletin, 95. **CONTACT ADDRESS** Theology Dept, Georgetown Univ, New North 120, Box 571135, Washington, DC 20057-1135. **EMAIL** lammj@georgetown.edu

LAMM, NORMAN
PERSONAL Born 12/19/1927, Brooklyn, NY, m, 1954, 4 children **DISCIPLINE** JEWISH PHILOSOPHY **EDUCATION** Yeshiva Col, BA, 49; Yeshiva Univ, PhD, 66. **CAREER** Jacob Michael prof of Jewish philos, Yeshiva Univ, 66- ; pres, Yeshiva Univ, 76- . **HONORS AND AWARDS** Abramowitz Zeitlin Awd, 72; Hon Dr Hebrew Letters, 77; Corning Glass Higher Educ Leadership Awd, 86. **RESEARCH** Hasidism; Talmud. **SELECTED PUBLICATIONS** Auth, The Royal Reach, 70; A Hedge of Roses, 70; Torah Lishmah, 72; Torah Umadda, 90; Halakhot Ve'halikhot, 91; Shema: Spirituality and Law in Judaism 98; The Religious Thought of Hasidism, 99. **CONTACT ADDRESS** Office of the President, Yeshiva Univ, 500 West 185th St, New York, NY 10033. **EMAIL** nlamm@attglobal.net

LAMOTHE, KIMERER L.
PERSONAL Born 07/25/1963, New York, NY, m, 1992, 2 children **DISCIPLINE** RELIGION **EDUCATION** Willaims Col , BA, 85; Harvard Divinity School, MTS, 84; Harvard Univ, PhD, 96. **CAREER** Vis asst prof, Brown Univ, 96-97; Lectr, Head Tutor, Harvard Univ, 97-. **HONORS AND AWARDS** Phi Beta Kappa; Bok Center Teaching Awd; Nat Merit Scholar; Graves Prize; Mellon Dissertation Fel; Center for the Study of World Rels Fel; Radcliffe Fel, Bunting Fel Prog, Radcliffe Inst for Advanced Studies, 00-01. **MEMBERSHIPS** AAR; Phi Beta Kappa; Soc for Dance Hist Scholar. **RESEARCH** Religion and the performing arts; Philosophy of religion; Modern dance; Feminist and postmodern theory. **SELECTED PUBLICATIONS** Passionate Madonna: the Christian Turn of American Dancer Ruth St Denis, J of am Acad Of Rel, 98. **CONTACT ADDRESS** Harvard Univ, 12 Quincy St, Cambridge, MA 02138. **EMAIL** klamothe@fas.harvard.edu

LAMPE, PHILIP
PERSONAL Born 07/25/1934, St Louis, MO, w, 1961, 3 children **DISCIPLINE** PHILOSOPHY, SOCIOLOGY **EDUCATION** Conception Sem, BA, 58; Southern Ill Univ, MA, 67; La State Univ, PhD, 73. **CAREER** Bi-Nat Cult Inst, Morelia, Michoacan, Mex, 60-65; Southern Ill Univ, Carbondale Community Develop Serv, 65-67; Teacher, Southwestern La Univ, 67-70; Univ of Incarnate Word, 70-. **MEMBERSHIPS** Soc for Sci Study of Relig: Southwest. **RESEARCH** Mexican Americans, Religion. **SELECTED PUBLICATIONS** Auth, "Adultery," in Family Life (Pasadena, CA: Salem Press, 98); co-ed, Our Changing Culture, Univ of Incarnate Word (San Antonio), 98; auth, "Culture & Change: An Introduction," in Our Changing Culture, ed. Philip Lampe and Roger Barnes (San Antonio: Univ of Incarnate Word, 98); auth, "Marriage & Sex or Sex & Marriage," in Our Changing Culture, ed. Philip Lampe and Roger Barnes (San Antonio: Univ of Incarnate Word, 98); auth, "Stereotypes," in Aging in America (Pasadena, CA: Salem Press, 99); auth, "Capital Punishment," in African American Encyclopedia (Pasadena, CA: Salem Press, 99); auth, "Chicano Movement," in The Sixties in America (Pasadena, CA: Salem Press, 99); co-ed, Violence in America, Univ of Incarnate Word (San Antonio), 99; auth, "Anatomy of Violence: An Introduction," in Violence in America, ed. Philip Lampe and Roger Barnes (San Antonio: Univ of Incarnate Word, 99); auth, "Violent to the Core," in Violence in America, ed. Philip Lampe and Roger Barnes (San Antonio: Univ of Incarnate Word, 99). **CONTACT ADDRESS** Dept Sci, Univ of the Incarnate Word, 4301 Broadway, San Antonio, TX 78209.

LANCASTER, HERMAN BURTRAM
PERSONAL Born 03/06/1942, Chicago, IL, m **DISCIPLINE** LAW **EDUCATION** Chicago State Univ, BS 1965; Rosary Coll, MA 1968; DePaul Univ, JD 1972. **CAREER** Chicago Bd of Ed, teacher 1965-66; DePaul Univ Law School, asst dir law library 1966-70; Univ of Chicago, psychiatric dept dir of info, 70-72, legal counsel 1972-73; Glendale Univ Law School, Prof, Dir of Research 1973-; The Legal Inst, Law Consultant, 76-. **HONORS AND AWARDS** Omega Psi Phi Scholarship 1963; Grad Fellowship 1966; DePaul Law School Scholarship 1968; DePaul Law Review Scholarship 1969-72; Blue Key Law Hon Soc 1968; Man of the Year Omega Psi Phi 1966. **MEMBERSHIPS** AAA, arbitrator, 1986-; The Subcontractors Inst, advisor, 1984-; Glendale Law Review 1976-; NAACP 1975-. **SELECTED PUBLICATIONS** Has published numerous articles **CONTACT ADDRESS** Legal Inst, 3250 W Wilshire Blvd, Ste 958, Los Angeles, CA 90010.

LANCE, MARK
DISCIPLINE PHILOSOPHY **EDUCATION** Univ Pittsburgh, PhD. **CAREER** Prof. **RESEARCH** Political philosophy; philosophy of language; epistemology; logic; metaphysics. **SELECTED PUBLICATIONS** Auth, pubs on logic, Normativity, meaning, and Bayesianism. **CONTACT ADDRESS** Dept of Philosophy, Georgetown Univ, 37th and O St, Washington, DC 20057.

LANCTOT, CATHERINE J.
DISCIPLINE CONSTITUTIONAL LAW, LEGAL PROFESSION **EDUCATION** Brown Univ, BA, 78; Georgetown Univ Law Ctr, JD, 81. **CAREER** Prof; Villanova Univ, 88-. **RESEARCH** Legal ethics, employment law. **SELECTED PUBLICATIONS** Auth, The Defendant Lies and the Plaintiff Loses: The Fallacy of the Pretext-Plus' Rule in Employment Discrimination Cases, 43 Hastings L J 59, 91, **CONTACT ADDRESS** Law School, Villanova Univ, 800 Lancaster Ave, Villanova, PA 19085-1692. **EMAIL** lanctot@law.vill.edu

LANDERS, RENEE M.
PERSONAL Born 07/25/1955, Springfield, IL, m, 1980 **DISCIPLINE** LAW **EDUCATION** Radcliffe Coll of Harvard Univ, AB, 1977; Boston Coll Law School, JD, 1985. **CAREER** Massachusetts Secretary of State, Bookstore Div, program development specialist, 78, admin asst to secretary of state, 79-80, deputy secretary of state, 80-82; Supreme Judicial Court of Massachusetts, law clerk, 85-86; Ropes & Gray, associate, 86-88; Boston Coll Law School, asst prof, 88-93; Office of Policy Development, US Department of Justice, deputy assistant attorney general, 93-96; US Department of Health & Human Services, deputy general counsel, 96-97; Ropes & Gray, counsel, 97-. **HONORS AND AWARDS** Radcliffe College Alumnae Assn, Distinguished Service Awd, 1992; Elected Honorary Mem, Iota of Massachusetts Chap, Phi Beta Kappa, Radcliffe College, 1995. **MEMBERSHIPS** Harvard Univ, bd of overseers, 1991-95, pres bd of overseers, 1996-97; Massachusetts Eye and Ear Infirmary, dir, 1993-96; Metropolitan District Commission, assoc commissioner, 1991-93; Big Sister Assoc of Greater Boston, vp and dir, 1988-93; Massachusetts Supreme Judicial Court, gender bias study committee, sub-committee chair, 1986-1989, racial and ethnic bias study, 1990-94; Boston Bar Assoc, council member, 1988-91, chair committee on gender and justice, 1989-93. **CONTACT ADDRESS** Ropes & Gray, One International Pl, Boston, MA 02110-2624. **EMAIL** rlanders@ropesgray.com

LANDES, GEORGE MILLER
PERSONAL Born 08/02/1928, Kansas City, MO, m, 1953, 1 child **DISCIPLINE** OLD TESTAMENT **EDUCATION** Univ Mo, AB, 49; McCormick Theol Sem, BD, 52; Johns Hopkins Univ, PhD(Semitic studies), 56. **CAREER** From instr to assoc prof, 56-70, Baldwin prof sacred lit, 72-80, Davenport Prof Hebrew, Union Theol Sem, NY, 81-, Am Coun Learned Soc fel, 67-68; annual prof, Am Sch Orient Res, Jerusalem, 67-68. **MEMBERSHIPS** Soc Bibl Lit; Am Orient Soc; Am Schs Orient Res. **RESEARCH** Old Testament history and archaeology; the semitic and cognate languages; Semitic studies. **SELECTED PUBLICATIONS** Auth, A Student's Vocabulary of Biblical Hebrew, Scribner, 61; Teaching the Biblical languages, Theol Educ, 67; coauth, Report on Archaeological Work at Suwannet eth-Thaniya, Tananir, and KhMinha, Scholars, 75; auth, Creation and liberation, Union Sem Quart Rev, 78; Jona: A Mashal?, In: Israelite Wisdom, Scholars, 78; Linguistic criteria and the date of The Book of Jonah, In: Eretz Israel, Vol 17, 82. **CONTACT ADDRESS** Union Theol Sem, New York, 3041 Broadway, New York, NY 10027.

LANDESMAN, CHARLES
PERSONAL Born 12/17/1932, Brooklyn, NY, m, 1955, 3 children **DISCIPLINE** PHILOSOPHY **EDUCATION** Wesleyan Univ, AB, 54; Yale Univ, MA, 56, PhD, 59. **CAREER** Instr philos, Yale Univ, 57-59; from asst prof to assoc prof, Univ Kans, 59-65; assoc prof, 65-70, Prof Philos, Hunter Col, 70-, Prof Emeritus, 99-; Chmn Dept, 67-71, 79-82, Dir, Fac Sem Interdisciplinary Studies, 77-78. **HONORS AND AWARDS** Fulbright lectr, Ben Gurion Univ, Israel, 92-93. **MEMBERSHIPS** Am Philos Asn; Am Fedn Teachers. **RESEARCH** Philosophy of language; philosophy of mind; political philosophy; epistemology. **SELECTED PUBLICATIONS** Auth, Discourse and its Perspective, Yale Univ Press, 72; Color and Consciousness, Temple Univ Press, 89; The Eye and the Mind, Kluwer Acad Publ, 93; An Introduction to Epistemology, Blackwell, 97. **CONTACT ADDRESS** Dept of Philos, Hunter Col, CUNY, 695 Park Ave, New York, NY 10021-5085. **EMAIL** clandesm@msn.com

LANDINI, GREGORY
PERSONAL Born 12/27/1955, Miami Beach, FL, m, 2 children **DISCIPLINE** PHILOSOPHY **EDUCATION** Ind Univ, BA, 78; MA, 81; PhD, 86. **CAREER** Instructor, Indiana/Purdue Univ, 84-85; Instructor, Indiana Univ, 83-85; Asst Prof of Philosophy, Ball State Univ, 85-89; Asst Prof, Univ of Iowa, 89-92; Assoc Prof of Philosophy, Univ of Iowa, 92-. **HONORS AND AWARDS** Bertrand Russell Book Awd, 99. **MEMBERSHIPS** Amer Philosophical Assoc; Assoc of Symbolic Logic; Bertrand Russell Society; Central States Philosophical Assoc. **RESEARCH** Twentieth Century Analytic Philosophy; Philosophy of Logic and Mathematics; Bertrand Russell; Philosophy of Mind & Language. **SELECTED PUBLICATIONS** Auth, "How to Russell Another Meinongian: An Early Russellian Account of Fictional Objects Versus Zalta's Abstract Objects," Grazer Philosphische Studien 37, 90: 93-122; coauth, "The Persistence of Counterexample: Re-examining the Debate Over Leibniz Law," co-author:Tom Foster, No us 25, 91: 43-61; auth, "A New Interpretation of Russell's Multiple-Relation Theory of Judgment," History and Philosophy of Logic 12, 91: 37-69; auth, "Decomposition and Analysis in Frege's Grundgesetze," History and Philosophy of Logic, 17, 96: 121-139; auth, "Logic in Russell's Principles of Mathematics," Notre Dame Journal of Formal Logic, 37, 96: 554-584; auth, "The Definability of the Set of Natural Numbers in the 1925 Principia Mathematica," Journal of Philosophical Logics," 25, 96: 597-615; auth, "On Denoting' Against Denoting," Russell, 18, 98: 43-80; auth, "Russell's Intensional Logic of Propositions: A Resurrection of Logicism?" in (eds.) F. Orilia & W. Rapaport, Thought, Language and Reality--Essays in Honor of Hector-Neri Castaneda, (Kluwer), 98: 61-93; auth, "Russell's Hidden Substitutional Theory, Oxford Univ Press, 98. **CONTACT ADDRESS** Dept Philosophy, The Univ of Iowa, 269 English Philosophy Bldg, Iowa City, IA 52242-1408. **EMAIL** gregory-landini@uiowa.edu

LANE, MARC J.
PERSONAL Born 08/30/1946, Chicago, IL, m, 1971, 3 children **DISCIPLINE** LAW **EDUCATION** Univ of Ill, BA, 67; Northwestern Univ, JD, 71; Int Asn of Registered Financial Planners, 87; Int Asn of Prof Financial Consults, 94; Int Asn of Registered Financial Consults, 95. **CAREER** Pres and atty, Law Offices of Marc J. Lane, 71- ; chemn and ceo, Marc J. Lane & Co., 85- ; pres, Longmeadow Assocs, Ltd., 84- ; pres, Longmeadow Insurance Servs, 84- ; adj prof, Univ of Ill, 96- . **HONORS AND AWARDS** Lincoln Awds, Ill State Bar Asn, 73, 77; Disting. Serv Awd, Grant A Wish, Inc., 90; Crystal Globe Awd, Tax Execs Inst, 92; Cert of Spec Congressional Recognition, U.S. Cong, 95; Cert of Recognition for Outstanding Contribs to the White House Conf on Small Bus, Pres William J. Clinton, 95; Recognition as a Business Leader, Small Bus Survival Comt, 96; Cert in Recognition and Appreciation of Outstanding Serv, Ill State Bar Asn, 96; Awd in Appreciation for Disting. Membership, Int Asn for Financial Planning, 96; Cert of Congressional Recognition, U.S. Cong, 96; Cert in Appreciation for Serv as a mem of the Bus Advice and Financial Planning Section Coun, 97; Awd for contributing immeasurably to the Center's growth and development, 97; Incl as a subject of biographical record, Contemporary Auths, Who's Who in American Law, Who's Who in Finance and Industry, Who's Who in the Midwest, Bar Register of Preeminent Attys, International Who's Who, International Who's Who of Professionals, National Directory of Who's Who in Executives and Professionals, National Registry of Who's Who, American Directory of Who's Who in Executives and Businesses, Int Auths and Writers Who's Who, Cambridge Who's Who Registry of Business Leaders, Who's Who Among Top Executives; AV (highest) rating: very high legal ability, Martindale-Hubbell, Inc.; Cert of Merit for Disting. Serv to the Community, Dictionary of Internat Biography. **MEMBERSHIPS** Int Bar Asn; ABA; Ill State Bar Asn; Chicago Bar Asn; Chicago Coun of Lawyers; Int Asn of Prof Financial Consults; Nat Acad of Elder Law Attys, Inc.; Ill Chap of the Nat Acad of Elder Law Attys; AARP; Medico-Legal Inst, Inc.; NASD; Int Asn for Financial Planning; Nat Asn of Corp Dirs; Int Trade Asn of Greater Chicago; Chicagoland Chamber of Com; NORBIC; Attys Title Guarantee Fund, Inc.; U.S. Securities and Exchange Comn and Ill Secy of State; Ill Dept of Prof Regulation; Int Asn of Registered Financial Planners; Nat Asn of Securities Dealers, Inc. **RESEARCH** Corp law; Finance; Taxation. **SELECTED PUBLICATIONS** Auth, Contracting for Communications Services, Nonprofit World, Jan-Feb, 90; Exempt Status Options--Which is Best?, Nonprofit World, Jul-Aug, 90; Challenges to Nonprofits' Tax Status: Is There Cause for Alarm?, Nonprofit World, Jul-Aug, 91; Partnerships, parts 1 and 2, Optometric Economics, Oct-Nov, 91; Does it Matter Where We Incorporate?, Nonprofit World, Nov-Dec, 91; Purchase and Sale of Small Business, 91; Purchase and Sale of Small Business: Forms, 91; Why is our Property-Tax Exemption Being Challenged?, Nonprofit World, Jan-Feb, 92; Can We Exclude Certain People from Membership?, Nonprofit World, Mar-Apr, 92; Can Our Organization Issue Stock?, Nonprofit World, May-June, 92; Can Fellowship Money Be Considered Income?, Nonprofit World, Jul-Aug, 92; Can Personal Lobbying Jeopardize Your Organization?, Nonprofit World, Nov-Dec, 92; Fundraising for Foreign Charities, Nonprofit World, Jan-Feb, 93; Exec Pay Options Ease Equity Dilemma, Crain's Small Bus, Sept, 93; Your Employees and your Retirement Plan, Nonprofit World, Nov-Dec, 93; It Might Not Pay to Delay Director's Fees, Crain's Small Bus, May, 94; Property for Profit, Winning Strategies, 1:2, sum, 94; For Exporters, Routing Goods Via Israel Can Yield Big Savings, Crain's Small Bus, Sept, 94; Lease Inducements Help Attract New Tenants, The Metro-Chicago Office Guide, 4th Quarter, 94; Partnerships Can Register With LCC Option, Crain's Small Bus, Dec-Jan, 94/95; GATT Lowers Tariffs But Raises New Taxing Questions, Crain's Small Bus, Mar, 95; Don't Buy Off-the -Shelf Power of Attorney, Crain's Small Bus, Sept, 95; This Trust Allows Charity To Begin at Home, Crain's Small Bus, Dec-Jan, 95-96; Don't Tell It to the Judge, Try a Mediator, Crain's Small Bus, Apr, 96; Clicking on Internet Stock Plays, Crain's Small Bus, Nov, 96; New Job Reference Law Is No Blank Check, Crain's Small Bus, Feb, 97; Portable Health Care Insurance Gets Rolling, Crain's Small Bus, May, 97; Look for Integrity in Board Members, Crain's Chicago Bus, Feb 9, 98; publ, A Summary of the Family and Medical Leave Act of 1993 (P.L. 1-3.3), 93, Key Features of the Revenue Reconciliation Act of 1993, 93; Incentives and Opportunities for Israeli Companies to Do Business in the United States, 94; U.S. Credit Facilities Available to Argentine Enterprises Doing Business in the United States, 94; Long-Term Care Insurance: The New Tax Benefits, The New Design Choices, 97; coauth, Business Advice & Financial Planning for Lawyers, 95; Elder Law: Meeting the New Challenges When Advising Elderly Clients, 97. **CONTACT ADDRESS** Marc J. Lane, 180 North LaSalle St., Ste 2100, Chicago, IL 60601. **EMAIL** mlane@marcjlane.com

LANG, BEREL
PERSONAL Born 11/13/1933, Norwich, CT, m, 1972, 2 children **DISCIPLINE** HISTORY, PHILOSOPHY **EDUCATION** Yale Univ, BA, 54; Columbia Univ, PhD, 61. **CAREER** Prof, Univ of CO, 61-84; prof, SUNY Albany, 84-97, prof, Trinity Col, 97-. **HONORS AND AWARDS** Fel, NEH;Fel, ACLS; Fel, Univ of Pa; Bauugardt Fel, APA: Remarque Fel, NYU. **MEMBERSHIPS** APA; MLA; Am Soc for Aesthetics; Assoc for Jewish Studies; Thoreau Soc. **RESEARCH** Political Philosophy, Aesthetics, Holocaust Studies. **SELECTED PUBLICATIONS** Auth, Hiidegger's Silence, Cornell Univ Pr, 96; auth, The Future of the Holocaust, Cornell Univ Pr, 99; ed, Race and Racism in Theory and Practice, Rowman and Littlefield, 00. **CONTACT ADDRESS** Dept Humanities, Trinity Col, Connecticut, 300 Summit St., Hartford, CT 06106-3100. **EMAIL** berel.lang@trincoll.edu

LANG, MARTIN ANDREW
PERSONAL Born 05/02/1930, Brooklyn, NY, 3 children **DISCIPLINE** THEOLOGY, RELIGION **EDUCATION** Marist Col, BA, 51; Cath Univ Am, MA, 60, PhD, 64. **CAREER** Asst prof theol, Marist Col, 64-68; assoc prof, St Norbert Col, 68-70; Prof Theol, Grad Div Relig Educ, Fairfield Univ, 77-, Dir, 70-; Union Theol Sem fel, Columbia Univ, 66-67; Fairfield Univ Fac res grant, 76. **MEMBERSHIPS** Am Acad Relig; Cath Bibl Asn Am; Relig Educ Asn; Dirs Grad Progs Relig Educ (vpres, 74-75). **RESEARCH** Religious and psychological development; religion and human sexuality; psychological and religious interrelationships in the development of God images. **SELECTED PUBLICATIONS** Auth, The Inheritance: What

Catholics Believe, Pflaum, 70; contribr, Continuing Christian Development, Twenty-Third Publ, 73; auth, Prayer, The Lamp, 1/73; Maturity of thought and religious alternatives, Relig Teachers J, 1/73; contribr, Faith as a learned lifestyle, in Emerging Issues in Religious Education, 76; Acquiring Our Image of God, Paulist, 83. **CONTACT ADDRESS** Relig Studies, Fairfield Univ, 1073 N Benson Rd, Fairfield, CT 06430-5195. **EMAIL** malang@fairi.fairfield.edu

LANG, MICHAEL B.
PERSONAL 2 children **DISCIPLINE** LAW **EDUCATION** Harvard Col, AB; Univ Pa, JD. **CAREER** Prof, Univ Maine Law Sch, 83-; assoc dean, Univ Maine Law Sch, 93-96; taught at: Utah, Ill Inst Technol/Chicago Kent Col Law, Wash Univ St. Louis Law and Univ San Diego Col Law; prac tax law, Philadelphia and Chicago. **HONORS AND AWARDS** res fel, Yale Univ. **MEMBERSHIPS** Amer Bar Asn Sect Taxation; Am Col of Tax Counsel: Order of the Coif. **SELECTED PUBLICATIONS** Collab on 1st ed, Bittker's multivolume Federal Taxation of Income, Estates and Gifts; co-compiler, Index to Federal Tax Articles; coauth, treatise on federal tax elections. **CONTACT ADDRESS** School of Law, Univ of So Maine, 96 Falmouth St, PO Box 9300, Portland, ME 04104-9300.

LANGAN, JOHN P.
PERSONAL Born 08/10/1940, Hartford, CT, s **DISCIPLINE** PHILOSOPHY **EDUCATION** Loyola Univ - Chicago, AB, 64, PhL, 64, MA, 66; Woodstock Col, BD, 70; Univ Mich, PhD, 79. **CAREER** Instr, St. Ignatius High Sch, 64-65; Instr, Univ Detroit, 65-67; Teaching Fel, Univ Mich, 71-72; Lectr Theol, 75-79, Lectr Philos, Georgetown Univ, 79-; Res Fel, 75-83, Sr Fel, Woodstock Theol Ctr, 83-, Actg Dir, 86-87; Vis Asst Prof Soc Ethics, Yale Divinity Sch, 83; Rose F. Kennedy Prof Christian Ethics, Kennedy Inst of Ethics, Georgetown Univ, 87-99; visting prof, Loyola Univ Chicago, 95-97; Joseph Cardinal Bernardin prof, Kennedy Institute of Ethics, Georgetown Univ, 99-. **HONORS AND AWARDS** Nat Merit Schol, 57; Rackham Prize Fel, Univ Mich, 72-73; Vis Fel, Jesuit Inst, Boston Col, 93-94. **MEMBERSHIPS** Am Acad Relig; Am Cath Philos Asn; Am Philos Asn; Asn Applied Professional Ethics; Cath Theol Soc Am; Int Studies Asn; Soc Christian Ethics; Soc Christian Philos; Coun Christian Approaches Disarmament; Soc Bus Ethics; Soc Medieval Renaissance Philos. **RESEARCH** Catholic social thought, moral theology, ethics of war and peace, human rights, capital punishment, ethics and economics. **SELECTED PUBLICATIONS** Ed, Catholic Universities in Church and Society: A Dialogue on Ex Corde Ecclesiae, Georgetown Univ Press, 93; auth, Just War Doctrine, The Harper Collins Encyclopedia of Catholicism, Harper, 95; Capital Punishment, The Harper Collins Encyclopedia of Catholicism, Harper, 95; Religious Pacifism and Quietism: A Taxonomic Approach and a Catholic Response, Pacifism and Quietism in the Abrahamic Traditions, Georgetown Univ Press, 96; author of numerous other publications and articles; ed, A Moral Vision for America: Addresses of Cardinal Joseph Bernardin, Georgetown Univ Press, 98; auth, "Humanitarian Intervention: From Concept to Reality," Close Calls, Ethics and Public Policy Center, 98; auth, "The Past and the Future of Intervention," Some Corner of a Foreign Field, Macmillan, 98. **CONTACT ADDRESS** The Joseph and Rose Kennedy Inst Ethics, Georgetown Univ, Room 424, Healy Bldg, Washington, DC 20057. **EMAIL** langanj@gunet.georgetown.edu

LANGER, MONIKA
DISCIPLINE PHILOSOPHY **EDUCATION** Univ Toronto, BA, MA, PhD; Univ McGill, MLS. **CAREER** Instr, Univ Toronto; Yale Univ; Univ Alberta; Dalhousie Univ; assoc prof, Univ if Victoria, 82-. **RESEARCH** Continental European philosophy; feminist philosophy; social/political issues and philosophy in literature. **SELECTED PUBLICATIONS** Auth, Merleau-Ponty's Phenomenology of Perception: A Guide and Commentary; pub(s), articles in Philos Today, Can Jour of Polit and Soc Theory, Tchg Philos, Thesis Eleven, The Trumpeter, Library of Living Philosophers, Philos of Jean-Paul Sartre; coed, The New Reality: The Politics of Restraint, Brit Columbia. **CONTACT ADDRESS** Dept of Philosophy, Univ of Victoria, PO Box 3045, Victoria, BC, Canada V8W 3P4. **EMAIL** mechthil@uvic.ca

LANGER, RUTH
PERSONAL Born 03/30/1960, Pittsburgh, PA, m, 1986, 2 children **DISCIPLINE** RELIGION **EDUCATION** Hebrew Union Col, Jewish Inst of Religion, PhD 94. **CAREER** Boston Col, asst prof 95-. **MEMBERSHIPS** AJS; WUJS; AAR; SBL. **RESEARCH** Jewish liturgy and ritual. **SELECTED PUBLICATIONS** Auth, "Beardless Rabbis," Bryn Mawr Alumnae Magazine (82); auth, "Birksat Betulim: A Study of the Jewish Celebration of Briday Virginity," Proceedings of the American Acad for Jewish Research LXI (95): 53-94; auth, "Communications Theory and Worship: James W. Carey's Communication as Culture and its Reception," Proceedings of the North America Acad of Liturgy (97): 147-163; coauth, "The Language and Experience of Tefillah," in Exploring Issues of Gender and Jewish Day School Education (97); auth, "Approaching Divine Holiness: Issues in the Liturgical Use of the Kedushah," in The Rabbinical Assembly: Proceedings, 97 (The Rabbinical Assembly, 98): 147-148; auth, "From Study to Scripture to Reenactment of Sinai," Worship 72.1 (98): 43-67; auth, To Worship God Properly: Tensions Between Liturgical Custom and Halakhah in Judaism, Heb Union Col Press, 98; auth, "Revisiting Early Rabbinic Liturgy: The Recent Contributions of Ezra Fleischer," Prooftexts 19.2 (99): 179-194; coed, Liturgy and the Life of the Synagogue, Duke Univ Press, forthcoming; auth, "Liturgy, History of," "Liturgy Reform," and "Synagogue" in Readers Guide to Judaism, ed. Michael Terry (Fitzroy Dearborn Pub, forthcoming). **CONTACT ADDRESS** Dept of Theology, Boston Col, Chestnut Hill, Chesnut Hill, MA 02467. **EMAIL** langerr@bc.edu

LANGERAK, EDWARD ANTHONY
PERSONAL Born 05/01/1944, Grand Rapids, MI, m, 1966, 2 children **DISCIPLINE** PHILOSOPHY, INTERDISCIPLINARY STUDIES **EDUCATION** Calvin Col, BA, 66; Univ Mich, MA, 72; Princeton Univ, PhD(relig), 72. **CAREER** Asst prof, 72-78, Assoc Prof, 78-86, prof, Philos, St Olaf Col, 87-, Nat Humanities Inst fel, Univ Chicago, 78-79. **MEMBERSHIPS** Am Philos Asn; Soc Values Higher Educ; Am Soc Value Inquiry; Inst Soc, Ethics & Life Sci. **RESEARCH** Medical ethics; values and technology; tolerance. **SELECTED PUBLICATIONS** Auth, Abortion: Listening to the middle, Hastings Ctr Report, 10/79; coauth, Christian Faith, Health, and Medical Practice, Eerdmans, 89; auth, Duties and Conventanal Ethics, Duties to Others, Kluwer, 94; auth, Theism and Toleration, Companion to Philosopy of Religion, Blackwell, 96; auth, Disagreement: The Dark Side of Tolerance, Philosophy, Religion, and the Question of Intolerance, SUNY, 97. **CONTACT ADDRESS** St. Olaf Col, 205 Manitou St, Northfield, MN 55057. **EMAIL** langerak@stolaf.edu

LANGFORD, MICHAEL J.
PERSONAL Born 06/29/1931, London, England **DISCIPLINE** PHILOSOPHY **EDUCATION** Oxford Univ, BA, 54, MA, 57; Univ London, England, PhD(philos), 66. **CAREER** Asst prof, 67-72, Assoc Prof Philos, Mem Univ NFld, 72-. **MEMBERSHIPS** Can Philos Asn. **RESEARCH** Philosophy of religion; moral philosophy. **SELECTED PUBLICATIONS** Auth, Fideist Responses to Atheism and Positivism--the Rationality of Belief Revisited, Stud in Rel-Sci Religieuses, Vol 0023, 94. **CONTACT ADDRESS** Dept of Philos, Mem Univ of Newfoundland, Saint John's, NF, Canada A1C 5S7.

LANGILL, RICHARD L.
PERSONAL Born 10/10/1942, Brooklyn, NY, m, 1 child **DISCIPLINE** INTERNATIONAL RELATIONS, COMPARATIVE POLITICS **EDUCATION** CA State Univ, BA, 65, MA, 67; Am Univ, PhD, 74. **CAREER** Peace Corps Vol, 67-69; Instr, Am Univ, 72-74; Dir, Blackburn Col, 80-86; Chair, Polit Sci Dept, Blackburn Col, 75-86; Dir, Soc sci div, Blackburn Col, 81-86; Vice-Pres, Acad Affairs, Saint Martin's Col , 86-97; prof, Saint Martin's Col, 97-98. **HONORS AND AWARDS** Cote Awd , 60; Nat Defense For Lang Fel , 69-72, Am Univ Tchg fel, 72-74; Malone Fel Prog , 92, 98. **MEMBERSHIPS** Am Polit Sci Asn; Int studies Asn; Wash Comt US-Arab Relations; Olympia World Affairs Coun. **SELECTED PUBLICATIONS** Auth, Americans in Southeast Asia, Potomac Rev, 75; Book Review of The Giants: Russia and America by Richard Barnet in Magill's Literacy Annual, Salem Int Publ, 78; Reunification of Vietnam, Great Events From History, Salem Int Publ, 79; The Fall of Saigon, Great Events From History, Salem Int Publ, 79; The Problem of Civic Illiteracy in American Education, Burnian Mag, 83. **CONTACT ADDRESS** Saint Martin's Col, 5300 Pacific Ave, Lacey, WA 98503-1297. **EMAIL** rlangill@stmartin.edu

LANGIULLI, NINO FRANCIS
PERSONAL Born 10/09/1932, Brooklyn, NY, m, 1959, 3 children **DISCIPLINE** PHILOSOPHY, ENGLISH **EDUCATION** Maryknoll Col, AB, 55; Hunter Col, MA, 60; NYork Univ, MA, 65, PhD(philos), 73. **CAREER** Instr English, St Augustine's High Sch, Brooklyn, 57-60; instr theol, 61-65, asst prof philos, 66-71, assoc prof, 72-76, Prof Philos, St Francis Col, NY, 76-, Danforth Assoc, 66-72. **HONORS AND AWARDS** Fulbright 60-61; Sears Roebuck Teaching Exc, 91; assoc ed, Measure, 89-96; book rev ed, Telos, 98. **MEMBERSHIPS** The Metaphysics Soc; Nat Asn of Scholars. **RESEARCH** Contemporary philosophy; history of philosophy; metaphysics. **SELECTED PUBLICATIONS** Auth, Machiavelli, In: Shakespeare Encycl, Crowell, 66; ed & translr, Critical Existentialism, 69 & ed, The Existentialist Tradition, 71, Doubleday; translr, Existentialism, In: Encycl Britannica, Univ Chicago, 73; Possibility, Necessity, and Existence, Temple, 92; European Existentialism, Transaction, 97; auth, Beauty: " The Qualities of the Beheld and the Eye of the Beholder, "Awer, Arts Quart, W of Sp, 00; auth, "Liberal Education: What to Resist," Academic Questions Summer, 00. **CONTACT ADDRESS** 32 Farnum St, Lynbrook, NY 11563.

LANGLINAIS, J. WILLIS
PERSONAL Born 08/12/1922, San Antonio, TX **DISCIPLINE** THEOLOGY **EDUCATION** Univ of Dayton, OH, BS, 43; Univ of Fribourg, Switzerland, STB, 50, STL, 52, STD, 54. **CAREER** Dir, Marianist Novitiate, Galesville, WI, 59-63; Dean of Arts and Sciences, 64-75, Academic Vice-Pres, 75-81, Dir of Institutional Self Study for Accreditation, St. Mary's Univ, San Antonio, 70-72, 82-. **MEMBERSHIPS** College Theol Soc; Cath Theol Soc of Am; Mariological Soc Am. **RESEARCH** Ethics; ecumenics; comparative religions. **CONTACT ADDRESS** 1 Camino Santa Maria, San Antonio, TX 78228. **EMAIL** jwillis@alvin.stmarytx.edu

LANGUM, DAVID J.
PERSONAL m, 2 children **DISCIPLINE** LAW **EDUCATION** Dartmouth Col, AB, 62; Stanford Univ, JD, 65; San Jose State Univ, MA, 76; Univ Mich Law School, LLM, 81, SJD, 85. **CAREER** Res clerk, Hon Murray Draper, Cal Court Appeals, San Fran, CA, 65-66; assoc, Dunne, Phelps & Mills, San Fran, CA, 66-68; partner, Christenson, Hedemark, Langum & O'Keefe, San Jose, CA, 68-78; fac, San Fran Law School, 66-67, Lincoln Univ School Law, 68-78, Detroit College of Law, 78-83; prof Law, 83-85, dean, 83-84, Nevada School of Law; prof of law, 85- , chemn doctoral prog law, relig & cult, 94- , co-chemn Cumberland Colloquim Am Legal Hist, 95- , Cumberland School Law, Samford Univ. chemn, Rushton Distinguised Lect Prof, 97. **HONORS AND AWARDS** Fel, Intercultural Commun Soviet Union, 62; James Willard Hurst Prize, 88; Golieb fel, NYU, 91; Ucross Found res writing fel, 98. Caroline Bancroft Hist Prize, 91; Herbert Eugene Bolton Awd, 78; Lawyers Title Awd, 64-65. **MEMBERSHIPS** Calif State Bar; US Supreme Court Bar; Mich State Bar; Am Soc Legal Hist; Am Hist Asn; Al Hist Asn; Ala Asn Hist; W Hist Asn; Cal Hist Soc. **SELECTED PUBLICATIONS** Auth, Law and Community on the Mexican Calif Frontier: Anglo-Am Expatriates and the Clash of Legal Traditions, Univ Okla Pr, 87; auth, Thomas O. Larkin: A Life of Patriotism and Profit in Old Calif, Univ Okla Pr, 90; auth, Crossing Over the Line: Legislating Morality and the Mann Act, Univ Chicago Press, 94; The Legal System of Spanish California: A Preliminiary Study, W Legal Hist, 94; From Maverick to Mainstream: Cumberland School of Law, 1847-1997, Univ Georgia Press, 97; Memoir of a Book: Writing the History of Cumberland, Cumberland Law Rev, 97; auth, William M. Kunstler: the Most Hated Lawyer in Am, NYork Univ Pr, 99. **CONTACT ADDRESS** Cumberland School of Law, Samford Univ, 800 Lakeshore Dr., Birmingham, AL 35229. **EMAIL** djlangum@samford.edu

LANIAK, TIMOTHY
PERSONAL Born 09/27/1958, MA, m, 1981, 3 children **DISCIPLINE** RELIGION **EDUCATION** Wheaton Coll, BA, 80; Gordon-Conwell Sem, MDiv, 89; Harvard Divinity Sch, ThD, 97. **CAREER** Asst prof, Gordon-Conwell Sem. **MEMBERSHIPS** AAR; SBL; IBR; BAS. **RESEARCH** Old Testament; anthropology; Judaism; archaeology. **SELECTED PUBLICATIONS** Auth, Shame and Honor in the Book of Esther, Scholars, 98. **CONTACT ADDRESS** 2324 Wedgewood Dr, Matthews, NC 28105. **EMAIL** tlaniak@gcts.edu

LANNING, BILL L.
PERSONAL Born 10/31/1944, Kansas City, MO, m, 1966, 2 children **DISCIPLINE** RELIGION **EDUCATION** Baylor Univ, PhD, 76; Wichita State Univ, P-doc, 89-90. **CAREER** Butler Com Col, inst, 93,96-97; Bethany Col, inst, 90-91, 93-94; Hutchinson Com Col, inst, 91-97, Blinn Col, inst, 79-88. **MEMBERSHIPS** AAR, APA, INS, IANDE, CTNS, ITEST **RESEARCH** Mind and consciousness; relig, philo and science; near-death experiences; vedic indo-euro stud. **SELECTED PUBLICATIONS** Contrib, Daily Book of Prayer, United Church Press, forthcoming yr 2000; articles in: Northwest Houston Leader, Mt. Hope Clarion and Haven Jour, McPherson Sentinel; bk reviews, in: Bryan Eagle, Jour of Church and State, and Jour of Near Death Studies. **CONTACT ADDRESS** 4606 Mangum Rd, Houston, TX 77092. **EMAIL** billanni@swbell.net

LANZILLOTTI, ROBERT F.
PERSONAL Born 06/19/1921, Washington, DC, m, 1945, 2 children **DISCIPLINE** ECONOMICS **EDUCATION** Dartmouth College, 43-44; Columbia Univ, US Navy Midshipman Sch, 44; Am Univ, BA, 46, MA, 47; Univ Calif, Berkeley, PhD, 53. **CAREER** Tchng Fellow, Univ Calif Berkeley, 47-49; Asst to Assoc to Prof of Econ, Wash State Univ, 49-61; Res Assoc, Brookings Inst, 56-57, 74-75; Prof & Ch, Mich State Univ, 61-69; Vis Prof, Cornell Univ, 65-82; Dean, Grad Sch Bus, Univ Fla, 69-86; Member, US Price Commission, 71-73; Dean Emeritus & Dir, Pub Policy Res Ctr, Grad Sch of Bus, Univ Fla, 86-; Eminent Scholar Prof of Am Economic Institutions, 86-97. **HONORS AND AWARDS** Phi Beta Kappa; Beta Gamma Sigma; Omicron Delta Kappa; Fla Blue Key; Am Men in Sci; Fellow, Swift & Co, 53; Fellow, US Steel Corp, 54; Fellow, Merrill Ctr for Econ, 56; N Atl Treaty Org Res Fellow, 64; Member, Vis Sci Prog, Am Econ Assoc, 68-71; D. Litt, Tampa Univ (hon), 79; DSc, Fla Inst of Tech (hon), 79. **MEMBERSHIPS** Am Econ Asn; S Econ Asn; Am Bar Asn, Antitrust Section; Fla Council of 100, 73-88,91-; Int Joseph A Schumpter Soc, Bd of Mgmt (pres-elect); Bd of Dir, Univ Fla Foundation Bd, 83-; Am Law & Econ Asn. **RESEARCH** Antitrust economics & industrial organization. **SELECTED PUBLICATIONS** Co-auth, Measuring Damage in Commercial Litigation: Present Value of Lost Opportunities, J of Acctng, Auditing & Finance, Winter/Spring 90; auth, The Great Milk Conspiracies of the 1980s, Rev of Ind Org, vol II, 413-458, 8/96; auth, Coming to Terms With Daubert in Sherman Act Complaints: A Suggested Economic Approach, Neb Law Rev, 98. **CONTACT**

ADDRESS Col of Bus Admin, Univ of Florida, PO Box 117154, Gainesville, FL 32611-7154. **EMAIL** lanz@dale.cba.ufl.edu

LAPOMARDA, VINCENT ANTHONY
PERSONAL Born 02/28/1934, Portland, ME **DISCIPLINE** UNITED STATES HISTORY, AMERICAN DIPLOMACY, AMERICAN RELIGIOUS HISTORY **EDUCATION** Boston Col, AB, 57, MA, 58, STL, 65; Boston Univ, PhD, 68. **CAREER** Teacher English, hist, Latin & relig, Boston Col High Sch, 58-61; asst prof, 69-74, assoc prof hist, Col of the Holy Cross, 74-, Dir, The Jesuits of Holy Cross Col, Inc, 71-87, secy, 72-87, mem educ policy comt, Col of the Holy Cross, 72-74, dir Washington internship prog, 74-75, coordr, Holocaust Collection, Col of the Holy Cross, 79-, dir, Italian Am Collection, Col of the Holy Cross; chmn comt hist memorials, Int Order Alhambra, 81-; state historian, Mass Knights of Columbus, 81-. **HONORS AND AWARDS** Coe Fel, 59; Phi Alpha Theta, 66; Batchelor Fel, 69, 70; Knight of Holy Sepulchre, 87; Alhambran of the Year, 87; Fac Service Awd, Col of the Holy Cross, 95. **MEMBERSHIPS** AHA; Am Cath Hist Asn; Orgn Am Historians; Am Ital Hist Asn. **RESEARCH** Jesuits in history; Italian Americans; The Holocaust. **SELECTED PUBLICATIONS** Auth, The Jesuit Heritage in New England, Worcester, 77; The Knights of Columbus in Massachusetts, Needham, 82, 2nd ed, Norwood, 92; The Jesuits and the Third Reich, Lewiston, 89; The Order of Alhambra, Baltimore, 94; The Boston Mayor Who Became Truman's Secretary of Labor, NY, 95; Charles Nolcini, Worcester, 97; author of numerous journal articles, letters, and reviews. **CONTACT ADDRESS** Col of the Holy Cross, 1 College St, Worcester, MA 01610-2322. **EMAIL** vlapomar@holycross.edu

LAPORTE, JOSEPH F.
PERSONAL Born 01/08/1968, Seattle, WA, m, 1994, 3 children **DISCIPLINE** PHILOSOPHY **EDUCATION** Franciscan Univ, BA, 91; Univ London, MA, 93; Univ Mass, 98; PhD, 98. **CAREER** Instr and Teaching Asst, Univ Mass, 94-97; Asst Prof, Hope Col, 98-. **HONORS AND AWARDS** NEH Fel, 00. **RESEARCH** Philosophy of language; Philosophy of science; Metaphysics. **SELECTED PUBLICATIONS** Auth, "Selection for Handicaps," Biology and Philosophy, forthcoming; auth, "Rigidity and Kind," Philosophical Studies, (00): 293-316; auth, "Living Water," Mind, (98): 451-455; auth, "Essential Membership," Philosophy of Science, (97): 95-112; auth, "Locke's Semantics and the New Theory of Reference to Natural Kinds," Locke Newsletter, (96): 41-64; auth, "Chemical Kind Term Reference and the Discovery of Essence," NOUS, (96): 112-132; auth, "In Search of Pigeonholes," The Philosophical Quarterly, (95): 499-505. **CONTACT ADDRESS** Dept Philos, Hope Col, 17 E 12th St, Holland, MI 49423-3607.

LAPORTE, ROBERT, JR.
PERSONAL Born 02/12/1940, Detroit, MI, m, 1962, 2 children **DISCIPLINE** POLITICAL SCIENCE, PUBLIC ADMINISTRATION **EDUCATION** Wayne State Univ, BA, 62, MA, 63; Syracuse Univ, PhD, 67. **CAREER** Asst prof, 66-69, assoc prof, 69-75, prof of public admin, 75-94; prof of public admin & political sci, The Pa State Univ, 94-. **MEMBERSHIPS** Am Political Sci Asn; Am Soc for Public Admin; Asn of Asian Studies. **RESEARCH** Public administrative systems; South Asian studies; development studies; comparative politics and government; political/governmental institutions. **SELECTED PUBLICATIONS** Auth, Pakistan: A Nation Still in the Making, India and Pakistan, Woodrow Wilson Center Press/Cambridge Univ Press, 98; Another Try at Democracy, Contemporary Problems of Pakistan, Westview Press, 93; Pakistan in 1996: Starting Over Again, Asian Survey, Feb 97; Pakistan in 1995: The Continuing Crises, Asian Survey, Feb, 96; Elements of unity, Dawm, Aug 97; coauth, Liberalization of the Economy Through Privatization, Pakistan in 1997, Westview Press, 98; Public Enterprise Management: Pakistan, Public Enterprise Management: Int Case Studies, Greenwood Press, 93. **CONTACT ADDRESS** Pennsylvania State Univ, Univ Park, Box 314, University Park, PA 16802. **EMAIL** rql@psu.edu

LAPSLEY, JAMES N.
PERSONAL Born 03/16/1930, Clarksville, TN, m, 1990, 2 children **DISCIPLINE** RELIGION **EDUCATION** Rhodes Col, BA, 52; Union Theol Seminary, BD, 55; Univ Chic, PhD, 61 **CAREER** Fac, Princeton Theol Seminary, 61-92; Prof Pastoral Theol, 76-92; Acad Dean, 84-89; Prof Emeritus, 92-. **HONORS AND AWARDS** Phi Beta Kappa; Rockefeller Bros Fellow, 59-61; Danforth Fellow, Menninger Fnd, 60-61. **MEMBERSHIPS** Soc for Pastoral Theol; Am Soc on Aging; Am Acad of Relig. **RESEARCH** Theological anthropology; personality characteristics and aging. **SELECTED PUBLICATIONS** Auth, Reconciliation, Forgiveness, Lost Contracts, Theol Today, XXIII, 2, 44-59, 7/66; auth, Salvation and Health, Westminster, 72; auth, The Self, Its Vicissitudes and Possibilities: An Essay in Theological Anthropology, Pastoral Psychology, 35, 23-45, 86; auth, Renewal in Late Life through Pastoral Counsleing, Paulist, 92; auth, Vengeance: The Half Hidden Pillager of Our Lives, Pastoral Psychol, 46, 4, 255-266, 3/98. **CONTACT ADDRESS** 16610 Meadow Park Dr, Sun City, AZ 85351. **EMAIL** lapsley@interacs.com

LARKIN, ERNEST ELDON
PERSONAL Born 08/19/1922, Chicago, IL **DISCIPLINE** THEOLOGY **EDUCATION** Mt Carmel Col, PhB, 43; Pontif Univ St Thomas Aquinas, STL, 49, STD, 54. **CAREER** Instr theol, Whitefriars Hall, Washington, DC, 51-60; lectr, Cath Univ Am, 60-61, from instr to assoc prof, 61-72; Prof Spiritual Theol and Pres, Kino Inst, 72-80; Lectr and Writer, 80-. **MEMBERSHIPS** Theol Soc Am. **RESEARCH** Spiritual theology; prayer, comtemplation, Carmelite spirituality. **SELECTED PUBLICATIONS** Auth, John of the Cross--an Appreciation, Horizons, Vol 0022, 95; John of the Cross--Conferences and Essays by Members of the Institute of Carmelite Studies and Others, Horizons, Vol 0022, 95. **CONTACT ADDRESS** Kino Inst of Theol, Phoenix, AZ 85020-4295.

LAROSILIERE, JEAN DARLY MARTIN
PERSONAL Born 02/04/1963, Port-au-Prince, Haiti, m, 1988 **DISCIPLINE** LAW **EDUCATION** Fairfield University, AB, 1985; Tulane University School of Law, JD, 1988; Georgetown University Law Center, LLM, 1990. **CAREER** Georgetown University Law Center, graduate teaching fellow, 88-90; Seton Hall University School of Law, adjunct professor of law, 92-; US Department of Justice, assistant US attorney, 90-. **HONORS AND AWARDS** Tulane University, senior trial competition finalist, 1988; Black Law Students Association, Frederick Douglass Moot Court Champion, 1988. **MEMBERSHIPS** US Department of Justice, hiring committee, 1992-; Garden State Bar Association, 1990-; American Bar Association, 1988-; Natl Bar Assn, 1985-. **CONTACT ADDRESS** Assistant US Attorney, US Department of Justice, 970 Broad St, Rm 502, Newark, NJ 07102.

LARRABEE, MARY JANE
PERSONAL Born 02/09/1943, Sacramento, CA, m, 1973, 2 children **DISCIPLINE** PHILOSOPHY **EDUCATION** Holy Names Col, BA, 65; Ind Univ, MA, 69; Univ Toronto, PhD, 74. **CAREER** Lectr, York Univ, 74-77; asst prof to prof, DePaul Univ, 75-. **HONORS AND AWARDS** Kappa Gamma Pi; Fac Res Grants, DePaul Univ, 83, 86, 88, 90, 95, 98. **MEMBERSHIPS** Am Philos Assoc; Soc for Phenomenology and Existential Philos; Soc for the Study of Husserl's Philos; Soc for Women in Philos; Husserl Circle, Metaphysical Soc of Am. **RESEARCH** Phenomenology, Existentialism, Postmodernism, Race Studies, Women's Studies, Time, Gender, Consciousness and Subjectivity. **SELECTED PUBLICATIONS** Auth, "The Contexts of Phenomenology as Theory", Human Studies 13, (90): 195-208; auth, "Inside Time-Consciousness: Diagramming the Flux", Husserl Studies 10, (94): 181-210; auth, "The Time of Trauma: Husserl's Phenomenology and Post-Traumatic Stress Disorder", Human Studies 18, (95): 351-366; auth, "Gender and Moral Development: A Challenge for Feminist Theory", An Ethics of Care: Feminist and Interdisciplinary Perspectives 3.16; auth, "Toward a Feminine Imaginary: Irigaray and Voices of the Crone?", Her Voices: Hermeneutics of the Feminine, eds Fabio DaSilva and M Kanjirathinkal, Univ Pr of Am (Landam, MD), 96; auth, "Searching for Voice: towards a Phenomenology of Autonomy and Connectedness", Feminist Phenomenology, ed Lester Embree, Kluwer Acad, (Boston, 00); auth, "There's No Time Like the Present: How to Mind the Now", Phenomenology of Time, eds John Brough and Lester Embree, Kluwer Acad, (Boston, 00); auth, "Existentialism", "Existential Feminism", "Phenomenological Feminism", and "Life-World", Routledge Encycl of Feminist Theories, Routledge, (NY, 00). **CONTACT ADDRESS** Dept Philos, DePaul Univ, 25 E Jackson Blvd, Chicago, IL 60604-2289. **EMAIL** mlarrabe@wppost.depaul.edu

LARSEN, ALLAN W.
PERSONAL Born 03/15/1936, NYC, NY, m, 1962, 3 children **DISCIPLINE** PHILOSOPHY **EDUCATION** CUNY Brooklyn Col, BA, 62; Univ Delaware, MA, 64; Duquesne Univ, PhD, 71. **CAREER** Univ Penn Slippery Rock, inst, asst prof, assoc prof, prof, 63-94; Westminister Col, part-time prof. **HONORS AND AWARDS** Professor Emeritus, 3 times Outstanding Philos Prof. **MEMBERSHIPS** APA, SPEP. **RESEARCH** Phenomenology; existential and environment philosophy; philosophy of technology. **SELECTED PUBLICATIONS** Auth, Nietzsche on the Legacy of Socrates, History of European Ideas, 96; auth,The flight from the Earth to the Universe, European Legacy, 98; auth, The Phenomenology of Mircea Eliade, An Eliade Anthology, 98. **CONTACT ADDRESS** Dept of Philosophy, Slippery Rock Univ of Pennsylvania, Slippery Rock, PA 16057-2125. **EMAIL** allan.larsen@sru.edu

LARSON, DAVID A.
PERSONAL m, 1 child **DISCIPLINE** LABOR LAW **EDUCATION** DePauw Univ, BA, 76; Univ Ill, JD, 79; Univ Pa, LLM, 87. **CAREER** Prof, Creighton Univ, 87-99; past managing ed, Recent Decisions Sect, Ill Bar J; pvt pract Minneapolis, Minn; Asst prof, Loyola Univ Chicago Sch Bus; Assoc prof, Millsaps Col; prof in residence, Equal Employ Opportunity Comn, Appellate Div in Wash DC, 90-91; vchmn, Employ Law Comt, Int Law and Pract Sect, Am Bar Asn; vchmn, Educ Comt, Dispute Resolution Sect, Am Bar Asn; Prof of Law and Dir of Dispute Resolution Inst, Hamline Univ, 00-; Ed-in-Chief, J of Alternative Dispute Resolution in Employ, CCH Inc, 00-. **HONORS AND AWARDS** Phi Beta Kappa; Fac Awd of Excellence, Am Bus Law Asn, 86; **MEMBERSHIPS** Education Comm Dispute Resloution Section; Employment Law Comm, Intl Law and Practice Section, Am Bar Asn. **RESEARCH** Employment discrimination. **SELECTED PUBLICATIONS** Pub(s) in, Yale J Int Law; Mo Law Rev; NY Univ Rev Law and Soc Change; La Law Rev; Memphis State Univ Law Rev; Labor Law J; Seton Hall Legislative J; Univ Detroit Mercy Law Rev; Amer J Trial Advocacy. **CONTACT ADDRESS** School of Law, Hamline Univ, 1536 Hewitt Ave, Saint Paul, MN 55104. **EMAIL** dlarson@gw.hamline.edu

LARSON, GERALD J.
DISCIPLINE RELIGIOUS STUDIES **EDUCATION** Columbia Univ, PhD, 67. **CAREER** Rabindranath Tagore Prof of Indian Cult and Civilizations, Ind Univ, Bloomington. **RESEARCH** Indian Philosophy; cross cultural philosophy of religion; history of religions; classical and Vedic Sanskrit studies. **SELECTED PUBLICATIONS** Auth, India's Agony Over Religion, State Univ NY, 95; Classical Samkhya: An Interpretation of Its History and Meaning, Banarsidass, 79; coauth, Samkhya: A Dualist Tradition in Indian Philosophy, Princeton, 86; Interpreting Across Boundaries: New Essays in Comparative Philosophy, Princeton, 87. **CONTACT ADDRESS** Dept of Religious Studies, Indiana Univ, Bloomington, Sycamore Hall 230, Bloomington, IN 47405.

LARUE, LEWIS HENRY
PERSONAL Born 01/30/1938, Bartley, WV, m, 1962, 2 children **DISCIPLINE** AMERICAN CONSTITUTIONAL LAW, JURISPRUDENCE **EDUCATION** Washington & Lee Univ, AB, 59; Harvard Univ, LLB, 62. **CAREER** Trial atty, US Marine Corps Reserve, 62-65 & US Dept Justice, 65-67; asst prof, 67-70, assoc prof, 70-74, Prof Law, Washington & Lee Univ, 74-. **RESEARCH** Literature. **SELECTED PUBLICATIONS** Auth, A Comment on Fried, Summers, and the Value of Life, Cornell Law Rev, Vol 57, 72; A Jury of One's Peers, Washington & Lee Law Rev, Vol 33, 76; Politics and the Constitution, Yale Law J, Vol 86, 77; The Rhetoric of Powell's Bakke, Washington & Lee Law Rev, Vol, 38, 81; A Student's Guide to the Study of Law: An Introduction, Matthew Bender & Co, 87; Political Discourse: A Case Study of the Watergate Affair, Univ of GA Press, 88; Constitutional Law as Fiction: Narrative in the Rhetoric of Authority, PA State Press, 95. **CONTACT ADDRESS** Sch of Law, Washington and Lee Univ, Lexington, VA 24450-0303. **EMAIL** lhl@wlu.edu

LASS, TRIS
PERSONAL Born 09/28/1972, Okinawa, Japan **DISCIPLINE** PHILOSOPHY **EDUCATION** Univ Portland, BA, 97. **CAREER** Guest lectr, Univ Portland; tchg asst, hist and res, Portland State Univ. **HONORS AND AWARDS** Cum laude, 97; Capstone presentor, Univ Portland. **MEMBERSHIPS** APA; Am Hist Soc. **RESEARCH** German and French phenomenology; existentialism; philosophy and history of science; Russian history; East Asian history; contemporary European history; Eastern philosophy; history of Christianity and Taoism. **SELECTED PUBLICATIONS** Auth, Outsider's Call to Thought, Three Days in Exile, Baobab, 96; auth, Necessary Lie, Science as Culture, 98; auth, Merleau-Ponty and Wittgenstein, A Synthesis, Univ Portland Philos J, 98; auth, Paradox: The Historical Tradition, Univ Portland Philos J, 98. **CONTACT ADDRESS** 710 Webster St, New Orleans, LA 70118-5846. **EMAIL** tlass@earthlink.net

LASSEK, YUN JA
PERSONAL Born 06/07/1941, Korea, 2 children **DISCIPLINE** PHILOSOPHY OF EDUCATION **EDUCATION** NYork Univ, PhD, 85 **CAREER** Adjunct prof, 93-94, Rosemont Col; managing dir, 93-94, 94- , program chair, The Board of Governors, The Greater Philadelphia Philosophy Consortium. **HONORS AND AWARDS** Boston Univ, Teaching Assistanship, 65-66; The first prize award in the Liberal Arts Col for the chung-Ang Univ Sch, 63-64. **MEMBERSHIPS** APA; SAAP **RESEARCH** Critical thinking; Perception and cognition; Visual arts education **SELECTED PUBLICATIONS** Auth,Ecology and the 18th century world view, Children: Thinking in Philosophy Proceedings of the 5th International Conf on Philosphy for Children, 92. **CONTACT ADDRESS** 415 Barclay Rd., Bryn Mawr, PA 19010. **EMAIL** 102165.3562@compuserve.com

LASSON, KENNETH
PERSONAL Born 03/24/1943, Baltimore, MD, m, 1974, 3 children **DISCIPLINE** LAW **EDUCATION** Johns Hopkins Univ, AB, 63; MA, 67; Univ Md, JD, 66. **CAREER** Asst to the Dean, Univ Md, 67-69; Asst to the Pres, Goucher Col, 70-71; Asst Prof, Loyola Col, 72-78; Lecturer, Univ Md, 77; Vis Scholar, Cambridge Univ, 85; Director, Haifa Summer Law Inst, 99-; Prof, Univ Baltimore, 76-. **MEMBERSHIPS** Member of Bar, Md; Md Am Civil Liberties Union, Am Zionist Movement, Baltimore Jewish Coun **SELECTED PUBLICATIONS** Auth, Trembling in the Ivory Tower. Excesses in the Pursuit of Truth and Tenure, Bancroft Press, forthcoming; auth, Mousetraps and Muffling Cups. 100 Brilliant and Bizarre US Patents, Arbor House, 86; auth, Your Rights as a Vet, Simon and Schuster, 80; auth, Proudly We Hail. Profiles of Public Citi-

zens in Action, Viking Press, 75; auth, The Workers. Portraits of Nine American Jobholders, Viking Press, 71; auth, "Hate Speech," in Group Defamation and Freedom of Speech, Greenwood Pub, 95; auth, "Controversial Speakers on Campus: Liberties, Limitations, and Common-Sense Guidelines," St Thomas Law Review, forthcoming; auth, "Political Correctness Askew: Excesses in the Pursuit of Minds and Manners," 63 Tennessee Law Review, 96; auth, "Radfems and the First Amendment," The Defender, 95; auth, "Lawyering Askew: Excesses in the Pursuit of Fees and Justice, Boston University Law Review, 94. **CONTACT ADDRESS** School of Law, Univ of Baltimore, 1420 N Charles St, Baltimore, MD 21201-5720. **EMAIL** klasson@ubmail.ubalt.edu

LATCOVICH, MARK A.
PERSONAL Born 04/15/1955, Ridgeway, PA **DISCIPLINE** THEOLOGY **EDUCATION** St Mary's Sem Wickliffe, MDiv, 81, MA, 86, Case Western Reserve Univ, PhD, 96. **CAREER** Ordained Priest, 81; St Mary's Sem, assoc prof, acad dean, 96-. **MEMBERSHIPS** ASA, GSA, RRA / SSR. **RESEARCH** Issues in Roman Catholic theology and their social impact. **SELECTED PUBLICATIONS** Auth, Ecclesial Empowerment: A Study of Roman Catholic Permanent Deacons and Their Spouses, Society for the Scientific Study of Religion, Annual Confer, 95; auth, The Emerging Role of Roman Catholic Permanent Deacons: An Application of the Role Theory of R.H. Turner, Am Socio Assoc, Annual Confer, 94; Extrinsic Religiosity as a Generalized Resistance Resource of an Older Person's Sense of Coherence, coauth, Gerontological Society of Am, Annual Confer, 93; auth, The Clergyperson and the Fifth Step, Spirituality and the Fifth Step, ed. R. Kus, Hayworth Pr, 95; auth, Special Groups and Alcoholics Anonymous, coauth, in Jour of Gay and Lesbian Studies, Hayworth Pr, 93. **CONTACT ADDRESS** Acad Dean, St. Mary Graduate Sch, 28700 Euclid Ave, Wickliffe, OH 44092. **EMAIL** frmalatc@mail.cle-dioc.org

LATHAM, WELDON HURD
PERSONAL Born 01/02/1947, Brooklyn, NY, m **DISCIPLINE** LAW **EDUCATION** Howard Univ, BA business admin 1968; Georgetown Univ Law Ctr, JD 1971; George Washington Univ Natl Law Ctr, advanced legal courses 1975-76; Brookings Inst, exec educ prog 1981. **CAREER** Checchi & Co, mgmt consultant 1968-71; Covington & Burling, atty 1971-73; Howard Univ Sch of Law, adj prof 1972-82; The White House Ofc of Mgmt & Budget, asst genl counsel 1974-76; Hogan & Hartson, atty 1976-79; Univ of VA Law Sch, guest prof 1976-91; US Dept of Housing & Urban Develop, genl deputy asst sec 1979-81; Sterling Systems Inc, vice pres genl cnsl 1981-83; Planning Research Corp, executive assistant, counsel to the chairman and CEO, 83-86; Reed Smith managing partner, McLean VA office 1986-92; Minority Business Entrepreneur Magazine, columnist, 91-; Civilian Aide to the Secretary of the Army, 94-99; Shaw, Pittman, senior partner, 92-00; Holland & Knight UP, Senior partner, 00-. **HONORS AND AWARDS** Advocate of the Year, Minority Enterprise Development Week, US Department of Commerce, 1996; Small Business Administration, Private Industry Advocate of the Year, 1992; Northern VA Min Business & Professioal Assn Awd, 1990; National Association of Equal Opportunity in Higher Education Achievement Awd, 1987; Outstanding Performance Awd, US Department of HUD, Sr Exec Serv Washington DC, 1980. **MEMBERSHIPS** Bd dirs Washington Hosp Center Foundation, 1996; Capital Area Advisory Board of First Union National Bank, 1995-; Burger King Corp Diversity Action Council, 1996-99; Small Business Administration National Advisory Council, 1994-; Maryland Economic Development Commission, 1996-98; general counsel, National Coalition of Minority Businesses, 1993-; Decomcratic National Committee, 1996; Platform Drafting Committee, 1996; trustee, Democratic National Committee, 1995-; bd dirs District of Columbia Foundation, Inc, 1982-88; Bar Association membership, 1972-: apptee VA Gov's Business Adv Comm on Crime Prevention 1983-86; apptee VA Gov's Regulatory Adv Bd 1982-84; Washington steering comm NAACP Legal Defense & Educ Fund 1976-96; Professional Services Council, board of directors 1984-88; editorial advisory bd Washington Business Journal 1985-88; VA Commonwealth Univ, board of directors 1986-89; Democratic Natl Committee Business Council 1986-90, and vice chair, 1994-; Washington Urban League, board of directors 1986-90; Am Univ, metropolitan Wash Airports Authority; Joint ctr for Political & Economic Studies; Congressional Black Caucus Found, Corporate Advisory Coun; numerous others. **CONTACT ADDRESS** Holland & Knight UP, 2099 Pennsylvania Ave, NW, Ste 100, Washington, DC 20006.

LATHROP, GORDON W.
PERSONAL Born 09/02/1939, Glendale, CA, m, 1987, 4 children **DISCIPLINE** LITURGY **EDUCATION** Occidental Col, BA, 61; Luther Sem, BD, 66; Univ Nijmegen, ThD, 69. **CAREER** Charles A. Schieren prof. **HONORS AND AWARDS** Past pres, N Amer acad of Liturgy. **MEMBERSHIPS** Mem, Societas Liturgica. **RESEARCH** Links between liturgy and culture, liturgy and ethics, liturgy and mission. **SELECTED PUBLICATIONS** Auth, Holy Things: A Liturgical Theology, Fortress, 93; auth, Holy People: A Liturgical Ecclesiology, Fortress, 99; gen ed, series Open Questions in Worship. **CONTACT ADDRESS** Dept of Practical Theology, Lutheran Theol Sem at Philadelphia, 7301 Germantown Ave, Philadelphia, PA 19119-1794. **EMAIL** glathrop@ltsp.edu

LATIOLAIS, CHRISTOPHER
PERSONAL Born 06/11/1957, m, 1985, 1 child **DISCIPLINE** PHILOSOPHY **EDUCATION** Univ Calif, BA, 80; MA, 87; PhD, 92. **CAREER** Univ Calif, 83-87; Univ San Diego, 87, 89-91; Kalamazoo Col, 91-; Univ Chicago, 97-98. **HONORS AND AWARDS** Deutsher Akademischer Austauschdienst Stipendium, 87-89; Dissertation Fel, UCSD, 87; Dissertation Travel Grant, UCSD, 86; Educ Aboard Prog, UCB, 87-88; Redfield Fel, Univ Chicago, 97-98. **RESEARCH** Philosophy of Language; Critical Social Theory; Philosophy and Film; Moral Psychology; Literary Criticism; Habermas's Critical Social Theory; Philosophical Conceptions of the body. **SELECTED PUBLICATIONS** Rev, of "The Inclusion of the Other: Essay in Political Theory," Ethics, forthcoming; rev, of "Habermas on Law and Democracy: Critical Exchanges," Ethics, forthcoming; rev, of "Heidegger and the Ground of Ethics: A Study of Mitsein," Ethics, ; auth, "The Eclipse of Reason: The Occlusion of Being: Is Habermas's Critique of Reason Complete?' Philosophy and Social Criticism, 97; auth, "Honneth's Renewal of Hegel's social Theory: Recognition in Early Childhood development," European Journal of Philosophy, 97; auth, "Natural Born Levellers: A Kierkegaardian Critique of Post-modern cinematography," Philosophy and Film, 97; auth, "Is the Speech Act the Actual Unit of Linguistic Exchange:?: a Proposal for Reorienting Pragmatics," Linguistics and Philosophy, 97; auth, "How Not to Conceive a Discourse Ethic: Young's Debilitation of Difference," Constellations, 97; auth, "Reconstructing and Deconstructing the Ideals of Reason: Habermas and the Constructive Role of Narrative," European Journal of Philosophy, 97. **CONTACT ADDRESS** Dept Philos, Kalamazoo Col, 1200 Acad St, Kalamazoo, MI 49006-3268.

LAU, SUE
PERSONAL Born 03/25/1935, St. Joseph, MO, m, 1955, 2 children **DISCIPLINE** RELIGIOUS STUDIES **EDUCATION** Univ Pittsburgh, PhD, 81. **CAREER** Lectr, Univ Pittsburgh, 81-; Asst Prof, Ind Univ of Pa, 91; Vis Asst Prof, WVa Univ, 98. **HONORS AND AWARDS** Phi Beta Kappa; Apple for the Teacher Awd, Univ Pittsburgh, 84, 87, 93. **MEMBERSHIPS** Service Int de Documentation Judeo-Chretienne; Am Acad Relig; Soc Bibl Lit; Bibl Archaeol Soc. **RESEARCH** Women in religion. **SELECTED PUBLICATIONS** Auth, Women and Religion: A Bibliography (available on the Internet). **CONTACT ADDRESS** 540 Leger Rd., North Huntington, PA 15642. **EMAIL** flsclau@aol.com

LAUDER, ROBERT EDWARD
PERSONAL Born 07/06/1934, Brooklyn, NY **DISCIPLINE** PHILOSOPHY **EDUCATION** Cathedral Col, BA, 56; Cath Univ Am, MA, 65; Marquette Univ, PhD(philos), 68. **CAREER** Lectr theol, St Joseph's Col, 63-64; lectr relig studies, Queens Col, 71-75; assoc prof, 75-79, Prof Philos, Cathedral Col Sem, 80-. **MEMBERSHIPS** Am Cath Theol Soc; Am Cath Philos Soc; AUP. **RESEARCH** Existentialist philosophy; personalist philosophy. **SELECTED PUBLICATIONS** Contribr, Ingmar Bergman: Essays in Criticism, Oxford Univ, 75; auth, Loneliness is for Loving, Ave Maria, 78; The Love Explosion: Human Experience and the Christian Mystery, Living Flame, 1/79. **CONTACT ADDRESS** Cathedral Col Sem, 7200 Douglaston Pkwy, Douglaston, NY 11362.

LAUER, EUGENE F.
PERSONAL Born 10/07/1935, Pittsburgh, PA, s **DISCIPLINE** THEOLOGY AND HISTORICAL THEOLOGY SYSTEMATICS **EDUCATION** St. Fidelis Col, 53-55; St. Vincent Col, BA, 57; St. Mary Sem and Univ, STB, 59, STL, 61; Gregorian Univ, Rome, STD, 66; Cath Univ of Amer, 84-85. **CAREER** Asst prof, relig, LaRoche Col, summer, 67; lectr, relig, Carlow Col, 66-68; assoc prof, relig, LaRoche Col, 68-73; adjunct facul mem, Duquesne Univ, 68-69; adjunct facul mem, St. Vincent Sem, 69-70; part-time asst prof, Ind Univ of Penn, 71-72; prof, relig, LaRoche Col, 73-75; ed, Middle States Report, 73; pres, acad senate, 73-75; acting acad dean, LaRoche Col, 74-75; assoc prof, theol, Duquesne Univ, 75-81; mem one-year all-univ planning comn, 78; mem search comt, 80; visiting prof, relig, Seton Hill Col, 81-82; assoc prof, theol/relig, 82-86; dir MA prog in relig educ, Wheeling Jesuit Col, 82-86; adjunct facul, Cath Univ of Amer, 84-85; prof, theol/relig, dir MA prog, Wheeling Jesuit Col, 86-87; dir, Ctr for Continuing Formation in Ministry, assoc prof specialist, Univ Notre Dame, 87-98, chair, special prof facul asn, Univ Notre Dame, 96-97; dir, Hesburgh Ctr for Continuing Formation in Ministry Cath Theol Union, 98-. **HONORS AND AWARDS** Chair, Special Professional Facul, Notre Dame, 97; chair, Nat Cath Coalition on Preaching, 92-97; chair, Facul Senate and Assembly, Wheeling Jesuit Univ, 86-87; Outstanding Facul Person award, Wheeling Jesuit Univ, 86, 87; facul rep, all-univ planning comn, 78-79; chair, facul senate, LaRoche Col, 73-75; outstanding educ award, LaRoche Col, 72. **MEMBERSHIPS** Amer Acad of Relig; Amer Asn for Higher Educ; Cath Theol Soc of Amer; Col Theol Soc. **RESEARCH** Sacraments; Religion and public affairs. **SELECTED PUBLICATIONS** Article, For What Shall We Ask: A Biblical-Theological Critique of Prayer of Petition, Studies in Formative Spirituality, XI, 2, 145-156, may, 90; rev, New Experiment in Democracy, Social Thought, XIV, 4, 60-61, fall, 88; reb, Faithful Dissent, Soc Thought, XIII, 1, 64-67, winter, 87; article, Overcoming Resistance in Power-Sharing, Health Progress, 67, 3, 46-48, 71, apr, 86; article, New Approaches to Decision-Making in Moral Theology, Health Progress, 67, 1, 42-46, 56, jan-feb, 86; article, The Holiness of Marriage: Some New Perspectives from Recent Sacramental Theology, Studies in Formative Spirituality, VI, 2, 215-226, may, 85; book rev, When Health Care Employees Strike, Health Progress, 66, 4, 66, may, 85; article, Service Strikes: The New Moral Dilemma, Issues in the Labor-Mgt Dialogue, Church Perspectives, Cath Health Asn of US, 82; auth, A Christian Understanding of the Human Person, Paulist Press, 82; auth, Sunday Morning Insights, Liturgical Press, 84; auth, Human Services Strikes: A Contemporary Ethical Dilemma, Catholic Health Asn Press, 86. **CONTACT ADDRESS** Hesburgh Center, Catholic Theol Union at Chicago, 5401 S. Cornell Av., Chicago, IL 60615. **EMAIL** elauer@ctu.edu

LAUGHLIN, JOHN C. H.
PERSONAL Born 09/05/1942, Asheboro, NC, m, 1965, 1 child **DISCIPLINE** HEBREW BIBLE STUDIES, NEAR EASTERN ANTHROPOLOGY AND PHILOSOPHY **EDUCATION** Wake Forest Univ, BA, Greek, 67; Southern Bapt Theol Sem, M Div, 71; PhD, 75. **CAREER** Pastor, Col Ave Bapt Church, Bluefield, WV, 75-76; asst prof relig, Hardin-Simmons Univ, Abilene, TX, 76-77; asst prof relig, Palm Beach Atlantic Col, West Palm Beach, Fla, 77-79; prof relig and cha, dept relig, Averett Col, Danville, Va, 79-. **MEMBERSHIPS** Nat Asn Bapt Prof of Relig; Amer Sch of Oriental Res; Soc of Bibl Lit; Bibl Archaeo Soc. **RESEARCH** Archaeology and the Bible; Near Eastern Archaeology; Biblical Studies. **SELECTED PUBLICATIONS** Articles, Mercer Dict of the Bible, 90; Capernaum from Jesus' Time and After, Bibl Archaeol Rev, 54-61, 90, 93; Joshua, Mercer Commentary on the Bible, 95; Israel and the Liberation of Canaan, Joseph A. Callaway's Faces of the Old Testament, Mercer Univ Press, 95; Digging Archaeology, The Bibl Illusr, fall, 97; Samaria the Strong, The Bibl Illusr, fall, 98; auth, Archaeology and the Bible, Routledge, 00. **CONTACT ADDRESS** Averett Col, 420 W. Main St., Danville, VA 24541. **EMAIL** laughlin@averett.edu

LAUMAKIS, STEPHEN J.
DISCIPLINE MEDIEVAL PHILOSOPHY: ST. THOMAS AQUINAS **EDUCATION** St. Charles Sem, BA, 82; Villanova Univ, MA, 84; Univ Notre Dame, PhD, 91. **CAREER** Phil, St. John Vianney Col Sem **MEMBERSHIPS** MN Philos Soc; Am Philos Asn; Am Catholic Philos Asn; Soc Christian Philos. **SELECTED PUBLICATIONS** Auth, Is Christian Science Possible?,Science & Theology, Univ St Thomas, 96; The Role of Chance in the Philosophy of Teilhard De Chardin, Villanova Univ, 84. **CONTACT ADDRESS** St. John Vianney Col Sem, 2115 Summit Ave, Saint Paul, MN 55105-1095.

LAURSEN, JOHN CHRISTIAN
PERSONAL 2 children **DISCIPLINE** POLITICAL THEORY **EDUCATION** Harvard Univ, JD, 77; Johns Hopkins Univ, PhD, 85. **CAREER** Prof polit sci, Univ Calif, Riverside. **SELECTED PUBLICATIONS** Auth, The Politics of Skepticism: in the Ancients, Montaigne, Hume, and Kant, Leiden, 92; ed, New Essays on the Political Thought of the Huguenots of the Refuge, Leiden, 95; co-ed, Difference and Dissent: Theories of Toleration in Medieval and Early Modern Europe, Rowman & Littlefield, 96; co-ed, Beyond the Persecuting Society: Religious Toleration Before the Enlightenment, Univ Pa Press, 98; ed, Religious Toleration: 'The Variety of Rites' from Cyrus to Defoe, St. Martin's, 99; co-ed, The Edict of Religion, Lexington, 00. **CONTACT ADDRESS** Dept Polit Sci, Univ of California, Riverside, Riverside, CA 92521. **EMAIL** Laursen@wizard.ucr.edu

LAWEE, ERIC J.
PERSONAL Born 01/12/1963, Toronto, ON, Canada **DISCIPLINE** JEWISH STUDIES **EDUCATION** Univ Toronto, BA, 86; Harvard Univ, PhD, 93. **CAREER** Asst Prof, Stanford Univ, 97-99; Asst Prof, York Univ, 99-. **HONORS AND AWARDS** Ray D. Wolfe Postdoc Fel, Univ Toronto, 93-94; Fel, Soc Sci and Humanities Res Coun, 94-96; Yad Hanadiv Fel, 96-97; Van Courtlandt Elliott Prize, Medieval Acad of Am, 97; Koret Found Pub Subsidy. **MEMBERSHIPS** Medieval Acad of Am; Asn for Jewish Studies. **RESEARCH** Late medieval Spain; Judaism in the medieval and early modern periods; History of premodern biblical interpretation. **SELECTED PUBLICATIONS** Auth, "On the Threshold of the Renaissance: New Methods and Sensibilities in the Biblical Commentaries of Isaac Abarbanel," Viator, 95; auth, "Israel Has No Messiah in Late Medieval Spain," J of Jewish Thought and Philos, 95; auth, "The Path to Felicity: Teachings and Tensions in Even Shetiyyah of Abraham ben Judah, Disciple of Hasdai Crescas," Mediaeval Studies, 97; auth, Isaac Abarbanel's Stance Toward Tradition: Defense, Dissent, and Dialogue, SUNY Press, 01. **CONTACT ADDRESS** Div Humanities, York Univ, Div Humanities, Toronto, ON, Canada M3J 2P3. **EMAIL** lawee@yorku.ca

LAWHEAD, WILLIAM F.
PERSONAL m, 2 children **DISCIPLINE** HISTORY OF PHILOSOPHY, PHILOSOPHY OF RELIGION **EDUCATION** Wheaton Col, BA; Univ TX, Austin, PhD. **CAREER** Prof, Univ MS, 80-. **RESEARCH** History of philosophy, God and time. **SELECTED PUBLICATIONS** Auth, The Voyage of Discovery: A History of Western Philosophy, Wadsworth Publ Co, 96; auth, The Philosophical Journey, Mayfield Publ Co, 00. **CONTACT ADDRESS** Univ of Mississippi, Oxford, MS 38677. **EMAIL** wlawhead@olemiss.edu

LAWLESS, CHARLES E.
PERSONAL Born 01/07/1961, m **DISCIPLINE** EVANGELISM AND CHURCH GROWTH **EDUCATION** Cumberland Col, BS; S Baptist Theol Sem, MDiv, PhD. **CAREER** Lectr, Univ Cincinnati; assoc prof, coord, Dr Ministry Prog, S Baptist Theol Sem. **SELECTED PUBLICATIONS** Contrib, articles to denominational periodicals; auth, curriculum for the Sunday Sch Bd, S Baptist Convention. **CONTACT ADDRESS** Billy Graham Sch Missions, Evangel and Church Growth, So Baptist Theol Sem, 2825 Lexington Rd, Louisville, KY 40280. **EMAIL** clawless@sbts.edu

LAWLOR, JOHN I.
PERSONAL Born 12/16/1941, Winona Lake, IN, m, 1965, 3 children **DISCIPLINE** OLD TESTAMENT STUDIES **EDUCATION** Cedarville Col, BA, 63; Grace Theological Seminary, BD, 66, THM 69; Drew Univ, MPhil, 89, PhD 91. **CAREER** Asst prof, 70-80, prof 80-99, Baptist Bible Col; adjunct prof, 92-99 , Penn State Univ; Grand Rapids Baptist Seminary, prof, 99-. **MEMBERSHIPS** ASOR, ETS, SBL. **RESEARCH** Archaeology: Ammonites and Moatsites; Hebrew Bible: Narrative. **SELECTED PUBLICATIONS** Auth, Violence, Evangelical Dictionary of Biblical Theology, 96; auth, Tel el-'Umeiri: Field A: The Ammonite Citadel, 1989, in Madaba Plains Project, 3: The 1989 Season at Tell el-'Umeiri and Vicinity, 97; auth, Karak Resources Project, 1997, American Journal of Archaeology, 98; auth, orthcoming: The Kerak Resources Project, 1997, Annual of the Department of Antiquities of Jordon; Tel el-'Umeiri: The Western Citadel: 1996, 1998, in Madaba Plains Project, 4: The 1994 Season at Tell el-'Umeiri and Vicinity; Tel el-'Umeiri: The Western Citadel: 1992, 1994, in in Madaba Plains Project, 4: The 1992 Season at Tell el-'Umeiri and Vicinity; A Corpus of Bone Carvings from the Excavation of the Esbus North Church, in a Festschrift for James A. Sauer. **CONTACT ADDRESS** Grand Rapids Baptist Sem, 1001 E Beltline NE, Grand Rapids, MI 49525. **EMAIL** John_Lawlor@Cornerstone.edu

LAWRENCE, JOHN SHELTON
PERSONAL Born 03/30/1938, Amarillo, TX, m, 1961, 2 children **DISCIPLINE** PHILOSOPHY **EDUCATION** Stanford Univ, BA, 60; Tex Univ, PhD(philos), 64. **CAREER** From instr to asst prof philos, Univ Devner, 64-66; asst prof, 66-69, assoc prof, 69-79, Prof Philos, Morningside Col, 80-, Head Dept, 66-. **MEMBERSHIPS** Am Philos Asn. **RESEARCH** Ethics; value theory; aesthetics. **SELECTED PUBLICATIONS** Auth, Whitehead's failure, Southern J Philos, winter 69-70; Violence, Social Theory & Pract, fall 70; coauth, The American Monomyth, Anchor & Doubleday, 77; co-ed, Fair Use and Free Inquiry: Copyright Law and the New Media, Commun & Info Sci (in press). **CONTACT ADDRESS** Dept of Philos, Morningside Col, Sioux City, IA 51106.

LAWRENCE, LARY
DISCIPLINE LAW **EDUCATION** Univ Calif, Los Angeles, BA, 70; Univ Calif, Berkeley, JD, 73. **CAREER** Prof, Loyola, 84-; prof & Harriet L. Bradley Ch Contract Law Contracts, Sales and Payments; Bigelow tchg fel; instr, Univ Chicago Sch of Law; assoc prof, Univ Mo-Columbia Sch of Law, 77-79; fac, Univ NC Sch of Law, attened rank tenured assoc prof, 79-84; vis prof, Hofstra; Univ San Diego; Univ Hawaii; Univ Bus and Econ(s), Beijing; Monash Univ, Melbourne, Australia. **SELECTED PUBLICATIONS** Published on, commercial law. **CONTACT ADDRESS** Law School, Loyola Marymount Univ, 7900 Loyola Blvd, Burns 425, Los Angeles, CA 90045. **EMAIL** llawrenc@lmulaw.lmu.edu

LAWRENCE, RICHARD
PERSONAL Born 01/19/1944, ND, m, 1 child **DISCIPLINE** CRIMINAL JUSTICE SCIENCES **EDUCATION** Bethel Col, BA, 66; St Mary's Univ, MA, 72; Sam Houston State Univ, PhD, 78. **CAREER** Probation Off, Bexar Cnty, 68-72; instr, San Antonio Col, 72-74; res trn dir, Bexar Cnty, 72-75; asst prof, Cen Missouri State Univ, 78-79; assoc prof, Univ Tex, 79-88; prof, St Cloud State Univ, 88-. **MEMBERSHIPS** ACJS; ASC. **RESEARCH** Juvenile delinquency; juvenile justice; criminal justice and correction. **SELECTED PUBLICATIONS** Auth, "Reexamining Community Corrections Models," Crime and Delinquency 37 (91): 449-464; auth, "The Effects of School Performance and Peers on Self-Reported Delinquent Behavior," Juv Fam Court J 42 (91): 59-69; auth, "The Impact of Sentencing Guidelines on Corrections," Crim Just Policy Rev (91); auth, "Classrooms vs. Prison Cells: Funding Policies for Education and Corrections," J Crime Justice 18 (95):113-126; auth, "Controlling School Crime: An Examination of Interorganizational Relations of School and Juvenile Justice Professionals," Juv Fam Court J 46 (95): 3-15; coauth, "Prison Riots," in Encyclopedia of American Prisons , eds. MD McShane, FP Williams III (Garland Publishing, Inc, 95); coauth, "Media and Mayhem in Corrections: The Role of the Media in Prison Riots," Prison J 76 (96): 42-441; auth, "Shared Goals, Resources Unite Probation and Schools," School Safety (97): 25-26; coauth, "Women Corrections Officers in Men's Prisons: Acceptance and Perceived Job Performance," Woman & Criminal Justice 9)98): 63-86; rev of, 'Chaos, Criminology, and Social Justice," by Dragan Milovanovic (forthcoming). **CONTACT ADDRESS** Dept Criminal Justice, St. Cloud State Univ, 720 4th Ave S, Saint Cloud, MN 56301. **EMAIL** lawrence@stcloudstate.edu

LAWRY, EDWARD GEORGE
PERSONAL Born 02/25/1944, Pittsburgh, PA, d, 2 children **DISCIPLINE** EXISTENTIALISM **EDUCATION** Fordham Univ, BA, 66; Univ Pittsburgh, MA, 67; Univ Tex, Austin PhD (philos), 71. **CAREER** Asst prof to assoc prof, 71-89, Prof Philos, Okla State Univ, 89-; Chm, Mountain-Plains Philos Conf, 77-78 & 80-81; vis fel, Dept Art Hist, Yale Univ, 78-79; fel, Ctr for Prof Ethics, Case Western Univ, 00-01; pres, Southwestern Philos Soc, 01. **MEMBERSHIPS** Am Philos Asn; Southwestern Philos Soc; Mountain-Plains Philos Conf(secy-treas, 73-74); Int Asn Philos & Lit. **RESEARCH** Aesthetics; ethics. **SELECTED PUBLICATIONS** Auth, The work-being of the work of art in Heidegger, Man & World, Vol II, No 1 & 2; Did Kant refute idealism?, Idealistic Studies, 1/80; Literature as philosophy, Moviegoer, 10/80; auth, On Not Needing a Fix: The Essence of Essence, Southwest Philosphy Rev, vol 12, No 2, 96; auth, Philosophy as Argument, Philosophy as Conversation, Philosophy in the Contemporary World, vol 5, No 1, 99. **CONTACT ADDRESS** Dept of Philos, Oklahoma State Univ, Stillwater, Stillwater, OK 74078-5064. **EMAIL** elawry@okway.okstate.edu

LAWSON, ANGUS KERR
DISCIPLINE PHILOSOPHY **EDUCATION** McMaster Univ, PhD, 63. **RESEARCH** Philos of George Santayana; foundations of math. **SELECTED PUBLICATIONS** Ed, Overhead in Seville: Bulletin of the Santayana Society; auth, Canadian Journal of Mathematics, The Transactions of the Charles S. Peirce Society, Dialogue, The Southern Journal of Philosophy; and two recent anthologies. **CONTACT ADDRESS** Dept of Philosophy, Univ of Waterloo, 200 University Ave W, Waterloo, ON, Canada N2L 3G1. **EMAIL** kerrlaws@uwaterloo.ca

LAWSON, E. THOMAS
PERSONAL Born 11/27/1931, Capetown, South Africa, m, 1966, 2 children **DISCIPLINE** RELIGION **EDUCATION** Univ Chicago, PhD, 63. **CAREER** Western Mich Univ, 61-; prof and chair, comparative relig, 76-. **HONORS AND AWARDS** Distinguished facul sch; excellence in teaching award. **MEMBERSHIPS** Northern Amer Asn for the study of relig; Amer Soc for the study of relig; Soc for philos psychol. **RESEARCH** Cognitive science; African religions. **SELECTED PUBLICATIONS** Auth, Rethinking Religion: Connecting Cognition and Culture, with Robert N. McCauley, Cambridge Univ Press, 90, 93; auth, "Cognitive Categories, Cultural Aspects of Religious Symbolism, ed P. Boyer, Cambridge Univ Pr, 92; auth, "Connecting the Cognitive and the Cultural: Artificial Minds as Methodological Devices in the Study of the Socio-cultural," with Robert N. McCauley, in Minds: Natural and Artificial, ed, Rober Burton, State Univ of New York Pr, 93; auth, Religions of Africa: Traditions in Transformation, Waveland Press, 98; auth, Religious Ideas and Practices, MIT Encyclopedia for Cognitive Science, MIT Press, 98. **CONTACT ADDRESS** Dept of Comparative Religion, Western Michigan Univ, 1903 W Michigan Ave, Kalamazoo, MI 49008. **EMAIL** e.thomas.lawson@wmich.edu

LAWSON MACK, RANETA
DISCIPLINE CRIMINAL LAW **EDUCATION** Univ Toledo, BA, 85, JD, 88. **CAREER** Prof, Creighton Univ; assoc, Davis, Graham & Stubbs, Denver, 88-91; USWEST fel, Creighton Univ, 97. **HONORS AND AWARDS** Outstanding Advocate awd; Amer Jurisp awd, Univ Toledo; Alumni Excellence in Law awd, Univ Toledo Black Law Stud Asn, 94. **SELECTED PUBLICATIONS** Auth, A Lay Person's Guide to Criminal Law, 98; pub(s) in, Ind Int and Comp Law Rev; Creighton Law Rev; Ariz State Law J; St Thomas Law Rev; Thurgood Marshall Law Rev; Creighton Lawyer. **CONTACT ADDRESS** School of Law, Creighton Univ, 2500 California Plaza, Omaha, NE 68178. **EMAIL** mack@culaw.creighton.edu

LAYMAN, FRED DALE
PERSONAL Born 09/27/1931, Marshfield, MO, m, 1952, 1 child **DISCIPLINE** THEOLOGY, BIBLICAL THEOLOGY **EDUCATION** Asbury Col, AB, 54; Asbury Theol Sem, BD, 56; Princeton Theol Sem, ThM, 57; Univ Iowa, PhD(relig), 72. **CAREER** Prof Bible and philos, Friends Univ, 58-63; assoc prof New Testament Greek, Asbury Col, 67-68; Prof Bibl Theol, Asbury Theol Sem, 68-98 **MEMBERSHIPS** Soc Bibl Lit. **RESEARCH** Old Testament theology; New Testament theology. **CONTACT ADDRESS** 2501 Lees Rd., Sevierville, TN 37876. **EMAIL** fredlayman@aol.com

LAYWINE, ALISON
DISCIPLINE PHILOSOPHY **EDUCATION** Univ Ottawa, BA, 84; Univ Montreal, MA, 86; Univ Chicago, PhD, 91. **RESEARCH** Hist of pol philos; Jewish philos; ancient Greek philos. **SELECTED PUBLICATIONS** Auth, Kant's Early Metaphysics and the Origins of the Critical Philosophy, Ridgeview, 95; art, Intellectual Appearances, British Jour Hist Philos, 95. **CONTACT ADDRESS** Philosophy Dept, McGill Univ, 845 Sherbrooke St, Montreal, QC, Canada H3A 2T5. **EMAIL** alaywine@leacock.lan.mcgill.ca

LAZAROFF, DANIEL E.
DISCIPLINE LAW **EDUCATION** State Univ NYork at Stony Brook, BA, 71;, NYork Univ, JD, 74. **CAREER** Prof, Loyola, 83-; prof & Leonard E. Cohen ch Law & Econ(s); fac, Univ Detroit Mercy Sch of Law, attained rank tenured assoc prof, 78-83. **SELECTED PUBLICATIONS** Publ on, antitrust and sports law. **CONTACT ADDRESS** Law School, Loyola Marymount Univ, 7900 Loyola Blvd, Burns 345, Los Angeles, CA 90045. **EMAIL** dlazarof@lmulaw.lmu.edu

LEA, THOMAS DALE
PERSONAL m, 3 children **DISCIPLINE** NEW TESTAMENT **EDUCATION** Miss State Univ, BS, 60; Southwestern Baptist Theol Sem, BD, 64, ThD, 67. **CAREER** Prof, 79-. **HONORS AND AWARDS** Pastor, Vineyard Grove Baptist Church, 64-66; asst pastor, Cliff Temple Baptist Church, 66-68; pastor, Liberty Baptist Church, 68-72; Hunter St Baptist Church, 72-79. **MEMBERSHIPS** Evangel Theol Soc; Inst Biblical Res; Soc Biblical Lit. **SELECTED PUBLICATIONS** Auth, The New Testament: Its Background and Message, Broadman & Holman, 96; Saved by Grace, Convention Press, 94; 1, 2 Timothy, Broadman & Holman, 92; Step by Step Through the New Testament, Baptist Sunday Sch Bd, 92. **CONTACT ADDRESS** Sch Theol, Southwestern Baptist Theol Sem, PO Box 22000, Fort Worth, TX 76122-0418. **EMAIL** tdalel@swbts.swbts.edu

LEAHY, MARGARET E.
PERSONAL Born 06/28/1945, San Franciso, CA, m, 1978, 2 children **DISCIPLINE** INTERNATIONAL RELATIONS THEORY, INTERNATIONAL POLITICAL ECONOMY, THIRD WORL **EDUCATION** San Francisco State Univ, BA, MA; Univ Southern CA, PhD. **CAREER** Prof ch, dept Public Affairs and Int Rel, Golden Gate Univ. **MEMBERSHIPS** Exec comt, Int Stud Asn. **SELECTED PUBLICATIONS** Auth, Development Strategies and the Status of Women; The Harassment of Nicaraguanists and Fellow Travelers. **CONTACT ADDRESS** Golden Gate Univ, San Francisco, CA 94105-2968. **EMAIL** mleahy@ggu.edu

LEAMAN, GEORGE R.
PERSONAL Born 05/26/1958, New Orleans, LA **DISCIPLINE** PHILOSOPHY **EDUCATION** Williams Col, BA, 80; Univ Mass, MA, 86; MA, 87; PhD, 91. **CAREER** Adj prof, Univ Md, 91-93; adj prof, Bowling Green State Univ, 94-01-. **HONORS AND AWARDS** DAAD Res Fel, 87-89; Puryear Fel, 84-85; Smith-Futransky Prize, 79. **MEMBERSHIPS** APA; MLA; SSP; SPEP. **RESEARCH** 20th-century German philosophy; social and political philosophy; sociology of philosophy. **SELECTED PUBLICATIONS** Auth, Heidegger im Kontext, Argument Verlag, 93; auth, The Holdings of the Berlin Document Center, BDC, 94; co-auth, "Die Kant-Studien im Dritten Reich," Kant-Studien (94). **CONTACT ADDRESS** Philos Doc Ctr, Bowling Green State Univ, PO Box 7147, Charlottesville, VA 22906-7147. **EMAIL** leaman@pdcnet.org

LEAR, ELIZABETH T.
DISCIPLINE LAW **EDUCATION** Univ NC, BA; Univ Mich, JD. **CAREER** Prof, Univ Fla, 90-; vis prof, Univ San Diego & Calif Western Sch Law; past assoc, Williams and Connolly, Wash, DC; clerk, Judge J. Edward Lumbard, US Ct Appeals, 2nd circut, NY; pvt pract. **MEMBERSHIPS** Order of the Coif; Pa Bar. **RESEARCH** Federal sentencing and the 11th amendment, criminal law, federal practice, civil procedure. **CONTACT ADDRESS** School of Law, Univ of Florida, PO Box 117625, Gainesville, FL 32611-7625. **EMAIL** lear@law.ufl.edu

LEARY, DAVID E.
PERSONAL Born 05/05/1945, Los Angeles, CA, m, 1972, 3 children **DISCIPLINE** HISTORY & PHILOSOPHY OF PSYCHOLOGY **EDUCATION** San Luis Rey Col, CA, BA, 68; San Jose State, CA, MA, 71; Univ Chicago, IL, PhD, 77. **CAREER** Vis asst prof of Psychology, Graduate Theol Union, Berkeley, CA, 71-72; instr Psychol, Holy Names Col, Oakland, CA, 72-74; instr psychol, San Francisco State Univ Ext Services and Univ CA Ext Services, 73-74; instr of Psychol, Univ Chicago, 75; asst prof of the History and Philos of Psychol, Univ NH, Durham, 77-81, co-dir, grad prog in the Theory and History of Psychol, 77-89, assoc prof Psychol & Humanities, 81-87; fel, Center for Advanced Study in the Behavioral Sciences, Stanford, CA, 82-83, co-dir, summer inst on the Hist of Social Scientific Inquiry, 86; assoc prof Humanities, Cambridge Univ Summer prog, 84; Chairperson, Dept of Psychol, 86-89, prof of Psychol, Hist, and the Humanities, Univ NH, Durham,

87-89; prof of Psychology, dean of Arts and Sciences, Univ Richmond, VA, 89-. **HONORS AND AWARDS** San Luis Rey College Memorial Fund Scholarship, 63-68; Special Honors, PhD dissertation, 77; Univ NH Merit Awd, 78, 82; Asn of Am Pubs Awd, 85; Phi Beta Kappa, 87; numerous grants, fellowships, and stipends from the NEH, Univ NH, Nat Sci Found, Mellon Found, and others. **MEMBERSHIPS** Am Asn of Higher Ed; Am Conf of Academic Deans (member of the bd, 93-2000, chair of the bd, 98-99); Am Hist Asn; Am Psychol Asn (Pres, Div of History of Psychology; 83-84, Pres, Div of Theoretical and Philos Psychol, 94-95); Am Psychol Soc; Asn of Am Colleges and Universities; Cheiron: Int Soc for the History of the Behavioral and Social Sciences; Forum for the Hist of Human Science; Hist of Science Soc; Soc for the Hist of Science in Am. **RESEARCH** The intellectual, social, and cultural history of psychology, with a special focus on the relations between psychology and the humanities (eg, literature, philosophy, and religion) and the other sciences. **SELECTED PUBLICATIONS** Auth, An Introduction to the Psychology of Guilt, Lansford Co, 75; A Century of Psychology as Science, co-ed with Sigmund Koch, MacGraw-Hill, 85 (recipient of the Asn of Am Pubs Award, 85), 2nd ed reissued with a new postscript, Am Psychol An, 92; Metaphors in the History of Psychology, Cambridge Univ Press, 90, paperback, 94; William James, the Psychologist's Dilema, and the Historiography of Psychology: Cautionary Tales, Hist of Human Sciences, 8, 95; Naming and Knowing: Giving Forms to Things Unknown, Social Res 62, 95; William James and the Art of Human Understanding, in Ludy T Benjamin, Jr, ed, A History of Psychology: Original Sources and Contemporary Research, 2nd ed, McGraw-Hill, 97 (reprinted from 92); Sigmund Koch (1917-1996), co-auth with Frank Kessel and William Bevan, Am Psychologist 53, 98; numerous other publications. **CONTACT ADDRESS** Dean of Arts and Sciences, Univ of Richmond, Richmond, VA 23173. **EMAIL** dleary@richmond.edu

LECK, GLORIANNE MAE
PERSONAL Born 07/28/1941, Tomahawk, WI **DISCIPLINE** PHILOSOPHY **EDUCATION** Univ Wis, BS, 63; MS, 66; PhD(educ philos), 68. **CAREER** Social fac residence halls, Univ Wis, 65-66, teaching asst, 65-67; instr, Wis State Univ, 67-69; asst prof, Pa State Univ, 69-73; assoc prof, 74-80, Prof Educ & Philos, Youngstown State Univ, 80-, Sect chairperson, Cultural Found of Educ, Pa State, 70-71; vis asst prof educ & philos, NY Univ, summer, 72; chairperson, Dept Educ Found, Youngstown State Univ, 75-77; chair, Comt Acad Standards & Accreditation, Am Educ Studies Asn, 78-79. **HONORS AND AWARDS** O E A Holloways/Human and Civil Rights Commission Awd, 94; Proclamation from Mayor and City Council for service on Human Relations Commission, 96; Distinguished Professorship for Community Service, Youngstown State, University Honors, Convocation, 97; **MEMBERSHIPS** Am Educ Studies; Am Philos Asn; Soc Women Philos; Philos Educ Soc; NEA; Am Educ res Asn. **SELECTED PUBLICATIONS** Coauth, Philosophical Assumptions of Research on Gender Differences of: Two by Two and We'll Never Get Through, Speech Commun Asn, summer 75; auth, Standards for Academic and Professional Instruction in Foundations of Education, Educational Studies & Educational Policy Studies, Educ Studies Press, 77; auth, Teacher Education and Social Action Concerns, J Ohio Asn Supv & Curric Develop, spring 79; auth, Review of Jean-Paul Sartre by Himself, Educ Studies, summer 80; auth, A Reflection on Consequences, J Ohio Coun Elementary Sc Sci, 1/81; auth, Other Cultural Perspectives: Field Experiences and Opportunities, The Forum, spring 81; auth, "The Politics of Adolescent Sexual Identity and Queer Responses," in The Gay Teen, ed. Gerald Unks, Routledge, 95; auth, "A Lavender-tongued Reliably Queer Lesbian Does Language on Language," in Beyond the Lavender Lexicon: Authenticity, Imagination, and Appropriation in Lesbian and Gay Literature, ed., William Leap, Gordon and Breach, 96; auth, "An Oasis: The LGBT Student Group on a Commuter Campus," in Working with Lesbian, Gay, Bisexual and Transgendered, College Students: A guide for Faculty, Staff and Administrators, ed., Ronni Sanlo, Greenwood, 98; auth, "Heterosexual or Homosexual? Reconsidering Binary Narratives on Sexual Identities in Urban Schools," in Education and Urban Society 32(3) (00); auth, "School Uniforms, Baggy Pants, Barbie Dolls, and Business Suit Cultures on School Boards," in Thinking Queer, ed. Susan Talbot and Shirley Steinberg (Peter Lang, 00. **CONTACT ADDRESS** Research & Founds, Youngstown State Univ, One Univ Plz, Youngstown, OH 44555-0002. **EMAIL** f0036363@cc.ysu.edu

LEDDY, T.
PERSONAL Born 09/30/1949, Oakland, CA, m, 1985 **DISCIPLINE** PHILOSOPHY **EDUCATION** Boston Univ, PhD, 83; San Francisco State, MA 74; Univ Cal Santa Cruz, BA 71; Col San Mateo, AA 69. **CAREER** San Jose State Univ, asst prof, assoc prof, prof, 83-95-; Alfred Univ, asst prof, 82-83; Napa Col, inst, 75-77; Chabot Col, inst, 74-75. **HONORS AND AWARDS** ASA Mem Bd Trustees **RESEARCH** Aesthetics; philo of art. **SELECTED PUBLICATIONS** Auth, Analytic Anti-Essentialism, The Encycl of Aesthetics, ed Michael Kelly, OUP, 98; Sparkle and Shine, Brit Jour of Aesth, 97; rev, Caroline Van Eck, Organicism in Nineteenth Century Architecture, in: The Jour of Aesth and Art, 97; rev, Jean Babbert Harrell, Profundity: A Universal Value, PUP 92, in: Jour of Aesth and Crit, 96; Everyday Surface Aesthetic Qualities: Neat Messy Clean Dirty, Jour of Aesth and Art Crit, 95; Metaphor and Metaphysics, Metaphor and Symbolic Activity, 95; Nietzsche On Unity of Style, Hist Reflections, 95; A Pragmatist Theory of Artistic Creativity, The J of Value Inq, 94; Dialogical Architecture, Philo and Arch, ed, Michael H. Mitias, Amster, Rudolpi, 94; American Society for Aesthetics: 50th Anniversary Meeting, The Jour of Value Inq, 94. **CONTACT ADDRESS** Dept of Philosophy, San Jose State Univ, San Jose, CA 95192. **EMAIL** twleddy@email.sjsu.edu

LEDER, DREW L.
PERSONAL Born 12/22/1954, New York City, NY, m, 1986, 2 children **DISCIPLINE** PHILOSOPHY **EDUCATION** Yale Univ, BA, MD; SUNY, PhD. **CAREER** Full prof; first Scholars-in-Residence on Aging, Chicago's Park Ridge Center. **RESEARCH** Pheomenology, Asia Thought, World Spirituality, Aging, Prison Work. **SELECTED PUBLICATIONS** Auth, Spiritual Passages: Embracing Life's Issues, Sacred Journey,Tarcher-Putnam, 97; The Absent Body, Univ Chicago Press, 90; ed, The Body in Medical Thought and Practice, Kluwer, 92; asst ed, The Encyclopedia of Bioethics, Macmillan, 95; auth, Games for the Soul, Hyperion, 98; auth, The Soul Knows No Bars: Imates Reflect on Life, Death, and Hope, Rowman and Littlefield, 00. **CONTACT ADDRESS** Dept of Philosophy, Loyola Col, 4501 N Charles St, Baltimore, MD 21210. **EMAIL** dleder@loyola.edu

LEDERLE, HENRY
PERSONAL Born 01/22/1946, Durban, South Africa, m, 1982, 3 children **DISCIPLINE** THEOLOGY **EDUCATION** Univ Orange Free State, BA, 66; MA, 69; Univ Stellenbosch, BTh, 72; Univ South Africa, ThD, 85. **CAREER** Seminary Teach, Zomba Theol Col Malawi, 76-77; Sen Lecturer, Univ South Africa, 78-80; Visiting Prof, Calvin Col, 80-81; Assoc Prof, Univ South Africa, 81-90; Prof, Oral Roberts Univ, 90-95; Assoc Pastor, First Presbyterian Church, 95-98; Prof, Oral Roberts Univ, 98-. **HONORS AND AWARDS** Von Humboldt Post doctoral Fel, German Govt. **MEMBERSHIPS** Am Acad of Relig, Soc for Pentecostal Studies. **RESEARCH** Pentecostal and Charismatic Movements; Doctrine of the Holy Spirit; Ecumenical Theology. **SELECTED PUBLICATIONS** Auth, Treasures Old and New: Interpretations of Spirit-Baptism, Peabody, 88; auth, Initial Evidence, Peabody, 91. **CONTACT ADDRESS** Dept Theol, Oral Roberts Univ, 7777 S Lewis Ave, Tulsa, OK 74171-0003. **EMAIL** hlederle@aol.com

LEDFORD, KENNETH F.
PERSONAL Born 08/17/1953, Gulfport, MS, m, 1977, 2 children **DISCIPLINE** HISTORY; LAW **EDUCATION** Univ NC, BA, 75, JD, 78; Johns Hopkins Univ, MA, 84, PhD, 89. **CAREER** Adjunct asst prof history, Univ MD, 88-89; vis asst prof history, Johns Hopkins Univ, 89, lectr Paul H. Nitze School Adv Int Studies, 88-91, Johns Hopkins Univ; res fel/ed, German Hist Inst, 89-91; asst prof history & law, 91-97, Assoc Prof History & Law, 97-, Case Western Reserve Univ; German Marshall Fund US res fel, 98-99; Fulbright fel, 97-98; ed bd Law Hist Rev, 96-; DAAD fel, 85-86; Mellon Found fel, 82-84; John Motley Morehead fel Univ NC, 75-78; Phi Beta Kappa, 74; Phi Eta Sigma, 72. **HONORS AND AWARDS** John Snell Mem Essay Prize S Hist Asn, 83; Seymour W Wurfel Prize Int Law Univ NC, 78. **MEMBERSHIPS** Am Hist Asn; Am Soc Legal Hist; Conf Grp Cent Europ Hist; S Hist Asn; Ger Stud Asn; Law Soc Asn; VA State Bar. **RESEARCH** German social history; German and European legal history; history of Central European professions; history of the German Burgertum; historiography of Germany. **SELECTED PUBLICATIONS** Conflict within the Legal Professions: Simultaneous Admission and the German Bar 1903-1927, German Professions, 1800-1950, Oxford Univ Press, 90; Lawyers, Liberalism, and Procedure: The German Imperial Justice Laws of 1877-79, Central European History, 93; "German Lawyers and the State in the Weimar Republic," Law and History Review, 95; "Identity, Difference, and Enlightenment Heritage: Comment on The Right to Be Punished," Law and History, 98; Lawyers and the Limits of Liberalism: The German Bar in the Weimar Republic, Lawyers and the Rise of Western Political Liberalism, Clarendon Press, 98; From General Estate to Special Interest: German Lawyers 1878-1933, Cambridge Univ Press, 96. **CONTACT ADDRESS** Dept of History, Case Western Reserve Univ, Cleveland, OH 44106-7107. **EMAIL** KXL15@po.cwru.edu

LEDOUX, ARTHUR O'BRIEN
PERSONAL Born 09/01/1948, Melrose, MA, m, 1982, 1 child **DISCIPLINE** PHILOSOPHY **EDUCATION** Tufts Univ, AB, 70; Univ Notre Dame, PhD, 77. **CAREER** Assoc Prof Philos, Merrimac Col, 75-; Dean of Liberal Arts, 97-98; interim dean, fac of lib arts; coor, hum prog. **HONORS AND AWARDS** Fulbright fel to Sri Lanka, 86. **MEMBERSHIPS** Am Philos Asn. **RESEARCH** Asian philos; comparative philos; philos of relig. **SELECTED PUBLICATIONS** Auth, review, The Middle Works of John Dewey, vols 1-2, in The New Scholasticism J of Am Cath Philos Asn, 9/78; Dewey on Meditation, in Insights, J of the John Dewey Soc, 12/78; Meditation in the Classroom: A Reply, AAPT News, Newsletter of the Am Asn Philos Teachers, 94; paper anthologized, On the Complementary Core Pradoxes of Faith and Effort in Theravada Buddhism and Christianity, in East-West Encounters in Philosophy and Religion, Long Beach Pubs, 96. **CONTACT ADDRESS** Dept of Philosophy, Merrimack Col, North Andover, MA 01845. **EMAIL** ALedoux@Merrimac.edu

LEE, CHERYL R.
PERSONAL Born 03/29/1960, Pittsburgh, PA **DISCIPLINE** LAW **EDUCATION** Northeastern Univ, BS, 81; Duquesne Univ, JD, 85. **CAREER** Aviation Law Clerk, Great Pittsburgh Int Airport, 82-85; asst corp counsel, Great Am Bank, 85-91; adj prof, San Diego City Col/San Diego State University/ Grossmont Col/Miramar Col, 89-99; partner, Thompson, Williams & Associates, 93-96; prof & prog consult, San Diego Col of Retailing, 94-96; asst prof, Thomas M. Cooley Law Sch, 96-99; vis assoc prof, dir of acad support & dir of diversity affairs, Thomas Jefferson Sch of Law, 99-. **HONORS AND AWARDS** The Saddler Scholar; The Oliver L. Johnson Book Scholar, Outstanding Young Women of Am, 82-84; Who's Who Among Am Law Students, 82-85. **MEMBERSHIPS** Nat Asn of Urban Bankers, Nat Bar Asn; Ingham County Bar Asn, Wolverine Bar Asn, San Diego County Bar Asn, Homer S. Brow Bar Asn, Lawyers Club of San Diego. **RESEARCH** Cyberbanking, Banking, Race Matters. **SELECTED PUBLICATIONS** Auth, "Elect or Appoint; Juris Talks to the Judges," JURIS 18.2 (83): 18; auth, "The Amalgamation of the Southern California Banking Industry: San Diego a Microcosm 35.1, Calif Western Law Rev (98); auth, "Cyberbanking: A New Frontier for Discrimination?," Rutgers Computer and Law Technol J (forthcoming). **CONTACT ADDRESS** Thomas Jefferson Sch of Law, 2121 San Diego Ave, San Diego, CA 92128. **EMAIL** cheryl@tjsl.edu

LEE, DONALD SOULE
PERSONAL Born 09/02/1933, New Orleans, LA, d, 1962, 3 children **DISCIPLINE** PHILOSOPHY **EDUCATION** Tulane Univ, BS, 55; MA, 58; Yale Univ, PhD, 61. **CAREER** From instr to asst prof philos, Wash Univ, 60-64; asst prof to assoc prof, Tulane Univ, 64-. **MEMBERSHIPS** Southern Soc Philos & Psychol (secy, 78-81 & pres, 81-82); Southwestern Philos Soc; Soc Advan Am Philos. **RESEARCH** Philosophy of science; epistemology; pragmatism. **SELECTED PUBLICATIONS** Auth, The construction of empirical concepts, Philos & Phenomenol, 12/66; Ultimacy and the philosophic field of Metaphysics, Tulane Studies Philos, 66; Scientific method as a stage process, Dialectics, 1/68; Hypothetic inference in systematic philosophy, Int Philos Quart, 9/69; Pragmatic ultimates: Contexts and common sense, Southern J Philos, winter 77; The structure of substitution, Southern J Philos, summer 80. **CONTACT ADDRESS** Dept of Philos, Tulane Univ, 6823 St Charles Ave, New Orleans, LA 70118-5698.

LEE, GRANT S.
DISCIPLINE PHILOSOPHY **EDUCATION** Temple Univ, PhD, 75. **RESEARCH** Oriental philosophy. **SELECTED PUBLICATIONS** Auth, Life and Thought of Yi Kwang-su, 84. **CONTACT ADDRESS** Philosophy Dept, Colorado State Univ, Fort Collins, CO 80523.

LEE, JOHNG O.
PERSONAL Born 11/20/1948, Kyung-Buk, S Korea, m, 1974 **DISCIPLINE** RELIGIOUS, BIBLE **EDUCATION** Trinity Intl Univ, BA, 79; Southwestern Baptist Theo Sem, M Ed, 82; PhD, 90; Liberty Univ, MA, 94. **CAREER** Adj prof, Reformed Theol Sem, N Bap Sem, Canaan Theol Sem; asst prof, Univ Virginia; prof, Moody Bible Inst. **HONORS AND AWARDS** Deans Hon Roll; Who's Who Am Coll. **MEMBERSHIPS** NAPCE. **RESEARCH** Religious Biblical education. **SELECTED PUBLICATIONS** Auth, Major Educational Characteristics of Asian-American, Moody Press; auth, Global Cultures, Moody Press (forthcoming). **CONTACT ADDRESS** Dept Christian Education, Moody Bible Inst, 820 N Lasalle St, Chicago, IL 60610. **EMAIL** jlee@moody.edu

LEE, JUNG YOUNG
PERSONAL Born 07/20/1935, Sunchun, Korea, m, 1965 **DISCIPLINE** SYSTEMATIC THEOLOGY, ASIAN RELIGIONS **EDUCATION** Findlay Col, BA, 57; Garrett Theol Sem, BD, 61; Western Reserve Univ, MS, 62; Boston Univ, ThD(syst theol), 68. **CAREER** Assoc minister, Alderstate United Methodist Church, Ohio, 60-61; minister, Oehloff Methodist Church, 61-63; actg librn, Howard Univ Sch Relig, 63-64; assoc minister, Ohmer Park Methodist Church, 65-66; asst prof relig and philos, Otterbein Col, 68-72; Prof Relig Studies, Univ N Dak, 72-, Fulbright-Hays sr fel, 77; Dir, Far Eastern Cult Inst, 77-; vis lectr, Seoul Nat Univ, Ewha Woman's Univ, 77, San Francisco Theol Sem and Grad Theol Union, 79-80, Ilift Sch Theol, 80 and Gerrett-Evangelical Theol Sem, 82; vis scholar, Univ Calif, Berkeley, 79-80. **MEMBERSHIPS** Am Acad Relig; Asn Asian Studies; Am Philos Asn; Korean Soc Relig Studies in NAm (pres, 77-). **RESEARCH** Comparative religion (Christian encounter with other religions); Korean religion (Shamanism); Chinese philosophy (I Ching). **SELECTED PUBLICATIONS** Auth, Eating + the Significance about the Lotus in the 'Pisan Cantos', Paideuma-J Devoted to Ezra Pound Scholarship, Vol 0022, 93; A Lotus of Another Color--an Unfolding of the South Asian Gay and Lesbian Experience, Amerasia J, Vol 0020, 94. **CONTACT ADDRESS** Univ of California, Berkeley, Berkeley, CA 94720. **EMAIL** jungylee@uclink4.berkeley.edu

LEE, K. SAMUEL
PERSONAL Born 12/20/1957, Korea, m, 1982, 2 children **DISCIPLINE** PASTORAL COUNSELING; PASTORAL THEOLOGY **EDUCATION** Yale Univ, MDiv, 83; Ariz State Univ, PhD, 95. **CAREER** Assoc Dean, 95-98, Asst Prof, Wesley Theol Seminary, 97-. **MEMBERSHIPS** APA; AAR, SPT. **RESEARCH** Cross-cultural psychology; pastoral care. **CONTACT ADDRESS** Wesley Theol Sem, 4500 Massachusetts Ave. NW, Washington, DC 20016. **EMAIL** RevSL@aol.com

LEE, MI KYOUNG
DISCIPLINE PHILOSOPHY **EDUCATION** Col of Columbia Univ, BA, 89; Harvard Univ, PhD, 96 **CAREER** Asst Prof 96-, Univ of IL. **HONORS AND AWARDS** Whiting Dissertation Fel, 94-5; NEH Summer Res Stipend, 99; fel Ctr for Hellenic Studies in Wash, DC, 99-00. **MEMBERSHIPS** Am Philos Assoc **RESEARCH** History of Ancient Greek and Roman Philosophy **SELECTED PUBLICATIONS** Auth, "Thinking and Perception in Plato's Theaetetus," Apeiron 32 (99): 37-54; auth, "The Secret Doctrine: Plato's Defense of Protagoras in the Theaetetus," Oxford Studies in Ancient Philosophy, (00). **CONTACT ADDRESS** Dept of Philos, Univ of Illinois, Chicago, 1423 University Hall, 601 S Morgan, Chicago, IL 60607-7114. **EMAIL** mmlee@uic.edu

LEE, MILTON C., JR.
DISCIPLINE CRIMINAL LAW & PROCEDURE, EVIDENCE, WILLS & ESTATES, TRIAL ADVOCACY **EDUCATION** Am Univ Sch Justice, BS, 82; Cathc Univ Sch Law, JD, 85. **CAREER** Assoc prof; supvr, Juvenile Justice Clin; staff atty, Publ Defender Serv, 85-90 & Dep Trial Ch, 90-93; vis assoc prof, Georgetown Univ Law Ctr, 90-91; adj fac, Georgetown Univ; Bd Dir, Law Stud in Court Prog. **MEMBERSHIPS** DC Bar Comt, Individual Rights & Criminal Law. **SELECTED PUBLICATIONS** Auth, Criminal Discovery, 98. **CONTACT ADDRESS** School of Law, Univ of District of Columbia, 4200 Connecticut Ave Northwest, Washington, DC 20008. **EMAIL** commtlee@aol.com

LEE, RICHARD
DISCIPLINE ETHICAL THEORY **EDUCATION** Stanford Univ, PhD. **CAREER** Philos, Univ Ark. **SELECTED PUBLICATIONS** Auth, "Gordon on Freedom and Introspection," Southwest Philosophical Studies VIII, no. 1, 82; auth, "Preference and Transitivity," 'analysis 44, no. 3, 84; auth, "Goodness and the Will," Values and Moral Standing: Bowling Green Studies in Applied Philosophy VIII, 86; auth, "Williams, Ought, and Logical Form," Analysis, 47, no. 3, 87; auth, "WordStar 5.5: A User's Report," Am Philosophical Asn Newsletter on Computer Use in Philosophy, 89:2, 90; auth, "What Berkeley's Notions Are," Idealistic Studies, 20, 90; auth, "Teaching Without telling: The Lessons of Plato's Meno," agora: A Journal of Interdisciplinary Discourse, 6 no. 2, 94; auth, "Let's be honest about this" relative to teaching, 99. **CONTACT ADDRESS** Dept of Philos, Univ of Arkansas, Fayetteville, 1446 Viewpoint Dr., Fayetteville, AR 72701. **EMAIL** rlee@comp.uark.edu

LEE, SANDER H.
PERSONAL Born 01/30/1951, Dallas, TX, m, 1984, 1 child **DISCIPLINE** PHILOSOPHY **EDUCATION** George Wash Univ, BA, 73; Univ Wien-Sommer Hoshsch, Dipl, 74; Georgetown Univ, MA, 76; PhD, 78; Brit Studies Prog in Philos and Criminal Justice, Inst of Anglo-Am Studies, London, 81; **CAREER** Prof, Keenes Coll, 86-; fac adv, 86-; asst prof, Howard Univ, 80-86; pres, The Intl Soc for Value Inquiry, 88-93;pres, Soc for the Philos Study of the Contemp Vis Arts, 89-; ch, Acad Overview Subcomm on the Grad Prog, 91-92; intl coord, Intl Soc for Value Inquiry, Finland and Russia, 93; ch, Philos Search Comm, 93; assoc ed, The Jour of Value Inquiry, 90-93; ed, Jour of Value Inquiry on Philos and Film, 95; ch, Admin Comm and Adv Act, 96-98; consult ed, The Jour of Value Inquiry and the Value Inquiry Bk Series, 93-; consult ed, Philos and Film, 93-; pres and Intl Cord for the Conf of Philos Soc, 96-; Chair, Dept of Communication, 01-. **HONORS AND AWARDS** Bd of Trustee's Scholar, George Wash Univ, 69-73; spec honors in philos, George Wash Univ, 73; Phi Beta Kappa, George Wash Univ 73; Univ Fel(s), Georgetown Univ, 73-76; Fel, Univt Wien-Summer Hoshsch, 74; Tchg Asstship, Georgetown Univ, 76-77; intl coord, soc for the philos study of the contemp vis arts, conf of philos soc, usa, 98; proj hum, the crisis in bosnia: political responsibility, history and cultural understanding, 95. **MEMBERSHIPS** Mem, Hist/Philos DPEC Subcomm, 95; mem, Commun Maj Comm, 93-; mem, VP, Acad Aff Search Comm, 94-95; mem, Hist/Philos DPEC Subcomm, 96; mem, Commun Search Comm, 95; mem, Commun Maj Comm, 94-;. **RESEARCH** Film and video aesthetics, phenomenology and existentialism. **SELECTED PUBLICATIONS** Co-auth, Philos Self-Study for the Prog Rev, 91-92; auth, Woody Allen's Angst: Philosophical Commentaries on his Serious Films, published by McFarland Publishing Co., 97; ed, of Inquiries into Values: The Inaugural Session of the International Society for Value Inquiry, Volume 11 in the series "Problems in Contemporary Philosophy" published by The Edwin Mellen Press, 88. **CONTACT ADDRESS** Dept of Philos, Keene State Col, 229 Main St, Keene, NH 03405-1402. **EMAIL** slee@keene.edu

LEE, STEVEN PEYTON
PERSONAL Born 05/19/1948, Schenectady, NY, m, 1981, 3 children **DISCIPLINE** PHILOSOPHY **EDUCATION** Univ Del, BA, 70, MA, 73; York Univ, Toronto, PhD(philos), 78. **CAREER** Asst prof Philos, Bowling Green State Univ, 78-80; asst prof Philos, Hobart & William Smith Col, Geneva, NY, 81-, Nat Endowment for Humanities fel, Ind Univ, 80-81; asst prof, 81-85; assoc prof to prof, 85-91, Hobart and William Smith Colls. **HONORS AND AWARDS** Faculty Research Awd, Hobart and William Smith Colleges, 91; Harvard Fell in Law and Lib Arts, 94-95, Harvard Law School. **MEMBERSHIPS** Am Philos Asn. **RESEARCH** Ethics; social philosophy; action theory. **SELECTED PUBLICATIONS** Auth, Poverty alnd Violence, Social Theory and Practice 22, no 1, Spring, 96; Democracy and the Problem of Persistent Minorities, in Larry May et al, eds Groups and Group Rights, Lawrence, KS, Univ of Kansas Press, 97. **CONTACT ADDRESS** Philosophy Dept, Hobart & William Smith Cols, Geneva, NY 14456. **EMAIL** lee@hws.edu

LEE, SUKJAE
DISCIPLINE PHILOSOPHY **EDUCATION** Seoul Natl Univ, BA, 90, MA, 92; Yale Univ, PhD program, 94- . **CAREER** Author **HONORS AND AWARDS** Korean Found for Advanced Stud Prize Fel, 94; Jacob Cooper Prize, Yale Univ, 97; tchg fel, Yale Univ, 98. **SELECTED PUBLICATIONS** Auth, Scotus on the Will: The Rational Power and The Dual Affection, Vivarium, 98. **CONTACT ADDRESS** 405 Canner St, #3, New Haven, CT 06511. **EMAIL** sukjae.lee@yale.edu

LEE, SUNGHO
PERSONAL Born 04/21/1959, South Korea, m, 1987, 2 children **DISCIPLINE** RELIGION, THEOLOGY **EDUCATION** Northwester Univ, PhD, 97. **CAREER** Pastor, United Methodist Church, Northern Ill Conf, 93- . **HONORS AND AWARDS** Am Bible Soc Awd for Excellence in Bible Studies (Old Testament), 88-89; Dr. & Mrs. Edgar Faust Preaching Awd, Garrett-Evangelical Theological Seminary, 89-90. **MEMBERSHIPS** SBL **RESEARCH** Old Testament Theol, Immigrants. **SELECTED PUBLICATIONS** Auth, A Theory and Practice of Rhetorical Criticism, Word Publ Company (Seoul, Korea), 99. **CONTACT ADDRESS** No Illinois Conf, 13530 Circle Dr., Orland Park, IL 60462. **EMAIL** sle312@megsinet.net

LEE, WONKEE "DAN"
PERSONAL Born 03/12/1963, Seoul, Korea, m, 1991, 2 children **DISCIPLINE** THEOLOGY; PHILOSOPHY **EDUCATION** Baylor Univ, BA, 86, MA, 87; Southern Baptist Theol Sem, MDiv, 90; Trinity Evangel Div School, PhD, 94. **CAREER** Asst prof pract theory, N Baptist Theol Sem, 99- . **RESEARCH** Multiculturalism, Postmodernism, Theological analysis of culture, Cross-cultural communication. **CONTACT ADDRESS** Dept Relig, No Baptist Theol Sem, 660 E Butterfield Rd, Lombard, IL 60148-5604. **EMAIL** dlee@northern.seminary.edu

LEE, YOUNG SOOK
DISCIPLINE PHILOSPHY **EDUCATION** Temple Univ, PhD, 93. **CAREER** Asst prof, Eastern Ill Univ, 94-. **MEMBERSHIPS** Int Soc of Chinese Philos, The Am Acad ofRelig, Int Inst of Field Bieng **RESEARCH** Chinese Philosophy, Indian Philsophy, Buddhism, Comparative Philosophy, Spinoza. **SELECTED PUBLICATIONS** Auth, A Comparative Study of Taoism and Spinoza on Three Ethical Questions; auth, Spirit and Beauty; auth, Tao in the Aesthetic Context. **CONTACT ADDRESS** Dept Philos, Eastern Illinois Univ, 600 Lincoln Ave, Charleston, IL 61920-3011.

LEEB, CAROLYN
PERSONAL m, 6 children **DISCIPLINE** HEBREW SCRIPTURES **EDUCATION** Mass Inst Tech, BS; San Francisco Theol Sem, MDiv, 93; Lutheran Sch Theol, ThM, 96; PhD, 98. **CAREER** Adj asst prof, McCormick Theol Sem, Lutheran Sch Theol, 98-99; vis asst prof, Valparaiso Univ, 99-. **MEMBERSHIPS** SBL. **RESEARCH** Social world of ancient Israel. **SELECTED PUBLICATIONS** Auth, Away From the Father's House: The Social Location of the Na'ar and Na'arah in Ancient Israel, Sheffield Acad (Sheffield), 00. **CONTACT ADDRESS** Dept Theology, Valparaiso Univ, 651 College Ave, Valparaiso, IN 46383-6461.

LEEDS, STEPHEN J.
PERSONAL Born 05/06/1943, New York, NY, m, 1974, 2 children **DISCIPLINE** PHILOSOPHY **EDUCATION** Harvard Univ, AB, 64; MIT, PhD, 69. **CAREER** Asst Prof, Brown Univ, 69-76; Assoc Prof to Full Prof, Univ Colo, 77-. **MEMBERSHIPS** Philos of Sci Asn. **RESEARCH** Philosophy of Science; Metaphysics; Epistemology. **CONTACT ADDRESS** Dept Philos, Univ of Colorado, Boulder, 504 Marine St, Boulder, CO 80309. **EMAIL** leeds@stripe.colorado.edu

LEFCOE, GEORGE
DISCIPLINE LAW **EDUCATION** Dartmouth Col, BA,59; Yale Univ, LLB,62. **CAREER** Florine & Ervin Yoder prof Real Estate Law, Univ Southern Calif; past pres, Los Angeles City Plan Comn; past ch, Los Angeles Co Regional Plan Comn and Commissioner of the Los Angeles Convention Ctr; ch, USC Law School's Property Forum; **RESEARCH** Urban redevelopment; affordable housing; real estate lending; financing major real estate transactions. **SELECTED PUBLICATIONS** Auth, Land Development in Crowded Places: Lessons from Abroad & Real Estate Transactions. **CONTACT ADDRESS** School of Law, Univ of So California, University Park Campus, Los Angeles, CA 90089.

LEFEBURE, LEO D.
PERSONAL Born 11/20/1952, Chicago, IL **DISCIPLINE** CHRISTIAN SYSTEMATIC THEOLOGY **EDUCATION** Univ Chicago PhD, 87; St Mary of the Lake Seminary STL, Mdiv, 78. **CAREER** Univ of St Mary of the Lake, Dean of the Eccle Fac of Theol, 92-98, Chair dept Syst Theo, 89-92, Prof Syst Theol, 94-, Assoc prof, 91-94; Assoc Visiting Prof, Fordham Univ, 99-. **HONORS AND AWARDS** ATS Jr Scholars Prog, 89; Louisville Inst, Christian Faith Life Sabb Grant, 98. **MEMBERSHIPS** AAR; CTSA; COVER; Soc Buddhist Christ Stud. **RESEARCH** Buddhist Christian Dialogue; revelation; interreligious dialogue; Christology **SELECTED PUBLICATIONS** The Budda and the Christ: Explor in Budd-Christ Dialo, Maryknoll NY, Orbis Books, 93; Life Transformed: Meditations on the Christian Scriptures in Light of Buddhist Perspectives, Chicago, ACTA pub, 89; Toward a Contemporary Wisdom Christology: A Study of Karl Rahmer and Norman Pittenger, Lanham MD, Univ Press Am, 88; Christianity and Other Religions in the Year 1000, forthcoming, Chicago Studies 37, 98; Beyond Scapegoating: A Conversation with Rene Girard and Ewert Cousins, The Christian Century 115/11, 98; 200 Years in Tibet: Glimpses of Fact and Film, The Christian Century, 115/8, 98; Awakening and Grace: Rel Ident in the Thought of Masao Abe and Karl Rahner, Cross Currents 47/4, 98; Report on Hindu-Catholic Dialogue, Pro Dialogo 9, 98; Approaches to Revelation and Theology, Chicago Studies, 36/2, 97; auth, Revelations, the Religious, and Violence, Mary Knoll, NY: Orbis Books, 00. **CONTACT ADDRESS** Theology Dept, Fordham Univ, 441 E Fordham Rd, Bronx, NY 10458. **EMAIL** lefebure@fordham.edu

LEFTOW, BRIAN
PERSONAL Born 09/25/1956, Brooklyn, NY, m, 1980 **DISCIPLINE** PHILOSOPHY **EDUCATION** Grove City Col, BA, 77; Yale, MA, 78; MPhilos, 81; PhD, 84. **CAREER** Vis asst prof, Reed Col, 84-85; Fordham Univ, 85-; assoc prof to prof, Fordham Univ, 92-. **HONORS AND AWARDS** Distinguished Scholar Fel, Univ Notre Dame, 92-93; Evangel Scholars' Grant, 91-92. **MEMBERSHIPS** Am Philos Asn; Soc of Christian Philos; Soc for Medieval and Renaissance in Philos; Philos of Time Soc. **RESEARCH** Philosophical Theology; Analytic Metaphysics; Medieval Philosphy. **SELECTED PUBLICATIONS** Auth, Anselm on the Necessity of the Incarnation, Rel Studies, 95; Can Philosphy Argue God's Existence?, The Rationality of Belief and the Plurality of Faith, 95; Anselm on the Beauty of the Incarnation, The Modern Schoolman, 95; Anselm on Cost of Salvation, Medieval Philos and Theol, 97; Divine Action and Embodiment, Proceedings of the ACPA, 97; Eternity, The Cambridge Companion to Philos of Rel, 97; Omnipresence; Necessary Being; Divine Simplicity; Concepts of God, The Encycl of Philos, 98; A God Beyond Space and Time, Theos, Antropos, Christos, 98; The Eternal Present, god and Time, 99; Anti Social Trinitarianism, The Trinity, 99; Aquinas on the Infinite, Preceedings of the XX World Congress of Philos, forthcoming; Divine Ideas, forthcoming; auth, Aquinas on Metaphysics, forthcoming. **CONTACT ADDRESS** 66 Wood Ave, Ardsley, NY 10502. **EMAIL** leftow@murray.fordham.edu

LEHMANN, SCOTT K.
PERSONAL Born 11/28/1942, Ancon, Canal Zone, m, 1964, 1 child **DISCIPLINE** PHILOSOPHY **EDUCATION** Swarthmore Col, BA, 64; Univ Chicago, PhD, 70. **CAREER** From Asst Prof to Assoc Prof, Univ Conn, 70-. **MEMBERSHIPS** Asn for Symbolic Logic. **RESEARCH** Free logic, environmental ethics and poetry. **SELECTED PUBLICATIONS** Auth, "Strict Frefean Free Logic," J Philos Logic 23 (94): 307-336; auth, Privatizing Public Lands, Oxford UP, 95. **CONTACT ADDRESS** Dept Philos, Univ of Connecticut, Storrs, 344 Mansfield Rd, Storrs, CT 06269-2054. **EMAIL** lehmann@uconnvm.uconn.edu

LEHRBERGER, JAMES
PERSONAL Born 12/08/1943, San Francisco, CA, s **DISCIPLINE** MEDIEVAL PHILOSOPHY, PHILOSOPHY OF RELIGION **EDUCATION** Univ SF, BA; Univ Dallas, MA, PhD; further advan stud, S Methodist Univ; Anselmianum Gregoriana, Augustinianum, Rome. **CAREER** Dept Philos, Univ Dallas; Guest Prof at Regina Apostorum, Rome **MEMBERSHIPS** Am Cath Phil Assoc; Am Acad of Relig; Nat Assoc of Scholars; Univ Fac for Life. **RESEARCH** Thomas Aquinas; Leo Strauss; Frederick Nietzsche; reason and revelation. **SELECTED PUBLICATIONS** Auth, Intelligo ut Cream: St. Augustine's Confessions, The Thomist, 88; auth, Crime Without Punishment: Thomistic Natural Law and the Problem of Sanctions, Law and Philos: The Practice of Theory, Ohio State Univ Press, 92; coed, Saints, Sovereigns, and Scholars: Studies in Honor of Frederick D. Wilhelmsen, Peter Lang, 93; Deontology, Teleology,

and Aquinas' Virtue Ethic in Saints, Sovereigns, and Scholars, Peter Lang, 93; Dialectical and Demonstrative Arguments in Aristotle's Account of the Eternal Cosmos, il cannocchiale, rivista di studi filosofici, 96; auth, "Christendom's Troubadour: Frederick D. Wilhelmsen," The Intercollegiate Review, (97); auth, "The Anthropology of Aquinas' De Ente et Essentia," Review of Metaphysics, 98. **CONTACT ADDRESS** Dept of Philos, Univ of Dallas, 1845 E Northgate Dr, Irving, TX 75062. **EMAIL** frjames@acad.udallas.edu

LEIBOWITZ, CONSTANCE
PERSONAL Born New York, NY **DISCIPLINE** PHILOSOPHY **EDUCATION** New York Univ, BA, 60, MA, 64, PhD, 73. **CAREER** Asst prof, 67-74, Assoc Prof Philos, Univ NH, 74-85, prof philos, Plymouth State Col Univ NH, Chmn, Philos Dept, 83. **HONORS AND AWARDS** Univ Hons Scholar, New York Univ, 60 & 74. **MEMBERSHIPS** Am Philos Asn; Am Asn Philos Tchr(s), Northern New England Philos Asn. **RESEARCH** Ethics, death, law. **CONTACT ADDRESS** Dept of Philos, Plymouth State Col of the Univ System of New Hampshire, 15 Holderness Rd, Plymouth, NH 03264-1600. **EMAIL** Constancel@psc.plymouth.edu

LEIBOWITZ, FLORA L.
PERSONAL Born 01/22/1955 **DISCIPLINE** PHILOSOPHY **EDUCATION** State Univ NY at Stony Brook, BA; Johns Hopkins Univ, MA, 73; PhD, 79. **CAREER** From asst prof to prof, Ore State Univ, 77-; dir of grad studies, Ore State Univ, 94-. **HONORS AND AWARDS** Phi Kappa Phi; L. L. Stewart Fac Development Awd. **MEMBERSHIPS** Am Philos Asn, Am Soc for Aesthetics, British Soc for Aesthetics. **RESEARCH** Hist of Aesthetics, Contemporary Aesthetic Theory, Aesthetics of Film and Mass Art. **SELECTED PUBLICATIONS** Auth, "Apt Feelings, or Why Women's Films Aren't Turial," in Post-Theory, eds. David Bond-Well and Noel Carroll (WI: Univ Wis Pr, 96); auth, "Pianists in the Movies," Philos and Lit 21.2 (97); auth, "Theories of Expression and the Movies," in Film Theory and Philosophy, eds. Murry M. Smith and Richard Allen (Oxford Univ Pr, 97). **CONTACT ADDRESS** Dept Philos, Oregon State Univ, 208 Hovland Hall, Corvallis, OR 97331-8543. **EMAIL** fleibowitz@orst.edu

LEIES, JOHN A.
PERSONAL Born 04/24/1926, Chicago, IL, s **DISCIPLINE** THEOLOGY **EDUCATION** Univ Dayton, BS, 48; Univ Fribourg, STB, 54; STL, 56; STD, 59. **CAREER** Fac, St Mary's Univ, 74-. **HONORS AND AWARDS** Fel, Nat Cath Bioethics Ctr; Distinguished Fac of the Year Awd, St Mary's Univ, 98, 00. **MEMBERSHIPS** Fel of Cath Scholars, Univ Fac for Life, Nat Cath Med Soc. **RESEARCH** Biomedical ethics, foundation moral theology. **SELECTED PUBLICATIONS** Auth, Religion and Sanctity According to St Thomas Aquinas; auth, Handbook on Critical Sexual Issues; auth, Handbook on Critical Life Issues; auth, Human Sexuality and Personhood. **CONTACT ADDRESS** Dept Theol, St. Mary's Univ of San Antonio, 1 Camino Santa Maria St, San Antonio, TX 78228-5433. **EMAIL** theojohn@stmarytx.edu

LEIGHTON, PAUL S.
DISCIPLINE SOCIOLOGY, LEGAL STUDIES **EDUCATION** State Univ NY at Albany, BA, 86; Am Univ, MS, 90; PhD, 95. **CAREER** Asst Prof, Univ of San Francisco, 95-96; Adj Fac/Lectr, The Am Univ, 90-94, 96; Asst Prof, Eastern Mich Univ, 97-. **MEMBERSHIPS** Am Soc of Criminol, Acad of Criminal Justice Sci. **RESEARCH** Criminology, Penology, prison and social control, White collar, corporate and crimes of domination, Violence, hate, prejudice and genocide, Theory and public policy, Gender and race. **SELECTED PUBLICATIONS** Auth, "Industrialized Social Control," Peace Rev: A Transnational Quart 7-3/4 (Dec 95); coauth, "Black Genocide? Prelimanry Thoughts on the Plight of America's Poor Black Men," J of African Am Men 1-2 (95); coauth, "American Genocide?: The Destruction of the Black Underclass," in Collective Violence: Harmful Behavior in Groups and Government, ed. Craig Summers and Erik Markusen (Rowman & Littlefield, 99); auth, "Television Execution, Primetime 'Live'," The Justice Prof 12-2 (99): auth, "Migrant Labor in the Ivory Toweer: The Crossroads and Crapshoots of a New Professor," in Inside Jobs: A Realistic Guide to Criminal Justice Careers for College Graduates, ed. Stuart Henry, 2nd ed (Sheffield, WI: Salem, 00); coauth, Class, Race, Gender: The Social Realities of Justice in America, Roxbury, 00; co-ed, Criminal Justice Ethics and Morality, Prentice-Hall, 01. **CONTACT ADDRESS** Dept Sociol and Anthrop, Eastern Michigan Univ, 712 Pray Harrold, Ypsilanti, MI 48197. **EMAIL** SOC_Leighton@online.emich.edu

LEIGHTON, STEPHEN
DISCIPLINE PHILOSOPHY **EDUCATION** Univ Alberta, BA; MA; Univ Tex Austin, PhD. **CAREER** Dept Philos, Queen's Univ **RESEARCH** Ancient philosophy; philosophical psychology; ethics. **SELECTED PUBLICATIONS** Auth, Aristotle and the Emotions, Garland, 95; "What We Love," Australasian J Philos, 93; "Relativizing Moral Excellence in Aristotle," Apeiron, 92; "On Feeling Angry or Elated," J Philos, 88. **CONTACT ADDRESS** Philos Dept, Queen's Univ at Kingston, Kingston, ON, Canada K7L 3N6. **EMAIL** leighton@post.queensu.ca

LEIGHTON, TAIGEN DANIEL
PERSONAL Born 01/23/1950, Baltimore, MD, d **DISCIPLINE** EAST ASIAN BUDDHISM **EDUCATION** Columbia Col, BA, 77; Calif Inst Integral Studs, MA, 88; Berkeley Grad Theol U, PhD. **CAREER** Adj prof, John F. Kennedy Univ, Oriada, Calif, 93; adj prof, Univ San Francisco, 96; adj prof, Calif Inst Integral Stud, 96-99; adj prof, Inst Buddhist Stud, Berkeley Grad Theol Union, 94-00. **HONORS AND AWARDS** Pres Scholar, Grad Theol Union. **MEMBERSHIPS** Am Acad Rel. **RESEARCH** Soto Zen; Dogen; East Asian Mahayana praxis and its contemporary implications; interfaith dialogue. **SELECTED PUBLICATIONS** Ed, transl, Cultivating the Empty Field: The Silent Illumination of Zen Master Hongzhi, N Point Press, 91, 00; Review of The Book of Serenity, The Eastern Buddhist, 91; ed, transl, Dogen's Pure Standards for the Zen Community: A Translation of 'Eihei Shingi,' State Univ of NY Press, 96; Being Time Through Deep Time, Tricycle, 96; Now is the Past of the Future, Shambhala Sun, 96; Comparative Review of Transmission of Light and The Record of Transmitting the Light, The E Buddhist, 97; ed, transl, The Wholehearted Way: A Translation of Eihei Dogen's Bendowa and Commentary by Kosho Uchiyama Roshi, Tuttle, 97; Bodhisattva Archetypes: Classic Buddhist Guides to Awakening and their Modern Expression, Penguin, 98; Masters of Spirit and Words, Dogen and Dylan, Kyoto Jour, 98; auth, Facing the Millenial Daze, Turning Weel, 99. **CONTACT ADDRESS** 94 Laurel Dr, Fairfax, CA 94930. **EMAIL** taigen@sirius.com

LEIMAN, SID ZALMAN
PERSONAL Born 11/03/1941, New York, NY **DISCIPLINE** HISTORY, RELIGION **EDUCATION** Brooklyn Col, BA, 64; Mirrer Yeshivah, BRE, 64; Univ Pa, PhD(Orient studies), 70. **CAREER** Lectr Jewish hist and lit, Yale Univ, 68-70, from asst prof to assoc prof relig studies, 70-78; prof Jewish hist and dean, Vervard Revel Grad Sch, Yeshiva Univ, 78-81; Prof and Chmn Dept Judaic Studies, Brooklyn Col, 81-, Nat Found Jewish Cult res grant, 67-68; Morse fel, Yale Univ, 71-72; vis scholar Jewish law and ethics, Kennedy Inst Ethics, Georgetown Univ, 77-78; Mem Found Jewish Cult res grant, 81-82. **MEMBERSHIPS** Am Schs Orient Res; Soc Bibl Lit; Am Acad Relig; Asn Jewish Studies; Am Jewish Hist Soc. **RESEARCH** Jewish history; Jewish ethics; Biblical studies. **SELECTED PUBLICATIONS** Auth, Horowitz, Jacob on the Study of Scripture--From the Pages of 'Tradition', Tradition-J Orthodox Jewish Thought, Vol 0027, 92; From the Pages of Tradition--Friedman, David of Karlin--the Ban on Secular Study in Jerusalem, Tradition-J Orthodox Jewish Thought, Vol 0026, 92; Dwarfs on the Shoulders of Giants + the Study of Torah Despite a Theology of Generational Regression, Tradition-J Orthodox Jewish Thought, Vol 0027, 93; Carlebach, Joseph, Wuerzburg and Jerusalem--a Conversation Between Bamberger, Seligmann, Baer and Salant, Shmuel, Tradition-J Orthodox Jewish Thought, Vol 0028, 94; Ha Kohen Kook, Abraham, Isaac--Invocation at the Inauguration of the Hebrew-University--Excerpt From the Pages of Tradition April-1, 1925, Tradition-J Orthodox Jewish Thought, Vol 0029, 94; Rabbi Schwab,Shimon + Respone on the Torah and Derekh-Eretz Movement Concerning Jewish Education--a Letter Regarding the Frankfurt Approach--From the Pages of 'Tradition', Tradition-J Orthodox Jewish Thought, Vol 0031, 97. **CONTACT ADDRESS** Dept of Judaic Studies, Brooklyn Col, CUNY, Brooklyn, NY 11367.

LEISER, BURTON
PERSONAL Born 12/12/1930, Denver, CO, m, 1984, 3 children **DISCIPLINE** PHILOSOPHY **EDUCATION** Univ of Chicago, BA, 51; Yeshiva Univ, MHL, 56; Brown Univ, PhD, 68; Drake Univ, JD, 81. **CAREER** Assoc prof, SU NY Col at Buffalo, 65-69; assoc prof, Sir George Univ, 69-72; prof, Drake Univ, 72-83; prof & adjunct prof, Pace Univ, 83-. **MEMBERSHIPS** APA, Amintaphil, Int Soc fpr Philos & Law **RESEARCH** Ethics, legal philosophy. **CONTACT ADDRESS** Dept Relig & Philos, Pace Univ, Pleasantville, 105 Dow Hall, Pleasantville, NY 10570. **EMAIL** bleiser@pace.edu

LEITH, JOHN HADDON
PERSONAL Born 09/10/1919, Due West, SC, m, 1943, 2 children **DISCIPLINE** THEOLOGY **EDUCATION** Erskine Col, AB, 40; Columbia Theol Sem, BD, 43; Vanderbilt Univ, MA, 46; Yale Univ, PhD, 49. **CAREER** Minister, Second Presby Church, Nashville, Tenn, 44-46 and First Presby Church, Auburn, Ala, 48-59; Prof Hist Theol, Union Theol Sem, VA, 59-, Lectr relig, Auburn Univ, 49-58; vis prof, Columbia Theol Sem, 55-57 and Univ Edinburgh, 74; Folger Shakespeare Libr fel, 65. **HONORS AND AWARDS** DD, Erskine Col, 72 and Davidson Col, 78. **RESEARCH** History of theology; reformation. **SELECTED PUBLICATIONS** Auth, Luther and Calvin on Secular Authority, 16TH Century J, Vol 0024, 93; Christian Confessions--a Historical Introduction, Theol Today, Vol 0054, 97. **CONTACT ADDRESS** Union Theol Sem, Virginia, 3401 Brook Rd, Richmond, VA 23227.

LEITICH, KEITH A.
PERSONAL Born 12/24/1965, Chicago, IL **DISCIPLINE** POLITICAL SCIENCE **EDUCATION** Iowa State Univ, BA, 90; Ark State Univ, MA, 94; EdS, 95; Wash State Univ, MA, 01. **CAREER** Tutor, Seattle Cent Cmty Col, 00-. **HONORS AND AWARDS** Fel, Korea Found, 95. **RESEARCH** Asian Politics; Central Asia; Comparative Politics. **SELECTED PUBLICATIONS** Auth, "The Future of Korean community Colleges: Problems and Possibilities," Intl Educ Forum, 97; auth, "At Issue: Religion and the community college," Contemporary Education, 97; auth, "Sexual Harassment in Higher Education," Education, 99; auth, "Korea and Koreans," in World War II in the Pacific: An encyclopedia, 00; auth, "The Korean Peninsula: A Fifty-Year Struggle for Peace and Reconciliation," in History Behind the Headlines, 00. **CONTACT ADDRESS** Dept Basic Studies, Seattle Central Comm Col, PO Box 20322, Seattle, WA 98102-1322. **EMAIL** asian_education@hotmail.com

LELAND, CHARLES WALLACE
PERSONAL Born 03/22/1928, Culver, IN **DISCIPLINE** ENGLISH LITERATURE, SCANDANAVIAN DRAMA **EDUCATION** Oberlin Col, AB, 50; Oxford Univ, BA, 53, MA, 56; Univ Toronto, STB, 58. **CAREER** Lectr English, 59-62, asst prof, 62-69, Assoc Prof English, Univ Toronto, 69-, Roman Cath priest, Congregation of St Basil, 59-. **MEMBERSHIPS** Asn Advan Scand Studies Can; Ibsen Soc Am; Soc Advan Scand Study. **RESEARCH** Ibsen; Strindberg; literature of the English Renaissance. **SELECTED PUBLICATIONS** Auth, Catiline and the Burial Mound, Mod Drama, Vol 0038, 95. **CONTACT ADDRESS** St. Michael's Col, Toronto, ON, Canada M5S 1J4.

LELWICA, MICHELLE M.
PERSONAL Born 03/13/1964, San Francisco, CA, m, 2000, 1 child **DISCIPLINE** RELIGIOUS STUDIES; WOMEN'S STUDIES **EDUCATION** Col of St. Benedict, BA, 86; Harvard Divinity School, MTS, 89, ThD, 96. **CAREER** Asst prof of religious studies & women's studies, St Mary's Col, Calif. **MEMBERSHIPS** AAR **RESEARCH** Women and religion; Religion and culture; Religion and the body. **SELECTED PUBLICATIONS** Auth, Starring for Salvation: The Spiritual Dimensions of Eating Problems Among American Girls and Women, (Oxford Univ Press, 99); Nudity, Encyclo of Women & World Relig, Macmillan Publ, 98; Losing Their Way to Salvation: Women, Weight-Loss, and the Salvation Myth of Culture Life, Religion and Popular Culture in America, Univ Calif Press, 98; From Superstition, to Enlightenment, to the Race for Pure Consciousness: Anti-Religious Currents in Popular and Academic Feminist Discourse, Jour Feminist Studies Relig, 98; auth, "Liberating Learning and Deepening Understanding: Reflections on Feminist Pedagogy--as a Student, as a teacher" in Journal of Women and Religion, Vol 17, (99): 77-84. **CONTACT ADDRESS** 2536 College Ave., #9B, Berkeley, CA 94704. **EMAIL** mlelwica@stmarys-ca.edu

LEMIEUX, LUCIEN
PERSONAL Born 04/30/1934, St-Remi, PQ, Canada **DISCIPLINE** HISTORY, RELIGION **EDUCATION** St-Jean Col, BA, 54; Univ Montreal, LTh, 58; Gregorian Univ, DHist, 65. **CAREER** Prof hist, St-Jean Col, 65-68; asst prof church hist, Univ Montreal, 67-73, Assoc Prof, 73-79. Mem, Centre Hist Relig Can, 67-. **HONORS AND AWARDS** Prix Litteraire Du Quebec, 68. **MEMBERSHIPS** Can Soc Theol. **RESEARCH** Religious history of citizens of Quebec, 1760-1840. **SELECTED PUBLICATIONS** Auth, Leger, Paul, Emile--Evolution of his Philosophy, 1950-1967, Revue D Histoire De L Amerique Francaise, Vol 0048, 95; The Seminaire-De-Quebec From 1800 to 1850, Revue D Histoire De L Amerique Francaise, Vol 0049, 96. **CONTACT ADDRESS** Dept of Theol, Univ of Montreal, Montreal, QC, Canada H3C 3J7.

LEMKE, WERNER ERICH
PERSONAL Born 01/31/1933, Berlin, Germany, m, 1959, 3 children **DISCIPLINE** OLD TESTAMENT, ANCIENT HISTORY **EDUCATION** Northwestern Univ, BA, 56; NPark Theol Sem, BD, 59; Harvard Univ, ThD(Old Testament), 64. **CAREER** Asst prof Bibl interpretation & lectr ancient hist, NPark Col & Theol Sem, 63-66; assoc prof, 66-69, actg dean, 73-74, Prof Old Testament Interpretation, Colgate Rochester Divinity Sch, 69-, Archaeol fel, Hebrew Union Col, Jerusalem, 69-70; prof, W F Albright Inst Archaeol Res Jerusalem, 72-73; vis prof in relig studies, Univ Rochester, 70, 74, 77. **MEMBERSHIPS** Colloquium Old Testament Res (secy-treas, 69-); Soc Bibl Lit; Am Schs Orient Res. **RESEARCH** Hebrew; Old Testament interpretation; ancient Near Eastern languages, literatures and history. **SELECTED PUBLICATIONS** Auth, The snyoptic problem in the chronicler's history, Harvard Theol Rev, 10/65; Nebuchadrezzar, my servant, Cath Bibl Quart, 1/66; Magnalia Dei: The Mighty Acts of God, Essays on the Bible and Archaeology presented to G Ernest Wright, Doubleday, 76; The way of obedience: I Kings 13 and the structure of the Deuteronomistic history, In: Magnalia Dei, Doubleday, 76; The near and distant God, J Bibl Lit, 12/81; Revelation through history in recent Biblical theology, Interpretation, 1/82; auth, "Theology, OT" in Anchor Bible Dictionary, Doubleday, 92; auth, "The Harper Collins Study Bible," Harper Collins, 93. **CONTACT ADDRESS** Colgate Rochester Divinity Sch/Bexley Hall/Crozer Theol Sem, 1100 S Goodman St, Rochester, NY 14620-2530. **EMAIL** wlemke@crds.edu

LEMONCHECK, LINDA
PERSONAL Born 07/15/1954, Los Angeles, CA, m, 1984 **DISCIPLINE** PHILOSOPHY; FEMINIST THEORY **EDUCATION** Occidental Col, AB, 76; UCLA, MA, PhD, 81. **CAREER** Lctr, Occidental Col, 78-81, UCLA, 81-83, Calif State Univ, LongBeach, 81-83, 90-92, 94-96, USC 96 & 98-99. **HONORS AND AWARDS** Phi Beta Kappa; Women's Studies Awd, Calif State Univ, Long Beach, 93; Editor, Oxford Univ Press, 98-. **MEMBERSHIPS** Am Philos Asn; Soc Women Philos; Nat Coun Res Women. **RESEARCH** Feminist applied ethics, specifically womens sexual and reproductive issues: promiscuity, sexual preference and deviance, pornography and prostitution, sexual harassment and sexual violence, new reproductive technologies. **SELECTED PUBLICATIONS** Auth, Dehumanizing Women: Treating Persons as Sex Objects, Rowman & Littlefield, 85; auth, Loose Women. Lecherous Men: A Feminist Philosophy of Sex, Oxford Univ Press, 97; coauth, Sexual Harassment: A Debate, Rowman & Littlefield, 97; coedi, Sexual Harassment: Issues and Answers, Oxford Univ Pr, forthcoming. **CONTACT ADDRESS** 128 6th St., Seal Beach, CA 90740. **EMAIL** llemon@msn.com

LEMOS, JOHN P.
PERSONAL Born 10/02/1963, Miami, FL, m, 1993, 2 children **DISCIPLINE** PHILOSOPHY **EDUCATION** Univ of the South, BA, 85; Duke Univ, PhD, 93. **CAREER** Vis instr, Univ NC, 92-93; asst prof, Coe Col, 93-. **RESEARCH** Ethical theory, Philosophy of Religion, Darwinism **SELECTED PUBLICATIONS** Auth, "A Defense of Darwinian Accounts of Morality," Philosophy of the social Sciences, (forthcoming); auth, "Evolution and Ethical Skepticism: Reflections on Ruse's Meta-Ethics," (forthcoming); auth, "The Problems with Emotivism: Reflections on Some MacIntyrean Arguments," Journal of Philosophical Research, 00; auth, "Bridging the Is/Ought Gap with Evolutionary Biology: Is This a Bridge Too Far?," The Southern Journal of Philosophy, (99): 559-577; auth, "An Agnostic Defense of Obligatory Prayer," Sophia: An International Journal for Philosophical Theology, (98): 70-87; auth, "Virtue, Happiness, and Intelligibility," Journal of Philosophical Research, (97): 307-320; auth, "Moral Crutches and Nazi Theists: A Defense of And Reservations About Undertaking Theism," Southwest Philosophy Review, (97): 147-154. **CONTACT ADDRESS** Dept Relig & Philos, Coe Col, 1220 1st Ave NE, Cedar Rapids, IA 52402-5008. **EMAIL** jlemos@coe.edu

LEMOS, RAMON M.
PERSONAL Born 07/07/1927, Mobile, AL, m, 1994, 4 children **DISCIPLINE** PHILOSOPHY **EDUCATION** Univ Alabama, BA, 51; Duke Univ, MA, 53, PhD, 55. **CAREER** Instr, asst prof, assoc prof, prof, philos, Univ Miami, 56-99, chamn, 71-84, Prof Emeritus, 99. **HONORS AND AWARDS** Phi Beta Kappa; Fulbright Scholar, 55-56; Outstanding Teacher, 68; Distinguished Fac Scholar, 97. **MEMBERSHIPS** APA; Southern Soc for Philos and Psychol. **RESEARCH** Metaphysics; philosophy of mind, moral and political; philosophical theology; history of philosophy. **SELECTED PUBLICATIONS** Auth, Experience, Mind, and Value: Philosophical Essays, Brill, 69; auth, Rousseau's Political Philosophy: An Exposition and Interpretation, Georgia, 77; auth, Hobbes and Locke: Power and Consent, Georgia, 78; auth, Rights, Goods, and Democracy, Delaware, 86; auth, Metaphysical Investigations, Associated Univ Presses, 88; auth, The Nature of Value: Axiological Investigations, Florida, 95. **CONTACT ADDRESS** Dept of Philosophy, Univ of Miami, Coral Gables, FL 33124.

LEMPERT, RICHARD O.
PERSONAL Born 06/02/1942, Hartford, CT, d, 1 child **DISCIPLINE** LAW **EDUCATION** Oberlin Col, AB, 64; Univ Mich, JD, 68; PhD, 72. **CAREER** Asst, assoc, full, and Francis A. Allen Collegiate Prof of Law, Univ Mich, 68-, prof of Sociol, 85-. **HONORS AND AWARDS** Phi Beta Kappa; mem, Am Acad of Arts and Scis; Harry Kalvin Prize, Law and Soc Asn. **MEMBERSHIPS** Law and Soc Asn, Am Social Asn. **RESEARCH** Sociology of law, evidence. **SELECTED PUBLICATIONS** Coauth, A Modern Approach to Evidence, 3rd ed; coauth, An Introduction to Law and Social Science; auth, "After the DNA Wars, Skirmishes with NRC II," Jurimetars Journal; coauth, "Cultural Discrimination: Sar. Before a Public Housing Eviction Board," Am Sociol Rev; coauth, "The Riviera Runs Through Law School: Michigan Minority Graduates in Practice," Law and Soc Inquiry. **CONTACT ADDRESS** Dept Sociol, Univ of Michigan, Ann Arbor, 500 S State St, Ann Arbor, MI 48109. **EMAIL** ROL25@hotmail.com

LENAGHAN, MICHAEL J.
PERSONAL Born Oak Park, IL, m, 1982 **DISCIPLINE** HISTORY, GOVERNMENT **EDUCATION** Georgetown Univ, BS, 65; Grad Sch Govt, MA, 69; Va Polytech Inst & State Univ, CAGS, 75; Va Polytech Inst & State Univ, EdD, 78. **CAREER** Intern, Am Red Cross, 65-66; Exec Dir, Pax Romana Secretariat for N Am, 66-68; Dir, Nat Asn of Partners of the Americas, 70-71; Assoc Adminr, Univ DC, 71-75; Sen Professional Staff, Am Red Cross, 75-86; Pres, The Lenaghan Group, 86-88; Pres, Am Humanics Found, 88-91; Fac, Miami-Dade Community Col, 92-. **HONORS AND AWARDS** Kiwanas DC Urban Fel, 73-78; Fel, Georgetown Univ, 95-96; Educ Innovator of the Year, 96; Fel, Southern Methodist Univ, 97; Educ of the Year, Univ Mich, 98; Fel, Kettering Found, 95-00. **MEMBERSHIPS** FPSA, WFS, APSA, S Fla Cult Coalition, NCCA. **RESEARCH** Application of "multiple intelligences," theory to college student course success, negotiating styles in non-violent conflict resolution, American political economy, inter-cultural communication patterns as a barrier to consensus decision-making. **SELECTED PUBLICATIONS** Coauth, Give the Gang Our Best, Marknoll Publ (Ossining, NY), 65; coauth, Human Rights and the Liberation of Man, Notre Dame Pr (South Bend, IN), 68; auth, The Social Environment: An Anthology, Prentice-Hall Publ, 96; coauth, The Social Environment, Forbes Publ, 00. **CONTACT ADDRESS** Dept Hist & Govt, Miami-Dade Comm Col, 11380 NW 27th Ave, Miami, FL 33167-3418.

LENNON, THOMAS M.
DISCIPLINE PHILOSOPHY **EDUCATION** Manhattan Col, BA; Ohio State Univ, PhD. **RESEARCH** Early modern philosophy. **SELECTED PUBLICATIONS** Auth, The Battle of the Gods and Giants: The Legacies of Descartes and Gasendi 1655-1715, Princeton, 93; co-auth, Bibliographia Malebranchiana: A Critical Guide to the Malebranche Literature into 1989, 92; The Cartesian Empiricism of Francois Bayle, Garland, 92. **CONTACT ADDRESS** Dept of Philosophy, Univ of Western Ontario, London, ON, Canada N6A 5B8. **EMAIL** tlennon@julian.uwo.ca

LENNOX, JAMES GORDON
PERSONAL Born 01/11/1948, Toronto, ON, Canada, m, 1969, 1 child **DISCIPLINE** ANCIENT PHILOSOPHY, PHILOSOPHY OF BIOLOGY **EDUCATION** York Univ, BA(hons), 71; Univ Toronto, MA, 73, PhD(philos and Greek), 78. **CAREER** Asst Prof Hist and Philos Sci, Univ Pittsburgh, 77-83; assoc prof, 83-92; prof, 92-; director, center for philosophy of science, 97-. **HONORS AND AWARDS** Fel, Center for Hellenic Studies, 83-84; fel, Clare Hull, Cambridge Univ, 87. **MEMBERSHIPS** Am Philos Asn; Soc Ancient Greek Philos; Philos Sci Asn; His Sci Soc. **RESEARCH** Ancient Greek metaphysics and science; medical ethics; history and philosophy of biology. **SELECTED PUBLICATIONS** Auth, "Robert Boyle's Defense of Teleological Inference in Experimental Science," Isis 74 (83): 38-52; auth, "Darwin Was a Telelogist," Biology and Philos (93); auth, "Darwinian Thought Experiments: A Funcition for Just So Stories," in Thought Experiments in Science and Philosophy, ed. Tamara Horowitz and Gerald Massey (Savage, MD, 91), 173-195; auth, "Natural-Selection and the Struggle for Existence," Stud in Hist and Philos of Sci (94); auth, "Health as an Objective Value," The Journal of Medicine and Philosophy 20 (95): 499-511; auth, "Aristotle's Biological Development: The Balme Hypothesis," in Aristotle's Philosophical Development, ed. W. Wians (Savage, MD, 96); auth, "Greek Science," in The Encyclopedia of Classical Philosophy, ed. Donald Zeyl (Princeton, 97), 476-484; auth, "Aristotle on the Biological Roots of Human Virtue," in Biology and the Foundations of Ethics, ed. Jane Maienschein and Michael Ruse (Cambridge, 99); auth, "The Place of Mankind in Aristotle's Zoology," Philosophical Topics 27(1) (99): 1-16; auth, Aristotle's Philosophy of Biology: Studies in the Origins of Life Science, Cambridge Univ Press (Cambridge), 00. **CONTACT ADDRESS** Dept of Hist and Philos of Sci, Univ of Pittsburgh, 1017 Cathedral/Learn, Pittsburgh, PA 15260-0001. **EMAIL** jglennox@pitt.edu

LENNOX, STEPHEN J.
PERSONAL Born 12/17/1957, Philadelphia, PA, m, 1982, 2 children **DISCIPLINE** THEOLOGY **EDUCATION** Drew Univ, PhD, 92. **CAREER** Asst prof to assoc prof to abstractor and assoc ed to dir, 94-. **HONORS AND AWARDS** Who's Who in Am Educ, 95; Doctoral Dissertation Awd, 92; Outstanding Young Man of Am. **MEMBERSHIPS** Soc Bibl Lit; Wesleyan Theolog Society. **RESEARCH** Biblical Interpretation **SELECTED PUBLICATIONS** Auth, art, The Eschatology of George D. Watson, 94; auth, Commentary on Proverbs, 98; auth, art, Biblical Interpretation in the American Holiness Movement, 98. **CONTACT ADDRESS** Indiana Wesleyan Univ, 4201 S Washington St, Marion, IN 46953. **EMAIL** slennox@indwes.edu

LENTNER, HOWARD H.
PERSONAL Born 09/08/1931, Detroit, MI, d, 3 children **DISCIPLINE** POLITICAL SCIENCE **EDUCATION** Miami Univ, BS, 58; Syracuse Univ, MA, 59, PhD, 64. **CAREER** Instr, 62-63, Asst Prof, 63-68, Western Reserve Univ; Assoc Prof, McMaster Univ, 68-72; Assoc Prof, 73-76, Prof Polit Sci, 77-, Baruch Col and the Graduate School of CUNY. **MEMBERSHIPS** Am Polit Sci Asn; Int Polit Sci Asn; Int Stud Asn; NE Polit Sci Asn; Acad Coun on the UN System. **RESEARCH** International politics; comparative politics; globalization; East Asian politics. **SELECTED PUBLICATIONS** Auth, Foreign Policy Analysis: A Comparitive and Conceptual Aproch, Merrill Pub Co, 74; auth, "The Role of the United States in the Maintenance of Peace and Security in East Asia," Peace Beyond the East-West Conflict: Northeast Asian Security and World Peace in the 1990's Kyung Hee Univ Press, (90): 47-69; auth, State Formation in Central America: The Struggle for Autonomy, Development, and Democracy, Greenwood Pub Co, 93; auth, International Politics: Theory and Practice, West Publishing Co, 97; auth, Realism and Asian Studies, Asian Stud in Am, 10, 3, 7, 98; auth, "Implications of the Economic Crisis for East Asian Foreign Policies," Journal of East Asian Affairs XIII, (99): 1-32; auth, "Globalization and Power," Rethinking Globalizations: From Corporate Transnationalism to Local Interventions, Macmillan Press, (00): 56-72; auth, "Politics, Power, and States in Globalization," Power in Contemporary Politics: Theories, Practices, Globalizations, forthcoming , 00; coed, Power in Contemporary Politics: Theories, Practices, Globalizations, forthcoming, 00. **CONTACT ADDRESS** 19 Abeel St, 6H, Yonkers, NY 10705. **EMAIL** HowardH.Lentner@worldnet.att.net

LEONARD, ELLEN M.
PERSONAL Born 08/26/1933, Toronto, ON, Canada **DISCIPLINE** THEOLOGY **EDUCATION** Reaching Certificate, Toronto Teacher's Coll, 55; Univ Toronto, BA, 67; Manhattan Coll, MA, 71; St Micheal's Coll, PhD, 78. **CAREER** Tchr, Holy Rosary School Toronto, 55-57; tchr, St James School Colgan, 57-59; St Joseph School Merriton, 59-62; tchr, principal, Holy Spirit Toronto, 62-69; tchr, Metropolitan Separate School Bd, 70-73; tchg asst, Univ Toronto, 74-75; tchg asst, St Michael's Coll,77-78; lectr, St Michael's Coll, 77-78; asst prof, 78-82; assoc prof, 82-91; Advanced Degree Fac, Toronto School of Theol, 83-; Prof to Prof Emer, St Michael's Col, 91-; Fac, Centre for the study of Rel Univ Toronto, 94-. **HONORS AND AWARDS** Vis fel, St Edmund's Coll, Cambridge, 88, 91; numerous grants from SSHRC. **MEMBERSHIPS** Am Acad of Rel; Can Theol Soc; cath Theol Soc of Am. **RESEARCH** Roman Catholic Modernism; Feminist Theory; Chritology. **SELECTED PUBLICATIONS** Auth, George Tyrrell and the Catholic Tradition, 82; Unresting Transformation: the Theology and Spirituality of Maude Petre, 91; Creative Tension: The Spiritual Legacy of Friedrich von Hugel, 97; numerous chapters in books and articles in refereed journals. **CONTACT ADDRESS** Faculty of Theology, Univ of St. Michael's Col, 81 St Mary St, Toronto, ON, Canada M5S 1J4. **EMAIL** leonard@chass.utoronto

LEONARD, KIMBERLY K.
DISCIPLINE CRIMINOLOGY **EDUCATION** Univ Nebr, BS, 80; Pa State Univ, MS, 82; Wharton Sch, Univ Pa, MA, 83; PhD, 86. **CAREER** Vis Scholar, London Sch of Economics and Polit Sci, 87; Youth Fel, Mo Youth Initiative, Univ of Mo and W.K. Kellogg Found, 90-94; Res Fel, The Center for Metropolitan Studies, Pub Policy Res Centers, Univ of Mo St. Louis, 87-99; Asst Prof, Kent State Univ, 86-87; Asst/Assoc Prof, Univ of Mo St. louis, 87-00; Prof, Univ of Tex Dallas, 00-. **HONORS AND AWARDS** Gustavus Myers Awd for Human Right in N Am, 97. **MEMBERSHIPS** Am Soc of Criminol, Acad of Criminal Justice Sci, Am Civil Liberties Union. **SELECTED PUBLICATIONS** Co-ed, Minorities in Juvenile Justice, Sage (Thousand Oaks, CA), 95; coauth, Continuity & Discontinuity in Criminal Careers, Plenum (NY), 96; auth, "Equity and Juveniles: What is Justice?," Corrections Management Quart (98): 25-35; coauth, "Sanctioning Serious Juvenile Offenders: A Review of Alternative Methods," 8 Advances in Criminological Theory (98): 135-171; coauth, "A Matter of Life and Death: The Failure of Juror Instructions in Capital Class," The Justice Prod 12-1 (99): 173-189; coauth, "The Gender Effect among Serious, Violent, and Chronic Juvenile Offenders: A Difference of Degree Rather than Kind," in It's a Crime: Women and Justice, 2nd ed, ed. R. Muraskin (NY: Prentice Hall, 99), 453-478; coauth, "Expanding Realms of the New Penology: The Advent of Actuarila Justice for Juveniles," Punishment and Soc 2-1 (00): 69-99; coauth, "Disparity Based on Sex: Is Gender-Specific Treatment Warranted?," Justice Quart 17-1 (00): 301-340. **CONTACT ADDRESS** Dept Criminol, Univ of Missouri, St. Louis, 8001 Natural Bridge, Saint Louis, MO 63121.

LEONARD, THOMAS M.
PERSONAL Born 11/08/1937, Elizabeth, NJ, m, 1968, 6 children **DISCIPLINE** HISTORY, PHILOSOPHY **EDUCATION** Mt St Mary's Col, BS, 59; Georgetown Univ, MA, 63; Am Univ, PhD, 69. **CAREER** From Instr to Assoc Prof, St Joseph Col, 62-73; From Assoc Prof to Prof, Univ N Fla, 73-. **HONORS AND AWARDS** Phi Alpha Theta; Phi Kappa Phi; Two Thousand Men Achievement Awd; Outstanding Educr Awd; Outstanding Young Men of Am Awd; Am Hist Asn Awd, 85; NEH Fel, 85, 89; Fulbright Fel, 90; Andrew W Mellon Found Res Awd, 94; U S Information Serv Awd, 94. **MEMBERSHIPS** ATWS, BSA, CLAH, LASA, NASSH, SHAFR, SCLAS. **RESEARCH** United States relations with Latin America, Central America. **SELECTED PUBLICATIONS** Auth, Central America and the United States: The Search for Stability, Univ Ga Pr, 91; auth, Panama and the United States: Guide to Issues and Sources, Regina Books, 93; auth, Guide to Archival Material in the United States on Central America, Greenwood Pr, 94; auth, "The Quest for Central American Democracy Since 1945," in Democracy in Latin Am, Westview Publ (98); auth, Castro and the Cuban Revolution, Greenwood Pr, 99; auth, "The New Pan Americanism in United States-Central American Relations 1933-1954," in Beyond the Ideal: Pan Americanism in Inter-American Affairs (Greenwood Pr, forthcoming). **CONTACT ADDRESS** Dept Hist & Philos, Univ of No Florida, 4567 St Johns Bluff Rd S, Jacksonville, FL 32224-2646. **EMAIL** tleonard@unf.edu

LEONARD, WALTER J.
PERSONAL Born 10/03/1929, Alma, GA, m **DISCIPLINE** LAW **EDUCATION** Savannah State Coll, 1947; Morehouse Coll Atlanta, 1959-60; Atlanta Univ Grad Schl of Business, 1961-62; Howard Univ Sch of Law, JD 1968; Harvard Univ Inst of Educ Mgmt, 1974; Harvard Univ, AMP 1977. **CAREER** Ivan Allen Jr Atlanta, asst campaign mgr 1961; The Leonard Land Co Atlanta, owner/operator 1962-65; Sam Phillips McKenzie, campaign asst 1963; Dean Clarence Clyde Ferguson Jr Sch of Law Howard Univ, legal rsch asst 1966-67; Washington Tech Inst, admin asst to pres 1967-68; Howard Univ Sch of Law, asst dean & lectr 1968-69; Harvard Univ Law Sch, asst dean/asst dir admiss & finan aid 1969-; US Office of Econ Oppty, hearing examiner 1969-70; Univ of CA/ Univ of VA, visit prof summers 1969-72; Harvard Univ, asst to pres 1971-77; Fisk Univ, pres 1977-84; Howard Univ, disting sr fellow 1984-86; US Virgin Islands, executive assistant to governor, 87-89; private consulting, 89-90; Cities in Schools, Inc. (National/International), executive director, 90-94. **HONORS AND AWARDS** Awd for Disting Serv to Assn & Office of Pres 1972; Apprec Awd Harvard Black Students' Assn 1971; Walter J Leonard Day and key to city of Savannah, GA 1969; 1st Annual Melnea A Cass Comm Awd Boston YWCA 1977; New England Tribute Dinner to Walter J Leonard spons by Hon Thomas P O'Neill Jr, Hon Edw M Kennedy, Hon Edw W Brooke, Pres Derek Bok of Harvard Univ 1977; Paul Robeston Awd Black Amer Law Students Assn 1977; Frederick Douglass Pub Serv Awd Greater Boston YMCA 1977; Special Orator Celebration of 50th Birthday of Martin Luther King Jr Boston, MA 1979; Alumni Achievement Awd Morehouse Alumni Club of New England 1977; Apprec Dinner and Awd Urban League of Eastern MA 1977; Exemplary Achieve Awd Faculty Resolution Grad Sch Educ Harvard Univ 1976; Service Awd and Appreciation Citation, Governor of US Virgin Islands; Oxford Scholar, 1997; more than 250 other awards, citations, and 5 honorary degrees. **MEMBERSHIPS** Mem Assn of Amer Law Schs; Council on Legal Educ Oppty; Law Sch Admissions Council; Amer Assn of Univ Prof; Howard Univ Law Sch Alumni Assn; bd of visitors USN Acad; bd trustees Natl Urban League; bd trustees Natl Pub Radio; Intl Assn of Y's Men's Club Inc; NAACP; pres Natl Bar Assn; consult The Ford Found NY 1969-71; Committee on Policy for Racial Justice, Joint Center for Economic and Political Studies; Harvard Alumni; NAACP life member; Omega Psi Phi Fraternity; Sigma Pi Phi Fraternity; board of trustees, US Naval Academy Foundation; board of directors, Cities in Schools, Inc. **SELECTED PUBLICATIONS** "Our Struggle Continues-Our Cause is Just" The Crisis, May 1978; "Reflecting on Black Admissions in White Colleges" The Morning After A Retrospective View, 1974; articles in, The Boston Globe, USA Today, The Harvard Law School Bulletin. **CONTACT ADDRESS** Howard Univ, 2400 Sixth St NW, Washington, DC 20059.

LEONE, MATTHEW C.
PERSONAL Born 08/16/1958, San Diego, CA, m, 1983, 1 child **DISCIPLINE** CRIMINAL JUSTICE **EDUCATION** San Diego State Univ, Ba, 82; Univ Calif, MA, 86; Phd, 90. **CAREER** Lecturer, Calif State Univ, 88-89; Asst Prof, to Assoc Prof, Univ Nev, 90-. **MEMBERSHIPS** Am Soc of Criminol, Western Soc of Criminol, Acad of Criminal Justice Sci, Western and Pacific Asn of Criminal Justice Educators. **RESEARCH** Juvenile justice, Corrections, Policy making in criminal justice. **SELECTED PUBLICATIONS** Auth, "Representing O.J.," Journal of Criminal Justice and Popular Culture, 99; auth, "Disjunction and function: Parole Board decision Making Processes," Federal Probation, 99; auth, Filling the Gap: Essential Readings in Criminal Justice, Simon & Schuster, 98; auth, "Focus Groups and Criminal Justice program Evaluation: A Methodological Note," Journal of Criminal Justice Education, 98; auth, "Conjugal Visitation and Prison Privatization: A Nexus of Opportunity," in Privatization and the Provision of Correctional Services, Anderson Pub, 96; auth, "A Transitional State: Gangs, Gang Members, and Social Change in Nevada," Nev Public Affairs Review, 96; auth, "Jails, Justice, and Minorities: Stacking the Deck in nevada," Nev Public Affairs Review, 96; auth, "To Smoke or Not to Smoke: The Experience of a Northern Nevada County Jail," American Jails, 96; ed, "Sex, Crime, and Justice," Journal of Contemporary Criminal Justice, 96. **CONTACT ADDRESS** Dept Crim Justice, Univ of Nevada, Reno, N Va Ave, Reno, NV 89557-0001. **EMAIL** mleone@unr.edu

LEONTIADES, MILTON
PERSONAL Born 11/25/1932, Athens, Greece, m, 1968, 2 children **DISCIPLINE** BUSINESS **EDUCATION** Indiana Univ, BA, 54, MBA, 57; Am Univ, PhD, 66. **CAREER** Management Consultant, 66-71; Dir, Econ Dev, IU Int, 71-73; Sr Planner, Gen Electric, 73-74; Dean & Prof, Rutgers Univ, 74-. **RESEARCH** Corporate strategy; company diversification & change. **SELECTED PUBLICATIONS** Auth, Strategies for Diversification & Change, Little Brown, 80; Management Policy, Strategy and Plans, Little Brown, 82; Policy, Strategy, and Implementation, Random Hse, 83; Managing the Unmanageable, Addison-Wesley, 86; Mythmanagement, Basil Blackwell, 89. **CONTACT ADDRESS** 14 Tallowood Dr, Voorhees, NJ 08043. **EMAIL** miltonl@crol.rutgers.edu

LEPARD, BRIAN
DISCIPLINE LAW **EDUCATION** Princeton Univ, BA; Yale Univ, JD. **CAREER** Asst prof **HONORS AND AWARDS** Ed, Yale J Int Law. **RESEARCH** Income taxation; international human relations. **SELECTED PUBLICATIONS** Co-auth, Unrelated Business Income Tax Issues in Health Care, 86. **CONTACT ADDRESS** Law Dept, Univ of Nebraska, Lincoln, 103 Ross McCollum Hall, PO Box 830902, Lincoln, NE 68588-0420. **EMAIL** blepard@unlserve.unl.edu

LEPLIN, JARRETT
PERSONAL Born 11/20/1944, Houston, TX **DISCIPLINE** HISTORY AND PHILOSOPHY OF SCIENCE **EDUCATION** Amherst Col, BA, 66; Univ Chicago, MA, 67, PhD(philos), 72. **CAREER** Instr philos, Ill Inst Technol, 67-70 and Univ Md Baltimore County, 70-71; asst prof, 71-76, Assoc Prof Philos, Univ NC, Greensboro, 76-. **MEMBERSHIPS** Am Philos Asn; Hist Sci Asn; AAAS; Brit Soc Hist Sci; Philos Sci Asn. **RESEARCH** Scientific methodology; theory comparison, philosophy of space and time. **SELECTED PUBLICATIONS** Auth, Kitcher, Philip the Advancement of Science--Science Without Legend, Objectivity Without Illusion, Philos of Sci, Vol 0061, 94. **CONTACT ADDRESS** Dept of Philos, Univ of No Carolina, Greensboro, Greensboro, NC 23412.

LEPOFSKY, DAVID M.
DISCIPLINE LAW **EDUCATION** Osgoode Hall Law Shc, LLB, 79; Harvard Univ, LLM, 82. **CAREER** Secondment, Crown Law Office - Criminal Division, 93-; adj prof, Univ of Toronto. **MEMBERSHIPS** Canadian Association for Visually Impaired Lawyers **RESEARCH** Constitutional and human rights law. **SELECTED PUBLICATIONS** Auth, Open Justice-the Constitutional Right to Attend and Speak about Criminal Proceedings in Canada. **CONTACT ADDRESS** Fac of Law, Univ of Toronto, 78 Queen's Park, Toronto, ON, Canada M5S 2C5.

LERMAN, LISA G.
PERSONAL Born 04/04/1955, Denver, CO, m, 1985, 2 children **DISCIPLINE** LAW **EDUCATION** Columbia Univ, BA, 76; NY Univ Sch Law, JD, 79; Georgetown Univ Law Ctr, LLM, 84. **CAREER** Vis Asst Prof, WVa Univ, 84-85; Vis Assoc Prof, Am Univ, 95; Vis Prof, George Wash Univ, 97-98; Assoc Prof, Cath Univ of Am, 90-. **HONORS AND AWARDS** Eugene R Byrne Hist Prize, 76; Advocacy Fel, Georgetown Univ, 82-84. **MEMBERSHIPS** LEC, LCC, ABA, AALS. **RESEARCH** Lawyers and the legal profession. **SELECTED PUBLICATIONS** Auth, Learning from Practice: Proposals for Development Text for Legal Externs, West Publ Co, 98; auth, "Teaching Moral Perception and Moral Judgement in Legal Ethics Courses: A Dialogue About Goals," 39 William & Mary Law Rev 457 (98); auth, "Scenes from a Law Firm,' 50 Rutgers Law Rev 2153 (98); auth, "Professional and Ethical Issues in Legal Externships: Fostering Commitment to Public Service," 67 Fordham Law Rev 2295 (99); auth, "Blue-Chip Bilking: Regulation of Billing and Expense Fraud by Lawyers," 12 Georgetown J of Legal Ethics 205 (99). **CONTACT ADDRESS** Law, Catholic Univ of America, 620 Michigan Ave NE, Washington, DC 20064-0001.

LERNER, ANNE LAPIDUS
PERSONAL m, 2 children **DISCIPLINE** RELIGION **EDUCATION** Harvard Univ, AB, 64, MA, 65, PhD, 77. **CAREER** Prof; dean, List College; vice chancellor, Jewish Theol Sem, 69. **HONORS AND AWARDS** Co-dir, Gender and Text Conf, 90; ed, prog adv, MA prog in Jewish Women's Studies, Jewish Theol Sem Am; dir, Ctr Conv to Judaism; ed bd, Women's League Outlook, Hadassah, Judaism, and Lilith. **RESEARCH** Study of modern Jewish literature particularly modern poetry; the reinterpretation of texts by modern writers; and the position of women in Judaism. **SELECTED PUBLICATIONS** Auth, Who Has Not Made Me a Man: The Movement for Equal Rights for Women in American Judaism; Passing the Love of Women: A Study of Gide's Saul' and its Biblical Roots; ed, Gender and Text: Feminist Approaches To Modern Hebrew and Yiddish Literature, Harvard Univ Press. **CONTACT ADDRESS** Dept of Jewish Lit, Jewish Theol Sem of America, 3080 Broadway, PO Box 3080, New York, NY 10027. **EMAIL** anlerner@jtsa.edu

LEROY CONRAD, ROBERT
DISCIPLINE EDUCATIONAL MINISTRY **EDUCATION** Concordia Sem, MDiv, STM; Wash Univ, MA; Princeton Sem, PhD. **CAREER** Dir, Extension Educ; prof. **HONORS AND AWARDS** Educ Comm ch, Commn for Church and Youth Agency Relationships. **SELECTED PUBLICATIONS** Auth, What Planners and Teachers Need to Know About Today's Adults, Lifelong Learning: A Practical Guide to Adult Education in the Church, Augsburg Fortress, 97. **CONTACT ADDRESS** Dept of Educational Ministry, Lutheran Sch of Theol at Chicago, 1100 E 55th St, Chicago, IL 60615.

LESCHER, BRUCE
PERSONAL Born 06/07/1945, Corpus Christi, TX, m, 2000 **DISCIPLINE** THEOLOGY **EDUCATION** Univ of Notre Dame, BA, 68; Univ of MI, MA, 73; Univ of San Fran, MAS, 82; Grad Theol Union, Berkeley, PhD **CAREER** Asst Prof, 90-95, St Edwards Univ; Assoc Prof, 95-98, Cath Theol Union; Dir, 98-, Inst for Spirit and Worship, Jesuit Sch of Theol **MEMBERSHIPS** Am Acad of Relig; Cath theol Soc of Am **RESEARCH** Spiritual formation **CONTACT ADDRESS** Jesuit Sch of Theol, Berkeley, 1735 LeRoy Ave, Berkeley, CA 94709. **EMAIL** blescher@jstb.edu

LESCHERT, DALE
PERSONAL Born 12/31/1954, Camrose, AB, Canada **DISCIPLINE** HERMENEUTICS **EDUCATION** Providence Theo Sem, MDiv, 80; Western Sem Portland, MTh, 81, Fuller Theo Sem, PhD, 91. **CAREER** Asst Prof, 83-85, Mountainview Bib Coll; faculty, bible & theo, 87-88, Briercrest Bible Coll; adj fac, 91, Can Bap Sem, Langley; adj Prof NT, 95, Capital Bible Sem; independent research & writing, 96-. **MEMBERSHIPS** SBL, ETS. **RESEARCH** Hermeneutics, New Testament, theology, epistemology. **SELECTED PUBLICATIONS** Auth, Hermeneutical Foundations of Hebrews, in: Nat Assoc BPRDS, 94; Entries, Age, Mediator and Witness, in: Eerdmans Dictionary of the Bible, eds D N Freedman, A C Myers & A B Beck, Grand Rapids Wm b Eerdmans Pub Co, forthcoming; Hebrews, Eschatology of, in: Dictionary of Premillennial Theology, ed, M Couch, Grand Rapids Kregel Pub, 96; Why Should We Think About God and the Bible? in: First People, Thanksgiving, 93. **CONTACT ADDRESS** 2013 Seventh Ave, New Westminster, BC, Canada V3M 2L5.

LESHER, JAMES
DISCIPLINE GREEK PHILOSOPHY **EDUCATION** Univ VA, BA; Univ Rochester, PhD. **CAREER** Mem, philos dept, 67; prof, dept(s) class and philos, 93; asst to the pres of the Univ. **HONORS AND AWARDS** ACLS Study fel for postdoc res; jr fel, Ctr Hellenic Stud, 81-82. **SELECTED PUBLICATIONS** Auth, Xenophanes of Colophon: Text, Translation, and Commentary, Univ Toronto Press, 92; Early Interest in Knowledge, Cambridge Companion to Early Greek Philos; auth, more than 30 articles on various aspects of ancient Greek philos and lit. **CONTACT ADDRESS** Dept of Philosophy, Univ of Maryland, Col Park, 1107 B Skinner Bldg, College Park, MD 20742-1335. **EMAIL** jlesher@arhu.umd.edu

LESKE, ADRIAN M.
PERSONAL Born 04/14/1936, Gumeracha, Australia, m, 1961, 3 children **DISCIPLINE** NEW TESTAMENT **EDUCATION** Concordia Sem, STM, 67, ThD,71. **CAREER** Min, Wellington, NZ, 60-65, Walkerie, S Australia, 66-69; prof relig stud, Concordia Univ, 71-. **HONORS AND AWARDS** Exch study schol, Concordia Sem, St. Louis, 58-60, 69-71; Allan Schendel Awd, 90. **MEMBERSHIPS** Soc of Bibl Lit; Can Soc of Bibl Stud; Asn for Res in Rel Stud & Theol. **RESEARCH** Gospel of Matthew; exile and post-exile prophets. **SELECTED PUBLICATIONS** Auth, "Influence of Isaiah 40-66 on Christology in Matthew and Luke: A Comparison," SBL 1994 Seminar Papers; "Influence of Isaiah on Christology in Matthew and Luke," Crisis in Christology: Essays in Quest of Resolution, Dove, 95; "Isaiah and Matthew: The Prophetic Influence in the First Gospel-A Report on Current Research," Jesus and the Suffering Servant: Isiah 53 and Christian Origins, Trinity, 1998; "Matthew," International Bible Commentary, Liturgical, 1998. **CONTACT ADDRESS** Concordia Univ Col of Alberta, 7128 Ada Blvd, Edmonton, AB, Canada T5B 4E4. **EMAIL** aleske@concordia.ab.ca

LESLIE, BENJAMIN C.
PERSONAL Born 05/02/1957, Anniston, AL, m, 1980, 2 children **DISCIPLINE** SYSTEMATIC THEOLOGY **EDUCATION** Samford Univ, BA, 79; Southern Baptist Theol Sem, MDiv, 83; Baptist Theol Sem, Ruschlikon, ThM, 86; Univ Zurich, D Theol, 90. **CAREER** Prof Systematic Theology and Christian Ethics, North American Baptist Sem, 90-00. **MEMBERSHIPS** Am Academy Relig; Soc of Christian Ethics; Nat Asn Baptist Professors of Relig. **RESEARCH** Christian theology general; Barth studies; Baptist studies. **SELECTED PUBLICATIONS** Auth, Trinitarian Hermeneutics, Peter Lung, 90; Barth, Karl, A New Dictionary of Christian Theologians, Abingdon, 96. **CONTACT ADDRESS** No American Baptist Sem, 1525 S. Grange Ave., Sioux Falls, SD 57105-1599. **EMAIL** bleslie@nabs.edu

LESSARD, HESTER A.
DISCIPLINE LAW **EDUCATION** Dalhousie Univ, LLB, 85; Univ Columbia, LLM, 89. **CAREER** Asst prof, 89-94; assoc prof, 94-. **HONORS AND AWARDS** Co-ed, Can Jour Women Law. **RESEARCH** Constitutional law; feminist legal theories; family law; and legal process. **SELECTED PUBLICATIONS** Auth, pubs on feminist critiques of constitutional rights. **CONTACT ADDRESS** Fac of Law, Univ of Victoria, PO Box 2400, Victoria, BC, Canada V8W 3H7. **EMAIL** hlessard@uvic.ca

LESTER, GILLIAN
PERSONAL Born 10/30/1964, Maple Ridge, BC, Canada, m, 1998, 1 child **DISCIPLINE** LAW **EDUCATION** Univ BC, BSc, 86; Univ Toronto, LLB, 90; Stanford Univ, JSM, 93; JSD, 98. **CAREER** Teaching fel, Stanford Law Sch, 92-93; acting prof to prof, UCLA, 94-; vis prof, Georgetown Univ, 00. **HONORS AND AWARDS** Sloan Found Scholar, Georgetown Univ, 00. **RESEARCH** Employment law (intellectual property, unemployment insurance, contingent employment, an-

tidiscrimination theory). **SELECTED PUBLICATIONS** Auth, "Toward the Feminization of Collective Bargaining Law," McGill L J, 91; auth, "Careers and Contingency," Stanford L Rev, 98; auth, "Restrictive Covenants, Employee Training, and the Limits of Transaction-Cost Analysis," Ind L J, 01; auth, "Unemployment Insurance and Wealth Redistribution, (forthcoming). **CONTACT ADDRESS** Sch of Law, Univ of California, Los Angeles, PO Box 951476, Los Angeles, CA 90095-1476. **EMAIL** lester@mail.law.ucla.edu

LESTER, ROBERT CARLTON
PERSONAL Born 02/01/1933, Lead, SD, m, 1954, 3 children **DISCIPLINE** COMPARATIVE RELIGION **EDUCATION** Mont State Univ, BA, 55; Yale Univ, BD, 58, MA, 59, PhD(comp relig), 63. **CAREER** From asst prof to assoc prof philos and relig, Am Univ, DC, 62-70; assoc prof, 70-72, Prof Relig Studies, Univ Colo, Boulder, 72-, Vis lectr, Foreign Serv Inst, US Dept State, 67-; vis prof Asian studies, Cornell Univ, 68-69; Fulbright-Hays sr res fel, India, 74-75. **MEMBERSHIPS** Asn Asian Studies; Am Acad Relig; fel Soc Relig Higher Educ. **RESEARCH** Buddhism in Southeast Asia; Hinduism; South Indian Vaishnavism. **SELECTED PUBLICATIONS** Auth, Ramanuja on the Yoga, Adyar Library, Madras, 75; auth, Theravada Buddhism in Southeast Asia, U of Mich Pr, 73; auth, The Srivacana Bhushana of Pillai Lookacharya, Madras, 78; auth, Buddhism: The Path to Nirvana, Harper, 87; auth, The Sattada Srivaisnavas, J Amer Oriental Soc, Vol 0114, 1994. **CONTACT ADDRESS** Relig Studies, Univ of Colorado, Boulder, Boulder, CO 80309. **EMAIL** Robert.Lester@Colorado.edu

LETTS, CHRISTINE WEBB
PERSONAL Born, OH, m, 2 children **DISCIPLINE** BUSINESS ADMINISTRATION **EDUCATION** Conn Col, BA, 70; Harvard, MBA, 76. **CAREER** Secretary, Project Manager, NY City Dept Sanitation, 70-73; Analyst, State Charter Revision Commission NY City, 74; Dir, Production Control Columbus Engine Plant, 76-87; VP, Cummins engine Co, 76-88; Commissioner, Ind Dept of Transportation, 89-91; Secretary, Ind Fam & Soc Service Admin, 91-92; Exec Dir, Hauser Ctr for Nonprofit Org, Harvard Univ, 92-; Lecturer, Harvard Univ, 92-. **HONORS AND AWARDS** Distinguished Service Awd, Nat Governonrs' Asn, 91; Honoree, YWCA Tribute to Women in Intl Industry, 87. **SELECTED PUBLICATIONS** Co-auth, "Virtuous Capital: What Foundations Can Learn from Venture Capitalists," Harvard Business Review, 97; co-auth, High Performance Nonprofit Organizations: Managing Upstream for Greater Impact, John Wiley and Sons, 99. **CONTACT ADDRESS** John F Kennedy Sch of Govt, Harvard Univ, 79 John F. Kennedy St, Cambridge, MA 02138. **EMAIL** christine_letts@harvard.edu

LEUBSDORF, JOHN
PERSONAL Born 02/11/1942, New York, NY, m, 1998, 1 child **DISCIPLINE** LAW, LITERATURE **EDUCATION** Harvard Univ, BA, 63; Stanford Univ, MA, Eng, 64; Harvard Law Sch, JD, 67. **CAREER** Assoc prof and prof, Boston Univ, 75-84; vis prof, Columbia Univ, 90-91; Univ Calif Berkeley, 93; Cornell Univ, 95; prof, Rutgers Law Sch, Newark, 84-. **HONORS AND AWARDS** Fulbright scholar, Paris, 95. **MEMBERSHIPS** Amer Law Inst. **RESEARCH** Legal Ethics, Civil Procedure, and Law & Literature. **SELECTED PUBLICATIONS** Auth, Civil Procedure, 4th ed, with F. James and G. Hazard, 92; auth," Man In His Original Dignity," Legal Ethics In France, 00; auth, " Restatement of the Law Governing Lawyers," Assoc Reporter, 00. **CONTACT ADDRESS** Rutgers, The State Univ of New Jersey, Newark, 15 Washington St., Newark, NJ 07102. **EMAIL** leubsdorf@kinoy.rutgers.edu

LEVEN, CHARLES LOUIS
PERSONAL Born 05/02/1928, Chicago, IL, m, 1971, 5 children **DISCIPLINE** MATHMATICS, ECONOMICS **EDUCATION** Northwestern Univ, BS 50, MA 56, PhD 57. **CAREER** Consult, Pub Pol Inst Cal, 98-; Consult, Pulmonary Diseases, Wash Univ Sch Med, 96-; Trustee, Univ City MO Pen Funds, 94-; Adv, Reg Econo Analysis Lab, 93-; Dist Vis Teacher, Reg Sci, Univ Reading, UK, 92-; Distg Prof Pub Pol, Univ MO-St Louis, 91-; Prof Econo Emer, Washington Univ, 91-; Prof Econo, Wash Univ, 65-91; Mem Exec Council, Soc Prof Emer, Wash Univ, 95-98; Mem Intl Adv Bd, Handbook Urban Stud, 95-97; Prof In Res, Arch Plan, Tech Univ, 95; Consult, Munic Rotterdam, 94; Consult, Spirit St Louis Airport, 94; Adv, Ukrain Nat Cen for Mkts Entreprshp, 92; Consult, Behavioral Med, Jewish Hosp, 91-95; Consult, Boatmen's Bank, 91-93; Adv, Metro St Louis Sewer Dist, 92; Prof in Res, Univ Lodz Poland, Dept Urban Econo, 91; Consult, Cardio Div, Jewish Hosp, 90-95; Mem, Bd Electors Land Econo, Cambridge Univ, 90-91; Vis Dist Scholr, Pub Pol Res Cent, Univ MO, 90-91; Consult, St Louis Civic Prog, 90, 96-97; Adv, Polish Found Local Democ, 90-91; Adv, Pol Min Plan Const, 89-91; Consult, IL, Office of the Auditor Gen, 87-89; Consult, Stockholm Reg Plan Off, 87; Chmn, Dept Econo, Wash Univ, 75-80; Chmn, Urban Studies, Wash Univ, 70-71, 82-85. **HONORS AND AWARDS** Walter Isard Awd Dist Scholar Reg Sci, 95; RIA Res Awd, Univ MO-St Louis, 93; Donald Robertson Mem Lect, Univ Glasgow, 91; Dist Fel So Reg Sci Asn, 91; Am Plan Asn, Mo ch, Excellence in Planning, 86; Nat Inst Health Grant, 85; US Dept Housing Urban Devel Grant, 78; Mercantile Bancorp Symp Grant, 76; Nat Sci Foun Res Grant, 68,73; Comm Urban Econo Res Grant, 65, 66; Soc Sci Res Council, Grant-in-aid-of-Res, 60; Alumni Achiev Fund Awd, Iowa State Col, 58; Soc Sci Res Council Res Train Fellowshp, 56; BS with Honors Mathematics, Northwestern Univ, 50. **MEMBERSHIPS** AEA; Midwest Econo Asn; So Econo Asn; **RESEARCH** Urban reg economs; health economs; quality of life measurement. **SELECTED PUBLICATIONS** An analytical Framework for regional Development, with J Legler and P Shaprio, MIT press, 70; Spatial Regional and Population Economics: Essays in Honor of Edgar M Hoover, ed with Mark Perlman and Benjamin Chintz, NY London, Gordon and Breach, 72; Neighborhood Change: Lessons in the Dynamics of Urban Decay, with J Little, H Nourse and R Read, NY, Praeger, 76; The Mature Metropolis, Ed, Lexington, DC, Heath, 78; Gaming in the Us: Taxation Revenues and Economic Impact, with D Phares and c Louishomme, in W B Hildreth and J A Richardson, eds, Handbook on Taxation, NY, forthcoming; Casino Gaming in Missouri: The Spending Displacement Effect and Gamings Net Economic Impact, with D Phares, Proceedings of the National Tax Asn, forthcoming; Economic Impact of Casino Gaming in Missouri, with D Phares and C Luishomme, St Louis, Civic Progress, 98. **CONTACT ADDRESS** Washington Univ, 1 Brookings Dr, Campus Box 1208, Saint Louis, MO 63130. **EMAIL** leven@wuecon.wustl.edu

LEVESQUE, PAUL J.
PERSONAL Born 06/17/1962, Santa Monica, CA **DISCIPLINE** RELIGIOUS STUDIES **EDUCATION** Catholic Univ of Amer, Philos, BA, 84, MA, 85; Catholic Univ of Louvain, Belgium, Rel Stud, BA, 87, MA, 88, STB, 88, Masters in Morals and Rel Sic, 89, PhD, 95. **CAREER** Instr, 97-, California State Univ, Fullerton; Adjunct Prof, 93-, Mount St Mary's Coll. **HONORS AND AWARDS** Theodore T. Basselin Scholar, Cath Univ Amer, Sch of Philos. **MEMBERSHIPS** Amer Acad Rel; Amer Philos Assoc; Soc for the Sci Stud of Rel; Assoc for the Sociology of Rel; North Amer Assoc for the Stud of Rel; Assoc Rel and Intellectual Life; Cath Theol Soc Amer. **RESEARCH** Christianity and Culture, Philosophy of Religion, Catholic Studies. **SELECTED PUBLICATIONS** Auth, Symbols of Transcendence, Religious Expression in the Thought of Louis Dupre, Louvain Theological and Pastoral Monographs 22, Leuven, Peeters Press, Grand Rapids, W.B. Eerdmans, 97; A Symbolical Sacramental Methodology, Questions Liturgiques Studies in Liturgy, 95; Eucharistic Prayer Posture, From Standing to Kneeling, Questions Liturgiques/Studies in Liturgy, 93. **CONTACT ADDRESS** Dept of Comparative Relig, California State Univ, Fullerton, P.O. Box 6868, Fullerton, CA 92834. **EMAIL** plevesque@fullerton.edu

LEVI, ISAAC
PERSONAL Born 06/30/1930, New York, NY, m, 1951, 2 children **DISCIPLINE** PHILOSOPHY **EDUCATION** NYork Univ, BA, 51; Columbia Univ, MA, 54; PhD, 57. **CAREER** From instr to asst prof philos, Case Western Reserve Univ, 57-62; asst prof, City Col NY, 62-64; from assoc prof to prof, Case Western Reserve Univ, 64-70, chmn dept, 68-70; prof philos, Columbia Univ, 70-, John Devoey Prof, 91-; Nat Sci Found awards, 63-65 & 67-69; Guggenheim fel, 66-67; Fulbright res fel, UK, 66-67; vis scholar, Corpus Christi Col, Cambridge, 73. **HONORS AND AWARDS** Vis scholar Darwin Col, Cambridge, 80, 92; vis fel, All Souls Col Oxford, 88; vis fel, Wolfson Col, Cambridge, 96; Doctor honorus causa, Lund Univ, Sweden. **MEMBERSHIPS** Am Philos Asn; Philos Sci Asn; Brit Soc Philos Sci. **RESEARCH** Philosophy of science; philosophy of social science. **SELECTED PUBLICATIONS** Auth, Must the Scientist Make Value Judgements?, J Philos, 60; auth, On the Seriousness of Mistakes, Philos Sci, 62; auth, Probability Kinematics, Brit J Philos Sci, 67; auth, Gambling With Truth, Knopf, 67; auth, On Indeterminate Probabilities, 74 & Direct inference, 77, J Philos; auth, The Enterprise of Knowledge, MIT, 80; auth, Decisions and Revisions, Cambridge, 84; auth, Hard Choices, Cambridge, 86; auth, The Fixation of Belief and its Undoing, Cambridge, 91; auth, For the Sake of the Argument, Cambridge, 96; auth, The Covenant of Reason, Cambridge, 97. **CONTACT ADDRESS** Dept of Philosophy, Columbia Univ, New York, NY 10027-6900. **EMAIL** levi@columbia.edu

LEVI, MARGARET
PERSONAL Born 03/05/1947 **DISCIPLINE** POLITICAL SCIENCE **EDUCATION** Bryn Mawr Col, AB, 68; Harvard Univ, PhD, 74. **HONORS AND AWARDS** Woodrow Wilson in Polit Sci, 68; German Marshall Fund Fel, 88-89; Fel, Ctr for Adv Study in the Beh Sci, Palo Alto, 93-94; Fel, Exeter Col; Honorable Mention, Allan Sharlin memorial Prize, Soc Sci Hist Asn, 98. **SELECTED PUBLICATIONS** Auth, Bureaucratic Insurgency: The Case of Police Unions, Lexington Books, 77; co-ed, The Political Economy of French and English Development, 88; co-ed, the Limits of Rationality, Univ Chicago Press, 90; contrib, Schools of Thought in Politics: Marxism 2 vols, Edward Elgar Pub, 91; auth, Of Rule and Revenue, Univ CA, 88; auth, Consent, Dissent, and patriotism, Cambridge Univ Press, 97; co-ed, Trust and Governance, Russell Sage Foundation, 98; co-auth, analytic Narratives, Princeton Univ press, 98; co-ed, competition and Cooperation: Conversations with Nobelists about Economics and Political Science, Russell Sage Foundation, 99; co-auth, "STRIKES! Past and Present: The Battles in Seattle," Politics & Society, forthcoming. **CONTACT ADDRESS** Dept Polit Sci, Univ of Washington, PO Box 353530, Seattle, WA 98195-3530. **EMAIL** mlevi@u.washington.edu

LEVIE, HOWARD SIDNEY
PERSONAL Born 12/19/1907, Wolverine, MI, m, 1934 **DISCIPLINE** LAW **EDUCATION** Cornell Univ, AB, 28, JD, 30; George Washington Univ, LLM, 57. **CAREER** From assoc prof to prof, 63-77, Emer Prof Law, Law Sch, St Louis Univ, 77-, Int law consult, Naval War Col, 65-71, Charles H Stockton chmn int law, 71-72; vpres, St Louis Coun World Affairs, 68-70. **MEMBERSHIPS** Int Soc Mil Law and Law of War; Am Bar Asn; Fed Bar Asn; Am Soc Int Law; Int Law Asn. **RESEARCH** International law. **SELECTED PUBLICATIONS** Auth, Some constitutional aspects of selected regional organizations, Columbia J Transnational Law, fall 66; Maltreatment of prisoners of war in Vietnam, Boston Univ Law Rev, summer 68; Some major inadequacies in the existing law relating to the protection of individuals during armed conflict, (working paper XIVth Hammarskjold Forum), In: When Battle Rages, How Can Law Protect?, Oceana, 71; Prisoners of War in International Armed Conflict, 79 & ed, Documents on Prisoners of War, 79, NWC Press; Protection of War Victims (4 vols), Oceana, 79-81. **CONTACT ADDRESS** Sch Law, Saint Louis Univ, Saint Louis, MO 63103.

LEVIN, DAVID M.
PERSONAL Born 06/04/1939, New York City, NY, s **DISCIPLINE** PHILOSOPHY **EDUCATION** Harvard Univ, BA, 61; Columbia Univ, PhD, 67. **CAREER** Asst Prof, Philosophy Dept, MIT, 68-72; Assoc Prof, Philosophy Dept, Northwestern Univ, 72-84; Prof, Philosophy Dept, Northwestern Univ, 84-. **HONORS AND AWARDS** Fulbright Exchange Grant 61-62, **MEMBERSHIPS** Society for Phenomenology & Existential Philosophy; International Heidegger Conference; International Merleau-Ponty Circle; International Assoc for Philosophy and Literature. **RESEARCH** Phenomenology; Frankfurt School Critical Social Theory; Aesthetics; post-modernism; twentieth century continental philosophy; psychoanalysis and psychotherapy. **SELECTED PUBLICATIONS** Auth, "The Body's Recollection of Being," Routledge, 85; auth, "The Opening of Vision, Routledge," 87; auth, "The Listening Self," Routledge, 89; auth, "Pathologies of the Modern Self," NYU Press, 88; auth, "Modernity and the Hegemony of Vision," Univ of California Press, 93; auth, "Sites of Vision," MIT Press, 97; auth, "Language Beyond Postmodernism," Northwestern Univ Press, 97; auth, "The Philosopher's Gaze," Univ of California Press, 99. **CONTACT ADDRESS** Dept Philosophy, Northwestern Univ, 633 Clark St., Evanston, IL 60208-0001. **EMAIL** d-levin@nwu.edu

LEVIN, RONALD MARK
PERSONAL Born 05/11/1950, St. Louis, MO, m, 1989 **DISCIPLINE** LAW **EDUCATION** Yale Univ, BA, 72; Univ Chicago, JD, 75. **CAREER** Law clerk, US Court of Appeals, 5th Circuit, 75-76; assoc, Sutherland, Asbill & Brennan, 76-79; from Asst Prof to Assoc Prof, 79-85, Prof Law, Washington Univ, 85-00, Assoc Dean, 90-93; consult, Admin Conf U.S., 79-81, 93-95; chair, Asn Am Law Sch Sect on Admin Law, 93, Sect on Legis, 95; chair, Am Bar Asn Sect Admin Law & Reg Pract, 00-01; Henry Hitchcock Prof, 00-. **RESEARCH** Administrative law; legislative process. **SELECTED PUBLICATIONS** Auth, Understanding unreviewability in administrative law, Minn Law Rev, 90; Judicial review and the uncertain appeal of certainty on appeal, Duke Law J, 95; Direct final rulemaking, George Washington Law Rev, 95; Congressional Ethics and Constituent Advocacy, Mich Law Rev, 96; coauth, State and Federal Administrative Law, West, 2nd ed, 98; Administrative Law and Process, West, 4th ed, 97. **CONTACT ADDRESS** Sch of Law, Washington Univ, Campus Box 1120, Saint Louis, MO 63130-4899. **EMAIL** levin@wulaw.wustl.edu

LEVINE, ANDREW
PERSONAL Born 11/28/1944, Philadelphia, PA, s **DISCIPLINE** PHILOSOPHY **EDUCATION** Columbia Univ, PhD, 71 **CAREER** Prof, UW, Madison **RESEARCH** Social and Political Philosophy **SELECTED PUBLICATIONS** Auth, Rethinking Liberal Equality, Cornell, 98; Auth, The General Will, Cambridge, 93 **CONTACT ADDRESS** Dept of Philos, Univ of Wisconsin, Madison, Madison, WI 53706. **EMAIL** alevine@macc.wisc.edu

LEVINE, JULIUS B.
PERSONAL Born 02/08/1939, Waterville, ME, d, 3 children **DISCIPLINE** LAW **EDUCATION** Harvard Univ, BA Summa Cum Laude, 60, JD Cum Laude, 64; Oxford Univ, PhD(law), 69. **CAREER** Instr law, Bd Student Adv, Harvard Law Sch, 63-64; law clerk, US Dist Ct, 64-65; assoc prof, 69-72, Prof Law, Boston Univ Sch Law, 72-, Law pract, Levine Brody & Levine, Attorneys at Law, 65-; adv uniform probate code, Law Sch Adv Coun, Am Bar Asn, 71-78; contribr ed, Am Bar Asn Sect Litigation, 76-80; legal ed, Nat Col Probate Judges Quart Newsletter, 80-81. **HONORS AND AWARDS** Omicron Chi Epsilon, 59; Phi Beta Kappa, 59; Rhodes Scholar, 60-61 & 67-69. **MEMBERSHIPS** Am Asn Law Sch. **RESEARCH** Law of procedure and litigation; wills, trusts, estates and prop-

erty law. **SELECTED PUBLICATIONS** Contribr, Higher Education: Resources and Finance, McGraw-Hill, 62; coauth, Uniform probate code: Analysis and comments, Nat Col Probate Judges, 70; auth, Abuse of discovery .. are we suffering a true crisis of overdiscovery?, Am Bar Asn J, Vol 67, 81; Living probate, Nat Col Probate Judges Quart Newsletter, spring 81; Discovery: A Comparison Between English and American Civil Discovery Law with Reform Proposals, Oxford Univ Press, 82; coauth, Enforcement of Secret and Semi-Secret Trusts, 5 Probate Law Journal 7, 83; Winning Trial Advocacy, Prentice Hall, 89; auth, Lawyer's Online: Discovery, Privilege, and the Prudent Practitioner, 3, B.U. Journal of Scientific and Technological Law 5, 97. **CONTACT ADDRESS** Sch of Law, Boston Univ, 765 Commonwealth Ave, Boston, MA 02215-1401. **EMAIL** rcoulson@lec.okcu.edu

LEVINE, MARTIN L.
PERSONAL Born 06/01/1939, New York, NY, m, 1978, 1 child **DISCIPLINE** CRIMINAL LAW **EDUCATION** Brandeis Univ, BA; Yale Univ, JD; LA Psychoanalytic Soc & Inst, grad. **CAREER** UPS Found prof Law, Gerontology, Psychiatry, and the Behavioral Sci Univ; Vprovost, Fac Aff; clerked for, Honorable J. Skelly Wright, Judge US Ct Appeals DC Circuit; dir, Oxford-USC Inst for Legal Theory; vis prof, Columbia, UC San Diego; vis academic Oxford. **MEMBERSHIPS** Former Pres, Coun for the Advancement of Psychoanalytic Education, Nat Senior Citizens Law Ctr, Western Ctr on Law and Poetry. **RESEARCH** Elderlaw, Psychoanalysis and law. **SELECTED PUBLICATIONS** Auth, Age Discrimination and the Mandatory Retirement Controversy; ed, Law and Aging: International Variations; Psychology and Law; auth, Legal Education. **CONTACT ADDRESS** Bovard Administration Bldg, Univ of So California, Los Angeles, CA 90089-4019. **EMAIL** levine@usc.edu

LEVINSON, JERROLD
PERSONAL Born 07/11/1948, Brooklyn, NY, m, 1985, 1 child **DISCIPLINE** PHILOSOPHY **EDUCATION** MIT, BS, 69; Univ Mich, PhD, 74 **CAREER** Asst Prof, SUNY, 74-75; Asst Prof to Prof, Univ Md, 76-. **HONORS AND AWARDS** NEH Fel, 80. **MEMBERSHIPS** Am Soc for Aesthetics; Am Philos Asn, British Soc for Aesthetics. **RESEARCH** Aesthetics, Metaphysics, Value theory, Philosophy of music. **SELECTED PUBLICATIONS** Auth, Music, Art, and Metaphysics, Cornell Univ Press, 90; auth, The Pleasures of Aesthetics, Cornell Univ Press, 96; auth, Music in the Moment, Cornell Univ Press, 98; auth, L'art, la musique, et l'histoire, Editions de L'Eclat, 98; auth, Musique de film: Fiction et narration, Presse Universitaire de Pau, 00; ed, Aesthetics and Ethics: Essays at the Intersection, Cambridge Univ Press, 98; ed, Oxford Handbook of Aesthetics, Oxford Univ Press, forthcoming; co-ed, Aesthetic concepts: Essays after Sibley, Oxford Univ Press, forthcoming. **CONTACT ADDRESS** Dept Philos, Univ of Maryland, Col Park, 1125 Skinner Bldg A, College Park, MD 20742-7615. **EMAIL** jl32@umail.umd.edu

LEVIT, NANCY
DISCIPLINE LAW **EDUCATION** Bates Col, BA; Univ Kans, JD. **CAREER** Prof **RESEARCH** Sex segregation; feminism; constitutional law; criminal law. **SELECTED PUBLICATIONS** Auth, The Gender Line: Men, Women, and the Law, Univ NY, 98; co-auth, Jurisprudence Contemporary Readings, Problems and Narratives. **CONTACT ADDRESS** Law Dept, Univ of Missouri, Kansas City, 5100 Rockhill Rd, Kansas City, MO 64110-2499. **EMAIL** levitn@umkc.edu

LEVMORE, SAUL
DISCIPLINE LAW **EDUCATION** Columbia Univ, BA, 73; Yale Univ, PhD, 78, JD, 80; Kent Univ, LLD, 95. **CAREER** Vis prof. **RESEARCH** Commercial Law, Comparative Law, Contracts, Corporate Tax, Corporations, Public Choice and the Law, and Torts **SELECTED PUBLICATIONS** Auth, pubs on commercial law, comparative law, contracts, and corporate tax. **CONTACT ADDRESS** Sch of Law, Univ of Chicago, 1111 E 60th St, Chicago, IL, Canada 60637-2776.

LEVY, IAN CHRISTOPHER
PERSONAL Born 02/24/1967, New York, NY **DISCIPLINE** HISTORICAL THEOLOGY **EDUCATION** Univ of New Mexico, BA, 89; Vanderbilt, MA, 91; Marquette Univ, PhD, 97. **CAREER** Marquette Univ, tchg asst, 94-96, Nashotah House Episcopal Sem, adj prof, 97; Marquette Univ, adj prof, 97-, Carroll Col, adj prof, 98-; Visiting Asst. Prof, Marquette Univ; Ed Assoc, Luther Digest; Ed with Reformation Texts in Translation. **HONORS AND AWARDS** Phi Beta Kappa, Marquette Univ, Schmitt fell. **MEMBERSHIPS** MAA, MAMW, SBL, ASCH **RESEARCH** Medieval Theol; esp biblical interpretations and sacraments. **SELECTED PUBLICATIONS** Auth, John Wyclif and Augustinian Realism, in: Augustiniana, 98; Biographical Dictionary of Christian Theologians, contributing auth, eds P. Carey, J. Lienhard, Greenwood Pub Co, 00; auth, Was John Wyclif's Theology of the Eucharist Donatistic? in: Scottish Jour of Theol, forthcoming; auth, "Christus qui Mentiri Non Potest: John Wyclif's Rejection of Transubstantiation Rechercher de Theologie et Philosophie Medievale, 99. **CONTACT ADDRESS** Dept of Theology, Marquette Univ, 5400 W Washington Blvd, Milwaukee, WI 53208. **EMAIL** ian.levy@marquette.edu

LEVY, ROBERT J.
DISCIPLINE PHILOSOPHY **EDUCATION** Boston Univ, BA, MA; Duke Univ, PhD. **CAREER** Prof, 67-; **RESEARCH** Philosophy of logic, philosophy of science, contemporary philosophy, non deductive reasoning. **SELECTED PUBLICATIONS** Auth, Introductory to Logic. **CONTACT ADDRESS** Wittenberg Univ, Springfield, OH 45501-0720.

LEWIS, BRADLEY
PERSONAL Born 02/20/1965, Wayne, MI, m, 1999 **DISCIPLINE** POLITICAL SCIENCE, GOVERNMENT **EDUCATION** Univ Md, BA, 87; Univ Notre Dame, MA, 89; PhD, 97. **CAREER** Asst Prof, Valparaiso Univ, 92-93; Teaching Fel, Instr, Adj Assist Prof, Col of Arts and Letters, Univ of Notre Dame, 94-97; Asst Prof, Sch of Philos, The Cath Univ of Am, 97-. **MEMBERSHIPS** Am Philos Asb, Soc for Ancient Greek Philos, Am Cath Philos Asn. **RESEARCH** Classical Political Philosophy, Natural Law. **SELECTED PUBLICATIONS** Auth, "Natural Law in Irish Constitutional Jurisprudence," Cath Soc Sci Rev 2 (97): 166-177; auth, "The Nocturnal Council and Platonic Political Philosophy," Hist of Polit Thought 19 (98): 1-20; auth, "'Politeia kai Nomoi': On the Coherence of Plato's Political Philosophy," Polity 31 (98): 331-349; auth, "The Rhetoric of Philosophical Politics in Plato's 'Seventh Letter'," Philos and Rhetoric (forthcoming); auth, "The 'Seventh Letter' and the Unity of Plato's Political Philosophy," Southern J of Philos (forthcoming). **CONTACT ADDRESS** Dept Philos, Catholic Univ of America, 620 Michigan Ave NE, Washington, DC 20064-0001. **EMAIL** lewisb@cua.edu

LEWIS, CARY B., JR.
PERSONAL Born 09/13/1921, Chicago, IL, m **DISCIPLINE** LAW **EDUCATION** Univ of IL, AB 1942; Univ of Chicago, MBA 1947; Univ of IL, CPA 1950; DePaul Univ, JD 1966; Harvard Univ, AMP 1971; Teaching Certificates & Licenses, HS 1951, Jr Coll 1967, Coll 1958, Supervisory 1967. **CAREER** KY State Univ, asst prof 1947-50; So Univ, assoc prof 1950-; CPA, 50-75; MT Washington & Co CPA's Chicago, sr auditor 1951-53; Chicago Pub Sch, 51-57; Collier-Lewis Realty Co, auditor 1953-71; Chicago Tchrs Coll, 57-65; AA Rayner & Sons, auditor 1960-72; Budget Coord, 66-67; Atty at Law, 66-; Chicago State Univ, spec asst to vice pres 1967, prof law & acctg 1957-, **HONORS AND AWARDS** Wisdon Hall of Fame, 1972; Worldwide Acad of Scholars 1975; Natl Hon Soc 1938; Sachem 1941; first black to practice as CPA LA 1951; first black atty & CPA State of IL 1966. **MEMBERSHIPS** Budgetary consult office of econ oppor 1967-69; educ consult to dept hlth educ & welfare 1968-69; auditing consult to dept of labor 1967-69; mgmt consult to Black Econ Union 1969; chmn educ adv comm Chicago NAACP; mem Amer Bar Assn, IL Bar Assn; Chicago Bar Assn; Cook Co Bar Assn; Amer Judicare Soc; Amer Bus Law Assn; Amer Inst CPA's; IL Soc CPA's; Natl Soc CPA's; Amer Acct's Assn; Amer Assn of Univ Prof's; City Club of Chicago. **CONTACT ADDRESS** 95 St at King Dr, Chicago, IL 60628.

LEWIS, DANIEL J.
PERSONAL Born 04/07/1950, Billings, MT, m, 1970, 3 children **DISCIPLINE** WESTERN RELIGION **EDUCATION** William Tyndale Col, BRE, 84; Univ Detroit Mercy, MA, 86. **CAREER** Sr pastor, Troy Christ Chapel, 81-, guest lectr, Univ of the Nations, 91-; adjunct facul, part-time facul, Robert H. Whitaker Sch of Theol, 87-89; adjunct facul, William Tyndale Col, 87-. **HONORS AND AWARDS** Who's Who in Amer Relig, 93; Who's Who in Amer Univ and Col, 84. **MEMBERSHIPS** Soc of Bibl Lit. **RESEARCH** Biblical theology; American railroads. **SELECTED PUBLICATIONS** Article, Building a Sellios Gas Station, N-Scale, Hundman Publ, jul/aug, 98; article, Bunker C..at Harlowton, N-Scale, Hundman Publ, may/jun, 98; article, Thinking Vertically, The Hobtox, NCR/NMRA, winter, 98; article, SW1200, N-Scale, Hundman Publ, nov/dec, 97; article, DPM Comes to Life, N-Scale, Hundman Publ, jul/aug, 97; article, Moving Toward the Prototype, The Hotbox, NCR/NMRA, spring, 96; article, Capturing a Mood, N-Scale, Hundman Publ, mar/apr, 96; article, Evolving Operations on a Small Railroad, Model Railroader, Kalmbach Publ, feb, 96; article, Modeling a Milwaukee Road Superdome, N-Scale, Hundman Publ, may/jun, 95; article, A Ride on the Tuscola and Saginaw Bay, The Hotbox, NCR/NMRA, fall, 95; article, Kitbashing the Bachmann Watertank, N-Scale, Hundman Publ, nov/dec, 94; article, The Three Sisters Railroad, N-Scale, Hundman Publ, mar/apr, 94; mongr; Ezra-Nehemiah, 98; mongr, The Book of Hebrews, 98; monogr, The Book of Daniel, 98; monogr; The Book of Isaiah, 97; monogr, Holy Space and Holy Time, 97; monogr, The Gospel of the Beloved Disciple, 96; monogr, Eschatology, 96; monogr, New Testament Survey, 96; monogr, Bible Characters, 96; monogr, Spiritual Life and Discipleship, 96; monogr, D-History, 96; monogr, Letters to Timothy, 95; monogr, Voices from the North, 95; monogr, The Church Catholic, 94; monogr, The Burden of Disillusionment, 94; monogr, Things That Matter Most, 94; monogr, Ezekiel: Message of Doom and Hope, 94; monogr, Christians and Culture, 94; auth, Three Crucial Questions About the Last Days, Grand Rapids: Baker, 98. **CONTACT ADDRESS** 400 E. Long Lake Rd., Troy, MI 48098. **EMAIL** tcchapel@aol.com

LEWIS, DAVID BAKER
PERSONAL Born 06/09/1944, Detroit, MI, m, 2 children **DISCIPLINE** LAW **EDUCATION** Oakland Univ, BA 1965; Univ of Chicago, MBA 1967; Univ of MI, JD 1970. **CAREER** Northern Trust Co, administrative dept, 66; Morgan Guaranty Trust Co, corporate research analyst, 67; Lewis & Thompson Agency Inc, 68; Miller Canfield Paddock & Stone, summer law clerk 1969; Univ of MI, lectr Afro-Am and African Studies Dept 1970; Hon Theodore Levin US Dist Ct, law clerk 1970-71; Patmon Young & Kirk, assoc atty 1971-72; Detroit College of Law, associate professor, 72-78; David Baker Lewis Atty at Law, sole practitioner 1972; Lewis, White & Clay, president, 72-82, chairman of the board, founding shareholder, director, 72-. **HONORS AND AWARDS** University of Detroit-Mercy, honorary LHD, 1991; American Jewish Comm, Learned Hand Awd, 1995. **MEMBERSHIPS** Lewis & Thompson Agency, Inc., board of directors, 67-; Am Bar Assoc, 70-; State Bar of Mich, 70-; Wolverine Bar Assoc, 70-; Detroit Bar Assoc, 70-; Nat Assoc of Bond Lawyers, 79-; Michigan Opera Theatre, board of trustees, 82-99; Ctr for Creative Studies, bd of directors, 83-96; Detroit Symphony Orchestra, bd directors, 83-; Music Hall Str for Performing Arts, bd directors, 83-94; Metropolitan Affairs Corp., bd directors, 84-92; Nat Assoc of Securities Professionals, 85-; Oakland Univ Found, 85-; Institute of Am Business, 85-; Am Bar Found, 87-; Booker T Business Assoc, 88-90; Consolidated Rail Corp., 89-98; Greater Detroit and Windsor Japan-Am Soc, 90-92; Arts Commission of the City of Detroit, 92-97; Nat Bar Assoc; NAACP. **CONTACT ADDRESS** Lewis & Munday, PC, 1300 First National Bldg, Detroit, MI 48226. **EMAIL** dbl@lewis-pc.com

LEWIS, DAVID LANIER
PERSONAL Born 04/05/1927, Bethalto, IL, m, 1953, 4 children **DISCIPLINE** BUSINESS HISTORY **EDUCATION** Univ Ill, BS, 48; Boston Univ, MS, 55; Univ Mich, MA, 56, PhD(hist), 59. **CAREER** Reporter, Edwardsville Intelligencer, Ill, 48; state ed, Alton Telegraph, 48-50; ed publ, Ford Motor Co, 50-51; press rel rep, Borden Co, 52; supvr, Indust Arts Awards, Ford Motor Co, 52-55; pub rel staff exec, Gen Motors Corp, 59-65; assoc prof, 65-68, Prof Bus Hist, Univ Mich, 68-, Contrib ed, Model T Times, 71-, V-8 Times, 71-, Horseless Carriage, 72-, Model A News, 72- and Old Car Illustrated, 76-; consult indust properties, Div Hist, Mich Dept State, 73-; assoc ed, Cars and Parts, 73-; feature ed, Bulb Horn, 74-; trustee, Nat Automotive Hist Collection, 75- **HONORS AND AWARDS** Cuqnot Awd, Soc Automotive Historians, 77; Duryea Awd, Antique Automobile Club Am, 77; Awd of Merit, Mich Hist Soc, 77. **MEMBERSHIPS** AHA; Econ Hist Asn; Soc Automotive Historians (dir, 74-, pres, 82-). **RESEARCH** Henry Ford; auto history; entrepreneurial history. **SELECTED PUBLICATIONS** Auth, International public relations, in: Handbook of Public Relations, McGraw, 60; Automobile industry, Collier's Encycl, 67; Automobile industry, Collier's Encycl Year Bk, annually, 68-; The Square Dancing Master, Am Heritage, 72; Milton Snavely Hershey, Dict of Am Biog, 73; The Public Image of Henry Ford, Wayne State Univ, 76; guest ed, Mich Quart Rev, fall 80 and winter 81. **CONTACT ADDRESS** Grad Sch of Bus Admin, Univ of Michigan, Ann Arbor, 435 S State St, Ann Arbor, MI 48109-1003.

LEWIS, DOUGLAS
DISCIPLINE PHILOSOPHY **EDUCATION** Univ Iowa, PhD. **RESEARCH** Early modern European philosophy. **SELECTED PUBLICATIONS** Auth, On the Aims and the Method of Spinoza's Philosophy, SW J Philos, 77; Spinoza on Extension, Studies Hist Philos, 76; The Existence of Substances and Locke's Way of Ideas, Theoria, 69; auth, Marie de Journay and the Engendering of Equality, Teaching Philosophy, 99; co-auth, Locke on Mixed Modes, Knowledge and Substances, J Hist Philos, 70; co-auth, Black Elk Speaks . . . , Teaching Philosophy, 98. **CONTACT ADDRESS** Philosophy Dept, Univ of Minnesota, Twin Cities, 271 19th Ave S, 845 Heller Hall, Minneapolis, MN 55455. **EMAIL** lewis002@tc.umn.edu

LEWIS, ERIC
DISCIPLINE PHILOSOPHY **EDUCATION** Univ Cornell, BA; Univ Ill Chicago, PhD. **CAREER** Dept Phil, Mcgill Univ, 00-. **RESEARCH** Ancient philos; hist and philos of science; ancient natural philos. **SELECTED PUBLICATIONS** Auth, Alexander of Aphrodisias; auth, The Stoic Theory of Identity; auth, "The Problem of the Void, Classical Theories of Time, and Andronicus of Rhodes," in The Encyclopedia of Classical Philosophy. **CONTACT ADDRESS** Philosophy Dept, McGill Univ, 855 Sherbrooke St, Montreal, QC, Canada H3A 2T5. **EMAIL** eric@atsphilo.mcgill.ca

LEWIS, GORDON RUSSEL
PERSONAL Born 11/21/1926, NY, m, 1948, 3 children **DISCIPLINE** THEOLOGY PHILOSOPHY **EDUCATION** Baptist Bible Seminary, 44-46; BA, Gordon Col, 48; M.Div Faith Seminary, 51; MA, Syracuse Univ, 53; Cornell Univ, 54; PhD, Syracuse Univ. **CAREER** Prof of Apologetic, Baptist Bible Seminary, 51-58; Prof of Theol/Philos, Denver Seminary, 58-93, Sr Prof, 93; Visiting Prof, Young Life Institute, 67; Cir Christan Training Inst, Denver Seminary, 60-70; VP and Pres of Evangelical Theol Soc, 77-78; Board Cam of Christian Res Assoc, 79-83; Founder and Board Chm Evangelical Ministries

to New Rel, 82-92; Contributing Ed to Journal of Psychol and Theol. **HONORS AND AWARDS** Theta, Beta Phi Hon Philosophical Soc, Syracuse Univ; Lausanne Asso Lusanne Comm On World Evangelism; Biographical sketch in Ref book,such as Who's Who in Amer; Pres of Ecangelical Philosophical Soc, 77-87; Pres of Evangelical Theol Soc, 92; Member of Evangelical Fellowship Theol Commn, 90-96. **MEMBERSHIPS** Amer Academy of Rel; Soc of Christian Philos; Evangelical Theol Soc; World Evangelical Fellowship Commn, 90-96. **RESEARCH** Philo; Theol; Rel; Cults. **SELECTED PUBLICATIONS** Integrative Theology, 3 vol in 1, 1544pp Zondervan, 96; Testing Christianity's Truth Claims, 363pp, Univ Press of Amer, 90; What Everyone Should Know About Transcendental Meditation, 92pp, Regal, 75; Decide For Yourself: A Theological Workbook, 174pp, InterVarsity Press, 70; Confronting the Cults, 198pp, Presbyterian and Reformed Publishing Co, 66. **CONTACT ADDRESS** Denver Conservative Baptist Sem, PO Box 10000, Denver, CO 80250. **EMAIL** Grlewis@aol.com

LEWIS, HAROLD T.
PERSONAL Born 02/21/1947, Brooklyn, NY, m, 1970, 1 child **DISCIPLINE** THEOLOGY **EDUCATION** McGill Univ, BA, 1967; Yale Divinity School, M Div, 1971; Cambridge Univ, research fellow, 1972-73; University of Birmingham (Eng), PhD, 1994. **CAREER** NYC Dept of Social Serv, social worker, 67-68; Overseas Missionary, Honduras, 71-72; St Monica's Church, rector, 73-82; St Luke's Episcopal Church, assoc priest, 83-96; Mercer School of Theology, prof of homiletics, 88-96; Episcopal Church Cent, staff officer, 83-94; NY Theological Seminary, prof of Homiletics, 95-96; Calvary Episcopal Church, Pittsburgh, PA, rector, 96-; Pittsburgh Theological Seminary, adj prof, 96-. **HONORS AND AWARDS** Berkeley Divinity Schhol at Yale, Doctor of Divinity, 91; Episcopal Church Foundation, Research Fellowship, 78; Yale Univ, Research Fellowship, 90; Operation Crossroads Office, Distinguished Alumnus Awd, 85; Seabury Western Theol Sem Doctor of Canon Law, Hon, 01. **MEMBERSHIPS** Sigma Pi Phi, sec, 1991-; Prophetic Justice Unit, Natl Council of Churches, exec committee, 1988-96; Racial Justice Working Group, Natl Council of Churches, 1986-96. **SELECTED PUBLICATIONS** Editor, Recruitment, Training & Devel of Black Clergy, 80; Lift Every Voice and Sing II, 93; Author, In Season, Out of Season, A Collection of Sermons, 93; Yet With a Steady Beat: The Afro-Amer Struggle for Recognition in the Episcopal Church, 96; auth, Christian Social Witness, Conley, 01; auth, Elijah's Mantle, Church Publ, Co., 01. **CONTACT ADDRESS** Calvary Episcopal Church, Pittsburgh, PA 15206. **EMAIL** hlewis@calvarypgh.org

LEWIS, JACK PEARL
PERSONAL Born 03/13/1919, Midlothian, TX, m, 1978, 2 children **DISCIPLINE** RELIGION **EDUCATION** Abilene Christian Col, AB, 41; Sam Houston State Teacher's Col, MA, 44; Harvard Univ, STB, 47, PhD, 53; Hebrew Union Col, PhD, 62. **CAREER** From asst prof to assoc prof, 53-57, prof bible & grad sch relig, Harding Col, 57-, Thayer fel, Am Sch Orient Res, Jerusalem, 67-68; senior fel, Albright Inst for Arch Res, Jerusalem, 87-88. **HONORS AND AWARDS** Christian Education Awd, 20th Century Christian, 68; Distinguished Christian Service Awd, Harding Univ, 88, Pepperdine Univ, 91. **MEMBERSHIPS** Soc Bibl Lit; Nat Asn Prof Hebrew; Am Acad Relig; Evangel Theol Soc; Near East Arch Soc. **RESEARCH** The minor Prophets. **SELECTED PUBLICATIONS** Ed, The Last Thing, 72; ed, The Minor Prophets, Baker Bk, 66; A Study of the Interpretation of Noah and the Flood in Jewish and Christian Literature, Brill, 68; Historical Backgrounds to Bible People, Baker Bk, 71; Exegesis of Difficult Passages, Resource Publications, 88; Questions You've Asked About Bible Translations, Resource, 91; The Major Prophets, Hester Pub, 99; "Selah Merrill: 19th Century Am Explorer-Diplomat", NEASB, 97; "'Sun of Righteousness' (Malachi 4:2): A History of Interpretation," Stone-Campbell Journal, 99; "Desire of the Nations (Hag. 2:7): A messianic Title?" in A Heart to Study and Teach, Essays Honoring Clyde M. Woods, 00; auth, The Offering of Abel (Gen. 4:4): A Historical Interpretation, JETS 37, 94; The Gates of Hell Shall Not Prevail Against It (Matt. 16:18): A Study of the History of Interpretation, JETS 38, 95; Claude R. Conder, Surveyor of Palestine, NEASB, 95; Sire Charles William Wilson Discoverer of Wilson's Arch, NEASB, 96; Clermont-Ganneau and 19th Century discovery, NEASB, 96. **CONTACT ADDRESS** Grad Sch of Relig, Harding Univ, 1000 Cherry Rd, Memphis, TN 38117-5499. **EMAIL** jackplewis@juno.com

LEWIS, JAMES F.
PERSONAL Born 06/21/1937, m, 1958, 3 children **DISCIPLINE** HISTORY OF RELIGIONS **EDUCATION** Bethel Col, BA, 60; Bethel Theol Sem, BD, 63; Univ Iowa, PhD, 76. **CAREER** Asst prof and dept chair, world relig, Union Bibl Sem, Pune, Maharashtra, India, 77-81; assoc prof and dept chair, world relig, St. Bonifacius, 81-94; assoc prof, world relig, Wheaton Col, 94-. **MEMBERSHIPS** Evang Theol Soc; Asn of Asian Studies; Amer Acad of Relig. **RESEARCH** Religion in Vietnam; Religion in Modern India. **SELECTED PUBLICATIONS** Co-auth, Religious Traditions of the World, Zondervan, 91. **CONTACT ADDRESS** 501 College Av., Wheaton, IL 60187. **EMAIL** james.f.lewis@wheaton.edu

LEWIS, JEFFREY E.
DISCIPLINE LAW **EDUCATION** Duke Univ, BA, JD. **CAREER** Dean emer, Univ Fla, 88-96; prof, Univ Fla, 72-; dean to assoc dean, 82-96; instr, Univ Akron, 70-72; ch, ABA Accreditation Comt, 96-; ch, Planning Comt, Asn Amer Law Schools, 95 Workshop for New Teachers; vis prof, Escuela Libre de Derecho, Mexico City and Fachbereich Rechtswissenschaft, Johann Wolfgang Goethe-Univ, Frankfurt, Ger. **HONORS AND AWARDS** Ful sch, Cambridge Univ. **MEMBERSHIPS** Ohio Bar; Omicron Delta Kappa; Phi Kappa Phi; Fla Bar. **RESEARCH** Evidence, remedies. **CONTACT ADDRESS** School of Law, Univ of Florida, PO Box 117625, Gainesville, FL 32611-7625. **EMAIL** lewis@law.ufl.edu

LEWIS, KEVIN
PERSONAL Born 07/13/1943, Asheville, NC, m, 1976, 2 children **DISCIPLINE** ARTS, LITERATURE, RELIGION; RELIGIOUS STUDIES **EDUCATION** Harv Col, BA, 65; St Johns Col, BA, 67; MA, 71; Univ Chic, MA, 69, PhD, 80. **CAREER** Instr, Valpar Univ, 70; asst prof, assoc prof, Univ S Car, 73-; prin, Prest Res Col, 95-98. **HONORS AND AWARDS** Fulbright Sr Lectr, Poland, 88, Gaza, 98; Vis Res Fel Trev Coll, Wolfson Coll. **MEMBERSHIPS** AAR; MLA; SLA; ASA. **RESEARCH** Images of lonesomeness in the American Arts; Muggletonians; Biblical literalism; 19th and 20th century British and American poets. **SELECTED PUBLICATIONS** Auth, The Appeal of Muggletonianism, 86; co-ed, The Changing Shape of Protestantism in the South, 96. **CONTACT ADDRESS** Dept Religious Studies, Univ of So Carolina, Columbia, Columbia, SC 29208. **EMAIL** kevin@sc.edu

LEWIS, NEIL
DISCIPLINE PHILOSOPHY **EDUCATION** Univ Melbourne, BA; Univ Pittsburgh, PhD. **CAREER** Assoc prof. **RESEARCH** Medieval philosophy. **SELECTED PUBLICATIONS** Auth, William of Auvergne's Account of the Enuntiabile: Its Relations to Nominalism and the Doctrine of Eternal Truths, 95; Robert Grosseteste and the Church of Fathers, Brill, 97; Power and Contingency in Robert Grosseteste and Duns Scotus, Brill, 96; The First Recension of Robert Grosseteste's De libero arbitrio, Mediaeval Studies, 91. **CONTACT ADDRESS** Dept of Philosophy, Georgetown Univ, 37th and O St, Washington, DC 20057.

LEWIS, PETER
DISCIPLINE COMPARATIVE POLITICS **EDUCATION** Univ Calif, Berkeley, BA; Princeton Univ, MA, PhD. **CAREER** Prof, Am Univ. **RESEARCH** International political economy, and Third World development. **SELECTED PUBLICATIONS** Articles, World Polit, World Develop & Jour Modern African Studies. **CONTACT ADDRESS** American Univ, 4400 Massachusetts Ave, Washington, DC 20016.

LEWIS, PETER J.
PERSONAL Born 12/01/1966, Luton, England, m, 1996 **DISCIPLINE** PHILOSOPHY **EDUCATION** Oxford Univ, BA, 88; U C Irvine, MA, 92, PhD, 96. **CAREER** Texas Tech Univ, 95-00; visting instr, visting asst prof, asst prof, 95-; Visting Lecturer, Univ of Miami, 00-01. **RESEARCH** Philo of Physics and science; epistemology. **SELECTED PUBLICATIONS** Auth, Quantum Mechanics and Ontology, Kriterion, 93; GRW and the Tails Problem, Topoi, 95; auth, Quantum Mechanics, Orthogonality and Counting, Brit Jour for Philo of Science, 97; auth, "What is it like to be Schrodinger's Cat?", Analysis, 00. **CONTACT ADDRESS** Dept of Philosophy, Univ of Miami, Coral Gables, FL 33124-4670. **EMAIL** plewis@ttacs.ttu.edu

LEWIS, RANDY LYNN
PERSONAL Born 07/02/1947, Brownfield, TX, m, 1975 **DISCIPLINE** PHILOSOPHY **EDUCATION** Tex Tech Univ, BA, 69; Univ Tex, Austin, PhD(philos), 75. **CAREER** Instr philos, Tex Tech Univ, 70-71 and Univ Tex, Asutin, 75-76; asst prof, Tex Tech Univ, 76-77; Asst Prof Philos, Univ Tex, Austin, 77-80. **MEMBERSHIPS** Western Am Philos Asn. **RESEARCH** History of modern philosophy; analytic philosophy; Marxism. **SELECTED PUBLICATIONS** Auth, Perception: a representative theory, J Interdisciplinary Study Mind, 3/78. **CONTACT ADDRESS** Univ of Texas, Austin, 5812 Blythewood Dr, Austin, TX 78745.

LEWIS, WILLIAM A., JR.
PERSONAL Born 08/15/1946, Philadelphia, PA, m **DISCIPLINE** LAW **EDUCATION** Amer Univ, 1967-68; Susquehanna Univ, BA 1968; Boston Univ Law School, JD 1972. **CAREER** City of Philadelphia PA, asst dist atty 1972-75; US Civil Rights Commission, Atty 1975-80, dir cong lia div 1980-85, dir congressional & community relations div 1985-86, acting asst staff dir for congressional & public affairs 1987, Senate Judiciary Committee, Washington, DC, counsel, 87-89; Equal Employment Opportunity Comm, Washington, DC, supervisory atty, 89-92; Office of Admin and Mgt, US Dept of Energy, exec asst to dir, 92-94; Office of Sci Educ Programs, dir, 94-96; Office of Employee Concerns, 96-. **HONORS AND AWARDS** Legal Defense Fund Scholarship NAACP 1971-72. **MEMBERSHIPS** Pres, Blacks in Govt US Civil Rights Comm 1977-80; exec comm Susquehanna Univ Alumni Assoc 1980-83, 2nd vice pres 1987, pres, 1988-90; mem PA Bar Assoc 1972-, Eastern Dist Court PA 1974-; del Legal Rights & Justice Task Force White House Conf on Youth Estes Park Co 1970; pres Susquehanna Univ Alumni Assoc 1988-91; bd of directors, Susquehanna Univ, 1988-. **SELECTED PUBLICATIONS** "Black Lawyer in Private Practice" Harvard Law School Bulletin 1971. **CONTACT ADDRESS** Office of Employee Concerns, US Dept of Energy, Washington, DC 20585. **EMAIL** bill.lewis@hq.doe.gov

LEYERLE, BLAKE
PERSONAL Born 08/16/1960, Boston, MA, s **DISCIPLINE** HISTORY OF CHRISTIANITY **EDUCATION** Duke Univ, PhD 91. **CAREER** Univ Notre Dame, asst prof, assoc prof, 91 to 98-. **MEMBERSHIPS** NAPS; AAR. **RESEARCH** Social Hist of Early Christianity; John Chrysostom; Pilgrimage; Monasticism. **SELECTED PUBLICATIONS** Auth, Meal Customs in the Greco-Roman World, Passover and Easter: The Liturgical Structuring of a Sacred Season, eds, Paul Bradshaw, Lawrence A. Hoffman, Univ Notre dame Press, forthcoming; Appealing to Children, The Jour of Early Christian Studies, 97; auth, Landscape as Cartography in Early Christian Pilgrimage Narratives, Jour of Amer Acad Relig, 96; auth, Clement of Alexandria on the Importance of Table Etiquette, The Jour of Early Christian Studies, 95; auth, John Chrysostom on Almsgiving and the Use of Money, Harv Theol Rev, 94; auth, John Chrysostom on the Gaze, The Jour of Early Christian Studies, 93. **CONTACT ADDRESS** Dept of Theology, Univ of Notre Dame, 327 O'Shaughnessy Hall, Notre Dame, IN 46556. **EMAIL** Leyerle@nd.edu

LI, CHENYANG
PERSONAL Born, China, m, 2 children **DISCIPLINE** PHILOSOPHY **EDUCATION** Univ Conn, PhD. **CAREER** Assoc prof, Monmouth Col. **HONORS AND AWARDS** Best Diss Essay Awd, Philo Ed Soc, 93. **MEMBERSHIPS** Asn Chinese Philosophers in Am; Amer Philos Assoc **RESEARCH** Comparative philosophy, metaphysics, ethics. **SELECTED PUBLICATIONS** Auth, "What-being," Int Philos Q, 93; "Natural Kinds," Rev of Metaphysics, 93; "Mind-Body Identity Revised," Philos: Philos Q Israel, 94; "Confucian Concept of Jen and the Feminist Ethics of Care," Hypatia, 94; "How Can One Be A Taoist-Buddhist-Confucian," Int Rev Chinese Rel & Philos, 96; "Shifting Perspectives," Philos E & W, 97; "Confucian Value and Democratic Value," J of Value Inquiry, 97; "Tao Encounters the West," SUNY, 99. **CONTACT ADDRESS** 700 E Broadway, Monmouth, IL 61462. **EMAIL** chenyang@monm.edu

LIBO, KENNETH HAROLD
PERSONAL Born 12/04/1937, Norwich, CT **DISCIPLINE** JEWISH AMERICAN STUDIES **EDUCATION** Dartmouth Col, BA, 59; Hunter Col, MA, 68; City Univ NYork Grad Ctr, PhD(Eng), 74. **CAREER** Asst prof Eng, City Col, City Univ NY, 71-78; ED, Jewish Daily Forward, 78-; Natl Museum of Am Jewish Hist, 86-89; Museum of Jewish Heritage, 89-92. **HONORS AND AWARDS** Nat Bk Awd, Am Acad & Inst Arts & Lett, 77. **MEMBERSHIPS** Gomez Foundation **RESEARCH** Jewish immigration; Lower East Side; Am Jewish Hist. **SELECTED PUBLICATIONS** Auth, World of Our Fathers, Harcourt Brace Jovanovich, 76; How We Lived, Richard Marek Publ, 79; We Lived There Too, St. Martin's Press, 84; All in a Life Time, John Loeb Publishers, 96; auth, "One Seixao-Kursheedts: Champions of Early American Judaism, American Jewish Historical Society, 00. **CONTACT ADDRESS** 365 W 20th St, New York, NY 10011. **EMAIL** kenlibo@aol.com

LIBONATI, MICHAEL E.
PERSONAL Born 05/24/1944, Chicago, IL, m, 1967, 2 children **DISCIPLINE** LEGAL STUDIES **EDUCATION** Yale Univ, LLB, 67. **CAREER** Vis Prof, Univ of Ala, 76; Vis Prof, Cornell Univ, 77; Vis Prof, Law Col of William & Mary, 88; Prof/Laura H. Carnell Prof, Temple Univ Law Sch, 90-; **MEMBERSHIPS** Am Law Inst. **RESEARCH** State and Local Government Law. **SELECTED PUBLICATIONS** Coauth, Local Government Law, 4 Volumes, 81-82; auth, Local Government Autonomy, 93; coauth, Legislative Law and Process, 93. **CONTACT ADDRESS** Sch of Law, Temple Univ, 1719 N Broad St, Philadelphia, PA 19122-6002.

LICHTENBERT, ROBERT H.
PERSONAL Born 12/26/1945, Chicago, IL, m, 1972, 2 children **DISCIPLINE** PHILOSOPHY **EDUCATION** DePaul Univ, BA, 68; Tulane Univ, MA, 70, PhD, 75. **CAREER** Adj prof, twelve col. **HONORS AND AWARDS** Several articles in newspapers on his journal, The Meaning of Life. **MEMBERSHIPS** APA; Asn for the Develop of the Philos Teaching, pres, 91- . **RESEARCH** The meaning of life; personal philosophy in daily life; aesthetics; teaching philosophy. **SELECTED PUBLICATIONS** Auth, "Motivating Students in Philos," 93; "Developing My Philosophy Teaching," 94; "The Mystery of Getting the Point Across," 95; "Philosophical Journals," 96; J for the Develop Philos Teaching; "A Kantian Indecent Proposal," 95; "Economic Determinism in Zola's Germinal," forthcoming; Soc for the Philos Study of the Contemp Visual Arts Rev; "The Meaning of Life," 88- . **CONTACT ADDRESS** 1823 W Barry Ave, Chicago, IL 60657. **EMAIL** boblichte@aol.com

LIDDICK, DONALD R.
PERSONAL Born 02/15/1965, Harrisburg, PA, m, 1991, 4 children **DISCIPLINE** LEGAL STUDIES **EDUCATION** Penn State, PhD, 95. **CAREER** Asst Prof, Univ Pittsburgh at Greensburg, 95-. **MEMBERSHIPS** Acad of Criminal Justice Sci, Int Asn for the Study of Organized Crime. **RESEARCH** Organized Crime. **SELECTED PUBLICATIONS** Auth, The Mob's Daily Number, Univ Press of Am, 99; auth, An Empirical, Theoretical, and Historical Overview of Organized Crime, Edwin Mellen Press, 00. **CONTACT ADDRESS** Dept Soc Sci, Univ of Pittsburgh, Greensburg, 1150 Mt Pleasant Rd, Greenburg, PA 15601.

LIDERBACH, DANIEL
PERSONAL Born 03/17/1941, Stow, OH, s **DISCIPLINE** THEOLOGY **EDUCATION** Regis Col Toronto, STL, 83; Toronto Sch Theol, PhD, 79. **CAREER** Asst Prof, John Caroll Univ, 78-83; Prof, Canisius Col, 83-. **MEMBERSHIPS** Col Theol Soc. **RESEARCH** Relation between faith and contemporary physics. **SELECTED PUBLICATIONS** Auth, The Theology of Grace and American Mind; auth, The Numinous Universe; auth, Why Do We Suffer?; auth, Christ in Early Christian Hymns. **CONTACT ADDRESS** Dept of Relig Studies, Canisius Col, 2001 Main St, Buffalo, NY 14208-1035. **EMAIL** liderbac@gort.canisius.edu

LIDSKY, LYRISSA C. BARNETT
DISCIPLINE LAW **EDUCATION** Tex A&M Univ, BA; Univ Tex, JD. **CAREER** Assoc prof, Univ Fla, 94-; clerk, Judge Joseph Sneed, US Ct of Appeals, 9th Circuit; articles ed, Tex Law Rev. **HONORS AND AWARDS** Ful sch, Cambridge Univ. **MEMBERSHIPS** Order of the Coif; Phi Kappa Phi; Fla Bar; 8th Judicial Circuit Bar Asn. **RESEARCH** Torts, professional responsibility, jurisprudence, media law. **SELECTED PUBLICATIONS** Coauth, Torts: The Civil Law of Reparation for Harm Done by Wrongful Act. **CONTACT ADDRESS** School of Law, Univ of Florida, PO Box 117625, Gainesville, FL 32611-7625. **EMAIL** lidsky@law.ufl.edu

LIDZ, JOEL W.
PERSONAL Born 03/17/1952, Wilkes-Barre, PA, s **DISCIPLINE** PHILOSOPHY **EDUCATION** Penn State, B Phil, 74, MA, 75; Tulane Univ, PhD, 79. **CAREER** Adj prof, 87-, Bentley Col, Waltham, MA. **MEMBERSHIPS** APA. **RESEARCH** Plato; ethics; affirmative action. **SELECTED PUBLICATIONS** Ed, Philosophy, Being and the Good, Univ Press Am, 83; auth, Reflections on and in Plato's Cave, Interpretation, vol 21, 93/94; auth, Medicine as Metaphor in Plato, J of Med & Philos, vol 19, 94; auth, 12 Angry Men, Tchng Philos, vol 18, 95. **CONTACT ADDRESS** 234 Marlborough St, Boston, MA 02116. **EMAIL** rascalj@yahoo.com

LIEBERMAN, JETHRO K.
PERSONAL Born 10/23/1943, Washington, DC, m, 1990, 2 children **DISCIPLINE** LAW **EDUCATION** Yale Univ, BA, 64; Harvard Univ, JD, 67; Columbia Univ, PhD, 95. **CAREER** Lieut, Judge Advocate General's Corps, US Navy, 68-71; assoc, Arent Fox Kintner Plotkin & Kahn, 71-72; vice pres, gen counsel & dir, Stein & Day Publ, 72-73; legal affairs ed, Business Week, 73-82; vice pres and dir of publ, Center for Public Res, 82-85; vis assoc prof, Fordham Law Sch, 83-85; prof law, dir of Writing Program, NY Law Sch, 85- ;adj prof polit sci, Columbia Univ, 98- ; assoc dean for academic affairs, NY Law School, 00- . **HONORS AND AWARDS** Silver Gavel Awd, ABA, 82, 88. **MEMBERSHIPS** ABA; Ny State Bar Asn; Law and Soc Asn; Am Polit Sci Asn; Typophiles. **RESEARCH** Constitutionalism; specialization and expertise; theory of harm. **SELECTED PUBLICATIONS** Auth, The Tyranny of the Experts: How Professionals and Specialists are Closing the Open Society, Walker, 70; auth, Milestones! 200 Years of American Law, West, 76; auth, Crisis at the Bar: Lawyers' Unethical Ethics and What To Do About It, Norton, 78; auth, The Litigious Society, Basic, 81; coauth, The Lawyer's Guide to Writing Well, McGraw-Hill, 89; auth, The Evolving Constitution: How the Supreme Court Has Ruled on Issues from Abortion to Zoning, Random, 92, rev ed, A Practical Companion to The Constitution, Univ Calif, 99. **CONTACT ADDRESS** New York Law Sch, 57 Worth St, New York, NY 10013. **EMAIL** jlieberman@nyls.edu

LIEBERT, ELIZABETH
PERSONAL Born 07/28/1944, Seattle, WA, s **DISCIPLINE** RELIGION AND PERSONALITY **EDUCATION** Vanderbilt Univ, PhD, 86. **CAREER** Prof spiritual life and dir christ spirituality, San Francisco Theol Sem, 87-; Grad Theol Union. **MEMBERSHIPS** Am Acad of Relig; Cath Theol Soc of Am; Spiritual Dir Intl; Soc for the Study of Christian Spirituality. **RESEARCH** Spiritual care of women; Spiritual exercises of Ignatius of Loyola; Discernment. **SELECTED PUBLICATIONS** Auth, Changing Life Patterns: Adult Development in Spiritual Direction, Chalice Press, 00; auth, "Seasons and Stages: Models and Metaphors of Human Development," in Her Own Time, Women and Developmental Issues in Pastoral Care, Fortress Press, 00; auth, Accompaniment in Ministry: Supervision as Spiritual Formation, Jour of Supervision in Training in Ministry, 97; auth, Linking Faith and Justice: Remarks on the Occasion of Installation, Christ Spirituality Bull, 97, Pastoral Psychol, 46, 207-212, 98; chap, Coming Home to Themselves: Women's Spiritual Care, Through the Eyes of Women: Insights for Pastoral Care, Fortress Press, 96; co-auth, The Spirituality of the Teacher, The Way Suppl, 95; auth, The Thinking Heart: Developmental Dynamics in Etty Hillesum's Diaries, Pastoral Psychol, 95; auth, The Eighteenth Annotation of the Spiritual Exercises: A Developmental Perspective and Contemporary Adaptations of the Eighteenth Annotation, A Symposium: Ignatian Spirituality: Summary of Proceedings, Loyola House, 94. **CONTACT ADDRESS** 2 Kensington Rd., San Anselmo, CA 94960. **EMAIL** eliebert@sfts.edu

LIECHTY, DANIEL
PERSONAL Born 05/02/1954, Beatrice, NE, m, 1996, 1 child **DISCIPLINE** RELIGION, ETHICS **EDUCATION** Univ Vienna, Austria, PhD, 83; Grad Theol Found, DMin, 94. **CAREER** Group specialist, Inst Penn Hospital, 90-94; Psychosocial Coord, Montgomery Hospital Hospice Prog, 95-99; Prof of Social Work, IL State Univ, 99-. **HONORS AND AWARDS** Marquis' Who's Who in America. **MEMBERSHIPS** Asn Death Educ & Coun; Ernest Becker Found; Nat Asn Soc Workers; Acad Certified Soc Workers; Nat Coun Hospice Professionals; Am Acad Relig. **RESEARCH** Values in medicine; death and dying; effects of cultural beliefs on behavior. **SELECTED PUBLICATIONS** Auth, Abstracts of the Complete Writings of Ernest Becker, 96; Transference and Transcendence, 95; Early Anabaptist Spirituality, 94; Sabbatarianism in the Sixteenth Century, 92; Theology in Post Liberal Perspective, 90; Andreas Fischer & the Sabbatarian Anabaptists, 88. **CONTACT ADDRESS** Dept of Pastoral Counseling, Illinois State Univ, 210 S Prospect Rd, Apt T191, Bloomington, IL 61704-4578. **EMAIL** dliecht@ilstu.edu

LIENHARD, JOSEPH T.
PERSONAL Born 05/07/1940, Bronx, NY, s **DISCIPLINE** HISTORICAL THEOLOGY **EDUCATION** Fordham Univ, BA, MA,; Woodstock Col, PhL, BD, STM; Freiburg Dr Theol Habil. **CAREER** Prof, 90, Fordham Univ. **RESEARCH** Augustine's late works. **SELECTED PUBLICATIONS** Auth, The Bible, the Church, and Authority: The Canon of the Christian Bible, Hist and Theol, Collegeville, 95; transl, Gospel according to Luke, Origen: Homilies on Luke; Fragments on Luke, Wash, 96. **CONTACT ADDRESS** Dept of Theol, Fordham Univ, 441 E Fordham Rd, New York, NY 10458. **EMAIL** lienhard@fordham.edu

LIGHTNER, ROBERT P.
PERSONAL Born 04/04/1931, Cleona, PA, m, 1952, 3 children **DISCIPLINE** THEOLOGY, MODERN HISTORY **EDUCATION** Baptist Bible Col, Sem, 55; Dallas Theol Sem, ThM, 59, ThD, 64; Southern Methodist Univ, MLA, 72. **CAREER** Instructor, 59-61; Asst Prof, Chairman, 63-66; Assoc Prof, 67-68; Asst Prof, 68-74; Assoc Prof, 74-84; Prof, 84-98; Prof Emer, 98-; Adjunct Prof, 84-. **HONORS AND AWARDS** Who's Who in Am Educ, 70; Outstanding Educators of Am, and Community Leaders of Am; Outstanding Alumnus of the Year 2000 Baptist Bible Col; started churches in ny and ar; pastor and interim pastor in ny, pa, ar, ok, la, and tx; mission trips to paraguay, venezuela, and peru. **MEMBERSHIPS** Grace Evangelical Soc; Conservative Theol Soc; Pre-Trib Study Group. **RESEARCH** Pre-millennial, A-millennial, and post-millennial theology. **SELECTED PUBLICATIONS** Auth, The Toungues Tied, Speaking in Tongues and Divine Healing; The Death Christ Died: A Case for Unlimited Atonement; Prophecy in the Ring; Truth for the Good Life; James: Apostle of Practical Christianity; The God of the Bible; The Saviour and the Scriptures; Triumph though Tragedy; Neo-Liberalism; Neo-Evangelicalism Today; Church-Union: A Layman's Guide; The God of the Bible and other gods; Last Days Handbook; author of numerous other publications and articles. **CONTACT ADDRESS** 324 Clear Springs Dr, Mesquite, TX 75150-0000.

LIGHTSTONE, JACK
DISCIPLINE RELIGION **EDUCATION** Carlton Univ, BA, 72; Brown Univ, MA, 74; Brown Univ, PhD, 77. **CAREER** Teaching Asst, Brown Univ, 75-76; Asst Prof Relig, Concordia Univ, 76-81; Assoc Prof Relig, Concordia Univ, 81-87; Prof Relig, Concordia Univ, 87-. **HONORS AND AWARDS** Soc Sci and Humanities Res coun of Can, Res Grant, 87-89; Soc Sci and Humanities Res Coun of Can, Res Grant, 91-94; Soc Sci and Humanities Res Coun of Can, Res Grant, 94-97. **MEMBERSHIPS** Early rabbinic religion and literature; Late Biblical religion; Palestinian Judaism in Graeco-Roman Times; Judaism in Late Antiquity; contemporary North American Judaism. **RESEARCH** Literature of Ancient Judaism, contemporary North American Judaism. **SELECTED PUBLICATIONS** Ed, Essays in the social scientifec Study of Judaism and Jewish society, (Montreal: Department of religion, concordia Unv; U.S. and int distributrion: Hoboken, New Jersey: ktav Publishing Co., 90), 333; auth, "The Modern study of Ancient Judaiam: scholoarship and Contemporary North American Jeswish Identity," in K. Kloestermaire and L. Hurtado ed(s), relig studies: Issues, Prospects and Proposals, (Atlanta: scholars Press, 91), 211-224; auth, "The Sociological Study of Groups on Ancient Judaism: a Prolegonmenon," in Schoenfeld and S. Fishbane ed(s), Essays in the Social Scientific Study of Judaism and Jewish Society, vol 2, (Hoboken, New Jersey: Ktav Publishing co., 92), 20-45; auth, "The Institutionalization of the Rabbinic adademy and the Redation of the Babylonian Talmud," Studies in Relig, (93), 167-186; auth, "The Rhetoric of the Balbylonian Talmud, its Social Meaning and Context, (Waterloo: Wilfrid Laurier Univ Press, 94), 14+320; co-auth, "ritual and Ethnic Identiyt: A Comparative Study of the social Meaning of Liturgical Ritual in Synagogues, Waterloo: Wilfrid Laurier Univ Press, (95), 12+266; auth, "Form, Formularies and Meaning in the Babylonian Talmud: the Case of b. Bekorot 2a-b," Approaches to ancient Judaism, vol 7, (Atlanta: sholoars Press, 95), 3-31; auth, "The Rhetoric of the Mishnah and the Babylonian Talmud: From rabbinic Priestly scribes to Scholastic Rabbis," Hist reflections, (95), 1-27; auth, "Whence the Rabbis? From coherent Description to Fragmented reconstructions," Studies in Relig, (97), 275-295. **CONTACT ADDRESS** Dept of Rel, Concordia Univ, Montreal, 1455 de Maisonneuve W, Montreal, QC, Canada H3G 1M8. **EMAIL** lightst@vax2.concordia.ca

LILLIE, BETTY JANE
PERSONAL Born 04/11/1926, Cincinnati, OH, s **DISCIPLINE** BIBLICAL STUDIES **EDUCATION** Col of Mt. St. Joseph, BSEd, 55, BA 61; Providence Col, MA Theology, 67, MA Biblical Studies, 75; Hebrew Union Col, PhD, 82. **CAREER** Fac, Athenaeum of OH, 82-; instr, Providence Col, 79-86; Univ of Cincinnati, 84-; Col of Mt. St. Joseph, 80. **HONORS AND AWARDS** Lifetime Achievement Award, ABI, 97 **MEMBERSHIPS** Cathol Biblical Asn; Soc for Biblical Lit; Biblical Archaeology Soc; Eastern Great Lakes Biblical Soc; Coun on the Study of Religion; OH Humanities Coun. **RESEARCH** Biblical Studies; Biblical Archaeology; Religious Studies. **SELECTED PUBLICATIONS** Auth, A History of the Scholarship on the Wisdom of Solomon from the Nineteenth Century to Our Time. **CONTACT ADDRESS** Mt. St. Mary's Seminary, Athenaeum of Ohio, 6616 Beechmont Ave, Cincinnati, OH 45230-2091.

LIMBURG, JAMES
PERSONAL Born 03/02/1935, Redwood Falls, MN, m, 1957, 4 children **DISCIPLINE** RELIGION **EDUCATION** Luther Col, BA, 56; Luther Theol Sem, BD, 61; Union Theol Sem, Va, ThM, 62, PhD, 69. **CAREER** Teacher, High Sch, Minn, 56-57; prof relig, Augustana Col, SDak, 62-78; Prof Old Testament, Luther Sem, 78- **HONORS AND AWARDS** Distinguished Service Awd, Luther Col, 78. **MEMBERSHIPS** Soc Bibl Lit; Cath Bibl Soc. **RESEARCH** Old Testament. **SELECTED PUBLICATIONS** Auth, The Prophets and the Powerless, John Knox, 77; The Old Testament for US, Augsburg, 82; Old Stories for a New Time, John Knox, 83; Psalms for Sojourners, Augsburg, 86; Hosea-Micah, in Interpretation: A Bible Commentary, John Knox, 88; Jonah: A Commentary, in The Old Testament Library, Westminster/John Knox, 93. **CONTACT ADDRESS** Dept of Bible, Luther Sem, 2481 Como Ave, Saint Paul, MN 55108-1445. **EMAIL** jlimburg@luthersem.edu

LIMPER, PETER FREDERICK
PERSONAL Born 06/26/1939, Chicago, IL **DISCIPLINE** PHILOSOPHY **EDUCATION** Yale Univ, BA, 61, MA, 65, PhD, 75. **CAREER** Asst prof philos, Calif State Univ, Hayward, 66-71; vis instr philos, Bowdoin Col, 74-75; asst prof, 77-80, assoc prof philos, 80-91, prof philos, Christian Brothers Univ, 91-; Dean of Arts, 93-99. **MEMBERSHIPS** Am Philos Asn; Soc Philos & Tech; AAAS. **RESEARCH** Process philosophy; American philosophy; science, technology and values. **SELECTED PUBLICATIONS** Auth, Process, Creativity, and Technology: Reflections on The Uncertain Phoenix, Process Stud, 86; Technology and Value: A Process Perspective, Contemp Philos, 89; Process Themes in Frederick Ferre's Philosophy of Technology, Philos and Tech, Kluwer Acad Publ, 90; Albert Borgmann and John Dewey on Everyday Technology, Research in Philos and Tech, JAI Press, 94; Of Algorithms and Apple Pie: A Pragmatist Critique of AI, Tx A&M Stud in Philos, Tx A&M Univ, 96. **CONTACT ADDRESS** Dept Religion and Philos, Christian Brothers Univ, 650 E Parkway S, Memphis, TN 38104-5519. **EMAIL** plimper@cbu.edu

LINCOLN, BRUCE K.
PERSONAL Born 03/05/1948, Philadelphia, PA, m, 1971, 2 children **DISCIPLINE** RELIGION **EDUCATION** Haverford Col, BA, 70; Univ Chicago, PhD, 76. **CAREER** Asst Prof, to Prof, Univ of Minn, 76-94; Prof, Univ Chicago, 93-. **HONORS AND AWARDS** Phi Beta Kappa, 70; Guggenheim Fel, 85; Scholar of the Col, Univ Minn, 90-93; Scholar of the Col, Univ Minn, 90-93; Bush sabbatical Fel, 91-92; NEH summer Res Grant, 82-83; Guggenheim Memorial foundation Res Grant, 82-83; Am Coun of Learned Soc Res Grant, 82-83; Rockefeller Foundation Res conf Grant, 81; Am Coun of Learned soc Travel Grant, 79; Roundy Scholar, Univ Chicago, 75-76; Phi Beta Kappa, Haverford Col, 70. **SELECTED PUBLICATIONS** auth, Theorizing Myth: Narrative, Ideology, and Scholarship, Univ Chicago Press, 99; auth, authority: construction and corrosion, Univ Chicago Press, 94; auth, Death, War, and Sacrifice: Studies in Ideology and Practice, Univ of Chicago Press, 91; auth, discourse and the construction of Society: comparative studies of Myth, Ritual, and classification, Oxford Univ press, 89; auth, Myth, Cosmos and society: indo-European themes of Creation and destruction, Harvard Univ Press, 86; auth, Emerg-

ing from the Chrysalis: Studies in Rituals of Women's Initiation, Harvard Univ Press, 81; auth, "Ritual, Change and Marked Categories," Journal of the American Academy of Religion; forthcoming; auth, "Retheorizing Myth," in Myth and symbol: symbolic Phenomena in ancient culture, forthcoming; auth, "Death By Water: Strange Events at the Strymon and the categorical Opposition of East and west," classical Philology, forthcoming **CONTACT ADDRESS** Divinity School, Univ of Chicago, 1025 E 58th St, Chicago, IL 60637-1509. **EMAIL** blincoln@midway.uchicago.edu

LINCOLN, C. ERIC
PERSONAL Born 06/23/1924, Athens, AL, m **DISCIPLINE** RELIGIOUS STUDIES **EDUCATION** LeMoyne Coll, AB 1947; Fisk Univ, AM 1954; Univ of Chicago, BD 1956; Boston U, MEd, PhD 1960; Carleton Coll, LLD 1968; St Michael's Coll, LHD 1970. **CAREER** Duke Univ, prof of religion 1976-; Fisk Univ, prof & chmn 1973-76; Union Theol Sem, prof 1967-73; Portland State Univ, prof 1965-67; Clark Coll, prof 1954-65; Dartmouth Coll, lectr 1962-63; Vassar Coll, adj prof 1969-70; State Univ of NY, visiting prof 1970-72; Queens Coll, visiting prof 1972; Vanderbilt Univ, adj prof 1973-76; Change Magazine, consultant; Rev of Religious Research Soc, assoc editor for scientific study of religion. **HONORS AND AWARDS** Fellow Amer Acad of Arts & Sciences; Lilly Ednowment Grant; author of The Black Church Since Frazier 1974, The Black Experience in Religion 1974, A Profile of Martin Luther King Jr 1969, The Black Americans 1969, Is Anybody Listening? 1968, Sounds of the Struggle 1967, The Negro Pilgrimage in America 1967, My Face is Black 1964, The Black Muslims in America 1961; co-author of A Pictorial History of the Negro in America 1968; Lillian Smith Book Awd, 1989, for first novel, The Avenue, Clayton City; author, This Road Since Freedom, poetry, 1989; author, The Black Church in the African American Experience, 1990-; William R Kenan, Jr Distinguished Professor, 1991; Teacher of the Year, Duke Univ; 11 hon degrees. **MEMBERSHIPS** Amer Sociol Assn; Authors League of Amer; founding pres, emeritus, Black Acad of Arts & Letters; NY Acad of Arts & Scis; Soc for Study of Black Religion; American Academy of Arts asnd Sciences; 32 Degree Mason; life member, NAACP; life member, Kappa Alpha Psi; Boule, Sigma Pi Phi; Fellowship of Southern Writers. **SELECTED PUBLICATIONS** Co-author, The Black Church in the African-American Experience, 1991; author, Coming through the Fire: Surviving Race and Place in America, 1996; Hymnodist; hymns appear in "United Methodist Hymnal," "Songs of Zion, (UMC)," "Lift Every Voice, (Episopalian)," etc. **CONTACT ADDRESS** Dept of Religion, Duke Univ, Durham, NC 27706.

LINCOURT, JOHN M.
DISCIPLINE BIOMEDICAL ETHICS, AMERICAN PHILOSOPHY, MEDIEVAL PHILOSOPHY **EDUCATION** St Anselm Col, BA, 63; Niagara Univ, MA, 64; SUNY, Buffalo, PhD, 72. **CAREER** Prof Philos, Bonnie E Cone Distinguished Prof Tchg, dir, Ctr for Prof and Appl Ethics, Univ NC, Charlotte. **HONORS AND AWARDS** John Huske Anderson Awd, NC Med Soc; Nations Bank Awd for Excellence in Tchg; Case Prof of the Yr for NC. **RESEARCH** Anselm of Canterbury; Charles S. Peirce's epistemology and its rel to areas in the Soc Sci(s). **SELECTED PUBLICATIONS** Auth, Costs of Care: Two Vexing Cases in Health Care Ethics, Strategic Management of Health Care Organizations by Duncan, Ginter & Swayne, Blackwell Publ, 94; Case # 12: The Costs of Care, in Instr's Manual, 95; Ethics Without a Net: A Case Workbook in Bioethics, 2nd ed, Kendall/Hunt, 95. **CONTACT ADDRESS** Univ of No Carolina, Charlotte, Charlotte, NC 28223-0001. **EMAIL** jmlincou@email.uncc.edu

LIND, MILLARD C.
PERSONAL Born 10/10/1918, Bakersfield, CA, m, 1943, 7 children **DISCIPLINE** BIBLICAL THEOLOGY, OLD TESTAMENT **EDUCATION** Goshen Col, BA, 42; Goshen Bibl Se, BD, 47; Pittsburgh-Xenia Theol Sem, ThM, 55; Pittsburgh Theol Sem, ThD(Old Testament), 63. **CAREER** Pastor, Hopewell Mennonite Church, Kouts, Ind, 43-47; writer, Mennonite Publ House, Pa, 47-60, ed mag, 55-60; actg dean Assoc Mennonite Bibl Sem, 70-71, Prof Old Testament, Goshen Bibl Sem, 60-, Am Asn Theol Schs fac fel, 68-69. **MEMBERSHIPS** Am Schs Orient Res; Soc Bibl Lit. **RESEARCH** Warfare in ancient Israel; worship in the Old Testament; theology of politics in the Old Testament. **SELECTED PUBLICATIONS** Auth, Theology of the Old Testament, Vol 1--Jhwh Election and Obligation, Cath Bibl Quart, Vol 0055, 93; Theology of the Old Testament, Vol 2--Israel Path With Jhwh, Cath Bibl Quart, Vol 0056, 94; The Patriarchate in Israel in Deuteronomy, Cath Bibl Quart, Vol 0056, 94; Rudiments of Old Testament Hermeneutics, Cath Bibl Quart, Vol 0057, 95. **CONTACT ADDRESS** Associated Mennonite Biblical Sem, 1123 S 8th St, Elkhart, IN 46517.

LINDBERG, CARTER HARRY
PERSONAL Born 11/23/1937, Berwyn, IL, m, 1960, 3 children **DISCIPLINE** THEOLOGY, HISTORY OF CHRISTIAN THOUGHT **EDUCATION** Augustana Col, AB, 59; Lutheran Sch Theol, BD, 62; Univ Iowa, PhD, 65. **CAREER** Asst prof relig, Susquehanna Univ, 65-67; asst prof theol, Col Holy Cross, 67-72; asst prof, 72-79, assoc prof, 80-84, Prof Church Hist & Theol, Sch Theol, Boston Univ, 85-. **MEMBERSHIPS** Am Soc Reformation Res; Am Soc, Church Hist; Soc 16th Century Studies (vpres, 77); Luther-Ges. **RESEARCH** Luther; ethics; historical theology in the 16th and 19th century. **SELECTED PUBLICATIONS** Auth, Martin Luther: Copernican Revolution or Ecumenical Bridge?, Una Sancta, Vol 24, No 1; Luther and Feuerbach, In:Sixteenth Century Essays and Studies, St Louis, 70; Prierias and his Significance for Luther's Development, Sixteenth Century J, 72; Luther's Theology of the Demonic, In: Disguises of the Demonic, Asn Press, 75; Theology and Politics: Luther the Radical and Muntzer the Reactionary, Encounter, 76; Luther's Views on Papal Authority, Andover Newton Quart, 77; Karlstadt, Luther and the Origins of Protestant Poor Relief, Church Hist, 77; Conflicting Models of Ministry, Concordia Theol Quart, 77; auth, The Third Reformation?, Macon: Mercer Univ Press, 83; ed and contrib, Piety, Politics, and Ethics: Reformation Studies in Honor of George W. Forell, Kirksville: Sixteenth Century J Pubs, 84; auth, Martin Luther, Nashville: United Methodist Pub House, 88; Korean Tr, Seoul: Concordia, 90; Beyond Charity: Reformation Initiatives for the Poor, Minneapolis: Fortress Press, 93; coauth, with Emily Albu Hanawalt, Through the Eye of the Needle: Judeo-Christian Contributions to Social Welfare, Kirksville: Thomas Jefferson Univ Press, 94; auth, The European Reformations, Oxford: Blackwell, 96; coauth, with Howard C. Kee, et al, Christianity: A Social and Cultural History, 2nd ed, Prentice-Hall, 98; over 60 articles and book chapters about reformation history and theology; ed, The European Reformations Sourcebook, Blackwell, 00. **CONTACT ADDRESS** Sch of Theol, Boston Univ, 745 Commonwealth Ave, Boston, MA 02215-1401. **EMAIL** clindber@bu.edu

LINDBERG, DEBRA
DISCIPLINE CRIMINAL JUSTICE **EDUCATION** Augustara Col, Sioux Falls, SD, BA, 81; MAT, 84; Portland State Univ, PhD, 96. **CAREER** Ore Dept of Corrections, Couns; Asst Prof, Radford Univ, 98-00. **MEMBERSHIPS** Acad of Criminal Justice Sci. **RESEARCH** Juvenile Crime. **SELECTED PUBLICATIONS** Coauth, Evaluating Columbia Villa/Tamaracks Community Service, Portland State Univ (Portland), 90; auth, Violent Youth Jongs in Portland: A Study of The City's Response, Portland State Univ (Portland), 96. **CONTACT ADDRESS** Dept Criminal Justice, Radford Univ, PO Box 6934, Radford, VA 24142.

LINDBERG, JORDAN
PERSONAL Born 04/21/1969, Traverse City, MI, m, 1993 **DISCIPLINE** PHILOSOPHY **EDUCATION** Albion Col, AB, 91; Mich State Univ, MA, 93; Univ of Mo, Columbia, PhD, 97. **CAREER** Asst prof, Central Mich Univ, 98-. **HONORS AND AWARDS** Jack Padgett Philos Awd, Albion Col, 91; Outstanding Grad Student Achievement Awd, Univ of Miss, 94. **MEMBERSHIPS** Am Philos Assoc. **RESEARCH** History of Contemporary Analytic Philosophy, Epistemology. **SELECTED PUBLICATIONS** Ed, Analytic Philosophy: Beginnings to Present, Mayfield Publishing, 00. **CONTACT ADDRESS** Dept Relig and Philos, Central Michigan Univ, 100 W Preston Rd, Mount Pleasant, MI 48859-0001. **EMAIL** wildtrout@yahoo.com

LINDER, ROBERT DEAN
PERSONAL Born 10/06/1934, Salina, KS, m, 1957, 4 children **DISCIPLINE** EUROPEAN HISTORY, HISTORY OF CHRISTIANITY **EDUCATION** Emporia State Univ, BS, 56; Cent Baptist Theol Sem, MDiv, MRE, 58, Univ IA, MA, 60, PhD, 63. **CAREER** Instr western civilization, Univ IA, 58-61; asst prof hist, William Jewell Col, 63-65; from asst prof to assoc prof, 65-73, prof KS State Univ, 73-, Sr res fel, The Centre for the Study of Christianity, Macquarie Univ, Sydney, Australia, 95-, Ed, Fides et Historia, Conf Faith & Hist, 68-78; Mayor, Manhattan, KS, 71-72, 78-79; Dir, Relig Studies Prog, KS State Univ, 79-82. **HONORS AND AWARDS** KS State Univ Distinguished Tchg Awd, 68; Phi Kappa Phi Outstanding Scholar, 1980; Sr Fac Awd for Res Excellence, Inst for Soc & Behav Res, KS State Univ, 97. **MEMBERSHIPS** AHA; Am Soc Church Hist; Am Soc Reformation Res (secy, 71-79); Renaissance Soc Am; Rocky Mountain Soc Sci Asn; Conf Faith & Hist. **RESEARCH** Reformation and Renaissance hist; hist of Christianity; Australian relig hist. **SELECTED PUBLICATIONS** Auth, The Political Ideas of Pierre Viret, Droz, Geneva, 64; co-ed, Protest and Politics: Christianity and Contemporary Politics, Attic, 68; coauth, Calvin and Calvinism: Sources of Democracy?, Heath, 70; ed, God and Caesar: Case Studies in the Relationship between Christianity and the State, Conf Faith & Hist, 71; co-ed, The Cross and the Flag, Creation House, 72; coauth, Politics and Christianity, InterVarsity, 73; co-ed, The Eerdman's Handbook to the History of Christianity, Eerdmans, 77; coauth, Twilight of the Saints: Biblical Christianity and Civil Religion in America, InterVarsity, 78; coauth, Civil Religion and the Presidency, Zonervan, 88; co-ed, The Dictionary of Christianity in America, InterVarsity, 90; co-ed, The History of Christianity, Fortress, 90; co-ed, A Concise Dictionary of Christianity in America, InterVarsity, 95; auth, The Long Tragedy: Australian Evangelical Christians and the Great War, 1914-1918, Open Book Pub, 00. **CONTACT ADDRESS** Dept of Hist, Kansas State Univ, 208 Eisenhower Hall, Manhattan, KS 66506-1002. **EMAIL** rdl@ksu.edu

LINDGREN, JOHN RALPH
PERSONAL Born 10/08/1933, Oak Park, IL, m, 1958, 5 children **DISCIPLINE** PHILOSOPHY **EDUCATION** Northwestern Univ, BS, 59; Marquette Univ, MA, 61, PhD(philos), 63. **CAREER** Teaching asst philos, Marquette Univ, 60-62; from instr to asst prof, Col Holy Cross, 62-65; asst prof, 65-69, assoc prof, 69-79, Prof Philos, Lehigh Univ, 79, Chmn Dept, 73-, Vis scholar, Law Sch, Univ Pa, 77-78. **MEMBERSHIPS** Eastern Div Am Philos Asn; Philos and Pub Affairs; Conf Studies Polit Thought; Int Asn Philos Law and Social Philos. **RESEARCH** Philosophy of law; social philosophy; political economy. **SELECTED PUBLICATIONS** Auth, Kant's conceptus cosmicus, Dialogue, 63; The Early Writings of Adam Smith, Kelley, 67; Cassirer's theory of concept formation, New Scholasticism, 68; Adam Smith's theory of inquiry, J Polit Econ, 69; The Social Philosophy of Adam Smith, M Nijhoff, 73; contribr, Adam Smith and the Wealth of Nations, 1776-1976, Richmond, Ky, 76; auth, Adam Smith e o estado minimalista, Documentaqao E Atreolidade Polit, 77; The irrelevance of philosophical treatments of Affirmative Action, Social Theory & Practice, 77. **CONTACT ADDRESS** Dept of Philos, Lehigh Univ, Bethlehem, PA 18015.

LINDQUIST, LARRY
DISCIPLINE RELIGION **EDUCATION** Trinity Intl Univ, BA; Trinity Evangel Divinity Sch, MA; Northern Ill Univ, DEd. **CAREER** Adj prof, Trinity Intl Univ; Moody Bible Inst; asst prof, Denver Sem, 98-. **RESEARCH** Youth and family ministries and educational ministry **SELECTED PUBLICATIONS** Auth, Reader's Guide; contrib auth, Reaching a Generation for Christ. **CONTACT ADDRESS** Denver Conservative Baptist Sem, PO Box 10000, Denver, CO 80250.

LINDSEY, WILLIAM D.
PERSONAL Born 03/30/1950, Little Rock, AR **DISCIPLINE** RELIGIOUS STUDIES **EDUCATION** Loyola Univ, BA, 72; Univ St Michael's Col, Toronto School of Theol, MA, 80, PhD, 87; Tulane Univ, MA, 89. **CAREER** Asst prof, Theol Dept, Xavier Univ, 84-91; asst prof, Theol Dept, Belmont Abbey Col, 91-93; assoc prof religion and philos, Philander Smith Col, 99-, Dean of Instruction. **HONORS AND AWARDS** Fel, Loyola Univ, 68-72; Alpha Sigma Nu, 69; Phi Delta Pi, 76; C Douglas Jay award, Toronto School of Theol, 83; Charles Dana grant, 86; fel, Center for the Humanities, Oregon State Univ, 89; Bush Found Fac Develop Grant, 90; winning essay, Ctr for the Study of Relig and Am Culture Awds, 92. **MEMBERSHIPS** Am Acad Relig; Catholic Theol Soc of Am; Col Theol Soc; Highlands Inst of American Religious and Philosophical Thought. **RESEARCH** Social gospel movement; social ethics; development of conscience and ethical awareness. **SELECTED PUBLICATIONS** Auth, Ethics and Morality, Loyola Inst, 89; auth, Singing in A Strange Land: Praying and Acting with the Poor, Sheed & Ward, 91; auth, The Problem of Great Time: A Bakhtinian Ethics of Discourse, J of Relig, 93; auth, Richard Rorty: The Homelessness of Liberalism, The Ecumenist, 93; auth, James Joyce's The Dead, Eschatology and the Meaning of History, Toronto J of Theol, 95; auth, Shailer Mathews' Lives of Jesus: The Search for a Theological Foundation for the Social Gospel, SUNY, 96; auth, The AIDS Crisis and the Church: A Time to Heal, in Thatcher, ed, Christian Perspectives on Sexuality and Gender, Eerdmans, 96; auth, Prophetic Neopragmatism and the Double Intentionality of Religious Symbols: A Theological Response to Cornel West's Keeping Faith: Philosophy and Race in America, Toronto J of Theol, 97; auth, Crossing the Postmodern Divide: Some Implications for Academic Theology, Theol and Sexuality, 97; auth, "'Somebody, Somehow, Somewhere, and Somewhen': Shailer Matthews and the Socio-Historical Interpretation of Doctrine," Am Jrnl of Theology and Philos 20 (99): 191-215. **CONTACT ADDRESS** 519 Ridgeway Dr, Little Rock, AR 72205. **EMAIL** indsch19@idt.net

LINDT, GILLIAN
DISCIPLINE RELIGION **EDUCATION** London Univ, BS, 54, MA, 55, PhD, 65. **CAREER** Prof. **RESEARCH** Social theory; sociology of religion; comparative history of religion in America and Western Europe from the eighteenth century to the present. **SELECTED PUBLICATIONS** Auth, Moravians in Two Worlds: A Study of Changing Communities. **CONTACT ADDRESS** Dept of Religion, Columbia Col, New York, 2960 Broadway, New York, NY 10027-6902. **EMAIL** gl9@columbia.edu

LINEBACK, RICHARD HAROLD
PERSONAL Born 06/05/1936, Cincinnati, OH, m, 1957, 2 children **DISCIPLINE** PHILOSOPHY **EDUCATION** Univ Cincinnati, BA, 58; Ind Univ, MA, 62, PhD, 63. **CAREER** Lectr philos, Ind Univ, 62-63; asst prof, Wichita State Univ, 63-65; from asst prof to assoc prof, 65-72, chmn dept, 68-72, prof philos, Bowling Green State Univ, 72-, Bowling Green State Univ grant computer applications in philos, 67-; ed, The Philosopher's Index, 67-; Nat Endowment for Humanities grants, 76, 77, 78 & 79. **MEMBERSHIPS** Am Philos Asn. **RESEARCH** Ethics; computers. **SELECTED PUBLICATIONS** Coauth, Encounter: An Introduction to Philosophy, Scott, 69; co-ed, International Directory of Philosophy, Philos Doc Ctr, 72, 74, 78 & 82. **CONTACT ADDRESS** Philosophers Information Ctr, 1616 E Wooster St, Bowling Green, OH 43402.

LINEHAN, ELIZABETH ANN
PERSONAL Born 03/19/1940, Des Moines, IA **DISCIPLINE** PHILOSOPHY **EDUCATION** Mount St Agnes Col, BA, 64; Fordham Univ, MA, 70, PhD(Philos), 76. **CAREER** From instr to asst prof Philos, Spring Hill, Col, 73-76; asst prof Philos, St Joseph's Univ, 76-; chmn, Philosophy Dept, 83-92; 97-. **MEMBERSHIPS** Am Philos Asn; Hastings Ctr Soc, Ethics & Life Sci; CTSA; ACPA. **RESEARCH** American philosophy; ethics; restorative justice. **SELECTED PUBLICATIONS** Auth, Neocortical tests and personal death: A reply to Robert Veatch, Omega, 81-82; Ignorance, self-deception and moral accountability, J Value Inquiry 16 (82): 101-115; auth, "The Duty Not to Kill Oneself," Proceedings of the am Catholic Philosophical Asn, 84; auth, "Moral Reflection and Moral Life," Proceedings of the Jesuit Philosophical Asn, 92; auth, "La peine de mort aux Etats-Unis," Etudes (00): 303-311; "Executing the Innocent" The Paideia On-Line Project: Proceedings of the 20th World Congress of Philosophy, Human Rights Volume, Philosophy Docementation Ctr, 99. **CONTACT ADDRESS** Saint Joseph's Univ, 5600 City Ave, Philadelphia, PA 19131-1376. **EMAIL** elinehan@sju.edu

LINENTHAL, EDWARD TABOR
PERSONAL Born 11/06/1947, Boston, MA, m, 1974, 1 child **DISCIPLINE** RELIGIOUS STUDIES, AMERICAN HISTORY **EDUCATION** Western Mich Univ, BA, 69; PACIFIC Sch Relig, MDiv, 73; Univ Calif, Santa Barbara, PhD(relig studies), 79. **CAREER** Lectr Am relig, Univ Calif, Santa Barbara, 78-79; Asst Prof Relig Studies, Univ Wis-Oshkosh, 79-, asst ed bk rev sect, Relig Studies Rev, 81-. **MEMBERSHIPS** Am Soc Church Hist; Am Acad Relig. **RESEARCH** Religion and war; religion and American culture; history of religions. **SELECTED PUBLICATIONS** Auth, From hero to anti-hero: The transformation of the warrior in modern America, Soundings, spring 80; Nostalgia for clarity: The memory of Patton, Studies Popular Cult, spring 82; Ritual drama at the Little Big Horn: The persistence and transformation of a national symbol, J Am Acad Relig (in press); The Warrior as a Symbolic Figure in America, Edwin Mellen Press (in press). **CONTACT ADDRESS** Dept of Relig, Univ of Wisconsin, Oshkosh, 800 Algoma Blvd, Oshkosh, WI 54901-8601.

LINGIS, ALPHONSO
DISCIPLINE PHILOSOPHY **EDUCATION** Loyola Univ, BA, 54; Cath Univ Louvain, Lic, 58, PhD, 61. **CAREER** From instr to assoc prof philos, Duquesne Univ, 60-66; assoc prof, 66-80, prof philos, PA State Univ, 80-. **MEMBERSHIPS** Soc Phenomenol & Existential Philos. **RESEARCH** Phenomenology and existentialist philos; hist of modern philos; ontology. **SELECTED PUBLICATIONS** Auth, Excesses: Eros and Culture, SUNY, 84; Libido: The French Existential Theories, Ind Univ, 85; Phenomenological Explanations, Martinus Nijhoff, 86; Deathbound Subjectivity, Ind Univ, 89; The Community of Those Who Have Nothing in Common, Ind Univ, 94; Abuses, Univ Calif, 94; Foreigh Bodies, Routledge, 94; Sensation: Intelligibility in Sensibility, NY Hum, 95; The Imperative, Ind Univ, 98; Dangerous Emotions, Univ Calif, 00. **CONTACT ADDRESS** Dept Philos, Pennsylvania State Univ, Univ Park, 240 Sparks Bldg, University Park, PA 16802-5201. **EMAIL** axl7@psu.edu

LINGSWILER, ROBERT DAYTON
PERSONAL Born 06/05/1927, Buffalo, NY, m, 1948, 2 children **DISCIPLINE** PHILOSOPHY **EDUCATION** Heidelberg Col, AB, 49; Iliff Sch Theol, ThM, 52, ThD(philos relig), 64. **CAREER** Asst prof philos, SDak Sch Mines & Technol, 63-66; assoc prof, 66-77, Prof Philos & Chmn Dept, Baldwin-Wallace Col, 77- **MEMBERSHIPS** Am Philos Asn. **RESEARCH** Philosophy of religion and science; political philosophy; ethics. **CONTACT ADDRESS** Baldwin-Wallace Col, 275 Eastland Rd, Berea, OH 44017-2088. **EMAIL** rlingswi@baldwinw.edu

LINKER, MAUREEN
PERSONAL Born 10/04/1963, New York, NY, m, 2000 **DISCIPLINE** PHILOSOPHY **EDUCATION** CUNY, PhD, 96. **CAREER** Asst prof philos, Univ Mich, Dearborn, 96- . **HONORS AND AWARDS** Rackham Jr Fac fel, 97. **MEMBERSHIPS** APA; Soc for Anal Feminism. **RESEARCH** Epistemology; logic; feminist philosophy; philosophy of law. **SELECTED PUBLICATIONS** Auth, "Sentencing Circles and the Dilemma of Difference," Criminal Law Quart 42 (99): 116-128; auth, "A coherentist epistemology with integrity," Philos and Soc Criticism 25 (99): 121-124. **CONTACT ADDRESS** Dept of Philosophy, Univ of Michigan, Dearborn, 4901 Evergreen Rd, Dearborn, MI 48128. **EMAIL** mlinker@umich.edu

LINSENBARD, GAIL E.
PERSONAL Born 10/06/1959, Los Angeles, CA **DISCIPLINE** PHILOSOPHY **EDUCATION** Univ Colo Boulderm, PhD, 96. **CAREER** Asst prof, Mass Coll of Liberal Arts, 96-; asst adj prof, NY Univ. **HONORS AND AWARDS** Dean's Small Grant Awd. **MEMBERSHIPS** Am Philos Asn; Soc for Women in Philos; Soc for Phenomenol and Existential Philos; N Am Sartre Soc; Simon de Beauvoir Circle. **RESEARCH** 19th and 20th Century Continental Philosophy; Human Rights; Ethics; Feminist Philosophy. **SELECTED PUBLICATIONS** Auth, Women's Rights as Human Rights, Women Rights as Human Rights: Activism and Social Change in Africa; An Investigation of Sartre's Notebooks for an Ethics, forthcoming. **CONTACT ADDRESS** 231 Clinton St. Apt. 5, Hoboken, NJ 07030-2555.

LINSS, WILHELM CAMILL
PERSONAL Born 03/21/1926, Erlangen, Germany, m, 1953, 3 children **DISCIPLINE** NEW TESTAMENT **EDUCATION** Univ Erlangen, BD, 50; Boston Univ, ThD(New Testament textual criticism), 55. **CAREER** Asst prof philos and Christianity, Gustavus Adolphus Col, 54-57; prof New Testament, Cent Lutheran Theol Sem, 57-67; dir admis, 68-78, registr, 68-70, Prof New Testament, Lutheran Sch Theol Chicago, 67-92, Res, Univ Munster, 63. **MEMBERSHIPS** Soc Bibl Lit. **RESEARCH** Textual criticism; New Testament theology; exegesis. **SELECTED PUBLICATIONS** Transl, of Matthew 1-7 by V. Luz. **CONTACT ADDRESS** Lutheran Sch of Theol at Chicago, 1100 E 55th St, Chicago, IL 60615. **EMAIL** wclinss@mcs.com

LINTS, RICHARD
PERSONAL m, 3 children **DISCIPLINE** THEOLOGY, APOLOGETICS **EDUCATION** Westminster Col, BA; Univ Notre Dame, MA, PhD; Univ Chicago, AM. **CAREER** Instr, Trinity Col, Bristol, 84-86; Westminster Col, 82-83; sr tchg fel, Univ Notre Dame, 81; prof, Gordon-Conwell Theol Sem, 86-. **HONORS AND AWARDS** Grant, Ass Theol Sch(s) and Pew Charitable Trusts; minister, presbyterian church in am; pastor, redeemer presbyterian church. **RESEARCH** Theological and cultural upheavals of the 1960's. **SELECTED PUBLICATIONS** Auth, The Fabric of Theology: A Prolegomena to Evangelical Theology, Eerdmans, 93. **CONTACT ADDRESS** Gordon-Conwell Theol Sem, 130 Essex St, South Hamilton, MA 01982.

LIOTTA, PETER H.
PERSONAL Born 09/16/1956, Burlington, VT, m, 1979, 1 child **DISCIPLINE** INTERNATIONAL RELATIONS, SECURITY STUDIES **EDUCATION** Oklahoma Univ, MA, 84; Cornell Univ, MA, 87; MFA, 87; Naval War Col, MA, 97; Salve Regina, PhD, 99. **CAREER** Greek Lang Training, US Dept of State, 91-93; Attache, Am Embassy Athens, 93-96; prof, chair, US Naval Col, 97-. **HONORS AND AWARDS** Pushcart Prize; Erika Mumford Award; Acad of Am Poets Prize; Colo Lit Award; Daniel Varoujan Award; Robert H Winner Mem Award; Fulbright Fel, 88-89; MacDowell Colony Fel, 89; Helene Wurlitzer Found Fel, 94; NEA Fel, 93-95; Inst for Nat Security Studies Fel, 99; RI State Coun on Arts Fel, 00. **MEMBERSHIPS** Asn for the Study of Nationalities, Int Peace Res Asn, Int Studies Asn, PEN Int, Fulbright Found, Bosnia Book Fund, Int Forum Bosnia, Authors Guild. **RESEARCH** Security affairs for Southeastern Europe, post-Soviet space, the Caspian Region, and the Euro-Mediterranean. **SELECTED PUBLICATIONS** Auth, Learning to Fly: A Season with the Peregrine Falcon, Algonquin Books, 89; auth, Rules of Engagement, Cleveland State Univ Pr, 91; auth, Diamond's Compass, Algonquin Books, 93; auth, The Ruins of Athens: A Balkan Memoir, Garden St Pr, 99; auth, Mediterranean Security at the Crossroads, Duke Univ, 99; auth, Unity and Diversity: Mutual Perceptions of Mediterranean Security, Unidad de Investigacion sobre (Madrid), 99; auth, The Wreckage reconsidered: Five Oxymorons, Lexington Books, 99; auth, Euro-Mediterranean Partnership for the 21st Century, Macmillan, 00; auth, Dismembering the State: The Death of Yugoslavia and Why It Matters, Lexington Books, 01; transl of The Wolf at the Door: A Poetic Cycle, by Bogomil Gjuzel, Xenos Books, 01. **CONTACT ADDRESS** Naval War Col, 686 Cushing Rd, Newport, RI 02841-1207.

LIPMAN, MATTHEW
PERSONAL Born 08/24/1923, Vineland, NJ, 1 child **DISCIPLINE** PHILOSOPHY **EDUCATION** Columbia Univ, BS, 50, PhD, 54. **CAREER** From instr to prof philos, Columbia Univ, 54-72; Prof Philos, Montclair State Col, 72, Dir Inst Advan Philos Children, 74-, Instr contemp civilization, Columbia Col, 54-63; lectr philos, City Col New York, 53-66, adj assoc prof, 66-75; mem fac, Sarah Lawrence Col, 63-64; Am Coun Learned Soc grant-in-aid, 67; Nat Endowment Humanities grants, 70-73; Rockefeller grant, 78-82. **HONORS AND AWARDS** Matchette Prize, 55. **MEMBERSHIPS** Am Philos Asn; Am Soc Aesthetics; Soc Advan Am Philos. **RESEARCH** Philosophy for children; aesthetics; metaphysics. **SELECTED PUBLICATIONS** Ed & contribr, Contemporary Aesthetics, Allyn & Bacon, 73; auth, Harry Stottlemeier's Discovery, 74; co-ed, Instructional Manual to Accompany Harry Stottlemeier's Discovery, 75; auth, Lisa, 76; co-ed, Instructional Manuel to Accompany Lisa, 77; coauth, Philosophy in the Classroom, 77, & auth, Suki, 78, Inst Advan Philos Children; co-ed, Growing Up With Philosophy, Temple Univ 78. **CONTACT ADDRESS** Inst Advan Philos, Montclair State Univ, Upper Montclair, NJ 07043. **EMAIL** lipmanm@mail.montclair.edu

LIPPY, CHARLES
PERSONAL Born 12/02/1943, Binghamton, NY, s **DISCIPLINE** RELIGION **EDUCATION** Dickinson Col, BA, 65; Union Theol Sem, MDiv, 68; Princeton Univ, MA, 70, PhD, 72 **CAREER** Prof, Univ of TN, 94-pres; Asst Prof, Assoc Prof, Prof, 76-94, Clemson Univ; Visit Asst Prof, 74-75, Miami Univ; Asst Prof, 72-74, Oberlin Col; Visit Prof, 90-91, Emory Univ **HONORS AND AWARDS** Fulbright Scholar, India, 88; Summer Fel, Louisville Inst, 98; NEH Summer Stipends; NEH Summer Seminars **MEMBERSHIPS** Am Acad of Relig; Am Soc of Church Hist; Am Stud Assoc; Org of Am Historians; Soc for Scientific Study of Relig **RESEARCH** Religion in American Culture **SELECTED PUBLICATIONS** Coauth, The Evangelicals A Historical, Thematic and Biographical Guide, Greenwood Press, 99; Auth, Modern American Popular Religion A Critical Assessment and Annotated Bibliography, Greenwood Press, 96; ed, Popular Religious Magazines of the United States, Greenwood Press, 94; auth, Pluralism Comes of Age: American Religious Culture in the 20th Century, M.E. Sharpe, 00. **CONTACT ADDRESS** Dept of Philos and Relig, Univ of Tennessee, Chattanooga, 615 McCallie Ave, Chattanooga, TN 37403. **EMAIL** charles-lippy@utc.edu

LIPSEY, ROBERT E.
PERSONAL Born 08/14/1926, New York, NY, m, 1948, 3 children **DISCIPLINE** ECONOMICS **EDUCATION** Columbia Univ, BA, 44, MA, 46, PhD, 61. **CAREER** Res assoc, 60-, dir NY off, 77-, Natl Bur Econ Res; prof econ, 67-95, emer, 95-, Queens Col and Grad Ctr, CUNY. **HONORS AND AWARDS** Fulbright fel, 83; fel, Am Statist Asn; fel, NY Acad Sci. **MEMBERSHIPS** Am Econ Asn; Acad Int Bus; Eastern Econ Asn; Econometric Soc; Cliometric Soc; European Econ Asn; Conf on Income and Wealth; Western Econ Asn; Int Asn for Res in Income and Wealth. **RESEARCH** Foreign direct investment; price measurement; international comparisons of prices, output and investment; prices and international trade. **SELECTED PUBLICATIONS** Auth, Price and Quantity Trends in The Foreign Trade of The United States, Princeton, 63; coauth, Studies in The National Balance Sheet of the United States, Princeton, 63; coauth, Source Book of Statistics Relating to Construction, National Bureau of Economic Research, 66; coauth, Price Competitiveness in World Trade, National Bureau of Economic Research, 71; coauth, The Financial Effects of Inflation, National Bureau of Economic Research, 78. **CONTACT ADDRESS** National Bureau of Economic Research, 365 Fifth Ave, #5FL, New York, NY 10016-4309. **EMAIL** rlipsey@email.gc.cuny.edu

LIPSON, CHARLES
PERSONAL Born 02/01/1948, m, 2 children **DISCIPLINE** POLITICAL SCIENCE, INTERNATIONAL AGREEMENTS **EDUCATION** Yale Univ, BA, 70; Harvard Univ, AM, 74; PhD, 76. **CAREER** Res assoc, vis schl, Harvard Univ, 76-80; vis fel, London Sch Econ, 88-89; asst prof, Univ Chicago, 77-84; assoc prof, 84-. **HONORS AND AWARDS** Macarthur Fond Grant, 85-92, 94-; Ford Found Grant; German Marshall Fund Fel; Rockefeller Fel; Who's Who Midwest; Univ Chicago Fac Awd; RIR Chase Prize. **MEMBERSHIPS** APSA; ASIL; BACSG; CCFR; CC; IISS; IRCPB; ISA; RIIA. **SELECTED PUBLICATIONS** Co-ed, Theory and Structure in International Political Economy: An International Organization Reader, MIT Press (Cambridge, MA), 99; co-ed, Issues and Agents in International Political Economy: An International Organization Reader, MIT Press (Cambridge, MA), 99; auth, "International Finance," in The Oxford Companion to Politics of the World (NY: Oxford Univ Press, 93); auth, "Nationalization," The Oxford Companion to Politics of the World (NY: Oxford Univ Press, 93); auth, "Is the Future of Collective Security Like the Past?" in Collective Security Beyond the Cold War, ed. George Downs (Ann Arbor, MI: Univ Mich Press, 94): 105-31; auth, "Are Security Regimes Possible? Historical Cases and Modern Issues," in Regional Security Regimes: Israel and Its Neighbors, ed. Ephraim Inbar (Albany, NY: SUNY Press, 95); auth, "Forward" to Kenneth P. Thomas, Capital Beyond Borders (NY: Macmillan, 97); auth, "American Support for Israel: History, Sources, Limits," in American-Israeli Relations and the "New World Order," ed. Gabriel Sheffer, Israel Affairs 2 (96): 128-46, reprinted in U.S.-Israeli Relations at the Crossroads, ed. Gabriel Sheffer (London and Portland, OR: Frank Cass, 97): 128-46; auth, Nationalization of Investments," in Routledge Encyclopedia of International Political Economy, ed. RJB Jones (London: Routledge, forthcoming); auth, European Recovery Program (Marshall Plan Aid)," in Routledge Encyclopedia of International Political Economy, ed. RJB Jones (London: Routledge, forthcoming). **CONTACT ADDRESS** Dept Political Science, Univ of Chicago, 5828 University Ave, Chicago, IL 60637. **EMAIL** c-lipson@uchicago.edu

LISSKA, ANTHONY JOSEPH
PERSONAL Born 07/23/1940, Columbus, OH, m, 1968, 2 children **DISCIPLINE** PHILOSOPHY **EDUCATION** Providence Col, AB, 63; St S Stephen's Col, MA, 67; Ohio State Univ, PhD(philos), 71. **CAREER** Asst prof, 69-76, chmn dept, 73-78, assoc prof, 76-81, Prof Philos, Denison Univ, 81-, Dean Col, 78-. **MEMBERSHIPS** Am Philos Asn; Am Cath Philos Asn; Soc Medieval and Renaissance Philos; Asn Am Cols. **RESEARCH** Medieval philosophy; history of perception; ethical naturalism. **SELECTED PUBLICATIONS** Auth, Deely and Geach on abstractionism in thomistic epistemology, Thomist, 7/73; Phantasms and sense data in Aquinas's theory of perception (abstract), J Philos, 8/73; Aquinas's use of Phantasia, Thomist, 4/76; Axioms of intentionality in Aquinas's Theory of Knowledge, Int Philos Quart, 12/76; Philosophy Matters, C E

Merrill, 77. **CONTACT ADDRESS** Dept of Philos, Denison Univ, 1 Denison University, Granville, OH 43023-1359.

LIST, PETER C.
PERSONAL Born 10/22/1939, WI, m, 2 children **DISCIPLINE** PHILOSOPHY **EDUCATION** Mich St Univ, PhD,69. **CAREER** Instr, 67-69, ast prof, 69-75, assoc prof, 74-94, prof, 94-, Oregon St Univ. **HONORS AND AWARDS** Phi Kappa Phi, Recognition Awd for Excellence in Tchg, Am Philos Asn, 95. **MEMBERSHIPS** APA; Int Soc for Environ Ethics; Soc for Philos Contemp World. **RESEARCH** Ethical issues in the natural resource sciences; public attitudes about nature; environmental ethics. **SELECTED PUBLICATIONS** Ed, Radical Environmentalism, Philosophy and Tactics, Wadworth, 93; "Some Philosophical Assessments of Environmental Disobedience," in Philosophy and the Natural Environment, Cambridge, 94; "The Land Ethic in American Forestry: Pinchot and Leopold," in The Idea of the Forest, Lang, 95; "Moving Toward an Expanded Land Management Ethic," in Nature and the Human Spirit, Venture, 96; auth, Spiritual Values in Leopold's Land Ethic: the Noumeual Integrity of Forest Ecosystems," Proceedings of the Society of American Foresters, 99 National Convention, Portland, Oregon, September 11-15, 99, Bethesda, MD, SA7,00; ed, Environmental Ethics and Forestry: A Reader, Temple Univ Press, 00. **CONTACT ADDRESS** Dept of Philosophy, Oregon State Univ, Corvallis, OR 97332. **EMAIL** plist@orst.edu

LISZKA, JAMES
PERSONAL Born 03/18/1950, Pittsburgh, PA, m, 2 children **DISCIPLINE** PHILOSOPHY **EDUCATION** Indiana Univ of Pa, BS, 72; Univ of So Carolina, MA, 74; New Sch for Soc Res, PhD, 78. **CAREER** Hum Fel, Scarborough Col, Univ Toronto, 85-86; Univ Alaska, Anchorage, 80- . **HONORS AND AWARDS** Teaching Excellence Award, 98. **MEMBERSHIPS** APA; Semiotic Soc of Am; Charles S. Peirce Soc. **RESEARCH** Ethics; aesthetics; semiotics. **SELECTED PUBLICATIONS** Auth, The Semiotic of Myth, Indiana, 90; auth, A General Introduction to the Semeiotic of Charles S. Peirce, Indiana, 96; auth, Moral Competence, Prentice-Hall, 99; auth, Chanecllor's Award for Excellence in Research, 99; auth, Moral Competence, 2nd edition, Prentice Hall, 01. **CONTACT ADDRESS** Dept of Philosophy, Univ of Alaska, Anchorage, 3211 Providence Dr, Anchorage, AK 99508. **EMAIL** afjjl@uaa.alaska.edu

LITCH, MARY
DISCIPLINE PHILOSOPHY **EDUCATION** Univ Mass, PhD. **CAREER** Prof, Univ Ala Birmingham, 96-. **RESEARCH** Philosophy of artificial intelligence. **SELECTED PUBLICATIONS** Auth, Computation, Connectionism and Modelling the Mind, Philos Psychol 10, 97. **CONTACT ADDRESS** Dept of Philosophy, Univ of Alabama, Birmingham, 1400 University Blvd, Birmingham, AL 35294-1150. **EMAIL** litch@uab.edu

LITTLE, DANIEL E.
PERSONAL Born 04/07/1949, Rock Island, IL, d, 2 children **DISCIPLINE** PHILOSOPHY **EDUCATION** Univ Ill, BA, BS, 71; Harvrd Univ, PhD, 77. **CAREER** Asst prof, Univ Wisc, Parkside, 76-79; vis assoc prof, Wellesley Col, 85-87; vis scholar, 89-91, assoc, 91-95, Ctr Int Aff, Harvard Univ; asst prof, 79-85, assoc prof, 85-92, prof, 92-96, chemn, dept philos and relig, 92-93, assoc dean fac, 93-96, Colgate Univ; vpres acad aff, Bucknell Univ, 96- . **HONORS AND AWARDS** Phi Beta Kappa; Woodrow Wilson Grad fel, 71-72; res grant NSF, 87; Soc sci res postdoctoral fel, MacArthur Found, 89-91. **MEMBERSHIPS** APA; Am Soc for Polit and Legal Philos; Asn Asian Stud; Int Asn Philos of Law and Social Philos; Int Devel Ethics Asn. **SELECTED PUBLICATIONS** Auth, The Scientific Marx, 86; auth, Understanding Peasant China: Case Studies in the Philosophy of Social Science, 89; auth, Varieties of Social Explanation: An Introduction to the Philosophy of Social Science, 91; auth, On the Reliability of Economic Models, 95; auth, Microfoundations Method and Causation: On the Philosophy of the Social Sciences, 98. **CONTACT ADDRESS** VPAA Marts Hall, Bucknell Univ, Lewisburg, PA 17837. **EMAIL** dlittle@bucknell.edu

LITTLE, JOSEPH W.
DISCIPLINE LAW **EDUCATION** Duke Univ, BSME; Worcester Polytech Inst, MSME; Univ Mich, JD. **CAREER** Prof; alumni res scholar; Univ Fla, 67-; vis prof, Monash Univ, Australia, Univ Auckland, New Zealand, Univ Natal, Univ Stellenbosch, S Africa, Peking Univ, China; past assoc, Sutherland, Asbill Brennan, Atlanta; fmr mayor/commnr, Gainesville City Comn. **HONORS AND AWARDS** Vis fel, Wolfson Col, Oxford, England. **MEMBERSHIPS** Michigan Bar; DC Bar; Ga Bar; Fla Bar; Amer Law Inst; Phi Beta Kappa; Sigma Xi. **RESEARCH** Local government law, workers' compensation, torts, US & Fla constitutional law. **SELECTED PUBLICATIONS** Coauth, Torts: The Civil Law of Reparation for Harm Done by Wrongful Act. **CONTACT ADDRESS** School of Law, Univ of Florida, PO Box 117625, Gainesville, FL 32611-7625. **EMAIL** little@law.ufl.edu

LITTLEFIELD, NEIL OAKMAN
PERSONAL Born 02/12/1931, North Conway, NH, m, 1958, 3 children **DISCIPLINE** LAW **EDUCATION** Univ Maine, BS, 53; Boston Univ, LLB, 57; Univ Mich, LLM, 59, SJD, 61. **CAREER** Asst prof law, Sch Law, Creighton Univ, 59-61; from assoc prof to prof, Sch Law, Univ Conn, 61-70; Prof Law, Col Law, Univ Denver, 70-, Dir Bus Planning Prog, 71-, Vis prof, Ind Univ, 66-67; consult, Food and Drug Admin, Consumer Access Prog, 77-78. **MEMBERSHIPS** Am Bar Asn. **RESEARCH** Commercial law; consumer law; bankruptcy law. **SELECTED PUBLICATIONS** Auth, Negotiable Instruments, Bank Deposits and Collections, and Other Payment Systems, Bus Lawyer, Vol 0048, 93; Payments--Article-3, Article-4 and Article-4a/, Bus Lawyer, Vol 0049, 94; Payments--Article-3, Article-4 and Article-4a, Bus Lawyer, Vol 0051, 96; Payments--Article-3, Article-4 and Article-4a, Bus Lawyer, Vol 0052, 97. **CONTACT ADDRESS** Col of Law, Univ of Denver, 200 W 24th Ave, Denver, CO 80208.

LITTLEJOHN, EDWARD J.
PERSONAL Born 05/05/1935, Pittsburgh, PA, d, 2 children **DISCIPLINE** LAW **EDUCATION** Wayne State Univ, BA 1965; Detroit Coll of Law, JD (cum laude) 1970; Columbia Univ Law Sch, LLM 1974, JSD 1982. **CAREER** City of Detroit, varied Gov serv 1959-70; Detroit Coll of Law, prof, 70-72; Wayne State Law Sch, assoc prof & asst dean 1972-76, assoc dean & prof of law 1976-78, prof of law 1972-96, prof emeritus of law, 96-; Univ of Utrecht Netherlands, visiting prof, 74; Wayne State Center for Black Studies, fac res assoc; The Damon J Keith Law Collection for History of African-American Lawyers and Judges of Wayne State University, founder/director, 93-97. **HONORS AND AWARDS** Charles Evans Hughes Fellow Columbia Univ Law School 1973-74; WEB Dubois Scholarship Awd Phylon Soc Wayn State Univ 1986; Special Alumni Awd Wolverine Student Bar Assoc Detroit Coll of Law 1986; Trailblazer Awd, Wolverine Bar Assn 1988;Black Educator of 1991 (MI & Ohio), Detroit Peace Corps; Alumni Faculty Service Awd, Wayne St Alumni Assn, 1991; DH Gordon Excellence in Teaching Awd, Alumni and Friends of the Law School, 1994; Champion of Justice Awd, State Bar of Michigan, 1995. **MEMBERSHIPS** Apptd to Bd Police Commrs Detroit 1974-78, chmn 1977-78; mem MI Bar Asn, NBA, ABA, Wolverine Bar Asn, Alpha Phi Alpha; ed bd The Urban Educator and the Compleat Lawyer; hearing officer MI Dept of Civil Rights; consult Police Civil Liability and Citizen Complaints; reporter Am Bar Asn; task force on Minorities in the Legal Profession; chair, City of Detroit Board of Ethics, 1994-; trustee, Kurdish Museum and Library of NY, 1990-96; Michigan Correctional Officers, training council, 1990-93; Michigan Committee on Juvenile Justice, 1987-90; Arts Commission, Detroit Institute of Arts, 00-. **SELECTED PUBLICATIONS** Publications in various legal journals. **CONTACT ADDRESS** 1300 E Lafayette Blvd, #609, Detroit, MI 48207. **EMAIL** ejl1300@aol.com

LIU, JUNG-CHAO
PERSONAL Born 02/09/1929, Taiwan, m, 1984, 5 children **DISCIPLINE** ECONOMICS **CAREER** McGill Univ, 64-70; SUNY, 70- . **MEMBERSHIPS** Am Econ Asn **CONTACT ADDRESS** SUNY, Binghamton, Vestal Pky E, Binghamton, NY 13901. **EMAIL** jungliu@binghamton.edu

LIVEZEY, LOWELL W.
PERSONAL Born 02/15/1943, Erie, PA, m, 1970 **DISCIPLINE** RELIGIOUS SOCIAL ETHICS, ECONOMICS **EDUCATION** Swarthmore Col, BA, 66; Univ Chicago, DMin, 70. **CAREER** Dir, World Without War Coun, 70-81; admin dir Undergrad Prog, Woodrow Wilson School, Princeton, 83-88; exec asst to pres, Chicago State Univ, 88-92; vis prof, Res prof, Univ Ill at Chicago, 92-. **MEMBERSHIPS** Am Acad Relig; Soc Christian Ethics; Relig Res Asn; Am Sociol Asn; Asn Sociol Relig. **RESEARCH** Public religion, urban studies, congregational studies. **SELECTED PUBLICATIONS** Ed, Public Religion and Urban Transformation, NYU Press, 00. **CONTACT ADDRESS** Rel in Urban Am Prog, Univ of Illinois, Chicago, 1007 W Harrison St, Chicago, IL 60607-7136. **EMAIL** livezey@uic.edu

LIVINGSTON, DONALD W.
DISCIPLINE HISTORY OF MODERN PHILOSOPHY **EDUCATION** WA Univ, PhD, 65. **CAREER** Prof, Philos, Emory Univ. **HONORS AND AWARDS** Nat Endowment Hum fel, 78-79. **RESEARCH** History of modern philosophy (especially Hume and the Scottish Enlightenment), philosophy of history, political philosophy **SELECTED PUBLICATIONS** Auth, Hume's Philosophy of Common Life; auth, Philosophical Melancholy and Delirium; Coed Hume, A Re-evaluation; Liberty in Hume's "History of England"; Hume as Philosopher of Society, Politics, and History **CONTACT ADDRESS** Emory Univ, Atlanta, GA 30322-1950. **EMAIL** dliving@emory.edu

LIVINGSTON, JAMES CRAIG
PERSONAL Born 07/12/1930, Grand Rapids, MI, m, 1954, 2 children **DISCIPLINE** RELIGION **EDUCATION** Kenyon Col, BA, 52; Union Theol Sem, NYork City, MDiv, 56; Columbia Univ, PhD(relig), 65. **CAREER** Asst prof relig, Southern Methodist Univ, 63-68; dean undergrad prog, 73-78, assoc prof Relig & chmn dept, Col William & Mary, 68-78, prof relig, 78-86, WALTER G. MASON PROF RELIG, 86-; Grad Coun Humanities Danforth fel, 65; vis fel, Clare Hall, Cambridge, 67-68; Am Coun Learned Soc fel, 72-73; Nat Endowment for Humanities fel, 79-80, 89-90; Busch fel, 79-80; Woodrow Wilson Int Center for Scholars, fel, 90. **HONORS AND AWARDS** Phi Beta Kappa; Brose Found Decemial Prize, 80; State Council of Higher Education for Virginia, Outstanding Faculty Awd, 89; The Thomas Jefferson Awd, Col of William and Mary, 94. **MEMBERSHIPS** Am Acad Relig. **RESEARCH** Modern religious thought; contemporary theology; Victorian religious studies. **SELECTED PUBLICATIONS** Auth, William Golding's The Spire, Seabury, 67; Paul Tillich's Christology and Historical Research, In: Paul Tillich: Retrospect and Future, Abingdon, 67; ed, M. Arnolds's Literature and Dogma, Ungar, 70; auth, Modern Christian Thought, Macmillan, 71, 2nd ed, 2 vols, 97, 99; Henry Dodwell's Christianity Not Founded on Argument, 1742, revisited, J Theol Studies, 71; Matthew Arnold on the Truth of Christianity: A Reappraisal, J Am Acad Relig, 73; The Religious Creed and Criticism of Sir James Fitzjames Stephen, Victorian Studies, 3/74; The Ethics of Belief. An Essay on the Victorian Religious Conscience, Scholars, 74; Matthew Arnold and Christianity: His Religious Prose Writings, Univ NC Press, 84; Anatomy of the Sacred, Macmillan, 89, 2nd ed, 93, 3rd ed, 98, 4th ed, 00; Tradition and the Critical Spirit: Catholic Modernist Writings of George Tyrrell, Fortress Press, 91. **CONTACT ADDRESS** Dept of Relig, Col of William and Mary, Williamsburg, VA 23187. **EMAIL** tacoop@fac.staff.wm.edu

LLEWELLYN, DON W.
DISCIPLINE LAW, INTERNATIONAL TAXATATION **EDUCATION** Dickinson Col, BA, 57; Dickinson Sch Law, JD, 61; NYork Univ Sch Law, LLM, 67. **CAREER** Prof;Villanova Univ, 80-; dean grad Legal Stud, Villanova Univ, 86-88; dir gard Tax Prog, Villanova Univ, 80-86. **MEMBERSHIPS** Amer and Philadelphia Bar Ass Tax Sections; Int Fiscal Asn. **RESEARCH** Taxation,estate planning. **SELECTED PUBLICATIONS** Auth, Tax Planning for For Persons Investing in and Disposing of US Assets, Int J, 96; The Evolution of Sophisticated Tax Planning for Lifetime Gifts-What Planning Techniques Continue to be Effective, Real Prop Prob & Tr. J, 95; coauth, Planning Pitfalls and Opportunities for For Owned Corporations Under the Earnings Stripping Rules, 47 Tax Law 641, 94; Tax Planning for Lifetime and Testamentary Dispositions-Prototype Plans, ALI-ABA, 97; contrib, Tax Aspects of For Investment in US Real Estate, Real Estate Financing, 93 & Partnerships, in Advan Bus Tax Plan, 85. **CONTACT ADDRESS** Law School, Villanova Univ, 800 Lancaster Ave, Villanova, PA 19085-1692. **EMAIL** llewelly@law.vill.edu

LLOYD, ELISABETH A.
PERSONAL Born 03/03/1956 **DISCIPLINE** HISTORY, PHILOSOPHY OF SCIENCE **EDUCATION** Queen's Univ, 74-75; Univ Colo-Boulder, BA, Sci/Polit Theory, 76-80; Princeton Univ, PhD, 80-84. **CAREER** Vis instr, Exper Stud, Univ Colo-Boulder, 80; vis scholar, Genetics, Harvard Univ, 83-84; vis lectr, Philos, Univ Calif-San Diego, 84-85; asst prof, Philos, Univ Calif-San Diego, 85-88; asst prof, Univ Calif-Berkeley, 88-90; assoc prof, Univ Calif-Berkeley, 90-97; prof, Philos, Univ Calif-Berkeley, 97-; PROF, BIOL, IND UNIV, 98-; visiting prof, Harvard, 98; prof, History & phil of sci dept, Ind Univ, 98-. **MEMBERSHIPS** Nat Endow Hum; Nat Sci Found; Am Philos Asn; Philos Sci Asn; Int Soc Hist, Philos, & Soc Stud of Biol **SELECTED PUBLICATIONS** The Structure and Confirmation of Evolutionary Theory, Princeton UP 94; co-edr, Keywords in Evolutionary Biology, Harvard Univ Press, 92; "The Anachronistic Anarchist," Philosophical Studies 81, APA West Div Sympos, 96; "Science and Anti-Science: Objectivity and its Real Enemies," Feminism, Science, and the Philosophy of Science, Kluwer, 96; "Feyerabend, Mill, and Pluralism," Philosophy of Science, Supplemental Issue: PSA 96 Symposium Papers, 97. **CONTACT ADDRESS** Hist & Philos Sci Dept, Indiana Univ, Bloomington, Goodbody Hall 130, Bloomington, IN 47405-2401. **EMAIL** ealloyd@indiana.edu

LO, JIM
PERSONAL Born 06/26/1954, New York, NY, m, 1974, 2 children **DISCIPLINE** THEOLOGY **EDUCATION** Bartiesville Wesleyan Col, BA, 78; Ind Wesleyan Univ, MA, 82; Wheaton Grad Sch, MA, 92; Univ South Africa, PhD, 98. **CAREER** Pastor, 78-82; missionary, bible sch tchr, Wesleyan Church, Africa, 82-95; missionary, dir, bible sch tchr, Wesleyan Church, Cambodia, 95-96; asst prof, Ind Wesleyan Univ, 96-99; assoc prof 99-. **HONORS AND AWARDS** W. Hilbert Norton Awd, 92, Wheaton Col; Tch Excellence Awd, 97-98; Who's Who among Am Tchrs, 98,99; IWU Prof of the year 98, 99. **MEMBERSHIPS** Evangelical Missiological Soc. **RESEARCH** Missions; intercultural issues; bible. **SELECTED PUBLICATIONS** Auth, art, Unique and United: a partnership in South Africa, 96; auth, art, When God Rocks the Boat, 97; auth, art, Staying True to God, 98; auth, art, Infanticide, 97; auth, art, Balancing Fear with Love, 97, auth, art, Christian College-An Answer to Prayer, 97. **CONTACT ADDRESS** 4201 S Washington St, Marion, IN 46953. **EMAIL** jlo@indwes.edu

LOBEL, DIANA
DISCIPLINE RELIGIOUS STUDIES **EDUCATION** Oberlin Col, BA, 79; Harvard Divinity School, MTS, 82; Harvard Univ, PhD, 95. **CAREER** Vis fel, instr, Univ Md, 96-97; Anna Smith Fine asst prof Judaic Stud, Rice Univ, 97; asst prof, Boston Univ. **HONORS AND AWARDS** Memorial Found for Jewish Culture grant; Danforth Awd; Combined Jewish Philanthropies award; Phi Beta Kappa; Harry Starr Fel, Harvard. **MEMBERSHIPS** APA; Asn for Jewish Stud; Am Acad Relig. **RESEARCH** Jewish and Islamic philosophy and the Classical Tradition; Judeo-Arabic thought; negative theology; comparative religious thought. **SELECTED PUBLICATIONS** Auth, Between Mysticism and Philosophy: Sufi Language of Religious Experience, SUNY, 98; auth, "A Dwelling Place of the Shekhina," Jewish Quarterly Review (forthcoming). **CONTACT ADDRESS** Religion Dept, Boston Univ, 745 Commonwealth Ave, Rm 624, Boston, MA 02215. **EMAIL** dnlobel@bu.edu

LOBO, ALFONSO GOMEZ
DISCIPLINE PHILOSOPHY **EDUCATION** Univ Munich, PhD, 66. **CAREER** Prof. **RESEARCH** Greek philosophy; Greek historiography; early Christian thought; history of ethics; contemporary natural law theory. **SELECTED PUBLICATIONS** Auth, The Foundations of Socratic Ethics; pubs on Herodotus, Thucydides, Plato and Aristotle. **CONTACT ADDRESS** Dept of Philosophy, Georgetown Univ, 37th and O St, Washington, DC 20057.

LOCHTEFELD, JAMES G.
DISCIPLINE CONTEMPORARY EUROPEAN CONTINENTAL PHILOSOPHY **EDUCATION** Colgate Univ, BA; Harvard Divinity Sch, MTS; Univ Wash, MA; Columbia Univ, PhD. **CAREER** Instr, St. Olaf Col, 91-92; Asst prof, Carthahe Col,92-97; Assoc prof, Carthage Col, 97-. **HONORS AND AWARDS** Robinson Prize, 79; Hindi Language Program Fel, 85, FLAS fel, 84, 86, 87; Fulbright-IIE, 89; Charlotte W. Newcombe Doctoral Dissertation fel, 90; pres fel, 88, 89, 91; Fac summer res Grant, 96; Senior Res fel, 97-98. **MEMBERSHIPS** AOS, AAR/SBL, ASIANetwork. **SELECTED PUBLICATIONS** Auth, Reflected Splendor: The Regional Appropriation of 'All-India' Tirthas, The Vishva Hindu Parishad And The Roots Of Hindu Militancy, JAAR LXII 2, 94; New Wine, Old Skins: The Sangh Parivar and the Transformation of Hinduism, Rel, 96; The Saintly Camar: Perspectives on the Life of Ravidas, ARC: The Jour Fac Relig Studies, 98. **CONTACT ADDRESS** Carthage Col, 2001 Alford Dr., Kenosha, WI 53140.

LOCKE, MAMIE EVELYN
PERSONAL Born 03/19/1954, Brandon, MS, s **DISCIPLINE** POLITICAL SCIENCE **EDUCATION** Tougaloo College, Tougaloo, MS, BA, 1976; Atlanta University, Atlanta, GA, MA, 1978, PhD, 1984. **CAREER** Dept of Archives & History, Jackson, MS, archivist, 77-79; Atlanta Historical Soc, Atlanta, GA, archivist, 79-81; Hampton Univ, Hamton,, VA, Prof, 97-; assistant dean, 91-96, Dean, 96-; Mayor, City of Hampton, 00-04. **HONORS AND AWARDS** Lindback Awd for Distinguished Teaching, Hampton University, 1990; Rodney Higgins Awd, National Conference Black Political Scientists, 1986; Fulbright-Hays Awd, Department of Education, 1986; Ford Foundation Grant, College of William & Mary, 1988; Ford Foundation Grant, Duke University, 1987; NEH Fellowship, National Endowment for the Humanities, 1985; Distinguished Public Service Awd, Conf of Minority of Public Administrators; Martin Luther King Awd, Old Dominion Univ. **MEMBERSHIPS** National Conference of Black Political Scientists, 1976-, executive council, 1989-92, president elect, 1992-93, president, 1993-94; Alpha Kappa Alpha Sorority Inc; American Political Science Association, 1990-; Southeastern Women's Studies Association, 1987-; advisor, member, Alpha Kappa Mu National Honor Society, 1990-; editorial board, PS: Politics and Political Science, 1992-95; editorial board, National Political Science Review, 1994-; Hampton City Council; commissioner, Hampton Planning Commission; commissioner, Hampton Roads Planning District Commission; commissioner, Hampton Redevelopment & Housing Authority; VA Municipal League, Government Affairs Committee; National Black Caucus of Local Elected Officers, dir, Region 3; Women in Municipal Government, bd mem, 1998-. **RESEARCH** Race and gender politics. **CONTACT ADDRESS** Hampton Univ, 119 Armstrong Hall, Hampton, VA 23668. **EMAIL** mamie.locke@hamptonu.edu

LOCKETT, JAMES
DISCIPLINE POLITICAL SCIENCE **EDUCATION** Morehouse Col, BA; Atlanta Univ, MS; Case Western Reserve Univ, MA; Atlanta Univ , PhD. **CAREER** Full Prof, Stillman Col, 90-. **HONORS AND AWARDS** NEH Fel, Univ Kans, 93-94; NEH Fel, Harvard Univ, 95; Mellon Grant, 97. **RESEARCH** American history; afro-American history; Political science, with stress on international politics, and American government-national, state, and local); Geography. **SELECTED PUBLICATIONS** Auth, "A Critical Analysis of the Black Man in the American system," U.S. Black and the News, (81): 26-27, 68-71; auth, ""Alexander Sergeyevich Pushkin: An Interpretation of the Russian renaissance," Negro History Bulletin, *82): 81-82; auth, "Persistence Gave Birth to a Quality College: Charles Allen Stillman," Presbyterian Survey, (82): 32-33; auth, "Abraham Lincoln's attempt to establish a colony for free blacks at L'Ile A Vache, Haiti in 1863-1864," The Western Journal ob Black Studies, (88): 176-184; auth, "Lucius Davenport Amerson: The First Black Sheriff in the south Since the Reconstruction Era," Alabama sheriffs Star, (96): 143-147; auth, The Growth and Development of the Stillman Institute into an Outstanding Senior College from Charles Allen Stillman and Andrew Flinn Dickson to Samuel Burney Hay, 1876-1976, Portal Press, 96; auth, "Stillman College and Brewster Hardy," The Christian Observer, (96): 24-25; auth, "The Lynching Massacre of Black and White Soldiers at Fort Pillow, Tennessee, April 12, 1864," The Western Journal of Black Studies, (98): 84-93; auth, "The Last Ship that Brought Slaves from Africa to America: The Landing of the Clotilde at Mobile in the Autumn of 1859," The Western Journal of Black Studies, (98): 159-163. **CONTACT ADDRESS** Dept Hist & Polit Sci, Stillman Col, PO Box 1430, Tuscaloosa, AL 35403-1430.

LOCKWOOD, KIMBERLY MOSHER
DISCIPLINE PHILOSOPHY **EDUCATION** Univ Dayton, BA, 91; Univ Cincinnati, MA, 95. **CAREER** Part-time Instr, Univ Cincinnati, Wittenberg Univ, Univ Dayton. **HONORS AND AWARDS** Charles P. Taft Fel, 97-98 **MEMBERSHIPS** Amer Phil Assoc; Amer Soc for Aesthetics **RESEARCH** Art; metaphor; language **CONTACT ADDRESS** 1150 Epworth Ave., Dayton, OH 45410. **EMAIL** mosherlockwood@yahoo.com

LODGE, JOHN G.
PERSONAL Born 08/07/1947, Chicago, IL, s **DISCIPLINE** BIBLICAL THEOLOGY, MATTHEW AND PAUL **EDUCATION** Pontifical Bibl Inst, Rome, SSL, 81; Pontifical Gregorian Univ, Rome, STD, 96. **CAREER** Parish priest and assoc pastor, 73-78; instr and assoc prof, Bible dept, Mundelein Sem, 81-; acad dean, Mundelein Sem, 84-88, 97-. **MEMBERSHIPS** Cath Theol Soc of Amer; Cath Bibl Asn; AAR/SBL. **RESEARCH** St. Paul; Romans; Gospel of Matthew. **SELECTED PUBLICATIONS** Auth, Romans 9-11: A Reader Response Analysis, Scholars Press, 96; auth, The Apostle's Appeal and Readers' Response: 2 Corinthians 8 and 9, Chicago Studies 30, 59-76, 91; auth, Matthew's Passion-Resurrection Narrative, Chicago Studies 25, 3-20, 86; auth, All Things to All: Paul's Pastoral Strategy, Chicago Studies 24, 291-306, 85; auth, The Salvation Theologies of Paul and Luke, Chicago Studies 22, 83; auth, James and Paul at Cross-Purposes? James 2,22, Biblica 62, 81. **CONTACT ADDRESS** Mundelein Sem, 1000 E Maple Ave, Mundelein, IL 60060-1174. **EMAIL** jlodge@usml.edu

LODGE, PAUL A.
PERSONAL Born 01/18/1968, Leeds, England, s **DISCIPLINE** PHILOSOPHY **EDUCATION** Oxford Univ, BA, 90; Leeds Univ, MA, 91; Rutgers Univ, PhD, 98. **CAREER** From vis asst prof 1998-99; to asst prof, Tulane Univ, 99-. **HONORS AND AWARDS** Fitzgerald Prize, Oxford Univ, 90; Final Exams Prize, Oxford Univ, 90; State Studentship, British Acad, 90-91; Univ Fel, Rutgers Univ, 96-97; Res Grant, DAAD, 97; Annual Essay Comp Winner, Leibniz Soc of N Am, 96 & 98; Summer Res Fel, 99. **MEMBERSHIPS** APA, HOPOS, Leibniz Soc of N Am, Gottfried-Wilhelm-Leibmiz-Gesellschaft. **RESEARCH** History of modern philosophy, Leibniz, medieval philosophy. **SELECTED PUBLICATIONS** Co auth, "Stepping Back Inside Leibniz's Mill," The Monist 81 (98): 554-573; auth, "Leibniz's Heterogeneity Argument Against the Cartesian Conception of Body," Studia Leibnitiana XXX/I (98): 83-102; auth, "The Failure of Leibniz's Correspondence with De Volder," Leibniz Soc Review 8 (98): 47-67; auth, "Leibniz's Commitment to the Pre-established Harmony in the Late 1670s and Early 1680s," Archiv fur Geschichte der Philos 80 (98): 292-320; auth, "The Debate over Extended Substance in Leibniz's Correspondence with De Volder," in HOPOS 98, eds. C. Pinnick and W. Schmaus (forthcoming). **CONTACT ADDRESS** Dept Philos, Tulane Univ, 6823 St Charles Ave, 105 Newcomb Hall, New Orleans, LA 70118-5665. **EMAIL** plodge@tulane.edu

LOEB, LOUIS EDWARD
PERSONAL Born 06/25/1945, St. Louis, MO **DISCIPLINE** PHILOSOPHY **EDUCATION** Wesleyan Univ, BA, 67; Oxford Univ, BPhil, 69; Princeton Univ, PhD, 75. **CAREER** Asst prof, 74-80, assoc prof, 80-89, prof philos, Univ MI, 89, chmn, Dept Philos, 93-99; Mem bd trustees, Wesleyan Univ, CT, 74-77. **MEMBERSHIPS** Am Philos Asn; Hume Soc; Leibniz Soc. **RESEARCH** Hist of mod philos. **SELECTED PUBLICATIONS** Auth, Causal theories and causal overdetermination, J Philos, 9/74; Hume's moral sentiments and the structure of the Treatise, J Hist Philos, 10/77; From Descartes to Hume: Continental Metaphysics and the Development of Modern Philosophy, Cornell Univ Press, 81; Is there radical sisimulation in Descartes' Meditations?, In: Amelia O Rorty, ed, Essays on Descartes' Meditations, Univ Calif Press, 86; Was Descartes sincere in his appeal to the light of nature?, Jour Hist Philos, 7/88; The priority of reason in Descartes, Philos Rev, 1/90; Stability, justification, and Hume's propensity to attribute identity to related objects, Philos Topics, spring 91; The Cartesian circle, In: Cambridge Companions to Philosophy: Descartes (John G Cottingham, ed), Cambridge Univ Press, 92; Causation, extrinsic relations, and Hume's second thoughts about personal identity, Hume Studies, 11/92; Hume on stability, justification, and unphilosophical probability, Jour Hist Philos, 1/95; Instability and uneasiness in Hume's theories of belief and justification, Brit Jour Hist Philos, 9/95; Causal inference, associationism, and skepticism in Part III of Book I of Hume's Treaties, In: Logic and the Workings of the Mind (Patricia Easton, ed), North Am Kant Soc Studies in Philos, vol 5, Ridgeview, 97; Sextus, Descartes, Hume, and Peirce: On securing settled doxastic states, Nous, 3/98. **CONTACT ADDRESS** Dept of Philos, Univ of Michigan, Ann Arbor, 435 S State St, Ann Arbor, MI 48109-1003. **EMAIL** lloeb@umich.edu

LOEWE, WILLIAM PATRICK
PERSONAL Born 11/28/1941, New Rochelle, NY, d, 1977, 2 children **DISCIPLINE** THEOLOGY **EDUCATION** Fordham Univ, BA, 65, MA, 66; Loyola Scn, PhL, 66; Marquette Univ, PhD(theol), 74. **CAREER** Asst prof, 73-80, Assoc Prof Theol, Cath Univ Am, 80-. **MEMBERSHIPS** Am Acad Relig; Cath Theol Soc Am; Col Theol Soc. **RESEARCH** Lonergan studies; contemporary foundational and systematic theology; theology within interdisciplinary perspective. **SELECTED PUBLICATIONS** Auth, College Students Introduction to Christology, Liturgical, 96; co-ed, Jesus Crucified and Risen, Liturgical, 98; auth, "From the Humanity of Christ to the Historical Jesus," Theological Studies 61 (00). **CONTACT ADDRESS** Dept of Relig and Relig Educ, Catholic Univ of America, 620 Michigan Ave NE, Washington, DC 20064-0002. **EMAIL** loewee@cua.edu

LOEWY, ERICH H.
PERSONAL Born 12/31/1927, Vienna, Austria, m, 1974, 3 children **DISCIPLINE** HEALTH CARE ETHICS **EDUCATION** NYork Univ, BA, 50; State Univ NYork, PhD Med, 54. **CAREER** Demonstrator, Case Western Reserve Univ, Ohio, 60-64; clin instr, 64-70; sr clin instr, 70-77; clin asst prof, Albany Med Coll Union Univ, 77-8 -81; lectr, Adirondack Community Coll, 74-81; asst prof, Univ Connecticut School Med, 81-84; assoc grad fac, Univ Ill Grad School, 86-95; asst prof, uni Ill Coll Med, 84-87; assoc prof, 87-93; prof, 93-95; asst prof, Univ Ill Chicago, 84-89; assoc prof, 89-93; prof, 93-95; Prof, Chair Biethics Dept, Univ Calif Sacramento, 96-. **HONORS AND AWARDS** Advisor of the Year, Univ Ill, 86; Convocation Speaker, 86; Golden Apple Tchg Awd, 88; Selected to hood Graduating Sr, 89, 90, 92; Marquis Who's Who in the Midwest; Marquis Who's Who in Am Law; Marquis Who's Who in Sci and Engineering; Woodrow Wilson Nat Fel. **MEMBERSHIPS** WHO Network Monitoring; Am Asn for the Advancement of Sci; NY Acad of Sci; Fel Am Coll of Physicians; Hist of Sci Soc; Paleopathology Soc; Soc of Hist of Med; Physicians for Human Rights; Int Physicians for the Prevention of Nuclear War; Physicians for Soc Responsibility; Am Philos Asn; inst Asn of Bioethics; Int Bioethics Inst; Akademie fr Ethik in der Medizin; Europ Soc fot eh Philos of Med and Health Care; Soc of Health & Human values; Hastings Center of Ethics & Life Sci. **RESEARCH** Health-care Ethics; Social Justice; Relation of individual freedom to communal needs; Allocation of service resources. **SELECTED PUBLICATIONS** Auth, numerous publications on health care ethics, 54-97; auth, Textbook of Health-Care Ethics, Plenum, 97; auth, Moral Strangeous, Moral Acquaintance, Moral Friends: connectedness and its conditions, SUNY Pub, 97; Of Cultural Practises, Ethics and Education: Thoughts about affecting changes in cultural practices, Health-Care Analysis, 98; Curiosity, Imagination, Science, compassion and Ethics: Do Curiosity and Imagination serve a central function? Theoretical Med, 98; Orchestrating the End of Life, Dignity and Physician Assisted Dying: Dangers, Opportunities and Prior Neglected Conditions, Med, Health and Philos, 98; Of Curiosity, Imagination, Justice and Health-Care Systems: What would an "ideal" health0care system look like? Health-Care Analysis, 98; Of Health-Care Professionals, Ethics and Strikes, Cambridge Quart, 98; coauth, Ethics and Managed care: Reconstructing a System and Refashioning a Society, Archive of Internal Med, 98; auth, With RS Loewy: Ethics of Terminal Care-Orchestrating the end of life, Plenum, 00. **CONTACT ADDRESS** Medical Ctr, Univ of California, Davis, 2221 Stockton Blvd, Sacramento, CA 95817. **EMAIL** ehloewy@ucdavis.edu

LOEWY, ROBERTA S.
PERSONAL Born 11/22/1945, OH, m, 1974, 3 children **DISCIPLINE** ETHICS **EDUCATION** Skidmore Coll, BA, 81; Loyola Univ Chicago, MA, 92; PhD, 97. **CAREER** Instr, Ill Central Coll, 88-89; consultant, Pekin Hospital, 93-94; co-fac, Methodist Med Center, 93-97; consultant, co-chair, Ethics Team, Sacramento County Dept of Health and Human Serv, 96-98; Asst Clin Prof, Univ Calif, 97-. **HONORS AND AWARDS** State Univ NY Tchg Asst ship, 81; State Univ NY Tchg Fel, 81-82; Univ Conn, non-tchg fel; 82-83; Loyola Univ Med Center Clin Fel, 90-92; NEH Diss grant, 93; Loyola Univ Diss Fel, 94-95. **MEMBERSHIPS** Am Asn of Univ Women, Am Philos Asn; Am Soc of Bioethics and Humanities; Int Asn of Bioethics; Int Bioethics Inst; Europ Soc for Philos of Med and Health Care; Concerned Philosophers for Peace. **RESEARCH** Ethical Obligations in Medical Relationships; Hospice; Cord Blood Salvage; Palliative Care and under Managed Care. **SELECTED PUBLICATIONS** Auth, Teamwork, Cambridge Quart of Healthcare Ethics, 93; The Relationship of Medically-Assisted Nutrition and Hydration to Respect for Human Persons, Cam-

bridge Quart of Healthcare Ethics, 93; A Critique of Tradition Relationship Models, Cambridge Quart of Healthcare Ethics, 94; Relationships in Health Care Revisited, Healthcare Ethics: Critical Issues, 94; rev, Health care Ethics Committees: The Next Generation, Doody's Health Sci Book Rev J, 94; Of Cultural Practices, Ethics and Education: Thoughts About Affecting Changes in Cultural Practices, Health Care Analyses; auth, Integrity and Personhood: Looking at Patients from a Bio/Psycho/Social Perspective, Kluwer/Plenum Publ, 00; coauth, The Ethics of Terminal Care: Orchestrating the End of Life, Kluwer/Plenum, forthcoming, 00. **CONTACT ADDRESS** 11465 Ghirardelli Ct, Gold River, CA 95670. **EMAIL** roberta.loewy@ucdms.ucdavis.edu

LOGAN, SAMUEL TALBOT, JR.
DISCIPLINE CHURCH HISTORY **EDUCATION** Princeton Univ, BA, 65; Westminster Theol Sem, MDiv, 68; Emory Univ, PhD, 72. **CAREER** Tchg asst, Emory Univ, 69; instr, DeKalb Jr Col, 70; dir, Dept Amer Stud, Barrington Col, 70-79; asst prof, 70-1978; prof, Barrington Col, 78-79; prof, Westminster Theol Sem, 79-. **SELECTED PUBLICATIONS** Auth, Academic Freedom at Christian Institutions, Christian Scholar's Rev; Shoulders to Stand On, Decision, 93; Theological Decline in Christian Institutions and the Value of Van Til's Epistemology, Westminster Theol Jour, 95; ed, The Preacher and Preaching: Reviving the Art in the Twentieth Century. **CONTACT ADDRESS** Westminster Theol Sem, Pennsylvania, PO Box 27009, Philadelphia, PA 19118. **EMAIL** slogan@wts.edu

LOKKEN, LAWRENCE
DISCIPLINE LAW **EDUCATION** Augsburg Col, BA; Univ Minn, JD. **CAREER** Hugh F. Culverhouse Eminent scholar in Taxation; prof, Univ Fla, 74-82 and 94-; instr, NY Univ, 80-93; instr, Univ Ga, 68-70; vis prof, NY Univ, Duke Univ, Univ Minn, Leiden Univ, Neth; vis scholar, Harvard Univ; ed, Fla Tax Rev, 94-96; ed-in-ch, Tax Law Rev, 83-87; past res consult, Harvard Law Sch Intl Tax Prog; note and comment ed, Minn Law Rev; spec adv to UN on Intl Tax Matters, 95-. **MEMBERSHIPS** Order of the Coif. **RESEARCH** Tax issues and policy, international tax treaties. **SELECTED PUBLICATIONS** Coauth, federal taxation of income, estates and gifts; fundamentals of intl taxation. **CONTACT ADDRESS** School of Law, Univ of Florida, PO Box 117625, Gainesville, FL 32611-7625. **EMAIL** lokken@law.ufl.edu

LOMAX, JOHN PHILLIP
PERSONAL Born 05/09/1952, Omaha, NE, d, 2 children **DISCIPLINE** HISTORY, CRIMINAL JUSTICE, POLITICAL SCIENCE **EDUCATION** Nebraska Wesley Univ, BA, 74; Univ Chicago, MA, 75; Univ Kansas, PhD, 87. **CAREER** Vis Instr of History, Univ of Nebr at Omaha, 86-87; Lecturer in History, Univ of Tex at Austin, 87-88; Asst Prof of History, Oh Northern Univ, 88-93; Assoc Prof of History, 93-00; Prof of History, 00-. **HONORS AND AWARDS** Fulbright-Hays Junior Fellow, 84-85. **MEMBERSHIPS** American Historical Assoc, Medieval Academy of America, Society for Medieval Canon Law. **RESEARCH** Medieval Politics and Law. **SELECTED PUBLICATIONS** Auth, "A Canonistic Reconsideration of the Crusade of Frederick II," Monumenta Iuris Canonici 9: 206-226; auth, "Frederick II, his Saracens, and the Papacy, " in Medieval Christian Perceptions of Islam (Garland, 96); auth, "Spolia as property," Res Publica Litterarum 20: 83-94. **CONTACT ADDRESS** Dept History, Political Science, and Criminal Justice, Ohio No Univ, 525 S Main St, Ada, OH 45810-6000. **EMAIL** j-lomax@onu.edu

LOMBARD, LAWRENCE B.
PERSONAL Born 11/24/1944, New York, NY, d **DISCIPLINE** PHILOSOPHY **EDUCATION** Cornell Univ, AB, 65; Stanford Univ, PhD, 74. **CAREER** Asst prof to prof, Wayne State Univ, 69-79; Chair, 96-. **MEMBERSHIPS** Am Philos Assoc; AAUP. **RESEARCH** Metaphysics, events and change. **SELECTED PUBLICATIONS** Auth, Events: A Metaphysical Study, Routledge and Kegan Paul, (London), 86; auth, "Sooner or Later", Nous 29.3 (95); auth, "Unless, Until and the Time of a Killing", Philos Quarterly, 89; auth, "Causes, Enablers and the Counterfactual Analysis" Philos Studies, 90. **CONTACT ADDRESS** Dept Philos, Wayne State Univ, 51 W Warren, Detroit, MI 48202. **EMAIL** l.b.lombard@wayne.edu

LOMBARDI, JOSEPH L.
PERSONAL Born 12/01/1939, Brooklyn, NY **DISCIPLINE** PHILOSOPHY **EDUCATION** Manhattan Col, BA, 61; Woodstock Col, PhL, 65, BD, 70; Fordham Univ, MA, 67; New York Univ, PhD, 75. **CAREER** Instr, Fordham Univ, 65-67; assoc prof philos, St Joseph's Univ, 74-. **HONORS AND AWARDS** NEH summer stipend, 85, 90. **MEMBERSHIPS** APA; Am Catholic Philos Asn; Jesuit Philos Asn; AAUP. **RESEARCH** Analytic philosophy; ethics; philosophy of religion. **SELECTED PUBLICATIONS** Various articles in Ethics, Relig Stud, Am Catholic Philos Quart, Jour of Relig Ethics, Am Jour of Jurisp. **CONTACT ADDRESS** Dept of Philosophy, Saint Joseph's Univ, 5600 City Ave, Philadelphia, PA 19131. **EMAIL** jlombard@sju.edu

LOMBARDI, MARK O.
PERSONAL Born 12/14/1960, Providence, RI **DISCIPLINE** POLITICAL SCIENCE, INTERNATIONAL RELATIONS **EDUCATION** Purdue Univ, BA, 82; Ohio State Univ, MA, 86; PhD, 89. **CAREER** Grad instr, Ohio State Univ, 83-87; vis instr, Wittenberg Univ, 87-88; assoc dir, Consortium for Int Studies Educ, 83-85; coord of Interdisciplinary Studies Prog, Univ Tampa, 93-94; dir of Baccalaureate Experience, Univ Tamp, 92-95; chair, Dept of Govt, Univ Tampa, 96-; assoc dir of Office of Int Prog and Development, Univ Tampa, 97-98; exec dir of US-Africa Educ Found, 97-98; dir of Office of Int Prog and Development, Univ Tampa, 99-. **HONORS AND AWARDS** Outstanding Grad Teaching Awd, Ohio State Univ, 85; NDFL Russian Lang Fel. **MEMBERSHIPS** African Studies Asn, Int Studies Asn, Am Political Sci Asn, Inst for African Affairs, NAFSA Asn of Int Educators, Nat Comt of Int Studies and Prog Adminr, Acad of Polit Sci, Am Asn for the Advancement of Core Curriculum, Coun on Int Educ Exchange. **RESEARCH** US Foreign Policy, Political Development, African Politics, Third World Development, Curriculum Reform. **SELECTED PUBLICATIONS** Rev, of "Superpower Foreign policy in Sub-Saharan Africa," The J of Modern African Studies 28.4 (90); Rev, of "South Africa and a Post-Apartheid Southern Africa in the 1990's," The J of Modern African Studies 29.2 (91); coauth, "Before We Connect: What Really Matters to Students in Core Curriculum," Asn for the Advancement of Core Curriculum Bullet (93); auth, "Third World Problem Solving and the 'Religion' of Sovereignty: Trends and Prospects," in Perspectives on Third World Sovereignty: The Post-Modern Paradox (London: Macmillan Press, 96); coauth, "Perspectives on Third World Sovereignty: Problems Without Borders," in Perspectives on Third World Sovereignty: The Post-Modern Paradox (London: Macmillan Press, 96); co-ed, Perspectives on Third World Sovereignty: The Post-Modern Paradox (London: Macmillan Press, 96); coauth, "International Financial Institutions and the Politics of Structural Adjustment: The African Experience," in Global Economic Policy Among and Within Nations (Macmillan Press, forthcoming). **CONTACT ADDRESS** Dept Soc Sci, The Univ of Tampa, 401 W Kennedy Blvd, Tampa, FL 33606-1450. **EMAIL** mol96@aol.com

LONE, JANA MOHR
PERSONAL Born 04/28/1960, New York, NY, m, 3 children **DISCIPLINE** PHILOSOPHY **EDUCATION** Univ Mass, BA, 82; George Wash Law Sch, JD, 85; Univ Wash, MA, 90, PhD, 96. **CAREER** Dir, Northwest Ctr for Philos for Children, 96-; affiliate asst prof, Univ Wash, 98-. **HONORS AND AWARDS** Amer fel, Amer Asn of Univ Women Educ Found, 93-94; JD with honors; BA, magna cum laude. **MEMBERSHIPS** Am Philos Asn Committee on Pe-Col Instruction in Philos; Northwest Women's Law Ctr; Vashon Island Connections Mentorship Prog; The Children's Alliance; Books for Kids; Seattle Jewish Family Svc; Shelters for Battered Women and Their Children. **RESEARCH** Ethics; Philosophy of education; Philosophy of childhood; Philosophy of law; Philosophy of feminism; Environmental ethics. **SELECTED PUBLICATIONS** Auth, Poetry and the Philosophical Understanding of Children, Bookbird: World of Children's Books, 96; auth, Are We All Mystery Creatures? Talking Philosophy With Children Who Are At Risk, Thinking, 97; auth, Voices in the Classroom: Girls and Philosophy for Children, Thinking, 97; auth, "Philos and Learning at Home," Home Educ Magazine, 99; auth, "Moral Philos with Children," Int J of Applied Philos, 00; auth, "Does Philos for Children Belong in School at All?," Analytic Teaching, 00. **CONTACT ADDRESS** 22024 Monument Rd. SW, Vashon Island, WA 98070. **EMAIL** jmohrlone@compuserve.com

LONG, BURKE O'CONNOR
PERSONAL Born 09/17/1938, Richmond, VA, m, 1964, 2 children **DISCIPLINE** RELIGION, BIBLICAL STUDIES **EDUCATION** Randoph-Macon Col, BA, 61; Yale Univ, BD, 64, MA, 66, PhD, 67. **CAREER** Instr relig, Yale Univ, 65-67 & Wellesley Col, 67-68; asst prof, 68-73, assoc prof, 73-82, Prof Relig, Bowdoin Col, 82-, Consult, Bd Educ, United Presby Church, 67-70; ed, Sources for Bibl Study, Soc Bibl Lit, 77-85; Soc Bibl Lit res fel, 79-80; vis prof, Emory Univ, 82; The Hebrew University, 83-84; Writing, From The Ancient World, 88-93. **HONORS AND AWARDS** Senior Fulbright Lecturer, Israel, 83-84; ACLS Fellow, 97-98. **MEMBERSHIPS** Soc Bibl Lit; World Union Jewish Studies; Inst Antiquity & Christianity. **RESEARCH** Old Testament; ancient Near East; folklore; history of biblical criticism, Bible and Culture. **SELECTED PUBLICATIONS** Auth, The Problem of Etiological Narrative in the Old Testament, Walter de Gruyter, Berlin, 69; Two question and answer schemata in the prophets, J Bibl Lit, 71; 2 Kings iii and genres of prophetic narrative, Vetus Testamentum, 73; contribr, Language in Religious Practice, Newbury, 76; auth, Recent field studies in oral literature and Old Testament form criticism, Vetus Testamentum, 76; co-ed & contribr, Canon and Authority: Essays in Old Testament Religion and Theology, Fortress, 77; ed & contribr, Images of Man & God: Old Testament Stories in Literary Focus, Almond, 81; auth, Social world of ancient Israel, Interpretation, 82; auth, I Kings with an Introduction To Historical Literature, Eerdmans, Grand Rapids, 84; auth, 2 Kings, Eerdmans, Grand Rapids, 91; auth, Planting and Reaping Albright: Politics, Ideology and Interpreting the Bible, University Park PA, Penn State University, 97. **CONTACT ADDRESS** Dept of Relig, Bowdoin Col, 7300 College Station, Brunswick, ME 04011-8473. **EMAIL** blong@bowdoin.edu

LONG, DOUGLAS C.
PERSONAL Born 05/25/1932, Ann Arbor, MI, m, 1961, 2 children **DISCIPLINE** PHILOSOPHY **EDUCATION** Univ Mich, BA, 54; Harvard, MA, 55, PhD, 63. **CAREER** Instr, UCLA, 60-62, asst prof, 62-67; assoc prof, Univ NC, Chapel Hill, 67-79, prof, 79-, chair of dept, 96-. **HONORS AND AWARDS** Phi Beta Kappa, NEH Fel, 76-77; NSF Grant, 67. **MEMBERSHIPS** Am Philos Asn, NC Philos Soc, Duke-UNC Med Ethics Res Group. **RESEARCH** Philosophy of mind, epistemology, action theory. **SELECTED PUBLICATIONS** Auth, "The Philosophical Concept of a Human Body," Philos Rev (July 64): 321-327; auth, "Particulars and Their Qualities," The Philos Quart (July 68): 193-206; auth, "Descartes' Argument for Mind-Body Dualism," Philos Forum, Boston Univ (spring 69): 259-273; auth, "The Bodies of Persons," The J of Philos, LXXI, No 10 (May 30, 74): 291-304; auth, "Agents, Mechanisms, and Other Minds," in Body, Mind, and Method, a collection of essays honoring Prof Virgil Aldrich, ed by Donald Gustafson and Bangs Tapscott, D. Reidl Pub Co, Dordrecht: Holland, (79): 129-148; auth, "The Self-Defeating Character of Skepticism," Philos and Phenomenological res, 52:1 (March 92): 67-84; auth, "Why Machines Can Neither Think Nor Feel," in Language, Mind, and Art: Essays in Appreciation and Analysis, in Honor of Paul Ziff, ed by Dale Jamieson, Synthese Library, vol 240, Dordrecht, Holland: Kluwer (94): 101-119; coauth with Dorit Bar-On, "Knowing Selves: 'Grammar' and Epistemology, Philosophy and Phenomenological Research (forthcoming). **CONTACT ADDRESS** Dept Philos, Univ of No Carolina, Chapel Hill, CB #3125, Chapel Hill, NC 27599-3125.

LONG, EUGENE T.
PERSONAL Born 03/13/1935, Richmond, VA, m, 1960, 2 children **DISCIPLINE** PHILOSOPHY **EDUCATION** Randolph Macon Col, BA, 57; Duke Univ, BD, 60; Univ of Glasgow, PhD, 64. **CAREER** Asst to assoc prof, Randolph Macon Col, 64-70; assoc to prof, Univ of SC, 70-; Chair, 72-87. **HONORS AND AWARDS** NEH Summer Res Fel; Duke/Univ of NC Humanities Fel. **MEMBERSHIPS** Metaphysical Soc of Am; Soc for the Philos of Relig; Am Philos Assoc. **RESEARCH** 19th/20th Century European Philosophy, Phenomenology and Existentialism, Philosophy of Religion. **SELECTED PUBLICATIONS** Auth, Jaspers and Bultmann: A Dialogue Between Philosophy and theology in the Existentialist Tradition, Duke Univ Pr, (Durham), 68; ed, God, Secularization and History: Essays in Memory of Ronald Gregor Smith, Univ of SC Pr, (Columbia), 74; ed, Experience, Reason and God: Essays in the Philosophy of Religion, Cath Univ Pr, of Am, (Washington, DC), 80; coed, God and Temporality, Paragon House, (NY), 84; auth, Existence, Being and God: An Introduction to the Philosophical Theology of John Macquarrie, Paragon House, (NY), 85; coed, Being and Truth: Essays in Honor of John Macquarrie, SCM Pr, (London), 86; ed, Prospects for Natural theology, Cath Univ of Am Pr, (Washington, DC), 92; ed, God, Reason and Religions, Kluwer Acad Pub, (Dordrecht), 95; auth, Twentieth Century Western Philosophy of Religion, Kluwer Acad Pub, (Dordrecht), 00. **CONTACT ADDRESS** Dept Philos, Univ of So Carolina, Columbia, Columbia, SC 29225. **EMAIL** longg@sc.edu

LONG, JAMES L.
PERSONAL Born 12/07/1937, Wintergarden, FL, s **DISCIPLINE** CRIMINAL JUSTICE **EDUCATION** San Jose State Coll, BA, 1960; Howard Univ Law School, JD, 1967. **CAREER** Legislative Counsel Bureau CA State Legislature, grad legal asst; Legal Aid Soc of Sacramento Co, grad legal asst; NAACP Western Region, special counsel; Private Practice, atty; Superior Court Bar Assn Liaison Comm, mem; Superior Court, Judge; California State Univ, Sacramento, CA, Asst Prof, Criminal Justice. **HONORS AND AWARDS** The Law and Justice Awd Sacramento Branch NAACP; Outstanding Contribution Awd in the Field of Civil Rights Riverside Branch NAACP; sat as Pro Tem Justice of the Supreme Court Dec 9, 1985; assigned Justice Pro Tem to the Court of Appeal Third Appellate Dist 1987. **MEMBERSHIPS** Hon mem, Wiley W Manual Bar Assn, Sacramento, CA; mem, Appellate Dept Superior Court of Sacramento Co, 1987; mem, Sacramento City/County Commn of the Bicentennial of the US Constitution. **SELECTED PUBLICATIONS** Co-author "Amer Minorities, The Justice Issue," Prentice Hall Inc, 1975. **CONTACT ADDRESS** Sacramento County Superior Court, 720 9th St, Sacramento, CA 95814.

LONG, JEROME HERBERT
PERSONAL Born 00/00/1931, Little Rock, AR, m, 1959, 2 children **DISCIPLINE** HISTORY OF RELIGIONS **EDUCATION** Knox Col, AB, 56; Univ Chicago Divinity Sch, BD, 60, MA, 62, PhD(hist of relig), 73. **CAREER** From instr to assoc prof relig, Western Mich Univ, 64-70; vis assoc prof, 70-71, Assoc Prof Relig, Wesleyan Univ, 71-, Mem, Comt on Reorgn of Curric of Relig Dept, Western Mich Univ, 65-67, mem, African Studies Comt, 65-70, secy, 66-67, mediator, Black Am Studies Prog, 68-70; mem, African Studies Comt, Wesleyan Univ, 74-75, chmn, 75-76, chmn, Search Comt for Dir for Ctr

for Afro-Am Studies and interim curric coordr, Ctr for Afro-Am Studies, 75-76; Vis Scholar, Inst African Studies, Legon, Ghana, West Africa, Univ Ghana, 77-. **RESEARCH** Prehistoric and primitive religions; historical approaches to religion and culture; religions of African peoples. **SELECTED PUBLICATIONS** Auth, Symbol and reality among the Trobriand Islanders, in: Essays in Divinity, Vol 1: the History of Religion, Univ Chicago, 69. **CONTACT ADDRESS** Wesleyan Univ, Middletown, CT 06457.

LONG, JOHN EDWARD
PERSONAL Born 03/16/1941, Philadelphia, PA, m **DISCIPLINE** RELIGIOUS STUDIES **EDUCATION** Temple U, BA 1963; Theol Sem of the Reformed Episcopal Ch, BD 1966; Westminister Theol Sem, Th M 1970; Brandeis U, MA PhD 1978. **CAREER** Western KY Univ, assoc prof of religious studies present. **HONORS AND AWARDS** Dissertation Research Fellowship Fulbright-Hays Research Fellow in Algeria 1974-75; Grad Study Fellowship Ford Found Advanced Study Fellowship for Black Am 1972-73; Fellowship to Study Arabic in Tunisia N African Cntr for Arabic Studies 1972. **MEMBERSHIPS** Mem Am Assn of Tchrs of Arabic 1979; mem Middle East & Studies Assn 1975; mem Middle East Inst 1975; Dissertation Research Fellowship Fulbright-Hays Research Fellow in Algeria 1974-75; Grad Study Fellowship Ford Found Advanced Study Fellowship for Black Am 1972-73; Fellowship to Study Arabic in Tunisia N African Cntr for Arabic Studies 1972. **CONTACT ADDRESS** Dept Philos, Relig, Western Kentucky Univ, Bowling Green, KY 42101.

LONG, PAUL
DISCIPLINE MISSIONS **EDUCATION** Fuller Theol Sem, PhD. **CAREER** Prof emeri. **HONORS AND AWARDS** Hubbard Awd. **SELECTED PUBLICATIONS** Auth, The Man in the Leather Hat; Citizen Soldiers of World War II. **CONTACT ADDRESS** Dept of Missions, Reformed Theol Sem, Mississippi, 5422 Clinton Blvd, Jackson, MS 39209-3099.

LONG, R. JAMES
PERSONAL Born 12/15/1938, Rochester, NY, m, 1974, 3 children **DISCIPLINE** HISTORY OF MEDIEVAL PHILOSOPHY **EDUCATION** Pontif Inst Med Studies, LMS, 66; Univ Toronto, PhD(Medieval studies), 68. **CAREER** From asst prof to assoc prof, 69-78, prof philos, Fairfield Univ, 78-, Fulbright scholar medieval philos, Fulbright Comn, US Govt, 68-69; Can Coun fel philos, 68-69; Am Coun Learned Socs & Am Philos Soc grant-in-aid, 77; Nat Endowment for Humanities scholarly publ grant, 79; vis fac fel, Yale Univ, 82-83, dir hon prog, 82-91; liason faculty, program in Greek and Roman Studies, Ffld univ, 81-. **HONORS AND AWARDS** Fellow of Massey Col, Toronto, 65-68; Province of Ontario Graduate Fellowships, 66-68; Canada Council Doctoral Fellowship, 67-68; Fulbright Scholarship, Italy and U.K., 68-69; Canada Council Postdoctoral Fellowship, 69; NEH Summer Stipend, 74; Am Council of Learned Socs Grant-in-Aid, 77; Am Philos Soc Grant, 77; Assoc of Clare Hall, Cambridge Univ, 77; NEH Scholarly Publications Grant, 79; NEH Summer Seminar for College Teachers, Fordham Univ, 81; Yale Visiting Faculty Fellowship, 82-83; NEH Summer Seminar for College Teachers, Yeshiva Univ, 84; Am Philos Soc Grant, 84; Fairfield Univ Summer Stipends, 86, 89, 92; NEH Summer Seminar for College Teachers, Columbia Univ, 87; NEH Summer Stipend, 88; Warren W. Wooden Citation, PMR Conference, 89; NEH Editions/Texts Grant, ed of Richard Fishacre's Sentences-Commentary, 1-2, $130,000, 92-94; Yale Visiting Fellowship, Philosophy Dept, 96-98. **MEMBERSHIPS** Medieval Acad Am; Am Cath Philos Asn (life member); Soc Textual Scholarship; Soc Medieval & Renaissance Philos, secrt-treas, 91-; Catholic Comm on Intellectual and Cultural Affairs; Consociatio cultorum historiae Ordinis Praedicatorum; International Soc for Napoleanic Studies; Societe Internationale pour l'Etude de la Philosophie Medievale. **RESEARCH** Early thirteenth-century philosophy, particularly Oxford; 13th-century science, particularly medicine and botany; works of Richard Fishacre. **SELECTED PUBLICATIONS** Auth, Utrum iurista vel theologus plus proficiat ad regimen ecclesie . . ., 68; The Science of Theology according to Richard Fishacre: Ed of the Prologue to his Commentary on the Sentences, 72, Mediaeval Studies; In Defense of the Tournament: an ed of Pierre Dubois' De torneamentis . . ., 73; A Note on the Dating of MS Ashmole 1512, 74, Manuscripta ; Richard Fishacre and the Problem of the Soul, Mod Schoolman, 75; Richard Fishacre's Quaestio on the Ascension of Christ: An Edition, Mediaeval Studies, 78; ed, Bartholomaeus Anglicus, On the Properties of Soul and Body, Toronto Medieval Latin Texts IV, 79; auth, Botany in the High Middle Ages: An introduction, Res Publica Litterarum, 81; The Virgin as Olive-Tree: A Marian Sermon of Richard Fishacre and Science at Oxford, Archivum Fratrum Praedicatorum 52: 77-87, 82; Alfred of Sareshel's Commentary on the Pseudo-Aristotelian De plantis: A Critical Edition, Mediaeval Studies 47: 125-67, 85; The Question "'Whether the Church Could Better be Ruled by a Good Canonist than by a Theologian' and the Origins of Ecclesiology, Proceedings of the PMR Conference 10: 99-112, 85; Richard Fishacre, Dictionnaire de Spiritualite 13, cols 563-65, 87; Richard Fishacre's Way to God, A Straight Path: Studies in Medieval Philosophy and Culture, Essays in Honor of Arthur Hyman, eds Ruth Link-Salinger et al, 174-82, Washington, D.C.: The Catholic Univ of Am Press, 88: with Joseph Goering, Richard Fishacre's Treatise De fide, spe, et caritate, Bull de Philos Medievale 31; 103-11, 89; Adam of Buckfield and John Sackville: Some Notes on Philadelphia Free Library MS Lewis European 53, Traditio 45: 364-67, 89-90; The Reception and Interpretation of the Pseudo-Arostolian De Plantis at Oxford in the Thirteenth Century, Knowledge and the Sciences in Medieval Philosophy (proceedings of the Eighth Intnl Congress of Medieval Philos: S.I.E.P.M, eds Reijo Tyorinoja, Anja I. Lehtinen, & Dagfinn Follesdal: Annuals of the Finnish Soc for Missiology and Ecumenics, 55, pp 111-23, Helsinki, 90; The Moral and Spiritual Theory of Richard Fishacre: Edition of Trinity Col, MS 0.1.30, Archivum Fratrum Praedicatorum 60, 5-143, 90; The Anonymous Peterhouse Master and the Natural Philosophy of Plants, Traditio 46: 313-26, 91; Richard Fishacre, Medieval Philosophers, ed Jeremiah Hackett, Dictionary of Literary Biography, vol 115, pp 195-200, Detroit: Bruccoli Clark Layman, Inc, 92; A Thirteenth-Century Teaching Aid: An Edition of the Bodleian Abbreviatio of the Pseudo-Aristolian De Plantis, in Aspectus et Affectus: Essays and Editions in Grosseteste and Medieval Intellectual Life in Honor of Richard C. Dales, ed Gunar Freibergs with an intro by Richard Southern, AMS Studies in the Middle Ages: no 23: 87-103, New York: AMS Press, 93; Richard Fishacre's Super S. Augustini librum de haeresibus adnotationes: An Edition and Commentary, Archives d'histoire doctrinale et litteraire du moyen age 60: 207-79, 93; Botany, in Medieval Latin: An Introduction and Bibliographical Guide, ed F.A.C. Mantello and A.G. Rigg, 401-05, Washington, D.C.: The Catholic Univ of America Press, 96; Richard Fishacre's Treatise De libero arbitrio, Moral and Political Philosophies in the Middle Ages, proceedings of the 9th Itnl congress of Medieval Philos, ed B. Carlos Bazan, Eduardo Andujar, Leonard Sbrocchi, 2: 879-91, Ottawa, 17-22, Aug 92, Ottawa: Legas, 95; with Margaret Jewett, A Newly Discovered Witness of Fishacre's Sentences-Commentary: Univ of Chicago MS 156, Traditio 50: 342-45, 95; The Reception and Use of Aristotle by the Early English Dominicans, Aristotle in Britain During the Middle Ages, ed John Marenbon, pp 51-56, Turnhout (Belgium): Brepols, 96; Roger Bacon on the Nature and Place of Angels, Vivarium 35/2: 266-82, 97; Richard Fishacre, in the New Dictionary of National Biography, (in press); Adam de Buckfield, ibid; Geoffrey de Aspale, ibid; The Cosmic Christ: The Christology of Richard Fishacre, OP, Christ Among the Medieval Dominicans, UND Press (in press); Of Angels and Pinheads: The Contributions of the Early Oxford Masters to the Doctrine of Spiritual Matter, Franciscan Studies, Essays in Honor of Girard Etzkorn, ed Gordon A. Wilson and Timothy B. Noone, 56: 237-52, 98; The First Oxford Debate on the Eternity of the World, Recherches de Philosophie et Theologie Medievale 65/1: 54-98, 98; with Timothy B. Noone, Fishacre and Rufus on the Metaphysics of Light: Two Unedited Texts, Melanges Leonard Boyle (in press); The Role of Philosophy in Richard Fishacre's Theology of Creation, proceedings of the 10th Inl Congress of Medieval Philosophy, Erfurt, 25-30 August 97: 571-78, in press; auth, "Fischacre and Rufus on the Metaphysics of Light: Two Unedited Texts," Roma, magistra mundi, Itineraria culturae medievalis, Melanges offerts au Pere L.E. Boyle a l'occasion de son 75 anniversire, Textes et Etudes du moyen age, with Timothy B. Noone, (Louvain-la-Neuve: Federation Internationale des Instituts d' Etudes Medievales, 98), 517-48; auth, "Richard Fishacre," Lexikon fur Theologie and Kirche 8, 99, 1171; auth, "The Integrative Theology of Richard Fishacre OP," New Blackfriars 80 no 941/42 (99): 354-60; auth, "Scholastic Texts and Orthography: A Response to Roland Hissette," Bulletin de Philosophie Medieval 41 (99), in press. **CONTACT ADDRESS** Dept of Philos, Fairfield Univ, 1073 N Benson Rd, Fairfield, CT 06430-5195. **EMAIL** long@fair1.fairfield.edu

LONG, RODERICK T.
PERSONAL Born 02/04/1964, Los Angeles, CA **DISCIPLINE** PHILOSOPHY **EDUCATION** Harvard Col, AB, 85; Cornell Univ, MA, 88, PhD, 92. **CAREER** Instr, asst prof, 90-98, Univ NC, Chapel Hill; instr, asst prof, Auburn Univ, 98-00. **RESEARCH** Ancient philosophy; moral and political philosophy. **SELECTED PUBLICATIONS** Auth, art, Mill's Higher Pleasures and The Choice of Character, 92; auth, art, Abortion, Abandonment, and Positive Rights: The Limits of Compulsory Altruism, 93; auth, art, Immanent Liberalism: The Politics of Mutual Consent, 95; auth, art, Aristotle's Conception of Freedom, 96; auth, art, Toward a Libertarian Theory of Class, 98, auth, art, The Irrelevance of Responsibility, 99. **CONTACT ADDRESS** Dept of Philosophy, Auburn Univ, 6080 Haley Ctr, Auburn, AL 36849. **EMAIL** longrob@auburn.edu

LONG, STEVEN A.
PERSONAL Born 07/26/1959, OH, m, 3 children **DISCIPLINE** PHILOSOPHY **EDUCATION** Trinity Int Univ, MA, 86; Marquette Univ, PhD, 95. **CAREER** Affil prof & fac and curric coordr, St Ambrose Univ, 95-98; ctr dir, Spring Arbor Col, 98-. **MEMBERSHIPS** Soc Christian Philos; Am Philos Asn. **RESEARCH** Logic of Christian doctrine; Public policy. **CONTACT ADDRESS** 860 Dolphin Ave, Kissimmee, FL 34744-4805.

LONGENECKER, RICHARD NORMAN
PERSONAL Born 07/21/1930, Mishawaka, IN, m, 1955, 3 children **DISCIPLINE** NEW TESTAMENT THEOLOGY **EDUCATION** Wheaton Col, Ill, BA, 53, MA, 56; Univ Edinburgh, PhD, 59. **CAREER** Instr Bible, Wheaton Col, Ill, 56-57, asst prof theol, 60-62, grad sch theol, 62-63; from assoc prof to prof New Testament, Trinity Evangel Divinity Sch, 63-73; prof new testament, wycliffe col, univ toronto, 72-, Am Asn Theol Schs fac fel, 66-67; mem sch bd, Ill Unit Dist 95, Lake Zurich, 70-72; prof emer, Wycliffe Col; dist prof, New Testament, McMaster Univ. **MEMBERSHIPS** Evangel Theol Soc (secy, 62-64, treas, 64-65, vpres, 73, pres, 74); Soc Bibl Lit; Studiorum Novi Testamenti Soc; Just Bibl Res. **RESEARCH** Pauline theology; early Jewish Christianity; inter-testamental period. **SELECTED PUBLICATIONS** Auth, Paul, Apostle of Liberty, New York: Harper & Row, 64, rev ed, 00; auth, The Christology of Early Jewish Christianity, London: SCM Press, 70; auth, The Ministry and Message of Paul, Grand Rapids: Zondervan, 71; auth, Biblical Exegesis in the Apostolic Period, Grand Rapids: Eardmans, 75, rev ed, 98; auth, New Testament Social Ethics for Today, Grand Rapids: Eerdmans, 84; ed, The Road from Damascus: The Impact of Paul's Conversion on his Life, Thought, and Ministry, McMaster New Testament Studies 2, ed, R.N. Longenecker, Grand Rapids: Eerdmans, 97; ed, Life in the Face of Death: The Resurrection Message of the New Testament, McMaster New Testament Studies 3, ed, R.N. Longenecker, Grand Rapids: Eerdmans, 98; auth, "New Wine into Fresh Wineskins": Contextualizing the Early Christian Confessions, Peabody, MA: Hendrickson, 99; ed, The Challenge of the Parables, McMaster New Testament Studies 4, ed, R. N. Longenecker, Grand Rapids: Eerdmans, 00; ed, Into God's Presence: Prayer in the New Testament, McMaster New Testament Studies 5, ed, R.N. Longenecker, Grand Rapids: Eerdmans, 00. **CONTACT ADDRESS** McMaster Univ, Hamilton, ON, Canada L8S 4K1. **EMAIL** longenec@caninet.com

LONGINO, HELEN
DISCIPLINE PHILOSOPHY **EDUCATION** Barnard Col, BA, 66; Univ Sessex, MA, 67; Johns Hopkins Univ, PhD, 73. **CAREER** Asst Prof, Univ Calif, 71-75; Asst Prof to Assoc Prof, Mills Col, 75-90; Assoc to Full Prof, Rice Univ, 90-95; Prof, Univ Minn, 95-. **HONORS AND AWARDS** Fel, Nat Sci Foundation; Fel, Mellon Foundation; Fel, Rockefeller Foundation; Fel, McKnight Foundation; Winton Scholar, Univ MN, 93-95; Fulbright Sen Scholar, 00. **MEMBERSHIPS** Am Philos Asn; Philos of Sci Asn; Soc for Soc Studies of Sci; Nat Women's Studies Foundation; Soc for Women in Philos. **RESEARCH** Philosophy of Biology; Social Dimensions of Scientific Knowledge; Gender and Science. **SELECTED PUBLICATIONS** Auth, Science as Social Knowledge, Princeton Univ, 90; auth, Feminism and Science, Oxford Univ Press, 96; auth, The Fate of Knowledge, Princeton Univ Press, forthcoming. **CONTACT ADDRESS** Univ of Minnesota, Twin Cities, 224 Church St SE, 425 Ford Hall, Minneapolis, MN 55455. **EMAIL** hlongino@tc.umn.edu

LONGMAN, TREMPER, III
PERSONAL Born 09/08/1948, Princeton, NJ, m, 1973, 3 children **DISCIPLINE** THEOLOGY **EDUCATION** Ohio Wesleyan Univ, BA, 74; Westminster Theol Sem, MDiv, 77; Yale Univ, MA, 80, PhD, 83. **CAREER** Westminster Theol Sem, prof, 81-98; Westmont Col, prof, 98-. **MEMBERSHIPS** SBL, IBR. **RESEARCH** Old Testament; ancient near east. **SELECTED PUBLICATIONS** Coauth, Cry of the Soul: How Our Emotions Reveal Our Deepest Questions About God, Nav Press, 94; auth, Psalms, Geneva Study Bible, Thomas Nelson, 95; coauth, When God Declares War, Christianity Today, 96; auth, How to Read the Psalms, Discipleship Jour, 97; auth, Reading the Bible with Heart and Mind, Nav Press, 97; auth, Guilt and Compassion: Old Testament versus New Testament?, Modern Reformation, 97; coauth, Bold Purpose: Exchanging Counterfeit Happiness for the Real Meaning of Life, Tyndale House Pub, 98. **CONTACT ADDRESS** Dept of Old Testament, Westmont Col, 955 La Paz Rd, Santa Barbara, CA 93108. **EMAIL** longman@westmont.edu

LONGSTAFF, THOMAS R. W.
PERSONAL Born 10/09/1935, Nashor, NH, m, 1969, 5 children **DISCIPLINE** RELIGION **EDUCATION** Univ ME, BA, 64; BD, Bangor Theol Sem, 64; Columbia Univ, PhD, 73. **CAREER** Visiting Prof, Bangor Theol Sem, 74-75; Interim Chaplain, Colby Col, 76, 79-81; Visiting Scholar, Ashmolean Museum and the Oriental Inst of Oxford Univ, 77-78; Asst Prof to Assoc Prof, Colby Col, 73-84; Visiting Res Scholar, MIT, 84-85; Prof and Dept Chair, Colby Col, 84-. **HONORS AND AWARDS** Jonathan F. Morris Prize, Bangor Theol Sem, 61, 63; Fac Prize, Bangor Theol Sem, 61, 63; Woodrow Wilson Fel, 64. **MEMBERSHIPS** Am Sch of Oriental Res; Catholic Biblical Asn of Am; Israel Exploration Soc; ME Archaeol Asn; Soc of Biblical Lit; N Eng Reg Soc of Biblical Lit; Studiorum Novi Testamenti Societas. **RESEARCH** Biblical archaeology and Christian origins; Judaism and Christianity in the roman and Byzantine periods; computer and technological applications in Biblical and archaeological research; The Synoptic Gospels. **SELECTED PUBLICATIONS** Auth, "Hypertext as a Medium for archaeological Publication," Archaeological Computing Newsletter, (93): 1-2; co-auth, "Excavations at Sepphoris: The Location and Identification of Shikhin, Part II," Israel Exploration Journal, (95): 171-87; co-auth, "Excavations at Sepphoris: The Location and Identification of Shikhin, Part I," Israel Exploration Journal, (94): 216-227; co-auth, "Zippori--1991," in Excavations and Surveys in Israel, Vol 13, (Jerusalem, 95), 29-

30; auth, "The digmaster Database: http://www.cobb.msstate.edu/figurines/", Biblical Archaeologist, (96): 128-129; auth, "Computer Recording, Analysis, and Interpretation," The Oxford Encyclopedia of Archaeology in the Near East, (Oxford Univ Press, 97), 57-59; contrib, Sepphoris in Galilee: Crosscurrents of Culture, Raleigh, 96; auth, "Sepphoris, The Ornament of All Galilee," in Many faces to the bible: Papers from the first Bates college symposium on Religion and contemporary Issues, (Bates Col Press, 97), 146-154. **CONTACT ADDRESS** Dept Relig, Colby Col, 150 Mayflower Hill Dr, Waterville, ME 04907-4799. **EMAIL** t_longst@colby.edu

LOOFBOURROW, RICHARD C.
PERSONAL Born 06/10/1940, Loma Linda, CA, d, 1 child **DISCIPLINE** PHILOSOPHY, ETHICS, LOGIC **EDUCATION** Long Beach State Univ, BA, 63; San Jose State Univ, MA, 65. **CAREER** San Jose State Univ, Long Beach City Col, 64-65; Antelope Valley Col, 66-. **HONORS AND AWARDS** NEH, 74-75; NEH, 79. **RESEARCH** Ethics; philosophy of mind. **SELECTED PUBLICATIONS** Auth, Puzzles, Principles and Philosophies, McGraw Hill, 99; auth, Paradoxes, Puzzles, and Possibilities, McGraw Hill, 98. **CONTACT ADDRESS** Dept Social Science, Antelope Valley Col, 3041 West Ave K, Lancaster, CA 93536-5402. **EMAIL** realzippy@aol.com

LOPACH, JAMES JOSEPH
PERSONAL Born 06/23/1942, Great Falls, MT, d, 2 children **DISCIPLINE** POLITICAL SCIENCE **EDUCATION** Carroll Col, AB 64; Univ MT, law sch, 64; Univ Notre Dame, MA 67, MAT 68, PhD 73. **CAREER** John Adams HS, teacher 67-68; Pac Tele Co, asst mgr mgr 68-69; South Bend Manpwr asst dir and Admin Aide to Mayor 71-73; Univ Notre Dame, instr dir dept govt intl studies 72-73; Univ MT, asst prof 75-78, ch 77-84, 85-87, assoc prof 78-83, prof 83-, act dir 84-88, 91, assoc dean 87-88, spec asst to pres 88-92, assoc provost 92-95, spec asst to provost 95-96. **RESEARCH** Am Constitutional Law, Am Indian Govt and Law, Montana Politics. **SELECTED PUBLICATIONS** Auth, We the People of Montana, Mountain Press, 83; Tribal Government Today: Politics on Montana Indian Reservations, Univ Press Colorado, rev ed, 98; Planning Small Town America-Observations, Sketches, and A Reform Proposal, with Kristina Ford and Dennis O'Donnell, Amer Plan Assn, 90; The Anomaly of Judicial Activism in Indian Country, Amer Ind Cult and Res Journal, 97. **CONTACT ADDRESS** Dept of Polit Sci, Univ of Montana, Missoula, MT 59812. **EMAIL** lopach@selway.umt.edu

LOPES, DOMINIC MCIVER
PERSONAL Born 07/03/1964, Aberdeen, Scotland, d **DISCIPLINE** PHILOSOPHY **EDUCATION** McGill Univ, BA, 86; Oxford Univ, DPhil, 92. **CAREER** Vis asst prof Philos, Purdue Univ, 91-92; asst prof Philos, 92-97, assoc prof Philos, Ind Univ-Kokomo, 97- ; Assoc prof Philos, Univ of British Columbia, 00-. **HONORS AND AWARDS** Philosophical Quarterly Essay Prize, 97; Fellow National Humanity Center, 00. **MEMBERSHIPS** Amer Soc Aesthetics; Amer Philos Asn. **RESEARCH** Philosophy of art, Philosophy of mind, ethics. **SELECTED PUBLICATIONS** Auth, Understanding Pictures, Oxford Univ Pr, 96; Ed, Routledge Companion to Aesthetics, Routledge, 00. **CONTACT ADDRESS** Dept of Philosophy, Univ of British Columbia, Vancouver, BC, Canada V6T 1Z1. **EMAIL** dlopes@bitwalla.com

LORD, TIMOTHY C.
PERSONAL Born 11/05/1960, Elizabethtown, KY, m, 1995, 1 child **DISCIPLINE** PHILOSOPHY **EDUCATION** Cedarville Col, BA, 85; Iowa State Univ, MA, 87; Purdue Univ, MA, 91; PhD, 95. **CAREER** Prof, Heartland Community Col, 93-. **HONORS AND AWARDS** Purdue Dissertation Res Fel, 91-93; Purdue Interdisciplinary Prog Res Awd, 92. **MEMBERSHIPS** Am Philos Asn, Am Soc for Aesthet, Soc for Phenomenol and Existential Philos, Int Asn for Philos and Lit, Asm Asn of Philos Teachers. **RESEARCH** Philosophy of history, History of modern philosophy, Aesthetics, Philosophy and literature, Contemporary continental philosophy. **SELECTED PUBLICATIONS** Rev, of "The Ideology of the Aesthetics," by Terry Eagleton, Philos and Lit 16.2 (92): 374-376; auth, "Hegel, Marx, and Shoeless Joe: Religious Ideology in Kinsella's Baseball Fantasy," Aethlon: The J of Sport Lit 10.1 (92): 43-51; rev, of "Philosophy and Its History: Issues in Philosophical Historiography," by Jorge J.E. Gracia, CLIO: A J of Lit, Hist and Philos of Hist 22.4 (93): 396-399; auth, "A Paradigm Case of Polemic History: Terry Eagleton's 'The Ideology of the Aesthetic'," CLIO: A J of Lit, Hist and Philos of Hist 22.4 (93): 337-356; rev, of "Philosophical Historicism and the Betrayal of First Philosophy," by Carl Page, CLIO: A J of Lit, Hist and Philos of Hist 26.3 (97): 390-397; auth, "Introducing Philosophy: The Challenge of Scepticism," by D.Z. Phillips, APA Newsletter on Teaching Philos 98.2 (99): 169-170; auth, "R.G. Collingwood: C Continental Philosopher," rev essay of "R.G. Collingwood", by Peter Johnson, CLIO: A J of Lit, Hist and Philos of Hist (forthcoming). **CONTACT ADDRESS** Dept Humanities, Heartland Comm Col, 1226 N Towanda Ave, Bloomington, IL 61701-3424. **EMAIL** tim@hcc.cc.il.us

LOREK, ROBERT
PERSONAL Born 05/02/1966, Chicago, IL, s **DISCIPLINE** PHILOSOPHY **EDUCATION** Univ Dayton, BS, bus adm, 88; Univ Nebr, MA, philos, 94. **CAREER** Adjunct prof, Elmhurst Col, Col of Dupage, Univ St. Francis. **MEMBERSHIPS** Amer Philos Asn. **RESEARCH** Ethics; Epistemology; Metaethical theory. **SELECTED PUBLICATIONS** Auth, Intuition: A Foundation for Moral Principles, Quest For Goodness, Krasemann, Simon & Schuster, 98. **CONTACT ADDRESS** 1504 W. Jackson, Chicago, IL 60607. **EMAIL** robertl@elmhurst.edu

LOSONCY, THOMAS A.
DISCIPLINE PHILOSOPHY **EDUCATION** Sacred Heart Sem, BA, 61; Univ Detroit, MA, 63; Univ Toronto, PhD, 72. **CAREER** Assoc prof,Villanova Univ. **RESEARCH** Ancient & Medieval philosophers-ethics, philosophy of man, metaph. **SELECTED PUBLICATIONS** Auth, St Augustine, in Ethics in the History of Western Philos, NY; St Martin's Press, Chap 3, 89; The Soul-Body Problem in the Thirteenth Century: Countering the Trend Toward Dualism, Stud in Medieval Cult XII, 78; St Anselm's Rejection of the 'Ontological Argument' - A Review of the Occasion and Circumstances, Amer Cath Philos Quart, LXIV, 90; Plato's Meno Argument for Recollection: Correct and Incorrect, Methexis, Etudes Neoplatoniciennes Presentees au Professeur Evanghelos A. Moutsopoulos, Athenes: Ctr Int d'Etudes Platoniciennes et Aristoleciennes, 92 & Giles of Rome (Aegidius Romanus), Dictionary of Literary Biog Vol 115: Medieval Philos, Detroit and London: Gale Res Inc, 92; auth, "Anselm's Proslogion-Unum argumentum sed tres quaestiones: On Right Answer, One Wrong Answer, One Unanswered," Saint Anselm Bishop and Thinker, ed. R. Majeran & E.I. Zielinski, (Lublin): Univ Press, Cath Univ of Lublin, 99. **CONTACT ADDRESS** Dept of Philosophy, Villanova Univ, 800 Lancaster Ave, Villanova, PA 19085-1692.

LOSONSKY, MICHAEL
PERSONAL Born 02/21/1953, Salzburg, Austria, m, 1982, 2 children **DISCIPLINE** PHILOSOPHY **EDUCATION** Earlham Col, BA, 75; Univ of Rochester, MA, 78, PhD, 82. **CAREER** Asst prof, Univ of Minn, 87-89; assoc prof, Colo State Univ, 89-. **HONORS AND AWARDS** Rush Rhees Fel, 75-8; Lewis White Beck Fel, 80. **MEMBERSHIPS** Am Philos Assoc; Brit Soc for the Hist of Philos. **RESEARCH** History of Modern Philosophy, Metaphysics. **SELECTED PUBLICATIONS** Auth, "Reference and Rorty's Veil", Philos Studies 47, (85): 291-4; auth, "No Problem for Actualism", Philos Rev 95 (86): 95-7; auth, "Leibniz's Adamic Language of Thought", J of the Hist of Phil 30, (92): 523-543; auth, "Meaning and Signification in Locke's Essay", in Locke's Philosophy: Content and Context, ed G.A.J. Rogers, Ox Univ Pr (Oxford), 94; auth, "John Locke on Passion, Will and Belief", Brit J for the Hist of Philos 4 (96): 267-83; coed, Readings in Language and Mind, Blackwell, 96; auth, "Self-Deceivers: Intentions and Possessions", Peer Commentary, Behav and Brain Sci 20 (97): 121-2; coauth, coed, Beginning Metaphysics: Introductory Text with Readings, Blackwell, 98; ed, W.V. Humboldt, On Language, Cambridge Univ Pr, 99; auth, "On Wanting to Believe" in Essays on Belief and Acceptance, ed, P. Engel, Philos Studies Libr, Kluwer Pr, 00. **CONTACT ADDRESS** Dept Philos, Colorado State Univ, Fort Collins, CO 80523-0001. **EMAIL** losonsky@lamar.colostate.edu

LOTT, JOHN BERTRAND
DISCIPLINE RELIGION **EDUCATION** Washington Univ, St Louis, BA, 89; Univ Pa, PhD, 95. **CAREER** Asst prof; lect, Amer Philol Asn, Chicago, 97, York Univ, Ont, 96; Amer Philol Asn, San Diego, 95; invited lect, Phi Alpha Theta lect His, Wichita State Univ, 97, Pomona Col, Wichita State Univ & Vassar Col, 97; Swarthmore Col, 95; Union Col, Schenectady, 95. **RESEARCH** The age of Augustus; Silver age Latin; ancient religion; Greek and Roman history. **SELECTED PUBLICATIONS** Auth, Philip II, Alexander and the Two Tyrannies at Eresos of IG XII 2 526, Phoenix 50 1, 96; An Augustan Sculpture of August Justice, ZPE 96; **CONTACT ADDRESS** Classics Dept, Vassar Col, Box 244, Poughkeepsie, NY 12604. **EMAIL** jolott@vassar.edu

LOTZ, DAVID WALTER
PERSONAL Born 07/01/1937, Houston, TX, m, 1965 **DISCIPLINE** CHURCH AND EARLY MODERN EUROPEAN HISTORY **EDUCATION** Concordia Sr Col, BA, 59; Concordia Theol Sem, MDiv, 63; Wash Univ, MA, 64; Union Theol Sem, STM 65, ThD, 71. **CAREER** Instr relig, Concordia Sr Col, 63-64; from instr to assoc prof, 68-76, Washburn Prof Church Hist, Union Theol Sem, 76-, Lectr church hist, Woodstock Col, NY, 71-74 and Gen Theol Sem, New York, 74-; consult, Inter-Lutheran Comn Worship, 73-74; theol consult, Atlantic Dist, Lutheran Church-Mo Synod, 74-. **MEMBERSHIPS** AHA; Am Acad Relig; Am Soc Church Hist; Am Soc Reformation Res; Am Cath Hist Asn. **RESEARCH** Reformation history and theology; 19th century religious thought; historiography. **SELECTED PUBLICATIONS** Auth, Christ Person and Life Work in the Theology of Ritschl,Albrecht With Special Attention to Munus Triplex, J Rel, Vol 0073, 93; The Harvest of Humanism in Central Europe--Essays in Honor of Spitz, Lewis, W, 16th Century J, Vol 0025, 94. **CONTACT ADDRESS** Dept of Church Hist, Union Theol Sem, New York, 3061 Broadway, New York, NY 10027-5710.

LOUCH, ALFRED
PERSONAL Born 02/14/1927, Fresno, CA, m, 1951, 2 children **DISCIPLINE** PHILOSOPHY **EDUCATION** Univ Calif, Berkeley, BA,49, MA, 51; Cambridge Univ, PhD, 56. **CAREER** Teaching asst, Univ Calif, Berkeley, 49-52; instr philos, Oberlin Col, 57-59; from asst prof to assoc prof, Syracuse Univ, 59-65; Prof Philos, Claremont Grad Sch, 65-, Vis assoc prof, Univ Calif, Los Angeles, 63-64. **RESEARCH** Philosophy of mind; philosophy of the social sciences and psychology; philosophy of law. **SELECTED PUBLICATIONS** Auth, The Myth of theory, Philos and Lit, Vol 0020, 96; The Reign of Ideology, Philos and Lit, Vol 0021, 97; Opera--Desire, Disease, Death, Philos and Lit, Vol 0021, 97; Reclaiming Truth--Contributions to a Critique of Cultural Relativism, Philos and Lit, Vol 0021, 97. **CONTACT ADDRESS** Dept of Philos, Claremont Graduate Sch, Claremont, CA 91711.

LOUDEN, ROBERT B.
PERSONAL Born 04/08/1953, Lafayette, IN, m, 1987, 2 children **DISCIPLINE** PHILOSHOPY **EDUCATION** Univ of Calif, Santa Cruz, BA, 75; Univ of Chicago, MA, 76; PhD, 81. **CAREER** From Asst to Full Prof, Univ of Southern Maine, 82-; Vis Prof, Gottingen Univ, Ger, 92; Vis Prof, Emory Univ, 95. **HONORS AND AWARDS** ACLS Fel, 89-90; Alexander von Humboldt Res Fel, 91-92, 96-97; NEH Fel for Col Teachers, 96. **SELECTED PUBLICATIONS** Auth, Morality and Moral Theory, Oxford Univ Press, 92; auth, The Greeks and US, Univ of Chicago Press, 96; auth, Kant's Impure Ethics, Oxford Univ Press, 00; ed, Kant, Lectures on Anthropology, Cambridge Univ Press, forthcoming; ed, Kant, Anthropology, History, Education, Cambridge Univ Press, 00; (ed.) The Greeks and Us, Univ of Chicago, 96 **CONTACT ADDRESS** Dept Philos, Univ of So Maine, Po Box 9300, Portland, ME 04104-9300. **EMAIL** louden@maine.edu

LOUGHRAN, JAMES N.
PERSONAL Born 03/22/1940, Brooklyn, NY **DISCIPLINE** PHILOSOPHY **EDUCATION** Fordham Univ, BA, 64; MA, 65; PhD, 85. **CAREER** Joined SJ, 58; ordained priest, 70; instr, St. Peter's Col, 65-67; ast dean Fordham Univ, 70-73; tchr, Fordham Univ, 74-79, 82-84, dean 79-82; pres, Loyola Marymount Univ, 84-91; act pres, Brooklyn Coll, 92; Miller prof, John Carroll Univ, 92-93; interim pres, Mount St Mary's Coll, 93-94; interim acad vpres, Fordham Univ, 94-95; pres, St. Peter's College, 95- . **HONORS AND AWARDS** PhD, hon, Loyola Col, 85. **MEMBERSHIPS** APA; Am Catholic Philos Asn. **RESEARCH** Moral philosophy. **SELECTED PUBLICATIONS** "Reasons for Being Just," Value of Justice, Fordham Univ, 79; "The Moral Ideal of the Person," Int Philos Q, 86; "Francis Hutcheson," Hist of Philos Q, 86. **CONTACT ADDRESS** President's Off, Saint Peter's Col, 2641 Kennedy Blvd., Jersey City, NJ 07305. **EMAIL** loughran_j@spcvxa.spc.edu

LOUNIBOS, JOHN
PERSONAL Born 03/21/1934, Petaluma, CA, m, 1970, 2 children **DISCIPLINE** RELIGIOUS STUDIES, PHILOSOPHY **CAREER** Tchng, 61-, Bellarmine HS, San Jose, Calif; prof, relig stud, 71-00, Dominican Col, Blauvelt **HONORS AND AWARDS** 3 NEH summer fellowships for college teachers: with John Gager, Princeton Univ, 79; with Arthur Hyman, Columbia/Yeshiva Univ, 84; with William Dever, Univ AZ, Tuscon, 95. **MEMBERSHIPS** AAR; Col Theol Soc CTSA; Int Soc for Neoplatonic Stud; Soc for Medieval Renaissance Philos. **RESEARCH** Philos and relig texts, histories, and interpretation. **SELECTED PUBLICATIONS** Co-ed, The College I Experience: Integrating Work, Leisure and Service, (ASC), 80; co-ed, Pagan and Christian Anxiety: A Response to E. R. Dodds, UAP, 84. **CONTACT ADDRESS** Dominican Col of Blauvelt, 470 Western Hwy, Orangeburg, NY 10962. **EMAIL** JLounibos@aol.com

LOUX, MICHAEL
DISCIPLINE PHILOSOPHY **EDUCATION** Col of St. Thomas, BA, 64; Univ Chicago, MA, 65, PhD, 68. **CAREER** Prof. **RESEARCH** Ancient philosophy; metaphysics. **SELECTED PUBLICATIONS** Auth, Primary Ousia, 91; Understanding Process: Reflections on Physics, 94; Composition and Unity, 94; Kinds and Predication: Aristotle's Categories, Philos Papers, 97; Beyond Substrata and Bundles, Cont Metaphysics, 97; An Introduction to Metaphysics, 97. **CONTACT ADDRESS** Philosophy Dept, Univ of Notre Dame, 336/7 O'Shaughnessy, Notre Dame, IN 46556. **EMAIL** loux.1@nd.edu

LOVEJOY, GRANT I.
PERSONAL m, 2 children **DISCIPLINE** THEOLOGY **EDUCATION** Baylor Univ, BA, 80; Southwestern Baptist Theol Semi, MDiv, 84, PhD, 90. **CAREER** Assoc prof, Southwwestern Baptist Theol Sem, 88-. **HONORS AND AWARDS** Col Minister, Emmanuel Baptist Church, 78-83; pastor, Kingswood ISU, 84-85; Shady Shores Baptist Church, 85-88. **MEMBERSHIPS** Acad Homiletics; Rel Speech Commun Assn; Evangel Homiletic Soc. **SELECTED PUBLICATIONS** Auth, Biblical Hermenuetics, Broadman & Holman, 96; Pastoral Preaching, Leadership Handbooks of Practical Theol, Word & Worship, Baker Bk House, 92; Pulpit Humor, Leadership handbooks of

Practical Theol: Word & Worship, Baker Bk House, 92; Emotion in Preaching, Leadership Handbooks of Practical Theol: Word & Worship, Baker Bk House, 92. **CONTACT ADDRESS** Sch Theol, Southwestern Baptist Theol Sem, PO Box 22000, Fort Worth, TX 76122-0418. **EMAIL** glovejoy@swbts.swbts.edu

LOVETT, LEONARD
PERSONAL Born 12/05/1939, Pompano Beach, FL, m **DISCIPLINE** THEOLOGY **EDUCATION** Saints Jr Coll, AA 1959; Morehouse Coll, BA 1962; Crozer Theological Seminary, MDiv 1965; Emory Univ Candler's Grad Sch of Theology, PhD 1979. **CAREER** Meml COGIC, pastor 1962-70; Health & Welfare Council Philadelphia New York City Proj, coord 1965-67; Stephen Smith Towers 202 Senior Citizens, proj mgr 1967-70; Ch Mason Theological Seminary, pioneer pres 1970-74; Fuller Theological Seminary, assoc dir Black Ministries 1977-81. **MEMBERSHIPS** Pres Soc for Pentecostal Studies 1975; mem Soc for the Study of Black Religion 1972-; reactor Vatican-Pentecostal Dialogue W Germany 1974; visit prof Grad Theological Union Berkeley 1975; prof of Ethics & Theology Ecumenical Cntr for Black Church Studies 1978-; prof of Ethics & Theology Amer Bapt Seminary of the West 1984; visiting fellow Human Behavior Amer Inst of Family Relations 1982-85; bd mem, Watts Health Foundation, United Health Plan 1985-; columnist, Black Perspective, Ministries Today Magazine 1988-. **SELECTED PUBLICATIONS** Conditional Liberation Spirit Journal 1977; What Charismatics Can Learn from Black Pentecostals Logos Journal 1980; Tribute to Martin Luther King in Outstanding Black Sermons Vol 2 Judson Press 1982; contrib Aspects of the Spiritual Legacy of the Church of God in Christ in Mid-Stream An Ecumenical Journal Vol XXIV No 4 1985, Black Witness to the Apostolic Faith Eardmans 1988; Black Holiness-Pentecostalism, Black Theology, Positive Confession Theology, Dictionary of the Pentecostal Charismatic Movement, Zondervan 1988; Doctor of Laws, Saints Jr College, 1972. **CONTACT ADDRESS** Church at the Crossroads COGIC, 9216 Parmelee Ave, Los Angeles, CA 90002.

LOW, ROY
PERSONAL Born 11/14/1953, San Francisco, CA, m, 1985, 2 children **DISCIPLINE** BIBLICAL STUDIES; OLD TESTAMENT **EDUCATION** Univ Cal Berkeley, BS, 76; Dallas Theol Sem, ThM, 84; Golden Gate Baptist Theol Sem, PhD, 95. **CAREER** Civil engr, 77-84; asst to assoc pastor, Cumberland Presby Chinese Church, 84-92; asst to assoc prof of Old Testament, W Sem, 92-99. **HONORS AND AWARDS** Who's Who Among Stud, Amer Univ & Col, 92-93. **MEMBERSHIPS** Soc Bibl Lit; Asn Prof Hebrew; Evangel Theol Soc. **RESEARCH** Poetic literature (Biblical); Rhetoric **CONTACT ADDRESS** 359 Michelle Ln., Daly City, CA 94015. **EMAIL** Roy1amylow@aol.com

LOWE, EUGENE Y., JR.
PERSONAL Born 08/18/1949, New York, NY, m, 4 children **DISCIPLINE** RELIGION; CHURCH HISTORY **EDUCATION** Princeton Univ, AB, 71; Union Theol Sem, M Div, 78; Union Theol Sem, PhD, 87. **CAREER** Res assoc and consult, Andrew W. Mellon Found, 93-97; lectr, dept of relig, Princeton Univ, 93-95; dean of students, Princeton Univ, 83-93; assoc provost, Northwestern Univ, 95-99, asst to the pres, 99-. **HONORS AND AWARDS** Phi Beta Kappa; Protestant fel; fund for Theol Educ, 76-77; Harold Willis Dodds Prize, Princeton Univ, 71; grad fel, Episcopal Church Found, 78-81. **MEMBERSHIPS** Amer Acad of Relig; Amer Soc of Church Hist; Lilly Seminar on Relig and Higher Educ. **RESEARCH** Religion in American History, Higher Education Policy. **SELECTED PUBLICATIONS** Auth, Mordecai Kaplan, Twentieth-Century Shapers of American Popular Religion, 210-217, Greenwood, 89; auth, Racial Ideology, Encycl of Amer Social Hist, 335-346, Charles Scribner's Sons, 93; auth, From Social Gospel to Social Science at the University of Wisconsin, The Church's Public Role: Retrospect and Prospect, 233-251, Eerdmans, 93; auth, Walter Righter, Dict of Heresy Trials in American Christianity, Greenwood Press, 320-326, 97; ed, Promise and Dilemma: Perspectives in Racial Diversity and High Education, Princeton Univ Press, 99. **CONTACT ADDRESS** Office of the Provost, Northwestern Univ, Crown Center 2-154, Evanston, IL 60208.

LOWENFELD, ANDREAS F.
PERSONAL Born 05/30/1930, Berlin, Germany, m, 1962, 2 children **DISCIPLINE** INTERNATIONAL LAW **EDUCATION** Harvard Univ, AB, 51; Harvard Law Sch, LLB, 55. **CAREER** Law practice with Hyde and de Vries, New York, 58-61; U.S. Dept of State, 61-66; vis prof, Stanford Law Sch, summer 69, 72; prof, Inst on Int and Comparative Law, Paris, summer 76, London, summer 80, Dublin, summer 83, Moscow, Leningrad, Warsaw, summer 91; prof, New York Univ Sch of Law; 67-, Charles L. Denison Prof of Law, 81-94, Herbert and Rose Rubin Prof of Int Law, 94-. **MEMBERSHIPS** Am Soc of Int Law, Am Law Inst, Am Bar Asn, Coun on Foreign Relations. **RESEARCH** International law, international trade, arbitration. **SELECTED PUBLICATIONS** Auth, International Litigation and Arbitration, West (93); auth, International Litigation and the Quest for Reasonableness, Oxford (96); auth, International Private Trade, M. Bender, ed (97); auth, Conflict of Laws: Federal, State, and International Perspectives, M. Bender, 2nd ed (98); auth, Revolutionary Days: The Iran Hostage Crisis and the Hague Claims Tribunal, Juris Pubs (99). **CONTACT ADDRESS** Sch of Law, New York Univ, 40 Washington Sq S, New York, NY 10012-1005. **EMAIL** andreas.lowenfeld@nyu.edu

LOWENSTEIN, DANIEL H.
PERSONAL Born 10/25/1943, New York, NY, m, 1970, 2 children **DISCIPLINE** LAW **EDUCATION** Yale Col, AB, 64; Harvard Law Sch, LLB, 67. **CAREER** Atty, Calif Rural Legal Assistance, 68-71; Dept Secretary of State, Calif, 71-75; Chair, Calif Fair Polit Practices Commission, 75-79; Prof, UCLA, 79-. **HONORS AND AWARDS** Sheldon Traveling Fel, Harvard Univ, 67-68. **RESEARCH** Election Law; Literature **SELECTED PUBLICATIONS** Auth, "A Patternless Mosaic: Campaign Finance and the First Amendment after Austin," Capital L Rev, 92; auth, "Associational Rights of Political Parties," Tex L Rev, 93; auth, "The Failure of the Act," Cardozo L Rev, 94; auth, "Are Congressional Term Limits Constitutional?," Harvard J of Law & Public Policy, 94; auth, Election Law, Carolina Acad Press, 95; auth, "You Don't Have to be Liberal to Hate the Racial Gerrymandering Cases," Stanford L Rev, 98. **CONTACT ADDRESS** Sch of Law, Univ of California, Los Angeles, 405 Hilgard, Los Angeles, CA 90095-1476. **EMAIL** lowenste@mail.law.ucla.edu

LOWERY, MARK
PERSONAL Born, WI, m, 8 children **DISCIPLINE** THEOLOGY **EDUCATION** Marquette Univ, PhD. **CAREER** Prof, Dallas Univ. **RESEARCH** Importance and complementary nature of theological education, spiritual formation and pastoral training. **SELECTED PUBLICATIONS** Faith and Reason; Irish Theol Quart; New Oxford Rev; Catholic Faith; Homiletic and Pastoral Rev; Soc Justice Rev and Envoy. **CONTACT ADDRESS** Instit for Religious and Pastoral Studies, Univ of Dallas, 1845 E Northgate Dr, Irving, TX 75062.

LOWRY, WILLIAM R.
DISCIPLINE POLITICAL SCIENCE **EDUCATION** IN Univ, BS 79; Univ IL, Chicago, MBA 83; Stanford Univ, MA 85, PhD 88. **CAREER** Dept Pol Sci, WA Univ **HONORS AND AWARDS** Polit Sci Prof of the Yr, 98, 96; Facul Res Gnt; Mortar Bd Tch Awd; Golden Key Nat Hon Soc; Women's Panhellenic Tch Awd; IFC tchr of the yr; MBT Awd; Brookings Inst Fell; Stanford Univ Fell; Univ IL Fell; Beta Gamma Sima Hon Bus Frat; Pi Sigma Alpha Hon PS Frat. **RESEARCH** Environmental policy, public lands. **SELECTED PUBLICATIONS** Preserving Public Lands for the Future: The Politics of Intergenerational Goods, Wash DC, Georgetown 98; The Capacity for Wonder: Preserving National Parks, Wash DC, Brookings Inst, 94; The Dimensions of Federalism: State Governments and Pollution Control Policies, Durham, Duke Univ Press, 92; Public Provision of Intergenerational Goods, in Amer Jour Pol Sci, 98; Paradise Lost?, Forum for Applied Res and Public Policy, 97; National Parks policy, in: Charles Davis, ed, Western Public Lands and Environ Pol, Lawrence KS, Univ Press KS, 97. **CONTACT ADDRESS** Dept of Polit Sci, Washington Univ, Saint Louis, MO 63130. **EMAIL** lowry@artsci.wustl.edu

LU, MATTHIAS
PERSONAL Born 06/02/1919, China **DISCIPLINE** PHILOSOPHY, THEOLOGY **EDUCATION** Pontifical Urbanian Univ, Rome, PhD, 46. **CAREER** Prof philos, theol, Fujen Univ, Peking, 46-48; chemn Educ Comt for Parish Co-Operatives, Ontario, 51-56; instr philos Univ Notre Dame, 56-58; vis lectr St Bonaventure Univ, 58-59; asst prof St John's Univ, 59-62; res assoc Univ Calif, Berkeley, 62- ; asst prof, 62-72, res assoc philos, 72- , scholar in res, 73- , St Mary's Col of Calif; vicar for Chinese and East Asian people, Oakland CA, 69-86; dir St Thomas Aquinas Int Ctr, 74-. **HONORS AND AWARDS** Pro Ecclesia et Pontefice Medal, Pope Pius XII, 39; Gold Medal for Distinguished Service, Pope John Paul II, 85; honorary PhD, Scicluna Int Univ Found, 87; Einstein Medal, 88; honorary ThD, Albert Einstein Int Acad Found, 93. **MEMBERSHIPS** APA; Am Cath Philos Asn; Am Oriental Soc; AAAS; Am Acad Polit and Soc Sci; Cath Theol Soc Am; Chinese Hist Soc of Am; Int Soc of St Thomas Aquinas; Int Jacques Maritain Soc; Int Soc of Metaphysics; Int Asn of Symbolic Logic; Int Soc of Chinese Philos. **SELECTED PUBLICATIONS** Auth, Common People Need the Common Doctor, Moraga, 79; auth, Einstein for Peace and Harmony between Science and Religion, Int Acad of Albert Einstein, 91; auth, Human Family and Human Children for a Human World, World Forum of NGO's, U.N., 93; auth, Dialogue of Christianity with Cultures in China in Francis, ed, Christian Humanism, International Perspectives, Peter Lang, 95; Martyrdom for Truth and Liberty in the People's Republic of China: a 1949-1996 report to the Fifth World Congress of Christian Philosophy, Euntes Docete, 96; auth, Hypocrisy or Tactful Machination? Cath Int, 96; auth, A Plea for Freedom, Cath Int, 98. **CONTACT ADDRESS** St. Thomas Aquinas Center, Saint Mary's Col, California, PO Box 3014, Moraga, CA 94575. **EMAIL** mlu@silcon.com

LU, SUPING
DISCIPLINE LIBRARY SCIENCE, INTERNATIONAL RELATIONS **EDUCATION** Ohio Univ, MA, 92; Univ SC, MLIS, 94. **CAREER** ASST PROF, UNIV NEB, 94-. **CONTACT ADDRESS** Lincoln Love Libr, Univ of Nebraska, Lincoln, 319 Love, City Campus 0410, Lincoln, NE 68588-0410. **EMAIL** slu1@unl.edu

LUBBERS, JEFFREY S.
PERSONAL Born 01/26/1949, Madison, WI **DISCIPLINE** HISTORY AND GOVERNMENT **EDUCATION** Cornell Univ, BA, 71; Univ Chicago Law Sch, JD, 74. **CAREER** Instr, Univ Miami Sch of Law, 74-75; atty, 75-82; res dir, Admin Conf of US, 82-95; fel in Admin Law, Amer Univ Wash Col of Law, 95-. **HONORS AND AWARDS** Pres rank of meritorious exec, 91; Outstanding govt svc award, Amer Bar Asn, 94; Walter Gellhorn award for admin law, Fed Bar Asn, 97. **MEMBERSHIPS** Amer Bar Asn; DC Bar. **RESEARCH** Administrative law; Regulation; Alternative dispute resolution. **SELECTED PUBLICATIONS** Auth, A Guide to Federal Agency Rulemaking, 3rd ed, Amer Bar Asn Book Publ, 98; If It Didn't Exit, it Would Have to Be Invented--Reviving the Administrative Conference, 30, Ariz State Law Jour, 147, 98; The ABA Section of the Administrative Law and Regulatory Practice--From Objector to Protector of the APA, 50, Admin Law Rev, 157, 98; The Administrative Law Agenda for the Next Decade, 49, Admin Law Rev, 159, 97; Testimony on H.R. 2592, The Private Trustee Reform Act of 1997, before the Subcomt of Com and Admin Law, Comt on the Judiciary, US House of Rep, 9 Oct, 97; Ombudsman Offices in the Federal Government--An Emerging Trend?, 22, Admin & Regulatory Law News, 6, summer, 97; Paperwork Redux: The Stronger Paperwork Reduction Act of 1995, 49, Admin Law Rev, 111, 97; APA Adjudication: Is the Quest for Uniformity Faltering?, 10, The Admin Law Jour of the Amer Univ, 65, 96; The Regulatory Reform Recommendations of the National Performance Review, 6, RISK: Health Safety and Environ, 145, Franklin Pierce Law Ctr, spring, 95; Justice Stephen Breyer: Purveyor of Common Sense in Many Forums, part of Symposium: Justice Stephen Breyer's Contribution to Administrative Law, 8, The Admin Law Jour of the Amer Univ, 775, 95; Reinventing Chinese Administrative Law, 19, Admin Law News, 1, spring, 94; Better Regulations: The National Performance Review's Regulatory Reform Recommendations, paper presented to the Duke Law Jour Twenty-Fifth Annual Admin Law Conf, Durham, NC, 20 Jan, 94, publ, 43, Duke Law Jour, 94; Anatomy of a Regulatory Program: Comments on Strategic Regulators and the Choice of Rulemaking Procedures, Hamilton and Schroeder, 56, Law and Contemporary Problems, 161, 94;ed, Developments in Administrative Law and Regulatory Practice, 98-99; ed, Developments in Administrative Law and Regulatory Practice, 99-00; coauth, Federal Administrative Procedure Sourcebook, 3rd ed, with William Funk and Charles Pou, Jr., Amer Bar Asn Book Publ, 00; ed, Developments in Administrative Law and Regulatory Practive, 98-99, Am Bar Asn Book Publ, 00. **CONTACT ADDRESS** 4801 Massachusetts Av. NW, Washington, DC 20016. **EMAIL** jsl26@aol.com

LUBECK, RAY
PERSONAL Born 05/29/1954, Waco, TX, m, 1981, 2 children **DISCIPLINE** OLD TESTAMENT STUDIES **EDUCATION** Multnomah Bible Col, BS, 79; Trinity Evangel Divinity Sch, MA, 86; Univ of South Africa, DTh, cand. **CAREER** Lectr, Ecola Bible Sch, 8 yrs; adj prof, Western Sem, 6 yrs; prof, Multnomah Bible Col, 10 years. **HONORS AND AWARDS** Cum laude, 86. Who's Who Among America's Tchrs, 98-00. **MEMBERSHIPS** Evangel Theol Soc; Soc of Bib Lit. **RESEARCH** Old Testament; hermeneutics; Biblical theology. **SELECTED PUBLICATIONS** Auth, Studies in the Literary Structure of Johah, Trinity Evangel Divinity Sch, 86; "Prophetic Sabotage," Trinity J, 88; rev, Hermeneutics as Theological Prolegomena by Scalise, Intepretation and the Bible by McEvenue, J of the Evangel Theol Soc, 96. **CONTACT ADDRESS** Multnomah Bible Col and Biblical Sem, 8435 NE Glisan St., Portland, OR 97220. **EMAIL** rlubeck@multnomah.edu

LUBETSKI, EDITH
PERSONAL Born 07/16/1940, Brooklyn, NY, m, 1968, 3 children **DISCIPLINE** LIBRARY SCIENCE, JEWISH STUDIES **EDUCATION** Brooklyn Col, BA, 62; Columbia Univ, MSL, 65; Yeshiva Univ, MA, 68. **CAREER** Judaica Librarian, Stern Col for Women, 65-66, acquistion librarian, 66-69, head librarian, 69-. **HONORS AND AWARDS** Asn of Jewish Libraries Fanny Goldstein Merit Awd, in recognition of Outstanding Contribution to the Asn and Judaica librarianship, 93; Asn of Jewish Libraries: Nat Corresp Sec, 80-84, Pres, NY Chapter, 84-86, Nat Pres, 86-88. **MEMBERSHIPS** ALA, Asn of Jewish Libr. **RESEARCH** Judaica. **SELECTED PUBLICATIONS** Coauth with Meir Lubetski, Building a Judaica Library Collection (83); auth, The Jewish Woman: Recent Books (95); contributed articles to professional journals. **CONTACT ADDRESS** Hedi Steinberg Libr, Head Librarian, Stern Col for Women, 245 Lexington Ave, New York, NY 10016.

LUBIC, ROBERT B.
PERSONAL Born 03/09/1929, Pittsburgh, PA, m, 1959, 3 children **DISCIPLINE** LAW **EDUCATION** Univ Pittsburgh, BA,

50; JD, 53; Georgetown Univ, MPL, 59. **CAREER** Att, PA, DC, 55-63; asst prof, Duquesne Univ, 63-65; assoc prof, American Univ, 65-70; assoc dean, 70-71; prof, 71-; vis prof, Tokyo, 88-89; vis prof, Puer Ric, 93; vis prof, China, 94; vis prof, Pola, 95; vis prof, Ital, 96. **MEMBERSHIPS** DCBA; ABA; FCBA; Who's Who in Am, World, Am Law, Am Edu. **SELECTED PUBLICATIONS** Auth, "The 1988 US Trade Act and Its Effect Upon the Coming Trade Wars," Diplo Rev Philipp; auth, "The Effects of the Omnibus Trade and Competitiveness Act of 1988 Upon Trade Relations Between the United States and the Republic of Korea," Seoul Nat Univ Law Rev; auth, "The Growth of International Commercial Arbitration and its Effects in Japan," J Japan Comm Arbitr Asn (91); auth, "A New Proposal For International Arbitration In Japan," Am Rev Intl Arbitr Parker Sch of For Comp Law of Colum Univ (91). **CONTACT ADDRESS** School of Law, Washington Col, 4801 Massachusetts Ave, Washington, DC 20016-8181.

LUCAS, RAYMOND E.
PERSONAL Born 06/26/1932, Richmond, VA, m, 1962, 1 child **DISCIPLINE** PHILOSOPHY **EDUCATION** Univ Va, BA, 58, MA, 63; Tulane Univ, PhD, 67. **CAREER** Asst prof, 66-67, assoc prof, 67-70, E Tenn State Univ; assoc prof, 70-73, prof, 73-93, chr Dept Philoso, 79-90, prof Emer, 93-, Kutztown Univ. **MEMBERSHIPS** APA; S Soc Philos & Psychol. **RESEARCH** Epistemology; Social and political philosophy. **CONTACT ADDRESS** 321 Spring St, Fleetwood, PA 19522.

LUCASH, FRANK S.
PERSONAL Born 02/06/1938, Belleville, IL, m, 1966, 2 children **DISCIPLINE** PHILOSOPHY **EDUCATION** Southern Illinois Univ, BA, 59, MA, 66, PhD, 70. **CAREER** Univ Nevada Reno, lectr, 68-70; asst prof, 70-80; assoc prof, 80-. **MEMBERSHIPS** APA, NASS **RESEARCH** Baruch Spinoza; Philo of Mind; The Passions. **SELECTED PUBLICATIONS** Ed, "Justice and Equality," Cornell, 86; articles: "On the Finite and Infinite in Spinoza," Southern Journal of Philosophy, 82; "What Spinoza's View of Freedom Should Have Been, Philosophy Research Archives, 84; Ideas, Images, and Truth, History of Philosophy Quarterly, 89; Spinoza on the Eternity of the Human Mind, Philosophy and Theology, 90; Spinoza's Philosophy of Immanence, Journal of Speculative Philosophy, 94; Does Self-Knowledge Lead to Self-Esteem?" Studia Spinozana, 92; Essence and Existence in Part 3 of Spinoza's Ethics, Manuscrito, 94; Spinoza's Dialectical Method, Dialogue, 95; Intuitive Knowledge in Spinoza, North American Spinoza Society Monograph 7, 98. **CONTACT ADDRESS** Dept of Philosophy, Univ of Nevada, Reno, Reno, NV 89557. **EMAIL** lucash@unr.edu

LUCE, DAVID R.
PERSONAL Born 02/22/1927, Boston, MA, m, 1962, 2 children **DISCIPLINE** PHILOSOPHY **EDUCATION** Dartmouth Col, BA, 50; Univ of Michigan, MA, 52, PhD, 57. **CAREER** Univ of Arkansas, inst, 57-59; Univ of Minnesota, inst, 59-60; Univ of Chicago, vis asst prof, 60; Univ of Wisconsin Milwaukee, asst prof, assoc prof, prof, 60-. **HONORS AND AWARDS** Phi Beta Kappa, Thayer Prize Math. **MEMBERSHIPS** APA, ASL, AAUP, PBK. **RESEARCH** Ethics; Social philosophy; philosophy of religion. **SELECTED PUBLICATIONS** Auth, Causal Relations Between Mind and Body: A New Formulation of the Mind Body Problem, Ann Arbor: Univ Microfilms, 57; auth, The Smith Act, Nixon's Smith Act and the Smith Act in the McClellan-Hruska Criminal Code Bill, in: Loyola of L. A. Law Rev, vol 9, no 2, 76; auth, A Proposal Even More Radical Than Proxmire's Bill to De-Regulate the Broadcasting Industry Entirely, Free Speech, 77; auth, Potential Personhood and the Rights of the Unconceived, in: Conscience: A Newsjournal of Prochoice Catholic Opinion, 86; auth, Civil Liberties and the Citizen, 1993 Viewpoints on War, Peace and Global Cooperation: The Annual Jour, 93; The Sociobiologist is Wearing No Clothes, Shepherd Express, 98. **CONTACT ADDRESS** 2914 N Downer Ave, Milwaukee, WI 53211. **EMAIL** luce@csd.uwm.edu

LUCK, DONALD G.
PERSONAL Born 01/02/1933, Portchester, NY, d, 3 children **DISCIPLINE** THEOLOGY **EDUCATION** Gettysburg Col, BA, 54; Lutheran Theol Sem, BD, 57; Union Theol Sem, STM, 66, PhD, 78. **CAREER** Parish pastor, metro NY, 58-65; from asst prof to assoc prof relig, Concordia Col, 69-82; from assoc prof systematic theol to T.A. Kantonen prof systematic theol, Trinity Lutheran Sem, 82-. **HONORS AND AWARDS** Vis res fel, Nanzan Institute for Rel and Culture, Nagoya, Japan, 99 **MEMBERSHIPS** Am Acad Relig; Soc Buddhist/Christian Studies. **RESEARCH** Doctrinal theology; philosophical theology; Christian-Buddhist dialogue. **SELECTED PUBLICATIONS** Auth, Taking a Page from Paul: Facing Contemporary Temptations of Acculturated Ministry, Trinity Sem Rev, Fall/Winter, 97; auth, Anonymous Extravagance, Trinity Sem Rev, Fall, 95; auth, Reaffirming the Image of God as Father, Trinity Sem Rev, Fall, 94; auth, The New Passover, Lutheran Partners, March/April, 93; auth, Why Study Theology? St. Louis: Chalice Press, 99. **CONTACT ADDRESS** Dept of Theology, Trinity Lutheran Sem, 2199 E Main St., Columbus, OH 43209. **EMAIL** dluck@trinity.capital.edu

LUCKERT, KARL WILHELM
PERSONAL Born 11/18/1934, Winnenden-Hoefen, Germany, m, 1957, 3 children **DISCIPLINE** HISTORY OF RELIGIONS **EDUCATION** Univ Kans, BA, 63; Univ Chicago, MA, 67, PhD, 69. **CAREER** Vis lectr, rel, NCent Col, 68-69; asst prof humanities, Northern Ariz Univ, 69-79; assoc prof, 79-82, prof relig studies, Southwest Mo State Univ, 82-; gen ed, Am Tribal Relig series, Univ Nebr Press, 77-. **HONORS AND AWARDS** NEH res fel anthrop, Okla Univ, 72-73; Rockefeller Found Humanities res fel, 77-78; res assoc, Mus Northern Ariz, 77-; Burlington Northern Found Fac Achievement Awd for Schol, 88; named hon prof, Univ Ningxia, China, 90; Excellence in Res Awd, SMSU Found, 95. **MEMBERSHIPS** Am Acad Relig. **RESEARCH** American Indian religions; religion in evolution. **SELECTED PUBLICATIONS** Auth, The Navajo Hunter Tradition, Univ Ariz, 75; Olmec Religion: A Key to Middle America and Beyond, Okla Univ, 76; Navajo Mountain and Rainbow Bridge Religion, Mus Northern Ariz Press, 77; A Navajo Bringing-Home Ceremony, Mus Northern Ariz Univ, 78; Coyoteway, A Navajo Holyway Healing Ceremonial, Univ Ariz, 79; Egyptian Light and Hebrew Fire: Theological and Philosophical Roots of Christendom in Evolutionary Perspective, State Univ NY Press, 91; coauth, Myths and Legends of the Hui, a Muslim Chinese People, State Univ NY Press, 94; Kazakh Traditions in China, Univ Press Am, 98; Uighur Stories from Along the Silk Road, Univ Press Am, 98; author numerous journal articles. **CONTACT ADDRESS** Dept Relig Studies, Southwest Missouri State Univ, Springfield, 901 S National, Springfield, MO 65804-0088. **EMAIL** luckert@dialnet.net

LUCKHARDT, C. GRANT
PERSONAL Born 10/25/1943, Palm Beach, FL, m, 1967, 1 child **DISCIPLINE** PHILOSOPHY **EDUCATION** St John's Col, AB, 65; Emory Univ, PhD(philos), 72. **CAREER** Asst prof, 71-76, assoc prof, 76-87, PROF PHILOS, GA STATE UNIV, 88-, DIR HONORS PROG, 89-; Vis tutor, St John's Col, summer, 76 & 77. **MEMBERSHIPS** Am Philos Asn. **RESEARCH** Wittgenstein; Native American thought. **SELECTED PUBLICATIONS** Wittgenstein: Investigations 50, Southern J of Philos, 77; Beyond Knowledge: Paradigms in Wittgenstein's Later Philosophy, Philos and Phenomenol Res, 78; Wittgenstein and His Impact on Contemporary Thought, 78 & Language, Logic and Philosophy, 80, Holder-Pichler-Tempsky; ed, Wittgenstein: Sources & Perspectives, Cornell Univ Press, 80; co-transl, L Wittgenstein: Remarks on the Philosophy of Psychology, Vol II, Blackwell's & Univ Chicago Press, 81; L Wittgenstein: Last Writings on the Philosophy of Psychology, vol I, Blackwell's, 82, vol II, 93; auth, Wittgenstein and Behaviorism, Synthese, 83; Lion Talk, Philos Investigations, 95; co-transl, The Big Typescript, by Ludwig Wittgenstein (Blakwell Pub, 01). **CONTACT ADDRESS** Dept of Philos, Georgia State Univ, University Plaza, Atlanta, GA 30303-3080. **EMAIL** dascgl@panther.gsu.edu

LUDWIG, JAN KEITH
PERSONAL Born 03/15/1942, Harrisburg, PA, m, 1965, 2 children **DISCIPLINE** PHILOSOPHY OF SCIENCE **EDUCATION** Gettysburg Col, BA, 63; Johns Hopkins Univ, PhD(philos), 71. **CAREER** Instr, Am Univ, 67-69; from instr to asst prof, 69-75, Assoc Prof Philos, Union Col, NY, 75-, Chmn Dept, 73-, Res fel, Harvard Univ, 76-77. **MEMBERSHIPS** Am Philos Asn; Philos Sci Asn; Hist Sci Soc. **RESEARCH** Analytic philosophy; philosophy of mind; history of science. **SELECTED PUBLICATIONS** Auth, Zero-remarks and the numbering system of the Tractatus, J Critical Anal, 75; Substance and simple objects in Tractatus, J Critical Anal, 75; Substance and simple objects in Tractatus 2 02ff, Philos Studies, 76; ed, Philosophy and Parapsychology, Prometheus Bks, 78. **CONTACT ADDRESS** Dept of Philos Humanities Ctr, Union Col, New York, 807 Union St, Schenectady, NY 12308-3107.

LUDWIG, KIRK
PERSONAL Born 05/11/1959, Tulsa, OK, m **DISCIPLINE** PHILOSOPHY **EDUCATION** Univ of Calif Santa Barbera, BS, 81; Univ of Calif Berk, PhD, 90. **CAREER** Univ of Fla, asst prof, assoc prof, 90-. **HONORS AND AWARDS** R. M. Griffith Memorial Awd, 2 NEH grants, IREX grant. **MEMBERSHIPS** APA, SPP, ESPP, SSPP, FPA. **RESEARCH** Philo of mind and language; epistemology. **SELECTED PUBLICATIONS** Auth, Duplicating Thoughts, Mind & Language, 96; auth, Singular Thought and the Cartesian Theory of Mind, Nous, 96; auth, The Truth About Moods, in: Protosozioloie, Cognitive Semantics I: Concepts of Meaning, 97; auth, Truth Conditional Semantics for Tense, coauth, Tense, Time and Reference, ed. Q. Smith, Oxford: Oxford Univ Press, 98; auth, Functionalism, Causation and Causal Relevance, Psyche, 98; Semantics for Opaque Contexts, coauth, Philos Perspectives, 98; auth, Meaning, Truth and Interpretation, & Introduction to Reading Davidson, Discussions with Donald Davidson on Truth, Meaning and Knowledge, ed., U. Zeglen, Routledge, 99; auth, The Semantics and Pragmatics of Complex Demonstrations, coauth, mind, 00. **CONTACT ADDRESS** Dept of Philosophy, Univ of Florida, Gainesville, FL 32611-8545. **EMAIL** kludwig@phil.ufl.edu

LUDWIG, THEODORE MARK
PERSONAL Born 09/28/1936, Oxford, NE, m, 1960, 4 children **DISCIPLINE** HISTORY OF RELIGIONS, ASIAN RELIGIONS **EDUCATION** Concordia Sem St Louis, BA, 58, MDiv, 61, STM, 62, ThD, 63; Univ Chicago, PhD(Hist Relig), 75. **CAREER** Asst prof, 68-73, assoc prof 74-83, prof, Theol, Valparaiso Univ, 83-; Surjit Patheja prof of Wold Religions and Ethics, 98- **HONORS AND AWARDS** Research professorship, 79-80; Nat. Endow. For Humanities fel, 81-82; Distinguished teaching award, Valparaiso Univ, 79-80. **MEMBERSHIPS** Soc Bibl Lit; Am Acad Relig; Asn Asian Studies; Soc for Study of Japanese Regions. **RESEARCH** Buddhist Studies; Japanese religions; Comparative Religious Studies. **SELECTED PUBLICATIONS** Auth, The way of tea: a religioaesthetic mode of life, Hist Relig, 74; co-ed (with Frank Reynolds), Transitions and Transformations in the History of Religions: Essays in Honor of Joseph M Kitagawa, 80 & auth, Remember not the former things: Disjunction and transformation in Ancient Israel, In: Transitions and Transformations in the History of Religions: Essays in Honor of Joseph M Kitagawa, 80, E J Brill, Leiden; Christian self-understanding and other religions, Currents in Theol & Mission, 80; Before Rikyu: Religious and aesthetic influences in the early history of the tea ceremony, Monumenta Nipponica, 81; auth, Chanoyu and Momoyama, in Tea in Japan, 89, U of Hawaii Press; The Sacred Paths: Understanding the Religions of the World, 01; auth, Sacred Paths of the East, 01. **CONTACT ADDRESS** Dept of Theology, Valparaiso Univ, Valparaiso, IN 46383-6493. **EMAIL** Ted.Ludwig@valpo.edu.

LUDWIKOWSKI, RETT R.
PERSONAL Born 11/06/1943, Skawina-Krakow, Poland, m, 1995, 2 children **DISCIPLINE** COMPARATIVE AND INTERNATIONAL LAW **EDUCATION** The Jagiellonian Univ, MA, 66, PhD, 71. **CAREER** Vis prof, Elizabethtown Col, Pa, 82-83; vis scholar, The Hoover Inst, Stanford Univ, 83; vis prof, Alfred Univ, fall 83; vis prof, The Cath Univ of Am, 84-85, prof, 85-86; vis scholar, Max-Planck-Inst fur auslandisches and internationales, Privatrecht, Hamburg, Germany, fall 90; Dir, The Cath Univ of Am Int Business and Trade Summer Prog in Poland, Dir, Comparative and Int Law Inst, 87-; Sr Fulbright Scholar, Jagiellonian Univ, Cracow, Poland, fall 97. **HONORS AND AWARDS** Res Grant, Earhart Found, 87, 88, 91-92; Res Grant, Wilbur Found, 89; Res Grant, Rosenstiel Found, 89, 90; Res Grant, Batory Found, 90; Residential Fel, Max-Planck-Inst, 90; Res Grant, Bradley Found, 92; Sr Fulbright grant, 97. **SELECTED PUBLICATIONS** Co-ed, Constitutionalism and Human Rights, Miller Center, Univ Va (91); auth, America and the World of Business, Cracow's Industrial Soc (91); coauth, The Beginning of the Constitutional Era. A Comparative Study of the First American and European Constitution, CUA Press (93); auth, Regulations of International Trade and Business, Vol I, International Trade, ABC (96); auth, Constitution Making in the Countries of Former Soviet Dominance, Duke Univ Press (96); ed and coauth, Regulations of International Trade and Business, Vol II, International Business Transactions, ABC (98); auth, " 'Mixed' Constitutions-Product of an East-Central European Constitutional Melting Pot," Boston Univ Int Law J, Vol 16, No 1 (spring 98); auth, Comparative Constitutional Law, TNOIK, Warsaw (99); auth, Constitutional Culture in East-Central Europe, paper for conf in Warsaw (99); **CONTACT ADDRESS** Sch of Law, Catholic Univ of America, 620 Michigan Ave NE, Washington, DC 20064-0001. **EMAIL** Ludwikowski@law.edu

LUEBKE, NEIL ROBERT
PERSONAL Born 09/15/1936, Pierce, NE, m, 1957, 2 children **DISCIPLINE** PHILOSOPHY **EDUCATION** Midland Col, BA, 58; Johns Hopkins Univ, MA, 62, PhD(philos), 68. **CAREER** Asst prof, 61-71, assoc prof, 71-76, assoc prof & chairperson, 76-81, Prof & Head Philos, Okla State Univ, 81-84, 89-87, Regents Service Prof, 97-98, prof emer, 98-; Dir Exxon critical thinking proj, Exxon Educ Found, 71-74. **HONORS AND AWARDS** National Pres, Honor Soc of Phi Kappa Phi, 98-01. **MEMBERSHIPS** Am Philos Asn; Am Sect Int Asn for Philos Law & Social Philos; Soc Bus Ethics; N Am Soc for Social Philos. **RESEARCH** Theories of social authority and trust; Thomas Hobbes; engineering ethics. **SELECTED PUBLICATIONS** Auth, Is Hobbes's view of property bourgeois?, Philos Topics, 81; Conflict of Interest as a Moral Category, Bus and Prof Ethics J, vol 6, no 1. **CONTACT ADDRESS** 616 W. Harned Ave., Stillwater, OK 74075-1303. **EMAIL** nluebke_osu@ionet.net

LUKE, BRIAN A.
DISCIPLINE ENVIRONMENTAL ETHICS, POLITICAL PHILOSOPHY **EDUCATION** Pittsburgh Univ, PhD, 92. **CAREER** Dept Philos, Univ Dayton **RESEARCH** Feminist theory. **SELECTED PUBLICATIONS** Auth, Solidarity Across Diversity: A Pluralistic Rapprochement of Environmentalism and Animal Liberation, Soc Theory and Pract, 95; Justice, Caring, and Animal Liberation, Beyond Animal Rights: A Feminist Caring Ethic for the Treatment of Animals, Continuum, 96; A Critical Analysis of Hunters' Ethics, Environmental Ethics , 97. **CONTACT ADDRESS** Dept of Philos, Univ of Dayton, 300 Col Park, Dayton, OH 75062. **EMAIL** luke@checkov.hm.udayton.edu

LULL, TIMOTHY F.
DISCIPLINE SYSTEMATIC THEOLOGY **EDUCATION** Williams Col, BA; Yale Divinity Sch, BD; Yale Grad Sch, MPhil, PhD. **CAREER** Tchg pastor, Harvard Divinity Sch; vis lectr, Stonehill Col; vis scholar, St Edmund's Col, Cambridge, Eng; asst prof, assoc prof, prof, Lutheran Theol Sem at Philadelphia; lectr, Churchwide Assembly, 93; Hein-Fry lectr, 96; ch, GTU Coun of Deans, 90-92; prof, 89-; pres. **HONORS AND AWARDS** GTU Core Doctoral Fac; co-ch, Lutheran/Reformed Dialogue; GTU fac trustee, 92-95; actg pres, PLTS, 94; GTU Bd Acad Comm, 1992-. **SELECTED PUBLICATIONS** Auth, Called to Confess Christ; This Church Confesses; ed, Martin Luther's Basic Theological Writings, Fortress, 89; A Common Calling, 93. **CONTACT ADDRESS** Dept of Systematic Theology, Pacific Lutheran Theol Sem, 2770 Marin Ave, Berkeley, CA 94708-1597. **EMAIL** tlull@plts.edu

LUMPP, RANDOLPH
DISCIPLINE PERSONALITY AND SPIRITUALITY, RELIGIOUS STUDIES, CHRISTIANITY THROUGH THE C **EDUCATION** Seattle Univ, BA, 63; Marquette Univ, MA, 68; Univ Ottawa, Canada, PhD, 76. **CAREER** Prof Relig Stud, ch, dept Relig Stud, Regis Col, 72-. **HONORS AND AWARDS** Regis Col Fac Lectr of the Year, 92. **MEMBERSHIPS** Am Acad of Relig; Am Asn of Univ Prof. **RESEARCH** Psychology of religion; biblical studies. **SELECTED PUBLICATIONS** Auth, A Biographical Portrait of Walter Jackson Ong, in Oral Tradition 2, 87; Literacy, Commerce and Catholicity: Two Contexts of Change and Invention, in Oral Tradition 2, 87; Introduction to the Study of Native American Religious Traditions, in Module for RC 410 Native American Religious Traditions, RECEP II, 91; Term and Method Problems in the Study of Native American Religious Traditions, AAR/SBL Rocky Mountain - Great Plains Reg, 93; Tradition and Common Sense in the Academy: An Odyssey in Search of Dialogue, Adducere II, Regis Univ, 95. **CONTACT ADDRESS** Dept of Relig Stud, Regis Univ, 3333 Regis Blvd, Denver, CO 80221. **EMAIL** rlumpp@regis.edu

LUNCEFORD, JOE E.
PERSONAL Born 01/20/1937, State Springs, MS, m, 1960, 2 children **DISCIPLINE** NEW TESTAMENT **EDUCATION** Mississippi Col, BA, 62; New Orleans Baptist Theol Sem, BD, 66; Baylor Univ, PhD, 79. **CAREER** Asst prof, 81-87, assoc prof, 87-94, prof relig, 94-, Georgetown Col. **HONORS AND AWARDS** Outstanding Young Men of America, 84; Cawthorne Award for Excellence in Teaching, 97. **MEMBERSHIPS** Soc of Biblical Lit; Nat Asn of Baptist Profs of Religion; Christians for Biblical Equality. **RESEARCH** The revelation, Johannine studies. **SELECTED PUBLICATIONS** Auth, "An Historical and Exegetical Inquiry into the New Testament Meaning of the Hilaskomai Cognates," Georgetown Col Fac Studies XI (83-84); auth, "Matthew (Part 2)," Bible Book Study for Adult Teachers, Sunday School Board of the Southern Baptist Convention (Nashville), 88; auth, "1, 2 Peter, 1, 2, 3 John, Jude," Bible Book Study Commentary, Sunday School Board of the Southern Baptist Convention (Nashville), 93; auth, "Zechariah," "The Unpardonable Sin," "Herodian Fortresses," and "Transjordan," in Mercer Dictionary of the Bible; auth, "Mithra, Mithraism" and "Congregation," in Holman Dictionary of the Bible; auth, "Meredith, James," in The Encylopedia of Civil Rights in America, Salem Press; auth, "Deism," "Millenialism," and "Free Exercise Clause (U.S. Constitution)," in The Encyclopedia of Contemporary Social Issues, Salem Press; auth, "Surrogate Mothers," in Encyclopedia of Family Life, Salem Press. **CONTACT ADDRESS** Georgetown Col, Box 254, Georgetown, KY 40324. **EMAIL** Joe_Lunceford@georgetowncollege.edu

LUND, ERIC
PERSONAL Born 09/06/1948, New Haven, CT, m, 1974, 2 children **DISCIPLINE** HISTORY OF CHRISTIANITY **EDUCATION** Brown Univ, AB, 70; Yale Divinity School, MDiv, 74; Yale Univ, MA, 76; PhD, 79. **CAREER** Dept relig, St Olaf Col, 79- . **HONORS AND AWARDS** Phi Beta Kappa, 69. **MEMBERSHIPS** Am Acad Relig; Am Soc Church Hist; Sixteenth Cent Student; Soc Student Christian Spirituality. **RESEARCH** Religion in 16th & 17th Century Europe, Religious conflict in the Middle East. **SELECTED PUBLICATIONS** Co-ed, Word, Church and State-Tyndale Quincentenary Essays, Wash, DC: Cath Univ Press. **CONTACT ADDRESS** Dept Relig, St. Olaf Col, 1520 Saint Olaf Ave, Northfield, MN 55057-1574. **EMAIL** lund@stolaf.edu

LUNDBOM, JACK R.
PERSONAL Born 07/10/1939, Chicago, IL, m, 1964, 2 children **DISCIPLINE** BIBLICAL STUDIES **EDUCATION** North Park Theological Seminary, BD, 67; San Francisco Theological Seminary and Graduate Theological Union, Berkeley, PhD, 73. **CAREER** Asst Prof/Lectr, 74, 76,-77, Univ California-Berkeley; Visiting Prof, 74-75, Andover Newton Theological School; Visiting Prof, 83, Yale Divinity School; Visiting Prof, 90, 92-93, Lutheran School of Theology, Chicago; Life Member, 96-, Univ Cambridge. **HONORS AND AWARDS** Sr Fulbright Prof, Universitat Marbury, Germany, 88-89; NEH Fel, Uppsda Univ and Cambridge Univ, 91-92; NEH Fel, Albright Inst of Archaeological Research, Jerusalem and Cambridge Univ, 97-98; Mem, Princeton Ctr of Theological Inquiry, 98-99. **MEMBERSHIPS** Soc of Biblical Lit; Catholic Biblical Assoc; American Schools of Oriental Research **RESEARCH** Old Testament/Hebrew Bible; Hebrew Prophets; Jeremiah; rhetorical criticism **SELECTED PUBLICATIONS** Auth, Jeremiah 15/15-21 and the Call of Jeremiah, Scandanavian Journal of the Old Testament, 95; Mary Magdalene and Song of Songs 3: 1-4, Interpretation 49, 95; Section Markings in Bible Scrolls, Genizah Fragments 32, 96; The Inclusio and Other Framing Devices in Deuteronomy I-XXVIII, Vetus Testamentum 46, 96; Warner Sallman and His Head of Christ, Swedish-American Historical Quarterly 47, 96; Scribal Contibutions to Old Testament Theology, To Hear and Obey: Essays in Honor of Frederick Carlson Holmgren, 97; Jeremiah: A Study in Ancient Hebrew Rhetoric, 97; Coauth, Haplography in Jeremiah 1-20, Frank Moore Cross Volume, 98; Parataxsis, Rhetorical Structure, and the Dialogue over Sodom in Genesis 18, World of Genesis: Persons, Places, Perspectives, 98; Masterpainter: Warner E. Sallman, 99; Jeremiah 1-20, 99. **CONTACT ADDRESS** 5254 N. Spaulding Ave., Chicago, IL 60625.

LUNDE, JONATHAN M.
PERSONAL Born 06/09/1960, Cameroon, m, 1984, 3 children **DISCIPLINE** BIBLICAL STUDIES **EDUCATION** Moorehead State Univ, BS (summa cum laude), 83; Lutheran Brethren Sem, MDiv (highest ranking senior), 86; Trinity Evangelical Divinity School, ThM (academic distinction), 89, PhD, 96. **CAREER** Adjunct Fac for The Grading of New Testament Extension Courses, Trinity Evangelical Divinity School, 91-; Asst Prof of Biblical Studies, Trinity Int Univ, Col of Arts and Sciences, 96-. **MEMBERSHIPS** Soc of Biblical Lit; Evangelical Theol Soc **RESEARCH** Life of Jesus; apocalyptic lit; NT use of the OT. **SELECTED PUBLICATIONS** Auth, Heaven and Hell & Repentance, in Dictionary of Jesus and the Gospels, ed J. B. Green, S. McKnight, I. H. Marshall, InterVarsity Press, 92; Repentance, in New Dictionary of Biblical Theology, InterVarsity Press, forthcoming. **CONTACT ADDRESS** Trinity Intl Univ, Col of Arts and Sciences, 2065 Half Day Rd., Deerfield, IL 60015. **EMAIL** jlunde@trin.edu

LUPER, STEVEN
DISCIPLINE PHILOSOPHY **EDUCATION** Baylor Univ, BA, 77; Harvard Univ, PhD, 82. **CAREER** Asst prof, 82-88; assoc prof, 88-94; PROF, 94-. **RESEARCH** Epistemology; Social and Political Philosophy; Ethics. **SELECTED PUBLICATIONS** Auth, Internalism, Synthese, 88; Morality and The Self, The Monist, 91; The Possibility of Knowledge: Nozick and his Critics, 87; Problems of International Justice, 88; Invulnerability: On Securing happiness, 96; Social Ideas and Policies: Readings in Social and Political Philosophy, 98; Existing: An introduction to Existentialist Thought, 2000, coauth, Drugs, Morality and the Law, 94; The Moral Life, 97. **CONTACT ADDRESS** Philosophy Dept, Trinity Univ, 715 Stadium Dr, San Antonio, TX 78212-7200. **EMAIL** sluper@trinity.edu

LURIE, HOWARD R.
DISCIPLINE ADMINISTRATIVE LAW **EDUCATION** W Va Univ, AB, 60; Univ Mich Law Sch, JD, 63. **CAREER** Prof; Villanova Univ, 68-. **HONORS AND AWARDS** Army Commendation Medal, 66. **MEMBERSHIPS** Amer Bar Asn; Philadelphia Patent Law Asn; Int Asn for the Adv of Tchg and Res in Intellectual Property. **RESEARCH** Trade regulation, intellectual property and copyright law. **SELECTED PUBLICATIONS** Auth, What is Fair Use, Synthesis, Law and Policy in Higher Education, Univ Md, 89; The Ownership of Copyright in Journal Articles, 1 3 Technical serv Quart 31, 84 & Consumer Complaints: A Proposed Fed Trade Regulation Rule, 5 Mich. J. Law Reform 426, 72. **CONTACT ADDRESS** Law School, Villanova Univ, 800 Lancaster Ave, Villanova, PA 19085-1692. **EMAIL** lurie@law.vill.edu

LUTER, A. BOYD
PERSONAL Born 07/10/1949, Dallas, TX, m, 1977, 3 children **DISCIPLINE** BIBLICAL STUDIES, NEW TEASTAMENT, THEOLOGY **EDUCATION** Miss State Univ, BS, 71; Dal Theol Sem, ThM, 76; PhD, 85. **CAREER** Asst prof, Let Univ, 83-84; assoc prof, Dal Sch Theol, 88-95; assoc prof, Criswell Col, 97-98; prof, 99-. **HONORS AND AWARDS** Inst Bib Res, Fel; Fac Res Gnt; Outstand Yng Man; Who's Who Religion, Bib Soc; Men Dist; Intl Dict. **MEMBERSHIPS** SBL; ETS. **RESEARCH** Literature; Hebrew; Revelation. **SELECTED PUBLICATIONS** Coauth, "Women Disciples and the Great Commission," Trinity J (95); coauth, Disciplined Living: what the New Testament Teaches about Recovery and Disciple-ship, Baker (96); auth, "Partnership in the Gospel: The Women in the Church at Philippi," J Evang Theol Soc (96); auth, Martyrdom" and "Savior," in Dictionary of the Later New Testament and its Developments, eds. Ralph Martin, Peter Davids (IVP, 97); coauth, Women as Christ's Disciples, Baker (97); auth, "Galatians" and "Revelation" in Nelson Study Bible, ed. Earl Radmacher , Thomas Nelson (97); auth, "Galatians" and "Apocalyptic Literature," in Holman Concise Bible Commentary, ed. David Dockery (B & H, 98); auth, "Matthew," "2 Corinthians," "Hebrews," "Revelation," in Spiritual Renewal Bible, ed. Steve Arterburn (Grand Rapids: Zondervan, 98); auth, "Interpreting the Book of Revelation," in Interpreting the New Testament, eds. David Black, David Dockery (B & H, 00); auth, "Israel and the Nations in God's Redemptive Plan," in Israel: The Land and the People, ed. H Wayne House (Kregel, 98); auth, "Church Polity and Mission," "End Times and Mission," "Homiletics and Mission," Evangel Dictionary World Missions, Baker, 00. **CONTACT ADDRESS** Dept Religious Studies, Criswell Col, 4010 Gaston Ave, Dallas, TX 75246-1585. **EMAIL** bluter@criswell.edu

LUYSTER, ROBERT W.
DISCIPLINE PHILOSOPHY **EDUCATION** Dartmouth Col, BA, 58; Univ Chicago, MA, 61, PhD, 64. **CAREER** Dept Philos, Univ Conn **RESEARCH** Religious myth and symbol, peace and social justice. **SELECTED PUBLICATIONS** Auth, King ego and the doublesex dancer, J of Relig and Health 19(2), (80): 121-29; auth, Cosmogonic Symbolism in the Old Testament, Zeitschrift fur die Alttestamentliche Wissenchaft, 93(1), (81): 110; auth, Warrier and farmer: Fundamental religious paradigms, Arc, IX, No 2, 82; auth, Foundation for a Scientific phenomenology of religion J. of Rel. Stud., 10(2), (83): 32-44; auth, The phenomenology of Hamlet and the evolution of consciousness, The Iliff Rev, 84; auth, "The Wife's Lament" in the Context of Scandinavian Myth and Ritual, Philosophical Quarterly, (98): 243-70; auth, The Meaning of Peace in the Bhagavad Gita and the New Testament, The International Journal of Humanities and Peace, 15, (99): 39-41; auth, Hamlet and Man's Being: The Phenomenology of Nausea, Univ Press Am, 84; Dionysos: The masks of madness, Parabola, 95; co-auth, Living Religions, Englewood Cliffs, Prentice Hall, 91. **CONTACT ADDRESS** Dept of Philos, Univ of Connecticut, Storrs, 1266 Storrs Rd, Manchester Hall, Unit 2054, Storrs, CT 06269. **EMAIL** robert.luyster@uconn.edu

LYLE, KENNETH
DISCIPLINE NEW TESTAMANT STUDIES **EDUCATION** Southern Baptist Theol Sem, PHD, 95; M DIV 91; Mississippi Col, BS, 84 **CAREER** Asst Prof of Relig, 96-pres, Bluefield Col; Adj Prof, 95-96, Southern Baptist Theol Sem **MEMBERSHIPS** Soc of Bibl Lit **RESEARCH** Apocalyptic Literature; Ethics **SELECTED PUBLICATIONS** Auth, Ethical Admonition in the Epistle of Jude, Peter Lang Press, 98 **CONTACT ADDRESS** Bluefield Col, 3000 College Dr, Box 27, Bluefield, VA 24605. **EMAIL** klyle@mail.bluefield.edu

LYMAN, J. REBECCA
PERSONAL Born 10/21/1954 **DISCIPLINE** CHURCH HISTORY **EDUCATION** W Mich Univ, BA; Cath Univ Am, MA; Univ Oxford, DPhil. **CAREER** Samuel M. Garrett prof, Church Divinity Sch Pacific **HONORS AND AWARDS** Henry Luce Fel, 96. **SELECTED PUBLICATIONS** Auth, Christian Traditions, Cowley, 99; auth, The Making of a Heretic: The Life of Origen in Epiphanius' Panarion 64, Studia Patristica, 97; A Topography of Heresy: Mapping the Rhetorical Creation of Arianism, Arianism after Arius, Edinburgh, 93; Lex Orandi: Heresy, Orthodoxy, and Popular Religion, The Making and Remaking of Christian Doctrine, Oxford, 93; Christology and Cosmology: Models of Divine Action in Origen, Eusebius, and Athanasius, Oxford UP, 93. **CONTACT ADDRESS** Church Divinity Sch of the Pacific, 2451 Ridge Rd, Berkeley, CA 94709-1217.

LYNCH, JOSEPH HOWARD
PERSONAL Born 11/21/1943, Springfield, MA, m, 1965, 3 children **DISCIPLINE** MEDIEVAL & CHURCH HISTORY **EDUCATION** Boston Col, BA, 65; Harvard Univ, MA, 66, PhD, 71. **CAREER** Vis asst prof hist, Univ Ill, Urbana, 70-71; asst prof & asst dir Ctr Medieval & Renaissance Studies, 71-77, assoc prof hist, 77-85, dir ctr Medieval & Renaissance Studies, 78-83, prof hist, Ohio State Univ, 85; Joe R. Engle Prof of the Hist of Christianity, 00; Ohio State Distinguished Univ Prof, 00. **HONORS AND AWARDS** Am Coun Learned Soc fel, 75, Inst Advanced Study, 88, NEH Fel, 87-88; ACLS Fel, 99-00; Guggenheim Fel, 00-01. **MEMBERSHIPS** Mediaeval Acad Am; Soc Relig Higher Educ; AHA; Am Cath Hist Assoc; Int Sermon Studies; Am Soc of Church Hist. **RESEARCH** History of monasticism; Medieval church history. **SELECTED PUBLICATIONS** Auth, Simoniacal Entry into Religious Life, 76; auth, Godparents and Kinship in Early Medieval Europe, 86; auth, Spiritale Vinculum: the Vocabulary of Spiritual Kinship in Early Medieval Europe, 87; The Medieval Church: A Brief History, 92; auth, Christianizing Kinship: Ritual Sponsorship in Anglo-Saxon England, 98. **CONTACT ADDRESS** Dept of History, Ohio State Univ, Columbus, 230 W 17th Ave, Columbus, OH 43210-1361. **EMAIL** lynch.1@osu.edu

LYNCH, JOSEPH J.
PERSONAL Born 08/28/1953, Decatur, AL, d, 1 child **DISCIPLINE** PHILOSOPHY **EDUCATION** Claremont Grad School, PhD, 92. **CAREER** Lectr in Philos, Cal Polytechnic State Univ, 90- . **MEMBERSHIPS** Am Philos Asn; Soc Philos & Psychol; Soc for Study Ethics & Animals; Soc Study Philos & Martial Arts. **RESEARCH** Philosophy of religion; philosophy of mind. **SELECTED PUBLICATIONS** Auth, Harrison and Hick on God and Animal Pain, Sophia, 94; Is Animal Pain Conscious?, Between the Species, 95; Reply to Professor Russow, Between the Species, 97; Wittgenstein and Animal Minds, Between the Species, 97; A Reply to Professor Comstock, Between the Species, 98; Theodicy and Animal Pain, Between the

Species, 98. **CONTACT ADDRESS** Philosophy Dept, California Polytech State Univ, San Luis Obispo, San Luis Obispo, CA 93405. **EMAIL** jlynch@calpoly.edu

LYNCH, MICHAEL P.
DISCIPLINE EPISTEMOLOGY, PHILOSOPHY OF MIND, EPISTEMOLOGY **EDUCATION** SUNY, Albany, BA, summa cum laude, 90; Syracuse Univ, MA, 92, PhD, 95. **CAREER** Mng tchg assoc, 92-94, sr tchg assoc, 92-94, instr, Syracuse Univ, 94-95; asst prof, Univ MS, 95-00; asst prof, Conn Col, 00-. **HONORS AND AWARDS** Phi Beta Kappa, 89; SUNYA Undergrad Awd for Distinguished Work in Philos, 90; tchg fel, Syracuse Univ, 94-95; Outstanding TA Awd, Syracuse Univ, 94; Syracuse Univ cert of univ tchg, 95; summer grant, Univ Miss Off of Res, 96, 97; Cora L Graham Oustanding Tchr of Freshman, Univ Miss, 98; Griffith Mem Awd. Southern Soc of Philos and Psychol, 98. **RESEARCH** Pluralism and objectivity. **SELECTED PUBLICATIONS** Auth, Expanding the Graduate Student's Role in Instructional Development, Tchg Philos. 18, 95; Hume and the Limits of Reason, Hume Stud, 22, 96; Truth and Relativism: A Reply to Rappaport, Philos, 25, 97; Minimal Realism or Realistic Minimalism?, Philos Quart, 97; Three Models of Conceptual Schemes, Inquiry. 40, 97; coauth, Videotaping as a Tool for Instructional Development, in Teaching: A Guide for Graduate Students, Syracuse UP, 94; guest ed, Real Knowing: Feminist Epistemology and the Coherence Theory, Soc Epistemology, Vol 12:3, 98; auth, Truth in Context, MIT Pr, 98. **CONTACT ADDRESS** Dept Philos, Connecticut Col, CB 5625, New London, CT 06320. **EMAIL** mplyn@conncoll.edu

LYNN, RICHARDSON R.
DISCIPLINE CIVIL PROCEDURE **EDUCATION** Abilene Christian Univ, BA, 73; Vanderbilt Univ, JD, 76. **CAREER** Adjunct prof, Vanderbilt Univ Sch Law, 76-80; prof, Pepperdine Univ Sch Law, 80-86; vis prof, Campbell Univ Sch Law, 86; assoc ed, Litigation, 90-95; prof, 86-89 admin, LA West Am Inn Court, 92-93; prof, dean. **HONORS AND AWARDS** Res fel, Belmont Univ, 89-90. **MEMBERSHIPS** Mem, Am, TN, Nebr Bar Assn(s). **SELECTED PUBLICATIONS** Auth, Appellate Litigation, 93; Jury Trial Law & Practice, 86; Honest Goverunient, 92; contrib, Fed Litigation Guide; Thompson on Real Property. **CONTACT ADDRESS** Sch of Law, Pepperdine Univ, 24255 Pacific Coast Hwy, Malibu, CA 90263.

LYON, GORDON W.
PERSONAL Born 11/09/1966, Durban, South Africa, m, 1997, 1 child **DISCIPLINE** PHILOSOPHY **EDUCATION** Univ Cambridge, PhD, 94. **CAREER** Lectr, Rhodes Univ, 94-97; vis ast prof, Florida St Univ, 97-. **HONORS AND AWARDS** S African Human Sci Res Coun Doctoral Merit Award, 91-93. **MEMBERSHIPS** Am Philos Asn; Fl Philos Asn; Southern Soc Philos & Psych. **RESEARCH** Wittgenstein, philosophy of psychology, philosophy of mind; ADD Applied Ethics. **SELECTED PUBLICATIONS** Auth, "Experience of Perceptual Familiarity," Philos, 96; auth, "Language and Perceptual Experience", Philosophy, 99; auth, "Philosophical Perspectives on Metaphor", Language Sciences, 00. **CONTACT ADDRESS** Dept of Philosophy, Florida State Univ, Tallahassee, FL 32306-1500. **EMAIL** glyon@mailer.fsu.edu

LYON, ROBERT WILLIAM
PERSONAL Born 03/15/1929, Peoria, IL, m, 1954, 2 children **DISCIPLINE** NEW TESTAMENT **EDUCATION** Ohio Univ, BS, 51; Asbury Theol Sem, BD, 54; Princeton Theol Sem, ThM, 56; Univ St Andrews, PhD(New Testament), 59. **CAREER** Vis lectr New Testament, Princeton Theol Sem, 58-59; pastor, LePorte United Methodist Church, Elyria, Ohio, 59-66; assoc prof New Testament lang and lit, 66-72, Prof New Testament Lang and Lit, Asbury Theol Sem, 72-, Res asst, Am Bible Soc, 58-59. **MEMBERSHIPS** Soc Bibl Lit; Studiorum Novi Testamenti Soc. **RESEARCH** Textual criticism; Greek paleography. **SELECTED PUBLICATIONS** Auth, Jesus--a Revolutionary Biog, J Church and State, Vol 0037, 95. **CONTACT ADDRESS** Asbury Theol Sem, Wilmore, KY 40390. **EMAIL** ryon31529@aol.com

LYON, STEVE
PERSONAL m, 2 children **DISCIPLINE** PASTORAL MINISTRY **EDUCATION** Univ Houston, BA, 68; Southwestern Baptist Theol Sem, MDiv, 71, PhD, 78. **CAREER** Adj prof, Midwestern Baptist Theol Sem; Baptist Theol Sem Costa Rica; prof, Baptist Theol Sem Venezuela, 88-93; prof, Southwestern Baptist Theol Sem, 93-. **SELECTED PUBLICATIONS** Auth, Should Baptist Churches Have Elders?, The Baptist Standard, 97; Deberian las Iglesias Bautistas Tener un Cuerpo de Ministros o Pastores Ancianos?, Luminar Bautista, Venezuela, 97; What About the Pastor's Family, Christian Family Mag, 97. **CONTACT ADDRESS** Sch Theol, Southwestern Baptist Theol Sem, PO Box 22000, Fort Worth, TX 76122-0418. **EMAIL** sml@swbts.swbts.edu

LYON, THOMAS D.
DISCIPLINE LAW **EDUCATION** Dartmouth Col, BA,83; Harvard Univ, JD,87; Stanford Univ, PhD,94. **CAREER** Assoc prof,Univ Southern Calif,97-; res assoc, Harbor-UCLA Med Ctr; atty, Children's Serv Div, Los Angeles Co Coun; instructor, Stanford Univ. **MEMBERSHIPS** American Psychological Association; American Psychological Society; Society for Research in Child Development; Member, Board of Directors, &Chair of the Legal Subcommittee, American Professional Society on the Abuse of Children; Editorial Board. **RESEARCH** Law & psychology; family law; evidence. **SELECTED PUBLICATIONS** Auth, The Relevance Ratio: Evaluating the Probative Value of Expert Testimony in Child Sexual Abuse Cases; The Effects of Threats on Children's Disclosure of Sexual Abuse; False Allegations and False Denials of Child Sexual Abuse; Children's Decision-making Competency: Misunderstanding Piaget; coauth, Young Children's Understanding of Forgetting over Time. **CONTACT ADDRESS** School of Law, Univ of So California, University Park Campus, Los Angeles, CA 90089. **EMAIL** tlyon@law.usc.edu

LYONS, DANIEL D.
PERSONAL Born 09/01/1930, Cresco, IA, m, 1963, 3 children **DISCIPLINE** PHILOSOPHY **EDUCATION** Univ Chicago, PhD, 67. **CAREER** Prof Emer. **RESEARCH** Ethical theory; social and political philosophy; logic; Ethics of Tech. **SELECTED PUBLICATIONS** Co-auth, Strutting and Fretting, 91; auth, Democracy, Rights and Freedoms, 00. **CONTACT ADDRESS** Philosophy Dept, Colorado State Univ, Fort Collins, CO 80523. **EMAIL** dlyons@lamar.colostate.edu

LYONS, DAVID
PERSONAL Born 02/06/1935, New York, NY, m, 1955, 3 children **DISCIPLINE** PHILOSOPHY **EDUCATION** Brooklyn Col, BA, 60; Harvard Univ, MA, 63, PhD, 63. **CAREER** Susan Linn Sage prof of philos emer, prof of law emer, Cornell Univ, 64-95; prof law, 95- , prof philos, 98- , Boston Univ. **HONORS AND AWARDS** Guggenheim Found fel, 70-71; Soc for Hum fel, 72-73; Clark award for dist tchg, Cornell Univ, 76; NEH fel, 77-78, 93-94; NEH Const fel, 84-85. **RESEARCH** Moral, political and legal theory. **SELECTED PUBLICATIONS** Auth, Moral Aspects of Legal theory: Essays on Law, Justice, and Political Responsibility, Cambridge, 93; auth, Normal Law, Nearly Just Societies, and other Myths of Legal Theory, in Archiv fur Rechts- und Sozialphilosophie, 93; auth, Rights, Welfare, and Mill's Moral Theory, Oxford, 94; auth, Ethics and the Rule of Law, Cambridge, 84; auth, In the Interest of the Governed, Oxford, 73/91; auth, Forms and Limits of Utilitarianism: Oxford, 65; auth, Moral Judgment, Historical Reality, and Civil Disobedience, Philos & Public Affairs, 98. **CONTACT ADDRESS** School of Law, Boston Univ, 765 Commonwealth Ave, Boston, MA 02215. **EMAIL** dbl@bu.edu

LYONS, JOSEPH
PERSONAL Born 08/17/1955, Wilkes-Barre, PA, m, 1980, 2 children **DISCIPLINE** ACCOUNTING **EDUCATION** BS, acctg, Univ Scranton, 77; MA, Univ Penn, 97. **CAREER** Vpres finance and internal auditor, Allied Services, 81-87; cert pub acct, McDonnell Smith & Assoc, 77-81; assoc exec dir finance, clinical pract, Univ Penn, 87-93; exec dir, Lehigh Valley Physician Grp, 94-. **HONORS AND AWARDS** Cert Pub Acct; Cert Internatl Auditor; Cert Info Systems Auditor; MLA degree. **MEMBERSHIPS** Amer Soc of Law; Med & Ethics; Amer Inst of CPAs; Penn Inst of CPAs; Info Syst Auditors Asn. **RESEARCH** Sociology of medicine; Medical & business ethics; Professions and society; Alternative medicine. **SELECTED PUBLICATIONS** Auth, The American Medical Doctor in the Current Milieu: A matter of trust, Perspectives in Bio and Med, 37, 3, 442-459, spring, 94. **CONTACT ADDRESS** 1007 Quill Ln., Oreland, PA 19075. **EMAIL** lions4@earthlink.net

LYONS, ROBIN R.
PERSONAL Born 12/09/1956, Salem, IL, m, 1992, 2 children **DISCIPLINE** RELIGIOUS STUDIES; PASTORAL THEOLOGY **EDUCATION** W Ky Univ, BA, 79; Drew Univ, M.Div, 82. **CAREER** Pastor, Murphysboro United Meth Church, 95-. **HONORS AND AWARDS** Various Seminary Awds; various Community Service Awds. **MEMBERSHIPS** AAR/SBL; Conf Board of Ordained Ministry **RESEARCH** Bonhoeffer Studies; Historical Jesus; Pastoral Theology; Church Growth Studies. **CONTACT ADDRESS** 1514 Pine St, Murphysboro, IL 62966. **EMAIL** faith1@globaleyes.net

LYSAUGHT, M. THERESE
DISCIPLINE RELIGIOUS STUDIES **EDUCATION** Duke Univ, PhD. **CAREER** Asst prof, Univ Dayton. **MEMBERSHIPS** Recombinant DNA Adv Comt, Nat Inst Health. **RESEARCH** Theological ethics and medical ethics. **CONTACT ADDRESS** Dept of Religious Studies, Univ of Dayton, 300 College Park, 302 Humanities, Dayton, OH 45469-1679. **EMAIL** lysaught@udayton.edu

LYTLE, TIMOTHY F.
PERSONAL Born 05/15/1959, Williamsburg, PA, s **DISCIPLINE** PHILOSOPHY **EDUCATION** Toccoa Falls Col, BA, 80; Western Kentucky Univ, MA, 81; Univ Georgia, PhD, 89. **CAREER** Vis asst prof, 89-90, Sweet Briar Col; vis asst prof, 90-92, Mississippi St Col; vis asst prof, 92-95, Arkansas St Univ; asst prof, 95-00, dept hdm phil & relig, 95-98, assoc prof, 00-, Dir of the Honors Col, 00-, Piedmont Col. **HONORS AND AWARDS** BA, summa cum laude Phi Sigma Tau, Phil Hon Soc, Vulcan Materials Comp Teachjng Excellence Awd, AY 1998-99. **RESEARCH** Philosophy of relig, epistemology **CONTACT ADDRESS** Mississippi State Univ, PO Box 362, Demorest, GA 30535. **EMAIL** tlytle@piedmont.edu

M

M'GONIGLE, R. MICHAEL
DISCIPLINE LAW **EDUCATION** Univ British Columbia, BA, 69; Univ London, MS, 70; Univ Toronto, LLB, 76; Yale Univ, LLM, 79, JD, 82. **CAREER** Assoc prof. **MEMBERSHIPS** Co-founder, Greenpeace Intl **SELECTED PUBLICATIONS** Auth, pubs on international law, law of the sea, and environmental issues; co-auth, Forestopia: A Practical Guide to the New Forest Economy. **CONTACT ADDRESS** Fac of Law, Univ of Victoria, PO Box 2400, Victoria, BC, Canada V8W 3H7. **EMAIL** mgonigle@uvic.ca

MABE, ALAN R.
PERSONAL Born 08/21/1942, Pilot Mountain, NC, m, 1982, 1 child **DISCIPLINE** PHILOSOPHY **EDUCATION** Guilford Col, BA, 64; Syracuse Univ, MA, 67, PhD(philos), 71. **CAREER** Asst prof philos & pub affairs, Syracuse Univ, 71-72; asst prof, 72-76, chmn ed comt, Social Theory & Pract, 73-76, Assoc Prof Philos, Fla State Univ, 76-, Chmn Dept, 77-, Dean Grad Stu, 93-, Ed, Law & Philos, Inter J Jurisp Legal Philos, 81-96. **MEMBERSHIPS** Am Philos Asn; Am Soc Polit & Legal Philos. **RESEARCH** Philosophy of law; ethics; philosophy of social science. **SELECTED PUBLICATIONS** Auth, Hart and the moral content of law, spring 72, The Relationship of Law and morality, spring 74 & Fuller and the Internal Morality of Law, 75, Southern J Philos; Coerced therapy, Social Protection, and Moral Autonomy, 75 & ed, New Techniques and Strategies of Social Contro, 75, Am Behav Sci; auth, Morality, Force and Democratic Theory, Philos Forum, 77. **CONTACT ADDRESS** Dept of Philosophy, Florida State Univ, 600 W College Ave, Tallahassee, FL 32306-1096. **EMAIL** amabe@mailer.fsu.edu

MABERY, LUCY
PERSONAL Born 04/14/1937, Dallas, TX, m, 1997, 3 children **DISCIPLINE** THEOLOGY **EDUCATION** Dallas Theol Sem, MABS, 85, ThM, 89; Texas Womens Univ, PhD, 94. **CAREER** Prof, Dallas Theol Sem. 8 yrs. **MEMBERSHIPS** AAMFT; AACC; Am Psychotherapy Asn. **SELECTED PUBLICATIONS** Auth, Ministering to Today's Women, Word, 99. **CONTACT ADDRESS** Dallas Theol Sem, 3909 Swiss Ave, Dallas, TX 75204. **EMAIL** lmabery@aol.com

MACARTHUR, JOHN
PERSONAL Born 06/19/1939, Los Angeles, CA, m, 4 children **DISCIPLINE** THEOLOGY **EDUCATION** Los Angeles Pacific Col, BA, 61; Talbot Theol Sem, BD, 64; MD, 70; Grace Grad School, LittD, 76; Talbot Theol Sem, 77, DD. **CAREER** Assoc pastor, Calvary Bible Church, Calif., 64-66; asst prof, Los Angeles Baptist Col, 65; fac rep, Talbot Theol Sem, 66-69; pastor of Grace Commun. Church, Sun Valley, Ca., 69- ; adj prof, Talbot Theol Sem, 70-78; pres and tchr on nat syndicated radio prog, Grace to You, 70- ; pres and tchr for Grace to You tape ministry, 70- ; adj prof, Dallas Theol Sem, 82; pres of The Master's Col, Newhall, Ca., 85- ; pres of The Master's Sem, 86-. **HONORS AND AWARDS** Grace to You, nationally syndicaticated radio program and tape ministry, is broadcast more than 750 times daily across America. Numerous tapes and books have been translated into more than 35 languages. Grace Community Church is the largest Protestant Congregation in LA County. **MEMBERSHIPS** Indep. Fundamental Churches of Am; Coun on Biblical Manhood and Womanhood; Stewardship Services Found; Joni and Friends. **SELECTED PUBLICATIONS** Auth, The Art of Giving and Recieving Forgiveness, Nelson Word Publishers, 99; auth, Ashamed of the Gospel, Crossway Books, 99; auth, I Believe in Jesus, Leading Your Child to Christ, Tommy Nelson, 99; auth, The MacArthur Topical Bible, Word, 99; auth, Nothing but the Truth, Crossway Books, 99; auth, The Second Coming, Crossway Books, 99; auth, Revelation 1-11, Vol 1, Moody Press, 99; auth, Biblical Parenting for Life, Word, 00; auth, The Gospels According to the Apostles, Word, 00; The Murder of Jesus, Word, 00; auth, Whose Money is it, Anyway?, Word, 00. **CONTACT ADDRESS** Grace Comm Church, PO Box 1642, Canyon Country, CA 91351. **EMAIL** patsky@gracechurch.org

MACARTHUR, STEVEN D.
PERSONAL Born 11/25/1949, Bronxville, NY, m, 1999, 2 children **DISCIPLINE** RELIGION; PHILOSOPHY **EDUCATION** Princeton Theol Sem, MDiv, 75; Univ Glasgow, PhD, 80. **CAREER** Assoc Prof of Relig and Philos, Sterling Col. **HONORS AND AWARDS** Phi Beta Kappa **MEMBERSHIPS** Soc of Biblical Lit; Evangelical Theol Soc. **CONTACT ADDRESS** Dept of Relig and Philos, Sterling Col, Kansas, Box 149, Sterling, KS 67579. **EMAIL** smacarthur@sterling.edu

MACAULAY, STEWART
PERSONAL Born 04/07/1931, Atlanta, GA, w, 1954, 4 children **DISCIPLINE** LAW **EDUCATION** Stanford Univ, AB, 52, LLB, 54. **CAREER** Instr law, Univ Chicago, 56-57; from asst prof to assoc prof, 57-65, Prof Law, Univ Wis Madison, 65-, Mem adv comt, Am Law Inst, 60-; fel, Ctr Advan Studies Behav Sci, 66-67; dir Chile law prog, Int Legal Ctr, 70-72. **RESEARCH** Law and behavioral science; law and exchange in large-scale industry; free speech in theory and in practice. **SELECTED PUBLICATIONS** Auth, "Non-Contractual Relations and Business: A Preliminary Study," Am Sociol Rev 28 (63): 55-69; auth, "Law and the Behavioral Sciences: Is There Any There There?," Law & Policy 6 (84): 149-187; auth, "Crime and Custom in Business Society," J of Law and Soc 22 (95): 248; auth, "Organic Transactions: Contract, Frank Lloyd Wright and the Johnson Building," Wis Law Rev (96): 75. **CONTACT ADDRESS** Law Sch, Univ of Wisconsin, Madison, 975 Bascom Mall, Madison, WI 53706-1301. **EMAIL** smacaula@facstaff.wisc.edu

MACCORMICK, CHALMERS
PERSONAL Born 04/17/1928, Framingham, MA, m, 1953, 5 children **DISCIPLINE** RELIGION **EDUCATION** Bowdoin Coll, AB, 52; Harvard Univ, AM, 53, PhD, 59. **CAREER** From instr to asst prof relig, 58-67, chmn dept hist and philos relig, 62-71, assoc prof, 67-71, Prof Hist and Philos Relig, Wells Col, 71-92. **MEMBERSHIPS** Am Acad Relig; Soc Values Higher Educ. **RESEARCH** CHURCH HIST; religions of India; comparative study of religions. **SELECTED PUBLICATIONS** Auth, We Are People Full of Hope--Interviews With the 14th Dalai Lama, J Ecumenical Stud, Vol 0029, 92; 3rd Eye Theology--Theology in Formation in Asian Settings, J Ecumenical Stud, Vol 0029, 92; The Story of Christianity in India, Vol 4, Pt 2--the History of Christianity in Tamil Nadu From 1800 to 1975, J Ecumenical Stud, Vol 0031, 94; A New Indian Translation of the Bhagavadgita in Relation With Christian Belief, J Ecumenical Stud, Vol 0031, 94; Making All Things New--Dialogue, Pluralism, and Evangelization in Asia, J Ecumenical Stud, Vol 0032, 95; World Religions in Dialogue--Cooperating to Transform Society, J Ecumenical Stud, Vol 0032, 95; Is My God Your God--a Critical Discussion, J Ecumenical Stud, Vol 0033, 96; Great God, Hear us--Prayers of the World, J Ecumenical Stud, Vol 0033, 96. **CONTACT ADDRESS** Dept of Relig, Wells Col, Aurora, NY 13026.

MACCOULL, LESLIE
PERSONAL Born 08/07/1945, New London, CT, s **DISCIPLINE** CLASSICS; SEMITICS (COPTIC) **EDUCATION** Vassar Col, AB, 65, summa cum laude; Yale Univ, MA, 66; Catholic Univ of Amer, PhD with distinction, 73. **CAREER** Curator, 74-78, Inst of Christian Oriental Research, Catholic Univ; dir of studies, 78-84, Soc for Coptic Archaeology Cairo; senior research scholar (North Am), 84- , adjunct, 97, AZ Ctr for Medieval and Renaissance Studies, AZ State Univ. **HONORS AND AWARDS** Phi Beta Kappa 64; Dumbarton Oaks jr fel 69-71; summer fel, 83; fel, 90-91; fel, Ameri Research Ctr in Egypt, 78-79; NEH Fel, 93-94. **MEMBERSHIPS** Amer Soc of Papyrologists; Intl Assn for Coptic Studies; US Natl Committee for Byzantine Studies, Mensa. **RESEARCH** Coptic papyrology; Byzantine papyrology; social and cultural hist of lat antiquity. **SELECTED PUBLICATIONS** Auth, Dated and datable Coptic documentary hands before A.D. 700, Le Museon, 97; auth, The Triadon: an English translation, Greek Orthodox Theological Review, 97; auth, Chant in Coptic pilgrimage, in Pilgrimage and Holy Space in Late Antique Egypt, 98; auth, BM 1075: A Sixth-Century Tax Register from the Hermopolite, in press; coauth, Catalogue of the Illustrated Manuscripts in the Coptic Museum, in press; auth, The Historical Background of John Philoponus' De Opificio Mundi in the Culture of Byzantine-Coptic Egypt, Zeitshrift fur Autkes Christeutum, in press. **CONTACT ADDRESS** 914 E Lemon St, #137, Tempe, AZ 85281. **EMAIL** haflele@imap4.asu.edu

MACCRIMMON, MARILYN
DISCIPLINE LAW **EDUCATION** Univ Ca, BS, 62; Univ British Columbia, LLB, 75. **CAREER** Asst prof, 76-81; assoc prof, 81-90; prof, 90-. **RESEARCH** Process of proof, feminism and procedural rights under the Charter, and the role of social science evidence in judicial decision-making. **SELECTED PUBLICATIONS** Auth, "Developments in the Law of Evidence: The 1988-89 Term: The Process of Proof: Schematic Constraints," (90): 345-403; auth, "Social Construction of Reality and the Rules of Evidence," in A Forum on Lavallee v.R.: Women and Self-Defence," eds. Boyle, Grant, MacCrimmon and Martinson, (U.B.C. Law Rev, 91): 23-68; auth, Filtering and Analyzing Evidence in an Age of Diversity, Canadian Institute for the Administration of Justice, (94): 437; coauth, "Equality, Fairness and Relevance: Disclosure of Therapists Records in Sexual Assault Trials," in Filtering and Analyzing Evidence in an Age of Diversity, eds. Marilyn MacCrimmon and Monique Ouellet, Canadian Institute for the Administration of Justice, (94): 81-106; coauth, "Operational and Strategic Improvements for a Major Environmental Problem: Application of Computer Models and Expert Judgment Driven byb Legal Requirements," in Verso Un Sistema Esperto Giuridico Integrale, eds. Ciampi, C, F. Socci Natali, and G. Taddei Elmi, (96): 139-150; auth, "Fair Traials, equality Rights and Privacy: The Accused's Right to Disclosure of Therpeutic Rcoords," in Proceedings of the First World Conference on New Trends in Criminal Investigation and Evidence, (97): 569-589; auth, "Developments in the Law of Evidence: The 1995-96 Term: Regulating Fact Determination and Commonsense Reasoning," 8 Supreme Court Law Review, (97): 367-446; coauth, "The Constitutionality of Bill C-49: Analyzing Sexual Assault Law as if Equality Really Mattered," 41 Criminal Law Quarterly, (98): 1-40; auth, "Generalizing about Racism," 10 Canadian Journal of Women and Law/Revue Femmes et Droit, (98): 184-199; auth, The Law of Evidence: Fact Finding, Fairness and Advocacy, Emond Montgomery Publications, (99): 967. **CONTACT ADDRESS** Fac of Law, Univ of British Columbia, 1822 East Mall, Vancouver, BC, Canada V6T 1Z1. **EMAIL** maccrimmon@law.ubc.ca

MACDONALD, MARY N.
PERSONAL Born 12/29/1946, Maleny, Australia, s **DISCIPLINE** HISTORY OF RELIGION **EDUCATION** Univ Chicago, PhD, 88 **CAREER** Lctr, Melanesian Inst, New Guinea, 80-83; prof Hist Relig, LeMoyne Col, 88-98 **HONORS AND AWARDS** Newcombe Dissertation Fel, 87-88 **MEMBERSHIPS** Amer Acad Relig; Assoc Social Anthropology in Oceania **RESEARCH** Religions of Oceania; Religious Movements; Ecology and Religion **SELECTED PUBLICATIONS** "Magic and the Study of Religion in Melanesia," Religiologigues, 95; "Youth and Religion in Papua New Guinea," Catalyst, 96; "Religion and Human Experience," Introduction to the Study of Religion, Orbis, 98 **CONTACT ADDRESS** Relig Studies Dept, Le Moyne Col, Syracuse, NY 13214-1399. **EMAIL** macdonald@maple.lemoyne.edu

MACDONALD, SCOTT C.
PERSONAL Born 03/17/1956, Colorado Springs, CO, m, 1979, 2 children **DISCIPLINE** PHILOSOPHY **EDUCATION** Cornell Univ, BA, 78; PhD, 86; Univ St. Andrews, BD, 81. **CAREER** Instr to assoc prof, Univ of Iowa, 85-95; prof, Cornell Univ, 95-. **HONORS AND AWARDS** Norma K. Regan Prof, 96. **RESEARCH** Medieval philosophy, Philosophy of Religion. **SELECTED PUBLICATIONS** Ed, Being and Goodness: The Concept of the Good in Metaphysics and Philosophical Theology, Cornell Univ Pr, 91; auth, "What is Philosophical Theology?", Presumption of Presence, ed Peter McEnhill and George B. Hall, Scottish Acad Pr, (96): 61-84; auth, "Primal Sin", Augustinian Tradition, ed Gareth B. Matthews, Univ of Calif Pr, (98): 110-39; auth, "Aquinas's Libertarian Account of Free Choice", Revue Int de Philos 52 (98): 309-328; auth, "Practical Reasoning and Reason-Explanations: Aquinas's Account of Reason's Role in Action", Aquinas's Moral Theory, eds Scott MacDonald and Eleonore Stump, Cornell Univ Pr, 98): 133-60; auth, "Gilbert of Poitiers' Metaphysics of Goodness", Recherches de Theologie et Philosophie medievales, (July 99): 57-77; coed, Aquinas's Moral Theory: Essays in Honor of Norman Kretzmann, Cornell Univ Pr, 99; auth, "The Divine Nature", Cambridge Companion to Augustine, eds Norman Kretzmann and Eleonore Stump, Cambridge Univ Pr, (forthcoming); ed, Cambridge Translations of Medieval Philosophical Texts: Metaphysics, (forthcoming); transl, Robert Grosseteste's Commentary on Aristotle's Posterior Analytics, Yale Univ Pr, (forthcoming). **CONTACT ADDRESS** Dept Philos, Cornell Univ, 218 Goldwin Smith Hall, Ithaca, NY 14853-3201.

MACDOUGALL, BRUCE
DISCIPLINE LAW **EDUCATION** Acadia Univ, BA, 82; Oxford Univ, BA, 84; BCL, 86; Dalhousie Univ, LLB, 85. **CAREER** Law Clerk, Justice Gerald Le Dain, Supreme Court Can, 86-87; asst prof, 87-93; prof, Univ of British Columbia, 93-. **HONORS AND AWARDS** Rhodes Scholar. **RESEARCH** Law of obligations; sexual orientation and the law; secured transactions; commercial transactions. **SELECTED PUBLICATIONS** Auth, pubs about contracts, commercial transactions, secured transactions and sexual orientation. **CONTACT ADDRESS** Fac of Law, Univ of British Columbia, 1822 East Mall, Vancouver, BC, Canada V6T 1Z1. **EMAIL** bmacdougal@law.ubc.ca

MACFARQUHAR, RODERICK
PERSONAL Born 12/02/1930, Lahore, India, m, 1964, 2 children **DISCIPLINE** GOVERNMENT **EDUCATION** Oxford Univ, BA, 53; Harvard Univ, MA, 55; London Sch Economics, PhD, 81. **CAREER** Harvard Univ, ch Dept Gov, 98-, Walter Channing Cabot Fel, 93-94, FCEAR, Dir 86-92, Prof 84-; WWC WA Fel, 80-81; Member of Parliament, 74-79; RIIA Fel, 71-74; BBC 24 Hours, founding co-presenter, 71-74, 79-80; RICAEAI Fel, 69; BBC TV, Panorama, reporter, 63-64; The China Qtly, founding editor, 59-68; Daily Telegraph, Sunday Telegraph, China specialist, 55-61. **HONORS AND AWARDS** Smith Richardson Foun Gnt; Chiang Ching-kuo Foun Gnt; Walter Channing Cabot Fel; Leverhulme Res Fel; Ford Foun Gnt; Rockefeller Fun Res Gnt; Levenson Prize for Books on 20th Century China, Asn for Asian Studies, 99. **MEMBERSHIPS** AAAS; RIIA; AAS; BACS; APSA. **RESEARCH** China, Asia. **SELECTED PUBLICATIONS** Coed, contrib, The Politics of China 1949-89, 93, new edition, 97; coed, Perspectives on Modern China: Four Anniversaries, 91; coed, The Secret Speeches of Chairman Mao, 89; coed, The Cambridge History of China, 87; auth, The Origins of the Cultural Revolution, 1, 1974: 2, 1983; 3, 97. **CONTACT ADDRESS** Dept of Government, Harvard Univ, Cambridge, MA 02138. **EMAIL** rkolodne@latte.harvard.edu

MACHADO, DAISY L.
PERSONAL Born, Cuba, m, 1984 **DISCIPLINE** CHRISTIAN HISTORY **EDUCATION** Brooklyn Coll, BA, 74; Hunter Coll School of Social Work, MSW, 78; Union Theo Sem, MDiv, 81; Univ Chi Div School, PhD, 96. **CAREER** Ordained minister, 79-92, Disciples of Christ; Asst Prof Hispanic stud & church hist, 92-96, Texas Christian Univ, Brite Div School; Prog Dir Hispanic Theo Initiative, 96-, Emory Univ, Atlanta. **HONORS AND AWARDS** O E Scott Scholarship, TE Fund Doc Scholarship, E S Ames Scholarship, TE Fund Diss Fel. **MEMBERSHIPS** AAR **RESEARCH** History of latin Protestant church in USA, history Protestant Missions to Mexico, Caribbean, & Central Latin America. **SELECTED PUBLICATIONS** Auth, Jesus loves me..more than you? The Bible and Racism, in: J of the Christian Church, 97; From Anglo-American Traditions to a Multicultural World, in: Discipliana Hist J Disciples of Christ Hist Soc, 97; El Cantico de Maria, in: J for Preachers, 97; Kingdom Building in the Borderlands, The Church and Manifest Destiny, in: Hispanic/Latino Theology, Challenge and Promise, eds, A M Isasi-Diaz & F Segovia, Mineapolis Fortress Press, 96; Latinos in the Protestant Establishment, Is There a Place for Us at the Feast Table?, in: Protestantes/Protestants, eds, J L Gonzalez & D Maldonado, Nashville Abingdon forthcoming. **CONTACT ADDRESS** Brite Divinity Sch, Texas Christian Univ, 2800 S University Dr, Fort Worth, TX 76129. **EMAIL** d.machado@tcu.edu

MACHAFFIE, BARBARA J.
PERSONAL Born 11/29/1949, Philadelphia, PA, m, 1972 **DISCIPLINE** RELIGIOUS STUDIES; ECCLESIASTICAL HISTORY **EDUCATION** Col of Wooster, BA, 71; Univ of Edinburgh, Scotland, BD, 74, PhD, 77. **CAREER** Ref Libr, Princeton Theol Sem, 77-80; vis asst prof, Cleveland State Univ, 81-83; instr, Marietta Col, 83-87; assoc prof, Hist and Relig, Marietta Col, 92- . **HONORS AND AWARDS** Molly C. Putnam and Israel Ward Andrews Assoc prof Relig. **MEMBERSHIPS** Phi Beta Kappa; Scottish Ecclesiastical Hist Soc; Amer Acad Rel. **RESEARCH** 19th Century British Ecclesiastical History; Women and Religion. **SELECTED PUBLICATIONS** Auth, Her Story: Women in Christian Tradition, Fortress, 86; Readings in Her Story: Women in Christian Tradition, Fortress, 92. **CONTACT ADDRESS** Dept of History and Religion, Marietta Col, Marietta, OH 45750. **EMAIL** machaffb@marietta.edu

MACHAMER, PETER KENNEDY
PERSONAL Born 10/20/1942, Cleveland, OH, 3 children **DISCIPLINE** PHILOSOPHY **EDUCATION** Columbia Univ, AB, 64; Cambridge Univ, BA, 66, MA, 70; Univ Chicago PhD(philos), 72. **CAREER** Instr philos, Ill Inst Technol, 67-69; from asst prof to assoc prof, Ohio State Univ, 69-76; assoc prof, 76-78, Prof Hist & Philos Sci Dept, Univ Pittsburgh, 79-, Nat Endowment for Humanities curric develop grant & asst dir, Prog Hist Philos & Hist Sci Theories, Ohio State Univ, 72-74. **HONORS AND AWARDS** NSF Scis and Values, 98 **MEMBERSHIPS** Philos Sci Asn (governing bd, 80-84); Hist Sci Soc; Am Philos Asn; AAAS **RESEARCH** History of 17th century philosophy and science; rationality in science; philosophy of psychology. **SELECTED PUBLICATIONS** Coauth, A theory of critical reasons, In: Language and Aesthetics, Kans State Univ, 73; auth, Feyerabend and Galileo: The the interaction of theories and the reinterpretation of experience, Studies Hist & Philos Sci, 73; Causality and explanation in the philosophy of Descartes, In: Matter Space and Motion, 74 & co-ed, Matter Space and Motion, 74, Ohio State Univ; co-ed, Mindscapes, Univ Pittsburgh, 97; ed, Cambridge Companion to Galiteo, Cambridge Univ, Science and Values, Critical Qrt, 98. **CONTACT ADDRESS** Dept of Hist & Philos of Sci, Univ of Pittsburgh, 1017 Cathedral/Learn, Pittsburgh, PA 15260-0001. **EMAIL** pkmacht@pitt.edu

MACHAN, TIBOR R.
PERSONAL Born 03/18/1939, Budapest, Hungary, d, 3 children **DISCIPLINE** PHILOSOPHY **EDUCATION** Claremont McKenna Col, BA, 65; NYork Univ. MA, 66; Univ Cal at Santa Barbara, PhD, 71. **CAREER** Cal State at Bakersfield, asst prof, 70-72; State Univ of NY at Fredonia, 72-82, tenured 78; Univ of Cal at Santa Barbara, vis assoc prof, 79-84; Franklin Col, Switzerland, 83,85-86 & 97; Univ of San Diego vis dist prof, 84-85; USMA West Point, v prof, 92-93; Adelphi Univ, sr J. M. Olin prof, 94; Chapman Univ, dist fel & prof, 97-, Auburn Univ, prof, 86-99. **HONORS AND AWARDS** Koch Foundation, Confer dir, 70, 72 & 80; Reason Foundation, edu pro dir, 79-84, US dept of edu, JJNGFBM, 85-90; Freedom Comm Inc, advisor, 97-. **MEMBERSHIPS** AAPS, APA, MTPS, Phila Society **RESEARCH** Political philo; meta-ethics; ethics, philo; soc; sciences. **SELECTED PUBLICATIONS** Auth, Ayn Rand, Peter Lang, 99 f/c; Classical Individualism, Routledge, 98; Generosity: Virtue in the Civil Society, Cato Institute, 98; A Primer of Ethics, Univ of Oklahoma Press, 97; Capitalism and Individualism: Reframing the Argument for the Free Society, St Martin's Pub. Co, 90; Marxism: A Bourgeois Critique, MCB Univ Press Ltd, 88. **CONTACT ADDRESS** Sch of Business and Economics, Chapman Univ, PO Box 64, Silverado, CA 92676. **EMAIL** machan@chapman.edu

MACHINA, KENTON F.
PERSONAL Born 04/23/1942, Denver, CO **DISCIPLINE** PHILOSOPHY **EDUCATION** Valparaiso Univ, BS, math and philos, 63; Univ Calif Los Angeles, MA, philos, 66, PhD, philos, 68. **CAREER** Asst prof, philos, Ind Univ, 68-73; asst to assoc to full prof, philos, Ill State Univ, 73-. **HONORS AND AWARDS** Danforth grad fel; Outstanding sr humanities prof, Ill State Univ, 95. **MEMBERSHIPS** Amer Philos Asn; Ill Philos Asn; AAUP. **RESEARCH** Free will and determinism and moral responsibility; Vagueness and semantics. **SELECTED PUBLICATIONS** Article, Challenges for Compatibilism, Amer Philos Quart, 31, 213-333, 94; article, Induction and Deduction Revisited, Nous, 19, 571-578, 85; article, Freedom of Expression in Commerce, Law and Philos, 3, 375-406, 84; auth, Basic Applied Logic, Scott, Foresman and Co, 82; article, Belief, Truth and Vagueness, Jour Philos Logic, 5, 47-78, 76, reprinted, Vagueness: a Reader, MIT Press, 97; article, Vague Predicates, Amer Philos Quart, 9, 225-33, 72; article, Kant, Quine, and Human Experience, Philos Rev, 484-497, Oct, 72. **CONTACT ADDRESS** Illinois State Univ, Campus Box 4540, Normal, IL 61790-4540. **EMAIL** kfmachin@ilstu.edu

MACHLE, EDWARD JOHNSTONE
PERSONAL Born 09/29/1918, Canton, China, m, 1942, 3 children **DISCIPLINE** PHILOSOPHY **EDUCATION** Whitworth Col, AB, 39; San Francisco Theol Sem, BD, 42, AM, 44; Columbia Univ, PhD, 52. **CAREER** Instr philos, Columbia Univ, 46-47; asst prof, 47-52, assoc prof, 53-63, prof, 63-81, chmn dept, 66-69, Emer Prof Philos, Univ Colo, Boulder, 81-; Pastor, churches, Concrete, Wash, San Francisco, Calif and Mineola, NY. **MEMBERSHIPS** Am Philos Asn; Am Acad Relig; Soc Asian and Comp Philos. **RESEARCH** Oriental and comparative philosophy; religious symbols; ethics. **SELECTED PUBLICATIONS** Auth, The Mind and the Shen-Ming in 'Xunzi', J Chinese Philos, Vol 0019, 92. **CONTACT ADDRESS** 515 Simmons St, Port Angeles, WA 98362.

MACIEROWSKI, E. M.
PERSONAL Born 11/01/1948, Springfield, MA, m, 1994, 10 children **DISCIPLINE** PHILOSOPHY; MEDIEVAL STUDIES **EDUCATION** St. John's Col, BA, 70; Pontifical Inst of Mediaeval Studies, MSL, 76; Univ Toronto, MA, 73, PhD, 79. **CAREER** Tutor, Latin prog, St. Michael's Col & Univ Toronto, 78-79; lectr & asst prof, philos, Univ St. Thomas, 79-83; visiting asst prof, philos, Cath Univ of Amer, 83-86; res grant transl, Nat Endow for the Humanities, 86-87; assoc prof and chair, philos, Christendom Col, 87-93; lectr II, logic, Lord Fairfax Community Col, spring, 93; Benedictine Col, 93-. **HONORS AND AWARDS** Woodrow Wilson fel, 70-71; Can Coun Doctoral fel, 75-76; NEH Seminar in Arabic Paleography, Univ Penn, 76; Imperial Iranian Acad of Philos, Tehran, 76-77; NEH Transl grant, 86-87; guest cur, Smithsonian Inst, 87; NEH summer seminar, Columbia Univ, 93; Second Summer Thomistic Inst, Univ Notre Dame, 94; NEH Study grant, 95; pres, Kans City Area Philos Soc, mar, 97-98; World Congress of Mulla Sadra, 99. **MEMBERSHIPS** Amer Cath Philos Asn; Amer Philos Asn; Fel of Cath Scholars; Kans City Area Philos Asn. **RESEARCH** History of Philosophy; Logic; Greek Mathematics; Philosophy of Nature; Moral Philosophy; Metaphysics; Mnemonics; History of Cryptology; Hermeneutics. **SELECTED PUBLICATIONS** Auth, Thomas Aquina's Earliest Treatment of the Divine Essence, Ctr for Medieval and Renaissance Studies & Inst of Global Cultural Studies at Binghamton Univ; auth, On Cutting Off A Ratio, Apollonius of Perga, Critical Translation of the Treatise From the Two Extant MSS of the Arabic Version of the Lost Greek Original, The Golden Hind Press, 87; article, Latin Averroes on the Motion of the Elements, Archiv fur Geschichte der Philosophie, Band 74, Heft 2, 127-157, 92; article, John Philoponus on Aristotle's Definition of Nature: A Translation from the Greek with Notes, Ancient Philos, VIII, 73-100, Spring, 88; transl, Aquinas's Exposition of Aristotle's De Memoria et reminiscentia, Catholic Univ Press, forthcoming. **CONTACT ADDRESS** Dept. of Philosophy, Benedictine Col, 1020 N 2nd St, Atchison, KS 66002. **EMAIL** edwardm@benedictine.edu

MACINTOSH, DUNCAN
DISCIPLINE PHILOSOPHY OF LANGUAGE AND SCIENCE **EDUCATION** Queen's Univ, BA, 79; Univ Waterloo, MA, 81; Univ Toronto, PhD, 86. **CAREER** Assoc prof. **RESEARCH** Epistemology, metaethics, decision and action theory, metaphysics. **SELECTED PUBLICATIONS** Auth, Preference-Revision & the Paradoxes of Instrumental Rationality, CJP, 92; "Persons and the Satisfaction of Preferences," Jour Philos, 93; "Partial Convergence & Approximate Truth," Brit Jour Philos Sci, 94; "Could God Have Made the Big Bang?," Dialogue, 94. **CONTACT ADDRESS** Dept of Philos, Dalhousie Univ, Halifax, NS, Canada B3H 3J5. **EMAIL** duncan.macintosh@dal.ca

MACINTOSH, JOHN JAMES
PERSONAL Born 07/30/1934, North Bay, ON, Canada **DISCIPLINE** PHILOSOPHY **EDUCATION** Univ Auckland, BA, 57, MA, 58; Oxford Univ, BPhil, 61, MA, 63. **CAREER** Jr lectr philos, Univ Auckland, 59; res lectr, Merton Col, Oxford Univ, 61-63, lectr and fel, St John's Col, 63-66, CUF lectr literae humaniores, Oxford Univ, 64-66; assoc prof, 66-70, Prof Philos, Univ Calgary, 70-. **RESEARCH** Identity theory, 17th Century Physics and Philosophy, philosophy of mind, epistemology, philosophy of relig, hist of philosophy and hist of science. **SELECTED PUBLICATIONS** Auth, "Animals, Morality, and Robert Boyle," Dialogue 35, 96; auth, "Is Pascal's Wager Self-Defeating?" Sophia, (forthcoming); auth, "Boyle, Bentley and Clarke on God, Necessity, Frigorifick Atoms, and the Void," International Studies in the Philosophy of Science, (forthcoming); auth, "Aquinas on Necessity," American Catholic Philosophical Quarterly 72, 98; auth, "Aquinas on Ockham on Time, Predestination and the Unexpected Examination," Franciscan Studies 55, 98; auth, "The Argument from the Need for Similar or 'Higher' Qualities: Cudworth, Locke, and Clarke on God's Existence," Enlightenment and Dissent 16, 98. **CONTACT ADDRESS** Dept of Philos, Univ of Calgary, 2500 Univ Dr NW, Calgary, AB, Canada T2N 1N4. **EMAIL** macintos@ucalgary.ca

MACINTYRE, JAMES
DISCIPLINE LAW **EDUCATION** Univ British Columbia, BC, 56, LLB, 57; Harvard Univ, LLM, 58. **CAREER** Assoc prof, 64-68; prof, 68-. **RESEARCH** Labour law; labour arbitration law; trusts; evidence. **SELECTED PUBLICATIONS** Auth, pubs about evidence in income tax, equity, labour law and labour arbitration. **CONTACT ADDRESS** Fac of Law, Univ of British Columbia, 1822 East Mall, Vancouver, BC, Canada V6T 1Z1. **EMAIL** macintyre@law.ubc.ca

MACK, ERIC M.
DISCIPLINE PHILOSOPHY **EDUCATION** Univ Rochester, PhD, 73. **CAREER** Prof, Tulane Univ. **SELECTED PUBLICATIONS** Auth, Personal Integrity, Practical Recognition, and Rights, The Monist; pub(s) in, Philos and Public Aff; Ethics; Philos Stud; Soc Philos and Policy. **CONTACT ADDRESS** Dept of Philosophy, Tulane Univ, 6823 St Charles Ave, New Orleans, LA 70118. **EMAIL** emack@mailhost.tcs.tulane.edu

MACK, KENNETH W.
PERSONAL Born 12/14/1964, Harrisburg, PA **DISCIPLINE** LAW **EDUCATION** Drexel Univ, BEEE, 87; Harvard Law Sch, JD, 91; Princeton Univ, MA, 96. **CAREER** Assoc, Covington & Burling Law Firm, 92-94; Reginald F. Lewis Fel to Asst Prof, Harvard Law Sch, 99-. **HONORS AND AWARDS** Earl Warren Fel, NAACP Legal Defense and Educ Fund, 88-91; Woodrow Wilson Soc of Fel, Princeton Univ, 97-99; Reginald F. Lewis Fel, Harvard Law Sch, 99-00. **MEMBERSHIPS** Org of Am Hist; Am Soc for Legal Hist; Dist of Columbia Bar. **RESEARCH** American Legal History; Civil Rights History; African-American History; History of the American Legal Profession; History of African-American Lawyers. **SELECTED PUBLICATIONS** Auth, "Case Note, Legality of Divestment Statutes," Harvard Law Review, (90): 817; auth, "Law, Society, Identity and the Making of the Jim Crow South: Travel and Segregation on Tennessee Railroads, 1875-1905," Law and Soc Inquiry, (99): 377. **CONTACT ADDRESS** Dept Law, Harvard Univ, 1525 Massachusetts Ave, Cambridge, MA 02138.

MACKEY, LOUIS HENRY
PERSONAL Born 09/24/1926, Sidney, OH, d, 4 children **DISCIPLINE** PHILOSOPHY, COMPARATIVE LITERATURE **EDUCATION** Capital Univ, BA, 48; Yale Univ, MA, 53, PhD(philos), 54. **CAREER** From instr to asst prof philos, Yale Univ, 53-59; from assoc prof to prof, Rice Univ, 59-67; vis prof, 67-68, prof Philos, Univ Tex, Austin, 68-, Morse fel, Yale Univ, 57-58; vis prof, Haverford Col, 71-72; Nat Endowment for Humanities res fel, 76-77; vis prof, Univ of Tulsa, 83. **HONORS AND AWARDS** Harry Ransom Awd for Undergraduate Teaching, 87; President's Assoc Teaching Excellence Awd, 91; Awd for Outstanding Grad Teaching, 94. **MEMBERSHIPS** Amer Comparative Lit Assoc, Inter Assoc for Philo and Lit. **RESEARCH** Literary theory; medieval philosophy; Kierkegaard. **SELECTED PUBLICATIONS** Auth, Kierkegaard: A Kind of Poet, Univ Pa, 71; auth, Points of View: Readings of Kierkegaard, Florida State, 86; auth, "Fact, Fiction, and Representation: Four Novels by Gilbert Sorrentino, Camden House, 97; auth, "Peregrinations of the Word: Essays on Medieval Philosophy," Michigan, 97; Theory and Practic in the Rhetoric of I A Richards, Rheoric Soc Quarterly, 97. **CONTACT ADDRESS** Univ of Texas, Austin, Austin, TX 78712-1180.

MACKINNON, JAMES
PERSONAL Born 01/04/1951, Charlottetown, PEI, Canada, m, 1985, 1 child **DISCIPLINE** ECONOMICS **EDUCATION** York Univ, BA, 71; Princeton Univ, MA, 74; PhD, 75. **CAREER** Asst prof to prof, Queen's Univ, 75-. **HONORS AND AWARDS** Fel, Econometric Soc; Fel, Royal Soc of Can, Queen's Univ Prize for Excellence in Res, 95. **MEMBERSHIPS** Am Econ Asn; Can Econ Asn; Econometric Soc; Inst of Math Statistics. **RESEARCH** Econometrics: specification testing, simulation, bootstrap. **SELECTED PUBLICATIONS** Co-auth, "Transforming the dependent variable in regression models," Intl Econ Rev, (90): 315-339; co-auth, "Regression-based methods for using control variants in Monte Carlo experiments," J of Econometrics, (92): 203-222; co-auth, Estimation and Inference in Econometrics, Oxford Univ Press, 93; auth, "Numerical distribution functions for unit root and cointegration tests," J of Applied Econometrics, (96): 601-618; co-auth, "Approximate bias correction in econometrics," J of Econometrics, (98): 205-230; co-auth, "The size distortion of bootstrap tests," Econometric Theory, (99): 361-376. **CONTACT ADDRESS** Dept Econ, Queen's Univ at Kingston, 99 University Ave, Kingston, ON, Canada K7L 3N6. **EMAIL** jgm@qed.econ.queensu.ca

MACKINNON, PETER
DISCIPLINE LAW **EDUCATION** Dalhousie Univ, BA, 69; Queen's Univ, LLB, 72; Univ Saskatchewan, LLM, 76. **CAREER** Asst dean, 79-81; prof, 75- **HONORS AND AWARDS** Pres, Can Coun Law Deans, 94. **MEMBERSHIPS** Law Soc Saskatchewan; Can Asn Law Tchr. **SELECTED PUBLICATIONS** Auth, Costs and Compensation for the Innocent Accused, Can Bae Rev, 88; co-ed, After Meech Lake, Fifth House, 91; Drawing Boundaries: Legislatures, Courts and Electoral Values, Fifth House, 92. **CONTACT ADDRESS** Col of Law, Univ of Saskatchewan, 15 Campus Dr, Saskatoon, SK, Canada S7N 5A6. **EMAIL** peter.mackinnon@usask.ca

MACKLER, AARON L.
PERSONAL Born 12/09/1958, Chicago, IL, m, 1986, 3 children **DISCIPLINE** THEOLOGY, PHILOSOPHY **EDUCATION** Yale Univ, BA, 80; Hebrew Univ, Grad Studies, 81-82; Jewish Theological Seminary, MA, 85; Georgetown Univ, PhD, 92. **CAREER** Staff ethicist, NY State Task Force on Life and the Law, 90-94; vis asst prof, Jewish Theological Seminary, 92-94; from asst prof theol to assoc prof, Duquesne Univ, 94-. **MEMBERSHIPS** Am Acad of Religion; Am Philos Asn; Am Soc for Bioethics and Humanities; Asn for Jewish Studies; Catholic Theological Soc of Am; Col Theology Soc; Rabbinical Assembly; Soc of Christian Ethics. **RESEARCH** Bioethics; Jewish ethics; Jewish thought; Catholic moral theology; religious ethics. **SELECTED PUBLICATIONS** Auth, Judaism, Justice, and Access to Health Care, Kennedy Inst of Ethics J, 91; auth, Symbols, Reality, and God: Heschel's Rejection of a Tillichian Understanding of Religious Symbols, Judaism, 91; auth, Cases and Principles in Jewish Bioethics: Toward a Holistic Model, Contemporary Jewish Ethics and Morality, Oxford Univ Press, 95; auth, An Expanded Partnership with God? In Vitro Fertilization in Jewish Ethics, J of Religious Ethics, 97; auth, Universal Being and Ethical Particularity in the Hebrew Bible: A Jewish Response to Voegelin's Israel and Revelation, J of Religion, 99; ed, Life and Death Responsibilities in Jewish Biomedical Ethics, JTS Pr (NYork), forthcoming. **CONTACT ADDRESS** Dept Theol, Duquesne Univ, Pittsburgh, PA 15282. **EMAIL** mackler@dug.edu

MACKLIN, RUTH C.
PERSONAL Born 03/27/1938, Newark, NJ, 2 children **DISCIPLINE** PHILOSOPHY **EDUCATION** Cornell Univ, BA, 58; Case Western Reserve Univ, MA, 66, PhD, 68. **CAREER** From instr to assoc prof philos, Case Western Reserve Univ, 67-76, dir moral probs in med proj, 73-74; assoc behav studies, Hastings Ctr, 76-80; assoc prof, 80-84, Prof Bioethics, Albert Einstein Col Med, 84-, Shoshanah Trachtenberg Frackman Fac Scholor, biomedical ethics, 91, head, Div Philos and Hist Med, Dept Epidemiology and Soc Med, 93-; consult ed, Ethics & Behaviors, 90-; ed advis bd, Jour Med Ethics, 95. **MEMBERSHIPS** Eastern Div Am Philos Asn; APHA; ASBH, IAB. **RESEARCH** Bioethics, AIDS; reproductive health. **SELECTED PUBLICATIONS** Auth, Moral concerns and appeals to rights and duties, Hastings Ctr Report, 10/76; co-ed, Moral Problems in Medicine, Prentice-Hall, 76; auth, Consent, coercion, and conflicts of rights, Perspectives in Biol & Med, spring 77; Moral progress, Ethics, 8/77; Moral issues in human genetics: Counseling or control?, Dialogue, 77; co-ed, Violence and the Politics of Research, 81 & Who Speaks for the Child: The Problems of Proxy Consent, 82, Plenum Press; auth, Man, Mind, and Morality: The Ethics of Behavior Control, Prentice-Hall, 82; Predicting dangerousness and the public health response to AIDS, Hastings Center Report, 86; co-auth, AIDS research: The ethics of clinical trials, Law, Med & Health Care, 12/86; Mortal Choices: Bioethics in Today's World, Pantheon Books, 87; Mortal choices: Ethical dilemmas in moder medicine, rep, Houghton Mifflin Co, 88; Is there anything wrong with surrogate motherhood? An ethical analysis, Law, Med & Health Care, spring/summer 88, In: Surrogate Motherhood: Politics and Privacy, Ind Univ Press, 90; Ethics and human values in family planning, In: Ethics and Human Values in Family Planning, CIOMS, 89; HIV infection in children: some ethical conflicts: Tech Report on Develop Disabilities and HIV Infection, 9/89; The paradoxical case of payment as benefit to reserach subjects: IRB: A Rev of Human Subjects Res, 11-12/89; Ethics and human reproduction: International perspectives, Social Problems, 90; HIV-infected psychiatric patients: Beyond confidentiality, Ethics & Behavior, 91; Universality of the Nuremberg code, In: The Nazi Doctors and the Nuremberg Code: Human Rights in Human Experimentation, Oxford Univ Press, 92; Privacy of genetic information and control of it, In: Gene Mapping, Oxford Univ Press, 92; Antiprogestins: Ethical issues, In: Proceedings of the International Symposium on Angiprogestins, Bangladesh Asn for Prevention of Septic Abortion, 6/92; Women's health: An Ethical perspective, Jour Law, Med & Ethics, spring 93; Enemies of Patients, Oxford Univ Press, 93; Surrogates and Other Mothers, The Debates over Assisted Reproduction, Temple Univ Press, 94; Reversing the presumption: The IOM report on women in health research, Jour Am

Women's Med Asn, 94; Cloning without prior approval: A response to recent disclosures of noncompliance, Kennedy Inst Ethics Jour, 95; Maternal-fetal conflict, In: Ethics and Perinatology, Oxford Univ Press, 95; Reproductive technologies in developing countries, Bioethics, 7/95; Rights in bioethics, In: Encyclopedia of Bioethics, 2nd ed, Macmillan, 95; Ethics, informed consent and assisted reproduction, Jour Assisted Reproduction and Genetics, 95; Trials and tribulations: The ethics of responsible research, In: Pediatric Ethics: From Principles to Practice, Harwood Acad Publ, 96; Disagreement, consensus and moral integrity, Kennedy Inst Ethics Jour, 96; Cultural differences and long-acting contraception, In: Controversial Contraception: Moral and Policy Challenges of Long-Acting Birth Control, Georgetown Univ Press, 96; Ethics and reproductive health: A principled approach, World Health Statist Quart, 96; Ethical relativism in a multicultural society, Kennedy Inst Ethics Jour, 98; Justice in international research, In: Beyond Consent: Seeking Justice in Research, Oxford Univ Press; auth, Against Relativism: Cultural Diversity and the Search for Ethical Universals in Medicine, Oxford Univ Press (New York), 99; auth, "Is Ethics Universal? Gender, Science, and Culture in Reproductive Health Research," in Reexamining Research Ethics: From Regulations to Relationships, eds Nancy M.P. King, Gail E. Henderson, and Jane Stein, Univ of NC Press (Chapel Hill), 99, 23-44; auth, "Understanding Informed Consent," Acta Oncologica 38 (99): 83-87; auth, "Ethics, Epidemiology, and Law: The Case of Silicon Breast Implants," Am Jrnl of Public Health, vol 89, no 4, (99): 487-489; auth, "A Defense of Fundamental Principles and Human Rights: A Response to Baker," Kennedy Inst of Ethics Jrnl, vol 8, no 4, (99): 403-422; auth, The Ethical Problems with Sham Surgery in Clinical Research," New England Jrnl of Medicine, vol 341, no 13, (99): 992-996; co-ed, International Collaborative Research: Recent Developments, Research on Human Subjects: International Experience, Publication Series 99, Regional Prog on Bioethics, Pan Am Health Org, WHO, 45-58; auth, "International Research: Ethical Imperialism or Ethical Pluralism?" Accountability in Research, vol 7, no 1 (99); coauth, "Ethical Considerations in International HIV Vaccine Trial: summary of a consultative process by the joint United Nations Programme on HIV/AIDS (UNAIDS)," Jrnl of Medical Ethics, vol 26, no 1 (00): 37-43. **CONTACT ADDRESS** Dept of Epidemiology & Soc Med, Albert Einstein Col of Med, 1300 Morris Pk Ave, Bronx, NY 10461-1926. **EMAIL** macklin@aecom.yu.edu

MACLEAN, IAIN STEWART
PERSONAL Born 01/06/1956, Bellville, Cape Raince, S Africa, m, 1991, 2 children **DISCIPLINE** RELIGION **EDUCATION** Univ Cape Town, BA, 76; Rhodes Univ, BD, 80; Univ S Africa, BA, 81; Princeton Theol Sem, ThM, 85; Univ S Africa, BTh, 86; Harvard Divinity Sch, ThD, 96. **CAREER** Sen Teaching Fel, Harvard Univ, 92-95; Adj Prof, Simmons Col, 95; Visiting Asst Prof to Adj Prof, Roanoke Col, 95-97; Visiting Asst Prof, Washington and Lee Univ, 97-98; Asst Prof, James Madison Univ, 98-. **HONORS AND AWARDS** Prizewinner, South African Historia, 73; Nationale Taalbond bilingualism Awd, 73; Rotary Scholarship, Cape Province Rotarians, 77-79; Grad Writing Fel Prog, Harvard Univ, 91; Distinction in Teaching Awd, Harvard Col, 90-91, 92-93, 94-95; Dean's Dissertation Awd, Harvard Div Sch, 93-94; Grant, James Madison Univ, 98. **RESEARCH** Religion and Society; Religion and Democracy; Comparative african and Latin american religions; Religion and Ethnic/Nationalist conflict; Historical Theology; Reformed/Catholic Theology and Ethics. **SELECTED PUBLICATIONS** Co-ed, God, Meaning and Morality, Harcourt Brace, 98; auth, "Participatory democracy: The case of the Brazilian ecclesial Base communities, 1981-1991," Religion and Theology, (98): 78-101; auth, "Religion and Democracy," "African American Churches," "Calvinism," "Fundamentalism," "Millennialism," "Secularization Thesis," "Jonathan Edwards," "Reinhold Niebuhr," "Persecution of Christians," "Presbyterian Church," "Race Relations," and "Just War Theory," in Encyclopedia of Religion in American Politics, Oryx Press, 99; auth, "Truth and Reconciliation: Irreconcilable Differences? An Ethical Examination of the south African Truth and Reconciliation Commission," in Religion and Theology, (99): 269-302; auth, Opting for Democracy: Liberation Theologians, the Catholic church and the Struggle for Democracy in Brazil, Peter Lang Pub, 99; co-ed, encyclopedia of Religion in American Politics, Oryx Press, 99; auth, "Bahia and Zion: Religions and Races in Conflict. Afro-Brazilian Religions and African Indigenous Churches in the Process of Democratization," in African Religions and the State, Eerdmans, forthcoming; auth, "From Africa to Bahia: afro-Brazilian Religions: Symbol of survival?," in Religions in the African Diaspora: Rhythms of the Motherland, forthcoming; auth, "Millennial Expectations: Jehovah Witnesses and 1918," and "The Origins of dispensational End Time Theory," in The Princeton Reader in American Religions, forthcoming; auth, "Beyond the Condition of (Post)-Modernity. Does Liberation Theology Still Have a Politics?," in Festschrift for Harvey Cox, Pilgrim Press, forthcoming. **CONTACT ADDRESS** Dept Relig & Philos, James Madison Univ, 800 S Main St, Harrisonburg, VA 22807-0001. **EMAIL** macleaix@jmu.edu

MACLEOD, COLIN
DISCIPLINE PHILOSOPHY **EDUCATION** B.A. Queens, M.A. Dalhousie, Ph.D. Cornell. **CAREER** Instr, Univ Brit Columbia; Simon Fraser Univ; asst prof, Univ of Victoria, 98. **HONORS AND AWARDS** Vis fel, Ctr for Law and Soc, Univ Edinburgh. **RESEARCH** Contemporary political philosophy, ethics, and philosophy of law. **SELECTED PUBLICATIONS** Auth, Liberalism, Justice, and Markets: A Critique of Liberal Equlaity, OUP, 98; pub(s), Polit and Soc; Can Jour for Law and Jurisprudence; Law and Philos; Dialogue. **CONTACT ADDRESS** Dept of Philosophy, Univ of Victoria, PO Box 3045, Victoria, BC, Canada V8W 3P4. **EMAIL** cmacleod@uvic.ca

MACNEIL, IAN RODERICK
PERSONAL Born 06/20/1929, New York, NY, m, 1952, 4 children **DISCIPLINE** LAW **EDUCATION** Univ Vt, BA, 50; Harvard Univ, JD, 55. **CAREER** Law clerk, Hon Peter Woodbury, US Court Appeals, Manchester, NH, 55-56; assoc, Sulloway Hollis Godfrey & Soden, Concord, NJ, 56-59; from asst prof to prof law, Cornell Univ, 59-72; vis prof law, Duke Univ, 71-72; prof, Univ Va, 72-74; prof law, Sch Law, Cornell Univ, 74-76, Ingersoll prof, 76-80; John Henry Wigmore Prof Law, Sch Law, Northwestern Univ, 80-99; vis prof, Harvard Univ, 88-89; prof emeritus, Northwestern Univ, 99-. **HONORS AND AWARDS** Fulbright vis prof law, Univ Col, Dar es Salaam, Univ EAfrica, 65-67; Emil Brown Prev Law Awd, 71; Guggenheim fel, 78-79. **MEMBERSHIPS** Am Bar Asn; Am Law Inst; Standing Coun Scottish Chiefs. **RESEARCH** Contracts, arbitration; Scottish hist. **SELECTED PUBLICATIONS** Auth, Bankruptcy Law in East Africa, Legal Publ & Oceana, 66; Contracts: Instruments of Social Cooperation--East Africa, Rothman, 68; coauth, Formation of Contracts: A Study of the Common Core of Legal Systems, Oceana & Stevens, 68; Students and Decision Making, Pub Affairs Press, 70; auth, The many future of contracts, Southern Calif Law Rev, 74; Adjustment of long term economic relations, Northwestern Univ Law Rev, 78; Contracts: Exchange Transactions & Relations, Foundation, 2nd ed, 78; auth, The New Social Contract, Yale Univ, 80; American Arbitration Law, Oxford Univ, 90; coauth, Federal Arbitration Law, Little Brown, 94. **CONTACT ADDRESS** Sch of Law, Northwestern Univ, 357 E Chicago Ave, Chicago, IL 60611-3069.

MACURDY, ALLAN
PERSONAL Born 11/24/1960, Arlington, MA, m **DISCIPLINE** LAW **EDUCATION** Boston Univ, BA, 84; JD, 86. **CAREER** Lectr, Boston Univ, 88-98; lectr, Boston Col, 94-96; lectr, Northeastern Univ, 92-94; lectr, New Eng Sch of Law, 95; adj prof to vis assoc prof, Boston Univ, 98-. **HONORS AND AWARDS** Petra Human Rights Fel, Washington, 94. **MEMBERSHIPS** RRTC; Asn for Higher Educ and Disability; Am Bar Asn; Mass Bar Asn; Boston Bar Asn. **RESEARCH** Legal theory; Felix Cohen and Realism's uses in normative justice; Federal civil rights enforcement; Law and disability. **SELECTED PUBLICATIONS** Auth, "Classical Nostalgia: Race, Class and Formalist Legal Reasoning in Patterson v. McLean Credit Union," NY Univ Rev of Law and Soc Change, 90; auth, "The Americans with Disabilities Act of 1990: A Time for Celebration or A Time for Caution," B.U. Public Interest L J, 91; auth, "Disability Ideology and the law School Curriculum," B.U. Public Interest L J, 95; auth, "Mastery of Life," in The Patient's Voice, reprinted in Bay State Nurse, 97. **CONTACT ADDRESS** Sch of Law, Boston Univ, 765 Commonwealth Ave, Boston, MA 02215. **EMAIL** amacurdy@bu.edu

MACY, GARY A.
DISCIPLINE RELIGIOUS HISTORY **EDUCATION** Univ Cambridge, PhD. **CAREER** Dept Theo, Univ San Diego **SELECTED PUBLICATIONS** Publ on, medieval theol and rel, espec the theol of the Eucharist. **CONTACT ADDRESS** Dept of Theological and Relig Studies, Univ of San Diego, 5998 Alcal Park, Maher 282, San Diego, CA 92110-2492. **EMAIL** macy@acusd.edu

MACZKA, ROMWALD
DISCIPLINE REFORMATION HISTORY, CHRISTIAN MARXIST ENCOUNTER, INTERRELIGIOUS DIALOGUE **EDUCATION** Wheaton Col, BA, 75; Wheaton Grad Sch, MA, 83; Leipzig Univ, PhD, 87. **CAREER** Instr, Inst Slavic Studies, 79-84; prof, Carthage Col, 89-; Res affiliate,Inst Study Christianity Marxism, 89-91; vis asst prof, Trinity College, 88-89; vis prof, Bangalore Theol Col, 95. **HONORS AND AWARDS** Grants: Evangelical Lutheran Church Am; Am Ctr Int Leadership; Lilly Found AmCtr Int Leadership; David C. Cook Foundation (Elgin, IL); academic sch; Stewards' Found. **MEMBERSHIPS** Mennonite Central Comt; Am Hist Asn; Conference Faith & Hist; Am Chemical Soc; American Asn Advancement Slavic Studies. **SELECTED PUBLICATIONS** Auth, Scholarly rev, Theology without Boundaries: Encounters of Eastern Orthodoxy and Western Tradition; The Rise and Decline of Thomas Muentzer, Lutheran Quart;Ed, Christianity and Marxism in U. S. Higher Education: A Handbook of Syllabi, Yesterday's Dissidents -- Tomorrow's Vanguard, 90; Glasnost and the Church; Re-theologizing Thomas Muentzer in the German Democratic Republic, Mennonite Quart Rev; Christian/Marxist Dialogue and Thomas Muentzer. **CONTACT ADDRESS** Carthage Col, 2001 Alford Dr., Kenosha, WI 53140. **EMAIL** rom@carthage.edu

MADDEN, DANIEL PATRICK
PERSONAL Born 09/29/1931, Chicago, IL **DISCIPLINE** PHILOSOPHY, RELIGION **EDUCATION** DePaul Univ, BSC, 53; Aquinas Inst, BA, 57, MA, 63; Ment Health Inst, Iowa, cert, 61; St Paul Univ, STL, 68, STD, 72; Univ Ottawa, MTh, 68, PhD, 72. **CAREER** Prof theol, chmn dept philos & theol, counselor & chaplain, Sacred Heart Dominican Col, 61-63; instr relig, Univ Dallas, 63-64; prof theol & philos, chmn dept & dean of men, Col St Joseph on the Rio Grande, 64-66; asst prof theol, Univ Albuquerque, 66-68; dir & pastor, Aquinas Newman Ctr, Univ NMex, 68-71; asst prof theol & chaplain, St Mary's Dominican Col, 71-73; Assoc Prof Theol/Relig Studies & Campus Ministry Adj, Barry Univ, 73-. **HONORS AND AWARDS** Archbishop Lamy Awd, Archdiocese of Santa Fe, 65. **MEMBERSHIPS** Col Theol Soc; Nat Cath Guidance Conf; Cath Theol Soc Am; Nat Liturgy Comn; Cath Campus Ministry Asn **RESEARCH** Scripture; counseling and guidance; Quakers & Catholics; spirituality of imperfection (12 steps) programs. **SELECTED PUBLICATIONS** Coauth, Teach Us to Love, Herder, 64. **CONTACT ADDRESS** Dept of Theol/Philos, Barry Univ, 11300 N E 2nd Ave, Miami, FL 33161-6695. **EMAIL** dmadden@mail.barry.edu

MADDEN, EDWARD H.
PERSONAL Born 05/18/1925, Gary, IN, m, 1946, 2 children **DISCIPLINE** PHILOSOPHY **EDUCATION** Oberlin Col, AB 46, MA 47; Univ of IA, PhD, 50 **CAREER** Asst Prof, 50-59, Univ of Connect; Assoc Prof, 59-64, San Jose St; Prof, St Univ of NY at Buffalo; Adj Prof, 92-98, Univ of KY **HONORS AND AWARDS** Herbert Schneider Awd; Phi Kappi Phi; Fulbright Prof; Vis Res Fel, Linacre Col, Oxford, England **MEMBERSHIPS** Am Philos Assoc; Soc for the Advancement of Am Philos; CS Pierce Soc; Am Council of Learned Soc **RESEARCH** American Philosophy; Philosophy of Science; Metaphysics **SELECTED PUBLICATIONS** Coauth, Theories of Scientific Method, U of WA Press, 60; Auth, Philosophical Problems of Psychology, Odyssey Press, 62; Auth, Chauncey Wright and the Foundations of Pragmatism, U of WA Press, 63; auth, Civil Disobedience and Moral Law, Univ Wisconsin Pr, 68; auth, Causal Powers, Blackwells (Oxford), 75; coauth, Causing, Perceiving, and Believing, D Reidel (Dordrecht), 75. **CONTACT ADDRESS** 4 Sanctuary Circle, White River Junction, VT 05001-2960.

MADDEN, PATRICK
PERSONAL Born 07/19/1948, Long Beach, CA, s **DISCIPLINE** BIBLICAL STUDIES **EDUCATION** Cath Univ of Am, PhD, 95 **CAREER** Asst Prof, 95-98, St. Mary's Sem; Adj Prof, 98-, Greco Inst **MEMBERSHIPS** Cath Bibl Assoc; Notre Dame Ctr for Past Liturgy **CONTACT ADDRESS** Our Lady of Fatima Church, PO Box 4136, Monroe, LA 71211-4136. **EMAIL** revpjmadden@csi.com

MADDOX, TIMOTHY D. M.
PERSONAL Born 09/14/1953, Riverside, CA, m, 1982, 2 children **DISCIPLINE** PHILOSOPHY, CHRISTIAN STUDIES **EDUCATION** Hardin Sim Univ, BA, 77; South Bap Theol Sem, M Div, 82; ThM, 92; PhD, 97. **CAREER** Pastor, Lanai Bap Chap, 83-84; dir col min, Metro Bap Stud Un, 86-88; dir chap serv, Kent Corr Psych Cen, 89-93; grp lead, SBTS, 96-97; instr, Camps Univ, Westn Ken Univ, Jeff Comm Col, 95-98; instr, Beller Col, 97-99; asst prof, chap, Alderson Broaddus, 99-. **HONORS AND AWARDS** Garrett Fel, 89-94; South Bap Arch Res Grnt. **MEMBERSHIPS** AAR, SBL, BAPT, SCP, NABPR. **RESEARCH** Post modernism and Christianity; Ricoeurian thought; hermeneutic philosophy; Baptist history; American Christianity; philosophy; biblical studies. **SELECTED PUBLICATIONS** Auth, "Revisioning Baptist Principles: A Ricoeurian Postmodern Investigation," Nat Asn Bap Prof Relig (97); auth, "E.Y. Mullins: Mr Baptist for the 20th and 21st Century," Rev Expositor (99). **CONTACT ADDRESS** Philo Dept., Alderson-Broaddus Col, PO Box 2067, Philippi, WV 26416. **EMAIL** maddox@ab.edu

MADDY, PENELOPE
DISCIPLINE PHILOSOPHY **EDUCATION** Univ Calif Berkeley, BA, math, 72; Princeton Univ, PhD, 79. **CAREER** Asst prof, philos, Univ Notre Dame, 78-83; assoc prof, philos, Univ Ill Chicago, 83-87; assoc prof, philos, Univ Calif Irvine, 87-89; prof, philos, Univ Calif Irvine, 89-00; prof, logic and philosophy of science, Univ Calif Irvine, 00-. **HONORS AND AWARDS** Westinghouse Sci Scholar, 68-72; Marshall fel, 72-73; NSF Scholar award, 86, 88-89, 91-92, 94-95; election, Amer Acad of Arts and Sci, 98. **MEMBERSHIPS** Amer Philos Asn; Asn for Symbolic Logis; Philos of Sci Asn. **RESEARCH** Philosophy and foundations of mathematics; Philosophy of logic. **SELECTED PUBLICATIONS** Auth, Naturalism in Mathematics, Oxford Univ Press, 97; auth, Realism in Mathematics, Oxford Univ Press, 90. **CONTACT ADDRESS** Dept. of Logic and Philosophy of Science, Univ of California, Irvine, Irvine, CA 92697. **EMAIL** pjmaddy@uci.edu

MADISON, GARY BRENT
PERSONAL Born 09/13/1940, Kankakee, IL **DISCIPLINE** PHILOSOPHY **EDUCATION** St Joseph's Col, Ind, BA, 62; Marquette Univ, MA, 64; Univ Paris, PhD(philos), 68. **CAREER** Lectr English, Univ Nantes, 65-67; asst philos, Univ

Paris, 68-70; asst prof, 70-75, assoc prof, 75-80, Prof, McMaster Univ, 80-, Can Coun fel, 76-77; affiliated prof comp lit, Univ Toronto, 79-. **MEMBERSHIPS** Can Philos Asn; Soc Phenomenol and Existential Philos. **RESEARCH** Contemporary European Philosophy, Phenemenology, Existentialism, Pragmatism, Hermeneutics, Political and Economic Theory, Philosophy of Social Sciences, Postmodern Thought. **SELECTED PUBLICATIONS** Auth, The Transition From Modernity to Postmodernity, and a Postmodern Interpretation of History, Progress, Revolution, Universality, Rationality, Humanism, and Civil Society, Etudes Litteraires, Vol 0027, 94. **CONTACT ADDRESS** Dept of Philosophy, McMaster Univ, Univ Hall 209, Hamilton, ON, Canada L8S 4K1. **EMAIL** madison@mcmaster.ca

MADSEN, CHARLES CLIFFORD
PERSONAL Born 02/13/1908, Luck, WI, m, 1934, 2 children **DISCIPLINE** THEOLOGY, PSYCHOLOGY OF RELIGION **EDUCATION** Univ Minn, AB, 31; Trinity Theol Sem, Nebr, BD, 34; Cent Baptist Theol Sem, ThD, 49. **CAREER** Pastor, Our Savior's Lutheran Church, Kansas City, Kans, 34-42; prof practical theol, Trinity Theol Sem, Nebr, 46; chmn dept Christianity, 46-56, pres, 56-71, consult, 71-73, Emer Pres, Dana Col, 73-, Knight, Royal Order Dannebrog, 68. **HONORS AND AWARDS** DD, Midland Lutheran Col, 65; LHD, Dana Col, 71. **RESEARCH** The relationship between Christian doctrine and current psychiatric practices; the doctrinal dynamics of Christian psychotherapy; psychiatry. **CONTACT ADDRESS** 2519 College Dr, Blair, NE 68008.

MADSEN, TRUMAN GRANT
PERSONAL Born 12/13/1926, Salt Lake City, UT, m, 1953, 3 children **DISCIPLINE** PHILOSOPHY, RELIGION **EDUCATION** Univ Utah, BS, 50, MS, 51; Harvard Univ, AM, 57, PhD, 60. **HONORS AND AWARDS** Schiller Essays Prize, Univ Southern Calif, 52; Honors Prof of the Year, Brigham Young Univ, 66, Karl G Maeser Distinguished Teacher, 67, Outstanding Teacher Awd, 71; teaching asst philos, harvard univ, 55; from asst prof to assoc prof philos and relig, 57-71, chmn dept hist and philos relig, 60-72, dir, inst mormon studies, 66-72, richard l evans prof christian understanding, 71-77, prof philos and dir, judeo-christia **MEMBERSHIPS** Am Philos Asn. **RESEARCH** Philosophy of language; contemporary philosophy of religion. **SELECTED PUBLICATIONS** Auth, Eternal Man, 68; Four Essays on Love, Bookcraft, 72; Christ and the Inner Life, Common Workshop, Provo, 73; The Highest in Us, Bookcraft, 78; ed, Nibley on the Timely and the Timeless, BYU Relig Studies Ctr, 78. **CONTACT ADDRESS** Brigham Young Univ, 165 Joseph Smith Bldg, Provo, UT 84602.

MAFFIE, JAMES
DISCIPLINE PHILOSOPHY **EDUCATION** UCLA, BA, 73; Univ Mich, MA, 76; PhD, 88. **CAREER** Asst prof, North Carolina State Univ, 88-90; asst prof, Calif State Univ Northbridge, 90-95; asst prof, Colo State Univ, 98-. **HONORS AND AWARDS** Phi beta kappa; Postdoctorate Fel. **MEMBERSHIPS** Am Philos Asn; radical Philos; Asn of Philos of Sci Asn. **RESEARCH** Epistemology; Philosophy of Science; Mesoamerican Philosophy; Feminism. **SELECTED PUBLICATIONS** Auth, Realism, Relativism, and Naturalized Meta - Epistemology, Metaphilosophy, 93; Naturalism, Scientism, and the Independence of Epistemology, Erkenntnis, 95; Towards and Anthropology of Epistemology, The Philos Forum, 95; 'Just-So' Stories about 'Inner Cognitive Africa' : Some Doubts about Sorensen's Evolutionary Epistemology of Thought Experiments, Biol and Philos, 97; Atran's Evolutionary Psychology: 'Say It Ain't Just-So, Joe', Behavioral and Brain Sci, 98; Naturalism and Epistemological Authority: Beyond Pragmatism and Absolutism, Intellectual Hist Newsletter, 98. **CONTACT ADDRESS** Dept of Philosophy, Colorado State Univ, Fort Collins, CO 80523-1781. **EMAIL** maffiej@spot.colorado.edu

MAGEE, GLENN A.
PERSONAL Born 04/10/1966, Norfolk, VA, s **DISCIPLINE** PHILOSOPHY **EDUCATION** Emory Univ, PhD, 98. **CAREER** Lectr, GA State Univ, fall 00-; Georgia State Univ. **MEMBERSHIPS** Amer Philos Assoc. **RESEARCH** German idealism; ancient philos. **SELECTED PUBLICATIONS** Auth, Hegel and the Hermetic Tradition, Cornell Univ Pr, 01. **CONTACT ADDRESS** 510 Coventry Rd #19-D, Decatur, GA 30030. **EMAIL** gamagee@mindspring.com

MAGEE, S. P.
PERSONAL Born 03/17/1943, Wichita, KS, m, 1988, 4 children **DISCIPLINE** ECONOMICS **EDUCATION** Tex Tech, BA, 65; MA, 66; MIT, PhD, 69. **CAREER** Asst prof, Univ Cal Berkeley, 69-71; assoc prof, Univ Chicago, 71-76; prof, Univ Tex, 76- . **HONORS AND AWARDS** Top Researcher, Grad Sch of Business, Univ Tex, 90; Who's Who in Am; Beasley Teaching Awd for best MBA Teacher, Univ Tex, 00. **MEMBERSHIPS** Am Econ Asn. **RESEARCH** International political economy (endogenous protection); the economic effects of lawyers; industrial organization. **CONTACT ADDRESS** Dept. of Finance, Univ of Texas, Austin, Austin, TX 78712. **EMAIL** magee@mail.utexas.edu

MAGER, DONALD
PERSONAL Born 08/24/1942, Santa Rita, NM, d, 2 children **DISCIPLINE** ENGLISH, PHILOSOPHY **EDUCATION** Drake Univ, BA, 64; Syracuse Univ, MA, 66; Wayne State Univ, PhD, 86. **CAREER** Prof of English, Johnson C. Smith Univ, 86-. **HONORS AND AWARDS** The Mott Univ Distinguished Prof, 99; Winner, Union County Writers Club 1998 Chapbook Contest for Borderins, 98; Finalist for Beholders in the Brickhouse Books annual Stonewall Chapbook Contest for Borderings, 97; Associate Artist Residency, Atlantic Cente For The Arts, New Smyrna Beach, Florida, 6-26, March 94; Reader on the Blumenthal Readers and Writers Series of the North Carolina Poetry Network, 94; Par Excellence Teaching Awd, Divisional Nominee, 96; Par Excellence Teaching Awd, Divisional Nominee, 95; Par Excellence Teaching Awd Divisional Nominee, 94; Par Excellence Teaching Awd, Divsional Nominee, 93; First Prize, The Lyricist Statewide Poetry Competition, Campbell Univ, 92; Par Excellence Teaching Awd, Divisional Nominee, 92; Par Excellence Teaching Awd, Divisional Nominee, 91; Tompkins Awd, first prize for poetry, Wayne State University, 86; Thomas A. Rumble Graduate Fel, Wayne State Univ, 84, 85, 86; Michigan Organization for Human Rights Awd for community service, 77. **MEMBERSHIPS** MLA; NC Poetry Society; Phi Beta Kappa, 64; Poetry Society of America, 99; Charlotte Writers Club, 96; North Carolina Poetry Society, Raleigh, NC, 95; Appointed to The Academy of American Poets as an Assciate, 94; The Writers' Workshop, Asheville, North Carolina, 94; Modern Language Assoc, 84. **RESEARCH** Renaisance Drama; Gay/Lesbian Studies; Twentieth Century Czech; Russian Poetry. **SELECTED PUBLICATIONS** Auth, "To Track The Wounded: A Journal," Poetry chapbook, (Roseville, MI): Ridgeway Press; auth, "John Bale and Early Tudor Sodomy Discourse," Queering The Renaissance, Ed, Jonathan Goldberg, Durham: Duke Univ Press, 93; auth, "Glosses: Twenty-four Preludes and Etudes," Poetry volume, St. Andrews Presbyterian College Press; auth, "Teaching About Homophobia at a Historically Black University: A Role Play for Undergraduate Students," with Robert Sulek, Overcoming Heterosexism and Homophobia: Strategies That Work, ed, James T. Sears and Walter L. Williams, (New York): Columbia U. Press, 97: 182-196; auth, "That Which Is Owed To Death," Poetry bolume, (Charlotte, NC): Main Street Rag Press; auth, "Borderings," Poetry volume, (Monroe, NC): Union County Writers Press, 98 Winter of the Union County Writers Press National Chapbook Contest; auth, "Deathwatch," Chapter in The Isherwood Century: Essays on the Life and Work of Christopher Isherwood, ed, James J. Berg and Chris Freeman, (Madison): Univ of Wisconsin Press, 00. **CONTACT ADDRESS** Dept English & Philosophy, Johnson C. Smith Univ, 100 Beatties Ford Rd, Charlotte, NC 2816-5302. **EMAIL** dmager@jcsu.edu

MAGGS, PETER B.
PERSONAL Born 07/24/1936, Durham, NC **DISCIPLINE** LAW **EDUCATION** Harvard Univ, AB, 57; Harvard Law School, JD, 61. **CAREER** Asst Prof to Prof and Acting Dean, Univ Ill, 64-. **HONORS AND AWARDS** Fulbright Fel; Guggenheim Fel **MEMBERSHIPS** District of Columbia Bar, Intl Acad of Comparative Law. **RESEARCH** Intellectual property, Russian law, Kazakhstan law. **SELECTED PUBLICATIONS** Trans & ed, Civil Code of the republic of Armenia, Iris, 99; trans & ed, The Civil Code of the Russian Federation, M.E. Sharpe, 97; co-auth, 1996 Supplement to Computer Law, Cases-Comments-Question, West Pub, 96; auth, The Mandelstam file, the Der Nister File: An Introduction to Stalin-Era Prison and labor Camp Records, M.E. Sharpe, 96; auth, "The Process of codification in Russia: Lessons Learned form the Uniform Commercial code," McGill Law Review, (99): 281-300; auth, "The Impact of the Internet on Legal Bibliography," American Journal of Comparative law, (98): 665-675; auth, "Civil Law Reform and Privatization in the Newly Independent states," Rule of Law consortium Newsletter, (98); 3-4; auth, "Consumer Protection on the Internet," Ajuris, (98): 105-112; auth, "The Russian courts and the Russian constitution,'" Indiana International and comparative Law Review, (97): 99-117. **CONTACT ADDRESS** Col of Law, Univ of Illinois, Urbana-Champaign, 504 E Penn Ave, Champaign, IL 61820-6909. **EMAIL** p-maggs@uiuc.edu

MAGID, LAURIE
PERSONAL Born 07/30/1960, New York, NY **DISCIPLINE** CRIMINAL LAW AND CRIMINAL PROCEDURE, LEGAL WRITING AND APPELLATE ADVOCACY **EDUCATION** Wharton Sch Bus, Univ Pa, BS, 82; Columbia Law Sch, JD, 85. **CAREER** Instr, Villanova Univ, 97-; asst district atty, Delaware Count, PA, 97-; clerked, Honorable James Hunter III Ct Appeals Third Circuit; asst dist atty, Philadelphia Dist Attorney's Off, 86-95; past prosecutor, tried cases, wrote briefs; argued in the Pa Supreme and Superior Courts; past adj prof, Temple Law Sch; assoc prof and co-dir Legal Writing Dept, Widener Law Sch, 95-97. **MEMBERSHIPS** Commissioner, Penn Commission on Sentencing. **SELECTED PUBLICATIONS** Publi in, Columbia Law Rev, Ohio State Law J, Houston Law Rev, Wayne Law Rev & San Diego Law Rev, on Miranda Rights, Discriminatory Selection of Juries, Legal Writing Pedagogy and First Amendment Protections. **CONTACT ADDRESS** Law School, Villanova Univ, 800 Lancaster Ave, Villanova, PA 19085-1692. **EMAIL** magid@law.villanova.edu

MAGILL, GERARD
PERSONAL Born 10/09/1951, Scotland **DISCIPLINE** THEOLOGICAL ETHICS **EDUCATION** Gregorian Univ, Rome, PhB, STB, STL; Edinburgh Univ, PhD. **CAREER** Drygrange Col, Scotland, 76-86; Loyola Univ, 81-88; St. Louis Univ, 88- . **MEMBERSHIPS** AAUP; SCE; AAR; CTSA; CTT; ASLME; ASBH. **RESEARCH** Health care ethics. **SELECTED PUBLICATIONS** Ed, Discourse and Context: An Interdisciplinary Study, Southern Ill Univ, 93; ed, Personality and Belief: Interdisciplinary Essays; Univ of Am, 94; co-ed, Values and Public Life: An Interdisciplinary Study, Univ of Am, 95; co-ed, Abortion, Catholicism, and Public Policy: An Interdisciplinary Investigation, Univ Creighton, 96. **CONTACT ADDRESS** Saint Louis Univ, 1402 S Grand Blvd, Saint Louis, MO 63104.

MAGNET, JOSEPH E.
DISCIPLINE LAW **EDUCATION** Univ Long Island, BA; McGill Univ, LLB, LLM, PhD. **CAREER** Distinguished vis prof, Univ of Calif; vis prof, Univ of Haifa, Israel; prof, Univ of Ottawa. **SELECTED PUBLICATIONS** Auth, Cases, Notes and Materials on Property, Ottawa: Faculty of Law, 79; auth, Implementing official Bilingualism in Manitoba, Winnipeg S. F.M., 82; auth, Withholding Treatment form Defective Newborn Children, Montreal, Brown Legal Publications, 85; auth, Official Languages of Canada: Perspectives from Law, Policy and the Future, Montreal: Edition Blais, 95; auth, Economic and Linguistic Competition in Canada's Federal System, in Towards a Language adgenda: Futurist Outlook on th eUnited Nations, ed. Leger, Canadian entre for Linguistic Rights, (96): 99-111; auth, Multiculturalism in the Canadian Charter of Rights and Freedoms, in The Canadian Charter of Rights and Freedoms, ed. Beaudoin and Mendez, (96): 1029-81; auth, Constitutional Law of Cnada, Kingston: QL Systems, 97; auth, Federalism for the Future: Essential Reforms, Monteal: Wilson & LaFleur, 98; auth, Language Rights Theory in Canadian Perspective in Language and Politics in Canada and the United States, N.J., ed. Ricento, (N.J., Lawrence Erlbaum, 98): 185-206; auth, Constitutional Law of Canada, 2 vols., Edmonton: Juriliber, 98. **CONTACT ADDRESS** Fac Common Law, Univ of Ottawa, 57 Lousi Pasteur St, PO Box 450, Stn A, Ottawa, ON, Canada K1N 6N5. **EMAIL** jmagnet@uottawa.ca

MAGNUS, BERND
PERSONAL Born 12/28/1937, Danzig, Germany, m, 1972, 2 children **DISCIPLINE** NINETEENTH AND TWENTIETH-CENTURY EUROPEAN PHILOSOPHY **EDUCATION** Columbia Univ, PhD. **CAREER** Prof, Univ Calif, Riverside. **RESEARCH** Critical literary theory; History of modern philosophy; post modernism. **SELECTED PUBLICATIONS** Auth, Nietzsche's Case: Philosophy as/and Literature, Routledge, 93; "Reading Ascetic Reading: Toward the Genealogy of Morals and the Path Back to the World," Nietzsche, Genealogy, Morality, Univ Calif Press, 94; "Postmodern Pragmatism," Pragmatism: From Progressivism to Postmodernism, Praeger, 95; Postmodern Philosophy, The Cambridge Dictionary of Philos, Cambridge Univ Press, 95; "Holocaust Child," Contemp Continental Philos in the US: A Photogrammic Presentation, 96; ed, Specters of Marx, Routledge, 94; Whither Marxism?, Routledge, 95; co-ed, The Cambridge Companion to Nietzsche, Cambridge Univ Press, 96. **CONTACT ADDRESS** Dept of Philos, Univ of California, Riverside, Humanities Bldg, Room 1604, Riverside, CA 92521-0201. **EMAIL** magnus@ucracl.ucr.edu

MAGUIRE, DANIEL C.
PERSONAL Born 04/04/1931, Philadelphia, PA, m, 1 child **DISCIPLINE** RELIGIOUS AND PHILOSOPHICAL ETHICS **CAREER** Prof Ethics, Marquette Univ; vis prof, Univ Notre Dame, 83-84. **HONORS AND AWARDS** Best Scholarly Book of the Year, for The Moral Choice, The Council of WI Writers, Inc, 78; Torch Bearer Awd, Cream City Business Assoc, Milwaukee; listed by MS Magazine, 82; voted one of the ten best teachers, Univ Notre Dame, 84. **MEMBERSHIPS** Soc Christian Ethics, pres, 81; The Religious Consultation on Population, Reproductive Health, and Ethics, pres, 98. **RESEARCH** Justice Theory; population; ecology; feminism. **SELECTED PUBLICATIONS** Auth, Death By Choice, 74; The Moral Choice, 75; A New American Justice: Ending the White Male Monopolies, 80; The New Subversives: Anti-Americanism of the Religious Right, 82; The Moral Revolution, 86; On Moral Grounds: The Art/Science of Ethics, 91; The Moral Core of Judaism and Christianity, 93; Ethics For a Small Planet, 98. **CONTACT ADDRESS** Marquette Univ, Milwaukee, WI 53233. **EMAIL** 6609maguired@vms.csd.mu.edu

MAGURSHAK, DANIEL J.
DISCIPLINE CONTEMPORARY EUROPEAN CONTINENTAL PHILOSOPHY **EDUCATION** Northwestern Univ, PhD. **CAREER** English, Carthage Col. **HONORS AND AWARDS** DAAD sch, Alexander von Humboldt Fel. **SELECTED PUBLICATIONS** Areas: Heidegger and Kierkegaard. **CONTACT ADDRESS** Carthage Col, 2001 Alford Dr., Kenosha, WI 53140. **EMAIL** magurs1@carthage.edu

MAHAN, HOWARD F.
PERSONAL Born 10/14/1923, New York, NY, m, 1946, 3 children **DISCIPLINE** HISTORY, POLITICAL SCIENCE **EDUCATION** Drew Univ, BA, 48; Columbia Univ, MA, 51, PhD(hist and govt), 58. **CAREER** Assoc prof hist, Univ Ala, 54-64; PROF HIST AND CHMN DEPT, UNIV S ALA, 64-. **MEMBERSHIPS** AHA; Orgn Am Historians; Am Studies Asn; Southern Hist Asn. **RESEARCH** Origins of United States declarations of war; early republic, intellectual history. **SELECTED PUBLICATIONS CONTACT ADDRESS** 4158 Holly Springs Dr, Mobile, AL 36688.

MAHAN, SUSAN
PERSONAL Born 04/13/1949, San Jose, CA, m, 1997, 3 children **DISCIPLINE** HISTORIC THEOLOGY **EDUCATION** Univ South FL, BA, 71, MA, 77; Marquette Univ, PhD, 88. **CAREER** Adjunct prof: San Jose State Univ, 88-97, Santa Clara Univ, 92-97, Univ of San Francisco, 92-98; Adjunct Prof, Loyola-Marymount, 98-. **MEMBERSHIPS** AAR; CTSA; CTS. **RESEARCH** Amer spirituality; women mystics; Asceticism; spirituality and work; spirituality and marriage. **CONTACT ADDRESS** 181 Rainbow Lane, Watsonville, CA 95076. **EMAIL** smahan@got.net

MAHER, PATRICK L.
PERSONAL Born 05/09/1949, Sydney, Australia, m, 1979 **DISCIPLINE** PHILOSOPHY **EDUCATION** Univ of Sydney, BS, 72; BA, 78; Univ of Pittsburg, MA, 82; PhD, 84. **CAREER** Administrative officer, Univ of New South Wales, 78-9; asst instr, teaching fel, Univ of Pittsburgh, 80-84; postdoctoral scholar/asst prof, Univ of Mich, 87-90; visiting lectr, Univ of Sydney, 94; asst prof, Univ of Ill, 84-92; assoc prof, 92-00; prof, Univ of Ill, 00-. **HONORS AND AWARDS** Univ Medal, Univ of Sydney, 78; Provost's Humanities Fel, 79-80; Hannah Fullerton Scholarship, 79-81; Michael Bennett Essay Prize, 81; Andrew Mellon Pre-Doctoral Fel, 82-3; Humanities Released Time Awd, 87; NEH, Summer Stipend, 87; Michigan Soc of Fel, Univ of Mich, 87-90; Fel, Mich Soc of Fel, 87-90; Australian Res Council Grant, 90; Univ Scholar, Univ of Ill, 95-98; . **MEMBERSHIPS** Am Philos Asn, Philos of Sci Asn. **RESEARCH** Philosophy of science, probability and induction. **SELECTED PUBLICATIONS** Auth, 'Framing of Decisions under Ambiguity' with Yoshihisa Kashima, Journal of Behavioral Decision Making 8, (95): 33-49; auth, 'Probabilities for New Theories,' Philosophical Studies 77, (95): 103-115; auth, 'Subjective and Objective Confirmation,' Philosophy of Science 63, (96): 149-174; auth, 'The Hole in the Ground of Induction,' Australasian Journal of Philosophy 74, (96): 423-432; auth, 'Preference Reversal in Ellsberg Problems' with Yoshihisa Kashima, Philosophical Studies 88, (97): 187-207; auth, 'Depragmatized Dutch Book Arguments,' Philosophy of Science 64, (97): 291-305; auth, 'Inductive Inference,' in The Routledge Encyclopedia of Philosophy, 98; auth, 'Inductive Logic and the Ravens Paradox,' Philosophy of Science 66, (99): 50-70; auth, 'The Confirmation of Black's Theory of Lime,' Studies in History and Philosophy of Science 30, (99): 335-353; auth, 'Probabilities for Two Properties,' Erkenntnis 52, (00): 63-91. **CONTACT ADDRESS** Dept Philos, Univ of Illinois, Urbana-Champaign, 810 S Wright St, Urbana, IL 61801-3611. **EMAIL** p-maher@uiuc.edu

MAHERN, CATHERINE
DISCIPLINE LAW **EDUCATION** Purdue Univ, BS, 75; Ind Univ-Indianapolis, JD, 80. **CAREER** Assoc prof & dir, Law Sch Legal Clinic, Creighton Univ; dir Elder Law Clinic Creighton Univ, Thurgood Marshall Sch Law, 85-92; legal svc(s) atty, Tex, 83-85; legal svc(s), In, 80-82. **RESEARCH** Consumer law; family law. **SELECTED PUBLICATIONS** Pub(s), legal problems of the elderly, Tex Bar J. **CONTACT ADDRESS** Sch of Law, Creighton Univ, 2500 California Plaza , Omaha, NE 68178. **EMAIL** mahern@culaw.Creighton.edu

MAHONEY, EDWARD P.
DISCIPLINE PHILOSOPHY **EDUCATION** Columbia Univ, PhD, 66. **CAREER** Fulbright tchg fel, Univ Rome; vis prof, Univ CA, Cath Univ Am; prof, Duke Univ. **HONORS AND AWARDS** Pres, Soc Medieval Renaissance Philos. **MEMBERSHIPS** Soc Medieval Renaissance Philos. **RESEARCH** Medieval psychology. **SELECTED PUBLICATIONS** Ed, Medieval Aspects of Renaissance Learning, Duke Univ, 74; Philosophy and Humanism, Columbia Univ, 76. **CONTACT ADDRESS** Philos Dept, Duke Univ, West Duke Bldg, Durham, NC 27706. **EMAIL** emahoney@acpub.duke.edu

MAHONY, WILLIAM K.
PERSONAL Born 10/06/1950, Denver, CO, m, 1984, 2 children **DISCIPLINE** RELIGION **EDUCATION** Williams Col, BA, 73; Yale Univ, MDiv, 76; Univ Chicago, PhD, 82. **CAREER** MacArthur Asst Prof Relig, 82-88, assoc prof, 88-96, prof, Davidson Col 96-. **HONORS AND AWARDS** Nat Endowment Hum Fel Col Tchr; Hamilton-Hunter Love of Tchg Awd; ODK Tchg Awd. **MEMBERSHIPS** Am Acad Relig; Soc Tantric Stud. **RESEARCH** Religions originating in India. **SELECTED PUBLICATIONS** Auth, Meditation Revolution, Agama, 1997; Artful Universe, SUNY, 1998. **CONTACT ADDRESS** Department of Religion, Davidson Col, PO Box 1719, Davidson, NC 28036-1719. **EMAIL** bimahony@davidson.edu

MAIDMAN, MAYNARD PAUL
PERSONAL Born 08/07/1944, Philadelphia, PA, m, 1971, 2 children **DISCIPLINE** ANCIENT HISTORY, BIBLICAL STUDIES **EDUCATION** Columbia Univ, AB, 66; Univ Pa, PhD(Oriental studies), 76. **CAREER** Lectr, 72-76, asst prof, 76-78, ASSOC PROF HIST AND HEBREW, YORK UNIV, 78-. **MEMBERSHIPS** Am Oriental Soc; Soc Bibl Lit. **RESEARCH** Private economic records from Late Bronze Age Iraq and their significance; the dynamics of ancient archive keeping; ancient Israelite political history. **SELECTED PUBLICATIONS** Auth, Reallexikon of Assyriology and Near Eastern Archaeology, Vol 8, Fascicles 1-2, Meek Miete, Fascicles 3-4, Miete Moab, J Amer Oriental Soc, Vol 0116, 96; Uncovering Ancient Stones--Essays in Memory of Richardson, H. Neil, J Amer Oriental Soc, Vol 0116, 96. **CONTACT ADDRESS** York Univ, North York, ON, Canada M3J 1P3. **EMAIL** mmaidman@yorku.ca

MAIER, HAROLD GEISTWEIT
PERSONAL Born 03/25/1937, Cincinnati, OH, d, 1963, 2 children **DISCIPLINE** LAW **EDUCATION** Univ Cincinnati, BA, 59, JD, 63; Univ Mich, LLM, 64. **CAREER** From asst prof to assoc prof law, 65-70, Prof Law, Vanderbilt Univ, 70, Dir Transnat Legal Studies, 73-99, David Daniels Allen Distinguished Chair in Law, 88-; US State Dept deleg, Asn Am Law Schs Conf Yugoslavian-US Trade, Belgrade, 68; guest scholar, Brookings Inst, Washington, DC, 76-77; consult Panama Canal treaties, Off Secy of Army, 76; Counr on Int Law, Office of the Legal Advisor, U.S. Dept of State, 83-84. **HONORS AND AWARDS** Order of the Coif, 63; Ford Inst Studies fel, Max Planck Inst Foreign & Int Patents, Univ Munich, 64-65; Paul J Hartman Outstanding Teaching Awd, 76. **MEMBERSHIPS** Am Soc Int Law; Am soc Comp Law. **RESEARCH** United States foreign relations law; private international law; international civil litigation. **SELECTED PUBLICATIONS** Coauth, Private internatioanl law and its sources, Vanderbilt Law Rev, 63; auth, The bases and range of federal common law in private international matters, Vanderbilt J Transnat Law, 71; Coordination of laws in a national federal state: An analysis of the writings of Elliott Evans Cheatham, Vanderbilt Law Rev, 73; Cooperative federalism in international trade: Its constitutional parameters, Mercer Law Rev, 76; Extraterritorial jurisdiction at a cross-roads: An intersection between public and private international law, Am J Int Law, 82; Interest Balancing and Extraterritorial Jurisdiction, Am J Comp Law 31, 83; coauth, A Unifying Theory for Judicial Jurisdiction and Choice of Law, Am J Comp Law 39, 91; Finding the Trees in Spite of the Metaphorist: The Problem of State Interests in Choice of Law, Alb Law Rev 56, 93. **CONTACT ADDRESS** Law Sch, Vanderbilt Univ, 2201 W End Ave S, Nashville, TN 37240-0001.

MAIER, WALTER A., III
PERSONAL 1 child **DISCIPLINE** RELIGION **EDUCATION** Concordia Theol Sem, MDiv, 78; Harvard Univ, MA, PhD, 84. **CAREER** Concordia Univ, River Forest, IL, asst, assoc prof, 84-89; Concordia Theol Sem, Ft. Wayne, IN, 89-. **MEMBERSHIPS** SBL, ETS, IBR **RESEARCH** Cult of Anc Near East; Bib Stud. **SELECTED PUBLICATIONS** Auth, Asherah: Extrabiblical Evidence, 86; The Healing of Namaan in Missiological Perspective, Concordia Theol Quart, 97; A Hermeneutics Text for the Advanced Student, Concordia Theol Quart, 98. **CONTACT ADDRESS** Dept of Theology, Concordia Theol Sem, 6600 N Clinton St, Fort Wayne, IN 46825-4996. **EMAIL** MAIERWA3@mail.ctsfw.edu

MAITZEN, STEPHEN
DISCIPLINE PHILOSOPHY **EDUCATION** Northwestern Univ, BA, 85; Yale Univ, Law Sch, 85-86; Cornell Univ, MA, 90, PhD, 92. **CAREER** Adj prof, Dalhousie Univ. **RESEARCH** Epistemology, applied ethics, philosophy of religion. **SELECTED PUBLICATIONS** Auth, "The Ethics of Statistical Discrimination," Soc Theory and Practice, 91; "Two Views of Religious Certitude," Rel Stud, 92; "Our Errant Epistemic Aim," Philos & Phenomen Res, 95; God and Other Theoretical Entities, Topoi, 95; The Knower Paradox and Epistemic Closure, Synthese, 98; "Closing the Is-Ought Gap," Can Jour of Philos, 98. **CONTACT ADDRESS** Dept of Philos, Dalhousie Univ, Halifax, NS, Canada B3H 4P9. **EMAIL** stephen.maitzen@dal.ca

MAKARUSHKA, IRENA
PERSONAL Born 10/01/1946, Munich, Germany, m, 1999, 3 children **DISCIPLINE** PHILOSOPHY OF RELIGION **EDUCATION** St John's Univ, BA, 67; Boston Univ, MA, 79; Boston Univ, PhD, 86 **CAREER** Instr, Boston Col, 85-86; asst prof, Holy Cross Col, 86-90; asst prof, Bowdoin Col, 90-93; assoc prof, Bowdoin Col, 94-; chair, Religious Dept, Bowdoin Col, 95-98; assoc dean acad affairs, Goucher Col, 98- **HONORS AND AWARDS** Faculty Res Grant, Bowdoin Col, 90, 91, 93, 96, 97; Faculty Development Fund, Bowdoin Col, 91, 96 **MEMBERSHIPS** Soc for Values in Higher Education; Intl Nietzsche Soc; Amer Philos Assoc; Amer Acad Relig; Member Steering Committee, Amer Acad Relig, 90-93; Member Prog Committee, Amer Acad Relig, 90-93; Program Dir, Amer Acad Relig New England, 90-92; Member Steering Committee, Film Prog Unit, Amer Acad Relig **SELECTED PUBLICATIONS** Auth, "Transgressing Goodness in Breaking the Waves," Imag(in)ing Otherness: Filmic Visions of Living Together, Scholar's Press, 99; auth, "Transgressing Goodness in Breaking the Waves," Jrnl Relig & Film, 98; auth, "Dualism," Encycl Women & World Relig, Macmillan, 98; auth, Religious Imagination and Language in Emerson and Nietzsche, Macmillan UK. **CONTACT ADDRESS** Goucher Col, 1021 Dulaney Valley Road, Baltimore, MD 21204-2794. **EMAIL** imakarus@goucher.edu

MAKAU, JOSINA M.
PERSONAL Born 04/11/1950, Oostzahn, Netherlands **DISCIPLINE** RHETORIC, PHILOSOPHY **EDUCATION** Calif State Univ, Northridge, BA, 73; Univ Calif, Los Angeles, MA, 73; Univ Calif, Berkeley, MA, 76, PhD(rhetoric), 80. **CAREER** Asst Prof Commun, Ohio State Univ, 79-. **MEMBERSHIPS** Speech Commun Asn; Rhetoric Soc Am; Int Soc Hist Rhetoric; Cent States Speech Asn. **RESEARCH** Rhetoric and philosophy of law; modern theories of argumentation; rhetorical criticism. **SELECTED PUBLICATIONS CONTACT ADDRESS** Dept of Commun, Ohio State Univ, Columbus, Columbus, OH 43210.

MAKKREEL, RUDOLF A.
PERSONAL Born 05/29/1939, Antwerp, Belgium, m, 1967, 1 child **DISCIPLINE** PHILOSOPHY **EDUCATION** Columbia Coll, BA, 60; PhD, 66. **CAREER** Instr, Rutgers Univ, 63-64, 65-66; asst prof, Univ California, 66-73; asst prof, 73-76; assoc prof, 76-85; prof, 85-91-, Emory Univ. **HONORS AND AWARDS** Pulitzer Prize Nom, 75; Nat Bk Awd, 75; DAAD; Alexander von Humboldt Fel; Fritz Thyssen Found Gnt; NEH Gnt; Volkswagen Found Gnt. **MEMBERSHIPS** Assoc of the Ctr for Advanced res in Phenomenology; APA; ASA; SPEP; SSHP; SOPHIA. **RESEARCH** History of philosophy from Kant to present; aesthetics; philosophy of history; phenomenology; hermeneutics. **SELECTED PUBLICATIONS** auth, Dilthey Philosopher of the Human Studies, Prin Univ Press (Princeton, NJ), 75; Co-ed, Dilthy and Phenomenology, Cen Adv Res Phen and Univ Press Am (Washington, DC), 87; auth, Imagination and Interpretation in Kant: The Hermeneutical Import of the Critique of Judgment, Chic Univ Press (Chicago, IL), 90; auth, "Kants Responses to Skepticism in The Skepticism Tradition Around 1800, Klower Academic Publishers, 1998; auth, From Simulation to Structural Transportation, in Empathy and Agency, Westview Press, 2000. **CONTACT ADDRESS** Dept Philosophy, Emory Univ, 1364 Clifton Rd NE, Atlanta, GA 30322. **EMAIL** philrm@emory.edu

MAKOWSKI, LEE
PERSONAL Born 04/10/1951, Norristown, PA, s **DISCIPLINE** THEOLOGY, RELIGIOUS STUDIES **EDUCATION** Villanova, MA, 81; Cath Univ, PhD, 92. **CAREER** Asst prof, Theol and Relig Studies, Villanova Univ, 90-. **HONORS AND AWARDS** Lindback Awd for Teaching Excellence, 98. **MEMBERSHIPS** Cath Theol Soc of Am. **RESEARCH** Developmental spirituality. **SELECTED PUBLICATIONS** Auth, Horace Bushnell on Christian Character Development, UPA (99). **CONTACT ADDRESS** Dept Relig Studies, Villanova Univ, 800 E Lancaster Ave, Villanova, PA 19085-1603. **EMAIL** Lee.Makowski@Villanova.edu

MAKUCH, STANLEY M.
DISCIPLINE LAW **EDUCATION** Univ Toronto, BA, 67; Univ Carleton, MA, 68; Osgoode Hall Law Sch, LLB, 71; Harvard Univ, LLM, 72. **CAREER** Assoc dean, 81-85; prof, Univ of Toronto, 76-85; partner, Cassels Brock & Blackwell; adj prof, Univ of Toronto. **RESEARCH** Municipal planning law; environmental law. **SELECTED PUBLICATIONS** Auth, Canadian Municipal and Planning Law, Carswell; Regulation by Municipal Licensing, Univ Toronto; Spill's Bill: Duties Rights and Obligations, Butterworth's. **CONTACT ADDRESS** Fac of Law, Univ of Toronto, 78 Queen's Park, Toronto, ON, Canada M5S 2C5.

MALAMENT, DAVID BARUCH
PERSONAL Born 12/21/1947, New York, NY, m, 2000 **DISCIPLINE** PHILOSOPHY OF SCIENCE **EDUCATION** Columbia Univ, BA, 68; Rockefeller Univ, PhD(philos), 75. **CAREER** Asst prof, 75-78, assoc prof, 78-82, prof philos, 82-89, David B & Clara E Stern Prof, Univ Chicago, 89-99; vis assist prof philos, Princeton Univ, spring 77; Visting Asst Prof of Philosophy at Princeton Univ, 77; chair, Comm on the Conceptual Foundations of Science, Univ Chicago, 95-98; Visiting Prof of Philosophy, Carnegie Mellon Univ, 98. **HONORS AND AWARDS** N S F res Fellowship, 79-80, 86-87; Whitehead Lecturer, Harvard Univ, fall 80; fel, Center for the Philos of Science, Univ Pittsburgh, fall 83; fel, Center for Advanced Study in the Behavioral Sciences, Palo Alto, 89-90; Quantrell Awd for Excellence in Undergraduate Teaching, Univ Chicago, June 91; UCI Distinguished Prof of Logic and Philosophy of Science, Univ of CA, Irvine, 99-. **MEMBERSHIPS** Elected to the Am Academy of Arts and Sciences, spring 92. **RESEARCH** Mathematical and conceptual foundations of modern physics. **SELECTED PUBLICATIONS** Auth, Minimal Acceleration Requirements for Time Travel in Godel Spacetime, J Mathematical Physics, vol 26, no 4, 85; A Modest Remark on Reichenbach, Rotation, and General relativity, Philos of Science, vol 52, no 4, 85, reprinted in J Butterfield, M Hogarth, &

G Belot, eds, Spacetime in the Int Res Libr of Philos, Dartmouth Pubs Co, 96; Newtonian Gravity, Limits, and the Geometry of Space, in R Colodny, ed, From Quarks to Quasars, Univ Pittsburgh Press, 86; Gravity and Spatial Geometry, in R Marcus, et al, eds, Logic, Methodology, and Philos of Science VII (proceedings of the 1983 Salzburg Congress), Elsevier Science Pubs, 86; Time Travel in the Godel Universe, PSA 1984, vol 2 (proceedings of the Philos of Science Asn meetings, Chicago, 1984), 86; A Note About Closed Timelike Curves in Godel Spacetime, J Mathematical Physics, vol 28, no 10, 87; Critical Notice: Itamar Pitowsky, Quantum Probability--Quantum Logic, Philos of Science, vol 59, no 2, 92; Introductory essay to a previously unpublished lecture by Kurt Godel on "rotating universes" in vol III of Godel, Kurt, Collected Works, ed S Feferman et al, Oxford Univ Press, 95; Is Newtonian Cosmology Really Inconsistent?, Philos of Science, vol 62, no 4, 95; In Defense of Dogma--Why There Cannot Be a Relativistic Quantum Mechanical Theory of (Localized) particles in R Clifton, ed, Perspectives on Quantum Reality, Kluwer, 96. **CONTACT ADDRESS** Dept of Logic and Philosophy of Science, Univ of California, Irvine, 3151 Social Science Plz, Irvine, CA 92697-5100. **EMAIL** dmalamen@uci.edu

MALAVET, PEDRO A.

DISCIPLINE LAW **EDUCATION** Emory Univ, BBA; Georgetown Univ, JD, LLM. **CAREER** Assoc prof, Univ Fla, 95-; adj prof, Georgetown Univ Law Ctr, 95, Pontifical Cath Univ Puerto Rico, 91-92; jr partner, Bufete Malavet Ayoroa, Ponce, Puerto Rico, 89-93; clerk, Honorable Raymond L. Acosta, US Dist Ct, San Juan, PR. **HONORS AND AWARDS** Future law prof fel, Georgetown Univ Law Ctr, 93-94. **MEMBERSHIPS** PR Bar; Order of the Coif. **RESEARCH** Comparative law, civil law, civil procedure, European union. **CONTACT ADDRESS** School of Law, Univ of Florida, PO Box 117625, Gainesville, FL 32611-7625. **EMAIL** malavet@law.ufl.edu

MALBON, ELIZABETH STRUTHERS

PERSONAL Born 01/24/1947, Orlando, FL, m, 1979, 2 children **DISCIPLINE** BIBLICAL STUDIES, NEW TESTAMENT **EDUCATION** Fla State Univ, BA, 69, MA, 70, PhD(humanities), 80. **CAREER** Teaching asst humanities, Fla State Univ, 76-77; vis instr relig, Vassar Col, 78-79; adj lectr, Fla State Univ, 79-80; asst prof relig, Va Polytech Inst & State Univ, 80-85, assoc prof, 85-92, prof, 92-, dir Religious Studies Program, 94-. **HONORS AND AWARDS** ACLS Research Fellowship, 84; NEH Summer Seminar, 87; ACLS Travel Grant, 88. **MEMBERSHIPS** Soc Bibl Lit; Am Acad Relig; Cath Bibl Assoc; Soc Values in Higher Ed; Studiorum Novi Testamenti Societas. **RESEARCH** Gospel of Mark; literary approaches; gospels. **SELECTED PUBLICATIONS** Auth, Mythic Structure and Meaning in Mark: Elements of a Levi-Straussian Analysis, Semeia, Vol 16, 79; Galilee and Jerusalem: History and literature in Marcan interpretation, Cath Bibl Quart, 82; Structuralism, Hermeneutics and Contextual Meaning, J Am Acad Relig, 83; No need to have any one Write?: A Structural Exegesis of 1 Thessalonians, Semeia,Vol 26, 83; Fallible Followers: Women and Men in the Gospel of Mark, Semeia, Vol 28, 83; The spiral and the Square: Levi-Strauss's Mythic Formula and Greimas's Constitutional Model, Linguistica Biblica, 84; The Jesus of Mark and the Sea of Galilee, J Bibl Lit, 84; Auth, The Text and Time: Levi-Strauss and New Testament Studies, in Anthropology and the Study of Religions, ed Frank E. Reynolds and Robert L. Moore, Council for the Scientific Study of religion, 84. Joint Auth, Parabling as a via Negativa: A Critical Review of the work of John Dominic Crossan, J Relig, 84. Auth, The Theory and Practice of Structural Exegesis: A review article, Perspectives in Religious Stud, 84; Te oikia autou: Mark 2:15 in Context, New Testament Studies, 85; Mark: Myth and Parable, Bibl Theol Bul, 86; Disciples/Crowds/Whoever: Markan Characters and Readers, Novum Testamentum, 86; The Jewish Leaders in the Gospel of Mark: A Literary Study of Marcan Characterizations, J Bibl Lit, 89; Ending at the Beginning: A response, Semeia, Vol 52, 90; Echoes and Foreshadowings in Mark 4-8: Reading and Rereading, J Bibl Lit, 93; Texts and Contexts: Interpreting the Disciples in Mark, Semeia, Vol 62, 93; The Poor Widow in Mark and Her Poor Rich Readers, Cath Bibl Quart, 91: Auth, Narrative Space and Mythic Meaning in Mark, Harper & Row, 86, Sheffield Academic Press, 91;Narrative Criticism: How Does the Story Mean?, in Mark and Method: New Approaches in Biblical Studies, ed Janice Capel Anderson and Stephen D. Moore, Fortress Press, 92. Joint ed, Characterization in Biblical Literature, Semeia, Vol 63, 93; Joint auth, Literary critical methods, in Searching the Scriptures, Vol 1, A Feminist Introduction, ed Elisabeth Schussler Fiorenza, Crossroad Press, 93. Auth, Echoes and foreshadowings in Mark 4-8: Reading and rereading, J Bibl Lit, 93; Texts and contexts: Interpreting the disciples in Mark, Semeia, Vol 62, 93; The New Literary Criticism and the New Testament, Sheffield Academic Press, 94, Trinity Press Int, 94; The Major Importance of the Minor Characters in Mark, in The New Literary Criticism and the New Testament, ed Elizabeth Struthers Malbon and Edgar V. McKnight, Sheffield Academic Press, 94, Trinity Press Int, 94; Literary Contexts of Mark 13, in Biblical and Humane: A Festschrift for John F. Priest, ed Linda Bennett-Elder, David Barr, and Elizabeth Struthers Malbon, Scholars Press, 96; Biblical and Humane: A Festschrift for John F. Priest, Scholars Press, 96. Auth, Fourteen entries on New Testament topics for The Harper Collins Dictionary of Religion, 95; Twelve entries for Women in Scripture: A Dictionary of Named and Unnamed Women in the Hebrew Bible, Apocrypha, and New Testament, ed by Carol Meyers, Toni Craven, and Ross Kraemer, in press. **CONTACT ADDRESS** Relig Studies Program, Virginia Polytech Inst and State Univ, 205 Major Williams Hall, Blacksburg, VA 24061-0135. **EMAIL** Malbon@vt.edu

MALDARI, DONALD

PERSONAL Born 05/10/1952, Malverne, NY, s **DISCIPLINE** THEOLOGY **EDUCATION** Georgetown Univ, BA, 74; Katholieke Univ Leuven (Belgium), MA, STB, 77, PhD, 87. **CAREER** Asst prof, St. Peter's Col, 86-91; assoc novice dir, St. Andrew Hall, 91-94; prof, Centre Pedro-Arrupe (Port-au-Prince, Haiti), 95-97; assoc pastor, St. ignatius Parish (Brooklyn), 97-98; asst prof, Le Moyne Col, 98-. **HONORS AND AWARDS** Founder, Le Bulletin de Liason, Theology Journal in Haiti; Cross keys, St. Peter's Col. **MEMBERSHIPS** Catholic Theol Soc of Am. **RESEARCH** Ecclesiology. **SELECTED PUBLICATIONS** Auth, "The Identity of Religious Life: the Contributions of Jean-Marie Tillard Critically Examined," in Louvain Studies 14, 325-345 (89); rev, "The Golden Legend: Readings on the Saints by Jacob de Voragine," in America 171, 26-27 (Oct. 15, 1994); auth, "Le radicalisme de la vie religieuse," in Le Bulletin de Liason (Centre Pedro-Arrupe, Port-au-Prince, Haiti) I, 25-35 (96); auth, "Haiti Since Aristide," in America 177, 3-4 (Oct. 25, 97); auth, "Les deux etapes de l'engagment chretien dans les Exercices spirituels de S. Ignace," in Le Bulletin de Liason II, 6-14 (97); rev, "Heart of Flesh: A Feminist Spirituality for Women and Men" by Joan D. Chittister, in America 179, 23-24 (Sept. 12, 98); rev, "In Search of Belief" by Joan Chittister, in America 180 no. 18, 29-31 (May 22, 99). **CONTACT ADDRESS** Dept Religion, Le Moyne Col, 1419 Salt Springs Rd, Syracuse, NY 13214-1302. **EMAIL** maldardc@maple.lemoyne.edu

MALHOTRA, ASHOK KUMAR

PERSONAL Born 04/01/1940, Ferozepur, India, w, 1966, 2 children **DISCIPLINE** PHILOSOPHY **EDUCATION** Univ Rajasthan, BA, 61, MA, 63; Univ Hawaii, PhD(philos), 69. **CAREER** Asst prof, 67-70, assoc prof, 70-80, chm dept, 76-78, Prof Philos, State Univ NY Col Oneonta, 80-, Chm Gen Studies, 75-, Campus coordr, NY State Five-Col Sem on India, 68-69; consult ed, J Humanistic & Interdisciplinary Studies, 77-; dir, India Intersession Prog, State Univ NY Col, 79-80 & 81-82; reviewer, Nat Endowment for Humanities grant proposals. **HONORS AND AWARDS** Gold Medal for obtaining the highest GPA in MA Philosophy; Suny Chancellor's Awd for excellence in teaching; Certificate of Recognition for bringing cultural interchange between East and West, Univ Hawaii. **MEMBERSHIPS** Soc Asian & Comp Philos; Am Asian Studies; Am Philos Asn; Asn for Asian Studies; Soc for Comparative Study of Civilizations; Jean-Paul Sartre Soc; Int Phenomenol Soc. **RESEARCH** Comparative philosophy and religion; existentialism and phenomenology; Indian philosophy. **SELECTED PUBLICATIONS** Auth, Sartre's Existentialism in Nausea & Being and Nothingness, Writers Workshop, Calcutta, 76; Hinduism's second shot at becoming a missionary religion, Bharata Manisha, An Ing J, India, 10/76; Samkhya-yoga versus Sartre's philosophy, Asian Thought & Soc, 4/78; Tagore's Aesthetics, Asian Studies Spec Ser, 79; coauth (with Nina Malhotra), Perspectives on Meditation and Personality, New Delhi, India, 80; auth, Hesse's Novel Siddhartha: A Rare Synthesis of Hinduism, Buddhism and Existentialism, 80 & coauth (with Nina Malhotra), Guru Business: A Study of Muktananda and Rajneesh, 81, Asian Res, Hong Kong; auth, Pathways to Philosophy, 95; author of over 30 other publications. **CONTACT ADDRESS** Dept of Philos, SUNY, Col at Oneonta, PO Box 4015, Oneonta, NY 13820-4015. **EMAIL** malhotak@oneonta.edu

MALIK, HAFEEZ

PERSONAL Born Lahore, Pakistan, m, 2 children **DISCIPLINE** POLITICAL SCIENCE **EDUCATION** BA Govt Col, Lahore Pakistan, 49; Graduate Diploma, Jour Univ of the Punjab, 52; MS 55, Syracuse Univ, MA 57, PhD 61. **CAREER** Asst Prof, 61-63, Polit Sci Villanova Univ, Assoc Prof, 63-67, Prof, 67-. **MEMBERSHIPS** Assoc Asian Studies; Pi Sigma Alpha-Natl Polit Sci Hon Soc; Am Assoc Univ Profs; Am Polit Sci Assoc; Am Hist Assoc; Pakistan Council, Asia Soc, NY Chm; Member Nstl Seminar on Pakistan/Bangladesh Columbia Univ. **SELECTED PUBLICATIONS** Central Asia: Its Strategic Importanc and Future Prospect, London: Macmillan and NY: St Martin's Pres, 93-94; Soviet_Pakistan Relations and Current Dynamics London: Macmillan and NY: St Martin's Press, 93; Encyclopedia of the Modern Islamic World, 93-94; Interests and Influence in the Gulf, Brookings Inst Wash DC, 87; Conf ib Relations Between Sussia, the Commonwealth of Independent States as a Whole and Pakistan in Moscow, 92; Interview with Assoc Press corresp on the UN-US challenge to Iraq to remove missiles from the no-fly zone, 93; Channel 3 taping for Newsmakers regarding the peace process in the Middle East. **CONTACT ADDRESS** Villanova Univ, 416-421 SAC, Villanova, PA 19085. **EMAIL** Hmalik@email.vill.edu

MALINO, FRANCES

PERSONAL Born 03/06/1940, Danbury, CT, d, 2 children **DISCIPLINE** EARLY MODERN FRENCH & JEWISH HISTORY **EDUCATION** Skidmore Col, BA, 61; Brandeis Univ, MA, 63, PhD(Judaic studies), 71. **CAREER** From asst prof to prof hist, Univ Mass, Boston, 70-89; assoc prof hist, Harbor Camput, Univ Mass, 70; Vis prof, Brandeis Univ, 71 & Yale Univ, 74; mem, Commission Francaise des Archives Juives, 77-; fel, Mary Ingraham Bunting Inst, Radcliff Col, 79-80, scholar-in-residence, Tauber Inst, Brandeis Univ, spring 83; vis prof Jewish Studies, Mount Holyoke Col, 86-87; Ecole des Haute Etudes en Sciences Sociales, Paris, 89; SOPHIA MOSES ROBINSON PROF JEWISH STUDIES AND HIST, WELLSLEY COL, 89-. **HONORS AND AWARDS** ACLS res grant, 79-80; ACLS travel grant, 87; Healey res grant, 88; guest fel, Wolfson Col, Oxford, 88; Wellsley Col res grant, 91, 96; Littauer Fdn res grant, 93, 96; Alumni Periclean schol award, Skidmore Col, 97; Barnett Miller Fac Dev grant for Int Studies, 98. **MEMBERSHIPS** AHA; Asn Jewish Studies; Soc French Hist Studies; Edit Bd, Jewish Soc Studies; Acad Adv Bd, Int Res Inst on Jewish Women. **RESEARCH** Jewish autonomy and citizenship in 18th century France; nationalism and modern national movements; contemporary Middle East; Jewish women teachers of the Alliance Israelite Universelle. **SELECTED PUBLICATIONS** Auth, Memoires d'un Patriole Proscrit, In: Michael IV, Diaspora Res Inst, Tel Aviv, 76; The Sephardic Jews of Bordeaux: Assimilation and Emancipation in Revolutionary and Napoleonic France, Univ Ala Press, 78; Furtado et les Portugais, Annales Hist Revolution Francaise, 1-3/79; Zalkind Hourwitz-Juif Polonais, Dix-Huitieme Siecle, 81; From patriot to Israelite: Abrahkam Furtado in revolutionary France, In: Essays in Jewish Intellectual History in Honor of Alexander Altmann, Duke Univ Press, 82; Attitudes toward Jewish communal autonomy in pre-revolutionary France, In: Essays in Modern Jewish History: A Tribute to Ben Halpern, Fairleigh Dickinson Univ Press, 82 & ed, Essays in Modern Jewish History; co-ed, The Jews in Modern France, Univ Press New England, 85; co-ed, From East and West: Jews in a changing Europe, Basil Blackwell, 90; ed, Profiles in Diversity: Jews in a Changing Europe, Wayne State Univ Press, 98; auth, A Jew in the French Revolution: The Life of Zalkind Hourwitz, Basil Blackwell, 96; auth, "Women teachers of the Alliance Israelite Universelle," in Jewish Women in Historical Perspective, Wayne State Univ Press, 98; auth, "Jewish Emancipation in France," in Religious Minorities, State and Society in Nineteenth-Century Europe, Manchester Univ Press, 98; auth, "Resistance and Rebellion: The Jews in Eighteenth Century France," in Jewish Historical Studies, No. 30, 89; auth, "Jewish Women in Early Modern Europe," in Women's Studies Encyclopedia, Greenwood Press, 91; auth, Un Juif rebelle dans la Revolution et sous l'Empire Zalkind Hourwitz (1751-1812), Berg Intl, 00. **CONTACT ADDRESS** Dept Hist, Wellesley Col, Wellesley, MA 02481. **EMAIL** fmalino@wellesley.edu

MALINOWSKI, MICHAEL J.

DISCIPLINE LAW **EDUCATION** Tufts Univ, BA, 87; Yale Law School, JD, 91. **CAREER** Adj prof law, Univ Houston Law Ctr, 93; assoc, Kirkpatrick & Lockhart LLP, 93-97; mem, Special Comn Genetic Info Policy, Mass Leg, 95-97; mgr gov affairs & commun, Mass Biotech Counc, 97-98; counselm, Foley, Hoag & Eliot LLP, 98-00; assoc prof, Widener Univ, 00-. **HONORS AND AWARDS** Phi Beta Kappa **MEMBERSHIPS** Ethics Comn & Biomedical Working Group: Biotech Ind Org; Res fel: Eunice Shriver Ctr for Mental Retardation: Genome Radoio Proj. **RESEARCH** Bioethcis; Commercialization of Life Scis; Health law and policy. **SELECTED PUBLICATIONS** auth, "The First Circuit: District Courts May Decide What is 'Unusual' But Will They Take the Hint?" 6 Fed Sent R 279 (March/April 94); auth, "Coming into Being: Law, Ethics, and the Practice of Prenatal Genetic Screening," 45 Hastings L J 1435 (94); auth, "Bringing Human Genome-Related Biotechnology to Market: A Matter of Survival," The Health Lawyer: ABA Forum on Health Law vol 8, no 2 (Spring 95); coauth, "Square Pegs and Round Holes: Dowes the Sentencing of Corporate C itizens for Environmental Crimes Fit Within Guidelines?" 8 Fed Sent R 230 (Jan/Feb 96); coauth, "A False Start? The Impact of Federal Policy on the Genotechnology Industry," 13 Yale J Reg 163 (Winter 96); auth, "Capitation, Advances in Medical Technology, and the Advent of a New Era in Medial Ethics, 22 Am J Law & Med 335 (96); auth, "Globalization of Biotechnology and the Public Health Challenges Accompanying It, 60 Albany Law Rev 119 (Oct 96); coath, "Commercialization of Genetic Testing Services: The FDA, Market Forces, and Biological Tarot Cards," 71 Tulane Law Rev 1211 (97); co-found & co-ed, The Journal of BioLaw & Business, Aspen Law & Bus, Feb 97-July 98; auth, Biotechnology: Law, Business and Regulation, Aspen Law & Bus, 99. **CONTACT ADDRESS** Sch of Law, Widener Univ, Delaware, 4601 Concord Pike, PO Box 7474, Wilmington, DE 19803-0474. **EMAIL** Michael.J.Malinowski@law.widener.edu

MALKIEL, BURTON GORDON

PERSONAL Born 08/28/1932, Boston, MA, m, 1988, 1 child **DISCIPLINE** ECONOMICS **EDUCATION** Boston Latin Sch, 43-49; Harvard Col, BA 49-53; Harvard Grad Sch of Bus, MBA 53-55; Princeton Univ, PhD 60-64. **CAREER** Smith Barney & Co, assoc 58-60; Council Econ Adv, mem 75-77; Princeton Univ, asst prof 64-66, dir fin res 66-81, assoc prof 66-

68, prof 68-81, Gordon S Rentschler Memorial Prof 69-81, chair 74-75, chair 77-81; Yale School of Org Mgmt, dean 81-88; Princeton Univ, Chem Bank Chmn Prof 88. **HONORS AND AWARDS** H D Humane Letters; Phi Beta Kappa; Alumni Achv Awd. **MEMBERSHIPS** AFA; AEA. **RESEARCH** Financial markets. **SELECTED PUBLICATIONS** A Random Walk Down Wall Street, W W Norton & Co, NY, 73, rev, 75, 81, 85, 90, 93, 96, translated into several languages; Global Bargain Hunting: An Investors Guide to Profits in Emerging Markets, with J P Mei, Simon & Schuster, NY 98; The Inflation Beaters Guide, W W Norton & Co, NY 80, rev paperback ed, Winning Investment Strategies, 82; numerous pub articles. **CONTACT ADDRESS** Dept Economics, Princeton Univ, Princeton, NJ 08544.

MALLARD, WILLIAM
PERSONAL Born 05/28/1927, New York, NY, m, 1961, 3 children **DISCIPLINE** RELIGION; CHURCH HISTORY **EDUCATION** Randolph-Macon, BA, 49; Duke Div School, Duke Univ, BD, 52; Duke Grad School, Duke Univ, PhD, 56. **CAREER** Instr Relig, Sweet Briar Col, 55-57; asst to full prof church hist, Candler School Theol, Emory Univ, 57- . **HONORS AND AWARDS** Dempster Grad fel, 54-55; Am Asn Theol Schools Fel, 62-63; Cross Disciplinary Fel Soc Relig, 69-70; Emory Wms Distinguished Teaching Awd, Emory Univ, 81; Thomas Jefferson Awd for Service, Emory Univ, 89; Chandler School Theol Serv Awd, 97 & 98. **RESEARCH** St. Augustine of Hippo, Theology and literary criticism. **SELECTED PUBLICATIONS** Auth, The Reflection of Theology in Literature, Trinity Univ Press, 77; auth, "The Incarnation in Augustine's Conversion," Recherches Augustiniennes XV, Paris, (80); auth, Language and Love: Introducing Augustine's Religious Thought through the Confessions Story, Penn State, 94; auth, "Jesus Christ," St Augustine through the Ages: an Encyclopedia, Erdman, (99). **CONTACT ADDRESS** School Theol, Emory Univ, 1364 Clifton Rd NE, Atlanta, GA 30322-1061. **EMAIL** wmallar@emory.edu

MALLER, MARK
PERSONAL Born 10/19/1947, Chicago, IL **DISCIPLINE** PHILOSOPHY **EDUCATION** Southern Ill Univ, BA, 70; Univ of Pittsburgh, MLS, 76; Dequesne Univ, MA, 73; PhD, 96. **CAREER** Instr, W.R. Harper Col, 92-97; instr, Col of DuPage, 96-; instr, Columbia Col, 99-. **MEMBERSHIPS** Am Philos Asn. **RESEARCH** Ethics, metaphysics, Sartre. **CONTACT ADDRESS** Center Independent Learning, Col of DuPage, 425 22nd St, Glen Ellyn, IL 60137-6784. **EMAIL** marlopal@yahoo.com

MALLOY, EDWARD A.
PERSONAL Born 05/03/1941, Washington, DC **DISCIPLINE** CHRISTIAN ETHICS, THEOLOGY **EDUCATION** Univ Notre Dame, BA, 63, MA, 67, MTh, 69; Vanderbilt Univ, PhD, 75. **CAREER** From Instr to Assoc Prof, 74-81, Prof Theol, Univ Notre Dame, 81, Dir Mdiv Prog, 77, Assoc Provost, 82-87, Pres, Univ Notre Dame, 87. **MEMBERSHIPS** Am Soc Christian Ethics; Cath Theol Soc Am. **SELECTED PUBLICATIONS** Auth, Natural law theory and Catholic moral theology, 75 & Typological analysis in Christian ethics, 75, Am Ecclesiastical Rev; The ethics of responsibility--a comparison of the moral methodology of H Richard Niebuhr and Charles Curran, Iliff Rev, 77; Robert Johann--an ontological basis for an ethics of responsibility, Horizons, 77; Ethical issues in the zoning controversy, Chicago Studies, 77; The problem of methodology in contemporary Roman Catholic ethics, St Luke's J Theol, 78; Homosexuality and the Christian Way of Life, Univ Press Am, 81. **CONTACT ADDRESS** Office of the President, Univ of Notre Dame, Notre Dame, IN 46556. **EMAIL** edward.a.malloy.5@nd.edu

MALM, HEIDI
DISCIPLINE PHILOSOPHY **EDUCATION** Univ Calif, Santa Barbara, BA; Univ Ariz, PhD. **CAREER** Assoc prof; fac, Univ Nebr-Lincoln & Univ Nebr Med Sch; 6 yrs dir undergrad Stud, Philos; 5 yrs vice-chp, Acad Coun; ed bd, Public Affairs Quart & Exec Comt, Am-Int Soc for Philos and Law. **RESEARCH** Ethical theory, medical ethics, philosophy of law. **SELECTED PUBLICATIONS** Publ in, Philos & Public Affairs, Ethics, Am Philos Quart, Philos Stud, Legal Theory and Public Affairs Quart, Law & Philosophy. **CONTACT ADDRESS** Dept of Philosophy, Loyola Univ, Chicago, 6525 N Sheridan Rd, Chicago, IL 60626. **EMAIL** hmalm2@home.com

MALONEY, ELLIOTT CHARLES
PERSONAL Born 04/17/1946, Pittsburgh, PA **DISCIPLINE** NEW TESTAMENT STUDIES, BIBLICAL LANGUAGES **EDUCATION** St Vincent Col, AB, 68; Pontifical Atheneum of St Anselm, Rome, STL, 72; Fordham Univ, PhD(New Testament), 79. **CAREER** Instr, 76-81, Assoc Prof New Testament Studies & Bibl Lang, 81-92; Professor New Testament Studies & Bibl Lang, 92-, St Vincent Sem, 76. **MEMBERSHIPS** Soc Bibl Lit; Cath Bibl Asn. **RESEARCH** Greek language of the New Testament; Gospel of Mark; Epistles of Paul. **SELECTED PUBLICATIONS** Auth, Semitic interference in Marcan Syntax, Soc Bibl Lit Dissertation Series, 81; transl, Epistles of James, 1-2 Peter, Jude, In: New American Bible, rev New Testament, 86. **CONTACT ADDRESS** Saint Vincent Col, 300 Fraser Purchase, Latrobe, PA 15650-2690. **EMAIL** emaloney@stvincent.edu

MALONEY, FRANCIS J.
PERSONAL Born 03/23/1940, Melbourne, Australia, s **DISCIPLINE** BIBLICAL STUDIES **EDUCATION** Univ Melbourne, BA, 60; Salesian Pontifical Univ, STL, 70; Pontifical Bibl Inst, SSL, 72; Univ Oxford, PhD, 75. **CAREER** Lectr to prof, Univ of Melbourne, 76-94; prof, Australian Cath Univ, 95-99; prof, Cath Univ of Am, 96-. **HONORS AND AWARDS** Fel, Australian Acad of the Humanities; Member, Order of Australia. **MEMBERSHIPS** Cath Bibl Assoc of Australia, Soc for the Study of the NT, Soc of Bibl Lit, Cath Bibl Assoc of Am. **RESEARCH** Historical Jesus, Gospels. **SELECTED PUBLICATIONS** Auth, Reading John. Introducing the Johannine Gospel and Letters, Harper-Collins (Melbourne), 95; auth, Signs and Shadows. Reading John 5-12, Fortress Pr, (Minneapolis), 96; auth, A Body Broken for a Broken People. Eucharist in the New Testament, Hendrickson, (Peabody), 97; auth, Glory not Dishonor. Reading John 13-21, Fortress Pr, 98; auth, The Gospel of John, Liturgical Pr, (Collegeville), 98; auth, From James to Jude, Bible Reading Commentary, 99; auth, "Salesians Beyond 2000," Jour of Salesian Studies 10, (99): 3018; auth, "The Fourth Gospel and the Jesus of History," New Testament Studies 46, (00): 42-58; auth, "The Scriptural Basis of Jubilee, Part I: The First Testament - the End of Servitude," Irish Theol Quart 64, (00): 99-110; auth, "Where Does One Look? Reflections on some recent Johannine scholarship," Salesianum 62 (00): 223-51. **CONTACT ADDRESS** Dept Bibl Studies, Catholic Univ of America, 620 Michigan Ave NE, Washington, DC 20064-0001. **EMAIL** maloney@cua.edu

MALONEY, J. CHRISTOPHER
PERSONAL Born 10/07/1949, Youngstown, OH **DISCIPLINE** PHILOSOPHY **EDUCATION** Cleveland State Univ, BA, 71; Ind Univ, Bloomington, MA, 75, PhD(philos), 78. **CAREER** Assoc instr philos, Ind Univ, Bloomington, 74-77, vis instr, 78; Asst Prof Philos, Oakland Univ, 78-. **HONORS AND AWARDS** Former fel, National Endowment for the Humanities. **MEMBERSHIPS** Am Philos Asn. **RESEARCH** Metaphysics; epistemology. **SELECTED PUBLICATIONS** Auth, The Mundane Matter of the Mental Language (Cambridge), 89; auth, "Connectionism and Conditioning," in Connectionism and the Philosophy of Mind (Kuwer, 91); auth, "Saving Psychological Solipism," Philosophical Studies (91); auth, "Content: Control, Contingency, and Covariation," Synthese (94); auth, "The Language of Thought," in A Companion to the Philosophy of Mind (Blackwell, 94). **CONTACT ADDRESS** Dept of Philos, Univ of Arizona, Tuscon, AZ 85721-0027. **EMAIL** maloney@u.arizona.edu

MALONEY, MAUREEN A.
DISCIPLINE LAW **EDUCATION** Warwick Univ, LLB, 77; Univ Toronto, LLM, 81. **CAREER** Asst prof, 81-93; prof, 93-; fac dean, , Univ of Victoria, 90-93. **MEMBERSHIPS** British Columbia Bar; Law Soc of England and Wales; Lawyers for Social Responsibility. **SELECTED PUBLICATIONS** Auth, pubs on tax law, tax policy, women and the law, and aspects of the law on disadvantaged groups. **CONTACT ADDRESS** Fac of Law, Univ of Victoria, PO Box 2400, Victoria, BC, Canada V8W 3H7.

MALONEY, THOMAS
DISCIPLINE MEDIEVAL PHILOSOPHY AND THE PHILOSOPHY OF RELIGION **EDUCATION** Gregorian Univ, Rome, PhD. **CAREER** Dept Philos, Univ Louisville **RESEARCH** 13th-century logic, espec semantics. **SELECTED PUBLICATIONS** Publ(s), transl on of three treatises on universals by Roger Bacon along with an edition and annotated transl of Bacon's Compendium studii theologiae; transl, Bacon's Summulae dialectices. **CONTACT ADDRESS** Dept of Philos, Univ of Louisville, 2301 S 3rd St, Louisville, KY 40292. **EMAIL** tsmalo01@ulkyvm.louisville.edu

MAMARY, ANNE
PERSONAL Born 11/02/1964 **DISCIPLINE** PHILOSOPHY **EDUCATION** State Univ Nyork, Binghamton, PhD. **CAREER** Vis Prof, Clarkson Univ. **MEMBERSHIPS** SAGP; SWIP; APA. **RESEARCH** Feminist philosophy; post colonial studies; multi cultural studies; ancient Greek philosophy. **SELECTED PUBLICATIONS** Auth, Not the Same Difference: a Review Essay of Luce Irigaray's Thinking the Difference, Int Studies Philo; Mint, Tomatoes and the Grapevine; co-ed, Cultural Activisms: Poetic Voices, Political Voices, SUNY, 99; auth, "Katharsis and Pharmakon," in Methexio; auth, "Live and Learn," in Feminist Studies. **CONTACT ADDRESS** Center for Liberal Studies, Clarkson Univ, Box 2000, Pobdam, NY 13676. **EMAIL** mamary@snycorva.cortland.edu

MAMO, NATHAN
PERSONAL Born 12/06/1952, Pasadena, CA **DISCIPLINE** NEW TESTAMENT STUDIES **EDUCATION** Jesuit Sch Theol, Berkeley, STL, 94. **CAREER** Pastor, 98-, St John the Apostle Cath Parish HI; rect, 94-98, Cathedral Our Lady Of Peace HI; Pastor, 78-91, St John V Parish HI. **MEMBERSHIPS** CBA; SBL. **RESEARCH** St Paul; Corinthian Correspondence. **CONTACT ADDRESS** 95-370 Kuahelani Ave, Mililani, HI 96789-1103.

MANDELKER, DANIEL ROBERT
PERSONAL Born 07/18/1926, Milwaukee, WI, d, 2 children **DISCIPLINE** LAW **EDUCATION** Univ Wis, BA, 47, LLB, 49; Yale Univ, JSD, 56. **CAREER** Asst prof law, Drake Univ, 49-51; atty & adv, Housing & Home Finance Agency, Washington, DC, 52-53; from asst prof to assoc prof law, Ind Univ, 53-62; from assoc prof to prof, 62-75, Stamper Prof Law, Washington Univ, 74-; Ford Found law fac fel, London, England, 59-60; mem comn soc & behav urban res, Nat Acad Sci, 68; consult housing, bldg, planning, UN Centre, 72-73; consult, Hawaii Dept Planning & Econ Develop, 72-; mem, Am Bar Asn Adv Comn Housing & Urban Growth, 75-77. **HONORS AND AWARDS** Phi Kappa Phi; Phi Beta Kappa; Order of the Coif; Sr Fel, Urban Land Inst, 89-95; Vis Fel, Fac of Laws, Univ Col, London, 89; Vis Fel, Univ of Copenhagen, Denmark, 89; John C. Vance Award, Most Outstanding Paper on Transportation Law Submitted to Transportation Res Board, 88; Vis Scholar, Dept of Urban Planning, Technion, Haifa, Israel, 83; Vis Scholar, Inst of State and Law, Moscow, Russia, 78; Urban Sem Fac, Salzburg Sem in Am Studies, 77; Brookings Inst Urban Program Fac, 65-73; Res Fel, Urban Land Inst, 76-89. **MEMBERSHIPS** Nat Center for the Revitalization of Central Cities; APA; Development Regulations Coun, Urban Land Inst; Comm on Environmental Law, Int Union for the Conservation of Nature. **SELECTED PUBLICATIONS** Auth, Environment and Equity: A Regulatory Challenge, 81; auth, Federal Land Use Law, 86 & Supp. 97; auth, Street Graphics and the Law, 88; auth, Housing and Community Development: Cases and Materials, 89; auth, Environmental Protection: Law and Policy, 90; auth, NEPA Law and Litigation, 92 & Supp. 97; auth, Planning and Control of Land Development, 95; auth, State and Local Government in a Federal System, 96; auth, Property Law and the Public Interest, 98. **CONTACT ADDRESS** School of Law, Washington Univ, Campus Box 1120, Saint Louis, MO 63130. **EMAIL** mandelker@wwlaw.wustl.edu

MANDLE, JONATHAN
DISCIPLINE PHILOSOPHY **EDUCATION** Univ Pitt, PhD. **CAREER** Asst prof, Univ Pitt. **RESEARCH** Ethics and political theory and their history. **CONTACT ADDRESS** Dept of Philosophy, SUNY, Albany, Albany, NY 12222. **EMAIL** mandle@cnsunix.albany.edu

MANDT, ALMER J., III
PERSONAL Born 01/29/1950, Urbana, IL **DISCIPLINE** PHILOSOPHY **EDUCATION** Trinity Col , BA, 72; Vanderbilt Univ, MA; PhD, 78. **CAREER** Coordr of Gen Edu, Wichita State Univ, 85-88; asst and assoc prof, 76-; dir of honors program, Wichita State Univ, 95-. **HONORS AND AWARDS** Phi Beta kappa, 71; Machette Found Dissertation Fel, 75-76; Council Awd for Distinguish Merit, Souther Soc for Philos nad Psychol; 81; Faculty Leadership Awd, Wichita State Univ, 92. **MEMBERSHIPS** Am Philos Asn; Metaphysics Soc of Am; Soc for the Advancement of Am Philos; Am Asn of Univ Profs. **RESEARCH** Philosophy of Culture; History of Philosophy; 19th Century Philosophy; Political Philosophy. **SELECTED PUBLICATIONS** Auth, The Inconceivability of Kant's Transcendental Subject, Int Philos Quart, 83; Mill's Two View On Belief, Philos, 84; The Inevitability of Pluralism: Philosophical Practice and Philosophical Excellence, Institution of Philosophy: A Discipline in Crisis?, 89; Religious Liberty, School Prayer, and the Constitution, Soundings, 89; Fichte, Kant's Legacy, and the Meaning of Modern Philosophy, Rev of Metaphysics, 97; ed, Fichte and Contemporary Philosophy, Philos Forum, 87-88. **CONTACT ADDRESS** Dept of Philosophy, Wichita State Univ, Wichita, KS 67260-0074. **EMAIL** mandt@twsuvm.uc.twsu.edu

MANESS, LONNIE E.
PERSONAL Born 07/30/1929, Henderson Co, TN, m, 1951, 2 children **DISCIPLINE** HISTORY, GOVERNMENT **EDUCATION** Univ Wis, BS, 61; Univ Wis, MS, 64; Memphis State Univ, PhD, 80. **CAREER** From Asst Prof to Prof, Univ Tenn, 68-. **HONORS AND AWARDS** Phi Kappa Phi, Phi Alpha Theta, Outstanding Teacher Awd, Univ Tenn, 84. **MEMBERSHIPS** THS, WTHS, Jackson Purchase Hist Soc, Southeastern Coun on Latin Am Studies. **RESEARCH** Nathan Bedford Forrest, Henry Emerson Etheridge. **SELECTED PUBLICATIONS** Auth, "Jefferson Davis as War Leader: The case of Fort Donelson Through the Kentucky Invasion of 1862," in The W Tenn Hist Soc Papers, vol XLIX (95); auth, "The Most Important Campaign of the American Revolution," in the Colonel Courier, vol XLII, no 3 (97); auth, "Congressman Henry Emerson Etheridge on the Slavery Question and the Kansas-Nebraska Act," in The W Tenn Hist Soc Papers (98); auth, "Alexander P Stewart," in Tenn Encycl of Hist and Cult (98); auth, "Henry Emerson Etheridge," in Tenn Encycl of Hist and Cult (98); rev, "Secessionists and Other Scoundrels: Selections from Parson Brownlow's Book," in NC Hist Rev (99); auth, "Nathan Bedford Forrest: Controversial Aspects of His Career," in J of the Jackson Purchase Hist Soc (99). **CONTACT ADDRESS** Dept Hist & Govt, Univ of Tennessee, Martin, 554 University St, Martin, TN 38238-0001. **EMAIL** lmaness@utm.edu

MANFRA, JO ANN
PERSONAL Born Schenectady, NY, m, 1980 **DISCIPLINE** AMERICAN HISTORY, LAW **EDUCATION** State Univ

NYork at Cortland, BS, 63, MS, 67; Univ Iowa, PhD(hist), 75; Suffolk Univ Law Sch, JD, 77; Harvard Law Sch, LLM, 79. **CAREER** Teacher hist, Kingston High Sch, 64-66; instr Am hist, Ball State Univ, 66-67; asst prof, 72-75; Assoc Prof, 76-82; Full Prof Am Hist; Worcester Polytechnk Inst., 83-; Res fel, Nat Endowment for Humanities, summer 76, Mary Ingraham Bunting Inst, 77-79. **HONORS AND AWARDS** NAT Endowment for humanities Interpretive Research/Projects Grant, 88-90; Brinkley-Stephenson Awd, OAH, 86. **MEMBERSHIPS** Am Soc Legal Hist; Orgn Early Am Historians; Orgn Am Historians; Am Cath Studies Asn. **RESEARCH** American religious history; American social history; American legal history. **SELECTED PUBLICATIONS** Coed, "Law and Bioethics: Text with Commentary on Major U.S. Court Decisions," New York: Paulist Press, 82; auth, "The Politics of Ultimate Ends," in An American Church," ed. David J. Alvarez Moraga, California: St. Mary's College Press, 79, pp. 43-52; auth, "Serial Marriage and the Origins of the Black Stepfamily: The Rowanty Evidence, " Journal of American History, 72, June 85: 18-44; auth, "An Emendation on the Church-State Problematic: The French Connection, in The Lively Experiment Continued," ed. Jerald C. Brauer, Macon, Georgia: Mercer University Press, 87, pp. 185-202; auth, "The Selection of the American Catholic Hierarchy, 1789-1851," Mid-America, 76, Winter 94: 27-52; auth, "Hometown Politics and the American Protective Association, 1887-1890," Annals of Iowa 55, Spring 96: 138-66. **CONTACT ADDRESS** Worcester Polytech Inst, 39 Waterford Dr, Worcester, MA 01602. **EMAIL** jmanfra@wpi.edu

MANGRUM, FRANKLIN M.

PERSONAL Born 06/01/1925, Mayfield, KY, m, 1945 **DISCIPLINE** PHILOSOPHY **EDUCATION** Washington Univ, AB, 49; Univ Chicago, PhD, 57. **CAREER** Teacher philos & humanities, Shimer Col, 56-59; distinguished fac award, ATMSU 68-69, prof, Morehead State Univ, 95, Head Dept, 66-84, prof philos emer, 95-, Fac mem bd regents, 68-71. **MEMBERSHIPS** Metaphys Soc Am; NEA; Western Div Am Philos Asn. **RESEARCH** Epistemology; metaphysics. **CONTACT ADDRESS** Dept of Philosophy, Morehead State Univ, 150 University Blvd, Morehead, KY 40351-1684.

MANGRUM, R. COLLIN

DISCIPLINE LAW **EDUCATION** Harvard Univ, BA, 72; Univ Utah, JD, 74; Oxford Univ, Bachelor of Civil Laws, 78; Harvard Univ, Doctor of Judicial Sci, 83. **CAREER** Pvt prac, Salt Lake City, 75-77; assoc ed, Utah Law Rev; Rotary Int Found fel, 77 and 78; vis scholar, Univ Edinburgh, 86, prof Creighton Univ, 79-; Yossem Prof of Jurisprudence, 99. **HONORS AND AWARDS** National Alpha Sigma Nu Bk awd, 89. **SELECTED PUBLICATIONS** Auth, Zion in the Courts: A Legal History of The Church of Jesus Christ of Latter-Day Saints 1830-1900, Univ Ill Press, 88; publ in, Creighton Law Rev; Duke Law J; Utah Law Rev; BYU Stud; Morman Hist J. **CONTACT ADDRESS** Sch of Law, Creighton Univ, 2500 California Plaza , Omaha, NE 68178. **EMAIL** mangrum@culaw.Creighton.edu

MANIATES, MARIA RIKA

PERSONAL Born 03/30/1937, Toronto, ON, Canada **DISCIPLINE** MUSICOLOGY, PHILOSOPHY **EDUCATION** Univ Toronto, BA, 60; Columbia Univ, MA, 62, PhD(musicol), 65. **CAREER** From lectr to assoc prof, 65-74, chmn dept, 73-78, PROF MUSICOL, UNIV TORONTO, 74-, Am Coun Learned Socs grant-in-aid musicol, 66-67; vis prof music, Columbia Univ, 67 and 76; appln appraiser musicol, Can Coun, 69-, res fel, 70-72; Einstein Award Comt, Am Musicol Soc, 76-79; Can Coun travel grants, 73, 75, 77, 78, 79, and 80; Univ Toronto humanities res grants, 78-79 and 79-80. **MEMBERSHIPS** Int Musicol Soc; Am Musicol Soc; Renaissance Soc Am; Can Renaissance Soc; Int Soc Hist Rhetoric. **RESEARCH** Renaissance music and culture; mannerism; philosophy and aesthetics. **SELECTED PUBLICATIONS** Auth, Musica Scientia--Musical Scholarship in the Italian Renaissance, Notes, Vol 0050, 93; The Politicized Muse--Music for Medici Festivals, 1512-1537, Renaissance and Reformation, Vol 0018, 94; Music in Renaissance Magic--Toward a Historiography of Others, J Amer Musicol Soc, Vol 0048, 95; **CONTACT ADDRESS** Fac of Music, Univ of Toronto, Toronto, ON, Canada M5S 1A1.

MANIER, A. EDWARD

DISCIPLINE PHILOSOPHY OF SCIENCE **EDUCATION** Univ Notre Dame, BS, 53; St Louis Univ, AM, 56, PhD, 61. **CAREER** Prof. **RESEARCH** History and philosophy of biology; neuromedical sciences. **SELECTED PUBLICATIONS** Auth, The Young Darwin and His Cultural Circle, 78; Reductionist Rhetoric: Expository Strategies and the Development of the Molecular Neurobiology of Behavior, 89; Walker Percy: Language, Neuropsychology and Moral Tradition, 91. **CONTACT ADDRESS** History and Philosophy of Science Dept, Univ of Notre Dame, Notre Dame, IN 46556. **EMAIL** A.E.Manier.1@nd.edu

MANIKAS, WILLIAM T.

PERSONAL Born 09/24/1938, Herkimer, NY, m, 1991, 2 children **DISCIPLINE** US HISTORY, POLITICAL SCIENCE **EDUCATION** Boston Univ, BA, 63; Colgate Univ, MA, 64; Fla Atlantic Univ, EdS, 70; EdD, 74. **CAREER** Instr, Marymount Jr Col, 68-74; instr, Gaston Col, 74-. **HONORS AND AWARDS** Liberal Arts and Sci Instr of the Year, 91; Fulbright Scholar, China, 95. **MEMBERSHIPS** Blue and Gray Educ Soc; NEA; NC Assoc of Educ. **RESEARCH** Life in textile mill villages in the early 20th century. **SELECTED PUBLICATIONS** Auth, "Isolationism", Ready Ref: Ethics, Salem Pr, 93; auth, "Joyce Diane Brothers", Great Lives from History: Am Women, Salem Pr, 94; auth, "Brown v Board of Education, 1954", Latino Encycl, Salem Pr, 94; auth, "Everson v Board of Education", Ready Ref: Am Justice, Salem Pr, 95; auth, "Jewish Women", Ready Ref: Women's Issues, Salem Pr, 95; auth, "Lobbying and Lobbyists", Encycl of Contemp Soc Issues, Salem Pr, 95; auth, "Raleigh's Attempts at Colonization in the New World, 1584-1591", Great Events from Hist: N Am, Salem Pr, 95; auth, "Swann v Charlotte-Mecklenburg Board of Educ, 1971", Encycl of Mod Soc Issues, Salem Pr, 95; auth, "Nullification Controversy, 1832-1833", Great Events from Hist: N Am, Salem Pr, 95; auth, "Garibaldi's Thousand Read Shirts Land in Italy, 1860-1865", Great Events from Hist: Europ Series, Salem Pr, 96. **CONTACT ADDRESS** Dept Soc Sci, Gaston Col, 201 Highway 321 S, Dallas, NC 28034-1402. **EMAIL** manikas.bill@gaston.cc.nc.us

MANN, GURINDER SINGH

DISCIPLINE RELIGION **EDUCATION** Columbia Univ, PhD, 93. **CAREER** Assoc prof. **SELECTED PUBLICATIONS** Auth, Studying the Sikhs: Issues for North America, SUNY, 93; The Goindval Pothis, Harvard, 96. **CONTACT ADDRESS** Dept of Religion, Columbia Col, New York, 2960 Broadway, New York, NY 10027-6902.

MANN, WILLIAM EDWARD

PERSONAL Born 05/06/1940, Los Angeles, CA, m, 1966, 2 children **DISCIPLINE** HISTORY OF PHILOSOPHY, PHILOSOPHY OF RELIGION **EDUCATION** Stanford Univ, BA, 62; MA, 64; Univ Minn, Minneapolis, PhD(Philos), 71. **CAREER** From instr to asst prof Philos, St Olaf Col, 67-72; asst prof, Ill State Univ, 72-74; assoc prof, 74-80, prof Philos, Univ VT, 80-; chmn dept, 80-91. **HONORS AND AWARDS** 1971 Dissertation Essay Competition, The Rev of Metaphys, 72. **MEMBERSHIPS** Am Philos Asn, div sec-treas, 94-; Soc Medieval Renaissance Philos. **RESEARCH** Philosophical theology; medieval philosophy, ancient philosophy. **SELECTED PUBLICATIONS** Auth, "The Best of All Possible Worlds," in Being and Goodness: The Concept of the Good in Metaphysics and Philosophical Theology, ed. Scott MacDonald (Ithaca, NY, Cornell Univ Press, 91), 250-277; auth, "Jephthah's Plight: Moral Dilemmas and Theism," Philosophical Perspectives 5 (91): 617-647; auth, "Duns Scotus, Demonstration, and Doctrine," Faith and Philosophy 9 (92): 436-462; auth, "Hope," in Reasoned Faith: Essays in Philosophical Theology in Honor of Norman Kretzmann, ed. Eleonore Stump (Ithaca, NY, Cornell University Press, 93), 251-280; auth, "Piety: Lending a Hand to Euthyphro," Philosophy and Phenomenological Research 58 (98): 123-142; auth, "Perplexity and Mystery," Metaphilosophy 29 (98): 209-222; auth, "Inner-Life Ethics," in The Augustinian Tradition, ed. Gareth B. Matthews (Berkeley, Univ of Calif Press, 99), 140-165; auth, "Believing Where We Cannot Prove: Duns Scotus on the Necessity of Supernatural Belief," in The Proceedings of the Twentieth World Congress of Philosophy: Volume 4: Philosophies of Religion, Art, and Creativity, ed. Kevin L. Stoehr (Bowling Green State Univ, Philosphy Documentation Center, 99), 58-68; auth, "Augustine on Evil and Original Sin," in The Cambridge Companion to Augustine, ed. Norman Kretzmann and Eleonore Stump (Cambridge, Cambridge Univ Press, forthcoming); auth, "Duns Scotus on Natural and Supernatural Knowledge of God," in The Cambridge Companion to Duns Scotus (Cambridge, Cambridge Univ Press, forthcoming). **CONTACT ADDRESS** Dept of Philosophy, Univ of Vermont, 70 S Williams St, Burlington, VT 05401-3404. **EMAIL** wmann@zoo.uvm.edu

MANNING, BLANCHE MARIE

PERSONAL Born 12/12/1934, Chicago, IL, m, 1957 **DISCIPLINE** LAW **EDUCATION** Chicago Tchrs Coll, BE 1961; John Marshall Law Sch Chicago, JD 1967; Roosevelt Univ Chicago, MA 1972; Univ of VA, Charlottesville, VA, LLM, 1992. **CAREER** Chicago Bd of Educ, teacher 1961-68; Cook Co State's Attys Office, asst states atty 1968-73; Equal Employment Oppor Commn, supervisory trial atty 1973-77; United Airlines, gen atty 1977-78; US Attys Office, asst US atty 1978-79; Circuit Ct of Cook Co, assoc judge 1979-86; 1st Municipal Dist Circuit Ct of Cook Co, supervising judge 1984-86, supervising circuit judge 1986-87; Justice of the Illinois Appellate Court, 1st District 1987-94; judge US District Court, ND IL, 94-; Harvard Law School, Univ of Chicago Law School, Trial Advocacy Workshops, teaching team member, 91-; De Paul University Col of Law, adjunct professor, 92-; Dept of Justice, Atty Gen Adv Inst, adj faculty mem, 79. **HONORS AND AWARDS** Edith Sampson Meml Awd 1985; Awd of Appreciation The Intl Assoc of Pupil Personnel Workers 1985; IL Judicial Council; Kenneth E Wilson Judge of the Year Awd Cook County Bar Assn; Disting Alumna Awd Chicago State Univ 1986; Awd of Excellence in Judicial Admin Women's Bar Assn 1986; Black Rose Awd, League of Black Women 1987; Thurgood Marshall Awd, IIT Kent Law School BALSA 1988; Professional Achievement Awd, Roosevelt Univ 1988; We Care Role Model Awd, Chicago Police Department 1987-94; Distinguished Service Awd, John Marshall Law School, 1989; We Care Outstanding Role Model Awd, Chicago Public Schools & Chicago Police Dept, 1992-99; National Black Prosecutors Association, Distinguished Service Awd, 1991; The Guardians Police Organization, Citizen's Awd, 1991; Fel, ABA Found, 91; Honorary Doctor of Humane Letters Degree, Chicago State Univ, 1998. **MEMBERSHIPS** Mem Natl Assn of Women Judges; Cook County Bar Association; Il Judicial Council; lecturer IL Judicial Conf New Judges Seminar, Professional Devel Prog for New Assoc Judges, IL Judicial Conf Assoc Judges Sem 1982-86; New Judges Seminar, faculty; Chicago Bar Assn Symphony Orchestra; Chicago State Univ Community Concert Band, and Jazz Band. **SELECTED PUBLICATIONS** Auth, Legal Malpractice: Is it Tort or Contract?, Univ Chicago, L.J. 741, 90. **CONTACT ADDRESS** United States District Court, 219 S Dearborn St, Ste 2156, Chicago, IL 60604.

MANNING, CHRISTEL

PERSONAL Born 11/11/1961, Long Beach, CA, m **DISCIPLINE** SOCIOLOGY OF RELIGION **EDUCATION** Tufts Univ, BA, economics (Magna cum laude), 84; Univ CA, Santa Barbara, MA, relig studies, 91, PhD, relig studies, 95. **CAREER** Teacher, Social Studies, Noble and Greenough School, 86-89; lect, Elderhostel, Santa Barbara, 94; instr, dept of philos and relig, Hollins Col, 94-95; Asst Prof, Dept of Philos and Religious Studies, Sacred Heart Univ, 95-. **HONORS AND AWARDS** Omnicron Delta Epsilon (Int Honor Soc in Economics), 84; Phi Beta Kappa, 84; Distinguished Scholars fel, 89-90; CA State grad fel, 91-92, 92-93; nominated for UCSB Outstanding Teaching Asst Awd, 94; Thomas O'Day Awd for the Study of Religion and Soc, 94; Soc for the Scientific Study of Religion, Res Awd, 94. **MEMBERSHIPS** Am Academy Relig; Asn for Soc of Relig; Soc for the Scientific Study of Relig, Nat prog chair, 97; Governing Coun of SSSR, 99. **RESEARCH** Gender and religion; fundamentalism; new religions. **SELECTED PUBLICATIONS** Auth, Review of Margaret Lamberts Bendroth, Fundamentalism and Gender, J for the Scientific Study of Religion 33.3, 94; Cultural Conflicts and Identity: Second Generation Hispanic Catholics in the United States, with Wade Clark Roof, Social Compass, 94; Embracing Jesus and the Goddess: Towards a Reconceptualizing of Conversion to Syncretistic Religion, in Magical Religion and Modern Witchcraft, ed by James Lewis, State Univ NY Press, 95; Review of Miriam Therese Winter, Defecting in Place: Women Claiming Responsibility for Their Own Spiritual Lives, J for the Scientific Study of Relig, 96; Women in a Divided Church: Liberal and Conservative Catholic Women Negotiate Changing Gender Roles, Sociology of Relig, 97; Review of Martin Marty & Scott Appleby, Fundamentalisms Comprehended, Review of Relig Res, 97; Women in New Religious Movements, in Encyclopedia of Women and World Religions, ed by Serinity Young, Macmillan, forthcoming, 98; Return to Mother Nature: The Politics of Paganism in America and Western Europe, in The Encyclopedia of Politics and Religion, ed by Robert Wuthnow, Congressional Quart Books, forthcoming, 98; God Gave Us the Right: Conservative Catholic, Evangelical Protestant, and Orthodox Jewish Women Grappel with Feminism, Rutgers Univ Press, 99; Conversations Among Women: Gender as a Bridge between Religious and Ideological Cultures, in Reflexive Ethnography: Remembering for Whom We Speak, ed by Lewis Carter, JAI Press, forthcoming, 99; auth, Sex & Religion, forthcoming, 02. **CONTACT ADDRESS** Dept Philos & Relig Studies, Sacred Heart Univ, 5151 Park Ave., Fairfield, CT 06432. **EMAIL** manningc@sacredheart.edu

MANNING, ELLIOTT

PERSONAL Born 06/07/1935, Atlanta, GA, m, 1959, 3 children **DISCIPLINE** LAW **EDUCATION** Columbia Col, AB, 55; Harvard Law Sch, JD, 58. **CAREER** Associate to Partner, Cleary, Gottlieb, Steen & Hamilton, 58-80; prof, Univ of Miami, 80. **MEMBERSHIPS** Am Law Inst; Am Col Tax Counsel; NY County Lawyers Assoc; Assoc of the Bar of NY. **RESEARCH** Tax Law, Corporate and Business Law. **SELECTED PUBLICATIONS** Auth, "Corporate Buy-Sell Agreements", CCH Tax Transactions Libr, 90; auth, coauth, "Family Deferred Payment Sales: Installment Sales, SCINs, Private Annuities Sales, OID and Other Enigmas", 26 Philip E Heckerling Inst on Est Plan, (91); coauth, "Intrafamily Sales and OID Safe Harbor: Transfer Tax Anomalies", 17 Tax Mgmt Est Gifts and Tr J 131, (92); coauth, "Partnership Capital Interest for Services: What, How Much and When", 10 Tax Mgmt Real Est J, (94); coauth, "The 1996 Marginal Federal Income Tax Rates: The Image and the Reality", 73 Tax Notes 1585, (96); coauth, "Deferred Payment Sales to Grantor Trusts, GRATs and Net Gifts: Income and Transfer Tax Elements", 24 Tax Mgmt Est Gifts and Tr J, (99); coauth, "Partnerships, Formation", TM Port 711, (forthcoming). **CONTACT ADDRESS** Sch of Law, Univ of Miami, PO Box 248087, Miami, FL 33124-8087. **EMAIL** emanning@law.miami.edu

MANNS, JAMES WILLIAM

PERSONAL Born 10/16/1944, South Weymouth, MA, m, 1967 **DISCIPLINE** PHILOSOPHY **EDUCATION** Lafayette Col, BA, 66; Boston Univ, MA, 70, PhD(philos), 72. **CAREER** Instr philos, Boston Univ, 70-71; asst prof, 71-76, Assoc Prof Philos, Univ KY, 76-. **MEMBERSHIPS** Am Philos Asn; Am Soc Aesthet. **RESEARCH** Aesthetics; epistemology. **SELECTED PUBLICATIONS** Auth, Reid and His French Disciples, Brill, 94; auth, Aesthetics, M.E. Sharpe, 98. **CONTACT ADDRESS** Dept of Philos, Univ of Kentucky, 1415 Patterson Off Tower, Lexington, KY 40506-0027. **EMAIL** manns@atspop.uky.edu

MANSFIELD, MECKLIN ROBERT
PERSONAL Born 08/11/1938, Crenshaw, MS, m, 1960, 3 children **DISCIPLINE** RELIGION, NEW TESTAMENT **EDUCATION** Rhodes College, BA, 60; Duke Divinity Sch, M. Div, 63; Vanderbilt Univ, MA & PhD(Bibl Studies), 70. **CAREER** Instr Philos, Cumberland Col, 68-70; asst prof Relig & chaplain, Mt Union Col, 70-78; assoc prof, 78-80, prof New Testament, Oral Roberts Univ, 80-, minister, United Methodist Church, Tenn Conf, 65-91; OK conf, 91. **MEMBERSHIPS** Soc Bibl Lit. **RESEARCH** New Testament Gospel studies; Mark; Johannine studies. **SELECTED PUBLICATIONS** Auth, Wind and Flame: Living Faith Series, United Methodist Publ House, 78; Gospel of John: Persons who Encountered Jesus, 80 & The Person and Work of Jesus, In: Adult Bible Studies, 82, United Methodist Publ House; Spirit and Gospel in Mark, Hendrickson, 87. **CONTACT ADDRESS** Dept Relig & Philosophy, Oral Roberts Univ, 7777 S Lewis, Tulsa, OK 74171-0001. **EMAIL** rmansfield@oru.edu

MANSUETO, ANTHONY
PERSONAL Born 08/07/1958, New York, NY, m, 1991 **DISCIPLINE** PHILOSOPHY **EDUCATION** Univ Chicago, BA, 77; Yale Univ, MA, 79; Grad Theol Union, PhD, 85. **CAREER** Res Asst, Univ Ill, 79-80; Tutor, Univ Calif, 82-84; Coordinator to lecturer and Adj Fac Member, Grad Theol Union, 83-88; Adj Asst Prof, Univ Dallas, 88-91; Res Assoc, Univ Ill, 93-94; Director, Calumet Col, 95-96; Prof, Centro de Estudios Regionales Universidad autonoma de Juarez, 96-97; President and Res Director, Inst for Philos, 91-. **HONORS AND AWARDS** Emiliano Zapata Awd, Mex am Democrats, 90. **MEMBERSHIPS** Inst for Strategic Studies and soc Progress, Acad of Humanistic Studies. **SELECTED PUBLICATIONS** Auth, Towards Synergism: The cosmic significance of the Human civilizational Project, Univ Press of Am, 95; auth, "The Catholic Right in the New South: Opus Dei in the Diocese of Dallas," in The Radical Right in the New south, Univ Ark Press, forthcoming; auth, "Organization in the Universe," in The Evolution of complexity, Kluwer Academic, 99; auth, "From Hermeneutical Circle to Dialectical spiral: Philosophy and Ideological Criticism," culture and Power, (99): 25-33; auth, "Organization, Teleology, and Value," Journal of Religion, (97): 68-86; auth, "From dialectic to Organization: Bogdanov's Contribution to Social Theory," Studies in East European Thought, (96): 37-61; auth, "Beyond Postmodernism: The contributions of anthropic cosmology and complex systems Theory to the social Sciences," Filosofskie nauki, (94): 45-73; auth, "The Current situation in the European countries of the former soviet Blo9c," in Russian and the West: a dialogue of Cultures, Tver Stat Univ, 94; auth, "religion, solidarity and Class Struggle: Marx, Durkheim, and Gramsci on the religious Question," social Compass, (88): 261-277. **CONTACT ADDRESS** Inst for Philos & Soc Progress, 5521 Greenville Ave, Dallas, TX 75206. **EMAIL** dialectic@britannica.com

MANZIG, JOHN G. W.
DISCIPLINE LAW **EDUCATION** Dalhousie, LLB, LLM; Cologne, Lic Jur, Dr Iur. **CAREER** Prof emer, Univ of Windsor; Osgoode Hall, Barrister-at-Law & Bar NS; dir, Can Inst of Env Law and Policy. **SELECTED PUBLICATIONS** Assoc ed, Env Law Reports. **CONTACT ADDRESS** Col of Business Administration, Education and Law, Univ of Windsor, 401 Sunset Ave, Windsor, ON, Canada N9B 3P4. **EMAIL** jmanzig@uwindsor.ca

MARANGOS, FRANK
PERSONAL Born 04/12/1954, Lowell, MA, m, 1977, 1 child **DISCIPLINE** RELIGION **EDUCATION** Hellenic Col, BA, 76; Holy Cross Sch Theol, MDiv, 79; Southern Methodist Univ, DMin, 86; Nova Southeastern Univ, EdD; Holy Cross Greek Orthodox School of Theology, MA, 99-. **CAREER** Asst Priest, Annunciation Cathedral, Huston, Tex, 79-83; Diocese of Denver Youth Dir, 81-83; Parish Priest, Annunciation Church, Pensacola, Fla, 83-89; Dioceseof Atlanta Clergy Syndesmo, Sec, 85-92; Rel Ed Comm, Diocese of Atlanta Recording Sec, 85-87; Editor, Praxis: National Clergy Mag, 85-95; Writer, Column: Liturgical Year, Orthodox Observer, 86-89; Rel Ed Dir, Diocese of Atlanta, 87-97; Dir, Sch Orthodox Stud, Palm Beach Comm Col, 88-97; Editor, Manna: Rel Ed Mag, 88-95; Parish Priest, St. Mark, Boca Raton, Fla, 89-97; Adj prof Orthodox Stud, Pope Vincent DePaul Theol Sch, Boynton Beach, Fla, 95-97; Dir Rel Ed for the Greek Orthodox Archdiocese of Am, present; Exec Ed, 99-; Project Dir, 99-. **HONORS AND AWARDS** Pres, Stud Coun, Hellenic Col, 76; Cum Laude, Hellenic Col, 76; Who's Who in Amer Univ, 77; Boston Theol Inst Rep, 77-78; Cum Laude, Holy Cross Sch Theol, 79; Amer Bible soc awd, Holy Cross, 79; Who's Who-Clergy in Amer, 85; High Honors, Doc Diss, Perkins Theol Sch, SMU, 86; Cum Laude, Perkins Theol Sch, 86; Hon Mention, Scholars Paper Competition, NOVA, 96; Pres, grad stud coun, NOVA Southeastern Univ, 96; built holy sanctuary of st mark in boca raton, fl, 95-97. **RESEARCH** Distance Learning, Instructional Technologies, Constructivism. **SELECTED PUBLICATIONS** Auth, An Examination of the Orthodox Funeral Service, Master Divinity Thesis, 79; Christ Is Risen!..Now What?, New Calif (Natl Greek Newspaper), April 10, 80; Ape or Adam , Orthodox Observer, 82; What's So New About New Week?, Orthodox Observer, April 7, 82, 10; After He Says Goodbye, Orthodox Observer, June 2, 82, 2; The Youth Rush, Orthodox Observer, Oct 20, 82, 7; Christmas: A Holiday Heresy?, Orthodox Observer, Dec 15, 82, 9; Was Jesus born Again?, Orthodox Observer, Jan 12, 83, 5; Pascha: Passion or Passage?, Orthodox Observer, Feb 24, 82, 3; Pre-Lent: Reach Out and Touch Somebody, Orthodox Observer, March 9, 83, 2; What's Become of the Light?, Theosis Mag, April 84, and Orthodox Observer; Going Home for Christmas, Orthodox Observer, Dec 84; Pentecost Revisited, Theosis Mag, June 85; Heart to Heart: A Pentecost Reflection, Orthodox Observer; Unwrapping the Indescribable Gift, Orthodox Observer; The Epitaphios: Flower or Power, Orthodox Observer; Do Your Compete with God?, Orthodox Observer; Shared Christian Praxis and Religious Education, Greek Orthodox Theol Rev, 85; Liberation Theology and Christian education Theory, Greek Orthodox Theol Rev, Winter, 85; Rev of Freedom in Mission, emilio Castro, WCC Publ, Greek Orthodox Theol Rev, 86; A Praxis of Liturgical Catechesis, Doc Diss, SMU, 86; How to Save the World Without Worshipping Nature, Greek Orthodox Theol Rev, 85; Liberation Theology and Christian Education, in ed, Jeff Astley, Theological Perspectives on Christian Education, Univ Wales, Eng, 95; **CONTACT ADDRESS** Dept of Religious Education, Greek Orthodox Archdiocese, 50 Goddard Ave, Brookline, MA 02445. **EMAIL** frfrank@omaccess.com

MARASINGHE, M. LAKSHMAN
DISCIPLINE LAW **EDUCATION** Univ Col, London, LLB, LLM; Sch Oriental and African Stud, London, PhD. **CAREER** Prof; Osgoode Hall, Barrister-at-Law & Inner Temple, Eng; past scholar, Max-Planck-Inst. **MEMBERSHIPS** Bd directors, Third World Legal Stud. **SELECTED PUBLICATIONS** Ed, Third World Legal Stud. **CONTACT ADDRESS** Col of Business Administration, Education and Law, Univ of Windsor, 401 Sunset Ave, Windsor, ON, Canada N9B 3P4. **EMAIL** lmarasi@uwindsor.ca

MARCH, WALLACE EUGENE
PERSONAL Born 07/08/1935, Dallas, TX, m, 1957, 2 children **DISCIPLINE** THEOLOGY; ANCIENT LANGUAGES **EDUCATION** Austin Col, BA, 57; Austin Presby Theol Sem, BD, 60; Union Theol Sem, NYork, PhD(Old Testament), 66. **CAREER** From instr to assoc prof, Austin Presby Theol Sem, 64-73, prof, 73-82; Arnold B Rhodes Prof Old Testament, Louisville Presby Theol Sem, 82-, Dean, 92-99. **HONORS AND AWARDS** Rockefeller Schol, 64; Advanced Rel Study Fel, 66, 74; Asn Theol Schs Theol Scholar res grant, 80. **MEMBERSHIPS** Soc Bibl Lit; Am Acad of Rel. **RESEARCH** Prophetic literature, particularly the sixth and eighth centuries; form criticism and literary criticism; Biblical theology. **SELECTED PUBLICATIONS** Contribr, Laken: its functions and meanings, In: Rhetorical Criticism, Pickwick, 74; Prophecy, In: Old Testament Form Criticism, Trinity Univ, 74; auth, Basic Bible Study, German Press, 78; Ed, Texts and Testaments: Critical Essays on the Bible and Early Church Fathers, Trinity Univ, 80; auth, Biblical Theology, authority and the Presbyterians, J Presby Hist, 81; Israel and the Politics of Land, John Knox Press, 94; Haggai, The New Interpreter's Bible, Abingdon Press, 96. **CONTACT ADDRESS** Louisville Presbyterian Theol Sem, 1044 Alta Vista Rd, Louisville, KY 40205-1758. **EMAIL** emarch@lpts.edu

MARCHENKOV, VLADIMIR
PERSONAL Born 06/24/1957, Leningorsk, USSR, m, 1981, 2 children **DISCIPLINE** PHILOSOPHY **EDUCATION** Ohio State Univ, MA, 94; PhD, 98. **CAREER** Transl, Postfactum Newsgency Moscow Russia, 89-91; grad res assoc, Ohio State Univ, 92-98. **MEMBERSHIPS** Am Philos Asn; Am Soc for Aesthetics; Am Asn of the Advancement of Slavic Studies; Am Asn of Tchrs of Slavic and Eastern Europ Lang. **RESEARCH** German Idealist Philosophy; Music Aesthetics; Russian Religious - Idealist Thought; Myth Theory; Philosophy of Art; Dialectical Logic. **SELECTED PUBLICATIONS** Auth, Conservative Ideas in Modern Russia, Slavic Almanach, 95; from The Dialectics of Myth, 96; rev of round-table Philosophy of Philology, Symposion. J of Russian Thought, 97; introd to Diasophic Odysseys: Odysses the First, Symposion. J of Russian Thought, 97; Orpheus and Vyacheslav Ivanov's Philosophy of Art, Symposion. J of Russian Thought, 97. **CONTACT ADDRESS** Sch of Comp Arts, Ohio Univ, Lindley Hall 120, Athens, OH 45701-2979. **EMAIL** marchenkov.2@osu.edu

MARCIN, RAYMOND B.
PERSONAL Born 02/25/1938, CT, m, 1965, 4 children **DISCIPLINE** PHILOSOPHY AND THEOLOGY OF LAW **EDUCATION** St John's Sem, AB, 59; Fairfield Univ, AB, 61; Fordham Univ, JD, 64. **CAREER** Staff coun legis, Conn State Legis, 64-67; atty poverty law, Neighborhood Legal Serv Inc, 67-68, law reform dir, 69-71; staff coun civil rights, Conn Comn on Human Rights, 68-69; atty civil rights, Ctr Nat Policy Rev, 71-72; from asst to assoc prof, 72-79, Prof Jurisp and Const Law and Legis, Cath Univ Sch Law, 79-, Mem, Proj Study and Appl of Humanistic Educ Law, 80-; vis prof, Delaware Law Sch, Widener Univ, 82-83. **MEMBERSHIPS** Am Law Inst. **RESEARCH** Rawlsian and other Kantian interpretations of justice; the interpretation of legislation; the nonresistancd-to-evil ethic and the litigative mind. **SELECTED PUBLICATIONS** Auth, Schopenhauer Theory of Justice, Cath Univ Law Rev, Vol 0043, 94. **CONTACT ADDRESS** Catholic Univ of America, Washington, DC 20064.

MARCUS, DAVID
PERSONAL Born 06/24/1941, Dublin, Ireland, m, 3 children **DISCIPLINE** BIBLE AND ANCIENT SEMITIC LANGUAGES **EDUCATION** Trinity Col Dublin, BA; Cambridge Univ, MA; Columbia Univ, PhD. **CAREER** Fac, Columbia Univ; prof, chr, Bible and Ancient Semitic Languages, Jewish Theol Sem Am. **MEMBERSHIPS** Soc of Biblical Lit; Columbia Univ Hebrew Bible Seminar. **RESEARCH** The Bible and the Ancient Near East; presently working with an international team of scholars revising the critical edition of the Hebrew Bible. **SELECTED PUBLICATIONS** Auth, From Balaam to Jonah: Anti-prophetic Satire in the Hebrew Bible, Brown Judaic Studies series; numerous scholarly articles; two language manuals, Akkadian, the ancient language of Mesopotamia, Tthe Aramaic of the Babylonian Talmud. **CONTACT ADDRESS** Jewish Theol Sem of America, 3080 Broadway, New York, NY 10027. **EMAIL** damarcus@jtsa.edu

MARCUS, RUTH BORCAN
PERSONAL d, 4 children **DISCIPLINE** PHILOSOPHY **EDUCATION** NYork Univ, BA, 41; Yale Univ, MA, 42; PhD, 46. **CAREER** Prof and Dept Head, Univ Ill, 64-70; Prof, Northwestern Univ, 70-73; Prof, Yale Univ, 73-; Visiting Distinguished Prof, Univ Calif, 73-. **HONORS AND AWARDS** Guggenheim Fel, 53; Fel, Am Acad of Arts and Sci; Medal, Col de France, 86; Machette Awd, Yale Univ, 86; Wilbur Cross Medal, Yale Univ, 00. **MEMBERSHIPS** Am Philos As; Inst de Philos. **RESEARCH** Philosophy: Logic, Epistemology, Ethics, Metaphysics. **SELECTED PUBLICATIONS** Auth, "A Backward Look at Quine's Animadversions on Modalities," in Perspectives on Quine, 90; auth, "Some Revisionary Proposals About Belief and Believing," Philosophy and Phenomenological Research, 90; auth, "Ontological Implications of the Barcan Formula," Philosophia: Handbook of Metaphysics and Ontology, 92; auth, Modalities: Philosophical Essays, Oxford Univ Press, 93; ed, The Logical Enterprise, Yale, 95; auth, "The Anti-Naturalism of Some Language Centered Accounts of Belief," Dialectica, 95; auth, "More on Moral Conflict," in Moral Conflict and Moral Theory, 96; auth, "Are Possible Non-Actual Objects Real," Revue Internationale de Philosophie, 97. **CONTACT ADDRESS** Dept Philos, Yale Univ, PO Box 208306, New Haven, CT 06520-8306. **EMAIL** Ruth.Marcus@yale.edu

MARDER, NANCY S.
DISCIPLINE LAW **EDUCATION** Yale Univ, BA; Univ Cambridge, England, MPhil; Yale Univ, JD. **CAREER** Assoc prof,Univ Southern Calif; clerked for, Honorable John Paul Stevens, Assoc Justice US Supreme Ct; Honorable William A. Norris, Judge US Ct Appeals 9th Circuit & Honorable Leonard B. Sand, Judge US Dist Ct Southern Dist NY; private practice, NY City. **MEMBERSHIPS** American Judicature Society; National Association of Women Judges (Judicial academic Network); Society of American Law Teachers; Law and Society Association. **RESEARCH** Civil Procedure; Advanced Civil Procedure: Judges, Juries, & Trials; & a seminar on Law, Literature, & Feminism. **SELECTED PUBLICATIONS** Auth, Deliberations and Disclosures: A Study of the Post-Verdict Interviews of Jurors; Beyond Gender: Peremptory Challenges & the Roles of the Jury & Gender Dynamics & Jury Deliberations **CONTACT ADDRESS** Sch of Law, Univ of So California, 699 Exposition Blvd, Los Angeles, CA 90089-0040.

MARDIN, SERIF
DISCIPLINE INTERNATIONAL STUDIES **EDUCATION** Stanford Univ, BA, Johns Hopkins Sch Adv Int Studies, MA; Stanford Univ, PhD. **CAREER** Prof, Am Univ; Vis Prof, Columbia; Vis Prof, Princeton; Vis Prof, UCLA. **HONORS AND AWARDS** Islamic Chair, Am Univ. **RESEARCH** Middle East. **SELECTED PUBLICATIONS** Auth, Religion and Social Change in Modern Turkey, State Univ NY Press, 89. **CONTACT ADDRESS** American Univ, 4400 Massachusetts Ave, Washington, DC 20016.

MARENCO, MARC
PERSONAL Born 09/15/1952, Uriah, CA, s **DISCIPLINE** PHILOSOPHY **EDUCATION** Oxford, DPhil, 92 **CAREER** ASSOC PROF, MORAL PHILOSOPHY, PACIFIC UNIV **SELECTED PUBLICATIONS** various **CONTACT ADDRESS** Dept Philosophy, Pacific Univ, 2043 College Way, Forest Grove, OR 97116. **EMAIL** marencom@pacificu.edu

MARGOLIS, JOSEPH
PERSONAL Born 05/16/1924, Newark, NJ, m, 1968, 5 children **DISCIPLINE** PHILOSOPHY **EDUCATION** Drew Univ, BA, 47; Columbia Univ, MA, 50, PhD(philos), 53. **CAREER** From instr to asst prof philos, Long Island Univ, 47-56; asst prof, Univ SC, 56-58; assoc prof dept philos and sr res assoc dept psychiat, Univ Cincinnati, 59-64, prof philos, 64-65;

prof and head dept, Univ Western Ont, 65-67; vis prof, Univ Toronto, 67-68; Prof Philos, Temple Univ, 68-, Lectr, Cooper Union, 53; reader, Columbia Univ, 53-54, lectr, 54; vis asst prof, Trinity Col, Conn, 55 and 56; vis assoc prof Northwestern Univ, 58, Columbia Univ, 65, Univ Minn, 64, Western Reserve Univ, 64-65, Univ Calgary, 68, Univ Utah, 68 and NY Univ, 70-71; Nimh spec fel, 62-63; Can Coun fel, 67; assoc ed, Mt Adams Rev, 70-71; mem adv bd, Social Theory and Practice, 72-; contrib ed, Bk Forum, 72-; consult, J Critical Analysis, 73-; ed, Philos Monogr, 75-; consult ed, Behaviorism, 76- and J Theory of Social Behaviour, 76-. **MEMBERSHIPS** Am Philos Asn. **RESEARCH** Theory of knowledge; philosophical psychology; value theory. **SELECTED PUBLICATIONS** Auth, Psychotherapy and Morality, Random, 66; An Introduction to Philosophical Inquiry, Knopf, 68, 78; Fact and Existence, Univ Toronto & Blackwell, 69; Values and Conduct, Clarendon & Oxford Univ, 71; Knowledge and Existence, Oxford Univ, 73; Arts, criticism of the, In: Encycl Britannica, 74; Negativities The Limits of Life, Charles Merrill, 75G Persons & Minds, Reidel, 77. **CONTACT ADDRESS** Dept of Philosophy, Temple Univ, 1114 W Berks St, Philadelphia, PA 19122-6029.

MARIETTA, DON E.
PERSONAL Born 11/01/1926, Montgomery, AL, m **DISCIPLINE** PHILOSOPHY **EDUCATION** Vanderbilt Univ, PhD, 59. **CAREER** FL Atlan Univ, asst prof, assoc. prof, prof, dist prof, 65-98; FL Atlan Univ, prof emeritus, 98-. **HONORS AND AWARDS** FL Atlan Univ, var tchg awards **MEMBERSHIPS** APA, FPA **RESEARCH** Ethical theory and environmental ethics. **SELECTED PUBLICATIONS** Auth, For People and the Planet, 95; Philosophy of Sexuality, 97; Introduction to Ancient Philosophy, 98; Environmental Philosophy and Environmental Activism, co-ed, 98; Pluralism in Environmental Ethics, in: Topoi, 93; Reflection and Environmental Activism, in: Enviro Philo and Enviro Act, 95. **CONTACT ADDRESS** Dept of Philosophy, Florida Atlantic Univ, Apt 562, Delray Beach, FL 33483. **EMAIL** marigord92@aol.com

MARINA, JACQUELINE
PERSONAL Born 06/28/1961, Bronx, NY, m, 1994, 2 children **DISCIPLINE** PHILOSOPHY OF RELIGION **EDUCATION** Yale Univ, PhD, 93. **CAREER** Asst prof of Philos, Purdue Univ. **HONORS AND AWARDS** Purdue Research Foundation, Summer Faculty Grant, 99; Fac incentive grant, Fall 97; Purdue res found, 94 summer grant; Yale Univ Paul C. Gignilliat fel for outstanding Stud (s) Hum, 88-89; Yale Div Sch Julia A. Archibald High scholar prize. **MEMBERSHIPS** Amer Philos Asn; Amer Acad Rel; N Amer Kant Soc; Schleiermacher Group. **RESEARCH** Kant and the 19th century; esp Schleiermacher. **SELECTED PUBLICATIONS** Coauth, Faith in Philosophy, in Handbook of Faith, James Michael Lee, ed, Religious Education Press, Birmingham, 90, 47-70; The Role of Limits in Aristotle's Concept of Place, The S Jour of Philos, XXXI,2, Summer 93, 205-216; Schleiermacher's Christology Revisited: A Reply to his Critics, The Scottish Jour Theol, 49,2, 96, 177-200; Kant's Deduction of the Categorical Imperative, Kant -Studien 89, Heft 2, 98, 167-178; A Critical-interpretive Analysis of Some Early Writings by Schleiermacher on Kant's Views of Human Nature and Freedom (1789-1799), with Translated Texts, New Athanaeum/Neues Athenaeum, 5, 11-31; Kant on Grace: A Reply to his Critics, rel stud (s), 33, 379-400; The Theological and Philosophical Significance of the Markan Account of Miracles, Faith and Philos, 13, 3, July 98; auth, "Schleiermacher on the Philsophers's Stone: The Shaping of Schleiermacher's Early Ethics by the Kantian Legacy," Journal of Religion (99): 193-215; auth, "Transformation and Personal Identity in Kant," to appear in the issue of Faith and Philosophy, 00; auth, "Aristotle as A-Theorist: Overcoming the Myth of Passage," with Franklin Mason, forthcoming, Journal of the History of Philosophy. **CONTACT ADDRESS** Dept of Philosophy, Purdue Univ, West Lafayette, 1360 Liberal Arts and Education Bldg, West Lafayette, IN 47907-1360. **EMAIL** marinaj@purdue.edu

MARION, LAURIE COWAN
PERSONAL Born 04/23/1961, Burlington, NC, m, 1996, 1 child **DISCIPLINE** PHILOSOPHY **EDUCATION** Emory Univ, MA, 90, PhD, 96; Bryn Mawr Col, AB, 83 **CAREER** Course Devel, Digital Lrn Grp, 97-00. **HONORS AND AWARDS** Univ Fel, Emory Univ, 85-89; Richard W Weaver Fel, 85; fel, Global Dialogue Institute, 00-. **MEMBERSHIPS** Am Philos Assoc **RESEARCH** Hist of Philosophy **SELECTED PUBLICATIONS** Auth, Dissertation: The Interpretation of Scripture in Hobbes's Leviathan, 96 **CONTACT ADDRESS** 208 Willow Ln, Decatur, GA 30030. **EMAIL** marionlec@cs.com

MARKIE, PETER J.
PERSONAL Born 04/04/1950, New York, NY, m, 1975 **DISCIPLINE** PHILOSOPHY **EDUCATION** NYork Univ, BA, 72; Univ MA, MA, 75; PhD, 77. **HONORS AND AWARDS** William T Kemper Teaching Fel, Univ MO. **MEMBERSHIPS** Am Philos Asn. **RESEARCH** Epistemology; Ethics. **SELECTED PUBLICATIONS** Auth, A Professor's Duties, Rowman & Littlefield, 95. **CONTACT ADDRESS** Dept Philos, Univ of Missouri, Columbia, 438 Gen Classroom Bldg, Columbia, MO 65211-4160. **EMAIL** markiep@missouri.edu

MARKOVITZ, IRVING LEONARD
DISCIPLINE POLITICAL SCIENCE **EDUCATION** Brandeis Univ, BA, 56; Boston Univ, MA, 58; Univ of Calif at Berkeley, PhD, 67. **CAREER** Teaching asst, 59-60, head teaching asst, Dept of Political Sci, Univ of Calif at Berkeley, 60-61; res asst for prof Peter Odegarde, N.B.C. Television, 61-62; vis asst prof, NY Univ, 62-63; fel of the Foreign Area Prog, 64-66; LECTR, DEPT OF POLITICAL SCI, 66-67, ASST PROF, 67-70, ASSOC PROF, 70-71, PROF, QUEENS COL, 72-; affiliated res scholar, Inst of African Studies, 68; Univ of Ghana, 73; vis adjunct prof, Dept of Political Sci & Inst of African Studies, Columbia Univ, 96. **HONORS AND AWARDS** Doctoral Res Grant, 68-69 & 69-70 (declined), Summer Res Grant, CUNY, 69; grants 80-81, 82-83, 84-85, 85-86, 89-90, & 94-95, Jr Fac Grant, Nat Endowment for the Humanities, 69; presidential res award, Queens Col, 86; Ford Fel, Am Coun of Learned Soc, 89-90 & 93; Presidential Innovation in Teaching Awd, 92-93; Fac Res Awd, CUNY, 72-74, 83-84, 85, 86, & 90; Mellon Fel, 83-84. **MEMBERSHIPS** Fel of the African Studies Asn; Am Political Sci Asn. **SELECTED PUBLICATIONS** Auth, An Uncivil View of Civil Society in Africa, forthcoming; Constitutions, Civil Society, and the Federalist Papers, Constitutionalism: Reflections and Recommendations, The InterAfrica Group, 94; Camels, Intellectuals, Origins, and Dance in the Invention of Somalia: A Commentary, The Invention of Somalia, The Red Sea Press, 95; Checks and Balances, Civil Society and the Federalist Papers, Constitutions and Constitution-Making in Eritrea, Univ of NC Press, forthcoming; coauth, African Literature and Social Science in the Teaching of World Studies, Soc Studies, 93. **CONTACT ADDRESS** Dept of Political Sci, Queens Col, CUNY, 6530 Kissena Blvd, Flushing, NY 11367. **EMAIL** markovitz@prodigy.net

MARKS, HERBERT J.
DISCIPLINE RELIGIOUS STUDIES **EDUCATION** Yale Univ, PhD, 85. **CAREER** Assoc prof. **RESEARCH** Hebrew Bible; history and theory of biblical interpretation; Bible in western literature. **SELECTED PUBLICATIONS** Auth, The Book of the Twelve, Lit Guide Bible; On Prophetic Stammering, The Book and the Text; co-ed, Indiana Studies in Biblical Literature. **CONTACT ADDRESS** Dept of Religious Studies, Indiana Univ, Bloomington, Sycamore Hall 230, Bloomington, IN 47405. **EMAIL** marks@indiana.edu

MARKS, JOEL HOWARD
PERSONAL Born 10/13/1949, New York, NY, d, 2 children **DISCIPLINE** PHILOSOPHY **EDUCATION** Cornell Univ BA, 72; Univ Conn, MA, 78, PhD, 82. **CAREER** Instr, dir lib arts, 73-75, Portland Schl Art; vis ast prof, 82-83, St John Fisher Col; 83-84; Univ of Rochester; asst prof, 84-88; assoc prof, 88-94, prof, phil, 94-, Univ New Haven. **HONORS AND AWARDS** Phi Bet Kappa **MEMBERSHIPS** APA; Amer Assoc of Phil Tchrs. **RESEARCH** Ethical theory, professional ethics. **SELECTED PUBLICATIONS** Ed, The Ways of Desire, 86; co-ed, Emotions in Asian Thought, 95; coed, Gerard Hoffnung Festschrift, 92; auth, Moral Moments, 96. **CONTACT ADDRESS** Dept of Philosophy, Univ of New Haven, West Haven, CT 06516.

MARLER, GRANT A.
PERSONAL Born 12/22/1957, Inglewood, CA, m, 1993, 1 child **DISCIPLINE** PHILOSOPHY **EDUCATION** Arizona State Univ, BA, 86; Old Dominion Univ, MA, 96; Claremont Grauduate University, MA, 00; PhD, in progress. **CAREER** Musicaian, 77-80; Imagery anal and proj mgr, USAF, 80-94; sr anal, Science Applications Int Corp. 95-96; adj instr, religion, Riverside Commun Col, 97; res asst, philos prog, Claremont Grad Univ, 98-99; res asst, philos prog, Pomona College, 00-. **HONORS AND AWARDS** USAF Intelligence Civilian of the Year, 88, 90, 91. **MEMBERSHIPS** APA; Assoc for Symbolic Logic, (ASL). **RESEARCH** Philosophical logic; early analytical philosophy; philosophy of mathematics. **SELECTED PUBLICATIONS** Auth, Wittgenstein on Freedom of the Will, MA thesis, 96; auth, Gottlob Frege, Selected Essays, in World Philosophers and Their Works, John Roth, ed. (Pasadena: Salem Press, 00. **CONTACT ADDRESS** 782 Stanislaus Circle, Claremont, CA 91711. **EMAIL** grant.marler@cgu.edu

MARLIN-BENNETT, RENEE
DISCIPLINE INTERNATIONAL POLITICAL ECONOMY **EDUCATION** Pomona Col, BA; Mass Inst Technol, PhD. **CAREER** Prof, Am Univ. **RESEARCH** Intellectual property rights, trade relations, conflict resolution. **SELECTED PUBLICATIONS** Auth, Foodfights: International Regimes and the Politics of Agricultural Trade Disputes, Gordon & Breach, 93. **CONTACT ADDRESS** American Univ, 4400 Massachusetts Ave, Washington, DC 20016.

MARMURA, MICHAEL ELIAS
PERSONAL Born 11/11/1929, Jerusalem, Palestine, m, 1962, 3 children **DISCIPLINE** ISLAMIC PHILOSOPHY, ARABIC **EDUCATION** Univ Wis, BA, 53; Univ Mich, MA, 55, PhD(-Near Eastern studies), 59. **CAREER** Lectr Islamic philos and theol, 59-62, from asst prof to assoc prof, 62-69, assoc chmn dept Mid E and Islamic studies, 69-78, Prof Islamic Philos and Theol, Univ Toronto, 69, Chmn Dept Mid E and Islamic Studies, 78-. **MEMBERSHIPS** Am Orient Soc; Can Philos Asn. **RESEARCH** Islamic theology. **SELECTED PUBLICATIONS** Auth, Islamic Theology and Philosophy; ed, Islamic Theology and Philosophy: Studies in Honor of George F. Hourani, ed, Michael E. Marmura, Hardcover, 84; cotransl, The Incoherence of the Philosophers (Islamic Translation Series), Al-Ghazali, Michael E. Marmura, Hardcover, 98; coauth, The Incoheence of the Philosophers (Islamic Translation Series), 00. **CONTACT ADDRESS** Dept of Near & Mid E Civilizations, Univ of Toronto, 4 Bancroft Ave, Toronto, ON, Canada M5S 1C1.

MARQUIS, DONALD BAGLEY
PERSONAL Born 11/02/1935, Elkhart, IN, d, 2 children **DISCIPLINE** PHILOSOPHY **EDUCATION** Ind Univ, BA, 57, MA, 64, PhD(philos), 70; Univ Pittsburgh, MA, 62. **CAREER** Actg asst prof philos, 67-70, asst dir, Western Civilization Prof, 67-71, asst prof, 70-76, assoc prof, 76-90, Prof Philos, Univ Kans, 90-. **MEMBERSHIPS** Am Philos Asn; Southwestern Philos Soc **RESEARCH** Medical ethics; ethics. **SELECTED PUBLICATIONS** Leaving Therapy to Chance: An Impasse in the Ethics of Randomized Clinical Trials, Hastings Center Report, 83; An Argument that All Prerandomized Clinical Trials Are Unethical, Jour Med and Philos, 86; Why Abortion Is Immoral, Jour Philos, 89; Four Versions of Double Effect, Jour Med and Philos, 91; Fetuses, Futures and Values: A Reply to Shirley, Southwest Philos Rev, 95; Reiman on Abortion, Jour Soc Philos, 98; Why Most Abortions are Immoral, Bioethics Med Ed, JAI Press, 98; The Weakness of the Case for Legalizing Physician-Assisted Suicide, In: Physician-Assisted Suicide: Expanding the Debate, Routledge, 98. **CONTACT ADDRESS** Dept of Philosophy, Univ of Kansas, Lawrence, Lawrence, KS 66045-2145. **EMAIL** dmarquis@falcon.cc.ukans.edu

MARRAS, AUSONIO
DISCIPLINE PHILOSOPHY **EDUCATION** Colgate Univ, BA, 63; Duke Univ, PhD, 67. **RESEARCH** Philosophy of mind; foundations of cognitive science. **SELECTED PUBLICATIONS** Co-ed, Agent, Action, and Reason, Univ of Toronto Press and Blackwell's, (71): 202; ed, Intentionality, Mind, and Language; co-ed, Forms of Representation, North Holland, (75): 245; ed, Language Learning and Concept Acquisition, Ablex Publishing Co, 86; auth, Nonreductive Materialism and Mental Causation, Canadian Journal of Philosophy 24, (94): 465-494; auth, The Causal Relevance of Mental Properties, Philosophia 25, (97): 389-400; auth, The Debate on Mental Causation: Davidson and His Critics, Dialogue 36, (97): 177-95; auth, Davidson on Intentional Causation, (forthcoming); auth, Action Explanation and Mental Causation, in Filosoifia della Mente e Scienze Cognitive, Napoli, dizioni Scientifiche Italiane, (97): 233-254; auth, Metaphysical Foundations of Action-Explanation, in Contempoary Action Theory: Vol 1: General Theory of Action, Kluwer Academic Publishers, 97. **CONTACT ADDRESS** Dept of Philosophy, Univ of Western Ontario, London, ON, Canada N6A 5B8. **EMAIL** amarras@julian.uwo.ca

MARROW, STANLEY BEHJET
PERSONAL Born 02/10/1931, Baghdad, Iraq **DISCIPLINE** NEW TESTAMENT **EDUCATION** Boston Col, BA, 54, MA, 55; Weston Col, PhL, 55, STL, 62; Pontifical Bibl Inst, Rome, SSL, 64; Gregorian Univ, Rome, STD, 66. **CAREER** Asst prof relig, Al-Hikma Univ, Baghdad, 66-68; asst prof New Testament, Pontifical Bibl Inst, 68-71; PROF NEW TESTAMENT, WESTON SCH THEOL, 71-; Assoc ed, Biblica, 68-71, New Testament Abstracts, 71- & Cath Bibl Quart, 78-87. **MEMBERSHIPS** Cath Bibl Asn; Soc Bibl Lit; Am Acad Relig; Soc New Testament Studies. **RESEARCH** Theology of the New Testament. **SELECTED PUBLICATIONS** Co-ed, AlFarabi's Commentary on Aristotle's Peri Hermeneias, Imprimerie Cath, Beyrouth, 60, 2nd ed, 71; auth, The Christ in Jesus, Paulist Press, 68; Index to Biblica 1945-1969, 70 & Basic Tools of Biblical Exegesis, 76 & 78, Biblical Inst, Rome; The Words of Jesus in Our Gospels, Paulist Press, 79; Speaking the Word Fearlessly: Boldness in the New Testament, NY: Paulist Press, 82; Paul, His Letters and His Theology, NY: Paulist Press, 86; The Gospel of John: A Reading, NY: Paulist Press, 95. **CONTACT ADDRESS** 3 Phillips Place, Cambridge, MA 02138-3495.

MARRS, RIOCK R.
PERSONAL Born 05/28/1952, Tucson, AZ, m, 2 children **DISCIPLINE** RELIGION **CAREER** Grad tchg asst, Abilene Christian Univ, 73-79; adjunct prof, Johns Hopkins Univ, 82-83; pt time instr, St. Mary's Sem, Univ, Ecumenical Inst, 79-81; asst prof, Abilene Christian Univ, 84-86; assoc prof, Pepperdine Univ, 87-; ch, Admission and Scholar Comm Rel, 91-92. **SELECTED PUBLICATIONS** Auth, What's Wrong with this Picture?, 21st Century Christian, 94; In the Beginning: Male and Female, Essays on Women in Earliest, Christianity, Col Press, 94; The Prophetic Faith: A Call to Ethics and Community, RQ 36, 94; rev, T. Lenchak, Choose Life!, A Rhetorical-Critical Investigation of Deuteronomy, Rel Studies Rev 20/4, 94; Gordon Mitchell, Together in the Land, A Reading of the Book of Joshua, Rel Studies Rev 20/4, 94. **CONTACT ADDRESS** Dept of Relig, Pepperdine Univ, 24255 Pacific Coast Hwy, Malibu, CA 90263. **EMAIL** rmarrs@pepperdine.edu

MARSCHALL, JOHN PETER
PERSONAL Born 12/11/1933, Chicago, IL **DISCIPLINE** AMERICAN RELIGIOUS HISTORY **EDUCATION** Loyola Univ, Ill, AB, 56; St Louis Univ, MA, 61; Cath Univ Am, PhD(hist), 65. **CAREER** Lectr relig hist, Cath Univ Am, 65; asst prof, Viatorian Sem, Washington, DC, 61-65; asst prof Am relig hist, Loyola Univ, Ill, 66-69, mem grad fac, 68; dir, Ctr Relig and Life, 69-72, prog coordr, Ctr Relig and Life, 73-76; lectr, 69-80, ASSOC PROF AM HIST, UNIV NEV, RENO, 80-, Schmitt Found travel grant, Europe, 63-64; dir, Self-Studies Sisters of Charity, BVM, 66-68; co-dir, Self-Studies New Melleray Trappist Abbey, 68-69; mem subcomt hist, life and ministry priests, Nat Coun Bishops, 68-72; Western dir, Nat Inst for Campus Ministries, 75-79; ed consult, NICM J for Christian and Jews in Higher Educ, 75-79; asst to pres, Univ Nev, Reno, 80-. **MEMBERSHIPS** Cath Campus Ministry Asn (pres, 75-76); Am Acad Relig; Orgn Am Historians; Am Cath Hist Asn; Am Acad Polit and Soc Sci. **RESEARCH** Nineteenth century American Catholic history; history of religion in Nevada. **SELECTED PUBLICATIONS** Auth, The Premier See--a History of the Archdiocese-of-Baltimore, Church Hist, Vol 0065, 96. **CONTACT ADDRESS** Dept of Hist, Univ of Nevada, Reno, Reno, NV 89557-0001.

MARSDEN, G. M.
PERSONAL Born 02/25/1939, m, 1969, 2 children **DISCIPLINE** HISTORY OF CHRISTIANITY **EDUCATION** Haverford College, BA, honors, 59; Westminster Theol Sem, BD, 63; Yale Univ MA, 61, PhD, 65. **CAREER** Francis A McAnaney Prof of Hist, 92-, Univ Notre Dame; Prof 86-92, Duke Univ; vis Prof 86, 90, Univ Cal Berkeley; vis Prof 76-77, Trinity Evang Div Schl; Dir 80-83, Calvin College; Instr, Asst Prof, Assoc Prof, Prof, 65-86, Calvin College; Asst Instr, 64-65, Yale Univ. **HONORS AND AWARDS** Lippincott Prize; YHF for NEH; Calvin Cen Christ Schl fel; Eternity Book of the Year; Calvin Res Fel; J Howard Pew Freedom Gnt; Guggenheim Fel. **MEMBERSHIPS** ASCH. **SELECTED PUBLICATIONS** Auth, Fundamentalism and American Culture, NY: Oxford, 80; coed, The Secularization of the Academy, NY, Oxford Univ Press, 92; The Soul of the American University: From Protestant Establishment to Established Nonbelief, NY, Oxford Univ Press, 94; Understanding Fundamentalism and Evangelicalism, Grand Rapids, W B Eerdmans, 91, collection of previously pub essays; Reforming Fundamentalism: Fuller Seminary and the New Evangelicalism, Grand Rapids, W b Eerdmans, 87, reissued pbk, 95; Auth, The Outrageous Idea of Christian Scholarship, NY, Oxford Univ Press, 97; auth, American Culture, 1st ed, 1990, rev, (00), second ed. **CONTACT ADDRESS** Dept of History, Univ of Notre Dame, Notre Dame, IN 46556. **EMAIL** marsden.1@nd.edu

MARSH, JAMES L.
DISCIPLINE PHILOSOPHY **EDUCATION** Northwestern Univ, PhD. **CAREER** Prof, Fordham Univ. **RESEARCH** Aesthetics, phenomenology and hermeneutics. **SELECTED PUBLICATIONS** Auth, Post-Cartesian Meditations, Fordham UP, 88; Critique, Action, and Liberation, SUNY, 95; co-auth, Modernity and Its Discontents, Fordham UP, 92. **CONTACT ADDRESS** Dept of Philos, Fordham Univ, 113 W 60th St, New York, NY 10023.

MARSH, LUCY A.
DISCIPLINE LAW **EDUCATION** Smith Col, BA, 63; Univ Mich Law Sch, JD, 66. **CAREER** From asst prof to prof, Univ of Denver Col of Law, 76-. **SELECTED PUBLICATIONS** Auth, Practical Applications of the Law: Real Estate Transactions, Little, Brown, 92; auth, Practical Applications of the Law: Wills, Trusts, and Estates, Aspen Law & business, 98. **CONTACT ADDRESS** Col of Law, Univ of Denver, 1900 Olive St, Denver, CO 80220.

MARSHALL, ROBERT J.
DISCIPLINE THEOLOGY **EDUCATION** Wittenberg Univ; Chicago Lutheran Theol Sem, PhD; Univ Chicago. **CAREER** Pres, Lutheran Church in Am; pres, Lutheran World Relief; sr sch in residence-. **MEMBERSHIPS** Mem, Bd of Trustees, Muhlenberg Col. **SELECTED PUBLICATIONS** Auth, On Being a Church Member in the ELCA; The Mighty Acts of God, Augsburg Fortress Press. **CONTACT ADDRESS** Dept of Theology, Lutheran Sch of Theol at Chicago, 1100 E 55th St, Chicago, IL 60615. **EMAIL** rmarshal@lstc.edu

MARTEL, LEON C.
PERSONAL Born 06/14/1933, Providence, RI, m, 1956, 2 children **DISCIPLINE** POLITICAL SCIENCE **EDUCATION** Dartmouth Col, BA, 55; Columbia Univ, MA, 57; PhD, 77. **CAREER** Off, U S Navy, 57-64; Fac, Hofstra Univ, 65-74; Dir, Hudson Inst, 74-84; Self-employed writer and lect, 81-89; Sen Feel, The Conf Board, 89-. **HONORS AND AWARDS** Secy Navy Achievement Awd; Teacher of the Year, Hofstra Univ. **MEMBERSHIPS** Am Polit SCI Assoc., World Future Soc, Naval Reserve Assoc. **RESEARCH** Business practices, long-range forecasting, chance management. **SELECTED PUBLICATIONS** Coauth, The Next 200 Years: A Scenario for America and the World, William Morrow (New York, NY), 76; auth, Lend-Lease, Loans and the Coming of the Cold War, Westview Pr (Boulder, CO), 79; auth, Mastering Change: The Key to Business Success, Simon & Schuster (New York, NY), 86. **CONTACT ADDRESS** 600 W 111th St, New York, NY 10025. **EMAIL** leonmartel@aol.com

MARTENS, ELMER ARTHUR
PERSONAL Born 08/12/1930, Main Centre, SK, Canada, m, 1956, 4 children **DISCIPLINE** RELIGION, OLD TESTAMENT **EDUCATION** Univ Sask, BA, 54; Univ Man, BEd, 56; Mennonite Brethren Bibl Sem, CA, BD, 58; Claremont Grad Sch, PhD, 72. **CAREER** Assoc prof, 70-80, pres, Mennonite Brethren Bibl Sem, 77-86, prof Old Testament, 80-95, Prof Emeritus, Mennonite Brethren Bibl Sem, 95-; Co-translr, New Am Standard Bible, 69-70; New Living Translation, 89-96. **HONORS AND AWARDS** First Award (an expense-paid trip to Israel), Sermon writing contest sponsored by Nat Asn of Evangelicals, 62. **MEMBERSHIPS** Soc Bibl Lit; Evangelical Theological Soc; Institute of Biblical Research. **RESEARCH** Old Testament theology; Prophets. **SELECTED PUBLICATIONS** Contribr, The Church in Mission, Bd Christian Lit, 67; God's Design: A Focus on Old Testament Theology, Baker, 81, 3rd ed, Bibal Press, 98; Jeremiah, Herald Press, 86; ed, along with B. C. Ollenburger and G. Hasel, The Flowering of Old Testament Theology: A Reader in Twentieth Century Theology 1930-1990, Eisenbraun, 92; Old Testament Theology, Institute of Biblical Research Bibliographies #13, Baker, 97. **CONTACT ADDRESS** Mennonite Brethren Biblical Sem, 4824 E Butler, Fresno, CA 93727-5014. **EMAIL** eamartens@compuserve.com

MARTHALER, BERARD LAWRENCE
PERSONAL Born 05/01/1927, Chicago Heights, IL **DISCIPLINE** RELIGIOUS EDUCATION **EDUCATION** Pontif Fac Theol, San Bonaventura, Rome, STL, 52, STD, 53; Univ Minn, MA, 56, PhD(ancient hist), 68. **CAREER** Instr church hist, Assumption Sem, 53-61; asst prof theol, Bellarmine Col, Ky, 61-63; asst prof relig educ, 63-67, assoc prof and head dept, 67-72, pres, 74-75, Prof Relig Educ, Cath Univ Am, 73, Chmn Dept, 74-. Exec ed, the Living Light, 72-; Prof Emeritus, Cath Univ am, 98-. **HONORS AND AWARDS** Professed member of Order Affairs, Minor Conventual Ordained Rome, 52; Benemerenti from Pope John Paul II, 88; Johannes Quasten Medal, 98. **MEMBERSHIPS** Col Theol Soc (vpres, 68-70); Am Acad Relig; Asn Prof and Researchers Relig Educ (pres, 74-75); Cath Theol Soc Am; Relig Educ Asn. **RESEARCH** Religious education as socialization. **SELECTED PUBLICATIONS** Auth, The Creed: The Apostolic faith in Contemporary Theology, 93; auth, The Catechism Yesterday and Today: The Evolution of a Genre, 95. **CONTACT ADDRESS** Dept of Relig and Relig Educ, Catholic Univ of America, Washington, DC 20064.

MARTI, GENOVEVA
DISCIPLINE PHILOSOPHY **EDUCATION** Stanford Univ, PhD. **CAREER** Assoc prof, Univ Calif, Riverside; Vis Prof, Birkbeck Coll, Eng, 98-00; lectr, LSE, Eng, 00-. **RESEARCH** Study of the connection between language and the world we talk about. **SELECTED PUBLICATIONS** Auth, "Aboutness and Substitutivity," Midwest Stud, 89; "The Source of Intensionality," Philos Perspectives, 93; "Do Modal Distinctions Collapse in Carnap's System?," Jour of Philos Logic, 94; "The Essence of Genuine Reference," Jour of Philos Logic, 95; auth, "Rethinking Quine's Argument on the Collapse of Modal Distinctions," Notre Dame Jrn l of Formal Logic (97); auth, "Sense and Reference," New Routledge Encyclopedia of Philos, 98. **CONTACT ADDRESS** Dept Philosophy, Logic and Scientific Method, London School of Economics, London WC2A 2AE. **EMAIL** gmarti@ucrac1.ucr.edu

MARTIN, CHARLES BURTON
PERSONAL Born 05/24/1924, Chelsea, MA, 4 children **DISCIPLINE** PHILOSOPHY OF MIND, METAPHYSICS **EDUCATION** Boston Univ, BA, 48; Cambridge Univ, PhD(philos), 59. **CAREER** From lectr to sr lectr & reader philos, Univ Adelaide, 54-66; prof, Univ Sydney, 66-71; prof philos, Univ Calgary, 71-01, prof emeritus, 01-; Vis assoc prof, Columbia Univ, summer, 61; vis asst prof, Harvard Univ, fall, 61; vis prof, Columbia Univ, 62, Univ Mich, 68 & Harvard Univ, 70, 75 & 80; vis lectr, Oxford Univ, 78. **HONORS AND AWARDS** Burney Studentship, Cambridge Univ, 51; vis fel, Lowell House, Harvard Univ, 70; Social Sciences & Humanities Res Council Travel Fel, 78, 83, 96-99; British Council Vis Scholar, 90, 95; vis fel, Wolfson Col, Oxford Univ, 90; Distinguished Vis Scholar, Flinders Univ, 90; Distinguished Vis Scholar, Univ of Adelaide, 90; vis fel, St. Peter's Col, Univ of Adelaide, 90; Sr Vis Scholar, Macquarie Univ, June-Aug, 93; Overseas Vis Scholar, St. John's Col, Cambridge Univ, Jan-June, 95; vis fel, Dunmore Lang Col, Macquarie Univ, 98; vis fel, Exeter Col, Oxford, 98. **MEMBERSHIPS** Australasian Philos Asn (pres, 68); Can Philos Asn. **RESEARCH** The role of sensory experience in concept formation; realism and anti-realism. **SELECTED PUBLICATIONS** Auth, "The Need for Ontology: Some Choices," Philos (93); auth, "Dispositions and Conditionals," Philosophical Quarterly (94); auth, "How It Is: Entities, Absences, and Void," Australasian Jour of Philos (96); coauth, Properties and Dispositions: A Debate, Routledge (London), 96; auth, "The Need for Properties: The Road to Pythagoreanism and the Way Back," Synthese, 97; coauth, "Rules and Powers" Philosophical Perspectives (98); coauth, "The Ontological Turn," Midwest Studies in Philos (99); auth, "An Event Remembered," Brain and Mind (00). **CONTACT ADDRESS** Univ of Calgary, 101 5th St NW, Calgary, AB, Canada T2N 2A8. **EMAIL** cmartin@ucalgary.ca

MARTIN, CHARLOTTE JOY
PERSONAL Born 05/26/1963, Brooklyn Park, MN, s **DISCIPLINE** THEOLOGY **EDUCATION** Col St Benedict, BA, 85; Vanderbilt Univ, MA, 90; PhD, 94. **CAREER** Asst prof, 91-, assoc prof, 97-, Mount Mercy Col, Cedar Rapids IA. **HONORS AND AWARDS** Who's Who in Am Tchrs, 96. **MEMBERSHIPS** Am Acad of Religion. **RESEARCH** Eschatology; Pedagogy; Jewish Christian Dialogue. **CONTACT ADDRESS** Religious Studies Dept, Mount Mercy Col, 1330 Elmhurst Drive NE, Cedar Rapids, IA 52402-4907. **EMAIL** chmartin@mmc.mtmercy.edu

MARTIN, D. MICHAEL
PERSONAL m, 2 children **DISCIPLINE** NEW TESTAMENT INTERPRETATION **EDUCATION** Dallas Baptist Col, BA; Southwestern Baptist Theol Sem, MDiv, PhD; addn stud, Tyndale House; Cambridge Univ, 94. **CAREER** Tchg asst, tchg fel, Southwestern Baptist Theol Sem; vis prof, 80-81; adj prof, Golden Gate's S Calif Campus, 81-84; instr, Calif Baptist Col; ch, Div Rel, Calif Baptist Col, 82; prof, Golden Gate Baptist Theol Sem-; assoc acad dean. **SELECTED PUBLICATIONS** Pub(s), Christian Century; Biblical Illustrator; Sunday Sch Bd; contrib, Holman Bible Dictionary; auth, Vol 33, 1 & 2 Thessalonians, New American Commentary, Broadman. **CONTACT ADDRESS** Golden Gate Baptist Theol Sem, 201 Sem Dr, Mill Valley, CA 94941-3197. **EMAIL** MichaelMartin@ggbts.edu

MARTIN, DEAN M.
PERSONAL Born 08/04/1942, Lebanon, MO, m, 1965, 2 children **DISCIPLINE** RELIGION **EDUCATION** William Jewell Col, BA, 64; Yale Univ Divinity Sch, BD, 67; Baylor Univ, PhD, 72. **CAREER** Asst prof, US Int Univ, 71-74; from asst prof to assoc prof, Campbell Univ, 74-92; vis prof Philos, Baylor Univ, 92; prof, Campbell Univ, 93-. **MEMBERSHIPS** Am Acad Relig; Soc Philos Relig; Baptist Asn Philos Tchrs; Asn Baptist Prof Relig; Soren Kierkegaard Soc. **RESEARCH** Religion and philosophy of language; Ludwig Wittgenstein; Soren Kierkegaard; religion/theology; philosophy of religion. **SELECTED PUBLICATIONS** Auth, God and Objects: Beginning with Existence, Int Jour Philos Relig, Feb, 97; auth, Learning to Become a Christian, Relig Educ, Winter, 87; auth, On Certainty and Religious Belief, Relig Studies, Dec, 84; auth, Language, Thinking, and Religious Consciousness, Int Jour Philos Relig, Fall, 79; auth, Language, Theology, and the Subject Life, Perspectives in Relig Studies, Fall, 78. **CONTACT ADDRESS** PO Box 487, Buies Creek, NC 27506. **EMAIL** dmartin@camel.campbell.edu

MARTIN, EDWARD N.
PERSONAL Born, MI, m, 1993, 1 child **DISCIPLINE** PHILOSOPHY **EDUCATION** Hillsdale Col, BA, 88; Trinity Evang Divinity Sch, MA, 90; Purdue Univ, PhD, 95. **CAREER** Prof, Trinity Col & Sem, 96-. **MEMBERSHIPS** Soc of Christian Phil; APA; Evangelical Theol Soc; Phil of Time Soc **RESEARCH** Contemporary Christian Philosophy of Religion; Ethics; G E Moore; Analytic Philosophy. **SELECTED PUBLICATIONS** Rev, Our Idea of God, The Crucible 2, 91; Proper Function, Natural Reason, and Evils as Extrinsic Goods, Global Jour of Classic Theol 1, 98; On Behalf of the Fool: G E Moore and Our Knowledge of the Existence of Material Objects, Sorites 2, 96; Rev, The Evidential Argument from Evil, Intl Jour for Phil of Religion, 97. **CONTACT ADDRESS** Dr, Trinity Col and Sem, 4233 Medwel Drive, Newburgh, IN 47629-0717. **EMAIL** enmartin@compuserve.com

MARTIN, ERNEST L.
PERSONAL Born 04/20/1932, Meeker, OK, m, 1987, 3 children **DISCIPLINE** THEOLOGY **EDUCATION** Ambassador Univ, BA, 58, MA, 60, PhD, 66. **CAREER** Sec of Bd, 60-72, Registrar, 60-65, Dean of Faculty, 65-72, Ambassador Univ, England; Chm, Dept of Theol, 73-74, Ambassador, Univ, Pasadena, CA. **HONORS AND AWARDS** Head of Coll Students for 5 yrs at the Jerusalem Excavations under Prof Benjamin Mazar, Hebrew Univ. **MEMBERSHIPS** SBL; ASOR; Planetarian Soc. **RESEARCH** Theology, chronology, history, astronomy. **SELECTED PUBLICATIONS** Auth, The Star That Astonished the World, 78; Secrets of Golgotha, 88; Restoring the Bible, 84; 101 Bible Secrets That Christians Do Not Know, 93; The People That History Forgot, 91; The Tithing Dilemma, 74; NEW: The Temples That Jerusalem Forgot, Jan 00. **CONTACT ADDRESS** Acad of Scriptural Knowledge, PO Box 25000, Portland, OR 97225. **EMAIL** doctor@asklem.com

MARTIN, FRANCIS DAVID
PERSONAL Born 03/29/1920, Johnstown, PA, m, 1942, 4 children **DISCIPLINE** PHILOSOPHY **EDUCATION** Univ Chicago, AB, 42, PhD, 49. **CAREER** From asst prof to prof philos, 49-72, John Howard Harris Prof, Bucknell Univ, 72-, Fulbright res scholar, Italy, 57-59; Lilly Found fel, 66-67.

HONORS AND AWARDS Christian Lindback Awd Distinguished Tchg, 69. **MEMBERSHIPS** Am Philos Soc; Am Soc Aesthet; Nat Soc Studies Educ. **RESEARCH** Aesthetics; the philos of A N Whitehead; the philos of Martin Heidegger. **SELECTED PUBLICATIONS** Auth, Unrealized possibility in the aesthetic experience, J Philos; On the supposed incompatibility between formalism and expressionism, J Aesthet & Art Criticism; Naming paintings, Art J; Art and the Religious Experience, Bucknell Univ, 72; Sculpture and Enlivened Space: Aethetics and History, Univ Press Ky, 81; The Humanities Throught the Arts, McGraw-Hill, 74, 5th ed, 97. **CONTACT ADDRESS** Dept of Philosophy, Bucknell Univ, Lewisburg, PA 17837.

MARTIN, GLEN T.
PERSONAL Born 01/21/1944, Rochester, NY, m, 1978, 1 child **DISCIPLINE** PHILOSOPHY **EDUCATION** SUNY, BA, 70; Hunter Col, MA, 76; CUNY, PhD, 85. **CAREER** Adj Lecturer to Adj Asst Prof, Hunter Col, 74-84; Prof, Radford Univ, 85-. **HONORS AND AWARDS** Alpha Lambda Delta; Intl Advisory Board, Radio for Peace Intl; Pres, Intl Philos for Peace, 96 **MEMBERSHIPS** Intl Philos for Peace, Am Philos Asn, Concerned Philos for Peace, Soc for process Philos of Educ. **RESEARCH** The foundations of world peace (philosophical, spiritual and social). **SELECTED PUBLICATIONS** Auth, "A Planetary Paradigm for Global Government," in Toward Genuine Global Governance: Critical Reactions to Our Global Neighborhood, Praeger Books, 99; auth, "A Buddhist Response to Institutional Violence," Institutional violence, Rodopi Press, 99; auth, "Freedom, Ethics, and Compassion," in Culture and Quest, ISISAR, 97; auth, "Eschatological Ethics and Positive Peace," in Perspectives on Power and domination, Rodopi Press, 96; auth, "Wittgenstein, Language, and Education for Creativity," Teaching Philosophy, (96): 31-46; auth, "Wittgenstein and Time," and "Kierkegaard and Time," in International Encyclopedia of Time, Garland Press, 94; auth, "deconstruction and Breakthrough in Nietzsche and Nagarjuna," in Nietzsche and Asian Thought, Univ Chicago Press, 91; auth, From Nietzsche to Wittgenstein - The Problem of Truth and Nihilism in the Modern World, Peter Lang Pub, 89. **CONTACT ADDRESS** Dept Relig & Philos, Radford Univ, PO Box 6943, Radford, VA 24142-6943. **EMAIL** gmartin@runet.edu

MARTIN, JAMES AUGUST
PERSONAL Born 03/18/1938, Sarasota, FL, m, 1962, 2 children **DISCIPLINE** PHILOSOPHY **EDUCATION** Fla State Univ, BA, 61; Univ Mich, MA, PhD(philos), 69. **CAREER** Res instr philos, Dartmouth Col, 67-69, asst prof, 69-73; asst prof, 73-77, Assoc Prof Phlios, Univ Wyo, 77-. **MEMBERSHIPS** Am Philos Asn. **RESEARCH** Epistemology; analytic philosophy; philosophy, logic and science. **SELECTED PUBLICATIONS** Auth, How not to define truth functionality, Logique Analyse, 12/70; Arc there truth functional connectives?, Metaphilos, 7/73; coauth, What a man does he can do?, Analysis, 4/73; Outcomes and abilities, Analysis, 6/73; Objective knowledge: A review, Philos Rev, 1/75; Proving necessity, Philos Res Arch, 76. **CONTACT ADDRESS** Dept of Philosophy, Univ of Wyoming, P O Box 3392, Laramie, WY 82071-3392.

MARTIN, JAMES LUTHER
PERSONAL Born 07/22/1917, Lone Wolf, OK **DISCIPLINE** RELIGION **EDUCATION** Oklahoma City Univ, BA, 38; Yale Univ, BD, 41, PhD(theol), 51. **CAREER** From assoc prof to prof philos & relig, Col Idaho, 46-57; Prof Relig & Chmn Dept, Denison Univ 57-85, Fund Advan Educ fel, 54-55; fac training fel, Am Inst Indian Studies, 63-64. **MEMBERSHIPS** Am Acad Relig; Asn Asian Studies. **RESEARCH** History of Christian thought; Oriental religions; Hindu temple administration. **SELECTED PUBLICATIONS** Auth, The economy of the Tiru Jeer math, Studies on Asia, 66; Hindu orthodoxy in a South Indian village, J Am Acad Relig, 12/67; Variations on Tergalai orthodoxy, India Cult Quart, 12/70. **CONTACT ADDRESS** Dept of Relig, Denison Univ, Granville, OH 43023.

MARTIN, JANE ROLAND
PERSONAL Born 07/20/1929, New York, NY, m, 1962, 2 children **DISCIPLINE** PHILOSOPHY, EDUCATION **EDUCATION** Radcliffe Col, AB, 51; Harvard Univ, M Ed, 56; Radcliffe Col, PhD, 61. **CAREER** From assoc prof philos to prof emerita, Univ MA, Boston, 72-. **HONORS AND AWARDS** Hon doct: Univ of Umea, Sweden; Salem St Univ, MA; Guggenheim fel, 87; NSF, 84; Bunting, inst fel, 81. **MEMBERSHIPS** APA; Philos of Ed Soc; Soc for Women in Philos; Am Ed Res Asn. **RESEARCH** Philos of ed; feminist theory and philos. **SELECTED PUBLICATIONS** Auth, Reclaiming a Conversation: The Ideal of the Educated Woman, Yale Univ Press, 85; auth, Science in a Different Style, Am Philos Quart, 25, 88; auth, Idealogical Critique and the Philosophy of Science, Philos of Science, 56, 89; auth, The Schoolhome: Rethinking Schools for Changing Families, Harvard Univ Press, 92; auth, Changing the Educational Landscape: Philosophy, Women, and Curriculum, Routledge, 94; auth, Methodological Essentalism, False Difference, and Other Dangerous Traps, Signs, 19, 94; auth, Aerial Distance, Esotericism, and Other Closely Related Traps, Signs, 21, 96; auth, Bound for the Promised Land: the Gendered Character of Higher Education, Duke J of Gender Law & Pol, 4, 97; auth, Coming of Age in Academe: Rekindling Women's Hopes and Reforming the Academy, Raitledge, 00. **CONTACT ADDRESS** 8 Gerry's Landing Rd, Cambridge, MA 02138. **EMAIL** mlmartin@bu.edu

MARTIN, JANICE R.
DISCIPLINE LAW **EDUCATION** University of Louisville, BS (with honors), political science; University of Louisville Law School, JD. **CAREER** Instructor, Univ of Louisville; Private practice, attorney; Jefferson County Attorney's Office, Juvenile Division, head; Jefferson County District Court, district judge, 92-. **HONORS AND AWARDS** Distinguished Law School Alumni Awd, 1992; Continuing Legal Educ Awd, 1994, 1996; Kentucky Women's Leadership Class, 1994. **MEMBERSHIPS** Kentucky Task Force on Racial Bias; Women's Lawyers Assn; NAWJ. **CONTACT ADDRESS** Judge, Jefferson County District Court, Hall of Justice, 600 W Jefferson Ave, Louisville, KY 40202.

MARTIN, JERRY LEE
PERSONAL Born 10/16/1941, Turkey, TX **DISCIPLINE** PHILOSOPHY **EDUCATION** Univ Calif, Riverside, AB, 63; Univ Chicago, MA, 66; Northwestern Univ, Evanston, PhD(philos), 70. **CAREER** Instr philos, eve div, Northwestern Univ, 65-67; asst prof, 67-73, chmn dept, 79-81, Assoc Prof Philos, Univ Colo, Boulder, 73-, Dir, Ctr Study Values & Social Policy, 81-, Mellon Congfel, 82-83. **MEMBERSHIPS** Am Philos Asn; Soc Phenomenol & Existential Philos; Soc Historians Early Am Repub; AAUP. **RESEARCH** Epistemology; ethics and public policy; political philosophy. **SELECTED PUBLICATIONS** Auth, Has Strawson Refuted Scepticism About Other Minds?, Philos Asn; contribr, New Essays in the philosophy of mind, Can J, 75; auth, A dialogue on criteria, Philos Forum; The duality of time, Man & World; ed, the Concept of the Quality of Life: Problems of Definition and Evaluation, 82. **CONTACT ADDRESS** Dept of Philos, Univ of Colorado, Boulder, Boulder, CO 80302.

MARTIN, JOAN M.
PERSONAL Born 06/23/1952, Englewood, NJ **DISCIPLINE** CHRISTIAN SOCIAL ETHICS **EDUCATION** Elmhurst Col, BA, 73; Princeton Theol Sem, M Div, 76; Temple Univ, MA, 89; Temple Univ, PhD, 96. **CAREER** Ordained Presbyterian minister, 76-; assoc prof, Christian ethics, Episcopal Divinity Sch, 94-; William W. rankin Assoc Prof of Christian Ethics, 98-. **HONORS AND AWARDS** Mary Grove Col, 89, dr of humane letters; Hamilton Col, dr of humane letters, 00. **MEMBERSHIPS** Am Acad of Relig; Soc for Christ Ethics. **RESEARCH** Christian ethics--economics, humane labor, womanist/feminist theory, economic ethics. **SELECTED PUBLICATIONS** Auth, Still Making The Road As We Go, Your Daughters Shall Prophesy: Feminist Alternatives in Theol Educ, The Pilgrim Press, 80; auth, We Can't Win For Losin' or Can We?, The Acceptable Year: Sermons From Liberation Theol, Judson Press, 82; auth, African American Women's Embodiment and Moral Agency, Probe, NARW, Spring, 93; auth, "The Notion of Difference for Emerging Womanist Ethics: The Writings of Audre Lorde and Bell Hooks," Jour Feminist Studies in Relig (Spring, 93); auth, "Re-Imagining the Church as Spiritual Institution: Affirming Diversity and Life Sustaining Relationships," Church and Soc: Jour of the Presbyterian Church 84, no 5 (May/June, 94); auth, "Perspectives on Womanist Theol," Black Church Scholars Series, vol VII, Spring, 95; auth, "The Work Ethic of Enslaved Women in The Antebellum, 1830-1865," Jour of the Interdenominational Theol Ctr (Spring, 95); auth, Sisterhood, Work, Womanist, Dict of Feminist Theol, Westminster/John Knox Press, 96; auth, "Sources for Womanist Ethics: The Slave Narrative as Historical and Sacred Text," Jour of the Proceedings of the Europ Soc of Women in Theol Res, Thessaloniki, Greece (98); auth, More than Chains and Toil: A Christian Work Ethics of Enslaved Women, Westminster/John Knox Press, 00. **CONTACT ADDRESS** Episcopal Divinity Sch, 99 Brattle St., Cambridge, MA 02138. **EMAIL** jmartin@episdivschool.org

MARTIN, JOEL
DISCIPLINE RELIGION **EDUCATION** Duke Univ, PhD **CAREER** ASSOC PROF, FRANKLIN MARSHALL COL, 88-. **CONTACT ADDRESS** PO Box 3003, Lancaster, PA 17604-3003.

MARTIN, JOSEPH RAMSEY
PERSONAL Born 10/15/1930, Paducah, KY, m, 1955, 2 children **DISCIPLINE** PHILOSOPHY **EDUCATION** Univ Va, PhD(philos), 67. **CAREER** Master English, Brooks Sch, Mass, 58-60, chmn dept, 60-62; instr, Lib Arts Sems & Dept English, Univ Va, 62-63; asst prof philos, Transylvania Col, 67-68; asst prof, 68-73, assoc prof, 73-78, Prof Philos, Washington & Lee Univ, 78-. **MEMBERSHIPS** Am Philos Asn. **RESEARCH** Epistemology; philosophy of mind and language. **SELECTED PUBLICATIONS** Conceptual obsolescence and land use policy, Towards a Land Use Ethic, Piedmont Environ Coun, 79. **CONTACT ADDRESS** Dept of Philosophy, Washington and Lee Univ, Lexington, VA 24450.

MARTIN, JUDITH G.
PERSONAL Born Buffalo, NY, s **DISCIPLINE** RELIGIOUS STUDIES **EDUCATION** McMaster Univ, MA, PhD; Union Theol Sem in NYork City, MA. **CAREER** Assoc prof; past dir, Women's Stud Prog, Univ Dayton. **RESEARCH** Feminist theology, religions of the world, religion and politics in Middle East. **SELECTED PUBLICATIONS** Auth, Why Women Need a Feminist Spirituality, Women's Stud Quart. **CONTACT ADDRESS** Dept of Religious Studies, Univ of Dayton, 300 College Park, 327 Humanities, Dayton, OH 45469-1679. **EMAIL** martin@checkov.hm.udayton.edu

MARTIN, MARTY
PERSONAL Born 02/05/1928, West Point, NE, m, 1982, 7 children **DISCIPLINE** RELIGIOUS HISTORY **EDUCATION** Lutheran School of Theol, Chicago, STM, 54; Univ of Chicago, PhD, 56. **CAREER** Lutheran Pastor, 49-63; prof, Univ Chicago, 63-98; sr, ed, Christian Century, 56-98; George B. Caldwell Sr Scholar in Residence, Park Ridge Center for Health, Faith and Ethics, 81-. **HONORS AND AWARDS** Natl Medal of Hum; Natl Book Awd; Medal of the Amer Acad of Arts and Sci; 64 honorary degrees. **MEMBERSHIPS** Past Pres Amer Acad of Rel; Amer Soc of Church Hist; Amer Catholic Hist Assoc. **RESEARCH** American Religious History, 18th and 20th centuries; comparative international studies of movements such as fundamentalism and ethnonationalism. **SELECTED PUBLICATIONS** Auth, Righteous Empire: The Protestant Experience in America, Dial, 70; Pilgrims in Their Own Land: 500 Years of Religion in America, Little Brown, 84; Religion and Republic: The American Circumstance, Beacon, 87; The One and the Many: America's Struggle for the Common Good, Harvard, 97; 3 volume Modern American Religion: The Irony of It All: 1893-1919, Univ of Chicago, 86; The Noise of Conflict, 1919-1941, Univ of Chicago, 91; Under God, Indivisible, 1941-1960, Univ of Chicago, 96. **CONTACT ADDRESS** 239 Scottswood Rd, Riverside, IL 60546.

MARTIN, MICHAEL LOU
PERSONAL Born 02/03/1932, Cincinnati, OH, m, 1962, 2 children **DISCIPLINE** PHILOSOPHY **EDUCATION** Ariz State Univ, BS, 56; Univ Ariz, MA, 58; Harvard Univ, PhD(-philos), 62. **CAREER** Asst prof philos, Univ Colo, 62-65; asst prof, 65-68, assoc prof, 68-75, prof Philos, 75-97, prof emer, 97- , Boston Univ. **HONORS AND AWARDS** Fel, Inst Theoretic Psychol, Univ Alta, 69-70; lib arts fel law & philos, Harvard Law Sch, 79-80. **MEMBERSHIPS** Am Philos Asn; Philos Sci Asn. **RESEARCH** Philosophy of science; philosophy of law; philosophy of religion. **SELECTED PUBLICATIONS** Coauth, Probability, Confirmation and Simplicity, Odyssey, 66; auth, Concepts of Science Education, Scott-Foresman, 72; auth, The Legal Philosophy of H.L.A. Hart: A Critical Appraisal, Temple, 87; auth, Atheism: A Philosophical Justification, Temple, 90; auth, The Case against Christianity, Temple, 91; coauth, Readings in the Philosophy of Social Science, MIT, 94; auth, The Big Domino in the Sky and Other Atheistic Tales, Prometheus, 96; auth, Legal Realism: American and Scandinavian, Peter Lang, 97; auth, Verstehen: The Use of Understanding in Social Science, Transaction, 00. **CONTACT ADDRESS** 8 Gerry's Landing Rd, Cambridge, MA 02138. **EMAIL** mlmartin@bu.edu

MARTIN, MIKE W.
PERSONAL Born 11/06/1946, Salt Lake City, UT, m, 1968, 2 children **DISCIPLINE** PHILOSOPHY **EDUCATION** Univ of Ut, BS, 69; MA, 72; Univ of Calif Irving, PhD, 77. **CAREER** Prof, Chapman Univ, 86. **HONORS AND AWARDS** NEH Fel, 81; IEEE Book Awd, 92; Staley, Rolseson, Ryan, St. Lawrence Book Awds. **MEMBERSHIPS** Am Philos Assoc. **RESEARCH** Applied Ethics, Moral Psychology. **SELECTED PUBLICATIONS** Auth, Self-Deception and Morality, Univ Pr of Kans, 86; auth, Virtuous Giving: Philanthropy, Voluntary Service and Caring, Ind Univ Pr, 94; auth, Love's Virtues, Univ Pr of Kans, 96; coauth, Ethics in Engineering, McGraw Hill, 96; auth, Meaningful Work: Rethinking Professional Ethics, Oxford Univ Pr, 00. **CONTACT ADDRESS** Dept Philos, Chapman Univ, 333 N Glassell St, Orange, CA 92866-1011. **EMAIL** mwmartin@chapman.edu

MARTIN, RANDY
DISCIPLINE SOCIOLOGY; POLICY STUDIES **EDUCATION** Univ Calif Berkeley, BA, 79; Univ Wis Madison, MS, 80; CUNY Grad Cen, PhD, 84. **CAREER** Asst prof to assoc prof to prof to dept chmn, Pratt Inst, 89-00; prof to assoc dean, NYork Univ Sch Arts, 00-. **HONORS AND AWARDS** Inst Prof, Distinguished Teacher, 94; HRI Fel, Univ Calif, 93. **MEMBERSHIPS** Co-ed, Social Text, ed col, 84-; co-ed, Socialism and Democracy, 90-98. **RESEARCH** Writing a book, Financialization of Daily Life for Temple UP. **SELECTED PUBLICATIONS** Auth, Performance or Political Art: The Embodied Self, Bergen/Garvey, 90; auth, Socialist Ensembles: Theater and State in Cuba and Nicaragua, Minn UP, 94; auth, On Your Marx: Relinking Socialism and the Left, Univ Minn Pr, 01; auth, Critical Mover: Dance Standing in Theory and Politics, Duke UP, 98; ed, Chalk Lines: The Politics Of Work in the Managed University, Duke UP, 99; co-ed, Sportcult, Minn UP, 99; co-ed, "Globalization?" Soc Text (99). **CONTACT ADDRESS** Sch of Art, New York Univ, 721 Broadway, New York, NY 10003. **EMAIL** randy.martin@nyu.edu

MARTIN, RAYMOND ALBERT
PERSONAL Born 11/03/1925, m, 1949, 4 children **DISCIPLINE** BIBLE **EDUCATION** Wartburg Col, BA, 47; Wartburg Theol Sem, BD, 51; Princeton Theol Sem, ThM, 52, PhD(Old Testament), 57, Harvard Divinity School Post-doctoral Study (N.T.), 63-64. **CAREER** Instr Greek, Wartburg Col, 52-54; Missionary prof Old Testament & New Testament, Gurukul Luth Theol Col, India, 57-69; prof Bibl & Intertestamental Studies to prof emeritus, Wartburg Theol Sem, 69-. **MEMBERSHIPS** Soc Bibl Lit; Soc Bibl Studies, India (secy, 65-69); Int Orgn Septuagint & Cognate Studies; Chicago Society of Biblical Research. **RESEARCH** Greek language; Gospel origins; Intertestamental literature, Historical Jesus; Early Paul; Septuagint Studies; translation Greek. **SELECTED PUBLICATIONS** Auth Some Syntactical Criteria of Translation Greek, VT, 60; Syntactical Evidence of Aramaic Sources in Acts I-XV, NTS, 64; Some Recent Developments in the Study of Discoveries Near the Dead Sea, IJT, 65; The Earliest Messianic Interpretation of Genesis 3:15, JBL, 65; The Date of the Cleansing of the Temple in John, IJT 2:13-22, 65; Syntax of the Greek of Jeremiah 57, India List of Theological Periodicals, 67; Syntactical Evidence of Semitic Sources in Greek Documents, 74; Job in Indian Commentary on the Bible, 74; Syntax Criticism of the LXX Additions to Esther, JBL, 75; Syntactical Evidence of a Semitic Vorlage of the Testament of Joseph in Studies on the Testament of Joseph, 75; Syntax Criticism of the Testament of Abraham in Studies on the Testament of Abraham, 76; Introduction to N.T. Greek, 76,78, & 80; Syntactical and Critical Concordance to the Greek text of Baruch and the Epistle of Jeremiah, Vol XII of The Computer Bible, 77; Introduction to Biblical Hebrew, 87; Syntax Criticism of the Synoptic Gospels, 87; Syntactical Concordance to the Correlated Greek & Hebrew Text of Ruth, Vol XXX of The Computer Bible, 88; Syntactical Concordance to the Correlated Greek and Hebrew Texts of Ruth, Part 2, Vol XXX of The Computer Bible, 89; Syntax Criticism of Johannine Literature, The Catholic Epistles and the Gospel Passion Accounts, 90; Studies in the Life and Ministry of the Early Paul and Related Issues, 93; Computer Generated Tools for the Study of the Greek and Hebrew Texts of Ruth, Part 3, V XXXC of The Computer Bible, 94; Computer Generated Tools for the Study of the Greek and Hebrew Texts of Obadiah in The Computer Bible, 95; Studies in the Life and Ministry of the Historical Jesus, 95; Computer Generated Tools for the Study of the Greek and Hebrew Texts of Jonah in The Computer Bible, 98; Computer Generated Tools for the Sudy of the Greek and Hebrew Texts of Nahum in The Computer Bible, 98. **CONTACT ADDRESS** Dept of Biblical Studies, Wartburg Theol Sem, 333 Wartburg Place, Dubuque, IA 52004-5004. **EMAIL** RAMartin7@aol.com

MARTIN, RAYMOND FREDERICK
PERSONAL Born 08/21/1941, Rochester, NY, m, 1961, 2 children **DISCIPLINE** PHILOSOPHY **EDUCATION** Ohio State Univ, BA, 62, MA, 64; Univ Rochester, PhD(philos), 68. **CAREER** Asst prof philos, Davidson Col, 67-69; asst prof, 69-72, assoc prof Philos, Univ MD, Col Park, 72-, Teaching & res fel, Macalester Col, 70-71. **HONORS AND AWARDS** Received the Univ of Maryland highest award from the Center for Teaching Excellence; received Nat Academic Honor Society Phi Kappa Phi's Mentor of the Year Awd. **MEMBERSHIPS** Am Philos Asn. **RESEARCH** Causal explanation; philosophy of history; objectivity. **SELECTED PUBLICATIONS** Auth, The Past Within Us: An Empirical Approach to Philosophy of History, Princeton: Princeton Univ Press, 89; co-ed, Self and Identity: Contemporary Philosophical Issues, New York: Macmillan, 91; coauth, "Hazlett on the Future of the Self," Journal of the History of Ideas, v. 56, (95): 463-81; auth, "Fission Reguvenation," Philosophical Studies, v. 80, (95): 17-40; auth, "The Essential Difference Between History and Science," History and Theory, v. 36, (97): 1-14; auth, "Progress in Historical Studies," History and Theory: Contemporary Reading, Oxford: Blackwells, 98; coauth, "Fission Examples in the Eighteenth and Early Nineteenth Century Personal Identity Debate," History of Philosophy Quarterly, v. 15, (98): 377-403; auth, Self-Concern; An Experiential Approach to What Matters in Survival, New York: Cambridge Univ Press, 98; auth, The Elusive Messiah: A Philosophical Overview of the Quest for the Historical Jesus, Boulder: Westview Press, 99; co-ed, Wisdom Without Answers: A Brief Introduction to Philosophy, 4th Ed., Belmont, Calif: Wadsworth Publishing Co., 99. **CONTACT ADDRESS** Dept of Philos, Univ of Maryland, Col Park, Skinner Bldg, Rm 1125, College Park, MD 20742-0001. **EMAIL** rm13@umail.umd.edu

MARTIN, REX
PERSONAL Born 07/12/1935, Marion, IN, m, 1956, 2 children **DISCIPLINE** PHILOSOPHY **EDUCATION** Rice Univ, BA, 57; Columbia Univ, MA, 60, PhD, 67. **CAREER** Lectr philos, Columbia Univ, 61-62; instr polit sci, Purdue Univ, 62-65; asst prof philos, Lycoming Col, 66-68; from asst prof to assoc, prof, 68-73, chmn dept, 72-78, Prof Philos, Univ Kans, 73-, prof Polit Theory and Govt, Univ Wales, Swansea, 95-00 (joint with Univ Kans); vis prof philos, Univ Auckland, summer, 81; fac Law, Univ Sydney, Australia, fall 92; vis res fel, School Hist Studies, Inst Advan Studies, Princeton, 84, and Centre for Philos and Public Affairs, Univ St Andrews, Scotland, 91; pres, Am Sect, Inst Asn Philos Law & Social Philos, 91-99, vpres, 95-99; chmn Am Philos Asn Comt Philos & Law, 92-95. **HONORS AND AWARDS** Fulbright res scholar, Univ Helsinki, 72-73; Nat Endowment for Humanities res fel, 76; scholar in residence, Rockefeller Found, Bellagio Study Ctr, Italy, 80; grant, Acad of Finland, 00. **MEMBERSHIPS** Am Philos Asn; Am Soc Polit & Legal Philos; Int Asn Philos Law & Social Philos; Soc Philos & Pub Affairs. **RESEARCH** Polit and legal philos; philos of hist; philos of R G Collingwood. **SELECTED PUBLICATIONS** Auth, Historical Explanation: Re-enactment and Practical Inference, Cornell Univ, 77; Rawls and Rights, Univ Press KS, 85; A System of Rights, Oxford Univ Press, 93; co-ed (with Mark Singer), G C macCallum, Legislative Intent, and Other Essays on Law, Politics and Morality, Univ Wis Press, 93; ed, R G Collingwood's Essay on Metaphysics, rev ed, Clarendon Press/Oxford Univ Press, 98. **CONTACT ADDRESS** Dept of Philos, Univ of Kansas, Lawrence, Lawrence, KS 66045-2145. **EMAIL** rexmartin@compuserve.com

MARTIN, RICHARD C.
PERSONAL Born 07/24/1938, Des Moines, IA, m, 1980, 1 child **DISCIPLINE** HISTORY OF RELIGIONS **EDUCATION** Princeton Theol Sem, ThM, 66; NYork Univ, PhD, 75. **CAREER** Chmn 83-89, Dept of Religious Stud, 75-95, Ariz State Univ; Chmn Relig Stud Prog, 95-96 Iowa State Univ; Prof, Chmn dept of Relig, 96-99; Emory Univ, 96-. **MEMBERSHIPS** ASSR **RESEARCH** Islamic religious thought, comparative religions. **SELECTED PUBLICATIONS** Co-auth, Defenders of Reason in Islam, Mu'tazilism from Medieval School to Modern Symbol, London, Oneworld, 97; auth, Islamic Studies, A History of Religious Approach, Englewood Cliffs NJ, Prentice Hall, 95; Public Aspects of Theology in Medieval Islam, The Role of Kalam in Conflict Definition and Resolution, in: J for Islamic Studies, 93. **CONTACT ADDRESS** Dept of Religion, Emory Univ, Atlanta, GA 30322. **EMAIL** rcmartin@emory.edu

MARTIN, ROBERT K.
PERSONAL Born 08/12/1959, Alexandria, LA, m, 1989, 2 children **DISCIPLINE** THEOLOGICAL STUDIES **EDUCATION** Louisiana Col, Ba, 81; Princeton Theol Sem, MDiv, 85; Harvard Univ Divinity Sch, ThM, 88; Princeton Theol Sem, PhD, 95. **CAREER** Asst Prof, Congregational Leadership. **HONORS AND AWARDS** Louisville Inst grant, 97-98; Wabash Ctr for Tchg and Learning in Theol and Relig grant, 98; Louisville Inst Grant, 00-01. **MEMBERSHIPS** United Methodisc Scholars in Christian Educ; Asn of Prof and Res in Relig Educ; N Am Prof of Christian Educ; Am Acad Relig. **RESEARCH** Systematic, practical, pastoral theology; organizational principles of Christian community; critical social theory; foundations of educational theory; liberation movements; postmodernism; epistemological correspondences between science and theology; theological education. **SELECTED PUBLICATIONS** Auth, Congregational Studies and Critical Pedagogy in Theological Perspective, Theol Educ, 97; auth, Theological Education in Epistemological Perspective: The Significance of Michael Polanyi's Personal Knowledge for a Theological Orientation of Theological Education, Tchg Theol and Relig, 98; auth, The Incarnate Ground of Christian Faith: Toward a Christian Theological Epistemology for the Educational Ministry of the Church, Univ Press of Am, 98; auth, Having Faith in Our Faith in God: Toward a Critical Realist Epistemology for Christian Education, Relig Educ, forthcoming; auth, Education and the Liturgical Life of the Church, Relig Educ, forthcoming; auth, Christian Ministry as Communion, J of Ecumenical Stud, 98. **CONTACT ADDRESS** 5123 E Truman Rd, Kansas City, MO 64127. **EMAIL** robert.martin@spst.edu

MARTIN, ROBERT M.
DISCIPLINE PHILOSOPHY **EDUCATION** Columbia Univ, BA, 63; .Univ Mich, MA, 66, PhD, 71. **CAREER** Prof. **RESEARCH** Philosophy of language, metaphysics, practical ethics. **SELECTED PUBLICATIONS** Auth, The Meaning of Language, 87; The Philosopher's Dictionary, 91; There are Two Errors in the the Title of This Book, 92; Scientific Thinking, 97. **CONTACT ADDRESS** Dept of Philos, Dalhousie Univ, Halifax, NS, Canada B3H 3J5. **EMAIL** r.m.martin@dal.ca

MARTIN, SEAN CHARLES
PERSONAL Born 02/24/1954, San Francisco, CA, s **DISCIPLINE** THEOLOGY **EDUCATION** Univ of Dallas, BA, 76; Univ of Notre Dame, MA, 77; Pontifical Gregorian Univ, STL, 92; STD, 94. **CAREER** Asst Prof, 93-98, Univ of St. Thomas Sch of Theol; Vis Asst Prof, 98-pres, Univ of Dallas **MEMBERSHIPS** Am Acad of Relig; Soc of Bibl Lit; Cath Bibl Assoc **RESEARCH** Deutero-Pauline Literature **SELECTED PUBLICATIONS** Auth, Pauli Testamentum 2 Timothy and the Last Words of Moses, Editrice Pontifica Universita Gregoriana, 97; auth, "1 Timoteo, 2 Timoteo, Tito," in Comentario Ibero-Americano, gen ed, Armando Levorratti, Editorial Verbo Divino (Navarre, 01). **CONTACT ADDRESS** Dept Theology, Univ of Dallas, 1845 E Northgate Dr, Irving, TX 75062. **EMAIL** martin@acad.udallas.edu

MARTIN, THOMAS
PERSONAL Born 04/12/1949, East Lansing, MI, m, 1974, 4 children **DISCIPLINE** PHILOSOPHY **EDUCATION** Univ Missouri, PhD. **CAREER** Chmn, dept of philos, Univ Nebraska, Kearney, 86- . **MEMBERSHIPS** Am Chesterton Soc. **RESEARCH** Dostoyevsky; Solzhenitsyn and Chesterton. **CONTACT ADDRESS** Dept of Philosophy, Univ of Nebraska, Kearney, Kearney, NE 68849. **EMAIL** martin@unk.edu

MARTIN, TROY W.
PERSONAL Born 03/15/1953, Seminole, TX, m, 1974, 2 children **DISCIPLINE** BIBLE STUDIES **EDUCATION** Univ Chicago, PhD, 90, **CAREER** Assoc Prof, 10 yrs, ST Xavier Univ. **HONORS AND AWARDS** Teacher/Scholar Awd; Excell Schlshp Awd; Sabb; DAAD Gnt. **MEMBERSHIPS** SBL; CSDR. **RESEARCH** Pauline Epistles. **SELECTED PUBLICATIONS** Auth, By Philosophy and Empty Deceit, Colossians as Response to a Cynic Critique, j for Stud of the New Test Supp Ser, Sheffield, Sheffield Acad Press, 96; Metaphor and Composition in First Peter, Soc of Bib Lit, Atlanta, Scholars Press, 92; auth, "The Voice of Emotion: Paul's Pathetic Persuasion (Gal 4:12-20)," in Paul and the Passions (forthcoming); auth, "Scythian Perspective or Elusive Chiasm: A Reply to Douglas A. Campbell," Novum Testamentum, 99; auth "The TestAbr and the Background of 1 Pet 3.6," Zeitschrift fur die Neutestamentliche Wessenschaft, 99; aut, "Whose Flesh? What Temptation? (Gal 4.13-14)," Jrnl for Stud of the New Test, 99; Assessing the Johannine Epithet The Mother of Jesus, 98; The Christian's Obligation Not to Forgive, Expository Times, 97; Pagan and Judeo-Christian Time-keeping Schemes in Gal 4:10 and Col 2:16, New Test Stud, 96; Apostasy to Paganism: The Rhetorical Stasis of the Galatian Controversy; of Bib Lit, 95; The Scythian Perspective in Col 3:11, Novum Testamentum, 95; But Let Everyone Discern the Body of Christ, J Bib Lit, 95. **CONTACT ADDRESS** Saint Xavier Univ, 3700 W 103rd St, Chicago, IL 60655. **EMAIL** martin@sxu.edu

MARTIN, WAYNE M.
DISCIPLINE HISTORY OF PHILOSOPHY **EDUCATION** Univ Calif-Berkeley, PhD, 93. **CAREER** Undergrad Adv, Univ Calif, San Diego. **RESEARCH** Post-Kantian idealists; Phenomenology. **SELECTED PUBLICATIONS** Auth, "Without a Striving, No Object is Possible:Fichte's Striving Doctrine and the Primacy of Practice," New Perspectives on Fichte, Hum Press, 96; Fichte's Anti-Dogmatism, Ratio V:2,92. **CONTACT ADDRESS** Dept of Philos, Univ of California, San Diego, 9500 Gilman Dr, La Jolla, CA 92093.

MARTINEZ, H. SALVADOR
PERSONAL Born 03/31/1936, Leon, Spain **DISCIPLINE** MEDIEVAL SPANISH LITERATURE, PHILOSOPHY OF HISTORY **EDUCATION** Univ Rome, Dr Laurea, 60; Gregoriana Univ, Rome, Laurea, 68; Univ Toronto, PhD, 72. **CAREER** Prof Span lit & philos, Angelo State Univ, 72-76; Prof Medieval Span Lit, NY Univ, 76-. **MEMBERSHIPS** Soc Rencesvals; Asoc Int Hispanistas; Mediaeval Acad Am; MLA; Am Acad Res Historians Medieval Spain. **CONTACT ADDRESS** Dept of Span & Port, New York Univ, 19 University Pl, New York, NY 10003-4556. **EMAIL** hsm1@is.nyu.edu

MARTINEZ, ROY
PERSONAL Born 01/25/1947, Dangriga, Belize, m, 1987, 1 child **DISCIPLINE** PHILOSOPHY **EDUCATION** Univ de Montreal, BA, 70; PhD, 86; Sir George Williams Univ, MA, 73. **CAREER** Prof & chair of Dept of Philos & Relig, Spelman Col. **HONORS AND AWARDS** 0BK; Presidential Awd in Scholarly Achievement. **MEMBERSHIPS** Am Philos Asn; Int Asn for Philos and Lit. **RESEARCH** Kierkegaard, Hermeneutics. **SELECTED PUBLICATIONS** Ed, The Very Idea of Radical Hermeneutics, Humanities Press, 97. **CONTACT ADDRESS** Dept Philos & Relig, Spelman Col, 350 Spelman Lane Soutwest, Atlanta, GA 30314-4346. **EMAIL** rmartine@spelman.edu

MARTINICH, ALOYSIUS P.
PERSONAL Born 06/28/1946, Cleveland, OH, m, 1973, 3 children **DISCIPLINE** PHILOSOPHY **EDUCATION** Univ of Windsor, BA, 69; Univ of Calif at San Diego, MA, 71; PhD, 73. **CAREER** Asst Prof to Roy Allison Vaughan Centennial Prof of Philos, Univ of Tex at Austin, 73-; vis assoc prof, Univ of San Diego, 84. **HONORS AND AWARDS** Woodrow Wilson Dissertation Fel, 72-73; Fac Res Awd, 77, 83, 89, 95, 00; NEH, 80, 90. **MEMBERSHIPS** Am Philos Asn, N Am Conf of British Studies. **RESEARCH** Philosphy of language, history of modern philosophy, Thomas Hobbes. **SELECTED PUBLICATIONS** Auth, A Hobbes Dictionary, Blackwell Publ (Oxford), 95; auth, "On the Proper Interpretation of Hobbes's Philosophy," J of the Hist of Philos 34 (96): 273-283; auth, "Rhetoric and Unreason in Skinner's Reason and Rhetoric," Int Hobbes Asn Newsletter (96): 23-28; auth, Thomas Hobbes Perspectives on British History, Macmillan (London, Eng), 97, St. Martin's Press (New York, NY), 97; auth, "Thomas Hobbes in Ben Jonson's Entertainment at Welbeck," Notes and Queries 243 (98): 370-371; auth, "Ordinary Language Philosophy," Routledge Encycl of Philos vol 7 (98): 143-147; auth, "Francis Andrewes's Account of Thomas Hobbes's Trip to the Peak," Notes and Queries 243 (98): 436-440; auth, Hobbes: A Biography, Cambridge Univ Press (New York, NY), 99. **CONTACT ADDRESS** Dept Philos, Univ of Texas, Austin, Austin, TX 78712-1013. **EMAIL** martinich@mail.utexas.edu

MARTINSON, PAUL V.
PERSONAL Born, China **DISCIPLINE** CHRISTIAN MISSIONS; WORLD RELIGIONS **EDUCATION** St Olaf Col, BA, 57; Luther Sem, BD, 61; Univ Chicago Divinity Sch, MA, 69, PhD, 73. **CAREER** Instr, 65-67; asst prof, 72; prof, 84-. **HONORS AND AWARDS** Bd ch, Midwest China Study Resource Center; asst pastor, Truth Lutheran Church, 63-67; supervis, Lutheran Middle Sch(s), Kowloon, Yuen-long, 66-67. **MEMBERSHIPS** Mem, Assn for Asian Stud (s); Amer Acad of Rel; Amer Soc of Missiology; Intl Assn for Mission Stud (s); Assoc prof(s) of Missions; Intl Assn of Buddhist Stud (s); founding mem, Soc for Stud of Chinese Rel. **SELECTED PUBLICATIONS** Auth, A Theology of World Religions: Interpreting God, Self, and the World Semitic, Indian, and Chinese Thought, 87; Islam: An Introduction for Christians, 95. **CONTACT ADDRESS** Dept of Christian Missions and World Religions, Luther Sem, 2481 Como Ave, Saint Paul, MN 55108. **EMAIL** pmartins@luthersem.edu

MARTINSON, ROLAND
DISCIPLINE PASTORAL THEOLOGY; MINISTRY **EDUCATION** Luther Sem, BD, 68; San Francisco Theol Sem, STD, 78. **CAREER** Scholar-in-residence, Inst Rel and Wholeness, 85-86; asst prof, 77; prof, 82-. **HONORS AND AWARDS** Pastor, Salem Lutheran Church, 68-74; Hope Lutheran Church, 74. **MEMBERSHIPS** Mem, Nat Coun on Family Rel(s). **RESEARCH** Pastoral care. **SELECTED PUBLICATIONS** Auth, Gearing Up for Youth Ministry in the 21st Century, 92; Effective Youth Ministry, A Congregational Approach, 88; Bringing Up Your Child and Ministries with Families, 86; A Joyful Call to Ministry, 82. **CONTACT ADDRESS** Dept of Pastoral Care, Luther Sem, 2481 Como Ave, Saint Paul, MN 55108. **EMAIL** rmartins@luthersem.edu

MARTLAND, T(HOMAS) R(ODOLPHE)
PERSONAL Born 05/29/1926, Port Chester, NY, m, 1952, 2 children **DISCIPLINE** PHILOSOPHY, RELIGION **EDUCATION** Fordham Univ, BS, 51, magna cum laude; Columbia Univ, MA, 55, PhD, 59. **CAREER** Asst prof, Lafayette Col, 59-65, Jones distinguished fac, lectr, 63; assoc prof philos, Southern IL Univ, 65-66; Assoc Prof Philos, Univ at Albany, 66-84; Fac exchange scholar, State Univ NY, 76-77; mem advisory comt, Literature and the Arts, MN Conf on Comparative Lit, 76-77, mem advisory comt Conf on the Epistemological Relations between the Sci and Humanitities, Miami Univ, Oxford, Ohio, 76; Assoc dir, reg resource center for the Nat Asc for Humanitities Ed, 79-82; Guest ed, Annuals of Scholar, 81; Dir Conf on Representation, Univ Albany, 81, Prof, 84-97; Prog chair, Conf on Art, Myth and Religion, James Mason Univ, Fairfax, Va, 86; Distinguished Jeannette K Watson vis prof of Relig, Syracuse Univ, 87; Dir Conf on Spaces: In Architecture & Dance, Univ Albany, 88; Dir, Relig Studies prog, 80-87, dir grad studies prog of Phil, 89-91, dir master of arts in Liberal studies, 95-97, res prof, phil, Univ at Albany 97. **HONORS AND AWARDS** Jones Fund Awd for Superior Tchg, Lafayette Col, 62-63; Fac res award, Lafayette Col, 63, 64, Southern IL Univ, 65, Univ at Albany, 67, 68, 71, 87; Signum Laudis Awd for Excellence in Tchg and Res, Univ at Albany, 86. **MEMBERSHIPS** Mem, Prog Comt, Am Soc for Aestheics, 79; Chair, Exec Comt Int Assoc for Phil and Relig, 80-81, mem 76-81; Mem, Advisory Comt, Conf on Deconstructionism, Univ at Stony Brook, 83; Mem, Advisory Comt Conf on Philosophy as Lit: Lit as Philos, Univ IA, IA City, 84; Ch, Eastern Div Am Soc for Aesthetics, 87-88, mem 85-88. **RESEARCH** Philos of relig; aesthetics; philos of the hum. **SELECTED PUBLICATIONS** Auth, The Metaphysics of William James and John-Dewey, 69; Religion as Art: An Interpretation, 81 (4th print); Essays in books, Religion as an Aspect of the Various Disciplines, In: The Status of Religious Studies in Public Universities (Milton D. McLean, ed), 67; When is Religion Art? Answer: When It Is a Jar, In: Art, Creativity and the Sacred (Diane Apostolos-Cappadona, ed), 84; Quine's Half Entities', and Gadamer's Too, In: Philosophy as Literature: Literature as Philosophy (Donald Marshall, ed), 87; The Sublime, The Encyclopedia of Religion (Mircea Eliade, ed), 87; Other articles have appeared in Jour of Phil, Am Phil Quart, Jour Aesthetic and Art Criticism, Jour Comparative Lit and Aesthetics, Jour Am Acad of Relig, Phil and Phenomenological Res, Rev of Metaphysics, Brit Jour of Aesthetics, Relig Studies, and The Monist. **CONTACT ADDRESS** Dept of Philos, SUNY, Albany, 1400 Washington Ave, Albany, NY 12222. **EMAIL** t.marthand@albany.edu

MARTOS, JOSEPH
PERSONAL Born 06/11/1943, New York, NY **DISCIPLINE** RELIGIOUS STUDIES **EDUCATION** Gregorian Univ (Rome), STB, 66; DePaul Univ, PhD, 73. **CAREER** Assoc Prof & Chmn Theol Dept, Allentown Col, PA, 85-92; Prof & Chmn, Russell Inst, Spalding Univ, LA, 92-. **MEMBERSHIPS** AAR; CTSA; CTS; NALM **RESEARCH** History; ritual; culture. **SELECTED PUBLICATIONS** Doors to the Sacred: A Historical Introduction to Sacraments in the Catholic Church, Triumph Bks, 91; Sacrament of Reconciliation, Modern Catholic Ency, 94; The Wild Man's Journey: Reflections on Male Spirituality, St Anthony Messenger Press, 96; Equal at the Creation: Sexism, Society, and Christian Thought, Univ of Toronto Press, 98; auth, Catholic Divorce, Crossroad, 00. **CONTACT ADDRESS** Spalding Univ, Louisville, KY 40203. **EMAIL** jmartos@spalding.edu

MARTY, MARTIN EMIL
PERSONAL Born 02/05/1928, West Point, NE, m, 1952, 5 children **DISCIPLINE** MODERN RELIGIOUS HISTORY **EDUCATION** Concordia Sem, BA, 49, MDiv, 52; Lutheran Sch Theol, Chicago, STM, 54; Univ Chicago, PhD(church hist), 56. **CAREER** From assoc prof to prof relig hist, 63-78, assoc dean divinity sch, 70-75, F M CONE DISTINGUISHED SERV PROF, UNIV CHICAGO, 78-, Vis assoc prof, Lutheran Sch Theol, Chicago, 61 & Union Theol Sem, New York, 65; bd mem, Nat Humanities Ctr, 76-; assoc ed, Christian Century, ed newslet, Context & coed, Church Hist. **HONORS AND AWARDS** Nat Humanities Medal; Nat Bk Awd; Medal of the Am Acad of Arts and Sciences, the Univ of Chicago Alumni Medal; Distinguished Serv Medal of the Asn of Theological Schools; nineteen from us cols & univs. **MEMBERSHIPS** Fel Am Acad Arts & Sci; Soc Am Historians; Soc Values Higher Educ. **RESEARCH** Nineteenth century religious history of United States, Great Britain and Western Europe; effects of political-industrial revolutions on religion; history of religious behavior in America. **SELECTED PUBLICATIONS** Auth, American Religious History in the 80s, Church Hist, vol 0062, 93; Dictionary of American Religious Biography, 2nd ed, Cath Hist Rev, vol 0079, 93; From the Centripetal to the Centrifugal in Culture ind Religion, Theol Today, vol 0051, 94; Religion and Radical Politics, J Relig, vol 0074, 94; Defending the Faith, J Amer Hist, vol 0082, 95; Evangelicalism, J Southern Hist, vol 0061, 95; God in the Wasteland, J Relig, vol 0076, 96; Neale, J.M. and the Quest for Sobornost, J Relig, vol 0076, 96; Religion, Public Life, and the American Polity, J Relig, vol 0077, 97. **CONTACT ADDRESS** Divinity Sch Swift Hall, Univ of Chicago, 239 Scottswood Rd., Riverside, IL 60546. **EMAIL** memarty@aol.com

MARTYN, JAMES LOUIS
PERSONAL Born 10/11/1925, Dallas, TX, m, 1950, 3 children **DISCIPLINE** NEW TESTAMENT **EDUCATION** Tex Agr & Mech Col, BS, 46; Andover Newton Theol Sch, BD, 53; Yale Univ, MA, 56, PhD, 57. **CAREER** Instr Bibl hist, Wellesley Coll, 58-59; from asst prof to assoc prof New Testament, 59-67, Edward Robinson Prof Bibl Theol, Union Theol Sem, NY, 67-87, Fulbright fel, Univ Gottingen, 57-58; Guggenheim fel, 63-64. **MEMBERSHIPS** Soc Bibl Lit. **RESEARCH** The Fourth Gospel; Jewish Christianity. **SELECTED PUBLICATIONS** Auth, Notes and Comments on the Letter of James Paul, United Christian Youth Movement, 62; co-ed, Studies in Luke-Acts, Abingdon, 66; auth, Epistemology at the turn of the ages, In: Christian History and Interpretation, Cambridge, 67; Attitudes ancient and modern toward tradition about Jesus, Student World, 67; History and Theology in the Fourth Gospel, Harper, 68, rev ed, Abingdon, 78; Source criticism and religionageschichte in the Fourth Gospel, Perspective, 70; The Gospel of John in Christian History, Paulist, 78; auth, Galatians, A.B., New York: Doubleday, 97; Theological Issues in the Letters of Paul, Nashville: Abingdon, 97. **CONTACT ADDRESS** 124 Downs Rd., Bethany, CT 06524. **EMAIL** lmartyn@pantheaen.yale.edu

MARTYN, SUSAN
PERSONAL Born 11/24/1947, Fairbanks, AK, m, 1969, 2 children **DISCIPLINE** LAW **EDUCATION** St Olaf Col, BA, MArquette Univ, JD. **CAREER** Prof. **MEMBERSHIPS** Am Law Institute, Am Bar Asn, Mich State Bar Asn. **RESEARCH** Legal Ethics and Bioethics. **SELECTED PUBLICATIONS** Auth, Informed Consent in the Practice of Law, Geo Wash Law Rev, 80; Peer Review and Quality Assurance for Lawyers, Univ Toledo, 88; Coming to Terms with Death: The Cruzan Case, Hastings, 91; auth, Visions of the Eternal Law Firm: The Future of Law Firm Screens, 45, S. Car. L., Rev 1, 94; auth, Substituted Judgment, Best Interests and the Need for Best Respect, 3, Cambridge Quarterly of Healthcare Ehtincs, 194, 94; Physician Assisted Suicide: The Lethal Flaws of the Ninth and Second Circuit Decisions, U Calif Law Rev, 97; auth, Now is the moment to Reflect: Two Yeas of Experience with Oergon's Physician-Assisted Suicide Law, 8 Elder Law, J. 1, 00. **CONTACT ADDRESS** Col Law, Univ of Toledo, Toledo, OH 43606. **EMAIL** smartyn@uoft02.utoledo.edu

MARUNA, SHADD
PERSONAL Born Canton, OH, 1 child **DISCIPLINE** LAW **EDUCATION** Ill State Univ, BA; Northwestern Univ MA; PhD. **CAREER** Asst prof, State Univ NYork at Albany, 98-. **HONORS AND AWARDS** Fulbright Scholar; Guggenheim Fel. **MEMBERSHIPS** Am Soc of Criminology, Am Psychol Asn, Peace Studies Asn. **RESEARCH** Offender Rehabilitation, Criminal Careers, Community Corrections. **SELECTED PUBLICATIONS** Auth, Making Good: How Ex-convicts Reform and Reclaim Their Lives, Am Psychol Asn Books (Washington, DC), 00. **CONTACT ADDRESS** Dept Criminal Justice, SUNY, Albany, 135 Western Ave, Albany, NY 12222-1000. **EMAIL** shadd@csc.albany.edu

MARX, ANTHONY W.
PERSONAL Born 02/28/1959, New York, NY, m, 1992, 2 children **DISCIPLINE** POLITICAL SCIENCE **EDUCATION** Yale Univ, BA, 81; Princeton Univ, MPA, 84, MA, 86, PhD, 90. **CAREER** Asst Prof of Polit Sci, Columbia Univ, 90-96; Assoc Prof, 96-; Dir, Ctr for Hist and Social Sci, Columbia Univ, 00-. **HONORS AND AWARDS** APSA Ralph Bunche Awd, 99; Guggenheim Fellow, 94, 98; US Inst of Peace Grant, 92-93; Nat Hum Ctr Fellow, 97-98; Howard Foundation Fellow, 97-98. **MEMBERSHIPS** APSA; SSHA. **RESEARCH** Comparative politics. **SELECTED PUBLICATIONS** Auth, Lessons of Struggle, Oxford Univ Press, 92; auth, Contested Images and Implications of South African Nationhood, The Violence Within: Cultural and Political Analyses of National Conflicts, Westview Press, 93; The State, Economy and Self-Determination in South Africa, Polit Sci Quart, 107:4, 93; auth, Contested Citizenship The Dynamics of Racial Identity and Social Movements, Int Rev of Soc Hist, vol 40, 95; auth, Race Making and the Nation-State, World Polit, vol 48, 1/96; auth, Apartheid's End: South Africa's Transition from Racial Domination, Ethnic and Racial Stud, 20:3, 7/97; auth, Making Race and Nation: A Comparison of the United States, South Africa and Brazil, Cambridge Univ Press, 98. **CONTACT ADDRESS** 420 W 118th St, Rm 701, New York, NY 10027. **EMAIL** awm4@columbia.edu

MASCHKE, TIMOTHY
PERSONAL Born 12/24/1947, Decatur, AL, 3 children **DISCIPLINE** THEOLOGY **EDUCATION** Concordia Sem, MDiv, 74, STM, 81; Trinity Evang Div Sch, DMin, 84; Marquette Univ, PhD, 93. **CAREER** Asst prof, 82-87, assoc prof, 88-97, PROF, 97-, CONCORDIA UNIV. **HONORS AND AWARDS** Faculty Laureate, 93. **MEMBERSHIPS** AAR; Am Society of Church History; Lutheran Liturgical Renewal; Sixteenth Century Scholars; Society of Reformation Research. **RESEARCH** Lutther and Angels; Worship Theory and Practice. **CONTACT ADDRESS** Concordia Univ, Wisconsin, 12800 N Lake Shore Dr, Mequon, WI 53097-2402. **EMAIL** tmaschke@cuw.edu

MASHBURN, AMY R.
DISCIPLINE LAW **EDUCATION** Eckerd Col, BA; Univ Fla, JD. **CAREER** Prof, Univ Fla, 90-; past assoc, Dean, Mead, Egerton, Bloodworth, Capouano Bozarth, Orlando, Fla; articles ed, Fla Law Rev. **MEMBERSHIPS** Fla Bar; Order of the Coif; mem, Fla Bar Prof Ethics Comt; mem. Fla Bar Standing Comt on Professionalism. **RESEARCH** Civil procedure, professional responsibility, administrative law. **CONTACT ADDRESS** School of Law, Univ of Florida, PO Box 117625, Gainesville, FL 32611-7625. **EMAIL** mashburn@law.ufl.edu

MASK, E. JEFFEREY
PERSONAL Born 01/22/1956, New Orleans, LA, m, 1980, 2 children **DISCIPLINE** THEOLOGY **EDUCATION** Univ Mississippi, BA, 77; Southeastern Baptist Theol Sem, MDiv, 81; Emory Univ, PhD, 90. **CAREER** Asst Prof, Wesley Col, 91-95, ASSOC PROF WESLEY COL, 95-. **HONORS AND AWARDS** Pres Awd for Excellence,98. **MEMBERSHIPS** Am Acad of Relig; Nat Assoc of Baptist Prof of Relig. **RESEARCH** American Theology and Religion; Relation of Religion and Culture. **SELECTED PUBLICATIONS** Auth, At Liberty Under God: Toward a Baptist Ecclesiology, Univ Press of Am, 97. **CONTACT ADDRESS** Wesley Col, Delaware, 120 N. State St., Dover, DE 19901. **EMAIL** maskje@mail.wesley.edu

MASOLO, D. A.
DISCIPLINE PHILOSOPHY **EDUCATION** Gregorian Univ, Rome, PhD. **CAREER** Justus Bier prof of hum. **RESEARCH** The impact of cult(s) on moral and conceptual knowledge. **SELECTED PUBLICATIONS** Auth, bk chapters on ethics, social and political philos, and African philosophy; ed, co-ed, several bk(s), Philosophy and Cultures; African Philosophy In Search of Identity, Ind Univ Press, Edinburgh UP, 94. **CONTACT ADDRESS** Dept of Philos, Univ of Louisville, 2301 S 3rd St, Louisville, KY 40292. **EMAIL** damaso01@ulkyvm.louisville.edu

MASON, DAVID RAYMOND
PERSONAL Born 11/06/1936, Hagerstown, MD, m, 1963, 3 children **DISCIPLINE** PHILOSOPHICAL & CONTEMPORARY THEOLOGY **EDUCATION** WVA Univ, AB, 59; Gen Theol Sem, MDiv, 62; Univ Chicago, MA, 69, PhD, 73. **CAREER** Instr philos, Cent YMCA Community Col, 68-70 & 71-72; asst prof relig studies, 72-76, Assoc Prof Relig Studies John Carroll Univ, 77, Prof, 82, Dir Tuohy Chair, 97, Grauel fac, fel, John Carroll Univ, 79, 86. **MEMBERSHIPS** Am Acad Relig; Soc Studies Process Milos; Metaphys Soc Am. **RESEARCH** Whitehead studies; correlation of concepts of time and providence, particularly historically and present possibilities; the logic of God-lang. **SELECTED PUBLICATIONS** Auth, Three recent treatments of the ontological argument, Ohio J Relig, spring 74; An examination of Worship as a key for reexamining the God problem, J Relig, 1/75; auth, "Time in Whitehead Heidegger," Process Studies, 75; Can we speculate on how God acts?, J of Relig, 1/77; auth, Analysis of Perception, Zygon, 75; Some abstract yet crucial thoughts about suffering, Dialog, spring 77; What sense does it make to say God knows future contingent things?, J Relig Studies, spring 79; Time and Providence, Univ Press Am, 82; ed, Talking About God, Seabury, 83; Can God be both perfect and free, Relig Studies, 2/82; Selfhood, Transcendence, & the Experience of God, Modern Theology, 87; Gilkeyon God and the World, Am Jour of Theol & Philos, 95; The Self and Its Body: A Model for

the God-World Relation, Jour of Relig Studies, 95. **CONTACT ADDRESS** Dept of Relig Studies, John Carroll Univ, 20700 N Park Blvd, Cleveland, OH 44118-4581. **EMAIL** dmason@jcu.edu

MASON, H. E.
DISCIPLINE PHILOSOPHY **EDUCATION** Harvard Univ, PhD. **RESEARCH** Moral and political philosophy; philosophy of the mind; Wittgenstein. **SELECTED PUBLICATIONS** Auth, Realistic Interpretations of Moral Questions, Univ Minn, 88; On the Many Faces of Morality: Reflections on Fear and Trembling, 88; AIDS: Some Ethical Considerations, Minn Medicine, 87; On the Treatment of the Notion of the Will in Wittgenstein's Later Writings, 86; On Wittgenstein's Use of the Notion of a Language Game, 78; co-auth, Some Thought Experiments about Mind and Meaning, Stanford, 90. **CONTACT ADDRESS** Philosophy Dept, Univ of Minnesota, Twin Cities, 355 Ford Hall, 224 Church St SE, Minneapolis, MN 55455. **EMAIL** hmason@tc.umn.edu

MASON, JEFFREY A.
PERSONAL Born 05/26/1945, Galveston, TX, d, 1977, 2 children **DISCIPLINE** PHILOSOPHY **EDUCATION** Birbeck Col, London, PhD, 75. **CAREER** Middlesex Polytech, London, 72-75, 76-82; Calif State, 75-76; Calif State, San Diego, 82-83; Middlesex Univ, 93-98; Irvine Valley College, 99-. **MEMBERSHIPS** APA. **RESEARCH** Philosophy and rhetoric; Distance philosophy teaching. **SELECTED PUBLICATIONS** Auth, Philosophical Rhetoric, Routledge, 89; auth, The Future of Thinking, Routledge, 92; auth, The Philosopher's Address, Lexington, forthcoming; auth, "The Philosophy Is Address," Lexington Books, Summer 99. **CONTACT ADDRESS** 825 12th St, Huntington Beach, CA 92648. **EMAIL** jeff4@surfside.net

MASON, SHEILA
DISCIPLINE ADVANCED ETHICS PHILOSOPHY, PHILOSOPHY OF LEISURE **EDUCATION** McGill Univ, BA, 65; Purdue Univ, MA, 67, PhD, 72. **CAREER** Assoc prof, Concordia Univ. **SELECTED PUBLICATIONS** Auth, "Inclusive Philosophy: Feminist Strategies for the Recoverry of Persons," in A Reader in Feminist Ethics, ed. Debra Shogan, (Canadian Scholars Press: Toronto, 93); auth, "Moral Talk," in A Reader in Feminist Ethics, ed. Debra Shogan, (Canadian Scholars Press: Toronto, 93); auth, Enseigner l'ethique selon le paradigme du 'moi moralement lie, Philosopher No. 16, 94; auth, "Education for Leisure: Moving towards Community," Leisure and Ethics: Reflections on the Philosophy of Leisure, Vol II, American Assoc for Leisure and Recreation, 95; auth, "The Self and the Ethics of Care," in The Conceptual Self in Context, eds. Ulrich Neisser and Robyn Fivush, Cambridge Univ Press; auth, "L'Intelligence Morale," Actes du Colloque: De L'Ethique aux ethiques, Ethica, Vol. 9, no. 2, 97; auth, "L'ethique Narrative et la compassion," ERES Groupe de Recherche en Ethiue Sociale, 98. **CONTACT ADDRESS** Dept of Philos, Concordia Univ, Montreal, 1455 de Maisonneuve W, Montreal, QC, Canada H3G 1M8.

MASON, STEVE
PERSONAL Born 09/14/1957, Toronto, ON, Canada **DISCIPLINE** EARLY JUDAISM AND CHRISTIAN ORIGINS **EDUCATION** McMaster Univ, BA, 80, MA, 81; Univ St Michaels Col, PhD, 86. **CAREER** Vis asst prof, Mem Univ NF, 87-89; prof and head, Dept Classics & Ancient Mediter Stud, Penn State Univ, 96-96; asst prof, 89-92, assoc prof, 92-98, prof, 98-, York Univ-Toronto. **MEMBERSHIPS** Soc Bibl Lit; Am Philol Asn; Studiorum Novi Testamenti Soc; Can Soc Bibl Stud. **RESEARCH** Philosophy and religion in the Greco-Roman world, especially Judaism (specialization: Flavius Josephus) and early Christianity. **SELECTED PUBLICATIONS** Coed An Early Christian Reader, Can Scholars Press, 90; auth Flavius Josephus on the Pharisees, E J Brill, 91; Josephus and the New Testament, Hendrickson, 92; ed Understanding Josephus: Seven Perspectives, Sheffield Acad Press, 98. **CONTACT ADDRESS** York Univ, 219 Vanier Col, Toronto, ON, Canada M3J 1P3. **EMAIL** smason@yorku.ca

MASSANARI, RONALD LEE
PERSONAL Born 06/04/1941, Champaign, IL, m, 1963, 2 children **DISCIPLINE** HISTORY OF CHRISTIAN THOUGHT **EDUCATION** Goshen Col, BA, 63; Univ Wis-Madison, MA, 65; Garrett Theol Sem, BD, 66; Duke Univ, PhD(relig), 69. **CAREER** Vis asst prof church hist, Divinity Sch, Duke Univ, 69-70; from asst prof to assoc prof, 70-80, Prof Relig, Alma Col, 80-, Adj prof, San Francisco Theol Sem, 77-. **MEMBERSHIPS** Am Soc Church Hist; Am Acad Relig **RESEARCH** Religion and imagination; myth and ritual; political theology. **SELECTED PUBLICATIONS** Auth, " Sexual Imagery and Religion: An Intercultural Exploration," Gender in World Religions, Vol II, (91); auth, "Dualism, Nondualism, and the Human Problem: An Exploration into Worldview Contexts of Western and Eastern Religions," Journal of Religious Studies, Vol 18, (92): 1-2; auth, "Nondualism Not Monism: A Response to Mark Wigierski," This World, 28, 93; auth, "Re-Imagining God: In the Very Presence Therof" Journal of the Interdenominational Theological Center, Vol. XXIII, 2, 96; auth, "Carnal Spirituality: A Nondual Response to Traditional Dualism: Journal of Religious Taditions, Vol 20, 97; auth, "When Mountains are Mountains and Gardens are Gardens: Explorations into Sacred Space, Worldviews, and Ethics," Journal of Developing Societies, Vol XIII, (97): 3-4; auth, "The Pluralisms of American 'Religious Pluralism: Journal of Church and State, Vol. 40, 3, 98; auth, "For Questioning is the Piety of Thought,' But, Not Without Consequences in Technocratic Society," Teaching Ttheology and Religion, Vol 1, 3, 98; auth, "A Problem in Environmental Ethics: Western and Eastern Styles," Journal of Christian-Buddhist Studies, Vol. 18, 98; auth, "The Net of Tantra On-line," Nova Religio, Vol 2, No 4, 99. **CONTACT ADDRESS** Dept of Relig, Alma Col, 614 W Superior St, Alma, MI 48801-1511. **EMAIL** massanari@alma.edu

MASSEY, GERALD J.
PERSONAL Born 02/11/1934, Wauseon, OH, m, 1957, 4 children **DISCIPLINE** PHILOSOPHY OF SCIENCE, SYMBOLIC LOGIC **EDUCATION** Univ Notre Dame, BA, 56, MA, 60; Princeton Univ, MA, 62, PhD(philos), 64. **CAREER** From Asst prof to prof philos, Mich State Univ, 63-70; chmn dept philos, 70-76, Prof Philos, Hist & Philos Sci, Univ Pittsburgh, 76, Sr Res Assoc, Ctr Philos Sci, 76-, Mellon fel, Univ Pittsburgh, 69-70. **MEMBERSHIPS** Philos Sci Asn (secy-treas, 65-70); Asn Symbolic Logic; Am Philos Asn; Am Cath Philos Asn; AAUP. **RESEARCH** Modal logic, philosophy of physical geometry; philosophical logic. **SELECTED PUBLICATIONS CONTACT ADDRESS** Dept of Philos, Univ of Pittsburgh, Pittsburgh, PA 15260.

MASSEY, JAMES EARL
PERSONAL Born 01/04/1930, Ferndale, MI, m **DISCIPLINE** THEOLOGY **EDUCATION** Detroit Bible Coll, BRE, BTh 1961; Oberlin Grad School of Theol, AM 1964; Asbury Theol Seminary, DD 1972; Pacific School of Religion, addit study 1972; Univ of MI; Boston Coll Grad School; Ashland Theological Seminary, DD, 1991; Huntington Coll, DD, 1994; Tuskegee Univ, Hum D, 1995; Warner Pacific College, DD, 1995; Anderson University, Litt D, 1995; Washington & Jefferson College, DD, 1997; North Park Thological Seminas, DD, 99. **CAREER** Church of God of Detroit, assoc minister 1949-51, 53-54; Metro Church of God, sr pastor 1954-76; Anderson Coll, School of Theol, campus minister, prof of religious studies 1969-77; Christian Brotherhood, speaker 1977-82; Anderson University, School of Theol, prof of new testament 1981-84; Tuskegee Univ Chapel & Univ Prof of Religion, dean 1984-89; Anderson Univ, School of Theology, Dean, professor of preaching and Biblical studies, 90-95, Dean Emeritus, 00. **HONORS AND AWARDS** Danforth Foundation, Underwood Fellow, 1972-73; Staley Foundation, Staley Distinguished Christian Scholar, 1977; Wesleyan Theological Society, Lifetime Achievement Awd, 1995. **MEMBERSHIPS** Lecturer Gautschi Lectures Fuller Theol Sem 1975-1986; Freitas Lectures Asbury Theol Sem 1977, Rall Co-Lecturer Garrett-Evangelical Sem 1980, Mullins Lectures So Bapt Sem 1981, Swartley Lectures Eastern Baptist Sem 1982, Jameson Jones Lecturer Iliff School of Theol 1983, Rom Lectures Trinity Evangelical DivSchool 1984; northcutt lectures Southwestern Bapt Theol Sem 1986;l bd of dir Detroit Council of Churches; theol study commiss Detroit Council of Churches; corp mem Inter-Varsity Christian Fellowship; matl comm Black Churchmen; mem Wesleyan Theol Soc; ed bd Christian Scholars Review; bd of dir Warner Press Inc; vchmn Publ Bd of the Church of God; ed adv Tyndale House Publisher 1968-69; comm chmn Christian Unity; mem Natl Assoc of Coll & Univ Chaplains; bdof dir Natl Black Evangelical oc; life mem NAACP; Lausanne Continuation Comm 1974-; pres Anderson Civil Serv Merit Commiss 1975-81; ed bd Leadership Mag; bd of dir Natl Religious Broadcasteers; ed bd Preaching Mag 1987; Resource Scholar, Christianity Today Inst 1985; sr editor, Christanity Today, 1993-95. **CONTACT ADDRESS** Sch of Theology, Anderson Univ, 367 Beverly Rd., Greensboro, AL 36744.

MASTERS, ROGER D.
PERSONAL Born 05/08/1933, Boston, MA, m, 1984, 3 children **DISCIPLINE** POLITICAL SCIENCE **EDUCATION** Harvard Col, AB, 55; Univ Chicago, MA, 58, PhD, 61. **CAREER** Asst prof, Yale Univ, 61-67; Assoc to full prof, Dartmouth Col, 67-98; Nelson A Rockefeller Prof Emeritus, 98-. **HONORS AND AWARDS** Fulbright Fellowship to France, 58-59; Joint Yale-SSRC Fellow, 64-65; John Simon Guggenheim Fellow, 67-68; John Sloan Dickey Third Cent Prof of Govt, Dartmouth Col, 79-85; Dir d'Etudes Assoc, Ecole des Hautes Etudes en Sci Soc, Paris France, 86. **MEMBERSHIPS** Am Asn Adv of Sci; Am Polit Sci Asn. **RESEARCH** Political philosophy, Biology and Human Social Behavior. **SELECTED PUBLICATIONS** Auth, Beyond Relativism: Science, Philosophy, and Human Nature, Univ Press of NE, 93; co-ed, The Neurotransmitter Revolution, S Ill Univ Press, 93; co-ed, Rousseau's Social Contract, with Discourse on Virtue of Heroes, Geneva Manuscript and Fragments Collected Writings of Rousseau, vol 4, Univ Press of NE, 94; gen ed, Gruter Institute Reader: Biology, Human Social Behavior, and Law, McGraw Hill, primis; auth, Machiavelli, Leonardo and the Science of Power, Univ Notre Dame Press, 96; auth, Fortune is a River: Leonardo da Vinci and Niccolo Machiavelli's Magnificent Dream to Change the Course of Florentine History, Free Press, 98. **CONTACT ADDRESS** Dept of Govt, Dartmouth Col, Silsby 6108, Hanover, NH 03755.

MATASAR, RICHARD
PERSONAL Born 06/04/1952, m, 1975, 2 children **DISCIPLINE** LAW **EDUCATION** Univ Pa, BA, 74; Univ Pa, JD, 77. **CAREER** Law Clerk, Judge Max Rosenn, U.S. Court of Appeals for the Third Circuit, 77-78; assoc atty, Arnold & Porter, 78-80; assoc prof, Univ of Iowa, 80-91; Dean, Chicago art college of Law, 91-96; DEAN, COL OF LAW, UNIV FLA, 96-99; Pres, Dean, New York Law School, 00-. **HONORS AND AWARDS** Phi Beta Kappa; Pi gamma Mu; Order of the Coif. **MEMBERSHIPS** ABA; AALS. **RESEARCH** Civil procedure; legal ethics; federal courts; professionalism; legal educ. **SELECTED PUBLICATIONS** Auth, "Rediscovering 'One Constitutional Case': Procedural Rules and the Rejection of Gibbs Test for Supplemental Jurisdiction", in 71 Calif L Rev, 83; auth, "A Pendent and Ancillary Jurisdiction Primer: The Scope and Limits of Supplemental Jurisdiction", in 17 U.C. Davis L. Rev 103, 83; coauth, "Procedural Common Law, Federal Jurisdictional Policy, and Abandonment of the Adequate and Independent State Grounds Doctrine", in 86 Colum L Rev, 86; auth, "Personal Immunities Under Section 1983: The Limits of the Court's Historical Analysis", in 40 Ark L Rev, 87; auth, "Commercialist Manifesto: Entrepreneurs, Academics, and Purity of the Heart and Soul", in 48 Fla L Rev, 96. **CONTACT ADDRESS** New York Law Sch, 57 Worty St, New York, NY 10013. **EMAIL** rMatasar@NYLS.edu

MATEJKA, GEORGE
PERSONAL Born 11/28/1950, Cleveland, OH, s **DISCIPLINE** PHILOSOPHY **EDUCATION** Cath Univ of Am, MA, 73 Philos; Gregorian Univ of Am, 81 Theol **CAREER** Asst Prof Philos, 91, Borromes Col of OH; Assoc Prof of Philos, 92-present, Notre Dame Col of OH **MEMBERSHIPS** Am Philos Assoc **RESEARCH** Umberto Eco **CONTACT ADDRESS** Dept of Philos, Ursuline Col, Pepper Pike, OH 44124. **EMAIL** gmatejka@ursuline.edu

MATHENY, PAUL DUANE
PERSONAL Born 07/13/1953, Conroe, TX, m, 1983, 1 child **DISCIPLINE** RELIGION **EDUCATION** Clarke Univ, BA; Goddard Col, MA, Princeton Theol Sem, MDiv, Yale, STM, Univ Heidelberg, DTh. **CAREER** Bellarmine Col, vis lectr; Barton Col, asst prof; Westhampton Christian Church Roanoke, VA, sr minister; First Christian Church Conroe, TX, sr minister. **MEMBERSHIPS** KBS of NA, AAR, IBS **RESEARCH** K. Barth's theology and ethics; Dietrich Bonhoeffer's life and work; theology and science. **SELECTED PUBLICATIONS** Ed. The Young Bonhoeffer, Fortress Press, forthcoming, ed. Renaissance and Reformation, T&T Clark, 92, auth, Dogmatics and Ethics, Peter Lang, 90. **CONTACT ADDRESS** First Christian Church, 549 Stephen F. Austin Dr, Conroe, TX 77302. **EMAIL** paul.matheny.div.83@aya.yale.edu

MATHER, HENRY S.
DISCIPLINE CONTRACTS, JURISPRUDENCE, AND SECURED TRANSACTIONS **EDUCATION** Univ Rochester, BA, 59; Columbia Univ, MA, 61; Cornell Univ, JD, 70. **CAREER** Prof, Univ of SC. **SELECTED PUBLICATIONS** Publ on, contract law. **CONTACT ADDRESS** School of Law, Univ of So Carolina, Columbia, Law Center, Columbia, SC 29208. **EMAIL** law0149@univscvm.csd.scarolina.edu

MATHEWES, CHARLES
PERSONAL Born 07/09/1969, Montclair, NJ, s **DISCIPLINE** RELIGIOUS STUDIES **EDUCATION** Univ Chicago, PhD 97, MA 92; Georgetown Univ, BA 91. **CAREER** Univ Virginia, 97-. **MEMBERSHIPS** AAR; SCE; APSA; SCP; APA. **RESEARCH** Theology; Ethics; Politics; Mural Psychology; Nature; Evil and Sin; Tradition. **SELECTED PUBLICATIONS** Auth, Augustine's Demythologizing of Evil in De Civitate Dei, in: The Unity of Belief and Practice in Early Christianity, Blackwell, forthcoming; Theology and Cultur, in: Blackwell Companion to Theol, forthcoming; Augustinian Anthropology: A Proposal and a Partial Map, Jour of Religious Ethics, forthcoming; Pluralism Otherness and the Augustine Tradition, Modern Theol, 98; rev, The Rebirth of Tragedy, Martha Nussbaum, Jonathon Lear, Bernard Williams, Anglican Theol Rev, 97. **CONTACT ADDRESS** Dept of Religious Studies, Univ of Virginia, Charlottesville, VA 22903. **EMAIL** ctmathewes@virginia.edu

MATHEWS, EDWARD G., JR.
PERSONAL Born 06/10/1954, Albany, NY, m, 1985 **DISCIPLINE** THEOLOGY **EDUCATION** Cath univ Am, BA, 82; MA, Semitic Lang and Lit; 82; Columbia Univ NYork, MA, Armenian Hist and Lit, 91; M Philos, 94; PhD, 96. **CAREER** ADJ FAC, Our lady Lebanon Maronite Sem Wash, 85; inst, Cath Univ Am Wash, 85-87; adj prof, 93; adj, Hebrew Univ Israel, 94; Evangel Theol Sem Armenia, 98; Instrm Univ Scranton, PA, 89-. **HONORS AND AWARDS** Cardinal Gibbons Scholarship, 78-82; Phi Beta Kappa, 82; Cath Univ Scholar, 84087; Cath Univ Grad Student Assoc Scholar, 86; App Pres Fel of the Fac, Columbia Univ, 90-94; Zohrab Fel, Columbia Univ, 94-96; Vis Res Fel, Hebrew Univ Jerusalem, 94-95. **MEMBERSHIPS** Soc for Bibl Lit; Asn Int des etudes armeniennes; Soc for Armenian Studies; Nat asn for Armenian Studies and Res; cath Bibl Asn; N Am Patristic Soc. **RESEARCH** History; Literature and Theology of Early Eastern

Christianity; Historical biblical Exegesis; Greek Patristics. **SELECTED PUBLICATIONS** Auth, The Armenian Literary Corpus Attributed to St Ephrem the Syrian: Prolegomena to a Project, StNersess Theol Rev, 96; The Armenian Version of Ephrem's Commentary on Genesis, The Book of Genesis in Jewish and Oriental Christian Interpretation, 97; The Armenian Commentary on the Book of Genesis attributed to Ephrem the Syrian, 98. **CONTACT ADDRESS** Dept of Foreign Languages, Univ of Scranton, Scranton, PA 18510. **EMAIL** egm381@vofs.edu

MATHEWS, MARK WILLIAM
PERSONAL Born 06/03/1955, Allentown, PA, d, 2 children **DISCIPLINE** PHILOSOPHY **EDUCATION** Colgate Univ, BA, 77; Univ Minn, PhD, 93. **CAREER** Metropolitan State Univ, asst prof, 91-. **HONORS AND AWARDS** Outstanding Tchr of the Yr. **MEMBERSHIPS** APA, ACJS. **RESEARCH** Ethics; Professional and law enforcement ethics. **CONTACT ADDRESS** Dept of Philosophy, Metropolitan State Univ, 1770 James Ave S #2, Minneapolis, MN 55403-2827. **EMAIL** mark.mathews@metrostate.edu

MATHIAS, WILLIAM J.
PERSONAL Born 10/06/1938, Atlanta, GA, m, 1981, 2 children **DISCIPLINE** CRIMINAL JUSTICE **EDUCATION** Univ Ga, BBA, 61; MS, 66; EdD, 69. **CAREER** From Asst Prof to Prof, Univ SC, 75-. **HONORS AND AWARDS** Nat Defense Fel, 3 years. **MEMBERSHIPS** Acad of Criminal Justice Sci, ASC, SCHA. **RESEARCH** Juvenile justice, youth at risk, children's and juvenile history. **SELECTED PUBLICATIONS** Auth, "Police Education," in The Ambivalent Force, 2nd ed (Hinsdale, IL: Dryden Pr, 76); coauth, Foundations of Criminal Justice, Prentice-Hall Publ (Englewood Cliffs, NJ), 80; coauth, The History of the South Carolina Penitentiary, Ohio St UP (Columbus, OH), 00. **CONTACT ADDRESS** Dept Criminal Justice, Univ of So Carolina, Columbia, Columbia, SC 29225-0001. **EMAIL** wjm@sc.edu

MATHIS, ROBERT
PERSONAL m, 1 child **DISCIPLINE** CHURCH ADMINISTRATION **EDUCATION** Univ Tex, MEd, 76; Southwestern Baptist Theol Sem, MRE, 78, PhD, 84; Univ Miss, EdD, 95. **CAREER** Instr, Hale Ctr ISD, 69-70; prof, NOBTS, 86-98. **HONORS AND AWARDS** S Baptist res fel; Outstanding res award, SBRF, 95; min edu, mountainview baptist church, 74-77; ridglea baptist church, 77-81; assoc pastor, 81-86. **MEMBERSHIPS** Rel Res Assn, SBREA. **SELECTED PUBLICATIONS** Auth, Teacher Preparation Material, The Adult Teacher, 94; Submission, Theol Educator, 92. **CONTACT ADDRESS** Sch Edu Ministries, Southwestern Baptist Theol Sem, PO Box 22000, Fort Worth, TX 76122-0418. **EMAIL** rrm@swbts.swbts.edu

MATICICH, KAREN K.
PERSONAL Born Portland, OR **DISCIPLINE** BIBLICAL STUDIES **EDUCATION** Univ Ore, BS, 85; Dallas Theol Sem, ThM, 90; Cambridge Univ, PhD, 93. **CAREER** Assoc prof, Int Sch of Theol, 95-. **MEMBERSHIPS** Soc for Old Testament Study, Soc of Biblical Lit. **CONTACT ADDRESS** Dept Bible, Intl Sch of Theol, 7623 East Ave, Fontana, CA 92336.

MATOVINA, TIMOTHY M.
PERSONAL Born 10/13/1955, Hammond, IN, m, 1996, 1 child **DISCIPLINE** THEOLOGY, RELIGION **EDUCATION** Cath Univ of Am, PhD, 93. **CAREER** Asst prof, 95-00, Loyola Marymount Univ; assoc prof, Univ Notre Dame, 00-. **MEMBERSHIPS** Am Acad of Relig; Acad of Cath Hispanic Theol; Am Hist Asn. **RESEARCH** Religion; Cultural studies; Latino studies; Catholicism; Ethnicity. **SELECTED PUBLICATIONS** Ed, Beyond Borders: Writings of Virgilio Elizondo and Friends, 00; auth, "San Fernando Cathedral and the Alamo: Sacred Place, Public Ritual, and Construction of Meaning," J of Ritual Studies, 98; coauth, San Fernando Cathedral: Soul of the City, 98; Mestizo Worship: A Pastoral Approach to Liturgical Ministry, 98; auth, Tejano Religion and Ethnicity: San Antonio, 1821-1860, 95; The Alamo Remembered: Tejano Accounts and Perspectives, 95; co-ed, Defending Mexican Valor in Texas: Jose Antonio Navarro's Historical Writings, 1853-1857, 95; auth, "New Frontiers of Guadalupanismo" in J of Hispanic/Latin Theol, 97; "Sacred Place and Collective Memory: San Fernando Cathedral, San Antonio, Texas" in U.S. Cath Historian, 97; "Guadalupan Devotion in a Borderlands Community" in J of Hispanic/Latino Theol, 96; "Lay Initiatives in Worship on the Texas Frontera, 1830-1860" in U.S. Cath Historian, 94. **CONTACT ADDRESS** Dept of Theology, Univ of Notre Dame, Notre Dame, IN 46556. **EMAIL** matovina.1@nd.edu

MATSEN, HERBERT S.
PERSONAL Born 03/15/1926, Portland, OR, m, 1987 **DISCIPLINE** PHILOSOPHY **EDUCATION** Wash State Col, BS, 50; Columbia Univ, MA, 61, PhD, 69. **CAREER** Instr, Wash Col, 60-61; instr, 62-65, asst prof, 66-68, Converse Col; asst prof, 69-72 assoc prof, 72-82, Univ S Carolina; Phi Beta Kappa; Phi Kappa Phi; Irwin Edman Scholar philos; Fulbright grant Italy, 58-60. **MEMBERSHIPS** Medieval Acad Am; Renaissance Soc Am; SIPPM. **RESEARCH** Philosophy of medicine at Bologna from 1300-1600; Alessandro Achillini (1463-1512); History of European Universities in the Middle Ages and Renaissance. **SELECTED PUBLICATIONS** Alessandro Achillini (1463-1512) and his Doctrine of Universals and Transcendentals: A Study in Renaissance Ockhamism, Bucknell Univ Press, 74; The Influence of Duns Scotus and his Followers on the Philosophy of A Achillini, Regnum Hominis et Regnum Dei, vol 2, Rome, 78; Students "Arts" Disputations at Bologna around 1500, Renaissance Quart, 94; auth, " Achillini, Alessandro (1463-1512)," Encyclopedia of the Renaissance, vol 1, NY, pp 9a-10a, 99. **CONTACT ADDRESS** 605 S 34th Ave, Yakima, WA 98902-3928. **EMAIL** hmatsen@nwinfo.net

MATTEI, UGO A.
PERSONAL Born 04/22/1961, Turin, Italy, m, 1986, 2 children **DISCIPLINE** LAW, ECONOMICS **EDUCATION** Univ Torino Italy, JD 83; Univ Cal Berk, LLD 89. **CAREER** Lectr, 85-86, asst prof, 87-90, prof, Facolta di Giurispudenza, Univ di Trento, 90- ; Alfred & Hanna Fromm Prof of Int & Comp Law, Univ Calif, Hastings Col of Law, 94- ; prof, European Univ Inst, 01-05. **HONORS AND AWARDS** Duilio Miccoli Fel, Inst Comp Law, 84; L.Einaudi Fel, 85, 86; Fulbright Fel, 87, 93; Consiglio Nazionale delle Ricerche Fel, 84, 88, 89; Order of the Coif, 94. **RESEARCH** Comparative law and law economics. **SELECTED PUBLICATIONS** Co-auth, The Common Core Approach to European Priate Law, Columbia J of European Law, 97; co-auth, The Function of Trust Law. A Comparative legal and Economic Analysis, NYork Univ Law Rev, 98; auth, Trust Law in the United States, spec iss of Am J Comp Law, 98; auth, The Issue of Civil Codification and European Legal Scholarship. Biases, Strategies and Developments, 21 Hastings Int & Com Law Rev 883 (98); auth, "Legal Pluralism, Legal Change and Economic Development, in New Law for New States, eds, Favali, Grande, & Guadagni (Politica del Diritto in Eritrea, 98); auth, An Opportunity not to be Missed. The Future of Comparative Law in the United States, 46 Am J of Comp Law, 98; auth, Efficiency and Equal Protection in the New European Contract Law. Mandatory, Enforcement and Default Rules, 39 Va J Int Law 537, 99; auth, "The Legal Profession as an Organization. Understanding Changes in Civil Law and Common Law," in Lawyers Practice and Ideals: A Comparative View, 157, eds Cramton & Barcelo, 99; auth, "The Comparative Jurisprudence of R. B. Schlesinger and R. Sacco. A Study in Legal Influence, in Rethinking the Masters of Comparative Law, ed A. Riles, 01; co-auth, The Art and Science of Citical Scholarship. Postmodernism and International Style in the Legal Architecture of Europe, Tulane Law Rev, 01, European Rev of Private Law, 01. **CONTACT ADDRESS** Hastings Coll of Law, Univ of California, San Francisco, San Francisco, CA 94102. **EMAIL** matteiu@uchastings.edu

MATTER, EDITH ANN
PERSONAL Born 12/29/1949, Ft Smith, AR **DISCIPLINE** HISTORY OF CHRISTIANITY **EDUCATION** Oberline Col, AB, 71; Yale Univ, MA, 75, Mphil, 75, PhD(relig studies), 76. **CAREER** Vis prof, Universita degli Studi di Trento, 93; vis assoc prof, Haverford Col, 83-86, 87-90; vis scholar, Weston Sschool of Theology, 79; asst prof, Univ of Pa, 76-82; assoc prof, Univ of Pa, 82-90. **HONORS AND AWARDS** Whiting Fel for the Humanities, Yale Univ, 75-76; Am Philos Soc Grants, 77, 80, 84; Am Council of Learned Societies, Summer Grant, 78; auth, Univ of Pennsylvania Res Coun Grants, 78, 886, 89, 90, 92; NEH fel, 79, 88; Annenberg Res Institute Fel, 92; John Simon Guggenheim Fel, 96; Lindback Awd for Distinguished Teaching, Univ of Pa, 81; Outstanding Teaching Awd, Col Alumni Soc, Upenn, 95; . Jean Brownlee Term Prof of Religious Studies, 96. **MEMBERSHIPS** Am Acad Relig, Women's Caucus; Mediaeval Acad Am; Del Valley Medieval Asn; Am Asn of Univ Profs; Am Asn of Univ Women. **RESEARCH** History of Christian culture, from the middle ages to the 17th century; history of interpretation of the Bible; spirituality nd mysticism in the Christian tradition from the middle ages to the present; women in Christian history; sexuality in Christian history; medieval textual studies; music in the history of Christianity. **SELECTED PUBLICATIONS** Auth, The Voice of My Beloved: The Song of Songs in Western Medieval Christianity, Philadelphia: Univ of Pennsylvania Press, 90; co-ed, Creative Women in Medieval and Early Modern Italy: A Religious and Artistic Renaissance, Philadelphia: Univ of Pennsylvania Press, 94; auth, "Il matrimonio mistico," in Dome e Fede: santita e vita relitiosa, eds. L. Scaraffia and G. Zarri, (Bari and Rome: Laterza Editore, 94): 43-60; auth, "Political Prophecy as Reperssion: Lucia Brocadeli da Narni and Ercole d'Este," in Christendom and its Discontents, ed. S. Waugh, (Cambridge: Cambridge Univ Press, 95): 168-76; auth, "The Academic Culture of Disbelief: Religious Studies at the University of Pennsylvania," in Method and Theory in The Study of Relig 7, (95): 389-98. **CONTACT ADDRESS** Dept of Relig Studies, Univ of Pennsylvania, Col Hall, PO Box 36, Philadelphia, PA 19104-6303. **EMAIL** amatter@ccat.sas.upenn.edu

MATTHAEI, SONDRA
PERSONAL Born 08/29/1942, Clay Center, KS, 1 child **DISCIPLINE** THEOLOGY **EDUCATION** Kans State Univ, BA, 64; Saint Paul School of Theol, MRE, 69; School of Theol at Claremont, PhD, 89. **CAREER** From Instr to Prof, Christian Rel Edu, 89-, Saint Paul School of Theo; Outreach Min, 86-87, Dir of Christian Edu 69-, Los Feliz United Methodist Church. **HONORS AND AWARDS** Consecrated Diaconal Minister; Member Kansas West Annual Conf; Member of the Joint Candidacy Task Force of Higher Edu and Ministry of the United Methodist Church. **MEMBERSHIPS** Am Acad of Rel; Asn of Prof and Res in Rel Edu; Christian Edu Fellowship; Rel Edu Asn; United Methodist Asn of Scholars in Christian Edu. **RESEARCH** Methodist History, Adult Christian Education. **SELECTED PUBLICATIONS** Auth, Transcripts of the Trinity, Communion and Community in: Formation for Holiness of Heart and Life, Quarterly Review, vol 18, 98; co-auth, Candidacy Guidebook for Deacons, Elders and Local Pastors, Nashville, Board of Higher Education and Ministry, 97; auth, Faith Matters Faith-Mentoring in the Faith Community, Valley Forge PA, Trinity Press International, 96; A Healing Ministry: The Educational Forms of Parish Nursing, Journal of Religious Education, 95; auth, Making Disciples: Faith Formation in the Weslayan Tradition, Abington, 00. **CONTACT ADDRESS** Saint Paul Sch of Theol, 5123 Truman Rd, Kansas City, MO 64127. **EMAIL** matthaci@spst.edu

MATTHEWS, A. WARREN
DISCIPLINE OLD TESTAMENT, NEW TESTAMENT **EDUCATION** Univ St Andrews, PhD, 59. **CAREER** Chair, dept, 79-85, 91-94; Dean, Student Affairs, 70-74; Vice Pres Student Services, 74-77. **SELECTED PUBLICATIONS** Auth, World Religions ;Abraham Was Their Father ;The Development of St. Augustine from Neoplatonism to Christianity. **CONTACT ADDRESS** Old Dominion Univ, 4100 Powhatan Ave, Norfolk, VA 23058. **EMAIL** WMathews@odu.edu

MATTHEWS, GARETH BLANC
PERSONAL Born 07/08/1929, Buenos Aires, Argentina, m, 1958, 3 children **DISCIPLINE** PHILOSOPHY **EDUCATION** Franklin Col, AB, 51; Harvard Univ, AM, 52, PhD, 61. **CAREER** Asst prof philos, Univ Va, 60-61; from asst prof to assoc prof, Univ Minn, Minneapolis, 61-69; Prof Philos, Univ Mass, Amherst, 69-, George Santayana fel, Harvard Univ, 67- 68; vis lectr, Cambridge Univ, 76; Mead-Swing lectr, Oberlin Col, 76; dir, Nat Endowment for Humanities summer sem, 80, 85, 88, 98; contrib ed, Thinking. **HONORS AND AWARDS** Doctor of Humane Letters, Franklin Col, 85; NEH Res Fel, 82-3, 89-90. **MEMBERSHIPS** Am Philos Asn; Mind Asn; Institute for Advanced Study, 86. **RESEARCH** Mediaeval philos; ancient philos; philos and children. **SELECTED PUBLICATIONS** Auth, Thought's Ego in Augustine and Descartes, Cornell Univ Press, 92; auth, The Philosophy of Childhood, Harvard Univ Press, 94; Philosophy and the Young Child, Harvard Univ Pres, 80; auth, Socratic Perplexity and the Nature of Philosophy, Oxford Univ Press, 99. **CONTACT ADDRESS** Dept of Philosophy, Univ of Massachusetts, Amherst, Amherst, MA 01003-0525. **EMAIL** matthews@philos.umass.edu

MATTHEWS, PATRICIA
DISCIPLINE PHILOSOPHY **EDUCATION** Knox Col, BA; Univ Iowa, PhD. **CAREER** Assoc prof, Fla State Univ. **HONORS AND AWARDS** Tchg Incentive Prog Awd, 96. **RESEARCH** Kant aesthetics. **SELECTED PUBLICATIONS** Kant's Theory of Imagination: Bridging Gaps in Judgment and Experience (rev), Oxford, 94; Kant on Cognition and Taste, Marquette Univ, 95; "Kant's Sublime: A Form Of Pure Aesthetic Reflective Judgment," Journal of Aesthetics and Art Criticism, 54, 165-80, 96; auth, The Significance of Beauty: Kant on Feeling and the System of the Mind, Kluwer Acad, 97; Feeling and Aesthetic Judgment: A Rejoinder to Tom Huhn, Jour Aesthet, 97; "Hutchenson on the Idea of Beauty," Journal of the History of Philosophy, 36. 233-59, 98; "Scientific Knowledge and the Aesthetic Appreciation of Nature," The Journal of Aesthetics and Art Criticism, forthcoming; "The Role of Disinteresteness in Kant's Theory of Taste," Proceedings of the Ninth International Kant Congress, forthcoming. **CONTACT ADDRESS** Dept of Philosophy, Florida State Univ, 211 Wescott Bldg, Tallahassee, FL 32306. **EMAIL** pmatthew@mailer.fsu.edu

MATTHEWS, ROBERT JOSEPH
PERSONAL Born 05/19/1943, Lubbock, TX **DISCIPLINE** PHILOSOPHY **EDUCATION** Cornell Univ, BS, 65, MS, 67, PhD(French lit & philos), 74; Georgetown Univ, MA, 70. **CAREER** Asst Prof Philos, Rutgers Univ, 74-, Andrew W Mellon fac fel humanities, Harvard Univ, 77-78; Adj Prof, Inst Aesthet, Temple Univ, 77-; assoc, Behav & Brain Sci, 77-. **MEMBERSHIPS** Am Philos Asn; Am Soc Aesthet; Soc Philos & Psychol. **RESEARCH** Aesthetics; philosophy of language; philosophy of science. **SELECTED PUBLICATIONS** Auth, 3 Concept Monte--Explanation, Implementation and Systematicity, Synthese, vol 0101, 94; Border Disputes--Response to Johnston, Penelope, Hist Today, vol 0046, 96; Can Connectionists Explain Systematicity, Mind and Lang, vol 0012, 97. **CONTACT ADDRESS** Dept of Philos, Rutgers, The State Univ of New Jersey, New Brunswick, P O Box 270, New Brunswick, NJ 08903-0270.

MATTHIS, MICHAEL
PERSONAL Born 11/22/1947, Austin, TX, m, 1974 **DISCIPLINE** PHILOSOPHY **EDUCATION** Unix Tex Austin, BA, 69; Ariz State Univ, MA, 73; Fordham Univ, PhD, 76. **CAREER** Asst Prof, Gonzaga Univ, 77-84; Vis Asst Prof, Kute-

town Univ, 90-92; Lectr, Lamar Univ, 95-00. **HONORS AND AWARDS** Teaching Bonus Awd, Lamar Univ, 98; Who's Who Among Am Teachers, 00. **MEMBERSHIPS** Am Philos Asn, NMex /W Tex Philos Soc. **RESEARCH** Metaphysics, Ethics, Aesthetics, Existentialism. **SELECTED PUBLICATIONS** Auth, "Unutointy in the Knowledge of Art and Persons," Men and World, 79; auth, "Nietesche as Anti-Naturalist," Philos Today, 92; auth, "Keirkegaard and the Social Othis," Philos Today, 94. **CONTACT ADDRESS** Dept English and Lang, Lamar Univ, Beaumont, Po Box 10023, Beaumont, TX 77710-0023. **EMAIL** matthismj@hal.lamar.edu

MATTINGLY, RICHARD EDWARD
PERSONAL Born 01/01/1938, Wichita, KS, m, 1963, 1 child **DISCIPLINE** PHILOSOPHY **EDUCATION** Univ Kans, BA, 61; Univ Tex, Austin, PhD, 71. **CAREER** Asst prof philos, 63-72, chmn joint dept philos, Westminster Col & William Woods Col, 73-77, Assoc Prof Philos, 72-, chair, Westminister Col, Philos dept, 96-, Westminster Col, 72, Dean Fac, 77-95, VP, 78-95. **MEMBERSHIPS** Central Div Am Philos Asn; Central States Philos Asn. **RESEARCH** Theory of knowledge; philosophy of science; political philosophy. **CONTACT ADDRESS** Dept of Philosophy, Westminster Col, Missouri, 501 Westminster Ave, Fulton, MO 65251-1299. **EMAIL** mattinre@jaynet.wcmo.edu

MATTINGLY, SUSAN SHOTLIFF
PERSONAL Born 10/12/1941, Kansas City, MO, m, 1963, 1 child **DISCIPLINE** PHILOSOPHY **EDUCATION** Univ KS, BA, 63; Univ TX, PhD, 68. **CAREER** Inst of Phil, 67-69, asst prof, 69-72, head phil dept, 72-77, assoc prof 72-94, prof philos Lincoln Univ, 94-00, Lectr, Westminster Col, MO, 66-67, Head Dept of Eng for Lang & Philos, 94-99. **HONORS AND AWARDS** NEH Summer Seminar fel, 81, Woodrow Wilson fel, Phi Beta Kappa. **MEMBERSHIPS** Am Philos Asn; Soc Women in Philos; AAUP. **RESEARCH** Medical ethics, philos of medicine. **SELECTED PUBLICATIONS** The Right to Health Care & the Right to Die, Philos Res Arch, 79; Viewing Abortion from the Perspective of Transplanatation: The Ethics of the Gift of Life, Soundings, 84; Fetal Needs, Physicians Duties, Midwest Medical Ethics, 91; Professional Ethics & the Maternal-Fetal Dyad: Exploring the Two-Patient Obstetric Model, Hastings Center Report, 92; Co-auth, Family Involvement in Medical Decision Making, Family Medicine, 96; The Mother-Fetal Dyad & the Ethics of Care, Physical & Occupational Therapy in Pediatrics, 96. **CONTACT ADDRESS** Dept of Philos, Lincoln Univ, Missouri, 820 Chestnut St, Jefferson City, MO 65102-0029. **EMAIL** mattings@lincolnu.edu

MATUSTIK, MARTIN J. BECK
PERSONAL Born, Czechoslovakia **DISCIPLINE** PHILOSOPHY **EDUCATION** Fordham Univ, PhD, 91. **CAREER** Prof, Purdue Univ, 00-01. **HONORS AND AWARDS** Fulbright, 98, 95. **MEMBERSHIPS** APA; SPEP; RPA. **RESEARCH** Critical theory; nineteenth and twentieth century continental philosophy. **SELECTED PUBLICATIONS** Auth, Postnational Identity, Guilford, 93; Specters of Liberation, SUNY, 95; co-ed, Kierkegaard in Post/Modernity, Indiana, 95; auth, Jurgen Habermasia Philosophical-Political Profile, forthcoming. **CONTACT ADDRESS** Dept of Philosophy, Purdue Univ, West Lafayette, West Lafayette, IN 47907-1360. **EMAIL** mmatustk@purdue.edu

MAULE, JAMES EDWARD
PERSONAL Born 11/26/1951, Philadelphia, PA, 2 children **DISCIPLINE** LAW **EDUCATION** Wharton Sch, Univ Pa, BS, 73; Villanova Univ Sch Law, JD, 76; Nat Law Ctr, George Washington Univ, LLM, 79. **CAREER** Prof, Villanova Univ; Owner, TaxJEM Inc, JEMBook Pub Co; past atty, Legislation and Regulations Div, Off Ch Coun to the Internal Revenue serv; past atty-adviser, Honorable Herbert L. Chabot, US Tax Ct; taught at, Dickinson Sch Law. **HONORS AND AWARDS** Order of the Coif, BNA Tax Mgmt Distinguished Author Awd, 93. **MEMBERSHIPS** Adv Bd, US Income, BNA Tax Mgt, Inc; Amer Bar Asn; past ed adv bd, J. ltd Liab Co; past ed adv bd, S Corp: J Tax, Legal, and Bus Strategies. **RESEARCH** Taxation, computer law. **SELECTED PUBLICATIONS** Contrib, BNA Tax Management Portfolio ser; publ on, Taxation and First Amendment History. **CONTACT ADDRESS** Law School, Villanova Univ, 800 Lancaster Ave, Villanova, PA 19085-1692. **EMAIL** maule@law.villanova.edu

MAXEY, B. ANN
DISCIPLINE BUSINESS ORGANIZATIONS, SECURITIES REGULATIONS, CORPORATE POLICY ISSUES **EDUCATION** Tulane Univ, BS, 63, JD, 78. **CAREER** Prior to coming to the WVU College of Law in 1991, Porfessor Maxey was Sr partner, Tucson, Ariz firm of O'Connor, Cavanaugh, Anderson, Westover, Killingsworth & Beshears, 88-91; partner, Hecker, Phillips & Hooker, 81-88; law clk, US Court of Appeals for the Ninth Circuit, SF, 79-81; prof, 91. **HONORS AND AWARDS** Morrison law rev award, Order of the Coif; cumulative index ed, mem, tulane law rev. **MEMBERSHIPS** Mem, AALS; Amer Bar Assn; Secy Comm Couns Responsibility; Comm Legal Bus Ethics; State Bar Calif; ArizState Bar Assn; Ariz Bar Found; W Va Bar Assn. **SELECTED PUBLICATIONS** Auth, SEC Enforcement Actions Against Securities Lawyers: New Remedies vs. Old Policies, 22 Delaware J. Corp. Law, 97; Competing Duties? Securities Lawyers' Liability After Center Bank, 64 Fordham L Rev 2185, 96. **CONTACT ADDRESS** Law Sch, West Virginia Univ, Morgantown, PO Box 6009, Morgantown, WV 26506-6009.

MAY, CHRISTOPHER N.
PERSONAL Born 03/05/1943, Evanston, IL, m **DISCIPLINE** AMERICAN LAW **EDUCATION** Harvard Univ, AB, 65; Yale Univ, LLB, 68. **CAREER** Dir res, Nat Inst Educ Law & Poverty, Sch Law, Northwestern Univ, 68-69; Staff atty, San Francisco Neighborhood Legal Assistance Found, 70-73; instr, Sch Law, Golden Gate Univ, 71-73; prof Law, Loyola Law Sch, Ca, 73-. **HONORS AND AWARDS** Alpha Sigma Nu Natl Jesuit Book Awd, 89. **RESEARCH** Supreme Court & congressional exercises of the war powers; Presidential noncompliance with the law. **SELECTED PUBLICATIONS** Auth, A Manual on the Laws & Administrative Regulations of the General Assistance & ADC Programs in the State of Illinois, Am Civil Liberties Union, 67; Withdrawal of Public Welfare: The right to a prior hearing, 76 Yale Law J 1234, 67; coauth (with Daniel William Fessler), Amicus Curiae brief in Goldberg versus Kelly, 397 US 254, 70; auth, Supreme Court holds residency test unconstitutional, Vol 3, No 1, Administration unveils welfare reform package: Recipients must work, Vol 3, No 89 & Supreme Court approves maximum grants, Vol 3, No 321, Clearinghouse Rev; coauth (with Daniel William Fessler), The Municipal Services Equalization Suit: A Cause of Action in Quest of a Forum, Public Needs, Private Behavior, and the Metropolitan Political Economy, Resources Future, Cambridge Univ, 75; In The Name of War: Judicial Review and the War Powers since 1918, Harvard Univ, 89; coauth, The Law of Prime Numbers, NY Univ Law Rev, 73; auth, Presidential Defiance of Unconstitutional Laws: Reviving the Royal Prerogative, Hastings Const Law Quart, 94; What Do We Do Now?: Helping Juries Apply the Instructions, Loyola Los Angeles Law Jour, 95; coauth, The Jurisprudence of Yogi Berra, Emory Law Jour, 97; coauth, Constitutional Law: National Power and Federalism, Aspen Law and Bus, 98; coauth, Constitutional Law: Individual Rights, Aspen Law and Bus, 98; auth, Presidential Defiance ofUnconstitutional Laws: Reviving the Royal Prerogative, Greenwood, 98. **CONTACT ADDRESS** Law Sch, Loyola Marymount Univ, 919 S Albany St, Los Angeles, CA 90015-0019. **EMAIL** christopher.may@lls.edu

MAY, DAVID M.
PERSONAL Born 11/18/1958, Monett, MO, m, 1980 **DISCIPLINE** NEW TESTAMENT **EDUCATION** Northwest MO State Univ, BS, 80; Southern Baptist Theol Sem, MDiv, 83, PhD, 87. **CAREER** Baptist chair of Bible, Central MO State Univ, Warrensburg, MO, 87-90; vis prof of New Testament, Midwestern Baptist Theol Sem, Kansas City, MO, 91-94; Assoc Prof of New Testament, Central Baptist Theol Sem, Kansas City, MO, 94-. **HONORS AND AWARDS** Regional Scholar nominee, 96. **MEMBERSHIPS** Soc of Biblical Lit; Nat Assoc Baptist Profs of Relig. **RESEARCH** Social scientific criticism of the New Testament. **SELECTED PUBLICATIONS** Auth, Mark 3:20-35 from the Perspective of Shame/Honor, Biblical Theol Bull, vol 17, summer 87; The Social Scientific Study of the New Testament: A Bibliography, vol 4, Mercer Univ Press, 91; Mark 2:15: The House of Jesus or Levi?, New Testament Studies, vol 39, 93; Drawn from Nature and Everyday Life: Parables and Social Scientific Criticism, Rev and Expositor, vol 94, no 2, spring 97; The Straightened Woman,(Luke 1310-17): Paradise Lost and Regained, Perspectives in Religious Studies, vol 24, no 3, fall 97. **CONTACT ADDRESS** Central Baptist Theol Sem, 741 N 31st St., Kansas City, KS 66102-3964. **EMAIL** davidmay@cbts.edu

MAY, JOHN RICHARD
PERSONAL Born 09/16/1931, New Orleans, LA, m, 1977, 4 children **DISCIPLINE** LITERATURE & RELIGION, FILM CRITICISM, ENGLISH **EDUCATION** Loyola Univ, La, BBA, 51; Spring Hill Col, MA, 57; St Louis Univ, STL, 65; Emory Univ, PhD(Lit & Theol), 71. **CAREER** Lectr Humanities, Spring Hill Col, 65-68; from asst prof to assoc prof Relig Studies, Loyola Univ, La, 71-76, dir Mat Social Studies, 74-76; assoc prof & chmn Freshman English, 76-81, prof English, La State Univ, Baton Rouge, 81-; dept chmn, 83-92; alumni prof, 88; assoc ed, Horizons, 74-80; prog dir, La Comt on Humanities, 75-77. **HONORS AND AWARDS** Alpha Sigma Nu; Phi Kappa Phi. **MEMBERSHIPS** Col Theol Soc; Conf Christianity & Lit; Southeastern Am Acad Relig; Walker Percy Soc; Flannery O'Connor Soc. **RESEARCH** Theological literary criticism; American literature; religion and film. **SELECTED PUBLICATIONS** Auth, Toward a New Earth; Apocalypse in the American Novel, Univ Notre Dame, 72; contribr, Mark Twain, 74; Disguises of the Demonic, Association, 75; auth, The Pruning Word: The Parables of Flannery O'Connor, Univ Notre Dame, 76; coauth, Film Odyssey: The Art of Film as Search for Meaning, 76 & The Parables of Lina Wertmuller, 77, Paulist; ed, The Bent World: Essays on Religion and Culture, Scholars Press, 81; co-ed, Religion in Film, Univ Tenn Press, 82; ed, Image and Likeness: Religious Visions in Am Film Classics, Paulist, 92; ed, New Image of Religious Film, Sheed & Ward, 97. **CONTACT ADDRESS** Dept of English, Louisiana State Univ and A&M Col, Baton Rouge, LA 70803-0001. **EMAIL** jmay2@lsu.edu

MAY, MELANIE A.
PERSONAL Born 01/06/1955, Washington, DC **DISCIPLINE** THEOLOGY **EDUCATION** Manchester Col, BA, 76; Harvard Divinity Sch, Mdiv, 79; Harvard Univ, AM, 82, PhD, 86. **CAREER** Assoc gen secy, ecumenical off, Church Brethren General Board, 86-92; prof, dean, Colgate Rochester Divinity Sch, 92-. **HONORS AND AWARDS** Decade Awd, Harvard Divinity Sch, 94; edward c. hopkins honor scholar, 78-79. **MEMBERSHIPS** Vice-Moderator, World Council Churches Standing Commission on Faith and Order; Nat council Churches, Faith and Order. **RESEARCH** Women and Church; women's theolog; ecumenism; global christianity **SELECTED PUBLICATIONS** auth, Bond of Unity: Women, Theology, and the Worldwide Church, 89; auth, For All the Saints: The Practice of Ministry in the Faith Community, 90; auth, Women and Church: Ecumenical Challenge of Solidarity in the Age of Alienation, 91; auth, A Body Knows: A Theopoetics of Death and Resurrection, 95. **CONTACT ADDRESS** 1100 Goodman St, Rochester, NY 14620. **EMAIL** mmay@crds.edu

MAY, RICHARD WARREN
PERSONAL Born 03/01/1944, Marlborough, MA, m **DISCIPLINE** PHILOSOPHY **EDUCATION** Univ Mass, BS 68, Cal State Univ, MA, 91. **CAREER** Res Assoc, adv bd mem, 85-, Point One Advisory Gp. **HONORS AND AWARDS** ISPE Diplomat; Who's Who in the World, 4 editions; us patent # 4739992, 88. **MEMBERSHIPS** NCIS; AAR; ISPE; JGS. **RESEARCH** Religious studies vis-a-vis Jewish genealogy. **SELECTED PUBLICATIONS** Auth, The Online Buddha and the Stars, Telicom, J the Intl Soc for Philo Enq, 95; Thinking About Mozart's Minuet K 355, Telicom. 95; Four Eastern Philosophies, in: Thinking on the Edge, Burbank CA, Agamemnon Press, 93. **CONTACT ADDRESS** 279 Highland Ave, Buffalo, NY 14222-1748. **EMAIL** ferdlilac@yahoo.com

MAYER, DON
PERSONAL Born 03/27/1948, CA, m, 1987, 4 children **DISCIPLINE** INTERNATIONAL & ENVIRONMENTAL LAW AND BUSINESS ETHICS **EDUCATION** Duke Univ Law School, JD, 73; Georgetown Univ Law Center, LLM, 85. **CAREER** Office of the Staff Judge Advocate, Francis E Warren Air Force Base, Cheyenne, WY, 73-75; private law practice, Asheville, NC, 75-83; Chief Clerk for Legal Res, Wilkes, Artis, Hendrick and Lane, Chartered, Washington, DC, 84-85; asst prof of Business Law, School of Business, Western Carolina Univ, Cullowhee, NC, 85-90; asst prof of Management, School of Business Administration, Oakland Univ, Rochester, MI, 90-94; asst adjunct prof of Law, History, and Commun, Univ MI School of Business Administration, 94; assoc prof of Management, Oakland Univ School of Business Administration, 95-. **HONORS AND AWARDS** Ralph Bunde Awd, Academy of Legal Studies in Business, Int Law Section, 98. **MEMBERSHIPS** Academy of Legal Studies in Business. **RESEARCH** Ethics; international law; the environment. **SELECTED PUBLICATIONS** Auth, Foreign Corrupt Practices Act, International Free Trade, International Arbitration, Negligence, Sex Discrimination, and International Law, in the Encyclopedia of Business, Gale Pub Co, 96; Arbitration of Employment Discrimination Claims and the Challenge of Contemporary Federalism, 47 South Carolina Law Rev, no 3, spring 96; Boundaries of the Moral Community, in Blackwell's Encyclopedic Dictionary of Business Ethics, Pat Werhane and Ed Freeman, eds, 98; Institutionalizing Overconsumption, in Westra and Werhane, eds, Consumption and the Environment, Rowman and Littlefield, forthcoming; Arbitral Alternatives to Injunctive Relief for International Letter of Credit Fraud, with Mark S Blodgett, Am Business Law J, vol 35, no 3; Environmental Law in Context: Integrating Ethics, Economics, and the International Dimension, J of Legal Studies ed, vol 16:1, 1-8, winter/spring 98; Lessons in Law from A Civil Action, J of Legal Studies Ed, vol 16:1, 113-148; Greenhouse Gas Emissions and the Social Responsibility of Automakers, in the Business and Society Review, vol 105:3, 347, 360, fall 00. **CONTACT ADDRESS** School of Business Administration, Oakland Univ, Rochester, MI 48309. **EMAIL** mayer@oakland.edu

MAYERFELD, JAMIE
DISCIPLINE POLITICAL SCIENCE **EDUCATION** Princeton Univ, PhD, 92. **CONTACT ADDRESS** Political Science, Univ of Washington, PO Box 353530, Seattle, WA 98195.

MAYNARD, ARTHUR HOMER
PERSONAL Born 08/28/1915, Centerville, MI, m, 1941, 2 children **DISCIPLINE** RELIGION **EDUCATION** Cornell Col, BA, 36; Boston Univ, MA, 38, STB, 39; Univ Southern Calif, PhD(Bible lit), 50. **CAREER** Minister, Methodist Churches, Wis & Calif, 39-50; vis prof relig, Willamette Univ, 50-52; from assoc prof to prof, Univ Miami, 52-58, chmn dept, 52-58; chmn dept relig studies, 62-75, Prof Bible, Univ Pac, 58-. **MEMBERSHIPS** Soc Bibl Lit; Am Acad Relig. **RESEARCH** Gospel of John; Old Testament prophets. **SELECTED PUBLICATIONS** The enduring word--a study of Old Testament literature in historical perspective, Self, 64 & 68. **CONTACT ADDRESS** Dept of Religious Studies, Univ of the Pacific, Stockton, Stockton, CA 95211.

MAYNARD, PATRICK
DISCIPLINE PHILOSOPHY **EDUCATION** Univ Chicago, BA; Cornell Univ, PhD. **CAREER** Assoc prof **SELECTED PUBLICATIONS** Auth, The Engine of Visualization: Thinking Through Photography, Cornell, 97; ed, Perspectives on the Arts and Technology, 97. **CONTACT ADDRESS** Dept of Philosophy, Univ of Western Ontario, London, ON, Canada N6A 5B8. **EMAIL** pmaynard@julian.uwo.ca

MAYNARD, THERESE H.
DISCIPLINE LAW **EDUCATION** Univ Calif, Irvine, BA, 78; Univ Calif, Los Angeles, JD, 81. **CAREER** Prof & William M. Rains fel; Loyola Univ, 83-; practiced, Gibson, Dunn & Crutcher. **RESEARCH** Securities litigation. **SELECTED PUBLICATIONS** Publ on, securities law. **CONTACT ADDRESS** Law School, Loyola Marymount Univ, 7900 Loyola Blvd, Burns 404, Los Angeles, CA 90045. **EMAIL** tmaynard@lmulaw.lmu.edu

MAYNARD-REID, PEDRITO U.
PERSONAL Born 07/10/1947, Kingston, Jamaica, m, 1970, 2 children **DISCIPLINE** NEW TESTAMENT **EDUCATION** Andrews Univ, ThD, 81 **CAREER** Pof bibl studies, W Indies Coll, Jamaica, 70-85; prof bibl studies, Antillian Univ, Puerto Rico, 85-89; prof bibl studies, WA, 91-. **HONORS AND AWARDS** Zarara Awdard for Teaching, 93. **MEMBERSHIPS** Soc of Bibl Studies. **RESEARCH** Epistle of James. **SELECTED PUBLICATIONS** Auth, Caribbean Worship, The Complete Libr of Christian Worship, 95; African-American Worship, Libr of Christian Worship, 95; James, 96; Complete Evangelism: The Luke-Acts Model, 97; James, Introducing the Bible, 97; Samaria, Dictionary of the Later New Testament and Its Development, 97; Forgiveness, Dictionary of the Later New Testament and Its Development, 97; auth, Diverse Worship: African American, Caribbean and Hispanic Perspectives, 00. **CONTACT ADDRESS** Walla Walla Col, 204 S. College Ave, College Place, WA 99324. **EMAIL** maynped@wwc.edu

MAYR, FRANZ KARL
PERSONAL Born 03/12/1932, Linz, Austria, m, 1968, 2 children **DISCIPLINE** PHILOSOPHY OF RELIGION & LANGUAGE; METAPHYSICS; LEGAL PHILOSOPHY **EDUCATION** Univ Innsbruck, LPh, 56, PhD(philos), 57, MLaw, 62. **CAREER** Asst prof philos, Univ Innsbruck, 63-64 & 65-68; asst prof relig & philos, 64-65, assoc prof, 68-76, Prof Philos, Univ Portland, OR, 76- . **RESEARCH** Political philosophy; Philosophy of religion. **SELECTED PUBLICATIONS** auth, Lenguaje: Dicconario de Hermenentica, Univ de Deusto Bilbao, 77; auth, El Matriarcalismo Vasco, Bilbao, 80; auth, Simbolos, Mitos Y Archetypos, Antropologia Vasca: Gran Encyclopedia Vasco, Bilbao, 80; auth, Sprache, Sprachphilosophie, Herders Theologisches Taschenlexikon, 81; coauth, El Inconsciente Colectivo Vasco, San Sebastian, 82; auth, La mitologia Occidental, Barcelona, 89; auth, Wort grgen bild, Zur Friihgeschichte der Symbolik des Horens: Das Buch von Horen Freiburg, 91; coauth, Arquetipos y Simbolos Colectivos: Circulo Eranos I, Barcelona, 94; auth, Seeing and Hearing in Pheno-Menology, Analytic Philosophy and Hermeneutics, Frebourg, 00; auth, M Heidegger, Zollikon Seminars, Northwestern Univ Press, 00. **CONTACT ADDRESS** Dept of Philosophy, Univ of Portland, 5000 N Willamette, Portland, OR 97203-5798.

MAZLISH, BRUCE
PERSONAL Born 09/15/1923, New York, NY, m, 1960, 4 children **DISCIPLINE** HISTORY, POLITICAL SCIENCE **EDUCATION** Columbia Univ, BA, 44, MA, 47, PhD, 55. **CAREER** Instr hist, Univ Maine, 46-48; lectr, Columbia Univ, 49-50; instr, 50-53, 55-56, from asst prof to assoc prof, 56-65, chmn sect, 65-70, head dept humanities, 74-79, Prof ist, Mass Inst Technol, 65-. **HONORS AND AWARDS** Soc Sci Rs Coun Fel, 67-68; Toynbee Prize, 86. **MEMBERSHIPS** Fel Am Acad Arts & Sci, AHA. **RESEARCH** Modern intellectual and social history, personality and politics, psychoanalysis and history. **SELECTED PUBLICATIONS** Auth, In Search of Nixon : A Psychohistorical Study, Basic Books (New York City), 72; auth, Kissinger: The European Mind in American Policy, Basic Books, 76; coauth, Jimmy Carter: An Interpretive Biography, Simon & Schuster (New York City), 79; auth, The Meaning of Karl Marx, Oxford Univ Pr (New York City), 84; auth, A New Science: The Breakdown of Connections and the Birth of Sociology, Oxford Univ Pr, 89; auth, The Leader, the Led, and the Psyche: Essays in psychohistory, Univ Pr New England (Hanover, NH), 90; auth, The Fourth Discontinuity: The Co-Evolution of Humans and Machines, Yale Univ Pr (New Haven, CT), 93; coauth, The Global Imperative: The Spread of Humans Across the Earth, Westview (Boulder, CO), 97; coauth, Progress: Fact or Illusion?, Univ of Mich Pr (Ann Arbor), 98; auth, The Uncertain Sciences, Yale Univ Pr, 98. **CONTACT ADDRESS** Massachusetts Inst of Tech, 77 Massachusetts Ave, Cambridge, MA 02139.

MAZOR, LESTER JAY
PERSONAL Born 12/12/1936, Chicago, IL, m, 1992, 3 children **DISCIPLINE** PHILOSOPHY OF LAW, LEGAL HISTORY **EDUCATION** Stanford Univ, AB, 57, JD, 60. **CAREER** Instr law, Univ Va, 61-62; from asst prof to prof, Univ Utah, 62-70; Henry R Luce prof, 70-75, Prof Law, Hampshire Col, 75-, Reporter, Am Bar Asn Proj Standards Criminal Justice, 65-69; vis assoc prof law, Stanford Univ, 67-68; vis prof, State Univ NY Buffalo, 73-74; proj dir mat study, Am Bar Found Study Legal Educ, 74-. **MEMBERSHIPS** Law & Soc Asn; Int Soc Asn; Am Legal Studies Asn; Int Asn Philos Law & Soc Philos. **RESEARCH** Legal hist; legal and polit theory; future studies. **SELECTED PUBLICATIONS** Ed, Prosecution and Defense Functions, 67 & Providing Defense Services, 70, American Bar Asn; coauth, Introduction to the Study of Law, Found Press, 70; auth, Power and responsibility in the attorney-client relation, Stanford Law Rev, 68; The crisis of liberal legalism, Yale Law J, 72; Disrespect for law, In: Anarchism, NY Univ, 78. **CONTACT ADDRESS** Sch of Soc Sci, Hampshire Col, 893 West St, Amherst, MA 01002-3359. **EMAIL** lmazor@hampshire.edu

MAZOUE, JIM
DISCIPLINE AMERICAN PHILOSOPHY, ETHICS, EPISTEMOLOGY **EDUCATION** Tulane Univ, PhD, 83. **CAREER** Vis instr, Univ Ala, 80; vis instr, 81-82, vis asst prof, Univ SC, Columbia, 82-83; vis asst prof, 84, Tulane Univ, 86; vis asst prof, Eastern Ky Univ; vis asst prof, Univ Tenn, Knoxville, 86-90; adj asst prof, Univ New Orleans, 91-; clin consult, Med Ctr, Univ Tenn, Knoxville, 86-90; Ethics comt, Lakeview Reg Med Ctr, Covington, La, 95-97. **HONORS AND AWARDS** NEH summer sem, Ind Univ, 86; La Educ Qual Sup Fund Enhancement grant, Philos Dept Acad Comput Lab, 97-98; City Nat Bank Awd, La State Univ, 98. **RESEARCH** American philosophy; epistemology. **SELECTED PUBLICATIONS** Auth, Nozick on Inferential Knowledge, Philos Quart 35, 85; Some Remarks on Luper-Foy's Criticism of Nozickian Tracking, Australasian J of Philos 64, 86; Self-Synthesis and Self-Knowledge, in Polrocznik Filozoficzny Mlodych, Piotr Boltuc, ed, Warsaw UP, 87; Self-Synthesis, Self-Knowledge, and Skepticism, Logos, 11, 90; Diagnosis Without Doctors, J of Med and Philos 15, 90; Should Human Diagnosticians Be Replaced by Automated Diagnostic Systems?:Yes, in Controversial Issues in Mental Health, Stuart A Kirk and Susan D Einbinder, eds, Brown & Allyn, 94. **CONTACT ADDRESS** Univ of New Orleans, New Orleans, LA 70148.

MAZUMDAR, RINITA
PERSONAL Born 10/11/1959, Calcutta, India, m, 1987, 1 child **DISCIPLINE** PHILOSOPHY, ETHICS, WOMEN'S STUDIES **EDUCATION** Calcutta Univ, BA; Brock Univ, MA; Univ Mass, PhD. **CAREER** Inst, St Phillips Coll; adj prof, Univ NMex, Valencia. **HONORS AND AWARDS** Fel, Brock Univ, Canada; **MEMBERSHIPS** APA; NWSA. **RESEARCH** Ethics, political philosophy, feminist theory. **SELECTED PUBLICATIONS** Auth, Karma and Utilitarianism, S W Philos Soc; auth, Women and Hindu Rights, NWSA, 99. **CONTACT ADDRESS** Dept Womans Studies, Univ of New Mexico, Albuquerque, Albuquerque, NM 87131-0001. **EMAIL** rinita@nmt.edu

MAZUR, DENNIS J.
PERSONAL Born 04/11/1949, Kittanning, PA, m, 1979, 2 children **DISCIPLINE** PHILOSOPHY **EDUCATION** Stanford Univ, BA, 73, MA, 74, MD, 79, PhD, 83. **CAREER** Assoc Prof Med, Ore Health Sci Univ, 91-; Chair, Inst Rev Bd, Dept Veterans Affairs Med Ctr, 91- Prof of Medicine. **HONORS AND AWARDS** Post-Doctoral Awd, Soc Med Decision Making, 83. **RESEARCH** Informed consent; risk disclosure; patient-physician decision making; how patients interpret data and use information in medical decision making; patients preferences for information and role in decision making, particularly in the area of invasive medical interventions. **SELECTED PUBLICATIONS** Coauth, How older patients' treatment preferences are influenced by disclosures about therapeutic uncertainty: Surgery vs. expectant management for localized prostate cancer, J Am Geriatrics Soc, 96; The influence of physician explanations on patient preferences about future health care states, Med Decision Making, 97; Patients' preferences for risk disclosure and role in decision making for invasive medical interventions, J General Internal Med, 97; auth, How older patient preferences are influenced by consideration of future health outcomes, J Am Geriatrics Soc, 97; Medical Risk and the Right to an Informed Consent in Clinical Care and Clinical Research, Am Col Physician Execs, 98; author of numerous other articles and publications. **CONTACT ADDRESS** Med Service, Dept of Veterans Affairs Med Ctr, 3710 SW US Veterans Hospital Rd, Portland, OR 97201.

MAZUR, DIANE H.
DISCIPLINE LAW **EDUCATION** State Univ NYork- Binghamton, BA; Penn State Univ, MS; Univ Tex, JD. **CAREER** Assoc prof, Univ Fla, 94-; Bigelow tchg fel & lectr, Univ Chicago, 93-94; adj fac, Widener Univ, 92-93; fmr assoc, Modrall law firm, Albuquerque, NM; staff, Rev Litigation. **MEMBERSHIPS** NM Bar; Order of the Coif; Univ Tex Chancellors. **RESEARCH** Evidence, corporations, women in military service. **CONTACT ADDRESS** School of Law, Univ of Florida, PO Box 117625, Gainesville, FL 32611-7625. **EMAIL** mazur@law.ufl.edu

MC GRANE, BERNARD
PERSONAL Born 08/23/1947, New York, NY, d, 1 child **DISCIPLINE** SOCIOLOGY, ANTHROPOLOGY, PHILOSOPHY **EDUCATION** New York Univ, PhD, 76; Fairfield Univ, BA, 69. **CAREER** Assoc Prof, Chapman Univ, 89-; Lecturer, UC Irvine, 85-; Lecturer, Univ Calif, Los Angeles, 83-85. **RESEARCH** Buddhist Sociology; Ethnomethodology; Media Studies. **SELECTED PUBLICATIONS** Auth, "This Book is Not Required, An Emotional Survuval Guide for Students," Pine Forge Press, 99; auth, "The UN-TV and the 10MPH car, Exploriments in Personal Freedom and Everyday Life," Small Press, 94; auth, "Beyond Anthropology: Society and the Other," Columbian Press, 89; auth, "Videos: The Ad and the Id-Sex, Death and Advertising, Univ of Calif, 92; auth, "The Ad and the Ego," California Newsreel, 96. **CONTACT ADDRESS** Dept Sociology, Chapman Univ, 333 N Glassell St, Orange, CA 92866-1011. **EMAIL** mcgrane@chapman.edu

MCAFFEE, THOMAS B.
DISCIPLINE CONSTITUTIONAL LAW **EDUCATION** Univ Utah, JD, 79. **CAREER** Articles ed, Utah Law Rev; instr, Southern Ill Univ; prof, Univ Nev, Las Vegas. **HONORS AND AWARDS** Fac Achievement Awd for Scholar, Univ Nev, Las Vegas, 97. **SELECTED PUBLICATIONS** Published numerous articles in law journals including the Harvard J of Law and Pub Policy, Columbia Law Rev, Brigham Young Univ Law Rev, and Temple Law Rev. **CONTACT ADDRESS** Univ of Nevada, Las Vegas, Las Vegas, NV 89154.

MCALISTER, ELIZABETH
DISCIPLINE PHILOSOPHY OF MIND **EDUCATION** Vassar Col, BA; Yale Univ, MA, Mphil, PhD. **CAREER** Asst prof, 90-97; Assoc prof, 97-; Chair, 98-; Wesleyan Univ. **HONORS AND AWARDS** Fel, Indiana Univ; Visitor, Mellon Seminar, Yale Univ Ctr Global Migration; Post-doctoral Fel, Rutgers Ctr Hisl Analysis; Dissertation Fel, Univ Ill, Yale Univ; Henry Hart Rice Adv Res fel. **SELECTED PUBLICATIONS** Auth, Haitian Vodou meets Italian Catholicism in Spanish Harlem: The Madonna of 115th Street Revisited; Congregations as Cultural Spaces: Immigration, Ethnicity and Religion in the United States, Temple Univ Press, 98, Angels in the Mirror: Vodou Music of Haiti. Roslyn, NY: Ellipsis Arts Publ, 97; New York, Lavalas, and the Emergence of Rara, Jour Haitian Studies, 96; A Sorcerer's Bottle: The Visual Art of Magic in Haiti, Sacred Arts of Haitian Vodou, UCLA Fowler Mus Cult Hist, 95, Vodou Music and Ritual Work, Rhythms of Rapture: Sacred Musics of Vodou, Smithsonian/Folkways, 95; 'Men Moun Yo; Here Are The People:" Haitian Rara Festivals and Transnational Popular Culture in Haiti and New York City, Yale Univ, 95; Sacred Stories from the Haitian Diaspora: A Collective Biography of Seven Vodou Priestesses in New York City, Jour Caribbean Studies, 93; Walking with the Mardi Gras Indians. FACES: Mag About People, 93; Rara Demonstrations: Traditional Ritual Turns Political Weapon in Haitian New York, Int Forum Yale, 92; Serving the Spirits Across Two Seas: Vodou Culture in Haiti and New York, Aperture, 92; Home Away From Home: Haitian Life in New York, FACES: Mag About People, 92; Haitians Make Some Noise in Brooklyn, Beat, 91; Ton Ton Club, Haiti since Duvalier, Mirabella, 90; Vodou in New York City: New Creolizations: The Economizing of Ritual Time and Space in Haitian Religion, Yale Univ, 90; Voodoo, NY Woman, 88. **CONTACT ADDRESS** Wesleyan Univ, Middletown, CT 06459.

MCALISTER, LINDA L.
PERSONAL Born 10/10/1939, Long Beach, CA **DISCIPLINE** PHILOSOPHY **EDUCATION** Barnard Col , BA, 62; Cornell Univ, PhD, 69. **CAREER** Asst/assoc prof, Brooklyn Coll, 68-77; Dean, San Diego State Univ Imperial Valley Campus, 77-82; Dean, Fort Myers Campus Univ S Fla, 82-85; Asst to Vice Chancellor, 85-87; Prof, Univ S Fla, 87-99; Prof Emerita, 00. **HONORS AND AWARDS** Sr Fulbright Res Fel, 73-74; Distinguished Woman Philosopher, Soc for Women in Philos, 98. **MEMBERSHIPS** Soc for Women in Philos; Am Philos Asn; Int Asn of Women Philosphers. **RESEARCH** Feminist Philos; History of Women In Philosophy. **SELECTED PUBLICATIONS** Auth, On the Possibility of Feminist Philosophy, Hypatia, 94; Gerda Walther, Hist of Women Philosophers, 95; Feminist Cinematic Depictions of Violence Against Women: Three Representational Strategies, Krieg/War, 97; My Grandmother's Passing, Whiteness: Feminist Philos Reflections, 99; coauth, Edith Stein, Hist of Women Philosophers, 95; Psychology From and Empirical Standpoint, 95; ed, Hypatia's daughters: 1500 Years of Women Philosphers, 96. **CONTACT ADDRESS** Women's Studies Program, Univ of So Florida, Tampa, FL 33820. **EMAIL** mcalister@chuma1.cas.usf.edu

MCANINCH, ROBERT D.
PERSONAL Born 05/12/1942, Wheeling, WV, d, 5 children **DISCIPLINE** POLITICAL SCIENCE, PHILOSOPHY **EDUCATION** W Liberty State Col, BA, 69; W VA Univ, MA, 70. **CAREER** Prof, Prestonburg Community Col, 70-. **HONORS AND AWARDS** KY Colonel **MEMBERSHIPS** Am Polit Sci Assoc; Ohio Valley Hist Assoc. **RESEARCH** Church and State Relations. **SELECTED PUBLICATIONS** Auth, Introduction to Philosophy, Justice Publ, 96; auth, American Government, Justice Publ, 97. **CONTACT ADDRESS** Dept Soc Sci, Prestonburg Comm Col, 1 Bert T Combs Dr, Prestonburg, KY 41653-1815. **EMAIL** robert.mcaninchjr@kctcs.net

MCANINCH, WILLIAM S.
DISCIPLINE CONSTITUTION AND CRIMINAL LAW **EDUCATION** Tulane Univ, BA, 62; Univ AR, LLB, 65; Yale Univ, LLM, 69. **CAREER** Solomon Blatt prof, Univ of SC. **SELECTED PUBLICATIONS** Auth or coauth, 3 bks on criminal law. **CONTACT ADDRESS** School of Law, Univ of So Carolina, Columbia, Law Center, Columbia, SC 29208. **EMAIL** Bill@law.law.sc.edu

MCARTHUR, ROBERT L.
PERSONAL Born 02/18/1944, San Mateo, CA, m, 1995, 2 children **DISCIPLINE** PHILOSOPHY, LAW, LOGIC & PHILOSOPHY OF SCIENCE **EDUCATION** Villanova Univ, BA, 67, MA, 68; Temple Univ, PhD(Philos), 72. **CAREER** Instr Philos, Villanova Univ, 69-72; from Assoc Prof to Prof Philos, 72-98, VPres and Dean of Fac, 88-98, Christian A. Johnson Prof of Integrated Learning, 98-. **HONORS AND AWARDS** Am Conn Educ fel acad admin, 75-76. **MEMBERSHIPS** Am Philos Asn; Philos Sci Asn. **RESEARCH** Logic; philosophy of language; philosophy of religion; philosophy of law. **SELECTED PUBLICATIONS** Coauth, Peter Damian and undoing the past, Philos Studies, 2/74 & Non-assertoric inference, Notre Dame J Formal Logic, 4/74; auth, Factuality and modality in the future tense, Nous, 9/74; Tense and temporal neutrality, Australasian J Philos, 5/75; Tense Logic, Reidel, 76; From Logic to Computing, Wadsworth, 91. **CONTACT ADDRESS** Dept of Philos, Colby Col, 150 Mayflower Hill, Waterville, ME 04901-4799. **EMAIL** rlmcarth@colby.edu

MCAULIFFE, J. D.
DISCIPLINE RELIGION **EDUCATION** Univ Toronto, BA, 68, MA, 79, PhD, 84. **CAREER** Asst prof, dept stud relig, Univ Toronto, 81-86; assoc prof, hist relig & Islamic stud, Candler Sch Theol, Emory Univ, Atlanta, 86-92; assoc dean, 90-92, assoc prof, 92-, Chair, Dept Stud Relig, Dir, Ctr Stud Relig, Univ Toronto 92-. **HONORS AND AWARDS** Thesis Awd, Mid East Stud Asn; Guggenheim Fel, 96. **MEMBERSHIPS** Am Soc Stud relig; Am Acad Relig; Am Oriental Soc; Can Soc Stud Relig; Soc Values Higher Educ. **SELECTED PUBLICATIONS** Auth, Qur'anic Christians: An Analysis of Classical and Modern Exegesis, 91; auth, Abbasid Authority Affirmed: The Early Years of al-Mansur, 94. **CONTACT ADDRESS** Dept of Relig Studies, Univ of Toronto, 73 Queens Park Crescent E, Toronto, ON, Canada M5S 1K7. **EMAIL** jane.mcauliffe@utoronto.ca

MCAVOY, JANE
PERSONAL Born 05/23/1957, Burlington, IA, m, 1985 **DISCIPLINE** THEOLOGY **EDUCATION** Drake Univ, BME, 79; Lexington Theol Sem, MDiv, 85; Univ Chicago, PhD, 91. **CAREER** Assoc prof, Rel Stud (s), Hiram Col, 90-97; assoc prof, Theol, Lexington Theol Sem, 97- . **HONORS AND AWARDS** Hiram nominee for TA Abbot awd for Outstanding Disciples prof, 91; Martin awd for Outstand Contrib to Hiram Col, 92; Gerstecker-Gund scholar fel from Hiram Col, 91-95; Louisville Inst Summer Scholar Stipend, 98. **MEMBERSHIPS** Amer Acad Rel; Forrest-Moss Inst for Disciples Women Scholars of Rel; Asn Disciples Theol Discussion. **RESEARCH** Feminist Theology; Christian Mysticism. PUB Auth, God-Talk: Three Modern Approaches, Lexington Theol Quart, 22, Oct 87, 106-117; The Changing Image of Parish ministry, Lexington Theol Quart, 25, July 90, 65-80; Biblical Images of the Call to Ministry, in Celebrating God's Call to Ministry, 10-13, eds, William B. Drake and Terry Ewing, Lexington, Lexington Theol Sem, 91; In Search of a Blessing, in Bread Afresh, Wine Anew: Sermons by Disciples Women, 151-144-155, eds, Joan Campbell and David Polk, St. Louis, Chalice Press, 91; ed, Table Talk: Resources for the Communion Meal, St. Louis, Chalice Press, 93; God With Us: From Language to Liturgy, in Setting the Table: Women in Theological Conversation, eds, Rita Brock, Claudia Camp, and Serene Jones, St. Louis, Chalice Press, 95; Hospitality: A Feminist Theology of Education, in Teaching Theology and Religion, 1,1, Feb 98, 20-26. **SELECTED PUBLICATIONS** Auth, "The Satisfied Life: Medieval women Mystics on Atonement," Cleveland, Pilgrim Press, 00. **CONTACT ADDRESS** Dept of Theology, Lexington Theol Sem, 631 S Limestone, Lexington, KY 40508. **EMAIL** jmcavoy@lextheo.edu

MCBAIN, JAMES F., JR.
PERSONAL Born 07/09/1971, St. Louis, MO, s **DISCIPLINE** PHILOSOPHY **EDUCATION** Northeast Missouri State Univ, BA, 94; Univ Missouri, St Louis, BA, 95; Univ Missouri, Columbia, PhD program. **CAREER** Dept Philos, Univ Missouri **MEMBERSHIPS** APA; Southwestern Philos Soc; Central States Philos Asn; Philos of Science Asn. **RESEARCH** Philosophy of science; epistemology; philosophy of mind. **SELECTED PUBLICATIONS** Auth, "The Role of Theory Contamination in Instutitions," Southwest Philosophy Review (99): 197-204. **CONTACT ADDRESS** Dept of Philosophy, Univ of Missouri, Columbia, 435 General Classroom Bldg, Columbia, MO 65211-4160. **EMAIL** c696666@showme.missouri.edu

MCBETH, HARRY LEON
PERSONAL m **DISCIPLINE** CHURCH HISTORY **EDUCATION** Wayland Baptist Univ, BA, 54; Southwestern Baptist Theol Sem, MDiv, 57, ThD, 61. **CAREER** Distinguished prof, Southwestern Baptist Theol sem, 60-. **HONORS AND AWARDS** Outstanding Young Men Am, 66; pastor, first baptist church, 55-60. **MEMBERSHIPS** S Baptist Hist Soc; Amer Soc Church Hist. **SELECTED PUBLICATIONS** Auth, The Baptist Heritage: Four Centuries of Baptist Witness, Broadman Press, 87; A Sourcebook for Baptist Heritage, Broadman Press, 90; Texas Baptists: A Sesquicentennial History, Baptist Way Press, 98. **CONTACT ADDRESS** Sch Theol, Southwestern Baptist Theol Sem, PO Box 22000, Fort Worth, TX 76122-0418. **EMAIL** hlm@swbts.swbts.edu

MCBRIDE, WILLIAM LEON
PERSONAL Born 01/19/1938, New York, NY, m, 1965, 2 children **DISCIPLINE** PHILOSOPHY **EDUCATION** Georgetown Univ, AB, 59; Yale Univ, MA, 62, PhD(philos), 64. **CAREER** From instr to assoc prof philos, Yale Univ, 64-73; assoc prof, 73-76, Prof Philos, Purdue Univ, West Lafayette, 76-, Morse fel philos, Yale Univ, 68-69; fel, Ctr for Humanistic Studies, Purdue Univ, 81-87, 93 ; Fulbright lecturer. Sofia Univ, Bulgaria, 97. **HONORS AND AWARDS** Chevalier, Ordre des Palmes Academiques. **MEMBERSHIPS** Am Philos Asn; Soc Phenomenol & Existential Philos (exec co-secy, 77-80); Am Soc Polit & Legal Philos; Am Sartre Soc; North Am Soc for Social Philos; Soc Am de Philos de Langue Francaise; Steering Committee; Intl Fed of Philos Societies. **RESEARCH** Social, political, and legal philosophy; Marx and Marxism; existentialist thought, especially the philosophy of Sartre. **SELECTED PUBLICATIONS** Auth, Fundamental Change in Law and Society: Hart and Sartre on Revolution, 70; auth, The Philos of Marx, 77; auth, Social Theory at a Crossroads, 80; auth, Demokrati og Autoritet, 80; auth, Sartre's Political Theory, 91; auth, Social and Political Philos, 94; auth, Philosophical Reflections on the Changes in Eastern Europe, 99; ed, Sartre and Existentialism, 97. **CONTACT ADDRESS** Purdue Univ, West Lafayette, West Lafayette, IN 47907. **EMAIL** wmcbride@purdue.edu

MCBRIEN, RICHARD PETER
PERSONAL Born 08/19/1936, Hartford, CT, S **DISCIPLINE** THEOLOGY **EDUCATION** St Thomas Sem, AA, 56; St John Sem, MA, 62; Pontifical Gregorian Univ, Rome, STL, 64, STD, 67. **CAREER** Prof theol & dean of studies, Pope John XXIII Nat Sem, 65-70; assoc prof, 70-72, prof, 72-80, dir, Inst Relig Educ, 75-80, Boston Col; Crowley-O'Brien-Walter Prof Theol, Univ Notre Dame, 80-; Assoc pastor, Our Lady of Victory Church, 62-63; chaplain, Southern Conn State Col, 62-63; syndicated columnist, Essays in Theol, 66-; chmn, Adv Coun, Notre Dame's Ecumenical Inst for Advan Theol Res, Tantur-Jerusalem, 82-87. **HONORS AND AWARDS** John Courtney Murray Awd, Cath Theol Soc Am, 76; Christopher Awd, The Christophers, 81. **MEMBERSHIPS** CTSA, AAR, CTS, AAUP. **SELECTED PUBLICATIONS** Auth, The Remaking of the Church: An Agenda for Reform, Harper & Row, 73; auth, Has the Church Surrendered?, Dimension Books, 74; auth, Roman Catholicism, Cathedral Publ, 75; auth, In Search of God, Dimension Books, 77; auth, Basic Questions for Christian Educators, St Mary's Press, 77; auth, Catholicism, Winston Press, 80, rev ed, HarperCollins, 94; Caeser's Coin: Religion and Politics in America, McMillan, 87; gen ed HarperCollins Encyclopedia of Catholicism, 95; auth, Responses to 101 Questions on the Church, Paulist Press, 96; auth, Lives of the Popes, HarperSanFrancisco, 97. **CONTACT ADDRESS** Dept of Theol, Univ of Notre Dame, 327 O'Shaugnessy Hall, Notre Dame, IN 46556.

MCCABE, DAVID
DISCIPLINE MORAL PHILOSOPHY, POLITICAL PHILOSOPHY **EDUCATION** Northwestern Univ, PhD, 95. **CAREER** From Vis asst prof to Assocc prof, Colgate Univ. **SELECTED PUBLICATIONS** Auth, var articles in moral and polit theory. **CONTACT ADDRESS** Dept of Philos and Relig, Colgate Univ, 13 Oak Drive, Hamilton, NY 13346. **EMAIL** dmccabe@mail.colgate.edu

MCCABE, KIMBERLY A.
PERSONAL m **DISCIPLINE** CRIMINAL JUSTICE **EDUCATION** Va Tech, BA, 87; Univ SC, MCJ, 90; PhD, 96. **CAREER** Teaching Asst to Instr to Asst Prof, Univ SC, 89-. **MEMBERSHIPS** Am Soc Criminol, Acad of Criminal Justice Sci, Southern Criminal Justice Asn. **RESEARCH** Victimization, Rural and small-town policing. **SELECTED PUBLICATIONS** Auth, "Disease as a Deviant Disability," in Encyclopedia of Criminology and Deviant Behavior, Vol 4, in press; auth, "Agency Professionalization - Accreditation," in Contemporary Police Organization and Management: Issues and Trends, 00; auth, "Law enforcement Accreditation: A National Comparison of Accredited Versus Non-Accredited Agencies," Journal of Criminal Justice, in press; auth, "Child Pornography and the Internet," Social Science Computer Review, 00: 73-76; auth, "Recognizing Illegal Activities of computer Users," Social Science Computer Review, (98): 419-422; auth, "Elderly Victimization: An Examination Beyond the FBI's Index Crimes," Research on Aging, (98): 363-372; auth, "Users' Perceptions of Internet Regulation: An Exploratory Study," social Science Computer Review, (97): 237-241; auth, "A Comparative Analysis of Female Offenders," Corrections Today, (97): 28-30, auth, "Using the Michigan Alcoholism Screening Test to Identify Problem Drinkers Under Federal Supervision," Federal Probation, (96): 38-42; auth, "Inmate Leaders in the Jail environment," American Jails, (97): 53-55. **CONTACT ADDRESS** Col of Crim Justice, Univ of So Carolina, Columbia, Columbia, SC 29225-0001. **EMAIL** kmccabe@sc.edu

MCCAFFERY, EDWARD J.
DISCIPLINE LAW **EDUCATION** Yale Univ, BA; Harvard Univ, JD; Univ Southern Calif, MA. **CAREER** Maurice Jones, Jr., prof; clerked for, Honorable Robert N. Wilentz, Ch Justice Supreme Ct NJ; off consult, Russian Fed; private practice, San Francisco. **SELECTED PUBLICATIONS** Auth, Taxing Women; Cognitive Theory and Tax; Slouching Towards Equality: Gender Discrimination, Market Efficiency, Social Change; coauth, Framing the Jury: Cognitive Perspectives on Pain and Suffering Awards. **CONTACT ADDRESS** School of Law, Univ of So California, University Park Campus, Los Angeles, CA 90089.

MCCAGNEY, NANCY
DISCIPLINE RELIGIOUS STUDIES **EDUCATION** Univ Wisc, Madison, BA, MA; Univ Calif Santa Barbara, MA, PhD. **CAREER** Asst prof, philos, Univ Delaware. **HONORS AND AWARDS** NEH fel; Regents fel. **MEMBERSHIPS** AAR; APA; ASAP; ISEE; IABS. **RESEARCH** Religion and environment. **SELECTED PUBLICATIONS** Auth, Nagarjuna and the Philosophy of Openness, Rowman & Littlfield, 97. **CONTACT ADDRESS** Pollution Ecology Lab, Rm 104, Univ of Delaware, 700 Pilottown Rd, Lewes, DE 19958.

MCCALL, EMMANUEL LEMUEL, SR.
PERSONAL Born 02/04/1936, Sharon, PA, m, 1958, 2 children **DISCIPLINE** THEOLOGY **EDUCATION** Univ of Louisville, BA 1958; So Bapt Theol Sem, BD 1962, MRE 1963, MDiv 1967; Emory Univ, DMinistry 1975. **CAREER** Simmons Bible Coll Louisville, prof 1958-68; 28th St Bapt Church Louisville, pastor 1960-68; Cooperative Ministries w/Natl Bapt So Bapt Conv, assoc dir, 68-74; So Bapt Theol Sem Louisville, adj prof 1970-96; So Baptist Convention, dir dept of black church relations home missions bd 1974-88; Black Church Extension Division, Home Mission Board, SBC, director 1989-91; Christian Fellowship Baptist Church, College Park, GA, Pastor, 91-; McAfee School of Theology, Adjunct Prof, 96-. **HONORS AND AWARDS** Hon DD Simmons Bible Coll 1965; Ambassador of Goodwill City of Louisville 1967; Hon DD United Theol Sem 1977; Victor T Glass Awd Home Mission Bd So Bapt Conv 1979; E Y Mullins Denominational Service Awd, Southern Bapt Theological Seminary, 1990, E Y Mullins Humanitarian Awd; American Baptist College, 1990. **MEMBERSHIPS** Bd of dir Morehouse Sch of Religion 1972-85; mem Amer Soc of Missiology 1975-80; bd of trustees Interdenominational Theol Ctr 1978-; president elect, National Alumni Assn SBTS 1990-91, president 1991-92; co-chairman, Interdenomenational Theological Center, 1990-93, chair, 1993-96; Atlanta University Center, trustee, 1993-96; Truett McConnell College, trustee, 1994-; Baptist World Alliance, 1980-. **RESEARCH** Black church history; ethics. **SELECTED PUBLICATIONS** Auth, Black Church Lifestyles. **CONTACT ADDRESS** 1500 Norman Dr, College Park, GA 30349. **EMAIL** cfbc@worldnet.att.net; emccallsr@juno.com

MCCALL, STORRS
DISCIPLINE PHILOSOPHY **EDUCATION** McGill Univ, BA; Oxford Univ, BA, PhD. **RESEARCH** Philosophy of law. **SELECTED PUBLICATIONS** Auth, Aristotle's Modal Syllogisms, North-Holland, 63; auth, Polish Logic 1920-39, Clarendon, 67; auth, A Model of the Universe, Clarendon, 94. **CONTACT ADDRESS** Philosophy Dept, McGill Univ, 855 Sherbrooke St, Rm 908, Montreal, QC, Canada H3A 2T7. **EMAIL** mccall@philo.mcgill.ca

MCCANN, EDWIN
DISCIPLINE PHILOSOPHY **EDUCATION** Univ Pa, PhD, 75. **CAREER** Assoc prof & dir, Sch Philos,Univ Southern Calif; Univ Southern Calif, 83-; asst prof, Harvard Univ, 75-78; asst prof, MIT, 78-83; past vis prof, UCLA, UC Irvine, and Claremont Grad Sch. **HONORS AND AWARDS** Fac of the Month, Mortar Brd Honors Soc, 93; USC Associate s' awd for Excellence in Tchg, 97. **RESEARCH** History of modern philosophy. **SELECTED PUBLICATIONS** Auth, The Conditional Analysis of 'Can': Goldman's 'Reductio' of Lehrer, Philos Stud 28, 75; Skepticism and Kant's B Deduction, Hist Philos Quart 2, 85; Lockean Mechanism, in Its History and Historiography, Dordrecht: D. Reidel, 85; Cartesian Selves and Lockean Substances, Monist 69, 86; Locke on Identity: Matter, Life, and Consciousness, Archiv fuer Geschichte der Philos 69, 87; rep in Essays on Early Modern Philos Vol 8: John Locke: Theory of Knowledge, NY: Garland, 92; Locke's Philosophy of Body, chap in The Cambridge Companion to Locke, Cambridge: Cambridge UP, 94; History: Philosophy of Mind in the Seventeenth and Eighteenth Centuries, chap in the Blackwell Companion to the Philosophy of Mind, Oxford: Blackwell, 94. **CONTACT ADDRESS** Dept of Philosophy, Univ of So California, 3709 Trousdale Pkwy, Los Angeles, CA 90089-0451. **EMAIL** mccann@bcf.usc.edu

MCCANN, HUGH JOSEPH
PERSONAL Born 12/27/1942, Philadelphia, PA, m, 1965, 4 children **DISCIPLINE** PHILOSOPHY **EDUCATION** Villanova Univ, BA, 64; Univ Chicago, MA, 65, PhD, 72. **CAREER** Instr, Northern IL Univ, 67-68; Prof Philos, TX A&M Univ, 68-, Dept Head, 81-85, Danforth fel, 64. **HONORS AND AWARDS** Danforth Graduate Fel, 64-68; NEH Summer Seminar, 76; NEH Summer Seminar, 80; NEH Fellowship, 87-88; Distinguished Scholar Fellowship, Univ of Notre Dame, 97-98 **MEMBERSHIPS** AAUP; Am Philos Asn; Mind Asn; Southwestern Philos Soc; Soc Christian Philosophers. **RESEARCH** Philos of action; metaphysics of time and events; causation and explanation. **SELECTED PUBLICATIONS** Coauth, "The Occasionalist Proselytizer: A Modified Catechism," coauthored with Kvanvig, in J. E. Tomberlin, ed., Philosophical Perspectives 5, Philosophy of Religion, Atascadero, California: Ridgeview Publishing Co., 91, pp. 587-615; auth, "The God Beyond Time," in L.P. Pojman, ed., Philosophy of Religion, second edition, Belmont, California: Wadsworth, 93, pp. 231-245, Revised for third edition, 97; auth, "Dretske on the Metaphysics of Freedom," Canadian Journal of Philosophy 23, 93, 617-628; auth, "Intenzione e Forza Motivazionale," Discipline Filosofiche 2, 93, 251-272; auth, "Paralysis and the Springs of Action," Philosophia 23, 93, 193-205; auth, "Action, Philosophy of," "Practical Reason," "Practical Reasoning," and Reasons for Action," in R. Audi, ed., The Cambridge Dictionary of Philosophy, New York: Cambridge University Press, 95; auth, "Divine Sovereignty and the Freedom of the Will," Faith and Philosophy 12, 95, 582-598; auth, "Creation and Conservation," in C. Taliaferro and P. L. Quinn, eds., A Companion to the Philosophy of Religion, Oxford: Basil Blackwell, 97, pp. 306-312; auth, "On When the Will Is Free," in G. Holmstre-Hintikka and R. Tuomela, eds., Contemporary Action Theory, vol. I. Dordrechts, Netherlands: Kluwer Academic Publishers, 97, pp. 219-232; auth, The Works of Agency: On Human Action, Will and Freedom, Ithaca, New York: Cornell University Press, 98. **CONTACT ADDRESS** Dept of Philos, Texas A&M Univ, Col Station, 1 Texas A and M Univ, College Station, TX 77843. **EMAIL** h-mccann@tamu.edu

MCCARTHY, J. THOMAS
PERSONAL Born 07/02/1937, Detroit, MI **DISCIPLINE** LAW **EDUCATION** Univ Detroit, BS, 60; Univ Mich, Ann Arbor, JD, 63. **CAREER** Atty, San Francisco, 63-66; from asst prof to assoc prof law, 66-72, prof law, Univ San Francisco, 72-, consult, Limbach & Limbach, San Francisco, Calif, 83-. **HONORS AND AWARDS** Patishall Medal, Brand Names Educational Foundation, 2000; Centennial Awd, Am Intellectual PropertyLaw Asn, 97; Jefferson Medal, N.J. Intellectual Property Assoc, 94. **MEMBERSHIPS** Am Intellectual Prop Law Asn; Inst Elec & Electronics Engrs; Int Asn Advan Teaching & Res Intellectual Property. **RESEARCH** Trademark law; unfair competition law; antitrust law. **SELECTED PUBLICATIONS** Auth, Trademarks and Unfair Competition (6 vols), West, 4th edition, 96; Rights of Publicity & Privacy (2 vols), 2nd ed West, 00. **CONTACT ADDRESS** Law Sch, Univ of San Francisco, 2130 Fulton St, San Francisco, CA 94117-1080. **EMAIL** mccarthyt@usfca.edu

MCCARTHY, THOMAS
DISCIPLINE PHILOSOPHY **EDUCATION** Nat Univ Ireland, PhD. **CAREER** Face, Univ Col Dublin and Merrimack Col; instr, Endicott Col, 95-. **RESEARCH** The nature of consciousness and perception. **SELECTED PUBLICATIONS** Auth, The Transcendental Ego and Its Legacy in Phenomenology. **CONTACT ADDRESS** Endicott Col, 376 Hale St, Beverly, MA 01915.

MCCARTHY, THOMAS A.
PERSONAL Born 03/06/1940, Springfield, MA, m, 1963, 2 children **DISCIPLINE** PHILOSOPHY **EDUCATION** Holy Cross Col, BS, 61; Univ Notre Dame, MA, Phil, 63; Univ Louvain, PhD, 68. **CAREER** Instr, Univ Munich, 68-72; from asst prof to assoc prof, Boston Univ, 72-85; from prof to John Shaffer Distinguished Prof in the Humanities, Northwestern Univ, 85-. **HONORS AND AWARDS** Guggenheim Fel; NEH Fel; ACLS Fel; Humboldt Fel. **MEMBERSHIPS** Am Philos Asn, Kant Soc of Am, Soc for Phenomenology and Existential Philos. **RESEARCH** Classical and Contemporary German Philosophy, Social and Political Philosophy. **SELECTED PUBLICATIONS** Auth, The Critical Theory of Jurgen Habermeas, MIT Press, 78; auth, Ideals and Illusions, MIT Press, 91; coauth, "Critical Theory, Blackwell Publ, 94; general ed, Studies in Contemporary German Social Thought, MIT Press. **CONTACT ADDRESS** Dept Philos, Northwestern Univ, 633 Clark St, Evanston, IL 6028-0001. **EMAIL** t-mccarthy@nwu.edu

MCCARTHY, TIMOTHY
DISCIPLINE PHILOSOPHY **EDUCATION** Johns Hopkins Univ, PhD, 79. **CAREER** Assoc prof, Univ Ill Urbana Champaign. **RESEARCH** Philosophical logic; philosophy of language; metaphysics; philosophy of mathematics; metaphysical issues in the philosophy of science. **SELECTED PUBLICATIONS** Auth, The Idea of a Logical Constant; Truth Without Satisfaction; Modality, Invariance, and Logical Truth. **CONTACT ADDRESS** Philosophy Dept, Univ of Illinois, Urbana-Champaign, 52 E Gregory Dr, Champaign, IL 61820. **EMAIL** tgmccart@staff.uiuc.edu

MCCARTNEY, DAN GALE
PERSONAL Born 01/27/1950, Clarksburg, WV, m, 1971, 2 children **DISCIPLINE** NEW TESTAMENT **EDUCATION** Carnegie-Mellon Univ, BFA, 71; Gordon-Conwell Theol Sem, MDiv, 74; Westminster Theol Sem, ThM, 77, PhD, 89. **CAREER** Instr, Manna Bible Inst, 78-81; prof, Westminster Theol Sem, 83-. **MEMBERSHIPS** SBL; IBR; ETS. **SELECTED PUBLICATIONS** Auth, "Biblical and Allegorical Interpretation in Origen's Contra Celsum," Westm Theol Jrnl 48 (86); auth, Let the Reader Understand: A Guide to Interpreting and Applying the Bible, Why Does It Have To Hurt?: The Meaning of Christian Suffering; "Logikos in 1 Peter 2:2," Zeitschrift fur neutestamentiche Wissenschaft, 82.1/2 (91); "Ecce Homo: The Coming of the Kingdom as the Restoration of Human Vicegerency," Westminster Theol Jour, 56:1 (94); auth, "No Grace without Weakness," Westm Theol Jrnl 61:1 (99). **CONTACT ADDRESS** Westminster Theol Sem, Pennsylvania, PO Box 27009, Philadelphia, PA 19118. **EMAIL** dmccartney@wts.edu.

MCCARTNEY, JAMES J.
PERSONAL Born 09/01/1943 **DISCIPLINE** PHILOSOPHY **EDUCATION** Villanova Univ, BA, 66; Wash Theol Union-Augustinian Col, MA, 71; Cath Univ Am, MS, 72; Georgetown Univ, PhD, 81. **CAREER** Tenured assoc prof & dept ch, Villanova Univ; ethicist consult, Holy Redeemer Health Syst; ethicist consult, Cath Health E. **MEMBERSHIPS** Amer Soc for Bioethics and Humanities; Hastings Ctr; Kennedy Inst Ethics; Amer Philos Asn; Soc for Phenomenological and Existential Philos; Cath Theol Soc Am; ed bd, Catholic Studies in Bioethics & HEC Forum. **SELECTED PUBLICATIONS** Auth, Mergers and Sterilization: Ethics in the Board Room, Health-Care Ethics Committee Forum 9:3, 97; The Social Implications of Abortion, J for Peace and Justice Stud 7:1, 96; Consensus Statement on the Triage of Critically Ill Patients, J of the Amer Medl Assn 271:15, 94; Attitudes of Critical Care Medicine Professionals Concerning Distribution of Intensive Care Resources, Critical Care Med 22:2, 94 & Abortion, Social Implications of, in the New Dictionary of Catholic Social Thought, , A Michael Glazier Book, Collegeville, MN: The Liturgical Press, 94. **CONTACT ADDRESS** Dept of Philosophy, Villanova Univ, 800 Lancaster Ave, Villanova, PA 19085-1692. **EMAIL** james.mccartney@villanova.edu

MCCARTNEY, SHARON
DISCIPLINE LAW **EDUCATION** Pomona Col, BA; Univ Iowa, MFA; Univ Victoria, LLB. **CAREER** Law, Univ Victoria. **SELECTED PUBLICATIONS** Auth, pubs on creative writing. **CONTACT ADDRESS** Fac of Law, Univ of Victoria, PO Box 2400, Victoria, BC, Canada V8W 3H7. **EMAIL** sharonmc@uvic.ca

MCCARTY, DORAN CHESTER
PERSONAL Born 02/03/1931, Bolivar, MO, m, 1952, 4 children **DISCIPLINE** PHILOSOPHY, THEOLOGY **EDUCATION** William Jewell Col, AB, 52; Southern Baptist Theol Sem, BD, 56, ThD(theol, philos), 63. **CAREER** Instr relig, William Jewell Col, 66-67; Prof Philos & Theol, Midwestern Baptist Theol Sem, 67-. **MEMBERSHIPS** Soc Bibl Lit; Am Acad Relig; Am Philos Asn. **SELECTED PUBLICATIONS** **CONTACT ADDRESS** Dept of Theol & Christian Philos, Midwestern Baptist Theol Sem, Kansas City, MO 64118.

MCCAULEY, ROBERT N.
PERSONAL Born 06/01/1952, Gassaway, WV, m, 1975, 1 child **DISCIPLINE** PHILOSOPHY **EDUCATION** Western Mich Univ, Ba, 74; Univ Chicago, MA, 75; PhD, 79. **CAREER** Asst prof, Univ Indianapolis, 79-83; adu asst prof, Purdue Univ, 82-83; asst prof to adj prof, Emory Univ, 83-. **HONORS AND AWARDS** Emory Williams Distinguished Teaching Awd, 96; Massee-Martin Nat Endowment, 94-98; Am Ac of Relig grant, 93-94; Henry R. Luce fac Sem, 93; Phi Beta Kappa, 91-94; Nat Endowment for the Humanities, 90; Lilly Endowment Post-doc teaching award, 85-86; Am Coun of Learned Soc study Fel, 82-83; Coun for Philos Studies summer Inst, 81; Danforth Grad Fel, 74-79; Mrs. Giles Whiting Found Dissertation Fel, 78-79. **MEMBERSHIPS** Soc Philos and Psychol, Southern Soc for Philos and Psychol, Am Philos Asn, Ga Philos Soc, N Am Asn for the Study Relig, Soc for the Sci Study of Relig. **RESEARCH** Philosophy of psychology, Philosophy of cognitive science, philosophy of science, naturalized epistemology, cognitive approaches to the study of religion. **SELECTED PUBLICATIONS** Auth, "Ritual, Memory and Emotion: Comparing Two Cognitive Hypotheses," Religion in Mind: Cognitive Perspectives on Religious Experience, Cambridge, (forthcoming); auth, "The Naturalness of Religion and the Unnaturalness of Science," Explanation and Cognition, (00): 61-85; auth, "Heuristic Identity Theory (or Back to the Future): The Mind-Body Problem Against the Background of Research Strategies in Cognitive Neuroscience," Proceedings of the Twenty-First Meeting of the Cognitive Science Society, (99): 67-72; auth, "The Cognitive Foundations of Religion and Science," Religion im Wandel der Kosmologien, (99): 55-67; auth, "Levels of Explanation and Cognitive Architectures," Blackwell companion to Cognitive Science, (98): 611-624; auth, "Who Owns Culture?" Method and Theory in the Study of Religion (96): 171-190; auth, "Explanatory Pluralism and the Coevolution of Theories in Science," The Churchlands and Their Critics, (96): 171-190; ed The Churchlands and Their Critics, Oxford, 96; auth, "Crisis of conscience, Riddle of Identity: Making Space for a Cognitive Approach to Religious Phenomena," Journal of the American Academy of Religion, (93): 210-223; auth, "Why the Blind Can't Lead the Blind: Dennett on the Blind Spot, Blindsight, and Sensory Qualia," Consciousness and Cognition, (93): 155-164. **CONTACT ADDRESS** Dept Philos, Emory Univ, 1364 Clifton Rd NE, Atlanta, GA 30322-1061. **EMAIL** philrnm@emory.edu

MCCLAIN, JOHN O.
DISCIPLINE OPERATIONS RESEARCH **EDUCATION** Yale Univ, PhD, 70. **CAREER** Sch Management, Cornell Univ **CONTACT ADDRESS** SC Johnson Grad Sch of Management, Cornell Univ, Sage Hall, Ithaca, NY 14853.

MCCLAIN, T. VAN
PERSONAL Born 06/10/1952, Dallas, TX, m, 1977, 3 children **DISCIPLINE** OLD TESTAMENT AND HEBREW **EDUCATION** SW Baptist Theol Sem, MDiv, 77, PhD, 85. **CAREER** Assoc Prof, Dir library serv, 89-, Mid-Amer Baptist Theol Sem. **MEMBERSHIPS** ETS; SBL. **RESEARCH** Old Testament and New Testament; Semitic Languages; Cults; Hermeneutics. **SELECTED PUBLICATIONS** Auth, The Use of Amos in the New Testament, Mid-America Theol J, 95; Hosea's Marriage to Gomer, Mid-Amer Theol J, 93; Introduction to the Book Of Isaiah, Mid-Amer Theol J, 91. **CONTACT ADDRESS** Northeast Branch, Mid-America Baptist Theol Sem, Northeast, 2810 Curry Rd, Schenectady, NY 12303. **EMAIL** VMcClain@mabtsne.edu

MCCLAMROCK, RON
DISCIPLINE PHILOSOPHY **EDUCATION** Mass Inst Tech, PhD. **CAREER** Assoc prof, Univ Albany, State Univ NY. **RESEARCH** Philosophy of psychology, foundations of artificial intelligence and cognitive science, philosophy of the mind and philosophy of science. **SELECTED PUBLICATIONS** Auth, Existential Cognition: Computational Minds in the World, Univ Chicago Press, 95. **CONTACT ADDRESS** Dept of Philosophy, SUNY, Albany, Albany, NY 12222. **EMAIL** ron@cnsunix.albany.edu

MCCLEAN, ALBERT
DISCIPLINE LAW **EDUCATION** Queen's Univ, LLB, 57; Cambridge Univ, PhD, 63. **CAREER** Prof, 68-. **HONORS AND AWARDS** Ed, Can Bar Rev, 84-94. **RESEARCH** Property law. **SELECTED PUBLICATIONS** Auth, pubs about advanced real property, equity and trusts, property and restitution. **CONTACT ADDRESS** Fac of Law, Univ of British Columbia, 1822 East Mall, Vancouver, BC, Canada V6T 1Z1. **EMAIL** mcclean@law.ubc.ca

MCCLELLAND, WILLIAM LESTER
PERSONAL Born 08/25/1924 **DISCIPLINE** HISTORY OF CHRISTIANITY **EDUCATION** Westminster Col, BA, 48; Pittsburgh Theol Sem, BD, 51, ThM, 56; Princeton Theol Sem, PhD(hist theol), 67. **CAREER** Pastor, Knox United Presby Church, Des Moines, 51-53; pastor, Avalon United Presby Church, Pittsburgh, 53-56; from asst prof to assoc prof, 56-71, dir honors, 67-72, trustee, Bd Trustees, 76-77, chmn dept, 68-74, Prof Relig, Muskingum Col, 71, Chmn Dept Relig & Philos, 77, Coordr, Div Arts & Humanities, 81-, Vis lectr, Westminster Col, Eng, 67; Am Col Switz, 69. **MEMBERSHIPS** Am Soc Church Hist; Am Acad Relig; Soc Liturgica; AAUP. **RESEARCH** American religious experience as compared with European religious experience; Reformation history; liturgical history. **SELECTED PUBLICATIONS** Auth, Underhill, Evelyn--Artist of the Infinite Life, Church Hist, vol 0063, 94. **CONTACT ADDRESS** Dept of Relig & Philos, Muskingum Col, New Concord, OH 43762.

MCCLENDON, JAMES WILLIAM, JR.
PERSONAL Born 03/06/1924, Shreveport, LA, m, 1983 **DISCIPLINE** THEOLOGY **EDUCATION** Univ Tex, BA, 47; SW Baptist Theol Sem, BD, 50; ThD, 53; Princeton Theol Sem, ThM, 52. **CAREER** Asst Prof to Prof, Golden Gate Baptist Theol Sem, 54-66; Prof, Church Divinity Sch, 71-90; Assoc Prof, Univ San Francisco, 66-69; Prof, Church Divinity Sch, 71-90; Prof, Fuller Theol Sem, 90-. **HONORS AND AWARDS** Phi Beta Kappa; Recognized Stud, Oxford Univ. **MEMBERSHIPS** Am Soc of Church Hist; Am Philos Asn; Faith and Order Colloquium; Nat Coun of Churches; Inst for Ecumenical and Cultural Res; PAC Coast Theol Soc; Philos of Relig and Theol; Am Acad of Relig; Nat Asn of Baptist Prof of Relig; **RESEARCH** Systematic Theology; Philosophy of Religion; Ethics. **SELECTED PUBLICATIONS** Auth, Is God GOD?, Abingdon Press, 81; auth, Ethics: Systematic Theology Volume I, Abingdon Press, 86; auth, Biography as Theology, Trinity Press Intl, 90; co-auth, Convictions: Defusing Religious Relativism, Trinity Press Intl, 94; auth, Doctrine: Systematic Theology Volume II, Abingdon Press, 94; co-ed, Baptist Roots: A Reader in the Theology of a Christian People, Judson Press, 99; auth, Witness: Systematic Theology Volume III, forthcoming. **CONTACT ADDRESS** Dept Theol, Fuller Theol Sem, 135 N Oakland Ave, Pasadena, CA 91182.

MCCLOSKEY, DEIRDRE
PERSONAL Born 09/11/1942, Ann Arbor, MI, d, 2 children **DISCIPLINE** ECONOMICS **EDUCATION** Harvard Col, BA, 64; Harvard Univ, PhD, 70. **CAREER** From asst prof to assoc prof, Univ Chicago, 68-80; prof hist & econ, Univ Iowa, 80-. **HONORS AND AWARDS** Guggenheim and NEH Fel; David A. Wells Prize for "Economic Maturity". **MEMBERSHIPS** Econ Hist Asn. **RESEARCH** British history; rhetoric of history. **SELECTED PUBLICATIONS** Auth, Economic Maturity and Entrepreneurial Decline: British Iron and Steel, 1870-1913, Harvard Univ Press, 73; auth, Enterprise and Trade in Victorian Britain: Essays in Historical Economics, Allen and Unwin, 81; auth, The Rhetoric of Economics, Univ Wis Press, 85; auth, Econometric History, Macmillan, 87; auth, If You're So Smart: The Narrative of Economic Expertise, Univ Chicago Press, 90. **CONTACT ADDRESS** Dept Econ, Univ of Iowa, 108 Pappajohn Bus Admin Bldg., Ste. 5336, Iowa City, IA 52242. **EMAIL** deirdre-mccloskey@uiowa.edu

MCCLURG, ANDREW
PERSONAL Born 10/15/1954, East Lansing, MI, d, 1 child **DISCIPLINE** LAW **EDUCATION** Univ Fla, BS, 77; JD, 80. **CAREER** Associate, Bedell, Dittmar, DeVault & Pillans, 82-86; vis prof, Golden Gate Univ, 91-92; asst prof to prof, Univ of Ark, 86-. **HONORS AND AWARDS** Faculty Excellence Awd for Teaching; Teacher of the Year Awd; UALR School of Law's Fac Excellence Awd for Res; Nadine H Baum Distinguished Prof. **MEMBERSHIPS** Am Bar Assoc. **RESEARCH** Tort law, firearms policy, privacy law. **SELECTED PUBLICATIONS** Auth, "The Danger Posed by Handguns Outweighs Their Effectiveness", Gun Control, eds Bruno Leone et al, (92): 176-81; auth, "Poetry in Commotion: Katko v Briney and the Bards of First-Year Torts, 74 Ore Law Rev (95): 823-848; auth, "100% Guarantee", ABA J, (97): 18; auth, "Final Footnote to Foster Tragedy: Supreme Court Recognizes Posthumous Attorney-Client Privilege", ATLA Docket, (98): 4; auth, "Supreme Court Gives Green Light To Police Chances", ATLA Docket, (98): 6; auth, "Good Cop, Bad Cop: Using Cognitive dissonance Theory To Reduce Police Lying", 32 Univ of Calif Davis Law Rev (99): 389-453; auth, "The Ten Commandments of (The First-Year Course of Your Choice) and Paying Respects to law School's First Year", Techniques for Teaching Law, eds Gerald F Hess and Steve Friedland, 99; auth, "Hiring Squeeze", ABA J, (99): 12; coauth, Gun Control and Gun Rights, NY Univ Pr, (forthcoming). **CONTACT ADDRESS** Sch of Law, Univ of Arkansas, Little Rock, 1203 McAlmont St, Little Rock, AR 72202-5142. **EMAIL** ajmcclurg@ualr.edu

MCCOLLOUGH, C. THOMAS
DISCIPLINE RELIGION **EDUCATION** Univ Fla, BA; Duke Univ, MDiv; Univ Notre Dame, MA and PhD. **CAREER** Fac, 80-; prof, current. **RESEARCH** History of Christianity and Christian thought; Biblical history and archaeology; contemporary Middle East. **SELECTED PUBLICATIONS** Auth, contribu, Studi Patristica, Relig Studies Rev; co-ed, Archaeology and the Galilee: Text and Context in the Graeco-Roman and Byzantine Periods, Scholars Press, 97. **CONTACT ADDRESS** Centre Col, 600 W Walnut St, Danville, KY 40422. **EMAIL** mccollog@centre.edu

MCCOLLOUGH, THOMAS ELMORE
PERSONAL Born 06/26/1926, Birmingham, AL, m, 1956, 2 children **DISCIPLINE** RELIGION **EDUCATION** Univ Tex, BBA, 47; Southern Baptist Theol Sem, BD, 50, ThD, 55. **CAREER** Asst prof relig, Stetson Univ, 55-58; assoc prof theol, Baptist Theol Sem, Switz, 58-61; asst prof, 61-66, Assoc Prof Relig, Duke Univ, 66-, Teaching fel theol, Southern Baptist Theol Sem, 50-52; Soc Relig Higher Educ cross disciplinary fel, London Sch Econ, 67-68. **MEMBERSHIPS** Am Soc Christian Ethics; Am Acad Relig; fel Soc Relig Higher Educ. **RESEARCH** Theology; ethics. **SELECTED PUBLICATIONS** Auth, Realized Eschatology and C H Dodd, Relig in Life, summer 57; The ontology of Tillich and Biblical personalism, Scottish J Theol, 9/62; Reinhold Niebuhr and Karl Barth on the relevance of theology, J Relig, 1/63. **CONTACT ADDRESS** Dept of Relig, Duke Univ, Durham, NC 27706.

MCCONNAUGHAY, PHILIP J.
DISCIPLINE LAW **EDUCATION** Univ Ill, BA; JD. **CAREER** Assoc prof, Univ Ill Urbana Champaign, 95-. **MEMBERSHIPS** Phi Beta Kapp;Univ Ill Law Forum. **RESEARCH** Copyright; evidence; international business transactions; and international litigation and arbitration. **SELECTED PUBLICATIONS** Auth, pubs on international commercial dispute resolution, commercial law reform in emerging nations, and comparative legal ethics. **CONTACT ADDRESS** Law Dept, Univ of Illinois, Urbana-Champaign, 52 E Gregory Dr, Champaign, IL 61820. **EMAIL** pmcconna@law.uiuc.edu

MCCONNELL, JEFF
PERSONAL Born 06/10/1953, Newport, RI **DISCIPLINE** PHILOSOPHY **EDUCATION** Harvard, AB, 77; MA Inst of Tech, PhD, 94 **CAREER** Lect, 88-pres, Tufts Univ **MEMBERSHIPS** Am Philos Assoc; Philos of Sci Assoc; Soc for Philos & Psychol **RESEARCH** Metaphysics; Philosophy of Mind **SELECTED PUBLICATIONS** Auth, In Defense of the Knowledge Argument, Philosophical Topics 22, 94 **CONTACT ADDRESS** Dept of Philos, Tufts Univ, Medford, Medford, MA 02155. **EMAIL** jmcconne@emerald.tufts.edu

MCCONNELL, TERRANCE C.
PERSONAL Born 12/19/1948, Zanesville, OH, m, 1970 **DISCIPLINE** PHILOSOPHY **EDUCATION** Wittenberg Univ, BA, 71; Univ of Minn, PhD, 75. **CAREER** Asst prof to prof, Univ of NC Greensboro, 76-. **HONORS AND AWARDS** NEH Fel, 89-90, 95-96. **MEMBERSHIPS** Am Philos Assoc. **RESEARCH** Medical Ethics, Political Philosophy, Ethical Theory. **SELECTED PUBLICATIONS** Auth, Gratitude, Temple Univ Pr, 93; Moral Issues in Health Care, Wadsworth Publ, 97; Inalienable Rights, Oxford Univ Pr, 00. **CONTACT ADDRESS** Dept Philos, Univ of No Carolina, Greensboro, 1000 Spring Garden, Greensboro, NC 27402-6170. **EMAIL** tcmcconn@uncg.edu

MCCONNELL, WILLIAM HOWARD
PERSONAL Born 07/02/1930, Aylmer East, PQ, Canada, m, 1963, 2 children **DISCIPLINE** LAW, POLITICAL SCIENCE **EDUCATION** Carleton Univ, BA, 55; Univ NB, BCL, 58; Univ Toronto, PhD(polit sci), 68; Univ Sask, LLM, 70. **CAREER** Lectr polit sci, Bishop's Univ, 66-69; from asst prof to assoc prof law, 70-75, Prof Law, Univ Sask, 75-98, Assoc prof law, Univ Windsor, 74-75; consult const law, Govt Northwest Territories, 75-78 & Govt Sask, 77-81; prof emer, 98-. **MEMBERSHIPS** Can Bar Asn; Can Asn Law Teachers. **RESEARCH** Constitutional law; comparative federalism; international law. **SELECTED PUBLICATIONS** Auth, Commentary on the British North America Act, Macmillan of Can, (Toronto, ON), 77; auth, William R. McIntyre: paladin of the common law, McGill-Queen's Univ Press, (Montreal, QC), 00. **CONTACT ADDRESS** Col of Law, Univ of Saskatchewan, 15 Campus Dr, Saskatoon, SK, Canada S7N 5A6.

MCCORD, JOAN
PERSONAL Born 08/04/1930, New York, NY, w, 1970, 2 children **DISCIPLINE** CRIMINAL JUSTICE **EDUCATION** Stanford Univ, PhD, 68. **CAREER** Prof of Criminal Justice, Temple Univ. **HONORS AND AWARDS** President, Am Soc of Criminology, 88-89; Herbert Bloch Awd, 91; Prix Emile Durkheim, 93; Edwin H. Sutherland, 94. **MEMBERSHIPS** Am Soc for criminology, Int Soc of Criminology, Life Hist Res Soc, Am Sociol Asn, Int Soc for Res on Aggression. **RESEARCH** Personality development, socialization, deviant behavior. **SELECTED PUBLICATIONS** Ed, Violence and Childhood in the Inner City, New York: Cambridge Univ Press (97); coauth, Youth Violence: Children at Risk, Washington, DC: Am Sociol Asn (98); ed, Coercion and Punishment in Long-term Perspectives, New York: Cambridge Univ Press (95); auth, "Understanding Childhood and Subsequent Crime," Aggressive Behavior, 25, 4 (99): 241-253; coauth, "When Interventions Harm: Peer Groups and Problem Behavior," Am Psychol, 54, 9 (99): 1-10; auth, "Interventions: Punishment, Diversion, and Alternative Routes to Crime Prevention," in The Handbook of Forensic Psychology, eds. A. K. Hess and I. B. Weiner (NY: Wiley (99): 559-579; auth, "Crime: Taking an Historical Perspective," in Where and When: Historical and geographical aspects of psychopathology, eds. P. Cohen, C. Slomkowski, and L. N. Robins (NJ: Lawrence Erlbaum Associates, 99). **CONTACT ADDRESS** Dept Criminal Justice-Gladfelter, Temple Univ, 1115 W Berks St, Philadelphia, PA 19122. **EMAIL** mccord@astro.temple.edu

MCCOY, FRANCIS T.
DISCIPLINE LAW **EDUCATION** Univ Fla, AB, MA, JD. **CAREER** Asst prof to prof emer, Univ Fla, 56-; past Vice Consul, US For Serv; vis prof, Johann Wolfgang Goethe Univ, Ger. **MEMBERSHIPS** Fla Bar; Phi Beta Kappa. **RESEARCH** Admiralty, legal history, family law. **CONTACT ADDRESS** School of Law, Univ of Florida, PO Box 117625, Gainesville, FL 32611-7625. **EMAIL** McCoy@law.ufl.edu

MCCOY, GARY W.
PERSONAL m, 3 children **DISCIPLINE** CHURCH MUSIC **EDUCATION** Cent Mo State Univ, BME; Southwestern Baptist Theol Sem, MCM; Southwestern Baptist Theol Sem, DMA; addn stud, Midwestern Baptist Theol Sem; Myong Dong Inst, Seoul, degree Korean Lang Stud. **CAREER** Prof, Korea Baptist Col/Sem, 85-89; dir, Area Mus Dept, Korea Baptist Col/Sem, 86-89; church mus consult, 75-79; assoc prof, 91; dir, Bill and Pat Dixon Sch of Church Mus, Golden Gate Baptist Theol Sem. **HONORS AND AWARDS** Missionary, For Mission Bd, 74; minister of mus, Concord Korean Baptist Church. **SELECTED PUBLICATIONS** Auth, Come to the Manger; Easter Praises and Jesus; the Very Thought of Thee, Jordan Press Seoul, Korea; Hymn Arrangements for the Korean Church Pianist and His Only Son: God's Gift at Christmas; pub(s), S Baptist keyboard mag; Pedalpoint. **CONTACT ADDRESS** Golden Gate Baptist Theol Sem, 201 Sem Dr, Mill Valley, CA 94941-3197. **EMAIL** GaryMcCoy@ggbts.edu

MCCOY, JERRY
DISCIPLINE RELIGION AND PHILOSOPHY **EDUCATION** DePauw Univ, BA; Northwestern Univ, MA; Christian Theol Sem, MDiv; Columbia Univ/Union Theol Sem, PhD. **CAREER** Prof, Eureka Col. **HONORS AND AWARDS** Rep Christian Church, World Coun Churches, 95. **RESEARCH** Western relig traditions and Asian relig(s). **SELECTED PUBLICATIONS** Auth, book on Christianity and ecology. **CONTACT ADDRESS** Eureka Col, 300 E College Ave, PO Box 280, Eureka, IL 61530.

MCCOY, PATRICIA A.
PERSONAL Born 06/20/1954, Cortland, NY **DISCIPLINE** LAW **EDUCATION** Univ Cal Berk, JD 83; Oberlin Col BA 76. **CAREER** Cleveland State Univ Col of Law, Assoc, Prof, 97; asst prof, 92-97; Mayer Brown Platt DC, partner, 91-92, assoc 84-90, sum assoc 83; Hon Robert S. Vance, law clk, 83-84. **HONORS AND AWARDS** Prof of the Year; Howard L. Oleck Awd; 6 Clev Marsh Fac Res Gnts; Ger Marshall Fund; Named DC Pro Bono Lawyer. **MEMBERSHIPS** DCB **RESEARCH** Banking regulation; corp law; corp finance; post-socialist econ reforms. **SELECTED PUBLICATIONS** Auth, Special Factors Making Small Post-Socialist Economies Susceptible to Bank System Risk, in: Global Trends and Changes in East European Banking, ed, Ewa Miklaszewka, Jagiellonian Univ, 98; The Demise of the Common Law Doctrine in D'Oench Duhme, Matthew Bender, 98; Banking Law Manual, 2nd ed, Matthew Bender, forthcoming 00; Levers of Law Reform: Public Goods and Russian Banking, Cornell Intl Law Jour, 97; A Political Economy of the Business Judgment Rule in Banking: Implications for Corporate Law, Case W Res L Rev, 96; The Notional Business Judgment Rule in Banking, Cath U L Rev, 95; auth, Technology Shifts and the Law: Year 2000 Liability for Banks, Ann. Rev. Banking L., 00; auth, Banks and Thifts, Matthew Bender, 1996-2000 Releases. **CONTACT ADDRESS** Dept of Law, Cleveland State Univ, 1801 Euclid Ave, Cleveland, OH 44115. **EMAIL** pagricia.mccoy@law.csuohio.edu

MCCOY, THOMAS RAYMOND
PERSONAL Born 04/14/1943, Cincinnati, OH, m, 1968, 2 children **DISCIPLINE** CONSTITUTIONAL LAW **EDUCATION** Xavier Univ, BS, 64; Univ Cincinnati, JD, 67; Harvard Univ, LLM, 68. **CAREER** Asst prof, 68-71, assoc prof, 71-75, assoc dean, 71-75, prof law, Sch of Law, Vanderbilt Univ, 75-. **RESEARCH** The religion clauses in the First Amendment; judicial jurisdiction and conflict of laws; alternative dispute resolution; conceptual language and syllogistic reasoning. **SELECTED PUBLICATIONS** Auth, Commentary on Katzenbach v McClung, The Oxford Companion to the Supreme Court of the United States, 92; coauth, Conditional Spending, Encyclopedia of the American Constitution, 92; art, The Sophisticated Consumer's Guide to Alternative Dispute Resolution Techniques: What You Should Expect (or Demand) from ADR Services, Proc of the Surety Claims Inst, 92 & 26 U.Memphis L Rev, 96; art, The Whys and Ways of Mediation -- A Guide for the Sophisticated User, Business Law Today, 92; art, A Coherent Methodology for First Amendment Speech and Religion Clause Cases, 48 Vand L Rev 1335, 95. **CONTACT ADDRESS** Sch of Law, Vanderbilt Univ, 2201 West End Ave S, Nashville, TN 37240-0001. **EMAIL** thomas.mccoy@law.vanderbilt.edu

MCCRACKEN, CHARLES JAMES
PERSONAL Born 04/17/1933, Los Angeles, CA, m, 1956, 2 children **DISCIPLINE** PHILOSOPHY **EDUCATION** Univ Calif, Los Angeles, BA, 55; Fordham Univ, MA, 59; Univ Calif, Berkeley, PhD, 69. **CAREER** From instr to asst prof, 65-71, assoc prof, 71-80, prof philos, Mich State Univ, 80-99; prof philos emer, Mich State Univ, 99-. **HONORS AND AWARDS** MSU distinguished faculty award, 98. **MEMBERSHIPS** AAUP; Am Philos Asn. **RESEARCH** History of modern philosophy; epistemology; metaphysics. **SELECTED PUBLICATIONS** Auth, Malebranche and British Philosophy, Oxford Univ Press, 83; auth, Berkeley's Principles and Dialogues: Background Source Materials, Cambridge Univ Press, 00. **CONTACT ADDRESS** Dept of Philosophy, Michigan State Univ, 1738 Calle Boca del Canon, Santa Barbara, CA 93101. **EMAIL** mccrack2@msu.edu

MCCULLAGH, MARK
DISCIPLINE PHILOSOPHY **EDUCATION** Philos, Math, BA; Philos, PhD. **CAREER** Asst Prof, SMU, 97-. **HONORS AND AWARDS** Soc Sci and Humanities Res Council Doctoral Fel; Alan Ross Anderson Fel. **MEMBERSHIPS** Am Philos Asn. **RESEARCH** Philosophy of language; Philos of Mind. **SELECTED PUBLICATIONS** Auth, Mediality and Rationality in Aristotle's Account of Excellence of Character, Aperion, 95; auth, "Self-knowledge failures and first person authority," Philosophy and Phenomenological Research, forthcoming; auth, "Fuctionalism and self-consciousness," Mind & Language, forthcoming; auth, "Wittgenstein on rules and practices," Journal of Philosophical Research; auth, "Solitary and embedded knowledge," The Southwest Philosophy Review 16: 161-9. **CONTACT ADDRESS** Dept of Philosophy, So Methodist Univ, Box 750142, Dallas, TX 75175. **EMAIL** mark_mcculagh@yahoo.com

MCCULLOCH, ELIZABETH
DISCIPLINE LAW **EDUCATION** Univ Mich, BGS; Duke Law Sch, JD. **CAREER** Dir, soc pol ctr govt responsibility; governors comn on child support; state Fla human subjects rev coun; co health care bd; pres, sexual and physical abuse resource ctr; dir, Fla bar found public serv law fellows; atty, VISTA Jacksonville legal aid; staff atty & dir, family law unit, JALA. **HONORS AND AWARDS** Grant recipient, Dept Hea and Rehab Svcs, Dept Educ, State WAGES bd, AvMed, Fla Bar Found. **RESEARCH** Poverty law and policy, family law, legal

services to the poor. **CONTACT ADDRESS** School of Law, Univ of Florida, PO Box 117625, Gainesville, FL 32611-7625. **EMAIL** McCulloc@law.ufl.edu

MCCULLOH, GERALD WILLIAM
PERSONAL Born 05/03/1941, St. Paul, MN, m, 1967, 2 children **DISCIPLINE** THEOLOGY, HISTORY AND STRUCTURE OF RELIGIOUS THOUGHT, PHILOSOPHY OF RELIGION **EDUCATION** Vanderbilt Univ, BA, 62; Harvard Univ, MDiv, 65; Univ Chicago, MA, 68, PhD(hist & systematic theol), 73. **CAREER** Instr humanities, Cent YMCA Community Col, 68; instr theol, 69-73, asst prof, 73-80, Assoc Prof Theol, Loyola Univ Chicago, 80-, Ed, th Century Theol Work Group Diss Set, 73-75; ed, Texts, 79; mem steering comt, th Century Theol Work Group, 76-; assoc Protestant Chaplain, Loyola Univ, 74-89; res leave, Gottingen Univ, 81; assoc dir res services, Loyola Univ Chicago, 90-96; actg dir res services, 93-95. **HONORS AND AWARDS** Alfred P. Sloan Fel, 58-62; Engl-Speaking Union Fel, 70-71; Nat Endowment for the Humanities Fel, 78-79; Loyola Univ Res Leave, 81. **MEMBERSHIPS** Am Acad Relig; Am Acad Polit & Soc Sci; AAUP; Phi Beta Kappa; Am Soc of Church Hist. **RESEARCH** Nineteenth century theology; American religious experience; history and structure of religious thought. **SELECTED PUBLICATIONS** Rev, of "Three Essays," by Albrect Ritschl, J of Relig 54 (Jan 74): 93-94; auth, A Bibliography of Dissertations in Nineteenth Century Theology: 1960-1976, Loyola Univ, 76; rev, of "Romantic Idealism and Roman Catholicism: Schelling and the Theologians," by Thomas F. O'Meara, TSF Bulletin 6 (May-June 83): 28; coed, Papers of the Nineteenth Century Theology Working Group AAR 1986 Annual Meeting, Grad Theol Union, 86; auth, Christ's Person and Life-work in the Theology of Albrecht Ritschl, Univ Press of Am, 90; auth, "The Theological Legacy of Albrecht Ritschl," in Ritschl in Retrospect: History, Community, and Science, ed. Darrell Jodock (Augsburg Fortress Press, 95), 31-50; rev, of "In Good Company: The Church as Polis," by Stanley Hauerwas, Am 173 (Nov 95): 26-27; rev, of "La Foi des Eglises Lutheriennes: Confessions et Catechismes," by Andre Birmele and Marc Lienhard, Church Hist 64 (June 95): 343; rev, of "Brief Introduction to the Study of Theology: With Reference to the Scientific Standpoint and the Catholic System," by Johann Sebastian Drey, Church Hist 65 (June 96): 343; auth, "Creation to Consumption: The Theology of Wolfhart Pannenberg," Anglican Theol Rev 83 (01): 115-128. **CONTACT ADDRESS** Dept of Theol, Loyola Univ, Chicago, 6525 N Sheridan Rd, Chicago, IL 60626-5385. **EMAIL** gmccull@luc.edu

MCCULLOUGH, LAURENCE B.
PERSONAL Born 08/02/1947, Philadelphia, PA, m, 1977 **DISCIPLINE** MEDICAL ETHICS **EDUCATION** Williams Col, BA, 69; Univ Texas, Austin, PhD, 75. **CAREER** Asst prof, hum and med, Texas A & M Univ, 76-79; asst prof, 79-82, assoc prof, 82-87, prof, of Family and Commun Med, Georgetown Univ; prof, med and med ethics, Baylor Col of Med, 88-. **HONORS AND AWARDS** Post-doctoral fel, 75-76; Am Coun of Learned Soc Fel, 95-96. **MEMBERSHIPS** Am Soc for Bioethics and Hum; Gerontological Soc of Am. **RESEARCH** Bioethics; history of medical ethics; Leibniz. **SELECTED PUBLICATIONS** Coauth, Ethics in Obstretics and Gynecology, Oxford, 94; ed, Long-Term Care Decisions: Ethical and Conceptual Dimensions, Johns Hopkins, 95; auth, Leibniz on Individuals and Individuation: The Persistence of Premodern Ideas in Modern Philosophy, Kluwer, 96; auth, John Gregory and the Invention of Professional Medical Ethics and the Profession of Medicine, Kluwer, 98; co-ed, Surgical Ethics, Oxford, 98; ed, John Gregory's Writings on Medical Ethics and Philosophy of Medicine, Kluwer, 98; coauth, Medical Ethics: Codes and Statements, BNA, 2000. **CONTACT ADDRESS** Center for Medical Ethics and Health Policy, Baylor Col of Med, One Baylor Plz, Houston, TX 77030. **EMAIL** mccullou@bcm.tmc.edu

MCCULLOUGH, RALPH C., II
DISCIPLINE TORTS, LAW AND MEDICINE, DAMAGES, AND TRIAL ADVOCACY **EDUCATION** Erskine Col, BA, 62; Tulane Univ, JD, 65. **CAREER** Am Col Trial Lawyers prof, Univ of SC. **SELECTED PUBLICATIONS** Coauth, bk(s) on civil litigation in the fed courts and on SC torts law. **CONTACT ADDRESS** School of Law, Univ of So Carolina, Columbia, Law Center, Columbia, SC 29208. **EMAIL** law0150@univscvm.csd.scarolina.edu

MCCURDY, HOWARD EARL
PERSONAL Born 12/18/1941, Atascadero, CA, d **DISCIPLINE** PUBLIC ADMINISTRATION AND POLITICAL SCIENCE **EDUCATION** Univ Wash, BA, 62; Univ Wash, MA, 65; Cornell Univ, PhD, 69. **CAREER** Prof, Amer Univ, 68-. **HONORS AND AWARDS** Henry Adams prize (for Inside NASA), 94; Eugene M. Emme Astronautical Literature Awd (for Space and the American Imagination), 99. **MEMBERSHIPS** Am Soc for Public Adminstration **RESEARCH** Public policy; Public management; Space exploration. **SELECTED PUBLICATIONS** Auth, Space and the American Imagination, Smithsonian Inst Press, 97; auth, Spaceflight and the Myth of Presidential leadership, Univ Ill Press, 97; auth, Inside NASA, Johns Hopkins univ Press. **CONTACT ADDRESS** School of Public Affairs, American Univ, Washington, DC 20016. **EMAIL** mccurdy@american.edu

MCCUSKER, JOHN J.
PERSONAL Born 08/12/1939, Rochester, NY, m **DISCIPLINE** ECONOMICS **EDUCATION** Saint Bernards Sem and Col, BA, 61; Univ Rochester, Mass, 63; Univ Pittsburgh, PhD, 70. **CAREER** Vis lectr, Mount Allison Univ, 63; lectr, St Francis Xavier Univ, 65-66; from lectr to asst prof to assoc prof to prof, Univ Md, 68-92; lectr, Univ Md, Univ Col, European Div, 71-72, 76-77; vis asst prof, Col William and Mary Va, 72-73; vis res prof, Katholieke Univ, 84-85; dist prof, prof, Trinity Univ, 92-; adj prof, Univ TX, 94-. **HONORS AND AWARDS** Vis res assoc, 69-70, Smithsonian Inst; Grants in Aid, Am Philos Soc, 69, 70, 72, 75, 82; res grants, Economic Hist Asn, 69, 72, 77; fac res fel and awards, Univ Md, 71, 74, 80, 81, 84, 85, 88, 89, 90; fel, Omohundro Inst, 71-73; Royal Hist Soc, 76; Nat Endow Hum fel, 76-77, 78-79, 88-89; Guggenheim Fel, 82-83; Vis Senior Mellon Scholar, Univ Cambridge, 96-97; John Adams Fel, Univ London, 96-97; fel, The British Libr, 96-97; Leverhulme Trust vis fel, Univ Cambridge, 96-97; Helen Cam vis fel, Univ Cambridge, 96-97; Fulbright Senior Scholar, Great Britian, 96-97; Scholar in Residence, Rockefellow Ctr 97; new york state scholar, 57-61, 62-63; grad tchg fel, univ pittsburgh, 63-65; andrew mellon pre-doctoral fel, univ pittsburgh, 66-67. **MEMBERSHIPS** Am Hist Asn; Organization Am Historians; Am Antiquarian Soc; Va Hist Soc; NY State Hist Asn; Pa Hist Soc; Economic Hist Soc; Bibliographical Soc; Md Hist Soc. **RESEARCH** Economic history of the Atlantic World during the seventeenth and eighteenth centurys. **SELECTED PUBLICATIONS** Coauth, The Economy of British America, 1607-1789, 91; coauth,The Beginnings of Commercial and Financial Journalism: The Commodity Price Currents, Exchange Rate Currents, and Money Currents of Early Modern Europe, 91; auth, The Italian Business Press in Early Modern Europe, 92; auth, Money and Exchange in Europe and America, 1600-1775: A Handbook, 92; auth, The Role of Antwerp in the Emergence of Commercial and Financial Newspapers in Early Modern Europe, 96; auth, Essays in the Economic History in the Atlantic World, 97. **CONTACT ADDRESS** Dept of History, Trinity Univ, 715 Stadium Dr, San Antonio, TX 78212. **EMAIL** jmccuske@trinity.edu

MCDANIEL, JOHN B.
DISCIPLINE RELIGION **EDUCATION** Vanderbilt Univ, BA, 72; Claremont Sch Theol, PhD, 78. **CAREER** Prof, Hendrix Col. **RESEARCH** Buddhism. **SELECTED PUBLICATIONS** Auth, Of God and Pelicans. **CONTACT ADDRESS** Hendrix Col, Conway, AR 72032.

MCDANIEL, JUDITH M.
DISCIPLINE HOMILETICS **EDUCATION** Univ Tex-Austin, BA, 61; Diocesan Sch of Theol, Seattle, Cert of Grad, 77; Gen Theol Sem, MDiv, 85; Univ Wash, PhD, 94. **CAREER** Parish admin, 77-78, deacon, St Barnabas Parish, Bainbridge Island, Wash, 78-79; deacon, 79-83, priest assoc, St Mark's Cathedral, Seattle, Wash, summer 84; assoc rector, St John's Parish, Olympia, Wash, 85-86; rector, St John's Parish, Gig Harbor, Wash, 87-90; asst prof, 90-93, assoc prof, 93-00, prof, Va Theol Sem, 00- . **SELECTED PUBLICATIONS** Auth, "What Do You Seek?" Va Sem J, 93; auth, "Speakingon Controversial Issues," in A Wholesome Example, ed Robert Prichard (Bristol Pr, 93) auth, The Rhythm of Rhetoric: Cach of the Middle Ages, Univ Microfilms Int, 94; auth, "What You See is what you Get," in Sermons that Work V (Forward Movement Pubs, 95); auth, "Disciples and Discipline," Va Sem J, 96; auth, "Let Every Heart Prepare Him Room, 'Advent'," The Living Pulpit, 97; auth, "Rhetoric Reconsidered: Preaching as Persuasion," Sewanee Theol Rev, 98; auth, "He Came to Proclaim a Message: A Sermon on Mark 1:21-28," in Preaching Mark: the Recovery of a Narrative Voice, by Robert Stephen Reid (Chalice Pr, 99); auth, "The Preacher as Theologian and Teacher," in Preaching through the Year of Mark: Sermons that Work VII (Morehouse Pub, 99). **CONTACT ADDRESS** Virginia Theol Sem, 3737 Seminary Rd, Alexandria, VA 22304. **EMAIL** JMcDaniel@vts.edu

MCDANIEL, THOMAS F.
PERSONAL Born Baltimore, MD, m **DISCIPLINE** OLD TESTAMENT STUDIES AND HEBREW **EDUCATION** Univ Richmond, BA; E Baptist Theol Sem, BD; Univ Pa, MA, 56; Johns Hopkins Univ, PhD, 66. **CAREER** Prof, E Baptist Theol Sem. **SELECTED PUBLICATIONS** Auth, rev, Deborah Never Sang: A Philol Commentary on Judges 5, Makor Press, Jerusalem, 83. **CONTACT ADDRESS** Eastern Baptist Theol Sem, 6 Lancaster Ave, Wynnewood, PA 19096.

MCDERMOTT, A. CHARLENE
PERSONAL Born 03/11/1937, Hazelton, PA, m, 1988, 3 children **DISCIPLINE** PHILOSOPHY **EDUCATION** Univ Penn, BA, 56, PhD, 64. **CAREER** Prof philos, 76-86, assoc dean, dir Asian Stud, 78-81, dean grad stud, 81-86, Univ New Mexico; prof philos 86-91, provost and vice-pres Acad Affairs, 86-89, CCNY; dean in residence, consultant, Council of Grad Sch, 85-86; dean for acad and student affairs, consultant, Albuquerque Acad, 91-93; acad consultant, grant writer, vis prof, 93- . **HONORS AND AWARDS** Phi Beta Kappa; Univ New Mexico res allocations comm grant; NEH fel, AAUW fel; listed, Who's Who in Am, Who's Who in Am Educ, Dict of Int Biog. **SELECTED PUBLICATIONS** Auth, An Eleventh Century Logic of Exists, Reidel of Dordrecht, Netherlands; auth, Beothius of Dacia's Treatis on the Modes of Signifying, John Benjamins, Netherlands, 80; auth, Comparative Philosophy: Selected Essays, University Press, 83. **CONTACT ADDRESS** PO Box 1814, Corrales, NM 87048.

MCDERMOTT, GERALD D.
PERSONAL Born 10/26/1952, m, 1976, 3 children **DISCIPLINE** RELIGION **EDUCATION** Univ Chicago, BA, New Testament and early Christian studies, 74; North Dakota State Univ, BS, history, edu, 82; Grand Rapids Baptist Seminary, MRE, 82; Univ Iowa, PhD, 89. **CAREER** Assoc prof religion & philos, Roanoke Coll, 88-. **HONORS AND AWARDS** Fellowship for Young Scholars in American Religion, Center for the Study of Religion and American Culture, 92-93; Woodrow Wilson Awd for outstanding scholarly article: "Jonathan Edwards, the City on a Hill, and the Redeemer Nation: A Reappraisal", 93; selected by Roanoke Coll student body to give "Last Lecture," 93; member, Center Theol Inquiry, Aug 95 - July 96; Mednick Fellowship, Virginia Found Independent Colls, 95. **RESEARCH** Jonathan Edwards; relationship between Christianity and the world religions. **SELECTED PUBLICATIONS** Auth, One Holy and Happy Society: The Public Theology of Jonathan Edwards, 92; coauth, A Medical and Spiritual Guide to Living with Cancer, 93; coauth, Dear God, It's Cancer, 97; auth, Jonathan Edwards Confronts the Gods: Christian Theology, Enlightenment Religion, and Non-Christian Religions, forthcoming; auth, Can Evangelicals Learn from the Buddha? Jesus, Revelation and the Religions, 99. **CONTACT ADDRESS** Dept of Religion, Roanoke Col, Salem, VA 24153. **EMAIL** mcdermott@roanoke.edu

MCDERMOTT, JOHN J.
PERSONAL Born 02/18/1960, Britt, IA, s **DISCIPLINE** RELIGIOUS STUDIES **EDUCATION** Harvard Univ, BA, 82; St. Meinrad Sch of Theol, 86; Pontifical Bibl Inst, 1992 **CAREER** Asst Prof, 92-pres, Loras Col **MEMBERSHIPS** Cath Bibl Assoc; Soc of Bibl Lit **RESEARCH** Early Israelite History **SELECTED PUBLICATIONS** Auth, "Multipurpose Genealogies," The Bible Today, 97; Auth, "What are they saying about the formation of Ancient Israel," Paulist Press, 98 **CONTACT ADDRESS** Dept of Religious Studies, Loras Col, 1450 Alta Vista, Dubuque, IA 52001. **EMAIL** mcdermot@loras.edu

MCDERMOTT, JOHN J.
DISCIPLINE PHILOSOPHY **EDUCATION** Fordham, PhD. **CAREER** Univ Distinguished prof, Texas A&M Univ. **SELECTED PUBLICATIONS** Auth, The Culture of Experience: Philosophical Essays in the American Grain, NYU, 76; Streams of Experience: Reflections on the History and Philosophy of American Culture, Mass, 86; ed, The Writings of William James, Chicago, 77 & The Philosophy of John Dewey, Chicago, 81. **CONTACT ADDRESS** Dept of Philosophy, Texas A&M Univ, Col Station, College Station, TX 77843-4237.

MCDEVITT, ANTHONY
PERSONAL Born 07/25/1925, Birmingham, AL, s **DISCIPLINE** THEOLOGY; CANON LAW **EDUCATION** St Mary's Univ, Baltimore, BA, 45, StL, 49; Lateran Univ, Rome, JCD, 53. **CAREER** Expert at II Vatican Council, 63-65; Judicial Vicar, Diocese of Mobile, 62-98. **MEMBERSHIPS** Cath Theol Soc Am; Canon Law Soc Am; Amer Acad Religion **RESEARCH** Theology; Canon Law **CONTACT ADDRESS** 958 Henckley Ave, Drawer D, Mobile, AL 36609. **EMAIL** Tonymcd@aol.com

MCDONALD, PATRICIA M.
PERSONAL Born 06/12/1946, Scarborough, England **DISCIPLINE** RELIGION **EDUCATION** Catholic Univ of America, PhD 89; Pontifical Biblical Inst Rome, LSS 86; Univ Cambridge, MPhil 83; Heythrope Col, Univ London, BD 72; Univ Cambridge England, BA, MA 68/71. **CAREER** Catholic Univ of America, asst prof, 89-90; Mount St. Mary's Col MD, asst prof, assoc prof, 90 to 96-. **MEMBERSHIPS** CBA; SBL; CTS **SELECTED PUBLICATIONS** Auth, Biblical Brinkmanship: Francis Gigot and the New York Review, in: William L. Portier and Sandra Yokum Mize, eds, American Catholic Traditions: Resources for Renewal, Col Theol Soc, Maryknoll NY, Orbis Press, 97; Three entries in: The Pastoral Dictionary of Biblical Theology, Liturgical Press, 96; Romans 5:1-11 as a Rhetorical Bridge, Jour for the Stud of the New Testament, 90. **CONTACT ADDRESS** Theology Dept, Mount Saint Mary's Col and Sem, Emmitsburg, MD 21727. **EMAIL** mcdonald@msmary.edu

MCDONALD, PETER J. T.
PERSONAL Born 02/04/1956, Germany, m, 1988, 2 children **DISCIPLINE** PHILOSOPHY **EDUCATION** Catholic Univ, MA, 80; Freiburg Univ, PhD, 97. **CAREER** Asst prof Philos, Dominican House Studies, 97-. **MEMBERSHIPS** Am Philos Asn; Martin Heidegger Gesellschaft. **RESEARCH** Phenomenology. **SELECTED PUBLICATIONS** Auth, Daseinsanalytik und Grundfrage. Zur Einheit und Ganzheit von Heideggers Sein und Zeit, 97. **CONTACT ADDRESS** 487 Michigan Ave NE, Washington, DC 20017. **EMAIL** PMcDonald@compuserve.com

MCDONALD, WILLIAM
PERSONAL Born 09/07/1967, Daytona Beach, FL, m, 1992, 3 children **DISCIPLINE** HISTORICAL THEOLOGY **EDUCATION** Lenoir-Rhyne Col, AB, 85; Duke Univ, MTS, 91; Vanderbilt Univ, MA, 96; PhD, 98. **CAREER** Asst prof, chaplin, Tenn Wesleyan Col, 97-. **MEMBERSHIPS** AAR; AMPS; ASCH. **RESEARCH** Historical theology; liturgy; ecumenism. **SELECTED PUBLICATIONS** Ed, Gracious Voices: Shouts and Whispers for God Seekers, Discipleship Resources, 97. **CONTACT ADDRESS** Dept Religious Studies, Tennessee Wesleyan Col, Box 40, Athens, TN 37371-0040. **EMAIL** mcdonald@usit.net

MCDONOUGH, SHEILA
DISCIPLINE RELIGION **EDUCATION** McGill Univ, PhD, 63. **CAREER** Prof. **RESEARCH** 19th and 20th century South Asian Islam, Muslim/Christian relations. **SELECTED PUBLICATIONS** Auth, Gandhi's Responses to Islam, New Delhi, D.K. Printworld, 94; The Muslims of Montreal, Muslim Communities of North America, New York: SUNY, 95; Typology of Religion and State, Religion, Law and Society, WCC Press, 95; The Impact of Social Change on Muslim Women, Gender Genre and Religion, Wilfred Laurier UP: 95; India 1857-1947, Muslim and Other Religions, Oxford UP, 96; Poetry and Ethics, The Legacy of Fazlur Rahman, Univ Edmonton Press, 96; Visions du future des musulmansm, Religiologiques, 96. **CONTACT ADDRESS** Dept of Rel, Concordia Univ, Montreal, 1455 de Maisonneuve W, Montreal, QC, Canada H3G 1M8. **EMAIL** donou@vax2

MCDORMAN, TED L.
DISCIPLINE LAW **EDUCATION** Univ Toronto, BA, 76; Dalhousie Univ, LLB, 79, LLM, 82. **CAREER** Assoc prof, Univ of Victoria, 85-. **RESEARCH** Ocean law and policy, trade law and comparative constitutional law. **CONTACT ADDRESS** Fac of Law, Univ of Victoria, PO Box 2400, Victoria, BC, Canada V8W 3H7. **EMAIL** tlmcdorm@uvic.ca

MCDOWELL, MARKUS
PERSONAL Born 07/21/1960, Chattanooga, TN, m, 1986, 2 children **DISCIPLINE** RELIGION **EDUCATION** Abilene Christian Univ, BS, 83; Pepperdine Univ, MS, 92, Mdiv, 96, MA, 97; Fuller Theol Sem, PhD, ABD. **CAREER** Assoc min, Camarillo Church of Christ, 95-96; youth min, Camarillo Church of Christ, 88-; bk rev ed, Leaven, 95-; teaching asst, 95; adj prof, Fuller Theol Sem and Pepperdine Univ, 96-; translations consult, 99-. **HONORS AND AWARDS** J P, Gloria Sanders scholar, Pepperdine Univ, 89-96; Howard A. White scholar, 89; Partial Grad Fel, 97-98, 98-99; Outstanding Young Men of Am Award, 98; Grad Student Res Grant, 97; Who's Who Among Students in Am Cols and Universities, 94-95. **MEMBERSHIPS** Soc Bibl Lit; Cath Bibl Asn Am. **SELECTED PUBLICATIONS** Auth, George Eldon Ladd, Scribner's American Biography, Vol 1, Scribner & Sons, 98; L. Ron Hubbard, Scribner's American Biography, Vol 2, Scribner & Sons, 99; What Are Human Being That You Are Mindful Of Them?: A worship service based on Psalm 8, Leaven, 96; Preaching Biblical and Modern, Leaven, 95; Cyberspace Helps Spread the Gospel,Ventura County Star, 95; auth, "Preaching Biblical and Modern," Leaven, (95): 30-34; auth, "The Christian and the State---A Biblical Perspective," Ventura County Star, (Nov 96); auth, "Critical Methodologies and the Bible as the Word of God," Leaven (00): 66-69; rev, Bondi, Roberta C. "A Place to Pray: Reflections on the Lord's Prayer," Restoration Quarterly 42 (00): 190-191; auth, "Peale, Norman Vincent," In The Scribner Encyclopedia of American Lives, Volume Two, Scribner's Sons, forthcoming; rev, Rosner, Brian S. "Paul, Scripture, & Ethics," forthcoming; **CONTACT ADDRESS** Dept of Relig, Pepperdine Univ, 24255 Pacific Coast Hwy, Malibu, CA 90263. **EMAIL** markus.mcdowell@gte.net

MCELENEY, NEIL JOSEPH
PERSONAL Born 08/08/1927, Charlestown, MA **DISCIPLINE** BIBLICAL STUDIES **EDUCATION** St Paul's Col, DC, AB, 50, MA, 53; Cath Univ Am, STL, 54; Pontif Bibl Inst, Rome, SSB, 55, SSL, 56. **CAREER** Ordained as Paulist father, 53; prof sacred scripture, St Paul's Col, DC, 56-73; prof New Testament & Greek, St Patrick's Sem, 75-78; Adj Assoc Prof, Cath Univ Am, DC, 79-, Ed & contribr, Pamphlet Bible Ser, Paulist, 60-73; vis prof, Cath Univ Am, 61, Marist Col, 64, Univ Dayton, 65 & 66 & St Louis Univ, 69; res assoc, William Foxwell Albright Inst Archaeol Res in Jerusalem, 73-74. **HONORS AND AWARDS** CBA Prof, Pontif Bibl Inst, Rome, 82. **MEMBERSHIPS** Am Acad Relig; Soc Bibl Lit; Soc Old Testament Study Gt Brit; Cath Bibl Asn England; Cath Theol Soc Am; Cath Bus Assoc of Am Liturgical Conf. **RESEARCH** Scriptural studies; Bible. **SELECTED PUBLICATIONS** Auth, The Growth of the Gospels Paulist, 79; auth, Cath Bibl Quart, vol 0055, 93; The Unity and Theme of Matthew VII,1-12 + Exegetical Diversity Within New Testament Gospel Passages, Cath Bibl Quart, vol 0056, 94; 192 items. **CONTACT ADDRESS** Dept of Philos Cath, St. Paul's Col, Washington, DC 20017.

MCELHANEY, JAMES WILLSON
PERSONAL Born 12/10/1937, New York, NY, m, 1961, 2 children **DISCIPLINE** LAW **EDUCATION** Duke Univ, AB, 60, LLB, 62. **CAREER** Atty, Wis, 62-63; from asst prof to prof law, Sch Law, Univ Md, Baltimore, 66-73; prof, Sch Law, Southern Methodist Univ, 74-76; vis Joseph C Hostetler prof trial pract & advocacy, 76-77, Joseph C Hostetler Prof Trial Pract & Advocacy, Sch Law, Case Western Reserve Univ, 77-, Atty, Wickham, Borgelt, Skogstad & Powell, Wis, 66; mem adv comt landlord-tenant laws, Nat Conf Comnrs on Uniform State Laws, 69-73; reporter, Governor's Comn Landlord-Tenant Law, Md, 70-73; consult, Md Comprehensive Health Planning Agency, 71-73; vis prof law, Southern Methodist Univ, 76. **MEMBERSHIPS** Am Bar Asn; Asn Am Law Sch. **RESEARCH** Conflict of laws; landlord-tenant law; litigation and evidence. **SELECTED PUBLICATIONS** Auth, Publishing the Exhibit, ABA J, vol 0079, 93; Authentication, ABA J, vol 0079, 93; The Real Message, ABA J, vol 0079, 93; Jury Voir Dire--Getting the Most Out of Jury Selection, ABA J, vol 0079, 93; Highlighting, ABA J, vol 0079, 93; Helping the Witness--Techniques for Keeping Witnesses Out of Trouble, ABA J, vol 0079, 93; Limited Admissibility--Keeping Evidence on Track, ABA J, vol 0079, 93; Focusing the Deposition--Using Your Goals to Guide Your Deposition Techniques, ABA J, vol 0079, 93; Rehabilitation, ABA J, vol 0079, 93; Understanding Character Evidence, ABA J, vol 0079, 93; Staying Out of Jail, ABA J, vol 0079, 93; Its Happening Now, ABA J, vol 0079, 93; Using the Exhibit, ABA J, vol 0080, 94; Good Ways to Lose, ABA J, vol 0080, 94; The Human Factor, ABA J, vol 0080, 94; Creative Objecting, ABA J, vol 0080, 94; Breaking the Rules of Cross--Fast Thinking Will Lift Inquiry Beyond Mediocrity, ABA J, vol 0080, 94; Showtime for the Jury, ABA J, vol 0080, 94; Liar, vol 80, Pg 74, Yr 1994, ABA J, vol 0080, 94; The Absent Witness, ABA J, vol 0080, 94; Working the File, ABA J, vol 0080, 94; Composting Files, ABA J, vol 0080, 94; The Varying Terrain of Impeachment, ABA J, vol 0080, 94; Liar, ABA J, vol 0080, 94; Blind Cross-Examination, ABA J, vol 0080, 94; How You Argue Will Affect Whether the Judge Sees Things Your Way, ABA J, vol 0081, 95; Litigating in Theory, ABA J, vol 0081, 95; Writing to the Ear, ABA J, vol 0081, 95; Advocacy in Other Forums, ABA J, vol 0081, 95; Putting the Case Together, ABA J, vol 0081, 95; Mongo on the Loose, ABA J, vol 0081, 95; Witness Profiles, ABA J, vol 0081, 95; Jury Instructions, ABA J, vol 0081, 95; Opening Statements--to Be Effective With the Jury, Tell a Good Story, ABA J, vol 0081, 95; Making Evidence, ABA J, vol 0081, 95; Finding the Right Script, ABA J, vol 0081, 95; When Admissibility Is the Issue, ABA J, vol 0081, 95; A Shot in the Foot, ABA J, vol 0082, 96; 12 Ways to a Bad Brief, ABA J, vol 0082, 96; The Case Wont Settle--Things Are Different When You Know Youre Going to Trial, ABA J, vol 0082, 96; The Art of Persuasive Legal Writing, ABA J, vol 0082, 96 ; Prepping the Ceo, ABA J, vol 0082, 96; Making the Most of Motions, ABA J, vol 0082, 96; A Matter of Style, ABA J, vol 0082, 96; Organizing the Witness List, ABA J, vol 0082, 96; Hung by Dangling Facts, ABA J, vol 0082, 96; Gestapo Impeachment, ABA J, vol 0082, 96; Reasonable Arguments, ABA J, vol 0082, 96; Winning Arguments, ABA J, vol 0082, 96; Evasive Witnesses, ABA J, vol 0083, 97; Winning Deposition Tactics, ABA J, vol 0083, 97; Disarming Tactics, ABA J, vol 0083, 97; Strategy for Dragonslayers, ABA J, vol 0083, 97; How I Solved My Evidence Problem, ABA J, vol 0083, 97; Gizmos in the Courtroom, ABA J, vol 0083, 97; Litigation--Ducking the Artful Dodger--Ethics Problems Within the Law Firm Require Special Care, ABA J, vol 0083, 97; Dont Take the Bait, ABA J, vol 0083, 97; Tactical Timing, ABA J, vol 0083, 97; Briefs That Sing, ABA J, vol 0083, 97; On Admissibility, ABA J, vol 0083, 97; Exposing Fatal Flaws, ABA J, vol 0083, 97; Terms of Enlightenment, ABA J, vol 0083, 97. **CONTACT ADDRESS** Sch of Law, Case Western Reserve Univ, 11075 East Blvd, Cleveland, OH 44106-1769.

MCELWAIN, HUGH THOMAS
PERSONAL Born 10/24/1931, Weirton, WV, m, 1973, 3 children **DISCIPLINE** RELIGION, PHILOSOPHY **EDUCATION** Stonebridge Priory, BA, 53; Marianum Theol Fac, Rome, BD, 55, STD, 59. **CAREER** Instr theol, Stonebridge Priory, 59-61, asst prof theol & acad dean, 61-65; assoc prof philos & theol, St Mary of the Lake Col, 65-68; prof hist theol & acad dean, Cath Theol Union, 68-72; chmn dept, 73-76, asst dean grad studies, 77-81, Assoc Prof Relig Studies, Rosary Col, 73-, Am Asn Theol Schs fac fel, Divinity Sch, Univ Chicago, 72. **MEMBERSHIPS** AACU **RESEARCH** Peace studies; religion and science. **SELECTED PUBLICATIONS** Auth, Theology in an age of renewal, Chicago Studies, 66; Implications of evolution for theology, Barat Rev, 67; An Introduction to Teilhard de Chardin, Argus Commun, 67; contribr, The They May Live: Reflections on Ecology, Alba, 72; St Augustine's Doctrine on War, Abbey Press, 72. **CONTACT ADDRESS** Dean Col of Arts and Sciences, Rosary Col, 7900 W Division, River Forest, IL 60305-1099. **EMAIL** mcelwnhu@email.dom.edu

MCFADDEN, DANIEL L.
PERSONAL Born 07/29/1937, Raleigh, NC, m, 1962, 3 children **DISCIPLINE** ECONOMICS **EDUCATION** Univ Minn, BS, 57; PhD, 62. **CAREER** Instr, Univ of Minn, 57-58, 61-62; res asst, 59-60; asst prof, Univ of Pittsburgh, 62-63; asst prof to prof, Univ of Calif Berkeley, 63-79, 90-, chair, 95-96; prof, MIT, 78-91. **HONORS AND AWARDS** Ford Found Fel, 58-62, 66-67; Earhart Fel, 60-61; Mellon Fel, 62-63; fel, Econometrics Soc, 69; John Bates Clark Medal, 75; Outstanding Teacher Awd, MIT, 81; Frisch Medal, 86; Univ of Chicago, LLD, 92; Prize, Am Agric Econ Assoc, 94; Nemmers Prize, Northwestern Univ, 00, Nobel Prize in Econ, 00. **MEMBERSHIPS** Tau Beta Phi, Am Econ Assoc, Econometric Soc, Am Statist Asssoc, Math Assoc of Am, TRB. **RESEARCH** Production Theory, Transportation, Econometrics, Economic Growth and Development, Economic Theory and Mathematical Economics, Energy, Health Economics, Environmental Economics. **SELECTED PUBLICATIONS** Auth, "The Measurement of Urban Travel Demand," Jour of Publ Econ 3.4, (74): 303-328; auth, "Conditional Logit Analysis of Qualitative Choice Behavior," Frontiers in Econometics, ed P. Zarembka, Acad Pr, (NY, 74): 105-142; coauth, Urban Travel Demand: A Behavioral Analysis, North Holland, (Amsterdam), 75; auth, "The Revealed Preferences of a Government Bureaucracy: Theory," Bell Jour of Econ and Mgt Sci 62. (75): 401-416; auth, "The Revealed Preferences of a Government Bureaucracy; Empirical Evidence," Bell Jour of Econ and Mgt Sci 71. (76): 55-72; coed, Production Economics: A Dual Approach to Theory and Applications, North Holland (Amsterdam), 78; auth, "Modeling the Choice of Residential Location," Spatial Interaction Theory and Planning Models, ed A. Karlqvist, L. Lundqvist, F. Snickars and J. Weibull, North Holland, (Amsterdam, 78); coed, Structural Analysis of Discrete Data with Econometric Applications, MIT Pr, (Cambridge, MA), 81; coauth, "Specification Tests for the Multinomial Logit Model," Econometrica 52.5, (84): 1219-1240; coauth, "Referendum Contingent Valuation, Anchoring, and Willingness to Pay for Public Goods," Resource and Energy Econ 20, (98): 85-116. **CONTACT ADDRESS** Dept of Econ, Univ of California, Berkeley, 549 Evans Hall #3880, Berkeley, CA 94720-3880. **EMAIL** mcfadden@econ.berkeley.edu

MCFAGUE, SALLIE
PERSONAL Born 05/25/1933, Quincy, MA **DISCIPLINE** THEOLOGY, RELIGION AND LITERATURE **EDUCATION** Smith Col, BA, 55; Yale Divinity Sch, BD, 59; Yale Grad Sch, PhD(theol), 64. **CAREER** Asst prof, 72-75, dean, 75-79, assoc prof, 75-79, Prof Theol, Vanderbilt Divinity Sch, 80-. Ed, Soundings, 67-75; Nat Endowment for Humanities fel, Oxford, 80-81. **MEMBERSHIPS** Am Acad Relig; Soc Values Higher Educ; Soc Arts, Relig & Contemp Cult; Am Theol Soc. **RESEARCH** Religious language; contemporary theology, religion and literature. **SELECTED PUBLICATIONS** Auth, Barbour, Ian--Theologians Friend, Scientists Interpreter, Zygon, vol 0031, 96; The Loving Eye Versus the Arrogant Eye--Christian Critique of the Western Gaze on Nature and the Third World, Ecumenical Rev, vol 0049, 97. **CONTACT ADDRESS** Vanderbilt Univ, 221 Kirkland Hall, Nashville, TN 37232.

MCFARLAND, DOUGLAS D.
PERSONAL Born 07/18/1946, Portland, OR, m, 1973, 4 children **DISCIPLINE** LAW, SPEECH **EDUCATION** Macalester Col, BA, 68; NY Univ, JD, 71; Univ Minn, PhD, 83. **CAREER** Lawyer, Dorsey & Whitney, 71-74; prof Hamline Univ, 74-; admin asst to Chief Justice, Supreme Court of US, 84-86. **HONORS AND AWARDS** Phi Beta Kappa; Professor of the Year (2). **RESEARCH** Civil procedure, evidence. **SELECTED PUBLICATIONS** Coauth, Minnesota Civil Practice, 79; "Diversity Jurisdiction: Is There Fear of Local Prejudice?, 7 Lit 38, Fall 80; auth, "Lerias: A Socratic Dialogue", 67 ABAJ 867, 81; auth, "Dead Men Tell Tales: Thirty Times Three Year of the Judicial Process After Hillmon", 30 Vill L. Rev 1, 85; auth, "Self-Images of Law Professors: Rethinking the Schism in Legal Education, 35 J. Legal Educ 232, 85; auth, "Students and Practicing Lawyers Identify the Ideal Law Professor", 36 J. Legal Educ 93, 86; coauth, "The Need for a New National Court,", 100 Harv L Rev 1400, 87; auth, "The Unconstitutional Stub of 1441", 54 Ohio St LJ 1059 (93); auth, "Chief Justice Warren E. Burger: A Personal Tribute", 19 Hamline L. Rev 1, 95. **CONTACT ADDRESS** School of Law, Hamline Univ, 1536 Hewitt Ave, Saint Paul, MN 55104-1205. **EMAIL** dmcfarland@gw.hamline.edu

MCGARY, HOWARD
PERSONAL Born 07/22/1947, Texarcana, TX, m, 1985, 2 children **DISCIPLINE** AFRICAN AMERICAN PHILOSOPHY, SOCIAL AND POLITICAL PHILOSOPHY **EDUCATION** Calif State Univ, Los Angeles, BA; Univ Minn, PhD. **CAREER** Prof of Philos, Rutger, The State Univ of NJ, New Brunswick. **HONORS AND AWARDS** Alain Locke Award fro Distinguished Scholarship in African Am Philos. **MEMBERSHIPS** Editorial Bds: Encyclopedia of Ethics, The Philosophical Forum, and Social Identities. **RESEARCH** Race and social justice, democratic theory, the emotions, and distributive justice. **SELECTED PUBLICATIONS** Auth, Rawls' Logic of Political Arguments: Political Justification Without Truth, in E. M. Barth and E. C. W. Krabbe, eds, Logic and Political Culture, Royal Neth Acad of Arts and Sci, 92; Alienation and the African American Experience, in Richard Schmitt and Thomas Moody, eds, Alienation and Social Criticism, Hum Press, 94; Police Discretion and Discrimination, in John Kleinig, ed, Handled with Discretion, Rowman & Littlefield, 96; Racism, Social Justice, and Interracial Coalitions, The J of Ethics, 1, 3, 97; coauth, Between Slavery and Freedom: Philosophy and American Slavery, Ind UP, 92; auth, Race and Social Justice, Blackwel Publishers, Oxford & New York, 99. **CONTACT ADDRESS** Dept of Philos, Rutgers, The State Univ of New Jersey, Douglass Col, 141 Davison Hall, 26 Nichol Ave, New Brunswick, NJ 08903. **EMAIL** hmcgary@rci.rutgers.edu

MCGEE, HENRY W., JR.
PERSONAL Born 12/31/1932, Chicago, IL, m **DISCIPLINE** LAW **EDUCATION** NW Univ, BS 1954; DePaul Univ, JD 1957; Columbia Univ, LLM 1970. **CAREER** Cook Co, asst state's atty 1958-61; Great Lakes Region USOEO, regional legal servs dir 1966-67; Univ of Chicago Ctr for Studies in Crim Justice Juv Delinq Rsch Proj, legal dir 1967-68; Wolfson Col Oxford Univ England, vis fel, 73; Vis Prof, Univ of Florence Italy Inst of Comparative Law 1976, Univ of Puerto Rico 1979, Univ of Madrid (complutense) 1982; Fed Univ Rio de Janeiro Brazil, grad planning prog, 87; Nat Autonomous Univ of Mex, 88; UCLA, prof of law, emer and Prof of Law, Seattle Univ. **HONORS AND AWARDS** Blue Key Nat Honor Frat 1957; num publ; Fulbright Prof, Spain, 82. **MEMBERSHIPS** Mem Nat Bar Asn; Mem Nat Conf of Black Lawyers; draftsman Nat Conf of Bar Examiners 1974-; consult City Poverty Com London England 1973; consult & lectr Urban Planning USIS Italy 1976; past editor in chief DePaul Law Rev. **RESEARCH** Environmental Land; Land Use Planning; Housing and Community Development. **SELECTED PUBLICATIONS** Auth, Housing and Community Development, 3rd ed., 99. **CONTACT ADDRESS** Seattle Univ, 900 Broadway, Seattle, WA 98122-4338. **EMAIL** mcgee@seattleu.edu

MCGEEVER, PATRICK
PERSONAL Born 05/07/1938, Johnstown, PA, m, 1970, 3 children **DISCIPLINE** POLITICAL SCIENCE **EDUCATION** St Louis Univ, AB, 63; MA, 64; Univ Penn, PhD, 71. **CAREER** Vis lectr, Nat Univ of Ireland, 78; prof, Ind Univ, 71-. **HONORS AND AWARDS** Outstanding Fac Awd, IUPUI Lib Arts Sch, 80; Teaching Excellence Awd, Am Pol Sci Awd, 99; Teaching Excellence Recognition Awd, Ind Univ, 99. **MEMBERSHIPS** Am Pol Sci Asn, Midwest Pol Sci Asn, Ind Pol Sci Asn. **RESEARCH** Teaching political science, US catholic social history, US welfare policy. **SELECTED PUBLICATIONS** Auth, The United States Governmental System: A Compact Introduction, 78; auth, Apostle of Contradiction: Rev Charles Owen Rice, 89; auth, Discovering Politics in Your Own Life, 00. **CONTACT ADDRESS** Dept Pol Sci, Indiana Univ-Purdue Univ, Indianapolis, 1100 W Michigan St, Indianapolis, IN 46202-5208. **EMAIL** iztd100@iupui.edu

MCGILLIVRAY, ANNE
DISCIPLINE LAW **EDUCATION** Saskatchewan Univ, BA, LLB, 86; Univ Toronto, LLM, 88. **CAREER** Lectr, 89-90; asst prof, 90-94; assoc prof, 94-, Univ of Manitoba. **RESEARCH** Children and the law; law and literature; criminal law. **SELECTED PUBLICATIONS** Auth, Different Voices, Different Choices: Playing at Law and Literature, Can Journal Law Soc, 92; Reconstructing Child Abuse: Western Definition and Non-Western Experience; Ideologies Children's Rights, 92; Abused Children in the Courts: Adjusting the Scales After Bill C-15, Manitoba Law Jour, 91. **CONTACT ADDRESS** Fac of Law, Univ of Manitoba, Robson Hall, Winnipeg, MB, Canada R3T 2N2. **EMAIL** anne@atsms.umanitoba.ca

MCGILVRAY, JAMES
DISCIPLINE PHILOSOPHY **EDUCATION** Univ Toronto, PhD. **RESEARCH** Time and tense; color perception; semantics of natural languages. **SELECTED PUBLICATIONS** Auth, Constant Colors in the Head, Synthese, 94; auth, Tense, Reference, and Worldmaking, 91. **CONTACT ADDRESS** Philosophy Dept, McGill Univ, 855 Sherbrooke St, Montreal, QC, Canada H3A 2T5. **EMAIL** mim@philo.mcgill.ca

MCGINLEY, JOHN WILLARD
PERSONAL Born 05/11/1944, Philadelphia, PA, m, 1968, 7 children **DISCIPLINE** PHILOSOPHY, RELIGION **EDUCATION** Holy Cross Col, BA, 66; Boston Col, PhD(philos), 71. **CAREER** From asst prof to assoc prof, 70-78, prof philos, Univ Scranton, 78, chmn dept, 76-. **RESEARCH** Platonic philosophy; Jewish-Christian dialogue; Schelling. **SELECTED PUBLICATIONS** Auth, The essential thrust of Heidegger's thought, 71 & Nous poetikas, 76, Philos Today; Commentary on Plato's Parmenides, Univ Scranton, 76; The doctrine of the good in Plato's Philebus, Apeiron, 77; Does God exist?, Philos Today, 78; Aristotle's Notion of the Voluntary, Apeiron, 80; Catechism for Theologians, Univ Press Am, 81; auth, SHAME! (another Guide for the Perplexed), Univ Press of America, Fanham, MD, 93; MIASMA: Haecceitas in SCOTUS, The Esoteric in Plato, and Other Related Matters, Universtiy Press of America, Lanham Maryland, 96; What Does Others Have to do with Jerusalem?; Brother John Publications, Dunmone, Pa, 97; auth, The Walking, Talking, Wounded: Episodic Rominations Concerning Things Jewish, Things Greek and Things Human, Golem Enterprises, Dalton, Pa, 00. **CONTACT ADDRESS** Dept of Philosophy, Univ of Scranton, 800 Linden St, Scranton, PA 18510-4501.

MCGINN, BERNARD JOHN
PERSONAL Born 08/19/1937, Yonkers, NY, m, 1971, 2 children **DISCIPLINE** HISTORY OF CHRISTIANITY **EDUCATION** St Joseph's Sem, BA, 59; Pontif Gregorian Univ, STL, 63; Brandeis Univ, PhD, 70. **CAREER** Instr theol, Cath Univ Am, 68-69; instr theol & hist Christiantiy, 69-70, asst prof hist Christianity, 70-75, assoc prof, 75-78, Prof Hist Theol & Christianity, Univ Chicago, 78-, Am Asn Theol Schs res fel, 71. **MEMBERSHIPS** AHA; Medieval Acad Am; Am Cath Hist Asn; Am Acad Relig; Am Soc Church Hist. **RESEARCH** Hist of theol; intellectual and cult hist of the Middle Ages. **SELECTED PUBLICATIONS** Auth, The abbot and the doctors, Church Hist, 71; The Golden Chain, Cistercian Publ, 72; The Crusades, Gen Learning Press, 73; Apocalypticism in the Middle Ages, Mediaeval Studies, 75; ed, Three Treatises on Man, Cistercian Publ, 77; auth, Visions of the End, Columbia, 79; transl, Apocalyptic Spirituality, 79 & coauth (with E Colledge), Meister Eckhart, 81, Paulist; Foundations of Mysticism, Crossroad, 91; Growth of Mysticism, Crossroad, 94; Flowering of Mysticism, Crossroad, 98. **CONTACT ADDRESS** Divinity Sch, Univ of Chicago, 1025-35 E 58th St, Chicago, IL 60637-1577. **EMAIL** bmcginn@midway.uchicago.edu

MCGINN, SHEILA E.
PERSONAL Born Dubuque, IA, m, 1980, 2 children **DISCIPLINE** RELIGION **EDUCATION** Northwestern Univ, BA, 78; Univ Dallas, MA, 81; Northwestern Univ, PhD, 89. **CAREER** Tchng asst, 82, Garrett-Evangelical Theol Sem, Evanston; instr, 84; lect of theol, 84-88, 90-91, Loyola Univ Chicago; lect in Relig Studies, 87, , asst prof, 87-91, Mundelein Col, Chicago; asst prof of Theol, 91-92, Loyola Univ Chicago; asst prof of Relig Studies, 92-97, assoc prof, 97-., John Carroll Univ, Cleveland. **HONORS AND AWARDS** Univ Dallas Merit Scholar, 80-81; Northwestern Univ Res Fel, 82-85; Kahl Endowment for Intl the Curric, 96, 98; Reg Scholar for the Eastern Great Lakes & Midwest Biblical Societies, 96. **MEMBERSHIPS** AAR; Asn Int d'Etudes Patristiques, Lyons; Cath Bibl Asn; Eastern Great Lakes Bibl Soc; N Am Patristic Soc; Soc for Bibl Lit. **RESEARCH** Early Christianity, New Testament studies, Hebrew bible, relig studies and Catholic theology **SELECTED PUBLICATIONS** Auth, Galations 3:26-29 and the Politics of the Spirit, Proceed: EGL & MWBS, 93; auth, The Acts of Thecla, in Searching the Scriptures, vol 2: A Feminist Ecumenical Commentary and Translation, Crossroads, 94; auth, Matthew's Gospel, in the Study Bible for Women: The New Testament, HarperCollins, 95, Baker 96; auth, "Divine Man," auth, "Division in Synagogues," auth, Eight Beatitudes and the Seven Woes,", auth, "Jesus' commissioning of the women," auth, "Matthew's understanding of marriag and divorce," auth," auth, Priorities in the family," auth, Tax Collectors and Prostitutes," in the Study Bible for Women: The New Testament, ed. By Catherine Clark Kroeger, Mary Evans & Elaine Storkey, London: HarperCollins & Grand Rapids, MI: Baker, 95; auth, Not Counting [the] Women: A Feminist Reading of Matthew 26-28, SBL 1995 Sem Papers, ed Gene H. Lovering, Scholars Press, 95; auth, 1 Cor 11:10 and the Ecclesial Authority of Women, Listening/J of Relig & Cult, Lewis Univ, vol 31, 96; auth, The Montanist Oracles and Prophetic Theology, Studia Patristica, 97; auth, Why Now the Women? Social-Historical Insights on Gender Roles in Matthew 26-28, Proceedings: EGLBS 17, 97; co-auth, Bibliographies for Biblical Research: Revelation, New Testament Series 21, Mellon Biblical Press, 97. **CONTACT ADDRESS** Dept of Relig Studies, John Carroll Univ, 20700 N Park Blvd, University Heights, OH 44118. **EMAIL** smcginn@jcu.edu

MCGINNIS, JAMES W.
PERSONAL Born 07/08/1940, Fairfield, AL, m, 1988 **DISCIPLINE** LAW **EDUCATION** Wayne State Univ, BS 1963; San Francisco State Univ, MA 1965; Yeshiva Univ, PhD 1976; Wayne State Univ Law School, JD 1977. **CAREER** Coll Entrance Examination Bd, asst dir 1967-69; Univ of California Berkeley, instructor, 70-72; Far West Lab for Educ Research, research assoc 1972-73; Oakland Univ, asst prof 1976-81; Private Practice, lawyer. **HONORS AND AWARDS** Fellowship Project Beacon, Yeshiva Univ 1965-66; Ford Found Fellowship Language Soc of Child, Univ of CA 1968. **MEMBERSHIPS** Pres Kappa Alpha Psi Frat Wayne State Univ 1961-62; mem Assn of Black Psychologist 1963-73; researcher Black Studies Inst Wayne State Univ 1975-76; office counsel Hall & Andary Law Firm 1982-84; chmn PAC 1982-85, mem 1982-, Natl Conf of Black Lawyers. National Bar Association 1989-. **CONTACT ADDRESS** Bell & Gardner P C, 561 E Jefferson Ave, Detroit, MI 48226.

MCGINTY, MARY PETER
PERSONAL Born 03/02/1925, Chicago, IL **DISCIPLINE** SYSTEMATIC THEOLOGY **EDUCATION** St Xavier Col, Ill, AB, 45; Marquette Univ, MA, 58, PhD, 67. **CAREER** From lectr to asst prof theol, 62-68, Rosary Col; asst prof syst theol, St Mary of the Lake Sem, 68-73; asst prof, 73-82, dir grad theol, 74-81, assoc prof Theol, 82-, Loyola Univ, Chicago; consult relig, Scholastic Testing Serv, 58-68; lectr, Marquette Univ, 69. **HONORS AND AWARDS** Mellon Grant, 81; research grants, 82, 84-85, Loyola. **MEMBERSHIPS** Cath Theol Soc Am; Col Theol Soc; Am Acad Relig. **RESEARCH** Contemporary theology, ecclesiology, Christology, secularization, Yves Congar. **SELECTED PUBLICATIONS** Auth, The Sacrament of Christian Life, 92; auth, Secularization: Our Destiny or Our Demon?, Jesuit Assembly, 89. **CONTACT ADDRESS** Dept of Theol, Loyola Univ, Chicago, 6525 N.Sheridan Rd, Chicago, IL 60626-5385. **EMAIL** mmcgint@wpo.it.luc.edu

MCGLONE, MARY M.
PERSONAL Born 08/28/1948, Denver, CO, s **DISCIPLINE** THEOLOGY **EDUCATION** Univ San Francisco, MA, 81; St Louis Univ, PhD, 91. **CAREER** Assoc prof theol, Avila Col, 91-98; leadership, The Sisters of St. Joseph of Carondulist, 98-. **HONORS AND AWARDS** Catholic Press Asn Best Hist, 98. **MEMBERSHIPS** CTSA; USCMA. **RESEARCH** Latin America **SELECTED PUBLICATIONS** Auth, Shining Faith Across The Hemisphere, Orbis Press, 97. **CONTACT ADDRESS** 2307 S Lindbergh, Saint Louis, MO 63131. **EMAIL** marymcgcsj@aol.com

MCGOVERN, ARTHUR F.
DISCIPLINE PHILOSOPHY **EDUCATION** Georgetown Univ, BA; Loyola Univ, MA; Univ Paris, PhD. **CAREER** Prof; past ch, Univ Core Curric Comt; prof, Univ of Detroit Mercy, 70-. **RESEARCH** Ethics, epistemology, Marxism and Christianity, social justice issues, and history of modern philosophy. **SELECTED PUBLICATIONS** Auth, Marxism: An American Christian Perspective; Ethical Dilemmas and the Modern Corporation Liberation Theology and its Critics. **CONTACT ADDRESS** Dept of Philosophy, Univ of Detroit Mercy, 4001 W McNichols Rd, PO Box 19900, Detroit, MI 48219-0900. **EMAIL** MCGOVEAF@udmercy.edu

MCGOVERN, WILLIAM M.
PERSONAL Born 07/09/1934, Evanston, IL, m, 1958, 3 children **DISCIPLINE** LAW **EDUCATION** Princeton Univ, AB, 55; Harvard Univ, LLB, 58. **CAREER** Prof, Northwestern Univ, 63-71; vis prof, Univ Minn, 79-80; vis prof, Univ Va, 83; prof to prof emeritus, UCLA, 71-94; vis prof, Univ of Jena and Erlangen, 01 **HONORS AND AWARDS** Fulbright Fel, 01. **RESEARCH** Wills and Trusts; Contracts; Legal history. **SELECTED PUBLICATIONS** Auth, "Nonprobate Transfers under the Revised Uniform Probate Code," Albany L Rev, (92): 1329-1353; auth, "Trusts, Custodianships and Durable Powers of Attorney," Real Property Probate and Trust J, (92): 1-47; auth, "Undue Influence and Professional Responsibility," Real Property, Probate and Trust J, (94): 643-681; auth, Annotated California Probate Code, 95; co-auth, Trusts and Estates: Wills, Trusts, Future Interests and Taxation, 2nd ed, 01. **CONTACT ADDRESS** Dept Law, Univ of California, Los Angeles, Box 951476, Los Angeles, CA 90095-1476. **EMAIL** mcgovern@law.ucla.edu

MCGOWAN, ANDREW
PERSONAL Born 08/17/1961, Melbourne, Australia, m, 1982, 1 child **DISCIPLINE** RELIGION **EDUCATION** Univ Western Australia, BA, 83; Melbourne Col Divinity, BD, 86; Univ Notre Dame, MA, 95, PhD, 96. **CAREER** Lectr, Univ Notre Dame, Australia, 96-98; asst prof, Episcopal Divinity Sch, 98-99, assoc prof, 99-. **HONORS AND AWARDS** Kavanagh Lectr, Yale Divinity Sch, 2000. **MEMBERSHIPS** Am Acad of Relig, North Am Patristic Soc, Soc of Biblical Lit. **RESEARCH** Early Christianity. **SELECTED PUBLICATIONS** Auth, "Eating People: Accusations of Cannibalism against Christians in the Second Century," J of Early Christian Studies 2 (94): 413-442; auth, " 'First Regarding the Cup': Papias and the Diversity of Early Eucharistic Practice," J of Theol Studies, n.s. 46 (95): 569-73; auth, "Ecstasy or Charity: Augustine with Nathanael Under the Fig Tree," Augustinian Studies, 27 (96): 27-38; auth, "Valentinus Poeta: Notes on Oepos," Vigiliae Christianae, 51 (97): 158-78; auth, "Naming the Feast: The Agape and the Diversity of Early Christian Ritual Meals," Studia Patristica, 30 (ed E. Livingstone; Leuven: Peeters, 97): 314-18; auth, " 'Is There a Liturgical Text in this Gospel?': The Institution Narratives and Their Early Interpretive Communities," J of Biblical Lit, 118 (99): 77-89; auth, Ascetic Eucharists: Food and Drink in Early Christian Ritual Meals, Oxford Early Christian Studies, Oxford: Clarendon (99). **CONTACT ADDRESS** Episcopal Divinity Sch, 99 Brattle St, Cambridge, MA 02138-3402. **EMAIL** amcgowan@episdivschool.org

MCGUCKIN, JOHN A.
PERSONAL Born 06/21/1952, England, m, 1990, 3 children **DISCIPLINE** CHURCH HISTORY **EDUCATION** London Univ, BD, 75; Univ Durham, PhD, 80; MA, 86. **CAREER** Lect, LSU Col, 87-89; Lect, Univ Leeds, 89-94; Reader, Univ Leeds, 94-96; Prof, Union Theolog Sem, 96-. **HONORS AND AWARDS** Fel, London Royal Hist Soc. **MEMBERSHIPS** Soc for the Prom of Byzantine Studies, Church Hist Soc. **RESEARCH** Christian thought in Lake Antiquity. **SELECTED PUBLICATIONS** auth, "The Non-Cyprianic Scripture Texts in Lactantius' Divine Institutes," Vigiliae Christianae 36 (82): 145-163; auth, Symeon the New Theologian, Chapters and Discourses, Cistercian Publ (Kalamazoo), 82; auth, "The Theopaschite Confession: A Study in the Cyrilline Reinterpretation of Chalcedon," J of Ecclesiastical Hist 35,2 (84): 239-255; auth, St Gregory Nazianzen: Selected Poems, SLG Pr (Oxford, UK), 86; auth, The Transfiguration of Christ in Scripture and Tradition, Mellen Pr (Lewiston, NY), 87; auth, St Cyril of Alexandria and the Chistological Controversy, Brill (Leiden), 94; auth, St Cyril of Alexandria: On The Unity of Christ, SVS Pr (New York, NY), 95; auth, At the Lighting of the Lamps: Hymns From the Ancient Church, SLG Pr (Oxford, UK), 95. **CONTACT ADDRESS** Dept Church Hist, Union Theol Sem, New York, 3041 Broadway, New York, NY 10027-5710. **EMAIL** jmcguckn@uts.columbia.edu

MCGUIRE, ANNE M.
PERSONAL Born 10/05/1951, New Haven, CT, m, 1980, 2 children **DISCIPLINE** RELIGIOUS STUDIES **EDUCATION** Barnard Col, BA, 73; Columbia Univ, MA, 75; Yale Univ, MPhil, 80, PhD, 83. **CAREER** Instr, Villanova Univ, 80-82; asst prof, 82-90, assoc prof, 90- , Haverford Col. **HONORS AND AWARDS** Fac res grant, Haverford Col; Ford Grant for development of social justice courses. **MEMBERSHIPS** Soc of Bibl Lit. **RESEARCH** Ancient religions; Gnosticism; early Christianity; New Testament; comparative religions. **SELECTED PUBLICATIONS** Auth, Virginity and Subversion: Norea against the Powers in The Hypostasis of the Archons, in King, ed, Images of the Feminine in Gnosticism, Fortress, 88; auth, Equality and Subordination in Christ: Displacing the Powers of the Household Code in Colossians, in Gower, ed, Annual Publication of the College Theology Society, Univ Press of Am, 90; auth, Thunder, Perfect Mind, in Fiorenza, ed, Searching the Scriptures, v.2: A Feminist Commentary, Crossroad, 94; co-ed, The Nag Hammadi Library after Fifty Years: Proceedings of the 1995 Society of Biblical Literature Commemoration, Brill, 97; auth, Women and Gender in Gnostic Texts and Traditions, in Kraemer, ed, Women and Christian Origins: A Reader, Oxford, 98. **CONTACT ADDRESS** Dept of Religion, Haverford Col, Haverford, PA 19041. **EMAIL** amcguire@haverford.edu

MCHALE, VINCENT EDWARD
PERSONAL Born 04/17/1939, Jenkins Twp, PA, m, 1963, 1 child **DISCIPLINE** POLITICAL SCIENCE, INTERNATIONAL RELATIONS **EDUCATION** Wilkes Univ, BA, Polit Sci, 64; Pa State Univ, MA, 66, PhD, 69. **CAREER** Asst prof, polit sci, Univ of Pa, 69-75; assoc prof. Polit sci, Case Western Reserve Univ, 75-84; Prof, Polit Sci, Case Western Reserve Univ, 84-. **HONORS AND AWARDS** Nominee Wittke Undergraduate Tchg Awd; ch, case western reserve univ polit sci dept, 77-. **RESEARCH** European mass politics **SELECTED PUBLICATIONS** Vote, Clivages Socio - Politiques et Developpment Regional en Belgique, 74; Political Parties of Europe, 83; Evaluating Transnational Programs in Government and Business, 80. **CONTACT ADDRESS** Dept of Polit Sci, Case Western Reserve Univ, Cleveland, OH 44106. **EMAIL** vem@po.cwru.edu

MCHATTEN, MARY TIMOTHY
PERSONAL Born 10/20/1931, Castle Hill, ME **DISCIPLINE** BIBLICAL STUDIES **EDUCATION** Univ Ottawa Can, PhD, 79. **CAREER** Dir of Bibl Studies, Kino Inst Phoenix Ariz, 73-89; chair of Bible Studies Dept, Mount Angel Sem St Benedict Ore, 89-. **MEMBERSHIPS** Cath Bibl Asn; Soc of Bibl Lit; Bibl Archaeol Soc. **RESEARCH** Biblical Women; Prophets; Wisdom Literature. **CONTACT ADDRESS** Mount Angel Sem, Saint Benedict, OR 97373. **EMAIL** mtmchatten@mtangel.edu

MCHENRY, LEEMON
PERSONAL Born 09/01/1956, NC, s **DISCIPLINE** PHILOSOPHY **EDUCATION** Univ S Miss, BA, 78; MA, 81; Univ Edinburgh, PhD, 84. **CAREER** Teaching Asst, Univ S Miss, 79-81; Instr, Univ Edinburgh, 83-84; Adj Asst Prof, Old dominion Univ, 85-86; Res Assoc, Johns Hopkins Univ, 86-87; vis Asst Prof, Davidson Col, 86-88; Vis Asst Prof, Central Mich Univ, 88-90; Asst Prof, Wittenberg Univ, 90-95; Vis Asst Prof, Univ Pa, 95-96; Vis Scholar, Univ Calif, Los Angeles, 96-97; Lecturer, Loyola Marymount Univ; Calif State Univ; Pasadena City Col, 97-99. **HONORS AND AWARDS** Vans Dunlop Scholarship, Edinburgh; NEH Univ Haw, 89; NC Philos Soc Annual Essay Prize, 87; Vans Dunlop Scholarship, Univ Edinburgh, 81-84; Overseas Res Students Awd, United Kingdom, 82-84; Scholarship, Jackson Miss, 81-84. **MEMBERSHIPS** Am Philos Asn, Center for Process Studies. **RESEARCH** Logic, Metaphysics, Philosophy of Science, American Philosophy, Process Philosophy. **SELECTED PUBLICATIONS** Co-ed, Reflections on Philosophy: Introductory Essays, St. Martin's Press, 93; auth, Whitehead and Bradley: A Comparative Analysis, SUNY Press, 92; "Alfred North Whitehead," in Twentieth-Century British Philosophers, Gale Pub, forthcoming; auth, "Naturalized and Pure Metaphysics: A Reply to Hutto," Bradley Studies, (98): 67-101; auth, "Quine and Whitehead: Ontology and Methodology," Process Studies, The forum, (97): 2-12; auth, "Bradley's Conception of Metaphysics," in Perspectives on the Logic and Metaphysics of F H Bradley, Thoemmes Press, 96; auth, "Descriptive and Revisionary Theories of Events," Process Studies, (96): 90-103; auth, "Whitehead's Panpsychism as the subjectivity of Prehension," Process Studies, (95): 1-14; auth, "Quine's Pragmatic Ontology," The Journal of speculative Philosophy, (95): 147-158; auth, Substance and Events: A Revisionary Metaphysics; forthcoming. **CONTACT ADDRESS** Dept Philos, California State Univ, Northridge, 18111 Nordhoff St, Northridge, CA 91330-0001. **EMAIL** lmchenry@lmumail.lmu.edu

MCHUGH, MICHAEL P.
PERSONAL Born 06/07/1933, Lackawanna, NY, m, 1961, 4 children **DISCIPLINE** CLASSICAL PHILOLOGY, PATRISTIC STUDIES **EDUCATION** Cath Univ Am, AB, 55, MA, 56, PhD(classics), 65. **CAREER** From instr to asst prof classics & humanities, Howard Univ, 58-68; from asst prof to assoc prof, 68-77; Prof Classics, Univ Conn-Storrs, 77-97; Prof Emer, Univ Conn-Storrs, 97- . **MEMBERSHIPS** NAm Patristic Soc; Am Philol Asn; Vergilian Soc; Am Class League; Medieval Acad Am. **RESEARCH** St Ambrose; Prosper of Aquitaine; textual studies. **SELECTED PUBLICATIONS** Auth, The Carmen de Providentia Dei: A Revised Text with Introduction, Translation and Notes, Cath Univ Pr (Washington, DC), 64; auth, St. Ambrose: Seven Exegetical Works, Cath Univ Pr (Washington, DC), 72; assoc ed, The Encyclopedia of Early Christianity, Garland Pub (New York), 90, 97. **CONTACT ADDRESS** 274 Hanks Hill Rd, Storrs, CT 06268.

MCINERNEY, PETER K.
PERSONAL Born 12/12/1948, m, 1 child **DISCIPLINE** PHILOSOPHY **EDUCATION** Yale Univ, BA, 71; Univ of TX, PhD, 76 **CAREER** Chm, 86-89, 97-; Prof, 91-, Assoc Prof, 84-91, Oberlin Col; Visit Asst Prof, 81, Univ of MI; Asst Inst, 76, Univ of TX **HONORS AND AWARDS** NEH Fel, 85-86 **SELECTED PUBLICATIONS** Auth, Time and Experience, Temple Univ Press, 91; Introduction to Philosophy, HarperCollins Publishers, 92; Coauth, Ethics, HarperCollins, 94 **CONTACT ADDRESS** Dept of Philosophy, Oberlin Col, Oberlin, OH 44074. **EMAIL** peter.mcinerney@oberlin.edu

MCINERNY, RALPH
PERSONAL Born 02/24/1929 **DISCIPLINE** PHILOSOPHY **EDUCATION** Laval Univ, PhD. **CAREER** Michael P Grace Prof, Univ Notre Dame. **HONORS AND AWARDS** Fulbright Fel; NEH Fel; NEA Fel. **MEMBERSHIPS** Am Cath Philos Assoc; Fel of Cath Scholars; Am Metaphysical Soc. **RESEARCH** Medieval philosophy; ancient philosophy; Kierkegaard. **SELECTED PUBLICATIONS** Ed, The Degrees of Knowledge, Vol VII, Collected Works of Jacques Maritain, Univ of Notre Dame Pr, 95; auth, Aquinas and Analogy, Cath Univ of Am Pr, 96; auth, Ethica Thomistica, Cath Univ of Am Pr, 97; auth, Thomas Aquinas, Penguin Classics, 98; auth, The Red Hat, Ignatius Pr, 98; auth, What Went Wrong with Vatican II, Sophia Inst Pr, 98; auth, The Lack of the Irish, St Martin's Pr, 98; auth, Irish Tenure, St Martin's Pr, 99. **CONTACT ADDRESS** Dept Philos, Univ of Notre Dame, 336 O'Shaugnessy Hall, Notre Dame, IN 46556-5639. **EMAIL** mcinerny.1@nd.edu

MCINTIRE, CARL THOMAS
PERSONAL Born 10/04/1939, Philadelphia, PA, 2 children **DISCIPLINE** MODERN HISTORY, PHILOSOPHY OF HISTORY **EDUCATION** Univ Pa, MA, 62, PhD(hist), 76; Faith Theol Sem, MDiv, 66. **CAREER** Instr hist, Shelton Col, 65-67; asst prof hist, Trinity Christian Col, 67-71; vis scholar, Cambridge Univ, 71-73; Sr Mem Hist, Inst Christian Studies, Toronto, 73-, Am Philos Soc res grant, 81; Soc Sci & Humanities Res Coun Can res grant, 81-82; lectr, Trinity Col, Univ Toronto, 82-. **MEMBERSHIPS** AHA; Conf Faith & Hist; Am Cath Hist Asn; Am Soc Church Hist. **RESEARCH** Secularization of modern thought and society; comparative views of history: Christian, Hindu, Jewish, Marxist, Liberal and African Tribal; English politics in relation to the papacy, especially 19th century. **SELECTED PUBLICATIONS** Auth, England against the Paapacy, 1858-1861, 83; auth, History and Historical Understanding, 84; auth, The Legacy of Herman Dooyeweerd, 85; auth, Toynbee: Reappraisal, 89; auth, Butterfield as Historian, forthcoming; auth, "Changing Religious Establishments and Religious Liberty in France, Part I: 1787-1879", 97; auth, "Changing Religious Establishments and Religious Liberty in France, Part II: 1879-1908"; coauth, The Parish and Cathedral of St. James, Toronto, 1797-1997, 98; auth, Women in the Life of St. James' Cathedral , Toronto, 1935-1998, 98; auth, "Secularization, Secular Religions, and Religious Pluralism in European and North American Societies," 99. **CONTACT ADDRESS** Dept of History, Univ of Toronto, 100 St George St, Room 2074, Toronto, ON, Canada M5S 3G3.

MCINTOSH, PHILLIP L.
PERSONAL Born 10/15/1954, MS, m, 1989, 1 child **DISCIPLINE** LAW **EDUCATION** La State Univ, BS, 77; JD, 78; NY Univ, LLM, 81. **CAREER** Assoc to partner, Snellings, Breard, Sartor Dnabnett & Traucher, 81-91; assoc prof to prof, Miss Col, 91-. **MEMBERSHIPS** Am Soc of Comparative Law; Am Bar Assoc; La State Bar Assoc. **RESEARCH** Products liability, torts, youth court/juvenille court, comparative law. **SELECTED PUBLICATIONS** Auth, When Surgeons Have HIV - What to Tell Patients About the Risk of Exposure and the Risk of Transmission, 42 KS L Rev 315 (96); auth, Tort Reform in Mississippi: An Appraisal of the New Law of Products Liability, Part I, 16 Miss C.L. Rev 393 (96); auth, Tort Reform in Mississippi: An Appraisal of the New Law of Products Liability, Part II, 17 Miss C.L. Rev 277 (97). **CONTACT ADDRESS** School of Law, Mississippi Col, Jackson, 151 E Griffith Way, Jackson, MS 39201-1302. **EMAIL** mcintosh@mc.edu

MCINTOSH, SIMEON CHARLES
PERSONAL Born 07/14/1944, Carriacou, Grenada **DISCIPLINE** LAW **EDUCATION** York U, BA 1971; Howard U, JD 1974; Columbia U, LlM 1975. **CAREER** Howard U, asst prof of law; Univ of OK, asst prof of law 1975-76. **MEMBERSHIPS** Soc of Am Law Tchrs; Am Legal Studies Assn. **CONTACT ADDRESS** 2935 Upton St, Washington, DC 20008.

MCINTYRE, LEE C.
PERSONAL Born 01/02/1962, Portland, OR, m, 1986, 2 children **DISCIPLINE** PHILOSOPHY **EDUCATION** Wesleyan Univ, BA 84; Univ Michigan, MA 87, PhD 91. **CAREER** Colgate Univ, asst prof, 93-; Boston Univ, res assoc, 91-93; Tufts Experimental Col, vis lectr, 92. **HONORS AND AWARDS** Phi Beta Kappa **MEMBERSHIPS** APA; PSA **RESEARCH** Philo of natural and social sciences. **SELECTED PUBLICATIONS** Auth, Complexity: A Philosopher's Reflections, Complexity, 98; Gould on Laws in Biological Science, Biology and Philo, 97; The Case for the Philosophy of Chemistry, coauth, Synthese, 97; Readings in the Philosophy of Social Science, coed, Cambridge, MIT Press, 94; Laws and Explanation in the Social Sciences: Defending a Science of Human Behavior, Boulder CO, Westview Press, 96. **CONTACT ADDRESS** Dept Philosophy and Religion, Colgate Univ, Hamilton, NY 13346. **EMAIL** Lmcintyre@center.colgate.edu

MCINTYRE, MONI
PERSONAL Born 02/12/1948, Detroit, MI **DISCIPLINE** THEOLOGY, CHRISTIAN ETHICS **EDUCATION** St Michael's Col, Toronto, PhD, 90. **CAREER** Asst prof, Duquesne Univ, 90-. **MEMBERSHIPS** CTE; AAR; CTSA; CTA. **RESEARCH** Feminist theol; ecological ethics; social ethics. **SELECTED PUBLICATIONS** Auth, Ethnicity and Religious Experience in the Social Ethics of Gibson Winter, in Ethnicity, Nationality and Religious Experience, ed Peter C Phan, Annual Pub of the Col Theol Soc, 91, Univ Press Am, 95; On Choosing the Good in the Face of Genocide, the Genocide Forum, 1, March 95; ed with Mary Heather Mackinnon, Readings in Ecology and Feminist Theology, Sheed & Ward, 95; auth, Capital Punishment in the Catholic Christian Tradition, New Theology Rev 9, Aug 96; review, An Agenda for Sustainability: Fairness in a World of Limits, by William M Bueler, Cross Cultural Pubs, 97, in Religious Studies Rev 24, July 98; ed with Mary Heather MacKinnon and Mary Ellen Sheehan, Light Burdens, Heavy Blessings: Essays from the Church in Honor of Margaret Brennan, IHM, Sheed & Ward, forthcoming 98; numerous other publications. **CONTACT ADDRESS** 507 Shady Ave, Apt A-6, Pittsburgh, PA 15206. **EMAIL** mcintyre@duq3.cc.duq.edu

MCINTYRE, RONALD TREADWELL
PERSONAL Born 05/01/1942, New Orleans, LA, m, 1984, 1 child **DISCIPLINE** PHILOSOPHY **EDUCATION** Wake Forest Col, BS, 64; FL State Univ, MA, 66; Stanford Univ, PhD(-philos), 70. **CAREER** Asst prof philos, Case West Reserve Univ, 70-77; assoc prof, 77-81, PROF PHILOS, CA STATE UNIV, NORTHRIDGE, 81-, DEPT CHAIR, 96-. **HONORS AND AWARDS** Nat Endowment for the Humanities Fel, 80; Woodrow Wilson Fel, 64; Phi Beta Kappa, 64. **MEMBERSHIPS** Am Philos Asn. **RESEARCH** Philosophy of language; phenomenology; contemporary metaphysics. **SELECTED PUBLICATIONS** Coauth, Intentionality via intensions, J Philos, 9/71; Husserl's Identification of Meaning and Noema, Monist, 1/75; Intending and Referring, in Hussert, Intentionality, and Cognitive Science, ed by H. Dreyfus, MIT Press, Bradford Books, 82; Husserl's Phenomenological Conception of Intentionality and its Difficulties, Philosophia, 11, 82; Searle on Intentionality, Inquiry, 27, 84; ed, Symposium on The Intentionality of Mind, Synthese, 61, 84; Husserl and the Representational Theory of Mind, Topoi, 5, 86, reprinted in: Perspectives on Mind, ed by H. Otto and J. Tuedio, D. Reidel, 88, Historical Foundations of Cognitive Science, ed by J-C Smith, Kluwer, 90, and trans by J. Jaze in Les Etudes Philosophiques, Phenomenologie et Psychologie Cognitive, Presses Univ de France, 91; Husserl and Frege, J of Philos, 84, 88; The Theory of Intentionality in Phenomenology and Analytic Philosophy, in Topics in Philosophy and Artificial Intelligence, ed by L. Albertazzi and R. Poli, Bozen, Italy: Inst Mitteleuropeo di Cultura, 91; Naturalizing Phenomenology?, Dretske on Qualia, in Naturalizing Phenomenology: Contemporary Phenomenology and Cognitive Science, ed by B. Pachoud et al, Stanford Univ Press, 99; co-ed four other publications. **CONTACT ADDRESS** Dept of Philos, California State Univ, Northridge, 18111 Nordhoff St, Northridge, CA 91330-8253. **EMAIL** ronald.mcintyre@csun.edu

MCKAGUE, CARLA A.
DISCIPLINE LAW **EDUCATION** Guelph Univ, BA, 70; MSC, 72; Univ Toronto, LLB, 80. **CAREER** Legal Counsel, Office of the Public Guardian and Trustee; adj prof, Univ Toronto. **SELECTED PUBLICATIONS** Co-auth, Mental Health Law in Canada, Butterworth's, 87. **CONTACT ADDRESS** Fac of Law, Univ of Toronto, 78 Queen's Park, Toronto, ON, Canada M5S 2C5.

MCKALE, MICHAEL
PERSONAL Born Piqua, OH, m, 1995, 2 children **DISCIPLINE** WORLD RELIGIONS **EDUCATION** Univ Notre Dame, BA; Jesuit Sch Theol, MA; Grad Theol Union, PhD. **CAREER** St Francis Col **HONORS AND AWARDS** Ch, Philos & Relig Studies Dept; Dir, Pastoral Ministry Ctr Inst Ethics. **MEMBERSHIPS** Am Acad Relig, Soc Christian Ethics, Asn Catholic Cols & Univ. **SELECTED PUBLICATIONS** Areas: Global Catholicism, Social Ethics, Justice and Peace, World Religion, Contemporary Islam, Religion in Mexico, Ethics &

Sports, Religion and Personality **CONTACT ADDRESS** Saint Francis Col, Pennsylvania, PO Box 600, Loretto, PA 15940. **EMAIL** mmckale@sfcpa.edu

MCKEE, PATRICK M.
DISCIPLINE PHILOSOPHY **EDUCATION** Univ Md, PhD, 71. **CAREER** Prof. **SELECTED PUBLICATIONS** Auth, Philosophical Foundations of Gerontology, 81; The Art of Aging, 87; pubs on epistemology and aesthetics. **CONTACT ADDRESS** Philosophy Dept, Colorado State Univ, Fort Collins, CO 80523. **EMAIL** pmckee@lamar.colostate.edu

MCKELWAY, ALEXANDER JEFFREY
PERSONAL Born 12/08/1932, Durham, NC, m, 1960, 3 children **DISCIPLINE** THEOLOGY **EDUCATION** Davidson Col, AB, 54; Princeton Theol Sem, BD, 57; Univ Basel, ThD, 63. **CAREER** Instr, Dartmouth Col, 63-65; asst prof, 65-68, assoc prof, 68-81, Prof Relig, Davidson Col, 81-, Nat Endowment Humanities younger scholar fel, 69-70. **MEMBERSHIPS** Am Acad Relig; Karl Barth Soc NAm; Duodecim Soc. **RESEARCH** Contemporary theology; modern theology, systematic theology, historical theology. **SELECTED PUBLICATIONS** Auth, The Gottingen Dogmatics--Instruction the Christian Religion, vol 1, Interpretation-J Bible and Theol, vol 0047, 93; Humanization and the Politics of God--The Koinonia Ethics of Lehmann, Paul, Interpretation-J Bible and Theol, vol 0049, 95; How to Read Barth, Karl--The Shape of His Theology, Interpretation-J Bible and Theol, vol 0050, 96; Defending the Faith--Machen, J.,Gresham and the Crisis of Conservative Protestantism in Modern America, Theol Today, vol 0053, 96; Barth, Karl Critically Realistic Dialectical Theology, Interpretation-J Bible and Theol, vol 0051, 97. **CONTACT ADDRESS** Dept of Relig, Davidson Col, Po Box 1719, Davidson, NC 28036-1719.

MCKENNA, JOHN H., C.M.
PERSONAL Born 05/25/1936, Brooklyn, NY, s **DISCIPLINE** THEOLOGY, RELIGIOUS STUDIES **HONORS AND AWARDS** Honorary mem, Golden Key Honor Soc, 95; St John's Univ Vincent dePaul Teacher/Scholar Awd, 99. **RESEARCH** Systemic theology and liturgy. **SELECTED PUBLICATIONS** Auth, "Symbol and Reality: Some Anthropological Considerations," Worship 65 (Jan 91): 2-27; auth, Book Chap 19, "Eucharistic Prayer, Epiclesis," in A. Heinz and H. Rennings, eds, Gratias Agamus: Studies zum eucharistichen Hochgebet, Herder: Freiburg (92): 283-91; auth, "Watch What You Pray: It Says What You Believe," an essay on lex orandi, lex credendi, Liturgical Ministry, 4 (summer 95): 127-31; auth, "From 'Berakah' to 'Eucharistia' to Thomas Talley and Beyond" pub in the Proceedings of the North American Academy of Liturgy (95): 87-99; auth, "Infant Baptism: Theological Reflections," Worship 70 (May 96): 194-210; auth, "Setting the Context for Eucharistic Presence," in Proceedings of the North American Academy of Liturgy (98): 81-99; auth, "Eucharistic Presence: An Invitation to Dialogue," Theol Studies, 60 (99): 294-317. **CONTACT ADDRESS** Dept Theol, St. John's Univ, 8000 Utopia Pkwy, Jamaica, NY 11439-0001. **EMAIL** mckennaj@stjohns.edu

MCKENNA, MICHAEL S.
PERSONAL Born 05/20/1963, Franklin, PA, s **DISCIPLINE** PHILOSOPHY **EDUCATION** Univ VA, PhD, 93. **CAREER** Lecturer, CA State Univ, Long Beach, 93-94; Asst Prof, Ithaca Col, 94-. **RESEARCH** Free will; moral responsibility; ethics. **SELECTED PUBLICATIONS** Auth, R. J. Wallace, Responsibility and the Moral Sentiments, review, The Philos Rev, 105, 96; A Reply to the MacDonald: A Defense of the Presumption in Favor of Requirement Conflicts, J of Social Philos, vol 28, no 1, spring 97; Alternative Possibilities and the Failure of the Counter-Example Strategy, J of Social Philos, vol 28, no 3, winter 97; John Martin Fischer's The Metaphysics of Free Will, review article, Legal Theory 3, 97; Moral Theory and Modified Compatibilism, J of Philos Res, vol 23, 98; Does Strong Compatibilism Survive Frankfurt-Style Counter-Examples?, Philos Studies, forthcoming; The Limits of Evil and the Role of Moral Address: A Defense of Strawsonian Compatibilism, J of Ethics, forthcoming. **CONTACT ADDRESS** Dept of Philos and Relig, Ithaca Col, Ithaca, NY 14850. **EMAIL** mmckenna@ithaca.edu

MCKENNA, WILLIAM R.
PERSONAL Born 08/30/1940, Worchester, MA, m, 1983 **DISCIPLINE** PHENOMENOLOGY, EPISTEMOLOGY, HISTORY OF PHILOSOPHY **EDUCATION** Clark Univ, BA; New Sch Soc Res, PhD. **CAREER** Prof & dept ch, Miami Univ **RESEARCH** How we experience and know ourselves and the world with present specific interests in perception; idea of truth; concept of rationality. **SELECTED PUBLICATIONS** Ed, Husserl Stud; Husserl's "Introductions to Philenomenology" (The Hague: Martin's Nijhoff) 81. **CONTACT ADDRESS** Dept of Philosophy, Miami Univ, Oxford, OH 45056. **EMAIL** mckennwr@muohio.edu

MCKENZIE, ELIZABETH M.
PERSONAL Born 06/27/1954, Lexington, KY, m, 1978, 2 children **DISCIPLINE** LAW **EDUCATION** Transylvania Univ, BA, 75; Univ Ky, JD, 81; MSLS, 84. **CAREER** Atty, Central Ky Legal Serv, 81-83; infor specialist, Ky Dept for Environmental Protection, 84-85; dept head, St. Louis Univ, 86-96; dir of libr serv, Suffolk Univ, 96-. **HONORS AND AWARDS** LLJ Article of the Year, Am Asn of Law Libr; Eli M. Oboler Award, Am Libr Asn; Beta Phi Mu; Reginald Heber Smith Community Lawyer Fel; Sigma Delta Pi; Nat Merit Scholar; Nat Honor Soc. **MEMBERSHIPS** Ky Bar Asn; Am Bar Asn; Am Asn of Law Libr; New Eng Law Libr Consortium; Asn Boston Law Libr. **RESEARCH** Computerized legal research; Law library administration; Freedom of speech; Adaptive technology. **SELECTED PUBLICATIONS** Auth, "The Feminist Attack on Pornography," in Erotica and Pornography, Oryx Press, 90; auth, "Using Adaptive Technology to Provide Access to Blind, Low-vision and Dyslexic Patrons," Law Libr J, 98; auth, "New Kid on the Block KeyCite Compared to Shepard's," AALL Spectrum, 98; auth, "Monopolies in the Law," in Legal Education in the 21st Century, 98; co-auth, "Leaving Paradise: Dropping Out of the Federal Depository Library Program," Law Libr J, (00): 305-319; co-auth, "A Law Librarian at Cooperstown," L Libr J, (01): 209-219. **CONTACT ADDRESS** Sch of Law, Suffolk Univ, 120 Tremont St, Boston, MA 02108-4977. **EMAIL** emckenzi@suffolk.edu

MCKEVITT, GERALD
PERSONAL Born 07/03/1939, Longview, WA, s **DISCIPLINE** AMERICAN HISTORY, THEOLOGY **EDUCATION** Univ San Fancisco, AB, 61; Univ Southern CA, MA, 64; Univ CA, Los Angeles, PhD(hist), 72; Pontif Gregorian Univ, Rome, STB, 75. **CAREER** Res asst prof hist, 75-77, asst prof, 77-92, prof hist, Univ Santa Clara, 93-, dir Univ Arch, 75-85; Historian, 85-. **HONORS AND AWARDS** Oscar O Wither Awd, 91. **MEMBERSHIPS** Calif Hist Society; Cath Hist Society; Western Hist Society. **RESEARCH** California history; Jesuit education in California; Italian Jesuit history. **SELECTED PUBLICATIONS** Auth, Gold Lake myth, J West, 10/64; The Jesuit Arrival in California and the Founding of Santa Clara College, Records Am Cath Hist Soc, 9-12/74; From Franciscan Mission to Jesuit College: a Troubled Transition at Mission Santa Clara, Southern CA Quart, summer 76; Progress Amid Poverty, Santa Clara College in the 1870s, Pac Hist, winter 76; The Beginning of Santa Clara University, San Jose Studies, 2/77; The University of Santa Clara, A History, 1851-1977, Stanford Univ, 79; Jump That Saved Rocky Mountain Mission, Pacific Hist Rev, 86; Jesuit Missionary Linguistics, Western Hist Quart, 90; Hispanic Californians and Catholic Higher education, CA Hist, 90-91; Jesuit Higher Education in US, Mis-America, 91; Italian Jesuits in New Mexico, NM Hist Rev, 92; Christopher Columbus as Civic Saint, CA Hist, winter 92-93; Art of Conversion: Jesuits and Flatheads, US Cath Hist, 94. **CONTACT ADDRESS** Dept Hist, Santa Clara Univ, 500 El Camino Real, Santa Clara, CA 95053-0001. **EMAIL** gmckevit@scu.edu

MCKIM, DONALD K.
PERSONAL Born 02/25/1950, New Castle, PA, m, 1976, 2 children **DISCIPLINE** THEOLOGY **EDUCATION** Westminster Col, 71; Pitts Theol Sem, MDiv, 74; Univ Pitts, PhD, 80. **CAREER** Vis fac, Relig Dept, Westminster Col; prof, Theology, Univ Dubuque Theol Sem, 81-88; acad dean & prof of theology, memphis theol sem, 94-. **HONORS AND AWARDS** Jamison Scholar; Marvin Scholar. **MEMBERSHIPS** Amer Acad Relig; Calvin Stud Soc; Karl Barth Soc; 16th Century Stud Soc **RESEARCH** Doctrine of scripture; John Calvin; Reformed theological tradition. **SELECTED PUBLICATIONS** Auth, Kerygma: The Bible and Theology I II III IV, 93; The bible in Theology and Preaching, Abingdon, 94; The Westminster Dictionary of Theological Terms, Westminster John Knox, 96; God Never Forgets: Faith, Hope, and Alzheimers Disease, Westminster John Knox, 97; ed, Historical Handbook of Major Biblical Interpreters, Inter-Varsity, 98. **CONTACT ADDRESS** Memphis Theol Sem, 168 E Parkway S, Memphis, TN 38104-4340. **EMAIL** dmckim@mtscampus.edu

MCKIM, ROBERT
DISCIPLINE RELIGIOUS STUDIES **EDUCATION** Trinity College Dublin, BA,1975;. Univ Calgary, 1977;Ph.D, Yale University, 1982. **CAREER** Assoc prof, Univ Ill Urbana Champaign,82-. **HONORS AND AWARDS** Templeton Foundation Awd, 1997; Arnold O. Beckman Research Awd, Research Board, Univ Ill, Spring 1998. **RESEARCH** Philosophy of religion; history of early modern philosophy; ethics. **SELECTED PUBLICATIONS** Auth, The Theological Notion of Anonymous Christianity, Calgary Inst Humanities, 82; The Significance of Religious Diversity, Fort Worth, 94; Environmental Ethics: The Widening Vision, Relig Studies Rev, 97; co-ed, National Identity and Respect among Nations, Oxford, 97; The Morality of Nationalism, Oxford, 97. **CONTACT ADDRESS** Religious Studies Dept, Univ of Illinois, Urbana-Champaign, 52 E Gregory Dr, Champaign, IL 61820. **EMAIL** r-mckim@uiuc.edu

MCKINION, STEVEN A.
PERSONAL Born 09/23/1970, Mobile, AL, m, 1995, 2 children **DISCIPLINE** CHURCH HISTORY, THEOLOGY **EDUCATION** Miss Col, BA, 92; Univ Mobile, MA, 97; Univ Aberdeen, PhD, 98. **CAREER** Asst prof, Southeastern Baptist Theol Sem, 98-. **MEMBERSHIPS** Evangel Theol Soc; Am Acad of Relig; N Am Patristics Soc. **RESEARCH** Patristics, Antiquity, Theology. **SELECTED PUBLICATIONS** Auth, Words, Pictures and Christology in Cyril of Alexandria, E.J. Brill, (forthcoming); auth, Life and Practice in the Early Church, NY Univ Pr, (forthcoming); auth, Ancient Christian Commentary on Scripture: Isaiah 1-39, Inter Varsity Pr, (forthcoming). **CONTACT ADDRESS** Dept Church Hist, Southeastern Baptist Theol Sem, PO Box 1899, Wake Forest, NC 27588-1889.

MCKINLEY, BARBARA L.
PERSONAL Born 10/26/1938, Bend, OH, m, 1995 **DISCIPLINE** MANAGEMENT SCIENCE **EDUCATION** Ohio Wesleyan Univ, BA, 60; Case Western Reserve Univ, MA, 65; Pa State Univ, PhD, 80. **CAREER** Asst prof, Baldwin-Wallace Col, 63-70; adj asst prof, Marshall Univ, 70-72; asst prof, Pa State Univ, 72-86; assoc prof to prof, Pfeiffer Univ, 86-95; instr, Fla Keys Community Col, 95-. **HONORS AND AWARDS** Nat Sci Found Grant, 68-71; Grant, Pa State Univ, 76; James Jordan Awd, 75; PSU Provost Fel, 78. **MEMBERSHIPS** DSI; SEDSI; Southern Bus Admin Assoc. **RESEARCH** Designing computer-based mathematical models for decision-making. **SELECTED PUBLICATIONS** Auth, "Planning Models in Higher Education: Historical Review and Survey of Currently Available Models", Higher Educ 10.2 (81): 153-168; auth, "The Academic Flow Model: A Markov-chain Model for Faculty", Decision Sci 12.2 (82): 194-106; rev of "Academic Administration: Planning, Budgeting, and Decision Making with Multiple Objectives", by SM Lee and JC Van Horn, J of Higher Educ 55.6, (84): 781-783; auth, "Faculty Contract Configurations: Probable Impact", Res in Higher Educ 23.3 (85): 293-306; auth, "BCS: Meeting the Challenge", Bus Facilities 18.9, (85): 44-51; auth, Forgotten Algebra, Second Edition, Barron's Educ Series, (Hauppauge, NY), 94; auth, Forgotten Calculus, A Refresher Course With Applications to Economics and Business, Second Edition, Barron's Educ Series, (Hauppauge, NY), 94. **CONTACT ADDRESS** Dept Bus and Tech, Florida Keys Comm Col, 5901 College Rd, Key West, FL 33040-4315.

MCKINNEY, GEORGE DALLAS, JR.
PERSONAL Born 08/09/1932, Jonesboro, AR, m **DISCIPLINE** THEOLOGY **EDUCATION** AR State AM& N Coll Pine Bluff, BA (magna cum laude) 54; Col, MA, 56; Univ of Mich, Grad Studies 57-58; CA Grad Sch of Theol, PhD, 74. **CAREER** St Stephen's Ch of God in Christ, Pastor 62-; Private Practice, Marriage Family & Child Counselor 71-; Comm Welfare Council, consult, 68-71; Econ Opportunity Com, asst dir 65-71; San Diego Co Probation Dept, sr probation officer 59-65; Family Ct Toledo, couns 57-59; Toledo State Mental Hosp, prot chaplain 56-57; Chargin Falls Park Comm Center, dir 55-56. **HONORS AND AWARDS** Recipient JF Kennedy Awd for servs to youth; outstanding pastor award San Diego State Univ Black Students; award for servs to youth Black Bus & Professional Women of San Diego; listed in Contemporary Authors; social worker of the yr award San Diego Co 1963; one of the ten outstanding men in San Diego Jr C of C 1966; outstanding man ot the yr award Intenat Assn of Aerospace Workers Dist 50 1969; outstanding contributions to the San Diego Comm in Field of Religious Activities NAACP 1975; achievement award for Religion Educ & Dedicated Serv to Youth So CA Ch of God in Christ; hon at Testimonial Dinner San Diego State Univ by the NewFriends of the Black Communications Center 1977; listed "Today" 1 of 20 hors Making Significant Contribution to Evangelical Christian Lit; named "Mr San Diego" by Rotary Club of San Diego. **MEMBERSHIPS** Mem CA Probation Parole & Correctional Assn; founder & chmn of bd of dirs St Stephen's Group Home; mem Sandiego Co Council of Chs; bd of trustees Interdenominational Theol Center Atlanta; bd of dirs C H Mason Theol Sem Atlanta; bd of dirs Bob Harrison Ministries; bd of elders Morris Cerillo World Evangelism; mem Sigma Rho Sigma Social Sci Frat; mem San Diego Rotary Club (1st black); mem Alpha Kappa Mu Nat Hon Society; mem Operation Push; vol chaplain at summer camp BSA; mem San Diego Mental Health Assn; mem NAACP; mem YMCA; mem San Diego Urban League; bd of advs Black Communication Center SanDiego State U; mem CA Mental Health Assn. **SELECTED PUBLICATIONS** "The Theol of the Jehovah's Witnesses" "I Will Build My Ch"; several other pubs; African American Devotional Bible, sr editor, 97. **CONTACT ADDRESS** St. Stephen's Church, 5825 Imperial Ave, San Diego, CA 92114.

MCKINNEY, LAUREN D.
DISCIPLINE THEOLOGY **EDUCATION** Dickinson Col, BA; Temple Univ, MA, PhD. **CAREER** Theol Dept, Eastern Mennonite Univ **SELECTED PUBLICATIONS** Contrib, Mary Mitford: Essays, Garland. **CONTACT ADDRESS** Eastern Mennonite Univ, 1200 Park Road, Harrisonburg, VA 22802-2462.

MCKINNEY, RICHARD I.
PERSONAL Born 08/20/1906, Live Oak, FL, m, 1967, 2 children **DISCIPLINE** PHILOSOPHY **EDUCATION** Morehouse Col, AB, 31; Andover Newton Theol Schl, BD, 34, STM, 37; Yale Univ, PhD, 42. **CAREER** Asst prof, phil & relig, 35-42 dean, schl of relig, 42-44, Virg Union Univ; Pres, 44-50, Storer Col; chmn, dept phil, 51-78, Morgan St Univ. **HONORS AND AWARDS** Phi Beta Kappa **MEMBERSHIPS** APA; Natl Ed

Assn; Soc for Rel Values. **RESEARCH** Philosophy of Religion **SELECTED PUBLICATIONS** Auth, Religion in Higher Education Among Negroes, Yale Univ Press, Relig in Amer, Arno Press, 72; auth, A Philosophical Paragraph: We Hold These Truths.., Common Ground, Essays in Honor of Howard Thurman, Hoffman Press, 76; auth, History of the Black Baptists of Florida 1850-1985, FL Mem Col Press, 87; auth, Keeping the Faith - A History of the First Baptist Church, 1863-1980, 1st Baptist Church, 81; art, Howard Thurman: Apostle of Sensitiveness - An Examination of his Autobiography, Toward Wholeness, J of Ministries to Blacks in Higher Ed, 83; art, American Baptist and Black Education in Florida, Amer Baptist Quart, 92; auth, Mordecai - The Man and his Message, The Story of Mordecai Wyatt Johnson, Howard Univ Press, 97; auth, Mordecai Wyatt Johnson, College President, Notable Black Amer Men, Fisk Univ Press, 98. **CONTACT ADDRESS** 2408 Overland Ave, Baltimore, MD 21214. **EMAIL** richmc0741@aol.com

MCKINSEY, MICHAEL
PERSONAL Born 08/19/1941, Fayette, MO, m, 1969, 2 children **DISCIPLINE** PHILOSOPHY **EDUCATION** S Methodist Univ, BA, 63; Kansas State Univ, MA, 66; Ind Univ, PhD, 76. **CAREER** Instr, Ohio Univ Chillicothe, 72-75; asst prof to prof, Wayne State Univ, 76-, Chair, 87-91. **HONORS AND AWARDS** ACLS Fel, 82-83; Career Develop Chair, Wayne State Univ, 84-85; Fulbright Lect, 91-92; Benjamin Meaker Vis Prof, Univ of Bristol, 98; Vis Philos, Oxford Univ, 98-99. **MEMBERSHIPS** Am Philos Assoc; AAUP. **RESEARCH** Philosophy of Language, Philosophy of Mind, Metaphysics, Epistemology, Ethics. **SELECTED PUBLICATIONS** Auth, "Names and Intentionality" Philos Rev 87, (78): 171-200; auth, Causality and the Paradox of Names", Midwest Studies in Philos 9, (84): 491-515; auth, "Mental Anaphora", Synthese 66 (86): 159-175; auth, "Apriorism in the Philosophy of Language", Philos Studies 52 (87): 1-32; auth, "Anti-Individualism and Privileged Access", Analysis 51 (91): 9-16; auth, "The Internal Basis of Meaning", Pacific Philos Quarterly 72, (91): 143-169; auth, "Curing Folk Psychology of Arthritis", Philos Studies 70 (93): 323-336; auth, "Individuating Beliefs", Philos Perspectives 8, Philos of Logic and Lang (94): 303-330; auth, "The Grammar of Belief", Thought, Language, and Ontology, Essays in Memory of Henri-Neri Castaneda, eds W. Rapaport and F. Orilia, Kluwer, 98; auth, "The Semantics of Belief Ascriptions" Nous 33 (Nov 99): 519-557. **CONTACT ADDRESS** Dept Philos, Wayne State Univ, Detroit, MI 48202. **EMAIL** t. m.mckinsey@wayne.edu

MCKIRAHAN, RICHARD D.
PERSONAL Born 07/27/1945, Berkeley, CA, m, 1989, 1 child **DISCIPLINE** ANCIENT PHILOSOPHY **EDUCATION** Univ Calif at Berkeley, AB, 66; Oxford Univ, BA, 69; MA, 78; Harvard Univ, PhD, 73. **CAREER** From asst prof to E.C. Norton Prof of Classics & Prof of Philos, Pomona Col, 73-; vis prof, Univ Calif at Berkeley, 80; vis prof, Univ Glasgow, 92. **HONORS AND AWARDS** Marshall Scholar; NEH Summer Stipends; NEH Fel; Fulbright Sr Scholar; Cambridge Overseas Vis Scholar, St. John's Col. **MEMBERSHIPS** Am Philol Asn; Soc for Ancient Greek Philos. **RESEARCH** Ancient Philosophy, Science, and Mathematics. **SELECTED PUBLICATIONS** Auth, Principles and Proofs: Aristotle's Theory of demonstrative Science, Princeton Univ Pr, 92; auth, "Epicurean Doxography in Cicero, De Natura Deorum, book I," in Epicureismo Greco e Romano, Atti del Congresso Internazionale, Napoli, 19-26 Maggio 1993, eds. G. Giannantoni and M. Gigante (Naples: Bibliopolis, 96): 865-878; auth, "Zeno," in Cambridge companion to the Early Greek Philosophers, ed. A.A. Long (Cambridge Univ Press, 99), 134-158. **CONTACT ADDRESS** Dept Classics, Pomona Col, 333 N College Way, Claremont, CA 91711-4429. **EMAIL** rmckirahan@pomona.edu

MCKISSICK, FLOYD B., JR.
PERSONAL Born 11/21/1952, Durham, NC, m, 1990 **DISCIPLINE** LAW **EDUCATION** Clark Univ, AB, 1974; Univ of NC at Chapel Hill, School of City and Regional Planning, MRP, 1975; Harvard Univ, Kennedy School of Government, MPA, 1979; Duke Univ School of Law, JD, 1983. **CAREER** Floyd B McKissick Enterprises, asst planner, 72-74; Soul City Com, director of planning, 74-79; Peat, Marwick, & Mitchell, management consultant, 80-81; Dickstein, Shapiro & Morin, Attorney, 84-87; Faison and Brown, Attorney, 87-88; Spaulding & Williams, Attorney, 88-89; McKissick & McKissick, Attorney, 89-. **MEMBERSHIPS** Durham City Council, 1994-; NC Center for the Study of Black History, president; Land Loss Prevention Project, past chairman, board member; Durham City-Council Planning Commission; St Joseph's Historical Society, board member; Museum of Life and Science, board member; Durham City of Adjustments; Rural Advancement Foundation International, board member. **SELECTED PUBLICATIONS** Co-author of Guidebook on Attracting Foreign Investment to the US, 1981; Author of When an Owner can Terminate a Contract Due to Delay, 1984; Author of Mighty Warrior, Floyd B McKissick, Sr, 1995. **CONTACT ADDRESS** McKissick & McKissick, 4011 University Dr, Ste 203, Durham, NC 27707-2549.

MCKNIGHT, EDGAR VERNON
PERSONAL Born 11/21/1931, Wilson, SC, m, 1955, 2 children **DISCIPLINE** RELIGION, CLASSICAL LANGUAGES **EDUCATION** Col Charleston, BS, 53; Southern Baptist Theol Sem, BD, 56, PhD, 60; Oxford Univ, MLitt, 78. **CAREER** Chaplain, Chowan Col, 60-63; from asst prof to assoc prof, 63-74, assoc dean acad affairs, 70-73, prof relig & classics, 74-82, chemn, dept classics, 78-80, chemn, dept relig, 91-95, William R Kenan Prof Relig, Furman Univ, 82-; vis prof, Southern Baptist Theol Sem, 66-67; Fulbright sr res prof, Univ Tubingen, 81-82, Univ Muenster, 95-96; NEH study grant, Yale Univ, summer, 80; Bye-fel Robinson Col, Univ Cambridge, 88-89. **HONORS AND AWARDS** Bk of Year Awd, MLA, 78. **MEMBERSHIPS** Soc Bibl Lit; Am Acad Relig; Am Schs Orient Res; Studiorum Novi Testamenti Soc. **RESEARCH** Biblical scholarship among American and Baptist scholars, espec A T Robertson; Biblical hermeneutics; structuralism and semiotics. **SELECTED PUBLICATIONS** Coauth, A History of Chowan College, Graphic Arts, 64; auth, Opening the Bible: A Guide to Understanding the Scriptures, Broadman, 67; coauth, Introd to the New Testament, Ronald 69; auth, What is Form Criticism?, In: Series on Introduction to Biblical Scholarship, Fortress, 69; coauth, Can the Griesbach Hypothesis be Falsified?, J Bibl Lit, 9/72; auth, Structure and Meaning in Biblical Narrative, Perspectives Relig Studies, spring 76; Meaning in Texts: The Historical Shaping of a Narrative Hermeneutics, Fortress, 78; The Bible and the Reader, Fortress, 85; Postmodern Use of the Bible, Abringdon, 88; ed, Reader Perspectives on the New Testament, Semeia 48, 89; NT ed, Mercer Dictionary of the Bible, 90; NT ed, Mercer Commentary on the Bible, Mercer, 94; co-ed, The New Literary Criticism and the New Testament, Sheffield and Trinity, 94. **CONTACT ADDRESS** Dept of Relig, Furman Univ, 3300 Poinsett Hwy, Greenville, SC 29613-1218. **EMAIL** edgar.mcknight@furman.edu

MCKNIGHT, JOSEPH WEBB
PERSONAL Born 02/17/1925, San Angelo, TX, m, 1975, 2 children **DISCIPLINE** LEGAL HISTORY, FAMILY LAW **EDUCATION** Univ Tex, Austin, BA, 47; Oxford Univ, BA, 49, BCL, 50, MA, 54; Columbia Univ, LLM, 59. **CAREER** Legal pract, Cravath, Swaine & Moore, New York, 51-55; from asst prof to prof, 55-63, assoc dean, 77-80, Prof Law, Sch Law, Southern Methodist Univ, 63-, Consult, Hemisfair, 67-69; dir, Family Code Proj, State Bar Tex, 66-75. **HONORS AND AWARDS** Phi Beta Kappa; Rhodes Scholar; Kent fel, 58-59; Academia Mexicana de Derecho Int, 88; State Bar of Texas Family Law Section Hall of Legends, 97. **MEMBERSHIPS** Am Soc Legal Hist (vpres, 67-69); Am Soc Int Law; Nat Legal Aid & Defenders Asn. **SELECTED PUBLICATIONS** Auth, Family Law: Husband and Wife, Annual Survey of Texas Law, SMU L Rev, 67-00; auth, Texas Community Property Law: Conservative Attitudes, reluctant Change, Law & Contemp Prob, 93; auth, The Mysteries of Spanish Surnames, El Campanario, 94; auth, Spanish Legitim in the United States: Its Survival and Decline, Am J Comp L, 96; auth, Survival and Decline of the Spanish Law of Descendent Succession on the Anglo-Hispanic Frontier of North America: Homenaje al Professor Alfonso Garcia-Gallo, 96; contribur, Tyler, ed, The New Handbook of Texas, 96; auth, Eugene L. Smith, 1933-1997, An Appreciation of His Achievements, Family Law Section Rept, 97; coauth, Texas Matrimonial Property Law, 2d ed, Lupus, 98. **CONTACT ADDRESS** Sch of Law, So Methodist Univ, Dallas, TX 75275. **EMAIL** mpmcknight@home.com

MCLAREN, JOHN P. S.
DISCIPLINE LAW **EDUCATION** St. Andrews Univ, LLB, 62; London Univ, LLM, 64; Univ Mich, LLM, 70; Calgary Univ, LLD, 97. **CAREER** Univ Saskatchewan, 66-71; fac of law, Univ Windsor, 71-75; Univ Calgay, 75-87; prof, Univ of Victoria 87-. **HONORS AND AWARDS** Founder, Can Law Soc Asn. **MEMBERSHIPS** Am Soc Legal Hist.; Canadian Law and Soc Assn. **RESEARCH** Tort law, insurance law, Canadian legal history, social history of the law, legal education, and legal theory **SELECTED PUBLICATIONS** Auth, Essays on Revisions, the State and the Law, 98; pubs on tort law, insurance law, Canadian legal history, social history of the law, legal education, and legal theory; co-auth, Fraser Committee Report on Pornography and Prostitution in Canada; co-ed, Law for the Elephant, Law for the Beaver: Essays in the Legal History of the North American West and Essays in the History of Canadian Law. **CONTACT ADDRESS** Fac of Law, Univ of Victoria, PO Box 2400, Victoria, BC, Canada V8W 3H7. **EMAIL** jmclaren@uvic.ca

MCLAUGHLIN, JOSEPH M.
PERSONAL Born 03/20/1933, Brooklyn, NY, m, 1959, 3 children **DISCIPLINE** LAW **EDUCATION** Fordham Univ, AB, 54, LLB, 59; NYork Univ, LLM, 64. **CAREER** Asst instr philos, Fordham Col, 54-55, from asst prof to assoc prof, 61-66, Prof Law, Sch Law, Fordham Univ, 66-, Dean, 71-, Lectr, Practicing Law Inst, 63-; consult, NY Law Revision Comn, 63-; NY Judicial Conf, 63-. **RESEARCH** Procedure; evidence, trail and appellate practice. **SELECTED PUBLICATIONS** Auth, Mulligan, William, Hughes--In Memoriam, Fordham Law Rev, vol 0065, 96. **CONTACT ADDRESS** Sch of Law, Fordham Univ, New York, NY 10023.

MCLAY, TIM
PERSONAL Born 01/17/1963, St. Stephen, NB, Canada, m, 1983, 3 children **DISCIPLINE** OLD TESTAMENT **EDUCATION** Durham, PhD, 94 **CAREER** Asst Prof, Acadia Divinity Col, 96-. **MEMBERSHIPS** Soc of Biblical Lit; Intl Org for Septuagint and Cognate Studies **RESEARCH** Septuagint; use of Septuagint; Daniel **SELECTED PUBLICATIONS** Auth, A Collation of variants from Papyrus 967 to Ziegler's Critical Edition of Susanna, Daniel, Bel et Draco, Textus 18, 95; Syntactic Profiles and the Characteristics of Revision: A Response to Karen Jobes, BIOSCS 26, 96; The OG and Th Versions of Daniel, 96; It's a Question of Influence: The Old Greek and Theodotion Texts of Daniel, Origen's Hexapla and Fragments, 98; Septuagint, Theodotion, Greek Versions, Chester Beatty Papyri, Eerdman's Dictionary of the Bible, forthcoming; Lexical Inconsistency: A Methodology for the Analysis of the Vocabulary in the Septuagint, 10th Congress of the IOCS, forthcoming. **CONTACT ADDRESS** Acadia Divinity Col, Wolfville, NS, Canada B0P 1X0. **EMAIL** tim.mclay@acadiau.ca

MCLEAN, EDWARD L.
DISCIPLINE ECONOMIC DEVELOPMENT **EDUCATION** Univ Wisc, Madison, BS, 61, MS, 64; Iowa State Univ, PhD, 68. **CAREER** Res analyst, State of Washington, 62-64; res assoc and instr, Iowa State Univ, 65-67; asst prof, Tex A & M Univ, 67-70; prof, Clemson Univ, 77-. **HONORS AND AWARDS** Acting head of dept, 86-88; res, instruction, curriculum adv and outreach appointments; Honor Role of Teachers, 94. **MEMBERSHIPS** Rural Sociol Soc. **RESEARCH** Demography, survey research, economic and social inequality. **SELECTED PUBLICATIONS** Coauth with Amy H. Garland and Suzanne Carr, "Characteristics of Mature Migrants," RR96-2, Carolina Power and Light Co and Clemson Univ (96); auth, "Demographic Characteristics and Forecasts for South Carolina," WP080897, Dept of Agriculture and Applied Economics, Clemson Univ (97); auth, "Mature Migrants to South Carolina: Selected Characteristics," RR98-3, Fac of Economic Development, Clemson Univ (98); coauth with Cindy G. Roper, "Demographic Information for the South Carolina Real Estate Industry," Center for Applied Real Estate Ed and Res, Univ SC, Columbia (99); coauth with Cindy G. Roper, "Causes of Different Growth Rates Between North and South Carolina," Center for Applied Real Estate Ed and Res, Univ SCm Columbia (99). **CONTACT ADDRESS** Fac of Economic Development, Clemson Univ, 263 Barre Hall, PO Box 340355, Clemson, SC 29634-0355. **EMAIL** emclean@clemson.edu

MCLEAN, GEORGE FRANCIS
PERSONAL Born 06/29/1929, Lowell, MA **DISCIPLINE** PHILOSOPHY **EDUCATION** Gregorian Univ, PhB, 51, PhL, 52, STB, 54, STL, 56; Cath Univ Am, PhD, 58. **CAREER** From instr to assoc prof, 58-67, dir philos workshop, 61-68, Prof Philos, 67-93, prof emeritus, 93- , Cath Univ Am, & Coordr, Acad Exchanges, 81-, Lectr-prof, Oblate Col, 56-92; metaphys & theodicy area ed, New Cath Encycl, 61-64; vis res prof, Univ Madras, 69, 77, Univ Paris, 70, Inst for Oriental Studies, Cairo, 91, 92. **HONORS AND AWARDS** Adv prof, Fordham Univ, 94; hon prof Shanghai Acad of Sci, 98. **MEMBERSHIPS** Am Cath Philos Asn (secy, 63-80); Am Philos Asn; Metaphys Soc Am; Int Soc Metaphys (secy, 78-98); World Union Cath Philos Soc (secy, 72-98); Coun for Res in Values and Philos (secy, 81-). **RESEARCH** Metaphysics; hist of philos; philos of relig. **SELECTED PUBLICATIONS** Auth, Man's Knowledge of God According to Paul Tillich, 58; auth, Perspectives on Reality, 66; auth, An Annotated Bibliography of Philosophy in Catholic Thought, 66; auth,A Bibliography of Christian Philosophy and Contemporary Issues, 66; ed, Readings in Ancient Western Philosophy, 70, 2d ed, 97; auth, Ancient Western Philosophy, 71; auth, Plenitude and Participation, 78; auth, Tradition and Contemporary Life: Hermeneutics of Perennial Wisdom and Social Change, 86; auth, Tradition, Harmony and Transcendence, 94; auth, Ways to God, 99; auth, Freedon, Cultrual Traditions and Progress, 00; Religion and Cooperation Between Civilizations, 00; auth, Faith Reason and Philosophy, 00. **CONTACT ADDRESS** Sch of Philos, Catholic Univ of America, Washington, DC 20064. **EMAIL** mclean@cua.edu

MCLELLAN, BRADLEY N.
DISCIPLINE LAW **EDUCATION** Univ Western Ontario, BA; Univ Toronto, LLB, 77. **CAREER** Spec lectr, Univ of Toronto, 82-85, 93-95, 97-98; Spec lectr, Osgoote Hall Law Sch, 85-88; Partner, Weir & Foulds; adj prof, Univ of Toronto. **SELECTED PUBLICATIONS** Auth, pubs on real estate law, condominium law and environmental law; co-auth, Real Estate Law (4th ed). **CONTACT ADDRESS** Fac of Law, Univ of Toronto, 78 Queen's Park, Toronto, ON, Canada M5S 2C5.

MCLELLAND, JOSEPH CUMMING
PERSONAL Born 09/10/1925, Scotland, m, 1947, 4 children **DISCIPLINE** PHILOSOPHY OF RELIGION **EDUCATION** McMaster Univ, BA, 46; Univ Toronto, MA, 49; Knox Col, Toronto, BD, 51; Univ Edinburgh, PhD, 53. **CAREER** Prof, Presby Col, Que, 57-64; Prof Philos Relig, McGill Univ, 64-92, Dean Fac Relig Studies, 75-85; prof emer, McGill Univ, 92-. **HONORS AND AWARDS** DD, Diocesan Col Montreal, 73 & Knox Col, Toronto, 76. **MEMBERSHIPS** Can Theol Soc

(pres, 63-64); Can Soc Studies Relig. **RESEARCH** Philosophy and theology of relationship; analogy and mythology; modern atheism. **SELECTED PUBLICATIONS** Auth, Toward a Radical Church, 61; auth, The Clown and the Crocodile, 70; auth, The New Man, with J. Meyendorff, 73; auth, God the Anonymous: Alexandrian Philosophical Theology, 76; ed, Peter Martyr Vermigli and Italian Reform, 80; auth, Celebration and Suffering, 84; auth, Prometheus Rebound: the Irony of Atheism, 88; auth, Life, Early Letters and Eucharistic Writings of Peter Martyr, with G. Duffield, 89; auth, Early Writings, Peter Martyr Library, Vol 1, 94; auth, Philosophical Writings, Peter Martyr Library, Vol 4, 96. **CONTACT ADDRESS** Fac of Relig Studies, McGill Univ, 3520 University St, Montreal, QC, Canada H3A 2T5. **EMAIL** cyjm@musica.mcgill.ca

MCLENNAN, SCOTTY
PERSONAL Born 11/21/1948, Chicago, IL, m, 1981, 2 children **DISCIPLINE** RELIGION **EDUCATION** Yale, BA, 70; Harvard, MDiv, 75; JD, 75. **CAREER** Dir, Unitarian Universalist Legal Ministry, 75-84; Univ Chaplain and Lecturer, Tufts Univ, 84-; Senior Lecturer, Harvard Business School, 88-. **HONORS AND AWARDS** Hotchkiss School Community Service Awd, 92, Rabbi Martin Katzenstein Awd, Harvard Divinity School, 94. **MEMBERSHIPS** Unitarian Universalist Ministers Assoc, National Assoc of College & Univ Chaplains **RESEARCH** Faith development, Business, Ethics, Spirituality in Business. **SELECTED PUBLICATIONS** Auth, Finding Your Religion: When the Faith You Grew Up With Has Lost Its Meaning, Harper (San Francisco), 99. **CONTACT ADDRESS** Dept Religion, Tufts Univ, Medford, Goddard Chapel, Medford, MA 02155. **EMAIL** smclenna@emerald.tufts.edu

MCLEOD, FREDERICK G.
PERSONAL Born 02/22/1932, Boston, MA, s **DISCIPLINE** THEOLOGY **EDUCATION** Boston Col, AB, 55; MA, 55; Licentiate in Theol, 63; Pontif Oriental Inst, DOES, 73. **CAREER** Instr, Baghdad Col, 56-59; asst prof, Al Hikma Univ, 68; superior/rector of Jesuit collegians, Boston Col, 69-73; assoc prof, St. Louis Univ, 73-. **MEMBERSHIPS** N Am Patristic Studies, The Col Theol Soc, Inst for Theol Encounter with Sci and Technol. **RESEARCH** Syriac and Greek Patrology with emphases upon the School of Antioch, Theodore of Mopsuestia, and the "image of God." **SELECTED PUBLICATIONS** Auth, The Soteriology of Narsai, Gregorian Press, 73; auth, narsai's metrical Homilies on Nativity, Epiphany, Passion, Ressurection, and Ascension, Patrologia Orientalis, 79; auth, The Image of God in the Antiochene Tradition, Catholic Univ Press, 99. **CONTACT ADDRESS** Dept Theol, Saint Louis Univ, 221 N Grand Blvd, Saint Louis, MO 63103-2006. **EMAIL** mcleodfg@slu.edu

MCLURE, CHARLES E., JR.
PERSONAL Born 04/14/1940, Sierra Bianca, TX, m, 1962 **DISCIPLINE** ECONOMICS **EDUCATION** Univ Kans, BA, 62; Princeton Univ, MA, 64, PhD, 66. **CAREER** Vice pres, Natl Bureau of econ res, 77- , Cline Prof, Rice Univ, 65-77; dep asst sec treasury, 83-85, US Treasure Dept; sr fel, presently, Hoover Inst, Stanford Univ. **RESEARCH** Intergovernmental fiscal relations; consumption-based taxes; and taxation of electronic commerce. **SELECTED PUBLICATIONS** Auth, Must Corporate Income Be Taxed Twice?, 79; ed, Tax Assignment in Federal Countries, 83; co-ed, Fiscal Federalism and the Taxation of Natural Resources, 83; ed, State Corporation Income Tax: Issues in Worldwide Unitary Taxation, 84; auth, Economic Perspectives on State Taxation of Multijurisdictional Corporations, 86; auth, The Value Added Tax: Key to Deficit Reduction, 87; co-ed, World Tax Reform, 90; coauth, The Taxation of Income from Business and Capital in Colombia, 90. **CONTACT ADDRESS** Hoover Inst, Stanford Univ, Stanford, CA 94022. **EMAIL** mclure@hoover.stanford.edu

MCMAHAN, JEFFERSON
PERSONAL Born 08/30/1954, GA, m, 1977, 2 children **DISCIPLINE** PHILOSOPHY **EDUCATION** Univ of the South, BA, 76; Oxford Univ, BA, MA, 79; Cambridge Univ, PhD, 85. **CAREER** Res fel, St. John's Col, Cambridge Univ, 83-86; asst prof, Univ Ill Urbana, 86-92; assoc prof, Univ Ill Urbana, 92-. **HONORS AND AWARDS** Rhodes scholar, 76. **SELECTED PUBLICATIONS** Co-auth, The Morality of Nationalism, Oxford Univ Press, 97; article, Wrongful Life; Paradoxes in the Morality of Causing People to Exist, Rational Commitment and Social Justice: Essays for Gregory Kavka, Cambridge Univ Pres, 208-247, 98; article, Brain Death, Cortical Death, and Persistent Vegetative State, A Companion to Bioethics, Blackwell, 250-260, 98; article, Preferences, Death, and the Ethics of Killing, Preferences, Walter de Gruyter & Co, 471-502, 98; article, A Challenge to Common Sense Morality, Ethics, 108, no 2, 394-418, 98; article, Intervention and Collective Self-Determination, Ethics and Intl Affairs, 10, 1-24, 96; article, Cognitive Disability, Misfortune, and Justice, Philos and Public Affairs, 25, no 1, 3-34, Winter, 96; article, Killing and Equality, Utilitas 7, no 1, 1-29, Apr 95; article, Innocence, Self-Defense, and Killing in War, Jour of Polit Philos, 2, no 3, 193-221, Sept 94; article, Self-Defense and the Problem of the Innocent Attacker, Ethics, 104, no 2, 252-290, Jan, 94; article, The Right to Choose an Abortion, Philos and Public Affairs, 22, no 4, 331-348, Fall, 93; article, Killing, Letting Die, and Withdrawing Aid, Ethics, 103, no 2, 250-279, Jan, 93. **CONTACT ADDRESS** Dept. of Philosophy, Univ of Illinois, Urbana-Champaign, 810 S. Wright St., 105 Gregor, Urbana, IL 61801.

MCMAHAN, OLIVER
PERSONAL Born 11/15/1954, Honolulu, HI, m, 1975, 2 children **DISCIPLINE** RELIGION **EDUCATION** Texas Christian Univ, DMin, 84; Ga State Univ, PhD, 97. **CAREER** Assoc prof, dean, Inst of External Studies, Church of God Theol Seminary. **MEMBERSHIPS** ACA. **CONTACT ADDRESS** Church of God Sch of Theol, 900 Wallcrest, Cleveland, TN 37311. **EMAIL** amintranet@aol.com

MCMAHON, MARTIN J., JR.
PERSONAL Born 05/03/1949, Philadelphia, PA, m, 1971, 2 children **DISCIPLINE** LAW **EDUCATION** Rutgers Col, BA; Boston Col, JD; Boston Univ, LLM. **CAREER** Clarence J. TeSelle prof, Univ Fla, 97-; prof, Univ Ky, 79-97; visting Hugh F. Culverhouse Eminent scholar in taxation, Univ Fla, 91. **MEMBERSHIPS** Amer Law Inst; Amer Col Tax Coun; Amer Bar Asn Tax Sect. **RESEARCH** Individual income taxation, corporate taxation, partnership taxation, tax policy. **SELECTED PUBLICATIONS** Coauth, Federal Income Taxation of Individuals; Federal Income Taxation of Business Organizations; auth, Federal Income Taxation of Corporations; auth, Federal Income Taxation of Partnerships and S Corporations; auth, Federal Income Taxation Cases and Molenols. **CONTACT ADDRESS** College of Law, Univ of Florida, PO Box 117625, Gainesville, FL 32611-7625. **EMAIL** mcmahon@law.ufl.edu

MCMAHON, ROBERT
DISCIPLINE EPIC, PLATONIST LITERATURE, PHILOSOPHY AND LITERATURE **EDUCATION** Univ Calif, Santa Cruz, PhD, 86. **CAREER** Prof, La State Univ. **HONORS AND AWARDS** Robert L (Doc) Amborski Awd, 87; Phi Kappa Phi Awd, 90; Awd for Excellence in Tchg Freshmen, 94; Alpha Lambda Delta, Nat Freshman Honor Soc; Amoco Awd, 95; Tiger Athletic Found Awd, Honors Col, 96. **RESEARCH** Voegelinian essays; Milton; Dante. **SELECTED PUBLICATIONS** Auth, Homer/Pound's Odysseus and Virgil/Ovid/Dante's Ulysses: Pound's First Canto and the Commedia, Paideuma, 87; Kenneth Burke's Divine Comedy: The Literary Form of The Rhetoric of Religion, PMLA, 89; Augustine's Prayerful Ascent: An Essay on the Literary Form of the Confession, 89; Satan as Infernal Narcissus: Interpretative Translation in the Commedia, in Dante and Ovid: Essays in Intertextuality, 91; 'Coloss. 3.3' as Microcosm, George Herbert J, 93; The Structural Articulation of Boethius' Consolation of Philosophy, Medievalia et Humanistica, 94; The Two Poets of Paradise Lost, 98. **CONTACT ADDRESS** Dept of Eng, Louisiana State Univ and A&M Col, 212K Allen Hall, Baton Rouge, LA 70803.

MCMAHON, WILLIAM EDWARD
PERSONAL Born 09/25/1937, Chicago, IL, m, 1962, 2 children **DISCIPLINE** PHILOSOPHY **EDUCATION** Univ Notre Dame, AB, 59, PhD(Philos), 70; Brown Univ, MA, 61. **CAREER** Instr philos, St Cincent Col, Pa, 61-64; asst prof, John Carroll Univ, 67-69; asst prof, 69-77, assoc prof Philos, Univ Akron, 77-; assoc prof, 77-83; prof Philos, 83-. **RESEARCH** Philosophy of language and linguistics; contemporary and medieval ontologies; contemporary analytic philosophy. **SELECTED PUBLICATIONS** Auth, The problem of evil and the possibility of a better world, J Value Inquiry, Summer 69; Hans Reichenbach's Philosophy of Grammar, Mouton, 76; The teaching of philosophy: Subject matter versus pedagogy, Teaching Philos, Fall 76; A generative model for translating from ordinary language into symbolic notation, Synthese, 77; Dreadnought Battleships and Battle Cruisers, Univ Am, 78; The semantics of Ramon Llull, Studies in the History of Logic: Proceedings of III Symposium of the Hist of Logic, de Gruyter, 96; Biographies in Biographical Dictionary of American Sports, Baseball II, Greenwood, 98. **CONTACT ADDRESS** Dept of Philosophy, Univ of Akron, 302 Olin Hall, Akron, OH 44325-1903. **EMAIL** mcmahon@uakron.edu

MCMANUS, EDGAR J.
PERSONAL Born 03/04/1924, New York, NY, w **DISCIPLINE** AMERICAN COLONIAL, LEGAL & CONSTITUTIONAL HISTORY **EDUCATION** Columbia Univ, BS, 52, MA, 53, PhD, 59; NY Univ, JP, 59. **CAREER** Lectr hist, Columbia Univ, 53-56; from lectr to assoc prof, 57-73, prof hist, Queens Col, NY, 73, Adj prof law, NY Law Sch, 62-66; Am Coun Learned Soc fel, 68-69. **HONORS AND AWARDS** Fulbright lectr, New Zealand, 82; Norway, 89; jd, ny univ, 59. **MEMBERSHIPS** AHA; NY State Bar. **RESEARCH** Am Negro slavery; legal origins of American Negro slavery; American Legal and constitutional history. **SELECTED PUBLICATIONS** Auth, The status of res ipsa loquitor in New York, NY Univ Intramural Law Rev, 11/47; Antislavery legislation in New York, J Negro Hist, 10/61; The enforcement of acceleration clauses in New York, NY Law Forum, 12/62; A History of Negro Slavery in New York, 66, Black Bondage in the North, 73, Syracuse Univ; Law and Libery in Early New England, Univ of MA, 93. **CONTACT ADDRESS** Dept of Hist, Queens Col, CUNY, 6530 Kissena Blvd, Flushing, NY 11367-1597.

MCMANUS, FREDERICK RICHARD
PERSONAL Born 02/08/1923, Lynn, MA **DISCIPLINE** CANON LAW **EDUCATION** St John's Sem, AB, 47; Cath Univ Am, JCD, 54. **CAREER** Prof moral theol & canon law, St John's Sem, 54-58; Prof Canon Law, Cath Univ Am, 58-, VProvost & Dean Grad Studies, 74-83, Ed, The Jurist, 58-; consult, Pontif Prep Comn Liturgy, 60-62; peritus, II Vatican Coun, 62-65, consult consilium execution const on liturgy, 64-69; dir secretariat of bishops' comt liturgy, Nat Conf Cath Bishops, DC, 65-75; treas, Int Comn English in Liturgy, 65-00; consult, Pontif Comn Revision of Code of Canon Law, Rome, 67-83; chmn bd, Asn Cath Col & Univ, 80-82; Acad Vice Pres, 83-85. **HONORS AND AWARDS** Pay Christi, St John's Univ, 64; Honorary Archimandrite of Jerusalem, 70; Role of Law Awd, Canon Law Soc, 73; Mathis award, Univ Notre Dame, 78; Berakah Awd, North Am Acad Liturgy, 79; Prelate of Honor, Pope John Paul II, 80; SJD, Holy Cross Col, 89; John Courtney Murray Awd, CTSA, 90; lld, st anselm's col, 64 & stonehill col, 65. **MEMBERSHIPS** Canon Law Soc Am; Cath Theol Soc Am; Liturgical Conf (pres, 59-62); NAm Acad Liturgy, Societas Liturgica; hon mem Guild Relig Archit. **RESEARCH** Liturgy **SELECTED PUBLICATIONS** Auth, The First Ordinary of the Royal Abbey of St Denis in France--Paris Bibliotheque Mazarine-526, Speculum-J Medieval Stud, vol 0068, 93. **CONTACT ADDRESS** Catholic Univ of America, Washington, DC 20064.

MCMULLEN, MIKE
PERSONAL Born 10/14/1965, Fremont, NE, m, 1989, 1 child **DISCIPLINE** RELIGION; SOCIOLOGY **EDUCATION** Emory Univ, PhD, 95 **CAREER** Asst prof Sociol, Univ Houston, 95- **HONORS AND AWARDS** Univ Houston Res Awd, 96, 97; SSSR Res Awd, 94; RRA Res Awd, 94; Emory Grad Tchg Awd, 93. **MEMBERSHIPS** Amer Acad Relig; Amer Sociol Assoc; Assoc Sociol Relig; Soc Sci Study Relig **RESEARCH** Baha'I Faith; Religious Denominations; Religion and Peace Issues; Conflict Resolution and Mediation. **SELECTED PUBLICATIONS** The Religious Construction of a Global Identity: The Baha'i Faith in Atlanta, Rutgers Univ, forthcoming; bk rev, Sacred Acts, Sacred Space, Sacred Time, by John Walbridge, Jour Baha'I Studies, forthcoming; bk rev, The Origins of the Baha'i Community of Can, 1889-1948, by Will C Van den Hoonaard, Soc Relig, 97. **CONTACT ADDRESS** Dept of Sociology, Univ of Houston, Clear Lake, 2700 Bay Area Blvd, Box 203, Houston, TX 77058. **EMAIL** mcmullen@cl.uh.edu

MCMULLIN, ERNAN
DISCIPLINE PHILOSOPHY OF SCIENCE **EDUCATION** Nat Univ of Ireland, BSc, 45; Maynooth Col, BD, 48; Univ Louvain, PhD, 54. **CAREER** Prof Emeritus, Univ Notre Dame, 94-. **HONORS AND AWARDS** Fel, Amer Acad of Arts & Sciences; Fel, Amer Assn for the Advn of Science; Fel, Intl Acad for the History of Science. **MEMBERSHIPS** APA; PSA; History of Science Soc; Metaphysical Soc of Amer; ACPA **RESEARCH** Issues in contemporary philosophy of science; history of scientific methodology; relationship of religion to the natural sciences. **SELECTED PUBLICATIONS** Auth, Newton on Matter and Activity, 78; The Inference that Makes Science, 92; Rationality and Paradigm Change in Science, 93; The Indifference Principle and the Anthropic Principle in Cosmology, 93; Religion and Cosmology, 93; Enlarging Imagination, 96; Galileo on Science and Scripture, 97; ed, Evolution and Creation, 85; Construction and Constraint: The Shaping of Scientific Rationality, 88; The Social Dimensions of Science, 92; co-ed, Philosophical Consequences of Quantum Theory, 89. **CONTACT ADDRESS** History and Philosophy of Science Dept, Univ of Notre Dame, Notre Dame, IN 46556. **EMAIL** Ernan.McMullin.1@nd.edu

MCNALLY, MICHAEL J.
PERSONAL Born 07/30/1947, Waterloo, NY, s **DISCIPLINE** THEOLOGY **EDUCATION** St Vincent de Paul Sem, Boynton Beach, Fla, BA, 69, MDiv, 72, MTh, 73; Univ Notre Dame, MA, 80, PhD, 83. **CAREER** Asst pastor, St John Bosco Parish, Miami, Fla, 73-74; asst pastor, Visitation Parish, Miami, Fla, 74-75; instr and Dean of Students, St John Vianney Col Sem, 75-79; archivist, Archdiocese of Miami, Fla, 83-84; asst prof, St Vincent de Paul Regional Sem, Boynton Beach, Fla, 82-83, archivist, 86-93, prof, 83-93; vis prof to prof, St Charles Borromeo Sem-Overbrook, Wynnewood, Pa, 93-. **HONORS AND AWARDS** Cushwa Fel, Cushwa Ctr for the Study of Am Catholicism, Univ Notre Dame, spring 82; Sabbatical Res Grant, St Vincent de Paul Regional Sem, Boynton Beach, Fl, fall 90; Curu of Ars Awd, St John Vianney Col Sem, Miami, Fl, May 5, 99. **MEMBERSHIPS** Am Cath Hist Asn, Am Hist Asn, Am Soc of Church Hist, Fla Hist Soc, Southern Hist Asn, U.S. Cath Hist Soc. **RESEARCH** Catholicism in the southern U.S., especially Florida. **SELECTED PUBLICATIONS** Auth, "Father Philippe de Carriere: Jesuit Pioneer on Florida's West Coast, 1888-1902," Tampa Bay Hist, 17 (fall/winter 95): 35-46; auth, Catholic Parish Life on Florida's West Coast, 1860-1968, St Petersburg, Fla: Cath Media Ministries (96); auth, "Presence and Persistence: Catholicism Among Latins in Tampa's Ybor City, 1885-1985," U.S. Catholic Historian, 14 (spring 96): 73-91; auth, "Florida, Catholic Church In (1865-1995)," in Encyclopedia of American Catholic History, by Michael Glazier and Thomas Shelly, gen eds, Collegeville, MN: Liturgical Press

(97): 520-22; auth, "Hurley, Joseph P.," in American National Biography, ed by John Garraty and Mark C. Carnes, Vol 11, New York: Oxford (99): 563-64; auth, "Florida," in Encyclopedia of the Irish in America, ed Michael Glazier, Notre Dame, IN: Univ of Notre Dame (99): 102-05. **CONTACT ADDRESS** Dept Theol, St. Charles Borromeo Sem, Overbrook, 100 E Wynnewood Rd, Wynnewood, PA 19096-3001.

MCNALLY, VINCENT J.
PERSONAL Born 02/06/1943, Philadelphia, PA, s **DISCIPLINE** CHURCH HISTORY **EDUCATION** St Charles Borromeo Col, BA, 65; Villanova Univ, MA, 71; Univ Dublib, trinity Col, PhD, 77; MSLS, 80; Catholic Univ, M Div, 82. **CAREER** Instr, Prince George Comm Col, 80-82; lectr, Seattle Univ, 82-83; adj prof, Simon Fraser Univ, CAN, 83-92; prof, Sacred Sch Theology, 92-. **HONORS AND AWARDS** Pew Charit Tr Res Awd; Lilly Found Res Awd; Lilly-Wabash Cen Teach Theol Awd; Western Canadian Pub Res Pub Awd; Soc Sci Hum Res Coun Awd, Canada. **MEMBERSHIPS** ACHA; CCHA; IAHA. **RESEARCH** Irish Catholic Church history; Canadian Catholic Church history. **SELECTED PUBLICATIONS** Auth, "Fighting for a Foundation: Oblate Beginnings in Far Western Canada, 1847-1864," in Western Oblate Studies 4/Etudes Oblate de L 'Ouest 4, Edmonton: Western Can Pub 96; auth, "Who is Leading? Archbishop John Thomas Troy and the Priests and People in the Archdiocese of Dublin 1787-1823," The Can Cath Hist Asn, Hist Studies, 61(95); auth, "Fighting City Hall: The Church Tax Exemption Baffle Between the City and the Roman Catholic Diocese of Victoria," J Can Church Hist Soc 34, (92); auth, "A Defence of the 'Durieu System,"' Bulletin, Western Canadian Pub 28 (98); auth, "A Question of Class? Relations between Bishops and Lay Leaders in Ireland and Newfoundland 1783-1807," The Canadian Catholic Hist Asn, Historical Studies, 64(98); auth, "Challenging the Status Quo: An Examination of the History of Catholic Education in British Columbia," The Canadian Cath Hist Asn, Historical Studies, 65 (99); auth, "Hope for the Future: Facing the Church's Challenges of the New Millennium," Centre de Patrimoine, Colloquium 99, Winnipeg: University of Manitoba, 00; auth, "The Lord's Distant Vineyard: A History of the Oblates and the Catholic Community in British Columbia," Univ Alberta Press, 00. **CONTACT ADDRESS** Dept Religion, Sacred Heart Sch of Theol, PO Box 429, Hales Corners, WI 53130-0429. **EMAIL** vmcnally@execpc.com

MCNAMARA, PAUL
PERSONAL s **DISCIPLINE** PHILOSOPHY **EDUCATION** Univ Mass, PhD, 90. **CAREER** Assoc prof. **HONORS AND AWARDS** Ed, Philos Studies. **MEMBERSHIPS** Am Philos Assoc and Soc for Exact Philos. **RESEARCH** Ethical theory; deontic logic; philosophy of language; philosophy of mind. **SELECTED PUBLICATIONS** Auth, pubs on Leibniz, metaphysics of modality, philosophy of AI, ethical theory, supererogation, and deonticlogic. **CONTACT ADDRESS** Philosophy Dept, Univ of New Hampshire, Durham, Hamilton Smith Hall, Durham, NH 03824. **EMAIL** paulm@cisunix.unh.edu

MCNEILL, SUSAN PATRICIA
PERSONAL Born 10/03/1947, Washington, DC, s **DISCIPLINE** LAW **EDUCATION** Wilson College, BA, 1969; Creighton University, JD, 1978; Pepperdine University, MBA, 1980. **CAREER** US Air Force: Edwards AFB, Assistant Staff Judge Advocate, contract attorney, 78-81; Norton AFB, Ballistic Missile Office, Asst Staff Judge Advocate, staff attorney, 81-84; Lindsey Air Station, Germany, Staff Judge Advocate, chief legal officer, 84-87; Dept of Justice, Defense Procurement Fraud Unit, trial attorney, 87-89; Pentagon, Air Force Contract Law Division, trial attorney, 89-91, Air Force General Counsel's Office, staff attorney, 91-92; Defense Systems Management Col, Acquisition Law Task Force, associate director, senior attorney, 92-93; AF General Counsels Office, civilian staff attorney, 93-95; Sawyer Myersburg, of counsel, currently. **HONORS AND AWARDS** Judge Advocate, Big Sisters of Omaha, Big Sister of the Year, 1978; Natl Coalition 100 Black Women, VA Commonwealth Chapter, Serwa Awd, 1993. **MEMBERSHIPS** Nebraska Bar Assn, 1978-; Big Sisters of Omaha, 1977-78; National Contract Management Assn, Wiesbaden, Germany, chapter president, 1985-87; Air Force Cadet Officer Mentor Program, executive board, 1991-; American Bar Assn, Government Contracts Section, 1991-. **CONTACT ADDRESS** Sawyer & Myerberg, 21689 Great Mills Rd, Lexington Park, MD 20653.

MCNULTY, JOHN K.
PERSONAL Born 10/13/1934, Buffalo, NY, m, 1955, 3 children **DISCIPLINE** LAW **EDUCATION** Swarthmore Col, AB, 56; Yale Law Sch, JD, 59. **CAREER** Law Clerk, Hon Hugo L Black, U S Supreme Ct, 59-60; Assoc, Jones Day Corkley & Reeves Law Firm, 60-64; Prof, Univ Calif, 64-. **HONORS AND AWARDS** Phi Beta Kappa; Guggenheim Fel, 77. **MEMBERSHIPS** Am Law Inst, Int Fiscal Asn, ABA. **RESEARCH** Law of taxation. **SELECTED PUBLICATIONS** Auth, Federal Income Taxation of Individuals, Corporations and Partnerships, 4th Ed, 85; auth, Federal Estate and Gift Taxation, 5th Ed, 94; auth, Federal Income Taxation of Individuals, 6th Ed, 99; auth, Flat Tax, Consumption Tax, Consumption-Type Income Tax Proposals, 00. **CONTACT ADDRESS** Dept Law, Univ of California, Berkeley, 355 Boalt Hall, Berkeley, CA 94720-0001. **EMAIL** mcnultyj@law.berkeley.edu

MCNUTT, PAULA M.
PERSONAL Born 03/12/1955, Denver, CO, s **DISCIPLINE** HEBREW BIBLE, ANTHROPOLOGY AND ARCHAEOLOGY **EDUCATION** Univ Colorado, BA, 78; Univ Montana, MA, 83; Vanderbilt Univ, PhD, 89. **CAREER** Prof, Canisius Col, 87-. **HONORS AND AWARDS** NEH Fel for Col Tchr, 94-95. **MEMBERSHIPS** Amer Acad Relig; Soc Bibl Lit, Cath Bibl Asn, Amer Sch Oriental Res, Archaeol Inst Amer **RESEARCH** Social world of ancient Israel; social roles and statuses of artisans; religion and technology. **SELECTED PUBLICATIONS** Reconstructing the Society of Ancient Israel, Libr of Ancient Israel Series, Louisville, Westminster John Knox Press, 99; The Kenites, the Midianites, and the Rechabites as Marginal Mediators in Ancient Israelite Tradition, Semeia 67, p 109-132, 94; coauth with James W. Flanagan, David W. McCreery and Khair Yassin, Preliminary Report of the 1993 Excavations at Tell Nimrin, Jordan, Ann of the Dept of Antiquities of Jordan, XXXVIII, pp 205-244, 94; Kenites, P. 407 in The Oxford Companion to the Bible, Bruce M. Metzger and Michael D. Coogan eds, Oxford Univ Press, 93; The Development and Adoption of Iron Technology in the Ancient Near East, Proceedings: The Eastern Great Lakes Bibilical Society, 12, pp 47-66, 92; The African Ironsmith as Marginal Mediator: A Symbolic Analysis, Journ of Ritual Studies, 5/2, pp 75-98, 91; The Forging of Israel: Iron Technology, Symbolism, and Tradition in Ancient Society, The Social World of Biblical Antiquity Series, 8, Sheffield, Almond Press, 90; Sociology of the Old Testament, pp 835-839, Mercer Dict of the Bible, Macon, GA, Mercer Univ Press, 90; Egypt as an Iron Furnace: A Metaphor of Transformation, pp 293-301, Society of Biblical Literature 1988 Seminar Papers, David J. Lull ed, Atlanta, Schol Press, 88; Interpreting Ancient Israel's Fold Traditions, Journ for the Study of the Old Testament, 39, pp 44-52, 87. **CONTACT ADDRESS** Canisius Col, 2001 Main St., Buffalo, NY 14208. **EMAIL** mcnutt@canisius.edu

MCPHERSON, JAMES ALAN
PERSONAL Born 09/16/1943, Savannah, GA, d, 1 child **DISCIPLINE** LITERATURE, HISTORY, LAW **EDUCATION** Morris Brown Col, BA, 65; Harvard Law School, LLB, 68; Writers Workshop, Univ IA, MFA, 71. **CAREER** Lect, Univ CA at Santa Cruz, 69-71; asst prof, Morgan State Univ, 75-76; assoc prof, Univ VA, 76-81; prof, Univ IA, 81-. **HONORS AND AWARDS** Pulitzer Prize, 78; MacArthur Prize Fellows Award, 81. **MEMBERSHIPS** ACLU; NAACP; Authors Guild; Am Acad of Arts and Scis; fel, Ctr for Advanced Studies, Stanford Univ, 97-98. **RESEARCH** Law. **SELECTED PUBLICATIONS** Auth, Hue and Cry, 69; auth, Railroad, 73; auth, Elbow Room, 77; auth, Crabcakes, 98; Fatherly Daughter, 98. **CONTACT ADDRESS** Dept of English, The Univ of Iowa, Iowa City, IA 52242.

MCQUAID, KIM
PERSONAL Born 11/02/1947, Boothbay, ME **DISCIPLINE** AMERICAN HISTORY, ECONOMIC HISTORY **EDUCATION** Antioch Col, BA, 70; Northwestern Univ, MA, 73, PhD, 75. **CAREER** Asst prof hist, Lake Erie Col, 77- **HONORS AND AWARDS** Woodrow Wilson Fel, 70; Marv Ball Wash Prof Am Hist, Univ Col Dublin, 85-86; Fulbright Overseas Teaching Awd, Malaysia, 95-96. **MEMBERSHIPS** Econ Hist Asn; Bus Hist Conf; Soc Hist Technol; Am Hist Asn. **RESEARCH** American economic history; 20th century American business; evolution of United States welfare policies; science, technology, and society. **SELECTED PUBLICATIONS** Coauth, Creating the Welfare State: The Political Economy of Twentieth Century Reform, Praeger Spec Studies, 80, rev ed, Univ Press Kans, 92; auth, The Roundtable: Getting Results in Washington, Harvard Bus Rev, 5-6/81; Big Business and Presidential Power: from Roosevelt to Reagan, William Morrow & Co, autumn 82; coauth, Bureaucrats as Social Engineers: Federal Welfare Programs in Herbert Hoover's America, Am J Econ & Sociol, 10/80; Welfare Reform in the 1950's, The Social Serv Rev, 3/80; auth, Big Business and Government Policy in Post-New Deal America: From Depression to Detente, Antitrust Law & Econ Rev, 79; Big Business and Public Policy in the Contemporary United States, Quart Rev Econ & Bus, summer 80; auth, The Anxious Years: America in the Vietnam-Watergate Era, Basic Books, 89; Uneasy Partners: Big Business in American Politics, 1945-1990, Johns Hopkins Univ Press, 94. **CONTACT ADDRESS** Lake Erie Col, 391 W Washington St, Painesville, OH 44077-3389.

MCRAE, DONALD M.
DISCIPLINE LAW **EDUCATION** Otago Univ, LLB, LLM. **CAREER** Prof. **RESEARCH** International law. **SELECTED PUBLICATIONS** Auth, pubs on international law. **CONTACT ADDRESS** Fac Common Law, Univ of Ottawa, Fauteux Hall, 57 Louis Pasteur, Ottawa, ON, Canada K1N 6N5. **EMAIL** dmcrae@uottawa.ca

MCRAE, JOHN R.
DISCIPLINE RELIGIOUS STUDIES **EDUCATION** Yale Univ, PhD, 83. **CAREER** Assoc prof, Indiana Univ-Bloomington. **HONORS AND AWARDS** Henry Luce Found grant; Teaching Excellence Recognition Awd, Indiana Univ, 00. **MEMBERSHIPS** Founded Collaborative Learning Archive Initiative (CLAI). **RESEARCH** East Asian Buddhism; Zen Buddhism. **SELECTED PUBLICATIONS** Auth, The Northern School and the Formation of Early Ch'an Buddhism, Univ Hawaii, 86; **CONTACT ADDRESS** Dept of Religious Studies, Indiana Univ, Bloomington, Sycamore Hall 230, Bloomington, IN 47405. **EMAIL** jmcrae@indiana.edu

MCRAY, JOHN ROBERT
PERSONAL Born 12/17/1931, Holdenville, OK, m, 1957, 3 children **DISCIPLINE** RELIGION **EDUCATION** David Lipscomb Col, BA, 55; Harding Col, MA, 56; Univ Chicago, PhD(New Testament & Early Christian lit), 67. **CAREER** Asst prof Bible, Greek & church hist, Harding Col, 58-66; assoc prof, David Lipscomb Col, 66-71; res prof archaeol & geog, Albright Inst Archaeol Res, Israel, 72-73; prof relig studies, Mid Tenn State Univ, 73-80; prof New Testament, Wheaton Col Grad Sch, 80-, Rockefeller grant, 62-63. **HONORS AND AWARDS** J W McGarvey Awd, 60; Christian Res Found Awd, 62; Outstanding Teacher of the Year, Mid Tenn State Univ, spring 77. **MEMBERSHIPS** Southeast Sect Soc Bibl Lit (vpres, 77-78, pres, 78-79); Inst Bibl Res; Am Schs Orient Res; Int Orgn Septuatint & Cognate Studies; North Am Patristic Soc. **RESEARCH** New Testament exegesis; New Testament backgrounds and archaeology; Pauline Studies. **SELECTED PUBLICATIONS** Auth, New Testament Introduction and Survey, Harding, 61; The Eternal Kingdom, Gospel Light, 61; auth, Scripture and tradition in Irenaeus, 67, The church fathers in the second century, 69 & To Teleion in I Corinthians 13:10, 71, Restoration Quart; Charismata in the second century, Studia Patristica, 75; Apocalyptic and atonement in the Epistle to the Hebrews, 80 & Stewardship and scholarship, 81, Restoration Quart; Archaeology and the New Testament, Baker, 91. **CONTACT ADDRESS** Dept of Relig, Wheaton Col, Illinois, 501 E College Ave, Wheaton, IL 60187. **EMAIL** John.R.McRay@wheaton.edu

MCROBERT, JENNIFER
DISCIPLINE PHILOSOPHY **EDUCATION** Mount Allison Univ, BA; Dalhousie University, MA; Univ Western Ontario, PhD. **CAREER** Asst prof, 94-. **MEMBERSHIPS** N Am Kant Soc, 93-; Can Philos Asn, 96-; Can Soc Hist Philos Sci, 95-. **RESEARCH** Early modern philosophy; history and philosophy of science. **SELECTED PUBLICATIONS** Auth, Stephen R. Palmquist. Kant's System of Perspectives: An architectonic interpretation of the Critical philosophy, Can Philos Rev, 94; I. Kant's afterword to Samuel Thomas Soemmerring's On the Organ of the Soul, 96. **CONTACT ADDRESS** Philosophy Dept, Acadia Univ, Wolfville, NS, Canada B0P 1X0. **EMAIL** jennifer.mcrobert@acadiau.ca

MCSHANE, MARILYN
PERSONAL Born, MA, m **DISCIPLINE** CRIMINAL JUSTICE **EDUCATION** Am Technol Univ, BS, 79; MS, 91; Sam Houston Univ, PhD, 85. **CAREER** Prof, Dept of Criminal Justice, Northern Ariz Univ, Flagstaff, 97-00, chair, 97-99; prof, Juvenile Justice, Prairie View, Tex, 00-. **HONORS AND AWARDS** Tex Prof Counseling Licensure, 83-84; CSUSB, Sch of Soc Scis Prof Growth Awd, 94; Outstanding Reference Source of 1997, Am Library Asn. **MEMBERSHIPS** Acad of Criminal Justice Scis, Am Soc of Criminol, Asn of Criminal Justice Res. **RESEARCH** Criminal justice management, corrections, correctional administration, criminological theory, community corrections, research methods, evaluation research, juvenile delinquency, sex offenders, domestic violence. **SELECTED PUBLICATIONS** Coauth with Frank P. Williams III, A Reader in Criminological Theory, 2nd ed, Cincinnati: Anderson (98); coauth with Frank P. Williams and Ronald Akers, "Worry about victimization: An alternative and reliable measure for fear of crime," Western Criminology Rev, 2, 2 (Sept 99); coauth with Frank P. Williams III and Michael Dolny, "Predicting Parole Absconders," in The Prison J (forthcoming); coauth with David Marshall, "First to Fight: An Analysis of the Marine Subculture and Domestic Violence," in Domestic Violence in the Military, Peter Mercier and Judith Mercier, eds, Charles C. Thomas Pub Co (forthcoming); auth, "Minorities and Employment, Ch 16 in M. Nielsen and B. Perry, eds, Discovering Difference: Human and Cultural Relations in Criminal Justice, Needham Heights, MA: Allyn & Bacon (2000): 207-218. **CONTACT ADDRESS** Juvenile Justice Prog, Prairie View A&M Univ, PO Box 4017, Prairie View, TX 77446-4017.

MCVANN, MARK
PERSONAL Born 08/28/1950, Washington, DC, s **DISCIPLINE** BIBLICAL STUDIES **EDUCATION** Emory Univ, PhD, 84 **CAREER** Prof Relig Studies, Lewis Univ, 79-; vis prof Relig Studies, Manhattan Col, 94-95; Chair of Relig Studies, Learning Resource Ctr, Lewis Univ. **HONORS AND AWARDS** Cordilio Excellence in Scholar Awd, 97. **MEMBERSHIPS** Cath Bibl Assoc; Amer Acad Relig; Context Group; Col Theolog Soc. **RESEARCH** Ritual and Literary Symbols **SELECTED PUBLICATIONS** Biblical Studies: A Brief Introduction, in Sacred Adventure: An Introduction to Theology, forthcoming; Rev of JB Gibson's The Temptation of Jesus in Early Christianity, Bibl Theology Bulletin, forthcoming; Rev of MD Hooker's The Gospel According to Saint Mark, Bibl Theology Bulletin, 97. **CONTACT ADDRESS** Dept of Religious Studies, Lewis Univ, Rt 53, Romeoville, IL 60446. **EMAIL** mcvannma@lewisu.edu

MEAD, LISA M.
PERSONAL 1 child **DISCIPLINE** LAW **EDUCATION** Univ Tex, BSW,84; Univ Southern Calif, JD,89. **CAREER** Asst dean; past dir atty, Homeless Assistance Proj Public Coun; past state off prog coordr, Texas Coalition for Juvenile Justice; co-founder and bd mem, Law School's Public Interest Law Found. **HONORS AND AWARDS** Student Bar Association Faculty Appreciation Awd, University of Southern California Law School, 1995-1996; University of Southern California Public Interest Law Foundation Outstanding Graduate, 1993. **MEMBERSHIPS** Member, National Association of Law Placement (NALP) since 1993; NALP Educational Programming Committee, Member 1997-98; NALP Public Service Committee, Chair 1996-97, Vice-Chair 1995-96; Los Angeles Count Bar Association (LACBA) Homeless Committee, Board Member 1989-93; LACBA Individual Rights Section, Treasurer, 1991-93, Member 1989-95; USC Public Interest Law Foundation, Board Member 1988-92, 1993-present; Women Lawyers Association of Los Angeles, member. **SELECTED PUBLICATIONS** Auth, Sharing the Obligation: How Legal Educators and Employers Engender Professionalism, Ethical Responsibility, & Accountability. **CONTACT ADDRESS** School of Law, Univ of So California, University Park Campus, Los Angeles, CA 90089. **EMAIL** lmead@law.usc.edu.

MEAD, WALTER BRUCE
PERSONAL Born 05/25/1934, Cedar Rapids, IA, 1 child **DISCIPLINE** POLITICAL PHILOSOPHY **EDUCATION** Carlton Col BA, 56; Yale Univ MA, 60; Duke Univ, MA PhD, 62-68. **CAREER** Asst Prof, Lake Forest Col, 63-67; Assoc Prof and Prof, Ill State Univ, 67-95, Prof Emer, 95-. **HONORS AND AWARDS** Lake Forest Col, Outstanding Prof; Ill State Univ, Numerous Fellowships, Research Grants. **MEMBERSHIPS** Am Pol Sci Asn; Midwest Pol Sci Asn; So Pol Sci Asn; ed bd, J Pol. **RESEARCH** Philos of Mind; Value Theory; Michael Polanyi. **SELECTED PUBLICATIONS** Extremism and Cognition, Kendall Hunt Pub, 71; The United States Constitution, Univ SC Press, 87. **CONTACT ADDRESS** 4 Kenyon Crt, Bloomington, IL 61701. **EMAIL** wbmead@ilstu.edu

MEADE, DENIS
PERSONAL Born 10/16/1930, Des Moines, IA **DISCIPLINE** THEOLOGY, CHURCH HISTORY **EDUCATION** St Benedict's Col, Kans, AB, 52; Pontif Univ St Anselmo, Rome, STL, 56; Pontif Lateran Univ, JCD, 60. **CAREER** From instr to asst prof theol, 60-71, assoc prof, 71-80, prof relig Studies, Benedictine Col, 80-. **MEMBERSHIPS** Canon Law Soc Am; Federation Catholic Schs. **RESEARCH** Medieval monastic history: moral theology. **SELECTED PUBLICATIONS** Auth, From Turmoil to Solidarity: The Emergence of the Vallumbrosan Monastic Congregation, Am Benedictine Rev, 68. **CONTACT ADDRESS** Dept of Religious Studies, Benedictine Col, 1020 N 2nd St, Atchison, KS 66002-1499. **EMAIL** dmeade@benedictine.edu

MEADE, E. M.
PERSONAL Born 04/27/1962, Cambridge, MA, m, 2 children **DISCIPLINE** PHILOSOPHY **EDUCATION** Boston Col, PhD, 93. **CAREER** Assoc prof, Cedar Crest Col, 93- . **MEMBERSHIPS** APA; SPEP. **RESEARCH** Moral judgment; axiology; biomedical ethics; ethics pedagogy. **SELECTED PUBLICATIONS** Auth, The Commodification of Values, in Hannah Arendt: Twenty Years Later, MIT, 96. **CONTACT ADDRESS** Cedar Crest Col, 100 College Dr, Allentown, PA 18104. **EMAIL** emeade@cedarcrest.edu

MEADOR, DANIEL JOHN
PERSONAL Born 12/07/1926, Selma, AL, m, 1955, 3 children **DISCIPLINE** LAW **EDUCATION** Auburn Univ, BS, 49; Univ Ala, JD, 51; Harvard Univ, LLM, 54. **CAREER** Law clerk, Justice Thomas S Lawson, Ala Supreme Court, 53 & Justice Hugo L Black, US Supreme Court, 54-55; atty at law, Birmingham, Ala, 55-57; from assoc prof to prof law, Univ Va, 57-66; dean, Sch Law, Univ Ala, 66-70; James Monroe Prof Law, Univ Va, 70-94, Mem, Judicial Conf Fourth Circuit; Fulbright lectr, UK, 65-66; Asst Atty Gen, US, 77-79. **MEMBERSHIPS** Am Law Inst; Am Bar Asn; Am Soc Legal Hist. **RESEARCH** Federal judiciary; civil procedure; legal hist. **CONTACT ADDRESS** Law School, Univ of Virginia, Charlottesville, VA 22903.

MEADORS, GARY T.
PERSONAL Born 06/03/1945, Connersville, IN, m, 1967 **DISCIPLINE** GREEK, NEW TESTAMENT **EDUCATION** Grace Coll and Theol Sem. ThD, 83. **CAREER** Asst Prof, 79-83, Piedmont Baptist Coll; Prof of NT, 83-93, Grace Theol Sem; Prof of NT, 93-95, Baptist Sem of PA; Prof of NT, 95-, Grand Rapids Baptist Sem; Dean of the School of Theology, 00-. **HONORS AND AWARDS** Homer A. Kent Sr. Awd in Church History, 75; Summa cum laude Mdiv, 76; Alumni Educational Achievement Awd, 96. **MEMBERSHIPS** ETS, IBR, SBL. **RESEARCH** New Testament; Ethics. **SELECTED PUBLICATIONS** Auth, "John R.W. Stott on Social Action," GTJ 1:2 NS, 80; auth, "The Poor in the Beatituder of Matthew and Luke," GTJ 6:2 NS, 85; auth, Can a Believer Fall from Grace?, Spire 14:2, 86; auth, "New Testament Essays," Winona: BMH Books, 91; Discipleship-Another Nuance to Consider, Exposition 4:3, 93; Evangelical Dictionary of Biblical Theology, ed by Walter Elwell, Grand Rapids, Baker Book House, 96; Love is the Law of Spiritual Formation, Presidential address to the Midwest Region Meeting of the Evangelical Theological Society, 98; Why Are They Looking At Jesus?, The Jesus Seminar, Baptist Bulletin, 97. **CONTACT ADDRESS** Grand Rapids Baptist Sem, 1001 E Beltline NE, Grand Rapids, MI 49525. **EMAIL** gary_t_meadors@cornerstone.edu

MEAGHER, ROBERT FRANCIS
PERSONAL Born 05/13/1927, Brooklyn, NY **DISCIPLINE** INTERNATIONAL LAW AND DEVELOPMENT **EDUCATION** City Col New York, BSS, 49; Yale Univ, LLB, 52. **CAREER** Leader specialist, Foreign Affairs Int Orgn State Dept grant, India, 53, Pakistan, 54; lawyer corp finance, Winthrop, Stimson, Putnam & Roberts, New York, 54-58; legal officer int law & contracts, UN, Beirut, 58-59; asst dir pub int develop finance foreign aid proj, Columbia Univ Law Sch, 61-65, assoc dir int legal res, 65-68; Prof Int Law, Fletcher Sch Law & Diplomacy, Tufts Univ, 67-, Int Legal Ctr grant, 71; Agency Int Develop grant, 72-74; adj prof law, Columbia Univ, 72; consult, Harvard Develop Adv Serv, 72-; Adj Prof Law, Columbia Univ, 72-; Rockefeller Found grant, 75-76; sr fel, Overseas Develop Corp, 75-76; Bellagie grant, 76; Am participant, Int Commun Agency India, Bangladesh, 79, Kuwait, Quatar, Nepal, Bangladesh, Thailand, Sri Lanka, Indonesia & Australia, 81; vis prof int law, Monash & Melbourne Univs, Australia, 81. **MEMBERSHIPS** African Law Asn Am (pres, 67-69); Am Foreign Law Asn; Int Law Asn; Am Bar Asn; Am Soc Int Law. **RESEARCH** Role of law in the development process; private investment and foreign aid; international economic and social organizations. **SELECTED PUBLICATIONS** Auth, The United Nations--Challenges of Law and Development--Introduction, Harvard Int Law J, vol 0036, 95. **CONTACT ADDRESS** Fletcher Sch of Law & Diplomacy, Tufts Univ, Medford, Medford, MA 02111.

MEANS, JAMES
PERSONAL Born 07/12/1932, Springfield, IL, m, 6 children **DISCIPLINE** PASTORAL MINISTRIES AND HOMILETICS **EDUCATION** Wheaton Col, BA; Denver Sem, BD; Univ Denver, MA; PhD. **CAREER** Prof, Denver Sem, 68-. **HONORS AND AWARDS** Gold Medallion Bk Awd winner; sr pastor, s gables evangel free church; pastor, evangel free churches in loomis and omaha, nebr. **MEMBERSHIPS** Soc for Pastoral Theol; Assn of Practical Theol. **SELECTED PUBLICATIONS** Auth, Leadership in Christian Ministry; auth, Effective Pastors for a New Century. **CONTACT ADDRESS** Denver Conservative Baptist Sem, PO Box 10000, Denver, CO 80250. **EMAIL** jimm@densem.edu

MEANY, MARY WALSH
DISCIPLINE RELIGIOUS STUDIES **EDUCATION** Spalding Univ, BA, 65; Fordham Univ, MA, 67, PhD, 75. **CAREER** Instr, Franciscan Inst, St Bonaventure Univ, 97; co-ch, Hist Christianity Sect, Am Acad Rel, 88-94; Col serv, ch, Core Rev Comt, 92-95 & Franciscan Tradition Comt, 90-96; mem, Jewish Christian Inst Plan Bd; 1st Yr Stud Adv. **HONORS AND AWARDS** Co-organizer, sessions on, The Appropriation of the Vita Christi Tradition in Off and Popular Piety, Kalamazoo, 90-92 & 94-96. **SELECTED PUBLICATIONS** Auth, Angela of Foligno: Destructuring of Identity, Divine Representations: Postmodernism and Spirituality, Paulist Press, 94. **CONTACT ADDRESS** Dept of Relig Studies, Siena Col, 515 Loudon Rd., Loudonville, NY 12211-1462.

MEDINE, CAROLYN JONES
PERSONAL Born 12/18/1958, Burlington, NC, m, 1997 **DISCIPLINE** RELIGIOUS STUDIES **EDUCATION** Univ NCar, Chapel Hill, BA, 80; MA, 83; Univ Va, PhD, 91. **CAREER** Adj fac, 87, Elon Col; vis lectr, 86, 87, 88, UNC Chapel Hill; acting asst prof, 88-91, asst prof, 91-98, assoc prof, La St Univ, 98-99; prof, Univ of Ga, 00-. **HONORS AND AWARDS** Ford Found Postdoctoral Fel, 93-94. **MEMBERSHIPS** Am Academy of Relig; Southeastern Commission for the Study of Relig; Toni Morrison Soc; Soc for Values in Higher Education. **RESEARCH** Religion & lit, African-Am lit, classical & modern lit. **CONTACT ADDRESS** Dept of Relig, Univ of Georgia, 206 Peabody Hall, Athens, GA 30602. **EMAIL** dr_cmjones@hotmail.com

MEDLEY, MARK S.
PERSONAL Born 04/10/1965, Graham, NC, m, 1988, 1 child **DISCIPLINE** RELIGIOUS STUDIES **EDUCATION** Univ NC at Chapel Hill, BS, 87; Southern Baptist Theol Sem, Mdiv, 90; PhD, 95; Univ Notre Dame, additional studies, 93. **CAREER** Adj prof, Lexington Theol Sem, 95-98; from adj prof to asst prof, Campbellsville Univ, 95-; adj prof, Ind Univ Southeast, 96-98. **HONORS AND AWARDS** Garret Teaching Fel, The Southern Baptist Theol Sem, 87 & 91-93; Rice-Judson Scholars Awd, The Southern Baptist Theol Sem. **MEMBERSHIPS** Am Acad of Relig, Nat Asn of Baptist Professors of Relig, Christian Theol Res Fel. **RESEARCH** Trinitarian Theology, Doctrine of God, Ecclesiology, Postmodernism/Postmodern Theology. **SELECTED PUBLICATIONS** Auth, "Emancipatory Solidarity: The Redemptive Significance of Jesus in Mark," Perspectives in Relig Studies Volume 21 (94): 5-22; auth, "Becoming Human Together: Imaging the Triune God," Perspectives in Relig Studies Volume 23 (96): 289-316; auth, "Art and Soul: A Town's Faith Communities Join for a Celebration of the Arts," The Christian Ministry Volume 29 (98): 25-26. **CONTACT ADDRESS** Dept Christian Studies, Campbellsville Univ, 1 University Dr, Campbellsville, KY 42718-2190. **EMAIL** mmedley@campbellsvil.edu

MEDLIN, S. ALAN
DISCIPLINE TRUSTS AND ESTATES, FIDUCIARY ADMINISTRATION, REAL ESTATE TRANSACTIONS AND **EDUCATION** Univ SC, BA, 76, JD, 79. **CAREER** Prof, Univ of SC. **SELECTED PUBLICATIONS** Coed, Probate Practice Reporter; ed, Amer Bar Asn, Real Property, Probate and Trust J. **CONTACT ADDRESS** School of Law, Univ of So Carolina, Columbia, Law Center, Columbia, SC 29208. **EMAIL** Alan@law.law.sc.edu

MEEHAN, M. JOHANNA
PERSONAL Born 02/01/1956, Winchester, MA, 2 children **DISCIPLINE** PHILOSOPHY **EDUCATION** Brandeis Univ, BA, 77; Boston Univ, MA, PhD, 90. **CAREER** Tchg asst, Instr, 79-83, Boston Univ; instr, 83-84, 89-90, Univ MS; inst, Bates Col, 86-87; instr, Brandeis Univ, 88; instr, Emerson Col, 89-90; asst prof, Grinnell Col, 90-99. **HONORS AND AWARDS** Machette Prize, 81; Borden Parker Bowne Scholar, 84; Col Lib Arts Awd, 84; Grad Sch Dissertation Scholar, 85; DAAD, 85; Peter Bertocci Fel, 86; GTE Grant, 90; NEH Speaker Grant, 93; Harris Fel, 94; Committee Status Women, 98. **MEMBERSHIPS** Am Philos Asn; Soc Phenomenology; Existentialist Philos; Critical Theory Round Table. **RESEARCH** Social political philosophy; continental philosophy; feminism pychoanalytic theory. **SELECTED PUBLICATIONS** Auth, Feminists Read Habermas: Gendering the Subject of Discourse, 95; ed, intro, Feminists Read Habermas: Gendering the Subject of Discourses, 95; auth, art, Communicative Ethics, 97; auth, art, Interpretation and the Social Sciences, 97; auth, art, Plurality, Autonomy and the Right to Die, 98. **CONTACT ADDRESS** Dept of Philosophy, Grinnell Col, Grinnell, IA 50112. **EMAIL** meehan@grinnell.edu

MEEKS, WAYNE ATHERTON
PERSONAL Born 01/08/1932, Aliceville, AL, m, 1954, 3 children **DISCIPLINE** RELIGION **EDUCATION** Univ Ala, BS, 53; Austin Presby Theol Sem, BD, 56; Yale Univ, MA, 63, PhD(New Testament studies), 65. **CAREER** Instr relig, Dartmouth Col, 64-65; from asst prof to assoc prof, Ind Univ, Bloomington, 66-69; assoc prof, 69-73, Prof Relig Studies, Yale Univ, 73-99, Guggenheim fel, 79-80; Emer 00-. **HONORS AND AWARDS** Fel, British Acad, 92-; Nat Endowment for Humanities fel, 75-76;. **MEMBERSHIPS** Soc Bibl Lit; Am Acad Relig; Soc New Testament Studies. **RESEARCH** New Testament studies; early Christian ethics; religions in Greco-Roman world. **SELECTED PUBLICATIONS** Co-ed, God's Christ and His People, Norwegian Univ Press, 77; coauth, Jews and Christians in Antioch, Soc Bibl Lit, 78; ed, Zur Soziologie des Urchristentums, Kaiser, 79; ed, The Library of Early Christianity (series), Westminster, 82-87; auth, The First Urban Christians, Yale Univ Press, 83; auth, The Moral World of the First Christians, Westminster, 86; assoc ed, Harper Bible commentary, Harper Collins, 88; co-ed, Greeks, Romans, and Christians, Fortress, 90; auth, The Origins of Christian Morality, Yale Univ Press, 93; co-ed, The Future of Christology, Fortress, 93; gen ed, Harper Collins Study Bible, Harper Collins, 93. **CONTACT ADDRESS** Dept of Relig Studies, Yale Univ, PO Box 208287, New Haven, CT 06520-8287. **EMAIL** wayne.meeks@yale.edu

MEERBOTE, RALF
PERSONAL Born 05/08/1942, Merseburg, Germany **DISCIPLINE** HISTORY OF MODERN PHILOSOPHY **EDUCATION** Univ Chicago, BS, 64; Harvard Univ, MA, 67, PhD(philos), 70. **CAREER** Asst prof philos, Univ Ill, Chicago Circle, 69-73, assoc prof, 73-80; Assoc Prof Philos, Univ Rochester, 80-, Fulbright sr res fel, 76-77; Prof philos, Univ of Rochester, 93-. **MEMBERSHIPS** Am Philos Asn; Kantgesellschaft, North Am Kent Soc. **RESEARCH** Kant's metaphysics and theory of knowledge; theory of knowledge; aesthetics. **SELECTED PUBLICATIONS** Auth, The unknowability of things in themselves, Proc Int Kant Cong, Holland, 72; Kant's use of the notions of objective validity and objective reality, Kant Studien, 72; The distinction between derivative and non-derivative knowledge, Philos Studies, 73; Erkenntnisvorschriften, Akten des 4 Int Kant Kongresses, de Gruyter, Berlin, 74; Fallibilism and the possibility of being mistaken, Philos Studies, 77; Radical Failure, Grazer Philos Studien, 78; Kant on Intuitivity, Synthese, 81; auth, Kant's Funchionalism, in Historical Foundations of Cognitive Science Reidel Dondrecht, 89; auth, The Singularity of Pure Judgments of Fasle, in Kant's Aesthetics, deGrytec, Berlin, 98; auth, Kant, in a Companion to the Philosophers, Blackwell, Oxford, 99. **CONTACT ADDRESS** Dept of Philosophy, Univ of Rochester, Rochester, NY 14627.

MEHL, PETER J.
PERSONAL Born 06/28/1956, m, 2 children **DISCIPLINE** PHILOSOPHY, RELIGION **EDUCATION** Univ Chicago, MA, 83, PhD, 89. **CAREER** Assoc prof, dir Interdisciplinary

Relig Stud, 94- , asst dean, Col Lib Arts, 96-98, interim dean, 98-00; dir of gen ed, 99- . **MEMBERSHIPS** APA; Am Acad Relig; Soc for Philos in Contemp World; Counc of Colleges of Arts and Sci. **RESEARCH** Philosophical and religious ethica; applied ethica; philosophy of religion; religion and culture; moral psychology; Kierkegaard. **SELECTED PUBLICATIONS** Auth, "The Self Well Lost," Philos in the Contemp World, 95; "Religion, Philosophy and Public Life," Theol and Public Policy, 95; "Moral Virtue, Mental Health and Happiness," International Kierkegaard Commentary on Kierkegaard's Either/Or, Pt 2, Mercer Univ, 95; "William James' Ethics and the New Causuistry," Int J of Applied Philos, 96. **CONTACT ADDRESS** Col of Liberal Arts, Univ of Central Arkansas, 201 Donaghey Ave, Conway, AR 72035-5003. **EMAIL** peterm@mail.uca.edu

MEHLMAN, MAXWELL
PERSONAL Born 11/04/1948, Washington, DC, m, 1979, 2 children **DISCIPLINE** POLITICAL SCIENCE, POLITICS AND ECONOMICS, AND LAW **EDUCATION** Reed Col, BA, 70; Oxford Univ, BA, 72; Yale Law Sch, JD, 75. **CAREER** Atty, Arnold & Porter, Wash, DC, 75-84; assoc prof of law, 87-90, asst prof, 84-87; dir, The Law Med Ctr, Case Western Reserve Univ, 88-; Arthur E. Petersilge prof of law, Case Western Reserve Univ, 97-; Prof of Biomedical Ehtnics, CWRU School of Medicine. **HONORS AND AWARDS** Rhodes Scholar, Ore, 70; Phi Beta Kappa, 70. **MEMBERSHIPS** Amer Soc of Law, Med and Ethics. **RESEARCH** Health care law and policy; Ethical, legal and policy issues in human genetics. **SELECTED PUBLICATIONS** Auth, Getting a Handle on Coverage Decisions: If Not Case Law, Then What?, 31, Ind Law Rev, 75, 98; co-auth, Genetic Testing for Cancer Risk: How to Reconcile the Conflicts, 279, JAMA, 179, 98; co-auth, Access to the Genome: The Challenge to Equality, Georgetown Univ Press, 98; co-auth, When Do Health Care Decisions Discriminate Against Persons With Disabilities? 22, Jour of Health Polit, Policy and Law, 1385, 97; co-auth, Enhancing Cognition in the Intellectually Intact: Possibilities and Pitfalls, 27, Hastings Ctr Report, 14, 97; auth, Access to the Genome and Federal Entitlement Programs, The Human Genome Project and the Future of Health Care, Ind Univ Press, 113-132, 96; auth, Historical Trends in Malpractice Litigation, Physician Exec and the Law: Issues and Trends in Liability, Amer Col of Physicians Exec, 21-44, 96; auth, Medical Advocates: A Call for a New Profession, 1, Widener Law Rev, 299, 96; co-auth, The Need for Anonymous Counseling and Testing, 58, Amer Jour Human Genetics, 393-397, 96; co-ed, Justice and Health Care: Comparative Perspectives, John Wiley & Sons, 95. **CONTACT ADDRESS** 11075 East Blvd., Cleveland, OH 44106.

MEHTA, MAHESH MAGANLAL
PERSONAL Born Bombay, India **DISCIPLINE** PHILOSOPHIES AND RELIGIONS OF INDIA **EDUCATION** Univ Bombay, BA, 53, MA, 55, LLB, 57, PhD(Sanskrit), 64. **CAREER** Prof Sanskrit, Gujarat Univ, India, 58-61; lectr, Mithibai Col, Univ Bombay, 61-63 and Wilson Col, 63-67; fel, Univ Pa, 67-68, lectr Indian philos and relig, 68-69; prof, 69-73, Univ Windsor, 73-99; prof emer, Univ Windsor, 99-. **MEMBERSHIPS** Am Orient Soc; Asn Asian Studies; Can Soc Asian Studies; Bhandarkar Orient Res Inst; All-India Orient Cong. **RESEARCH** Advaita Vedanta; Mahayana Buddhism: Madhyamika and Yogacara. **CONTACT ADDRESS** Dept of Asian Studies, Univ of Windsor, Windsor, ON, Canada N9B 3P4. **EMAIL** mmehta@uwindsor.ca

MEHURON, KATE
DISCIPLINE PHILOSOPHY **EDUCATION** Col Santa Fe, BA; Univ Denver, MA; Vanderbilt Univ, PhD. **CAREER** Prof, Eastern Michigan Univ. **HONORS AND AWARDS** Distinguished fac tchg awd, 92; Mich Governing Boards Distinguished fac awd, 95. **RESEARCH** History of philosophy; 19th and 20th century continental thought, feminist theory, HIV/AIDS issues. **SELECTED PUBLICATIONS** Ed, Free Spirits: Feminist Philosophers On Culture, Prentice-Hall, 95. **CONTACT ADDRESS** Dept of History and Philosophy, Eastern Michigan Univ, 701 Pray-Harrold, Ypsilanti, MI 48197. **EMAIL** kate.mehuron@emich.edu

MEIDINGER, ERROL ELDON
PERSONAL Born 04/28/1952, Bismarck, ND, m, 1981, 2 children **DISCIPLINE** LAW **EDUCATION** Univ ND, BA, 74; Northwestern Univ, MA, 77, JD, 79, PhD, 87. **CAREER** Legis aid, NDak State Legis, 73; resident assoc, Argonne Nat Lab, 76-77; Assoc Prof, 82-87, Prof Law & Jurisprudence, State Univ NY Buffalo, 87-, Vis prof, Syracuse Univ, 91-92; Vis prof, Univ of Wash, 93-94; Dir, Environmental Law & Policy Prog, 98, 01-; Vice Dean of Law for Interdisciplinary and International Initiatives **HONORS AND AWARDS** Sr Fel, Lewis & Clark Col, 79-82. **MEMBERSHIPS** Law & Soc Asn; Int Asn Study Common Property. **RESEARCH** Property syst and soc rel; environmental policy; "private" environmental standard setting. **SELECTED PUBLICATIONS** Co-auth, Applied Time Series Analysis, 80 & Interrupted Time Series Analysis, 80; Sage; coauth, Science Advocacy is Inevitable: Deal with It, Proceedings of the Soc of Am Foresters, 96; auth, Organizational and Legal Challenges for Ecosystem Management, In Creating a Forestry for the 21st Century: The Science of Ecosystem Management, Island Press, 97; Look Who's Making the Rules: The Roles of the FSC and ISO in International Environmental Policy, Human Ecol Rev, 97; Laws and Institutions in Cross-Boundary Stewardship, In Stewardship Across Boundaries, Island Press, 98; auth, "Reconstituting Haudenosaunee Law, Sovereignty, and Governance," Buffalo Law Review 46 (98): 799-804; auth, "Private Environmental Standard Setting, Human Rights, and Human Communities," Buffalo Environmental Law J 9 (99-00): 123-237; auth, "Incorporation of Private Environmental Certification Systems in Formal Legal Systems: the US Case," Environmental Law Network International (00): 71-86; auth, "Private Environmental Certification Systems and US Environmental Law: Closer than You May Think," Environmental Law Reporter 31 (01): 10162-10179. **CONTACT ADDRESS** Sch of Law, SUNY, Buffalo, 719 O'Brien Hall, North Campus, Buffalo, NY 14260-1100. **EMAIL** eemeid@buffalo.edu

MEIER, JOHN P.
PERSONAL Born 08/08/1942, New York, NY **DISCIPLINE** BIBLICAL STUDIES **EDUCATION** St Joseph Col, BA, 64; Gregorian Univ, STL, 68; Bibl Inst, SSD, 76. **CAREER** Prof of New Testament, St Joseph's Sem, 72-84; prof of New Testament, Catholic Univ of Am, 84-98; prof of New Testament, Univ of Notre Dame, 98- . **HONORS AND AWARDS** Summa Cum Laude with gold medal, 68, 76; Catholic Press Asn best book award 84; Bibl Archaeol Soc best book award, 93. **MEMBERSHIPS** CBA; SBL; SNTS; CTSA. **RESEARCH** Historical Jesus; New Testament Christology; Gospel of Matthew. **SELECTED PUBLICATIONS** Auth, Why Search for the Historical Jesus? Bible Rev, 93; auth, A Marginal Jew--Retrospect and Prospect, in Archbishop Gerety Lectures, 1992-1993, Seton Hall Univ, 93; auth, The Miracles of Jesus: Three Basic Questions for the Historian, in The Santa Clara Lectures, v.1, no.1, Santa Clara Univ, 94; auth, A Marginal Jew: Rethinking the Historical Jesus, v 2: Mentor, Message, and Miracles, Doubleday, 94; auth, Happy the Eyes That See: The Tradition, Message, and Authenticity of Luke 10:23-24 par, in Bartelt ed, Fortunate the Eyes That See: David Noel Freedman Festschrift, Eerdmans, 95; auth, Miracles and Modern Minds, Catholic World, 95; auth, The Eucharist at the Last Supper: Did It Happen? Theol Dig, 96; auth, Dividing Lines in Jesus Research Today: Through Dialectical Negation to a Positive Sketch, Interpretation, 96; auth, The Quest for the Historical Jesus as a Truly Historical Project, Grail: An Ecumenical J, 96; auth, The Miracles of Jesus: Three Basic Questions for the Historian, Dialogue: A J of Mormon Thought, 96; auth, four essays: John 1:1-18, John 20:19-23, The Jerusalem Council, The Conflict at Antioch, Mid-Stream, 97; auth, The Circle of the Twelve: Did It Exist During Jesus' Public Ministry, JBL, 97; auth, On Retrojecting Later Questions from Later Texts: A Reply to Richard Bauckham, CBQ, 97. **CONTACT ADDRESS** Dept of Theology, Univ of Notre Dame, Notre Dame, IN 46556. **EMAIL** meier.8@nd.edu

MEIKELJOHN, DONALD
PERSONAL Born 06/01/1909, Providence, RI, m, 1941, 4 children **DISCIPLINE** PHILOSOPHY **EDUCATION** Univ Wisconsin, AB, 30; Harvard Univ, PhD, 36. **CAREER** Instr, 36-38, Dartmouth; Assoc Prof, 38-46, WM & Mary; Assoc Prof to Prof, 46-63, Univ of Chicago Coll; Prof, 63-74, Syracuse Univ. **HONORS AND AWARDS** Bechtal Prize Essay, Harvard, 37; Excellence in Tchg, Chicago, 54. **MEMBERSHIPS** Amer Philos Assoc; AAUP. **RESEARCH** Political Theory. **SELECTED PUBLICATIONS** Auth, Freedom and the Public, 65; Articles in Philosophical and Legal Journals. **CONTACT ADDRESS** 822 Maryland Ave, Syracuse, NY 13210-2501.

MEILAENDER, GILBERT
DISCIPLINE PHILOSOPHY **EDUCATION** Concordia Col Ft Wayne, BA, 68; Concordia Sem St Louis, Mdiv, 72; Princeton Univ, PhD, 76. **CAREER** Philos, Valparaiso Univ. **HONORS AND AWARDS** NEH Fel Col Tchrs, 89-90 and 81-82; bd dir, soc christ ethics, 95-; ed adv bd, first things; assoc ed, j relig ethics, 92-; ed bd, dialog, 88-; ed bd, ann soc relig ethics, 88-90; assoc ed, relig studies rev, 85-91; ed bd, j relig ethics, 82-; fel, the hastings ctr. **MEMBERSHIPS** Am Theol Soc; Soc Christ Ethics. **SELECTED PUBLICATIONS** Auth, Body, Soul, and Bioethics, Notre Dame UP, 95; Faith and Faithfulness: Basic Themes in Christian Ethics, Notre Dame UP, 91; Veritatis Slendor: Reopening Some Questions of the Reformation, J Relig Ethics, 95; Products of the Will: Robertson's Children of Choice, Washington and Lee Law Rev, 95; When Harry and Sally Read the Nicomachean Ethics: Friendship Between Men and Women in The Changing Face of Friendship, Notre Dame UP, 94; Terra es animata: On Having a Life, Hastings Ctr Rpt, 93; 'Love's Casuistry': Paul Ramsey on Caring for the Terminally Ill, J Relig Ethics, 91; A View From Somewhere: The Political Thought of Michael Walzer, Rel Studies Rev, 90. **CONTACT ADDRESS** Valparaiso Univ, 1500 E Lincoln Way, Valparaiso, IN 46383-6493.

MEINWALD, CONSTANCE
DISCIPLINE PHILOSOPHY **EDUCATION** Princeton Univ, PhD, 87. **CAREER** Assoc prof, Univ IL at Chicago. **RESEARCH** Ancient philos. **SELECTED PUBLICATIONS** Auth, Plato's Parmenides, Oxford, 91; Good-bye to the Third Man, Cambridge, 92. **CONTACT ADDRESS** Philos Dept, Univ of Illinois, Chicago, S Halsted St, PO Box 705, Chicago, IL 60607.

MEISEL, ALAN
PERSONAL Born 12/24/1946, Newark, NJ, m, 2 children **DISCIPLINE** LAW **EDUCATION** Yale Univ, BA, 68; Yale Law School, JD, 72. **CAREER** Prof of Law, 76-; Dickie, McCamey & Chilcote prof of Bioethics, 95-; founder and dir, Ctr for Bioethics and Health Law, Univ Pittsburgh School of Law. **HONORS AND AWARDS** Am Asn of Publishers, Most Outstanding Book in Legal and Accounting Practice Category for The Right to Die, 89; Am Fed of Clinical Res, Nellie Westerman Prize in Medical Ethics for Ethical Factors in the Allocation of Experimental Medical Therapies: The Chronic Left-Ventricular Assist Device, 90; fel, Hastings Center. **MEMBERSHIPS** Am Bar Asn; Am Health Lawyers Asn; Am Socv of Bioethics and Humanities; Am Soc of Law, Medicine and Ethics; Int Asn of Bioethics. **RESEARCH** Health law; bioethics; informed consent; end-of-life decision making. **SELECTED PUBLICATIONS** Auth, Legal Myths About Terminating Life Support, Archives of Internal Medicine, 91; The Legal Concensus About Foregoing Life-Sustaining Treatment: Its Status and Its Prospects, Kennedy Inst of Ethics J, 92; Barriers to Foregoing Nutrition and Hydration in Nursing Homes, Am J of Law and Medicine, 95; The Right to Die, John Wiley & Sons, 95; The Right to Die: A Case Study in American Law Making, European J Health Law, 96; Legal Myths About Informed Consent, Archives of Internal Medicine, with M G Kucezewski, 96, condensed in Resident Physician, 97; Physician-Assisted Suicide: A Roadmap for State Courts, Fordham Urban L J, 97. **CONTACT ADDRESS** School of Law, Univ of Pittsburgh, Pittsburgh, PA 15260. **EMAIL** meisel@law.pitt.edu

MELCHIONNE, KEVIN
DISCIPLINE PHILOSOPHY **EDUCATION** SUNY, Stony Brook, PhD, 95. **CAREER** Dir, exhibits, Tyler Schl of Art, Temple Univ. **HONORS AND AWARDS** Renwick Fel, Natl Museum of Amer Art, Smithsonian Inst. **MEMBERSHIPS** Col Art Assn; Amer Assn of Museums. **RESEARCH** Aesthetics; cult stud; contemporary art. **SELECTED PUBLICATIONS** Rev, Werner Muensterberger's Collecting: An Unruly Passion: Psychological Perspectives, Phil 7 Lit, vol 20, 96; rev, Christopher Reed's Not at Home: the Suppression of the Domestic in Modern Art and Architecture, J of Aesthetics & Art Criticism, vol 55, 97; art, Living in Glass Houses: Decoration, Neatness and the Art of Domesticity, J of Aesthetics and Art Criticism, Spec issue on Environ Aesthetics, vol 56, 98; auth, Artistic Dropouts, Aesthetics: The Big Questions, Blackwell, 98; auth, Drawing upon Drawing: the Reclamation Drawings of Michael Lucero, Amer Ceramics, 98; art, Re-Thinking Site-Specificity in Public Art: some Critical and Philosophical Problems, Art Criticism, vol 12, 98; art, The Aesthetics of Collecting, Phil & Lit, 98; art, Of Bookworms and Busybees: Cultural Theory in the Age of Do-It-Yourselfing, J of Aesthetics & Art Criticism, 99. **CONTACT ADDRESS** Temple Univ, Beech & Penrose Aves, Elkins Park, PA 19027.

MELE, ALFRED R.
DISCIPLINE CLASSICS AND PHILOSOPHY **EDUCATION** Wayne State Univ, BA, 73; Univ MI, PhD, 79. **CAREER** Vail Prof Philos, Davidson Col; William H. and Lucyle T. Werkmeister Prof of Philos, Fla State Univ. **RESEARCH** Cognitive philos; hist of ancient philos. **SELECTED PUBLICATIONS** Auth, Irrationality, Oxford Univ Press, 87; auth, Springs of Action, Oxford Univ Press, 92; coed, Mental Causation, Clarendon, 93; auth, Autonomous Agents, Oxford Univ Press, 95; ed, The Philosophy of Action, Oxford Univ Press, 97; auth, Self-Deception Unmasked, Princeton Univ Press, 01. **CONTACT ADDRESS** Dept of Philos, Florida State Univ, 288 Dodd Hall, Tallahassee, FL 32306-1500. **EMAIL** almele@mailer.fsu.edu

MELLEMA, GREGORY
PERSONAL Born 06/22/1948, Chicago, IL, m, 1973, 2 children **DISCIPLINE** PHILOSOPHY **EDUCATION** Univ MI, MBA, 78; Univ MA, PhD, 74. **CAREER** Instr, 74-75, St. Olaf Col; asst prof, 75-76, assoc prof, prof, 78-, Calvin Col. **HONORS AND AWARDS** Who's Who in the World; Who's Who in Am Ed. **MEMBERSHIPS** APA; Soc of Christian Philos. **RESEARCH** Ethics. **SELECTED PUBLICATIONS** Auth, On Being Fully Responsible, Am Philos Quart, 84; auth, Quasi-Supererogation, Philos Stud, 87; auth, Individuals, Groups, and Shared Moral Responsibility, Peter Lang, Inc, 88; auth, Beyond the Call of Duty, SUNY Press, 91; auth, Offense and Virtue Ethics, Can J of Philos, 91; auth, Supererogation, Blame, and the Limits of Obligation, Philosophia, 94; auth, Collective Responsibility, Rodopi, 97; auth, Collective Guilt, Encycl of Applied Ethics, 98. **CONTACT ADDRESS** Dept of Philosophy, Calvin Col, Grand Rapids, MI 49546. **EMAIL** mell@calvin.edu

MELLI, MARYGOLD SHIRE
PERSONAL Born 02/08/1926, Rhinelandr, WI, m, 1950, 4 children **DISCIPLINE** LAW **EDUCATION** Univ Wis, Ba, 47, LLB, 50. **CAREER** Fel, res and criminal law, Univ Wis

Law Sch, 50-53; asst prof law, 61-66, assoc prof, 66-67, assoc dean admin, 70-72, Prof Law, Law Sch, Univ Wis-Madison. Mem Bd Mgrs, Nat Conf Bar Examrs, 80-; affil, Univ Wis Inst Res Poverty, 81-. **MEMBERSHIPS** Law and Soc Asn; Int Soc Family Law; Nat Coury Family Rel; Am Bar Asn Family Law Sect. **RESEARCH** Child support; divorce policy; legal problems of the elderly. **SELECTED PUBLICATIONS** Auth The United States-Child Support Enforcement for The 21st Century, Univ Louisville J Family Law, Vol 32, 94; The United States--Continuing Concern With the Economic Consequences of Divorce, Univ Louisville J Family Law, Vol 31, 93. **CONTACT ADDRESS** Law Sch, Univ of Wisconsin, Madison, Madison, WI 53706.

MELNICK, ATRHUR
DISCIPLINE PHILOSOPHY **EDUCATION** Univ Chicago, PhD, 71. **CAREER** Prof, Univ Ill Urbana Champaign. **RESEARCH** Metaphysics; history of modern philosophy; philosophy of science; philosophy of mathematics; logic. **SELECTED PUBLICATIONS** Auth, Kant's Analogies of Experience and Space; Time and Thought in Kant; pubs on Kant. **CONTACT ADDRESS** Philosophy Dept, Univ of Illinois, Urbana-Champaign, 52 E Gregory Dr, Champaign, IL 61820. **EMAIL** amelnick@staff.uiuc.edu

MELTZER, ALLAN H.
PERSONAL Born 02/06/1928, Boston, MA, m, 1950, 3 children **DISCIPLINE** ECONOMICS **EDUCATION** Duke Univ, AB, 48; Univ Cal, Los Angeles, MA 55, PhD 58. **CAREER** Carnegie Mellon Univ, assoc prof, prof, 57-; The Bank of Japan, Hon Advis, 86-; Am Ent Inst for Pub Pol Res, Vis Schol, 89-; The Allan Meltzer Univ Prof of Pol Econ, 97-; chmn, International Financial Institution Advisory Commission to the US Congress, 99-00. **HONORS AND AWARDS** Medal Outstanding Prof Ach Awd; Fellow, Nat Asn Bus Econ; Man Of the Year In fin; Templeton Honor Roll, Edu in a Free Soc; Distg Ach Awd Money Mkteers NY Univ. **MEMBERSHIPS** AEA; WEA; Nat Asn Bus. **RESEARCH** Monetary econo; Pol Econ; Hist Fed Reserve. **SELECTED PUBLICATIONS** Money Credit and Policy, Edward Elgar Pub, 95; Money and the Economy: Issues in Monetary Analysis, with K Brunner, Cambridge Press, 91; auth, Report of the International Financial Institutions Advisory Commission, Washington: GPO, 00; auth, A History of the Federal Reserve, vol. 1, 1913-51, Chicago: Univ of Chicago Press, (forthcoming, 01). **CONTACT ADDRESS** Carnegie Mellon Univ, Pittsburgh, PA 15213. **EMAIL** am05@andrew.cmu.edu

MELUSKY, JOSEPH
PERSONAL Born 06/02/1952, Pottsville, PA, m, 1976, 2 children **DISCIPLINE** HISTORY, POLITICAL SCIENCE **EDUCATION** W Chester State Col, BA, 74; Univ Del, MA, 78; Univ Del, PhD, 83. **CAREER** Lect, Univ Del, 79-80; Prof, St Francis Col, 80-. **HONORS AND AWARDS** Outstanding Fac Citation, Hon Soc, 83; Swatsworth Fac Merit Awd, 90; Distinguished Fac Awd, St Francis Nat Alumni Asn, 95; Who's Who in the East, 96; Who's Who in the World, 97; Who's Who Among Am Teachers, 96, 00. **MEMBERSHIPS** Pa Polit Sci Asn, Northeastern Polit Sci Asn, Am Polit Sci Asn, Pa Humanities Coun, Inst for Exp Learning. **RESEARCH** Presidential elections, American presidency, constitutional law. **SELECTED PUBLICATIONS** Auth, The Constitution: Our Written Legacy, Krieger Publ Co, 91; coauth, "To Preserve These Rights: The Bill of Rights 1791-1991," Pa Humanities Coun, 91; coauth, The Bill of Rights: Our Written Legacy, Krieger Publ Co, 93; auth, The American Political System: An Owner's Manual, McGraw-Hill, 00. **CONTACT ADDRESS** Dept Hist and Polit Sci, Saint Francis Col, Pennsylvania, Loretto, PA 15940-0600. **EMAIL** jmelusky@sfcpa.edu

MEMON, MUHAMMAD UMAR
PERSONAL Born 05/15/1939, Aligarh, India **DISCIPLINE** ISLAMIC STUDIES, URDU LANGUAGE & LITERATURE **EDUCATION** Karachi Univ, BA, 60, MA, 61; Harvard Univ, AM, 65; Univ Calif, Los Angeles, PhD, 71. **CAREER** Lectr Islamic hist, Sachal Sarmast Col, Pakistan, 62; lectr Arabic, Sind Univ, 62-64; instr Arabic, Persian & Urdu, 70-71, asst prof, 72-76, assoc prof Islamics, Persian & Urdu, Univ Wis-Madison, 76-; vis asst prof Urdu & Islamics, Dept SAsian Studies, Univ Minn, Minneapolis, 74-75; mem US adv comt, Berkeley Urdu Lang Prog in Pakistan, 75-; res grant, Grad Sch, Univ Wis-Madison, 77; SSRC, 84; assoc ed, SAsian Lit, 80-83; prof Islamic Studies, Persian & Urdu, Univ Wisc-Madison, 84-. **MEMBERSHIPS** Mid E Studies Assn N Am; Am Orient Soc; Assoc for Asian Studies. **RESEARCH** Islamic history and religion; Arabic and Urdu literature. **SELECTED PUBLICATIONS** Auth, The Seventh Door and Other Stories, Lynne Rienner, 89; auth, Hasan Manzar: A Requiem for the Earth, Oxford Univ Press, 98; auth, Abdullah Hussein: Storeis of Exile and Alienation, Oxford Univ Press, 98; auth, An Epic Unwritten: Penguin Book of Partition Stories, Penguin, 98. **CONTACT ADDRESS** Dept of South Asian Studies, Univ of Wisconsin, Madison, 1220 Linden Dr, Madison, WI 53706-1557. **EMAIL** mumemon@facstaff.wisc.edu

MENDELSON, ALAN
PERSONAL Born 07/30/1939, Washington, DC **DISCIPLINE** RELIGION **EDUCATION** Kenyon Col, AB, 61; Brandeis Univ, MA, 65; Univ Chicago, PhD(hist cult), 71. **CAREER** Vis lectr philos and relig, Hebrew Univ Jerusalem, 71-73; Asst Prof Relig, McMaster Univ, 76-. **MEMBERSHIPS** Philos Inst. **RESEARCH** Judaism and Christianity in Greco-Roman world. **SELECTED PUBLICATIONS** Auth, "Eusebius and the Posthumous Career of Apolonius of Tyana," in H.W. Attridge and G. Hata, ed, Eusebius, Christianity and Judaism, Detroit, Mich: Wayne State Univ Press, (92): 510-522; auth, "Did Philo Say the Shema?' and Other Reflections on E.P. Sanders'Judaism: Practice and Belief," Studia Philonica Annual 6, (94): 160-170; auth, "Philo's Dialectic of Reward and Punishment," Studia Philonica Annual 9, (97): 104-125. **CONTACT ADDRESS** Dept of Relig Stud, McMaster Univ, Univ Hall, Rm 105, Hamilton, ON, Canada L8S 4K1. **EMAIL** mendelsn@mcmaster.ca

MENDELSON, JOHANNA
DISCIPLINE POLITICAL SCIENCE **EDUCATION** Wash Univ, PhD; Am Univ, JD. **CAREER** Prof, Am Univ. **RESEARCH** Democracy and civil-military relations. **SELECTED PUBLICATIONS** Coauth, Lesson of the Venezuelan Experience, Johns Hopkins Press, 95. **CONTACT ADDRESS** American Univ, 4400 Massachusetts Ave, Washington, DC 20016.

MENDES, ERROL
DISCIPLINE LAW **EDUCATION** Exeter Univ, LLB; Univ Ill, LLM. **CAREER** Prof. **HONORS AND AWARDS** Ed, Nat Jour Const Law. **SELECTED PUBLICATIONS** Ed, Racial Discrimination: Law and Practice; co-ed, Canadian Charter of Rights and Freedoms. **CONTACT ADDRESS** Fac Common Law, Univ of Ottawa, 550 Cumberland St, PO Box 450, Ottawa, ON, Canada K1N 6N5. **EMAIL** emendes@uottawa.ca

MENDIETA, EDUARDO
PERSONAL Born 12/28/1963, Colombia, m, 1993, 2 children **DISCIPLINE** PHILOSOPHY **EDUCATION** Union Theol Sem, MA, 91; New School for Soc Res, PhD, 97. **CAREER** Vis prof, Univ Iberoamericans, 98; asst prof, Univ San Fran, 94-. **HONORS AND AWARDS** Nat Endowment for the Humanities Chair, Univ of San Francisco, 00-01. **MEMBERSHIPS** Amer Acad Relig; Amer Pholos Asn; Soc Phenomenol Existential Philos. **RESEARCH** German & Latin American philosophy; Moral philosophy; Postcolonist & globalization theory; Habermas; Dussel; Apel. **CONTACT ADDRESS** Philosophy Dept, Univ of San Francisco, 2130 Fulton St, San Francisco, CA 94117-1080. **EMAIL** mendietae@usfca.edu

MENDOLA, JOSEPH
PERSONAL Born 05/02/1957, 1 child **DISCIPLINE** METAPHYSICS, ETHICAL THEORY, AND PHILOSOPHY OF MIND **EDUCATION** Univ Mich, PhD, 83. **CAREER** Prof, ch, dept Philos, Univ Nebr, Lincoln. **SELECTED PUBLICATIONS** Auth, Normative Realism, or Bernard Williams and Ethics at the Limit, Australasian J of Philos 67, 89; Objective Value and Subjective States, Philos and Phenomenol Res L, 90; An Ordinal Modification of Classical Utilitarianism, Erkenntnis 33, 90; Human Thought. **CONTACT ADDRESS** Univ of Nebraska, Lincoln, Lincoln, NE 68588-0417.

MENDOSA, ANTONIO
DISCIPLINE CORPORATE FINANCE **EDUCATION** St Mary's Univ, BBA, 73, JD, 78. **CAREER** Prof, Pepperdine Col. **HONORS AND AWARDS** Rick J Caruso res fel, 94-95. **MEMBERSHIPS** Mem, Am Bar Assn; Am Soc Intl Lawyers; State Bar TX. **SELECTED PUBLICATIONS** Auth, The Creeping Breach Intl Law. **CONTACT ADDRESS** Sch of Law, Pepperdine Univ, 24255 Pacific Coast Hwy, Malibu, CA 90263.

MENKE, CHRISTOPH
DISCIPLINE PHILOSOPHY **EDUCATION** Free Univ Berlin, PhD, 55. **CAREER** Assoc prof, Eugene Lang Col. **RESEARCH** Nietzsche; Hegel; aesthetics; ethics. **SELECTED PUBLICATIONS** Auth, Tragedy in Daily Life: Freedom and Justice in Hegel, 96. **CONTACT ADDRESS** Eugene Lang Col, New Sch for Social Research, 66 West 12th St, New York, NY 10011.

MENN, STEPHEN
DISCIPLINE PHILOSOPHY **EDUCATION** Johns Hopkins Univ, MA, 82, PhD, 85; Univ Chicago, MA, 84; PhD, 89. **RESEARCH** Ancient philosophy; medieval philosophy; history and philosophy of mathematics. **SELECTED PUBLICATIONS** Auth, Aristotle and Plato on God as Nous and as the Good, Review of Metaphysics, 45, 92; auth, The Problem of the Thrid Meditation, American Catholic Philosophical Quarterly, Autumn, 93; auth, Metaphysics, Dialectic, and the Categories, Revue de Metaphysique it de Morale, 100, no. 3, 95; auth, Plato on God as Nous, Journal of the History of Philosophy Monograph Series, Southern Illinois Univ Press, 95. **CONTACT ADDRESS** Philosophy Dept, McGill Univ, 845 Sherbrooke St, Montreal, QC, Canada H3A 2T5. **EMAIL** spmenn@philo.mcgill.ca

MENSCH, JAMES
DISCIPLINE PHILOSOPHY **EDUCATION** Univ Md, BA, 67; Univ Toronto, PhD, 76. **CAREER** Instr, Univ Col, Univ of Toronto, 71-73; asst prof, Univ of Dallas, 82-83; from asst prof to full prof, St Francis Xavier Univ, 89-. **MEMBERSHIPS** Am Philos Asn; Soc Phenomenol Existential Philos; Can Soc Hermeneutics Post Modern Thought. **SELECTED PUBLICATIONS** Auth, The Question of Being in Husserl's Logical Investigations, Martinus Nijhoff Press, 81; auth, Intersubjectivity and Transcendental Idealism, SUNY Press, 88; auth, The Beginning of the Gospel of St. John: Philosophical Perspectives, Peter Lang Publ, 92; auth, After Modernity: Husserlian Reflections on a Philosophical Tradition, SUNY Press, 96; auth, Knowing and Being: A Post-Modern Reversal, Pa State Univ Press, 96; auth, "Post Normative Subjectivity," in The Ancients and Moderns, ed. Reginald Lilly (Bloomington: Ind Univ Press, 96), 311-321; auth, "What is a Self," in Husserl in the Contemporary Context: Prospects and Projects for Phenomenology, ed. B. Hopkins (Dordrecht: Kluwer Press, 97), 61-78; auth, "Cross-cultural Understanding and Ethics," in New Europe at the Crossroads I (NY: Peter Lang Publ, 99), 169-180; auth, "Rescue and the Face to Face: Ethics and the Holocaust," in New Europe at the Crossroads II (NY: Peter Lang Publ, 01); auth, Postfoundational Phenomenology: Husserlian Reflections on Presence and Embodiment, Pa State Univ Press, 01. **CONTACT ADDRESS** Dept of Philos, St. Francis Xavier Univ, PO Box 5000, Antigonish, NS, Canada B2G 2W5. **EMAIL** jmensch@stfx.ca

MENUGE, ANGUS
PERSONAL Born 06/23/1964, England, m, 1988, 2 children **DISCIPLINE** PHILOSOPHY **EDUCATION** Univ Warwick, BA, 85; Univ Wis at Madison, MA, 87; PhD, 89. **CAREER** From teaching asst to teaching fel, 85-89; computer programmer, 89-91; asst prof, 91-97; assoc prof, Concordia Univ, 97-. **HONORS AND AWARDS** Res Fel, 88-89. **MEMBERSHIPS** Soc of Christian Philosophers, Wis Philos Asn. **RESEARCH** Philosophy of Mind, Philosophy of Science, Christian Apologetics, Life and Works of C. S. Lewis, Christianity and Culture. **CONTACT ADDRESS** Dept Philos, Concordia Univ, Wisconsin, 12800 N Lake Shore Dr, Mequon, WI 53097-2418. **EMAIL** angus.menuge@cuw.edu

MENZEL, CHRISTOPHER
DISCIPLINE PHILOSOPHY **EDUCATION** Pacific Lutheran Univ, BA, 79; Univ Notre Dame, PhD, 84. **CAREER** Assoc prof, 91-, ass prof, 86-91 researcher, 87-91, Texas A&M Univ; vis res scientist, Commonwealth Scientific and Industrial Res Org, 96; actg asst prof, 85-86 & postdoctoral fel, 84-86, Stanford Univ. **RESEARCH** Artificial intelligence, Metaphysics, Logic, Knowledge representation. **SELECTED PUBLICATIONS** Auth, " Actualism, Outological Commitment, & Possible World Semantics," Synthese 85 (90); auth, " The True Modal Logic," J of Philos Logic 20 (91); auth, Modeling Method Ontologies: A Foundation for Enterprise Model Integration, in Ontological Engineering: Papers from the 97 AAAI Spring Symp, Menlo Park, AAAI Press, Technical Report SS-97-06; Entries on Alethic Modalities, Type Theory, Cambridge Dictionary of Philos, Cambridge Univ Press, 95; coauth, Situations and Processes, Concurrent Engineering: Research and Applications 3 (96); "IDEF3 Process Descriptions and Their Semantics," in Intelligent Systems in Design and Manufacturing, ASME Press, 94; auth, " The Objective Conception of Context and its Logic," Minds & Machines 9 (99). **CONTACT ADDRESS** Dept of Philosophy, Texas A&M Univ, Col Station, 510 Blocker, College Station, TX 77843-4237. **EMAIL** cmenzel@tamu.edu

MERCADANTE, LINDA A.
PERSONAL Born Newark, NJ, 1 child **DISCIPLINE** THEOLOGY AND HISTORY OF DOCTRINE **EDUCATION** Princeton Theol Sem, PhD, 86. **CAREER** Prof, theol, B. Robert Straker chair, Methodist Theol Sch in Oh, 87-. **HONORS AND AWARDS** Mem, Ctr of Theol Inquiry; scholar, Ecumenical Inst; grants, The Louisville Inst; grants, Asn of Theol Scholars. **MEMBERSHIPS** Amer Acad of Relig; Workgroup on Constructive Theol. **RESEARCH** Gender; Addiction; Doctrine of sin; Historical theology. **SELECTED PUBLICATIONS** Auth, Victims & Sinners: Spiritual roots of addiction & recovery, Westminster, 96; auth, Sin, Addiction & Freedom, Reconstructing Christ Theol; auth, Gender, Doctrine & God: The Shakers & contemporary theology, Abingdon, 90; auth, Hierarchy to Equality, GMH, 78. **CONTACT ADDRESS** 3081 Columbus Pk., Delaware, OH 43015. **EMAIL** lmercadante@mtso.edu

MERCER, MARK
PERSONAL Born 11/03/1957, London, ON, Canada, m, 1998 **DISCIPLINE** PHILOSOPHY; FILM STUDIES **EDUCATION** Carleton Univ, BA, 82, MA, 85; Univ Toronto, PhD, 91. **CAREER** Col prof, Okanagau Univ Col, 93-94; asst prof, Brandon Univ, 94-95; asst prof, Univ Calgary, 95-97; asst prof, Univ Manitoba, 98; asst prof, St Cloud State Univ, 98-99; St. Mary's Univ. **HONORS AND AWARDS** Soc Serv Hum fel, 91-93. **MEMBERSHIPS** Can Philos Asn; Amer Philos Asn **RESEARCH** Pholosophy of mind; Epistenology; Ethics. **SELECTED PUBLICATIONS** Auth, Grounds of Liberal Tolerance, Journal of Value Enquiry, 99; coauth, Meaning Holism

and Interpretability, Philos Quart, 91; auth, On a Pragmatic Argument Against Pragmatism in Ethics, Am Philos Quart, 93; Psychological Egoism and Its Critics, S Jour Philos XXXVI, 98. **CONTACT ADDRESS** Dept of Philosophy, St. Mary's Univ, Canada, 923 Robie St., Halifax, NS, Canada B3H 3C3. **EMAIL** mmercer@stmarys.ca

MERCHANT, CAROLYN
PERSONAL Born 07/12/1936, Rochester, NY, 2 children **DISCIPLINE** ENVIRONMENTAL HISTORY, PHILOSOPHY & ETHICS **EDUCATION** Vassar Col, AB, 58; Univ Wis, MA, 62, PhD, 67. **CAREER** Lectr hist of sci, Univ San Francisco, 69-74, asst prof, 74-78; asst prof environ hist, 79-80, assoc prof 80-86, Prof, 86-, Chancellor Prof Environ Hist, Philos & Ethics, Univ Calif, Berkeley, former chmn, Dept Conserv & Resource Studies; Vis prof, Ecole Normale Superieure, Paris, 6/86. **HONORS AND AWARDS** NSF, 76-78; NEH grant, 77, 81-83; Am Counc Learned Soc fel, 78; Center Advan Studies, Behavioral Sci, 78; Fulbright sr scholar, Umea Univ, Sweden, 84; Agr Exp Station, Univ Calif, Berkeley, 80-86, 86-92, 92-; Nathan Cummings Found, 92; Am Cultures fel, Univ Calif, Berkeley, 6/90; Vis fel, School Soc Sci, Murdoch Univ, Perth, Australia, 91; John Simon Guggenheim fel, 95; Doctor Honoris Causa, Umea Univ, Sweden, 95; National Humanities Center Fellow, 01. **MEMBERSHIPS** Hist Sci Soc; West Coast Hist Sci Soc; British Soc Hist Sci; Soc Hist Technol; Am Soc Environ Hist. **RESEARCH** Scientific revolution; American environmental history; women and nature. **SELECTED PUBLICATIONS** Auth, D'Alembert and the vis viva controversy, Studies in Hist and Philos of Sci, 8/70; Leibniz and the vis viva controversy, Isis, spring 71; The Leibnizian-Newtonian debates: Natural philosophy and social psychology, British J for the Hist of Sci, 12/73; Madame du Chatelet's metaphysics and mechanics, Studies in Hist and Philos of Sci, 5/77; The Death of Nature: Women, Ecology, and the Scientific Revolution, Harper and Row, San Francisco, 80, 2nd ed, 90; Earthcare: Women and the environmental movement, Environment, 6/81; Isis' consciousness raised, Isis, fall 82; Ecological Revolutions: Nature, Gender, and Science in New England, Univ NC Press, 89; Radical Ecology: The Search for a Liveable World, Routledge, 92; ed, Major Problems in American Environmental History: ed, Ecology, Humanities Press, 94; Earthcare: Women and the Environment, Routledge, 96; ed, Green Versus Gold: Sources in California's Environmental History, Island Press, 98; Reinventing Eden, in progress. **CONTACT ADDRESS** Dept of Environ Sci, Policy & Mgt, Univ of California, Berkeley, Berkeley, CA 94720-3310. **EMAIL** merchant@nature.berkeley.edu

MERKL, PETER HANS
PERSONAL Born 01/29/1932, Munich, Germany, m, 1954, 2 children **DISCIPLINE** POLITICAL SCIENCE **EDUCATION** Univ Cal Berkeley, PhD, 59. **CAREER** Lectr, asst prof, assoc prof, prof, 58-92, Dept Chmn, 72-73, EmeritusProf, 93-, Univ Calif Santa Barbara; vis Prof, 83, Univ Augsburg, 87, U of Istanbul, 88 Bogazici U, 90, U of Gottingen, 91, Free U of Berlin. **HONORS AND AWARDS** Rockefeller Fel; Ford Fnd Fel; DAAD Gnt; Volkswagen Fnd Gnt; NEH; Japan Soc Gnt; UCSB Fac Res Lectshp; West German Fed Order of Merit; Japan Soc Promotion Sci Gnt. **MEMBERSHIPS** APSA; IPSA; ISA; CES; CGGP. **RESEARCH** Comparative and European Politics; political parties; elections; right radicalism; political violence and terror. **SELECTED PUBLICATIONS** Auth, German Unification in the European Context, Penn State Press, 93; Coed, Encounters with the Contemporary Radical Right, Boulder CO, Westview, 93; ed, The Federal Rep At Forty-Five, London, Macmillan and NYU Press, 95; coed, The Revival of Rightwing Extremism in the Nineties, London, Frank Cass; ed, The Federal Rep at Fifty, London, Macmillan, NYU Press, 99; auth, A Coup Atempt in Washington? A European Mirror on the 1998-1999 Constitutional Crisis, New York: St. Martin's/Palgrave, 01. **CONTACT ADDRESS** Dept of Political Science, Univ of California, Santa Barbara, Santa Barbara, CA 93106. **EMAIL** merkl@sscf.ucsb.edu

MERKLE, JOHN CHARLES
PERSONAL Born 12/26/1946, Philadelphia, PA **DISCIPLINE** RELIGIOUS STUDIES AND THEOLOGY **EDUCATION** St Vincent de Paul Sem, BA, 69; Cath Univ Louvain, MA, 74, PhD(relig studies), 82. **CAREER** Instr Theol, Col St Benedict, 77-. **MEMBERSHIPS** Col Theol Soc; Relig Educ Asn. **RESEARCH** Modern and contemporary Jewish philosophy and theology; Jewish-Christian dialogue; faith development. **SELECTED PUBLICATIONS** Auth, Bound Together in God, Rel Edu, Vol 91, 96. **CONTACT ADDRESS** Dept of Theol, Col of Saint Benedict, 37 College Ave S, Saint Joseph, MN 56374-2001.

MERKUR, DAN
PERSONAL Born 05/26/1951, Toronto, ON, Canada, m, 1997, 3 children **DISCIPLINE** RELIGIOUS STUDIES **EDUCATION** Stockholm Univ, PhD, 85. **CAREER** Syracuse Univ, asst prof, 86-90; adj prof, Univ of Toronto, York Univ, McMaster Univ, Queens Univ, 92-. **MEMBERSHIPS** CSSR, CSBS, AAR, SBL. **RESEARCH** Religious uses of altered states of consciousness. **SELECTED PUBLICATIONS** Auth, Becoming Half-Hidden: Shamanism and Invitation Among the Inuit, 2nd ed, 92; auth, Gnosis: An Esoteric Tradition of Mystical Visions and Unions, 93; auth, The Ecstatic Imagination: Psychedelic Experiences and the Psychoanalysis of Self-Actualization, 98; auth, Mystical Moments and Unitive Thinking, 99; auth, The Mystery of Mana, 00. **CONTACT ADDRESS** Centre for the Study of Relig, Univ of Toronto, 123 St George St, Toronto, ON, Canada M5N 1J1. **EMAIL** dan.merkur@utoronto.ca

MERLING, DAVID
PERSONAL Born 06/14/1948, Pittsburg, PA, m, 1969, 2 children **DISCIPLINE** OLD TESTAMENT STUDIES, ARCHAEOLOGY, HISTORY OF ANTIQUITY **EDUCATION** Andrews Univ, PhD, 96. **CAREER** Assoc prof of Archaeol and Hist of Antiquities, Andrews Univ, 86-; Curator, Siegfried H. Horn Archaeol Museum, 91- . **HONORS AND AWARDS** Andrews Univ Fac Res Grant, 91-92, 94; Who's Who in Bibl Stud and Archaeol, 93; Zion Res found travel grant, 84, Tell e-Umeyri, Jordan. **MEMBERSHIPS** Adventist Theol Soc; Amer Sch Oriental Res; Bibl Archaeol Soc; Evangelical Theol Soc; Inst Bibl Res; Israel Exploration Soc; Near Eastern Archaeol Soc; Soc Bibl Lit. **RESEARCH** Archaeology and the Book of Joshua. **CONTACT ADDRESS** Dept of Archaeology, Andrews Univ, Berrien Springs, MI 49104-0990. **EMAIL** merling@andrews.edu

MERLINO, SCOTT A.
PERSONAL Born 08/23/1962, Erie, PA **DISCIPLINE** PHILOSOPHY **EDUCATION** Univ of Cal at Davis, PhD, 97. **CAREER** Amer River Col, instr; Cal State Univ, adj prof. **MEMBERSHIPS** APA, PSA, ISHP&SSB **CONTACT ADDRESS** Dept of Philosophy, American River Col, 3814 Arroyo Ave., Davis, CA 95616-7106. **EMAIL** samerlin@inreach.com

MERON, THEODOR
PERSONAL Born 04/28/1930, Kalisz, Poland **DISCIPLINE** INTERNATIONAL LAW, HUMAN RIGHTS **EDUCATION** Hebrew Univ, MJ, 54; Harvard Univ, LLM, 55, SJD, 57. **CAREER** Prof Law, Law Sch, NY Univ, 78- ; consult, World Bank, spring, 79; prof, Grad Inst of Int Studies, 91-95; co-ed, Am J of Int Law, 84-88; vis prof, Harvard Law Sch; counselor on Int Law, Dept of State, 00-01. **HONORS AND AWARDS** Israel Ministry for Foreign Affairs Prize, 58; Fel, Rockefeller Found, 75; Carnegie lectr, The Hague Acad Int Law, 80 **MEMBERSHIPS** Am Soc Int Law; Int Law Asn; French Soc Int Law. **RESEARCH** Public international law; international organization. **SELECTED PUBLICATIONS** Auth, Investment Insurance in International Law, Ociana-Sijthoff, 76; auth, The United Nations Secretariat, Lexington Books, 77; auth, Human Rights in International Law, Oxford Univ Pr, 84; auth, Human Rights Law-Making in the United Nations, Oxford Univ Pr, 86; auth, Human Rights in Internal Strife: Their International Protection, Grotius Pubs, 87; auth, Human Rights and Humanitarian Norms as Customary Law, Oxford Univ Pr, 89; auth, Henry's Wars and Shakespeare's Laws, Oxford Univ Pr, 93; auth, Bloody Constraint: War and Chivalry in Shakespeare, Oxford Univ Pr, 98; auth, War Crimes Law comes of Age: Essays, Oxford Univ Pr, 98. **CONTACT ADDRESS** Sch of Law, New York Univ, 40 Washington Sq S, New York, NY 10012-1005.

MERRILL, DANIEL DAVY
PERSONAL Born 06/01/1932, South Bend, IN, m, 1956, 2 children **DISCIPLINE** PHILOSOPHY **EDUCATION** Princeton Univ, BA, 54; Univ Minn, MA, 58, PhD, 62. **CAREER** Instr philos, Knox Col, 59-62; from asst prof to assoc prof, 62-75, chmn dept, 65-68, assoc dean, 70-73, Prof Philos, Oberlin Col, 75-, Mem comt on status and future profession, Am Philos Asn, 69-72 and prog comt Western Div, 83. **MEMBERSHIPS** Western Div Am Philos Asn; Western Conf Teaching Philos (chmn, 70-72); Asn Symbolic Logic; Philos Sci Asn. **RESEARCH** History and philosophy of logic; philosophy of language; philosophy of science. **SELECTED PUBLICATIONS** Auth, Making Sense of Sollys Syllogistic Symbolism, Hist Philos Logic, Vol 17, 96. **CONTACT ADDRESS** Dept of Philosophy, Oberlin Col, 135 W Lorain St, Oberlin, OH 44074-1076.

MERRILL, EUGENE H.
PERSONAL Born 09/12/1934, Anson, ME, m, 1960, 1 child **DISCIPLINE** OLD TESTAMENT **EDUCATION** Bob Jones Univ, BA, 57, MA, 60, PhD, 63; NYork Univ, MA 70; Columbia Univ, MPhil, 77, PhD, 85. **CAREER** Prof Old Testament Stud, Bob Jones Univ, 63-66; prof of the Bible, Berkshire Christian Col, 68-75; sr prof Old Testament Stud, Dallas Theol Sem, 75- . **HONORS AND AWARDS** Vis scholar, Union Theol Sem, 63, 64; travel-study grant, Israel, US State Dept, 65; listed Who's Who in Religion, 76, 78, Outstanding Educators of America, 81-82, International Scholars Directory, 71, 73, 75. **MEMBERSHIPS** Evangelican Theol Soc; Am Schools of Orient Res; Am Orient Soc; Soc of Bibl Lit. **RESEARCH** History of Israel; Old Testament theology. **SELECTED PUBLICATIONS** Auth, Royal Priesthood: An Old Testament Messianic Motif, Bib Sac, 93; auth, Deuteronomy, New Testament Faith, and the Christian Life, in Dyer, ed, Integrity of Heart, Skillfulness of Hands, Baker, 94; auth, Haggai, Zechariah, Malachi : An Exegetical Commentary, Moody, 94; auth, Deuteronomy, Broadman & Holman, 94; contribur to The Complete Who's Who in the Bible, ed Gardner, Marshall Pickering, 95; auth, History in Sandy, ed Cracking Old Testament Codes, Broadman & Holman, 95; auth, The Late Bronze/Early Iron Age Transition and the Emergence of Israel, Bib Sac, 95; contribur to Evangelical Dictionary of Biblical Theology, ed Elwell, Baker Book, 96; co-trans, Deuteronomy, in New Living Translation, Tyndale, 96; auth, The Peoples of the Old Testament According to Genesis, Bib Sac, 97; ed and contribur New International Dictionary of Old Testament Theology and Exegesis, ed Van Gemeren, Zondervan, 97; auth, Suicide and the Concept of Death in the Old Testament in Demy, ed, Suicide: A Christian Response, Kregel, 98. **CONTACT ADDRESS** Dallas Theol Sem, 3909 Swiss Ave, Dallas, TX 75204. **EMAIL** eugene_merrill@dts.edu

MERRILL, KENNETH ROGERS
PERSONAL Born 06/15/1932, Marshall, TX, m, 1954 **DISCIPLINE** PHILOSOPHY **EDUCATION** Bethany-Peniel Col, BA, 54; Northwestern Univ, MA, 56 PhD, 63. **CAREER** From instr to assoc prof, 58-77, chmn dept, 64-70, Prof Philos, Univ Okla, 77- **MEMBERSHIPS** Am Philos Asn; Hume Soc; Southwestern Philos Soc. **RESEARCH** Philosophy of Whitehead; British empiricism; American philosophy. **SELECTED PUBLICATIONS** Auth, "Hum's 'Of Miracles,' Peirce, and the Balancing of Likelihoods," J of the Hist of Philos, 29 (91); auth, "Hume on Suicide," Hist of Philos Quart, 16 (99). **CONTACT ADDRESS** Dept of Philosophy, Univ of Oklahoma, 455 W Lindsey St, Norman, OK 73019-2006. **EMAIL** kmerrill@ou.edu

MERRILL, RICHARD AUSTIN
PERSONAL Born 05/20/1937, Logan, UT, m, 1974, 2 children **DISCIPLINE** LAW **EDUCATION** Columbia Univ, AB, 59, LLB, 64; Oxford Univ, BA and MA, 61. **CAREER** Law clerk, Circuit Court Appeals, 64-65; attorney, Covington and Burning, 65-69; Prof Law, Univ VA, 69, Dean, 80-, Consult, Admin Conf US, 72-; gen coun US Food and Drug Admin, 75-77; Mem, Inst Med, 77-; Mem Lid Toxicol, Nat Acad Sci, 79- **SELECTED PUBLICATIONS** Auth, Introduction to the American Public Law System, West, 75; Food and Drug Law, Foundation Press, 80. **CONTACT ADDRESS** Law Sch, Univ of Virginia, Charlottesville, VA 22901.

MERRITT, FRANK S.
DISCIPLINE LAW **EDUCATION** Hiram Col, BA; Case Western Reserve Univ, JD. **CAREER** Prof. **HONORS AND AWARDS** Ed, Criminal Law J Ohio, 90-93. **SELECTED PUBLICATIONS** Co-auth, Federal Rules of Criminal Procedure, 97. **CONTACT ADDRESS** Col Law, Univ of Toledo, Toledo, OH 43606. **EMAIL** fmerrit@pop3.utoledo.edu

MERRYMAN, JOHN HENRY
PERSONAL Born 02/24/1920, Portland, OR, m, 1953, 3 children **DISCIPLINE** LAW **EDUCATION** Univ Portland, BS, 43; Univ Notre Dame, MS, 44, JD, 47; NYork Univ, LLM, 50, JSD, 55. **CAREER** Assoc prof law, Univ Santa Clara, 48-53; prof, 53-71, Sweitzer Prof Law, Stanford Univ, 71-, Vis prof comp law, Univ Rome, 63-64; vis res prof, Ctr Econ Res, Athens, Greece, 62 and 64; consult, Chile Law Prog, Ford Found and Int Legal Ctr, 66-70; vis res prof, Max Planck Inst Foreign St Int Pvt Law, Hamburg, 68-69; Fulbright res grant, Ger, 68-69. **HONORS AND AWARDS** Order of Merit, Italy, 70. **RESEARCH** Comparative law; art and the law; law and development. **SELECTED PUBLICATIONS** Auth, The Moral Right of Utrillo, Maurice, Am J Comparative Law, Vol 43, 95; The Wrath of Rauschenberg, Robert, J Copyright Soc USA, Vol 40, 92; The French Deviation, Am J Comparative Law, Vol 44, 96. **CONTACT ADDRESS** Crown Law, Stanford, CA 94305-1926.

MERSKY, ROY MARTIN
PERSONAL Born 09/01/1925, New York, NY, m, 1999, 3 children **DISCIPLINE** LAW **EDUCATION** Univ Wis, BS, 48, JD, 52, MALS, 53. **CAREER** Cataloger, US Govt Doc, Univ Wis Educ Libr, 51-52; readers' adv and ref and catalog librn, Milwaukee Publ Libr, Munic Ref Libr, City Hall, 53-54; asst librn and chief readers' and ref serv, Yale Law Libr, 54-59; dir, Wash State Law Libr, 59-63; prof law and law librn, Univ Colo, 63-65; Prof Law and Law Librn, Univ Tex, Austin, 65-, Atty, 52-54; exec secy judicial coun and comnr Wash court reporters, State of Wash, 59-63; consult, Nat Col State Trial Judges, var col law libr, legal serv prog, Off Econ Opportunity and ETexas Legal Serv; interim dir, Jewish Nat and Hebrew Univ Jerusalem Libr, 72-73; Consult, J Reuben Clark Sch Law, Brigham Young Univ, 72-73 and Oral Roberts Univ, 77-; Ed Consult, Trans-Media Publ Co, 72- **MEMBERSHIPS** Am Bar Asn; Am Libr Asn; Am Asn Law Libr; Am Civil Liberties Union; Asn Am Law Schs. **RESEARCH** Civil rights; legal history; legal research and writing. **SELECTED PUBLICATIONS** Auth, Aall and the Road to Diversity, Law Library Jour, Vol 85, 93. **CONTACT ADDRESS** 727 E Dean Keaton Street, Austin, TX 78705-3224. **EMAIL** rmersky@mail.law.utexas.edu

MERWIN, PETER MATTHEW
PERSONAL Born 06/20/1944, Chicago, IL **DISCIPLINE** PHILOSOPHY **EDUCATION** DePaul Univ, BA, 67, MA, 69,

PhD, 92. **CAREER** Instr, philos, DePaul Univ, 78-81; instr, English, Chicago Bd of Educ, 71-98. **HONORS AND AWARDS** Arthur J Schmitt Found fel, 78-79, 79-80; Who's Who in the Midwest, 98. **MEMBERSHIPS** APA; Soc for Phenomenological and Existential Philos; Newberry Lib Assoc; Westerners Int; Int Soc for Philos and Lit. **RESEARCH** Symbols of the American Indians; philosophy of symbolic forms of Ernst Cassiver. **SELECTED PUBLICATIONS** Auth, The People's Relationship to the Land, Univ of So Dakota, 79; auth, Revenge on the Reservation, Heartland J, 84; auth, The Philosophy of Symbolic Forms of Ernst Cassiver and the Lakotas, DePaul Univ, 92 (diss); ed, Brand Book, vol 44, 1, 2, Westerners Int, 97; ed, Brand Book, vol. 44, 3, Westerners Int, 98, ed, Brand Book, vol. 44, 4, Spring 99, ed, Brand Book, vol. 44, 5, Spring 00. **CONTACT ADDRESS** 8821 O'Brien Dr, Orland Hills, IL 60477.

MESLE, C. ROBERT
PERSONAL Born 12/18/1949, Independence, MO, m, 1970, 2 children **DISCIPLINE** PHILOSOPHY, RELIGION **EDUCATION** Graceland Univ, BA, 72; Univ Chicago, MA, 75; Northwestern Univ, PhD, 80. **CAREER** Prof, Graceland Univ. **HONORS AND AWARDS** Mellon Fel; Excell Teach Awd; NEH; Dist Auth Lect. **SELECTED PUBLICATIONS** Auth, John Hicks Theodicy: A Process Humanist Critique, Macmillan and St Martin's, 91; auth, Process Theology: A Basic Introduction, Calice Press, 93; auth, Supplement Religious Studies, Camb Univ Press; auth, Ethics, Univ Chicago Press; auth, Religious Studies Review, Cen Scientific Study of Rel, ed, Theology V: The Jesus Seminar, Graceland/Park Press (Independence, MO), 98; auth, The Bible as Story and Struggle, Herald House, 89; auth, "Pragmatism, Naturalism, and the Inner Life," Rel Hum (99); auth, "A Friend's Love: Why Process Theology Matters," Christ Cent (87); auth, "The Problem of Genuine Evil: A Critique of John Hick's Theodicy," J Rel (86). **CONTACT ADDRESS** Dept Humanities, Graceland Col, 700 College Ave, Lamoni, IA 50140. **EMAIL** bobmesle@graceland.edu

METZGER, BRUCE MANNING
PERSONAL Born 02/09/1914, Middletown, PA, m, 1944, 2 children **DISCIPLINE** NEW TESTAMENT LANGUAGE & LITERATURE **EDUCATION** Lebanon Valley Col, AB, 35; Princeton Theol Sem, ThB, 38, ThM, 39; Princeton Univ, MA, 40, PhD, 42. **CAREER** Teaching fel New Testament, 38-40, from instr to prof, 40-64, George L Collord Prof New Testament Lang & Lit, Princeton Theol Sem, 64-, Chmn Am comt versions, Int Greek New Testament Proj, 50-; vis lectr, Presby Sem, Campinas, Brazil, 52; mem panel transl, Rev Standard Version of the Apocrypha, Nat Coun Churches, 53-57 & Standard Bible Comt, 59-; hon fel & corresp mem, Higher Inst Coptic Studies, Egypt, 55-; mem Kuratorium, Vetus-Latina-Inst, Ger, 59-; mem adv comt, Inst New Testament Text Res, Univ Munster, 62-; mem managing comt, Am Sch Class Studies, Athens; mem, Inst Advan Studies, Princeton, 64-65 & 73-74; Soc Bibl Lit deleg, Am Coun Learned Soc, 64-67; consult, Nat Endowment for Humanities, 68-, vis fel, Clare Col, Cambridge Univ, 74; mem adv comt, Collected Works of Erasmus, 77-. **HONORS AND AWARDS** Christian Res Found Prizes, 55, 62 & 63; F C Burkitt Medal Bibl Stud, Br Acad, 94; dd, lebanon valley col, 51; lhd, findlay col, 62; dd, univ st andrews, 64; dtheol, univ munster, 70; dlitt, univ potchefstroom, 85. **MEMBERSHIPS** Am Philol Asn; Am Acad Relig; Soc Bibl Lit; Soc Study New Testament; Am Papyrological Asn. **RESEARCH** New Testament; early versions of the Bible; early Church history. **SELECTED PUBLICATIONS** Auth, Chapters in the History of New Testament Textual Criticism, Brill, Leiden, 63; The Text of the New Testament, Its Transmission, Corruption, and Restoration, Oxford, 64, Ger ed, 66, Japanese ed, 73, Italian ed, 96, Russian ed, 96; The New Testament, Its Background, Growth, and Content, Abingdon, 65, Chinese ed, 77; co-ed, The Greek New Testament, Am Bible Soc, 66; auth, Index to Periodical Literature on Christ and the Gospels, 66 & Historical and Literary Studies: Pagan, Jewish, and Christian, 68, Brill, Leiden; A taxtual commentary on the Greek New Testament, United Bible Soc London, 71; Manucripts of the Greek Bible, Oxford, 81. **CONTACT ADDRESS** 20 Cleveland Lane, Princeton, NJ 08540.

METZGER, DANIEL
PERSONAL Born 01/20/1954, Milwaukee, WI, m, 1976, 3 children **DISCIPLINE** RELIGION **EDUCATION** Mankato State Univ, MA, 85; Marquette, PhD, 94. **CAREER** Pastor, Our Savior's Lutheran Church, 80-82; instr, Bethany Lutheran College, 82-98. **MEMBERSHIPS** AAR; SBL. **RESEARCH** Fifteenth century justification theory; Eucharistic theology. **CONTACT ADDRESS** 336 N Redwood Dr, Mankato, MN 56001. **EMAIL** dmetzger@blc.edu

MEYER, BEN FRANKLIN
PERSONAL Born 11/05/1927, Chicago, IL **DISCIPLINE** BIBLICAL LITERATURE **EDUCATION** Gonzaga Univ, BA, 50; Mt St Michael's Col, PhL, 51; Univ Santa Clara, MST, 58; Pontif Bibl Inst, STL, 61 Gregorian Univ, STD(Theol), 65. **CAREER** Asst prof scripture and theol, Alma Col, Calif, 63-68; asst prof scripture, Grad Theol Union, 66-68; Prof Judaism and Christianity, McMaster Univ, 69-, Fulbright grant, Germany, 64-65. **MEMBERSHIPS** Cath Bibi Asn Am; Soc Bibl Lit; Studiorum novi Testamenti Soc. **RESEARCH** Historical Jesus; early Christian thought. **SELECTED PUBLICATIONS** Auth The 5 Gospels--The Search for the Authentic Words of Jesus, Interpretation J Bible Theol, Vol 48, 94; The Historical Jesus--The Life of a Mediterranean Jewish Peasant, Cath Biblical Quart, Vol 55, 93. **CONTACT ADDRESS** Dept of Religious Studies, McMaster Univ, 1280 Main St W, Hamilton, ON, Canada L7S 4K1.

MEYER, GEORGE H.
PERSONAL Born 02/19/1928, Detroit, MI, m, 1988, 2 children **DISCIPLINE** POLITICAL SCIENCE **EDUCATION** Univ Mich, BA, 49; Harvard Law, JD, 52; Oxford Univ, Certif, 55; Wayne St Univ, LLM, 62 **CAREER** 1st Lt, USAF, 52-55; Fischer, Franklin & Ford (assoc, 56-63, partner, 63-74); sr. member, Meyer, Kirk, Snyder & Lynch, PLLC, 74-; **HONORS AND AWARDS** Phi Beta Kappa; Pi Sigma Alpha; Wm Jennings Bryan Prize; Who's Who in Amer **MEMBERSHIPS** Amer Bar Assoc; Mich Bar Assoc; Amer Folk Art Soc; Cranbrook Writers Guild; Museum of Am Folk Art, NYC, trustee. **RESEARCH** American Folk Art **SELECTED PUBLICATIONS** Auth, "Property Tax Equalizations in Michigan," Gale, 62; "Folk Artists Biographical Index," Gale, 86; American Folk Art Canes, Univ of Wash Press, 92. **CONTACT ADDRESS** 1483 N Cranbrook Rd., Bloomfield Village, MI 48301. **EMAIL** gmeyer@meyerkirk.com

MEYER, LEROY N.
PERSONAL Born 02/04/1946, Arlington, VA, m, 1986, 3 children **DISCIPLINE** PHILOSOPHY **EDUCATION** Univ Va, PhD, 75. **CAREER** Asst prof, Philos, George Mason Univ, 76-77; vis schol, Philos, Univ Cambridge, 77-78; asst to assoc prof to Dir of Philos, Univ S Dakota, 88 -. **MEMBERSHIPS** Am Philos Asn; Iowa Philos Asn; Philos Science Asn; Realia. **RESEARCH** Philos Culture; Philos Science; Philos War, Peace. **SELECTED PUBLICATIONS** Auth, "The Shadows of August: Moral Reflections Fifty Years After Hiroshima and Nagasaki," Intl Quart 2, 95; co-auth, "Wakinyan Hotan: Inscrutability of Lakota/Dakota Metaphysics," in From Our Eyes: Learning From Indigenous People, 96; auth, "Pluralism, Perspectivism & the Enigma of Truth," Contemporary Philosophy, 97. **CONTACT ADDRESS** Dept of Philosophy, Univ of So Dakota, Vermillion, Vermillion, SD 57069. **EMAIL** lnmeyer@usd.edu

MEYER, MICHAEL ALBERT
PERSONAL Born 11/15/1937, Berlin, Germany, m, 1961, 3 children **DISCIPLINE** JEWISH HISTORY **EDUCATION** Univ Calif, Los Angeles, BA, 59; Hebrew Union Col, Ohio, PhD, 64. **CAREER** Asst prof Jewish hist, Hebrew Union Col, Calif, 64-67; from asst prof to assoc prof, 67-72, Prof Jewish Hist, Hebrew Union Col, Ohio, 72-, Vis asst prof, Univ Calif, Los Angeles, 65-67; vis lectr, Antioch Col, 68; Fel, Leo Baeck Inst, 69-; vis sr lectr, Haifa Univ, 70-71 and Univ Negev, Israel, 71-72; vis prof, Hebrew Univ, Jerusalem, 77-78; **HONORS AND AWARDS** Frank and Ethel Cohen Awd, Jewish Bk Coun Am, 68; Am Coun Learned Soc fel, 82. **MEMBERSHIPS** AHA; Asn Jewish Studies. **RESEARCH** Jewish intellectual history of modern Europe; history of Reform Judaism. **SELECTED PUBLICATIONS** Auth, The Origins of the Modern Jew: Jewish Identity and European Culture in Germany, 1749-1824, Wayne State Univ Press (Detroit, MI), 67; ed, Ideas of Jewish History, Behrman House, 74; auth, Response to Modernity: A History of the Reform Movement in Judaism, Oxford Univ Press (New York, NY), 88; auth, Jewish Identity in the Modern World, Univ Wash Press (Seattle, WA), 90; ed & contribur, German-Jewish History in Modern Times, 4 vols, Columbia Univ Press (New York, NY), 96-98. **CONTACT ADDRESS** Dept of Hist, Hebrew Union Col-Jewish Inst of Religion, Ohio, Cincinnati, OH 45220. **EMAIL** mameyer@cn.huc.edu

MEYER, MILTON WACHSBERG
PERSONAL Born 09/08/1951, Pittsburgh, PA, m, 1991, 2 children **DISCIPLINE** PHILOSOPHY **EDUCATION** Duke Univ, BA, 73; Oxford Univ, BPhil, 75; Princeton Univ, PhD, 83. **CAREER** Instr, Univ Notre Dame, 79-84; asst prof, Cornell Univ, 84-91; lecturer, Univ of Penn, 95, 97-. **HONORS AND AWARDS** Danforth fel, 73. **MEMBERSHIPS** APA. **RESEARCH** Ethics; political philosophy; feminist philosophy. **CONTACT ADDRESS** 316 Ogden Ave, Swarthmore, PA 19081. **EMAIL** mwmeyer@nous.phil.upenn.edu

MEYER, PAUL WILLIAM
PERSONAL Born 05/31/1924, Raipur, India, m, 1948, 2 children **DISCIPLINE** NEW TESTAMENT **EDUCATION** Elmhurst Col, BA, 45; Union Theol Sem, NYork, BD, 49, ThD, 55. **CAREER** Lectr New Testament, Union Theol Sent, NY, 51-52, instr, 52-54; asst prof, Divinity Sch, Yale Univ, 54-62, assoc prof, 62-64; prof, Colgate Rochester Divinity Sch, 64-70; prof New Testament, Divinity Sch, Vanderbilt Univ, 70-78; Helen H P Manson Prof New Testament Lit and Exegesis, Princeton Theol Sem, 78-89; Emer, 89-. **HONORS AND AWARDS** Fulbright res grant, Univ Gottingen, 61-62; Morse fel, Yale Univ, 61-62. **MEMBERSHIPS** Soc Bibi Lit; Soc New Testament Studies; Am Theol Soc; AAUP. **RESEARCH** New Testament theology and exegesis; history of New Testament interpretation. **SELECTED PUBLICATIONS** Auth, Christians and the New Creation--Genesis Motifs in the New Testament, J Biblical Lit, Vol 0115, 96. **CONTACT ADDRESS** Princeton Theol Sem, Princeton, NJ 08540.

MEYERS, CAROL L.
PERSONAL Born 11/26/1942, Wilkes-Barre, PA, m, 1964, 2 children **DISCIPLINE** WOMEN STUDIES **EDUCATION** Wellesley Col, AB, 64; Brandeis Univ, MA, 66; PhD, 75. **CAREER** Prof Religion, Duke Univ, 90-; dir Women's Studies Program, Duke Univ, 92; assoc dir Women's Studies Program, Duke Univ, 86-90, 92-98; consultant, DreamWorks production of Prince of Egypt, 97-98; Ntl Endowment Humanities Inst on Image & Reality of Women in Near East Soc, 95; vis fac, Univ Conn, 94-; Consultant, Lilith Publications Network, 94-; Consultant, "Mysteries of the Bible," for Cable TV, 93; Consultant, New Dominion Pictures, 92-93; Consultant, "Religion, Culture, and Family," Univ Chi Divinity School, 91-97; assoc prof, Duke Univ, 84-90; Res Fac, Duke Univ, 83-; co-dir, Duke Univ Summer Prog in Israel, 80-. **HONORS AND AWARDS** Wellesley Wellesey Col Alumnae Achievement Awd, 99; Intl Correspondence Fel, Bar Ilan Univ, 98-; Frankfurt am Main Res Assoc, Johann Wolfgang Goethe Universitat, 95; Alumni Distinguished Undergraduate Tchg Awd Nominee, 94; Severinghaus Awd, Wellesley Col, 91; Princeton Univ Vis Fel, 90-91; Princeton Univ Res Member, 90-91; Ntl Endowment Humanities, 82-83, 90-91; Howard Found Fel, 85-86; Duke Univ Res Council, 83-84, 85-86, 87-88, 90-91, 92-93, 93-94, 99-00; Oxford Univ Vis Res Fel, 82-83; Oxford Centre for Postgraduate Hebrew Studies Vis Scholar, 82-83; Duke Univ Fac Summer Fel, 82; Cooperative Program in Judaic Studies Publications Grant, 81. **MEMBERSHIPS** Amer Acad Relig; Amer Schools of Oriental Res; Archaeol Inst Amer; Archaeol Soc Jordan; Assoc Jewish Studies; British School of Archaeol in Jerusalem; Cath Bibl Assoc; Center for Cross-Cult Res on Women; Harvard Semitic Museum; Israel Exploration Soc; Palestine Exploration Soc; Soc Bibl Lit; Soc Values in Higher Ed; Wellesley Col Center for Res on Women; Women's Assoc of Ancient Near East Studies; Women's Caucus, Assoc for Jewish Studies. **RESEARCH** Syro-Palestinian Archaelogy; Hebrew Bible; Gender in the Biblical World **SELECTED PUBLICATIONS** Ed, Women in Scripture, Houghton-Mifflen, 00; Coauth, Families in Ancient Israel, Westminister/John Knox Pr, 97; co-ed, Sepphoris in Galilee: Cross-Currents of Culture, N Carolina Museum Art, 96; coauth, Zippori (Sepphoris) 1994, Excavations & Surveys in Israel, 97; "New Faces of Eve," Humanistic Judaism, 97-98. **CONTACT ADDRESS** Dept of Religion, Duke Univ, Box 90964, Durham, NC 27708-0964. **EMAIL** carol@.duke.edu

MEYERS, DIANA TIETJENS
DISCIPLINE ETHICS, FEMINIST THEORY, SOCIAL AND POLITICAL PHILOSOPHY **EDUCATION** Univ Chicago, AB, philosophical psychol, 69; City Univ New York Grad Center, MA, philosophy, 76, PhD, philosophy, 78. **CAREER** Visiting asst prof, State Univ New York Stony Brook, 78-79; asst prof, Government Dept , Cornell Univ, , 79-85; asst prof, Montclair State Coll, 85-87; assoc prof, 87-90, prof, 90-, Univ of Connecticut Storrs. **HONORS AND AWARDS** Univ Fellowship, 76-77; graduate fellow, res, 77-78; humanities faculty res grant, summer, 90; general educ development grant, 81; grant, Exxon Educ Found, 84-85; Rockefeller Residency Fellowship, Center for Philosophy and Public Policy (declined), 85-86; fellowship, ACLS/Ford Found, 86; Career Devel Grant, Montclair State Coll, 86-87; Special Achievements Awds, 90, 94, major res grants, 91, 93, Provost's Fellowship, spring 93, Univ Conn; Rockefeller Found Study Center at Bellagio, Italy, residency, summer 93; Who's Who in the East, 86-; Intl, Who's Who of Women, 86-; Who's Who of Amer Women, 98; Who's Who in America, 00. **MEMBERSHIPS** Ex officio member, Comt Status Women 92-97, chair, Eastern Div Program Comt, 94-96, Amer Philosophical Assn; treas, New York Group, 97-, natl hq, Exec Comt, 80-84, 91-95, exec sec, 84-91, Soc Philosophy and Public Affairs; co-chair, 87-, Women's Studies Exec Bd, Women's Studies Curriculum Courses Comt, 91-, chair, Grad Placement Comt, 96-, sexual harassment officer, 94-, Dept of Philosophy, Women's Studies/Psychol Search Comt for the Dir of Women's Studies, 97-, Univ Conn; Member Comt Status of Women, 00-. **RESEARCH** Philosophy of law; applied ethics. **SELECTED PUBLICATIONS** Ed, Feminist Social Thought: A Reader, 97; auth, "Inalienable Rights: A Defense (Columbia UP); Self, Society, and Personal Choice (Columbia UP); Subjection and Subjectivity (Routledge); Gender in the Mirror (Oxford UP, forthcoming). **CONTACT ADDRESS** Dept of Philosophy, Univ of Connecticut, Storrs, Storrs, CT 06269-2054. **EMAIL** diana.meyers@uconn.edu

MEYERS, ERIC MARK
PERSONAL Born 06/05/1940, Norwich, CT, m, 1964, 2 children **DISCIPLINE** BIBLE AND JUDAIC STUDIES **EDUCATION** Dartmouth Col, BA, 62; Brandeis Univ, MA, 64; Harvard Univ, PhD (Jewish hist, Bible and archaeol), 69. **CAREER** Asst prof relig, 69-71, assoc prof, 71-79, Prof Relig, Duke Univ, 79-, Dir joint exped to Khirbet Shema, Meiron and Gush Halav, Nabratein; Am Schs Orient Res, 70-82; Vis Assoc Prof, Univ NCar, Chapel Hill, 72-; dir coop prof Judaic studies, Duke Univ-Univ NC, Chapel Hill, ed, Present Tense, 73-75; Bibl Archaeologist, 81-; First Vpres Publ, Am Schs Orient Res, 82-90; Pres, Am Schs, 90-96; Bernice and Morton Lerner Prof

of Judaic Studies and Arch, 97. **MEMBERSHIPS** Asn Jewish Studies; Am Acad Relig; Am Schs Orient Res; Soc Religh Higher Educ; Soc Bibl Lit. **RESEARCH** Jewish history; archaeology; Bible. **SELECTED PUBLICATIONS** Auth, Jewish Ossuaries: Reburial and Rebirth, Bibl Press, Rome, 71; Theological implications of an ancient Jewish burial custom, Jewish Quart Rev, 71; The synagogue at Khirbet Shema, In: Perspectives in Jewish Learning, 73; coauth, Synagogue excavation at Khirbet Shema, Bibl Archaeologist, Duke Univ, 76; auth, Galilean regionalism as a factor in historical reconstruction, Bull Am Schs Orient Res, 76; coauth (with W C Meyers and J F Strange), Excavations at Ancient Meiron, Am Schs Orient Res, 81; (with J F Strange), Archaeology, the Rabbis and Early Christianity, Abingdon, 81; coauth, Cambridge Companion to Bible, 97; ed, The Oxford Encyclopedia of Archaeology in The Near East, 5 vols, 97. **CONTACT ADDRESS** Dept of Relig, Duke Univ, PO Box 90964, Durham, NC 27708-0964. **EMAIL** emc@duke.edu

MEYERS, MICHAEL
PERSONAL Born 02/16/1950, Manhattan, NY, s **DISCIPLINE** LAW **EDUCATION** Antioch Coll, BA 1972; Rutgers Law School, JD 1975. **CAREER** Marc Corp NYC, intern 1967,68, fellow 1968-75; Met Applied Rsch Ctr, asst to Dr Kenneth B Clark pres 1970-75; NAACP, asst exec dir 1975-84, dir res policy & planning 1977-84; RACE Inc NY, founder/dir/pres 1984-. **HONORS AND AWARDS** Staff Cit Comm Investigating Corpl Punishment in NYC's Publ School 1974; Law School Rep to Law Student Div Amer Bar Assoc 1972-75; Outstanding Young Men of Amer 1986. **MEMBERSHIPS** Mem spec comm HUD, Amer Bar Assoc 1974-75; bd dir Sponsors of Open Housing Investment Wash DC 1970-77; bd dir New Hope Housing Inc 1971-77; natl chmn comm of 25 SOHI 1972-74; exec comm SOHI 1970-77; bd dir Natl Child Labor Comm Inc 1976-82; bd dir NY Civil Liberties Union 1976-; exec comm Natl Coaltion Against the Death Penalty 1977-84, Amer Civil Liberties Union Equality Comm 1974-80, Acad Freedom Comm, Free Speech Assoc Comm; bd dir Amer Civil Liberties Union 1981-. **SELECTED PUBLICATIONS** Publs in Integrated Ed Mag, Youth & Soc Jrnl, Civil Liberties, Wall St Jrnl, Change Mag, LA Times, Crisis, NY Times, Wash Post, Christ Sci Monitor, Newsday, Daily News, NY Post, Village Voice; Esquire Register 1986. **CONTACT ADDRESS** RACE Inc, PO Box 1342, Riverdale, NY 10471.

MEYERS, ROBERT
PERSONAL Born 01/20/1937, Brooklyn, NY, m, 4 children **DISCIPLINE** PHILOSOPHY **EDUCATION** State Univ NYork, Buffalo, PhD. **CAREER** Prof, Univ Albany, State Univ NY. **RESEARCH** Theory of knowledge, history of modern empiricism, American pragmatism and Hume. **SELECTED PUBLICATIONS** Auth, The Likelihood of Knowledge, Dordrecht, 88; coauth, Early Influences on Peirce: A letter to Samuel Barnett, J Hist Philos, 93. **CONTACT ADDRESS** Dept of Philosophy, SUNY, Albany, Albany, NY 12222. **EMAIL** Rgm95@csc.Albany.edu

MEYLER, JOAN BERNADETTE
PERSONAL Born, NY, m, 1 child **DISCIPLINE** ENGLISH, LAW **EDUCATION** Marymount Col, BA, 65; St John's Univ Law Sch, JD, 75; CUNY Grad Cen, PhD, 98. **CAREER** Adj asst prof, John Jay Col Criminal Justice, 95-. **MEMBERSHIPS** MLA; ABA; BBA. **RESEARCH** Theories of interpretation, metaphor, allegory and meaning; 18th-century; human rights issues. **SELECTED PUBLICATIONS** Auth, "A Matter of (Mis) Interpretation: State Sovereign Immunity, the Eleventh Amendment and the Supreme Court's Reformation of the Constitution in Seminole Tribe and It's Progeny," Howard Law J 44 (forthcoming). **CONTACT ADDRESS** 10 Clinton St, Duplex 11, Brooklyn, NY 11201-2748. **EMAIL** jmeyler@attglobal.net

MEZEI, REGINA A.
PERSONAL Born 07/06/1942, Trenton, NJ, s **DISCIPLINE** POLITICAL SCIENCE **EDUCATION** Douglass Col, BA, 63; Fordham Univ, MA, 68; PhD, 74. **CAREER** Adjunct prof, Seton Hall Univ and Rider Univ; asst prof to prof, Mercer Community Col, 81-. **HONORS AND AWARDS** Fulbright Scholar to Mexico; NDEA Fel at Fordham Univ; started the ESL Prog at Mercer Community Col; chaired the curriculum comt at MCCC for 3 years; vice pres, NJ Fulbright Asn. **MEMBERSHIPS** NJ Fulbright Asn, Consortium on Revolutionary Europe, Soc for Spanish and Portuguese Hist Studies. **RESEARCH** Spanish Carlism, Basque studies. **SELECTED PUBLICATIONS** Auth, "El carlismo y la guerra entre Espana y los Estados Unidos: Luis Maria de Llauder y El Correo Catalan (enero-octubre 1898)," Aportes, Revista de Historia Contemporanea, IX, No 24 (Marzo 94): 67-78; auth, "Espana contemporanea en los Estados Unidos y Canada: la historiografia recients," Spagna Contemporanea, Turin Italy, IV, No 7 (95): 165-176; auth, "Great Britain and the First Carlist War: The Carlist Sympathizers in England 91833-1840)," Selected Papers 1995, Consortium on Revolutionary Europe, 1750-1850 (Inst on Napolean and the French Revolution, Fla State Univ, 95): 709-718; auth, "Carlism and the Spanish-American War," Mediterranean Studies, VI, Thomas Jefferson Univ Press, Kirksville, Mo (96): 113-128. **CONTACT ADDRESS** Dept Liberal Arts, Mercer County Comm Col, PO Box B, Trenton, NJ 08690. **EMAIL** mezei@mccc.edu

MICHAEL, ALOYSIUS
PERSONAL Born 09/28/1938, Dindigul, s **DISCIPLINE** COMPARATIVE AND CHRISTIAN ETHICS **EDUCATION** Col of the Jesuits, MPhil, 60; Univ Madras, BS, 64; DeNobili Col, MTh, 70; Loyola Marymount Univ, MEd, 72; Gregorian Univ, Rome, PhD, 75. **CAREER** DeNobili Col, 75-80; Flannery prof, Gonzaga Univ, 80-82; assoc prof, Mt St Marys Col, 82-. **HONORS AND AWARDS** Flannery Chair, Gonzaga Univ. **RESEARCH** Comparative religious ethics and theological ethics. **SELECTED PUBLICATIONS** Auth, Radhakrishnan on Hindu Moral LIfe, and Action, Concept Pub Co, 79; auth, Visions of Women, College Pub, 87; auth, American Virtues and Cultural Values from the 1820's to 1990's, Mellen, (forthcoming). **CONTACT ADDRESS** Dept Relig Studies, Mount St. Mary's Col, 12001 Chalon Rd, Los Angeles, CA 90049-1526.

MICHAEL, COLETTE
PERSONAL Born, France, d **DISCIPLINE** FRENCH, PHILOSOPHY **CAREER** Prof, N Ill Univ. **HONORS AND AWARDS** Ford Fel. **RESEARCH** Phenomenology. **CONTACT ADDRESS** Dept For Lang, No Illinois Univ, 1425 W Lincoln Hwy, Dekalb, IL 60115-2828. **EMAIL** cmichael@niu.edu

MICHAEL, COLETTE VERGER
PERSONAL Born Marseille, France, 6 children **DISCIPLINE** FRENCH AND PHILOSOPHY **EDUCATION** Univ Wash Seattle, fr and philos, BA, 69; Univ Wash Seattle, romance lang, MA, 70; Univ Wisc Madison, hist of sci, MA, 75; Univ Wisc Madison, fr and minor philos, PhD, 73. **CAREER** Tchg asst, Fr and Ital Dept, Univ Wisc Madison, 9/73-12/73; lectr, extension dept, Univ Wisc Madison, 7/74-8/74; lectr, fr and ital dept, Univ Wisc Madison, 2/74-8/74; prof, humanities, Shimer Col, Mt Carroll, Ill, 75-77; asst prof, foreign lang and lit, Northern Ill Univ, 77-84; assoc prof, foreign lang and lit, Northern Ill Univ, 84-90; prof, foreign lang and lit, Northern Ill Univ, 90-. **HONORS AND AWARDS** Consulat General de France Svc Culturel, Subvention for Bulletin de la Soc Amer de Philos, Jan, 92; Facul Develop grant, Hist and Tech of Fr Cinema, Fall, 91; Deans fund for res in the humanities, Spring, 87; Deans' Fund for Res, Grad Sch, Northern Ill Univ, asst for res on Negritude, Fall, 85; Deans's Fund for Res, Grad Sch, Northern Ill Univ, asst for res on The Marquis de Sade: The Man, His Works and His Critics, Fall, 83; Res award from Dean of Grad Sch, Northern Ill Univ, Topic: Choderlos de Laclos, The Man, His Works, and His Critics, Jan 80-Jun 80; Grad Sch Summer grant, NIU Topic: The Marquis de Condorcet, His Work, His Ideology, His Influence, 78; Nat Endow for the Humanities Summer Fel for Col Tchrs, Univ Ill Univ, Champaign, Topic: The European Enlightenment in the Amer Revolution, Summer, 77; Ford Found Fel, Fr and Ital Dept, Univ Wisc Madison, 71, 72, 73; Nonresident scholar, The Grad Sch, Univ Wisc Madison, 71-72. **RESEARCH** Philosophy, 18th Century. **SELECTED PUBLICATIONS** Articles, Camus, Science and Metaphors, Bull de la Soc Amer de Philos de Lang Fr VIII, 2, 78-88, 96; A la recherche de l'absolu: le neant des ecrivains maudits, Actes du Congres Intl des Soc de Philos de lang Fr, Poitiers, Fr, 167-169, 96; L'audiovisuel et la litterature francophone, Rev Francophone, VIII, 2, 73-83, 95; Justine ou la vertu devant la violence, Actes de Ile Congres mondial sur la violence et la coexistence humaine, Montreal, Vol VII, 429-435, 95; Billy Budd: An Allegory on the Rights of Man, Allegory Old and New: Creativity and Continuity in Culture, Analecta Husserliana, XLII, 251-258, 94; Light and Darkness and the Phenomenon of Creation in Victor Hugo, Analecta Husserliana: The Elemental Dialectic of Light and Darkness, XXXVIII, 131-149; Les Lettres de Doleances: Un Genre de Cahiers, ou Cahiers d'un nouveau Genre? Lang de la Revolution 1770-1815, Inst Nat de la Lang Fr: Lexicometrie et textes polit, Paris, Klimcksieck, 251-264, 95. **CONTACT ADDRESS** 635 Joanne Ln., De Kalb, IL 60115. **EMAIL** tc0cvm1@corn.cso.niu.edu

MICHAEL, EMILY
PERSONAL Born Baltimore, MD, m, 2 children **DISCIPLINE** PHILOSOPHY **EDUCATION** Univ Pa, PhD, 73. **CAREER** Prof, Brooklyn Col, 73-. **HONORS AND AWARDS** NEH fel, 82-83. **MEMBERSHIPS** Am Philos Asn; Hume Soc; British Soc for the Hist of Philos; Soc for Medieval and Renaissance Philos. **RESEARCH** History of Philosophy: Medieval, Renaissance, Early Modern, Scottish Englightenment; John Wyclif; Thomas Reid; Pierre Gassendi. **SELECTED PUBLICATIONS** Auth, "The Nature and Influence of Late Renaissance Paduan Psychology," History of Univ, (93); auth, "Gassendi's 1592-1992, (94); auth, "Francis Hutcheson's Confusing Univ Career"; auth, Gassendi's Modified Epicureanism and British Moral Philosophy," History of European Ideas, (95); auth, "Pierre Gassendi," Encyclopedia of Empiricism, Greenwood Press, (97); auth, Francis Hutcheson and the Glasgow School of Logic," Logic and the Workings of the Mind; auth, "Daniel Sennert On Matter and Form: At the Juncture of the Old and the New," Early Science and Medicine, (97); auth, "Descartes and Gassendi On Matter and Mind, From Aristotelian Pluralism to Early Modern Dualism" Meeting of the Minds, Brepols, (98); auth, "Reid's Critique of the Logic of Ideas," Reid Studies, (99); auth, "Renaissance Theories of Body, Soul and Mind," Psyche and Soma in the History of Western Medicine and Philosophy, Oxford, (00). **CONTACT ADDRESS** Dept of Philosophy, Brooklyn Col, CUNY, 2900 Bedford Ave., Brooklyn, NY 11210. **EMAIL** emichael@ brooklyn.cuny.edu

MICHAEL, RANDALL BLAKE
PERSONAL Born 08/17/1948, Lexington, NC, m, 1970, 1 child **DISCIPLINE** RELIGIOUS STUDIES **EDUCATION** Univ NC Chapel Hill, BA, 70; Harvard Divinity School, MDiv, 72; Harvard Univ, AM, 75, PhD, 79. **CAREER** Instr, 78; to prof, 91-; to assoc dean, 92-. **RESEARCH** Hindu bhakti movements. **CONTACT ADDRESS** Dept of Religion, Ohio Wesleyan Univ, 50 Henry St, Delaware, OH 43015-2377. **EMAIL** rbmichae@cc.owu.edu

MICHAELSEN, ROBERT SLOCUMB
PERSONAL Born 05/16/1919, Clinton, IA, m, 1941, 3 children **DISCIPLINE** RELIGION **EDUCATION** Cornell Col, BA, 42; Yale Univ, BD, 45, PhD(Christian soc ethics), 51. **CAREER** Asst prof religh Univ Iowa, 47-52; asst prof Am Christianity, Divinity Sch, Yale Univ, 52-54; prof relig and dir sch, Univ Iowa, 54-65, res prof, 63-64; chmn dept, 65-72, Prof Relig Studies, Univ Calif, Santa Barbara, 65-, Fulbright scholar, India, 61; proj consult, Soc Relig Higher Educ, 63-64. **HONORS AND AWARDS** DD, Cornell Col, 54. **MEMBERSHIPS** Fel Soc Relig Higher Educ; Am Soc Church Hist; Am Acad Relig (pres, 71-72). **RESEARCH** Religion in American; religion in higher education, especially in tax-supported universities. **SELECTED PUBLICATIONS** Coauth, The Ministry in Historical Perspective, 56 & Faith and Ethics, 57, Harper; Religious Education, Abingdon, 60; auth, The Study of Religion in American Universities; Ten Case Studies, Soc Relig Higher Educ, 65; Piety in the Public Schools, Macmillan, 70; contribr, The Religion of the Republic, Fortress, 71; New theology No 9, Macmillan, 72; The American Search for Soul, La State Univ, 75. **CONTACT ADDRESS** Dept of Religious Studies, Univ of California, Santa Barbara, Santa Barbara, CA 93106.

MICHEL, WALTER L.
DISCIPLINE OLD TESTAMENT **EDUCATION** Univ Vienna, MDiv; Univ Wis, MA, PhD; post-dr stud, Yale Univ; Pontifical Bibl inst, Rome. **CAREER** Campus pastor, Univ Wis; lectr, Adult Forums; vis prof, Univ Chicago Divinity Sch; Spertus Col of Judaica; North Park Theol Sem; prof-. **SELECTED PUBLICATIONS** Auth, Job In the Light of Northwest Semitic; Prologue and First Cycle of Speeches Job; Biblica et Orientalia, Bibl Inst Press, 87. **CONTACT ADDRESS** Dept of Old Testament, Lutheran Sch of Theol at Chicago, 1100 E 55th St, Chicago, IL 60615. **EMAIL** wmichel@lstc.edu

MICHELMAN, STEPHEN A.
PERSONAL Born 06/08/1962, New York, NY, m, 1999 **DISCIPLINE** PHILOSOPHY **EDUCATION** Vassar Col, AB, 85; SUNY, MA, 90; PhD, 94. **CAREER** Asst Prof, Wofford Col, 96-. **HONORS AND AWARDS** Chateaubriand Fel, 89; French Govt Dissertation Awd. **MEMBERSHIPS** Am Philos Asn. **RESEARCH** Philosophical Psychology; Continental Philosophy; Aesthetics. **SELECTED PUBLICATIONS** Auth, Historical Dictionary of Existentialism, Scarecrow Press, forthcoming. **CONTACT ADDRESS** Dept Philos, Wofford Col, 429 N Church St, Spartanburg, SC 29303-3612. **EMAIL** michelmansa@wofford.edu

MICHELSEN, JOHN MAGNUS
PERSONAL Born Bergen, Norway **DISCIPLINE** GREEK PHILOSOPHY **EDUCATION** Univ Wash, BA, 60, MA, 64, PhD(philos), 70. **CAREER** Lectr philos, Univ Alta, 65-66; lectr, 66-70, asst prof, 70-77, Assoc Prof Philos, Univ Victoria, BC, 77- **MEMBERSHIPS** Can Philos Asn; Int Husserl and Phenomenol Res Soc; Hegel Soc Am; Soc for Advan Am Philos; Can Archaeol Inst at Athens. **RESEARCH** Aristotle, Plato and Santayana; post-Kantian European philosophy. **SELECTED PUBLICATIONS** Auth, Bmw Trouble, Aba Jour, Vol 83, 97. **CONTACT ADDRESS** Dept of Philosophy, Univ of Victoria, Victoria, BC, Canada V8W 2Y2.

MICKIEWICZ, ELLEN PROPPER
DISCIPLINE POLITICAL SCIENCE **EDUCATION** Wellesley Col, BA; Yale Univ, PhD. **CAREER** James R Shepley Prof Pub Policy Studies, Duke Univ, 94-; dir, DeWitt Wallace Ctr for Com and Jour, Terry Sanford Inst of Pub Policy, Duke Univ, 94-; prof, dept polit sci, Duke Univ, 94-; fel, The Carter Ctr, 86-; prof polit sci, Emory Univ, 88-93; dir, int media com prog, Emory Univ, 86-93; prof, dept polit sci, Emory Univ, 85-88; dean, grad school of arts and sci, Emory Univ, 80-85; prof, dept polit sci, Mich State Univ, 73-80; assoc prof, Mich State Univ, 67-73. **HONORS AND AWARDS** Edelman Awd for Distinguished Scholar in Polit Com, Amer Polit Sci Asn, 97; Outstanding Service to Promote Democratic Media in Russia, Union of Jour of Russia, 94; Elec Media Book of the Year, Nat Asn Broadcasters and Broadcast Educ Asn, 88; Guggenheim Fel, 73-74. **MEMBERSHIPS** Amer Polit Sci Asn; Int Com Asn; Amer Asn for the Advan of Slavic Studies; Dante Soc of Amer. **RESEARCH** Political communication; comparative politics; public policy. **SELECTED PUBLICATIONS** Auth, Changing Channels: Television and the Struggle for Power in Russia, Oxford, 97; After Soviet-era Rule: The Role of Journalists in Democratizing Societies, The Politics of News, the News

of Politics, 98; Media, Transition, and Democracy: Television and the Transformation of Russia, Communications Cornucopia, 98; co-auth, Television, Campaigning, and Elections in the Soviet Union and Post-Soviet Russia, 96; auth, The Political Economy of Media Democratization, Russia in Transition, 95; Television and Political Change, Cambridge Encyclopedia of Russia and the Soviet Union, Cambridge Univ, 94; co-auth, Television/Radio News and Minorities, Emory Univ, 94. **CONTACT ADDRESS** Dept of Public Policy Studies, Duke Univ, Durham, NC 27708-0241. **EMAIL** epm@pps.duke.edu

MICKLER, MICHAEL L.
PERSONAL Born 10/21/1949, Providence, RI, m, 1982, 4 children **DISCIPLINE** HISTORICAL STUDIES **EDUCATION** Graduate Theological Union, PhD, 89 **CAREER** Asst Prof, Church History, 89-94, Assoc Prof, 95-, Academic Dean, 95-, Unification Theological Sem. **RESEARCH** Unification Church and tradition **SELECTED PUBLICATIONS** Auth, The Unification Church in America: A Bibliography and Research Guide, 87; auth, A History of the Unification Church in America, 59-74, 93; auth, Forty Years in America: An Intimate History of the Unification Movement, 1959-99, 00. **CONTACT ADDRESS** 30 Seminary Dr., Barrytown, NY 12507. **EMAIL** utsed@ulstn.net

MICKOLUS, EDWARD F.
PERSONAL Born 12/28/1950, Cincinnati, OH, m, 1983, 1 child **DISCIPLINE** POLITICAL SCIENCE **EDUCATION** Georgetown Univ, AB, 73; Yale Univ, MA, 74, MPhil, 75, PhD, 81. **CAREER** Tchng Asst, Yale Univ, 74-76; Asst to Dir, Yale Univ, 74; Dir, Summer Inst, Georgetown Univ, 71-73. **HONORS AND AWARDS** Mgr of the Yr in a Fed Govt Agency, 93; Exceptional Performance Awds in a Fed Agency, 3/90, 1/91, 4/91, 8/95, 9/97, 5/98, 6/00; Quality Step Increase, 89; Delta Tau Kappa Soc Sci Honors Soc, 75; Pi Sigma Alpha Polit Sci Honors Soc, Georgetown Univ, 72; Mensa; founder & pres, vinyard software, inc; granted cocktail ripr c-458 by bartender magazine via am bartender asn for ciana sunrise, 4/88. **MEMBERSHIPS** Acad of Polit Sci, 75-80; Am Acad of Polit & Soc Sci, 75-80; Am Polit Sci Asn; Am Soc for Int Law, 75-81; Int Soc for Contemp Legend Res, 91-93; Int Stud Asn, 73-81; Soc for Basic Irreproduceable Res, 73-; Disco Preservation Soc, 86-; Yale Int Relations Asn, Inc, (pres), 73-75. **RESEARCH** Terrorism & polit science; virtual communities. **SELECTED PUBLICATIONS** Auth, Terrorism, 1988-1991: A Chronology of Events and a Selectively Annotated Bibliography, Bibliographies & Indexes in Mil Stud, no 6, Greenwood Press, 93; co-auth, Terrorism, 1992-1995: A Chronology of Events and a Selectively Annotated Bibliography, Greenwood Press, 97. **CONTACT ADDRESS** 2305 Sandburg St, Dunn Loring, VA 22027-1124. **EMAIL** edmickolus@hotmail.com

MIDDLETON, DARREN J. N.
PERSONAL Born 10/06/1966, Nottingham, England, m, 1994 **DISCIPLINE** THEOLOGY **EDUCATION** Univ Manchester, 86-89; Oxford Univ, 89-91; Univ Glasgow, 92-96. **CAREER** Ast prof, Rhodes Col, 93-97; ast prof, Texas Chr Univ, 98-. **HONORS AND AWARDS** Southwest AAR Junior Scholar Awd, 00. **MEMBERSHIPS** AAR/SBL. **RESEARCH** Theology and literature; Rastafarianism; Baptist theology. **SELECTED PUBLICATIONS** Auth, "David Pailin's Theology of Divine Action," Process Stud, 93; "Nikos Kazantzakis and Process Theology," Jrnl of Mod Greek Stud, 94; "W. Norman Pittenger's The Word Incarnate," Mod Believing, 95; "Christ Recrucified," Notes in Contemp Lit, 95; "Nikos Kazantzakis and The Last Temptation of Christ," Christianity and the Arts, 96; "Vagabond or Companion: Kazantzakis and Whitehead on God," God's Struggler, Mercer Univ, 96; "Genesis: A Journey into Eden," Christianity and the Arts, 97; "Apophatic Boldness," Midwest Qrtly, 98; "Kazantzakis and Christian Doctrine," Jrnl of Mod Greek Stud, 98; "Chanting Down Babylon," This is How We Flow, Univ South Carolina, 99; auth, Novel Theology: Nikos Kazantzakis's Encounter with Whiteheadian Process Theism, Mercer Univ Press, 00. **CONTACT ADDRESS** Texas Christian Univ, PO Box 298100, Fort Worth, TX 76129. **EMAIL** d.middleton2@tcu.edu

MIECZKOWSKI, BOGDON
PERSONAL Born 11/08/1924, Poland, m, 1961, 3 children **DISCIPLINE** ECONOMICS **EDUCATION** Univ London, BS, 50; Univ Ill, MA, 53; PhD, 54. **CAREER** Asst prof, Univ Vt, 54-57; res assoc, Columbia Univ, 58-62; asst prof, Boton Col, 62-65; Assoc Prof and Prof, Ithaca Col, 65- . **HONORS AND AWARDS** ODE; Distinguished Fel of the NY State Econ Asoc. **MEMBERSHIPS** NY State Econ Asoc. **RESEARCH** Comparative economic systems; dysfunctional bureaucracy. **SELECTED PUBLICATIONS** Auth, The Rot at the Top: Dysfunctional Bureacracy in Academia, 95. **CONTACT ADDRESS** Dept of Econ, Ithaca Col, Ithaca, NY 14850. **EMAIL** bogdan@ithaca.edu

MIKVA, A. J.
PERSONAL Born 01/21/1926, Milwaukee, WI, m, 1948, 3 children **DISCIPLINE** LAW **EDUCATION** Univ Chicago Law Sch, JD, 51. **CAREER** Congressman, 69-79; judge & chief judge, US Ct Appeals, 79-94; White House coun, 94-95; visiting prof, Univ Chicago Law Sch, 96-98; visiting prof, Univ Ill Col of Law, 98-. **HONORS AND AWARDS** Order of COIF; Phi Beta Kappa. **MEMBERSHIPS** Amer Law Inst. **RESEARCH** Legislative process. **SELECTED PUBLICATIONS** Auth, Legislative Process, Little Brown & Co; auth, Introduction to Statutory Interpretation, Aspen Books. **CONTACT ADDRESS** 5020 S. Lake Shore Dr., Apt. 3608, Chicago, IL 60615. **EMAIL** amikva@uic.edu

MILES, DELOS
PERSONAL Born 11/20/1933, Florence Co, SC, m, 1953, 4 children **DISCIPLINE** THEOLOGY **EDUCATION** Furman Univ, BA, 55; Southeastern Baptist Theol Sem, BD, 58; San Francisco Theol Sem, STD, 73. **CAREER** Assoc pastor, West End Baptist Church, Va, 58-59; pastor, Crewe Baptist Church, Va, 59-63; assoc secy Evangel and assoc missions, Va Baptist Gen Bd, 63-66; dir evangel, Gen Bd SC Baptist Convention, 66-73, dir Evangel and Church serv div, 74-77; Assoc Prof Evangel, Midwestern Baptist Theol Sem, MO, 78- **MEMBERSHIPS** Acad Evangel Prof. **RESEARCH** Evangelism; church growth; neo-pentecostalism. **SELECTED PUBLICATIONS** Auth, A Line of Time--Approaches to Archaeology in the Upper and Middle Thames Valley, England, World Archaeol, Vol 29, 97; Political Experience and Anti Big Government--The Making and Breaking of Themes in Ford,Gerald 1976 Presidential Campaign, Mich Hist Rev, Vol 23, 97. **CONTACT ADDRESS** Midwestern Baptist Theol Sem, 5001 N Oak St Trafficway, Kansas City, MO 64118.

MILES, KEVIN THOMAS
PERSONAL Born 04/22/1956, Schenectady, NY, m, 1987, 2 children **DISCIPLINE** PHILOSOPHY **EDUCATION** DePaul Univ, PhD, 98. **CAREER** Asst Prof, Dept Philos, Villanova Univ, 94-. **HONORS AND AWARDS** Lindback Minority Faculty Research Awd, 98; Faculty summer research grant, Villanova Univ, 98. **MEMBERSHIPS** Soc for Phenomenology & Existential Philosophy; Int Soc for African & Ditspara Philos; Amer Philos Assoc, eastern div. **RESEARCH** Greek Social & Political Philosophy, African American Philosphy, Philosophy of Law. **SELECTED PUBLICATIONS** auth, Haunting Music in The Souls of Black Folk, Boundary 2, vol 27, no 23, (00); 199-214; auth, Body Badges: Race & Sex, in Race/Sex: Theis sameness, Difference, & Interplay, Routledge Pr, (97), 133-143; auth, Martin Luther King's Debt to W.E.B. Du Bois' Debt to Hegel, in The Owl Minerva, 27:2, (96), 227-230. **CONTACT ADDRESS** Villanova Univ, 800 Lancaster Ave., Villanova, PA 19085. **EMAIL** kmiles@email.vill.edu

MILES, MURRAY LEWIS
DISCIPLINE PHILOSOPHY **EDUCATION** Univ Toronto, BA; Albert-Ludwigs-Univ, Freiburg, Ger, PhD. **CAREER** Instr, Ryerson Polytech Inst, 77-80; asst prof, Univ Toronto, 83-84; asst prof, 84-88; assoc prof, 88-; dept ch, 84-89; adj prof, McMaster Univ, 97. **HONORS AND AWARDS** Ger Acadc Exchange Assn scholar, 71-72; Can Coun doc fel, 72-73, 73-74, 74-75, 75-76; postdoc fel, Soc Sci and Hum Res Coun, 81-82; ch, brock univ fac assn comm on the terms and conditions of employment, 86-87; brock univ fac assn comm on public aff and commun liaison, 92-93, 93-93; parent adv gp, niagara peninsula children's ctr, 94-. **MEMBERSHIPS** Mem, Exec Fac Bd, 87-88, 88-89; Sen Comm on Grad Stud and Res, 87-88, 88-89; Decanal Comm on the Image/Profile of the Hum, 88; Parent Adv Gp; Niagara Peninsula Children's Ctr; OCUFA Pol Rel(s) Comm, 92-93; Adv Comm, Neurodevelopmental Clinical Res Unit, 94-; Sen Comm on Res. **SELECTED PUBLICATIONS** Auth, Logik und Metaphysik bei Kant, Zu Kants Lehre vom zwiefachen Gebrauch des Verstandes und der Vernunft, Vittorio Klostermann Verlag, Frankfurt, Ger, 78; "Fundamental Ontology and Existential Analysis in Heidegger's Being and Time," Intl Philos Quart, 94; "Leibniz on Apperception and Animal Souls," Dialogue XXXIII, 94; "Philosophy and Liberal Learning," Queen's Quart 104/1, 97 **CONTACT ADDRESS** Dept of Philos, Brock Univ, 500 Glenridge Ave, Saint Catharines, ON, Canada L2S 3A1. **EMAIL** mmiles@spartan.ac.brocku.ca

MILETIC, STEPHEN F.
PERSONAL Born 11/23/1952, Windsor, ON, Canada, m, 1975, 4 children **DISCIPLINE** NEW TESTAMENT, THEOLOGY **EDUCATION** Academy of Music & Performing Arts, Vienna, Austria, 71-72; Univ Windsor, BA, 75-76; Univ Windsor, MA, 77; Univ Windsor, BEd, 78; Marquette Univ, PhD, 85. **CAREER** Dir, Nat Office of Relig Educ, Canadian Conf of Catholic Bishops, 86; consult, res & relig educ, 87-88; provost & academic dean, Notre Dame Inst, 88-96, assoc prof, Franciscan Univ of Steubenville, 96-; Dean of Faculty, 99. **MEMBERSHIPS** Soc of Biblical Lit; Canadian Soc of Biblical Studies; Catholic Biblical Asn. **SELECTED PUBLICATIONS** Translat, R. Le Doaut's The Message of the New Testament and the Aramaic Bible, Pontifical Biblical Inst Press, 82; auth, "One Flesh: Ephesians 5.22024, 31. Marriage and the New Creation", in Analecta Biblica 115, Pontifical Biblical Inst Press, 88; auth, 204 brief New Testament articles for the Catholic Encyclopedia, Our Sunday Visitor, 91; auth, commentaries on biblical texts for Sunday, Cycle C for Discover the Bible, No. 1166, 92; auth, commentaries on biblical texts for 4th & 5th Sundays of Easter, Cycle A for Discover the Bible, 93; auth, commentaries on biblical texts for 1st and 2nd Sundays of Lent, Year B for Discover the Bible, 94; auth, commentaries on biblical texts for All Saints and 31st Sunday of Ordinary Time, Year C for Discover the Bible, 98. **CONTACT ADDRESS** Office of the Dean of Faculty, Franciscan Univ of Steubenville, 1235 University Blvd., Steubenville, OH 43952-6701. **EMAIL** smiletic@franuniv.edu

MILGROM, JACOB
PERSONAL Born 02/01/1923, New York, NY, m, 1948, 4 children **DISCIPLINE** RELIGION **EDUCATION** Brooklyn Col, BA, 43; Jewish Theol Sem, BHL, 43, MHL, 46, DHL, 53;. **CAREER** From instr to prof Old Testament, Grad Sch Relig, Va Union Univ, 54-65; assoc prof Hebrew and Bible, 65-73, Prof Bibl Studies, Univ Calif, Berkeley, 73-, Mem staff, Encycl Judaica, 68-71; dir, Univ Calif Studies Ctr, Hebrew Univ Jerusalem, 69-71; Nat Found Jewish Cult fel, 69; Am Philos Soc and Am Coun Learned Soc grants-in-aid, 72; Jewish Mem Cult Found fel, 72-73; Univ Calif, Berkeley humanities res inst, 77; Guggenheim fel, 78. **HONORS AND AWARDS** DD, Jewish Theol Sem, 73. **MEMBERSHIPS** Soc Bibl Lit. **RESEARCH** Biblical and ancient Near Eastern culture; Cult and law of ancient Israel. **SELECTED PUBLICATIONS** Auth, Cult and Conscience, E J Brill, Leiden, 76; Israel's sanctuary: The priestly picture of Dorian Gray, Revue Biblique, 77; A shoulder for the Levites, In: The Temple Scroll, 77; articles in Encycl Biblica, Encycl Judaica & Interpreter's Dict of Bible, suppl, 71-77; Studies in the Temple Scroll, J Bibl Lit, 78; Furthur studies in Temple Scroll, Jewish Quart Rev, 80; The paradox of the red cow, Vetus Testamentum, 81; Sancta Contagion and Altar, City Asylum, Vetus Testamentum Suppl, 81. **CONTACT ADDRESS** Dept of Near Eastern Studies, Univ of California, Berkeley, Berkeley, CA 94720.

MILLEN, ROCHELLE L.
PERSONAL Born 02/26/1943, Brooklyn, NY, m, 1961, 3 children **DISCIPLINE** RELIGIOUS STUDIES **EDUCATION** Stern Col, BA, 65; McMaster Univ, MA, 75, PhD, 84. **CAREER** Instr, McMaster Univ, 72-74, 75-76; res assoc, Shalom Hartman Inst, Jerusalem, 76-77; lect, Pardes Grad Inst, Jerusalem, 77-79; ed consult, United Hebrew Sch of Detroit, 78-83; fac, Yeshiva Univ High Sch, 83-86; adj asst prof, Stern College for Women, 85-86; asst prof, Univ Nebr, Omaha, 87-89; fac, Wexner Heritage Found 87-89; assoc prof, Wittenberg Univ, 88- . **HONORS AND AWARDS** Samuel Belkin Mem Awd for Prof Achievement; McMaster Univ Benefactors Scholar; McMaster Univ Dept of Philos Fel; Stern Col Fac Awd for Academic Excellence and Character; B'Nai Zion Awd for Excellence in Hebrew. **MEMBERSHIPS** Am Acad of Relig; Asn for Jewish Stud; Canadian Soc for Stud in Relig; Coalition for Alternatives in Jewish Educ; Eastern Great Lakes Bibl Soc; Midwest Jewish Stud Asn; Soc for Bibl Lit; World Union of Jewish Stud. **RESEARCH** Women and religion, Nineteenth and twentieth century German-Jewish thought. **SELECTED PUBLICATIONS** Auth, "Birkhat HaGomel," Judaism, 94; auth, "B T Kiddushin 34a Revisited," Gender and Judaism, NYU, 95; auth, "Monarchy and Don Isaac Abravanel," Religion in the Age of Exploration, ed Menachem Mor, Creighton Univ, 96; ed, New Perspectives on the Holocaust; NYU, 96; ed, "Pitfalls of Memory," New Perspectives on the Holocaust, NYU, 96; auth, "Gardens of Innocence?" Nietzsche and Depth Psychology, ed Jacob Golomb, SUNY, 97; auth, "Seventy Faces," Hadassah Mag, 97; auth, "Christians and Pharisees," Death of God Movement and the Holocaust, ed Stephen R. Haynes, Greenwood, 98; auth, "The Desert as Focus for Ethical Exploration," Shofar, 98. **CONTACT ADDRESS** Dept of Religion, Wittenberg Univ, PO Box 720, Springfield, OH 45501. **EMAIL** rmillen@wittenberg.edu

MILLENDER, MICHAEL J.
DISCIPLINE LAW **EDUCATION** Duke Univ, BA; Oxford Univ, BA; Princeton Univ, PhD. **CAREER** Asst prof, Univ Fla, 96-. **HONORS AND AWARDS** Mellon fel in Humanities, Princeton Univ, 90-92, 95; Marshall scholar, Oxford Univ, 88-90. **RESEARCH** American legal history. **CONTACT ADDRESS** School of Law, Univ of Florida, PO Box 117625, Gainesville, FL 32611-7625. **EMAIL** Millender@law.ufl.edu

MILLER, A. R.
PERSONAL Born 01/27/1949, Wheeling, WV, m, 1971, 2 children **DISCIPLINE** PHILOSOPHY **EDUCATION** Mich State Univ, MA, 71; PhD, 75. **CAREER** Asst prof, 75-80, assoc prof, 80-90, full prof, 90-, philos, Univ Tex San Antonio. **HONORS AND AWARDS** NEH year-long seminar, Ind Univ; NDEA Title IV fel; Woodrow Wilson fel. **MEMBERSHIPS** Amer Philos Asn. **RESEARCH** Philosophy of mind; Philosophy of language; Ethics. **SELECTED PUBLICATIONS** Auth, Survival & Diminished Consciousness; auth, Bentham on Justifying the Principle of Utility; auth, Describing Unwitting Behavior; auth, Wanting, Intending & Knowing What One is Doing; others. **CONTACT ADDRESS** Div. of English, Classics, Philos & Communication, Univ of Texas, San Antonio, 6900 N. Loop 1604 W, San Antonio, TX 78249. **EMAIL** amiller@lonestar.jpl.utsa.edu

MILLER, ANTHONY
DISCIPLINE FAMILY LAW, PUBLIC SECTOR LABOR LAW, TORTS **EDUCATION** CA State Univ, BA, 67, MA, 72;

Pepperdine Univ, JD, 77. **CAREER** Pepperdine law rev, 75-77; tchg fel, 77-78; fac mem, 83; vis prof, Univ Calif, 91; assoc dean, acad, 89-93; prof-. **MEMBERSHIPS** Mem, arbitration panels; Am Arbitration Assn; Fed Mediation and Conciliation Serv; Employ Rel Bd; CA State Bar; Am Bar Assn. **SELECTED PUBLICATIONS** Auth, Cases and Materials on Family Law, Matthew Bender; California Government Codes, Forms and Commentary, 2d ed, W Publ. **CONTACT ADDRESS** Sch of Law, Pepperdine Univ, 24255 Pacific Coast Hwy, Malibu, CA 90263.

MILLER, BARBARA BUTLER
PERSONAL Born 05/17/1942, Chicago, IL, M, 1988, 1 child **DISCIPLINE** RELIGION **EDUCATION** Univ Mich, PhD, 94. **CAREER** Edgewood Col, assoc prof, chemn relig stud dept, 98-. **MEMBERSHIPS** SBL, CTS, CBA, NAWCHE, MBAS **RESEARCH** Women in the bible; feminist critique. **SELECTED PUBLICATIONS** Auth, Eve and Behind the Sex of God, in: Ready Reference: Women's Issues, Salem Press, 97; Bible: New Testament and Virgin Mary, in: Reader's Guide to Women's Studies, Chicago: Fitzroy Dearborn Press, 97; **CONTACT ADDRESS** Dept of Religious Studies, Edgewood Col, 1000 Edgewood Col Drive, Madison, WI 53711. **EMAIL** bmiller@edgewood.edu

MILLER, BENJAMIN
PERSONAL Born 06/27/1914, West Haven, CT **DISCIPLINE** PHILOSOPHY, RELIGION **EDUCATION** Occidental Col, BA, 35; Pac Sch Relig, MA, 38. **CAREER** Asst relig, Pomona Col, 38-40; vicar, St Mark's Episcopal Church, Downey, Calif, 41-46; rector, Grace Espiscopal Church, Glendora, 46-48; prof philos, Stephens Col, 48-54; vis prof, Univ Vt, 54-55; leader, Soc Ethical Cult, 55-60 and Philadelphia Ethical Soc, 60-61; asst prof philos, Lake Erie Col, 62-71; dir serv to mil families, Lake Co Chap, Am Red Cross, 73-77; Res and Writing, 77-, Men Nat Coun, Robinson Jeffers Comt, 62- **RESEARCH** Philosophy of religion; ethics; aesthetics. **SELECTED PUBLICATIONS** Auth, The elements of religious humanism, Humanist, 61; An empirical concept of the religious life, 63 & The ethical basis of religion, 64, J Relig; The Religious Response, privately publ, 77. **CONTACT ADDRESS** 315 1/2 E Walnut Ave, Painesville, OH 44077.

MILLER, C. DOUGLAS
DISCIPLINE LAW **EDUCATION** Univ Kans, BS, JD; NYork Univ, LLM. **CAREER** Prof,Univ Fla, 73-; pst Off Coun, Miller Rainey, Orlando, Fla and Lowndes, Drosdick Doster, Orlando; past partner, Clark, Mize, Linville Miller, Salina, Kans; vis prof, Leiden Univ, Neth and Ariz State Univ. **HONORS AND AWARDS** Harry J. Rudick mem awd, NY Univ, 66. **MEMBERSHIPS** Exec Coun, Fla Bar Gen Practt Sect, 0-94, and Tax Sect, 84-85; Adv bd, Univ Calif, San Diego, Estate Planning Inst, 79-82; Fla Bar Elder Law Sect, Tax Sect, Real Property, Probate Trust Law Sect; Amer Bar Asn Tax Sect Sect Real Property, Probate Trust Law; Kans Bar; Fla Bar; Beta Gamma Sigma. **RESEARCH** Estates and trusts, estate planning, professional responsibility, sports law, taxation. **CONTACT ADDRESS** School of Law, Univ of Florida, PO Box 117625, Gainesville, FL 32611-7625. **EMAIL** miller@law.ufl.edu

MILLER, CLARENCE
PERSONAL Born 08/05/1927, New York, NY, m, 1953, 2 children **DISCIPLINE** PHILOSOPHY **EDUCATION** New York Univ, PhD, 61; New School for Social Research, PhD, 68. **CAREER** Educr, New York Bd of Ed, Yeshiva Mesivta, Ladycliff Col, Ford Found Freedom Agenda Prog, 53-78; ed therapist and couns, SUNY, Downstate Med Ctr, Brooklyn, 77-78; writer, RGH Publ, New York, 62- ; playwright, FirstStage Theatre, Hollywood, 90- . **HONORS AND AWARDS** Deans list; Tchr of the year, 73, 74, 75, 76. **MEMBERSHIPS** APA; Dramatist Guild; FirstStage Theatre Asn; Ibsen Soc; The Shaw Project. **RESEARCH** Philosophical foundations of psychology; metaphysical implications of cosmology; philosophy of theatre; epistemology. **SELECTED PUBLICATIONS** Auth, Moore Dewey and the Problem of the Given, The Mod Schoolman, 62; auth, Body Washed Ashore, in The Mutilators, Windsor, 93; auth, Theoretical Perspectives for Directors and Actors, FirstStage, 94; auth, numerous parable plays staged yearly, FirstStage PlayWrights Express, 90-98. **CONTACT ADDRESS** 3057 Brighton 4th St, Brooklyn, NY 11235. **EMAIL** cmiller3@worldnet.att.net

MILLER, DANNA R.
DISCIPLINE PHILOSOPHY **EDUCATION** Harvard Univ, PhD. **CAREER** Asst prof, Fordham Univ. **RESEARCH** Matter, natural philos, and metaphysics. **SELECTED PUBLICATIONS** Auth, Sargis of Re 'aina on what the celestial bodies knew, Proc Vithum Symp Syriacum, Orientalia Christiana Analecta, 94; George, bishop of Arab tribes on true philosophy, Festschrift in Honor of Sebastian Brock, Oxford UP, 96. **CONTACT ADDRESS** Dept of Philos, Fordham Univ, 113 W 60th St, New York, NY 10023.

MILLER, DAVID
PERSONAL Born 12/16/1932, Chicago, IL **DISCIPLINE** COMPARATIVE RELIGION **EDUCATION** Harvard Divinity Sch, BD, 57-60; Univ Ill, BA, 51-55; Harvard Univ, PhD, 60-68. **CAREER** Assoc prof, 74-; assoc prof, Sir George Williams Univ, 72-74; asst prof, Sir George Williams Univ, 70-72; asst prof, Case W Reserve Univ, 68-70; lectr, Case W Reserve Univ, 65-68; vis lectr, Oberlin Col, 69-70. **RESEARCH** Study of contemporary Hindu monastics and gurus. **SELECTED PUBLICATIONS** co-auth, Hindu Monastic Life: The Monks and Monastics of Bhubaneswar, McGill-Queens UP, 76; Hindu Monastic Life, reprinted, Manamohar Press, New Delhi, 96; The Spiritual Descent of the Divine: The Life Story of Svami Sivananda, Hindu Spirituality, Vol II, 97; "Modernity in Hindu Monasticism," Intl Jour of Comparative Rel and Phil, 96; "The Chariot and the Phallus in the Temple Architecture of Orissa," Jour of Vaisnava Stud, 95. **CONTACT ADDRESS** Dept of Rel, Concordia Univ, Montreal, 1455 de Maisonneuve W, Montreal, QC, Canada H3G 1M8.

MILLER, DAVID LEROY
PERSONAL Born 02/25/1936, Cleveland, OH **DISCIPLINE** RELIGION **EDUCATION** Bridgewater Col, AB, 57; Bethany Theol Sem, BD, 60; Drew Univ, PhD, 63. **CAREER** Instr English, Drew Univ, 60-61; instr classics, Upsala Col, 62-63; asst prof relig, Drew Univ, 63-67; assoc prof, 67-74, Prof Relig, 74-, Syracuse Univ; Vis asst prof comp lit, Rutgers Univ, 66-67; mem adv coun, Danforth Assocs, 73-76; lectr, Eranos Conf, Switz, 75, 77, 78, & 80. **HONORS AND AWARDS** Chancellor's prize best teacher, Syracuse Univ, 81. **MEMBERSHIPS** Am Acad Relig. **RESEARCH** Theology in relation to mythology, literature & depth psychology. **SELECTED PUBLICATIONS** Co-ed, Interpretation: The poetry of Meaning, Harcourt, 67; auth, Gods & Games, Harper, 70; The New Polytheism, Harper, 74; Images of happy ending, Eranos Jahrbuch, 77; Silenos and the poetics of Christ, Eranos Jahrbuch, 78; Between God and the Gods-Trinity, Eranos Jahrbuch, 80; Christs-Archetypical images in theology, Seabury, 81; Three Faces of God-Traces of the Trinity in Literature and Life, Fortress, 86; Hells and Holy Ghosts-A Theopoetics of Christian Belief, Abingdon, 89. **CONTACT ADDRESS** Dept of Religion, Syracuse Univ, Syracuse, NY 13244-1170. **EMAIL** dlmiller@mailbox.syr.edu

MILLER, DONALD
DISCIPLINE SOCIOLOGY OF RELIGION **EDUCATION** Univ Southern Calif, BA, 68; USC, MA, 72, PhD, 75. **CAREER** Firestone prof; Univ Southern Calif, 75-. **RESEARCH** Sociology of religion; religion and social change in America; religion and community organizing/development; genocide. **SELECTED PUBLICATIONS** Auth or coauth, bk(s), Survivors: An Oral History of the Armenian Genocide, Univ Calif Press, 93; Homeless Families: The Struggle for Dignity, Univ Ill Press, 93; Writing and Research in Religious Studies, Prentice Hall, 92 & The Case for Liberal Christianity, Harper & Row, 81. **CONTACT ADDRESS** Dept of Religion, Univ of So California, University Park Campus, Los Angeles, CA 90089. **EMAIL** demiller@bcf.usc.edu

MILLER, DOUGLAS B.
PERSONAL Born 04/12/1955, Ft. Dodge, IA, 3 children **DISCIPLINE** OLD TESTAMENT **EDUCATION** Princeton Theol Sem, PhD, 96. **CAREER** Assoc prof, dept ch, Tabor College, 5 yrs. **MEMBERSHIPS** SBL; CBA. **RESEARCH** Wisdom Literature; Bible Theology. **SELECTED PUBLICATIONS** Auth, Meir Sternberg: Narrative Poetics and Bible Ideology, Koinonia, 91; coauth, Signs as Witnesses in the Forth Gospel: Reexamining the Evidence, Cath Bib Qtly, 94; auth, Power in Wisdom: The Suffering Servant of Ecclesiastes Four, Millard Lind festschrift, Pandora Press, 99; Qoheleth's Symbolic Use of Hebel, J of Biblical Lit, 98; coauth, Teaching the Bible: Paradigms for the Christian College, Direction, 95; coauth, An Akkadian Handbook, Eisenbrauns, 96; auth, Qoheleth's Symbolic Use of Hebel, J of Biblical Lit, 98; auth, Power in Wisdom: The Suffering Servant of Ecclesiastes Four, Millard Lind festschrift, Pandora Press, 99; auth, What the Preacher Forgot: The Rhetoric of Ecclesiastes, Biblical Quarterly, 00. **CONTACT ADDRESS** 601 Lincoln St S, Hillsboro, KS 67063. **EMAIL** dougm@tabor.edu

MILLER, DOUGLAS JAMES
PERSONAL Born 07/03/1941, Portland, OR, m, 1963, 2 children **DISCIPLINE** RELIGION AND SOCIETY **EDUCATION** Wheaton Col, Ill, AB, 63; Fuller Theol Sem, BD, 66; Claremont Grad Sch and Univ Ctr, PhD (relig and soc), 72. **CAREER** Ford Found teaching asst social ethics, Claremont Men's Col, 69; assoc prof, 70-80, Prof Christian Social Ethics, Eastern Baptist Theol Sem, 80- **MEMBERSHIPS** Am Soc Christian Ethics. **RESEARCH** Civil violence and social change; methodology in Christian ethics. **SELECTED PUBLICATIONS** Auth, The Human Science of Communicology--A Phenomenology of Discourse in Foucault and Merleauponty, Philos Rhetoric, Vol 28, 95; Pink Collar Trash--Semiotics of the Secretarial Position, Am J Semiotics, Vol 11, 94. **CONTACT ADDRESS** Dept of Christian Thought and Mission Eastern Baptis, Philadelphia, PA 19151.

MILLER, EDWARD L.
PERSONAL Born 04/06/1937, Los Angeles, CA, m, 1979, 4 children **DISCIPLINE** PHILOSOPHY; THEOLOGY **EDUCATION** Univ S Calif, BA, MA, PhD; Univ Basel, Dr Theol. **CAREER** Instr, Calif Lutheran Col, 62-64; asst prof, St Olaf Col, 64-66; prof, Univ Colo, 66-99; Dir Theol Forum, 67; Prof Emer, 00-. **MEMBERSHIPS** Amer Acad Relig; Soc for New Testament Studies; Soc of Christian Philos; Soren Kierkegaard Soc. **RESEARCH** Philosophical Theology; New Testament; Soren Kierkegaard. **SELECTED PUBLICATIONS** Coauth, Contemporary Theologies, Fortress Pr, 98; At the Centre of Kierkegaard: An Objective Absurdity, Religious Studies, 97; Question that Matter, McGraw Hill, 4th ed, 96. **CONTACT ADDRESS** Dept of Philosophy, Univ of Colorado, Boulder, Campus Box 232, Boulder, CO 80309. **EMAIL** Edlmiller@aol.com

MILLER, FRANKLIN
PERSONAL Born 07/15/1948, Washington, DC, m, 1968, 3 children **DISCIPLINE** PHILOSOPHY **EDUCATION** Columbia Univ, PhD, 77. **CAREER** Special Expert, Dept of Clinical Bioethics, National Institutes of Health, 99-;assoc prof of Medical Education, Univ VA 90-98. **HONORS AND AWARDS** Sr res fel, Kennedy Institute of Ethics; Soc of Biological Psychiatry. **MEMBERSHIPS** Am Philos Assoc, Am Soc of Bioethics and the Humanities. **RESEARCH** Ethics of Clinical research, death and dying, professional integrity, pragmatism and bioethics. **SELECTED PUBLICATIONS** Auth, Placebo-Controlled Trials in Psychiatric Research: An Ethical Perspective , Biological Psychiatry, Vol 47, April 15, 00; auth, The Concept of Medically Indicated Treatment, The Journal of Medicine and Philosophy, Vol 18, Feb 93; coauth, Assisted Suicide Compared with Refusal of Treatment: A Valid Distinction? Annals of Internal Medicine, Vol 132, Mar 21,00; coauth, Professional Integrity in Clinical Research, The Journal of the American Medical Association, Vol 280, Oct 28,98; coauth, End-of-Life Decision-Making in the Hospital: Current Practice Future Prospects, Journal of Pain and Symptom Management, Vol 17, Jan,99; coauth, Voluntary Death: A Comparison of Terminal Dehydration and Physician Assisted Suicide, Annals of Internal Medicine, Vol 128, Apr 1. 98; coauth, Psychiatric Symptom-Provoking Studies: An Ethical Appraisal, Biological Psychiatry, Vol 42, Sept 1 97; coauth, Clinical Pragmatism: A Method of Moral Problem Solving, Kennedy Institute of Ethics Journal, Vol 7, June 97; coauth, Clinical Pragmatism: John Dewey and Clinical Ethics, The Journal of Contemporary Health Law and Policy, Vol 13, issue I, 96; coauth, A Proposal to Restructure Hospital Care for Dying Patients, The New England Journal of Medicine, Vol 334, June 27, 96; coauth, Professional Integrity and Physician-Assisted Death, Hastings Center Report, Vol 25, May-June 95; coauth, Regulating Physician Assisted Death, New England Journal of Medicine, Vol 331m July 14, 94. **CONTACT ADDRESS** 3910 Underwood St, Chevy Chase, MD 20815. **EMAIL** fgm3910@aol.com

MILLER, J. MAXWELL
PERSONAL Born 09/20/1937, Kosciusko, MS, m, 1962, 2 children **DISCIPLINE** HEBREW BIBLE **EDUCATION** Millsaps Col, AB, 59; Emory Univ, PhD, 64; post-doctoral, Biblisch-arcaologisches Institut, Tubingen Univ, W Ger, 74-75, 81-82; Millsaps Col, hon DD, 84. **CAREER** Instr, old testament, Interdenominational Theol Ctr, Atlanta, 62-63; grad asst instr, Hebrew, Emory Univ, 63-64; asst prof, old testament, Birmingham-Southern Col, 64-67; asst prof, 71-78, full prof, 78-, dir, grad div of relig, 83-92, Candler Sch of Theol, Emory Univ. **HONORS AND AWARDS** Nat Defense Educ Act grad fel, 60-64; Nat Found of the arts and Humanities, summer res stipend, 66; Emory Univ summer res grant, 67, 69, 72, 78, 79, 82; Alexander von Humbolt Stiftung stipend, 74-75, 81-82; Woodruff Res Support Grant, 80; Asn of Theol Sch res grant, 81-82; Nat Endow for the Humanities res grant, 87-88. **MEMBERSHIPS** Soc of Bibl Lit; Amer Sch of Oriental Res; Palestine Exploration Soc; Deutsche Verein fur Erforschung Palastinas. **RESEARCH** History and archaeology of biblical times. **SELECTED PUBLICATIONS** Auth, Separating the Solomon of History from the Solomon of Legend, The Age of Solomon: Scholarship at the Turn of the Millenium, Leiden, The Netherlands, Brill, 97; auth, Biblical Archaeologist, 60/4, Ancient Moab: Still Largely Unknown, 194-204, 97; auth, Central Moab and History of Moab, Encycl of Near Eastern Archaeol, Oxford Univ Press, 96; auth, The Ancient Near East an Archaeology, Old Testament Interpretation: Past, Present and Future, Abingdon Press, 245-260, 95; auth, Explorations in Ancient Moab, Qadmoniot, 28, 77-82, 95; auth, Introduction to the History of Ancient Israel, The New Interpreter's Bible, Abingdon Press, 244-271, 94; auth, Israel, History of, Judah, Oxford Companion to the Bible, Oxford Univ Press, 93; auth, Reading the Bible Historically: The Historian's Approach, chap I, 11-28, To Each Its Own Meaning: An Introduction to Biblical Criticisms and Their Application, Westminster/John Knox Press, 93; ed, Archaeological Survey of the Kerak Plateau, Amer Sch of Oriental Res Archaeol Reports, 1, Scholars Press, 91; co-auth, A History of Ancient Israel and Judah, Westminster Press/SCM Press, 86. **CONTACT ADDRESS** Candler School of Theology, Emory Univ, Atlanta, GA 30322. **EMAIL** theojmm@emory.edu

MILLER, J. MITCHELL
PERSONAL Born 12/22/1965, Nashville, TN, s **DISCIPLINE** CRIMINAL JUSTICE **EDUCATION** Univ Tenn, PhD, 96. **CAREER** Asst Prof, Univ S C, 96-. **HONORS AND AWARDS** Anderson Paper Awd, Acad of Criminal Justice Sci, 93; Paper Awd Winner, Southern Criminal Justice Asn, 94. **MEMBERSHIPS** ADJS, AS, SCJA, MCJA. **RESEARCH** Drug enforcement, Substance abuse, Subcultures. **SELECTED PUBLICATIONS** Auth, "On Criminological Scholarship and Race: A Response to Professors Ross and Edwards," Journal of Criminal Justice, 99; auth, "Administrative Police Training for an Emerging Democracy: An Evaluation of the Moscow Police Command College - a Research Note," American Journal of Criminal Justice, 99; co-auth, "Critical Criminologists in Introductory Criminology Textbooks, 1992 to 1996," Critical Criminology, forthcoming; co-auth, "The Most cited Scholars and works in corrections," the Prison Journal, 99; co-auth, "The Most cited Scholars and works in Police Studies," Policing: an International Journal of Police strategies and Management, 98; auth, "The Most cited Scholars and works in Police Studies," Policing: an International Journal of Police strategies and Management, 98; co-auth, "Taboo Until today? The coverage of biological Criminology in Textbooks," Journal of Criminal Justice, 98; auth, "Ideology and gang Policy: beyond the False dichotomy," Journal of Gang Research, (97): 9-20; auth, "Routine activity and Labor Market segmentation: an empirical Test of a Revised approach," American Journal of Criminal Justice, (97): 71-100; co-auth, "On the demise and Morrow of Subcultural-based Theories of Crime and Delinquency," Journal of crime and Justice, (97): 167-178; auth, "Evaluating criminology and Criminal Justice: an Interview with Richard Wright," American Journal of Criminal Justice, (96): 105-116. **CONTACT ADDRESS** Col of Criminal Justice, Univ of So Carolina, Columbia, Columbia, SC 29225-0001.

MILLER, JAMES
PERSONAL Born 02/28/1947, Chicago, IL, m, 3 children **DISCIPLINE** POLITICAL SCIENCE **EDUCATION** Pomona Col, BA, 69; Brandeis Univ, PhD, 75. **CAREER** Inst, Univ Waterloo, 75-76; asst prof, Univ Tex at Austin, 76-80; vis asst prof, Boston Univ, 86, 88; lecturer, Harvard Univ, 87-89; vis asst prof, Brown Univ, 90; vis lamont prof, Union Col, 94; fac, Skidmore Col, 88, 92-; assoc prof & dir of Liberal Stud, grad fac of polit and soc sci, 92-94; prof, polit sci, dir liberal stud, NY School for Soc Res, 94-. **HONORS AND AWARDS** Woodrow Wilson Dissertation Fellow, 72-73; NEH Fellow, 79-80, 91; ASCAP_Deems Taylor Awd, 83, 84; Nat Book Critics Circle Finalist, 87, 93; Premio Letterario Giovanni Comisso Finalist, 94; Guggenheim Fellow, 97. **RESEARCH** Political & social science. **SELECTED PUBLICATIONS** Auth, History and Human Existence, California, 79; auth, Rousseau: Dreamer of Democracy, Yale, 84; auth, Democracy is in the Streets, Simon & Schuster, 87; auth, The Passion of Michael Foucalt, Simon & Schuster, 93; auth, Flowers in the Dustbin: The Rise of Rock and Roll, 1947-1977, Simon & Schuster, 99. **CONTACT ADDRESS** Comm on Liberal Stud, New Sch for Social Research, 65 Fifth Ave, New York, NY 10003. **EMAIL** millerje@newschool.edu

MILLER, JAMES BLAIR
PERSONAL Born 08/02/1916, Mt Vernon, OH, m, 1943, 3 children **DISCIPLINE** CHRISTIAN EDUCATION, PRACTICAL THEOLOGY **EDUCATION** Bethany Col, WVa, AB, 38; Yale Univ, BD, 41; Ind Univ, EdD(educ), 55. **CAREER** Pastor, First Christian Church, Plymouth, Pa, 41-44; instr relig, Bethany Col, WVa, 44-51; asst prof Christian educ, 51-55, prof, 55-80, Emer Prof Christian Educ, Christian Theol Sem, 80-, Pastor, Mem Church, Bethany, WVa, 44-51; consult educ dept, United Christian Missionary Soc, 62-63; chmn prof and res sect, Div Christian Educ, Nat Coun Churches, 62; mem curric and prog coun, Christian Churches, 64-68 and Comn Christian Educ, Am Asn Theol Schs, 65-67. **MEMBERSHIPS** Asn Professors and Researchers in Relig Educ; Asn Christian Church Educators. **RESEARCH** Theological foundations for Christian education; history of education; learning theory. **SELECTED PUBLICATIONS** Auth, Our Church's Story, 60 & coauth, Basics for Teaching in the Church, 68, Christian Bd Publ. **CONTACT ADDRESS** Christian Theol Sem, 1000 W 42nd St, Indianapolis, IN 46208.

MILLER, JEREMY M.
PERSONAL Born 04/02/1954, Boston, MA, m, 1998, 3 children **DISCIPLINE** LAW **EDUCATION** Yale Univ, BA, 76; Tulane Univ, JD, 80; Univ Penn, LLM, 81. **CAREER** Prof, Western State Univ, 83-94; Prof and Dean, Chapman Univ, 83-. **HONORS AND AWARDS** Who's Who in Am Law, 87; Outstanding Young Men of Am, 89; Best Teacher, CA State Univ, 91; Golden Apple Awd, 92; Best Prof, Chapman Univ, 96; Who's Who in the World, 97; Master of the Bench, 00; Intl Who's Who of Prof, 99, 00. **MEMBERSHIPS** MA Bar Asn; Orange Cty Bar Asn; Am Bar Asn. **RESEARCH** Criminal law; Legal theory. **SELECTED PUBLICATIONS** Auth, "Miranda Protection is no Longer Good Law", LA Daily Journal, 91; auth, "Conservative Court coddling Criminals?," LA Daily Journal, 91; auth, "How to Avoid the Pitfalls of Lawyer Discipline," LA Daily Journal, 91; auth, "If He Were Reborn, What Would Madison Say?", LA Daily Journal, 91; auth, "An Outline for a Model Penal Code II," Nat Dist Attorneys Asn, 91; auth, "The Bar Could Improve on Rules of conduct," LA Daily Journal, 91; auth, Constitutional Criminal Procedure: A Practitioner and Student Resource, 98; auth, Criminal Law: A Student's Survival Guide, 99; auth, The Exam Solution: Professional Responsibility, 99. **CONTACT ADDRESS** Sch of Law, Chapman Univ, 1 University Dr, Orange, CA 92866. **EMAIL** kayshva@aol.com

MILLER, JEROME A.
PERSONAL Born 08/24/1946, Pittsburgh, PA, m, 1969, 3 children **DISCIPLINE** PHILOSOPHY **EDUCATION** Georgetown Univ, PhD, 72. **CAREER** Prof, Chr Dept Philos, 72-98, Salisbury State Univ. **HONORS AND AWARDS** Outstanding Faculty Awd. **MEMBERSHIPS** Amer Philos Assoc. **RESEARCH** Philosophy of Religion; Theory of Knowledge. **SELECTED PUBLICATIONS** Auth, The Way of Suffering, Georgetown Univ Press, 89; In The Throe of Wonder, Santa Univ of NY Press, 92. **CONTACT ADDRESS** 303 New York Ave, Salisbury, MD 21801. **EMAIL** jamiller@ssv.edu

MILLER, JOHN DOUGLAS
PERSONAL Born 09/05/1940, Terrell, TX, m, 1996, 2 children **DISCIPLINE** PHILOSOPHY **EDUCATION** Midwestern State Univ, BA, 71; Univ Central Okla, MA, 83; Union Inst, PhD, 93. **CAREER** Instr, Univ of Regensburg, Germany, 70-71; instr, Rose State Col, 81-92; instr, Univ of Central Okla, 95-98; instr, Okla State Univ/OKC, 94-2000. **HONORS AND AWARDS** Alpha Chi Nat Honor Soc; Who's Who Among Am Students; Outstanding Psychology Student, MN, 70; Who's Who in Am. **MEMBERSHIPS** Southwest Philos Soc, Mensa. **RESEARCH** Ethics, particularly the ethics of Immanel Kant and virtue ethics. **SELECTED PUBLICATIONS** Auth, A Footnote to Plato: An Introduction to Western Philosophy. **CONTACT ADDRESS** Dept Humanities, Oklahoma State Univ, Oklahoma City, 900 N Portland Ave, Oklahoma City, OK 73107-6120. **EMAIL** janellel@worldnet.att.net

MILLER, JOHN F., III
PERSONAL Born 06/25/1938, Buffalo, NY **DISCIPLINE** PHILOSOPHY **EDUCATION** Gettysburg Col, BA, 60; Univ of MD, MA, 63; NYork Univ, PhD, 69. **CAREER** Instr, 65-66 Queens Coll, NY; Asst Prof, 65-66, Radford Coll, VA; Instr, 66-69, Univ of South FL, Tampa; Assoc Prof, 70-98, North Texas State Univ, Denton; Adjunct Prof in Philo, Univ of South FL. Hillsborough Comm Coll, Tampa, FL, St Leo Coll, St Leo FL, St Petersburg Jr C. **HONORS AND AWARDS** Phi Beta Kappa. **MEMBERSHIPS** APA, SPS, SSPP, New Mexico and West Texas Philo Soc, ARR. **RESEARCH** Ancient Philosophy, Philosophy of Religion, Parapsychology. **SELECTED PUBLICATIONS** Auth, On the Track of the Elephant: The Relevance of Psychical Research to Religious Experience for an Understanding of Reality, The J of Religion and Psychical Research, 95; American Culture and the Development of New Thought, The J Study of Metaphysical Religion, 96; Mind, Mind, What Therefore art Thou, Mind, The J of Religion and Metaphysical Research, 97; Birthmarks and Memory: Evidence for Mind-Body Dualism, The J of Religion and Physical Research, 98; Creation Meditation, Gateways to Higher Consciousness, Annual Conference Preceedings of the Academy of Religion and Psychical Research, 98. **CONTACT ADDRESS** 1004 Cedar Lake Dr, Tampa, FL 33612.

MILLER, MYRON
PERSONAL Born 12/12/1937, MI, m, 1959, 3 children **DISCIPLINE** PHILOSOPHY, THEOLOGY **EDUCATION** Wheaton Col, BA, 62; MA, 64; NY Univ, PhD, 77. **CAREER** Prof & President, St Petersburg Jr Col, 86-. **HONORS AND AWARDS** NSF Fel, St Johns Univ, 65; NSF Fel, Am Univ, 67; NEH Fel, Brown Univ, 78; Who's Who Among Am Teachers, 94, 96, 98, 99. **MEMBERSHIPS** APA, FPA, NLS. **RESEARCH** Philosophy of science, religion and ethics. **SELECTED PUBLICATIONS** Auth, "Plato's Modern Enemies and the Theory of Natural Law," Critical Rev (87): 20-23; auth, "From the Industrial to the Virtual University," Futures Studies Quart (97). **CONTACT ADDRESS** Dept Philos & Theol, St. Petersburg Junior Col, 10830 Navajo Dr, Saint Petersburg, FL 33708-3116. **EMAIL** pat-miller1@juno.com

MILLER, PATRICIA COX
PERSONAL Born 01/19/1947, Washington, DC, m **DISCIPLINE** RELIGION IN LATE ANTIQUITY **EDUCATION** Mary Washington Col of U Va, BA, 69; Univ Chicago, MA, 72; PhD, 79. **CAREER** Asst prof, Univ Wash, 75-76; asst prof, Syracuse Univ, 77-83; assoc prof, Syracuse Univ, 83-95; prof, Syracuse Univ, 95-; dir grad studies, dept relig, Syracuse Univ, 92-99. **HONORS AND AWARDS** Chair, Council of Grad Stud in Religion, 99-; pres, Namer Patristics Soc, 96-97; fel, NEH, 83; Kent fel, Univ Chicago, 72-75. **MEMBERSHIPS** Amer Acad Relig; Namer Patristics Soc. **RESEARCH** Religion and Aesthetics in Late Antiquity; Early Christian asceticism; Early Christian and Pagan hagiography. **SELECTED PUBLICATIONS** Auth, Dreams in Late Antiquity: Studies in the Imagination of a Culture, Princeton, Princeton Univ Press, 94; Biography in Late Antiquity: A Quest for the Holy Man, Berkeley, Univ Calif Press, 83; Articles, Differential Networks: Relics and Other Fragments in Late Antiquity, Jour of Early Christ Studies, 6, 113-38, 98; Strategies of Representation in Collective Biography: Constructing the Subject as Holy, Greek Biography and Panegyrics in Late Antiquity, ed Tomas Hagg and Philip Rousseau, Berkeley, Univ Calif Press, 98; Jerome's Centaur: A Hyper-Icon of the Desert, Jour of Early Christ Studies, 4, 209-33, 96; Dreaming the Body: An Aesthetics of Asceticism, Asceticism, ed Vincent Wimbush and Richard Valantasis, New York, Oxford Univ Press, 281-300, 95; Desert Asceticism and The Body from Nowhere, Jour of Early Christ Studies, 2, 137-53, 1994; The Blazing Body: Ascetic Desire in Jerome's Letter to Eustochium, Jour of Early Christian Studies, 1, 21-45, 93; The Devil's Gateway: An Eros of Difference in the Dreams of Perpetua, Dreaming, 2, 45-63, 92; Plenty Sleeps There: The Myth of Eros and Psyche in Plotinus and Gnosticism, Neoplatonism and Gnosticism, ed R. Wallis and J. Bregman, Stony Brook, State Univ of NY Press, 223-38, 92. **CONTACT ADDRESS** Dept of Religion, Syracuse Univ, 501 Hall of Languages, Syracuse, NY 13244-1170. **EMAIL** plmiller@syr.edu

MILLER, PETER
PERSONAL Born 09/06/1940, Dunkirk, NY, s, 4 children **DISCIPLINE** ENGLISH, RELIGION **EDUCATION** State Univ NY at Fredonia, BA, 66; MS, 70; CAS-SAS, 80; Holy Names Col, MA, 95. **CAREER** High Sch English, 66-89; Principal, 89-90; Trocaire Col, 92-00; Niagara Univ, 99-00. **HONORS AND AWARDS** Listed in Who's Who in College Teachers, 98-00. **MEMBERSHIPS** NCTE, St Luke's Guild, NYSCLA. **RESEARCH** World Religions. **SELECTED PUBLICATIONS** Auth, Right Rites--Right Rituals, Holy Names Col Press (Oakland, CA); auth, The Aurora Experiment, Univ Creation Spirituality Pr (Oakland, CA), forthcoming. **CONTACT ADDRESS** Dept Humanities, Trocaire Col, 360 Choate Ave, Buffalo, NY 14220-2003. **EMAIL** millerpetera@aol.com

MILLER, RICHARD B.
DISCIPLINE RELIGIOUS STUDIES **EDUCATION** Univ Chicago, PhD, 85. **CAREER** Assoc prof and dept chair, Ind Univ, Bloomington. **RESEARCH** Methods in religious ethics; history of Christian ethics; political and social ethics. **SELECTED PUBLICATIONS** Auth, Interpretations of Conflict: Ethics, Pacifism, and the Just-War Tradition, Univ Chicago, 91; auth, Casuistry and Modern Ethics: A Poetics of Practical Reasoning, Univ of Chicago Press, 96. **CONTACT ADDRESS** Dept of Religious Studies, Indiana Univ, Bloomington, Sycamore Hall 230, Bloomington, IN 47405. **EMAIL** rmiller@indiana.edu

MILLER, ROLAND
DISCIPLINE MISSIONS **EDUCATION** Concordia Sem, BA, MDiv; Kennedy Sch of Missions, MA, 54; Hartford Sem Found, PhD, 73. **CAREER** Instr, Concordia Sem, 66-67; vis sholar, Harvar Univ, 76-90; prof, Luther Col, Univ Regina, Can, 76-89; acad dean, Luther Col, 77-89; cord rel prog, Luther Col, 80-89; vis lectr, 91-92; vis prof, 93-99; prof emer, Luther Sem, 99- . **HONORS AND AWARDS** Lutheran missionary, Malappuram, Kerala, southern India, 53-76. **MEMBERSHIPS** Mem, W Conf Univ Deans of Arts and Sci; Shastri Indo-Can Inst. **SELECTED PUBLICATIONS** Auth, The Mappila Muslims of Kerala, A Study in Islamic Trends, 91; The Sending of God: Essays on the Mission of God and His People, 80; Religious Studies in Manitoba and Saskatchewan, 91. **CONTACT ADDRESS** Dept of Missions, Luther Sem, 2481 Como Ave, Saint Paul, MN 55108. **EMAIL** rmiller@luthersem.edu

MILLER, RONALD H.
PERSONAL Born 04/17/1938, St. Louis, MO, d, 3 children **DISCIPLINE** RELIGION **EDUCATION** St. Louis Univ, BA, 61; Jesuit Sch Phil, PhL, 62; St Louis Univ, MA, 63; Northwestern Univ, PhD, 78. **CAREER** Regis High School and Col, tchr, 62-65; Northwestern Univ, TA, 70-74; Lake Forest Col, lectr, 74-89, assoc prof, 89-, Dept chemn, 94-. **HONORS AND AWARDS** St. Louis Univ, BA, magna cum laude; Deutsche Akademische Austauschdienst Fel, 69-70; Clement Stone Schshp, 72; Lake Forest Col, Great Tchr Award, 86, Bird Award, 93, Charlotte Simmons Prize, 94, William R. Bross Professorial Ch, 95 **MEMBERSHIPS** IFCJ **RESEARCH** Jewish Christian dialogue; NT. **SELECTED PUBLICATIONS** Auth, The Spirituality of Franz Rosenzweig, in: Western Spirituality, ed Mathew Fox, Fides, 79; Pilgrimage Without End, in: Five Spiritual Journeys, ed by L. Zirker, Iroquois House, 81; Fireball and the Lotus: Emerging Spirituality from Ancient Roots, co-ed, Bear and Co, 87; Dialogue and Disagreement: Franz Rosenzweig's Relevance for Contemporary Jewish - Christian Understanding, Univ Press of Amer, 89; Space for the Spirit, in: Finding a Way: Essays on Spiritual Practice, ed by Lorette Zirker, Tuttle Press, 96. **CONTACT ADDRESS** Dept of Religion, Lake Forest Col, Lake Forest, IL 60045. **EMAIL** rmiller@lfc.edu

MILLER, STEPHEN R.
PERSONAL Born 09/25/1949, Jackson, TN, m, 1970, 2 children **DISCIPLINE** OLD TESTAMENT **EDUCATION** Union Univ, BS, 71; Mid-Amer Baptist Theol Sem, ThM, 76, PhD, 82. **CAREER** 82- OT/Hebrew Lang, Mid-Amer Baptist Theol Sem. **MEMBERSHIPS** Soc of Biblical Lit; Evangel Theol Sem. **SELECTED PUBLICATIONS** Auth, The Literary Style of the Book of Isaiah and the Unity Question, Mid-Amer Baptist Theol Sem, 82; art, Psalm 19: The Revelation of

God, Mid-Amer Theol J, vol 8:2, 84; art, The Authorship of Isaiah, Mid-Amer Theol J, vol 15:1, 91; art, Introduction to the Book of Hosea, Mid-Amer Theol J, vol 17, 93; auth, Daniel, New Amer Comm, vol 18, Broadman & Holman, 94; art, Introduction and Outline for the Prophecy of Amos, Mid-Amer Theol J, vol 19, 95; art, Christians and the Ten Commandments, Life & Work Advan Bibl Stud, Lifeway Christian Rsrcs, 96; art, An Introduction to Old Testament Wisdom Literature, Life & Work Directions Tchr Ed, Lifeway Christian Rscrs, 96; art, Tithes and Offerings, Bibl Illus, Lifeway Christian Rscrs, 97; art, The Prophecy of Jeremiah, Life & Work Advan Bibl Study, Lifeway Christian Rscrs, 98; auth, The Book of Daniel, Shepherd's Notes Series, Broadman and Holman, 98; art, Eerdmans Dictionary of the Bible, Eerdmans, 00; trans (Old Testament), Holman Christian Standard Bible, Broadman and Holman, New Testament to be released 00, Old Testament to be released later. **CONTACT ADDRESS** Mid-America Baptist Theol Sem, PO Box 381528, Germantown, TN 38183-1528. **EMAIL** smiller@mabts.edu

MILLER, TEDD
PERSONAL Born 01/04/1946, Washington, DC, m, 1976 **DISCIPLINE** LAW **EDUCATION** Bethune Cookman College, BA, 1968; Rutgers School of Law, JD, 1972. **CAREER** Rutgers Univ, adjunct faculty, 72-75; Essex County Legal Services, staff attorney, 72-75; Council on Legal Education Opportunity, asst director, 75-80; Georgetown Univ Law Center, director of admissions, 80-92; Howard Univ School of Law, asst dean of director of admissions, currently. **MEMBERSHIPS** Law School Admissions Council, board of trustees, 1994-97; Assn of American Law Schools, chair section on pre legal education and admission to law school, 1994-96. **CONTACT ADDRESS** Sch of Law, Howard Univ, 2900 Van Ness St NW, Ste 200, Holy Cross Mall, Washington, VT 20010.

MILLER, TELLY HUGH
PERSONAL Born 06/18/1939, Henderson, TX, m **DISCIPLINE** THEOLOGY **EDUCATION** Wiley Coll, BA 1962; Interdenom Theol Cntr, MDiv 1965; Vanderbilt U, DMin 1973; Prairie View A&M Univ, EdM 1980. **CAREER** St Paul Baptist Church St Albans WV, pastor 1965; WV State Coll, religious counselor 1967; Wiley Coll Marshall TX, coll minister 1968, financial aid dir 1970, assoc prof/chmn dept of religion 1973, vice pres for student affairs 1974, prof and chmn dept of religion and philosophy 1976-. **HONORS AND AWARDS** East TX Educ Oppors Ctr Awd 1980; Kappa Alpha Psi Achievement Awd 1980; Omega Psi Phi Man of the Year Awd 1983; elected first Black Commissioner for Harrison County 1983; apptd by Gov of TX to East TX Regional Review Comm for the State's Comm Develop Block Grant Prog. **MEMBERSHIPS** Relig consult Bapt WV St Coll Inst 1967; mem Am Assn Univ Profs; chmn Christmas Baskets for Needy St Albans 1967; bd dirs YMCA St Albans 1966-67; chmn mem drive NAACP 1967; mem exec com Kanawha Co chap 1967; v moder Mt Olivet Assn 1966-67; pres George Washington Carver Elem Sch PTA 1977; pres Gamma Upsilon Lambda Chap Alpha Phi Alpha Frat Inc 1977; mem Alpha Phi Alpha Frat Inc, Alpha Phi Omega Natl Serv Frat Kappa Pi Chapt, AAUP, Morgan Lodge No 10 St Albans WV, NAACP; fellowship of Christian Athletes; bd of dirs Harrison County United Way Fund Dr 1983, bd of dirs Harrison County Red Cross. **CONTACT ADDRESS** Dept of Relig/Philos, Wiley Col, 711 Rosborough Springs Rd, Marshall, TX 75670.

MILLER, WALTER, JR
PERSONAL Born 12/08/1932, Buffalo, NY, m, 1989, 2 children **DISCIPLINE** LAW **EDUCATION** Harvard Col, AB, 54; Lutheran Theol Sem, BD, 57; SUNY Buffalo, JD, 64; Harvard Law Sch, LLM, 65. **CAREER** Pastor, Lutheran Church in Am, 58-60; teacher, Buffalo, NY, 60-61; asst prof to prof, Boston Univ, 65-. **MEMBERSHIPS** Asn of Am Law Sch; Mass Bar Asn; NY Bar Asn. **RESEARCH** Contracts; Bankruptcy; Commercial law. **SELECTED PUBLICATIONS** Auth, "Bankruptcy's New Value Exception: No Longer a Necessity," Boston Univ L Rev, 97; auth, Contracts: Problems, Cases and Materials, Carolina Acad Press, 99. **CONTACT ADDRESS** Sch of Law, Boston Univ, 765 Commonwealth Ave, Boston, MA 02215. **EMAIL** wmiller@bu.edu

MILLER-MCLEMORE, BONNIE JEAN
PERSONAL Born 11/25/1955, Jacksonville, FL, m, 1980, 3 children **DISCIPLINE** THEOLOGY **EDUCATION** Kalamazoo Col, BA, 97; Univ Chi, MA, 80; Univ Chi, PhD, 86. **CAREER** Assoc prof Pastoral Theolog & Coun, Vanderbilt Univ, 95-; assoc prof Relig, Personality & Culture, Chi Theolog Sem, 92-95; asst prof Relig, Personality & Culture, Chi Theolog Sem, 87-92; vis asst prof Pastoral Care, Chi Theolog Sem, 86-87. **HONORS AND AWARDS** Hary Luce III Fellow, 99-00; Lilly Found Grant Recipient, 98-; Lilly Found Grant Recipient, 90-96; Assoc Theolog Schools Young Scholar Awd, 90-91; Ann E Dickerson Scholar, 80-84; Edward Scribner Aims Awd, 80-81; Stevens Memorial Scholar, 79-80. **MEMBERSHIPS** Amer Acad Relig; Soc Christian Ethics; Soc of Pastoral Theology. **RESEARCH** Practical & Pastoral Theology; Feminist Theology; Feminist Psychology; Theology and Culture of Work **SELECTED PUBLICATIONS** Co-ed, Feminist and Womanist Pastoral Theology: Implications for Care, Faith, and Reflection, Abingdon, 99; coauth, From Culture Wars to Common Ground: Religion and the American Debate, Westminster/John Knox, 98; Also A Mother: Work and Family as Theological Dilemma, Abingdon, 94; auth, Let the Children Come: Care of Children as a Religious Practice, Jossey-Bass, forthcoming, 2002. **CONTACT ADDRESS** Dept of Religion, Vanderbilt Univ, Nashville, TN 37240-2701. **EMAIL** bonnie.miller-mclemore@vanderbilt.edu

MILLGRAM, ELIJAH
DISCIPLINE PHILOSOPHY **EDUCATION** Harvard Univ, AB (philos), 84, PhD (philos), 91. **CAREER** Asst prof, Princeton Univ, 91-97; Assoc Prof, Vanderbilt Univ, 97-99; Assoc prof, Univ of Utah, 99-. **HONORS AND AWARDS** Nat Endowment for the Humanities fel, 96-97; Nat Humanities Center fel (declined), 96-97; Center for Advanced Studies in the Behavioral Sciences, Stanford Univ, fel for 99-00. **RESEARCH** Theory of Rationality; Truth; John Stuart Mill **SELECTED PUBLICATIONS** Auth, Was Hume a Humean?, Hume Studies21, April 95; Williams' Argument Against External Reasons, Nous 30, June 96; Hume on Practical Reasoning, Iyyun, July 97; Practical Induction, Cambridge, MA: Harvard Univ Press, 97; Varieties of Practical Reasoning, in G. Meggle, Analyomen 2, vol 3, Berlin: de Gruyter, 97; Incommensurability and Practical Reasoning, in R. Chang, Incommensurability, Incomparability, and Practical Reason, Cambridge, MA: Harvard Univ Press, 98; Deciding to Desire, in C, Fehige and U. Wessels, Preferences, Berlin: Walter de Gruyter, 98; book review, Iris Murdoch, Existentialists and Mystics, Boston Review, 23, Feb/March 98; auth, "What's the Use of Utility?" Philosophy and Public Affairs 29, Spring 00; auth, "Coherence: The Price of the Ticket" Journal of Philosophy 97, February 00; auth, "Mill's Proof of the Principle of Utility" Ethics 110, January 00. **CONTACT ADDRESS** Philosophy Dept, Univ of Utah, 260 Central Campus Dr., Rm. 341, Salt Lake City, UT 84112. **EMAIL** lije.millgram@m.cc.utah.edu

MILLIKAN, RUTH G.
DISCIPLINE PHILOSOPHY **EDUCATION** Oberlin Col, AB, 55; Yale Univ, PhD, 69. **CAREER** Prof, Dept Philos, Univ Conn. **RESEARCH** Philosophy of mind; Philosophy of language; philosophy of biology; ontology; philosophy; psychology; natural epistemology. **SELECTED PUBLICATIONS** Auth, Language, Thought, and Other Biological Categories, Bradford Books/MIT Press, (84): 355; auth, White Queen Psychology and Other Essays For Alice, Bradford Books/MIT Press, (93): 388; auth, "Wings, Spoons, Pills and Quills; A Pluralist Theory of Functions," The Journal of Philosophy 96.4, 191-206; auth, "Images of Identity," Mind 106, no. 423, (97): 499-519; ed, "Proper Function and Convention in Speech Acts," in ed. L.E. Hahn, The Philosophy of Peter F. Strawsn, The Library of Living Philosophers, LaSalle ILL: Open Court, (98): 25-43; auth, "A Common Structure for Concepts of Individuals, Stuffs, and Basic Kinds: More Mama, More Milk and More Mouse," Behavioral and Brain Sciences, 22.1, (98): 55-65; auth, "With Enemies Like these I Don't Need Friends," Behavioral and Brain Sciences, vol 22.1, (98): 89-100; auth, "Language Conventions Made Simple," Journal of Philosophy XCV, no 4, 98; auth, "How We Make Our Ideas clear," The Tenth Annual Patrick Romanell Lecture, Proceedings and Addresses of the American Philosophical Association, (98): 65-79; ed, "A More Plausible Kind of 'Recognitional Concept," In E. Villanueva, ed., Concepts; Philosophical Issues, vol 9, Atascadero CA: Ridgeview Publishing, (98): 35-41. **CONTACT ADDRESS** Dept of Philos, Univ of Connecticut, Storrs, 1266 Storrs Rd, Manshester Hall, Unit 2054, Storrs, CT 06269. **EMAIL** ruth.millikan@uconn.edu

MILLNER, DIANNE MAXINE
PERSONAL Born 03/21/1949, Columbus, OH, m, 1986 **DISCIPLINE** LAW **EDUCATION** Pasadena City Coll, AA 1969; Univ of CA at Berkeley, AB 1972; Stanford U, JD 1975. **CAREER** Hastings Coll of The Law, instructor 1977-78; Pillsbury Madison & Sutro Law Firm, Attorney 1975-80; Alexander, Millner & McGee, atty, 80-91; Steefel, Levitt & Weiss, Attorney, 91-94; CA Continuing Education of the Bar, atty, currently. **HONORS AND AWARDS** Pres Awd Womens Div Nat Bar Assn 1980; Phi Beta Kappa UC Berkeley 1975. **MEMBERSHIPS** Dir Youth for Serv 1978-80; mem Commnty Redevel Agencys Assn 1983-94; Nat Bar Assn; Black Woman Lawyers Assn; Charles Houston Bar Assn; mem, American Assn of Univ Women, 1990-92; comm chair, Parents Division of the Natl Federation of the Blind, 1988-; mem, American Bar Assn; mem, CA State Bar. **CONTACT ADDRESS** California Continuing Education of the Bar, 2300 Shattuck Avenue, Berkeley, CA 94704.

MILLS, CHARLES
DISCIPLINE PHILOSOPHY **EDUCATION** Univ Toronto, PhD. **CAREER** Assoc prof., Univ IL at Chicago **RESEARCH** Oppositional politl theory. **SELECTED PUBLICATIONS** Auth, The Moral Epistemology of Stalinism, Polit Soc, 94; Under Class Under Standings, Ethics, 94; Non Cartesian Sums: Philosophy and the African American Experience, Tchg Philos, 94. **CONTACT ADDRESS** Philos Dept, Univ of Illinois, Chicago, S Halsted St, PO Box 705, Chicago, IL 60607.

MILLS, CLAUDIA
PERSONAL Born 08/21/1954, New York, NY, m, 1985, 2 children **DISCIPLINE** PHILOSOPHY **EDUCATION** Wellesley Col, BA, 76; Princeton Univ, MA, 79; Univ Md, MLS, 88; Princeton Univ, PhD, 91. **CAREER** Ed, Inst for Philos and Pub Policy, Univ Md, 80-89; asst prof, Univ Md, 91-92; asst prof to assoc prof, Univ Colo Boulder, 92-. **HONORS AND AWARDS** SOAR Award, Univ Colo, 94. **MEMBERSHIPS** Am Philos Asn; Asn for Practical and Professional Ethics; Children's Lit Asn. **RESEARCH** Ethics; Social and political philosophy; Applied ethics; Children's literature. **SELECTED PUBLICATIONS** Ed, Values and Public Policy, Harcourt, 92; auth, "Politics and Manipulation," Soc Theory and Practices, (95): 97-112; auth, "Goodness as a Weapon," J of Philos, (95): 485-499; auth, "From Obedience to Autonomy: Moral Growth in the Little House Books," Children's Lit, (95): 127-140; auth, "The ethics of the Author/Audience Relationship in Children's Fiction," Children's Lit Asn Quart, (97): 184-190; auth, "Choice and Circumstance," Ethics, (98): 154-165; auth, "The Structure of the Moral Dilemma in 'Shiloh'," Children's Lit (99): 185-197; auth, "Passing: The Ethics of Pretending to Be What You Are Not," Soc Theory and Practice, (99): 29-51; auth, "Appropriating Others' Stories: Some Questions about the Ethics of Writing Fiction," J of Soc Philos, (00): 190-203. **CONTACT ADDRESS** Dept Philos, Univ of Colorado, Boulder, Campus PO Box 232, Boulder, CO 80309-0232. **EMAIL** cmills@colorado.edu

MILLS, JON L.
DISCIPLINE LAW **EDUCATION** Stetson Univ, BA; Univ Fla, JD. **CAREER** Prof and dir,Univ Fla, 88-. **MEMBERSHIPS** Fla Bar; Order of the Coif; Phi Kappa Phi; Fla Constitution Rev Comn, 97-98; chem, CRC Style and Drafting Comt. **RESEARCH** Florida Constitutional Law, Environmental Law, Legislative Drafting. **CONTACT ADDRESS** School of Law, Univ of Florida, PO Box 117625, Gainesville, FL 32611-7625. **EMAIL** mills@law.ufl.edu

MILLSTEIN, IRA M.
PERSONAL Born 11/08/1927, New York, NY, m, 1949, 2 children **DISCIPLINE** LAW **EDUCATION** Columbia School of Law, LL.B, 49; Columbia Univ School of Engineering, BS, 47. **CAREER** Sr Partner, Weil, Gotshal & Manges, NY, NY, present; Eugene F William Jr Vis Prof, Yale Univ, 96; Lester Crown Vis Fel, Yale Univ, 92; Ch, Inst Investory Proj, Columbia Univ School of Law, 87-; adjunct prof, Columbia Univ, 87-89; Fel Fac of Govt, Harvard Univ, 83-87; Distinguished Fac Fel, Yale Univ, 83; Sloan Fel, Yale Univ, 82; adjuct prof Law, NY Univ, 67-78. **HONORS AND AWARDS** Honorary Doctorate Humane Letters, Yeshiva Univ, 88; Awded by Fr Govt rank of"Chevalier (Knight) of the National Order of Merit. **MEMBERSHIPS** NY City Partnership Policy Center Ch; Yale School of Management Advisory Board Member; Org for Econ Develop Chair; Amer Acad Arts & Sci Fel; Ntl Assoc of Corporate Directors Brd Member; Japan Society; Appointed by Vice-Pres Gore and Russian Prime Minister Chernomyrdin to US-Russia Capital Markets Forum Working Group on Investory Protection, 97-; Amer Bar Assoc; NY State Bar Assoc; Assoc of Bar of City of NY. **SELECTED PUBLICATIONS** Coauth, The Active Board of Directors and Performance of the Large Publicly Traded Corporation, Columbia Law Rev, 98; The Responsible Board," Bus Lawyer, 97; The Professional Board, Bus Lawyer; The Evolution of the Certifying Board, Bus Lawyer, 93. **CONTACT ADDRESS** Dept of Management, Weil, Gotshal & Manges, 767 Fifth Ave, New York, NY 10153. **EMAIL** Ira.Millstein@weil.com

MINAR, EDWARD
DISCIPLINE WITTGENSTEIN AND THE HISTORY OF ANALYTIC PHILOSOPHY **EDUCATION** Harvard Univ, PhD. **CAREER** Philos, Univ Ark **SELECTED PUBLICATIONS** Articles; Synthese, Philos & Phenomenological Res, Pacific Philos Quart. **CONTACT ADDRESS** Dept of Philos, Univ of Arkansas, Fayetteville, Fayetteville, AR 72701. **EMAIL** eminar@comp.uark.edu

MINAS, ANNE C.
DISCIPLINE PHILOSOPHY **EDUCATION** Harvard Univ, PhD, 67. **RESEARCH** Social philos gender issues; feminism. **SELECTED PUBLICATIONS** Auth, Gender Basics: Feminist Perspectives on Women and Men, Wadsworth, 93. **CONTACT ADDRESS** Dept of Philosophy, Univ of Waterloo, 200 University Ave W, Waterloo, ON, Canada N2L 3G1. **EMAIL** aminas@watarts.uwaterloo.ca

MINNICH, ELIZABETH
DISCIPLINE PHILOSOPHY **EDUCATION** New Sch Soc Res, MA, PhD. **CAREER** Prof. **RESEARCH** Western philosophy. **SELECTED PUBLICATIONS** Auth, Can Virtue Be Taught? A Feminist Reconsiders, Boston Univ, 93; From Ivory Tower to Tower of Babel?, Duke Univ, 92; Judging in Freedom: Hannah Arendt On The Relation of Thinking and Judgment, 89. **CONTACT ADDRESS** Union Inst, 440 E McMillan St., Cincinnati, OH 45206-1925.

MINOGUE, BRENDAN PATRICK
PERSONAL Born 04/19/1945, Brooklyn, NY, m, 1970, 2 children **DISCIPLINE** PHILOSOPHY **EDUCATION** Cathedral Col, BA, 67; OH State Univ, MA, 70, PhD, 74. **CAREER** From Asst Prof to Prof Philos, Youngstown Univ, 74, Chmn Dept, 78. **HONORS AND AWARDS** Nat Endowment Hum fel, 76; vis scholar award, Col Grad Studies, Univ WVA,76. **MEMBERSHIPS** Am Philos Asn; Philos Sci Asn. **RESEARCH** Philos of Sci, Metaphysics, and philos of lang. **SELECTED PUBLICATIONS** Auth, Quine on analyticity and transl, Southern J Philos, summer 76; Numbers, properties and frege, Philos Studies, 6/77; Cartesian optics and Semantic rationalism, Proc XV Int Cong Hist Sci, 8/77; Realism and intensional reference, Philos Sci, winter 79; Bioethics: A Committee Approach, Jones & Bartlett, 96; ed, Reading Engelhardt: Essays on the Thought of H. Tristram Engelhardt, Kluwer, 96. **CONTACT ADDRESS** Dept of Philos, Youngstown State Univ, 1 University Plz, Youngstown, OH 44555-0002. **EMAIL** bpminogu@cc.ysu.edu

MINOR, KEVIN I.
PERSONAL Born 09/19/1959, Jasper, IN, m, 1988, 1 child **DISCIPLINE** JUSTICE **EDUCATION** Ind State Univ, BS, 82; Emporia State Univ, MS, 84; Western Mich Univ, PhD, 88. **CAREER** Asst prof, Southwest Miss State Univ, 88-92; assoc prof to prof, Eastern Ky Univ, 92-. **HONORS AND AWARDS** Fel, Western Mich Univ, 84-87. **MEMBERSHIPS** Am Soc of Criminol; Acad of Criminal Justice Sci. **RESEARCH** Adult Corrections, Juvenile Justice, Program Evaluation. **SELECTED PUBLICATIONS** Coed, Prisons around the world: Studies in international penology, Wm. C. Brown, (Dubuque, IA), 92; coed, Law-related education and juvenile justice, Charles C. Thomas (Springfield, IL), 97; coauth, "Predictors of juvenile court actions and recidivism", Crime and Delinquency 43, (97): 328-344; coauth, "An outcome study of the Diversion Plus Program for juvenile offenders", Federal Probation 61 (97): 51-57; coauth, "Distance learning: Examining new directions and challenges for criminal justice education", ACJS Today 16.2 (98): 3-5; coauth, "Distance education in criminal justice: Student evaluations of interactive, satellite television courses", Justice Prof 10, (98): 291-308; coauth, "Sentence completion and recidivism among juveniles referred to teen court", Crime & Delinquency 45, (99): 467-480; coauth, "Inaugural issue - Overview of the series", Ky Justice & Safety Res Bull 1.1 (99): 1-6; auth, "Rejoinder to Drs. Gehring and Eggleston", Controversial issues in corrections, ed C.B. Fields, Allyn and Bacon (Boston, MA, 99): 15-17; auth, "Is recidivism a valid measure of correctional success? Yes", Controversial issues in corrections, ed C.B. Fields, Allyn and Bacon (Boston, MA, 99): 1-8; coauth, "Corrections and the courts", Corrections: An introduction to corrections in America, eds J. Whitehead, J. Pollock and M. Brasell, Anderson (forthcoming). **CONTACT ADDRESS** Dept Correctional and Juv Justice Studies, Eastern Kentucky Univ, 521 Lancaster Ave, Richmond, KY 40475. **EMAIL** corminor@acs.eku.edu

MINOR, ROBERT NEIL
PERSONAL Born 10/02/1945, Milwaukee, WI, s, 1 child **DISCIPLINE** ASIAN RELIGION **EDUCATION** Trinity Col, BA, 67; MA, 69; Univ Iowa, PhD, 75. **CAREER** Asst prof relig, Allegheny Col, 75-77; asst prof, 77-81, assoc prof to prof, relig, Univ Kans, 88-. **MEMBERSHIPS** Am Acad Relig; Asn Asian Studies; Phi Beta Delta Honor Soc. **RESEARCH** Religious thought in modern India; the Bhagavad Gita; history of religions; methodology; gender and religion. **SELECTED PUBLICATIONS** Auth, Radhakrishnan: A Religious Biography, 87; auth, "The Response of Sri Aurobindo and the Mother," in Modern Indian Responses to Religious Pluralism, ed. Harold Coward (Albany, State Univ of NYork Press, 87), 85-104; auth, "The Bhagavadgita: as Sacred Literature, The Bhagavadgita as Secular Literature," in The Gita in World Literature, ed. C.D. Verma (New Delhi: Sterling Pub, 90): 37-46; auth, "Krishna and the Ethics of the Bhagavadgita," The Journal of the Bhagavadgita X-XI (90-91): 57-73; auth, "Sarvepalli Radhakrishnan and Religious Pluralism," Studia Missionalia XLII, (93): 307-327; auth, "Auroville and the Courts: Religious and Secular," in Relgion and Law in Independent India, ed. Robert D. Baird (Delhi, Manohar, 93), 293-312; auth, "Perennial Issues in Radhakrishnan Scholarship," in New Essays in the Philosophy of Sarvepalli Radhalrishnan, ed. S.S. Rama Rao Pappu (Delhi, Indian Books Centre, 94), 29-42; auth, "The Bhagavadgita and the Reified 'Hinduism,'" J of Vaisnava Studies III, No. 2 (95): 71-89; auth, "Radhakrishnan as Advocate of the Class/Caste System as a Universal Religio-Social System," International Journal of Hindu Studies I, No. 2, (97): 386-400; auth, The Religious, the Spiritual, and the Secular: Auroville & Secular India, 98. **CONTACT ADDRESS** Univ of Kansas, Lawrence, Lawrence, KS 66045-0001. **EMAIL** rminor@ukans.edu

MINOW, MARTHA
PERSONAL Born 12/06/1954, Highland Park, IL, m, 1 child **DISCIPLINE** LAW **EDUCATION** Univ of Mich, AB, 75; Harvard Grad School of Ed, EdM, 76; Yale Law School, JD, 79. **CAREER** Law clerk to Justice Thurgood Marshall, U.S. Supreme Court, 80-81; acting dir, Harvard Prog in Ethics and the Professions, 93-94; ASST PROF, 81-86, PROF, HARVARD LAW SCHOOL, 86-. **HONORS AND AWARDS** Honorary Doctor of Ed, Wheelock Col, 98. **MEMBERSHIPS** Fac Advisory Comt, Fac Hist and Ourselves; Board of Syndication, Harvard Univ Press; Board of Trustees, Revson Found; Sr Fel, The Prog of Ethics and the Professions, Harvard Univ; Chair of the Board, Radcliffe Public Policy Inst of Families, Children, Disabled Persons, Truth, and Reconsiliation Comns. **SELECTED PUBLICATIONS** Co-ed, Women and the Law, Foundation Press, 98; co-ed, Law Stories, Univ of Mich Press, 96; co-ed, Narrative, Violence and the Law: The Essays of Robert M. Cover, Univ of Mich Press, 92; auth, Between Vengeance and Forgiveness: Facing History After Genocide and Mass Violence, Beacon Press, forthcoming; auth, Not Only For Myself: Identity, Politics, and Law, The New Press, 97; auth, Making All the Difference: Inclusion, Exclusion, and American Law, Cornell Univ Press, 90; coauth, Civil Procedure: Doctrine, Practice and Context, Little Brown, forthcoming. **CONTACT ADDRESS** School of Law, Harvard Univ, 407 Griswold, Cambridge, MA 02138. **EMAIL** minow@law.harvard.edu

MINTS, GRIGORI
PERSONAL Born 06/07/1939, Leningrad, Russia, m, 1987, 1 child **DISCIPLINE** PHILOSOPHY **EDUCATION** Steklov Math Inst, PhD, 65; ScD, 90. **CAREER** Res Assoc, Steklov Math Inst, 61-79; Trans, Mir Publ Moscow, 80-84; Sen Res Assoc, Inst Cybernetics, 85-91; Prof, Stanford Univ, 91-. **MEMBERSHIPS** Asn for Symbolic Logic, AMS. **RESEARCH** Mathematical logic, foundations of mathematics, philosophy of mathematics. **SELECTED PUBLICATIONS** Auth, A Short Introduction to Modal Logic, Stanford UP, 92; auth, "Selected Papers on Proof Theory," Bibliopolis-N Holland (92); auth, A Short Introduction to Intuitionistic Logic, Plenum/Kluwer (New York, NY), 00. **CONTACT ADDRESS** Dept Philos, Stanford Univ, Stanford, CA 94305. **EMAIL** mints@turing.stanford.edu

MINTZ, JOEL A.
PERSONAL Born 07/24/1949, New York, NY, m, 1975, 2 children **DISCIPLINE** LAW **EDUCATION** Columbia Col, BA, 70; NY Univ, JD, 74; Columbia Univ, LLM, 82; JSD, 89. **CAREER** Asst prof to prof, Nova Southeastern Univ Shepard Broad Law Center, 82-. **HONORS AND AWARDS** Special Serv Awd, US EPA, 78; Bronze Medal, US EPA, 79; Who's Who in Am; Who's Who in Am Law. **MEMBERSHIPS** Phi Alpha Delta; Environ Law Inst Assoc; Environ and Land Use Law Center; Am Bar Assoc; Int Coun of Environ Law; Assoc of Am Law Sch; Int Union for the Conservation of Nature, Environ Law Comm. **RESEARCH** Environmental law and policy, State and local government, Taxation and finance. **SELECTED PUBLICATIONS** Auth, "Federal Environmental Regulation", Fla Real Estate Transactions, Matthew Bender, 89; auth, "Progress Toward a Health Sky: An Assessment of the London Amendments to the Montreal Protocol on Substances that Deplete the Ozone Layer", 16 Yale J Int L No 2, 571, (91); auth, "The Future of Environmental Enforcement: A Reply to Paddock, 21 Environ Law 1543 (92); auth, State and Local Government Environmental Liability, Clark Boardman Callaghan, 94; auth, Enforcement At the EPA: High Stakes and Hard Choices, Univ of Tex Pr, 95; auth, "Introduction to Symposium on Growth Management: A Plan for Florida's Future", 20 Nova L Rev 585, (96); auth, "Rebuttal: EPA Enforcement and the Challenge of Change", 25 Environ L Reptr 10538, (96); auth, "Potential Liabilities of Governments, State and Local Government Debt Financing, ed MD Gelfand, West Group, 98; coauth, Environmental Law: Cases and Problems Columbia Law Sch, (forthcoming); coauth, State and Local Taxation and Finance in a Nutshell, Tulane Law Sch, (forthcoming). **CONTACT ADDRESS** Col of Law, Nova Southeastern Univ, Davie, 3305 College Ave, Davie, FL 33314-7721. **EMAIL** mintzj@nsu.law.nova.edu

MIRANDA DE ALMEIDA, ROGERIO
PERSONAL Born 04/09/1953, Crato-CE, Brazil **DISCIPLINE** PHILOSOPHY; THEOLOGY; PSYCHOANALYSIS **EDUCATION** Univ of Strasbourg, PhD, 93; Univ Metz, PhD, 97. **CAREER** Instr, Univ of Campinas, Brazil, 94; asst prof, St. Vincent Col, Latrobe, PA, 95-; assoc prof, Ateno S. Anselmo, Rome, 97-; vis prof, Greggoriana Univ, 99-. **HONORS AND AWARDS** Two doctorates with Highest Honors, 93, 97; Scholarship from the Fr government by reason of intellectual performance, 89, 93. **MEMBERSHIPS** The Am Philos Asn, C.E.R.I.T., Univ of Strasbourg. **RESEARCH** Philosophy of language; Philosophy and psychoanalysis; History of philosophy; Lacanian thought; Am Philos Asn; C.E.R.I.T. **SELECTED PUBLICATIONS** "The True, the Non-True and Appearance According to Nietzsche," in Sintese, 94; "Foucault, Nietzsche and Interpretation," in Foucault e a Destruicao das Evidencias, 95; auth, "La Finalite, la Providence et le Hasard Selon Nietzsche," in Revue des Sci Relig, 97; auth, L'au-dela du plaisir, Unie lecture de Nietzsche et Freud, Lille: Universite de Lille III, 97; Auth, "Freud, Nietzsche: L'Enigme du Pere," in Le Portique, 98; auth, Nietzsche et le paradoxe, strasbourg: Presses Universitaires de Strasbourg, 99; auth, "Una filosofia al di la di bene e male," in Per la Filosofia, 00; auth, "La Grande Salute nel pensiero e nell'esperienza di Friedrich Nietzsche," in L'Arco di Giano, 00. **CONTACT ADDRESS** Saint Vincent Col, 300 Fraser Purchase Rd, Latrobe, PA 15650-2690. **EMAIL** rogerio@acad1.stvincent.edu

MIRECKI, PAUL A.
DISCIPLINE RELIGION **EDUCATION** Harvard Univ, ThD, 86 **CAREER** Vis asst prof, Univ Mich, 86-88; vis asst prof, Albion Col, 88-89; Assoc prof, Univ Kans, 89- . **HONORS AND AWARDS** NEH; ACLS, DAAD res & travel grants **MEMBERSHIPS** Amer Soc of Papyrologist; Amer Acad of Relig. **RESEARCH** Papyrology; coptic lang; ancient Mediterranean relig. **SELECTED PUBLICATIONS** Auth, The Coptic Wizard's Hoard, Harvard Theol Rev, 95; coauth, Manichaean Letter, Magical Spell, in Emerging from Darkness: Studies in the Recovery of Manichaean Sources, Brill, 97; Ancient Magic and Ritual Power, Brill, 95; The Gospel of the Savior: A New Ancient Gospel, Polebridge, 99; coed, Emerging from Darkness: Studies in the Recovery of Manichaean Sources, Brill, 97. **CONTACT ADDRESS** Dept of Relig Stud, Univ of Kansas, Lawrence, 103 Smith Hall, Lawrence, KS 66045-2164. **EMAIL** pmirecki@ukans.edu

MIROWSKI, PHILIP E.
DISCIPLINE PHILOSOPHY OF SCIENCE **EDUCATION** Mich State Univ, BA, 73; Univ Mich, MA, 76, PhD, 79. **CAREER** Prof. **RESEARCH** History and philosophy of economic theory. **SELECTED PUBLICATIONS** Auth, Mandelbrot's Economics After a Quarter-Century, 95; Three Ways of Thinking About Testing in Econometrics, 95; Harold Hotelling and the Neoclassical Dream, 97; Civilization and its Discounts, 95; The Economic Consequences of Philip Kitcher, 96; On Playing the Economics Trump Card in the Philosophy of Science: Why It Didn't Work for Michael Polanyi, 97; Do You Know the Way to Santa Fe?, 96; Machine Dreams: Economic Agent as Cyborg, 98; ed, Edgeworth's Writings on Chance, Probability and Statistics, 94; Natural Images in Economics: Markets Read in Tooth and Claw, 94; auth, "Machine Dreams: Economics Becomes a Cyborg Science," 01. **CONTACT ADDRESS** History and Philosophy of Science Dept, Univ of Notre Dame, Notre Dame, IN 46556. **EMAIL** Philip.E.Mirowski.1@nd.edu

MISNER, PAUL
PERSONAL Born 02/14/1936, Akron, OH, m, 2000, 1 child **DISCIPLINE** THEOLOGY **EDUCATION** St Charles Borromeo Sem, BA, 54-58; Gregorian Univ, Rome, STL, 58-62; Univ of Munich, Dr Theol. 65-69. **CAREER** Asst Prof, 69-75, Theol, Boston Coll; Fulbright Res Prof, 75-76, Univ of Marburg; Asst, Assoc, Prof, 79-, Theol, Marquette Univ; Fulbright Res Prof, 85-86, Inst for European Hist, Mainz; Vis Prof, 91, Univ of Cologne. **HONORS AND AWARDS** Fulbright Res Prof; Social Catholicism name d Book of the Year, 92; Awd from Bradley Inst for Democracy and Public Values for Sabbatical support. **MEMBERSHIPS** Amer Acad Rel; Amer Catholic Hist Assoc; Amer Hist Assoc; Catholic Theol Soc Amer; College Theology Soc; North Amer Acad of Ecumenists. **RESEARCH** Modern European Christianity and Christian Thought; Roman Catholic Studies. **SELECTED PUBLICATIONS** Auth, Social Catholicism in Europe, From the Onset of Industrialization to the First World War, NY, Crossroad, 91; Social Catholicism in Nineteenth-Century Europe, A Review of Recent Historiography, The Catholic Historical Review, 92; Contributor to The New Dictionary of Catholic Social Thought, Collegeville, MN, Liturgical Press, 94. **CONTACT ADDRESS** Dept Theology, Marquette Univ, Milwaukee, WI 53201-1881. **EMAIL** paul.misner@marquette.edu

MISSNER, MARSHALL HOWARD
PERSONAL Born 01/10/1942, Chicago, IL, m, 1969, 2 children **DISCIPLINE** PHILOSOPHY **EDUCATION** Univ Chicago, BA, 63, MA, 67, PhD, 70. **CAREER** Asst prof, 69-80, assoc prof philos, 80-, Univ Wis-Oshkosh; consult, Wis Humanities Comt, 77-. **MEMBERSHIPS** Am Philos Assn. **RESEARCH** Hobbes; social philosophy; philosophy of science. **SELECTED PUBLICATIONS** Art, Hobbes's Method in Leviathan, J Hist Ideas, 77; ed, Business and Ethics, Alfred Publ, 80; art, The Skeptical Basis Of Hobbe's Political Philosophy, J Hist Ideas, 83. **CONTACT ADDRESS** Dept of Philosophy, Univ of Wisconsin, Oshkosh, 800 Algoma Blvd, Oshkosh, WI 54901-8601. **EMAIL** missner@uwosh.edu

MITCHELL, ALAN C.
PERSONAL Born 11/16/1948, Brooklyn, NY, m, 1998 **DISCIPLINE** NEW TESTAMENT, CHRISTIAN ORIGINS **EDUCATION** Fordham Univ, AB, 72; Western Sch Theol, MDiv, 79; Yale Univ, MA, 81, MPhil, 83; PhD, 86. **CAREER** Instr, Wheeling Col, 73-76; teach fel, Yale Div Sch, Yale Col, 80-82; adj inst, Fairfield Univ, 83; asst prof, 86, Assoc Prof, Georgetown Univ, 92-. **HONORS AND AWARDS** Phi Beta Kappa; Alpha Sigma Nu; Yale Univ fel; Landegger Sr. fel, 96-97. **MEMBERSHIPS** Cath Bibl Asn; Soc Bibl Lit. **RESEARCH** New Testament soc world; Hellenistic moral philos and early Christianity; Paul; Hebrews. **SELECTED PUBLICATIONS** Auth, Looking to the Interests of Others: Friendship and Justice in New Testament Communities, in Let Justice Roll Down Like Waters: Distinguished Lectures in Jesuit Education, Georgetown Univ Press, 93; auth, Rich and Poor in the Courts of Corinth: Litigiousness and Status in 1 Corinthians 6.1-11, New Testament Stud 39, 93; auth, Friendship, in A Modern Catholic Encyclopedia, Liturgical Press, 94; auth, Holding on to Confidence, in Friendship, Flattery, and Frankness of Speech: Studies on Friendship in the Ancient World, Nov Supp 82, 96; auth,

Greet the Friends by Name: New Testament Evidence for the Greco-Roman Topon on Friendship, in Greco-Roman Perspectives on Friendship, Scholars Press, 97; auth, The Use of Scripture in Evangelium Vitae: A Response to James Keenan, in Choosing Life: A Dialogue on Evangelium Vitae, Georgetown Univ Press, 97; co-ed, Choosing Life: A Dialogue on Evangelium Vitae, Georgetown Univ Press, 97. **CONTACT ADDRESS** Georgetown Univ, Box 571135 - 123 New North Bldg, Washington, DC 20057-1135. **EMAIL** mitchela@georgetown.edu

MITCHELL, C. BEN
DISCIPLINE CHRISTIAN ETHICS **EDUCATION** Miss State Univ, BS; Southwestern Baptist Theol Sem, MDiv; Univ Tenn, PhD. **CAREER** Bioethics consult, S Baptist Ethics and Rel Liberty Commn; Senior fel, Ctr for Bioethics and Human Dignity; dir, Southern's Jordan Inst; asst prof, Trinity Int Univ, 99-. **HONORS AND AWARDS** Founding fel, Res Inst of Ethics and Rel Lib Comm; fel, Carl F.H. Henry Inst. **MEMBERSHIPS** Univ Fac for Life at Georgetown Univ. **RESEARCH** Ethical implications of new genetics. **SELECTED PUBLICATIONS** Co-ed, Prescription Ethics: Pharmaceutical Representative Interactions with Health Care Professionals; ed, Ctr's jour, Ethics and Medicine: A Christian Perspective on Bioethics; ed. New International Dictionary of Bioethics, 01. **CONTACT ADDRESS** Trinity Evangelical Divinity Sch, 2065 Half Day Rd., Deerfield, IL 60015. **EMAIL** bmitchell@sbts.edu

MITCHELL, DONALD
DISCIPLINE ASIAN AND COMPARATIVE PHILOSOPHY OF RELIGION **EDUCATION** Univ Hawaii, PhD. **CAREER** Prof, Purdue Univ; assoc ed, Buddhist-Christian Stud. **RESEARCH** The Buddhist-Christian dialogue. **SELECTED PUBLICATIONS** Auth, Spirituality and Emptiness: The Dynamics of Spiritual Life in Buddhism and Christianity. **CONTACT ADDRESS** Dept of Philos, Purdue Univ, West Lafayette, 1080 Schleman Hall, West Lafayette, IN 47907-1080.

MITCHELL, JEFF
PERSONAL Born 03/03/1964, Lancaster, PA, m, 1995 **DISCIPLINE** PHILOSOPHY **EDUCATION** Whitman Col, BA, 86; Vanderbilt Univ, MA, 90, PhD, 93. **CAREER** Vis prof, philos, Miss State Univ, 93-94; asst prof, philos, Ark Tech Univ, 94-99; assoc prof, philos, Ark Tech Univ, 99-. **MEMBERSHIPS** Amer Philos Asn; Soc for the Advan of Amer Philos; Am Soc for Philos, Counseling, and Psychotherapy. **RESEARCH** Moral and philosophical psychology; Pragmatism; Value theory. **SELECTED PUBLICATIONS** Auth, Reason's Different Tastes, The Southern Jour of Philos, 96; auth, Danto, Dewey and the Historical End of Art, Transactions of the Charles S. Peirce Society, 89; auth, "Neurosis and the Historic Quest for Security: A Social Role Analysis," Philosophy, Psychiatry, and Psychology, vol 5, no 4 (98): 317-328; auth, "Living a Lie: Self-Deception, Habit, and Social Roles," Human Studies (00). **CONTACT ADDRESS** Social Sciences & Philosophy, Arkansas Tech Univ, WPN 255, Russellville, AR 72801. **EMAIL** jeff.mitchell@mail.atu.edu

MITCHELL, R. LLOYD
PERSONAL Born 05/25/1940, Madison, ME, m, 1960, 2 children **DISCIPLINE** PHILOSOPHY **EDUCATION** Barrington Col, BA, 60; Boston Univ, AM, 64; Duquesne Univ, PhD, 78. **CAREER** Prof, Wash & Jefferson Col, 64-. **MEMBERSHIPS** APA, Am Assoc of Philos Teachers. **RESEARCH** Plato social and political philosophy. **SELECTED PUBLICATIONS** Auth, The Hymn to Eros, Univ Pr of Am, 93. **CONTACT ADDRESS** Dept Philos, Washington and Jefferson Col, 60 S Lincoln St, Washington, PA 15301-4812. **EMAIL** rmitchell@washieff.edu

MITCHELL, SANDRA D.
DISCIPLINE PHILOSOPHY OF SCIENCE **EDUCATION** Univ Pittsburgh, PhD, 87. **CAREER** Prof, HPS, Univ of Pittsburgh. **RESEARCH** Epistemological and metaphysical issues in biology and the social sciences. **SELECTED PUBLICATIONS** Auth, "Competing Units of Selection?: A Case of Symbiosis," Philos of Sci, 54, 87; "The Units of Behavior in Evolutionary Explanations," Interpretation and Explanation in the Study of Animal Behavior, Westview Press, 90; "On Pluralism and Integration in Evolutionary Explanations," Amer Zoologist, 92; "Dispositions or Etiologies? A Comment on Bigelow and Pargetter," Jour Philos, 93; "Function, Fitness and Disposition," Biol and Philos, 95; co-auth, Self Organization and Adaptation in Insect Societies, PSA, 90, Volume Two, 91; auth, Dimensions of Scientific Law" Philos of Sci, June 00. **CONTACT ADDRESS** Dept of History and Philosophy of Science, Univ of Pittsburgh, 1017 Cathedral of Learning, Pittsburgh, PA 15260.

MITIAS, MICHAEL HANNA
PERSONAL Born 07/23/1939, Swaydieh, Syria, m, 1966, 3 children **DISCIPLINE** VALUE THEORY, METAPHYSICS **EDUCATION** Union Col, Ky, BA, 63; Univ Waterloo, PhD, 71. **CAREER** From instr to full prof philos, 67-99, distinguished prof, 71-72, Prof Philos, Millsaps Col, 73-. **RESEARCH** Aesthetics; social and political philosophy. **SELECTED PUBLICATIONS** Auth, Another look at Hegel's concept of punishment, Hegel-Studies, 78; Law as the foundation of the state: Hegel, Interpretation, 82; auth, Moral Foundation of the State, Rodopi, 85; auth, What Makes an Experience Aesthetic?, Rodopi, 88; auth, Philosophy and Architecture, Rodopi, 96; auth, Architecture and Civilization, Rodopi, 99; Asethetic Experience of the Architectural Work, Journal of Aesthetic Education, 99. **CONTACT ADDRESS** Dept of Philosophy, Millsaps Col, 1701 N State St, Jackson, MS 39210-0001. **EMAIL** mitiamh@okra.millsaps.edu

MITTAL, SUSHIL
PERSONAL Born 03/04/1967, ON, Canada, m, 1996, 2 children **DISCIPLINE** RELIGION, ANTHROPOLOGY, SOUTH ASIAN STUDIES **EDUCATION** McGill Univ, BA, 90; Carleton Univ, MA, 93; Univ Montreal, PhD, 98. **CAREER** Vis asst prof, Univ Fla, 98-99; asst prof, Millikin Univ, 99-. **HONORS AND AWARDS** Millikin Univ Fac Summer Res Grant, 00; Millikin Univ Merit Awd, 00; Am Acad of Relig Individual res grant, 99-00; Soc sci and Humanities res coun of Canada Doctoral Fel, 93-97; Nominated for fac teaching Awd, Univ Fla, 98-99. **MEMBERSHIPS** Am Acad of Relig. **RESEARCH** Comparative history of religions, Hindu civilization, Hindu theories of social and human sciences, Mahatma Gandhi, Occidentalism, Structure, logic and meaning of Hindu worldviews. **SELECTED PUBLICATIONS** Ed, International Journal of Hindu Studies, Quebec: World Heritage Press, 97-. **CONTACT ADDRESS** Dept Relig, Millikin Univ, 1124 W Main St, Decatur, IL 62522-2084. **EMAIL** smittal@mail.millikin.edu

MITTELMAN, JAMES H.
DISCIPLINE INTERNATIONAL RELATIONS **EDUCATION** Mich State Univ, BA; Cornell Univ, MA, PhD. **CAREER** Prof, Am Univ; Prof and Dean, Grad Sch Int Studies, Univ Denver; Prof and Dean, Div Soc Sci, Queens Col, CUNY. **HONORS AND AWARDS** Pok Rafeah Chair in Intl Stud and Distinguished Vis Prof, Nat Univ of Malaysia; mem, Inst for Advanced Stud, Princeton, 98-99. **RESEARCH** Globalization; global political economy. **SELECTED PUBLICATIONS** Ed and contrib, Globalization: Critical Reflections, Lynne Rienner Publs, 96; co-auth, Out from Underdevelopment Revisited: Changing Global Structures and the Remaking of the Third World, St. Martin's Press, 97; Co-ed and contrib, Innovation and Transformation in International Studies, Cambridge Univ Press, 97; auth, The Globalization Syndrome: Transformation and Resistance, Princeton Univ Press, 00. **CONTACT ADDRESS** American Univ, 4400 Massachusetts Ave, Washington, DC 20016-8071.

MIZELL, K.
PERSONAL Born Colorado Springs, CO **DISCIPLINE** PHILOSOPHY **EDUCATION** Incarnate Word Col, BA, 74; Univ Okla, MA, 86; PhD, 97. **CAREER** Vis Instr, Brigham Young Univ, 94-96; Assoc Prof, Ut Valley State Col, 99-. **HONORS AND AWARDS** Who's Who Among Studs in Am Univs and Cols, 74; Outstanding Young Women of Am, 81; J C Penny Golden Rule Awd, 87; Scholar, Nat Endowment for the Humanities, 97-98; Teacher of the Semester, 99; Who's Who Among Am Teachers, 00. **MEMBERSHIPS** APA, Am Soc of Aesthetics, Am Asn of Mus. **RESEARCH** Philosophy of childhood, philosophical issues involving children, social philosophy, aesthetics, philosophy pedagogy. **CONTACT ADDRESS** Dept Philos, Utah Valley State Col, 800 W University Pkwy, Orem, UT 84097-8295. **EMAIL** mizellka@uvsc.edu

MIZZONI, JOHN M.
PERSONAL Born 04/04/1967, Bridgeport, CT, m, 1987, 3 children **DISCIPLINE** PHILOSOPHY **EDUCATION** Providence Col, BA, 89; Temple Univ, MA, 92; PhD, 96. **CAREER** Lectr, Rowan Col, Glassboro NJ, 91-92; Community Col of Philadelphia, Pa, 92-98; Chestnut Hill Col, Philadelphia, Pa, 92-94; Temple Univ, Philadelphia, Pa, 95; Ursinus Col, Colville, Pa, 96; Univ of St Francis, Joliet, Ill, 97-; Gwynedd-Mercy Col, Gwynedd Valley, pa, 97-; Del Co Community Col, Media, Pa,, 96; Pa State Univ, Abington, Pa, 96-; St. Joseph's Univ, Philadelphia, Pa, 96-; La Salle Univ, Philadelphia, Pa, 93-; Villanova Univ, Villanova, Pa, 94-. **HONORS AND AWARDS** John P. reid Philos Awd, Providence Col, 89. **MEMBERSHIPS** Am Philos Asn, AAUP, Int Soc for Environmental Ethics. **RESEARCH** Metaethics, Environmental Ethics. **SELECTED PUBLICATIONS** Auth, "Freedom in Kant's Antinomy," Kinesis XXI (94): 24-32; auth, "Moral Realism, Objective Values, and J.L. Mackie," Auslengung XX (95): 11-24; rev, of "Quasi Realism," by Simon Blackburn, Eidos XX (95): 58-62; rev, of "Environmental Ethics: An Introduction to Environmental Philosophy," by Joseph R. DesJardins, The Philos Quart 46 (Oct 96): 558-561; auth, "Maurice Mandelbaum," in The American National Biography Vol 14, ed. John A. Garraty and Mark C. Carnes (NY: Oxford Univ Press, 99), 397-398; auth, "May Brodbeck," in The American National Biography Vol 3, ed. John A. Garraty and Mark C. Carnes (NY: Oxford Univ Press, 99), 584-585; auth, "Transformative Value: Intrinsic or Instrumental?," in Inherent and Instrumental Value, ed. John Abbarno (Int Scholars Publ, forthcoming); rev, of "Readings on Human Nature," ed. Peter Loptson, Philos in Rev (forthcoming); rev, of "Commitment, Value, and Moral Realism," by Marcel S. Lieberman, Philos In Rev (forthcoming); auth, "Environ-Moral Realism: Some Prospects for Environmental Metaethics," The J of Philos Res (forthcoming). **CONTACT ADDRESS** 125 Summit Ave, Jenkintown, PA 19046.

MOBERLY, ROBERT B.
DISCIPLINE LAW **EDUCATION** Univ Wis, BS, JD. **CAREER** Fac, Univ of Tenn, 73-77; trustee res fel, prof and dir, Inst Dispute Resolution, Univ Fla, 77-. **MEMBERSHIPS** Arbitration Panels for Railway Mediation bd, Amer Arbitration Asn, and Fed Mediation Conciliation Serv; Wis Bar; Tenn Bar; Fla Bar Fac Affe. **RESEARCH** Labor law, negotiation, mediation, collective bargaining & arbitration. **CONTACT ADDRESS** School of Law, Univ of Florida, PO Box 117625, Gainesville, FL 32611-7625. **EMAIL** moberly@law.ufl.edu

MOBLEY, TOMMY W.
PERSONAL Born 07/12/1949, Harrodsburg, KY, m, 1973, 2 children **DISCIPLINE** RELIGION **EDUCATION** Cincinnati Bible Col and Sem, BS, 71; Southern Baptist Theol Sem, MRE, 73; DMin, 77. **CAREER** Instr, Col of the Scriptures, 74-77; Lectr, Cincinnati Bible Col, 78-89; prof, La Bible Col, 83-. **HONORS AND AWARDS** Christian Education Awd, 71; Homiletics Awd, 71. **MEMBERSHIPS** Fel of christian Peace Officers; Southern Ind Christian Ministers Assoc; Scottsburg Ministerial Assoc; N Am Christian Convention; Presidents Assoc of Christian Col. **SELECTED PUBLICATIONS** Auth, "The Restoration Movement Among the American Negro", Sem Rev XXIV.2, June 78; auth, "Camp - A Life Laboratory", Key to Christian Educ XVII.4, Summer 79; auth, "A Chaplain's Comments", Badge 9, March 77; coauth, Chaplaincy in Law Enforcement: What It Is and How to do It, Charles C. Thomas, (Springfield, IL), 89; auth, "My Kind of Brotherhood", Restoration Herald LXVII.1 Jan 93; auth, "Chaplain's Chat", Louisville Div of Police News, auth, "Reflections", Christian Standard CXXXIV.6, Feb 99. **CONTACT ADDRESS** Louisville Bible Col, PO Box 91046, Louisville, KY 40291-0046.

MOCKLER, ROBERT J.
PERSONAL s **DISCIPLINE** BUSINESS **EDUCATION** Harvard Univ, BA, 54, MBA, 59; Columbia Univ, PhD, 61. **CAREER** St John's Univ, Peter J. Tobin Col of Bus, Grad School, prof, 63-. **HONORS AND AWARDS** St. Johns Univ, Annual Merit Awd, 89-99, Joseph F.Adams prof, 98; personal audience with Pope John-Paul II, St. John's Univ, Thirty year Distinguished Service Awd; Concordia Univ. Case Study Competition; Best Paper Awd, Info. Resources Mgmt. Assn, 98; nyc marathon, ran and finished, at age 65, 97; dsi, 5th intl conf, coch, athens greece, 99; nacra, ed bd, of: case research jour, 94-, jour strat change, ed bd, 94-, nsf, lead review, 97; dsi, creating a strategic res plan, orig / organ, co-lead 95,96 & **MEMBERSHIPS** DSI, NACRA, IRMA, ECWA, IEEE / ACM **RESEARCH** Multinational strategic alliances; CIS/MIS sys; intl bus strategies; cross-cult mgmt; knowledge based sys; innov tchg methods; e-commerce. **SELECTED PUBLICATIONS** Auth, Multinational Strategic Alliances, John Wiley and Sons, 99; The Case Study Development Program of the Management Department at St. John's University, Strat Man Res Group, 00; Developing Knowledge-Based Systems Using an Expert System Shell: A Guide for General Business Managers and Computer Information System Technicians, 19 Sample Prototype Systems and a Development Shell, Prentice Hall / MacMillan, 92, trans to Chinese, China Railway Pub Corp, 98; Strategic Management, Idea Group Pub, 93, trans to Chinese, Intl Cult Pub Comp, 97; Computer Software to Support Strategic Management Decision Making: A Comprehensive Review of Available Existing Conventional and Knowledge-Based Applications, Prentice Hall / MacMillan, 92; Contingency Approaches to Strategic Management: Integrating Basic and Applied Research, SMRG, 92; Auth, Multinational Strategic Management, 01; Multinational Strategic Leaders and Management; Winning in Today's Rapidly Changing Markets: The Never Ending Quest for Newer, Better, Different, Faster, Cheaper; Learning How to Learn from Multinational Strategic Management Situations, 99. **CONTACT ADDRESS** Dept of Management, St. John's Univ, 114 East 90th St (1B), New York, NY 10128. **EMAIL** mocklerr@stjohns.edu

MODICA, JOSEPH BENJAMIN
PERSONAL Born 07/19/1957, Brooklyn, NY, m, 1981, 4 children **DISCIPLINE** BIBLICAL STUDIES **EDUCATION** Queens Col, City Univ New York, BA, 75; Alliance Theol Sem, MDiv, 86; MPhil, 91, PhD, 95, Drew Univ. **CAREER** Chaplain and Asst Prof, Biblical Studies, 93-, Eastern Col. **CONTACT ADDRESS** Eastern Col, 1300 Eagle Rd., Saint Davids, PA 19087-3696. **EMAIL** jmodica@eastern.edu

MODRAS, RONALD E.
PERSONAL Born 08/23/1937, Detroit, MI, m, 1991 **DISCIPLINE** THEOLOGY **EDUCATION** St Mary's Col, BA, 59; Cath Univ Am, STB, 63; Univ Tuebingen, ThD, 74. **CAREER** Assoc Prof, St John Sem, 72-79; Prof, St Louis Univ, 79-. **HONORS AND AWARDS** Micah Awd, Am Jewish Comt; Fel, Annenberg Res Inst; Book of the Year Awd, Col Theol Soc, 94. **MEMBERSHIPS** Cath Theol Soc of Am, Col Theol Soc, Polish Inst of Arts and Sci of Am. **RESEARCH** History of antisemitism, Catholic-Jewish relations, history of Jesuit spiritual humanism, the writing of Pope John Paul II. **SELECTED PUBLICATIONS** Auth, Paul Tillich's Theology of the Church, 76; auth, Human Sexuality: New Directions in American Catholic Thought, 79; auth, The Catholic Church and Anti-Semitism: Poland 1933-1939, 94. **CONTACT ADDRESS** Dept Theol, Saint Louis Univ, 221 N Grand Blvd, Saint Louis, MO 63103-2006. **EMAIL** modrasre@slu.edu

MOENSSENS, ANDRE A.
PERSONAL Born 01/13/1930, Hoboken, Belgium, s, 5 children **DISCIPLINE** LAW, CRIMINALISTICS, FORENSIC EVIDENCE **EDUCATION** Chicago-Kent Col Law of Ill Inst Technol, JD, 66; Northwestern Univ, LLM, 67. **CAREER** Head instr, Inst Appl Sci, 60-66; from instr to prof law, Chicago-Kent Col Law, 66-73, dir, Inst Criminal Justice, 67-71; Prof Law, Sch of Law, Univ Richmond, 73-95; chm, Law, W Va Univ, 93-95; emer prof law, Univ Richmond, 95- ; Doublas Stripp prof law and dir, Forensic Center Law, Med and Public Policy, Univ Mo, Kansas City, 96- . **HONORS AND AWARDS** Excellence in tchg awards, 73, 79, 84, 95; Harold A Feder Jurisp Awd, AAFS, 98. **MEMBERSHIPS** Fel Am Acad Forensic Sci (secy-treas, 75-76); Am Trial Lawyers Asn; Int Assoc for Identification; Can Identification Soc; Am Soc Law, Med and Ethics; Va State Bar; Ill State Bar Assn; KCMO Bar Assn. **RESEARCH** Criminal justice; scientific evidence; criminalistics. **SELECTED PUBLICATIONS** Auth, Fingerprints and the Law , 69 & Fingerprint Techniques, 70, Chilton; coauth, Scientific Police Investigation, 72; coauth, Scientific Evidence in Civil and Criminal Cases, 73, 2nd ed 78, to 4th ed, 95, 5th ed 01; coauth, Cases on Criminal Law, 73, to 6th ed, 98; Cases on Criminal Procedure, Bobbs-Merrill, 2d ed, 87; Problems & Cases in Trial Advocacy, 81, to 5th ed, 95. **CONTACT ADDRESS** School of Law, Univ of Missouri, Kansas City, 5100 Rockhill Rd, Kansas City, MO 64110-2499. **EMAIL** moenssensa@umkc.edu

MOFFAT, ROBERT C. L.
DISCIPLINE LAW **EDUCATION** Southern Methodist Univ, BA, MA, LLB; Univ Sydney, Australia, LLM. **CAREER** Prof, aff prof Philos, Univ Fla, 66-. **HONORS AND AWARDS** Lon Fuller Prize in Jurisp, 87. **MEMBERSHIPS** Texas Bar; Law and Soc Asn; Amer Soc for Polit and Legal Philos. **RESEARCH** Jurisp, criminal law, law and society, law and public policy. **SELECTED PUBLICATIONS** Co-ed, Radical Critiques of the Law, Kans, 97. **CONTACT ADDRESS** School of Law, Univ of Florida, PO Box 117625, Gainesville, FL 32611-7625. **EMAIL** moffat@law.ufl.edu

MOFFETT, SAMUEL HUGH
PERSONAL Born 04/07/1916, Pyongyang, Korea, m, 1942 **DISCIPLINE** HISTORY OF MISSIONS, ASIAN CHURCH HISTORY **EDUCATION** Wheaton Col, Ill, AB, 38; Princeton Theol Sem, ThB, 42; Yale Univ, PhD, 45. **CAREER** Lectr English & church hist, Yenching Univ, Peking, 48-49; asst prof church hist, Nanking Theol Sem, 49-50; vis lectr ecumenics, Princeton Theol Sem, 53-55; prof church hist, 60-81, dean Grad Sch, 66-70, assoc pres, 70-81, Presby Theol Sem, Seoul, Korea; pres, Asian Ctr Theol Studies & Mission, 74-81; prof missions & ecumenics, 81-87, Henry Winters Luce Prof of Ecumenics and Mission, emeritus, Princeton Theol Sem; bd dir, Yonsei Univ, Seoul, 57-81, Soongjun Univ, Seoul, 69-81 & Whitworth Col, Spokane, Wash, 73-79; mem, US Educ Comn, Korea, 66-67. **HONORS AND AWARDS** Order Civil Merit, Repub Korea, 81; DD, King Col, TN, 85; DD, Gordon Conwell Theol Sem, 95; DD, Presbyterian Col and Theol Sem, 96; hon PhD Soongsil Univ, SEoul, 97; littd, yonsei univ, seoul, korea, 81. **MEMBERSHIPS** Am Soc Missiology; Int Asn Missiological Studies; Korean Church History Soc; Royal Asiatic Soc (pres, Korean Br, 68-69). **RESEARCH** Asian church history; history of missions; Korean studies. **SELECTED PUBLICATIONS** Coauth, First Encounters: Korea 1880-1910, Dragon's Eye Press, Seoul, 82; auth, History of Christianity in Asia, Beginnings to 1500, Harper Collins, 92. **CONTACT ADDRESS** 150 Leabrook Ln, Princeton, NJ 08540.

MOHAN, BRIJ
PERSONAL Born 09/09/1939, Mursan, India, m, 1967, 2 children **DISCIPLINE** POLITICAL SCIENCE **EDUCATION** AGRA Univ, BA, 58; MSW, 60; Lucknow Univ, PhD, 64. **CAREER** Acad Specialist, Univ Wis Oshkosh, 75-76; from assoc prof to prof & dir of doctoral prog, La State Univ, 76-. **HONORS AND AWARDS** Univ Grants comn Scholar, Lucknow Univ, 60-63; CINESCO Fel, Danish Res Inst, 68; Brij Mohan Distinguished Prof Awd; Alumni Distinguished Fac Awd, La State Univ Sch of Soc Work, 97; Distinguished Fac Awd, La State Univ, 99. **MEMBERSHIPS** NA-SW, CSWE. **RESEARCH** Philosophy of Science, International/Comparative Social Welfare Systems, Mental Health, Diversity, Human Oppression. **SELECTED PUBLICATIONS** Auth, Global Development, Praeger, 92; auth, Eclipse of Freedom, Praeger, 93; auth, Democracies of Unfreedom, Praeger, 96; auth, Unification of Social Work, Praeger, 99. **CONTACT ADDRESS** Dept Soc Work, La State Univ at Baton Rouge, Baton Rouge, LA 70803-0001. **EMAIL** mohan.b@att.net

MOHAN, ROBERT PAUL
PERSONAL Born 10/25/1920, Ashley, PA **DISCIPLINE** PHILOSOPHY **EDUCATION** Cath Univ, AB, 42, AM, 47, PhD, 49, STL, 54. **CAREER** Instr English, St Mary's Sem, MD, 47-48; instr French & Latin, St Edward's Sem, Wash, 48-50; dean summer session & workshops, 60-72, univ marshal, 68, mem acad senate, prof Philos, Cath Univ Am, 50-, Assoc ed, Am Ecclesiastical Rev, 55; lectr ethics, sr sem, Dept of State, 80. **MEMBERSHIPS** Am Cath Philos Asn; Am Philos Asn, Case DC Prof of the Year, 90. **RESEARCH** Social philosophy; a Thomistic philosophy of civilization and culture. **SELECTED PUBLICATIONS** Auth, Philosophy of History, McMillan- Crowell, 70. **CONTACT ADDRESS** Dept of Philos, Catholic Univ of America, Washington, DC 20017. **EMAIL** mohan@cua.edu

MOHANTY, JITENDRA N.
DISCIPLINE PHENOMENOLOGY **EDUCATION** Univ Gottingen, PhD, 54; Univ Burdwan, DLitt, 88. **CAREER** Prof, Philos, Emory Univ. **HONORS AND AWARDS** Life Mem, Indian Acad Philos; Humboldt Prize, 92; pres, socy asian & comp philos, 93-95; vis fel, all souls col, oxford, 82. **RESEARCH** Phenomenology; transcendental philosophy; and Indian philosophy **SELECTED PUBLICATIONS** Auth, Edmund Husserl's Theory of Meaning; Phenomenology and Ontology; auth, Husserl and Frege; auth, The Possibility of Transcendental Philosophy; auth, Reason and Tradition in Indian Thought; and auth, Theory and Practice. **CONTACT ADDRESS** Emory Univ, Atlanta, GA 30322-1950. **EMAIL** jmohant@emory.edu

MOHLER, R. ALBERT, JR.
DISCIPLINE CHRISTIAN THEOLOGY **EDUCATION** Samford Univ, BA; S Baptist Theol Sem, MDiv, PhD. **CAREER** Prof, pres, S Baptist Theol Sem, 93-. **HONORS AND AWARDS** Listed, Time mag, fifty outstanding young leaders US, 94. **SELECTED PUBLICATIONS** Ed, Christian Index. **CONTACT ADDRESS** Christian Theol Dept, So Baptist Theol Sem, 2825 Lexington Rd, Louisville, KY 40280. **EMAIL** mohler@sbts.edu

MOHR, RICHARD
DISCIPLINE PHILOSOPHY **EDUCATION** Univ Toronto, PhD, 77. **CAREER** Prof, Univ Ill Urbana Champaign. **RESEARCH** Ancient philosophy ; social philosophy; arts. **SELECTED PUBLICATIONS** Auth, The Platonic Cosmology, 85; Gays/Justice: A Study of Ethics, Society and Law, 88; Gay Ideas: Outing and Other Controversies, 92; A More Perfect Union: Why Straight Americans Must Stand Up For Gay Rights, 94. **CONTACT ADDRESS** Philosophy Dept, Univ of Illinois, Urbana-Champaign, 52 E Gregory Dr, Champaign, IL 61820. **EMAIL** r-mohr@staff.uiuc.edu

MOHRLANG, ROGER L.
PERSONAL Born 12/05/1941, Hastings, NE, m, 1976, 2 children **DISCIPLINE** RELIGIOUS STUDIES, NEW TESTAMENT STUDIES **EDUCATION** Carnegie-Mellon Univ, BS, 63; Fuller Theol Sem, MA, 76; Univ Oxford, DPhil, 80. **CAREER** Wycliffe Bible Translators (Nigeria), 67-74; Whitworth Col, 78-. **HONORS AND AWARDS** Burlington-Northern Outstanding Teaching Awd, Whitworth Col Fac Outstanding Service Awd, Who's Who Among America's Teachers. **RESEARCH** New Testament ethics, Paul's letters, Bible translation. **SELECTED PUBLICATIONS** Auth, Vaca Yesu Kristi, the New Testament in the Kamwa (Higi) language, 1st ed, The Bible League (75); auth, Matthew and Paul: a comparison of ethical perspectives, SNTSMS 48, Cambridge (84); auth, "Love," Dictionary of Paul and His Letters, InterVarsity (93); rev and ed, Malifyi Klakawals Yesu Kristi, the New Testament in the Kamwa (Higi) language, The Bible League (97); auth, "Romans," Theological Commentary on the Bible, Tynoble (forthcoming). **CONTACT ADDRESS** Dept Relig & Philos, Whitworth Col, 300 W Hawthorne Rd, Spokane, WA 99251. **EMAIL** rmohrlang@whitworth.edu

MOKYR, JOEL
PERSONAL Born 07/26/1946, Lryren, Netherlands, m, 2 children **DISCIPLINE** ECONOMICS **EDUCATION** Hebrew Univ-Jerusalem; Yale Univ, PhD, 74. **CAREER** Vis prof, Harvard; vis prof, Univ Chicago; vis prof, Stanford Univ; vis prof, Hebrew Univ-Jerusalem; vis prof, Univ Tel Aviv; vis prof, Univ Coll Dublin; vis prof, Univ Manchester; PROF, ECON & HIST, NORTHWESTERN UNIV, 74-. **HONORS AND AWARDS** Nat Science Found Grant, 78-81, 86-87, 92-94; John Simon Guggenheim Mem Found Fel, 80-81. **MEMBERSHIPS** Fel, Am Acad of Arts and Science; Trustee, EHA. **RESEARCH** Economic History. **SELECTED PUBLICATIONS** Why Ireland Starved: An Analytical and Quantitative Study of the Irish Economy; the Lever of Riches: Technological Creativity and Economic Progress; The British Industrial Revolution: An Economic Perspective; sen edr, Journal of Economic History. **CONTACT ADDRESS** Dept Econ, Northwestern Univ, Evanston, IL 60208. **EMAIL** j-mokyr@nwu.edu

MOLETTE-OGDEN, CARLA E.
DISCIPLINE POLITICAL SCIENCE **EDUCATION** Spelman Col, BA, 91; WA Univ, PhD, 98. **CAREER** Prof, SUNY, 97-. **MEMBERSHIPS** Am Polit Sci Asn; Nat Conf of Black Polit Sci. **RESEARCH** Judicial politics. **CONTACT ADDRESS** Dept Polit Sci, SUNY, Stony Brook, Stony Brook, NY 11794-4392. **EMAIL** carla.molette-ogden@sunysb.edu

MOMEYER, RICK
DISCIPLINE BIOETHICS, ETHICS, POLITICAL PHILOSOPHY, JUSTICE AND HEALTH CARE **EDUCATION** Allegheny, BA; Univ Chicago, MA; Univ Wash, PhD. **CAREER** Dept Philos, Miami Univ **RESEARCH** Traditional and contemporary views on the value of life, both human and that of animals. **SELECTED PUBLICATIONS** Auth, Confronting Death, Ind UP, 88. **CONTACT ADDRESS** Dept of Philosophy, Miami Univ, Oxford, OH 45056. **EMAIL** momeyerw@muohio.edu

MONAN, JAMES DONALD
PERSONAL Born 12/31/1924, Blasdell, NY **DISCIPLINE** PHILOSOPHY **EDUCATION** Woodstock Col, AB, 48, PHL, 49, STL, 56; Cath Univ Louvain, PhD(philos), 59. **CAREER** Instr philos, St Peter's Col, 49-52; from instr to assoc prof, Le Moyne Col, NY, 60-68, chemn dept, 61-68, acad den, 68-72, from pres to chancellor, Boston Col, 72-. **HONORS AND AWARDS** LHD, Le Moyne Col, 73, St. Joseph's Col, 73, New England School of Law, 75, Northeastern Univ, 75, Univ Mass, 84; LLD, Harvard Univ, 82, Loyola Univ Chicago, 87, Nat Univ Ireland, 91, Boston Col, 96, Univ Mass, 97; LHD, Western New England Col, 00. **MEMBERSHIPS** Metaphys Soc Am; Jesuit Philos Asn US & Can; Mass Historical Soc. **RESEARCH** Metaphysics; ethics; epistemology. **SELECTED PUBLICATIONS** Coauth, Philosophy of Human Knowing, Newman, 53; auth, La connaissance morale, Rev Philos de Louvain, 5/60; Moral knowledge in the Nicomachaen ethics, Aritotle et les Ptoblemes de Methode, 61; coauth, Prelude to Metaphysics, Prentice-Hall, 67; auth, Moral Knowledge and its Methodology in Aristotle, Clarendon Press, Oxford, 68. **CONTACT ADDRESS** Off of the Chancellor, Boston Col, Chestnut Hill, 140 Commonwealth Ave, Chestnut Hill, MA 02467-3800. **EMAIL** monan@bc.edu

MONGOVEN, ANN
DISCIPLINE RELIGIOUS STUDIES **EDUCATION** Univ Va, PhD, 96. **CAREER** Asst prof, Ind Univ, Bloomington. **RESEARCH** History of Christian ethics; methods in religious and philosophical ethics; comparative ethics; gener issues in ethics. **CONTACT ADDRESS** Dept of Religious Studies, Indiana Univ, Bloomington, Sycamore Hall 230, Bloomington, IN 47405. **EMAIL** amongove@indiana.edu

MONOSON, S. SARA
DISCIPLINE CLASSICS AND POLITICAL SCIENCE **EDUCATION** Brandeis, BA, 81; London Sch Econ and Polit Sci, MSc, 82; Princeton Univ, PhD, 93. **CAREER** Asst prof, Northwestern Univ, 93-. **RESEARCH** Plato and Athenian democracy. **SELECTED PUBLICATIONS** Auth, Citizen as Erastes: Erotic Imagery and the Idea of Reciprocity in the Periclean Funeral Oration, Polit Theory, 94; Frank Speech, Democracy and Philosophy: Plato's Debt to a Democratic Strategy of Civic Discourse, Athenian Polit Thought and the Reconstruction of Am Democracy, Cornell, 94; auth, Plato's Democratic Entanglements: Athenian Politics and the Practice of Philosophy, Princeton Univ Press, 00. **CONTACT ADDRESS** Dept of Classics, Northwestern Univ, 1801 Hinman, Evanston, IL 60208. **EMAIL** s-monoson@nwu.edu

MONROE, KRISTEN R.
PERSONAL Born 05/17/1946, Princeton, IL, m, 1981, 3 children **DISCIPLINE** POLITICAL SCIENCE **EDUCATION** Smith Col, AB, 68; Univ Chicago, MA, 70; PhD, 74. **CAREER** Stony Brook; NYork Univ; Princeton; Univ Calif at Irvine. **HONORS AND AWARDS** Killian Fel; La Verne Noyes Fel; Earhart Fel; Best Book Awd, APSA Section in Polit Psychology. **MEMBERSHIPS** Int Soc of Polit Psychology, Am Polit Sci Asn, Women's Caucus for Polit Sci, Midwest Polit Sci Asn. **RESEARCH** Altruism, Genocide, Political Psychology, Political Theory, Holocaust. **SELECTED PUBLICATIONS** Auth, The Heart of Altruism; auth, Contemporary Empirical Political Theory; auth, Political Psychology, Lawrence Erlbaum; auth, The Economic Approach to Politics, Harper Collins; auth, Presidential Popularity and the Economy, Praeger; auth, The Political Process and Economic Change, Agatum. **CONTACT ADDRESS** Dept Polit Sci, Univ of California, Irvine, Irvine, CA 92697. **EMAIL** krmonroe@uci.edu

MONROE, THERESA M.
PERSONAL Born 08/28/1951, Buffalo, NY, s **DISCIPLINE** THEOLOGY **EDUCATION** Univ AZ, BA, 72; Western Jesuit Sch Theol, Mdiv, 76, ThM, 84; Harvard Univ, MPA, 87; Cath Univ Am, JCL, 89; Harvard Univ, EdD (cand.). **CAREER** Prog assoc, Lilly Endowment, Inc, 76-77; Dean of students, Cath Theol Union, Chicago, 77-82; prog dir and adjunct lect, John F. Kennedy Sch of Govt, Harvard Univ, 87-97; asst prof, Univ San Diego, 97-. **MEMBERSHIPS** Canon Law Soc of Am, Am Psychol Asn, A. K. Rice Inst. **RESEARCH** Leadership studies, group dymanics, org behavior, authority in religious organizations. **SELECTED PUBLICATIONS** Auth, "Theological Education for Lay Ministry," in Proceedings of Shared Ministry Conf, Washington, DC: US Cath Conf (80); auth, "Reclaiming Competence," Rev for Rel, 27:245-265 (May/June 92); auth, "Cooperation Between Clergy and Laity: Ambivalent Texts, Collaborative Context," Proceedings of the Canon Law Soc in Am (92); auth, "Leadership in Tough Times," Touchstone 12: 2,14-15 (winter 96); auth, "The Practice of Authority," In Trust, vol 1, no 2:3-5 (Jan 97); auth, "The Practice of Leadership and Authority: Contemporary Rhetoric and Reality," Priesthood:

Challenges of Pastoral Leadership, vol 3, no 3:25-44 (97), reprinted in Irish Province Bull (Feb 98). **CONTACT ADDRESS** Dept Ed, Univ of San Diego, 5998 Alcala Pk, San Diego, CA 92110. **EMAIL** Tmonroe@acusd.edu

MONTGOMERY, JOHN E.
DISCIPLINE TORTS AND PRODUCTS LIABILITY **EDUCATION** Univ Louisville, BChE, 64, JD, 69; Univ MI, LLM, 71. **CAREER** Dean & prof, Univ of SC. **SELECTED PUBLICATIONS** Coauth, casebk on products liability law. **CONTACT ADDRESS** School of Law, Univ of So Carolina, Columbia, Law Center, Columbia, SC 29208. **EMAIL** Johnm@law.law.sc.edu

MONTGOMERY, SHARON BURKE
PERSONAL Born 11/01/1937, Wilkes-Barre, PA **DISCIPLINE** PHILOSOPHY **EDUCATION** Univ Pa, BA, 59, MA, 62, PhD, 72. **CAREER** Inst philos, Ohio Univ, 64-65; asst prof, Fresno State Col, 67-69; teaching fel, Univ Pa, 69; actg chair & asst prof, Del State Col, 70-71; Prof Philos, Ind Univ PA, 71-, chmn, Dept Philos, 85-90. **HONORS AND AWARDS** Univ of Pa Scholarship, 55-59; NSF grant, Summer Ling Inst, 60; Woodrow Wilson Nat Fel, 60-62 **MEMBERSHIPS** Am Philos Asn **RESEARCH** Value theory; philosophy of language; logic; pragmatism **CONTACT ADDRESS** Dept of Philos, Indiana Univ of Pennsylvania, Indiana, PA 15705-0001. **EMAIL** smonty@grove.iup.edu

MOODY, LINDA A.
DISCIPLINE SYSTEMATIC & PHILOSOPHICAL THEOLOGY; PHILOSOPHY OF RELIGION **EDUCATION** Univ Mich, AB, 75, AM, 76; S Baptist Theol Sem, MDiv, 80; Grad Theol Union, PhD, 93. **CAREER** Sr chaplain, Brookville Lake Min, 79-80; Dir Curric English Ctr Int Women, 81-89, Robert F. Leavens Col chaplain & lectr, women' studies dept, Mills Col, 85-. **HONORS AND AWARDS** Quigley Summer Fel Womens Studies, 96; Stephen Bufton Nat Scholar Am Bus & Prof Women, 88; Amer Asn Univ Women Res Proj Grant. **MEMBERSHIPS** Amer Acad Relig; Soc Bibl Lit; Nat Women's Studies Asn; Nat Asn Col-Univ Chaplins. **RESEARCH** 19th and 20th Century theology; Women's Studies and Religion **SELECTED PUBLICATIONS** Auth, Paul Tillich and Feminist Theology: Echoes From the Boundary, Papers From the Annual Meeting of the North American Paul Tillich Society, 93; Your People Will Be My People, Songs of Miriam: A Women's Book of Devotions, Judson Press, 94; Constructive Theological Understandings of God: Methodological and Epistemological Contributions of Sallie McFague, New Theology Review, 95; Mills--For Women Agin: The Role of Women's Spirituality in the Effort to Remain a Women's College, Nat Womens Studiess Asn Jour, 95; Women Encounter God: Theology Across the Boundaries of Difference, Orbis Books, 96; Ties That Bind: A Response to Maria Archuleta's Review of Women Encounter God, Ctr for Women and Relig Mem Newsl, Grad Theol Union, 97; Designing A Mentoring Program for Students Interested in Graduate Studies in Religion, Women's Caucus--Religious Studies, 97; Priests, Pastors, Prophets, Preachers, and Professors of Religions: Women in Ecclesia and Academia, Jour Women and Relig, 98. **CONTACT ADDRESS** Mills Col, 5000 MacArthur Blvd, Oakland, CA 94613.

MOODY, PETER R.
PERSONAL Born 10/13/1943, San Francisco, CA, m, 1966, 6 children **DISCIPLINE** POLITICAL SIENCE **EDUCATION** Vanderilt, AB, 65; Yale Univ, PhD, 71. **CAREER** Prof, Notre Dame, 83-. **HONORS AND AWARDS** Peace Fel, Hodver Inst, 75; Chiang Ching Kuo Res Fel, 78. **MEMBERSHIPS** APSA. **RESEARCH** Chinese Politics; Asian Politics; Asian International Relations; Chinese Political Thought. **SELECTED PUBLICATIONS** Auth, Trends in the Study of Chinese Political Culture, China Quart, 94; Asian Values, J of Int Affairs, 96; Introduction, China Doc Annual 93: The End of the Post-Mao Era, 97; Four Powers Are Good, Six May Be Better, Diplomacy, 97; The Politics of Presidentialism on Taiwan, 1988-1997, Working Papers in Taiwan Studies, 98. **CONTACT ADDRESS** Dept of Government and International Studies, Univ of Notre Dame, Notre Dame, IN 46556-5644. **EMAIL** Peter.R.Moody.1@nd.edu

MOOR, JAMES H.
DISCIPLINE PHILOSOPHY **EDUCATION** IN Univ, PhD. **CAREER** Prof, Dartmouth Col. **MEMBERSHIPS** Soc Machines and Mentality. **RESEARCH** Logic, philos of artificial intelligence, philos of mind, and computer ethics. **SELECTED PUBLICATIONS** Auth, Towards a Theory of Privacy for the Information Age, Comput & Soc, 97; The Logic Book, 3rd ed, McGraw-Hill, 98; Reason, Relativity, and Responsibility in Computer Ethics, Comput & Soc, 98; co-ed, The Digital Phoenix: How Computers Are Changing Philosophy Basil Blackwell, 98. **CONTACT ADDRESS** Dartmouth Col, 6035 Thornton, Hanover, NH 03755-3592. **EMAIL** James.H.Moor@Dartmouth.edu

MOORE, BROOKE N.
PERSONAL Born 02/12/1943, Palo Alto, CA, m, 1970, 2 children **DISCIPLINE** PHILOSOPHY **EDUCATION** Antioch, BA, 66; Univ Cinn, PhD, 71. **CAREER** Asst prof, 70-74, assoc prof, 74-79, PROF, 80- , Calif State Univ Chico. **HONORS AND AWARDS** Master Tchr, 96-98; Outstanding prof, 97. **MEMBERSHIPS** Am Philos Asn; editl bd Teaching Philosophy. **RESEARCH** Critical thinking; epistemology **SELECTED PUBLICATIONS** Auth, Philosophical Possibilities Beyond Death, 81; coauth Critical Thinking, 87; The Power of Ideas, 90; The Cosmos, God and Philosophy, 92; Moral Philosophy, 93; The Power of Ideas: A Brief Edition, 95; Making Your Case, 95. **CONTACT ADDRESS** Dept of Philosophy, California State Univ, Chico, Chico, CA 95929. **EMAIL** bmoore@csuchico.edu

MOORE, CECILIA
PERSONAL Born 01/18/1966, Danville, VA, s **DISCIPLINE** RELIGIOUS STUDIES **EDUCATION** Sweet Briar Col, AB, 88; Univ VA, MA, 91, PhD, 97. **CAREER** Asst Prof Relig Studies, Univ Dayton, 96-. **HONORS AND AWARDS** Phi Beta Kappa; Anne Gary Punell Scholar; State Council of Higher Education in VA Scholar; Fund for Theological Education Scholar. **MEMBERSHIPS** Amer Academy Relig; Amer Cath Hist Assoc; Soc Church Hist; Black Cath Theological Symposium. **RESEARCH** Amer rel hist; US Cath hist; African Amer Cath hist. **CONTACT ADDRESS** 2615 Shroyer Rd., #4, Dayton, OH 45419. **EMAIL** moore@chekov.hm.udayton.edu

MOORE, DEBORAH D.
PERSONAL Born 08/06/1946, New York City, NY, m, 1967, 2 children **DISCIPLINE** RELIGIOUS STUDIES **EDUCATION** Brandeis Univ, BA, 67; Columbia Univ, MA, 68; PhD, 75. **CAREER** From Asst Prof to Prof, Vassar Col, 76-; Chair Dept of Relig, Vassar Col, 83-87; Dean, VIVO Inst for Jewish Res, 88-89; Dir Prog in Am Cult, Vassar Col, 92-95. **HONORS AND AWARDS** Res Grant, Mem Found for Jewish Cult, 83-84; Fulbright Fel in Am Jewish Studies, The Hebrew Univ of Jerusalem, Isreal, 84-85; Rapoport Fel in Am Jewish Studies, Am Jewish Arch, 87-88; Nat Endowment for Humanities, Fel for Col Teachers, 78-79, 89; Res Grant, Lucius N. Littauer Found, 90, 93, 95; Nat Jewish Book Awd Hon Book for To the Golden Cities, 94; Saul Viener Prize for Best Book in Am Jewish Hist, 94-95, for To the Golden Cities, 95; Skirball Vis Fel, Oxford Center for Hebrew and Jewish Studies, 96; Center for Judaic Studies Fel, Univ of Pa, 96-97; Asn of Jewish Librn ref book award, for Jewish Women in America: An Historical Encyclopedia, 97; Dartmouth Medal of the Am Libr Asn for best ref work in 97, for Jewish Women in America: An Historical Encyclopedia, 97; Choice Outstanding Acad Book in 98, for Jewish Women in America: An Historical Encyclopedia, 97; Nat Jewish Book Awd for best book in Women's Studies, for Jewish Women in America: An Historical Encyclopedia, 97. **MEMBERSHIPS** AJNS, AHA, ASA, AJS. **RESEARCH** American Jewish history, urban history - 20th century. **SELECTED PUBLICATIONS** Auth, At Home in America: Second Generation New York Jews, Columbia Univ Press (NY), 81, 83, chap 9 in the American Jewish Experience, ed. Jonathan D. Sarna (NY: Holmes & Meier, 97); auth, B'nai Brith and the Challenge of Ethnic Leadership, State Univ of NY Press (Albany), 81; auth, "Studying America and the Holy Land: Prospects, Pitfalls, and Perspectives," on With Eyes Towards Zion, ed. Moshe Davis (NY: Pantheon, 91), and in The American People and the Land of Isreal, ed. Menahem Kaufman (Jerusalem: Magnes Press, 97); auth, "Jewish Migration in Postwar America: The Case of Miami and Los Angeles," Studies in Contemp Jewry 8 (92), and in The American Jewish Experience, ed. Jonathan D. Sarna (NY: Holmes & Meier, 97); auth, "Class and Ethnicity in the Creation of New York City Neighborhoods, 1900-1930," in Budapest and New York: Studies in Metropolitan Transformation, ed. Thomas Bender and Carl E. Schorske (NY: Russell Sage, 94); auth, "Foreword," in Greenwich Village, 1920-1930, by Caroline Ware, Classics in Urban History (Berkeley: Univ of Calif Press, 94); auth, "Trude Weiss-Rosmarin and 'The Jewish Spectator," The 'Other' New York Jewish Intellectuals, ed. Carole Kessner (NY: NY Univ Press, 94); auth, To the Golden Cities: Pursuing the American Jewish Dream in Miami and L.A., The Free Press (NY), 94, Harvard Univ Press (Cambridge), 96, chap 4 reprinted in Religion and American Culture, ed. David G. Hackett, Routledge (NY), 95; co-ed, Jewish Women in America: An Historical Encyclopedia, Routledge (NY), 97; auth, "Jewish GIs and the Creation of the Judeo-Christian Tradition," Rel and Am Cult 8:1 (Winter 98). **CONTACT ADDRESS** Dept Rel, Vassar Col, 124 Raymond Ave, Poughkeepsie, NY 12604-0001. **EMAIL** moored@vassar.edu

MOORE, FRED HENDERSON
PERSONAL Born 07/25/1934, Charleston County, SC, m **DISCIPLINE** LAW **EDUCATION** SC State Coll 1952-56; Roosevelt Univ Chicago 1956; Allen U, BS 1956-57; Howard Episcopal, JD 1957-60; Teamers Sch of Religion, DD 1976; Stephens Christian Inst 1976; Reform Episcapal Seminary. **CAREER** Atty self-employed 1977. **HONORS AND AWARDS** Youth award NAACP 1957; memorial award Charles Drew 1957; Youth March for Integrated Schs 1958; stud body pres SC State Coll. **MEMBERSHIPS** Corp cncl NAACP 1960; mem Black Rep Party; mem Silver Elephant Club; 1st Dist Coun SC Conf of NAACP; asso pstr Payne RMUE Ch; asso cncl NC Mutual Ins Co; Mem Omega Psi Phy Frat. **SELECTED PUBLICATIONS** Co-auth, "Angry Black South" 1960. **CONTACT ADDRESS** 39 Spring St, Charleston, SC 29403.

MOORE, JOHN NORTON
PERSONAL Born 06/12/1937, New York, NY, m, 1981, 2 children **DISCIPLINE** LAW **EDUCATION** Drew Univ, BA, 59; Duke Law Sch, LLB, 62; Univ Ill, LLM, 65. **CAREER** Dir, Cen Ocean Law Policy, Cen Nat Security Law, Univ Vir, 65-72; prof, 76-; dir Grad Law Prog, 68-93; adj prof of law, Geotown Univ, Am Univ; lectr/consult, Nat War Col, Naval War Col, Army War Col, For Ser Inst; Judge Advo Gen Sch of Army. **HONORS AND AWARDS** Chmn, Bd Dir, US Inst Peace, Pres appt, 85-89, 89-91; Spec Coun US; Woodrow Wilson ICS Fel; Phi Beta Kappa; MTS Fel; Alum Achiev Awd; Geo Washington Medal Hon; Mem Bars, Fla, Ill, Vir, DC, US Sup Ct, US Ct Claims; Who's Who in World, Am, S SW, Govt, Am Law, Fin Indust, Writers, Ed and Poets, US and Can; Fed Staff Dir. **MEMBERSHIPS** ABILA; ALI; ILAB; IIL at Univ Kiel; ISC; NSIC; MPOE; WLF; IFPA; FPC; MENSA; Phi Delta Phi; CSISIRC; OPI; ICEL; MLAUS; ILS; AAA; WIFA. **RESEARCH** Security issues; foreign policy issues; international law issues; constitutions and the rule of law; resource and energy issues. **SELECTED PUBLICATIONS** Auth, Crisis in the Gulf: Enforcing the Rule of Law, Oceana Press, 92; ed, The Vietnam Debate: A Fresh Look at the Arguments, Univ Press Am, 90; co-ed, National Security Law, Cal Acad Press, 90; co-ed, Readings on International Law from the Naval War College Review: 1978-1994, Naval War Coll, 95; co-ed, Oceans Policy: New Institutions, Challenges and Opportunities, Carolina Acad Press, 99; co-ed, Current Maritime Issues and the International Maritime Organization, Carolina Acad Press, 99; co-ed, Strengthening the United Nations and Enhancing War Prevention, Carolina Acad Press, forthcoming; auth, "Enhancing Compliance with International Law: A Neglected Remedy," Vir J Intl Law 4 (99); auth, Remembrance of Myres S McDougal, Myres S McDougal, Appreciation of an Extraordinary Man, Yale Law Sch (99); auth, "Ambassador Max Kampelman Receives the Presidential Medal of Freedom," Intl Security Law Report (99); coauth, "Saddam, War Crimes and the Rule of Law," Jerusalem Post (91); auth, Maintain America's Leadership on the Oceans," LA Times (99). **CONTACT ADDRESS** School of Law, Univ of Virginia, 580 Massie Rd, Charlottesville, VA 22903-1738. **EMAIL** colp@virginia.edu

MOORE, JOSEPH G.
PERSONAL Born 10/03/1963, Boston, MA, s **DISCIPLINE** PHILOSOPHY **EDUCATION** Cornell Univ, PhD, 94. **CAREER** From asst prof to assoc prof, Amherst Col, 93-. **MEMBERSHIPS** APA **RESEARCH** Philosophy of mind; philosophy of language; metaphysics; environmental ethics. **CONTACT ADDRESS** Amherst Col, Philosophy, PO Box 5000, Amherst, MA 01002-5000. **EMAIL** jgmoore@amherst.edu

MOORE, KATHLEEN D.
PERSONAL Born 07/06/1947, Cleveland, OH, m, 1968, 2 children **DISCIPLINE** PHILOSOPHY **EDUCATION** Col of Wooster, BA, 69; Univ of Colo, MA, 72; PhD, 77. **CAREER** Spring Creek Proj Dir, Dept of Philosophy, Oregon State Univ, 00; Prof and Chair, Dept of Philosophy, Oregon State Univ, 92-00. **HONORS AND AWARDS** Hovland Service Awd; Coll of Liberal Arts; Oregon State Univ, 99; Master Teacher, Oregon State Univ, 99; Pacific Northwest Booksellers Awd, 96; Phi Kappa Phi Honarary Society, 1995; College of Liberal Arts Excellence Awd, OSU Faculty Teaching Awd, Excellence in Teaching Awd, all at Oregon State Univ. **MEMBERSHIPS** Amer Philosophical Assoc, Society for Philosophy in the Contemporary World, Assoc for the Study of Literature and the Environment. **RESEARCH** Philosphy of law; philosophy and nature; creative non-fiction; nature writing. **SELECTED PUBLICATIONS** Auth, "Holdfast, The Lyons Press, 99; auth, Riverwalking, Lyons and Burford, 95; Harcourt, 96; auth, "Pardons: Justice, Mercy, and the Common Good," Oxford Univ Press, 89, 97; auth, "Reasoning and Writing," Macmillan, 93; auth, "Pardon and Amnesty;" auth, "Encyclopedia of Ethics;" auth, "Philosophical Justifications for Pardoning;" auth, "U. of Richmond Law Rev, winter 93. **CONTACT ADDRESS** Dept Philosophy, Oregon State Univ, 208 Hovland Hall, Corvallis, OR 97331-8543. **EMAIL** kmoore@orst.edu

MOORE, MARGARET
DISCIPLINE PHILOSOPHY **EDUCATION** London Sch Econ, Polit Sci, PhD, 89. **RESEARCH** Contemporary political philos; liberal-communitarian debate; philos of nationalism; ethics of secession; citizenship in diverse societies. **SELECTED PUBLICATIONS** Auth, Foundations of Liberalism, Oxford, 93; ed, National Self-Determination and Secession, Oxford, 98. **CONTACT ADDRESS** Dept of Philosophy, Univ of Waterloo, 200 University Ave W, Waterloo, ON, Canada N2L 3G1. **EMAIL** mrmoore@watarts.uwaterloo.ca

MOORE, MAX
PERSONAL Born 01/29/1964, Bristol, England, m, 1996 **DISCIPLINE** PHILOSOPHY, POLITICS AND ECONOMICS **EDUCATION** St. Anne's Col, Oxford Univ, BA, 84-87; Univ Southern Calif, PhD, philos, 95. **CAREER** Pres, Extropy Inst, 91-. **RESEARCH** The consequences & implications of advanced technologies. **SELECTED PUBLICATIONS** Auth, Beyond the Machine: Technology and Posthuman Freedom, Proceedings of the Fleshfactor symposium of Ars Electronica,

97; auth, Virtue and Virtuality: From Enhanced Reality to Experience Machines, Proceedings from Sense of the Senses conference, 97; auth, Ways and Memes, Rage, 97; auth, Thinking About Thinking, Wired, 96; auth, Is God a Computer Nerd?, Rage, 96; auth, Live Freely, Live Longer, The Freeman: Ideas on Liberty, 95; auth, On Becoming Posthuman, Free Inquiry, 94; auth, Extropy: Death and Taxes Must Go, Calif Liberty, 94. **CONTACT ADDRESS** 13428 Maxella Ave,, #273, Marina del Rey, CA 90292. **EMAIL** max@maxmore.com

MOORE, RICKIE D.
PERSONAL Born 10/08/1953, Sikeston, MO, m, 1976, 2 children **DISCIPLINE** OLD TESTAMENT **EDUCATION** Lee Col, BA, 76; Vanderbilt Univ, MA, 82, PhD, 88. **CAREER** Ed, Lee Col, 73-76; Old Testament Bibliographer, Vanderbilt Divinity Libry, 80-82; prof, Church of God Theolog Sem, 82-. **HONORS AND AWARDS** Asn Theolog Sch Grant, 92-93; lee col dept award, rel, 76; vanderbilt univ tchg assistantship, 79-80. **MEMBERSHIPS** Soc Biblical Lit; Soc Pentecostal Stud. **RESEARCH** Old Testament Prophets. **SELECTED PUBLICATIONS** Auth, Didactic Salvation Stories in the Elisha Cycle: An Analysis of 2 Kings 5; 6:8-23: and 6:24-7:20, 88; auth, God Saves: Lessons from the Elisha Stories, 90; auth, art, Deuteronomy and the Fire of God, 95; auth, art, And Also Much Cattle?!': Prophetic Passions and the End of Jonah, 97; auth, art, Futile Labor Vs Fertile Labor: Observing the Sabbath in Psalm 127, 98. **CONTACT ADDRESS** Church of God Sch of Theol, 900 Walker St NE, Cleveland, TN 37311. **EMAIL** rdmoore777@aol.com

MOORE, RONALD
PERSONAL Born 05/04/1943, Framingham, MA, m, 1968, 1 child **DISCIPLINE** PHILOSOPHY **EDUCATION** Stanford Univ, AB, 64; Columbia Univ, PhD, 71. **CAREER** Preceptor, Columbia Col, Columbia Univ, 66-68; asst prof to assoc prof, Univ Hawaii, 69-79; assoc prof, Univ Wash, 79- ; Dir, Univ Wash Ctr for Hum, 87-94; **HONORS AND AWARDS** Phi Beta Kappa; Harvard Lib Arts fel Law & Philos, Univ Wash Distinguished Tchg Awd; Charles E Odegaard Awd. **MEMBERSHIPS** Am Philos Asn; Am Asn Univ Prof; Am Soc Aesthet; Am Soc Polit & Legal Philos; Int Soc Philos Law. **RESEARCH** Philosophy of law; aesthetics and philosophy of art. **SELECTED PUBLICATIONS** Auth, Kelsens Puzzling Descriptive Ought, UCLA Law Rev, 73; The Deontic Status of Legal Norms, Ethics, 73; Legal Norms and Legal Science, Univ Press Hawaii, 78; Puzzles About Art: A Casebook in Aesthetics, St Martin's Press, 89; The Aesthetic and the Moral, Jour of Aesthet Education, 95; ed Aesthetics for Young People, Nat Aret Education Asn, 95; auth, The Nightmare Science and its Daytime Uses, Jour of Aesthet Education, 96; Ugliness, Moral Rights of Art, History of Aesthetic Education, Encyclo Aesthet, Oxford Univ Press, 98. **CONTACT ADDRESS** Dept of Philosophy, Univ of Washington, Box 353350, Seattle, WA 98195-3350. **EMAIL** ronmoore@u.washington.edu

MOORE, TERRENCE L.
PERSONAL Born 04/27/1950, Hanover, PA, m, 1973, 2 children **DISCIPLINE** PHILOSOPHY **EDUCATION** Univ Pittsburgh, PhD, 87. **CAREER** USAF Acad, 81-96; Univ Colo, Colo Springs, 96-. **HONORS AND AWARDS** Fel, Harvard Ctr for Ethics and the Professions, 91-92. **MEMBERSHIPS** APA. **RESEARCH** Ethics; philosophy of religion; political theory. **CONTACT ADDRESS** Dept of Philosophy, Univ of Colorado, Boulder, PO Box 7150, Colorado Springs, CO 80930. **EMAIL** tmoore@brain.uccs.edu

MOORHEAD, JAMES HOWELL
PERSONAL Born 01/16/1947, Harrisburg, PA, m, 1969, 2 children **DISCIPLINE** AMERICAN RELIGIOUS HISTORY **EDUCATION** Westminster Col, PA, BA, 68; Princeton Theol Sem, MDiv, 71; Yale Univ, MPhil, 73, PhD(relig studies), 75. **CAREER** Asst prof, 75-80, Assoc Prof Relig, NC State Univ, 80-, Fel independent study & res, Nat Endowment for Humanities, 81-82. **HONORS AND AWARDS** Brewer Prize, Am Soc Church Hist, 76. **MEMBERSHIPS** Am Soc Church Hist; Am Acad Relig; Am Hist Asn. **RESEARCH** Nineteenth century and early twentieth century American Protestantism; Millennialism; views of death and after life. **SELECTED PUBLICATIONS** Auth, Joseph Addison Alexander: Common sense, romanticism and Biblical criticism at Princeton, J Presbyterian Hist, spring 75; American Apocalypse: Yankee Protestants and the Civil War, 1860-1869, Yale Univ Press, 78; Social reform and the divided conscience of antebellum Protestantism, Church Hist, 79; Softly And Tenderly Jesus Is Calling - Heaven And Hell In American Revivalism, 1870-1920 - Butler,Jm, Church History, Vol 0062, 1993; Glorious Contentment - The Grand Army Of The Republic, 1865-1900 - Mcconnell,S, J Of American History, Vol 0080, 1993; A Field Of Divine Wonders - The New-Divinity And Village Revivals In Northwestern Connecticut, 1792-1822 - Kling,Dw, Theology Today, Vol 0051, 1994; A Friend To Gods Poor - Smith,Edward,Parmalee - Armstrong,Wh, J Of American History, Vol 0081, 1995; Church People In The Struggle - The National- Council-Of-Churches And The Black-Freedom Movement, 1950-1970 - Findlay,JF, J Of Interdisciplinary History, Vol 0026, 95; Peddler In Divinity - Whitefield, George And The Transatlantic-Revivals, 1737-1770 - Lambert,F, Theology Today, Vol 0051, 1995; Arguing The Apocalypse - A Theory Of Millennial Rhetoric - Oleary,Sd, Theology Today, Vol 0051, 1994; No Sorrow Like Our Sorrow Northern Protestant Ministers And The Assassination Of Lincoln - Chesebrough,Db, American Historical Review, Vol 0100, 1995; auth, Consumer Rites - The Buying And Selling Of American Holidays - Schmidt,LE, Theology Today, Vol 0053, 1996; The Myth Of American Individualism - The Protestant Origins Of American Political-Thought - Shain,BA, J Of Religion, Vol 0076, 1996; Our Southern Zion - A History Of Calvinism In The South-Carolina Low Country, 1690-1990 - Clarke,E, J Of Presbyterian History, Vol 0075, 1997; Law And Providence In Bellamy, Joseph New-England - Valeri,M, American Presbyterians-J Of Presbyterian History, Vol 0074, 1996; Spreading The Word - The Bible Business In 19th- Century America - Wosh,PJ, American Presbyterians, J Of Presbyterian History, Vol 0074, 1996. **CONTACT ADDRESS** Church Hist, Princeton Theol Sem, PO Box 821, Princeton, NJ 08542-0803.

MOPPETT, SAMANTHA A.
PERSONAL Born 06/17/1969, Boston, MA **DISCIPLINE** LAW **EDUCATION** Bucknell Univ, BA, 91; Suffolk Univ, JD, 95. **CAREER** Instr, Suffolk Univ, 97-99; Prof, Ariz State Univ, 99-. **SELECTED PUBLICATIONS** Auth, "Warrantless Airport Luggage Search Constitutional When Conducted Subsequent to Establishment of Probable Cause and Continual Disclaimer of Ownership," Suffolk Univ L Rev, 94; auth, "The Age Discrimination in Employment Act Preempts State Regulation of Public Employees on the Basis of Age," Suffolk Univ L Rev, 94; auth, "Extending Eighth Amendment Protections to Prisoners Involuntarily Exposed to Unreasonable Levels of Environmental Tobacco Smoke," Suffolk Univ L Rev, 94; auth, Navigating the Internet: Legal Research on the World Wide Web, Rothman Pub, 00. **CONTACT ADDRESS** Sch of Law, Arizona State Univ, Box 877906, Tempe, AZ 85287. **EMAIL** samantha.moppett@asu.edu

MORALES, MARIA H.
DISCIPLINE PHILOSOPHY **EDUCATION** Univ Md, BA, 87; Univ Pa, PhD, 92. **CAREER** Assoc prof. **MEMBERSHIPS** Am Philos Asn; Soc Women Philos; Fla Philos Asn. **RESEARCH** Political and social philosophy; philosophy of law; ethics; competence in ancient philosophy and feminism. **SELECTED PUBLICATIONS** Auth, Perfect Equality (rev), Rowman & Littlefield, 96; The Corrupting Influence of Power, Rodopi, 96; pubs on Jeremy Bentham, Thomas Hobbes, and John Stuart Mill. **CONTACT ADDRESS** Dept of Philosophy, Florida State Univ, 211 Wescott Bldg, Tallahassee, FL 32306. **EMAIL** mmorales@garnet.acns.fsu.edu

MORAN, GERALD P.
DISCIPLINE LAW **EDUCATION** Univ Scranton, BS; Cath Univ Am, JD; George Wash Univ, LLM. **CAREER** IRS trial attny, tax athy before 74; prof 74-. **MEMBERSHIPS** Ohio Bar Assn. **SELECTED PUBLICATIONS** Auth, Tax Amnesty: An Old Debate as Viewed From Current Public Choices, Univ Fla Tax Law Rev, 93; co-auth, The Rule Against Perpetuity: The Case for Exemption of Trusts or the Repeal of the Rule, Law J, 95; A Radical Theory of Jurisprudence: The 'Decisionmaker' as the Source of Law, Akron Law Rev, 96; auth, co-auth, Ohio Joins With Other Jurisdictions in the Adoption of Spousal Election of UPC, Toledo Transcript, 97; **CONTACT ADDRESS** Col Law, Univ of Toledo, Toledo, OH 43606. **EMAIL** gmoran@pop3.utoledo.edu

MORAN, JON S.
PERSONAL Born 11/11/1941, Rock Island, IL, m, 1965, 3 children **DISCIPLINE** PHILOSOPHY **EDUCATION** St Louis Univ, BS, 63; Tulane Univ, PhD, 72. **CAREER** Asst prof, St Ambrose Coll, 68-73; prof, Southwest MO State Univ, 73-. **HONORS AND AWARDS** Woodrow Willion Fel, 63. **MEMBERSHIPS** Am Philos Asn; Soc of Christain Philos. **RESEARCH** Philosophy of Religion; American Philosophy. **SELECTED PUBLICATIONS** Auth, Mead on the Self and Moral Situations, Tulane Studies in Philos, 73; Divine Commands and Moral Autonomy, Philos In Context: Moral Truth, 86; Mead, Gadamer, and Hermeneutics, Frontiers in Am Philos, 92; Bergsonian Sources of Mead's Philosophy, Transactions of the Charles S Peirce Soc, 96. **CONTACT ADDRESS** Dept of Philosophy, Southwest Missouri State Univ, Springfield, Springfield, MO 65804-0094. **EMAIL** jsm174f@mail.smsu.edu

MORAN, RICHARD
DISCIPLINE PHILOSOPHY **EDUCATION** Cornell, PhD, 89. **CAREER** Prof; Harvard Univ, 95-; taught at, Princeton. **RESEARCH** Philosophy of mind and moral psychology; aesthetics and the philosophy of literature; Wittgenstein. **SELECTED PUBLICATIONS** Publ on, metaphor, imagination and emotional engagement with art & nature of self-knowledge. **CONTACT ADDRESS** Dept of Philosophy, Harvard Univ, 8 Garden St, Cambridge, MA 02138. **EMAIL** moran@fas.harvard.edu

MORAVCSIK, JULIUS M.
DISCIPLINE PHILOSOPHY **EDUCATION** BA, 53; Harvard Univ, PhD, 59. **CAREER** Prof, Stanford Univ. **HONORS AND AWARDS** Humboldt Human Prize; Fel Inst of Adv Stud, honorary citiz Rhodos. **MEMBERSHIPS** Am Phil Asn; Soc for Aesthetics; Soc for Ancient Greek Phil; phil of lang; metaphysics. **RESEARCH** Pre-Socratics; Plato; Aristotle. **SELECTED PUBLICATIONS** Auth, Plato and Platonism, 92; The Philosophic Background of Aristotle's AITIA, 95; ed/contrib, Plato's Theory of Art and Beauty, 81; auth, Meaning, Creativity, 98. **CONTACT ADDRESS** Stanford Univ, Bldg 20, Main Quad, Stanford, CA 94305. **EMAIL** julius@csli.stanford.edu

MORELAND, RAYMOND T., JR.
PERSONAL Born 03/12/1944, Baltimore, MD, m, 1980 **DISCIPLINE** PASTORAL THEOLOGY AND PSYCHOLOGY **EDUCATION** Randolph-Macon Col, BA, 66; Wesley Theological Sem, M Div, 70, D Min, 73; St Mary's Sem & Univ-Ecumenical Inst, MA, 91; Graduate Theol Found, PhD, 97. **CAREER** Pastor for 29 years in MD and WV; taught course of study at Wesley Theol Sem for 3 years; Academic Policy Committee, Ecumenical Inst of Theol, St Mary's Sem and Univ; currently exec dir, MD Bible Soc. **HONORS AND AWARDS** Who's Who in Am Colleges and Universities; Nat Preaching Fel, 71. **MEMBERSHIPS** AAR; Soc of Biblical Lit; Academy of Parish Clergy; Alban Inst, AGO; Asn for Relig and Intellectual Life; Network of Biblical Storytellers. **RESEARCH** Carl Jung's influence on Biblical hermeneutics; the thinking of Joseph Campbell on myth and the Bible. **SELECTED PUBLICATIONS** Auth, thesis abstract on The Beloved Journey-Psychospiritual Study of Persons Living, Struggling and Dying of HIV-AIDS-Sharing the Practice, J of the Academy of Parish Clegy; several book reviews for the Academy. **CONTACT ADDRESS** 9731 Hall Rd, Frederick, MD 21701-6736. **EMAIL** agape@erols.com

MORELAND-YOUNG, CURTINA
PERSONAL Born 03/05/1949, Columbia, SC, d, 1978 **DISCIPLINE** POLITICAL SCIENCE **EDUCATION** Fisk University, Nashville, TN, BA, 1969; University of Illinois, Urbana, Il, MA, 1975, PhD, 1976; Harvard University, Cambridge, MA, post-doctoral, 1982. **CAREER** Ohio State University, Dept of Black Studies, Columbus, OH, instructor asst prof, 71-78; Jackson State University, Mississippi College & University Consortium for International Study, Dept of Political Science, coord for MA program, assoc prof, 78-84, chair, public policy & administration dept, 84-. **HONORS AND AWARDS** Kellogg National Fellow, Kellogg Foundation, 1989-92; Rockefeller Foundation Feller, Rockefeller Foundation, 1983; DuBois Scholar, DuBois Institute, Harvard University, 1983; John Oliver Killen Writing Awd, Fisk University, 1969; Lilly Fellow, Lilly Foundation, 1979-80. **MEMBERSHIPS** Chair, pres, The Conference of Minority Public Administrators, 1989-90; member, exec board, National Conference of Black Political Scientist, 1989; member, National Council of American Society for Public Administrators, 1989-90; chair, The Committee on Organization Review & Evaluation, ASPA, 1990-91; member, exec board, Jackson International Visitors Center. **CONTACT ADDRESS** Public Policy & Administration Dept, Jackson State Univ, 3825 Ridgewood Rd, Box 18, Jackson, MS 39211.

MORELLI, MARIO FRANK
PERSONAL Born 02/03/1945, Poughkeepsie, NY, m, 1966, 3 children **DISCIPLINE** PHILOSOPHY **EDUCATION** Johns Hopkins Univ, BA, 66; Wash Univ, MA, 68, PhD(philos), 71. **CAREER** Instr philos, Univ Mo-St Louis, 68-70 & Kent State Univ, 70-72; from Asst Prof to Assoc Prof, 72-83, Prof Philos, Western Ill Univ, 83-; Dept. Chair, 99-. **MEMBERSHIPS** Am Philos Asn;. **RESEARCH** Moral philosophy; social philosophy; philosophy of law. **SELECTED PUBLICATIONS** Coauth, Beyond Wittgensteinian fideism: An examination of John Hick's Analysis of Religious Faith, Int J Philos Relig, Vol VIII, No 4, 77; Stanley Milgram and the obedience experiment: Authority, legitimacy, and human action, Polit Theory, Vol 7, No 3, 8/79; auth, The constitutional right of privacy: Autonomy and intrusion, In: Values in the law: Proceedings of the Fourteenth Conference on Value Inquiry, State Univ NY, Geneseo, 80; coauth, Inner Judgements and Blame, Southern J Philos, Fall 82; auth, Milgram's Dilemma of Obedience, Metaphilosophy, 85; coauth, Obedience to Authority in a Laboratory Setting: Generalizability and Context Dependency, Polit Studies, 85; auth, Education as a Right, In: Communitarianism, Liberalism, and Social Rsponsibility, Mellen Press, 91; Equal Educational Opportunity: Rodriguez Revisited, In: The Bill of Rights: Bicentennial Reflections, Mellen Press, 93; Race-Conscious Admissions and Individual Treatment, In: Rending and Renewing the Social Order, Mellen Press, 96; auth, Commerce in Organs: A Kantian Critique, Jrl of Social Phil., Summer '99. **CONTACT ADDRESS** Dept of Philosophy, Western Illinois Univ, 1 University Cir, Macomb, IL 61455-1390. **EMAIL** mario-morelli@ccmail.wiu.edu

MORENO, JOELLE
PERSONAL Born 11/21/1962, New York, NY, m, 1994, 2 children **DISCIPLINE** LAW **EDUCATION** Swarthmore Col, 84; Univ Pa Law Sch, 89. **CAREER** Atty, 89-91; trial atty, U.S.

Dept of Justice, 92-95; adj prof, Thomas Jefferson Sch of Law, 96-98; fac member, Nat Inst for Trial Advocacy, 96-. **SELECTED PUBLICATIONS** Auth, "Whoever Fights Monsters Should See To It That in the Process He Does Not Become a Monster: Hunting the Sexual Predator with Silver Bullets," Fed Rules of Evidence, (97): 413-415; auth, "A Stake through the Heart, Kansas v. Hendricks," Fla L Rev, 97; auth, "Beyond the Polemic Against Junk Science: Navigating the Oceans that Divide Science and Law with Justice Breyer at the Helm," Boston Univ L Rev, 01. **CONTACT ADDRESS** New England Sch of Law, 154 Stuart St, Boston, MA 02116. **EMAIL** jmoreno@fac.nesl.edu

MOREY, ANN-JANINE
PERSONAL Born 10/31/1951, Atlanta, GA, m, 1986, 2 children **DISCIPLINE** RELIGION, ETHICS **EDUCATION** Grinnell Col, BA, 73; USC, PhD, Relig & Ethics, 79. **CAREER** Asst/assoc prof, Southern Ill Univ-Carbondale, Relig Stud, 79-89; assoc prof, SIUC, Eng, 89-93; dir, SIUC, Univ Core Curric, 93-; PROF, SIUC, ENG, 93-. **MEMBERSHIPS** MLA; ALA; Am Relig & Lit Soc; AAR **RESEARCH** Religion & Literature **SELECTED PUBLICATIONS** Religion and Sexuality in American Literature, Cambridge UP, 92; "In Memory of Cassie: Child Death and Religious Vision in American Women's Novels," Religion and American Culture, 96; "Margaret Atwood and Toni Morrison: Reflections on Postmodernism and the Study of Religion and Literature," The Fiction of Toni Morrison, Garland Publ, 96; "The Literary Physician," In Good Company: Essays in Honor of Robert Detweiler, 94, "Naked Ladies," Spelunker Flophouse, 97; "Balancing the Blame: Mother Images in Margaret Deland's The Iron Woman," National Women's Studies Association Jour, 98; What Happened to Christopher. An American Family's Story of Shaken Baby Syndrome, SIU Press, 98. **CONTACT ADDRESS** Dept Eng, James Madison Univ, 800 S Main St, Harrisonburg, VA 22807. **EMAIL** moreyaj@jmu.edu

MORGAN, CHARLES G.
DISCIPLINE PHILOSOPHY **EDUCATION** Univ Memphis St, BS; Johns Hopkins Univ, MA, PhD; Alta Univ, MSc; Univ Victoria, MSc. **CAREER** Instr, Univ Alberta; prof, 75. **RESEARCH** Philosophy of science and logic. **SELECTED PUBLICATIONS** Pub(s), Jour Symbolic Logic; Philos of Sci; Zeitschrift fur Mathematische Logik; Artificial Intelligence. **CONTACT ADDRESS** Dept of Philosophy, Univ of Victoria, PO Box 3045, Victoria, BC, Canada V8W 3P4. **EMAIL** morgan@phastf.phys.uvic.ca

MORGAN, DONN F.
DISCIPLINE OLD TESTAMENT **EDUCATION** Oberlin Col, AB; Yale Divinity Sch, BD; Claremont Grad Sch, MA, PhD. **CAREER** Pres, dean, prof, Church Divinity School Pacific. **SELECTED PUBLICATIONS** Auth, How to Make the Bible User-Friendly: Challenges for Contemporary Teachers, Rel Edu Jour Hong Kong, 97; Searching for Biblical Wisdom: Recent Studies and their Pertinence for Contemporary Ministry, Sewanee Theol Rev, 94; Religious Educators: Professionals or Sages?, Rel Edu Jour Hong Kong, 93; Between Text and Community: The 'Writings' in Canonical Context, Augsburg-Fortress, 90; Wisdom in the Old Testament Traditions, John Knox, 81. **CONTACT ADDRESS** Church Divinity Sch of the Pacific, 2451 Ridge Rd, Berkeley, CA 94709-1217. **EMAIL** dmorgan@cdsp.edu

MORGAN, EDWARD M.
DISCIPLINE LAW **EDUCATION** Northwestern Univ, BA, 76; Univ Toronto, LLB, 84; Harvard Univ, LLM, 86. **CAREER** Law clerk, Madame Justice Bertha Wilson, Supreme Court Can, 84-85; Prof, Fac of Law, Univ of Toronto, 86-89. **RESEARCH** Corporate/commercial litigation; constitutional law; human rights; professional discipline defence work; conflict of laws and international litigation. **SELECTED PUBLICATIONS** Auth, International Law and the Canadian Courts, Carswell, 90; pubs on current legal issues. **CONTACT ADDRESS** Fac of Law, Univ of Toronto, 78 Queen's Park, Toronto, ON, Canada M5S 1A1.

MORGAN, JOSEPH
PERSONAL Born 07/09/1953, Chicago, IL, s **DISCIPLINE** HISTORY, GOVERNMENT **EDUCATION** Iona Col, BA, 75; Manhattan Col, MA, 81; Georgetown Univ, PhD, 93. **CAREER** Instr, Iona Col, 89-94; Asst Prof, Iona Col, 94-. **MEMBERSHIPS** Am Hist Asn, Asn of Asian Studies, Soc of Historians of Am For Rels. **RESEARCH** Vietnam War, American diplomacy, Chinese history. **SELECTED PUBLICATIONS** Auth, The Vietnam Lobby: The American Friends of Vietnam, 1955-1975, Univ of N Carolina Pr, 97. **CONTACT ADDRESS** Dept Hist and Govt, Iona Col, 715 North Ave, New Rochelle, NY 10801-1830. **EMAIL** jmorgan@iona.edu

MORGAN, MARTHA
DISCIPLINE LAW **EDUCATION** Univ Ala, BS, 72; George Washington Univ, JD, 77. **CAREER** Prof, Univ Ala, 79-. **MEMBERSHIPS** Order of the Coif; Bd, ACLU; bd, ACLU Ala; bd, Equal Justice Initiative of Ala. **RESEARCH** Constitutional law, civil rights legislation, and seminars on legal education and comparative constitutional law. **CONTACT ADDRESS** Law Dept, Univ of Alabama, Tuscaloosa, Box 870000, Tuscaloosa, AL 35487-0383. **EMAIL** mmorgan@law.ua.edu

MORICK, HAROLD
DISCIPLINE PHILOSOPHY **EDUCATION** Columbia Univ, PhD. **CAREER** Assoc prof, Univ Albany, State Univ NY **RESEARCH** Philosophy of the mind. **SELECTED PUBLICATIONS** Ed, Intr to the Philos of Mind. **CONTACT ADDRESS** Dept of Philosophy, SUNY, Albany, Albany, NY 12222. **EMAIL** vanderluyd@aol.com

MORRILL, BRUCE T.
PERSONAL Born 06/02/1959, Bangor, ME, s **DISCIPLINE** THEOLOGY **EDUCATION** Emory Univ, PhD, 96. **CAREER** Asst Prof Theol, Boston Col, 96-. **HONORS AND AWARDS** Phi Beta Kappa. **MEMBERSHIPS** Am Acad Relig; Cath Theol Soc Am; NAm Acad Liturgy; Societas Liturgica. **RESEARCH** Liturgical and sacramental theology. **SELECTED PUBLICATIONS** Coed, The Struggle for Tradition, Liturgy and the Moral Self: Humanity at Full Stretch Before God, Liturgical Press, 98; contrib & ed, Bodies of Worship: Explorations in Theory and Practice, Liturgical Press, 99; auth, "Walking the Labyrinth: Recovering Sacred Tradition," Liturgical Ministry 8, (99): 201-209; auth, Anamnesis as Dangerous Memory: Political and Liturgical Theology in Dialogue, Liturgical Press, 00; auth, "Anamnetic Action: The Ethics of Remembracing," Doxology 17, (00): 3-22; auth, "The Meaning of Confirmation: Searching with the Bishop, the Liturgy, and the Holly Spirit," Liturgical Ministry 9, (00): 49-62; auth, "Liturgical Music: Bodies Proclaiming and Responding to the Word of God," Worship 74, (00): 20-37. **CONTACT ADDRESS** IREPM, Boston Col, Chestnut Hill, 31 Lawrence Ave., Chestnut Hill, MA 02467-3931. **EMAIL** morrilb@bc.edu

MORRIS, CALVIN S.
PERSONAL Born 03/16/1941, Philadelphia, PA **DISCIPLINE** THEOLOGY **EDUCATION** Friends Select Schl, Philadelphia, PA, Diploma, 59; Lincoln Univ, AB, Amer Hist, 63; Boston Univ, AM, Amer Hist, 64; Boston Univ Schl of Theology, STB, 67; Boston Univ, PhD, Amer Hist, 82. **CAREER** SCLC Operation Breadbasket, assoc dir 67-71; Simmons Coll, dir Afro-Amer Studies/Simmons Coll 71-73; Urban Devel, Michigan State Univ, visitng lecturer 73-76; Martin Luther King, Jr Ctr for Social Change, exec dir 73-76; Howard Univ Divinity Schl, asst prof practical theology & dir min in church & soc 76-82; Howard Univ Divinity Schl, assoc prof pastoral theology & dir Urban Ministries 82-92; exec dir, Community Renewel Soc, 98; exec vice pres for Academic Services and Academic Dean, Interdenominational Theological Center, 92-98. **HONORS AND AWARDS** Distinguished Alumni Awd, Friends Select HS 74; Jr Chamber of Comm Awd One of Chicago's Ten Outstanding Young Men 70; Crusade Schlr United Methodist Church 63-66; Rockefeller Protestant Fellow 64-65; Whitney Young Fellow 71-72; Grad Fellowship for Black Amer, The Natl Fellowship Fund 79-80; Black Doctoral Dis The Fund for Theological Ed 79-80; Distinguished Alumni Awd, Lincoln Univ, Pennsylvania, 88; Published Reverdy C. Ransom: Black Advocate of the Social Gospel Univ Press of America, 90. **MEMBERSHIPS** Mem Amer Historical Assn, Amer Soc of Church History, Assn for the Study of Negro Life & History, Assn for Theological Field Educ, Soc for the Study of Black Religion, Amer Civil Lib Union, Amer Friends Serv Comm Amnesty Intl, NAACP-Life Mem, Natl Urban League; mem Omega Psi Phi; Intl Peace Research Assn 1987-; bd mem, Arts in Action, 1988; bd mem, The Churches Conference on Shelter and Housing 1988. **CONTACT ADDRESS** Community Renewal Society, 332 South Michigan Ave., Suite 500, Chicago, IL 60604.

MORRIS, DEREK
PERSONAL Born 03/28/1954, Bristol, England, m, 1977, 2 children **DISCIPLINE** PREACHING, PASTORAL THEOLOGY **EDUCATION** Columbia Union Col, BA, 76; Andrew Univ, M Div, 80; D Min, 87; Gord Con Theol Sem, D Min, 98. **CAREER** Prof, Southern Adventist Univ, 87-. **HONORS AND AWARDS** Zaparra Excell Teach Awd, 90, 93; Pres Awd, Teach Excell, 00. **MEMBERSHIPS** EHS. **RESEARCH** Preaching; interpersonal communication. **SELECTED PUBLICATIONS** Auth, "The Minister as a Spiritual Lender," in The Adventist Minister, ed. C Raymond Holmes, Douglas Kilcher (Andrew: Univ Press, 91; auth, "Are Your Children Spiritually Protected?" Parent Talk (96); auth, "Slowing Down to Pray," Ministry (97); auth, "Journey to the Cross," Adven Rev (98); rev of, "Classic Sermons of the Cross of Christ," Ministry (93); rev of, "The World of the Cross: A Contemporary Theology of Evangelism," Ministry (94); rev of, "Christianity With Power," Ministry (93). **CONTACT ADDRESS** School of Religion, Southern Adventist Univ, PO Box 370, Collegedale, TN 37315. **EMAIL** dmorris@southern.edu

MORRIS, GRANT H.
PERSONAL Born 12/10/1940, Syracuse, NY, m, 1967, 2 children **DISCIPLINE** LAW **EDUCATION** Syra Univ, AB, 62; JD, 64; Harv Univ, LLM, 71. **CAREER** Recod att, Inst Pub Admin, 64-66; asst prof, 67-68; assoc prof, 69-70; prof, 70-73; Wayne State Univ; prof, Univ San Diego, 73-; act dean, 77-78, 88-89, 97-98. **HONORS AND AWARDS** Res Recog Awd; Prof of Year, USD. **RESEARCH** Law and psychiatry. **SELECTED PUBLICATIONS** Ed, contr, The Mentally Ill and the Right to Treatment, 70; auth, The Insanity Defense: A Blueprint for Legislative Reform, 75; coauth, Mental Disorder in the Criminal Process. **CONTACT ADDRESS** School of Law, Univ San Diego, 5998 Alcala Park, San Diego, CA 92110-2429. **EMAIL** gmorris@acusd.edu

MORRIS, JEFFREY B.
DISCIPLINE LAW **EDUCATION** Princeton Univ, BA, 62; Columbia Univ, JD, 65, PhD, 72. **CAREER** Instr, CUNY, Univ PA, Brooklyn Law Schl; spec asst, Columbia Univ, 76-81; assoc prof Law, Touro Col. **RESEARCH** Hist of fed courts. **SELECTED PUBLICATIONS** Auth, Federal Justice in the Second Circuit; History of U.S. District Court for the Eastern District of New York. **CONTACT ADDRESS** Touro Col, New York, Brooklyn, NY 11230. **EMAIL** jeffreym@tourolaw.edu

MORRIS, NORVAL
PERSONAL Born 10/01/1923, Auckland, New Zealand, m, 1947, 3 children **DISCIPLINE** LAW CRIMINOLOGY **EDUCATION** Univ Melbourne, LLB, 46, LLM, 47; London Sch Econ, PhD(criminology), 49. **CAREER** Asst lectr law, London Sch Econ, 49-50; lectr, Univ Melbourne, 50-58, assoc prof criminol, 55-58, Bonython prof law & dean law sch, 58-62; dir criminal justice, UN Inst, Tokyo, 62- 64; Julius Kreeger prof law & criminol & dir ctr studies criminal justice, 64-76, Prof Law & Dean Law Sch, Univ Chicago, 76-, Ezra Ripley Thayer teaching fel, Harvard Univ, 55-56; chmn, Ceylon Govt Comm Capital Punishment, 58-59; mem, Soc Sci Res Coun Australia, 60-62; vis prof, Harvard Law Sch, 61-62. **HONORS AND AWARDS** Hutchinson Silver Medal, Univ London, 50; Japanese Order of the Sacred Treasure, 65. **MEMBERSHIPS** Criminal law; criminology. **SELECTED PUBLICATIONS** Auth, The Habitual Criminal, Longmans, 51; coauth, Cases in Torts, Law Bk Co, Australia, 62; Studies in Criminal Law, Oxford Univ, 64; The Honest Politician's Guide to Crime Control, 72, The Future of Imprisonment, 75, Letters to the President on Crime Control, 78 & Madness & the Criminal Law, 82, Univ Chicago Press; auth, The Brothel Boy, Oxford Univ Pr, 92; auth, The Oxford Hist of the Prison, Oxford Univ Pr, 96; Street-Level Purposes Of Punishment, Proceedings Of The American Philosophical Society, Vol 0140, 96. **CONTACT ADDRESS** Law School, Univ of Chicago, Chicago, IL 60637. **EMAIL** norval_morris@law.uchicago.edu

MORRIS, PAUL
PERSONAL m, 6 children **DISCIPLINE** THEOLOGY **EDUCATION** Univ SC; Grace Theol Sem, MDiv; Calif Grad Sch Theol, PhD. **CAREER** Exec VP, acad dean, instr, Bible Col, Pa, 94; educator/instr. **HONORS AND AWARDS** Nat fel, Grace Brethren churches; affil, presbyterian church; asst dirship, word of life island; dir youth ministries, first brethren church; pastorates, grace brethren church; cypress, calif; neighborhood family chapel; nat trng dir, prison fel; bd dir(s), ycibi, inc; thesis 96, inc; cha **RESEARCH** Redemptive therapy **SELECTED PUBLICATIONS** Auth, Love Therapy, Tyndale House Publ, 74; Shadow of Sodom, Tyndale House Publ, 78; Helping Others Grow, Tyndale House Publ, 80; Jour of Redemptive Therapy. **CONTACT ADDRESS** Sch Redemptive Stud, San Diego Theol Sem, PO Box 50-131, Lake Arrowhead, CA 92352. **EMAIL** Dr.Morris@fishernet.com

MORRIS, WILLIAM O.
PERSONAL Born 12/02/1922, Fairmont, WV, m, 1948, 2 children **DISCIPLINE** LAW **EDUCATION** Col William & Mary, AB, 44; Univ IL, LLB, 46, JD, 68; H.D.C. Nicholas Copernicus Univ, (Poland). **CAREER** Asst prof bus law, Univ IL, 46-55; assoc prof law, Stetson Univ, 55-58; PROF LAW, WV UNIV, 58-, PROF DENT JURISP, MED CTR, 59-; Law practice, Champaign, IL, 46-55; consult interim comt, WV Legis, 59; comptroller of currency, US Treasury Dept, 63-67; Fulbright prof, Univ Munster, 69, prof, 70; prof, Gutenberg Univ, 71 & 72, Stetson Univ, 71, 73 & 74 & Univ Oslo, 73. **HONORS AND AWARDS** Medel of Merit, Nicholas Copernicus Univ, Torun, Poland; MDC degree from Nicholas Copernicus Univ. **RESEARCH** Banking law; suretyship; law of dentistry. **SELECTED PUBLICATIONS** Auth, Accommodation Parties to Negotiable Instruments, Banking Law J, 59; Fictitious Payees on Checks Requiring Dual Signatures, WI Law Rev, 61; Negotiable Instruments Under Uniform Commerical Code, WV Law Rev, 62; Dental Litigation, 72 & The Law of Domestic Relations, 73, Michie; Cases and Statutes Relative to Domestic Relations, WV Univ, 74; Veterinarian in Litigation, V M Publ, 76; Dental Litigation, Michie, 2nd ed, 77; Revocation of Professional License by Governmental Agencies, 94; The Dentists' Legal Advisor, 95. **CONTACT ADDRESS** Law Bldg, West Virginia Univ, Morgantown, Morgantown, WV 26506.

MORRISON, CLAYTON T.
PERSONAL Born 03/12/1970, Sierra Madre, CA, m, 1997 **DISCIPLINE** PHILOSOPHY **EDUCATION** Occidental Coll, BA, 92; SUNY Binghamton, MA, 95, PhD, 98. **CAREER** Teacher intern, 94, J Hopkins Univ; teach Asst, 93-97, adj Lectr, 95-97, research Asst, 98-, Binghamton Univ. **HONORS AND AWARDS** Ford Fel, Disting Hon Sr Comprehensive Proj, Occidental Coll; Ringle Awd, Grad Student Awd Excellence in Teaching, Dissertation Yr Fel, Binghamton Univ. **MEMBERSHIPS** AAAI, APA, CSS, SMM, SPP. **RESEARCH** Nature of cognitive representation, artificial intelli-

gence, philosophy, psychology, cognitive science, autonomous agent epistemology, and philosophy of mind. **SELECTED PUBLICATIONS** Co-auth, Why Connectionist Nets Are Good Models - Commentary on Green on Connectionist-Explanation, in: Psychology, 98; auth, What it means to be Situated, in: Cybernetics & Sys, 98; Conceptual Change as Change of Inner Perspective, in: Papers from the 1996 AAAI Fall Symposium, Menlo Park CA AAAI Press, 96; Structure-Mapping vs High-level Perception, the mistaken fight over the explanation of analogy, in: Proceedings of the Seventeenth Annual Conference of the Cognitive Sciences Society, 95. **CONTACT ADDRESS** Dept of Philosophy PACCS Program, SUNY, Binghamton, Hinman 129, Binghamton, NY 13902-6000. **EMAIL** clayton@turing.paccs.binghamton.edu

MORRISON, FRED L.
PERSONAL Born 12/24/1939, Salina, KS, m, 1971, 4 children **DISCIPLINE** LAW **EDUCATION** Univ Kans, AB, 61; Oxford Univ, BA, 63; Princeton Univ, MA & PhD(polit), 66; Univ Chicago, JD, 67; Oxford Univ, MA, 68. **CAREER** Asst prof law, Univ Iowa, 67-69; assoc prof, 69-72, Prof Law, Univ Minn, Minneapolis, 72-; Fulbright vis prof, Univ Bonn, WGer, 75-76; counr, Counsel to Popham, Haik, Schnobrich, Kaufman & Doty, Minneapolis, Minn, 81-82; counr on int law, US Dept State, 82-83. **RESEARCH** Comparative public law; international law; American Constitutional law. **SELECTED PUBLICATIONS** Auth, Recognition in international law, Univ Chicago Law Rev, 67; chap, In: Frontiers of Judicial Research, Wiley, 69; Courts and the Political Process in England, 73; Limitations on alien investment in real estate, Minn Law Rev, 76; State corporate farming legislation, Univ Toledo Law Rev, 76; The right to fish for seacoast products, Supreme Court Rev, 77; The general competence of the municipality, Am J of Comp Law Suppl, 82. **CONTACT ADDRESS** Law Sch, Univ of Minnesota, Twin Cities, 229 19th Ave S, Room 285 Law, 7911, Minneapolis, MN 55455. **EMAIL** morri001@tc.umn.edu

MORSE, BRADFORD W.
DISCIPLINE LAW **EDUCATION** Rutgers Univ, BA; Univ British Columbia, LLB; Osgoode Hall Law Sch, LLM. **CAREER** Asst prof of law, Univ of Ottawa, 76-83; sessional lectr, Carleton Univ, 78-81; assoc prof of law, Univ of Ottawa, 83-86; Prof of law, Univ of Ottawa, 86-. **HONORS AND AWARDS** British Columbia Government Scholarship, 73-74, 74-75; SSHRCC International Travel Grants, 85-86; Canadian Visiting Fel, Macquarie Univ, Australia, 87; Univ of Ottawa International Travel Grants, 88, 91, 92; Canada-U.S. Fulbright Sr Scholar Fel, Oklahoma City Univ, 93; Fulbright Sr Scholar Fel, 97. **MEMBERSHIPS** Canadian Bar Asn, 73-94; Royal Commission on Family & Children's Law, 74-75; Civil Liberties Asn - Nat Capital Region, 76-93; Canadian Asn of Law Teachers, 76-; Board of Editors, Rights and Freedoms, 83-86. **SELECTED PUBLICATIONS** Coauth, The First Nations: Bill C-52 An Act Relating to Self-Government For Indian Nations, with Michael Posluns and Jerry Gambill, (Ottawa: Assembly of First Nations, 84); coauth, The First Nations: A Report on the Self-Government Bill, with Michael Posluns, (Ottawa: Assembly of First Nations, 84); coauth, Bill C-31 & The New Indian Act with, Robert Groves, (Ottawa: Native Council of Canada, 85); coauth, Bill C-31 & The New Indian Act Guidebook #2: Protecting Your Rights, with Robert Groves, (Ottawa: Native Council of Canada, 86); ed, Intoxication By-laws and the Indian Act, (Toronto: Chiefs on Ontario, 86); auth, Providing Land and Resources for Aboriginal Peoples, Kingston: Institute for Intergovernmental Relations, Queen's Univ, 87; co-ed, Indigenous Law and the State, with Gordon R.Woodman, (Dordrecht, The Netherlands: Foris Publications, 87); coauth, Native Offenders' Perceptions of the Criminal Justice System, with Linda Lock, (Ottawa: Department of Justice, 88); auth, Constitutionalizing Rights: Implications for Canadians, Australians and Aboriginal Peoples, The Macquarie Canadian Lecture 87, (North Sydney, Austalia: Macquarie Univ, 89); ed, Aboriginal Peoples and the Law: Indian, Metis and Inuit Rights in Canada, (Ottawa: Carleton Univ Press, 85). **CONTACT ADDRESS** Fac Common Law, Univ of Ottawa, Fauteux Hall, 57 Louis Pasteur, Ottawa, ON, Canada K1N 6N5. **EMAIL** bmorse@uottawa.ca

MORSE, EDWARD A.
PERSONAL Born 11/04/1962, Council Bluffs, IA, m, 1984, 5 children **DISCIPLINE** LAW **EDUCATION** Drake Univ, BS, 85; BA, 85; Univ Mich, JD, 88. **CAREER** Law Clerk, Hon Deanell R. Tacha, U S Ct of Appeals, 10th Dist, 88-89; Assoc Atty, Sutherland Asbill & Brennan, 89-94; From Asst Prof to Prof, Creighton Univ, 94-. **MEMBERSHIPS** ABA, Tax Acct and Environ Taxes Commt. **RESEARCH** Taxation, electronic commerce, retirement savings policy. **SELECTED PUBLICATIONS** Auth, "Demystifying LIFO: Towards Simplification of Inflation - Adjusted Inventory Valuation," Fla Tax Rev 559 (95); auth, "State Taxation of Internet Commerce: Something New Under the Sun?" Creighton Law Rev 1113 (97); Auth, "Reflections on the Rule of Law and Clear Reflection of Income: What Constrains Discretion?" Cornell J of Law and Publ, vol 445 (99). **CONTACT ADDRESS** Dept Law, Creighton Univ, 2500 California Plaza, Omaha, NE 68178-0001. **EMAIL** morse@culaw.creighton.edu

MORSE, OLIVER
PERSONAL Born 05/17/1922, New York, NY, m **DISCIPLINE** LAW **EDUCATION** St Augustine's Coll, BS 1947; Brooklyn Law Sch, LLB 1950; NYork Univ, LLM 1951; Brooklyn Law Sch, JSD 1952. **CAREER** Howard Univ School of Law, acting dean, 86, asso dean, prof (retired); Hunter Coll, instr 1959; So Univ School of Law, prof 1956-59; Brooklyn Law School, prof 1968-69; Morse Enterprises Inc, chairman, board of directors, 89-97. **HONORS AND AWARDS** Most Outstdng Law Prof Howard Law Sch 1967, 70-72 **MEMBERSHIPS** Vice-chmn HEW Reviewing Authority; Beta Lamba Sigma; Phi Alpha Delta; Omega Psi Phi; Am Assn of Law Schs; mem Nat Bar Assn; mem NY Bar Assn; 1st chmn of section on legal Educ of NBA 1971-72; sire archon, 1986-87, member, Sigma Pi Phi Fraternity, Maryland Boule, 1981-; board of trustees, St Augustine's College, 1991-. **SELECTED PUBLICATIONS** Pubs include 40 legal decisions of cases heard on appeal to HEW Reviewing Authority. **CONTACT ADDRESS** Morse Enterprises, Inc., 11120 New Hampshire Ave, Ste. 204, Silver Spring, MD 20904-3448.

MORT, DALE L.
PERSONAL Born 10/27/1954, St Louis, MO, m, 1977 **DISCIPLINE** BIBLE STUDIES **EDUCATION** Florida Bible Col, BA, 77; Luther Rice Sem, M Div, 78; Talbot Theol Sem, MA, 82; Texas AM Univ, PhD, 93. **CAREER** Chair, Texas Bible Inst, 83-84; dir, Cornerstone Comm Ch, 83-84; teach, Temple Baptist Christ Sch, 84-86; superv, CPP Pinkertons, 86-89; instr, Florida Bible Col, 90-04; prof, Lancaster Bible Col, 94-. **HONORS AND AWARDS** Kappa Tau Epsilon. **MEMBERSHIPS** PAACE; NAPCE; TDETA; ETA. **RESEARCH** Adult education. **SELECTED PUBLICATIONS** Auth, "Lead Your Team to the Top," Sec Manage (88); auth, "An Objective Approach," Sec Manage (88); auth, "the Training Buck Stops Here (But Should It?)," Sec Manage (88). **CONTACT ADDRESS** Dept Biblical Studies, Lancaster Bible Col, PO Box 3403, Lancaster, PA 17608-3403.

MORTON, CHARLES E.
PERSONAL Born 01/31/1926, Bessemer, AL, m **DISCIPLINE** PHILOSOPHY **EDUCATION** Morehouse College, Atlanta, GA, BA, 1946; Union Theological Seminary, New York, NYork, 1949; Heidelberg University, Heidelberg, Germany, 1955; Garrett Biblical Institute, Northwestern University, 1956; Columbia University, New York, NYork, PhD, 1958; Shaw College, Detroit, MI, LHD, 1970. **CAREER** Michigan Bd Edn, mem 1946-54; Div of Humanities & Philosophy Dillard Univ, former chmn; Albion Coll, assoc prof of philosophy; Ebeneze Baptist Ch Poughkeepsie, NY, minister; Metropolitan Baptist Church, Detroit, MI, pastor, 63-; Oakland University, Rochester, MI, professor of philosophy, 72-. **MEMBERSHIPS** President, board of directors, Metropolitan Baptist Church Non-Profit Housing Corporation, 1969-; member, board of directors, First Independence National Bank, Detroit, MI, 1970-; chairperson emeritus, Inner-City Business Improvement Forum of Detroit, 1972-; member, board of directors, Brazeal Dennard Chorale, 1988-; president, Michigan Progressive Baptist State Convention, 1990-92; board member, Gleaners Community Food Bank, 1990-; pres, Michigan Progressive Baptist Convention, Inc; chairperson, board of trustees, Wayne County Community College, 1990-93. **CONTACT ADDRESS** Metropolitan Baptist Church, 13110 14th St, Detroit, MI 48238.

MOSELEY, ALLAN
PERSONAL Born 11/18/1957, Montgomery, AL, m, 1979, 3 children **DISCIPLINE** OLD TESTAMENT STUDIES **EDUCATION** Samford Univ, BA, 80; New Orleans Baptist Sem, MDiv, 82, PhD, 87. **CAREER** Pastor, Big Level Baptist Church, 82-85; pastor, Bayou View Baptist Church, 85-90; pastor, First Baptist Church, Durham. 90-96; vice pres stud serv, dean stud, 96- , prof Old Testament, 98- , Southeastern Sem. **MEMBERSHIPS** Soc of Bibl Lit; Evangel Theol Soc. **SELECTED PUBLICATIONS** Auth, The Life-View of Qoheleth, Bibl Illusr, 94; auth, What in the World Should the Church Do? Preaching, 94; auth, Shadrach, Meshach, and Abednego: All We Know, Bibl Illusr, 95; auth, Christmas Greatness, Preaching, 95; auth,The Birth of the Church, Mothers Helper, and, Keep Climbing, Preaching, 96; auth, Survey of the Old Testament, SBC Sunday School Board, 96; auth, Beginnings: Thirteen Lessons in Genesis 1-26 for Explore the Bible teacher's book, 97; auth, Sermon Briefs, in Abingdon Preaching Annual, 99; auth, Worldviews at War, Davidson Press, forthcoming. **CONTACT ADDRESS** PO Box 1889, Wake Forest, NC 27588-1889. **EMAIL** amoseley@sebts.edu

MOSELEY, JAMES G.
PERSONAL Born 03/24/1946, Atlanta, GA, m, 1968, 2 children **DISCIPLINE** RELIGION; LITERATURE **EDUCATION** Stanford Univ, BA, 68; Univ Chicago Div Sch, MA, 71, PhD, 73. **CAREER** Cord Amer stud (s) prog, 73-79, Ch Hum div, 79-86, asst, assoc, full prof, 73-86, New Col, Univ S Fla; prof Relig, 86-91, dir honors prog, 89-91, VP acad affairs, Dean fac, 86-89, Chapman Col, Calif; VP, Dean, prof Relig, Transylvania Univ, Ky, 91- . **HONORS AND AWARDS** Fel in res Col tchrs, Natl Endowment Hum, Princeton, 76-77; Ed proj grant, NEH, for curric devel, New Col, 77; summer sem Col tchrs, NEH, 79, Univ Calif, Irvine; summer sem Col tchrs, NEH, 82, Harvard Univ; res and creative scholar awd, Univ S Fla, Summer, 83; Co-dir, summer sem sch tchrs, NEH, 84, New Col; Core Fac, Revisioning Am: Relig and the Life of the Nation, series, Ind Univ, Lilly Endowment, 84-90; Proj Dir, Power and Morality conf for commun leaders and sec sch tchrs, Fla endowment Hum, New Col, 85; dir, summer sem sch tchrs, NEH, New Col, 86; dir, summer sem sch tchrs, NEH, Univ Calif Irvine, 90; dir, summer sem sch tchrs, Transylvania Univ, 92; Core fac, Cultural Diversity and Civic Responsibility, Wye High Sch fac sem, Transylvania Univ, 93; Core Fac, Pub Expressions of Rel in Amer, series, Ind Univ, Lilly Endowment, 92-94. **MEMBERSHIPS** Amer acad Relig; Amer Stud Asn; Org Amer Hist; Amer soc Church Hist; Natl Col honors coun; Amer conf acad Deans; Asn Amer Col Univ; Amer Asn higher educ. **RESEARCH** History of Religion. **SELECTED PUBLICATIONS** Auth, A Complex Inheritance: The Idea of Self-Transcendence in the Theology of Henry James, Sr, and the Novels of Henry James, Amer Acad Relig Diss Series, vol 4, Missoula, MT, AAR and Scholar Press, 75; Conversion through Vision: Puritanism and Transcendentalism in The Ambassadors, Jour Amer Acad Relig, XLIII/3, Sept 75; Religious Ethics and the Social Aspects of Imaginative Literature, Jour Amer Acad Relig, XL vol 3, Sept 77; Religion and Modernity: A Case Granted, Bull of the Couns on the Stud Relig, IX/1, Feb 78; Literature and Ethics: Some Possibilities for Religious Thought, Perspect Relig Stud (s), VI/1, Spring 79; The Social Organization of Religion in America: Then and Now, SEASA '79 Proceedings, Tampa, Fla, Amer Stud (s) Press, 79; Culture, Religion, and Theology, Theol Today, XXXVII/3, Oct 80; auth, A Cultural History of Religion in America, Westport, Conn, Greenwood Press, 81; From Conversion to Self-Transcendence: Religious Experience in American Literature, SEASA '83 Proceedings, Tampa, Fla, Amer Stud (s) Press, 83; Inerrantism as Narcissism: Biblical Authority as a Cultural Problem, Perspectives in Relig Stud (s), Fall 83; An Occasion for Changing One's Mind: A Response to Charles Long, Relig Studs and Theol, vol 3, Sept 85; Winthrop's Journal: Religion, Politics, and Narrative in Early America, in Religion and the Life of the Nation: American Recoveries, Sherrill, Illinois UP, 90, reprinted in Literature Criticism from 1400-1800, LC, vol 31, Bostrom, Detroit, Gale, 95; auth, John Winthrop's World: History as a Story as History, Madison, U of Wisconsin P, 92; Civil Religion Revisited, Relig and Amer Cult: A Jour of Interpretation, 4/1, Winter, 94; rev essay: Jenny Franchot's Roads to Rome: The Antebellum Protestant Encounter with Catholicism, Relig Stud (s) Rev, 23/3, July 97. **CONTACT ADDRESS** Dept of Dean, Transylvania Univ, Lexington, KY 40508. **EMAIL** dean@transy.edu

MOSER, PAUL K.
PERSONAL Born 10/29/1957, Bismarck, ND, m, 1980, 2 children **DISCIPLINE** PHILOSOPHY **EDUCATION** Vanderbilt Univ, PhD, 82. **CAREER** Asst prof to assoc prof Philosophy, 83-89, Prof Philosophy, 89, Chr Philosophy Dept, 97-, Loyola Univ Chicago. **MEMBERSHIPS** Am Philos Asn **RESEARCH** Philosophy of Religion; Theory of Knowledge. **SELECTED PUBLICATIONS** auth Empirical Justification, Philosophical Studies Series in Philosophy, 85; Knowledge and Evidence, Cambridge Univ Press, 89; Philosophy After Objectivity, Oxford Univ Press, 93; The Theory of Knowledge: A Thematic Introduction, Oxford Univ Press, 97; ed Contemporary Approaches to Philosophy, Macmillan Publ Co, 93; Contemporary Materialism, Routledge Ltd, 95; Morality and the Good Life, Oxford Univ Press, 97. **CONTACT ADDRESS** Dept of Philosophy, Loyola Univ, Chicago, 6525 N Sheridan Rd, Crown Ctr , Chicago, IL 60626-5385. **EMAIL** PMOSER@LUC.EDU

MOSES, GREG
DISCIPLINE PHILOSOPHY **EDUCATION** Tex Am Univ, BA, 81; MA, 88; Univ Tex, Austin, PhD, 92. **CAREER** Lectr, Tex AM Univ, 88-95; asst prof, Marist Col, 95-. **HONORS AND AWARDS** Fac Of Year Awd, 97, 98. **MEMBERSHIPS** APA; AAVP; RPA; SAAP; SSAP. **RESEARCH** Social and political philosophy; nonviolence; racism. **SELECTED PUBLICATIONS** Auth, "Revolution of Conscience: Martin Luther King, Jr, and the Philosophy of Nonviolence," in Critical Perspectives Series, ed. Douglas Kelner (NY: Guilford Press, 97), ppbk, 99; auth, "Essays for Peace and Integration," in Bricks Without Straw: A Comprehensive History of African Americans in Texas, ed. David Williams (Austin: Eakin, 97); auth, "Two Lockes, Two Keys: Tolerance and Reciprocity in a Culture of Democracy," in The Critical Pragmatism of Alain Locke, ed. Leonard Harris (Lanham, MD: Rowman & Littlefield, 99); auth, "Back to Africa with Plato: Testing Diop's Thesis on the African Origins of the Timaeus," forthcoming; auth, "A Kingian Defense of Affirmative Action," APA NL Philo Black Experience (97); auth, "Begin Where We Have Not Yet Reached: Affirmative Action and the Philosophy of Martin Luther King, Jr," Nat Womens Stud Asn J (98); auth, "David Theo Goldberg, Racial Subjects: Writing on Race in America," Ethics 108 (98): 839-840; auth, "Michael J. White, Partisan or Neutral?: The Futility of Public Political Theory," H-Pol, H-Net Rev (97), http://www.h-net.msu.edu/reviews; auth, "CLR James, American Civilization," APA NL Phil and Black Exp (96): 24-25. **CONTACT ADDRESS** Dept Humanities, Marist Col, 290 North Rd, Poughkeepsie, NY 12601-1326.

MOSHA, RAYMOND S.
PERSONAL Born 05/02/1945, Moshi, Tanzania, m, 1994, 3 children **DISCIPLINE** THEOLOGY **EDUCATION** Makerere Univ, Uganda, BA; Maryknoll School Theol, Theology, 75; Univ Md, MA, 77; Duquesne Univ, MA, 84; PhD, 86. **CAREER** Asst prof, Kibosho Philos Col, Tanzania, 77-82; asst prof, Cath Univ of E Africa, 87-93; vis assoc prof, Duquesne Univ, Xavier Univ, Loyola Univ Chicago, 93-01; **HONORS AND AWARDS** Int Vis Fel, Georgetown Univ, 97-98; Ecumenical Awd, Ecumenical Chair in Theol Lect Series, Xavier Univ, 94; Int Res Fel, Georgetown Univ, 97-98. **MEMBERSHIPS** Indigenous Res Group. **RESEARCH** Research and writing in indigenous knowledge, spirituality and the relationship between spirituality and knowledge, science, technology. **SELECTED PUBLICATIONS** Auth, "The Inseparable Link Between Intellectual and Spiritual Formation in Indigenous Knowledge" in What is Indigenous Knowledge? Voices from the Academy, Garland Pub Co (NY) 99; auth, The Heartbeat of Indigenous Africa, Garland Pub Co (NY), 00. **CONTACT ADDRESS** Dept Theol, Loyola Univ, Chicago, 6525 N Sheridan Rd, Chicago, IL 60626-5344. **EMAIL** rmosha@luc.edu

MOSKOP, JOHN C.
PERSONAL Born 10/19/1951, IL, m, 1977, 2 children **DISCIPLINE** PHILOSOPHY **EDUCATION** Univ Notre Dame, BA, 73; Univ Texas at Austin, PhD, 79. **CAREER** Asst Prof, 79-84, Assoc Prof, 84-89, Prof, 89-, East Carolina Univ School of Med; Dir, 95-, Bioethics Ctr, Univ Health Systems of Eastern Carolina. **HONORS AND AWARDS** Fel, Inst on Human Values in Med, 77; Basic Sci Serv Awd, East Carolina Univ Sch of Med, 98; East Carolina Univ Founders' Day Serv Awd, 00. **MEMBERSHIPS** Am Soc for Bioethics and Humanities; Am Phil Assoc; Am Soc of Law, Med, and Ethics **RESEARCH** Bioethics, especially ethical issues in death and dying; allocation of healthcare; emergency medicine ethics **SELECTED PUBLICATIONS** Auth, Informed Consent and the Limits of Disclosure: A Response to Joel M. Zinburg, Current Surgery; Coauth, Knowing the Score: Using Predictive Scoring Systems in Clinical Practice, American Journal of Critical Care, 96; Auth, End-of-Life Decisions in Dutch Neonatal Intensive Care Units, Journal of Pediatrics, 96; Physician Assisted Suicide: What's the Answer, Medical Center Review, 96; Not Sanctity of Dignity, But Justice and Autonomy: Key Moral Concepts in the Allocation of Critical Care, The Concepts of Human Dignity and Sanctity of Life and Their Significance for Ethical Conflicts in Modern Medicine, 96; Persons, Property or Both: Engelhardt on the Moral Status of Young Children, Reading Engelhardt, 97; Coauth, Ethical and Legal Aspects of Teratogenic Medications: The Case of Isotretinoin, Journal of Clinical Ethics, 97; Auth, A Moral Analysis of Military Medicine, Military Medicine, 98; co-ed, Ethics and Mental Retardation; co-ed, Ethics and Critical Care Medicine; co-ed, Children and Health Care: Moral and Social Issues. **CONTACT ADDRESS** Dept of Medical Humanities, East Carolina Univ, 25-17 Brody Medical Sciences Bldg., Greenville, NC 27858. **EMAIL** moskopj@mail.ecu.edi

MOSKOVITZ, MYRON
PERSONAL Born 11/23/1938, San Francisco, CA, m, 2 children **DISCIPLINE** LAW **EDUCATION** Univ Calif, BS, 60. **CAREER** Chief Atty, Nat Housing Law Proj, 68-71; Dir of Litigation, Legal Aid Soc, 72; Prof, Golden Gate Univ, 72-. **HONORS AND AWARDS** John Gorgunkel Outstanding Prof Awd, Golden Gate Univ, 88. **MEMBERSHIPS** CSB, ABA. **RESEARCH** Appellate advocacy, civil procedure, comparative criminal procedure, constitutional law, contracts, criminal law, evidence, landlord-tenant law. **SELECTED PUBLICATIONS** Auth, "The O J Inquisition: A United States Encounter with Continental Criminal Justice, 28," Vanderbilt J of Transitional Law 1121 (95); rev, "You Can't Tell A Book By Its Title (Reviewing Uviller, 'Virtual Justice'), 8," Criminal Law Forum 125 (97); coauth, California Residential Landlord-Tenant Practice, 2nd Ed, CCEB, 97; auth, Cases and Problems in Criminal Procedure: The Police, 2nd Ed, with Teacher's Manual, Matthew Bender, 98; auth, Cases and Problems in Criminal Procedure: The Courtroom, 2nd Ed, with Teacher's Manual, Matthew Bender, 98; auth, Cases and Problems in California Criminal Law, with Teacher's Manual, Anderson Publ, 99; auth, Cases and Problems in Criminal Law, 4th Ed, with Teacher's Manual, Anderson Publ, 99. **CONTACT ADDRESS** Dept Law, Golden Gate Univ, 536 Mission St, San Francisco, CA 94105-2921. **EMAIL** mmoskovitz@ggu.edu

MOSOFF, JUDITH
DISCIPLINE LAW **EDUCATION** Univ Toronto, BA, 69; York Univ, MA, 70; Univ British Columbia, LLB, 83; LLM, 94. **CAREER** Prof, 91- **RESEARCH** Disability; mental health; public interest law. **SELECTED PUBLICATIONS** Auth, pubs about administrative law, clinical legal education and law and psychiatry. **CONTACT ADDRESS** Fac of Law, Univ of British Columbia, 1822 East Mall, Vancouver, BC, Canada V6T 1Z1. **EMAIL** mosoff@interchange.ubc.ca

MOSS, ALFRED A., JR.
PERSONAL Born 03/02/1943, Chicago, IL, d **DISCIPLINE** AFRICAN-AMERICAN, U.S. SOCIAL AND U.S. RELIGIOUS HISTORY **EDUCATION** Lake Forest College, Lake Forest, IL, BA, with honors, 1961-65; Episcopal Divinity School, Cambridge, MA, MA, divinity, 1965-68; University of Chicago, Chicago, IL, MA, 1972, PhD, 1977. **CAREER** Episcopal Church of the Holy Spirit, Lake Forest, IL, assistant minister for urban ministry, 68-70; University of Chicago, Episcopal Chaplaincy, Chicago, IL, associate chaplain, 70-75; Univ of Maryland, Dept of History, College Park, MD, lecturer, 75-77, assistant professor, 77-83, associate professor, 83-. **HONORS AND AWARDS** Franklin, which was chosen by the Gustav Myers Found as "An Outstanding Book on the Subject of Human Rights in the United States"; received an Awd for Excellence in Teaching from the Col of Arts and Humanities. **RESEARCH** African American, American Social, and American religious history. **SELECTED PUBLICATIONS** The American Negro Academy, Louisiana State Univ Press, 1981; Looking at History, People for the American Way, 1986; From Slavery to Freedom, Alfred A Knopf, 1988; The Facts of Reconstruction, Louisiana State Univ Press, 1991. **CONTACT ADDRESS** Professor, Dept of History, Univ of Maryland, Col Park, 1500 N Lancaster Str, Arlington, VA 22205. **EMAIL** am45@umail.umd.edu

MOSS, C. MICHAEL
PERSONAL Born 02/10/1950, Danville, IL, m, 1972, 3 children **DISCIPLINE** NEW TESTAMENT & GREEK **EDUCATION** Lipscomb Univ, BA; Harding Univ Grad Sch of Relig, MA; Southern Bapt Theol Sem, M Div, PhD. **CAREER** Prof and assoc dean, col of bible and ministry, Lipscomb Univ, 83-. **HONORS AND AWARDS** Outstanding Teacher, 98; Gospel Advocate, 98. **MEMBERSHIPS** Soc of Bibl Lit; Amer Acad of Relig; Evang Theol Soc. **RESEARCH** New Testament backgrounds; Greek; Hermeneutics; Johannine literature. **SELECTED PUBLICATIONS** auth, 1, 2, Timothy and Titus, Col Press New Intl Commentary, Joplin, Col Press, 94; transl, The NKSV Greek English Interlinear New Testament, Nashville, Word, 94; auth, The Exposition of Scripture, Man of God, Nashville, Gospel Advocate, 96; auth, But Lord, Sometimes I Don't Feel Saved: Studies in John's Epistles, Covenant Pr (Phoenix), 01. **CONTACT ADDRESS** 3901 Grannywhite Pike, Nashville, TN 37204-3951. **EMAIL** michael.moss@lipscomb.edu

MOSS, LENNY
PERSONAL Born 04/24/1952, Brooklyn, NY, d, 2 children **DISCIPLINE** PHILOSOPHY AND BIOCHEMISTRY **EDUCATION** San Francisco State Univ, BA, 81; Univ Calif Berkeley, PhD, 89; Northwestern Univ, PhD, 98. **CAREER** Genetic sci in soc fel, Univ Utah, 96-97; vis asst prof, philos, Univ Utah, 97-98; instr, philos, Northwestern Univ, 98-99. **HONORS AND AWARDS** Genesis fel, Utah Ctr for Human Genome Res, Univ Utah, 96; Univ fel, Northwestern Univ, 90; Regents fel, Univ Calif Berkeley, 81. **MEMBERSHIPS** Amer Asn for the Advan of Sci; Amer Asn of Bioethics; Amer Philos Asn; Amer Soc for Cell Bio; Critical Theory Roundtable; Hist of Sci Soc; Intl Asn of Bioethics; Intl Soc for the Hist, Philos, and Social Studies of Bio; Philos of Sci Asn; Soc for Phenomenol and Existential Philos; Soc for Philos and Psychol. **SELECTED PUBLICATIONS** Auth, Life, Origins of, Routledge Encycl of Philos, 98; auth, Ethical Challenges of the New Genetic Technologies, Ethics Grand Rounds, Med Col of Wisc, 98; auth, What Genes Can't Do or Prolegomenon to a Dynamically-Relational, Developmentally-Embodying Life-Philosophy, dept of philos, Univ Utah, 97; auth, What is Selecting What?, Intl Soc for the Hist, Philos, and Social Studies of Bio, Univ Wash, 97; auth, Critical Reflections on the Gene Concept, Genetic Sci in Soc Prog, Utah Ctr for Human Genome Res, Univ Utah, 96; auth, Understanding Life: From Ontogenesis and Final Cause to Genetic Information and Back, Philos Colloquium, City Col/CUNY, 96; auth, Epigenesis, Dynamic Developmental Systems and Cancer, Workshop on the Logic and Dynamics of the Higher Level Formations in Biology, 96; auth, Post-Mendelian Biology and the Theory of Evolving Developmental Systems, The Prog in Hist and Philos of Sci at Northwestern Univ, 96; auth, Timeley Mediations: Martin Heidegger and Postmodern Politics, ETHICS, 97; auth, Gene and Generalizations: Darden's Strategies and the Question of Context, Bio and Philos, 95; **CONTACT ADDRESS** Sci, Technol, and Values Program, Univ of Notre Dame, Notre Dame, IN 46556. **EMAIL** lenny.moss.9@mail.nd.edu

MOSS, MYRA ELLEN
PERSONAL Born 03/22/1937, Los Angeles, CA **DISCIPLINE** CONTEMPORARY ITALIAN PHILOSOPHY **EDUCATION** Pomona Col, BA, 58; Johns Hopkins Univ, PhD, 65. **CAREER** Asst prof, San Jose State Col, 66-68; lectr, 68-70, asst prof, 70-74, Santa Clara Univ; tutor, 75-82, adj assoc prof Philos, 82-92, prof philos, 92-, prof philos and govt, 98-, Claremont McKenna Col. **HONORS AND AWARDS** Phi Beta Kappa (hon); bogliasco fel, Italy, 00. **MEMBERSHIPS** Am Philos Asn; Metaphysical Soc; Am Soc Aesthetics; Vico Soc. **RESEARCH** Italian philosophers: Croce, Gentile, Gramsci; philosophy and psychology. **SELECTED PUBLICATIONS** Auth, Benedetto Croce's Coherence Theory of Truth, Filos, 68; auth, Petrarch and Modern Criticism: De Sanctis and Croce, Rivista Rosminiana Filos Cult, 77; auth, Croce's Theory of Intuition Reconsidered, Rivista Studi Crociani, 78; auth, Croce's Categorial Theory of Truth, Idealistic Studies, 80; auth, Benedetto Croce Reconsidered, 87; transl, Benedetto Croce's Essays on Literature and Literary Criticism, 90. **CONTACT ADDRESS** Dept of Philosophy, Claremont McKenna Col, 500 E 9th St, Claremont, CA 91711-6400. **EMAIL** myra_moss@mckenna.edu

MOSSER, KURT
DISCIPLINE PHILOSOPHY OF LOGIC AND LANGUAGE **EDUCATION** Univ Chicago, PhD, 90. **CAREER** Dept Philos, Univ Dayton **RESEARCH** Kant, epistemology and metaphysics. **SELECTED PUBLICATIONS** Auth, Stoff and Nonsense in Kant's First Critique, Hist Philos Quart, 93; Was Wittgenstein a neo-Kantian? A Response to Prof Haller, Grazer Philos Stud, 93; Kant's Critical Model of the Experiencing Subject, Idealistic Stud, 95. **CONTACT ADDRESS** Dept of Philos, Univ of Dayton, 300 Col Park, Dayton, OH 75062. **EMAIL** mosser@checkov.hm.udayton.edu

MOSTAGHEL, DEBORAH M.
DISCIPLINE LAW **EDUCATION** Univ Calif Berkeley, BA; Shiraz Univ, MA; Univ Utah, JD. **CAREER** Dir of Legal Writing and Res **SELECTED PUBLICATIONS** Auth, Mediating Status Offender Cases-A Successful Approach, Mediation Quarterly, 96; The Low-Level Radioactive Waste Policy Amendment Act-An Overview, DePaul, 94; Who Regulates the Disposal of Low-Level Radioactive Waste Under the Low-level Radioactive Waste Policy Act?, 88; State Reactions to the Trading of Emissions Allowances Under Title IV of the Clean Air Act Amendments of 1990, Boston Col, 95. **CONTACT ADDRESS** Col Law, Univ of Toledo, Toledo, OH 43606. **EMAIL** dmostag@utnet.utoledo.edu

MOTHERSILL, MARY
PERSONAL Born 05/27/1923, Edmonton, AB, Canada **DISCIPLINE** PHILOSOPHY **EDUCATION** Univ Toronto, BA, 44; Harvard Univ, PhD(philos), 54. **CAREER** Instr philos, Vassar Col, 47-51; instr, Sch Gen Studies, Columbia Univ, 51-53 & Univ Conn, 53-57; lectr, Univ Mich, 57- 58; asst prof, Univ Chicago, 58-61; assoc prof, City Col NY, 61-64; Prof Philos, Barnard Col, Columbia Univ, 64-. **MEMBERSHIPS** Am Philos Asn. **SELECTED PUBLICATIONS** Auth, Agents, critics and philosophers, Mind, 10/60; Is art a language?, J Philos, 10/65; ed, Ethics, Macmillan, 67. **CONTACT ADDRESS** Dept of Philosophy Barnard College, Columbia Univ, New York, NY 10027.

MOULDER, WILLIAM J.
DISCIPLINE BIBLE INTERPRETATION **EDUCATION** Columbia Bible Col, BA, 66; Trinity Evangelical Divinity Sch, Mdiv, 69; St. Andrews Univ, PhD, 74. **CAREER** Relig, Trinity Int Univ. **SELECTED PUBLICATIONS** Areas: the Old Testament and the New Testament. **CONTACT ADDRESS** Trinity Intl Univ, Col of Arts and Sciences, 2065 Half Day Road, Deerfield, IL 60015.

MOULTON, JANICE
DISCIPLINE ENGLISH, PHILOSOPHY **EDUCATION** Cornell Univ, BA, 63; Univ Chicago, MA, 68; PhD, 71. **CAREER** Asst prof, Univ Ky, 79-81; prof, Central China Tchrs Univ, 86-87; res fac, Smith Coll, 81-. **HONORS AND AWARDS** Executive Comm, Am Philos Asn, 78; Bd of Dir, Sino-Am Network for Educ Exchange. **MEMBERSHIPS** Am Philos Asn; Sino-Am Network for Educ Exchange; Soc for Women in Philos. **RESEARCH** Philosophy; Methodology; Ethics; Feminism; Philosophy Language; Research Methodology; Fraud. **SELECTED PUBLICATIONS** Auth, Plagiarism; Academic Freedom, Encycl of Ethics, 98; coauth, Scaling the Dragon, 94. **CONTACT ADDRESS** Dept of Philosophy, Smith Col, Northampton, MA 01063. **EMAIL** jmm93@cornell.edu

MOUNCE, WILLIAM D.
DISCIPLINE NEW TESTAMENT **EDUCATION** Bethel Col, BA; Fuller Theol Sem, MA; Aberdeen Univ, Scotland, PhD. **CAREER** Instr, Azuza Pacific Univ; prof, Gordon-Conwell Theol Sem, 97-; adv, Courseware Devel. **HONORS AND AWARDS** Producer, FlashWorks and ParseWorks, integrative cmpt prog(s) for lrng lang(s). **MEMBERSHIPS** Mem, Evangel Theol Soc; Soc Biblical Lit; Inst Biblical Res; Tyndale House. **RESEARCH** Greek and exegesis. **SELECTED PUBLICATIONS** Auth, The Basics of Biblical Greek; The Analytical Lexicon to the Greek New Testament; Profiles in Faith. **CONTACT ADDRESS** Gordon-Conwell Theol Sem, 130 Essex St, South Hamilton, MA 01982.

MOUNT, ERIC, JR.
PERSONAL Born 12/07/1935, Versailles, KY, m, 1958, 4 children **DISCIPLINE** ENGLISH, CHRISTIAN ETHICS AND RELIGION **EDUCATION** Rhodes Col, BA, 57; Union Theol Sem in Va, BD, 60; Yale Divinity Sch, STM, 61; Duke Univ, PhD, 66. **CAREER** Asst prof, 66-70, assoc prof, 70-75, prof, 75-96, Rodes prof, 96-, relig, Centre Col; dir, Centre-in-Europe, 92-93, 00; vpres and dean of students, Centre Col, 83-88; social studies div chair, 80-83, relig prog chair, 84-88, Centre Col; Dir., Centre in Strasburg, 92-93, 00. **HONORS AND AWARDS** BA with distinction; Phi Beta Kappa; Omicron Delta Kappa; NEH summer seminars, 76, 81; BD, second in class; Alsop fel; PhD two univ fel; one Kearns fel; Theologian-

in-residence, Amer Church in Paris, 74-75; pres, southeast region, Amer Acad of Relig, 87-88; David Hughes distinguished svc award, Centre Col, 77; Pres, SE, region, Am Acad of Religion, 87-88; Project on the Common Good, Center of Theological Inquiry, 00-03. **MEMBERSHIPS** Soc of Christrian Ethics; Amer Acad of Relig; Soc for Values in Higher Educ; Soc of Bus Ethics; Asn for Practical and Professional Ethics; Assoc of Aplied and Prof. Ethics **RESEARCH** Theological ethics; Social ethics; Contemporary theology; Medical ethics; Business ethics; Professional ethics; Christian social ethics **SELECTED PUBLICATIONS** Auth, Covenant, Community, and the Common Good, Pilgrim Pr, 99; Articles, Homing in on Family Values, The Family, Religion and Culture Series, Theol Today, 98; article, European Community and Global Community: A View from Alsace and Beyond, Soundings, 96; article, The Currency of Covenant, Annual of the Soc of Christ Ethics, 96; article, Metaphors, Morals and AIDS, Jour of Ethical Studies, 93; article, Can We Talk? Contexts of Meaning for Interpreting Illness, Jour of Med Humanities, vol 14, no 2, 93; auth, Professional Ethics in Context: Institutions, Images and Empathy, John Knox Press, 90; auth, The Feminine Factor, John Knox Press, 73; auth, Conscience and Responsibility, John Knox Press, 69. **CONTACT ADDRESS** Centre Col, 600 W. Walnut St., Danville, KY 40422. **EMAIL** mounte@centre.edu

MOUNTCASTLE, WILLIAM W.
PERSONAL Born 07/10/1925, Hanover, NH, m, 1979, 6 children **DISCIPLINE** PHILOSOPHY **EDUCATION** Whittier Col, BA, 51; Boston Univ, STB, 54; PhD. **CAREER** Asst Prof, High Point Col, 58-60; Assoc Prof to Prof and Dept Head, Neb Wesleyan Univ, 6-67; Prof, Fla Southern Col, 67-69; Prof, Univ W Fla, 69-. **HONORS AND AWARDS** Teaching Awd, Univ W Fla; Who's Who Among Am Teachers; Who's Who in Am. **MEMBERSHIPS** Am Acad of Relig, Am Philos Asn, United Faculty of Fla. **RESEARCH** Finding common themes in world religions; The future of religion in the space age; New paradigms for Science and Religion. **SELECTED PUBLICATIONS** Auth, Religion in Planetary Perspective, Abingdon Press, 79; auth, Science Fantasy Voices and Visions of cosmic Religion, Univ Press of America, 96. **CONTACT ADDRESS** Dept Philos, Univ of West Florida, 11000 Univ Pkwy, Pensacola, FL 32514-5732.

MOURELATOS, ALEXANDER PHOEBUS DIONYSIOU
PERSONAL Born 07/19/1936, Athens, Greece, d **DISCIPLINE** PHILOSOPHY, CLASSICAL PHILOLOGY **EDUCATION** Yale Univ, BA, 58, MA, 61, PhD(philos), 64. **CAREER** Instr, Yale Univ, 62-64; from asst prof to assoc prof, 65-71, Prof Philos, Univ Tex Austin, 71-, Jr fel, Inst Res Humanities, Univ Wis, 64-65; mem, Inst Advan Study, Princeton, NJ, 67-68; Nat Endowment for Humanities fel, 68 & 82-83; jr fel, Ctr Hellenic Studies, Washington, DC, 73-74; Am Coun Learned Soc fel, 73-74; vis fel, Humanities Res Ctr, Australian Nat Univ, Canberra, 78 and 91; Guggenheim Fellow, 88-89. **HONORS AND AWARDS** Dr phil. hon, Univ of Athens (Greece), 94. **MEMBERSHIPS** Am Philos Asn; Am Philol Asn; Can Philos Asn; Correspdg member of the Academy of Athens, 99. **RESEARCH** Pre-Socratic philosophy; Plato; Aristotle; philosophical linguistics. **SELECTED PUBLICATIONS** Auth, Aristotle's Powers and Modern Empiricism, Ratio, 67; The Route of Parmenides, Yale Univ, 70; co-ed, Exegesis and Argument: Studies Presented to Gregory Vlastos, Van Gorcum, Assen, Neth, 73; ed, The Pre-Socratics: A Collection of Critical Essays, Doubleday, 2nd ed., Princeton Univ Press, 93; 74; Events, processes, and states, Ling & Philos, 78; Astronomy and kinematics in Plato's project of rationalist explanation, Study Hist & Philos of Sci, 80; auth, Quality, Structure, and Emergence in Later Pre-Socratic Philosophy, Proceedings of the Boston Area Colloquium in Ancient Philosophy, 87. **CONTACT ADDRESS** Dept of Philos, Univ of Texas, Austin, Austin, TX 78712-1180. **EMAIL** apdm@mail.utexas.edu

MOUSTAKAS, CLARK
DISCIPLINE PHILOSOPHY **EDUCATION** Wayne State Univ, BS, MS; Union Inst, PhD. **CAREER** Philos, Union Inst. **RESEARCH** Clinical psychology and education; phenomenological existential humanistic psychology and psychotherapy; dream psychology; philosophy; human science; jurisprudence. **SELECTED PUBLICATIONS** Auth, Creativity and Conformity; Creative Life; Existential Child Therapy; Loneliness and Love; Phenomenology, Science, and Psychotherapy; Psychotherapy with Children; Rhythms, Rituals, and Relationships; The Touch of Loneliness; Turning Points; Phenomenological Research Methods. **CONTACT ADDRESS** Union Inst, 440 E McMillan St., Cincinnati, OH 45206-1925. **EMAIL** cmoustakas@tui.edu

MOYER, JAMES CARROLL
PERSONAL Born 11/30/1941, Norristown, PA, m, 1965, 3 children **DISCIPLINE** OLD TESTAMENT, ANCIENT HISTORY **EDUCATION** Wheaton Col, BA, 63; Gordon Divinity Sch, MDiv, 66; Brandeis Univ, MA, 68, PhD(Mediter studies), 69. **CAREER** Sachar Int fel, Brandeis Univ, 69-70; asst prof, 70-75, assoc prof hist, 75-78, assoc prof religious studies, 78-79, Prof Relig Studies, 79, Head of Relig Studies, 79--, Southwest MO State Univ; 85--Fel archaeol, Hebrew Union Col Bibl & Archaeol Sch, Jerusalem, 69-70. **MEMBERSHIPS** Soc Bibl Lit; Am Orient Soc; Am Schs Orient Res; Cath Bibl Asn; Nat Asn of Baptist Professors of Relig. **RESEARCH** Old Testament; Israelite historiography and chronology; Hittitology. **SELECTED PUBLICATIONS** Auth, Philistines and Samson, In: Zondervan Pictorial Encyclopedia of the Bible, 75; contribr 14 articles for the revision of Eerdman's Int Standard Bible Encycl, Vol I, 79, Vol II, 82; co-ed, Hittite and Israelite cultic practices: A selected comparison, In: Scripture in Context II, 82; Ashkelon Discovered - From Canaanites And Philistines To Romans And Moslems - Stager,Le, J Of Biblical Literature, Vol 0112, 1993; contribr, The Anchor Bible Dictionary, 5 articles, 93; History And Technology Of Olive-Oil In The Holy-Land - Frankel,R, Avitsur,S, Ayalon,E, Jacobson,J, Biblical Archaeologist, Vol 0059, 1996; Through The Ages In Palestinian Archaeology - An Introductory Handbook - Rast,We, Biblical Archaeologist, Vol 0057, 1994; Scripture And Other Artifacts - Essays On The Bible And Archaeology In Honor Of King,Philip,J. - Coogan,Md, Exum,Jc, Stager,Le, Biblical Archaeologist, Vol 0058, 1995; coed, The Old Testament Text and Context, 97; contribr, Eerdmans Dictionary of the Bible, 5 articles, 00. **CONTACT ADDRESS** Dept of Religious Studies, Southwest Missouri State Univ, Springfield, Springfield, MO 65802. **EMAIL** jcmb25f@smsu.edu

MOZUR, GERALD E.
PERSONAL Born 11/23/1956, Birmingham, AL, m, 1984 **DISCIPLINE** PHILOSOPHY **EDUCATION** Center Col of Kentucky, BA, 79; Univ of Kentucky, MA, 83; Washington Univ, St Louis, PhD, 90. **CAREER** Millsaps Col, asst prof, 89-90; SW Missouri State Univ, asst prof, 90-94; Webster Univ, adj prof, 94-97; Lewis & Clark Comm Col, asst prof, 97-. **HONORS AND AWARDS** SWMSU FSR Fel. **MEMBERSHIPS** APA, SAAP **RESEARCH** Philo of John Dewey; pragmatism; naturalism. **SELECTED PUBLICATIONS** Auth, Argument and Abstraction: An Introduction to Formal Logic, McGraw-Hill, 98, art, Sex, Race and the Privacy of Experience, in: Becoming Persons, Applied Theo Press, 94; Half-Hearted Pragmatism, in: Jour of Spec Philo, 94; Dewey on Time and Individuality, in: Transactions of the Charles S. Pierce Society, 91. **CONTACT ADDRESS** Dept of Philosophy, Lewis and Clark Comm Col, 5800 Godfrey Rd, Godfrey, IL 62035. **EMAIL** gmozur@lc.cc.il.us

MUELLER, DAVID L.
PERSONAL Born 10/05/1929, Buffalo, NY, m, 1959, 1 child **DISCIPLINE** RELIGION **EDUCATION** Baylor Univ, BA, 51; Southern Baptist Theol Sem, BD, 54; Duke Univ, PhD, 58. **CAREER** From asst prof to assoc prof relig, Baylor Univ, 57-61; asst prof theol, 61-62, assoc prof, 62-75, Prof Theol, retired, Southern Baptist Theol Sem, 75-. **MEMBERSHIPS** Am Acad Relig; Am Soc Church Hist. **RESEARCH** Systematic theology; 19th and 20th century Protestant theology. **SELECTED PUBLICATIONS** Auth, Karl Barth's critique of the anthropoligical starting point in theology, Diss Abstr, 58; Roger William's view of the church and ministry, Rev & Expositor, 58; The theology of Karl Barth and the 19th century, Relig in Life, 64-65; An Introd to the Theology of Albrecht Ritschl, Westminster, 69; Karl Barth, Word Bks, 72; Bonhoeffer,Dietrich - A Spoke In The Wheel - Wind,R, J Of Church And State. **CONTACT ADDRESS** So Baptist Theol Sem, 2825 Lexington Rd., Louisville, KY 40280.

MUELLER, HOWARD ERNEST
PERSONAL Born 08/04/1936, Danube, MN, m, 1959, 2 children **DISCIPLINE** HISTORY OF RELIGIONS **EDUCATION** NCent Col, BA, 58; Evangel Theol Sem, BD, 61; Yale Univ, Stm, 62; Northwestern Univ, PhD(relig), 73. **CAREER** Asst prof relig, Carleton Col, 73-76; asst prof Relig, 76-80, assoc prof, 81-85, Prof Relig, Ncent Col, 85-, Chmn Dept, 90-. **HONORS AND AWARDS** Toenniges Prof of Religious Studies, 92. **MEMBERSHIPS** Am Acad Relig. **RESEARCH** African traditional religions; death and dying; biblical studies. **CONTACT ADDRESS** Dept of Religious Studies, No Central Col, 30 N Brainard St, Naperville, IL 60566. **EMAIL** hem@noctrl.edu

MUESSE, MARK WILLIAM
PERSONAL Born 06/01/1957, Waco, TX, s **DISCIPLINE** RELIGION **EDUCATION** Baylor Univ, BA (English), 79; Harvard Divinity School, MTS (theol), 81; Harvard Univ, AM (The Study of Relig), 83, PhD (The Study of Relig), 87. **CAREER** Assoc dean, Col Of Arts and Sciences, Univ Southern ME, 87-88; asst prof, relig studies, Rhodes Col, 88-95; vis prof, Tamilnadu Theological Sem of South India, 90; Assoc Prof, Relig Studies, Rhodes Col, 95-98. **HONORS AND AWARDS** Phi Beta Kappa, 79; Roothbert fel, 85; Charlotte W. Newcombe fel, 86. **MEMBERSHIPS** Am Academy of Relig; Soc for Values in Higher Ed; Am Men's Studies Asn; Soc for Indian Philos and Relig. **RESEARCH** Asian relig and philos; gender studies; religion and sexuality. **SELECTED PUBLICATIONS** Auth, Redeeming Men: Religion and Masculinities, 96. **CONTACT ADDRESS** Rhodes Col, 2000 North Parkway, Memphis, TN 38112-1690. **EMAIL** muesse@rhodes.edu

MUIR, MALCOLM, JR
PERSONAL Born 04/24/1943, Williamsport, PA, m, 1965, 2 children **DISCIPLINE** HISTORY, PHILOSOPHY **EDUCATION** Emory Univ, BA, 65; Fla St Univ, MA, 66; Ohio St Univ, PhD, 76. **CAREER** From asst prof to chemn, 77-; Austin Peay State Univ; SecNay Res Ch, Naval Hist Ctr, 87-88; vis prof, US Military Acad, 88-90; vis prof, Air War Col, 96-97. **HONORS AND AWARDS** Outstanding Civilian Serv Medal, U S Dept of the Army, 90; Richard M Hawkins Awd, 92; John Lyman Prize, N Am Soc for Oceanic Hist, 96; Larry Rowen Remele Awd, 99; Phi Alpha Theta; Phi Kappa Phi. **MEMBERSHIPS** Hist Soc, Nat Asn of Scholars. **SELECTED PUBLICATIONS** Auth, rev, 49 articles, entries and essays and 34 book rev; auth, The Iowa-Class Battleships: Iowa, New Jersey, Missouri and Wisconsin, Blandford Pr (Dorset, UK), 87; auth, Black Shoes and Blue Water: Surface Warfare in the United States Navy 1945-1975, Naval Hist Ctr (Washington, DC), 96. **CONTACT ADDRESS** Dept Hist & Philos, Austin Peay State Univ, 601 College St, Clarksville, TN 37044-0001. **EMAIL** muirm@apsu.edu

MUIR, WILLIAM KER, JR.
PERSONAL Born 10/30/1931, Detroit, MI, m, 1960, 2 children **DISCIPLINE** POLITICAL SCIENCE **EDUCATION** Yale, PhD, 65. **CAREER** Prof Political Science, Univ Calif Berkeley, 68-. **HONORS AND AWARDS** Hadley Cantril Awd; Edward S Corben Awd; Distinguished Tchg Awd. **MEMBERSHIPS** Am Polit Sci Asn. **RESEARCH** Democracy; Power, American society and government. **SELECTED PUBLICATIONS** The Bully Pulpit; Legislature: California's School for Politics; Police: Street Corner Politicians; Law and Attitude Change. **CONTACT ADDRESS** Dept of Political Science, Univ of California, Berkeley, Berkeley, CA 94720-1950. **EMAIL** sandymuir@aol.com

MULDER, JOHN MARK
PERSONAL Born 03/20/1946, Chicago, IL, m, 1968, 2 children **DISCIPLINE** AMERICAN CHURCH HISTORY **EDUCATION** Hope Col, AB, 67; Princeton Theol Sem, MDiv, 70; Princeton Univ, PhD, 74. **CAREER** From ed asst to asst ed, Papers of Woodrow Wilson, 71-74; instr Am church hist, Princeton Theol Sem, 74-75, asst prof, 75-80, assoc prof, 80-81; Pres, Louisville Presby theol sem, 81-, Asst ed, Theology Today, 69-; fels hist, Asn Theol Schs in US & Can, 76 & Am Coun Learned Soc, 77. **HONORS AND AWARDS** D.Th, Institut de Portestant Theologie, Montpellier, 96; D D, Hanover College, 96; L H D, Bellarmine College, 90; D D, Rhodes College, 84; L H D, Centre College, 84. **MEMBERSHIPS** AHA; Orgn Am Historians; Am Soc Church Hist; Presby Hist Soc; Am Acad Relig. **RESEARCH** Woodrow Wilson; relig and polit in Am; relig in the Revolutionary and early national periods; 20th century Am relig. **SELECTED PUBLICATIONS** Coed, The Mainstream Protestand Decline: The Presbyterian Pattern, Louisville: Westminster/John Knox Press, 90; coed, The Presbyterian Predicament: Six Perspectives, Louisville: Westminster/John Knox Press, 90; coed, The Confessional Mosaic: Presbyterians in Twentieth-Century Theology, Lousiville: Westminster/John Knox Press, 91; coed, The Organizational Revolution: Presbyterians and American Denominationalism, Louisville: Westminster/John Knox Press, 91; coed, The Diversity of Discipleship: Presbyterians in Twentieth-Century Christian Witness, Louisville: Westminster/John Knox Press, 91; auth, Sealed in Christ: The Symbolism of th Seal of the Presbyterian Church U S A, Louisville: Presbyterian Publishing House, 91; coed, The Pluralistic Vision: Presbyterians in Mainstream Protestant Education and Leadership, Louisville: Westminster/John Knox Press, 92; coauth, the Re-forming Tradition: Presbyterians and Mainstream Protestantism, Louisville: Westminster/John Knox Press, 92; coauth, Vital Signs: The Promise of Mainstream Protestantism, Grand Rapides, Mich: Wm B Eerdmans, 95; coed, Woodrow Wilson: A Bibliography, Greenwood Press, 97. **CONTACT ADDRESS** Louisville Presbyterian Theol Sem, 1044 Alta Vista Rd, Louisville, KY 40205-1758. **EMAIL** jmmulder@lpts.edu

MULHOLLAND, KENNETH B.
PERSONAL Born 10/24/1937, Oak Park, IL, m, 1961, 3 children **DISCIPLINE** MISSIOLOGY **EDUCATION** Elmhurst Col, BA, 59; Lancaster Theol Sem, BD, 62; STM, 71; Fuller Theol Sem, DThP, 73. **CAREER** Pastor, Bethel United Church, 61-66; prof, Theol Inst of the Evangel and Reformed Church, Honduras, 67-70; Interim pastor, Downey Congregational Church, 71-72; prof, Latin Am Bibl Sem, 72-80; prof, dean, Columbia Bibl Sem, 80-. **HONORS AND AWARDS** Course of the Year Awd, Asn of Continuing Educ and Schools, 84; Schol in Residence, Fuller Theol Sem, 76, Res Fel, Yale Div School, 00. **MEMBERSHIPS** Am Soc of Missiology; Evangel Missiological Soc; Evangel Theol Soc; Int Assoc of Mission Studies. **RESEARCH** World Christianity, History of Missions, Missionary Life and Work, Contemporary Issues in Missions. **SELECTED PUBLICATIONS** Auth, Adventures in Training the Ministry, Presbyterian and Reformed Pub, (Philipsburg), 76; auth, "Getting Fitted with Mediterranean Glasses", Global Civilization: Module Two 11, William Carey Libr, (Pasadena, 95): 1-5; auth, "Paul Burgess", Biographical Directory of Christian Missions, ed, Gerald H Anderson, Simon & Shuster, (NY), 97; auth, "A Church for All Peoples", Perspectives on the World Christian Movement: A Reader, eds Ralph d Winter and Steven

Hawthorne, William Carey Lib, (Pasadena, 99); auth, "Teaching them to Obey All Things: Three Dots and a Pilgrimage", Teaching Them Obedience in all Things, ed Edgar J. Elliston, William Carey Libr, (Pasadena, 99); auth, "Working together to Shape the New Millennium", Evangel Missions Quarterly 35.3 (99): 317-320; auth, "Cross-cultural Counseling: Difficult/ Inescapable/Possible", Missionary Monthly 104, (Feb, 00): 4-6; auth, "More Reflections on Cross-Cultural Counseling", Missionary Monthly 104, (Mar, 00): 4-6; auth, "Guidelines for Cross-cultural Counseling", Missionary Monthly 104, (Apr 00): 8-10. **CONTACT ADDRESS** Dept Relig Studies, Columbia Intl Univ, PO Box 3122, Columbia, SC 29230-3122. **EMAIL** kenm@ciu.edu

MULLER, EARL
PERSONAL Born 08/18/1947, Columbia, SC, s **DISCIPLINE** THEOLOGY **EDUCATION** Spring Hill Col, BS, 71; Regis Col, MDiv, 77; Marquette Univ, PhD, 87. **CAREER** Instr, Spring Hill Col, 83-86; Asst Prof, Marquette Univ, 87-95; Prof, Gregorian Univ, 95-99; Prof, Sacred Heart Major Sem, 99-. **HONORS AND AWARDS** Univ Scholar, Marguette Univ, 77-79; Arthur J Schmitt Fel, 79-81. **MEMBERSHIPS** Cath Theol Soc of Am, N Am Patristics Socs, Cath Bibl Asn, Soc of Bibl Lit. **RESEARCH** Primarily topics in Trinity and Christology. **SELECTED PUBLICATIONS** Auth, Trinity and Marriage in Paul, Peter Lang Publ Co (New York, NY), 90; co-ed, Augustine: Presbyter Factors sum in Collectanea Augustianiana, Vol 12, Peter Lang Publ Co (New York, NY), 93; co-ed, Theological Education in the Catholic Tradition, (New York: Crossroad), 97. **CONTACT ADDRESS** Dept Theol, Sacred Heart Major Sem, 2701W Chicago, Detroit, MI 48206-1704.

MULLER, RALF
PERSONAL Born 06/01/1965, Mainz, Germany, 2 children **DISCIPLINE** PHILOSOPHY **EDUCATION** Mainz Univ, PhD, MA. **CAREER** Asst prof, Fordham Univ. **RESEARCH** Pragmatism, Peirce philos of mind, logic. **SELECTED PUBLICATIONS** On the Principles of Construction and the Order of Peirce's Trichotomies of Signs, Transactions of the Charles Sanders Peirce Society, 94; Peirce and Israel/Perry on the Conditions of Informational Flow, Proceedings of the Fifth Congress on the International Association for Semiotic Studies, Berkeley, 94; auth, "Die Dynamische Logik Des Eruennews von Charles S. Peirce Werzburg: Konigshausen & Neumann 97; auth, "Interpretations of Modality: Epistemic Logic and Peirce's Logic of Ibnorance in: Ihenomenology on Kant, Berman Idealism, Hermeneutics and Logic, ed. By ok Wiegand et al Dororcht: Kluwer, 00. **CONTACT ADDRESS** Dept of Philos, Fordham Univ, 113 W 60th St, New York, NY 10023. **EMAIL** muller@fordham.edu

MULLIN, AMY M.
PERSONAL Born 09/06/1963, Pittsburgh, PA, m, 1995, 3 children **DISCIPLINE** PHILOSOPHY **EDUCATION** Harvard Univ, AB, 85; Yale Univ, PhD, 90. **CAREER** Asst Prof to Assoc Prof, Univ Toronto, 90-. **HONORS AND AWARDS** Res Grant, Soc Sci and Humanities, 00-03; Connaught Grant, 90-93. **MEMBERSHIPS** And Philos Asn; Can Soc for Women in Philos; Am Soc of Aesthetics. **RESEARCH** Feminist philosophy; Aesthetics; Continental philosophy; Descartes. **SELECTED PUBLICATIONS** Auth, "Selves Diverse and Divided," Hypatia, 95; auth, "The Safeguarded Self," Dialogue, 95; auth, "As the Lights Go On," Philosophy Today, 95; auth, "Art, Politics and Knowledge," Metaphilosophy, 96; auth, "Purity and Pollution," J of the Hist of Ideas, 96; auth, "Whitman's Oceans, Nietzsche's Seas," Philosophy Today, 98; auth, "Descartes and the Community of Inquirers," Hist of Philos Quart, 00; auth, "Nietzsche's Free Spirit," J of the Hist of Philos, 00; auth, "Adorno, Art Theory and Feminist Practice," Philos Today, 00; auth, "Art, Understanding and Political Change," Hypatia, 00. **CONTACT ADDRESS** Dept Philos, Univ of Toronto, 22 Cragmuir Ct, Toronto, ON, Canada M5S 1A1. **EMAIL** mullin@chass.utoronto.ca

MULLIN, ROBERT BRUCE
PERSONAL Born 10/24/1953, Plainfield, NJ, m, 1960, 1 child **DISCIPLINE** RELIGIOUS HISTORY **EDUCATION** Col of William & Mary, AB, 75; Yale Divinity School, MAR, 79; Yale Univ, PhD. **CAREER** Instr, Yale Univ, 84-85; asst prof to prof, North Carolina State Univ, 85-98; Sprl Prof of Hist & World Mission, General Theological Seminary, 98-. **MEMBERSHIPS** AAR; ASCH; Hist Soc of the Episcopal Church. **RESEARCH** American religious history; modern intellectual history; Anglicanism. **SELECTED PUBLICATIONS** Auth, Episcopal Vision/American Reality: High Church Theology and Social Thought in Evangelical America, Yale Univ Press, 86; The Scientific Theist: A Life of Francis Ellingwood Abbot, Mercer Univ Press, 87; Moneygripe's Apprentice: The Personal Narrative of Samuel Seabury III, Yale Univ Press, 89; Reimagining Denominationalism: Interpretive Essays, Oxford Univ Press, 94; Miracles and the Modern Religious Imagination, Yale Univ Press, 96. **CONTACT ADDRESS** General Theol Sem, 175 Ninth Ave, New York, NY 10011-4977. **EMAIL** mullin@gts.edu

MULRONEY, MICHAEL
PERSONAL Born 02/26/1932, Chicago, IL, m, 1959, 5 children **DISCIPLINE** TAX LAW **EDUCATION** State Univ Iowa, BSC, 54; Harvard Law Sch, JD, 59. **CAREER** Atty, advisor US Tax Court, 59-61; appellate atty, US Dept of Justice Tax Div, 61-64; assoc partner of counsel, Lee, Toomey, and Kent, Wash DC, 64-88; adj prof, Georgetown Law Sch Grad Tax Prog, 86-; prof and dir, Villanova Law Sch Grad Tax Prog, 88-. **HONORS AND AWARDS** BNA Tax Management Distinguished Author, 96. **MEMBERSHIPS** ABA; DC Bar; Iowa Bar; Fed Bar Asn; Amer Asn Law Sch; Philadelphia Tax Conf; Int Fiscal Asn's USA Branch; Int Fiscal Res Inst Coun Experts & J. Edgar Murdock Inn Ct; Am Col of Tax Counsel. **RESEARCH** Taxation. **SELECTED PUBLICATIONS** Publ on, Fed Tax Examinations Manual and For Taxation. **CONTACT ADDRESS** School of Law, Villanova Univ, 299 Northspring Mill Rd., Villanova, PA 19085-1682. **EMAIL** mulroney@law.villanova.edu

MULVEY, BEN
PERSONAL Born 05/04/1954, Freeport, NY, m, 1995, 1 child **DISCIPLINE** PHILOSOPHY **EDUCATION** Mich State Univ, PhD, 93. **CAREER** Assoc prof, philos, Nova Southeastern Univ, 88-; dir, liberal arts, Nova Southeastern Univ, 97-. **MEMBERSHIPS** Amer Philos Asn; Fla Bioethics Network. **RESEARCH** Moral development; Bioethics. **SELECTED PUBLICATIONS** Auth, Response to The Case of Mr. B, Network News: The Newsletter of the Fla Bioethics Network, 98, 2, apr, 98; auth, Synopsis of a Practical Guide: Guidelines for Ethics Comittees, Jour of Fla Med Asn, v 84, n 8, nov, 97; auth, Autonomy and the Moral Tradition: The Foundation of the Patient Self-Determination Act of 1990, The Record, v 43, n 10, nov, 91; auth, Needs versus Rights: State Subsidized Abortions, The Mich Acad, v 18, n 3, jul, 86; co-auth, Guidelines for Ethics Committees, Fla Med Asn, 96. **CONTACT ADDRESS** Dept. of Liberal Arts, Nova Southeastern Univ, Fort Lauderdale, 3301 College Ave, Fort Lauderdale, FL 33314. **EMAIL** mulvey@nova.edu

MUMBY, DENNIS K.
DISCIPLINE ORGANIZATIONAL COMMUNICATION, PHILOSOPHY OF COMMUNICATION **EDUCATION** Southern Ill Univ, PhD, 84. **CAREER** Assoc prof, Purdue Univ. **SELECTED PUBLICATIONS** Auth, The Political Function of Narrative in Organizations, Commun Monogr, 87; Communication & Power in Organizations, Ablex, 88; ed, Narrative & Social Control, Sage, 93. **CONTACT ADDRESS** Dept of Commun, Purdue Univ, West Lafayette, 1080 Schleman Hall, West Lafayette, IN 47907-1080. **EMAIL** dmumby@purdue.edu

MUNEVAR, GONZALO
PERSONAL Born Barranquilla, Colombia, d, 1 child **DISCIPLINE** PHILOSOPHY OF SCIENCE **EDUCATION** Calif State Univ, BA, 70; MA, 71; Univ Calif Berkeley, PhD, 75. **CAREER** Lectr, San Francisco State Univ, 75-76; asst to prof, Univ Nebr Omaha, 76-85; prof, 85-89; vis assoc prof, Stanford Univ, 83-84; vis res prof, Univ Newcastle, 86; vis res prof, Instituto de Filosofia, Madrid, 87; vis res prof, Univ Barcelona, 88; vis res prof, Univ de Santiago de Compostel a, 88; vis prof, Kobe Univ of Commerce, 93; vis prof, Univ Wash, 94; prof, The Evergreen State Coll, 89-97; vis prof Univ Calif Irvine, 97-. **HONORS AND AWARDS** Distinguished Res Awd, Univ Nebr Omaha, 86; Nebr Found Professorship, Univ Nebr Omaha, 86-89. **MEMBERSHIPS** Am Philos Asn; Philos of Sci Asn; Am Asn for the Advan of Sci. **RESEARCH** Philosophy of sciences; Philosophy of Space Sciences; Philosophy of Technology; Philosophy of Mind; Ethics. **SELECTED PUBLICATIONS** Auth, Evolution and the Naked Truth, 98; The Master of Fate, 99; ed, Beyond Reason: Essays on the Philosophy of Paul K Feyerabend, 91; Spanish Studies in the Philosophy of Science, 96; co-ed, The Worst Enemy of Science? Essays on the Life and Thought of Paul Feyerabend, 99. **CONTACT ADDRESS** Dept of Philosphy, Univ of California, Irvine, Irvine, CA 92697. **EMAIL** munevarg@aol.com

MUNNEKE, GARY A.
PERSONAL Born 12/29/1947, IN, m, 1990, 4 children **DISCIPLINE** LAW **EDUCATION** Univ Tex, BS, 70; JD, 73. **CAREER** Ass Dean Univ Tex School of Law, 70-73; Prof, Widener Univ, 80-87; prof, Pace Univ, 98-. **HONORS AND AWARDS** Fel, Am Bar Asn, Fel, Col of Law Practice Management. **MEMBERSHIPS** Am Bar Asn, State Bar of Tex. **RESEARCH** Professional responsibility for lawyers, Legal profession. **SELECTED PUBLICATIONS** Auth, "King Canute's Last Stand: Will Model Rule 5.4 Turn the Tide," forthcoming; auth, "A Multidisciplinary Practice in Your Future?," Pace Chronicle, 00; auth, Law Practice Management in a Nutshell, forthcoming; auth, "Multidisciplinary Practice," New York Professional Responsibility Report, 99; auth, "What Have Ethics Got to Do With Legal Malpractice: The Relationship Between the Rules of Professional Conduct and the Standard of Care," Journal of the Legal Profession, 99; auth, "The Repugnant Client," New York Professional Responsibility Report, 98; auth, "Lawyers, Accountants and the Battle over Professional Services," Pace Law Review, (98): 63; auth, Changing Jobs: A Handbook for Lawyers in the 90's, American Bar Association, 99; auth, "Seize the Future: Forecasting and Influencing the Future of the Legal Profession," forthcoming; auth, "Report on the Seize the Future Conference," Law Practice Quarterly, 00. **CONTACT ADDRESS** School of Law, Pace Univ, White Plains, 78 N Broadway, White Plains, NY 10603-3710. **EMAIL** gmunneke@law.pace.edu

MUNSON, RONALD
PERSONAL Born 10/19/1939, Jasper, TX, m, 1966 **DISCIPLINE** PHILOSOPHY **EDUCATION** Southern Methodist Univ, BA, 61; Columbia Univ, PhD(philos), 67. **CAREER** Preceptor contemp, civilization, Columbia Col, 64-67; from asst prof to assoc prof philos, 67-77, Prof Philos, Univ MO-ST Louis, 77-, Nat Endowment for Humanities younger humanist fel, Dept Biol, Harvard Univ, 72-73, vis prof, 77-78. **MEMBERSHIPS** Philos Sci Asn; Am Philos Asn; AAAS. **RESEARCH** Philosophy of science; philosophy of biology; philosophy of medicine. **SELECTED PUBLICATIONS** Ed, Man and Nature: Philosophical Issues in Biology, Dell, 71; auth, Biological Adaptation, Philos Sci, 71; Essay review: Ruse's philosophy of biology, Hist & Philos Sci, 75; Is biology a provincial science?, Philos Sci, 75; The Way of Words, Houghton-Mifflin, 76; Mechanism, vitalism, reductionism and organismic biology, Encycl del Novenciento, Rome, 76; coauth, Philosophy of biology, Encycl Britannica, 76; auth, Intervention and Reflection: Basic Issues in Medical Ethics, Wadsworth, 78; Testing Normative Naturalism - The Problem Of Scientific Medicine, British J For The Philosophy Of Science, Vol 0045, 1994. **CONTACT ADDRESS** Dept of Philosophy, Univ of Missouri, St. Louis, 8001 Natural Bridge, Saint Louis, MO 63121-4499.

MUNZEL, GISELA FELICITAS
DISCIPLINE PHILOSOPHY **EDUCATION** Mercer Univ, BA, 83; Emory Univ, MA, 88; PhD, 90. **CAREER** Instr, Ga State Univ, 90-92; from asst prof to assoc prof, Univ of Notre Dame, 92-. **HONORS AND AWARDS** Am Fel, Am Asn of Univ Women Educ Found, 89-90; Heinrich Hertz Fel, Ger Ministry for Wissenschaft und Forschung, 90; Johnsonian Prize, 91; Res Support Summer Stipend, Univ of Notre Dame, 94; Fac Res Program Awd, Univ of Notre Dame, 99; Int Travel Grant, Univ of Notre Dame, 00; Fel Res Grant, Earhart Found, 00-01. **MEMBERSHIPS** N Am Kant Soc, Ger Kant-Gesselschaft, APA, Ger Studies Asn, Am Soc for Eighteenth Century Studies, Goethe Soc of N Am, Am Asn of Univ Women, Soc for Values in Higher Educ, Honor Soc of Phi Kappa Phi. **RESEARCH** Immanuel Kant (moral philosophy, anthropology, pedagogy, aesthetics), 18th century philosophical literature by other thinkers on these topics, German idealism. **SELECTED PUBLICATIONS** Auth, "'The Beautiful Is the Symbol of the Morally-Good': Kant's Philosophical Basis of proof For the Idea of the Morally-Good," J of the Hist of Philos 33 (95): 301-330; auth, "The Privileged Status of Interest in Nature's Beautiful Forms," in Proceedings of the Eighth Int Kant Congress, ed. Hoke Robinson (Milwaukee: Marquette Univ Press, 95): 787-792; auth, "Reason's Practical Idea of Perpetual Peace, Human Character, and the Pedagogical Function of the Republican Constitution," Idealistic Studies 26 (96): 101-134; auth, "Menschenfreundschaft: Friendship and Pedogogy in Kant," Eighteenth Century Studies 32 (98-99): 247-259; auth, Kant's Conception of Moral Character. The 'Critical' Link of Morality, Anthropology and Reflective Judgement, Univ of Chicago Press, 99. **CONTACT ADDRESS** Program of Lib Studies, Univ of Notre Dame, 358 Decio, Notre Dame, IN 46556. **EMAIL** Munzel.1@nd.edu

MUNZER, STEPHEN ROGER
PERSONAL Born 02/02/1944, Topeka, KS, m, 1982, 3 children **DISCIPLINE** LAW, PHILOSOPHY **EDUCATION** Univ Kans, BA, 66; Oxford Univ, BPhil, 69; Yale Univ Law Sch, JD, 72. **CAREER** Assoc, Covington & Burling, 72-73; Staff Atty, Legislative Drafting Res Fund, Columbia Law School, 73-74; Asst prof, Rutgers Col, Rutgers Univ, 74-77; Prof of Law, Univ of Minn, 80-81, Assoc prof, 77-80, Adj mem of Dept of Philos, 79-80; Vis prof of Law, UCLA, 80-81; Vis Prof of Law, Columbia Univ, 81-82; Prof of Law, UCLA, 82-. **HONORS AND AWARDS** Fel from the Nat Endowment for the Humanities, 91; David Baumgardt Memorial Fel (Am Philos Asn), 97-98, Berger Prize in the Philos of Law, 99. **MEMBERSHIPS** Am Soc Polit & Legal Philos. **RESEARCH** Property; legal and political philosophy; biotechnology **SELECTED PUBLICATIONS** Auth, Legal Validity, The Hague, Netherlands: Martinus Nijhoff, 72; auth, A Theory of Property, Cambridge: Cambridge Univ Press, 90; auth, "Transplantation, Chemical Inheritance, and the Identity of Organs," British Journal for the Philosophy of Science 45 (94): 555-70; auth, "An Uneasy Case Against Property Rights in Body Parts," Social Philosophy & Policy 11 (94): 259-86; auth, "Ellickson on Chronic Misconduct in Urban Spaces: Of Panhandlers, Bench Squatters, and Day Laborers," Harvard Civil Rights-Civil Liberties Law Review 32 (97): 1-48; auth, "Human Dignity and Property Rights in Human Body Parts," Property Problems: From Genes to Pension Funds, London: Kluwer Law International (97): 25-38; auth, "Property" Routledge Encyclopedia of Philosophy London and New York: Routledge (98): 757-61; auth, "The Special Case of Property Rights in Umbilical Cord Blood for Transplantation," Rutgers Law Review 51 (99): 493-568; auth, "Beggars of God: The Christian Ideal of Mendicancy," Journal of Religious Ethics 27 (99):

305-30; auth, "Poverty, Virtue, and Ideal," Angelicum 76 (99): 411-49. **CONTACT ADDRESS** Law Sch, Univ of California, Los Angeles, 405 Hilgard Ave, Los Angeles, CA 90095-1476. **EMAIL** munzer@mail.law.ucla.edu

MURDOCK, JONAH
PERSONAL Born 04/28/1969, New York, NY, m, 1998 **DISCIPLINE** PHILOSOPHY **EDUCATION** Northwestern Univ, PhD, 98 **CAREER** Research Asst, Northwestern Univ, present **MEMBERSHIPS** Amer Phil Assoc. **RESEARCH** Political philosophy; ethics; health care policy **CONTACT ADDRESS** Inst for Health Services Research and Policy Studi, Northwestern Univ, 629 Noyes St, Evanston, IL 60208-4170. **EMAIL** jmurdock@nwu.edu

MURNION, WILLIAM E.
PERSONAL Born 01/27/1933, New York, NY, m, 1969, 2 children **DISCIPLINE** PHILOSOPHY; RELIGIOUS STUDIES **EDUCATION** St Joseph's Sem, BA, 54; Gregorian Univ, STB, 56, STL, 58, PhD, 70. **CAREER** Instr, St John's Sem, 66-67; asst prof, Duquesne Univ, 67-68; fac fel, Boston Col, 68-69; asst prof, Newton Col, 69-72; Prof, Ramapo Col of NJ, 72-. **HONORS AND AWARDS** Fel, Inst for Ecumenical and Cultural Res, 74-75; dir, NEH Summer seminars for school teachers, 92, 95. **MEMBERSHIPS** Amer Philos Assoc; Amer Academy Relig; Soc for Ancient Greek Philos; Soc for Medieval Philos. **RESEARCH** Aquinas; philos of mind; philos of hist; philos of relig. **SELECTED PUBLICATIONS** Auth, Questions About the Family, in M. D. Bayles, R. C. Moffat, and J. Grcic, eds, Perspectives on the Family, Lewiston, NY: Edwin Mellon Press, 90; Aquinas on Revolution, in Werner Maihofer and Gerhard Sprenger, eds, Revolution and Human Rights, Archiv fur Rechts-und Sozialphilosophie, Beiheft 41, Stuttgart: Steiner Verlag, 90; The Foundations of Rights, in J. K. Roth and C. Peden, eds, Rights, Justice, and Community, Lewiston, NY: EDwin Mellon Press, 92; Multiculturalism and the Transformation of World History, J of Multicultural Ed of NJ 1, 93; The Phenomenology of Hegel's Concept of Religion, in Ugo Bianchi, ed, The Notion of Religion in Comparative Research: Selected Proceedings of the XVI IAHR Congress, Rome: L'Erma di Breitschneider, 94; Natural Law or Social Contract? The Foundation of Rights in Hobbes and Locke, in J. Ralph Lindgren, ed, Horizons of Justice: Critic of Institutions 8, NY: Peter Lang, 96; Aquinas's Earliest Philosophy of Mind: Mens in the Commentary on the Sentences and Other Contemporaneous Writings, in Jeremiah Hackett, ed, Aquinas on Mind and Intellect: New Essays, NY: Dowling Col Press, 96. **CONTACT ADDRESS** P.O. Box 23, Bellvale, NY 10912. **EMAIL** murnion@warwick.net

MURPHY, FREDERICK J.
DISCIPLINE RELIGIOUS STUDIES **EDUCATION** Harvard Univ, BA, 71, PhD, 84; Univ London, BD, 77. **CAREER** Tchg asst, Harvard Univ, 81-83; asst prof, 83-89; assoc prof, 89-94; prof, 94-. **MEMBERSHIPS** Soc Jesuit Col and Univ. **SELECTED PUBLICATIONS** Auth, The Structure and Meaning of Second Baruch, Scholars, 85; The Religious World of Jesus: An Introduction to Second Temple Palestinian Judaism, Abingdon, 91; Pseudo-Philo: Rewriting the Bible, Oxford, 93; The Book of Revelation, 94; Apocalypses and Apocalypticism: The State of the Question, 94; The Martial Option in Pseudo-Philo, 95. **CONTACT ADDRESS** Religious Dept, Col of the Holy Cross, Worcester, MA 01610-2395. **EMAIL** fmurphy@holycross.edu

MURPHY, JANE C.
PERSONAL Born 01/08/1953, Freeport, NY, m, 1979, 4 children **DISCIPLINE** LAW **EDUCATION** Boston Col, BA, 75; NYork Univ Sch Law, JD, 78. **CAREER** Instr, Georgetown Univ, 87-88; Adj Prof, Univ Md, 93; Asst Prof to Prof, Univ Baltimore, 88-. **HONORS AND AWARDS** Md Top 100 Women Awd, Daily Record, 99; Outstanding Teaching Awd, Univ Baltimore, 96; Rosalyn B. Bell Awd, Women's Law Ctr of Md, 95; Pro Bono Awd, Md Volunteer Lawyers Service, 89; Study Grant, Md Legal Services Corporation, 91-92; Grant, Kreiger Fund, 92-93 **MEMBERSHIPS** Am Asn of Law Schools, Clinical Legal Educ Asn, NY Univ School of Law Public Interest Law Foundation, Am Civil Liberties Union of Md, Women's Law Center of Md **RESEARCH** Domestic violence, Family law. **SELECTED PUBLICATIONS** Auth, Rules, Responsibility and Commitment to Children: The New Language of Morality in Family Law, Univ Pitt Law Review, 99; auth, Legal Images of Motherhood: Conflicting Definitions from Welfare Reform, Family and Criminal Law, Cornell Law Review, 98; auth, Legal Protections for Victims of Domestic Violence: A Guide for the Treating Physician, Maryland Medical Journal, 94; auth, "'M' is the Many Things that 'Mother' Means," The Baltimore Sun, 98; auth, "Assembly Bill to Speed Divorce After Abuse Will Save Many Lives," The Baltimore Sun, 98; auth, "The Myth of the Impartial Judge," Baltimore Sun, 93. **CONTACT ADDRESS** School of Law, Univ of Baltimore, 1420 N Charles St, Baltimore, MD 21201-5720.

MURPHY, JOHN F.
PERSONAL Born 04/25/1937, New York, NY, m, 1989, 2 children **DISCIPLINE** INTERNATIONAL LAW **EDUCATION** Cornell Univ, BA, 59; Cornell Law Sch, LLB, 62. **CAREER** Prof, Villanova Univ; taught, Aix-en Provence, London, Mexico City & Paris; past fel in the Afro-Asian Public serv Fel Prog, Govt India; past consult, Coun for Int Exchange Scholars; US Dept Justice; UN Crime Prevention Unit, Vienna, Austria; ABA Standing Comt on Law and Nat Security; US Dept State; UN Asn US Am; Comn on the Orgn Govt for the Conduct of For Policy; Int Task Force on Prevention of Nuclear Terrorism & Univ Microfilms Int. **HONORS AND AWARDS** Certificate of Merit, Amer Soc Int Law. **MEMBERSHIPS** ABA's Alternate Observer, US Mission to the UN; Coun ABA's Section Int Law and Practice, 94-96, 99; Intl Legal Scholar, 99-; exec coun, Amer Soc Int Law, 89-92; exec comt and vice pres, Amer Branch Int Law Asn; Panel of Arbitrators for the NY Stock Exchange. **RESEARCH** International law, international business transactions, international terrorism. **SELECTED PUBLICATIONS** Auth, Report of the Task Force on an International Criminal Court of the American Bar Association, 95; State Support of International Terrorism: Legal, Political, and Economic Dimensions, 89; Punishing International Terrorists: The Legal Framework for Policy Initiatives, 85; The United Nations and the Control of International Violence: A Legal and Political Analysis, 83 & Legal Aspects of International Terrorism: Summary Report of an International Conference, 80; coauth, The Constitutional Law of the European Union, 96; Instructor's Manual for the Constitutional Law of the European Union, 96; Teacher's Guide for the Regulation of International Business and Economic Relations, 92; The Regulation of International Business and Economic Relations, 91, 2nd ed, 99; & Legal Aspects of International Terrorism, 78. **CONTACT ADDRESS** Law School, Villanova Univ, 299 N. Springmill Rd., Villanova, PA 19085-1692. **EMAIL** murphy@law.vill.edu

MURPHY, JULIEN
DISCIPLINE PHILOSOPHY **EDUCATION** DePaul Univ, PhD, 82. **CAREER** Prof and assoc dean, Col of Arts and Sci; teaches in, women's stud prog and Honors prog. **RESEARCH** Contemporary continental philosophy; medical ethics; feminist theory. **SELECTED PUBLICATIONS** Publ chap, in 12 bk(s) on phenomenol, med, and recent French philosophy, unluding Feminist Interpretations of Simone de Beauvoir, Penn State UP, 95; auth, The Constructed Body: AIDS, Reproductive Technology, and Ethics, SUNY Press, 95; ed, Feminist Reinterpretations of Jean-Paul Sartre. **CONTACT ADDRESS** Dept of Philosophy, Univ of So Maine, 96 Falmouth St, PO Box 9300, Portland, ME 04104-9300. **EMAIL** jmurphy@usm.maine.edu

MURPHY, LARRY G.
PERSONAL Born 11/07/1946, Detroit, MI, m, 1967, 1 child **DISCIPLINE** AMERICAN AND AFRICAN AMERICAN RELIGIOUS HISTORY **CAREER** Lectr, African Amer studies, Univ Calif Berkeley, 72; lectr, hist dept, St. Mary's Col of Calif, 72-74; prof, hist of christ, Garrett-Evangelical Sem, 74-. **HONORS AND AWARDS** Henry McNeal Turner centennial lectr, Capetown, South Africa, 96. **MEMBERSHIPS** Soc for the Study of Black Relig; Oral Hist Asn; Amer Acad of Relig. **SELECTED PUBLICATIONS** Co-ed, Encyclopedia of African American Religions, Garland Press; ed, "Down by the Riverside": Readings in African Am Religion, NY Univ Press, 00. **CONTACT ADDRESS** 2121 Sheridan Rd., Evanston, IL 60201. **EMAIL** lmurphy1@nwu.edu

MURPHY, LAURENCE LYONS
PERSONAL Born 08/23/1948, New York, NY **DISCIPLINE** COMPARATIVE LITERATURE, PHILOSOPHY **EDUCATION** Rugers Univ, PhD, 90 **CAREER** Asst prof Intellectual Heritage, Philos, Temple Univ, Tyler Sch Art, 91- . **HONORS AND AWARDS** Merit Hons; Violet Keters awd for disting Srv and tchg. **MEMBERSHIPS** Amer Philos Asn **RESEARCH** Phenomenology, Hermeneutics. **SELECTED PUBLICATIONS** Exec ed, Ellipses, Jour Arts and Ideas. **CONTACT ADDRESS** Intellectual Heritage Prog, Col of Liberal Arts, Temple Univ, 214 Anderson Hall, 1114 W-Berks St, Philadelphia, PA 19122-6090. **EMAIL** laurence_murphy@hotmail.com

MURPHY, LIAM BERESFORD
PERSONAL Born 06/30/1960, Melbourne, Australia **DISCIPLINE** LAW, PHILOSOPHY **EDUCATION** Univ Melbourne, BA, 82; LLB, 84; Columbia Univ, MPhil, 90; PhD, 91. **CAREER** Assoc prof of Law, New York Univ, 98-00, prof, 00-. **HONORS AND AWARDS** Ed bd, Melbourne Univ Law Rev, 84; Commonwealth Postgraduate Res Awd, 85; Fulbright Travel Awd, 85-90; Whiting Fel in the Humanities, 89-90; Diss passed with distinction, 90. **MEMBERSHIPS** Auth, "The Demands of Beneficence," Philos and Public Affairs, 22 (93): 267-92; auth, "Liberty, Equality, Well-Being: Rakowski on Wealth-Transfer Taxation," Tax Law Rev, 51 (96): 473; auth, "A Relatively Plausible Principle of Beneficence: Reply to Mulgan," Philos and Public Affairs, 26 (97): 80-86; auth, "Help and Beneficence," in Edward Craig, ed, Routledge Encyclopedia of Philos, London and New York: Routledge (98); auth, "Comment on Scheffler's 'The Conflict Between Justice and Responsibility'," in Ian Shapiro and Lea Brilmayer, eds, Nomos XLI: Global Justice, NY: NY Univ Press (99): auth, "Institutions and the Demands of Justice," Philos and Public Affairs, 27 (98): 251-291; auth, "International Justice: Redistribution and Entitlement," to appear in a projected collection of papers from the conf on Cosmopolitanism and Nationalism, Stanford Univ, April 99, ed by Debra Satz (forthcoming); auth, "The Political Question of the Concept of Law," forthcoming in a collection of articles devoted to H. L. A. Hart's Postscript to the second edition of The Concept of Law, edited by Jules Coleman; auth, Moral Demands in Nonideal Theory, NY: Oxford Univ Press (2000). **CONTACT ADDRESS** Sch of Law, New York Univ, 40 Washington Sq S, New York, NY 10012-1005.

MURPHY, MARK CHRISTOPHER
PERSONAL Born 10/14/1968, Coral Gables, FL, m, 1992, 1 child **DISCIPLINE** PHILOSOPHY **EDUCATION** Univ Texas, BA, 88; Univ Notre Dame, MA, 92, PhD, 93. **CAREER** Asst prof Philos, Univ Hawaii, 93-95; asst prof Philos, Georgetown Univ, 95-; Erasmus fel, 98-99. **MEMBERSHIPS** APA; Soc Christian Philos; ACPA. **RESEARCH** Ethics; Political philosophy; Philosophy of law; History of early modern philosophy. **SELECTED PUBLICATIONS** Auth Deviant Uses of Obligation in Hobbes Leviathan, Hist of Philos Quart, 94; Acceptance of Authority and the Requirement to Comply with Just Institutions: A Comment on Waldron, Philos & Pub Affairs, 94; Philosophical Anarchism and Legal Indifference, Am Philos Quart, 95; Was Hobbes a Legal Positivist? Ethics, 95; Self-Evidence, Human Nature, and Natural Law, Am Cath Philos Quart, 95; Hobbes on Conscientious Disobedience, Archiv fur Geschichte der Philos, 95; Natural Law, Impartialism, and Others Good, Thomist, 96; Consent, Custon, and the Common Good in Aquinas Theory of Political Authority, Rev Politics, 97; Surrender of Judgment and the Consent Theory of Political Authority, Law and Philos, 97; Divine Command, Divine Will, and Moral Obligation, Faith and Philos, 98. **CONTACT ADDRESS** Philosophy Dept, Georgetown Univ, 215 New North, Washington, DC 20057. **EMAIL** murphym@gunet.georgetown.edu

MURPHY, NANCEY
PERSONAL Born 06/12/1951, Alliance, NE **DISCIPLINE** PHILOSOPHY; THEOLOGY **EDUCATION** Creighton Univ, BA, 73; Univ Calif Berkeley, PhD, 80; Graduate Theological Union, ThD, 87. **CAREER** Lecturer, Dominican School of Philosophy and Theology, 87-88; visiting asst prof of religion, Whittier Coll, 88-89; asst prof, 89-91, assoc prof, 91-98, prof, 98-, Christian philosophy, Fuller Theological Seminary. **HONORS AND AWARDS** Creighton Univ Alumni Achievement Awd, 98; Templeton Awd, for Theology in the Age of Scientific Reasoning; American Acad of Religion Book Awd for Excellence in the Constructive-Reflective Category, for Theology in the Age of Scientific Reasoning; National Science Found Fellow, 3 years; President's Scholar, Creighton Univ. **MEMBERSHIPS** Amer Philos Assn; Soc Christian Philosophers; Center Theology Natural Scis. **RESEARCH** Current Anglo-American philosophy; philosophy of religion; relation between science and religion. **SELECTED PUBLICATIONS** Coauth, On the Moral Nature of the Universe: Theology, Cosmology, and Ethics, 96; auth, Anglo-American Postmodernity: Philosophical Perspectives on Science, Religion, and Ethics, 97; auth, Reconciling Theology and Science: A Radical Reformation Perspective, 97; coauth, Virtues and Practices in the Christian Tradition: Christian Ethics after MacIntyre, 97; coauth, Whatever Happened to the Soul? Scientific and Theological Portraits of Human Nature, 98 **CONTACT ADDRESS** Fuller Theol Sem, 135 N Oakland Ave, Pasadena, CA 91182. **EMAIL** nmurphy@fuller.edu

MURPHY, ROMALLUS O.
PERSONAL Born 12/18/1928, Oakdale, LA, m **DISCIPLINE** LAW **EDUCATION** Howard Univ, BA 1951; Univ NC, JD 1956. **CAREER** Pvt law prac 1956-62; Erie Human Rel Commn, exec dir 1962-65; Mitchell & Murphy, 65-70; Mayor's Comm Rel Committee, exec secr 1968; Shaw Univ, spec asst to pres 1968-70; Shaw Coll at Detroit, pres 1970-82; Gen Counsel NC State Conf of Branches NAACP; gen practice emphasis on civil rights; private practice, atty 1983-. **HONORS AND AWARDS** Omega Man of the Year 1968; Detroit Howardite for Year Howard Univ Alumni 1974; Key to City Positive Futures Inc New Orleans 1974; Citizen of the Year Awd Omega Psi Phi 1977; Community Serv Awd Greensboro Br NAACP 1985; Tar Heel of the Week NC; Educator of the Year, Gamma Phi Delta Sorority, 1975; William Robert Ming Advocacy Awd, NAACP, 1990. **MEMBERSHIPS** Mem Intermittent consult conciliator 1966-69; Amer Arbitration Assoc, Arbitrators & Community Dispute Settlement Panel, ACE, AAHE, NBL, NEA, Positive Futures Inc, Task Force Detroit Urban League Inc, NAACP; bd mem Metro Fund Inc; mem Central Governing Bd & Educ Com Model Neighborhood Agency; charter mem Regional Citizens Inc; mem Greensboro Task Force One; bd mem Good News Jail & Prison Ministry; trustee, sec trust bd Shiloh Baptist Church; pres Laymen's League Shiloh Baptist Church; mem Omega Psi Phi; bd mem Greensboro Br NAACP; mem Foreign Travel for Intl Commun Agency & other govt agencies in South Africa, Zambia, Nigeria & Kenya; partic Smithsonian InstTravel Seminar in India; mem NC Assn Amer Bar Assn, NC Black Lawyers Assn. **CONTACT ADDRESS** PO Box 20383, Greensboro, NC 27420.

MURPHY, TIM
PERSONAL Born Kileen, TX **DISCIPLINE** THEORIES OF RELIGION **EDUCATION** Wichita State Univ, BA, 84; Univ Calif Santa Cruz, PhD, 97. **CAREER** Instr, Univ Calif Santa Cruz, 91-96; adjunct prof, San Jose State Univ, 96-97; fellow, Case Western Reserve Univ, 97-. **HONORS AND AWARDS** Undergraduate Student Govt Undergraduate Teaching Excellence Awd; mellon postdoctoral fel, cwru, 97-00. **MEMBERSHIPS** North Am Asn for the Study of Relig; Am Acad of Relig; North Am Nietzsche Soc **RESEARCH** Nineteenth-century German religious thought; Philosophy of religion; Religious theory; Postmodern cultural theory. **SELECTED PUBLICATIONS** Ed, Postmodernism and the Study of Religion: A Reader, 99; "Nietzsche's Jesus" in Epoche, 98; "The Concept of Entwicklung in German Religionswissenschaft Before and After Darwin," 98; auth, Nietzche, Metaphor, Relig, SUNY Press, 01. **CONTACT ADDRESS** Dept of Religion, Case Western Reserve Univ, 10900 Euclid Ave, Cleveland, OH 44106-7112. **EMAIL** txm55@po.cwru.edu

MURRAY, J. GLENN
PERSONAL Born 04/22/1950, Philadelphia, PA, s **DISCIPLINE** THEOLOGY **EDUCATION** St Louis University, BA, 1974; Jesuit School of Theology at Berkeley, MDiv, 1979; Aquinas Institute, MA, 1996; Catholic Theological Union of Chicago, DMin, 1996. **CAREER** St Frances Academy, asst principal, 81-88; Office for Pastoral Liturgy, asst dir, 89-; St Mary Seminary, homiletics professor, 92-. **HONORS AND AWARDS** Archdiocese of Baltimore, Youth Ministry Medal of Honor, 1988. **MEMBERSHIPS** National Black Catholic Clergy Caucus, 1979-; Catholic Assn of Teachers of Homiletics, 1992-; Academy of Homiletics, 1992-; North American Academy of Liturgy, 1993-; Black Catholic Theological Symposium, 1994-. **CONTACT ADDRESS** Office for Pastoral Liturgy, 1031 Superior Ave., Ste 361, Cleveland, OH 44114.

MURRELL, NATHANIEL SAMUEL
PERSONAL Born 02/20/1945, Grenada, m, 1982, 3 children **DISCIPLINE** RELIGION, PHILOSOPHY **EDUCATION** Wheaton Col, MA, 81; Drew Univ, MPhil, 86; PhD, 88; Rutgers Univ, EdM, 91. **CAREER** Vis Prof, CAribbean Grad Sch of Theol, 86-91; Asst Prof, Col of Wooster, 91-95; Asst Prof, Univ NC, 95-. **HONORS AND AWARDS** AAR Awd, 97; Prof of the Week, Univ NC, 98. **MEMBERSHIPS** AAR, SBL, ASR, SSBR. **RESEARCH** Caribbean studies and religion, Africana studies, Hebrew Bible. **SELECTED PUBLICATIONS** Auth, Chanting Down Babylon: The Rastifari Reader, Temple UP, 98; auth, Religious Politics and the Bible, St Martins Pr, 00; auth, Introduction to Afro-Caribbean Religions, Temple UP, forthcoming. **CONTACT ADDRESS** Dept Relig & Philos, Univ of No Carolina, Wilmington, 601 S College Rd, Wilmington, NC 28403-3201. **EMAIL** murrells@uncwil.edu

MURZAKU, INES A.
PERSONAL Born 06/02/1964, Tirana, Albania, m, 1987, 2 children **DISCIPLINE** ORIENTAL CHURCH HISTORY **EDUCATION** Ponitfical Oriental Institute, PhD, 95. **CAREER** Asst prof, Acad Arts, Tirana-Albania, 86-91; journalist, East Europe - Vatican Radio, 92-94; Adj Prof, St. John Fisher Col, 96- . **HONORS AND AWARDS** Prestigious Grant for Doctoral Studies, 91-95. **MEMBERSHIPS** AAUP, AAR, AHA, ACHA, AAASS, ASN. **RESEARCH** East Europe: religion, history and culture, Jesuit History, Albanian history, religious values and contemporary society, women in the church. **SELECTED PUBLICATIONS** Auth, Angazhimi yne Shoqeror, 94; auth, Religion in Post-Communist Albania, Missioni e Popoli, 94; auth, The Activity and the Role of the Jesuits in the Albanian History and Culture 1841-1946, 96; The Flying Mission (Missione Volante), Diakonia; The Beginning of the Jesuit Albanian Mission, Diakonia. **CONTACT ADDRESS** Religious Studies Dept, Seton Hall Univ, So Orange, 40 S Orange Ave, South Orange, NJ 07079. **EMAIL** murzakui@shu.edu

MUSCARI, PAUL G.
PERSONAL Born 11/09/1940, Brooklyn, NY, m, 1974, 2 children **DISCIPLINE** PHILOSOPHY **EDUCATION** NYork Univ, PhD, 73. **HONORS AND AWARDS** NEH Fel, Case Western Res; NEH Fel, State Univ NY,82; NEH Gnt, 86; SUNY Gnt, 86; Dist Prof Awd, 91; NEH Fel, Penn State, 94; IAP Res Awd; Chan Awd, State Univ NY; Teach Year Awd, Adirondack Comm Coll; Founders Day Awd. **MEMBERSHIPS** IAPR; APPE. **RESEARCH** Biomedical ethics; philosophy of mind. **SELECTED PUBLICATIONS** Auth, The Artist and the Madman," Man and World 20 (87): 385-397; auth, "Science and Creativity," Contem Philo 15 (93): 10-13; auth, "A Critique of "Changing The World," "J Mind and Behavior 16 (95): 99-102; auth, "Subjective Experience," Philosophical Inquiry, 34 (92):12-33; auth, "Plea for the Poetic Metaphor," J Mind and Behavior 13 (92): 233-246; auth, "The Depersonalization of Creativity," J of Mind and Behavior 15 (94) 311-322. **CONTACT ADDRESS** Dept Humanities, Adirondack Comm Col, 439 Bay Rd, Queensbury, NY 12804-1408.

MUSGROVE, PHILIP
PERSONAL Born 09/04/1940, Dallas, TX, m, 1989, 2 children **DISCIPLINE** MATHEMATICS, ECONOMICS **EDUCATION** Haverford Col , BA, summa cum laude, 62; Princeton Univ, MPA, 64; MIT, PhD, 74. **CAREER** Res asst , 64-68, res assoc, 71-76, 78-81, Brookings Institution; tech coordinator, ECIEL Program of Joint Studies of Latin Amer Integration, 66-68, 71-80; consultant, Banco Central de Venezuela and Corporacion Venezolana de Guayana, 75-79; assoc prof lecturer, Dept of Econ, George Wash Univ, 74, 76-78; vis asst prof, Dept of Economics, Univ Fla, 75; staff assoc, Resources for the Future, 77-78; adjunct prof, Latin Amer Program, applied economics, Amer Univ, 78-84; consultant, US Dept of Agriculture, Office of Nutrition Economics, 79-82; regional advisor in health economics, 82-90, Pan Amer Health Orgn; consultant, Development Res Center, 71-73, 74, Living Standards Measurement Study, 81, Tech Dept, Latin Am and Caribbean Region, 90-93, World Development Report, 92-93; health economist to sr economist to principal economist, 90-, Resident Mission in Brasilia, Brazil, 96-98, World Bank; seconded to World Health org, Geneva, 99-01. **MEMBERSHIPS** Scientific and Tech Advisory Coun, Brazilian Natl Food and Nutrition Inst, 86-90; Advisory Coun on Scientific Publications, Pan Amer Health Org, 87-91, chm, 89-90; Advisory Coun to Pres of the Maternal and Child Health Inst of Pernambuco (Recife), 89-. **RESEARCH** Health economics, with emphasis on Latin America. **SELECTED PUBLICATIONS** Ed, World Health Report 2000, World Health org, 00; auth, "Public Spending on Health Care: How are Different Criteria Related?," Health policy 47 (99); auth, "Economic Crisis and Health Policy Response," in Demographic Responses to Economic Adjustment in Latin America, 97; auth, "Equitable Allocation of Ceilings on Public Investment," Human Capital Development Working Paper, World Bank (96); auth, "Public and Private Roles in Health: Theory and Financing Patterns," Discussion Paper no. 339, World Bank (96); auth, "Cost-Effectiveness and the Socialization of Health Care," Health Policy 32 (95); auth, "Reformas al Sector Salud en Chile: Contexto, Logica y Posibles Caminos," in La Salud en el Siglo Veintiuno, Cambios Necesarios (95). **CONTACT ADDRESS** World Bank, 1818 H St, NW, Washington, DC 20433. **EMAIL** pmusgrove@worldbank.org

MUTCHLER, DAVID EDWARD
PERSONAL Born 06/21/1941, Lexington, KY, m, 1979, 3 children **DISCIPLINE** POLITICAL SCIENCE **EDUCATION** PhD WA Univ (ST Louis) 70. **CAREER** Sr Foreign Service Offical US Agency for Intl Devel USAID 27yrs Incl Sr Adv Cord for Cuba, 97-98; Mission Dir for Panama, 94-96. **MEMBERSHIPS** Assoc for the Study of the Cuban. **CONTACT ADDRESS** Sr Adv/Coordinator for Cuba, Ronald Reagan Building, 1300 Pennsylvania Ave. N.W. Fifth Floor 5 8A, Washington, DC 20523. **EMAIL** damutchler@usaid.gov

MUZOREWA, GWINYAL
PERSONAL Born, Zimbabwe, m, 1976, 4 children **DISCIPLINE** THEOLOGY **EDUCATION** Union Theol Sem, PhD, 83. **CAREER** Lectr, 81-84, acad dean, 85-85, 91-94, United Theol Col, Harare; assoc prof, United Theol Sem, 88-90; prof relig, Lincoln Univ, 98- ; Prof and dept chair. **HONORS AND AWARDS** Phi Theta Capa; Maslow Fel, 77-78. **MEMBERSHIPS** Clergy of the United Methodist Church; Ecumenical Asn of Third World Theol; Acad Am Relig. **RESEARCH** African and African American religion and theology. **SELECTED PUBLICATIONS** Auth, The Origin and Development of African Theology, Orbis; auth, An African Theology of Mission, Mellen. **CONTACT ADDRESS** Dept of Religion, Lincoln Univ, Pennsylvania, 1570 Old Baltimore Pike, PO Box 179, Lincoln University, PA 19352-0004. **EMAIL** gmuzorewa@lu.lincoln.edu

MYERS, CHARLES EDWARD
PERSONAL Born 02/01/1955, Pasadena, CA, m **DISCIPLINE** BIBLICAL STUDIES, ETHICS, THEOLOGY **EDUCATION** Univ Calif, Berkley, BA, 78; Grad Theol Union, Berkeley, MA, 84. **CAREER** Lectr, nonviolence, Sch of Applied Theol, 80; adj fac, liberation theol, Immaculate Heart Col, 86, 88; adj fac, ethics and New Testament, Sch Theol, Claremont, CA, 93; adj fac, ethics and New Testament, Fuller Sch Theol, Pasadena, 93-96; lect, Churches of Christ Theol Col, Melbourne, Australia, 97. **HONORS AND AWARDS** Phi Beta Kappa, 78. **MEMBERSHIPS** Soc for Bibl Lit. **RESEARCH** Ethics and the Bible. **SELECTED PUBLICATIONS** Auth, The Ideology and Social Strategy of Mark's Gospel, in Gottwald, ed, The Bible and Liberation: Political and Social Hermeneutics, Orbis, 93; auth, I Will Ask You A Question: Interrogatory Theology, in Hauerwas, ed, Theology Without Foundations: Religions Practice and the Future of Theological Truth, Abingdon, 94; co-auth, Say to This Mountain, Mark's Story of Discipleship, Proclamation 6, Year B, Pentecost 1, 96; auth, Who Will Roy Away the Stone? Queries for First World Christians, Mayknoll: Orbis, 94; co-auth, The American Journey, 1492-1992: A Call to Conversion, Eerie, PA: Pax Christi Pr, 94; co-auth, Resisting the Serpent: Palau's Struggle for Self-Determination, Baltimore: Fortkamp Pr, 90; auth, Binding the Strong Man: A Political Reading of Mark's Story of Jesus, Maryknoll: Orvis, 88; auth, Beyond the Addict's Excuse: Public Addiction and Ecclesial Recovery, The Other Side of Sin, NY: SUNY Pr, 01; auth, Proclaiming Good News in Hard Times: Reflections on Evangelism and the Bible, Athol Gill Festschrift, Melbourne, Australia, 01. **CONTACT ADDRESS** 706 Burwood Terr, Los Angeles, CA 90042. **EMAIL** chedmyers@igc.apc.org

MYERS, DAVID
DISCIPLINE RELIGIOUS HISTORY **EDUCATION** Yale Univ, PhD. **CAREER** Assoc prof, Fordham Univ. **HONORS AND AWARDS** Herzog Aug Bibliothek Res Fel 99-00; Nat Endowment for the Humanities Fel, 01-02; reviewer, chicago tribune bk rev. **RESEARCH** History of sin and crime in early modern Europe. **SELECTED PUBLICATIONS** Auth, Poor, Sinning Folk: Confession and the Making of Consciences in Counter-Reformation Germany, Cornell UP, 96; Die Jesuiten die Beichte, und die katholische Reformation in Bayern, Beitge zur altbayerischen Kirchengeschichte 96; Ritual, Confession, and Religion in Early Sixteenth-Century Germany, Arch fur Reformationsgeschichte, 97. **CONTACT ADDRESS** Dept of Hist, Fordham Univ, Bronx, NY 10458. **EMAIL** dmyers@fordham.edu

MYERS, DAVID G.
PERSONAL Born 02/27/1952 **DISCIPLINE** ENGLISH, JEWISH STUDIES **EDUCATION** Univ Calif at Santa Cruz, BA, 74; Wash Univ, AM, 77; Northwestern Univ, PhD, 89. **CAREER** From asst prof to assoc prof, Tex A&M Univ, 89-. **MEMBERSHIPS** Asn for Jewish Studies. **RESEARCH** Holocaust literature and reception and their interaction with the history of ideas. **SELECTED PUBLICATIONS** Auth, The Elephants Teach: Creative Writing Since 1880, Prentice Hall, 96; co-ed, Unrelenting Readers: The New Poet-Critics, Story Line Press, forthcoming. **CONTACT ADDRESS** Dept English, Texas A&M Univ, Col Station, College Station, TX 77843-0001. **EMAIL** dgmyers@tamu.edu

MYERS, GERALD E.
PERSONAL Born 06/19/1923, Central City, NE, m, 1948, 1 child **DISCIPLINE** PHILOSOPHY **EDUCATION** Haveland Col, AB, 47; Brown Univ, MA, 49, PhD, 54. **CAREER** Inst/Asst Prof, Williams Col, 52-61; Assoc Prof, Chmn Phil Dept, Kerry Col, 61-65; Prof, LIU, 65-67; Prof, Deputy Exec Off, Queens Col, CUNY, 67-91; Phil in Residence, Hon Dir, Amer Dance Festival, Durham, NC, 77-; Retired Emeritus Prof, 91. **HONORS AND AWARDS** NEH fel, 82-83. **MEMBERSHIPS** APA, Phi Beta Kappa **RESEARCH** Philosophy of psychology; american philosophy; aesthetics. **SELECTED PUBLICATIONS** Echoes From the Holocaust; Phil Reflect on a Dark Time, 88; The Black Tradition in American Modern Dance, 88-90; Reflections on the Home of An Art Form, Amer Dance Fest 65th Ann, 98. **CONTACT ADDRESS** 36 Gardner Ave, New London, CT 06320.

MYERS, JOHNNIE D.
PERSONAL Born 12/18/1948, Macon, GA, d, 2 children **DISCIPLINE** CRIMINAL JUSTICE **EDUCATION** Clark Atlanta Univ, BA, 70; Ga State Univ, 76; Clark Atlanta Univ, PhD, 95. **CAREER** Instr, Kennesaw State Univ, 77-83; Asst Prof, Albany State Col, 83-88; Assoc Prof/Chair, Morris Brown Col, 88-. **HONORS AND AWARDS** Patricia Roberts Harris Fel; Golden Key Nat Hon Soc. **MEMBERSHIPS** Am Correctional Asn, Nat Asn of Blacks in Criminal Justice. **RESEARCH** Women in Criminal Justice, Black Women Judges. **SELECTED PUBLICATIONS** Auth, "Criminal Justice," Ga Legislative Rev, 93-00. **CONTACT ADDRESS** Dept Criminal Justice, Morris Brown Col, 643 Martin King Jr Dr, Atlanta, GA 30314. **EMAIL** jmyers@morrisbrown.edu

MYERS, MICHAEL W.
PERSONAL Born 12/27/1951, Spokane, WA, d, 3 children **DISCIPLINE** PHILOSOPHY **EDUCATION** Univ Wash, BA, 74; Gonzaga Univ, MA, 81; Univ Haw, PhD, 90. **CAREER** Assoc prof, Wash State Univ, 91-. **MEMBERSHIPS** Soc for Asian & Comparative Philos. **RESEARCH** Philosophy of Religion, Indian Philosophy, Comparative Philosophical Theology. **SELECTED PUBLICATIONS** Auth, Let the Cow Wander: modeling the Metaphors in Veda and Vedanta, Univ of Haw Press (Honolulu, HI), 95; auth, Brahman: A Comparative Theology, Curzon Press, 00. **CONTACT ADDRESS** Dept Philos, Washington State Univ, PO Box 645130, Pullman, WA 99164-5130.

MYERS, ROBERT
DISCIPLINE PHILOSOPHY **EDUCATION** Queen's Univ, Canada, BA, 80; Univ Cal Berkeley, PhD, 89. **CAREER** Vis asst prof, NYork Univ, 88-89; vis asst prof, Barnard Col, 89-92; asst prof, Barnard Col, 92-. **RESEARCH** Moral philosophy. **SELECTED PUBLICATIONS** Auth, " Prerogatives and Restrictions from the Cooperative Point of View," Ethics 105 (94): 128-152; auth, :On the Explanation, the Justification and the Interpretation of Action," Nous 29 (95): 212-231; auth, "The Inescapability of Moral Reasons," Philos Phenomenol Res 59 (99): 281-307; auth, Self-Governance and Cooperation, Oxford Univ Press (Oxford), 99. **CONTACT ADDRESS** Dept Philos, Barnard Col, 3009 Broadway, New York, NY 10027-6501. **EMAIL** rmyers@barnard.edu

MYERS, WILLIAM R.
PERSONAL Born 06/19/1942, Oil City, PA, m, 1964, 3 children **DISCIPLINE** THEOLOGY **EDUCATION** Westminster Col, BA, 64; Pittsburgh Theological Sem, Mdiv, 67; MA.ed, Rhode Island Col; Ed.d, 81, Loyola Univ. **CAREER** Dir of

Leadership Education, The Association of Theological Schools in The United States and Canada, 99-; Academic Dean and Prof, Religious Education, 81-99, Chicago Theological Sem. **CONTACT ADDRESS** Chicago Theol Sem, 10 Summit Park Dr., Pittsburgh, PA 15275-1103. **EMAIL** myers@ats.edu

MYRICKS, NOEL
PERSONAL Born 12/22/1935, Chicago, IL, w **DISCIPLINE** LAW **EDUCATION** San Francisco State Univ, BA 1965, MS 1967; Howard Univ, JD 1970; The American Univ, EdD 1974. **CAREER** Howard Univ, prof 67-69; Univ of Dist of Columbia, educ administrator 69-72; Private Practice, attorney 73-; (admitted to practice before US Supreme Court); Univ of Maryland, prof beginning 72, Assoc Prof, currently. **HONORS AND AWARDS** Appointed by Pres Jimmy Carter Natl Adv Council on Extension and Cont Educ 1978-81; Outstanding & Dedicated Serv to Youth & Community Easton, PA NAACP 1984; Outstanding Citizen of the Year Omega Psi Phi Frat Columbia, MD 1979; Faculty Minority Achievement Awd, President's Commission on Ethnic Minority Issues, Univ of Maryland, 1990; Outstanding Advisor for a Student Organization, Campus Activities Office of Maryland, 1990; Superior Teaching Awd, Office of the Dean for Undergraduate Studies, Univ of Maryland, 1990; Outstanding Mentor, UMCP, 1992; Outstanding Teacher of the Year, UMCP, 1992; Univ of MD at Coll Park Natl Championship Intercollegiate Mock Trial Team, coach/dir, 1992, 1993, 1996, 1998; Outstanding Teacher, Coll of Health & Human Performance, 1998; Outstanding Mentor, Omicron Delta Kappa, 1998. **MEMBERSHIPS** Certified agent NFL Players Assn 1984-; assoc editor Family Relations Journal 1978-82; mem, Kappa Upsilon Lambda, Alpha Phi Alpha, Reston, MD, 1984-; mem, American Bar Assn; mem, Groves Assn; educator, attorney coach, National Intercollegiate Mock Trial Champions, UMCP, 1992; Omicron Delta Kappa Honor Society, 1992. **RESEARCH** Family law, children's legal rights, and mediation. **SELECTED PUBLICATIONS** Auth, Race and child custody disputes, Family Relations, 35,(2), (86): 325-328; auth, Legalizing gay and lesbian marriages: Trends and policy implications, American Journal of Family Law, 9(1), (95): 35-44; auth, Same-sex marriage: An idea whose time has come? In Wiley Family Law Update 1997, New York: John Wiley & Sons, Inc, 97. **CONTACT ADDRESS** Univ of Maryland, Reston, Marie Mount Hall, Rm 1218, Reston, VA 20742. **EMAIL** nm24@umail.umd.edu

MYRVOLD, WAYNE C.
DISCIPLINE PHILOSOPHY **EDUCATION** McGill Univ, BS, 84; Boston Univ, PhD, 94. **CAREER** Asst prof, Univ of Western Ontario. **RESEARCH** Philosophy of physics; philosophy of mathematics; philosophy of biology. **SELECTED PUBLICATIONS** Auth, The Decision Problem for Entanglement, Kluwer, 97; Bayesianism and Diverse Evidence: A Reply to Andrew Wayne, Philos Sci, 96; Computability in Quantum Mechanics, Kluwer, 95; Peirce on Cantor's Paradox and the Continuum, 95; Tractatus 4.04: (Compare Hertz' Mechanics, on Dynamical Models, Verlag Holder-Pichler-Tempsky, 90. **CONTACT ADDRESS** Dept of Philosophy, Univ of Western Ontario, London, ON, Canada N6A 5B8. **EMAIL** wmyrvold@julian.uwo.ca

N

NADEAU, RANDALL
PERSONAL Born 04/30/1956, Lancaster, PA, m, 1987, 2 children **DISCIPLINE** RELIGION **EDUCATION** Oberlin Col, BA, 78; Princeton Univ, MA, 80; Univ British Columbia, PhD, 90. **CAREER** Assoc prof East Asian Relig, Trinity Univ, 90-. **MEMBERSHIPS** Asn Asian Studies; Am Acad Relig. **RESEARCH** Chinese religions; Buddhism; comparative religion. **SELECTED PUBLICATIONS** Auth, Dimensions of Sacred Space in Japanese Popular Culture, Intercultural Commun Studies, 97; auth, Frederick Streng, Madhyamika, and the Comparative Study of Religion, Buddhist-Christian Studies, 96; auth, Xunzi, Wang Chong, Wang Yang-ming, Great Thinkers of the Eastern World, 95; auth, The Domestication of Precious Scrolls: The Ssu-ming Tsao-chun pao-chuan, Jour Chinese Relig, 94; auth, Genre Classifications of Chinese Popular Religious Literature: Pao-chuan, Jour Chinese Relig, 93. **CONTACT ADDRESS** Dept of Religion, Trinity Univ, 715 Stadium Dr., San Antonio, TX 78212-3422. **EMAIL** rnadeau@trinity.edu

NAFZIGER, E. WAYNE
PERSONAL Born 08/14/1938, Bloomington, IL, m, 1966, 2 children **DISCIPLINE** ECONOMICS **EDUCATION** Goshen Col, BA, 60; Univ Mich, MA, 62; Univ Ill, PhD, 67. **CAREER** Res Assoc, Univ Nigeria, 64-65; from asst prof to Univ Distinguished Prof, Kans St Univ, 66-; vis prof, Intl Univ Japan, 83; Commerce Bank Distinguished Grad Fac, Kans St Univ, 96-. **HONORS AND AWARDS** East-West Center Fel, 72-73; Fulbright prof, Andhra Univ, India, 70-71; Mid_Amer Univ Assoc Honor Lctr, Kans St Univ, 84-85; Commerce Bank Distinguished Grad Fac, Kans St Univ, 96-; Sen Res Fel, UN Univ/World Inst for Develop Economics Res, 96-98; Hewlett Vis Fel, Carter Center Emory Univ, 91; Choice Outstanding Acad Book Awd, 89-90. **MEMBERSHIPS** Amer Econ Assoc; Amer Assoc Univ Professors; Assoc Evolutionary Econ; Assoc Indian Economics Studies; Assoc Asian Studies; Fulbright Assoc **RESEARCH** Economics of Conflict; Economic Development and Income Distribution; Comparative Economic Development. **SELECTED PUBLICATIONS** auth, Poverty and Wealth: Comparing Afro-Asian Development, JAI Pr, 94; auth, Learning from the Japanese: Japan's Prewar Development and the Third World, ME Sharpe, 95; auth, The Economics of Developing Countries, Prentice Hall, 97; auth, Fathers, Sons, and Daughters: Industrial Entrepreneus During India's Liberalization, JAI Pr, 98; ed, War, Hunger, and Displacement, Oxford Univ Pr, 00. **CONTACT ADDRESS** Dept of Economics, Kansas State Univ, 327 Waters Hall, Manhattan, KS 66506. **EMAIL** nafwayne@ksu.edu

NAFZIGER, JAMES A. R.
PERSONAL Born 09/24/1940, Minneapolis, MN **DISCIPLINE** INTERNATIONAL LAW **EDUCATION** Univ Wis, BA, 62, MA, 69; Harvard Univ, JD, 67. **CAREER** Clerk, US District Ct, 67-69; fel, Am Soc Int Law, 69-70 & admin dir, 70-74; vis assoc prof law, Univ Ore, 74-77; Prof Law, Willamette Univ, Ore, 77-, lectr, Sch Law, Cath Univ, 70-74; Fulbright vis prof, Nat Univ Mex, 78; lectr & tutor, Inst Pub Int Law & Int Relations, Univ Thessaloniki, Greece, 82; Thomas B Stoel prof law & dir intl progs, Willamette University Coll of Law, 98. **HONORS AND AWARDS** Burlington Northern Awd for Excellence in Teaching & Scholar; Univ Resident's Awd for Excellence in Scholar. **MEMBERSHIPS** Assn Am Law Schs; Am Soc Int Law; Int Law Assn. **RESEARCH** Public international law; immigration law and policy; conflict of laws, international business transactions. **SELECTED PUBLICATIONS** Auth, Conflict of Laws 85; auth, International Sports Law, 88. **CONTACT ADDRESS** Col of Law, Willamette Univ, 245 Winter St, SE, Salem, OR 97301-3900.

NAG, MONI
PERSONAL Born 04/01/1925, India, m, 1964, 1 child **DISCIPLINE** ANTHROPOLOGY; PUBLIC HEALTH; POPULATION; STATISTICS **EDUCATION** Calcutta Univ, M.SC, 46; Yale Univ, MA, 59, Yale Univ, PhD, 61 **CAREER** Adjunct prof Anthropol, Columbia Univ, 76-; senior assoc, Population Council, 76-92 **HONORS AND AWARDS** Fyfe Scholar, Scottish Church Col Calcutta, 42-44; Fulbright Travel Grant, 57-61; Brady, Boies Fel, Yale Univ, 57-58; Univ Fel, Yale Univ, 58-59; Boies Fel, Yale Univ, 59-60; Fel from Committee of Res on Sex, National Res Coun, 60-61 **RESEARCH** Statistics; Anthropology; Population; Health. **SELECTED PUBLICATIONS** Auth, Sexual Behavior and AIDS in India, Vikas, 96; auth, "Sexual behaviour in India with risk of HIV/AIDS transmission," Health Transmission Rev; coauth, Listening to Women Talk about Their Health: Issues and Evidence from India, Har-Anand, 94 **CONTACT ADDRESS** 260 Garth Rd., 5E5, Scarsdale, NY 10583-4051. **EMAIL** mn1925@yahoo.com

NAGAN, WINSTON P.
PERSONAL Born, South Africa **DISCIPLINE** LAW **EDUCATION** Univ S Africa, BA; Oxford Univ, BA, MA; Duke Univ, LLM, MCL; Yale Univ, JSD. **CAREER** Trustee res fel, prof Law,aff prof Anthrop, Univ Fla 75-. **HONORS AND AWARDS** Co-founded, 1st Human Rights & Peace Ctr in Uganda; jointly organizing int conf in Sarajevo that produced the Sarajevo Declaration. **MEMBERSHIPS** Amer Soc Int Law. **RESEARCH** Conflict of laws, international law, human rights, jurisprudence. **CONTACT ADDRESS** School of Law, Univ of Florida, PO Box 117625, Gainesville, FL 32611-7625. **EMAIL** nagan@law.ufl.edu

NAGARAJAN, VIJAYA
PERSONAL Born 06/02/1961, Enangudi, India, m, 1991, 2 children **DISCIPLINE** RELIGIOUS STUDIES RELIGIOUS STUDIES **EDUCATION** Univ Calif, Berkeley, PhD. **CAREER** Asst prof, theol & rel stud, Univ San Francisco, 97-. **HONORS AND AWARDS** Fulbright Res Fel , 92-94; Chancellors Dissert Writing Fel, 95-96; Louise Davies Chair, Fall 1999; Res Assoc and Visit Fel, Women's Studies in Rel Prog, Harvard Univ, 2001-2002. **MEMBERSHIPS** AAR. **RESEARCH** Gender; ecology; art; nonviolence; memory. **SELECTED PUBLICATIONS** Hosting the Divine: the Kolam in Tamil Nadu. In Mud, Mirror and Thread: Folk Traditions of Rural India, Nora Fischer, Ed. Santa Fe, NM: Museum of Folk Art, 93; auth, The Earth as Goddess Blui Devi, Toward a Theory of Embedded Ecologies, In Lance Nelson, ed Hinduism, Purifying the Earthly Body of God: Religion & Ecology in Hindu India, SUNY Press, 98; Rituals of Embedded Ecologies: Drawing Kolams, Marrying Trees, and Generating Auspiciousness. In Mary Evelyn Tucker and Christopher Chapple, Hinduism and Ecology, Harvard Univ Press, 00. **CONTACT ADDRESS** Dept of Theology and Religious Studies, Univ of San Francisco, 2130 Fulton St., San Francisco, CA 94117-1080. **EMAIL** nagarajan@usfca.edu

NAGEL, MECHTHILD E.
PERSONAL Born 06/08/1966, Germany **DISCIPLINE** PHILOSOPHY **EDUCATION** Albert-Ludwigs-Univ, Germany, BA, 87; Univ of Mass-Amherst, MA, 91; PhD, 96. **CAREER** Instr, Mount Holyoke Col, 93; vis asst prof, Minn State Univ, 96-99; asst prof, SUNY-Col at Cortland, 99- . **HONORS AND AWARDS** Fac Res Grant, 98-99. **MEMBERSHIPS** Rad Phil Assn; APA; AAUW; Soc Women in Phil; Natl Women Stud Asn; ASA; TASP **RESEARCH** Feminist; postmodernism **SELECTED PUBLICATIONS** auth, "Of Monsters and Transgression," in Alterity, Excess, Community, Toronto, 93; auth, "Critical Theory Meets the Ethic of Care: Engendering Social Justice and Social Identities," Soc Theo & Prac, 97; auth, "Play in Culture and the Jargon of Primordiality: A Critique of Huizinga's Homo Ludens," in Play Writes: Diversions & Divergences in Fields of Play, 98; auth, "Reclaiming Affirmative Action," in E Wind, W Wind, Mankato Quart Jour, 98. **CONTACT ADDRESS** Dept of Philos, SUNY, Col at Cortland, Cortland, NY 13045. **EMAIL** nagelm@cortland.edu

NAGEL, NORMAN E.
PERSONAL Born 09/30/1925, Kuling, China, m, 1953, 3 children **DISCIPLINE** SYSTEMATIC THEOLOGY **EDUCATION** Univ Adelaide, S Australia, BA, 45; Concordia Sem, BA, 49, MDiv, 53; Univ Cambridge, England, PhD, 62. **CAREER** Instr, Concordia Col, 47; pastor, Luther-Tyndale, London, 54-57; pastor and preceptor, Westfield House, Cambridge England, 57-68; vis prof, Concordia Sem, 62-63, summers 81-83; univ preacher and dean, prof of theol, 68-83, Valparaiso Univ; vis prof Martin Luther Sem, Papua New Guines, 75; prof systematic theology, 83-92, graduate prof, 92- chemn dept, 86-92, 94-95, Concordia Sem. **HONORS AND AWARDS** D.D., 99; LL.D. 00. **RESEARCH** Office of the Ministry; Lutheran confessions. **SELECTED PUBLICATIONS** Auth, Externum Verbum: Testing Augustana on the Doctrine of the Holy Ministry, Lutheran Theol J, 96; auth, Consubstantiation, in, Stephenson, ed, Hermann Sasse: A Man for Our Times? Concordia, 98. **CONTACT ADDRESS** Concordia Sem, 801 DeMun Ave, Saint Louis, MO 63105. **EMAIL** nageln@csl.edu

NAGEL, ROBERT F.
PERSONAL Born 01/17/1947, Dover, DE, m, 1970, 4 children **DISCIPLINE** LAW **EDUCATION** Swarthmore Col, BA, 68; Yale Law Sch, JD, 72. **CAREER** Vis assoc prof, Cornell Law Sch, 80-81; vis prof, Univ Mich Law Sch, 84; distinguished vis prof, Marshall-Wythe Sch of Law, 89; assoc prof to prof, Univ Colo, 75-. **MEMBERSHIPS** Bar of Colo; Bar of the Supreme Court of the U.S. **RESEARCH** Free speech; Federalism; Judicial power; Interpretation; Constitutional law. **SELECTED PUBLICATIONS** Auth, Judicial Power and American Character: Censoring Ourselves in an Anxious Age, Oxford, 94; ed, Intellect and Craft: The Contributions of Justice Hans Linde to American Constitutionalism, Westview, 95; auth, The Implosion of American Federalism, Oxford, 01. **CONTACT ADDRESS** Sch of Law, Univ of Colorado, Boulder, Campus Box 403, Boulder, CO 80309-0403. **EMAIL** Robert.Nagel@Colorado.edu

NAGEL, THOMAS
PERSONAL Born 07/04/1937, Belgrade, Yugoslavia **DISCIPLINE** PHILOSOPHY **EDUCATION** Cornell Univ, BA, 58; Oxford Univ, BPhil, 60; Harvard Univ, PhD, 63. **CAREER** Asst prof philos, Univ CA, Berkeley, 63-66; from asst prof to assoc prof, Princeton Univ, 66-72, prof philos, 72-80; chmn dept, 81-86, Prof Philos, NY Univ, 80-, Prof of Philos and Law, 86-; Fels, Guggenheim, 66-67, Nat Sci Found, 68-70 & NEH, 78-79, 84-85; Am Academy of Art and Sciences, 80-, British Academy, 88-, Honorary Fel Corpus Christi Col, Oxford, 92-; Assoc ed, Philosophy & Public Affairs, 70-82. **HONORS AND AWARDS** Tanner Lecturer, Stanford Univ, 77; Tanner Lecturer, Oxford Univ, 79; Howison Lecturer, Johns Hopkins Univ, 87; Thalheimer Lecturer, Johns Hopkins Univ, 89; John Locke Lecturer, Oxford Unv, 90; Hempel Lecturer, Priceton Univ, 95; Whitehead Lecturer, Harvard Univ, 95; Immanuel Kant Lecturer, Stanford Univ, 95. **MEMBERSHIPS** Am Philos Asn; Am Acad Arts & Sci; Soc Philos & Pub Affairs. **RESEARCH** Ethics; Philosophy of mind, Epistemology, and Political Philosophy. **SELECTED PUBLICATIONS** Auth, The Possibility of Altruism, Oxford Univ, 70; Mortal Questions, Cambridge Univ, 79; The View From Nowhere, 86; What Does It All Mean?, 87; Equality and Partiality, 91; Other Minds: Critical Essays, 1969-1994, 95; The Last Word, 97. **CONTACT ADDRESS** Dept of Philos, New York Univ, 100 Washington Sq E, New York, NY 10003-6688. **EMAIL** NAGELT@TURING.LAW.NYU.EDU

NAGIN, DANIEL S.
DISCIPLINE PUBLIC POLICY **EDUCATION** Carnegie Mellon Univ, PhD, 76. **HONORS AND AWARDS** Sigma Xi; Honorable mention, Psychology Today's 1976 Social Issues Dissertation Contets; North Eastern State Tax Officials Asn Awd for Excellence in Tax Admin, 85; fourteen grants from the following: Nat Sci Found, Nat Inst of Justice; Nat Consortium on Violence Res; and the Urban Mass Transit Authority. **MEMBERSHIPS** Editorial boards: Criminology, 92-; Evaluation Rev, 95-; J of Criminal Law and Criminology, 96-; Policy Sciences, 96-; J of Quantitative Criminology, 97-; Member of Committee on Law and Justice, Nat Res Coun, Nat Academy of Sciences, 97-; Brd of the PA Governor's Energy Coun, 86-90; Bd Pittsburgh Filmakers, 88-91. **RESEARCH** Crime; statistical methodology. **SELECTED PUBLICATIONS** Auth, Life-Course Trajectories of Different Types of Offenders, with

D Farrington and T Moffitt, Criminology, 95; The Effects of Criminality and Conviction on the Labor Market Status of Young British Offenders, with J Waldfogel, Int Rev of Law and Economics, 95; A Comparison of Poisson, Negative Binomial, and Semiparametric Mixed Poisson Regression Models With Empirical Applications to Criminal Careers Data, with K Land and P McCall, Sociol Methods and Res, 96; Micro-Models of Criminal Careers: A Synthesis of the Criminal Careers and Life Course Approaches via Semiparametric Mixed Poisson Models with Empirical Applications, J of Quantitative Criminology, 96; The Effect of Sexual Arousal on Expectations of Sexual Forcefulness, with G Loewenstein and R Paternoster, J of Res in Crime and Delinquency, 97; Adolescent Mothers & the Criminal Behavior of Their Children, with G Pogarsky and D Farrington, Law and Soc Rev, 97; Do Right-to-Carry Laws Deter Violent Crime?, with Dan Black, J of Legal Studies, 98; Trajectories of Change in Criminal Offending: Good Marriages and the Desistance Process, with John Laub and Robert Sampson, Am Sociol Rev, 98; numerous other publications, several forthcoming. **CONTACT ADDRESS** Carnegie Mellon Univ, 2105 Hamburg Hall, Pittsburgh, PA 15213.

NAGY, PAUL
PERSONAL Born 01/02/1937, Shelton, CT, m, 1965, 4 children **DISCIPLINE** PHILOSOPHY **EDUCATION** Fairfield Univ, BS, cum laude, 58; Boston Col, MA, 60; Fordham Univ, PhD, 68. **CAREER** Otto Salgo Prof Am Studs, Univ Budapest, 84-86; vis prof Am studs, Warsaw Univ, 77-78; prof Philos, prof Am studs, adj prof Philanthropic stud, Indiana Univ, 67-98. **MEMBERSHIPS** Amer Philos Asn; Amer Studs Asn; Soc Advance Amer Philos; Soc Values in Higher Educ; Polanyi Soc N Amer and Eng; Amer Asn Univ prof. **RESEARCH** Classical American philosophy; Ethics; Michael Polanyi. **SELECTED PUBLICATIONS** Auth, Cultural Origins of Pragmatism, Amer Studs, vol 3, Warsaw Univ, 81, 5-14; George Santayana and the American National Character, Atlantis, vol 4, Madrid, Asn Espanola de Estudios Anglo-Nortamericanos, 82, 81-91; Pragmatism and the American Frontier Experience, Annales Univ Sci Budapest de Rolando Eotvos Nominatae Sectic Philologia Moderna, vol XVI, Budapest, Eotvos Lorand Univ, 85, 89-99; Television: A Pervasive Presence in the American Cultural Landscape, USA Mag, Vienna and Budapest, US Info Agency, 86, 86-93; Some Traces of Pragmatism and Humanism in Michael Polanyi's Personal Knowledge, Polanyiana: The Periodical of the Michael Ploanyi Lib Philos Assn, vol 1, no 2, Budapest, 93, 137-147; Philosophy in a Different Voice: Michael Polanyi on Liberty and Liberalism, Tradition and Discovery, vol XXII, no 3, 96, 17-27; **CONTACT ADDRESS** Dept of Philosophy, Indiana Univ-Purdue Univ, Indianapolis, 425 University Blvd, Indianapolis, IN 46202. **EMAIL** pnagy@iupui.edu

NAILS, DEBRA
PERSONAL Born 11/15/1950, Shreveport, LA, w, 1983 **DISCIPLINE** PHILOSOPHY **EDUCATION** Univ of the Witwatersrand, S Africa, PhD, 93. **CAREER** Lect/researcher, 86-92, Univ Witwatersrand; assoc prof, 94-00, Mary Wash Coll; assoc prof, Mich State Univ, 00-. **HONORS AND AWARDS** Univ P-DR Fel, Univ Witwatersrand. **MEMBERSHIPS** APA, SAGP, Intl Plato Soc, NA Spinoza Soc. **RESEARCH** Plato, Spinoza, rationalism **SELECTED PUBLICATIONS** Auth, Agora Academy and the Conduct of Philosophy, Philo Stud Series, Dordrecht, Kluwer Acad Pub, 95; Mouthpiece Schmouthpiece, in: Who Speaks for Plato, ed, G A Press, Lanham Rowman & Littlefield, 98; The Dramatic Date of Plato's Republic, in: Classical J, 98; Tidying the Socratic Mess of a Method, in: SW Philo Review, 97; Socrates and Plato, Understanding the World and Changing It, in: Sci, Mind & Art, eds K Gavroglu, J Stachel & M W Wartofsky, Boston Kluwer, 95; Plato's Middle Cluster, in: Phoenix, 94; Problems with Vlastos's Platonic Developmentalism, in: Ancient Philo, 93; Platonic Chronology Reconsidered, in: Bryn Mawr Classical Review, 92. **CONTACT ADDRESS** Dept of Philos, Michigan State Univ, East Lansing, MI 48824-1032. **EMAIL** nails@msu.edu

NAIM, ELISSA BEN
PERSONAL Born 11/03/1969, Chicago, IL, m, 1996 **DISCIPLINE** RELIGIOUS STUDIES **EDUCATION** Hebrew Union Col, MA, 96; MA, 97. **CAREER** Rabbi. **HONORS AND AWARDS** Fulbright Scholar. **MEMBERSHIPS** CCAR; Fulbright Asn; Nat Asn of Temple Educators. **RESEARCH** Religious studies; Hebrew; Education. **CONTACT ADDRESS** 1055 S Sherbourne Dr, Los Angeles, CA 90035.

NAIRN, CHARLES E.
PERSONAL Born 08/26/1926, Columbus, OH, m, 1952, 5 children **DISCIPLINE** PHILOSOPHY, RELIGION **EDUCATION** Kent State Univ, BA, 51, MA, 52; Oberlin Coll, BD, 58; Vanderbilt Univ, MA, 72. **CAREER** Librarian Philo & Relig Div, 51-53, Cleveland Pub Library; Head Lib & teach, 60-64, Upper Iowa Univ; Hd Lib & teach, 64-68, Findlay Coll; Dir of Lib, teach & Ref/DLL librarian, 68-88, Lake Superior State Univ, Sault Ste Marie. **MEMBERSHIPS** SBL, AAR, APA, ALA, MLA, SCP, MSA. **RESEARCH** Mysticism, history of philosophy & religion, ethics, Christology as related to theology, poetry, painting & the Arts. **SELECTED PUBLICATIONS** Book review, Man as the Christian Problem, review of Dumery's Problem of God, in: Pacific Philo Forum, 67; auth, Absolutism, the Theistic Dilemma, in: Humanist's Speak, ed by S V Pehl, 74. **CONTACT ADDRESS** 903 Prospect Ave, Sault Ste. Marie, MI 49783-1725.

NAKAMURA, C. LYNN
PERSONAL Born Summit, NJ, s, 1 child **DISCIPLINE** OLD TESTAMENT **EDUCATION** Susquehanna Univ, BA, 78; Lutheran Theol Sem, MDiv, 83; Princeton Theol Sem, PhD, 92. **CAREER** Asst prof, 88-93; assoc prof, Trinity Lutheran Sem, 93-; sec fac, 94-96; dir, Learning Tech, 96-; act mgr, Cmpt Svc, 96-98. **SELECTED PUBLICATIONS** Co-auth, A Nation Turns to God, Augsburg Adult Bible Stud, 95; Mission90 Bible Study/Witness: Witnesses to the Word, Augsburg, 91; auth, Monarch, Mountain, and Meal: A Traditio-Historical Investigation of the Eschatological Banquet of Isaiah 24:21-23, PhD dissertation, Princeton Theol Sem, 92; co-ed, Lutherans and the Challenge of Religious Pluralism, Augsburg, 90. **CONTACT ADDRESS** Bible Dept, Trinity Lutheran Sem, 2199 E Main St, Columbus, OH 43209-2334. **EMAIL** lnakamur@trinity.capital.edu

NAKASONE, RONALD
PERSONAL Born 07/13/1969, HI, m, 1998, 1 child **DISCIPLINE** BUDDHIST STUDIES **EDUCATION** Univ of Wis, PhD, 80; Ryuoka Univ, MA, 75 **CAREER** Grad Theol Un, 89-98; Inst of Buddhist Stud, 87-89 **HONORS AND AWARDS** Fulbright, 78-79 **MEMBERSHIPS** Am Acad of Relig; Am Soc for Bioethics & Humanities; Japan Assoc for Bioethics; Assoc for Asian Amer Studies; Amer Soc on Aging **RESEARCH** Buddhist Studies, Aging; Asian American Religious Experience; Okinawan Spirituality **SELECTED PUBLICATIONS** Auth, Buddhist view on Biotechnology, Encyclopedia of Ethical, Legal and Policy Issues in Biotechnology, 99; Auth, Buddhist Issues in End of Life Decision Making, Sage Publications, 99 **CONTACT ADDRESS** Ronald Y Nakasone, 43109 Gallegos Ave, Fremont, CA 94539. **EMAIL** rynakasone@aol.com

NAKHAI, BETH ALPERT
PERSONAL Born 07/05/1951, New York, NY, m, 1986, 1 child **DISCIPLINE** NEAR EASTERN ARCHAEOLOGY, BIBLICAL STUDIES **EDUCATION** Conn Col, BA, 72; Harvard Div Sch, MTS, 79; Univ Ariz, MA, 85, PhD, 93. **CAREER** Univ Ariz, 83-86, 88-89; adj instr, Prescott Col, 95; asst prof, Univ Ariz, 94- . **HONORS AND AWARDS** Robert H. Pfeiffer Found Trust, 78; Zion Res Found Travel Scholar, 79; Univ Ariz Grad Tuition Scholar, 82-83; Maurice Cohen Awd in Judaic Stud, 83; Bernard Ivan Amster Mem Awd, 83; tchg asst, Dept Oriental Stud, 1st yr Hebrew, 83-87; Samuel H. Kress found fel, 86-87; Univ Ariz Grad Acad Scholar, 87-89; Dorot Found doctoral fel, 88-89; Tchg asst, Dept Near East Stud, Ancient Civilizations Near East, 88-89; Res Asst, Dept Near East Stud, 90; Mem found Jewish Cult Doctoral Scholar, 86-91; Amer Sch Oriental Res Comm Archaeol Policy Endow Bibl Archaeol grant, 97; Amer Sch Oriental Res Comm Archaeo Policy Endow Bibl Archael grant, 97; Assoc Women fac travel grant, Univ Ariz, 97-98; American Assoc of Univ Women Summer Research grant, 00. **MEMBERSHIPS** Amer Sch Oriental Res; Soc Bibl Lit; Ctr Middle East Stud; Assn Women Fac, Univ Ariz. **RESEARCH** Canaanite and Israelite Religion; women in antiquity issues. **SELECTED PUBLICATIONS** Auth, Tell el-Wawiyat, Revue biblique, 95/2, 88, 247-251; Tell el-Wawiyat, 1987 Israel Exploration Jour, 39.1-2, 102 Tell el-Wawiyat, Encyclopedia of Archaelolgical Excavations in the Holy Land, 2nd ed, E. Stern, ed, Jerusalem, Israel Exploration Soc, 92; What's a Bamah? How Sacred Space Functioned in Ancient Israel, Bibl Archaeol Rev, 20, 18-19, 77-78; Wawiyat, Jell el-, Encyclopedia of Archaeology in the Bibl World, vol 5, 333-334, Eric M. Meyers, ed, New York, Oxford UP, 97; Syro-Palestinian Temples, Encyclopedia of Near Eastern Archaeology, vol 5, E.M. Meyers, ed, New York, Oxford UP, 169-174, 97; Locus, Encyclopedia of Near Eastern Archaeology, vol 3, E.M. Meyers, ed, NY, Oxford UP, 97, 383-384; Kitan, Tel., Encycolpedia of Near Eastern Archaeology, vol 3, E.M. Meyers, ed, New York, Oxford Univ Press, 97, 300; Furniture and Furnishings: Furnishings of the Bronze and Iron Ages, Encyclopedia of Near eastern Archaeology, vol 2, E.M. Meyers, ed, NY, Oxford UP, 97, 354-356; Beth Zur, Encyclopedia of near Eastern Archaeology vol 1, E.M. Meyers, ed, NY, Oxford UP, 97, 314; Featured in Written in Stones, People, Places and Society: A Publication for Alumni and Friends of the College of Social and Behavioral Sciences, Univ Ariz, Spring, 3, 98; Rev article, Jerusalem: An Archaeological Biography, Shofar, 16,3, 98, 174-176; auth, Iraelite Religion Beyond the Temple; The Archaeological Witness, The World of the Bible 1, (99): 38-43; auth, Archaelogy, Encyclopedia of Women and World Religions, vol 1, New York, Macmillan Reference, (99): 50-51; coauth, A Landscape Comes to Life: The Iron I Period, Near Eastern Archaelolgy 62/2, (99): 62-92, 101-127. **CONTACT ADDRESS** 905 N Tenth Ave, Tucson, AZ 85705-7623. **EMAIL** bnakhai@u.arizona.edu

NAKHNIKION, GEORGE
PERSONAL Born 11/12/1920, Varna, Bulgaria, m, 1983, 4 children **DISCIPLINE** PHILOSOPHY **EDUCATION** Harvard, AB, 44, MA, 48, PhD, 49. **CAREER** Instr to Prof, 49-68, Departmental Chr, 57-68, Wayne State Univ; Chr, 68-72, Indiana Univ, Bloomington, Emeritus, 88-. **HONORS AND AWARDS** Vis Asst Prof, Brown Univ; Fulbright Lectr, Univ St., Andrews **MEMBERSHIPS** APA **RESEARCH** Epistemology & Epistemology of Theism. **SELECTED PUBLICATIONS** Co-ed, Readings in Twentieth Century Philosophy, W.P. Alston, 63; co-ed, Morality and the Language of Conduct, 63; auth, An Introduction to Philosophy, 67; Bertrand Russell's Philosophy, 74. **CONTACT ADDRESS** Dept of Philosophy, Indiana Univ, Bloomington, Bloomington, IN 47405. **EMAIL** LHARL@Indiana.edu

NALLA, MAHESH K.
DISCIPLINE CRIMINAL JUSTICE **EDUCATION** State Univ NY at Albany, PhD, 88. **CAREER** Asst prof, Northern Ariz Univ, 88-92; from asst prof to prof, Mich State Univ, 92-; grad chair, Mich State Univ Sch of Criminal Justice, 99-. **MEMBERSHIPS** Acad for Criminal Justice Sci, Am Soc of Criminology, Am Soc for Industrial Security. **RESEARCH** Public and Private Policing, Comparative Criminal Justice Issues, Domestic Violence. **SELECTED PUBLICATIONS** Coauth, "Benchmarking Study of Workplace Violence Prevention and Response Programs," Security J 7.1 (96): 89-99; coauth, "Security Training Needs: A Study of the Perceptions of Security Guards in Singapore," Security J 7.4 (96): 287-293; coauth, "Security Guards' Perceptions of Their Relationship With Police Officers and the Public in Singapore," Security J 7.4 (96): 281-286; coauth, "A Study of Security Challenges and Practices in Emerging Markets," Security J 8.3 (97): 247-253; coauth, "Determinants of Police Growth in Phoenix, 1950-1988," Justice Quart 15.1 (97): 115-143; coauth, "Attitudes of White and Minority Delinquent Youth Toward Police: An Examination of the Intervening Effects of Delinquent Youth," Justice Quart 15.1 (98): 151-173; auth, "Opportunities in an Emerging Market," Security J 10.1 (98): 15-21; coauth, "Relations Between Police Officers Security Professionals: A Study of Perceptions," Security J 12 (99): 31-40; coauth, "Mexican American Homicide in Phoenix: A Comparative and Descriptive Analysis," Int J of Comparative and Applied Criminal Justice 23.1 (99): 25-43; coauth, "Assessing Strategies for Improving Law Enforcement/Security Relationships: Implications for Community Policing," Int J of Comparative and Applied Criminal Justice 23.2 (99): 227-239. **CONTACT ADDRESS** Sch of Criminal Justice, Michigan State Univ, 560 Baker Hall, East Lansing, MI 48824-1118.

NANCARROW, PAUL S.
PERSONAL Born 09/09/1956, Ontonagon, MI, m, 1982, 2 children **DISCIPLINE** RELIGION **EDUCATION** Seabury-Western Theol Sem, MDiv, 86; Univ Minn, MA, 84; Vanderbilt Univ, PhD, 00. **CAREER** Rector, St. George's Episcopal Church. **RESEARCH** Sacramental theology; process theology; theology and science. **SELECTED PUBLICATIONS** Auth, Wisdom's Information: Rereading a Biblical Image in the Light of Some Contemporary Science and Speculation, Zygon: Jour Relig Sci, March, 97; auth, Realism and Anti-Realism: A Whiteheadian Response to Richard Rorty Concerning Truth, Propositions, and Practice, Process Studies, 95. **CONTACT ADDRESS** 10849 Forestview Cir, Eden Prairie, MN 55347. **EMAIL** deervale44@mn.rr.com

NANDA, VED P.
PERSONAL Born 11/20/1934, Gujranwala, India **DISCIPLINE** LAW **EDUCATION** Panjab Univ, India, BA, 52, MA, 53; Univ Delhi, LLB, 55, LLM, 56; Northwestern Univ, LLM, 62. **CAREER** From asst prof to assoc prof, 65-70, Prof Law, Col Law, Univ Denver, 70, Dir Int Legal Studies Prog, 72-, Chairperson, sect int legal exchange, Asn Am Law Schs; vis prof law, Col Law, Univ Iowa, 74-75, Col Law, Fla State Univ, summer, 73 & Int Law Inst, Paris, summers, 79, 80 & 81; distinguished vis prof int law, Ill Inst Technol, Chicago-Kent Col Law, 81; dir & mem exec coun, Asn US Mem Int Inst Space Law; mem adv coun, US Inst Human Rights. **MEMBERSHIPS** Am Asn Law Schs; Am Soc Int Law; Asn US Mem Int Inst Space Law; Int Law Asn; World Asn Law Professors (secy-gen, 79-). **SELECTED PUBLICATIONS** Auth, The Pubic Trust Doctrine: A viable approach to international environmental protection, Ecol Law Quart, 76; The world food crisis and the role of law in combating hunger and malnutrition, JInt Law & Econ, 76; Emerging trends in the use of international law and institutions for the management of international water resources, Int Law & Policy, 77; ed, Water Needs for the Future, Westview, 77; Ocean Thermal Energy Conversion (OTEC) development, Denver Law J, 79; ed, The Law of Transnational Business Transactions, Clark Boardman, 81; co-ed, Global Human Rights, 81 & ed, Global Climate Change, 82, Westview; Ethnic-conflict in Fiji And International Human-rights Law, Cornell International Law J, Vol 0025, 1992; New Legal Foundations For Global Survival - Security Through The Security Council - Ferencz,bb, American J of International Law, Vol 0089, 1995. **CONTACT ADDRESS** Col of Law, Univ of Denver, 200 W 14th Ave, Denver, CO 80204. **EMAIL** vnanda@law.du.edu

NANOS, MARK D.
PERSONAL Born 07/31/1954, Corpus Christi, TX, m, 1974, 2 children **DISCIPLINE** RELIGION **EDUCATION** Univ of Missouri, BA, 81; Univ of St Andrews, Scotland, PhD, 00. **CA-**

REER Vis lect, 97, 99, Central Baptist Sem, KS; Vis Schol, 94, Westhill Col, UK; Co-Founder/Pres, 74-, Nanos & Gray Inc. **HONORS AND AWARDS** Nat Jewish Book Awd for Jewish-Christian Relations, 96. **MEMBERSHIPS** Soc of Bibl Lit **RESEARCH** Greek, Roman, Jewish and Christian Studies of 200 bce-200ce. **SELECTED PUBLICATIONS** The Mystery of Romans The Jewish Context of Pauls Letter, Fortress Press, 96. **CONTACT ADDRESS** 313 NE Landings Dr, Lees Summit, MO 64064.

NANTAMBU, KWAME
PERSONAL Born 09/23/1942, Trinidad, d **DISCIPLINE** POLITICS **EDUCATION** BA, 72; MA, 74; MBPA, 78; PhD, 81. **CAREER** Assoc prof, Kent State Univ, 74-81; lectr to asst prof, Howard Univ, 74-88. **HONORS AND AWARDS** Phi Beta Kappa; Omega Delta Epsilon. **MEMBERSHIPS** ASCAC. **RESEARCH** Afrocentricity, Afro-centric Geopolitical analysis of international issues affecting African peoples, Ancient Kemet, Geo-politics/European supremacy. **SELECTED PUBLICATIONS** Auth, Decoding European Geopolitics, Afrocentric Perspectives, 94; auth, Egypt & Afrocentric Geo-politics, Afrocentric Perspectives, 96. **CONTACT ADDRESS** Dept Pan African Studies, Kent State Univ, PO Box 5190, Kent, OH 44242-0001. **EMAIL** knantamb@kent.edu

NARDIN, TERRY
PERSONAL Born 01/19/1942, New York, NY, m, 1962, 2 children **DISCIPLINE** PHILOSOPHY **EDUCATION** NYork Univ, BA, 63; Northwestern Univ, PhD, 67. **CAREER** State Univ of NY Buffalo, prof, 67-85; Univ of Wisconsin, Milwaukee, prof, 85-. **HONORS AND AWARDS** Rockefeller Foun Human Fel, 78-79; Princeton, IAS, visitor, 91-92, Harvard Univ, vis scholar, 98-99. **MEMBERSHIPS** ASPLP, CSPT, Collingwood Soc **RESEARCH** Polit philo; hist of polit thought; ethics and intl relations. **SELECTED PUBLICATIONS** Auth, Private and Public Roles in Civil Society, in Toward a Global Civil Society, ed by M. Walzer, Berghahn Books, 95; The Philosophy of War and Peace, Routledge Encycl of Philosophy, Routledge, 98; Law, Morality, and the Relations of States, Princeton Univ Press, 83, Portuguese trans, 87; Traditions of International Ethics, co-ed, Cambridge Univ Press, 92; The Ethics of War and Peace: Religious and Secular Perspectives, Ethikon Series, Princeton Univ Press, 96; co-ed, International Society: Diverse Ethical Perspectives, Ethikon Series, Princeton Univ Press, 98; auth, The Philosophy of Michale Oakeshott, Penn State Univ Press, 02. **CONTACT ADDRESS** Dept of Political Science, Univ of Wisconsin, Milwaukee, PO Box 413, Milwaukee, WI 53201. **EMAIL** nardin@uwn.edu

NARDONE, RICHARD MORTON
PERSONAL Born 06/21/1929, Orange, NJ **DISCIPLINE** HISTORICAL THEOLOGY **EDUCATION** Seton Hall Univ, BA, 50; Cath Univ Am, STL, 54; Univ St Michael's Col, PhD(theol), 72. **CAREER** Assoc Prof Relig Studies, Seton Hall Univ, 68-, Judge, Matrimonial Tribunal-Archdiocese of Newark, NJ, 77-. **MEMBERSHIPS** Cath Theol Soc Am; Am Acad Relig. **RESEARCH** Patristics; liturgical studies; ecumenical studies. **SELECTED PUBLICATIONS** Auth, The Roman calender in ecumenical perspective, Worship, 5/76; coauth, The Church of Jerusalem and the Christian Calender, Standing Before God, KTAV Publ House, 81; auth, Liturgical change: A reappraisal, Homiletic & Pastoral Rev, 11/81; The Story of the Christian Year, Paulist Press, 91. **CONTACT ADDRESS** Dept of Relig Studies, Seton Hall Univ, So Orange, 400 S Orange Ave., South Orange, NJ 07079-2697.

NASER, CURTIS R.
DISCIPLINE PHILOSOPHY **EDUCATION** Univ Pittsburgh, BA, 86; SUNY Stony Brook, PhD, 93. **CAREER** Assoc dir, Inst Med Contemp Soc, SUNY Stony Brook, 91-95; to assoc course dir Med in Contemp Soc, 93-95; asst prof philos, Fairfield Univ, 95-. **HONORS AND AWARDS** Fellow, Univ IA Col Med, 96; Human Inst Fellow, SUNY Stony Brook, 88-89. **RESEARCH** Biomedical ethics; philos of sci; biology; Ger Idealism; Hegel; Kant; hist of philos. **SELECTED PUBLICATIONS** Auth, Patient Dignity--Physician Dignity, Trends Health Care Law Ethics, 94; The Dialectics of Self-organization and Nonlinear Systems, Dialectic, Cosmos and Soc, 95; coauth, The First Patient: Reflections and Stories about the Anatomy Cadaver, Tchg Lrng Med, 94. **CONTACT ADDRESS** Dept Philos & Prog in Applied Ethics, Fairfield Univ, 1073 N Benson Rd, 315 Donnar, Fairfield, CT 06430. **EMAIL** cnaser@funrsc.fairfield.edu

NASH, ROBERT N.
PERSONAL Born 04/04/1959, Salisbury, NC, m, 1984, 2 children **DISCIPLINE** RELIGION **EDUCATION** Ga Col, BA, MA; Southern Baptist Theol Sem, MDiv, PhD. **CAREER** Assoc prof; Shorter's dir, Rel Act. **SELECTED PUBLICATIONS** Auth, An 8-Track Church in a CD World: The Modern Church in the Postmodern World, Smyth & Helwys; auth, The Bible in English Translation: An Essential Guide, Abingdon Press; auth, Choosing a Bible: A guide to Modern English Translations, Abingdon Press. **CONTACT ADDRESS** Div of Relig and Philos, Shorter Col, Georgia, 315 Shorter Ave., Rome, GA 30165-4267. **EMAIL** rnash@shorter.edu

NASH, ROGER
DISCIPLINE PHILOSOPHY **EDUCATION** Exeter Univ, PhD. **RESEARCH** Nature of creativity and imagination in the arts; relation between ethics, religion and the arts. **SELECTED PUBLICATIONS** Auth, "Poetry, mysticism and the indirectness of God," Quarry, 41, (91): 105-106; auth, The poetry of prayer, Norfolk, EN: Brynmill Press, (94): 60; auth, "Strategies: how to get written by a poem," in Poets in the classroom, ed. by Betsy Sturthers and Sarah Klassen, (Markham, ON: Pembroke Publishers Limited, (95): 81-87; auth, "The world umbrella," in Quarry, 43, (95): 128; auth, "Wind-bells can overcome jealousy, in Windsor Review: A Journal of the Arts, 28, (95): 33; auth, "Wedding in the garden," in Malahat Review, 112, (95): 77-79; auth, "Trying to balance the books," in The Garden of Life, Owings Mills, ON: Watermark Press, (95): 620; auth, "Borders," in Outlook 34, (96): 25. **CONTACT ADDRESS** Philosophy Dept, Laurentian Univ, 935 Ramsey Lake Rd, Sudbury, ON, Canada P3E 2C6.

NASH, RONALD H.
PERSONAL Born 05/27/1936, Cleveland, OH, m, 1957, 2 children **DISCIPLINE** PHILOSOPHY, THEOLOGY **EDUCATION** Barrington Col, BA, 58; Brown Univ, MA, 60; Syracuse Univ, PhD, 64. **CAREER** Instr, Barrington Col, 58-60; instr, Houghton Col, 60-62; instr, Syracuse Univ, 63-64; prof, W. Ky Univ, 64-91; vis prof, Fuller Theo Sem, 83; advisor, US Civil Rights Comn, 88-91; vis prof, Reformed Theol Sem, Trinity Int Univ, Fuller Theol Sem, 89; prof, Reformed Theol Sem, 91-; prof, S. Baptist Theol Sem, 99-. **HONORS AND AWARDS** Grant, NEH, 69. **RESEARCH** History of Philosophy, Philosophy of Religion, Theology Economics. **SELECTED PUBLICATIONS** Auth, Choosing a College, Wolgemuth & Hyatt, (Brentwood, TN), 89; auth, The Closing of the American Heart: What's Really Wrong with America's Schools, Probe, 90; auth, The Word of God and the Mind of Man, Presbyterian & Reformed, (Phillipsburg, NJ), 92; auth, Poverty and Wealth: Why Socialism Doesn't Work, Probe, (Richardson, TX), 92; auth, The Gospel and the Greeks, Probe, (Richardson, TX), 92; auth, Worldviews in Conflict, Zondervan, (Grand Rapids) 92; auth, Is Jesus The Only Savior?, Zondervan, (Grand Rapids), 94; auth, The Meaning of History, Broadman & Holman, (Nashville), 98; auth, When a Baby Dies, Zondervan, (Grand Rapids), 99; auth, Life's Ultimate Questions: An Introduction to Philosophy, Zondervan, (Grand Rapids), 99. **CONTACT ADDRESS** Dept Theol & Philos, Reformed Theol Sem, Florida, 1231 Reformation Dr, Oviedo, FL 32765-7197. **EMAIL** ronnsh@aol.com

NASR, SAYED H.
PERSONAL Born 04/07/1933, Tehran, Iran, m, 1958, 2 children **DISCIPLINE** RELIGION **EDUCATION** MIT, BS, 54; Harvard Univ, MS, 56; PhD, 58. **CAREER** Prof, Tehran Univ, 58-79; Vis Prof, Harvard Univ, 62, 65; Prof, Am Univ of Beirut, 64-65; Vis Prof, Univ Utah, 79; Prof, Temple Univ, 79-84; Prof at Large, Cornell Univ, 91-97; Prof, George Washington Univ, 84- **HONORS AND AWARDS** Royal Book Awd of Iran, 63. **MEMBERSHIPS** Federations Internationales des Societes Philosophiques, Institut International de Philosophie, Royal Acad of Jordan, Greek Acad of Philos. **RESEARCH** Islamic studies; Comparative religion and philosophy; Religion and the environmental crisis. **SELECTED PUBLICATIONS** Ed, The Essential Writings of Frithjof Schuon; ed, Expectation of the Millennium 2 Vols; co-ed, The History of Islamic Philosophy, 2 Vols; auth, Introduction to Islamic cosmological doctrines; auth, Islamic Art and spirituality; ed, Islamic spirituality - Manifestations Vol II; auth, Muhammad - Man of Allah; auth, The Need for a Sacred Science; ed, Shi'ism - doctrines, Thought, spirituality; auth, Three Muslim Sages. **CONTACT ADDRESS** Dept Relig, The George Washington Univ, 2035 H St NW, Washington, DC 20052-0001.

NASU, EISHO
PERSONAL Born 02/14/1961, Japan, m, 1996 **DISCIPLINE** CULTURAL AND HISTORICAL STUDY OF RELIGIONS; BUDDHIST STUDIES **EDUCATION** Kobe City Univ For Studies, BA, 83; Ryukoku Univ, MA, 86; Grad Theol Union, MA, 90, PhD, 96. **CAREER** Asst res, Jodo Shinshu Seiten Hensan Iinkaa, Jodo Shinshu Hongwanji, 85-88; adj prof, Inst of Buddhist Studies, Grad Theol union, 96-97; res fel, dept e asian lang, Univ Calif Berkeley, 96-98; acad ed, numata ctr buddhist transl res, 97-; asst prof, shin buddhism, inst buddhist studies, grad theol union; Henry Mayo Newhall Res Fel, 92-93. **HONORS AND AWARDS** Int Asn Buddhist Cult Scholar, 88-92; Horai Asn Scholar, 93-96. W E Friends Awd Outstanding Res Encounters W/E Cult, 90. **SELECTED PUBLICATIONS** Auth, A Critical Review of Joseph Kitagawa's Methodology of History of Religions in the Field of Japanese Religious Studies, Pacific World, 94; Popular Pure Land Teachings of the Zenkoji Nyorai and Shinran, The Pure Land, 95; Ocean of the One Vehicle: Shinran's View of the ekayana Ideal, Watanabe Takao kyoju kanreki kinen ronshu: Bukkyoshiso bunkashi ronso, Nagata bunshodo, 97; coed, Engaged Pure Land Buddhism: Challenges Facing Jodo Shinshu in the Contemporary World, Studies in Honor of Prof Alfred Bloom, WisdomOncean Publ, 98; auth, Ordination Ceremony of the Honganji Priests in Premodern Japanese Society, Engaged Pure Land Buddhism: Challenges Facing Jodo Shinshu in the Comtemporary World, 98. **CONTACT ADDRESS** 1821 Carleton St, Berkeley, CA 94703. **EMAIL** nasu_ibs@msn.com

NATHAN, DANIEL O.
DISCIPLINE PHILOSOPHY **EDUCATION** Univ MI, AB; Univ IL, Chicago, MA, PhD. **CAREER** Assoc prof, chp, dept Philos, TX Tech Univ. **RESEARCH** Aesthetics; ethics; philos of law. **SELECTED PUBLICATIONS** His work has appeared in the Australasian J of Philos, The J of Aesthet and Art Criticism, Public Aff Quart, Erkenntnis and The Brit J of Aesthet. **CONTACT ADDRESS** Texas Tech Univ, Lubbock, TX 79409-5015. **EMAIL** dnathan@ttu.edu

NATHANSON, STEPHEN L.
PERSONAL Born 08/19/1943, Port Chester, NY, m, 1966, 2 children **DISCIPLINE** PHILOSOPHY **EDUCATION** Swarthmore Col, BA, 65; Johns Hopkins Univ, PhD, 69. **CAREER** Asst prof, SUNY, 69-72; asst prof to prof, Northeastern Univ, 72-. **HONORS AND AWARDS** Woodrow Wilson Fel, 68-69; Phi Beta Kappa, 69; Martin Luther King Peace Awd, Northeastern Univ, 83; NEH Fel, 89, 92; Fel, Summer Inst on Global Conflict & Security, Univ Calif, Los Angeles, 90. **SELECTED PUBLICATIONS** Auth, The Ideal of Rationality, Humanities Pr Int, 85; auth, An Eye for an Eye? - The Immorality of Punishing by Death, Rowman and Littlefield, 87; auth, Should We Consent to be Governed? - A Short Introduction to Political Philosophy, Wadsworth, 92; auth, Patriotism, Morality, and Peace, Rowman and Littlefield, 93; auth, "How (Not) to Think about the Death Penalty", Int J of Applied Philos 11 (97): 7-10; auth, "Are Special Education Programs Unjust to Nondisabled Children? - An Essay on Justice, Equality, and the Distribution of Education", J of Educ 180.2 (98): 17-40; auth, Economic Justice, Prentice-Hall, 98; auth, "The Death Penalty as a Peace Issue", Institutional Violence, eds D. Curtin, and R. Litke, Rodopi (99): 53-59; auth, "Is the Death Penalty What Murderers Deserve?", Living Morally, ed S. Luper, Harcourt Brace, (00): 543-53; auth, "Capital Punishment", The Philosophy of Law: An Encyclopedia, ed C. Gray, Garland, 00. **CONTACT ADDRESS** Dept Philos and Relig, Northeastern Univ, 360 Huntington Ave, Boston, MA 02115-5005. **EMAIL** s.nathanson@nunet.neu.edu

NAUCKHOFF, JOSEFINE C.
PERSONAL Born 04/07/1965, Stockholm, Sweden **DISCIPLINE** PHILOSOPHY **EDUCATION** Stanford Univ, BA, 87; Univ of Penn, PhD, 94. **CAREER** Asst prof, Wake Forest Univ, 94-. **MEMBERSHIPS** APA. **RESEARCH** Kant; history of ethics and aesthetics. **SELECTED PUBLICATIONS** "Objectivity and Expression in Thomas Reid's Aesthetics," JAA, 94. **CONTACT ADDRESS** Wake Forest Univ, PO Box 7332, Winston-Salem, NC 27127. **EMAIL** nauckhjc@wfu.edu

NAYLOR, ANDREW
PERSONAL Born Des Moines, IA, m, 1964, 2 children **DISCIPLINE** PHILOSOPHY **EDUCATION** Yale Univ, BA, 62; Univ Chicago, MA, 63, PhD, 66. **CAREER** Asst prof, San Fernando Valley State Col, 66-71; from asst prof philos to prof, 71- , chair dept, 71-77, 90-91, 92- , Indiana Univ South Bend. **HONORS AND AWARDS** NEH summer sem, 75, 83; NEH summer Inst on Theory of Knowledge, 86; pres, Indiana Philos Asn, 87-88. **MEMBERSHIPS** APA; Philos Sci Asn; Soc Business Ethics; AAUP. **RESEARCH** Theory of knowledge; metaphysics; philosophy of mind. **SELECTED PUBLICATIONS** Auth, B Remembers that P from Time T, J of Philos, 71; auth, On the Evidence of One's Memories, Analysis, 73; auth, Justification in Memory Knowledge, Synthese, 83; auth, In Defense of a Nontraditional Theory of Memory, The Monist, 85; auth, Remembering without Knowing--Not without Justification, Philos Stud, 86. **CONTACT ADDRESS** Dept of Philosophy, Indiana Univ, South Bend, PO Box 7111, South Bend, IN 46634-7111. **EMAIL** ANaylor@iusb.edu

NEALE, DAVID
PERSONAL Born 07/05/1953, Twin Falls, ID, m, 1974, 2 children **DISCIPLINE** THEOLOGY **EDUCATION** Idaho State Univ, BA, 76; Fuller Theol Sem, MA, 87; Univ Sheffield, PhD, 91. **CAREER** Canadian Nazarene Col, prof, acad dean, 90-. **HONORS AND AWARDS** Tyndale fel, Overseas res award. **MEMBERSHIPS** SBL. **RESEARCH** Gospels. **SELECTED PUBLICATIONS** Auth, None But the Sinners, Sheffield Acad Pr, 92; auth, Was Jesus a Mesith?, Tyndale Bulletin, 93. **CONTACT ADDRESS** Can Nazarene Col, 610, 833 4th Ave SW, Calgary, AB, Canada T2P 3T5. **EMAIL** dave.neale@cnaz.ab.ca

NEALE, PHILIP WHITBY
PERSONAL Born 02/10/1945, Brooklyn, NY, m, 1973, 1 child **DISCIPLINE** PHILOSOPHY, RELIGION **EDUCATION** Col Wooster, BA, 67; Union Theol Sem, NYork, BD, 70; Vanderbilt Univ, MA, 73, PhD, 75. **CAREER** Instr philos, Columbia State Community Col, 72-74; from asst prof to assoc prof to prof of philos, McKendree Col, 74-. **HONORS AND AWARDS** Assoc, Danforth Found, 78; Phi Beta Kappa, 67; Grandy Scholar Awd, 82 **MEMBERSHIPS** Am Philos Assn; Soc Study Process Philos; Ill Philo Assoc Central States Philo Assoc. **RESEARCH** Whiteheadian metaphysics; theories of the self; ethics. **CONTACT ADDRESS** Dept of Philosophy, McKendree Col, 701 College Rd, Lebanon, IL 62254-1299. **EMAIL** pneale@atlas.mckendree.edu

NEANDER, K.
DISCIPLINE PHILOSOPHY **EDUCATION** LaTrobe Univ, PhD, 84. **CAREER** Assoc Prof, Dept philo, John Hopkins Univ. **RESEARCH** Philosophy of Mind; Philo of Biology. **CONTACT ADDRESS** Dept of Philosophy, Johns Hopkins Univ, Baltimore, 3400 N Charles St, Baltimore, MD 21218. **EMAIL** karen.neander@jhu.edu

NEEDLEMAN, JACOB
PERSONAL Born 10/06/1934, Philadelphia, PA, m, 1989, 2 children **DISCIPLINE** PHILOSOPHY; RELIGION **EDUCATION** Harvard Univ, BA, 56; Yale Univ, PhD, 61. **CAREER** Res assoc philos, Rockefeller Inst, 61-62; from asst prof to assoc prof, 62-70, chmn dept, 68-69, Prof Philos, San Francisco State Univ, 70-, Clin assoc gen med, med sch, Univ Calif, 67; vis scholar & Soc Relig Higher Educ cross-disciplinary grant, Union Theol Sem, 67-68, ed, Penguin Metaphys Libr, 71-; Rockefeller fel humanities, 77; dir, Ctr Study New Relig Movements, Grad Theol Union, Berkeley, 77- **MEMBERSHIPS** Am Philos Asn; Am Acad Relig. **RESEARCH** Comparative religion; philosophy of religion; philosophy of science. **SELECTED PUBLICATIONS** Auth, The New Religions, Doubleday, 70; ed, Religion for a New Generation, Macmillan, 73; The Sword of Gnosis, Penquin, 73; auth, On the Way to Self Knowledge, Knopf, 75; A Sense of the Cosmos, 75 & Lost Christianity, 80, Doubleday; Consciousness and Tradition, Crossroads, 82; The Heart of Philosophy, Knopf, 82; Sorcerer, 86; Sin and Sciantism, 86; Money and the Meaning of Life, 91; Modern Esoteric Spirituality, 92; The Way of the Physician, 93; The Indestructible Question, 94; A Little Book on Love, 96; Gurdjieff: Essays and Relections, 97; Time and the Soul, 98. **CONTACT ADDRESS** Dept of Philos, San Francisco State Univ, 1600 Holloway Ave, San Francisco, CA 94132-1740. **EMAIL** jneedle@sfsu.edu

NEELEY, G. STEVEN
PERSONAL Born 11/08/1957, Cincinnati, OH **DISCIPLINE** PHILOSOPHY **EDUCATION** Xavier Univ, BSBA; Univ Cincinnati, MA, PhD, JD. **CAREER** Assoc prof Philos, Saint Francis Col, 97-; Philos psychotherapist, 97-; adj prof, Union Inst, 89-; atty, 85-; asst prof Philos, Saint Francis Col, 92-97; adj prof Philos, Col Mt St. Joseph, 92-93; vis asst prof Philos, Xavier Univ, 89-92; law clk, Law Off TD Shackleford, 82-84. **HONORS AND AWARDS** Who's Who Among Am Tchrs, 98, 96; Swatsworth Fac Awd, 97; Saint Francis Hon Soc Distinguished Fac Awd, 94; Am Philos Asn Excellence Tchg Awd, 94; Bishop Fenwick Tchr Yr Awd, 91; Greater Cincinnati Consortium Col Univ Celebration Tchg Awd, 91; Charles Phelps Taft Mem Fel, 87-88, 88-89; Univ Res Coun Fel, 87. **MEMBERSHIPS** Am Philos Asn; Am Cath Philos Asn; AMINTAPHIL; APA Sartre Cir; Am Soc Philos, Couns, Psychotherapy; Asn Death Educ Couns; Ill Philos Asn; Ind Philos Asn; Int Asn Philos Law Soc Philos; Ky Philos Asn; N Am Nietzsche Soc; N Am Schopenhauer Soc; Ohio Philos Asn; Ohio State Bar Asn; Post-Socratic Soc; Soc Philos Psychic Res; Soc Rt Die/Choice Dying; WVa Philos Soc. **RESEARCH** Philosophy of Law; Modern Philosophy; 19th Century European Philosophy; Constitutional Privacy; Health Care Ethics; Philosophical Thanatology; Philosophical Psychotherapy; Epistemology; Logic; Political Philosophy; History of Philosophy; Theoretical Ethics; Applied Ethics; Metaphysics; Philosophy of Religion; Critical Thinking; Existentialism; Death and Dying; Constitutional Law; Criminal Law; American Legal History; The Law of Torts; Philosophy of the Paranormal. **SELECTED PUBLICATIONS** Auth, Constitutional Right to Suicide, 94; auth, Patient Autonomy and State Intervention: Re-examining the State's Purported Interest, Northern Kentucky Law Review, vol 19; auth, A Critical Examination of Schopenhauer's Concept of Human Salvation, Schopenhauer-Jahrbuch, vol 75; auth, A Re-examination of Schopenhauer's Analysis of Bodily Agency: The Ego as Microcosm, Idealistic Studies, vol 22; auth, The Death of God in Nietzsche: Pity, Revenge and Laughter, Dialogos, vol 64; auth, The Knowledge and Nature of Schopenhauer's Will, Schopenhauer-Jahrbuch, vol 77; auth, The Constitutionality of Elective and Physician Assisted Death, Physician-Assisted Death, 1994; auth, Self-Directed Death, Euthanasia, and the Termination of Life-Support: Reasonable Decisions to Die, Campbell Law Review, vol 16; auth, The Right to Self-Directed Death: Reconsidering an Ancient Proscription, The Catholic Lawyer, vol 36; auth, The Constitutional Right to Suicide, The Quality of Life, and the Slippery Slope': An Explicit Reply to Lingering Concerns, Akron Law Review, vol 28; auth, Chaos in the Laboratory of the States': The Mounting Urgency in the Call for Judicial Recognition of a Constitutional Right to Self-Directed Death, Toledo Law Review, vol 26; auth, Dworkin, Vague Constitutional Clauses, and the Eighth Amendment?s Admonition Against Cruel and Unusual' Punishment, Contemporary Philosophy, vol 16; auth, The Absurd, the Self, the Future, My Death: A Reexamination of Sartre's Views on Suicide, Phenomenological Inquiry, forthcoming; auth, The Constitutional Right to Self-Directed Death and Reciprocal Responsibilities of Health Care Personnel, Contemporary Philosophy, vol 17; auth, Schopenhauer and the Limits of Language, Idealistic Studies, forthcoming; auth, Legal and Ethical Dilemmas Surrounding Prayer as a Method of Alternative Healing for Children, Alternate Medicine and Ethics, 98; auth, Nietzsche On Apostates' and Divine Laughter, Contemporary Philosophy, vol 18; auth, "The Grieving Motif in 'Legends of the Fall'," Contemp Philos; auth, "Schopenhauer and the Platonic Ideas: A Reconsideration," Idealistic Studies, forthcoming; auth, "The Psychological and Emotional Abuse of Children: Suing Parents in Tort for the Infliction of Emotional Distress," Northern Ky Law Rev, forthcoming. **CONTACT ADDRESS** Department of Philosophical and Religious Studies, Saint Francis Col, Pennsylvania, PO Box 600, Loretto, PA 15940. **EMAIL** sneeley@sfcpa.edu

NEELY, DAVID E.
PERSONAL Born Chicago, IL **DISCIPLINE** LAW **EDUCATION** Fayetteville State Univ, BA Sociology 75; Univ of ID, MA Sociology 78; Univ of IA School of Law, JD 81; Univ of IL at Chicago, PhD in Education, 97. **CAREER** Univ of IA, univ ombudsman 79-81; IL State Univ, assoc prof pol sci 81-83, dir of affirm action 81-83; Natl Bar Assoc, reg dir; John Marshall Law School, asst dean; John Marshall Law School, Practicing Atty, Prof of Law, Consultant, K-12, Colleges and Universities. **MEMBERSHIPS** Legal counsel IL Affirm Action Officer Assoc, IL Human Relations Assoc, IL Comm on Black Concern in Higher Ed, Chicago Southside Branch NAACP. **SELECTED PUBLICATIONS** Capital punishment discrimination An Indicator of Inst Western Jrnl of Black Studies 79; innovative approach to recruiting minority employees in higher ed EEO Today 82; Blacks in IL Higher Ed A Status Report Jrnl for the Soc of Soc & Ethnic Studies 83; The Social Reality of Blacks Underrepresentation in Legal Ed Approach Toward Racial Parity 85. Author of articles, "Pedagogy of Culturally Biased Curriculm in Public Education," 94; "Social Reality of African American Street Gangs," 97. Capital punishment discrimination An Indicator of Inst Western Jrnl of Black Studies 79; innovative approach to recruiting minority employees in higher ed EEO Today 82; Blacks in IL Higher Ed A Status Report Jrnl for the Soc of Soc & Ethnic Studies 83; The Social Reality of Blacks Underrepresentation in Legal Ed Approach Toward Racial Parity 85. **CONTACT ADDRESS** John Marshall Law Sch, 315 S Plymouth Ct, Chicago, IL 60604. **EMAIL** deneely1@prodigy.net

NEELY, WRIGHT
DISCIPLINE PHILOSOPHY **EDUCATION** Yale Univ, PhD, 67. **CAREER** Assoc prof, Univ Ill Urbana Champaign. **RESEARCH** Philosophy of mind; philosophy of action; American pragmatism; history of modern philosophy. **SELECTED PUBLICATIONS** Auth, Transitive Action, Intervention, and Prevention; Freedom and Desire. **CONTACT ADDRESS** Philosophy Dept, Univ of Illinois, Urbana-Champaign, 52 E Gregory Dr, Champaign, IL 61820. **EMAIL** w-neely@staff.uiuc.edu

NEHAMAS, ALEXANDER
PERSONAL Born 03/22/1946, Athens, Greece, m, 1983, 1 child **DISCIPLINE** PHILOSOPHY **EDUCATION** Swarthmore Col, BA, 67; Princeton Univ, PhD, 71. **CAREER** Asst prof to prof, Univ of Pittsburgh, 71-86; prof, Univ of Pa, 86-89; prof, Princeton, Univ, 89-. **HONORS AND AWARDS** Hon PhD, Univ of Athens; Behrman Awd, Princeton, Univ; Lindback Distinguished Teaching Awd, univ of Pa; Guggenheim Fel; NEH Fel. **RESEARCH** Greek philosophy, Nietzsche, Philosophy of Art, Literary Theory. **SELECTED PUBLICATIONS** Auth, Nietzsche: Life as Literature, Harvard Univ Pr (Cambridge), 85; co-trans, Plato's "Symposium", (Indianapolis: Jackett, 89); ed, cotrans, Socrates: Ironist and Moral Philosopher by Gregory Vlastos, (Athens: Estia, 93); coed, Aristotle's Rhetoric: Philosophical Essays, Princeton Univ Pr, 94; co-trans, of Plato's "Phaedrus", (Indianapolis: Hackett, 89); auth, The Art of Living: Socratic Reflections from Plato to Foucault, Univ of Calif Pr (Berkeley), 98; auth, Virtues of authenticity: Essays on Plato and Socrates, Princeton Univ Pr, (Princeton), 99. **CONTACT ADDRESS** Dept Philos, Princeton Univ, 217 - 1879 Hall, Princeton, NJ 08544-0001.

NEILL, WARREN
PERSONAL Born 10/27/1962, Montreal, QC, Canada, s **DISCIPLINE** PHILOSOPHY **EDUCATION** McGill Univ, MA, 92; Univ of GA, PhD, 97. **CAREER** Vis asst prof, State Univ of W Ga, 97-98; asst prof, Marist Col, 98-; Asst Prof, Marist Col, 98-00; Asst Prof, Univ of NB, 00-. **MEMBERSHIPS** APA; Amer Assn of Philo Tchrs; Int Soc for Env Ethics. **RESEARCH** Ethics; environmental ethics; philosophy of education. **SELECTED PUBLICATIONS** Auth, An Interest-Satisfaction Theory of Value, Ethics & the Environ; auth, An Emotocentric Theory of Interests, Environ Ethics, 98. **CONTACT ADDRESS** 487 Charlotte St, No 1, Fredericton, NB, Canada E3B 1L9. **EMAIL** wneill@attcanada.ca

NEILSON, WILLIAM A. W.
DISCIPLINE LAW **EDUCATION** Univ Toronto, BC, 60; Univ British Columbia, LLB, 64; Harvard Univ, LLM, 65. **CAREER** Prof, 71-. **RESEARCH** International trade and business law; competition policy; regulatory modeling. **SELECTED PUBLICATIONS** Auth, Law & Economic Development: Cases and Materials from Southeast Asia; The Vietnam Investment Manual. **CONTACT ADDRESS** Fac of Law, Univ of Victoria, PO Box 2400, Victoria, BC, Canada V8W 3H7. **EMAIL** wneilson@uvic.ca

NEITHERCUTT, MARC G.
PERSONAL Born 06/23/1939, Hobbs, NM, m, 1962, 2 children **DISCIPLINE** CRIMINAL JUSTICE **EDUCATION** Baylor Univ, BA, 61; Univ Calif, MCrim, 64; DCrim, 68. **CAREER** Probation & Parole Offices, US Courts, 64-69; Res Criminologist, 69-88; Prof, Calif State Univ, 77-. **HONORS AND AWARDS** Psy Chi; Who's Who in Am Law. **MEMBERSHIPS** Am Corrections Asn, Nat soc Sci Asn. **RESEARCH** Effectiveness, particularly of corrections programs. **CONTACT ADDRESS** Dept Criminal Justice, California State Univ, Hayward, 25800 Carlos Bee Blvd, Hayward, CA 94542-3044.

NELSON, HERBERT JAMES
PERSONAL Born 08/26/1938, Grand Forks, ND, m, 1964, 2 children **DISCIPLINE** PHILOSOPHY **EDUCATION** Gregorian Univ, PhB, 60, PhL, 61; State Univ NYork, Buffalo, PhD, 69. **CAREER** Instr philos, Niagara Univ, 63-66; asst prof, 68-74, assoc prof, 74-82, Prof Philos, Canisius Col, 82-, Chmn Dept, 76-90, Vice-Pres Acad Affairs, 96-. **MEMBERSHIPS** Am Philos Asn; Am Cath Philos Asn. **RESEARCH** Philosophy of religion; 17th and 18th century philosophy; American philosophy. **SELECTED PUBLICATIONS** Auth, The resting place of process theology, Harvard Theol Rev, 79; The epistemic availability of Hartshorne's Experience, Int Philos Quart, 81; Experience, Dialect, and God, Proces Studies, 82; Time(s), Eternity, and Duration, Int J Philos Relig, 87; Kant on Arguments Cosmological and Ontological, Am Cath Philos Quart, 93. **CONTACT ADDRESS** Acad Affairs, Canisius Col, 2001 Main St, Buffalo, NY 14208-1098. **EMAIL** nelson@canisius.edu

NELSON, JAMES DAVID
PERSONAL Born 02/13/1930, Luray, KS, m, 1957, 2 children **DISCIPLINE** HISTORY OF CHRISTIAN THOUGHT **EDUCATION** Westmar Col, AB, 52; United Theol Sem, BD, 59; Univ Chicago, MA, 61, PhD(church hist), 63. **CAREER** Asst prof & librn, 63-65, from asst prof to prof hist theol, 65-77, Prof Church Hist, United Theol Sem, 77-98, Mem comn arch & hist, United Methodist Church, 72-78; Dir, Ctr for Evangelical United Brethren Heritage, 96-. **HONORS AND AWARDS** Sr Scholar, Lily Found (ATS) 58-59; Rockefeller Doctoral Fel, 62-63. **MEMBERSHIPS** Am Acad Relig; Am Hist Asn; Am Soc Church Hist. **RESEARCH** German Lutheran Pietism; theological enlightenment in Germany; German romanticism; Moravians; Wesley. **SELECTED PUBLICATIONS** Auth, Piety and invention, In: The Impact of Christianity on its Environment, Univ Chicago, 68; Responsible Grace - Wesley,john Practical Theology - Maddox,rl, Theological Studies, Vol 0056, 1995. **CONTACT ADDRESS** 20 Greenmount Blvd, Dayton, OH 45419. **EMAIL** jnelson@united.edu

NELSON, JAMES L.
PERSONAL Born 04/02/1954, Williamsport, PA, m, 1986, 6 children **DISCIPLINE** PHILOSOPHY **EDUCATION** Canisius Col, BA, 74; State Univ NYork, PhD, 80. **CAREER** Assoc prof, Mich State Univ, 89-90; asst prof, 80-87; assoc prof, St. John's Univ, 87-90; prof, 90-. **HONORS AND AWARDS** Sr Res & Creative Achievement Awd, Univ Tenn, 97. **MEMBERSHIPS** Am Philos Asn; Am Asn Univ Prof; Am Soc Bioethics Hum; Brit Soc Ethical Theory; Am Soc Politics & Life. **RESEARCH** Contemporary moral theory; bioethics. **SELECTED PUBLICATIONS** Auth, Alzheimer's Answers to Hard Questions for Families, 96; auth, The Patient in the Family, 95; ed, Meaning and Medicine: A Reader in the Philosophy of Health Care, 98; auth, The Meaning of the Act: Reflections on the Expressive Meaning of Prenatal Screening, Kennedy Inst Ethics Jour, 98; auth, Death's Gender, Mother Time: Women, Aging and Ethics, 99; auth, Moral Teachings from Unexpected Quarters, Hastings Center Report, 00;auth, Unlike Calculating Rules? Clinical Judgement, Formalized Decisionmaking and Wittgenstein, Slow Cures and Bad Philos: Wittgenstein and Bioethics, 00; auth, The Silence of the Bioethicists: Ethical and Political Aspects of Managing Gender Dysphoria, Gay & Lesbian Quart, April, 98; auth, Everything Includes Itself in Power: Power and Coherence in Englehardt's Foundations of Bioethics, Reading Englehardt, 97; auth, Measured Fairness, Situated Justice: Feminist Reflections on Health Care Rationing, Kennedy Inst Ethics Jour, March, 96; auth, Other Isms Aren't Enough: Feminism, Social Policy, and Long-Acting Contraception, Coerced Contraception: The Ethics of Long-Term Contraception, 96; auth, Critical Interests and Sources of Familial Decisionmaking Authority for Incapacitated Patients, Jour Law, Med, & Ethics, Summer, 95; auth, Publicity and Pricelessness: Grassroots Decisionmaking and Justice in Rationing, Jour Med & Philos, Aug, 94; auth, Moral Sensibilities and Moral Standing, Bioethics, July, 93. **CONTACT ADDRESS** Dept of Philosophy, Michigan State Univ, 503 S Kedzie Hall, East Lansing, MI 48824. **EMAIL** jlnelson@msu.edu

NELSON, LANCE E.
DISCIPLINE THEOLOGICAL AND RELIGIOUS STUDIES **EDUCATION** McMaster Univ, PhD. **CAREER** Dept Theo, Univ San Diego **RESEARCH** Vedanta and devotional traditions of Hinduism; relig and ecology in South Asia; Hindu-Christian dialogue. **SELECTED PUBLICATIONS** Publ on, res interest. **CONTACT ADDRESS** Dept of Theological and Relig Studies, Univ of San Diego, 5998 Alcal Park, Maher 282, San Diego, CA 92110-2492. **EMAIL** lnelson@acusd.edu

NELSON, LONNIE R.
PERSONAL Born 01/17/1961, Kirkville, MO, m, 1981, 2 children **DISCIPLINE** PHILOSOPHY; THEOLOGY **EDUCATION** New Orleans Baptist Theological Seminary, MDiv, 89; Tulane Univ, MA, 91, PhD, 98. **CAREER** Author **MEMBERSHIPS** APA; Soc of Christian Philosophers; Baptist Assn of Philosophy Teachers **RESEARCH** Philosophy of Religion **CONTACT ADDRESS** 1332 11th St SE, Cullman, AL 35055. **EMAIL** l&knelson@pobox.com

NELSON, LYNN HANKINSON
PERSONAL Born 01/07/1948, Brooklyn, NY **DISCIPLINE** PHILOSOPHY **EDUCATION** Temple Univ, PhD, 87. **CAREER** Asst, assoc and prof, Rowan Univ, 89-97; prof, Univ Missouri, St Louis, 98- . **MEMBERSHIPS** APA; Philos of Sci Asn; Soc for Women in Philos. **RESEARCH** Philosophy of science; history and philosophy of biology; feminist philosophy of science. **SELECTED PUBLICATIONS** Auth, Who Knows: From Quine to a Feminist Empiricism, Temple, 90; auth, A Question of Evidence, Hypatia 8, 93; auth, Epistemological Communities, in Alcoff, ed, Feminist Epistemologies, Routledge, 93; coauth, No Rush to Judgment, The Monist, 94; auth, The Very IDea of Feminist Epistemology, Hypatia, 95; coauth, Feminist Values and Cognitive Virtues, PSA, 95; auth, Feminist Naturalized Philosophy of Science, Synthese, 95; ed, Synthese, Special Issue on Feminism and Science, 95; co-ed and contribur, Feminism, Science, and the Philosophy of Science, Kluwer Academic, 96; auth, Who Knows? in Garry, ed, Women, Knowledge, and Reality, 2d ed, Routledge, 96; auth, Empiricism, in Jaggar, ed, Blackwell Companion to Feminist Philosophy, Oxford, 97; co-ed and contribur, Re-Reading the Canon: Feminist and Other Contemporary Interpretations of Quine, Penn State, 98; auth, On Quine, Wadsworth, 99. **CONTACT ADDRESS** Philosophy Dept, Univ of Missouri, St. Louis, Saint Louis, MO 63121. **EMAIL** hankinson-nelson@umsl.edu

NELSON, MICHAEL P.
PERSONAL Born 06/15/1966, Richland Center, WI **DISCIPLINE** PHILOSOPHY **EDUCATION** Univ Wisc, BA 86; Mich State Univ, MA, 90; Lancaster Univ, UK, PhD, 98. **CAREER** Assoc lectr, asst prof, Univ Wisc, Stevens Point, 93- . **HONORS AND AWARDS** Vice Chancellor's Merit for Tchg Excellence. **MEMBERSHIPS** APA; Int Soc for Environ Ethics; Soc for Philos in the Contemp World; Forest Service Employees for Environ Ethics; Int Asn of Environ Philos. **RESEARCH** Environmental philosophy. **SELECTED PUBLICATIONS** Auth, A Defense of Environmental Ethics, Environ Ethics, 93; auth, Rethinking Wilderness: The Need for a New Idea of Wilderness, Philos in the Contemp World, 96; auth, Holists and Fascists and Paper Tigers..Oh My! Ethics and the Environ, 96; co-ed, The Great New Wilderness Debate, Univ Georgia, 98. **CONTACT ADDRESS** Dept of Philosophy, Univ of Wisconsin, Stevens Point, Stevens Point, WI 54481. **EMAIL** m2nelson@uwsp.edu

NELSON, PAUL T.
PERSONAL Born 11/29/1952, Hinsdale, IL, m, 1977, 2 children **DISCIPLINE** RELIGIOUS STUDIES **EDUCATION** Princeton Univ, AB, 74; Yale Univ, M Div, 77, MA, 79, M Phil, 81, PhD, 84. **CAREER** Res assoc, Lutheran Church in Amer, NY, 82-84; visiting asst prof, theol, Univ Notre Dame, 84-85; asst prof, relig, Wittenberg Univ, 85-91; assoc prof and chair, relig, Wittenberg Univ, 91-97; prof and chair, relig, Wittenberg Univ, 97-. **MEMBERSHIPS** Amer Acad of Relig; Soc of Christ Ethics. **RESEARCH** Religious ethics; Bioethics. **SELECTED PUBLICATIONS** Articles, Lutheran Bioethics, Bioethics Yearbook, vol I, 91; vol III, 93; vol V, 97, Kluwer Acad Publ; auth, Narrative and Morality, Penn State Press, 87. **CONTACT ADDRESS** Wittenberg Univ, PO Box 720, Springfield, OH 45501. **EMAIL** pnelson@wittenberg.edu

NELSON, STANLEY A.
PERSONAL Born 08/19/1931, Turon, KS, m, 1956, 2 children **DISCIPLINE** THEOLOGY **EDUCATION** Va Commonwealth Univ, BA; Southwestern Baptist Theol Sem, MDiv, PhD; advan grad stud, Union Theol Sem; Grad Theol Union; Univ Nigeria; dan; sabbatical leaves, Oxford Univ; Regent's Park Col; Spiritual Dirs' Inst, prog spiritual direction, Mercy Ctr Burlingame, 95. **CAREER** Prof, Nigerian Baptist Theol Sem; prof, 84-98; sr prof, Golden Gate Baptist Theol Sem, Taiwan Baptist Theological Seminary, 00; Wayland Univ. Extension Center 98-00. **HONORS AND AWARDS** Assoc, Personnel Selection Dept, S Baptist For Mission Bd; dir, Missionary Journeyman Prog, S Baptist For Mission Bd; pastor, pastor of Benicia Fel. **MEMBERSHIPS** AAR **RESEARCH** Cross cultural communication, Spirituality **SELECTED PUBLICATIONS** Contrib, Baptist Prog; Student; World Mission Jour; Baptist Faith and Heritage; auth, Journey in Becoming, Broadman, 83; A Believer's Church Theology, re-pub, 96. **CONTACT ADDRESS** Golden Gate Baptist Theol Sem, 15559 W. Coral Pointe Dr., Surprise, AZ 85374. **EMAIL** StanNelson@aol.com

NELSON, WILLIAM N.
PERSONAL Born 02/18/1945, Oakland, CA, m, 1968, 2 children **DISCIPLINE** PHILOSOPHY **EDUCATION** Harvard Col, AB, 67; Cornell, PhD, 72. **CAREER** Prof, 71-, Univ Houston. **MEMBERSHIPS** APA; AAUP; Amintaphil. **RESEARCH** Moral & political phil. **SELECTED PUBLICATIONS** Auth, On Justifying Democracy, Routledge & Kegan Paul, 80; art, Equal Opportunity, Soc Theory & Prac, 84; art, Evaluating the Institutions of Liberal Democracy, Pol & Process, Cambridge, 89; auth, Morality: What's in it for Me? A Historical Introduction t **CONTACT ADDRESS** Dept of Philosophy, Univ of Houston, Houston, TX 77204-3785. **EMAIL** wnelson@uh.edu

NEMZOFF, RUTH
PERSONAL Born 12/10/1940, Boston, MA, m, 1964, 4 children **DISCIPLINE** GOVERNMENT, GENDER ISSUES **EDUCATION** Columbia Univ, Barnard Col, BA, 62; MA, 64; Harvard Univ, EdD, 79. **CAREER** Lectr, Rivier Col, 79; vis res scholar, Wellesley Center for Res, Wellesley Col, 91-93; adjunct asst prof, Regis and Lesley Cols, 91-93; vis scholar, Women Studies, Brandeis Univ, 97-98; adjunct assoc prof, Govt, Bentley Col, 93-, Gender Issues Coordr, 96-. **HONORS AND AWARDS** Phi Delta Kappa; Who's Who in Am Politics; New Hampshire Coun for Better Schools Awd for Outstanding Innovative Progs; Regional Wise Awd, Outstanding Contribution to Enlarging Opportunities for Women; "Hers" Program at Management Inst for Women in Higher Educ at Wellesley Col, Wellesley. **MEMBERSHIPS** Nat Asn Jewish Legislators, Nat Orgn of Women, Nashua Asn for Retarded Citizens, Nat and Mass Women's Political Caucuses, Women's Action for New dirs, Hadassah. **RESEARCH** Gender issues in Jewish education. **SELECTED PUBLICATIONS** Auth, "Ignoring the Mothers Voice: Sex Bias in Individual Education Plans," in AAUW, eds, "Classroom on the Campus: Focusing on the 21st Century" (95); coauth, "A Tale of Two Professions: Women in Business and Politics," Business and the Contemporary World, vol 7, no 3 (95); coauth, "The Greening of Advertising: A Twenty-five year Look at Environmental Advertising," J of Marketing Theory and Practice (winter 96): 20; coauth, "Derech Eretz in the Classroom: Gender Issues in Classroom Management Conference Proceedings," Conference Proceeding: Exploring Issues of Gender and Jewish Day School Education, Brandeis Institute for Community and Religion and Cohen Center for Modern Jewish Studies, Brandeis Univ (97): 23-29. **CONTACT ADDRESS** Dept Govt, Bentley Col, 175 Forest St, Waltham, MA 02452. **EMAIL** rnemzoff@bentley.edu

NENON, THOMAS J.
DISCIPLINE PHILOSOPHY **EDUCATION** Regis Col, BA, 72; Boston Col, MA; Univ Freiburg, Germany, PhD, 83. **CAREER** ASST VPROVOST ACAD AFF, 97-, PROF PHILOS, 97-, UNIV MEMPHIS. **CONTACT ADDRESS** Dept Philosophy, Univ of Memphis, Memphis, TN 38152. **EMAIL** tnenon@memphis.edu

NERENBERG, BRUCE EDWARD
PERSONAL Born 06/05/1948, Cincinnati, OH, m, 1989, 1 child **DISCIPLINE** PHILOSOPHY **EDUCATION** Mich State Univ, BA, 70; New Sch for Social Res, grad fac, PhD, 83; Univ Wisc Milwaukee, PhD, 93. **CAREER** Lect, Univ Wisc Milwanker, (Psychotherapy). **MEMBERSHIPS** Amer Philos Asn; Amer Psychol Asn; North Amer Kant Soc. **SELECTED PUBLICATIONS** Auth, Extraneous Reason(s): A Critical Social-Psychological and Historical Analysis of Radical Behaviorism, 93; auth, The Phantom of the Opera: Subjectivity and Antimentalism in Radical Behaviorism, 90; auth, An Enquiry into the Structure of Kant's First Two Critiques: Ethics Within the Bounds of the Idea of Technology Alone, 83; transl, Why We Can Only Use Natural Language to Talk about Principles of the Political Realm, 78; article, The Logic of Parts and Wholes: Husserl and Gurwitsch, Grad Fac Philos Jour, 4, 1, 74. **CONTACT ADDRESS** 1910 E. Menlo Blvd., Shorewood, WI 53211-2518. **EMAIL** nerenbrg@csd.uwm.edu

NESSAN, CRAIG L.
PERSONAL Born 06/09/1952, Lansing, MI, m, 1972, 6 children **DISCIPLINE** THEOLOGY **EDUCATION** Mich State Univ, BA, 74; Wartburg Theol Sem, MDiv, 78; Univ Munich, ThD, 86. **CAREER** Pastor, Trinity Lutheran Church, Philadelphia, 78-82; univ official, Univ Regensburg, Ger, 82-86; pastor, St. Mark Lutheran Church, MD, 87-94; prof, Wartburg Theol Sem, 94-. **HONORS AND AWARDS** Phi Beta Kappa. **MEMBERSHIPS** Am Acad of Relig, Bonhoeffer Soc, Tillich Soc. **RESEARCH** Ecclesiology, science and theology, liberation theology. **SELECTED PUBLICATIONS** Auth, Orthopraxis or Heresy, 89; auth, Wer Bist du Jesus?, 98; auth, Beyond Maintenance to Mission, 99. **CONTACT ADDRESS** Watburg Theol Sem, 333 Wartburg Pl, Dubuque, IA 52003-7769. **EMAIL** cnessan@wartburgseminary.edu

NESSON, CHARLES ROTHWELL
PERSONAL Born 02/11/1939, Boston, MA, m, 1961, 2 children **DISCIPLINE** LAW **EDUCATION** Harvard Univ, AB, 60, LLB, 63. **CAREER** Prof Law, Harvard Law Sch, 66, Assoc Dean, 80-. **SELECTED PUBLICATIONS** Auth, Earnings and profits discontinuities, Harvard Law Rev, 64; Constitutional Hearsay - Requiring Foundational Testing And Corroboration Under The Confrontation Clause, Virginia Law Review, Vol 0081, 1995; The 5th-amendment Privilege Against Cross-examination, Georgetown Law J, Vol 0085, 1997. **CONTACT ADDRESS** 1525 Massachusetts Ave., Cambridge, MA 02138-2903. **EMAIL** nesson@law.harvard.edu

NESTINGEN, JAMES A.
DISCIPLINE CHURCH HISTORY **EDUCATION** Concordia Col, BA, 67; Luther Sem, MDiv, 71; MTh, 78; St. Michael's Col, Univ Toronto, ThD, 84. **CAREER** Instr, 76-78; asst prof, 80; prof, 92-. **HONORS AND AWARDS** Bruce prize in New Testament, 71; pastor, faith lutheran church, 71-74; curriculum ed, augsburg publ house, 74-76; asst to the pastor, st. ansgar lutheran church, can, 78-80. **SELECTED PUBLICATIONS** Auth, The Faith We Hold, 83; Martin Luther: His Life and His Writings, 82; Roots of Our Faith, 78; coauth, Free to Be, 75. **CONTACT ADDRESS** Dept of Church History, Luther Sem, 2481 Como Ave, Saint Paul, MN 55108. **EMAIL** jnesting@luthersem.edu

NETA, RAM
PERSONAL Born 07/15/1966, Tel Aviv, Israel **DISCIPLINE** PHILOSOPHY **EDUCATION** Harvard Univ, BA, 88; Univ Pittsburgh, PhD, 97. **CAREER** Asst prof, Univ Utah, 98- . **HONORS AND AWARDS** Mellon predoctoral fel, 88-89; NSF grad fel, 90-93; Southwest Philos Soc prize, 98; NEH summer sem, 98; Awarded Univ of Utah Fac Fel, 00. **MEMBERSHIPS** APA. **RESEARCH** Epistemology; philosophy of language; philosophy of mind. **SELECTED PUBLICATIONS** Auth, Stroud and Moore on Skepticism, Southwest Philos Rev, 97; auth, How Can There be Semantic Facts? Southwest Philos Rev, 98; auth, "Contextualism and the Problem of the External World," in Philosophy and Phenomenological Res, (Forthcoming). **CONTACT ADDRESS** Dept of Philosophy, Univ of Utah, 260 Central Campus Dr, Rm 341, Salt Lake City, UT 84112. **EMAIL** ramneta@yahoo.com

NEU, JEROME
PERSONAL Born 06/23/1947, New York, NY **DISCIPLINE** PHILOSOPHY **EDUCATION** Princeton Univ, AB, 67; Oxford Univ, DPhil, 73. **CAREER** Prof Philos, Univ CA, Santa Cruz, 72-, vis prof law, Univ TX Sch Law, 76. **HONORS AND AWARDS** Fel law & philos, Harvard Law Sch, 75-76; Soc Sci Res Coun res training fel, 75-76; Rockefeller hum fel, 78-79; NEH Fel, 94-95; ACLS fel, 95-96. **MEMBERSHIPS** Am Philos Asn. **RESEARCH** Philos of law; philos of mind; psychoanalytic theory. **SELECTED PUBLICATIONS** Auth, Emotion, Thought and Therapy, Univ Calif, 77; ed, Cambridge Companion to Freud, 91; auth, A Tear is an Intellectual Thing: The Meanings of Emotion, Oxford Univ Pr, 00. **CONTACT ADDRESS** Philos Bd, Univ of California, Santa Cruz, 1156 High St, Santa Cruz, CA 95064-0001. **EMAIL** neu@cats.ucsc.edu

NEUFELD, DIETMAR
PERSONAL Born 05/03/1949, m, 1977, 4 children **DISCIPLINE** CHRISTIAN ORGINS; RELIGIOUS STUDIES **EDUCATION** Univ Winnipeg, BA; Mennonite Biblical Seminary, MA; McGill Univ, PhD. **CAREER** Asst prof, Univ of British Columbia, 94- . **MEMBERSHIPS** CBA; CSBS; AAR/SBL; Context Group. **RESEARCH** Religious Rivalry - Pagans, Jews, Christians in Ancient Sardis and Smynna; States of Ecstasy in the Ancient Near East; The Social Sciences and the New Testament. **SELECTED PUBLICATIONS** Auth, Eating, Ecstasy and Exorcism, Biblical Theology Bulletin, 96; auth, Apocalypticsm: Context, Whose Historical Jesus, 97; auth, And When That One Comes: Aspects of Johannine Messianism, Eschatology, Messianism, and the Dead Sea Scrolls, 97. **CONTACT ADDRESS** Dept of Classical, Near East, and Religious Studie, Univ of British Columbia, 1866 Main Mall Buch C 270, Vancouver, BC, Canada V6T 1Z1. **EMAIL** dneufeld@interchange.ubc.ca

NEUHOUSER, FREDERICK
PERSONAL Born 05/26/1957 **DISCIPLINE** 19TH CENTURY GERMAN PHILOSOPHY **EDUCATION** Columbia Univ, PhD, 88. **CAREER** Harvard Univ; Univ Calif, San Diego; Assoc Prf, Cornell Univ. **HONORS AND AWARDS** Humboldt fel. **RESEARCH** Social and political phil, psychoanalysis. **SELECTED PUBLICATIONS** Auth, Fichte's Theory of Subjectivity, Cambridge Univ Press, 90; "Freedom, Dependence, and the General Will," The Philos Rev, 93; "Fichte and Foundatios of Hegel's Social Theory and the Relation between Right and Morality," Fichte: Historical Context/Contemporary Controverseries, Hum Press, 94; "The First Presentation of Fichte's Wissenschaftslehre (94/95)," The Cambridge Companion to Fichte, Cambridge Univ Press, 00. **CONTACT ADDRESS** Cornell University, Cornell Univ, 218 Goldwin Smith Hall, Ithaca, NY 14853. **EMAIL** fwn1@cornell.edu

NEUJAHR, PHILIP JOSEPH
PERSONAL Born 01/24/1944, San Jose, CA, 1 child **DISCIPLINE** PHILOSOPHY **EDUCATION** Stanford Univ, BA, 65; Yale Univ, MPhil, 72, PhD(philos), 73. **CAREER** Asst prof, 73-77, Assoc Prof Philos, Oglethorpe Univ, 77-. **MEMBERSHIPS** Am Philos Asn. **RESEARCH** Metaphysics, personal identity; histor of philosophy. **SELECTED PUBLICATIONS** Auth, Subjectivity, Philos Res y Arch, 12/76; Hume on identity, Hume Studies, 4/78; Kant's Idealism, Mercer Univ Press, 96. **CONTACT ADDRESS** Dept of Philosophy, Oglethorpe Univ, 4484 Peach Tree Rd, Atlanta, GA 30319-2797.

NEUMANN, HARRY
PERSONAL Born 10/10/1930, Dormoschel, Germany, m, 1959 **DISCIPLINE** POLITICAL PHILOSOPHY, ETHICS **EDUCATION** St Johns Col, Md, BA, 52; Univ Chicago, MA, 54; Johns Hopkins Univ, PhD, 62. **CAREER** Asst prof philos, Mich State Univ, 62-63 & Lake Forest Col, 63-65; fel, Ctr Hellenic Studies, 65-66; assoc prof philos & govt, 66-69, Prof Philos & Govt, Scripps Col & Claremont Grad Sch, 69-, Res assoc, Rockefeller Inst, 62; res fel, Henry Salvatori Ctr Studies Individual Freedom in Mod World, 70-71, Earhart Found, 73-74, 78, 82, 86-90-94; adv, Scripps Asn Study Freedom, 75-. **MEMBERSHIPS** AAUP **RESEARCH** Political philosophy and humanities; classical philosophy; religion and philosophy. **SELECTED PUBLICATIONS** Auth, Liberalism, Carolina Acad Press, 91; Eternal and Temporal Enemies, Polit Commun, vol 9, 92; Political Theology?, Interpretation, Fall 95; Political Philosophy or Self-Knowledge, Interpretation, Fall 96. **CONTACT ADDRESS** Dept of Philos, Scripps Col, 1030 Columbia Ave, Claremont, CA 91711-3948.

NEUSNER, JACOB
PERSONAL Born 07/28/1932, Hartford, CT, m, 1964, 4 children **DISCIPLINE** RELIGIOUS STUDIES **EDUCATION** Harvard College, BA magna cum laude 53; Jewish Theol Sem, Master Hebrew Letters, 60; Columbia Univ, PhD 60. **CAREER** Uppsala Univ Swed, vis prof 96; Univ Gottingen Ger, Von Humboldt res prof, 95; Inst Judaicum Aboense Finland, vis prof 93; Cambridge Univ Eng, vis fel 92; Univ Frankfort Ger, Von Humboldt fel 90-91; Bard Col NY, prof 94-99; Univ S FL, Dist res prof 90-00; Princeton Univ Inst Adv Stud, mem 90-; Univ Minn, vis prof 78-79; Jewish Theol Sch, vis prof 76; Brown Univ, prof, Ungerleider Dist Sch, 68-90; Dartmouth Col, asst prof, assoc prof, 64-68; Brandeis Univ, res assoc 62-64; Univ WI Milwaukee, asst prof 61-62; Columbia Univ, instr, 60-61; res prof, Bard Col, 00-. **HONORS AND AWARDS** Phi Beta Kappa; Abraham Berliner Awd; LDH; Fellner Prize; Medal of Col de France; Ecumenical Medal; Comm Medal of the Cardinal of Milano; Ambassador for the Arts; Queen Christina of Sweden Medal; Guggenheim fel; Fulbright fel; Lown fel; NEH. **SELECTED PUBLICATIONS** Auth, The Encyclopaedia of Judaism, three volumes, organizer and Editor-in-Chief, E. J. Brill, forthcoming, 1999; The Talmud of Babylonia, An American Translation, Chico, Atlanta, Scholars Press for Brown Judiaic Studies, 84-95; Invitation to the Talmud: A Teaching Book, NY Harper & Row, 2nd printing of 2nd edition, Atlanta, Scholars Press for S FL Studies in the History of Judaism, 98; The Talmud: Close Encounters, Minneapolis, 91, Fortress Press, 2nd printing, 96; The Transformation of Judaism, From Philosophy to Religion, Champaign, 92, Univ IL Press, pbk ed, Baltimore, John Hopkins Univ Press, 99; Rabbinic Judaism, Structure and System, Minneapolis, Fortress Press, 96; The Theology of the Oral Torah, Revealing the Justice of God, Kingston and Montreal, McGill-Queens Univ Press, 98; Judaism in the Mainstream: Interpreting the History of a Religion, London, Routledge, 99; Religious Norms of the Oral Torah in Practice: Sanctifying the Social Order, Atlanta, Scholars Press S FL St in the Hist of Judaism, 2001, Summary of The Religious Commentary; Judaism and Islam, Comparing Religions Through Law, with Tamara Sonn, London, Routledge, forthcoming, 2000. **CONTACT ADDRESS** Dept of Relig and Theol, Bard Col, Annandale, NY 12504. **EMAIL** neusner@bard.edu

NEVILLE, ROBERT C.
PERSONAL Born 05/01/1934, St. Louis, MO, m, 1963, 3 children **DISCIPLINE** PHILOSOPHY; THEOLOGY **EDUCATION** Yale, BA (magna cum laude), 60, MA, 62, PhD, 63. **CAREER** Dean, Prof of Philos, Relig, and Philos, Boston Univ School of Theology. **HONORS AND AWARDS** DD, Lehigh Univ, 93; Doctoris honoris causa, Russian Academy of Sciences, Inst of Far Eastern Studies, 96. **MEMBERSHIPS** Am Academy Relig, pres 92; Am Theol Soc; Metaphysical Soc Am; Asn of Theol Schools. **RESEARCH** Chinese religion & philos; pragmatism; metaphysics. **SELECTED PUBLICATIONS** Auth, A Theology Primer, SUNY, 91; The High Road Around Modernism, SUNY, 92; Eternity X Time's Flow, SUNY, 93; Normative Culture, SUNY, 95; The Truth of Broken Symbols, SUNY, 95. **CONTACT ADDRESS** Boston Univ, 745 Commonwealth Ave., Boston, MA 02215. **EMAIL** rneville@bu.edu

NEWBY, GORDON D.
PERSONAL Born 12/16/1939, Salt Lake City, UT, m, 1992, 4 children **DISCIPLINE** MIDDLE EASTERN STUDIES, HISTORY OF RELIGIONS **EDUCATION** Univ Utah, BA, 62; Brandeis Univ, MA, 64, PhD, 66. **CAREER** Affl prof hist dept/chemn dept Near Eastern Judaic Langs Lits. **HONORS AND AWARDS** Founding ed; Medieval Encounters, Fulbright Scholar (Malaysia); founding ed, medieval encounters. **MEMBERSHIPS** Am Soc for the Study of Religion, Am Oriental Soc, Am Academy of Religion, Middle East Studies Asn, Asn of Jewish Studies. **RESEARCH** Islamic history; medieval Jewish history; Muslim/non-Muslim relations; Comparative religions. **SELECTED PUBLICATIONS** Auth, A History of the Jews of Arabia; auth, The Making of the Last Prophet. **CONTACT ADDRESS** Middle Eastern Studies, Emory Univ, S-312 Callaway Ctr, 537 Kilgo Cir, Atlanta, GA 30322. **EMAIL** gdnewby@emory.edu

NEWELL, ROGER
PERSONAL Born 05/30/1952, Erie, PA, m, 1975, 2 children **DISCIPLINE** SYSTEMATIC THEOLOGY **EDUCATION** Westmont Col, BA, 74; Fuller Sem, MDiv, 77; Univ Aberdeen, PhD, 83. **CAREER** Pastor, Claypath United Reformed Church, Durham, UK, 84-92; assoc pastor, Lake Grove Presby Ch, Ore, 92-97; asst prof, George Fox Univ, 97- . **RESEARCH** Theology and science; theological epistemology; Christian education; pastoral theology. **SELECTED PUBLICATIONS** Auth, Passion's Progress: The Meanings of Love, SPCK, 94. **CONTACT ADDRESS** 104 Pinehurst Dr, Newberg, OR 97132. **EMAIL** rnewell@georgefox.edu

NEWELL, WILLIAM H.
PERSONAL Born 11/27/1943, Springfield, VT, d, 2 children **DISCIPLINE** ECONOMICS **EDUCATION** Amherst Col, AB, 65; Univ Pa, PhD, 71. **CAREER** Instr, Temple Univ, 69-70; Asst Prof, St Olaf Col, 70-74; From Asst Prof to Prof, Miami of Ohio Univ, 74-. **HONORS AND AWARDS** Excellence in Teaching Awd, GCCCU, 91; Alumni Enrichment Awd, 93; Who's Who in Am Educ, 97-98. **MEMBERSHIPS** AIS. **RESEARCH** Interdisciplinary studies, complex systems theory, integrative higher education. **SELECTED PUBLICATIONS** Auth, "Interdisciplinary Studies into the 21st Century," J of Gen Educ 45:2 (96): 152-169; coauth, "Advancing Interdisciplinary Studies," Handbk of the Undergrad Curric, Jossey-bass (96): 393-415; coauth, "What Can Public Administration Learn from Complex Systems Theory?" Admin Theory & Praxis 19:3 (97): 318-330; auth, "Professionalizing Interdisciplinarity: A Literature Review and Research Agenda," in Interdisciplinarity: Essays from the Lit (New York: Col Board Pr, 98), 529-563; ed, Interdisciplinarity: Essays from the Literature, Col Board Pr (New York), 98; auth, "The Promise of Integrative Learning," About Campus 4:2 (99): 17-23; auth, "Integrating the College Curriculum," in K-16 Interdisciplinarity: Integrating the Sch and Col Curric (New York: Col Board Pr, 00); auth, "Powerful Pedagogies," in Reinventing Ourselves: Interdisciplinary Educ, Collaborative Learning and Exp in Higher Educ (Anker Pr, 00). **CONTACT ADDRESS** Dept Interdisciplinary Studies, Miami Univ, 500 E High St, Oxford, OH 45056-1602. **EMAIL** newellwh@muohio.edu

NEWMAN, ANDREW
PERSONAL Born 12/24/1948, Bournemouth, Dorset, England, m, 4 children **DISCIPLINE** PHILOSOPHY **EDUCATION** King's Col, London, BSc; Birkbeck Col, London, PhD (physics), 76; Univ Col, London, PhD (philos), 84. **CAREER** Asst prof, Univ Tulsa, 85-90; asst prof, Univ Neb, Omaha, 90-92; assoc prof, 92-01; prof, 01-. **RESEARCH** Metaphysics; Philosophy of Science. **SELECTED PUBLICATIONS** Auth, The Physical Basis of Predication, Cambridge Univ Pr, 92; auth, The Correspondence Theory of Truth: An Essay on the Metaphysics of Predication, Cambridge Univ Pr, 02. **CONTACT ADDRESS** Dept of Philos & Relig, Univ of Nebraska, Omaha, Omaha, NE 68182-0285. **EMAIL** andrewnewman@mail.unomaha.edu

NEWMAN, BARBARA J.
PERSONAL Born 08/14/1953, Chicago, IL, m, 1986 **DISCIPLINE** ENGLISH, LITERATURE, RELIGION **EDUCATION** Oberlin Col, BA, 75; Univ of Chicago Divinity School, MA, 76; Yale Univ, Phd, 81. **CAREER** Prof of English & Religion, Northwestern Univ, 92-; Asst Prof, 81-87; Assoc Prof, 87-92; Prof, 92-. **HONORS AND AWARDS** Guggenheim Fellow, 00-01; ACLS Fellow, 87-88; Fellow of the Medieval Academy, elected 99; Distinguished Teaching Awd, 91; Outstanding Academic Book Awd, 87. **MEMBERSHIPS** Medieval Academy of America; Modern Lang Assn; Amer Society of Church History; AAVP **RESEARCH** Medieval Religion and literature; History of Spirituality; Women Mystics. **SELECTED PUBLICATIONS** Auth, Sister of Wisdom: St. Hildegard's Theology of the Feminine, Berkeley: Univ of Calif Press, 87; auth, Symphonia Armoni Celestium Revelationum, Ithaca; Cornell Univ Presss, 88; auth, From Virile Woman to Woman Christ: Studies in Medieval Religion and Literature, Philadelphia: Univ of Pennsylvania Press, 95; auth, Voice of the Living Light: Hildegard of Bingen and Her World, Berkeley: U of California Press, 98. **CONTACT ADDRESS** Dept English, Northwestern Univ, University Hall 215, 1897 Sheridan Rd, Evanston, IL 60208-2240. **EMAIL** bjnewman@northwestern.edu

NEWMAN, DAVID
DISCIPLINE PHILOSOPHY OF MIND **EDUCATION** Pomona Col, BA, 84; Univ Tex-Austin, PhD, 95. **CAREER** Asst prof, Philos, W Mich Univ 96- . **RESEARCH** Congitive science. **SELECTED PUBLICATIONS** Auth, "Vandevert's Solution to the Mind-Body Problem: A Response to Vandevert," New Ideas in Psych 13(2) (95): 129-134; auth, "Emergence and Strange Attractors," Phlos of Sci 63(2) (96): 244-260; auth, Chaos, Classification, and Intelligence," in Origine Della Vita Intelligente Nell'Universo: Atti del Convegno Internazionale, ed, Roberto Columbo, (Como: Edizione New Pr, 99), 93-106; auth, "Chaos, Emergence, and the Mind-Body Problem," Australasian J of Philos 79(2) (01): 180-196; auth, "Impersonal Interaction and Ethics on the World-Wide-Web" in Ethics and Information Technology, forthcoming. **CONTACT ADDRESS** Philos Dept, Western Michigan Univ, 320 Moore Hall, 1903 W Michigan Ave, Kalamazoo, MI 49008-5328. **EMAIL** David.Newman@wmich.edu

NEWMAN, JOEL S.
PERSONAL Born 10/21/1946, Oceanside, NY, m, 1970, 2 children **DISCIPLINE** LAW **EDUCATION** Brown Univ, 68; Univ Chicago, JD, 71. **CAREER** Assoc, Shearman & Sterling, 71-73 & Fredrickson Law Firm, 73-76; asst prof, 76-78, assoc prof tax & ethics, law sch, Wake Forest Univ, 78-. **HONORS AND AWARDS** Nat Endowment for Humanities fel, summer 80. **RESEARCH** Personal tax deductions; estate and gift taxation; legal ethics. **SELECTED PUBLICATIONS** Auth, Research and Development Allocations Under Sections 861 and 864: An Author's Query, 60 Tax Notes, 93; art, On Section 107's Worst Feature: The Teacher-Preacher, 61 Tax notes 1505, 93; art, A Truly Moving Experience, 64 Tax Notes 261, 94; art, A Comparative Look at Three British Tax Cases, 67 Tax Notes 1509, 95; art, Legal Advice Toward Illegal Ends, 28 University of Richmond Law Review, 94; auth, Federal Income Taxation: Cases, Problems and Materials, West Publishing Company, 98 **CONTACT ADDRESS** Box 7206, Winston-Salem, NC 27109-7206. **EMAIL** jnewman@law.wfu.edu

NEWMAN, LEX
DISCIPLINE THE HISTORY OF MODERN PHILOSOPHY **EDUCATION** Irvine, PhD, 94. **CAREER** Asst prof, Univ Nebr, Lincoln, 94-; vis asst prof, Univ Pittsburgh, 96. **SELECTED PUBLICATIONS** Auth, Descartes on Unknown Faculties and Our Knowledge of the External World, Philos Rev 103, 94; Descartes' epistemology, in The Stanford Encyclopedia of Philosophy, ed, Edward N Zalta, an online publication of Ctr for Stud of Lang and Infor, Stanford Univ, http://plato.stanford.edu/entries/descartes-epistemology, 97. **CONTACT ADDRESS** Univ of Utah, 260 Central Campus Dr., Room 341, Salt Lake City, UT 84112-9156.

NEWMAN, LOUIS E.
PERSONAL Born 07/10/1956, St. Paul, MN, m, 1996, 2 children **DISCIPLINE** JEWISH ETHICS **CAREER** Religion, Carleton Univ. **SELECTED PUBLICATIONS** Auth, "Post Imperatives: Studies in the History, Theory of Jewish Ethics, 98; Contemporary Jewish Ethics and Morality, 95. **CONTACT ADDRESS** Carleton Col, 100 N College St., Northfield, MN 55057-4016. **EMAIL** lnewman@carleton.edu

NEWMAN, MURRAY L.
PERSONAL Born 07/22/1924, Checotah, OK, m, 1946, 4 children **DISCIPLINE** OLD TESTAMENT **EDUCATION** Phillips Univ, AB, 45, MA, 47; Union Theol Sem, NYork, BD, 51, ThD, 60. **CAREER** Tutor asst Old Testament, Union Theol Sem, NY, 50-51, instr, 53-54; instr refig, Vassar Col, 52-53; asst prof, Smith Col, 54-55; from asst prof to assoc prof Old Testament, 55-63, prof, 63-96, Catherine McBurney Prof of Old Testament, Protestant Episcopal Theol Sem, 80-; adjunct prof of Old Testament, Howard Divinity School, Howard Univ, Washington, D.C.; adjunct prof of Old Testament, Trinity School for Ministry, Ambridge, Pa. **MEMBERSHIPS** Soc Bibl Lit; Cath Bibl Soc; Soc Bibl Theol. **RESEARCH** Old Testament; Biblical archaeology. **SELECTED PUBLICATIONS** Auth, The People of the Covenant, 62 & contribr, The Interpreter's Dictionary of the Bible, 62, Abingdon; The Prophetic Call of Samuel, In: Israel's Prophetic Heritage, Harper, 62; Rahab and the Conquest; The Continuing Quest for the Historical Covenant, 90; The Pentateuch, The Psalms, and other articles in the Encyclopedia of the Episcopal Church, 98. **CONTACT ADDRESS** 3812 King St, Alexandria, VA 22302-1906. **EMAIL** mlnewman@aol.com

NEWMAN, PETER C.
PERSONAL Born 05/10/1929, Vienna, Austria **DISCIPLINE** HISTORY, POLITICAL SCIENCE **EDUCATION** Univ Toronto, BA, 50, Inst Bus Admin, MCom, 54. **CAREER** Asst ed to prod ed, Financial Post, 51-55; asst ed to nat affairs ed, 56-63, ed, Maclean's mag, 71-83; ed to ed-in-chief, Toronto Star, 64-71; vis prof, polit sci, McMaster Univ, 69-71; vis prof, polit sci, York Univ, 79-80. **HONORS AND AWARDS** Nat Newspaper Awd Jour, 71; Achievement Life Awd, Encycl Britannia Publs, 77; off, 79, companion, Order Can, 90; Can Authors Asn Lit Awd Non-fiction, 86. **RESEARCH** Canadian economic and political history. **SELECTED PUBLICATIONS** Auth, Flame of Power, 59; auth, Renegade in Power: The Diefenbaker Years, 63; auth, The Distemper of Our Times, 68; auth, Home Country-People, Places and Power Politics, 73; auth, The Canadian Establishment-Vol I, The Great Business Dynasties, 75; auth, Bronfman Dynasty: The Rothschilds of the New World, 78; auth, The Acquisitors: The Canadian Establishment, Vol II, 81; auth, The Establishment Man: A Portrait of Power, 82; auth, True North: Not Strong and Free-Defending the Peaceable Kingdom in the Nuclear Age, 83; auth, Company of Adventurers: An Unauthorized History of the Hudson's Bay Company, 3 vols, 85-91; auth, Sometimes A Great Nation: Will Canada belong to the 21st Century?, 88; auth, Empire of Bay, 89; auth, Portrait of a Promised Land: The Canadian Revolution from Deference to Defiance, 95; auth, Defining Moments: Dispatches from an Unfinished Revolution, 97; gen ed, Debrett's Illustrated Guide to the Canadian Establishment, 83. **CONTACT ADDRESS** 2568 W 1st Ave, Vancouver, BC, Canada V6K 1G7.

NEWMAN, ROBERT CHAPMAN
PERSONAL Born 04/02/1941, Washington, DC **DISCIPLINE** NEW TESTAMENT **EDUCATION** Duke Univ, BS, 63; Cornell Univ, PhD, 67; Faith Theol Sem, MDiv, 70; Bibl Theol Sem, Pa, STM, 75. **CAREER** Assoc prof math & phys sci, Shelton Col, 68-71; assoc prof New Testament, 71-77, prof New Testament, Bibl Theol Sem, 77-; fel, Barton Res Found, Franklin Inst, 67-68. **HONORS AND AWARDS** Pres, Evangelical Theological Society, 95-96. **MEMBERSHIPS** Evangel Theol Soc; Am Sci Affil. **RESEARCH** Interaction of science and theology. **SELECTED PUBLICATIONS** Auth, Scientific and Religious Aspects of the Origins Debate, Perspectives on Science and Christian Faith 47, September, 95; auth, Scientific Problems for Scientism, Presbyterian 21/2, 95; auth, Fulfilled Prophecy as Miracle, In Defense of Miracles: A Comprehensive Case for God's Action in History, Downers Grove, IL: InterVarsity, 97; auth, "Word Group 'Star,'" New International Dictionary of Old Testament Theology and Exegesis, 97; auth, Three Views of Creation and Evolution, Grand Rapids, MI: Zondervan, 99; coauth, What's Darwin Got to Do with It?, Downers Grove, IL: InterVarsity, 00. **CONTACT ADDRESS** Biblical Theol Sem, 200 N Main St, Hatfield, PA 19440-2421. **EMAIL** rcnewman@erols.com

NEWPORT, J.
PERSONAL Born 06/16/1917, Buffalo, MO, m, 1941, 3 children **DISCIPLINE** BIBLICAL STUDIES, PHILOSOPHY **EDUCATION** William Jewell Col, BA, 38; Southern Baptist Theol Sem, ThM, 42; ThD, 46; Univ Edinburgh, PhD, 53; Tex Christian Univ, MA, 68. **CAREER** Assoc prof & dir grad studies, Baylor Univ, 49-51; assoc prof, New Orleans Baptist Theol Sem, 51-52; from assoc prof to prof, Southwestern Baptist Theol Sem, 52-76; assoc field work dir & lectr, Boston Univ Sch of Theol, 58-59; prof, Rice Univ, 76-79; provost & vpres for Acad Affairs, Southwestern Theol Sem, 70-90; Princeton Theol Sem, 82; Rockwell vis prof, Univ of Houston, 84 & 92. **HONORS AND AWARDS** Rockefeller Fel, Harvard Univ; Rockwell Vis Prof, Univ Houston. **MEMBERSHIPS** Am Acad of Relig, Evangelical philos Asn, Southwestern philos Soc, Nat Asn of Baptist Professors of Relig. **RESEARCH** Philosophy of Religion, Apologetics, Hermeneutics, New Age Movement. **SELECTED PUBLICATIONS** Auth, Theology and contemporary Art Forms; auth, Demons, Demons, Demons; auth, Why Christians Fight Over the Bible; auth, Christianity and Contemporary Art Form; auth, Nineteenth Century Devotional Thought; auth, Makers of the Modern Theological Mind: Paul Tillich; auth, What is Christian Doctrine?; auth, The Lion and the Lamb: The Book of Revelation for Today; auth, Life's Ultimate Questions: A Contemporary Philosophy of Religion; auth, The New Age Movement and the Biblical Worldview: Conflict and Dialogue. **CONTACT ADDRESS** Dept Theol, Southwestern Baptist Theol Sem, 2001 W Seminary Dr, Fort Worth, TX 76115-1153. **EMAIL** jnewp@swbts.edu

NEWSOME, CLARENCE GENO
PERSONAL Born 03/22/1950, Ahoskie, NC, m, 1972 **DISCIPLINE** THEOLOGY **EDUCATION** Duke Univ, BA 1971; Duke Divinity School, M Div 1975; Duke U, PhD 1982. **CAREER** Duke U, asst pro & dean of minority affairs 1973-74; Mt Level Baptist Church, Durham, NC Dem Nat'l Comm, asst staff dir demo charter comm 1974-75; Duke Divinity School, instructor 1978-82, asst prof 1982; Mt Level Baptist Church, Durham, NC Democratic Nat'l Comm 1974-75; Duke Univ, asst prof of Amer religious thought; Howard Univ DC Assistant Dean School of Divinity 1986-89, assoc dean, School of Divinity, 89-. **HONORS AND AWARDS** 1st Black to receive Athletic Grant-in-Aid (Scholarship) Duke Univ 1968-72; 1st Black to be named to the All Atlantic Coast Conf Acad Team Duke Univ 1970-71; 1st Black stud Comm Speaker Walter Cronkite was the Keynote Duke Univ 1972; Rockfellow Doct Fellowship, Natl Fellowship, James B Duke Dissertation Fellowship, 1975-78. **MEMBERSHIPS** Mem American Society of Church History 1980-; mem of finance comm Creative Ministries Assoc 1981; chrmn of the brd NC Gen Baptist Found, Inc 1982; mem of comm on educ Durham Comm on the Affairsof Black People 1983; co-chairman of comm on educ Durham Interdenominational Ministerial Alliance 1983-84; Planning Coordinator, Euro-American Theology Consultation Group, American Academy of Religion 1987-; pres Society for the Study of Black Religion 1989-. **SELECTED PUBLICATIONS** Number of articles and completed book length manuscript on Mary McLeod Bethund, A Religious Biography **CONTACT ADDRESS** Dean of Theology, Howard Univ, 1400 Sheperd St., NE, Washington, DC 20017.

NEWTON, LISA HAENLEIN
PERSONAL Born 09/17/1939, Orange, NJ, m, 1972, 5 children **DISCIPLINE** PHILOSOPHY **EDUCATION** Columbia Univ, BS, 62, PhD(philos), 67. **CAREER** Asst Prof Philos, Hofstra Univ, 67-69; from Asst Prof to Assoc Prof, 69-77, Prof Philos, Fairfield Univ, 77-, Dir, Prog Applied Ethics, 82-, Dir, Prog Environmental Studies, 86-; Lectr Medicine, Yale Medical Sch, 83-. **MEMBERSHIPS** Am Philos Asn; Am Soc Polit & Legal Philos; Soc Values Higher Educ; Soc Study Prof Ethics; Am Soc Bioethics & Humanities; Soc Business Ethics. **RESEARCH** Business and professional ethics; medical ethics and health care policy; environmental ethics & policy; biotechnology. **SELECTED PUBLICATIONS** Auth, Ethics in America: Study Guide, Prentice Hall, 89; ed, Ethics in America: Source Reader, Prentice Hall, 89; co-ed, Taking Sides: Clashing Views on Controversial Issues in Business Ethics, Dushkin Pub Group, 90, 6th ed, 00; coauth, Wake-up Calls: Classic Cases in Business Ethics, Wadsworth, 95; auth, "A Passport for the Corporate Code," in A Companion to Business Ethics, Backwell Pub 98; coauth, Watersheds: Cases in Environmental Ethics 3rd ed , 01. **CONTACT ADDRESS** Dept of Philos, Fairfield Univ, 1073 N Benson Rd, Fairfield, CT 06430-5195. **EMAIL** lhnewton@fair1.fairfield.edu

NEYREY, JEROME H.
PERSONAL Born 01/05/1940, New Orleans, LA **DISCIPLINE** NEW TESTAMENT STUDIES **EDUCATION** Yale Univ, PhD, 77. **CAREER** Asst prof, assoc prof, prof, Weston Sch of Theol, 77-92; prof, Univ Notre Dame, 92- . **HONORS AND AWARDS** Pres, New England region, SBL. **MEMBERSHIPS** Catholic Bibl Asn; Soc of Bibl Lit; The Context Gp. **RESEARCH** Rhetoric; social-scientific criticism; prayer and sacrifice; God in the New Testament; Gospel of John. **SELECTED PUBLICATIONS** Auth, Paul, In Other Words: A Cultural Reading of His Letters, Westminster, 90; auth, The Social World of Luke-Acts: Models for Interpretation, Hendrickson, 91; auth, 2 Peter and Jude, Doubleday, 93; auth, What's Wrong With This Picture? John 4, Cultural Stereotypes of Women, and Public and Private Space, Bibl Theol Bull, 94; auth, Josephus' Vita and the Encomium: A Native Model of Personality, J for the Stud of Judaism, 94; auth, The Footwashing in John 13:6-11: Transformation Ritual or Ceremony? in White, ed, The Social World of the First Christians: Essays in Honor of Wayne A. Meeks, Fortress, 95; auth, Loss of Wealth, Loss of Family and Loss of Honor: A Cultural Interpretation of the Original Four Makarisms, in Esler, ed, Modelling Early Christianity: Social-Scientific Studies of the New Testament in Its Context, Routledge, 95; coauth, Portraits of Paul: An Archaeology of Ancient Personality, Westminster, 96; auth, Luke's Social Location of Paul: Cultural Anthropology and the Status of Paul in Acts, in Witherinton, ed, History, Literature, and Society in the Book of Acts, Cambridge, 96; auth, Despising the Shame of the Cross: Honor and Shame in the Johannine Passion Narrative, Semeia, 96; auth, The Trials (Forensic) and Tribulations (Honor Challenges) of Jesus: John 7 in Social Science Perspective, Bibl Theol Bull, 96; auth, Meals, Food and Table Fellowship, in Rohrbaugh, ed, The Social Sciences and New Testament Interpretation, Hendrickson, 96; auth, Clean/Unclean, Pure/Polluted and Holy/Profane, in Rorhbaugh, ed, The Social Sciences and New Testament Interpretation, Hendrickson, 96; coauth, It Was Out of Envy that They Handed Jesus Over (Mark 15:10): The Anatomy of Envy and the Gospel of Mark, JSNT, 98; auth, Honor and Shame: Matthew and the Great Code, Westminster, 98. **CONTACT ADDRESS** Dept of Theology, Univ of Notre Dame, 163 Decio Faculty Hall, Notre Dame, IN 46556. **EMAIL** neyrey.1@nd.edu

NG, ON-CHO
PERSONAL Born 01/29/1953, Hong Kong, m, 1995 **DISCIPLINE** HISTORY, RELIGIOUS STUDIES **EDUCATION** Univ HI, PhD, 86. **CAREER** Vis asst prof, Univ CA, Riverside, 86-89; asst prof, 89-95, assoc prof, PA State Univ, 95-. **MEMBERSHIPS** Am Academy of Relig; Asn for Asian Studies; Soc for Comparative and Asian Philos; Soc of Chinese Religions. **RESEARCH** Intellectual hist of late Imperial China; 16th-18th centuries; Confucian tradition. **SELECTED PUBLICATIONS** Auth, Revisiting Kung Tzu-chen's (1792-1841) Chin-wen (New Text) Precepts: An Excursion in the History of Ideas, J of Oriental Studies, 31-2, fall 93; A Tension in Ch'ing Thought: Historicism in Seventeenth and Eighteenth Century Chinese Thought, J of the History of Ideas, 54-4, Oct 93; Hsing (Nature) as the Ontological Basis of Practicality in Early Ch'ing Ch'eng-Chu Confucianism: Li Kuang-ti's (1642-1718) Philosophy, Philos East and West 44-1, Jan 94; Mystical Oneness and Meditational Praxis: Religiousness in Li Yong's (1627-1703) Confucian Thought, J of Chinese Religions, no 22, fall 94; Mid-Ch'ing New Text (Chin-wen) Classical Learning and Its Han Provenance: The Dynamics of a Tradition of Ideas, East Asian History, no 8, Dec 94; Interpreting Qing Thought in China as a Period Concept: On the Construction of an Epochal System of Ideas, Semiotica: J of the Int Asn for Semiotic Studies, 107-3/4, 95; Is Emotion (Qing) the Source of a Confucian Antimony?, J of Chinese Philos, 98; Imagining Boundaries: Changing Confucian Doctrines, Texts, and Hermeneutics, co-ed with Kai-wing Chow and John Henderson, SUNY, March 99; and six book chapters. **CONTACT ADDRESS** History Dept, Pennsylvania State Univ, Univ Park, University Park, PA 16802. **EMAIL** oxn1@psu.edu

NGAN, LAI LING E.
PERSONAL Born, Hong Kong, s **DISCIPLINE** THEOLOGY **EDUCATION** California Baptist Col, BS, 76; Loma Linda Univ, MA, 79; MDiv, 82, PhD, 91, Golden Gate Baptist Theological Seminary. **CAREER** Assoc Minister, 91-93, Stockton Chinese Baptist Church; Instr, 87-89, Asst Prof, 93-95, Assoc Prof, 95-96, Golden Gate Baptist Theological Seminary; Assoc Prof, 96-, George W. Truett Seminary, Baylor Univ. **HONORS AND AWARDS** Selected for participation in NEH Summer Seminar and ATS Seminar; Intl Who's Who among professional and business women **MEMBERSHIPS** Amer Schools of Oriental Religion; Soc of Biblical Lit; Natl Assoc of Professors of Hebrew; Ethnic Chinese Biblical Colloquim **RESEARCH** Literary study of Biblical narratives **SELECTED PUBLICATIONS** Auth, 2 Kings 5, Review and Exposition, 94; A Teaching Outline of the Book of Joshua, Review and Exposition, 98. **CONTACT ADDRESS** George W. Truett Theological Seminary, Baylor Univ, Waco, Waco, TX 76798-7126. **EMAIL** lai_ngan@baylor.edu

NI, PEIMIN
PERSONAL Born 10/22/1954, Shanghai, China, m, 1984, 1 child **DISCIPLINE** PHILOSOPHY **EDUCATION** Univ Conn, PhD, 91. **CAREER** Vis asst prof, Mont State Univ, 91-92; asst prof, Mont State Univ, 92-97; assoc prof, Grand Valley State Univ, 97-. **HONORS AND AWARDS** Outstanding Teaching Award, Mont State Univ, 92. **MEMBERSHIPS** Asn of Chinese Philosophers in Am; Am Philos Asn. **RESEARCH** East-West comparative philos; Philos of causation. **SELECTED PUBLICATIONS** Auth, "Changing the Past," 92; "Taoist Concept of Freedom," 96; "A Qigong Interpretation of Confucianism," 96; Thomas Reid, 96; auth, "Teaching Chinese Philosophy On-site," 99; auth, "Moral and Philosophical Implications of Chinese Calligraphy," 99; auth, "How is Qigong Science Possible?" 01; auth, "Toward a Broader Notion of Causation (and Technology)," 01; auth, On Confucius, 01. **CONTACT ADDRESS** 600 Prestwick Dr SE, Grand Rapids, MI 49546-2252. **EMAIL** NIP@GVSU.edu

NICE, JULIE A.
DISCIPLINE LAW **EDUCATION** Northwestern Univ, BS 82, JD 86. **CAREER** Univ Denver, asst prof, assoc prof, 91-97-; assoc prof, Univ of Denver Col of Law, 97; asst prof, 91-97; Northwestern Univ, clinical teaching fell, 89-91; Legal Asst Foun Chicago, staff att, 86-89; visiting prof, Univ of Mich Law School, 99-00; visiting prof, Univ of Conn School of Law, 00. **HONORS AND AWARDS** 4 Years Prof of the year for teaching excellence; Hughes Res Professorship; Univ of Denver Scholar/Teacher of the Year, 99. **MEMBERSHIPS** LSA; SALT. **RESEARCH** Poverty and welfare reform; constitutional law. **SELECTED PUBLICATIONS** Auth, Poverty Law: Theory and Practice, West Pub, 97; Making Conditions Constitutional by Attaching Them to Welfare, Den Univ Law, 72, rev 95; Welfare Servitude, Georgetown Jour on Fighting Poverty, 94; auth, Poverty Law: Theory and Practice, 1997 and 1999 Supplement (West Group); auth, Equal Protection's Antinomies and the Promise of a Co-Constitutive Approach, 85 Cornell Law Rev 1392, 00; auth, The Emerging Third Strand in Equal Protection Jurisprudece: Recognizing the Co-Constitutive Nature of Rights and Classes, Univ of Illinois Law Review 101, 99; auth, Making Conditions Constitutional by Attaching Them towelfare, 72 Denver Univ Law Review 971, 95; auth, Welfare Servitude, 1 Georgetown Journal on Fighting Poverty 340, 94. **CONTACT ADDRESS** Dept of Law, Univ of Denver, 1900 Olive St, Denver, CO 80220. **EMAIL** jnice@mail.law.du.edu

NICHOLAS, JAMES C.
DISCIPLINE LAW **EDUCATION** Univ Miami, BBA, MA; Univ Ill, PhD. **CAREER** Prof, Univ Fla, 85-. **MEMBERSHIPS** Amer Econ Asn; Amer Planning Asn; Urban Land Inste Exec Coun; Southern Econ Asn; Amer Real Estate Urban Econ Asn; Omicron Delta Epsilon; Pi Mu Epsilon. **CONTACT ADDRESS** School of Law, Univ of Florida, PO Box 117625, Gainesville, FL 32611-7625. **EMAIL** nicholas@law.ufl.edu

NICHOLAS, JOHN M.
DISCIPLINE PHILOSOPHY **EDUCATION** Sussex Univ, BS; MS; Univ Pittsburgh, PhD. **CAREER** Assoc prof, Univ of Western Ontario, 71-. **SELECTED PUBLICATIONS** Auth, Images, Perception and Knowledge, Reidel, Dordrecht, Holland, (77): 309; auth, Cartesianism 1650-1750, McGill-Queens Press, 83; auth, Moral Priorities in Medical Research, Toronto: Hannah Institute, 88; auth, "Planck's Quantum Innovation," in Scrutinizing Science: Empirical studies of Scinetific Change, eds. Donovan, A., L. Laudan, and R. Laudan, Dordrecht: Reidel Press, (88): 317-335; auth, "Realism for Shopkeepers: Behaviouralist Notes on Constructive Empiricism," in An Intimate Relation, eds. Brown, J.R. and J. Mittelstrass, Dordrecht: Kluwer, (89): 459-476. **CONTACT ADDRESS** Dept of Philosophy, Univ of Western Ontario, London, ON, Canada N6A 5B8. **EMAIL** jnichola@julian.uwo.ca

NICHOLS, MARY P.
PERSONAL Born Opelousas, LA, m, 1979, 2 children **DISCIPLINE** POLITICAL SCIENCE **EDUCATION** Chicago Univ, PhD. **CAREER** Prof, Fordham Univ. **HONORS AND AWARDS** Leo Strauss Dissertation Awd, 77. **RESEARCH** Ancient political philosophy; politics and literature; gender and political psychology. **SELECTED PUBLICATIONS** Auth, Socrates and the Political Community: An Ancient Debate, 87; Citizens and Statesmen: A Study of Aristotle's Politics, 92; auth, Reconstructing Woody: Art, Love, and Life in the Films of Woody Allen, 98. **CONTACT ADDRESS** Dept of Political Science, Fordham Univ, Bronx, NY 10458. **EMAIL** 73504.2024@compuserve.com

NICHOLS, P. M.
PERSONAL Born 09/16/1960, OR, m, 1990, 3 children **DISCIPLINE** INTERNATIONAL LAW **EDUCATION** Harvard Univ, BA, 82; Duke Univ, JD, 88, LLM, 88. **CAREER** Asst prof, assoc prof, 98-, Univ Penn Wharton Sch. **HONORS AND AWARDS** 9 Teach Awds. **MEMBERSHIPS** ALSB; ACG; ASIL. **RESEARCH** Emerging Economies; Intl Trade and Investment. **SELECTED PUBLICATIONS** Auth, A Legal Theory of Emerging Economies, VA J Intl L, 99; auth, Forgotten Linkages-Historical Institutionalism and Sociological Institutionalism and Analysis of the World Trade Organization, U of Penn J Intl Econ L, 98; auth, Creating a Market Along the Silk Road: A Comparison of Privatization Techniques in Central Asia, NY U J Intl L and Politics, 98; auth, The Viability of Transplanted Law: Kazakhstani Reception of A Transplanted Foreign Investment Code, U of Penn J Intl Econ L, 97; auth, Trade Without Values and the World Trade Organization, U of Penn J Intl Econ L, 96; GATT Doctrine, VA J Intl L, 96; auth, Swapping Debt for Development: A Theoretical Application of Swaps to the Creation of Microenterprise Lending Institutions in Sub-Saharan Africa, NY U J Intl L and Politics; auth, Regulating Transnational Bribery in Times of Globalization and Fragmentation, Yale J Int L, 99; auth, Increasing Global Security by Controlling Transnational Bribery, Mich J Int L, 99; auth, Electronic Uncertainty in the International Trade Regime, Am U Int L Rev, 00. **CONTACT ADDRESS** Dept of Legal Studies, Univ of Pennsylvania, 2100 SH-DH, Philadelphia, PA 19104-6369. **EMAIL** nicholsp@wharton.upenn.edu

NICHOLSON, L.
PERSONAL Born 01/13/1947, Philadelphia, PA **DISCIPLINE** PHILOSOPHY, HISTORY, WOMEN'S STUDIES **EDUCATION** Univ Penn, BA 68; Brandais Univ, MA 70, PhD 75. **CAREER** Fom Lectr to distinguished prof, SUNY, Albany. **HONORS AND AWARDS** Rockefeller Fel; SVPL Fel; **MEMBERSHIPS** APS; SWP; APSA **RESEARCH** Political philosophy; social theory; feminist theory. **SELECTED PUBLICATIONS** Auth, Gender and History: The Limits of Social Theory in the Age of the Family, CUP, 86; The Play of Reason: From the Modern to the Postmodern, Ithaca NY, CUP, 98; Feminism and Postmodernism, ed, NY, Routledge, 90; The Second Wave, NY, ed, Routledge, 97; Social Postmodernism, co-ed, Cambridge Eng, CUP, 95; Thinking Gender, ed, Routledge Press, 98. **CONTACT ADDRESS** Dept of Philosophy, Washington Univ, One Brookings Dr, PO Box 1062, Saint Louis, MO 63130 63130. **EMAIL** lnichols@artsci.wustl.edu

NICKEL, JAMES W.
PERSONAL Born 03/12/1943, CA, 2 children **DISCIPLINE** PHILOSOPHY **EDUCATION** Tabor Col, BA, 64; Univ Kans, PhD, 68. **CAREER** Asst Prof to Full Prof, Wichita State Univ, 68-80; Vis Prof, Univ Calif Berkeley, 80-82; Prof, Univ Colo, 82-. **HONORS AND AWARDS** NEH, 73-74; ACLS, 76-77; Nat Humanities Ctr, 78-79; Rockefeller Found Fel, 81. **RESEARCH** Moral, political, and legal philosophy. **SELECTED PUBLICATIONS** Auth, Making Sense of Human Rights, Univ Calif Press, 87. **CONTACT ADDRESS** Dept Philos, Univ of Colorado, Boulder, Dept Philos, Boulder, CO 80309-0232. **EMAIL** james.nickel@colorado.edu

NICKELSBURG, GEORGE WILLIAM ELMER
PERSONAL Born 03/15/1934, San Jose, CA, m, 1965, 2 children **DISCIPLINE** NEW TESTAMENT & CHRISTIAN ORIGINS, EARLY JUDAISM **EDUCATION** Valparaiso Univ, BA, 55; Concordia Sem, St Louis, BD, 60, STM, 62; Harvard Div Sch, ThD, 68. **CAREER** From Asst Prof to Prof Relig, 69-98; Guest lectr, Concordia Sem, St Louis, 68, instr, 69; guest prof, Christ-Sem-Seminex, 79; vis scholar, Univ Munster, 74; assoc ed, Cath Bibl Quart, 79-87; Daniel J. Krumm Distinguished Prof New Testament and Reformation Studies, Univ Iowa, 98-00; Prof Emeritus, 00-. **HONORS AND AWARDS** Fel, John Simon Guggenheim Mem Found, 77-78; Fel, Netherlands Inst Advan Study, 80-81; Fel, Human Sci Res Coun of SAfrica, 93. **MEMBERSHIPS** Soc Bibl Lit; Studiorum Novi Testamenti Societas; Cath Bibl Asn. **RESEARCH** The synoptic gospels; New Testament christology; history and literature of early post-biblical Judaism. **SELECTED PUBLICATIONS** Auth, Resurrection, Immortality and Eternal Life in Intertestamental Judaism, Harvard/Oxford, 72; ed, Studies on the Testament of Abraham, Scholars Press, 76; auth, Apocalyptic and myth in 1 Enoch 6-11, J Bibl Lit, 77; collabr, A Complete Concordance to Flavius Josephus, Vol 3, Brill, 79; auth, The genre and function of the markan passion narrative, Harvard Theol Rev, 80; Jewish Literature between the Bible and the Mishnah, Fortress, 81; Enoch, Levi and Peter, recipients of revelation in Upper Galilee, J Bibl Lit, 81; coauth, Faith and Piety in Early Judaism, Fortress, 83. **CONTACT ADDRESS** 4691 Running Deer Woods, Iowa City, IA 52240. **EMAIL** george-nickelsburg@uiowa.edu

NICKLES, THOMAS
PERSONAL Born 02/14/1943, Charleston, IL, m, 3 children **DISCIPLINE** HISTORY AND PHILOSOPHY OF SCIENCE **EDUCATION** Princeton Univ, PhD, 69. **CAREER** Prof, Univ Nev, Reno. **MEMBERSHIPS** Philosophy of Science Assn; Am Assn for the Advancement of Science; History of Science Society; Society for Social Studies of Science **RESEARCH** History and philosophy of science and technology **SELECTED PUBLICATIONS** Edited SCIENTIFIC DISCOVERY, LOGIC, AND RATIONALITY and SCIENTIFIC DISCOVERY: CASE STUDIES (both Reidel, 1980) and THOMAS KUHN the Philosophy of Science, Philosophy of Science, Biology and Philosophy, Configurations, etc. **CONTACT ADDRESS** Philosophy (102), Univ of Nevada, Reno, Reno, NV 89557. **EMAIL** nickles@unr.edu

NICKOLI, ANGELA M.
PERSONAL Born 12/15/1970, Fort Wayne, IN, m, 1992, 2 children **DISCIPLINE** CRIMINOLOGY **EDUCATION** Ball State Univ, BS, 93; MA, 96. **CAREER** Personnel Practices Off, Muncie, 93-97; Instr to Asst Prof, Ball State Univ, 97-. **RESEARCH** Infusion of affirmative Action in Introductory Criminal Justice Courses; Pop Culture, Crime and Pedagogy. **SELECTED PUBLICATIONS** Co-auth, "Multicultural Issues and Perspectives," in Multicultural Perspectives in Criminal Justice Criminology 2nd ed, (Charles C. Thomas, 00). **CONTACT ADDRESS** Dept Criminal Justice/Criminol, Ball State Univ, 1416 N Buckeye, Muncie, IN 47306. **EMAIL** anickoli@wp.bsu.edu

NICOLE, ROGER R.
PERSONAL Born 12/10/1915, Charlottenburg, Germany, m, 1946 **DISCIPLINE** SYSTEMATIC THEOLOGY **EDUCATION** Gymhese Classique, AB, 35; Sorbonne, MA, 37; Gordon Divinity Sch, MA & BD, 39; STM, 40; ThD, 43; Harvard Univ, PhD, 67. **CAREER** Prof, Gordon Divinity Sch, 46-69; prof, Gordon-Conwell Theol Sem, 69-86; vis prof, Reformed Theol Sem, 89-00. **MEMBERSHIPS** Evangelical Theol Soc. **RESEARCH** Reformed Theology, History of Doctrine. **SELECTED PUBLICATIONS** Auth, Moyse Amyraut: A Bibliography, Garland, 81. **CONTACT ADDRESS** Dept Theol & Philos, Reformed Theol Sem, Florida, 1231 Reformation Dr, Oviedo, FL 32765-7197. **EMAIL** rnicole@rts.edu

NIDITCH, SUSAN
PERSONAL Born 07/10/1950, Boston, MA, m, 1974, 2 children **DISCIPLINE** RELIGIOUS STUDIES **EDUCATION** Radcliffe Col , AB, 72; Harvard Univ, PhD, 77. **CAREER** Asst Sr Tutor, Harvard Univ, 74-77; asst prof, Univ Cincinnati, 77-78; asst prof, Amherst Coll, 78-84; vis prof, Williams Coll, 80-81; assoc prof, Amherst Coll, 84-90; Chair Dept Rel, Amherst Coll, 86-87 and 91-93; Elizabeth Bruss Readership, 87-90; prof, Amherst Coll, 90-; Samuel Green prof, Amherst Coll, 92-. **HONORS AND AWARDS** Phi Beta Kappa; Briggs Fel for Grad Study, 72-73; NEH Fel, 85-86, 90-91, 95. **MEMBERSHIPS** Soc of Bibl Lit; Am Acad of Relig; Am Folklore Soc. **RESEARCH** Ancient Israel and Early Judaism. **SELECTED PUBLICATIONS** Auth, Short Stories: The Book of Esther and the Theme of Women as a Civilizing Force, in Old Testament Interpretation, Past, Present, and Future, 95; War in the Hebrew Bible and Contemporary Parallels, in Word and World, 95; Oral World and Written Word, Ancient Israelite Literature, 96; Ancient Israelite Religion, 97. **CONTACT ADDRESS** Relig Dept, Amherst Col, Amherst, MA 01002. **EMAIL** sniditch@amherst.edu

NIEDNER, FREDERICK A.
PERSONAL Born 05/05/1945, Lander, WY, m, 1986, 3 children **DISCIPLINE** THEOLOGY, HEBREW BIBLE AND LANGUAGE **EDUCATION** Christ Sem, ThD, 79. **CAREER** Visiting instr, Christ Sem, 76-77; instr to asst prof to assoc prof to prof, dept theol, Valparaiso Univ, 73-. **HONORS AND AWARDS** Caterpillar Awd for Excellence in Teaching, 96. **MEMBERSHIPS** Soc of Bibl Lit. **RESEARCH** Hatred and war in the biblical world; Rhetoric of polarization. **SELECTED PUBLICATIONS** Auth, Keeping the Faith, Fortress, 81. **CONTACT ADDRESS** Dept. of Theology, Valparaiso Univ, Valparaiso, IN 46383-6493. **EMAIL** fred.niedner@valpo.edu

NIEHAUS, JEFFREY J.
DISCIPLINE OLD TESTAMENT **EDUCATION** Yale Univ, BA; Harvard Univ, AM, PhD; Gordon-Conwell Theol Sem, MDiv. **CAREER** Prof, Gordon-Conwell Theol Sem, 82-. **SELECTED PUBLICATIONS** Pub(s), Jour Biblical Lit; Vetus Testamentum; Jour Evangel Theol Soc; Tyndale Bulletin; auth, Amos, Obadiah; God at Sinai; No Other Gods, forthcoming. **CONTACT ADDRESS** Gordon-Conwell Theol Sem, 130 Essex St, South Hamilton, MA 01982.

NIELSEN, HARRY A.
DISCIPLINE PHILOSOPHY **EDUCATION** Rutgers, AB; Univ Conn, MA; Univ Nebr, PhD. **CAREER** Prof emer, Univ of Windsor. **SELECTED PUBLICATIONS** Pub (s), Kierkegaard; Ethics & Philosophy of Science. **CONTACT ADDRESS** Dept of Philosophy, Univ of Windsor, 401 Sunset Ave, G105 Chrysler Hall North, Windsor, ON, Canada N9B 3P4.

NIELSEN, KAI
DISCIPLINE PHILOSOPHY **EDUCATION** Univ Duke, PhD. **CAREER** Adj prof, Concordia Univ. **RESEARCH** Metaphilosophy, contemporary ethical and political theory, and marxism. **SELECTED PUBLICATIONS** Auth, 22 bk(s) and 415 articles; Transforming Philosophy, 95; Naturalism Without Foundations, 96. **CONTACT ADDRESS** Dept of Philos, Concordia Univ, Montreal, 1455 de Maisonneuve W, Montreal, QC, Canada H3G 1M8.

NIETO, JOSE CONSTANTINO
PERSONAL Born 04/07/1929, El Ferrol, Spain, m, 1959, 2 children **DISCIPLINE** HISTORY OF RELIGIOUS THOUGHT **EDUCATION** Univ Santiago, BS, 49; United Evangel Sem, Madrid, BD, 56; Princeton Theol Sem, ThM, 62, PhD(relig), 67. **CAREER** Pastor, Span Evangel Church, 58-61; from asst prof to assoc prof, 67-78, prof relig, 78-82, Mary S Geiger Prof Relig & Hist, Juniata Col, 82-. **MEMBERSHIPS** Am Soc Reformation Res; Sixteenth Century Studies Conf; Am Acad Relig; AAUP. **RESEARCH** Spanish 16th century religious thought, particularly reformation, humanism and mysticism. **SELECTED PUBLICATIONS** Auth, Juan de Valdes and the Origins of the Spanish and Italian Reformation, Librairie Droz, Geneva, 70 & transl, Madrid-Mexico, Fondo de Cultura Economica, 79; Mystic, Rebel, Saint: A study of St John of the Cross, Geneva, Droz, 79 & Spanish ed, Mistico, poeta, rebelde, Santo, En torno a San Juan de Cruz, Marid-Mexico, Fondo de Cultura Economica, 82; ed and auth introd notes, Valdes Two Catechisms, The Dialogue on Christian Doctrine and the Christian Instruction for Children, Coronado Press, 81, 2nd. Enlarged ed. 93; auth, San Juan de la Cruz, poeta del amor profano, Ed Swan, Madrid, 88; auth, Religious Experience and Mysticism. Otherness as Experience of Transcedence, Univ Press of America, Lanham, 97; auth, El Renacimiento y la Otra Espana. Vision Cultural Socioespiritual, Librairie Droz, Geneva, 97. **CONTACT ADDRESS** Dept History, Juniata Col, 1700 Moore St, Huntingdon, PA 16652-2196. **EMAIL** nieto@juniata.edu

NIEVA, CONSTANTINO S.
PERSONAL Born 07/09/1929, Boac, Philippines, s **DISCIPLINE** RELIGIOUS STUDIES **EDUCATION** San Jose Sem, AB, 58; Univ Philippines, LLB, 53; Pontifical Gregorian Univ, STL, 65; STD, 70. **CAREER** Assoc pastor, Roman Cath Diocese Rockville Center, 74-. **MEMBERSHIPS** Medieval Acad of Am; MLA **RESEARCH** 14th Century English Mystics **SELECTED PUBLICATIONS** Auth, This Transcending God, London, 71; auth, The Cloud of Unknowing and St. John of the Cross, Mount Carmel, 78. **CONTACT ADDRESS** Roman Cath Diocese of Rockville Center, 16 Browns Ln, Bellport, NY 11713-2733.

NIGOSIAN, SOLOMON ALEXANDER
PERSONAL Born 04/23/1932, Alexandria, Egypt **DISCIPLINE** HISTORY OF RELIGION **EDUCATION** Univ Toronto, BA, 68; McMaster Univ, MA, 70, PhD(relig), 75. **CAREER** Teaching asst relig, McMaster Univ, 69-71; lectr, 72-75, Asst Prof Relig, Univ Toronto, 75-, Lectr relig, Ctr Christian Studies, Toronto, 71-74 & York Univ, 71-73; consult films relig, Ont Educ Commun Authority, Toronto, 72-73; assoc ed, Armenian Missionary Asn Am, Inc, Paramus, NJ, 72-76; asst prof, Ont Col Art, Toronto, 78-79. **MEMBERSHIPS** Int Asn Hist Relig; Can Soc Study Relig; Am Acad Relig. **RESEARCH** History of interreligious interactions with specialization in the Near East. **SELECTED PUBLICATIONS** Auth, World religions, S.A. Nigosian; auth, Judaism: The Way of Holiness, Solomon Nigosian; auth, Islam: The Way of Submission, Solomon Nigosian; auth, The Zoroastrian Faith: Tradition and Modern Research, S.A. Nigosian, Hardcover, 93; auth, World Faiths, S.A. Nigosian, 94; auth, The Zoroastrian Faith: Tradition and Modern Research, S.A. Nigosian, Paperback, 93; auth, World Religions: A Historical Approach, S.A. Nigosian, Paperback, 99. **CONTACT ADDRESS** Dept of Relig Studies, Univ of Toronto, 73 Queen's Park Crescent, Toronto, ON, Canada M5S 1K7. **EMAIL** nigosian@chass.utoronto.ca

NIKULIN, DMITRI
PERSONAL Born 01/13/1962, Novosibirsk, Russia, m, 2 children **DISCIPLINE** PHILOSOPHY **EDUCATION** Institute for Philosophy of the Academy of Sciences of Moscow, MA, 85; Inst for Philos of the Acad of Sci, Moscow, PhD, 90. **CAREER** Res Scholar, Inst of Philos of the Acad of Sci Moscow, 90; Res Scholar, Inst for Philos and Law of the Acad of Sci, Univ of Novosibirsk, 91-94; Vis Prof, Univ of Oslo, Norway, 92, 98; Vis Prof, Istituto italiano per gli studi filosofici, Naples, Italy, 92; Asst Prof, Univ of Essen, Ger, 94; Postdorctoral Res Assoc, Univ of Notre Dame, 94-95; Res Fel, Alexander von Humboldt Found, Univ of Tubingen, 97-98; Asst Prof, Grad Fac of Polit and Soc Sci, New Sch Soc Sci, 95-. **RESEARCH** Philosophy and history of science of late antiquity and early modernity (17th century). **SELECTED PUBLICATIONS** Auth, Space and Time in the Metaphysics of the XVIIth Century, Nauka (Novosibirsk), 93 (in Russian lang); Metaphysics and Ethic. Theoretical and Practical Philosophy in Antiquity and Modernity, C.H. Beck (Munchen), 96. **CONTACT ADDRESS** Dept Philos, New Sch for Social Research, 65 5th Ave, New York, NY 10003-3003. **EMAIL** nikulind@newschool.edu

NILSON, JON
PERSONAL Born 09/03/1943, Chicago, IL, m, 1998, 3 children **DISCIPLINE** THEOLOGY **EDUCATION** St Mary of the Lake Sem, AB, 65, STB, 67; Univ Notre Dame, MA, 68,

PhD(theol), 75. **CAREER** Asst prof theol, Ill Benedictine Col, 70-74 & Univ Dallas, 74-75; asst prof, 75-80, Assoc Prof Theol, Loyola Univ Chicago, 80-, Lonergan Trust Fund Pub subsidy, 77. **HONORS AND AWARDS** Best First Article in Patristics, NAm Patristic Soc, 77. **MEMBERSHIPS** Cath Theol Soc Am. **RESEARCH** Ecclesiology, ecumenism. **SELECTED PUBLICATIONS** Auth, Transcendent knowledge in insight: A closer look, Thomist, 73; To whom is Justin's dialogue with Trypho addressed?, Theol Studies, 77; Hegel's Phenomenology and Lonergan's Insight, Verlag Anton Hain, 78; Receiving the Vision - the Anglican Roman-catholic Reality Today - Bird,d, Theological Studies, Vol 0057, 1996; Progress in Unity - 50 Years of Theology Within the World-council-of-churches, 1945- 1995 - a Study Guide - Brinkman,me, Theological Studies, Vol 0057, 1996; Gods Spirit - Transforming a World in Crisis - Mullerfahrenholz,g, Horizons, Vol 0024, 1997. **CONTACT ADDRESS** Dept of Theol, Loyola Univ, Chicago, 6525 N Sheridan Rd, Chicago, IL 60626-5385. **EMAIL** jnilson@luc.edu

NISSEN, LOWELL A.
PERSONAL Born 01/10/1932, Fargus Falls, MN, m, 1960, 1 child **DISCIPLINE** PHILOSOPHY **EDUCATION** Univ of Minn, BA, 54; MA, 58; PhD, 62. **CAREER** Instr, Concordia Teachers Col, River Forest Ill, 60-61; From Instr to Prof, Univ of Ark, 63-. **HONORS AND AWARDS** Phi Beta Kappa; Regents Fel; Wolfe Fel. **MEMBERSHIPS** Am Philos Asn, Philos of Sci Asn, Brit Soc for the Philos of Sci. **RESEARCH** Teleological explanation in science, functions in biology, the relation of scientific theory to observation, realism-instrumentalism issue in theories. **SELECTED PUBLICATIONS** Auth, Teleological Language in the Life Sciences; coauth, Reflective Thinking: the Fundamentals of Logic; auth, John Dewey's theory of Inquiry and Truth. **CONTACT ADDRESS** Dept Philos, Univ of Arkansas, Fayetteville, 318 Old Main, Fayetteville, AR 72701-1201. **EMAIL** lnissen@comp.uark.edu

NISSIM-SABAT, MARILYN
PERSONAL Born 07/30/1938, Brooklyn, NY, m, 1967, 1 child **DISCIPLINE** PHILOSOPHY **EDUCATION** Brooklyn Col, BA, 59; DePaul Univ, PhD, 77; Univ Illinois, Chicago, MSW, 93. **CAREER** Prof philos, Lewis Univ, 79-. **MEMBERSHIPS** APA; Husserl Circle; Soc for Phenomenology and Existential Psych; Soc for Women's Philos. **RESEARCH** Integration of Husserlian phenomenology; psychoanalysis; Marxism; feminism. **SELECTED PUBLICATIONS** Auth, Freud, Feminism, and Faith, Listening, 85; auth, Psychoanalysis and Phenomenology: A New Synthesis, Psychoanalytic Rev, 96; auth, Kohut and Husserl: The Emphatic Bond, in, Self Psychology: Comparisons and Contrasts, Analytic, 89; auth, Autonomy, Empathy, and Transcendence in Sophocles' Antigone: A Phenomenological Perspective, Listening, 90; auth, The Crisis in Psychoanalysis: Resolution Through Husserlian Phenomenology and Feminism, Human Stud, 91; auth, Towards a Phenomenology of Empathy, Am Jour of Psychotherapy, 95; auth, An Appreciation and Interpretation of the Work of Lewis Gordon, C L R James Jour, 97; auth, Victims No More, Radical Philos Rev, 98. **CONTACT ADDRESS** Dept of Philos, Lewis Univ, Romeoville, IL 60446. **EMAIL** nissimma@lewisu.edu

NITSCHKE, BEVERLEY A.
DISCIPLINE RELIGION **EDUCATION** Carleton Univ, Canada, BA, 73; Yale Univ, Divinity Sch, M Div, 76; St Johns Univ, MA, 82; Univ Notre Dame, PhD, 88. **CAREER** Asst pastor, St John Lutheran Church, Conn, 77-79; assoc pastor, First English Lutheran Church, Ind, 85-87; campus pastor, Wayne State Col, 87-90; int pastor, Prince Peace Lutheran Church, Ind, 91-92; int pastor, Good Shepherd Lutheran Church, Ind, 94-96; int pastor, Holy Trinity Lutheran Church, Pa, 96-97; chap, fac mem, Thiel Col, 97-. **HONORS AND AWARDS** Pre-Doc Fel, Ed Found Am Asn Univ Women, 86-87. **RESEARCH** Liturgical, sacramental, and ecumenical theology. **SELECTED PUBLICATIONS** Coauth, With This Bread and Cup, Fortress/ Parish Life Press (Philadelphia), 85; auth, "The Sacrament of Penance: A Lutheran Perspective," Worship 63 (89), 327-340; auth, "The Eucharist: For the Forgiveness of Sins," Ecumenical Trends 20 (91), 92-93; auth, "Eucharist: Forgiveness of Sins or Reconciliation?" Liturgical Ministry 1(92), 85-92; auth, "By Water and The Spirit - - A United Methodist Understanding Of Baptism A Lutheran Response," Ecumenical Trends 22 (93), 3-7; auth, "Confession and Forgiveness: The Continuing Agenda," Worship 68 (94), 353-368; auth, "Twenty-five Years Later: A Goal in Question," Dialog 35 (96), 58-59; auth, 'The Use Of the Means of Grace: A Response," Ecumenical Trends 24 (95), 7-11; auth, "The Use of the Means of Grace -- The Final Proposal," Ecumenical Trends 27(98), 1-7. **CONTACT ADDRESS** Dept Religion, Thiel Col, 75 College Ave, Greenville, PA 16125-2186.

NNAM, NKUZI
DISCIPLINE POLITICAL SCIENCE, PHILOSOPHY **EDUCATION** Depaul Univ, BA, 81; Depaul Univ, MA, 82; Depaul Univ, PhD, 85. **CAREER** Assoc Prof, Dominican Univ, 85-. **HONORS AND AWARDS** Excellence in Teaching Awds, Depaul Univ, 88-89; Excellence in Teaching Awd, Dominican Univ, 93; Phi Sigma Tau; Alpha Lambda Delta. **RESEARCH** African culture and philosophy. **SELECTED PUBLICATIONS** Auth, Anglo-American and Nigerian Jurisprudence, 89; auth, Magnani: African Culture and Philosophy, forthcoming. **CONTACT ADDRESS** Dept Polit Sci & Philos, Dominican Univ, 7900 Division St, River Forest, IL 60305-1066.

NNORUKA, SYLVANOS I.
PERSONAL Born 06/16/1953, Enugu, Nigeria **DISCIPLINE** PHILOSOPHY **EDUCATION** Urban Univ, Rome, BA, 78, BD, 82; Univ Catholique de Louvain, Belgium, MA philos, 87, MA lit, 88, PhD, 90; Katholieke Univ Leuven, Belgium, STL, 91. **CAREER** Lectr, dean of philos, St. Joseph Major Sem, Nigeria (on sabbatical). **MEMBERSHIPS** Nigeria Philos Assoc; APA. **RESEARCH** Phenomenological-Hermeneutical analysis of African values; human personality. **SELECTED PUBLICATIONS** Auth, Have Women a Voice in the Church, The Times, J of St. Augustine's School of Mass Commun, 93; auth, Personal Identity: A Philosophical Survey, 95; auth, Alfred Schutz on the Social Distribution of Knowledge, Darshana Int, 96; auth, Multiplicity of Ethnic Groups in Nigeria: A Challenge to the Nigerian Church, in Oguejiofor, ed, Ecclesia in Africa, The Nigerian Repsonse, Fulladu, Nigeria, 97. **CONTACT ADDRESS** 117 Valley Rd, Katonah, NY 10536. **EMAIL** ifeanyinno@aol.com

NOAH, LARS
DISCIPLINE LAW **EDUCATION** Harvard Univ, AB, JD. **CAREER** Assoc prof, Univ Fla, 94-; past assoc, Covington Burling, Wash, DC. clerk, Ch Judge Abner J. Mikva, US Ct Appeals, DC Circuit; ed, Harvard Law Rev. **MEMBERSHIPS** DC Bar; Pa Bar; Food and Drug Law Inst. **RESEARCH** Administrative law, conflict of laws, food and drug law, products liability, torts. **CONTACT ADDRESS** School of Law, Univ of Florida, PO Box 117625, Gainesville, FL 32611-7625. **EMAIL** noah@law.ufl.edu

NOBLE, WILLIAM P.
PERSONAL Born 01/25/1932, New York, NY, m, 1998, 2 children **DISCIPLINE** LAW & HISTORY **EDUCATION** Lehigh Univ, BA, 54; Univ Penn, JD, 61. **CAREER** Instr, 86- , writing assessment mentor, 94- , Commun Col of Vermont; Ver Hum Scholar, Ver Coun on Hum, 91- ; adj fac, external degree prog, Johnson State Col, 93- . **HONORS AND AWARDS** Nominated for Eli Oboler Awd, ALA Intellectual Freedom Roundtable, 92. **MEMBERSHIPS** Authors Guild; Freedom to Read Comt. **RESEARCH** Law; history; writing. **SELECTED PUBLICATIONS** Auth, Bookbanning in America, Eriksson, 90; auth, Show Don't Tell, Eriksson, 91; auth, Twenty-Eight Most Common Writing Blunders, Writer's Digest, 92; auth, Conflict, Action & Suspense, Writer's Digest, 94; auth, The Complete Guide to Writers' Conferences and Workshops, Eriksson, 95; auth, Three Rules for Writing a Novel, Eriksson, 97; auth, Writing Dramatic Nonfiction, Eriksson, 00. **CONTACT ADDRESS** PO Box 187, Island Heights, VT 05769. **EMAIL** bn777@voice.net

NOBLES, PATRICIA JOYCE
PERSONAL Born 06/16/1955, St. Louis, MO, 1 child **DISCIPLINE** LAW **EDUCATION** Southwest Baptist Coll, BA, 1976; Univ of AK, JD, 1981. **CAREER** US District Judge, law clerk, 81-83; Southwestern Bell Telephone Co, Attorney, 83-99. **HONORS AND AWARDS** Mem of UALR Law Review 1980-81; mem of 1988 Class of Leadership America; author with Alexander C. Larson, Calvin Manson. **MEMBERSHIPS** Mem of the executive bd, Urban League 1981-84; mem Amer Assoc of Trial Attorneys 1983-87; mem AK Bar Assn 1983-87; pres AK Assn of Women Lawyers 1985-86; mem of bd KLRE Public Radio Station 1986-87; mem NAACP 1989-; mem, Missouri Bar Assn, 1981-; Board of Literacy Instructor for Texas, 00-. **SELECTED PUBLICATIONS** "Competitive Necessity and Pricing In Telecommunications Regulation," Federal Communications Law Journal, 1989. **CONTACT ADDRESS** SBS Communications, Inc, 201 S Arkard, Rm 3021, Dallas, TX 75202.

NODA, KEISUKE
PERSONAL Born, Japan, m, 2 children **DISCIPLINE** PHILOSOPHY **EDUCATION** New School for Soc Res, PhD, 96. **CAREER** Adj prof, philos, SUNY Westchester Commun Col, 96- . **MEMBERSHIPS** APA. **RESEARCH** Phenomenology; Eastern thoughts. **CONTACT ADDRESS** 1137 Crescent Dr., Tarrytown, NY 10591-5816.

NOGALES, PATTI
PERSONAL Born 02/08/1961, Caracas, Venezuela, m, 1991, 2 children **DISCIPLINE** PHILOSOPHY OF LANGUAGE **EDUCATION** St Johns Col, BA, 82; N Arizona Univ, MA, 98; Stanford, PhD, 93. **CAREER** Tchr, ORME School, 82-84; writing lab instr, 84-85, instr spec lrng asst ctr, 85-88, N Arizona Univ; tchg asst, Stanford Univ, 89-91; instr, Col Dupage, 95-96. **MEMBERSHIPS** Asn Am Philos **RESEARCH** Philosophy of language; psycholinguistics. **SELECTED PUBLICATIONS** Auth, adj workshop prog critical classes, Jour Reading & Lrng, 87; Appleworks for Tchrs, 97; Appleworks for Stud, 91; Works for Stud, 91; Metaphorically Speaking, CSLI Press. **CONTACT ADDRESS** 270 Vereda Pradera, Goleta, CA 93117. **EMAIL** pno@juno.com

NOGEE, JOSEPH LIPPMAN
PERSONAL Born 06/16/1929, Schenectady, NY, m, 1960, 2 children **DISCIPLINE** POLITICAL SCIENCE **EDUCATION** Georgetown Sch of Foreign Serv, BSFS, 50; Univ Chicago, MA, 52; Yale Univ, PhD, 58. **CAREER** Prof, polit sci, Univ Houston, 58- ; vis prof NY Univ, 63, 64, Vanderbilt Univ, 69-70, US Army War Col, 79, 80, 84, 85, Rice Univ 82, 86, 87, 90, Univ Va, 88, 89; Political Science, emeritus, Univ Houston, 99. **HONORS AND AWARDS** NY State Regents fel; Overbrook Fel & Sterling Fel, Yale; Rockefeller grant; Carnegie Endowment grant; tchg excellence award, Univ Houston. **RESEARCH** Russian foreign policy. **SELECTED PUBLICATIONS** Auth, Soviet Policy Toward International Control of Atomic Energy, Notre Dame, 61; coauth, The Politics of Disarmament, Praeger, 62; ed, Man, State, and Society in the Soviet Union, Praeger, 72; co-ed, Congress, The Presidency, and American Foreign Policy, Pergamon, 81; ed, Soviet Politics: Russia after Brezhnev, Praeger, 85; coauth, Peace Impossible/War Unlikely, Little Brown, 88; coauth, Soviet Foreign Policy since World War II, Macmillan, 92; coauth, Russian Politics: The Struggle for a New Order, Allyn & Bacon, 97; coauth, Russian Foreign Policy, ME Sharpe, 98. **CONTACT ADDRESS** Dept of Political Science, Univ of Houston, Houston, TX 77204. **EMAIL** jnogee@uh.edu

NOHRNBERG, JAMES CARSON
PERSONAL Born 03/19/1941, Berkeley, CA, m, 1964, 2 children **DISCIPLINE** RENAISSANCE & MEDIEVAL LITERATURE, BIBLE STUDIES **EDUCATION** Harvard Col, BA, 62; Univ Toronto, PhD, 70. **CAREER** Tch fel Eng, Univ Toronto, 63-64; Jr fel, Soc of Fel, Harvard Univ, 65-68; adj Eng, Harvard Univ, 67-68; Actg instr Eng, Yale Univ, 68-69, lectr, 69-70, asst prof, 70-75; Prof English, Univ VA, 75-; lectr, 74-00, Yale, Princeton, MLA, Columbia, Hopkins, Kenyon, NEH Seminars, Cornell, Univ VA, Georgetown, Emory, Univ Calif Irvine, Ind Univ, Newberry Libr, Loyola Balitmore, Univ South. **HONORS AND AWARDS** Robert Frost Poetry Prize, Kenyon Col 60; Acad of Am Poets Prize, harvard Col, 62; Woodrow Wilson Fel, Univ of Toronto, 62-63; Queen Elizabeth II Ontario Scholarship, 64-65; Soc of Fels, Harvard Univ, 65-68; Morse Fel, Yale Univ, 74-75; Center for Advanced Studies, Univ of VA, 75-78; Guggenheim Fel, 81-82; Gaus Seminar lectures, Princeton Univ, 87; Institute for Advanced Study, Indiana Univ, 91. **MEMBERSHIPS** MLA; Spenser Society, ACLA, PBK. **RESEARCH** Bible, Dante, Spenser, Shakespeare, Milton, allegory. **SELECTED PUBLICATIONS** Auth, Allegories of scripture, Shofar, winter 93; Like unto Moses: The Constituting of an Interruption, Ind Univ, 95; The Descent of Geryon: the Moral System of Inferno XVI-XXXI, Dante Studies, 98; Allegory De-Veiled: A New Theory for Construing Allegory's Two Bodies, Modern Philol, 11/98; Fortune and romance: Boiardo in America, In: Orlando's Opportunity: Chance, Luck, Fortune, Occasion, Boats, and Blows in Boiardo's Orlando Innamorato, Ariz State Univ, 98; Lectura Dantis, Inferno, In: Inferno XVIII: Introduction to Malebolge, Univ CA, 98; auth, Earthly Love, Spiritual Love, Love of Saints, The Love That Moves the Sun and Other Stars in Inferno XVIII, Univ Souht, 99; auth, Health, Sickness, and Death in the Middle Ages, Dante's Adam's Dropsy: A Case-Study in the Literary Etiology of the Sickness of Sin, Univ South, 99; Sparks and Seeds: Medieval Literature and Its Afterlife: Essays Honor of John Freccero, The Love That Moves the Sun and Other Stars in Dante's Hell, Brepol, 00. **CONTACT ADDRESS** Dept of Eng, Univ of Virginia, 219 Bryan Hall, Charlottesville, VA 22903. **EMAIL** jnc@virginia.edu

NOLAN, JOHN JOSEPH
PERSONAL Born 11/01/1928, Derby, CT, m, 1976, 5 children **DISCIPLINE** LAW **EDUCATION** Holy Cross Col, BS, 50; Suffolk Univ, JD, 55; Harvard Univ, LLM, 62. **CAREER** From asst prof to assoc prof, 57-62, prof law, 62-75, partner, Vinci & Nolan, 75-78, Prof Law, Suffolk Univ, 78-, Ford Found teaching fel, Law Sch, Harvard Univ, 62; lectr, Boston Univ Law Sch, 77. **MEMBERSHIPS** Am Bar Asn; Mass Bar Asn. **RESEARCH** Administrative law; workman's compensation. **CONTACT ADDRESS** Sch of Law, Suffolk Univ, 120 Tremont St., Boston, MA 02108-4977. **EMAIL** jjnolan@acad.suffolk.edu

NOLAN, RICHARD T.
PERSONAL Born 05/30/1937, Waltham, MA, m, 1955 **DISCIPLINE** PHILOSOPHY OF RELIGION **EDUCATION** Trinity Col, BA, 60; Hartford Sem, MDiv, 63; Yale Univ, MA, 67; NYork Univ, PhD, 73. **CAREER** Instr, Latin and English, Watkinson Sch, 61-62; instr Math, Cathedral Choir School, 62-64; instr, math and religion, Cheshire Acad, 65-67; instr, philos and educ, 67-68, asst acad dean, 68-70, Hartford Sem; prof philos and soc sci, Mattatuck Commun Col, 69-92; adj lectr philos and theology, 73, 89-92, 97-98, Barry Univ; adj prof philos, Florida Atlantic Univ, 98-99; Adjunct philosophy prof, Palm Beach Comm College, 00- . **HONORS AND AWARDS** Hon Canon, Christ Church Cathedral, Hartford Conn. **MEMBERSHIPS** APA; Authors Guild; Interfaith Alliance; Anglican Asn of Bibl Scholars; AAUP; Am Acad of Relig; Hemlock Soc; Integrity; English-Speaking Union. **RESEARCH** Philosophical theology; systematic theology; ethics. **SELECTED PUBLICATIONS** Ed and contribur, The Diaconate Now, 68; auth, The Significance of the Religious Thought of Edmond La B.

Cherbonnier for a Basic Objective of Religious Education, NYU, 73; coauth, Living Issus in Ethics, Wadsworth, 82, Newed, 2000, Universe; ed, Occasional Papers from Christ Church Cathedral, 91-94; coauth, Living Issues in Philosophy, 9th ed, Wadsworth, 95; ed, www.philosophy-religion.org, 00-. **CONTACT ADDRESS** 2527 Egret Lake Dr, West Palm Beach, FL 33413-2181. **EMAIL** canonn@adelphia.net

NOLAN, RITA
DISCIPLINE PHILOSOPHY **EDUCATION** Univ Penn, PhD 65; Boston College, MA 60, BSc 58. **CAREER** Assoc Prof, Prof, 79 to 93-, SUNY Stony Brook; vis acad, 87-88, Oxford Univ; G. Santayana fel, 80, Harvard Univ; vis Assoc Prof, 78-79, Columbia Univ; Assoc Prof, 73-78, Univ N C Chapel Hill; vi Prof, 75, Univ Warwick Eng; ten Assoc Prof, act head, Asst Prof, vis Prof, 70-73, Univ N C Greensboro; vis Asst Prof, 68-70, Univ IL; Asst Prof, 65-68, Univ Wisc Madison; vis Asst Prof, 66-67, Univ Wisc Milwaukee; Instr, 63-65, Chestnut Hill College; vis Lectr, teach fel ed Asst, res Asst, teach Asst, 61-64, Univ Penn. **MEMBERSHIPS** APA; SPP; ESPP. **RESEARCH** Theory of knowledge, philos of lang, philos of psychology. **SELECTED PUBLICATIONS** Auth, Cognitive Practices: Human Language and Human Knowledge, Oxford UK, Cambridge, USA, Blackwell, 94; Distinguishing Perceptual from Conceptual Categories, in Philo and the Cognitive Sciences, 94; The Unnaturalness of Grue, in Lang Art and Mind, 94; Anticipatory Themes in the Writings of Lady Welby, in Essays on Significs, 90; rev, Communicative Processes in Human Development: One Philo Perspective, in Perspective Comments and Background Articles, Inst for Hum Comm Res, 95; rev, Consciousness in Action, 98, in Philosophical Books, forthcoming. **CONTACT ADDRESS** Philosophy Dept, SUNY, Stony Brook, Stony Brook, NY 11794-3750. **EMAIL** RDNOLAN@ccmail.sunysb.edu

NOLL, MARK ALLAN
PERSONAL Born 07/18/1946, Iowa City, IA, m, 1969, 3 children **DISCIPLINE** HISTORY OF CHRISTIANITY (NORTH AMERICAN) **EDUCATION** Wheaton Col, Ill, BA, 68; Univ Iowa, MA, 70, Trinity Evangel Divinity Sch, MA, 72; Vanderbilt Univ, PhD(church hist), 75. **CAREER** Asst prof hist, Trinity Col, Ill, 75-78; from assoc prof hist to McManis prof of Christian Thought, Wheaton Col, Ill, 78-, vis prof Regent Col, Vancouver, 90, 95, 97; vis prof Harvard Divinity School, spring 98. **HONORS AND AWARDS** Fels, Nat Endowment for Humanities 78-79, 87-88, Pew Charitable Trusts, 93-94. **MEMBERSHIPS** Am Cath Hist Asn; AHA; Am Soc Church Hist; Canadian Soc of Church Hist; Conf Faith & Hist; OAH. **RESEARCH** Theology, politics, society in America 1730-1860; Protestants in the North Atlantic region; cultural history of the Bible. **SELECTED PUBLICATIONS** Auth, Christians in the American Revolution, Eerdmans, 77; Between Faith and Criticism: Evangelicals, Scholarship, and the Bible in America, Harper & Row, 86; One Nation Under God? Christian Faith and Political Action in America, Harper & Row, 88; Princeton and the Republic, 1768-1822, Princeton Univ Press, 89; A History of Christianity in the United States and Canada, Eerdmans, 92; The Scandal of the Evangelical Mind, Eerdmans, 92; Turnung Points: Decisive Moments in the History of Christianity, Baker Books, 98. Co-ed and contrib, The Bible in America, Oxford Univ Press, 82; Religion and American Politics, Oxford Univ Press, 89; coauth, The Search for Christian America, 2nd ed, Helmers & Howard, 89; Evangelicalism: Comparative Studies of Popular Protestantism in North America, the British Isles, and Beyond, Oxford Univ Press, 93; Evangelicals and Science in Historical Perspective, Oxford Univ Press, 99. **CONTACT ADDRESS** Hist Dept, Wheaton Col, Illinois, Wheaton, IL 60187-5593. **EMAIL** Mark.Noll@wheaton.edu

NORDBY, JON JORGEN
PERSONAL Born 11/14/1948, Madison, WI **DISCIPLINE** PHILOSOPHY, LOGIC **EDUCATION** St Olaf Col, BA, 70; Univ Mass, Amherst, MA, 76, PhD philos, 77. **CAREER** Assoc prof, Pacific Lutheran Univ, Tacoma, WA, 77-present; former dept chmn, Philos, 95-98; med investigator, Pierce County Med Examiner, 88-92; consult, Coroner's Serv Forensic Unit, BC Canada, 88-; cons, King County Medical Examiner, Seattle, WA, 93-; cons, Pierce County Medical Examiner, 92-97; cons, Puyallup Police Dept, Pullayup, WA, 95-; cons, Final Analysis, Tacoma, WA, 85-; sr res fel, Dept Forensic Med, Guy's Hosp, London, 94; Metorius Serv Award, Amer Acad of Forensic Sciences, Boston, 94; Presentations Serv Award, Intl Assoc of Bloodstain Pattern Analysts, Seattle, 97. **HONORS AND AWARDS** Phi Beta Kappa; Wilson Fel; Rockefeller Fel. **MEMBERSHIPS** Am Philos Asn; Am Lutheran Church; Philos Sci Asn. **RESEARCH** Philosophy of forensic science, evidence, logic. **SELECTED PUBLICATIONS** Auth, Dead Reckoning: The Art of Forensic Detection, CRC Press, 99. **CONTACT ADDRESS** Dept of Philosophy, Pacific Lutheran Univ, 12180 Park Ave S, Tacoma, WA 98447-0014. **EMAIL** finalanalysis@msn.com

NORDENHAUG, ERIK
DISCIPLINE PHILOSOPHY **EDUCATION** Mercer Univ, BA, 85; Emory Univ, MA, 89; PhD, 94. **CAREER** Asst Prof, Armstrong Atlantic State Univ, 95-. **MEMBERSHIPS** APA **RESEARCH** Philosophy of Technology; Ethics; History of Philosophy. **CONTACT ADDRESS** Dept Lang, Lit & Philos, Armstrong Atlantic State Univ, 11935 Abercorn St, Savannah, GA 31419-1909. **EMAIL** nordener@mail.armstrong.edu

NOREN, STEPHEN J.
PERSONAL Born 12/16/1938, New York, NY, m, 1972, 2 children **DISCIPLINE** PHILOSOPHY **EDUCATION** Ohio Univ, BS; Univ Mass, MA, PhD. **CAREER** Assoc prof, Calif State Univ, Long Beach, 68-77; assoc prof, Univ Wisc, 75-77. **HONORS AND AWARDS** ACLS fel, 75; Gugenheim fel, 75. **MEMBERSHIPS** APA. **RESEARCH** Philosophy of the mind; philosophical sciences. **CONTACT ADDRESS** 469 Hampstead Way, Santa Cruz, CA 95062. **EMAIL** snoren@got.net

NORMAN, ANDREW
PERSONAL Born 09/03/1963, Washington, DC, m, 1992, 1 child **DISCIPLINE** PHILOSOPHY **EDUCATION** Wesleyan Univ, BA, 86; Northwestern Univ, PhD, 92. **CAREER** Asst prof, 93-98, Hamilton Col, vis asst, 92-93, Purdue Univ. **MEMBERSHIPS** APA; DSA. **RESEARCH** The narrative structure of dialogue; the hist of science; complexity theory. **SELECTED PUBLICATIONS** Auth, Teaching Wisdom, Knowledge, Teaching and Wisdom, Kluwer, 96; Regress and the Doctrine of Epistemic Original Sin, The Philosophical Quarterly, 97. **CONTACT ADDRESS** 198 College Hill rd, Clinton, NY 13323. **EMAIL** anorman@hamilton.ed

NORMAN, JUDITH
DISCIPLINE PHILOSOPHY **EDUCATION** Univ Wisc, Madison, PhD, 95. **CAREER** Asst prof, Trinity Univ, 97-. **RESEARCH** Nineteenth century human philosophy. **SELECTED PUBLICATIONS** Transl, "Ages of the World," by F.W.J. Schelling, Univ Mich, 97; auth, "Schelling," A Companion to the Philosophers, Blackwell, 98; "Utilitarianism," Living Well, Harcourt Brace, 99; "Ages of the World," Schelling: Between Fichte and Hegel, Gruner Verlag, 99; "Squaring the romantic Circle," Hegel and Aesthetics, SUNY, forthcoming. **CONTACT ADDRESS** Dept of Philosophy, Trinity Univ, San Antonio, TX 78212-7200. **EMAIL** jnorman@trinity.edu

NORMAN, KEN
DISCIPLINE LAW **EDUCATION** Univ Saskatchewan, BA, 63, LLB, 65; Oxford Univ, BCL, 67. **CAREER** Prof, 68-**HONORS AND AWARDS** Dir, Int Comn Jurists. **MEMBERSHIPS** Law Soc Saskatchewan. **SELECTED PUBLICATIONS** Auth, Your Clients and The Charter: Liberty and Equality, 88; Equality and Judicial Neutrality, 87. **CONTACT ADDRESS** Col of Law, Univ of Saskatchewan, 15 Campus Dr, Saskatoon, SK, Canada S7N 5A6. **EMAIL** Norman@law.usask.ca

NORMORE, CALVIN GERARD
PERSONAL Born Corner Brook, NF, Canada **DISCIPLINE** PHILOSOPHY, MEDIEVAL STUDIES **EDUCATION** McGill Univ, BA, 68; Univ Toronto, MA, 69, PhD(philos), 76. **CAREER** Lectr philos, York Univ, 72-74; Killam fel, Univ Alta, 76-77; Mellon Asst Prof Philos, Princeton Univ, 77-. **MEMBERSHIPS** Am Philos Asn; Can Medieval Acad Am; Soc Medieval & Renaissance Philos. **RESEARCH** Medieval philosophy; social and political philosophy; philosophy of time. **SELECTED PUBLICATIONS** Auth, Future contingents, In: Cambridge History of Later Medieval Philosophy, 82; Walter Burley on continuity, In: Infinity & Continuity in Ancient & Medieval Thought, 82; the Necessity in Deduction - Cartesian Inference and its Medieval Background, Synthese, Vol 0096, 1993. **CONTACT ADDRESS** Dept Philosophy, Univ of Toronto, Toronto, ON, Canada M5S 1A1. **EMAIL** normore@chass.utoronto.ca

NORRIS, JAMES D.
PERSONAL Born 11/02/1930, Richmond, MO, m, 1957, 3 children **DISCIPLINE** AMERICAN FRONTIER & ECONOMIC HISTORY **EDUCATION** Univ Mo-Columbia, BS, 56, MA, 58, PhD, 61. **CAREER** Asst prof hist, Hiram Col, 61-65; vis assoc prof, Univ Wis, 65-66; assoc prof hist, Univ Mo-St Louis, 66-69, prof, 69-79; Dean, Col Lib Arts & Sci, 79-95, Prof Hist, Northern Ill Univ, 95-; Am lectr, Fulbright-Hays prog, Univ Ghana, 72-73. **MEMBERSHIPS** Orgn Am Historians; Bus Hist Asn. **RESEARCH** Business history; American frontier; American economic history. **SELECTED PUBLICATIONS** Auth, One price policy in antebellum country stores, Bus Hist Rev, 62; Frontier Iron: The Meramec Iron Works 1826-1876, 64; Business longevity and the frontier iron industry, Ann Bus Hist, 65; The Missouri and Kansas Zinc Miner's Association, Bus Hist, 66; History of American Zinc, 68, co-ed, Politics and Patronage in the Gilded Age, 70 & R G Dun & Co, 1841-1900: The Development of Credit Reporting in 19th Century America, 78; coauth, Advertising & the Transformation of the American Economy, 1865-1920, Building a Tradition of Excellence, 91; The James Foundation in Missouri, 1941-1991, 96. **CONTACT ADDRESS** Col Lib Arts & Sci, No Illinois Univ, 1425 W Lincoln Hwy, De Kalb, IL 60115-2825.

NORRIS, JOHN
DISCIPLINE LAW **EDUCATION** Carleton Univ, BA, 82; Univ Western Ontario, MA, 84; Univ Toronto, LLB, 91. **CAREER** Assoc, Ruby & Edwardh; adj prof, Univ of Toronto. **RESEARCH** Criminal and constitutional law. **SELECTED PUBLICATIONS** Coauth, Myths, Hidden Facts and Common Sense: Expert Opinion Evidence and the Assessment of Credibility, 95; coauth, Sentencing for Second-Degree Murder: R v. Shropshire, 96; coauth, Developments in Criminal Procedure and Sentencing: The 1995-96 Term, 8 Sup Ct Lr (2nd), (97): 233. **CONTACT ADDRESS** Fac of Law, Univ of Toronto, 78 Queen's Park, Toronto, ON, Canada M5S 2C5.

NORRIS, JOHN MARTIN
PERSONAL Born 04/04/1962, Albuquerque, NM, s **DISCIPLINE** THEOLOGY **EDUCATION** Univ Dallas, BA, 84; Marquette Univ, PhD, 90. **CAREER** Dir, Rome prog, Univ Dallas, 93-95; Asst Prof Theology, Univ Dallas, 91-. **HONORS AND AWARDS** Schmitt fel, 88-90. **MEMBERSHIPS** Am Acad of Religion; North America Patristics Soc. **RESEARCH** Augustine; patristic exegesis. **SELECTED PUBLICATIONS** Auth, "The Theological Structure of Augustine's Exegesis in the Tractatus in Iohannis Euangelium," in Collectanea Augustiniana III: Augustine, Presbyter Factus Sum (Peter Lang, 93); auth, Macribius: A Classical Contrast to Christian Exegesis, Augustinian Studies, 97; auth, Augustine and Sign in the Tractates on John, Collectanea Augustiniana V; auth, "Abyss in the Confessions: Cosmic Darkness and Spiritual Depravity," in Studia Patristica, forthcoming. **CONTACT ADDRESS** Theol Dept, Univ of Dallas, 1845 E Northgate Dr., Irving, TX 75062. **EMAIL** jnorris@acad.udallas.edu

NORRIS, ROBERT
DISCIPLINE THEOLOGY **EDUCATION** Kings Col, London, BA; Univ St Andrews, MTh, PhD. **CAREER** Adj prof **HONORS AND AWARDS** Sr pastor, Fourth Presbyterian Church, Md; exec pastor, First Presbyterian Church, Hollywood. **SELECTED PUBLICATIONS** Ed, Themelios. **CONTACT ADDRESS** Dept of Theology, Reformed Theol Sem, No Carolina, 2101 Carmel Rd, Charlotte, NC 28226.

NORTHEY, RODNEY
DISCIPLINE LAW **EDUCATION** Queen's Univ, BA, 83; Dalhousie Univ, LLB, 87; York Univ, MA, 88; Osgoode Hall Law Sch, LLM, 88. **CAREER** Partner, Birchall Northey; adj prof, Univ of Toronto. **RESEARCH** Environmental law. **SELECTED PUBLICATIONS** Auth, The 1995 Annotated Canadian Environmental Assessment Act; auth, EARP Guidelines Order, Carswell, 94. **CONTACT ADDRESS** Fac of Law, Univ of Toronto, 78 Queen's Park, Toronto, ON, Canada M5S 2C5.

NORTHUP, LESLEY A.
PERSONAL Born 12/02/1947, New York, NY, 1 child **DISCIPLINE** RELIGIOUS STUDIES **EDUCATION** Catholic Univ of Amer, PhD, 91, MA, 84; Episcopal Divinity School, MDiv, 80; Univ of Wisconsin, BA, 70. **CAREER** Instr, Univ Md, 87-93; asst prof, 93-98, assoc prof, Fla Int Univ, 98- . **HONORS AND AWARDS** Florida Hum Council Master Scholar, 98; State of Florida Tchg Incentive Prog Awd, 97. **MEMBERSHIPS** Am Acad of Rel; N Am Acad of Lit; Societas Liturgica. **RESEARCH** Ritual Studies, Women's Ritualizing, 20th century American Religion, Episcopal Prayer Book Studies. **SELECTED PUBLICATIONS** Auth, Ritualizing Women: Patterns and Practices, Pilgrim Press, 97; co-ed, Leaps and Boundaries, Liturgical Revision in the Twenty-first Century, Morehouse Pub Co, 97; co-ed, Women and Religious Ritual, Pastoral Press, 93; co-ed, The 1892 Book of Common Prayer, Edwin Mellen Press, 93. **CONTACT ADDRESS** Dept of Relig Studies, Florida Intl Univ, Miami, FL 33199. **EMAIL** northupl@fiu.edu

NORTON, BRYAN G.
PERSONAL Born 07/19/1944, Marshall, MI, s **DISCIPLINE** PHILOSOPHY **EDUCATION** Univ Mich, BA, 66; PhD, 70. **CAREER** Prof, New Col of Univ S Flor, 70-87; prof, Ga Institute of Technology, 87-91; prof, Ga Insititute of Technology, 91-; assoc scientist, Zoo Atlanta, 90-. **HONORS AND AWARDS** Pi Sigma Alpha; BA with Distinction in Pol Sci; Gilbert White Fel, Resources for the Future. **MEMBERSHIPS** Am Philos Asn; Int Soc Ecol Econ; Int Soc Environ Ethics; Hastings Center Fel. **RESEARCH** Environmental Ethics; Sustainability Concepts and Measures; Environmental Valuation. **SELECTED PUBLICATIONS** Auth, Toward Unity Among Environmentalists, Oxford Univ Press, 91; Improving Ecological Communication: The Role of Ecologists in Environmental Policy Formation, Ecol Applications, 98; coauth, Sustainability: Ecological and Economic Perspectives, Land Econ, 97; coauth, Environmental Values: A Place-Based Theory, Environ Ethics, 97; coauth, Ethics on the Ark: Zoos, Animal Welfare, and Wildlife Conservation, Smithsonian Pr, 95; co-ed, Wolves and Human Communities, Island Press, 00. **CONTACT ADDRESS** School of Public Policy, Georgia Inst of Tech, Atlanta, GA 30332. **EMAIL** bryan.norton@pubpolicy.gatech.edu

NORTON, DAVID FATE
DISCIPLINE PHILOSOPHY **EDUCATION** Claremont Grad Sch, MA, 64; Univ Calif San Diego, PhD, 66. **CAREER** Prof emer. **RESEARCH** Early modern philosophy; Hume. **SELECTED PUBLICATIONS** Auth, David Hume: Common-Sense Moralist, Sceptical Metaphysician, Princeton: Prineton Univ Press, 82; auth, The Cambridge Companion to Hume, ed. Cambridge: Cambridge Univ Press, 93; auth, How a Sceptic May Live Scepticism in Faith, Scepticism and Personal Identity, ed. J.J. MacIntosh and H. Meynell, Edmonton: Univ of Alberta Press, 94; auth, David Hume in Cambridge Dictionary of Philosophy, Cambridge: Cambridge Univ Press, 95; auth, The David Hume Library, with M.J. Norton, Edinburgh: Edinburgh Bibliographical Soc, 95. **CONTACT ADDRESS** Philosophy Dept, McGill Univ, 845 Sherbrooke St, Montreal, QC, Canada H3A 2T5. **EMAIL** dnorton@philo.mcgill.ca

NORTON, ELEANOR HOLMES
PERSONAL Born 06/13/1937, Washington, DC, d **DISCIPLINE** LAW **EDUCATION** Antioch Coll, attended; Yale Univ, MA 1963; Yale Law School, JD 1964. **CAREER** American Civil Liberties Union, assistant legal director, 65-70; New York University Law School, adjunct assistant professor of law, 70-71; New York City Commission on Human Rights, chair, 70-77; US Equal Employment Opportunity Commission, chair, 77-81; The Urban Institute, senior fellow, 81-82; Georgetown University Law Center, professor of law beginning 1982; US House of Representatives, Washington, DC, nonvoting member, currently. **HONORS AND AWARDS** One Hundred Most Important Women, Ladies Home Journal, 1988; One Hundred Most Powerful Women in Washington, The Washingtonian Magazine, 1989; Distinguished Public Service Awd, Center for National Policy, 1985. **SELECTED PUBLICATIONS** "Equal Employment Law: Crisis in Interpretation, Survival against the Odds," Tulane Law Review, v. 62, 1988; "The Private Bar and Public Confusion: A New Civil Rights Challenge," Howard Law Journal, 1984; "Public Assistance, Post New-Deal Bureaucracy, and the Law: Learning from Negative Models," Yale Law Journal, 1983; author, Sex Discrimination and the Law: Causes and Remedies. **CONTACT ADDRESS** US House of Representatives, 1424 Longworth House Office Bldg, Washington, DC 20515.

NORTON, H. WILBERT, SR.
DISCIPLINE MISSIONS **EDUCATION** Wheaton Col, BA; Columbia Bible Col, MA, ThM; N Baptist Theol Sem, ThD. **CAREER** Dean, Wheaton Col Grad Sch, 72-80; prof. **HONORS AND AWARDS** Dir, Doctor of Missiology prog at RTS/Jackson, 89-93; interim dir, Stud Foreign Missions Fel-Intervarsity Christian Fel Missions Dept, 45; founder, Bible Inst Ubangi, Zaire; missions prog, Trinity Col/Evangel Divinity Sch, 50; pres, TEDS, 57-64; founding principal, JOS, ECWA Theol Sem, Nigeria; Dir, Comm to Assist Ministry Edu Overseas, 83-89; founding pres, Evangel Missiological Soc. **MEMBERSHIPS** Mem, Amer Missiological Soc. **SELECTED PUBLICATIONS** Auth, The European Background and History of the Free Church of America Missions; Twenty-five Years in the Ubangi; To Stir the Church; coauth, What's Gone Wrong with the Harvest?; ed, The Jubliee Story. **CONTACT ADDRESS** Dept of Missions, Reformed Theol Sem, No Carolina, 2101 Carmel Rd, Charlotte, NC 28226.

NORTON-SMITH, THOMAS M.
PERSONAL Born 08/02/1954, Springfield, IL, m, 1983, 2 children **DISCIPLINE** PHILOSOPHY **EDUCATION** Mo Southern State Col, BS, 79; Pittsburgh State Univ, Kans, MS, 81; Univ Ill, Urbana-Champaign, PhD, 88. **CAREER** Assoc and asst prof, Kent State Univ Stark Campus, 88-. **HONORS AND AWARDS** Kent State Univ Stark Teaching Campus Distinguished Teaching Awd, 91. **MEMBERSHIPS** Am Philos Asn, Am Indian Philos Asn, Am Asn of Philos Teachers, Ohio Philos Asn, Central States Philos Asn. **RESEARCH** Philosophy of mathematics, American Indian philosophy, logic, metaphysics. **SELECTED PUBLICATIONS** Auth, "An Arithematic of Action Kinds," Philos Studies, 63 (91): 217-230; auth, "A Note on Philip Kitcher's Conception of Mathematical Truth," Notre Dame J of Symbolic Logic, 33 (92): 136-139. **CONTACT ADDRESS** Dept Philos, Kent State Univ, Stark, 6000 Frank Ave NW, North Canton, OH 44720-7548. **EMAIL** tnorton-smith@stark.kent.edu

NORWOOD, KIMBERLY JADE
PERSONAL Born 08/18/1960, New York, NY, m, 1988 **DISCIPLINE** LAW **EDUCATION** Fordham Univ, BA, 1982; Univ of Missouri-Columbia, JD, 1985. **CAREER** Hon. Clifford Scott Green, law clerk, 85-86; Bryan Cave et al, litigation assoc, 86-90; Univ of MO-Columbia, visiting lecturer, Cleo Program, 90; Washington Univ School of Law, prof of law, 90-. **HONORS AND AWARDS** American Jurisprudence Awd, 1983; Bernard T Hurwitz Prize, 1984; Judge Shepard Barclay Prize, 1984-85. **MEMBERSHIPS** Greeley Comm Assn, bd mem, 1993-94; St Louis Women Lawyers Assn, bd mem, 1993-94; Mound City Bar Assn, 1986-; Jack & Jill of America, 1994-96; Girls, Inc, bd mem, 1994; Bar Assn of Metro St Louis, 1986-; Illinois Bar Assn, 1987-; American Bar Assn, 1986-; American Assn of Law Schools, 1993-. **SELECTED PUBLICATIONS** "Shopping for a Venue: The Need for More Limits on Choice," Miami Law Review, v 50, p 267, 1996. **CONTACT ADDRESS** Sch of Law, Washington Univ, Anheuser-Busch Hall, One Brookings Dr, Saint Louis, MO 63130. **EMAIL** norwood@wulaw.wustl.edu

NOTZ, JOHN K., JR.
PERSONAL Born 01/05/1932, Chicago, IL, m, 1966, 2 children **DISCIPLINE** MATHEMATICS, LAW **EDUCATION** Williams Col, BA, 53; Northwestern Univ, JD, 56. **CAREER** United States Air Force, 57-60; LAWYER, 60-95; ARBITRATOR/MEDIATOR, 96-. **MEMBERSHIPS** Am Law Inst; many other memberships in legal organizations. **RESEARCH** Chicago/Milwaukee history, 1885-1915. **SELECTED PUBLICATIONS** Auth, Edward G. Uihlein, Advocate for Landscape Architect Jens Jensen, Wis Acad Rev, 98; several other publications in legal journals. **CONTACT ADDRESS** 399 Fullerton Pkwy, Chicago, IL 60614-2810. **EMAIL** jnotz@gcd.com

NOVAK, DAVID
DISCIPLINE LAW **EDUCATION** Univ Chicago, BA, 61, MHL, 64; Georgetown Univ, PhD, 71. **CAREER** Prof, Univ Toronto **SELECTED PUBLICATIONS** Auth, The Election of Israel: The Idea of the Chosen People, Cambridge, 95. **CONTACT ADDRESS** Fac of Law, Univ of Toronto, 78 Queen's Park, Toronto, ON, Canada M5S 1A1.

NOVAK, JOSEPH A.
DISCIPLINE PHILOSOPHY **EDUCATION** Univ Notre Dame, PhD, 77. **RESEARCH** Ancient philos; medieval philos. **SELECTED PUBLICATIONS** Auth, pub(s) on ancient philosophy, Greek mathematics and method, Greek ethics and New Testament, and concept of immateriality. **CONTACT ADDRESS** Dept of Philosophy, Univ of Waterloo, 200 University Ave W, Waterloo, ON, Canada N2L 3G1. **EMAIL** jnovak@watserv1.uwaterloo.ca

NOVAK, PHILIP CHARLES
PERSONAL Born 12/28/1950, Chicago, IL, m, 1979 **DISCIPLINE** RELIGIOUS STUDIES **EDUCATION** Univ Notre Dame, BA, 72; Syracuse Univ, MA, 75, PhD, 81. **CAREER** Instr to PROF, PHILOS & RELIG, 80-, CHAIR, 83-, DOMINICAN COL. **MEMBERSHIPS** American Academy of Religion. **SELECTED PUBLICATIONS** Auth, The World's Wisdom, 94; auth, The Vision of Nietzsche, 95. **CONTACT ADDRESS** Dept of Philos, Relig, Dominican Col of San Rafael, 50 Acacia Ave, San Rafael, CA 94901. **EMAIL** novak@dominican.edu

NOWAK, JOHN E.
DISCIPLINE LAW **EDUCATION** Marquette Univ, BA; Univ Ill, JD. **CAREER** Prof, Univ Ill Urbana Champaign. **HONORS AND AWARDS** Ed, Univ Ill Law Forum. **MEMBERSHIPS** Nat Collegiate Athletic Asn. **SELECTED PUBLICATIONS** Auth, pubs on constitutional law. **CONTACT ADDRESS** Law Dept, Univ of Illinois, Urbana-Champaign, 52 E Gregory Dr, Champaign, IL 61820. **EMAIL** jnowak@law.uiuc.edu

NOWELL, IRENE
PERSONAL Born 06/08/1940, Dallas, TX, s **DISCIPLINE** BIBLICAL STUDIES; OLD TESTAMENT **EDUCATION** Mount St Scholastica, BA, 61; Cath Univ, MA, 64, PhD, 83; St John's, MA, 78. **CAREER** Prof, Dean Acad Aff, 87-88, Dean Students, 70-71, Mount St Scholastica/Benedictine Col, 64-72, 75-78, 83-94; adj prof, St John's Univ, 83-. **MEMBERSHIPS** SBL; CBA **RESEARCH** Biblical women; Psalms; Old Testament wisdom; Monasticism. **SELECTED PUBLICATIONS** Auth Sing A New Song: Responsorial Psalm in the Sunday Lectionary, Liturgical Press, 93; Women in the Old Testament, Liturgical Press, 97. **CONTACT ADDRESS** 801 S 8th, Atchison, KS 66002. **EMAIL** nowell@benedictine.edu

NOZICK, ROBERT
PERSONAL Born 11/16/1938, Brooklyn, NY, m, 1987, 2 children **DISCIPLINE** PHILOSOPHY **EDUCATION** Columbia Col, AB, 59; Princeton Univ, AM, 61, PhD(philos), 63; AM (honorary), Harvard Univ, 69; DHL (honorary), Knox Col, 83. **CAREER** Instr philos, Princeton Univ, 62-63, asst prof, 64-65; asst prof, Harvard Univ, 65-67; assoc prof, Rockefeller Univ, 67-69; Prof Philos, Harvard Univ, 69-, chmn dept, 81-84, Arthur Kingsley Porter Prof, 85-98, Pellegrino Univ Prof, 98-; Fulbright scholar, Oxford Univ, 63-64; fel, Ctr Advan Studies Behav Sci, 71-72; Rockefeller Foundation humanities fel, 79-80; NEH fel, 87-88; Guggenheim fel, 96-97. **MEMBERSHIPS** Am Philos Asn, pres, eastern div, 97-98; Am Acad Arts and Sciences; Council of Scholars, Library of Congress; Corresponding fel, British Academy. **RESEARCH** Philosophical explanations. **SELECTED PUBLICATIONS** Auth, Anarchy, State, and Utopia, Basic Books, 74 (Nat Book Award, 75); Philosophical Explanations, Harvard Univ Press, 81 (Ralph Waldo Emerson Award, Phi Beta Kappa, 82); The Examined Life, Simon & Schuster, 89; The Nature of Rationality, Princeton Univ Press, 93; Socratic Puzzles, Harvard Univ Press, 97. **CONTACT ADDRESS** Dept of Philos, Harvard Univ, Emerson Hall, Cambridge, MA 02138-3800. **EMAIL** nozick@fas.harvard.edu

NUFFER, RICHARD T.
PERSONAL Born 10/28/1946, Toledo, OH, m, 1967, 4 children **DISCIPLINE** THEOLOGY **EDUCATION** Valparaiso Univ, BA, 68; Baylor Univ, JD, 75; Concordia Theol Sem, MDiv, 93. **CAREER** Attorney, 75-89; Pastor, 92-97; Prof, Concordia Theol Sem, 97-. **MEMBERSHIPS** Mo Synod, Lutheran Church. **RESEARCH** Confessional Lutheran Homiletics. **CONTACT ADDRESS** Dept Pastoral Ministry, Concordia Theol Sem, 6600 N Clinton St, Fort Wayne, IN 46825-4916. **EMAIL** nufferrt@mail.ctsfw.edu

NUGENT, DONALD CHRISTOPHER
PERSONAL Born 12/31/1930, Lousiville, KY, s **DISCIPLINE** HISTORY, THEOLOGY **EDUCATION** PhD Univ of IA, 65; MA Theol, Univ of San Francisco, 82. **CAREER** Asst Prof, Univ KY, 66-95; Vis Prof, Univ Col Dublin, 72-73; Univ Alberta, 61-62. **RESEARCH** Msyticism; Spirituality, esp St John of the Cross. **SELECTED PUBLICATIONS** Ecummenism in the Age of the Reformation, Harvard, 74; Masks of Satan: The Demonic in History, Sheed & Ward, 83; Mysticism, Deathe and Dying, Albany: SUNY, 94; Satori in St John of the Cross: The Eastern Buddhist, Kyoto, 95; Pax Sexuals: The Month, London, 98. **CONTACT ADDRESS** Dept Hist, Univ of Kentucky, Lexington, KY 40506.

NUGENT, PATRICK
PERSONAL Born 05/26/1965, Evanston, IL, m, 1991, 2 children **DISCIPLINE** RELIGION **EDUCATION** Xavier Univ,HAB, 87; Univ Chicago, MDiv, 99. **CAREER** Visiting Asst Prof, Earlham Col, 96-99; Director of Institute for Quaker Studies, Earlham Col, 99-. **MEMBERSHIPS** Am Acad Relig; Am Hist Asn; Friends Hist Asn; Medieval Acad of Am; Hagiography Soc. **RESEARCH** Medieval Hagiography; Ritual Theory; Quakerism. **CONTACT ADDRESS** Earlham Col, 801 Nat Rd W, Richmond, IN 47374-4021. **EMAIL** nugenpa@earlham.edu

NUNN, KENNETH B.
DISCIPLINE LAW **EDUCATION** Stanford Univ, AB; Univ Calif, Berkeley, JD. **CAREER** Prof, Univ Fla, 90-. **MEMBERSHIPS** Exec Comt, Nat Asn Public Interest Law; Calif Bar; DC Bar. **CONTACT ADDRESS** School of Law, Univ of Florida, PO Box 117625, Gainesville, FL 32611-7625. **EMAIL** Nunn@law.ufl.edu

NUTBROWN, RICHARD A.
DISCIPLINE PHILOSOPHY **EDUCATION** Carleton Univ, PhD, 85. **CAREER** Assoc prof **RESEARCH** Political philosophy. **SELECTED PUBLICATIONS** Auth, History, Language and Time; pub(s) on political philosophy. **CONTACT ADDRESS** Dept of Philosophy, Univ of Waterloo, 200 University Ave W, Waterloo, ON, Canada N2L 3G1. **EMAIL** nutbrown@uwaterloo.ca

NUTT, R.
PERSONAL Born 07/31/1953, Kansas City, MO, m, 1978, 2 children **DISCIPLINE** US RELIGIOUS HISTORY **EDUCATION** Vanderbilt Univ, PhD, 86 **CAREER** Asst prof, 88-94, Assoc prof, 94-, Muskingum Coll. **HONORS AND AWARDS** Wm Rainey Harper Awd for Outstanding Scholarship, 94, 98 **MEMBERSHIPS** Amer Soc of Church Hist; Presbyterian Historical Soc; Amer Acad of Relig **RESEARCH** American Religious Hist; Church-State Issues; Presbyterian Hist **SELECTED PUBLICATIONS** Auth, Contending for the Faith: The First Two Centuries of the Presbyterian Church in Cincinnati Area, 91; Toward Peacemaking: Presbyterians in the South and National Security, 1945-1983, 94; Presbyterians and Nuclear Weapons: Fifty Years of a Life-and-Death Issue, American Presbyterians, Summer 95; The Whole Gospel for the Whole World: G Sherwood Eddy and American Protestant Social Mission, 97; G. Sherwood Eddy and Attitudes of the Protestants in the US toward Global Mission, Church History, 97. **CONTACT ADDRESS** Brown Chapel, Muskingum Col, New Concord, OH 43762. **EMAIL** rnutt@muskingum.edu

NUZZO, ANGELICA
PERSONAL Born, Italy **DISCIPLINE** HISTORY OF PHILOSOPHY **EDUCATION** Liceo Classico, BA, 83; Univ Heidelberg, PhD, 91; Scuola Normale Superiore, PhD, 91. **CAREER** Vis asst prof, Univ Heidelberg, 93-94, 94-95; invest, Univ Studi dell'Aquila, 95-96; vis asst prof, DePaul Univ, 96-97; asst prof, 97-. **HONORS AND AWARDS** DAAD Fel; Postdoc Fel; TransCoop Res Grant; DU Res Grant. **MEMBERSHIPS** APA; HAS; NAKS; NAFS; NASS; SPEP; IPS; IHV; IHG. **RESEARCH** German idealism; political philosophy; ethics' logic; theory of translation. **SELECTED PUBLICATIONS** Auth, Rappresentazione a concetto nella 'logica' della Filosofia del diritto di Hegel, Guida (Napoli), 90; auth, Logica a sistema: Sull'idea hegeliana di filosofia, Pantograf (Genova), 92; auth, La logica a la metafisica di Hegel: Guida alla critica, a cura di A. Nuzzo, La Nuova Italia Scientifica (Roma), 93; auth, "Per una metodologia della storia della filosofia secondo Hegel: Le introduzioni berlinesi alle lezioni sulla storia della filosofia, 1819-1831, Il Cannocchiale 1 (97): 49-56; auth, "An Outline of Italian Hegelianism (1832-1998), Owl of Minerva 29 (98): 165-205; auth, "Nachklange der Fichte-Rezeption Jacobis

in der Schrift, Von den gottlichen Dingen and ihrer Offenbarung," in Fichte and Jacobi, hrsg. V. K. Hammacher (Amsterdam, Rodophi: Fichte Studien, 98): 121-137; auth, "The Idea of 'Method' in Hegel's Science of Logic: A Method for Finite Thinking and Absolute Knowing," Hegel Soc Bull Gt Brit 39/40 (99): 1-18; rev of, Hegel's Idea of a Phenomenology of Spirit, European J Philo (99); auth, "Ding/Eigenschaft," "Idee," "Ganzes/Teil," "Gattung/Gattungswesen," "Spekulation," "Theorie," in Enzyklopadie Philosophie, ed. HJ Sandkuhler (Hamburg, Meiner, 00); auth, "Geschichte der Philosophie als Ubersetzungsproze," in Ubersetzung: Sprache and Interpretation, hrsg. W Buttemezer, HJ Sandkuhler, Peter Lang, 00; transl of, B. Bourgeois, Il destino francese dei Lineamenti di Filosofia del diritto di Hegel (Le destin francais des Principes de la Philosophie du Droit de Hegel), Giornale critico della filosofia italiana, 67 (88): 321-347. **CONTACT ADDRESS** Dept Philosophy, DePaul Univ, 2320 North Kenmore Ave, Chicago, IL 60614-3210.

NYE, ANDREA
DISCIPLINE PHILOSOPHY **EDUCATION** Radcliffe Col, BA, 61; Univ Ore, PhD, 77. **CAREER** Prof, Univ Wis, 78-. **RESEARCH** Feminist theory, history of philosophy, philosophy of language. **SELECTED PUBLICATIONS** Auth, Feminist Theory and the Philosophies of Man, Croom Helm (London, UK), 97; auth, Feminist Theory and the Philosophies of Man, Routledge, Chapman, Hall (New York, NY), 88; auth, Words of Power: A Feminist Reading of the History of Logic, Routledge, Chapman, Hall (New York, NY), 90; auth, Philosophia: The Thought of Rosa Luxemburg, Simone Weil, Hannah Arendt, Routledge (New York, NY), 94; auth, Philosophy and Feminism: At the Border, Twayne Publs (New York, NY), 95; auth, The Philosophy of Language: The Big Questions, Blackwell (New York, NY); 99; auth, The Princess and the Philosopher: The Letters of Elisabeth Palatine to Rene Descartes, Rowman and Littlefield (Latham, MD), 99. **CONTACT ADDRESS** Dept Philos, Univ of Wisconsin, Whitewater, 800 W Main, Whitewater, WI 53190.

NYSSE, RICHARD W.
DISCIPLINE OLD TESTAMENT **EDUCATION** Concordia Senior Col, BA, 68; Concordia Sem, MDiv, 72; Harvard Divinity Sch, ThD, 84. **CAREER** Fac mem, Pacific Lutheran Sem; asst prof, 78; prof, 93-. **HONORS AND AWARDS** Asst pastor, Christ Lutheran Church, 74-76; bk ed, World & World, 80-84, 84-91. **SELECTED PUBLICATIONS** Auth, An Analysis of the Greek Witnesses to the Text of the Lament of David, The Hebrew and Greek Texts of Samuel, 80. **CONTACT ADDRESS** Dept of Old Testament, Luther Sem, 2481 Como Ave, Saint Paul, MN 55108. **EMAIL** rnysee@luthersem.edu

NYSTROM, DAVID P.
PERSONAL Born 04/27/1959, San Mateo, CA, m, 1982, 1 child **DISCIPLINE** NEW TESTAMENT; ROMAN HISTORY **EDUCATION** UC Davis, BA, 81, PhD, 92; Fuller Theol Sem, MDiv, 86. **CAREER** Prof & chr bibli & theol student, N Park Univ. **HONORS AND AWARDS** Phi Beta Kappa; Outstanding Teaching Awd, UC Davis; Outstanding Teaching Awd, n Park Col. **MEMBERSHIPS** Soc for Prom Roman Studenties; Soc Bibl Lit; fel, Inst Bibl Res. **RESEARCH** New Testament, Gospel of John & James, Slavery, Women in the Roman Prov. **SELECTED PUBLICATIONS** Auth, James, (97); auth, "Josephus," NIDNTT, (97). **CONTACT ADDRESS** Bibl & Theol Stud, No Park Univ, 3225 W Foster Ave, Chicago, IL 60625-4823. **EMAIL** dnystrom@northpark.edu

O

O'BRIEN, J. WILLARD
PERSONAL Born 10/19/1930, New York, NY **DISCIPLINE** AMERICAN LEGAL SYSTEM **EDUCATION** Fordham Univ, BS, 52; Fordham Univ Sch Law, JD, 57. **CAREER** Prof; Villanova Univ, 65-98 & dean, Law Sch, 72-83. **MEMBERSHIPS** Canon Law Soc; Order of the Coif; Amer Bar Asn; Pa Bar Asn; bd dir, Interfaith Coun on the Holocaust. **RESEARCH** Human rights, holocaust. **SELECTED PUBLICATIONS** Contrib, The Subversion of Justice: Lessons in Legal Ethics, in the Holocaust Forty Years Later, 89 & The Obligation of a Law School to Instruct Students on Morality, in Holocaust Education, 85. **CONTACT ADDRESS** Law School, Villanova Univ, 299 N. Springmill Rd., Villanova, PA 19085-1692. **EMAIL** obrien@law.vill.edu

O'CONNELL, ROBERT H.
PERSONAL Born 12/04/1955, Kitchener, ON, Canada, m, 1982, 2 children **DISCIPLINE** RELIGION **EDUCATION** Univ of Western Ontario, BA, 78; Dallas Theol Sem, ThM, 82, DTS, ThD, 89; Univ of Cambridge UK, PhD 93. **CAREER** Co Christian Univ, prof, 91-95; Web Developer, 96-99; Hastings Col, prof, 99-00. **HONORS AND AWARDS** ORS AWARD, 88-91; Lamb Foundation Shipley Award, 88-89; Fitzwilliam Col Cambridge UK Crosse Award 89-91 **MEMBERSHIPS** AAR, NAPH, SBL, SOTS **RESEARCH** Hebrew Bib; Anc Mid-East Stud; Philo Lang; Cosmology. **SELECTED PUBLICATIONS** Auth, Concentricity and Continuity: The Literary Structure of Isaiah, Jour for Stud OT, Sheffield Acad Press, 94; The Rhetoric of the Book of Judges, Vetus Testamentum 96; Telescoping N+1 Patterns in the Book of Amos, Vetus Test, 96; Deuteronomy ix 7-x7,10-11: Paneled Structure, Double Rehearsal and the Rhetoric of Covenant Rebuke, Vetus Test, 92; Proverbs vii 16-17: A Case of Fatal Deception in a 'Woman and the Window' Type Scene, Vetus Test, 91. **CONTACT ADDRESS** 1120 Pleasant St., Hastings, NE 68901-4153. **EMAIL** rhoconnell@wordsmyth.com

O'CONNOR, DANIEL D.
PERSONAL Born 03/26/1931, Detroit, MI, m, 1959, 2 children **DISCIPLINE** PHILOSOPHY **EDUCATION** Univ Detroit, BA, 55; Univ Toronto, MA, 58; Yale Univ, PhD, 61. **CAREER** From asst prof to assoc prof, 61-76, Prof Philos, Williams Col, 76-, Dean of Col, 80-. **MEMBERSHIPS** Am Philos Asn; Soc Phenomenol & Existential Philos. **RESEARCH** Phenomenology; history of philosophy. **SELECTED PUBLICATIONS** Coauth, Readings in Existential Phenomenology, Prentice-Hall, 67 & Creation: Impact of an Idea, Scribner's, 69. **CONTACT ADDRESS** Dept of Philos, Williams Col, 36 Hawthorne Rd, Williamstown, MA 01267-2600.

O'CONNOR, DAVID
PERSONAL Born 07/02/1949, Cork, Ireland, d, 3 children **DISCIPLINE** ANALYTIC PHYLOSOPHY, PHILOSOPHY OF RELIGION **EDUCATION** Nat Univ Ireland, BA, 71, MA, 73; Marquette Univ, PhD, 79. **CAREER** Asst philos, Villanova Univ, 79-80; Prof Philos, Seton Hall Univ, NJ, 80. **MEMBERSHIPS** Am Philos Asn. **RESEARCH** Analytical philos of relig; Hume. **SELECTED PUBLICATIONS** Auth, On the viability of Macquarrie's God-talk, Philos Studies Vol 23, 75; Remarks of Macquarrie's philosophy of death, Expository Times, Vol 88, 77; Identification and description in Ayer's sense-datum theory, Mod Schoolman, Vol 57, 80; Moore and the Paradox of analysis, Philosophy, Vol 57, 82; The Metaphysics of G E Moore, Reidel, 82; contribr, Etienne Gilson, Nelson Goodman, Charles Morris, In: Twentieth Century Thinkers, Macmillan & Gale Res; God and Inscrutable Evil, Rowman & Littlefield, 98; Hume on Religion, Routledge. **CONTACT ADDRESS** Dept of Philos, Seton Hall Univ, So Orange, 400 S Orange Ave, South Orange, NJ 07079-2696. **EMAIL** Oconnoda@shy.edu

O'CONNOR, DAVID
DISCIPLINE PHILOSOPHY **EDUCATION** Univ Notre Dame, BA, 80; Stanford Univ, PhD, 86. **CAREER** Assoc prof. **RESEARCH** Ancient philosophy; ethics. **SELECTED PUBLICATIONS** Auth, Socrates and the Socratics, Columbia Hist W Philos, 97; Aristotle's Audience and Political Ambition, 98; Socrates and Political Ambition, Ancient Philos, 98; co-ed, Essays on the Foundations of Aristotelian Political Science, 91. **CONTACT ADDRESS** Philosophy Dept, Univ of Notre Dame, 336/7 O'Shaughnessy, Notre Dame, IN 46556. **EMAIL** o'connor.2@nd.edu

O'CONNOR, DENNIS
DISCIPLINE PHILOSOPHY **EDUCATION** Univ St. Louis, PhD. **CAREER** Assoc Prof, Concordia Univ. **RESEARCH** Phenomenology, hermeneutics and philosophy of the social sciences. **SELECTED PUBLICATIONS** Auth, Ecart and Difference: Seeing and Writing in Merleau-Ponty and Derrida. **CONTACT ADDRESS** Dept of Philos, Concordia Univ, Montreal, 1455 de Maisonneuve W, Montreal, QC, Canada H3G 1M8.

O'CONNOR, JUNE ELIZABETH
PERSONAL Born Chicago, IL **DISCIPLINE** RELIGIOUS ETHICS **EDUCATION** Mundelein col, BA, 64; Marquette Univ, MA, 66; Temple Univ, MA, 72, PhD, 73. **CAREER** Instr theol, Mundelein Col, 65-69; asst prof, 73-79, assoc prof, 79-90, Prof Relig Studies, Univ Calif, Riverside, 90-. **HONORS AND AWARDS** Distinguished Teaching Award, Univ Calif, Riverside, 79; Fac Public Serv Award, Univ Calif, Riverside, 93. **MEMBERSHIPS** Col Theol Soc; Am Acad Relig; Soc Christian Ethics; Pac Coast Theol Soc. **RESEARCH** Religious ethics; theology of liberation; women and religion; contemporary western religious thought. **SELECTED PUBLICATIONS** Auth, The Quest for Political and Spiritual Liberation: A Study in the Thought of Sri Aurobindo Ghose, Farleigh Dickinson Univ Press, 77; On Doing Religious Ethics, J Relig Ethics, spring 79; The Moral Vision of Dorothy Day, Crossroad Publ, 91; Does a Global Village Warrant a Global Ethic?, Relig, 94; On Being Bi-Religious in Efroymson and Rainer, The Open Church, 97; Ritual Recognition of Abortion: Japanese Buddhist Practices and U S Jewish and Christian Proposals in Cahill and Farley, Embodiment, Morality, and Medicine; auth, "Teachers of Reality: Voices of Resistance and Reconstruction," in Sumner B. Twiss and Bruce Grelle; auth, "Explorations in Global Ethics: Comparative Religious Ethics and Interreligious Dialogue, Westview Press (Boulder, CO), 98. **CONTACT ADDRESS** Dept Relig Studies, Univ of California, Riverside, 900 University Ave, Riverside, CA 92521. **EMAIL** june.oconnor@ucr.edu

O'CONNOR, PATRICIA
DISCIPLINE PHILOSOPHY **EDUCATION** Gustavus Adolphus Col, BA, 84; Univ Exeter, MA, 85; PhD, 90. **CAREER** Asst prof, City Univ NYork Queens Col, 92-; assoc provost, City Univ NYork Queens Col, 98-. **MEMBERSHIPS** Am Philos Asn, Soc for the Study of Women Philosophers, Soc for Women in Philos. **RESEARCH** Ethics, Business Ethics, Philosophy of Literature, Feminist Philosophy, Problem of Evil. **SELECTED PUBLICATIONS** Auth, To Love the good: The Moral Philosophy of Iris Murdoch, Peter Lang, 96; coauth, "How not to Make Ethical Decisions: 'Guidelines' from Management Textbooks," Teaching Business Ethics 3.1 (99): 69-86; auth, "Iris Murdoch: Love and The Bell," in Presenting Women Philosophers, ed. Tougas, Cecile and Sara Ebenreck (Temple Univ Press, 00). **CONTACT ADDRESS** Dept Philos, Queens Col, CUNY, 6530 Kissena Blvd, Flushing, NY 11367-1575.

O'DEA, JANE
DISCIPLINE PHILOSOPHY **EDUCATION** Univ Alberta, PhD, 90. **CAREER** Porf, Univ of Lethbridge. **HONORS AND AWARDS** Univ of Lethbridge Distinguished Teaching Award, 95. **SELECTED PUBLICATIONS** Auth, pubs on music, aesthetics, education and feminism. **CONTACT ADDRESS** Dept of Philosophy, Univ of Lethbridge, 4401 University Dr W, Lethbridge, AB, Canada T1K 3M4. **EMAIL** jane.odea@uleth.ca

O'DONOVAN-ANDERSON, MICHAEL
PERSONAL Born 08/07/1968, m, 1992 **DISCIPLINE** PHILOSOPHY; SCIENCE **EDUCATION** Yale Univ, PhD, 96; Univ Notre Dame, BS, 90. **CAREER** Tutor, St John's Col, 96-98; Biomedical Systems Scientist, Digene Res & Develop, 98-99; Programmer, AAPM, 99-; Area Editor, Ancient Philosophy, The Internet Encyclopedia of Philosophy 99-. **MEMBERSHIPS** Amer Philos Assoc; Amer Assoc for Advancement of Sci. **RESEARCH** History of Philosophy; Cognition & Embodiment. **SELECTED PUBLICATIONS** Auth, Content and Comportment: On Embodiment and the Epistemic Availability of the World, Rowman & Littlefield, 97; ed, The Incorporated Self: Interdisciplinary Perspectives on Embodiment, Rowman & Littlefield, 96. **CONTACT ADDRESS** 1 Physics Ellipse, College Park, MD 20740. **EMAIL** m_o'donovan-anderson@post.harvard.edu

O'HARA, MARY L.
PERSONAL Born 05/28/1923, Indianapolis, IN **DISCIPLINE** PHILOSOPHY **EDUCATION** Col of St. Catherine, BA, 46; Catholic Univ of Am, MA, 48, PhD, 56. **CAREER** Col of St. Catherine, Col of St. Mary, prof, 48-91. **HONORS AND AWARDS** Phi Beta Kappa **MEMBERSHIPS** APA; ACPA; Metaphysical Soc. **RESEARCH** The human person; wisdom; religious life. **SELECTED PUBLICATIONS** Auth, The Future of Religious Life, Collegeville Liturgical Pr, 90; auth, The Logic of Human Personality, Humanities, 97; Substances and Things, Univ Press of Amer. **CONTACT ADDRESS** 1870 Randolph Ave, Saint Paul, MN 55105-1796. **EMAIL** mlohara@stkate.edu

O'HYUN, PARK
PERSONAL Born 03/15/1940, Taegu, South Korea, 3 children **DISCIPLINE** RELIGION **EDUCATION** Educ: Yonsei Univ, Korea, BTh, 64; Knox Col, NZ, dipl, 65; Bible Col, dipl, 65; Temple Univ, PhD(relig), 72. **CAREER** From asst prof to assoc prof, 71-81, Prof Orient Relig & Philos, Appalachian State Univ, 81-. **MEMBERSHIPS** Am Acad Relig. **RESEARCH** Buddhism, Zen Buddhism and Chinese religions. **SELECTED PUBLICATIONS** Auth, The World of Nothingness, Knox Collegian, 64; Paul van Buren and Theology, Theol Rev, 65; Oriental Ideas in Recent Religious Nought, 74 & Religion and the Life of Man, CSA Press; Zen as the Cosmic Psychotherapy, Pastoral Coun, 77; Invitation to Dialogue between East and West, 97. **CONTACT ADDRESS** Dept of Philos & Relig, Appalachian State Univ, 1 Appalachian State, Boone, NC 28608-0001. **EMAIL** parko@appstate.edu

O'MEARA, THOMAS F.
PERSONAL Born 05/15/1935, Des Moines, IA, s **DISCIPLINE** THEOLOGY **EDUCATION** Univ Munich **CAREER** Teacher, Aquinas Inst, 67-78; vis prof, Weston School of Theol, Sem of Sts. Peter and Paul, Wartburg Theol Sem; Dir, Univ Notre Dame, 81-84; Chair, 85-86; William K. Warren Prof, Univ Notre Dame. **HONORS AND AWARDS** John Courtney Murray Awd, Catholic Theological Soc, 91. **MEMBERSHIPS** Cath Theol Soc of Am; N Am Paul Tillich Soc; Comm on the Intellectural Life of the Dominican Order for 1980 to 1984. **SELECTED PUBLICATIONS** Auth, "Fundamental Theology and Intelligent Extraterrestrials", Theol Studies 60 (99):3-30; auth, "Reflections on Yves Congar and Theology in the US", U.S. Cath Hist 17 (99):91-105; auth, "Teaching Karl Rahner", Philos and Theol 8 (98):16-30; auth, "The Presence of Thomas Aquinas", Theol Today 55 (98):46-88; auth, "Ministry in the Catholic Church Today. The Gift of Some Historical Trajectories", Together in God's Service, (98):7-86; auth, Tarzan, Las Casas, and Rahner", Theol Digest 45 (98):319-328; auth, "The Expansion of Ministry: Yesterday, Today, and Tomorrow", The Renewal That Awaits Us, (97):91-103; auth, Thomas Aquinas, Theologian, Univ of Notre Dame Pr, 97; auth, Seeing Theologi-

cal Forms, Archives of Modern Christian Art: Monograph Number Six, Belmont, The Archives of Modern Christian Art, 97. **CONTACT ADDRESS** Dept Theology, Univ of Notre Dame, 327 O Shaugnessy Hall, Notre Dame, IL 46556-5639.

O'NEILL, WILLIAM GEORGE
PERSONAL Born 07/03/1943, Evergreen Park, IL, m, 1972, 2 children **DISCIPLINE** PHILOSOPHY OF SCIENCE; BUSINESS ETHICS **EDUCATION** Iona Col, BA, 64; Boston Col, MA, 67, PhD(philos), 70. **CAREER** Instr, 68-71, asst prof, 71-78, Assoc Prof Philos, Iona Col, 78- **MEMBERSHIPS** Am Philos Asn; Metaphys Soc Am; Am Cath Philos Asn. **RESEARCH** History of science; business ethics; theory of knowledge; moral theory. **CONTACT ADDRESS** Dept of Philosophy, Iona Col, 715 North Ave, New Rochelle, NY 10801-1890. **EMAIL** woneill@iona.edu

O'ROURKE, MAUREEN
PERSONAL Born 10/18/1963, Poughkeepsie, NY, m, 1998 **DISCIPLINE** LAW **EDUCATION** Marist Col, BS, 85; Yale Law Sch, JD, 90. **CAREER** Assoc accounting analyst to atty, IBM Co, 85-93; vis prof, Univ Victoria Law Sch, 99; vis prof, Columbia Univ, 99; assoc prof to prof and assoc dean, Boston Univ, 93-. **HONORS AND AWARDS** Metcalf Award, Boston Univ. **MEMBERSHIPS** NY State Bar Asn. **RESEARCH** Commercial law; Antitrust; Intellectual property; Law on the Internet. **SELECTED PUBLICATIONS** Auth, "Drawing the Boundary Between Copyright and Contract: Copyright Preemption of Software License Terms," Duke L J, 95; co-auth, "A False Start?: The Impact of Federal Policy on the Genotechnology Industry," Yale J on Regulation, 96; auth, "Copyright Preemption After the Procd Case: A Market Based Approach," Berkeley Technol L J, 97; auth, "Rethinking Remedies at the Intersection of Intellectual Property and Contract: Toward a Unified Body of Law," Iowa L Rev, 97; auth, "Defining the Limits of Free-Riding in Cyberspace: Trademark Liability for Metatagging," Gonzaga L Rev, 98; auth, "Striking a Delicate Balance: Intellectual Property, Antitrust, Contract and Standardization in the computer Industry," Harvard J of L and Technol, 98; auth, "Fencing Cyberspace: Drawing Borders in a Virtual World," Minn L Rev, 98; auth, "Toward a Doctrine of Fair Use in Patent Law," Columbia L Rev, 00; auth, "Shaping Competition on the Internet: Who Owns Product and Pricing Information?" Vanderbilt L Rev, 00; auth, "Property Rights and Competition on the Internet: In Search of an Appropriate Analogy," Berkeley Technol L J, (forthcoming). **CONTACT ADDRESS** Sch of Law, Boston Univ, 765 Commonwealth Ave, Boston, MA 02215. **EMAIL** mo1@bu.edu

O'SULLIVAN, MICHAEL
PERSONAL Born 04/10/1948, Ft. Wayne, IN, m, 1 child **DISCIPLINE** RELIGION; SOCIAL ETHICS **EDUCATION** Univ Southern Cal, PhD, 81. **MEMBERSHIPS** Amer Acad Religion **RESEARCH** New Religious Movements; Popular Religion **CONTACT ADDRESS** 4717 Lowell Ave., La Crescenta, CA 91214-1636. **EMAIL** mosull@voa.gov

OAKES, EDWARD T.
DISCIPLINE RELIGION **EDUCATION** St Louis Univ, BA, 71, MA, 76; Jesuit School Theol, MDiv, 79; Union Theol Sem, MPhil, 84, PhD, 87. **CAREER** Adj instr, Fordham Univ, 85-87; vis asst prof, 87-90 & 93-94, adj asst prof, 90-92, NYU; res fel, Deutscher Akademischer Austauschdienst, 92-93; scholar res, Cambridge Univ, 95 & Immaculate Conception Sem, Seton Hall Univ, 96; Assoc Prof, Regis Univ, 96-. **HONORS AND AWARDS** Res grant Marguerite Eyer Wilbur Found, 92-93; Bakers Dozen Distinguished Tchr Awd 1989 Stud Coun, NYU. **SELECTED PUBLICATIONS** Auth, Discovering the American Aristotle, First Things, 93; Cardinal Newman on the Season of Lent, America, 93; Jewish Ethics Engaged, First Things, 93; The Paradox of the Literal: Protestant and Roman Catholic Confrontations with the Biblical Canon in the Sixteenth and Seventeenth Centuries, Reform and Counter-Reform: Dialectics of the Word in Western Christianity Since Luther, Mouton de Gruyter, 94; A Life of Allegory: Type and Pattern in Historical Narratives, Through a Glass Darkly: Essays in the Religious Imagination, Fordham Univ Press, 96; German Essays on Religion, Continuum, 94; The Achievement of Alasdair MacIntyre, First Things, 96; Pattern of Redemption: The Theology of Hans Urs von Balthasar, Continuum; 97; Exposed Being, Jour of Relig, 98; The Blind Programmer, First Things, 98. **CONTACT ADDRESS** Jesuit Commun, Regis Univ, 3333 Regis Blvd., Denver, CO 80221. **EMAIL** oakesedw@regis.edu

OAKES, JAMES L.
PERSONAL Born 02/21/1924, Springfield, IL, m, 1999, 3 children **DISCIPLINE** LAW **EDUCATION** Harvard Col, AB, 45; Harvard Law School, LLB, 47. **CAREER** Atty Gen VT, 67-69; US Dist Judge, VT, 70-71; US Circuit Judge, Second Circuit, 71-, chief judge, 89-92, sr status, 92-; adj prof, Duke Univ Law School, 85-90, 92-96; adj prof Iowa Univ Col Law, 93-97. **HONORS AND AWARDS** Hon LLD New Eng Col, 76, Suffolk Univ, 80, Vermont Law School, 95; Learned Hand Awd Excellence Jurisp, 83; Environ Law Inst Awd, 89; Louis Dembitz Brandeis Medal Distinguished Legal Serv; 91; William J Brennan Awd for Commitment to Indiv Rights & Civil Liberties, 92; Gold Medal Awd Distinguished Serv In Law, NY State Bar Asn, 92; Edward Weinfeld Awd for distinguished contrib to Admin Justice, 92 & Distinguished Publ Serv Awd, 94 both from NY Cty Law Asn. **SELECTED PUBLICATIONS** Auth, commentary on Judge Edwards Growing Disjunction Between Legal Education and the Legal Profession, Mich Law Rev, 93; rev, The Tenth Justice, Learned Hand: The Man and the Judge, Brooklyn Law Rev, 94; Personal Reflections on Learned Hand and the Second Circuit, Stanford Law Rev, 95; Tribute to Thomas Debevoise, VT Law Rev, 95; On Appeal: Courts, Lawyering, and Judging, Yale Law Jour, 95; Developments in Environmental Law: What to Watch, 95; rev Intellect and Craft: The Contributions of Justice Hans Linde to American Constitutionalism, Oregon Law Rev, 96. **CONTACT ADDRESS** US Court of Appeals, Second Circuit, PO Box 696, Brattleboro, VT 05302-0696.

OAKLANDER, L. NATHAN
DISCIPLINE PHILOSOPHY **EDUCATION** Univ of Iowa, BA, 67; MA, 70; PhD, 73. **CAREER** Prof of Philosophy, Univ of Mich, 95; Prof of Philosophy and Chair, The Dept of Philosophy, Univ of Mich, 92-95; David M. French Prof and Prof of Philosophy, Univ of Mich, 90-92; Prof of Philosophy and Chair, The Dept of Philosophy, Univ of Mich, 85-90; Prof of Philosophy, Univ of Mich, 82-85; Assoc Prof of Philosophy and Chair, The Dept of Philosophy, Univ of Michigan, 78-82; Assoc Prof of Philosophy, Univ of Mich, 77-78; Asst Prof of Philosophy, Univ of Michigan, 73-77; Instructor of Philosophy, Univ of Michigan, 72-73. **HONORS AND AWARDS** Visiting Fellowship, Cambridge Univ, England, Fall 01. **MEMBERSHIPS** Amer Philosophical Assoc; Philosophy of Time; and MIND Association. **RESEARCH** Philosophy of Time; Metaphysics; Existentialism; Philosophy of Religion; Early Modern Philosophy; Personal Identity; Universals and Particulars. **SELECTED PUBLICATIONS** Auth, "God Evil and Death: Questions in the Philosophy of Religion," Belmont, California: Wadsworth Publishing Company, forthcoming 01; auth, "Existentialist Philosophy: An Introduction," Upper Saddle River, NJ: Prentice Hall, Inc., 92, second edition, 96: xi + 402, coauth, "Time, Change and Freedom: An Introduction to Metaphysics," New York and London: Routledge, 95, vi + 215, co-authored with Quentin Smith; auth, "The New Theory of Time," New Haven, CT: Yale Univ Press, 94, xiv + 378, co-edited with Quentin Smith; auth, "Metaphysics: Classic and Contemporary Readings," Belmont, California: Wadsworth Publishing Company, 91, second edition, forthcoming, x + 542, Co-edited with Ronald Hoy; auth, "Temporal Relations and Temporal Becoming: A Defense of a Russellian Theory of Time," Lanham, MD: Univ Press of America, 84, 238. **CONTACT ADDRESS** Dept Philosophy, Univ of Michigan, Flint, 303 East Kearsley St., Flint, MI 48502-1907. **EMAIL** lno@umich.edu

OAKLEY, JOHN BILYEU
PERSONAL Born 06/18/1947, San Francisco, CA, m, 1974, 2 children **DISCIPLINE** LAW & PHILOSOPHY **EDUCATION** Univ Calif, Berkeley, BA, 69; Yale Univ, JD, 72. **CAREER** Law clerk, Supreme Ct Calif, 72-73; sr law clerk, US Dist Ct, Conn, 73-74 & Supreme Ct Calif, 74-75; actg prof, 75-79, Prof Law, Univ Calif Davis, 79-; Pub mem, New Motor Vehicle Bd Calif, 76-82; Federal Judicial Code Revision Project, Am Law Ins, 95-; reporter, Comt on Federal-State Jurisdiction, U S Judicial Conf, 91-96; reporter, Civil Justice Reform Act Ad Group, U S Dist Ct, Ed Calif, 91-94; reporter, Speedy Trial Planning Group, US Dist Ct, Ed Calif, 78-82; scholar-in-residence, Civil Rights Div, US Dept Justice, 79-80; mem, Duke Univ Primate Center Bd of Visitors, 98-00, (with Rex R. Parsch Bacher) Civil Procedure, 90,96; (with Charles A. Wright) Federal Courts-Cases and Materials, 99; mem, Calif Judicial Counc Appellate Process Task Force, 97-01, Board of Directors, Amer Judicature Soc, 96-98. **MEMBERSHIPS** Am Law Ins; Amintaphil; Phi Beta Kappa **RESEARCH** Legal philosophy; anthropology; law. **SELECTED PUBLICATIONS** Coauth (with Edgar Bodenheimer and Jean C Love), An Introduction to the Anglo-American Legal System, West Publ Co, 80,88; (with Robert S Thompson), Law Clerks and the Judicial Process, Univ Calif Press, 80; fac visitor, Oxford Univ, 82-83. **CONTACT ADDRESS** Sch of Law, Univ of California, Davis, King Hall, Davis, CA 95616-5201. **EMAIL** jboakley@ucdavis.edu

OAKMAN, DOUGLAS E.
PERSONAL Born 02/11/1953, Des Moines, IA, m, 1976, 2 children **DISCIPLINE** RELIGION **EDUCATION** Univ Iowa, BA, 75; Christ Sem, MDiv, 79; Grad Theol Union, PhD, 86. **CAREER** Instr, San Francisco Theol Sem, 84-86; Lectr, Univ San Francisco, 85; Vis Asst Prof, Santa Clara Univ, 86-87; From Asst Prof to Assoc Prof, Pac Lutheran Univ, 88-. **HONORS AND AWARDS** Who's Who Among Students in Am Univ and Col, 78-79; Phi Beta Kappa; Regency Advan and Fac Excellence Awds, Pac Lutheran Univ; Who's Who in the West; Who's Who in Am Educ, 5th Ed; Who's Who in Bibl Studies and Archaeol; Dict of Int Biog, 22nd Ed; Who's Who in Relig, 4th Ed. **MEMBERSHIPS** Soc of Bibl Lit, Cath Bibl Asn, The Context Group. **RESEARCH** Social-scientific criticism of the Bible, historical Jesus studies, ancient economy, Hermeneutics. **SELECTED PUBLICATIONS** Auth, Jesus and the Economic Questions of His Day, Edwin Mellen Pr, 86; auth, "The Archaeology of First-Century Galilee and the Social Interpretation of the Historical Jesus," Soc of Bibl Lit 1994 Seminar Papers, Scholars Pr (94): 220-251; auth, "The Ancient Economy," in The Soc Sci and New Testament Interpretation, Hendrickson Publ (96): 126-143; auth, "The Lord's Prayer in Social Perspective," in Authenticating the Words of Jesus, E J Brill (98): 137-186; auth, Palestine in the Time of Jesus: Social Structures and Social Conflicts, Fortress Pr, 98; auth, "Economics of Palestine," in Dict of New Testament Background, InterVarsity Pr (forthcoming). **CONTACT ADDRESS** Dept Relig, Pacific Lutheran Univ, 12180 Park Ave S, Tacoma, WA 98447-0001. **EMAIL** oakmande@plu.edu

OBAYASHI, HIROSHI
PERSONAL Born 12/03/1934, Osaka, Japan, m, 1960, 3 children **DISCIPLINE** THEOLOGY, PHILOSOPHY OF RELIGION **EDUCATION** Doshisha Univ Col, Japan, BA, 57, BD, 59; Andover Newton Theol Sch, STM, 63; Univ Pa, PhD(relig), 67. **CAREER** Minister, United Church of Christ, Japan, 59-62; from instr to asst prof relig, 67-73, assoc prof, 73-82, Prof Relig, Rutgers Univ, New Brunswick, 82- **MEMBERSHIPS** Am Acad Relig, AAUP. **RESEARCH** Contemporary theology; religion and politics; history of religion. **SELECTED PUBLICATIONS** Auth, Ernst Troeltsch and Contemporary Theology, Kyodan Press, Tokyo, 72; Agape and history: A theological essay on historical consciousness, Univ Press Am, 81; auth, Death and Afterlife: Perspectives of World Religions, Greenwood Pr, 92; auth, Death and Eternal Life: A Christian Theological Understanding, Jordan Pr, Tokyo, 94; Towards a Trinitarian Theology of Religions - a Study of Tillich,paul Thought - Lai,pc, J of Ecumenical Studies, Vol 0033, 1996; Out of Silence - Emerging Themes in Asian-American Churches - Matsuoka,f, J of Ecumenical Studies, Vol 0034, 1997. **CONTACT ADDRESS** Dept of Religion Douglass College, Rutgers, The State Univ of New Jersey, New Brunswick, P O Box 270, New Brunswick, NJ 08903-0270. **EMAIL** abayahk@rci.rutgers.edu

OBERDIEK, HANS FREDRICK
PERSONAL Born 08/04/1937, Portage, WI, 4 children **DISCIPLINE** PHILOSOPHY **EDUCATION** Univ Wis-Madison, BS, 59, PhD, 65. **CAREER** Teaching asst philos, 61-63, lectr, 64-65, Univ Wis-Madison; asst prof, 65-69, assoc prof, 70-80, prof philos, 80-, Swarthmore Cor; Old Dom res fel, 68-69; Nat Endowment Humanities fel, 72-73; vis lectr philos, 72-73, Balliol Col, Oxford, England; vis Ring prof social ethics, 76-77, Univ Fla. **HONORS AND AWARDS** Henry C & Charlotte Turner Professor, 98-. **MEMBERSHIPS** Am Philos Soc. **RESEARCH** Moral philosophy; philosophy of law; political philosophy. **SELECTED PUBLICATIONS** Art, Foresight and Intention in Criminal Law, Mind, 7/72; art, John Rawl's Theory of Justice, NY Law J, 11/73; art, Who is to judge?, Ethics, 10/76; art, The Role of Sanctions and Coercion in Understanding Law and Legal Systems, Am J Jurisp, 76; co-auth, Living in a Technological Age, Routledge, 95. **CONTACT ADDRESS** Dept of Philosophy, Swarthmore Col, 500 College Ave, Swarthmore, PA 19081-1306. **EMAIL** hoberdi1@swarthmore.edu

OBERST, MICHAEL A.
DISCIPLINE LAW **EDUCATION** Univ Fla, BSBA, JD. **CAREER** Prof, Univ Fla, 79-; vis prof, Leiden Univ, Neth; past legislative counl, US Cong Joint Comt on Taxatiabout Wash, DC; past assoc, Buchalter, Nemer, Fields Chrystie, Los Angeles; past assoc, Ervin, Cohen Jessup, Los Angeles; past atty adv, US Tax Ct, Wash, DC. **MEMBERSHIPS** DC Bar; Calif Bar. **RESEARCH** Taxation. **SELECTED PUBLICATIONS** Auth, Florida Tax Review: Tax Analysts, Arlington, Va. **CONTACT ADDRESS** School of Law, Univ of Florida, PO Box 117625, Gainesville, FL 32611-7625. **EMAIL** oberst@law.ufl.edu

OBITTS, STANLEY RALPH
PERSONAL Born 09/04/1933, Denver, CO, m, 1960, 3 children **DISCIPLINE** PHILOSOPHY, PHILOSOPHICAL THEOLOGY **EDUCATION** Wheaton Col, AB, 55, BD, 58; Univ Edinburgh, PhD(philos), 62. **CAREER** Instr Bible, Wheaton Col, 56-57; asst prof philos, Nyack Col, 62-65; from asst prof to assoc prof, 65-72, prof philos, Westmont Col, 72-, prof philos of relig, Trinity Evangel Divinity Sch, 69-70; exchange prof philos, Wheaton Col, 75-76; vis prof theol, Denver Theol Sem, 79-80. **MEMBERSHIPS** Evangel Philos Soc (secy-treas, 78-79, pres 79-80); Am Philos Asn; Am Sci Affil; Evangel Theol Soc; Soc Christian Philosophers. **RESEARCH** Religious epistemology; 18th century philosophy; attributes of God. **SELECTED PUBLICATIONS** Auth, The Plight of the Christian Liberal-Arts College, Christianity Today, 4/70; contribr, Toward a Theology For the Future, Creation House, 71; auth, The Scientist and Ethical Decision, Intervarsity, 73; Current Issues in Biblical and Patristic Interpretation, Eerdmans, 75; Tensions in Contemporary Theology, Moody, 76. **CONTACT ADDRESS** Dept of Philos, Westmont Col, 955 La Paz Rd, Santa Barbara, CA 93108-1099. **EMAIL** obitts@westmont.edu

OCHIE, C.
PERSONAL Born 08/12/1957, Agulesi, Nigeria, m, 1990, 4 children **DISCIPLINE** CRIMINAL JUSTICE **EDUCATION** Albany State Univ, BS, 87; Valdosta State Univ, MS, 89, Okla State Univ, PhD, 93. **CAREER** Asst prof, Troy State Univ, 93-95; asst prof, W Va State Col, 95096; asst prof, Albany State Univ, 97-. **MEMBERSHIPS** Acad of Criminal Justice Sci; Am

Soc of Criminol. **RESEARCH** Recidivism, Women Crime, Differential Treatment, Police Areas and Corrections. **SELECTED PUBLICATIONS** Auth, "Mandatory International Students Insurance Policy: Oklahoma State University", Daily O'Collegian, Nov 89; auth, "The Effects of Incarceration On the Children of Incarcerated Mothers: The Case of Oklahoma", Daily O'Collegian, Mar 92: 12A; auth, Female Offenders and the Criminal Justice System: Examining the Patterns of Differential Treatment of Female Offenders in Oklahoma, UMI (Ann Arbor), 93; auth, "The Effects of Recidivism on the Sentencing Outcome for Female Recidivists", Jof the Ala Acad of Sci, 66. 1-2, 95; auth, "Myths Slow Down Drugs Solutions", Albany Herald, June, 97; auth, "Jailed Parents' Children Often Troubled", Albany Herald, Dec 97; auth, "Judicial Attitudes on Feminist Ideas and Female Felons: The Impact on Female Crime Patterns, Jof the Okla Criminal Justice Res Consortium 3 (97): 135-142; auth, "School Crime Demands National Response", Albany Herald, Nov 98: 7A; auth, "Revisiting the Debate of Voluntary versus Mandatory HIV/AIDS Testing in U.S. Prisons", Jof Health and Human Ser Admin, 99; auth, "Costing the Black Image Problem", The Comet 1.39 (Aug 99): 24. **CONTACT ADDRESS** Dept Criminal Justice, Albany State Univ, 504 College Dr, Albany, GA 31705. **EMAIL** cochie@asurams.edu

OCHOA, TYLER T.
DISCIPLINE LAW **EDUCATION** Stanford Univ, AB, 83; JD, 87. **CAREER** Clerk, US Courts of Appeals Ninth Circuit, 87-88; assoc, Brown & Bain, 88-93; from asst prof to assoc prof, Whittier Law Sch, 94-. **HONORS AND AWARDS** Charles Seton Awd, J of the Copyright Soc of the USA, 98; Order of the Coif; Phi Beta Kappa. **MEMBERSHIPS** State Bar of Calif, Am Bar Asn, Orange County Patent Law Asn. **RESEARCH** Copyright law, statute of limitations. **SELECTED PUBLICATIONS** Coauth, "Limitation of Legal Malpractice Actions: Defining Actual Injury and the Problem of Simultaneous Litigation," 24 Sw. U.L. rev 1 (94); coauth, "Unraveling the Tangled Web: Choosing the Proper Statute of Limitation for Breach of the Implied Covenant of Good Faith and Fair Dealing," 26 Sw. U.L. rev 1 (96); coauth, "Defiling the Dead: Necrophilia and the Law, " 18 Whittier L. rev 539 (97); **CONTACT ADDRESS** Sch of Law, Whittier Col, 3333 Harbour Blvd, Costa Mesa, CA 92626-1501. **EMAIL** tochoa@law.whittier.edu

OCKER, CHRISTOPHER
PERSONAL m **DISCIPLINE** RELIGION **EDUCATION** Princeton Theological Seminary, PhD, 91; Princeton Theological Seminary, THM, 85; Fuller Theological Seminary, MDIV, 83 **CAREER** San Francisco Theological Seminary 91-95; Asst Prof, 95-; Assoc Prof, Graduate Theological Union, 92-; Member of the Core Doctoral Faculty. **HONORS AND AWARDS** Alexander von Humboldt Fellowship in History; Institut fur Europaische Geschichte Fellowship; Deutscher Akademischer Austanschdienst Research Awd. **MEMBERSHIPS** Amer Historical Assoc; Amer Society of Church History; Medieval Academy of Amer. **RESEARCH** Religion in late Medieval; Early Modern Europe. **SELECTED PUBLICATIONS** Auth, "Johannes Klenkok: A Friar's Life, c. 1310- 1374, Philadelphia: Amer Philosophical Society, 93; auth, "rechte Arme and Bettler Orden: Eine neue Sicht der Armat und die Deligitimierung der Bettelmonche;" auth, Kalturelle Reformation: Sinnformationen in Umbruch, 99. **CONTACT ADDRESS** Dept Religion, San Francisco Theol Sem, 2 Kensington Rd, San Anselmo, CA 94960-2905.

ODDIE, GRAHAM JAMES
PERSONAL Born 03/24/1954, Timaru, New Zealand, m, 1975, 3 children **DISCIPLINE** PHILOSOPHY **EDUCATION** Univ Otago, BA, 76; London Univ, PhD, 79. **CAREER** Prof Philos, Otago Univ, 79-87, Massey Univ, 88-96, Univ Co-Boulder, 94-96, Univ Canterbury, 96-97; PROF & CHR OF PHILOS, UNIV CO-BOULDER, 97-; Imre Lakatos vis fel Univ London, 86; Claude McCarty fel Prague Acad Sci ci, 92; vis fel Australian Nat Univ, 90; vis prof Univ Sydney, 93. **MEMBERSHIPS** Australian Asn Philos (pres 90); New Zealand Acad Hum (vpres 93). **RESEARCH** Metaphysics; Ethics; Logic. **SELECTED PUBLICATIONS** Auth, Likeness to Truth, Western Ontario Series in Philosophy of Science, Dordrecht: Reidel, 86; ed, Justice, Ethics and New Zealand Society, with R. Perrett, Auckland: Oxford Univ Press, 92; auth, "Axiological Atomism," Australasian Journal of Philosophy, 01. **CONTACT ADDRESS** Philosophy Dept, Univ of Colorado, Boulder, Campus Box 232, Boulder, CO 20309-0232. **EMAIL** oddie@spot.colorado.edu

ODELL, MARGARET S.
PERSONAL Born 01/18/1955, Norfolk, VA, d **DISCIPLINE** BIBLICAL STUDIES **EDUCATION** Meredith Col, BA, 77; Yale Univ Divinity School, MAR, 79; Univ Pittsburgh, PhD, 88. **CAREER** Asst prof, Hollins Col, 88-89; asst prof, Converse Col, 89-94; asst prof, St. Olaf Col, 94-. **MEMBERSHIPS** Soc of Bibl Lit. **RESEARCH** Ancient Israelite prophecy; Book of Ezekiel. **SELECTED PUBLICATIONS** Auth, "The City of Hamoniah in Ezekiel 39: 11-16," in CBQ, 94; "I Will Destroy Your Mother: The Obliteration of a Cultic Role in Hosea 4:4-6," 95; auth, "The Prophets and the End of Hosea," 96; auth, "Who Were the Prophets in Hosea?," 96; auth, "History or Metaphor: Contributions to Old Testament Theology in the Works of Leo G. Perdue," in Relig Studies Review, 98; "The Particle and the Prophet: Observations on Ezekiel II 6," in Vetus Testamentum, 98; "You Are What You Eat: Ezekiel and the Scroll, in JBL, 98. **CONTACT ADDRESS** St. Olaf Col, 1520 St. Olaf Ave., Northfield, MN 55057. **EMAIL** odell@stolaf.edu

OGDEN, GREGORY L.
DISCIPLINE LAW **EDUCATION** Univ CA, LA, BA, 70; Univ CA, Davis, JD, 73; Temple Univ, LLM, 78; Columbia Univ, LLM, 81. **CAREER** Sr res ed, Univ CA; private practice, 75-76; lectr, Assoc Prof, Pepperdine Univ Sch of Law, 78-82; Prof, 82-present; vis prof, Notre Dame Law Sch, 88-89; Valparaiso Univ Sch Law, 89-90; Univ CA, 90; USC Law Ctr, 96; consult, Admin Conf US, 82-84, 87-89; fac dir, Ira Sherman ctr ethical awareness; prof, 82-. **HONORS AND AWARDS** Reginald Heber Smith fel, San Mateo Legal Aid Soc, 73-75; Law and Hum tchg fel, Temple Univ, 76-78; Chamberlain fel Legis, Columbia Univ, 80-81. **MEMBERSHIPS** Mem, Phi Kappa Phi; CA State Bar; Am Bar Assn; Christian Legal Soc. **SELECTED PUBLICATIONS** Co-auth, West's California Code Forms, Civil Procedure, 3rd ed, 81, 4th ed, 88; ed, contrib auth, Calif Public Agency. **CONTACT ADDRESS** Sch of Law, Pepperdine Univ, 24255 Pacific Coast Hwy, Malibu, CA 90263.

OGDEN, SCHUBERT MILES
PERSONAL Born 03/02/1928, Cincinnati, OH, m, 1950, 2 children **DISCIPLINE** SYSTEMATIC THEOLOGY **EDUCATION** Ohio Wesleyan Univ, AB, 50; Univ Chicago, DB, 54, PhD, 58. **CAREER** From instr to prof theol, Perkins Sch Theol, Southern Methodist Univ, 56-69; univ prof, Divinity Sch, Univ Chicago, 69-72; Prof Theol Perkins Sch Theol, Southern Methodist Univ, 72-93, Dir Grad Prof Relig Studies, 74-90, Soc Values Higher Educ Kent fel, 51-; Fulbright res fel & Guggenheim Mem fel, Univ Marburg, 62-63; vis fel, Coun of Humanities, Princeton Univ, 77- 78. **HONORS AND AWARDS** Merrick lectr, Ohio Wesleyan Univ, 65; LittD, Ohio Wesleyan Univ, 65; L.H.D. Univ of Chicago, 83; L.H.D. Southern Methodist Univ, 94; Sarum lectr, Univ Oxford, 80-81. **MEMBERSHIPS** Am Philos Asn; Am Acad Relig (pres, 76-77); Am Theol Soc; Am Acad of Arts and Sciences. **RESEARCH** Philosophical theology. **SELECTED PUBLICATIONS** Transl, Existence and Faith: Shorter Writings of Rudolf Bultmann, Meridian, 60; The Reality of God and Other Essays, Harper, 66, 2nd ed, 77; auth, Christ Without Myth: A Study Based on the Theology of Rudolf Bultmann, Harper, 61, 2nd ed, Southern Methodist Univ Press, 79; Faith and Freedom: Toward a Theology of Liberation, Abingdon, 79; The Point of Christology, Harper, 82; auth, On Theology, Harper 86; auth, Is There Only One True Religion or Are There Many? Southern Methodist Univ Press, 92; auth, Doing Theology Today, Trinity Press International, 96. **CONTACT ADDRESS** 9652 W. 89th Cir., Westminster, CO 80021-4406.

OGLETREE, CHARLES J., JR.
PERSONAL Born 12/31/1952, Merced, CA, m, 1975 **DISCIPLINE** LAW **EDUCATION** Stanford University, Stanford, CA, BA, 1974, MA, 1975; Harvard Law School, Cambridge, MA, JD, 1978. **CAREER** District of Columbia Public Defender Service, Washington, DC, staff attorney, 78-82, director of staff training, 82-83; American University/Washington College of Law, Washington, DC, adjunct professor, 82-84; Antioch Law School, Washington, DC, adjunct professor, 83-84; District of Columbia Public Defender Service, Washington, DC, deputy director, 84-85; Jessamy, Fort & Ogletree, Washington, DC, partner, 85-89; Harvard Law School, Cambridge, MA, visiting professor, 85-89, director, introduction to trial advocacy workshop, 86-, assistant professor, 89-93, professor of law, 93-; Jessamy, Fort & Botts, Washington, DC, of counsel, 89-; Harvard Law School, Criminal Justice Institute, Cambridge, MA, director, Jesse Climenko Professor of Law, currently. **HONORS AND AWARDS** Hall of Fame, California School Boards Foundation, 1990; Nelson Mandela Service Awd, National Black Law Students Association, 1991; Richard S Jacobsen Certificate of Excellence in Teaching Trial Advocacy, 1990; Honoree, Charles Hamilton Houston Institute, 1990; Awd of Merit, Public Defender Service Associaton, 1990; Personal Achievement Awd, NAACP and The Black Network, 1990; "Supreme Court Jury Discrimination Cases and State Court Compliance, Resistance and Innovation," Toward a Usable Past, 1990; "Justice Marshall's Criminal Justice Jurisprudence: The Right Thing to Do, the Right Time to Do It, The Right Man and the Right Place," The Harvard Blackletter Journal, Spring 1989; Boston Museum of Afro-American History, Man of Vision Awd, 1992; Harvard Law School, Albert M Sacks-Paul A Freund Awd for Excellence in Teaching, 1993; Criminal Practice Inst, A Champion of Liberty Awd, 1994; NY State Bar Assn-Criminal Justice Sect, honoree, Awd for Outstanding Contribution in Criminal Law Education, 1992; Transafrica-Boston Chapter, Outstanding Service Awd, 1992; co-author: Beyond the Rodney King Story; "Just Say No! A Proposal to Eliminate Racially Discriminatory Uses of Peremptory Challenges," 31 American Criminal Law Review 1099, 1994; "The Quiet Storm: The Rebellious Influence of Cesar Chavez," Harvard Latino Review, vol 1, 1995. **MEMBERSHIPS** Member, American Bar Association; member, National Conference of Black Lawyers; member, National Bar Association; member, American Civil Liberties Union; member, Bar Association of DC; member, Washington Bar Association; defender committee member, National Legal Aid and Defender Association; Assn of American Law Schools; DC Bar; Southern Ctr for Human Rights Committee, chairperson. **SELECTED PUBLICATIONS** Moderator of television programs including: "Surviving the Odds: To Be a Young Black Male in America," Public Broadcasting System, 1994; "Political Correctness and the Media," C-Span, 1994; "Don't Say What You Think!; Limits to Free Speech," C-Span, 1994. **CONTACT ADDRESS** Dept of Law, Harvard Univ, Cambridge, MA 02138. **EMAIL** ogletree@law.harvard.edu

OHNUMA, REIKO
PERSONAL Born 04/10/1963, New Haven, CT, m, 1993, 1 child **DISCIPLINE** ASIAN STUDIES, BUDDHIST STUDIES **EDUCATION** Univ Calif, Berkeley, BA, 86; Univ of Michigan, Ann Arbor, MA, 93; PhD, 97. **CAREER** Vis lectr, 96-98, Univ of TX, Austin; Asst Prof, 98-99, Univ of AL, Tuscaloosa; asst prof, Dartmouth Col. **HONORS AND AWARDS** Charlotte Newcombe Doctoral Dissertation Fellowship. **MEMBERSHIPS** Intl Assoc of Buddhist Stud; Amer Acad of Rel. **RESEARCH** Indian Buddhist Literature, especially narrative literature; Women and Literature; Hagiography. **SELECTED PUBLICATIONS** Auth, The Gift of the Body and the Gift of Dharma, History of Religions, 98. **CONTACT ADDRESS** Dept of Religion, Dartmouth Col, Hanover, NH 03755. **EMAIL** reiko.ohuma@dartmouth.edu

OKHAMAFE, IMAFEDIA
PERSONAL s **DISCIPLINE** PHILOSOPHY,. ENGLISH **EDUCATION** Purdue Univ, PhD, Philosophy and English, 1984. **CAREER** Univ of NE at Omaha, prof of philosophy & English 1993-. **MEMBERSHIPS** Modern Language Association of America; American Philosophical Association. **SELECTED PUBLICATIONS** Articles have appeared in periodicals such as Black Scholar, Journal of the British Soc for Phenomenology, UMOJA, Intl Journal of Social Educ, Auslegung, Rsch in African Literatures, Soundings, Philosophy Today, and Africa Today. **CONTACT ADDRESS** Prof of Philosophy & English, Univ of Nebraska, Omaha, Annex 39, Omaha, NE 68182-0208.

OLBRICHT, THOMAS H.
PERSONAL Born 11/03/1929, Thayer, MO, m, 1951, 5 children **DISCIPLINE** BIBLICAL THEOLOGY, RHETORIC **EDUCATION** Northern IL, BS, 51; Univ IA, MA 53, PhD, 59; Harvard Divinity School, STB, 62. **CAREER** Chair speech, Univ Dubuque, 55-59; assoc prof speech and humanities, Pa State, 62-67; prof biblical theol, Abilene Christian Univ, 67-86; dean, Col of Liberal and Fine Arts, Abilene Christian Univ, 81-85; chair, relig div, Pepperdine Univ, 86-96; from distinguished prof relig to distinguished prof emeritus, Pepperdine Univ, 94-. **MEMBERSHIPS** Soc of Biblical lit; Nat Commun Asn; Am Academy Relig. **RESEARCH** Rhetorical analysis of scripture; history of Biblical interpretation. **SELECTED PUBLICATIONS** Co-auth, with Stanley E Porter, Rhetoric and the New Testament 1991 Heidelberg Conference, Sheffield Academic Press, 93; auth, Hearing God's Voice: My Life with Scriptures in Churches of Christ, ACU Press, 96; co-auth, with Stanley E Porter, Rhetoric, Theology and the Scriptures, Pretoria Conf, Sheffield Academic Press, 96; with Stanley E Porter, The Rhetorical Analysis of Scripture: Essays from the 1995 London Conference, Univ of Sheffield, 97. **CONTACT ADDRESS** 14 Beaver Dam Rd, South Berwick, ME 03908-1818. **EMAIL** Tolbrich@gw1.net

OLCOTT, MARTHA
DISCIPLINE NATIONALISM, ETHNIC POLITICS, AND ETHNO-NATIONALISM **EDUCATION** SUNY Buffalo; Univ Chicago, PhD, 78. **CAREER** Vis instr, UC Berkeley; dept ch, prof-. **HONORS AND AWARDS** Res fel, Truman Inst, Hebrew Univ, Jerusalem; Bunting Inst, Radcliffe; Russ Res Ctr, Harvard Univ, East-West Ctr, Duke Univ; sr assoc, Carnegie Endowment for Intl Peace, Moscow; dir, Moscow Study Group, 96, 97. **SELECTED PUBLICATIONS** Publ, articles in scholar jour(s), bk(s); auth, The Kazakhs, Hoover Inst, 96; Central Asias New States, USIP, 96. **CONTACT ADDRESS** Dept of Russ Stud, Colgate Univ, 13 Oak Drive, Hamilton, NY 13346.

OLCZAK, JOSEPH M.
PERSONAL Born 03/19/1940, Poland, s **DISCIPLINE** THEOLOGY **EDUCATION** Drew Univ, DMin, 92. **CAREER** Adj Prof, Holy Apostles Col, 86-. **MEMBERSHIPS** Theol Soc of Am; Menological Soc of Am. **CONTACT ADDRESS** Dept Theol, Holy Apostles Col and Sem, 33 Prospect Hill Rd, Cromwell, CT 06416. **EMAIL** olczadjoseph@emal.msn.com

OLIKER, MICHAEL A.
PERSONAL Born 01/09/1946, Philadelphia, PA, m, 1982 **DISCIPLINE** PHILOSOPHY OF EDUCATION, LIBRARY AND INFORMATION SCIENCE, ENGLISH **EDUCATION** Kutztown Univ of Pa, BA, 67; Temple Univ, EdM, 69; Univ Ill-Urbana, PhD, 76; Drexel Univ, MS, 80. **CAREER** Tchg asst, Syracuse Univ, 69-70; adj fac, Phila Commun Col, 70; vis fac, 70-71, adj fac, 83-84, Glassboro State Col; adj fac, Bloomsburg State Col, 74; tchg asst, 71-72, 73-75, adj fac, 76, Univ Ill-

Urbana; vis fac, 76-77, adj fac, 80, 89-91, Loyola Univ Chicago; adj fac, 80 & 83, Temple Univ; adj fac, Ill State Univ, 84; asst prof, E Ill Univ, 95-97; adj fac, NE Ill Univ, 97-. **MEMBERSHIPS** Midwest Philos Educ Soc; Am Educ Stud Asn; Am Libr Asn; Am Philos Asn; Mod Lang Asn; Philos Educ Soc; Popular Cult Asn. **RESEARCH** Applied critical thinking to: (1) Popular culture, (2) Educational administration and policy; Douglas McGregors 'Theory Y' approach to administration; Philosophy of Plato and John Dewey; History of American educational thought. **SELECTED PUBLICATIONS** Auth On the Images of Education in Popular Film, Educ Horizons, 93; Analytical Philosophy and the Discourse of Institutional Democracy, Proceedings of the Midwest Philosophy of Education Society 1991-92, The Society, 93; Popular Film as Educational Ideology: A Framework for Critical Analysis, Proceedings of the Midwest Philosophy of Education Society 1993-94, The Society, 95; Educational Policy and Administration, 96; Censorship, in Philosophy of Education, Garland, 96; Superman, Adolescents, and the Metaphysics of Popular Culture, 97; The Language of Educational Policy and Administration, Proceedings of the Midwest Philosophy of Education Society, The Society, 97; Toward an Intellectual Understanding of Anti-Intellectual Popular Culture, Jour of Thought, 98. **CONTACT ADDRESS** 5006 W Grace St, Chicago, IL 60641. **EMAIL** moliker@sprynet.com

OLIPHINT, K. SCOTT
DISCIPLINE APOLOGETICS **EDUCATION** W Tex State Univ, BA, 78; Westminster Theol Sem, ThM; Westminster Theol Sem, PhD, 94. **CAREER** Assoc prof , Westminster Theol Sem. **SELECTED PUBLICATIONS** Co-auth, If I Should Die Before I Wake: Help for Those who Hope for Heaven; auth, Jonathan Edwards: Reformed Apologist, Westminster Theol Jour, 95; Plantinga on Warrant, Westminster Theol Jour, 95. **CONTACT ADDRESS** Westminster Theol Sem, Pennsylvania, PO Box 27009, Philadelphia, PA 19118. **EMAIL** soliphint@wts.edu.

OLIVER, HAROLD HUNTER
PERSONAL Born 10/09/1930, Mobile, AL, m, 1951 **DISCIPLINE** RELIGION, PHILOSOPHY **EDUCATION** Samford Univ, AB, 52; Southern Baptist Theol Sem, BD, 54; Princeton Theol Sem, ThM, 55; Emory Univ, PhD, 61. **CAREER** From instr to assoc prof New Testament, Southeastern Baptist Theol Sem, 57-65; assoc prof theol, 65-70, Prof New Testament & Theol, Sch Theol, Boston Univ, 70-, Res asst, Int Greek New Testament Proj, 55-57; Christian Res Found award, 56; Am Asn Theol Schs fac fel, 63-64; res ed New Testament, J Bible & Relig, 65-67 & J Am Acad Relig, 68-; chmn Am Textual Criticism Sem, 67; fel cross-disciplinary studies, 71-72; vis fel, Inst Theoret Astron, Cambridge Univ, 71-72; consult & panelist, Nat Endowment for Humanities, 76-; Chavanne vis prof relig studies, Rice Univ, 80-81. **MEMBERSHIPS** Am Acad Relig; Soc Values Higher Educ; fel, Royal Astron Soc; Am Philos Asn; Metaphys Soc Am. **RESEARCH** Philosophy of religion; cosmology. **SELECTED PUBLICATIONS** Transl, Theory of Existence, Attic, 65; Thinking Faith, 68; auth, Hope and knowledge: The epistemic status of religious language, Cult Hermeneutics, 74; The impact of 19th century philosophy on Biblical authority, Perspectives Relig Studies, 74; Theses on the relational self and the genesis of the Western ego, Theol Z, 77; The complementarity of theology and cosmology, Zygon: JRelig & Sci, 78; Relational metaphysics and the human future, In: The Sources of Hope, Pergamm, 79; A Relational Metaphysic, Nijhoff, 81; The Neglect And Recovery of Nature in 20th-century Protestant Thought, J of The American Academy of Religion, Vol 0060, 1992. **CONTACT ADDRESS** Sch Theol, Boston Univ, Boston, MA 02215.

OLKEN, SAMUEL R.
DISCIPLINE LAW **EDUCATION** Harvard Univ, AB, 82; Emory Univ, JD, 85. **CAREER** Asst prof, John Marshall Law Sch, 89-97; assoc prof, 98-. **HONORS AND AWARDS** Hughes-Gossett Prize. **MEMBERSHIPS** ABA; ASLH. **RESEARCH** Constitutional law; constitutional history. **SELECTED PUBLICATIONS** Coauth, "An Historical Study of Their Conflict over United States Supreme Court Appellate Jurisdiction," J Supreme Court Hist 125 (90); auth, "Charles Evans Hughes and the Blaisdell Decision: A Historical Study of Contract Clause Jurisprudence," Ore Law Rev (93); auth, :Justice George Sutherland and Economic Liberty: Constitutional Conservatism and the Problem of Factions," William and Mary Bill of Rights J 1 (97); auth, "Chief Justice John Marshall in Historical Perspective," John Marshall Law Rev 137 (97); auth, "The Business of Expression: Economic Liberty, Political Factions and the Forgotten First Amendment Legacy of Justice George Sutherland," forthcoming; auth, "Chief Justice John Marshall and the Course of Constitutional History," forthcoming. **CONTACT ADDRESS** John Marshall Law Sch, 315 S Plymouth Ct, Chicago, IL 60604-3969. **EMAIL** 7olken@jmls.edu

OLNEY, MARTHA L.
PERSONAL Born 11/27/1956, Oakland, CA, p, 1 child **DISCIPLINE** ECONOMICS **EDUCATION** Univ Redlands, BS, 78; Univ Calif Berkeley, MA, 80; PhD, 85. **CAREER** Instr to assoc prof, Univ Mass, 84-95; vis assoc prof, Univ Calif Berkeley, 92-; vis assoc prof, Stanford Univ, 01. **HONORS AND AWARDS** Jonathan Hughes Prize, Econ Hist Asn, 97; Distinguished Teaching Awd, Univ Mass, 90-91; Fel, Univ Mass, 91; Lilly Endowment Teaching Fel, Univ Mass, 87-88. **MEMBERSHIPS** Am Econ Asn; Bus Hist Conf; Cliometric Soc; Committee for the Status of Women in the Econ Profession; Econ Hist Asn; Soc Sci Hist Asn. **RESEARCH** United States Economic History; Economics of Discrimination. **SELECTED PUBLICATIONS** Auth, "Demand for Consumer Durable Goods in Twentieth Century America," Explorations in Economics History, (90): 322-349; auth, Buy Now, Pay Later: Advertising, Credit, and Consumer Durables in the 1920s, Univ NC Press, 91; auth, "When Your Word is not Enough: Race, Collateral, and Household Credit," J of Econ Hist, (98): 408-431; auth, "Avoiding Default: The Role of Credit in the Consumption Collapse of 1930," Quart J of Econ, (99): 319-335. **CONTACT ADDRESS** Dept of Econ, Univ of California, Berkeley, 549 Evans Hall, No 3880, Berkeley, CA 94720-3880. **EMAIL** Molney@econ.berkeley.edu

OLSHEWSKY, THOMAS MACK
PERSONAL Born 11/20/1934, Springfield, MO, m, 1956, 4 children **DISCIPLINE** PHILOSOPHY **EDUCATION** Wabash Col, AB, 56; McCormick Theol Sem, BD, 60; Emory Univ, PhD(philos), 65. **CAREER** Asst prof philos, Parsons Coll 62-63 & Coe Col, 63-66; asst prof, 66-69, Assoc Prof Philos, Univ KY, 69-. **MEMBERSHIPS** Am Philos Asn; Am Soc Value Inquiry; Soc Ancient Greek Philos; Soc Advan Am Philos; Ling Soc Am. **RESEARCH** Ancient Greek philosophy; philosophy of language; philosophy of mind. **SELECTED PUBLICATIONS** Auth, Problems in the Philosophy of Language, Holt, 69; Deep structure: Essential, transcendental, or pragmatic?, Monist, 73; The analogical argument .. revisited, Am Philos Quart, 74; On competence and performance, Linguistics, 74; Depositions and reductionism in psychology, J Theory Social Behav, 75; On the notion of a rule, Philosophia, 76; On the relations of soul to body in Plato and Aristotle, J Hist Philos, 76; Self-movers And Unmoved Movers in Aristotle 'Physics Vii', Classical Quarterly, Vol 0045, 1995. **CONTACT ADDRESS** Dept of Philos, Univ of Kentucky, 500 S Limestone St, Lexington, KY 40506-0003. **EMAIL** tmolshew@pop.uky.edu

OLSON, CARL
PERSONAL Born 11/12/1941, Newark, NJ, m, 1967, 2 children **DISCIPLINE** RELIGION **EDUCATION** Penn State Univ, BA, 67; Drew Theol Sch, MDiv, 70; Drew Univ, PhD, 77. **CAREER** Asst Prof, S Ill Univ, 78-79; Asst Prof, Univ NDak, 79-80; Prof, Allegheny Col, 81-. **MEMBERSHIPS** Am Acad of Relig; Am Asian Asn; Am Oriental Soc; Soc for Asian & Comparative Philos; World Asn for Vedic Studies. **RESEARCH** Religion and philosophy of India. **SELECTED PUBLICATIONS** Auth, The Mysterious Play of Kali: An Interpretive Study of Ramakrishna, Scholarly Press, 90; auth, The Theology and Philosophy of Eliade: A Search for the Centre, Macmillan, 92; auth, The Indian Renouncer and Postmodern Poison: A Cross-Cultural Encounter, Peter Lang, 98; auth, Zen and the Art of Postmodern Philosophy: Two Paths of Liberation from the Representational Mode of Thinking, SUNY Press, 00; auth, Indian Philosophers and Postmodern Thinkers: dialogues on the Margins of Culture, Oxford Univ Press, 00. **CONTACT ADDRESS** Dept Relig, Allegheny Col, 520 N Main St, Meadville, PA 16335-3903. **EMAIL** colson@alleg.edu

OLSON, RICHARD P.
PERSONAL Born 07/19/1934, Rapid City, SD, m, 1957, 3 children **DISCIPLINE** RELIGION **EDUCATION** Sioux Falls Col, BA, 56; Andover Newton Theol Sch, BD, 59, STM, 60; Boston Univ, PhD, 72. **CAREER** Christian minister, 59-98; Adjunct Tchr, Sioux Falls Col, Holy Redeemer Col, Col of Racine, Cent Baptist Theol Seminary; Vis Prof, Cent Baptist Seminary, 98-. **HONORS AND AWARDS** Ten most important books for clergy, Am Acad of Parish Clergy, 91. **MEMBERSHIPS** Am Asn of Pastoral Counselors. **RESEARCH** The changing family; the changing American religious consciousness. **SELECTED PUBLICATIONS** Co-auth, Discoveries: Expanding Your Child's Vocational Horizon, United Church Press, 95; auth, Privileged Conversations: Dramatic Stories for Christmas, United Church Press, 96; co-auth, A New Day for Family Ministry, Alban, 96; auth, Midlife Journeys: A Traveler's Guide, Pilgrim Press, 96; auth, A Different Kind of Man, Judson, 98; auth, Families of the Futum, Mariners, 99. **CONTACT ADDRESS** 9112 Slater Dr, Overland Park, KS 66212. **EMAIL** rpolson@planetkc.com

OLSON, ROGER E.
PERSONAL Born 02/02/1952, Des Moines, IA, m, 1973, 2 children **DISCIPLINE** CHRISTIAN HISTORICAL THEOLOGY **EDUCATION** Open Bible Col, BA, 74; North Amer Baptist Sem, MA, 78; Rice Univ, MA, 82, PhD, 84; Stud Univ of Munich, Germany, 81-82. **CAREER** Asst Prof, Theol, 82-84, Oral Robert Univ; Prof Theol, 84-99, Bethel Col & Sem; Ed, Christian Scholar's Review, 94-; prof, Truett Theol Sem, 99- . **HONORS AND AWARDS** Bethel Col Fac Schlrshp Awd; Gold Medallion, Evangelical Christian Pub Asn, 99. **MEMBERSHIPS** ATS, AAR. **RESEARCH** History of Christian Theology and Contemporary Christian Thought. **SELECTED PUBLICATIONS** Co-auth, 20th Century Theology: God and the World in a Transitional Age, InterVarsity Press, 92; Who Needs Theology? An Invitation to the Study of God, InterVarsity Press, 96; auth, The Story of Christian Theology, Twenty Centuries of Tradition and Reform, forthcoming, 99. **CONTACT ADDRESS** Truett Theol Sem, PO Box 97126, Waco, TX 76798. **EMAIL** olsrog@aol.com; roger_olson@baylor.edu

OMATSEYE, JIM
PERSONAL Born 07/31/1946, Warri, Nigeria, m, 1972, 4 children **DISCIPLINE** PHILOSOPHY, EDUCATION **HONORS AND AWARDS** Vis Fulbright Scholar, Univ of Ky, Ky State Univ 85-86; Vis Prof, Fla International Univ, 94. **MEMBERSHIPS** Am Educ Studies Asn, Mid S Educ Res Asn. **RESEARCH** Phenomenology of Schooling and Education, Multicultural Education. **SELECTED PUBLICATIONS** Auth, "Moral Education: A Saga of Nigeria's Ethical Revolution," in PEAN Yearbook: 1st Education. The Teaching of Moral Values in Nigerian Education, ed. J.A. Akinpelu, Philos of Educ Asn in Nigeria, 84; auth, "Between Development and Educational Policy," J of Educ in Developing Areas, Univ of Port Harcourt (Jan 85); auth, "Philosophy and Education Policy," in J or Educ Policy and J of Educ Studies 1,2, Univ of Jos (88); auth, "Wazobia and Democratic Pluralism," NJEP, Philos of Educ Asn of Nigeria, 91; coauth, "Pre-School and Primary Education in Nigeria," in History and Organization of School and Primary Education - A New International Reference Book, Sch of Early Childhood Educ, Ryerson Polytech Inst Toronto, Ontario, Can, 91; auth, "Towards An Integrated Philosophy of Teacher Education," The Nigerian Teachers, Nat Comn on Col Educ, 94. **CONTACT ADDRESS** Dept Educ Admin, Eastern Kentucky Univ, 521 Lancaster Ave, Richmond, KY 40475. **EMAIL** eduomats@acs.euk.edu

OMOLE-ODUBEKUN, OMOLOLA E.
PERSONAL Born, Nigeria **DISCIPLINE** CRIMINAL JUSTICE **EDUCATION** Ahmadu Bello Univ, Zaria, Nigeria, LLB, 80; Nigerian Law Sch, Lagos, BL, 81; Rutgers Univ, MA, 88, PhD, 91. **CAREER** Legal coun, Nat Youth Service Corps and Ministry of Justice, Jos, Plateau State, Nigeria, 81-82; State Coun, Ministry of Justice, Jos, Plateau State, Nigeria, 82-84; res assoc, Prog Resources Center, Rutgers, The State Univ, Newark, NJ, 85-86, teaching asst, 86-89; Public Policy Assoc, The Correctional Asn of NY, 88-90; Res Analyst, Criminal Disposition Commission of NJ, Newark, 90-92; Project Dir, Vera Inst of Justice, NY, 92-93, Sr Res Assoc, 94-95; Res Consult, The Center for Public Service, Seton Hall Univ, South Orange, NJ, 98-99; Res Consult, The Violence Inst of NJ, Univ of Med and Dentistry, Newark, 7/99-9/99; asst prof of Law and Justice, The Col of NJ, Ewing, 95-. **HONORS AND AWARDS** Teaching assts, Sch of Criminal Justice, Rutgers, 86-89; Walter C. Russell Scholar, Rutgers, 90; 225th Anniversary Awd for Excellence, Rutgers, 91; Dean's Diss Awd for Outstanding Doctoral Diss, Rutgers, 91; Fac Fel Awd for Outstanding Fac Contrib to the First Year Undergrad Experience, The Col of NJ, Ewing, 98. **MEMBERSHIPS** Am Soc of Criminology, NJ Asn of Criminal Justice Educr, Acad of Criminal Justice Scis. **RESEARCH** Transnational crime; women, race and crime; crime mapping. **SELECTED PUBLICATIONS** Coauth with C. Shapiro and A. Schuman, "The colaborative relationship between Victims and Probation: Is it Working?," Crime Victims Digest, 3, 1 (86): 1-3; auth, "Having a say in criminal justice policy [Opinion]," The New York Amsterdam News (July 15, 89): 15; auth, "Let's have a say in criminal justice policy [Viewpoint]," The City Sun (Aug 23-29, 89): 32; auth, Clarifying the role of gender in court dispositions: A LISREL model of pretrial release, Doctoral Diss, Rutgers Univ, Diss Abstracts Int (91); auth, "A structural approach to differential gender sentencing," Criminal Justice Abstracts, 23, 2 (92): 343-360; auth, The Vera Institute Atlas of Crime and Justice in New York City, Vera Inst of Justice, NY (93). **CONTACT ADDRESS** Dept Law & Justice, The Col of New Jersey, PO Box 7718, Ewing, NJ 08628-0718. **EMAIL** odubekun@tcnj.edu

ONWUDIWE, IHEKWOABA
DISCIPLINE CRIMINAL JUSTICE **EDUCATION** Central State Univ, Wilberforce, Oh, BA, 88; Fla State Univ, MSC, 89, PhD, 93. **CAREER** Asst prof, Barber Scotia Col, Concord, NC, 93-94; asst prof, Univ SC, Spartanburg, 94-97; asst prof, Univ Md, Eastern Shore, 2000-. **HONORS AND AWARDS** Recipient, Scholastic All-Am Awd; Nat Deans List; Awd for Grad Sr with Highest GPA; developed a Master's Program at UMES; developed new courses at UMES and USCS. **MEMBERSHIPS** Am Soc of Criminology, Acad of Criminal Justice Scis. **RESEARCH** Terrorism, Policing, Race and Crime, Theoretical Criminology. **SELECTED PUBLICATIONS** Coauth, "A Contextual Analysis of Political Violence in America," in Konrad, Adenauer Stifflung, Violence in South Africa (98); auth, The Globalization of Terrorism, Ashgate Pub Co (2000); auth, "Decentralization of the Nigerian Police Force," J of Int African Studies (accepted for pub, 2000). **CONTACT ADDRESS** Dept Criminal Justice, Univ of Maryland, Eastern Shore, 11868 Academic Oval, Princess Anne, MD 21853. **EMAIL** e-mail-ionwudiwe@mail.umes.edu

OOSTERHUIS, TOM
PERSONAL Born 03/11/1943, Bradford, ON, Canada, m, 1968, 2 children **DISCIPLINE** THEOLOGY; NEW TESTA-

MENT; PAULINE STUDIES **EDUCATION** Free Univ of Amsterdam, Doctor of Theology, 92. **CAREER** Campus Minister, Univ Alberta, 75-. **MEMBERSHIPS** Soc of Biblical Lit **RESEARCH** New Testament; Pauline studies; Jewish-Christian relationships **SELECTED PUBLICATIONS** The Strong and the Weak: An Exegetical Study of the Romans **CONTACT ADDRESS** Univ of Alberta, Sub 158f, Edmonton, AB, Canada T6G 2J7. **EMAIL** toosterh@ualberta.ca

OPHARDT, MICHAEL
DISCIPLINE PHILOSOPHY **EDUCATION** Duquesne Univ, PhD, 92. **CAREER** Lectr, Malone Col, 96- . **MEMBERSHIPS** APA; Am Cath Philos Asn; Soc of Christian Philos. **RESEARCH** Ethics; aesthetics. **CONTACT ADDRESS** 3849 Silverwood Dr, Stow, OH 44224. **EMAIL** mophardt@malone.edu

OPPENHAIM, MICHAEL
DISCIPLINE RELIGION **EDUCATION** Univ of Southern Calif, BA, 68; Univ Calif, Santa Barbara, MA, 73; PhD, 76. **CAREER** Asst prof, Concordia Univ, 74-79; assoc prof, Concordia Univ, 80-. **MEMBERSHIPS** Am Academy of Relig; Asn for Jewish Studies; Canadian Soc for the Study of Relig; Am Philos Asn. **RESEARCH** Modern Jewish philosophy and identity. **SELECTED PUBLICATIONS** Auth, Mutual Upholding: Fashioning Jewish Philosophy Through Letters, Peter Lang, New York, 92; auth, "Eliezer Schweid, Interpreters of Judaism in the Late Twentieth Century, B'nai B'rith Books, (93): 301-324; auth, "Welcoming the Other: The Philosophical Foundations for Pluralism in the Works of Charles Davis and Emmanuel Levinas," Wilfrid Laurier Univ Press, (95): 93-116; auth, "Franz Rosenzweig and Emmanuel Levinas: A Midrash or Thought-Experiment, Judaism 42:2, (95): 177-192; auth, "Feminism, Jewish Philosophy, and Religious Pluralism," Modern Judaism 16, (96): 147-160; auth, Speaking/Writing of God: Jewish Philosophical Reflections on the Life with Others, State Univ of New York Press, 97; auth, Foreword: Into Life, Franz Rosenzweig: God, Man, and the World Syracuse Univ Press, 98; auth, The Halevi Book, Modern Judaism, 19, (99): 83-93; auth, Judaism, in The Dictionary of Existentialism, Greenwood Press, (99): 231-35. **CONTACT ADDRESS** Dept of Rel, Concordia Univ, Montreal, 1455 de Maisonneuve W, Montreal, QC, Canada H3G 1M8. **EMAIL** oppm@vax2.concordia.ca

OPPENHEIM, FRANK M.
PERSONAL Born 05/18/1925, Coldwater, OH **DISCIPLINE** PHILOSOPHY **EDUCATION** Loyola Univ, AB, 47, MA, 52; St Louis Univ, PhD, 62; Loyola Univ, PhL, 49, STL, 56. **CAREER** Prof, Xavier Univ, 57- . **HONORS AND AWARDS** Exec Comm, Soc Advancement of Amer Philos; Herbert Schneider Awd, Soc Advancement of Am Philos, 99. **MEMBERSHIPS** Amer Philos Assn, Eastern Div; Soc Advance Amer Philos; Jesuit Philos Asn. **RESEARCH** Josiah Royce (1855-1916); Classic American Philsophy. **SELECTED PUBLICATIONS** Auth, Josiah Royce's Intellectual Development: An Hypothesis, Idealistic Stud, 6, Jan 76, 85-102; Royce's Community: A Dimension Missing in Freud and James?, Jour Hist Behavioral Sci, 13, 77, 173-190; Graced Communities: A Problem in Loving, Theol Stud, 44, Dec 83, 605-624; Royce's Voyage Down Under: A Journey of the Mind, Lexington, UP of Kentucky, 80; The Idea of Spirit in the Mature Royce Transactions of the Charles S. Peirce Soc, 19, Fall 83, 381-395; The Mature Royce's Idea of God, Papers in Nineteenth Century Theology Working Group, Amer Acad Rel, 85, I, 12-22; Hermeneutics and the Mature Royce, Proceedings of the Ohio Philos Assn, 86, 43-56; ed, The Reasoning Heart: Towards a North American Theology, Wash DC, Georgetown UP, 86; A Report on Nicarague, Am, 154, March 8, 86, 183-185; Gullible Media Swallow Reagan's Whoppers, Nat Cath Reporter, June 6, 86, 9; Philosophy Royce's Mature of Religion, U of Notre Dame P, 87; coauth, The Mustard Seed Process: Twelve Practical Exercises on Social Justice, for Groups and Individuals, New York, Paulist, 87; None Dare Call it Disobedience-Not Even the Author, LANDAS, 11, Jan 97, 64-81; A Roycean Response to the Challenge of Individualism, in Beyond Individualism: Toward a Retrieval of Moral Discourse in America, ed Donald L. Gelpi, SJ, U of Notre Dame P, 87, 87-119; coauth, New Documents on Josiah Royce, Transactions of the Charles S. Peirce Soc, 26, Winter 90, 131-145; Josiah Royce and Rudolph Steiner: A Comparison and Contrast, Revision, 13-14, Spring-Summer 91; Major Developments in Royce's Ethics after the Problem, in Frontiers in American Philosophy, College Station, TX, Texan A&M Univ Press, 92, I, 346-356; How Can a Philosopher's Specialization Inerdigitate with his or her Teaching of Philosophy?, Proceedings of the Fifty-Fourth Jesuit Philosophical Assn Mtg, San Diego, March 92; Royce's Mature Ethics, U of Notre Dame P, 93; Royce Project Report, Newsl no 78 of the Soc for the Advancement of Amer Philos, Oct 97, 10-11; The Peirce-Royce Relationship-Part I, The Jour Speculative Philos, 11, 97, 256-279; The Peirce-Royce Relationship-Part II, The Jour Speculative Philos, 12, 98, 35-46; coauth, Behind the Bits: Managing the Media Maze, Univ Pr Am (Lantham, Maryland), 98; co-ed, Metaphysics, 1915-1916, State Univ New York Pr (Albany), 98; auth, "The Personal Temperments of William James and Josiah Royce," Int Philos Quart 29 (99), 291-303. **CONTACT ADDRESS** Xavier Univ, Ohio, 5367 S Milford Rd, Milford, OH 45150-9744. **EMAIL** oppenhei@xavier.xu.edu

ORBACH, ALEXANDER
PERSONAL Born 02/16/1945, Dzalal Abad, USSR, m, 1967, 2 children **DISCIPLINE** MODERN JEWISH HISTORY **EDUCATION** Queens Col, New York, BA, 66; Univ Wis, MA, 69, PhD Hist, 75. **CAREER** Asst prof Relig, Oberlin Col, 73-76; asst prof Hist, Ind Univ, Bloomington, 76-77; assoc prof Relig Studies, Hist, Univ Pittsburgh, 77-. **MEMBERSHIPS** AHA; Am Asn Advan Slavic Studies; Asn Jewish Studies. **RESEARCH** Russian Jewry 19th century; modern Jewish thought. **SELECTED PUBLICATIONS** Auth, Jewish intellectuals in Odessa in the late 19th century: The nationalist theories of Ahad Ha'am and Simon Dubnov, Nationalities Papers, VI: 109-123; The Jewishness of Soviet-Jewish culture: Historical considerations, J Jewish Communal Serv, Vol L VII, No 2; New Voices of Russian Jewry: A Study of the Russian-Jewish Press in the Era of the Great Reforms, 1860-1871, Brill Press, Leiden, Holland, 80; The Saul M Ginsburg Archival Collection: A major source for the study of Russian-Jewish life and letters, Soviet Jewish Affairs, Vol XI, No 2. **CONTACT ADDRESS** Dept of Relig Studies, Univ of Pittsburgh, 2604 Cathedral/Learn, Pittsburgh, PA 15260-0001. **EMAIL** orbach@pitt.edu

ORDOWER, HENRY M.
PERSONAL Born Chicago, IL, 3 children **DISCIPLINE** TAXATION LAW, MEDIEVAL LITERATURE **EDUCATION** Washington Univ, St Louis, AB, 67; Univ Chicago, MA, 70, JD, 75. **CAREER** Instr law, Univ Chicago Law Sch, 75-76; assoc atty, Sonnenschein, Calin, Nath & Rosenthal, 75-77; asst prof, 77-80, assoc prof Law, St Louis Univ Law Sch, 80-83. **MEMBERSHIPS** Soc Advan Scand Studies. **RESEARCH** United States taxation of income, estates and gifts; the Icelandic family saga. **SELECTED PUBLICATIONS** Art, Separating Statutory Frameworks: Incompatibility of the Complete Liquidation & Reorganization Provisions of the Internal Revenue Code, St Louis Univ Law J, 81; auth, Tax Act Offers New Choices: Planning the Large Estate, Trusts & Estates, 82. **CONTACT ADDRESS** Law School, Saint Louis Univ, 3700 Lindell Blvd, Saint Louis, MO 63108-3412. **EMAIL** ordoweh@slu.edu

OREND, BRIAN
DISCIPLINE PHILOSOPHY **EDUCATION** Univ NY, PhD, 98. **RESEARCH** Moral and Political Philos, and Applied Ethics; international relations and foreign policy, especially human rights issues and questions of war and peace. **SELECTED PUBLICATIONS** Auth, War and International Justice: A Kantian Perspective, Wilfrid Laurier Univ Press, 00; auth, Michael Walzer on War and Justice, Univ of Wales Press, 00; auth, Politics, Law and Philosophy, The Kournal of Social Philosophy, Kantian Review, The Journal of the Hist of Philosophy and The Canadian Journal of Law and Jurisprudence. **CONTACT ADDRESS** Dept of Philosophy, Univ of Waterloo, 200 University Ave W, Waterloo, ON, Canada N2L 3G1. **EMAIL** bdorend@watarts.uwaterloo.ca

ORGAN, BARBARA
DISCIPLINE RELIGIOUS STUDIES **EDUCATION** Univ of Western Ontario, BA, 69; Univ of Ottawa, MA, 75; St Michael's Coll, PhD, 87. **CAREER** Asst prof, 87-90, chair, dept of Religious Studies, 90-92, Univ of Sudbury; coordinating chair, Joint dept of Religious Studies, Laurentian Univ, 92-95; asst prof, 95-96, assoc prof, 96-, dept of Religious Studies, Univ of Sudbury. **MEMBERSHIPS** Canadian Soc of Biblical Studies; Canadian Soc of the Study of Religion; Catholic Bible Asn; Soc of Biblical Lit. **RESEARCH** Literary composition of the Hebrew Bible. **SELECTED PUBLICATIONS** Auth, "Text and Translation," Canadian Catholic Review (93): 9-17; auth, Judaism for Gentiles, BIBAL Press (N Richland, Tex), 96; auth, "The Sabbath in the Book of Leviticus," in The Bible Today (98), 11-16. **CONTACT ADDRESS** Religious Studies Dept, Univ of Sudbury, 935 Ramsey Lake Rd, Sudbury, ON, Canada P3E 2C6.

ORNSTEIN, JACK
DISCIPLINE BIOMEDICAL ETHICS AND PHILOSOPHY OF MIND **EDUCATION** Univ Calif, San Diego, PhD. **CAREER** Prof; undergrad adv. **RESEARCH** Biomedical Ethics and Philos of Mind. **SELECTED PUBLICATIONS** Auth, The Mind and the Brain. **CONTACT ADDRESS** Dept of Philos, Concordia Univ, Montreal, Sir George William Campus, 2100 Mackay St., Montreal, QC, Canada H3G 1M8. **EMAIL** jackorn@alcor.concordia.ca

OROPEZA, B. J.
PERSONAL Born 12/21/1961, Oakland, CA, m, 1986, 2 children **DISCIPLINE** NEW TESTAMENT **EDUCATION** Univ Durham England, PhD 98. **CAREER** Victory Outreach Sch, lectr 89-97; George Fox Univ, vis asst prof, 98-99. **MEMBERSHIPS** SBL; BNTS. **RESEARCH** Pauline studies; Apostasy and Perseverance; Christian Use of Jewish Traditions. **SELECTED PUBLICATIONS** Auth, Paul and Apostasy: Eschatology, Perseverance and Falling Away, Tubingen, JCB, Paul Siebeck, 00; Situational Immortality: Paul's Vice Lists at Corinth, Expository Times, 98; auth, Laying to Rest the Midrash: Paul's Message on Meat Sacrificed to Idols in Light of the Deuteronomic Tradition, Biblica 98; auth, 99 Answers to Questions About Angels, Eastbourne UK, Kingsway, 98. Auth, Downers Grove, IVP, 97; auth, A Time to Laugh: The Holy Laughter Phenomenon Examined, Peabody, Hendrickson, 95. **CONTACT ADDRESS** Dept of Religion, George Fox Univ, 414 North Meridian St, Newberg, OR 97132. **EMAIL** boropeza@georgefox.edu

ORR, JANICE
PERSONAL Born 08/10/1944, St. Louis, MO, s **DISCIPLINE** LAW **EDUCATION** Roosevelt Univ, BA, 1966; Boston Univ School of Law, JD, 1972. **CAREER** Chicago Bd of Educ, teacher, 66-69; US Dept of Labor, law clerk, 72-73; US Dept of Housing & Urban Development, Attorney, 73-74; International Communication Group, general counsel, 74-75; Natl labor Relations Bd, LAW, 75-76; Equal Employment Opportunity Commission, 76-83; US Dept Health & Human Services, 83-; Self Employed, Law, entertainment, visual arts law, 75-. **HONORS AND AWARDS** Natl Bar Assn, Best Section, 1993, Outstanding Achievement, 1987, 1991; US Dept Health & Human Services, Outstanding Achievement, 1993, 1995. **MEMBERSHIPS** Natl Bar Assn, bd of dirs, 1973-79, 1986-, chair, Legislation Comm, 1994-, chair, International Law Section, 1989-94, chair, Committee on Southern Africa, 1986-89; Emarrons, general counsel, 1989-; DC Music Ctr, general counsel, 1982-90; Ctr for Independent Living, bd mem, 1995-; GWAC Women Lawyers Assn, NBA, bd mem, 1990-92. **CONTACT ADDRESS** Orr & Associates, 1815 E St NE, Washington, DC 20002.

ORR, LESLIE
PERSONAL Born 04/29/1948, Ann Arbor, MI **DISCIPLINE** HISTORY OF RELIGIONS, ASIAN RELIGIONS **EDUCATION** McGill Univ, BS, 70, MA, 81-82, PhD, 93. **CAREER** Full-time lectr, asst, assoc prof, 91-; full-time lect, McGill Univ, 89-91; part-time lectr, McGill Univ, 84-89; tchg asst, McGill Univ, 82-83; ch, dept of Relig, Concordia Univ, 99-. **HONORS AND AWARDS** Social Sciences and Humanities Res Council of Canada grant, 94-97; Am Academy of Relig grant, 98-99. **MEMBERSHIPS** Canadian Soc for the Study of Relig; Canadian Asian Stud Asn; Am Academy of Relig; Asn for Asian Stud; Am Oriental Soc. **RESEARCH** Women in the religions of India (Hinduism, Buddhism, and Jainism). **SELECTED PUBLICATIONS** Auth, "Women of Medieval South India in Hindu Temple Ritual: Text and Practice," Annual Rev of Women in World Religions, 3, (93): 107-141; ed, "The Concept of Time in ankara's Brahma-sutra-bhasya," In Hermeneutical Paths to the Sacred Worlds of India, eds. Katherine K. Young, Atlanta: Scholar's Press, 94; auth, "The Vaisnava Community at rirangam: The Testimony of the Early Medieval Inscriptions," The Journal of Vaisnava Stud, 3/3: (95): 109-136; auth, "Jain and Hindu Religious Women' in Early Medieval Tamilnadu," In Open Boundaries: Jain Communities and Cultures in Indian History, ed. John E. Cort, State Univ of New York Press, 98; ed, "Women's Wealth and Worship: Female Patronage of Hinduism, Jainism, and Buddhism in Medieval Tamilnadu," In the Captive Subject: A Social and Cultural Casebook for Indian Women, vol. 2: The Medieval Period, ed. Mandakranta Bose, New York: Oxford Univ Press, 99. **CONTACT ADDRESS** Dept of Rel, Concordia Univ, Montreal, 1455 de Maisonneuve W, Montreal, QC, Canada H3G 1M8. **EMAIL** orr@vax2.concordia.ca

ORSI, ROBERT A.
DISCIPLINE RELIGIOUS STUDIES **EDUCATION** Yale Univ, PhD, 82. **CAREER** Assoc prof, Ind Univ, Bloomington. **RESEARCH** Religion and society; social theory; history of religions in America; field methods in religion. **SELECTED PUBLICATIONS** Auth, The Madonna of 115th Street: Faith and Community in Italian Harlem 1880-1950, Yale, 85; The Cult of Saints and the Reimagination of the Space and Time of Sickness in Twentieth Century American Catholicism, Johns Hopkins, 89; 'He Keeps Me Going': Women's Devotion to Saint Jude and the Dialectics of Gender in American Catholicism 1929-1965, Univ Notre Dame, 90; auth, Thank You, Saint Jude: Women's Devotion to the Patron Saint of Hopeless Causes, Yale Univ Press, 96; auth, Gods of the City: Religion and the American Urban Landscape, Ind Univ Press, 99. **CONTACT ADDRESS** Dept of Religious Studies, Indiana Univ, Bloomington, Sycamore Hall 230, Bloomington, IN 47405. **EMAIL** rorsi@indiana.edu

ORT, LARRY V.
PERSONAL Born 08/13/1947, Wauseon, OH, m, 1995, 2 children **DISCIPLINE** PHILOSOPHY **EDUCATION** Spring Arbor Col, BA, 69; Mich St Univ, MA, 76, PhD, 97. **CAREER** Assoc prof, adult stud and phil, 83-00, Spring Arbor Col; vpres acad affairs & exec vpres, Russ-Am Christian Univ, 00-. **HONORS AND AWARDS** Fac Merit Awd, Spring Arbor Col, 98; Honorary Prof, St Petersburg St Techn Univ of Plant Polymers, St Petersburg Russia. **MEMBERSHIPS** Soren Kierkegaard Soc; Amer Phil Asn. **RESEARCH** Kierkegaardian and Wittgensteinian studies; justice and righteousness. **SELECTED PUBLICATIONS** Wittgenstein's Kierkegaardian Heritage, Univ Micro Dis. **CONTACT ADDRESS** Russ-Am Christian Univ, PO Box 2007, Wheaton, MD 20915-2007.

ORTH, JOHN VICTOR
PERSONAL Born 02/07/1947, Lancaster, PA, m, 1972, 2 children **DISCIPLINE** HISTORY OF LAW, PROPERTY LAW

EDUCATION Oberlin Col, AB, 69; Harvard Univ, JD, 74, PhD(hist), 77. **CAREER** Law clerk, US Ct Appeals, 77-78; asst prof, 78-81, Assoc Prof Law, Univ NC, 81-; assoc dean, UNC-Chapel Hill, 85-86. **MEMBERSHIPS** AAUP; Am Soc Legal Hist; Am Bar Asn; Selden Soc; Conf Brit Studies. **RESEARCH** American constitutional history; history of labor law. **SELECTED PUBLICATIONS** Auth, The Judicial Power of the United States: The Eleventh Amendment in Am History, 87; auth, Combination and Conspiracy: The Legal History of Trade Unionism, 1721-1906, 91; auth, The North Carolina State Constitution: A Reference Guide, 93. **CONTACT ADDRESS** Sch of Law, Univ of No Carolina, Chapel Hill, 5116 Van Hecke-Wettach Hall, Chapel Hill, NC 27514. **EMAIL** jvorth@email.unc.edu

ORTIZ, MANUEL
DISCIPLINE MINISTRY AND URBAN MISSION **EDUCATION** Philadelphia Col Bible, BS, 71; Wheaton Grad Sch Theol, MA, 75; Westminster Theol Sem, DMin, 89. **CAREER** Tchr, Philadelphia Assn for Christian Sch(s); headmaster, Humboldt Community Christian Sch, 79-87; founder, dir, Apprenticeship Sch for Urban Ministry, 81-87; bd mem, fac, Sem Consortium for Urban Pastoral Edu, 82-; bd mem, InterVarsity Fel and World Relief, 94; vis prof, E Baptist Sem, 94; instr, 86; prof, Westminster Theol Sem, 95-. **SELECTED PUBLICATIONS** Auth, The Hispanic Challenge: Opportunities Confronting the Church; One New People: Models for Developing a Multiethnic Church; My Commitment to Intercultural Christian Community: An Hispanic Pilgrimage, Urban Mission, 94. **CONTACT ADDRESS** Westminster Theol Sem, Pennsylvania, PO Box 27009, Philadelphia, PA 19118.

ORTIZ, VICTOR
PERSONAL Born 12/12/1946, New York, NY, s **DISCIPLINE** LAW **EDUCATION** BBA, marketing, 1970; JD, 1973. **CAREER** Private practice, civil & criminal law, 77-78, 81-85; Office of District Attorney, Dallas County, TX, asst district attorney, 78-81; Dallas County Mental Health Center, hearing officer, 84-85; City of Dallas, TX, asst city attorney, 74-77, associate municipal judge, 77-78, 84-85, municipal judge, 85-. **HONORS AND AWARDS** Natl Council of Negro Women, Man of the Year, 1986; Bancroft Witney Co., American Jurisprudence Awd/Trusts, 1972; St Paul AME Church, Usher Board #2, Extra Mile Awd, 1985; United Negro College Fund, Community Service Awd, 1975; Natl Council of Negro Women, Man of the Year; St Paul AME Church, Man of the Year, 1997; Charles Rice Learning Center Hall of Fame, 00. **MEMBERSHIPS** Dallas Minority Repertory Theatre, board of directors, 1976-81; Committee of 100, vice pres, membership director, 1976-82; Dallas Black Chamber of Commerce, board of directors, 1979-81; Park South YMCA, board of directors, 1978-81; Progressive Voters League, 1975-86; Natl Bar Assn, 1982-; J L Turner Legal Assn, 1974-; St Paul AME Church, stewards board, 1978-. **CONTACT ADDRESS** Municipal Judge, City of Dallas, 2014 Main St, Suite 210, Dallas, TX 75201. **EMAIL** victorortiz@msn.com

ORTS, ERIC W.
PERSONAL Born 01/11/1960, m, 1 child **DISCIPLINE** LAW **EDUCATION** Oberlin Col, BA, 82; New Schl for Soc Res, MA, 85; Univ Mich Law Schl, JD, 88; Columbia Law Schl, JSD, 94. **CAREER** Assoc, 88-90, Paul, Weiss, Rifkind, Wharton & Garrison, NY; Chem Bank Fel, Corp Soc Respon, 90-91, Columbia Law Schl; adj asst prof, law, 95, Univ Penn Law Schl; vis prof, law, 97, Univ Mich Law Schl; vis prof, law, Fulbright res schlr, 98, Univ Leuven, Belgium; fac mem, ethic prog, 94-, Nelson Peltz Term asst prof, 91-96, dir, environ manag prog, 98, assoc prof, 96-, Univ Penn, Wharton Schl, Legal Stud Dept. **MEMBERSHIPS** Amer Bar Assn; Amer Law Inst; Amer Soc for Pol and Legal Phil; Carnegie Coun on Ethics & Intl Affairs; Environ Law Inst; Intl Assn for Phil of La and Soc Phil. **SELECTED PUBLICATIONS** Art, Positive Law and Systemic Legitimacy: A Comment on Hart and Habermas, Ratio Juris, vol 6, 93; art, The Complexity and Legitimacy of Corporate Law, Wash & Lee Law Rev Vol 50, 93; auth, The Legitimacy of Multinational Corporations, Progress Corp Law, Westview Press, 95; art, A Model of Reflexive Environmental Regulation, Bus Ethics Quart, vol 5, 95; art, Reflexive Environmental Law, Nwestern Univ Law Rev, vol 89, 95; auth, A North American Legal Perspective on Stakeholder Management Theory, Persp on Co Law: 2, 97; coauth, Environmental Disclosure and Evidentiary Privilege, Univ IL law Rev, vol 1997, 97; art, Quality Circles in Law Teaching, J of Legal Ed, vol 47, 97; coauth, Informational Regulation of Environmental Risks, Risk Analysis, vol 18, 98; art, Shirking and Sharking: A Legal Theory of the Firm, Yale Law & Policy Rev, vol 16, 98. **CONTACT ADDRESS** Legal Studies Dept, Univ of Pennsylvania, The Wharton School, Philadelphia, PA 19104. **EMAIL** ortse@wharton.upenn.edu

OSBORNE, KENAN BERNARD
PERSONAL Born 05/29/1930, Santa Barbara, CA **DISCIPLINE** RELIGION, THEOLOGY **EDUCATION** San Luis Rey Col, BA, 52; Old Mission Theol Sem, STB, 56; Cath Univ Am, STL, 65; Ludwig Maximilians-Univ, Munich, Dr theol, 67. **CAREER** Instr Greek & hist, St Anthony's High Sch, Santa Barbara, 56-57; asst dir, Hour of St Francis Radio & TV, Los Angeles, 57- 58; dir admin, Cent Off, Franciscan Prov, Calif, 58-64; acting pres, 69-71, Prof Theol & Dean, Franciscan Sch Theol, 68, Pres, 71-; Prof Theol, Grad Theol Union, 68-. **MEMBERSHIPS** Western Am Acad Relig (pres, 73-74); Pac Coast Theol Soc; Cath Theol Soc Am (vp, 77-78, pres, 78-79). **RESEARCH** Phenomenology, Heidegger, Merleau-Ponty & Ricoeur; Sacramental theology and christology. **SELECTED PUBLICATIONS** Auth, New Being: A Study of Paul Tillich, Martinus Nijhoff, The Hague, 69; Methodology and the Christian Sacraments, Worship, 74; coauth, The renewal of the Sacrament of Penance, Cath Theol Soc Am, 75; auth, Theology in 1977 and beyond, Christian Century, 77; Ministry as Sacrament Ministerium Ecclesia, Leiturgia, Luther- Agricol Soc, 77; Sacramental theology & Theology of the Sacraments, In: New Cath Encycl, Vol XVII, 79; The Laity in The Middle-ages - Religious Beliefs And Devotional Practices - Vauchez,a, Theological Studies, Vol 0055, 1994; The Lay-person in The Church - Focus on Damian,peter, Anselm-of-canterbury, Ivo-of-chartres - French - Grandjean,m, Theological Studies, Vol 0056, 1995; Ecumenical Wedding Celebration - German - Candolfi,bj, Editor, J of Ecumenical Studies, Vol 0033, 1996; b Hear What The Spirit Says to The Churches - Towards Missionary Congregations in Europe - Linn,g, Editor, J of Ecumenical Studies, Vol 0033, 1996; Imago-dei - Approaches to The Theological Anthropology of Bonaventure,saint - Spanish - Chaveroblanco,fda, Speculum-a J of Medieval Studies, Vol 0072, 1997; Imago-dei - Approaches to The Theological Anthropology of Bonaventure,saint - Spanish - Chaveroblanco,fda, Speculum-a J of Medieval Studies, Vol 0072, 1997. **CONTACT ADDRESS** Franciscan Sch of Theol, 1712 Euclid Ave, Berkeley, CA 94709-1294.

OSBORNE, ROBERT E.
PERSONAL Born 06/26/1920, Sherbrooke, PQ, Canada, m, 1947, 4 children **DISCIPLINE** RELIGION **EDUCATION** Sir George Williams Univ, BA, 50; McGill Univ, BD, 53, STM, 54; Univ Edinburgh, PhD(divinity), 66. **CAREER** Assoc prof New Testament, Emmanuel Col, Victoria Univ, Ont, 61-68; assoc prof Bibl studies, 68-75, Prof Bibl Studies, Carleton Univ, 74-. **HONORS AND AWARDS** Teaching Awd, OCUFA, 78. **MEMBERSHIPS** Can Soc Bibl Studies; Soc New Testament Studies; Soc Bibl Lit. **RESEARCH** St Paul; New Testament archeology. **SELECTED PUBLICATIONS** Auth, St Paul's silent years, 65 & Paul and the wild beasts, 66, J Bibl Lit; coauth, Forgar: The occurrence of Gar as one of the first four words in sentences: A test of authorship for Greek writers, Sci & Archaeol, 1-371. **CONTACT ADDRESS** Dept of Religion, Carleton Univ, 1125 Colonel By Dr, Ottawa, ON, Canada K1S 5B6.

OSBURN, CARROLL D.
PERSONAL Born 09/02/1941, Arkansas City, KS, m, 1966, 2 children **DISCIPLINE** BIBLICAL CRITICISM **EDUCATION** Vanderbilt Univ, D Min, 70; Univ St Andrews Scotland, PhD, 74. **CAREER** Prof, Harding Grad School of Rel; 73-83; prof, Pepperdine Univ; 83-87; Carmichael-Walling Distinguished prof, Abilene Christian Univ, 87-. **HONORS AND AWARDS** 20th Century Christian Educator of the Year, 83; Abilene Christian Univ, Honors Prof of the Year, 92, 96. **MEMBERSHIPS** Soc of Bibl Lit; Asn Internationale d'etudes patristiques; Int Asn of Coptic Studies. **RESEARCH** New Testament textual criticism. **SELECTED PUBLICATIONS** Auth, Women in the Church: Refocusing the Discussion, 94; The Greek Lectionaries of the New Testament, The Text of the New Testament in Contemporary Res: Essays on the Status Quaestionis-A Volume in Honor of Bruce M Metzger, 95; 1 Cor 11:2-16 - Public or Private?, Essays on Women in Earliest Christianity, 95; The Search for the Original Text of Acts, New Testament Text and Language, 96; The Epistle of Jude; The Epistle of Second Peter; Codex Alexandrinus; Codex Claromontanus; Gothic Version; Old Latin Versions; Oxyrhynchus Frgaments; Textus Receptus; Vulgate, Eerdmans Dictionary of the Bible, 98; coauth, A Note on Luke 18: 29-30; Essays on Women in Earliest Christianity, 95; ed, Essays on Women in Earliest Christianity, 95. **CONTACT ADDRESS** Abilene Christian Univ, ACU Station, PO Box 29425, Abilene, TX 79699.

OSTERTAG, GARY
PERSONAL Born 01/06/1960, New York, NY, s **DISCIPLINE** PHILOSOPHY **EDUCATION** Graduate School of the City Univ of NYork, PhD, 94. **CAREER** Vis Scholar to Adj Asst Prof, Dept of Philo, 96-00, NY Univ. **HONORS AND AWARDS** CUNY Res Found Fellowships; Best Masters Thesis, Hum, Northeast Assoc of Grad Schools Awd. **MEMBERSHIPS** APA **RESEARCH** Philosophy of Language; Philosophy of Mind. **SELECTED PUBLICATIONS** Auth, A Scorekeeping Error, Philosophical Studies, 99; Definite Descriptions: A Reader, Cambridge: Bradford Books, MIT Press, 98; auth, "Descriptions and Logical Form," in The Blackwell Companion to Philosophical Logic, 00. **CONTACT ADDRESS** 666 West End Ave, Apt 18X, New York, NY 10025. **EMAIL** go2@is6.nyu.edu

OSWALT, JOHN N.
PERSONAL Born 06/21/1940, Mansfield, OH, m, 1962, 3 children **DISCIPLINE** BIBLE, OLD TESTAMENT **EDUCATION** Taylor Univ, BA, 61; Asbury Theol Sem, BD, 64; ThM, 65; Brandeis Univ, MA, 66; PhD, 68. **CAREER** Asst prof, Barrington Col, 68-70; asst prof, assoc prof, prof, Asbury Theol Sem, 70-82; pres, Asbury Col, 83-86; prof, Trinity Evang Div Sch, 86-89; prof, Asbury Theol Sem 86-89; prof, Wesley Bib sem, 99-. **HONORS AND AWARDS** Nat Def For Lang Fel; Teach of the Year, Barrington Coll, 70. **MEMBERSHIPS** SBL; IBR; WTS. **RESEARCH** Book of Isaiah; ancient near eastern religion; Hebrew religion. **SELECTED PUBLICATIONS** Auth, Called to Be Holy, Evangel Press (99); auth, The Book of Isaiah, Chapters 1-39, Erdmans (86); auth, The Book of Isaiah, Chapters 40-66, Erdmans (98); auth, Where are You, God? (Evangel, 99). **CONTACT ADDRESS** Dept Religion, Wesley Biblical Sem, PO Box 9938, Jackson, MS 39286-0938. **EMAIL** joswalt@wbs.edu

OTTATI, DOUGLAS FERNANDO
PERSONAL Born 06/17/1950, Indianapolis, IN, m, 1979, 2 children **DISCIPLINE** THEOLOGY; ETHICS **EDUCATION** Univ PA, AB, 72; Univ Chicago, MA, 74, PhD(theol), 80. **CAREER** Instr in Relig, Concordia Col, MN, 77; Instr in Theol and Ethics, Union Theol Seminary in Virginia, 77-81; Asst Prof of Theol and Ethics, Union Theol Sem in Virginia, 81-84; Assoc Prof of Theol and Ethics, Union Theol Sem in Virginia, 84-89; Prof of Theol and Ethics, Union Theol Sem in Virginia, 89-. **HONORS AND AWARDS** Louisville Inst, Summer Stipend, 93; Louisville Faith and Life Sabbatical Grant, 01-02. **MEMBERSHIPS** Soc of Christian Ethics; Am Acad of Relig; Am Theol Soc. **RESEARCH** Am contemporary theology; theological ethics. **SELECTED PUBLICATIONS** Auth, Meaning and Method in H Richard Niebuhr's Theology, Univ Press Am, 82; Jesus Christ and Christian Vision, Westminster John Knox Press, 95; Reforming Protestantism: Christian Commitment in Today's World. Westminster John Knox Press, 95; auth, "Reforming Protestantism: Reclaiming The Poetry of Theology," Pilgrim Press, 99; ed, "The Library of Theological Ethics," Westminster John Knox Press. **CONTACT ADDRESS** Union Theol Sem, Virginia, 3401 Brook Rd, Richmond, VA 23227. **EMAIL** dottati@union-psce.edu

OTTESON, JAMES R.
DISCIPLINE PHILOSOPHY **EDUCATION** Univ Chicago, PhD, 97. **CAREER** Asst prof philos, Univ Ala, 97-. **RESEARCH** Modern philosophy; Scottish Enlightenment; political philosophy. **CONTACT ADDRESS** Dept of Philosophy, Tuscaloosa, AL 35487. **EMAIL** jotteson@tenhoor.as.ua.edu

OTTLEY, BRUCE L.
PERSONAL Born 05/02/1947, MO, m, 1975 **DISCIPLINE** LAW **EDUCATION** Univ Mo at Kans City, BA, 69; Univ Iowa, JD & MA, 72; Columbia Univ, LLM, 78. **CAREER** From lectr to sr lectr, Univ Papua New Guinea, 72-77; prof & assoc dean, DePaul Univ Col of Law, 78-. **RESEARCH** Torts (personal injury law) and law in developing countries. **SELECTED PUBLICATIONS** Coauth, Illinois Tort Law 2nd ed, LEXIS Law Pub, 92; coauth, The Investigation and Prosecution of Arson, LEXIS Law Pub, 99. **CONTACT ADDRESS** Col of Law, DePaul Univ, 25 E Jackson Blvd, Chicago, IL 60604-2289. **EMAIL** bottley@wppost.depaul.edu

OTTO, DAVID
PERSONAL Born 06/14/1961, Denver, CO **DISCIPLINE** THEOLOGY **EDUCATION** Centenary Col, BA, 83; Scarritt Grad School, MA, 85; Vandervilt Univ, EdD, 93. **CAREER** Assoc prof, 90-; chm, 96-. **MEMBERSHIPS** Asn of Prof and Res in Relig Educ; Relig Educ Asn. **RESEARCH** Practical theology; Religious education. **CONTACT ADDRESS** Dept of Religion, Centenary Col of Louisiana, PO Box 41188, Shreveport, LA 71134-1188. **EMAIL** dotto@centenary.edu

OUDERKIRK, WAYNE
PERSONAL Born 01/08/1947, Albany, NY, d, 2 children **DISCIPLINE** PHILOSOPHY **EDUCATION** Univ of Albany (SUNY), PhD, 84. **CAREER** Mentor and Unit Coordinator, Assoc prof, 85- , SUNY Empire State Col. **MEMBERSHIPS** Intl Soc for Environmental Ethics; APA; Adirondack Mountain Club. **RESEARCH** Environmental Ethics and Philosophy; Pragmatism. **SELECTED PUBLICATIONS** Auth, Earthly Thoughts: An Essay on Environmental Philosophy, Choice: Current Reviews for Academic Libraries, 97; auth, Review of Kate Soper, What Is Nature? Culture, Politics and the non-Human, Environmental Ethics, 98; auth, Mindful of the Earth: A Biblographical Essay on Environment Philosphy, Centennial Review, 98; auth, Review of Val Plumwood, Feminism and the Mystery of Nature, Ethics, Place, and Environment, forthcoming; auth, Can Nature Be Evil? Rolson, Disvalue, and Theodicy, Environment Ethics, Summer 99; ed, with Jim Hill, Land, Community, Value: Cellicett & Environmental Philosophy, Suny Press, (forthcoming). **CONTACT ADDRESS** SUNY, Empire State Col, Cobleskill, NY 12043. **EMAIL** wouderkirk@sescua.esc.edu

OUREN, DALLAS
PERSONAL Born 11/13/1940, Pope Co, MN, s **DISCIPLINE** PHILOSOPHY **EDUCATION** Univ Minn, PhD, 73. **CAREER** Lect, Univ Minn, 73-. **HONORS AND AWARDS** Phi

Beta Kappa. **MEMBERSHIPS** APA. **RESEARCH** Philosophy, genealogy. **SELECTED PUBLICATIONS** Auth, Mill on Hamilton, Mellon, 92. **CONTACT ADDRESS** Univ of Minnesota, Twin Cities, 831 Heller Hill, 26783 Hwy 104, Minneapolis, MN 55455.

OUTKA, GENE HAROLD
PERSONAL Born 02/24/1937, Sioux Falls, SD, m, 3 children **DISCIPLINE** RELIGION **EDUCATION** Univ Redlands, BA, 59; Yale Univ, BD, 62, MA, 64, PhD, 67. **CAREER** From instr to assoc prof relig, Princeton Univ, 65-75; assoc prof, 75-81, Dwight Prof of Philos & Christian Ethics, Yale Univ, 80-; Am Coun Learned Soc fel, Oxford Univ, 68-69; Soc Values Higher Educ cross-disciplinary studies fel; serv fel, Off Spec Proj, Health Serv & Ment Health Admin, US Dept Health, Educ & Welfare, 72-73; vis scholar, Kennedy Ctr Bioethics, Georgetown Univ, 72-73; dir sem for col teachers, NEH, 77-78; fel, Woodrow Wilson Int Center for Scholars, DC, 83; Honorary member of the High Table, Queens' Col, Cambridge, England, 91. **HONORS AND AWARDS** Phi Beta Kappa; lhd, univ redlands, 78. **MEMBERSHIPS** Soc Values Higher Educ; Am Theol Soc; Am Soc Christian Ethics; Am Acad Relig. **RESEARCH** Theological, philosophical, and social ethics. **SELECTED PUBLICATIONS** Co-ed, with Paul Ramsey, Norm and Context in Christian Ethics, Scribner, 68; co-ed,with John P Reeder, Jr, Religion and Morality, Doubleday Anchor, 73; auth, Care Settings and Values: A Response, In: Ethics of Health Care, Inst Med, Nat Acad Sci, 74; Respite for Hallowing, Reflection, 1/78; Agape: An Ethical Analysis, Yale Univ Press, New Haven & London, 72; Character, Vision, and Narrative, Religious Studies Rev, 4/80; Discontinuity in the Ethics of Jacques Ellul, In: Jacques Ellul: Interpretive Essays, Univ IL Press, 80; On Harming Others, Interpretation, 10/80; Social Justice and Equal Access to Health Care, In: Biomedical Ethics, McGraw-Hill, 81; Universal Love and Impartiality, in The Love Comandments, Georgetown Univ Press, 92; co-ed, with John P Reeder, Jr, Prospects for a Common Morality, Princeton Univ Press, 93. **CONTACT ADDRESS** Dept Relig Studies, Yale Univ, PO Box 208287, New Haven, CT 06520-8287. **EMAIL** gene.outka@yale.edu

OVERALL, CHRISTINE D.
DISCIPLINE PHILOSOPHY **EDUCATION** Univ Toronto, BA; MA; PhD. **CAREER** Dept Philos, Queen's Univ **HONORS AND AWARDS** Awd for teaching excellence, 96; Ontario Confederation of University Faculty Associations. **RESEARCH** Feminist theory; applied ethics; philosophy of religion; philosophy of education. **SELECTED PUBLICATIONS** Coed, Perspectives on AIDS: Ethical and Social Issues, coedited with William Zion (Toronto: Oxford University Press, 91; reprinted 92); auth, What's Wrong With Prostitution? Evaluating Sex Work", Signs: Journal of Women in Culture and Society 17:4 (summer, 92): 705n724; auth, Human Reproduction: Principles, Practices, Policies, (Toronto: Oxford University Press, 93); auth, "Nowhere at Home': Toward a Phenomenology of Working Class Consciousness", in This Fine Place So Far From Home: Voices of Academics From the Working Class, edited by C. L. Barney Dews and Carolyn Leste Law (Philadelphia, Pennsylvania: Temple University Press, 95): 209-220; auth, "Reflections of a Sceptical Bioethicist", in Philosophical Perspectives on Bioethics, edited by L. W. Sumner and Joseph Boyle (Toronto: University of Toronto Press, Toronto Studies in Philosophy Series, 96): 163-186; auth, "Miracles and God: A. Reply to Robert A. H. Larmer", Dialogue: Canadian Philosophical Review, 36 #4 (Fall, 97): 741-752; auth, "Monogamy, Non-Monogamy, and Identity", Hypatia: A Journal of Feminist Philosophy 13 #4 (fall, 98): 1-17; auth, A Feminist I: Reflections From Academia. Peterborough: Broadview Press, 98; auth, Critical Notice of The Rejected Body: Feminist Philosophical Reflections on Diability, by Susan Wendell, Canadian Journal of Philosophy, 28 #3 (September, 98): 435-452. **CONTACT ADDRESS** Philosophy Dept, Queen's Univ at Kingston, Kingston, ON, Canada K7L 3N6. **EMAIL** cdo@post.queensu.ca

OVERBECK, JAMES A.
PERSONAL Born 09/11/1940, Eau Claire, WI, m, 1966, 3 children **DISCIPLINE** ECCLESIASTICAL HISTORY **EDUCATION** Univ of Chicago, MA, PhD, Grad Library Sch, MALS. **CAREER** Librarian, professor. **MEMBERSHIPS** Amer Library Assn, Amer Acad of Religion. **RESEARCH** History of Religious Journalism **SELECTED PUBLICATIONS** Auth, The Rise and Fall of Presbyterian Official Journals 1925-1985, Diversity of Discipleship, Westminister Press, 91. **CONTACT ADDRESS** 517 Ridgecrest Rd, NE, Atlanta, GA 30307-1845. **EMAIL** Joverbec@ce1.af.public.lib.ga.us

OVERBECK, T. JEROME
PERSONAL Born 11/21/1946, Cincinnati, OH, s **DISCIPLINE** LITURGICAL THEOLOGY, COUNSELING PSYCHOLOGY **EDUCATION** Loy Univ, AB, 70; Xavier Univ, M Ed, 72; Jes Sch Theol, M Div, 74; ThM, 75; STL, 82; Grad Theol Union, PhD, 83. **CAREER** Liturgist, Loy Univ, 83-. **HONORS AND AWARDS** Fac Fel, Univ Cal; Who's Who, Midwest, Religion; Alpha Epsilon Delta; W Daniel Conroyd Awd; Outstand Ser to Stud Awd; Excell in Teach Awd; Golden Key Hon Soc; Fav Fac Mem Recog, 97, 98; Dist Fac, 92, 93; Dir Am Schls; Alpha Sigma Nu. **MEMBERSHIPS** ACA; ASCA; AJL; LC; NAAL; SL. **RESEARCH** How culture impacts the warp people formulate their myth and ritual. **SELECTED PUBLICATIONS** Auth, "The Cross," "Sacred Vessels," "Eucharistic Chapel, ""Reconciliation Room," in The New Dictionary on Sacramental Worship (Collegeville: Liturgical Press, 90); auth, "Theses on Art and Environment for Christian Worship Space," Mod Lit 18 (91): 20-23; auth, Liturgical consultant for Come, Follow Me, Benzinger Pub (Mission Hills, CA), 91; auth, "Building and Renovating a Church: Well Begun Is More Than Half Done," Mod Lit 19 (92): 14-16; auth, "The Way We Pray," Loyola (95): 16-19; auth, "How Sacred Is Your Sacred Space?" Mod Lit 25 (98): 6-8; auth, Ancient Fonts Modern Lessons, Liturgy Training Pub (Chicago), 98; coauth, "Unhealthy Attitudes: Colleges Try to Make Student Care A More Popular Subject," Chic Tribune, Edu Today 5 (00): 18; coauth, Preparing a Catholic Wedding: Contemporary Parables, forthcoming. **CONTACT ADDRESS** Dept Theology, Loyola Univ, Chicago, 6526 N Sheridan Rd, Chicago, IL 60626-5344.

OVERHOLT, THOMAS WILLIAM
PERSONAL Born 08/09/1935, Bucyrus, OH, m, 1957, 2 children **DISCIPLINE** BIBLICAL STUDIES, HISTORY OF RELIGIONS **EDUCATION** Heidelberg Col, BA 57; Chicago Theol Sem, BD, 61; Univ Chicago, MA, 63, PhD, 67. **CAREER** Prof relig studies, Yankton Col, 64-75; assoc prof, 75-80, prof relig studies, Univ Wis-Stevens Point, 80-99. **HONORS AND AWARDS** Soc Values Higher Educ fel anthrop, Univ Ariz, 73-74. **MEMBERSHIPS** Am Acad Relig; Soc Bibl Lit; Soc Values Higher Educ. **RESEARCH** Old Testament; American Indian religions. **SELECTED PUBLICATIONS** Auth, Prophecy in Cross-Cultural Perspective: A Sourcebook for Biblical Researchers, Atlanta: Scholars Press, 86; auth, Jeremiah, Harper's Bible Commentary, San Francisco: Harper and Row, 88; auth, Channels of Prophecy: The Social Dynamics of Prophetic Activity, Minneapolis: Fortress Press, 89; auth, Cultural Anthropology and the Old Testament, Minneapolis: Fortress Press, 96. **CONTACT ADDRESS** Dept of Philosophy, Univ of Wisconsin, Stevens Point, 2100 Main St, Stevens Point, WI 54481-3897. **EMAIL** toverhol@uwsp.edu

OWEN, DAVID G.
PERSONAL Born 11/28/1945, Boston, MA, m, 1987, 3 children **DISCIPLINE** TORTS AND PRODUCTS LIABILITY **EDUCATION** Univ PA, BS, 67, JD, 71. **CAREER** Carolina Distinguished Prof of Law, Univ SC. **HONORS AND AWARDS** Res prize, Univ SC. **MEMBERSHIPS** Am Law Institute. **RESEARCH** Tort Theory. **SELECTED PUBLICATIONS** Coauth, a treatise & casebk on products liability law, a treatise on tort law; ed, bk on tort law theory; publ on, tort law, products liability & punitive damages. **CONTACT ADDRESS** School of Law, Univ of So Carolina, Columbia, Columbia, SC 29208. **EMAIL** owen@sc.edu

OWENS, DOROTHY M.
PERSONAL Born 12/02/1943, Atlanta, GA, d, 2 children **DISCIPLINE** THEOLOGY, PSYCHOLOGY **EDUCATION** Emory Univ, BA, 66; Summa cum laude, MDiv, 91; Vanderbilt Univ, MA, 94; PhD, 96. **CAREER** Pastoral psychotherapist, 92-, Pastoral Coun Ctr,TN; res instr, med, 96-, Vanderbilt Univ; parish assoc, 96-, Westminster Presbyterian Church, TN. **HONORS AND AWARDS** Intl Soc of Theta Phi **MEMBERSHIPS** Am Acad on Phys & Patient; AAR; Fellow Am Asn of Pastoral Coun; Soc of Pastoral Theol; Amer Coun Asn; Mental Health Asn; Nashville Psychotherapy Inst; TN Asn of Pastoral Therapists; Am Soc for Bioethics & Hum; Functional Brain-Gut Res Group; Emory Univ Comm on Biomed Ethics, 88-90; Licensed Certified Clinical Pastoral Therapist (TN); ordained Minister of Word: Sacrament Presbyterian Church (USA); Presbytery of Middle Tenn. **RESEARCH** Interface of relig/psycho/med; quality of life issues; physician/patient relationship **SELECTED PUBLICATIONS** Auth, Hospitality to Strangers: Empathy and the Physician-Patient Relationship, Oxford Univ Press, 99; coauth, The Irritable Bowel Syndrome: Long term prognosis an th Physician-Patient Interaction, Ann Int Med vol 122, 95; auth, Emotional Stress and the Holiday Season, Peachtree Papers, 80. **CONTACT ADDRESS** 807 Huntington Cir, Nashville, TN 37215-6112. **EMAIL** dorothy.m.owens@worldnet.att.net

OWENS, JOSEPH
DISCIPLINE PHILOSOPHY **EDUCATION** Univ Calif Los Angeles, PhD. **RESEARCH** Philosophy of the mind; mental state; philosophy of language. **SELECTED PUBLICATIONS** Auth, Pierre and the Fundamental Assumption, Mind Lang, 95; Contradictory Belief and Cognitive Access, Midwest Studies Philos, 89; The Failure of Lewis' Functionalism, Philos Quarterly, 87; In Defense of a Different Doppelganger, Philos Rev, 87; Synonymy and the Non-Individualistic Model of the Mental, Synthese, 86; Functionalism and Propositional Attitudes, 83; ed, Propositional Attitudes: The Role of Content in Logic, Lang Mind, 90. **CONTACT ADDRESS** Philosophy Dept, Univ of Minnesota, Twin Cities, 355 Ford Hall, 224 Church St SE, Minneapolis, MN 55455. **EMAIL** owens002@tc.umn.edu

OWENS, KATHLEEN MARIE
PERSONAL Born 05/05/1948, Detroit, MI **DISCIPLINE** PHILOSOPHY **EDUCATION** Ohio State Univ, BA, 70; Univ Pittsburgh, MA, 71; PhD, 77. **CAREER** Instr, Southern Ill Univ, 75-76; asst, assoc prof, Canisius Coll, Buffalo, NY, 77-. **HONORS AND AWARDS** Tenure: Canisius Coll Philo Dept, 82. **MEMBERSHIPS** Am Philos Asn; Am Asoc of Univ Prof. **RESEARCH** Epistemology; Philosophy of Social Sciences; Informal Logic; Feminism. **CONTACT ADDRESS** Ellicott Sta, PO Box 305, Buffalo, NY 14205-0305.

OWENS, RICHARD C.
DISCIPLINE LAW **EDUCATION** McGill Univ, BA, 80; Univ Toronto, LLB, 87. **CAREER** Partner, Smith Lyons, Barristers and Solicitors **HONORS AND AWARDS** Recognized at one of Canada's leading computer lawyers in 1999 Leading 500 Lawyers in Canada guide published by Lexpert. **MEMBERSHIPS** Int Bar Asn; Comput Law Asn; Toronto Comput Lawyers Group. **SELECTED PUBLICATIONS** Auth, pubs on provision of on-line services, electronic data interchange, opinions in copyright matters, and law and the Internet. **CONTACT ADDRESS** Fac of Law, Univ of Toronto, 78 Queen's Park, Toronto, ON, Canada M5S 2C5.

OZAR, DAVID T.
DISCIPLINE PHILOSOPHY **EDUCATION** Loyola Uniov, BA, MA; Yale Univ, PhD. **CAREER** Prof & dir, Center for Ethics; fac, Loyola Univ, 72-; co-dir, Grad Stud in Health Care Ethics, dept Philos at Loyola Univ Chicago; adj prof, Med Humanities in Loyola's Stritch Sch of Med; actg dir, Medical Humanities at Loyola, 84; lectr, Loyola's sch of law, dent, nursing, & soc work; initiated & tchg, Loyola Philos Dept's undergrad course in health care ethics,75; 7 yrs dir & designer now co-dir, Philos Dept's Grad Prog in Health Care Ethics; assoc member, Professional Staff & assoc dir, Medical Ethics Program; member, Instnl Ethics Comt; consult ethicist, Evanston Hospital, Ill; served on, Res Rev Comt, Chicago Dept of Health, 86-93; consult ethicist, Palliative Care Center of the North Shore; member, Ethics Bd of the Ill Dept of Children and Family Services; dir, Soc for Health and Human Values & Am Philos Asn. **HONORS AND AWARDS** Founder & first pres, Prof Ethics in Dent Network. **RESEARCH** Health care ethics; professional ethics; metaethics; normative ethics; history of ethics; soc contract theory; soc-Polit philosophy; philosophy of law. **SELECTED PUBLICATIONS** coauth, Dental Ethics at Chairside: Professional Principles and Practical Applications, Mosby-Yearbk, 94; co-ed, Philosophical Issues in Human Rights: Theories and Applications, Random House, 85. **CONTACT ADDRESS** Dept of Philosophy, Loyola Univ, Chicago, 820 N. Michigan Ave., Chicago, IL 60611.

P

PACHOW, WANG
PERSONAL Born 06/01/1918, Chungking, China, m, 1956, 1 child **DISCIPLINE** ASIAN CIVILIZATION, BUDDHIST STUDIES **EDUCATION** Mengtsang Col, BA, 36; Visva-Bharati Univ, MA, 42; Univ Bombay, PhD, 48. **CAREER** Lectr, Visva-Bharati Univ, 41-47; lect & head dept, Univ Allahabad, 47-53; sr lectr, Univ Ceylon, 54-65, reader, 66-68; assoc prof, 68-75, Prof, prof emer, Sch Relig, Univ Iowa, 75-. **HONORS AND AWARDS** Res fel, Yale Univ, 61; Acad Hospitality Awd, Univ London, 61-62; vis prof, Visva-Bharati Univ, 62; hon consult for the Humanities, Washington, 77; external examr, Univ Delhi, India, 78-. **MEMBERSHIPS** Am Acad Relig; Am Orient Soc; Asn Asian Studies; Maha-Bodhi Soc; Soc Study Chinese Relig. **RESEARCH** Chinese thought and literature; Sino-India culture. **SELECTED PUBLICATIONS** Auth, A Comparative Study of Pratimoksa, On the Basis of Its Chinese, Tibetan, Sanskrit and Pali Versions, Comp Sino- Indian Cult Soc, 55; A study of the Dotted Record, J Am Orient Soc, 7-965; Tripitaka, Encycl Britannica, 68; Gautama Buddha: Man or superman?, In: Malalasekera Commemoration Volume, Colombo, Ceylon, 76; The controversy over the immortality of the soul in Chinese Buddhism, J Orient Studies, Univ Hong Kong, 1278; A Study of the Twenty-Two Dialogues on Mahayana Buddhism, The Chinese Culture, 79; Chinese Buddhism: Aspects of Interaction and Reinterpretation, Univ Am Press, 80; Arahant, Bhavacakra, Paticcasamuppada, In: Abingdon Dict of Living Religions, 81; Tan,yun-shan And Cultural-relations Between China And India, Indian Horizons, Vol 0043, 1994; Tan,yun-shan And Cultural-relations Between China And India, Indian Horizons, Vol 0043, 1994. **CONTACT ADDRESS** 3600 Wonderland Park Ct, Kissimmee, FL 34746. **EMAIL** wang-pacho@uiowa.edu

PACIOCCO, DAVID
DISCIPLINE LAW **EDUCATION** Univ Western Ontario, LLB, 79; Oxon, BCL, 81. **CAREER** Prof, Univ of Ottawa, 90. **RESEARCH** Criminal law; evidence; law of trusts. **SELECTED PUBLICATIONS** Coauth, "Essentials of Canadian Law", The Law of Evidence, Concord, Ontario: Irwin Law, 96; coauth, Jury Selection in Criminal Trials: Skills, Science and the Law, Concord, Ontario: Irwin Law, 97; coauth, "Essentials of Canadian Law," The Law of Evidence, Toronto, Ontario: Irwin Law,

99; auth, Getting Awary with Murder: The Canadian Criminal Justice System, Toronto: Irwin Law, 99. **CONTACT ADDRESS** Fac Common Law, Univ of Ottawa, Fauteux Hall, 57 Louis Pasteur, Ottawa, ON, Canada K1N 6N5. **EMAIL** dpaciocc@uottawa.ca

PACKEL, LEONARD
DISCIPLINE CRIMINAL LAW **EDUCATION** Univ Pa, BS, 57; Harvard Law Sch, JD, 60. **CAREER** Prof; Villanova Univ, 73-. **RESEARCH** Evidence, trial pract. **SELECTED PUBLICATIONS** Coauth, Pennsylvania Evidence, 95; Trial Advocacy: A Systematic Approach, 84 & Trial Practice For The General Practitioner, 80. **CONTACT ADDRESS** Law School, Villanova Univ, 800 Lancaster Ave, Villanova, PA 19085-1692. **EMAIL** packel@law.vill.edu

PACWA, MITCH
DISCIPLINE SCRIPTURE, SPIRITUALITY **EDUCATION** Vanderbilt Univ, PhD. **CAREER** Prof, Dallas Univ; Entered Soc of Jesus, 68; ordained, 76. **SELECTED PUBLICATIONS** Auth, Catholics and the New Age, 92; Father Forgive Me, For I Am Frustrated, 97. **CONTACT ADDRESS** Inst for Religious and Pastoral Studies, Univ of Dallas, 1845 E Northgate Dr, Irving, TX 75062. **EMAIL** irps@acad.udallas.edu

PADGETT, ALAN G.
PERSONAL Born 09/23/1955, Washington, DC, m, 1977, 1 child **DISCIPLINE** THEOLOGY & PHILOSOPHY **EDUCATION** S CA Col, BA, 77; Drew Univ, MDiv, 81; Oxford Univ, Dphil, 90 **CAREER** Asst Prof, Bethel Col; Prof, Azusa Pac Univ **HONORS AND AWARDS** John Wesley Scholar; Christian Theolog Res Fel **MEMBERSHIPS** AAR, SBL, Am Philos Assoc; Philos of Sci Assoc **RESEARCH** Christian philosophy; systemmatic Theology; Philosophy of Science **SELECTED PUBLICATIONS** Auth, God, Eternity and the Nature of Time, MacMillan, 92; Coauth, Christianity and Western Thought, Intervarsity Press, 99 **CONTACT ADDRESS** Dept of Relig & Philos, Azusa Pacific Univ, PO Box 7000, Azusa, CA 91702-7000. **EMAIL** padgett@apu.edu

PADILLA, ALVIN
PERSONAL Born 03/11/1954, Ponce, PR, m, 1983, 4 children **DISCIPLINE** NEW TESTAMENT **EDUCATION** Drew Univ, PhD, 96. **CAREER** Academic Dean, Gordon-Conwell Theol Sem, Boston. **MEMBERSHIPS** AAP/SBL. **CONTACT ADDRESS** Gordon-Conwell Theol Sem, 130 Essex St., South Hamilton, MA 01982. **EMAIL** apadilla@gcts.edu

PAFFENROTH, KIM
PERSONAL Born 03/07/1966, Manhasset, NY, m, 1986, 2 children **DISCIPLINE** THEOLOGY **EDUCATION** St John's Col, BA, 88; Harvard Divinity Sch, MTS, 90; Univ of Notre Dame, PhD, 95. **CAREER** Instr, 93, Southwestern Michigan Col; tutor, 93-95, teaching fel, 94-95, adjunct asst prof, 95-96, visiting asst prof, 96-97, Univ of Notre Dame; teaching fel, 97-99, Villanova Univ. **HONORS AND AWARDS** St. John's Col Mathematics Prize, 85 and 88; NEH Summer Seminar Participant, Yale Univ, 96; Salvatori Fel, The Heritage Found, 97; Arthur Ennis Fel, Villanova Univ, 97-99; Research Fel, The Acton Institute, 98. **MEMBERSHIPS** Soc of Biblical Literature; Amer Acad of Relig; Catholic Biblical Assn of Amer; North Amer Patristic Soc **SELECTED PUBLICATIONS** Auth, The Story of Jesus according to L, Journal for the Study of the New Testament Supplement Series 147. Sheffield: Sheffield Academic Press, 97; auth, Tears of Grief and Joy, Confessions, Book 9: Chronological Sequence and Structure, Augustinian Studies, 97; auth, The Testing of the Sage: 1 Kings 10:1-13 and Q 4:1-13, The Expository Times, 96. **CONTACT ADDRESS** Villanova Univ, Villanova, PA 19085. **EMAIL** kpaffenr@email.vill.edu

PAGE, BENJAMIN BAKEWELL
PERSONAL Born 06/16/1939, Pittsburgh, PA, m, 1965, 4 children **DISCIPLINE** PHILOSOPHY, HEALTH PLANNING **EDUCATION** Harvard Univ, BA, 62; Fla State Univ, MA, 69, PhD, 70, MS, 72. **CAREER** Teacher English, Col St Pierre, Haiti, 60-61; internship, Tenn Off Comprehensive Health Planning, Nashville, 71; asst prof health planning & ethics, Meharry Med Col, 71-72; asst prof, 72-80, Assoc Prof Philos & Health Serv, Quinnipiac Col, 80-; Dir, Sleeping Giant Health Group Study Proj, Conn, 73-74; Int Res & Exchange Bd fel, Inst Philos & Sociol, Czech Acad Soc Sci, 75-76; secy, Quinnipiac fac fed, 76-80; hon vis fac mem, Univ Manchester, England, 80-81. **MEMBERSHIPS** Am Philos Asn; Christians Asn Rel East Europe; Am-Korean Friendship & Info Ctr; Inst Soc, Ethics & Life Sci; Soc Health & Human Values. **RESEARCH** Socialism and technological civilization; ethics in biomedical research and health care delivery; philosophy of health healing and medicine. **SELECTED PUBLICATIONS** Transl, Thoughts of a Czech Pastor, SCM Press, 71; auth, The Czechoslovak Reform Movement, 1963-68; A Study in the Theory of Socialism, Gruner, 73; Who owns the professions, Hastings Ctr Report, 10/76; Scientific medicine and health: The case for a reappraisal, World Outlook, summer 77; Biomedical ethics in East Europe, in Encycl Biocthics, 78; ed & auth, Marxism & Spirituality: An International Anthology, Bergin & Garvey, 93; Four Summers: A Czech Kaliedoscope, IREX Res papers, 93; Conversations with Bondy, in Monthly Rev; Tiger Still at the Gates, or The Cold War Is Not Yet Over, in Rethinking Marxism. **CONTACT ADDRESS** Dept of Fine Arts Lang & Philos, Quinnipiac Col, 275 Mt Carmel Ave, Hamden, CT 06518-1908. **EMAIL** page@quinnipiac.edu

PAGE, JEAN-GUY
PERSONAL Born 01/17/1926, Montreal, PQ, Canada **DISCIPLINE** ECCLESIOLOGY, PASTORAL THEOLOGY **EDUCATION** Laval Univ, BA, 48; Inst Int Lumen Vitae, Brussels, dipl, 65; Pontif Gregorian Univ, Doct, 67. **CAREER** Asst priest pastoral care, N D du Chemin Parish, 52-55; chaplain, Montcalm Sch, Que, 56-59; moral adv, Young Students Cath Action, 59-63; Prof Theol, Laval Univ, 67-, Mem, Pastoral Coun, 68-74; super pastoral care, Major Sem of Diocese of Que, 69-72; mem, Presbyteral Council, Diocese of Que, 69-73. **MEMBERSHIPS** Can Corp for Studies Refig; Soc Can Theol. **RESEARCH** Church Dogmatic; ecclesiastical ministries; pastoral theology in general, as a science. **SELECTED PUBLICATIONS** Auth, Reflections Sur L'Eglise du Quebec, 76; auth, Foi on Liberte?, 77; auth, Qui est l'Eglise, Vol III, 79; auth, Une Eglise Sans Laics?, 80; auth, L'Eglise a son printemps, 90. **CONTACT ADDRESS** Dept of Theol, Univ of Laval, Tour des Arts, Ste. Foy, QC, Canada G1K 7P4.

PAGE, JOSEPH ANTHONY
PERSONAL Born 04/13/1934, Boston, MA **DISCIPLINE** LAW **EDUCATION** Harvard Univ, AB, 55, LLB, 58, LLM, 64. **CAREER** From asst prof to assoc prof law, Lat Ctr, Univ Denver, 64-68; assoc prof, 68-73, Prof Law, Law Ctr, Georgetown Univ, 73, Chmn, Torts Round Table Coun, Am Asn Law Schs, 68-69; mem, Adverse Drug Effect Study Adv Panel. Off Technol Assessment, US Cong, 76; dir, Pub Citizen, Inc, 77-; dir, Nat Comt Citizen Broadcasting, 81-; Dir, Am Mus Tort Law, 98-. **RESEARCH** Tort law; government regulation of food, drugs, cosmetics, automobiles and household products. **SELECTED PUBLICATIONS** Auth, State law and the damages remedy under the Civil Rights Act, Denver Law J, fall 66; coauth, Automobile design and the judicial process, Calif Law Rev, 8/67; auth, Of mace and men: Tort law as a means of controlling domestic chemical warfare, Georgetown Law J, 6/69; The Revolution That Never Was: Northeast Brazil, 1955-1964, 72 & coauth, Bitter Wages: The Nader Report on Disease and Injury on the Job, 73, Grossman; Occupational health and the Federal Government, Law & Contemp Problems, summer-autumn 74; auth, Law of Premises Liability, Anderson, 76; coauth, Behind the looking glass: Administrative, legislative and private approaches to cosmetics safety substantiation, Univ Calif, Los Angeles Law Rev, 4/77; auth, Peron: A Biography, Random House, 83; auth, The Brazilians, Addison-Wesley, 95; co-auth, Automobile-Design Liability and Compliance with Federal Standards, George Wash Law Rev, 3/96; auth, Liability for Unreasonably and Unavoidably Unsafe Products: Does Negligence Doctrine Have a Role to Play? Chi-Kent Law Rev, 96; auth, Federal Regulation of Tobacco Products and Products that Treat Tobacco Dependence: Are the Playing Fields Level? Food & Drug Law J, Supp 98. **CONTACT ADDRESS** Law Ctr, Georgetown Univ, 600 New Jersey NW, Washington, DC 20001-2075. **EMAIL** page@law.georgetown.edu

PAGE, PATRICIA
PERSONAL Born 11/11/1923, Melrose, MA **DISCIPLINE** SOCIOLOGY; RELIGIOUS EDUCATION **EDUCATION** Smith Coll, AB 45; Harvard Graduate School of Education, EdM, 74; NYork Univ, PhD, 86 **CAREER** Dir of Christian Education Episcopal Church Parishes in North Carolina and Maine 46-55; Chaplain, Episcopal Church Smith Coll, 55-63; Advisor in Christian Education Dioces of Zamia, 63-73; Dir, Natl Inst Lay Training New York, 75-80; Prof Educ and Dir of Continuing Educ, Church Divinity Sch of the Pacific, 80-89. **HONORS AND AWARDS** Honorary Doctor of Divinity, 89; Nat Network of Lay Professionals at the Episcopal Church Ruth Schmidt Awd. **MEMBERSHIPS** Assoc of Profs and Researchers in Religious Educ; Network of Lay Profs of the Episopal Church; Ministry in Daily Life **RESEARCH** Adult Religions Educ; History of Episcopal Church Women; Theology and practice of ministry. **SELECTED PUBLICATIONS** All God's People Are Ministers, Augsburg Press, 93. **CONTACT ADDRESS** 715 Shepherd St., Durham, NC 27701. **EMAIL** pnpage@juno.com

PAGE, SYDNEY
PERSONAL Born 11/27/1944, London, ON, Canada, m, 1968, 2 children **DISCIPLINE** NEW TESTAMENT **CAREER** Asst Prof, New Testament, 77-79, Assoc Prof, 79-80, N Amer Baptist Coll; Assoc Prof, 80-86, Prof, 86-, Acad Vice Pres, 81-, New Testament, Edmonton Baptist Seminary. **MEMBERSHIPS** Soc of Biblical Lit; Canadian Soc of Biblical Studies; Inst for Biblical Res; Evangelical Theol Soc; Canadian Evangelical Theol Assoc. **RESEARCH** Biblical Demonology. **SELECTED PUBLICATIONS** Auth, Powers of Evil: A Biblical Study of Satan and Demons, Grand Rapids, Baker, 95; Marital Expectations of Church Leaders in the Pastoral Epistles, J Study of the New Testament, 93; review, Dictionary of the New Testament, by X Leon-Defour, in: Westminster Theo J; Reading the Corinthian Correspondence, by K Quast, in: Christian Week, 95; Worship: Then and Now, Baptist Herald, 89. **CONTACT ADDRESS** Edmonton Baptist Sem, 11525 23 Ave, Edmonton, AB, Canada T6J 4T3. **EMAIL** spage@nabcebs.ab.ca

PAGEL, ULRICH
PERSONAL Born 06/02/1963, Bonn, Germany, 1 child **DISCIPLINE** BUDDHIST STUDIES **EDUCATION** SOAS-London, BA, 88, PhD, 92. **CAREER** Cur Tibetan Collection, 93-97, British Library; Asst Prof, 97-99, Univ of Washington; lectr, lang and relig, Univ London, 99-. **MEMBERSHIPS** PTS, AOS, IABS, Royal Asiatic Society. **RESEARCH** Mahayana Buddhism **SELECTED PUBLICATIONS** Auth, The Bodhisattvapitaka, Its Doctrines, Practices and their Postion in Mahayana Literature, The Institute of Buddhist Stud, Tring, 95; co-auth, The Buddhist Forum III, School of Oriental & African Stud, 94; co-auth, Location List of the Shel dkar, London, Manuscript Kanur, The British Library, London, 96; auth, The Bodhisattvapitaka and Aksayamatinirdesa, Continuity and Change in Buddhist Sutras, in: The Buddhist Forum, School of Oriental and African Stud, 94; Buddhist Scriptures, Themes in Religious Studies, Cambridge, 94; auth, "The Tibetica of the British Library: A Historical Survey," in Tibetan Studies: Proceedings of the 7th Seminar of the International Association for Tibetan Studies, Schloss Segau 1995, (Vienna: Verlag der Osterreichischen Akademie der Wissenschaften, 97), 725-732; auth, "Three Tabo Manuscripts of the Bodhisattvapitaka: A Tradition of West Tibetan Manuscript Transmission," Journal of the International Association of Buddhist Studies, 22.1 (99): 165-210; auth, "Buddhas, Kings and Bodhisattvas: The Buddhist Ideal of Statecraft in Mahayana Sutra Literature," Buddhist Studies Review, forthcoming. **CONTACT ADDRESS** Sch of Oriental & African Studies, Univ of London, Thornhaugh St., Russell Sq., London, England WC1 H0XG.

PAINCHAUD, LOUIS
PERSONAL Born 03/10/1950, Quebec, PQ, Canada, m, 1975, 4 children **DISCIPLINE** THEOLOGY **EDUCATION** Laval Univ, PhD, 79. **CAREER** Prof, Ste-Foy Coll, 77-; Assoc Prof, Laval Univ, 88-. **MEMBERSHIPS** Canadian Soc of Patriotic Studies; Societe quebecoise l'eterde de la religion; Intl Assoc for Coptic Studies; Assoc internationale de esterdes patristiques; SBL. **RESEARCH** Early Christianity **SELECTED PUBLICATIONS** Auth, The Literary Contacts Between the Writing Without Title, On the Origin of the World and Eugnostos the Blessed, 95; The Use of Scripture in Gnostic Literature, Journal of Early Christian Studies 4, 96; coauth, The Kingless Generation and the Polemical Rewriting of Certain Nag Hammadi Texts, The Nag Hammadi Library after 50 Years: Papers from the 1995 Society of Biblical Literature Commemoration of the 50th Anniversary of the Discovery of the Nag Hammadi Library, 97. **CONTACT ADDRESS** Faculte De Theology, Cite Universitaire, Ste. Foy, QC, Canada G1K 7P4. **EMAIL** louis.painchaud@ftsr.ulaval.ca

PAINTER, MARK A.
PERSONAL Born 02/11/1959, Huntsville, TX, m, 1984, 2 children **DISCIPLINE** PHILOSOPHY **EDUCATION** Evergreen State College, BA, 81; Univ N Texas, MA, 88; Univ Missouri, PhD, 93. **CAREER** From asst prof to assoc prof, 93-, College Misericordia PA. **MEMBERSHIPS** APA; SWPS; HAS; EPPA. **RESEARCH** Ethics; History of Philosophy; Kant; Hegel. **SELECTED PUBLICATIONS** Auth, The Depravity of Wisdom: The Protestant Reformation and the Disengagement of Knowledge from Virtue in Modern Philosophy, Ashgate Pub, 99; The Profane Became Sacred: The Protestant Ethics of Kant and Sarte, Southwest Philo Rev, 99; Language and Moral Justification in Pre-Reformation Philosophy, J of Philo Res, 98; Phaedo 99d-101d: Gadamer's and Socrates Second Way, SW Philo Rev, 98; Virtue Depravity and Another Disquieting Suggestion About Contemporary Moral Reasoning, SW Philo Rev, 96; The Loss of Practical Reason and Some Consequences for the Idea of Post-Modernism, SW Philo Rev, 97. **CONTACT ADDRESS** Dept of Philosophy, Col Misericordia, 301 Lake St, Dallas, PA 18612. **EMAIL** mpainter@miseri.edu

PAINTER, RICHARD W.
PERSONAL Born 10/03/1961, Philadelphia, PA, m, 1987 **DISCIPLINE** LAW **EDUCATION** Harvard Univ, BA, 84; Yale, JD, 87. **CAREER** Vis prof, Cornell Univ; Vis prof, Boston Univ; assoc prof, Univ Ore, 93-97; prof, Univ Ill, 98-. **HONORS AND AWARDS** Phi Beta Kappa. **MEMBERSHIPS** Am Law Institute. **RESEARCH** Legal Ethics; Securities Regulation. **SELECTED PUBLICATIONS** Auth, The Moral Interdependence of Corporate Lawyers and Their Clients, Southern Calif Law Rev, 94;Toward A Market for Lawyer Disclosure Services: In Search of Optimal Whistleblowing Rules, George Washington Law Rev, 95; Litigating on a Contingency: A Monopoly of Champions or a Market for Champerty?, Chicago Kent Law Rev, 95; Game Theoretic and Contractarian Paradigms in the Uneasy Relationship Between Regulators and Regulatory Lawyers, Fordham Law Rev, 96; coauth, Personal and Professional Responsibilities of the Lawyer, Foundation Pr, 97; Proposal to Amend Model Rule 1.13, The Professional Lawyer, 98; Sounding a False Alarm: The Congressional Initiative to Preempt State Securities Fraud Causes of Action, Cornell Law Rev, 98; rev, Open Chambers?,

Michigan Law Rev, 99; and other numerous articles on law. **CONTACT ADDRESS** Univ of Illinois, Urbana-Champaign, 504 E Pennsylvania Ave, Champaign, IL 61820. **EMAIL** rpainter@law.uiuc.edu

PALECZNY, BARBARA
PERSONAL Born Hamilton, ON, Canada **DISCIPLINE** THEOLOGY **EDUCATION** St Jerome's Univ, BA, 71; Univ Windsor, MA, 72; Regis Col, MDiv, Bach Sacred Theol, Lic, Sacred Theol, 89, MA, 89, PhD, 94. **CAREER** Vis prof, Incarnate Word Univ, 98-00; coordr, Justice Peace and Integrity of Creation, School Sisters of Notre Dame, 00-; prof, Our Lady of the Lake Univ, 01-. **MEMBERSHIPS** AAR; Can Assn for Res in Home Econ; Can Soc for the Stud of Practical Ethics; Can Soc for the Stud of Relig; Can Res Inst for the Advan of Women; Can Theol Soc; Can Women's Stud Assn; Catholic Theol Soc of Amer; Col Theol Soc; Soc for Intl Devel; Soc of Bibl Lit. **RESEARCH** Religion & socio-economic transformation; eco-feminist advan in econ & ecology; new spiritual sensitivities; cultural transformation; cross-cultural communication, images, symbols, religious practice; Democratization of knowledge, social movements and faith communities; Eucharistic living & celebrating, linked with ecology, inclusive communities, economics. **SELECTED PUBLICATIONS** Coauth, Becoming Followers of Jesus, Burlington, Trinity Press, 83; coauth, From the Double Day to the Endless Day, Can Ctr for Policy Altern, 94; coauth, Justice-seeking-Faith, Jesuit Ctr for Soc Faith & Justice, 96; auth, Teaching Ethical Foundations in a Postmodern Era: Context, Meaning and Applications, Proceed of Laurier Conf on Bus & Prof Ethics, Wilfrid Laurier Univ, ON, 98; Systemic Wealth and Debt Accumulation and Jubilee 2000, Prof Ethics J, 98; Waves of Globalization and the New Millennium, Univ Incarnate Word, San Antonio TX, 98; auth, Clothed in Integrity: Weaving Just Cultural Relations and the Garment Industry, Wilfrid Laurier Press, 00. **CONTACT ADDRESS** Depr of Religious Studies, Our Lady of the Lakes Univ, 411 SW 24th St., San Antonio, TX 78207-4689. **EMAIL** paleczny@universe.uiwtx.edu

PALLARD, HENRI
DISCIPLINE LAW **EDUCATION** Univ Alberta, BA, 72; Univ Ottawa, BA, 75, MA, 76; McGill Univ, LLB, 84. **CAREER** Prof. **RESEARCH** Philos of law; legal theory. **SELECTED PUBLICATIONS** Auth, Precis de droit commercial pour les petites entreprises, Sudbury, ON: Institut des technologies telematiques, (91): 158; auth, "La question ontologique et la Phenomenologie de la perception," Man and World 24, (91): 373-393; rev, "Judges and judging: inside the Canadian judicial system, by Peter McCormick and Ian Green," in Canadian Book Rev Annual, (90): 373; auth, "Reflections on sentencing and corrections," Numero speciale, Canadian Journal of Law and Jurisprudence, (92): 174; auth, "Liberalisme, individualisme et les obliga-gations contractuelles," Dans Law I. Vancouver, BC: CGA Canada, (93): 6; rev, "Provincial justice: Upper Canadian legal portraits from the Dictionary of Canadian biography, ed. By R.L. Fraser," in Candian Book Review Annual, (92): 390; rev, "School law under the Charter of Rights and Freedoms, by E.L. Hurlbert and M.A. Hurlbert," in Canadian Book Rev Annual, (92): 385-386; rev, "Judicial power and the Charter: Canada and the paradox of liberal constitutionalism, by C.P. Manfredi", in Canadian Book Review Annual, no. 4096, (93); auth, "Peine, justification et hermeneutique", Revue Interntionale de Philosophie penale et de Criminologie de l'Acte, 5, (94): 179-190; auth, "Quelques reperes pour comprendre le Critical Legal Studies Movement," Eudikia, (95): 3-4, 25-36. **CONTACT ADDRESS** Law and Justice Dept, Laurentian Univ, 935 Ramsey Lake Rd, Sudbury, ON, Canada P3E 2C6. **EMAIL** hpallard@nickel.laurentian.ca

PALM, CRAIG W.
DISCIPLINE LAW **EDUCATION** Univ Vermont, BA, 78; Cornell Law Sch, JD, 81. **CAREER** Prof, Villanova Univ, 87-99; coordr, Villanova Law Sch Minority Stud Orientation Prog, 94-99; fac, Villanova Univ Grade Sch Educ; assoc, Davis Wright Tremaine LLP, Seattle, Wash, 00-. **MEMBERSHIPS** Order of the Coif; Colorado and the ABA Litigation, Bus Law, Criminal Justice & Alternative Dispute Resolution sect. **RESEARCH** Corporations and securities. **SELECTED PUBLICATIONS** Coauth, The Informative Process in Medical Care: Preliminary Multivariate Analysis for the Nat Center for Health servs Research; publ on, corporate, securities and constitutional law, in Cornell Law Rev, Pittsburgh Law Rev & Villanova Law Rev. **CONTACT ADDRESS** Davis Wright Tremaine LLP, 1501 Fourth Ave, 2600 Century Square, Seattle, WA 98101-1688. **EMAIL** craigpalm@dwt.com

PALMER, DAVID SCOTT
PERSONAL Born 07/16/1937, Boston, MA, m, 1998, 7 children **DISCIPLINE** POLITICAL SCIENCE **EDUCATION** Dartmouth Col, BA, 59; Univ Chile, Cert, 60; Stanford Univ, MA, 62; Cornell Univ, PhD, 73. **CAREER** Volunteer, Peace Corps, 62-64; asst dean, Dartmouth Col, 64-68; vis prof, Catholic Univ, 71-72; asst prof, Bowdoin Col, 72-76; vis prof, George Wash Univ, 82-83; lectr, Johns Hopkins Univ, 77-88; vis assoc prof, Princeton Univ, 79; vis prof, Georgetown Univ, 84-86; chair to assoc dean, For Service Inst, 76-88; prof to dept chair, Boston Univ, 88-. **HONORS AND AWARDS** Daniel Webster Nat Scholar; Edward John Noble Found Leadership Grant; Phi Sigma Delta; Latin Am Teaching Fel; Fulbright Travel Grant; Phi Delta Pi; Nat Defense Education Act Fel; Who's Who in Am Educ; State Depet Meritorious Honor Awd; For Service Inst Outstanding Service Awd; Fulbright Sen Res Fel; Belgrano Found Grant; Who's Who in the East; Who's Who in AM; Who's Who in the World. **MEMBERSHIPS** New Eng Coun of Latin Am Studies; Am Polit Sci Asn; World Affairs Coun; Inter-Am Dialogue Assoc. **RESEARCH** Latin American Redemocratization; Peru; Latin American Guerrilla Movements; Civil-Military Relations; Ecuador-Peru Border Dispute; Drug Production and Trafficking; U.S.-Latin American Relations. **SELECTED PUBLICATIONS** Auth, "U.S.-Latin American Relations," Ciencia Politica, 94; auth, "Peru-Ecuador Border Conflict: Missed Opportunities, Misplaced Nationalism, and Multilateral Peacekeeping," J of Interamerican Studies and World Affairs, 97; auth, "Drug Trafficking and U.S. Policy," in Drug Trafficking Research in the Americas, 97; auth, "The Latin American Military," in Latin America: Perspectives on a Region, Holmes and Meier, 98; auth, "U.S.-Peru Relations in the 1990s: Dynamics, Antecedents, and Future," Rev de la Acad Diplomatica del Peru, 98; auth, "Citizen Responses to Conflict and Political Crisis in Peru: 'Informal Politics' in Ayacucho," Univ Calif Press, 02. **CONTACT ADDRESS** Dept Polit Sci, Boston Univ, 232 Bay State Rd, Boston, MA 02215. **EMAIL** dspalmer@bu.edu

PALMER, LARRY ISAAC
PERSONAL Born 06/18/1944, St. Louis, MO, m, 1976, 3 children **DISCIPLINE** LAW **EDUCATION** Harvard Univ, AB, 66; Yale Univ, LLB, 69. **CAREER** Asst prof, Rutgers Univ, Camden, 70-73; from Assoc Prof to Assoc Prof, 73-79, Prof Law, Cornell Univ, 79-, Vice-Provost, 79-84, Vice-Pres, 87-94; Consult, Ctr Rape Concern, Philadelphia, 73-75 & Nat Inst Educ, 79-81; vis prof law, Univ Va, 79; Vis Fel, Cambridge Univ, 84-85. **MEMBERSHIPS** Am Law Inst. **RESEARCH** Law and medicine; health policy; legislation. **SELECTED PUBLICATIONS** Auth, Ethical and Legal Implications of Diabetes Self-Management, Practical Diabetology 8, 89; Law, Medicine, and Social Justice, Westminster/John Knox Press, 89; Who Are the Parents of Biotechnological Children?, Jurimetrics 35, Fall 94; Paying for Suffering: The Problem of Human Experimentation, Md Law Rev 56, 97; In Vitro Fertilization as a Social Experiment, Human Reproduction 12, 97; Institutional Analysis and Physicians' Rights after Vacco v Quill, Cornell J Law and Public Policy 7, 98; auth, Patient Safety, Park Reduction, and the Law, Hauton Law Rev 36, 99; auth, Endings and Beginnings: Law, Medicine and Society in Assisted Life and Death, Praeger Publishers, 00. **CONTACT ADDRESS** Law Sch, Cornell Univ, Myron Taylor Hall, Ithaca, NY 14853-4901. **EMAIL** lip1@cornell.edu

PALMER, RICHARD E.
PERSONAL Born 11/06/1933, Phoenix, AZ, m, 1956, 3 children **DISCIPLINE** PHILOSOPHY & RELIGION **EDUCATION** Univ Redlands, BA, 55, MA, 56, PhD, 59. **CAREER** Asst prof humanities, 59-64, assoc prof humanities & world lit, 64-69, dir humanities core lit prog, 65-76, prof humanities & world lit, 69-71, prof philos & lit, 72-80, Chmn Dept Philos & Relig, MacMurray Col, 80-. **HONORS AND AWARDS** Am Coun Learned Soc fel, 64-65; NEH younger humanist fel philos, Univ Heidelberg, 71-72, and grant, summer 78; Fulbright res grants, Germany, 91-92, 95-96; Awds for excellence in teaching, 89, 92; Jospeh R Harker Prof Philos, 93. **MEMBERSHIPS** Am Philos Asn; Soc Phenomenol & Existential Philos; Heidegger Conf Scholars; Intl Asn Philos & Lit; Conference of Gadamer Scholars. **RESEARCH** Philosophical hermeneutics, existentialism and phenomenology. **SELECTED PUBLICATIONS** Auth, Hermeneutics: Interpretation Theory in Schleiermacher, Dilthey, Heidegger, and Gadamer, Northwestern Univ, 69; Husserl's Brittanica article: A retranslation, J Brit Soc Phenomenol, 5/71; Toward a postmodern interpretive self-awareness, J Relig, 7/75; The postmodernity of Heidegger, winter 76 & Postmodernity and hermeneutics, winter 77, Boundary 2; contribr, Toward a postmodern hermeneutics of performance, in Performance in Postmodern Culture, Coda, 78; Allegorical, philological, and philosophical hermeneutics, Univ Ottawa Quart, 5/81; contribr, Hermeneutics 1966-78 - Review of research, in Vol 2, Contemporary Philosophy: A New Survey, Nijhoff, 82; co-ed & co-transl, Dialogue and Deconstruction: The Gadamer-Derrida Debate, SUNY, 89; co-transl, Edmund Husserl, Psychological and Transcendental Phenomenology and the Confrontation with Heidegger (1927-1931), Kluwer Acad Publ, 97; Husserl's debate with Heidegger in the margins of Kant and the Problem with Metaphysics, Man and World, 4/97; contrib, Two Late Essays of Gadamer, in The Philosophy of Hans-Georg Gadamer, Open Court Press, 97; transl, Reflections on a Philosophical Journey, and compiled bibliography; auth, Havermas versus Gadamer? Some Remarks, Perspectives on Habermas, Open Court, 00, Gadamer in Conversation, Yale, 01. **CONTACT ADDRESS** Dept of Philos & Relig, MacMurray Col, 477 E College Ave, Jacksonville, IL 62650-2590. **EMAIL** rpalmer@mac.edu

PALMER, RUSS
PERSONAL Born 05/04/1936, Detroit, MI **DISCIPLINE** BIBLICAL STUDIES, THE HISTORY OF CHRISTIAN THOUGHT, AND CHRISTIAN ETHICS **EDUCATION** Wayne State Univ, BA; Dallas Theol Sem, MA; Univ Iowa, PhD. **CAREER** Instr, Univ Nebr, Omaha, 65-; ed, Karl Barth Soc Newsl. **MEMBERSHIPS** Exec bd, Karl Barth Soc of N Am; steering comt, Reformed Theol and Hist Consultation, Am Acad of Relig. **SELECTED PUBLICATIONS** Auth, Introduction to World Religions Study Guide, Kendall-Hunt Publ. **CONTACT ADDRESS** Univ of Nebraska, Omaha, Omaha, NE 68182.

PANDHARIPANDE, RAJESHWARI
DISCIPLINE RELIGIOUS STUDIES **EDUCATION** Univ Ill Urbana Champaign, PhD. **CAREER** Prof, Univ Ill Urbana Champaign. **RESEARCH** Asian mythology; Hinduism; Hinduism in the United States; language of religion; language variation; Sanskrit; Hindi literature. **SELECTED PUBLICATIONS** Auth, The Eternal Self & the Cycle of Samsara: Introduction to Asian Mythology and Religion, Ginn; Intermediate Hindi, Motilal Banarsidass; Never is a Long Time Aur Anya Kavitayen: A Collection of her Original Hindi Poems, Banahatti. **CONTACT ADDRESS** Dept Religion Studies, Univ of Illinois, Urbana-Champaign, 3010 Foreign Language Bldg; 707 S Mathews Ave, MC-166, Urbana, IL 61801. **EMAIL** raj-pan@staff.uiuc.edu

PANFORD, KWAMINA
PERSONAL Born 04/17/1955, Ghana, m, 1980, 2 children **DISCIPLINE** POLITICAL SCIENCE **EDUCATION** Univ Ghana, BA, 78; Grad Diploma, 80; McMaster Univ, MA, 82; Cornell Univ, MILR, 83; Northeastern Univ, PhD, 89. **CAREER** Assoc Prof and Acting Chair, Northeastern Univ, 98-. **HONORS AND AWARDS** Senegal Fel, Dakar, 95-98; Fel, US Inst of Peace, 97; Teaching Fel, Brandeis Univ, 86; Frances Perkins Fel, Cornell Univ, 81-82. **MEMBERSHIPS** Intl Industrial Relations Asn, CODESRIA, Afri Studies Asn. **RESEARCH** International/African public/labor policies; Social-economic development and International organizations. **SELECTED PUBLICATIONS** Auth, "Ghana's Industrial Relations and Labor Laws," in The International Encyclopedia of Laws: Labor Law and Industrial Relations Series, Kluwer Law and Taxation Pub, forthcoming; auth, Ghana's Labor Relations: Testing Africa's Global Competitiveness, Praeger Pub, forthcoming; auth, Labor's Role in the Transition to Parliamentary/Democratic Governance in Ghana, CODESRIA, in press; auth, African Labor Relations and Workers' Rights: Assessing the Role of the International Labor Organization, Greenwood Press, 94; auth, "Structural adjustment Programs, Human Resources and The Organizational Challenges Facing Labor and Policy Makers in Ghana," Ashgate Intl Pub, forthcoming; auth, "British Colonial rule and contemporary Industrial relations in Ghana," Research in Organizations, Cornell Press, forthcoming; auth, "Elections and Democratic Transition in Ghana: 1991-196," in Democratization in Late Twentieth Century Africa, Greenwood Press, 98; auth, "The ILO and Employment in Sub-Saharan Africa," African Development Perspectives Year Book, 98. **CONTACT ADDRESS** African-Am Studies, Northeastern Univ, 360 Huntington Ave, Boston, MA 02115-5005. **EMAIL** kwpanfor@lynx.neu.edu

PANICCIA, PATRICIA L.
DISCIPLINE ADMINISTRATIVE LAW **EDUCATION** Univ HI, BA, 77; Pepperdine Univ Sch Law, JD, 81. **CAREER** Reporter, weekend anchor, KEYT-ABC, 83-85; reporter, KCOP, 85-88; reporter CNN 89-93; media consult, 88-present; ABA Nat Conf Lawyer and Rep(s) Media, 88-91; vchmn Affairs Comm, 85-87; CA State Bar Fair Trial Free Press Comm, 84-85; Acad Television Arts and Sci, 87; contrib ed, consult, preview U.S. Supreme Court Cases, Public edu div, ABA, 85-95; adj prof. **HONORS AND AWARDS** Women in commun nat Clarion award; emmy nomination for mini-doc invest ser, 87. **MEMBERSHIPS** Mem, CA State Bar; HI State Bar; Am Bar Assoc. **SELECTED PUBLICATIONS** Auth, Gender and the Law, Communications LawPractice, Matthew Bender, 88. **CONTACT ADDRESS** Sch of Law, Pepperdine Univ, 24255 Pacific Coast Hwy, Malibu, CA 90263.

PANIKKAR, RAIMUNDO
PERSONAL Born 11/03/1918, Barcelona, Spain **DISCIPLINE** COMPARATIVE PHILOSOPHY & RELIGION **EDUCATION** Univ Barcelona, MSc, 41; Univ Madrid, MA, 42, PhD (philos), 46, DSc(chem), 58; Pontif Lateran Univ, ThL, 54, ThD(theol), 61. **CAREER** Prof Indian cult, Theol Sem, Madrid, 46-51 & Int Univ Social Studies, Rome, 62-63; vis prof compt relig, Harvard Univ, 67-71; Prof Relig Studies, Univ Calif, Santa Barbara, 71-, Fel, Inst Philos Luis Vives, Coun Sci Res, Madrid, 42-57; prof, Inst Leon XIII, 50-51; docent, Univ Rome, 63-; mem acad coun, Ecumenical Inst Advan Theol Studies, Jerusalem, 65-; Henry Luce vis prof, Union Theol Sem, NY, 70. **HONORS AND AWARDS** Teape lectr, Cambridge Univ, 66; Gifford Lectures, Edimburg, 89. **MEMBERSHIPS** Am Soc Studies Relig; Int Soc Medieval Philos; Inst Int Philos, Paris; Am Acad Relig; UNESCO; Sociedad Espanola de Gengas de Las Religiones; Center for Intercultural Studies. **RESEARCH** Philosophy of science. **SELECTED PUBLICATIONS** Auth, Kerygma und Indien, Reich, Hamburg, 67; Worship and Secular Man, 73 & Trinity and the Religious Experience of Man, 73, DLT, London; The Vedic Experience, Univ Calif, Berkeley, 77; Myth, Faith and Hermeneutics, 78,

79; Fortress, A Dwelling Place for Wisdom, Westminster/John Knox, 93; Disarmament, Westminster/John Knox, 95; Invisible Harmony, 95; The Cosmotheandric Experience, Orbis, Marknoll, 98; La Pienezza Dell'Umomo Una Cristofania, Jaca Book, 99; The Intrareligous Dialogue, 99, Paulist; The Unknown Christ of Hinduism, Orbis Bks, rev ed, 81; El silencio del Buddha Scruela, Madrid, 99. **CONTACT ADDRESS** Can Felo, Univ of California, Santa Barbara, E-08511 Taveret, Catalunya, Spain. **EMAIL** iboada@pie.xtec.es

PANKEY, WILLIAM J.
DISCIPLINE THEOLOGY **EDUCATION** Central Bible Col, BA, 82; Assem God Theol Sem, MA, 98; Trinity Int Univ, MDiv, 96, DMin, 94; Dominican Univ, MILS, 97. **CAREER** DIR, COL LIBR, CHRISTIAN LIFE COL **MEMBERSHIPS** ALA, ACRL **RESEARCH** Hermeneutics, philosophy of religion, Buddhism **SELECTED PUBLICATIONS** Auth, Role of the Holy Spirit in the Exegetical Process, The Pneuma Rev, 2:1, winter 99. **CONTACT ADDRESS** Christian Life Col, 400 E Gregory St, Mount Prospect, IL 60056. **EMAIL** wpankey@christianlifecollege.edu

PAPAZIAN, MICHAEL
PERSONAL Born 03/13/1965, Englewood, NJ, s **DISCIPLINE** PHILOSPHY **EDUCATION** Johns Hopkins Univ, BA, 83; Univ of Va, MA, 91; Oxford Univ, M St, 95; Univ of Va, PhD, 95. **CAREER** Vis prof, Hampden-Sydney Col, 97-98; asst prof, Berry Col, 98-. **MEMBERSHIPS** Am Philos Assoc; Soc of Ancient Greek Philos; Am Cath Philos Assoc; Soc for Armenian Studies. **RESEARCH** Ancient philosphy; logic; metaphysics. **SELECTED PUBLICATIONS** Auth, Stoie Ontology and the Reality of Time in Ancient Philosophy, Vol. 19; auth, The Authorship of a Sixth Century Armenian Commentary on Aristotles 'Prior' Analytics' in Jour of the Soc for Armenian Studies, Vol 10. **CONTACT ADDRESS** Dept Relig & Philos, Berry Col, 1 Mt Berry Sq NE, Rome, GA 30165-7736. **EMAIL** mpapazian@berry.edu

PAPER, JORDAN
PERSONAL Born 12/03/1938, Baltimore, MD **DISCIPLINE** HISTORY OF RELIGIONS, EAST ASIA **EDUCATION** Univ Chicago, AB, 60; Univ Wis-Madison, MA, 65, PhD(Chinese), 71. **CAREER** Asst prof hist, Ind State Univ, 67-72; asst prof, 72-78, Assoc Prof Humanities, York Univ, 78-, Vis prof Am lit, Ching I Col, Taiwan, 73-74. **MEMBERSHIPS** Asn Asian Studies; Am Orient Soc; Soc Studies Pre-Han China; Soc Study Chinese Relig; Can Soc Study Relig. **RESEARCH** East Asian aesthetics; Chinese intellectual history; East Asian and Amerindian religion. **SELECTED PUBLICATIONS** Auth, The Spirits are Drunk: Comparative Approaches to Chinese Religion, Albany: State Univ of New York Press, 95; auth, "Chinese Religion," Harold Coward, ed, Population and the Environment: Population Pressures, Resource Consumption, Religions and Ethics, Albany: SUNY Press, (95): 173-91; auth, "Religions in Contact: The Effects of Domination from a Comparative Perspective," Iva Dolezalova, Bretislav Horyna, & Dalibor Papousek, eds, Religions-in Contact: Selected Proceedings of the Special IAHR Conference, Brno, 94, Brno: Czech Society for the Study of Religion: (96): 39-56; auth, "Communicating the Intangible: An Anishnabe Story," American Indian Ouarterly, Kenn Pitawanakwat, 20, (96): 451-67; auth, Through the Early Darkly: Female Spirtuality in Comparative Perspective, New York: Continuum, 97; auth, Chinese Way in Religion, 2nd ed, Belmont, Calif, Wadsworth, 98; auth, "Introduction -- Ascetic Culture: Renunciation and Wordly Engagement," "Eremitism in China," Journal of Asian and African Philosophy, 34, (99)1-3, 46-55; auth, "Chinese Religion, 'Daoism', and Deep Ecology," David Barnhill & Roger Gottlieb, eds, Deep Ecology and World Religions, Albany: State Univ of New York Press, (forthcoming). **CONTACT ADDRESS** Div of Humanities, York Univ, 4700 Keele St, Downsview, ON, Canada M3J 1P3. **EMAIL** jpaper@yorku.ca

PAPPAS, GEORGE SOTIROS
PERSONAL Born 05/04/1942, Philadelphia, PA, m, 1963, 2 children **DISCIPLINE** PHILOSOPHY **EDUCATION** Gettysburg Col, BA, 63; Univ Pa, MA, 66, PhD(philos), 74. **CAREER** Asst Prof, Vis Prof, Univ of Western Ontario, Vis Assoc Prof, Univ of Tex; Vis Prof, Western Wash Univ, Vis Prof, Dalousie Univ. **HONORS AND AWARDS** Turbayne Prize, 93; Exemplary Fac Awd, Col of Humanities, 98. **MEMBERSHIPS** Can Philos Asn; Am Philos Asn. **RESEARCH** Epistemology, hist of modern philosophy, metaphysics. **SELECTED PUBLICATIONS** Co-ed and contrib, Essays on Knowledge and Justification, Cornell Univ Press, with Marshall Swain, 78; ed and contrib, Justification and Knowledge: New Studies in Epistemology, Dordrecht: D. Reidel, 79; transl, Problemas y Argumentos Filosoficas, Spanish translation of 3rd edition of previously cited book, Mexico City, 90; coauth, Philosophical Problems and Arguments, 4th edition, with Keith Lehrer and James Cornman, Hackett, 92; auth, "Experts," Acta Analytica, 95; auth, "Experts, Knowledge, and Perception," in Warrant in Contemporary Epistemology, ed., J. Kvanvig, Rowman and Littlefield, 96; auth, "Epistemology in the Empiricists," History of Philosophy Quarterly, Vol 15, (98): 285-302; auth, "Berkeley and Scepticism," Philosophy and Phenomenological Res, Vol LIX, 99; auth, "Internalism and Externalism in Epistemology," to appear in the Stanford On-Line Encyclopedia, 99; auth, "The Philosophy of Berkeley," to appear in Blackwell Guide to Modern Philosophy, ed., S. Emmanuel, (forthcoming 99/00). **CONTACT ADDRESS** Dept of Philos, Ohio State Univ, Columbus, 230 N Oval Mall, Columbus, OH 43210-1335. **EMAIL** pappas.1@osu.edu

PAPPAS, GREGORY F.
PERSONAL Born 02/09/1960 **DISCIPLINE** PRAGMATISM, ETHICS **EDUCATION** Univ PR, BA, 81; Univ Wyo, MA, 83; Univ Tex at Austin, PhD, 90. **CAREER** Assoc prof, Tex A & M Univ; lectr and asst instr, Univ Tex. **HONORS AND AWARDS** Ford Foun postdoc fel, National Res Coun, 91-92; Douglas Greenlee Prize, 92; William James Prize, 90. **RESEARCH** American philosophy. **SELECTED PUBLICATIONS** Auth, Dewey's Philosophical Approach to Racial Prejudice, Journal of Social Philosophy, 96; William James Virtuous Believer, Transactions of the Charles Peirce Society, 94; Dewey and Feminism: The Affective and Relationships in Dewey's Ethics, Hypatia vol.8, 93; William James and The Logic of Faith, Transactions of the Charles Peirce Society, 92; rev, The Community Reconstructs: The Meaning of Pragmatic Social Thought, Vol.8, J Speculative Philos. **CONTACT ADDRESS** Dept of Philosophy, Texas A&M Univ, Col Station, 309E Bolton Hall, College Station, TX 77843-4237. **EMAIL** pappase@io.com

PAPPU, RAMA RAO
DISCIPLINE ORIENTAL PHILOSOPHY, PHILOSOPHY OF LAW, ETHICS **EDUCATION** Punjab, BA; Delhi, MA; Southern Ill Univ at Carbondale, PhD. **CAREER** Prof, Miami Univ **MEMBERSHIPS** Conf dir, 9th Int Cong of Vedanta, Rishikesh UP India, 97. **RESEARCH** Philosophy of law; ethics; Indian and Comparative Philosophy. **SELECTED PUBLICATIONS** Ed, Indian Philosophy: Past and Future; Dimensions of Karma & Perspectives on Vedanta. **CONTACT ADDRESS** Dept of Philosophy, Miami Univ, Oxford, OH 45056. **EMAIL** pappuss@muohio.edu

PAPRZYCKA, KATARZYNA
PERSONAL Born 01/15/1967, Poznan, Poland, m, 1988, 2 children **DISCIPLINE** PHILOSOPHY **EDUCATION** Harvard, BA, 89; Univ Pittsburg, PhD, 97. **CAREER** Teaching asst, 90-93, teaching fel, 94-95, Univ of Pittsburg; adjunct faculty member, 96, 97, Univ TX of the Permian Basin; adjunct faculty member, 98, Univ of Southern Mississippi. **HONORS AND AWARDS** Honorary Immatriculation, 85; Merit Scholarship, 85-86; Open Society Found Scholarhsip, Oxford Univ, 86-87; Harvard Col Scholarship, Harvard University, 87-88; Graduated Magna Cum Laude from Radcliffe Col, 89; Andrew Mellon Predoctoral Fel, University of Pittsburgh, 89-90; Sloan Fel, Univ of Pittsburgh, 93-94; Andrew Mellon Predoctoral Fel, Univ of Pittsburgh, 94-95; **MEMBERSHIPS** Amer Philosophical Assn, 87-; Assoc member of The Southern Soc for Philosophy and Psychology, 92-. **RESEARCH** Philosophy of action, mind, psychology and social sciences. **SELECTED PUBLICATIONS** Auth, Collectivism on the Horizon: A Challenge to Pettit's Critique of Collectivism, Australasian Journal of Philosophy 76 (98), 165-181; auth, Normative Expectations, Intenrions and Beliefs, The Southern Journal of Philosophy 37-4 (99), 629-652; auth, Idealization in Unitarian Metaphysics, Axiomathes, 00; auth, Meets Carnap: Explications in the Theaetetus, Logical Analysis and History of Philosophy 2 (99), 87-108; auth, Must False Consciousness Be Rationally Caused?", Philosophy of the Social Science 28-1 (98), 69-82; auth, Flickers of Freedom and Frankfurt-Style Cases in the Light of the New Incompatibilism of the Stit Theory, forthcoming in Journal of Philosophical Res; auth, "The Master and Slave Configuration in Hegel's System," in Social Systems, Rationally and Revolution (Amsterdam: Rodopi, (93), 83-104; auth, "How Do Enslaved People Make Revolutions," in Soc Systems, Rationality and Revolution (Amsterdam: Rodopi, (93), 251-263; auth, "Carnap and Leibniz on the Problem of Being," in Poznan Studies in Philo of the Sci and the Humanities 28 (92), 163-177. **CONTACT ADDRESS** 117 Continental Dr, Hattiesburg, MS 39402-1071. **EMAIL** paprzyck@pitt.edu

PARCHMENT, STEVEN
DISCIPLINE HISTORY OF MODERN PHILOSOPHY, SPINOZA, ANCIENT AND MEDIEVAL PHILOSOPHY **EDUCATION** Emory Univ, PhD, 96. **CAREER** Lectr, Ga State Univ. **SELECTED PUBLICATIONS** Published an article on Spinoza in Hist of Philos Quart. **CONTACT ADDRESS** Georgia State Univ, Atlanta, GA 30303. **EMAIL** phlsgp@panther.gsu.edu

PARENS, JOSHUA
DISCIPLINE PHILOSOPHY OF BEING **EDUCATION** St John's Col, BA; Univ Chicago, MA, PhD. **CAREER** Dept Philos, Univ Dallas **SELECTED PUBLICATIONS** Auth, Theory and Practice in Medieval Aristotelianism, Polity,93; Multiculturalism and the Problem of Particularism, Amer Polit Sci Rev, 94; Whose Liberalism, Which Islam? Leonard Binder's Islamic Liberalism, PS, 94; Metaphysics as Rhetoric: Alfarabi's Summary of Plato's Laws, SUNY Press,95. **CONTACT ADDRESS** Dept of Philos, Univ of Dallas, 1845 E Northgate Dr, Irving, TX 75062. **EMAIL** parens@acad.udallas.edu

PARENT, MARK
PERSONAL Born 08/25/1954, Halifax, NS, Canada, m, 1974, 3 children **DISCIPLINE** RELIGIOUS STUDIES **EDUCATION** York Univ, BA, 76; Acadia Div Col, MDiv, 79; McGill Univ, PhD, 91. **CAREER** Fac, MTh sem, 84-85, instr, Queen's Theol Col, 89; lectr Atlantic Baptist Col, 92; fel, relig stud, Mount Allison Univ, 92-93; instr, New Brunswick Commun Col, 94; instr, Mount Allizon Univ 92- , hon res assoc, Acadia Univ, 94-96; asst prof, Mount Allizon Univ, 98- . **HONORS AND AWARDS** Edward Manning Saunders Prize, Diefenbaker Awd, Acadia Univ. **MEMBERSHIPS** Can Evangel Theol Asn; Can Theolog Soc; Faith and Hist Soc. **RESEARCH** Christianity and culture; fundamentalism; liberation theology. **SELECTED PUBLICATIONS** Auth, Enigmatic Answers, Church Leadership Unltd, 93; auth, Strange New Movements, Atlantic Baptist, 94; auth, T T Shields and the Irony of Fundamentalism, in Fides et Historia, 94; auth, Religion at Three Maritime Universities, in Aspects of Education in the Small University, McGill-Queens, 96; auth, Spiritscapes: Mapping the Spiritual and Scientific Terrain at the Dawn of the New Millennium, Northstone, 98. **CONTACT ADDRESS** Mount Allison Univ, 65 York St, Sackville, NB, Canada E4L 1E4. **EMAIL** mparent@glinx.com

PARENTE, WILLIAM
PERSONAL Born 07/07/1937, Chicago, IL, m, 1970, 9 children **DISCIPLINE** POLITICAL SCIENCE **EDUCATION** Xavier Univ, AB, 61; Georgetown Univ, PhD, 70. **CAREER** Asst prof to assoc Dean, Antioch Col, 66-70; prof, Univ of Scranton, 73-; Dean, 70-85. **HONORS AND AWARDS** Woodrow Wilson Fel, 61; Fel, Union for Experimenting Col and Univ, 65-66; Fulbright, Korea, 74-75; Fulbright, Indonesia, 78-79; Fulbright, Thailand, 86-87; NEH Summer Grants, 76, 85, 88, 90-94, 96. **MEMBERSHIPS** APSA. **RESEARCH** Proscription of racist speech in constitutional law, etc. **SELECTED PUBLICATIONS** Auth, "The Racial Factor in the Sino-Soviet Dispute", Jour of E and W Studies, Seoul, Vol III, 1; auth, "Campus Radicalism and a Relevant Political Science", Jour of Higher Educ, Vol XXX1X, 6; auth, "The Introduction and Structure of Political Science", W Polit Quarterly, Vol XXII, 2, 69; auth, "The Contribution of Communist States to the Proscription of Racist Speech", The Europ Legacy, 1.1 (MA: MIT Pr, 96). **CONTACT ADDRESS** Dept Polit Science, Univ of Scranton, 800 Linden St, Scranton, PA 18510-2429. **EMAIL** parentewl@uofs.edu

PARIS, ROLAND C.
PERSONAL Born 06/29/1967, Toronto, ON, Canada **DISCIPLINE** POLITICAL SCIENCE **EDUCATION** Univ Toronto, BA, 89; Cambridge Univ, MPhil, 90; Yale Univ, PhD, 99. **CAREER** Asst Prof, Univ Colo, 99-. **CONTACT ADDRESS** Dept Polit Sci, Univ of Colorado, Boulder, CB 333, Boulder, CO 80309. **EMAIL** rcp040@email.com

PARK, EUNG CHUN
PERSONAL Born 07/21/1958, Seoul, Korea, m, 1982, 2 children **DISCIPLINE** BIBLICAL STUDIES **EDUCATION** Seoul Natl Univ, BA, 81; Presbyterian Theol Sem, MDiv, 84; Yale Univ Div, STM, 86; Univ Chicago, PhD, 91. **CAREER** Ast prof, 96-99, asoc prof, 99- , San Francisco Theol Sem. **MEMBERSHIPS** Soc of Bibl Lit. **RESEARCH** Biblical hermeneutics; Gospel of Matthew; universalism in the New Testament. **SELECTED PUBLICATIONS** Auth, "The Nicene Creed and the New Testament," Church and Theol, 93; "The Pentecost Event Through Luke's Eyes," Bibl Ground, 93; "The Image of the Rabbi in New Testament Times," Educ and Church, 93; "Paul's Philosophy of Ministry," Bible and Ministry, Korean Inst Bibl Stud, 94; "Jewish Particularism and Universalism in New Testament Churches," Church and Theol, 94; "Paul's Appropriation and Transformation of Culture, Christian Culture and Female Leadership in the Church," Inst of the Stud of Women in Korean Church, 94; "Fruit Worthy of Repentance," Bibl Stud for Preachers and Lay Persons, 94; "The Terms of Defining Self-identity of the Early Christianity Reflected in the Areopagus Address in Acts 17:22-31," Church and Theol, 95; The Mission Discourse in Matthew's Interpretation. JCB Mohr, 95; The Gospel for the World, Inst Bibl Stud, 97; "Savior," Encyclopedia of Theology, Korean Inst for Catholic Stud, forthcoming; "Book Note on Mitzi Minor, The Spirituality of Mark: Responding to God," Theol Tod, forthcoming; "The Lord's Supper Turned into Disaster," Jrnl Case Tchg, 98. **CONTACT ADDRESS** San Francisco Theol Sem, 2 Kensington Rd, San Anselmo, CA 94960-2905. **EMAIL** ecpark@sfts.edu

PARK, HONG-KYU
PERSONAL Born 03/07/1938, Kyungbuk, Korea, m, 1968, 1 child **DISCIPLINE** HISTORY; POLITICAL SCIENCE **EDUCATION** Kent Wesleyan Col, BA, 62; Univ Tenn, MA, 64; Univ N Tex, PhD, 81. **CAREER** Instr to assoc prof, Wiley Col, 65-76; asst prof to prof, Jarvis Christian Col, 77-93; prof, Kilgore Col, 93- . **HONORS AND AWARDS** UNCF Distinguished Schol Awd, 85-86. **MEMBERSHIPS** Am Hist Asn; Asn Asian Student; Orgn Am Hist; Soc Hist Am For Relations; SW Sco Sci Asn. **RESEARCH** American-East Asian relations since 1945. **SELECTED PUBLICATIONS** Auth, The Korean War: An Annotated Bibliography, Demmer Co, (71); auth, "The Korean War Revisited: A Survey of Historical Writings,"

World Affairs 137, pp336-344, (75); auth "American-Sovient Rivalry in Korea, 1945-1948," Korea J 22, pp 4-15, (82); auth, "From Pearl Harbor to Cairo: America's Korean Diplomacy, 1941-43," Diplomatic Hist 13, pp 343-358, (89); auth, " America's Response to the Korean Problem, 1941-1945," Asian Profile 21, pp 23-30, (93). **CONTACT ADDRESS** Dept Soc & Behav Sci, Kilgore Col, 729 Pam Dr, Tyler, TX 75703-4852. **EMAIL** ProfHP@aol.com

PARK, JIN Y.
PERSONAL Born 05/31/1962, Seoul, Korea, m, 1996 **DISCIPLINE** COMPARATIVE STUDIES, RELIGION **EDUCATION** SUNY Stony Brook, PhD, 98. **CAREER** Yonsei Univ Seoul, lectr, 87; SUNY Stony Brook, tchg asst, adj lect, 93-99; Vassar Col, Mellon Post Doctoral Fellow, 99-. **HONORS AND AWARDS** Yonsei Univ, Grad & Undergrad Fel, SUNY Stony Brook Grad Fel, Mellon Post Doctoral fellow, NY Lit Young Writers Awd; Buddhist Grants. **MEMBERSHIPS** AAR; APA; AAS; IAPL; KWAA, KWWA; KNA; SACP; SPEP; IIFB; ISCP. **RESEARCH** Asian and comparative thought; deconstruction and Buddhism; Korean and E Asian Zen Buddhism; contemp continental philosophy. **SELECTED PUBLICATIONS** Co-trans, Mother and Dove: Korean-American Poetry Anthology (Flushing) Pringing & AD Express, Inc., 97; auth, Postmodernism-the Endgame of Literature?, Study of English Language and Literature, 91; auth, Buddhism and Won Buddhism, Journal of Won Buddhist Study, 98; auth, Buddhism and Won Buddhism, Journal of Won Buddhist Study, 98; auth, Religious Conflict or Religious Anxiety: New Buddhist Movements in Korea and Japan, Religious Studies and Theology, 98; trans, Getting Familiar with Death (Philadelphia), Won Publication, 99; auth, Hwadu and Hwaom in Chinul- A Postmodern Perspective, in Son Buddhism and Western Philosophy in the Era of Deconstruction, 00. **CONTACT ADDRESS** Dept of Religion, Vassar Col, PO Box 242, Poughkeepsie, NY 12604-6242. **EMAIL** jypark@vassar.edu

PARK, KYEONG-SOOK
PERSONAL Born Pusan, S Korea, 2 children **DISCIPLINE** MISSIOLOGY **EDUCATION** Hankuk Univ, BA, 80; Moody Bible Inst, Cert, 83; Wheaton Col, MA, 85; Biola Univ, DM, 96. **CAREER** Prof, Evangel Theol Sem of Indonesia, 90-97; prof, Moody Bible Inst, 97-. **HONORS AND AWARDS** Summa Cum Laude; Korean Prime Minister Awd. **MEMBERSHIPS** Evangel Missiological Soc. **RESEARCH** Anthropology, Social Organization, Intercultural Communication. **CONTACT ADDRESS** Dept Missions, Moody Bible Inst, 820 N Lasalie St, Chicago, IL 60610-3284.

PARK, ROGER COOK
PERSONAL Born 01/01/1942, Atlanta, GA **DISCIPLINE** LAW **EDUCATION** Harvard Univ, BA, 64, JD, 69. **CAREER** Prof Law, Univ Minn Law Sch, 73-. **HONORS AND AWARDS** Julius E Davis prof, Univ Minn Law Sch, 81. **RESEARCH** Evidence; computer aided instruction; legal education. **SELECTED PUBLICATIONS** Auth, The entrapment controversy, J Minn Law Rev, 76; Computer Aided Instruction in Law, West Pub Co, 76; Computer aided instruction in law: Theories, techniques and trepidations, J Am Bar Found, 78; coauth, Teaching Law with Computers, West View Press, 80; auth, McCormick on evidence and the concept of hearsay, J Minn Law Rev, 81; the 22nd Annual Hodson,kenneth,j. Lecture - Uncharged Misconduct Evidence in Sex Crime Cases - Reassessing the Rule of Exclusion, Military Law Review, Vol 0141, 1993. **CONTACT ADDRESS** Law Sch, Univ of Minnesota, Twin Cities, Minneapolis, MN 55454.

PARK, TIMOTHY K.
PERSONAL Born 11/19/1948, Seoul, Korea, m, 1975, 3 children **DISCIPLINE** MINISTRY **EDUCATION** Chongshin Univ, BA, 72; Presbyterian Gen Assembly Theol Sem, MDiv, 76; Asian Center for Theol Studies and Mission, ThM, 82; Fuller Theol Sem, PhD, 91. **CAREER** Asst Prof to Pres, Presbyterian Theol Sem, 83-96; Assoc Prof and Director of Korean Studies, 96-. **MEMBERSHIPS** Am Soc of Missiol. **RESEARCH** Asian Mission/Korean Mission; Cross-cultural Church Planting. **SELECTED PUBLICATIONS** Auth, Missionary Movement of the Korean Church, 99. **CONTACT ADDRESS** Dept Pastoral Ministry, Fuller Theol Sem, 135 N Oakland Ave, Pasadena, CA 91182-0001. **EMAIL** timpark@fuller.edu

PARK, WILLIAM WYNNEWOOD
PERSONAL Born 07/02/1947, Philadelphia, PA **DISCIPLINE** LAW **EDUCATION** Yale Univ, BA, 69; Columbia Univ, JD, 72; Cambridge Univ, England, MA, 75. **CAREER** Atty, Coudert Freres, Paris, 72-75 & Hughes, Hubbard & Reed, Paris, 77-79; fel, Selwyn Col, Cambridge Univ, England, 75-77; prof Law, Boston Univ, 79-, adjunct prof Int Law, Fletcher Sch Law & Diplomacy, 80-86; vis prof, Inst Universitaire de Hautes Etudes Int Geneva, 83; vis prof, Univ Dijon, 84; vis prof, Univ Hong Kong, 90. **HONORS AND AWARDS** Vice pres, London Court of Int Arbitration; Arbitrator; Claims Resolution Tribunal for Dormant Accounts in Switzerland. **MEMBERSHIPS** Am Soc Int Law; Int Fiscal Asn; British Inst Int & Comp Law; Brit Chartered Inst Abitrators. **RESEARCH** International business transactions; taxation; arbitration. **SELECTED PUBLICATIONS** Auth, Fiscal jurisdiction and accrual basis taxation, Columbia Law Rev, 12/78; Le nouveau statut des banques etrangeres aux Etats-Unis, Rev Int de Droit Compare, 1/80; Tax characterization of international leases, Cornell Law Rev, 11/81; coauth, French codification of a legal framework for international commercial arbitration, Georgetown J Law & Policy in Int Bus, 11/81; International Forum Selection, 95; International Commercial Arbitration with W M Reisman, 97; Arbitration in Banking & Finance, 17 Ann Rev, Banking Law 213, 98. **CONTACT ADDRESS** Law Sch, Boston Univ, 765 Commonwealth Ave, Boston, MA 02215-1401.

PARKER, JOSEPH C., JR.
PERSONAL Born 09/25/1952, Anniston, AL, m, 1975 **DISCIPLINE** LAW **EDUCATION** Morehouse Col, BA, 74; Univ of Ga, M Public Admin, 76; Univ of Tex at Austin, JD, 82. **CAREER** City of Dallas, admin asst mgmt serv 1976-77, admin asst office of the city mgr 1977-79, mgr summer youth employment program 1979; Travis Co Attorney Office, trial attorney 1983-84, chief trial div 1985-86; David Chapel Missionary Baptist Church, assoc pastor 1984-; Long, Burner, Parks & Sealy PC, attorney, dir, vice pres, 86-; Univ of TX at Austin, instructor in trial advocacy, 91-. **HONORS AND AWARDS** Man of the Year Spelman College Student Govt Assn 1973-74; Univ of GA Fellowship 1974-76; Pi Sigma Alpha Honor Soc 1976; Dallas Jaycees Rookie of the Yr 1978-79, Presidential Awd 1978-79; Outstanding Achievement Awd Natl Conf of Minority Public Administrators 1979; Gene Woodfin Awd Univ of TX 1982; Leadership Austin 1984-85; Distinguished Morehouse Coll Alumni Citation of the Year 1986; Baptist General Convention of TX Theological Scholarship 1986-87; Benjamin E Mays Fellowship in Ministry, Fund for Theological Studies; publication "Prosecuting the DWI", True Bill Vol 6 No 4 TX Prosecutor Council. **MEMBERSHIPS** Mem Natl Conf of Minority Public Administrators 1974-80; mem Amer Soc for Public Admin; bd dirs Morehouse Coll Natl Alumni Assn; bd dirs Austin Child Guidance and Evaluation Ctr; mem Conference of Christians and Jews; mem Black Austin Democrats; mem Urban League, NAACP, Austin Jaycees; mem Travis County Public Defender Task Force; mem State Bar of TX, TX and Austin Young Lawyers Assns, Natl Bar Assns; mem Austin Black Lawyers Assn and Federal Bar Assn; mem Association of Trial Lawyers of America. **CONTACT ADDRESS** School of Law, Univ of Texas, Austin, Austin, TX 78712. **EMAIL** joe@resolutionarchitects.com

PARKER, KELLY A.
PERSONAL Born 10/22/1963, Osborne, KS, m, 1984, 2 children **DISCIPLINE** PHILOSOPHY **EDUCATION** Vanderbilt Univ, PhD, 92. **CAREER** Asst prof, 92-98, assoc prof, 98-, Grand Valley St Univ. **HONORS AND AWARDS** Vanderbilt Grad Stud Res Day, First Prize, 89; Diss Enhancement Awd, Vanderbilt Grad School, 90; Harold Stirling Vanderbilt Fel, 87-91; Mellon Diss Yr Fel, 91-92; Charles S. Pierce Soc Essay Contest Winner, 91; Soc for the Advancement of Am Philos, Douglas Greenlee Essay Prize, 94; GVSU Center on Philanthropy and Non-Profit Leadership Curriculum Development Grant (Ethics and Professions), 96. **MEMBERSHIPS** APA; Charles S. Pierce Soc; Soc for the Advancement of Am Philos; The Metaphysical Soc of Am; Int Soc for Environ Ethics; Asn for Pract & Profes Ethics; North Am Merleau-Ponty Cir; Am Asn of Univ Profs, GVSU Chap; Ctr for Acad Integrity. **SELECTED PUBLICATIONS** Auth, Economics, Sustainable Growth, and Community, Environmental Values vol 2, 93; autn, Pierce's Semeiotic and Ontology, Transactions of the Charles S. Pierce Soc, vol 30, 94; auth, Pragmatism and Environmental Thought, Chap 1 Environ Pragmatism, Routledge Press, 96; auth, The Ascent of Soul to Nous: Charles S. Pierce as Neoplatonist, in Neoplatonism and Contemporary Thought, SUNY Press, forthcoming; auth, The Ethics Committee: A Concensus-Recommendation Model, in Pragmatic Bioethics, Vanderbilt Univ Press; The Continuity of Pierce's Thought, The Lib of Am Philos, Vanderbilt Univ Press, 98; auth, William James: Experience and Creative Growth, in Classical American Philosophy: Its Contemporary Vitality, Univ IL Press, 98. **CONTACT ADDRESS** Dept of Philosophy, Grand Valley State Univ, 210 Lake Superior Hall, Allendale, MI 49401-9403. **EMAIL** parkerk@gvsu.edu

PARKER, LISA S.
PERSONAL Born 09/22/1962, South Bend, IN **DISCIPLINE** BIOETHICS **EDUCATION** Univ Pittsburgh, PhD, 90. **CAREER** Asst prof, Univ Tenn, 90-91; assoc prof, Univ Pittsburgh, 91-98; assoc prof, Univ Pittsburgh, 98-. **HONORS AND AWARDS** Nellie Westerrman Prize in Ethics, 90. **MEMBERSHIPS** Am Soc of Bioethics and Humanities; Am Philos Asn; Sigma Xi. **RESEARCH** Bioethics. **SELECTED PUBLICATIONS** Auth, Social Justice, federal paternalism, and feminism: Breast implantation in the cultural context of femaule beauty, Kennedy Inst of Ethics J, 93; Bioethics for human geneticists: Models for reasoning and methods for teaching, Am J of Human Genetics, 94; Beauty and breast implantation: How candidate selection affects autonomy and informed consent, Hypatia, 95; Breast cancer genetic screening and bioethics' critical gaze, J of Med and Philos, 95; coauth, Standards of care and ethical concerns in genetic testing and screening, Clinical Obstetrics and Gynecology, 96. **CONTACT ADDRESS** Ctr for Bioethics and Health Law, 3708 Fifth Ave, Pittsburgh, PA 15213. **EMAIL** lisap@pitt.edu

PARKER, PAUL P.
PERSONAL Born 08/25/1953, Louisville, KY, m, 1993, 3 children **DISCIPLINE** THEOLOGY **EDUCATION** Univ F, BS, 75; SBTS, MDiv, 81, PhD, 86. **CAREER** Relig, Elmhurst **RESEARCH** Theology; social ethics. **CONTACT ADDRESS** Elmhurst Col, 190 Prospect Ave., Elmhurst, IL 60126. **EMAIL** paulp@elmhurst.edu

PARKER, THOMAS D.
PERSONAL Born 12/22/1931, Los Angeles, CA, m, 1978, 5 children **DISCIPLINE** THEOLOGY **EDUCATION** Calif State Col, Los Angeles, BA, 54; San Francisco Theol Sem, BD, 57; Princeton Theol Sem, PhD, 65. **CAREER** Asst prof, 68-71, Assoc prof, 71-74, prof, 74-94, Cyrus McCormick prof, 94-98, emer prof, 98- , McCormick Theol Sem. **HONORS AND AWARDS** Cum laude, 57; summa cum laude, 65; Rockefeller Doctoral Fel, 64-65; AATS Fac Fel, 70-71. **MEMBERSHIPS** Am Theol Soc; Am Acad of Relig; Sof for the Sci Stud of Relig; Soc of Christian Philos; Highlands Institute for Am Philosophical & Religious thought. **RESEARCH** Religious experience and belief; Christology; religion and science. **SELECTED PUBLICATIONS** Auth, "Promise," McCormick Q, 70; "On Doing Theology," Teachers Guide: Christian Faith and Action, 71; ed, Christian Theology, 76; auth, "The Political Meaning of the Trinity," J of Relig, 80; "Can There be a Covenant Community that is Genuinely Inclusive," Miller, ed, A Covenant Challenge to a Broken World, 82; "Spirituality and Peacemaking," Peace, War and God's Justice, 89; "Immediacy and Interpretation," Am J of Theol and Philos, 91. **CONTACT ADDRESS** PO Box 1778, Hendersonville, NC 28793. **EMAIL** ktparker20@aol.com

PARKER, VERNON B.
PERSONAL Born 11/16/1959, Houston, TX, m, 1991 **DISCIPLINE** LAW **EDUCATION** Bilingual and Cultural Institute of Cuernavaca, Mexico, 1980; California State Univ at Long Beach, BS, 1980-83; Georgetown Univ, JD, 1988. **CAREER** Rockwell International, financial analyst, 83-85; US Office of Personnel Management, counselor to the dir/dir of policy, 89-91, general counsel, 92; White House, special asst to the pres, 92-93; Kenny Rogers Roasters of Chicago, vice pres, 93-94; Multinational Legal Services, partner, 94-; Parian International, president & CEO; Parker, Farringer, Parker, Attorney, currently; Belsante International, pres and ceo, co-founder, currently. **HONORS AND AWARDS** Georgetown Univ Law Center, Outstanding Leader, 1988; Georgetown Univ Law Center, Outstanding Tutor, 1988, Foreign Language Scholarship recipient, 1980. **MEMBERSHIPS** National Bar Association, 1991-; District of Columbia Bar, 1989-; Virginia Bar Association, 1995; Student Bar Association, Georgetown Univ Law Center, vice pres, 1986-87. **SELECTED PUBLICATIONS** Editor-in-chief, Georgetown American Criminal Law Review; Author, "Annual Survey of White-Collar Crime Attorney Client Privilege," American Criminal Law Review, Winter 1986-1987. **CONTACT ADDRESS** Parker, Farringer, Parker, 1825 I St NW, Ste 400, Washington, DC 20006.

PARKS, EDWARD Y.
PERSONAL Born 02/05/1951, Thomson, GA, m, 1975, 2 children **DISCIPLINE** LAW **EDUCATION** Otterbein College, BA, 1973; Howard Univ, JD, 1979. **CAREER** Ohio Public Interest campaign, assoc dir, 79-81; Legal Aid Society, Attorney, 81-83; Public Utilities Commission, Attorney examiner, 83-86; Ohio Dept Health, legal counsel, 86-89; Law Office, Edward YA Parks, president, 89-. **HONORS AND AWARDS** Welfare Rights, Outstanding Legal Advocate, 1983; NAACP, Community Service Awd, 1985; Shiloh Baptist Church, Outstanding Service-Softball Program, 1987 & 1988. **MEMBERSHIPS** Assoc Juvenile Laws, presiding officer, 1989-; NAACP, 1979-; Urban League, 1991-; Columbus Bar Assoc, 1980-; Natl Conference Black Lawyers, 1980-; Shiloh Baptist Church, trustee, 1993; Legal Aid Society Lawyer Referral, 1989-; Natl Bar Assn, 1993-. **SELECTED PUBLICATIONS** Shiloh Baptist Church Plan, 1990; Book of Poems. **CONTACT ADDRESS** Law Office, Edward Y A Parks, 8 E Long St, Ste 225, Columbus, OH 43215. **EMAIL** edwarparks@aol.com

PARKS, JENNIFER A.
PERSONAL Born 12/31/1968, Kingston, ON, Canada, m, 1999 **DISCIPLINE** PHILOSOPHY **EDUCATION** Queen's Univ, BA, 90; MA, 90; McMaster Univ, PhD, 96. **CAREER** Asst prof, Loyola Univ, 97-. **HONORS AND AWARDS** Loyola Summer Res Awd, 97-00; Woman in Leadership, Loyola Univ, 00. **MEMBERSHIPS** Am Philos Assoc; Feminist Approaches to Bioethics. **RESEARCH** Ethics, Health Care Ethics, Feminist theory, Feminist Bioethics (special interest in reproductive technologies and feminist ethica). **SELECTED PUBLICATIONS** Rev, of "Misconceptions: The Social Construction of Choice and the New Reproductive and Genetic Technologies", eds Gwynne Basen, Margrit Eichler, and Abby Lippman, Res for Feminist Res, 241.1, 66-67; auth, "A Closer Look at Reproductive Technology and Postmenopausal Motherhood", Can Med Assoc J 154.8 (Apr 96): 1189-1191; auth, "A Contextualized Approach to the Therapeutic Relationship", J of Med Humanities 19.4 (98); auth, On the Use of IVF by Post-Menopausal Women", Hypatia, 14.1 (99): 77-96; auth, "Ethical Androcentrism and Maternal Substance Addiction: Concerns of

a Feminist Ethicist", Int J of Applied Philos 13.2 (99): 165-175; auth, "Why Gender Matters to the Euthanasia Debate: On Reason, Decisional Capacity, and the Rejection of Women's Death Requests", Hastings Center Report (forthcoming). **CONTACT ADDRESS** Dept Philos, Loyola Univ, Chicago, 6525 N Sheridan Rd, Chicago, IL 60626-5344. **EMAIL** jparks1@luc.edu

PARKS, SHARON DALOZ
DISCIPLINE THEOLOGY, HUMAN DEVELOPMENT **EDUCATION** Harvard, ThD, 80 **CAREER** Assoc dir, fac, The Whidbey Inst. **HONORS AND AWARDS** D.D.; D.D.; D.H.L. **MEMBERSHIPS** Am Acad of Relig. **RESEARCH** Leadership and ethics. **SELECTED PUBLICATIONS** Auth, The Critical Years, 86; auth, Common Fire: Leading Lives of Commitment in a Complex World, 96; auth, Big Questions, Worthy Dreams: Mentoring Young Adults in their Search for Meaning, Purpose and Faith, 00. **CONTACT ADDRESS** Whidbey Inst, PO Box 57, Clinton, WA 98236-9520.

PAROT, JOSEPH JOHN
PERSONAL Born 06/04/1940, Hammond, IN, m, 1962, 2 children **DISCIPLINE** AMERICAN RELIGIOUS & URBAN ETHNIC HISTORY **EDUCATION** Maryknoll College, 58; IN Univ, 59-60; St Joseph's Col, Ind, BA, 63; DePaul Univ, MA, 67; Northern IL Univ, PhD, 71. **CAREER** Instr hist, St Augustine High Sch, Chicago, 63-67; from instr to asst prof hist & bibliog, 67-74, assoc prof, 75-82, prof hist & head hist ctr, Northern IL Univ, 82-, prof hist & head soc sci dept, 84; Instr soc sci, Chicago Comt Urban Opportunity Prog, 66-67; vis prof urban/ethnic studies, George Williams Col, 72-73; assoc ed, Polish-Am Studies, 73. **HONORS AND AWARDS** Ed Emer Awd, St Joseph's Col, 63; Lions Int, Outstanding Teacher Awd, Chicago rea, 66; Pi Gamma Mu, DePaul Univ, 67; Oscar Halecki Awd from Polish Am Hist Asn for outstanding book, 83; grants from Am Philos Soc, NEH; Honorariums from Multicultural Hist Soc of Ontario, 78; Pa Hist Comm, 76; Univ Notre Dame 82; Multicultural Curr Transformation Ins, 95. **MEMBERSHIPS** AHA; Polish-Am Hist Asn; Phi Gamma Mu (Natl Soc Sci Honor Soc); Friends of NIU Libraries, 90-. **RESEARCH** Immigration hist; urban hist; religious hist in Am. **SELECTED PUBLICATIONS** Auth, Ethnic versus Black metropolis: Origins of Polish Black housing tensions in Chicago, 71, Unthinkable thoughts on unmeltable ethnics, 74 & Racial dilemma in Chicago's Polish neighborhoods, 1920-1970, 75, Polish Am Studies; contribr, Bishop Francis Hodur, suppl five, In: Dict of American Biography, 77; Strangers in the city: Immigrant Catholics and the black community in Twentieth century Chicago, Black History Conference, Lincoln Univ, 4/78; Immigrant Labor and the Paradox of Pluralism in American Urban Society, 1860-1930: A Comparative Study and Census Analysis of Polish, German, Irish, Bohemian, Italian and Jewish Workers in Chicago, Polish Res Inst of the Jagiellonian Univ, Cracow, 79; Sources of community conflict in Chicago Polonia: A comparative analysis and historigraphical appraisal, Ethnicity, vol 7, winter 80; Polish Catholics in Chicago, 1850-1920: A Religious History, Northern Ill Univ Press, 81; The Serdeczna Matko of the sweatshops: Marital and family crises of immigrant working-class women in late nineteenth century Chicago, Poles in North America Conference, Multicult Hist Soc of Ont, 82; Steelmills, sweatshops, stockyards, and slums: The social fabric of the immigrant Catholic working class in Chicago, 1870-1930, Perspectives in American Catholicism, Univ Notre Dame, 11/82; Catholic manuscript and archival sources in the Greater Chicago area, Mdwest Archives Conf, Chicago 5/83; The urbanization and suburbanization of the ethnic working class in Chicago, 1870-1980, Celebrate Illinois: Its Cultural Heritage, Ill Humantities Counc, 4/85; Family and social history in the immigrant community, Polish Genealogical Soc, 11/88; auth, Praca Imigranta I Paradoks Pluralizmu w Amerykanskim Spoleczenstwie Miejskim w Latach, 1860-1930: Studium Porownaczne, Wroclaw: Ossolineum, 88; co-ed (with James Pula, et al), Polish History in America to 1908, vol 1-4; Catholic Univ of Am Press, 94-98, Kruszka Transl Proj; ed board of Ill Hist Jour, 95-98; The German immigrant in Illinois, 1840-1930, Elmhurst Hist Soc, 3/98; Reverend Vincent Barzynski, In: American National Biography, 99; Multicultural difficulties in the Polish Catholic community in Chicago, Ill Hist Teacher, 99; auth, "The Polish Roman Catholic Union," "The Polish National Alliance," and "Dziennik Zwiazkowy," in Enclyclopedia of Chicago History (00); numerous rev essays in Am Hist Rev, Cath Hist Rev, Ill Hist Jrnl, Ind Magazine of Hist, Intl Migration Rev, and Polish Am Studies. **CONTACT ADDRESS** Social Sci Dept; Dept of History, No Illinois Univ, Founders Libr, De Kalb, IL 60115-2825. **EMAIL** c60jjpl@wpo.cso.niu.edu

PARR, CHRIS
DISCIPLINE RELIGION **EDUCATION** Univ Canterbury, NZ, BA, 77, MA, 80; Boston Univ, PhD, 92. **CAREER** Tchg fel, 84-90, gallery asst, 87, assoc dir, Video Icons & Values Conf, 87, lectr and instr, Boston Univ, 89-92; asst prof, Webster Univ, 92-; steering comt, 90-92, co-ch Arts, Lit and Relig sect, Am Acad Relig, 92-95; gallery asst, Inst Contemp Art, Boston, 87-89. **HONORS AND AWARDS** Wilma and Roswell Messing, Jr, fac Awd. **MEMBERSHIPS** Am Acad Relig, 87-; MLA, 88-90. **SELECTED PUBLICATIONS** Auth, Introducing James K. Baxter, Longman Paul, 83; Cars are Part of Nature Too, Illeagle Press, 92; Taking Boston as Given, & Giving Back: Bill Corbett's Quality of Attention, lift 15/16, 94; coauth, Ecologic and Symbiotic Approaches to Animal Welfare, Animal Rights, and Human Responsibility,' J of Am Vet Med Asn, 191, 6, 87; coed, Video Icons & Values, State Univ NY Press, 91. **CONTACT ADDRESS** Webster Univ, Saint Louis, MO 63119. **EMAIL** parrch@websteruniv.edu

PARRENT, ALLAN MITCHELL
DISCIPLINE CHRISTIAN ETHICS **EDUCATION** Georgetown Col, BA, 52; Vanderbilt Univ, MA, 55; Vanderbilt Univ, MDiv, 61; Duke Univ, PhD, 69. **CAREER** Lt, US Naval Reserve, 56-59; for svc off, Dept of State, 62-64; asst coord, stud act, asst dir, Stud Union, Duke Univ, 64-67; dir, Prog in Wash, Dept Intl Aff, Nat Coun of Churches, 67-72; prof, 72-83; assoc dean for acad aff, VP, Clinton S. Quin prof, Va Theol Sem, 83-97; adj prof, School of Theol, Univ of the South. **HONORS AND AWARDS** Fulbright scholar, Durham Univ, 52-53; Danforth Grad Fel, 52-62; Rockefeller Theol Fel, 59-60; Gurney Harriss Kearns Fel, Duke Univ, 66-67. **SELECTED PUBLICATIONS** Auth, Jesus' Messiahship and Our Discipleship, Best Sermons II, Harper and Row, 89; The War in the Persian Gulf and the Episcopal Church, Sewanee Theol Rev, 91; The Distorted and the Natural, Best Sermons IV, Harper and Row; On War, Peace and the Use of Force, The Crisis in Moral Teaching in the Episcopal Church, Morehouse Publ, 92. **CONTACT ADDRESS** Virginia Theol Sem, 3737 Seminary Rd, Alexandria, VA 22304. **EMAIL** aparrent@sewanee.edu

PARRISH, STEPHEN E.
PERSONAL Born 03/22/1952, Detroit, MI, m, 1981, 3 children **DISCIPLINE** PHILOSOPHY **EDUCATION** Schoolcraft Col, AA, 72; Eastern Mich Univ, BS, 75; Univ Mich, MLS, 79; Wayne State, MA, 84, PhD, 91. **CAREER** Instr, Wayne State Univ, 88-; William Tyndale Col Libr and asst prof Philos, 91-. **MEMBERSHIPS** Amer Philos Asn; Soc Christian Philos; Evangel Philos Soc. **RESEARCH** Philosophy of Religion; Nietzsche; Philosophy of mind; objectivism. **SELECTED PUBLICATIONS** Auth, The Mormon God, Omniscience, and eternal progression: A Philosophical Analysis, Trinity Jour 12NS, Fall, 91, 127-138; Mormon Theism and the Argument from Design: Philosophical Analysis, Criswell Theol Rev, spring 91; Yandell on Temptation and Necessity, Philosophia Christi, Jour of the Evangelical Philos Soc, vol 20:2, winter 97, 57-62; coauth, See the Gods Fall, The Col Press, Fall 97; Fod and Necessity, UP of Am, May 97; Auth, The Mormon Concept of God: A Philosophical Analysis, Mellen, 91. **CONTACT ADDRESS** Dept of Philosophy, William Tyndale Col, 35700 W Twelve Mile Rd, Farmington Hills, MI 48331.

PARROTT, ROD
PERSONAL Born 03/26/1942, Ontario, OR, m, 1964, 1 child **DISCIPLINE** RELIGION **EDUCATION** Northwest Christ Col, BTh, 65; Phillips Univ Grad Sem, MDiv, 69, MTh, 70; Claremont Grad School, PhD, 80. **CAREER** Disciples Sem Found, asst dean, 79-89, assoc dean, 89-00; prof, Disciples Studies and New Testament, 00-. **HONORS AND AWARDS** Ecumenical Serv Award, 84 **MEMBERSHIPS** SBL, SACEM, CCU, DCHS **RESEARCH** Adult learn theol; congreg stud and lead; soc formations; soclgy of relig; soclgy of conflict in Pauline churches. **SELECTED PUBLICATIONS** Auth, Impact, Semeia and Forum, revs: The Disciple, Encounter and Midstream, coauth the Ministry of Elders, Oikodome Pub, 90; coed, Impact, 00-. **CONTACT ADDRESS** Disciples Sem Foundation, 300 W Foothill Blvd, Claremont, CA 91711-2709. **EMAIL** rparrott@dsf.edu

PARRY, RICHARD D.
PERSONAL Born 06/30/1939, Easton, PA, m, 1966, 2 children **DISCIPLINE** PHILOSOPHY **EDUCATION** Georgetown Univ, BA, 61; Yale Univ, MA, 63; Univ NC, PhD, 68. **CAREER** Instr, Univ SCar, 64-65; From Asst Prof to Prof, Agnes Scott Col, 67-. **HONORS AND AWARDS** Woodrow Wilson Fel, 61; Sterling Jr Fel, 62; Richard M Griffin Awd, S Soc for Philos and Psychol, 70; Vis Fel, Oriel Col (Oxford), 81-82; President's Awd for Excellence in Teaching, Agnes Scott Col, 90. **MEMBERSHIPS** APA, Southern Soc for Philos and Psychol, Soc for Ancient Greek Philos, Am Cath Philos Asn. **SELECTED PUBLICATIONS** Auth, Plato's Craft of Justice, SUNY Press, 96; auth, "Morality and Happiness: Book IV of Plato's 'Republic'," J of Educ (96); auth, "The Uniqueness Proof for Forms in 'Republic' 10," Great Polit Thinkers: Plato (97); auth, "Philosopher Kings and Forms," Plato's Polit Philos and Contemp Democratic Theory (97); auth, "Death, Dignity and Physician Asisted Suicide," Am (98). **CONTACT ADDRESS** Dept of Philosophy, Agnes Scott Col, 141 E College Ave, Decatur, GA 30030. **EMAIL** rparry@agnesscott.edu

PARSONS, CHARLES D.
PERSONAL Born 04/13/1933, Cambridge, MA, m, 1968, 2 children **DISCIPLINE** PHILOSOPHY **EDUCATION** AB, 54, AM, 56, Harvard Univ; PhD, 61. **CAREER** Asst Prof, 61-62, Cornell Univ; Assoc Prof, 65-69, Prof, 69-89, Columbia Univ; Asst Prof, 62-65, Prof, 89-91, Edgar Pierce Prof, 91-, Harvard Univ. **HONORS AND AWARDS** Henry Fel, 54-55; NEH Fel, 79-80; Guggenheim Fel, 86-87; Fel, NIAS, 87; Fel, Ctr for Advanced Study in Behavioral Sciences, 94-95; Fel, Am Acad of Arts and Sciences, 82-. **MEMBERSHIPS** Assoc for Symblic Logic; Am Phil Asn. **RESEARCH** Logic; philos of logic and mathematics; Kant. **SELECTED PUBLICATIONS** Auth, Mathematics in Philosophy, 83; auth, The Structuralist View of Mathematical Objects, Synthese 84, 90; The Uniqueness of the Natural Numbers, Iyyun 39, 90; The Transcendental Aesthetic, The Cambridge Companion to Kant, 92; On Some Difficulties Concerning Intuition and Intuitive Knowledge, Mind N.S. 102, 93; Intuition and Number, Mathematics and Mind, 94; Structuralism and the Concept of Set, Modality, Morality, and Belief: Essays in Honor of Ruth Barcan Marcus, 95; Platonism and Mahematical Intuition in Kurt Godel's Thought, The Bulletin of Symbolic Knowledge, 95; What Can We Do in Principle, Logic and Scientific Mehtods, 97; Finitism and Intuitive Knowledge, The Philosophy of Mathematics Today, 98. **CONTACT ADDRESS** Dept of Philosophy-Emerson Hall, Harvard Univ, Cambridge, MA 02138. **EMAIL** parsons2@fas.harvard.edu

PARSONS, KEITH M.
PERSONAL Born 08/31/1952, Macon, GA, s **DISCIPLINE** HISTORY & PHILOSOPHY OF SCIENCE; PHILOSOPHY OF RELIGION **EDUCATION** Queens Univ, PhD, 86; Univ Pitts, PhD, 96. **CAREER** Asst Prof Univ Houston-Clear Lake; Ed, Philo, Jour Soc Humanist Phil **MEMBERSHIPS** Philos Sci Asn; Am Philos Asn. **RESEARCH** Rationality & theory change in science; history of the earth sciences; Darwinism; science and religion. **SELECTED PUBLICATIONS** Auth, God and the Burden of Proof, Prometheus Books, 89; Drawing Out Leviathan: Dinosaurs and the Science Wars, Ind Univ Press. **CONTACT ADDRESS** Univ of Houston, 2700 Bay Area Blvd., Houston, TX 77058-1098. **EMAIL** parsons@cl.uh.edu

PARTAN, DANIEL GORDON
PERSONAL Born 08/02/1933, Gardner, MA, m, 1957, 5 children **DISCIPLINE** LAW **EDUCATION** Cornell Univ, AB, 55; Harvard Univ, LLB, 58, LLM, 61. **CAREER** Fac asst law, Harvard Univ, 59-61; res assoc, 61-62; res assoc rule of law res ctr, Duke Univ, 62-65; assoc prof, 65-68, Prof Law, Boston Univ, 68-; Fulbright fel, Law Fac, Univ Cologne, 58-59; assoc prof law, Univ NDak, 64-65; chmn, Comt Charter UN, Am Br Int Law Asn, 71-75; consult, Law & Pop Prog, Fletcher Sch Law, Tufts Univ, 71-75; consult, Am Acad Arts & Sci, 74-75, US Dept State, 76-77 & UN Develop Prog, 77-78. **HONORS AND AWARDS** App Chpt 19 Binat Panel Roster, U S-Canada Free Trade Agreement & NAFTA, 92-; App Dispute Settlement Roster, WTO, 97-. **MEMBERSHIPS** Am Soc Int Law; Int Law Asn; Am Law Inst; UN Asn; Comn Study Orgn Peace; Acad Counc UN System; European Community Studies Asn. **RESEARCH** International law and organization; international trade law; admiralty and maritime law; arms control and legal problems in the development of world order; international adjudication and human rights. **SELECTED PUBLICATIONS** Coauth, Legal Problems in International Administration, Harvard Law Sch, 68; auth, Population in the United Nations System, Sijthoff, the Netherlands, 73; auth, Documentary Study of the Politicizaion of UNESCO, 2 vol, Am Acad Arts & Sci, 75; auth, The United States and the Internationalal labor organization, Comn study Orgn, Peace, 79; coed, "Corporate Disclosure of Environmental Risks: US and European Law," Butterworth Legal Pub, 90; auth, the International Law Process: Cases and Materials, Carolina acad Press, 92; auth, "Report on improving the effectiveness of the United Nations in advancing the rule of law in the world," Rapporteur, 8/94, Intl Lawyer, (95); auth,"The justiciability of subsidarity," The State of the European Union, (95); auth, The International Law Process: 1999 Documents Supplement, Carolina Acad Press, 99. **CONTACT ADDRESS** Sch of Law, Boston Univ, 765 Commonwealth Ave, Boston, MA 02215-1401. **EMAIL** partan@bu.edu

PARTLETT, DAVID FREDERICK
PERSONAL Born 08/10/1947, Sydney, Australia, m, 2 children **DISCIPLINE** LAW **EDUCATION** Univ Sydney, LLB; Univ Mich, LLM; Univ Va, SJD. **CAREER** Vis asst prof, Univ Ala Sch of Law, Tuscaloosa, 72-73; lectr, Sr lectr, Fac of Law, Australian Nat Univ, Canberra, 78-87; John Sparkman Distinguished Vis Prof of Law, Univ of Ala, 86-87; vis assoc prof, Vanderbilt Univ Sch of Law, 87-88, prof, Sch of Law, and Sr Fel, Vanderbilt Inst for Public Policy Studies, Vanderbilt Univ, 88-2000, acting dean, Vanderbilt Univ Law Sch, 96-97; Dean of the Law Sch, Washington & Lee Univ, Lexington, Va, 2000-. **HONORS AND AWARDS** Cook Grad Fel, Univ Mich, 73-74; Distinguished Service Awd, Vanderbilt Univ Sch of Law, 96; The Thomas Jefferson Awd, Vanderbilt Univ, 98. **MEMBERSHIPS** Southeastern Asn of Am Law Schs, Tenn Governor's Comn for Revision of title 33, Acad Advisory Comt to Am Bar Asn (Torts & Insurance Law Section), Seldon Soc, Am Soc of Law & Med. **SELECTED PUBLICATIONS** Coauth, coauth, Suing for Medical Malpractice, Univ Chicago Press (93); coauth, Torts: Cases and Materials, 9th Ed, Foundation Press, NY (94); coauth, Child Mental Health and the Law, Macmillan Free Press, NY (94); coauth, Modern Remedies: Cases, Practical Problems and Exercises, West Pub Co, St Paul, Mn (97); auth, "Tort liability and the American Way: Reflections on Liability for Emotional Distress," 45 Am J Comp Lit, 601 (97); coauth with Barry Nurcombe, "Recovered Memories of Child Sexual Abuse and Liability: Society, Science, and The Law in a Comparative Setting," 4 Psychol, Public Policy, and Law 1 (98); auth, "Punitive Damages: Legal Hot Zones," 56 La Law Rev,

781 (96), reprinted in Davies, et al, A Torts Anthol, 2nd ed (99): 508-529; auth, Defamation and Free Speech: A Study of Different Cultures, Anderson Pubs (under contract); coauth, Torts: Cases and Materials, 10th ed, Foundation Press, NY (in prep). **CONTACT ADDRESS** Sch of Law, Washington and Lee Univ, Sydney Lewis Hall, Lexington, VA 24450. **EMAIL** partlettd@wlu.edu

PASCH, ALAN
PERSONAL Born 12/01/1925, Cleveland, OH, m, 1950, 1 child **DISCIPLINE** PHILOSOPHY **EDUCATION** Univ Mich, BA, 49; New Sch Soc Res, MA, 52; Princeton Univ, PhD, 55. **CAREER** Bamford fel, Princeton Univ, 55-56; from instr to asst prof philos, Ohio State Univ, 56-60; assoc prof, 60-67, prof philos, prof emer, 97- , Univ Md-College Park, 67-. **MEMBERSHIPS** Am Philos Asn (exec dir, 69-72); Metaphys Soc Am; Soc Philos & Pub Affairs; Wash Philos Club (pres, 78-79); Eastern Div Am Philos Asn (secy-treas, 65-68); Wash Rare Book Gp. **RESEARCH** Metaphysics of human sexuality; philosophy of logic. **SELECTED PUBLICATIONS** Auth, Experience and the Analytic, Univ Chicago, 58. **CONTACT ADDRESS** Dept of Philosophy, Univ of Maryland, Col Park, College Park, MD 20742-7615. **EMAIL** ap3@umail.umd.edu

PASCUZZI, MARIA
PERSONAL Born 07/18/1951, Brooklyn, NY **DISCIPLINE** BIBLICAL STUDIES **EDUCATION** Pontifical Bibl Inst, Rome, SSL, 87; Gregorian Univ, Rome, STD, 97. **CAREER** Asst prof, St. Joseph's Sem & Grad Sch of Theology, Yonkers NY, 87-92; asst prof, Immaculate Conception Sem & Graduate Sch of Theology, Huntington NY, 92-96; asst prof theol, St. Peter's Col, Jersey City, NJ, 98-00; Asst Prof of New Testament, Univ of San Diego, 00. **HONORS AND AWARDS** Kenny Fellowship. **MEMBERSHIPS** AAR/SBL; CBA. **RESEARCH** New Testament; Paul; Greco-Roman rhetoric. **SELECTED PUBLICATIONS** Auth, Ethics, Ecclesiology and Church Discipline: A Rhetorical Analysis of 1 Corinthians 5, Gregorian Univ Pr, 97. **CONTACT ADDRESS** 5998 Alcala Park, San Diego, CA 92110-2492. **EMAIL** pascuzzi@acusd.edu

PASHA, MUSTAPHA
DISCIPLINE POLITICAL ECONOMICS **EDUCATION** Forman Christian Col, BA; Punjab Univ, Pakistan LLB; Univ Denver, MA, PhD. **CAREER** Prof, Am Univ. **HONORS AND AWARDS** Wilma and Roswell Messing Jr. Faculty Awd, Webster Univ. **RESEARCH** Global political economy and the comparative politics of the Third World. **SELECTED PUBLICATIONS** Auth, Colonial Political Economy: State-Building and Underdevelopment in the Punjab, Oxford Univ Press, 97. **CONTACT ADDRESS** American Univ, 4400 Massachusetts Ave, Washington, DC 20016.

PASKOW, ALAN
PERSONAL Born 06/11/1939, Elizabeth, NJ, m, 1967, 1 child **DISCIPLINE** PHILOSOPHY **EDUCATION** Haverford Col, BA, 61; Northwestern Univ, MA, 63; Yale Univ, PhD(philos), 71. **CAREER** Instr philos, Antioch Col, 67-68; from instr to asst prof, Univ Vt, 68-74; asst prof, Prescott Col, 74, mem fac, Prescott Ctr Col, 75-76; mem fac, Deep Springs Col, 76-80, Assoc Prof Philos, St Mary's Col, Md, 81-, Danforth teaching assoc humanities, 67-68; Nat Endowment Humanities grant spec humanities prog, 73; vis assoc prof philos, Haverford Col, 80-81. **HONORS AND AWARDS** Sr Res Fulbright Grant. **MEMBERSHIPS** Am Philos Asn. **RESEARCH** Phenomenology and existentialism, philosophy of art. **SELECTED PUBLICATIONS** Auth, Are College Students Educable?, J Higher Educ, 3/74; auth, "The Meaning of my Own Death," Int Philos Quart, 3/74; "A Phenomenological View of the Beetle in my Box," New Scholasticism, summer 74; auth, What do I Fear in Facing my Death?, 5/75 & Towards a Theory of Self-deception, Vol 12, No 2, Continental Philosophical Review. **CONTACT ADDRESS** Div Human Develop, St. Mary's Col of Maryland, Saint Mary's City, MD 20686-0222. **EMAIL** apaskow@osprey.smcm.edu

PASKOW, SHIMON
PERSONAL Born 06/21/1932, Newark, NJ, m, 1962, 1 child **DISCIPLINE** RELIGIOUS STUDIES **EDUCATION** Brooklyn Col, BA; Hebrew Union Col, MA, 59. **CAREER** Instr, Hebrew Union Col; instr, Univ of Judaism. **HONORS AND AWARDS** Hebrew Union Col, fel, 59-60. **MEMBERSHIPS** Cent Conf of Am Rabbis; Military Chaplains Asn; Asn of Jewish Chaplains; Soc of Bibl Lit; Am Jewish Hist Soc. **RESEARCH** Religious studies; Hebrew; Judaism. **CONTACT ADDRESS** 1080 Janss Rd, Thousand Oaks, CA 91360.

PASS, MARTHA WHITE
PERSONAL Born 02/19/1946, AL, m, 1968, 2 children **DISCIPLINE** ECONOMICS **EDUCATION** Randolph-Macon Woman's Col, BA, 67; Bryn Mawr Col, PhD, 81. **CAREER** Lectr, Univ of Md, Europ Campus, 70-72; From Instr to Prof Carleton Col, 75-77, 78-. **HONORS AND AWARDS** Phi Beta Kappa, Fulbright Fel, 68; Andrew W. Mellon Teaching Fel, Carleton Col, 77-78; Sr Fulbright Fel, 88, 96. **MEMBERSHIPS** Asn of Cult Econ, Econ Hist Soc, Econ Hist Asn. **RESEARCH** European economic history, economics of arts. **SELECTED PUBLICATIONS** Auth, Population Change, Labor Supply and Agriculture in Augsburg, 1480-1618: A Study of Early Economic-Demographic Interactions, Arno Press (NY), 81; auth, "The Economics of Population Change and Agricultural Response in Fifteenth-Century Germany," Fifteenth Century Studies 6 (83): 187-204; auth, "Demographic Change and Market Structure in Early Modern Germany," in The Structure of Internal Trade, 15th-19th Century, ed. J. Chartres and S. Gyimesi (Bern: Nineth Int Econ Hist Congress, 86), 4-13; auth, "Family Labor Strategies in Early Modern Swabia," J of Family Hist 17 (92): 233-240, and in The European Peasant Family and Society: Historical Studies, ed. Richard Rudolph (Liverpool: Univ of Liverpool Press, 93), 146-153; auth, "Nurnbers Wirtschaft im 17. Jahrhundert," in "Der Franken Rom": Nurnbergs Blutezeit in der zweiten Halfte des 17. Jahrhunderts (Wiesbaden: Harrassowitz, 95), 46-61. **CONTACT ADDRESS** Dept of Econ, Carleton Col, 1 N Col St, Northfield, MN 55057-4001.

PASSELL, DAN
PERSONAL Born 10/08/1928, Cleveland, OH, m, 1954, 4 children **DISCIPLINE** PHILOSOPHY **EDUCATION** Univ Chicago, PhB, 49, MA, 54; Stanford Univ, PhD, 64. **CAREER** Instr philos, Fresno State Col, 61-63; asst prof, 64-72, prof philos, Portland State Univ, 72-. **RESEARCH** Theory of meaning. **CONTACT ADDRESS** Dept of Philosophy, Portland State Univ, PO Box 751, Portland, OR 97207-0751. **EMAIL** dan@nh1.nh.pdx.edu

PATEL, RAMESH
DISCIPLINE EASTERN AND WESTERN PHILOSOPHY, WORLD RELIGIONS **EDUCATION** St Xavier Col, BA, MA; Govt Law Col, LLB; Univ NM, MA, PhD. **CAREER** Prof, Antioch Col. **RESEARCH** The philos of Mahatma Gandhi. **SELECTED PUBLICATIONS** Auth, Philosophy of the Gita, Peter Lang Publ, 91; The Numinous and the Mystical; Gandhi's Dual Concept of Truth; Brahma's Philosophical Synthesis According to Ojha. **CONTACT ADDRESS** Antioch Col, Yellow Springs, OH 45387.

PATERSON, ROBERT
DISCIPLINE LAW **EDUCATION** Univ New Zeland, LLB, 69; Stanford Univ, JSM, 72. **CAREER** Prof, 81-. **RESEARCH** Corporations; securities regulation; international trade and investment; international commercial arbitration; cultural property and law. **SELECTED PUBLICATIONS** Auth, International Trade and Investment Law in Canada, 94; pubs about corporations, securities regulation, international trade, international arbitration and cultural property; co-ed, UNCITRAL Model Law in Canada, 89. **CONTACT ADDRESS** Fac of Law, Univ of British Columbia, 1822 East Mall, Vancouver, BC, Canada V6T 1Z1. **EMAIL** paterson@law.ubc.ca

PATRICK, ANNE E.
PERSONAL Born 04/05/1941, Washington, DC, s **DISCIPLINE** RELIGION **EDUCATION** Medaille Col, BA, 69; Univ Maryland, MA, 72; Univ Chicago, MA, 76, PhD, 82. **CAREER** Lectr, religion & lit, 78-80, Univ Chicago Divinity School; Warren Dist Vis Prof, 89, Univ Tulsa; Paul E McKeever vis prof, moral theology, 97-98, St John's Univ, NY; instr, 80-82, asst prof, 82-86, assoc prof, 86-91, dept chmn, 86-88, 90-91, 00-; prof, 91-, Carleton Col. **MEMBERSHIPS** AAR; Amer Asn Univ Prof; CTSA, Pres, 89-90; Col Theology Soc; Intl Network of Soc for Catholic Theology; Vice-Pres, 96-02; Soc of Christian Ethics. **RESEARCH** Christian feminist ethics; moral theology; George Eliot; fiction and ethics. **SELECTED PUBLICATIONS** Art, Publications of the Park Ridge Center for Health, Faith, and Ethics, Religious Stud Rev, 93; art, Veritatis Splendor, Commonweal, 93; art, Mass Media and the Enlargement of Moral Sensibility: Insights from Theology and Literary History, Mass Media and the Moral Imagination, Sheed & Ward, 94; art, Is Theodicy an Evil? Response to The Evils of Theodicy, Proceedings of the Catholic Theological Soc of Amer Vol 50, 95; art, From Hearing to Collaboration: Some Steps for the Privileged Toward a Praxis of Solidarity, Women and Theology, Maryknoll, Orbis, 95; auth, Liberating Conscience: Feminist Explorations in Catholic Moral Theology, NY Continuum 96; art, Creative Fiction and Theological Ethics: The Contributions of James M. Gustafson, Ann of the Soc of Christian Ethics 17, 97; art, Markers, Barriers, and Frontiers: Theology in the Borderlands, Theology: Expanding the Borders, 23rd Pub, 98; art, Imaginative Literature and the Renewal of Moral Theology, New Theology Review, 5/98; auth, Art, His Dogs More Than Us: Virtue in Situations of Conflict, Practice What You Preach, Sheed and Ward, 99; auth, art, A Ministry of Justice, What's Left: Liberal American Catholics, Indiana Univ Press, 99; auth, art, American Spirituality, Religion & American Culture vol. 9, 99; auth, art, Feminist Ethics and the New Millennium, Ethics and the New Millenium I, Villanova University Press, 00. **CONTACT ADDRESS** Dept of Religion, Carleton Col, One North College St., Northfield, MN 55057-4228. **EMAIL** apatrick@carleton.edu

PATRICK, DALE
PERSONAL Born 10/02/1938, Eugene, OR, m, 1961, 1 child **DISCIPLINE** THEOLOGY **EDUCATION** Lewis & Clark Col, BS, 60; Union Theol Sem, 61; School of Theol, Drew Univ, BD, 63; Grad Theol Union/San Francisco Sem, ThD, 71. **CAREER** Asst to assoc prof, Mo Sch of Rel, 68-81; vis assoc prof, Univ Mo, 81-82; assoc prof to Prof, Endowed Hum Chair, Drake Univ, 82-. **HONORS AND AWARDS** RockeFeler Fel, 60-61. **MEMBERSHIPS** Soc Bibl Lit; Am Acad Rel. **RESEARCH** Bibl law, rhetoric, Bibl Theol. **SELECTED PUBLICATIONS** Auth, The Rendering of God in the Old Testament, 81; Auth, Old Testament Law: An Introduction, 84; coauth, Rhetoric and Biblical Interpretation, 90; auth, "God's Commandment," in God in the Fray: A Tribute to Walter Brueggemann, 98; "The First Commandment in the Structure of the Pentateuch," in Vetus Testamentum XLV/1, 95; "The Rhetoric of Collective Responsibility in Deuteronomic Law," in Pomegranates and Golden Bells: Studies in Biblical, Jewish and Near Eastern Ritual, Law, and Literature in Honor of Jacob Milgrom, 95; Auth, The Rhetoric of Revelation in Hebrew Scripture, 99. **CONTACT ADDRESS** Dept of Philos/Rel, Drake Univ, Des Moines, IA 50311. **EMAIL** dale.patrick@drake.edu

PATRY, WILLIAM F.
DISCIPLINE LAW **EDUCATION** SF State Univ, BA, 74; MA, 76; Univ Houston, JD 80. **CAREER** Ed-in-chief, J of the Copyright Soc, 88-97; policy planning adv to the register of copyrights, US Copyright Off, 88-92; counsel, US House of Reps, comm on the judiciary, subcomm on Intellectual Prop & the Admin of Just, 92-95; dir, LLM Prof in Intel Prop, 98-00, assoc prof, Law, Benjamin N. Cardozo Law Sch, 95-00. **HONORS AND AWARDS** Asst coun, House Judiciary Subcomt, 92-95; advisor, US Copyright Off. **SELECTED PUBLICATIONS** Auth, The Copyright Term Extension Act of 1997, 72 Notre Dame Law Rev 907, 97; auth, The Enumerated Powers Doctrine and Intellectual Property, 67 George Wash Law Rev 359, 99; auth, Choice of Law & International Copyright, 48 Am J of Comp Law, 00. **CONTACT ADDRESS** Skadden, Arps, Slate, Meagher, & Flom LLP, Four Times Sq, New York, NY 10036. **EMAIL** patry@ymail.yu.edu

PATSAVOS, LEWIS J.
PERSONAL Born 06/04/1937, Everett, MA, s **DISCIPLINE** THEOLOY **EDUCATION** Athens Univ , Lic Theol, 61; Univ Munich, 65; Athens Univ School Theol, Dr Theol, 74. **CAREER** Vis Lecturer, Boston Col, 79-84; Prof, Hellenic Col, 85-. **HONORS AND AWARDS** World Coun of churches Scholarship, Taylor Foundation Scholarship, Bavarian State Ministry of Educ Awd, Catholic Committee for Cultural Collaboration Awd, ATS-Lilly Grant, Holy Cross Alumni Asn Citation, Archbishop Iakovos Fac Awd, Three Hierarchs Medal, Who's Who in the East Listing, Men of Achievement Listing. **MEMBERSHIPS** Soc Law of the Eastern Churches, Orthodox Theol Soc in Am, Canon Law Soc of Am, Asn for Theol Field Educ, BTI Directors' of Field Educ Asn. **SELECTED PUBLICATIONS** Auth, "Third International Conference of Orthodox Schools of Theology: Icon and Kingdom," Greek Orthodox Theological Review, (93): 1-4; auth, "Holy Cross Conference: The Council 'in Trullo'," Greek Orthodox Theological Review, (95): 1-2; auth, Primacy and Conciliarity, Holy Cross Press, 95; auth, entry into the clergy during the first fie Centuries, Athens, 73; auth, "Lived Experience and Theoretical differences in the approach to law and discipline in the eastern and Western Churches," in Rightly Teaching the word of Your truth, Holy Cross press, 95; auth, "The Interface of Pastoral ministry and the Holy canons," Kirchenrecht und Oikumene: Festgabe Panteleimon, 99. **CONTACT ADDRESS** Dept Theol, Hellenic Col, 50 Goddard Ave, Brookline, MA 02445-7415.

PATTE, DANIEL
PERSONAL Born 01/17/1939, France, m, 1960, 3 children **DISCIPLINE** BIBLICAL STUDIES **EDUCATION** Univ Grenoble, France, BA, 58; Faculte de Theol Protestante, France, BD, 60; Univ Geneva, M Th, 64; Chicago Theol Sem, ThD, 71. **CAREER** Asst min, 63-64, Reformed Church of Meyrin, Switzerland; prof, 64-66, Col Hammar, Rep of Congo; instr, 68-71, Syracuse Univ; assoc prof, 74-80, chmn, dept relig stud, 77-98, prof, relig stud, 80-, Vanderbilt Univ. **RESEARCH** Comparative stud of interpretations of the Bible through hist & cultures. **SELECTED PUBLICATIONS** Auth, Paul's Faith and the Power of the Gospel, Philadelphia: Fortress Press, 83; auth, Preaching Paul, Philadelphia; Forrtress Press, 84; auth, Paul, Sa Foi, et la Puissance de l'Evangile, 85; auth, Paulo, Sua Fe e a Forca do Evangelo, Sao Paulo: Edicoes Paulinas, 87; auth, The Gospel acording to Matthew: A Sturctural Commentary on Matthew's Faith, Philadelphia: Fortress Press, 87; auth, structural Eegesis for New Testament Critics, Minneapolis: Fortress Press, 90; auth, The Religious Dimensions of Biblical Tets: Geimas's Structural Semiotics and Biblical Eegesis, 90; auth, Ethics of Biblical Interpretation: A Reevaluation, Westminister/John Knox, 95; auth, Discipleship According to the Sermon on the Mount: Four Legitimate Readings, Four Plausible Views of Discipleship, and Their Relative Values, Harrisburg, PA: Trinity Press Internaitonal: 96; auth, The Challenge of Discipleship: A Critical Study of the Sermon on the Mount as Scripture, Harrisburg, PA: Trinity Press International, 99. **CONTACT ADDRESS** Vanderbilt Univ, Box 1585, Station B, Nashville, TN 37235. **EMAIL** Daniel.M.Patte@Vanderbilt.edu

PATTERSON, BECKY H.
DISCIPLINE CRITICAL CREATIVE THINKING **EDUCATION** Fielding Inst, PhD. **CAREER** Prof, Univ Alaska, Anchorage, English. **SELECTED PUBLICATIONS** Auth, Concentration, 93; Coauth, Developing Reading Versatility, 97. **CONTACT ADDRESS** Dept of English, Univ of Alaska, Anchorage, 3211 Providence Dr., Anchorage, AK 99508.

PATTERSON, BOB E.
PERSONAL Born 08/29/1931, Kings Mountain, NC, m, 1953, 2 children **DISCIPLINE** LITERATURE AND THEOLOGY **EDUCATION** Gardner-Webb Univ, AA, 50; Baylor Univ, BA, 52, MA, 57; Southern Baptist Theol Seminary, Mdiv, 56, PhD, 60. **CAREER** Distinguished Prof of Rel, Dept of Rel, 61-, Baylor Univ. **HONORS AND AWARDS** Alpha Chi Scholastic Fraternity; Outstanding Educ Of Amer; Outstanding Faculty Member; Permanent Distinguished Prof of Rel; Regional Pres of AAR; Natl Pres of N.A.B.P.R. **MEMBERSHIPS** AAR, A.A.U.D., NABPR. **RESEARCH** Theology, Faith and Science, Biblical Studies, Philosophy of Religion. **SELECTED PUBLICATIONS** Auth, Science, Faith and Revelation; Perspectives on Theology; Discovering Ezekiel and Daniel; Discovering Matthew; Discovering Revelation; Theologians, Carl F. H. Henry, Reinhold Niebuhr; Who is Jesus Christ?, ed, 18 vol series, Makers of Modern Theological Mind. **CONTACT ADDRESS** Dept of Religion, Baylor Univ, Waco, Waco, TX 76798. **EMAIL** Bob_Patterson@baylor.edu

PATTERSON, D.
PERSONAL Born 09/29/1955, New York, NY, m, 1978, 2 children **DISCIPLINE** PHILOSOPHY LAW **EDUCATION** SUNY Buffalo, PhD, JD, 80, MA 78, BA 76. **CAREER** Rutgers Univ, assoc prof, prof, dist prof, 90 to 95-; Western New Eng College, asst prof, 87-90; Univ Maine, lect, 85-86; Loyd Bumgardner Field and Patterson, att, partner, 82-87; Preti Flaherty Beliveau, assoc, 81-82. **HONORS AND AWARDS** RUBT Awd for Excell; ACLS Sr Res Awd; Fulbright Sr Lect Gnt; Alexander von Humbolt Stifung Sr Res Gnt; Dean's Sch Rutgers; Phi Beta Kappa; visiting prof at: univ vienna 95; georgetown univ law cen 94-95; univ texas 93; karl-franzens-univ 92; bar admissions to: nj 96, supreme court usa 84, usdc ma 82, maine 81, ny 81. **MEMBERSHIPS** ABA; AALS; APA. **SELECTED PUBLICATIONS** Auth, The Philosophy of Law: An Introduction, with Jeffery White, Oxford Univ Press, in production; Recht and Wahrheit, translation of Law and Truth, Nomos Verlag, 00; Introduction to Commercial Law, with Richard Hyland, West Pub, 99; Introduction to Contemporary Jurisprudence, Blackwell, in prep; Blackwell Anthology for Philosophy of Law and Legal Theory, Blackwell ed, in prep; Post Modern Law, Dartmouth and NY Univ Press, 94; Theory Practice and Jurisprudence: Reflections on the Work of Frederick Schauer, Hart Pub, forthcoming; Response to Critics: Symposium on Law and Truth, SMU Law Rev, forthcoming; Karl Llewellyn, in: The Philosophy of Law: An Encycl, ed, Christopher Gray, NY, NY Garland Pub, 97; Postmodernism, in: Blackwell Companion to the Philo of Law and Legal Theory, ed, 96; Law as a Social Fact: A Reply to Professor Martinez, Loyola LA, L Rev 96; Uniform Commercial Code, rev sec 1-205, Auth, pending public comment; Legality and Legitimacy: Carl Schmitt, Hans Kelsen and Hermann Heller, in: Wiemar, Jurist, forthcoming; Jorge J. E. Gracia, A. Theory of Textuality: The Logic and Epistemology, Rev of Metaphysics, 97. **CONTACT ADDRESS** Dept of Law, Rutgers, The State Univ of New Jersey, Camden, 40 Regan Lane, Voorhees, NJ 08043. **EMAIL** dpatters@camden.rutgers.edu

PATTERSON, DAVID SANDS
PERSONAL Born 04/26/1937, Bridgeport, CT, m, 1968, 1 child **DISCIPLINE** AMERICAN DIPLOMATIC HISTORY, INTERNATIONAL RELATIONS **EDUCATION** Yale Univ, BA, 59; Univ Calif, Berkeley, MA, 63, PhD(hist), 68. **CAREER** Instr hist, Ohio State Univ, 65-69; asst prof, Univ Ill, Chicago Circle, 69-71; asst prof, Rice Univ, 71-76; vis assoc prof US hist, Colgate Univ, 76-78; Historian, Dept of State, 80-; John Hopkins-Nanjing Univ Ctr, 90-91; Dep Hist & Gen Ed Foreign Relations Series, 96-00; Acting Historian, 00-. **HONORS AND AWARDS** Mershon Soc Sci fel, 66; Nat Endowment for Humanities summer fel, 71-; Bernath lectr Am diplomatic hist, Soc Hist Am Foreign Rel, 78. **MEMBERSHIPS** Peace Hist Soc, pres 86-89; Soc Hist Am Foreign Rel, council 98-. **RESEARCH** American diplomatic history; national security affairs; arms control. **SELECTED PUBLICATIONS** Auth, "Woodrow Wilson and the mediation movement, 1914-17," Historian, 8/71; auth, Toward a Warless World: The Travail of the American Peace Movement, 1887-1914, Ind Univ, 76; auth, "The United States and the origins of the world court," Polit Sci Quart, summer 76; auth, "What's wrong (and right) with American diplomatic history: A diagnosis and prescription," Soc Hist Am Foreign Rel Newslett, 78; auth, "A historical view of American security," Peace & Change, Fall 81; auth, "President Eisenhower and Arms Control," Peace & Courage, No 3/4, 86; auth, "The Department of State: The Formative Years, 1775-1800," Prologue, winter 92; auth, The Legacy of President Eisenhower's Arms Control Policies, The Military-Industrial Complex: Eisenhower's Warning Three Decades Later, Peter Lang, 92; auth, Pacifism and Arms Limitation, Encyclopedia of the United States in the Twentieth Century, Scribner's, 96; auth,"Expanding the Horizons of the Foreign Relations Series", The Soc for Hist of Am Foreign Rel Newsletter, June 99. **CONTACT ADDRESS** 9011 Montgomery Ave, Chevy Chase, MD 20815. **EMAIL** pattersonds@state.gov

PATTERSON, ELIZABETH G.
DISCIPLINE PROPERTY, HEALTH LAW, AND FAMILY LAW **EDUCATION** Agnes Scott Col, BA, 68; Univ AZ, JD, 76. **CAREER** Prof, Univ of SC. **RESEARCH** Health law; children and the law. **SELECTED PUBLICATIONS** Publ on, res interest. **CONTACT ADDRESS** School of Law, Univ of So Carolina, Columbia, Law Center, Columbia, SC 29208. **EMAIL** Libba@law.law.sc.edu

PATTERSON, ELIZABETH HAYES
PERSONAL Born 06/25/1945, Boston, MA, m **DISCIPLINE** LAW **EDUCATION** Sorbonne Univ of Paris, diploma with honors 1966; Emmanuel Coll, AB with distinction in French 1967; Stanford U, 1967-68; Columbus Sch of Law Cath Univ of Am, JD 1973. **CAREER** Georgetown Ul Law Cntr, assoc dean JD & graduate programs, 93-97, asso prof 1980-; DC Pub Sev Commn, chmn 1978-80; DC Pub Serv Commn, commr 1977-80 Columbus Sch of Law Cath U, adj prof 1976; Hogan & Hartson Law Firm, asso 1974-77; Hon Ruggero Aldisert US Ct of Appeals, law clk 1973-74. **HONORS AND AWARDS** Woodrow Wilson Fellow Woodrow Wilson Soc 1967; A Salute to Black Women in Gov Iota Phi Lambda Sor Gamma Cht 1978; **MEMBERSHIPS** National Florence Crittenton Mission Foundation Board, trustee, 1995-; bd of dirs, Child Welfare League of America, 1997; Amer Law Institute, 1995-; Trst Family & Child Sev Wash DC 1977-; bd of dirs, Frederick B Abramson Foundation, 1992-; trst, Emmanuel Coll, 1994-; ACLU Litigation Screening Com 1977-80; DC Bar Div I Steering Com 1980-82, DC Bar Screening Comm 1985-86; bd editors Washington Lawyer 1986-91; Sec of State's Adv Comm on Private Intl Law; study group on the Law Applicable to the Intl Sale of Goods 1983-85; adv comm Procedures Judicial Council of the DC Circuit 1981-84; DC Law Revision Comm, 1990-93; treas, District of Columbia Bar, 1987-88. **SELECTED PUBLICATIONS** "UCC 2-612(3): Breach of an Installment Contract and a Hobson's Choice for the Aggrieved Party," 48 Ohio State Law Journal 227, 1987; "UN Convention on Contracts for the Intl Sale of Goods: Unification and the Tension Between Compromise and Domination," 22 Stanford Journal of Intl Law 263, 1986. **CONTACT ADDRESS** Law Ctr, Georgetown Univ, 600 New Jersey Ave NW, Washington, DC 20001.

PATTERSON, JAMES A.
PERSONAL Born 12/01/1947, Camden, NJ, m, 1971, 2 children **DISCIPLINE** CHURCH HISTORY **EDUCATION** Rutgers Univ, BA, 70; Gordon-Conwell Theol Sem, MDiv, 73; Princeton Theol Sem, PhD, 80. **CAREER** From asst prof to prof, Toccoa Falls Col, 77-89; from assoc prof to prof, Mid-America Baptist Sem, 89-99; prof, Union Univ, 99-. **HONORS AND AWARDS** Recipient of a dedication in Toccoa Falls Col Yearbook, 89. **MEMBERSHIPS** Am Soc of Church Hist, Confr on Faith and Hist, Evangelical Theol Soc, Southern Baptist Hist Soc. **RESEARCH** American Christianity, History of Missions, Religion and Politics. **SELECTED PUBLICATIONS** Auth, "The Loss of a Protestant Missionary Consensus: Foreign missions and the Fundamentalist-Modernist Conflict," in Earthen Vessels: American Evangelicals and Foreign Missions, 1880-1890, eds. Joel A. Carpenter and Wilbert S. Shenk, (Wm. B Eerdmans Pub Co., 97); contribur, The Dictionary of Christianity in America, ed. Daniel Reid, et al. (IL: InterVarsity Press, 90); auth, "The Kingdom and the Great Commission: Social Gospel Impulses and American Protestant Missionary Leaders, 1890-1920," Fides et Historia 25 (93): 48-61; auth, "Robert P. Wilder, 1863-1938: Recruiting Students for World Mission," in Mission Legacies, ed. Gerald H. Anderson (NY: Orbis Books, 94); auth, "The Theocratic Impulse in American Protestantism: The Persistence of the Puritan Tradition," in God and Caesar, eds. Michael Bauman and David Hall (PA: Christian Pub, 94); auth, To All the World: A History of Mid-America Baptist Theological Seminary, 1972-1997, Disciple Press (Memphis, TN), 97; contribur, Biographical Dictionary of Christian Missions, ed. Gerald H. Anderson (NY: Simon & Schuster Macmillan, 98). **CONTACT ADDRESS** Christian Studies, Union Univ, 1050 Union University Dr, Jackson, TN 38305. **EMAIL** jpatters@uu.edu

PATTERSON, MARK R.
DISCIPLINE ANTITRUST LAW **EDUCATION** OH State Univ, BSEE, 78, MS, 80; Stanford Law Sch, JD, 91. **CAREER** Assoc, Choate, Hall & Stewart, Boston, 91-93; clk, Sup Judicial Court of Mass, 93-94; Bigelow tchg fel, lectr, Univ Chicago Law Sch, 94-95; assoc prof, 95-. **RESEARCH** Law and sci research. **SELECTED PUBLICATIONS** Auth, Antitrust Liability for Collective Speech: Medical Society Practice Standards, 27 Ind Law Rev 51, 93; Product Definition, Product Information, and Market Power: Kodak in Perspective, 73 NC Law Rev 185, 94; Is Unlimited Liability Really Unattainable?: Of Long Arms and Short Sales, 56 Ohio State Law Jour 815, 95; Coercion, Deception, and Other Demand-Increasing Practices in Antitrust Law, 66 Antitrust Law Jour 1, 97. **CONTACT ADDRESS** Law Sch, Fordham Univ, 113 W 60th St, New York, NY 10023. **EMAIL** mpatterson@mail.lawnet.fordham.edu

PATTERSON, RICHARD
DISCIPLINE ANCIENT PHILOSOPHY **EDUCATION** Univ PA, PhD, 75. **CAREER** Philos, Emory Univ. **HONORS AND AWARDS** Assoc mem, Am Sch Clas Studies, Athens, 74-75; Fel, Ctr Hellenic Studies, 78-79; Nat Ctr Hum Fel, 85-86; Fel, Inst Adv Study, 89; Dir, Prog Clas Studies, Emory Univ, 87-93. **SELECTED PUBLICATIONS** Auth, Image and Reality in Plato's Metaphysics; Aristotle's Modal Logic: Essence and Entailment in the Organon. **CONTACT ADDRESS** Emory Univ, Atlanta, GA 30322-1950.

PATTERSON, SAMUEL C.
PERSONAL Born 11/29/1931, Omaha, NE, m, 1956, 3 children **DISCIPLINE** POLITICAL SCIENCE **EDUCATION** Univ SD, BA 53; Univ Wis, MS 56, PhD 59. **CAREER** Asst prof 59-61; Univ IA, Prof 67-85; Assoc prof 64-67; asst prof 61-64; Carver Distg prof 85-86; OK State Univ, prof 86-98; OH State Univ, prof emer 98-, **HONORS AND AWARDS** Phi Eta Sigma; Phi Beta Kappa; Phi Kappa Phi; ML Huit teach Awd; Hon Deg Doctor Of Humane Letters; Richard F Fenno Prize; Distg Scholar Awd; Fulbright Bologna Italy; Listed in Who's Who in Am; Amer Men and Women of Sci; Who's Who in the Midwest; Contemporary Authors; World Who's Who of Authors. **MEMBERSHIPS** IPSA; APSA; MPSA. **RESEARCH** Comp polit institutions, parliaments and legislatures, polit leadership. **SELECTED PUBLICATIONS** Parliaments and Legislatures, in: G T Kurian, ed, World Encyclopedia of Parliaments and Legislatures, Congress Quart Press, Wash, 98; Congress and Gun Control, in: J M Bruce & C Wilcox, eds, The Changing Politics of Gun Control, Rowman and Littlefield, MD, 98; Senates and the Theory of Bicameralism, in: S C Patterson & A Mughan, eds, Senates: Bicameralism in the Contemporary World, OH State Univ Press, 99. **CONTACT ADDRESS** Dept of Polit Sci, Ohio State Univ, Columbus, 2140 Derby Hall, Columbus, OH 43210-1373. **EMAIL** patpat851@aol.com

PATTERSON, WAYNE KIEF
PERSONAL Born 12/20/1946, Philadelphia, PA, m, 1977 **DISCIPLINE** HISTORY, INTERNATIONAL RELATIONS **EDUCATION** Swarthmore Col, BA, 68; Univ Pa, MA, 69 & 74, PhD(int rels), 77. **CAREER** Prof hist, St Norbert Col, 77-. **MEMBERSHIPS** Asn Asian Studies; Int Studies Asn; Immigration Hist Soc; AHA; Soc Historians of Am Foreign Relat. **RESEARCH** Korean immigration to, and Koreans in, America; Korean-American relations; modern Korean and East Asian history. **SELECTED PUBLICATIONS** Co-ed, The Koreans in America, 1882-1974: A Chronology and Fact Book, Oceana, 74; coauth, The Koreans in America, Lerner, 77. **CONTACT ADDRESS** Dept of Hist, St. Norbert Col, 100 Grant St, De Pere, WI 54115-2099. **EMAIL** pattwk@mail.snc.edu

PATTON, CORRINE
PERSONAL Born 01/19/1958, Sacramento, CA, m, 1986, 2 children **DISCIPLINE** THEOLOGY **EDUCATION** Univ San Francisco, BA, 80; Grad Theol Union, Berkeley, MA, 84; Yale Univ, PhD, 91. **CAREER** Asst Prof, Florida State Univ, 91-96; Asst Prof, Univ of St Thomas, 96-. **MEMBERSHIPS** SBL, CBA. **RESEARCH** Ezekiel, Prophets, History of Biblical Interpretation. **SELECTED PUBLICATIONS** Auth, Contribute to Chronicles and Its Synoptic Parallels in Samuel, Kings and Related Biblical Texts, Liturgical Press, 98; The Old Testament Canon in Catholic Tradition, For Theological Exegesis: Essays in Conversation with Brevard S Childs, ed C Seitz and K Greene-McCreight, in press, 1999; Hugh and Andrew of St Victor and Nicholas of Lyra, Historical Handbook of Major Biblical Interpreters, ed, K K McKim, InterVarsity Press, 98; Psalm 132, A Methodological Inquiry, Catholic Biblical Quarterly, 95. **CONTACT ADDRESS** Univ of St. Thomas, Minnesota, 2115 Summit Ave, Saint Paul, MN 55105. **EMAIL** clpatton@stthomas.edu

PATTY, STACY L.
PERSONAL 4 children **DISCIPLINE** THEOLOGICAL ETHICS **EDUCATION** Lubbock Christian Univ, Lubbock, Tex, BA, 79; Harding Univ Grad Sch Rel, Memphis, Tenn, MTh, 83; Union Theol Sem, NYork, STM, 88; Baylor Univ,Waco, Tex, PhD, 94. **CAREER** Assoc prof rel stud, Lubbock Christian Univ, 95-; ch, Southern Asn Accreditation Rev-Fac Issues, 96-98; Tenure Policy Rev, 96-97; Core Curr Rev, 95-97; Fac Senate, 95-98; asst prof Bible, 92-94; ch, Chapel, 94-95; Liberal Arts Curr Rev, 93-94; Acad Policy, 92-93; grad asst, Baylor Univ, Waco, Tex, 89-92; res asst, grader exams & papers, Hill Col, Hillsboro, Tex; instr, 83-85; Lilly Found, Inc. & Rhodes Col, fel, 98-99; Amer Acad Rel, consult fel, 96-97; Lilly fel, 96; Amer Acad Rel-Lilly Endowment-Nat Endowment for the Humanities, Lilly fel, 95-96; Lubbock Christian Univ grad fel, 91-92; Baylor Univ grad fel, 90-92; Christian Scholar Found, Atlanta, GA, Who's Who Among Stud in Amer Col(s) & Univ(s), listed for the acad yrs 90-91, 81-82, 78-79, & 77-78 Alpha Chi Honor Soc Elected to membership, 78; ch, Philos Relig & Theol Sect, Amer Acad Relig, sw region, 96-98; member, bd dir Christian Scholars' Confe, 96- & Corp Bd, Restoration Quart jour, 96-; lect, Abilene Christian Univ, Abilene, Tex, Jl 97; Lubbock Christian Univ, Lubbock, Tex), Aug 97; Amer Acad Relig-sw Region Meeting, Dallas, Tex, Mar 97; David Lipscomb Univ, Nashville, Tenn, Jl 96; Lubbock Christian Univ, Lubbock, Tex), Jl 95; church related presentations,

Lubbock Christian Univ, Oct,97; Nat Youth Min Sem, Lubbock, Tex, Oct 94; Ann Lectureship, Lubbock Christian Univ, Oct 93; Ann Lectureship, Pepperdine Univ, Malibu, Calif, Apr 93; church activ, adult Bible class tchr, Vandelia Church of Christ, Lubbock, Tex, 97; col Min, Monterey Church of Christ, Lubbock, Tex, 93-95; Min, Elm Mott Church of Christ, Elm Mott, Tex, 89-92. **HONORS AND AWARDS** Trinity Univ L.R. Wilson ,sr tchg awd, 96. **MEMBERSHIPS** Amer Acad Relig; Soc Christian Ethics. **RESEARCH** Pedagogy in Religion and Theology; contemporary and Postmodern Philosophy and Theology; World Religions; Religion and Society; Religion and Science; Environmental Ethics; Medical Ethics & Business Ethics. **SELECTED PUBLICATIONS** Rev, Leonardo and Clodovis Boff's Introducing Liberation Theology and Robert McAfee Brown's Gustavo Gutierrez: An Introduction to Liberation Theology, Restoration Quart 33, 91. **CONTACT ADDRESS** Bible Dept, Lubbock Christian Univ, 5601 19th St, Lubbock, TX 79407-2099. **EMAIL** stacypat@lcu.edu

PATZIA, ARTHUR G.
DISCIPLINE NEW TESTAMENT **EDUCATION** Univ of Manitoba, BA, 59; North Amer Baptist Sem, BO, 62; Princeton Theol Sem, ThM, 63; McMaster Univ, PhD, 70. **CAREER** Assoc Prof, 70-74, Biblical Lit, North Amer Baptist Sem; Assoc Prof NT, 79-82, Bethel Theol Sem; Temp App, 82-84, Dept Class, Univ of Minnesota; Assoc Prof, NT, 85-, Fuller Theol Sem. **HONORS AND AWARDS** Ontario Grad Fellowships; Canada Council Doctoral Fellowship. **MEMBERSHIPS** Soc of Biblical Lit; Inst of Biblical Res. **RESEARCH** Pauline Studies; Intertestamental; New Testament Church. **SELECTED PUBLICATIONS** Auth, Knowledge, Mystery, and Wisdom, Dictionary of the Later New Testament and Its Developments, ed, Ralph P. Martin and P. Davids. Downers Grove, IVP, 97; The Making of the New Testament, Origin, Collection, Text and Canon, Downers Grove, IVP, 95; Canon and Philemon, Epistle to, in Dictionary of Paul and His Letters, ed, Gerald Hawthorne, Ralph Martin and Daniel Reid, Downers Grove, IVP Press, 93; Ephesians, Colossians, Philemon, NIB Commentary, Hendrickson, 91. **CONTACT ADDRESS** 320 Middlefield Rd, Box 906, Menlo Park, CA 94026-0906. **EMAIL** apatzia@fuller.edu

PAUL, GARRETT E.
PERSONAL Born 11/10/1949, Chicago Heights, IL, m, 3 children **DISCIPLINE** CHRISTIAN THEOLOGY **EDUCATION** Wabash Col, AB, 71; Univ Chicago, MA, 73, PhD, 80. **CAREER** Asst prof Relig, St Andrews Presbyterian Col, 76-83; Regent Prof Relig, Gustavus Adolphus Col, 83-. **MEMBERSHIPS** Am Academy Relig; Soc of Christian Ethics; Ernst Troeltsch Gesellschaft; Paul Tillich Soc. **RESEARCH** 19th and 20th century theology; philosophy, sociology, and history of religion; Ernst Troeltsch; religion and politics. **SELECTED PUBLICATIONS** Auth, Translation of Ernst Troeltsch, The Christian Faith, Glaubenslehre, Fortress, 91; Forming an Emphatic Christian Center: A Call to Political Responsibility, with Kyle Pasewark, in Christian Century 111, Aug 94, forthcoming, Abingdon Press, July 99; Theological Themes, in Lectionary Homiletics 6, no 7, June 95; Taste, Natural Law, and Biology: Connections and Separations between Ethics and Biology, in James Hurd, ed The Biology of Morality, Lewiston, NY: Edwin Mellon Press, 96; Jesus' Ethics of Perfection, review of Hans Dieter Betz, The Sermon on the Mount, in Christian Century 113, March 96; History and Ontology in Tension: Troeltsch's Glaubenslehre and Tillich's Dogmatik of 1925, forthcoming in a volume of papers on Troeltsch and Tillich, ed by Jean Richard and Robert Scharleman, to be published by Editions du Cerf, Paris; Translation of Ernst Troeltsch, Der Historismus und seine Probleme, with David Reid, Scholars Press, USA, Seigakuin Univ Press, Japan. **CONTACT ADDRESS** Dept of Relig, Gustavus Adolphus Col, 800 W College Ave, Saint Paul, MN 56082-1498. **EMAIL** gpaul@gac.edu

PAUL, HARRY W.
PERSONAL Born 09/21/1933, NF, Canada **DISCIPLINE** MODERN EUROPEAN RELIGIOUS & INTELLECTUAL HISTORY **EDUCATION** Univ Nfld, BA, 54; Columbia Univ, MA, 58, PhD(hist), 62. **CAREER** Asst prof hist, Md State Col, 62-63 & Newark State Col, 63- 66; assoc prof, 66-73, Prof Hist, Univ FL, 73-, Nat Endowment for Humanities fel, 71-72; NSF grants soc sci, 77, 81-90. **MEMBERSHIPS** AAHM. **RESEARCH** History of medicine; history of science. **SELECTED PUBLICATIONS** Auth, The Second Ralliement: The Rapprochement Between Church and State in France in the 20th Century, Cath Univ Am, 67; The Sorcerer's Apprentice: The French Scientist's Image of German Science, 1840-1919, Univ Fla, 72; Religion and Darwinism, In: The Comparative Reception of Darwinism, Univ Tex, 74; The Edge of Contingency: French Catholic Reactions to Scientific Change from Darwin to Duhem, Univ Fla, 79; Apollo courts the Vulcans: The applied science institutes in nineteenth-century French science faculties, In: The Organization of Science and Technology in France, 1808-1914, Cambridge Univ Press, 80; The role and reception of monographs in nineteenth-century French science, In: Development of Science Pubishing in Europe, Elsevier, 80; coauth (with T W Shinn), The state and structure of science in France, Contemp Fr Civilization, fall 81-winter 82; auth, From Knowledge to Power, The Rise of the Science Empire in France 1860-1939, Cambridge Univ Press, 85; auth, Science, Vine, and Wine in Modern France, Cambridge Univ Press, 96. **CONTACT ADDRESS** Dept of Hist, Univ of Florida, Gainesville, FL 32611. **EMAIL** hpaul@history.ufl.edu

PAULIEN, JON
PERSONAL Born 06/05/1949, New York, NY, m, 1973, 3 children **DISCIPLINE** NEW TESTAMENT **EDUCATION** Andrews Univ, M Div, 76, PhD, 87. **CAREER** Pastor, NY City, 72-81; prof, Andrews Univ, 84-. **HONORS AND AWARDS** Scholarly Publ Awd, Andrews Univ, 92, 97, 00. **MEMBERSHIPS** Soc of Bibl Lit; Chicago Soc for Bibl Res. **RESEARCH** The Apocalypse; Gospel of John; Contemporary culture issues. **SELECTED PUBLICATIONS** Auth, John, Bible Amplifier Series, Pacific Press Publ Asn, 95; auth, What the Bible Says About the End-Time, Review and Herald Publ Asn, 94; auth, Decoding Revelation's Trumpets, Andrews Univ Sem Doctoral Dissertation Series, vol 11, Andrews Univ Press, 88; article, The Role of the Hebrew Cultus, Sanctuary, and Temple in the Plot and Structure of the Book of Revelation, Andrews Univ Sem Studies, 33, 2, 245-264, 95; articles, The Anchor Bible Dict, NY, Doubleday, 92; article, The Seven Seals, Symposium on Revelation--Book I, 199-243, Bibl Res Inst, 92; article, Interpreting Revelation's Symbolism, Symposium on Revelation--Book I, 73-97, Bibl Res Inst, 92; Elusive Allusions: The Problematic Use of the OT in Revelation, Bibl Res, 33, 37-53, 88; article, Recent Developments in the Study of the Book of Revelation, Andrews Univ Sem Studies, 26, 2, 159-170, 88; auth, Knowing God in the Real World, Nampa, ID, Pacific Pr, 00; auth The Book of Revelation and the Old Testament, Biblical Res 43, 98, 61-69; auth, The Millennium is Here Again: Is It Panic Time? Andrews Univ Seminary Studies 2, 99, 167-178. **CONTACT ADDRESS** Andrews Univ, Berrien Springs, MI 49104-1500. **EMAIL** jonp@andrews.edu

PAULO, CRAIG N.
PERSONAL Born 01/01/1968, Philadelphia, PA, M, 1999, 1 child **DISCIPLINE** PHILOSOPHY **EDUCATION** LaSalle Univ, BA; Villanova Univ, MA; Pontifical Gregorian Univ, PhD, PhL. **CAREER** Asst prof philos, Pontifical Gregorian Univ, Rome. **HONORS AND AWARDS** Scholar in residence, Augustinianum, Rome. **MEMBERSHIPS** APA; ACPA. **RESEARCH** History of philosophy; Augustine; Heidegger; phenomenology. **SELECTED PUBLICATIONS** Auth, Being and Conversion, UMI, 97; auth, Out of the Garden: A Collection of Poetry, Spruce St Press, 98. **CONTACT ADDRESS** 1946 Durfor St, Philadelphia, PA 19145. **EMAIL** craigjnp@aol.com

PAULSELL, WILLIAM O.
PERSONAL Born 08/26/1935, Miami, FL, m, 1957, 2 children **DISCIPLINE** RELIGION **EDUCATION** Tex Christian Univ, BA, 57; BD, 59; MA, 61; Vanderbilt Univ, PhD, 65. **CAREER** Prof, Barton Col, 62-81; Prof, Lexington Theol Sem, 81-. **HONORS AND AWARDS** Sheperd Prize in Church Hist, Vanderbilt Univ. **MEMBERSHIPS** Am Soc of Church Hist, Disciples of Christ Hist Soc. **RESEARCH** The history of Christian spirituality, Cistercian history, women in the history of Christianity. **SELECTED PUBLICATIONS** Auth, Letters from a Hermit, Templegate, 78; auth, Tough Minds, Tender Hearts: Six Prophets of Social Justice, Paulist Pr, 90; auth, Taste and See: A Personal Guide to the Spiritual Life, Chalice Pr, 92; auth, Rules of Prayer, Paulist Pr, 93; auth, Disciples at Prayer, Chalice Pr, 95. **CONTACT ADDRESS** Dept Relig, Lexington Theol Sem, 631 S Limestone, Lexington, KY 40508-3400. **EMAIL** wpaulsell@aol.com

PAULSEN, DAVID L.
PERSONAL Born 11/13/1936, Ephraim, UT, m, 1967, 6 children **DISCIPLINE** PHILOSOPHY, LAW **EDUCATION** Brigham Young Univ, BS, 61; Univ Chicago, JD, 64; Univ Mich, PhD(philos), 75. **CAREER** Atty, Kirton & Bettilyon, 65-68; instr, 72-75, asst prof, 75-78, Assoc Prof Philos, Brigham Young Univ, 78-. **RESEARCH** Thought of Soren Kierkegaard; philosophy of religion; William J Ames. **SELECTED PUBLICATIONS** **CONTACT ADDRESS** 225 East 300 North, Orem, UT 84057.

PAULSON, STANLEY LOWELL
PERSONAL Born 05/16/1941, Fergus Falls, MN, m, 1965 **DISCIPLINE** PHILOSOPHY **EDUCATION** Univ Minn, Minneapolis, BA, 64; Univ Wis-Madison, MA, 66, PhD(philos), 68; Harvard Univ, JD, 72. **CAREER** Instr philos, Univ Wis-Madison, 68-69; vis lectr, 72-73, asst prof, 74-78, Assoc Prof Philos, Wash Univ, 78-, Fels, Nat Endowment Humanities, Harvard Law Sch, 73-74 & Alexander von Humboldt Found, Law Fac, Free Univ Berlin, 76-77. **MEMBERSHIPS** Am Philos Asn; Am Soc Polit & Legal Philos; Int Asn Philos Law & Soc Philos. **RESEARCH** Philosophy of law **SELECTED PUBLICATIONS** Auth, Two types of motive explanation, Am Philos Quart, 4/72; Classical legal positivism at Nuremburg, Philos & Pub Affairs, winter 75; Jus Non Scriptum and the reliance principle, Mich Law Rev, 11 /76; Neue grundlagen fuer einen begriff der rechtsgeltung, Arch Fuer Rechts--und Sozialphilos, 1/79; Material and formal authorisation in Kelsen's Pure Theory, Cambridge Law J, 4/80; Zum problem der Normenkonflikte, Arch fuer Rechtsund Sozialphilos, 4/80; Naturgesetze und die rechte Vernunft in Hobbes Rechtsphilosophie, Rechtstheorie, 4/81; Subsumption, derogation and noncontradiction in Legal Science, Univ Chicago Law Rev, summer 81. **CONTACT ADDRESS** Dept of Philos, Washington Univ, 1 Brookings Dr, Saint Louis, MO 63130-4899.

PAULSON, STEVEN
DISCIPLINE SYSTEMATIC THEOLOGY **EDUCATION** St. Luther Sem, BA, 84; Lutheran Sch Theol, ThM, 88, ThD, 92. **CAREER** Res librarian, JKM Library; psychiatric counselor, Fairview Hospitals, Minn; asst prof, Concordia Col, 93-; assoc prof, 98-. **HONORS AND AWARDS** Goethe Inst scholar, 85; N Amer Ministerial fel, 80-84; pastor, trinity lutheran church, 90-93. **SELECTED PUBLICATIONS** Pub(s), ed bd, Lutheran Quart. **CONTACT ADDRESS** Dept of Systematic Theology, Luther Sem, 2481 Como Ave, Saint Paul, MN 55108. **EMAIL** spaulson@luthersem.edu

PAVESICH, VIDA
PERSONAL Born San Diego, CA **DISCIPLINE** PHILOSOPHY **EDUCATION** USCD, MA, 73. **CAREER** Diablo Valley Col, 92-. **MEMBERSHIPS** Am Philos Asn; Col Art Asn. **RESEARCH** Continental philosophy; History of skepticism. **SELECTED PUBLICATIONS** Gender and Hans Blumenbergs Theory of Myth, Int Stud Philos. **CONTACT ADDRESS** 2934 Ford St, #24, Oakland, CA 94601. **EMAIL** vpavesic@viking.dvc.edu

PAVLICH, DENNIS
PERSONAL Born, Zimbabwe **DISCIPLINE** LAW **EDUCATION** Witwatersrand Univ, BA, 68; Yale Univ, LLM, 75. **CAREER** Asst prof, 75-78; assoc prof, 78-84; prof, 84-. **HONORS AND AWARDS** Tchg Excellence Awd. **RESEARCH** Real Property. **SELECTED PUBLICATIONS** Auth, pubs about condominium law. **CONTACT ADDRESS** Fac of Law, Univ of British Columbia, 1822 East Mall, Vancouver, BC, Canada V6T 1Z1. **EMAIL** pavlich@law.ubc.ca

PAWELSKI, JAMES
PERSONAL Born 09/01/1967, Greenville, OH **DISCIPLINE** PHILOSOPHY **EDUCATION** Cedarville Col , BA, 89; Penn State, MA, 91; PhD, 97. **CAREER** Asst prof Albright Coll, 97-; Dir of Honors Program, 99-. **HONORS AND AWARDS** Phi Kappa Phi Honor Soc, Penn State, 91; Edwin Erle Sparks Grad Fel, Penn State, 92-93; Fulbright Grant Germany, 94-95. **MEMBERSHIPS** Am Philos Asn; Soc for the Advancement of Am Philos. **RESEARCH** American Philosophy; Pragmatism; Philosophy of Religion; Philosophy of Education. **SELECTED PUBLICATIONS** Auth, Attention, Extension and Ecstasies in Augustine's Account of Time, J of Contemporary Philos, 93; Rev of Heaven's Champion: William James's Philosophy of Religion, J of Speculative Philos, forthcoming; auth, "William James and Epiphand Experience," forthcoming in the Proceedings of the 3rd International Conference of the Highlands Institute for American Religious and Philosophical Thought. **CONTACT ADDRESS** Albright Col, Box 15234, Reading, PA 19612. **EMAIL** jamesp@alb.edu

PAWLIKOWSKI, JOHN
PERSONAL Born 11/02/1940, Chicago, IL **DISCIPLINE** SOCIAL ETHICS, JEWISH-CHRISTIAN RELATIONS **EDUCATION** Loyola Univ Chicago, AB, 63; Wheeling Col, dipl Jewish studies, 67; Oxford Univ, cert ecumenical studies, 68; Univ Chicago, PhD, 70. **CAREER** From asst prof to assoc prof, 68-76, actg pres, 75-76, Prof Social Ethics, Cath Theol Union, Chicago Cluster Theol Schs, 76-, Mem adv comt, Secretariat for Cath-Jewish Rels, Nat Conf Cath Bishops, 71-73; bd dirs, Nat Cath Conf Interracial Justice, 72-73; chmn, Nat Coun Churches Faith & Order Study Comn on Israel, 72-73 & Chicago Inst Interrelig Res, 73; mem staff, Nat Cath Coalition for Responsible Investment, 73-75; bd mem, Nat Inst on Holocaust, 77-; US Holocaust Mem Coun, 80-. **HONORS AND AWARDS** Interfaith Awd, Am Jewish Comt, 72; Founders' Citation, Nat Cath Conf Interracial Justice, 73; Off Cross of Merit, Govt Poland, 95; Person of Year Awd, 94; Polish Coun of Christians and Jews, Warsaw. **MEMBERSHIPS** Am Soc Christian Ethics; Cath Theol Soc Am; Am Acad Relig. **RESEARCH** Christian-Jewish relations in Second Temple Period and in modern times; theology of revolution; foundations of social ethics; Holocaust. **SELECTED PUBLICATIONS** Auth, On renewing the revolution of the Pharisees, Cross Currents, fall 70; Jesus and the revolutionaries, Christian Century, 12/72; Catechetics and Prejudice, Paulist Press, 73; Sinai and Calvary: The Meeting of Two Peoples, Bruce, 76; Christ and the Jewish-Christian dialogue, Chicago Studies, fall 77; Judaism in Christian education and liturgy, Auschwitz: Beginning of a New Era, 77; What Are They Saying About Christian-Jewish Relations, 78 & Christ in Light of the Christian-Jewish Dialogue, 82, Paulist; Jesus and the Theology of Israel, 89; auth, Reinterpreting Tradition and Revelation: Jews and Christians in Conversation, 00. **CONTACT ADDRESS** Catholic Theol Union at Chicago, 5401 S Cornell Ave, Chicago, IL 60615-6200. **EMAIL** jtmp@ctu.edu

PAYNE, JULIEN
DISCIPLINE LAW **EDUCATION** London Univ, LLD. **CAREER** Prof, Univ of Ottawa. **SELECTED PUBLICATIONS** Auth, pubs on family law, children and the law, dispute resolution processes, and family conflict resolution. **CONTACT ADDRESS** Fac Common Law, Univ of Ottawa, 57 Louis Pasteur St, PO Box 450 Stn A, Ottawa, ON, Canada K1N 6N5.

PAYNE, PHILIP B.
PERSONAL Born 07/02/1948, Rockville Center LI, NY, m, 1976, 3 children **DISCIPLINE** NEW TESTAMENT STUDIES **EDUCATION** Cambridge Univ UK, PhD 76; Trinity Evange Div Sch, MDiv summa cum laude, 73, MA summa cum laude, 72. **CAREER** Cambridge Univ, suprv New T stud, 74-75; Trinity Evange Div Sch, vis prof, 76; Gordon Conwell Theol Sem, vis prof, 85-87; Fuller Theol Sem, adj prof, 88-. **HONORS AND AWARDS** Higgins Schshp. **MEMBERSHIPS** SBL; TF; IBR; ETS. **RESEARCH** Man and woman in the Bible; The Parables, of Jesus; Christology. **SELECTED PUBLICATIONS** Auth, Man & Woman One in Christ, Grand Rapids, Zondervan, 01, forthcoming; auth, LaserGreek for Windows 95 NT, 98, 00, and 3.1; Edmonds, Linguist's Software, 00; J. Barton Payne, Handbook for Evangelical Theologians, ed, Walter Elwell, Grand Rapids, Baker, 98; auth, New American Standard Bible for Windows, Edmonds, Linguist's Software, 97; auth, New American Standard Bible for Macintosh, Edmonds, Linguist's Software, 97; Computer Aided Biblical Research, Twentieth Century Encycl of Religious Knowledge, 2nd edition, ed, J.D. Douglas, Grand Rapids, 95; auth, "Fuldensis, Sigla for Variants in Vaticanus, and 1 Cor 14.34-5," NTS 41 (95): 240-262; auth, "Ms. 88 as Evidence for a Text without 1 Cor 14.34-5," NTS 44 (98): 152-158; auth, "The Originality of Text-Critical Symbols in Codex Vaticanus," NovT 42 (00), forthcoming. **CONTACT ADDRESS** Dept of New Testament, Fuller Theol Sem, PO Box 580, Edmonds, WA 98020. **EMAIL** phil@linguistsoftware.com

PAYNE, RODGER M.
PERSONAL Born 06/14/1955, Morganton, NC, m, 1974, 2 children **DISCIPLINE** RELIGION **EDUCATION** Harvard Divinity Sch, MTS, 83; Univ of Va, MA, 88; PhD, 89. **CAREER** Instr, Univ of Va, 86; lectr, Hampden-Sydney Col, 88; lectr, Univ of Va, 89-91; asst prof to prof, La State Univ, 91-; ed, J of Southern Relig, 97-. **HONORS AND AWARDS** Young Scholars in Am Relig, Center for the Study of Relig and Am Culture, 92-94. **MEMBERSHIPS** Asn for the Study of Relig in the S, Am Acad of Relig, Am Soc of Church Hist. **RESEARCH** American Catholicism; religion in the South, especially Catholicism in Lousiana. **SELECTED PUBLICATIONS** Auth, "Metaphors of the Self and the Sacred: The Spiritual Autobiography of the Reverend Freeborn Garrettson," Early Am Lit 27 (92): 31-48; auth, "New Light in Hanover County: Evangelical Dissent in Piedmont Virginia 1740-1755," J of S Hist 61 (95): 665-694; auth, "On Teaching Religion: A Symposium," J of the Am Acad of Relig 65 (97): 745-762; auth, The Self and the Sacred: Conversion and Autobiography in Early American Protestantism, Univ of Tenn Press (Knoxville, TN), 98. **CONTACT ADDRESS** Dept Philos & Relig Studies, La State Univ at Baton Rouge, Baton Rouge, LA 70803-3901. **EMAIL** rmpayne@lsu.edu

PAYNE, STEVEN
PERSONAL Born 07/25/1950, Ames, IA, s **DISCIPLINE** PHILOSOPHY, THEOLOGY **EDUCATION** Cornell, PhD, 82; Catholic Univ of Am, PhD., 00. **CAREER** Instr, Washington Theol Univ, 96-. **MEMBERSHIPS** AAR, CTSA. **CONTACT ADDRESS** ICS Publications, 2131 Lincoln Rd NE, Washington, DC 20002-1199.

PAZMINO, ROBERT W.
PERSONAL Born 06/15/1948, Brooklyn, NY, m, 1969, 2 children **DISCIPLINE** RELIGIOUS EDUCATION: CURRICULUM AND TEACHING **EDUCATION** Gordon-Conwell Theol Sem, M Div; Teachers Col, Columbia Univ in coop with Union Sem, Ed D. **CAREER** Asst prof of Christian Education, Gordon-Conwell Theol Sem, 81-86; assoc prof, 86-90, prof of relig ed, 90-96, Valeria Stone prof of Christian Education, Andover Newton Theol School, 96-. **HONORS AND AWARDS** Phi Beta Kappa; Psi Chi; Phi Eta Sigma; Phi Alpha Chi; Nat Dean's List; Hispanic Doctoral fel of the Fund for Theol Ed. **MEMBERSHIPS** North Am Professors of Christian Education. **RESEARCH** Theol foundations of Christian education. **SELECTED PUBLICATIONS** Auth, Principles and Practices of Christian Education: An Evangelical Perspective, Baker, 92, trans, Editorial Caribe, 95; Foundational Issues in Christian Education: An Introduction in Evangelical Perspective, Baker, 88, 2nd ed, Baker, 97; Latin American Journey: Insights for Christian Education in North America, United Church Press, 94; By What Authority Do We Teach? Sources for Empowering Christian Educators, Baker, 94; Nurturing the Spiritual Lives of Teachers, in The Christian Educator's Handbook on Spiritual Formation, eds Kenneth O Gangel and James C Wilhoit, Victor Books, 94; Designing the Urban Theological Education Curriculum, in The Urban Theological Education Curriculum: Occasional Papers, eds, Eldin Villafane and Bruce Jackson, CUTEEP, 96, Christian Ed J, fall 97; review of Jesuit Education and Social Change in El Salvador by Charles D Beirne in J of Res on Christian Ed 5, fall 96; Basics of Teaching for Christians: Preparation Instruction and Evaluation, Baker, 98; numerous other publications. **CONTACT ADDRESS** Andover Newton Theol Sch, 210 Herrick Rd, Newton, MA 02459-2243. **EMAIL** rpazmino@arts.edu

PEACOCK, KENT
DISCIPLINE PHILOSOPHY **EDUCATION** Univ Toronto, PhD, 91. **CAREER** Prof, Univ of Lethbridge. **RESEARCH** Philosophy of science; environmental and professional ethics. **SELECTED PUBLICATIONS** Auth, Living with the Earth: An Introduction to Environmental Philosophy, Harcourt Can, 96. **CONTACT ADDRESS** Dept of Philosophy, Univ of Lethbridge, 4401 University Dr W, Lethbridge, AB, Canada T1K 3M4. **EMAIL** kent.peacock@uleth.ca

PEACOCK, KEVIN
PERSONAL Born 03/28/1962, Natchez, MS, m, 1988, 2 children **DISCIPLINE** OLD TESTAMENT **EDUCATION** Southwestrn Baptist Theol Sem, PhD, 95 **CAREER** Prof, 97-pres, Can Southern Baptist Sem **HONORS AND AWARDS** Am Bibl Soc Awd, 95 **MEMBERSHIPS** Soc of Bibl Lit; Am Acad of Relig; Ntl Assoc of Baptist Professors of Relig; In-Service Guidance Assoc **RESEARCH** Pentateuch; Prophets **SELECTED PUBLICATIONS** Auth, "Vanity; The Meaning," Biblical Illustrator, 98, 27-29 **CONTACT ADDRESS** PO Box 512, Cochrane, AB, Canada T0L 0W0. **EMAIL** kpeacock@csbs.ca

PEARCE, RUSSELL G.
PERSONAL Born 10/18/1956, Brooklyn, NY, m, 1980, 2 children **DISCIPLINE** LEGAL ETHICS **EDUCATION** Yale Univ, BA, 78; Yale Univ, JD, 81. **HONORS AND AWARDS** Sanford D Levt Memorial Awd of the N Y State Bar Assoc, 97; Baker & Mckenzie Lecture on Legal Ethics, Loyola Univ Chicago School of Law, 97. **RESEARCH** Legal Profession, Judaism. **SELECTED PUBLICATIONS** Auth, Law Day 2050: Post-Professionalism, Moral Leadership and the Law as Business Paradign, 27 Florida State L Review 9, 99; auth, the Jewish Lawyer's Question, 27 Texas Tech L Rev 1259, 96; auth, the Professionalism Paradigm Shift: Why Discarding Professional Idealogy Will Improve the Conduct and Reputation of the Bar, 70 N Y U l Rev 1229, 95. **CONTACT ADDRESS** Law Sch, Fordham Univ, 140 W 62nd St., New York, NY 10023. **EMAIL** rpearce@maillawnet.fordham.edu

PEARSON, ANNE
PERSONAL Born 07/23/1957, London, ON, Canada, m, 1987, 3 children **DISCIPLINE** RELIGIOUS STUDIES **EDUCATION** McMaster Univ, PhD, 93 **CAREER** Inst, 87, McMaster Univ; Inst, 94 Wilfrid Laurier Univ; Inst, 97, Univ of Waterloo **MEMBERSHIPS** Am Acad of Relig; Can Soc for Study of Relig **RESEARCH** Hinduism; Faith; Women in Hinduism; Diaspora Hinduism; Religion & Popular Culture **SELECTED PUBLICATIONS** Auth, Because it gives me peace of mind Ritual Fasts in the Religioius Lives of Hindu Women, State Univ of NY Press, 96; Auth, Aspects of Hindu Women's Vrat Tradition as Constitutive for an Eco spirituality, Journal of Dharma, 98, 228-236 **CONTACT ADDRESS** 107 Victoria St, Dundas, ON, Canada L9H 2C1. **EMAIL** apearson@worldchat.com

PEARSON, BIRGER ALBERT
PERSONAL Born 09/17/1934, Turlock, CA, m, 1966, 6 children **DISCIPLINE** HISTORY OF RELIGIONS **EDUCATION** Upsala Col, BA, 57; Univ Calif, Berkeley, MA, 59; Pac Lutheran Sem, BDiv, 62; Harvard Univ, PhD(Christian origins), 68. **CAREER** Instr Greek, Pac Lutheran Sem, 59-62; lectr New Testament, Episcopal Theol Sch, 65-66; from instr to asst prof relig, Duke Univ, 66-69; from asst prof to assoc prof relig studies, 69-75, assoc dir, Educ Abroad Prog, 74-76, Prof Relig Studies, Univ Calif, Santa Barbara, 75-, Fel, Humanities Inst, Univ Calif, 70-71, 72-73; Am Philos Asn grant, 72; chmn dept, 76-79, dir, Univ Calif Study Ctr, Lund, Sweden,79-81; emer, UCSB, 94-. **MEMBERSHIPS** Soc Bibl Lit; Am Acad Relig; Archaeol Inst Am; Soc New Testament Studies; Soc Coptic Archaeol. **RESEARCH** Gnosticism; Early Christianity; Hellenistic religions. **SELECTED PUBLICATIONS** Auth, The Pneumatikos-Psychikos Terminology in I Corinthians, Soc Bibl Lit, 73, Scholars, 76; ed & transl, The Gnostic Attitude, Univ Calif Inst Relig Studies, 73; ed & contribr, Religious Syncretism in Antiquity, Scholars, 75; contribr, The Nag Hammadi Library in English, BrillHarper, 77, 3rd ed 88; coed, & contribr, The Roots of Egyptian Christianity, Fortress, 86, 92; auth, Gnosticism, Judaism, and Egyptian Christianity, Fortress, 90; ed, Naghammad, Codex VII, Brill, 96; auth, The Emergence of the Christian Religion, Trinity Press International, 97. **CONTACT ADDRESS** Dept of Relig Studies, Univ of California, Santa Barbara, 27345 E Vine Ave, Escalm, CA 95320. **EMAIL** bpearson@thevision.net

PEARSON, ERIC
PERSONAL Born 02/24/1960, Washington, DC, m, 1994, 1 child **DISCIPLINE** PHILOSOPHY **EDUCATION** Cornell Col, BPh, 82; Syracuse Univ, PhD, 89. **CAREER** Instr, 90-91, Ithaca Col; asst prof, 91-99, Berea Col. **MEMBERSHIPS** Amer Philos Soc **RESEARCH** Philos of lang **CONTACT ADDRESS** Berea Col, CPD 1933, Berea, KY 40404. **EMAIL** eric-pearson@berea.edu

PEARSON, SAMUEL C.
PERSONAL Born 12/10/1931, Dallas, TX, m, 1955, 2 children **DISCIPLINE** HISTORY OF CHRISTIANITY **EDUCATION** TX Christian Univ, AB, 51; Univ Chicago, DB, 53, MA, 60, PhD, 64. **CAREER** Asst prof, 64-69, assoc prof, 69-74, prof, hist stud, 74-, dept chmn, 72-77 & 81-83, act dir, 86-87, Reg Res & Develop Serv, Dean, Sch of Soc Sci, 83-95, dean emeritus, 95-, Southern Ill Univ, 74-98; prof emeritus, 98. **HONORS AND AWARDS** Phi Eta Sigma; Phi Kappa Phi (Emeritus Lifetime Member); Phi Alpha Theta; Outstanding Foreign Expert Northeast Normal Univ, 95, appointed vis prof, 96; Nat Endowment for the Hum Sum Sem grants to Yale Univ, 76, and Univ Hawaii, 98; Fulbright Prof of Am Hist, Nanjing Univ, 00-01. **MEMBERSHIPS** Am Soc Church Hist; Am Hist Asn; Org of Am Hist; Am Academy of Relig. **RESEARCH** Religions in the modern world. **SELECTED PUBLICATIONS** Auth, From Church to Denomination: American Congregationalism in the Nineteenth Century, Church Hist, XXXVIII, 69; auth, Enlightenment Influence on Protestant Thought in Early National America, Encounter, XXXVII, 77; auth, The Great Awakening and Its Impact on American History, Forum Press, 78; auth, The Campbell Institute: Herald of the Transformation of an American Religious Tradition, The Scroll, LXII, 78; auth, Rationalism in an Age of Enthusiasm: The Anomalous Career of Robert Cave, The Bul of MO Hist Soc, XXXV, 79; auth, The Cave Affair: Protestant Thought in the Guilded Age, Encounter, XLI, 80; auth, The Religion of John Locke and the Character of His Thought, John Locke: Critical Assessments, 4 vols, Routledge, 91; Alexander Campbell, 1788-1866, Makers of Christian Theology in America, Abingdon Press, 97. **CONTACT ADDRESS** Dept of Historical Studies, So Illinois Univ, Edwardsville, Edwardsville, IL 62026-1454. **EMAIL** spearso@siue.edu

PECK, WILLIAM DAYTON
PERSONAL Born 07/12/1934, New York, NY, m, 1961, 2 children **DISCIPLINE** PHILOSOPHY **EDUCATION** Yale Univ, BA, 56, PhD, 74. **CAREER** From instr to asst prof, 61-67, assoc prof philos & humanities, 67-75, Prof 75-, Reed Coll. **RESEARCH** Modern European philosophy. **CONTACT ADDRESS** Dept of Philosophy, Reed Col, 3203 SE Woodstock Blvd, Portland, OR 97202-8199. **EMAIL** bill.peck@reed.edu

PECORINO, PHILIP ANTHONY
PERSONAL Born 10/10/1947, New York, NY, m, 1968, 1 child **DISCIPLINE** PHILOSOPHY, PSYCHOLOGY **EDUCATION** Boston Col, BA, 69; Fordham Univ, MA, 70, PhD, 80. **CAREER** From Instr to Assoc Prof, 72-88, Prof Philos, City Univ New York, 88-. **MEMBERSHIPS** Am Asn Philos Teachers (vpres, 80-82, pres, 82-84); Community Col Humanities Asn (Eastern vpres, 81-83); Am Philos Asn; Soc Study Process Philos; AILACT. **RESEARCH** Critical reasoning; applied ethics; metaphysics and scientific inquiry. **SELECTED PUBLICATIONS** Auth, The midwife's trickery, Vol 3, No 2 & Philosophy and interdisciplinary studies, Vol 4, No 3, Aitia; Nursing ethics, technical training and values, Process, Vol VI, No 2; Evil as direction in Plotinus, Philos Res Arch, 82; ed, Perspectives on Death and Dying, Ginn Publ Co, 2nd ed, 82; coauth, Philosophy and science fiction, in The Intersection of Philosophy and Science Fiction, Greenwood Press, 88. **CONTACT ADDRESS** Social Sci Dept, Queensborough Comm Col, CUNY, 22205 56th Ave, Flushing, NY 11364-1497. **EMAIL** ppecorino@qcc.cuny.edu

PEDEN, WILLIAM CREIGHTON
PERSONAL Born 07/25/1935, Concord, NC, m, 1961, 2 children **DISCIPLINE** PHILOSOPHY, RELIGION **EDUCATION** Davidson Col, BA, 57; Univ Chicago, MA, 60, BD, 62; Univ St Andrews, PhD(philos relig), 65. **CAREER** Asst prof philos, St Andrews Presby Col, 64-65; prof & chmn dept, Radford Col, 65-68; prof & chmn dept, Millikin Univ, 68- 69; Fuller E Callaway Prof Philos, Augusta Col, 69-, Ed, J Social Philos, 70; assoc mem, Inst Social Philos, 72-; assoc, Danforth Found, 73-. **MEMBERSHIPS** Am Philos Asn; Am Acad Relig; Soc Studies Process Philos; Soc Social Philos; Am Asn Higher Educ. **RESEARCH** Social philosophy; process philosophy; American philosophy. **SELECTED PUBLICATIONS** Rights In a Changing Society, 81, Values In Our Developing World, 81 & Women's Liberation, 81, In: Philosophy for a Changing Society, Advocate Press; coauth (with Charles Hartshorne), Whitehead's View of Reality, Pilgrim Press, 81; auth, Immature Liberalism, Vol 3, No 1 & Liberal Religion and Education, Vol 3, No 1, Am J Theol & Philos; Philosophy for a Changing Society, Advocate Press, 82; Creative Freedom: Vocation of Liberal Religion, Pilgrim Press, 82; The Foundations of Potter,William, Religion of Humanity, Religious Humanism, Vol 0027, 1993. **CONTACT ADDRESS** Dept of Philos, Augusta State Univ, Augusta, GA 30904.

PEDERSON, WILLIAM DAVID
PERSONAL Born 03/17/1946, Eugene, OR **DISCIPLINE** AMERICAN HISTORY & GOVERNMENT **EDUCATION** Univ Ore, BS, 67, MA, 72, PhD(polit sci), 79. **CAREER** Teaching & res asst polit sci, Univ Ore, Eugene, 75-77; instr govt, Lamar Univ, Beaumont, Tex, 77-79; asst prof polit sci, Westminster Col, Fulton, Mo, 79-80; asst prof & head, dept polit sci, Yankton Col, Univ SDak, 80-81; prof, Am Studies Chmn, coordr polit sci, dir am studies, dept soc sci, La State

Univ, Shreveport, 81-; Intern, Operations Ctr, Dept State, Washington, DC, summer 71; prog analyst, off of the dir, Nat Inst Health, Bethesda, Md, summer, 74; vis res prof, NY Univ, summer, 81; res assoc, Russian & East Europe Ctr, Univ Ill, Urbana, summer, 82-. **HONORS AND AWARDS** Westcoast Lumbermen's Assoc Scholar, 65; Eugene Educ Assoc Scholar, 65; Oregon State Scholar Comn Scholars, 65; Nat Inst of Health Training Awd, 74; Deutsche Sommerschule am Pazifik Scholar, 75; Coun for Eurpoean Studies/DAAD Grant, 75; Kosciuszko Found Grant, 79; Westminister Col Student Gov Assoc Outstanding Leadership and Service Awd, 80; NY Univ, 81, Harvard Univ, 85, Nat Endowment for the Humanities Fel; Fac Res Grant on Soviet and Russian Military Amnesties, 82; Kappa Alpha Fraternity Prof of the Month, 9/85; Fac Excellence Awd, 94-95, La State Univ in Shreveport; Essay Competition for Colum on the Bicentennial of the US Constitution, 87; Special Humanities Awd, 98, La Endowment for the Humanities; Annual Awd of Achievement, Abraham Lincoln Assoc, Springfield, IL, 2/94; Cultural Olympiad, Regional Designation Awd in the Humanities, 95-96; The Times Journal page Shreveport Rose Awd, 9/95; Phi Kappa Phi, 96. **MEMBERSHIPS** Am Asn Advan Slavic Studies; Am Polit Sci Asn; Int Soc Polit Psychol; Int Lincoln Assoc; La Hist Asn; North La Hist Asn; Acad of Criminal Justice Sci; Lincoln Fel of Wisconsin; Center for the Study of the Presidency; Presidency Res Group; Ger Studies Asn; Amnesty Int; Am Studies Prog; Am Soc Public Admin; Smithsonian Inst. **RESEARCH** American politics; presidental behavior; human rights. **SELECTED PUBLICATIONS** Co-ed, Abraham Lincoln: Sources and Style of Leadership, Greenwood Press, 94, 95; Ambraham Lincoln: Contemporary, Savas Woodbury, 95; FDR and the Modern Presidency. Leadership and Legacy, Praeger, 97; co-ed, International Abraham Lincoln Journal, 00-; Journal of Contemporary Thought, 97; The New Deal and Public Policy, St Martin's Press, 98; A Comparative Test of Jimmy Carter's Character, The Presidency and Domestic Policies of Jimmy Carter, Greenwood Press, 94; Preface to Lincoln and Leadership Summer Teachers Institute, The 1993 ILA Annals, International Lincoln Assoc, 94; Preface in Abraham Lincoln: Sources and Style of Leadership, Greenwood Press, 94; Congressman Thomas Hale Boggs, Encyclopedia of the US Congress Vol 3, Simon and Schuster, 95; guest ed, Quarterly Journal of Ideology, 6/94. **CONTACT ADDRESS** Dept of Soc Sci, Louisiana State Univ, Shreveport, 1 University Pl, Shreveport, LA 71115-2301. **EMAIL** wpederso@pilot.lsus.edu

PEDRICK, WILLARD HIRAM
PERSONAL Born 10/01/1914, Ottumwa, IA, m, 1939, 4 children **DISCIPLINE** LAW **EDUCATION** Parsons Col, BA, 36; Northwestern Univ, JD, 39. **CAREER** Instr law, Univ Cincinnati, 40-42; asst prof, Sch Law, Univ Tex, 41-42; from assoc prof to prof, Sch Law, Northwestern Univ, 46-66; dean, 66-75, Prof Law, Col Law, Ariz State Univ, 66-, Carnegie grant, Australia & Fulbright prof, Univ Western Australia, 56-57; Ford grant, Australia & George Turner vis prof, Univ Melbourne, 62; J DuPratt White vis prof, Cornell Univ, 64; consult, Am Acad Arbit & Am Law Inst; Fulbright vis prof, Univ Western Australia, 73. **HONORS AND AWARDS** LLD, Parsons Col, 64 & Calif Western Law Sch, 82. **MEMBERSHIPS** Am Bar Asn; Am Law Inst. **RESEARCH** Law of torts; federal taxation; international business investments. **SELECTED PUBLICATIONS** Coauth, Cases on Torts, 68 & Injuries to Relations, 68, West Pub; auth, Estate and Gift Taxation, 77 & Death, Taxes & the Living, 80, Commerce Clearing House; Aals Musical - Time For Revival, J of Legal Education, Vol 0043, 1993. **CONTACT ADDRESS** Col of Law, Arizona State Univ, Tempe, AZ 85287. **EMAIL** willard.pedrick@asu.edu

PEEBLES, I. HALL
PERSONAL Born 01/09/1930, Augusta, GA, m, 1962, 3 children **DISCIPLINE** RELIGION **EDUCATION** Univ Ga, AB, 50; Yale Univ, BD, 53, MA, 55, PhD(relig), 59. **CAREER** From instr to assoc prof, 58-77, prof, 77-80, Evans Prog Relig, Wabash Col, 80-, Ford Found fac fel non-western studies & res fel, Divinity Sch, Yale Univ, 63-64. **MEMBERSHIPS** Am Theol Soc Midwest Div; AAUP; Soc Bibl Lit; Am Acad Relig. **RESEARCH** History of religions. **CONTACT ADDRESS** Dept of Relig, Wabash Col, PO Box 352, Crawfordsville, IN 47933-0352. **EMAIL** peeblesh@wabash.edu

PEITZ-HILLENBRAND, DARLENE
PERSONAL Born 02/04/1947, Yankton, SD, m, 1984, 2 children **DISCIPLINE** THEOLOGY **EDUCATION** Notre Dame, MA, 79; St. John's Sem, MDiv, 83; St. Michael's Col-Univ Toronto, PhD, 90. **MEMBERSHIPS** Cath Theol Soc; Am Asn of Relig. **RESEARCH** Political theology; American religion. **SELECTED PUBLICATIONS** Auth, Solidarity as Hermeneutic: A Revisionist Reading of the Social Theology of Walter Rauschenbusch," 92. **CONTACT ADDRESS** 9309 Edenberry Ct, Elk Court, CA 95758. **EMAIL** peitz@law.com

PEJOVICH, SVETOZAR
PERSONAL Born 03/22/1931, Yugoslavia, m, 1982, 4 children **DISCIPLINE** ECONOMICS **EDUCATION** Univ Belgrade, LLB, 55; Georgetown Univ, PhD (economics), 63. **CAREER** Prof of Economics, TX A&M; fel, Int Center of Economics Res, Turin, Italy; vis prof, Univ of Podgorica. **HONORS AND AWARDS** Templeton Awd of Excellence in Higher Ed, 97. **MEMBERSHIPS** AEA. **RESEARCH** Economics of property rights; economics of systems. **SELECTED PUBLICATIONS** Auth, "Why has the Labor-Managed Firm Failed?," Cato Journal, 92; auth, "A Propery Rights Analysis of the Inefficiency of Investment Decisions by Labor-Managed Firms," Journal of Institutional and Theoretical Economics, 92; auth, "Institutions, Nationalism and the Transition Process in Eastern Europe," Social Philosophy and Policy, Journal, 93; auth, "The Market of Institution vs. Capatalism by Fiat: The Case of Eastern Europe," Kuklos, 94; auth, Economic Analysis of Institutions and Systems, Kluwer Academic Publishers, 95. **CONTACT ADDRESS** Dept of Economics, Texas A&M Univ, Col Station, College Station, TX 77843. **EMAIL** s-pejovich@tamu-edu

PELCHAT, MARC
PERSONAL Born 05/03/1950, PQ, Canada, s **DISCIPLINE** ECCLESIOLOGY **EDUCATION** Univ Gregorienne, Rome, doctorate in theol, 86. **CAREER** Asst prof, 87, full prof, 92, dean of fac, 98, Univ Laval, Quebec. **MEMBERSHIPS** AAR; Can Soc of Theol; Acad of Practical Theol; Soc Intl de Theol Pratique. **RESEARCH** Practical theology; Ministry; Church. **SELECTED PUBLICATIONS** Co-auth, La Ville. Defis Ethiques, Ecclesiaux et Theologiques, Novalis, 98; co-auth, Gesti d'Amore. Sacramenti e Riti, Preghiera e Contemplazione, Edizioni Messaggero Padova, 94; chap, Les Implantations Ecclesiales Dans l'Espace Urbain: Nouvelles Frontieres, La Ville. Defis Ethiques, Ecclesiaux et Theologiques, Novalis, 98; chap, Les Revues Canadiennes-Francaises de Devotion et le Concile Vatican II, L'Eglise Canadienne et Vatican II, Fides, 165-188, 97; chap, Qu'est-ce Donc au Juste Que l'Education de la foi des Adultes?, L'Education de la foi des Adultes, L'Experience du Quebec, Mediaspaul, 229-249, 96; chap, Etapes de la Vie Adulte et Cheminement de Foi, L'Education de la Foi des Adultes, L'Experience du Quebec, Mediaspaul, 273-314, 96; chap, La Pastorale des Vocations: une Lecture Theolgique, La Pastorale des Vocations, Situation Actuelle, Enjeux et Defis, Diocese de Quebec, 11-13, 96; chap, La Paroisse, une Realite Deplacee? La Paroisse en Eclats, Novalis, 119-120, 95; chap, Les Priorites Pastorales du Diocese de Quebec: un Probleme de Communication? La Communication et le Monde de la Foi, Ed Pastor, 241-284, 94; chap, Le Magistere et la Loi, Loi et Autonomie Dans la Bible et la Tradition Chretienne, Fides, 249-285, 94. **CONTACT ADDRESS** Faculte de theologie, Univ of Laval, Pavillon Felix-Antoine-Savard,, local 846, Quebec, QC, Canada G1K7P4. **EMAIL** marc.pelchat@ftsr.ulaval.ca

PELLEGRINO, EDMUND DANIEL
PERSONAL Born 06/22/1920, Newark, NJ, 7 children **DISCIPLINE** PHILOSOPHY OF MEDICINE **EDUCATION** St John's Univ (NYork), BS, 41; NYork Univ, MD, 44. **CAREER** Prof & chmn, Dept Med, & dir med serv, Col Med, Univ Ky, 59-66; prof & chmn, Dept Med & dean, Sch Med, Health Sci Ctr, State Univ NY, Stony Brook, 66-73; chancellor, Ctr Health Sci, vpres health affairs & prof med & humanities in med, Univ Tenn, 73-75; pres & chmn, Med Ctr & prof med, Sch of Med, Yale Univ, 75-78; prof philos & biol & pres, Cath Univ Am, 78-82; prof clinical & community med, Sch of Med, 78-82, John Carroll Prof Med & Med Humanities, Med Ctr, Georgetown Univ, 82-, Consult & panelist, Nat Found Arts & Humanities & Nat Endowment for Humanities, 74-; nat bd consult, Nat Endowment for Humanities, 74-; nat adv comt, trial Humanities in Med, Univ Tex, 74-; chmn, Successor Generation Comt, Atlantic Coun US, 79-; mem int bd adv, Ctr Advan Res Phenomenol, 80-; mem coun adv, Inst Humanities Salado, 80-; mem coun scholars, Libr Cong, 82-84. **HONORS AND AWARDS** St John's Pres Medal, 79; Walter C Alvarez Awd, Am Med Writer's Asn, 81; Encycl Brittanica Achievement in Life Awd, 79; recipient of 41 honorary doctorates; numerous from am cols & univs. **MEMBERSHIPS** Soc Health & Human Values (pres, 69-70); Am Asn Advan Humanities; Am Philos Asn; Inst Med, Nat Acad Sci; Medieval Acad Am. **RESEARCH** Philosophy and ethics of medicine; mineral metabolism. **SELECTED PUBLICATIONS** Auth, Philosophy of medicine: Problematic and potential, J Med & Philos 1: 5-31; Toward a reconstruction of medical morality: The primacy of the act of profession and the fact of illness, J Med & Philos, Univ Chicago Press, 3/79; The anatomy of clinical judgments: Some notes on right reason and right action, in Philosophy and Medicine, Vol VI, D Reidel, Dordrecht, Netherlands, 77; Humanism and the Physician, Univ Tenn Press, 79; coauth (with D C Thomasma), A Philosophical Basis of Medical Practice, Toward a Philosopohy and Ethic of the Healing Professions, Oxford Univ Press, 81. **CONTACT ADDRESS** Med Ctr, Georgetown Univ, 4000 Reservoir Rd NW, Washington, DC 20007-2195.

PELLETIER, LUCIEN
DISCIPLINE PHILOSOPHY **EDUCATION** Univ Montreal, PhD. **RESEARCH** Philos anthropology; social and political philos; philos of relig. **SELECTED PUBLICATIONS** Auth, Socialisme religieux et communaut chez Martin Buber, 93; auth, L'imergence du concept de totalit chez Lukas, 92; auth, Bloch lecteur de Schelling, 91. **CONTACT ADDRESS** Philosophy Dept, Laurentian Univ, 935 Ramsey Lake Rd, Sudbury, ON, Canada P3E 2C6. **EMAIL** lpelleti@nickel.laurentian.ca

PELLETIER, SAMUEL R.
PERSONAL Born 06/20/1965, Philadelphia, PA, 1 child **DISCIPLINE** NEW TESTAMENT **EDUCATION** Hannibal-LaGrange Col, BA, 88; Westminster Theol Sem, MAR, 90; Univ MO-Columbia, MA, 92; Southern Baptist Theol Sem, PhD, 97. **CAREER** Adj Inst, Hannibal-LaGrange Col, 90-92; Garrett Tchg Fel, 93-95; Adj Inst/Prof, 95-98, Asst Prof, Southern Baptist Theol Sem, 98-. **MEMBERSHIPS** IBR, SBL, AAR **RESEARCH** Luke-Acts, New Testament Backgrounds, Hermenuetics **CONTACT ADDRESS** 17 Coachlight Dr, #A, Hannibal, MO 63401-2516. **EMAIL** spelletier@sbts.edu

PELLI, MOSHE
PERSONAL Born 05/19/1936, Israel, m, 1961, 2 children **DISCIPLINE** JUDAIC STUDIES **EDUCATION** NY Univ, BS, 60; Rice Univ, PhD. **CAREER** Asst prof, Univ of Tex, 67-71; lectr, Ben-Gurion Univ, Israel, 71-74; assoc prof, Cornell Univ, 74-78; assoc prof, Yeshiva Univ, 78-84; assoc prof to prof, Univ of Central Fla, 85-. **HONORS AND AWARDS** Grant, Lucius N. Littauer Found, 90; Fla-Israel Inst Grant, 91; Joseph Meyerhoff Fund Grant, 91; Abraham Friedman Prize for Hebrew Culture in Am, 92; Univ of Central Fla Distinguished Res of the Year, 96; Col of Arts and Sci Excellence Awd, 96; President of Israel's Amos Fund Awd, 97; Professional Excellence Awd, Univ of Central Fla; I. Edward Libr Found Grant, 99. **MEMBERSHIPS** Assoc for Jewis Studies; Am Acad of Relig; Am Soc of 18th-Centry Studies; Nat Assoc of Prof of Hebrew; World Union of Jewish Studies; Am Acad for Jewish Res. **SELECTED PUBLICATIONS** Auth, Moses Mendelssohn: Bonds of Tradition, Alef, (Tel Aviv), 72; auth, The Age of Haskalah, (Brill, (Leiden), 79; auth, Getting By In Hebrew, Barron (NY), 84; auth, Struggle for Change, Univ Pub, (Tel Aviv), 88; auth, Hebrew Culture in America, 80 Years of Hebrew Culture in the United States, Reshafim Pub, (Tel Aviv), 98; auth, Kinds of Genres in Haskalah Literature: Types and Topics, Hakibutz Hame'uchad Pub House, (Tel Aviv), 99. **CONTACT ADDRESS** Dept Judaic Studies, Univ of Central Florida, PO Box 160001, Orlando, FL 32816-0001. **EMAIL** pelli@pegasus.cc.ucf.edu

PENASKOVIC, RICHARD
PERSONAL Born 02/11/1941, Bayonne, NJ, m, 1974, 3 children **DISCIPLINE** PHILOSOPHY; THEOLOGY **EDUCATION** St Hyacinth Col, BA, 63; Univ Wurzburg, BA, 65, MA, 67; Univ Munich, PhD, 73. **CAREER** Asst to assoc prof, Col of St Rose, Albany, NY, 74-84; prof relig student, Auburn Univ, 84- . **HONORS AND AWARDS** Marquis Who's Who for the Yr 2000; Who's Who Among Am Tchrs; Scholar in Residence Inst Ecumenical Cultural Affairs, St John's Univ, 01. **MEMBERSHIPS** Am Acad Relig; Col Theol Soc; Cath Theol Soc Am. **RESEARCH** Augustine & Newman studies, Ecumenism, Critical thinking. **SELECTED PUBLICATIONS** Ed, Theology & Authority, Hendrickson Publ, 87; auth, Critical Thinking & the Academic Study of Relig, Schol Press, 97. **CONTACT ADDRESS** Dept Philos, Auburn Univ, Auburn, AL 36849-2900. **EMAIL** penasri@auburn.edu

PENCE, GREGORY E.
DISCIPLINE PHILOSOPHY **EDUCATION** Col William and Mary, MA, 70; NYork Univ, PhD, 74. **CAREER** Prof, Univ Ala Birmingham, 76-; joint app, UAB Sch Med; dir, Early Med Sch Acceptance Prog, Univ Ala at Birmingham. **HONORS AND AWARDS** Ingalls awd for Best Teaching, 94. **RESEARCH** Bioethics **SELECTED PUBLICATIONS** Auth, Classic Cases in Medical Ethics: Accounts of the Cases that Shaped Medical Ethics, McGraw-Hill, 2nd ed, 95; Who's Afraid of Human Cloning, Rowman & Littlefield, 97; Flesh of My Flesh: The Ethics of Cloning Humans, Rowman & Littlefield, 98; coauth, Seven Dilemmas in World Religions, Paragon House, 94; ed, Classic Works in Medical Ethics: Core Philosophical Readings, McGraw-Hill, 97. **CONTACT ADDRESS** Dept of Philosophy, Univ of Alabama, Birmingham, 1400 University Blvd, Birmingham, AL 35294-1150. **EMAIL** pence@uab.edu

PENCHANSKY, DAVID
PERSONAL Born 12/03/1951, Brooklyn, NY, d, 2 children **DISCIPLINE** HEBREW BIBLE **EDUCATION** Vanderbilt Univ, PhD, 88. **CAREER** Instr, Evangel Col, 79-84; instr, Western Ky Univ, 85-89; assoc prof, Univ of St. Thomas, 89-. **MEMBERSHIPS** Soc of Bibl Lit; Cath Bibl Asn; Amer Asn of Univ Prof. **RESEARCH** Wisdom literature; Hermeneutics; Literary criticism. **SELECTED PUBLICATIONS** Auth, The Betrayal of God, Westminster/John Knox, 90; auth, Storyteller's Companion, vol III, Abingdon Press, 92; auth, Up for Grabs: A Tentative Proposal for Ideological Criticism, Semeia, 59, 92; auth, Staying the Night, Reading Between Texts, Westminster/John Knox, 92; auth, Proverbs, The Mercer Bible Commentary, Mercer Press, 94; auth, The Politics of Biblical Theology, Studies in American Biblical Hermeneutics Series, Mercer Press, 95; auth, God the Monster, The Monstrous and the Unspeakable, Sheffield Acad Press, 97; auth, What Rough Beast, Westminster/John Knox, 99; co-ed, Shall Not the Judge of All the Earth Do What is Right?, Eisenbraun, 00. **CONTACT ADDRESS** Mail #4328, 2115 Summi, Saint Paul, MN 55105. **EMAIL** d9penchansky@stthomas.edu

PENCZEK, ALAN
PERSONAL Born 06/23/1956, Chicago, IL, s **DISCIPLINE** PHILOSOPHY **EDUCATION** Johns Hopkins Univ, PhD, 98. **CAREER** Asst prof, philos, Villa Julie Col, 98-. **MEMBERSHIPS** Am Philos Asn; Am Asn of Philos Teachers; Humanities and Technology Asn. **RESEARCH** Metaphysics; Philosophy of mind. **SELECTED PUBLICATIONS** Auth, Disjunctive Properties and Causal Efficacy, Philos Studies, 97; auth, Counterfactuals with True Components, Erkenntnis, 97; auth, Introductory Logic: First Day, Teaching Philos, 96. **CONTACT ADDRESS** Philosophy Dept., Villa Julie Col, Stevenson, MD 21153. **EMAIL** f-pencze@mail.vjc.edu

PENELHUM, TERENCE M.
PERSONAL Born 04/26/1929, Bradford-on-Avon, England **DISCIPLINE** RELIGIOUS STUDIES **EDUCATION** Univ Edinburgh, MA, 50; Oriel Col Oxford, BPhil, 52; Univ Lethbridge, DHu, 82; Univ Waterloo, DLitt, 90; Univ Calgary, LLD, 91. **CAREER** Lectr to assoc prof philos, Univ Alta, 53-63; prof philos, 63-78, head philos, 63-70, dean arts & sci, 64-67, Prof Emer, Religious Studies, Univ Calgary, 88-. **HONORS AND AWARDS** Can Coun Molson Prize Hum, 88 **SELECTED PUBLICATIONS** Auth, Survival and Disembodied Existence, 70; auth, Religion and Rationality, 71; auth, Problems of Religious Knowledge, 71; auth, Hume, 75; auth, God and Skepticism, 83; auth, Butler, 85; auth, David Hume: an Introduction to his Philosophical System, 92; auth, Reason and Religious Faith, 95; ed, Immortality, 73; ed, Faith, 89; co-ed, The First Critique, 69. **CONTACT ADDRESS** Dept Rel Stud, Univ of Calgary, Calgary, AB, Canada T2N 1N4. **EMAIL** penelhum@ucalgary.ca

PENNELL, JEFFREY N.
PERSONAL Born 09/05/1949, Evanston, IL, m, 1995 **DISCIPLINE** LAW **EDUCATION** Northwestern State Univ, BS, 71; JD, 75. **CAREER** Adj prof, Loyola Univ, 78; asst prof to prof, Univ of Okla, 78-86; Richard H Clark Prof, Emory Univ, 86-. **MEMBERSHIPS** Am Law Inst; Int Acad of Estate and Trust Law; Am Col of Trust and Estate Coun; Am Bar Assoc; Ga Bar Assoc; IL Bar Assoc. **SELECTED PUBLICATIONS** Auth, "Marital Deduction Planning Potpourii", Estate Planning 1993 321-382; auth, "Representations Involving Fiduciary Entities: Who Is the Client?", 62 Fordham L Rev (94): 1319-1356; auth, "TAM Rejects Death Bed Family Limited Partnership Discounts", 2 J Asset Protection (97): 9-13; auth, "Current Wealth Transfer Tax Developments", 49 Major Tax Pallning 21-1 to 21-50, Univ of Southern Calif, 97; auth, Income Taxation of Trusts, Estates, Grantors and Beneficiaries, West 87; auth, "Estate Tax Marital Deducation", 843 Estates, Gifts, and Trusts Portfolio, Tax Mgmt 96; coauth, Federal Taxation of gifts, Trusts and Estates, West, 97; coauth, Estate Planning, Aspen, 98; coauth, Wills, Trusts and Estates, Aspen, 00. **CONTACT ADDRESS** Sch of Law, Emory Univ, 1301 Clifton Rd NE, Atlanta, GA 30322-2770.

PENNER, HANS HENRY
PERSONAL Born 01/29/1934, Sacramento, CA, m, 1959 **DISCIPLINE** HISTORY OF RELIGIONS **EDUCATION** Univ Chicago, DB, 58, MA, 62, PhD, 65. **CAREER** Instr hist of relig, Univ VT, 62-65; asst prof, 65-72, assoc prof relig, 72-74, John Phillips prof, & chmn dept, 74-79, Dean Fac, Dartmouth Col, 81-, Fulbright res scholar, India, 66; Soc Relig Higher Educ-Danforth Cross-disciplinary fel, 68-69; Dartmouth fac fel, 68-69. **MEMBERSHIPS** Asn Asian Studies; Soc Sci Studies Relig; Am Acad Relig; Int Asn Hist Relig. **RESEARCH** Methodological approaches to understanding relig; myth and ritual-phenomenology; relig traditions of India. **SELECTED PUBLICATIONS** Auth, Cosmogony as Myth in Vishnu Purana, Hist Relig, 66; The Study of Religion According to Jan de Vries, J Relig, 1/69; Myth and Ritual: Wasteland or Forest of Symbols, Hist & Theory, 69; The poverty of functionalism, Hist Relig, 71; Ritual, In: Encyl Britannica; Creating a Brahman & The problem of semantics in the study of religion, Method Issues Relig Studies, 75; Impasse & Resolution: A Critique of the Study of Religion, 89; Why Does Semantics Matter to the Study of Religion, Method and Theory in the Study of Religion, 7/95. **CONTACT ADDRESS** Dept Relig, Dartmouth Col, 6036 Thornton Hall, Hanover, NH 03755-3592. **EMAIL** Hans.Penner@Dartmouth.edu

PENNER, ROLAND
DISCIPLINE LAW **EDUCATION** Univ Manitoba, BA, 49, LLB, 61. **CAREER** Lectr, 68-72 prof, 72; assoc prof, 67; dean, 89-94, Univ of Manitoba. **MEMBERSHIPS** Pres, C.A.U.T., 79-80; Chair, Legal Aid Manitoba, 72-78 **RESEARCH** Constitutional law; criminal law; labour law; evidence; charter of rights. **SELECTED PUBLICATIONS** Auth, Illegally Obtained Evidence and the Right to Privacy: Some Policy Considerations, Butterworths, 80; Making Law in a Cynical Society, Carswell, 85; Constraints on the Political Will, 84. **CONTACT ADDRESS** Fac of Law, Univ of Manitoba, Robson Hall, Winnipeg, MB, Canada R3T 2N2. **EMAIL** roland_penner@umanitoba.ca

PENNICK, AURIE ALMA
PERSONAL Born 12/22/1947, Chicago, IL, s **DISCIPLINE** LAW, CIVIL RIGHTS **EDUCATION** Univ of IL, BA 1971, MA 1981; John Marshall Law Sch, JD 1986. **CAREER** Coalition of Concerned Women Inc, exec dir 76-78; Chicago Abused Women Coalition, exec dir 78-81; Citizens Alert, exec dir 81-82; Chicago Comm Trust Fellowship, staff assoc 82-84; John D & Catherine T MacArthur Foundation, asst dir spec grant; Chicago Transit Authority Chief Adminstrative Atty; managing attorney/administration; Leadership Council for Metropolitan Open Communities, Pres, Chief Exec Officer, currently; part time Faculty Roosevelt Univ, 86-; **HONORS AND AWARDS** Ten Outstanding Young Citizens Chicago Jr Assoc of Commerce & Industry 1984; Kizzy Image & Achievement Awd 1985; Natl Council of Negro Women, Chicago Midwest Section, Ida B Wells Education Awd, 1992. **MEMBERSHIPS** Part time trainer Vista/Action Region V 1980-81; mem Chicago Police Bd, Chicago Women in Philanthropy, Chicago Blacks in Philanthropy, Phi Alpha Delta Legal Frat; mem Cook County Bar Assoc 1988-; mem American Bar Assoc 1988-. **CONTACT ADDRESS** Sch for New Learning, DePaul Univ, 1 E Jackson, Chicago, IL 60604.

PENNOCK, ROBERT T.
PERSONAL Born 05/07/1958, Ithaca, NY, m, 1998 **DISCIPLINE** PHILOSOPHY **EDUCATION** Earlham Col, BA, 80; Univ Pittsburgh, PhD, 91. **CAREER** Asst prof, Univ Texas at Austin, 91-99; prof, Mich State Univ, 00- . **HONORS AND AWARDS** Mellon fel, 85, 88; NEH summer fel, 93; Templeton Found prize, 97; NSF/NEH fel, 96. **MEMBERSHIPS** APA; Philos of Sci Asn; Sigma Xi; AAAS; Lone Star Hist of Sci Soc; Nat Ctr for Sci Educ; Soc for the Study of Evolution. **RESEARCH** Philosophy of biology; science and values; scientific explanation and evidence. **SELECTED PUBLICATIONS** Auth, Moral Darwinism: Ethical Evidence for the Descent of Man, Biol and Philos, 95; auth, Death of the Self: Changing Medical Definitions in Japan and the US, Obirin Rev of Int Stud, 95; auth, Epistemic and Ontic Theories of Explanation and Confirmation, Philos of Sci-Japan, 95; auth, Naturalism, Evidence and Creationism: The Case of Phillip Johnson, Biol and Philos, 96; auth, Inappropriate Authorship in Collaborative Scientific Research, Public Affairs Q, 96; auth, Naturalism, Creationism and the Meaning of Life: The Case of Phillip Johnson Revisited, Creation/Evolution, 96; auth, Is a Necessity-and-Sufficiency Account of Causation Contradictory? in Weingartner, ed, The Roles of Pragmatics in Contemporary Philosophy, Austrian Wittgenstein Soc, 97; auth, Pre-Existing Conditions: Disease Genes, Causation and the Future of Medical Insurance, in Magnus, ed, Contemporary Genetic Technology: Scientific, Ethical, and Social Challenges, Krieger, 98; auth, Creationism's War on Science, Environ Rev, 98; auth, Death and Taxes: On the Justice of Conscientious Objection to War Taxes, J of Acct, Ethics & Public Policy, 98; auth, Evidential Relevance and the Grue Paradox, Philos of Sci-Japan, 98; auth, The Prospects for a Theistic Science, Perspectives on Sci and Christian Faith, 98; auth, Tower of Babel: The Evidence Against the New Creationism, MIT, 99; auth, Ruts, Roots and Branches: On Learning and Teaching an Environmental Ethic With Help from Thoreau, in Aleksiuk, ed, Nature, Environment & Me: Explorations of Self in a Deteriorating World, in press. **CONTACT ADDRESS** Dept of Philosophy, Michigan State Univ, E-30 Holmes Hall, East Lansing, MI 48825-1107. **EMAIL** pennock5@msu.edu

PENROD, STEVEN D.
DISCIPLINE PSYCHOLOGY; LAW **EDUCATION** Yale Col, BA; Harvard Univ, JD; PhD. **CAREER** Vis prof, Law and Psychol, Univ of Minn, 88-89; prof of Law, Univ of Minn, 89-96; dir, Conflict and Change Ctr, Univ of Minn, 91-95; prof of Psychol Program, Univ of Nebr, 95-01; Gallup prof, Univ of Nebr, 99-00. **HONORS AND AWARDS** Yale Col: Political Science Honor Soc; Harvard Law School: Taft Scholarship; Harvard Univ: Nat Sci Found Dissertation Res Grant: Law and Social Sciences; Co-winner of Soc for the Psychol Study of Social Issues Dissertation Awd, 80; Soc for Experimentl Social Psychol Dissertation Awd, 80; Cattell Dissertation Awrd, 80; Second Prize Am Psychol Asn Diision 13 Meltzer Res Awd, 81; Am Psychol Asn Distinguished Scientific Awd for and Early Career Contribution to Applied Psychology, 86; Davis Professorship in Law, Univ of Minn, 94-95; Gallup Professorship, Univ of Nebr, 99-00. **MEMBERSHIPS** Soc for the Psychol Study of Social Issues; Soc for Experimental Social Psychol; Textbook Authors Asn; International Asn of Conflict Management; Psychonomic Soc; Midwestern Psychol Asn; Law & Soc Asn; International Asn for Applied Psychol; European Asn of Psychology and Law; Am Sociological Asn; Am Psychology-Law Soc; Am Psychol Soc; Am Psychol Asn. **RESEARCH** Jury decsionmaking, eyewitness reliability, media effects, Alternative dispute resolution. **SELECTED PUBLICATIONS** Auth, pubs on eyewitness reliability and jury decisionmaking. **CONTACT ADDRESS** Psychol Dept, John Jay Col of Criminal Justice, CUNY, 899 Tenth Ave, New York, NY 10019. **EMAIL** spenrod@unlinfo.unl.edu

PENTIUC, EUGENE
PERSONAL Born 12/08/1955, Romania, m, 1977, 2 children **DISCIPLINE** SEMITIC PHILOSOPHY **EDUCATION** Harvard Univ, PhD, 98. **CAREER** Tchng Fel, Harvard Univ, 94-96; Inst, Holy Cross Greek Orthodox Schl of Theol, 98. **MEMBERSHIPS** SBL, AOS, CBA **RESEARCH** Old Testament and Semitic Philology **CONTACT ADDRESS** 16 Romanian Ave, Southbridge, MA 01550. **EMAIL** epentiuc@aol.com

PEPERZAK, ADRIAAN THEODOOR
PERSONAL Born, Indonesia **DISCIPLINE** PHILOSOPHY **EDUCATION** Licenciate in philos, Higher Inst Philos, Louvain Univ, Belgium; Univ Paris-Sorbonne, PhD. **CAREER** Arthur J. Schmitt prof; fac, Amsterdam Univ, Utrecht Univ & Nijmegen Univ; vis prof, Bandung Univ, Indonesia, Mallorca Univ, Spain, Scuola Normale of Pisa, Italy, Istituto Superiore di Filosofia of Naples, Italy, Nice Univ, France, Dusquesne Univ, (ittsburgh, Pa State Univ at State Col, Boston Col & Loyola Univ Chicago. **RESEARCH** Ethics and Polit philosophy; philosophy of religion; metaphilosophy; Hegel; French phenomenology; Levinas. **SELECTED PUBLICATIONS** Auth, Le jeune Hegel et la vision morale du monde; auth, Hegels praktische Philosophie; auth, To the Other; auth, Ethics as First Philosophy; auth, Before Ethics; auth, Beyond: The Philosophy of Emmanuel Levinas; Platonic Transformations; auth, Selbsterkenntnis des Absoluten: Grundlinien der Hegelschen Philosophie des Geistes, auth, Reason in Faith, Paulist Pr (New York), 99; auth, Modern Freedom: Hegel's Legal, Moral, and Political Philosophy, Dordrecht (Boston), 01. **CONTACT ADDRESS** Dept of Philosophy, Loyola Univ, Chicago, 6525 N Sheridan Rd, Chicago, IL 60626. **EMAIL** apeperz@wpo.it.luc.edu

PEPPER, GEORGE B.
PERSONAL Born 06/17/1926, Jersey City, NJ, s **DISCIPLINE** PHILOSOPHY **EDUCATION** Fordham Univ, MA, 48, PhD, 58. **CAREER** Lectr, Fordham Univ & Col New Rochelle & Cape Cod Commun Col; vis prof, Talladega Col, 68-89; prof emer, 93-, Iona Col, 50-93; NEH Summer Inst Columbia Univ, 86; Roberta C Rudin Fel Jewish Christian Rel, 89-90; vis scholar, Columbia Univ, 89-90. **MEMBERSHIPS** Amer Asn Univ Prof; Amer Philos Asn; Karl Jaspers Soc N Amer; Soc Advan Amer Philos. **RESEARCH** Philosophy of religion; Ethics; Political philosophy; M Heidegger. **SELECTED PUBLICATIONS** Auth, Peter Berger on Modernization and Religion, Cross Currents, 88-89; Die Relevanz von Jasper's Achenzeit fur interkulterelle Studien, Karl Jaspers: Zur Aktualitat Seines Denkens, Verlag; 91; rev, The Architecture of Meaning, Philosophy East and West, 88; coauth, Jewish-Christian Dialogue: A Jewish Justification, and Beyond Occupation: American Jewish, Christian and Palestinian Voices for Peace, Cross Currents, 90-91; auth, Karl Jaspers: Basic Philosophical Writings, Humanities Press, 94; The Boston Heresy Case in View of the Secularization of Religion, Edwin Mellen Press, 88. **CONTACT ADDRESS** 470 Halstead Ave, Apt 2-P, Harrison, NY 10528. **EMAIL** GPEPPER@gis.net

PEPPER, STEPHEN L.
DISCIPLINE LAW **EDUCATION** Stanford Univ, AB, 69; Yale Law School, JD, 73. **CAREER** Prof of law, Col of Law, Univ Denver. **RESEARCH** Professional ethics **SELECTED PUBLICATIONS** Auth, The Lawyers Amoral Ethical Role: A Defense, A Problem, and Some Possibilities, Am Bar Found Res Jour, 86; Autonomy, Community, and Lawyers Ethics, Cap Univ Law Rev, 90; Conflicting Paradigms of Religious Freedom: Liberty Versus Equality, Brigham Young Univ Law Rev, 93; Counseling at the Limits of the Law: An Exercise in the Jurisprudence and Ethics of Lawyering, Yale Law Jour 1545, 95. **CONTACT ADDRESS** 1900 Olive St, Denver, CO 80222. **EMAIL** SPepper@mail.law.du.edu

PEPPET, SCOTT R.
PERSONAL Born 12/11/1969, Minneapolis, MN **DISCIPLINE** LAW **EDUCATION** Cornell Univ, BA, 91; Harvard Law Sch, JD, 96. **CAREER** Lectr, Harvard Law Sch, 97-99/ **HONORS AND AWARDS** CPR Inst Dispute Resolution Book Awd, 00. **MEMBERSHIPS** Mass Bar Asn; ABA; CBA. **RESEARCH** Negotiation; ADR; Ethics and the Legal Profession. **SELECTED PUBLICATIONS** Co-auth, Beyond Winning: Negotiating to Create Value in Deals and Disputes, Harvard Univ Press, 00. **CONTACT ADDRESS** Sch of Law, Univ of Colorado, Boulder, CB 401, Boulder, CO 80309.

PEREIRA, JOSE V.
PERSONAL Born 01/22/1931, Bombay, India, m, 1965, 5 children **DISCIPLINE** THEOLOGY **EDUCATION** Siddharth Col, BA, 51; St. Xavier's Col, PhD, 59. **CAREER** Vis Prof of East-West Cultural Relationships, Instituto Superior de Estudos Ultrormarinos, 59-60; Research Asst, Univ of London, 61; Research Fellow in the History of Indian Art Studies, Univ of London, 62-66; Research Assoc in the History of Indian Art, The Am Academy of Benares, 67-69; Asst Prof Fordham Univ, 70-76; Assoc Prof Fordham Univ, 76-86; Prof, Fordham Univ, 86-. **RESEARCH** Theologies of Catholicism, Hinduism, Buddhism and Islam/ Scholasticism, Suarez, History of Baroque, Indian and Islamic architecture, Konkani literature and traditional song. **SELECTED PUBLICATIONS** Rev, "The Portrait of Christ in the Koran, The Canadian Catholic Review Saskatoon, Canada (Mar 95): 6-12; auth, Badarayana, in Ian P. McGreal (ed.) Great Thinkers of Eastern World, New York: Harper Collins Publishers (95): 170-174; auth, Goan Secular Architecture of the Eighteenth Century in Narendra K. Wagle & George Coelho, Goa: Continuity and Change, Toronto: Univ of Toronto, Centre for South Asian Studies (95); 204-212; auth, "Infallible Papal Pronouncements," Homiletic and Pastoral Review, New York (Mar 96): 55-60; auth, John of St. Thomas and

Suarez, Acta Philosophica 5, Rome, fasc 1 (96): 115-136; auth, Resonances of Buddhism and Christianity, Buddhist-Christian Studies, University of Hawaii (96): 115-127; auth, The Human Person, Ideal and Fallen, in Classical Catholic Theology, Dialogue & Alliance, New York 10-2 (96): 41-55; auth, The Signifiance of the Indic Religions for the West, in S.N. Sridhar & Nirmal Mattoo (eds.), Ananya. A Portrait of India, New York, The Association of Indians in America (97): 125-136; Are Eeumneical Councils Infallible? Josephinum Journal of Theology (Columbus, OH, 97), 40-50; auth, Ranakpur: Climax of the Jain Temple, Marg, Bombay 49 (97): 88-91; auth, O integralismo existencial de Suarez, in calumniatorem Doctoris Eximii, Revista Filosofica de Coimbra 7 (98): 295-312. **CONTACT ADDRESS** Dept Theology, Fordham Univ, 441 East Fordham Rd, Bronx, NY 10458-5149. **EMAIL** eximirom@hotmail.com

PERELMUTER, HAYIM GOREN
PERSONAL Born 06/02/1914, Montreal, PQ, Canada, m, 1940, 2 children **DISCIPLINE** JEWISH HISTORY **EDUCATION** McGill Univ, BA, 35; Jewish Inst Relig, MHL, 39; Hebrew Union Col Jewish Inst Relig, DHL, 79. **CAREER** Rabbi, Beth Israel, Waltham MAss, 39-41; rabbi, Beth Zion Temple, Johnstown Penn, 41-57; rabbi, KAM Isaiah Israel, 57-79; prof Jewish Stud, Catholic Theol Union, 49- . **MEMBERSHIPS** Am Acad Relig; Conf of Am Rabbis; North Am Acad of Liturgy; Soc of Bibl Lit; Am Jewish Hist Soc. **SELECTED PUBLICATIONS** Trans, Song of the Steps and In Defense of Preachers, Hebrew Union Col, 84; auth, This Immortal People: A Short History of the Jews, Paulist, 85; coauth, Von Kanaah nach Israel, Deutsche Tascherbuch Verlag, 86; auth, Siblings: Rabbinic Judaism and Early Christianity at Their Beginnings, Paulist, 89; coauth, Paul the Jew: Jewish-Christian Dialogue, Center for Hermeneutical Stud, Grad Theol Union, 90; auth, Do Not Destroy in the Ecological Challenge, Liturgical, 94; coauth, Harvest of a Dialogue, Ktav, 97. **CONTACT ADDRESS** Catholic Theol Union at Chicago, 5401 S Cornell Ave, Chicago, IL 60615. **EMAIL** goodper@ctu.edu

PERHAC, RALPH M.
PERSONAL Born 12/17/1953, Albuquerque, NM, m, 1978, 3 children **DISCIPLINE** PHILOSOPHY **EDUCATION** Univ MN, PhD, 89. **CAREER** Asst prof, Univ AL, 89-92; Res Assoc, Univ Tenn, 93-99; Economist, TVA, 99-. **MEMBERSHIPS** Am Philos Asn. **RESEARCH** Environmental risk policy; environmental philos. **SELECTED PUBLICATIONS** Auth, Defining Risk: Normative Considerations, Human and Ecological Risk Assessment, June 96; Does Risk Aversion Make a Case for Conservatism?, Risk--Health, Safety & Environment, fall 96; Comparative Risk Assessment: Where Does the Public Fit In?, Science, Technology, & Human Values, spring 98; Environmental Justice: The Issues of Disproportionality, Environmental Ethics, forthcoming; Medical Costs and Lost Productivity from Health Conditions at Volatile Organic Compound Superfund Sites, with J. Lybarger, R. Lee, D. Vogt, R. Spengler, and D. Brown, Environmental Res, forthcoming. **CONTACT ADDRESS** TVirginia, HRT 11B, PO Box 292409, Nashville, TN 37229. **EMAIL** rmperhac@tva.gov

PERILLO, JOSEPH M.
PERSONAL Born 01/02/1933, New York, NY, m, 1963, 3 children **DISCIPLINE** CONTRACT LAW **EDUCATION** Cornell Univ, AB, 53, JD, 55. **CAREER** Assoc, Proj Int Procedures, Columbia Univ, 60-63; asst prof, 63-66, assoc prof, 66-68, actg dean, 81-82, Prof Contracts, Law Sch, Fordham Univ, 68-, Fulbright grant, Univ Florence, 60-61. **RESEARCH** Law of remedies. **SELECTED PUBLICATIONS** Coauth, Civil Procedure in Italy, Mortinus Nijhoff, 65; The Italian Legal System, Stanford Univ Press, 67; The Law of Contracts, 70, 4th ed, 98 & co-ed, Cases and Problems on Contracts, 78, 3rd ed, 00, West Publ Co. **CONTACT ADDRESS** Law Sch, Fordham Univ, 140 W 62nd St, New York, NY 10023-7407. **EMAIL** JPerillo@mail.lawnet.fordham.edu

PERKINS, DOROTHY
DISCIPLINE RELIGION **EDUCATION** Gettysburg Col, BA, 68; Temple Univ, PHD, 82. **CAREER** Teach asst, Temple Univ, 71-74; lectr, La Salle Univ, 74-77; Commonwealth Speakers Prog, Pa Hum Counc, 84-85, 86; INDEPENDENT SCHOLAR, WRITER, 77-. **CONTACT ADDRESS** 220 Locust St, Apt 29-A, Philadelphia, PA 19106.

PERKINS, DWIGHT HEALD
PERSONAL Born 10/20/1934, Chicago, IL, m, 1957, 3 children **DISCIPLINE** ECONOMICS **EDUCATION** Cornell Univ, BA, 56; Harvard Univ, AM, 61, PhD, 64. **CAREER** Inst, Asst Prof Econ, 63-66; Assoc Prof Modern China Studies and Econ, 66-69, Assoc Dir EARC, 73-77, Prof Modern China Studies and Econ, Assoc of the East Asian Res Center, 69-77; Chm Dept of Econ, 77-80; Dir Harvard Inst for Intl Devel HUD, 80-95; Harold Hitchings Burbank Prof of Poli Econ, 81-. **HONORS AND AWARDS** Phi Beta Kappa; Pi Kappa Phi; BA with Distinction and High Hon; Woodrow Wilson Fel(honorary). **MEMBERSHIPS** Soc Sci Res Council(NY). **RESEARCH** Econ Hist and Contemporary Devel of East and SEast Asia. **SELECTED PUBLICATIONS** China: Asia's Economic Giant? Univ Wash Press, 86; Agricultural Development in China, 1368-1968, Aldine, 69; co-ed, Reforming Economic Systems in Developing Countries, Cambridge: Harvard Univ Press, 91; co-ed, Social Capability and Long-Term Economic Growth, 95; co-ed, Industrialization and the State: Korea's Heavy and Chemical Industry Drive, Harvard Institute for Intl Devel, 97; ed, Assisting Development in a Changing World: The Harvard Institute for International Development, 1980-1995, Harvard Studies in International Affairs, 97; auth, Economics of Development, 97. **CONTACT ADDRESS** Dept Econ, Harvard Univ, Cambridge, MA 02138. **EMAIL** dwight_perkins@harvard.edu

PERKINS, EDWARD JOSEPH
PERSONAL Born 00/00/1928, Sterlington, LA, m, 1962 **DISCIPLINE** POLITICAL SCIENCE **EDUCATION** Univ of MD, BA 1968; Univ of Southern CA, MPA 1972, PhD 1978. **CAREER** AID Far East Bureau Washington, asst general serv officer; US Operations Mission to Thailand Bangkok, asst genl serv officer, 67-69, mgmt analyst, 69-70, deputy asst dir for mgmt, 70-72; Office of the Dir General of the Foreign Serv Washington, staff assistant, 72, personnel officer; Bureau of Near Eastern & South Asian Affairs, admin officer, 74-75; Office of Mgmt & Opers, mgmt analysis officer, 75-78; Accra, counselor for polit affairs, 78-81; Monrovia, deputy chief of mission, 81-83; Bureau Of African Affairs Office of West African Affairs, dir, 83-85; Dept of State, ambassador to Liberia, 85-86, ambassador to South Africa, 86-89, dir general The Foreign Service, 89-92; United Nations and UN Security Council, ambassador, 92-93; US ambassador to Australia, 93-96; Univ of Oklahoma, Exec Dir, Intl Prog Center, William J Crowe Chair Prof of Geopolitics, 96-. **HONORS AND AWARDS** Honoree of the Beta Gamma Sigma Chapter of the Univ of Oklahoma, 1998; Univ of Southern California, Distinguished Alumni Awd, 1991; Southern Univ, Achievement Awd, 1991; Kappa Alpha Psi, C Rodger Wilson Leadership Conference Awd, 1990; The Links, Inc, Living Legend Awd, 1989; Eastern Province, Kappa Alpha Psi, Awd for Distinguished Service as US Ambassador to South Africa, 1989; Presidential Distinguished Service Awd, 1989; Una Chapman Cox Foundation Awd, 1989; Presidential Meritorious Service Awd, 1987; Kappa Alpha Psi Fraternity Awd for Outstanding Achievement in the Foreign Service, 1986; Dept of State, Superior Honor Awd, 1983; Agency for Intl Development, Meritorious Honor Awd, 1967; National Academy of Public Administration, fellow; Statesman of the Year, George Washington Univ, 1992; Distinguished Honor Awd, Department of State, 1992; St Augustine College, Doctor of Humane Laws, Honoris Causa, 1993; Beloit College, Doctor of Humanities, 1990; and numerous other honorary degrees. **MEMBERSHIPS** Epsilon Boule of Sigma Pi Phi Fraternity; Kappa Alpha Psi Fraternity; Navy League; Honor Society of Phi Kappa Phi; American Society for Public Administration, 1971-; Veterans of Foreign Wars, Chevy Chase Chapter; American Academy of Diplomacy; American Foreign Service Assn; American Political Science Assn; World Affairs Councils of Central OK and Washington, DC; Cranlana Programme, bd; Asia Society, bd of trustees; Joint Center for Political and Economic Studies, bd of govs; numerous other organizations, councils, and boards; American Legion, Chester A. Arthur Society, Council on Foreign Relations, Foreign Policy Assn, Intl Studies Assn, Pacific Council on Intl Policy, Public Service Commission, American Consortium for Intl Public Administration, Center for the Study of the Presidency bd of dirs, Assn for Diplomatic Studies & Training; bd of trustees, Inst of Intl Education; adv bd, Inst for Intl Public Policy; bd of trustees, Lewis & Clark College; adv council Univ Ofc of Intl Programs, Pennsylvania State Univ. **SELECTED PUBLICATIONS** Author, "New Dimensions in Foreign Affairs: Public Administration Theory in Practice," Public Administration Review, July-August 1990; "Divsersity in US Diplomacy," The Bureaucrat, Vol 20, No 4, 1991-92; "The United States and the UN", Yale Univ Law Journal, 1993; "Global Institutions (Action for the Future)," U.S. Catholic Conference, 1995; "Resolution of Conflict, the Attainment of Peace", University of Sydney, Centre for Peace and Conflict Studies, 1996; "An International Agenda for Change," American Behavorial Scientist, Vol 40, Number 3, Sage Publishers, 1997; "The Psychology of Diplomacy: Conflict Resolution in a Time of Minimal or Unusual Small-Scale Conflicts, "Chapter 4, The Psychology of Peacekeeping, edited by Harvey J. Langholtz, Westport, CT: Praeger, 1998. Distinguished Jerry Collins Lecturer in Public Administration, Florida State Univ; presidential appointment to the Presidential/Congressional Commission on Public Service, 1992-93. **CONTACT ADDRESS** International Programs Ctr, Univ of Oklahoma, 339 W Boyd St, Rm 400, Norman, OK 73019-5144.

PERKINS, MORELAND
PERSONAL Born 04/16/1927, Richmond, VA, 2 children **DISCIPLINE** PHILOSOPHY **EDUCATION** Harvard Univ, AB, 48, AM, 49, PhD, 53. **CAREER** Prof Emeritus of Philos, Univ MD, College Park. **HONORS AND AWARDS** Johnsonian Prize in Philosophy for Sensing the World, 82. **MEMBERSHIPS** Amer Philos Assoc. **SELECTED PUBLICATIONS** Auth, Sensing the World, Hackett Pub Co, 83; Reshaping the Sexes in Sense and Sensibility, Univ Press VA, 98. **CONTACT ADDRESS** 410 Auburn Dr., Daytona Beach, FL 32118.

PERLIN, MARC G.
PERSONAL Born 07/15/1948, Brookline, MA, m, 1970, 2 children **DISCIPLINE** LAW **EDUCATION** Boston Univ, BA, 70; Northeastern Univ, JD, 73. **CAREER** Law clerk, Super Ct of Mass, 73-74; legal asst to Chief Justice, Boston Munic Ct, 74-75; instr legal writing & res, 75-77, asst prof to prof, Law Sch, Suffolk Univ, 77-; lectr, Sch of Law, Northeastern Univ, 74-76; speaker & panelist, Mass Continuing Legal Educ, Inc, 75; ed, Mass Rules Serv, 80-; reporter, Standing Adv Comt on Rules of Civil Proc of Supreme Judicial Ct of Mass, 94-; assoc dean, Suffolk Univ, 99-. **MEMBERSHIPS** Am Bar Asn. **RESEARCH** Family law; civil practice and procedure; constitutional law. **SELECTED PUBLICATIONS** Auth, Sum and Substance Quick Review of Family Law, 92, 97, 99; auth, Mottla's Proof of Cases in Massachusetts, 3rd ed, vol 1, 92, vol 2, 93, coauth, vol 3, 95; coauth, Handbook of Civil Procedure in the Massachusetts District Court, 80, 90; Massachusetts Collection Law, 84, 92. **CONTACT ADDRESS** Sch of Law, Suffolk Univ, 120 Tremont St., Boston, MA 02108-4977. **EMAIL** mperlin@acad.suffolk.edu

PERLMAN, HARVEY
DISCIPLINE LAW **EDUCATION** Univ Nebr, BA, JD. **CAREER** Prof, Univ Neb, Law Sch, 98- . **RESEARCH** Torts; unfair business practices. **SELECTED PUBLICATIONS** Coauth, Legal Regulation of the Competitive Process; Federal Criminal Jury Instructions. **CONTACT ADDRESS** Law Dept, Univ of Nebraska, Lincoln, 103 Ross McCollum Hall, PO Box 830902, Lincoln, NE 68588-0902. **EMAIL** hsperlman@unl.edu

PERLMAN, MARK
PERSONAL Born New York, NY, m **DISCIPLINE** PHILOSOPHY **EDUCATION** Ohio St Univ, BA, 87, MA, 89; Univ Ariz, PhD, 94. **CAREER** Grad tchng asst, 88-89, Ohio St Univ; grad tchng assoc, 89-93, Univ AZ; lectr, phil, 93-97, vis asst prof, 97-98, Ariz St Univ; asst prof, 98-, Western Oregon Univ. **RESEARCH** Phil of mind; metaphysics; phil of law. **SELECTED PUBLICATIONS** Art, Punishing Acts and Counting Consequences, AZ Law Rev, Vol 37, 95; art, The Trouble with Two-Factor Conceptual Role Theories, Minds and Machines, 97; auth, Conceptual Flux: Mental Representation, Misrepresentation, and Concept Change, Kluwer Academic Publ, 00. **CONTACT ADDRESS** Dept of Philosophy and Religious Studies, Western Oregon Univ, 345 N. Monmouth Ave, Dept of Phil and Religious Studies, Humanities Div, Monmouth, OR 97361. **EMAIL** perlman@wou.edu

PERLMUTTER, RICHARD MARK
PERSONAL Born 12/03/1942, Cambridge, MA, m, 1966, 2 children **DISCIPLINE** LAW **EDUCATION** Tufts Univ, AB, 64; Harvard Univ, LLB, 67. **CAREER** Prof Law, Suffolk Univ Law Sch, 75-, pvt pract Law, Boston, 68-; vis prof Law, Boston Univ Law Sch, 82-. **MEMBERSHIPS** AAUP; Am Asn Law Schs. **RESEARCH** General contracts. **SELECTED PUBLICATIONS** Coauth, Contracts: Contemporary Cases & Materials, Callaghan & Co, 80. **CONTACT ADDRESS** Law Sch, Suffolk Univ, 41 Temple St, Boston, MA 02114-4241. **EMAIL** rperlmut@acad.suffolk.edu

PERO, ALBERT
PERSONAL Born 12/14/1935, St. Louis, MO, m, 1988 **DISCIPLINE** SYSTEMATIC THEOLOGY AND CULTURE **EDUCATION** St. Paul Col, BA, 57; Concordia Sem, B Th, 62; Univ of Det, Grad, 68; Lutheran Sch of Theol, PhD, 75; Univ of Chicago, Post Doc Study, 85; Univ of Zimbabwe, Post Doc Study, 86 **CAREER** Prof, Lutheran School of Theology, 75-pres **HONORS AND AWARDS** Ach Awd, Afr Am Lutheran Assoc; Staley Distinguished Christian Scholar, St. Olaf Col; Disciple for Justice Awd, Commission for Multicultural Ministries-Evangelical Lutheran Church in Amer; Milwaukee Theolog Inst -- Distinguished Service; Chicago "We Do Care": Humanitarian Awd. **MEMBERSHIPS** Intl Afro-Am Museum; Assoc for Study of Negro Life & History; Lutheran Human Relation Assoc of Am; Ntl Committee of Black Churchmen; Lutheran Council in USA; African Am Lutheran Assoc; Theology of the Americas; Amer Acad Relig; Conf of Intl Black Luths. **SELECTED PUBLICATIONS** Auth, Cultural/Self Transcendence, Lutheran School of Theology, 93; Auth, Black and Lutheran, Trinity Lutheran Sem, 90 **CONTACT ADDRESS** Lutheran Sch of Theol at Chicago, 1100 E 55th St, Chicago, IL 60615. **EMAIL** apero@lstc.edu

PERREIAH, ALAN RICHARD
PERSONAL Born 04/11/1937, Los Angeles, CA, m, 1958, 5 children **DISCIPLINE** LOGIC, HISTORY OF PHILOSOPHY **EDUCATION** Loyola Univ, Los Angeles, BA, 59; Marquette Univ, MA, 61; Ind Univ, Bloomington, PhD(philos), 67. **CAREER** Asst prof philos, Univ Wis-Whitewater, 66-67; asst prof, 67-69, Assoc Prof Philos, Univ Ky, 69-82, prof, 82-. **HONORS AND AWARDS** Fulbright Fel, 65-66; Am Coun of Learned Societies and Social Science Res Coun-Joint Grant, 68; int Res and Exchanges Bd grant, 70; Afro-Am Traineeship, 70; coun for Philol Studies-Inst in the Philos of Language, Univ of Calif, Carnegie Foundation, 71; fel, Inst Advan Studies, Princeton Univ, 73-74; Am Coun of Learned Societies Res Grant, 73-74; Nat Endowment for Humanities Award, 74; Nat Endowment for Humanities Awards, 74, 78, 79, 80-81; fel, Villa i Tatti, Harvard Univ Ctr Ital Renaissance Studies, 80-81. **MEMBERSHIPS** Am Philos Asn, Southeastern Medieval Asn, Soc

Int Pour L'Etude Philos Medievale, Ky Philos Asn. **RESEARCH** History of logic, particularly 14th and 15th century; history of science; Paul of Venice. **SELECTED PUBLICATIONS** Auth, George Santayana and recent theories of man, Philos Today, 69; Approaches to supposition-theory, New Scholasticism, 71; ed, Treatise on Suppositions From the Logica Magna by Paul of Venice, Text Ser 15, Franciscan Inst, 71; auth, Buridan and the definite description, J Hist Philos, 72; transl, Paul of Venice: Logics Parva Philosophia Verlag, Munich, 82; Paul-of- venice, 'Logica Magna', Vol 2 Pt 4 - Capitula-de-conditionali- et-de-rationali - Latin And English - Hughes,ge, Editor And Translator, Speculum-a J of Medieval Studies, Vol 0068, 1993; Medieval Mereology - Henry,dp, History And Philosophy of Logic, Vol 0014, 1993; Aristotle Axiomatic Science, Peripatetic Notation or Pedagogical Plan, History And Philosophy of Logic, Vol 0014, 1993; Sophisms in Medieval Logic And Grammar - Read,s, History And Philosophy of Logic, Vol 0015, 1994; Buridanus,iohannes Summulae in Praedicamenta - Latin - Bos,ep, History And Philosophy of Logic, Vol 0017, 1996; Semantics And Speculative Grammar in Scholarly Discourse - Paris, Bologna, And Erfurt, 1270-1330 - The Modist Semiotics - Italian - Marmo,c, Speculum-a J of Medieval Studies, Vol 0071, 1996; Buridanus,iohannes Questiones-elencorum - Latin - Vanderlecq,r, Braakhuis,hag, History And Philosophy of Logic, Vol 0017, 1996; Buridanus,iohannes Summulae-de-praedicabilibus - Latin - Derijk,lm, History And Philosophy of Logic, Vol 0017, 1996; Semantics And Speculative Grammar in Scholarly Discourse - Paris, Bologna, And Erfurt, 1270-1330 - The Modist Semiotics - Italian - Marmo,c, Speculum-a J of Medieval Studies, Vol 0071, 1996. **CONTACT ADDRESS** Dept of Philos, Univ of Kentucky, 1415 Patterson Office Tower, Lexington, KY 40506-0027. **EMAIL** peera@pop.uky.edu

PERRIN, DAVID
PERSONAL Born 09/26/1956, Chiliwack, BC, Canada, s **DISCIPLINE** THEOLOGY **EDUCATION** Univ Ottawa/St Paul Univ, PhD, 95; Pontifical Gregorian Univ, Rome, STL, 87; Pontifical Gregorian Univ, Rome, STB, 85; W Ontario Univ, B.Sc, 78. **CAREER** Interim Dean Theology, St Paul Univ, Ottawa, 98-; asst prof Theology, St Paul Univ, Ottawa, 96-; lctr Theology, St Paul Univ, Ottawa, 94-96; Distance Educ Coord, St Paul Univ, Ottawa, 94-96; part-time lctr Theology, St Paul Univ, 91-94; Pastor, St Agnes Parish, Thunder Bay, Ontario, 89-90; asst pastor, St Mary's Parish, Fort Frances, Ontario, 87-89; part-time lctr, Ontario Eastern Cath Tchrs Assoc, 87-96. **MEMBERSHIPS** Ed, Between the Lines, 93-96; Amer Acad Relig. **SELECTED PUBLICATIONS** The Sacrament of Reconciliation: An Existential Appproach, Edwin Mellon Pr, 98; For Love of the World: The Old and New Self of John of the Cross, Intl Scholars Publ, 97; Canciones entre el alma y el esposo of Juan de la Cruz: A Hermeneutical Interpretation, Intl Scholars Publ, 96. **CONTACT ADDRESS** Dept of Theology, Saint Paul Univ, 223 Main St, Ottawa, ON, Canada K1S 1C4. **EMAIL** dperrin@ustpaul.uottawa.ca

PERRITT, HENRY H., JR.
DISCIPLINE COMPUTER LAW, CIVIL PROCEDURE, ADMINISTRATIVE LAW **EDUCATION** Mass Inst Technol, BS, 66, MS, 70; Georgetown Univ Law Ctr, JD, 75. **CAREER** Prof, Villanova Univ; White House Staff; past Dep Under Sec Labor in the Ford Admin; past mem, Pres Clinton's Transition Team; past adv, Europ Comn and OECD. **HONORS AND AWARDS** Founder, Villanova Ctr for Inf Law and Policy; dir, Proj Bosnia, effort to extend the Rule of Law in Ctrl Europe by tying civic inst together through the Internet. **MEMBERSHIPS** Bars mem, Va, Pa, Dist Columbia, Md & US Supreme Ct; Past chem Sec on Law and Comput, Assoc Amer Law Sch; Nat Acad Public Admin; chem Comt on Regulatory Initiatives and Information Technol, ABA Sec on Admin Law and Regulatory Practice; VP and mem bd dir, Ctr for Comput Aided Legal Instr; Adv Comt on Internet Dissemination, SEC EDGAR data under an NSF grant to NYU and IMS. **RESEARCH** Law and the information superhighway; fed electronic information policy,international legal issues arising from internet use, reforming legal institutions through the internet. **SELECTED PUBLICATIONS** Auth, Internet Basics for Lawyers, Practising Law Institute, 111 pgs., 96; ed, Wiley Employment Law Update, ed, John Wiley & Sons, 96; ed, Law and the Information Superhighway, ed, John Wiley & Sons, 740 pgs., 96; ed, Wiley Employment Law Update, ed, John Wiley & Sons, 97; ed, Employee Dismissal Law and Prectice, 4th ed., John Wiley & Sons, with supplements every six months, 3 vols, 97; ed, Americans with Disabilities act Handbook - 3rd edition, ed, John Wiley & Sons, with supplements every six months, 3 vols, 97; ed, Wiley Employment Law Update, ed, Aspen Law and Business, 98; ed, How to Practice Law with Computers, 3D, Ed, Practising Law Institute, 98; ed, Employment Law Update, Ed, Aspen Law and Business, 99; Employment Law Update, ed, Aspen Law and Business, 00. **CONTACT ADDRESS** Law School, Illinois Inst of Tech, 565 W Adams St, Chicago, IL 60661-3691. **EMAIL** hperritt@kentlaw.edu

PERRY, BARBARA
PERSONAL Born 02/23/1962, Picton, ON, Canada, m, 1996 **DISCIPLINE** CRIMINAL JUSTICE **EDUCATION** Queen's Univ, BA, 85; MA, 87; Carleton Univ, PhD, 92. **CAREER** Asst Prof, Univ of Southern Maine, 92-96; Asst Prof to Assoc Prof, Northern Ariz Univ, 96-; Director of Grad Program, Northern Ariz Univ, 97-. **HONORS AND AWARDS** Nat Inst of Justice Grant, 99; Nat Sci Foundation Grant, 98; Harry Frank Guggenheim Foundation Grant. **MEMBERSHIPS** Soc for the Study of Soc Problems, Am Soc of Criminol **RESEARCH** Criminal and social justice policy, Hate crimes; Difference, identity and justice, Civil and human rights, sociology of law, feminist criminology, Rural criminology, Intl/comparative justice policy, History of crime, law and social control, Neoconservatism. **SELECTED PUBLICATIONS** Auth, "Defending the Color Line: Racially and Ethnically Motivated Hate Crime," American Behavioral Scientist, (forthcoming); auth, "Beyond Black and White: Interethnic Minority violence," Sociology of Crime, Law and Deviance, (forthcoming); auth, "Button-Down Terror: the Metamorphosis of the Hate Movement," Sociological focus, (forthcoming); auth, "Violence Against and Harassment of Women in Canadian Public Housing: An Exploratory Study," Canadian Review of sociology and Anthropology, (99): 499-516; auth, "Introduction: Investigating difference," in Investigating Difference: Human and Cultural Relations in Criminal Justice, Boston, 99; auth, "Exclusion, Inclusion and Violence: Immigrants and Criminal Justice," in Investigating Difference: Human and Cultural Relations in Criminal Justice, Boston, 99; auth, "Perpetual Outsiders: Criminal Justice and the Asian American Experience," in Investigating Difference: Human and Cultural Relations in Criminal Justice, Boston, 99; auth, "Constructing Sexual Identities: Gay Men and Lesbians in the Criminal Justice System," in Investigating Difference: Human and Cultural Relations in Criminal Justice, Boston, 99; auth, "In Whose God We Trust? Religious Difference, Persecution and Violence," in Investigating Difference: Human and Cultural Relations in Criminal Justice, Boston, 99; auth, "Irreconcilable Differences? Understanding the Crime Victim/Criminal Justice Worker Relationship," in Investigating Difference: Human and Cultural Relations in Criminal Justice, Boston, 99. **CONTACT ADDRESS** Dept Crim Justice, No Arizona Univ, PO Box Nau, Flagstaff, AZ 86011-0001. **EMAIL** barbara.perry@nau.edu

PERRY, CONSTANCE K.
PERSONAL Born 05/15/1965, Huntington, NY, m, 1990 **DISCIPLINE** PHILOSOPHY **EDUCATION** Univ Buffalo, PhD, 94. **CAREER** Sr instr, 92-93, Hahnemann Univ; asst prof, 94-, Allegheny Univ of The Health Professions **HONORS AND AWARDS** Member of Alpha Eta, nat honor soc for allied health profes. **MEMBERSHIPS** Am Philos Asn; Am Soc for Bioethics and Humanities. **RESEARCH** Ethical issues in pregnancy; feminist ethics; personhood and its connection to care of animals and incompetent humans; clinical and research ethics. **SELECTED PUBLICATIONS** Auth, Maternal-Fetal Conflict and Principles of Biomedical Ethics, Fostering a Relationship Between Flexibility & Stability, Univ Microfilms Int, 93; auth, Unreliable Results, Commentary to Protocol Review: An Investigator Considers an Animal's Experience, Lab Animal, 24:10, 95. **CONTACT ADDRESS** CN HP-Humanities and Sciences, MCP Hahnemann Univ, Bellet Bldg, 1505 Race St, MS 503, Philadelphia, PA 19104. **EMAIL** constance.perry@drexel.edu

PERRY, EDMUND
PERSONAL Born 05/18/1923, GA, m, 3 children **DISCIPLINE** HISTORY OF RELIGIONS **EDUCATION** Univ Ga, AB, 44; Emory Univ, BD, 46; Northwestern Univ, PhD(bibl theol, hist of relig), 50. **CAREER** Dir Wesley Found, GA State Col Women, 46-48; from instr to asst prof Bible & hist of relig, Duke Univ, 50-54; assoc prof, 54-62, Prof Hist Of Relig, Northwestern Univ, 62-, Chmn Dept, 54-, Mem univ senate, Methodist Church, 54-60; educ consult, Am Tel & Tel Co, 60-62; Fulbright prof, Vidyodaya Univ Ceylon, 67- 68. **HONORS AND AWARDS** DLitt, Vidyodaya Univ Ceylon, 68. **MEMBERSHIPS** Am Orient Soc; Am Theol Soc; Am Acad Relig; Soc Bibl Lit; Int Soc Buddhist-Christian Friends (exec secy, 68-). **RESEARCH** History and methods of studying religions; history and the history of religions; a Christian theology of religion. **SELECTED PUBLICATIONS** Coauth, Jews and Christians in North America, Westminster, 65; auth, The Study and Practice of Religion Today, Vidyodaya Univ Ceylon, 68; Buddhist Studies in Honour of Walpola Rahula, Fraser, London, 80; Theravada Buddhism - a Social-history From Ancient Benares to Modern Colombo - Gombrich,rf, J of The American Oriental Society, Vol 0117, 1997. **CONTACT ADDRESS** Dept of Hist & Relig, Northwestern Univ, Evanston, IL 60201.

PERRY, GLENN
PERSONAL Born 01/28/1940, Barbourville, KY, m, 1963, 5 children **DISCIPLINE** POLITICAL SCIENCE **EDUCATION** Union Col, BA, 60, Univ Va, PhD, 64. **CAREER** Instr, Union Col, 60; asst prof, Univ of Southwestern La, 63-66; vis asst prof, Am Univ Cairo, 68-70; asst prof to prof, Ind State Univ, 66-. **HONORS AND AWARDS** Woodrow Wilson Fel; NDEA Fel; NDFL, Fel, Fulbright Scholar. **MEMBERSHIPS** Middle East Studies Assoc of N Am; Am Polit Sci Assoc; Middle East Inst. **RESEARCH** Middle East politics and international relations. **SELECTED PUBLICATIONS** Auth, Palestine: Continuing Dispossession, AAUG, 86; auth, The Palestine Question: An Annotated Bibliography, AAUG, 90; auth, The Middle East: Fourteen Islamic Centuries, Prentice-Hall, 97. **CONTACT ADDRESS** Dept Polit Sci, Indiana State Univ, 210 N 7th St, Terre Haute, IN 47809-0001.

PERRY, RICHARD J., JR.
DISCIPLINE CHURCH; SOCIETY **EDUCATION** Lutheran Sch Theol at Chicago, ThD. **CAREER** Asst prof-. **HONORS AND AWARDS** Mem, treasurer, LSTC Alumni Senate; dir, Black Ministries for the ELCA; Inclusive Ministries for the North Carolina Synod of the LCA; ch, Working Group on Racism in Church and Society at the 7th Assembly in Budapest, Hungary. **RESEARCH** Urban and cross-cultural ministry. **SELECTED PUBLICATIONS** Auth, Justification by Grace and Its Social Implications, Theol and the Black Experience, Fortress Press, 88. **CONTACT ADDRESS** Dept of Church and Society, Lutheran Sch of Theol at Chicago, 1100 E 55th St, Chicago, IL 60615. **EMAIL** rperry@lstc.edu

PERRY, TIM
PERSONAL Born 04/06/1969, Ottawa, ON, Canada, s **DISCIPLINE** THEOLOGY **EDUCATION** Univ of Durham, PhD, 96 **CAREER** Asst Prof, Providence Col, 98-pres **MEMBERSHIPS** Soc of Christian Philos; Am Acad of Relig **RESEARCH** Development of Doctring; John Hick's Philosophy of Religion **SELECTED PUBLICATIONS** Auth, Anti Judaism, The Historical Jesus and the Christology of Hebrews A Theological Reflection, Didaskalia, forthcoming; Auth, The Significance of Hendrik Kraemers Theology of Religions, Didaskalia, 98, 37-59; Auth, Beyond the Threefold Typology, Canadian Evangelical Review, 97, 1-8. **CONTACT ADDRESS** Dept Bibl and Theol Studies, Providence Col, Division of Bibl & Theolog Studies, Otterburne, MB, Canada R0A 1G0. **EMAIL** tperry@providence.mb.ca

PERSONS, W. RAY
PERSONAL Born 07/22/1953, Talbottan, GA, m, 1977 **DISCIPLINE** LAW **EDUCATION** Armstrong State Col, BS, 75; Oh State Univ, JD, 78. **CAREER** Armstrong State Coll, coll prof 79-80; Natl Labor Rel Bd, attny 80-82; Wells Braun Persons Law Firm, partner/owner 82-; Cong Lindsay Thomas, legislative counsel; Arrington & Hollowell, PC, attorney 86-; adj prof, Col of Law, Ga State Univ, 89-; State of Georgia, special asst attorney general, 89-. **HONORS AND AWARDS** Regents Scholar Armstrong State Col, 73-75; Silver "A" Awd Armstrong State Col, 75. **MEMBERSHIPS** State Bar of GA; Leadership GA Found; Legal Advisor to Brook Glen Neighborhood Asn; Oh State Univ Alumni Asn; Ga Defense Lawyers Asn; Lawyers Club of Atlanta; Am Bar Asn; Emory Univ Law School, Master Lamar Inn of Court; State Bar Disciplinary Bd. **SELECTED PUBLICATIONS** Coauth, Ohio Civil Rules Supplement, 78. **CONTACT ADDRESS** Hunton & Williams, 600 Peachtree St, NE Ste 4100, Bank of Am Plaza, Atlanta, GA 30308-2216. **EMAIL** rpersons@hunton.com

PESANTUBBEE, MICHELENE
DISCIPLINE RELIGIOUS STUDIES **EDUCATION** Univ Calif Santa Barbara, PhD. **CAREER** Asst prof, Relig Studies Dept, Univ of Colorado-Boulder. **MEMBERSHIPS** Native Traditions in the Americans, Am Acad of Relig, Soc for the Study of Native Am Relig Traditions **RESEARCH** American Indian religious movements; southeastern American Indian religious traditions **SELECTED PUBLICATIONS** Auth, When the Earth Shakes: The Cherokee Prophecies of 1811-1812; auth, "Cult of Domesticity or cultural Continuity?" Choctaw Women and the Prostestant Church," J of Am Acad of Religion, (99), 387-409; auth, "The Wounded knee massacre," Millennialism, Persecution, and Violence, Syracuse Univ Press, 00; auth, Honors and Awards: Research Associate in womens's Studies in Religion and Socirety, Harvard Univ the Divinity school, 01-02. **CONTACT ADDRESS** Religious Studies Dept, Univ of Colorado, Boulder, Boulder, CO 80309. **EMAIL** Michelene.Pesantubbee@Colorado.edu

PESSIN, SARAH
PERSONAL Born 07/23/1970, New York, NY **DISCIPLINE** MEDIEVAL PHILOSOPHY **EDUCATION** Yeshiva Univ, BA, 91; Columbia Univ, MA, 94; OH State Univ, doctoral candidate, 2000. **CAREER** Graduate student/fellow, OH State Univ. **HONORS AND AWARDS** Melton Center for Jewish Studies Graduate Fellowship. **RESEARCH** Neoplatonism; Jewish and Islamic Medieval Philosophy. **CONTACT ADDRESS** Dept of Philos, Ohio State Univ, Columbus, 230 N. Oval Mall, 350 Univ H, Columbus, OH 43209. **EMAIL** pessin.4@osu.edu

PESTANA, MARK
PERSONAL Born 02/14/1953, Fresno, CA, m, 1994, 2 children **DISCIPLINE** PHILOSOPHY **EDUCATION** Univ Chicago, PhD, 86. **CAREER** Assoc prof; assoc prof, Grand Valley State Univ. **MEMBERSHIPS** Am Philos Asn; Am Cath Philos Asn. **RESEARCH** Philosophical Psychology; Theory of Mind. **SELECTED PUBLICATIONS** Auth, Conscience; Guilt and Shame; Envy; Self Deception, Magill's Ready Reference: Ethics, 94; Second Order Desires and Strength of Will, The Modern Schoolman, 96; The Three Species of Freedom a nd the Six Species of will Acts; The Modern Schoolman, 96; Moral Virtue or Mental Health, 98. **CONTACT ADDRESS** Dept of Philosophy, Grand Valley State Univ, Allendale, MI 49401. **EMAIL** PestanaM@gvsu.edu

PETER, DAVID J.
PERSONAL Born 04/11/1960, Grand Island, NE, m, 1999 **DISCIPLINE** THEOLOGY **EDUCATION** Univ Nebr, BA, 82; Concordia Sem, MDiv, 87; Trinity Evangelical Divinity Sch, DMin, 99. **CAREER** Vis instr, Concordia Col, 87-88; assoc pastor, Trinity Lutheran Church, 88-95; sr pastor, Trinity Lutheran Church, 95-98; asst prof & dir ministry prog, Concordia Sem, 98-. **MEMBERSHIPS** Asn of Doctor of Ministry Educators. **RESEARCH** Homiletics, Pastoral Leadership. **SELECTED PUBLICATIONS** Auth, Christ Our Passover, Concordia Publ House, 94; auth, "A Lutheran Perspective on the Inward Call to the Ministry," Concordia J 12.4: 121-129; auth, "Five Standards for Effective Sermons," Concordia Pulpit Resources 10.2: 2-4; auth, "Evaluating the Sermon Using CARPE Standards," Concordia Pulpit Resources 10.3: 2-3. **CONTACT ADDRESS** Dept Practical Theol, Concordia Sem, 801 De Mun Ave, Saint Louis, MO 63105-3168. **EMAIL** peterd@csl.edu

PETERS, AULANA LOUISE
PERSONAL Born 11/30/1941, Shreveport, LA, m **DISCIPLINE** LAW **EDUCATION** Notre Dame School for Girls, diploma 1959; College of New Rochelle, BA Philosophy 1963; Univ of S CA, JD 1973. **CAREER** Publimondial Spa, secty/English corres 1963; Fibramianto Spa, secty/English corres 1963-64; Turkish Delegation to Org for Economic Coop and Develop, English corres 1965; Cabinet Braconnier AAA Translation Agency, translator/interpreter 1966; Organ for Economic Coop and Develop Scientific Rsch Div, admin asst 1966-67; Gibson Dunn & Crutcher, Attorney 1973-84; US Securities and Exchange Comm, comm 1984-88; Gibson, Dunn & Crutcher, partner, 88-. **HONORS AND AWARDS** Natl Assoc of Bank Women Inc Washington Achiever Awd 1986; Natl Women's Economic Alliance Foundation, Director's Clt Awd, 1994; Hollywood Chamber of Commerce, Women in Business Awd, 1995; Natl Law Journal one of the 50 most influential women attorneys in USA. **MEMBERSHIPS** Los Angeles Co Bar Assn, State of CA Bar Assn, Langston Hughes Assn; Black Women Lawyers Assn, Amer Bar Assoc; mem Univ of S CA Law Sch Law Alumni Assn; Council on Foreign Relations Inc NY; Bd of Dirs: Mobil, Merrill Lynch, 3M, Northrop Grumman Corp. **CONTACT ADDRESS** Gibson, Dunn & Crutcher, 333 S Grand Ave, Los Angeles, CA 90071-1504.

PETERS, ELLEN ASH
PERSONAL Born 03/21/1930, Berlin, Germany, m, 1979, 3 children **DISCIPLINE** LAW **EDUCATION** Swarthmore Col, BA, 51; Yale Univ, LLB, 54. **CAREER** Law clerk, US Court of Appeals, 54-55; assoc law, Univ Calif, Berkeley, 55-56; from asst prof to prof, Yale Univ, 56- 75, Southmayd prof, 75-78; Justice, Conn Supreme Court, 78-00, now judge trial referee, Adv, Am Law Inst Restatement of Restitution, 63-; mem bd managers, Swarthmore Col, 70-81; adj prof law, Yale Univ, 78-; trustee, Yale New Haven Hosp, 81-83, fellow Yale Corporation, 84-90. **HONORS AND AWARDS** Conn Law Rev Award, Univ Conn Sch Law, 78; Distinguished Achievement Award, Conn Bar Asn, 81; Ella Grasso Distinguished Serv Medal, 82, Ma, Yale Univ, 64; 13 honorary degrees; ma, yale univ, 64. **MEMBERSHIPS** Am Law Inst, Am Philos Soc AARP. **RESEARCH** Contracts; commercial transactions; government contracts federalism. **SELECTED PUBLICATIONS** Auth, Remedies for breach of contracts relating to the sale of goods under the Uniform Commercial Code, 1263, Suretyship under Article 3 of the Uniform Commercial Code, 468 & Quest for uncertainty, 478, Yale Law J; Commercial Transactions, Cases Text and Problems, Bobbs, 71; Reconsidering Gilmore,grant The Death-of-contract - Symposium - Foreword, Northwestern University Law Review, Vol 0090, 1995; The William-8-Lockhart- lecture - Getting Away From The Federal Paradigm - Separation of Powers in State Courts, Minnesota Law Review, Vol 0081, 1997. **CONTACT ADDRESS** Judge Trial defense Superior Court, 185 Washington St, Hartford, CT 06106.

PETERS, FRANCIS EDWARD
PERSONAL Born 06/23/1927, New York, NY, m, 1957, 1 child **DISCIPLINE** CLASSICS, ISLAMIC STUDIES **EDUCATION** St Louis Univ, AB, 50, MA, 52; Princeton Univ, Ph-D(Orient studies), 61. **CAREER** Instr English, Latin & Greek, Canisius High Sch, Buffalo, NY, 52-54; instr English, Scarborough Country Day Sch, NY, 55- 56; from asst prof to assoc prof classics, 61-69, Prof Hist & Near Eastern Lang & Lit & Chmn Dept Near Eastern Lang & Lit, New York Univ, 70-. **MEMBERSHIPS** Am Orient Soc; Mid E Studies Asn. **RESEARCH** Social and intellectual history of Late Antiquity and Early Islam; Near Eastern urbanism. **SELECTED PUBLICATIONS** Auth, Greek Philosophical Terms, 67 & Aristotle and the Arabs, 68, New York Univ; Aristoteles Arabus, Brill, 68; The Harvest of Hellenism, 71 & Allah's Commonwealth, 74, Simon & Schuster; Ours, R Mareck, 81; The Children of Abraham: Judaism, Christianity, Islam, Princeton Univ Press, 82. **CONTACT ADDRESS** Dept of Near Eastern Lang & Lit, New York Univ, New York, NY 10003.

PETERS, THEODORE FRANK
PERSONAL Born 04/03/1941, Wayne, MI, m, 1964, 3 children **DISCIPLINE** PHILOSOPHY, RELIGION **EDUCATION** Mich State Univ, BA, 63; Capital Sem, BD, 67; Univ Chicago, MA, 70, PhD, 73. **CAREER** Pastor, Trinity Lutheran Church, Chicago, 70-72; asst prof relig & philos, Newberry Col, 72-76; assoc prof relig, Loyola Univ of the South, 76-78; Prof Syst Theol, Pac Lutheran Sem & Grad Theol Union; ed, Dialog, A J of Theol. **HONORS AND AWARDS** Prof of the Year Award, Newberry Col, 75. **MEMBERSHIPS** Am Acad Relig; SC Soc Philos (pres, 75-76); World Future Soc; Mutual UFO Network; AAAS. **RESEARCH** Philosophical theology; science and religion. **SELECTED PUBLICATIONS** Auth, God - The World's Future, Fortress, 92; For the Love of Children, Westminster/John Knox, 96; Playing God? Genetic Determinism and Human Freedom, Routledge, 97. **CONTACT ADDRESS** Pacific Lutheran Theol Sem, 2770 Marin Ave, Berkeley, CA 94708-1530. **EMAIL** tpeters2ct@aol.com

PETERSEN, CYNTHIA
DISCIPLINE LAW **EDUCATION** Queen's Univ, Ba, LLB; Harvard Univ, LLM. **CAREER** Assoc prof. **RESEARCH** Property law; family law; consititutional law; lesbian and gay legal issues. **SELECTED PUBLICATIONS** Auth, pubs on human rights, anti-discrimination law, and lesbian and gay equality rights. **CONTACT ADDRESS** Fac Common Law, Univ of Ottawa, 550 Cumberland St, PO Box 450, Ottawa, ON, Canada K1N 6N5.

PETERSON, BRIAN
PERSONAL Born 07/17/1959, Alexandria, MN, m, 3 children **DISCIPLINE** NEW TESTAMENT STUDIES **EDUCATION** Union Theological Seminary in Virginia, 97 **CAREER** Instr, 84, 86, Luther Theological Seminary; visiting instr, 91-94, Union Theological Seminary in Virginia; asst prof, 98-, Lutheran Theological Southern Seminary. **HONORS AND AWARDS** Bruce Prize, Luther Theological Seminary, 96 **MEMBERSHIPS** Soc of Biblical Lit, Catholic Biblical Assoc. **RESEARCH** Pauline epistles; rhetorical analysis, 4th Gospel, Apocalypse. **SELECTED PUBLICATIONS** Auth, Review of David L. Barlett's Romans (Westminister Bible Companion), Interpretation, 97; Between Text and Sermon: 2 Corinthians 6: 1-13, Interpretation, 97; Conquest, Control, and the Cross: Paul's Self-Portrayal in 2 Corinthians 10-13, Interpretation, 98; Eloquence and the Proclamation of the Gospel in Corinth, Society of Biblical Literature Dissertation Series #163, 98; Review of Paul Barnett's The Second Epistle to the Corinthians (NICNT), Catholic Biblical Quarterly, Oct 98. **CONTACT ADDRESS** 4201 N. Main St., Columbia, SC 29203. **EMAIL** bpeterson@ltss.edu

PETERSON, COURTLAND H.
PERSONAL Born 06/28/1930, Denver, CO, m, 1966, 3 children **DISCIPLINE** LAW **EDUCATION** Univ CO, BA, 51, LLB, 53; Univ Chicago, MCL, 59; Univ Freiburg, DJur, 63. **CAREER** From asst prof to assoc prof, 59-63, actg dean sch law, 73-74, dean sch law, 74-79, Prof Law, Univ Colo, Boulder, 63-96, Nicholas Doman Prof Int Law Emer, 96-; Vis prof, UCLA, 65, Max Planck Inst, Ger, 69-70, Univ TX, 73-74. **HONORS AND AWARDS** Robert L Stearns Award; William Lee Knous Award. **MEMBERSHIPS** International Academy of Comparative Law, Studies Law (treas, 79-90, hon pres, 96-98); Am Law Inst. **RESEARCH** Comp law; for judgments; conflict of law theory. **SELECTED PUBLICATIONS** Auth, Die Anerkennung Auslindischer Urteile, Frankfurt, 64; An introduction of the history of continental civil procedure, Colo Law Rev, 69; Developments in American conflicts law: Torts, Ill Law Forum, 69; Foreign country judgments and the second restatement of conflict of law, Columbia Law Rev, 72; Particularism in conflict of laws, Hofstra Law Rev, 82; auth, "Private Interational Law at the End of the 20th Century: Progress of Regress?," Am Journal Comp Law, (98); auth, "Restating Conflicts Again: A Cure for Schizphrenia?," Ind Law Journal, (00); auth, "Choice of Law and forum Clauses and Recognition of Foreign Country Judgments," Revisited Through the Lloyd's of London Cases, Louisiana Law Rev, (00). **CONTACT ADDRESS** Sch of Law, Univ of Colorado, Boulder, PO Box 401, Boulder, CO 80309-0401. **EMAIL** court.peterson@worldnet.att.net

PETERSON, GREGORY R.
PERSONAL Born 05/06/1966, Minneapolis, MN, m **DISCIPLINE** RELIGION, PHILOSOPHY **EDUCATION** Univ Minn, BA, 88; Luther Sem, MA, 90; Denver Univ, PhD, 96. **CAREER** Asst prof, Univ Minn, 96-97; asst prof, Thiel Col, 97-. **HONORS AND AWARDS** Templeton Course Prog Prize, 98; Templeton Awd for Exemplary Papers in Sci and Relig, 98. **MEMBERSHIPS** Am Acad of Relig, Am Philos Asn, Inst for Relig in an Age of Science, Philos of Sci Asn, Am Asn for the Advancement of Sci. **RESEARCH** Science & religion, religion & popular culture, philosophy of mind, philosophy of science. **SELECTED PUBLICATIONS** Auth, "Minds and Bodies: Human and Divine," Zygon, 32 (97): 189-206; auth, "Cognitive Science: What One Needs to Know," Zygon, 32 (97): 615-627; auth, "The Scientific Status of Theology: Imre Lakatos, Method and Demarcation," Perspectives in Sci and Christian Faith (spring 98); auth, "Where Do We Go From Here? A Review of 'Beginning with the End,' " Zygon, 34 (99): 139-150; auth, "The Evolution of Consciousness and the Theology of Nature," Zygon, 34 (99): 283-306; auth, "Three Crises: Science, History, and Plurality," Zygon, 34 (99): 683-694; auth, "Religion and Science in 'Star Trek: The Next Generation': God, Q, and Evolutionary Eschatology on the Final Frontier," in Star Trek and Sacred Space: Essays on Star Trek, Religion, and American Culture, ed by Jennifer Porter, New York: State Univ of New York Press (99); auth, "Going Public-Science and Religion at a Crossroads," Zygon (forthcoming 2000); auth, "Whose Evolution, Which Theology?" Zygon (forthcoming 2000). **CONTACT ADDRESS** Dept Relig, Thiel Col, 75 Col Ave, Greenville, PA 16125-2186. **EMAIL** gpeterson@thiel.edu

PETERSON, MICHAEL LYNN
PERSONAL Born 01/07/1950, Linton, IN, m, 1970, 2 children **DISCIPLINE** PHILOSOPHY **EDUCATION** Asbury Col, BA, 72; Univ Ky, MA, 74; State Univ NYork, Buffalo, PhD, 76. **CAREER** From instr to asst prof philos, Roberts Wesleyan Col, 74-78; Assoc Prof Philos, Asbury Col, 78, Head Philos Dept, 80-, Nat Endowment Humanities fel philos, 78; mem adv & ref bd, John Witherspoon Inst, Princeton Univ, 78-; fel philos, Inst Advan Christian Studies, 79 & 80; lectr, Univ Ky & Georgetown Col, 81-82; managing ed, J Soc Christian Philosophers, 82- **HONORS AND AWARDS** Pew Found Fel, 92-93; Distinguished Schol in Residence, Greenville Col, 96-97; Templeton Sci and Relig Awd 01-02. **MEMBERSHIPS** Am Philos Asn; Soc Christian Philosophers; Wesleyan Theol Soc; Am Sci Affil. **RESEARCH** Philosophy of religion; philosophy of science; modern philosophy. **SELECTED PUBLICATIONS** Coauth, Reason and Religious Belief: An Introduction to the Philosophy of Religion, Oxford Univ Press, 2nd ed, 98; co-ed, Philosophy of Religion: Selected Readings, Oxford Univ Press, 2nd ed., 01; auth, The Problem of Evil, in Companion to the Philosophy of Religion, Blackwell Publ, 97; auth, God and Evil: An Introduction to the Issues, HarperCollins/Westview, 98; ed, Blackwell series, Exploring the Philosophy of Religion; author of numerous other articles and book chapters. **CONTACT ADDRESS** Asbury Col, 1 Macklem Dr, Wilmore, KY 40390-1198. **EMAIL** mike.peterson@asbury.edu

PETERSON, MORGAN
PERSONAL Born 08/15/1934, San Francisco, CA, m, 1962, 2 children **DISCIPLINE** PUBLIC SAFETY **EDUCATION** Col San Mateo, AA, 60; Golden Gate Univ, BA, 75; Dominican Col, MS, 85; Univ San Francisco, Ed D, 91. **CAREER** Adj assoc prof, Skyline Col, 76-94; assoc prof, Golden Gate Univ, 88-94; assoc prof, Palomar Col, 94-. **HONORS AND AWARDS** PSI CHI Nat Hon Soc; Dist Fac Mem; Excel Awd, NISOD. **MEMBERSHIPS** CAAJE; IFCC. **RESEARCH** Police violence; juvenile delinquency. **SELECTED PUBLICATIONS** Auth, Crisis Counseling for a Quality School Community, Acc Devel, 98; auth, Street Gangs: Coping With Violence in Schools. **CONTACT ADDRESS** Dept Public Safety, Palomar Col, 1140 Mission Rd, San Marcos, CA 92069. **EMAIL** mpeterson@palomar.edu

PETERSON, PHILIP LESLIE
PERSONAL Born 03/12/1937, San Francisco, CA, m, 1967, 2 children **DISCIPLINE** PHILOSOPHY, LINGUISTICS **EDUCATION** Col William & Mary, AB, 59; Duke Univ, PhD (philos), 63. **CAREER** From asst prof to assoc prof, 63-76, Prof Philos, Syracuse Univ, 76-, Res assoc, Century Res Corp, 59-63, consult, 63-; Woodrow Wilson fel, 60-63; proj leader ling, Info Processing Systs Res, US Air Force Contracts, 66-71; partic, Early Mod Philos Inst, R Williams Col, 74. **MEMBERSHIPS** Am Philos Asn; AAAS; AAUP; Ling Soc Am. **RESEARCH** Philosophy of language; semantics; epistemology. **SELECTED PUBLICATIONS** Auth, Concepts and Language, Mouton, The Hague, 73; An abuse of terminology, Found Lang, 76; On specific reference, Semantikos, 76; How to infer belief from knowledge, Philos Studies, 77; On representing event reference, In: Presupposition, Acad Press, 79; On the logic of few, many, and most, Notre Dame J Formal Logic, 79; What causes effects?, Philos Studies, 81; Philosophy of Language, Social Res, 81. **CONTACT ADDRESS** 222 Buckingham Ave, Syracuse, NY 13210.

PETERSON, SANDRA
DISCIPLINE PHILOSOPHY **EDUCATION** Princeton Univ, PhD. **RESEARCH** Aristotle's ethics and metaphysics; Plato's metaphysics and philosophy of language. **SELECTED PUBLICATIONS** Auth, Plato's Parmenides: A Principle of Interpretation and Seven Arguments, J Hist Philos, 96; Apparent Circularity in Aristotle's Account of Right Action in the Nicomachean Ethics, Apeiron, 92; Horos (Limit) in Aristotle's Nicomachean Ethics, Phronesis, 88; Substitution in Aristotelian Technical Contexts, Philos Studies, 85; Remarks on Three Formulations of Ethical Relativism, Ethics, 85; Zeno's Second Argument against Plurality, J Hist Philos, 78. **CONTACT ADDRESS** Philosophy Dept, Univ of Minnesota, Twin Cities, 355 Ford Hall, 224 Church St SE, Minneapolis, MN 55455. **EMAIL** peter009@maroon.tc.umn.edu

PETERSON, THOMAS V.
PERSONAL Born 04/14/1943, Everett, WA, m, 1980, 1 child **DISCIPLINE** RELIGIOUS STUDIES **EDUCATION** Stanford Univ BA, 65, PhD, 75; Harvard Div Sch, MTS, 69. **CAREER** Prof rel stud, 75-, Alfred Univ. **HONORS AND AWARDS** 3 NEH Fel. **MEMBERSHIPS** AAR; SCTL. **RESEARCH** Ritual Studies; Religion and the Arts. **SELECTED**

PUBLICATIONS Auth, Ham and Japheth: The Mythic World of Whites in the Antebellum South, Metuchen NJ, Scarecrow Press, 78; editor of spec issue, Historical Reflections/Reflexions Historiques, 97; auth, The Prophetic Challenge of Cherokee Artist Jimmie Durham: Colonialism and Dehumanizing Images of Native Americans, in: The Future of Prophetic Christianity: Essays in Honor of Robert McAfee Brown, ed, John Carmody, Denise Carmody, NY, Orbis, 93. **CONTACT ADDRESS** Division of Human Studies, Alfred Univ, Alfred, NY 14802. **EMAIL** FPETT@alfred.edu

PETIT, PHILIP
PERSONAL Born 12/20/1945, Ireland, m, 1978, 2 children **DISCIPLINE** PHILOSOPHY **EDUCATION** Nat Univ Ireland, BA, 66; MA, 67; Queens Univ, Belfast, PhD, 70; Cambridge Univ, MA. **CAREER** Lectr, Univ Col, Dublin, 68-72, 72-75; res fel, Cambridge, 72-75; prof, Univ of Bradford, UK, 77-85; prof, Australian Nat Univ, 83-; vis prof, Columbia Univ, 97-. **HONORS AND AWARDS** DLitt, (Hon Causa), Nat Univ of Ireland, 00. **RESEARCH** Philosophical Foundations of Human Sciences, Moral and Political Philosophy. **SELECTED PUBLICATIONS** Auth, The Common Mind: An Essay on Psychology, Society and Politics, Oxford Univ Pr, (NY), 93; auth, Republicanism: A Theory of Freedom and Government, Oxford Univ Pr, (Oxford), 97; auth, Three Methods of Ethics: A Debate with Marcia Baron and Michael Slote, Blackwell, (Oxford), 97; coauth, "A Problem for Expressivists", Analysis 58, (98): 239-51; auth, "Republican Freedom and Contestatory Democratisation", Democracy's Value, eds Ian Shapiro and Casiano Hacker-Cordon, Cambridge Univ Pr, (99): 163-190; auth, "A Theory of Normal and Ideal Conditions", Philos Studies 96, (99): 21-44; auth, "Winch's Double-edged Idea of a Social Science", Hist of the Human Sci, (00): 63-77; auth, From Metaphysics to Political Theory, Oxford Univ Pr, (forthcoming); auth, The Fundamentals of Freedom: A Psychological and Political Theory, Polity Pr, (forthcoming). **CONTACT ADDRESS** Dept Philos, Columbia Univ, 2960 Broadway, New York, NY 10027-6944.

PETRAS, JAMES FRANK
PERSONAL Born 01/17/1937, Lynn, MA, m, 1959, 2 children **DISCIPLINE** POLITICAL SCIENCE **EDUCATION** Boston Univ, BA 58; Univ CA Berkeley, MA 63, PhD 67. **CAREER** PA State Univ, asst prof 67-70, assoc prof 70-72; SUNY Binghamton, prof 73. **HONORS AND AWARDS** Ford Found; Vis Scholar Chinese Academy. **MEMBERSHIPS** Latin Am Stud Assn. **RESEARCH** Latin Am, US fire arm policy. **SELECTED PUBLICATIONS** Class Conflict in Neoliberalism in Latin America, co auth, Macmillan, 97; Empire or Republic, co auth, Pontledge, 95; The Left Strikes Back, Westview, 98; Poverty and Democracy in Chile, Westview, 94; Latin America in the Time Of Cholera, Pontledge, 93. **CONTACT ADDRESS** Dept of Sociology, SUNY, Binghamton, Binghamton, NY 13901.

PETTER, ANDREW J.
DISCIPLINE LAW **EDUCATION** Univ Victoria, LLB, 81; Cambridge Univ, LLM, 82. **CAREER** Asst prof, 86-88; assoc prof, 88-. **RESEARCH** Constitutional law, legal and political theory, legislative and regulatory processes, contracts, and legal education. **CONTACT ADDRESS** Fac of Law, Univ of Victoria, PO Box 2400, Victoria, BC, Canada V8W 3H7. **EMAIL** lawadmss@uvic.ca

PETUCHOWSKI, JAKOB JOSEF
PERSONAL Born 07/30/1925, Berlin, Germany, m, 1946, 3 children **DISCIPLINE** THEOLOGY, LITURGY **EDUCATION** Univ London, England, BA, 47; Hebrew Union Col, Ohio, MA, 52, PhD(theol), 55. **CAREER** Rabbi, Beth Israel Congregation, Pa, 55-56; asst prof rabbinics, 56-59, assoc prof, 59-63, prof, 63-65, prof rabbinics & theol, 65-74, res prof theol & liturgy, 74-81, Res Prof Judeo- Christian Studies, Hebrew Union Col, Ohio, 81-, US citizen Vis prof, Antioch Col, 6 1; dir Jewish studies, Hebrew Union Col, Israel, 63-64; vis prof, Tel-Aviv Univ, Israel, 71. **HONORS AND AWARDS** Dr phil, Univ Cologne, West Ger, 78. **MEMBERSHIPS** Am Acad Relig; fel Am Acad Jewish Res. **RESEARCH** Jewish theology in the classical Rabbinic and in the modern periods; Jewish liturgy; the Christian-Jewish dialogue on a theological level. **SELECTED PUBLICATIONS** Auth, Prayer book Reform in Europe, World Union of Progressive Judaism, 68; Heirs of the Pharisees, Basic Books, 70; The Theology of Haham David Nieto, Ktav, second ed, 70; Understanding Jewish Prayer, Ktav, 72; Theology and Poetry, Routledge & Kegan Paul, London, 78; Metchisedech-Urgestalt der Okumene, Herder, Freiburg, 79; Ever Since Sinai, B Arbit Books, third ed, 79; co-ed, Studies in Memory of Joseph Heinemann, Magnes Press, Jerusalem, 81; 100 Years of American Conservative Judaism - a Review-essay, American Jewish History, Vol 0080, 1991. **CONTACT ADDRESS** 7836 Greenland Pl, Cincinnati, OH 45237.

PFEIFFER, RAYMOND SMITH
PERSONAL Born 10/11/1946, New York, NY, m, 1999, 3 children **DISCIPLINE** PHILOSOPHY **EDUCATION** Kenyon Col, AB, 68; Washington Univ, AM, 72, PhD, 74. **CAREER** Asst prof, Alma Col, MI, 74-75; prof, Delta Col, 75-. **HONORS AND AWARDS** Kenyon Col, AB, cum laude, High Honors in philos, 68; Univ Fel and Teaching Assistantship, Washington Univ, 71-73; NEH Fel, Summer Sem, 77, 87; Fel, Am Philos Asn, 86; Who's Who in the Humanities, 92; The Barstow-Frevel Awd, Delta Col, 94; Am Asn of Univ Prof Awd for Service to Delta Col, 98. **MEMBERSHIPS** Am Philos Asn; Mich Acad of Sci, Arts, and Letters; Soc for Philos and Public Affairs; Soc for Health, Ethics, and Life Scis (Hastings Center); Sigma Xi; Int Asn for the Philos of Law and Soc Philos. **RESEARCH** Philosophy of technology, philosophy of science, applied philosophy, ethical theory, business ethics, medical ethics. **SELECTED PUBLICATIONS** Auth, "Is Motivation Management Manipulative?," Ethical Theory and Business, 3rd ed, ed Tom L. Beauchamp and Norman E. Bowie, Englewood Cliffs, NJ: Prentice Hall (88): 287-292; auth, "The Meaning and Justification of Collective Moral Responsibility," Public Affairs Quart, 2, no 3 (88): 69-83; auth, "The Central Distinction in the Theory of Corporate Moral Personhood," J of Business Ethics, 9 (90): 473-480; auth, "Owing Loyalty to One's Employer," J of Business Ethics, 11 (92): 387-396; auth, Teaching Ethical Decision-Making: The Case Study Method and the RESOLVEDD Strategy," Teaching Philos, 15 (92): 175-184; coauth, Ethics on the Job: Cases and Strategies, Belmont, CA: Wadsworth Pub Co (93); auth, Why Blame the Organization? A Pragmatic Analysis of Collective Moral Responsibility, Lanham, Md: Rowman and Little field (95); auth, "Obligations of Loyalty" (forthcoming); coauth, "Tellling Nurses Their Patients Have AIDS," (forthcoming); coauth, Ethics in the Hospital (forthcoming). **CONTACT ADDRESS** Dept Humanities, Delta Col, 6263 Mackinaw Rd, University Center, MI 48710-0001. **EMAIL** rspfeiff@alpha.delta.edu

PFUND, PETER H.
PERSONAL Born 10/06/1932, Bryn Mawr, PA, m, 1959, 2 children **DISCIPLINE** HISTORY, LAW **EDUCATION** Amherst Col, BA, 54; Univ of PA Law Sch, JD, 59. **CAREER** US Dept of St, Office of the Legal Adviser, full-time, 59-97; asst legal adviser for private int law, 79-97; special adviser for pvt int law, 97-. **HONORS AND AWARDS** Am Bar Asn, Sect for Int Law & Pract, Leonard J. Theberge Prize for Pvt Int Law, 87; Commendation, ABA Section of Intl Law Practice, 97; Awd of Appreciation, Joint Council on Intl Children's Services, 99; Special Achiev Awd, New York State Bar Assoc, 99; Hall of Fame Awd, Nat Council for Adoption, 00 . **MEMBERSHIPS** Am Law Inst; German-American Lawyers Asn, Bonn, Ger. **SELECTED PUBLICATIONS** Auth, Contributing to Professional Development of Private International Law: The International Process and the United States Approach, 249 Receuil des cours 9-144, 94-V; and other publications. **CONTACT ADDRESS** 10419 Pearl St, Fairfax, VA 22032-3824. **EMAIL** pfund.ph@gateway.net

PHELAN, JIM
PERSONAL Born 05/10/1944, Boston, MA, m, 1974, 2 children **DISCIPLINE** LIBERAL ARTS, LEGAL STUDIES **EDUCATION** Govt Suffolk Univ Boston Mass, AB; Lawyer Suffolk Law Sch Boston Mass, JD. **CAREER** Instr RAI Acad, 69-84; Serv Special Agent, FBI; Assoc Prof, Mc Intosh Col. **HONORS AND AWARDS** Rolor Grad Mem Awd. **MEMBERSHIPS** ASIS, ABT. **SELECTED PUBLICATIONS** Auth, Terrorism, Firefighting Magazine, 91. **CONTACT ADDRESS** Dept Lib Arts, McIntosh Col, 23 Cataract Ave, Dover, NH 03820.

PHELAN, MARILYN E.
PERSONAL Born 07/12/1938, Lubbock, TX, m, 3 children **DISCIPLINE** LAW, HUMANITITES **EDUCATION** Tex Tech Univ, BA, 58; MBA, 68; PhD, 71; Univ Tex, JD, 72. **CAREER** Assoc dean, 73-77, Tex Tech Univ; prof, Tex Tech Univ, 74-; general counsel, Tex Tech Univ and Tex Tech Univ Health Sci Ctr, 77-84. **HONORS AND AWARDS** Pres Excellence in Teaching Awd; Pres Acad Achievement Awd for Excellence in Teaching, Res, & Service; Res Awd, Sch of Law. **MEMBERSHIPS** Am Bar Asn, Am Ist of Certified Public Accountatns, Am Museum Asn, Int Coun of Museums, Tex Bar Asn, Tex Board of Legal Specialization. **RESEARCH** Nonprofit Organizations, Art and Museum Law. **SELECTED PUBLICATIONS** Auth, Museum Law, Kalos Kapp Press; Nonprofit Enterprises (3 vols), West Group; Law of Cultural Property and Natural Heritage, Kalos Kapp Press. **CONTACT ADDRESS** Sch of Law, Texas Tech Univ, Lubbock, TX 79409-0999.

PHELPS, TERESA GODWIN
PERSONAL Born 05/29/1944, Bournemouth, England, m, 1964, 3 children **DISCIPLINE** LEGAL WRITING **EDUCATION** Univ Notre Dame, BA, 73, MA, 75, PhD(English), 80. **CAREER** Asst Prof Legal Writing, Law Sch, Univ Notre Dame, 80-, Ed, Notre Dame English J, 78-80. **MEMBERSHIPS** MLA; Law & Humanities Inst; Asn Am Law Sch. **RESEARCH** Legal language; law and humanities. **SELECTED PUBLICATIONS** Auth, Problems and Cases for Legal Writing, Nat Inst Trial Advocacy, 82; the Power of Persuasion, University of Cincinnati Law Review, Vol 0063, 1994. **CONTACT ADDRESS** Law Sch, Univ of Notre Dame, Notre Dame, IN 46556.

PHENIX, PHILIP HENRY
PERSONAL Born 03/01/1915, Denver, CO, m, 1943, 2 children **DISCIPLINE** PHILOSOPHY, RELIGION **EDUCATION** Princeton Univ, BA, 34; Union Theol Sem, MDiv, 42; Columbia Univ, PhD, 50; LHD, Alderson-Broaddus Col, 70. **CAREER** Asst prof philos & relig, Carleton Col, 46-48; assoc prof relig, 50-53; assoc prof educ, Teachers Col, Columbia Univ 54-58; dean, Carleton Col, 58-60; prof philos & educ, 60-73, Arthur I Gates prof, 73-80, Arthur I Gated Emer Prof Philos & Educ, 80-Teachers Col, Columbia Univ; Brown & Haley lectures, Col Puget Sound, 64. **HONORS AND AWARDS** Harbison Awd, 64; Butler Silver Medal, Columbia Univ, 81. **MEMBERSHIPS** Philos Educ Soc (pres, 71-72); Relig Educ Asn; Soc Values Higher Educ; NEA. **RESEARCH** Philosophy of educaton; value education; religious education. **SELECTED PUBLICATIONS** Auth, Education and the Common Good, Harper, 61; auth, Realms of Meaning, McGraw, 64; auth, Man and His Becoming, Rutgers Univ, 64; auth, Education and the Worship of God, Westminster, 66; transl, Jorge Manach, Frontiers in the Americas, Teachers Ltd Press, 75. **CONTACT ADDRESS** 127 Rosewood Cir, Bridgewater, VA 22812.

PHILLIPS, CLARENCE MARK
PERSONAL Born 09/18/1960, Key West, FL **DISCIPLINE** PHILOSOPHY **EDUCATION** Univ Warwick, Coventry, Eng, MA, 91; Tulane Univ, PhD, 98. **CAREER** Lectr, phil, 91-, Calif St Univ; lectr, 91-92, Justus-Liedig Volkshorchschule, Germany; lectr, 94-, Tulane, Univ New Orleans, Xavier & Dillard Univ. **HONORS AND AWARDS** French Honor Soc. **MEMBERSHIPS** APA **RESEARCH** Pragmatism, evolutionary psychology, phil of economics. **SELECTED PUBLICATIONS** Homo Natura: Influence of Emerson's Conception of Nature on Nietzche's Will to Power, Hist of Phil Quart, 97. **CONTACT ADDRESS** UNO - Lakefront, LA 383, New Orleans, LA 70118. **EMAIL** cphillip@uno.edu

PHILLIPS, CRAIG A.
PERSONAL Born 07/01/1954, Tulsa, OK, m, 1977, 2 children **DISCIPLINE** THEOLOGY; ETHICS **EDUCATION** Brown Univ, AB, 76; Harvard Univ, M Div, 79; Duke Univ, PhD, 93. **CAREER** Visiting lectr, Univ NC Chapel Hill, 93; visiting instr, Duke Univ, 94; asst prof, Temple Univ, 94-97; rector, Incarnation/Holy Sacrament Episcopal Church, 97-; instr, Rosemont Col, 98-. **HONORS AND AWARDS** Amer Asn of Col Jr Teaching fel, 91-92; Outstanding Young Men of Amer, 86. **MEMBERSHIPS** Amer Acad of Relig; Soc of Bibl Lit. **RESEARCH** Methodology of the study of relig; Colonial and postcolonial theory; Critical social theory; Modern Christian traditions. **SELECTED PUBLICATIONS** Auth, From Aesthetics to Redemptive Politics: A Political Reading of the Theological Aesthetics of Hans Urs von Balthasar and the Materialist Aesthetics of Walter Benjamin, Univ Mich, 93. **CONTACT ADDRESS** 317 Grayling Av., Narberth, PA 19072-1905. **EMAIL** craigphillips@mac.com

PHILLIPS, DEWI ZEPHANIAH
PERSONAL Born 11/24/1934, Wales, m, 1959, 3 children **DISCIPLINE** PHILOSOPHY **EDUCATION** Univ Col of Swansea, BA, MA; St Catherine's Col, Oxford, BLitt. **CAREER** Asst lectr & lectr, Queen's Col Dundee, 61-63; lectr, Univ Col N Wales, 63-65; from lectr to prof, philos, 65-96, Univ Wales, Swansea; Danforth Prof Philos of Relig, 92- , Claremont Grad Univ; Rush Rhees Res Prof, Univ Wales, Swansea, 96- . **HONORS AND AWARDS** Hon PhD, Abo Akademi, Finland, 98. **MEMBERSHIPS** Aristotelian Soc; APA; AAR. **RESEARCH** Philosophy of religion; ethics; literature; Wittgenstein; metaphilosophy. **SELECTED PUBLICATIONS** Auth, Through a Darkening Glass, 82; Dramau Gwenlyn Parry, 82; auth, Belief Change and Forms of Life, 86; auth, R.S. Thomas: Poet of the Hidden God, 86; auth, Faith After Foundationalism, 88; auth, From Fantasy to Faith, 91; auth, Interventions in Ethics, 92; auth, Wittgenstein and Religion, 93; auth, Writers of Wales: J.R. Jones, 95; auth, Introducing Philosophy, 96; auth, Recovering Religious Concepts, 99; auth, Philosophy's Cool Place, 99. **CONTACT ADDRESS** Dept of Religion, Claremont Graduate Sch, Claremont, CA 91711. **EMAIL** Jacquelyn.Huntzinger@cgu.edu

PHILLIPS, L. EDWARD
PERSONAL Born 09/24/1954, Jackson, TN, m, 1976, 3 children **DISCIPLINE** RELIGION **EDUCATION** Univ Tenn, BS; Emory Univ, MDiv; Univ Notre Dame, PhD. **CAREER** Asst prof religion, 91-94, assoc prof religion, 94-97, chair hum, 95-97, Union Col; assoc prof hist theol, Garrett Evangel Theol Sem, 97-. **HONORS AND AWARDS** James Still Fel, 94; Fac Scholars Fel, Appalachain Col Asn, 95. **MEMBERSHIPS** N Am Acad Liturgy; Am Acad Relig; Soc Liturgica; North Am Patristic Soc. **RESEARCH** History of liturgy. **SELECTED PUBLICATIONS** Auth, Ritual Kiss in Early Christian Worship, 96; auth, In Spirit and Truth, 00. **CONTACT ADDRESS** Garrett-Evangelical Theol Sem, 2121 Sheridan Rd., Evanston, IL 60201. **EMAIL** lephillips@nwu.edu

PHILLIPS, RANDALL R.
PERSONAL Born 01/13/1957, Detroit, MI, s **DISCIPLINE** THEOLOGY **EDUCATION** Pontifical Gregorian Univ, PhD, 88. **CAREER** St. Ephrem Church, assoc pastor, 89-92; Sacred

Heart Sem, adj prof, 89-92; Our Lady of Victory Church, Pastor, 92-95; St. Linus Church, 95-. **MEMBERSHIPS** AAR, CTS **RESEARCH** Liberation theology **CONTACT ADDRESS** St. Linus Church, 6466 N Evangeline St, Dearborn Heights, MI 48127-2029.

PHILLIPS, ROBERT L.
DISCIPLINE PHILOSOPHY **EDUCATION** Queen's Univ, MA; Oxford Univ, PhD. **CAREER** Sr instr, Queen's Univ at Kingston, Canada, 64-65; col lectr, Lincoln Col, Oxford, 65-67; asst prof, Wesleyan Univ, 67-74; dir, Prog War and Ethics, Univ Conn; prof-. **SELECTED PUBLICATIONS** Auth, Jus In Bello: Combatancy, Non-Combatancy, and Non-Combatant Immunity, Johnson and Kelsay, The Justification and Limitation of War in Western and Islamic Cultural Traditions, Greenwood Press, 90; Terrorism: Historical Roots and Moral Justifications, Crisp and Warner, Terrorism, Protest, and Power, Pergamon Press: 90; Ethics and Grand Strategy in the Gorbachov Era, Ethics and Intl Aff Annual, 90. **CONTACT ADDRESS** Dept of Philos, Univ of Connecticut, Hartford, 85 Lawlor Rd, West Hartford, CT 06117.

PHILLIPS, THOMAS
PERSONAL Born 07/21/1964, Seymour, IN, m, 1985, 2 children **DISCIPLINE** THEOLOGY **EDUCATION** Olivet Nazarene Univ, BA, 87; MA, 88; Nazarene Theol Sem, Mdiv, 91; Southern Methodist Univ, PhD, 98. **CAREER** Asst prof, Eastern Nazarene Col, 98-. **MEMBERSHIPS** Wesleyan Theol Soc; Cath Biblical Asn; Soc of Biblical Lit; Am Acad Relig. **SELECTED PUBLICATIONS** Auth, Literary Studies in Luke-Acts, Macon: Mercer Univ Press (98). **CONTACT ADDRESS** Dept Relig & Philos, Eastern Nazarene Col, 23 E Elm Ave, Quincy, MA 02170-2905.

PHILPOTT, MARK
PERSONAL Born 11/29/1968, London, England **DISCIPLINE** PHILOSOPHY **EDUCATION** Univ Bristol, B V Sc, 90; Univ Hull, MA, 94; Univ Bristol, M Litt, 96. **HONORS AND AWARDS** Univ Bristol scholar, 94; Brit Acad fel, 95; Stanford Univ fel, 96. **MEMBERSHIPS** APA. **RESEARCH** Genetics and identity; medical ethics; philos of lang; metaphysics. **SELECTED PUBLICATIONS** Auth, Not Guilty by Reason of Genetic Determinism, Punishment, Excuses & Moral Develop, Henry Tam, 96. **CONTACT ADDRESS** Dept of Philosophy, Stanford Univ, Stanford, CA 94305-2155. **EMAIL** mark.philpott@stanford.edu

PHIPPS, WILLIAM EUGENE
PERSONAL Born 01/28/1930, Waynesboro, VA, m, 1954, 3 children **DISCIPLINE** RELIGION, PHILOSOPHY **EDUCATION** Davidson Col, BS, 49; Union Theol Sem, Va, MDiv, 52; Univ St Andrews, PhD(Bibl criticism), 54; Univ Hawaii, MA, 63. **CAREER** Prof Bible, Peace Col, 54-56; Prof Emer Relig & Philos, Davis & Elkins Col, 56-95, Minister, Presby USA Church, 52-; vis fel, Princeton Theol Sem, 69-70; vis scholar, Emory Univ, 77-78. **HONORS AND AWARDS** MLitt, Davis and Elkins Col, WV, 72. **RESEARCH** Bibical interpretation; religion and sexuality; thanatology; religious biography. **SELECTED PUBLICATIONS** Cremation is Gaining, NY Times, 2/4/81; auth, Death: Confronting the Reality, John Knox, 87; auth, Genesis and Gender, Praeger, 89; auth, Assertive Biblical Women, Greenwood, 92; auth, Wisdom and Wit of Rabbi Jesus, Westminster, 93; auth, Muhammad and Jesus, Continuum, 96; auth, The Sexuality of Jesus, Pilgrim, 96; auth, Amazing Grace in John Newton, Mercer, 01; auth, African-American Livingstone, Geneva, forthcoming. **CONTACT ADDRESS** 1217 Rennie Ave, Richmond, VA 23227. **EMAIL** mphipps@attglobal.net

PIAR, CARLOS R.
PERSONAL Born 06/05/1956, Santurce, Puerto Rico, m, 1986, 2 children **DISCIPLINE** RELIGION **EDUCATION** Biola Col, BA, 77; Talbot Theol Sem, MDiv, 80, ThM, 82; Univ S Cal, PhD, 91. **CAREER** Assoc prof, Cal State Univ, 90-. **MEMBERSHIPS** Am Acad Relig; Soc Christian Ethics; Pac Coast Theol Soc. **RESEARCH** Ethnicity & religion; Christian social ethics. **SELECTED PUBLICATIONS** Auth Jesus and Liberation, Peter Lang, 94; Cesar Chavez and La Causa: Toward a Hispanic Christian Social Ethic, Ann Soc Christian Ethics, 96. **CONTACT ADDRESS** 11405 Harrisburg Rd, Los Alamitos, CA 90720. **EMAIL** crpiar@csulb.edu

PICART, CAROLINE (KAY) J. S.
PERSONAL Born 01/31/1966, Philippines, m, 1995 **DISCIPLINE** PHILOSOPHY & RELIGIOUS STUDY **EDUCATION** Ateneo de Manila Univ, Philippines, BS, 87, MA, 89; Cambridge Univ, England, MPhil, 91; Pa St Univ, PhD, 96. **CAREER** Instr, 87-89, Ateneo de Manila Univ; instr, 92-93, Yonsei Univ, Korea; instr, teaching asst, 93-96, Pa St Univ; instr, 96-97, Fl Atlantic Univ; instr, 97-99, Univ Wisc Eau Claire; asst prof, St Lawrence Univ, 99-00; asst prof, Fla State Univ, 00- . **HONORS AND AWARDS** Ateneo de Manila Univ Merit Schol, 84-87; Ateneo Scholar Found Grant, 84-87; Acad Excellence & Extra-Acad Involvement Awd, 87; Magna Cum Laude, 87; Univ Scholar, 87-89; Overseas Res Student Awd, 89-90; Sir Run Run Shaw Awd, 89-91; Rueben Levy Travel Awds Scheme award, 89, 91; Wolfson Prize for Acad Excellence, 91; XIIIth Int Cong on Logic, Methodology & Philos of Sci Awd, 95; Grad Res Exhib, 96; Vis Minority Scholar/Artist, 97; Network for Excellence in Teaching Awd, 97, 98; Faculty-Student Res Collaboration Grant, 97; Internal Res Grant, 97; Off of Univ Travel Awd, 98; Univ Res & Creative Activity Awd, 98; Inst on Race & Ethnicity Reading Sem Grant, 98. **MEMBERSHIPS** Nietzsche Soc; Amer Philos Assoc; Soc for Phenomenology & Existential Philos; NA Soc for Soc Philos; Int Assoc for Philos & Lit; Pa St Filipino Stud Assoc; Amer Conf on Romanticism; Int Group of Poets & Artists, Int Writers' Group; Pa St Ballroom Dance Club; Int Dance Club. **RESEARCH** Aesthetics; philos/sociology of sci; soc & polit philos/ethics; feminist philos; nineteenth & twentieth century continental philos. **SELECTED PUBLICATIONS** Auth, "Scientific Controversy as Farce: The Benveniste-Maddox Counter-Trials," Soc Studies of Sci 24 (94): 7-37; auth, "Metaphusics in Gaston Bachelard's 'Reverie'," Human Studies: A J for Philos and the Soc Scis 20 (97): 59-73; auth, "Blurring Boundaries: A Reply to Fadlon and Lewin-Epstein," Soc Studs of Sci 27 (97): 142-46; auth, "Nietzsche as Masked Romantic," J of Aesthetics & Art Crit 55 (97): 273-92; auth, "Gayelord Hauser," in Am Nat Biog (Oxford Univ Pr, 98); auth, Resentment and "the Feminine" in Nietzsche's Politico-Aesthetics, Penn State Univ Pr (State Col, PA), 99; auth, Thomas Mann and Friedrich Nietzshe: Eroticism, Death, Music and Laughter, Rodopi (Dordrecht, Netherlands), 99; auth, "Through the Lens of an Insider-Outsider: Gender Race and (Self) Representation in Science," in A New Generation of Feminist Science Studies, eds, Maralee Mayberry, Banu Subramaniam, & Lisa Weasel (Routledge, 01); auth, "Gender, Authority and the Politics of Representation in Science and Art," in A New Generation of Feminist Science Studies, eds, Maralee Mayberry, Banu Subramaniam, & Lisa Weasel (Routledge, 01); auth, The Cinematic Rebirths of Frankenstein: Universal, Hammer and Beyond, Greenwood, forthcoming; co-auth, A Frankenstein Film Sourcebook, Greenwood, forthcoming. **CONTACT ADDRESS** Dept of Philos, Florida State Univ, 216 William Johnston Bldg, Tallahassee, FL 32306-1580. **EMAIL** kpicart@english.fsu.edu

PICIRILLI, ROBERT EUGENE
PERSONAL Born 10/06/1932, High Point, NC, m, 1953, 5 children **DISCIPLINE** BIBLICAL STUDIES, THEOLOGY **EDUCATION** Free Will Baptist Bible Col, BA, 53; Bob Jones Univ, MA, 55, PhD, 63. **CAREER** Registrar, 60-79, teacher Bible & Greek, Free Will Baptist Bible Col, 55-, acad dean, 79-98, dean Grad Sch, 82-84, writer, Sunday Sch Dept, Nat Asn Free Will Baptists, 61-81; pastor, Cofer's Chapel Free Will Baptist Church, 62-64; gen ed, Randall House Commentary, 86-. **HONORS AND AWARDS** DD, Bob Jones Univ, 67. **MEMBERSHIPS** Evangel Theol Soc; Inst Bibl Res. **RESEARCH** Biblical studies; Free Will Baptist history. **SELECTED PUBLICATIONS** Auth, By what authority?, in Presby J, 66; He Emptied Himself: Philippians 2: 5-11, in Bibl Viewpoint, 69; The Book of Galatians, Randall House Publ, 73; The Book of Romans, Randall House Publ, 75; The Meaning of Epignosis, in Evangel Quart, 75; ed & contribr, History of Free Will Baptist State Associations, Randall House Publ, 76; auth, A Study of Separate Free Will Baptist Origins in Middle Tennessee, in Quart Rev Southern Baptists, 77; contribr, Christian Education: An Introduction to Its Scope, Randall House Publ, 78; 1,2 Corinthians, Randall House Publ, 87; Ephesians and Phillipians, Randall House Publ, 88; 1,2 Thessalonians, Randall House Publ, 90; 1,2 Peter, Randall House Publ, 92; coauth, The NKJV Greek English Interlinear New Testament, Thomas Nelson Publ, 94; auth, Arminius and the Deity of Christ, in Evangel Quart, 97; auth, "Allusions to 2 Peter in the Apostolic Fathers," Jour Stud NT(98); auth, "Free Will Baptists in Tennessee," Tenn Bapt Hist (99). **CONTACT ADDRESS** 3606 West End Ave, Nashville, TN 37205-2403. **EMAIL** repic@fwbbc.edu

PICKARD, DEAN
PERSONAL Born 03/12/1947, Geneva, NY **DISCIPLINE** PHILOSOPHY **EDUCATION** Univ Calif, Riverside, BA, 73; Calif State Univ, Long Beach, MA, 77; Claremont Grad Univ, PhD, 92. **CAREER** Phys educ dept, Pomona Col, 75-82; philos, phys educ, Moorpark & Ventura Col, 78-82; prof, philos, hum, phys educ, Los Angeles Mission Col, 79-83; philos, Calif State Univ, 88-99; prof philos, Los Angeles Pierce Col, 83-. **HONORS AND AWARDS** Phi Beta Kappa, cum laude, 73; fel Claremont Grad Univ, 88-89; Golden Apple Awd tchg, 86, 88, 92, 95, 96, 97; Who's Who Among America's Teachers, 96, 98, 00; NEH grant, 95; Liberty Fund Grant, 98. **MEMBERSHIPS** Los Angeles Ara Nietzsche Soc, APA; North Am Nietzsche Soc; Nietzsche Soc. **RESEARCH** Nietzsche; Kant; nineteenth and twentieth century continental philosophy; interdisciplinary humanities; philosophy and literature; contemporary philosophy; Heidegger; Wittgenstein; philosophy of martial arts; Asian/Buddhist philosophy; world religions. **SELECTED PUBLICATIONS** Auth, Martial Arts and Meditative Disciplines, Black Belt Mag, 79; auth, Mystical Experience, Language & Ontological Claims, Jour of the Los Angeles Commun Col, 82; auth, The Problem of Reflexivity in Habermasian Universalism, Auslegung, 93; auth, Logic, Truth, and Reasoning: A Textbook in Critical Thinking, Pierce Col, 97; auth, Nietzsche, Emancipation, & Truth, in Babich, ed, New Nietzsche Studies, 97; Rev, of The Art of Living, by Alexander Nehemas, in Babich, ed New Nietzsche Studies, 99. **CONTACT ADDRESS** Dept of Philosophy, Pierce Col, 6201 Winnatka Ave, Woodland Hills, CA 91371. **EMAIL** deanpickard@cs.com

PICKENS, GEORGE F.
PERSONAL Born 02/26/1958, Parkersburg, WV, m, 1980, 2 children **DISCIPLINE** INTERCULTURAL STUDIES, MISSION STUDIES **EDUCATION** Ky Christian Col, BA, 80; Ohio Univ, MA, 84; Univ Birmingham, Eng, PhD, 97. **CAREER** Lectr, Daystar Univ, Nairobi, Kenya; prof Intercult Studs, Ky Christian Col, 97- . **HONORS AND AWARDS** Overseas Studs Res Scheme, UK, 94-97, Neville Chamberlain prize, Univ Birmingham, UK, 94-95. **MEMBERSHIPS** Amer Acad Rel; Amer Soc Missiology. **RESEARCH** Oral history; African religion and Historical studies. **CONTACT ADDRESS** Dept of Intercultural Studies, Kentucky Christian Col, 100 Academic Pkwy, PO Box 2050, Grayson, KY 41143-2205. **EMAIL** gpickens@email.kcc.edu

PICKENS, RUPERT TARPLEY
PERSONAL Born 02/20/1940, High Point, NC, m, 1963, 2 children **DISCIPLINE** ROMANCE PHILOLOGY, MEDIEVAL FRENCH **EDUCATION** Univ NC, Chapel Hill, AB, 61, MA, 64, PhD(Romance philol), 66. **CAREER** Asst prof French, Univ NC, Chapel Hill, 66-69; from asst prof to assoc prof, 69-78, Prof French, Univ KY, 78-, Managing ed, Fr Forum, 75-. **MEMBERSHIPS** MLA; Soc Rencesvals; Am Asn Teachers Fr. **RESEARCH** The Bestiaire and Cumpot of Philippe de Thaun; Old French courtly literature; medieval lyric poetry. **SELECTED PUBLICATIONS** Auth, The concept of the feminine ideal in Villon's Testament: Huitain 89, Studies Philol, 73; Thematic Structure of Marie de France's Guigemar, Romania, 74; Somnium and Interpretation in Guillaume de Lorris, Symposium, 74; Estoire, Lai and romance: Chretien's Erec et Enide and Cliges, Romanic Rev, 75; The Welsh Knight: Paradoxicality in Chretien's Conte del Graal, FS Forum, 77; Jafure Rudel et la poetique de la mouvance, Çahiers Civilisation Medievale, 77; The Songs of Jaufre Rudel, Pontif Inst Mediaeval Studies, 78; La Poetique de Marie de France d'apres les prologues des Lais, Les Lett Romanes, 78. **CONTACT ADDRESS** Dept of French, Univ of Kentucky, 1021 Patterson Office Tower 0027, Lexington, KY 40506. **EMAIL** rtp@pop.uky.edu

PICKERING, GEORGE W.
DISCIPLINE RELIGIOUS STUDIES **EDUCATION** Bates Col, AB; Univ Chicago, BD, MA, PhD. **CAREER** Prof, Univ Detroit Mercy, 70-. **MEMBERSHIPS** Amer Soc Christian Ethics; Amer Acad Rel. **RESEARCH** American civil rights movement, development of American religious liberalism, ethical issues in contemporary society. **CONTACT ADDRESS** Dept of Religious Studies, Univ of Detroit Mercy, 4001 W McNichols Rd, PO Box 19900, Detroit, MI 48219-0900. **EMAIL** PICKERGW@udmercy.edu

PIECK, MANFRED
DISCIPLINE PUBLIC INTERNATIONAL LAW **EDUCATION** NYork Univ, BS, 52; Columbia Univ, JD, 55, LLM, 58. **CAREER** Prof, Creighton Univ; pvt pract NY City, 55-57; fac adv, Int Moot Ct bd; Jessup Int Moot Ct team; Int Law Soc; Ger transl for Vera Lex. **MEMBERSHIPS** US and Int Asn(s), Semiotics Law; Int Soc Legal Philos; Ger-Amer Lawyers Asn; Omaha Comt Coun on For Relations. **SELECTED PUBLICATIONS** Pub(s), Rev Socialist Law; Nebr Law Rev; Amer J Comp Law; Villanova Law Rev; Amer J Int Law; Critic of Institutions, Vol 1, Codes and Customs, Lang, 94. **CONTACT ADDRESS** School of Law, Creighton Univ, 2500 California Plaza, Omaha, NE 68178.

PIEKALKIEWICZ, JAROSLAW
PERSONAL Born 07/24/1926, Poland, m, 1957, 2 children **DISCIPLINE** POLITICAL SCIENCE **EDUCATION** Trinity Col, Ire, BA, 58; Ind Univ, PhD, 63. **CAREER** Lectr, Ind Univ, 63; lectr, US Army Com Col, 67-71, 79-81; asst prof, Univ Kans, 63-68; assoc prof, 68-73; dist lectr, 94-98; prof, 73-00. **HONORS AND AWARDS** Brit Min Edu Schlp; Kosciuszko Found Fel; Ford Found Fel; Ind Univ Fel; Fulbright-Hays Fel, 75, 91; NEH; Sab Lve. **MEMBERSHIPS** TCDA; APSA; AAASS; CSC; KPSA; Amnesty Intl. **RESEARCH** Politics of Ideocracy; politics of Post-Communist Europe; comparative politics; political theory; Western Civilization. **SELECTED PUBLICATIONS** Co-ed, The Soviet Invasion of Czechoslovakia: Is Effects on Eastern Europe, Praeger (NY), 72; auth, Public Opinion Polling in Czechoslovakia 1968-1969: An Analysis of Surveys Conducted During the Dubcek Era, Praeger (NY), 72; auth, Communist Local Government - A Study of Poland, Oh Univ Press (Athens, OH), 75; co-ed, Public Bureaucracies Between Reform and Resistance: Legacies, Trends and Effects in China, USSR, Poland and Yugoslavia, Berg Pub (Oxford, Eng), 91; coauth, Politics of Ideocracy, NY State Univ Press (Albany, NY), 95. **CONTACT ADDRESS** Dept Political Science, Univ of Kansas, Lawrence, Lawrence, KS 66045-0001. **EMAIL** keraj@falcon.cc.ukans.edu

PIERARD, RICHARD VICTOR
PERSONAL Born 05/29/1934, Chicago, IL, m, 1957, 2 children **DISCIPLINE** MODERN EUROPEAN HISTORY, HISTORY OF CHRISTIANITY **EDUCATION** CA State Univ, Los Angeles, BA, 58, MA, 59; Univ IA, PhD, 64. **CAREER** Tchg asst Western civilization, Univ IA, 59-64; from asst prof to assoc prof, 64-72, prof hist, IN State Univ, Terre Haute, 72-00, emer, 00; Vis prof, Greenville Col, 72-73; vis prof, Fuller Theol Seminary, 88, 91; Fulbright prof, Univ Frankfurt, Ger, 84-85; Univ Halle-Wittenberg, Ger, 89-90; vis prof, Gordon Col, 00-01. **HONORS AND AWARDS** Research and Creativity award, In-State Univ, 94; Eternal Flame award, Scholars' conf on the Holocaust and the Churches, 00. **MEMBERSHIPS** AHA; Conf Faith & Hist (secy-treas, 67-); Am Soc Church Hist; Am Soc Missiology. **RESEARCH** Europ polit and relig expansion into Africa since 1800; mod Germany; conservative relig and polit ideas. **SELECTED PUBLICATIONS** Ed, The Revolution of the Candles, Mercer, 96; auth, Shaking the Foundations: World War I, The Western Allies, and German Protestant Missions, International Bulletin of Missionary Research, 98; auth, Informers or Resisters? The East German Secret Police and the Church, Christian Scholars Rev, 98; auth, Christianity Outside North American, In World War II in Asia and the Pacific and the War's Aftermath, Greenwood, 98; auth, Evangelical and Ecumenical: Missionary Leaders in Mainline Protestantism, In Re-forming the Center, Ecrdmans, 98; auth, The Coming of the New Millennium, Evangelical Rev of Theology, 99; auth, The New Millenium Manual, Baker, 99; auth, The Globalization of Baptist History, American Baptist Quarterly, 00. **CONTACT ADDRESS** 633 Hollowbrook Ct, Terre Haute, IN 47803. **EMAIL** CharRichP@aol.com

PIETSCH, PAUL ANDREW
PERSONAL Born 08/08/1929, New York, NY, m, 1950, 4 children **DISCIPLINE** ANATOMY, BIOLOGY, & PHILOSOPHY **EDUCATION** Syracuse Univ, AB, 54; Univ of Pa, PhD, 60. **CAREER** Instr in nursing, School of Nursing, Univ of Pa, 59; instr in anatomy, The Bowman Gray School of Medicine, Wake Forest Col, 60-61; asst prof of anatomy, School of Medicine, School of Dentistry and the Grad School, SUNY, 61-64; senior res molecular biologist, Biochemical Res Lab, The Dow Chemical Co, 64-70; assoc prof, 70-78, chair, Dept of Basic Health Sci, School of Optometry, 75-83, prof, 78-94, prof emer, 94-, Ind Univ. **HONORS AND AWARDS** Medical Journalism Awd, AMA, 72; res featured on 60 Minutes, 73; 14 teaching awards, 73-94. **MEMBERSHIPS** Am Asn of Anatomists; AAAS; Soc Dev Biol (emeritus); Am Federation of Teachers; Am Asn of Univ Profs; Sci Handicapped Asn. **RESEARCH** Neurosciences: memory; developmental biology: regeneration; science journalism: publishing on the World Wide Web. **SELECTED PUBLICATIONS** Auth, Shufflebrain, Houghton-Mifflin, 81; auth, The Mind of a Microbe, Sci Digest, 83; auth, The Effects of Retinoic Acid on Mitosis During Tail and Limb Regeneration in the Axolotl Larva, Ambystoma mexicanum, Roux's Arch Dev Biol, 87; coauth, C.W. Vision and the Skin Camouflage Reactions of Ambystoma Larvae: the Effects of Eye Transplants and Brain Lesions, Brain Res, 85; coauth, The Dermal Melanophore of the Larval Salamander, Ambystoma tigrinum, Cytobios, 92; coauth, Phototaxic Behavior and the Retinotectal Transport of Horseradish Perxidase (HRP) in Surgically Created Cyclopean Salamander Larvae (Ambystoma), Neuroscience Res, 93. **CONTACT ADDRESS** School of Optometry, Indiana Univ, Bloomington, Bloomington, IN 47405-3680. **EMAIL** pietsch@indiana.edu

PILANT, CRAIG WESLEY
PERSONAL Born 08/26/1952, San Francisco, CA **DISCIPLINE** THEOLOGY, AMERICAN RELIGIOUS STUDIES, HISTORICAL THEOLOGY **EDUCATION** Loyola Univ, Chicago, BA, 74; Univ Ill, Chicago, MA, 83; Fordham Univ, MSEd, 87, PhD, 97. **CAREER** Dir of admissions, GSAS, 90-97, asst dean, GSAS, 97-, Fordham Univ. **MEMBERSHIPS** AAR; CHS; NAGAP. **RESEARCH** American religious history; hagiography; music and theology; Social Gospel; Orestes A. Brownson. **SELECTED PUBLICATIONS** Auth, Inward Promptings: Orestes A. Brownson, Outsidership and Roman Catholicism in the United States, 96. **CONTACT ADDRESS** Fordham Univ, 216 Keating Hall, 441 E Fordham Rd, Bronx, NY 10458-5161. **EMAIL** cwphd@aol.com

PILCH, JOHN J.
PERSONAL Born 08/07/1936, Brooklyn, NY, w, 1975 **DISCIPLINE** THEOLOGY **EDUCATION** St. Francis Col, BA (summa cum laude), 59; Marquette Univ, MA, 67, PhD, 72. **CAREER** Inst, Bishop Neuman High School, 64-65; vis prof of Liturgy, Sisters of Saint Casimir, Marymount Col, 65; acting chair and inst, St. Francis Col, 65-68; vis prof of Theology and New Testament, Mount Saint Scholastica Col, 69 & 70; vis prof of Hebrew Scriptures, Marquette Univ, 71; vis prof of New Testament, 71-72, asst prof of Hebrew Scriptures, Univ of Saint Mary of the Lake, 72-74; New Testament Renewal Prog for the Sisters of Providence, Col of Great Falls, 73; vis prof, St. John's Univ; lectr, Milwaukee Area Tech Col, 74-76; prog coord, Uni of Wis, 77-79; adjunct prof, Univ of Wis-Platteville, 78; vis prof, Old St. Mary's Seminary and Univ, 84; vis prof, Theological Inst at the Univ of Albuquerque, 86; speaker, Sinsinawa Biblical Inst, 87; speaker, th Annual Scripture Inst, Col Misericordia, 87; vis prof, Pacific Lutheran Univ, 91; vis prof, Ecumenical Inst of St. Mary's Seminary and Univ, 93; vis prof of Bible, Univ of San Francisco, 95; adjunct asst prof, 93-94, vis asst prof, 94-97, adjunct asst prof of biblical lit, Georgetown Univ, 97-; vis prof of Old Testament, Loyola Univ, 98. **HONORS AND AWARDS** St. Francis Col Scholar, 55-59; Teaching fel, Christ the King Seminary, 59-64; Franciscan Scholar, 66-70; Marquette Univ Scholar, 70-71. **MEMBERSHIPS** Catholic Biblical Asn of Am; Soc of Biblical Lit; Am Acad of Religion; Soc for Ancient Medicine; Soc for Cross-Cultural Res; The Context Group. **RESEARCH** Utilizing social scientific methods and sources to analyze ancient documents; health, sickness and healing in antiquity; secrecy, deception, and lying in the ANE; experiences in alternate reality/altered states of consciousness; aspects of ancient, Eastern Mediterranean cultures. **SELECTED PUBLICATIONS** Auth, Cultural Dictionary of the Bible, Liturgical Press, 99; auth, Healing in the New Testament: Insights from Medical and Mediterranean Anthropology, Fortress Press, 99; auth, The Cultural World of Jesus Sunday by Sunday: Cycle C: Luke, Liturgical Press, 97; auth, The Cultural World of Jesus Sunday by Sunday: Cycle B: Mark, Liturgical Press, 96; auth, The Cultural World of Jesus Sunday by Sunday: Cycle A: Matthew, Liturgical Press, 95; auth, Appearances of the Risen Jesus in Cultural Context: Experiences of Alternate Reality, Biblical Thology Bulletin, 98; auth, A Window into the Biblical World: Caves, The Bible Today, 98; A Window into the Biblical World: Walking on the Sea, The Bible Today, 98; auth, A Window into the Biblical World: The Art of Insult, The Bible Today, 98; auth, A Window into the Biblical World: Games, Amusement, and Sport, The Bible Today, 98; co-ed & contribur, Handbook of Biblical Social Values, Hendrickson Pub, 98. **CONTACT ADDRESS** 1318 Black Friars Rd., Cantonsville, MD 21228. **EMAIL** pilchj@georgetown.edu

PILGRIM, RICHARD B.
PERSONAL Born 01/19/1938, Rochester, MN, m, 2 children **DISCIPLINE** RELIGION **EDUCATION** Hamline Univ, AB, 60; Yale Div Sch, BD, 63; Univ Chicago, PhD, 70. **CAREER** Prof to Asst Dean, Syracuse Univ, 70-. **MEMBERSHIPS** AAR. **CONTACT ADDRESS** Dept Relig, Syracuse Univ, 501 Hall of Lang, Syracuse, NY 13244-1170. **EMAIL** rbpilgri@syr.edu

PILGRIM, WALTER
PERSONAL Born 03/26/1934, St Paul, MN, m, 1957, 3 children **DISCIPLINE** RELIGION **EDUCATION** Wartburg Col, BA, 56; Wartburg Theol Sem, ThM, 60; Princeton Theol Sem, PhD, 66. **CAREER** Exec Dir, Lutheran Inst Theol Educ, 73-93; Prof, Pac Lutheran Univ, 71-99. **HONORS AND AWARDS** Lutheran World Fedn Scholar, 78-79. **MEMBERSHIPS** Soc Bibl Lit. **RESEARCH** New Testament, biblical studies, apocalyptic literature. **SELECTED PUBLICATIONS** Auth, Good News to the Poor, 88; auth, Unit 20: Revelation Search Series, 88; auth, The Pastoral Epistles: Inspire Series, 98; auth, Uneasy Neighbors: Church and State in the New Testament, 99. **CONTACT ADDRESS** Dept Relig, Pacific Lutheran Univ, 12180 Park Ave S, Tacoma, WA 98447-0001. **EMAIL** pilgrimew@plu.edu

PINCHES, CHARLES R.
PERSONAL Born 11/06/1955, Niagara Falls, NY, m, 1978, 4 children **DISCIPLINE** RELIGION **EDUCATION** Wheaton Col, BA, 76; Univ Notre Dame, MA, 83; PhD, 84. **CAREER** Adj Prof, Univ Ark, 85-89; Asst Prof, Univ Cent Ark, 84-89; Visiting Assoc Prof, Princeton, 91-92; Assoc Prof to Prof, Univ Scranton, 90-. **MEMBERSHIPS** Soc of Christian ethics; Am Acad of Relig; Soc Christian Philos; AR Philos Asn; Mid-South Philos Asn. **RESEARCH** Christian ethics. **SELECTED PUBLICATIONS** Auth, "Action," in The Encyclopedia of Bioethics rev ed, (Macmillan, 95), 56-63; auth, "Cookbooks: Journey Through the Wilderness," Pro Ecclesia, (97): 488-495; co-auth, Christians Among the Virtues: conversations with Ancient and Modern Ethics, Univ Notre Dame Press, 97; auth, "Ecominded: Faith and Action," The Christian Century, (98): 755-757; auth, "Virtue," in Oxford Companion to Christian Thought, Oxford Univ Press, forthcoming. **CONTACT ADDRESS** Dept Religious Studies, Univ of Scranton, 800 Linden St, Scranton, PA 18510-2429.

PINKARD, TERRY
DISCIPLINE PHILOSOPHY **EDUCATION** Univ Tex, BA; SUNY, Stone Brook, PhD, 74. **CAREER** Prof. **RESEARCH** Ethics, political philosophy; philosophy of history; German idealism. **SELECTED PUBLICATIONS** Auth, Hegel's Phenomenology: The Sociality of Reason, Cambridge, 94; auth, Hegel: A Biography, Cambridge, 00. **CONTACT ADDRESS** Dept of Philosophy, Northwestern Univ, Brentano Hall, 1818 Hinman Ave, Evanston, IL 60208.

PINN, ANTHONY B.
PERSONAL Born 05/12/1964, Buffalo, NY **DISCIPLINE** RELIGIOUS STUDIES **EDUCATION** Columbia Univ, BA, 86; Harvard Divinity School, Mdiv, 89; Harvard Univ, MA, PhD, 94. **CAREER** Macalester Col, 94-present. **MEMBERSHIPS** AAR, Soc for the study of Black Rel. **RESEARCH** Liberation Theology, Humanism, Popular Culture, non Christian Religions. **SELECTED PUBLICATIONS** Auth, Why Lord?, Suffering and Evil in Black Theology, Continuum Publishing Group, 95; Varieties of African American Religious Experience, Fortress Press, 98; coed, Studies in African-American Religious Thought and Life, Trinity Press International, forthcoming, 99; Studies in The History of African-American Religions, Univ Press of Florida, forthcoming, 2000; Protest Thought in The African Methodist Episcopal Church, 1863-1939, Vol 1, Univ Of Tennessee Press, spring, 99; Anybody There?: Reflections on African American Humanism, Religious Humanism, vol xxxi, 97. **CONTACT ADDRESS** Dept of Religious Studies, Macalester Col, 1600 Grand Ave, Saint Paul, MN 55105. **EMAIL** pinn@macalester.edu

PINTCHMAN, TRACY
PERSONAL Born 09/21/1962, White Plains, NY, m, 1995, 1 child **DISCIPLINE** RELIGIOUS STUDIES **EDUCATION** Cornell Univ, BA, 84; Boston Univ, MA, 87; Univ CA, Santa Barbara, PhD, 92. **CAREER** Teaching fel and lectr, 85-87, Boston Univ; teaching asst and lectr, 87-91, Univ CA, Santa Barbara; vis prof, 96, Northwestern Univ; dir, Religion, Culture, and Society Minor Program, Loyola Univ Chicago, 97-; Assoc Prof, 98-. **HONORS AND AWARDS** Graduation Magna Cum Laude with distinction in all subjects, Cornell Univ, 84; Loyola Endowment for the Humanities Faculty Development Awd, 94; Loyola Summer Research Fel, 97; Sujack Awd for Teaching Excellence, Loyola Univ Chicago, 97; Amer Insti of Indian Studies Senior Research Fel, 97; Natl Endowment for the Humanities Fel, 98. **MEMBERSHIPS** Amer Acad of Religion, Assn for Asian Studies. **RESEARCH** Hindu Studies **SELECTED PUBLICATIONS** Auth, The Ambiguous Female: The Conception of Female Gender in the Brahmanical Tradition and the Roles of Women in India, Ethical and Political Dilemmas of Modern India, 93; auth, The Rise of the Goddess in the Hindu Tradition, 94; auth, Gender Complementarity and Gender Hierarchy in Puranic Accounts of Creation, Journal of the American Academy of Religion, 98; auth, contributions to this volume include two chapters, Seeking Mahadevi: Constructing the Identities of the Hindu Great Goddess, forthcoming; auth, Is The Hindu Goddess Tradition a Good Resource for Western Feminism? Working Goddesses, forthcoming. **CONTACT ADDRESS** Dept of Theology, Loyola Univ, Chicago, 6525 N Sheridan Rd, Chicago, IL 60620. **EMAIL** tpintd@luc.edu

PINZINO, JANE M.
PERSONAL Born 04/27/1958, Chicago, IL, s **DISCIPLINE** CHRISTIANITY **EDUCATION** Colgate Univ, BA, 81; Duke Univ, MDiv, 86; Univ Pa, PhD, 96. **CAREER** Instr Bibl Stud, 88-91 & 92-94 & 95-96, tchg asst, 90-92, tchg & res asst, Univ Pa, 94-96; peer evaluator, Thomas Jefferson Univ, 92-96; vis asst prof Relig Stud, Grinnell Col, 96-97; asst prof Relig, Univ Puget Sound, 97-. **HONORS AND AWARDS** Merit Scholar, Duke Univ, 84-86; Boardman fel, Univ Pa, 92-95; Dean's Scholar, Univ Pa, 94-95. **MEMBERSHIPS** Am Acad of Relig; exec comt bd-mem, Mid-Atlantic Region, 92-95; women's caucus co-moderator, Mid-Atlantic Region, 94-96. **RESEARCH** Medieval canon law; religions of Near Eastern origin and women and religion. **SELECTED PUBLICATIONS** Auth, Speaking of Angels: A 15th-Century Bishop in Defense of Joan of Arc's Mystical Voices, Fresh Verdicts on Joan of Arc, Garland Press, 96; Valerie Hotchkiss, Clothes Make the Man: Female Cross-Dressing in Medieval Europe, Arthuriana, vol 7.4, 98; ed, Some Skeptical Thoughts About Active Euthanasia and Assisted Suicide, Relig Stud Dept of Univ Pa; co-ed, The Culture of Disbelief, Relig Stud Dept of Univ Pa. **CONTACT ADDRESS** Dept of Relig, Univ of Puget Sound, 1500 North Warner, Tacoma, WA 98416. **EMAIL** jpinzino@ups.edu

PIPER, ADRIAN MARGARET SMITH
PERSONAL Born 09/20/1948, New York, NY, s **DISCIPLINE** PHILOSOPHY **EDUCATION** School of Visual Arts, NYork, AA, fine arts, 69; City Col of NYork, BA, philos, 74; Harvard Univ, Cambridge, MA, philos, 77, PhD, philos, 81. **CAREER** Harvard University, graduate teaching asst, 76-77; Univ of Mich, asst prof, 79-86; Georgetown Univ, assoc prof, 86-88; Univ of Calif, San Diego, assoc prof, 88-90; Wellesley Col, prof, 90-. **HONORS AND AWARDS** Sperling Prize for Excellence in Philos, 74, Phi Beta Kappa Medal for the Best Honors Essay in the Social Sciences, 74, Res Honors in Philos, 74, City Col of New York; First Prize in Drawing, Annual Student Exhibition, 68, School of the Visual Arts; Stanford Univ, Mellon Post-Doctoral Res Fel, 82-84; Woodrow Wilson International Scholars' Fellowship, 89-90; NEA, Visual Artists' Fellowship, 79, 82; Guggenheim Fellowship, 88-89; Awds in the Visual Arts Fellowship, 90; California Institute of the Arts, Honorary Doctorate of Arts, 91; NEH Coll Teacher's Res, Fel, 98; Getty Res Inst, Distinguished Scholar, 98-99. **MEMBERSHIPS** Am Philos Asn, 1979-; AAUP, 1979-; Asn for Legal and Political Philos, 1979-; Col Art Asn, 1983-; North Am Kant Soc, 1979-. **RESEARCH** Metaethics; moral psychology; history of ethics; Kant's metaphysics; Kant's ethics; Kant's aesthetics; philosophy of social science; philosophy of law; Indian philosophy (Vedanta, Yoga, Samkhya); political philosophy; philosophy of action. **SELECTED PUBLICATIONS** Auth, "Hume on Rational Final Ends," Philosophy Research Archives XIV(88): 193-228; auth, "Higher-Order Discrimination," in Identity, Character and Morality, eds. Amelie O. Rorty and Owen Flanagan, (Cambridge, Mass: MIT Press, 90): 285-309;

auth, "Seeing Things," Southern Journal of Philosophy XXIX, Supplementary Volume: Moral Epistemology, (90): 29-60; auth, "Impartiality, Compassion, and Modal Imagination," Ethics 101, 4, Symposium on Impartiality and Ethical Theory, (91): 726-757; auth, "Government Support for Unconventional Works of Art," in Culture and Democracy: Social and Ethical Issues in Public Support for the Arts and Humanities, ed. Andrew Buchwalter, (Boulder: Westview Press, 92); auth, "Xenophobia and Kantian Rationalism," Philosophical Forum XXIV, 1-3, 92-93; auth, "Two Kinds of Discrimination," Yale Jouranl of Criticism 6, 1, (93): 25-74; auth, "Making Sense of Value," Ehtics 106, 2, (96): 525-537; auth, "Kant on the Objectivity of the Moral Law," in Reclaiming the History of Ehtics: Essays for John Rawls, eds. Andrews Reath, Christine M. Korsgaard, and Barbara Herman, (Cambridge Univ Press, 97); auth, "The Enterprise of Socratic Metaethics," in Nonwhite Women and Philosophy: A Critical Reader, ed. Naomi Zack, (Blackwell, 00). **CONTACT ADDRESS** Dept of Philosophy, Wellesley Col, 106 Central St, Wellesley, MA 02181-8249.

PIPER, RICHARD
PERSONAL Born 10/02/1946, Sewickley, PA, m, 1970, 1 child **DISCIPLINE** POLITICAL SCIENCE **EDUCATION** Penn State Univ, BA, 68; Cornell Univ, MA, 71; PhD, 72. **CAREER** prof, Backburn Col, 72-76; asst prof to prof, Univ Tampa, 76-. **HONORS AND AWARDS** Louise Loy Hunter Teaching Awd; Ful Awd; Sears-Roebuck Outstanding Educator Awd. **MEMBERSHIPS** Am Pol Sci Asn, Nat Col Hon Coun, Southern Reg Hon Counc, FL Col Honors Coun. **RESEARCH** West European Politics, American politics. **SELECTED PUBLICATIONS** Auth, Ideologies and Institutions: American Conservative and Liberal Governance Prescriptions since 1933, Rowman & Littlefield, 97; auth, "The European Parliament Simulation," Ecsa Review (Spring 2000). **CONTACT ADDRESS** Dept Soc Sci, The Univ of Tampa, 401 W Kennedy Blvd, Tampa, FL 33606-1450.

PIPPIN, TINA
PERSONAL Born 09/10/1956, Kinston, NC, m, 1984, 1 child **DISCIPLINE** RELIGIOUS STUDIES **EDUCATION** Marshill Col, BA, 78; Candler School of Theol, MDiv, 80; S Baptist Theol Sem, ThM, 82, PhD, 87. **CAREER** Asst prof to assoc prof, chair, Agnes Scott Col, 89- **RESEARCH** Bible & culture; critical theory & ethics **SELECTED PUBLICATIONS** Auth, The Bible and Culture Collective, The Postmodern Bible, Yale Univ Press, 95; Death and Desire: The Rhetoric of Gender in the Apocalypse of John, John Knox Press, 92; coed, The Monstrous and the Unspeakable: The Bible as Fantastic Literature, Sheffield Acad Press, 97; Violence, Utopia, and the Kingdom of god, Routledge Press, 98; auth, Apocalyptic bodies: The Biblical End of the World in Text and Image, Routledge, 99. **CONTACT ADDRESS** Dept of Religious Studies, Agnes Scott Col, 141 E College Ave, Decatur, GA 30030. **EMAIL** tpippin@agnesscott.edu

PIRAU, VASILE
PERSONAL Born 02/20/1955, Fagaras, Romania, m, 1989, 3 children **DISCIPLINE** PHILOSOPHY **EDUCATION** Univ of Bucharest, ABD, MA, 80; Michigan State Univ, PhD, 98. **CAREER** Prof, philos, Caragiale Col, Bucharest, 80-85; lectr, hum, Norwalk Commun Col, 91; adj prof, hum, Lansing Commun Col, 93; tchg asst, instr, philos, Michigan State Univ, 92, 93, 94, 95, 97; adj prof, hum, Mott Commun Col, 98-99; instr, Washtenaw Commun Col, 00-; vis asst prof, Mich State Univ, 00-. **HONORS AND AWARDS** Magna Cum Laude, 80; Michigan State Col of Arts and LettsVarg-Sullivan Awd, outstanding grad stud, Dean's Awd. **MEMBERSHIPS** APA. **RESEARCH** Philosophy of social sciences; continental philosophy; philosophy of science. **SELECTED PUBLICATIONS** Auth, Ways of Understanding in Social Sciences, Cultura Militans, 86; auth, The Relationship between Age and Creativity from Cognitive Sociology of Science Perspective, Youth Problems, 87; auth, Social and Behavioral Factors Responsible for the Idiosyncrasy toward the Implementation of Technological Innovations, Youth and Educ, 88; auth, Are There Irrational People or Only Mistranslated Ones?, Sci Bull of Baia Mare Univ, 96. **CONTACT ADDRESS** 1313 Daylilly Dr., Holt, MI 48842-8735. **EMAIL** pirauvas@pilot.msu.edu

PITCHER, GEORGE WILLARD
PERSONAL Born 05/19/1925, Newark, NJ **DISCIPLINE** PHILOSOPHY **EDUCATION** US Naval Acad, BS, 46; Harvard Univ, MA, 54, PhD, 57. **CAREER** From instr to assoc prof, 56-70, Prof Philos, Princeton Univ, 70-81, Emer Prof Philos, Princeton Univ 81-. **HONORS AND AWARDS** Guggenheim fel, 65-66. **MEMBERSHIPS** Am Philos Asn. **RESEARCH** Epistemology; Wittgenstein; philos of mind. **SELECTED PUBLICATIONS** Auth, The Philosophy of Wittgenstein, 64 & ed, Truth, 64, Prentice-Hall; ed, Wittgenstein: A Collection of Critical Essays, 66 & co-ed, Ryle, 70, Doubleday; auth, A Theory of Perception, Princeton Univ, 71; Berkeley, Routledge & Kegan, 77. **CONTACT ADDRESS** Dept of Philosophy, Princeton Univ, Princeton, NJ 08544.

PITOFSKY, ROBERT
PERSONAL Born 12/27/1929, Paterson, NJ, m, 1961, 3 children **DISCIPLINE** LAW **EDUCATION** NYork Univ, BA, 51; Columbia Univ, LLB, 54. **CAREER** Prof law, NY Univ, 64-70; dir, Bur Consumer Protection, Fed Trade Comn, 70-73 ; prof law, Georgetown Univ, 73-77; comnr, Fed Trade Comn, 78-81; Prof Law, Georgetown Univ, 81-. **RESEARCH** Antitrust and economic regulation. **SELECTED PUBLICATIONS** Coauth, Antitrust Law: Cases and Materials, Found Press, 67; auth, Joint ventures under the antitrust laws, Harvard Law Rev, 3/69; coauth, Trade Regulation: Cases and Materials, Found Press, 75; Beyond Nader: Consumer protection and the regulation of advertising, Harvard Law Rev, 2/77; Proposals for Revised United-states Merger Enforcement in a Global Economy, Georgetown Law J, Vol 0081, 1992; the Scholar as Advocate - Comment/, J of Legal Education, Vol 0043, 1993; Healy,timothy,s. - In-memoriam, Georgetown Law J, Vol 0081, 1993. **CONTACT ADDRESS** Law Center, Georgetown Univ, 600 New Jersey NW, Washington, DC 20001-2022.

PITT, DAVID
DISCIPLINE PHILOSOPHY OF LANGUAGE, FORMAL SEMANTICS, AND THE PHILOSOPHY OF MIND **EDUCATION** CUNY, PhD, 94. **CAREER** Vis asst prof, Univ Nebr, Lincoln. **SELECTED PUBLICATIONS** Published in music and the philosophy of mind. **CONTACT ADDRESS** Univ of Nebraska, Lincoln, Lincoln, NE 68588-0417.

PITT, JACK
PERSONAL Born 09/14/1928, Montreal, PQ, Canada, m, 1953, 2 children **DISCIPLINE** PHILOSOPHY **EDUCATION** Sir George Williams, BSc, 50; McGill, BA, 52, MA, 53; Yale Univ, PhD, 57. **CAREER** Cal State Univ-Fresno, 57-97. **MEMBERSHIPS** Am Philos Asn. **RESEARCH** Analytical Marxism; Logical atomism. **SELECTED PUBLICATIONS** Russell on Religion, Critical Essays, Routledge. **CONTACT ADDRESS** 1135 E Santa Ana, Fresno, CA 93704. **EMAIL** jpitt@csufresno.edu

PITT, JOSEPH C.
PERSONAL Born 09/12/1944, Hempstead, NY, m, 1966 **DISCIPLINE** PHILOSOPHY **EDUCATION** Col of William and Mary, AB, 66; Duke Univ, advan study, 96-98; Univ Western Ontario, MA, 70, PhD, 72. **CAREER** Teaching fel, Univ Western Ontario, 70-71; instr, Va Polytech Inst & State Univ, 71-72; asst prof, philos, Va Polytechnic Inst & State Univ, 72-78; vis asst prof, Univ Pittsburgh, 74; assoc prof, philos, Va Polytechnic Inst & State Univ, 78-83; adjunct prof, Ctr for the Study of Sci in Soc, 81-; prof, philos, Va Polytech Inst & State Univ, 83-. **HONORS AND AWARDS** Eta Sigma Phi, 66; Can Cound Doctoral fel, 70, 71; teaching excellence award, Va Polytech Inst & State Univ, 74, 75, 76, 77, 85; acad of teaching excellence, Va Polytech Inst & State Univ, 78, 85; sr vis fel, Ctr for Philos of Sci, Univ Pittsburgh, 84; alumni teaching award, Va Polytech Inst & State Univ, 85; acad of univ svc, Va Polytech Inst & State Univ, 86; Sigma Xi, 88; res assignment, Va Polytech Inst & State Univ, 91; trustee, Amer Philos Inst, 97; Who's Who Amer Men & Women of Sci; Who's Who in Tech. **MEMBERSHIPS** Amer Philos Asn; Amer Asn for the Advan of Sci; Can Soc for Hist and Philos of Sci; Hist of Sci Asn; Intl Soc for Hist, Philos, and Social Studies of Bio; Philos of Sci Asn; Sigma Xi; Soc for Philos and Tech; Soc for Hist of Tech; Southern Soc for Philos and Psychol. **SELECTED PUBLICATIONS** Auth, Thinking About Technology, Seven Bridges Press, 00; auth, Philosophical Methodologies and the Philosophy of Technology, Soc for Philos and Tech Quart Elec Jour, 97; rev, Galilio Courtier, Physis, Nuova Serie, 97; auth, Developments in the Philosophy of Science 1965-1995, The Encycl of Philos, suppl vol, Macmillan, 97; ed, New Directions in the Philosophy of Technology, Philos & Tech, 95; rev, The Discovery of Kepler's Laws; The Interaction of Science, Philosophy, and Religion, Isis, 95; ed, New Directions in the Philosophy of Technology, Philos & Tech, Kluwer, 95; auth, Galileo, Human Knowledge and the Book of Nature, Kluwer, 92; auth, Pictures, Images & Conceptual Change, Kluwer, 81; auth, Theories of Explanation, Oxford, 88; . **CONTACT ADDRESS** Dept. of Philosophy, Virginia Polytech Inst and State Univ, Blacksburg, VA 24061-0126. **EMAIL** jcpitt@vt.edu

PITTS, BILL
PERSONAL Born 12/27/1937, Winfield, KS, m, 1961, 2 children **DISCIPLINE** RELIGION; CHURCH HISTORY **EDUCATION** Baylor Univ, BA, 60; Vanderbilt Divinity School, MD, 63; Vanderbilt, PhD, 69. **CAREER** Instr, Mercer Univ, 66-69; asst prof, Houston Baptist Univ, 69-70; assoc prof, Dallas Baptist Univ, 70-75; assoc prof & prof, Baylor Univ, 75- . **HONORS AND AWARDS** Luke Acts Prize & Hist Prize, Vanderbilt, 63; Lilly Scholar, 64-65; Piper Prof Nominee, 74; Mortar Bd Distinguished Prof, 93. **MEMBERSHIPS** Soc Study Christian Spirituality; Am Acad Relig; Am Soc Church Hist; Nat Asn Baptist Prof Relig; Conf Faith & Hist. **RESEARCH** New religious movements; historiography; spirituality; Baptist history. **SELECTED PUBLICATIONS** Auth, Millennial Spirituality of the Branch Davidians, Christian Spirituality Bull, 93; The Mount Carmel Davidians: Adventist Reformers, 1935-1959, Syzgy, 93; The Davidian Tradition, The Coun Soc for Study Relig Bull, 93; The Davidian Tradition, From the Ashes: Making Sense of Waco, Rowman & Littlefield Publ, 94; Davidians and Branch Dividians: 1929-1987, Armageddon in Waco, Univ Chicago Press, 95; Davidians and Branch Davidians, New Cath Encycl, Cath Univ Press, 95; The Persistence of the Millennium, Medieval Perspectives, 97. **CONTACT ADDRESS** Religion Dept, Baylor Univ, Waco, Waco, TX 76798. **EMAIL** william_pitts@baylor.edu

PLACHER, WILLIAM C.
PERSONAL Born 04/28/1948, Peoria, IL, s **DISCIPLINE** THEOLOGY **EDUCATION** Wabash Col, AB, 70; Yale Univ, M Phil, 74, PhD, 75. **CAREER** Wabash Col, inst, asst prof, assoc prof, prof, dept ch, 72-. **HONORS AND AWARDS** Danforth Grad Fellow. **MEMBERSHIPS** APA, AAR. **RESEARCH** Christian Theology. **SELECTED PUBLICATIONS** Auth, A History of Christian Theology, Westminster, 83; auth, Readings in the History of Christian Theology, Westminster, 88; auth, Unapologetic Theology, Westminster John Knox, 89; Belonging to God, coauth, Westminster John Knox, 92; auth, Narratives of a Vulnerable God, Westminster John Knox, 94; auth, The Domestication of Transcendence, Westminster John Knox, 96; Why Are We Here?, coauth, Trinity Press Intl, 98. **CONTACT ADDRESS** Dept of Philosophy, Wabash Col, Crawfordsville, IN 47933. **EMAIL** placherw@wabash.edu

PLANEAUX, CHRISTOPHER
PERSONAL Born 04/10/1967, Atlanta, GA, m, 1996 **DISCIPLINE** PHILOSOPHY; HISTORY; CLASSICS GREEK **EDUCATION** Ind Univ, AB, 93, AB, 94; Univ Cambridge, MPhil, 97. **CAREER** Dept For Lang, Ind Univ **HONORS AND AWARDS** Fac Develop Mentorship grant, Ind Univ, 94; Sur Grant, Ind Univ, 93; Univ Cambridge Res Grant, 94. Thelander Mem Awd, Ind Univ, 94. **MEMBERSHIPS** Amer Philol Asn; Class Asn Mid W & S; Asn Ancient Hist; Soc Greek Philos; Univ London Inst Class Studies; Cambridge Philol Soc; Darwin Col Soc. **RESEARCH** Dramatic settings of Platos Dialogues; Athens (ca.470-399 BCE); Peloponnesian War; Thirty Tyrants; Athenian calendar; Athenian Cultic societies; Philosophical schools; Alcibiades. **SELECTED PUBLICATIONS** Auth, Socrates, Alcibiades, and Plato's: Does the Charmides Have an Historical setting?, Mnemosyne, 99; coauth, "Who's Who in the Timaeus-Critias and Why," Review of Metaphysics, 98; auth, "The Date of Bendis' Entry into Attica," Classical Jrnl, 00. **CONTACT ADDRESS** Dept of Foreign Languages & Cultures, Indiana Univ-Purdue Univ, Indianapolis, 425 Univ Blvd, Indianapolis, IN 46202. **EMAIL** cplaneau@iupui.edu

PLANK, KARL A.
PERSONAL Born 11/18/1951, Raleigh, NC, m, 1989, 1 child **DISCIPLINE** RELIGION **EDUCATION** Hanover Col, BA, 74; Vanderbilt Univ, M.Div, 77, MA, 80, PhD, 83. **CAREER** From instr to asst prof to assoc prof to prof to JW Cannon prof, 82-, Davidson Col; Dept Chair, 96-. **HONORS AND AWARDS** The Founder's Medal, The Divinity School, Vanderbilt Univ, 77; Thomas Carter Prize for Non Fiction Prose, 93. **MEMBERSHIPS** Soc Biblical Lit, Am Acad Relig, Coun for Liberal Arts Depts of Relig, Int Thomas Merton Soc. **RESEARCH** Biblical intertextuality and hermeneutics; modern Jewish lit. **SELECTED PUBLICATIONS** Auth, Paul and The Irony of Affliction, 87; "Thomas Merton and Hannah Arendt: Contemplation after Eichmann," Merton Annual, 90; "The Eclipse of Difference: Merton's Encounter with Judaism," Cistercian Studies, 93; Mother of the Wire Fence; Inside and Outside the Holocaust, 94; "Ascent to Darker Hills: Psalm 121 and its Poetic Revision," Lit and Theol, 97; auth, "Reynolds Price and the Struggle of 'People in Rooms,'" The Quarterly Review, 99; auth, "Thomas Merton and the Ethical Edge of Contemplation," in Anglican Theological Review, forthcoming. **CONTACT ADDRESS** Dept of Religion, Davidson Col, PO Box 1719, Davidson, NC 28036. **EMAIL** kaplank@davidson.edu

PLANTINGA, ALVIN
DISCIPLINE PHILOSOPHY **EDUCATION** Calvin Col, AB, 54; Univ Mich, MA, 55; Yale Univ, PhD, 58. **CAREER** Prof. **RESEARCH** Epistemology; metaphysics; philosophy of religion. **SELECTED PUBLICATIONS** Auth, Justification in the 20th Century, 90; Warrant: the Current Debate, 93; Warrant and Proper Function, 93; Methodological Naturalism?, 95; auth, Warranted Christian Belief, New York: Oxford Univ Press, 00. **CONTACT ADDRESS** Philosophy Dept, Univ of Notre Dame, 336/7 O'Shaughnessy, Notre Dame, IN 46556. **EMAIL** plantinga.1@nd.edu

PLANTINGA, RICHARD
PERSONAL Born 01/13/1959, Winnipeg, Canada, m, 1982, 3 children **DISCIPLINE** RELIGIOUS STUDIES **EDUCATION** Calvin Col, AB, 82; McMaster Univ, MA, 85; PhD, 90. **CAREER** Asst prof to tenural prof relig, Calvin Col, 90- . **HONORS AND AWARDS** Soc Sci Hum Res Council of Can fel; Deutschor Akademischer Austanschdienst fel. **MEMBERSHIPS** Am Acad Relig. **RESEARCH** Christian theology & religious pluralism, Approaches to the study of religion. **SELECTED PUBLICATIONS** Ed, Christianity and Plurality, Blackwell Publ, 99. **CONTACT ADDRESS** Dept Relig, Calvin Col, 3201 Burton St SE, Grand Rapids, MI 49546-4301. **EMAIL** plar@calvin.edu

PLATT, DAVID S.
PERSONAL Born 04/22/1924, China, m, 1969 **DISCIPLINE** PHILOSOPHY **EDUCATION** Univ Penn, PhD, 58. **CAREER** Prof Emeritus Philos, Wilson Col, 33 years. **HONORS AND AWARDS** Lindback disting tchg awd, 69. **MEMBERSHIPS** APA; Metaphysical Soc; N Am Nietzsche Soc; Hegel Soc. **RESEARCH** Philosophy of Religion. **SELECTED PUBLICATIONS** Auth, Intimations of Divinity, 89; The Gift of Contingency, 91. **CONTACT ADDRESS** Dept of Philosophy, Wilson Col, 914 Wallace Ave, Chambersburg, PA 17201.

PLATT, ELIZABETH ELLAN
PERSONAL Born 02/11/1936, Orange, NJ, s **DISCIPLINE** THEOLOGY **EDUCATION** College of Wooster, Ohio, BA, 57; Columbia Univ and Union Theol Sem, MA, 61; Harvard Univ, PhD, 73. **CAREER** Asst prof Bibl Stud, Rutgers Col, State Univ NJ, 73-80; assoc pastor, Presbyterian Church, Westfield, NJ, 81-88; assoc prof, Bibl Stud, 88-98, Prof of Old Testament, 98- , Univ Dubuque Theol Sem. **HONORS AND AWARDS** Vis prof in archaeol res, Andrews Univ, Mich, 76-83. **MEMBERSHIPS** Am Acad Relig; Am Schools of Oriental Res. **RESEARCH** Biblical archaeology; ancient Near Eastern jewelry; Old and New Testament studies; women in ancient Near East; Object Registry for Madaba Plains project, Jordan. **SELECTED PUBLICATIONS** Auth, The Ministry of Mary of Bethany, Theol Today, 74; auth, Jewelry, Anchor Bible Dictionary, 95; Madaba Plains Project, Jordan publications in jewelry and objects. **CONTACT ADDRESS** Div of Biblical Studies, Univ of Dubuque, 2000 University Ave, Dubuque, IA 52001-5099.

PLESTINA, DIJANA
DISCIPLINE POLITICAL SCIENCE **EDUCATION** Carleton Univ, Canada, BA, 70, MA, 73; Univ Calif-Berkeley, PhD, 87. **CAREER** Assoc prof. **RESEARCH** Economic development and democratization in East and West Europe, and the former Soviet Union. **SELECTED PUBLICATIONS** Auth, Regional Development in Communist Yugoslavia: Success, Failure and Consequences. **CONTACT ADDRESS** Dept of Russ, The Col of Wooster, Wooster, OH 44691.

PLOTKIN, HOWARD
DISCIPLINE PHILOSOPHY **EDUCATION** Univ Mich, BA, 64; Univ Wis, MA, 66; Johns Hopkins Univ, PhD, 72. **CAREER** Prof **RESEARCH** History of Science; history of astronomy and astrophysics; history of meteoritics; history of American science; institutional history. **SELECTED PUBLICATIONS** Auth, "Edward C. Pickering," Journal for the History of Astronomy, vol. 21, (90): 47-58; auth, "Harvard College Observatory's Boyden Station in Peru: Origin and Formative Years, 1879-1898," Mundializacion de la ciencia y cultura nacional, in Actas del Congreso Internacional, "Ciencia, descubrimiento y mundo colonial," (93): 689-705; auth, "William H. Pickering in Jamaica: The Founding of Woodlawn and Studies of Mars," Journal for the History of Astronomy, vol. 24, (93): 101-122; auth, The Port Orford Meteorite Hoax," Sky and Telescope, vol. 86, no. 3, (93): 35-38; auth, The Port Orford Meteorite Hoaz, in The Port Orford, Oregon, Meteroite Mystery, Smithsonian Contributions to the Earth Sciences, no. 31, (93): 24; auth, "The Henderson Network vs. the Prairie Network: The Dispute Between the Smithsonian's National Museum and the Smithsonian Astrophysical Observatory Over the Acquisition and Control of Meteorites, 1960-1970," Journal of the Royal Astronomical Society of Canada, vol. 91, (97): 32-38. **CONTACT ADDRESS** Dept of Philosophy, Univ of Western Ontario, London, ON, Canada N6A 5B8. **EMAIL** hplotkin@julian.uwo.ca

PLUHAR, EVELYN BEGLEY
PERSONAL Born 07/08/1947, Harlan, KY, m, 1971 **DISCIPLINE** PHILOSOPHY **EDUCATION** Univ Denver, BA, 69; Univ Mich, PhD(philos), 76. **CAREER** Teaching asst philos, Univ Mich, 70-73; instr, Grinnell Col, 73-76, asst prof, 76-78; Asst Prof Philos, PA State Univ, Fayette, 78-. **HONORS AND AWARDS** Horan H Rackham Prize, Univ Mich, 71. **MEMBERSHIPS** Am Philos Asn; Soc Study Ethics & Animals; Am Soc Aesthetics; Am Asn Univ Women. **RESEARCH** Ethics; philosophy of science; philosophy of mind; philosophy of mind; ethics. **SELECTED PUBLICATIONS** Auth, Emergence and Reduction, Studies in the History and Philosophy of Science, 78; Physicalism and the identity theory, J Critical Analysis, 79; Preferential hiring and unjust sacrifice, Philos Forum, Vol XII, 81; Must an opponent of Animal Rights also be an opponent of Human Rights?, Inquiry, 81; On Replaceability, Ethics and Animals, 82; The Justification of an Environmental Ethic, Environmental Ethics; On Vegetarianism, Morality, and Science - a Counter Reply, J of Agricultural & Environmental Ethics, Vol 0006, 1993. **CONTACT ADDRESS** Dept of Philos, Pennsylvania State Univ, Fayette, P O Box 519, Uniontown, PA 15401-0519.

PLUHAR, WERNER S.
PERSONAL Born 05/29/1940, Berlin, Germany, m, 2000, 2 children **DISCIPLINE** PHILOSOPHY **EDUCATION** Univ of Calif Berk, BA, 68; Univ Mich, Ann Arbor, PhD, 73. **CAREER** Grinnell Col, asst prof, 73-78; Penn State Univ, lectr, asst prof, affil prof, 78-. **HONORS AND AWARDS** Horace H. Rackman Prize, PSU, Eleanor L. Coldren Exllence in Teaching Award; PSU, Res and Scholarly Excellence Award. **MEMBERSHIPS** APA, Phi Beta Kappa. **RESEARCH** Immanuel Kant; ethics; aesthetics. **SELECTED PUBLICATIONS** Auth, Translation of Immanuel Kant's Critique of Judgment 1790, Indianapolis and Cambridge MA, Hackett Pub Co, 87; Auth, Translation of Immanuel Kant's Critique of Pure Reason of 1781,1787, Indianapolis & Cambridge MA: Hackett Pub Co, 96; auth, Abridgment of my translation of Immaunuel Kandt's Critique of Pure Reason, Indianapolis & Cambridge, MA: Hackett Pub Co, 99. **CONTACT ADDRESS** Dept of Philosophy, Pennsylvania State Univ, Fayette, One Univ Dr, Uniontown, PA 15401. **EMAIL** WPluhar@psu.edu

PODET, ALLEN HOWARD
PERSONAL Born 12/18/1934, Cleveland, OH, m, 1981 **DISCIPLINE** MODERN JEWISH HISTORY **EDUCATION** Univ Ill, Urbana, BA, 56; Hebrew Union Col, BHL, 58, MA, HL, 62, DHL, 64; Univ Wash, PhD(hist), 79. **CAREER** Lectr, Dept Near Eastern Lang & Lit, Univ Wash, Seattle, 70-73; asst prof, 69-73, prof, Dept Philos & Relig Studies, State Univ NYork Col Buffalo, 80-, Consult, Jewish Collection, Folklore Archives, Buffalo, 80-; contrib ed, Am Books by Europ Judaism J, 77-; Univ lectr, Univ Vienna, Austria, 98. **HONORS AND AWARDS** Fulbright-Hays fel, Jerusalem, 95-96. **MEMBERSHIPS** Cent Conf Am Rabbis; Asn Jewish Studies. **RESEARCH** Rabbinics. **SELECTED PUBLICATIONS** Auth, The Sephardim of Seattle, Jewish Digest, 9/68; Secular studies and religious uniqueness: A view of Hanukkah, Relig Educ, Vol 71, No 6, 11-12/76; The Jew as witness to history, Europ Judaism, Vol II, No 1, winter 77; Ein historischer Zuzang zu einem Philsophen: Moses Maimonides in seiner Zeit, Emuna, Vol 4, No 77, winter 77; The unwilling midwife: Ernest Bevin and the birth of Israel, Europ Judaism, Vol II, No 2, winter 77; Anti-Zionism in a key United States Diplomat: Loy Henderson at the end of World War II, Am Jewish Archives, Vol 30, No 2, 11/78; The Al-Barazi Testimony: a Secret Syrian Peace Proposal Recognizing the State of Israel, Mid East Studies Anthology; The Soviet Jewish problem, J Assembly of Rabbis; auth, Success & Failure of the Anglo-American Comm of Inquiry, 1945-1946, Mellon Press, Lewiston NY, 87; auth, A Translation of the Magen Wa-Hereb of Leon Woodoner, 1571-1648, Union Press, Lewiston, NY, 00. **CONTACT ADDRESS** Dept of Philos & Relig Studies, SUNY, Buffalo, 1300 Elmwood Ave, Buffalo, NY 14222-1095. **EMAIL** podetah@buffalostate.edu

POETHIG, EUNICE BLANCHARD
PERSONAL Born 01/16/1930, Hempstead, NY, m, 1952, 5 children **DISCIPLINE** OLD TESTAMENT **EDUCATION** DePauw Univ, BA, 51; Union Theol Sem, MA, 52m Phd, 85; McCormick Theol Sem, MDiv, 75, STM, 77. **CAREER** Missionary with United Church of Christ (Philippines), Philippine Womens Univ, 56-72; assoc exec, Presby of Chicago, 79-85; ex presbyter, Presby of W NY, 86-93; DIR, CONGREGATIONAL MIN DIV, GEN ASSEMBLY COUN, Presbyterian Church (USA), 94-98; Nettie F McCormick fel Old Testament Hebrew, McCormick Sem. **MEMBERSHIPS** SBL; AAR; Int Assn Women Min. **RESEARCH** Early Israelite history; Womens history-Biblical, mission, contemporary; Music, especially Biblical traditions. **SELECTED PUBLICATIONS** Auth Sing, Shout, and Clap for Joy, United Meth Womens Bd, 85; Good News Women, Presby Women, 87; many Bible studies and curricula and articles for church publ. **CONTACT ADDRESS** 3606 Trail Ridge Rd, Louisville, KY 40241. **EMAIL** ebpoethig@unidial.com

POHLHAUS, GAILE
PERSONAL Born 11/04/1938, Jamaica, NY, m, 1969, 2 children **DISCIPLINE** RELIGIOUS STUDIES **EDUCATION** Col of St. Elizabeth, BA, 61; Boston col, MA, 65, Villanova Univ, MA, 77; Temple Univ, PhD, 87 **CAREER** Tchr, 61-71; Adj Inst, 77-87, Villanova Univ; Asst Prof, 87-pres, Villanova Univ; dir of women's stud, Villanova Univ, 99-. **MEMBERSHIPS** AAR/SBL, CTS, NWSA; AAUP; CTSA **RESEARCH** Marriage; Sexuality; Feminist Ethics **SELECTED PUBLICATIONS** Essays on marriage in various collections. **CONTACT ADDRESS** Theology and Relig Studies Dept, Villanova Univ, 800 Lancaster Ave, Villanova, PA 19080. **EMAIL** gaile.pohlhaus@villanova.edu

POJMAN, LOUIS
PERSONAL Born 04/22/1935, Chicago, IL, m, 1962, 2 children **DISCIPLINE** PHILOSOPHY **EDUCATION** Columbia Univ, MA, 67; Union Theol Sem, PhD, 72; Oxford Univ, DPhil, 77. **CAREER** Lecturer, Oxford Univ, 73-77; Asst Prof, Univ Notre Dame, 77-79; Asst Prof, Univ Tex, 79-84; Assoc Prof, Univ MI, 84-95; Prof, US Military Acad, 95. **HONORS AND AWARDS** Outstanding Teacher in the Humanities, MS Coun for the Humanisites, 94; NEH Sem, 93; Bufrington Northern Awd, 88; Kent Fel, 69-71; Fulbright Fel, 69-71; Fochester Fel, 70-71. **MEMBERSHIPS** APA; Aristotelian Soc and Mind Asn; Soc for Environmental Ethics; Soc for Philos of Relig. **RESEARCH** Ethical Theory; Environmental Ethics; Political Philosophy; Epistemology; Philosophy of Religion; Kierkegaard Soc; Am Soc for Value Inquiry. **SELECTED PUBLICATIONS** Auth, Life and Death: Grappling with the Moral Dilemmas of Our Time, Wadsworth Pub Co, 99; auth, Life and Death: A Reader, Wadsworth Pub, Co, 99; co-auth, Desert: A Reader; Oxford Univ Press, 98; auth, Kierkegaard's Philosophy of Religion, Intl Scholars Press, 99; auth, Global Environmental Ethics, Mayfield Pub Co, 99; auth, Environmental Ethics, Wadsworth, 00; auth, The Moral Life, Oxford Univ Press, 00; auth, What Can We Know? An Introduction to the Theory of Knowledge, Wadsworth Pub Co, 00; auth, Classics of Philosophy: The Twentieth Century, Oxford Univ Press, 00; auth, Philosophy of Religion, Mayfield Pub Co, 00. **CONTACT ADDRESS** Dept Eng & Philos, United States Military Acad, 600 Thayer Rd, West Point, NY 10996-1707. **EMAIL** cl5338@exmal.usma.edu

POLAND, LYNN
DISCIPLINE RELIGION **EDUCATION** Bates College, AB; Univ Chicago, AM and PhD. **CAREER** Fac, 91-; assoc prof, Davidson Col. **HONORS AND AWARDS** Ed bd, Lit and Theol and Bibl Interpretation. **RESEARCH** Hist of bibl interpretation, gender, and ecology. **SELECTED PUBLICATIONS** Auth, Literary Criticism and Biblical Hermeneutics, 85; numerous essays on Augustine, biblical interpretation, and the sublime. **CONTACT ADDRESS** Davidson Col, 102 N Main St, PO Box 1719, Davidson, NC 28036.

POLANSKY, RONALD M.
PERSONAL Born 08/06/1948, Okinawa, RI, m, 1971, 2 children **DISCIPLINE** PHILOSOPHY **EDUCATION** Yale Univ, BA, 70; Boston Col, PhD, 74. **CAREER** Asst prof, Purdue Univ, 74-75; asst to full prof , Duquense Univ, 74-; Ed of Ancient Philos, 79-. **MEMBERSHIPS** Am Philos Soc; Soc for Ancient Greek Philos; Int Plato Soc. **RESEARCH** Ancient philosophy; political philosophy. **SELECTED PUBLICATIONS** Auth, Philosophy and Knowledge: A Commentary on Plato's Theaetetus, Bucknell Univ Press, 92; The Unity of Plato's Crito, Scholia, 97; Foundationalism in Plato?, Foundationalism Old and New, Temple Univ Press, 92; coauth, The Viability of Virtue in the Mean, Apeiron, 96; Locating Justice through Process of Elimination on Plato's Republic, forthcoming. **CONTACT ADDRESS** Dept of Philosophy, Duquesne Univ, Pittsburgh, PA 15282. **EMAIL** polansky@duq3.cc.duq.edu

POLASKI, SANDRA HACK
PERSONAL Born 11/25/1964, Louisville, KY, m, 1991, 2 children **DISCIPLINE** RELIGION **EDUCATION** Furman Univ, BA summa cum laude, 87; Vanderbilt, MDiv 90; Duke Univ, PhD 95. **CAREER** St. Mary's Col NC, instr 94; Elon Col NC, instr 94; Furman Univ, asst prof, 95-96; Baptist Theol Sem, asst prof, 96-. **HONORS AND AWARDS** Wabash Cen Prog Gnt. **MEMBERSHIPS** AAR; SBL; NABPR. **RESEARCH** New Testament Interpretation; Pauline Studies; Feminist Biblical Interpretation. **SELECTED PUBLICATIONS** Auth, Paul and the Discourse of Power, Sheffield Eng, Sheffield Acad Press, 99; 2 Corinthians, IVP Women's Bible Commentary, Inter-Varsity Press, forthcoming. **CONTACT ADDRESS** Baptist Theol Sem, 3400 Brook Rd, Richmond, VA 23227. **EMAIL** sandra.hack.polaski@btsr.edu

POLE, NELSON
PERSONAL Born 10/13/1941, Detroit, MI, m, 1963, 4 children **DISCIPLINE** PHILOSOPHY OF SCIENCE, LOGIC **EDUCATION** Wayne State Univ, BPhil, 63; Ohio State Univ, PhD(philos), 71. **CAREER** From instr to assoc prof, 68-92, Prof Philos, Cleveland State Univ, 93-. **MEMBERSHIPS** Am Philos Asn; Philos Sci Asn; AAAS; Am Asn Philos Teachers (pres, 86-88). **RESEARCH** Logic; philosophy of religion and technology. **SELECTED PUBLICATIONS** Auth, Logic-Coach Software. **CONTACT ADDRESS** Dept of Philos, Cleveland State Univ, 1983 E 24th St., Cleveland, OH 44115-2440. **EMAIL** n.pole@popmail.csuohio.edu

POLHILL, JOHN B.
PERSONAL Born 01/06/1939, Americus, GA, m, 1966, 2 children **DISCIPLINE** THEOLOGY **EDUCATION** Univ Richmond, BA, 60; Southern Baptist Theolog Sem, Mdiv, 63, PhD, 69. **CAREER** James B. Harrison chemn; assoc dean, 90-99; director, Ph.D. studies, 95-99; fal member, 69-; Southern Baptist Theological Sem. **MEMBERSHIPS** Society Biblical Lit; Asn Baptists Prof of Relig; Evangelical Theolog Society. **RESEARCH** Greek language and literature; pauline studies; Acts. **SELECTED PUBLICATIONS** Auth, Acts, New American Commentary, 92; auth, Paul and His Letters, 99. **CONTACT ADDRESS** So Baptist Theol Sem, 2825 Lexington Rd, Louisville, KY 40280. **EMAIL** jpolhill@sbts.edu

POLING, JAMES N.
PERSONAL Born 12/14/1942, Greene County, VA, m, 1963, 2 children **DISCIPLINE** PASTORAL THEOLOGY **EDUCATION** Bridgewater Col, BA, 64; Bethany Theol Sem, M Div, 68; Claremont School Theol, PhD, 80. **CAREER** Exec Dir, Camp Eder, 69-73; Pastor, W York Church of the Brethren, 69-76; assoc prof, Bethany Theol Sem, 79-87; assoc prof to prof, Colgate Rochester Div School, 87-91; prof, Garrett Evangel Theol Sem, 96-. **HONORS AND AWARDS** Award for Acad Achievement, Claremont School of Theol, 80; Res Grant, Asn of Theol Schools, 84-89; Distinguished Alumni Awd, Claremont Col, 96. **MEMBERSHIPS** Soc for Pastoral Theol; Int

Acad of Practical Theol; Am Acad of Relig; Assoc for Practical Theol; Am Assoc of Pastoral Counselors; Am Assoc of Marital and Family Therapists. **RESEARCH** Pastoral Theology, Care and Counseling, Practial Theology, Theology, Domestic and Sexual Violence, Sexuality. **SELECTED PUBLICATIONS** Auth, "Sexuality: A Crisis for the Church, in Pastoral Care in a Society in Conflict, ed Pamela Couture and Rodney Hunter, (Nashville: Abingdon Pr, 95); coauth, "Calling to Accountability: The Church's Response to Abusers", in Violence Against Women and Children: A Christian Theol Source Book, ed Carol J. Adams and Marie M. Fortune, (NY: Continuum), 95; auth, "Child Sexual Abuse: A Rich Context for Thinking about God, Community and Ministry", in Christian Perspectives on Sexuality and Gender, ed Elizabeth Stuart and Adrian Thatcher, (MI: Eerdmans, 96), 396-399; coauth, "Perspectives on Practical Theologies and Methodologies", in Globalization and Difference: Practical Theology in a World Context, ed Pam Couture, and Paul Ballard, (UK: Cardiff Acad Pr, 99), 193-212; auth, "Preaching to Perpetrators of Violence", in Telling the Truth: Preaching About Sexual and Domestic Violence, ed John S. McClure and Nancy J. Ramsay, (Cleveland: United Church Pr, 99), 71-82; coed, The Care of Men, Abingdon (Nashville, 97); auth, Deliver Us from Evil: Resisting Racial and Gender Oppression, Fortress (Minneapolis), 96; coauth, Galm for Gilead: Pastoral Care for African American Families Experiencing Abuse, Abingdon, (Nashville), 98. **CONTACT ADDRESS** Dept Pastoral Minsitry, Garrett-Evangelical Theol Sem, 2121 Sheridan Rd, Evanston, IL 60101-2926. **EMAIL** jpoling@northwestern.edu

POLISCHUK, PABLO
DISCIPLINE PASTORAL COUNSELING, PSYCHOLOGY **EDUCATION** Univ Calif, BA; SF State Univ, MA; Fuller Theol Sem, MA, PhD. **CAREER** Adj prof, S Calif Col; Fuller Theol Sem; instr, Harvard Med Sch; prof, Gordon-Conwell Theol Sem, 80-. **HONORS AND AWARDS** Ch psychologist, Chelsea Health Ctr; dir, Willowdale Ctr for Psychol Svc. **SELECTED PUBLICATIONS** Auth, Depression and its Treatment; The Therapeutic Counseling; Dotting the I's. **CONTACT ADDRESS** Gordon-Conwell Theol Sem, 130 Essex St, South Hamilton, MA 01982.

POLK, ELMER
DISCIPLINE CRIMINOLOGY AND CRIMINAL JUSTICE **EDUCATION** Sam Houston Sate Univ, PhD. **CAREER** Asst prof, Univ of TX at Arlington. **RESEARCH** Juvenile justice; probation; correctional issues. **SELECTED PUBLICATIONS** Auth, Police Training and Violence, Contemp J of Criminal Justice, 96; The Effects of Ethnicity on Career Paths of Advanced/Specialized Law Enforcement Officers, Police Stud, 95; coauth, Intensive Supervision Probation--Fad or For Keeps, in Correctional Theory and Practice, 92. **CONTACT ADDRESS** Criminology and Criminal Justice Prog, Univ of Texas, Arlington, 303 Univ Hall, PO Box 19595, Arlington, TX 76019-0595. **EMAIL** epolk@uta.edu

POLK, TIMOTHY H.
PERSONAL Born 04/22/1946, Harrisburg, PA, m, 1970, 3 children **DISCIPLINE** OLD TESTAMENT STUDIES **EDUCATION** Wesleyan Univ, BA, 68; Yale Divinity Sch, MDiv, 74; Yale Univ, PhD, 82. **CAREER** Prof, Hamline Univ, 82- . **HONORS AND AWARDS** Agnes Conger Awd for Scholar in Hum, 84; Master of Arts in Liberal Stud Tchg Awd, 92; Burton Teaching Prize, 92. **MEMBERSHIPS** AAR; SBL; Kierkegaard Soc; Karl Barth Soc of North Am. **RESEARCH** Kierkegaard and Barth's use of scripture. **SELECTED PUBLICATIONS** Auth, The Biblical Kierkegaard: Reading by the Rule of Faith, Mercer, 97. **CONTACT ADDRESS** 1388 Englewood Ave, Saint Paul, MN 55104-1903. **EMAIL** tpolk@gw.hamline.edu

POLLAK, LOUIS HEILPRIN
PERSONAL Born 12/07/1922, New York, NY, m, 1952, 5 children **DISCIPLINE** LAW **EDUCATION** Harvard Univ, AB, 43; Yale Univ, LLB, 48. **CAREER** Vis lectr law, Law Sch, Howard Univ, 53; from asst prof to prof, Law Sch, Yale Univ, 55-74, dean, 65-70; Greenfield prof law, 74-78, dean law sch, 75-78, Lectr Law, Univ Pa, 79-; Judge, US Dist Ct, Pa, 78-. **RESEARCH** Constitutional law; civil liberties. **SELECTED PUBLICATIONS** Ed, The Constitution and the Supreme Court: A Documentary History, World Pub, 66. **CONTACT ADDRESS** US Courthouse, 601 Mkt St, Ste. 16613, Philadelphia, PA 19106.

POLLARD, ALTON BROOKS, III
PERSONAL Born 05/05/1956, St Paul, MN, m **DISCIPLINE** THEOLOGY **EDUCATION** Fisk Univ, BA 1978; Harvard Univ Divinity School, MDiv 1981; Duke Univ, PhD 1987. **CAREER** John St Baptist Church, pastor 1979-82; Clark Univ, dir 1981-82; New Red Mountain Baptist Church, pastor 1984-86; St Olaf Coll, asst prof 1987-88; Wake Forest Univ, asst prof, beginning 1988, assoc prof, 92-98; Emory Univ, Candler School of Theology, Black Church Studies, dir, assoc prof of religion and culture currently. **HONORS AND AWARDS** Thomas J Watson Fellowship Fisk Univ 1978; Fund for Theological Educ Fellowships Princeton NJ 1978-81, 1983-86; Andrew Mellon Fellowship Duke Univ 1986-87; article "Religion, Rock, & Eroticism," The Journal of Black Sacred Music 1987; "The Last Soul Singer in Amer," Black Sacred Music 1989. **MEMBERSHIPS** Mem Soc for the Scientific Study of Religion 1984-, Assoc for the Sociology of Religion 1985-; mem (clergy) Amer Baptist Convention; mem NAACP, Amer Acad of Religion 1987; Religious Research Assn 1988-; member, Society for the Study of Black Religion, 1989-. **SELECTED PUBLICATIONS** review of "The Color of God" and "Black Theology in Dialogue," Perspectives in Religious Studies 1989; "Howard Thurman and the Experience of Encounter," Journal of Religious Thought, 1990; "Of Movements and Motivations," AME Zion Quarterly Review, 1991; "The Promise and Peril of Common Ground," BRIDGES, 1991; Mysticism and Social Change, Peter Lang, 1992. **CONTACT ADDRESS** Director of Black Church Studies, Emory Univ, Atlanta, GA 30322. **EMAIL** abpolla@emory.edu

POLLEY, MAX EUGENE
PERSONAL Born 06/03/1928, South Bend, IN, m, 1950 **DISCIPLINE** RELIGION **EDUCATION** Albion Col, AB, 50; Duke Univ, BD, 53, PhD(Old Testament), 57. **CAREER** Asst prof Bible & relig, 56-66, Prof Relig, Davidson Col, 66-. **MEMBERSHIPS** Soc Bibl Lit; Am Acad Relig. **RESEARCH** Biblical theology. **SELECTED PUBLICATIONS** Auth, Bibliography of H Wheeler Robinson's Writings, 472 & The Place of Henry Wheeler Robinson Among Old Testament Scholars, 472, Baptist Quart; H Wheeler Robinson and the Problem of Organizing an Old Testament Theology, In: The Use of the Old Testament in the New and Other Essays: Studies in Honor of William Franklin Stinespring, Duke Univ, 72; Revelation in the writings of H Wheeler Robinson and Eric Rust: A comparative study, In: Science, Faith, and Revelation, Broadman press, 79; Hebrew prophecy within the council of Yahweh, examined in its ancient Near Eastern setting, In: Scriptures in Context: Essays on the Comparative Method, Pickwick Press, 80; Amos - a Commentary on the Book of Amos - Paul,sm, J of Biblical Literature, Vol 0112, 1993; Isaiah-xlvi, Isaiah-xlvii, and Isaiah-xlviii - a New Literary-critical Reading - Franke,C, J of Biblical Literature, Vol 0115, 1996. **CONTACT ADDRESS** Dept Relig, Davidson Col, Davidson, NC 28036.

POLLOCK, JOHN LESLIE
PERSONAL Born 01/28/1940, Atchison, KS **DISCIPLINE** PHILOSOPHY **EDUCATION** Univ MN, BA, 61; Univ CA, Berkeley, PhD, 65. **CAREER** From asst prof to assoc prof philos, State Univ NY Buffalo, 65-71; from assoc prof to prof, Univ Rochester, 71-78; Prof Philos, Univ AZ, 78-, ed-in-chief, Philosophical Studies, 80-87. **RESEARCH** Artificial intelligence; epistemology; logic; philosophical logic. **SELECTED PUBLICATIONS** Auth, Introduction to Symbolic Logic, Holt, 69; Knowledge and Justification, Princeton Univ, 74; Subjunctive Reasoning, D Reidel, 76; Language and Thought, Princeton Univ, 82; The Foundations of Philosophical Semantics, Princeton Univ, 84; Contemporary Theories of Knowledge, Rowman and Littlefield, 86; How to Build a Person, MIT, 90; Nomic Probability and the Foundations of Induction, Oxford, 90; Technical Methods in Philosophy, Westview, 90; Cognitive Carpentry, MIT, 95. **CONTACT ADDRESS** Dept of Philos, Univ of Arizona, Tucson, AZ 85721-0001. **EMAIL** pollock@arizona.edu

POLS, EDWARD
PERSONAL Born 02/01/1919, Newark, NJ, m, 1942, 6 children **DISCIPLINE** PHILOSOPHY **EDUCATION** Harvard Univ, AB, 40, AM, 47, PhD, 49. **CAREER** Asst philos, Harvard Univ, 47-48; instr, Princeton Univ, 48-49; from asst prof to assoc prof, 49-62, chmn dept, 55-75, Prof Philos, 62- , Kenan Prof Humanities, 75-84, res prof, 84-94, Kenan Prof Philos & Hum Emeritus, 94- , Bowdoin Col **MEMBERSHIPS** Am Philos Asn. **RESEARCH** Metaphysics; epistemology. **SELECTED PUBLICATIONS** Auth, To live at east ever after, Sewanee Rev, 58; The Recognition of Reason, Southern Ill Univ, Carbondale, 63; Whitehead's Metaphysics: A Critical Examination of Process and Reality, Southern Ill Univ, Carbondale & Edwardsville, 67; Consciousness-makers and the autonomy of consciousness, Yale Rev, 71; Meditation on a Prisoner: Towards Understanding Actiona and Mind, Southern Ill Univ, Carbondale & Edwardsville, 75; The Acts of Our Being: A Reflection on Agency and Responsibility, Univ Mass, Amherst, 82; auth, Radical Realism: Direct Knowing in Science and Philosophy, Cornell, 92; auth, Mind Regained, Cornell, 98. **CONTACT ADDRESS** Dept of Philosophy, Bowdoin Col, Brunswick, ME 04011. **EMAIL** epols@polar.bowdoin.edu

POMERLEAU, WAYNE PAUL
PERSONAL Born 12/19/1946, Shreveport, LA, m, 1968, 1 child **DISCIPLINE** PHILOSOPHY **EDUCATION** Georgetown Univ, AB, 68; Northwestern Univ, MA, 72, PhD(philos), 77. **CAREER** Instr philos, Evening Div, Northwestern Univ, 73-77 & Ill Inst Tech, 76-77; asst prof, 77-82, assoc prof Philos, Gonzaga Univ, 82-98, prof, 98, chmn Dept, 80-85. **RESEARCH** History of modern philosophy; philosophy of religion, philosophy of human nature. **SELECTED PUBLICATIONS** Auth, The accession and dismissal of an upstart handmaid, Monist, 5/77; Twelve Great Philosophers, 97, Western Philosophies of Religion, 98. **CONTACT ADDRESS** Dept of Philosophy, Gonzaga Univ, 502 E Boone Ave, Spokane, WA 99258-0050. **EMAIL** pomerleau@gonzaga.edu

PONTON, LIONEL
PERSONAL Born 06/14/1930, East Angus, PQ, Canada **DISCIPLINE** PHILOSOPHY **EDUCATION** Univ Montreal, BA, 50; Univ Laval, BPh, 51, LPh, 53; Angelicum, Rome, PhD(philos), 70. **CAREER** Prof philos, Ecole Normale Laval, 59-70; assoc prof, 70-78, vdean, 77-78, Prof Philos, Fac Philos, Univ Laval, 78-, Co-ed, Laval Theol Philos, 82-. **MEMBERSHIPS** Can Philos Asn. **RESEARCH** Aristotle and Hegel. **SELECTED PUBLICATIONS** Auth, 1789-1989, les droits de l'homme et les philosophies. **CONTACT ADDRESS** Fac Philos Tour des Arts, Univ of Laval, Laval, QC, Canada G1K 7P4.

POOL, JEFF B.
PERSONAL Born 12/18/1951, Seminole, TX, m, 2 children **DISCIPLINE** SYSTEMATIC THEOLOGY, PHILOSOPHY OF RELIGION, THEOLOGICAL ETHICS **EDUCATION** Wayland Baptist Univ, BA, 75; Southwestern Baptist Theol Sem, MDiv, 79; Tex Christian Univ, MA, 80; Univ Chicago, PhD, 94. **CAREER** Minister to Youth, First Baptist Church, Muleshoe, Tex, 74; teaching asst, Tex Christian Univ, 75-76; teaching asst, Southwestern Baptist Theol Sem, 78-79; Pastor, Hugoton Baptist Church, Kans, 80-82; instr, Seward County Community Col, Liberal, Kans, 80-81; instr, DeLourdes Col, Des Plaines, Ill, 82-83; reference librarian, Jesuit-Krause-McCormick Library, Chicago, Ill, 83-84; Resident Head of Dewey House, Univ of Chicago, Office of Student Housing, 84-89; res asst to the Theol Area, Univ Chicago, The Divinity Sch, 86-87; col advisor, Univ Chicago, Office of the Col Dean of Students, 88-89; instr, Phillips Theol Sem, Tulsa, Okla, 89-92; asst prof, Southwestern Baptist Theol Sem, Fort Worth, 92-98; vis prof, Int Baptist Theol Sem, Prague, Czech Republic, 98; Dir of Annual Fund and Lectr in Theol, Brite Divinity Sch, Fort Worth, 98-99, special asst to the Pres and Lectr in Theol, 99-. **HONORS AND AWARDS** Philos Awd, Wayland Baptist Univ, 74-75; grad assistantship, Tex Christian Univ, 75-76; grad assistantship, Southwestern Baptist Theol Sem, 78-79; Divinity Sch Fel, Univ Chicago, 84-85, Res Assistantship, 86-87, Univ Fel, 87-88, Jr Fel in the Inst for the Advanced Study of Relig, 87-88. **MEMBERSHIPS** Am Acad of Relig, Soc of Christian Ethics, Nat Asn of Baptist Profs of Relig. **RESEARCH** Theologies of divine suffering, liberation theology, ecclesiology, theodicy, rhetorical and hermeneutical studies in religion, theological anthropology. **SELECTED PUBLICATIONS** Auth, "Baptist Infidelity to the Principle of Religious Liberty," Perspectives in Religious Studies, 17 (spring 90): 13-20; ed, Through the Tempest: Theological Voyages in a Pluralistic Culture, by Langdon Gilkey, Minneapolis: Fortress Press (91); auth, " 'Sacred Mandates of Conscience': A Criteriology of Credalism for Theological Method among Baptists," Perspectives in Religious Studies, 23 (winter 96): 353-386; ed, Sacred Mandates of Conscience: Interpretations of the Baptist Faith and Message, Macon, GA: Smyth & Helwys Pub Co (97); auth, "Christ, Conscience, Canon, Community: Web of Authority in the Baptist Vision," Perspectives in Religious Studies, 24 (winter 97): 417-45; auth, "Conscience and Interpreting Baptist Tradition," and "Chief Article of Faith: The Preamble of The Baptist Faith and Message (1963)," in Sacred Mandates of Conscience: Interpreting the Baptist Faith and Message, ed by Jeff B. Pool, Macon, Ga: Smyth & Helwys Pub Co (97); auth, "Southwestern Baptist Theol Sem," in Encyclopedia of Religious Controversies in the United States, ed by George H. Shriver and Bill J. Leonard, Greenwood Pub Group (97); auth, Against Returning to Egypt: Exposing and Resisting Credalism in the Southern Baptist Convention, Macon: Mercer Univ Pres (98); co-ed with Kyle A. Pasewark, The Theology of Langdon Gilkey, Macon: Mercer Univ Press (99); auth, "Beyond Postliberal Foundationalism: The Theological Method of Langdon Gilkey," in The Theology of Langdon Gilkey, co-ed with Kyle A. Pasewark, Macon: Mercer Univ Press (99). **CONTACT ADDRESS** Brite Divinity Sch, Texas Christian Univ, PO Box 298130, Fort Worth, TX 76129. **EMAIL** j.pool@tcu.edu

POPE, STEPHEN J.
PERSONAL Born 05/26/1955, San Francisco, CA, m, 1980, 3 children **DISCIPLINE** THEOLOGICAL ETHICS **EDUCATION** Univ Chicago, PhD, 98. **CAREER** Assoc Prof, Boston Col. **MEMBERSHIPS** Soc Christian Ethics. **RESEARCH** Evolution of theological ethics; charity in Thomas Aquinas. **SELECTED PUBLICATIONS** Auth, The Evolution of Altruism and the Ordering of Love, Georgetown Univ Press, 94; Love in Contemporary Christian Ethics, J of Relig Ethics 23, 95; Finding God in All Things: Essays in Honor of Michael J Buckley, S J, co-ed with Fr Michael J Himes, Crossroad Pubs, 96; Knowability of the Natural Law: A Foundation for the Ethics of the Common Good, Religion, Ethics, and the Common Good, ed James Donahue and M Theresa Moser, RSCJ, Twenty-Third Pubs, 96; Descriptive and Normative Uses of Evolutionary Theory, in Christian Ethics: Problems and Prospects, ed Lisa Sowle Cahill and James Childress, Pilgrim Press, 96; Neither Enemy nor Friend: Nature as Creation in the Theology of St Thomas, Zygon: J of Relig and Science 32, spring 97; Scientific and Natural Law Assessments of Homosexuality, J of Relig Ethics 2 5 spring 97; 'Equal Regard' vs 'Special Relations'? Reaffirming the Inclusiveness of Agape, J of Relig 77 3, July 97; Sociobiology and Human Nature: A Perspective from Catholic Theology, Zygon: J of Relig and Science 33, June 98; Response to Outka, J of Relig Ethics 78, Dec 98; Essays on the Ethics of St Thomas Aquinas, ed, Georgetown Univ Press, forthcoming;

Christian Ethics and Evolutionary Theory, Cambridge Univ Press, forthcoming; numerous scholarly articles and other publications. **CONTACT ADDRESS** Theology Dept, Boston Col, Chestnut Hill, Chestnut Hill, MA 02167-3806. **EMAIL** stephen.pope.1@bc.edu

POPIDEN, JOHN ROBERT
PERSONAL Born 11/02/1949, Pittsburgh, PA, m, 1972, 2 children **DISCIPLINE** THEOLOGY, MORAL THEOLOGY **EDUCATION** Rice Univ, BA, 72; Univ Notre Dame du Lac, MA, 77, PhD, 80. **CAREER** Assoc prof Theological Stud, Loyola Marymount Univ, 77-. **MEMBERSHIPS** Soc Christian Ethics; Cath Theol Soc Am; Col Theol Soc; Soc Christian Ethics. **RESEARCH** Christian social ethics; constructive moral theology; war and peace; marriage and sexuality. **SELECTED PUBLICATIONS** Auth, Choice and Conscience: Abortion in Perspective, Choice and Conscience Comt, 80; An American Catholic Moralist and World War II: John Ford on Obliteration Bombing, Irish Theol Quart, 90; Saturdays of Competition and Christianity; Reformed Rev, 94. **CONTACT ADDRESS** Dept of Theol Stud, Loyola Marymount Univ, 7900 Loyola Blvd, Los Angeles, CA 90045-8400. **EMAIL** jpopiden@popmail.lmu.edu

POPKIN, RICHARD
DISCIPLINE PHILOSOPHY **EDUCATION** Columbia Univ, Ba, 43, MA, 47, PhD, 50. **CAREER** Instr, Univ Conn, 46-47; prof, Univ Iowa, 47-60; prof, Harvey Mudd Col, 60-63; prof, Univ Calif, San Diego, 63-73; prof, 73-86, PROF EMER, 86-, WASH UNIV; ADJ PROF, PHILOS, HIST, UNIV CALIF, LOS ANGELES, 85-. **SELECTED PUBLICATIONS** Auth, History of Scepticism, 60, 4th ed, 80; ed, Readings in the History of Philosophy, 16th and 17th Century, Free, 66; The Second Oswald, Avon, 66, rev ed, Andre Deutsch & Sphere, 67 & Lisbon, 68; Les assassins de Kennedy, Gallimard, Paris, 67; coauth, Introductory Readings in Philosophy, Holt, 72; auth, High Road to Pyrrhorism, 80; over 300 articles on history of philosophy and Jewish intellectual history; New Views on the Role of Skepticism in the Enlightenment, Modern Language Quarterly, Vol 0053, 1992; The Olympian Dreams and Youthful Rebellion of Descartes,rene - Cole,JR, American Historical Review, Vol 0098, 1993; Sources of Knowledge of Sextus-empiricus in Hume Time, J of the History of Ideas, Vol 0054, 1993; Defenders of the Text - the Tradition of Scholarship in an Age of Science, 1450-1800 - Grafton,A, J of Interdisciplinary History, Vol 0024, 1993; Columbia History of Western Philosophy (US), Pimlico History of Western Philosophy (UK), 99; Messianic Revolution, co-auth David S. Katz still & Wang; Penquin (UK), 99; Newton and Religion, ed By James Force and Richard H. Popkin, Kluwer 99. **CONTACT ADDRESS** 15340 Albright St, #204, Pacific Palisades, CA 90272. **EMAIL** rpopkin@humnet.ucla.edu

POPPE, SUSAN
DISCIPLINE PHILOSOPHY **EDUCATION** Univ Notre Dame, PhD, 95. **CAREER** Asst Prof, Philosophy, 95-, Concordia Col. **CONTACT ADDRESS** Concordia Col, Minnesota, 901 S. Eight St., Moorhead, MN 56562. **EMAIL** poppe@cord.edu

POPPER, ROBERT
PERSONAL Born 05/22/1932, New York, NY, m, 1963, 2 children **DISCIPLINE** LAW **EDUCATION** Univ Wis, BA; Harvard Univ, LLB; New York Univ, LLM. **CAREER** Prof and dean emer. **MEMBERSHIPS** Missouri Bar **RESEARCH** Criminal law and procedure; constitutional law. **SELECTED PUBLICATIONS** Auth, Post Conviction Remedies in a Nutshell, W, 78; pubs on professional responsibility, law and mental illness, and criminal, juvenile and prisoners' rights. **CONTACT ADDRESS** Law School, Univ of Missouri, Kansas City, 5100 Rockhill Rd, Kansas City, MO 64110-2499. **EMAIL** popperr@umkc.edu

PORTER, ANDREW P.
PERSONAL Born 10/05/1946, Boston, MA, s **DISCIPLINE** APPLIED SCIENCE; PHILOSOPHICAL THEOLOGY **EDUCATION** Harvard Col, BA, 68; MS, 68, PhD, 76, Univ California-Davis; Church Divinity School, Berkeley, MTS, 80; Graduate Theological Union, PhD, 91. **CAREER** Teaching Asst, 83, Church Divinity School of the Pacific; Instr, 80-87, The School for Deacons of the Episcopal Church; Instr, 92, Los Medanos Col; Physicist, 68-94, Special Studies Group, Lawrence Livermore Natl Lab; Physicist, 94-, Physics and Space Div, Lawrence Livermore Natl Lab; Instr, 96-, Las Positas Col. **MEMBERSHIPS** Amer Acad of Religion; Mathematical Assoc of Amer. **RESEARCH** Theology and religious studies; philosophy of religion; phenomenological philosphy; Bible introduction; history of philosophy; Martin Heidegger; H. Richard Niebuhr **SELECTED PUBLICATIONS** Science, Religious Language and Analogy, Faith and Philosophy, 96; When Failure is Success: Counter-Performative Speech Acts, Amer Acad of Religion Western Regional Meeting, 94; The Fertility of Niebuhr's Idea of Monotheism, Pacific Coast Theological Soc, 94; Extending Merold Westphal's Typology of Basic Religious Options, Soc of Christian Philosophers Meeting, 95; The Logic of Confessional Speech Acts, Amer Acad of Religion Western Regional Meeting, 96; Critical and Confessional Responsibility in Theology, Pacific Coast Theological Soc, 96. **CONTACT ADDRESS** 774 Joyce St., Livermore, CA 94550. **EMAIL** app@jedp.com

PORTER, BURTON F.
PERSONAL Born 06/22/1936, New York, NY, m, 1980, 2 children **DISCIPLINE** PHILOSOPHY **EDUCATION** Univ Md, BA, 59; Univ St Andrews, PhD, 61; Oxford Univ, postdoctorate, 63. **CAREER** Prof, Russel Sage Col, 71-87; prof, Drexel Univ, 87-91; dean, Western New Eng Col, 91-. **HONORS AND AWARDS** Outstanding Educator of Am, 75; Special Awd for Teaching Excellence. **MEMBERSHIPS** Am Philos Asn **RESEARCH** Ethical theory, contemporary moral issues, critical thinking, philosophy in literature. **SELECTED PUBLICATIONS** Auth, Fundamentals of Critical Thinking, Oxford Univ Press, 01; auth, The Good Life: Alternatives in Ethics, Macmillan, 94; auth, Philosophy: A Literary and Conceptual Approach, Harcourt Brace, 95; auth, Religion and Reason, St. Martin's Press, 92; auth, Reasons for Living, A Basic Ethics, Macmillan, 88; auth, Personal Philosophy: Perspectives on Living, Harcourt Brace, 76; auth, Deity and Morality, Humanities Press, 68. **CONTACT ADDRESS** Dept Humanities & English, Western New England Col, 1215 Wilbraham Rd, Springfield, MA 01119-2612. **EMAIL** bporter@wnec.edu

PORTER, DAVID L.
PERSONAL Born 02/18/1941, Holyoke, MA, m, 1970, 2 children **DISCIPLINE** HISTORY, POLITICAL SCIENCE **EDUCATION** Franklin Col, BA, 63; Ohio Univ, MA, 65; Pa State Univ, PhD (hist), 70. **CAREER** Asst prof hist, Rensselaer Polytech Inst, 70-75; educ admin asst, Troy Civil Ser Comn, NY, 75-76; from asst prof to prof, 76-86, Louis Tuttle Shangle Prof Hist, William Penn Univ, 86-, Dir Pre-Law Prog, 79-; Co-dir Am studies, Rennselaer Polytech Inst, 72-74; chmn hist, Troy Area Bicentennial Comt, 75-76; consult, Midwest Rev, 77-78; acting chair, Social and Behavioral Sciences Div, Wm Penn Univ, 00. **HONORS AND AWARDS** President's Schol, 59-63; Franklin's Schol, 62-63; Lancers; Blue Key; Alpha; Phi Alpha Theta, advisor, 77; Kappa Delta Pi; Nat Sci Found Grant, 67; Fac Travel Grants, 74, 77, 81, 86; NEH grant, 79; Eleanor Roosevelt Inst Grant, 81; Distinguished Service Awd, United Nations Asn, 81; Prof Development Grant, 86, 89, 92; Choice Outstanding Academic Book, 88, 89. **MEMBERSHIPS** AHA; Orgn Am Historians; Soc Hist Am Foreign Rels; North Am Soc Sport Hist; Soc Am Baseball Res; Ctr for the Study of the Presidency; State Hist Soc Iowa; Professional Football Res Asn; Col Football Res Asn. **RESEARCH** United States political history; United States diplomatic history; United States sport history. **SELECTED PUBLICATIONS** Auth, The Seventy-Sixth Congress and World War II, 1939-1940, Univ Mo Press, 79; Congress and the Waning of the New Deal, Kennikat Press, 80; Biographical Dictionary of American Sports: Baseball, Greenwood Press, 87; Biographical Dictionary of American Sports: Football, Greenwood Press, 87; Biographical Dictionary of American Sports: Outdoor Sports, Greenwood Press, 88; Biographical Dictionary of American Sports: Basketball and Other Indoor Sports, Greenwood Press, 89; Biographical Dictionary of American S ports: 1989-1992 Supplement for Baseball, Football, Basketball, and Other Sports, Greenwood Press, 92, (92-95 supplement, 95); compiler, A Cumulative Index to the Biographical Dictionary of American Sports, Greenwood Press, 93; auth, African-American Sports Greats, Greenwood Press, 95; author of numerous book and journal articles and book reviews; auth, Biographical Dictionary of Am Sports: Baseball, Revised and Expanded Edition, 3 vols. Greenwood Press, 00; co-auth, San Diego Padres Encyclopedia, Sports Publishing, 00 Assoc ed (with others) Am National Biography, 24 vols. Oxford Univ Press, 99. **CONTACT ADDRESS** Soc and Behav Sci Div, William Penn Univ, 201 Trueblood Ave, 110C Penn , Oskaloosa, IA 52577-1799. **EMAIL** porterd@wmpenn.edu

PORTER, KWAME JOHN R.
PERSONAL Born 04/02/1932, Mineral Springs, AR, m **DISCIPLINE** THEOLOGY **EDUCATION** IO Wesleyan Coll, BA 1959; Garrett Evan Theol Sem, MDiv 1962; Union Grad Sch, PhD 1975. **CAREER** Christ United Meth Ch, pastor 1962-71 & 1979-95; Urban Young Life, vice pres 1974-79; Chicago Cntr Black Religious Studies, dir 1971-74; Sch of Human Dignity, dir, 67-70; Fellowship United Methodist Church, pastor, 96-; National Urban Black Church Growth Institute, Chicago, dean. **HONORS AND AWARDS** Three awards for work in 7th District's CAPS projects; Alumnus of the year, 1996 Iowa Wesleyan College, 1994-95. **MEMBERSHIPS** Adj prof Garrett Theol Sem; mem Intl Black Writers 1980; pres Student Assn Garrett Theol Sem 1961; community trainer, JCPT/CAPS, Chicago Alliance for Neighborhood Safety, 1995-96; founding mem, Operation Breadbasket PUSH, 1966. **SELECTED PUBLICATIONS** Research writer, proposal developer, chair, Englewood's New Village, EZEC project, 1994-95; author, "The Dating Habits of Young Black Americans," 1979; Pending publications "Black Male Violence," 1997; "How Blackfolk and Others Die," 1997; "Basic Training Manual for 21st Century Christians." Pub book "Dating Habits of Young Black Ams" 1979; pub articles best black sermons Vol II Judson Press 1979; pub articles Metro Ministry David C Cook Pub 1979. **CONTACT ADDRESS** Fellowship United Methodist Church, 447 W 120th St, Chicago, IL 60628.

PORTER, SAMUEL C.
PERSONAL Born 09/25/1952, Eugene, OR, d, 1 child **DISCIPLINE** RELIGION; SOCIOLOGY OF RELIGION AND CULTURE IN THE US **EDUCATION** Emory Univ, PhD, 96. **CAREER** Instr, Univ OR, 98-. **HONORS AND AWARDS** Graduate fellowships, tuition scholarships, Emory Univ. **MEMBERSHIPS** Am Academy of Relig; Asn for the Sociology of Relig; Soc for the Scientific Study of Relig; Asn of Religious Res. **RESEARCH** Sociology of religion and culture; religion in the US; history and theory of religion; morality and society; religion and ecological politics. **SELECTED PUBLICATIONS** Auth, Review, The Future of Religion: Secularization, Revival, and Cult Formation, by Rodney Stark and William Sims Bainbridge, in the J for the Am Academy of Relig 54, 86; submission under review, The Paufre Northwest Forest Debate: Bringing Religion Back In?, Worldviews: Environment, Culture, and Religion, ed, Clare Palmer, Univ Greenwich, 98. **CONTACT ADDRESS** Dept of Sociology, Univ of Oregon, 1291 Univ of Oregon, Eugene, OR 97403-1291. **EMAIL** sporter@oregon.uoregon.edu

PORTERFIELD, AMANDA
PERSONAL Born 02/06/1947, Bronxville, NY, m, 1979, 1 child **DISCIPLINE** RELIGIOUS STUDIES **EDUCATION** Mt. Holyoke Col, BA, 69; Columbia Univ, MA, 71; Stanford Univ, PhD, 75. **CAREER** Asst prof, 75-81, assoc prof, 81-90, prof, 91-94, Syracuse Univ; prof, 94-98, IUPUI; prof, 98-, Univ Wyoming. **HONORS AND AWARDS** Phi Betta Kappa; Sarah Willington Scholar. **MEMBERSHIPS** AAR; ASCH; ASA; SSSR. **RESEARCH** Am religious hist. **SELECTED PUBLICATIONS** Auth, Female Piety in Puritan New England, 92; Mary Lyon and the Mt Holyoke Missionaries, 97; The Power of Religion, 97; auth, The Transformation of American Religion, 00. **CONTACT ADDRESS** Religious Studies Program, Univ of Wyoming, Hoyt Hall 201, Laramie, WY 82071. **EMAIL** ap@uwyo.edu

PORTIER, WILLIAM L.
PERSONAL Born 07/08/1945, Englewood, NJ, m, 1971, 3 children **DISCIPLINE** THEOLOGY **EDUCATION** Loyola Univ, BA, 69; Washington Theological Union, MA, 72; Faculty of Theology, St. Michael's Col, PhD, 80 **CAREER** Henry J Knott Prof of Theol, Mt Saint Mary's Col, 97-; prof, Mt Saint Mary's Col 89-; assoc prof, Mt Saint Mary's Col, 86- **MEMBERSHIPS** Amer Acad Relig; Cath Theol Soc Amer; Col Theol Soc; Amer Cath Hist Assoc **RESEARCH** Historical Theology, Nineteen-Century American Catholic History, US-Vatican Relations **SELECTED PUBLICATIONS** Tradition and Incarnation, Foundations of Christian Theology, 94; Isaac Hecker and The First Vatican Council, 85; co-ed, American Catholic Traditions, Resources for Renewal, 97 **CONTACT ADDRESS** Dept of Theology, Mount Saint Mary's Col and Sem, Emmitsburg, MD 21727. **EMAIL** wportier@msmary.edu

PORTON, GARY GILBERT
PERSONAL Born 03/12/1945, Reedley, CA, m, 1968, 2 children **DISCIPLINE** HISTORY OF JUDAISM **EDUCATION** UCLA, BA, 67; Hebrew Union Col, MA, 69; Brown Univ, PhD, 73. **CAREER** Asst prof, 73-80, assoc prof Relig Studies, 80-84, prof relig studies, Univ IL, 84-, prof Dept Hist, 91, prof Prog Comp Lit, Guggenheim fel, 82-83; assoc, Ctr Advan Study, Univ Ill, 82-83. **MEMBERSHIPS** Soc Bibl Lit; Europ Asn Jewish Studies. **RESEARCH** Rabbinic lit; Jewish Bibl exegesis; hist of Rabbinic Judaism. **SELECTED PUBLICATIONS** Auth, The Traditions of Rabbi Ishmael I, 76, II, 77, III, 78 & IV, 82, E J Brill; The Grape Cluster in Jewish art and literature in late antiquity, J Jewish Studies, 76; Midrash: The Bible and the Palestinian Jews in the Greco-Roman period, Aufsteig Niedergang Romischen Welt, 78; Understanding Rabbaic Midrash, KTAU, 85; Goyim: Gentiles and Israelites in Moshrah-Csefla, Scholars Press, 88; The Stranger within Your Gates: Converts and Conversion in Rabbinic Literature, Chicago, 94. **CONTACT ADDRESS** Univ of Illinois, Urbana-Champaign, 707 S Mathews Ave, Urbana, IL 61801-3625. **EMAIL** g_porton@uiuc.edu

POSEN, BARRY R.
DISCIPLINE POLITICAL SCIENCE **EDUCATION** Univ Calif, Berkeley, PhD, 81. **CAREER** Prof, Mass Inst of Tech, 87-. **HONORS AND AWARDS** Edward J Furniss Jr Bk Awd, Oh State Univ, 84; Woodrow Wilson Found Bk Awd, APSA, 85; Levitan Prize in Hum, MIT, 91; ed bd for security studies, international security, and orbis. **MEMBERSHIPS** Int Inst for Strategic Stud; Coun on For Rel. **RESEARCH** US military strategy and force structure; Nationalism. **SELECTED PUBLICATIONS** Auth, The Sources of Military Doctrine: France, Britain, and Germany Between the World Wars, Cornell Univ Press, 84; auth, Inadvertent Escalation: Conventional War and Nuclear Risks, Cornell Univ Press, 91; auth, "The Security Dilemma and Ethnic Conflict," Survival 35(1)(93): 27-47; auth," Nationalism, the Mass Army and Military Power," Int Sec, 18(2)(93): 80-124; auth, "A Defense Concept for Ukraine," in Ukraine: Issue of Security (96), 85-136; auth," Military Responses to Refugee Disasters," Int Sec, 21(1)(96): 72-111; auth, "Competing Visions for U.S. Grand Strategy," Int Sec, 21(3)(97): 5-53; auth, "U.S. Security Policy in a Nuclear Armed World," Sec Stud, 6(3)(97): 1, 31; auth, "The War for Kosovo,"

Int Sec, 24(4)(00): 39-84. **CONTACT ADDRESS** CIS/DACS E38-616, Massachusetts Inst of Tech, 292 Main St, Cambridge, MA 02139. **EMAIL** posen@mit.edu

POSPESEL, HOWARD
PERSONAL Born 01/25/1937, Dayton, OH, m, 1960, 3 children **DISCIPLINE** PHILOSOPHY **EDUCATION** Wittenberg Univ, BA, 59; Univ FL, MA, 61; Univ NC at Chapel Hill, 67. **CAREER** Asst prof, 65-71, assoc prof 71-77, prof, 77- , Univ Miami. **HONORS AND AWARDS** Phi Eta Sigma; Alpha Lambda Delta; Phi Kappa Phi; Phi Beta Kappa; Phi Sigma Tau; James W. Mchamore Outstanding Service Awd. **MEMBERSHIPS** FL Philosophical Assn; Southern Soc for Philosphy and Psychology; APA. **RESEARCH** Logic; Plato; Continental Rationalism. **SELECTED PUBLICATIONS** Auth, Arguments: Deductive Logic Exercises, Prentice-Hall, 71; auth, Propositional Logic, Prentice-Hall, 74; auth, Predicate Logic, Prentice-Hall, 76; auth, The Method of Propositional Analogues, Teaching Philosophy, 93; coauth, Premises and Conclusions: Symbolic Logic for Legal Analysis, Prentice-Hall, 97; auth, Toward a Legal Deontic Logic, Notre Dame Law Review, 98. **CONTACT ADDRESS** Dept of Philosophy, Univ of Miami, Coral Gables, FL 33124. **EMAIL** pospesel@miami.edu

POST, DEBORAH W.
DISCIPLINE LAW **EDUCATION** Hofstra Univ, BA (Cum Laude), 71; Harvard Univ, JD, 78. **CAREER** Assoc, Bracewell & Patterson, Houston, TX; asst prof, Univ Houston; prof Law, Touro Col. **SELECTED PUBLICATIONS** Auth, Continuity and Change: Partnership Formation Under the Common Law, Villanova Law Rev, 87; Reflections on Identity, Diversity, and Morality, Berkeley Women's Law J, 90-91; Race, Riots and the Rule of Law, Denver Law Rev, 93; Profit, Progress and Moral Imperatives, Touro Law Rev, 93; Critical Thoughts About Race, Exclusion, Oppression and Tenure, Pace Law Rev, 94; Power and Morality of Grading: A Case Study and a Few Critical Thoughts on Grade Normalization, Univ Mo, Kansas City Law Rev, 97; coauth, Cultivating Intelligence: Power, Law and the Politics of Teaching, NY UP; Contracting Law, Carolina Acad Press. **CONTACT ADDRESS** Touro Col, New York, Brooklyn, NY 11230. **EMAIL** DeborahP@tourolaw.edu

POSTEMA, GERALD JAY
PERSONAL Born 11/26/1948, Chicago, IL, m, 1969, 1 child **DISCIPLINE** LEGAL & MORAL PHILOSOPHY **EDUCATION** Calvin Col, AB, 70; Cornell Univ, MA, 73, PhD(philos), 76. **CAREER** Tutor jurisp, Queen's Col, Oxford, England, spring, 74; instr philos, Cornell Univ, 74-75; asst prof, Johns Hopkins Univ, 75-80; Assoc Prof Philos, Univ Nc, Chapel Hill, 80-, Fel, Am Coun Learned Soc & Nat Endowment for Humanities, 78; hon res assoc, Dept Philos, Univ Col, London, 78; vis asst prof, Sch Law, Univ Calif, Berkeley, 79; vis assoc prof, Univ Mich, 82. **MEMBERSHIPS** Am Philos Asn; Am Soc Polit & Legal Philos; Soc Legal & Social Philos. **RESEARCH** Philosophy of law, Bentham, positivism, and judicial reasoning; professional ethics, law and medicine; moral and political philosophy, international justice and Marxism. **SELECTED PUBLICATIONS** Auth, the principle of utility and the law of procedure: Bentham's theory of adjudication, Ga Law Rev, 77; The expositor, the censor and the common law, Can J Philos, 79; Bentham and Dworkin on positivism and adjudication, & Nozick on liberty, compensation and the individual's right to punish, Social Theory; Moral responsibility and professional ethics, NY Univ Law Rev, 80; Coordination and convention at the foundations of law, J Legal Studies, 82; Bentham's early reflections on law, justice and adjudication, Rev Int Philos, 82; Facts, fictions and law: Bentham on the foundations of evidence, Arch Legal & Social Philos (in press). **CONTACT ADDRESS** Dept of Philos, Univ of No Carolina, Chapel Hill, Chapel Hill, NC 27514.

POSTLEWAITE, PHILIP F.
PERSONAL Born 06/30/1945, Modesto, CA, 2 children **DISCIPLINE** LAW **EDUCATION** Univ Calif, Berkeley, JD, 70; New York Univ, LLM, 71. **CAREER** Instr law, New York Univ, 71-73; assoc prof law, Notre Dame Univ, 76-81; assoc prof, 81-82, Prof Law, Northwestern Univ, 82-; Mem, Tax Adv Group, Am Law Inst, 82, 98. **RESEARCH** Law taxation, federal individual, partnerships, international. **SELECTED PUBLICATIONS** Auth, Partnership Taxation, 6th ed, Warren, gorham, and Lamont, 97; International Taxation: Corporate and Individual, 3rd ed, Carolina Acad Press, 98; Taxation of Intellectual Property and Intangible Assets, Warren, Gorham, amd Lamont, 97. **CONTACT ADDRESS** Sch of Law, Northwestern Univ, 357 E Chicago Ave, Chicago, IL 60611-3069.

POSTON, LARRY A.
PERSONAL Born 09/25/1952, Leesburg, VA, m, 1975, 1 child **DISCIPLINE** CHRISTIAN STUDIES **EDUCATION** Grace Col, BA, 77; Trinity Evan Div Sch, MA, 78; Northwestern Univ, MA, 86; PhD, 88. **CAREER** Dept chair, assoc prof, Nyack Col, 89-95; inst dir, assoc prof, Wheaton Col, 95-96; prof, Nyack Col, 96-. **HONORS AND AWARDS** Who's Who, Am Teach; Who's Who, Intl Auth Writers; Contemp Auth. **MEMBERSHIPS** AAR; EMS; ASM. **RESEARCH** Islam in America; Islamic Missiology; Religious pluralism; Christian Missiology; Religious supernaturalism. **SELECTED PUBLICATIONS** Auth, Islamic Da'wah in the West: Muslim Missionary Activity and the Dynamics of Conversion to Islam, Oxford Univ Press (NY), 92; coauth, The Changing Face of Islam in America, Horizon Books (Camphill, PA), 00; auth, "Christian Reconstructionism and the Christian World Mission," Missiology (95); auth, "Christianity as a Minority Religion," in Christianity and the Religions: A Biblical Theology of Working Religions, ed. Edward Rommen, Harold Netland, William Carey Library Press (Pasadena), 95; auth, "American Ijtihad: The Influence of Western Converts Upon Contemporary Islamic Theology and Praxis," in Towards a New Understanding of Conversion, ed. Ulf Gorman (Relig 50, 99); auth, "The Future of Da'wah in North America," in Muslims and Islamization in North America: Problems and Prospects, ed. Amber Haque (Beltsville, MD: Amana Pub, 99); auth, "The Role of Higher Education in the Christian World Mission: Past, Present, and Future," in Teaching Them Obedience in All Things: Equipping for the 2 I" Century, ed. Edgar J Elliston (Pasadena, CA: William Carey Library, 99); also pub in, The Alliance Academic Rev (99). **CONTACT ADDRESS** Dept Christian Studies, Nyack Col, 1 South Blvd, Nyack, NY 10960-3604. **EMAIL** postonla@nyack.edu

POSY, CARL J.
DISCIPLINE PHILOSOPHY **EDUCATION** Yale Univ, PhD, 71. **CAREER** Prof, 81-, Duke Univ. **RESEARCH** Philos of mathematics; logic; hist of philos; contemp metaphysics. **SELECTED PUBLICATIONS** Ed, Kant's Philosophy of Mathematics: Modern Essays, Kluwer, 92; Autonomy, Omniscience and the Ethical Imagination, Kluwer, 89; pubs on math intuitionism. **CONTACT ADDRESS** Philos Dept, Duke Univ, West Duke Bldg, Durham, NC 27706. **EMAIL** posy@h2.hum.huji.ac.il

POTESTA, WOODROW A.
DISCIPLINE TRIAL ADVOCACY **EDUCATION** St John Fisher Col, BA, 70; Claremont Grad Sch, MA, 71; Univ S Calif, JD, 74. **CAREER** Atty and Smith Poverty law fel, Appalachian res and defense fund, 74-78; Bigelow tchg fel, Univ Chicago Law Sch, 78-79; prof, 79-. **HONORS AND AWARDS** Prof yr, 86, 90, 94; outstanding tch, WVU Found; Hale Posten award; Roscoe Pound found, 95; Richard S Jacobson award; founder, w va fund for law in the public interest. **SELECTED PUBLICATIONS** Auth, articles on civil disobedience, jury selection, faith and the law, bioethics and technology. **CONTACT ADDRESS** Law Sch, West Virginia Univ, Morgantown, PO Box 6009, Morgantown, WV 26506-6009.

POTTER, KARL HARRINGTON
PERSONAL Born 08/19/1927, Oakland, CA **DISCIPLINE** PHILOSOPHY **EDUCATION** Univ Calif, BA, 50; Harvard Univ, MA, 52, PhD(philos), 55. **CAREER** Instr philos, Carleton Col, 55-56; from instr to prof, Univ Minn, Minneapolis, 56-71, chmn dept, 64-67; Prof Philos & S Asia Studies, Univ Wash, 71-, Fulbright res fel, India, 59-60; res fel, Am Inst Indian Studies, 63-64; vis prof, Univ Hawaii, 78 & Jadavpur Univ, 81. **MEMBERSHIPS** Am Philos Asn; Western Div Am Philos Asn; Asn Asian Studies; Am Orient Soc. **RESEARCH** Indian philosophy; Sanskrit. **SELECTED PUBLICATIONS** Auth, The Padarthatattvanirupanam of Reghunatha Siromani, Harvard Univ, 57; Presuppositions of India's Philosophies, Prentice-Hall, 63; Bibliography of Indian Philosophies, Motilal Banarsidass, Delhi, 70; Indian Metaphysics and Epistemology, 77 & Advaita Vedanta to Samkara and his Pupils, 81, Motilal Banarsidass, Princeton Univ. **CONTACT ADDRESS** Dept of Philos, Univ of Washington, Seattle, WA 98195.

POTTER, NANCY
DISCIPLINE ETHICS **EDUCATION** Univ MN, PhD. **CAREER** Dept Philos, Univ Louisville **RESEARCH** Philosophical analysis of trust. **SELECTED PUBLICATIONS** Auth, The Severed Head and Existential Dread: The Classroom as Epistemic Community and Student Survivors of Incest. **CONTACT ADDRESS** Dept of Philos, Univ of Louisville, 2301 S 3rd St, Louisville, KY 40292. **EMAIL** nlpott01@ulkyvm.louisville.edu

POTTER, NELSON
PERSONAL Born 09/22/1939, Freeport, IL, m, 1979, 1 child **DISCIPLINE** ETHICS AND KANT **EDUCATION** Johns Hopkins Univ, PhD, 69. **CAREER** Prof, Univ Nebr, Lincoln. **MEMBERSHIPS** Amer PhilAssn. **RESEARCH** Kant's philosophy. **SELECTED PUBLICATIONS** Auth, What is Wrong with Kant's Four Examples, J of Philos Res 43, 93; Kant on Obligation and Motivation in Law and Ethics, Jahrbuch fur Recht and Ethik 2, 94; Kant and the Moral Worth of Actions, Southern J of Philos 34, 96. **CONTACT ADDRESS** Univ of Nebraska, Lincoln, Lincoln, NE 68588-0321. **EMAIL** npotter@unlserve.unl.edu

POTTER, PITMAN
DISCIPLINE LAW **EDUCATION** Univ Wash, BA, 78; MA, 75; JD, 85; PhD, 86. **CAREER** Assoc prof, 86-; assoc dean, 97-; prof law and dir of Chinese Legal Studies, Univ British Columbia Fac of Law. **RESEARCH** Chinese law; comparative law; international law; international business transactions; law and society. **SELECTED PUBLICATIONS** Auth, "Legitimation and Contract Autonomy in the PRC: The Contract Law of China," (92). **CONTACT ADDRESS** Fac of Law, Univ of British Columbia, 1822 East Mall, Vancouver, BC, Canada V6T 1Z1. **EMAIL** potter@law.ubc.ca

POTTS, DONALD R.
PERSONAL Born 06/10/1930, St. Louis, MO, m, 1951, 2 children **DISCIPLINE** THEOLOGY **EDUCATION** OK Baptist Univ, BA, 50; Southwestern Baptist Theol Sem, BD, 55, ThD, 59, M Div, 73. **CAREER** Instr, Homiletics, Southwestern Baptist Theol Sem, 59-60; prof, Humanities, Cameron Col, 60-64; adjunct prof and Pastor, 60-75; Prof/Chairman, Religion Dept, East TX Baptist Univ, 76-. **HONORS AND AWARDS** Postdoctoral study grant at Oxford, England, 85; Most Scholarly Prof, ETBU, 85; Eleventh Annual Andy Reavis Lecturer at Marshall Memorial Hospital, 92; guest prof, fosham education col, fosham, china, 92; guest prof, ecole baptiste de theologie, lome, togo, 94. **MEMBERSHIPS** Am Academy of Relig; Biblical Archaeology Soc; Asn of Baptist Teachers of Relig. **RESEARCH** Theology; ethics; homiletics; archaeology. **SELECTED PUBLICATIONS** Auth, articles for various periodicals, 76-98; articles for Holman Bible Dictionary, 95; articles for Eerdman Bible Dictionary, 97; Biblical Stewardship Studies for Baptist Conventions in MS. AR, and MO, 98; Bible Studies for Baptist Standard, May-Nov, 98. **CONTACT ADDRESS** Dept of Relig, East Texas Baptist Univ, 1109 N. Grove, Marshall, TX 75670. **EMAIL** dpotts@etbu.edu

POTTS, MICHAEL
PERSONAL Born 12/25/1961, Murfreesboro, TN, m, 1987 **DISCIPLINE** PHILOSOPHY **EDUCATION** David Lipscomb Col, BA, 83; Harding Univ Grad Sch Relig, MTh, 86; Vanderbilt Univ, MA, 87; Univ Ga, PhD, 92. **CAREER** Instr, Univ of Ga, 92-93; temporary asst prof, Kennesaw Col, 93-94. **MEMBERSHIPS** Am Philos Asn, Am Catholic Philos Asn, Soc of Christian Philosophers, The Hastings Center. **RESEARCH** Philosophy of Religion, Medieval Philosophy, Biomedical Ethics. **SELECTED PUBLICATIONS** Auth, "Hopkins and the Theory of Metaphor," Am Catholic Philos Quart 68 (94): 501-513; auth, "The Spatio-Temporal Theory of Individuation," The Thomist 59 (95): 59-68; auth, "C.S. Lewis, Aquinas' Theory of Habituation, and the Fall," Am Catholic Philos Quart (Supplement) 71 (97): 151-162; auth, "Morals, Metaphysics, and Heart Transplantation: Reflections on Richard Selzer's 'Whither Thou Goest'," Perspectives in Biol and Medicine 41 (98): 212-223; auth, Aquinas, Hell, and the Resurrection of the Damned," Faith and Philos 15 (98): 341-351; coed, Beyond Brain Death: The Case Against Brain Based Criteria for Human Death, Kluwer Academic Pub (Dordrect, The Netherlands), forthcoming. **CONTACT ADDRESS** Dept Relig & Philos, Methodist Col, 5400 Ramsey St, Fayetteville, NC 28311-1420. **EMAIL** mpotts20@hotmail.com

POTUTO, JOSEPHINE R.
DISCIPLINE LAW **EDUCATION** Douglass Univ, BA; Seton Hall Univ, MA; Rutgers Univ, JD. **CAREER** Prof **RESEARCH** Constitutional law; federal jurisdiction; criminal procedure. **SELECTED PUBLICATIONS** Auth, Prisoner Collateral Attacks: Habeas Corpus; Federal Prisoner Motion Practice, Clark Boardman; Winning Appeals; co-auth, Federal Criminal Jury Instructions, Michie. **CONTACT ADDRESS** Law Dept, Univ of Nebraska, Lincoln, 103 Ross McCollum Hall, PO Box 830902, Lincoln, NE 68588-0420. **EMAIL** jpotuto@unlinfo.unl.edu

POTVIN, THOMAS R.
PERSONAL Born 09/22/1934, Worcester, MA **DISCIPLINE** THEOLOGY **EDUCATION** Univ Montreal, BPh, 54; Univ Ottawa, MTh, 64; Fribourg (Suisse) DTh, 75. **CAREER** Secy treas, 67-88, Prior, St-Jean-Baptiste Priory, 87-93; prof, 74, prof titulaire, 84, doyen, fac theol, College Dominicain de Philosophie et de Theologie, 93; Provincial Prior, Dominicans of Canada, 93-97. **MEMBERSHIPS** Soc can Theologie; Can soc theol; Cath Theol Soc Am; Relig Educ Asn; Societas Liturgica. **SELECTED PUBLICATIONS** Auth, The Theology of the Primacy of Christ According to St. Thomas and its Scriptural Foundations, 73; coauth, L'experience comme lieu theologie, 83; coauth, Questions actuelles sur la foi, 84. **CONTACT ADDRESS** 96 Empress Ave, Ottawa, ON, Canada K1R 7G3. **EMAIL** thomasraymond.potvin@sympatico.ca

POULIN, ANNE BOWEN
DISCIPLINE CRIMINAL LAW **EDUCATION** Radcliffe Col, Harvard Univ, BA, 69; Univ Maine Sch Law, JD, 73; Univ Mich Law Sch, LLM, 75. **CAREER** Prof, Villanova Univ, 81-. **RESEARCH** Evidence, criminal procedure. **SELECTED PUBLICATIONS** Auth, Double Jeopardy and Judicial Accountability: When is an Acquittal not an Acquittal, 27 Ariz St L. J 953, 95; Female Delinquents: Defining Their Place in the Justice System, Wisc. L. Rev 543, 96;The Jury: The Criminal Justice System's Different Voice, 62 U Cin. L. Rev 1377, 94 & The Fourth Amendment: Elusive Standards, Elusive Review, 67 Chi.-Kent L. Rev 127, 92; coauth, Pennsylvania Evidence, 87; auth, The Plain Feel Doctrine and the Evolution of the Fourth Amendment, 42 Villanova Law Review 741, 97; auth, Prosecutorial Discretion and Selective Prosecution: Enforcing

Protection after United States v. Armstrong, 34 American Criminal Law Review 1071, 97; auth, The Psychotherapist-Patient Privilege after Jaffee v. Redmond: Where Do We Go From Here?, 76 Washington Univ. Law Quaterly 1341, 98; auth, L. Packel and A. Poulin, Pennsylvania Evidence, 2d Edition (West 99); auth, The Role of Standby Counsel in Criminal Cases: In the Twilight Zone of the Criminal Justice System, 75 New York University Law Review 676, 00; auth, Prosecutorial Inconsistency, Estoppel and Due Process: Making the Prosecution Get its Story Straight, California Law Review, 01. **CONTACT ADDRESS** Law School, Villanova Univ, 299 North Spring Mill Rd., Villanova, PA 19085. **EMAIL** poulin@law.villanova.edu

POVARSKY, CHAIM
DISCIPLINE JEWISH AND AMERICAN LAW **EDUCATION** Hebrew Univ, LLB, 66; Tel Aviv Univ, LLM, 78, JSD, 86. **CAREER** Pvt pract, Israel; instr, Tel Aviv Univ; instr, dir, Inst of Jewish Law, Touro Col. **MEMBERSHIPS** Dir, Jewish Law Asn **SELECTED PUBLICATIONS** Author of scholarly articles in the field of Jewish law and philos; ed of the Institute's Jewish Law Rpt, co-editor of the Dine-Israel J. **CONTACT ADDRESS** Touro Col, New York, Brooklyn, NY 11230. **EMAIL** ChaimP@tourolaw.edu

POWELL, BURNELE VENABLE
DISCIPLINE LAW **EDUCATION** Univ Mo Kans City, BA; Univ Wis, JD; Harvard Univ, LLM. **CAREER** Prof **RESEARCH** Legal ethics; administrative law. **SELECTED PUBLICATIONS** Auth, The Problem of the Parachuting Practitioner, 92; Open Doors, Open Arms, and Substantially Open Records, Valparaiso Law Rev, 94. **CONTACT ADDRESS** Law Dept, Univ of Missouri, Kansas City, 5100 Rockhill Rd, Kansas City, MO 64110-2499. **EMAIL** powellb@umkc.edu

POWELL, CEDRIC MERLIN
PERSONAL Born 11/08/1961, Cleveland, OH, m, 1993, 1 child **DISCIPLINE** LAW **EDUCATION** Oberlin Col, BA, 84; New York Univ, JD, 87. **CAREER** Judicial Clerk, DC Court of Appeals, 87-88; Karpatkin Fel, ACLU, 88-89; Litigation Assoc, New York, 89-93; Asst Prof to Prof, Univ Louisville, 93-. **HONORS AND AWARDS** Exemplary Multicultural Teaching Awd, 00; Ferrari Family Fel, 98. **MEMBERSHIPS** Louisville Bar Asn, Am Bar Asn. **RESEARCH** First Amendment (Hate Speech, Religion); Fourteenth Amendment (Scope of national power under 65, race, affirmative action, colorblind constitutionalism, critical race theory). **CONTACT ADDRESS** Louis D Brandeis Sch of Law, Univ of Louisville, 2301 S 3rd St, Louisville, KY 40292-0001. **EMAIL** cedric.powell@louisville.edu

POWELL, JOUETT L.
PERSONAL Born 12/02/1941, Dallas, TX, m, 1964, 1 child **DISCIPLINE** PHILOSOPHY, RELIGION **EDUCATION** Baylor Univ, BA, 64; S Baptist Theol Sem, BD, 67; Yale Univ, MPhil, 70; PhD, 72. **CAREER** Instr to asst prof, Univ NC, 71-78; asst prof to dean, Christopher Newport Univ, 78-. **HONORS AND AWARDS** Rockefeller Doct Fel, Yale Univ, 69-70; Nat Endowment for the Humanities, 81; Summer Res Stipend, NEH, 82; Smith-Reynolds Foundation grantee, 74. **MEMBERSHIPS** Am Acad of Relig, Am Philos Asn, Am Asn for Higher Educ, AAUP. **RESEARCH** John Henry Cardinal Newman, Philosophy of Religion. **SELECTED PUBLICATIONS** Auth, "The Problem of Evil: Introduction to Formal and Material Elements in the Study of Religion," Academic Study of Religion: 1974 Proceedings, Tallahassee, 74; auth, "Three Uses of Christian Discourse in John Henry," American Academy of Religion, 75; auth, "The Work of John Henry Cardinal Newman: The Complex Unity of Religious Reflection," Heroldsberg bei Nurnberg: Glock and Lutz, (78): 68-79; auth, "Newman on Faith and Doubt: The Role of Conscience," The Downside Review, (81): 137-148; auth, "Advising as Acculturation: An Early Report on a Freshman Advising Program at a Four Year Commuter College," Proceedings of the National Academic Advising Association Annual Meeting, 89. **CONTACT ADDRESS** Dept Philos, Christopher Newport Univ, 1 Univ Place, Newport News, VA 23606-2949. **EMAIL** jpowell@cnu.edu

POWELL, MARK ALLAN
DISCIPLINE NEW TESTAMENT **EDUCATION** Tex Lutheran Col, BA, 75; Trinity Lutheran Sem, MDiv, 80; Union Theol Sem, PhD, 87. **CAREER** Asst prof, 87-92; dir, Cont Edu, Post-Grad Stud, 89-92; assoc prof, 92-; Robert and Phyllis Leatherman prof; assoc ed, Catholic Biblical Q, 95- ; ed, Soc of Biblical Lit Diss Series (New Testament), 98- ; ch, Historical Jesus Sect, Soc of Biblical Lit, 00- . **HONORS AND AWARDS** Outstanding Young Grad Awd, Tex Luth Col, 89; Leatherman Ch in New Testament, Trinity Luth Sem, 98. **MEMBERSHIPS** E Great Lakes Biblical Soc; Cath Biblical Assn. **SELECTED PUBLICATIONS** Auth, What Are They Saying About Luke?, Paulist Pr (New York), 89; auth, What Is Narrative Criticism? Guides to Biblical Scholarship Series, Fortress Pr (Minneapolis), 90; auth, What Are They Saying About Acts?, Paulist Pr (New York), 91; auth, THe Bible and Modern Literary Criticism: A Critical Assessment and Annotated Bibliography, Greenwood Pr (New York), 92; auth, God With Us: Toward a Pastoral Theology of Matthew's Gospel, Fortress Pr (Minneapolis),95; auth, A Fortress Introduction to..The Gospels, Fortress Pr (Minneapolis), 98; auth, Jesus As A Figure in History: How Modern Historians View the Man from Galilee, Westminster/John Knox Pr (Louisville), 98; auth, Chasing hte Eastern Star: Adventures in Biblical Reader-Response Criticism, Westminster/John Knox Pr (Louisville), 01. **CONTACT ADDRESS** Bible Dept, Trinity Lutheran Sem, 2199 E Main St, Columbus, OH 43209-2334. **EMAIL** mapowell@trinity.capital.edu

POWELL, SAM
PERSONAL Born 02/23/1956, San Bernardino, CA, m, 1976, 2 children **DISCIPLINE** PHILOSOPHY AND RELIGION **EDUCATION** Point Loma Nazarene Univ, BA, 78; Nazarene Theol Sem, MDiv, 81; Claremont Grad Univ, PhD, 87. **CAREER** Lectr Theol, Nazarene Theol Col, 94-95; Prof Philos & Relig, Point Loma Nazarene Univ, 86-. **HONORS AND AWARDS** Templeton Found Sci-Relig Course Prog Award, 96-97; Wesley Ctr Fel 21st Century Stud, 98-99. **MEMBERSHIPS** Am Acad Relig; Soc Bibl Lit. **RESEARCH** German philosophy and religious thought; the doctrine of the Trinity. **SELECTED PUBLICATIONS** Auth, The Doctrine of the Trinity in 19th Century American Wesleyan Theology, Wesleyan Theol Jour, 83; Religious Experience and Myth: The Philosophy of C H Weisse, Annals of Scholar, 89; Thinking About Economics and Ethics as a Wesleyan, Grace in the Academic Community, Festschrift for Dr Cecil Paul, Point Loma Press, 96; Committing Christianity in Public, Maps and Models for Ministry, Point Loma Press, 96; The Fear of the Lord is the Beginning of Wisdom: Thoughts on the Relation between Holiness and Ethics, 99; Holiness and Community, Intervarsity Press, 99; auth, The Trinity in German Theololgy, Cambridge Univ Press, 00; auth, " History and Eschatology in the Thought of Wolfhart Pannenberg," Fideset Historiea 32, (00). **CONTACT ADDRESS** Point Loma Nazarene Col, 3900 Lomaland Dr, San Diego, CA 92106. **EMAIL** spowell@ptloma.edu

POWER, GARRETT
PERSONAL Born 10/16/1938, Baltimore, MD, m, 1960, 3 children **DISCIPLINE** LAW **EDUCATION** Duke Univ, AB, 60, LLB, 62; Univ Ill, LLM, 65. **CAREER** Prof Law, Univ Md, Baltimore City, 63-, Prin investr, Chesapeake Res Consortium, 71-; assoc ed, Coastal Zone Mgt J, 72- **RESEARCH** Environmental law; coastal zone planning. **SELECTED PUBLICATIONS** Coauth, Chesapeake Bay In Legal Perspective, 70 & Legal Problems Of Coal Mine Reclamation, 72, US Govt Printing Off; contribur, Federal Environmental Law, West Pub, 74; The Case Of The 1989 Bordeaux, J Of Legal Ed, Vol 44, 94. **CONTACT ADDRESS** 107 Longwood Rd, Baltimore, MD 21210. **EMAIL** gpower@law.umaryland.edu

POWER, MARGARET
PERSONAL Born 08/15/1953, Nashville, TN, s **DISCIPLINE** PHILOSOPHY, FRENCH, HISTORY **EDUCATION** Georgetown Univ, BA, 75; San Francisco State Univ, MA, 79; Univ Ill Chicago, PhD, 97. **CAREER** Vis Asst Prof/Asst Prof, Ill Inst of Technology, 98-. **HONORS AND AWARDS** Orgn of Am States, Res, 93-94; Woodrow Wilson Women Studies, 95; Guggenheim, 96-97. **MEMBERSHIPS** AHA, Latin Am Studies Asn, Congress on Latin Am Hist. **RESEARCH** Women, gender, the Armed Forces, technology, the right in Chile and Latin America. **SELECTED PUBLICATIONS** Auth, Right-using Women in Chilean Politico, 1964-1973, Penn State Press, forthcoming; auth, Right-using Women Across the Ilahe, Routledge Press, forthcoming. **CONTACT ADDRESS** Dept Humanities, Illinois Inst of Tech, 3300 S Federal St, Chicago, IL 60616-3795. **EMAIL** Power@iit.edu

POWER, WILLIAM L.
PERSONAL Born 08/02/1934, Biloxi, MS, m, 1970, 4 children **DISCIPLINE** PHILOSOPHY OF RELIGION, PHILOSOPHICAL THEOLOGY **EDUCATION** Univ Miss, BA, 56; Emory Univ, MDiv, 59, PhD, 65. **CAREER** Prof, Lambuth Col, 65-67; prof, Univ Ga, 67-. **HONORS AND AWARDS** Vice Pres and Pres of SE Region of the Am Acad of Relig, 90-91, 91-92; Vice Pres and Pres of Soc for Philos of Relig, 93-94, 94-95. **MEMBERSHIPS** Am Acad of Relig, Soc for the Philos of Relig, Soc for the Study of Process Philos, The Highlands Inst for Am, Relig and Philos Thought. **RESEARCH** Hist and Systematic Theol; Philos of Relig. **SELECTED PUBLICATIONS** Rev, "On Divine Perfection," Anglican Theol Rev, LXXV, no. 1, (Winter 93): 34-47; auth, "Our Konwledge of God," Perspectives in Religious Stud, 21, no. 3, (94): 231-243; auth, "Divine Poeisis and Abstract Entities," Religious Stud, 30, no. 3, (94): 335-341; auth, "Imago Dei -Imatitio Dei," International Journal for Phlosophy of Relig, 42, No. 3, (97): 131-141. **CONTACT ADDRESS** Dept Relig, Univ of Georgia, 0 Ga Univ, Athens, GA 30602-0002. **EMAIL** power@uga.edu

POWERS, BRUCE P.
PERSONAL Born 05/25/1940, Savannah, GA, m, 2 children **DISCIPLINE** RELIGION **EDUCATION** Mercer Univ, BA, 64; Southern Baptist Sem, MRE, 67, PhD, 71. **CAREER** Dir, Church Prog Training Center, Sunday Sch Bd, Nashville TN, 71-77; prof, Southeastern Baptist Theol Sem, Wake Forest, NC, 78-95; assoc dean, Campbell Univ, 96- . **HONORS AND AWARDS** Awd for Fac Excellence, 89; Dean's Excellence Awd, 96. **MEMBERSHIPS** Intl Relig Educ Asn; North Am Prof of Christian Educ; World Future Soc. **RESEARCH** Christian Leadership, Growing Faith. **SELECTED PUBLICATIONS** Auth, "How to Handle Conflict in the Church," Convention, 91; "Christian Education Handbook," rev, "Broadman & Holman," 96; "Church Administration Handbook," rev ed, Broadman & Holman, 97; auth, Covenant Ministry, NC Convention, 99. **CONTACT ADDRESS** Divinity Sch, Campbell Univ, Buies Creek, NC 27506-4050.

POWERS, DAVID STEPHEN
PERSONAL Born 07/23/1951, Cleveland, OH, m, 1984, 3 children **DISCIPLINE** ISLAMIC HISTORY, LAW **EDUCATION** Yale Univ, BA, 73; Princeton Univ, MA & PhD(Islamic hist), 79. **CAREER** Prof Arabic & Islamics, Cornell Univ, 79-. **MEMBERSHIPS** Am Oriental Soc; Mid Eastern Studies Asn. **RESEARCH** Islamic law; Islamic history; medieval social history. **SELECTED PUBLICATIONS** Auth, Studies in Quran and Hadith: The Formation of the Islamic Law of Inheritance, Berkeley, 86; Islamic Legal Interpretation: Muftis and Their Fatwas, Harvard, 86; The History of al-Tabari, volume XXIV The Empire in Transition, tras, David Stephen Powers, Suny Press, 89. **CONTACT ADDRESS** Cornell Univ, Rockefeller Hall, Ithaca, NY 14853-0001. **EMAIL** dsp4@cornell.edu

POWERS, MADISON
DISCIPLINE PHILOSOPHY **EDUCATION** Oxford Univ, PhD. **CAREER** Assoc prof. **RESEARCH** Political, legal, and moral philosophy; genetics and reproductive ethics. **SELECTED PUBLICATIONS** Co-auth, Aids, Women and the Next Generation. **CONTACT ADDRESS** Dept of Philosophy, Georgetown Univ, 37th and O St, Washington, DC 20057.

POYTHRESS, VERN S.
PERSONAL Born 03/29/1946, Madera, CA, m, 1983, 2 children **DISCIPLINE** THEOLOGY, MATHEMATICS **EDUCATION** Cal Tech, BS, 66; Harvard Univ, PhD, 70; Westminster Theological Seminary, MDiv, 74, ThM, 74; Cambirdge Univ, MLitt, 77; Univ of Stellenbosch, ThD, 81. **CAREER** Tchg asst, 69, asst prof, Fresno State Col, 70-71; tchg fel, Harvard Univ, 70-71; lectr, summer 74, adjunct asst prof, Univ of Okla, 77; Asst Prof, 76-81, Assoc Prof, 81-87, Prof, Westminster Theological Seminary, 87-. **MEMBERSHIPS** Evangelica Theol Soc; Ling Asn of Can and U.S. **RESEARCH** Hermeneutics; New Testament. **SELECTED PUBLICATIONS** Auth, Symphonic Theology, Korean Lang, Compass House Pub, 93; Divine Meaning of Scripture, The Right Doctrine from the Wrong Texts? Essays on the Use of the Old Testament in the New, Baker, 94; Understanding Dispensationalists, Presbyterian and Reformed, 94; Reforming Ontology and Logic in the Light of the Trinity: An Application of Van Til's Idea of Analogy, Westminster Theological J, 95; Indifferentism and Rigorism in the Church: With Implications for Baptizing Small Children, Westminster Theological J, 97; Linking Small Children with Infants in the Theology of Baptizing, Westminster Theological J, 97; Gender in Bible Translation: Exploring a Connection with Male Representatives, Westminster Theological J, 98; Keep On Praying!, Decision, 98; contribur, Notes on Revelation, New Geneva Study Bible, Thomas Nelson, 95. **CONTACT ADDRESS** Westminster Theol Sem, Pennsylvania, PO Box 27009, Philadelphia, PA 19118-0009.

POZZO, RICCARDO
PERSONAL Born 06/07/1959, Milan, Italy, m, 1992, 1 child **DISCIPLINE** KANT AND HEGEL **EDUCATION** Univ Trier, PhD; Universitaet des Saarlandes, PhD; Universitaet Trier, Dr.phil.habil. **CAREER** Universitaet Trier, Philos, Cath Univ Am. **HONORS AND AWARDS** Alexander von Humboldt Fel, 90-91 and 98. **MEMBERSHIPS** Am Cath Philos Assoc; Deutscher Hochschulverband; Hegel Soc of Am; Kant-Gesellschaft; North Am Kant Soc; Societa Italiana di Studi Kantiani. **RESEARCH** Renaissance; Enlightenment; German Idealism; Contemporary Philosophy. **SELECTED PUBLICATIONS** Auth, Karl-Heinz Iltings Edition und Interpretation der Hegelschen Rechtsphilosophie, Hegel-Jahrbuch, 94; Philosophische Terminologie zwischen Leibniz und Meier, In VI. Internationaler Leibniz-Kongress, Vortrage, Hannover, Leibniz-Gesellschaft, 94, Coed, Norbert Hinske, Kant-Index. Bd. 6: Stellenindex und Konkordanz zur 'Logik; Transl, Henry S. Harris, La fenomenologia dell'autocoscienza in Hegel, 95; Wissenschaft und Reformation. Die Beispiele der Universitaten Konigsberg und Helmstedt, 95; Tracce zabarelliane nella logica kantiana, 95; Formal Logic versus Epistemic Logic between 1500 and 1800, 95; Coed, John Locke, Anleitung des menschlichen Verstandes. Eine Abhandlung von den Wunderwerken. In der ubersetzung Konigsberg 1755 von Georg David Kypke - Of the Conduct of the Understanding. A Discourse of Miracles. Nach der ersten Werkausgabe London 1714. Festgabe fur Norbert Hinske zum 65. Geburstag, 96; Theodor F. Geraets, La logica di Hegel fra religione e storia, 96; Vorlesungsverzeichnisse als Quelle der Universitatsgeschichte Preussens, 97; 18 Seiki Kenihisuberuku Daigakushi (The History of the University of Konigsberg in the 18th Century), 97; 18 Seiki Kenihisuberuku Daigaku no Kougiyoukou (Course Announcments at the University of Konigsberg in the 18th Century), 97; auth, El giro kantiano, Translated by Jorge Perez de Tudela, Madrid: Ediciones Akal, 98, 64p.; auth, Res considerata and modus considerandi rem: Averroes, Aquinas, Jacopo, Zabearel-

la, and Cornelius Martini on Reduplication, In Medioevo 24, 98, 251-67; auth, Kant Within the Tradition of Modern Logic: The Role of the Introduction: Idea of a Transcendental Logic, In Review of Metaphysics, 52, 98, 4 issue 206, 295-310; auth, Die Etablierung des naturwissenschafftlichen Unterrichts unter dem Einflub Melanchthons, In Melanchthon und die Naturwissenschaften seiner Zeit, Edited by Gunther Frank and Stefan Rehein, Sigmaringen: Jan Throbecke, 98, 273-87; coed, Vorlesungsverzeichnisse der Universitat Konigsberg, 1720-1804: Reprint mit einer Einleitung und Registern, edited by Michael Oberhausen and Riccardo Pozzo, Stuttgart-Bad Cannstatt: Frommann-Holzboog, 99, LXVIII-778P; auth, The Philiosophic Works by Antonio Rosmini in English Translation, American Catholic Philosophical Quarterly, 73, Autumn 99, Forthcoming; auth, Vorlesungsverzeichnisse als Quelle der Universitatsgeschichte PreuBens, In Studien zur Entwicklung PreuBischer Universitaten, Edited by Reinhard Brandt and Werner Stark, Wiesbaden: Otto Harrassowitz, 99, p. 59-80; auth, Hegels Kantverstandnis im Manuskript zur Psychologie und Transzendentalphilosophie aus dem Jahre 1794, In Hegels Denkentwicklung in der Berner und Frankfurter Zeit, Edited by Martin Bondeli and Helmut Linneweber-Lammerskitten, Munchen: Wilhelm Fink, 99, 15-29; auth, Johann Amos Comenius, Christian August Crusius, Christian Garve, Martin Luther, Gottfried Ploucquet, Ehrenfried Water von Tschirnhaus, Giambattista Vico, In Grobes Werklexikon der Philosophie, Edited by Franco Volpi, Stuttgart: Kroner Verlag, 99, 322-23, 343-45, 542-43, 960-62, 1202-03, 1513-14, 1528-32. **CONTACT ADDRESS** Catholic Univ of America, 620 Michigan Ave Northeast, Washington, DC 20064. **EMAIL** pozzo@cua.edu

PRADES, JOSE ALBERT
PERSONAL Born 11/01/1929, Valencia, Spain, m, 1971 **DISCIPLINE** SOCIOLOGY OF RELIGION **EDUCATION** Cath Univ Louvain, lic econ, 57, lic soc sci, 63, PhD(soc sci), 65. **CAREER** Asst soc sci, Cath Univ Louvain, 65-70; asst prof sociol relig, Cath Inst Paris, 70-71; vis prof, 71-74, Prof Sociol Relig, Univ Que, Montreal, 74-, Dir Dept Relig, 78-, Mem, Coun Sci Res, Spain, 65-; Conf Learned Socs, Can, 71- **MEMBERSHIPS** Fr-Can Asn Advan Sci. **RESEARCH** Contemporary industrial society; ultimate concerns and social class in Canada today. **SELECTED PUBLICATIONS** Auth, Valeurs Religieuses En Milieu Urbain, Social Compass, 66; La Cociologie De La Religion Chez Max Weber, Nauwelaerts, Louvain, 69; Sur Le Concept De Religion, Relig Studies, 73; Renouveau Communantaire Et Utopie Autogestionnaire, In: Renouveau Communantaire Au Quebec, Ed Fides, 74. **CONTACT ADDRESS** Dept of Relig, Univ of Quebec, Montreal, C P 8888, Montreal, QC, Canada H3C 3P8. **EMAIL** prades.jose_a@uqam.ca

PRADO, C. G.
PERSONAL Born Guatemala **DISCIPLINE** PHILOSOPHY **EDUCATION** Univ Berkeley, BA; MA; Queen's Univ, PhD. **CAREER** Dept Philos, Queen's Univ **RESEARCH** Bioethics while doing research on the decline of interpretive flexibility in advanced age; the rationality of suicide and the permissibility of physician-assisted suicide; health-care policy. **SELECTED PUBLICATIONS** Auth, Starting With Foucault: An Introduction to Genealogy; Descartes and Foucault: A Contrastive Introduction to Philosophy; The Last Choice: Preemptive Suicide in Advanced Age; The Limits of Pragmatism; Rethinking How We Age: A New View of the Aging Mind; Making Believe: Philosophical Reflections on Fiction; Illusions of Faith: A Critique of Noncredal Religion. **CONTACT ADDRESS** Philos Dept, Queen's Univ at Kingston, Kingston, ON, Canada K7L 3N6. **EMAIL** pradocg@post.queensu.ca

PRAGER, JONAS
PERSONAL Born New York, NY, 2 children **DISCIPLINE** ECONOMICS **EDUCATION** Yeshiva Col, NYork City, AB (magna cum laude), 59; Columbia Univ, PhD, 64. **CAREER** Instr, 62-64, asst prof, 64-69, assoc prof, New York Univ, 69-, Dir Graduate Studies, Dept of Economics, 77-81, 86-89; vis sr economist, res dept, The Bank of Israel, 65-67; observer, US Delegation, CENTO Symposium on Central Banking, Monetary Policy, and Economic Development, 71; consult, United Nations Development prog; lect, US Information Service, India, 83, Yugoslavia, West Germany, 84, France, Hungary, 89; part, Fed Reserve Bank of NY, Central Banking Sem, 70, 74, 86; vis scholar, The Bank of Israel, 80, 82-83; vis prof, Hebrew Univ of Jerusalem, 82-83. **HONORS AND AWARDS** New York State Regents Teaching Fel, 59-61; Columbia Univ Fac Scholarship, 61-62; Am Philos Soc grant, 74-75, 75-76; Fulbright-Hays Fac Res Fel, 71, 82-83. **MEMBERSHIPS** Am Economic Asn; Hagop Kervorkian Center for Near Eastern Studies, NY Univ; C V Starr Center for Applied Economics, NY Univ; United Nations Development Program, Interregional Network on Privatization; Center for the Study of Central Banks. **RESEARCH** Privatization, banking regulation. **SELECTED PUBLICATIONS** Auth, Applied Microeconomics: An Intermediate Text, Irwin, 93; Contracting Out Government Services, Public Administration Rev, March/April 94; Banking Privatization in Israel, 1983-1994: A Case Study in Political Economy, Banco Nazionale del Lavoro Quart Rev, June 96; Privatizing Local Government Operations: Lessons from Federal Contracting Out Methodology, with S Desai, Public Productivity and Management Rev, Dec 96; Contracting Out: Half Speed Ahead, J of Int Affairs, winter 97; Banking Privatization: How Compelling is the Case? in Anthony Bennett, ed, How Does Privatization Work? Essays in Honor of V V Ramanadham, Routledge, 97; Balancing the Scales: Halakha (Jewish Law), The Firm, and Information Asymmetries, in A Levine and M Pava, Jewish Business Ethics: The Firm and Its Stakeholders, Aronson, 99; numerous other publications. **CONTACT ADDRESS** Dept of Ecomonics, New York Univ, 269 Mercer St, New York, NY 10003. **EMAIL** jonas.prager@nyu.edu

PRATICO, GARY D.
DISCIPLINE OLD TESTAMENT **EDUCATION** Berkshire Christian Col, BA; Gordon-Conwell Theol Sem, MDiv; Harvard Divinity Sch, ThD. **CAREER** Assoc prof, Gordon-Conwell Theol Sem, 82-; dir, Hebrew Lang Prog. **HONORS AND AWARDS** Cur, Harvard Semitic Mus, 82-93. **SELECTED PUBLICATIONS** Auth, Nelson Glueck's 1938-1940 Excavations at Tell el-Kheleifeh: A Reappraisal; pub(s), on topics concerning biblical and ancient Near Eastern studies. **CONTACT ADDRESS** Gordon-Conwell Theol Sem, 130 Essex St, South Hamilton, MA 01982.

PRATT, RICHARD L., JR.
PERSONAL Born 10/17/1953, Roanoke, VA, m **DISCIPLINE** RELIGION **EDUCATION** Covenant Col, 73; Roanoke Col, BA, 77; Westminster Theol Sem, 79; Union Theol Sem, MDiv, 81; Harvard Univ, ThD, 87. **CAREER** Pulpit supply & conf speaker, 84-; from asst prof to assoc prof to prof, Reformed Theol Sem, 84-; instr, Chesapeake Theol Sem, 83-84. **SELECTED PUBLICATIONS** Auth, 1 and 2 Chronicles, New Geneva Study Bibl, 95; auth, Designed for Dignitym 93. **CONTACT ADDRESS** 1231 Reformation Dr., Oviedo, FL 32765-7197. **EMAIL** RichPratt@aol.com

PREBISH, CHARLES STUART
PERSONAL Born 10/11/1944, Chicago, IL, m, 1968, 2 children **DISCIPLINE** BUDDHIST STUDIES **EDUCATION** Case Western Reserve Univ, BA, 66, MA, 68; Univ Wis, PhD, 71. **CAREER** Asst prof, 71-77, Assoc Prof Relig Studies, Pa State Univ, University Park, 77-99; ed, J Buddhist Ethics, 94-; ed, Critical Rev Bks Relig, 94-98; series ed, Critical Studies in Buddhism, 96; Full Prof, PA State Univ, 99-. **HONORS AND AWARDS** Nat Sci Found grant, 72-73; Yehan Numata (visiting) Chair in Buddhist Studies, Univ Calgary, Fall 93; Am Acad Relig grant, 94; Rockefeller Found Hum Fel, 97-98. **MEMBERSHIPS** Am Acad Relig; Asn Asian Studies; Am Orient Soc; Int Asn Buddhist Studies. **RESEARCH** Buddhist monastic lit; early Buddhist hist and doctrine; Buddhism in Am. **SELECTED PUBLICATIONS** Auth, Theories concerning the Skandhaka: An appraisal, 8/73 & A review of scholarship on the Buddhist councils, 2/74, J Asian Studies; The Pratimoksa puzzle: Fact versus fantasy, J Am Orient Soc, 74; Co-ed & contribr, Introduction to the Religions of the East: Reader, 74, Kendall/Hunt; ed & contribr, Buddhism: A Modern Perspective, 75 & transl, Buddhist Monastic Discipline, 75, Pa State Univ Press; auth, American Buddhism, Duxbury Press, 79; Religion and Sport, Greenwood Press, 92; Historical Dictionary of Buddhism, Scarecrow Press, 93; A Survey of Vinaya Literature, Curzon Press, 94; co-ed, The Faces of Buddhism in America, Univ CA Press, 98; auth, Luminous Passage: The Practice and Study of Buddhism in America, Univ CA Press, 99. **CONTACT ADDRESS** Relig Studies Program, Pennsylvania State Univ, Univ Park, 216 Weaver Bldg, University Park, PA 16802-5503. **EMAIL** csp1@psu.edu

PREISSER, THOMAS
PERSONAL Born 04/12/1939, New Orleans, LA, m, 1964, 2 children **DISCIPLINE** HISTORY, POLITICAL SCIENCE **EDUCATION** Stanford Univ, BA, 64; Northwestern Univ, MA, 68; Col of William and Mary, PhD, 77. **CAREER** Instr, Oakland Community Col, 68-70; Prof and Chair, Sinclair Community Col, 73-. **HONORS AND AWARDS** NEH Fel, 84, 99. **MEMBERSHIPS** Am Hist Asn, Ohio Acad of Hist, Nat Coun for Hist Educ. **RESEARCH** European History especially Renaissance, Reformation and Early Modern Europe. **SELECTED PUBLICATIONS** Auth, "The Virginia Decision to Use Negro Soldiers in the Civil War, 1864-1965," Virginia Magazine of History and Biography, 75; auth, "The 'Precarious Trade' of a Virginia tobacco Merchant: Harry Piper of Alexandria, 1749-1776," Alexandria History, 78; auth, "Alexandria and the Evolution of the Northern Virginia Economy, 1749-1776," Virginia Magazine of History and biography, 81; auth, "White Servant labor in Colonial Alexandria, 1749-1776," Northern Virginia Heritage, 82; auth, "Working on the Hot Side of the Lights: Several Techniques for Effective Television Instruction," social Science Perspectives Journal, 89; auth, "Strengthening Our Community Ties: Corporate Training Programs," Journal of the Ohio Association of Two-Year Colleges, 94. **CONTACT ADDRESS** Dept Humanities, Sinclair Comm Col, 444 W 3rd St, Dayton, OH 45402-1421. **EMAIL** tpreisse@sinclair.edu

PRELL, RIV-ELLEN
PERSONAL Born 10/15/1947, Los Angeles, CA, m, 1970, 2 children **DISCIPLINE** AMERICAN STUDIES, JEWISH STUDIES, ANTHROPOLOGY **EDUCATION** Univ S Calif, BA; Univ Chicago, MA; PhD. **CAREER** From assoc prof to prof of Am Studies, Univ Minn, Twin Cities. **HONORS AND AWARDS** Phi Beta Kappa; Nat Jewish Bk Awd, 89. **MEMBERSHIPS** ASA; ASSJ; JSA. **RESEARCH** Ethnicity, 20th century American Jews, ritual, religion. **SELECTED PUBLICATIONS** Auth, Fighting to Become Americans: Jews, Gender and the Anxiety of Assimilation; auth, Prayer and Community: The Hauura in American Judaism; coed, Interpreting Women's Lives: Personal Narratives and Feminist Theory. **CONTACT ADDRESS** Dept Am Studies, Univ of Minnesota, Twin Cities, 72 Pleasant St SE, 203 Scott Hall, Minneapolis, MN 55455. **EMAIL** prell001@tc.umn.edu

PRENTISS, KAREN PECHILIS
DISCIPLINE RELIGIOUS STUDIES **EDUCATION** Bowdoin Col, AB, 84; Univ Chicago, AM, 86, PhD, 93. **CAREER** ASST PROF, DREW UNIV, 94-. **CONTACT ADDRESS** Relig Stud, Drew Univ, 36 Madison Ave, Madison, NJ 07940.

PRESS, GERALD
PERSONAL Born 01/04/1945, San Diego, CA, m, 1 child **DISCIPLINE** PHILOSOPHY **EDUCATION** Univ Calif Berkeley, AB, 66; Univ Calif San Diego, MA, 69;PhD, 74. **CAREER** Instructor, Grossmont Col, 7-73; Asst Prof, Penn State Univ, 73-75; Instructor, Contra Costa Col, 75-76; Lecturer, Univ Calif Riverside, 76-79; Instructor, Stanford Univ, 80-85; Visiting Asst Prof to Prof, Hunter Col, 85-. **MEMBERSHIPS** APA; SAGP; IPS; ISNS. **RESEARCH** Ancient Philosophy; History of Philosophy; Plato; Aristotle. **SELECTED PUBLICATIONS** Ed, Plato's Dialogues: New Studies and Interpretations, Rowman and Littlefield, 93; auth, "The State of the Question n the Study of Plato," The Southern Journal of Philosophy 34, (96): 507-532; auth, "Continuities and Discontinuities in the History of Republic Interpretation," International Studies in Philosophy 28, (96): 61-78; auth, "Principles of Dramatic and Non-Dogmatic Plato Interpretation," in Plato's Dialogues: New Studies and Interpretation, (G Press, 93), 107-127; auth, "Plato's Dialogues as Enactment," in The Third Way: New Directions in Platonic Studies, (Rowman & Littlefield, 95), 133-152; auth, "The Dialogical Mode in Modern Plato Studies," in Plato's Dialogues: The Dialogical Approach, (Edwin Mellen Press, 97), 1-28; auth, "Origins of Western Philosophic Thinking," in The Columbia History of Western Philosophy, (Columbia Univ Press, 98), 1-6; auth, "A Brief Summary of Aristotle's Writings," in The Columbia History of Western Philosophy, (Columbia Univ Press, 98), 72-74; auth, "Plato" in The Columbia History of Western Philosophy, (Columbia Univ Press, 98), 35-52; ed, Who Speaks for Plato? Studies in Platonic Anonymity, Rowman and Littlefield, 00; auth, "The Logic of Attributing Characters' Views to Plato," in Who Speaks for Plato, (G Press, 00), 27-38; auth, "The Elenchos in Charmides 162-175," in Re-Examining the Socratic Elenchos, Penn State Univ Press, forthcoming. **CONTACT ADDRESS** Dept Philos, Hunter Col, CUNY, 695 Park Ave, New York, NY 10021-5024. **EMAIL** gerald.press@hunter.cuny.edu

PRESSEAU, JACK R.
PERSONAL Born 11/16/1933, Curtisville, PA, m, 1955, 4 children **DISCIPLINE** RELIGIOUS EDUCATION **EDUCATION** IN State Tchr(s), Col PA, BS, 55; Pittsburgh-Xenia Sem, MDiv, 58; Presby Sch Christian Educ, MCE, 59; Univ Pittsburgh, PhD, 65. **CAREER** Assoc pastor, North Presby Church, Elmira, NY, 59-62; studies asst relig educ, Univ Pittsburgh, 63-65; assoc prof relig & psychol, 65-69, prof psychol, 69-75, counselor, 72-75, Prof Relig, Presby Col, SC, 69-98, retired, 98. **RESEARCH** Faith development; recruiting and training for church vocations. **SELECTED PUBLICATIONS** Auth, I'm Saved, You're Saved--Maybe, John Knox Press, 77; Gospel illustrations: What's memorable may be irrelevant, Duke Divinity Sch Rev, winter 78; Life maps, Harvard Educ Rev, 11/80; Tradition, trends, and tomorrow, Presby Survey, 9/81; Pendulum swings and pre-ministerial preparation, The Presby Outlook, 4/12/80; Teach-niques, John Knox Press, 82. **CONTACT ADDRESS** Rt 2, Box 327, Clinton, SC 29325-2865.

PRESSMAN, H. MARK
PERSONAL Born 07/07/1968, m, 1998 **DISCIPLINE** PHILOSOPHY **EDUCATION** U C Davis, PhD, 97. **CAREER** Adj Instr, Philosophy, Fresno City Col & Calif State Univ, Fresno. **MEMBERSHIPS** Am Philos Asn. **RESEARCH** Hume; philosophy of Religion **SELECTED PUBLICATIONS** Auth, Hume on Geometry, Hume Studies, 97. **CONTACT ADDRESS** 1136 N. Columbus Ave No. 206, Glendale, CA 91202. **EMAIL** markpressman@netzero.net

PRESTON, CHERYL B.
PERSONAL Born 11/23/1952, Provo, UT, m, 1976, 3 children **DISCIPLINE** LAW **EDUCATION** Brigham Young Univ, BA, summa, cum laude, 75, JD, 79. **CAREER** Assoc Prof, 89-95, Prof, 95-, BYU Rueben Clark Law Sch; VP, Sr Counl, 87-89, Fst Interstate Bank SLC; Assoc, 84-87, Holme Roberts and Owen SLC; Assoc, 81-83, O'Melveny and Myers LA; law clerk, 79-80, Hon Monroe G McKay Ct of Appeals. **HONORS AND AWARDS** Phi Delta Phi; Order of the Coif; ISR Gnt David M Kennedy Cen; BYU Women's Res Gnt; UT Court of Appeals nom. **MEMBERSHIPS** NAWJ; BYUFWA; AALS; ABA; USB; CBA; ALI. **SELECTED PUBLICATIONS** Auth, Joining Traditional Values and Feminist Legal Scholarship, J

Legal Edu, 93; This Old House: A Blueprint for Constructive Feminism, Geo L J, 95; It Moves Even if We Don't: A Reply to Arthur Austin, The Top Ten Politically Correct Law Reviews, Tenn L Rev, 96; Feminist Legal Theory: Concepts Applications and Bibliography, Utah State Bar Annual Meeting Source Book, 96; auth, Consuming Sexism: Pornography Suppression in the Larger Context of Commercial Images, GA L Rev, 97; coed, Conflict Resolution: Come Let Us Reason Together, in: Talks Selected from the 97 LDS Women's Conf, 98; auth, Significant Bits and Pieces: Learning from Fashion Magazines About Violence Against Women, 9 UCLA Women's Law Jour, 98. **CONTACT ADDRESS** Brigham Young Univ, 424 JRCB, Provo, UT 84602. **EMAIL** prestonc@lawgate.byu.edu

PREUS, ANTHONY
PERSONAL Born 07/05/1936, Perth Amboy, NJ, m, 1984, 3 children **DISCIPLINE** PHILOSOPHY **EDUCATION** Luther Col, BA, 58; Oxford Univ, BA, 62; MA, 66; Johns Hopkins Univ, PhD, 68. **CAREER** Prof, Binghamton Univ, 64-. **HONORS AND AWARDS** Woodrow Wilson Fel; Rhodes Scholar; Fels Fellow. **MEMBERSHIPS** Soc for Ancient Greek Philos. **RESEARCH** Ancient philosophy and science; Medical ethics. **SELECTED PUBLICATIONS** Auth, "The Priority of the Intelligible," Apeiron XXVIII, (95): 239-249; auth, "Some Ancient Ecological Myths and Metaphors," in the Greeks and the Environment, (Roman & Littlefield, 97), 11-18; auth, "Greek Philosophy in Egypt: From solon to the Arab conquest," in Greeks and Barbarians: Essays on the Interactions between Greeks and Non-Greeks in antiquity and the Consequences for Eurocentrism, CDL Press, 97; auth, "Polemon of Athens," "Sotion of Alexandria," "Hermetica: Egyptian Religious and Philosophical Texts," in Encyclopedia of Ancient Philosophy, (Greenwood Pub, 97), 439, 524, 263-265; auth, "Thoth and Apollo. Greek Myths of the Origin of Philosophy," Methexis XI, (98): 113-125; auth, "Hellenic Philosophy of Law: Conceptual Framework," in Encyclopedia of Philosophy of Law, (Garland Press, 99), 353-360; auth, "Hellenic Philosophy of Law: Sources for the Earlier Period," in Encyclopedia of Philosophy of Law, (Garland Press, 99), 356-360. **CONTACT ADDRESS** Dept Philos, SUNY, Binghamton, PO Box 6000, Binghamton, NY 13902-6000. **EMAIL** Apreus@binghamton.edu

PRIALKOWSKI, KRISTOFF
PERSONAL Born 06/13/1958, Warsaw, Poland **DISCIPLINE** PHILOSOPHY **EDUCATION** Univ of Lublin, MA, Christian Philos; Temple Univ, MA, 91, PhD, 97. **CAREER** Lectr, CCP, 90-; Adjunct Prof, 86-94, Villanova Univ; Adjunct Prof, 94-96, St Joseph's Univ. **HONORS AND AWARDS** Pres Scholarship, Villanova Univ; Tchg Asst, Temple Univ. **MEMBERSHIPS** APA. **RESEARCH** Epistemology/Metaphysics. **CONTACT ADDRESS** 762 Rugby Rd, Bryn Mawr, PA 19010.

PRICE, CHARLES EUGENE
PERSONAL Born Apalachicola, FL, m **DISCIPLINE** LAW **EDUCATION** Johnson C Smith U, BA 1946; Howard U, AM 1949; Johns Hopkins U, further study 1951-52; Boston U, further study 1956; John Marshall Law Sch JD, 1967; Harvard Law Sch, CS, 1980. **CAREER** NC Mutual Life Ins, ins mgr 1949-50; Butler Coll, dean of coll 1950-53; FL Mem Coll, dean of coll 1953-55; NAACP (assgnd to GA), field dir 1955-57; Livingstone Coll, asst prof 1957-59; Morris Brown Coll, assoc prof/atty. **HONORS AND AWARDS** Ldrshp Awrd GA NAACP 1965-66; schlrshp Alpha Kappa Mu 1954; artcls pub Atlanta Daily Wrld & Pittsbrgh Courier 1955-57; Tchr of Yr Morris Brown Coll 1972, 1980-81. **MEMBERSHIPS** Bd dir Hemphill Food Serv 1982-; cnsltnt Thomas & Russell 1979-; atty at law State Bar of GA Fed Bars 1968-; bd dir Dekalb, GA EOA 1965-70; pres Dekalb, GA NAACP Chptr 1962-70; adv bd Sm Bsns Adm GA 1968-82. **CONTACT ADDRESS** Morris Brown Col, 643 MLK Dr NW, Atlanta, GA 30314.

PRICE, DANIEL
PERSONAL Born 10/03/1965, Houston, TX, m, 2000 **DISCIPLINE** PHILOSOPHY **EDUCATION** DePaul Univ, PhD, 99; teaching, Honors Col, Univ of Houston, 01-. **CAREER** Dept Philos, De Paul Univ **SELECTED PUBLICATIONS** Auth, Without a Woman to Read: Toward the Daughter in Post modernism, St. Univ of NY Press, 97; art, Negotiated Escape, Cimarron Review, 93; Who Owns the Lie? The Problem of Presentation in Shakespeare's Troilus and Cressida, in Man and World, 94; Stein's Audiences: Gertrude Stein and the Philosophical Exemplar, in: Jour for the Brit Soc of Phenomenology, 96. **CONTACT ADDRESS** Dept of Philos, DePaul Univ, 1150 W Fullerton Ave, Chicago, IL 60614. **EMAIL** dprice3@mail.uh.edu

PRICE, MARJORIE S.
DISCIPLINE PHILOSOPHY **EDUCATION** Barnard Col, BA; NYork Univ, PhD. **CAREER** Prof, Univ Ala Birmingham, 77-. **RESEARCH** Metaphysics, philosophy of mathematics, philosophy of language. **CONTACT ADDRESS** Dept of Philosophy, Univ of Alabama, Birmingham, 1400 University Blvd, Birmingham, AL 35294-1150. **EMAIL** price@uab.edu

PRICE, MONROE E.
DISCIPLINE LAW **EDUCATION** Yale Univ, BA, 60; LLB, 64. **CAREER** Prof, UCLA, 68; Joseph and Sadie Danzinger Prof, Yeshiva Univ. **HONORS AND AWARDS** Pres, Calif Found Community Service Cable Television; dep dir, Sloan Commission Cable Comm. **RESEARCH** Communications policy; Native American land and water rights; copyright and the arts. **SELECTED PUBLICATIONS** Auth, Law and the American Indian. **CONTACT ADDRESS** Yeshiva Univ, 55 Fifth Ave, New York, NY 10003-4301.

PRICE, ROBERT GEORGE
PERSONAL Born 06/01/1934, New York, NY, m, 1955, 2 children **DISCIPLINE** HISTORY OF LOGIC, ETHICS **EDUCATION** Yale Univ, BA, 55, MA, 57, PhD(philos), 63. **CAREER** From instr to asst prof, 59-66, Assoc Prof Philos, PA State Univ, University Park, 66- **MEMBERSHIPS** Am Philos Asn; Asn Symbolic Logic; Mind Asn. **RESEARCH** History of logic; moral and political philosophy; Greek philosophy. **SELECTED PUBLICATIONS** Auth, Some Antistrophes To The Rhetoric, Philos & Rhet, 68; Ockham And Supposito Personalis, Franciscan Studies, 71; A Refutative Demonstration In Metaphysics Gamma, Philos And Rhetoric, Vol 29, 96. **CONTACT ADDRESS** Dept Philos, Pennsylvania State Univ, Univ Park, 240 Sparks Bldg, University Park, PA 16802-5201.

PRICE, ROBERT M.
PERSONAL Born 07/07/1954, Jackson, MS, m, 1984, 2 children **DISCIPLINE** PHILOSOPHY **EDUCATION** Montclair State Col, BA, 76; Gordon-Cromwell Theol Sem, S Hamilton, MA, Theol, 78; Drew Univ, Madison, NJ, PhM, 80, PhD, 81, PhM, 92, PhD 93. **HONORS AND AWARDS** Phi Kappa Phi; Phi Alpha Theta; Phi Alpha Chi; Who's Who in Biblical Stud and Archaeol; Dissertation Awded Distinction. **MEMBERSHIPS** Soc of Biblical Lit; The Westar Inst; Collegium. **RESEARCH** Christian Origins; Hist Jesus; Auth of Pauline Epistles; Deconstruction. **SELECTED PUBLICATIONS** Auth, Beyond Born Again: Towards Evangelical Maturity, Hypatia Press, 93; The Widow Traditions in Luke-Acts: A Feminist-Critical Scrutiny, Scholars Press, 97; Mystic Rhythms: The Philosophical Vision of RUSH, Borgo Press, 98; Apocryphal Apparitions: 1 Corinthians 15:3-11 as a Post-Pauline Interpolation, Journal of Higher Criticism, 2, #2, 95; Protestant Hermeneutical Axiomatics: A Deconstruction, Christian New Age Quarterly 4-6, 97. **CONTACT ADDRESS** 30 Stockton St, Bloomfield, NJ 07003-5016. **EMAIL** criticus@aol.com

PRICHARD, ROBERT W.
PERSONAL Born 05/14/1949, Washington, D.C., m, 1973, 2 children **DISCIPLINE** CHURCH HISTORY, LITURGY **EDUCATION** Princeton Univ, AB, 71; Berkeley at Yale Divinity Sch, MDiv, 74; Emory Univ, PhD, 83. **CAREER** Asst to the rector, St George's Episcopal Church, 74-77; stud colloquy leader, Emory Univ, 77-79; rector, Clarke Episcopal Parish, 80-83; instr, 80-81; asst prof, 83-89; assoc prof, 89-94; Arthur Lee Kinsolving prof, Va Theol Sem, 94. **HONORS AND AWARDS** Univ Scholar Program, Princeton Univ; Fel, of Episcopal Church Found; interim vicar, st martin's episcopal church, 79-80; la iglesia de san jose, 90. **MEMBERSHIPS** Am Soc of Church Hist; Hist Soc of the Episcopal Church; Conference of Anglican Church Historians. **RESEARCH** 19th century Am Church Hist; 19th century Latin Am Protestantism; Liturgy. **SELECTED PUBLICATIONS** Auth, Readings from the Hist of the Episcopal Church, Morehouse-Barlow, 86; auth, The Bat and the Bishop, Morehouse, 89; auth, A History of the Episcopal Church, Morehouse, 91, rev ed, 99; auth, A Wholesome Example, Bristol, 92; auth, The Nature of Salvation: Theological Consensus in the Episcopal Church, 1801-1873, Univ Ill Press, 97. **CONTACT ADDRESS** Virginia Theol Sem, 3737 Seminary Rd, Alexandria, VA 22304. **EMAIL** RPrichard@vts.edu

PRIEBE, DUANE A.
PERSONAL Born 06/29/1934, Rhinelander, WI, m, 1960, 2 children **DISCIPLINE** THEOLOGY **EDUCATION** Univ Washington, BSc in Physics, 56, dean, 83-99; Luther Sem, BD, 61; Sch of Theol at Claremont, ThD, 65. **CAREER** Pastor, St. Paul Lutheran Church, Garrison ND, 65-67; dir, Great Plains Inst of Theol, 66-70; instr, 63-64, prof, 70- , dean, 83- , Wartburg Sem. **MEMBERSHIPS** Soc of Bibl Lit. **RESEARCH** Theology and Biblical theology; Hermeneutics; the systematic power of simple structures of thought; Christian faith and religious pluralism. **CONTACT ADDRESS** Wartburg Theol Sem, 333 Wartburg Pl, Dubuque, IA 52004. **EMAIL** dapriebe@mwci.net

PRIMACK, MAXWELL
PERSONAL Born 06/04/1934, Brooklyn, NY, m, 1955, 4 children **DISCIPLINE** PHILOSOPHY; INTELLECTUAL HISTORY **EDUCATION** Brandeis Univ, BA, 56; John Hopkins Univ, PhD, 62. **CAREER** Erie Community Col, 26 years; Univ Buffalo (SUNYAB); Lincoln Univ in Pennsylvania; Illinois Inst Tech; Bloomsburg State College. **HONORS AND AWARDS** Cume Laude; Phi Betta Kappa **MEMBERSHIPS** Amer Phil Assoc. **RESEARCH** Marx; Lenin; The Bible Biomedical Ethics. **SELECTED PUBLICATIONS** Auth, A Reinterpretation of Francis Bacon's Philosophy, 68; The Last American Frontier: Education, 72. **CONTACT ADDRESS** 20 Marjann Ter., Buffalo, NY 14223. **EMAIL** mprinted@aol.com

PRIMEAUX, PATRICK
PERSONAL Born 02/01/1947, Abbeville, LA **DISCIPLINE** THEOLOGY **EDUCATION** Univ La, BA, 71; Univ Toronto, MA, 74; Univ Toronto, PhD, 79; Southern Methodist Univ, MBA, 89. **CAREER** Asst Prof, Notre Dame Sem and Grad Sch of Theol, 77-80; Adj Prof, Loyola Univ S, 82-88; Adj Prof, Southern Methodist Univ, 90-91; From Asst Prof to Assoc Prof, St Johns Univ, 92-. **HONORS AND AWARDS** Grant for Innovative Teaching, St Johns Univ, 96; Int Fac Grant, St Johns Univ, 98; Summer Grant, St Johns Univ, 98; Fac Merit Awd, St Johns Univ, 98; Summer Grant, St Johns Univ, 99. **MEMBERSHIPS** Soc for Bus Ethics, Am Asn of Univ Profs, Col Theol Soc, Am Acad of Relig. **RESEARCH** Business ethics. **SELECTED PUBLICATIONS** Coauth, Profit Maximization: The Ethical Mandate of Business, Austin & Winfield Publ (New York, NY), 95; auth, The Moral Passion of Bruce Springsteen, Int Scholars Pr (San Francisco, CA), 96; auth, "A Management Primer for Pastors: 'It's Time to Factor in the Spiritual Bottom Line'," The priest 52-3 (96): 37-42; auth, "Determining Parishioner Satisfaction," The Priest 53-6 (97): 12-20; ed, Humanizing the City: Religion, Politics and the Arts in Critical Conversation, Cath Scholars Pr (San Francisco, CA), 97; ed, Research in Ethical Issues in Organizations, Volume 1, JAI Pr (Stamford), 99; coauth, "Double Bookkeeping: Hierarchical Obedience and Participative Cooperation," J of Bus Ethics 19-1 (99); coauth, "Transformation and Interdependence for Spirituality in Business," Res in Ethical Issues in Orgns 1:1 (99). **CONTACT ADDRESS** Dept Theol, St. John's Univ, 8150 Utopia Pkwy, Jamaica, NY 11439-0001.

PRIMIANO, LEONARD NORMAN
DISCIPLINE RELIGIOUS STUDIES; FOLKLORE AND FOLKLIFE **EDUCATION** Harvard Univ, MTs; Univ Pennsylvania, PhD. **CAREER** Asst Prof, Religious Studies, 93-, Cabrini Col. **CONTACT ADDRESS** Dept of Relig, Cabrini Col, 610 King of Prussia Rd., Radnor, PA 19087-3698. **EMAIL** primiano@cabrini.edu

PRINCE, ARTHUR
PERSONAL Born 08/30/1938, Memphis, TN, s **DISCIPLINE** PHILOSOPHY **EDUCATION** Univ of Memphis, BA, 64, MA, 70; Univ of Tenn, MS, 87; Univ of Okla, PhD, 96. **CAREER** Tchng Asst, Instr, 68-71, Univ of Memphis; Instr, 77-87, Univ of TN; Instr, 86-88, Maryville Univ; Instr, 89-91, Rhodes Col; Instr, 92-, Dyersburg St Univ, Instr, 97-, Mid-South Com Col; Adj Asst Prof, 98-, Christian Bros Univ; Instr, 00-, Baptist College of Health Sciences. **HONORS AND AWARDS** Hon Sargent-At-Arms TN House of Repr; Colonel Aide de Camp Governors Staff; Community Leaders and Noteworthy Amer Awd; Presidential Achievement Awd (Ronald Reagan), Personalities of the South Awd;Paper Accpt Tenth Interamerican Cong of Philos; Paper Accpt Twentieth World Cong of Philos; Security Bank Outstanding Adjunct Faculty Awd at Dyersburg State; The Memphis Flyer's list of Good Things About Memphis. **MEMBERSHIPS** APA **RESEARCH** Philosophy, especially political and social philosophy, ethics. **SELECTED PUBLICATIONS** Auth, Unseen Scars, 94; auth, A Matter Of Freedom, 94; auth, Abusers Rampant, 95; auth, Heroes Should Heed Dr. Kings Words on Violence, 95; auth, Coach Saluted, 96; auth, Cutbacks Not Worthy of A Great State, 97; auth, Welcome Laughter, 97; auth, The Stigma Remains, 99; auth, Cardinal's Example, 00; auth, A Perspective on Knight, 00. **CONTACT ADDRESS** 1446 Snowden Ave, Memphis, TN 38107.

PRINCE, JOHN R.
DISCIPLINE LEGAL WRITING AND APPELLATE ADVOCACY **EDUCATION** Okla Baptist Univ, BA, 79; Duke Univ Sch Law, JD, 83. **CAREER** Prof, Villanova Univ; clerked, Honorable Thomas N. O'Neill, Jr. US Dist Ct Eastern Dist Pa; past assoc, firms in Philadelphia; private pract in his own firm; taught at, Rutgers-Camden Sch Law & St Thomas Univ Sch Law. **MEMBERSHIPS** Amer, Philadelphia & Dela Co Bar Asn. **CONTACT ADDRESS** Law School, Villanova Univ, 800 Lancaster Ave, Villanova, PA 19085-1692. **EMAIL** prince@law.vill.edu

PRINDLE, DAVID F.
PERSONAL Born 04/10/1948, Los Angeles, CA, m **DISCIPLINE** POLITICAL SCIENCE **EDUCATION** Univ Calif at Santa Cruz, BA, 70; Univ Calif at Los Angeles, MA, 72; PhD, 77. **CAREER** Prof, Univ Tex at Austin, 76-. **HONORS AND AWARDS** U. O. Key, Jr Awd, Southern Polit Sci Asn, 82; Harry Ransom Awd, Col of Liberal Arts, 94. **MEMBERSHIPS** Am Polit Sci Asn. **RESEARCH** American Politics, American Political Thought, Politics of Media. **SELECTED PUBLICATIONS** Auth, Petroleum Politics and the Texas Railroad Commission, 81; auth, The Politics of Glamour: Ideology and Democracy in the Screen Actors Guild, 88; auth, Risky Business: The Political Economy of Hollywood, 93. **CONTACT ADDRESS** Dept Govt, Univ of Texas, Austin, Austin, TX 78712-1013. **EMAIL** dprindle@mail.la.utexas.edu

PRITCHARD, MICHAEL
DISCIPLINE PHILOSOPHY **EDUCATION** Univ Wisc, PhD. **CAREER** Prof, Philos, West Mich Univ; dir, WMU Ctr for the Study of Ethics in Soc, West Mich Univ. **RESEARCH** Professional ethics, philosophy for children. **SELECTED**

PUBLICATIONS Co-ed, Responsible Communication: Ethical Issues in Business, Industry, and the Professions, Hampton Pr; co-ed, Profits and Professions; co-auth, Practicing Engineering Ethics, Inst Electrical & Electronic Engineeres; auth, On Becoming Responsible, Univ Pr of Kans; auth, Reasonable Children, Univ Pr of Kans; co-auth, Ethics in Engineering, Wadworth; co-auth, Communication Ethics, Wadsworth. **CONTACT ADDRESS** Philos Dept, Western Michigan Univ, 320 Moore Hall, 1903 W Michigan Ave, Kalamazoo, MI 49008-5328. **EMAIL** michael.pritchard@wmich.edu

PRITZL, KURT
PERSONAL Born Milwaukee, WI **DISCIPLINE** PHILOSOPHY **EDUCATION** Marquette Univ, BA, 74; Univ Toronto, MA, 75, PhD, 82. **CAREER** Assoc prof, philos, Catholic Univ, 80- . **MEMBERSHIPS** APA; Am Catholic Philos Asn; Soc for Ancient Greek Philos; Metaphysical Soc of Am. **RESEARCH** Ancient philosophy; theory of knowledge. **SELECTED PUBLICATIONS** Auth, Ways of Truth and Ways of Opinion in Aristotle, The Importance of Truth: Proceedings of the American Catholic Philosophical Association, 93; auth, Opinions as Appearances: Endoxa in Aristotle, Ancient Philos, 94; auth, The Significance of Some Structural Features of Plato's Crito, in van Ophuijsen, Plato and Platonism, Washington DC, 98; auth, Being True in Aristotle's Thinking, Proceedings of the Boston Area Colloquium in Ancient Philosophy, forthcoming. **CONTACT ADDRESS** School of Philosophy, Catholic Univ of America, Washington, DC 20064. **EMAIL** pritzl@cua.edu

PROCTER, HARVEY THORNTON, JR.
PERSONAL Born 12/29/1945, Monongahela, PA, d **DISCIPLINE** LAW **EDUCATION** Southern IL Univ, BA 1967; Roosevelt Univ, MA 1970; Wayne State Univ, JD 1976. **CAREER** Chicago Comm on Youth Welfare, asst zone dir, 66, dir special events, 67; Ford Motor Company, Human Res, 68-; Univ of Mich, School of Business, Lead Prog, Lect, 86-; National Urban League, Black Exec Exchange Prog, Visit Prof, 88-. **HONORS AND AWARDS** Univ of IL Law Fellowship; IL General Assembly Scholarship; Vice President's Awd - Youth Motivation, Vice President of the United States, 1970; Citation of Merit, City of Detroit Police Dept, 1990, 1991; Awd of Merit, Jarvis Christian College, 1990, 1992. **MEMBERSHIPS** Mem Amer, MI State, Detroit Bar Assocs, Assoc of Trial Lawyers of Amer; mem Amer Mgmt Assoc; Society of Human Resource Management; Midwest Co-op Educ Assoc, Employer Management Assoc; life mem Alpha Phi Alpha Inc, NAACP; parish council St Thomas the Apostle Church; assy & comm chmn Midwest Coll Placement Assoc 1983-; pres bd of dirs Earhart Village Homes; pres, exec bd, Midwest College Placement Assoc 1988-; mem Business Advisory Council Univ of MI Comprehensive Studies Program 1989-; mem Business Advisory Council Clark-Atlanta University Center 1988-89; mem Business Advisory Council GMI Mgt Instit 1987-90; president, National Association of Colleges & Employers, 1997-; vp, employer relations, board of governors, College Placement Council, 1991-; task force mem, National Governor's Assn, 1990-. **CONTACT ADDRESS** Ford Motor Co, The American Rd, Rm 367, Dearborn, MI 48121.

PROFFITT, ANABEL C.
PERSONAL Born 12/18/1956, Yonkers, NY, m, 1984, 1 child **DISCIPLINE** RELIGION **EDUCATION** Hood Col, BA, 79; Presbyterian Sch of Christ Ed, MA, 81; Princeton Theol Sem, PhD, 90. **CAREER** Vis Inst, Presbyterian Schl of Christ Ed, 86; Adj Prof, United Theol Sem, 92; Hon Sr Res Fel, Univ, Birmingham UK, 97; Dean, Assoc Prof, Lancaster Theol Sem, 89-. **MEMBERSHIPS** Assoc of Prof and Res in Relig Ed, Assoc for Supvr and Curric Dev, Intl Sem on Rel Ed and Values, Rel Ed Assoc **RESEARCH** The role of wonder in education and religion, teaching and learning, theological education. **SELECTED PUBLICATIONS** A Sense of Wonder, In Season, 95; Mystery Metaphor and Religious Education: The Challenge of Teaching in a Postmodern World, Salt Jour of the Rel and Moral Ed Coun, 95; Reclaiming Piety as a Goal of Religious Education, 95; Wonder as an Attitude, 96; Playing in the Presence of God: Wonder, Wisdom and Education, Intl Jour of Child Spirit, 98. **CONTACT ADDRESS** Lancaster Theol Sem, 555 W James St, Lancaster, PA 17603. **EMAIL** aproffitt@lts.org

PROKURAT, MICHAEL
PERSONAL Born 02/08/1950, Detroit, MI, m, 1970, 3 children **DISCIPLINE** THEOLOGY **EDUCATION** Univ Mich, BA, 70; St Vladimir Orthodox Theol Sem, MDiv, 73; MTh, ABD, 74; Grad Theol Union, Berkeley, Calif, PhD, 88. **CAREER** Dir, Lectr, Late Vocations Prog, Diocese of the West, OCA, 80-83, 88-91; lectr, Univ Calif, Berkeley, 89-90; lectr, Dominican Col, San Raphael, Calif, 91; adjunct fac, Pacific Lutheran Theol Sem, Berkeley, Calif, 91-94; vis scholar, Univ Houston, 96-97; assoc prof of Sacred Scripture, Univ St Thomas, Sch of Theol, Houston, 94-. **MEMBERSHIPS** Am Acad of Relig, Am Schools of Oriental Res, Cath Biblical Asn of Am, Cath Theol Soc of Am, Soc of Biblical Lit. **RESEARCH** Auth, "Orthodox Interpretation of Scripture," in The Bible in the Churches, 2nd ed with Revisions, Kenneth Hagen, ed, Milwaukee: Marquette Univ Press (94): 59-99; coauth, A Historical Dictionary of the Orthodox Church. Historical Dictionaries of Religions, Philosophies, and Movements, No 9, Jon Woronoff, series ed, Lanham, MD & London: Scarecrow Press (96); coauth with a comt, "A Treasure in Earthen Vessels: Hermeneutical Reflections for a Growing Koinonia," World Coun of Churches Comn on Faith and Order (Nov 97): 1-22; auth, "WCC Programme Unit 1-Unity and Renewal: Ecclesial Unity--Commission on Faith and Order: 'Consultation on Ecumenical Hermeneutics',” St Vladimir's Theol Quart, Vol 41, No 4 (97): 353-5; auth, "Orthodox Interpretation of Scripture," in The Bible in the Churches, 3rd ed, Kenneth Hagen, ed, Milwaukee: Marquette Univ Press (98): 61-100; auth, "NRSV: Preliminary Report," St Vladimir's Theol Quart, Vol 43, No 3-4 (99): 359-74; auth, The Orthodox Church: A Critical Assessment and Annotated Bibliography, Series Bibliographies and Indexes in Religious Studies, Westport, Ct/London: Greenwood Press (forthcoming); auth, "The Pneumatological Dimension of Ecumenical Hermeneutics," Faith and Order Comn of the WCC (forthcoming); auth, "What difference do orthodox traditions make in Bible translation?," NCC Bible Translation and Utilization Prof Pub (forthcoming); auth, several entries in The Encyclopedia of Monasticism, William M. Johnston, ed, Chicago: Fitzroy Dearborn Pubs (forthcoming). **CONTACT ADDRESS** Sch of Theol, Univ of St. Thomas, Texas, 9845 Memorial Dr, Houston, TX 77024. **EMAIL** prokurat@stthom.edu

PROOPS, IAN
DISCIPLINE PHILOSOPHY **EDUCATION** Oxford Univ, BA, 89; Harvard Univ, PhD, 98. **CAREER** Asst prof, Univ Mich, 98-. **HONORS AND AWARDS** Rm. Martin Prize Fel, Harvard Univ, 96-97. **MEMBERSHIPS** Am Philos Asn. **RESEARCH** Philosophy of language; metaphysics; analytical philosophy; Wittgenstein; Kant. **SELECTED PUBLICATIONS** Auth, The Early Wittgenstein on Logical Assertion, Philos Topics, Fall, 97. **CONTACT ADDRESS** Dept of Philosophy-2215 Angell Hall, Univ of Michigan, 435 S State St., Ann Arbor, MI 48109-1003. **EMAIL** iproops@umich.edu

PROSSER, PETER E.
PERSONAL Born 12/16/1946, Birmingham, England, m, 1970, 2 children **DISCIPLINE** CHURCH HISTORY; ETHICS **EDUCATION** Univ Montreal, MDiv, 75, MA, 78, PhD, 89. **CAREER** Lectr, Inst Biblique Beree, Montreal, 72-75; fel, Univ Montreal, 82-83; asst prof, Church Hist, Regent Univ, 83-90; Assoc prof, 91-97; prof, 98- . **HONORS AND AWARDS** Who's Who in Am, 79, 84, 90-92, 98; Int Men of Distinction, 79; Silver medal, Cambridge Biographical Institute, UK; International Scholar Awd 00, (Cambridge) Int. Order of Merit, UK, Fellowship, Westminister College, Oxford, 00; International Who's Who, 01 **MEMBERSHIPS** AAR/SBL; SPS; ETS. **RESEARCH** Millennialism; Reformation; apocalypticism; Methodist history. **SELECTED PUBLICATIONS** Auth, Prophecy: A Vital Gift to the Church, Including Yours, Acts 29 Mag, 92; Spirit-Filled Life Bible, Sections on 1 and 2 John, Thomas Nelson publ; auth, Dispenstional Eschatology, Mellen Press (486 pgs), The Papacy, Chi Hist, Magazine, 00. **CONTACT ADDRESS** School of Divinity, Regent Univ, 1000 Regent Dr, Virginia Beach, VA 23464-9800. **EMAIL** petepro@regent.edu

PROSTERMAN, ROY L.
PERSONAL Born 07/13/1935, Chicago, IL **DISCIPLINE** LAW **EDUCATION** Univ Chicago, AB, 54; Harvard Univ, LLB, 58. **CAREER** Assoc, Sullivan & Cromwell, 59-65; from asst prof to assoc prof law, 65-70, Prof Law, Univ Wash, 70-, Mem bd dirs, World Without War Coun, US, 71-; consult, Stanford Res Inst, 67; adv, Ctr War/Peace Studies, 67-; consultant to World Bank and USAID on various projects in formerly centrally planned economies, 92-. **HONORS AND AWARDS** Ralph Bunche Awd, Seattle-King County Bar Asn, 73. **RESEARCH** Land tenure reform; lethal violence; international legal order. **SELECTED PUBLICATIONS** Auth, Surviving to 3000, Duxbury, 72; coauth, Land Reform and Democratic Development, Johns Hopkins, 87; coauth, Land Reform and Grassroots Development: 10 Cases Studies, Lynne Rienner, 90; ed, Legal Impediments to Effective Rural Land Relations in Eastern Europe and Central Asia, A Comparative Perspective, World Bank, 99; coauth, "Implementation of 30-year Land Use Rights for Farmers Under China's 1998 Land Management Law: An Analysis and Recommendations Based on a 17 Province Survey," Pacific Rim Law and Policy Journal (00). **CONTACT ADDRESS** Sch of Law, Univ of Washington, Seattle, WA 98195. **EMAIL** royp@u.washington.edu

PROUDFOOT, WAYNE
DISCIPLINE RELIGION **EDUCATION** Yale Univ, BS, 61; Harvard Univ, PhD, 66. **CAREER** Prof. **HONORS AND AWARDS** Am Acad Relig Awd, 86. **SELECTED PUBLICATIONS** Auth, God and Self, Bucknell, 76; Religious Experience, Berkeley, 85. **CONTACT ADDRESS** Dept of Religion, Columbia Col, New York, 2960 Broadway, New York, NY 10027-6902. **EMAIL** wlp2@columbia.edu

PRUETT, GORDON EARL
PERSONAL Born 10/16/1941, Raton, NM, m, 1966, 1 child **DISCIPLINE** HISTORY OF RELIGION **EDUCATION** Yale Univ, BA, 63; Oxford Univ, BA & MA, 65; Princeton Univ, PhD, 68. **CAREER** Asst prof relig, Lehigh Univ, 68-69; asst prof, 69-74; acting chmn dept eng, 76-80; assoc prof philos & relig, Northeastern Univ, 74- . **RESEARCH** History of Christianity; Sociology of religion; Mysticism and psychoanalysis. **SELECTED PUBLICATIONS** Auth, A note on Robert Bellah's theory of religious evolution: The early modern period, Sociol Analysis, 73; History, transcendence, and world community in the work of Wilfred Cantwell Smith, Jour Am Acad Relig, 73; Christianity, history and culture in Nagaland, Contribs to Indian Sociol, 74; A Protestant doctrine of the Eucharistic presence, Calvin Theol Jour, 75; Thomas Cranmer's progress in the doctrine of the Eucharist, 1535-1548, Hist Mag Protestant Episcopal Church, 76; Will and freedom: Psychoanalytic themes in the work of Jacob Boehme, Studies Relig & Sci Relig, 77; Religion in higher education, Int Encycl Higher Educ, 78; The escape from the Seraglio: Anti-orientalist trends in modern religious studies, Arab Studies Quart, 80; Preparatio Evangelii: Religious Studies and Secondary Education, Nat Asn of Episcopal Schools Jour 1:1, 84; Islam and Orientalism, Orientalism, Islamists and Islam, ed Asaf Hussain, Robert Olson, and Jamil Qureshi, Amana, 84; Through a Glass Darkly: Knowledge of the Self in Dreams in Ibn Khaldun's Mugaddima, The Muslim World LXXV:1, 85; The Meaning and End of Suffering for Freud and the Buddhist Tradition, 87; World Theology and World Community: The Vision of Wilfred Cantwell Smith, Studies in Religion 19:4, 1990; Theravadin Buddhist Commentary on the Current State of Western Epistemology, Buddhist-Christian Studies 10, 1990; As a Father Loves His Children: The Image of the Supreme Being as Loving Father in Judaism, Christianity and Islam, 94. **CONTACT ADDRESS** Dept of Philosophy and Religion, Northeastern Univ, 360 Huntington Ave, Boston, MA 02115-5000.

PRUST, RICHARD CHARLES
PERSONAL Born 04/21/1939, Milwaukee, WI **DISCIPLINE** PHILOSOPHY; RELIGION **EDUCATION** Univ Wis, BA, 61; Yale Univ, BD, 64; Duke Univ, PhD, 70. **CAREER** Assoc prof Philos, St Andrews Presby Col, 67-. **HONORS AND AWARDS** Sears Awd for Excellence in Tchg, 91. **MEMBERSHIPS** Am Acad Relig; Am Philos Asn; N.C. Philos Soc; Am Assoc of Univ. Profs; Intl. Personalist Assoc. **SELECTED PUBLICATIONS** Auth, Was Calvin a Biblical literalist, Scottish J Theol, 9/67; The self as saved, Personalist, 7/78; Personal Integrity and Moral Value, The Personalist Forum, 12/96; When She Comes into a Room: Reflections on Wholeness and Personal Presence, Soundings, 80/97; Soul Talk and Bowne's Ontology of Personhood, The Personalist Forum, 13/97. **CONTACT ADDRESS** 1700 Dogwood Mile, Laurinburg, NC 28352-5521. **EMAIL** rcp@tartan.sapc.edu

PUBANTZ, JERRY
PERSONAL Born 05/07/1947, Elgin, IL, m, 1970, 4 children **DISCIPLINE** POLITICAL SCIENCE **EDUCATION** Georgetown Univ, BSFS, 69; Duke Univ, MA, 72; PhD, 73. **CAREER** Dept of History and Govt, Salem Col, Winston Salem, NC. **HONORS AND AWARDS** Phi Beta Kappa; Sears-Roebuck Found Excellence in Teaching Awd; nominee, Change Mag Nat Teaching Awd; Inst Fel, Islamic and Arabian Develop Studies, Duke Univ; Pi Sigma Alpha; Pi Gamma Mu; Fel, Ctr for European Studies, Univ NC; Fel, Ctr for Theoretical Studies, Univ of Miami; Exxon Educ Fund Grant, Shell Corp Grant; NDEA-IV Fel, Georgetown Univ Scholar. **MEMBERSHIPS** Am Political Sci Asn, Am Hist Asn, Southern Asn for the Advancement of Slavic Studies, Southern Asn of Pre-Law Advisors, NC Political Sci Asn, Middle East Policy Coun. **RESEARCH** The United Nations, American foreign relations, US-Russian relations, Middle East politics. **SELECTED PUBLICATIONS** Auth of several entries in Modern Encyclopedia of Russian and Soviet History; auth, "Succeeding in Lilliput, Pre-law Advising in the Small Liberal Arts Institution," revised ed in The Pre-law Adviser's Handbook, ed by Gerald L. Wilson, Duke Univ Press (95): 17-23; coauth, To Create a New World? US Presidents and the United Nations, Peter Lang Pub, NY (99); auth, "Beyond Good and Evil, American Politics and Iran," Arabies TRENDS, No 19, Paris (April 99): 66; auth, "China and the Middle East," Arabies TRENDS, Paris (Nov 99); auth, "Russia and the Middle East," Arabies TRENDS, Paris (99); co-ed with John Allpin Moore, Jr, The Encyclopedia of the United Nations, Facts on File Pubs (forthcoming spring 2002). **CONTACT ADDRESS** Dept Hist & Govt, Salem Col, 601 S Church St, Winston-Salem, NC 27101-5318. **EMAIL** pubantz@salem.edu

PUCKETT, PAULINE N.
PERSONAL Born 03/18/1928, Dayton, OH, s **DISCIPLINE** PASTORAL SUPERVISION **EDUCATION** United Theological Sem, D.Min, 95; United Theological Sem, MARE, 85; Wright St Univ, Med, 74; Miami Univ of Ohio, BS Ed, 66. **CAREER** Air Force, Logistics Command, Wright-Patterson AFB, 33 years. **MEMBERSHIPS** Amer Bus Women's Assoc; League of Women Voters; Church Women United. **CONTACT ADDRESS** Dept of The Air Force, Wright Patterson AFB, 5838 Troy Villa Blvd, Huber Heights, OH 45424-2650.

PUDSELL, F. DAVID
PERSONAL Born 07/09/1934, Baltimore, MD, d, 3 children **DISCIPLINE** HISTORY, PHILOSOPHY **EDUCATION** Tuscuhum Col, BA; Ind Univ, MA; Pittsburgh Theol Sem, MTh. **CAREER** Assoc Prof, Fairmont State Col, 68-. **RESEARCH** Greek Philosophy; Medical Ethics; Cosmology; Russian History. **CONTACT ADDRESS** Dept Soc Sci, Fairmont State Col, 1201 Locust Ave, Fairmont, WV 26554-2451.

PUE, WESLEY W.
DISCIPLINE LAW **EDUCATION** Oxford Univ, BA, 77; BA, 79; Univ Alberta, LLM, 80; Osgoode, JD, 89. **CAREER** Prof, 93-. **HONORS AND AWARDS** Pres, Can Law Soc Asn. **MEMBERSHIPS** Pres, Can Law Soc Asn. **RESEARCH** Legal pluralism; cultural history approaches to the history of law. **SELECTED PUBLICATIONS** Co-ed, Glimpses of Canadian Legal History, Legal Research Institute, Univ of Manitoba, 91; auth, "Towards Geo-Jurisprudence? - Formulating Research Agendas in Law and Geography," Windsor Review of Legal & Social Issues, 3, (91): 71-93; auth, "Trajectories of Professionalism: Legal Professionalism after Abel," in Manitoba Law Annual, 1989-1990, ed. Alvin Esau, (Winnipeg: Legal Research Institute, 91): 57-92; auth, "A Profession in Defense of Capital?" Canadian Journal of Law & Society, 7:2, 92; auth, "Revolution by Legal Means," Contemporary Law 1994 Droit contemporain, ed. Patrick Glenn, (Montreal: Editions Yvons Blais, 94): 1-30; auth, "In Pursuit of Better Myth: Lawyers' Histories and Histories of Lawyers," Alberta Law Review, 33, (95): 730-767; auth, Law School: The Story of Legal Education in British Coumbia, Vancouver: Continuing Legal Education Society of British Columbia & Faculty of Law, Univ of British Columbis, (95): 285; co-ed, Canada's Legal Inheritances, Legal Research Institute, Univ of Manitoba, 97; ed, Lawyering for A Fragmented World, International Journal of the Legal Profession, Vol. 5, No. 2/3, (98): 125-288; co-ed, Misplaced Traditions: British Lawyers, Colonial Peoples, Law in Context, 16, 99. **CONTACT ADDRESS** Fac of Law, Univ of British Columbia, 1822 East Mall, Vancouver, BC, Canada V6T 1Z1. **EMAIL** pue@law.ubc.ca

PUGSLEY, ROBERT ADRIAN
PERSONAL Born 12/27/1946, Mineola, NY, d **DISCIPLINE** LAW **EDUCATION** State Univ NYork, Stony Brook, BA, 68; NYork Univ, JD, 75, LLM, 77. **CAREER** Coordr, Peace Educ Prog, The Christophers, 71-78; assoc prof, 78-81, Prof Law, Sch of Law, Southwestern Univ, 81-; Lectr sociol, New Sch Social Res, 71; res asst, Crime Deterrence & Offender Career Proj, 74; adj asst prof criminal justice, Southhampton Col, Long Island Univ, 75-76; mem exec comt, Non-Govt Orgn, Off Pub Info, UN, 75; Robert Marshall fel civil liberties, Criminal Law Educ & Res Ctr, Sch Law, NY Univ, 76-78 & actg dep dir, 77-78; producer, Inside LA, KPFK, Los Angeles, 79-; mem bd adv, Ctr Legal Educ, City Col, City Univ New York, 78-. **HONORS AND AWARDS** Paul E. Treusch Prof of Law, 00-01 **MEMBERSHIPS** Am Legal Studies Asn; Am Soc Polit St Legal Philos; Inst Study Bioethics & Life Sci; Am Soc Criminol. **RESEARCH** The rationales for and practice of criminal punishment and sentencing; moral, constitutional, and practical questions raised by capital punishment; the education, organization, and discipline of the legal profession. **SELECTED PUBLICATIONS** Auth, Kill for peace?, Cath Worker, 3-4/71; Embattled prelate: Review of Cardinal Mindszenty's memoirs, New Leader, 3/3/75; Capital punishment: Bringing back death, Commonweal, 8/13/76; Reflections on January 17, 1977, Christianity & Crisis, 2/7/77; coauth, Peace--Justice Curriculum Unit for Grade 12, Arcdiocese of NY, 78; auth, Retributivism: A just basis for criminal sentences, 7:379-405 & A retributivist argument against capital punishment, 9: 1501-1523, Hofstra Law Rev; coauth, Current leading issues in criminal law: A panel, Southwestern Univ Law Rev, 12:431-448. **CONTACT ADDRESS** Southwestern Univ Sch of Law, 675 S Westmoreland Ave, Los Angeles, CA 90005-3905. **EMAIL** rpugsley@swlaw.edu

PULCINI, THEODORE
PERSONAL Born 05/11/1954, Sewickley, PA, s **DISCIPLINE** RELIGIOUS STUDIES **EDUCATION** Harvard Coll, BA, 76; Univ Notre Dame, MA, 79; Harvard Divinity School, ThM, 82; Cath Univ Am, DMin, 85; Univ Pittsburgh, PhD, 94. **CAREER** Tchg asst, Univ Notre Dame, 78; Jr Tutorial Instr, Harvard Univ, 82; tchg fel, Univ Pittsburgh, 92-94; instr, Chatham Coll, 93-94; vis prof, St Vladimir's Orthodox Theol Sem NY, 94-95; asst prof, Dickinson Coll Carlisle PA, 95-. **HONORS AND AWARDS** Ganoe Awd for Inspirational Teaching, Dickinson College, 98-99. **MEMBERSHIPS** Am Acad of Rel; Soc of Bibl Lit; Middle East Studies Asn. **RESEARCH** Eastern Orthodoxy; Islam; Interreligious Dialogue; Religious Polemic. **SELECTED PUBLICATIONS** Auth, Orthodoxy and Catholicism: What Are the Differences?, 95; Appreciating Islam, New Theol Rev, 96; Eastern Orthodox-Oriental Orthodox relations: Practical Steps Toward Unity, St Nerses Theol Rev, 96; Of Flesh and Faith: Abraham as a Principle of Inclusion and Exclusion in Christian Thought, Abrahamic Faith, Ethnicity, and Ethics Conflicts, 97; Reasserting Boundaries: Another View of 'Ecumenical Jihad', in Reclaiming the Great Tradition: Evangelicals, Catholics, and Orthodox in Dialogue; Exergesis as Polemic Discourse: Ibn Hazm on Jewish and Christian Scriptures, 98; Cultivating Christian Anger: A Warning from the Fifth Century, Touchstone, 98. **CONTACT ADDRESS** Dept of Religion, Dickinson Col, Box 1773, Carlisle, PA 17013. **EMAIL** pulcini@dickinson.edu

PULIGANDLA, RAMAKRISHNA
PERSONAL Born 09/08/1930, Nellore, India, m, 1949, 5 children **DISCIPLINE** PHILOSOPHY **EDUCATION** Rice Univ, PhD, 66. **CAREER** Prof, Univ of Toledo,Ohio, 70-; lectured in U.S.A., Europe, India, and China. **HONORS AND AWARDS** Fulbright Lecturing Fel, 92 (India), 97 (Russia). **MEMBERSHIPS** APA; Soc for Asian and Comparative Philo **RESEARCH** Logic; phil of science; comparative philo and religion. **SELECTED PUBLICATIONS** Coed, Buddhism and th Emerging World Civilization: Essays in Honor of Nolan Pliny Jacobson, 96; Fundamentals of Indian Philosophy, 97; Jnana-Yoga (The Way of Knowledge): An Analytical Interpretation, 97; Reality and Mysticism: Perspectives in the Upanishads, 97. **CONTACT ADDRESS** 4138 Beverly Dr, Toledo, OH 43614. **EMAIL** Rpuliga@aol.com

PURCELL, E. A.
PERSONAL Born 07/20/1941, Kansas City, MO, m, 1982, 2 children **DISCIPLINE** HISTORY, LAW **EDUCATION** Rockhurst Col, AB 62; Univ Kansas, MA 64; Univ Wisconsin, PhD 68; Harvard Law, JD 79. **CAREER** Univ Cal Berk, asst prof, 67-69; Univ Missouri Col, asst prof, assoc prof 69-77; New York Law Sch, prof law, 89-. **HONORS AND AWARDS** Louis Peltzer Awd; Frederick Jackson Turner Prize. **MEMBERSHIPS** OAH; ASLH; ABNY **RESEARCH** 19th, 20th Century Amer Social Intellectual and Legal Hist. **SELECTED PUBLICATIONS** Auth, The Crisis of Democratic Theory, 73; Litigation and Inequality, 92; auth, Brandeis and the Progressive Constitution, 00. **CONTACT ADDRESS** New York Law Sch, 57 Worth St, New York, NY 10013-2960.

PURTILL, RICHARD L.
PERSONAL Born 03/12/1931, Chicago, IL, m, 1959, 3 children **DISCIPLINE** PHILOSOPHY **EDUCATION** Univ Chicago, BA, 58; MA, 60; PhD(philos), 65. **CAREER** Assoc prof, 62-72; actg chmn dept, 70-71; prof philos, Western Wash Univ, 72-96; prof emeritus, 96-; vis lectr philos, San Francisco State Col, 68-69. **HONORS AND AWARDS** Western Wash Univ res off res grants. **MEMBERSHIPS** Am Philos Asn. **RESEARCH** Logic, metaphysics, ethics and aesthetics; Modal logic; arguments for God's existence. **SELECTED PUBLICATIONS** Auth, Logic for Philosophers, 71 & Logical Thinking, 72, Harper; auth, Lord of the Elves and Eldils, Zondervan, 74; auth, Reason to Believe, Eerdmans, 74; auth, Philosophically Speaking, 75, auth, Thinking About Ethics, 76 & Thinking About Religion, 78, Prentice Hall; auth, Logic: Argument, Refutation and Proof, Harper, 79; auth,C.S. Lewis' Case for the Christian Faith, Harper, 81; auth, A Logical Introduction to Philosophy, Prentice Hall, 88; author of 6 novels, 8 short stories, and over 30 journal articles. **CONTACT ADDRESS** 1708 Douglas Ave, Bellingham, WA 98225-6709. **EMAIL** purtill@cc.wwu.edu

PUTNAM, HILARY
PERSONAL Born 07/31/1926, Chicago, IL, m, 1962, 4 children **DISCIPLINE** PHILOSOPHY **EDUCATION** Univ Pa, AB, 48; Univ Calif, Los Angeles, PhD, 51. **CAREER** Rockefeller fel, 51-52; instr philos, Northwestern Univ, 52-53; from asst prof to assoc prof, 53-61, Princeton Univ; prof, Mass Inst Technol, 61-65; prof philos, 65-, Walter Beverly Pearson Prof mod math & math logic, 76, Harvard Univ; Nat Sci Found fel, Minn Ctr Philos Sci, 57; Guggenheim fel, 60-61; Nat Sci Found fel, 68-69; NEH fel, 75-76; John Locke lectr, Oxford Univ, 76; Cogan Univ Prof, 95. **HONORS AND AWARDS** Fel Acad Arts & Sciences; Fel of Brit Acad. **MEMBERSHIPS** Am Math Soc; Am Philos Assn; Assn Symbolic Logic; Philos Sci Assn. **RESEARCH** Mathematical logic. **SELECTED PUBLICATIONS** Auth, Renewing Philosophy, Harvard University, 92; auth, Pragmatism, Blackwell, 94; auth, Words and Life, Harvard University, 94. **CONTACT ADDRESS** Dept of Philosophy, Harvard Univ, Emerson Hall, Cambridge, MA 02138-3800. **EMAIL** hputnam@fas.harvard.edu

PUTNEY, DAVID P.
PERSONAL Born 07/23/1949, Seattle, WA, m, 2 children **DISCIPLINE** ASIAN PHILOSOPHY AND RELIGION **EDUCATION** Univ Hawaii, PhD, 90. **CAREER** Philos, Old Dominion Univ. **RESEARCH** Buddhist Philosophy and Religion; Japanese Philosophy and Religion; Chinese Philosophy and Religion; Indian Philosophy and Religion. **SELECTED PUBLICATIONS** Area; Buddhist philosophy: Dogen (Chan/Zen Buddhism), Early Buddhism. **CONTACT ADDRESS** Dept of Philos & Religious Studies, Old Dominion Univ, Norfolk, VA 23529-0083. **EMAIL** dputney@odu.edu

PYLES, JOHN E.
PERSONAL Born 01/11/1927, Memphis, TN, m **DISCIPLINE** LAW **EDUCATION** BCL 1951; JD 1968. **CAREER** Office of John E Pyles, Attorney 1968-; municipal judge 1979-81. **MEMBERSHIPS** Mem Wichita Bar Assn; Sedgwick County Bar Assn; Wichita Bd of Realtors 1960-; Multilist Serv of Wichita 1967-; MS Trial Lawyer Assn 1967-. **CONTACT ADDRESS** 2703 E 13th, Wichita, KS 67214.

PYNN, RONALD EARL
PERSONAL Born 09/11/1942, Eau Claire, WI, m, 1961, 3 children **DISCIPLINE** POLITICAL SCIENCE **EDUCATION** Univ Mich. PhD, 70. **CAREER** Asst prof, Lake Super State Col, 70-71; Prof, 71-99, prof emer, Univ N Dakota, 99- . **HONORS AND AWARDS** Univ Outstanding Tchg Awd, 75; Michael Keedy Awd, 94; Spirit of Sioux Awd, 95. **MEMBERSHIPS** Am Polit Sci Asn; Midwst Polit Sci Asn; Text Acad Auth Asn. **RESEARCH** American government; Political theory. **SELECTED PUBLICATIONS** auth Watergate and the American Political Process, Praeger, 75; American Political Economy, Brooks/Cole, 88; American Politics: Changing Expectations, Simon & Schuster, 97. **CONTACT ADDRESS** Dept of Political Science, Univ of No Dakota, Grand Forks, ND 58201. **EMAIL** Pynn@badlands.nodak.edu

Q

QUANDER, ROHULAMIN
PERSONAL Born 12/04/1943, Washington, DC, m, 3 children **DISCIPLINE** LAW **EDUCATION** Howard Univ, BA 1966, JD 1969. **CAREER** Neighborhood Legal Serv, 69-71; Geo Wash Univ, 70-72; Intl Investors, Inc, market cons, Attorney, state dir 1973-; private practice 1975-86; Office of Adjudication DC Govt 1986-; geneological hist and researcher for private groups; DC Dept of Consumer & Regulatory Affairs, administrative law, 86-. **HONORS AND AWARDS** Man of Yr Awd Omega Psi Phi Frat 1965 & 1968; Spl Awd Howard Univ Outstdg Serv to Law Sch, the Community and the Univ 1969; Dean's List Howard Univ 1964, 1965, 1968; Travel Fellowship to 13 foreign countries 1964; Outstanding Service Awd, Quanders United, Inc, 1991; author, The History of the Quander Family, 1984; have published numerous articles for Howard Univ Alumni newspaper. **MEMBERSHIPS** Mem Superior Ct of DC 1975; US dist Ct of DC 1976; mem Amer Bar Assn; Natl Bar Assn; DC Bar Assn; Bar of Supreme Ct of PA; US Dist Ct for Eastern PA; Ct of Appeals DC; Phi Alpha Delta Law Frat 1967; Phi Alpha Theta His Soc; founder Howard Univ Chap of Black Amer Law Students Assn 1968; mem Omega Psi Phi Frat 1964-; pres Student Bar Assn 1968-69, vice pres 1967-68; mem bd of dir The Wash DC Parent & Child Center 1977-81; chief archivist Quander Family History 1977-; reg chmn Howard Univ Alumni 1979-87; chmn Educ Inst Licensure Commn of DC 1979-; bd dir Wash Urban League 1969-70; pres Howard Univ Alumni Club for Wash DC 1970-71; guest lecturer on the geneology hist & contributions of the Quander Family (America's oldest documntd black fam); member, MLK Holiday Commission for DC, 1987-89;s Quanders United, Inc 1983-; mem of, Columbia Hist Soc, Int'l Platform Speakers Assoc 1985-, Republican Party of DC; bd of dir Pigskin Club 1986-; pres, founder, Quanders Historical Society, Inc, 1985-; co-chair, founder, Benjamin Banneker Memorial Comm, Inc, 1991; dir and vp, Torruella-Quander Gallery, Ltd, 1988-; founder and pres, IliRoFa International, Inc, 1991-. **CONTACT ADDRESS** 1703 Lawrence St NE, Washington, DC 20018.

QUANDT, RICHARD E.
PERSONAL Born 06/01/1930, Hungary, m, 1955, 1 child **DISCIPLINE** ECONOMICS **EDUCATION** Princeton, BA 52; Harvard Univ, MA 55, PhD 57. **CAREER** Princeton Univ, asst prof 56-59, assoc prof 59-64, prof 64-95, prof emeritus 95; A W Mellon Fond, Sr Advisor 90. **HONORS AND AWARDS** Guggenheim Fell, McCosh Fel; Ford Found Fell; Econometric Soc Fell; Nat Sci fell; Hugh-Rogers Fell; ASA Fell; APS Fell; Hon Doc Budapest; Gold Medal Budapest; Merit Cit Jagiellonian Univ; AAAS Fell; Medal of Merit Copernicus Univ; Hon Doc Comenius Univ; Hon Doc Queens Univ; Order of Merit Govt Hungary. **MEMBERSHIPS** ASA; AES; ESI. **RESEARCH** Economies **SELECTED PUBLICATIONS** Electronic Publishing and Virtual Libraries: Issues and an Agenda for the Andrew W Mellon Foundation, Serials Review, 96; Betting Bias and Market Equilibrium in Racetrack Betting, with S Chadha, Applied Financial Economics, 96; The Kornai Effect with Partial Bailouts and Taxes, with Karen L Magee, Economics of Planninf, 94; Optimal Decisions in Markets and Planned Economies, ed with D Triska, Boulder CO, WestView Press, 90; numerous books and articles. **CONTACT ADDRESS** Dept of Economics, Princeton Univ, Princeton, NJ 08544-1017. **EMAIL** reg@quandt.com

QUEEN, EVELYN E. CRAWFORD
PERSONAL Born 04/06/1945, Albany, NY, m, 1971, 2 children **DISCIPLINE** LAW **EDUCATION** Howard University, BS, 1963-68, JD, 1972-75. **CAREER** National Institute of Health, support staff, 68-75; Metropolitan Life Insurance Co, attorney, 75-77; United States Department of Commerce, Maritime Adm, Attorney-Advisor, 77-79; United States Attorneys Office, Assistant United States Attorney, 79-81; DC Superior Court, Commissioner, 81-86; judge, 86-; Adjunct Prof, Howard Univ Law School, 89-90; DC School of Law, adjunct professor, 91-92. **HONORS AND AWARDS** Hudson Valley Girl Scout, Trefoil Awd, 1988; Director of Distinguished Americans, Achievement in Law, 1985; Personalities of America, Contributions to Government and Justice, 1986; Department of Justice, Special Achievement Awd, 1981; Department of HEW, Special Achievement Awd, 1975. **MEMBERSHIPS** ABA, 1975-; NBA, 1975-. **RESEARCH** Civil Rights, Criminal Law. **SELECTED PUBLICATIONS** Auth, "Corporate Sentencing Guidelines," in Corporate Misconduct: The Legal, Societal and Management Issues, ed. Margaret P. Spencer and Ronald R. Sims (95). **CONTACT ADDRESS** Judge, DC Superior Court, 500 Indiana Ave NW, H Carl Moultne I Courthouse, Ste 1510, Washington, DC 20001. **EMAIL** queenie@dcsc.gov

QUERE, RALPH WALTER
PERSONAL Born 09/26/1935, Cleveland, OH, m, 1957, 3 children **DISCIPLINE** HISTORY OF CHRISTIAN THOUGHT **EDUCATION** Princeton Univ, AB, 57; Trinity Sem, Columbus Ohio, BD, 64; Princeton Theol Sem,, 70. **CAREER** From instr to assoc prof, 69-84, Prof Hist & Theol, Wartburg Theol Sem, 84-. **MEMBERSHIPS** Am Soc Reformation Res; Am Soc Church Hist; Acad Evangel Theol Educ; Sixteenth Century Cong; Concordia Acad. **RESEARCH** Melanchthon's eucharistic thought; history of Christological thought; history of worship. **SELECTED PUBLICATIONS** Auth, Confrontation at Marburg, Harvard Case Study Inst, 73; Superstar and Godspell, Dialogue, summer 73; Evangelical Witness, Augsburg, 75; The spirit and the gifts are ours.., ordination rites, Lutheran Quart, 11/75; Melanchthonian motifs in the formula, in Dialogue, Discord and Concord, Fortress, 77; Melanchthon's Christum Cognoscere, DeGraaf, 77; Christ's efficacious presence in The Lord's Supper, Lutheran Quart, 2/77. **CONTACT ADDRESS** Wartburg Theol Sem, 333 Wartburg Pl, Dubuque, IA 52004-5004. **EMAIL** quere@mwci.com

QUICK, ALBERT T.
DISCIPLINE LAW **EDUCATION** Univ Ariz, BA; Central Mich Univ, MA; Wayne State Univ, JD; Tulane Univ, LLM. **SELECTED PUBLICATIONS** Auth, 'Against the Framers' Intent: The Court's Fourth Amendment Jurisprudence, 91; co-auth, Federal Rules of Criminal Procedure, New York, Clark Boardman Callaghan, 94; Retention of Minority Professors: Dealing with the Failure to Presume Competence, 91. **CONTACT ADDRESS** Col Law, Univ of Toledo, Toledo, OH 43606. **EMAIL** aquick@uoft02.utoledo.edu

QUIGLEY, JOHN M.
PERSONAL Born 02/12/1942, New York, NY **DISCIPLINE** ECONOMICS **EDUCATION** U.S. Air Force Acad, BS, 64; Univ Stockholm, MSc, 65; Harvard Univ, AM, 70. **CAREER** Asst prof to assoc prof, Yale Univ, 72-81; prof, Univ Calif Berkeley, 79-. **HONORS AND AWARDS** Fulbright Fel; NSF Fel; Woodrow Wilson Nat Fel; Thord-Gray Fel; SSRC Fel; Walter Isard Awd; George Bloom Awd. **MEMBERSHIPS** Am Econ Asn; Econometric Soc; Am Real Estate & Urban Econ Asn; Reg Sci Asn; Asn for Public Policy & Management. **RESEARCH** Local Public Finance; Housing and labor Markets. **CONTACT ADDRESS** Dept Econ, Univ of California, Berkeley, 549 Evans Hall, No 3880, Berkeley, CA 94720-3880. **EMAIL** quigley@econ.berkeley.edu

QUIGLEY, TIM
DISCIPLINE LAW **EDUCATION** Univ Saskatchewan, BSC, 70, LLB, 74, LLM, 86. **CAREER** Prof, 85- **HONORS AND AWARDS** Ed, Can Criminal Law Rev. **MEMBERSHIPS** Law Soc Saskatchewan. **SELECTED PUBLICATIONS** Auth, Some Issues in Sentencing of Aboriginal Offenders, 94; Battered Women and the Defence of Provocation, 91; Reform of the Intoxication Defence, 87; Specific and General Nonsense, 87; Procedure in Canadian Criminal Law, Carswell, 97. **CONTACT ADDRESS** Col of Law, Univ of Saskatchewan, 15 Campus Dr, Saskatoon, SK, Canada S7N 5A6. **EMAIL** Quigley@law.usask.ca

QUIGLEY, TIMOTHY R.
DISCIPLINE PHILOSOPHY **EDUCATION** Univ of Wisconsin-Madison, BS ART, 80, MFA ART, 83, MA Philosophy, 84; PhD Philosophy, 91. **CAREER** Instr, 80-83, Univ of Wisconsin-Extension; lectr, 83-84, teaching asst, 84-86, Univ of Wisconsin-Madison; adjunct instr, 87-88, Kenyon Col; vis asst prof, 88-91, Oakland Univ; instr, 91-95, Wayne State Univ; instr, 91-95, College of Art and Design; adjunct asst prof, 96-98, New York Univ; instr, 95-98, School of Visual Arts; core faculty, 95- , acting dir, BA Prog, 98- , New School for Social Research. **HONORS AND AWARDS** Univ of Wisconsin Graduate Sch Research Grant, 81; European Foreign Travel Fel, Univ of Wisconsin Graduate Sch, 86; Mellon Found Grant, The Postmodern Perspective, 88, Kenyon Col. **MEMBERSHIPS** Amer Philosophical Assn; College Art Assn of Amer; Radical Philosophy Assn. **RESEARCH** Metaphysics; visual and cultural studies. **SELECTED PUBLICATIONS** Auth, The Ethical and the Narrative Self, Philosophy Today, 94; auth, Shooting at the Father's Corpse: The Feminist Art Historian as Producer, Journal of Aesthetics and Art Criticism, fall 94; auth, Review of Alain Finkielkraut, The Defeat of the Mind, Canadian Philosophical Reviews, 95. **CONTACT ADDRESS** The New School, 89 Butler St., Apt. 4, Brooklyn, NY 11231-4776. **EMAIL** quigleyt@newschool.edu

QUILLIAN, WILLIAM F.
PERSONAL Born 04/13/1913, Nashville, TN, m, 1940, 4 children **DISCIPLINE** PHILOSOPHY **EDUCATION** Emory Univ, AB, 35; Yale Univ, BD, 38, PhD, 43. **CAREER** Asst Prof, 41-45, Gettysburg Col; Prof, 45-52, Ohio Wesleyan Univ; Pres, 52-78, Randolph-Macon Womans Col. **HONORS AND AWARDS** LLD Ohio-Wesleyan Univ, 52; Hampden-Sydney Col, 78; Randolph-Macon Col, 67; LTTD Emory Univ, 59; LHD Randolph-Macon Womans Col. **MEMBERSHIPS** APA; Amer Acad of Religion **RESEARCH** The nature of moral obligation; what and where is God. **SELECTED PUBLICATIONS** The Moral Theory of Evolution Naturalism, Yale Univ Press, 45; Evolution and Moral Theory in America, Evolutionary Thought in America, Yale Univ Press, 50. **CONTACT ADDRESS** Pres, 1407 Club Dr, Lynchburg, VA 24503.

QUINN, JOHN F.
PERSONAL m, 4 children **DISCIPLINE** BUSINESS ETHICS, PHILOSOPHY OF LAW, MEDIEVAL PHILOSOPHY **EDUCATION** Univ Dayton, JD, 82. **CAREER** From asst prof to prof, Univ Dayton, 70-. **SELECTED PUBLICATIONS** Co-auth, The Christian Foundations of Criminal Responsibility, Mellon, 91; co-auth, Indonesian Deforestation: A Policy Framework for Sustainable Development, Jour of Asian Bus, 94; auth, Development in the Underdeveloped World: A New Challenge for Business Ethics, Who's Business Values?: Some Asian and Cross-Cultural Perspectives, Hong Kong UP, 95; auth, Anthropocentric Modernism and the Search for a Universal Environmental Philosophy, Dialogue and Universalism, 95; co-auth, Management Ethics: Integrity at Work, Sage & Response Presses, 97. **CONTACT ADDRESS** Dept of Philos, Univ of Dayton, Dayton, OH 45469-1546. **EMAIL** john.quinn@notes.udayton.edu

QUINN, PHILIP L.
DISCIPLINE PHILOSOPHY OF SCIENCE **EDUCATION** Georgetown Univ, AB, 62; Univ Del, MS, 66; Univ Pittsburgh, PhD, 69. **CAREER** John A. O'Brien Prof of Philos. **MEMBERSHIPS** Am Philos Asn, Philos of Sci Asn. **RESEARCH** Philosophy of space and time; issues in ethics and science. **SELECTED PUBLICATIONS** Auth, Creation, Conservation and the Big Bang, 93; Moral Objections to Pascalian Wagering, 94; Religious Pluralism and Religious Relativism, 95; Political Liberalisms and Their Exclusions of the Religious, 95; The Divine Command Ethics in Kierkegaard's Works of Love, 96; Relativism About Torture: Religious and Secular Responses, 96; Tiny Selves: Chisholm on the Simplicity of the Soul, 97; Augustinian Learning, 98. **CONTACT ADDRESS** Dept of Philos, Univ of Notre Dame, 336/7 O'Shaugnessy Hall, Notre Dame, IN 46556. **EMAIL** philip.L.quinn.2@nd.edu

QUINN, THOMAS MICHAEL
PERSONAL Born 08/05/1924, New York, NY, m, 1972, 2 children **DISCIPLINE** LAW **EDUCATION** Holy Cross Col, AB, 47; Harvard Univ, LLB, 50 & LLM, 56; Bellarmine Col, PhL, 55; Woodstock Col, STL, 62. **CAREER** Assoc prof, 63-66, asst prof, 66-70, prof Law, Law Sch, Fordham Univ, 70-; prof of law; lectr, Practising Law Inst, 64-70; auth, Uniform commercial code law letter, monthly, 67- & auth, coauth & ed, The banker's letter of the law, monthly, 75-80; chmn, Community Serv Comt, Asn Am Law Sch, 69-70 & Paralegal Comt, 73-75; dir, NY City Legal Serv Corp, 68-70 & chmn of bd, 70-71. **HONORS AND AWARDS** Lefkowitz award; keefe award. **RESEARCH** Commercial law; banking law; consumer law. **SELECTED PUBLICATIONS** Coauth, Modern Banking Forms, 2 vols, 70 & Uniform Commercial Code Commentary & Law Digest, 1 vol supplemented 2 times per yr, 78, Warren, Gorham & Lamont. **CONTACT ADDRESS** Law Sch, Fordham Univ, 140 W 62nd St, New York, NY 10023-7407.

QUIRK, WILLIAM J.
DISCIPLINE LEGAL RESEARCH **EDUCATION** Princeton Univ, AB, 56; Univ VA, LLB, 59. **CAREER** Prof, Univ of SC. **SELECTED PUBLICATIONS** Publ on, tax and financial policy. **CONTACT ADDRESS** School of Law, Univ of So Carolina, Columbia, Law Center, Columbia, SC 29208. **EMAIL** law0159@univscvm.csd.scarolina.edu

QUITSLUND, SONYA ANTOINETTE
PERSONAL Born 03/08/1935, Portland, OR **DISCIPLINE** RELIGION **EDUCATION** Seattle Univ, BA, 58; Cath Univ Am, MA, 64, PhD(relig), 67. **CAREER** From grad asst to instr relig, Cath Univ Am, 64-67; Asst Prof Relig, George Washington Univ, 67-, Mem nat bd, Col Theol Soc, 77-79; mem subcomt discriminatory lang, Inst Comn English in Liturgy 77-8- **MEMBERSHIPS** Am Acad Relig; Cath Bibl Asn; Col Theol Soc; AAUP. **RESEARCH** Modern Roman Catholicism, especially Lambert Beauduin; Bible and religious thought; woman in Western religious tradition. **SELECTED PUBLICATIONS** Auth, Les idees fondamentales de l'ecclesiologie de dom Lambert Beauduin, Nouvelle Rev Theol, 12/69; United not absorbed: Does it still make sense? J Ecumenical Studies, spring 71; The continuing pastoral relevance of Lambert Beauduin, Am Benedictine Rev, 12/73; Beauduin, a Prophet Vindicated, Newman, 73; Social implications of the Biblical Covenant and the Holy Year, Bible Today, 3/75; Unity-vision or reality?, The Third Hours, 1/76; A theological case for the ordination of women, In: Theology Confronts a Changing World, 23 Publ, 77; In the image of Christ, In: Women Priests: A Catholic Commentary on the Vatican Declaration, Paulist, 77. **CONTACT ADDRESS** Dept of Relig, The George Washington Univ, Washington, DC 20052.

R

RAABE, PAUL R.
PERSONAL Born 04/09/1953, Fairview, KS, m, 1996, 1 child **DISCIPLINE** EXEGETICAL THEOLOGY **EDUCATION** Concordia Tchrs Col, BS, 75; Concordia Sem, MDiv, 79; Washington Univ, MA, 79; Univ Michigan, PhD, 89. **CAREER** Instr, Concordia Col, 79-83; from asst prof to assoc prof, 83-97, prof exegetical theol, 97- , chemn dept, 98- , Concordia Sem. **MEMBERSHIPS** Am Schs of Oriental Res; Bibl Archeol Soc; Soc of Bibl Lit; Cath Bibl Asn. **RESEARCH** Prophecy; Psalms; eschatology; Old Testament theology. **SELECTED PUBLICATIONS** Auth, Psalm Structure: A Study of Psalms with Refrains, Sheffield Academic, 90; auth, Obadiah, Doubleday, 96. **CONTACT ADDRESS** Concordia Sem, 801 DeMun Ave, Saint Louis, MO 63105. **EMAIL** raabep@csl.edu

RAABE, WILLIAM A.
PERSONAL Born 12/14/1953, Milwaukee, WI, m, 1989, 2 children **DISCIPLINE** ACCOUNTING, TAXATION, PUBLIC FINANCE, LAW, ECONOMICS **EDUCATION** Univ of Ill, PhD, 79. **CAREER** Prof, Samford, 97- ; prof, Univ Wis-Milwaukee, 79-97; Ariz State Univ, 84. **HONORS AND AWARDS** Wis Disting Prof, 89-97; Amer Acctg Assn Fellow; Ernst & Young Fellow; Deloitte & Touche Fellow; Natl Ctr for Tax Ed and Res Fel; Ed of the Yr, WI Soc of CPAs, 87. **MEMBERSHIPS** AAUP, Am Acctg Asn, Am Taxation Asn. **RESEARCH** Economic Impact of Arts, and of Sports/Stadiums; Tax Policy; Taxpayer Behavior; Federal, State, Local, International Tax Issues; Adult Learning Styles and Techniques; Integration of Technology into Adult Learning Systems. **SELECTED PUBLICATIONS** Books: West's Federal Taxation; West's Federal Tax Research; Income Tax Fundamentals; Multistate Corporate Tax Guide; The Capital Asset Pricing Model in Tax Litigation; Talking Tax; Eliminating Writing Errors by Professsionals; Taxation of the Virtual Office; Combined Reporting for the Alabama Corporate Income Tax. **CONTACT ADDRESS** Sch of Business, Samford Univ, 800 Lake Shore Dr, Birmingham, AL 35229. **EMAIL** waraabe@samford.edu

RABIN, ROBERT LEONARD
PERSONAL Born 08/09/1939, Chicago, IL, m, 1966, 3 children **DISCIPLINE** LAW **EDUCATION** Northwestern Univ, BS, 60, JD, 63, PhD (polit sci), 67. **CAREER** Asst prof, law, Univ Wisc-Madison, 66-69; assoc prof, 70-71; Prof, Stanford Law Sch, 71- ; vis prof, Harvard law, 87-88; vis prof, Northwestern Univ, 98; vis prof, NYU, 99-00. **HONORS AND AWARDS** Vis Fel, Ctr for Sociol Stud, Oxford Univ, 82; Fel, Ctr for Advanc Study in the Behav Scis at Stanford, 82-83; sr prog consult, Sub Abuse Pol Res Prog, Robert Wood Johnson Found, 96- . **RESEARCH** Empirical research on the administrative process. **SELECTED PUBLICATIONS** Co-auth, Smoking Policy: Law, Politics, and Culture, Oxford Univ Pr (NYork, NY), 93; auth, Perspectives on Tort Law, 4th ed, Little, Brown (Boston), 95; co-auth, Regulating Tobacco, Oxford Univ Pr (NYork, NY) 01; auth, Tort Law and Alternatives, 7th ed, Foundation Pr (Wetbury, NY), 01. **CONTACT ADDRESS** Sch of Law, Stanford Univ, Stanford, CA 94305-1926.

RABINOWITZ, MAYER E.
PERSONAL Born 01/31/1939, New York City, NY, m, 1965, 3 children **DISCIPLINE** TALMUD AND RABBINICS **EDUCATION** Yeshiva Univ, BA, BHL, MA; Jewish Theol Sem Am, MHL ordination, PhD. **CAREER** Libn, assoc prof, dean grad schl, dir Saul Lieberman Inst Talmudic Res, 93-97, Jewish Theol Sem; Chmn, Joint Bet Din Conser Mvmt; secy and res consult, Comm Jewish Law and Stds Rabbinical Assembly. **HONORS AND AWARDS** Nat Def Foreign Lang Fel; grant, Mem Found; fel, Herbert Lehman Inst Talmudic Ethics. **MEMBERSHIPS** Comm Jewish Law and Stds Rabbinical Assembly; AJL; AJS. **RESEARCH** Halakha (Jewish Law). **SELECTED PUBLICATIONS** Auth, Sefer Hamordekhal-Gittin-A Critical and annotated edition; auth, Sefer Hamordekhal-Megiuah-A Critical and annotated edition. Articles in Conservative Judaism, Reconstructionist Magazine, Sinai; responsa, Comm on Jewish Law and Stds, Proceedings Comm Jewish Law and Stds, 80-85; ed/transl, Jewish Law in the State of Israel, Proceedings Rabbinical Assembly, 74. **CONTACT ADDRESS** Jewish Theol Sem of America, 3080 Broadway, New York, NY 10027. **EMAIL** marabinowitz@jtsa.edu

RABOUIN, E. MICHELLE
PERSONAL Born 11/07/1956, Denver, CO, d, 1 child **DISCIPLINE** LAW **EDUCATION** University of Colorado, BS, 1977; University of Denver, MBA, 1984, JD, 1984. **CAREER** Coal Employment Project, assistant director, 83-85; Colorado Office of Attorney General, assistant attorney general, 86-89; Colorado Education Association, legal counsel, 89-90; Community Col of Denver, management chair, faculty, 91-94; Texas Southern Univ, visiting prof of law, 94-95; Washburn Univ School of Law, assoc prof of law, 94-. **HONORS AND AWARDS** Colorado Energy Research Fellow, 1983; Colorado Black Women for Political Action, Community Service Awd, 1981; University of Colorado, President's Academic Scholarship, 1974-77. **MEMBERSHIPS** Soc of Prof in Dispute Reso-

lution, 1990-; Colorado Bar Association, 1984-; Colorado Women's Bar Association, 1988-;Colorado Chapter, National Association of Black Women Attorney, Founding Member, 1987-; American Civil Liberties Union, board member, 1991-92; Junior League of Denver, 1988-1991; Northeast Women's Center, board member, 1980-82; Colorado Black Women for Political Action, board member, editor, 1979-. **SELECTED PUBLICATIONS** Co-author with Anthony Leo, "1992 Tenth Circuit Court of Appeals Survey of Corporate and Commercial Law", Denver University Law Review, 1601; author, Valuing Diversity: Train the Trainer Manual, Mahogany Mountain Press, 1992; author, "The Legal Dimensions of Diversity: the Civil Rights Act of 1991, and the ADA," City of Boulder, Department of Social Services, 1992; lecturer, "Pro Bono: Enforceable Duty of Voluntary Obligation," "Intersection of Race and Poverty, Common Issues," Statewide Legal Services Conference, 1992; auth, "Transforming Law Students Info Ethical Transactional attorneys," Depaul Bus. Law Journal 9 (97); auth, "Gifting children of Promise: Re-Imaging the Margins As Transformative Legal Space, Journal of Gender, Race, & Justice, 59 (00). **CONTACT ADDRESS** 19211 E 45th Ave, Denver, CO 80249.

RACE, JEFFREY
PERSONAL Born 07/29/1943, Norwalk, CT **DISCIPLINE** POLITICAL SCIENCE **EDUCATION** Harvard College, BA 65; Harvard Univ, MA 71, PhD 73. **CAREER** Inst of Current World Affairs, Fellow, 72-76; Industry, Government, and Intl Orgs, Consultant, 77-. **RESEARCH** Technology transfer; econ political development; legal systems. **SELECTED PUBLICATIONS** Auth, War Comes to Long An: Revolutionary Conflict in a Vietnamese Province, Univ Cal Press, 72; Toward an Exchange Theory of Revolution, in: Peasant Rebellion and Communist Revolution in Asia, ed, John W Lewis, Stanford Univ Press, 74; auth, "The Hardware and Software of Development," in From Alliance to Interdependence: An Overview of the Third U.S.-Thailand Bilateral Forum, ed. Clark Neher and Wiwat Mungkandi, 90. **CONTACT ADDRESS** 20 Chester St, Somerville, MA 02144.

RACHELS, JAMES
DISCIPLINE PHILOSOPHY **EDUCATION** Mercer Univ, BA; Univ NC at Chapel Hill, PhD. **CAREER** Prof, Univ Ala at Birmingham, 77-; dean, Univ Ala at Birmingham Sch of Arts and Humanities, 78-83; instr, Univ Richmond, NY Univ & Univ Miami. **SELECTED PUBLICATIONS** Auth, The End of Life: Euthanasia and Morality, Oxford UP, 86; Created from Animals: The Moral Implications of Darwinism, Oxford UP, 91; The Elements of Moral Philosophy, McGraw-Hill, 3rd ed, 98; Can Ethics Provide Answers? And Other Essays in Moral Philosophy, Rowman and Littlefield, 97. **CONTACT ADDRESS** Dept of Philosophy, Univ of Alabama, Birmingham, 1400 University Blvd, Birmingham, AL 35294-1150. **EMAIL** rachels@uab.edu

RACHELS, STUART
PERSONAL Born 09/26/1969, s **DISCIPLINE** PHILOSOPHY **EDUCATION** Syracuse Univ, PhD, 98 **CAREER** Instr, Univ Colorado at Boulder, 98-99 **HONORS AND AWARDS** Marshall Scholar, Oxford Univ, 91-93 **MEMBERSHIPS** Amer Phil Assoc. **RESEARCH** Ethics **SELECTED PUBLICATIONS** Auth, Counterexamples to the Transitivity of Better Than, Australasian Journal of Philosophy, 98; Intrasitivity, Encyclopedia of Ethics, 2nd ed, 98; Is Unpleasantness Intrinsic to Experience, Philosophical Studies, forthcoming. **CONTACT ADDRESS** Philos Dept, Univ of Alabama, Tuscaloosa, Box 870268, Tuscaloosa, AL 35487-0268. **EMAIL** srachels@tenhoor.as.ua.edu

RACHLINSKI, J. J.
PERSONAL Born 06/22/1966, Buffalo, NY, m, 1991 **DISCIPLINE** LAW **EDUCATION** Stanford Univ, JD 93, PhD 94. **CAREER** Cornell Law Sch, asst prof, assoc prof, 94 to 96-. **CONTACT ADDRESS** Law School, Cornell Univ, Ithaca, NY 14853-4901.

RADDEN, JENNIFER
PERSONAL Born 09/10/1943, Melbourne, Australia, m, 1971, 3 children **DISCIPLINE** PHILOSOPHY **EDUCATION** Univ Melbourne, BA, 68; Oxford Univ, B Phil, 71, D Phil, 76. **CAREER** Lectr, 72-74, Tufts Univ; lectr, 75-84, asst prof, 84-89, assoc prof, 90-97, prof, 97-, Univ Mass. **MEMBERSHIPS** APA; AAPP. **RESEARCH** Philosophical issues in the theory and practice of psychiatry, philosophy of mind, moral philosophy and professional ethics. **SELECTED PUBLICATIONS** Auth, Madness & Reason, 85; auth, Divided Minds & Successive Selves, 96; auth, The Nature of Melancholy, 00. **CONTACT ADDRESS** Dept Philosophy, Univ of Massachusetts, Boston, Boston, MA 02125. **EMAIL** jennifer.radden@umb.edu

RADER, ROSEMARY
PERSONAL Born St Leo, MN, s **DISCIPLINE** HISTORY OF CHRISTIANITY **EDUCATION** Col St Catherine, BA; Univ Minn, MA; Stanford Univ, PhD. **CAREER** Religion, Carleton Univ. **HONORS AND AWARDS** Fulbright Schlr, Italy, 66-67; Whiting Fel, Italy, 76-77; Res Grant, Oxford, England, 92-94. **MEMBERSHIPS** AAR. **SELECTED PUBLICATIONS** Auth, Breaking Boundaries: Male/Female Friendship in Early Christian Communities; Coauth, Women Writers of the Early Church. **CONTACT ADDRESS** Carleton Col, 100 S College St., Northfield, MN 55057-4016. **EMAIL** rrader@carleton.edu

RADIC, RANDALL
PERSONAL Born 12/20/1952, NM, s **DISCIPLINE** THEOLOGY **EDUCATION** Agape Sem, STD, 95. **CAREER** First Congregational Church, Pastor; Grace Notes, writer. **MEMBERSHIPS** SBL **RESEARCH** Old and New Testament word studies. **CONTACT ADDRESS** First Congregational Church, 137 N Elm Ave, Ripon, CA 95366. **EMAIL** drradic@sprynet.com

RADOMSKI, HARRY B.
DISCIPLINE LAW **EDUCATION** Univ Toronto, BC, 72, LLB, 75; Univ Ca, LLM, 76. **CAREER** Lectr, 88-. **RESEARCH** General commercial and insurance related litigation; administrative law practice. **SELECTED PUBLICATIONS** Co-auth, The Insurance Act of Ontario; pubs on insurance policy. **CONTACT ADDRESS** Fac of Law, Univ of Toronto, 78 Queen's Park, Toronto, ON, Canada M5S 2C5.

RADZIK, LINDA
PERSONAL Born 08/03/1970, Raleigh, NC, m, 1999 **DISCIPLINE** PHILOSOPHY **EDUCATION** Univ NC at Chapel Hill, BA, 92; Univ Ariz, MA, 96, PhD, 97. **CAREER** Asst prof, Tex A&M Univ, 97-. **HONORS AND AWARDS** Univ Fel, Univ Ariz, 96; Fink Prize for Outstanding Grad Stud in Philos, Univ Ariz, 96; Univ Fel, Univ Ariz, 92-93; Phi Beta Kappa, Univ NC, 91. **RESEARCH** Ethics; Epistemology. **SELECTED PUBLICATIONS** Coauth, "Contested Commodities," Law and Philos 16 (97); auth, "Advocacy and Genuine Autonomy: The Lawyer's Role When the Client Has a Right to Do Wrong," S Tex Law Rev 40 (99): 255-267; auth, "A Normative Regress Problem," Am Philos Quart 36 (99): 35-47; auth, "Incorrigible Norms," Southern J of Philos, 00; auth, "Justification and the Authority of Norms," J of Valve Inquiry, 00. **CONTACT ADDRESS** Dept of Philosophy, Texas A&M Univ, Col Station, College Station, TX 77843-4237. **EMAIL** lradzik@philosophy.tamu.edu

RAE, BOB
DISCIPLINE LAW **EDUCATION** Univ Toronto, BA, 69, LLB, 77; Oxford Univ, BPhill, 71. **CAREER** Premier of Ontario, 90-95; elected to federal and provincial parliaments eight times; partner, Goodman Phillips & Vineberg. **HONORS AND AWARDS** Hon degrees from the Law Soc of Upper Canada and the Univ of Toronto. **SELECTED PUBLICATIONS** Auth, From Protest to Power; auth, The Three Questions. **CONTACT ADDRESS** Dept Polit Sci, Univ of Toronto, 78 Queen's Park, Toronto, ON, Canada M5S 1A1. **EMAIL** raeb@tor.gpv.org

RAELIN, JOSEPH A.
PERSONAL Born 04/10/1948, Cambridge, MA, m, 1974, 2 children **DISCIPLINE** POLICY STUDIES **EDUCATION** SUNY Buff, PhD, 77. **CAREER** Prof, 76-, Boston College; vis Prof, 90, Lancaster Univ. **HONORS AND AWARDS** John Wiley Best Paper Awd; Who's Who Intl Authors and Writers; Dir Intl Bus & Mgmt Schls; Dir of Intl Biography; Inducted as faculty member into Beta Gamma Sigma National business Honor Society. **MEMBERSHIPS** Acad of Mgmt; Soc of Org Learning. **RESEARCH** Developing the emerging field of work-based learning. **SELECTED PUBLICATIONS** The Persean Ethic: Consistency of Belief and Action in Managerial Practice, Human Relations, 93; coauth, Open the Door for Joint Ventures with Business, Sch Admin, 94; coauth, From Generic to Organic Conpetercics, Human Res. Planning, 95; auth, A Model of Work-Based Learning, Org Science, 97; Action Learning and Action Science: Are They Different?, Org Dynamics, 97; Internal Career Development in the Age of Insecurity, Bus Forum, 97; Executive Professionalism and Executive Selection, Human Resource Plan, 97; Individual and Situational Precursors of Successful Action Learning, J Mgmt Edu, 97; auth, The Design of the Action Project in Work-Based Learning, Human Resource Planning, 99; auth, The Action Dimersion in Management: Different Approaches to Research, Teaching, and Development, Mgmt Learning, 99; Auth, Work-Based Learning: The New Frontier of Management Development, The OD Series, Prentice-Hall, 00. **CONTACT ADDRESS** Carroll Sch of Management, Boston Col, Chestnut Hill, Chestnut Hill, MA 02467. **EMAIL** raelin@bc.edu

RAEPPLE, EVA MARIE
PERSONAL Born 02/19/1959, Frankfurt, Germany, m, 1986, 2 children **DISCIPLINE** THEOLOGY **EDUCATION** Univ Frankfurt, 83; Cath Theol Union, MA, 95. **CAREER** Instr, Col Du Page, 98-; instr, Tepeyac Inst, 95-98; instr, Bible Inst, 85-87. **MEMBERSHIPS** Soc Bibl Lit. **RESEARCH** Biblical literature; religious studies. **CONTACT ADDRESS** Dept of Theology, Col of DuPage, 425 Fawell Blvd, Glen Ellyn, IL 60137-6599. **EMAIL** raepple@cdnet.cod.edu

RAFALKO, ROBERT J.
DISCIPLINE PHILOSOPHY **EDUCATION** Univ Scranton, AB, 71; Tufts Univ, MA, 73; Temple Univ, PhD, 83. **CAREER** Asst Prof Univ of NC, 84-88; Asst Prof, Calif State Univ, 88; Vis Asst Prof, Wash Univ, 91-92; instr, St. Louis Univ, 94-97; Consultant, 92-94; Asst Prof, Univ of New Haven, 97-. **HONORS AND AWARDS** Scholarship for Research in theologic of Jan Lukasiewicz, 71, Robert Schalkerbach Foundation Grant for Henry George research, 83, Am Philosophical Asn Fellowship in the Teaching of Philosophy, 90. **MEMBERSHIPS** Am Philsosphical Asn. **RESEARCH** Ethics, Professional Ethics, Logic, Social and Political Philosophy. **SELECTED PUBLICATIONS** Auth, "On Terror," in the Annals, The American Academy of Political and Social Science 463 (82); auth, "Henry George and the Trend Toward Protectionism," The American Journal of Economics and Sociology, 47 (88): 111-125; auth, "Henry's George's Labor Theory of Value,", The American Journal of Economics and Sociology 48 (89); auth, "Corporate Punishment: A Proposal," The Journal of Business Ethics, 90; auth, "An Embargo on Food is a Cruel Weapon," News Analysis, The St. Louis Post Dispatch, 90; auth, Logic for an Overcast Tuesday, Wadsworth Publishing, 90; auth, "Remaking the Corporation: The 1991 U.S. Sentencing Guidelines," The Journal of Business Ethics 13 (94): 625-636; auth, "Corporate Punishment" an entry for the Blackwell Encyclopedia of Business Ethics, London: Blackwell Publishing Co, 97. **CONTACT ADDRESS** Dept Visual & Performing Arts, Univ of New Haven, 300 Orange Ave, West Haven, CT 06516-1916. **EMAIL** rafalko@chargov.newhaven.edu

RAINER, THOM S.
DISCIPLINE EVANGELISM AND CHURCH GROWTH **EDUCATION** Univ Ala, BS; S Baptist Theol Sem, MDiv, PhD. **CAREER** Dean, Billy Graham Sch Missions, Evangel and Church Growth, S Baptist Theol Sem. **MEMBERSHIPS** Mem, Acad Evangel in Theol Edu; Amer Soc for Church Growth. **SELECTED PUBLICATIONS** Auth, The Bridger Generation; The Book of Church Growth: History, Theology, and Principles; Eating the Elephant; Giant Awakenings. **CONTACT ADDRESS** Billy Graham Sch Missions, Evangel and Church Growth, So Baptist Theol Sem, 2825 Lexington Rd, Louisville, KY 40280. **EMAIL** trainer@sbts.edu

RAITT, JILL
PERSONAL Born 05/01/1931, Los Angeles, CA, s **DISCIPLINE** THEOLOGY **EDUCATION** Radcliffe Col, Latin/Eng, 49-51; Inst Hist, Rome, Italy, Philos/Theol, 51-52; San Francisco Col for Women, BA, Philos, 53; San Francisco Col for Women, Eng, 64; Inst Pontificum, Rome, Italy, Theol; Marquette Univ, Theol, MA, 67; Univ Chicago, theol, MA, 67; Univ Chicago, theol, PhD, 70. **CAREER** Instr and asst prof, San Francisco Col for Women, 63-64; Marywood Col, theol dept, summer, 66; Immaculate Heart Col, theol and eng, summer, 67; instr and asst prof, theol dept, St Xavier Col, 66-68; asst prof, Univ Calif Riverside, 69-73; assoc prof and mem grad facul, hist theol, Duke Univ, Divinity Sch, 73-81; Iliff Sch of Theol, summer, 79, 80; prof and chair, dept relig studies, Univ Mo Columbia, 81-87, 90-95. **HONORS AND AWARDS** Radcliffe Scholar, 49-51; scholar, San Francisco Col for Women, 52-53; tuition grant, Marquette Univ, 64-65; DAAD scholar, Goethe Inst, Germany, summer, 65; full tuition grant, Univ Chicago, 65-68; jr fel, Foun for Reformation Res, summer, 68; univ fel, Univ Chicago, 68-69; facul fel, Univ Calif Riverside, summer, 70; SRHE for Lilly-Johnson project, 72-73; Humanities Inst fel, Univ Calif, 72-73; ACLS grant-in-aid, res, summer, 74; Duke Res Coun Grant, 74-76; ACLS and ATS fel, 75-76; Radcliffe Inst fel, 75-76; NEH fel, 75-76; Alumna of the Year, Divinity Sch of Univ Chicago, 80; ACLS grant-in-aid, summer, 81; NEH fel, 81-82; Fel of Nat Humanities Ctr, 81-82; Fleming Scholar, Southwestern Univ, fall, 81; UMC Res Coun res grant and travel grant; Amer Coun of Learned Soc grant, Intl Congress for Calvin Studies, sep 6-9, 82; Comt for Fulbright Scholar, relig, jul 84-jun 87, chair; 85-87; Nat Endow for the Humanities grant, 83-85; Alpha Sigma Nu, Nat Jesuit Honor Soc, 84; Exxon Educ Foun grant, 85-87; Alexander Robertson lectr, Univ Glasgow, apr-jun, 85; Univ Mo Columbia res coun leave, 87-88; fel, Nat Humanities Ctr, 87-88; outstanding teacher, Sect of Acad Teaching and Study of Relig, Amer Acad Relig, 90; NEH speaker, Whittier Col, feb 25-28, 92; key note address, Central States Reg Mtg, apr, 93; Plenary address, Col Theol Teachers Annual Mtg, jun, 93; fel, East-West Ctr, jan and jun, 91-93; commencement speaker, Col of Arts and Sci, MU, aug 6, 93; Catherine Paine Middlebush Prof in the Humanities, 90-95; respondent to keynote, Calvin Studies Soc, mar, 95; visiting scholar, Grad Theol Union, mar, 96; facul intl travel award, jul, 96; summer stipend, Lilly Foun for the Valparaiso Project, summer, 96; renewal 97 participant, Fairfield Univ, summer, 97; Collegium Mentor, Univ San Diego, jun, 98. **MEMBERSHIPS** Amer Acad of Relig, 81; Amer Soc of Church Hist; Amer Soc for Reformation Res; Bishops Comm for Inter-Relig and Ecumenical Affairs; Duke Univ Comt on Medieval Renaissance Studies; Soc for Calvin Studies; Univ Chicago Nat Alumni Cabinet; Univ Chicago Divinity Sch Alumni Asn; Univ Mo Columbia Mus of Art and Archeol; Univ Mo Columbia Sinclair Comparative Med Res Farm; Univ Mo Columbia. **SELECTED PUBLICATIONS** Auth, The Colloquy of Montbeliard: Religion and Politics in the Sixteenth Century, NY, Oxford Univ Press, mar, 93; ed and contrib, Saints and Sinners, Christian

Spirituality: High Middle Ages and Reformation, vol 17, World Spirituality Series, NY, Crossroad/Continuum Publ Co, jun, 87; ed, Theodore Beza, transl, Lambert Daneau, Shapers of Traditions in Germany, Switzerland and Poland, 1560-1600, New Haven, Yale Univ Press, 81; auth, The Eucharistic Theol of Theodore Beza: The Development of the Reformed Tradition, AAR Studies in Relig, no 4, 72; article, Two Spiritual Directors of Women in the Sixteenth Century: St. Ignatius Loyola and St. Teresa of Avil, In Laudem Caroli: Renaissance and Reformation Studies for Charles G. Nauert, Sixteenth Century Studies, 98; article, Contemplatives in Action, the World Christian Life Community, Doors of Understanding: Conversations in Global Spirituality, Franciscan Press, 98; article, Transformations and Traditions: Augustine's Teaching on the Transformation of Christians in the Liturgy and the Use of these Teachings in the Sixteenth Century, The Australasian Cath Record, apr, 97. **CONTACT ADDRESS** Dept. of Religious Studies, Univ of Missouri, Columbia, 405 GCB, Columbia, MO 65211-4140. **EMAIL** raittj@missouri.edu

RAITT, RONALD D.
DISCIPLINE LAW **EDUCATION** Univ Nebr, BS, JD. **CAREER** Prof. **SELECTED PUBLICATIONS** Auth, Evidence Cases and Problems, Harrison, 95; The Preemption and Economic Loss Provisions of the Ohio Product Liability Code, Univ Dayton Law Rev, 91; The Ohio Product Liability Code: The Mechanical Problems Involved in Applying Strict Tort Remedies to Economic Loss in Commercial Cases, Univ Dayton Law Rev, 91; Personal Knowledge Under the Federal Rules of Evidence: A Three-Legged Stool, Rutgers Law J, 87. **CONTACT ADDRESS** Col Law, Univ of Toledo, Toledo, OH 43606. **EMAIL** rraitt@pop3.utoledo.edu

RAJ, VICTOR A. R.
PERSONAL Born 03/22/1948, Trivandrum, India, m, 1976, 3 children **DISCIPLINE** EXEGETICAL THEOLOGY **EDUCATION** Kerala Univ, India, BSc, 67; Gurukul Col, India, BD, 71; Concordia Sem, STM, 76, ThD, 81. **CAREER** Pastor, Cochin, India, 71-74; pastor, Trivandrum, India, 75-78; pastor, Gospel, Trivandrum, India, 81-84; dir, Renewal Prog, India Evangel Lutheran Church, 84-88; pres, 88-90, Concordia Theol Sem, Nagercoil, India; prof, chemn div theol, 90-95, Concordia Univ, Mequon, Wisc; mission prof of exegetical theol, asst dir of Inst for Mission Stud, Concordia Sem, 95- . **RESEARCH** Missions; world religions and their influence on Christian theology and culture; New Testament studies. **SELECTED PUBLICATIONS** Auth, The Hindu Connection: Roots of the New Age, Concordia, 95; ed, "Missio Apostolica," Journal of the Lutheran society for Missiology. **CONTACT ADDRESS** Concordia Sem, 801 DeMun Ave, Saint Louis, MO 63105. **EMAIL** rajv@csl.edu

RAJASHEKAR, J. PAUL
DISCIPLINE SYSTEMATIC THEOLOGY **EDUCATION** Univ Mysore, BA, 68; United Theol Col, BD, 71; Concordia Sem-Seminex, STM, 74; Univ Iowa, PhD, 81. **CAREER** Prof **RESEARCH** Christian ecumenism, cross-cultural dialogue, social and political ethics. **SELECTED PUBLICATIONS** Pub(s), on authentic forms of Christian witness/mission in a multi-religious world. **CONTACT ADDRESS** Dept of History and Systematic Theology, Lutheran Theol Sem at Gettysburg, 7301 Germantown Ave, Philadelphia, PA 19119 1794. **EMAIL** Rajashekar@ltsp.edu

RAKUS, DANIEL T.
PERSONAL Born 03/05/1958, Philadelphia, PA, s **DISCIPLINE** PHILOSOPHY **EDUCATION** La Salle Col, BS, 80; St. Charles Borromeo Sem, MA, 85; Villanova Univ, MA, 90; Univ of Toronto, PhD, 97. **CAREER** Unaffiliated Scholar. **MEMBERSHIPS** APA **RESEARCH** Medieval philo; philo of religion; ethics and philosophical anthropology. **SELECTED PUBLICATIONS** Auth, Towards an Anselmian Theodicy, Ottawa: Nat Lib of Can, 98; Augustinian Libertas: The Foundations of an Ethics of Being, in: Downside Review, 97; Alter Augustinus and the Question of Moral Knowledge: Answering Philosophically as an Anselmian, in: Revue des Etudes Augustiniennes, 97; auth, "Anselmian Libertas--'Freedom of Choice' of the Free and Ratioonal Will: The Foundation of an Ethics of Being," American Benedictine Review, 98. **CONTACT ADDRESS** PO Box 17165, Philadelphia, PA 19105-7165. **EMAIL** dtrakus@hotmail.com

RAMEY, GEORGE
PERSONAL Born 08/17/1938, Dixon, MO, m; 1959, 2 children **DISCIPLINE** THEOLOGY **EDUCATION** Southwest Baptist Col, AA, 58; William Jewel Col, BA, 60; Midwestern Baptist Theo Seminary, BD, 63; Southern Baptist Theo Seminary, ThM, 65, Phd, 68. **CAREER** Prof, 68-98, vice president, 75-98, Cumberland Col. **MEMBERSHIPS** Soc of Biblical Literature; Amer Acad of Relig; Internation Organization for Study of Old Testament; Amer Schs of Oriental Research; Natl Assn of Col & Univ Business Officers; Southern Assn of Col & Univ Business Officers; Council of Independent Kentucky Col & Univ Business Officers. **CONTACT ADDRESS** Cumberland Col, 75 Hemlook St., Williamsburg, KY 40769-1793. **EMAIL** gramey@cc.cumber.edu

RAMP, STEVEN W.
DISCIPLINE HOMILETICS **EDUCATION** Col William and Mary, BA, 71; Vanderbilt Univ Sch, JD, 75; Princeton Theol Sem, MDiv, 90, PhD, 97. **CAREER** Assoc prof, 98-. **HONORS AND AWARDS** Sr pastor, J.J. White Memorial Presbyterian Church, 93-97; interm pastor, Hope Presbyterian Church, 90-93. **MEMBERSHIPS** Mem, Presbytery Comm; bd mem, Habitat for Humanity. **SELECTED PUBLICATIONS** Auth, The Uniform Commercial Code in Tennesse, 87. **CONTACT ADDRESS** Dept of Homiletics, Luther Sem, 2481 Como Ave, Saint Paul, MN 55108. **EMAIL** sramp@luthersem.edu

RAMRAS-RAUCH, GILA
PERSONAL Born Tel-Aviv, Israel **DISCIPLINE** JUDAIC STUDIES **EDUCATION** Hunter Col, MA, Bar-Ilan Univ, PhD. **CAREER** Col Prof; Lecturer. **HONORS AND AWARDS** NEH Grant, Skirball Fel, Centre for Post-Graduate Hebrew Studies at Oxford, Lewis H. Weinstein Chair of Hebrew and Jewish Literature, Hebrew College. **MEMBERSHIPS** Pam America, MLA, AJS, NAPA, ACLA **RESEARCH** Holocaust Literature, Women in the Bible, Modern Hebrew Literature. **SELECTED PUBLICATIONS** Auth, Protagonist in Transition (published by Peter Lang Verlag, Berne, Switzerland, 82); auth, Holocaust: Facing the Holocaust (published by the Jewish Publication Society, Philadelphia, Pennsylvania, 85); auth, The Arab in Israeli Literature, Indiana Univ Press, 89; auth, L.A. Arieli, Papyrus, Tel-Aviv Univ, 92; auth, Aharon Appelfeld: The Holocaust and Beyond, Indiana Univ Press, 94. **CONTACT ADDRESS** Dept Judaic Studies, Hebrew Col, 43 Hawes St, Brookline, MA 02446-5412.

RAMSEY, JEFF
DISCIPLINE HISTORY AND PHILOSOPHY OF SCIENCE **EDUCATION** Kans State Univ, BA; Univ Chicago, MS (chem), PhD (hist & plilos science). **CAREER** Asst prof, Ore State Univ, 94-. **RESEARCH** Three-dimensional molecular shape, interaction of science and policy. **SELECTED PUBLICATIONS** Area: how approximations and idealizations affect our notions of justification and reduction. **CONTACT ADDRESS** Dept Philos, Oregon State Univ, Hovland Hall 102E, Corvallis, OR 97331-3902. **EMAIL** jramsey@orst.edu

RAMSEY, WILLIAM M.
DISCIPLINE PHILOSOPHY OF SCIENCE **EDUCATION** Univ Ore, BS, 82; Univ Calif San Diego, PhD, 89. **CAREER** Assoc prof. **RESEARCH** Cognitive science; philosophy of psychology. **SELECTED PUBLICATIONS** Auth, Parallelism and Functionalism, 89; Connectionism, Eliminativism and the Future of Folk Psychology, 90; Where Does the Self-refutation Objection Take Us?, 91; Prototypes and Conceptual Analysis, 92; Connectionism and the Philosophy of Mental Representation, 93; Prototypes and Conceptual Analysis, 94; Investigating Common Sense Psychology, 96; co-auth, Connectionism and Three Levels of Nativism, 90; co-ed, Philosophy and Connectionist Theory, 91. **CONTACT ADDRESS** History and Philosophy of Science Dept, Univ of Notre Dame, Notre Dame, IN 46556. **EMAIL** William.M.Ramsey.1@nd.edu

RAMSHAW, ELAINE JULIAN
DISCIPLINE PASTORAL CARE **EDUCATION** Valparaiso Univ, BA, 78; Univ Chicago Divinity Sch, MA, 79, PhD, 89. **CAREER** Fac mem, Methodist Theol Sch, 86; assoc prof, 95-. **HONORS AND AWARDS** Danforth fel, 78-82; Theol scholar, Assn Theol Sch(s); res grant for younger scholars, 93-95; intern in pastoral psychotherapy, ctr rel and psychotherapy, 82-85. **MEMBERSHIPS** Mem, Soc Pastoral Theol; Evangel Lutheran Church, Confirmation Ministry Task Force, 89-93; Consult Comm S Ohio Synod of the ELCA, 88-94; Family Violence Policy Panel, Ohio State Univ, 86-89. **RESEARCH** Religion and psychological studies. **SELECTED PUBLICATIONS** Auth, Ritual and Pastoral Care, 87. **CONTACT ADDRESS** Dept of Pastoral Care, The Church Divinity School of the Pacific, 2451 Ridge Rd, Berkeley, CA 94709-1217. **EMAIL** eramshaw@cdsp.edu

RANDALL, KENNETH C.
DISCIPLINE LAW **EDUCATION** Hofstra Univ, JD, 81; Yale Univ, MA, 82; Columbia Univ Sch Law, MA, 85, SJD, 88. **CAREER** Prof, Univ Ala, 85. **HONORS AND AWARDS** Outstanding fac mem, Univ Ala, 87-88; outstanding law grad, Hofstra Univ. **RESEARCH** Public international law, international business transactions,and constitutional law. **SELECTED PUBLICATIONS** Auth, Int Law Bk, Duke UP. **CONTACT ADDRESS** Law Dept, Univ of Alabama, Tuscaloosa, Box 870000, Tuscaloosa, AL 35487-0383. **EMAIL** kcrandal@law.ua.edu

RANDALL, SUSAN LYONS
DISCIPLINE LAW **EDUCATION** Univ NC-Chapel Hill, BA, 78; Columbia Univ Sch Law, JD, 82. **CAREER** Prof, Univ Ala, 92-. **MEMBERSHIPS** Phi Beta Kappa. **RESEARCH** Torts I and II, insurance, and jurisprudence. **CONTACT ADDRESS** Law Dept, Univ of Alabama, Tuscaloosa, Box 870000, Tuscaloosa, AL 35487-0383. **EMAIL** srandall@law.ua.edu

RANKIN, DUNCAN
DISCIPLINE THEOLOGY **EDUCATION** Clemson Univ, BS; Reformed Theol Sem, MDiv; Univ Edinburgh, PhD. **CAREER** Prof **SELECTED PUBLICATIONS** Auth, articles in the Jour Amer Ceramic Soc; Christian Observer; contrib, James Henley Thornwell; Westminster Confession of Faith. **CONTACT ADDRESS** Dept of Theology, Reformed Theol Sem, Mississippi, 5422 Clinton Blvd, Jackson, MS 39209-3099.

RANKIN, STEVE
PERSONAL Born 11/25/1954, Ashland, KS, m, 1979, 4 children **DISCIPLINE** RELIGIOUS STUDIES **EDUCATION** Kans State Univ, BS, 78; MDiv, St Paul Sch Theol, 86; Trinity Evangelical Divinity Sch, ThM, 92; Northwestern Univ, PhD. **CAREER** Asst prof & Campus Minister, Southwestern Col, 95-. **HONORS AND AWARDS** John Wesley Fel, Found for Theol Educ. **MEMBERSHIPS** Am Acad of Relig, Am Soc of Church Hist, Wesley Hist Soc, Wesleyan Theol Soc. **RESEARCH** Eighteenth-Century (Enlightenment), Theology and Popular Culture. **SELECTED PUBLICATIONS** Auth, "Forward," in Importance of E. Stanley Jones Chairs of Evangelism in United Methodist Seminaries, 92. **CONTACT ADDRESS** Dept Philos & Relig Studies, Southwestern Col, Kansas, 100 College St, Winfield, KS 67156-2443. **EMAIL** srankin@sckans.edu

RANSDELL, JOSEPH M.
DISCIPLINE PHILOSOPHY **EDUCATION** San Francisco State Univ, BA, 61; Columbia Univ, PhD, 66. **CAREER** Assoc prof emer, Tex Tech Univ. **RESEARCH** Socrates and Plato; early mod philos, Charles Peirce. **SELECTED PUBLICATIONS** Publ(s) are chiefly on var aspects of the philos of the Am philosopher Charles Peirce, espec his semiotic or theory of representation; Ransdell has also authored an introductory work on the hist of philos. **CONTACT ADDRESS** Dept of Philos, Texas Tech Univ, Box 43092, Lubbock, TX 79409-5015. **EMAIL** joseph.ransdell@ttu.edu

RAPAPORT, WILLIAM J.
PERSONAL Born 09/30/1946, Brooklyn, NY, m, 1993, 4 children **DISCIPLINE** PHILOSOPHY; COMPUTER SCIENCE **EDUCATION** Univ of Rochester, BA, 68; Indiana Univ, AM, 74, PhD, 76; SUNY Buffalo, MS, 84. **CAREER** Inst, Inwood Jr High Sch, 68-69; Dir, Math Prog, Walden Schl, 69-71; Assoc Inst Phil, 71-72, Assoc Inst Math, 75, Res Ass Phil, 72-75, Indiana Univ; Asst Prof, 76-83, Assoc Prof 83-84, SUNY Fredonia; Vis Asst Prof, 84-86, Asst Prof, 86-88, Assoc Prof 88-98, Computer Science, Adj Prof, Phil, 94-, Assoc Prof, Computer Science & Eng, 98-, SUNY Buffalo. **HONORS AND AWARDS** Dist Alumnus, Indiana Univ, 90; Steelman Vis Scientist Dist Let, Lenoir-Rhyne Col, 89; Northeastern Assoc of Grad Schl Masters Scholar Awd, 87; APA Quarterly Essay Prize, 92; SUNY Chancellor's Awd for Exc in Tchg, 81. **MEMBERSHIPS** Amer Assoc for Artificial Intel; APA; Assoc for Comutational Linguistics; Assoc for Computing Machinery; Assoc for Symbolic Logic; Congnitive Science Soc **RESEARCH** Artificial inelligence, cognitive science; computational linguistics; knowledge representation; logic philosophy of mind; philosophy of language; critical thinking; cognitive development. **SELECTED PUBLICATIONS** Understanding Understanding Syntactic Semantics and Computational Cognition, Philo Persp, Conn and Philo Psychol, 95; Cognition and Fiction, & An Introduction to a Computational Reader of Narratives, Deixis in Narrative A Cogn Science Persp, 95; Quasi-Indexicals and Knowledge Reports, Cognitive Science, 97; Thought Language and Ontology Essays in Memory of Hector-Neri Castaneda, Philo Stud Series, 98. **CONTACT ADDRESS** SUNY, Buffalo, Dept of Computer Science, 226 Bell Hall, Box 602000, Buffalo, NY 14260-2000. **EMAIL** rapaport@cse.buffalo.edu

RAPOPORT, DAVID C.
PERSONAL Born 01/07/1929, Pittsburgh, PA, m, 1959, 2 children **DISCIPLINE** POLITICAL SCIENCE **EDUCATION** Univ Calif, BA, 50; MA, 52; PhD, 60. **CAREER** Res Fel, Columbia Univ, 59-62; Lectr, Barnard Col, 61-62; Asst Prof to Prof Emeritus, 62-. **HONORS AND AWARDS** UC Chancellor's Fel, 70; LSE Vis Fel, 66; Ford Found Fel, 68-69; NIMH Res Grant, 71-74; Reason Found Fel, 80; H.F. Guggenheim Fel, 89-91. **MEMBERSHIPS** APSA; IPSA; ISA; ISPP. **RESEARCH** Political Violence; Religion; Political Theory. **SELECTED PUBLICATIONS** Co-ed, The Democratic Experience and Violence, London: Frank Cass, 01. **CONTACT ADDRESS** Dept Polit Sci, Univ of California, Los Angeles, 4289 Bunche, PO Box 951472, Los Angeles, CA 90095-1472. **EMAIL** Rapoport@polisci.ucla.edu

RAPPAPORT, STEVEN D.
PERSONAL Born 08/09/1945, New York, NY, m, 1983 **DISCIPLINE** PHILOSOPHY **EDUCATION** Univ Calif, Berkeley, BA, 67; San Jose State Univ, MA, 83; Univ Toronto, PhD, 72. **CAREER** Vis asst prof, McGill Univ, 72-73; vis asst prof, Ryerson Polytechnical Inst, 73-74; prof, De Anza Col, 74-. **MEMBERSHIPS** APA; Philos of Sci Assoc. **RESEARCH** Philosophy of economics; philosophy of social science; epistemology. **SELECTED PUBLICATIONS** Auth, Must a Metaphysical Relativist be a Truth Relativist? Philosophia, 93; auth, Basic Beliefs and the Regress of Justification: A Reply to Yal-

cin, Southern Jour of Philos, 93; auth, Is Economics Empirical Knowledge? Econ and Philos, 95; auth, Economic Models and Historical Explanation, Philos of Soc Sci, 95; auth, Inference to the Best Explanation: Is It Really Different from Mill's Methods? Philos of Sci, 96; auth, Abstraction and Unrealistic Assumptions in Economics, Jour of Econ Methodology, 96; auth, Relativism and Truth: A Rejoinder to Lynch, Philosophia, 97; auth, Relativism and Truth: A Reply to Davson-Galle, Philosophia, 98; auth, Models and Reality in Economics, Elgar, 98. **CONTACT ADDRESS** Dept of Philosophy, De Anza Col, Cupertino, CA 95014.

RASER, HAROLD E.
PERSONAL Born 03/09/1947, Altadena, CA, m, 1968, 2 children **DISCIPLINE** RELIGION **EDUCATION** Pasadena Col, BA, 68, MA, 70; Nazarene Theol Sem, MDiv, 74; Penn State Univ, PhD, 87. **CAREER** Adj grad prof relig studies, Univ Mo, 96-; adj lectr, S Nazarene Univ, 96-97; adj lectr, Point Loma Nazarene Univ, 93-94; adj lectr, Fuller Theol Sem, 89; vis prof, Europ Nazarene Bibl Col, 86-87; adj lectr, St. Paul Sch Theol, 84-87; from asst prof to assoc prof to prof, Nazarene Theol Sem, 80-. **MEMBERSHIPS** Am Acad Relig; Am Soc Church Hist; Wesleyan Theol Soc. **RESEARCH** History of the American Holiness Movement; American revivalism and evangelicalism; 19th century American religion; new religious movements in America. **SELECTED PUBLICATIONS** Auth, Phoebe Palmer: Her Life and Thought, 87; auth, More Preachers and Better Preachers: The First Fifty Years of Nazarene Theological Seminary, 95; Views of Last Things in the American Holiness Movement, Second Coming: Wesleyan Perspective on Eschatology, 95; auth, Forming and Reforming Worship, Worshipping God: The Church's First Call, 96; auth, Worship Since the Reformation, Worshipping God: The Church's First Call, 96. **CONTACT ADDRESS** Nazarene Theol Sem, 1700 E Meyer Blvd, Kansas City, MO 64131. **EMAIL** heraser@nts.edu

RASKIN, JAMIN
DISCIPLINE CONSTITUTIONAL LAW; CRIMINAL LAW **EDUCATION** Harvard Col, BA, 83; Harvard Law Sch, JD, 87; **CAREER** Prof, Am Univ; Benjamin Trustman Fel; Harvard Univ Carnochan Nat Scholar, Presidential Scholar WCL Pauline Ruyle Moore Scholar, 96; Tchg fel, Harvard Univ. **HONORS AND AWARDS** First Circuit Court Appeals Prize; asst atty gen, commonwealth mass, 87-89; gen counsel, natl rainbow coalition, 89-90; mem, clinton-gore justice dept transition team, 92; codir wcl prog law & government; ed, harvard law rev. **SELECTED PUBLICATIONS** Ed, Harvard Law Rev; Contrib, Columbia Law Rev; Univ Pa Law Rev; American Univ Jour Gender & the Law; Yale Law & Policy Rev; Hastings Law Jour; Howard Law Jour; Catholic Univ Law Rev **CONTACT ADDRESS** American Univ, 4801Massachusetts Ave, Washington, DC 20016. **EMAIL** raskin@wcl.american.edu

RASKIN, JAY
PERSONAL Born 08/16/1953, New York, NY, m, 1987, 1 child **DISCIPLINE** PHILOSOPHY **EDUCATION** School of Visual Arts, BFA Filmmaking, 76; Univ S Fla, MA, 95, PhD, 97. **CAREER** Adj prof, Rollins Col; vis instr, Univ of Central Fla. **MEMBERSHIPS** Amer Philos Asn; Fla Philos Asn. **RESEARCH** Film; Marxism; Technology; Classical History. **CONTACT ADDRESS** Dept of Philos, Univ of Central Florida, HFA 411, Orlando, FL 32816-1352. **EMAIL** jraskin@pegasus.cc.ucf.edu

RAST, WALTER EMIL
PERSONAL Born 07/03/1930, San Antonio, TX, m, 1955, 4 children **DISCIPLINE** OLD TESTAMENT, ARCHEOLOGY **EDUCATION** St John's Col, BA, 52; Concordia Theol Sem, MDiv, 55, STM, 56; Univ Chicago, MA, 64, PhD(Old Testament), 66. **CAREER** From asst prof to assoc prof, 61-73; Prof Old Testament & Archaeol, Valparaiso Univ, 73-, James Alan Montgomery fel, Am Schs Orient Res, Jerusalem, 66-67; res prof, Albright Inst Archaeol Res, Jerusalem, 71-72; Danforth assoc, 73-; co-dir, Excavations at Bab edh-Dhra & Numeira, 75-; Nat Endowment for Humanities res grants, 75, 77, 79 & 81; Univ Chicago fel, 76; vis prof Old Testament, Univ Notre Dame, 77-78 & 82; pres, Am Ctr of Orental Res Amman, 78-82; prof, Albright Inst Archaeol Res, Jerusalem, 82-83; Am Coun Learned Soc fel, 71-72; Nat Endowment for Humanities fel, 82. **MEMBERSHIPS** Archaeol Inst Am; Am Schs Orient Res; Soc Bibl Lit; Israel Explor Soc. **RESEARCH** Old Testament; Syro-Palestinian archeology; Semitic languages. **SELECTED PUBLICATIONS** Auth, Tradition History and the Old Testament, Fortress, 72; coauth, Survey of the Southeastern plain of the Dead Sea, Ann Dept Antiq Jordan, 74; A preliminary report of excavations at Bab edh, Dhra, 1975, Ann Am Schs Orient Res, 76; auth, Tannach I: Studies in the Iron Age Pottery, Am Scholars Orient Res, 78; Joshua, Judges, Samuel and Kings, Fortress, 78; An Ostracon from Tell el-Ful, 78 &; co-ed, The Southeastern Dead Sea Plain Expedition: An Interim Report of the 1977 Season, 79, Annals Am Scholars Orient Res; coauth, Preliminary Report of the 1979 Expedition to the Dead Sea Plain, Jordan, Bull Am Scholars Orient Res, 240. **CONTACT ADDRESS** Dept of Theol, Valparaiso Univ, Valparaiso, IN 46383.

RATCLIFFE, CAROLYN
PERSONAL Born 03/04/1940, Lubbock, TX, m, 1959, 4 children **DISCIPLINE** BIBLICAL STUDIES **EDUCATION** Tex Tech Univ, BS, 66; Wayland Baptist Univ, MA, 89; Baylor Univ, PhD, 95. **CAREER** From adj prof to asst prof, Wayland Baptist Univ, 93-. **MEMBERSHIPS** Soc of Biblical Literature, Baptist Women in Ministry, Baptist Professors. **RESEARCH** Intertextuality in Scripture. **CONTACT ADDRESS** Dept Relig & Philos, Wayland Baptist Univ, 1900 W 7th St, Plainview, TX 79072-6900. **EMAIL** ratcliff@mail.wbu.edu

RATES, NORMAN M.
PERSONAL Born 01/01/1924, Owensboro, KY, m **DISCIPLINE** THEOLOGY **EDUCATION** KY State Coll, AB 1947; Lincoln Univ, BD 1950; Oberlin Coll, MDiv 1952; Yale Univ, MAR 1961; Vanderbilt Univ, DMin 1974; Oberlin Coll, STM 1953; Harvard Univ, independent study 1968-69. **CAREER** Camac Comm Ctr Phila, student counselor 1947-48; Philadelphia Gen Hosp, asst to protestant chaplain 1948-49; St Paul Bapt Ch W Chester PA, asst to pastor 1949-50; Div of Home Missions Natl Council for Ch of Christ in USA NY FL DE, missionary to agricultural migrants 1948-56; Morris Coll, minister dean of men tchr 1953-54; Morehouse Spelman Coll Pre-Coll Prog summers, counselor & minister 1966-67; Central Brooklyn Model Cities Summer Acad Spelman Coll summer, couns 1972; Interdenom Theol Ctr, guest lectr & part-time tchr 1971; Westhills Presb Ch GA summer, interim pastor 1963; Spellman Col GA Dept of Religion, Coll Minister & Chmn 1954-. **HONORS AND AWARDS** C Morris Cain Prize in Bible Lincoln Univ 1949; Samuel Dickey Prize in New Testament Lincoln Univ 1949; Campus Christian Worker Grant Danforth Found 1960-61; Atlanta Univ Ctr Non-Western Studies Prog Grant for Travel & Study Ford Found 1968-69. **MEMBERSHIPS** Mem Natl Assn of Coll & Univ Chaplains; mem Ministry to Blacks in Higher Educ; mem Amer Assn of Univ Profs; mem Natl Assn of Biblical Instr; mem Univ Ctr in GA Div of Tchr of Religion; Petit Juror Fulton Co Superior Ct 1971, 1973; grand juror Fulton Co Superior Ct 1972; ministerial standing The United Ch of Christ; Fellow Conf on African & African-Amer Studies Atlanta Univ Campus; bd mem Camping Unlimited Blue Star Camps Inc; bd dir Planned Parenthood Assn of Atlanta; chmn Religious Affairs Com Planned Parenthood Assn of Atlanta; mem Com on the Ministry The United Ch of Christ; mem The Metro Atlanta Christian Council; mem GA-SC Assn of the United Ch of Christ SE Conf; mem Alpha Phi Alpha Frat. **CONTACT ADDRESS** Dept Religion, Spelman Col, 350 Spelman Lane SW, Atlanta, GA 30314.

RATHEL, MARK
PERSONAL Born 11/19/1957, Panama City, FL, m, 1977, 2 children **DISCIPLINE** RELIGION **EDUCATION** William Carey Col, BA, 79; New Orleans Baptist Theol Sem, MDiv, 81; PhD, 88. **CAREER** Asst prof, Fla Baptist Theol Col, 98-. **MEMBERSHIPS** Evangelical Theol Soc, Fla Baptist Hist Soc. **RESEARCH** New Testament, Theology, Christian History. **SELECTED PUBLICATIONS** Auth, "Temptation: Meaning and Usage," The biblical Illustrator (97); auth, "Word Studies," Pursuits: Live and Work (98); auth, "Gergaza," The Biblical Illustrator (98); auth, "The Influence of J. R. Graves on Florida Baptists," Fla Baptist Witness (98); auth, "The Importance of Baptist Heritage," Fla Baptist Witness (99); auth, "The History of Baptist Confessions," Fla Baptist Witness (00); auth, "Herod Agrippa II," The Biblical Illustrator (forthcoming). **CONTACT ADDRESS** Dept Relig, Florida Baptist Theol Col, 5400 College Dr, Graceville, FL 32440-1831.

RATLIFF, CHARLES EDWARD
PERSONAL Born 10/13/1926, Morven, NC, m, 1945, 3 children **DISCIPLINE** ECONOMICS **EDUCATION** Davidson Col, BA, 47; Duke Univ, AM, 51, PhD, 55. **CAREER** V-12, 44-45, aviation supply officer, U.S. Navy, 45-46; Instr to Kenan Prof of ecomomics, Davidson College, 47-92; Kenan Prof emeritus, Davidson College, Prof of economics, Forman Christian College, Pakistan (United Methodist Bd Global Ministries, 63-66, 69-70. **HONORS AND AWARDS** Ford Found award; Fulbright-Hays award; CASE Prof of the Year, 85. **MEMBERSHIPS** Nat Tax Asn; Southern Economic Asn; Am Economic Asn. **RESEARCH** Idea of a world development fund, an approach to financing world development. **SELECTED PUBLICATIONS** Auth, Interstate Apportionment: Business Income, UNC Press, 62, Oxford Univ Press, 63; auth, A World Development Fund, World Acad of Development & Cooperation, 87; auth, Economics at Davidson: A Serguicentenial History, Davidson Col, 87; contribur, Rural Development in Pakistan, Carolina Acad Press, 80; auth, Articles in Professional Journals in USA and Pakistan. **CONTACT ADDRESS** 29 Lake Hunter Dr, Lakeland, FL 33803-1288.

RATNER, STEVEN RICHARD
PERSONAL Born 12/09/1959, New York, NY, m, 1995, 2 children **DISCIPLINE** INTERNATIONAL LAW **EDUCATION** Princeton Univ, AB, 82; Yale Law School, JD, 86; Institut Universitaire de Hautes Etudes Internationales Geneva, MA, 93. **CAREER** Atty adv, Off of Legal Advs, US Dept of State, 86-93; Int Affairs Fel, Council of Foreign Rels, 92-93; asst prof Univ Tex School Law, 93-97; prof, Univ Tex School Law, 97-; Vis Prof, Columbia Law School, 00. **HONORS AND AWARDS** Certificate of Merit for Best Scholarly book, Am Soc of Int Law, 97; Bd of Ed of Am J of Int Law; Fulbright Scholar, 98-99. **MEMBERSHIPS** Am Soc of Int Law; Acad Council of the UN Syst; Asn of Am Law Schools. **RESEARCH** International Law; Human Rights; United Nations; Foreign Investment. **SELECTED PUBLICATIONS** Auth, The New Un Peacekeeping: Building Peace in Lands of Conflict After the Cold War, 95; Accountability for Human Rights Atrocities In International Law: Beyond the Nuremberg Legacy, 97; numerous articles in law journals, 84-00. **CONTACT ADDRESS** Univ of Texas, Austin, 727 E 26th St, Austin, TX 78705. **EMAIL** sratner@mail.law.utexas.edu

RATUSHNY, EDWARD J.
DISCIPLINE LAW **EDUCATION** Univ Saskatchewan, BA, LLB; London Univ, LLM; Univ Mich, LLM. **CAREER** Prof. **HONORS AND AWARDS** Mem, Order of Canada, 91; Commemorative Medal, 92; Justice Awd, 99 **MEMBERSHIPS** Canadian Bar Asn; Am Arbitration Asn; Canadian Institute for the Administration of Justice; International Commission of Jurists; Asn of Canadian Law Teachers; Sports Law years Asn. **RESEARCH** Sports and entertainment law. **SELECTED PUBLICATIONS** Auth, pubs on transportation, environmental, labour, competition, immigration, refugee and human rights law. **CONTACT ADDRESS** Fac Common Law, Univ of Ottawa, Fauteux Hall, 57 Louis Pasteur, Ottawa, ON, Canada K1N 6N5. **EMAIL** eratushn@uottawa.ca

RAUCH, DOREEN E.
PERSONAL Born 07/17/1947, Port of Spain, Trinidad and Tobago, m, 1969 **DISCIPLINE** LAW **EDUCATION** Univ of Cincinnati, BA, 1976; Howard Univ School of Law, JD, 1984. **CAREER** Emerson Law School, faculty, 84-89; Univ of Massachusetts-Boston, instructor, 85-86; Massachusetts Bay Comm Col, instructor, 85-86; Murray State Univ, dir of equal opportunity & affirm action, 91-93; Northern Michigan Univ, afirmative action officer, 93-. **HONORS AND AWARDS** Howard Univ, Amer Jurisprudence Awd in Commercial Paper, 1983; Amer Jurisprudence Awd in Criminal Law, 1982; Amer Jurisprudence Awd in Contracts, 1983; Amer Jurisprudence Awd in Municipal Law, 1982; Univ of Cincinnati, Dean's List, 1974-76. **MEMBERSHIPS** Natl Organization of Women, 1990-; Amer Assn of Univ Women, 1990-; Amer Assn of Univ administrators, 1995; Amer Assn of Affirmative Action, 1990-. **CONTACT ADDRESS** Affirmative Action Officer, No Michigan Univ, 1401 Presque Isle Avenue, Marquette, MI 49855.

RAUHUT, NILS
PERSONAL Born 10/05/1965 **DISCIPLINE** PHILOSOPHY **EDUCATION** Univ Regensburg, Germany, BA, 87; Univ Colo, MA, 90; Univ Wash, PhD, 97. **CAREER** Vis asst prof, Webster State Univ, 97-98; asst prof Coastal Carolina Univ, 98-. **MEMBERSHIPS** Am Philos Asn. **RESEARCH** Ancient Philosophy; Plato. **CONTACT ADDRESS** Dept of Philos and Relig, Coastal Carolina Univ, PO Box 261954, Conway, SC 29528-6054. **EMAIL** nrauhut@coastal.edu

RAUSCH, THOMAS P.
PERSONAL Born 02/12/1941, Chicago, IL **DISCIPLINE** THEOLOGY **EDUCATION** Gonzaga, BA, 66; MA, 67; Jesuit School of Theol Berkeley, STM, 72; Duke Univ, PhD, 76. **CAREER** Prof and Chair, Dept of Theol Studies, Loyola Marymount Univ. **MEMBERSHIPS** Cath Theol Soc of Am; Am Acad of Rel; N Am Acad of Ecumenists; Cath/ Southern Baptist Conversation. **RESEARCH** Contemporary theological issues; ecclesiology; authority; priesthood; ecumenism. **SELECTED PUBLICATIONS** Auth, The Roots of Catholic Tradition, 86; Authority and Leadership in the Church: Past Directions and Future Possibilities, 89; Radical Christian Communities, 90; Priesthood Today: An Appraisal, 92; Wspotczesne Kaptastwo, 96; Catholicism at the Dawn of the Third Millenium, 96; ed, The College Student's Introduction to Theology, 92. **CONTACT ADDRESS** Jesuit Comm, Loyola Marymount Univ, 7900 Loyola Blvd, Box 45041, Los Angeles, CA 90045-0041. **EMAIL** trausch@lmumail.lmu.edu

RAVEN-HANSEN, PETER
PERSONAL Born 06/05/1946, Copenhagen, Denmark, m, 1974, 2 children **DISCIPLINE** LAW **EDUCATION** Harvard Col, BA, 68; Harvard Law Sch, JD, 74. **CAREER** Assoc prof of law, George Wash Univ Law Sch, 80-85; prof of law, George Wash Univ Law Sch, 85-96; Glenn Earl Weston res prof of law, George Wash Univ Law Sch, 92-. **HONORS AND AWARDS** Phi Beta Kappa. **MEMBERSHIPS** Civil Procedure Sect; Asn Amer Law Sch. **RESEARCH** Law of the Presidency; National security; Civil procedure. **SELECTED PUBLICATIONS** Coauth with W. Banks, A Berney & S. Dycus, National Security Law, Little Brown, 2nd ed, 97; coauth with G. Shreve, Understanding Civil Procedure, Matthew Bender, 2nd ed, 94; Coauth with W. Banks, National Security Law and the Power of the Purse, Oxford Univ Press, 94. **CONTACT ADDRESS** Law Sch, The George Washington Univ, Washington, DC 20052. **EMAIL** praven@main.nlc.gwu.edu

RAVENELL, WILLIAM HUDSON
PERSONAL Born 05/31/1942, Boston, MA **DISCIPLINE** LAW **EDUCATION** Lincoln Univ PA, BA 1963; State Coll at Boston, MEd 1965; Howard Univ Sch of Law, JD 1968. **CAREER** John Hancock Ins Co, analyst 1968-71; Housing Inspection Dept, admin 1971-72; State Dept of Comm Affairs, dep sec 1972-75; FL Dept of Comm Affairs, sec 1975-79; FL A&M Univ, prof 1979; FL Office of the Atty Gen, special asst 1979-80; US Dept of Transportation Fed Hwy Admin, chief counsel 1980-81; State of FL, asst attorney general 1982-85; Florida A&M Univ, Attorney, Professor 1985-. **MEMBERSHIPS** Chmn FL Commn on Human Relations 1975-77; chmn FL Manpower Serv Council 1975-80; FL, DC, VA, Natl, Amer Bar Assns; mem Phi Alpha Delta, Omega Psi Phi, FL Council of 100; First Union Bank, board of directors, 1990-; NAACP, life member. **CONTACT ADDRESS** Florida A&M Univ, Tallahassee, FL 32303.

RAVVEN, HEIDI
PERSONAL Born 04/28/1952, Boston, MA, m, 1988, 1 child **DISCIPLINE** PHILOSOPHY **EDUCATION** Brandeis Univ, BA, 74, PhD, 84. **CAREER** Jewish Chaplain, Wellesley Col, 79-82; assoc prof, Hamilton Col, 83-; Stroum vis prof Jewish studies, Univ Wash, 97; prof, Dept of Relig Studies, Hamilton Col, 00-. **MEMBERSHIPS** Am Philos Asn; Acad Jewish Philos; N Am Spinoza Soc; Hegel Soc Am. **RESEARCH** Spinoza; feminist philosophy; Hegel; Jewish philosophy. **SELECTED PUBLICATIONS** Auth, Has Hegel Anything to Say to Feminists?, Int Libr Critical Essays Hist Philos Ser: Vol II Hegel, 98; co-ed & contribur, Spinoza and Judaism: A Collection of Essays, 99; auth, Spinoza's Rupture with Tradition, Spinoza & Jewish Philos: A Collection of Essays, 99; auth, Observations on Jewish Philosophy and Feminist Thought, Judaism: Quart Jour Jewish Life & Thought, Fall, 97; auth, Spinoza's Individualism Reconsidered: Some Lessons from the Short Treatise on God, Man, and His Well-Being, Iyyun: Jerusalem Philos Quart, July, 98; auth, Response to James Pinkerton: Hegel and Nazism, The Owl of Minerva: Jour Hegel Soc Am; auth, "Some Thoughts on What Spinoza Learned from Maimonides about the Prophetic Imagination," The Journal of the Hist of Philos, 01; auth, "Hegel and Feminism-Further Thoughts," Owl of Minerva: Journal of the Hegel Society of Am, (forthcoming, 01), auth, "Spinoza's Ethic of the Liberation of Desire," in On Being Human: Women in Jewish Philosophy, Hava Tirosh-Samuelson, ed., Indiana Univ Press, (forthcoming). **CONTACT ADDRESS** Dept of Religious Studies, Hamilton Col, New York, Clinton, NY 13323. **EMAIL** hravven@hamilton.edu

RAVVIN, NORMAN
PERSONAL Born 08/26/1963, Calgary, AB, Canada, m **DISCIPLINE** RELIGION **EDUCATION** Univ BC, BA, 85; MA, 88; Univ Toronto, PhD, 94. **CAREER** Asst prof, Univ NBrun, 97-99; asst prof and chair, Concordia Univ, 99-. **HONORS AND AWARDS** Morris Winemaker Prize, 98; Emerging Artists Prize, Ont Arts Coun, 96; Scholar, Soc Sci and Humanities Res Coun of Canada, 89; Albta Culture and Multiculturalism New Fiction Award, 90. **MEMBERSHIPS** Asn of the Can Col and Univ Teachers of English; Asn for Can Jewish Studies; MLA; Albta Writers Guild. **RESEARCH** Contemporary American and Canadian literature; Jewish Studies; Holocaust Studies; Literary Theory; Ethics; Landscape and Memory; Memoir. **SELECTED PUBLICATIONS** Auth, Cafe des Westens: A Novel, Red Deer Press, 91; auth, Sex, Skyscrapers, and Standard Yiddish, 97; auth, A House of Words: Jewish Writing, Identity, and Memory, McGill Univ Press, 97; auth, Hidden Canada: An Intimate Travelogue, Red Deer Press, 01; auth, Lola by Night, (forthcoming). **CONTACT ADDRESS** Dept Relig, Concordia Univ, Montreal, 1455 de Maisonneuve Blvd. W., Montreal, QC, Canada H3G 1M8. **EMAIL** ravvinbutler@sprint.ca

RAWLING, J. PIERS
DISCIPLINE DECISION THEORY, LOGIC, ETHICAL THEORY, PHILOSOPHY OF MATHEMATICS **EDUCATION** Cambridge Univ, Eng, BA, 81; Cornell Univ, MS, 86; Univ Calif, Berkeley, PhD, 89. **CAREER** Asst prof, Univ Ga, 89-91; invited vis lectr, Keele Univ, Eng, 93-94; asst prof, Univ Mo, St Louis; bd of counsult ed, Theory and Decision, 96. **HONORS AND AWARDS** Richard M Griffith Mem Awd in Philos, Southern Soc for Philos and Psychol, 90; NEH summer inst, 90; summer res grant, Univ Ga, 90; summer res grant, Univ Mo, St Louis, 91; NEH summer inst, 92; NEH summer sem, 93; NEH summer fel, 93; Univ Mo Syst Res Bd Awd, 95; Univ Mo Syst Inst for Instruct Develop Awd, 96-97. **SELECTED PUBLICATIONS** Auth, A Note on the Two Envelopes Problem, Theory and Decision 36, 94; Psychology and Newtonian Methodology, J of Mind and Behav 16(1), 95; coauth, Value and Agent-Relative Reasons, Utilitas 7(1), 95; Agent-Relativity and Terminological Inexactitudes, Utilitas 7(2), 95. **CONTACT ADDRESS** Univ of Missouri, St. Louis, Saint Louis, MO 63121.

RAWLS, JOHN
PERSONAL Born 02/21/1921, Baltimore, MD, m, 1949, 4 children **DISCIPLINE** PHILOSOPHY **EDUCATION** Princeton Univ, BA, 43; PhD, 50. **CAREER** Instr philos, Princeton Univ, 50-52; Oxford Univ, 52-53; asst prof, 53-56, assoc prof, 56-60, Cornell Univ; vis prof, Harvard Univ, 59-60; prof, MIT, 60-62; prof, 62-74, John Cowles Prof Philos, Harvard Univ, 74-79, James Bryant Conant Univ prof, 79-91, Conant Univ prof emeritus, 91-; Fulbright fel, . **HONORS AND AWARDS** Rolf Schock Prize in logic and Philos, Royal Swedish Acad, 99; Nat Humanities Award, awarded by Pres Bill Clinton, 99; Hon degrees, Oxford Univ, 83; Princeton Univ, 87; Harvard Univ, 97. **MEMBERSHIPS** Am Philos Asn; Am Soc for Legal and Political Philos; Am Philosophical Soc; British Acad. **RESEARCH** Moral and political philosophy; philosophical analysis. **SELECTED PUBLICATIONS** Auth, A Theory of Justice, 71; auth, Political Liberalism, 93; auth, Collected Papers, 99; auth, The Law of the Peoples, with the Idea of Public Reason Revisited, 99; auth, Lectures on the History of Moral Philosophy, 00; auth, Justice as Fairness - A Restatement, 01. **CONTACT ADDRESS** Dept of Philos, Harvard Univ, Cambridge, MA 02138.

RAY, DOUGLAS E.
DISCIPLINE LAW **EDUCATION** Univ Minn, BA; Harvard Univ, JD. **CAREER** Dean, prof, vpres of Law Ctr, Widener Univ, Sch of Law, 99- . **SELECTED PUBLICATIONS** Auth, Sexual Harassment, Labor Arbitration and National Labor Policy, Nebr Law Rev, 94; Some Overlooked Aspects of the Strike Replacement Issue, Kansas Law Rev, 92; Labor Management Relations: Strikes, Lockouts and Boycotts, Clark Boardman Callaghan, 92. **CONTACT ADDRESS** Sch of Law, Widener Univ, Delaware, 4601 Concord Pike, PO Box 7474, Wilmington, DE 19803-0474.

RAY, GREG
DISCIPLINE PHILOSOPHY **EDUCATION** Univ of Calif, Berkley, PhD, 92. **CAREER** Asst Prof, Univ Florida, 92-97; Vis Assoc Prof, Univ of MI, 98; Assoc Prof, Univ of FL, 98-. **MEMBERSHIPS** Amer Philo Asn; Asn for Symbolic Logic; Soc for Exact Phil; Florida Philo Asn **RESEARCH** Philosophical logic; metaphysics; philosophy of language. **CONTACT ADDRESS** Prof, Univ of Florida, Dept of Philosophy, Gainesville, FL 32611-8545. **EMAIL** gray@phil.ufl.edu

RAY, REGINALD
DISCIPLINE RELIGIOUS STUDIES **EDUCATION** Univ Chicago, PhD. **CAREER** Senior instr. **RESEARCH** Buddhist saints; Tantric Buddhism; Tibetan Buddhism; Vajrayana. **SELECTED PUBLICATIONS** Auth, Buddhist Saints in India. **CONTACT ADDRESS** Religious Studies Dept, Univ of Colorado, Boulder, Boulder, CO 80309. **EMAIL** Reginald.Ray@Colorado.edu

RAYE, VANCE WALLACE
PERSONAL Born 09/06/1946, Hugo, OK, m **DISCIPLINE** LAW **EDUCATION** Univ of OK, BA 1967, JD 1970. **CAREER** Bulla and Horning, attorney; US Air Force, asst staff judge advocate, Beale AFB chief of military justice, chief of civil law, judge advocate, 70-74; CA Attorney General, civil division, deputy atty general 74-80, sr asst atty general 80-82, deputy legislative scty 82-83; Governor of CA, legal affairs secretary, advisor, legal counsel, 83-89; Sacramento County Superior Court, judge, 89-90; California Court of Appeal, Third District, Assoc Justice, 91-; Lincoln Law School, Prof. **MEMBERSHIPS** State Bar of CA 1972-; vice chair CA Exec Emergency Council 1984-; CA Assn of Black Lawyers; NAACP; Urban League; CA State Bar Commn on Malpractice Insurance; chmn Staff Adv Council Natl Governors Assn Comm on Criminal Justice and Public Safety; Government's Emergency Operations Executive Council, vice chairman; National Institute of Justice, peer reviewer; Martin Luther King Holiday Commission, vice chairman; California Health Decisions; 100 Black Men of Sacramento; National Bar Association; Wiley Manuel Bar Association; California Judges Association; Judicial Council Committee on Family Law, chairman; Amer Bar Assn, criminal justice standards comm; CA Commission on the Future of the Courts, Family Relations Comm, chair; Judicial Council Appellate Standards Committee, chair legislative subcommittee; CA Commission on the Status of the African American Male; Univ of CA, Davis Med School Leadership Council. **SELECTED PUBLICATIONS** Publications: Contributor, "California Public Contract Law;" co-author: California Family Law Litigation, 3 volumes. **CONTACT ADDRESS** California Court of Appeal, 3rd Appellate District, 914 Capitol Mall, Sacramento, CA 95814.

RAYFIELD, DAVID
PERSONAL Born 04/10/1940, Miami, FL **DISCIPLINE** PHILOSOPHY **EDUCATION** Earlham Col, AB, 62; Duke Univ, PhD(philos), 66. **CAREER** Asst prof philos, Univ Akron, 66-68; mem fac, Univ Nfld, 68-70; assoc prof, 70-77, Prpf Philos, Saginaw Valley State Col, 77-, Chmn Dept, 70-. **RESEARCH** Philosophy of action. **SELECTED PUBLICATIONS** Auth, Action, Nous, 5/68; On describing actions, Inquiry, 70; Action: An Analysis of the Concept, Nijhoff, The Hague, 72; Cody's categories, 74 & On Miller's paradoxes and circles, winter 74, Inquiry. **CONTACT ADDRESS** Saginaw Valley State Univ, 7400 Bay Rd, University Center, MI 48710-0001. **EMAIL** rayfield@atssvsu.edu

RAYMOND, DIANE
DISCIPLINE PHILOSOPHY **EDUCATION** Vassar Col, BA; NYork Univ, PhD. **CAREER** Prof; dir, Women's Stud Prog; mem, GALA & Curric Comt. **MEMBERSHIPS** Am Philos Asn; Socr Women in Philos. **RESEARCH** Feminist theory; critical race theory; applied ethics; cult studies. **SELECTED PUBLICATIONS** Auth, Existentialism and the Philosophical Tradition, Prentice Hall; coauth, Looking at Gay and Lesbian Life, Beacon Press; ed, Sexual Politics and Popular Culture, Bowling Green UP; articles in, feminist theory, app ethics & popular cult theory. **CONTACT ADDRESS** Dept of Philos, Simmons Col, 300 The Fenway, Boston, MA 02115. **EMAIL** draymond@simmons.edu

REA, MICHAEL C.
DISCIPLINE PHILOSOPHY **EDUCATION** UCLA, BA, 91; Univ Notre Dame, MA, 94, PhD, 96. **CAREER** Asst Prof, 96 to 98-, Univ Delaware. **HONORS AND AWARDS** Vis Schl, 99, Univ Notre Dame; Pew Evan Fel; UD U Gnt; Diss Yr Fel; John A O'Brien Fel; Robert E Gordon Gnt; Phi Beta Kappa; Magna Cum Laude. **MEMBERSHIPS** SCP; APQ; PPR. **RESEARCH** Metaphysics, Philosophy of Religion, Ancient Philosophy. **SELECTED PUBLICATIONS** Ed, Material Constitution: A Reader, Lanham MD, Rowman and Littlefield, 97; coauth, Personal Identity and Psychological Continuity, Philo and Phenomenological Res, forthcoming; auth, Temporal Parts Unmotivated, Philo Rev, forthcoming; In Defense of Mereological Universalism, Philo and Phenom Res, 98; Supervenience and Co-location, Amer Philo Qtly, 97; ed, Introduction, in Material Constitution: A Reader, Lanham MD, Rowman and Littlefield, 97; auth, The Problem of Material Constitution, Philo Rev, 95. **CONTACT ADDRESS** Dept of Philosophy, Univ of Delaware, Newark, DE 19718. **EMAIL** mcrea@udel.edu

REASONER, MARK
PERSONAL Born 08/11/1960, Tokyo, Japan, m, 1992, 4 children **DISCIPLINE** NEW TESTAMENT **EDUCATION** Bethel Col, BA, 82; Trinity Evangelical Div Sch, MA, 85; MDiv, 85; Univ Chicago, PhD, 90. **CAREER** Assoc prof, Bethel Col, 88. **MEMBERSHIPS** Soc of Biblical Lit, Catholic Biblical Asn **RESEARCH** Romans. **SELECTED PUBLICATIONS** Auth, The Strong and the Weak: Romans 14:1-15:13 in Context, Cambridge Univ Press, 99. **CONTACT ADDRESS** Dept Bible Studies, Bethel Col, Minnesota, 3900 Bethel Dr, Saint Paul, MN 55112-6902. **EMAIL** m-reasoner@bethel.edu

REATH, ANDREWS
PERSONAL Born 06/15/1951, Philadelphia, PA **DISCIPLINE** SOCIAL AND POLITICAL PHILOSOPHY **EDUCATION** Harvard Univ, PhD. **CAREER** Prof, Ch, Univ Calif, Riverside. **RESEARCH** Kant's moral and political philosophy; Contemporary moral theory; History of ethics. **SELECTED PUBLICATIONS** Auth, "Legislating the Moral Law," Nous, 94; "Agency and the Imputation of Consequences in Kant's Ethics," Jahrbuch for Recht und Ethik, Vol 2, 94; "Autonomy and Practical Reason: Thomas Hill's Kantianism," Jahrbuch for Recht und Ethik, Vol 3, 95; Reclaiming the History of Ethics: Essays for John Rawls, Cambridge Univ Press, 97; "Introduction to the Critique of Practical Reason," Kant, Critique of Practical Reason, Cambridge Univ Press, 97; "Legislating for a Realm of Ends: the Social Dimensions of Autonomy," Reath, Herman & Korsgaard, 97. **CONTACT ADDRESS** Dept of Philos, Univ of California, Riverside, 1156 Hinderaker Hall, Riverside, CA 92521-0209. **EMAIL** reath@citrus.ucr.edu

RECK, ANDREW JOSEPH
PERSONAL Born 10/29/1927, New Orleans, LA, m, 1987 **DISCIPLINE** PHILOSOPHY **EDUCATION** Tulane Univ, BA, 47, MA, 49; Yale Univ, PhD, 54. **CAREER** Reader econ, Tulane Univ, 45-47; instr, Univ Conn, 49-50; asst instr philos, Yale Univ, 50-51, part-time instr, 51-52, instr, 55-58; from asst prof to assoc prof, 58-64, Prof Philos, Tulane Univ, 64-, Chmn Dept, 69-89, Dir, Master Liberal Arts Prog, 83-; mem adv comt Am Studies, 71-; Howard Found fel, 62-63; Am Philos Soc grantee, 72; vis fel, Huntington Libr, San Marino, Calif, 73; adv ed, Southwestern J Philos, 72 & Southern J Philos, 78; vis prof, Fordham Univ, 79; vis scholar, Inst Soc, Ethics and the Life Sci, Hastings on the Hudson, New York, 81; sr scholar, Inst Humane Studies, 82; Ed, Hist Philos Quart, 93-98; Acad Specialist, U.S. Information Agency (Brazil), 93. **HONORS AND AWARDS** Am Coun Learned Soc grant, 61-62; LEQSF grant, 94-96; The Outstanding Graduate of the Class of 1947, Emeritus Club, Tulane Univ, 97. **MEMBERSHIPS** Central Div Am Philos Asn; Metaphys Soc Am (pres, 77-78); Southwestern Philos Soc (vpres, 71-72, pres, 72-73); Southern Soc Philos & Psychol (treas, 68-71, pres, 76-77); Soc Adv Am Philos (exec coun, 80-83, pres, 98-00); Charles S. Peirce Soc (secy-treas, 85-86, vpres, 86-87, pres, 87-88). **RESEARCH** American philosophy; metaphysics; history of philosophy. **SELECTED PUBLICATIONS** Auth, Recent American Philosophy, Pantheon, 64; Introduction to William James, Ind Univ, 67; The New American Philosophers, La State Univ, 68; Speculative Philosophy, Univ NMex, 72; ed, Knowledge and Value, Essays in Honor of H N Lee, M Nijhoff, 72; co-ed, Studies on Santayana, Southern J Philos, 72; ed, George Herbert Mead, Selected Writings, Univ Chicago Press, 81; co-ed, American Philosophers' Ideas of Ulti-

mate Reality and Meaning, Univ Toronto Press, 93. **CONTACT ADDRESS** Dept of Philos, Tulane Univ, 6823 St Charles Ave, New Orleans, LA 70118-5698. **EMAIL** areck@mailhost.tcs.tulane.edu

RECK, ERICH H.

PERSONAL Born 05/01/1959, Riedlingen, Germany **DISCIPLINE** PHILOSOPHY **EDUCATION** Univ of Bonn, Germany, MS, 86; Univ Chicago, MA, 87; PhD, 92. **CAREER** Postdoctoral Res Fel, Univ Minn, 92-93; instr, Univ Chicago, 93-95; asst prof, Univ Calif Riverside, 95-. **MEMBERSHIPS** APA; PSA; ASL; GAP. **RESEARCH** Philosophy of Mathematics; Logic; History of Analytical Philosophy. **SELECTED PUBLICATIONS** Auth, Frege's Influence on Wittgenstein: Reversing Metaphysics via the Context Principle, 97; auth, Freges Platonismus im Kontext, 00; auth, Stuctures and Structuralism in Contemporary Philosophy of Mathematics, with MPPrice, 00. **CONTACT ADDRESS** Dept of Philosophy, Univ of California, Riverside, Riverside, CA 92521-0201. **EMAIL** reck@citrus.ucr.edu

REDDISH, MITCHELL GLENN

PERSONAL Born 08/13/1953, Jesup, GA, m, 1975, 3 children **DISCIPLINE** RELIGIOUS STUDIES **EDUCATION** Univ Georgia, BA, 75; Southern Baptist Theol Sem, MDiv, 78, PhD, 82. **CAREER** Instr, 80-83, New Testament, adj prof, 82-83, Southern Baptist Theol Sem and Sem Evening School; asst prof, 83-89, assoc prof, 89-95, prof, 95- , relig, chmn, 92-, Stetson Univ. **HONORS AND AWARDS** Phi Beta Kappa, Magna Cum Laude, 75; Fac summer res grant, 86; listed, Who's Who in Religion, 92-93; listed, Who's Who in Bibl Stud and Archaeol, 93; Homer and Dolly Hand Fac Res Awd, 98. **MEMBERSHIPS** Am Acad Relig; Soc of Bibl Lit; Natl Assoc Baptist Prof of Relig. **RESEARCH** New Testament studies; apocalyptic literature. **SELECTED PUBLICATIONS** Auth, Apocalyptic Literature: A Reader, Abingdon, 90; coauth, An Introduction to The Bible, Abingdon, 91; auth, Daniel, Revelation, in Mercer Commentary on The Bible, Mercer, 94; auth, Reclaiming the Apocalypse, Perspectives in Relig Stud, 97; auth, An Introduction to the Gospels, Abingdon, 97; auth, Apocalyptic Literature and Western Culture, Tchg Apocalypse, Scholars, forthcoming; auth, Revelation, Smyth & Helwys, forthcoming. **CONTACT ADDRESS** Dept of Religious Studies, Stetson Univ, De Land, 421 N Woodland Blvd, Unit 8354, DeLand, FL 32720. **EMAIL** mreddish@stetson.edu

REDDITT, PAUL L.

PERSONAL Born 08/08/1942, Little Rock, AR, m, 1965, 2 children **DISCIPLINE** RELIGION **EDUCATION** Ouachita Baptist Col, BA, 63; Southern Baptist Theol Sem, MDiv, 67; Vanderbilt Univ, MA, 71; PhD, 72. **CAREER** Otterbein Col, 72-86; Chair, Georgetown Col, 86-. **MEMBERSHIPS** Soc of Bibl Lit; Cath Bibl Assoc; Nat Assoc of Baptist Prof of Relig. **RESEARCH** Post-exile era, post-exile prophets, apocalyptic literature. **SELECTED PUBLICATIONS** Auth, "The Book of Malachi in Its Social Setting", CBQ 56 (94): 240-255; auth, "Nehemiah's First Mission and the Date of Zechariah 9-14", CBQ 56, (94): 664-678; auth, "Haggai, Zechariah, Malachi", New Century Bible, 95; auth, "Zechariah 9-14, Malachi, and the Redaction of the Book of the Twelve", Forming Prophetic Literature: Essays on Isaiah and the Twelve in Honor of John D.W. Watts, Sheffield Acad Pr, (Sheffield, 96): 245-268; auth, "Nebuchadnezzar as the Head of Gold: Politics and History in the Theology of the Book of Daniel", PRS 24.4, (97): 399-416; auth, "Daniel 11 and the Sociohistorical Setting of the Book of Daniel", CBQ 60 (98): 463-474; auth, "Calculating the Times: Daniel 12:5-12", PRS 25.4, (98): 373-9; auth, "Daniel", New Century Bible, 99; coed, Shall Not the Judge of All the Earth Do What Is Right? Studies on the Nature of God Presented to James L. Crenshaw, Eisenbrauns, (Winona Lake, IN), 00; auth, "Daniel 9: Its Structure and Meaning", CBQ 62, (00): 269-283. **CONTACT ADDRESS** Dept Relig, Georgetown Col, 400 E College St, Georgetown, KY 40324-1628. **EMAIL** predditt@georgetowncollege.edu

REDENBARGER, WAYNE JACOB

PERSONAL Born 11/27/1945, Alton, IL, m, 1993, 2 children **DISCIPLINE** ROMANANCE LINGUISTICS, LATIN, PORTUGUESE **EDUCATION** Ind Univ, BA, 71; Harvard Univ, MA, 75, PhD, 76. **CAREER** Lectr Port, Boston Univ, 74-76; asst prof, 76-82, Assoc Prof Port & Romance Ling, 82- , asst dean, Col of Human, dir comput, 86-90, Ohio State Univ. **HONORS AND AWARDS** Pres, Omicron Chap Phi Beta Kappa; Woodrow Wilson Fel; vis sci, MIT RLE speech grp. **MEMBERSHIPS** Ling Soc Am. **RESEARCH** Morphology of Latin, Portuguese, and Western Romance. **SELECTED PUBLICATIONS** Auth, Vowel lowering and i-epenthesis in Classical Latin, In: Current Studies in Romance Linguistics, Georgetown Univ, 76; Lusitanian Portuguese is advanced tongue root and constricted pharynx, In: Studies in Romance Linguistics, Newbury House, 77; Portuguese vowel harmony and the elsewhere condition, In: Contemporary Studies in Romance Linguistics, Georgetown Univ, 78; Portuguese evidence for the non-unitary nature of syllable parsing, Georgetown Univ, 81; Articulator Features and Portuguese Vowel Height, Harvard Univ, 81; auth, Apocopy and Lenition in Portuguese, Issues in the Phonology and Morphology of the Major Iberian Languages, Georgetown U, 97. **CONTACT ADDRESS** Dept of Spanish and Portuguese, Ohio State Univ, Columbus, 1841 Millikin Rd, Columbus, OH 43210-1229. **EMAIL** redenbarger.2@osu.edu

REED, GREGORY J.

PERSONAL Born 05/21/1948, MI, m **DISCIPLINE** LAW **EDUCATION** MI State Univ, BS 1970, MS 1971; Wayne State Univ, JD 1974, LLM 1978. **CAREER** Gregory J Reed & Assocs PC, Attorney specializing in corporate, taxation and entertainment law, currently; Wayne State Univ, Detroit MI, prof 1988-89; AHR Packaging Consultant Corp, Detroit MI, pres/developer 1987-. **HONORS AND AWARDS** Graduate Professional Scholarship 3 consecutive years; Distinguished Alumni of the Yr Awd MI State Univ 1980; Resolution for Achievement State of MI Senate, City of Detroit; one of the top ten blacks in the law profession, Detroit News 1985; implemented Gregory J Reed Scholarship Foundation 1986; Awd for Contributions to the arts Black Music Month State of MI House of Rep 1987; govt appointment Martin Luther KingCommn of Michigan 1989-; 1992 Hall of Fame inductee by BESLA. **MEMBERSHIPS** Chairperson, Martin Luther King Statue Committee; bd of dirs MI Assn of Community Arts Agencies; mem Natl Bar Assn; MSU Foundation, board of directors; comm mem of entertainment sports, taxation, corp and real estate sects Amer Bar Assn; mem Amer Bar Assn; mem Accounting Aide Soc of Metro Detroit; bd comm New Detroit Inc; tax and corp advisor BUF; mem MI State Bar Taxation and Corporate Div; mem Amer Arbitration Assn; bd of dir BESLA Entertainment Law Assn; bd of dirs MI Assn of Community Arts Agencies; mem State Bar Law Media Comm; first black Attorney adv bd mem US Internal Revenue Serv; founder Advancement Amateur Athletics Inc 1986; first black chmn in US State Bar of MI Arts Communication Sports and Entertainment Sect 1987; speaker, lecturer US & foreign countries; MSU Foundation, vice chairperson, 1996-97. **SELECTED PUBLICATIONS** Author: Tax Planning and Contract Negotiating Techniques for Creative Persons; Professional Athletes and Entertainers (first book of its kind cited by American Bar Association); This Business of Boxing & Its Secrets, 1981; This Business of Entertainment and Its Secrets, 1985; Negotiations Behind Closed Doors, 1987; Economic Empowerment through the church, American Book Award, 1994; "Quiet Strength," co-author with Rosa Parks; "Dear Mrs Parks," co-author with Rosa Parks. **CONTACT ADDRESS** Gregory J. Reed & Associates, PC, 1201 Bagley, Detroit, MI 48226.

REED, ROSS CHANNING

PERSONAL Born 11/23/1961, Lancaster, PA, s **DISCIPLINE** PHILOSOPHY **EDUCATION** Millersville Univ, BA, 83; Baylor Univ, MA, 86; Loyola Univ Chicago, PhD, 94. **CAREER** Sr Lect, 86-97, Loyola Univ of Chicago; Vis Fac, 94-97, Schl of the Art Inst of Chicago; Instr, 94-97, Columbia Col Chicago; Instr, 970, Univ of Memphis. **HONORS AND AWARDS** M MU In Jazz and Studio Music, Univ of Memphis, 00. **MEMBERSHIPS** APA; Amer Soc for Philos; Counseling and Psychotherapy; Amer Fed of Musicians; Soc for the Advancement of Amer Philos, American Philosophical Practitioner's Assoc. **RESEARCH** Philosophical psychology, existentialism, phenomenology, phil of religion, ethics, history and theor of jazz/comercial music. **CONTACT ADDRESS** 5060 Sea Isle Rd, Memphis, TN 38117. **EMAIL** doctorreed@yahoo.com

REEDER, HARRY P.

DISCIPLINE PHILOSOPHY **EDUCATION** Univ Ill, Urbana, BA, 68; Univ Waterloo, MA, 74; PhD, 77. **CAREER** Lectr, Univ Guelph, 78-79, vis asst prof, 79-80; vis asst prof, Univ Alberta, 81-82; asst prof, Univ Tex Arlington, 82-86, assoc prof, 86-. **HONORS AND AWARDS** Organized Res Grant, Univ of Tex, Arlington, 84-85; Res Grant, Univ Tex, Arlington, 87-90; Nominated for Univ of Tex System Chancellor's Coun Awd for Excellence in Teaching, 90, recipient, 91; Dict of Int Biography, 95; invited to nominate candidates for the 1996 Kyoto Prizes, Inamori Found, 95; Who's Who in the World, 96; Who's Who in America, 96; Who's Who in Am Educ, 96-97; Asn of the Ctr for Advanced Res in Phenomenology, 99-. **MEMBERSHIPS** Am Philos Asn, Can Philos Asn, Husserl Circle, Japanese/Am Phenomenology Conf, Soc for Phenomenology and Existential Philos, N Tex Philos Asn, N Mex and W Tex Philos Soc. **RESEARCH** Phenomenology, hermeneutics, epistemology, philosophy of language, history of philosophy (ancient, early modern), philosophy of science. **SELECTED PUBLICATIONS** Auth, Language and Experience: Descriptions of Living Language in Husserl and Wittgenstein, Current Continental Res, No 301, NY: Univ Press of Am (84); auth, The Theory and Practice of Husserl's Phenomenology, NY: Univ Press of Am (86); coauth, The Literate Mind: Reading, Writing, and Critical Thinking, Dubuque, Iowa: Kendall-Hunt (87, 2nd ed, revised, 90); auth, The Work of Felix Kaufmann, Current Continental Res Series, No 220, NY: Univ Press of Am and the Centre for Advances Res in Phenomenology (91); Chinese transl of "Husserl and Wittgenstein on the 'Mental picture Theory of Meaning'," transl by Prof Wang Tang Jia, Fudan Univ, Huishou Soc Scis (96); auth, "Ludwig Wittgenstein," and "Felix Kaufmann," in Lester Embree, et al, ed, The Encyclopedia of Phenomenology, Contributions to Phenomenology, Vol 18, Boston: Kluwer Acad Pubs (97): 732-736, 382-285; auth, "Husserl's Phenomenology and Contemporary Science," in Burt Hopkins, ed Husserl in Contemporary Context: Prospects and Projects for Phenomenology, Contributions to Phenomenology, Boston: Kluwer Acad Pub (97); auth, "Quantum Phenomenology," in Young-Ho Lee and Soon-Young Park, eds, Phenomenology of Nature: Festschrift in Honor of Kah Kyung Cho, Seoul: Koren Soc for Phenomenology (98): 207-235. **CONTACT ADDRESS** Dept Philo, Univ of Texas, Arlington, Box 19527, Arlington, TX 76019. **EMAIL** reeder@uta.edu

REEDER, JOHN P., JR.

PERSONAL Born 07/11/1937, Charlotte, NC, m, 1965, 2 children **DISCIPLINE** RELIGIOUS STUDIES **EDUCATION** Yale Univ, PhD, 68. **CAREER** Prof, Brown Univ. **RESEARCH** Ethics & religious thought. **SELECTED PUBLICATIONS** Killing and Saving: Abortion, Hunger and War, Penn State Press, 96. **CONTACT ADDRESS** Dept Relig Stud, Brown Univ, PO Box 1927, Providence, RI 02912. **EMAIL** john_reeder@brown.edu

REESE, CATHERINE C.

PERSONAL Born 04/10/1962, Nashville, TN, d **DISCIPLINE** POLITICAL SCIENCE **EDUCATION** Rhodes Col, BA, 84; Univ Memphis, MPA, 89; Univ Ga, DPA, 95. **CAREER** Asst Prof, N Mex State Univ, 95-97; Asst Prof, Ark State Univ, 97-. **MEMBERSHIPS** Am Soc for Pub Admin; Govt Finance Officers Asn; Pi Alpha Alpha. **RESEARCH** Public budgeting & finance; State government. **SELECTED PUBLICATIONS** Auth, "The Line-Item Veto in Practice in Ten Southern States," Public Administration Review, 97; co-auth, "Budgeting Essentials for Human Resource Managers," in Handbook of Human Resource Managemnt in Government, 98; co-auth, "The Line-Item Veto in Georgia: Incidence and Fiscal Effects," Public Administration Review, forthcoming. **CONTACT ADDRESS** Dept Polit Sci, Arkansas State Univ, PO Box 1750, State University, AR 72467-1750. **EMAIL** ccreese@inet-direct.com

REESE, MIKE

PERSONAL Born 09/19/1945, Columbus, GA, m, 1979, 3 children **DISCIPLINE** LEGAL STUDIES **EDUCATION** Troy State Col, BS, 67; Univ Ala, JD, 72; Emory Univ, LLM, 78; Ga State Univ, PhD, 86. **CAREER** Asst Prof, Univ of Alaska Anchorage, 85-87; Assoc Prof, Ga Southern Univ, 88-93; Assoc Prof, N Ga Col and State Univ, 94-. **HONORS AND AWARDS** McBrayer Awd, outstanding paper, Meeting of the Ga Polit Sci Asn, 91. **MEMBERSHIPS** Acad of Criminal Justice Sci, Ala Bar Asn, Ga Asn of Historians, Ga Polit Justice Asn, Southern Criminal Justice Asn. **RESEARCH** Law, Criminal, Constitutional, Native American. **SELECTED PUBLICATIONS** Auth, "Obstacles to the Psychological Development of American Indian Children," Family Law Quart IX (75): 573-593; auth, "The Indian Civil Rights Act: Conflict Between Constitutional Assimilation and Trial Self-Determination," Southeastern Polit Rev XX (92): 29-61; auth, "Judicial Approaches to Consent Searches: The Georgia Experience," J of Ga Asn of Historians XVI (95): 52-83; auth, "Disciplinary Exclusion of Public School Students Under the Education for All Handicapped Children Act, 1975-1988: Intersection or Legislative Intent and Judicial Interpretation," J of Ga Asn of Historian XIX (98): 184-218. **CONTACT ADDRESS** Polit Sci/Criminal Justice, No Georgia Col, 100 College Circle, Dahlonega, GA 30597-1001. **EMAIL** mreese@ngcsu.edu

REESE, THOMAS

PERSONAL Born 01/11/1945, Altadena, CA, s **DISCIPLINE** POLITICAL SCIENCE; RELIGION **EDUCATION** St. Louis Univ, MA, 68; Jesuit Sch of Theology, Mdiv, 74; Univ CA, Berkeley, PhD, 76. **CAREER** Instr, 68-70, St. Ignatius Col Prep; Univ San Francisco, spring 69; asst to the president, 70-71, Univ Santa Clara; assoc ed, 78-85; sr fel, 85-98, Woodstock Theological Ctr at Georgetown Univ; ed-in-chief, June 98, at America magazine. **SELECTED PUBLICATIONS** Auth, The Politics of Taxation, 80; Archbishop: Inside the Power Structure of the American Catholic Church, 89; A Flock of Shepherds: The National Conf of Catholic Bishops, 92; Inside the Vatican: The Politics and Organization of the Catholic Church, 97; 2001 and Beyond: Preparing the Church for the Next Millenium, 97, America; Synod of America, America, 97; Synod for America Ends, 98, America. **CONTACT ADDRESS** America Magazine, 106 W 56th St, New York, NY 10019.

REESE, WILLIAM L.

PERSONAL Born 02/15/1921, Jefferson City, MO, m, 1945, 3 children **DISCIPLINE** PHILOSOPHY **EDUCATION** Drury Col, AB, 42; Univ Chicago, BD, 45; PhD, 47. **CAREER** Asst to assoc prof and chair, Drake Univ, 47-57; assoc to full prof, Grinnell Col, 57-60; vis prof, Iowa State Univ, 58; prof and chair, Univ Del, 60-67; prof, Univ Albany, SUNY, 67-99, chair, Dept Philos, 68-74, acting chair, spring 84, Prof of Philos Emeritus and Res Prof in Philos, 99-; vis prof, Iztapalapa Campus, Nat Univ of Mex, spring 80. **HONORS AND AWARDS** Ford Found Study Awd, 67-68; Chancellor's Awd for Multi--Campus Sem in Philos of the Soc Scis, 68-74; NEH Grant, 69-74; Consultant, NEH; Fulbright Lectr, Argentina, summer 71; Who's Who in the World; Sr Fel, Inst for Humanistic Studies, Univ Albany, 77-. **MEMBERSHIPS** Am Asn of Univ Profs,

Am Philos Asn, Metaphysical Soc of Am, Peirce Soc, Soc for Iberian and Latin Am Thought. **RESEARCH** Metaphysics, philosophy of religion, history of philosophy. **SELECTED PUBLICATIONS** Ed, The Best in the Literature of Philosophy and World Religions, Vol IV, 13th ed, The Reader's Advisor, NY: Bowker (88); contribur of eighteen essays to the Biographical Dictionary of Twentieth-Century Philosophers, ed, Stuart Brown, Diane Collinson, and Robert Wilkinson, London: Routledge (96); auth, "Epitomization and the Hermeneutic Circle," Hypotheses (fall 97): 17-20; coauth, Philosophers Speak of God (with Charles Hartshorne) Univ of Chicago Press, 5, 2nd ed, Humanity Books, 00; auth, Dictionary of Philosophy and Religion, 3rd ed, Humanity Books (spring 00); auth, Freedom. Fundamental Issues of Philosophy: a Study Guide with Readings, Humanity Books (spring 00); auth, Freedom, Humanities Book, 00. **CONTACT ADDRESS** Dept Philos, SUNY at Albany, 1400 Washington Ave, Albany, NY 12222-0100. **EMAIL** reesewl@cs.com

REEVES, JOHN C.
PERSONAL Born 12/01/1954, Fayetteville, NC, m, 1985, 1 child **DISCIPLINE** RELIGIOUS STUDIES **EDUCATION** Univ NC, BA, 76; Southeastern Sem, MDiv, 82; Hebrew Union Col, PhD, 89. **CAREER** Asst prof to assoc prof, Winthrop Univ, 89-96; prof, Univ NC, 96-. **MEMBERSHIPS** Am Acad of Relig, Am Oriental Soc, Soc of Biblical Lit, Asn for Jewish Studies. **RESEARCH** Ancient Near Eastern Languages and literature, biblical literature, Jewish studies. **SELECTED PUBLICATIONS** Auth, Jewish Lore in **CONTACT ADDRESS** Dept Religious Studies, Univ of No Carolina, Charlotte, 9201 University City Blvd, Charlotte, NC 28223-0001. **EMAIL** jcreeves@email.uncc.edu

REGAN, PATRICK J.
PERSONAL Born 01/18/1938, New Orleans, LA, s **DISCIPLINE** LITURGY **EDUCATION** St John's Univ, MA, 66; Inst Cath de Paris, STD, 71. **CAREER** Instr, St Joseph's Sem Col, 71-; sum prof, St John's Univ, 72-81; Abbott, St Joseph's Abbey, 82-. **MEMBERSHIPS** NAAL; SCL. **RESEARCH** Feasts and seasons' early Christian and medieval art. **SELECTED PUBLICATIONS** Auth, "Homily," Worship 50 (1976), 353-354; auth, "Pneumatological and Eschatological Aspects of Liturgical Celebration," Worship 51 (77): 332-350; auth, "Veneration of the Cross," Worship 2 (78): 2-13; auth, "The Three Days and the Forty Days," Worship 54 (80), 2-18; auth, "Restoring the Cross to Good Friday," Liturgy 1 (80): 55-59; auth, "The Fifty Days and the Fiftieth Day," Worship 55 (81): 194-218; auth, "The Candle, the Sign of the Crucifix," Liturgy 3 (82): 18-21; auth, "How Did Liturgical Change Get Started . . . and Why?" Pastoral Music 8 (84): 27-33; auth, "Congress of Benedictine Abbots. Synthesis of the Congress," A.I.M. Monastic Bulletin No. 53 (92), 7-14. **CONTACT ADDRESS** Dept Religion, Saint Joseph Sem Col, General Delivery, Saint Benedict, LA 70457-9999. **EMAIL** abbot@neosoft.com

REGNISTER, BERNARD
PERSONAL Born 07/16/1961, Belgium, s **DISCIPLINE** PHILOSOPHY **EDUCATION** Univ Penn, PhD, 92. **CAREER** Loyola Marymont Univ, asst prof, 92-94; Brown Univ, asst prof, 94-. **HONORS AND AWARDS** L. S. Rockefeller fel, J. R. Workman Award for tchg Excellence; Nationl Humanities Center Fel, 99-00. **MEMBERSHIPS** APA, NANS, NAKS. **RESEARCH** 19th -20th Century Germany & French Philosophy; ethics & moral psychology. **SELECTED PUBLICATIONS** Auth, Papers in Philosophy and Phenomenological Res, Hist of Philosophy Quarterly, The European Journal of Philosophy; auth, The Affirmation of Life, Nietzsche on Overcoming Nihilsm, Harvard Univ Press, (forthcoming, 02). **CONTACT ADDRESS** Dept of Philosophy, Brown Univ, PO Box 1918, Providence, RI 02912. **EMAIL** bernard_reginster@brown.edu

REGUER, SARA
PERSONAL Born Brooklyn, NY, 2 children **DISCIPLINE** MIDDLE EAST & JEWISH HISTORY **EDUCATION** City Col New York, BA, 66; Yeshiva Univ, BReligEduc, 66; Columbia Univ, MA, 69, PhD(MidE hist), 76. **CAREER** Instr, 74-77, asst prof to prof Judaic Studies, Brooklyn Col, 77-, chp, 87-; Consult, Fed Off Educ, 76-; vis asst prof Jewish hist, Yeshiva Univ, 77-78; vis distinguished prof, Univ Naples, 97. **HONORS AND AWARDS** Res fel, City Univ New York, 78-79. **MEMBERSHIPS** AHA; MidE Studies Asn; Asn for Jewish Studies; Coord Comt Women Hist Prof. **RESEARCH** Contemporary Middle East; Jews of the Middle East. **CONTACT ADDRESS** Dept of Judaic Studies, Brooklyn Col, CUNY, 2901 Bedford Ave, Brooklyn, NY 11210-2813.

REHER, MARGARET MARY
PERSONAL Born Reading, PA **DISCIPLINE** HISTORICAL THEOLOGY, CHURCH HISTORY **EDUCATION** Immaculata Col, BA, 60; Providence Col, MA, 64; Fordham Univ, PhD, 72. **CAREER** Asst prof theol, Immaculata Col, 60-64; asst prof, 73-76, assoc prof, 76-80, Prof Relig, Cabrini Col, 80-93, Prof Emerita, 93. **MEMBERSHIPS** Col Theol Soc Am; Cath Hist Soc; Am Cath Hist Asn. **RESEARCH** Domestic and for outreach of communities of women relig established in Philadelphia. **SELECTED PUBLICATIONS** Auth, Pope Leo XIII and Americanism, In: The Inculcation of American Catholicism 1820-1900, Garland Publ Inc, 88; Americanism and Modernism -- Continuity or Discontinuity?, In: Modern American Catholicism, 1900-1965, Garland Publ Inc 88; Catholic Intellectual Life in America: A History of Persons and Movements, Macmillan Co, 89; Den[n]is J Dougherty and Anna M Dengle: The Missionary Alliance, Records Am Cath Hist Soc of Philadelphia, spring 90; Bishop John Carroll and Women, Archbishop Gerety Lectures, 1988-89, Seton Hall Univ, 89; Get Thee to a [Peruvian] Nunnery: Cardinal Dougherty and the Philadelpha IHM's, Records Am Cath Hist Soc of Philadelphia, winter 92; Phantom Heresy: A Twice-Told Tale, U S Cath Hist, summer 93; Review Symposium on Begin Catholic: Commonweal from the Seventies to the Nineties, Loyola Univ Press, 93, Horizons, spring 94; co-auth, From St Edward's School to Providence Center: A Story of Commitment, Records Am Cath Hist Soc of Philadelphia, spring-summer, 96; Mission of America: John J Burke in Peru, U S Cath His, fall 97. **CONTACT ADDRESS** Dept of Relig, Cabrini Col, 610 King of Prussia, Radnor, PA 19087-3698. **EMAIL** margaret.mcguinness@cabrini.edu

REHNQUIST, WILLIAM HUBBS
PERSONAL Born 10/01/1924, Milwaukee, WI, m, 3 children **DISCIPLINE** LAW **EDUCATION** Stanford Univ, BA & MA, 48, LLB, 52; Harvard Univ, MA, 50. **CAREER** Law clerk, US Supreme Court Justice Robert H Jackson, 52-53; pvt pract law, Phoenix, Ariz, 53-69; asst atty gen, Off Legal Coun, 69-72; Assoc Justice, US Supreme Court, 72-86; Chief Justice of US, 86-. **RESEARCH** General practice of law, especially civil litigation. **CONTACT ADDRESS** US Supreme Court, One First St NE, Washington, DC 20543.

REIBETANZ, S. SOPHIA
PERSONAL Born 11/27/1972, Toronto, ON, Canada **DISCIPLINE** PHILOSOPHY **EDUCATION** Univ Toronto, BA, 94; Oxford Unic, BPhil, 96; Harvard Univ, PhD, 96- . **CAREER** Grad stud, philos, Harvard Univ, 96- . **HONORS AND AWARDS** Frank Knox Mem Fel, 96-97, 97-98; Commonwealth Scholar, Balliol Col, Oxford Univ, 94-96. **RESEARCH** Ethics; metaphysics; philosophy of mind. **SELECTED PUBLICATIONS** Auth, Contractualism and Aggregation, Ethics, 98; auth, A Problem for the Doctrine of Double Effect, Proc of the Aristotelian Soc, 98. **CONTACT ADDRESS** Emerson Hall, Harvard Univ, Cambridge, MA 02138. **EMAIL** reibetan@fas.harvard.edu

REICH, LOUIS
PERSONAL Born 11/30/1947, Jersey City, NJ, s **DISCIPLINE** PHILOSOPHY **EDUCATION** Calif State Univ, Fullerton, BA, 84; Univ Calif, Riverside, MA, 86, PhD, 93. **CAREER** Lectr, Calif State Univ, San Bernardino, 90-. **MEMBERSHIPS** Am Philos Asn, Home Soc, Calif Fac Asn. **RESEARCH** David Hume's philosophy; philosophy of religion; history of empiricism; metaphysics; epistemology. **SELECTED PUBLICATIONS** Auth, Hume's Religious Naturalism, Univ Press of Am (98); auth, "On Mystic Experience: Is the 'Argument From Unanimity' Possible," HSIN: The Int J of Philos and Psychotherapy (2000). **CONTACT ADDRESS** Dept Philos, California State Univ, San Bernardino, 5500 University Pkwy, San Bernardino, CA 92407-2318. **EMAIL** Lreich@pacbell.net

REICH, PETER L.
PERSONAL Born 03/20/1955, Los Angeles, CA, m, 1985, 2 children **DISCIPLINE** LAW **EDUCATION** UCLA, BA, 76; UCLA, MA, 77, PhD, 91; UC Berkeley, JD, 85. **CAREER** Vis lectr, UC Riverside, 81; asst prof, 88-91, assoc prof, 91-93; prof, Whittier Law Sch 93-; Vis. Prof, UCIrvine, 99,00. **HONORS AND AWARDS** Fulbright-Hays Fellowship, 79-80; Hubert Herring Mem Awd, Pacific Coast Coun on Latin Am Studies, 91; Ray Allen Billington Awd, Western Hist Asn, 95; Huntington Library Res Fel, 97. **MEMBERSHIPS** Am Soc Legal Hist; Calif Bar Asn. **RESEARCH** Legal history of U.S. Southwest, Mexico; environmental and natural resource policy. **SELECTED PUBLICATIONS** Auth, Mexico's Hidden Revolution: Catholic Church in Law & Politics Since 1929, Univ Notre Dame Press, 95; auth, Mission Revival Jurisprudence: State Courts and Hispanic Water Law Since 1950, Washington Law Review, Vol 69: 869, 95; auth, Western Courts and the Privatization of Hispanic Mineral Rights Since 1850: An Alchemy of Title, Columbia Jour of Environ Law, Vol 23: 57, 98. **CONTACT ADDRESS** Law Sch, Whittier Col, 3333 Harbor Blvd, Costa Mesa, CA 92626. **EMAIL** preich@law.whittier.edu

REICH, WARREN T.
PERSONAL Born 12/21/1931, Paterson, NJ, m, 1995, 2 children **DISCIPLINE** BIOETHICS **EDUCATION** St Joseph Col, Holy Trinity, AL, BA, 54; Catholic Univ Amer, Washington, DC, STB, 58, STL, 59; Gregorian Univ, Rome, Italy, STD, 62. **CAREER** Res Assoc Prof, Assoc Prof, Prof, Prof Emer, Dist Res Prof, 71-, Sr Res Scholar, Kennedy Inst, 71-, Sr Res Scholar, Center for Clin Bioethics, 71-, Dir, Div of Health and Hum, Dept Family Med, 77-97, Georgetown Univ; Lectr to Assoc Prof, Sch Theol, 66-71, Catholic Univ Amer, Washington, DC; Asst Prof, 62-68, Holy Trinity Mission Sem, Silver Spring, MD. **HONORS AND AWARDS** Royal Natl Acad Med of Spain, Honorary Foreign Member; Amer Lib Assoc; Soc Health and Hum Values; Georgetown Univ The Vicennial Medal; Natl Hum Center, Fellow; Acad of Med of Washington, DC, Dir; Amer Lib Assoc, Dartmouth Medal, 1st ed of Encyclopedia of Bioethics; Univ Wurzburg, Post-doctoral Fellow. **MEMBERSHIPS** Amer Assoc Bioethics and Hum; Alexander von Humboldt Assoc Amer; Amer Philos Assoc; Acad Med of Washington, DC; Soc Health and Hum Values; Inst Soc, Ethics and the Life Sci; Amer Acad Rel; Council on the Stud of Rel; Soc of Christian Ethics; Catholic Theol Soc Amer. **RESEARCH** Ethics Methodology; Philosophy and History of care; Applied ethics: assisted suicide. **SELECTED PUBLICATIONS** Ed in Chief, Bioethics, Sex, Genetics and Human Reproduction, Macmillan Compendium, Sel from the 5 vol Encyclopedia of Bioethics, NY, Simon & Schuster Macmillan, 97; Encyclopedia of Bioethics, ed Chief, rev ed, 5 vol, NY, Simon & Schuster Macmillan, 95; Encyclopedia of Bioethics, ed Chief, 4 vol, NY, The Macmillan Co., The Free Press, 78. **CONTACT ADDRESS** Georgetown Univ, 415 Kober-Cogan, Washington, DC 20007. **EMAIL** wreich1@attglobal.com

REICHBERG, GREGORY M.
DISCIPLINE PHILOSOPHY **EDUCATION** Emory Univ, PhD. **CAREER** Assoc prof, Fordham Univ. **RESEARCH** Metaphysics, theories of knowledge, and ethics. **SELECTED PUBLICATIONS** Auth, La Communication de la Nature Divine en Dieu Selon Thomas d'Aquin, Revue Thomiste 93, 93; Thomas Aquinas on Moral Responsibility in the Pursuit of Knowledge, Thomas Aquinas and his Legacy, Cath UP, 94; Contextualizing Theoretical Reason: Thomas Aquinas and Postmodern Thought, Aquinas 38, 95. **CONTACT ADDRESS** Dept of Philos, Fordham Univ, 113 W 60th St, New York, NY 10023.

REICHEL, PHILLIP
PERSONAL Born 10/08/1946, Bakersfield, CA, m, 1983, 2 children **DISCIPLINE** CRIMINAL JUSTICE **EDUCATION** Nebr Wesleyan Univ, BS, 69; Kans State Univ, MS, 72, PhD, 79. **CAREER** Assoc prof, Augusta State Univ, Ga, 72-83; prof, Northwestern Colo Univ, 83-. **MEMBERSHIPS** Am Soc of Criminol, Acad of Criminal Justice Soc. **SELECTED PUBLICATIONS** Auth, Comparative Criminal Justice Systems, Prentice Hall: Needham Heights, MA (99); auth, Corrections, Allyn & Bacon: Needham Heights, MA (2000). **CONTACT ADDRESS** Dept Sociol, Univ of No Colorado, 501 20th St, Greeley, CO 80639-0001. **EMAIL** Reichel@CJED.com

REICHENBACH, BRUCE ROBERT
PERSONAL Born 12/13/1943, Staten Island, NY, m, 1965, 2 children **DISCIPLINE** PHILOSOPHY **EDUCATION** Wheaton Col, Ill, AB, 65; Northwestern Univ, MA, 67, PhD, 68. **CAREER** Assoc prof, 68-80, prof philos, Augsburg Col, 80-, vis prof New Testament, Morija Theol Sem, Lesotho, 76-77; vis distinguished prof Evangelical Christianity, Juniata Col, 85-86; vis prof, Daystar Univ, Nairobi, Kenya, 98. **HONORS AND AWARDS** NEH Summer Sem, 78; NEH Summer Inst, 84; Res Grant Inst Advan Christian Study, 84; Fulbright-Hays Sem India, 86; Fulbright-Hays Sem Pakistan, 91; John Templeton Found Grant, 95. **MEMBERSHIPS** Am Philos Asn; Soc of Christian Philosophers. **RESEARCH** Philosophy of religion; Medical Ethics; Critical Thinking. **SELECTED PUBLICATIONS** Auth, The Cosmological Argument: A Reassessment, CC Thomas, 72; The cosmological argument and the causal principle, Int J Philos Relig, 75; Natural evils and natural laws, Int Philos Quart, 76; Is Man the Phoenix: A Study of Immortality, Eerdmans, 78; Why is God Good, J Religion, 80; The inductive argument from evil, Am Philos Quart, 80; CS Lewis on the desolation of de-valued science, Christian Scholar's Rev, 82; Evil and a Good God, Fordham Univ, 82; The Law of Karma: A Philosophical Study, MacMillan, 90; coauth, Reason and Religious Belief: An Introduction to the Philosophy of Religion, Oxford Univ, 91, 2 ed, 98; coauth, On Behalf of God: A Christian Ethic for Biology, Wm B Eerdmans, 95; coauth, Philosophy of Religion: Selected Readings, Oxford Univ, 96, 2 ed, 01; auth, "On Obligations to Future Generations," Public Affairs Quart (92); auth, "Inclusivism and Atonement," Faith and Philos (99); An Introduction to Critical Thinking, McGraw Hill, 01. **CONTACT ADDRESS** Dept of Philos, Augsburg Col, 2211 Riverside Ave, Minneapolis, MN 55454-1350. **EMAIL** reichen@augsburg.edu

REICHENBACH, MARIA
PERSONAL Born 03/30/1909, Berlin, Germany, w, 1946, 1 child **DISCIPLINE** PHILOSOPHY **EDUCATION** Freiburg, PhD. **CAREER** Univ Calif Los Angeles City Col, 48-74. **HONORS AND AWARDS** Nat Sci Found fel, 65. **MEMBERSHIPS** Amer Philos Asn. **RESEARCH** Science. **SELECTED PUBLICATIONS** Auth, Ger ed, Collected Works in Wiesbaden, Germany. **CONTACT ADDRESS** 456 Puerto del Mar, Pacific Palisades, CA 90272.

REICHMANN, JAMES B.
PERSONAL Born 01/14/1923, Everett, WA, s **DISCIPLINE** PHILOSOPHY **EDUCATION** Gonzaga Univ, BA, 46, MA, 47; Gregorian Univ, STL, 54, PhD, 60. **CAREER** From instr to asst prof Philos, Seattle Univ, 55-62; assoc prof Mt St Michael's Sem, 64-65; assoc prof, 65-71, chmn dept, 69-79, prof Philos, Seattle Univ, 71-93; Prof Emeritus, 93-. **MEMBER-**

SHIPS Northwestern Philos Asn (pres, 64-65); Am Cath Philos Asn. **RESEARCH** Philosophical psychology; Aristotle's philosophy of God; immanent and subsistent esse in Aquinas, Evolutinary theory, Nature and origin of Rights, Principle of Individuation. **SELECTED PUBLICATIONS** Auth, St Thomas, Capreolus, Cajetan and the Created Person, New Scholasticism, 1-2/59; Logic and the method of metaphysics, 10/65, The transcendental method and the psychogenesis of being, 10/68 & Immanently transcendent and subsistent esse: A comparison, 4/74, Thomist; Hegel's ethics of the epochal situation, Proc Am Cath Philos Asn, 75; The Philosophy of the Human Person, Loyola Univ Press, 85; The "Cogito' in St. Thomas: Truth in St. Thomas and Descartes, Internation Philosophyical Quarterly, 86; Language and the Interpretation of Being in Gadamer and Aquinas, Proceedings of the American Catholid Philosophical Assoc, 88; Evolution, Animal 'Rights' and the Environment, The Catholic Univ of America Pres, 99. **CONTACT ADDRESS** Dept of Philosophy, Seattle Univ, 900 Broadway, Seattle, WA 98122-4340.

REID, GARNETT
PERSONAL Born 12/15/1955, Nashville, TN, m, 1976, 2 children **DISCIPLINE** OLD TESTAMENT INTERPRETATION **EDUCATION** Bob Jones Univ, PhD, 91. **CAREER** Prof of Bible, Free Will Baptist Bible Col, 82- . **MEMBERSHIPS** Soc Bibl Lit; Evangelical Theol Soc; Near E Archaeol Soc; Nat Asn Prof of Hebrew. **RESEARCH** Bible, primarily Old Testament; history. **SELECTED PUBLICATIONS** Auth, articles for the Greek-English Dictionary, Complete Biblical Library, 90, the Hebrew-English Dictionary, 94-98, The Complete Biblical Library, 90; Jeremiah30-33: Heart of Jeremiah's Covenantal Message, Bibl Viewpoint, 91; Defending Christianity in a Pluralistic Society, Contact, 92; Minimalism & Biblical History; Bibliotheca Sacra, 98. **CONTACT ADDRESS** Free Will Baptist Bible Col, 3606 West End Ave, Nashville, TN 37205. **EMAIL** greid@fwbbc.edu

REID, INEZ SMITH
PERSONAL Born 04/07/1937, New Orleans, LA **DISCIPLINE** LAW **EDUCATION** Tufts Univ, BA 1959; Yale Univ Law Sch, LLB 1962; UCLA, MA 1963; Columbia Univ, PhD 1968. **CAREER** Barnard Coll Columbia Univ, assoc prof 1969-76; NY State Div for Youth, genl counsel 1976-77; Dept of Health Educ & Welfare, deputy genl counsel 1977-79; Environmental Protection Agency, inspector genl 1979-80; Dist of Columbia Govt, corp counsel. **HONORS AND AWARDS** Numerous articles published; numerous awds. **MEMBERSHIPS** Past bds Antioch Univ Bd of Trustees, United Ch of Christ Bd for Homeland Ministries. **CONTACT ADDRESS** Corporation Counsel, Dist of Columbia Govt, Dist Bldg Ofc of Corp Coun, Rm 329, Washington, DC 20004.

REID, JOHN P.
PERSONAL Born 05/17/1930, Weehawken, NJ, s **DISCIPLINE** LAW **EDUCATION** Georgetown Univ, BSS, 52; Harvard Law School, LLB, 55; Univ NHamp, MA, 57; NYork Univ, LLM, 60; JSD, 62. **CAREER** Instr to Prof, New York Univ, 60-. **HONORS AND AWARDS** Fel, Guggenheim Foundation, 80; Fel, Huntington Library, 80; NEH Fel, 84. **MEMBERSHIPS** Am Soc for Legal Hist, Org of Am Hist, Am Hist Asn. **RESEARCH** American Legal History. **SELECTED PUBLICATIONS** Auth, Constitutional History of the American revolution: abridged Ed, Univ Wisc Press, 95; auth, "Introduction," separate pamphlet accompanying laws of the Cherokee Nation, Legal classics Library, 95; auth, "Beneath the Titans," New York University Law Review, (95): 653-676; auth, Policing the Elephant: Crime, Punishment, and Social Behavior on The Overland Trail, Huntington Library Press, 97; auth, Patterns of Vengeance: Retaliation by Fur Trappers and Fur Traders Against Indians for Homicides in the Transboundary North American West, Ninth Judicial Circuit Hist Press, in press. **CONTACT ADDRESS** School of Law, New York Univ, 40 Washington Square South, New York, NY 10012-1005. **EMAIL** john.reid@nyu.edu

REID, STEPHEN B.
PERSONAL Born Dayton, OH, m, 4 children **DISCIPLINE** RELIGON **EDUCATION** Manchester Col, BS, 73; Bethany Theol Sem, MDiv, 76; Emory Univ, PhD, 81. **CAREER** Assoc prof, Pacific Sch of Relig, 81-90; assoc prof, Austin Presby Theol Sem, 90-. **HONORS AND AWARDS** Fel, Fund for Theol Educ, 76-78, 80-81.[**MEMBERSHIPS** Soc of bibl Lit; Cath Bibl Assoc; Pacific Coast theol Soc; Am Sch of Oriental Res. **RESEARCH** Old Testament, Psalms. **SELECTED PUBLICATIONS** Auth, "The Art of Marc Chagall: An Interpretation of Scripture", Visual Art as Religious: Using Visual Arts as Primary Texts in Teaching Religious Studies, eds D Apostolos-Cappadona and D Adams, Crossroads, (NY, 87); auth, Daniel and Enoch: A Form Critical and Sociological Study, Bibal Pr, (Berkeley), 89; auth, Experience and Tradition: A Primer in Black Biblical Hermeneutics, Abingdon, (Nashville), 91; auth, "Worth the Wait, or Reasonable People Don't Wait for Nothing", Psalm 130: 5-8, The Bible in Theology and Preaching: How Preachers Use Scripture, ed Donald K McKim, Abingdon, (Nashville, 94); auth, "The Role of Reading in Multicultural Exegesis", Test and Experience: Toward Cultural Exegesis of the Bible, ed Daniel Smith-Christopher, Sheffield Acad Pr, 95; auth, "The Theology of the Book of Daniel and the Political Theory of WEB DuBois", The Recover of Black Presence: An Interdisciplinary Exploration, eds Randall C Bailey and Jacquelyn Grant, Abingdon, (Nashville, 95): 37-49; auth, "Reading Scripture as an African-American', Bible today 34.6, (96); auth, "Abraham" and "Ashkelon", New Harper Collins Bible Dict, ed P Achtemeier, Harper Collins (San Francisco, 96); ed, Prophets and Paradigms: Essays in Honor of Gene M Tucker, Sheffield Acad Pr, 96; auth, Listening In: A Multicultural Reading of the Psalms, Abingdon, (forthcoming). **CONTACT ADDRESS** Dept Relig, Austin Presbyterian Theol Sem, 100 E 27th St, Austin, TX 78705-5711.

REIDE, JEROME L.
PERSONAL Born 04/23/1954, New York, NY, s **DISCIPLINE** LAW **EDUCATION** SUNY, New Paltz, BA, 1977; Hofstra University Law School, JD, 1981; Columbia University Graduate Journalism School, MS, 1982; Michigan State University, PhD, 1991. **CAREER** American Civil Liberties Union, Access to Justice, coordinator, 86-87; Center for Labor Studies, SUNY, political science lecturer, 86-87; Eastern Michigan University, African-American studies lecturer, 87-88; Detroit City Council, special projects assistant, 87-88; Michigan State University, Dean of Urban Studies, research assistant, 88-90; Wayne State University, School of Education, lecturer, 92-93; NAACP, Special Contribution Fund Midwest, development director, 90-93; Wayne County Commission, Chair of Ways and Means, legislative aide, 93-94; Wayne State Univ, Interdisciplinary Studies, asst prof, 94-; Raheem Fuckemeyer & Reide PLLC. **HONORS AND AWARDS** NAACP, Religious Affairs, Back to School/Stay in School, 1992; University of Michigan, Flint, College Bound, Most Inspirational Teacher, 1992; Jackson Fair Housing Commission, Fair Housing Awd, 1992; Governor of Kentucky, Order of the Kentucky Colonels, 1991; Committee on Institutional Cooperation, Social Science Fellow, 1988; State Legislature of Michigan, Special Tribute, 1994; Wayne State Univ, ISP, CLL Teaching Excellence Awd, 1997. **MEMBERSHIPS** Urban League, Michigan, 1988-; Dispute Resolution Coordination Council, board of directors, 1991-95; NAACP, life member, 1975-; Boniface Community Action, board of directors, 1991-95; Urban Affairs Graduate Studies Association, president, 1989-90; National Conference of Black Lawyers, press secretary, 1986-87; Black Law Students Association, national press secretary, 1980-81; Sutton for Mayor, press aide, 1977; Global Economic Development Conf, pres, 1993; Wayne State Univ, Ctr for Peace & Conflict Studies, Exec Committee, 1994; State Bar of Michigan, 1996; American Bar Assn, 1997-; Wolverine Bar Assn, 1997-; Team Justice, 1997. **SELECTED PUBLICATIONS** Author, Justice Evicted, American Civil Liberties Union, 1987; executive producer/moderator, "The State of Black Michigan," 1989-; editor, Mulitcultural Education Resource Guide, Michigan State Board of Education, 1990; executive producer, "Human Rights and Civil Wrongs," Museum of African-American History, 1991; writer, "NAACP Community Economic Development," The Crisis Magazine, 1992. **CONTACT ADDRESS** Wayne State Univ, 2220 Academic/Administrative Bldg, Detroit, MI 48202.

REIDENBERG, JOEL R.
DISCIPLINE INFORMATION TECHNOLOGY LAW, COMPARATIVE LAW **EDUCATION** Dartmouth, AB, 83; Columbia, JD, 86; Univ de Paris, DEA, 87. **CAREER** Assoc, Debevoise and Plimpton, Wash DC, 87-90; vis prof, AT&T Lab(s) Pub Policy Res, 96; guest lectr, Univ de Paris, 97; vis prof, Univ de Paris I (Panth,on-Sorbonne), 96-97; ch, Assn Am Law Sch, 96; ch, sect defamation and privacy, Assn Amer Law Sch, 98; prof, 90-. **HONORS AND AWARDS** Friedmannfel, Promethee, Paris, 86-87; **SELECTED PUBLICATIONS** Auth, Rules of the Road on Global Electronic Highways: Merging the Trade and Technical Paradigms, 6 Harvard J Law & Tech 287, 93; Information Flows on the Global Infobahn, New Information Infrastructure: Strategies for US Policy, Twentieth Century Fund Press, 95; Setting Standards for Fair Information Practice in the US Private Sector, 80 Iowa L Rev 497, 95; Governing Networks and Rule-Making in Cyberspace, 45 Emory L Jour 911, 96; Multimedia as a New Challenge and Opportunity in Privacy, 22 Materialien Zum Datenschutz 9, 96; The Use of Technology to Assure Internet Privacy: Adapting Labels and Filters for Data Protection, Lex Electronica, 97; Lex Informatica: The Formulation of Information Policy Rules through Technology, 76 Texas L Rev 553, 98; co-auth, The Fundamental Role of Privacy and Confidence in Networks, 30 Wake Forest L Rev 105, 95. **CONTACT ADDRESS** Law Sch, Fordham Univ, 113 W 60th St, New York, NY 10023. **EMAIL** reidenberg@sprynet.com

REIDY, DAVID A.
PERSONAL Born 09/11/1962, Chicago, IL, m, 1990, 1 child **DISCIPLINE** PHILOSOPHY, LAW **EDUCATION** DePauw Univ, BA, 84; Ind Univ Sch of Law, JD, 87; Univ Kans, PhD, 97. **CAREER** Lectr, Ind Univ Sch of Law, 87-90; grad instr, Univ Kans, 90-97; vis asst prof, Ind Univ-Purdue Univ, Indianapolis, 97-00. **HONORS AND AWARDS** Osborne Fel, Univ Kans, 94; Univ Dissertation Fel, Univ Kans, 95; James Wilbur Prize, Am Soc for Value Inquiry, 95. **MEMBERSHIPS** Am Philos Asn, Am Soc for Polit & Legal Philos, Am Polit Sci Asn, N Am Soc for Soc Philos, Int Soc for Soc Philos & Philos of Law. **RESEARCH** Philosophy of Law, Contemporary Theories of Justice, History of Political Philosophy. **SELECTED PUBLICATIONS** Auth, "Antigone, Hegel, and the Law," Legal Studies Forum (95): 239-261; auth, "Education for Citizenship in a Just and Stable Pluralist Democracy," J of Value Inquiry (96): 25-42; auth, "Citizenship and Educational Institutions," Archives for Philos of Law and Soc Philos (97): 88-102; auth, "False Pleasures and Plato's Philebus," J of Value Inquiry (98): 343-356; auth, "Postmodern Philosophy of Law," in Philosophy of Law: An Encyclopedia (Garland Publ, 99), 668-672; auth, "Rawl's Idea(l) of Public Reason," Polis: A Rev of Polit Sci (99): 93-113; auth, "Rawl's Wide View of Public Reason: Not Wide Enough," Res Publica (00): 1-25; auth, "Pluralism, Liberal Democracy and Compulsory Education," J of Soc Philos (forthcoming). **CONTACT ADDRESS** Dept Philos, Indiana Univ-Purdue Univ, Indianapolis, 1100 W Michigan St, Indianapolis, IN 46202-5208. **EMAIL** dreidy@iupui.edu

REIGSTAD, RUTH
PERSONAL Born 04/24/1923, Minneapolis, MN **DISCIPLINE** CLINICAL PHYSICAL THERAPY, HISTORY OF ENGLISH, SCIENCE **EDUCATION** St Olef Coll, BA, 45; Univ Minn, RTP, 47. **CAREER** Consultant, Wash State Health Dept, 41-73; clin phys therapist, 47-61; volunteer activities. **HONORS AND AWARDS** Stipends for Post Grad Study, UCLA, USC, NYU; Children's Bureau; US Public Health. **MEMBERSHIPS** Public Health Asn; Am Phys Therapy Asn; Am Acad of Rel; AF Asn. **RESEARCH** Correlations between studies of science and religion; Early childhood development. **CONTACT ADDRESS** Box 4237, Tacoma, WA 98438-0001.

REIMER, JAMES A.
DISCIPLINE RELIGIOUS STUDIES **EDUCATION** University Toronto, MA, 74; Univ St. Michael's Col, PhD, 83. **CAREER** Prof, Conrad Grebel Col. **RESEARCH** Nineteenth-century European intellectual history; modern theology; technology and theology, modern theology, Mennonite theology and German theology in the Hitler era. **CONTACT ADDRESS** Dept of Religious Studies, Univ of Waterloo, Conrad Grebel Col, 200 Westmount Rd, Waterloo, ON, Canada N2L 3G6. **EMAIL** ajreimer@uwaterloo.ca

REISCH, GEORGE
PERSONAL Born 12/25/1962, NJ **DISCIPLINE** HISTORY AND PHILOSOPHY OF SCIENCE **EDUCATION** Univ Chicago, MA, 90, PhD, 95. **CAREER** res fel, Northwestern Univ, 95-96; Vis asst prof, Il Inst Tech, 96-97; columnist, Stereophile, 96; technical writer, Shure Inc, 98-. **HONORS AND AWARDS** Phi Beta Kappa. **MEMBERSHIPS** Philos of Sci Assoc; Hist of Sci Soc; Hist of Philos of Sci Working Group. **RESEARCH** Philosophy of science; philosophy of history; history of physics and astronomy; history of philosophy; general history of science. **SELECTED PUBLICATIONS** Auth, "Did Kuhn Kill Logical Empiricism?" Philosophy of Science, 58 (91): 264-277; auth, "Planning Science: Otto Neurath and the International Encyclopedia of Unified Science," British Journal for the History of Science 27 (94): 153-175; auth, "Scientism Without Tears: A Reply to Roth and Ryckman," History and Theory 34 (95): 45-58; auth, "Terminology in Action," in Encyclopedia and Utopia, Kluwer, 96; "How Postmodern was Neurath's Idea of Unified Science," Stud in Hist and Philos of Sci, 97; "Epistemologist, Economist..and Censor: On Otto Neurath's Infamous Index Verborum Prohibitorum," Perspectives on Sci, 97; auth, "Pluralism, Logical Empiricism, and the Problem of Pseudoscience," Philosophy of Science 65 (98): 333-348; coauth, "The Nature of Science: A Perspective from the Philosophy of Science," Journal of Research in Science Teaching 36 (99): 107-116; auth, "The Neurath-Carnap Disputes in the Context of World War Two," in proceedings of Analytical and Continental Aspects of Logical Empiricism: Historical and Contemporary Perspectives, (Univ of Pittsburgh Press, Paolo Parrini, ed), forthcoming; auth, "Logical Empiricism and the Unity of Science Movement," Cambridge Companion to Logical Empiricism, (Cambridge Univ Press), forthcoming. **CONTACT ADDRESS** 5246 N. Kenmore Ave., 1N, Chicago, IL 60640. **EMAIL** reischg@ripco.com

REISMAN, W. MICHAEL
PERSONAL Born 04/23/1939, Philadelphia, PA, 4 children **DISCIPLINE** INTERNATIONAL LAW, JURISPRUDENCE **EDUCATION** Johns Hopkins Univ, BA, 60; Hebrew Univ, LLB, 63; Yale Univ, LLM, 64, JSD, 65. **CAREER** Prof Law, Yale Univ, 68-, Fulbright fel, Netherlands, 66-67. **HONORS AND AWARDS** Gherini Prize, Yale Univ, 64; World Acad Arts & Sci Awd, 81. **MEMBERSHIPS** Int Law Asn; Coun Foreign Rel; ASIL; Co-Editor-in-Chief of AJIL; Elected to the Institut de Droit Int. **SELECTED PUBLICATIONS** Auth, Nullity and Revision, Yale Univ Press, 71; Art of the Possible, Princeton Univ, 71; Puerto Rico and the International Process, West Publ Co, 75; co-ed, Toward World Order and Human Dignity, Free Press, 75; auth, Folded Lies, Free Press, 75 & Span tranal, Fundo Cult Econ, Mex, 82; coauth, International law in contemporary perspective, 81 & International Law Essays, 81; coauth, Regulating Covert Action, 92; auth, The Supervisory Jurisdiction of the International Court of Justice: International Arbitration and International Adjudication, 97; auth, Law in Brief Encounters, 99; auth, Jurisdiction in International Law, 99. **CONTACT ADDRESS** Yale Univ, P O Box 208215, New Haven, CT 06520-8215. **EMAIL** michael.reisman@yale.edu

REITER, DAVID DEAN
DISCIPLINE PHILOSOPHY **EDUCATION** Univ Nebraska, PhD. **CONTACT ADDRESS** Philosophy Dept, Univ of St. Thomas, Minnesota, Saint Paul, MN 55105. **EMAIL** davidreiter@juno.com

REITZ, CHARLES
PERSONAL Born 03/10/1946, Buffalo, NY, m, 1987, 2 children **DISCIPLINE** PHILOSOPHY OF EDUCATION **EDUCATION** Canisius Col, BA, 68; SUNY Buffalo, PhD, 83. **CAREER** Prof philos, Kansas City Commun Col, 87- . **HONORS AND AWARDS** Tchg awards, 90, 00. **MEMBERSHIPS** APA; Soc for Ger-Am Stud. **RESEARCH** Critical theory of society and education. **SELECTED PUBLICATIONS** Auth, Art, Alienation and the Humanities: A Critical Engagement with Herbert Marcuse, SUNY, 00. **CONTACT ADDRESS** 2 East 58th St, Kansas City, MO 64113. **EMAIL** creitz@toto.net

REITZ, CURTIS R.
PERSONAL Born 11/20/1929, Reading, PA, m, 1983, 3 children **DISCIPLINE** LAW **EDUCATION** Univ PA, AB, LLB, 56. **CAREER** From asst prof to assoc prof, 57-63, prof law, Univ PA, 63-; Frances Lewis Schol-in-Res, Sch Law, Washington & Lee Univ, 82. **MEMBERSHIPS** Am Law Inst; Nat Conf Comnr Uniform State Laws. **RESEARCH** International trade and investment; commercial law; commercial credit; construction contracts. **SELECTED PUBLICATIONS** Ed, Cases and Materials on Contracts as Basic Commercial Law, West Publ, 75; auth, Consumer Protection Under the Magnuson-Moss Warranty Act, Am Law Inst, 78; Cases, Problems and Materials on Sales Transactions: Domestic and International Law, 92. **CONTACT ADDRESS** Sch Law, Univ of Pennsylvania, 3400 Chestnut St, Philadelphia, PA 19104-6204. **EMAIL** creitz@law.upenn.edu

REJAI, MOSTAFA
PERSONAL Born 03/11/1931, Tehran, Iran **DISCIPLINE** POLITICAL SCIENCE **EDUCATION** Calif State Univ, BA, 59, MS, 61; UCLA, PHD, 64. **CAREER** Tchg fel UCLA, 63-64; asst prof, polit sci, 64-67, assoc prof, 67-70, prof, 70-83, distinguished prof, 83- , Miami Univ; vis scholar Ctr for Int Affairs, Harvard Univ, 72, Hoover Inst on War, Revolution and Peace, Stanford Univ, 73, Inst Int Stud, Iran, 74-75; vis prof Western Col, Oxford, 71, 72. **HONORS AND AWARDS** Assoc ed, J Polit and MilSociol, 73- ; contribur articles to prof journals & book chapters; Outstanding Teaching award, 70. **MEMBERSHIPS** Am Polit Sci Asn; Am Sociol Asn; Int Polit Sci Asn; Int Soc Polit Psychol; Int Stud Asn; Inter-Univ Sem on Armed Forces and Soc; Conf for Study Polit Thought; Midwest Polit Sci Asn; So Polit Sci Asn; Western Polit Sci Asn; Pi Gamma Mu; Pi Sigma Alpha. **SELECTED PUBLICATIONS** Auth, World Military Leaders: A Collective and Comparative Analysis, 66; auth, The Strategy of Political Revolution, 73; auth, The Comparative Study of Revolutionary Strategy, 77; auth, Comparative Political Ideologies, 84; coauth, Loyalists and Revolutionaries: Political Leaders Compared, 88; coauth, Demythogizing an Elite: American Presidents in Empirical, Comparative, and Historical Perspectives, 93; auth, World Military Leaders: A Collective and Comparative Analysis, 96; auth, Leaders and Leadership: An Appraisal of Theory and Research, 97. **CONTACT ADDRESS** Department of Political Science, Miami Univ, Oxford, OH 45056. **EMAIL** rejaip@miavx1.muohio.com

RENICK, TIMOTHY MARK
PERSONAL Born 03/16/1959, Camden, NJ **DISCIPLINE** PHILOSOPHY **EDUCATION** Dartmouth Col, BA, 82; Princeton Univ, MA, 84; PhD, 86. **CAREER** Lect, Dartmouth Col, 80-81; Teaching Asst, Princeton Univ, 83-84; From Dir to Asst Prof, Georgia State Univ, 86-. **HONORS AND AWARDS** Phi Beta Kappa; Princeton Grad Alumni Teaching Awd; Distinguished Hon Prof, Georgia State Univ; Outstanding Teacher Awd, Col of Arts and Sci; Outstanding Teacher, Blue Key Nat Hon Soc. **MEMBERSHIPS** Am Acad of Relig, Soc of Christian Ethics. **RESEARCH** Religion and ethics, just-war tradition, Aquinas, religious pluralism and ethical discourse. **SELECTED PUBLICATIONS** Auth, "Toward Recapturing the Virtue of Charity in the Just-War Tradition: Deterrence, Proportionality and the Use of Minimum Means," J of Relig Studies, vol 18, no 2 (92): 94-113; auth, "Charity Lost: The Secularization of the Principle of Double Effect in the Just-War Tradition," The Thomist, vol 58, no 3 (94): 441-462; auth, "A Cabbit in Sheep's Clothing: Exploring the sources of Our Moral Disquiet About Cloning," The Annual of the Soc of Christian Ethics, vol 18 (98): 259-274; rev, "Explorations in Global Ethics -- Comparative Religious Ethics and Interreligious Dialogue," Relig Studies Rev, 25, 3 (99): 273; auth, "The Time is Now: The Living Eschaton as Unifying Theme in Contemporary Christian Thought," in Apocalypse, Am Acad of Relig Ser (00); auth, Aquinas: An Introduction, Westminster Pr, forthcoming. **CONTACT ADDRESS** Dept Philos, Georgia State Univ, Atlanta, GA 30303. **EMAIL** trenick@gsu.edu

RENNIE, BRYAN
PERSONAL Born 12/13/1954, Scotland, m, 1990 **DISCIPLINE** PHILOSOPHY **EDUCATION** Univ of Edinburgh, PhD, 91. **CAREER** To Assoc Prof, Westminster Col, 90-. **MEMBERSHIPS** AAR, NAASR, SSSR, APA. **RESEARCH** Eliade, Theory and Methos in the Study of Religion. **SELECTED PUBLICATIONS** Auth, "Actualitatea lui Mircea Eliade," Origini: A Rev of Lit, Ideas, and the Arts Vol 1 (Nov/Dec 97): vii, ix; auth, "Mircea Eliade," in The Routledge Encyclopedia of Philosophy, ed. Edward Craig (Routledge, 98); auth, "Manufacturing the Sui Generis Discourse: A Response to Russell McCutcheon's Review of 'Reconstructing Eliade'," Rel 28-4 (98): 413-414; rev, of "East-West Encounters in Philosophy and Religion," ed. Ninian Smart and B. Srinivasa Murthy, Dialogue: Can Philos Rev 38-2 (99); auth, "The View of the Invisible World: An Elaboration on Ninina Smart's Analysis of the Dimensions of Religion and of Religious Experience," The Bull of Coun of Soc for the Study of Relig 28-3 (99): 63-68; auth, "Mircea Eliade: A Secular Mystic in the History of Religions?," in Method as Path: Religious Experience and Hermeneutical Reflection, Vol in the Ser NY Univ Annual Conf in Comp Relig, ed. Elliot R. Wolfson and Jeffrey J. Kripal (NY: Seven Bridges Press, forthcoming); auth, "A Response to 'Mircea Eliade, Postmodernism, and the Problematic Nature of Representational Thinking' by Carl Olson," Method and Theory in the Study of Rel 13-3 (forthcoming); rev, of "Manufacturing religion: The Discourse on Sui Generis Program and the Politics of Nostalgia," by Russell McCutcheon, Zygon (forthcoming); rev, of "Myth and Religion in Mircea Eliade," by Douglas Allen, Rel 30-1 (forthcoming); auth, "Manufacturing McCutcheon: The Failure of Understanding in the Academic Study of Religion," Culture and Relig 1-1 (forthcoming). **CONTACT ADDRESS** Dept Relig and Philos, Westminster Col, Pennsylvania, 319 S Market St., New Wilmington, PA 16172-0002. **EMAIL** brennie@westminster.edu

RESCHER, NICHOLAS
PERSONAL Born 07/15/1928, m, 1967, 3 children **DISCIPLINE** PHILOSOPHY **HONORS AND AWARDS** Five Hon Degrees; Alexander von Humboldt Humanities Prize, 83; Elected Academia Europaea, 97. **RESEARCH** Philosophy. **SELECTED PUBLICATIONS** Auth, Rationality, Clarendon Press, 88; auth, Objectivity, Univ Notre Dame Pr, 97; auth, Complexity, Transaction Publ, 98; auth, The Limits of Science, Univ Pittsburgh Pr, 99. **CONTACT ADDRESS** Dept Philos, Univ of Pittsburgh, 1001 Cathedral of Learning, Pittsburgh, PA 15260-6299. **EMAIL** rescher@pitt.edu

RESIG, MICHAEL D.
PERSONAL Born 04/06/1968, Eugene, OR, s **DISCIPLINE** CRIMINAL JUSTICE **EDUCATION** Washington State Univ, PhD, 96. **CAREER** Asst prof, Mich State Univ, 96-. **MEMBERSHIPS** Am Soc Criminology, Am Sociol Asn, Acad of Criminal Justice Sciences. **RESEARCH** Organizations, survey research, and applied statistical models. **SELECTED PUBLICATIONS** Coauth, with Mark E. Correia and Nicholas P. Lovrich, "Public Perceptions of State Police: An Analysis of Individual-Level and Contextual Variables," J of Criminal Justice,24(1): 17-28 (96); coauth with Quint C. Thurman, Andrew L. Giacomazzi, and David G. Mueller, "A Community Based Gang Intervention and Prevention Program: A Process Evaluation of the Neutral Zone," Crime & Delinquency, 42(2): 279-295 (96); coauth with Quint C. Thurman, Community Oriented Research in an Era of Community Oriented Policy," Am Behav Sci, 39(5): 570-586 (96); coauth with Mark E. Correia, "Public Evaluations of Police Performance: An Analysis Across Three Levels of Policing," Policing:An Int J of Police Strategy and Management 20(2):311-325 (97); auth, Rates of Disorder in Higher-Custody State Prison Management Personnel: A Comparative Analysis of Managerial Practices," Crime & Delinquency, 44(2): 229-244 (98); coauth with Nicholas P. Lovrich,"Job Attitudes Among Higher-Custody State Prison Management Personnel: A Cross-Sectional Comparative Assessment," J of Criminal Justice 26(2):213-226 (98); coauth with Andrew L. Giacomazzi,"Citizen Perceptions of Community Policing: Are Attitudes Toward Police Important?," Policing: An Int J of Police Strategy and Management, 21(3):547-561 (98); coauth with Christopher E. Smith and Lara Pellegrini," Party Affiliation and Support for Capital Punishment: An Assessment of Lawmakers from Canada and the United States," Int J of Comparative and Applied Criminal Justice, 22(2):225-234 (98); coauth with Merry Morash and Yoon Ho Lee, "Powerlessness, Isolation, and Future Expectations: A Gender-Based Analysis of Korean Inmates," Int J of Comparative and Applied Criminal Justice, 23(2):215-226 (99); coauth with Bert Useem, "Collective Action in Prison: Protests, Disturbances, and Riots," Criminology, 37(4):735-760 (99). **CONTACT ADDRESS** Sch of Criminal Justice, Michigan State Univ, 560 Baker Hall, East Lansing, MI 48824.

RESNICK, IRVEN M.
PERSONAL Born 11/22/1952, Rochester, NY, m, 1989, 3 children **DISCIPLINE** RELIGION **EDUCATION** Tulane Univ, BA, 74; Catholic Univ Amer, MA, 80; Univ Va, PhD, 83. **CAREER** Acting asst prof, 82-83, Univ Va Charlottesville; lectr, 84, Smith Col; asst prof, 83-84, Mt Holyoke Col; asst prof, 87-90, Louisiana State Univ assoc prof to prof, chair, , 90- Univ Tn Chattanooga. **HONORS AND AWARDS** NEH Summer Sem, 85; NEH Summer Stipend, 88; NEH Travel to Collections Grant, 89; NEH Summer Inst, Univ Notre Dame, 89; Summer Res Coun Grant, La St Univ, 89; DAAD, Res Visit Grant, Germany, 92; Jerusalem Trust Fel, Oxford Univ, 95; co-dir, Nat Endow for the Humanities, 96; Corresponding Fel, Bar-Ilan Univ, Israel; knights of columbus fel, 79-80; dupont fel, 77-79, 80-81; andrew w. mellon fel, 81-82; summer fel, harvard univ, 82. **MEMBERSHIPS** Midwest Jewish Stud Assoc; Soc for Medieval & Renaissance Philos; Assoc for Jewish Stud. **RESEARCH** Medieval Judaism & Christianity; Jewish-Christian polemics. **SELECTED PUBLICATIONS** Auth, "Albertus Magnus On Animal, A Medieval Summa Zoologica," An annotated English translation of this monumental work, produced in collaboration with Professor Kenneth Kitchell, Baltimore, MD: John Hopkins University Press, 99, 2 vols, p. 32; auth, "Two Theological Treatises of Odo of Tournai: On Original Sin, and a Debate with the Jew, Leo, Concerning the advent of Christ, the Son of God," Philadelphia: University of Pennsylvania Press, 94; auth, "Power, Penance, and Possibility in St. Peter Damian's De divina omnipotentia," Leiden: E.J. Brill publishers, 92. **CONTACT ADDRESS** Dept of Philos & Relig, Univ of Tennessee, Chattanooga, 615 McCallie Ave, Chattanooga, TN 37403-2598. **EMAIL** Irven-resnick@utc.edu

RESNIK, JUDITH
PERSONAL Born 06/27/1950, Orange, NJ **DISCIPLINE** LAW **EDUCATION** Bryn Mawr Col, AB, 72; New York Univ, JD, 75. **CAREER** Lectr & supvy atty, Yale Univ, 77-79, actg dir, Guggenheim Prog Criminal Justice, 79-80; asst prof, 80-82, Assoc Prof Law, Univ Southern Calif, 82-, Lectr, Nat Inst Corrections, 80-; consult, Inst Civil Justice, Rand Corp, 81-. **RESEARCH** Courts in the United States; procedure and process of dispute resolution; women prisoners. **SELECTED PUBLICATIONS** Coauth, Prisoners of their sex: Women's health in jails and prisons, In: Prisoners' Rights Sourcebook, Vol II, Clark Boardman, 80; auth, Women's prisoners, men's prisons: Should prisoners be segregated by sex?, In: Criminal Corrections: Ideals and Realities, Lexington Bks, 82; Managerial Judges, Harvard Law Rev, 12/82; Gender Bias--From Classes To Courts, Stanford Law Rev, Vol 45, 93; Aggregation, Settlement, And Dismay, Cornell Law Rev, Vol 80, 95; Procedural Innovations, Sloshing Over--A Comment On Hensler,Deborah, A Glass Half Full, A Glass Half Empty--The Use Of Alternative Dispute Resolution In Mass Personal-Injury Litigation, Texas Law Rev, Vol 73, 95; Multiple Sovereignties--Indian Tribes, States, And The Federal-Government, Judicature, Vol 79, 95; Whose Judgment--Vacating Judgments, Preferences For Settlement, And The Role Of Adjudication At The Close Of The 20th-Century, UCLA Law Rev, Vol 41, 94. **CONTACT ADDRESS** Law Ctr, Univ of So California, Los Angeles, CA 90007.

RESNIK, MICHAEL D.
PERSONAL Born 03/20/1938, New Haven, CT, m, 1960, 3 children **DISCIPLINE** PHILOSOPHY, LOGIC **EDUCATION** Yale Univ, BA, 60; Harvard Univ, AM, 62, PhD(philos), 64. **CAREER** Mathematician, US Air Force Cambridge Res Labs, 61-63; asst prof philos, Univ Hawaii, 64-67; assoc prof, 67-75, Prof Philos & Chmn Dept, Univ NC, Chapel Hill, 75-, Vis asst prof, Wash Univ, 66-67; dir summer sem for col teachers, Nat Endowment for Humanities, 80; pres, NC Philos Soc, 80-81. **MEMBERSHIPS** Asn Symbolic Logic; Am Philos Asn. **RESEARCH** Philosophy of mathematics; decision theory. **SELECTED PUBLICATIONS CONTACT ADDRESS** Dept of Philos, Univ of No Carolina, Chapel Hill, Chapel Hill, NC 27514.

RESSEGUIE, JAMES L.
PERSONAL Born 01/01/1945, Buffalo, NY, m, 1970, 3 children **DISCIPLINE** THEOLOGY **EDUCATION** Univ California-Berkeley, AB, 67; Princeton Theological Seminary, MDiv, 72; Fuller Theological Seminary, PhD, 78. **CAREER** Peace Corps volunteer, Cameroon, 67-69; from asst prof to J. Russell Bucher Prof, Winebrenner Theological Seminary, 76-; Dean of Academic & Student Affairs and Registrar, Winebrenner Theological Sem, 90-97. Peace Corps Volunteer, Cameroon, 67-69. **HONORS AND AWARDS** Natl Endowment for Humanities Fel, Indiana Univ, 79; Fel, Case Method Inst, 81; Natl Endowment for Humanities Fel, Stanford Univ, 82; Fel, Inst for Ecumenical & Cultural Research, Collegeville, MN, 83; Natl Endowment for Humanities Fel, Univ Florida, 85; Coolidge Research Fel, Episcopal Divinity School, Cambridge, 87; Natl Endowment for Humanities Fel, Univ California-Berkeley, 88; Fulbright Scholar, Univ Iceland, 90; Natl Endowment for Humanities Fel, Ohio State Univ, 91. **MEMBERSHIPS** SBL; Maumee Valley Presbytery **RESEARCH** New Testament **SELECTED PUBLICATIONS** Auth, Defamiliarization and the Gospels, Biblical Theology Bulletin, 90; Automatization and Defamiliarization in Luke 7:36-50, Literature and Theology: An Interdisciplinary Journal of Theory and Criticism, 91; Making the Familiar Strange, Interpretation: A Journal of Bible and Theology, 92; Revelation Unsealed: A Narrative Critical Approach to John's Apocalypse, 98; auth, "New Testament as Lit," Eerdmans Dictionary of the Bible, 00. **CONTACT ADDRESS** Winebrenner Theol Sem, 701 E. Melrose Ave., Findlay, OH 45839. **EMAIL** resseguiej@mail.findlay.edu

REUMANN, JOHN HENRY PAUL
PERSONAL Born 04/21/1927, Easton, PA, m, 1958, 3 children **DISCIPLINE** THEOLOGY **EDUCATION** Univ PA, MA, 50, PhD, 57; Lutheran Theol sem, STM, 51. **CAREER**

Asst prof New testament, 55-59, dean, 74-78, acting pres, 75-76, Prof New Testament, Lutheran Theol Sem, Philadelphia, 59-95, res assoc, sem New Testament studies, Columbia Univ, 60-72; mem bd trustees, Muhlenberg Col, 60-78, 95-; assoc ed, J Bibl Lit, 61-69, ed, 70; ed, Facet Bks Bibl ser, Fortress, 63-72; mem, Lutheran Coun in USA, 66-78; guest lectr, Princeton Theol Sem, 70, La Salle Col, 71 & United Theol Col, India, 72; mem adv coun, Interpretation, 71-78, 84-89; Fry fel, Lutheran Church in America, 72-73; mem bd, Inst Ecumenical Res, France, 74-86, U.S. Lutheran-Roman Catholic dialogue, 65-95, 98-. **HONORS AND AWARDS** Am Asn Theol Sem fac fel, Cambridge Univ, 59-60; Guggenheim fel, Univ Gottingen, 65-66. **MEMBERSHIPS** Soc Study New Testament; Soc Bibl Lit. **RESEARCH** New Testament; Greek; patristics; ecumenics. **SELECTED PUBLICATIONS** Coauth, Righteousness and Society, 67 & auth, Jesus in the Church's Gospels, 68, Fortress; ed & contribr, Understanding the Sacred Text, Judson, 71; Peter in the New Testament, Augsburg & Paulist, 73; auth, Creation and New Creation, Augsburg, 73; ed & contribr, The Church Emerging, Fortress, 77; coauth, Witness of the Word, Fortress, 86; co-ed & contribr, Peter in the New Testament, Fortress & Paulist, 73; Mary in the New Testament, Fortress & Paulist, 78; Ministries Examined, Augsburg, 87-, Variety and Unity in the New Testament, Oxford, 91; auth, Philippians, Anchor Bible, forthcoming. **CONTACT ADDRESS** Lutheran Theol Sem at Philadelphia, 7301 Germantown Ave, Philadelphia, PA 19119. **EMAIL** jreumann@aol.com

REUSCHER, JOHN
DISCIPLINE PHILOSOPHY **EDUCATION** Fordham Univ, PhD. **CAREER** Assoc prof. **RESEARCH** Development of Kant's thought. **SELECTED PUBLICATIONS** Auth, A Concordance to the Critique of Pure Reason. **CONTACT ADDRESS** Dept of Philosophy, Georgetown Univ, 37th and O St, Washington, DC 20057.

REVELOS, C. NICHOLAS
PERSONAL Born 03/01/1938, Middletown, OH, s **DISCIPLINE** LAW **EDUCATION** Bowdon Col, AB, 61; Duke Univ, JD, 65; Univ Calif at Berkeley, LLM, 71. **CAREER** Dean & assoc prof, Chase Law Sch, 67-70; prof, Detroit Col of Law, MSU, 71-. **MEMBERSHIPS** ABA, CLLA, Am Bankruptcy Inst, Mich Bar, Ohio State Bar Asn. **RESEARCH** Corporate and securities law. **SELECTED PUBLICATIONS** Auth, Michigan Practice, Business Organizations (3 vols), West Publ Co, 85. **CONTACT ADDRESS** Detroit Col of Law at Michigan State Univ, 364 Law College Bldg, East Lansing, MI 48824-1300. **EMAIL** revelos@msu.edu

REYDAMS-SCHILS, GRETCHEN
PERSONAL m, 3 children **DISCIPLINE** CLASSICS; ANCIENT PHILOSOPHY **EDUCATION** Katholieke Universiteit Leuven, Belgium, AB (classics, magna cum laude), 87; Univ Cincinnati, MA, 89; KU Leuven, Belgium, Inst of Philos, res, 91-92; Univ CA, Berkeley, Candidate Philos, 91, PhD, 94. **CAREER** Prog dir, Int House, Berkeley, 89-91; teaching asst, Univ Cincinnati, 88-89; press & info office, European Parliament, Brussels, summer 90; post-graduate sem moderator, KU Leuven, Inst for Philos, 91-92; grad student instr, Univ CA, Berkeley, 92-93; press office Brussels, Council of the European Communities, spring 94; asst prof, Prog Liberal Studies, Univ Notre Dame, 94-; vis prof, Spiritan Missionary Sem, Arusha, Tanzania, spring 98 (sabbatical); assoc prof, Univ of Notre Dame, 00-. **HONORS AND AWARDS** Fulbright fel, 87-92; Louise Semple-Taft fel, Univ Cincinnati, 87-89; Sather Assist, Univ CA, Berkeley, 89-91; Louise McKay Prize in Latin Prose Composition, Univ CA, Berkeley, 91; Mellon Dissertation Res grant, 91; fel, Center of Western European Studies, spring 93; Chancellor's Dissertation Year fel, Univ CA, Berkeley, 93-94; Scientific Council of the Found Hardt, Geneva, 96; Belgian Univ Found pub grant, 96; Fac Res Grant, Univ of Notre Dame, 99; Erasmus Institute Fac Workshop, Theol and Fiction, 99; Paul M. and Barbara Henkels Vis Scholars Series, Univ of Notre Dame, 99-00; Jr Fel at the Center for Hellenci Studies, Washington D.C., 00-01. **SELECTED PUBLICATIONS** Auth, Solon and the Hektemoroi, Ancient Soc 22, Leuven, 91; Plato's Myth of Er: the Light and the Spindle, l'Antiquite Classique 62, 93; Stoicized Readings of Plato's Timaeus in Philo of Alexandria, Soc Bib Lit, sem papers 94, Studia Philonica Annual 7, 95; The European Union and Cultural Policy, European Intergration and American Federalism: A Comparative Perspective, Richard Herr and Steven Weber, eds, Berkeley, 96; Plato's World Soul: Grasping Sensibles without Sense-Perception, Interpreting the Timaeus-Critias: Proceedings of the IV Symposium Platonicum, selected papers, Int Plato Studies 9, ed L. Brisson and T. Calvo, Sankt Augustin, 97; Posidonius and Plato's Timaeus: Off to Rhodes and Back to Plato?, Classical Quart 47, 97; Romand and Stoic, the Self as a Mediator, Dionysius, New Series 16, (98): 35-62; Demiurge and Providence, Stoic and Platonist Readings of Plato's Timaeus, Monotheismes et Philosophie, (Brepols Publishers: Turnhout, Belgium, 99); contrib, Socrates Request: Tim, 19B-20C in the Tradition of Platonism, forthcoming in The Ancient World, Conference Papers, 98; An Anthology of Snakebites, (Philosophy/Gender Studies, Seven Bridges Press, 01); ed, Plato's Timeus as Cultural Icon. **CONTACT ADDRESS** Prog Liberal Studies, Univ of Notre Dame, Notre Dame, IN 46556. **EMAIL** gretchen.j.reydams-schils.1@nd.edu

REYMOND, ROBERT L.
DISCIPLINE SYSTEMATIC THEOLOGY **EDUCATION** Bob Jones Univ, BA, MA, PhD. **CAREER** Prof, Knox Theol Sem. **SELECTED PUBLICATIONS** Auth, A New Systematic of the Christian Faith. **CONTACT ADDRESS** Knox Theol Sem, 5554 N Federal Hwy, Fort Lauderdale, FL 33308.

REYNOLDS, CLARK WINTON
PERSONAL Born 03/13/1934, Chicago, IL, m, 1977, 4 children **DISCIPLINE** ECONOMICS **EDUCATION** Claremont Men's Col, AB (magna cum laude), 56; MIT, Danforth fel, 58; Harvard Divinity School, Rockefeller Brothers Theological fel, 57-58; Univ of Calif at Berkeley, MA, PhD, 62. **CAREER** Asst prof, Occidental Col, 61-62; asst prof to assoc prof, Yale Univ, 62-67; assoc prof to full prof, Food Res Instr, 67-96, prof emer, Sr fel, Instr for International Studies, Standford Univ, 90-; vis prof of Economics, Hopkins-Nanjing Ctr, 99-00; fulbright ch, Univ of Tuscia, 01. **HONORS AND AWARDS** Ford Found Grant, 92-96; Canadian Consular Grants, 1980s & 92; Mellon Found Grants, US-Mex Project, 1980s & 92-96; MacArthur Found Grant, 88; Tinker Found Grant, 86-87; Hewlett Found Grants, 1980s & 90; Rockefeller Found Grants, 79-1980s; Inter-Am Dev Bank res grant, 1970s; Org of Am States res grants, 1970s; Soc Sci Res Coun Collaborative Res Grant, 70-72; Norman Buchanan Awd, 64; Doherty Found Fel, 60-61; Rockefeller Brothers Theological Fel, 57-58; Danforth Found Grad Fel, 56-60; Woodrow Wilson Grad Fel, 56-67. **MEMBERSHIPS** U.S.-Mex Consultative Group, Carnegie Endowment for Int Peace; North Am Economics and Finance Asn; Am Economics Asn. **RESEARCH** Economic dev, Mexico; NAFTA; and Latin America dev (including Asia and China in particular); international trade, finance, and migration; dev; regional economics; labor economics. **SELECTED PUBLICATIONS** Auth, The Political Economy of Open Regionalism, in Integrating Cities and Regions: North Am Faces Globalization, forthcoming; auth, Efficiency, Control, and Convergence: Lessons from Privatization of the Mexican Banking System, Quaderni di economia e finanza, 96; auth, Open Regionalism, Lessons from Latin America for East Asia, working paper, 97; auth, Open Regionalism and Social Access: Approaches to Integration in the Americas, Growth, Trade, and Integration in Latin America, 96; auth, The NAFTA and Wage Convergence: a Case of Winners and Losers, NAFTA as a Model of Development: the Benefits and Costs of Merging High and Low Wage Areas, 95; coauth, Japanese Investment in Mexico: A New Industrial Nexus?, The Effect of Japanese Investment on the World Economy, 96; auth, A Case for Open Regionalism in the Andes, forthcoming. **CONTACT ADDRESS** Institute for International Studies, Stanford Univ, Stanford, CA 94305-3056. **EMAIL** reynolds@stanford.edu

REYNOLDS, EDWARD
PERSONAL Born 01/23/1942, s **DISCIPLINE** THEOLOGY **EDUCATION** Wake Forest Univ, BA 1964; OH Univ, MA 1965; Yale Univ, MDiv 1968; London Univ PhD 1972. **CAREER** Christ United Presby, assoc pastor 1982-; Univ of CA San Diego, asst prof 1971-74, assoc prof 1974-83, prof 1983-; City of San Diego, planning commissioner, 89-93. **HONORS AND AWARDS** Books-Trade and Economic Change on the Gold Coast 1974; Stand the Storm A History of the Atlantic Slave Trade 1985; Focus on Africa, 1994; vice moderator Presbytery of San Diego, 1993; Excellence in Teaching Awd, University of California, San Diego, 1990-91; Moderator, Presbytery of San Diego, 1994; Director Univ of CA Study Center, 1994-96. **CONTACT ADDRESS** Dept of History 0104, 9500 Gilman Dr, La Jolla, CA 92093-0104.

REYNOLDS, FRANK E.
PERSONAL Born 11/13/1930, Hartford, CT, m, 1997, 3 children **DISCIPLINE** HISTORY OF RELIGION, BUDDHIST STUDIES **EDUCATION** Princeton; Oberlin Col, BA, 52; Yale Univ, BD, 55; Univ Chicago, MA, 64, PhD, 71. **CAREER** Prog dir, Student Christian Ctr, Bangkok, 56-59; minister to foreign students, Univ Chicago, 62-65; from instr to asst prof, 67-71, assoc prof, 72-79, Prof Hist Relig & Buddhist Studies; Univ Chicago, 79-, chmn, Comt Asian Southern Asian Studies, 78-83, dir, Inst Advan Studies Relig, 92-00; Lectr hist, Chulalonkorn Univ, 57-59; vis prof, Stanford Univ, 70-71; ed, Hist Relig J, 76-; Asn Asian Studies Monograph Series, 77-83; assoc ed, J Relig Ethics, 90-, assoc ed, J Relig, 88-. **HONORS AND AWARDS** Jacob L. Fox fellow, 52; Danforth fellow, 60-64; Fullbright senior research fellowship, 73-74; NEH senior research fellowship, 78-79; NEH translation grant, 90-91. **MEMBERSHIPS** Am Soc Study Relig; Am Acad Relig; Asn Asian Studies; NAm Soc Buddhist Studies; Int Asn Buddhist Studies; Law & Soc. **RESEARCH** Therauada Buddhism; Thailand; comparative ethics. **SELECTED PUBLICATIONS** Coauth, Two Wheels of Dhamma, Am Acad Relig, 72; co-ed, Religious Encounters with Death, Pa State Univ, 77; co-ed & contribr, The Biographical Process, Mouton, 76; Transitions and Transformations in the History of Religion, E J Brill, 80; auth, Guide to Buddhist Religion, 80; co-ed & transl, Those Worlds according to King Buang: A Thai Buddhists Cosmology, Asian Humanities Press, 82; co-ed, Cosmogony and Ethical Order, Chicago, 85; co-ed, Myth and Philosophy, SUNY, 90; co-ed, Discourse and Practice, SUNY, 92; co-ed, Religion and Practical Reason, 94; co-ed, Life of Buddhism, 00. **CONTACT ADDRESS** Swift Hall, Univ of Chicago, 1025-35 E 58th St, Chicago, IL 60637-1577. **EMAIL** mgp2@midway.uchicago.edu

REYNOLDS, J. ALVIN
PERSONAL Born 10/03/1929, Gaston, SC, m, 1961, 2 children **DISCIPLINE** RELIGION **EDUCATION** Univ SC, AB, 54; New Orleans Baptist Theol Sem, BD, 57, ThD, 62. **CAREER** Assoc prof relig & head dept, 62-72, Prof Relig & dept head, Univ Mary Hardin-Baylor, 72-97, Dir, In-Serv Guide, 75-88; Janey S Briscoe Chair Relig and Life, 97. **HONORS AND AWARDS** Honoray alumnus, UMHB, 85. **MEMBERSHIPS** Southwestern Asn Baptist Tchr(s) Relig (vpres, 72-73, pres, 73-74); Southern Baptist In-Serv Guidance Conf (charter mem, vpres, 83-84, pres, 84-85); Southern Baptist Hist Soc; Nat Asn Baptist Prof Relig; TX Baptist Hist Assoc. **RESEARCH** Church hist; Bible. **SELECTED PUBLICATIONS** Contribr, Wycliffe Bible Encyclopedia, Moody, 75; Mercer Dictionary of the Bible, Mercer Univ, 90; Holman Bible Dictionary, Holman, 91; Baptists Working Together, Baptist Gen Conv TX, 76; auth, Richard Furman: Denominational Architect, Quart Rev, 10-12/76. **CONTACT ADDRESS** Dept of Relig, Univ of Mary Hardin-Baylor, 900 College St, Belton, TX 76513-2599.

REYNOLDS, LAURIE A.
DISCIPLINE LAW **EDUCATION** Georgetown Univ, BA; Univ Ill, MA; JD. **CAREER** Prof, Univ Ill Urbana Champaign. **HONORS AND AWARDS** Ed, Univ Ill Law Forum. **RESEARCH** Property, state and local government; land use; and American Indian law. **SELECTED PUBLICATIONS** Auth, pubs about municipal annexation law. **CONTACT ADDRESS** Dept of Law, Univ of Illinois, Urbana-Champaign, 504 E Pennsylvania, Champaign, IL 61820-6909. **EMAIL** lreynold@law.uiuc.edu

REYNOLDS, NOEL BELDON
PERSONAL Born 02/26/1942, Los Angeles, CA, m, 1965, 11 children **DISCIPLINE** POLITICAL & LEGAL PHILOSOPHY **EDUCATION** Brigham Young Univ, AB, 67; Harvard Univ, AM, 68, PhD, 71. **CAREER** Chmn dept Philos, 71-76, assoc prof, 74-78, dir Gen Educ, 80, prof Govt & Philos, Brigham Young Univ, 80, assoc Acad VPres, 81-85, 98-, Vis fac philos Law, J Reuben Clark Law School, 74, 75 & 79; fel Law & Philos, Harvard, 76-77 & Lib Arts fel, Law Sch, 76-77. **MEMBERSHIPS** Int Asn Philos Law & Social Philos; Mont Pelerin Soc. **RESEARCH** Constitutionalism, Plato, philosophy of law, authorship studies, Mormon studies. **SELECTED PUBLICATIONS** Ed, Constitutionalism and rights, Brigham Young Univ, 87; auth, Grounding the rule of law, Ratio Juris, 2, 1, 89; auth, Law as convention, Ratio Juris, 2, 1, 89; auth, The moral responsibilities of universities, Moral values in higher education, Brigham Young Univ, 91; auth, The rule of law in eighteenth century revolutions, Revolution and enlightenment in Europe, Aberdeen Univ Pr, 91; auth, Thomas Hobbes, three discourses, Univ Chicago Pr, 95; auth, Religious Liberty in Western thought, Emroy Univ Ser Law and Religion, 96; auth, Book of Mormon authorship revisited: the evidence for ancient origins, Found Ancient Res and Mormon Stud, 97; auth, Prod, Dead Sea scrolls electronic library, E J Brill 1, 00. **CONTACT ADDRESS** Dept of Philosophy, Brigham Young Univ, D-380 ASB, Provo, UT 84602-1349. **EMAIL** nbr@email.byu.edu

REYNOLDS, STEVEN L.
PERSONAL Born 04/12/1956, UT, m, 1985, 3 children **DISCIPLINE** PHILOSOPHY **EDUCATION** UCLA, PhD, 88. **CAREER** Assoc prof, Ariz State Univ, 88-. **MEMBERSHIPS** Am Philso Asn. **RESEARCH** Epistemology; Perception; Metaphysics. **SELECTED PUBLICATIONS** Auth, Skeptical Hypotheses and 'Omniscient' Interpreters, Australasian J of Philos, 93; proxy Functions and Inscrutability of Reference, Analysis, 94; Evaluation Illusions and Skeptical Arguments, Philos and Phenomenol Res, forthcoming; Skills and Perceptual Justification, forthcoming. **CONTACT ADDRESS** Dept of Philosophy, Arizona State Univ, MC 2004, Tempe, AZ 85287. **EMAIL** steven.reynolds@asu.edu

RHEE, VICTOR
PERSONAL Born 06/10/1954, Korea, m, 1987 **DISCIPLINE** BIBLICAL STUDIES **EDUCATION** Univ Md, BS, 78; Capital Bible Sem, MDiv, 84; Talbot Sch Theol, THM, 89; Dallas Theol Sem, PhD, 96. **CAREER** Assoc prof, Talbot Sch of Theol, 93-. **MEMBERSHIPS** Evangelical Theol Soc. **RESEARCH** New Testament--primarily the books of Hebrews. **SELECTED PUBLICATIONS** Auth, Faith in Hebrews Analysis Within the Context of Christology, Eschatology, and Ethics, Peter Lang (New York), forthcoming. **CONTACT ADDRESS** Dept Bible Studies, Talbot Sch of Theol, 13800 Biola Ave, La Mirada, CA 90639-0002. **EMAIL** victor.rhee@truth.biola.edu

RHOADS, DAVID
PERSONAL Born 11/17/1941, Altoona, PA, m, 1964, 2 children **DISCIPLINE** RELIGION, BIBLICAL STUDIES **EDUCATION** Gettysburg Col, BA, 63; Oxford Univ, MA, 65; Gettysburg Luth Sem, BD, 66; Duke Univ, PhD, 73 **CAREER** Prof, 88-, Luth Sch of Theol; Prof, 73-88, Carthage Col; Pastor, 68-70, St John Luth Church **MEMBERSHIPS** Cath Bibl Asc; Chicago Soc for Bibl Res; The Context Group **SELECTED PUBLICATIONS** Auth, Israel in Revolution: 6-74 C.E. A Political History Based on the Writings of Josephus, Fortress, 76; auth, The Challenge of Diversity: The Witness of Paul and the

Gospels, Fortress, 96; coauth, Mark as Story: An Introduction to the Narrative of a Gospel, Fortress, 99 **CONTACT ADDRESS** Lutheran Sch of Theol at Chicago, 1100 E 55 St., Chicago, IL 60615. **EMAIL** drhoads@lstc.edu

RHODES, PAULA R.
PERSONAL Born 07/18/1949, New Orleans, LA, s **DISCIPLINE** LAW **EDUCATION** Amer Univ, BA cum laude, 1971; Harvard Univ, JD 1974. **CAREER** Legal Serv Corp, atty 1977-79; Mid Atlantic Legal Educ, prof 1980; Univ of San Diego Law School, visiting prof 1983-84; Howard Univ School of Law, assoc prof 1979-90; Univ of Bridgeport, adjunct prof 1985; Univ of Denver College of Law, Denver, CO, visiting prof, 89-90, professor, dir, LLM in Amer & Comparative Law Program, 90-. **HONORS AND AWARDS** Various conferences including Amer Friends Serv Committee Consultation on Korea, Los Angeles, CA 1983, Inst for Policy Studies/Transnatl Inst Intl Conf on "Meeting the Corporate Challenge" Washington DC 1984; Brown Univ, ACUNS/ASIL Summer Workshop on Intl Organization Studies, 1994; African American Leaders Meetings with Mexican Leaders, Mexico City, Mexico, delegation spokesperson, 1992; featured in Lisa Jones, The Path, Six Women Talk About Their Religious Faith Essence vol16 #9 Jan 1986; Phi Delta Phi Legal Fraternity; panelist, moderator, v of Denver Consortium on Rights Development, seminar, international debt, structural adjustment, development and human rights, 1990; panelist, Human Rights and the Underclass, CORD, 1990. **MEMBERSHIPS** Dist of Columbia Bas Assn; LA Bar Assn; American Bar Assn; InterWolsa; American Soc of Intl Law; Academic Council on United Nations Studies; former vice chair, American Friends Serv Committee. **SELECTED PUBLICATIONS** Auth, "Expanding NGO Participation in Intl Decision Making," World Debt and the Human Condition: Structural Adjustment and the Right to Development, 1993; "Devel of New Business Opportunities for Minorities in the Synthetic Fuels Program", Rsch & Legislative Narrative 1981; "Energy Security Act and its Implications for Economic Devel", Howard Law Journal 1981, "We the People and the Struggle for a New World," WSA Constitution on Human Rights 1987; Assoc Ed Fed Bar Assn Forum 1982-83; auth, "Regulation of Multinational Coporations: International Codes of Conduct," in Law of Transnational Business Transaction (V. Nanda ed., release #3, 84, release #5, 86, release #7, 88, release #10, 90); auth, Responsibilities of Transnational Corporations In Times of Globalization-Facts, Issues, Problems and Perspectives with regard to Labor & Human Rights Issues. **CONTACT ADDRESS** Professor, Univ of Denver, 1900 Olive St, Denver, CO 80220. **EMAIL** prhodes@law.ou.edu

RHODES, RON
DISCIPLINE APOLOGETICS **EDUCATION** Houston Baptist Univ, BA; Dallas Theol Sem, ThM, ThD. **CAREER** Adj prof. **SELECTED PUBLICATIONS** Auth, New Age Movement, Zondervan Publ House, 95. **CONTACT ADDRESS** So Evangelical Sem, 4298 McKee Rd, Charlotte, NC 28270.

RHYS, J. HOWARD W.
PERSONAL Born 10/25/1917, Montreal, Canada, m, 1954 **DISCIPLINE** THEOLOGY **EDUCATION** McGill Univ, BA, 39; Gen Theol Sem, STM, 49, ThD, 53. **CAREER** Asst prof, 53-61, prof, 61-83, Schl of Theol Univ of S Sewanee TN. **CONTACT ADDRESS** 75 Louisiana Circle, Sewanee, TN 37375.

RICCI, PAUL O.
PERSONAL Born 08/15/1932, Bristol, CT, m, 1963, 2 children **DISCIPLINE** PHILOSOPHY **EDUCATION** Univ Conn, BA, 54; Univ Ariz, MA, 62; Univ So Calif, grad study, 70-73. **CAREER** Pueblo Col, 59-61; Fullerton Col, 63-66; Cypress Col, 66-93. **MEMBERSHIPS** Sigma Pi Sigma. **RESEARCH** Philosophy of religion; philosophy of science; ethics. **SELECTED PUBLICATIONS** Auth, Humanism and Religion: Independent Thinking Review; Resources for Independent Thinking, 96. **CONTACT ADDRESS** 6157 James Alan St, Cypress, CA 90630. **EMAIL** poricci@earthlink.net

RICCIARDELLI, ANGELA R.
DISCIPLINE PHILOSOPHY **EDUCATION** Georgetown Univ, PhD, 86. **CAREER** Adj fac, , 89-, Notre Dame, Md; dir, devel, 97-, Mcauley Inst **MEMBERSHIPS** APA; Zorta Int; ASAE; NSFRE. **RESEARCH** Ethics and philos of relig. **SELECTED PUBLICATIONS** Auth, Reason and Faith in the Philosophy of Sacred Kwikegaard; auth, A Comparison of Wilfrid Desan's and Pierre L'eilkards de Chaudia's Concept of United World. **CONTACT ADDRESS** 4601 Park Ave, #404, Chevy Chase, MD 20815. **EMAIL** angela218@aol.com

RICE, BERRY
PERSONAL Born 03/23/1940, Birmingham, AL, m, 1962, 2 children **DISCIPLINE** ELEMENTARY EDUCATION, NURSING; DIVINITY **EDUCATION** Univ Ala, BSED, 61; Med Col Ga, BNursing, 89; Interdenominational Theol Ctr, MDiv, 96. **CAREER** Reg Nurse, Athens Reg Med Ctr, 89- . **HONORS AND AWARDS** Theta Phi; Briggs NT scholar awd; nurs hon soc. **MEMBERSHIPS** Ga Nurses Asn; Soc Bibl Studs. **RESEARCH** Prayer, Judaic and Christian; Healing. **CONTACT ADDRESS** Athens Regional Medical Ctr, 386 Milledge Cir, Athens, GA 30606. **EMAIL** price@negia.net

RICE, CHARLES E.
PERSONAL Born 08/07/1931, New York, NY, m, 1956, 10 children **DISCIPLINE** LAW, POLITICAL SCIENCE **EDUCATION** Col Holy Cross, AB, 53; Boston Col, JD, 56; NYork Univ, LLM, 59, JSD, 62. **CAREER** Prof law, Fordham Univ, 60-69; prof law, 69-, Univ Notre Dame, 69-; co-ed, American Journal of Jurisprudence; pres, Wanderer Forum Found. **SELECTED PUBLICATIONS** Auth, Freedom of Association, NY Univ, 62; The Supreme Court and Public Prayer, Fordham Univ, 64; The Vanishing Right to Live, 69 & Authority and Rebellion, Doubleday, 71; Beyond Abortion: The Theory and Practice of The Secular State, Franciscan Herald Press, 79; 50 Questions on the Natural Law, Ignatius Press, 93. **CONTACT ADDRESS** Sch of Law, Univ of Notre Dame, Notre Dame, IN 46556.

RICE, CHARLES L.
PERSONAL Born 12/12/1936, Chandler, OK, s **DISCIPLINE** THEOLOGY **EDUCATION** Baylor Univ, BA, 59; Southern Bapt. Theol Sem, BD, 62; Union Theol Sem, STM, 63; Duke Univ, PhD, 67. **CAREER** Prof, Drew Univ, 70- . **MEMBERSHIPS** Acad of Homiletics. **RESEARCH** Hist of preaching; Preaching and the arts . **SELECTED PUBLICATIONS** Auth, Interpretational and Imagination, 70; Preaching the Story, 80; The Embodied World, 91. **CONTACT ADDRESS** Theological School, Drew Univ, Madison, NJ 07940. **EMAIL** crice@drew.edu

RICE, HORACE WARREN
PERSONAL Born 02/14/1944, Huntsville, AL, d **DISCIPLINE** LAW **EDUCATION** Chicago City College, AA, 1964; Alabama A&M University, BS, 1966; University of Toledo, JD, 1972. **CAREER** Chicago Legal Assistance Foundation, attorney, 72-75; Univ of Alabama-Huntsville, prof, 76-82; self-employed, player representative, sports agent, 77-84; Alabama A&M Univ, Prof, 76-; Self-Employed, Arbitrator/Mediator, 77-. **HONORS AND AWARDS** Ohio State Impass Panel, appointed to Arbitration Panel, 1985; American Arbitration Association, National Panel, 1980; Federal Mediation & Conciliation Service, National Panel, 1982; United States Postal Service, National Panel, 1983; Citizens Ambassador Program, US State Department, educator, Europe, Russia, Africa, 1988-89. **MEMBERSHIPS** American Arbitration Association; Academy for Legal Studies in Business; American Management Association; Society of Professionals in Dispute Resolution. **SELECTED PUBLICATIONS** "Zoning: A Substantive Analysis," AAMU Faculty Research Journal, 1978; "Labor Arbitration: A Viable Method of Dispute Resolution," American Business Law Assn Journal, 1983; "Class Actions Under the 1964 Civil Rights Act," AAMU Faculty Res Journal, 1989; "What Consumers Should Know About Installment Buying," Business Newsletter, 1980; published 23 arbitration cases in Bureau of National Affairs, Commerce Clearinghouse, Labor Relations Reporter, Labor Arbitration In Government. **CONTACT ADDRESS** Department of Business Administration, Alabama A&M Univ, Normal, AL 35762.

RICE, PAUL R.
DISCIPLINE PUBLIC LAW **EDUCATION** Marshall Univ, BBA, 65; W Va Col Law, JD, 68; Yale Law Sch, LLM, 72. **CAREER** Prof, Am Univ; Lect, Practicing law Inst. **HONORS AND AWARDS** Fel, Am Bar Found; Pauline Ruyle Moore Scholar, 87-88; Reporter;DC; Law Revision Comn, Consultant: Fed Trade Comn; DC. **MEMBERSHIPS** Finnegan,Henderson, Farabow, Garrett and Dunner; Bar Asn Comn Court Improvement; Instit Advan Studies Justice. **RESEARCH** Evidence, civil procedure. **SELECTED PUBLICATIONS** Auth, Attorney-Client Privilege: State law, 96; Evidence, Common law and Federal Rules, 96; Attorney Clien Privilege in the U. S., 93; contribur, Am Univ Law Rev; Univ of Conn Law Rev; Duquesne Law Rev; Mercer Law Rev; Miss Law Jour; Northwestern Univ Law Rev; Temple Law Rev; Vanderbilt Law Rev; W Va Univ Law Rev. **CONTACT ADDRESS** American Univ, 4400 Massachusetts Ave, Washington, DC 20016.

RICH, ROBERT F.
DISCIPLINE LAW **EDUCATION** Oberlin Col, BA; Univ Chicago, MA; Ph.D. **CAREER** Prof, Princeton Univ, Prof, Carnegie-Mellon Univ, Prof, U of MI, Prof, Dir, Inst of Gov and Public Affairs, 86-97, Univ Ill Urbana Champaign, 86-. **RESEARCH** Health law and policy; federalism and the role of the states; environmental policy; and science policy **SELECTED PUBLICATIONS** Auth, pubs on health law and policy, federalism and the role of the states, environmental policy, and science policy. **CONTACT ADDRESS** Law Dept, Univ of Illinois, Urbana-Champaign, 1007 W. Nev, MC 037, Urbana, IL 61801. **EMAIL** rrich@law.uiuc.edu

RICHARDS, EDWARD P.
DISCIPLINE LAW **EDUCATION** Rice Univ, BA; Univ Houston, JD. **CAREER** Prof **RESEARCH** Public health; communicable diseases control; bioengineering; legal problems in health care delivery. **SELECTED PUBLICATIONS** Auth, Law and the Physician: A Practical Guide; pubs on medical and scientific issues, public health and communicable disease control, bioengineering, and legal problems in health care delivery. **CONTACT ADDRESS** Law Dept, Univ of Missouri, Kansas City, 5100 Rockhill Rd, Kansas City, MO 64110-2499. **EMAIL** richardse@umkc.edu

RICHARDS, JEFFREY
PERSONAL Born 07/02/1949, Columbus, OH, m, 1972, 2 children **DISCIPLINE** THEOLOGY **EDUCATION** Pfeiffer Univ, BA, 72; Dallas Theological Seminary, THM, 78; Drew Univ, MPHIL, 83; PhD, 85; Mellen Univ, DHabil, 96. **CAREER** Vis Prof of Religious Studies, Univ of NC, 86-88; Prof of Systematic Theology, Hood Theological Seminary, 87-. **MEMBERSHIPS** American Academy of Religion; Evangelical Theological Society. **RESEARCH** Ethics, Reformation Studies; Comtemporary Theology. **SELECTED PUBLICATIONS** Auth, "Contemporary Christian Options of the World's End", Edwin Mellen Press, 99; auth, "The Promise of Dawn," Univ Press of America," 91. **CONTACT ADDRESS** Dept Chair, Systematic Theology, Hood Theological Seminary, 800 W Thomas St, Salisbury, NC 28144-5245. **EMAIL** jjonrichards@aol.com

RICHARDS, JERALD H.
PERSONAL Born 01/22/1933, Pittsburgh, PA, m, 4 children **DISCIPLINE** PHILOSOPHY **EDUCATION** Univ TX at Arlington, 56-58; Univ KY, BA, philos, 61; Harvard Univ, philos, 61-62; Boston Univ, AM, 62-65, PhD, 66; Harvard Univ, post-doctoral scholar, relig studies, 67-68. **CAREER** Asst prof philos, Western KY Univ, 65-69, assoc prof philos, 69-72; assoc prof philos, Northern NY Univ, 72-76, Prof Philos, 76-; chair, Dept of Anthrop, Sociol, and Philos, 98-. **HONORS AND AWARDS** Phi Beta Kappa; BA "with high distinction" and "honors in philos;" Danforth grad fel, 61-65; grant from Soc for Values in Higher Ed to study at Harvard Univ, 67-68. **MEMBERSHIPS** Amer Soc Social Philos; Amer Philos Assoc; Concerned Philos for Peace. **RESEARCH** Ethics and int relations; value theory; social and political philos; peace studies; philos of war and peace; war and morality. **SELECTED PUBLICATIONS** Auth, Alan Donagan, Hebrew-Christian Morality, and Capital Punishment, The J of Relig Ethics, vol 8, no 2, fall 90; Raymond Moody, Near-Death Experiences, and Life After Death, Essence, vol 5, no 3, 82; Walzer's Just War Theory and Limited Nuclear First Strikes, Peace Res, vol 15, no 3, Sept 83; C. S. Lewis, Retributive Punishment, and the Worth of Persons, Christian Scholar's Rev, vol XIV, no 4, 85; Harmful Psychological and Moral Effects of US Nuclear Weapons Policy, Peace Res, vol 19. no 2, May 87; Limited Nuclear First Strikes and Just War Theory, Philosophy and Culture: Proceedings of the XVIIth World Congress of Philosophy, vol III, Montreal: Editions Montmorency, 88; On Saving the Bishops: Deterrence without Deterrence Doctrine, Philosophy in Context, vol 18, 88; Radhakrishan, Religion, and World Peace, Darshana International, vol XXVII, no 4, 89; Gene Sharp's Pragmatic Defense of Nonviolence, The Int J of Applied Philos, vol 6, no 1, summer 91; Gene Sharp, Nonviolence, and the Western Moral Tradition, in Werner, Richard, and Duane Cady, eds, Just War, Nonviolence and Nuclear Deterrence: Philosophers on War and Peace, Wakefield, NH: Longwood Academic, 91; George Bush, Justified War Morality, and the Gulf War, in Bove, Laurence, and Laura Duhan Kaplan, eds, In the Eye of the Storm: Philosophers Reflect on Militarism and Regional Conflict, Amsterdam/Atlanta: Rodopi Press, 95; Radhakrishnan, Religion, and World Peace, in Pappu, S.S. Rama Rao, ed, New Essays in the Philosophy of Sarvepalli Radhakrishnan, Delhi: Sri Satguru Pubs, 95; Gandhi's Qualified Acceptance of Violence, The Acorn, vol VII, no 2, fall 95; Power Imbalance and Human Worth, in Kaplan, Laura, and Laurence F. Bove, eds, Philosophical Perspectives on Power and Domination: Theory and Practice, Rodopi Press, 97; Ideological Intolerance: Causes, Consequences, and Alternatives, in Curtin, Deane, and Robert Litke, eds, Institutional Violence, Rodopi Press, forthcoming; Common Morality and Peacemaking, in Presler, Judith, and Sally J. Scholz, eds, Peacemaking: Lessons from the Past, Visions from the Future, Rodopi Press, forthcoming; Hiroshima, Morality, and Democracy, in Kultgen, John, and Mary Lenzi, eds, Problems for Democracy, Rodopi Press, 99. **CONTACT ADDRESS** Philos Program, No Kentucky Univ, Highland Heights, KY 41076. **EMAIL** RichardsJ@nku.edu

RICHARDS, KENT HAROLD
PERSONAL Born 07/06/1939, Midland, TX, m, 1960, 2 children **DISCIPLINE** OLD TESTAMENT **EDUCATION** Fresno State Col, BA, 61; Sch Theol Claremont, MTh, 64; Claremont Grad Sch, PhD(Old Testament), 70. **CAREER** Res assoc Old Testament, Inst Antiq & Christianity, 68-69; asst prof, Univ Dayton, 69-72; asst prof, 72-75, Assoc Prof Old Testament, Iliff Sch Theol, 75-, Researcher, Univ Heidelberg, 71; Asn Theol Schs Basic Theol Scholar & Res Award, 75-76; exec secy, Soc Bibl Lit, 81-; chmn bd of trustees, Scholars Press, 80- **MEMBERSHIPS** Soc Bibl Lit (tress, 76-); Cath Bibl Asn Am; Am Acad Relig; AAUP; Am Sch Orient Res. **RESEARCH** Old Testament form criticism; I and II Chronicles; Ezra and Nehemiah. **SELECTED PUBLICATIONS** Auth, A note on the bisection of Isaiah, Rev Qumran, 65; Correlating methods in the interpretation of the Old Testament, Univ Dayton Rev, 70; Changing contexts for Biblical interpretation, Christian Century, 73; Lament and praise in the Old Testament, 75 & Can we divorce fire?, 76, Cross-talk; Beyond bruxism, Soc Bibl Lit, 76; ed, Society of Biblical Literature Seminar Papers, 81 & 82. **CONTACT ADDRESS** Iliff Sch of Theol, 2201 S University Blvd, Denver, CO 80210.

RICHARDS, LEON
PERSONAL Born 06/07/1945, Montgomery, AL, m, 1969, 2 children **DISCIPLINE** INTERNATIONAL RELATIONS,

POLITICAL SCIENCE, ENGLISH **EDUCATION** Alabama State Univ, BS (summa cum laude), 1968; University of Hawaii-Manoa, MA, 1970, PhD, 1974, MA, 00. **CAREER** East-West Center, Univ of Hawaii, Honolulu, HI, res assistant, 70-71, 74-75; Leeward Community Col, Pearl City, HI, staff dev specialist, 75-77; Kapiolani Community Col, Honolulu, HI, asst dean of instruction, 77-81, acting provost, 83-84, dean of instruction, 83-. **HONORS AND AWARDS** Alpha Kappa Mu Scholastic Honorary Society, 1966-68; Sigma Rho Sigma Scholastic Honorary Soc for History Majors, 1966-68; Am Council on Education Fellow in Academic Administratiion, 1981-82; Summer In-Residence Fel at Nat Center for Res in Vocational Education, 1979; East-West Ctr Fellows, 1993-97; Field Study Fellows to Peking Univ; Fulbright Study Abroad, Korea Foundation, for Field Study in China and Korea; Field Study Fellow to Peking Univ, East - West Center, Fulbright study abroad to Vietnam, 99. **MEMBERSHIPS** Vice president, Hawaii Asn of Staff, Program & Organizational Development, 1978-90; member, Nat Committee of Black Political Scientist, 1979-; member, Nat Council of Resource Dev, 1980-. **CONTACT ADDRESS** Dean of Instruction, Univ of Hawaii, Manoa, 4303 Diamond Head Road, Honolulu, HI 96816.

RICHARDS, RANDY
PERSONAL Born 06/20/1958, Altus, OK, m, 1980, 2 children **DISCIPLINE** NEW TESTAMENT STUDIES **EDUCATION** Texas Wesleyan Col, BA, 80; Southwestern Baptist Theol Sem, MDiv, 83, PhD, 88. **CAREER** Tchg fel, New Testament Greek, Southwestern Baptist Theol Sem, 84-85; instr Latin, Sch for Sci and Engg Professions, 85-86; instr relig stud, Tarrant Co Jr Col, 86-88; prof New Testament, Bibl Theol, Indonesia Theol Col, 89-92; guest prof New Testament, Asia Baptist Grad Theol Sem, 92-94; missionary guest prof New Testament, SW Baptist Theol Sem, 93; prof New Testament and Bibl Theol, dean Grad Stud, Indonesia Grad Sch Theol, 93-96; guest lect ser, Indonesia, 94, 95; asst prof 96-98, assoc prof and chemn Dept of Relig and Philos, 98- , Williams Baptist Col. **MEMBERSHIPS** Soc of Bibl Lit; Inst for Bibl Res. **SELECTED PUBLICATIONS** Auth, Judgment Seat in the Theology of Paul, Bibl Illusr, 94; auth, Patience in Pauline Theology, Bibl Illusr, 95; auth, Peter, Babylon and Rome, Bibl Illusr, 98; auth, The Codex and the Early Collection of Paul's Letters, Bull for Bibl Res, 98; auth, Stop Lying, Bibl Illusr, 99; auth, The Greek Gymnasium and 1 Tim 4:8, Bibl Illusr, forthcoming. **CONTACT ADDRESS** Williams Baptist Col, PO Box 3426, Walnut Ridge, AR 72476. **EMAIL** RRichards@wbcoll.edu

RICHARDS, STEPHEN C.
PERSONAL Born 08/15/1951, Cleveland, OH **DISCIPLINE** SOCIOLOGY, CRIMINOLOGY **EDUCATION** Univ Wis, BS, 86; MA, 89; Iowa State Univ, PhD, 92. **CAREER** Assoc Prof, Northern Ky Univ. **MEMBERSHIPS** Am Sociol Asn, Am Soc for Criminol, Acad of Criminal Justice Sci. **SELECTED PUBLICATIONS** Auth, The Sociological Significance of Tattoos, 95; auth, The Structure of Prison Release, 95. **CONTACT ADDRESS** Dept Sociol and Anthrop, No Kentucky Univ, Newport, KY 41099-0001.

RICHARDS, WILLIAM M.
DISCIPLINE PHILOSOPHY **EDUCATION** Georgetown Univ, PhD, 70. **CAREER** Dept Philos, Univ Dayton **RESEARCH** Buddhist doctrine of annata; antirealism in ethics. **SELECTED PUBLICATIONS** Auth, A Case for Non-rigid Proper Names, Proc Ohio Philos Assn, 75; Self-Consciousness and Agency, Synthese, 84. **CONTACT ADDRESS** Dept of Philos, Univ of Dayton, 300 Col Park, Dayton, OH 75062. **EMAIL** richards@checkov.hm.udayton.edu

RICHARDSON, ANDRA VIRGINIA
PERSONAL Born 04/16/1954, Detroit, MI, m, 1984, 2 children **DISCIPLINE** LAW **EDUCATION** Wayne State Univ, BS, 84; Wayne State Univ Law School, JD, 87. **CAREER** Reservation sales agent, Delta Airlines, 77-86; asst prosecuting atty, Oakland County, 88-90; magistrate, 52nd-1st District Court, 90-; adjunct prof, Easten Mich Univ, 98-; attorney, part-time law practice. **HONORS AND AWARDS** Dollars and Sense Magazine, Outstanding Business and Professional Awd, 1993; National Assn of Negro Business and Professional Women Club, Inc, Professional Woman of the Year, 1993. **MEMBERSHIPS** Top Ladies of Distinction, Inc, exec board, recording secretary, 93-95; Top Ladies, president, 95-97; Jack & Jill of America, Inc, exec board, parlimentarian, 93-95, legislative liason, 98-; Oakland County Chap Child Abuse and Neglect Council, executive bd/chair, 90-94; Girl Scouts of America, board of directors, 91-94; The Doll League, 98-. **CONTACT ADDRESS** Magistrate Andra V Richardson, 52nd 1st District Court, 48150 Grand River Ave, Novi, MI 48374.

RICHARDSON, BRIAN C.
PERSONAL Born 11/18/1941, Amsterdam, NY, m, 3 children **DISCIPLINE** CHRISTIAN EDUCATION **EDUCATION** Campbell Univ, BA; Southwestern Baptist Theol Sem, MA, PhD. **CAREER** Prof, ch, Biblical Stud Div, Bryan Col; Basil Manly, Jr. prof, S Baptist Theol Sem. **HONORS AND AWARDS** Outstanding Ed of Am. **MEMBERSHIPS** NAPCE, YME. **RESEARCH** Youth. **SELECTED PUBLICATIONS** Auth, Christian Education: Foundations for the Future, Moody Press. **CONTACT ADDRESS** Sch Christian Edu and Leadership, So Baptist Theol Sem, 2825 Lexington Rd, Louisville, KY 40280. **EMAIL** brichardson@sbts.edu

RICHARDSON, DAVID M.
DISCIPLINE LAW **EDUCATION** Rensselaer Polytech Inst, BS; Columbia Univ, LLB; NYork Univ, LLM. **CAREER** Prof, Univ Fla, 84-. **HONORS AND AWARDS** Founding ed, Fla Tax Rev. **MEMBERSHIPS** Fla Bar. **RESEARCH** Taxation. **CONTACT ADDRESS** School of Law, Univ of Florida, PO Box 117625, Gainesville, FL 32611-7625. **EMAIL** richards@law.ufl.edu

RICHARDSON, DEAN M.
DISCIPLINE AMERICAN INDIAN LAW, CIVIL RIGHTS, PRODUCTS LIABILITY **EDUCATION** Univ Rochester, BA, 66; Syracuse Univ, JD, 69. **CAREER** Willamette Univ, Sch Law **HONORS AND AWARDS** NEH fel, Harvard Univ, 80; ch, northwest afrikan amer ballet, portland, oregon, 94. **MEMBERSHIPS** Mem, Justinian Hon Law Soc. **SELECTED PUBLICATIONS** articles ed, Syracuse Law Rev. **CONTACT ADDRESS** Sch of Law, Willamette Univ, 900 State St, Salem, OR 97301. **EMAIL** drichard@willamette.edu

RICHARDSON, HENRY
DISCIPLINE PHILOSOPHY **EDUCATION** Harvard Univ, BA, JD, 81, MPP, 81; PhD, 86. **CAREER** Prof. **SELECTED PUBLICATIONS** Auth, Practical Reasoning about Final Ends, Cambridge, 94; pubs on history of ethics, ethical theory, political philosophy, and practical reasoning. **CONTACT ADDRESS** Dept of Philosophy, Georgetown Univ, 37th and O St, Washington, DC 20057.

RICHARDSON, JOHN
DISCIPLINE RELATIONSHIPS BETWEEN POPULATION, RESOURCES AND ENVIRONMENT **EDUCATION** Univ Minn, PhD. **CAREER** Prof, Am Univ. **RESEARCH** Prevention,management and resolution of political conflict. **SELECTED PUBLICATIONS** Co-auth, Making it Happen: A Positive Guide to the Future, U.S. Asn Club Rome, 84; Ending Hunger: An Idea whose Time Has Come, Praeger, 84, 85. **CONTACT ADDRESS** American Univ, 4400 Massachusetts Ave, Washington, DC 20016.

RICHARDSON, KURT A.
PERSONAL Born 04/04/1957, m, 1983, 4 children **DISCIPLINE** SYSTEMATIC THEOLOGY AND ETHICS **EDUCATION** D Theo, 91. **CAREER** Assoc Prof, Theo and Ethics, 11 years, Gordon-Cromwell Theo Sem; Continuing Vis Prof of Theo, Theologische Fabuultat, Unive of Marburg. **HONORS AND AWARDS** Sci and Rel Scholar. **MEMBERSHIPS** AAR; ETS; CTWS. **RESEARCH** Theology of culture & Technology, Theology of Religion. **SELECTED PUBLICATIONS** Auth, The Epistle of James, NAC Broadman, 97. **CONTACT ADDRESS** Gordon-Conwell Theol Sem, 130 Essex St, South Hamilton, MA 01982.

RICHARDSON, PETER
PERSONAL Born 01/06/1935, Toronto, ON, Canada, m, 1959, 4 children **DISCIPLINE** PHILOSOPHY, ARCHITECTURE **EDUCATION** Univ Toronto, B Archit, 57; B Divinity, 62; Cambridge Univ, PhD Philos, 65. **CAREER** Asst/assoc prof, Loyola Montreal, 69-74; asst to the dean of arts, 71-72; asst to the acad vice-pres, 72-73; coordr,73-74; chemn, Univ of Toronto Scarborough Coll Div of Humanities, 74-77; prin, Univ Coll Univ Toronto, 77-89; prof, Univ Toronto, 80-. **HONORS AND AWARDS** Honorary Mem, Ontario Asn of Archits, 87. **MEMBERSHIPS** Studiorum Novi Testamenti Societas; Can Soc of Bibl Studies; Soc of Bibl Lit; Am Soc for Oriental Res; Am Inst of Archeol, Can Soc for Patristic Study; Am Soc for Greek and Latin Epigraphy. **RESEARCH** Second Temple Judaism; Early Christian history and literature; Architecture in the late Hellenistic and Roman periods. **SELECTED PUBLICATIONS** Auth, Herod, Friend of Romans and King of Jews, 96; co-ed, Gospel in Paul: Studies on Corinthians, Galatians and Romans in Honour of Richard N Longencker, 94; Judaism and Christianity in First-Century Rome, 98. **CONTACT ADDRESS** Univ of Toronto, 15 Kings College, Rm 173, Toronto, ON, Canada M5S 1A1. **EMAIL** prchrdsn@chass.utoronto.ca

RICHARDSON, ROBERT CALVIN
PERSONAL Born 04/22/1949, Pueblo, CO, m, 1972, 1 child **DISCIPLINE** PHILOSOPHY **EDUCATION** Univ Colo, BA, 71; Univ Chicago, MA, 72, PhD(philos), 76. **CAREER** Asst prof, 75-82, Assoc Prof Philos, Univ Cincinnati, 83-, Vis assoc prof philos, Ohio State Univ, 83. **MEMBERSHIPS** Am Philos Asn; Philos Sci Asn; Soc Philos & Psychol; Soc Interdisciplinary Study of Mind. **RESEARCH** Philosophy of mind/psychology; philosophy of science; epistemology. **SELECTED PUBLICATIONS** Auth, Functionalism and reductionism, Philos Sci, 79; Reductionist Research Programs in Psychology, Philos Sci Asn, 80; Internal representations: Prologue to a theory of intentionality, Philos Topics, 81; The scandal of Cartesian Interactionism, Mind, 82; How not to reduce a functional psychology, Philos Sci, 82; coauth (with G Muilenburg), Sellars and Sense Impressions, Ekenntnis, 82; auth, Grades of Organization and Units of Selection, Philos Sci Asn, 82; Brentano on the Distinction Between Mental and Physical Phenomena, Archiv fur die Geschichte die Philos (in prep). **CONTACT ADDRESS** Dept of Philos, Univ of Cincinnati, P O Box 210374, Cincinnati, OH 45221-0374.

RICHARDSON, STEPHEN R.
DISCIPLINE LAW **EDUCATION** Wayne State Univ, BA, 68; Univ Mich, MA, 70; Univ Toronto, LLB, 73. **CAREER** Lawyer, Tory Tory DesLauriers & Binnington **HONORS AND AWARDS** Dir, Tax Policy Legislation, 83-85. **SELECTED PUBLICATIONS** Auth, pubs on various aspects of taxation. **CONTACT ADDRESS** Fac of Law, Univ of Toronto, 78 Queen's Park, Toronto, ON, Canada M5S 1A1.

RICHEY, RUSSELL EARLE
PERSONAL Born 10/19/1941, Asheville, NC, m, 1965, 2 children **DISCIPLINE** CHURCH HISTORY **EDUCATION** Wesleyan Univ, BA (high honors), 63; Union Theol Sem, BD (M Div), 66; Princeton Univ, MA, 68, PhD, 70. **CAREER** Instr, asst prof, assoc prof, prof of church history, Drew Univ Theol and Graduate Schools, 69-86; assoc dean for academic progs and res prof of church hist, The Divinity School, Duke Univ, 86-92, assoc dean for Academic Progs and prof Church Hist, 92-, prof Church Hist, Duke Univ, 97-00; dean, Candler Sch of Theol, Emory Univ, 00-. **HONORS AND AWARDS** Wesleyan: High Honors, Distinction in Hist, Phi Beta Kappa, Sophomore, Junior, and Senior Honor Societies, French Prize in Relig, Honorary Woodrow Wilson; Union Theol Sem: Int Fels Prog, Columbia, Prize in Church Hist, Senior Honor Society; Princeton: Rockefeller Doctoral Fel (withdrew to be Univ Teaching Fel, 68-69), Frelinghuysen Fel, dissertation received with distinction; Ecumenical fac assoc grant, Gen Comm on Christian Unity and Interreligious Concerns, for Bossey conf on Teaching Ecumenics and subsequent three-year service as liason from Commision to United Methodist seminaries, ended 92; Lilly Endowment grant, 91; planning and implementation grant from the Lilly Endowment for a major study of US United Methodism. **MEMBERSHIPS** Am Soc of Church Hist (member, Council 76-78, 95-97); Am Academy of Relig; Hist Soc of the United Methodist Church; adv bd: Quart Rev, Christian Hist, Church Hist, and J of Southern Relig. **SELECTED PUBLICATIONS** Co-ed with Donald Jones, American Civil Religion, Harper & Row, 74, Mellon Res Univ Press, 90; ed and co-auth, Denominationalism, Abingdon Press, 77; co-ed with Kenneth E Rowe, Rethinking Methodist History, United Methodist Pub House, 85; auth, Early American Methodism, IN Univ Press, 91; co-auth and ed, Ecumenical and Interreligious Perspectives: Globalization in Theological Education, Quart Rev Imprint, 92; co-ed with Kenneth E Rowe and Jean Miller Schmidt, Perspectives on American Methodism, IN Univ Press, Kingswood/Abingdon, 93; co-ed and co-auth with R Bruce Mullin, Reimagining Denominationalism, Oxford Univ Press, 94; auth, The Methodist Conference in America: A History, Kingswood/Abingdon, 96; The Methodists, with James Kirby and Kenneth Rowe, Greenwood, 96; Connectionalism: Ecclesiology, Mission, and Identity, primary co-ed with Dennis M Campbell and William B Lawrence, UMAC, I, Abingdon, 97; The People(s) Called Methodist: Forms and Reforms of Their Life, co-ed with Dennis M Campbell and William B Lawrence, UMAC, II, Abingdon, 98; Doctrines and Discipline, co-ed with Dennis M Campbell and William B Lawrence, UMAC, III, Abingdon, forthcoming 99; Questions for the Twenty-First Century Church, co-auth and primary co-ed with Dennis M Campbell and William B Lawrence, UMAC, IV, forthcoming 99. **CONTACT ADDRESS** Candler School of Theology, Emory Univ, Atlanta, GA 30322. **EMAIL** rrichey@mail.duke.edu

RICHMAN, KENNETH A.
PERSONAL Born 09/25/1966, m, 1997 **DISCIPLINE** PHILOSOPHY **EDUCATION** Haverford Col, BA, 88; Rutgers Univ, MA, 93; PhD, 97. **CAREER** Special asst to Dean, Haverford Col, 88-89; asst examiner, Educ Testing Serv, 96-97; asst prof, Kalamazoo Col, 97-; asst prof, Bryn Mawr Col, 00-. **HONORS AND AWARDS** Who's Who Among Am Teachers; Rugters Univ Excellence Fel; Schwartz Prize in Philos. **MEMBERSHIPS** Am Philos Assoc; Hume Soc; Am Soc for Eighteen Century Studies; Mich Acad of Arts and Sci. **RESEARCH** Hume and Early Modern Philosophy, Epistemology, Medical Ethics, Philosophy of Medicine. **SELECTED PUBLICATIONS** Auth, "Epistemology, Community and Experts", Mich J of Community Serv Learning III, (Fall 96): 5-12; auth, "Empiricism, Natural Belief and the New Hume", Hist of Philos Quarterly XII.4, (Oct 95): 425-441; coed, Current Moral and Social Issues, Kendall/Hunt Pub Co, 96; coed, The New Hume Debate, Routledge (London), 00. **CONTACT ADDRESS** Dept Philos, Kalamazoo Col, 1200 Academy St, Kalamazoo, MI 49006-3268.

RICHMAN, PAULA
DISCIPLINE SOUTH ASIAN RELIGIONS **EDUCATION** Oberlin Col, BA, 74; Princeton Univ, MA, 77; Univ Chicago, MA, 80, PhD, 83. **CAREER** Irvin E. Houck prof, 85; chair, relig dept, Oberline Col. **RESEARCH** Tamil religious literature; Ramayana. **SELECTED PUBLICATIONS** Ed, Questing Ramayanas, A South Asian Tradition; ed, Many Ramayanas:

The Diversity of a Narrative Tradition in South Asia; A Gift of Tamil; transl from Tamil literature; auth, Extraordinary Child: Poems From a South Indian Devotional Game; auth, Women, Branch Stories, and Relig Rhetoric in a Tamil Buddhist Text. **CONTACT ADDRESS** Dept of Relig, Oberlin Col, Oberlin, OH 44074.

RICHMAN, WILLIAM M.
DISCIPLINE LAW **EDUCATION** Univ Pa, BA; Univ Md, JD. **CAREER** Prof. **SELECTED PUBLICATIONS** Co-auth, Cases and Materials on Conflict of Laws, Matthew Bender, 90; Understanding Conflict of Laws, Matthew Bender, 93; Elitism, Expediency and the New Certiorari, Cornell Law Rev, 96. **CONTACT ADDRESS** Col Law, Univ of Toledo, Toledo, OH 43606. **EMAIL** wrichma@uoft02.utoledo.edu

RICHTER, DUNCAN J.
PERSONAL Born 12/26/1966, Chester, England, m, 1994, 1 child **DISCIPLINE** PHILOSOPHY **EDUCATION** Univ of Virginia, PhD, 95; Univ Coll of Swansea, Wales, MPhil, 89; Oxford UnivBA, 88. **CAREER** Asst Prof, 95-, Virgina Military Inst. **HONORS AND AWARDS** Thomas Jefferson Tchg Awd, 98; V.M.I. **MEMBERSHIPS** Amer Philo Assoc, Southern Soc for Philo and Psych, VA Philos Assoc, Soc for Philo and Public Affairs. **RESEARCH** Wittgenstein, Anti-Theory in Ethics, Virtue, Theory of Applied Ethics. **SELECTED PUBLICATIONS** Auth, The Incoherence of the Moral Ought, Philosophy, 95; Nothing to be Said, Wittgenstein and Wittgensteinian Ethics, Southern Journal of Philosophy, 96; Is Abortion Vicious?, Journal of Value Inquiry, 98; auth, Virtue Without Theory, Jouranl of Value Inquiry, 99; auth, Ethics After Anscombe: Post Modern Moral Philosophy, Kluwer Academic Pub, 99; auth, Understanding Genocide: Wittgenstein and the Holocuast, Review Journal of Philosophy and Social Science, 00. **CONTACT ADDRESS** Dept of Psychology & Philosophy, Virginia Military Inst, Lexington, VA 24450. **EMAIL** richterdj@mail.vmi.edu

RICKETTS, THOMAS G.
PERSONAL Born 02/02/1949, Cleveland, OH **DISCIPLINE** PHILOSOPHY **EDUCATION** Oberlin Col, BA, 71; Univ Mich, MA, 74, PhD, 77. **CAREER** Instr & asst prof, Harvard Univ, 76-69; asst prof, 79-85, assoc prof, 85- , dept chemn, 89-92, Univ Penn. **HONORS AND AWARDS** ACLS fel, 83-84. **MEMBERSHIPS** APA; AAUP. **RESEARCH** History of analytic philosophy; Frege; Russell; Wittgenstein; Carnap; Quine. **SELECTED PUBLICATIONS** Auth, Carnap's Principle of Tolerance, Empiricism and Conventionalism, in Clark, ed, Reading Putnam, Blackwell, 94; auth, Logic and Truth in Grege, Aristotelian Soc Suppl, 96; auth, Pictures, Logic, and the Limits of Sense in Wittgenstein's Tractatus, in Sluga, ed, Cambridge Wittgenstein Companion, Cambridge, 96; auth, Carnap: From Logical Syntax to Semantics, in Giere, ed, Origins of Logical Empiricism: Minnesota Studies in Philosophy of Science, Univ Minneapolis, 96; auth, Truth-Values and Courses-of-Values in Frege's Grundgesetze, in Tait, ed, Early Analytic Philosophy: Essays in Honor of Leonard Linsky, Open Court, 97; auth, Frege's 1906 Foray into Metalogic, Philos Topics, 97; auth, Truth and Propositional Unity in Early Russell, in Floyd, ed, Future Pasts; Reflections on the History and Nature of Analytic Philosophy, Harvard, 99. **CONTACT ADDRESS** Logan Hall, Univ of Pennsylvania, Philadelphia, PA 19104. **EMAIL** ricketts@sas.upenn.edu

RICKLESS, SAMUEL
PERSONAL Born 09/22/1964, Paris, FRA, m, 1964 **DISCIPLINE** PHILOSOPHY **EDUCATION** Harvard Univ, BA, 86; Oxford Univ, BPhil, 88; UCLA, PhD, 96. **CAREER** Asst prof, Fla State Univ, 96-. **HONORS AND AWARDS** Marshall Scholar, 86-88; Univ Teaching Awd, Fla State Univ, 99-00. **MEMBERSHIPS** Am Philos Asn, Am Asn of Univ Professors, Soc for Ancient Greek Philos, Soc for Exact Philos. **RESEARCH** Metaphysics, Philosophy of Language, Ethics, History of Philosophy. **SELECTED PUBLICATIONS** Auth, "Lock on Primary and Secondary Qualities," Pacific Philos Quart 78 (97): 297-319; auth, "The doctrine of Doing and Allowing," Philos Rev 106 (97): 555-575; auth, "Socrates' Moral Intellectualism," Pacific Philos Quart 79 (98): 355-367; auth, "How Parmenides Saved the Theory of Forms," Philos Rev 107 (98): 501-554. **CONTACT ADDRESS** Dept Philos, Florida State Univ, PO Box 3061500, Tallahassee, FL 32306-1500. **EMAIL** srickles@mailer.fsu.edu

RICOEUR, PAUL
PERSONAL Born 02/27/1913, m, 1935, 5 children **DISCIPLINE** PHILOSOPHY **EDUCATION** Univ Paris, Agregation, 35, D es Lett, 50. **CAREER** Prof hist of philos, Univ Strasbourg, 48-56; prof, Univ Paris, 56-65; prof, 65-76, John Nuveen Prof Philos Theol & Prof Philos, Univ Chicago, 76- **HONORS AND AWARDS** Hon degrees from Univs Basil, Chicago, Montreal, Nijmegen, Zurich, Ohio State & DePaul. **RESEARCH** Philosophy of language; philosophy of action; hermeneutics. **SELECTED PUBLICATIONS** Auth, Fallible Man, Henry Regnery, 65; History and Truth, 65 & Freedom and Nature: The Voluntary and the Unvoluntary, 66, Northwestern Univ; The Symbolism of Evil, Harper, 67; Freud and Philosophy, Yale Univ, 70; Interpretation Theory, Tex Christian Univ Press, 76; The Crisis Of The Cogito, Synthese, Vol 106, 96. **CONTACT ADDRESS** Dept of Philos, Univ of Chicago, Chicago, IL 60637.

RIDGWAY, JOHN KARL
PERSONAL Born 12/13/1949, Seattle, WA **DISCIPLINE** RELIGION **EDUCATION** Marquette Univ, PhD, 95. **CAREER** Asst prof, Dept Relig Studies, Regis Univ. **MEMBERSHIPS** Cath Bibl Asn; Soc Bibl Lit. **RESEARCH** Gospel of Matthew; the Concepts of Healing and Peace in the Old and New Testaments; Johannine literature. **SELECTED PUBLICATIONS** Auth, Let Your Peace Come Upon It: Healing and Peace in Matthew 10:1-15, Peter Lang Publ, Inc., 99. **CONTACT ADDRESS** Dept of Religious Studies, Regis Univ, 3333 Regis Blvd., Denver, CO 80221-1099. **EMAIL** jridgway@regis.edu

RIEBER, STEVEN
DISCIPLINE PHILOSOPHY OF LANGUAGE, PHILOSOPHY OF MIND, METAPHYSICS, EPISTEMOLOGY, ETHI **EDUCATION** Princeton Univ, PhD, 91. **CAREER** Assoc prof, Ga State Univ. **SELECTED PUBLICATIONS** Author of eight recent articles in journals such as Analysis, Nous and Philos Stud. **CONTACT ADDRESS** Georgia State Univ, Atlanta, GA 30303. **EMAIL** phlsdr@panther.gsu.edu

RIESER, ALISON
DISCIPLINE LAW **EDUCATION** Cornell Univ, BS; George Washington Univ, JD; Yale Law Sch, LLM. **CAREER** Prof and dir, Marine Law Inst; res fel, Woods Hole Oceanographic Inst, 2 yrs; fac law sch, Louisiana Tech Univ, 80-; app prof, Maine Law, 93-; consult to state and fed agencies; fac adv, law student-edited Ocean and Coastal Law J; **MEMBERSHIPS** US Env Protection Agency; Nat Oceanic and Atmospheric Admin. **RESEARCH** World's oceans. **SELECTED PUBLICATIONS** Coauth, leading casebk in ocean and coastal law. **CONTACT ADDRESS** School of Law, Univ of So Maine, 96 Falmouth St, PO Box 9300, Portland, ME 04104-9300.

RIGALI, NORBERT JEROME
PERSONAL Born 12/29/1928, Los Angeles, CA **DISCIPLINE** MORAL THEOLOGY **EDUCATION** Gonzaga Univ, AB, 52, MA, 53; Innsbruck Pontif Col, STL, 60; Univ Munich, PhD(philos), 65. **CAREER** Asst prof philos, Mt St Michael Col Philos & Sci, Gonzaga Univ, 64-65 & Loyola Univ, Calif, 65-68; res assoc ethics & moral theol, Cambridge Ctr Soc Studies, 68-69; asst prof, 72-75, chmn dept relig studies, 74-78, assoc prof, 75-81, prof Moral Theol, Univ San Diego, 81-00, Prof Emer, 00-. **MEMBERSHIPS** Col Theol Soc; Catholic Theol Soc Am. **RESEARCH** Moral theology. **SELECTED PUBLICATIONS** Auth, Die Selbstkonstitution der Geschichte im Denken von Karl Jaspers, Anton Hain, Meisenheim, 68; Moral theology: Old and new, Chicago Studies, spring 69; A new axis of history, Int Philos Quart, 70; Toward a Moral Theology of Social Consciousness, fall 77 & Evil and Models of Christian Ethics, spring 81, Horizons; Reimaging Morality: A Matter of Metaphors, The Heythrop J, Jan 94; Christian Morality and Universal Morality: The One and the Many, Louvain Studies, Spring 94; Church Responses to Pedophilia, Theol Studies, March 94. **CONTACT ADDRESS** Dept of Theol and Relig Studies, Univ of San Diego, San Diego, CA 92110. **EMAIL** nrigali@acusd.edu

RIGBY, KENNETH
PERSONAL Born 10/20/1925, Shreveport, LA, m, 1951, 3 children **DISCIPLINE** LAW **EDUCATION** La State Univ, BA, JD. **CAREER** Adj prof Law, La State Univ Law Center, 90- , lect La State Univ annual bar review course. **HONORS AND AWARDS** Magna Cum Laude; Summa Cum Laude; Order of the Coif; Phi Delta Phi; Omicron Delta Kappa; listed in Best Lawyers of Am, Who's Who in the South and Southwest, Who's Who in American Law and Who's Who in the World; Am Acad of Matrimonial Lawyers Fel; Am Col of Trial Lawyers Fel **MEMBERSHIPS** Am Acad of Matrimonial Lawyers; Am Col of Trial Lawyers; La St Law Inst; La State Bar Asn. **RESEARCH** Family law; matrimonial regimes. **SELECTED PUBLICATIONS** Auth, Recent Developments: Matrimonial Regimes, LaLaw Rev, 99, 00; auth, Some Views, Old and New on Recent Developments in Family Law, in La Bar J, 82; auth, Alternate Dispute Resolution, in La Law Rev, 84; coauth, Louisiana's New Divorce Legislation: Background and Commentary, La Law R, 93; auth, The 1993 Custody and Child Support Legislation, La Law Rev, 94; auth, The 1997 Spousal Support Act, La Law Review, 98; auth, Divorce Forms, West LSA Civil Procedure, West, 96, 98. **CONTACT ADDRESS** 8916 Creswell Rd, Shreveport, LA 71106. **EMAIL** charli@prysm.net

RIGDON, V. BRUCE
PERSONAL Born 02/23/1936, Philadelphia, PA, m, 1959, 3 children **DISCIPLINE** RELIGION **EDUCATION** Wooster, BA, 58; Yale Divinity Sch, BD, 62; Yale Univ, MA, 63, PhD, 68. **CAREER** Asst prof/prof, McCormicle Theol Sem, 65-88; pastor, Grosse Pointe Mem Church, 88-; prof church hist, 89-, pres, 97-, Ecumenical Theol Sem. **CONTACT ADDRESS** Dept of Theology, Ecumenical Theol Sem, 1028 Yorkshire Rd., Grosse Pointe, MI 48230.

RIGGINS, THOMAS
PERSONAL Born 02/17/1942, West Palm Beach, FL, d, 2 children **DISCIPLINE** PHILOSOPHY **EDUCATION** FL State Univ, BA, MA; CUNY, MPhil, PhD. **CAREER** Adjunct Asst Prof, NYU; faculty, New Sch for Social Research **MEMBERSHIPS** APA **RESEARCH** Comparative philosophy; hist of philosophy; Marxism **SELECTED PUBLICATIONS** Various reviews in Philosophy East and West; International Journal of Philosophy; Korea Focus. **CONTACT ADDRESS** 150 E 2 St, #3B, New York, NY 10009. **EMAIL** jtr2@nyu.edu

RIKE, JENNIFER L.
DISCIPLINE RELIGIOUS STUDIES **EDUCATION** Univ Mich, BA; Univ Chicago Divinity Sch, MA, PhD. **CAREER** Ordained minister, Presbyterian Church, USA; asst prof, Univ Detroit Mercy, 95-. **RESEARCH** Paradoxical relationship between violence and religion. **CONTACT ADDRESS** Dept of Religious Studies, Univ of Detroit Mercy, 4001 W McNichols Rd, PO Box 19900, Detroit, MI 48219-0900. **EMAIL** RIKEJL@udmercy.edu

RIND, MILES
PERSONAL Born Seattle, WA **DISCIPLINE** PHILOSOPHY **EDUCATION** Univ Chicago, PhD, 98. **CAREER** Author **MEMBERSHIPS** APA; Am Soc for Aesthet; North Am Kant Soc. **RESEARCH** Kant; aesthetics; philosophy of music. **CONTACT ADDRESS** Dept of Philosophy, Univ of Cincinnati, Cincinnati, OH 45221-0374.

RINDERLE, WALTER
PERSONAL Born 08/31/1940, Vincennes, IN, m, 1974, 2 children **DISCIPLINE** CHURCH HISTORY, THEOLOGY, EURO HISTORY **EDUCATION** St Meinrad Col, AB 62; State Univ Innsbruck, Austria, STL 66, MA 67; Univ Notre Dame, MA 73, PhD 76; Ind State , MS, 00. **CAREER** Vincennes Univ, asst prof 90-94; Univ Southern IN, asst prof 94-97; Univ St Francis, instr 98; Instr, Ind State Univ, 00. **HONORS AND AWARDS** 2 NEH awds. **MEMBERSHIPS** Indiana Hist Soc; Catholic Hist Soc. **RESEARCH** Role of the Lutheran Church in the collapse of East Germany; Medical hist; Nazi Germany. **SELECTED PUBLICATIONS** Nazi Impact on a German Village; 200 Years of Catholic Education; Permanent Pastors in Knox County. **CONTACT ADDRESS** 2814 N Church Rd, Vincennes, IN 47591. **EMAIL** rinderle@charter.net

RING, NANCY C.
PERSONAL Born 08/26/1937, Memphis, TN, s **DISCIPLINE** THEOLOGY **EDUCATION** Marquette Univ, PhD, 80. **CAREER** Prof, Dept Chr, LeMoyne Coll, 79-. **MEMBERSHIPS** Catholic Theol Soc of Amer; Amer Acad of Relig; Coll Theol Soc **RESEARCH** Theol Method; feminist studies, spirituality **SELECTED PUBLICATIONS** An Introduction to the Study of Religion **CONTACT ADDRESS** Le Moyne Col, Syracuse, NY 13214. **EMAIL** Ring@Maple.Lemoyne.edu

RIPPLE, KENNETH FRANCIS
PERSONAL Born 05/19/1943, Pittsburgh, PA, m, 1968, 3 children **DISCIPLINE** LAW **EDUCATION** Fordham Univ, AB, 65; Univ Va, JD, 68; George Washington Univ, LLM, 72. **CAREER** Atty, IBM Corp, 68 & Judge Advocate General's Corps, US Navy, 68-72; legal officer, Supreme Ct US, 72-73, special asst to Chief Justice Burger, 73-77; Prof Law, Univ Notre Dame, 77-, Reporter, Adv Comt Fed Appellate Rules, 78-; mem, Nat Adv Comt to Chief Justice on Law Clerk Selection, 78 & Anglo Am Judicial Exchange, 80; United States Circuit Court Judge, South Bend, Ind, 85-. **HONORS AND AWARDS** Teacher of Year, Law Sch, Univ Notre Dame, 78-80, 84 & 85; Special Pres Awd, 85. **MEMBERSHIPS** Am Law Inst; Am Bar Asn; Fed Bar Asn; NY State Bar Asn; Phi Beta Kappa; Supreme Court Hist Soc. **RESEARCH** Constitutional law; conflicts of law; Supreme Court of the United States. **SELECTED PUBLICATIONS** Coauth, Extralegal standards in the process of constitutional adjudication in the Supreme Court of the United States, Zeitschrift fur Politik, 79; State sovereignty--A polished but slippery crown, 79 & World Wide Volkswagon Corporation versus Woodson: Relfections on the road ahead, 80, Notre Dame Lawyer; auth, The Supreme Court's workload: Some thoughts for the practitioner, Am Bar Asn J, 80; The entanglement test of the religion clauses: A ten year assessment, Univ Calif Los Angeles Law Rev, 80; coauth, The separate appendix in federal appellate practice: Necessary tool or costly luxury?, Southwestern Law J, 81; American constitutional law 1976-1981, Jahrbuch Des Offentlichen Rechts Der Gegenwart, 81; Sanctions Imposable for Violations of the Federal Rules of Civil Procedure, Fed Judicial Ctr, 81. **CONTACT ADDRESS** Sch of Law, Univ of Notre Dame, Notre Dame, IN 46556.

RISJORD, MARK
DISCIPLINE PHILOSOPHY OF LANGUAGE **EDUCATION** Univ NC, PhD, 90. **CAREER** Assoc Prof, Philos, Emory Univ **RESEARCH** Philosophy of science, philosophy of anthropology; philosophy of language; logic; and the philosophy of mathematics. **SELECTED PUBLICATIONS** Articles, Am Philos Quart, Jour Med & Philos, Canadian Jour Philos, Studies Hist & Philos Science; auth, Woodcutters and Witchcraft: Rationality and Interpretive Change in the Social Sciences. **CONTACT ADDRESS** Emory Univ, Atlanta, GA 30322-1950. **EMAIL** mrisjor@emory.edu

RISSER, JAMES C.
PERSONAL Born 08/23/1946, Allentown, PA, m, 2 children **DISCIPLINE** PHILOSOPHY **EDUCATION** Calif State Univ-Long Bch, BA, 71; Duquesne Univ, PhD, 78. **CAREER** Vis asst prof, Villanova Univ, 78-79; asst prof, 79-85, prof, 96-, Seattle Univ, 79-; Pigott McCone Chr Hum, 91-94. **MEMBERSHIPS** Am Philos Asn; Soc Phenomenol & Existential Philos. **RESEARCH** Hermeneutics; Aesthetics. **SELECTED PUBLICATIONS** Hermeneutics and the Voice of the Other, SUNY Press, 97. **CONTACT ADDRESS** Dept of Philosophy, Seattle Univ, Seattle, WA 98122. **EMAIL** jrisser@seattleu.ed

RISSI, MATHIAS
PERSONAL Born 09/29/1920, Wienacht, Switzerland, m, 1945, 4 children **DISCIPLINE** RELIGION **EDUCATION** Univ Basel, ThD, 52. **CAREER** Minister, Sargans, Hauptwil, Rheineck & Basel, Switz, 44-63; Prof New Testament to Prof Emer, Union Theol Sem, Va, 63-, Privat docent, Univ Basel, 56-63; guest lectr, Univ Hamburg, 67; dean studies, Ecumenical Sem, Vienna, Austria, 77- **MEMBERSHIPS** Soc Studies New Testament; Soc Bibl Lit. **RESEARCH** New Testament. **SELECTED PUBLICATIONS** Auth, The Kerygma Of The Revelation To John, Interpretation, 68; Studies Zum 2 Korintherbrief, Zwingli Verlag, 69; Die Logoslieder Im Prolog Des Vierten Evangeliums, Theol Zeitschrift, 75; The Eternal Word, Interpretation, 77; Voll Grosser Fische, Theoll Zcitschrift, 79; Coauth, Biblisch-Historisches Worterbuch, Vandenhoeck-Ruprecht, Gottingen, 62-79; Der Aufgau Des Johannesevangeliums, New Testament Studies, 82; Exegetisches Worterbuch Zum Neven Testament, Kohlhammer, 81-82; The Theology Of The Book Of Revelation, Interpretation-A J Of Bible And Theology, Vol 49, 95; Revelation--A Continental Commentary, Interpretation-A J Of Bible And Theology, Vol 49, 95; After The 1000 Years--Resurrection And Judgment In Revelation-XX, Interpretation-A J Of Bible And Theology, Vol 48, 94. **CONTACT ADDRESS** Union Theol Sem, Virginia, 3401 Brook Rd, Richmond, VA 23227.

RITSON, G. JOY
PERSONAL Born 12/18/1945, Highworth, England **DISCIPLINE** HISTORICAL THEOLOGY **EDUCATION** Graduate Theo Union, PhD, 97. **CAREER** Seeking first position. **MEMBERSHIPS** AAR/SBL, APA, SSSR. **RESEARCH** History of Christian Spirituality; Early and Medieval Church; Linguistic Issues involving Latin and Greek Text. **SELECTED PUBLICATIONS** Auth, Eros, Allegory and Spirituality, in preparation, based on PhD Dissertation; Shame in the Developing Though of Augustine, in preparation. **CONTACT ADDRESS** 1277 Sun Cir E, Melbourne, FL 32935. **EMAIL** MINDOX@ix.NETCOM.COM

RITTER, SUSAN
PERSONAL Born 01/07/1956, Lamar, CO, s **DISCIPLINE** CRIMINAL JUSTICE **EDUCATION** Tex Woman's Univ, BS, 80; Univ Tex, MA, 88; Sam Houston State Univ, PhD, 97. **CAREER** Correctional officer to sen officer, case manager, Fed Bureau of Prison, 90-99. **HONORS AND AWARDS** Superior Perf Awd, Sam Houston State Univ. **MEMBERSHIPS** Acad of Criminal Justice Sci, SW Asn of Criminal Justice Educators. **RESEARCH** Institutional corrections, Recidivism, Female offenders, Chronic juvenile offenders. **SELECTED PUBLICATIONS** Auth, Briefs of Leading Cases in Corrections, 2nd Ed, Anderson Pub Co: Cincinnati, 98. **CONTACT ADDRESS** Dept Criminal Justice, Texas Southmost Col, 80 Fort Brown, Brownsville, TX 78520. **EMAIL** ritter@utb1.utb.edu

RIVERA, JENNY
PERSONAL Born 12/08/1960, New York, NY, s **DISCIPLINE** LAW **EDUCATION** Princeton Univ, AB, 82; New York Univ, JD 85; Columbia Univ, LLM, 93. **CAREER** Asst Prof, Suffolk Univ, 94-96; Assoc Prof, CUNY, 97-. **MEMBERSHIPS** NY City Public Advocate's Accountability Project, An of the Bar of the city of NY, Grand Street Settlement, UN Fourth World Conf on Women. **RESEARCH** Civil Rights; Women's Rights. **SELECTED PUBLICATIONS** Auth, "Intimate partner violence strategies: Models for community Participation," Maine Law Review, 98; auth, "the availability of domestic violence services for Latinas in New York State," In The Public Interest, 98; auth, "Jenny Rivera, 'Panel-The diversity among Us'," W New England Law Review, (97): 31-35; auth, "The violence against Women Act and the construction of Multiple consciousness in the civil Rights and feminist Movements," Journal Law , 96; auth, "The Violence against women Act of 1994: A Promise Waiting to Be Fulfilled," Journal Law, 96; auth, "the Politics of Invisibility," Journal on fighting Poverty , 95. **CONTACT ADDRESS** School of Law, Queens Col, CUNY, 6521 Main St, Flushing, NY 11367-1358.

RIVERS, CLARENCE JOSEPH
PERSONAL Born 09/09/1931, Selma, AL **DISCIPLINE** RELIGION **EDUCATION** BA 1952; MA 1956; St Mary's Sem, Cincinnati; English Lit Xavier U; Cath Univ of Am; Union Grad Sch, PhD; Institut Catholique, Paris. **CAREER** Archdiocese of Cincinnati, priest 1956-; Purcell HS, tchr, English Lit 1956-66; St Joseph's & Assumption Parishes, asso pastor 1956-66; Dept of Culture & Worship Nat Ofc of Black Cath, founder first dir 1972, spl cons; Stimuli Inc, "Newborn Again", pres. **HONORS AND AWARDS** Recipient pub serv awards; 1966 Gold Medal of Cath Art Assn for "An Am Mass Prog". **MEMBERSHIPS** Mem bd dir Nat Liturgical Conf; N Am Academy of Liturgy; Martin Luther Kings Fellows; pub "Turn Me Loose"; mem worship comm Archdiocese of Cincinnati. **SELECTED PUBLICATIONS** Rec, "An Am Mass Prog," 1963; auth, books on worship; CBS Network, scripted/co-prod/starred "Freeing the Spirit" 1971; CBS Network Easter Special, prod cons/narrator/composer "The Feast of Life." **CONTACT ADDRESS** PO Box 20066, Cincinnati, OH 45220.

ROACH, KENT
DISCIPLINE LAW **EDUCATION** Univ Toronto, BA, 84, LLB, 87; Yale Univ, LLM, 87. **CAREER** Law clerk, Justice Bertha Wilson, Supreme Court Can, 88-89; prof, 98- **HONORS AND AWARDS** Walter Owen Prize, 84; ed, criminal law quarterly; assoc ed, dominion law reports. **MEMBERSHIPS** Law Soc Saskatchewan; Law Found Saskatchewan; Law Soc Upper Can. **SELECTED PUBLICATIONS** Auth, Constitutional Remedies in Canada, Can Law Bk, Criminal Law, Irwin Law, 96. **CONTACT ADDRESS** Col of Law, Univ of Saskatchewan, 15 Campus Dr, Saskatoon, SK, Canada S7N 5A6. **EMAIL** Roach@law.usask.ca

ROARK, DALLAS MORGAN
PERSONAL Born 12/15/1931, Birchwood, TN, m, 1955, 2 children **DISCIPLINE** PHILOSOPHY, RELIGION **EDUCATION** Northern Baptist Theol Sem, ThB, 54; Univ Iowa, MA, 58, PhD, 63. **CAREER** Pastor, Harrisburg & Downey Baptist Churches, 55-60; assoc prof relig, Wayland Baptist Col, 60-66; assoc prof Soc Sci, 66-80, Prof Philos & Chmn, Div Soc Sci, Emporia State Univ, 80-. **MEMBERSHIPS** Am Soc Church Hist; Am Acad Relig; Southwestern Philos Soc. **RESEARCH** History of doctrine; American theological thought; theology. **SELECTED PUBLICATIONS** Ed, Wayland Lectures, Wayland Press, 62; auth, The Christian Faith, Broadman, 69; Dietrich Bonhoeffer, Word Publ, 72; Introduction to Philosophy, Ginn, 82. **CONTACT ADDRESS** Dept of Soc Sci, Emporia State Univ, 1200 Commercial St, Emporia, KS 66801-5087. **EMAIL** roarkdal@yahoo.com

ROBBINS, IRA PAUL
PERSONAL Born 01/02/1949, Brooklyn, NY, m, 1970, 2 children **DISCIPLINE** LAW **EDUCATION** Univ PA, AB, 70; Harvard Univ, JD, 73. **CAREER** Law clerk, US Ct Appeals Second Circuit, 73-75; assoc prof law & dir, KS Defender Proj, Univ KS, 75-79; Prof Law & Justice, Am Univ, 79-; dir, joint degree prog, 80-; Vis prof law, Georgetown Univ, 82, 90. **HONORS AND AWARDS** Ethel & Raymond F. Rice Prize Fac Scholar, Sch Law, Univ KS, 78; Pauline Ruyle Moore Scholar, WA Col Law, Am Univ, 80, 89, Outstanding Scholar, 81 & Outstanding Tchr, 82-85, 94, 97, Tchr/Sch of the Year, 88; R. Brown Awd for Judicial Scholarship and Educ, 98. **MEMBERSHIPS** Am Law Inst **RESEARCH** Criminal law; penology; judicial process. **SELECTED PUBLICATIONS** Auth, Comparative Postconviction Remedies, DC Heath/Lexington Bks, 80; The Law and Processes of Post-Conviction Remedies: Cases and Materials, West Publ Co, 82; The Legal Dimensions of Private Incarceration, Am Bar Asn, 88; Toward a More Just and Effective System of Review in State Death Penalty Cases, Am Bar Asn, 90; Prisoners and the Law, West Group (4 vols), 98; Habeas Corpus Checklists, West Group, 98, 99, 00, 01; auth, "Managed Health Care in Prisons as Cruek and Unusual Punishment," Journal of Criminal Law and Criminology, 99; auth, "Semiotics, Analogical Reasoning, and the Cf. Citation; Getting Our Signals Uncrossed," Duke Law Journal, 99; auth, "Concurring in Result Without Written Opinion: A Condemnable Practice," Judicature, 00. **CONTACT ADDRESS** WA Col of Law, American Univ, 4801 Massachusetts Ave NW, Washington, DC 20016-8181. **EMAIL** robbins@wcl.american.edu

ROBERGE, RENE-MICHEL
PERSONAL Born 07/08/1944, Charny, PQ, Canada **DISCIPLINE** THEOLOGY, HISTORY **EDUCATION** Univ Laval, BA, 65, BTh, 67, LTh, 69, DTh, 71. **CAREER** PROF THEOLOGIE FONDAMENTALE ET D'HISTOIRE DE LA THEOLOGIE, UNIV LAVAL, 71-, prof titulaire, 83-, vice-doyen theol, 88-89, doyen, 89-97; dir de la revue Laval theologique et philosophique, 87-92. **MEMBERSHIPS** Int Asn Patristic Stud; Can Soc Patristic Stud; N Am Patristic Soc; Soc can de theologie. **SELECTED PUBLICATIONS** Auteur d'une cinquantaine de pubs et de nom communications en patristique, en theol fond et system, et en documentation spec. **CONTACT ADDRESS** Fac de Theologie, Univ of Laval, Laval, QC, Canada G1K 7P4. **EMAIL** Rene-Michel.Roberge@fes.ulaval.ca

ROBERSON, CHRISTOPHER
PERSONAL Born Binghamton, NY, m, 1991 **DISCIPLINE** PHILOSOPHY **EDUCATION** Yale Univ, BA, 86; Univ Mich, PhD, 96. **CAREER** Vis asst prof, Univ Mich, 96-97; instr, Roosevelt Univ, 98-. **MEMBERSHIPS** Am Philos Asn **RESEARCH** Political Philosophy; Ethics; 18th Century Philosophy. **SELECTED PUBLICATIONS** Auth, The State as Rational Authority," Oxford j of Legal Studies, vol 18, no 4, philos ed, The Eighteen Cenury: A Current Bibliography (98), 617-630. **CONTACT ADDRESS** 1303 Maple Ave #2-W, Evanston, IL 60201-4329. **EMAIL** robchr@enteract.com

ROBERTS, DON
DISCIPLINE PHILOSOPHY **EDUCATION** Univ Ill, PhD, 63. **RESEARCH** Logic; theory of knowledge; American philos. **SELECTED PUBLICATIONS** Auth, Logical Fragments, Univ Waterloo, 69; The Existential Graphs of Charles S. Peirce, Mouton, 73. **CONTACT ADDRESS** Dept of Philosophy, Univ of Waterloo, 200 University Ave W, Waterloo, ON, Canada N2L 3G1. **EMAIL** ddrob@serv1.uwaterloo.ca

ROBERTS, KATHRYN L.
PERSONAL Born 12/21/1949, Grand Haven, MI, m, 1994, 2 children **DISCIPLINE** OLD TESTAMENT **EDUCATION** Hope Col, BA magna cum laude, 85; Colgate Rochester Divinity School, MDiv, 88; Princeton Theo Sem, PhD, 96. **CAREER** Adj Prof, 94-98, SUNY Rutger; Asst Prof, 98-, Austin Presbyterian Theo Sem. **MEMBERSHIPS** SBL, AAUP, AAUW. **RESEARCH** Worship in Israel, religions of Israel, the prophets. **CONTACT ADDRESS** 6112 Harrogate Dr, Austin, TX 78759-4776. **EMAIL** kathlee@ix.netcom.comkroberts@austinseminary.edu

ROBERTS, LANI
PERSONAL Born 09/08/1946, The Dalles, OR **DISCIPLINE** PHILOSOPHY **EDUCATION** BA, 85, PhD, 93, Univ Oregon **CAREER** Sr. Instructor (indefinite tenure), Oregon State Univ, 94-01; Asst prof (indefinite tenure), Oregon State Univ, 01. **HONORS AND AWARDS** Col of Liberal Arts Master Teacher, 97-99, 99-01; Col of Liberal Arts, Meehan Excellence in Teaching, 97. **MEMBERSHIPS** Soc for Phil in the Contemporary World; Soc for Women in Phil. **RESEARCH** Philosophy of oppression; ethics; social and political philosophy; feminism **SELECTED PUBLICATIONS** Auth, Chapter IX, Duty, Virtue and the Victim's Choice, Duty to Others, 94; auth, One Oppression or Many, Philosophy in the Contemporary World, 97. **CONTACT ADDRESS** Dept of Philosophy, Oregon State Univ, 102B Hovland Hall, Corvallis, OR 97331-3902. **EMAIL** lroberts@orst.edu

ROBERTS, MELINDA
DISCIPLINE APPLIED ETHICS AND PHILOSOPHY OF LAW **EDUCATION** Vassar Col, 76; Univ MA, PhD, 83; Univ TX, JD, 86. **CAREER** Prof Philos, Col NJ. **MEMBERSHIPS** Soc for Philos and Public Affairs; Am Soc for Political and Legal Philos **SELECTED PUBLICATIONS** Auth, Human Cloning: A Case of No Harm Done?, Jour Med Philos, 96; Parent and Child in Conflict: Between Liberty and Responsibility, Notre Dame Jour Law, Ethics, & Public Policy, 96; auth, Child versus Childmaker: Future Persons and Present Duties in Ethics and the Law, Rowman & Littlefield, 98; auth, Cloning and Harming: Children, Future Persons, and the Best Interests Test, Notre Dame Journal of Law, Ethics & Public Policy, 99. **CONTACT ADDRESS** The Col of New Jersey, PO Box 7718, Ewing, NJ 08628-0718.

ROBERTS, RODNEY C.
DISCIPLINE PHILOSOPHY **EDUCATION** Univ Wisconsin, Madison, PhD, 97. **CAREER** Instr, Seattle Central Commun Col, 96-98; asst prof, philos, Univ Hawaii, Manoa, 98- . **MEMBERSHIPS** APA; Am Sect Int Asn for Philos of Law and Soc Philos; Soc for Ethics; AAUP. **RESEARCH** Injustice; Hume. **SELECTED PUBLICATIONS** Auth, Race, Family, and Obligation, Center for the Study of Ethics in Society, Western Michigan Univ, 95; rev, The Underclass Question by Lawson, ed, Black Scholar, 96; auth, Note on Imbo, ed, An Introduction to African Philosophy, Roman & Littlefield, 98; auth, Philos East & West, forthcoming; auth, Note on Eze, Blackwell 98; auth, ed, African Philosophy: An Anthology, Philosophy East & West, forthcoming. **CONTACT ADDRESS** Department of Philosophy, Univ of Hawaii, Manoa, 2530 Dole St, Sak B-306, Honolulu, HI 96822-2383. **EMAIL** rodneyr@hawaii.edu

ROBERTS, SAMUEL KELTON
PERSONAL Born 09/01/1944, Muskogee, OK, m **DISCIPLINE** THEOLOGY **EDUCATION** Univ de Lyon France, Diplome 1966; Morehouse Coll, BA 1967; Union Theol Sem, MDiv 1970; Columbia Univ, PhD 1974. **CAREER** New York City Mission Soc, summer proj dir 1967-70; S Hempstead Congregational Church, pastor 1972-73; Pittsburgh Theol Sem, asst prof 1973-76; Union Theol Sem, asst prof religion & soc 1976-80; VA Union Univ, dean 1980-. **HONORS AND AWARDS** Merril Overseas Study Awd Morehouse Coll 1965-66; Protestant Fellow Fund for Theol Educ 1967-70; Fellow Columbia Univ 1970-72. **MEMBERSHIPS** Mem Amer Acad of Rel; mem Soc for the Scientific Study of Rel; mem Soc for the Study of Black Relition. **SELECTED PUBLICATIONS** Auth, "George Edmund Haynes" 1978 **CONTACT ADDRESS** Dean, Virginia Union Univ, 1500 N Lombardy St, Richmond, VA 23220.

ROBERTS, VICTOR WILLIAM
PERSONAL Born 02/22/1942, Oklahoma City, OK **DISCIPLINE** PHILOSOPHY, THEOLOGY **EDUCATION** St John's Univ, MN, BA, 65; Univ Ottawa, MA & STL, 69; Fordham Univ, PhD, 73. **CAREER** Chmn hum div, 74-77, Prof Philos, St Gregory's Univ, 73-, V Pres Acad Affairs, 77. **MEM-**

BERSHIPS Am Philos Asn; Am Cath Philos Asn; Hegel Soc Am. **RESEARCH** Hegel; St Anselm of Canterbury; 19th century Europe. **SELECTED PUBLICATIONS** Auth St Anselm of Canterbury's tchg on faith, 9/70 & The rel of faith and reason in St Anselm of Canterbury, 12/74, Am Benedictine Rev. **CONTACT ADDRESS** St. Gregory's Col, 1900 W Macarthur, Shawnee, OK 74804-2499. **EMAIL** vwroberts@sgc.edu

ROBERTS, WENDY HUNTER
PERSONAL Born 01/15/1948, New York, NY, d **DISCIPLINE** RITUAL AND THEOLOGY **CAREER** Consultant in private practice, 81-, East West Healing Arts Center, Oakland CA; Adjunct fac, Grad Theol Union, Berkeley CA; Independent Scholar & Writer. **MEMBERSHIPS** AAR **RESEARCH** Moral Theology; Ancient Women's History. **SELECTED PUBLICATIONS** Auth, In Her Name, in: Women at Worship, ed, Proctor Smith and Walton, Lexington KY, WJK, 93; Celebrating Her, Cleveland, Pilgrim Press, 98. **CONTACT ADDRESS** East West Healing Arts Center, 4174 Park Blvd, Oakland, CA 94602. **EMAIL** whroberts1@earthlink.net

ROBERTS, WILLIAM
PERSONAL Born 07/24/1960, Weehawken, NJ, s **DISCIPLINE** HISTORY, GOVERNMENT **EDUCATION** Fairleigh Dickinson Univ, BA, 67; Fordham Univ, MA, 69; City Univ NY (CUNY), MPhil, 87; City Univ NY (CUNY), PhD, 88. **CAREER** Prof, Fairleigh Dickinson Univ, 88-. **HONORS AND AWARDS** EWC Outstanding Fac Awd, 92; Who's Who in the East, 93; FDU Outstanding Fac Awd, 94; FDU Distinguished Fac Awd for Serv, 99. **RESEARCH** Intellectual history, modern European history. **SELECTED PUBLICATIONS** Coauth, Mazzinianesimo nel Mondo, Pisa: Instituto Domus Mazziniana, 95; coauth, "Mazzini and Lamennais," Encycl of the Essay, Fitzroy Dearborn (97); auth, Controversial Concordats: The Church and the Dictators, CUA Pr (Washington, DC), 99. **CONTACT ADDRESS** Dept Hist & Govt, Fairleigh Dickinson Univ, Teaneck-Hackensack, 1000 River Rd, Teaneck, NJ 07666-1914.

ROBERTSON, BENJAMIN W.
PERSONAL Born 04/06/1931, Roanoke, VA, m, 1 child **DISCIPLINE** THEOLOGY **EDUCATION** VA Theol Seminary, BTh 1951; VA Union Univ, AB 1954; VA Seminary & Coll MDiv 1956, DD 1959, DMin 1968; Union Baptist Seminary, LLD 1971; Richmond VA Seminary LLD 1982; VA Union Univ, HLD 1997. **CAREER** Cedar St Memorial Bapt Ch of God, pastor 1955-; Radio Station WLEE, radio preacher 1961-; Natl Progressive Bapt Cong, tchr 1962-; Radio Station WANT, 65-; Robertson's Kiddie Coll, pres 1968-; First Union Bapt Ch Chesterfield, pastor; Piney Grove Bapt Ch, pastor; Richmond VA Seminary, pres, 81-; Virginia Theological Seminary & College, Lynchburg, VA, Pres, currently. **HONORS AND AWARDS** Afro-Amer Awd for Superior Public Serv without Thought of Gain 1981; Minister of Yr Hayes-Allen VTS&C 1975; Rich Com Hosps Humanitarian Awd 1975; Beta Gamma Lambda Chap Alpha Phi Alpha Frat Inc 1968; FOX Channel 35, television ministry. **MEMBERSHIPS** Bd dirs Commonwealth of VA Girl Scouts 1960-69, Brookland Branch YMCA 1963-75, Rich Met Blood Serv 1963-68, Rich Br NAACP 1964-68, vice pres Lott Carey Bapt Foreign Miss Conv 1976-83; treas Baptist Ministers Conf 1960-70; founder Progressive Natl Bapt Convention 1961; dean of preaching VA Theological Seminary 1965-75; pres VA Seminary & Coll 1980-81; Xi Delta Lambda Chap of Alpha Phi Alpha Frat Inc; tchr of leaders PNBC 1961-81; Founder and First Pres of Richmond VA Seminary 1981-State Board of Psychology, 1996-2000; mem VA State Board of Psychology; VA State Board of Health Professionals. **SELECTED PUBLICATIONS** Author, "Just As He Promised," Providence House Publisher. **CONTACT ADDRESS** Virginia Theol Sem, 2318-20 Cedar St, Richmond, VA 23223.

ROBERTSON, HEIDI GOROVITZ
PERSONAL Born 04/02/1964, Detroit, MI, m, 1993, 2 children **DISCIPLINE** LAW **EDUCATION** Tufts Univ, BA, 85; Univ Wis Law Sch, JD, 90; Columbia Univ Sch of Law, LLM, 95. **CAREER** Instr, Legal Writing & Res, Univ Wis, Law Sch, 88-90; assoc in law, Columbia Univ Sch of Law, 93-95; asst prof, 95-99, assoc prof law, Cleveland-Marshall Col of Law, Cleveland State Univ, 00- ; assoc prof environ studies, Col of Urban Aff, Cleveland State Univ, 00- . **HONORS AND AWARDS** Ruth B Doyle Awd, Univ WI Law School, 89; George H Young Memorial Awd, Univ WI Law School, 90; Teaching Enhancement Awd, Center for Teaching Excellence, Cleveland State Univ, 96, 97. **SELECTED PUBLICATIONS** Auth, Commentary: The EPA Propsed Rule on Lender Liability Under CERCLA, CA Environmental Law Reporter, Sept 91; Commentary: Western World Insurance Co v Dana, CA Environmental Law Reporter, Sept 91; Commentary: Shell Oil Co v EPA, CA Environmental Law Reporter, Feb 92; Commentary: Arkansas v Oklahoma, CA Environmental Law Reporter, April 92; Commentary: The EPA Final Rule On Lender Liability Under CERCLA, CA Environmental Law Reporter, June 92; Commentary: Chemical Waste Management v Hunt and Fort Gratiot Sanitary Landfill v Michigan Dept of Natural Resources, CA Environmental Law Reporter, July 92; Commentary: People v Blech, CA Environmental Law Reporter, Nov 92; If Your Grandfather Could Pollute, So Can You: Environmental 'Grandfather Clauses' and Their Role in Environmental Inequity, 45 Cath U L Rev 131, 95; Environmental Justice: The Social and Demographic Impact of Environmental Choices 9 09 in Frank Grad, Environmental Law Treatise, Matthew Bender, 95 update; Methods for Teaching Environmental Law: Some Thoughts on Providing Access to the Environmental Law System, 23 Colum J Envtl L 237, 98; One Piece of the Puzzle: Legislative Innovation and Other Barriers to the Success of Brownfields Redevelopment Efforts, forthcoming. **CONTACT ADDRESS** Cleveland-Marshall Col of Law, Cleveland State Univ, 1801 Euclid Ave, Cleveland, OH 44115. **EMAIL** Heidi.Robertson@law.csuohio.edu

ROBERTSON, O. PALMER
DISCIPLINE OLD TESTAMENT **EDUCATION** Belhaven Col, BA; Westminster Theol Sem, BDiv; Union Theol Sem, ThM, ThD. **CAREER** Prof, Knox Theol Sem. **SELECTED PUBLICATIONS** Auth, Psalms in Congregational Celebration. **CONTACT ADDRESS** Knox Theol Sem, 5554 N Federal Hwy, Fort Lauderdale, FL 33308.

ROBERTSON, TERESA
PERSONAL Born 05/23/1964, Ft. Hood, TX **DISCIPLINE** PHILOSOPHY **EDUCATION** Univ Wash, BA, 87; Princeton Univ, MA, 93. **CAREER** Instr and teaching asst, Princeton Univ, 92-94; Reed Coll, vis asst prof of philos and humanities, 95-98; asst prof, Univ of Kansas, 99. **HONORS AND AWARDS** Phi Beta Kappa. **MEMBERSHIPS** Am Philos Asn. **RESEARCH** Philosophy of Language; Metaphysics; History of Twentieth Century Analytic Philosophy. **SELECTED PUBLICATIONS** Auth, Possibilties and the Arguments for Origin Essentialism, Mind, 98. **CONTACT ADDRESS** Dept of Philosophy, Univ of Kansas, Lawrence, 3052 Wescoe Hall, Lawrence, KS 66045-2145. **EMAIL** teresa@eagle.cc.ukans.edu

ROBINSON, HADDON W.
PERSONAL Born 03/21/1931, New York, NY, m, 1951, 2 children **DISCIPLINE** PREACHING **EDUCATION** Dallas Theol Sem, ThM, 55; S Methodist Univ, MA, 60; Univ Ill, PhD, 64. **CAREER** Instr, Univ Ill, 60-62; Dallas Theol Sem; co-dir, DMin Prog; Harold John Ockenga Distinguished prof, Gordon-Conwell Theol Sem, 91-. **HONORS AND AWARDS** Hon degree, DD, Gordon Col; dir, dallas youth for christ, 52-55; assoc pastor, first baptist church, 56-58; pres, denver conservative baptist sem, 79; gen dir, christian med and dental soc, 70-79; tchr, radio bible class; pres, evangel theol soc, 83. **MEMBERSHIPS** Evangelical Homiletics Soc.; Evangelical Theological Soc. **SELECTED PUBLICATIONS** Ed, Theol Annual; contrib ed, Preaching; fel and sr ed, Christianity Today; ed, Christian Medical Soc Jour, Our Daily Bread; pub(s), Christianity Today; Bibliotheca Sacra; Moody Monthly; Amer Lutheran Mag; Leadership and Decision mag; auth, Psalm 23; Grief; Biblical Preaching; Biblical Sermons; What Jesus Said About Successful Living; Decisions by the Book. **CONTACT ADDRESS** Gordon-Conwell Theol Sem, 130 Essex St, South Hamilton, MA 01982.

ROBINSON, HOKE
PERSONAL Born 08/16/1942, Columbia, SC, 1 child **DISCIPLINE** PHILOSOPHY **EDUCATION** George Washington Univ, BA, 69; Univ Tex, MA, 71; State Univ NYork, Stony Brook, PhD(Philos), 78. **CAREER** Asst prof, Southern Methodist Univ, 78, Univ Tex, Tyler, 78-79 & Rice Univ, 79-81; prof Philos, Memphis State Univ, 81-83; from assoc prof to prof, 82-95; Deutscher Akademischer Austauschdienst fel, 72 & 73; Alexander von Humboldt-Stiftung fel, 82-90. **MEMBERSHIPS** Am Philos Asn; North Am Kant Soc; Southwestern Philos Soc; Southern Soc Philos & Psychol; Centro Superiore Logica Scienze Comparate. **RESEARCH** Kantian Exegesis; foundations of logic; classical metaphysics. **SELECTED PUBLICATIONS** Auth, Anschauung und Manigfaltiges in der Transzendentalen Duduktion & Incongruent counterparts and the refutation of idealism, Kant-Studien, 81; Two Perspectives on Kant's Appearances & Things in Themselves, J Hist Phil, 94. **CONTACT ADDRESS** Dept Philosophy, Univ of Memphis, 3706 Alumni St, Memphis, TN 38152-0001. **EMAIL** hrobinsn@latte.memphis.edu

ROBINSON, JAMES BURNELL
PERSONAL Born 09/07/1944, Indianapolis, IN, m, 1977, 1 child **DISCIPLINE** WORLD RELIGIONS, TIBETAN BUDDHISM **EDUCATION** Wabash Col, BA, 66; Univ Wis, MA, 68, PhD(Buddhist studies), 75. **CAREER** Assoc Prof Relig, Univ Northern Iowa, 71-, Coordr, Iowa Theol Soc, 76-82. **MEMBERSHIPS** Am Acad Relig; Am Theol Soc; Tibet Soc; Int Asn Buddhist Studies **RESEARCH** Tibetan Buddhism; the primordial tradition; religious symbolism **SELECTED PUBLICATIONS** Auth, The Buddha's Lions: The Lives of the 84 Siddhas, Dharma Publ Col, 79; The Siddhas: Saints & Sorcerers, Gesar Mag, spring 79; The Coming American Dictatorship, Humanities Newslett, 81; coauth, The Doctrine of Socialist Realism, J Social & Polit Studies, spring 81; Ahimsa: Trajectory of a Moral Ideal, In: Boeings & Bullock Carts, Canakya Publ, Delhi, 90; History of Religions & Primordial Tradition, In: Fragments of Infinity, Prism Press, Great Brit, 91; Lives of the Buddhist Saints: Biography, Hagiography & Myth, In: Tibetan Literature: Studies in Genre, Snow Lion Publ, 96. **CONTACT ADDRESS** Dept of Philos & Relig, Univ of No Iowa, Cedar Falls, IA 50614-0001. **EMAIL** james.robinson@atsuni.edu

ROBINSON, JOHN H.
PERSONAL Born 04/04/1943, Providence, RI, m, 1981, 2 children **DISCIPLINE** LAW AND PHILOSOPHY **EDUCATION** Boston Col, BA, 67; Univ Notre Dame, MA, 72; PhD, 75; Univ Calif Berkeley, JD, 79. **CAREER** Assoc prof, Univ of Notre Dame, 99-. **RESEARCH** Philosophy of law; legal ethics; education law. **SELECTED PUBLICATIONS** Auth, "The Compromise of '38 and the Federal Courts Today," Notre Dame Law Rev 4 (98); auth, "Physician Assisted Suicide: A Constitutional Crisis Resolved," Notre Dame J of Law, Ethics and Public Policy 4 (98); coauth, A Health Law Reader: An Interdisciplinary Approach, Carolina Acad Press, 99; auth, "A Symposium of the Implementation of 'Ex Corde Ecclesiae: Introduction,'" J of Col and Univ Law 23 (99). **CONTACT ADDRESS** Law School, Univ of Notre Dame, 123 Law School, PO Box R, Notre Dame, IN 46556. **EMAIL** john.h.robinson.1@nd.edu

ROBINSON, KEITH ALAN
PERSONAL Born 04/24/1963, London, England, m, 2 children **DISCIPLINE** PHILOSOPHY **EDUCATION** Univ Essex, BA, 87, MA 88; Univ Warwick, PhD, 95. **CAREER** Instr, Warwick Univ; instr, Open Univ adj in philos, Davenport Univ; vis Asst Prof in Philos, Grand Valley State Univ. **MEMBERSHIPS** Am Philos Asn. **RESEARCH** Continental philsophy; Twentieth-century French philosophy; American philosophy; Process thought; Ethics. **SELECTED PUBLICATIONS** Auth, "The Passion and the Pleasure: Foucault's Art of Not Being Oneself," J of the British Soc for Phenomenol, 99; "The Foucault/Deleuze Conjunction: Thought of the Outside" Philos Today, 99; auth, Michel Foucault's Freedom Thought: Thinking Otherwise Between Knowledge, Power & Self, Mellon Press, 00; auth Becoming Immortal: Deleuze, Whitehead and the Transformations of Science, Athlone Press (forthcoming). **CONTACT ADDRESS** 3959 Prairie SW, Grandville, MI 49418. **EMAIL** kar3959mjs@sprynet.com

ROBINSON, LYMAN R.
DISCIPLINE LAW **EDUCATION** Saskatchewan Univ, BA, 62, LLB, 63; Harvard Univ, LLM, 68. **CAREER** Law, Univ Victoria **RESEARCH** Debtor-creditor law; evidence; taxation; criminal law. **SELECTED PUBLICATIONS** Auth, British Columbia Debtor-Creditor Law and Precedents. **CONTACT ADDRESS** Fac of Law, Univ of Victoria, PO Box 2400, Victoria, BC, Canada V8W 3H7. **EMAIL** lrobinso@uvic.ca

ROBINSON, MARY ELIZABETH
PERSONAL Born 02/16/1946, Sallis, MS, d **DISCIPLINE** LAW **EDUCATION** Wartburg Coll Waverly IA, BA 1972; Univ of IA Coll of Law Iowa City, JD 1977-78. **CAREER** Mary E Robinson Law Office, atty 1979-; Coll of Law Univ of IA Iowa City, asst to dean of law 1977-79; Coll of Law Univ of IA, dir acad asst prog 1976-77; Martin Luther King Center for Vocational & Educ Training Waterloo IA, acting dir 1972-74; Educ Opportunity Prog Univ No IA Ceader Falls, dir on campus 1972-73. **HONORS AND AWARDS** Outstanding Black Grad Student Awd; AG Clark Awd Water Loo 1976; Achievement Awd NAACP Cedar Rapids Chap 1979; One of Top 10 Black Women Ldrs State of IA US Dept of Labor. **MEMBERSHIPS** Gov appointed bd mem IA State Dept of Pub Instr 1979-85; mem Nat Conf of Black Lawyers; mem Assn of Trial Lawyers of IA & Am; founder & pres Black Womens Civil Orgn Cedar Rapids IA 1978-; commr Human Rights Commn Cedar Rapids 1978-; dep IA-nE NAACP Legal Redress Commn; IA rep Nat Task Force to the White House Conf on Families 1980; IA del White House Conf on Families Minneapolis 1980; bd mem United Way of Linn Co Acad Ascholarship & Dean's List Wartburg Coll Waverly IA 1970-72; offered internship Washington Interns in Educ Inst for Educ Leadership Washington DC 1974-75. **CONTACT ADDRESS** Higley Bldg, Ste 315, Cedar Rapids, IA 52401.

ROBINSON, REGINALD L.
PERSONAL Born 12/02/1955, New York, NY, m **DISCIPLINE** LAW **EDUCATION** Howard Univ, BA, 81; Univ Chicago, MA, 83; Univ Pa, JD, 89. **CAREER** Staff Atty, Philadelphia City Coun, 89-90; Asst City Solicitor, Philadelphia, 90-91; Asst Prof, Whittier Law Sch, 91-93; Vis Asst Prof, Univ San Francisco Law Sch, 93; Vis Assoc Prof, Univ Conn Law Sch, 94; Assoc Prof to Prof, Howard Law Sch, 94-; Vis Prof, Ind Univ Sch of Law, 01-02. **HONORS AND AWARDS** Tinker Travel Grant, 84; Danforth-Compton Scholar, 81-84; Arthur Stadelmann Scholar, 84; Phi Beta Kappa; Charles N. Leighton Awd for Acad Excellence. **MEMBERSHIPS** Phi Beta Kappa; Am Bar Asn; Mid-Atlantic People of Color Legal Scholar Conf; Pa Bar Asn; Soc for Am Law Teachers; AALS. **RESEARCH** Understanding how individuals become cognitively aware of race and how such individuals acquire a race consciousness, using thus race and race thinking to find themselves in the world, to assess how others relate to them, and to determine in which degree they can succeed in the world. Understanding to what degree black or minority parents reinscribe their children not only with race but also with race consciousness, so that a

new generation becomes bounded, but not clearly determined, by racial affects and experiences, even if they have not personally suffered immediate forms of racial animus. Understanding the degree to which race and race consciousness, regardless of which social group relies upon them, erode or impede or undermine effective movements toward a color-blind or race neutral consciousness can take hold in America. Thus, understanding the degree to which blacks and other minorities play equally culpable roles in the perpetuation not only of racial conflict, but also of racism and race consciousness. **SELECTED PUBLICATIONS** Auth, "Impact of Hobbes' Empirical Natural Law on Title VII's Effectiveness: A Hegelian Critique," Conn Law Rev, 93; auth, "The Other Against Itself: Deconstruction the Violent Discourse between Koreans/African Americans," S Calif L Rev, 93; auth, "The Racial Limits of the Fair Housing Act: The Intersection of Dominant White Images, the Violence of Neighborhood Purity, and the Master Narrative of Black Inferiority," William and Mary L Rev, 95; auth, "White Cultural Matrix and the Language of Nonverbal Advertising in Housing Segregation: Toward an Aggregate Theory of Liability," Capital Univ L Rev, 96; auth, "Teaching from the Margins: Race as a Pedagogical Sub-Text," W New Eng L Rev, 97; auth, "Race, Myth, and Narrative in the Social Construction of the Black Self," Howard L J, 97; auth, "Race Consciousness: A Mere Means of Preventing Escapes from the Control of her White Masters," Touro L Rev, 00; auth, "Expert Knowledge: Introductory Comments on Race Consciousness," Boston Col Third World L J, 00; auth, "The Multiracial Category Movement and the Shift in the Race Consciousness Matrix: A Critical Reply to Professor Hernandez," Boston Col Third World L J, 00; auth, "Race Consciousness: Can Thick, Legal Contextual Analysis Assist the Poor, Low-Status Worker in Overcome Discriminatory Hurdle in the Fast Food Industry? A Critical Reply to Regina Austin," John Marshall L Rev, 01. **CONTACT ADDRESS** Sch of Law, Howard Univ, 2900 Van Ness St NW, Washington, DC 20008. **EMAIL** rrobinson@law.howard.edu

ROBINSON, WILLIAM SPENCER
PERSONAL Born 10/22/1940, Staten Island, NY, m, 1998, 2 children **DISCIPLINE** PHILOSOPHY **EDUCATION** Yale Univ, BA, 62; Ind Univ, PhD(Philos), 66. **CAREER** Asst prof Philos, Univ Iowa, 66-72; asst prof Philos, Iowa State Univ, 72-74; assoc prof Philos, Iowa State Univ; 74-83; prof Philos, Iowa State Univ, 83-; chmn of dept, 91-99. **MEMBERSHIPS** Am Philos Asn; Asn for the Sci Study of Consiousness. **RESEARCH** Philos of mind; analytical philos. **SELECTED PUBLICATIONS** Auth, Judgements involving identification, Analysis, 6/64; Brains and People, Temple, UP, 88; Computers, Minds and Robots, Temple, UP, 92. **CONTACT ADDRESS** Dept of Philos and Relig Studies, Iowa State Univ of Science and Tech, Ames, IA 50011-1306.

ROBSON, KENT E.
PERSONAL Born 10/11/1937, Ogden, UT, m, 1961, 4 children **DISCIPLINE** PHILOSOPHY **EDUCATION** Univ Utah, BA, 62; Stan Univ, PhD, 72. **CAREER** Res fel, Univ Warsaw, Pol, 63-64; prof, Ut State Univ, 64-. **HONORS AND AWARDS** Phi Beta Kappa; Phi Kappa Phi. **MEMBERSHIPS** APA. **RESEARCH** Philosophy of language; ethics; philosophy of religion; philosophy of history; history of philosophy. **SELECTED PUBLICATIONS** Auth, The Narrative Constitution, Rowman & Littlefield; auth, Readings in Philosophy, Simon & Schuster; auth, freedom and Responsibility, BYU; auth, Line Upon Line: Essays on Mormon Doctrine, Signature Press; auth, History and Objectivity, Signature Press. **CONTACT ADDRESS** Dept Languages, Philosophy, Utah State Univ, 720 University Blvd, Logan, UT 84322-0720. **EMAIL** kerobson@cc.usu.edu

ROCHE, MARK W.
PERSONAL Born 08/29/1956, Weymouth, MA, m, 1981 **DISCIPLINE** GERMAN LITERATURE, PHILOSOPHY **EDUCATION** Williams Col, BA, 78; Ederhard Karls Univ, MA, 80; Princeton Univ, MA, 82, PhD, 84. **CAREER** Teaching asst, Williams Col, 77-78; teaching asst, Phillips Andover Acad, 78; asst instr, Princeton Univ, 82-83; asst prof to assoc prof to dept chmn, Ohio State Univ, 84-96; dept chmn to prof to dean, Univ Notre Dame, 96-. **HONORS AND AWARDS** Alexander von Humboldt Fel, 97; Distinguished Vis Lectr, Wake For Univ, 95; DAAD Res Grant, 91; NEH, 91; ACLS Fel, 85; Fac Development Grant, 85; Whiting Fel, 83-84; Max Kade Fel, 81-82; Fulbright Fel, 78-80; Benedict Prize, 78; Phi Beta Kappa. **MEMBERSHIPS** AATG; AAUP; APA; GSA; HAS; MLA; SPSCVA; Lessing Soc. **RESEARCH** German literature; philosophy; film; higher education. **SELECTED PUBLICATIONS** Auth, "Laughter and Truth in Doktor Faustus: Nietzschean Structures in Mann's Novel of Self-cancellations," Deut Vierte Lit Geistes 60 (86): 309-32; auth, "Holiness and Justice: Lessing's Nathan der Weise in the Context of Plato's Euthyphro," Antike Abend 34 (88): 42-62; auth, "Schnitzler's Anatol as a Philosophical Comedy," Modern Austrian Lit 22 (89): 51-63; auth, Gottfried Benn's Static Poetry: Aesthetic and Intellectual-Historical Interpretations, Univ NCar Pr, 91; uth, Dynamic Stillness: Philosophical Conceptions of Ruhe in Schiller Holderlin Michner and Heine, Studies Deuts Lit, 92; auth, "Apel and Lessing--or: The Ethics of Communication and the Strategies of Comedy," Lessing Yearbk 25 (93): 41-54; co-auth, "Vico's Age of Heroes and the Age of Men in John Ford's Film The Man Who Shot Liberty Valance," CLIO 23 (94): 131-47; auth, Tragedy and Comedy: A Systematic Study and a Critique of Hegl, Univ NYork Pr, 98; auth, "Justice and the Withdrawal of God in Woody Allen's Crimes and Misdemeanors," Film Philol (00): 68-83. **CONTACT ADDRESS** 12418 Range Line Rd, Berrien Springs, MI 49103-9632. **EMAIL** mroche@nd.edu

ROCKEFELLER, STEVEN C.
DISCIPLINE HISTORY OF RELIGION, PHILOSOPHY OF RELIGION, AND RELIGION, ETHICS **EDUCATION** Princeton Univ, AB; Union Theol Sem, MDiv; Columbia Univ, PhD. **CAREER** Prof; Middlebury Col, 71-. **SELECTED PUBLICATIONS** Auth, John Dewey: Religious Faith and Democratic Humanism; co-ed, Spirit and Nature: Why the Environment is a Religious Issue-An Interfaith Dialogue. **CONTACT ADDRESS** Dept of Religion, Middlebury Col, Middlebury, VT 05753.

ROCKER, STEPHEN
PERSONAL Born 09/12/1953, Lowville, NY **DISCIPLINE** PHILOSOPHY **EDUCATION** Univ Ottawa, PhD, 90. **CAREER** Prof Philos, Wadhams Hall Sem Col, 82-. **MEMBERSHIPS** Hegel Soc Am; Am Philos Asn. **RESEARCH** Philosophy of religion; ethics; metaphysics; Hegel studies. **SELECTED PUBLICATIONS** Auth, Hegel's Rational Religion, 95; auth, The Integral Relation of Religion and Philosophy in Hegel's Philosophy of Religion, New Perspectives on Hegel's Philos of Relig, 92. **CONTACT ADDRESS** Dept of Philosophy, Wadhams Hall Sem-Col, 6866 State Hwy. 37, Ogdensburg, NY 13669-4420.

RODA, ANTHONY
PERSONAL Born 09/10/1939, Fossato Ionico, Calabria, Italy, d, 3 children **DISCIPLINE** PHILOSOPHY **EDUCATION** St Peter's Col, BA, 62; WA Univ, MA, 64; Southern IL Univ, PhD, 68. **CAREER** Instr, SUNY Oneonta, 67-69; assist prof, 69-70; assoc prof, 70-91; to prof, 91-; chmn of dept, 74-75; spring 80 (acting); 81-87, 91-93; dir of interdisciplinary studies 75-76; spring 80 (acting); 81-84; spring 91, SUNY, Col at Oneonta. **HONORS AND AWARDS** NEH Summer Inst, Yale Univ, 89; NEH Summer Inst, Dartmouth Col, 86; NEH Summer Inst, Yale Univ, 91; NEH Summer Sem, Yale Univ, 94. **MEMBERSHIPS** APA; Soc Asian Comp Philos; Dante Soc Am; Inst Vico Studies; NY State Found Educ Assn. **RESEARCH** Epistemology; Am philos; Giambattista Vico; Immanuel Kant. **SELECTED PUBLICATIONS** Trans, Dialectic of Abstract and Concrete in Whitehead, (Telos), 71; trans, History and Existence in Husserl's Manuscripts (Telos), 72; rev, Giuseppe Mazzotta's Dante's Vision and the Circle of Knowledge, Philosophy and Literature, 95; rev Berel Lang's Philosophy and the Art of Writing, Philosophy and Literature, 89; auth, The Federalist Papers: Political Principles and Educational Consequences, Educational Change, 87; De La Legitime Politique, Singuliers, 91; ed, Educational Change, 00, 99, 98, 97, 96, 95. **CONTACT ADDRESS** Dept of Philosophy, SUNY, Col at Oneonta, Oneonta, NY 13820. **EMAIL** rodaa@oneonta.edu

RODAS, M. DANIEL CARROLL
PERSONAL m, 1976, 2 children **DISCIPLINE** OLD TESTAMENT **EDUCATION** Dallas Theol Sem, ThM; Univ Sheffield, PhD. **CAREER** Prof, Denver Sem, 96-. **MEMBERSHIPS** Society of Biblical Literature, Inst for Biblical Res, Society for Old Testament Study, Evangelical Theo Society, Latin Am Studies Asn, Fratenidad Teologica Latinoamerica. **RESEARCH** Prophetic literature, Old Testament ethics, and the use of the Bible in the Third World **SELECTED PUBLICATIONS** Auth, Contexts for Amos: Prophetic Poetics in Latin Amer Perspective; co-ed, The Bible in Ethics and The Bible in Human Society: Essays in Honour of John Rogerson. **CONTACT ADDRESS** Denver Conservative Baptist Sem, PO Box 100000, Denver, CO 80250. **EMAIL** danny.carrollr@densem.edu

RODDEN, KIRK A.
DISCIPLINE POLITICAL SCIENCE **EDUCATION** NE State Univ, BA, 88; Okla State Univ, MA, 90. **CAREER** Instructor to Asst Prof, Murray State Col, 90-. **HONORS AND AWARDS** Neustadt Awd for Teaching Excellence, 96; Political Sci Teacher of the Year, 99. **MEMBERSHIPS** Okla Polit Sci Asn. **RESEARCH** Oklahoma Political History - State and Local Government. **SELECTED PUBLICATIONS** Rev, of "The Lost Promise of Progressivism," Journal of Oklahoma Politics, 95. **CONTACT ADDRESS** Dept Arts & Sci, Murray State Col, 1 Murray Campus St, Tishomingo, OK 73460-3137. **EMAIL** krodden@msc.cc.ok.us

RODDY, NICOLAE
PERSONAL Born 03/05/1954, Lincoln, NE, d, 1 child **DISCIPLINE** RELIGIOUS STUDIES **EDUCATION** Univ of Nebraska at Omaha, BA; St Vladimir's Orthodox Theol Seminary, Crestwood, NYork, MA; Univ of Iowa, PhD. **CAREER** Asst prof, Creighton Univ; lect, Univ Neb-Omaha, 95- . **HONORS AND AWARDS** Fulbright Scholar, 94-95, to Romania; Soc of Biblical Lit Regional Scholar Awd, 98. **MEMBERSHIPS** AAR, SBL. **RESEARCH** Pseudoepigraphical and Apocryphal Literature. **SELECTED PUBLICATIONS** Auth, The Campaign for Catholicity in the Letters of St Ignatius of Antioch, Coptic Church Review, 91; The Form and Function of the Protevangelium of James, Coptic Church Review, 93; Two Parts: Weeks of Seven Weeks: The End of the Age as Terminus ad Quem for 2, Syriac Apocalypse of Baruch, Journal for the Study of the Pseudepigrapha, 96. **CONTACT ADDRESS** Dept of Theology, Creighton Univ, 2500 California Plaza, Omaha, NE 68178. **EMAIL** nroddy@creighton.edu

RODES, ROBERT EMMET
PERSONAL Born 05/29/1927, New York, NY, m, 1953, 7 children **DISCIPLINE** LAW **EDUCATION** Harvard, LLB (JD), 52; Brown, AB, 47. **CAREER** Attorney, Lib Mut Ins Co, 52-54; Rutgers Univ, Asst Prof, 54-56; Notre Dame, Asst prof, Assoc prof, Prof, 56-. **RESEARCH** Law and Theology **SELECTED PUBLICATIONS** Pilgrim Law, 98; Premises and Conclusions, with H Pospesel, 97. **CONTACT ADDRESS** Univ of Notre Dame, School Law, Notre Dame, IN 46556. **EMAIL** rodes.1@nd.edu

RODGERS, SANDA
DISCIPLINE LAW **EDUCATION** Univ Case Reserve, BA; McGill Univ, LLB, LLM. **CAREER** Prof, Univ of Ottawa. **RESEARCH** Canadian health law; women's health. **SELECTED PUBLICATIONS** Auth, pubs on health law. **CONTACT ADDRESS** Fac Common Law, Univ of Ottawa, Fauteux Hall, 57 Louis Pasteur, Ottawa, ON, Canada K1N 6N5. **EMAIL** srodgers@uottawa.ca

RODRIGUES, HILLARY
DISCIPLINE RELIGIOUS STUDIES **EDUCATION** McMaster Univ, BA, 86; MA, 88; PhD, 93. **RESEARCH** Religions of India; anthropology of religion; philosophy and culture; medieval and modern hinduism. **SELECTED PUBLICATIONS** Auth, pubs on the contemporary religious teacher Jiddu Krishnamurti and popular Hindu goddess Durga. **CONTACT ADDRESS** Dept of Religious Studies, Univ of Lethbridge, 4401 University Dr W, Lethbridge, AB, Canada T1K 3M4. **EMAIL** rodrigues@hg.uleth.ca

RODRIGUEZ, ANGEL MANUEL
PERSONAL Born 05/06/1945, Cidra, PR, m, 1967, 2 children **DISCIPLINE** THEOLOGY **EDUCATION** Antillian Col, PR, BA, 68; Andrews Univ Theol Sem, MDiv, 70, ThD, 79. **CAREER** Dis Pastor, PR, 70-73; Acad Bible Tchr, PR, 73-75; asst prof, Antillian Col, 79-80, acad vice-pres, 81-82, pres, 83-87; prof, Southwestern Adventist Univ, 87-89, acad vice-pres, 89-92; assoc dir, Biblical Res Inst, 92- . **MEMBERSHIPS** Soc Bibl Lit; Am Acad Relig; Adventist Theol Soc. **RESEARCH** Hebrew cultus; wisdom literature. **SELECTED PUBLICATIONS** Auth, Substitution in the Hebrew Cultus, Andrews Univ, 82; auth, El rapto secreto de la iglesia, Pacific, 93; auth, Stewardship Roots, Church Ministries, 94; auth, Health and Healing in the Pentateuch, in Health 2000 and Beyond: A Study Conference of Adventist Theology, Philosophy, and Practice of Health and Healing, Home Study Int, 94; auth, Esther: A Theological Approach, Andrews Univ, 95; auth, Fin del mundo o muevo comienzo? Pacific, 96; auth, Leviticus 16: Its Literary Structure, Andrew Univ Sem Stud, 96; auth, Jewelry in the OT: A Description of Its Function, in Merling, ed, To Understand the Scriptures: Essays in Honor of William H. Shea, Inst of Archaeol, 97. **CONTACT ADDRESS** Biblical Research Inst, 12501 Old Columbia Pike, Silver Spring, MD 20904-6600.

RODRIGUEZ, JOSE DAVID
DISCIPLINE THEOLOGY **EDUCATION** Lutheran Sch Theol at Chicago, PhD. **CAREER** Dir, Hisp Ministry Prog; vis prof, Sem Evangel de Puerto Rico; Comunidad Teologica de Mexico; assoc prof-. **HONORS AND AWARDS** Co-ch, planner of the First Encuentro of Hispanic-Latina Theologians and Ethicists, Princeton Theol Sem. **SELECTED PUBLICATIONS** Pub(s), articles on Hispanics in the church to The Lutheran. **CONTACT ADDRESS** Dept of Theology, Lutheran Sch of Theol at Chicago, 1100 E 55th St, Chicago, IL 60615. **EMAIL** jrodrigu@lstc.edu

RODRIGUEZ-HOLGUIN, JEANETTE
PERSONAL Born 01/04/1954, NY, m, 1983, 2 children **DISCIPLINE** THEOLOGY **EDUCATION** Queens Col, BA, 76; Fordham Univ, MA, 78; Univ Guam, MA, 81; Grad Theol Union, PhD, 90. **CAREER** From asst prof to assoc prof to chemn, 90-, Seattle Univ. **HONORS AND AWARDS** Who's Who Among Hispanic Am, 91-92; Nat Hispana Leadership Inst Fel, 94; Assoc Status, 98, United Holocaust Mus; partial scholar, grad theol union, 84; nat hispana leadership inst fel, 94; summer fac fel award, 98. **MEMBERSHIPS** Am Asn Marriage and Family Therapy. **RESEARCH** US Hispanic theology; cultural memory; women's spirituality; religion and culture. **SELECTED PUBLICATIONS** Auth, Our Lady of Guadalupe: Faith and Empowerment Among Mexican-American Women, 94; auth, Stories We Live: Cuentos que Vivimos, 96; ed, Isasi-Diaz and Mujerista Theology, 96; ed, Cultural Memory: Source of Theological Insight, 96. **CONTACT ADDRESS** Dept of Theology and Religious Studies, Seattle Univ, Seattle, WA 98122. **EMAIL** jrodrigu@seattleu.edu

ROE, MARK J.
PERSONAL Born 08/08/1951, New York, NY, m, 1975, 2 children **DISCIPLINE** LAW **EDUCATION** Columbia Col, BA, 72; Harvard Law Sch, JD, 75. **RESEARCH** Corporate governance, Public choice, Bankruptcy. **SELECTED PUBLICATIONS** Auth, "Some Differences in Coporate Structure in Germany, Japan, and the United States," Yale Law J 1927 (93); auth, Strong Managers, Weak Owners: The Political Roots of American Corporate Finance, Princeton Univ Press, 94; auth, "Chaos and Evolution in Law and Economics," 109 Harvard Law Rev 641 (96); auth, "Blacklas," Columbia Law Rev 217 (98); auth, "Comparative Corporate Governance," in Palgrave Dictionary on Law and Economics (98); auth, "German Securities Markets and German Codetermination," 98 Columbia Bus Law Rev 167 (98); coauth, "The Political Economy of Japanese Lifetime Employment," in Employee's Role in Corporate Governance, by Margaret Blair & Mark Roe (Brookings Inst, 99); coauth, "A Theory Path Dependence in Corporate Ownership and Governance," 52 Stanford Law Rev 127 (99); auth, Corporate Bankruptcy and Reorganization: Legal and Financial Materials, Found Press, fortchoming; auth, Political Foundations to separations Ownershiip from Control, 52. **CONTACT ADDRESS** Sch of Law, Columbia Univ, 435 W 116th St, New York, NY 10027-7201. **EMAIL** more@law.columbia.edu

ROGERS, ISABEL WOOD
PERSONAL Born 08/26/1924, Tallahassee, FL **DISCIPLINE** RELIGION **EDUCATION** Fla State Univ, AB, 45; Univ Va, MA, 47; Presby Sch Christian Educ, MRE, 49; Duke Univ, PhD, 61. **CAREER** Dir student work, First Presby Church, Milledgeville, Ga, 49-52; instr relig & chaplain, Women's Col, Ga, 52-61; Prof Appl Christianity, Presby Sch Christian Educ, 61-98, Kent fel, Soc Relig Higher Educ, 58. **HONORS AND AWARDS** DD, Austin Col; LLD, Westminster Col; DD Centre Col. **RESEARCH** Christianity and politics; church and women; reformed theology. **SELECTED PUBLICATIONS** Auth, The Christian and World Affairs, 64 & In Response to God: How Christians Make Ethical Decisions, 69, CLC Press; Sing a New Song, United Presby Church US Am, 80; Our Shared Earth, CE:SA Press, 80. **CONTACT ADDRESS** 1214 Palanyra Ave, Richmond, VA 23227-4435.

ROGERS, W. KIM
DISCIPLINE PHILOSOPHY **EDUCATION** New Sch Soc Res, PhD. **CAREER** Prof emer, E Tenn State Univ. **RESEARCH** Contemporary continental philosophy. **SELECTED PUBLICATIONS** Auth, Hegel and Fukuyama, 87; Existentialism is not Irrationalism: A Challenge to the Common Interpretation of Existentialism, J British Soc Phenomenology, 89; Ortega's Development of an Ecological Philosophy, J Hist Ideas, 94. **CONTACT ADDRESS** Philosophy Dept, East Tennessee State Univ, Johnson City, TN 37614-1701. **EMAIL** rogersk@etsu.edu

ROGNESS, MICHAEL
DISCIPLINE HOMILETICS **EDUCATION** Augustana Col, BA; Luther Sem, SD, 56, BD, 60; Erlangen/Nurnberg Univ, ThD, 63. **CAREER** Instr, Inst for Ecumenical Res, Lutheran World Federation, Strasbourg, France, 67-70; assoc prof, 85; prof, 93-. **HONORS AND AWARDS** Fulbright scholar, Erlangen/Nurnberg Univ, 63; pastor, st john's lutheran church, 64-67; first lutheran church, 70-85. **SELECTED PUBLICATIONS** Auth, Philip Melanchthon, Reformer, 69; The Church Nobody Knows - The Shape of the Future Church, 71; Follow Me, 77; Lutheran Doctrine, 84; The Hand that Holds Me - How God's Grace Touches Our Lives, 84; Hope in a Threatening World, 91; Preaching to a TV Generation - The Sermon in the Electronic Age, 95. **CONTACT ADDRESS** Dept of Homiletics, Luther Sem, 2481 Como Ave, Saint Paul, MN 55108. **EMAIL** mrogness@luthersem.edu

ROHATYN, DENNIS ANTHONY
PERSONAL Born 04/21/1949, New York, NY, d, 2 children **DISCIPLINE** PHILOSOPHY **EDUCATION** Queens Col, BA, 68; City Col New York, MA, 69; Fordham Univ, PhD(Philos), 72. **CAREER** Asst prof Philos, Roosevelt Univ, 72-77; assoc prof Philos, Univ San Diego, 77-; prof, 82. **HONORS AND AWARDS** Lowell Davies Awd for Outstanding Faculty Achievement, 87; Class of 91 prof of the yr. **MEMBERSHIPS** Am Philos Asn; Am Cath Philos Assn; Soc for the Advancemtn of Am Philosophy; Am Soc for Value Inquiry; Phi Beta Kappa, 67-. **RESEARCH** History of philosophy; phd & lit;contemporary philosophy; ethics and value theory. **SELECTED PUBLICATIONS** Auth, Naturalism and Deontology: An Essay on the Problems of Ethics, Mouton, 76; Two Dogmas of Philosophy and other Essays on the Philosophy of Philosophy, Assoc Univ, 77; Bennett on Kant, Kant-Studien, 78; What are Kant's presuppositions, Brit J Phenomenol, 78; Resurrecting Peirce's Neglected Argument for God, 82 & Peirce and the Defense of Realism (in prep), Trans C S Peirce Soc; Hume's Dialectical Conceits: The Case of Dialogue XII, Philos & Phenomenol Res; Aristotle and the Limits of Philosophic Proof, Nature & System; Philosophy/History/Sophistry, Rodopi, 99. **CONTACT ADDRESS** Dept of Philosophy, Univ of San Diego, 5998 Alcala Park, San Diego, CA 92110-2492. **EMAIL** drohatyn@acusd.edu

ROHR, MICHAEL D.
PERSONAL Born 04/02/1940, Bronx, NY, m, 1987, 3 children **DISCIPLINE** PHILOSOPHY **EDUCATION** Harvard Col , AB, 62; Stanford Univ, PhD, 75. **CAREER** Instr, C/ W Post Coll, 66-68; instr, Univ Pittsburgh, 68-69; instr, Rutgers Univ 72-75; asst prof, 75-79; Assoc Prof, 79-. **MEMBERSHIPS** Am Philos Asn; Soc for Ancient Greek Philos; NY Ancient Philos Colloquium. **RESEARCH** Plato; Aristotle; Richard Rorty. **SELECTED PUBLICATIONS** Auth, Empty Forms in Plato, Arh for Geschichte der Philosophie, 78; Rorty Richard, Routledge Encycl of Philos, 98. **CONTACT ADDRESS** Rutgers, The State Univ of New Jersey, Newark, 427 Conklin Hall, Newark, NJ 07102. **EMAIL** rohr@alumni.stanford.orgMichael_Rohr_ab61@post.harvard.edu

ROHRBAUGH, RICHARD L.
PERSONAL Born 12/12/1936, Addis Ababa, Ethiopia, m, 1960, 2 children **DISCIPLINE** RELIGIOUS STUDIES **EDUCATION** Sterling Col, BA, 58; Pittsburgh Theol Sem, MDiv, 61; San Francisco Theol Sem, STD, 77. **CAREER** Pastor, Tri-City Presbyterian Church, Myrtle Creek, Ore, 61-68; pastor, St. Mark Presbyterian Church, Portland, Ore, 68-77; from asst prof to prof, Lewis and Clark Col, 77-. **HONORS AND AWARDS** James C. Purdy Sch, 59-60; Fund for Theol Educ Fel, 70-72; Outstanding Young Men of America, 72; Who's Who in Religion, 84; Who's Who in Biblical Studies and Archaeology, 85-. **MEMBERSHIPS** Am Acad of Relig; Soc of Bibl Lit; Cath Bibl Asn; Am Schs of Oriental Res; The Context Group. **RESEARCH** Social-scientific criticism of the New Testament; social world of early Christianity; New Testament hermeneutics. **SELECTED PUBLICATIONS** Auth, The Biblical Interpreter: An Agrarian Bible in an Industrial World, 78; Into All the World: A Basic Overview of the New Testament, 80; Methodological Considerations in the Debate over the Social Class Status of Early Christians, in J of the Am Acad of Relig, LII/3, 84; Parables: Occasions for the Unexpected, in Pacific Theol Rev, 84; Interpretation: An Introduction to the Study of the Bible, 85; Social Location of Thought as a Heuristic Device on New Testament Interpretation, in Jour for the Study of the New Testament 30, 87; Models and Muddles, in Foundations and Facets Forum 3,2, 87; Church Canon or Scholars' Canon?, in Fourth R 2,3, 89; The Patronage System in Roman Palestine, in Fourth R 3,1, 90; The City in the Second Testament: A Reader's Guide, in Bibl Theol Bull, 21/2, 91; The Social Location of the Markan Audience, in Bibl Theol Bull 23/3, 93; A Peasant Reading of the Parable of the Talents: A Text of Terror? In Bibl Theol Bull 22/4, 93; The Progress of the Gospel: From Jerusalem to Rome, in The Bible Today 31/1, 93; Social Science and Literary Criticism: What is at Stake?, in Hervormde Teologiese Studies 49/1, 93; Autobiographical Criticism: A Social-Scientific Response, in Semeia 72, 95; coauth, Social Science Commentary on the Synoptic Gospels, 92; Los evangelicos sinopticos y la cultura mediterranea del siglo I: Comentario desde las ciencias sociales, 96; Social Science Commentary on the Gospel of John, 98; ed, Using the Social Sciences in New Testament Interpretation, 96; rev, The Orphan Gospel: Mark's Perspective on Jesus, in Crit Rev of Books in Relig, 94; Feasting and Social Rhetoric in Luke 14, in Soc for New Testament Studies, Monograph Series 85, 95. **CONTACT ADDRESS** Religious Studies Dept, Lewis and Clark Col, Portland, OR 97219. **EMAIL** rbaugh@lclark.edu

ROHRER, JAMES
PERSONAL Born 05/13/1960, Canton, OH, m, 1994, 2 children **DISCIPLINE** RELIGIOUS STUDIES **EDUCATION** Kent State Univ, BA, 82; Ohio State Univ, MA, 85, PhD, 91; Univ Dubuque Theol Sem, MDiv, 95. **CAREER** Asst prof, Presbyterian Bible Col, 93-96; asst prof, Yushan Theol Sem, 96-98; asst prof, Northwestern Col, 98-. **HONORS AND AWARDS** Who's Who Among America's Teachers, 00. **MEMBERSHIPS** Am Acad of Relig; Am Soc of Church Hist; Asn for Asian Studies; Conf on Faith and Hist. **RESEARCH** History of Christian mission; Christianity in the non-western world; Taiwanese Christianity; Am religious hist. **SELECTED PUBLICATIONS** Auth, "Sunday Mails & The Church State Theme in Jacksonian America," Journal of the Early Republic, 87; auth, "The Origins of the Temperance Movement: A Reinterpretation," Journal of American Studies, 90; auth, Keepers of the Covenant: Frontier Missions and the Decline of Congregationalism, 1774-1818; "German Presbyterians or Christian Americans? Intercollegiate Sports and the Identity Crisis at the University of Dubuque, 1902-1927," in Am Presbyterians, 96; auth, "The Connecticut Missionary Society and Book Distribution in the Early Republic," Libraries & Culture, 99. **CONTACT ADDRESS** 101 7th St SW, Orange City, IA 51041-1996. **EMAIL** rohrer@esther.nwciowa.edu

ROLAND, GERARD
PERSONAL Born 10/03/1954, Jemappes, Belgium, m, 1980, 3 children **DISCIPLINE** ECONOMICS **EDUCATION** Univ Libre de Bruxelles, BA, 83; MA, 84; PhD, 88. **CAREER** Teaching asst to prof, ULB, 83-01; prof, Univ Calif Berkeley, 01-. **HONORS AND AWARDS** CEPR Res Fel, 91; Fel, William Davidson Inst, 97; Medal of the Univ Helsinki, 96; Off de l'Ordre de Leopold II, 97; Who's Who in Econ since 1776; Who's Who in the World. **MEMBERSHIPS** Asn for Comparative Econ; Europ Econ Asn. **RESEARCH** Economics of transition from socialism to capitalism; Political economics. **SELECTED PUBLICATIONS** Co-auth, "Economic Reform and Dynamic Political Constraints," Rev Econ Studies, (92): 703-730; co-auth, "The Design of Reform Packages under Uncertainty," Am Econ Rev, (95): 107-1223; co-auth, "The Breakup of Nations: A Political Economy Analysis," Quart J Econ, (97): 1057-1090; co-auth, "Separation of Powers and Political Accountability," Quart J Econ, (97): 1163-1202; co-auth, Federalism and the Soft Budget Constraint," Am Econ Rev, (98): 1143-1162; co-auth, "Reform Without Losers: An Interpretation of China's Dual-Track Approach to Reforms," J Polit Econ, 00; co-auth, "Comparative Politics and Public Finance," J Polit Econ, 00; auth, Transition and Economics: Politics, Markets and Firms, MIT Press, 00. **CONTACT ADDRESS** Dept Econ, Univ of California, Berkeley, 549 Evans Hall, No 3880, Berkeley, CA 94720-3880. **EMAIL** groland@econ.berkeley.edu

ROLL, SUSAN K.
PERSONAL Born Clarence Center, NY **DISCIPLINE** THEOLOGY **EDUCATION** Niagara Univ, BA, 74; Saint Bernard's Sem, MA, 80; Cath Univ Louvain, Leuven, Belgium, STB, 88; PhD, 93. **CAREER** Campus Minister, Ithaca Col, 76-85; Doctoral Asst, Cath Univ of Louvain, Leuven, Belgium, 89-95; Asst Prof, Christ the King Sem, 95-. **HONORS AND AWARDS** Walter J. Schmitz Chair in Liturgical Studies, Cath Univ of Am, Wash DC, 96; Vis Fel, Sanum Col Salisburg, Eng, 00. **MEMBERSHIPS** Am Acad of Rel, N Am Acad of Liturgy, Societas Liturgica, Cath Theol Soc of Am, Europ Soc of Women in Theol Res. **SELECTED PUBLICATIONS** Auth, Toward the Origins of Christmas, Liturgia Condenda 6, Kok Pharos (Kampen, The Netherlands), 95, and Peeters Press (Leuven); co-ed, Re-Visioning Our Sources. Women's Spirituality in European Perspectives, Kok Pharos (Kampen, The Netherlands), 97; auth, "The Future of the Eucharist: new thinking, fresh optimism," Jaarboek voor liturgie-onderzoek 13 (97): 167-174; auth, "The Debate on the Origins of Christmas," Archiv fur Liturgiewissenschaft 40/1-2 (98): 1-16; auth, "Christ as Sun/King: the historical roots of a perduring dualism," in Feminist Perspectives in Pastoral Theology, Yearbk of Europ Soc of Women in Theol Res Vol 6, ed. Hedwig Meyer-Wilmes, Lieve Troch and Riet Bons-Storm (Leuven: Peeters and Mainz: Matthias-Gruenwald, 98): 133-142; auth, "Risen to New Life. A feminist reading of the Easter Triduum," Papers of the LAUD Linguistics Agency, Universitat Gesamthochschule Eseen, Series A: General and Theoretical Papers (Essen: LAUD, 99), Paper 504; auth, "Christmas Then and Now. Reflections on its origins and contemporary pastoral problems," Worship 73-6 (Nov 99): 505-521; auth, "Weihnachten I. Liturgiegeschichtlich," in Lexikon fur Theologie und Kirche(Freiburg: Herder, forthcoming); auth, "Women's Liturgical Spirituality," in Handbook of Spirituality for Ministers Vol II, ed. Robert J. Wicks (Mahwah, NJ: Paulist Press, forthcoming); auth, "The Origins of Christmas. The State of the Question," in Between Memory and Hope. Readings on the Liturgical Year, ed. Maxwekk E. Johnson (Pueblo Books/ Liturgical Press, forthcoming). **CONTACT ADDRESS** Dept of Syst Theol and Liturgy, Christ the King Sem, PO Box 607, East Aurora, NY 14052-0607. **EMAIL** skroll1@juno.com

ROLLIN, BERNARD E.
PERSONAL Born 02/18/1943, New York City, NY, m, 1964, 1 child **DISCIPLINE** PHILOSOPHY **EDUCATION** Columbia Univ, PhD, 72; CCNY, BA. **CAREER** Prof. **HONORS AND AWARDS** Brownlee Awd for Animal Welfare Science; Colorado Vet Med Assoc Service Awd; Honors Prof, CSU. **RESEARCH** Traditional philosophy; applied philosophy. **SELECTED PUBLICATIONS** Auth, Natural and Conventional Meaning, 76; Animal Rights and Human Morality, 81; The Unheeded Cry: Animal Consciousness, Animal Pain and Scientific Change, 88; Farm Animal Welfare, 95; The Frankenstein Syndrome, 95; ed, The Experimental Animal in Biomedical Research, 95; auth, Veterinary Medical Ethics, 99. **CONTACT ADDRESS** Philosophy Dept, Colorado State Univ, Fort Collins, CO 80523. **EMAIL** berhard-rollin@colostate.edu

ROLLINS, RICHARD ALBERT
PERSONAL Born 11/30/1927, Philadelphia, PA, m **DISCIPLINE** THEOLOGY **EDUCATION** Lincoln Univ, AB 1952; Union Theological Seminary, MDiv 1955; Boston Univ School of Theology, STM 1960; Claremont School of Theology, RelD 1969. **CAREER** Bishop Coll, chmn div of rel 1958-67, assoc dean/admin 1969-70, dean of the college 1970-77, vice pres for pme/prof of religion 1977-83, exec asst to pres dean of chapel 1983-. **HONORS AND AWARDS** Danforth Foundation Teacher Awd 1960-62; Ford Foundation Fellowship Awd 1967; Dallas Citizenship Awd Radio Station KNOK 1970. **MEMBERSHIPS** Mem Goals for Dallas, Natl Urban League, NAACP, Natl Campus Ministry Assoc, Acad of Religion, TX Alcohol/Narcotics Assoc; bd of dirs Dallas YMCA; chmn-Moorland Branch YMCA 1969-85. **CONTACT ADDRESS** Exec Asst to the President, Bishop Col, 3837 Simpson Stuart Rd, Dallas, TX 75241.

ROLLINS, WAYNE GILBERT
PERSONAL Born 08/24/1929, Detroit, MI, m, 1953, 3 children **DISCIPLINE** RELIGION **EDUCATION** Capital Univ, BA, 51; Yale Univ, BD, 54, MA, 56, PhD, 60. **CAREER** Instr relig, Princeton Univ, 58-59; asst prof Bibl hist, Wellesley Col, 59-66; from assoc prof to prof New Testament, Hartford Sem Found, 66-74; prof Relig Studies, dir Ecumenical Inst & coordr

Grad Prog Relig Studies, Assumption Col, 74-99, minister, United Church of Christ, 58-; Huber Found fel, 60-61; vis prof, Colgate Rochester Divinity Sch, 68, dept relig studies, Yale Univ, 68-69, Greater Hartford Community Col, 69, St Joseph Col, 71, Mt Holyoke Col, 72 & Col of the Holy Cross, 76-77; Am Asn Theol Schs fel, 70. **HONORS AND AWARDS** Pope John Paul medal for ecumenical service, 00. **MEMBERSHIPS** Soc Bibl Lit; Am Acad Relig; AAUP; Soc New Testament Studies. **RESEARCH** Biblical theology; hermeneutics; psychology and Biblical studies. **SELECTED PUBLICATIONS** Auth, The Gospels, Portraits of Christ, Westminster, 64; God and the New Critics, Can Forum, 6/65; The New Testament and Apocalyptic, New Testament Studies, 7/71; De Pythiae Oraculis, In: Plutarch's Theological Writings and Early Christian Literature, Brill, 75; Slavery in the New Testament, In: Interpreter's Dictionary of the Bible Supplement, Abingdon, 76; Christological Tendenz in Colossians 1: 15-20: A Theologia Crucis, In: Christological Perspectives, 82; auth, Jung and the Bible, John Knox, 83; auth, Psychology, Hermeneutics, and the Bible, in, Jung and the Interpretation of the Bible, Continuum, 95; auth, The Bible and Psychology: New Directions in Biblical Scholarship, Pastoral Psychol, 97; auth, Soul and Psychel: The Bible in Psychological Perspective, Fortress, 99. **CONTACT ADDRESS** Assumption Col, 75 Craigmoor Rd, West Hartford, CT 06107-1212. **EMAIL** wrollins@worldnet.att.net

ROLNICK, PHILIP
PERSONAL Born 06/27/1949, Pittsburgh, PA, m, 1975, 2 children **DISCIPLINE** THEOLOGY **EDUCATION** Duke Univ, PhD, 89. **CAREER** Prof, 89-, dept relig, dir, Ethics Across Cur, 95-, Greensboro Col. **MEMBERSHIPS** AAR; Soc of Christian Ethics; Michael Polany Soc; Pen Trust Seminar in Christian Scholarship, 99; Center of Theological Inquiry, Princeton, 00-01. **RESEARCH** Religious lang; science & religion; social ethics. **SELECTED PUBLICATIONS** Auth, Analogical Possibilities: How Words Refer to God, Atlanta Scholars Press, 93; ed, Explorations in Ethics: Readings form Across the Curriculum, Greensboro Col Press, 98. **CONTACT ADDRESS** Dept of Religion & Philosophy, Greensboro Col, 815 W Market St, Greensboro, NC 27401-1875. **EMAIL** rolnickp@gborocollege.edu

ROLSTON, HOLMES
PERSONAL Born 11/19/1932, Staunton, VA, m, 1956, 2 children **DISCIPLINE** PHILOSOPHY **EDUCATION** Davidson Col, BS, 53; Union Theol Sem, BD, 56, Univ of Edinburgh, PhD, 58; Univ of Pittsburgh, MA, 68. **CAREER** Pastor, Walnut Grove Presby Church, 59-67; prof, Colo State Univ, 68-. **HONORS AND AWARDS** Gifford Lectr; Univ Distinguished Prof, Colo State Univ. **MEMBERSHIPS** Int Soc for Environ Ethics; Soc for Conserv Biology. **RESEARCH** Environmental Ethics, Science and Religion, Biology. **CONTACT ADDRESS** Dept Philos, Colorado State Univ, 1 Colorado State, Fort Collins, CO 80523-0001. **EMAIL** rolston@lamar.colostate.edu

ROLWING, RICHARD J.
PERSONAL Born 03/18/1929, Indianapolis, IN, m, 1964, 5 children **DISCIPLINE** THEOLOGY **EDUCATION** Cath Univ, BA, 55; Kennick Seminary, BD, 62; Notre Dame Univ, MA, 64. **CAREER** Asst prof, Univ Dayton, Xavier Univ. **MEMBERSHIPS** AAR, SBL, ACPA, CBA, SCP, SPR, Mantain Soc, Rahner Soc, Fel of Cath Scholars, Cardinal Newman Soc, Federalist Soc, CCICA. **RESEARCH** Political Philosophy. **SELECTED PUBLICATIONS** Auth, Israels Original Sin: A Catholic Confession, Intl Sch Publ, 94; auth, My Daily Constitution: a Natural Law Perspective, Xlibris Corporation, 00. **CONTACT ADDRESS** 7651 Burkey, Reynoldsburg, OH 43068. **EMAIL** dicrolwing@aol.com

ROMAN, ERIC
PERSONAL Born 03/26/1926, Bekescsaba, Hungary, m, 1953, 2 children **DISCIPLINE** MODERN HISTORY, WESTERN PHILOSOPHY **EDUCATION** Hunter Col, BA, 58; NYork Univ, MA, 59, PhD(Hist), 65. **CAREER** From instr to assoc prof, 65-77, prof Hist, Western Conn State Univ, 77-. **HONORS AND AWARDS** Americanism Medal, Nat Daughters Am Revolution, 70. **MEMBERSHIPS** AHA. **RESEARCH** Modern German history; immediate origins of World War II; diplomacy of interwar period. **SELECTED PUBLICATIONS** Auth, The Best Shall Die, Prentice-Hall, 61, Davies, London, 61 & Plaza & Janes, Madrid, 64; After the Trial, Citadel, 68 & Carl Scherz, Berne, 69; Munich and Hungary, Eastern Europ Quart, 74; Will, Hope and the Noumenon, J Philos, 2/75; A Year as a Lion, Stein & Day, 9/78; Hungary and the Victor Powers, New York, St Martin's Press, 96; auth, The Stalin Years in Hungary, The Edwin Mellen Press, 99. **CONTACT ADDRESS** 181 White St, Danbury, CT 06810-6826. **EMAIL** romane@wsu.ctstateu.edu

ROMANS, J. THOMAS
PERSONAL Born 12/26/1933, Yonkers, NY, m, 1979, 2 children **DISCIPLINE** ECONOMICS **EDUCATION** Cornell Univ, BS 55; Univ Tenn, MS 57; Brown Univ, PhD 63. **CAREER** State Univ of NY Buffalo, assoc prof. **HONORS AND AWARDS** New Eng Pub Prize **MEMBERSHIPS** AEA **RESEARCH** Law & Economics; Reg Economics. **SELECTED PUBLICATIONS** Auth, Incomplete Markets and the Calculation of Economic Loss, coauth, in: Jour of Forensic Econ, 96; The Annals of the Latin American Debt Crisis, coauth, in: Jour of For Ex and Intl Fin, 94; The Estimation of Retirement Age in the Calculation of Earning Loss, coauth, in: Jour of Leg Econ, 93. **CONTACT ADDRESS** Dept of Economics, SUNY, Buffalo, 423 Fronczak Hall, Amherst, NY 14260. **EMAIL** roman@acsu.buffalo.edu

ROOKS, CHARLES SHELBY
PERSONAL Born 10/19/1924, Beaufort, NC, m **DISCIPLINE** THEOLOGY **EDUCATION** VA State Coll, AB 1949; Union Theol Sem, MDiv 1953; Coll of Wooster, DD 1968; Interdenominational Theol Ctr, DD 1979; VA Union Univ, DD 1980. **CAREER** Shanks Vill Protestant Church Orangeburg, pastor 1951-53; Lincoln Meml Temple United Church of Christ Washington, pastor 1953-60; Fund for Theol Educ Princeton, assoc dir 1960-67, exec dir 1967-74; Chicago Theol Sem, pres 1974-84; United Church Bd for Homeland Ministries, exec vice pres, 84-92. **HONORS AND AWARDS** Distinguished Service Medal, Association of Theological Schools in the US and Canada, 1992; Numerous honorary degrees. **MEMBERSHIPS** Pres Commun Recruitment & Training Inc; bd of dir Office of Comm United Church of Christ; Pres, Soc for the Study of Black Religion, 1970-74, 1980-84. **SELECTED PUBLICATIONS** Author of Rainbows and Reality, Atlanta, The ITC Press 1984; The Hopeful Spirit, New York, Pilgrim Press 1987; Revolution in Zion; Reshaping African American Ministry, New York, Pilgrim Press, 1989. **CONTACT ADDRESS** United Church Board for Homeland Ministries, 700 Prospect, Cleveland, OH 44115-1100.

ROOP, EUGENE F.
PERSONAL Born 05/11/1942, South Bend, IN, m, 1963, 2 children **DISCIPLINE** HISTORY; BIBLE; OLD TESTAMENT; HEBREW BIBILE **EDUCATION** Manchester Col, BS, 64; Bethany Theological Seminary, MDiv 67; Claremont Graduate Univ, PhD, 72. **CAREER** Prof of Old Testament, 70-77, Earlham Sch of Relig; prof of Biblical Studies, 77-92, president, 72- , Bethany Theological Seminary. **HONORS AND AWARDS** Wieand professor of biblical studies, Bethany Theological Seminary; ordained minister, Church of the Brethren. **MEMBERSHIPS** Soc of Biblical Lit **RESEARCH** Narrative lit in the Hebrew bible. **SELECTED PUBLICATIONS** Coauth, A Declaration of Peace, 90; authm Master Dreamer, The Bible Today, January, 90; auth, Heard in Our Land, 91; auth, Let The Rivers Run, 91; auth, Esther, Covenant Bible Series, 97; auth, Commentary on Ruth, Jonah, and Esther, forthcoming. **CONTACT ADDRESS** Bethany Theol Sem, 615 National Rd W, Richmond, IN 47374-4019. **EMAIL** roopge@earlham.edu

ROOT, MICHAEL
DISCIPLINE SYSTEMATIC THEOLOGY **EDUCATION** Dartmouth Col, AB, 73; Yale Univ, MA, 74, MPhil, 76-77, PhD, 79. **CAREER** Instr, Davidson Col, 78-80; asst prof, Lutheran Theol S Sem, 80-84; assoc prof, Lutheran Theol S Sem, 84-88; res prof, Inst Ecumenical Res, Strasbourg, 88-98; dir, Inst Ecumenical Research, Strasbourg, 91-93, 95-98; prof, Trinity Lutheran Sem, 98-. **HONORS AND AWARDS** Consult, Lutheran-Cath Coord Comm; Anglican-Lutheran Intl Comm; ed coun, A Jour Theol. **MEMBERSHIPS** Faith and Order Commission Observer, Anglican-Roman Cath Intl Comm; ecumenical mem, Inter-Anglican Theol and Doctrinal Comm. **SELECTED PUBLICATIONS** Auth, Conditions of Communion: Bishops, the Concordat, and the Augsburg Confession, Inhabiting Unity: Theological Perspectives on the Proposed Lutheran-Episcopal Concordat, Eerdmans, 95; Full Communion between Episcopalians and Lutherans in the United States: What Would It Look Like?, Concordat of Agreement: Supporting Essays, Augsburg, Forward Movement, 95; The Immediate Ecumenical Task: A Response to William Rusch, 95; The Concordat and the Northern European Porvoo Common Statement: Different Paths to the Same Goal, A Commentary on Concordat of Agreement, Augsburg, Forward Movement, 94; The Ecumenical Identity of the Lutheran World Federation, Ecumenical Rev 46, 94; Ministry in the Lutheran-Methodist Dialogue, Lutheran Forum, 94; The Unity of the Church as a Moral Community: Some Comments on Costly Unity, Ecumenical Rev 46, 94. **CONTACT ADDRESS** Hist, Theol, Soc Dept, Trinity Lutheran Sem, 2199 E Main St, Columbus, OH 43209-2334.

ROOT, MICHAEL
DISCIPLINE PHILOSOPHY **EDUCATION** Univ Ill Urbana Champaign, PhD. **RESEARCH** Philosophy of language; metaphysics; philosophy of social sciences. **SELECTED PUBLICATIONS** Auth, Philosophy of Social Science: The Methods, Ideals, and Politics of Social Inquiry, Blackwell, 93; Miracles and the Uniformity of Nature, Am Philos Quarterly, 89; Davidson and Social Science, Blackwell, 86; co-auth, Meaning and Interpretation, J Formal Logic, 82. **CONTACT ADDRESS** Philosophy Dept, Univ of Minnesota, Twin Cities, 355 Ford Hall, 224 Church St SE, Minneapolis, MN 55455. **EMAIL** rootx001@maroon.tc.umn.edu

RORTY, AMELIE OKSENBERG
PERSONAL Born Antwerp, Belgium, 1 child **DISCIPLINE** PHILOSOPHY **EDUCATION** Univ Chicago, BA, Yale, MA, PhD. **CAREER** Rutgers Univ, instructor to Distinguished prof, Harvard Grad Sch, vis prof, Brandeis Univ, dir & prof. **HONORS AND AWARDS** Awds from Guggenheim, Woodrow Wilson Center, CASBS & IAS **MEMBERSHIPS** APA **RESEARCH** Aristotle; moral psychol; hist of polit theory; psychol anthro, art history. **CONTACT ADDRESS** 54 Hammond St, Cambridge, MA 02138. **EMAIL** rorty@binah.cc.brandeis.edu

RORTY, R.
PERSONAL Born 10/04/1931, New York, NY, m, 1972, 3 children **DISCIPLINE** PHILOSOPHY **EDUCATION** Univ of Chicago, BA, 49, MA, 52; Yale, PhD, 56. **CAREER** Instr/Asst Prof, 58-61, Wellesley Univ; Asst, Assoc, Prof, 61-82, Princeton Univ; Prof, 82-98, Univ of Virginia; Prof, 98-, Stanford Univ. **HONORS AND AWARDS** MacArthur Guggenheim; NEH; ACLS Fel; Amer Acad of Sciences. **MEMBERSHIPS** APA **RESEARCH** American Pragmatism **SELECTED PUBLICATIONS** Auth, Achieving Our Country, Harvard Univ Press, 98; auth, Truth and Progress, Campbridge Univ Press, 98. **CONTACT ADDRESS** Dept of Comparative Literature, Stanford, CA 94305-2031. **EMAIL** rrorty@leland.stanford.edu

ROSE, I. NELSON
DISCIPLINE LAW **EDUCATION** Univ Calif at Los Angeles, BA, 73; Harvard Law School, JD, 79. **CAREER** Attorney private practice, 79-82; Prof, Whittier Law School, 83-. **HONORS AND AWARDS** Visiting Scholar, Univ Nev; Reno's Inst for the Study of Gambling and Commercial Gaming. **MEMBERSHIPS** Intl Asn of Gaming Attorneys, Gaming Law Committee of ABA. **RESEARCH** Gaming Law: Gambling, Lotteries, Pari-mutuel wagers, Indian casinos, Internet betting. **SELECTED PUBLICATIONS** Auth, Gambling and the Law, 86; auth, Blackjack and the Law, 98. **CONTACT ADDRESS** School of Law, Whittier Law School, 3333 Harbor Blvd, Costa Mesa, CA 92626-1501. **EMAIL** rose@GamblingAndTheLaw.com

ROSE, KENNETH
PERSONAL Born 05/03/1951, m **DISCIPLINE** RELIGIOUS STUDIES & PHILOSOPHY **EDUCATION** OH State Univ, BA; Harvard Univ, MDiv, MA, PhD. **CAREER** Philos, Christopher Newport Univ. **MEMBERSHIPS** Am Academy of Religion **SELECTED PUBLICATIONS** Auth, Knowing the Real: John Hick on the Cognitivity of Relgions and Religious Pluralism, Peter Lang, 96. **CONTACT ADDRESS** Dept of Philos, Christopher Newport Univ, 1 University Place Newport News, Newport News, VA 23606. **EMAIL** krose@cnu.edu

ROSE, LEO E.
PERSONAL Born 01/02/1926, Hanford, CA, s **DISCIPLINE** POLITICAL SCIENCE **EDUCATION** Univ CA, Berkeley, PhD 51. **CAREER** Himalayan Border Countries Project, 62-69; Adjunt Prof 59-91; Univ CA, Berkeley, Ed, Asian Survey 62-97. **RESEARCH** South Asian Politics; International rels. **CONTACT ADDRESS** Dept of Polit Sci, Univ of California, Berkeley, Berkeley, CA 94720. **EMAIL** rosel@socrates.berkeley.edu

ROSE-ACKERMAN, SUSAN
PERSONAL Born 04/23/1942, Mineola, NY, m, 1967, 2 children **DISCIPLINE** LAW **EDUCATION** Wellesley Col, BA, 64; Yale Univ, PhD, 70. **CAREER** Instr, to prof, Yale Univ, 74-92; Henry R Luce Prof, 92-. **HONORS AND AWARDS** Guggenheim Fel; Fulbright Fel. **MEMBERSHIPS** AEA; APSA; APPM. **SELECTED PUBLICATIONS** Auth, "Public Law Versus Private Law in Environmental Regulation: European Union Proposals in the Light of United States and German Experience," in Law and Economics of the Environment, eds. Erling Eide, Roger van der Bergh (Oslo: Juridish Forlag, 96),13-39; auth "Political Corruption and Democracy," CT J Intl Law 14 (99):363-378; coauth, "Kleptocracy and Reform in African Regimes: 'Theory and Cases," in Corruption and Development in Africa: Lessons From Country Case Studies, eds. K.R. Hope, BC Chikulo (London: Macmillan Press, 99); coauth, "Corruption in a Paternalistic Democracy: Lessons from Italy for Latin America," Political Sci Quart 113 (98): 447-470; auth, "Corruption and the Global Economy" in United Nations Development Program, Corruption and Integrity," Improvement Initiatives in Developing Countries (New York, 98); auth, "Altruism, Ideological Entrepreneurs and the Non-profit Firm," Voluntas 8 (97):120-134; auth, "Altruism, Nonprofits, and Economic Theory," J Econ Lit 34(96): 701-728; auth, 'Inalienability," in New Palgrave Dictionary of Law and Economics, ed. Peter Newman (London: Macmillan Press, 98); auth, "Economics, Public Policy and Law," Victoria Univ Wellington Law Rev 26 (96):1-16; auth, "European Administrative and Regulatory Reform: Introduction to the Special Issue," Columbia J Euro Law 4 (98): 493-498; coauth, "Environmental Federalism in the United States: The Risks of Devolution," in Regulatory Competition and Economic Integration: Comparative Perspectives, eds. Daniel Esty, Damien Geradin (Oxford: Oxford Univ Press, forthcoming). **CONTACT ADDRESS** School of Law, Yale Univ, PO Box 208215, New Haven, CT 06520-8215. **EMAIL** susan.rose-ackerman@yale.edu

ROSELL, GARTH M.
PERSONAL Born 05/27/1939, Rochester, MN, m, 1965, 2 children **DISCIPLINE** CHURCH HISTORY **EDUCATION** Wheaton Col, BA; Princeton Theol Sem, MDiv, 64, ThM, 66; Univ Minn, PhD, 71. **CAREER** Prof, Bethel Theol Sem 70-78; acad dean, Conwell Theol Sem; prof, Gordon-Conwell Theol Sem, 78-; dir, Ockenga Inst. **MEMBERSHIPS** Mem, AAR, ASCH, AHA ETS. **SELECTED PUBLICATIONS** Co-auth, The Memoirs of Charles G. Finney: The Complete Restored Text, Zondervan, 89; American Christianity, Eerdmans, 86; The Millionaire and The Scrublady and Other Parables by William E. Barton, Zondervan, 90; auth, Shoeleather Faith, Bruce, 62; Cases in Theological Education, ATS, 86. **CONTACT ADDRESS** Gordon-Conwell Theol Sem, 130 Essex St, South Hamilton, MA 01982. **EMAIL** grosell@gcts.edu

ROSEMANN, PHILIPP W.
PERSONAL Born 02/24/1964, Frankfurt am Main, Germany, s **DISCIPLINE** PHILOSOPHY **EDUCATION** Univ Hamburg,, Candidatus philos, 87; Queen's Univ, Belfast, MA, 89; Univ Catholique de Louvain, Licence en philos, 91, PhD, 95. **CAREER** Tchg fel, Queen's Univ, Belfast, 89-90; chercheur sur fonds FDS, 90-93, maitre de conferences invite, 95-96, Univ Catholique de Louvain; lectr, Uganda Martyrs Univ, 96-97; asst prof, Univ Dallas, 97- . **HONORS AND AWARDS** Studienstiftung des deutschen Volkes grant, 83-87, 88-89, 93-95; Warburg scholar, Univ London, 87-88; Haggar Presidential Awd, Univ Dallas, 98; King/Haggar Scholar, Univ of Dallas, 01. **MEMBERSHIPS** Martin-Heidegger-Ges; Soc int pour l'etude de la philos medievale; APA; Soc for the Promotion of Eriugenian Stud; Uganda Soc; Am Catholic Philos Asn; AAUP; Texas Medieval Assoc. **RESEARCH** Medieval philosophy; Peter Lombard Thomas Aquinas; contemporary continental philosophy. **SELECTED PUBLICATIONS** Coauth, Alltagssprachliche Metakommunikation im Englischen und Deutschen, Peter Lang, 90; ed., Tabula, in Opera Roberti Grosseteste Lincolniensis, v 1, Brepols, 95; auth, Omne ens est aliquid: Introduction a la lecture du systeme philosophique de saint Thomas d'Aquin, Peeters, 96; auth, Omne agens agit sibi simile: A Repetition of Scholastic Metaphysics, Leuven, Univ. Press, 96; co-ed, Business Ethics in the African Context Today, Uganda Martyrs, 96; co-ed, Editer, traduire, interpreter: essais de methodologie philosophique, Peeters, 97; auth, Understanding Scholastic Thought with Foucault, St. Martin's Press, 99. **CONTACT ADDRESS** Philosophy Department, Univ of Dallas, 1845 E Northgate Dr, Irving, TX 75062-4736. **EMAIL** rosemann@acad.udallas.edu

ROSEMONT, HENRY, JR.
PERSONAL Born 12/20/1934, Chicago, IL, m, 1961, 5 children **DISCIPLINE** PHILOSOPHY **EDUCATION** Univ IL, AB, honors, 62; Univ Washington, PhD, 67. **CAREER** Oakland Univ, Instr, Asst Prof, philos, 65-69; MIT, post doctoral fellow in Linguistics, 69-72; Brooklyn Col, CUNY, Asst and Assoc Prof, 72-77; St Mary's Col, MD, Prof philos and rel studies, 77-, George B and Wilma Reeves Dist Prof Liberal Arts, 97-. **HONORS AND AWARDS** Post doctoral Fellowships from ACLS, NEH, NSF, Fulbright; Homer Dodge Excellence in Teaching Awd, St Mary's Col MD, 91; SACP, Distinguished Achievement Awd, 89; Eminent Scholar of Maryland, 01. **MEMBERSHIPS** Soc for Asian and Comparative Philos; Asn Asian Studies; Am Acad Religion. **RESEARCH** Classical Chinese philos, comparative philos, moral and political philos. **SELECTED PUBLICATIONS** A Chinese Mirror, Open Ct pub, 91; Chinese Texts and Philosophical Contexts, Open Ct Pub, 91; Leibniz: Writings on China, with Daniel J Cook, Open Ct Pub, 94; The Analects of Confucius, with Roger T Ames, Random House-Ballantine, 98; A Confucian Alternative, Univ Hawaii Press, 02; auth, Rationality & Religious Experience, Open Court, 01. **CONTACT ADDRESS** Dept Philosophy & Religious Studies, St. Mary's Col of Maryland, Saint Mary's City, MD 20686.

ROSEN, STANLEY H.
PERSONAL Born 07/29/1929, Warren, OH, m, 1955, 3 children **DISCIPLINE** SOCIAL THOUGHT **EDUCATION** Univ Chicago, BA, 49, PhD, 55. **CAREER** 55-93, Evan Pugh prof, 86-93, Penn State Univ; Borden Parker Bowne prof, 93- , Boston Univ. **HONORS AND AWARDS** Pres, Metaphysical Soc of Amer **MEMBERSHIPS** APA; MSA. **SELECTED PUBLICATIONS** Auth, The Question of Being, 93; auth, The Mask of Enlightenment, 95; auth, Plato Statermen, 95; auth, Metaphysics In Ordinary Language, 99; The Examined Life, 00. **CONTACT ADDRESS** Philosophy Dept, Boston Univ, 745 Commonwealth Ave, Boston, MA 02215. **EMAIL** srosen@acs.bu.edu

ROSENBERG, ALEXANDER
PERSONAL Born 08/31/1946, Austria **DISCIPLINE** PHILOSOPHY OF SCIENCE **EDUCATION** CCNY, BA, 67; Johns Hopkins Univ, PhD, 71. **CAREER** Vis asst prof, Univ Minn, 75; assoc prof, Syracuse Univ, 76-81; vis assoc prof, Univ Calif, Santa Cruz, 78-79; prof, Syracuse Univ, 81-86; prof, Univ Calif, Riverside, 86-95; vis lectr, Oxford Univ, 94-95; prof, Univ Ga, 95- . **HONORS AND AWARDS** Phi Beta Kappa, 67; Am Coun of Learned Soc Study-Fel, 81-82; Guggenheim Found Fel, 82-83; Nat Sci Found Sr Scholar Awd, 87; Lakatos Prize for Phil in Sci, 93. **MEMBERSHIPS** Am Phil Asoc; Phil of Sci Asoc. **RESEARCH** Philosophy of biology; philosophy of science. **SELECTED PUBLICATIONS** Coauth with T.L. Beauchamp, Hume and the Problem of Causation, 81; ath, The Structure of Biological Science, 85; auth, Philosophy of Social Science; 88; auth, Economics: Mathematical Politics or Science of Diminishing Returns?, 92; auth, Instrumental Biolgoy or the Disunity of Science, 94. **CONTACT ADDRESS** Honors Program, Univ of Georgia, 0117 Academic, Athens, GA 30602-6116. **EMAIL** alexrose@duke.edu

ROSENBERG, EMILY SCHLAHT
PERSONAL Born 07/21/1944, Sheridan, WY, m, 1966, 4 children **DISCIPLINE** AMERICAN HISTORY, INTERNATIONAL RELATIONS **EDUCATION** Univ NE, BA, 66; State Univ NYork Stony Brook, MA, 69, PhD, 73. **CAREER** Asst prof, Honors Prog, Cent Mich Univ, 73-74; asst prof, 74-80, assoc prof, Macalester Col, 80-85; prof hist, 86-93; Dewitt Wallace prof, 93-, Stanford prof hist, San Diego State Univ, 96-97. **HONORS AND AWARDS** Phi Beta Kappa, 66, AAUW Fel, 71-72; NEH Fel, 83-84; SSRC Fel, 91-92; Burlington-Northern Tchg Awd, 93; Thomas Jefferson Awd, 94. **MEMBERSHIPS** OHA; AHA; SHAFR. **RESEARCH** 20th century US for rel(s); US cult and economic rel(s). **SELECTED PUBLICATIONS** Auth, Dollar Diplomacy under Wilson: An Ecuadoran Case, Inter-American Econ Affairs, 71; Co-auth, America: A Portrait in History, Prentice-Hall, 73, rev ed, 78; World War I and Continental Solidarity, The Americas, 75; Economic Pressures in Anglo-American Diplomacy in Mexico, 1917-18, Jour of Inter-Am Studies and World Affairs, 75; Co-ed, Postwar America: Readings and Reminiscences, Prentice-Hall, 76; Anglo-American Economic Rivalry in Brazil during World War I, Diplomatic Hist, 78; Emergency Executive Controls over Foreign Comerce and United States Economic Pressure on Latin American during World War I, Inter-Am Econ Affairs, spring 78; Spreading the American Dream: American Economic and Cultural Expansion, 1890-1945, Hill and Wang, 82; Foundations of United States International Financial Power: Gold Standard Dipolmacy, 1900-1905, Bus Hist Rev, 85; The Invisible Protectorate: The United States, Liberia and the Evolution of Neocolonialism, 1909-1940, Diplomatic Hist, 85; World War I and the Growth of United States Predominance in Latin America, Garland, 86; Co-auth, From Colonialism to Professionalism: The Public-Private Dynamic in United States Foreign Financial Policy, 1898-1930, Jour Am Hist, 87; Gender in A Round Table: Explaining the History of American Foreign Relations, Jour Am Hist, 90; Walking the Borders, Diplomatic Hist, 90; Signifying the Vietnam Experience, Rev in Am Hist, 91; Walking the Borders, In: Explaining the History of American Foreign Relations, Cambridge Univ Press, 91; The Rocky Mountain West: Region in Transit, Mont Bus Quart, 92; NSC-68 and Cold War Culture, In: American Cold War Strategy: Interpreting NSC 68, St. Martin's Press, 93; The Cold War and the Discourse of National Security, Dplomatic Hist, 93; A Century of Exporting the American Dream, In: Exporting America: Essays on American Studies Abroad, Garland, 93; Economic Interest and US Foreign Policy, In: American Foreign Relations Reconsidered, Routledge, 94; Foreign Affairs after World War II: Connecting Sexual and International Politics, Diplomatic Hist, 94; Cultural Interactions, In: The Encyclopedia of the United States in the Twentieth Century, Scribners, 96; A Call to Revolution: A Roundtable on Early U.S. Foreign Relations, Diplomatic Hist, 98; Revisiting Dollar Diplomacy: Narratives on Money and Manliness, Diplomatic Hist, 98; Co-auth, In Our Times: America since 1945, Prentice-Hall, rev ed, 99; Co-auth, Liberty, Equality, Power: A History of the American People, Harcourt-Brace, rev ed, 99; auth, "Consuming Women: Images of Americanization in the 'American Century'," in Michael Hogan, ed., The Ambitious Legacy: U.S. Foreign Relations in the 'American Century,' (Cambridge University Press, 99) 437-62; auth, Financial Missionaries to the World: The Politics and Culture of Dollar Diplomacy, 1900-1930, Harvard Univ Press, 99; auth, "Turning to Culture," in Gilbert Joseph, et al, eds, Close Encounters of Empire (Duke University Press, 98). **CONTACT ADDRESS** 1600 Grand Ave, Saint Paul, MN 55105-1899. **EMAIL** rosenberg@macalester.edu

ROSENBLUM, VICTOR GREGORY
PERSONAL Born 06/02/1925, New York, NY, m, 1946, 8 children **DISCIPLINE** LAW, POLITICAL SCIENCE **EDUCATION** Columbia Univ, AB, 45, LLB, 48; Univ Calif, Berkeley, PhD(polit sci), 53. **CAREER** Asst prof polit sci, Univ Calif, Berkeley, 53-57; assoc count, US House Rep, 56-58; from assoc prof to prof law & polit sci, Northwestern Univ, 58-68; pres, Reed Col, 68-70; prof law & polit sci, Northwestern Univ, Chicago, 70-, sr legal consult, Brookings Inst, 65-69; Fulbright prof, Sch Law, Cath Univ Louvain, 66-67 & 78; consult, Admin Conf of US, 71-; mem bd dirs, Ctr Admin Justice, 72-80; consult, Nat Inst Law Enforcement & Criminal Justice, 73-; chmn, Admin Law Sect, Am Bar Asn, 77-78; Pres, Assoc Am Law Schools, 87. **HONORS AND AWARDS** DHL, Hebrew Union Col, 70; LittD, Siena Heights Col, 82; LLD Wabash Col, 98. **MEMBERSHIPS** Am Bar Asn; Am Polit Sci Asn; Law & Soc Asn (pres, 70-72). **RESEARCH** Interactions of legal and political factors in the development of public policy and the formulation of public law. **SELECTED PUBLICATIONS** Auth, Judicial reform & Courts and judges: Power and politics, In: The Fifty States and Their Local Governments, Knopf, 67; Legal dimensions of tenure, In: Faculty Tenure, Jossey-Bass, 73; coauth, Constitutional Law: Political Roles of the Supreme Court, Dorsey, 73; auth, Handling citizen initiated complaints: An introductory study of federal agency procedures, practices, Admin Law Rev, winter 74; Schoolchildren: Yes, Policemen: No--some thoughts about the Supreme Court's priorities concerning the right to a hearing in suspension & removal cases, Northwestern Law Rev, 77; coauth, The Making of a Public Profession, Am Bar Found, 81; auth, Administrative Law and the Regulatory Process, In: Contemporary Public Administration, Harcourt Brace, 81. **CONTACT ADDRESS** Sch of Law, Northwestern Univ, 357 E Chicago Ave, Chicago, IL 60611-3069. **EMAIL** v-rosenblum@northwestern.law.edu

ROSENFELD, MICHEL
DISCIPLINE CONSTITUTIONAL LAW **EDUCATION** Columbia Univ, BA, 69; MA, 71; MPhil, 78; PhD, 91; Northwestern Univ, JD, 74. **CAREER** Prof, Yeshiva Univ, 82-. **HONORS AND AWARDS** Asso, Skadden, Arps, Slate, Meagher & Flom, 77-80; Asso, Rosenman, Colin, Freund, Lewis & Cohen, 80-82. **RESEARCH** Comparative constitutionalism, jurisprudence, and the philosophy of human rights. **SELECTED PUBLICATIONS** Auth, Affirmative Action and Justice: A Philosophical and Constitutional Inquiry, Yale Univ Press, 91; Coed, Hegel and Legal Theory, Routledge Press, 91; Deconstruction and the Possibility of Justice, Routledge Press, 92; ed, Constitutionalism, Identity, Difference and Legitimacy: Theoretical Perspectives , Duke Univ Press, 94. **CONTACT ADDRESS** Yeshiva Univ, 55 Fifth Ave, New York, NY 10003-4301.

ROSENKRANTZ, GARY SOL
PERSONAL Born 07/12/1951, New York, NY **DISCIPLINE** PHILOSOPHY **EDUCATION** City Col New York, BA, 72; Brown Univ, PhD(philos), 76. **CAREER** From Asst Prof to Assoc Prof, 76-94, Prof Philos, Univ NC, Greensboro, 94-; head philos dept, 00-. **HONORS AND AWARDS** Bd of Editors Philos and Phenomenol Res, 97-02. **MEMBERSHIPS** Am Philos Asn. **RESEARCH** Epistemology; metaphysics; philosophy of religion. **SELECTED PUBLICATIONS** Auth, Haecceity: An Ontological Essay, Kluwer Acad Publ, 93; Substance Among Other Categories, Cambridge Univ Press, 94; Substance: Its Nature and Existence, Routledge, 97; Exploring the Divine Attributes, Basil Blackwell (under contract); author of numerous journal articles. **CONTACT ADDRESS** Dept of Philosophy, Univ of No Carolina, Greensboro, PO Box 26170, Greensboro, NC 27402-6170. **EMAIL** g_rosenk@uncg.edu

ROSENSTEIN, LEON
PERSONAL Born 07/04/1943, Newark, NJ, m, 1972 **DISCIPLINE** PHILOSOPHY **EDUCATION** Columbia Univ, BA, 65, PhD(philos), 72. **CAREER** Prof philos, San Diego State Unin, 69, chm Europ Studies prof, 78, chm Humanities Prog, 80-, Fulbright fel philos, US Govt, Univ Paris, 68-69. **MEMBERSHIPS** Pres, Classical Alliance of the Western States, 97-; Am Philos Asn; Am Soc Aesthet; Int Asn Philos & Lit; Int Soc Comp Study Civilizations. **RESEARCH** Existentialism; aesthetics; European intellectual and artistic culture. **SELECTED PUBLICATIONS** Auth, Metaphysical foundations of Hegel and Nietzsche's theories of tragedy, J Aesthet & Art Criticism, summer 70; Some metaphysical problems of Cassirer's symbolic forms, Man & World, 9/73; The ontological integrity of the art object from the Ludic viewpoint, J Aesthet & Art Criticism, spring 76; On Aristotle and thought in the drama, Critical Inquiry, spring 77; Mysticism as pre-ontology: A note on the Heideggerian connection, Philos & Phenomenol Res, 9/78; Rethinking Aristotle's thought, Critical Inquiry, spring 78; Heidegger and Plato and the good, Philos Today, fall 78; Hegelian sources of Freud's social and political philosophy (3 article ser), Kronos, fall 78-spring 79; The Last Word on Catharsis, Annales d'Esthetique, vol 23-24, 85; The Aesthetic of the Antique, J Aesthet and Art Criticism, summer 97. **CONTACT ADDRESS** Dept of Philos, San Diego State Univ, 5500 Campanile Dr, San Diego, CA 92182-8142.

ROSENTHAL, ABIGAIL L.
PERSONAL Born 03/02/1937, New York, NY, m, 1999 **DISCIPLINE** PHILOSOPHY **EDUCATION** Bernard Col, AB, 58; Sorbonne, Fulbright Scholar, 58-59; Columbia Univ, MA, 62; Univ London King's Col, 64-65; Pa State Univ, PhD, 68. **CAREER** Asst prof, SUNY at Stony Brook, 68-71; from asst prof to prof, CUNY Brooklyn Col, 71-; res affiliate, Univ Sydney, 82-83. **HONORS AND AWARDS** Fulbright Scholar, Sorbonne & Col de France, 58-59; fac res fel, State Univ NY at Stony Brook, 69; PSC-CUNY Res Awd, 87; Tow Awd for Fac Achievement, CUNY Brooklyn Col, 96-97; Fel Leave, CUNY Brooklyn Col, 99; listed in Who's Who of Am Women, 00-01. **MEMBERSHIPS** Am Philos Asn, Hegel Soc of Am. **RESEARCH** Moral Philosophy, Philosophy of History, Philosophy of Religion. **SELECTED PUBLICATIONS** Auth, Conversions: A Philosophic Memoir, 94; auth, "In 'Windowless Chambers'" Inquiry 41 (98). **CONTACT ADDRESS** Dept Philos, Brooklyn Col, CUNY, 2901 Bedford Ave, Brooklyn, NY 11210-2813.

ROSENTHAL, DAVID M.
PERSONAL Born 04/10/1939, New York, NY, 1 child **DISCIPLINE** PHILOSOPHY **EDUCATION** Univ Chicago, AB, 61; Princeton Univ, MA, 64, PhD, 68. **CAREER** Asst prof, Rutgers Univ, 67-71; asst prof, City Univ NY, 71-. **HONORS AND AWARDS** McDonnell-Pew Vis Fel, 96. **MEMBERSHIPS** Am Philos Asn; Soc for Philos and Psych; Asn for the Sci Study of Consciousness. **RESEARCH** Philosophy of the mind; Cognitive science; Philosophy of language; Ancient philosophy; Continental rationalism. **SELECTED PUBLICATIONS** Auth, Consciousness and Mind; "Consciousness and its Expression," in Midwest Studies in Philos, 98; "Consciousness and Metacognition," 98; "The Colors and Shapes of Visual Experiences," 98; "Perceptual and Cognitive Models of Consciousness," in J of the Am Psychoanalytic Asn, 97; "Apperception, Sensation, and Dissociability," in Mind and Language, 97; "A Theory of Consciousness," 97; "Multiple Drafts and Facts of the Matter," 95; "Moore's Pradox and Consciousness," in Philos Persepctives, 95; "First-Person Operationalism and Mental Taxonomy," in Philos Topics, 95. **CONTACT ADDRESS** 425 Riverside Dr, Apt 12F, New York, NY 10025. **EMAIL** dro@ruccs.rutgers.edu

ROSENTHAL, MICHAEL A.
PERSONAL Born 06/10/1962, Anaheim, CA, m, 1996, 2 children **DISCIPLINE** PHILOSOPHY **EDUCATION** Stanford Univ, AB, 86; Univ Chicago, AM, 88, PhD, 96. **CAREER** Lectr, Univ Delaware, 94-95, from instr to asst prof, 95-, Grinnell Col. **HONORS AND AWARDS** Mellon Fel, 87-91. **MEMBERSHIPS** Am Philos Asn; N Am Spinoza Soc; Iowa Philos Soc. **RESEARCH** Spinoza; early modern philosophy; ethics and political philosophy. **CONTACT ADDRESS** Dept of Philosophy, Grinnell Col, Box 805, Grinnell, IA 50112. **EMAIL** rosentha@grinnell.edu

ROSENTHAL, PETER
DISCIPLINE LAW **EDUCATION** Univ Ca, BS, 62; Univ Mich, MA, 63, PhD, 67; Univ Toronto, LLB, 90. **CAREER** Prof, Univ of Toronto, 67-. **SELECTED PUBLICATIONS** Auth, pubs on criminal law. **CONTACT ADDRESS** Fac of Law, Univ of Toronto, 78 Queen's Park, Toronto, ON, Canada M5S 2C5.

ROSIN, ROBERT L.
PERSONAL Born 02/12/1951, Lexington, MO, m, 1975 **DISCIPLINE** HISTORICAL THEOLOGY **EDUCATION** Concordia Tchrs Col, BA, 72; Concordia Sem, MDiv, 76; Stanford Univ, MA, 77, PhD, 86. **CAREER** From instr to assoc prof, 81-97, prof hist theol, 97- , chemn dept, 95- , Concordia Sem; guest instr, Martin Luther Sem, Papua New Guines, 83; actg dir lib services, 88-90, fac marshal, 89-97, ed, Concordia Sem Publ, 95- ; Exec dir Center for Reformation Res, 97- . **MEMBERSHIPS** Soc for Reformation Res; Sixteenth-Century Stud Conf; Renaissance Soc of Am; Luther-Gesellschaft; Am Soc of Church Hist; Lutheran Hist Conf; Am Friends of the Herzog August Biliothek. **RESEARCH** Reformation and education/curriculum in the sixteenth century. **SELECTED PUBLICATIONS** Auth, Christians and Culture: Finding Place in Clio's Mansions, in, Christ and Culture: The Church in Post-Christian(?) America, Concordia Sem, 96; auth, Bringing Forth Fruit: Luther on Social Welfare, in Rosin, ed, A Cup of Cold Water: A Look at Biblical Charity, Concordia Sem, 97; auth, Reformers, The Preacher, and Skepticism: Luther, Brenz, Melanchthon, and Ecclesiastes, Verlag Philipp von Zabern, 97. **CONTACT ADDRESS** Concordia Sem, 801 DeMun Ave, Saint Louis, MO 63105. **EMAIL** rosinr@csl.edu

ROSNER, JENNIFER
PERSONAL Born 04/08/1966, New York, NY, m, 1994, 1 child **DISCIPLINE** PHILOSOPHY **EDUCATION** Stanford Univ, PhD, 98. **CAREER** Acting Asst Prof, Stanford Univ. **HONORS AND AWARDS** Dept Fel Stanford Univ, 92-96; Mellon Dissertation Fel, Stanford Univ, 96-97. **MEMBERSHIPS** APA, APPE. **RESEARCH** Ethics; Moral Psychology. **SELECTED PUBLICATIONS** Auth, Quine's Global Structuralism, Dialectica, 96; Reflective Endorsement and the Self: A Response to Arpaly and Schroeder, Philos Studies, Vol 97, No 2, 00. **CONTACT ADDRESS** Dept of Philosophy, Stanford Univ, Stanford, CA 94305-2155. **EMAIL** rosner@csli.stanford.edu

ROSS, CHRISTOPHER F. J.
PERSONAL Born 06/17/1946, London, England, s, 1 child **DISCIPLINE** PSYCHOLOGY OF RELIGION **EDUCATION** Univ Durham, BA, 67; Univ Edinburgh, MSc, 69; Univ Calany, PhD, 73. **CAREER** Assoc Prof **HONORS AND AWARDS** Citation in Outstanding Young Men of Amer, 77. **MEMBERSHIPS** Clinical Psychologist, 69-71; clinical supervisor, 80-82, **RESEARCH** Relig and psychol issues; psychol and spiritual; dev; psychotherapy and spiritual direction; psychological type and spirituality; mysticism and spirituality; philosophical aspects of interdisciplinary studies in relig and the social sciences; relig and social change; the peace movement; new relig movements. **SELECTED PUBLICATIONS** Auth, The Intuitive Function and Religious Orientation, Journal of Analytical Psychology, 92; auth, Orientation to Religion and the Feeling Function in Jung's Personality Typology, Studies in Religion, 92; auth, Type Patterns Among Members of the Anglican Church: Comparisions with Catholics, Evangelicals and Clergy, Journal of Psychological Type, 93; auth, Type Patterns among Catholics: A Study of Four Anglophone Congregations with Comparisons to Protestants, Francophone Catholics and Priests, Journal of Psychological Type, 95; co auth, Relationship of Jungian Psychological Type to Religious Orientation and Spiritual Practices, International Journal for the Psychology of Religion, 97; auth, Experiencing Mother Meera, Canadian Woman Studies, 97; coauth, The Perceiving Function and Christian Spirituality: Distinguishing between Sensing and Intuition, Pastoral Sciences, forthcoming. **CONTACT ADDRESS** Dept of Relig and Culture, Wilfrid Laurier Univ, 75 Univ Ave W, Waterloo, ON, Canada N2L 3C5. **EMAIL** cross@wlu.ca

ROSS, JAMES F.
DISCIPLINE OLD TESTAMENT **EDUCATION** Doane Col, BA, 49; Union Theol Sem, BD, 52, ThD, 55; Amer Sch Oriental Res, Jerusalem, Jordan, 53-54. **CAREER** Instr, Dartmouth Col, 55-57; asst prof, Dartmouth Col, 57-59; asst prof, Drew Univ, 59-63; assoc prof, Drew Univ, 63-68; vis prof, Princeton Univ, 62-63; vis prof, Swarthmore Col, 64; prof, Va Theol Sem, 68-96; emeri, 96-. **SELECTED PUBLICATIONS** Auth, Reports on excavations in Field VI, Tell el-Hesi, 83; The Vounous Jars Revisited, BASOR 296, 94. **CONTACT ADDRESS** Virginia Theol Sem, 3737 Seminary Rd, Alexandria, VA 22304. **EMAIL** JRoss@vts.edu

ROSS, JAMIE
PERSONAL Born New York, NY **DISCIPLINE** PHILOSOPHY **EDUCATION** Univ Ore, PhD, 95. **CAREER** Asst prof, Portland State Univ. **MEMBERSHIPS** Am Philos Asn; Soc for Advancement Am Philos; Soc for Women in Philos. **RESEARCH** Am Pragmatism; Feminist Theory. **CONTACT ADDRESS** Portland, OR 97221-2634. **EMAIL** rossj@pdx.edu

ROSS, JEROME C.
PERSONAL Born 09/24/1953, Richmond, VA, m, 1977 **DISCIPLINE** RELIGIOUS STUDIES **EDUCATION** Randolph-Macon College, BA, 75; VA Union Univ, MDiv, 78; Univ Pitt, PhD, 97. **CAREER** Instr, Asst Prof, 82-, VA Union Univ; Pastor 83-93, Mt Olive Bap Church VA; Providence Pk Baptist Church VA, 93-. **HONORS AND AWARDS** Most Outstanding Stud of the New Testament; Asbury Christian Awd; Amer Bible Soc Awd. **MEMBERSHIPS** SBL **RESEARCH** Hebrew Law; Pentateuch; Worship; History. **SELECTED PUBLICATIONS** Coauth, Proclamation 6, Series B: Lent, Minneapolis, Fortress Press, 96; rev, Stony the Road We Trod, Interpretation, 93; auth, A History of Israel: A Compilation, 99; auth, " The Cultural Affinity Between the Ancient Yahwists and the African Americans: A Hermeneutic for Homiletics," in Born to Preach: Essays in honor of Henry & Ella Mitchell, Judson Press, 00. **CONTACT ADDRESS** 8211 Chipplegate Dr, Richmond, VA 23227. **EMAIL** jross@ruu.edu

ROSS, PATRICIA A.
PERSONAL Born 03/18/1961, Washington, PA, m, 1992 **DISCIPLINE** PHILOSOPHY **EDUCATION** Univ Ill, MA, 87; Univ Md, PhD, 96. **CAREER** Fel, Cent Philos Sci, Univ Minn, 96-98; vis asst prof, Univ Minn, 98-00. **MEMBERSHIPS** Philos Sci Asn; Am Philos Asn; Asn Advan Psychol Psychiat; Int Soc Theoret Psychol. **RESEARCH** Philosophy of science. **SELECTED PUBLICATIONS** Auth, The Limits of Physicalism, Philos Sci, 98; Values and Objectivity in Psychiatric Nosology, 00. **CONTACT ADDRESS** Dept of Philosophy, Univ of Minnesota, Twin Cities, 851 Heller Hall, Minneapolis, MN 55455. **EMAIL** rossx035@tc.umn.edu

ROSS, PETER W.
PERSONAL Born 05/27/1963, Canton, OH, m, 1995 **DISCIPLINE** PHILOSOPHY **EDUCATION** Oberlin Col, BA, 85; Graduate Sch of CUNY, PhD, 97. **CAREER** Lectr, Calif State Polytech Univ, Pomona, 97-98. **MEMBERSHIPS** APA; Soc for Philos and Psych; Southern Soc for Philos and Psychol. **RESEARCH** Color; color perception; consciousness. **SELECTED PUBLICATIONS** Auth, Trichromacy and the Neural Basis of Color Discrimination: Commentary on B.A.C. Saunders and J. Van Brakel, Are There Nontrivial Constraints on Colour Categorization? Behav and Brain Sci, 97. **CONTACT ADDRESS** Dept of Philosophy, California State Polytech Univ, Pomona, 3801 West Temple Ave, Pomona, CA 91768-4051. **EMAIL** pross@pomona.edu

ROSS, RALPH M.
PERSONAL Born 12/23/1936, Miami, FL, m **DISCIPLINE** THEOLOGY **EDUCATION** AB 1961; BD 1965; MDiv 1970; DMin, 1988. **CAREER** Beth Salem United Presb Church Columbus, GA, minister 1965-66; Eastern Airlines Atlanta, ramp agt 1965-66; Mt Zion Baptist Church Miami, assoc minister 1966-68; Urban League Miami, field rep 1967-68; Knoxville Col, campus minister 1968-70; UT Knoxville, lectr/relig dept 1969-; Naval Officer, Lieutenant Jr Grade, in the US Naval Reserve Chaplain Corps, 76; Knoxville Col, dean of students; NC A&T State Univ, dir relig activities, 78-86, asst dean student devel 1986-90; Mt Zion Baptist Church, Miami, FL, pastor/teacher, 90-; From Lieutenant to Lieutenant Comdr to Captain, retired 96. **HONORS AND AWARDS** YMCA Best Blocker Award Knoxville Col 1959; Rockefeller Fel Award 1964; Theta Phi Hon Soc 1965; First African Am to reach the rank of Captain in the US Navel Reserve, Chaplain Corps. **MEMBERSHIPS** Mem bd dir Ministries to Blacks in Higher Edn Knoxville; Knoxville Interdenominational Christian Ministeral Alliance; life mem Alpha Phi Alpha; NAACP; Baptist Ministers Coun & Faith In The City; ROA. **CONTACT ADDRESS** Pastor/Teacher, Mount Zion Baptist Church, 301 NE 9th St, Miami, FL 33136.

ROSS, ROSETTA E.
DISCIPLINE RELIGION, CHRISTIAN SOCIAL ETHICS **EDUCATION** Emory Univ, PhD, 95 **CAREER** Asst prof of ethics and public policy interdenominational theological ctr Atlanta GA **MEMBERSHIPS** Amer Acad of Religion; Soc of Christian ethics; Soc for the Study of Black Religion **RESEARCH** Womanist/feminist theology & ethics; social theory; ethics & public policy **CONTACT ADDRESS** Dept of Relig, United Theol Sem, 3000 5th St NW, New Brighton, MN 55112-2598. **EMAIL** rross@itc.edu

ROSS, STEPHEN D.
PERSONAL Born 05/04/1935, New York, NY, m, 1968, 1 child **DISCIPLINE** PHILOSOPHY **EDUCATION** Columbia Col, AB, 56; MA, 57; PhD, 61. **CAREER** Lecturer, Columbia Univ, 56-61; Instr, Queens Col, 61-63; Asst Prof, Univ Wisc, 63-65; Asst Prof, Univ Colo, 65-67; Asst Prof to Prof, Binghamton Univ, 67-. **HONORS AND AWARDS** Phi Beta Kappa; Res Fel, Univ Wisc, 64; Res Fel, SUNY, 68, 69, 74; Rockefeller Foundation Humanities Fel, 75-76; Humanities Res Fel, Australian Nat Univ, 77. **SELECTED PUBLICATIONS** Auth, Plenishment I the earth: an Ethic of Inclusion, SUNY, 95; auth, The Gift of Beauty: The Good as Art, SUNY, 96; auth, The Gift of Truth: Gathering the Good, SUNY, 97; auth, The gift of Touch: Embodying the Good, SUNY, 98; auth, The Gift of Kinds: The Good in Abundance, SUNY, 99; auth, The Gift of Property: Having the Good, betraying genitivity, economy and ecology, an ethic of the earth, SUNY, forthcoming. **CONTACT ADDRESS** Dept Philos, SUNY, Binghamton, PO Box 6000, Binghamton, NY 13902-6000.

ROSS, STEPHEN F.
DISCIPLINE LAW **EDUCATION** Univ Calif Berkeley, BA; JD. **CAREER** Law clerk, Judge Ruth Bader Ginsburg, US Court Appeals; prof, Univ Ill Urbana Champaign. **HONORS AND AWARDS** Ed, Calif Law Rev. **RESEARCH** Antitrust; sports law; statutory interpretation; Canadian law; and welfare law. **SELECTED PUBLICATIONS** Auth, Principles of Antitrust Law, Foundation, 93; pubs on general antitrust and competition policy in the USA and Canada, sports antitrust issues, and statutory interpretation. **CONTACT ADDRESS** Law Dept, Univ of Illinois, Urbana-Champaign, 52 E Gregory Dr, Champaign, IL 61820. **EMAIL** sross@law.uiuc.edu

ROSSELL, CHRISTINE H.
PERSONAL Born 01/22/1945, Brooklyn, NY, m, 1982, 1 child **DISCIPLINE** POLITICAL SCIENCE **EDUCATION** UCLA, AB, 67; Calif State Univ, MA, 69; Univ S Calif, PhD, 74. **CAREER** Asst Prof, Pitzer Col, 73-74; Res Assoc and Lectr, Univ Md, 74-75; Asst Prof to Prof, Boston Univ, 75-. **HONORS AND AWARDS** Fel, Univ S Calif, 70-72; Fel, Haynes Found, 72-73; Fel, Public Policy Inst of Calif, 99; Who's Who in Am, 95-; Who's Who in the World, 95-; Who's Who in Am Educ, 94-; Res Grant, Ford Found; Res Grant, Smith Richardson Found; Res Grant, Pioneer Inst. **MEMBERSHIPS** Am Polit Sci Asn; Am Educ Res Asn. **RESEARCH** Bilingual Education; School Desegregation; School Choice; Tracking and Ability Grouping. **SELECTED PUBLICATIONS** Auth, The Carrot or the Stick in School Desegregation Policy, Temple Univ Press, 90; auth, The Convergence of Black and White Attitudes on School Desegregation Issues During the Four Decade Evolution of the Plans, William and Mary Law Review, Vol 36, 95; co-auth, Bilingual Education in Massachusetts, Pioneer Inst, 96; co-auth, "The Effectiveness of School Desegregation Plans, ", Am Polit Quart, 96; co-auth, "The Educational Effectiveness of Bilingual Education," in Research in the Teaching of English, Vol 30, 96; auth, The Federal Bilingual Education Program: Title VII of the Elementary and Secondary Education Act, Brookings Inst Press, 00; auth, Teaching Language Minorities: Theory and Reality, Johns Hopkins Univ Press, 00. **CONTACT ADDRESS** Dept Polit Sci, Boston Univ, 44 High St, Brookline, MA 02445. **EMAIL** crossell@bu.edu

ROSSI, CHRISTOPHER
DISCIPLINE INTERNATIONAL LAW AND ORGANIZATION **EDUCATION** Wash Univ, BA, Univ Iowa, JD; Univ London, LLM; John Hopkins Univ, MA,PhD. **CAREER** Prof, Am Univ. **MEMBERSHIPS** Asso Dir, World Jurist Asn. **RESEARCH** International law and organization, human rights, international courts and tribunals. **SELECTED PUBLICATIONS** Auth, Equity and International Law: A Legal Realist Approach to International Decisionmaking,Transnational Publs, 93; coauth, Arms Control Treaties, Review and Revision, Bull Int Atomic Energy Agency. **CONTACT ADDRESS** American Univ, 4400 Massachusetts Ave, Washington, DC 20016.

ROSTHAL, ROBERT
PERSONAL Born 10/16/1923, New York, NY, m, 1952, 1 child **DISCIPLINE** PHILOSOPHY **EDUCATION** Univ Wis Madison, graduate, liberal studies, 43; Univ Chicago, MA, 54; Univ Mich, PhD, 61. **CAREER** Inst, NYork Univ, 53; instr, Brooklyn Col, 54; fel, instr, Univ Mich, 55-59; vis lectr, Ohio State Univ, 59; asst prof, Kenyon Col, 60; from asst prof to prof, Univ N Carolina, 61-93; ed, The North Carolina Scholar, 99-. **HONORS AND AWARDS** Hd of Philos Dept; Ford Foun Gnt; Pres NC Assoc Scholars 93-. **MEMBERSHIPS** APA; PPS; SA. **RESEARCH** Contemporary Philosophy; Aesthetics; Philosophy of mind; Value theory; Ethics. **SELECTED PUBLICATIONS** Auth, "The Asciption of Mental Predicates," Philosophical Studies, 61; auth, Gabriel Marcel, Creative Fidelity, translation and intro, Farrar Straus, 63; auth, Moral Weakness and Remorse, MIND, 67; auth, Philosophy in France Since 1945, World Philosophy: Contemporary Developments Since 1945, ed John Burr, Greenwood, 80; guest ed, "Action, Agency, and the Will," Erkenntnis, 82. **CONTACT ADDRESS** 4403 Graham Rd, Greensboro, NC 27410. **EMAIL** rrosthal@aol.com

ROTH, JEAN
PERSONAL Born 08/08/1939, Kunming, China, m, 1963, 2 children **DISCIPLINE** RELIGIOUS STUDIES **EDUCATION** Radcliffe Col, BA, 61; Union Theol Sem, MRE; Stanford Univ, PhD, 97. **CAREER** Tchg asst, 83, 85, lectr, 97-98, Stanford Univ. **HONORS AND AWARDS** Shared first prize for student papers at Am Acad of Relig W Regional Conf, 89. **MEMBERSHIPS** Am Acad Relig. **RESEARCH** Modern Western philosophy of religion, particularly the problems in the relationship between reason and faith in the Victorian period. **CONTACT ADDRESS** 12113 Foothill Ln, Los Altos Hills, CA 94022.

ROTH, JEFFREY I.
DISCIPLINE LAW **EDUCATION** Yeshiva Univ, BA, 68; Columbia Univ, MA, 69; Yale Univ, JD, 74. **CAREER** Fac fel, Columbia Univ, 68-69; Fulbright prof, Hungary, 91; assoc prof, NY Law Schl; assoc prof, Touro Col. **HONORS AND AWARDS** Nat Sci Found grad fel. **SELECTED PUBLICATIONS** Auth, The Justification for Controversy in Jewish Law, CA Law Rev, 88; Successor Trustees of Tentative Trusts: Trust Law Phantoms, St Louis Law J, 93. **CONTACT ADDRESS** Dept of Law, Touro Col, New York, Brooklyn, NY 11230. **EMAIL** jeffreyr@tourolaw.edu

ROTH, JOEL
PERSONAL Born 05/15/1940, Detroit, MI, m, 1965, 3 children **DISCIPLINE** TALMUDIC STUDIES **EDUCATION** Wayne State Univ, BA; Jewish Theol Sem Am, MA, 68; PhD, 73. **CAREER** Dean stud List Col; dir, Melton Res Ctr Jewish Educ; assoc dean and dean, Rabbinical Schl; prof 96-; Rosh Yeshiva, the Conservative Yeshiva of the United Synagogue, Jerusalem, 01-. **HONORS AND AWARDS** Chmn, Comm Jewish Law and Stds Rabbinical Assembly, 78-85. **MEMBERSHIPS** Asn for Jewish Studies; World Union of Jewish Studies; Jewish Law Asn; Rabbinical Assembly Committee on Jewish Law and Standards. **RESEARCH** Jewish Law. **SELECTED PUBLICATIONS** Auth, The Halakhic Process: A Systemic Analysis; auth, Sefer ha-Mordecai: Tractate Kiddushin; auth, articles and responsa, Law Comm Jewish Law and Stud. **CONTACT ADDRESS** The Fuchsberg Center, 2 Agron St., Jerusalem, Israel. **EMAIL** joroth@jtsa.edu

ROTH, PAUL A.
PERSONAL Born 11/18/1948, New York, NY, m, 1989, 1 child **DISCIPLINE** PHILOSOPHY **EDUCATION** Wesleyan Univ, BA, 70; Univ of Chicago, MA, 72; PhD, 78. **CAREER** Vis asst prof to prof, chair, Univ Miss St Louis, 78-. **HONORS AND AWARDS** NEH Grants, 78, 86-89, 98; ACLS Grant, 90; **MEMBERSHIPS** Am Philos Assoc; Philos of Sci Assoc. **SELECTED PUBLICATIONS** Auth, Meaning and Method in the Social Sciences: A Case for Methodological Pluralism, Cornell Univ Pr, (Ithaca, NY), 87; auth, "Will the Real Scientists Please Stand Up? Dead Ends and Life Issues in the Expiation of Scientific Knowledge", Studies in Hist and Philos of Sci 27, (96): 813-838; auth, "Microfoundations Without Foundations: comments on D Little's Causation in the Social Sciences", Southern J of Philos 34, (95): 57-64; auth, "Dubious Liaison: Review essay of Alvin Goldman's Liaisons: Philosophy Meets the Cognitive and Social Sciences", Philos Psychol 9, (96): 261-79; auth, "The Cure of Stories: Self-Deception, Danger Situations, and the Clinical role of Narratives in Roy Schafer's Psychoanalytic theory", Psychoanalytic Versions of the Human Condition, ed P. Marcus and A Rosenberg, NY Univ Pr, (98): 306-331; auth, "Naturalizing Goldman", Southern J of Philos (99): 89-109; auth, "The Full Hempel: review essay of Clayton Roberts, The Logic of Historical Explanation", Hist & Theory 38, (99): 249-63; auth, "The Epistemology of Epistemology Naturalized", Dialecta 53, (99): 87-109; auth, "The Object of Understanding", Empathy and Agency, ed K Stueber and B Kogler, Westview, (forthcoming); coed, Companion to the Philosophy of Social Science, Blackwell, (forthcoming). **CONTACT ADDRESS** Dept Philos, Univ of Missouri, St. Louis, 8001 Natural Bridge Rd, Saint Louis, MO 63121-4401. **EMAIL** roth@umsl.edu

ROTH, ROBERT J.
PERSONAL Born 11/28/1920, NJ **DISCIPLINE** PHILOSOPHY **EDUCATION** Boston Col, BA, 44; Fordham Univ, MA, 48, PhD, 61. **CAREER** From instr to assoc prof, 53-70, vice chmn dept, 60-64, chmn, 70-73, pres, fac senate, 72-74, dean, 74-79, Fordham Col; prof philos, 70-91, prof emeritus, 91-, Fordham Univ; res fel, Yale Univ, 68-69. **MEMBERSHIPS** Jesuit Philos Assn US & Can; Am Cath Philos Assn; Am Philos Assn. **RESEARCH** Philosophy of person; American pragmatism; British empiricism. **SELECTED PUBLICATIONS** Art, Locke on Ideas and the Intuition of the Self, Int Philos Quart, 90; auth, David Hume on Religion in England, Thought, 91; auth, British Empiricism and American Pragmatism, Fordham Univ, 93; auth, Radical Pragmatism: An Alternative, Fordham Univ, 99. **CONTACT ADDRESS** Dept of Philosophy, Fordham Univ, Bronx, NY 10458.

ROTH, WILLIAM
PERSONAL Born 06/01/1942, New Haven, CT, m, 1994, 1 child **DISCIPLINE** POLITICAL SCIENCE **EDUCATION** Yale Univ, BA, 64; Univ Calif, Berkeley, PhD, 70. **CAREER** Tchng Asst, Univ Calif, 67-68; Instr, San Francisco Art Inst, 69; Instr, Univ Calif, 69-70; Lectuerer, Dartmouth Col, 71; Asst Prof, Univ Vt, 71-72; Sr Res Assoc, Carnegie Counc on Children, 72-76; Res Assoc, Univ Wisc, 76-78; Ch, Dept of Public Aff & Policy, Grad Sch of Pub Aff, 82-84; Assoc, Inst for Govt & Policy Stud, 84-88; Exec Dir for Policy & res, 88-90; Founder & Dir, Ctr for Computing & Disability, SUNY, 84-88; Asn Prof, SUNY, 78-. **RESEARCH** Disability studies, children. **SELECTED PUBLICATIONS** Auth, The Handicaped Speak, Mcfarland & Co.; coauth The Unexpedted minority, Marcourt, Brace, Jovanovich; auth, Personal Computers for Persons with Disabilities, McFarland & Co, Inc, 92; co-auth, Job Analysis and The Americans With Disabilities Act, Business Horizons, Nov/Dec 96. **CONTACT ADDRESS** Dept of Soc Welfare, SUNY, Albany, 1400 Washington Ave, Albany, NY 12222. **EMAIL** wroth@csc.albany.edu

ROTHAUGE, ARLIN J.
DISCIPLINE RELIGION **EDUCATION** Univ Oregon, BA; Phillips Univ, BD; Univ Scotland, Glasgow, PhD; Berkeley Divinity Sch, DD. **CAREER** Prof, exec dir, Seabury-Western Theol Sem, 95-. **HONORS AND AWARDS** Nat coord, Congregational Develop on the Presiding Bishop's staff. **SELECTED PUBLICATIONS** Auth, Sizing Up a Congregation for New Member Ministry; A Church is Born: Basics for Developing a New Mission Congregation; Reshaping a Congregation for a New Future; An Overview of New Church Development; A Diocesan Strategy for New Church Development. **CONTACT ADDRESS** Seabury-Western Theol Sem, 2122 Sheridan Rd, Evanston, IL 60201.

ROTHBART, DANIEL
PERSONAL Born 09/05/1950, Newark, NJ, m, 1973, 2 children **DISCIPLINE** PHILOSOPHY **EDUCATION** Farleigh Dickinson Univ, BA, 72; State Univ NYork-Binghamton, MA, 75; Wash Univ, PhD, 79. **CAREER** Post-doctoral lectr, phil, Wash Univ, 78-79; vis asst prof to ASSOC PROF, PHIL, GEORGE MASON UNIV, 79-; vis research scholar, dept hist and phil of sci, Univ Cambridge, 90; vis research scholar, dept phil, Darmouth Col, 94. **HONORS AND AWARDS** Intensive Bioethics Course, Kennedy Inst of Ethics, 82; NEH Summer Seminiar: Agreement and Disagreement in Science, 85; Travel Grant, Am Counc of Learned Scholars, 88; Grant-in-Aid, Am Council of Learned Scholars, Univ of Cambridge, 90; Templeton Foundation Awd, 97; exec comm, int soc phil of chem, 94-; editorial board, foundations of chemistry and philosophical and historical studies in chemistry, 97-; scientific board, hyle: an international journal in the philosophy of chemistry, 97-. **SELECTED PUBLICATIONS** Auth, Explaining the Growth of Scientific Knowledge: Metaphors, Models and Meanings, Edwin Mellen Press, 97; ed, Science, Reason and Reality: Issues in the Philosophy of Science, Harcourt/Brace, 97; ed, Inquiry: Critical Thinking Across the Disciplines, Summer 96; auth, "Spectometers as Analogues of Nature," in PSA: 1994, Vol One, Phil of Sci Asn, 94; auth, "The Design of Nature through Chemical Instrumentation," in Chemistry and Philosophy, Koenigshausen und Neumann, 97; auth, "Flew on Popper and Popper on Properties," in Philosophy, Theology and Justice, Kluwer Academic Press, 98; auth, "The Epistemology of a Spectrometer," in Phil of Sci 61, 94; auth, "Extending Popper's Epistemology to the Laboratory," in Dialectica 51, 97; auth, "Kant's Critique of Judgment and the Scientific Investigation of Nature," in Hyle: An Int Jour in the Phil of Chemistry 3, 97; auth, "Substances Fuction in Chemical Research" in Molecules and Minds, (Oxford Univ Press, 00). **CONTACT ADDRESS** Dept Phil & Relig Studies, George Mason Univ, Fairfax, Fairfax, VA 22030. **EMAIL** drothbar@gmu.edu

ROTHBERG, DONALD JAY
PERSONAL Born 07/15/1950, Washington, DC **DISCIPLINE** PHILOSOPHY **EDUCATION** Yale Col, BA, 72; Boston Univ, PhD, 83. **CAREER** Vis instr philos, Bowling Green State Univ, 81-82; asst prof philos, Univ Ky, 82-86; asst prof philos, Kenyon Col, 86-89; mem exec fac, Saybrook Grad Sch, 90- . **HONORS AND AWARDS** NSF fel polit sci, Paris, 70; Magna Cum Laude, 72; Ger Acad Exchange Serv fel, Heidelberg Univ, 75-76; NEH sum sem fel, Berkeley, 85; one of twenty selected for Revisioning Philosophy, funded by L Rockefeller, 87-89. **MEMBERSHIPS** APA; Am Acad of Relig; Asn for Transpersonal Psych. **RESEARCH** Philosophy of the human sciences; spirituality and epistemology; spirituality and social action; transpersonal psychology; Buddhist philosophy and psychology; nineteenth and twentieth century continental philosophy. **SELECTED PUBLICATIONS** Auth, Toward an Integral Spirituality, ReVision, 96; auth, Structural Violence and Spirituality: Socially Engaged Buddhist Perspectives, ReVision, 97; coauth, Unlearning Oppression: Healing Racism, Healing Violence, ReVision, 97; auth, Responding to Violence: An Introduction, ReVision, 97; coauth, Directions for Transpersonal Inquiry: Reflections on the Conversation, and Ken Wilber and the Future of Transpersonal Inquiry: An Introduction to the Conversation, in Rothberg, ed, Ken Wilber in Dialogue: Conversations with Leading Transpersonal Thinkers, Quest, 98; coauth, ReVisioning ReVision: A Statement from the Executive Editors, ReVision, 98; auth, Spiritual Practice at Work: The Importance of Community: The Buddhist Peace Fellowship BASE Program, Inner Edge, 98; auth, Responding to the Cries of the World: Socially Engaged Buddhism in North America, in Prebish, ed, The Face of Buddhism in America, Univ Calif, 98; ed, Intimate Relationships and Spirituality, ReVision, 98; co-ed, Ken Wilber in Dialogue: Conversations with Leading Transpersonal Thinkers, Quest, 98. **CONTACT ADDRESS** Saybrook Graduate School and Research Center, 450 Pacific, 3rd Floor, San Francisco, CA 94133. **EMAIL** drothberg@igc.org

ROTHENBUSCH, ESTHER H.
DISCIPLINE CHURCH MUSIC **EDUCATION** Baldwin-Wallace Col, BM; Univ Mich, MA, PhD. **CAREER** Instr, Univ Mich, Adrian Col, Bowling Green State Univ; asst prof, S Baptist Theol Univ, 94-. **SELECTED PUBLICATIONS** Auth, The Joyful Sound: Women in the Nineteenth-Century United States Hymnody Tradition; Hallelujah! Handel Meets the Megachurch. **CONTACT ADDRESS** Sch Church Mus and Worship, So Baptist Theol Sem, 2825 Lexington Rd, Louisville, KY 40280. **EMAIL** erothenbusch@sbts.edu

ROTHMAN, FREDERICK P.
PERSONAL Born 11/14/1940, Baltimore, MD, 2 children **DISCIPLINE** CORPORATIONS, DECEDENTS' ESTATES AND TRUSTS, ELDER LAW, ESTDT PLANNING, FED TAXATION **EDUCATION** Cornell Univ, AB, 62; Cornell Law Sch, JD, 64. **CAREER** Prof, Villanova Univ, 71-. **RESEARCH** Corporate finance, probate, professional responsibility, taxation. **SELECTED PUBLICATIONS** Coauth, Probate Law and Taxation of Transfers, Trusts and Estates, Vol I and II, 80; auth, Corporate Finance Electronic Database, 98; auth, Wealth Tax Electronic Database, 99. **CONTACT ADDRESS** Law School, Villanova Univ, 299 N Sprwt Mill Rd, Villanova, PA 19085-1682. **EMAIL** rothman@law.villanova.edu

ROTHSTEIN, PAUL FREDERICK
PERSONAL Born 06/06/1938, Chicago, IL, m, 1963, 2 children **DISCIPLINE** LAW **EDUCATION** Northwestern Univ, BS, 59, LLB, 61. **CAREER** Instr law, Univ Mich, 63-64; from asst prof to assoc prof, Univ Tex, Austin, 64-71; Prof Law, Georgetown Univ, 71-, Guest lectr, Univ Wales, 63; co-dir, Univ Tex, Fed Defender Prog, 65-67; reporter-consult, comt rev penal code, State Bar Tex, 66-68 & Dist Columbia, 77; consult, Fed Trade Comn, US Dept Treas, US Dept Health, Educ & Welfare, Nat Acad Sci, Am Acad Judicial Educ, Nat Col State Judiciary, Comnr Uniform State Laws, US Senate Judiciary Comt, 67-; atty, Surrey, Karasik, Gould & Greene, Wash, DC, 67; chmn, Fed Bar Asn federal rules evidence comt, 76 & Asn Am Law Schs evidence sect, 77; mem, Nat Coun & Continuing Legal Educ Bd, Fed Barn Asn, 77-; secy, Nat Asn Criminal Injuries compensation bds, 77- **HONORS AND AWARDS** Chairman, Am Bar Assn, Evidence & Procedure Committee, 80-90; Council, Am Bar Assn, Criminal Justice Section; Various community & professional awards. **MEMBERSHIPS** Fed Bar Asn; Am Bar Asn. **RESEARCH** Trial law; constitution and supreme court; philosophy of law. **SELECTED PUBLICATIONS** Auth, A reevaluation of the privilege against adverse spousal testimony in the light of its purpose, Int & Comp Law Quart, 10/63; The new British Resale Prices Act, parts I and II (Part II: Recent developments), Am J Comp Law, spring & autumn 64; State compensation for criminally inflicted injuries, Univ Tex Law Rev, 11/65; Evidence in a Nutshell, West Publ, 97; Understanding the federal rules of evidence, Law J Press, 75; The Federal Rules of Evidence, West Publ Co, 99; auth, Evidence: Cases, Materials, and Problems, Matthew Bender Co., 2nd Ed, 98. **CONTACT ADDRESS** Law Ctr, Georgetown Univ, 600 New Jersey N W, Washington, DC 20001-2022. **EMAIL** rothstei@law.georgetown.edu

ROTTSCHAEFER, WILLIAM ANDREW
PERSONAL Born 06/20/1933, Tulsa, OK, m, 1974 **DISCIPLINE** PHILOSOPHY **EDUCATION** St Louis Univ, BA, 57, MA, 60, STL, 66; Univ IL, Urbana-Champaign, MS, 69; Boston Univ, PhD, 73. **CAREER** Asst prof philos, State Univ NY Col Oswego, 72-73 & State Univ New York Col Plattsburgh, 73-74; asst prof, 75-79, assoc prof, 79, Prof Philos, Lewis & Clark Col, 79. **MEMBERSHIPS** Am Philos Asn; Philos Sci Asn; Inst Relig in Age of Sci; Int Soc Hist, Philos, Soc Study

of Biol; Hist of Sci Soc; Ore Acad Sci; Soc Philos and Psychol. **RESEARCH** Relationships between theory and observation in sci and other modes of cognition; behaviorism and cognitive behavioral theory; biology, psychology and values; sci and values; sci and relig. **SELECTED PUBLICATIONS** Auth, Believing is seeing--sometimes, New Scholasticism, 75; Observation: Theory-laden, theory-neutral or theory free?, Southern J Philos, 76; Wilfrid Sellars and the demise of the manifest image, Mod Schoolman, 76; Cognitive characteristics of belief systems, Am Psychologist, 78; Ordinary knowledge and scientific realism, In: The Philosophy of Wilfrid Sellars: Queries and Extensions, Reidl, 78; coauth (with William Knowlton), A Social Learning Theory Perspective on Human Freedom, Behaviorism, 79; Is there a values expert in the house, Comtemp Philos, 82; The psychological foundations of value theory: B F Skinner's Science of Values, Zygon, 82; Religious Cognition as Interpreted Experience: An Examination of Ian barbour's Compaison of the Epistemic Structures of Science and Religion, Zygon, 85; Learning to Be a Moral Agent, Personalist Forum, 86; Wilfrid Sellars on the Nature of Though, In: Naturalistic Epistemology, Reide, 87; Roger Sperry's Science of Values, Jour Mind and Behavior, 87; The New Interactionism between Science and Religion, Relig Studies Rev, 88; The Ghost of the Given: A Case for Epistemological Ghostbusters or Ghostlovers?, Bridges, 89; Creation and Evolution: Some Epistemological Criteria for an Integration, Explorations, 90; co-auth, Really Taking Darwin Seriously: An Alternative to Michael Ruse's Darwinian Metaethics, Biol and Philos, 90; Evolutionary Naturalistic Justifications of Morality: A Matter of Faith and Works, Biol and Philos, 91; Some Philosophical Implications of Bandura's Social Cognitive Learning Theories of Personality, Zygon, 91; Social Learning Theories of Moral Agency, Behavior and Philos, 91; The Insufficiency of Supervenient Explanations of Moral Actions, Biol and Philos, 91; A Course in the History and Philosophy of Mathematics from a Naturalistic Perspective, Teaching Philos, 91; What if the Universe if Fine-Tuned for Life, Explorations, 93; The Interaction between Science and Religion: An Assessment of Polkinghorne's Amiable Interactionism, 95; Scientific Naturalistic Philosophy and Gustafason's Theocentrism: A Marriage Made in Heaven, Zygon, 95; B F Skinner and the Grand Inquisitor, Zygon, 95; Is Science Epistemically Dependent on Religious Knowedge? Center for Theol and the Natural Sci Bull, 95; Evolutionary Ethics: An Irresistibe Temptation: Some Reflections on Paul Farber's The Temptation of Evolutionary Ethics, Biol and Philos, 97; Road Runner and the Bunch of Carrots: Some Teleological Implications of Theory of Natural Selection, Bridges, 97; Adaptational Functional Ascriptions in Evolutionary Biology: A Critique of Schaffner's Views, Philos Sci, 97; Naturalizing Moral Agency: A Critical Review of Some Recent Works on the Bilogical and Psychological Bases of Human Morality, Bridges 97; The Biology and Psychology of Moral Agency, Cambridge Univ Press, 98; auth, Moral Learning and Moral Realism: How Empirical Psychology Illuminates Issues in Moral Ontology, Behavior and Philosophy, 99. **CONTACT ADDRESS** Dept of Philos, Lewis and Clark Col, 0615 SW Palatine Hill, Portland, OR 97219-7879. **EMAIL** rotts@lclark.edu

ROTUNDA, RONALD DANIEL
PERSONAL Born 02/14/1945, Blue Island, IL, s, 2 children **DISCIPLINE** LAW **EDUCATION** Harvard Univ, BA, 67, JD, 70. **CAREER** Law clerk, Second Circuit Court Appeals, 70-71; lawyer, Wilmer, Cutler & Pickering, Washington, DC, 71-73; asst coun law, Senate Watergate Comt, 73-74; asst prof, 74-77, assoc prof, 77-80, prof Law, Univ Ill, 80-. **MEMBERSHIPS** Am Law Inst; Am Bar Asn. **RESEARCH** Constitutional law; legal ethics; Federal jurisdiction. **SELECTED PUBLICATIONS** Co-auth, Treatise on Constitutional Law: Substance and Procedure, 2nd ed, West Pub (St Paul, MN), 92; auth, Modern Constitutuional Law: Cases and Notes, 4th ed, West Pub (St Paul, MN), 93; co-auth, Constitutional Law, 5th ed, West Pub (St Paul, MN), 95; co-auth, Problems and Materials on Professional Responsibility, 6th ed, Found Pr (Westbury, NY), 95; auth, Professional Responsibility, 4th ed, West Pub (St Paul, MN), 95; co-auth, Treatise on Constitutional Law: Substance and Procedure, CD Rom ed, West Pub (St Paul, MN), 95; auth, Modern Constitutional Law: Cases and Notes, West Pub (St Paul, MN), 97; co-auth, Treatise on Constitutional Law: Substance and Procedure, 3rd ed, West Pub (St Paul, MN), 99; coauth, Problems and Materials on Professional Responsibility, 7th ed, Found Pr (New York, NY), 00; auth, Legal Ethics: The Lawyer's Deskbook on Professional Responsibility, ABA-West Group (St Paul, MN), 00. **CONTACT ADDRESS** Col of Law, Univ of Illinois, Urbana-Champaign, 504 E Pennsylvania, Champaign, IL 61820-6996. **EMAIL** rrotunda@law.uiuc.edu

ROUNDS, CHARLES E., JR
PERSONAL Born 12/16/1946, Middletown, CT, m, 1975, 2 children **DISCIPLINE** LAW **EDUCATION** Columbia Univ, BA, 69; Suffolk Univ Law Sch, JD, 76. **CAREER** Assoc Trust Coun, First Nat Bank of Boston, 77-83; Prof, Suffolk Univ Law Sch, 83-. **MEMBERSHIPS** Am Col of Trust and Estate Coun; Beacon Hill Inst; Mass Bar Asn. **RESEARCH** The Law of Trusts. **SELECTED PUBLICATIONS** Auth, Loring A Trustee's Handbook, 7th ed, Little, Brown & Co, 94; auth, Loring A Trustee's Handbook, 1996 ed, Little, Brown & Co, 96; auth, Loring A Trustee's Handbook, 1997 ed, Little, Brown & Co, 97; auth, IOLTA, Interest without Principle, Cato Inst, 97; auth, Loring A Trustee's Handbook, 1998 ed, Panel Pub, 98; auth, Loring A Trustee's Handbook, 1999 ed, Panel Pub, 99; auth, Loring A Trustee's Handbook, 2000 ed, Panel Pub, 00; auth, Property Rights: The Hidden Issue of Social Security Reform, Cato Inst, 00; auth, Loring A Trustee's Handbook, 2001ed, Panel Pub, 01. **CONTACT ADDRESS** Sch Law, Suffolk Univ, 120 Tremont St, Boston, MA 02108-4977. **EMAIL** CRoundsJr@aol.com

ROUSE, JOHN JAY
PERSONAL Born 03/11/1955, New York, NY, s **DISCIPLINE** CRIMINAL JUSTICE **EDUCATION** State Univ NY at Birmingham, BA, 77; New Sch for Soc Res, MA, 80; City Univ NY, M Philos, 87; PhD, 88. **CAREER** Postdoctoral Fel, Narcotic and Drug Res Inc, 88-90; Dir of Res, Drug Serv Unit, NYork City Dept of Probtn, 90-95; Asst Prof, Sacred Heart Univ, 95-. **MEMBERSHIPS** ACUS. **RESEARCH** Criminology, Corrections, Comparative Criminal Justice. **SELECTED PUBLICATIONS** Auth, Alternatives to Prison and Their Effects on Recidivism Rates, Master's Thesis, The New Sch for Soc Res, Univ Microfilms Int (Ann Arbor, MI), 80; auth, "The Relationship between Police Presence and Crime Deterrence," The Police J 58-2 (Apr-June 85): 118-131; auth, "Deinstitutionalization and Its Impact on Swedish Corrections, " Int J of Comp and Appl Criminal Justice 9-2 (spring/winter 85): 71-83; auth, Citizen Crime Patrols and Their Effect on Fear of Crime in Urban Neighborhoods," PhD Dissertation, The City Univ of NY, Univ Microfilms Int (Ann Arbor, MI), 88; rev, "Marijuana: Costs of Abuse, Costs of Control, " J of Contemp Criminal Justice 6-1 (Feb 90): 46; coauth, "Hidden Paradigms of Morality in Debates About Drugs: Historical and Policy Shifts in British and American Drug Policies," in The Drug Legalization Debate, ed. James A. Inciardi (Sage, 90); auth, "Evaluation Research on Prison-Based Drug Treatment Programs and Some Policy Implications," The Int J of the Addictions 26-1 (91): 29-44; coauth, "A Historical Perspective on British and American Drug Policies," in Problems of Drug Dependence 1990: Proceedings of the 52nd Annual Meeting of the Committee on Problems of Drug Dependence (US Dept of Health and Human Serv, Alcohol, Drug Abuse, and Mental Health Admin, 91), 471-472. **CONTACT ADDRESS** Dept Soc and Behav Sci, Sacred Heart Univ, 5151 Park Ave, Fairfield, CT 06432.

ROUSH, SHERRILYN
DISCIPLINE PHILOSOPHY **EDUCATION** Penn St Univ, BS, 88, BA, 88; Harvard Univ, PhD, 99 **CAREER** Tch Fel, 91-98, Harvard Univ; Lect, 91-96, New Eng Conserv of Music **HONORS AND AWARDS** AAUW Dissert Fel, 95-96; Nat Sci Found Fel, 88-91; Mellon Fel in Humanities, 88 **MEMBERSHIPS** Am Philos Assoc; Philos of Sci Assoc **RESEARCH** Metaphysics and Epistemology; Kant; Philosophy of Science; Subjects & Objects; Anthropic Principle; Transcendental Arguments **SELECTED PUBLICATIONS** Auth, Alternate Possibilities and their Entertainment, Philosophy, 98 **CONTACT ADDRESS** Dept Philos, Harvard Univ, 208 Emerson Hall, Cambridge, MA 02138. **EMAIL** roush@rice.edu

ROWAN, ALBERT T.
PERSONAL Born 05/15/1927, Kansas City, MO, m, 1948 **DISCIPLINE** THEOLOGY **EDUCATION** MI State U, 1946; Western Baptist Bible Coll, BRE, BTh 1955-59; Ashland Theological Sem, MDiv 1976; Trinity Theol Sem, DMin 1987. **CAREER** First Baptist, Quincy IL, pastor 1955-60; Zion Baptist, Springfield IL, pastor 1960-61; Salem Baptist, Champaign IL, pastor 1961-64; Bethany Baptist, Cleveland OH, pastor 1964-; Trinity Theological Seminary, adjunct professor, 90-95, Course Assessor, 95-. **HONORS AND AWARDS** Proclamation "Rev Albert T Rowan Day" Mayor Carl B Stokes 1970; Certificate of Appreciation Champaign County Urban League 1963; elected to Lincoln High School Hall of Fame 1981; Hon Dr of Div Am Bible Inst 1969; Hon Dr of Div VA Seminary & Coll 1975; Outstanding Pastor of the Year, Baptist Ministers Conference of Cleveland, 1983; Hall of Fame, Lincoln High School, Kansas City, MO, 1981. **MEMBERSHIPS** 1st vice pres Baptist Minister's Conf of Cleveland; pres Northern OH Dist Congress 1955-60; past pres Cleveland Baptist Assn 1983-; mem exec bd OH General Baptist State Convention; mem Cleveland Library Bd of Trustees 1976-78; first vice moderator, Northern Ohio Baptist District Assn, 1987-; City Planning Commission of Cleveland, Ohio, chairman, mem, 1976-. **CONTACT ADDRESS** Bethany Baptist Church, 1201-1225 E 105th St, Cleveland, OH 44108.

ROWAN, BERNARD
PERSONAL Born 08/10/1964, Nashville, TN, s **DISCIPLINE** POLITICAL SCIENCE **EDUCATION** Vanderbilt Univ, BA, Political Science and Economics, 86; Univ York (UK), MA, Political Philosophy, 88; Univ Chicago, PhD, 93. **CAREER** Assoc Prof, Chicago State Univ 99-; Asst Prof, 96-99; Lecturer, 95-96. **HONORS AND AWARDS** Rotary Scholarship, 87; Univ Centennial Fel, 87-90; Phi Beta Kappa. **MEMBERSHIPS** Amer Political Science Assn; Midwest Political Science Assn; Institute for African-American Studies. **RESEARCH** Contemporary Political Theory; Korean Studies. **SELECTED PUBLICATIONS** Auth, "On the Ajumma: A Political and Economic Perspective," Journal of Asiatic Studies, December 99. **CONTACT ADDRESS** Dept History & Government, Chicago State Univ, 9501 South King Drive, Chicago, IL 60628-1501. **EMAIL** tb-rowan@csu.edu

ROWAN, JOHN R.
PERSONAL Born 03/06/1967, Philadelphia, PA, m **DISCIPLINE** PHILOSOPHY **EDUCATION** Univ of Virginia, PhD, 97. **CAREER** Asst Prof, Purdue Univ, Calumet, 97-. **MEMBERSHIPS** Amer Phil Assoc; Soc for Business Ethics; Assoc for Practical and Professional Ethics; Intl Assoc of Business and Soc; Intl Economics and Phil Soc; North Amer Soc for Social Phil. **RESEARCH** Business and professional ethics; ethical theory; issues in applied ethics; political and social philosophy; legal philosophy **SELECTED PUBLICATIONS** Auth, Philosophy on Messick and Social Conflict: Resolving the Reolution Conflict, 97; Grounding Hypernorms: Toward a Contractarian Theory of Business Ethics, 97; State Sponsored Abortion in a Property Rights Framework, 98; Moral Rights and Social Policy, 99. **CONTACT ADDRESS** Dept of Philosophy, Purdue Univ, Calumet, 2200 169th St, Hammond, IN 46323-2094. **EMAIL** jrowan@calumet.purdue.edu

ROWE, STEPHEN C.
PERSONAL Born 02/25/1945, Cincinnati, OH, m, 3 children **DISCIPLINE** ETHICS AND SOCIETY **EDUCATION** Colgate Univ, BA, 67; Univ Chicago Divinity Sch, MTh, 69, PhD, 74. **CAREER** Chemn Philos Dept, 88- , coordr Liberal Studies Prog, 95- , Grand Vallet State Univ. **HONORS AND AWARDS** Univ Fel, 71-72; Danforth Assoc, 77-84; Phi Kappa Phi; Distinguished Fac Awd, 83; Mich Hum Fac, 84- ; Outstanding Educr Awd, 97. **MEMBERSHIPS** Am Acad Relig; APA; Asn for General and Liberal Stud; Ctr for Process Stud; Chicago Social Ethics Sem; Soc for the Advanc of Am Philos; Soc for Buddhist-Christian Stud; Soc for Values in Higher Educ. **RESEARCH** Philosophy of religion; ethics. **SELECTED PUBLICATIONS** Auth, Living Beyond Crisis: Essays on Discovery and Being in the World, Pilgrim, 80; auth, Leaving and Returning: On America's Contribution to a World Ethic, Bucknell, 89; auth, Claiming a Liberal Education: Resources for Realizing the College Experience, Ginn, 90; auth, Rediscovering the West: An Inquiry into Nothingness and Relatedness, SUNY, 94; auth, The Vision of William James, Element/ Penguin, 96; auth, Toward a Postliberal Liberalism: James Luther Adams and the Need for a Theory of Relational Meaning, Am J of Theol & Philos, 96; auth, A Zen Presence in America: Dialogue As Religious Practice, in Mitchell, ed, Masao Abe: Zen Life in Dialogue, Tuttle, 98. **CONTACT ADDRESS** Philosophy Dept, Grand Valley State Univ, 1 Campus Dr, Allendale, MI 49401. **EMAIL** rowes@gvsu.edu

ROWE, WILLIAM L.
PERSONAL Born 07/26/1931, Detroit, MI, m, 1952, 3 children **DISCIPLINE** PHILOSOPHY **EDUCATION** Wayne State Univ, AB, 54; Chicago Theol Sem, BD, 57; Univ Mich, PhD, 62. **CAREER** Instr philos, Univ Ill, 60-62; from asst prof to assoc prof, 62-69, Prof Philos, Purdue Univ, W Lafayette, 69-. **HONORS AND AWARDS** Guggenheim Fel, 84-85; Nat Humanities Ctr Fel, 84-85. **MEMBERSHIPS** Soc Relig Higher Educ; Soc for Philos of Relig. **RESEARCH** Philosophy of religion; metaphysics. **SELECTED PUBLICATIONS** Auth, Religious Symbols and God: A Philosophical Study of Tillich's Theology, Univ Chicago, 68; co-ed, Philosophy of Religion: Selected Readings, Harcourt, 73; auth, The Cosmological Argument, Princeton Univ, 75; Philosophy of Religion, Dickenson, 78; Thomas Reid on Freedom and Morality, Cornell Univ, 95. **CONTACT ADDRESS** Dept of Philos, Purdue Univ, West Lafayette, West Lafayette, IN 47907-1968. **EMAIL** wlrowe@purdue.edu

ROWLAND, RICK
PERSONAL Born 06/20/1952, m, 1974, 3 children **DISCIPLINE** BIBLICAL STUDIES, OLD TESTAMENT **EDUCATION** Univ CA, BA, 74; Pepperdine Univ, MA, 87; Princeton theol sem, Mdiv, 90, PhD, 97. **CAREER** Mgr, Hebrew Lexicon proj, Princeton theol sem, 88-95; Dead Sea Scrolls proj, Princeton theol sem, 87-93; tchg fel, Princeton theol sem, 87-93; res asst, Princeton theol sem, 93; instr, Princeton theol sem, 93; adjunct inst, Princeton theol sem, 93-94; vis instr, 94-95; mgr, Acad proj design, 97-. **HONORS AND AWARDS** Pres's award, 77-80, 83-85; Henry Snyder Gehman award, Princeton theol sem, 88; George S. Green fel, Princeton theol sem, 90-91; one-yr fel award, Christian Scholar Found, 92-93, 93-94. **SELECTED PUBLICATIONS** Auth, Job's Humble Reply: Is the Question Really the Answer?, Difficult Texts in Job, Pepperdine Univ Annual Bible Lectures, 96; Religion 101 The History and Religion of Ancient Israel: Course Reader, 94; The Character and Identity of God in the Old Testament: Significance for Contemporary Christian Worship, Pepperdine Univ Annual Bible Lectures, 93; rev, E. Achtemeier, The Old Testament and the Proclamation of the Gospel, Leaven 3/1, 95. **CONTACT ADDRESS** Dept of Relig, Pepperdine Univ, 24255 Pacific Coast Hwy, Malibu, CA 90263. **EMAIL** rrowland@pepperdine.edu

ROWLETT, LORI
PERSONAL Born 01/26/1955, Dallas, TX, d **DISCIPLINE** RELIGIOUS STUDIES **EDUCATION** Univ Tex, BA, 76; Perkins Sch Theol at Southern Methodist Univ, MTS, 86; Cambridge Univ, PhD, 96. **CAREER** Vis asst prof, Col of William and Mary, 94-95; adj prof, Christopher Newport Univ, 95-97; asst prof, Univ of Wis at Eau Claire, 97-. **MEMBERSHIPS**

Am Acad of Relig, Soc for Biblical Lit, Soc for Critical Exchange, Nat Women's Studies Asn. **RESEARCH** Hebrew Bible, feminist studies in religion, religion and literature. **SELECTED PUBLICATIONS** Auth, Joshua and the Rhetoric of Violence: a New Historicist Analysis, Sheffield Univ Press (Sheffield, Eng), 96. **CONTACT ADDRESS** Dept Relig & Philos, Univ of Wisconsin, Eau Claire, PO Box 4004, Eau Claire, WI 54702-4004. **EMAIL** rowletl@uwec.edu

ROWOLD, HENRY
PERSONAL Born 07/10/1939, St. Louis, MO, m, 1962, 3 children **DISCIPLINE** THEOLOGY **EDUCATION** Concordia Sem, MDiv, 64, STM, 65; Christ Sem, ThD, 77. **CAREER** Dir res and plan, Lutheran Church, South Asia, 83-87; dir, Lutheran Church, China Coordinating Ctr, 87-95; prof, Concordia Sem, 95- . **HONORS AND AWARDS** Listed, Who's Who in Biblical Archaeology; listed, Who's Who in the Midwest. **MEMBERSHIPS** Cath Bibl Asn; Soc of Bibl Lit; Am Soc of Missiology; Lutheran Soc for Missiology. **RESEARCH** Wisdom and wisdom literature; history of Christianity in China. **SELECTED PUBLICATIONS** Auth, Educating for World Missions: A Missionary Perspective, Issues in Chr Educ, 93; auth, Lord of the Reach, Missio Apstolica, 94; auth, Arresting Developments in China's Religious Policies, Concordia J, 95; auth, Reflections on Leaving the Mission Field, Missio Apostolica, 96; auth, Teaching English as Ministry, Missio Apostolica, 97; auth, The Reunification of Hong Kong with China: Why? What's at Stake? What about the Church? Concordia J, 98; auth, Ministry at the Fringes: The Missionary as Marginal Person, Missio Apostolica, 98. **CONTACT ADDRESS** 801 DeMun Ave, Saint Louis, MO 63105-3199. **EMAIL** rowoldh@csl.edu

ROY, DONALD H.
PERSONAL Born 07/29/1944, Hartford, CT, s **DISCIPLINE** POLITICAL SCIENCE **EDUCATION** Bard Col, BA, 66; Georgetown Univ, MA, 70; Univ Notre Dame, PhD, 77. **CAREER** Assoc Prof, Ferris State Univ, 93-. **MEMBERSHIPS** Amnesty Int. **RESEARCH** American politics and public policy. **SELECTED PUBLICATIONS** Auth, Dialogues in American Politics, Kendall-Hent, 93; auth, Public Policy Dialogues, Univ Press of Am, 94. **CONTACT ADDRESS** Dept Soc Sci, Ferris State Univ, 820 Campus Dr, Big Rapids, MI 49307. **EMAIL** royd@ferris.edu

ROY, SUDIPTO
PERSONAL Born Calcutta, India, s **DISCIPLINE** CRIMINOLOGY **EDUCATION** Carleton Univ, MA, 80; Univ Okla, MA, 85; Western Mich Univ, PhD, 91. **CAREER** Vis asst prof, Del State Col, 90-91; asst prof, Ind Univ Nw, 91-94; asst to assoc prof, Ind State Univ, 94-. **HONORS AND AWARDS** Res Grant, Western Mich, Univ, 87; Grad Student Excellence Certificate, Western Mich Univ, 90; Grad Res and Creative Scholar Awd, Western Mich Univ, 90; Prof Develop Awd, Del State Col, 90, 91; Lambda Alpha Epsilon Awd; Summer Fac Res Fel, Ind Univ, 92, 93, 94, 95, 96; Alpha Phi Sigma. **MEMBERSHIPS** World Soc of Victimology; Am Soc of Criminol. **RESEARCH** Corrections, Program Evaluation, Victimology. **SELECTED PUBLICATIONS** Auth, "Adult Offenders in an Electronic Home Detention Program: Factors Related to Failure", J of Offender Monitoring, (Fall 94); coauth, "Manual and Electronic House Arrest Programs for Adults: An Evaluation of Factors Related To Failure" and "Juvenile Electronic Monitoring Program in Lake County, Indiana: An Evaluation", Intermediate Sanctions: Sentencing in the 1990s, eds J. Smykla and W. Selke, Anderson Pub, (Cincinnati, 95); auth, "Juvenile Restitution and Recidivism in a Midwestern County", Fed Probation, March 95; auth, "Juvenile Offenders in an Electronic Home Detention Program: A Study of Factors Related to Failure, J of Offender Monitoring, Spring, 95; coauth, "Juvenile Restitution in the United States: Bringing Justice for Victims?", Criminol and Soc Integration 4.1 (96); auth, "Five Years of Electronic Monitoring of Adults and Juveniles in Lake County, Indiana: A Comparative Study on Factors Related to Failure", J of Crime and Justice 20.1 (97); auth, "Violations of the Rights of the Accused and the Convicted in India", Criminol and Soc Integration 5.2 (97); coauth, "Perceptions of Alumni Concerning Their Level of Preparation for Careers in the Criminal Justice Field: A Pilot Study", J of Criminal Justice Educ 10.1 (99): auth, "An Analysis of the Exit Status of Adult Offenders in an Electronic Monitoring Home Detention Program in Indiana", J of Offender Monitoring, (Summer 99). **CONTACT ADDRESS** Dept Criminol, Indiana State Univ, Holmstedt Hall, Rm 228, Terre Haute, IN 47809-0002. **EMAIL** crroy@scifac.indstate.edu

RUBARTH, SCOTT M.
PERSONAL Born 07/21/1962 **DISCIPLINE** PHILOSOPHY **EDUCATION** Univ of Toronto, PhD, 97. **CAREER** Asst Prof, Rollins Col. **HONORS AND AWARDS** Cornell Scholar in Classical Philos. **MEMBERSHIPS** Amer Philos Asn; Amer Philol Asn **RESEARCH** Hellenistic philosophy; Greek moral theory. **CONTACT ADDRESS** Rollins Col, 1000 Holt Ave, Philosophy, Winter Park, FL 32789-4499. **EMAIL** srubarth@rollins.edu

RUBENSTEIN, ERIC M.
DISCIPLINE CONTEMPORARY ANGLO-AMERICAN PHILOSOPHY, MODERN PHILOSOPHY **EDUCATION** Univ NC, Chapel Hill, PhD, 96. **CAREER** Vis asst prof, Colgate Univ. **RESEARCH** Contemporary Anglo-American Philosophy, Modern Philosophy, Metaphysics. **SELECTED PUBLICATIONS** Auth, Absolute Processes: A Nominalist Alternative, The S Jour Philos; Color as Simple: Reply to Westphal, Philos; auth, "Experiencing the Future: Kantian Thoughts on Husserl," Idealistic Studies; auth, "Sellars Without Homogeneity," International Journal of Philosophical Studies; auth, "Individuation and Metaphysics"; auth, Experiencing the Ever Present Future. **CONTACT ADDRESS** Dept of Philos and Relig, Colgate Univ, 13 Oak Drive, Hamilton, NY 13346-1398. **EMAIL** erubenstein@mail.colgate.edu

RUBENSTEIN, RICHARD LOWELL
PERSONAL Born 01/08/1924, New York, NY, m, 3 children **DISCIPLINE** RELIGIOUS STUDIES **EDUCATION** Univ Cincinnati, AB, 46; Jewish Theol Sem, MHL, 52; Harvard Univ, STM, 55, PhD(hist & philos relig), 60. **CAREER** Prof, 70-77, Distinguished prof Relig, 77-95, prof emer, 95- , Fla State Univ; dir, Ctr Study Southern Cult & Relig, 73-95; pres, Univ of Bridgeport, 95- . **HONORS AND AWARDS** Nat Humanities Inst fel, Yale Univ, 76-77; Portico d'Ottavia Lit Prize, 77; Doctor of Hebrew Letters, honoris causa, Jewish Theol Sem of Am, 87. **MEMBERSHIPS** Am Acad Relig; Soc Bibl Lit; Soc Values Higher Edue; Soc Arts, Relig & Contemp Cult. **RESEARCH** Contemporary religious thought; Holocaust studies; values in contemporary society. **SELECTED PUBLICATIONS** Auth, After Auschwitz, Bobbs-Merrill, 68; The Religious Imagination, Beacon Paperbk, 68; Morality and Eros, McGraw Hill, 70; My Brother Paul, Harper & Row, 72; Power Struggle, Scribners, 74; The Cunning of History, Harper & Row, 75; auth, The Aft of Triage, Beacon, 83; ed, Modernization: The Humanist Response to Its Promise and Problems, Paragon, 84; coauth, Approaches to Auschwitz: The Holocaust and Its Legacy, Westminster, 87; ed, Spirit Matters: The World Wide Impact of Religion on Contemporary Politics, Paragon, 87; ed, The Dissolving Alliance: The United States and the NATO Alliance, Paragon, 87; co-ed, the Politics of Liberation Theology: North American and Latin American Views, Paragon, 88; auth, After Auschwitz: History, Theology and Contemporary Judaism, 2d ed, Johns Hopkins, 92; **CONTACT ADDRESS** Office of the President, Univ of Bridgeport, Bridgeport, CT 32306-6601.

RUBENSTEIN, WILLIAM
PERSONAL Born 09/03/1960, Pittsburgh, PA, p **DISCIPLINE** LAW **EDUCATION** Yale Col, BA, 82; Harvard Law Sch, JD, 86 **CAREER** Law clerk, U.S. District Court, 86-87; staff coun to dir, Am Civil Liberties Union, 87-95; lectr, Harvard Law Sch, 90-93, 94-96; lectr, Yale Law Sch, 93-95; acting assoc prof, Stanford Law Sch, 95-97; acting prof, UCLA, 97-. **HONORS AND AWARDS** John Bingham Hurlbut Award, Stanford Law Sch, 97; Top Twenty Calif Lawyers Under 40, 00. **MEMBERSHIPS** Nat Lesbian and Gay Law Asn; Commonwealth of Pa Bar Asn. **RESEARCH** Constitutional law; Complex adjudication; Sexual orientation law. **SELECTED PUBLICATIONS** Co-ed, AIDS Agenda: Emerging Issues in Civil Rights, New Press, 92; auth, Lesbians, Gay Men, and the Law, New Press, 93; auth, "Don't Ask, Don't Tell, Don't Believe It," NY Times, 93; auth, "Since When is the Equal Protection Clause Our Route to Equality?: some Reflections on the Construction of the Hate Speech Debate from a Lesbian/Gay Perspective," in Speaking of Race, Speaking of Sex: Hate Speech, Civil Rights and Civil Liberties, NYU Press, 94; coauth, The Rights of People Who Are HIV Positive, S Ill Univ Press, 96; auth, Cases and materials on Sexual Orientation and the Law, West Pub Co, 97; auth, "Divided We Litigate: Addressing Disputes Among Clients and Lawyers in Civil Rights Campaigns," Yale L J, 97; auth, "In Community Begins Responsibilities: Obligations at the Gay Bar," Hastings L J, 98; auth, "The Myth of Superiority," Constitutional Commentary, 99; auth, "A Transactional Model of Adjudication," Georgetown L Rev, 01. **CONTACT ADDRESS** Dept Law, Univ of California, Los Angeles, PO Box 951476, Los Angeles, CA 90095-1476. **EMAIL** rubenste@law.ucla.edu

RUBIN, ALFRED P.
PERSONAL Born 10/13/1931, New York, NY, m, 1960, 3 children **DISCIPLINE** INTERNATIONAL LAW **EDUCATION** Columbia Univ, BA, 52, JD, 57; Univ Cambridge, MLitt, 63. **CAREER** Atty adv, 61-66, dir trade control, 66-67, US Dept Defense; prof law, Univ Oregon, 67-73; prof, distinguished prof, int law, Fletcher Sch of Law and Diplomacy, Tufts Univ, 73-. **HONORS AND AWARDS** Chairman of the Exec Committee Branch, 00-; Pres, Am branch, Int Law Assoc, 00-; Charles H. Stockton Prof of Int Law, US Naval War College, 81-82. **MEMBERSHIPS** Am Soc of Int Law; Int Law Asn. **RESEARCH** Public international law. **SELECTED PUBLICATIONS** Auth, Enforcing the Rules of International Law, Harvard Int Law J, (93); auth, Ethics and Authority on International Law, Cambridge, 97; auth, Dayton and the Limits of Law, in National Interest, 97; auth, The Law of Piracy, 2d, Transnational, 98. **CONTACT ADDRESS** Fletcher School of Law and Diplomacy, Tufts Univ, Medford, Medford, MA 02155. **EMAIL** arubin@tufts.edu

RUBIN, PAUL H.
PERSONAL Born 08/09/1942, Boston, MA, m, 2 children **DISCIPLINE** LAW & ECONOMICS **EDUCATION** Univ Cinn, BA, 63; Purdue Univ, PhD, 70. **CAREER** Asst, assoc, & full prof of Econ, Univ Georgia, 68-82; Sr Staff Economist, President's Council of Economic Advisers, 81-82; prof, Baruch Col & Grad Ctr CUNY, 82-83; adj prof, VPI, 84, dir of Advertising Economics, Federal Trade Commission, 83-85; chief Economist, U.S. Consumer Product Safety Commission, 85-87; vpres, Glassman-Oliver Economic Consultants, 87-91; Goerge Wash Law Ctr, 85-89; Prof Econ, 91- , actg chr, 93-94, Emory Univ; adj scholar, Am Enterprise Inst, Cato Inst, 92-98; **HONORS AND AWARDS** Chemn Award, Consumer Prod Safety Comn, 87; grants & fel: William H Donner Found, 97-98, Pfizer, 97, IRIS, 92-93, Paul Oreffice Fund, 93, Liberty Fund, 79, CUNY, 83; Fel, Public Choice Soc. **MEMBERSHIPS** Am Econ Asn; Allied Soc Sci Asn; Am Law & Econ Asn; Int Soc New Inst Econ; Publ Choice Soc; S Econ Asn; W Econ Asn. **RESEARCH** Law and economics, industrial organization and antitrust; transactions cost economice, ecmonics of advertising and safety, price theory, law in post-Communist economies. **SELECTED PUBLICATIONS** Auth, The Expansion of Firms," Journal of Political Economy, 73; auth, "The Theory of the Firm and the Structure of the Franchise Contract," Journal of Law and Economics, 78; auth, Managing Business Transactions: Controlling the Costs of Coordinating, Communicating, and Decision Making, Free Press, 93; Tort Reform by Contract, Am Enterprise Inst, 93; auth, "The Assault on the First Amendment: Public Choice and Political Correctness," Cato Journal, (94): 23-37; auth, "The Role of Lawyers in Changing the Law," Journal of Legal Studies, 94; ed, Deregulating Telecommunications: The Baby Bells Case for Competition, Wiley, 95; Promises, Promises: Contrcts in Russia and Other Post-Communist Economies, Shaftesbury Papers, 98; Indicting Liability: How the Liability System Has Turned Against Itself, Am Enterprise Inst, 98; Lives Saved or Lives Lost: The Effect of Concealed Handgun Laws on Crime, Am Econ Rev, 98. **CONTACT ADDRESS** Dept of Economics, Emory Univ, 1635 N Decatur Rd., Atlanta, GA 30322-2240. **EMAIL** prubin@emory.edu

RUBINSTEIN, ERNEST
PERSONAL Born 07/11/1952, New York, NY **DISCIPLINE** RELIGION **EDUCATION** Northwestern Univ, PhD, 95. **CAREER** Adjunct Asst. Prof. In Humanities, NY Univ school of continuing ed, 96-; Librn, the interchurch center, 95-. **HONORS AND AWARDS** Awd for Teaching Excellence, NYU, 99; Constructing a Perfect Solitude in the Spirit of Poesy: Essays on Jewish & German Literature; and Thought in honor of German Literature and Thought in honor of Geza von Molnar Northwestern Univ Pr, 00. **MEMBERSHIPS** Am Acad of Relig. **RESEARCH** Jewish Theology; German Judaism; philosophy. **SELECTED PUBLICATIONS** Auth, A New German Jewish Identity, Aufbau, 98; auth, An Episode of Jewish Romanticism: Franz Rosenzweig's Star of Redemption, SUNY Press, 99; auth, "Constructing a Perfect Solitude," The Spirit of Poesy: Essays on Jewish & German Lit & Thought in honor of Geza Von Molnar, Northwestern Univ Press, 00. **CONTACT ADDRESS** 200 Cabrini Blvd, Apt 42, New York, NY 10033. **EMAIL** ehr3@nyu.edu

RUBSYS, ANTHONY L.
PERSONAL Born 11/05/1923, Lithuania, s **DISCIPLINE** BIBLICAL STUDIES **EDUCATION** Universita Gregoriana, Rome, STL, 49; Pontifical Bibl Inst, Rome, SSL, 51 and CD, 58. **CAREER** Prof Old Testament & New Testament, Immaculate Heart Sem, 53-57; prof relig stud, Manhattan Col, 59-92, prof emer, 93- ; vis prof sacred scripture, St Joseph's Sem, 69-82; vis prof, Vilnius Pedagogical Univ, 93-; vis prof, Vytautas Magnus University, Kaunas, 92-. **HONORS AND AWARDS** Nat award by Educ Dept of Lithuania for transl Old Testament into Lithuanian, 95; STD, Vytautas Magnus Univ. **MEMBERSHIPS** SBL; CBQ; ASOR; Lithuanian Catholic Acad of Sci. **RESEARCH** Pentateuchal studies; archaeology. **SELECTED PUBLICATIONS** Auth, Key to the Old Testament (in Lithuanian), 3 v, Vilnius, Kataliku Pasaulis, 95; auth, Key to the New Testament (in Lithuanian) 2 v, Vilnius, Kataliku Pasaulis, 97; auth, Sventojo Rasto Krastuose, 3 v, Vilnius, Kataliku Pasaulis, 98; transl and contribur to two ed of Bible (in Lithuanian) has been published by The Bible Soc, ecumenical ed, and The Bishop's Conf, Catholic ed., 99. **CONTACT ADDRESS** Manhattan Col, Riverdale, NY 10471-4098. **EMAIL** rtonis@aol.com

RUDENSTINE, DAVID
DISCIPLINE CONSTITUTIONAL LAW **EDUCATION** Yale Univ, BA, 63; MAT, 65; NYork Univ, JD, 69. **CAREER** Prof, Yeshiva Univ, 82-. **HONORS AND AWARDS** Staff atty, NY City Legal Services Prog, 69-72; Dir Citizen's Inquiry Parole & Criminal Justice, Inc, 72-74; counl Nat News Coun; Proj dir, assoc dir, acting exec dir, NY Civil Liberties Union; Guggenheim vis fel. **RESEARCH** The First Amendment, and labor arbitration. **SELECTED PUBLICATIONS** Auth, Prison Without Walls: Report on New York Parole; Rights of Ex-Offenders **CONTACT ADDRESS** Yeshiva Univ, 55 Fifth Ave, New York, NY 10003-4301.

RUDINOW, JOEL
PERSONAL Born 05/23/1947, Oakland, CA, d, 1 child **DISCIPLINE** PHILOSOPHY **EDUCATION** Univ Calif at Santa Barbara, BA, 68; Univ British Columbia, PhD, 73. **CAREER** Lectr, Carlton univ, 73; vis asst prof, Univ Western Ontario, 73; asst prof, Dartmouth Col, 73-81; lectr, Sonoma State Univ, 84-98; instr, Santa Rosa Jr Col, 84-. **HONORS AND AWARDS** Canada Coun Doctoral Fel; Hogg Found Bicentennial Fel in Hist & Philos of Mental Health. **MEMBERSHIPS** Am Philos Asn, Am Soc for Aesthetics. **RESEARCH** Applied Ethics, Philosophy of Music, Popular & Vernacular Culture. **SELECTED PUBLICATIONS** Auth, Invitation to Critical Thinking, Harcourt Brace, 90, 94, & 99. **CONTACT ADDRESS** Dept Philos, Santa Rosa Junior Col, 1501 Mendocino Ave, Santa Rosa, CA 95401-4332. **EMAIL** jrudinow@santarosa.edu

RUEGSEGGER, RONALD W.
PERSONAL Born 09/13/1946, m **DISCIPLINE** PHILOSOPHY **EDUCATION** Westmont Col, BA, 68; Trinity Evang Div Sch, 69; Univ Toronto, Canada, MA, 73; PhD, 77. **CAREER** Asst prof, dept hd, 77; assoc prof, 81; prof, 84; asst pres, 88; exec asst, 90; exec vice, 93; act trea, 93; dean, 93; vice, dean, 94-, Nyack Coll. **RESEARCH** Systematic philosophy. **SELECTED PUBLICATIONS** Auth, "The Propositional Attitude in Perception," Philo Res Arch (81); auth, "Francis Schaeffer on Philosophy," Christ Schl Rev (81): 238-254; auth, "A Reply to Gordon Clark," Christ Schl Rev (82): 150-152; auth, "Three Candidates for the Propositional Attitude in Perception: Judging, Believing and Taking," Philo Res Arch (82): 535-559; auth, Reflections on Francis Schaeffer, Zondervan (Grand Rapids), 86. **CONTACT ADDRESS** Chief Academic Dean, Nyack Col, 1 South Blvd, Nyack, NY 10960-3604.

RUETHER, ROSEMARY R.
PERSONAL Born 11/02/1936, St Paul, MN, m, 1957, 3 children **DISCIPLINE** RELIGION **EDUCATION** Scripps Col, BA, 58; Claremont Grad School, MA, 60; PhD, 65. **CAREER** Prof, Harvard Univ, 65-76; Prof, Harvard Univ Divinity School, 72-73; Prof, Garrett Theol Sem, 76- **HONORS AND AWARDS** Danforth Fel, 60-61; Kent Fel 62-65; Fulbright Fel, Sweden, 85; Honorary Doctorates: Denison Col, Emmanuel Col, Wittenberg Univ, Xavier Univ, Hamilton Col, St Olafs Col, Walsh Col, DePaul Univ, St Bernard's Sem, Edinburgh Univ. **MEMBERSHIPS** Am Acad of Relig. **RESEARCH** Feminism; Women's Issues in Christian history. **SELECTED PUBLICATIONS** Auth, "Christian Understandings of Human Nature," in religion, Feminism and the Family, John Knox Press, 96; auth, "Healing the world: the Sacramental Tradition," in Feminist Ethics and the Catholic Moral Tradition, Paulist Press, 96; auth, "Eco-feminism: first and Third World Women," in women Resisting Violence: Spirituality for Life, Orbis Press, 96; auth, "Eco-feminism: Symbolic and social Connections Between the Oppression of Women and the domination of Nature," in This sacred Earth: Religion, Nature and Environment, Routledge press, 96; auth, "The Unrealized Revolution: searching the Scriptures for a Model of the Family," in Christian Perspectives on Sexuality and Gender, Eerdmans Pub, 96; auth, "Theological Resources for Earth healing," in The Challenge of Global Stewardship: Roman Catholic Responses, Notre Dame Univ Press, 97; auth, "Gender Equity and Christianity Pre-Modern Roots, Modern and Post-Modern perspectives," in faith and praxis in a Post-Modern Age, Cassell Pres, 98; auth, "The Theological Vision of Letty Russell," in Liberating Eschatology Essays in Honor of Letty Russell, John Knox Press, 99. **CONTACT ADDRESS** Dept Theol, Garrett-Evangelical Theol Sem, 2121 Sheridan Rd, Evanston, IL 60201-2926. **EMAIL** rosemary.ruether@nwu.edu

RUFFING, JANET
PERSONAL Born 07/17/1945, Spokane, WA, s **DISCIPLINE** CHRISTIAN SPIRITUALITY AND SPIRITUAL DIRECTION **EDUCATION** Russell Col, BA, 68; Univ San Fran, MAS, 78; Jesuit Sch of Theol, Berkley, 84; Grad Theol Union, PhD, 86. **CAREER** Tchr, Sec Ed Mercy HS, Burlingame & San Fran, Marian HS, San Diego, 68-80; Assoc Prof, Fordham Univ, 86-. **HONORS AND AWARDS** Comprehensive Exams with Distinction, GTU. **MEMBERSHIPS** Amer Acad of Religion, Cath Theol Soc of Amer, Spiritual Dir Intl. **RESEARCH** Spiritual direction, Mysticism, religious life, spirituality. **SELECTED PUBLICATIONS** Auth, Uncovering Stories of Faith: Narrative Aspects of Spiritual Direction, Paulist Press, 89; Visiting a Scene of Election, Rev for Rel 56, 97; Celibacy and Contemplation, InFormation, 97; Supervision and Spiritual Development: the Conventional Post Conventional Divide, Jour of Supv and Trng in Ministry, 97; Knitting Together the Mind and the Body, and the Spirit: The Experience of Contemporary Christian Women, Stud in Spirit, 97; To Have Been One With The Earth: Nature in Contemporary Christian Mystical Experience, Presence 3, 97; Unacknowledged Conflicts: Prayer and Morality, The Way Sup 88, 97; Catherine McAuley's Quaker Connection: What Can We Know? What Do We Imagine?, Mast Jour, 97; Going Up Into the Gaps: Prophetic Life and Vision, InFormation, 98; auth, Spritual Direction: Beyond The Beginning, Paulist Press and St Pauls Press, 00. **CONTACT ADDRESS** Fordham Univ, Grad Sch of Religious Ed., Bronx, NY 10458. **EMAIL** Ruffing@fordham.edu

RUJA, HARRY
PERSONAL Born 02/26/1912, Paterson, NJ, m, 1940, 3 children **DISCIPLINE** PHILOSOPHY **EDUCATION** Univ Calif, Los Angeles, BA, 33; Univ Chicago, MA, 34; Princeton Univ, PhD, 36; San Diego State Col, MA, 53. **CAREER** Instr, psych and philos, Compton Col, 39-47; asst prof, assoc prof, prof, philos, San Diego State Col, 47-79; prof emer philos, San Diego State Univ, 79- ; vis prof philos, Univ Minnesota, 59, C W Post Col, 65, Penn State Univ, 64-65, Haifa Univ, 81. **HONORS AND AWARDS** Russell Scholar of the Year, 93, Bertrand Russell Soc. **MEMBERSHIPS** APA. **RESEARCH** Bertrand Russell; Zionism; Judaica; civil liberties. **SELECTED PUBLICATIONS** Auth, "Not so shrewd after all," The Jerusalem Post 14 (82): 22; auth, "Russell on the meaning of 'good'," in Intellect and Social Conscience, ed. Margaret Morana and Carl Spadoni (McMaster Univ Press, 84), 137-156; auth, "Justifying war," Newsweek 11 (91): 12-12; coauth, A Bibliography of Bertrand Russell, Routledge, 94; auth, "Visitor's Day Revisited," Univ of Calif Los Angeles Mag 6 (95): 5; auth, "Bertrand Russell's Life in Pictures," J of the Bertrand Russell Archives 15 (96): 101-152; auth, "Philosophically Speaking," Univ of Calif Los Angeles Alumni News 10 (98): 3; ed, Mortals and Others: American Essays, 1931-1935, Routledge, 98. **CONTACT ADDRESS** 4664 Troy Ln, La Mesa, CA 91941.

RUKMANI, T. S.
DISCIPLINE RELIGION **EDUCATION** Delhi Univ, BA, 52; MA, 54; PhD, 58, Dlitt, 91. **CAREER** Lectr and Sr lectr, Univ of Delhi, 64-81; dir, Univ of Delhi, 81-82; principal, Univ of Delhi, 82-93; prof, Univ of Durban, 93-95; prof; ch, Hindu Stud, Concordia, 96. **HONORS AND AWARDS** Awd by Nat Asn of Canadians of Indian Origin, 98; Res Grant by Concordia Univ, 97-99; ed, jour indological soc, s africa, 95; mem, consult comm intl asson for sanskrit stud, 94; adv bd for the xth world sanskrit conf, 97. **SELECTED PUBLICATIONS** Auth, A Critical Study of the Bhagavata Purana, Chowkhamba sanskrit Series Varanasi, India, 71; auth, Yogavarttika of Vijnanabhiksu, Munshiram Manoharlal Publishers, Delhi, 81-89; ed, Religious Consciousness and Life Worlds, Indian Institute of Advanced Study, Shimla, India, 88; auth, Sankara: The Man and his Philosophy, Indian Institute of Advanced Study: Shimla, India, 91; auth, Folk Traditions Related to the Mahabharata in South India in The Mahabharata in the Tribal and Folk Traditions of India, Indian Institute of Advanced Study, Shimla, India, 93; auth, The Concept of Jivanmukta in the Advaita and Sankhya-Yoga Traditions in Pandit N.R. Bhatt Felicitation vol, Pondicherry Univ, 94; auth, Sankaracarya: Publications Division, Government of India: Delhi, 94; auth, The Concept of the Self in Hindu thought Routledge Encyclopedia of Philosophy, released at the World Philosophy Conference, Boston, 98; auth, Vedanta and the Bhakti Traditions, (forthcoming, 99); ed, Hindu Diaspora: Global Perspectives, Ch in Hindu Stud, Concordia Univ, 99. **CONTACT ADDRESS** Dept of Rel, Concordia Univ, Montreal, 1455 de Maisonneuve W, Montreal, QC, Canada H3G 1M8. **EMAIL** rukmani@alcor.concordia.ca

RUNKEL, ROSS R.
DISCIPLINE ARBITRATION, CONTRACTS, DISPUTE RESOLUTION, EMPLOYMENT DISCRIMINATION **EDUCATION** Univ Wash, BS, 61; JD, 65. **CAREER** Tchg fel, Stanford Univ, 65-66; private practice, Seattle, 66-67; asst prof, 67-70; assoc prof, 70-74; prof, 74-; vis prof, Univ Wash, 85; dir, Ctr Dispute Resolution, 89-92. **HONORS AND AWARDS** Co-pres, Pacific Northwest Chapter, 92-93; v ch, Ore Dispute Resolution Comm, 89-93; dir, Portland Branch of the Fed Reserve Bank, 91-. **MEMBERSHIPS** Mem, Order of the Coif; IRRA; Soc Prof in Dispute Resolution. **SELECTED PUBLICATIONS** Assoc ed, Wash Law Rev. **CONTACT ADDRESS** Sch of Law, Willamette Univ, 900 State St, Salem, OR 97301. **EMAIL** rrunkel@willamette.edu

RUPRECHT, LOUIS A., JR.
PERSONAL Born 03/24/1961, Elizabeth, NJ, s **DISCIPLINE** ETHICS; COMPARATIVE RELIGION **EDUCATION** Duke Univ, AB, 83, MA, 85; Emory Univ, PhD, 90. **CAREER** Vis prof, 92-96, relig and classics, Emory Univ; vis prof, 96-97, relig department, Barnard Col; visiting prof, 97-98, Mercer Univ & GA State Univ; vis prof, 98, Princeton Univ. **HONORS AND AWARDS** Charlotte W. Newcombe Dissertation Fel; New Summer Institute Fels (twice). **MEMBERSHIPS** Amer Academy of Relig; Soc of Biblical Lit; Soc for Values in Higher Education; Woodrow Wilson Found; Amer Sch of Classical Studies in Athens. **RESEARCH** Comparative relig; classical antiquity; modern Greek studies; ethics **SELECTED PUBLICATIONS** Auth, Afterwards: Hellenism, Modernism, and the Myth of Decadence, 96; auth, Symposia: Plato, the Erotic and Moral Value, Homeric Wisdom and Heroic Friendship, South Atlantic Quarterly, 98; auth, The Virtue of Courage: The Penultimacy of the Political, forthcoming in Soundings, forthcoming; auth, Panamanian Peregrinations, recently submitted for review by Farrar; God Gardened in the East, forthcoming in South Atlantic Quarterly, Spring 99; auth, To The Gods of Hellas: A History of Greek Games at Barnard College, 1903-1968, forthcoming in Arion, Fall 99; auth, Classics at the Millennium: An Outsider's View of a Discipline, commissioned for Soundings, 99; auth, Are We Living in an Ethical Age? Instilling Ethics: The collected Papers of the Olmsted Symposium, forthcoming with Yale University Press, 99; auth, Why the Greeks? Agon" On the Democratic Future of the Classical, forthcoming 99. **CONTACT ADDRESS** Dept Relig, Duke Univ, PO Box 90964, Durham, NC 27708-0964. **EMAIL** larupre@emory.edu

RURA, SVETLANA
PERSONAL Born 11/23/1958, Yugoslavia, w **DISCIPLINE** PHILOSOPHY **EDUCATION** Univ Cincinnati, PhD, 97. **CAREER** Prof, Col of Mount St. Joseph, Cincinnati. **RESEARCH** Epistemology; Aesthetics. **CONTACT ADDRESS** 2856 Observatory Ave., #3, Cincinnati, OH 45208. **EMAIL** svetlanar@juno.com

RUSCO, ELMER R.
PERSONAL Born 05/06/1928, Haviland, KS, m, 1955, 2 children **DISCIPLINE** POLITICAL SCIENCE **EDUCATION** Univ Kansas, Ba, 51, MA, 52; Univ Calif, Berkeley, PhD, 60. **CAREER** San Diego State Col, 57-58; Univ Idaho, 59-60; Parsons Col, 61-63; from asst prof to prof, 63-86, prof emer, 86-, Univ Nev, Reno; dir Bureau of Govt Res, 66-76; vis prof Univ Nev, Las Vegas, 84. **HONORS AND AWARDS** Phi Beta Kappa; Pi Sigma Alpha. **MEMBERSHIPS** Am Polit Sci Asn; Am Soc for Ethnohistory. **RESEARCH** Law and public policy affecting ethnic racial groups. **SELECTED PUBLICATIONS** Auth, The Great Books, Multiculturalism, Political Correctness and Related Matters, Halcyon, 93; auth, Campaign Finance Reform in the Silver Era: A Puzzle, parts 1 & 2, Nev Hist Soc Q, 95; auth, A Fateful Time: The Background and Legislative History of the Indian Reorganization Act, Univ Nev, 00. **CONTACT ADDRESS** PO Box 8947, Reno, NV 89507.

RUSH, SHARON E.
PERSONAL Born, IN, s, 1 child **DISCIPLINE** LAW **EDUCATION** Cornell Univ, BA, JD. **CAREER** Irving Cypen prof, Univ Fla, 85-. **MEMBERSHIPS** Asn Amer Law Schools Sect on Women, Minorities, and Constitutional Law; Soc Amer Law Teachers; DC Bar; Phi Kappa Phi. **RESEARCH** Constitutional law, civil procedure, federal courts, outsider jurisprudence, fourteenth amendment . **SELECTED PUBLICATIONS** Auth, Loving Across the Color Line, Rowmant Littlefield, 00. **CONTACT ADDRESS** Levin College of Law, Univ of Florida, PO Box 117625, Gainesville, FL 32611-7625. **EMAIL** rush@law.ufl.edu

RUSSELL, BRUCE ALAN
PERSONAL Born 03/15/1945, San Francisco, CA, m, 1971, 2 children **DISCIPLINE** PHILOSOPHY **EDUCATION** Univ Calif, Davis, BS, 67, MA, 72 PhD(philos), 77. **CAREER** Sessional lectr philos, Univ Alta, 73-74; asst prof, 78-80, 80-82, assoc prof, 85-92, prof, 92- , Wayne State Univ; Andrew Mellon fel, Univ Pittsburgh, 80-81; Nat Endowment for Humanities, Princeton Univ, summer, 82; Western Wash, 86; Univ Neb 87; Univ Cal Berkeley, 93. **MEMBERSHIPS** Am Philos Asn. **RESEARCH** Ethics, epistemology, philosophy of religion. **SELECTED PUBLICATIONS** Auth, What is the ethical in fear and trembling, Inquiry, fall 75; Probability, utility and rational belief, Sophia, 3/76; On the relative strictness of negative and positive duties, Am Philos Quart, 4/77; Still a live issue, Philos & Publ Affairs, spring 78; On the relation between psychological and ethical egoism, Philos Studies, 82; auth, Two forms of Ethical Skepticism, Ethical Theory, 88; auth, Defenseless, The Evidential Argument from Evil, 96; auth, Justification and Knowledge, Knowledge, Teaching, and Wisdom, 96; auth, Critical Study of Reason, Ethics, and Society, Nous, 98. **CONTACT ADDRESS** Dept of Philosophy, Wayne State Univ, 3001 51 W Warren, Detroit, MI 48201. **EMAIL** bruce.russell@wayne.edu

RUSSELL, C. ALLYN
PERSONAL Born 09/03/1920, Bovina Center, NY, m, 1947 **DISCIPLINE** RELIGION **EDUCATION** Houghton Col, AB, 42; Eastern Baptist Theol Sem, BD, 44, ThM, 46; Univ Buffalo, MA, 55; Boston Univ, PhD, 59. **CAREER** Clergyman, 44-56; asst prof church hist, Southern Baptist Theol Sem, 59; from lectr to assoc prof relig, 59-73, travel grant sabbatical res, 68-69, Prof Relig, 73-88, PROF EMERITUS, BOSTON UNIV; Danforth assoc, 65- **HONORS AND AWARDS** Solon J Buck Awd, Minn Hist Soc, 73; Metcalf Cup and Prize, Boston Univ, 82. **MEMBERSHIPS** Am Acad Relig; Am Soc Church Hist; Am Baptist Hist Soc; AAUP. **RESEARCH** Religion in America; religious biography; fundamentalism. **SELECTED PUBLICATIONS** Auth, A History of the Fredonia Baptist Church, McClenathan, 55; Voices of American Fundamentalism: Seven Biographical Studies, Westminster, 76. **CONTACT ADDRESS** 43 Prospect St, Carlisle, MA 01741.

RUSSELL, IRMA S.
PERSONAL Born 03/22/1947, Pratt, KS, m, 1972, 2 children **DISCIPLINE** LEGAL STUDIES **EDUCATION** Univ Kansas, BA, 69; MA, 72; BS, 74; JD, 80. **CAREER** Reporter and Photographer, Pratt, Kansas, 66-68; Assoc editor, Prairie Village, Kansas, 69; Technical writer, Lawrence, Kansas, 74-75; Teacher, Lawrence, Kansas, 77-78; Teacher, Univ of Kansas, 77-78; Supervisor, State of Kansas, 77; Law Clerk, 78; instr, Univ of Kansas, 79; instr, Univ of Kansas, 78-79; Legal research, Univ of Kansas, 79-80; Judicial clerk, 80; Attorney/Associate, 81/82; Attorney, 82-84; Attorney, 85-89; vis Asst

Prof, Univ of Memphis, 86-89; Assoc/Attorney, 89-92; instr, Univ of San Diego, 93; Asst Prof, Univ of Memphis, 92-98; Assoc Prof, Univ of Memphis, 98-. **HONORS AND AWARDS** Chair, Ethics Committee; Env Section ABA, 99-00; Chair, Env Section, Tenn Bar Assoc, 92; Chair, Ethics Comm Memphis Bar, 91. **MEMBERSHIPS** ABA; Memphia Bar Assoc for Women Attorney. **RESEARCH** Environment; Ethics; Wetlands; Commercial Law. **SELECTED PUBLICATIONS** Auth, "An Annotation of the Federal Insecticide, Fungicide, and Rodenticide Act (FIFRA), in Pest Control in Museums," Russell, 80; auth, "Beyond Shooting Snaildarters in Porkbarrels: Endangered Species and Land Use in America," Coggins, Russell, 70 Georgetown Law Journal 1433, 82; auth, "The Political and Administrative History of the U.S. Court of Appeals for the Tenth Circuit," Stanley, Russell, 60 Denver Law Journal 119, 83; auth, "Tennessee's Surrogacy Statute," Russell, 4 Tennessee Family Law Letter 12, 89; " auth, "Modification of Custody: When May Pre-existing Evidence be Considered?" Russell, Pounders, 5 Tennessee Family Law Letter 10, 91; auth, "The Role of Public Opinion, Public Interest Groups, and Political Parties in Creating and Implementing Environmental Policy," Russell, 23 Environmental Law Reporter 10665, 93; auth, "An Autthentic Life in the Law: A Tribute to James K. Logan," Russell, 43 Kansas Law Review 609, 95; **CONTACT ADDRESS** School of Law, Univ of Memphis, 3715 Central Ave, Memphis, TN 38111-6042. **EMAIL** irussell@memphis.edu

RUSSELL, KATHRYN
DISCIPLINE PHILOSOPHY **EDUCATION** Univ Cincinnati, PhD. **CAREER** Prof, State Univ NY Cortland. **RESEARCH** Social and political philosophy; philosophy of science; Marxism; feminist theory. **SELECTED PUBLICATIONS** Auth, Birth, Social Reproduction and Abstract Labor, Sci Soc, 94; co-auth, Curriculum Reform Through General Education: A Requirement in Prejudice and Discrimination, 93. **CONTACT ADDRESS** Philosophy Dept, SUNY, Col at Cortland, Box 2000, Cortland, NY 13045-0900. **EMAIL** russellk@snycorva.cortland.edu

RUSSELL, WILLIAM R.
PERSONAL Born 10/01/1954, Iowa City, IA, m, 1979, 3 children **DISCIPLINE** RELIGION **EDUCATION** Univ Iowa, BA, 77; PhD, 89; Luther Sem, Master of Divinity, 81. **CAREER** Adj and/or vis appointments at various inst, 89-98; Asst Prof of Religion, Midland Lutheran Col. **HONORS AND AWARDS** Walker award, 77; Evangelisch-lutherische kirche in Deutschland award, ger lang study, 83; NEH sumer seminar for col teachers, 92. **MEMBERSHIPS** 16th century studies conf; Amer Acad of Relig; Luther Gesellschaft. **RESEARCH** Reformation history and theology. **SELECTED PUBLICATIONS** Rev, The Reformation, vol I and II, The Book Newsletter, 98; rev, Christian Confessions: A Historical Introduction, The Jour of the Amer Acad of Relig, 98; rev, Martinus Noster, Dialog: A Jour of Theol, winter, 98; article, Dusting off The Book of Concord, Lutheran Partners, 96; auth, How to Read Luther, Inquirere Jour, 96; auth, A Neglected Key to the Theology of Martin Luther, Word and World, 96; auth, The Theological Magna Charta of Confessional Lutheranism, Church Hist, 95; auth, Ash Wednesday, Living by Faith under the Cross, Immanuel Lutheran Church, 95; auth, Luther's Theological Testament: The Schmalkald Articles, Fortress Press, 95; auth, Topical Index to Luther's Works and the Lutheran Confessional Writings, Fortress Press, 95; rev, The Early Reformation in Europe, The Lutheran Quart, 95; rev, Kommentar zu Luthers Katechismen, vol I-V, The Sixteenth Century Jour, 91-95; ed and transl, The Schmalkald Articles by Martin Luther, Fortress Press, 95; ed, Martin Luther, Theologian of the Church by George W. Forell: Collected Essays in Honor of His Seventy-Fifth Birthday, word and world suppl vol II, Luther Sem, 94; auth, Luther's Understanding of the Pope as the Antichrist, Die Archiv fuer Reformationsgeschichte/The Arch for Reform Res, 94; rev, A Cry of Absence, The Lutheran Quart, 94. **CONTACT ADDRESS** Dept of Religion, Midland Lutheran Col, 900 N Clarkson St, Fremont, NE 68025. **EMAIL** wrussell@prairie.kodak.edu

RUSSO, DONALD T.
PERSONAL Born 04/05/1943, New York, NY, d, 1 child **DISCIPLINE** RELIGIOUS EDUCATION AND RELIGIOUS STUDIES **EDUCATION** Cathedral Col, Brooklyn, NYork, BA, Philos, 64; Gregorian Univ, Rome, theol, STB, 66, STL, 75; New York Univ, PhD, relig educ, 84. **CAREER** Tchr, relig and latin, Xaverian High Sch, Brooklyn, NY, 73-; asst prin for supv, Xaverian High Sch, Brooklyn, NY, 75-77; adjunct lectr, relig dept, Syracuse Univ, 79-; adjunct asst prof, develop reading, NY City Tech Col, Brooklyn, NY, 73-. **HONORS AND AWARDS** Who's Who among students in Amer Univ, 77-78; Educr of the Yr, Asn of Tchrs of NY, 86; Educr of the Yr, Xaverian Brothers Sponsored Sch, 95; Who's Who among Amer Tchrs, 98, 00. **MEMBERSHIPS** Amer Acad of Relig; Amer Class Leag; Asn of Prof and Res in Relig Educ; Asn for Supv and Curric Develop; Class Asn of the Empire State; Nat Cath Educ Asn; NY Metro Asn of Develop Educ; NY State Asn of Foreign Lang Tchrs; Relig Educ Asn of the US and Can. **RESEARCH** Religion and American culture; Religious education and ecumenism. **SELECTED PUBLICATIONS** Auth, Twenty-five Years of Religious Education in Catholic High Schools, PACE 25, Professional Approaches for Christ Educ, Mar, 96; auth, A Response to Dykstra: Youth and the Language of Faith, Relig Educ, 81, 188-193, 86; book rev, Ministries, James Dunning, Relig Educ, Summer, 81. **CONTACT ADDRESS** 7100 Shore Rd., Brooklyn, NY 11209. **EMAIL** drussodr@aol.com

RUSSON, JOHN E.
PERSONAL Born 06/11/1960, Regina, Canada, s **DISCIPLINE** PHILOSOPHY **EDUCATION** Univ Regina, BA, 85; Univ Toronto, MA, 86; PhD, 90. **CAREER** Vis asst prof, Univ of Toronto, 92-93; asst prof, Acadia Univ, 93-95; asst prof, Pa-State Univ, 95-99, assoc prof, 99-. **HONORS AND AWARDS** Postdoctoral fel in the Classics, Harvard Univ, 90-92; Res assoc, SUNY Stony Brook, 97. **MEMBERSHIPS** Can Philos Asn, Am Philos Asn, Hegel Soc Am, Soc for Phenomenal and Existential Philos. **RESEARCH** Ancient philosophy, Hegel, phenomenology. **SELECTED PUBLICATIONS** Auth, The Self and Its Body in 'Hegel's Phenomenology of Spirit', Univ Toronto Press (97); coed with Michael Bauer, Hegel and the Tradition, Univ Toronto Press (97); coed with John Salis, Retracing the Platonic Text, Northwestern Univ Press (99). **CONTACT ADDRESS** Dept Philos, Pennsylvania State Univ, Univ Park, 240 Sparks Bldg, University Park, PA 16802-5201. **EMAIL** jxr36@psu.edu

RUSSOW, LILLY-MARLENE
PERSONAL Born 05/24/1951, New York, NY **DISCIPLINE** THE PHILOSOPHY OF MIND, ETHICS **EDUCATION** Princeton Univ, PhD. **CAREER** Assoc prof, Purdue Univ. **HONORS AND AWARDS** Hastings Center, Fel. **RESEARCH** Ethics & animals, environmental ethics, philosophy of mind, artificial intelligence and coginitive scinece, Hume, Merleau-Ponty. **SELECTED PUBLICATIONS** Coauth, Principles of Reasoning. **CONTACT ADDRESS** Dept of Philos, Purdue Univ, West Lafayette, 1080 Schleman Hall, West Lafayette, IN 47907-1080. **EMAIL** lmrussow@purdue.edu

RUTHERFORD, DONALD P.
DISCIPLINE HISTORY OF MODERN PHILOSOPHY **EDUCATION** Univ CA, PhD, 88. **CAREER** Philos, Emory Univ. **SELECTED PUBLICATIONS** Auth, Leibniz and the Rational Order of Nature. **CONTACT ADDRESS** Dept of Hist, Emory Univ, Atlanta, GA 30322-1950. **EMAIL** phildr@emory.edu

RUTHVEN, JON M.
PERSONAL Born 06/22/1942, Truro, NS, Canada, m, 3 children **DISCIPLINE** SYSTEMATIC THEOLOGY **EDUCATION** Ctr Bible Col, BA; Trinity Evangel Divinity Sch, BD; Ctr Bible Col, MA; Inst Holy Land Stud, Hebrew Univ, Jerusalem; Marquette Univ, PhD. **CAREER** Pastor of the Lincoln Christian Fel Church 67-80; Assoc prof, 88; Prof, 97-; Actg Pres and Dean of Pan Africa Christian Col, 80-82; Marital and psycho-therapeutic co-counseling; Adjunct counselor, Loving Shepherd Counseling Center; Speaker-Lectr. **MEMBERSHIPS** Mensa, Soc for Pentecostal Studies, Evangelical Theol Soc. **SELECTED PUBLICATIONS** Auth, On the Cessation of the Charismata: The Protestant Polemic on Miracles, Sheffield, UK: University of Sheffield Academic Press, 93; auth, "Charismatic Theology and Biblical Emphases," Evangelical Quarterly, (97): 217-236; rev, "Was Jesus Also a Heretic?" (97); rev. "The Kingdom and the Power: Are Healing and Spiritual Gifts Used by Jesus and the Early Church Meant for the Church today?" A Biblical Look at How to Bring the Gospel to the World with Power, Ventura, CA: Regal Books, (93), Pneuma 20 (Fall 99): 221-26; rev, "Are Miraculous Gifts for Today? Four Views," Zondervan, 96 in Pneuma 21:1 (99); auth, "Early History of the Ruthven Clan," U.S. Scots, 8:1 (99); auth, "What's Right about the Faith Movement," Ministries Today, (99): 56-60; auth, "The Imitation of Christ in Christian Tradition: Its Missing Charismatic Emphasis," Journal of Pentecostal Theology 16 (00): 60-77; auth, "The Feckless Later Reign of David: A Case of Chronic Depressive Disorder?" Journal of Pastoral Care 54:1 (00); auth, "Answers about Continuing Spiritual Gifts for Your Non-Pentecostal Friends," Pneuma Review 3:1 (00): 8-20, Part II: 3:2 (00). **CONTACT ADDRESS** Dept of Systematic Theology, Regent Univ, 416--125 Bonis Ave, Scarborough, ON, Canada M1T 3R8. **EMAIL** ruthven@regent.edu

RUTTER, IRVIN C.
PERSONAL Born 11/08/1909, New York, NY, m, 1938, 2 children **DISCIPLINE** LAW **EDUCATION** Columbia Univ, AB, 29, JD, 31. **CAREER** Law secy, SDist NY, US Dist Ct, 31-33; asst US atty, SDist NY, US Dept Justice, 34-40, spec asst to Atty Gen US, 40-42; chief enforcement atty, Off Price Admin, 42-44, chief hearing comnr, 44-46; pvt pract, NY, 46-56; prof, 56-66, Distinguished Prof Law, Col Law, Univ Cincinnati, 66-, Lectr, Practising Law Inst, 46-50; mem curric comt, Asn Am Law Schs, 61-62, chmn, 62-63; vis prof, Sch Law, Columbia Univ, 64. **SELECTED PUBLICATIONS** Auth, Law, Language, And Thinking Like A Lawyer/, Univ Cincinnati Law Rev, 1993. **CONTACT ADDRESS** Col of Law, Univ of Cincinnati, Cincinnati, OH 45221.

RYAN, EILISH
PERSONAL Born 05/22/1943, Birmingham, England, s **DISCIPLINE** PASTORAL THEOLOGY; CHRISTIAN SPIRTUALITY **EDUCATION** Univ of St Michael's Col, ThD, 94. **CAREER** Instr, 81-86, asst prof, 86-89, asst prof, 94-97, assoc prof, 97- , Univ of the Incarnate Word. **MEMBERSHIPS** AAR; CTSA; CTS, AGPIM. **RESEARCH** Contemporary Christian spirituality and theology; Practical theology **SELECTED PUBLICATIONS** Auth, Rosemary Haughton: Witness to Hope, Sheed, 97. **CONTACT ADDRESS** Univ of the Incarnate Word, 4301 Broadway, San Antonio, TX 78209. **EMAIL** eryan@universe.uiwtx.edu

RYAN, EUGENE EDWARD
PERSONAL Born 11/27/1926, Chicago, IL, m, 1967, 2 children **DISCIPLINE** PHILOSOPHY **EDUCATION** St Mary of the Lake Sem, BA, 49; Gregorian Univ, PhL, 60, PhD(philos), 62. **CAREER** Instr philos, Marshall Univ, 67-68; from asst prof to assoc prof, 68-75, Prof Philos, East Carolina Univ, 75-, Chmn Dept, 79-, Vis fel, Inst Res Humanities, Univ Wis, 73-74; Nat Endowment of Humanities fel, 73-74. **MEMBERSHIPS** Am Philos Asn; Soc Ancient Greek Philos. **RESEARCH** Ancient Greek philosophy; Aristotle; medieval philosophy. **SELECTED PUBLICATIONS** Auth, The Notion of Good, Munksgaard, Copenhagen, 61; Aristotle and a refutation of naturalism, J Value Inquiry, 72; Aristotle's rhetoric and ethics and the ethos of society, Greek Roman & Byzantine Studies, 72; Pure form in Aristotle, Phronesis, 73; Ethical terms with negative evaluations, J Critical Anal, 77; Plato's Gorgias and Phaedrus and Aristotle's Theory of Rhetorical Argumentation, Athenaeum, 79; Aristotle on Proper Names, Apeiron, 80; Bartolomeo Cavalcanti as a Critic of Thomas Aquinas, Vivarium, 82 **CONTACT ADDRESS** Dept of Philos, East Carolina Univ, Greenville, NC 27834.

RYAN, FRANK X.
PERSONAL Born 08/03/1952, Morristown, NJ, m, 1987, 3 children **DISCIPLINE** PHILOSOPHY **EDUCATION** Univ Colorado, BS, 74; Univ S CO, BA, 83; Emory Univ, MA, 89, PhD, 96. **CAREER** Tchg assoc, Emory Univ, 88-91; instr, Georgia State Univ, 88-91; instr, Reinhardt Col, 88-91; instr, Auburn Univ, 92-97; asst prof, Kent State Univ, 97- . **HONORS AND AWARDS** Grad scholar and fel, 84-87; Outstanding Prof Awd, 96; tchg award, Auburn Univ Student Govt Asn, 97. **MEMBERSHIPS** APA; Soc for Advan Am Philos; Charles S Peirce Soc; John Dewey Discussion List. **RESEARCH** Am Philosophy, Epistemology, and applied Metaphysics. **SELECTED PUBLICATIONS** Auth, Primary Experience as Settled Meaning, Philos Today, 94; auth, The Extreme Heresy of John Dewey and Arthur F. Bentley I: A Star-Crossed Collaboration?, Trans of the Charles S Peirce Soc, 97; auth, The Extreme Heresy of John Dewey and Arthur F. Bentley II: Knowing Knowing and the Known, Trans of the Charles S Peirce Soc, 97; auth, Affirming Dewey's Philosophy, A Rejoinder, Trans of the Charles S Peirce Soc, 97; contribur, Ginsberg, ed, Pragmatism: An Annotated Bibliography, 1898-1940, Rodopi, 98; rev, John Dewey, Principles of Instrumental Logic: John Dewey's Lectures in Ethics and Political Ethics, 1859-1896; Jerome A. Popp, Naturalizing Philosophy of Educations: John Dewey in the Postanalytic Period; and Terry Hoy, The Politcial Philosophy of John Dewey: Toward a Constructive Renewal, Philosophy in Review 19.6 (Dec 99): 404-409; auth, The Chicago Pragmatists, Vol 3: Early Debates on Instrumentalism, ed, John R. Shook. History of American Thought: Pragmatism in American Thought Program, Bristol: Theommes Press, 00; auth, The Chicago Pragmatist, Vol 4: Later Debates on Instrumentalism, ed, John R. Shook. History of American Thought: Pragmatism in American Thought Program, Bristol: Thoemmes Press, 00; ed, The Evolutionary Philosophy of Chauncey Wright, Vol 1: Essays. History of American Thought: American Evolutionism Program, Bristol: Thoemmes Press, 00; ed, The Evolutionary Philosophy of Chauncey Wright, Vol 2: Correspondence. History of American Thought: American Evolutionism Program, Bristol: Thoemmes Press, 00; ed, The Evolutionary Philosophy of Chauncey Wright, Vol 3: Influence and Legacy. History of American Thought: American Evolutionism Program, Bristol: Theommes Press, 00. **CONTACT ADDRESS** Dept of Philosophy, Kent State Univ, PO Box 5190, Kent, OH 44242. **EMAIL** fryan@kent.edu

RYAN, HERBERT JOSEPH
PERSONAL Born 02/19/1931, Scarsdale, NY **DISCIPLINE** THEOLOGY, HISTORY **EDUCATION** Loyola Univ, Ill, AB, 54, MA, 60, PhL, 56; Woodstock Col, Md, STL, 63; Gregorian Univ, STD, 67. **CAREER** From asst prof to assoc prof hist theol, Woodstock Col, Md, 67- 74; assoc prof relig studies, 74-79, Prof Theol, Loyola Marymount Univ, 79-, Off Roman Cath observer, Lambeth Conf, 68; mem joint comn Anglican-Roman Cath relat, Roman Cath Bishops Comn Ecumenical, Affairs, 68-; convenor joint comn ministry & off observer Roman Cath Church, Gen Conv Episcopal Church, 69, 71 & 73; secretariat for promoting Christian unity, Anglican-Roman Cath Int Comn, 69-; vis lectr hist theol, Union Theol Sem, NY, 71-74; vis prof ecumenical & ascetical theol, Gen Theol Sem, 73-74. **HONORS AND AWARDS** Int Christian Unity Awd, Graymoor Ecumenical Inst, 74; Medal Order St Augustine, Archbishop Canterbury, London, 81; std, gen theol sem, 73. **MEMBERSHIPS** Am Acad Relig; Cath Hist Soc; Cath Theol Soc Am; Church

Hist Soc; N Am Acad Ecumenists; Mediaeval Acad Am. **RESEARCH** Anglican theological tradition; influence of St Augustine on Christian theology; methodology of ecumenical theology. **SELECTED PUBLICATIONS** Auth, Wolsey - Church, State And Art - Gunn,Sj, Lindley,Pg, Editors/, Theol Studies, Vol 0053, 1992; The Synods For The Carolingian Empire From Ad721 To Ad090 Held In France And In Italy - Ger - Hartmann,W/, Speculum-A J Of Medieval Studies, Vol 0067, 1992; The Renewal Of Anglicanism - Mcgrath,Ae/, Theol Studies, Vol 0055, 1994. **CONTACT ADDRESS** Dept of Theological Studies, Loyola Marymount Univ, 7900 Loyola Blvd, Los Angeles, CA 90045.

RYAN, ROBERT M.
DISCIPLINE BRITISH ROMANTICISM, RELIGION IN LITERATURE **EDUCATION** Columbia Univ, PhD. **CAREER** Instr, Rutgers, State Univ NJ, Camden Col of Arts and Sci. **MEMBERSHIPS** Bd dir, Keats-Shelley Asn of Am, 19th-Century Stud Asn. **SELECTED PUBLICATIONS** Auth, Keats: The Religious Sense, Princeton Univ Press, 76; contribu, Mod Philol, keats-Shelley Jour, Wordsworth Circle, Jour of Rel. **CONTACT ADDRESS** Rutgers, The State Univ of New Jersey, New Brunswick, Camden Col of Arts and Sci, New Brunswick, NJ 08903-2101. **EMAIL** rmryan@camden.rutgers.edu

RYAVEC, KARL WILLIAM
PERSONAL Born 01/29/1936, Cleveland, OH, m, 1957, 2 children **DISCIPLINE** POLITICAL SCIENCE **EDUCATION** Mimai Univ (Ohio), BA, 57; Columbia Univ, MA, 62, PhD, 68. **CAREER** FAC MEMBER, POLITICAL SCI DEPT, 64-, FULL PROF, 78-, UNIV OF MASS AT AMHERST. **HONORS AND AWARDS** William C. Foster Fel, U.S. Arms Control and Disarmament Agency, 95-96; Fel, Russian Res Center, Harvard Univ, 70-71; senior exchange participant, U.S.-Soviet senior scholarly exchange, 77. **MEMBERSHIPS** Am Asn for the Advancement of Slavic Studies; Soc for Slovene Studies. **RESEARCH** Russian politics and foreign policy; Slovene politics and foreign policy. **SELECTED PUBLICATIONS** Auth, United States-Soviet Relations, Longman, 89; auth, Implementation of Soviet Economic Reforms: Political, Orazizational and Social Processes, Praeger, 75; auth, Nikita Khrushchev and Soviet Politics, Governments and Leaders, Houghton-Mifflin, 78; auth, Slovenia and United States Policy on NATO Enlargement, Slovene Studies, 98; auth, Russo-Soviet Bureaucratism, Soviet and Post-Soviet Review, 98; auth, Gorbachev, Khrushchev, and Economic Reform, The Sons of Sergei: Khrushchev and Gorbachev as Reformers, Praeger, 92; ed, A Scholar's Odyssey: The Memoirs of Ferenc A. Vali, Iowa State Univ Press, 89; ed, Soviet Society and the Communist Party, Univ of Mass Press, 78. **CONTACT ADDRESS** Dept of Political Science, Univ of Massachusetts, Amherst, Thompson Hall, Amherst, MA 01003-7520. **EMAIL** ryavec@polsci.umass.edu

RYCHLAK, RONALD J.
PERSONAL Born 09/23/1957, Columbus, OH, m, 1985, 5 children **DISCIPLINE** ECONOMICS, LAW **EDUCATION** Wabash Col, BA, 80; Vanderbilt Univ Sch Law, JD, 83. **CAREER** Judicial Law Cleark, Harry W. Wellford at U.S. 6th Circuit Court of Appeals, 83-84; assoc, Jenner & Block, 84-87; from asst prof to prof, Univ Miss, 87-; assoc dean, Univ Miss, 98-. **HONORS AND AWARDS** Order of the Coif; Salvatori Fel. **MEMBERSHIPS** Ill Bar Asn, Nat Asn of Scholars, Federalist Soc, Int Asn of Gaming Attorneys. **RESEARCH** Criminal Law and Procedure, Environmental Law, Law and Gambling, Catholic History. **SELECTED PUBLICATIONS** Coauth, "To Tell the Truth: Accuracy in Demonstrative Evidence (Part 1)," The Practical Litigator (94); auth, "Changing the Face of Environmentalism," Fordham Environmental Law J (96); auth, "Ocean Aquaculture," Fordham Environmental Law J (97); coauth, "A Clear-Cut Case for Excommunication," New Oxford Rev (97); auth, "Why Pope Pius XII Was Right: The Holy See vs. The Third Reich," New Oxford Rev, 98; auth, Real and Demonstrative Evidence: Applications and Theory, The Michie Co., 95 and Supp. 96-99; auth, "Pete Rose, Bart Giamattie, and the Dowd Report," Miss Law J (99); auth, "Videotape and Casino Lawsuites, Gaming Law Rev (99); auth, "Vatican Chronicles: A Different Read," Brill's Content (00); auth, Hitler, the War, and the Pope, Genesis press, forthcoming. **CONTACT ADDRESS** Sch of Law, Univ of Mississippi, University, MS 38677-9999. **EMAIL** rrychlak@olemiss.edu

RYDEN, DAVID K.
PERSONAL Born 05/06/1959, MN, m, 1998 **DISCIPLINE** POLITICAL SCIENCE **EDUCATION** The Catholic Univ America, PhD, 95; Univ Minnesota Law School, JD, 85; Concordia Col, BA, 81. **CAREER** Assoc Prof, Hope Col, 94-. **HONORS AND AWARDS** Towsley Foundation Research Fel, 98-01; Aspen Institute Grant; Commissioned Scholar. **MEMBERSHIPS** ABA, Minnesota Bar Assn, American Political Science Assn, Midwest Political Science Assn. **RESEARCH** Election Law and Politics; Church-State Relations, Political Partiers, Dept of Political Science. **SELECTED PUBLICATIONS** Auth, The U.S. Supreme Court and Election Law, ed. Georgetown Univ Press, 00; auth, Representation in Crisis: The Constitution, Political Parties, and Interest Groups, SUNY Press, 96; **CONTACT ADDRESS** Dept Political Science, Hope Col, 137 E 12th St, Holland, MI 49423. **EMAIL** ryden@hope.edu

RYDER, JOHN
PERSONAL Born 09/29/1951, New York, NY, m, 1985 **DISCIPLINE** PHILOSOPHY **EDUCATION** SUNY Stony Brook, PhD, 82. **CAREER** Lectr to prof, SUNY Cortland, 80-; dean of arts and sci, SUNY Cortland, 96-. **HONORS AND AWARDS** Fulbright, Wroclaw Univ, Poland, 97. **MEMBERSHIPS** Am Philos Asn; Soc for the Adv of Am Philos; Soc for the Philos Study of Marxism; Alliance of Univ for Democracy; Bd of Directors, SUNY-Moscow Univ Res Center; Co-founder and Bd of Directors, Central European Pragamatist Forum. **RESEARCH** Hist of Am philosophy; Metaphysics; Philosophy of education. **SELECTED PUBLICATIONS** Ed, American Philosophic Naturalism in the 20th Century, Prometheus Books, Jul, 94; ed, Contemporary Philosophy in Eastern Europe, Metaphilosophy, v 25, n 2&3, 94; article, Yuri K. Melvil and American Pragmatism, Trans of the Charles S. Peirce Soc, vol XXXII, no 4, 598-632, 96; article, Cadwallader, Colden, Samuel Johnson, and the Activity of Matter: Materialism and Idealism in 18th Century Colonial American Thought, Trans of the Charles S. Peirce Soc, vol XXXII, no 2, 248-272, 96; article, The Use and Abuse of Modernity: Postmodernism and the American Philosophic Tradition, Jour of Speculative Philos, vol VII, no 2, 92-102, 93, reprinted, Philos in Experience: Amer Philos in Trans, Fordham Univ Press, 97; transl, Women and Patriarchy, Women's Studies Intl Forum, vol 16, no 1, 57-63, 93; article, Contradictions in American Culture, Frontiers in Amer Philos, Tex A&M Univ Press, 92; rev, Nature and Spirit, Metaphilosophy, vol 26, no 1&2, 138-146, 95; rev, Psychology and Nihilism, Jour of Speculative Philos, vol X, no 2, 153-159, 96; rev, War and Democracy, Soc for the Adv of Amer Philos Book Rev, 93; auth, Interpreting America; Russian and Soviet Studies of American Thought, Vanderbilt Univ Press, 00; coauth, Philosophical writings of Cadwallader Colden, Prometheus Books, (forthcoming). **CONTACT ADDRESS** Dean of Arts & Sciences, SUNY, Col at Cortland, Cortland, NY 13045. **EMAIL** ryderj@cortland.edu

RYOU, DANIEL H.
PERSONAL Born 10/12/1953, Seoul, Korea, m, 1980, 4 children **DISCIPLINE** OLD TESTAMENT **EDUCATION** Calvin Theol Sem, MDiv, 84; ThM, 86; Frei Univ, Amsterdam, PhD, 94. **CAREER** Assoc prof, OT & Hebrew, Christian Theol Sem, Seoul Korea, 95-. **MEMBERSHIPS** SBL **RESEARCH** Prophetic literature; Hebrew syntax (text-linguistic). **SELECTED PUBLICATIONS** Auth, Zephaniah's Oracles Against the Nations, Bibl Inter Ser 13, EJ Brill, 95; auth, The Book of Hebrews: A Literary & Theological Commentary, Christian Dig Press (Seoul, S Korea), 98; auth, The Book of Amos: A Literary & Theological Commentary, Christian Dig Press (Seoul, S Korea), 99. **CONTACT ADDRESS** 2231 Rowland Dr SE, Grand Rapids, MI 49546-5801. **EMAIL** dhryou@hotmail.com

RYSKAMP, GEORGE R.
PERSONAL Born 05/06/1950, Detroit, MI, m, 1975, 4 children **DISCIPLINE** LAW **EDUCATION** Brigham Young Univ, BA, 74, JD, 79. **CAREER** Acredited Genealogist, 75-, Spain; prvt law pract, 79-93, Riverside CA; cert estate plan & probate spec, 91-93, CA; City Attny, 82-92, Beaumont CA; asst prof, 93-, Brigham Young Univ. **RESEARCH** Family history in S Europe and Latin Amer; legal hist in the US as it relates to record creation, Spanish borderlands study. **CONTACT ADDRESS** 334 KMB BYU, Provo, UT 84602. **EMAIL** ryskamp@byu.edu

S

SAADOUN, MOHAMED
PERSONAL Born 01/14/1954, Lebanon, m, 1975, 2 children **DISCIPLINE** INTERNATIONAL RELATIONS **EDUCATION** FIU, BS, 84. **CAREER** Publisher **MEMBERSHIPS** MESA. **RESEARCH** Islamic Aqeedah-Hadith; Quran Sciences. **SELECTED PUBLICATIONS** Auth, Lebanon-The Crisis That Ceases To End. **CONTACT ADDRESS** 17 Hammond, #403, Irvine, CA 92618.

SAATKAMP, HERMAN J.
PERSONAL Born 09/29/1942, Knoxville, IN, m, 1964, 2 children **DISCIPLINE** PHILOSOPHY **EDUCATION** Vanderbilt Univ, PhD, 72. **CAREER** Dana Prof, 81-85, Chmn Humanities Div, 83-85, Univ of Tampa FL; Dept Head, Phil & Human, 85-94, Dept Head, Human in Med, 96-98, Texas A&M Univ; Dean, Prof, Indiana Univ, 98-. **HONORS AND AWARDS** NEH; faculty development grant, Univ of Tampa, 81; General Electric grant, 76; NDEA fel, 68-70; Vanderbilt Univ fel, 67-68; Phi Kappa Phi, 88; Phi Beta Delta, 87; Outstanding Educators of Amer, 73; Outstanding Fac Mem, 72. **MEMBERSHIPS** APA; Arts Coun of Brazos Valley; Assoc for Comp and the Human; Assoc for Documentary Editing; Assoc for Lit and Ling Comput; The Bibliographical Soc of the Univ of Virginia; Bryan-College Station Sister City Asn; Inst for the Humanities at Salado; Interdisciplinary Group for Hist Lit Stud Texas A&M Univ. **RESEARCH** American philosophy; genetics **SELECTED PUBLICATIONS** Coauth, Frontiers in American Philosophy, Vol I, Texas A&M Press, 92; The Works of George Santayana, MIT Press, 86; Coauth, Frontiers in American Philosophy, Vol II, Texas A&M Press, 96. **CONTACT ADDRESS** Dean, Indiana Univ-Purdue Univ, Indianapolis, 425 University Blvd, Rm 441, Indianapolis, IN 46202-5140. **EMAIL** hsaatkam@iupui.edu

SABATO, LARRY J.
PERSONAL Born 08/07/1952, Norfolk, VA **DISCIPLINE** POLITICAL SCIENCE **EDUCATION** Univ of Virginia, BA 74; Princeton Univ 75; Queen's Col Oxford, asst inst, 76-78; Univ Virginia, asst prof, assoc prof, prof, 78-. **CAREER** Univ Virginia, Robert Kent Gooch Prof. **HONORS AND AWARDS** Rhodes Sch; Danforth Fel; Phi Beta Kappa; NEH; Outstanding Young Teacher; Outstanding Prof Awd; Brookings Inst Guest sch; Downing College Cambridge Univ Eng, Thomas Jefferson Vis Fellow; served on many national and state commissions. **SELECTED PUBLICATIONS** Auth, Toward the Millennium: The Elections of 1996, Allyn and Bacon, 97; Dirty Little Secrets: The Persistence of Corruption in American Politics, Random House/Times Books, 96; Feeding Frenzy: How Attack Journalism Has Transformed American Politics, Free Press/Macmillan, 91, 93. **CONTACT ADDRESS** Univ of Virginia, 2020 Minor Rd, Charlottesville, VA 22903.

SABES, JANE
PERSONAL Born 03/02/1948, Omaha, NE, s **DISCIPLINE** PUBLIC ADMINISTRATION **EDUCATION** Columbia Union Col, BS, 71; Loma Linda Univ, MPH, 75; Auburn Univ, PhD, 99. **CAREER** Policy Analyst, Wyoming, 88-94; prof, Andrews Univ, 95-. **HONORS AND AWARDS** Harvard Univ Fel; US Pub Health Ser Fel. **MEMBERSHIPS** Am Soc for Pub Admin, Am Pol Sci Asn, Asn for Pub Policy Analysis & Man. **RESEARCH** International Public Policy. **CONTACT ADDRESS** Dept Hist & Govt, Andrews Univ, 100 US Highway 31, Berrien Springs, MI 49104-0001. **EMAIL** sabesja@andrews.edu

SABLE, THOMAS F.
PERSONAL Born 08/16/1945, Rochester, NY **DISCIPLINE** THEOLOGY **EDUCATION** Boston Col, BA, 69; Georgetown Univ, MS, 73; Jesuit Sch Theol, MDiv, 75; Graduate Theol Union, PhD, 83. **CAREER** Adj faculty, Fordham Univ, 82-85; assoc prof, Univ Scranton, 85- . **MEMBERSHIPS** Amer Cath Hist Assoc. **RESEARCH** American Catholic history; Byzantine theology. **SELECTED PUBLICATIONS** Auth, Uniate Churches, The Encyclopedia of Relig, Macmillan & Co, 85; Eastern-Rite Catholics, Kenrick, Peter Richard, Knights of Labor, McCloskey, John, McMaster, James Alphonsus, Satolli, Francesco, & Wimmer, Bonifact, in dictionary of Christianity in American, InterVarsity Press, 90; The Spirituality of the Christian East: A Systematic Handbook, rev, Diakonia, 94-95. **CONTACT ADDRESS** Univ of Scranton, T-362A, Scranton, PA 18510. **EMAIL** sable@uofs.edu

SACHS, JOHN R.
PERSONAL Born 12/09/1948, Chicago, IL **DISCIPLINE** SYSTEMATIC THEOLOGY **EDUCATION** Boston Col, AB, 69, MA, 73; Weston Jesuit School Theol, MDiv, 76; Tubingen, DTheol, 84. **CAREER** Asst prof, Fairfield Univ, 84-86; asst prof, 86-93, assoc prof, 94-, adac dean, 99-, Weston Jesuit School Theol. **MEMBERSHIPS** AAR; CTSA. **RESEARCH** Trinity; Creation; Eschatology; Spirituality. **SELECTED PUBLICATIONS** Auth The Christian Vision of Humanity: Basic Christian Anthropology, Liturgical Press, 91; And God saw it was good: Spirituality for an Ecological Age, Handbook of Spirituality for Ministers, Paulist Press, 95; Ignatian Mysticism, The Supplement to The Way, 95; Do not Stifle the Spirit: Karl Rahner, The Legacy of Vatican II, and its Urgency for Theology Today, CTSA Proceedings, 96; Trinity and Communications: the Mystery and Task of Self-Communication, Budhi, 97. **CONTACT ADDRESS** 3 Phillips Pl, Cambridge, MA 02138. **EMAIL** sachser@aol.com

SACHS, WILLIAM L.
PERSONAL Born 08/23/1947, Richmond, VA, m, 1986, 1 child **DISCIPLINE** HISTORY OF CHRISTIANITY **EDUCATION** Baylor, BA, 69; Vanderbilt Univ, MDiv, 72; Yale Univ, STM, 73; Univ Chicago, PhD, 81. **CAREER** Dir of Res, Episcopal Church Found; vis fel, Yale Univ. **RESEARCH** English and American evangelicism; religious leadership; Anglican communion. **SELECTED PUBLICATIONS** Auth, The Transformation of Anglicanism, Cambridge; auth, Of One Body, John Knox. **CONTACT ADDRESS** Episcopal Church Foundation, 815 Second Ave, New York, NY 10017. **EMAIL** bsachs@episcopalfoundation.org

SACKSTEDER, WILLIAM
PERSONAL Born 05/30/1925, Muncie, IN, d, 3 children **DISCIPLINE** PHILOSOPHY **EDUCATION** Univ Chicago, PhB, 46, MA, 49, PhD, 53. **CAREER** Instr in philos, 49-50, IL Inst Technology; asst in philos, 49-52, Univ Chicago; instr, asst prof, assoc prof, full prof, 52-90, prof emeritus, 90-, Univ Co; vis lect, 57, Univ CA, Berkeley; vis prof, 77, Univ Graz, Austria; prof, emer. **HONORS AND AWARDS** Phi Beta Kappa, 49. **MEMBERSHIPS** APA; Mt/Plains Philos Asn. **RESEARCH** Hist of philos; ethics; major philosophers. **SELECTED PUBLICATIONS** Auth, Hobbes Bibliography, 1879-1979; auth, The Philosopher in the Community. **CONTACT ADDRESS** 2525 Taft Rd, # 602, Boulder, CO 80302.

SADRI, HOUMAN A.
DISCIPLINE POLITICAL SCIENCE **EDUCATION** Univ Ariz, MA, 83; Univ Va, PhD, 93. **CAREER** Graduate teaching asst, Univ Va, 88-92; vis lecturer, Univ of Richmond, 93-95; asst prof, Univ Cen Fla, 95-. **HONORS AND AWARDS** Thomas Jefferson Foundation Fel, Monticello, 87-88; Dupont Research Fel, Univ Va, 88-90; Central Asian Foundation for Development, guest scholar, 94; Hoover Institution Res Fel, 97; Am Pol Sci grant, 97; Intl Res and Exchange Board, grant 97; Udmurt state Univ, (Russia), Res grant, 98; Intl Studies Asn grant, 98; Res grant for Gulf Cooperation Coun, 99; Fulbright Summer Res grant, 01; Excellence in Undergraduate Teaching Awd, Col of Arts & Sci, 00; Fac Asn Awd, Office of Intl Studies, 99-00. **MEMBERSHIPS** Am Iranian Coun, am Pol Sci Asn, Asn of Third world Studies, Cen for Iranian Res and Analysis, fla Pol Sci Asn, Intl coun of Cen Fla, Intl Studies Asn, The Middle East Inst, Middle East Studies Asn, Nat Pol Sci Honor soc (Pi sigma alpha), UN Asn of the USA. **RESEARCH** Foreign policy and relations among the Caspian Sea (including the former Soviet Republics of Central Asia & Caucasus) and Persian Gulf states. **SELECTED PUBLICATIONS** Auth, "An Islamic Perspective on Non-Alignment," in The Zen of International Relations, Macmillan: Hampshire, (forthcoming); auth, "A Holistic Approach to Central Asian Affairs," in The Middle East and the New World Order, St Martin's Press: New York, (forthcoming), auth "Trends in Foreign Relations of Kazakstan," Journal of Central Asian Studies, (forthcoming); auth, "An Islamic Perspective on Non-Alignment: Iranian foreign Policy in Theory & Practice," Journal of Third World Studies, 99; auth, "Integration in the Caspian Sea & the Russian Role and the Policy," Problems of the Regional Economy, 99; auth, Non-Alignment as a Foreign Policy Strategy: Dead or Alive," Mediterranean Quarterly, 99; auth, "Central Asia: Perspectives on Regional Integration," Political Chronicle, 98; auth, "Trends in the Foreign Policy of Revolutionary Iran," Journal of Third World Studies, 98; auth, "Integration in Central Asia: From Theory to Policy," Central Asian Survey, 97; auth, Revolutionary States, Leaders, and Foreign Relations: A Comparative Study of China, Cuba, and Iran, Praeger Pub: New York, 97. **CONTACT ADDRESS** Dept Pol Sci, Univ of Central Florida, PO Box 161356, Orlando, FL 32816-1356. **EMAIL** hsadri@pegasus.cc.ucf.edu

SAEED, KHALID
PERSONAL Born 07/03/1946, Pakistan, m, 3 children **DISCIPLINE** POLICY STUDIES, SYSTEM DYNAMICS **EDUCATION** MIT, PhD, 81. **CAREER** Vis Assoc Prof, Darthmouth Col, 83-84; Asst/Assoc/Full Prof, Asian Institute of Tech, 80-97; Prof Dept Head, Social Science WPI, 97-. **HONORS AND AWARDS** Jay Wright Forrester Awd, 95; President, System Dynamics Society, 95. **MEMBERSHIPS** System Dynamics Society. **RESEARCH** System Dynamics, Environment, Public Policy, Organizations. **SELECTED PUBLICATIONS** Auth, Development Planning and Policy Design: A System Dynamics Approach, Aldershot, England: Ashgate/Avebury Books, 94; rev, "Sustainable Development, Old Conundrums, New Discords, System Dynamics Review 12 (96); auth, "The Dynamics of Collegial Systems in the Developing Countries, Higher Education Policy, 9 (96); auth, "System Dynamics Review 12 (96); rev, "Contact Design for Profitability in Macro Engineering Projects, System Dynamics Review 12 (96); rev, "An Attempt to Operationalize the Recommendations of the "Limits to Growth" Study to Sustain Futrue of Mankind, System Dynamics Review 12 (96); auth, "A Re-evaluation of the Effort to Alleviate Poverty and Hunger, in G. P. Richardson ed., Modeling for Management, Aldershot, England: Darthmouth Publishing Company, 97; auth, "Slicing a Complex Problem for System Dynamics Modeling, in G.P. Richardson ed., Modeling for Management, Aldershot, England: Dartmouth Publishing Company, 97; auth, "Technological Development in a Dual Economy: Alternative Policy Levers for Economic Development, World Development 25 (97): 695-712; auth, "Contract Design for Profitability in macro-Engineering Projects, in P.E. Glaser, F.P. Davidson, Katinka Csigi eds., Solar Power Satelites, A Space Energy System for Earth, New York: John Wiley, 98; auth, "A dynamic model for managing civil engineering design projects, Computers and Structures 67 (98): 401-419. **CONTACT ADDRESS** Dept Social Science, Worcester Polytech Inst, 100 Institute Rd, Worcester, MA 01609. **EMAIL** saeed@wpi.edu

SAENZ, MARIO
PERSONAL Born 04/01/1956, Cali, Colombia, m, 1983, 1 child **DISCIPLINE** PHILOSOPHY **EDUCATION** Southern Ill Univ, PhD, 85 **CAREER** Instr, St Augustine Comm Col, 86-87; lctr, Loyola Univ, 87; visiting asst prof, Earlham Col, 87-89; prof, Le Moyne Col, 89- **HONORS AND AWARDS** Scholar of the Year, Le Moyne, 00. **MEMBERSHIPS** Amer Philos Assoc; Amer Acad Relig **RESEARCH** Contemporary Continental Philosophy, Nineteenth Century Philosophy; Latin American Philosophy **SELECTED PUBLICATIONS** Auth, "The Identity of Liberation in Latin American Thought," Lexington Books, 99; auth, "Cartesian Autobiography/Post Cartesian Testimonials," in Feminist Interpretations of Descartes, ed. By Susan Bordo, Penn State Press, 99; auth, "Dussel on Marx: Dussel's Conceptualization of Living Labor and the Materiality of Life," Thinking from the Underside of History: Enrique Dussel's Philosophy of Liberation, Rowman & Littlefield, forthcoming; "Rigoberta Menchu: "A quien muy pronto le nacio la conciencia," Las desobedientes: biografias sobre mujeres Latinoamericanas, ed. By M. Jaramillo Editorial Panamericana, 97; auth, "Philosophies of Liberation and Modernity: The Case of Latin America," Philos Today, 94 **CONTACT ADDRESS** Dept Philos, Le Moyne Col, Syracuse, NY 13214. **EMAIL** saenz@maple.lemoyne.edu

SAFFIRE, PAULA REINER
PERSONAL Born 09/05/1943, NJ, s, 2 children **DISCIPLINE** CLASSICS AND PHILOSOPHY **EDUCATION** Mount Holyoke Col, BA, 65; Harvard, PhD, 76. **CAREER** Assoc Prof, Butler Univ, 89-. **HONORS AND AWARDS** Writing Across the Curriculum Awd, Butler Univ; Creative Tchr Awd; Indiana Classical Conference. **MEMBERSHIPS** APA, ICC **RESEARCH** Sappho; tragedy; mythology; pedagogy; performance. **SELECTED PUBLICATIONS** Auth, Aristotle on Personality and Some Implications for Friendship, in: Ancient Phil, 91; auth, Ancient Greek Alive, Aldine Press, 92; Coauth, Deduke men a Selanna: The Pleiades Mid-Sky, Mnemosyne, 93; coauth, Ancient Greek Alive, Univ of North Carolina Press, Performer of Songs of Sappho, 93-; auth, Whip, Whipped and Doctors: Homers Iliad and Camus the Plague, Interpretations, 94. **CONTACT ADDRESS** Dept of Classics, Butler Univ, 4600 Sunset Ave, Indianapolis, IN 46208. **EMAIL** psaffire@butler.edu

SAFFORD, JOHN L.
PERSONAL Born 01/06/1947, Pasadena, CA, m, 1983, 2 children **DISCIPLINE** POLITICAL SCIENCE **EDUCATION** Univ Calif Riverside, PhD, 84. **CAREER** Prof, Univ SC, 84. **MEMBERSHIPS** Am Polit Sci Asn; Am Philos Assoc. **RESEARCH** Political Theory. **SELECTED PUBLICATIONS** Auth, Pragmatism and The Progressive Movement, 87; co-auth, Bhagavad Gita: A Philosophical System, 90; auth, "John C. Calhoun, Lani Guinier, and Minority Rights," PS: Political Science and Politics, 95. **CONTACT ADDRESS** Univ of So Carolina, Sumter, 200 Miller Rd, Sumter, SC 29150-2498. **EMAIL** jsafford@uscsumter.edu

SAFRAN, WILLIAM
PERSONAL Born 07/08/1930, Dresden, Germany, m, 1961, 2 children **DISCIPLINE** POLITICAL SCIENCE **EDUCATION** Columbia Univ, PhD, 64. **CAREER** Lectr & instr, CUNY, 60-65; vis prof, Hebrew Univ, Jerusalem, 73-74; asst prof, 65-68, assoc prof, 68-73, Prof of Political Sci, Univ of Colo, 73-; vis prof, Institut d'Etudes Politiques, Univ Grenoble, 91-92; vis prof, Institut d'Etudes Politiques, Univ of Bordeaux, spring 98. **HONORS AND AWARDS** Soc Sci Found, 66; Nat Endowment for Humanities, 80-81; Hanns-Seidel Found, 83; French Ministry of Culture, 86; Am Coun of Learned Socs, 88-89; Fulbright, 91-92; fac res fel, Univ Colo, 66, 69-70. **MEMBERSHIPS** Am Acad of Political Sci; Am Political Sci Asn; Asn Francaise de Sci Politique; Asn for the Study of Ethnicity and Nationalism; Conf Group on French Politics and Soc; Conf Group on German Politics; Sci Comm, Data Bank on Minorities, Centre National de Recherche Sci; Int Political Sci Asn; Int Studies Asn; Inter-Univ Consortium for Soc Res on France; Tocqueville Soc; Western Political Sci Asn. **RESEARCH** Comparative politics; industrial democracies; European politics; French politics; the politics of ethnicity; nationalism; language; citizenship; civil liberties. **SELECTED PUBLICATIONS** Auth, Veto-Group politics, 67; The French Polity, 77, 79, 85, 91, 95, & 98; coauth, Ideology and Politics: The Socialist Party of France, 79; Comparative Politics, 83; Politics in Western Europe, 93 & 98; co-ed, Ethnicity and Citizenship: The Canadian Case, 96; ed, Nationalism and Ethnoregional Identities in China, 98; coed, Identity and Territorial Antonomy in Plural Societies, 00; editor-in-chief, Nationalsim Ethnic Politics, contributor, Divided Nations, 94; Political Leaders in Western Europe, 95; Encyclopedia of Democracy, 95; Union Europea Y Estado Del Bienestar, 97; Fremde Freunde: Deutsche und Franzosen vor dem 21.Jahrhundert, 97; How France Votes: The Parliamentary Elections of 1997-99; auth, Handbook of Language and Ethnic Identity, 99; auth, Identites: Multiculturalism, Integration? 00. **CONTACT ADDRESS** Dept of Political Sci, Univ of Colorado, Boulder, Boulder, CO 80309-0333.

SAGER, ALLAN HENRY
PERSONAL Born 08/29/1934, Boerne, TX, m, 1959, 2 children **DISCIPLINE** THEOLOGY, SPEECH COMMUNICATIONS, SPIRITUALITY **EDUCATION** Tex Lutheran Univ, BA, 55; Wartburg Theol Seminary, BD, 59; Northwestern Univ, Evanston, MA, 60, PhD, 63. **CAREER** Assoc pastor, Trinity Lutheran Church, Ft Worth, Tex, 63-65, sr pastor, 65-72; prof contextual educ, Trinity Lutheran Sem, 72- **MEMBERSHIPS** Speech Commun Asn; Lutheran Acad Scholar; Asn Theol Field Educ; Enneagram Asn. **RESEARCH** Contextual education; homiletics; communications; spirituality. **SELECTED PUBLICATIONS** Auth, The fundamentalist-modernist controversy, 1918-1930, in Preaching in American History, 69 & Sermons in American History, 71, Abingdon; Modernists and fundamentalists debate restraints on freedom, in America in Controversy: History of American Public Address, W C Brown, 73; Augsburg Sermons: Epistles, Series A, 77, Old Testament, Series C, 79, Old Testament, Series A, 80 & Old Testament, Series B, 81, Augsburg Publ House; Gospel-Centered Spirituality, Augsberg, 90. **CONTACT ADDRESS** Trinity Lutheran Sem, 2199 E Main St, Columbus, OH 43209-2334. **EMAIL** asager@trinity.capital.edu

SAGOFF, MARK
PERSONAL Born 11/29/1941, Boston, MA, m, 1984, 2 children **DISCIPLINE** PHILOSOPHY **EDUCATION** Harvard Univ, BA, 63; Columbia Univ, MA, 65; Univ of Rochester, PhD, 70. **CAREER** Princeton Univ, lectr, 68-69; Univ of Pennsylvania, asst prof, 69-75; Univ of Wisconsin Madison, vis asst prof, 75-76; Cornell Univ, asst prof, 76-78; Center for Philos and Pub Policy, res scholar, 79-88; Maryland Law Sch, lectr, 82-84 & 89; Inst for Philos and Pub Policy, dir, sr res scholar, 88-95, 88-. **HONORS AND AWARDS** Pew Scholars Awd, Woodrow Wilson Center fel. **MEMBERSHIPS** ISEE, Hastings Center Fellow. **RESEARCH** International environmental ethics; philosophy; law and technology. **SELECTED PUBLICATIONS** Auth, The Economy of the Earth: Philosophy, Law and the Environment, New York: Cambridge Univ Press, 88; auth, On the Value of Endangered and other Species, Environmental Management, 96; auth, Patented Genes: An Ethical Appraisal, Issues in Science and Technology, 98; auth, Aggregation and Deliberation in Valuing Environmental Public Goods: A Look Beyond Contingent Pricing, Ecological Economics, 98; auth, Is the Economy Too Big for the Environment? Environmental Ethics and the Global Marketplace, eds. D. Dallmeyer and A. Ike, Athens GA: Univ of Georgia Press, 98. **CONTACT ADDRESS** Inst for Philosophy and Public Policy, Univ of Maryland, Col Park, Maryland School of Public Affairs, 3111 Van Munching, College Park, MD 20742. **EMAIL** msagoff@puafmail.umd.edu

SAHADAT, JOHN
PERSONAL Born 02/22/1936, Trinidad and Tobago, m, 1987 **DISCIPLINE** THEOLOGY **EDUCATION** Laurentian Univ, BA, 66; Banaras Hindu Univ (India), MA, 69; Univ of Lancaster (UK), PhD, 75. **CAREER** Prof, 70-, Univ Sudbury Col in Laurentian Univ. **HONORS AND AWARDS** The Thorneloe Univ Mitre Awd for Teaching Excellence, 97. **MEMBERSHIPS** Canadian Soc for the Study of Relig; Am Acad of Relig. **RESEARCH** Cross Cultural study of Salvation; interreligious dialogue. **SELECTED PUBLICATIONS** Auth, "The Call of the Ignatian Spiritual Exercises," Vidyajyoti: Journal of Theological Reflection, 55, (91): 385-392; auth, "Tawhid: the Affirmation of Affirmations and the Negation of Affirmations," Muslim education Quarterly, 10, (93): 24-34; auth, "Religion and the Metaphysics of the One," Vidyajyoti: Journal of Theological Reflection, 58, (94): 106-116; auth, "Unity in Diversity not Uniformity," in Canadian Diversity: 2000 and Beyond, ed. by Stephen Nancoo and Subhas Ramcharan, Mississauga: Canadian Educators Press, (95): 309-333; auth, "Religious Influence in the Ries of Indian Nationalism," Asian Thought and Society, 20, (95): 106-116; auth, "The Indian Contribution to Harmony in Diversity," Indo Caribbean Review, 3, (96): 1-14; auth, "Divine Revelation and the Status of the Qur'an," Muslim Eudcation Quarterly, 13, (96): 4-17; auth, "A Swidlerian and Jain Prolegomenon to Dialogue," Journal of Ecumenical Studies, 34, (97): 531-550; auth, "Islamic Eduation: A Challenge to conscience," The American Journal of Islamic Social Sciences, 14, (97): 19-34; auth, Ways to meaning and a Sense of Universality, Mississauga: Canadian Educators Press, vi, (98): 308. **CONTACT ADDRESS** Dept of Religious Studies, Laurentian Univ, Sudbury, ON, Canada P3E 2C6. **EMAIL** jsahadat@nickel.laurentian.ca

SAID, ABDUL AZIZ
DISCIPLINE INTERNATIONAL RELATIONS **EDUCATION** School Intl Serv, Amer Univ, PhD. **CAREER** Mohammed Said Farsi Prof, Islamic Peace; dir, Ctr Global Peace. **RESEARCH** Islamic Peace; Peace and Conflict Resolution; East and West Reconciliation. **CONTACT ADDRESS** School of Intl Serv, American Univ, Washington, DC 20016. **EMAIL** asaid@american.edu

SAKEZLES, PRISCILLA
PERSONAL Born 04/12/1962, Tampa, FL **DISCIPLINE** PHILOSOPHY **EDUCATION** Univ S Fla, BA, 86, MA, 89; Fla State Univ, PhD, 93. **CAREER** Asst prof, Mich State Univ, 93-94; asst prof, Millsaps Col, 94-95; asst prof, Univ Akron, 95-; Univ Akron Fac Res grant, 97 & 98. **MEMBERSHIPS** Am Philos Asn; Soc Ancient Greek Philos; Soc Women Philos. **RESEARCH** Ancient philosophy **SELECTED PUBLICATIONS** Auth Pyrrhonian Indeterminacy: A Pragmatic Interpretation, Apeiron, 93; Bringing Ancient Philosophy to Life: Teaching Aristotelian and Stoic Theories of Responsibility, Teaching Philosophy, 97; rev Stoics, Epicureans and Sceptics, Rphilos in Rev, 97; rev The Sceptics, Ancient Philos, 98; auth Aristotle and Chrysippus on the Physiology of Human Action, Apeiron, 98. **CONTACT ADDRESS** Dept of Philosophy, Univ of Akron, Akron, OH 44325-1903. **EMAIL** psakezles@uakron.edu

SAKS, ELYN R.
DISCIPLINE FAMILY LAW **EDUCATION** Vanderbilt Univ, BA, 77; Oxford Univ, MLitt, 81; Yale Univ, JD, 86. **CAREER** Instr, Univ of Bridgeport Sch of Law, 87-89; asst prof,

89-91; assoc prof, 91-93; assoc prof, law, psychiatry & behav scis, 93-94; prof, 94-98; Orrin B. Evans Prof of Law, USC, 98-; clinical assoc, Los Angeles Psychoanalytic Soc & Inst, 95-. **HONORS AND AWARDS** Phi Beta Kappa. **MEMBERSHIPS** Am Col of Forensic Exam; Am Psycho Asn; Int Soc of Law and Mental Health; Int Soc for the Study of Dissociation; Int Soc for the Study of Traumatic Stress; bd mem, Mental Health Advocacy Serv. **RESEARCH** Crim law; fam law; law and psychiatry; mental health law; mental health law and the crim just syst. **SELECTED PUBLICATIONS** Auth, "The Use of Mechanical Restraints in psychiatric Hospitals," in Mental health Law Project, Protection and Advocacy for People who are Labeled Mentall Ill 409 (87); auth, "Competency to Refuse Treatment," in Law and the Mental Health System: Civil and Criminal Aspects 2d ed, eds Ralph Reisner & Christopher Slobogin (90); coauth, Jekyll on Trial: Multiple Personality Disorder and Criminal Law, Nyork Univ Pr, 97; coauth, "Therapeutic Jurisprudence: Informed Consent as Clinical Indication for the Chronically Suicidal Patient with Borderline Personality Disorder," (Symposium: Mental Disability Law) 31 Loyola of Los Angeles Law Rev 945 (98); coauth, "Competency to Decide on Treatment and Research: MacArthur and Beyond," 10 J of Contemporary Legal Issues 103 (99); auth, "competency to Decide on Treatment and Research: The MacArthur Capacity Instruments," in Commissioned Papers by the National Bioethics Advisory Commission (99); auth, Interpreting Interpretation: The Limits of Hermeneutic Psychoanalysis, Yale Univ Pr, 99; auth, "Psychoanalysis: Past, Present, and the Future Contributions to the Law," Am Psychol Asn Pr, 00; auth, "MPD and Criminal Responsibility," Int J of Law & Pscyh (forthcoming); coauth, Law, Ethics, and the Seriously Disturbed Psychiatric Patient, forthcoming. **CONTACT ADDRESS** School of Law, Univ of So California, Los Angeles, CA 90089-0071. **EMAIL** esaks@law.usc.edu

SALE, MARY

PERSONAL Born 11/27/1929, New Haven, CT, m, 1991, 3 children **DISCIPLINE** PHILOSOPHY; CLASSICS **EDUCATION** BA, 51, MA, 54, PhD, 58, Cornell Univ. **CAREER** Instr, Yale Univ, 57-58; Instr, 58-59, Asst Prof, 59-64, Assoc Prof, 64-75, Prof, 75-, Washington Univ. **MEMBERSHIPS** London Inst of Classical Studies; Honorary Fel, Univ Wales, Univ College Cardiff. **RESEARCH** Philosophy; Classics **SELECTED PUBLICATIONS** Auth, Homer, Iliad, Odyssey, Reader's Guide to World Literature, 93; Homer and the Roland: the Shared Formulary Technique, Oral Tradition, 93; The Government of Troy: Politics in the Illiad, Greek, Roman and Byzantine Studies, 94; Homer and Avdo: Investigating Orality through External Consistency, Voice into Text, 96; In Defense of Milman Parry, Oral Tradition, 96; Virgil's Formularity and Pius Aeneas, Epos and Logos, 98. **CONTACT ADDRESS** 2342 Albion Pl, Saint Louis, MO 63104. **EMAIL** Aperkins@midwest.net

SALE, WILLIAM F.

PERSONAL Born 11/20/1938, Malvern, AR, m, 1962, 2 children **DISCIPLINE** ETHICS, BIOETHICS **EDUCATION** Univ N Tex, BA, 60; Southwestern Baptist Theol Sem, MDiv, 63; ThM, 65. **CAREER** Assoc Prof, Gulf Coast Community Col, 67-. **HONORS AND AWARDS** Outstanding Prof, 75. **MEMBERSHIPS** Wager Philos Soc, Community Bioethics Consortium, Fla Philos Asn, Nat Coun of Instructional Adminrs. **RESEARCH** Applied ethics and bioethics. **SELECTED PUBLICATIONS** Auth, Life Choices: A Hastings Center Introduction to Bioethics, 1st Ed, Georgetown UP, 95; auth, Life Choices: A Hastings Center Introduction to Bioethics, 2nd Ed, Georgetown UP, 00. **CONTACT ADDRESS** Dept Sco Sci, Gulf Coast Comm Col, 5230 W Highway 98, Panama City, FL 32401-1041. **EMAIL** fsale@ccmail.gc.cc.fl.us

SALIBA, JOHN A.

PERSONAL Born 04/16/1937, Valletta, Malta **DISCIPLINE** RELIGIOUS STUDIES, THEOLOGY **EDUCATION** Heythrop Col, England, Lic Philos, 60, Lic Theol, 66; Oxford Univ, England, Diploma in Anthropol, 62; Cath Univ of Am., PhD, 71. **CAREER** Asst prof, Univ Detroit, 70-78, assoc prof, 78-87, prof, 87-90; prof, Univ of Detroit Mercy, 90-2000. **MEMBERSHIPS** Am Acad of Relig, Soc for the Sci Study of Relig, Asn for the Sociol of Relig. **RESEARCH** New religious movements, contemporary religious and spiritual developments. **SELECTED PUBLICATIONS** Auth, Understanding New Religious Movements, Grand Rapids: Eerdman's (96); auth, Signs of the Times: The New Religious Movements in theological Perspective, Sherebrooke, Can: Mediaspaul (96); auth, "Dialogue with the International Society for Krishna Consciousness (ISKCON): A Roman Catholic Perspective," in Croyances et societes, ed by Betrand Ouellet and Richard Bergeron, Quebec: Fides (98): 321-39; auth, " 'Religious' Themes in the New Religious Movements," in Rethinking New Religious Movements, ed by Michael A. Fuss, Rome: Pontifical Gregorian Univ (98): 135-156; auth, Christian Responses to the New Age Movement: A Critical Assessment, London: Chapman, NY: Continuum (99); auth, "Understanding New Religious Sects in America: The Search for Community," Bull of the Royal Inst for Inter-Faith Studies, Aman, Jordan, 1 (spring 99): 160-179; auth, "The Earth is a Dangerous Place: The World View of the Aetherius Society," Marburg J of Relig, 4.2 (Dec 99): 1-10; auth, "Cults: An Overview," in Cults, ed by Jill Karson, San Diego: Greenhaven Press, Contemporary Issues Companion (2000): 13-31. **CONTACT ADDRESS** Dept Relig Studies, Univ of Detroit Mercy, PO Box 19900, Detroit, MI 48219-0900. **EMAIL** salibaja@udmercy.edu

SALIERS, DON E.

PERSONAL Born 08/11/1937, Fostoria, OH, m, 1959, 4 children **DISCIPLINE** PHILOSOPHICAL THEOLOGY **EDUCATION** Ohio Wesleyan Univ, BA, 59; Yale Divinity Schl, BD, 62; St Johns Cambridge Univ, grad fel, 64-65; Yale Univ, PhD, 67 **CAREER** Instr, asst, assoc prof, 66-74, Yale Divinity Schl; prof, theol & worship, 74-, Franklin Parker Chmn, 96-, dir MSM prog, Emory Univ, Chandler Schl of Theol; vis prof, liturgy, St Johns Univ, Notre Dame. **HONORS AND AWARDS** Phi Beta Kappa; Fulbright Fel, Emory Williams Tchng Awd; Berakah Awd (NAAL), Dist Alumnus (OWU); Henry Luce III Fel; Emory Scholar/Teacher, 99. **MEMBERSHIPS** N Amer Acad of Liturgy; Soc for Stud of Christian Spirituality; AAR; Societas Liturgica; Charles Wesley Soc; Assn of Anglican Musicians. **RESEARCH** Contemporary issues in liturgical theology; relig discourse and human emotion; theology and aesthetics: doxa, beauty, holiness. **SELECTED PUBLICATIONS** Auth, The Soul In Paraphrase: Prayer and the Religious Affections, OSL Pub, 92; auth, Worship as Theology: Foretaste of Glory Divine, Abingdon, 94; auth, Liturgy As Holy Play, Communion, Community, Commonweal, Upper RmBks, 95; auth, Worship and Spirituality, OSL Pub, 96; auth, Worship Come To Its Senses, Abingdon Press, 96; art, Divine Grace, Diverse Means: Sunday Worship in Unite Methodist Congregations, Sunday Svcs of the Methodists: 20th Century Worship in Worldwide Methodism, Abingdon: Kingswood Bks, 96; art, Singing Our Lives, Practicing Our Faith: A Way of Life for a Searching People, Jossey-Bass Pub, 96; art, Liturgy As Art, & David's Song In Our Land, Landscape of Praise: Readings in Liturgical Renewal, Trinity Press Intl, 96; art, Musique Liturgique et Techniques Electroniques, La Maison-dieu, 212, 97; coauth, Human Disability and the Service of God: Reassessing Religious Practice, Abingdon, 98; art, Afterword: Liturgy and Ethics Revisited, Liturgy and the Moral Self: Humanity at Full Stretch Before God, Liturgical Press 98. **CONTACT ADDRESS** Chandler Sch of Theology, Emory Univ, 302 Cannon Chapel Bldg, Atlanta, GA 30322. **EMAIL** dsalier@emory.edu

SALIH, HALIL IBRAHIM

PERSONAL Born 02/26/1939, Kyrenia, Cyprus, m, 1989, 4 children **DISCIPLINE** POLITICAL SCIENCE, GOVERNMENT, AREA STUDIES, MIDDLE EAST AREA STUDIES, INTERNATIONAL STUDIES, INTERNATIONAL ORGANIZATIONS AND LAW **EDUCATION** Univ of Pacific, BA, 63; Am Univ, MA, 65, PhD, 67. **CAREER** Asst prof, 68-71, assoc prof, 71-81, Chr Polit Sci Dept, 73-95, Chr Soc Sci Dept, 95, prof of Political Science, 81-, Texas Wesleyan Col, 68-; Hall of Nations Scholar, 65-66; Pi Sigma Alpha, 67; Danfort Assoc, 79; Malone fel, 95. **HONORS AND AWARDS** Outstanding Educ Am, 72; Texas Wesleyan Fac Recog Award, 81 & 94; Mortar Board, 96. **MEMBERSHIPS** Mid East Inst; Am Asn Univ Prof; W Soc Sci Asn; SW Sco Sci Asn; Int Studies Asn. **RESEARCH** International law and organizations; Middle East; Greco-Turkish crisis; Cyprus. **SELECTED PUBLICATIONS** Auth Cyprus: An Analysis of Cypriot Political Discord, 68; Cyprus: The Impact of Diverse Nationalism on a State, 78. **CONTACT ADDRESS** Dept of Social Science, Texas Wesleyan Univ, 1201 Wesleyan St, Fort Worth, TX 76105. **EMAIL** salihi@txwes.edu

SALISBURY, ROBERT H.

PERSONAL Born 04/29/1930, Elmhurst, IL, m, 1953, 3 children **DISCIPLINE** POLITICAL SCIENCE **EDUCATION** Wash and Lee Univ, AB, 51; Univ Ill, MA, 52; PhD, 55. **CAREER** Instr to prof emeritus, 55-. **HONORS AND AWARDS** Guggenheim Fel, 90; Eldersveld Career Achievement Award, 97; Walker Award, 89, 98. **MEMBERSHIPS** Am Polit Sci Asn; Midwest Polit Sci Asn; Mo Polit Sci Asn; Intl Polit Sci Asn. **RESEARCH** Interest groups; Political parties; Urban politics. **SELECTED PUBLICATIONS** Auth, Interests and Institutions, 92; co-auth, The Hollow Core, 93. **CONTACT ADDRESS** Dept Polit Sci, Washington Univ, One Brookings Dr, CB 1063, Saint Louis, MO 63130. **EMAIL** rhsalisb@artsci.wustl.edu

SALLA, MICHAEL

DISCIPLINE INTERNATIONAL LAW AND ORGANIZATION **EDUCATION** Univ Melbourne, BA, BS, MA; Univ Queensland, PhD. **CAREER** Prof, Am Univ; Lecturer, Australian Nat Univ. **RESEARCH** Peace and conflict studies; religious nationalism, and politics of nonviolent action. **SELECTED PUBLICATIONS** Auth, Islamic Radicalism, Muslim Nations and the West; Co-ed, Why the Cold War Ended; Essays on Peace:Paradigms for a New World Order; auth, the Hero's Journey of the Second American Century. **CONTACT ADDRESS** American Univ, 4400 Massachusetts Ave, Washington, DC 20016. **EMAIL** msalla@american.edu

SALLIS, JOHN C.

PERSONAL Born 06/08/1938, Poplar Grove, AK, m, 1959, 2 children **DISCIPLINE** PHILOSOPHY **EDUCATION** Univ Arkansas, BA, 59; Tulane Univ, MA, 62, PhD, 64. **CAREER** Instr, phil, 64-66, Univ South; assoc prof, 66-70, prof, 70-83, chmn, phil, 78-83, Duquesne Univ; Arthur J. Schmitt Prof, phil, 83-90, Loyola Univ; W. Alton Jones Prof, phil, 90-95, Vanderbilt Univ; prof, liberal arts, 96-, Penn St Univ. **HONORS AND AWARDS** Alexander von Humboldt-Stiftung grant, res Hegel Archiv, Ruhr-Univ Bochum, Germany; Amer Council of Learned Soc Fel, 83; Fritz Thyssen-Stiftung Res Grant, 79; Alexander von Humboldt-Stiftung Dozentenstipendium, 74-75. **MEMBERSHIPS** APA; Hegel Soc of Amer; Heidegger Conf; Metaphysical soc; Soc for Phenomenology & Existential Phil. **RESEARCH** Ancient phil; German idealism; contemp continental phil; phil of art. **SELECTED PUBLICATIONS** Auth, Echoes: After Heidegger, IN Univ Press, 90; auth, Crossings: Nietzsche and the Space of Tragedy, Univ Chicago Press, 91; ed, Reading Heidegger: Commemorations, IN Univ Press, 93; auth, Stone, IN Univ Press, 94; auth, Delimitations: Phenomenology and the End of Metaphysics, IN Univ Press, 95; auth, Double Truth, Albany SUNY Press, 95; auth, Being and Logos: The Way of Platonic Dialogue, IN Univ Press, 96; auth, Shades: Of Painting at the Limit, IN Univ Press, 98; auth, Chorology: On Beginning in Plato's "Timaeus," Indiana Univ Press, 99; auth, Force of Imagination: The Sense of the Elemental, Indiana Univ Press, 00. **CONTACT ADDRESS** Dept of Philosophy, Pennsylvania State Univ, Univ Park, 240 Sparks Bldg, University Park, PA 16802. **EMAIL** jcs29@psu.edu

SALLSTROM, JOHN EMERY

PERSONAL Born 04/28/1939, Quincy, IL, m, 1969, 2 children **DISCIPLINE** PHILOSOPHY, RELIGION **EDUCATION** Elmhurst Col, BA, 61; Union Theol Sem, NYork, MDiv, 64; Duke Univ, PhD(relig), 68. **CAREER** Assoc V.P., Academic Services, Prof Philos & Relig, GA Col & State Univ, 67-, Minister, United Church Christ, 67-. **MEMBERSHIPS** Am Acad Relig, Am Philos Asn; Soc Christian Philosophers **CONTACT ADDRESS** Academic Services, Ga Col and State Univ, Campus Box 029, Milledgeville, GA 31061-0490. **EMAIL** jsalstr@mail.gacsu.edu

SALMON, NATHAN

PERSONAL Born 01/02/1951, Los Angeles, CA, d, 1 child **DISCIPLINE** PHILOSOPHY **EDUCATION** Univ Calif, Los Angeles, BA, 73, MA, 74, CPhil, 77, PhD, 79. **CAREER** Lectr, Calif State Univ, Northridge, 77-78; asst prof, Princeton Univ, 78-82; vis sr res philos, Princeton Univ, summer 82; assoc prof, Univ Calif, 82-85, prof, Santa Barabara, 85-; vis prof, Univ Calif, Los Angeles, spring 99. **HONORS AND AWARDS** Phi Beta Kappa; First Prize, Rudolph Carnap Essay Competition, UCLA, 75-76, 76-77, 77-78; The Gustave O. Arlt Awd in the Humanities, Coun of Grad Schs in the US, 84; Fulbright Distinguished Prof Lect Grant, Yugoslavia, 86; Am Coun of Learned Socs Travel Grant, 90; Princeton Univ Res Grant, 79-80; Univ Calif Res Grant, 82-92; Received the Twentieth Century Awd for Achievement and nominated as an Int Man of the Year, Int Biographical Centre, Cambridge, England, 99-200 and 200-2001; listed in: Contemporary Authors, Int Directory of Distinguished Leadership, Outstanding People of the 20th Century, 2000 Outstanding Intellectuals of the 20th Century. **MEMBERSHIPS** Am Philos Asn, Bertrand Russell Soc, Soc for Ethics, Royal Inst of Philos **RESEARCH** Analytic metaphysics; philosophy of language; philosophy of logic. **SELECTED PUBLICATIONS** Auth, Reference and Essence, Princeton Univ Press (81), and Basil Blackwell (82); auth, Frege's Puzzle, Atascadero, Calif: Ridgeview (86, 91); co-ed, Propositions and Attitudes, Oxford Readings in Philos (88); auth, "Is De Re Belief Reducible to De Dicto?," in A. A. Kazmi, ed, Meaning and Reference, Can J of Philos Supplementary Vol 23, Univ of Calgary Press (98): 85-110; auth, "Kripke," in the Cambridge Dictionary of Philos, 2nd ed, Cambridge Univ Press (95, 99): 476; auth, "The Very Possibility of Language: A Sermon on the Consequences of Missing Church," C. A. Anderson and M. Zeleny, eds, Essays in Memory of Alonzo Church, Boston: D. Reidel (forthcoming); auth, "Tense and Intension," in A. Jokic, ed, Proceedings of the Santa Barbara City Col Int Conf on Time, Tense, and Reference, Cambridge Univ Press (forthcoming); auth, "The Doris and Rita Incidents," in J. Berg, ed, Proceedings of the Univ of Haifa Int Conf on the Work of Saul Kripke: Naming, Necessity, and More (forthcoming); auth, "The Limits of Human Mathematics," in J. Tomberlin, ed, Philosophical Perspectives, 15: Metaphysics, 2001 (forthcoming). **CONTACT ADDRESS** Dept Philos, Univ of California, Santa Barbara, Santa Barbara, CA 93106-0002. **EMAIL** nsalmon@humanities.ucsb.edu

SALMON, WESLEY CHARLES

PERSONAL Born 08/09/1925, Detroit, MI, 1 child **DISCIPLINE** PHILOSOPHY OF SCIENCE **EDUCATION** Univ Chicago, MA, 47; Univ Calif, Los Angeles, PhD, 50. **CAREER** Instr philos, Univ Calif, Los Angeles, 50-51; State Col Wash, 51-53, asst prof, 53-54; vis asst prof, Northwestern Univ, 54-55; asst prof, Brown Univ, 55-59, assoc prof, 59-63; prof philos sci & hist, Ind Univ, Bloomington, 63-67, Norwood Russell Hanson prof, 67-73; prof, Univ Ariz, 73-81; prof to univ prof philos, Univ Pittsburgh, 81-, vis lectr, Univ Bristol, 59; vis res prof, Univ Minn, 63; vis prof, Univ Pittsburgh, 68-69 & Univ Melbourne, 78. **HONORS AND AWARDS** MA, Brown Univ, 59; Fund Advan Educ fac fel, 53-54; Senior Res Awd from the Alexander von Humboldt Found of Ger; fel of the Am Asn for the Advancement of Sci; Fel of the Am Acad of Arts and Sciences.

MEMBERSHIPS Am Philos Asn; Philos Sci Asn; Pac Div Am Philos Asn; Int Union Hist & Philos Sci; Am Asn for Adv of Sci. RESEARCH Probability, induction and confirmation; causality and scientific explanation; philosophy of physical science. SELECTED PUBLICATIONS Auth, Logic, Prentice-Hall, 63, 3rd ed, 84; Foundations of Scientific Inference, Univ Pittsburgh, 67; ed, Zeno's Paradoxes, Bobbs-Merrill, 70; coauth, Statistical Explanation and Statistical Relevance, Univ Pittsburgh, 71; auth, Space, Time and Motion, Dickenson, 75, 2nd ed, 81; ed, Hans Reichenbach, Logical Empiricist, D Reidel Publ, 79; auth, Scientific Explanation and the Causal Structure of the World, Princeton, 84; co-ed, The Limitations of Deductivism, Calif, 88; auth, Four Decades of Scientific Explanation, Minn, 90; co-ed, Logic, Language, and the Structure of Scientific Theories, Konstanz, 94; co-ed, Scientific Explanation, Minn, 89; auth, Causality and Explanation, Oxford, 98. CONTACT ADDRESS Dept of Philos, Univ of Pittsburgh, 1001 Cathedral/Learn, Pittsburgh, PA 15260-0001. EMAIL wsalmon@pitt.edu

SALOMON, DAVID A.
PERSONAL Born 11/08/1963, Bronx, NY, m, 1993 DISCIPLINE ENGLISH, PHILOSOPHY, RELIGION EDUCATION Fairleigh Dickinson Univ, BA, 87; Herbert Lehman Col, CUNY, MA, 88; Univ Conn, PhD, 99. CAREER Adj lectr, Univ of Conn, 90-99; asst prof, Lyme Acad of Fine Arts, 97-99; asst prof, Black Hills State Univ, 99- MEMBERSHIPS Am Acad of Relig, Soc for Bibl Lit, MLA. RESEARCH Mysticism, Spirituality, Religion and Literature, Recusancy. SELECTED PUBLICATIONS Auth, "Forging a New Identity: Narcissism and Imagination in the Mysticism of Ignatius Loyola," Christianity and Literature, (98). CONTACT ADDRESS Black Hills State Univ, 1200 University, Unit 9063, Spearfish, SD 57799. EMAIL davidsalomon@bhsu.edu

SALTZMAN, JUDY DEANE
PERSONAL Born 02/02/1942, San Jose, CA, m, 1995 DISCIPLINE RELIGIOUS STUDIES, PHILOSOPHY OF RELIGION EDUCATION San Jose State Univ, BA, 63; Univ Calif, Berkeley, MA, 65; Univ Calif, Santa Barbara, MA & PhD, 77. CAREER Teaching asst social sci, Univ Calif, Berkeley, 65-66; Instr philos & sociol, Santa Barbara City Col, 66-67 & philos, 68-70; instr philos & relig, Ventura Community Col, 73-75; from Asst Prof to Assoc Prof, 75-85, Prof Philos, Calif Polytech State Univ, 85-. HONORS AND AWARDS Fulbright Schol, Freie Universitat, Berlin. MEMBERSHIPS Am Acad Relig; Soc Values Higher Educ; Soc Sci Study Relig; Western Asn Ger Studies; AAUP; Soc Asian and Comparative Philos. RESEARCH Neo-Kantian philosophy; German philosophy of religion and theology; sociology of religion; philosophies of India. SELECTED PUBLICATIONS Auth, The Young, Center Mag, 1/69; Simulation Gesellshaft Realitat, in Prioritaten Fur die Gesellshaft Politik, Verlag, 70; Paul Natorps philosophy of religion within the Marburg Neo-Kantian tradition, Olms Verlag, 81; The Individual and the Avatara in the Thought of Radhakrishman, India Books Centre, 95; Karma and Reincarnation in the West, 94, Transaction # 94 Indian Institute of World Culture; Plato and Vedanta: Tradition or Imagination? in Facets of Humanism, Indian Inst World Culture, Bangalore, 95; auth, Sat Chit Aranda in Greek and Indian Thought, Indian Inst of World Culture, 98; auth, "The Idea of Spritual Knowledge in the Philosophy of Seyyed Hossein NASR," in Library of Living Philosophers (IL: Southern Ill Univ Press, 00). CONTACT ADDRESS Philos Dept, California Polytech State Univ, San Luis Obispo, 1 Grand Ave, San Luis Obispo, CA 93407-0001. EMAIL jsaltzma@calpoly.edu

SALTZMAN, ROBERT M.
DISCIPLINE LAW EDUCATION Dartmouth Col, BA, 83; Harvard Univ, JD, 87. CAREER Adj asst prof, USC Law Sch, 80-81; sr deputy, Los Angeles County Supvr, Ed Edelman, 81-84; spec counsel, Dir, Health Services, Los Angeles County, 84-88; assoc dean, 88- ; adj assoc prof, 92-94; adj prof, USC Law Sch, 95- . MEMBERSHIPS Phi Beta Kappa; Am Asn of Law Schs; LSAC. RESEARCH Academic administration. He teaches Family Law, Property, Jurisprudence, and Community Property. SELECTED PUBLICATIONS Auth, "Judge with AIDS Will Enlighten Us About the Disease," The Los Angeles Daily J (12/25/91); auth, "Report of the Liaison tot he Pre-Law Advisors' National Council," Nat Asn for Law Placement Ann Rev (92-93); auth, "Report from the National Associaiton for Law Placement," Newsletter of the Pre-Law Advisors Nat Council 1 (Spring 93; Summer 93); "The Big Lie about Affirmative Action," Boston Globe (5/11/98); auth, "Affirmative Action in Law School Admissions and Legal Employment: Facts, Observations, and Suggestions for 'Gatekeepers'," Insights: Issues and Opportunities for Law Deans & Hiring Attorneys 12 (98); coauth, "Update on Admissions and Student Services," USC Law 24 (99). CONTACT ADDRESS School of Law, Univ of So California, University Park Campus, Los Angeles, CA 90089. EMAIL rsaltzma@law.usc.edu

SALYER, GREGORY
DISCIPLINE LITERATURE, RELIGION EDUCATION King Col, BA; West Ky Univ, MA; Emory Univ, PhD, 92. CAREER Asst prof Humanities, Huntingdon Col, 93-. HONORS AND AWARDS Lilly Tchg Fel. MEMBERSHIPS AAR; MLA; SHC. RESEARCH Native American literature and culture. SELECTED PUBLICATIONS Co-ed, Literature and Theology at Century's End, 95; auth, Leslie Marmon Silko, 97. CONTACT ADDRESS Dept of Humanities, Huntingdon Col, 1500 E Fairview Ave, Montgomery, AL 36106. EMAIL gsalyer@huntingdon.edu

SALZBERG, STEPHAN
DISCIPLINE LAW EDUCATION Rochester Univ, BA, 74; Univ British Columbia, MA, 83; Univ Wash, JD, 85. CAREER Prof. HONORS AND AWARDS Japanese Ministry of Education Graduate Research Fel, Kyoto Univ, 77-78, 1978-80 RESEARCH Comparative medical and mental health law; Japanese constitutional law; Japanese law and society. SELECTED PUBLICATIONS Auth, pubs about mental health law of Japan and Taiwan. CONTACT ADDRESS Fac of Law, Univ of British Columbia, 1822 East Mall, Vancouver, BC, Canada V6T 1Z1. EMAIL salzberg@law.ubc.ca

SALZMAN, JIM
DISCIPLINE U.S. AND INTERNATIONAL ENVIRONMENTAL LAW EDUCATION Yale Col, BA, 85; Harvard Law Sch, 89; Harvard Univ, Msc, JD, 90. CAREER Prof, Am Univ. HONORS AND AWARDS Fel, Royal Geog Soc, 95; Europ environ mgr, S.C. Johnson, 92-95; environ dir, OECD, 90-92; consult, UN Environment Program. RESEARCH Environmental law and policy. SELECTED PUBLICATIONS Auth, Environmental Labeling in OECD Countries, OECD, 91; Greener Product policy in Practice, Swedish Ministry Environ, 95; Setting Environmental Goals, Environmental Management, Croner Publ Ltd, 94. CONTACT ADDRESS American Univ, 4400 Massachusetts Avc, Washington, DC 20016.

SAMAR, VINCENT J.
PERSONAL Born 02/12/1953, Syracuse, NY, s DISCIPLINE PHILOSOPHY EDUCATION Syracuse Univ, BA, 75, JD, MPA, 78; Univ Chicago, PhD, 86. CAREER Adj prof philos, Loyola Univ, 84- ; adj prof law, Ill Inst Technol, Chicago/Kent Col of Law, 90-. HONORS AND AWARDS BA, cum laude; ACLU for service as director. MEMBERSHIPS NY State Bar; Ill State Bar. RESEARCH Philosophy of law; political philosophy; ethics and constitutional law. SELECTED PUBLICATIONS Auth, the Right to Privacy: Gays, Lesbians, and the Constitution, Temple, 91; auth, Privacy and AIDS, Univ of West Los Angeles Law Rev, 91; auth, AIDS and the Politician's Right to Privacy, in Cohen, ed, AIDS: Crisis in Professional Ethics, Temple, 94; auth, A Moral Justification for Gay and Lesbian Civil Rights Legislation, Jour of Homosexuality, 94; auth, Justifying Judgment: Practicing Law and Philosophy. Kansas, 98; auth, "Law: Criminal," Reader's Guide to Gay and Lesbian Studies, ed T. Murphy, Fitzroy-Dearborn, 00; auth, "Is the Right to Die Dead?" DePaul Law Review 50.1, forthcoming, 00; auth, "Same-Sex Marriage as Part of Human Dignity," in "Proceedings," Univ of Chicago Law School Roundtable, forthcoming, 00; ed, New York Times Century in Review: Gay Rights, Fitzroy-Dearborn, forthcoming, 00. CONTACT ADDRESS Dept of Philosophy, Loyola Univ, Chicago, 820 N Michigan Ave, Chicago, IL 60611. EMAIL vsamar@luc.edu

SAMPLE, MAXINE J.
PERSONAL Born Port Norris, NJ DISCIPLINE ENGLISH, PHILOSPHY EDUCATION Col NJ, BA, 72; Clark Atlanta Univ, MA, 77; Emory Univ, PhD, 90. CAREER Instr, Atlanta Public Schs; Assoc Prof, Dekalb Col; Assoc Prof, State Univ W Ga. HONORS AND AWARDS NISOD Excellence in Teaching Awd, 91, 94; Cole Fel, Dekalb Col, 94; CASE Prof of the Year, 94; Fulbright Fel, 95. MEMBERSHIPS MLA, NEA, Ga Asn Educ, Toni Morrison Soc, Nat Coun Black Studies, African Lit Asn. RESEARCH African women writers, African-American literature, women's studies. SELECTED PUBLICATIONS Co-ed, The Polishing Cloth, Kendall Hunt (Dubuque), 95; auth, "Behind the Gated Fence (from a Kenyan Journal)," Chattahoochee Rev 16.3 (96): 130-133; auth, "The Bridal 8:4:4: Graduation Day at the University of Nairobi (from a Kenyan Journal)," Chattahoochee Rev 17.2 (97): 100-104; auth, "Richard Bruce Nugent," African-American Authors 1745-1945: A Bio-Bibliog Critical Sourcebook, Greenwood Pr (Westport, CT), 00; rev, "Alice Walker's 'Possessing the Secret of Joy'," The Explicator (forthcoming); ed, Critical Essays on Bessie Head, Greenwood Pr (Westport, CT), forthcoming. CONTACT ADDRESS Dept English & Philos, State Univ of West Georgia, 1601 Maple St, Carollton, GA 30117-4116. EMAIL msample@westga.edu

SAMPLE, RUTH
PERSONAL Born 05/28/1964, Washington, DC, m, 1991 DISCIPLINE PHILOSOPHY EDUCATION Oberlin, BA; PhD. CAREER Asst prof and adj fac, Univ of NH. HONORS AND AWARDS DAAD scholar; Mellon fel. MEMBERSHIPS APA. RESEARCH Social philosophy. CONTACT ADDRESS Dept of Philosophy, Univ of New Hampshire, Durham, Durham, NH 03824. EMAIL rjsample@hopper.unh.edu

SAMUELSON, HAVA TIROSH
DISCIPLINE RELIGIOUS STUDIES EDUCATION Hebrew Univ Jerusalem, PhD, 78. CAREER Asst prof to prof, Ind Univ, Bloomington; assoc prof, Ariz State Univ. RESEARCH Medieval and early modern Jewish intellectual history; Jewish philosophy, Kabbalah; medieval European intellectual history. SELECTED PUBLICATIONS Auth, Between Worlds-The Life and Thought of Rabbi David ben Judah Messer Leon, SUNY, 91; Continuity and Revision in the Study of Kabbalah, AJS Rev, 91; auth, "'Dare to Know'--Feminism and Jewish Philosophy," in Feminist Perspective of Jewish Studies, ed. Shelly Tenenbaum and Lynn Davidman (Yale Univ Press, 94), 84-119; auth, "The Theology of Nature in Sixteenth-Century Jewish Philosophy," Sci in Context 10 (97): 529-570; auth, "A Jewish Perspective on Religious Pluralism," Macalester Int 8 (00): 73-112. CONTACT ADDRESS Dept of Hist, Arizona State Univ, Box 872501, Tempe, AZ 85287-2501. EMAIL hava.samuelson@asu.edu

SANDALOW, TERRANCE
PERSONAL Born 09/08/1934, Chicago, IL, m, 1955, 3 children DISCIPLINE LAW EDUCATION Univ Chicago, AB, 54, JD, 57. CAREER Prof law, Univ Minn, 61-66; prof, 66-78, Dean Law Sch, Univ Mich, Ann Arbor, 78-, Ctr Advan Studies Behav Sci fel, 72-73. RESEARCH Local government law; constitutional law; federal courts and the federal system. SELECTED PUBLICATIONS Auth, Soc-Justice And Fundamental Law - A Comment On Sager Constitution/, Northwestern Univ Law Rev, Vol 0088, 1993. CONTACT ADDRESS Law Sch, Univ of Michigan, Ann Arbor, 922 Legal Res Bldg, Ann Arbor, MI 48104.

SANDER, FRANK E. A.
PERSONAL Born 07/22/1927, Stuttgart, Germany, m, 1958, 3 children DISCIPLINE LAW EDUCATION Harvard Univ, BA, 49, LLB, 52. CAREER Law clerk, US Ct of Appeals, 52-53; US Supreme Ct, 53-54; atty, Tax Div, US Dept Justice, 54-56; assoc, Hill & Harlow, Boston, 56; asst prof, 59-62, prof, 62-80, Bussey Prof Law, Harvard Univ, 80-; Mem tax mission, Rep Colombia, 59; mem labor panel, Am Arbit Asn & Fed Mediation & Conciliation Serv, 60-; mem comt civil & polit rights, President's Comn Status Women, 61-63; consult, US Treas Dept, 67-68; chmn spec subcomt domestic relation probs, Am Bar Asn, 63-64; chmn, State Adv Bd Mass Dept Pub Welfare, 75-. HONORS AND AWARDS Phi Beta Kappa; Kutak Medal, ABA; CPR Int of Dep Res Prize. MEMBERSHIPS Am Bar Asn. RESEARCH Dispute Resolution. SELECTED PUBLICATIONS Co-ed, Readings in Federal Taxation, Foundation, 70; auth, Tax Aspects of Divorce, Bur Nat Affairs, 75; coauth, Cases and Materials in Family Law, Little, 76; Varieties of dispute processing, 70, Fed Rules Decision, III, 76; Report of Conference on minor disputes resolution, Am Bar Asn, 77; co-auth, Dispute Resolution, Aspen, 99. CONTACT ADDRESS Law Sch, Harvard Univ, 1525 Massachusetts, Cambridge, MA 02138-2903.

SANDERS, CHERYL J.
PERSONAL Born Washington, DC, m, 1982, 2 children DISCIPLINE APPLIED THEOLOGY EDUCATION Harvard Divinity School, M Div (cum laude), 80, ThD, 85. CAREER Asst prof to prof Christian Ethics, Howard Univ School of Divinity, 84-. HONORS AND AWARDS Minister of the Year Awd, Nat Asn of Negro Business and Professional Women's Clubs, 94; Outstanding Author award, Howard Univ, 95. MEMBERSHIPS Am Academy Relig; Soc Christian Ethics. RESEARCH Christian ethics; African Am relig studies; wanist studies; biamedical ethics. SELECTED PUBLICATIONS Auth, Living the Intersection, Fortress Press, 95; Empowerment Ethics for a Liberated People, Fortress Press, 95; Saints in Exile, Oxford Univ Press, 96; Ministry at the Margins, Intervarsity Press, 97. CONTACT ADDRESS 7704 Morningside Dr NW, Washington, DC 20012. EMAIL csanders@fac.howard.edu

SANDERS, DOUGLAS
DISCIPLINE LAW EDUCATION Univ Alberta, BA, 60; LLB, 61; Univ Ca, LLM, 63. CAREER Assoc prof, Windsor Univ, 69-72; assoc prof, 72-77; prof, Univ of British Columbia, 77-. RESEARCH Constitutional Law, First Nations legal issues, gays/lesbians and the law, and International Human Rights Law. SELECTED PUBLICATIONS Auth, pubs about constitutional law, First Nation's legal issues, gays/lesbians and the law, and international human rights law. CONTACT ADDRESS Fac of Law, Univ of British Columbia, 1822 East Mall, Vancouver, BC, Canada V6T 1Z1. EMAIL sanders@law.ubc.ca

SANDERS, JACK THOMAS
PERSONAL Born 02/28/1935, Grand Prairie, TX, m, 1959, 1 child DISCIPLINE RELIGION EDUCATION Tex Wesleyan Col, BA, 56; Emory Univ, MDiv, 60; Claremont Grad Sch & Univ Ctr, PhD(relig), 63. CAREER Asst prof New Testament, Emory Univ, 64-67, Garrett Theol Sem, 67-68 & McCormick Theol Sem, 68-69; assoc prof, 69-75, chmn dept, 73-76 & 77-80, Prof Relig Studies, Univ Ore, 75-, Fulbright fel, Univ Tubingen, 63-64; corresp mem Inst Antiq & Christianity, Claremont Grad Sch, 69-73; mem policy bd, Dept Higher Educ, Nat Coun Churches of Christ, USA, 71-73; Danforth assoc, 71-76; res grant, Ctr Bibl Res & Archives, Soc Bibl Lit, 76-77. MEMBERSHIPS Soc Bibl Lit; Studiorum Novi Testament Soc;

AAUP. **RESEARCH** New Testament; Judaism of second temple period. **SELECTED PUBLICATIONS** Auth, First Corinthians 13: Its interpretation since the First World War, Interpretation, 66; Tradition and redaction in Luke XV, 11-32, New Testament Studies, 69; The question of the relevance of Jesus for ethics today, J Am Acad Relig, 70; The New Testament Christological Hymns: Their Historical Religious Background, Cambridge Univ, 71; Ethics in the New Testament: Change and Development, Fortress Press, 75; Ben Sira's Ethics of Caution, Hebrew Union Col Annual, 80; Ben Sira and Demotic Wisdom, Scholars Press, 82. **CONTACT ADDRESS** Dept of Relig Studies, Univ of Oregon, Eugene, OR 97403-1205.

SANDERS, JAMES ALVIN
PERSONAL Born 11/28/1927, Memphis, TN, m, 1951, 1 child **DISCIPLINE** BIBLICAL STUDIES **EDUCATION** Vanderbilt Univ, BA, 48, BD, 51; Hebrew Union Col, PhD, 55. **CAREER** Hoyt prof Old Testament interpretation, Colgate Rochester Divinity Sch, 54-65; Auburn prof Bibl studies, Union Theol Sem, NY, 65-77; E H Bechtel Prof Intertestamemtal & Bible Studies, Sch Theol & Prof Relig, Claremont Grad Sch, 77-97-, Guggenheim Found fel & ann prof, Am Sch Orient Res, Jerusalem, 61-62; mem Dead Sea Scroll fund comt, Am Schs Orient Res, 62-; adj prof, Columbia Univ, 65-77; Guggenheim Found fel, 72-73; Ecumenical Inst Jerusalem fel, 72-73; trustee, Am Sch Orient Res, 77-80; pres, Ancient Bibl Manuscript Ctr for Preserv & Res, Claremont, 80-; Hebrew Old Testament Text Critical Proj United Bible Soc, Stuttgart, 69- **HONORS AND AWARDS** DLitt, Acadia Univ, 73; STD, Univ Glasgow, 75; plus four others 88-00. **MEMBERSHIPS** Soc Bibl Lit (pres, 78). **RESEARCH** Old Testament texts and canon; Hellenistic Judaism and New Testament; Biblical history, literature and theology. **SELECTED PUBLICATIONS** Fifteen books and over 250 articles. **CONTACT ADDRESS** PO Box 593, Claremont, CA 91711. **EMAIL** sandersja@aol.com

SANDERS, JOHN E.
PERSONAL Born 07/16/1956, Danville, IL, m, 5 children **DISCIPLINE** THEOLOGY, PHILOSOPHY OF RELIGION **EDUCATION** Trinity Col, BA, 79; Wartburg Theol Sem, MA, 87; Univ S Africa, ThD, 96. **CAREER** Head of Educ, Oak Hills Christian Col, 81-97; assoc prof, Huntigton Col, 98-. **HONORS AND AWARDS** Extraordinay Fel, Univ Notre Dame, 97-98. **MEMBERSHIPS** Am Acad of Relig, Soc of Christian Philos, christian Theolo Res, Am Theol Soc, Evangelical Theol Soc. **RESEARCH** Nature of God, Divine Providence, Religious Pluralism. **SELECTED PUBLICATIONS** Auth, The God Who Risks, Inter-Varsity Press, 98; auth, The Openness of God, Inter-Varsity Press, 95; auth, No Other Name, Eerdmans, 92. **CONTACT ADDRESS** Dept Humanities, Huntington Col, 2303 College Ave, Huntington, IN 46750-1237. **EMAIL** jsanders@huntington.edu

SANDERS, JOHN T.
PERSONAL Born 12/29/1945, Chicago, IL, m, 1986, 3 children **DISCIPLINE** PHILOSOPHY **EDUCATION** Purdue Univ, BA, 68; Boston Univ, MA, 72, PhD, 77. **CAREER** Social work/Psychology specialist, U.S. Army, 68-70; from asst prof to prof, Rochester Inst of Technol, 76-; consult to the Instruct Telecommunications Consortium Course Develop Proj of The Corp for Community Col Television in Cypress, Calif, 88-89; consult to the City Col of Loyola Univ, New Orleans, 95; vis prof, Univ of Helsinki, 95; vis prof, Polish Acad of Scis, 95-96; prof, U.S. Bus Sch in Prague, 97-; chr, Dept of Philos, RIT, 77-82-, 86-88, 01-. **HONORS AND AWARDS** Bronze Star for meritorious service, U.S. Army, 70; Eisenhart Annual Awd for Outstanding Teaching, Rochester Inst of Technol, 79-80. **MEMBERSHIPS** Am Philos Inst. **SELECTED PUBLICATIONS** Auth, The Ethical Argument Against Government, 80; The Attractiveness of Risk, in Am Soc for Value Inquiry Newsletter, fall, 94; An Ecological Approach to Cognitive Science, in The Electronic J of Analytic Philos, issue 4, 96; Risk and Value, in A.S.V.I. News: The Newsletter of the Am Soc for Value Inquiry, spring, 96; coed The State of Statelessness, in For and Against the State: New Philosophical Readings, 96; coed Comments on the Habermas/Rorty Debate, Comments on Philosophy and the Dilemmas of the Contemporary World, in Debating the State of Philosophy: Habermas, Rorty, and Kolakowski, 96; Stanislaw Lesniewski's Logical Systems, in Axiomathes, vol. vii, no. 3, 96; An Ontology of Affordances, in Ecological Psychology, vol. 9, no. 1, 97; Reflections on the Value of Freedom, in Taking the Liberal Challenge Seriously: Essays on Contemp Liberalism at the Turn of the 21st Century, 97; A Mixed Bag: Political Change in Central and Eastern Europe and its Impact on Philosophical Thought, in Philosophy in Post-Communist Europe, 98; Incommensurability and Demarcation, in Criticism and Defense of Rationality in Contemp Philos, 98; Contra Leviathan: On the Legitimacy and Propriety of the State, 99; ed, Niels Bohr: Essays and Papers, two vols., Manuscript archive, 87; coed, The Philosopher's Annual, vols. I-IV, 78-81; The Philosopher's Annual, vol. V, 84; For and Against the State: New Philosophical Readings, 96; Debating the State of Philosophy: Habermas, Rorty, and Kolakowski, 96. **CONTACT ADDRESS** Dept of Philosophy, Rochester Inst of Tech, 92 Lomb Memorial Dr, Rochester, NY 14623-5604. **EMAIL** jtsgsh@rit.edu

SANDS, KATHLEEN M.
PERSONAL Born 09/12/1954, New York, NY, s **DISCIPLINE** THEOLOGY **EDUCATION** Boston Univ, BA, 76; Harvard Div Sch, MTS; Boston Col, PhD. **CAREER** Assoc prof, relig stud, Univ Mass, Boston, 96- . **HONORS AND AWARDS** Summa Cum Laude; Harvard Univ res fel, 98; Res fellow, Ingraham Bunting Inst, 00-01. **MEMBERSHIPS** Am Acad Relig. **RESEARCH** Evil and tragedy; religion in American public life; religion and culture. **SELECTED PUBLICATIONS** Auth, Escape from Paradise: Evil and Tragedy in Feminist Theology, Augsberg/Fortress, 99; ed, contribur, Religion and Sex in American Public Life, Oxford, 00; auth, God Forbid: Religion and Sex in American Public Life, Oxford Univ Press, 00. **CONTACT ADDRESS** 89 Rossmore Rd, Jamaica Plain, MA 02130-3666. **EMAIL** kathleensands@umbsky.cc.umb.edu

SANFORD, DANIEL
DISCIPLINE INTERNATIONAL STUDIES **EDUCATION** Univ Denver, PhD. **CAREER** Dir, Grad Sch Intl Mg, Whitworth col; prof-. **HONORS AND AWARDS** Fulbright scholar, Univ Kiemyung, Daegu, Korea; res fel, Univ Calif, Berkeley.; former pres, world trade coun; northwest intl edu assn. **MEMBERSHIPS** Mem, Spokane Mayor's Comm Intl Devel; Spokane Chamber of Com Intl Steering Comm. **RESEARCH** International political economy with focus on trade politics in Northeast Asia. **SELECTED PUBLICATIONS** Auth, South Korea and the Socialist Countries; The Politics of Trade. **CONTACT ADDRESS** Dept of Hist, Whitworth Col, 300 West Hawthorne Rd, Spokane, WA 99251. **EMAIL** dsanford@whitworth.edu

SANFORD, DAVID HAWLEY
PERSONAL Born 12/13/1937, Detroit, MI, m, 1965, 2 children **DISCIPLINE** PHILOSOPHY **EDUCATION** Wayne State Univ, BA, 60; Cornell Univ, PhD(philos), 66. **CAREER** From instr to asst prof philos, Dartmouth Col, 63-70; assoc prof, 70-78, prof philos, Duke Univ, 78-, vis assoc prof philos, Univ Mich, 70; Nat Endowment Humanities fel selected fields, 74-75, fel, 82-83, 89-90; Nat Humanities Center, fel, 89-90. **MEMBERSHIPS** Mind Asn; Am Philos Asn; Soc Philos Psychol. **RESEARCH** Philosophical logic; metaphysics; theory of knowledge. **SELECTED PUBLICATIONS** Auth, The Direction of Causation and the Direction of Conditionship, J Philos, 76; Where was I?, Hofstadter and Dennett, eds, The Mind's I, 81; The Perception of Shape, Ginet and Shoemaker, eds, Knowledge and Mind, 83; Infinite Regress Arguments, Fetzer, ed, Principles of Philosophical Reasonong, 84; Self-Deception as Rationalism, A.O. Rorty and McLaughlin, eds, Perspectives on Self-Deception, 88; If P, then Q: Conditionals and the Foundations of Reasoning, Routledge, 89; paperback ed, 92; Causation and Intelligibility, Philosophy, 94; Temporal Parts, Temporal Portions, and Temporal Slices: An Exercise in Naive Mereology, Acta analytica, 96. **CONTACT ADDRESS** Dept of Philos, Duke Univ, P O Box 90743, Durham, NC 27708-0743. **EMAIL** dhs@acpub.duke.edu

SANKS, T. HOWLAND
PERSONAL Born 10/28/1933, Baltimore, MD, s **DISCIPLINE** THEOLOGY **EDUCATION** Loyola Col, AB, 55; Fordham Univ, PhL, 59; Woodstock Col, STB, 65; STL, 66; Univ Chicago, MA, 69; PhD, 71. **CAREER** Chairman, Col of Holy Cross, 71-75; res assoc, Woodstock Theol Center, 75-76; chairman, Canisius Col, 76-80; assoc prof to prof, Jesuit Sch of Theology, 80-; president, 97-. **MEMBERSHIPS** Am Acad of Relig; Assoc of Theol Schools. **SELECTED PUBLICATIONS** Auth, Authority in the Church: A Study in Changing Paradigms, Scholars Pr, 74; coed, Faithful Witness: Foundations of Theology for today's Church, Crossroad, 80; auth, "Forms of Ecclesiality: The Analogical Church", Theol Studies 49, (88): 695-708; auth, Salt, Leaven, and Light: The Community Called Church, Crossroad, 92; coed, Reading the Signs of the Times: Resources for Social and Cultural Analysis, 93; auth, "David Tracy's Theological Project: An Overview and Some Implications", Theol Studies 54, (93): 698-727; auth, "Postmodernism and the Church", New Theol Rev 11.3 (98): 51-59; auth, "The Church's Social Mission: Its Changing Context", Louvain Studies, (99): auth, "The Social Mission of the Church: Its Changing Context", The Gift of the Church, Festschrift for Patrick Granfield, Liturgical Pr, (forthcoming); auth, "Globalization and the Church's Social Mission", Theol Studies, (forthcoming). **CONTACT ADDRESS** Dept Theol, Jesuit Sch of Theol, Berkeley, 1735 Le Roy Ave, Berkeley, CA 94709-1115.

SANSON, JERRY P.
PERSONAL Born 03/13/1952, Alexandria, LA, m, 1991, 1 child **DISCIPLINE** HISTORY, POLITICAL SCIENCE **EDUCATION** La Col, BA, 74; La State Univ, MA, 75; PhD, 84. **CAREER** Instr to prof, La State Univ, 86-. **HONORS AND AWARDS** Huie-Dellmon Trust Prof, La State Univ, 98-00. **MEMBERSHIPS** La Hist Assoc; N La Hist Assoc; La Polit Sci Assoc; La Acad of Sci; Gulf S Hist Assoc. **RESEARCH** New Deal - World War II Era. **SELECTED PUBLICATIONS** Auth, Louisiana State and Local Government, Prentice-Hall, (Englewood Cliffs, NJ), 92; auth, Louisiana During World War II, La State Univ Pr, (Baton Rouge), 99. **CONTACT ADDRESS** Dept Lib Arts, Louisiana State Univ, Alexandria, 8100 Hwy 71 S, Alexandria, LA 71302-9119. **EMAIL** jsanson@pobox.lsua.edu

SANTA MARIA, DARIO ATEHORTUA
PERSONAL Born 06/19/1943, Medellin, Colombia, s **DISCIPLINE** RELIGION **EDUCATION** Univ St. Thomas Bogota, BD, BPh 65; Ashbury Sem, ThM 67; Univ Madrid, Lic comunicaciones 69; Episcopal Sem VA, cert theol, palaeography 71-74; Univ Lateranense Rome, ThD 75; Ecole Biblique Francaise Jerusalem, post grad 76; Oxford Univ, 82-84. **CAREER** NT Union Theol Sem Madrid, prof 67-70; Prot Theol Inst Fe y Secularidad Madrid, prof 67-70; Iglesia De Camillejas Madrid, pastor 68-70; Oikoumenikon Vatican City Italy, asst editor 72-76; Ed Clie Spain, ed 76-81; St. James Piccadilly Inst London, prof 81-84; United Bible Soc London, 76-85; Ch World Svc Geneva, 80-; British Lib London, man dept 81-; Inst Contemp Christianity, prof 95-; German Seamen's Mission NY, assoc pastor 96-. **HONORS AND AWARDS** Sion Col Fel; Dr. of Letters recp; ordained priest, roman catholic church. **MEMBERSHIPS** APC; ACL; ATE; AAH **SELECTED PUBLICATIONS** Auth, Diccionario Biblico Ilustrado, 82, revised ed 98; Los Manuscriptos Del Mar Muerto y su impacto En Los Estudios Biblicos, Madrid 97; La Reforma En La Iglesia Hoy, Barcelona 97; Yel Texto Griego Delabiblia, 83; The World After Columbus, 1492-1992, 91. **CONTACT ADDRESS** Seafarers and International House, 123 E 15th Street, New York, NY 10003.

SANTAS, GERASIMOS
PERSONAL Born 03/23/1931, Greece, m, 1979, 5 children **DISCIPLINE** PHILOSOPHY **EDUCATION** Cornell Univ, PhD. **CAREER** Prof, philos, Univ Calif Irvine. **HONORS AND AWARDS** Doctorate, Honoris Causa, Univ Athens, 94. **MEMBERSHIPS** Amer Philos Asn; Intl Asn of Greek Philos. **RESEARCH** Ancient Greek philosophy; History of ethics. **SELECTED PUBLICATIONS** Auth, Socrates, Greek ed, 97, new ed, 99, Routledge; auth, Pluto and Focero, Blackwell. **CONTACT ADDRESS** Philosophy, Univ of California, Irvine, Irvine, CA 92664. **EMAIL** gxsantas@uci.edu

SANTILLANA, FERNANDO
PERSONAL Born 02/09/1940, Lima, Peru, m, 1965, 3 children **DISCIPLINE** THEOLOGY **EDUCATION** Claremont Schl Theol, MDiv, DMin, 83; LaSalle Univ, PhD, 87. **CAREER** Rector, Comunidad Biblico-Theologica, Peru, 87-90; prof, Sem Metodista, Brazil, 90-94; coordr, Mission Ed, Univ Methodist Church, S Cent Jurisdiction, USA, 94-97; coordr, MDiv prog, Seminario Metodista, Mexico, 98-; assoc council dir, Latino Ministries and Relig and Race Calif-Pacific Annual Conference of the United Methodist Church, 99-. **HONORS AND AWARDS** Magna Cum Laude, PhD, LaSalle Univ. **MEMBERSHIPS** AAR; OEF. **RESEARCH** Misticism, liberation theology, liturgy. **SELECTED PUBLICATIONS** Auth, Modulo de Liturgia, Porto Alegre, ITJW, 93; auth, Miqueas: Profeta para Latinoamerica, Maryland Intl Scholars Pub, 98. **CONTACT ADDRESS** 829 Warwick Dr, Plano, TX 75023-6819. **EMAIL** fsantillana@cal-pac.org

SANTONI, ROLAND J.
DISCIPLINE BUSINESS LAW **EDUCATION** Univ Penn, BS, 63, JD, 66. **CAREER** Prof, Creighton Univ; pvt pract, Philadelphia, 66-77; ed, Annual Inst on Sec Reg for Practicing Law Inst, 81-87; arbitrator, National Asn Securities Dealers. **HONORS AND AWARDS** Creighton Univ Robert F. Kennedy Mem Outstanding Prof awd. **MEMBERSHIPS** Order of the Coif. **SELECTED PUBLICATIONS** Pub(s), Creighton Law Rev; Employee Relations Law J; J Corp Law. **CONTACT ADDRESS** Sch of Law, Creighton Univ, 2500 California Plaza , Omaha, NE 68178. **EMAIL** santoni@culaw.Creighton.edu

SANTONI, RONALD ERNEST
PERSONAL Born 12/19/1931, Arvida, QC, Canada, m, 1955, 6 children **DISCIPLINE** PHILOSOPHY **EDUCATION** Bishop's Univ, BA, 52; Brown Univ, MA, 54; Univ of Paris, Sorbonne, Boston Univ, PhD(philos), 61. **CAREER** Asst prof philos, Univ of the Pac, 58-61; Wabash Col, 62-64; assoc prof, 64-68, chmn dept, 71-73, prof philos, Denison Univ, 68- & Maria Theresa Barney Chair, 78-, Church Soc Col Work fel, 61-62; res fel, Yale Univ, 61-62 mem nat exec comt, Episcopal Peace fel, 69-79; Soc Relig Higher Educ fel, 71-; trustee, Margaret Hall Sch, 72-74; res fel, Yale Univ, 75; vis fel, Berkeley Col, Yale Univ, 75 & 81, 93-94, 97; vis fel, Clare Hall, Cambridge Univ, UK, 86; vis scholar in philos, Cambridge Univ, 86, 90, 94, 97, 99, 01; vis lecturer on Sartre's philosophy, Cambridge, 90; life member Clare Hall, Cambridge. **HONORS AND AWARDS** Mellon Awd for distinguished faculty, 72; Tchr of the Yr, 86-87; assoc fel, Berkeley Col, Yale Univ, 97- ; Who's Who in the World, 01- ; 2000 Outstanding Authors of the 21st Century, 01- ; Member, high Table, King's Col, Cambridge, 99; Robert C. Good Fellow (for research and writing at Cambridge), 86, 94, 01. **MEMBERSHIPS** Am Philos Asn; Int Phenomenol Soc; Soc Phenomonology & Existential Philos; Sartre Soc of North Am (exec comm95-); Sartre Circle, co-ord, 97; Concerned Philosophers for Peace, Pres, 96-97; Int Philosophers for Prevention of Nuclear Omnicide, Pres, 91-96. **RESEARCH** Philos of Jean-Paul Sartre; existentialism; philos of violence and non-violence; social and political philos; philos of relig. **SELECTED PUBLICATIONS** Co-ed, Social and Political Philosophy, Doubleday, 63; ed & contribr, Religious Language and The Problem of Religious Knowledge, Ind Univ, 68;

auth, Sartre on Sincerity: Bad Faith? or Equivocation? spring 72 & Ducasse's Criterion of Morality: An Exploration and Critique, fall 72, Personalist; Ducasse on cause: Another look, Current Philos Issues, 66; Bad Faith and Lying to Oneself, Philos & Phenomenol Res, 78; Sartre and Morality: Jeanson's Classic Revisited, Int Philos Quart, 81; Nurturing the Institution of War: Just War Theory's Justifications and Accomodations, 91; On the Existential Meaning of Violence, 91; Bad Faith, Good Faith, and Authenticity, Temple Univ, 95; auth, "On Monasterio's 'Vindication' of Sartre," Sartre Studies Int, 97; auth, "In Defense of Levy and 'Hope Now'," Sartre Studies Int, 98; auth, "On the Existential Meaning of War," Dialogue and Humanism, 98. **CONTACT ADDRESS** Dept of Philos, Denison Univ, 1 Denison University, Granville, OH 43023. **EMAIL** santoni@denison.edu

SANTOS, MANUEL S.
PERSONAL Born 03/15/1957, Spain **DISCIPLINE** ECONOMICS **EDUCATION** Univ Autonoma de Madrid, Licenciatura, 79; Univ Chicago, MA, 82; PhD, 84. **CAREER** Asst Prof to Assoc Prof, Univ Autonoma de Barcelona, 85-91; Vis Prof, Univ Calif Los Angeles, 91; Tinker Vis Prof, Univ Chicago, 91; Prof, Univ Carlos III de Madrid, 91-94; Vis Prof to Prof, ITAM, Mexico, 93-97; Prof, Univ Minn, 97-99; Prof, Ariz State Univ, 99-. **RESEARCH** Economic Theory; Computation; Growth and Development. **SELECTED PUBLICATIONS** Auth, "Smoothness of the Policy Function in Discrete-Time Economic Models," Econometrica, 91; co-auth, "On Expenditure Functions," J of Math Econ, 96; co-auth, "Competitive Equilibria for Infinite Horizon Economies with Incomplete Markets," J of Econ Theory, 96; co-auth, "J of Econ Theory, 97; co-auth, "Rational Asset Pricing Bubbles," Econometrica, 97; co-auth, "On the Speed of Convergence in Endogenous Growth Models," Am Econ Rev, 97; co-auth, "Analysis of Error for a Dynamic Programming Algorithm" Econometrica, 98; co-auth, "A Two-Sector Model of Endogenous Growth," Rev of Econ Studies, 99; auth, "Accuracy of Numerical Solutions Using the Euler Equation Residuals," Econometrica, 00; auth, "On Non-Existence of Markov Equilibria in competitive-Market Economies," J of Econ Theory, forthcoming. **CONTACT ADDRESS** Dept Econ, Arizona State Univ, Dept Econ, Tempe, AZ 85287. **EMAIL** Manuel.Santos@asu.edu

SANTOS, SHEROD
PERSONAL Born 09/09/1948, Greenville, SC, m, 1975, 2 children **DISCIPLINE** ENGLISH, PHILOSOPHY **EDUCATION** San Diego State Univ, BA, 71; MA, 74;, MFA, 78; Univ Utah, PhD, 82. **CAREER** Asst prof, Calif State Univ San Bernardino, 82-83; asst prof, Univ Mo Columbia, 83-86; vis prof, Univ Calif Irvine, 89-90; assoc prof, Univ Mo Columbia, 86-92; prof, Univ MO Columbia, 93-. **HONORS AND AWARDS** Utah Arts Coun Awd in Lit, 80; Discovery The Nat award, 78; Pushcart Prize in Poetry, 80; Oscar Blumenthal Prize, 81; Nat Poetry Series Selection, 82; Meralmikjen Fel in Poetry, Bread Loaf Writers' Conf, 82; Ingram Merrill Found Grant, 82; The Robert Frost Poet, 84; Mo Arts Coun Awd in Lit, 87; Fel to the Yaddo Center fort he Arts, 87; NBC Today Show Appearance, 87; Nat Endowment for the Arts Grant, 87; Weldon Springs Res Grant, Univ Mo, 91-92; Chancellor's Awd for Outstanding Fac Res, Univ Mo, 93; Pushcart Prize in the Essay, 94; British Arts Coun Int Travel Grant, 95; Appointed Mem, Nat Endowment for the Arts Lit Panel, 95; BF Conners Awd in Poetry, 98; Finalist, New Yorker Book Awd in Poetry, 99; Finalist, Nat Book Awd in Poetry, 99; Acad Awd in Literature, Am Acad of Arts & Letters, 99; Presidents Awd for Outstanding Res and Creativity Acitivity, Univ of Missouri, 99; The Poetry Society of Am Lyric Poetry Prize, 99. **MEMBERSHIPS** Acad Am Poets; Poetry Soc of Am; PEN Am Center; Robinson Jeffers Soc; Poets and Writers; Associated Writing Programs. **RESEARCH** Poetry and Poetics. **SELECTED PUBLICATIONS** Auth, The City of Women, 93; The Pilot Star Elegies, 99; auth, "A Poetry of Two Minds," (a collection of literary essays), 00. **CONTACT ADDRESS** Dept of English, Univ of Missouri, Columbia, 107 Tate Hall, Columbia, MO 65211. **EMAIL** santoss@missouri.edu

SANTUCCI, JAMES A.
PERSONAL Born 11/12/1942, Bronxville, NY, m, 1967, 2 children **DISCIPLINE** RELIGION **EDUCATION** Iona Col, BA, 64; Univ Haw, MA, 67; Australian Nat Univ, PhD, 71. **CAREER** From asst prof to prof, Calif State Univ Fullerton, 74-. **MEMBERSHIPS** Pali Text Soc, Am Oriental Soc, Am Acad of Rel, Royal Asiatic Soc, Int Asn of Buddhist Studies. **RESEARCH** New religious movements, theosophy, Buddhism. **SELECTED PUBLICATIONS** Auth, "Theosophy and the Theosophical Societies: An Overview," Syzyogy 1(2) (97); coauth, America's Religions, Teachers Ideas Press, 97; auth, La Societa Teosofica, Elledici (Torino), 99. **CONTACT ADDRESS** Dept Comparative Rel, California State Univ, Fullerton, 800 N State College Blvd, Fullerton, CA 92834-6868. **EMAIL** jsantucci@fullerton.edu

SAPONTZIS, STEVE FREDERIC
PERSONAL Born 02/09/1945, New York, NY **DISCIPLINE** PHILOSOPHY **EDUCATION** Rice Univ, BA, 67; Yale Univ, MPhil, 70, PhD(philos), 71. **CAREER** Asst prof, 71-76, assoc prof, 76-81, Prof Philos, Calif State Univ, Hayward, 81- **MEMBERSHIPS** Am Soc Value Inquiry; Am Philos Asn; Soc Study of Ethics & Animals. **RESEARCH** Ethics; animal rights; philosophical psychology. **SELECTED PUBLICATIONS** Auth, Anatomy Of A Defeat In Renaissance Italy - The Battle Of Fornovo In 1495/, Int Hist Rev, Vol 0016, 1994. **CONTACT ADDRESS** Dept of Philos, California State Univ, Hayward, 25800 Carlos Bee Bvd, Hayward, CA 94542-3001.

SARAO, KARAM TEJ S.
PERSONAL Born 04/01/1955, Sangrur, India, m, 1981, 2 children **DISCIPLINE** RELIGION **EDUCATION** Univ Delhi, PhD, 85; Univ Canfab, PhD, 89. **CAREER** Cambridge Univ, Commonwealth Fel, 85-89; Delhi Univ, prof, dept chemn, 93-. **HONORS AND AWARDS** Delhi Univ, Gold Medal, Commonwealth Fel. **MEMBERSHIPS** RAS London, IABS, Indian Hist Congress. **RESEARCH** Animal rights; thesavada Buddhism. **SELECTED PUBLICATIONS** Auth, Urbanization and Urban Centers as Reflected in the Sali Vinaya and Sutta Pitakas, Delhi: Vidyanidhi, 89; auth, Origin and Nature of Early Indian Buddhism, Delhi: Eastern Book Linkess, 89; auth, A Text Book of the History of Thesavada Buddhism, Delhi Univ, Delhi, 93. **CONTACT ADDRESS** Dept of Buddhist Studies, Delhi Univ, 1701-17 Knightsbridge Rd, Brampton, ON, Canada L6T 3X9. **EMAIL** ktsarao@hotmail.com

SARASON, RICHARD SAMUEL
PERSONAL Born 02/12/1948, Detroit, MI **DISCIPLINE** RELIGIOUS STUDIES, HISTORY OF RELIGIONS **EDUCATION** Brandeis Univ, AB, 69; Hebrew Union Col, MAHL, 74; Brown Univ, PhD(relig studies), 77. **CAREER** Instr relig studies, Brown Univ, 76-77, asst prof, 77-79; asst prof, 79-81, Assoc Prof Rabbinic Lit & Thought, Hebrew Union Col, 81- **MEMBERSHIPS** Am Acad Relig; Soc Bibl Lit; Asn Jewish Studies; Am Sch Orient Res; Soc Values Higher Educ. **RESEARCH** Judaism in late antiquity; early rabbinic Judaism, Mishnah-Tosefta, rabbinic midrash and liturgy. **SELECTED PUBLICATIONS** Transl, Joseph Heinemann's Prayer in the Talmud, Walter de Gruyter & Co, 77; auth, A History of the Mishnaic Law of Agriculture: Demai, E J Brill, 78; contribr, Approaches to Ancient Judaism, Scholars, 78 & 80; Joseph Heinemann Memorial Volume, Magnes, 81; ed, The Tosefta: An English Translation, I The Order of Seeds, Ktav, 83. **CONTACT ADDRESS** Hebrew Union Col-Jewish Inst of Religion, Ohio, 3101 Clifton Ave, Cincinnati, OH 45220.

SARAT, AUSTIN D.
PERSONAL Born 11/02/1947, Fall River, MA, m, 1993, 3 children **DISCIPLINE** LAW, POLITICAL SCIENCE **EDUCATION** Providence Col, BA, 69; Univ Wis, MA; PhD, 73; Yale Law Sch, JD, 88. **CAREER** Prof, Amherst Col, 74-. **HONORS AND AWARDS** Woodrow Wilson Fel, 69-70; Russell Sage Fel, 73-74; NEH, 78, 85; Vis Fel, Oxford Univ, 85-86; Harry Kalven Prize, Law & Soc Asn, 97. **MEMBERSHIPS** Am Polit Sci Asn; Law & Soc Asn; Asn for the Study of Law, Cult and the Humanities. **RESEARCH** Law and culture; Law and film; Capital punishment; The legal profession. **SELECTED PUBLICATIONS** Co-auth, Divorce Lawyers and Their Clients: Power and Meaning in the Legal Process, Oxford Univ Press, 95; ed, Race, Law and Culture: Reflections on Brown v. Board of Education, Oxford Univ Press, 97; co-ed, Cause Lawyering: Political Commitments and Professional Responsibilities, Oxford Univ Press, 98; co-ed, Law in the Domains of Culture, Ann Arbor, 98; ed, The Killing state: Capital Punishment in Law, Politics, and Culture, 98; co-ed, History, Memory, and the Law, Univ Mich Press, 99; ed, Law, Violence, and the Possibility of Justice, Princeton Univ Press, 01; ed, Pain, Death, and the Law, Univ Mich Press, 01; co-ed, Cause Lawyering and the State in a Global Era, Oxford Univ Press, 01; auth, When the State Kills: Capital Punishment and the American Condition, Princeton Univ Press, 01. **CONTACT ADDRESS** Dept Law/Polit Sci, Amherst Col, 76 Snell St, Amherst, MA 01002. **EMAIL** ADSarat@amherst.edu

SARGENTICH, THOMAS O.
PERSONAL Born 05/09/1950, Los Angeles, CA, m, 1981, 1 child **DISCIPLINE** ADMINISTRATIVE LAW, CONSTITUTIONAL LAW **EDUCATION** Harvard Univ, AB, 72; Oxford Univ, M Phil, 74; Harvard Law Sch, JD, 77. **CAREER** Prof, Am Univ. **HONORS AND AWARDS** Awd for Outstanding Res Scholar, 90; Elizabeth Cubberly Scholar, 99; Phi Beta Kappa; pauline ruyle moore scholar, 89; comt government org separation powers, aba section admin law regulatory practice, 90-; u.s. dept justice; law clerk, judge arlin m. adams, u.s. court appeals. **MEMBERSHIPS** ABA; SALT; Prettyman-Leventhall Inn of Court. **RESEARCH** Separation of Powers; constitutional interpretation; administrative reform. **SELECTED PUBLICATIONS** Contribur, Admin Law Rev; Cornell Law Rev; Harvard Law Rev; Iowa Law Rev; William & Mary Law Rev; Wisconsin Law Rev; ed, Administative Law Anthology, Anderson, 94. **CONTACT ADDRESS** American Univ, 4400 Massachusetts Ave, Washington, DC 20016. **EMAIL** sargentich@wcl.american.edu

SARNA, JONATHAN D.
PERSONAL Born 01/10/1955, Philadelphia, PA, m, 1986, 2 children **DISCIPLINE** AMERICAN JEWISH HISTORY **EDUCATION** Brandeis Univ, BA, 75, MA, 75; Yale Univ, MA, 76, MPhil, 78, PhD, 79. **CAREER** Joseph H. & Belle R. Braun Prof Amer Jewish Hist, 90- , Dept ch, 92-95, 98, Brandeis Univ; Prof Amer Jewish Hist, 88-90, assoc prof, 84-88, asst prof, 80-84, vis lectr, 79-80, Hebrew Union Col-Jewish Inst Rel; Ch of the Board, Judaica On-Line Network (H-Judaic), 96- ; Ch, Acad Coun, Amer Jewish Hist Soc, 92-95; Dir Boston Jewish Hist Proj, 92-95; Dir, Ctr Stud The Amer Jewish Experience, 86-90, Acad dir, 84-86, acad adv, 81-84; vis assoc prof, Hebrew Univ, 86-87; vis asst prof Judaic Stud, Univ Cincinnati, 83-84; asst Amer Hist, Yale Univ, 78; Dir, Am Jewish Experience Curriculum Proj, 82-90; assoc ed, Amer Natl Biog, ed J. Garraty; Consultant, Amram Nowak Assoc, Amer Jewish Hist Film Proj, 94- ; Consulting ed, Am: The Jewish Experience, by Sondra Leiman, UAHC Press, 92-94; Publ Committee, Jewish Publ Soc, 85-90; Ed Board, Univ Press New England, 92- ; ed, North Amer Judaism sec, Rel Stud Rev, 84-94; ed comm, Queen City Heritage, 85- ; ed board, Am Jewish Hist, 88- ;ed board, Rel and Amer Cult, 89-96; ed board, Contemporary Jewry, 92- ; ed board, Patterns of Prejudice, 94- ; ed committee, Jewish Soc Stud, 93- ; acad comm, Touro Natl Heritage Trust, 93- ; adv comm, Ctr for Amer Jewish Hist, Temple Univ, 91; adv comm, Ctr Stud N Amer Jewry, Ben-Gurion Univ, Israel, 91- ; Wexner Found Grad Fel Comm, 89-92; Adv board, Maurice Amado Found, 90-95. **HONORS AND AWARDS** NEH Sr fel, 96; Lilly Endow grants, 84-93; Pew Endow grant, 91-94; Lady Davis Endow 86-87; Amer Coun Learned Soc, 82; Mem Found Jewish Cult, 82-83; Bernard and Audre Rapoport Fel in Amer Jewish Hist, Amer Jewish Archives, 79-80; Mem Found Jewish Cult, 77-79; Natl Found Jewish Cult, 77-79; Loewenstein-Wiener Fel, Amer Jewish Archives, 77; Howard F. Brinton Fel, Yale Univ, 77-78; Seltzer-Brodsky Prize Essay, YIVO Inst, 77; Charles Andrews Fel, Yale Univ, 76-77; Hebrew Free Loan Assn Fel, Amer Jewish Hist Soc, 74-75. **MEMBERSHIPS** Amer Acad Rel; Amer Hist Assn; Amer Jewish Hist Soc; Assn Jewish Stud; Can Jewish Hist Soc; Cincinnati Hist Soc; Immigration Hist Soc; Org Amer Hist; Phi Beta Kappa; Soc Hist Early Am Rep. **RESEARCH** Judaism. **SELECTED PUBLICATIONS** Ed, Jews in New Haven, Jewish Hist Soc New Haven, 78; Mordecai Manuel Noah: Jacksonian Politician and American Jewish Communal Leader-A Biographical Study, PhD Theis, Yale Univ, 79; Jacksonian Jew: The Two Worlds of Mordecai Noah, Holmes & Meier, 81; People Walk on Their Heads: Moses Weinberger's Jews and Judaism in New York, Holmes & Meier, 82; co-ed, Jews and the Founding of the Republic, Markus Wiener, 85; The American Jewish Experience: A Reader, Holmes and Meier, 86, 2nd ed, 97; American Synagogue History: A Bibliography and State-of-the-Field Survey, with Alexandria S. Korros, Markus Wiener, 88; Yahadut Amerika: American Jewry: An Annotated Bibliography of Publications in Hebrew, with Janet Liss, Hebrew Univ, 91; JPS: The Americaniztion of Jewish Culture (A history of the Jewish publication Soc, 1888-1988), JPS, 89; The Jews of Cincinnati, with Nancy H. Klein, Ctr for the Stud Am Jewish Experience, 89; A Double Bond: The Constitutional Documents of American Jewry, ed with Daniel J. Elazar and Rela Geffen Monson, Univ Press of Am, 92; Ethnic Diversity and Civic Identity: Patterns of Conflict and Cohesion in Cincinnati Since 1820, ed with Henry D. Shapiro, U of Illinois P, 92; Yehude Artsot Ha-Berit, ed with Lloyd Gartner, Merkaz Shazar, 92; Observing America's Jews by Marshall Sklare, ed, with forword and headnotes, UP of New England, 93; The Jews of Boston, with Ellen Smith, Combined Jewish Philanthropies/Northeastern Univ Press, 95; The Evolution of the American Synagogue, in The Americanization of the Jews, ed Robert M. Seltzer & Norman J. Cohen, New York, NYU Press, 95, 215-229; When Jews Were Bible Experts, Moments, Oct 95, 4, 55.80; Perched Between Continuity and Discontinuity: American Judaism at a Crossroads, Proceedings of the Rabbinical Assembly, 56, 95, 74-79; Current Trends and Issues in American Jewish Religious Life, Gesher, 42, 132, 95, 111-117, in Hebrew; contribution to Rebuilding Jewish Peoplehood: Where Do We Go From Here? A Symposium in the Wake of the Rabin Assassination, Amer Jewish Comm, 96, 86-87; The American Jewish Community's Crisis of Confidence, Pamphlet, World Jewish Congress, 96; From Antoinette Brown Blackwell to Sally Priesand: An Historical Perspective on the Emergence of Women in the American Rabbinate, Women Rabbis: Exploration and Celebration, ed Gary P. Zola, Cincinnati, American Jewish Archives, 96, 43-53; A Projection of America as it Ought to Be: Zion in the Mind's Eye of American Jews, in Allon Gal, ed, Envisioning Israel: The changing Ideals and Images of North American Jews, Jerusalem & Detroit, Magnes Press & Wayne State Univ Press, 96, 41-59; If You Lend Money to My People, Learning Torah With. .3:18, Feb 8, 97, 1-4; Minority Faiths and the American Protestant Mainstream, ed. U of Illinois P, 97; Abba Hillel Silver and American Zionism, co-ed with Mark A. Raider and Ronald W. Zweig, Frank Cass, 97; Religion and State in the American Jewish Experience, with David G. Dalin, U of Notre Dame P, 97; Masterworks of Modern Jewish Writing, gen ed, 11 vol, Markus Wiener Publ; Amer Jewish Life, co-ed, 8 vol, Wayne State Univ Press; Brandeis Series in American Jewish History, Cult and Life, gen ed, 10 vol, Brandeis Univ Press/UP of New England; Contribution to One Year Later: The Rabin Symposium, Am Jewish Comm, 97; Two Traditions of Seminary Scholarship, in Jack Werheimer, ed, Tradition Renewed: A History of the Jewish Theological Seminary, Jewish Theol Sem, 97, 54-80; Structural Challenges to Jewish Continuity, American Jewry: Portrait and Prognosis, ed David M. Gordis and Dorit P. Gray, Wilstein Inst Behrman House, 97, 404-408; Back to the Center: The

Plain Meaning of A Statement on Jewish Continuity, Am Jewish Comm, 97; Jacob Rader Marcus, Am Jewish Year Bk, 97, 97, 633-640; Martha Wolfenstein, in Paula Hyman and Deborah D. Moore, eds, Jewish Women in Am, Routledge, 97, 1486-1487; Foreword to Gerry Cristol, A Light in the Prairie: Temple Emanu-El of Dallas, 1872-1997, TCU Press, 98; Committed Today, Divorced Tomorrow, JTS Mag, 7, Winter 98, 12, 23; Ten Ways That Israel Liberated American Jewry, Hadassah Mag, 79, June 98, 14-15; American Jewish Education in Historical Perspective, Jour Jewish Ed, 64, Fall 98, 8-21; **CONTACT ADDRESS** Dept of Near East and Judaic Studies, Brandeis Univ, MS 054, Waltham, MA 02454. **EMAIL** sarna@brandeis.edu

SARNA, NAHUM M.
PERSONAL Born 03/27/1923, London, England, m, 1947, 2 children **DISCIPLINE** BIBLICAL & SEMITIC STUDIES **EDUCATION** Univ London, BA, 44, MA, 46; Dropsie Col, PhD(Bibl studies & Semitics), 55. **CAREER** Asst lectr Hebrew, Univ Col, Univ London, 46-49; lectr Bible, Gratz Col, 51-57; librn & asst prof, Jewish Theol Sem, 57-63, assoc prof, 63-65; assoc prof, 65-67, chmn Dept Near Eastern & Judaic Studies, 69-75, Distinguished Prof of Jewish Studies, 95-00, Dora Golding Prof Bibl Studies, Brandeis Univ, 67-00, Vis assoc prof relig, Columbia Univ, 64-65; assoc trustee, Am Schs Orient Res, 65-67; ed & translr, Bible Transl Comt, Jewish Publ Soc Am, 65, ed-in-chief, Bible Commentary, 73-; vis prof Bible studies, Andover Newton Theol Sch, 66-67 & Dropsie Col, 67-68; mem B'nai B'rith Adv Bd Adult Jewish Educ, 67-; dept ed, Bible Div, Encycl Judaica, 68-72; trustee, Boston Hebrew Col, 68-75, mem exec comt, 70-75; Am Coun Learned Soc sr fel, 71-72; mem acad adv coun, Nat Found Jewish Cult, 73-; Inst for Advan Studies fel, Hebrew Univ, Jerusalem, 82-83; Scholar & Prof of Judaica, Fla Atlantic Univ, 00-. **HONORS AND AWARDS** Jewish Bk Coun Awd, 67. **MEMBERSHIPS** Fel Am Acad Jewish Res; Am Orient Soc; Soc Bibl Lit; Asn Jewish Studies (hon secy-trcas, 72-); fel Royal Asiatic Soc. **RESEARCH** History of the ancient Near East; Semitic literature and languages. **SELECTED PUBLICATIONS** Auth, Understanding Genesis, Schocken, 65; auth, Exploring Exodus, Schocken, 86; auth, On the Book of Psalms, Schocken, 94. **CONTACT ADDRESS** Dept of Near Eastern Studies, Brandeis Univ, Waltham, MA 02154.

SARRA, JANIS
DISCIPLINE LAW **EDUCATION** Univ Toronto, BA, MA, LLB, LLM. **CAREER** Labour arbitrator, Social Assistance Review Board; Faculty of Bus, Ryerson Univ; Vice-Chair of the Ontario Pay Equity Hearings Tribunal; Vice-Chair of the Social Assistance Review Board and the Ontario Labour Relations Board; co-taught, Univ of Toronto Faculty of Law, as well as York Univ. **SELECTED PUBLICATIONS** Auth, pubs on labour law, equality law and diversity management, and corporate governance. **CONTACT ADDRESS** Fac of Law, Univ of Toronto, 78 Queen's Park, Toronto, ON, Canada M5S 2C5.

SARRI, SAMUEL
PERSONAL Born 06/25/1957, Casablanca, m, 1985 **DISCIPLINE** ECONOMICS, PHILOSOPHY, POLITICAL SCIENCE **EDUCATION** Paris Univ, doctorate, 81; Mich State Univ, grad degrees, 88; Southwest Univ, PhD, 92. **CAREER** Researcher, Univ of Paris, 79-82; asst prof, Mich State Univ, 85-92; int translator/interpreter, 85-. **MEMBERSHIPS** Mich Acad. **RESEARCH** World Monetary Economics, Applied Financial Economics (Investment, Risk Management, Finance), Logic & Statistics, Mesoeconomics. **SELECTED PUBLICATIONS** Auth, Elements of Contemporary Logic, 87; auth, Prolegomena to Islamology, 88; auth, Poetic Reflections, Rosethorn Pub (Lansing, MI), 91; auth, Philosophico-Economic Anthology, 92; auth, Strategies to Financial & Investment Success, 94; auth, Human Emotions in Poetry, 95; auth Visions, 98; auth, Ethics of the International Monetary Systems, 99; auth, Macroeconomics 2000, 99; auth, Microeconomics 2000, 00. **CONTACT ADDRESS** Philos & Regional Studies, Comm Col of So Nevada, 3200 E Cheyenne Ave, Las Vegas, NV 89030-4228. **EMAIL** samuel_sarri@ccsn.nevada.edu

SARVER, VERNON T., JR.
PERSONAL Born 12/17/1943, Bluefield, WV, m, 1970, 2 children **DISCIPLINE** PHILOSOPHY **EDUCATION** Fla State Univ, BA, 66; Tufts Univ, Mdiv, 69; Boston Univ, STM, 71; Ohio State Univ, MA, 76; Univ Fla, PhD, 94. **CAREER** Adj instr, Fla Community Coll Jacksonville, 79-81; adj instr, Lake City Community Coll, 81-83; grad res asst, Univ Fla, 82-85; tchr of emotionally handicapped, Bradford County Schools Starke Fla, 85-86; tchr of gifted, Marion County Schools Ocala Fla, 86-; adj prof, Saint Leo Univ, 94-. **HONORS AND AWARDS** Rockefeller Prize, Am Philos Asn, 96; Who's Who in Am Educ, 96-97; Who's Who Among America's Teachers, 98. **MEMBERSHIPS** Am Philos Asn; Am Soc for Value Inquiry; Int Soc for Value Inquiry. **RESEARCH** Political Philosophy; Ethics. **SELECTED PUBLICATIONS** Auth, Ajzen and Fishbein's 'Theory of Reasoned Action': A Critical Assessment, J for the Theory of Soc Behavior, 83; Kant's Purported Social Contract and the Death Penalty, J of Value Inquiry, 97. **CONTACT ADDRESS** Box 605, Archer, FL 32618.

SASSEN, SASKIA
PERSONAL Born 01/05/1949, The Hague, Netherlands, m, 1 child **DISCIPLINE** SOCIOLOGY, POLITICAL ECONOMY **EDUCATION** Univ Notre Dame, Ind, PhD, 74; Post-Doctorate, Center for Int Affairs, Harvard Univ, 74-75. **CAREER** Prof, Queens Col and The Grad Sch, CUNY, NY, 76-88; prof, Columbia Univ, 85-98; prof, Univ Chicago, 98-; res fel, Am Bar Found, 98-. **HONORS AND AWARDS** Fels and res grants from Ford, Tinker, Russell Sage, Reuson, and other founds; Distinguished Profs and Endowed Lectureships at various institutions (Clark, SUNY-Binghampton, Inst for Advanced Studies Vienna, Univ of Toronto Law Sch, etc.; Resident Scholar, The Ctr for Advanced Behav Studies, The Russel Sage Found, The Woodrow Wilson Ctr for Scholars, The Ctr for Int Studies of Harvard Univ, etc. **MEMBERSHIPS** ASA, APSA, ISA. **RESEARCH** The global economy, cities, immigration, digitilization, the state and globalization. **SELECTED PUBLICATIONS** Auth, Migranten, Siedler, Fluchtlinge: Von der Massenauswanderung zur Festung Europa, Frankfurt: Fiuscher Verlag (96, English, The New Press, 99, Italian, Fetrinelli, 99); auth, "The New Centrality: The Impact of Telematics and Globalization," in W. S. Saunders, et al, eds, Reflections on Architectural Practices in the Nineties, Princeton Architectural Press (96): 206-218; auth, "New Employment Regimes in Cities: Impacts on Immigrant Workers," New Community, Vol 22, no 4 (Oct 96): 579-594); auth, "Toward a Feminist Analytics of the Global Economy," Indiana J of Global Legal Studies, Vol 4, No 1 (fall 96): 7-41; auth, Losing Control? Sovereignty in an Age of Globalization, The 1995 Columbia Univ Schoff Memorial Lectures, New York: Columbia Univ Press (96); auth, Globalization and Its Discontents, New York: New York Press (98); auth, "The De-Nationalization of Time and Space," invited contrib, Millenial Issue of Public Culture (forthcoming 2000); auth, invited contrib, Millenial Issue of The Annals of the British Asn of Geogs (forthcoming 2000); auth, "Immigration policy in a global economy," invited contrib, Millenial Issue of The Annals of the Am Acad of Arts and Scis (forthcoming 2000); auth, "The Global City" Theoretical and Methodological Elements," invited contrib, Milleneial Issue of the British J of Sociol (forthcoming 2000). **CONTACT ADDRESS** Soc Sci Bldg, Univ of Chicago, 1126 E 59th St, Chicago, IL 60637. **EMAIL** ssassen@midway.uchicago.edu

SASSON, JACK MURAD
PERSONAL Born 10/01/1941, Aleppo, Syria **DISCIPLINE** ASSYRIOLOGY, HEBREW SCRIPTURE **EDUCATION** Brooklyn Col, BA, 62; Brandeis Univ, MA, 63, PhD, 66. **CAREER** From asst prof to assoc prof, 66-77, Prof Relig, Univ NC, Chapel Hill, 77-91; assoc ed, J Am Orient Soc, 77; Mary Jane Werthan prof of Judaic and Bibl Studies, Divinity School, Vanderbilt Univ. **HONORS AND AWARDS** Soc Relig Higher Educ fel, 69-70. **MEMBERSHIPS** Soc Bibl Lit; Am Orient Soc; Israel Explor Soc; Dutch Orient Soc. **RESEARCH** Ancient Near Eastern societies. **SELECTED PUBLICATIONS** Auth, Circumcision in the ancient Near East, J Bibl Lit, 66; The Military Establishments at Mari, 69 & contribr, Hebrew-Ugaritic Studies, 71, Pontif Bibl Inst; Archive keeping at Mari, Iraq, 72; Literary motif in . . . Gilgamesh epic, Studies Philol, 72; Commentary to Ruth, Johns Hopkins Univ, 78; ed, Civilizations of the Ancient Near East, 95. **CONTACT ADDRESS** Divinity School, Vanderbilt Univ, Nashville, TN 37240. **EMAIL** jack.m.sasson@vanderbilt.edu

SASSON, VICTOR
PERSONAL Born 12/20/1937, Baghdad, Iraq, d, 1 child **DISCIPLINE** RELIGION; ENGLISH LITERATURE **EDUCATION** Univ London, BA honors, 73; New York Univ, PhD, 79. **CAREER** Univ S Africa, sr lectr, 81-85; Long Island Univ, asst prof, 90-91; Touro Col NY, asst prof, 90-96. **HONORS AND AWARDS** Thayer fel; AAR. **MEMBERSHIPS** Colum Univ Sem Hebrew Bible and Shakespeare; SOTS. **RESEARCH** Text and language of Hebrew bible; N W Semitic Epigraphy; tense and aspect in Biblical Hebrew and old Aramaic; ancient near east. **SELECTED PUBLICATIONS** Auth, The Literary and Theological Function of Job's Wife in the Book of Job, Biblica, 98; Some Observations on the Use and Original Purpose of the Waw Consecutive in Old Aramaic and Biblical Hebrew, VT, 97; The Inscription of Achish Governor of Eqron and Philistine Dialect, Cult and Culture, UF, 97; The Old Aramaic Inscription for Tell Dan: Philological Literary and Historical Aspects, JSS, 95; The Book of Oraccular Visions of Balaam from Deir Alla, UF, 86. **CONTACT ADDRESS** PO Box 971, Brooklyn, NY 11235.

SASSOWER, RAPHAEL
PERSONAL Born 09/26/1955, Israel, d, 2 children **DISCIPLINE** PHILOSOPHY **EDUCATION** Lake Forest Col, BA, 80; Boston Univ, MA, PhD, 85. **CAREER** Prof, Univ of Colo. **RESEARCH** Postmodern Technoscience, Critical Rationality, Aesthetics and Education. **SELECTED PUBLICATIONS** Auth, Cultural Collisions: Postmodern Technoscience, Routledge, 95; auth, Technoscience Angst: Ethics and Responsibility, Univ of Minn Pr, 97; coauth, The Golden Avant-Garde: Idolatry, Commercialism, and Art, Univ of Va Pr, 00; auth, A Sanctuary of Their Own: Intellectual Refugees in the Academy, Rowman and Littlefield, 00. **CONTACT ADDRESS** Dept Philos, Univ of Colorado, Colorado Springs, 1420 Austin Bluffs Pky, Colorado Springs, CO 80918-3733. **EMAIL** rsassowe@brain.uccs.edu

SATRIS, STEPHEN A.
PERSONAL Born 05/05/1947, New York, NY, m, 1975, 2 children **DISCIPLINE** PHILOSOPHY **EDUCATION** Univ Calif, BA, 69; Univ Hawaii, MA, 71; Cambridge Univ, PhD, 84. **CAREER** Vis instr Philos, Gustavus Adolphus Col, 78-80; from instr to assoc prof Philos, SE Mo State Univ, 80-86; from asst to assoc prof, Clemson Univ, 86-. **MEMBERSHIPS** Am Philos Asn; SC Soc Philos. **RESEARCH** Ethics; Wittgenstein. **SELECTED PUBLICATIONS** Ed, Taking Sides: Clashing Views on Controversial Moral Issues, 00. **CONTACT ADDRESS** Dept of Philosophy and Religion, Clemson Univ, Clemson, SC 29634-0528. **EMAIL** stephen@clemson.edu

SATTERFIELD, PATRICIA POLSON
PERSONAL Born 07/10/1942, Christchurch, VA, m, 1966 **DISCIPLINE** LAW **EDUCATION** Howard University, BME, 1964; Indiana University, MM, 1967; St Johns University, School of Law, JD, 1977. **CAREER** Sewanhaka High School District, vocal music teacher, 68-77; UCS Counsels Office of Court Administration, assistant deputy counsel, senior counsel, 78-90; Unified Court System of State of New York, judge, 91-94, acting supreme court justice, 94-98, supreme court justice, 98-. **HONORS AND AWARDS** Alpha Kappa Alpha, Epsilon Omega Chapter, Outstanding Community Leader of the Year, 1991; Queens County Women's Bar Association, Ascension to Bench, 1991; Alva T Starforth, Outstanding Teacher of the Year, 1976. **MEMBERSHIPS** St John's University, cultural diversity committee, School of Law, 1991-, board of directors, law alumni, 1991-; Queens Women's Network, co-chair, board of directors, 1983-90; Human Resources Center of St Albans, board of directors, 1990-; Association of Women Judges, 1991-; Metropolitan Black Lawyers Association, 1988-; Queens County Bar Association, 1989-; Jack and Jill of America Inc Queens Co, president, 1978-87; St Albans Congregational Church, United Church of Christ, moderator, 1996-; Greater Queens Chapt of the Links, Inc, pres, 1998-. **CONTACT ADDRESS** Supreme Court of the State of New York, 88-11 Sutphin Blvd, Jamaica, NY 11435.

SAUER, JAMES B.
PERSONAL Born 12/31/1948, Richmond, VA, m, 1968, 3 children **DISCIPLINE** PHILOSOPHY **EDUCATION** Univ Richmond, BA, 66; Union Theol Sem, MDiv, 74, DMin, 79; St Paul's Univ, MA, 90, PhD, 92. **CAREER** Prof, theol, Inst Superieur de Theol, 74-79; minister, Presby Church, 79-91; vis prof ethics, St Paul's Univ, 91-93; assoc prof philos, St. Mary's Univ, 93- . **HONORS AND AWARDS** Centennial mem fel, 80; distinguished fac award, 97; listed, Who's Who Among American Teachers, 98, 00. **MEMBERSHIPS** APA. **RESEARCH** Ethics; applied ethics; economic philosophy; environmental philosophy. **SELECTED PUBLICATIONS** Auth, Conscience and Deliberation: Notes for A Critical Realist Ethics, St Mary's, 93; auth, Faithful Ethics According to John Calvin: The Teachability of the Heart, Edwin Mellin, 97; ed, The Personalist Forum, 98-; ed, Philosophy in the Contemporary World, 99-; auth, Method in Theology: A Commentary, LWS Pr, 00. **CONTACT ADDRESS** One Camino Santa Maria, San Antonio, TX 78228-8566. **EMAIL** philjim@stmarytx.edu

SAUL, NORMAN E.
PERSONAL Born 11/26/1932, La Fontaine, IN, m, 1959, 3 children **DISCIPLINE** HISTORY, INTERNATIONAL RELATIONS **EDUCATION** Ind Univ, BA, 54; Columbia Univ, MA, 57; PhD, 65. **CAREER** Instr, Purdue Univ, 62-65; asst prof, Brown Univ, 65-68; Univ Kans, 70-. **HONORS AND AWARDS** Higuchi Res Awd, 97; Kans Humanities Coun Public Service Awd, 97; Inst for Advanced Study member, 00; IREX and Kennan Awds. **MEMBERSHIPS** Am Hist Asn, Am Asn for Advancement of Slavic Studies, Kans State Hist Soc. **RESEARCH** Russian-American Relations, Immigration of Germans from Russia, Russian Revolution. **SELECTED PUBLICATIONS** Auth, Russia and the Mediterranean 1797-1807, 70; auth, Sailors in Revolt in 1917, 78; auth, Distant Friends: The US and Russia 1763-1867; auth, Concord and Conflict: The US and Russia 1867-1914, 96. **CONTACT ADDRESS** Dept Hist, Univ of Kansas, Lawrence, Lawrence, KS 66045-0001. **EMAIL** normsaul@falcon.cc.ukans.edu

SAUNDERS, KURT M.
PERSONAL Born McKeesport, PA **DISCIPLINE** BUSINESS LAW, ECONOMICS **EDUCATION** Carnegie Mellon Univ, BS, 82; Univ Pittsburgh, JD, 85. **CAREER** Instr, 88-89, Dickinson Sch of Law; instr, 89-94, Univ of Pitts Sch of Law; adj prof of law,94-97,; clin prof of law, 97-98, Duquesne Univ Sch of Law; asst prof, law, 98-, Calif St Univ, Northridge, School of Bus Admin & Econ **MEMBERSHIPS** PA Bar Asn; Allegheny Co Bar Asn, 92-94, ed staff, Pitts Legal J, 87-93; Clin Legal Ed Asn; Acad of Legal Stud in Bus; Asn for Pract & Profes Ethics; The Federalist Soc for Law & Pub Pol Stud; Int Coun for Innovation in Higher Ed. **RESEARCH** Computer and internet law; advanced technology law; legal education; rhetoric. **CONTACT ADDRESS** Col of Business Administration and Economics, Dept of Business Law, California State Univ, Northridge, 18111 Nordhoff St, Northridge, CA 91330-8245. **EMAIL** kurt.saunders@csun.edu

SAVAGE, C. WADE
PERSONAL Born 09/01/1932, Tuscaloosa, AL, m, 1955, 3 children **DISCIPLINE** PHILOSOPHY **EDUCATION** Univ Al, AB, 53; Univ Iowa, MA, 55; Cornell Univ, PhD, 63. **RESEARCH** Epistemology; philosophy of cognitive sciences; philosophy of science. **SELECTED PUBLICATIONS** Auth, Foundationalism Naturalized, Univ Minn, 91; Epistemological Advantages of a Cognitivist Analysis of Sensation and Perception, Univ Am, 91; Sense-Data in Russell's Theories of Knowledge, Univ Minn, 89; An Old Ghost in a New Body, Plenum, 76; The Measurement of Sensation, Univ Calif, 70; ed, Perception and Cognition, Univ Minn. 78; Reading Russell, Univ Minn, 89. **CONTACT ADDRESS** Philosophy Dept, Univ of Minnesota, Twin Cities, 271 19th Ave S, 831 Heller, Minneapolis, MN 55455. **EMAIL** savag001@tc.umn.edu

SAWATSKY, RODNEY JAMES
PERSONAL Born 12/05/1943, Altona, MB, Canada, m, 1965, 3 children **DISCIPLINE** RELIGION, HISTORY **EDUCATION** Can Mennonite Bible Col, Winnipeg, B Christian Ed, 64; Bethel Col, Kans, BA, 65; Univ Minn, MA, 72; Princeton Univ, MA, 73 & Phd(relig), 77. **CAREER** Instr hist, Can Mennonite Bible Col, Winnipeg, 67-70; asst prof relig, 74-80, Dir Acad Affairs, Conrad Grabel Col, Univ Waterloo, 74-89, assoc prof Relig, Univ of Waterloo, 81-94; pres, Conrad Grebel Col, 89-94; pres, Messiah Col, 94-. **MEMBERSHIPS** Am Soc Church Hist; Am Acad Relig; Can Soc Study Relig; Can Protection Relig Freedom (pres, 78-). **RESEARCH** Mennonite history; evangelical and new religions; Canadian religious history. **SELECTED PUBLICATIONS** Coauth, Evangelical-Unification Dialogue, Rose of Sharon Pr (New York, NY), 79; co-ed, The Limits of Perfection, Inst of Anabaptist-Mennonite Studies (Waterloo, ON), 93. **CONTACT ADDRESS** President's Office, Messiah Col, One Col Ave, Grantham, PA, Canada 17027. **EMAIL** sawatsky@messiah.edu

SAWYER, MARY R.
PERSONAL Born, NE **DISCIPLINE** RELIGIOUS STUDIES **EDUCATION** Howard Univ Divinity, MA, 82; Duke Univ, PhD, 86. **CAREER** Assoc prof, IA State Univ, 86-. **MEMBERSHIPS** Am Acad of Relig, Relig Res Assoc, Asn of Sociol of Relig. **RESEARCH** Religious Movements for social change, African American Religion Spirituality. **SELECTED PUBLICATIONS** Auth, Black Ecumenism: Implementing the Demands of Justice. **CONTACT ADDRESS** Dept Phil & Relig Studies, Iowa State Univ, 413 Cott Hall, Ames, IA 50011-2010. **EMAIL** sawyerm@iastate.edu

SAX, JOSEPH L.
PERSONAL Born 02/03/1936, Chicago, IL, m, 1958, 3 children **DISCIPLINE** LAW **EDUCATION** Harvard Univ, AB, 57; Univ Chicago, JD, 59. **CAREER** Prof, Univ Mich, 66-86; Coun to Secy of Interior, 94-96; Prof, Univ Calif, 86-. **HONORS AND AWARDS** Fel, Standford Univ; Fel, Ill Inst Technol; Alumni Achievement Awd, Univ Chicago. **RESEARCH** Cultural property, water law, public lands, property rights, environmental law. **SELECTED PUBLICATIONS** Auth, Defending the Environment, Knopf, 70; auth, Mountains Without Handrails, Univ Mich Pr, 80; auth, Playing Darts with a Rembrandt, Univ Mich Pr, 99; auth, Legal Control of Water Resources, West Publ Co, 00. **CONTACT ADDRESS** Dept Law, Univ of California, Berkeley, 220 Boalt Hall, Berkeley, CA 94720-0001. **EMAIL** saxj@law.berkeley.ed

SAYRE, KENNETH MALCOLM
PERSONAL Born 08/13/1928, Scottsbluff, NE, m, 1983, 4 children **DISCIPLINE** PHILOSOPHY **EDUCATION** Grinnell Col, AB, 52; Harvard Univ, MA, 54, PhD, 58. **CAREER** Asst dean grad sch arts & lett, Harvard Univ, 53-56; mem staff syst anal, Lincoln Lab, 56-58; from instr to assoc prof, 58-71, prof philos, Univ Notre Dame, 71-, dir philos inst, 66-, vis scientist, Sylvania Elec Prod, Inc, 59; consult, Lincoln Lab, 61; vis fel, Princeton Univ, 67-68; vis prof, Bowling Green Univ, 81; vis fel, Merton Col, Oxford, 86; senior res fel, St. Edward's Col, Cambridge, 96. **RESEARCH** Plato; cybernetics; philosophy of mind. **SELECTED PUBLICATIONS** Auth, Recognition: A Study in the Philosophy of Artificial Intelligence, 65 & coauth, Philosophy and Cybernetics, 67, Univ Notre Dame; auth, Plato's Analytic Method, 69 & Consciousness: A Philosophic Study of Minds and Machines, 69, Random; Cybernetics and the Philosophy of Mind, Routledge & Kegan Paul, 76; Moonflight, 77 & Starburst, 77, Univ Notre Dame; auth, Plato's Literary Garden: How to Read a Platonic Dialogue, Univ Notre Dame, 95; Parmenides' Lesson: Translation and Explication of Plato's Parmenides, Univ Notre Dame, 96; Belief and Knowledge: Mapping the Cognitive Landscape, Ronmau and Littlefield, 97. **CONTACT ADDRESS** Dept of Philos, Univ of Notre Dame, 337 Oshaugnessy Hall, Notre Dame, IN 46556.

SAYRE, PATRICIA
PERSONAL Born 05/27/1958, Mt. Holly, NJ, m, 1983, 1 child **DISCIPLINE** PHILOSOPHY **EDUCATION** Wheaton Col, BA, 80; Univ Notre Dame, PhD, 87. **CAREER** Tutor, instr, Saint Olaf Col, 85-87; assoc prof, chair, Saint Marys Col, 87-. **HONORS AND AWARDS** Maria Piena Awd; vis scholar, St Edmunds Col, Cambridge; Executive Committee, Soc Christian Philosophers; Coolidge Res Fel; ed board, Personalist Forum. **MEMBERSHIPS** Am Philos Soc; Soc Christian Philosophers; Austrian Ludwig Wittgenstein Soc; Int Forum on Persons. **RESEARCH** Wittgenstein; metaphysics; moral psychology. **SELECTED PUBLICATIONS** Auth, "The Philosophical Life as Literature: Fictional Renditions of Wittgenstein," The Cresset, 93; "The Dialectics of Trust and Suspicion," Faith and Philosophy, 93; "Moral Psychology and Persons," Becoming Persons: Proceedings of the Second Conf on Persons, 96; "Personalism," in The Companion to the Philos of Rel, 97; "Socrates is Mortal: Formal Logic and the Pre-Law Undergraduate," Notre Dame Law Rev, 98. **CONTACT ADDRESS** Dept of Philosophy, Saint Mary's Col, Indiana, Notre Dame, IN 46556. **EMAIL** psayre@saintmarys.edu

SAYWARD, CHARLES
DISCIPLINE PHILOSOPHY OF LOGIC, PHILOSOPHY OF LANGUAGE, AND POLITICAL PHILOSOPHY **EDUCATION** Cornell Univ, PhD, 64. **CAREER** Prof, Univ Nebr, Lincoln. **RESEARCH** The philosophy of mathematics. **SELECTED PUBLICATIONS** Auth, Definite Descriptions, Negation and Necessitation, Russell 13, 93; coauth, Two Concepts of Truth, Philos Stud 70, 93; The Internal/External Question, Grazer Philosophische Studien 47, 94; Intentionality and truth: an essay on the philosophy of Arthur Prior. **CONTACT ADDRESS** Univ of Nebraska, Lincoln, Lincoln, NE 68588-0417.

SCAER, DAVID P.
PERSONAL Born 03/13/1936, Brooklyn, NY, m, 1960, 3 children **DISCIPLINE** THEOLOGY **EDUCATION** Concordia Sem, BA, 57, BD, 60, ThD(baptism), 63. **CAREER** From asst prof to assoc prof, 66-77, prof syst theol, Concordia Theol Sem, 77-, instr relig, Univ Ill, 66-76; John W Behnken fel, Univ Heidelberg, 69-70, 86-87; ed, Springfielder, 69-76; mem subcomt ordination, Inter-Lutheran Worship Comn, 73-76; ed, Concordia Theol Quart, 76-93;member, comm on Theology and Church Relations, The Lutheran Church-Missouri Synod, 98-; contrib ed, Christianity Today, 81-, Modern Reformation, and Logia. **MEMBERSHIPS** Evangel Theol Soc; Concordia Hist Inst; Soc Bibl Lit. **RESEARCH** Lutheran confessional theology; contemporary theology; quest for the historical Jesus studies. **SELECTED PUBLICATIONS** Auth, Lutheran World Federation Today, 71, The Apostolic Scriptures, 71; What Do You Think of Jesus?, 73 & Getting Into the Story of Concord, 77, Concordia; contribr, Tensions in Contemporary Theology, Moody, 76; History of Christian Doctrine, Baker, 79; auth, James the Apostle of Faith, Concordia Pub House, 83; Christology, Confessional Lutheran Dogmatics: The Int Foundation for Lutheran Confessional Research, 89; contrib, Evangelical Affirmations, Academie Books, 90; Doing Theology in Today's World, Harper and Row, 91; Handbook of Evangelical Theologians, Baker, 93; Evangelical Dictionary of Biblical Theology, Baker, 95; Eintraechtig Lehren, Verlag der Lutherischen Buchhandlung Heinrich Harms, Gross Oesingen, Germany, 97; The Pieper Lectures: The Office of the Ministry, Concordia Hist Institute, 97; auth, Baptism, Confessional Lutheran Dogmatics, The Int Found for Lutheran Confessional Research, 98; and articles in: The Lutheran Witness, Lutheran Forum, Forum Letter, Lutheran Quart, Modern Reformation, Logia, Concordia Journal, Grace Theological Journal, Lutheran Worship Notes, Journal of the Evangelical Theological Society, and Issues in Christian Education. **CONTACT ADDRESS** Dept of Syst Theol, Concordia Theol Sem, 6600 N Clinton St, Fort Wayne, IN 46825-4996. **EMAIL** dpscaer@juno.com

SCALES-TRENT, JUDY
PERSONAL Born 10/01/1940, Winston-Salem, NC **DISCIPLINE** LAW **EDUCATION** Oberlin Coll, BA 1962; Middlebury Coll, MA 1967; Northwestern Univ Sch of Law, JD 1973. **CAREER** Equal Empl Opp Commn, spec asst to vice chmn 1977-79, spec asst to gen counsel 1979-80, appellate Attorney 1980-84; SUNY Buffalo Law Sch, assoc prof of law 1984-90, professor of law, 90-. **MEMBERSHIPS** mem DC Bar; mem NY State Bar; US Ct of Appeals for the Fourth, Fifth, Sixth, Seventh, Ninth and Eleventh Circuits; mem Amer Bar Assn; mem bd dir Park School of Buffalo (1985-88 term); mem, bd of dirs, National Women and the Law Assn 1987-91; mem, bd of visitors, Roswell Park Memorial Cancer Institute, 1991-96; mem, bd of governors, Society of American Law Teachers, 1992-95. **SELECTED PUBLICATIONS** Auth, "Comparable Worth: Is This a Theory for Black Workers" 8 Women's Rights L Rptr 51 (Winter 1984); "Sexual Harassment and Race, A Legal Analysis of Discrimination," 8 Notre Dame J Legis 30 (1981); "A Judge Shapes and Manages Institutional Reform: School Desegregation in Buffalo," 12 NYU Review of Law and Social Change 19 (1989); "Black Women and the Constitution: Finding our Place, Asserting our Rights," 24 Harvard Civil Rights-Civil Liberties Law Review 9 (1989); "Women of Color and Health: Issues of Gender, Power and Community," 43 Stanford Law Review 1357, 1991; "The Law as an Instrument of Oppression and the Culture of Resistance," in Black Women in America: An Historical Encyclopedia 701, 1993; "On Turning Fifty," in Patricia Bell-Scott, ed, Life Notes 336, 1994; Notes of a White Black Woman: Race, Color, Community, 1995. **CONTACT ADDRESS** Law Sch, SUNY, Buffalo, O'Brian Hall, Buffalo, NY 14260.

SCALISE, CHARLES J.
PERSONAL Born 07/25/1950, Baltimore, MD, m, 1980, 2 children **DISCIPLINE** CHURCH HISTORY, CHRISTIAN THEOLOGY **EDUCATION** Princeton Univ, AB, summa cum laude, 72; Yale Div Sch, MDiv, magna cum laude, 75; S Baptist Theol Sem, PhD, 87; Univ Oxford, postgrad, 90-91. **CAREER** Baptist Chaplain, Yale, 75-82; lectr, Pastoral Theol, Yale Div Sch, 76-80; dir, dept Christian higher educ, Baptist Conven New Eng, 82-84; asst prof, S Baptist Theol Sem, 87-94; assoc and mang ed, Rev and expositor, 91-94; assoc prof, Fuller Theol Sem, 94- . **HONORS AND AWARDS** Sloan Scholar, 68-72; Ger bk prize, 71; Albert G. Milband mem scholar prize, 71; Phi Beta Kappa, 72; Tew prize, 73; Oliver Ellsworth Daggett prize, 74; Julia A. Archibald high scholar prize, 75; Outstanding young men Am, 75; Who's Who S and SW, 93-94. **RESEARCH** Theological hermeneutics; History of exegesis; History of doctrine; pastoral Theology. **SELECTED PUBLICATIONS** Auth, Allegorical Flights of Fancy: The Problem of Origen's Exegesis, The Greek Orthodox Theol Rev, 32, 87, 69-88; Origen and the Sensus Literalis, in Origen of Alexandria, Notre Dame, 88, 117-129; Developing a Theological Rationale for Ministry: Some Reflections on the Process of Teaching Pastoral Theology to MDiv Students, Jour Pastoral Theol, 1, 91, 53-68; Hermeneutics as Theological Prolegomena: A Canonical Approach, Mercer UP, 94; Canonical Hermeneutics: Childs and Barth, Scotish Jour Theol, 47, 94, 61-88; Teresa of Avila: Teacher of Evangelical Women? Cross Currents: The Jour of the Asn for Rel and Intel Life, 46, 96, 244-249; From Scripture to Theology: A Canonical Journey into Hermeneutics, InterVarsity Press, 96; Agreeing on where We Disagree: Lindbeck's Postliberalism and Pastoral Theology, Jour Pastoral Theol, 8, 98, 43-51. **CONTACT ADDRESS** Fuller Theol Sem, 101 Nickerson St, Ste 330, Seattle, WA 98109-1621. **EMAIL** cscalise@fuller.edu

SCALISI, JOSEPH M.
PERSONAL Born 01/28/1967, North Syracuse, NY, m, 1995, 1 child **DISCIPLINE** STATISTICS **EDUCATION** SUNY Cortland, MAT, 91, PhD candidate, spring 99. **CAREER** Prof, Bryant and Stratton Bus Inst, 92-; founder and director, Math Center, Bryant and Stratton Bus Inst, 97-; adjunct prof, Le-Moyne Col, 95-. **HONORS AND AWARDS** Deans List, 89, 90: curriculum revision of foundations program at Bryant and Stratton Bus Inst, 95. **MEMBERSHIPS** NY State Asn of Two-Year Collleges. **RESEARCH** Statistics, probability. **CONTACT ADDRESS** Dept Mathematics, Le Moyne Col, 1419 Salt Springs Rd, Syracuse, NY 13214. **EMAIL** scalisjm@maple.lemoyne.edu

SCANLAN, JAMES P.
PERSONAL Born 02/22/1927, Chicago, IL, m, 1948 **DISCIPLINE** PHILOSOPHY **EDUCATION** BA, 48, MA, 50, PhD, 56, Univ Chicago. **CAREER** Research Fel, Inst for Phil Research, 53-55; Ford Fdn Teaching Fel and Instr, Case Inst of Tech, 55-56; Instr to Assoc Prof, Goucher Col, 56-68; Prof and Dir, Ctr for Soviet and Eastern European Studies, Univ Kansas, 68-70; Dir, Ctr for Slavic and Eastern European Studies, 88-91, Prof, 71-, Prof. Emeritus, 92-, Ohio State Univ. **HONORS AND AWARDS** Resident Fel, Woodrow Wilson Intl Ctr for Scholars, 82; Fulbright-Hays Faculty Research Awd, 82-83; Visiting Research Scholar, Univ Fribourg, Switzerland, 82-83; Resident Scholar, Bellagio Study Ctr of Rockefeller Fdn, Balagio Italy, 83; Foreign Visiting Fel, Sapporo Japan, 87-88; Visiting Research Scholar, Moscow State Univ, 93; Visiting Research Scholar, Russian State Univ for the Humanities, 95. **MEMBERSHIPS** Amer Phil Assoc; Amer Assoc for the Advancement of Slavic Studies **RESEARCH** Russian philosophy; Soviet Marxism; social and political philosophy **SELECTED PUBLICATIONS** Auth, Marxism in the USSR: A Critical Survey of Current Soviet Thought, 85; ed, A History of Young Russia, 86; Technology, Culture, and Development: The Experience of the Soviet Model, 92; Russian Thought after Communism: The Recovery of a Philosophical Heritage, 94. **CONTACT ADDRESS** 1000 Urlin Ave., Apt. 206, Columbus, OH 43212. **EMAIL** scanlan.1@osu.edu

SCANLAN, MICHAEL
DISCIPLINE PHILOSOPHY OF SCIENCE **EDUCATION** SUNY-Buffalo, PhD. **CAREER** Philos, Oregon St Univ. **RESEARCH** Logic; artificial intelligence; Bertrand Russell; F.P. Ramsey. **SELECTED PUBLICATIONS** Area: Aristotle's logic; the American Postulate Theorists, and Wittgenstein's Tractatus. **CONTACT ADDRESS** Dept Philos, Oregon State Univ, Corvallis, OR 97331-4501. **EMAIL** scanlanm@ucs.orst.edu

SCANLON, T. M.
DISCIPLINE PHILOSOPHY **EDUCATION** Princeton, BA, 62; Harvard Univ, PhD. **CAREER** Prof; Harvard Univ, 84-; taught at, Princeton Univ, 66-84; Fulbright fel, Oxford. **SELECTED PUBLICATIONS** Auth, What We Owe to Each Other, Harvard UP, 98; publd papers on, freedom of expression, nature of rights, conceptions of welfare, theories of justice & foundational questions in moral theory. **CONTACT ADDRESS** Dept of Philosophy, Harvard Univ, 8 Garden St, Cambridge, MA 02138. **EMAIL** scanlon@fas.harvard.edu

SCAPERLANDA, MICHAEL
PERSONAL Born 04/29/1960, Austin, TX, m, 1981, 4 children **DISCIPLINE** LAW **EDUCATION** Univ TX, Austin, BA, 81, JD, 84. **CAREER** Judicial clerk, Chief Justice to Supreme Court, 84-85; assoc, Hogan & Hartson, DC, 85-86; assoc, Hughes & Luce, Austin, TX, 86-89; assoc prof, 89-95, prof, Univ OK, College of Law, 95-; Gene Elaine Edwards Family Chair in Law and prof of Law, 00. **HONORS AND AWARDS** James D Feller Awd for Outstanding Scholarship; Outstanding Young Man of America, 82, 88. **MEMBERSHIPS** Order of the COIF; Asn of Am Law Schools. **RESEARCH** Religious influence on law and society; The Constitution and the Am people; immigration. **SELECTED PUBLICATIONS** Auth, Judicial Solecism Repeated: An Analysis of the Oklahoma Supreme Court's Refusal to Recognize the Adjudicative Nature of Particularized Ratemaking, 47 OK Law Rev 601, 94; Justice Thurgood Marshall and the Legacy of Dissent in Federal Alienage Cases, 8 Georgetown Immigration Law J 1, 94; Are We That Far Gone?: Due Process and Secret Deportation Proceedings, 7 Stanford Law and Policy Rev 23, 96; A Godless Constitution?, Our Sunday Visitor, Nov 10, 96; Partial Membership: Aliens and the Constitutional Community, 81 IA Law Rev 707, 96; Who is My Neighbor?: An Essay on Immigrants, Welfare Reform, and the Constitution, 29 CT Law Rev 1587, 97; Church & Nation are Poorer Sans Religious Freedom Restoration Act, Nat Cath Register, July 20, 97; Kiryas Joel and the Need for Religious Accommodation, Nat Cath Register, Sept 21, 97; To Bind Up the Nation's Wounds: Lessons from Abraham Lincoln, Our Sunday Visitor, Nov 9, 97; Louisiana's Covenant Marriage Law Misses the Mark, Cath Parent, forthcoming. **CONTACT ADDRESS** College of Law, Univ of Oklahoma, 300 W Timberdell, Norman, OK 73019. **EMAIL** mscaperlanda@ou.edu

SCARBOROUGH, MILTON R.
PERSONAL Born 06/02/1940, Gulfport, MS, d, 2 children **DISCIPLINE** RELIGION **EDUCATION** Univ Miss, BA, eng, 62; New Orleans Bapt Theol Sem, BD, theol, 65; Duke Univ, PhD, relig, 72. **CAREER** Prof, philos and relig, Centre Col, 69-. **HONORS AND AWARDS** Nat Endow of Humanities Distinguished Prof of Humanities; Dana fel, Emory Univ, 91-92. **MEMBERSHIPS** Amer Acad of Relig. **RESEARCH** Myth; Phenomenology; Buddhism. **SELECTED PUBLICATIONS** Auth, Myth & Modernity: Postcritical Reflections, SUNY, 94. **CONTACT ADDRESS** Centre Col, 600 W Walnut St., Danville, KY 40422. **EMAIL** mscarb@centre.edu

SCARLETT, JAMES D.
DISCIPLINE LAW **EDUCATION** McGill Univ, BC, 75; Univ Toronto, LLB, 81. **CAREER** Partner, McMillan Binch **HONORS AND AWARDS** Dir, Capital Markets Branch. **RESEARCH** Corporate and securities law. **SELECTED PUBLICATIONS** Auth, pubs on public finance, mergers and acquisitions, and providing regulatory advice. **CONTACT ADDRESS** Fac of Law, Univ of Toronto, 78 Queen's Park, Toronto, ON, Canada M5S 1A1.

SCERRI, ERIC R.
DISCIPLINE PHILOSOPHY **EDUCATION** London Univ, BS, 74; Southampton Univ, M Phil; King's Col, London, hist of philos of sci, PhD, 92. **CAREER** Postdoctoral fel, Caltech, 95-97; asst prof, Bradley Univ, 97-98; asst prof, Purdue Univ, 98-. **MEMBERSHIPS** Amer Philos Asn; Philos of Sci Asn; Amer Chem Soc. **RESEARCH** History and philosophy of chemistry; Chemical education. **SELECTED PUBLICATIONS** Article, The Evolution of the Periodic System, Sci Amer, 78-83, Sept, 98; article, Popper's Naturalized Approach to the Reduction of Chemistry, Intl Studies in Philos of Sci, 12, 33-44, 98; article, Has the Periodic Table Been Successfully Axiomatized?, Erkentnnis, 47, 229-243, 97; article, The Periodic Table and the Electron, Amer Sci, 85, 546-553, 97; article, Interdisciplinary Research at the Beckman Institutes, Interdisciplinary Sci Rev, 22, 131-137, 97; article, Chemical Periodicity, Macmillan Encycl of Chem, Macmillan, vol 3, 23-33, 97; article, The Case for Philosophy of Chemistry, Synthese, 111, 213-232, 97; article, A Bibliography for the Philosophy of Chemistry, Synthese, 111, 305-324, 97; article, It All Depends What You Mean By Reduction, From Simplicity to Complexity, Information, Interaction, Emergence, Vieweg-Verlag, 97; article, Are Chemistry and Philosophy Miscible?, Chem Intelligencer, 3, 44-46, 97; article, Reduktion und Erklarung in der Chemie, Philosophie der Chemie - Bestandsaufnahme und Ausblik, Wurtzburg, Koningshausen & Neumann, 77-93, 96; article, Why the 4s Orbital Is Occupied before the 3d, Jour of Chem Educ, 73, 6, 498-503, 96; article, Stephen Brush, The Periodic Table and the Nature of Chemistry, Die Sprache der Chemie, Wurtzburg, Koningshausen & Neumann, 96; article, Why is There (Almost) No Philosophy of Chemistry?, Hist Grp of Royal Soc of Chem Newsletter and Summary of Papers, 19-24, Feb, 96; article, Philosophy of Chemistry Resurgens, Chem Heritage, 13, no 1, 33, Winter, 95-96; article, The Exclusion Principle, Chemistry and Hidden Variables, Synthese, 102, 165-169, 95; article, Has Chemistry Been at Least Approximately Reduced to Quantum Mechanics?, PSA, 1, 160-170, 94; article, Please Change (The Periodic Table), Chem in Britain, 30, no 5, 379-381, 94; article, Prediction of the Nature of Hafnium from Chemistry, Bohr's Theory and Quantum Theory, Annals of Sci, 51, 137-150, 94. **CONTACT ADDRESS** Dept. of Chemistry, Purdue Univ, West Lafayette, West Lafayette, IN 47907. **EMAIL** scerri@bradley.edu

SCHABERG, JANE D.
DISCIPLINE RELIGIOUS STUDIES AND WOMEN'S STUDIES **EDUCATION** Manhattanville Col, BA; Columbia Univ, MA; Union Theol Sem NYork City, PhD. **CAREER** Prof; Univ Detroit Mercy, 77-. **RESEARCH** Feminist interpretation, biblical studies, introductions to RS and WS **CONTACT ADDRESS** Dept of Religious Studies, Univ of Detroit Mercy, 4001 W McNichols Rd, PO Box 19900, Detroit, MI 48219-0900. **EMAIL** SCHABEJD@udmercy.edu

SCHACHT, RICHARD
DISCIPLINE PHILOSOPHY **EDUCATION** Princeton Univ, PhD, 67. **CAREER** Prof, Univ Ill Urbana Champaign. **RESEARCH** Post-Kantian continental philosophy; philosophical anthropology; social theory; value theory. **SELECTED PUBLICATIONS** Auth, Alienation, Hegel and After, Nietzsche; Classical Modern Philosophers: Descartes to Kant; The Future of Alienation and Making Sense of Nietzsche; ed, Nietzsche: Selections and Nietzsche, Genealogy, Morality. **CONTACT ADDRESS** Philosophy Dept, Univ of Illinois, Urbana-Champaign, 52 E Gregory Dr, Champaign, IL 61820. **EMAIL** rschacht@staff.uiuc.edu

SCHACHTER, GUSTAV
PERSONAL Born 05/27/1926, Botosani, Romania, m, 1958, 2 children **DISCIPLINE** ECONOMICS **EDUCATION** New York Univ, PhD 62, MA 56; City Col NYork, BS 54. **CAREER** Northeastern Univ, prof 65-98; City Col NY, asst prof 60-65; B&G Inc NY, prod mgr 51-59; IRO Rome, off mgr 49-51. **HONORS AND AWARDS** United Nations Sr Vis Sch Euro Econ Cen; Lowell Tchg Inst Hon Doc; NYC Founders Day Awd; Fulbright Dist Ch; Fulbright Sr Sch; Fulbright Lectr; Ital Gov Awd and Fulbright Gnt. **MEMBERSHIPS** AEA; EEA; ACE; RSA; ECA. **RESEARCH** Europe; Italy; Input output methodology. **SELECTED PUBLICATIONS** Auth, Economic Development in Boston in the 1990's, co-ed, 94; pattern Regionali di Convergenza Nell'Unione Europea e Performance Delle Regioni Alpine, coauth, F Bosacci, L Senn eds, Montagna, Area di Integrazione, F Angeli, 97; auth, The Impact of Mega Infrastructure Projects on Urban Development: Boston USA and Messina Streets Italy, coauth, Euro Plan Studies, 96; auth, The Impact of Redirection on the Transfer to the Italian South on Input Output and Employment to 2000, coauth, Jour of Sys Analysis and Model Simulation, 96; auth, Ell Mezzorgiorno: Cuando si vive al sur del Capitol, coauth, Horizonte Sindical, 95; auth, Structural Change and Regional Development, coauth, Jour of Sys Analysis and Model Simulations, 94; auth, Economic Growth Through Dependence in the Mezzogiorno: 1950-1990, Jour of Euro Econ History, 94. **CONTACT ADDRESS** Dept of Economics, Northwestern Univ, 301 Lake Hall, Boston, MA 02115.

SCHACK, HAIMO
DISCIPLINE LAW **EDUCATION** Univ Calif Berkeley, LL.M. **CAREER** Prof, Univ Ill Urbana Champaign. **RESEARCH** Comparative law, conflict of laws, and copyright law. **SELECTED PUBLICATIONS** Auth, Copyright Law, 97; International Civil Litigation, 96; Jurisdictional Minimum Contacts Scrutinized, Heidelberg, 83. **CONTACT ADDRESS** Law Dept, Univ of Illinois, Urbana-Champaign, 504 E Pennsylvania Ave, Champaign, IL 61820. **EMAIL** hschack@law.uiuc.edu

SCHAEFER, JAME
PERSONAL Born 01/07/1940, Syracuse, NY, m, 1962, 4 children **DISCIPLINE** SYSTEMATIC THEOLOGY, ETHICS; RELIGIOUS STUDIES **EDUCATION** PhD **CAREER** Marquette Univ, 95-; CTNS Quality & Excellence in Teaching Award; John Templeton Found Relig & Sci Award. **MEMBERSHIPS** Am Acad Relig; Soc Christian Ethics; Nat Asn Environ Ethics; Col Theol Soc; Int Soc Environ; Professionals Cath Theol Soc Am. **RESEARCH** Theological Foundations for environmental ethics; Theological discourse informed by the natural sciences. **SELECTED PUBLICATIONS** Auth Theistic Foundations for Environmental Ethics: Promising Patristic and Medieval Sources; auth, Appreciating the Beauty of Earth, Theological Studies; auth, Acting Reverentl in a Saramental World, Proceedings of The Theology Institute vol 33, Vileanova University, 00. **CONTACT ADDRESS** Theology Dept, Marquette Univ, 207 Coughlin Hall, Milwaukee, WI 53201-1881. **EMAIL** jame.schaefer@marquette.edu

SCHAEFFER, PETER MORITZ-FRIEDRICH
PERSONAL Born 05/14/1930, Breslau, Germany, m, 1968 **DISCIPLINE** GERMANIC STUDIES, CLASSICS, RELIGIOUS STUDIES. **EDUCATION** Univ Ottawa, Lic Theol, 59; Princeton Univ, PhD(Germanic studies), 71. **CAREER** From lectr to asst prof Germanic studies, Princeton Univ, 70-74; vis lectr Ger & comp lit, Univ CA, Berkeley, 74-76; Assoc Prof to Prof Ger, Univ CA, Davis, 76-. **HONORS AND AWARDS** Outstanding Advisor, 86; Outstanding Mentor of the Year, 93. **MEMBERSHIPS** ALSC; Renaissance Soc Am; Erasmus Soc; Tyndale Soc. **RESEARCH** Renaissance; Neo-Latin literature; Classical tradition. **SELECTED PUBLICATIONS** Auth, Joachim Vadianus, De poetica, Text, Translation & Commentary, Wilhelm Fink, Munich, 73; Hoffmannswaldau, De curriculo studiorum, Peter Lang, Bern, 91; Sapidus Consolator, Annuaire de Selestat, 96. **CONTACT ADDRESS** German Dept, Univ of California, Davis, One Shields Ave, Davis, CA 95616-5200. **EMAIL** pmschaeffer@ucdavis.edu

SCHAGRIN, MORTON L.
PERSONAL Born 11/22/1930, Wilmington, DE, m, 1956, 3 children **DISCIPLINE** PHILOSOPHY **EDUCATION** Univ Chicago, BA, 51, BS, 52, MA, 53, Univ Calif Berk, PhD, 65. **CAREER** Univ Calif Berk, tchg asst, lectr, 58-61; Univ Fla, asst prof, 61-63; Denison Univ, asst prof, assoc prof, pres DSA, chemn H&FAC, 63-70; Harvard Univ, res assoc., 65-66; SUNY Fredonia, assoc prof, chemn, prof, assoc dean, dean, 70-. **MEMBERSHIPS** GLCA, NSF, T-SPA, APA, Fulbright Assoc. **RESEARCH** 18th and 19th century experimental science; modern logic. **SELECTED PUBLICATIONS** Auth, The Resistance to Ohm's Law, Am Jour of Physics, 63; auth, The Language of Logic, Random House, 79; auth, Early Observations and Calculations on Light Pressure, Am Jour of Physics, 74; auth, More Heat than Light, Syntheses, 94; auth, Logic: A Computer Approach, coauth, McGraw-Hill, NY, 85; Rumford's Experiments on the Materiality of Light, Realism and Anti-realism in the Philosophy of Science, eds. R. S. Cohen, R. Hilpinen, Q. Renzong, Kluwer Academic Pub, Dordrecht, 95. **CONTACT ADDRESS** Dept of Philosophy, SUNY, Col at Fredonia, 54 Capitol St, Watertown, MA 02472. **EMAIL** schagrin@fredonia.edu

SCHALL, JAMES VINCENT
PERSONAL Born 01/20/1928, Pocahontas, IA, m **DISCIPLINE** POLITICAL PHILOSOPHY **EDUCATION** MA Philos, Fon309A Univ, 55; PhD Political Philos, Georgetown Univ, 60; MST Theol, Univ of Santa Clara, 64. **CAREER** Inst Soc, Georgian Univ, Rome, Italy, 65-77; Univ of San Francisco, 69-77; Georgetown Univ, 78-. **MEMBERSHIPS** Amer Political Sci Assoc. **SELECTED PUBLICATIONS** At These Limits of Political Philosophy(Was): The Catholic Univ of Amer Press, 96; Jacques Maritain: A Philosopher in Society, Lanham, Rowman and Littlefield, 98; The Death of Plato, The American Scholar, 65, pp 401-415, 96; On the Uniqueness of Socrates, Gregorianum, 76(#2 95); In the Place of Augustine in Political Philosophy, The Political Science Reviewer XXIII, 94; Post-Aristotelian Political Philosophy and Modernity, Aufstieg und Niedergang der Romischen Welt, Berlin: Gruyter 11 36.7, 94; Friendship and Political Philosophy, The Review of Metaphysics, L pp121-141, 96; The Role of Christian Philosophy in Politics, American Catholic Philosophical Quarterly (#1,95) 1-14; auth, Schall on Chesterton: Timely Essays on Timeless Paradoxes, Catholic Univ of Am Press (Washington), 00; auth, "Fides et Ratio: Approaches to Roman Catholic Political Philosophy," Rev of Politics 62 (00): 49-75. **CONTACT ADDRESS** Dept of Government, Georgetown Univ, 37th and 0 Sts NW, Washington, DC 20057. **EMAIL** schallj@gunet.georgetown.edu

SCHALLER, WALTER E.
DISCIPLINE PHILOSOPHY **EDUCATION** Univ CA, Berkeley, MA; Univ Wis, PhD, 84. **CAREER** Instr, Wheaton Col; instr, Univ KY; assoc prof, TX Tech Univ. **RESEARCH** Ethics; polit philos; the philos of law. **SELECTED PUBLICATIONS** Publ articles on Kant's ethics, utilitarianism, and the relationship between virtues and duties in Philos and Phenomenol Res, Ratio, Southern J of Philos, Dialogue and Hist of Philos Quart; auth, "Rawls", Journal of Political Philosophy, Pacific Philos Quarterly. **CONTACT ADDRESS** Texas Tech Univ, Lubbock, TX 79409-3092. **EMAIL** walter.schaller@ttu.edu

SCHALOW, FRANK H.
PERSONAL Born 02/23/1956, Denver, CO, s **DISCIPLINE** PHILOSOPHY **EDUCATION** Tulane Univ, PhD, 84. **CAREER** Assoc Prof, Loyola Univ New Orleans, 86-92; Vis Assoc Prof, Univ of New Orleans, 95-00. **HONORS AND AWARDS** Phi Beta Kappa. **MEMBERSHIPS** N Am Heidegger Conf, Hesel Soc, Southwestern Philos Soc. **RESEARCH** Heidegger, Kant, Phenomenology, German Idealism. **SELECTED PUBLICATIONS** Auth, Imagination and Existence, UPA, 86; coauth, Traces of Understanding, Editions Rodopi, 90; auth, Renewal of the Herdegger-Kant Dialogue, SUNY Press, 92; auth, Language and Deed, Editions Rodopi, 98. **CONTACT ADDRESS** Dept Philos, Univ of New Orleans, 2000 Lakeshore Dr, New Orleans, LA 70148-0001. **EMAIL** fschalow@uno.edu

SCHARLEMANN, ROBERT PAUL
PERSONAL Born 04/04/1929, Lake City, MN **DISCIPLINE** THEOLOGY **EDUCATION** Concordia Col & Sem, Mo, BA, 52, BD, 55; Heidelberg Univ, DrTheol, 57. **CAREER** Instr philos, Valparaiso Univ, 57-59; pastor, Bethlehem Lutheran Church, Carlyle, Ill, 60-61, Grace Lutheran Church, Durham, NC, 62-63; asst prof theol, Grad Sch Relig, Univ Southern Calif, 63-66; assoc prof theol, Univ Iowa, 66-68, prof, 68-81; Commonwealth Prof Philos Theol, Univ Va, 81-, Res fel, Yale Univ, 59-60; assoc ed, Dialog, 60-; Coun Int Exchange Scholars Fulbright sr res grant, 75-76; ed, J Am Acad Relig, 80- **MEM-**

BERSHIPS Am Acad Relig; NAm Paul Tillich Soc (vpres, 77, pres, 78); Am Theol Soc. **RESEARCH** History of thought; constructive theology; theology and science. **SELECTED PUBLICATIONS** Auth, From Text To Action - Essays In Hermeneutics, Vol 2 - Ricoeur,P/, Lang In Soc, Vol 0022, 1993; Can Religion Be Understood Philosophically/, Int J For Philos Of Rel, Vol 0038, 1995; The Quadrilog - Tradition And The Future Of Ecumenism - Essays In Honor Of Tavard,George,H. - Hagan,K, Editor/, J Of Ecumenical Studies, Vol 0033, 1996; The Royal Priesthood - Essays Ecclesiological And Ecumenical - Yoder,Jh, Cartwright,Mg/, J Of Ecumenical Studies, Vol 0033, 1996. **CONTACT ADDRESS** Dept Relig Studies, Univ of Virginia, Charlottesville, VA 22903.

SCHARPER, STEPHEN B.
PERSONAL Born 09/05/1960, Port Chester, NY, m, 1994, 1 child **DISCIPLINE** THEOLOGY **EDUCATION** Univ Toronto, BA, 82; Univ St. Michael's Col, MA, 88; McGill Univ, PhD, 97. **CAREER** The John A. O' Brien Chr, Univ Notre Dame, Visiting Instr, 94-97; Dir, English Publications, Novalis Publications, 97-. **HONORS AND AWARDS** Fel, Joan B. Kroc Inst for Intl Peace Studies **MEMBERSHIPS** Amer Acad of Religion; Catholic Theological Soc of Amer; College Theology Soc. **RESEARCH** Globalization; religion and environment; economic disparity **SELECTED PUBLICATIONS** Coauth, The Green Bible, 93; Auth, Four Books about Saving the Planet God Loves, National Catholic Reporter, 95; We are the World's Most Dangerous Animals, National Catholic Reporter, 95; And God Saw That it was Good: Catholic Theology and the Environment, Catholic New Times, 97; Redeeming the Time: A Political Theology of the Environment, 97. **CONTACT ADDRESS** Massey Col, 4 Devonshire Pl., Gatehouse , Toronto, ON, Canada M5S 2E1. **EMAIL** scharper@spu.stpaul.uottawa.ca

SCHAUB, MARILYN MCNAMARA
PERSONAL Born 03/24/1928, Chicago, IL, m, 1969, 1 child **DISCIPLINE** RELIGIOUS STUDIES, CLASSICAL LANGUAGES **EDUCATION** Rosary Col, BA, 53; Univ Fribourg, PhD(class philos), 57. **CAREER** Asst prof class lang, 57-62, assoc prof relig studies & class lang, 62-69, Rosary Col; assoc prof, 73-77, prof theol, 77-80, Duquesne Univ; hon assoc, Am Schs Orient Res, Jerusalem, 66-67; admin dir, expedition to the southeast end of the Dead Sea, Jordan, 77, 79, 81, 89-90. **HONORS AND AWARDS** Pres Awd for Faculty Excellence in Teaching, Duquesne Univ, 90. **MEMBERSHIPS** Soc Bibl Lit; Cath Bibl Asn; Am Acad Relig; Archaeol Inst Am. **RESEARCH** Old Testament; New Testament; early Bronze Age settlements at the southeast end of the Dead Sea, Jordan. **SELECTED PUBLICATIONS** Co-translr, Agape in the New Testament, Herder, 63-67; auth, Friends and Friendship in St Augustine, Alba, 65; contribr, Encyclopedic Dictionary of Religion, Corpus, 78; contrib, Harper Collins Bible Dictionary, 96; contrib, Collegeville Pastoral Dictionary of Biblical Theology, 96. **CONTACT ADDRESS** Theol Dept, Duquesne Univ, Pittsburgh, PA 15282. **EMAIL** schaub@duq3.cc.duq.edu

SCHAUB, R. THOMAS
PERSONAL Born 03/26/1933, South Bend, IN, m, 1969, 1 child **DISCIPLINE** RELIGIOUS STUDIES (BIBLICAL), HISTORY & ARCHAEOLOGY OF ANCIENT NEAR EAST **EDUCATION** Architecture, Univ Notre Dame, 49-52; MIT, construction & engineering, 52-53; Aquinas Inst of Philos, BA (madna cum laude), 57, MA (summa cum laude), 58; Aquinas Inst of Theol, MA (cum laude), 61, STD cand, 63; Cath Univ AM, Semitic Studies; Harvard Divinity School, Old Testament and Semitic Studies, 64-65; Ecole Biblique et Archeologique, SSB, 65, SSL, 67 (Pontifical Biblical Commission); Univ Pittsburgh, Pittsburgh Theol Sem, PhD, 73. **CAREER** Asst prof, Aquinas Inst Theol, 68-69; vis lect, Pittsburgh Theol Sem, 70-71; asst Prof, relig Studies, Indiana Univ of PA, 69-71, 73-76, asoc prof, 76-79; prof, Religious Studies, Indiana Univ of PA, 79-99; prof Emerins, 00. **HONORS AND AWARDS** Teaching fel, Pittsburgh Theol Sem, 69-70; Thayer fel, Am Schools of Oriental Res, 71-72; Ed Counsellor, Old Master, Purdue Univ, 75; Danforth Assoc, 75-; res assoc, Carnegie Museum Nat Hist, 79-; fel, Explorer's Club, 79-; NEH fel, 82-83; Distinguished Fac Awd for Res, Indiana Univ PA, 85; Fac Res Assoc, Inst of Applied Res and Public Policy, IUP, 88-89; Fulbright res fel, 89, 91; numerous res grants from the following: Indiana Univ PA, NEH, Nat Geographic Soc, Fulbright. **MEMBERSHIPS** Soc of Biblical Lit; Cath Biblical Asn; Am Schools of Oriental Res; Am Academy of Relig; Am Inst of Archaeology; Asn for Field Archaeology. **RESEARCH** Early Bronze Age, Near East. **SELECTED PUBLICATIONS** Auth, Review of the Jordan Valley Survey, 1953: Some Unpublished Soundings Conducted by James Mellaart, by Albert Leonard, Jr, Annual of the American Schools of Oriental Res, 50, Bul of the Am Schools of Oriental Res, 95; Pots as Containers, in Retrieving the Past, Essays on Archaeological Research and Methodology, in Honor of Gus W Van Beek, ed Joe D Seger, Cobb Inst of Archaeol, MS State Univ, Eisenbraun, 96; Southeast Dead Sea Plain, in The Oxford Encyclopedia of Archaeology in the Near East, ed Eric Meyers, Oxford Univ Press, vol 5, 97; Bab edh-Dhra' in the Oxford Encyclopedia of Archaeology in the Near East, ed Eric M Meyers, Oxford Univ Press, 97; The Southeastern Dead Sea Plain: Changing Shorelines and their Impact on Settlement Patterns of the Major Historical Periods of the Region, with Jack Donahue and Brian Peer, in Studies in the History and Archaeology of Jorgdan, 98; two books and numerous other publications. **CONTACT ADDRESS** Indiana Univ of Pennsylvania, 442 Sutton Hall, Indiana, PA 15705. **EMAIL** rtschaub@grove.iup.edu

SCHAUBER, NANCY ELLEN
PERSONAL Born 03/25/1960, White Plains, NY, m, 1987, 1 child **DISCIPLINE** PHILOSOPHY **EDUCATION** St. John's Col, BA, 81; Univ Va, MA, 87; Yale Univ, PhD, 93. **CAREER** Asst prof to assoc prof, 93-. **MEMBERSHIPS** Am Philos Asn. **RESEARCH** Moral Theory, Ancient Philosophy. **SELECTED PUBLICATIONS** Auth, "Hume on Moral Motivation: It's Almost Like Being in Love," History of Philosophy Quarterly; auth, "Persons, Perception and Particularity: The Moral Vision of Iris Murdoch," Cogito; auth, "Integrity, Commitment, and the concept of a Person," American Philosophical Quarterly. **CONTACT ADDRESS** Dept Philos, Univ of Richmond, 28 Westhampton Way, Richmond, VA 23173-0001. **EMAIL** nschauber@richmond.edu

SCHECHTMAN, MARYA
DISCIPLINE PHILOSOPHY **EDUCATION** Harvard Univ, PhD, 88. **CAREER** Assoc prof, Univ IL at Chicago. **RESEARCH** Philos of psychology; existentialism; philos of lit; Am philos. **SELECTED PUBLICATIONS** Auth, Personhood and Personal Identity, Jour Philos, 90; Consciousness, Concern, and Personal Identity, Logos, 91. **CONTACT ADDRESS** Philos Dept, Univ of Illinois, Chicago, S Halsted St, PO Box 705, Chicago, IL 60607.

SCHEDLER, GEORGE EDWARD
PERSONAL Born 12/22/1945, Fresno, CA, m, 1970, 3 children **DISCIPLINE** PHILOSOPHY **EDUCATION** St Mary's Col, Calif, BA, 67; Univ Calif, San Diego, MA, 70, PhD(philos), 73; South Ill Univ, JD, 87. **CAREER** Asst prof to assoc prof, 73-84, prof philos, Southern Ill Univ, Carbondale, 84-. **MEMBERSHIPS** Am Philos Asn; Am Cath Philos Asn; SW Philos Soc. **RESEARCH** Political philosophy; legal philosophy; ethics. **SELECTED PUBLICATIONS** Auth, On Punishing the Guilty, Ethics, 4/76; Capital Punishment and its Deterrent Effect, Social Theory & Pract, 12/76; Behavior Modification and Punishment of the Innocent, Gruner, 77; Justice in Marx, Engels and Lenin, Studies Soviet Thought, 8/78; Does Society Have the Right to Force Pregnant Drug Addicts to Abort their Fetuses?, Soc Theory and Pract, 11/91; Racist Symbols and Reparations, Rowman and Littlefield, 98. **CONTACT ADDRESS** Dept of Philos, So Illinois Univ, Carbondale, Carbondale, IL 62901-4505. **EMAIL** geosched@siu.edu

SCHEELE, RAYMOND H.
PERSONAL Born 11/18/1943, Glendale, CA, m, 1982, 3 children **DISCIPLINE** POLITICAL SCIENCE **EDUCATION** Valparaiso Univ, BA, 65; Univ Mo Columbia, PhD, 72. **CAREER** Instr, DePaul Univ, 70-73; asst prof to prof, Ball State Univ, 75-. **MEMBERSHIPS** Am Polit Sci Asn. **RESEARCH** Electoral and Voting Behavior; Political Biography; State and Local Government. **SELECTED PUBLICATIONS** Auth, Larry Conrad of Indiana: A Biography, IU Press, 97. **CONTACT ADDRESS** Dept Polit Sci, Ball State Univ, Ball State Univ, Muncie, IN 47306. **EMAIL** rscheele@bsu.edu

SCHEFFLER, ISRAEL
PERSONAL Born 11/25/1923, New York, NY, m, 1949, 2 children **DISCIPLINE** PHILOSOPHY **EDUCATION** Brooklyn COl, BA, 45, MA, 48; Jewish Theol Sem, MHL, 49; Univ Pa, PhD(philos), 52. **CAREER** From instr educ, to prof, 52-62, prof educ & philos, 62-64, Victor S. Thomas Prof Educ & Philos, Harvard Univ, 64-, Guggenheim fel, 58-59 & 72-73; NSF res grants, 62 & 65-66; chmn gen probs sect, Int Cong Logic; Methodol & Philos Sci, 64; hon res fel cognitives studies, Harvard Univ, 65-66; fel, Ctr Advan Studies Behav Sci, 72-73, co-dir, Philosophy of Education Res Ctr, Harvard, 83-98, dir, 98-. **HONORS AND AWARDS** Distinguished Serv Medal, Teachers Col Columbia, 80, AM (hon), Harvard Univ, 59, D.H.L. (hon) Jewish Theological Sem, 93. **MEMBERSHIPS** Eastern Div Am Philos Asn; Aristotelian Soc; Philos Sci Asn(pres, 73-75); Nat Acad Educ; Am Acad Arts & Sci, Charles S. Piece Soc, Pres, 98. **RESEARCH** Philosophy of science, language and education. **SELECTED PUBLICATIONS** Auth, The Language of Education, 60; auth, The Anatomy of Inquiry, 63; auth, Conditions of Knowledge, 65; auth, Science and Subjectivity, 67; auth, Four Progmatists, 74; auth, Beyond The Letter, 79; auth, Of Human Potential, 85; auth, In Praise of the Cognitive Emotions, 91; auth, Symbolic World, 97. **CONTACT ADDRESS** Dept of Philos, Harvard Univ, Cambridge, MA 02138. **EMAIL** israel_scheffler@harvard.edu

SCHEJBAL, DAVID
PERSONAL Born 02/12/1961, Prague, Czechoslovakia, d **DISCIPLINE** PHILOSOPHY **EDUCATION** Univ Conn, PhD, 92 **CAREER** Assoc dean cont educ & dir summer sessions spec prog, Northwestern Univ; Dir, Office of Continuing Educ. **HONORS AND AWARDS** Awd Merit Credit Prog; N Amer Asn Summer Sessions **MEMBERSHIPS** Amer Philos Asn; Asn Univ Summer Sessions; N Amer Asn Summer Sessions **RESEARCH** Environmental ethics; Philosophy of education. **SELECTED PUBLICATIONS** Auth, On the Notion of Following a Rule Privately, Ludwig Wittgenstein: A Symposium on the Centennial of His Birth, Longwood Acad, 90; The Aesthetics of Summer Session Administration, Summer Acad: A Jour of Higher Educ, 97-98; Summer Sessions: A Time in Change, Adv Quart, 98; Summer Session Homeostasis, Proceedings: 34th Annual Conference of the North American Association of Summer Sessions, 98; Summer Language Instruction, International Study Guides: Studying Abroad, 98. **CONTACT ADDRESS** Office of Continuing Educ, Univ of Illinois, Urbana-Champaign, Urbana, IL 61801. **EMAIL** schejbal@uiuc.edu

SCHEMAN, NAOMI
PERSONAL Born New York, NY **DISCIPLINE** PHILOSOPHY **EDUCATION** Harvard Univ, PhD. **RESEARCH** Politics of epistemology. **SELECTED PUBLICATIONS** Auth, Engenderings: Constructions of Knowledge, Authority, and Privilege, 93. **CONTACT ADDRESS** Philosophy Dept, Univ of Minnesota, Twin Cities, 271 19th Ave S, 831 Heller Hall, Minneapolis, MN 55455. **EMAIL** nschema@tc.umn.edu

SCHERER, IMGARD S.
PERSONAL Born 01/14/1937, Berlin, Germany, m, 1958, 4 children **DISCIPLINE** HISTORY OF PHILOSOPHY **EDUCATION** Amer Univ, PhD, 91. **CAREER** Asst Prof, 92-, Loyola Coll, MD; Vis Prof, 92, Amer Univ; Vis Prof, 88-91, George Mason Univ. **HONORS AND AWARDS** Amer Philos Assoc; North Amer Kent Soc. **MEMBERSHIPS** ASA, Phi Sigma Tan, IHSP. **RESEARCH** Science of Aesthetics, Theory of Judgement applied to Science, Morality and Art. **SELECTED PUBLICATIONS** Auth, The Crisis of Judgement in Kant's Three Critiques, In Search of a Science of Aesthetics, NY, Peter Lang Pub Co, 95; The Problem of the A Priori in Sensibility, Revisiting Kant's and Hegel's Theories of the Senses, forthcoming, The Review of Metaphysics; co-auth, Kant's Critique of Judgement and the Scientific Investigation of Matter, Universitat Karlsruhe, Germany, Inst Of Philos, Vol 3, 97; Kant's Eschatology in Zum ewigen Frieden: The Concept of Purposiveness to Guarantee Perpetual Peace, Proceedings of the 8th International Kant Congress, Memphis, 95. **CONTACT ADDRESS** Dept of Philosophy, Loyola Col, 4501 N Charles St, Baltimore, MD 21210-2699. **EMAIL** ischerer@loyola.edu

SCHIAVONA, CHRISTOPHER F.
PERSONAL Born 09/08/1958, Boston, MA, s **DISCIPLINE** PHILOSOPHY **EDUCATION** Georgetown Univ, MA, PhD, 92; St John's Seminary, BA, MA, M.Div. **CAREER** Asst prof, St John's Sem; Dean of Students, St John's Sem; Senior Consultant, Taylor Res Consulting Group; Pres, City Square Assoc. **MEMBERSHIPS** Amer Philos Assoc; Greater Boston Bus Council; Soc for Bus & Prof Ethics. **RESEARCH** Business Ethics; Philosophy of Religion; Media Studies; Popular Culture. **CONTACT ADDRESS** City Square Associates, 26 Prospect St, Charlestown, MA 02129. **EMAIL** cschiavone@citysquareassociates.com

SCHICK, FREDERIC
PERSONAL Born 08/27/1929, Brunn, Czechoslovakia, m **DISCIPLINE** PHILOSOPHY **EDUCATION** Columbia Univ, BA, 51, MA, 52, PhD, 58. **CAREER** Instr philos, CT Col, 54-57; lectr, City Col NY, 57-58; insts, Columbia Univ, 58-60; asst prof, Brandeis Univ, 60-62; from asst prof to assoc prof, 62-69, chmn dept, 65-68, 79-82, Prof Philos, Rutgers Univ, 69-, Lectr, New Sch Social Res, 57-59; ed, Theory & Decision, 74-82, adv ed, Theory & Decision Libr, 77-; adv ed, Econ & Philos, 87-; vis scholar, Corpus Christi Col, Cambridge Univ, 75. **HONORS AND AWARDS** Coun Res Humanities grant, 59; Nat Sci Found res grants, 63-64 & 73-74; vis fel, Clare Hall, Cambridge Univ, 94. **MEMBERSHIPS** Am Philos Asn. **RESEARCH** Philos of sci; inductive logic; decision theory. **SELECTED PUBLICATIONS** Auth, Beyond utilitarianism, 71 & A justification of reason, 72, J Philos; Democracy and interdependent preferences, Theory & Decision, 72; Some notes on thinking ahead, Social Res, 77; Self-knowledge, uncertainty and choice, British J Philos Sci, 79; Toward a logic of liberalism, J Philos, 80; Welfare, Rights and Fairness, In: Science, Belief and Behavior, 80 & Under Which Description? In: Beyond Utilitarianism, Cambridge Univ, 82; Having Reasons, Princeton Univ Press, 82; Understanding Action, Cambridge Univ Press, 91; Making Choices, Cambridge Univ Pres, 97. **CONTACT ADDRESS** Dept of Philos, Rutgers, The State Univ of New Jersey, New Brunswick, 139 Davison Hall, New Brunswick, NJ 08903-0270. **EMAIL** fschick@rci.rutgers.edu

SCHIEFEN, RICHARD JOHN
PERSONAL Born 05/09/1932, Rochester, NY **DISCIPLINE** MODERN CHURCH HISTORY, HISTORY OF RELIGION **EDUCATION** Univ Toronto, BA, 56, MA, 62; Univ St Michael's Col, STB, 61; Univ Rochester, MEd, 58; Univ London, PhD, 70. **CAREER** From asst prof to assoc prof hist, Univ St Thomas, Tex, 65-72, chmn dept, 70-72; assoc prof church hist, St Michael's Col, Univ Toronto, 72-81; Dean Sch Theol, Univ St Thomas, 81- **MEMBERSHIPS** AHA; Am Cath Hist Asn; Can Cath Hist Asn; Ecclesiastical Hist Soc. **RESEARCH** Victorian religion; 19th century Roman Catholicism. **SELECTED PUBLICATIONS** Auth, A Hist Commentary On The Major Catholic Works Of Newman,Cardinal - Griffin,Jr/, Cath Hist

Rev, Vol 0080, 1994; Trial Of Strength, Furtwangler,Wilhelm In The Third-Reich - Prieberg,Fk/, Biog-An Interdisciplinary Quart, Vol 0018, 1995; Cath Devotion In Victorian Eng - Heimann,M/, Cath Hist Rev, Vol 0083, 1997. **CONTACT ADDRESS** Sch of Theol, Univ of St. Thomas, Texas, Houston, TX 77024. **EMAIL** schiefen@stthom.edu

SCHIEVELLA, P. S.
PERSONAL Born 03/13/1914, Bayonne, NJ, m, 1965, 4 children **DISCIPLINE** PHILOSOPHY **EDUCATION** Columbia Univ, BS, 50, MA, 51, PhD, 67. **CAREER** Tchr, Brooklyn Acad, 54, E Islip, 54-55, Earl L Vandermeulen High School, 55-68; prof of Philosophy, Bemidji Univ, 68-70; prof philosophy & chr, Jersey City State Univ, 70-78; full prof of philosophy, Suffolk Community Col, 78-. **HONORS AND AWARDS** Wall of Fame, Earl L Vandermeulen High School, 98. **MEMBERSHIPS** Amer Philos Asn; Nat Coun Critical Anal; Long Island Philos Asn; NJ Reg Philos Soc. **RESEARCH** Clear, critical and analytical thinking. **SELECTED PUBLICATIONS** Auth, Critical Analysis: Language and Its Functions, Hum Press, 66; The Philosophy of Conwy Lloyd Morgan, Univ Microfilms, 67; ed, The Jour of Critical Analysis, 68; The Jour of Pre-Col Philos, 75; Emergent Evolution and Reductionism, Scientia, 73; auth, Hey! Is That You, God?, Sebastian Publ Co, 87. **CONTACT ADDRESS** Box 137, Port Jefferson, NY 11777. **EMAIL** passch@li.net

SCHINE, ROBERT S.
DISCIPLINE JEWISH STUDIES **EDUCATION** Kenyon Col, AB; Univ Freiburg, MA; Jewish Theol Sem Am, PhD. **CAREER** Dean of faculty, Silberman prof of Jewish Studies, Middlebury Col, 85-. **RESEARCH** 19th- and 20th-century European Jewish thought. **SELECTED PUBLICATIONS** Auth, Jewish Thought Adrift: Max Wiener 1882-1950. **CONTACT ADDRESS** Office of the Dean of Faculty, Middlebury Col, Middlebury, VT 05753.

SCHLAFLY, PHYLLIS STEWART
PERSONAL Born 08/15/1924, St. Louis, MO, w, 1949, 6 children **DISCIPLINE** POLITICAL SCIENCE **EDUCATION** Washington Univ, BA, 44; Harvard Univ, MA, 45; Washington Univ Law School, 78; Niagara Univ, LLD, 76. **CAREER** Broadcaster, CBS Radio Network, 73-78; commentator, Cable TV News Network, 80-83; host, Matters of Opinion, WBBM-AM, Chicago, 73-75; PRES, EAGLE FORUM, 75-; SYNDICATED COLUMNIST, COPLEY NEWS SERV, 76-. **HONORS AND AWARDS** Ten honor awards, Freedom Found; Brotherhood award, NCCJ, 75; Woman of Achievement in Public Affairs, St Louis Globe-Democrat, 63; voted one of the ten most admired women in the world, Good Housekeeping poll, 77-90; one of the most important women of the 20th century, Ladies' Home Jrnl, 99; ill bar, 79; dc bar, 84; mo bar, 85; u.s. supreme court, 87. **MEMBERSHIPS** ABA; DAR; Ill Bar Asn, Phi Beta Kappa; Pi Sigma Alpha. **RESEARCH** Education; national defense; feminism; politics. **SELECTED PUBLICATIONS** Auth, pub, Phyllis Schlafly Report, 67-; auth, A Choice Not an Echo, 64; auth, The Gravediggers, 64; auth, Strike From Space, 65; auth, Safe Not Sorry, 67; auth, The Betrayers, 68; auth, Mindszenty The Man, 72; auth, Kissinger on the Couch, 75; auth, Ambush at Vladivostok, 76; auth, The Power of the Positive Woman, 77; auth, First Reader, 94; ed, Child Abuse in the Classroom, 84; auth, Pornography's Victims, 87; auth, Equal Pay for Unequal Work, 84; auth, Who Will Rock the Cradle, 89; auth, Stronger Families or Bigger Government, 90; auth, Meddlesome Mandate: Rethinking Family Leave, 91. **CONTACT ADDRESS** Eagle Forum, 7800 Bonhomme Ave., Saint Louis, MO 63105. **EMAIL** phyllis@eagleforum.org

SCHLAGEL, RICHARD H.
PERSONAL Born 11/22/1925, Springfield, MA, m, 1962 **DISCIPLINE** PHILOSOPHY **EDUCATION** Springfield Col, BS, 49; Boston Univ , MA, 53, PhD, 55. **HONORS AND AWARDS** Borden Parker Bowne fel, Boston Univ, 54-55; Res Awd, George Wash Univ, 96. **MEMBERSHIPS** AAUP; Am Philos Asn. **RESEARCH** Epistemology; hist and philos of science; philos of mind. **CONTACT ADDRESS** Dept of Philosophy, The George Washington Univ, Washington, DC 20052. **EMAIL** schlagel@wis2

SCHLESINGER, JOSEPH ABRAHAM
PERSONAL Born 01/04/1922, Boston, MA, m, 1951, 2 children **DISCIPLINE** POLITICAL SCIENCE **EDUCATION** Univ of Chicago, BA, 42; Yale Univ, MA, 50; PhD, 55. **CAREER** Instr, Soc Sci, Boston Univ Gen Coll, 47-49; tchg fel, Pol Sci, Wesleyan Univ, 52-53; instr, Soc Sci/Polit Sci, Mich state Univ, 53-55; asst prof, Mich State Univ, 55-59; assoc prof, Mich State Univ, 59-63; vis prof, Polit Sci, Univ Calif, Berkeley, 64-65; prof, Mich State Univ, 63-91; Emer Prof, 91-. **MEMBERSHIPS** Am Polit sci Asn; Midwest Polit Sci Asn **RESEARCH** Study of Political Party Dev since 1960 in U.S., Britain, and France. **SELECTED PUBLICATIONS** Political Parties and the winning of Office, Univ Mich Press, 91; "Understanding Political Parties: Back to Basic," Am Rev Polit, 93; coauth, "French Parties and the Legislative Elections of 1993," Party Polit, 95; coauth, "Dual Ballot Elections and Political Parties, The French Presidential Election of 1995," Comp Polit Stud, 98; coauth, "The Stability of the French Party System: The Enduring Impact of the Two-Ballot Electoral Rules," How France Votes, 98. **CONTACT ADDRESS** Dept Polit Sci, Michigan State Univ, 303 S Kedzie Hall, East Lansing, MI 48824. **EMAIL** schlesi@pilot.msu.edu

SCHMALENBERGER, JERRY L.
DISCIPLINE PARISH MINISTRY **EDUCATION** Wittenberg Univ, BA; Hamma Sch Theol, MDiv; Consortium for Higher Edu Rel Stud, Dmin; Wittenberg Univ, DD. **CAREER** Roland Payne lectr, Gbarnga Sch Theol; lectur, Lutheran Theol Sem, Hong Kong; Theol Col of the West Indies, Jamaica; Belgum Memorial lectr, Calif Lutheran Univ, 89; prof, 88-96; prof, 96-; Pres, Pacific Lutheran Theol Sem, **HONORS AND AWARDS** Pastor, dir, consult, Evangel Outreach; co-dir, PLTS Ctr for Lutheran Church Growth and Mission; bd(s) of dir(s), Hamma Sch Theol; Wittenberg Univ; Lutheran Soc Serv Iowa; Grand View Col; pres, Downtown Revitalization Comm; **SELECTED PUBLICATIONS** Auth, Preparation for Discipleship: A Handbook for New Christians, C.S.S. Publ, 98; The Preacher's Edge, C.S.S. Publ, 96; Plane Thoughts on Parish Ministry, C. S. S. Publ, 94; Called to Witness, C.S.S. Publ, 93. **CONTACT ADDRESS** 162 Pelican Loop, Pittsburgh, CA 94565-2004. **EMAIL** r2ac@aol.com

SCHMALTZ, TED M.
PERSONAL Born 12/17/1960, Ft Wayne, IN, m, 1983, 2 children **DISCIPLINE** PHILOSOPHY **EDUCATION** Kalamazoo Col, BA, 83; Univ Notre Dame, PhD, 88. **CAREER** Tchg asst and grad asst, 83-88, adj asst prof, 88-89, Univ Notre Dame; asst prof, 89-96, assoc prof, 96- , Duke Univ. **HONORS AND AWARDS** Benjamin N. Duke Fel, Natl Human Ctr, 97-98; Andrew W. Mellon Asst Prof Philos, Duke Univ 94-95; Fel for Univ Tchrs, NEH, 93-94; Univ Res Coun Fac Res Grant, 90-97; Univ Res Counc Travel Grant, Duke Univ, 91, 94-97. **MEMBERSHIPS** Am Philos Soc; Leibniz Soc; Hume Soc; British Soc of Modern Philos. **RESEARCH** Early Modern Metaphysics and Epistemology; Historiography of Modern Philosophy. **SELECTED PUBLICATIONS** Auth, Human Freedom and Divine Creation in Malebranche, Descartes and the Cartesians, British Jour Hist Philos, 2, 2, (94): 3-50; auth, Malebranche on Descartes on Mind-Body Distinctness, Jour Hist of Philos, 32, 4 (94): 573-603; auth, Malebranche's Cartesianism and Lockean Colors, Hist of Philos Quart, 12, 4 (95): 387-403; auth, Malebranche's Theory of the Soul: A Cartesian Interpretation, New York, Oxford Univ Press, 96; auth, Spinoza's Mediate Infinite Mode, Jour Hist Philos, 35, 2 (97): 199-235; auth, Descartes on Innate Ideas, Sensation, and Scholasticism: The Response to Regius, in Studies in Seventeenth-Century European Philosophy, ed. MA Stewart, 33-73, Oxford Studies in the History of Philosophy, 2, Oxford, Clarendon Press, 97; auth, What has Cartesianism to do with Jansenism?, Jour Hist Ideas 60 (99): 37-56; auth, Spinoza on the Vacuum, Archiv fur Geschichte der Philosophie 81 Bd., Heft 2 (99): 174-205; auth, The Disappearance of Analogy in Descartes, Spinoza, and Regis, Canadian Jour Philos 30 (00): 85-114; auth, Malebranche, ed. S. Nadler (Cambridge University Press, 00), 59-86. **CONTACT ADDRESS** Dept of Philos, Duke Univ, Box 90734, Durham, NC 27708. **EMAIL** tad.schmaltz@duke.edu

SCHMANDT, JURGEN
DISCIPLINE PHILOSOPHY **EDUCATION** Univ Bonn, PhD, 56. **CAREER** Org Econ Coop & Dev, Paris, 58-65; Harvard Univ, 65, 71; HOUSTON ADV RES CTR, 87-; UNIV TEX, AUSTIN, 71-. **CONTACT ADDRESS** Ctr for Global Studies, Houston Advanced Research Ctr, 4800 Research Forest Dr, Woodlands, TX 77381. **EMAIL** jschmandt@harc.edu

SCHMAUS, WARREN STANLEY
PERSONAL Born 04/02/1952, Staten Island, NY, m, 1979, 2 children **DISCIPLINE** PHILOSOPHY & HISTORY OF SCIENCE **EDUCATION** Princeton Univ, AB, 74; Univ Pittsburgh, MA, 75, PhD(Hist & Philos of Sci), 80. **CAREER** Asst prof Philos, Ill Inst Technol, 80-, res assoc, Study Ethics in Professions, Ill Inst Technol, 80-; asst prof Phil, Ill Inst Technol, 80-85; from assoc prof to prof, 85-95; prof, 95-. **HONORS AND AWARDS** Vis fel, Center for Philosophy of Science, Univ of Pittsburgh, 96-97; vis scholar, Univ Chicago, 87-88. **MEMBERSHIPS** Am Philos Asn; Philos Sci Asn; Hist Sci Soc; Cheiron; Soc Social Studies Sci; HOPOS, Hist of the Philos of Science Working Group. **RESEARCH** Hist and philos of the social sciences. **SELECTED PUBLICATIONS** Auth, Durkheim's Philosophy of Science and the Sociology of Knowledge, Univ of Chicago Press, 94; auth, "Functionalism and the Meaning of Social Facts," Philosophy of Science 66, (99): 314-323; co-ed, Emile Durkheim: Critical Assessments, London, Routledge, 01; some 50 articles and reviews. **CONTACT ADDRESS** Dept of Humanities, Illinois Inst of Tech, 3301 S Dearborn, Chicago, IL 60616-3793. **EMAIL** schmaus@iit.edu

SCHMID, A. ALLAN
PERSONAL Born 03/12/1935, NE, m, 2 children **DISCIPLINE** AGRICULTURAL ECONOMICS **EDUCATION** Univ Nebr, BSc, 56; Univ Wis, PhD, 59. **CAREER** Asst prof, 59-64, assoc prof, 64-68, prof, 68-, Mich State Univ. **HONORS AND AWARDS** Univ Distinguished Prof. **MEMBERSHIPS** Amer Econ Assn; Amer Agric Econ Assn; Assn Evolutionary Econ. **RESEARCH** Institutional and behavioral economics. **SELECTED PUBLICATIONS** Ed, Beyond Agricultural and Economics, 97; coauth, The Economy As a Process of Evaluation, 97; coauth, "Costs and Power," in Nahid Aslanbeigui and Young Back Chois, 97; auth, "The Environment and Property Rights," in Handbook of Environmental Economics, 95; coauth, "Interest Groups, Selective Incentives, Cleverness, History and Emotion: The case of the American Soybean Association," Journ of Economic Behavior and Organization, vol 31, 97. **CONTACT ADDRESS** Dept of Agricultural Economics, Michigan State Univ, East Lansing, MI 48824. **EMAIL** schmid@msu.edu

SCHMID, W. THOMAS
PERSONAL Born 08/22/1946, Chicago, IL, m, 1980, 3 children **DISCIPLINE** PHILOSOPHY **EDUCATION** Yale Univ, BA, 68; PhD, 76. **CAREER** Asst Prof to Prof, Univ NCar, 79-. **HONORS AND AWARDS** Co-chair, 1898 Foundation. **MEMBERSHIPS** IPS, SAGP. **RESEARCH** Ancient Philosophy; Political Philosophy; Race and Social Justice. **SELECTED PUBLICATIONS** Auth, On Manly Courage: A Study of Plato's Laches, S IL Univ Press, 92; auth, Plato's Charmides and the Socratic Ideal of Rationality, SUNY Press, 98. **CONTACT ADDRESS** Dept Relig & Philos, Univ of No Carolina, Wilmington, 601 S Col Rd, Wilmington, NC 28403-3201. **EMAIL** schmidt@uncwil.edu

SCHMIDHAUSER, JOHN RICHARD
PERSONAL Born 01/03/1922, Bronx, NY, m, 1952, 7 children **DISCIPLINE** POLITICAL SCIENCE **EDUCATION** Univ Del, BA, 49; Univ Va, MA, 52; PhD, 54; res fel, 58, inst, judicial process, Univ Wisc; sr fel, law & behavioral sci, 59-60, Law Schl Univ Chicago. **CAREER** Grad instr, 52-54, Dupont Fel, 50-53, Univ Va; instr, 54-55, asst prof, 55-60, res prof, 59, assoc prof, 60-63, prof, 63-65, 67-73, Univ Iowa; res prof, Natl Sci Found Grant, 70-72; prof, 73-92, chmn, 73-75, 77-80, Univ S Calif; Proj '87, grantee, 80-81; Frank Talbot Vis Prof of Govern, 82-83, Univ Va; Wormuth Dist Scholar, 84, Univ Utah; dist vis prof, 84, Simon Fraser Univ, BC; dist vis prof, 85, So Ill Univ. **HONORS AND AWARDS** Phi Kappa Phi, 49; Phi Beta Kappa, 54; Raven Soc, 54; Univ Va Sesquicentennial Awd, pub svc, 69; Phi Sigma Alpha Fac Excel Awd, 84; Golden key Awd for Res, 91; Raubenheimer Awd, dist tchng & res, 91. **SELECTED PUBLICATIONS** Coauth, Age and Political Behavior, Concepts & Issues in Gerontology, Von Nostrand, 75; coauth, Political Corruption and Congress, Gen Lrng Press, 76; auth, Whales and Salmon: The Interface of Pacific Ocean and Cross-National Policy-Making, The Law of the Sea: Issues in Ocean Rsrc Mgt, Praeger Pub, 77; coauth, Whaling in Japanese-American Relations, Westview Press, 78; auth, Future International Shocks Related to Ocean Food Resources, Whaling in Japanese-American Rel, Westview Press, 78; auth, Judges and Justices, Little Brown & Co, 79; auth, Constitutional Law in American Politics, Brooks/Cole Pub, 84; auth, Comparative Judicial Systems: Challenging Frontiers in Conceptual and Empirical Analysis, Butterworths, 87. **CONTACT ADDRESS** Dept of Political Science, Univ of So California, Los Angeles, CA 90007.

SCHMIDT, DARYL DEAN
PERSONAL Born 08/12/1944, Sioux Falls, SD, m, 1993 **DISCIPLINE** NEW TESTAMENT STUDIES **EDUCATION** Bethel Col, BA, 66; Assoc Mennonite Bibl Sem, MDiv, 70; Grad Theol Union, PhD(bibl studies), 79. **CAREER** Instr New Testament, Pac Sch Relig, 77-78; Asst Prof Relig, Tex Christian Univ, 79-. **MEMBERSHIPS** Soc Bibl Lit; Soc New Test St. **RESEARCH** Synoptic gospels; Hellenistic Greek syntax; hist Jesus. **SELECTED PUBLICATIONS** Auth, "The Syntactical Style of 2 Thess: How Pauline is it?" in The Thessalonian Correspondence, ed. Raymond F. Collins, (Louvain Univ Press, 90): 383-93; auth, "Semitisms and Septuagintalisms in the Book of Revelation," New Testament Studies 37, (91): 592-603; auth, "Verbal Aspect in Greek: Two Approaches," in Biblical Greek Language and Linguistics: Open Questions in Current Research, ed. Dono A. Carson and Stanley E. Porter, (Sheffield Academic Press, 93); auth, The Sabbath Day: To Heal or Not to Heal," Dialogue 27, (94); auth, "The Jesus Tradition in the Common Life of Early Christian Communities," in Common Life in the Early Church: Essays Honoring Graydon F. Snyder, ed. Julian Hills, (Trinity Press International, 98); auth, "The Septuagintal Influence in Shaping the Passion Narratives: With Special Attention to Matthew," Forum 1, (9): 95-118; auth, "Sane Eschatology: Albert Schweitzer's Profile of Jesus," Fourm 1, (98): 241-60; auth, Anti-Judaism and the gospel of Luke," in Anti-Judaism and the Gospels, ed. Wm. R. Farmer, (Trinity Press International, 99); auth, "Luke's Preface and the Rhetoric of Hellenistic Historiography," in Jesus and the Heratige of Israel, ed. David P. Moessner, (Trinity Press International, 99). **CONTACT ADDRESS** Dept of Relig, Texas Christian Univ, TCU Box 298100, Fort Worth, TX 76129-0002. **EMAIL** dschmidt@tcu.edu

SCHMIDT, DENNIS
DISCIPLINE PHILOSOPHY **EDUCATION** Bucknell Univ, BA, 74; Boston Col, MA, 76, PhD, 80. **CAREER** Prof, Villanova Univ. **HONORS AND AWARDS** Univ Fac Res awd, 95; PDQWL awd, 93; Univ Res Semester awd; 88; Univ awd

for Excellence in Undergrad Tchg, SUNY, 87; Chancellor's awd for Excellence in Tchg, NY State Univ, 87; SUNY Fac Summer Res grant, 87; Experienced Fac Travel grant, 87; New Fac Develop awd, 85; SUNY Fac Summer Res grant, 84; Phi Beta Kappa, Bucknell Univ, 84; Fulbright-Hays Full Fel, Univ Freiburg, 78; Univ Dissertation awd, Boston Col, 78. **SELECTED PUBLICATIONS** Auth, The Ubiquity of the Finite: Hegel, Heidegger and the Entitlements of Philosophy, MIT Press: Cambridge, MA, 88; What We Owe the Dead, in Revue Philos, 96; Beauty, Encycl Philos Supp, Macmillian Publ Co, 96; The Ordeal of the For, Philos Today, Caputo and Berghofen, 96; What We Didn't See, in The Silverman Lectures, Duquesne UP, 95, rep in The Presocratics After Heidegger, SUNY Press, 96; Putting Oneself in Words.., in Library of Living Philosophers, Open Ct Press, 95; Heidegger and the Greeks / History, Catastrophe and Community, in Heidegger Toward the Turn: Essays on Texts of the 1930's, SUNY Press, 95 & Ruins and Roses: Hegel and Heidegger on Mourning, Sacrifice and History, in Endings: The Question of Memory in Hegel and Heidegger, Northwestern UP, 95; transl, Natural Law and Human Dignity, by Ernst Bloch, MIT Press: Cambridge, MA, 86; ed, Hermeneutics and the Poetic Motion, SUNY/CRIT, 90; auth, On Germans and Other Greeks: Tragedy and Ethnical Life, Indiana Univ Pr, 01. **CONTACT ADDRESS** Dept of Philosophy, Villanova Univ, 800 Lancaster Ave, Villanova, PA 19085-1692.

SCHMIDT, FREDERICK W.
PERSONAL Born 06/20/1953, Louisville, KY, m, 1975, 1 child **DISCIPLINE** NEW TESTAMENT STUDIES **EDUCATION** Asbury Coll, BA, 75; Asbury Theo Seminary, MDiv, 78; Oxford Univ, DPhil, 86. **CAREER** Teaching fel, New Testament Greek, Biblical Studies Dept, Asbury Theological Seminary, 78-80; instr in New Testament Theology, Oxford Univ, 84-86; tutor New Testament Studies, Keble Coll, 86; assoc prof, New Testament Studies, Dept Religion and Philosophy, Messiah Coll, 87-94; dean, Saint George's Coll, 94-95; special asst to the pres, La Salle Univ, 95-96; canon edu, dir, Programs Spirituality and Religious Educ and Acting Program Mgr, Washington Natl Cathedral, 97-00; Dir of Spritual Life and formation, Perkins Sch of Theol, Southern Methodist Univ, Dallas TX, 00-. **HONORS AND AWARDS** Amer Coun Educ Fel, Center Leadership Dev, 96; sr fel, W. F. Albright Inst Arch Res, 95; Young Scholars Fel, Catholic Bibl Assn, Catholic Univ, 93; Who's Who in Bibl Studies in Arch, Bibl Arch Soc, 93. **MEMBERSHIPS** Amer Acad Relig; mem, sec-treas, Anglican Assn Bibl Studies; Soc Bibl Lit; Soc Sci Study Relig; Mem Editorial Bd; LINKS; Episcopal Church Found; Mem Instnl Rev Bd; Nat Insts of Health; Off of Human Subjs Res; Mem The Oxford Soc; Mem The Wash Episcopal Clergy Asn. **RESEARCH** Historical Jesus; early Jewish apocalyptic literature; Spirituality and spiritual formation other theological topics. **SELECTED PUBLICATIONS** Auth, "Anchor Bible Dictionary," ed. by David N. Freedman, Doubleday, Inc. (NY: Doubleday, Inc, 92); auth, "Behind Orthodoxy and Beyond It: Recent Developments in Evangelical Christology," Scottish Journal of Theology 45 (93): 515-541; auth, "Beyond a Biblicistic Feminism: Hermeneutics and Ordained Women," Feminist Theology No. 11 (96): 55-71; auth, A Still Small Voice: Women, Ordination and the Church, Women and Gender in North American Religions, ed, Amanda Porterfield and Mary Farrell Bednarowski, Syracuse: Syracuse University Press, 96; ed, The Changing Face of God, Morehouse Publishing, 00. **CONTACT ADDRESS** So Methodist Univ, PO Box 750133, Dallas, TX 75275-0133. **EMAIL** fschmidt@mail.smu.edu

SCHMIDT, JAMES W.
PERSONAL Born 12/03/1949, Camden, NJ, m, 1975, 2 children **DISCIPLINE** POLITICAL SCIENCE **EDUCATION** Rutgers Univ, BA, 69; MIT, PhD, 74. **CAREER** Asst Prof, Univ Tex at Austin, 75-81; Asst Prof to Prof, Boston Univ, 81-. **HONORS AND AWARDS** Fel, Am Coun of Learned Soc, 78; Fel, NEH, 87-88, 89; James L. Clifford Prize, Am Soc for Eighteenth-Century Studies, 99. **MEMBERSHIPS** Am Soc for Eighteenth-Century Studies; N Am Kant Soc; Intl Soc for the Hist of Ideas; Conf for the Study of Polit Thought. **RESEARCH** The Enlightenment and its critics; Refugee intellectuals during World War II; The concept of 'civil society'. **SELECTED PUBLICATIONS** Auth, "What Enlightenment Was: How Moses Mendelssohn and Immanuel Kant Responded to the Berlinische Monatsschrift," J of the Hist of Philos, (92): 77-102; auth, "The Fool's Truth: Diderot, Goethe, and Hegel," J of the Hist of Ideas, (96): 625-644; ed, What is Enlightenment?: Eighteenth-Century Answers and Twentieth-Century Questions, Univ Calif Press, 96; auth, "Cabbage Heads and Gulps of Water: Hegel on the Terror," Polit Theory, (98): 4-32; auth, "Civility, Enlightenment, and Society: Conceptual Confusions and Kantian Remedies," Am Polit Sci Rev, (98): 419-427; auth, "Language, Mythology, and Enlightenment: Historical Notes on Horkheimer and Adorno's Dialectic of Enlightenment," Soc Res, (98): 807-838; auth, "Is Civility a Virtue?" in Civility, (Univ Notre Dame Press, 00); auth, "What Enlightenment Project?" Polit Theory, (00): 734-757. **CONTACT ADDRESS** Dept Polit Sci, Boston Univ, 745 Commonwealth Ave, Boston, MA 02215. **EMAIL** jschmidt@bu.edu

SCHMIDT, LAWRENCE
PERSONAL Born 02/10/1949, Rochester, NY, m **DISCIPLINE** PHILOSOPHY **EDUCATION** Reed Col, BA, 72; Univ NMex, MA, 78; Universitaet Duisburg, PhD, 83. **CAREER** Teacher, Volkshochschule, Duisburg, 81-83; Lehrbeauftragter, Univ Duisburg, 79-83; instr, Univ of NMex, 84; asst prof to prof, Hendrix Col, 84-. **HONORS AND AWARDS** Excellence in Scholarship, Reed Col, 68, 70, 71; Phi Beta Kappa; Fulbright Scholar, Germany, 79-80, 80-81; NEH Summer Seminar, 94; Fulbright Senior Res Scholar, 99. **MEMBERSHIPS** AAUP; Ark Philos Assoc. **RESEARCH** Primarily Hans-Georg Gadamer's philosophical hermenentics. **SELECTED PUBLICATIONS** Auth, "The Epistemology of Hans-Georg Gadamer: An Analysis of the Legitimization of Vorurteile", Peter D. Lang, (Frankfurt), 85; auth, "When the Text Speaks the Truth: The Preconception of Completion", Southern J of Philos 25.3 (87): 395-405; auth, "Jonathan Edwards' Idealistic Argument From Resistance", Southwest Philos Rev 4.2 (88): 39-47; auth, "The Enlightening Perspective: A Hermeneutic Truth Criterion", Southwest Philos Studies X.3 (88): 83-91; auth, "The Exemplary Status of Translating", Hermeneutics and the Poetic Motion: Translation Perspectives V, ed Dennis J. Schmidt, SUNY (Binghamton, NY, 90): 83-93; ed, The Specter of Relativism: Truth, Dialogue, and Phronesis in Philosophical Hermeneutics, Northwestern Univ Pr, (Evanston, IL), 95; transl, "Verstehen und Willen", by Keys Vuyk, The Specter of Relativism: Truth, Dialogue, and Phronesis in Philosophical Hermeneutics", Northwestern Univ Pr, (Evanston, IL), 95; auth, "Das Einleuchtende: The Enlightening Aspect of the Subject Matter", Phenomenology, Interpretation, and Community, eds Lenore Langsdorf and Stephen H. Watson, SUNY (Binghamton, NY, 96): 175-191; auth, "Effective History, Consciousness of", "Fusion of Horizons", Encyclopedia of Philosophy, Supplement, ed Donald M. Borchert, MacMillan (NY), 96; auth, "Recalling the Hermeneutic Circle", Philos Today 40.2 (96): 263-273; auth, "Tolerance: From A Hermeneutic Perspective", Existentia, VI.VII (96-97): 79-87. **CONTACT ADDRESS** Dept Philos, Hendrix Col, 1600 Washington Ave, Conway, AR 72032-4115. **EMAIL** schmidt@mercury.hendrix.edu

SCHMIDT, MARK
PERSONAL Born 11/17/1953, Dallas, TX, m, 1981, 6 children **DISCIPLINE** ENGLISH, LITERATURE, PHILOSOPHY **EDUCATION** Dallas Bible Col, BS, 76; Univ Tex at Dallas, MA, 80; Univ Tex at Arlington, PhD, 90. **CAREER** Asst prof, Univ of Ark at Monticello, 92-. **RESEARCH** The idea of human nature. **SELECTED PUBLICATIONS** Auth, Human Nature: Opposing Viewpoints, Greenhaven Press, 99; auth, The 1970s: American Decades, Greenhaven Press, 00. **CONTACT ADDRESS** Division Arts & Lang, Univ of Arkansas, Monticello, PO Box 3460, Monticello, AR 71656-3460. **EMAIL** schmidt@uamont.edu

SCHMIDT, PAUL F.
PERSONAL Born 09/14/1925, Rochester, NY, m, 1964 **DISCIPLINE** PHILOSOPHY **EDUCATION** Univ Rochester, BA, 47; Yale Univ, PhD, 51. **CAREER** Instr, Oberlin Col, 51-53; asst prof to prof, philos, chemn 65-76, Univ New Mexico, 53-89. **HONORS AND AWARDS** Phi Beta Kappa, 47. **MEMBERSHIPS** APA; AAUP. **RESEARCH** Whitehead; American philosophy; philosophy of science; Buddhism. **SELECTED PUBLICATIONS** Auth, Religious Knowledge, Free Press, 61; auth, Perception and Cosmology in Whitehead's Philosophy, Rutgers, 67; auth, Rebelling, Loving & Liberation, Hummingbird Press, 71; auth, Temple Reflections, Hummingbird Press, 80; auth, Buddhist Meditation on China, Hummingbird Press, 84. **CONTACT ADDRESS** 2400 Hannett NE, Albuquerque, NM 87106.

SCHMIDT, WILLIAM JOHN
PERSONAL Born 05/22/1926, Green Bay, WI, m, 1949 **DISCIPLINE** CHURCH HISTORY **EDUCATION** N Cent Col, BA, 51; Evangel Theol Sem, BD, 54; Columbia Univ, PhD (church hist), 66. **CAREER** Pastor, Wis Conf Evangel United Brethren Church, 52-62; tutor, Union Theol Sem, 62-65; from asst prof to assoc prof church hist, NY Theol Sem, 67-70; adj assoc prof church hist, 67-70, assoc prof, 70-78, Prof Theol, St Peter's Col, NJ, 78-, Res writer with Samuel McCrea Cavert on The American Churches in the Ecumenical Movement, 00-1968, 65-67; mem Gen Prog Coun, Reformed Church Am, 70-76. **MEMBERSHIPS** Am Soc Church Hist; N Am Acad Ecumenists (secy-treas, 68-72). **RESEARCH** American church history; history of the ecumenical movement; religous syncretism. **SELECTED PUBLICATIONS** Auth, COCU in the crucible, Cath World, 8/68; The morphology of ecumenism, Foundations, 7-9/69; Samuel McCrea Cavert: American bridge to the German church 1945-46, J Presby Hist, spring 73; The sheep market, New Pulpit Digest, 7-8/77; Evolution of an American mind, J Ecumenical Studies, spring 77; The Conciliar Renaissance, Mid-Stream, 4/78; Interpreters of the faith: Samuel McCrea Cavert, A D Mag, 5/78; Architect of Unity: A Biography of Samuel McCrea Cavert, Friendship, 78. **CONTACT ADDRESS** Dept of Theol, Saint Peter's Col, Kennedy Blvd, Jersey City, NJ 07306.

SCHMITT, FREDERICK FRANCIS
PERSONAL Born 04/20/1951, Indianapolis, IN, m, 1981, 1 child **DISCIPLINE** PHILOSOPHY **EDUCATION** Syracuse Univ, BS, 73; Univ Mich, MA, 76, PhD, 80. **CAREER** Vis instr, Univ Southern Calif, 77-78; vis lectr, Univ NC, Chapel Hill, 78-80; from Asst Prof to Assoc Prof, 80-92, Prof Philos, Univ IL, Urbana-Champaign, 92; prof Philos, Indiana Univ, 01-. **HONORS AND AWARDS** Fel, Ohio State Univ, 82; Fel, Ctr for Advanced Study, Urbana, 84; Fel, Univ Melbourne, 95. **MEMBERSHIPS** Am Philos Asn. **RESEARCH** Epistemology; metaphysics; hist of 17th and 18th century philos. **SELECTED PUBLICATIONS** Auth, Change, 78 & Justification as reliable indication or reliable process?, 81, Philos Studies; Knowledge justification and reliability, Synthese, 83; Against epistemic indolence, Mind, 84; Knowledge and Belief, Routledge, 92; ed, Socializing Epistemology: The Social Dimensions of Knowledge, Rowan & Littlefield, 94; auth, Truth: A Primer, Westview Press, 95. **CONTACT ADDRESS** Dept of Philos, Univ of Illinois, Urbana-Champaign, 105 Gregory Hall, Urbana, IL 61801-3611. **EMAIL** fschmitt@uiuc.edu

SCHMITT, RICHARD GEORGE
PERSONAL Born 05/05/1927, Frankfurt, Germany, m, 1961 **DISCIPLINE** PHILOSOPHY **EDUCATION** Univ Chicago, AB, 49, MA, 52; Yale Univ, PhD, 56. **CAREER** Instr, Yale Univ, 56-58; from asst prof to full prof, Brown Univ, 58-, vis assoc prof, Stanford Univ, 67-68; vis prof, Univ Calif, Santa Barbara, 71-72. **HONORS AND AWARDS** Alfred Hodder fel, Princeton Univ, 62-63; Guggenheim fel, 65-66; MA, Brown Univ, 66. **MEMBERSHIPS** Am Philos Asn, Rad Philos Asn. **RESEARCH** Phenomenology; existentialism. **SELECTED PUBLICATIONS** Auth, Maurice Meleau-Ponty, Rev Metaphys, 66; Phenomenology, In: Encycl of Philosophy, Collier-Macmillan, 67; Can Heidegger Be Understood?, Inquiry, 67; Martin Heidegger on Being Human, Random, 69; Alienation and Class, Schenkman, 82; Introduction to Marx and Engels, Westview, 87, 2nd ed, 97; with Tom Moody, Alienation and Social Criticism, Humanities, 94; Beyond Separateness, Westview, 95. **CONTACT ADDRESS** Dept of Philos, Brown Univ, Providence, RI 02912-9127. **EMAIL** rschmitt@net1plus.com

SCHMITTER, AMY
DISCIPLINE HISTORY OF EARLY MODERN PHILOSOPHY, HISTORY OF METAPHYSICS, PHILOSOPHY OF A **EDUCATION** Bryn Mawr Col, AB, 84; grad work, Univ Bonn, 88-89; Univ Pittsburgh, PhD, 93. **CAREER** Asst prof, Univ NMex. **SELECTED PUBLICATIONS** Auth, Representation, Self-Representation, and the Passions in Descartes, Rev of Metaphysics, Vol XVII, No 2, Dec 94; Formal Causation and the Explanation of Intentionality in Descartes, The Monist, Jl 96. **CONTACT ADDRESS** Univ of New Mexico, Albuquerque, Albuquerque, NM 87131. **EMAIL** amys@unm.edu

SCHNABEL, ECKHARD J.
PERSONAL Born 05/09/1955, Stuttgart, Germany, m, 1981, 2 children **DISCIPLINE** NEW TESTAMENT **EDUCATION** Staatsunabhaugige Hochschule, ThM, 79; Univ Aberdeen, PhD, 83. **CAREER** Asst prof, Asia Theol Sem Manila, 85-88; lecturer, Wiedemest Bible Col Ger, 88-94; prof, Freie Theol Acad Ger, 94-98; assoc prof, Trinity Evangelical Div Sch, 98-. **MEMBERSHIPS** Soc of New Testament Studies, Tyndale, Fel, Inst of Biblical Res, Evangelical Theol Soc, Soc of Biblical Lit. **RESEARCH** Early Judaism, Early Christianity, New Testament. **SELECTED PUBLICATIONS** Auth, "Law and Wisdom from Ben Sira to Paul: A Tradition Historical Enquiry into the relation of Law, Wisdom, and Ethics, WUNT 2/16, 85; auth, Inspiration und Offenbarung: Die Lehre vom Ursprung und Wesen der Bibel, 86; auth, Das Reich Gottes als Wirklichkeit und Hoffnung. Neuere Entwicklungen in der evangelikalen Theologie, 93; ed, "Wisdom", Dictionary of Paul and His Letters, Inter-Varsity Press: Downers Grove, 93; auth, Sind Evangelikale Fundamentalisten?, 95; auth, "How Paul Developed His Ethics," Understanding Paul's Ethics, Twentieth-Century Approaches, Grand Rapids (95): 267-297; auth, "Mission, Early Non-Pauline," Dictionary of the Later New Testament and Its Developments, (97): 752-775. **CONTACT ADDRESS** Dept New Testament, Trinity Intl Univ, Col of Arts and Sciences, 2065 Half Day Rd, Deerfield, IL 60015-1241. **EMAIL** eschnabel@trin.edu

SCHNAITER, SAMUEL E.
PERSONAL Born 02/11/1942, Martinsville, IN, m, 1968, 4 children **DISCIPLINE** NEW TESTAMENT LANGUAGE AND LITERATURE **EDUCATION** Purdue Univ, BA; MA; PhD. **CAREER** Prof, Bob Jones Univ, 32 years. **MEMBERSHIPS** ETS. **RESEARCH** New Testament textual criticism. **SELECTED PUBLICATIONS** Auth, Biblical Manuscripts and the Providence of God, forthcoming; auth of articles in Detroit Baptist J and Biblical Viewpoint. **CONTACT ADDRESS** Dept Ancient Languages, Bob Jones Univ, 1700 Wade Hampton Blvd, Greenville, SC 29614-1000. **EMAIL** sschait@bju.edu

SCHNEEWIND, JEROME B.
PERSONAL Born 05/17/1930, m, 3 children **DISCIPLINE** PHILOSOPHY **EDUCATION** Cornell Univ, BA, 51; Princeton Univ, MA, 53, PhD, 57. **CAREER** Prof, Johns Hopkins

Univ, 81-. **MEMBERSHIPS** APA, Am Acad of Arts and Sci. **RESEARCH** Philosophy; Victorian literature; Victorian morality. **SELECTED PUBLICATIONS** Auth, Backgrounds of English Victorian Literature, 70; "Moral Problems and Moral Philosophy in the Victorian Period," 71; "Moral Knowledge and Moral Principles," 70; Sidgwick's Ethics and Victorian Moral Philosophy, 86; Moral Philosophy from Montaigne to Kant: An Anthology, 90; "Classical Republicanism and the History of Ethics," 93; "Locke's Moral Philosophy," 94; "Voluntarism and the Foundations of Ethics," 96; Immanuel Kant: Lectures on Ethics, 97; The Invention of Autonomy: A History of Modern Moral Philosophy, 98. **CONTACT ADDRESS** Dept of Philosophy, Johns Hopkins Univ, Baltimore, 3400 N Charles St, Baltimore, MD 21218.

SCHNEIDER, CARL E.
PERSONAL Born 02/23/1948, Exeter, CT, m **DISCIPLINE** LAW **EDUCATION** Harvard Univ, BA, 72; Univ Mich Law Sch, JD, 79. **CAREER** Adv on educ policy, Mass Tchrs Asn, 72-75; law clerk, US Court of Appeals for the District of Columbia Circuit, 79-80; law clerk to Hon Potter Stewart, Assoc Justice, US Supreme Court, 80-81; prof law, Univ Mich Law School, 81- ; prof Internal Med, Univ Mich Med Sch, 98- . **MEMBERSHIPS** Fel, Hasting Ctr; Am Soc Law, Med, & Ethics; Int Asn of Bioethics; Acad Adv Bd, Inst for Am Values; Int Soc of Family Law; AALS; Order of the Coif. **RESEARCH** Moral culture of the American family; moral culture of medical decisions. **SELECTED PUBLICATIONS** Auth, The Tension Between Rules and Discretion in Family Law: A Report and a Reflection, Family Law Q, 93; auth, Bioethics with a Human Face, Indiana Law J, 94; auth, Bioethics in the Language of the Law, Hastings Ctr Rpt, 94; auth, Marriage, Morals, and the Law: No-Fault Divorce and Moral Discourse, Utah Law Rev, 94; auth, The Decision to Withdraw from Dialysis, Advan in Renal Replacement Therapy, 94; auth, The Frail Old Age of the Socratic Method, Law Quadrangle Notes, 94; auth, Triumph and Crisis: The Autonomy Principle in the American Law of Medicine, Jurisuto, 95; auth, The Socratic Method and the Goals of Legal Education: With Some Thoughts Inspired by Travel, Hogaku Kyoshitsu, 95; auth, Medical Decisions at the End of Life: Cruzan, Advance Directives, and Individual Autonomy, Jurisuto, 95; auth, From Consumer Choice to Consumer Welfare, Hastings Ctr Rpt, 95; coauth, Medical Decisions in the Moral Lives of Patients, Bull of the Europ Soc of Philos of Med and Health Care, 95; auth, On the Duties and Rights of Parents, Va Law Rev, 95; auth, The Law and the Stability of Marriage: The Family as a Social Institution, in Popenoe, ed, Promises to Keep: Decline and Renewal of Marriage in America, Rowman & Littlefield, 96; coauth, An Invitation to Family Law: Principles, Process, and Perspectives, West, 96; auth, Moral Discourse, Bioethics, and the Law, Hastings Ctr Rpt, 96; auth, Making Sausage, Hastings Ctr Rpt, 97; auth, Testing Testing, Hastings Ctr Rpt, 97; auth, Hard Cases, Hastings Ctr Rpt, 98; auth, The Book Review Issue: An Owner's Manual, Mich Law Rev, 98; auth, The Practice of Autonomy: Patients, Doctors, and Medical Decisions, Oxford, 98. **CONTACT ADDRESS** Law School, Univ of Michigan, Ann Arbor, 625 S State St, 341 HH, Ann Arbor, MI 48109-1215. **EMAIL** carlschn@umich.edu

SCHNEIDER, CATHY
DISCIPLINE COMPARATIVE POLITICS AND POLITICAL THEORY **EDUCATION** SUNY Albany, BA, MA; Cornell Univ, MA, PhD. **CAREER** Prof, Am Univ. **HONORS AND AWARDS** Aaron Diamond Post-Doctoral Fel, 93-96. **RESEARCH** Past dependency in social movements in neighborhood organization. **SELECTED PUBLICATIONS** Auth, Shantytown Protest in Pinochet's Chile,Temple Univ Press, 95. **CONTACT ADDRESS** American Univ, 4400 Massachusetts Ave, Washington, DC 20016.

SCHNEIDER, LAUREL
PERSONAL Born Newton, MA **DISCIPLINE** THEOLOGY **EDUCATION** Dartmouth Col, AB, 83; Harvard Univ, Mdiv, 90; Vanderbilt Univ, MA, 94; PhD, 97. **CAREER** Asst Prof of Theology, Ethics & Culture, The Chicago Theological Seminary, 99-; Asst Prof of Religious Studies, North Central Col, 96-99; Instr, Religious Studies, Colby Col, 95-96. **HONORS AND AWARDS** Dissinger Awd for Teaching, North Central Coll, 98; Graduate Awd for Dissertation Research, Vanderbilt,98; Harold Sterling Vanderbilt Fel, 91-94; Chase Peace Prize, 83. **MEMBERSHIPS** Amer Acad of Religion; Society for Study of Native Amer Religious Traditions; Water (Women's Alliance for Theology, Ethics, & Ritual). **RESEARCH** Feminist Theologies; Doctrines of God; Native Amer Religious Traditions. **SELECTED PUBLICATIONS** Auth, "The Courage to See and to Sin: Mary Daly's Elemental Transformation of Paul Tillich's Ontology," in Re-Reading the Canon: Feminist Interpretations of Mary Daly edited by Marilyn Frye and Sarah Lucia Hoagland, Philadelphia: Pennsylvania State Univ Press, 00; auth, "Queer Theory," in The Postmodern Handbook for Biblical Scholars, edited by A,K.M. Adam, St. Louis, Chalice Press, 00; auth, "Homosexuality, Queer Theory, and Christian Theology," in Religious Studies Review Volume 26, Number 1, 00: pp 3-12; rev, "The Serpent and the Goddess by Mary Condren," HarperCollins, 89, auth, "Re-Imaging the Divine: Confronting the Backlash to Feminist Theology, Cleveland: Pilgrim Press, 99. **CONTACT ADDRESS** Dept Theology, Chicago Theol Sem, 5757 S Univ Ave, Chicago, IL 60637-1507. **EMAIL** lschneider@chgosem.edu

SCHNEIDER, ROBERT J.
PERSONAL Born 02/28/1939, Saginaw, MI, m, 1997 **DISCIPLINE** MEDIEVAL STUDIES, RELIGIOUS STUDIES **EDUCATION** Univ of the South, BA, 61; Univ of Notre Dame, MSM, 63, DSM, 65. **CAREER** Asst prof, 65-68, Univ of Southern CA; asst prof, 68, assoc 72, prof, 81, distinguished prof of general studies, 98, Berea Col. **HONORS AND AWARDS** Seabury Awd for Excellence in Teaching, 89; Acorn Awd for excellence in teaching and scholarship, 93; Templeton Found Sci and Relig Course Prize, 97. **MEMBERSHIPS** Medieval Acad of Amer; Soc for Values in Higher Education; Episcopal Church Working Group on Science, Technology, and Faith. **RESEARCH** Issues in science and religion. **SELECTED PUBLICATIONS** Auth, Vincent of Beauvais' Opus universale de statu principis: A Reconstruction of Its History and Contents, in Vincent de Beauvais: intentions et receptions d'une oeuvre encyclopedique au moyen-age, 91; coauth, The Medieval Circulation of the De morali principis institutione of Vincent of Beauvais, Viator, 91; auth, Vincentii belvacensis De morali principis institutione, 95; auth, Vincent of Beauvais, Dominican Author: From Compilatio to Tractatus, in Lector et compilator, Vincent de Beauvais, Frere Precheur: un intellectuel et son milieu au XIIIe siecle, 97. **CONTACT ADDRESS** Dept of Foreign Lang, Berea Col, 113 Tremont Dr, Berea, KY 40403. **EMAIL** robert_schneider@berea.edu

SCHNEIDER, SAMUEL
PERSONAL Born 08/26/1907, Yonkers, NY, w, 1936, 3 children **DISCIPLINE** PHILOSOPHY **EDUCATION** NYork Univ, PhD, 69. **CAREER** Hunter Col, tchr, adj assoc prof, 54-58. **HONORS AND AWARDS** CCNY, Phi Beta Kappa, 1930 **MEMBERSHIPS** Philo of Edu Society **RESEARCH** Philosophy of Education **SELECTED PUBLICATIONS** Auth, An Identification, Analysis and Critique of Thorstein Veblen's Philosophy of Higher Education, Edwin Mellen Press, 98; Three American Economics Professors Battle Against Monopoly and Pricing Practices, Ripley, Fetter and Commons: Three for the People, Edwin Mellen Press, 98. **CONTACT ADDRESS** Dept Judaic Studies, Yeshiva Univ, 500 W 185th St, New York, NY 10033-3299.

SCHNEIDERS, SANDRA MARIE
PERSONAL Born 11/12/1936, Chicago, IL **DISCIPLINE** NEW TESTAMENT STUDIES, CHRISTIAN SPIRITUALITY **EDUCATION** Marygrove Col, BA, 60; Univ Detroit, MA, 67; Cath Inst, Paris, STL, 71; Gregorian Univ, Rome, STD, 75. **CAREER** Instr philos, Marygrove Col, 65-67, instr relig studies, 71-72; from asst prof to assoc prof, 76-89, prof New Testament & Spirituality, Jesuit Sch Theol, 89-. **HONORS AND AWARDS** Assoc Theol Sch res grant, 78; elected to Delta Epsilon Sigma, Nat Catholic Hon Soc, 87; Book-of-the-Year, for: New Wineskins, Human Development V.8:1, Spring 87; The Twentieth Century Awd for Achievement, Int Biog Ctr, 93; Honorary Degrees from St. Mary's Col, Lafayette Col, and St. Bernard's Inst; Christian Culture Gold Medalist, Assumption Univ, 94; Teresa of Avila Awd, Long Island Women's Ordination Conf, 94. **MEMBERSHIPS** Am Academy and Religion; Cath Bibl Asn; Soc Bibl Lit; Cath Theol Soc Am; Cath Comn on Intellectual and Cultural Affairs; Soc Study Christian Spirituality, vice-pres, 96, pres, 97; Soc New Testament Studies. **RESEARCH** Gospel of St John; Biblical hermeneutics; spirituality. **SELECTED PUBLICATIONS** Auth, Women and the Word: The Gender of God in the New Testament and the Spirituality of Women, Paulist Press, 86; New Wineskins: Re-Imagining Religious Life Today, Paulist Press, 86; Beyond Patching: Faith and Feminism in the Catholic Church, Paulist Press, 90; Feminist Spirituality: Christian Alternative or Alternative to Christianity?, in Women's Spirituality: Resources for Christian Development, Paulist Press, 2nd ed, 96; A Case Study: A Feminist Interpretation of John 4:1-42, in The Interpretation of John, T&T Clark, 2nd ed, 97; Biblical Spirituality: Life, Literature, and Learning, in Doors of Understanding: Conversations in Global Spirituality in Honor of Ewert Cousins, Franciscan Press, 97; author of numerous articles and other book chapters; auth, The Revelatory Text: Interpreting the New Testament as Sacred Scripture, 2nd edition Liturgical Press, 99; auth, Written That You May Believe, Crossroad/Herder, 99; auth, Finding the Treasure: Locating Catholic Religious Life in a New Ecclesial and Cultural Context Pawlist, 00; With Oil in Their Lamps: Faith, Feminism, and the Future, Pawlist, 00. **CONTACT ADDRESS** Jesuit Sch of Theol, Berkeley, 1735 LeRoy Ave, Berkeley, CA 94709-1193. **EMAIL** sschneide@jstb.edu

SCHNER, GEORGE
PERSONAL Born 05/22/1946, St. Boniface, MB, Canada, s **DISCIPLINE** PHILOSOPHY; THEOLOGY **EDUCATION** BA, 69, MA, 70, Gonzaga Univ; Mdiv, 74, Regis Col; PhD, 80, Yale Univ. **CAREER** Lectr, 69, 74, Gonzaga Univ; Lectr, 70, Concordia Univ; Prize Teach Fel, 77, Yale Univ; Lectr, 79, Asst Prof, 80, Dir of Basic Degree Studies, 81-88, Asst to the Pres of Academic Affairs, 84-85, Academic Dean, 85-89, Assoc Prof, 87, Dir of Advanced Degree Studies, 93-96, Acting Academic Dean, 94, Regis Col; Chr Basic Degree Council, 84-86, Chr Advanced Degree Council, 93-95, Chr Theology, 96, Toronto School of Theology. **MEMBERSHIPS** Amer Acad of Religion; Canadian Phil Assoc; Canadian Theological Soc; Catholic Theological Soc Amer; Jesuit Phil Assoc. **RESEARCH** Philosophy; Theology **SELECTED PUBLICATIONS** Auth, On Theology: A Speech to its Cultured Despisers, 90; Response to Issues Research Seminar, Thological Education, 90; McClelland and Buckley on Modern Athesim, Toronto Journal of Theology, 91; Hume's Dialogues and the Redefinition of the Philosophy of Religion, The Thomist, 91; The Eclipse of Biblical Narrative: Analysis and Critique, Modern Theology, 92; The Appeal to Experience, Theological Studies, 92; Education for Ministry, 93; Post Liberal Theology and Roman Catholic Theology, Religious Studies Review, 95; Christian Spirituality and the Culture of Modernity: The Thought of Louis Dupre, 98; Theological Method After Liberalism, forthcoming. **CONTACT ADDRESS** Regis Col, Ontario, 15 St. Mary St., Toronto, ON, Canada M4Y 2R5. **EMAIL** gschner@chass.utoronto.ca

SCHOEDEL, WILLIAM RICHARD
PERSONAL Born 01/10/1930, Stratford, ON, Canada, m, 1956, 3 children **DISCIPLINE** RELIGION **EDUCATION** Univ Western Ont, BA, 51, MA, 52; Univ Chicago, PhD (relig), 63. **CAREER** From instr to assoc prof relig, Brown Univ, 60-70; dir relig studies, Univ Ill, Urbana, 70-76, prof classics, 70-80. **MEMBERSHIPS** Am Acad Relig; Am Soc Church Hist; Am Soc Studies Relig; Soc Bibl Lit. **RESEARCH** Classical and early Christian literature. **SELECTED PUBLICATIONS** Auth, A blameless mind not on loan, J Theol Studies, 64; The Apostiolic Fathers, Nelson, Vol V, 67; Pauline thought, In: Essays in Divinity, Univ Chicago, Vol VI, 68; Topological theology and some monistic tendencies in gnosticism, In: Essays on the Nag Hammadi Texts in Honour of Alexander Bohlig, 72; Athenagoras: Legatio and De resurrectione, Clarendon, Oxford, 72. **CONTACT ADDRESS** 1207 S Race, Urbana, IL 61801.

SCHOEN, EDWARD LLOYD
PERSONAL Born 12/16/1949, Providence, RI **DISCIPLINE** PHILOSOPHY **EDUCATION** Wheaton Col, IL, AB, 71; Univ Southern CA, MA, 74, PhD, 76. **CAREER** From Asst Prof to Assoc Prof, 76-85, Prof Philos, Western KY Univ, 85; Contrib ed philos, J Psychol & Theol, 76-; ed consult philos, Pacific Philos Quart, 78-81. **MEMBERSHIPS** Am Philos Asn; Soc Philos Relig; Soc Christian Philos. **RESEARCH** Epistemology; Relig and Sci. **SELECTED PUBLICATIONS** Auth, Religious Explanations: A Model from the Sciences, Duke Univ Press, 85; auth, David Hume and the Mysterious Shroud of Turin, Relig Stud, 91; Galileo and the Church: An Untidy Affair, Philos in the Contemp World, Fall 95; Philosophy 310: Religion, Science, and Contemporary Life, Sci & Relig Courses (forthcoming); Between Addition and Difference: A Place for Religious Critiques of the Sciences, Zygon, 98; Perceiving an Imperceptible God, Relig Studies, vol. 34; auth of numerous other articles. **CONTACT ADDRESS** Dept of Philos & Relig, Western Kentucky Univ, 1 Big Red Way St, Bowling Green, KY 42101-3576. **EMAIL** edward.schoen@wku.edu

SCHOENFELD, MARCUS
PERSONAL Born 07/01/1933, New York, NY, 2 children **DISCIPLINE** LAW **EDUCATION** Harvard Univ, AB, 54, JD, 57; NYork Univ, LLM, 62. **CAREER** From instr to asst prof law, Cleveland-Marshall Law Sch, 63-66; assoc prof, 66-69, Prof Law, Villanova Univ, 69- ; Ford fel, NYU, 63 & 65. **MEMBERSHIPS** Am Bar Asn. **RESEARCH** Taxation. **SELECTED PUBLICATIONS** Auth, Tax Management Portfolio-Moving Expenses, Bur Nat Affairs, 70-76; contribr, Non Profit Organizations, Prentice-Hall, 68. **CONTACT ADDRESS** Sch of Law, Villanova Univ, 299 N Spring Mill Rd, Villanova, PA 19085-1597. **EMAIL** Schoenfe@law.vill.edu

SCHOENING, JEFFREY D.
PERSONAL Born 04/16/1953, Providence, RI, m, 1984 **DISCIPLINE** RELIGIOUS STUDIES **EDUCATION** Amherst Coll, BA, 76; Univ Wash, MA, 83; Univ Wash, MLS, 85; PhD, 91. **CAREER** Vis lectr, Univ Wash, 92, 94-96, 99-00; DIR, Virupa Ecumenical Inst, Seattle Wash, 98-. **HONORS AND AWARDS** Fulbright-Hays Doctoral Dissertation Fel, 87-88. **RESEARCH** Tibetan Buddhism; Mahayana Buddhism. **SELECTED PUBLICATIONS** Auth, The Salistamba Sutra and Its Indian Commentaries, Wien, 95; Sutra Commentaries in Tibetan Translation, Tibetan Lit: Studies In Genre, 96. **CONTACT ADDRESS** 6817 27th Ave NE, Seattle, WA 98115-7140. **EMAIL** jdschoe@juno.com

SCHOLER, DAVID M.
PERSONAL Born 07/24/1938, Rochester, MN, m, 1960, 2 children **DISCIPLINE** NEW TESTAMENT **EDUCATION** Wheaton College, BA 60, MA, 64; Gordon Divinity Sch, BD, 64; Harvard Divinity Sch, ThD, 80. **CAREER** Asst to assoc prof, Gordon-Conwell Theol Sem, 69-81; Dean, Prof, Northern Baptist Theol Sem, 81-88; Distinguished Prof, North Park Theol Sem, 88-94; prof, assoc dean, Fuller Theol Sem, 94-. **MEMBERSHIPS** Amer Acad of Rel; Chicago Soc of Biblical Res; Catholic Biblical Asn; Inst for Biblical Res; Natl Assoc of Baptist Prof of Rel; North Amer Patristic Soc; Soc of Biblical Lit; Studiorum Novi; Testamenti Soc. **RESEARCH** Women in

the early Church; Gnosticism; Separation of Church and Judaism; Eng Trans of the New Testament. **SELECTED PUBLICATIONS** Asst ed, The Encyclopedia of Modern Christian Missions: The Agencies, Camden Thomas Nelson and Sons, 67; Auth, Nag Hammadi Bibliography 1948-1969, Leiden, E.J. Brill, 71; The Caring God: Biblical Models of Discipleship, Valley Forge, Judson, 89; Gnosticism in the Early Church, Studies in Early Christianity 14, NY and London, ed, Garland, 93; Perspectives on Ethical and Social Issues: Essays in Honor of Culbert Gerow Rutenber, NABPR Festschrift Series 11, Macon, National Assoc of Baptist Prof of Rel, 94; Nag Hammadi Bibliography 1970-1994, Nag Hamadi and Manichaean Studies 32, Leiden, E.J. Brill, 97. **CONTACT ADDRESS** Fuller Theol Sem, Pasadena, CA 91182. **EMAIL** dscholer@fuller.edu

SCHOLZ, DANIEL J.
PERSONAL Born 07/31/1960, Milwaukee, WI, m, 1997, 3 children **DISCIPLINE** THEOLOGY **EDUCATION** Mundelein Col, MA, 85; Marquette Univ, PhD, 97. **CAREER** Pius XI High School, dept ch, 86-; Adjunct Faculty Member, Marquette Univ, St Francis Seminary. **MEMBERSHIPS** AAR, SBL, CBA. **CONTACT ADDRESS** Dept of Theology Chair, Pius XI High Sch, 2603 N 89th St, Wauwatosa, WI 53226. **EMAIL** dbscholz@execpc.com

SCHOLZ, SALLY J.
PERSONAL Born 04/05/1968, Eugene, OR, m, 1996 **DISCIPLINE** PHILOSOPHY; ETHICS **EDUCATION** Univ Portland, BA, 89; MA, 91, PhD, 93, Purdue Univ. **CAREER** Villanova Univ. **MEMBERSHIPS** Amer Phil Assoc; North Amer Soc for Social Phil; Intl Soc for Value Inquiry; Amer Soc for Value Inquiry; Soc for Phil in Contemporary World; Concerned Philosophers for Peace; Radical Phil Assoc. **RESEARCH** Social and political philosophy; ethics; feminist theory **SELECTED PUBLICATIONS** Auth, Civil Disobedience in the Social Theory of Thomas Aquinas, The Thomist, 96; A Feminist Look at Ferdinand Schoeman's Privacy and Social Freedom Rending and Renewing the Social Order, Social Philosophy Today Book series, 96; Coauth, Seven Principles for Better Practical Ethics, Teaching Philosophy, 96; Auth, Service Learning in Ethics: A New Pedagogical Approach to Old Theory v. Practice Problem, Beyond the Tower: Philosophy in Service Learning, 98; The Dignity of Work and Economic Concerns, Visions and Values, 98; Can Opressed Groups dialogue? Self-Determination, Power, and Coercion in Iris Young's Dialogic Community, Crossing Cultural Boundaries, forthcoming; Peacemaking in Domestic Violence: From and Ethics of Care to an Ethics of Advocacy, Journal of Social Philosophy, forthcoming; The Duty of Solidarity: Catholic Social Teaching and Feminist Moral Theory, Philosophy in the Contemporary World, forthcoming; Values and Language: Toward a Theory of Translation for Alain Locke, Alain Locke and Values, forthcoming; Catcalls and Military Strategy, Peacemaking: Lessons from the Past, Visions for the Future, forthcoming. **CONTACT ADDRESS** Dept of Philosophy, Villanova Univ, 800 Lancaster Ave, Villanova, PA 19085-1699. **EMAIL** sally.scholz@villanova.edu

SCHOLZ, SUSANNE
PERSONAL Born 03/14/1963, Frankfurt/Main, Germany **DISCIPLINE** THEOLOGY **EDUCATION** Univ of Heidelberg, Germany, Erstes Kirchliches Examen, 89; Union Theo Sem NYork, STM, 91, MA, 94, PhD, 97. **CAREER** Adj Prof, 97-98, Fordham Univ; Asst Prof, Biblical Studies, Coll of Wooster, Wooster OH. **HONORS AND AWARDS** WCC Scholarship. **MEMBERSHIPS** SBL, AAR, ESWTR, NAPH. **RESEARCH** Biblical cultural studies, feminist Biblical studies. **SELECTED PUBLICATIONS** Auth, Through Whose Eyes? A Right Reading of Genesis 34, in: Genesis, A Feminist Companion to the Bible, ed, A Brenner, Sheffield Univ Press Sheffield, 98; Exodus, Was Befreiung aus seiner Sicht bedeutet, in: Kompendium Feministische Bibelauslegung, eds L Schottroff & M-T Wacker, Gutersloh, Gutersloher Verlagshaus, 98; Was It Really Rape in Genesis 34? Biblical Scholarship as a Reflection of Cultural Assumptions, in: Escaping Eden; auth, New Feminist Perspectives on the Bible, eds H. Washington S L Graham & P Thimmes, Sheffield Academic Press, Sheffield, 99; Sodom and Gomorrah (Gen 19:1-29) on the Internet, The Implications of the Internet for the Study of the Bible, in: Journal of Religion and Society 1(99); auth, Restrospecting Rape in Christian Commentaries of Genesis 34, NY, Peter Lang, 00; coed, Zwischen-Raume, Deutsche feministische Theologinnen im Ausland, Munster, LIT-Verlag, 00. **CONTACT ADDRESS** Dept of Religious Studies, The Col of Wooster, Wooster, OH 44691. **EMAIL** sscholz@acs.wooster.edu

SCHONFELD, MARTIN
PERSONAL Born 02/20/1963, Regensburg, Germany, M, 2000 **DISCIPLINE** PHILOSOPHY **EDUCATION** Univ Regensburg, BA, 84; Ludwigs-Maximilian Universitat, Munich, BA, 86; Univ Georgia, MA, 88; Indiana Univ, PhD, 95. **CAREER** Asst prof, Univ S Fla, 95- . **HONORS AND AWARDS** Studienstiftung fel, 85-90; MacArthur Found Fel, 91; creative scholar grants, 96, 98; USF Teaching Awd, 98. **MEMBERSHIPS** APA; Fl Philos Assoc; N Am Kant Soc; Soc for Asian and Comp Philos; Int Soc for Environ Ethics; Soc for the Study of Ethics and Animals. **RESEARCH** History of philosophy and science: eighteenth century; Kant; current environmental philosophy; Chinese philosophy. **SELECTED PUBLICATIONS** "Who or What Has Moral Standing?," American Philosophical Quarterly 29 (92); auth, Dogmatic Metaphysics and E.W. v. Tschirnhaus's methodology, J of the Hist of Philos 36, 98; auth, "Was There A Western Inventor of Porcelain? Technol and Culture 39, (98); auth, The Philosophy of the Young Kant: The Precritical Project, Oxford, 00; "German Philosophy after Leibniz," in Blackwell Companion to Early Modern Philosophy, ed. S. Nader, (Blackwell, 01). **CONTACT ADDRESS** FAO 248, Univ of So Florida, Tampa, FL 33620. **EMAIL** mschonfe@chuma.cas.usf.edu

SCHOONER, STEVEN L.
PERSONAL Born 05/20/1960, Ft Lewis, WA, m, 1990, 1 child **DISCIPLINE** LEGAL STUDIES **EDUCATION** Rice Univ, BA, 82; William and Mary, JD, 85; George Washington Univ, LLM, 89. **CAREER** Assoc, Wickwire, Gavin & Gibbs, Vienna, Va, 85-86; Comn, Armed Serv Bd of Contract Appeals, Falls Church Va Army Jag Corps, 86-89; Assoc, Seyfarth, Shaw, Fairweather & Geraldson, Wash DC, 89-91; Trial Atty, Dept of Justice, Civil Div Com Litigation Br, Wash DC, 91-96; Assoc Adminr for Procurement Law and Legislation, Office of Fed Procurement Policy, Office of Management and Budget, Exec Office of the Pres, Wash DC, 96-98; Adj Prof, The Judge Advocate General's Sch of the Army, Charlottesville, Va, US Army JAG Corps Reserves, 91-; Assoc Prof, George Washington Law Sch, Wash DC, 98-. **HONORS AND AWARDS** Fed Bar Asn Young Fed Lawyer Awd, 89. **MEMBERSHIPS** Am Bar Asn Nat Contrast Management Asn. **RESEARCH** Government Contract Law, Federal Procurement Policy. **SELECTED PUBLICATIONS** Rev, of "Contracts Disputes Act: Annotated," by Robert T. Peacock and Peter D. Ting, 28 Public Contract Law J 117 (98) and VIV The Clause 9 (Jan 99); ed, "Protests Serve Public as Watchdog," Fed Comput Week 17 (Mar 99); auth, "Feature Comment -- The Future of 'Businesslike' Government: The CBD Asserts Its Rights Against Debtor Federal Agencies," 41 Govt Contractor 112 (Mar 99); auth, "The FTCA Discretionary Function Exception Nullifies $25 Million Malpractice Judgement Against DCAA: A Sigh of Relief Concludes the DIVAD Contract Saga," The Army Lawyer (Mar 99):17; auth, "Who's Watching Now?," Legal Times (Apr 26, 99): S27; auth, "Mixed Messages: Heightened Complexity In Social Policies Favoring Small Business Interests," 8 Public Procurement Law Rev CS78-3 (99); coauth, "The CDA At Twenty: A Brief Assessment of BCA Activity," 34 Procurement Lawyer 10 -4 (Summer 99); auth, "Pondering The Decline of Federal Government Contract Litigation in the United States," 8 Public Procurement Law Rev 242 (99); auth, "What next? A Heuristic Approach to Revitalizing the Contract Disputes Act of 1978," 28 Public Contract Law J 635 (99). **CONTACT ADDRESS** Sch of Law, The George Washington Univ, 2029 G St NW, Washington, DC 20006-4211. **EMAIL** sschooner@main.nlc.gwu.edu

SCHORSCH, ISMAR
PERSONAL Born 11/03/1935, Hanover, Germany, m, 1960, 3 children **DISCIPLINE** JEWISH HISTORY **EDUCATION** Ursinus Col, BA, 57; Columbia Univ, MA, 61, PhD(hist), 69; Jewish Theol Sem, MHL, 62. **CAREER** Instr Jewish hist, Jewish Theol Sem Am, 67-68; instr, Columbia Univ, 68, asst prof, 68-70; assoc prof, 70-76, prof, 76-80, Rabbi Herman Abramovitz Prof Jewish Hist, Jewish Theol Sem Am, 80-, Dean, Grad Sch, 75-; Mem Found Jewish Cult grant, 73-76. **HONORS AND AWARDS** Ansley Awd, Columbia Univ Press, 69; Litt D (hon), Wittenberg Univ, 89, Ursinus Col, 90, Gratz Col, 95, Russian State Univ, 96. **MEMBERSHIPS** Leo Baeck Inst (pres); fel Am Acad Jewish Res. **RESEARCH** Modern German Jewish history; Jewish historiography; modern Jewish history. **SELECTED PUBLICATIONS** Auth, The philosophy of history of Nachman Krochmal, Judaism, 61; Moritz Gudemann: Rabbi, historian and apologist, Leo Baeck Inst Yearbk, 66; Jewish Reactions to German Anti-Semitism, 1870-1914, Columbia Univ, 72; German antisemitism in the light of post-war historiography, Leo Baeck Inst Yearbk, Vol XIX, 74; translator & ed, Heinrich Graetz's, The Structure of Jewish History and Other Essays, Jewish Theol Sem Am, 75; auth, From Wolfenbuttel to Wissenschaft: The divergent careers of Isaac M Jost and Leopold Zunz, Leo Baeck Inst Yearbk, Vol XXI, 76; Historical reflections on the Holocaust, Conservative Judaism, fall-winter 76-77; auth, From Text to Context: The Turn to History in Modern Judaism, 94. **CONTACT ADDRESS** Dept of Hist, Jewish Theol Sem of America, 3080 Broadway, New York, NY 10027-4650. **EMAIL** isschorsch@jtsa.edu

SCHOTCH, PETER K.
PERSONAL Born 07/26/1946 **DISCIPLINE** PHILOSOPHY IN LITERATURE, INTERMEDIATE LOGIC, STOICISM. **EDUCATION** Waterloo Univ, PhD, 73. **CAREER** Prof, 84-. **RESEARCH** Formal logic and its applications, philosophy of Descartes, the early Stoa. **SELECTED PUBLICATIONS** Auth, Paraconsistent Logic: The View from the Right, PSA 92; Remarks on Copenhagen Semantics, Essays in Honour of R.E. Jennings, Simon Fraser Univ, 93; Hyperdeontic Logic: An Overview, Social Rules, Westview Press, Boulder, 96; co-auth, Logic on the Track of Social Change, Oxford, Clarenden, 95. **CONTACT ADDRESS** Dept of Philos, Dalhousie Univ, Halifax, NS, Canada B3H 3J5. **EMAIL** peter.schotch@dal.ca

SCHOUBORG, GARY
PERSONAL Born 03/02/1936, Beatrice, NB, d, 1978 **DISCIPLINE** PHILOSOPHICAL PSYCHOLOGY **EDUCATION** Univ Texas, Austin, PhD, 78. **CAREER** General partner and founder, Performance Consulting, 89-. **MEMBERSHIPS** APA; Am Psychol Assoc; Am Psychol Soc. **RESEARCH** Philosophy of mind, especially consciousness. **SELECTED PUBLICATIONS** Auth, It Ain't Whatcha Do, It's the Way Thatcha Do It, Inguiring Mind,99; auth, Review: Beyond Religion , by David N. Elkins, Dialogues, 99; auth, Review: Zen and the Brain, By James H. Austin, Journal of Consciousness Studies, 99; auth, Science and Soteriology: A Review of Fenner's Reasoning into Reality, Meta (online journal), 99; auth, Three Approaches to Consciousness: Phenomenology, Hermeneutics, and Systems-Cybernetics, Journal of Consciousness Studies, 99; auth, A Pragmatic View of Enlightenment: The Science of Enlightenment, by Nitin Trasi.network: The Scientific and Medical Network Review, 00; auth, What We Learn in the Dark, Realization.org magazine, 00; auth, Love Letter from the Abyss (poem), Journal of Consciousness Studies, in press: auth, Review: Why We Feel: The Science of Human Emotions, By Victor S. Johnston, Journal of Consciousness Studies, in press; auth, How You Can Increase Training Effectiveness by Systems Thinking, Pfeiffer Annual 01, Jossey-Bass/Pfeiffer, in press. **CONTACT ADDRESS** 1947 Everidge Ct, Walnut Creek, CA 94596-2952. **EMAIL** garyscho@att.net

SCHOULS, PETER A.
PERSONAL Born 12/01/1937, Netherlands, m, 1960, 2 children **DISCIPLINE** PHILOSOPHY **EDUCATION** Univ Toronto, BA, 60, MA, 62, PhD(epistemology), 67. **CAREER** Lectr philos, Univ Toronto, 64-67; from asst prof to assoc prof, 67-76, Prof Philos, Univ Alta, 76-, Can Coun leave fel, 72-73. **MEMBERSHIPS** Can Philos Asn; Mind Asn. **RESEARCH** Epistemology; history of philosophy; methodology. **SELECTED PUBLICATIONS** Auth, Descartes and the Enlightenment, McGill-Queen's Univ Pr, 89. **CONTACT ADDRESS** Dept of Philos, Massey Univ, Private Bag 11 222, Palmerston North, New Zealand 11 222. **EMAIL** p.schouls@massey.ac.nz

SCHOVILLE, KEITH NORMAN
PERSONAL Born 03/03/1928, Soldiers Grove, WI, 5 children **DISCIPLINE** HEBREW, BIBLICAL STUDIES **EDUCATION** Milligan Col, BA, 56; Univ Wis-Madison, MA, 66, PhD(Hebrcw & Semitic studies), 69. **CAREER** From instr to asst prof, 68-74, assoc prof, 74-81, chmn dept, 77-82, Prof Hebrew & Semitic Studies, Univ Wis-Madison, 81-95, Emer, 95. **MEMBERSHIPS** Am Orient Soc, Soc Biblical Lit, Am Schs Orient Res, Nat Asn Prof Hebrew (secy); Archaeol Inst Am, Near East Archaeol Soc. **RESEARCH** The human factor in archaeology; literary and historical illumination of biblical literature; the Intertestamental Period. **SELECTED PUBLICATIONS** Auth, Bab-Edh-Dhra - Excavations In The Cemetery Directed By Lapp,Paul,W 1965-67 - Schaub,Rt, Rast,Pw/, J Of The Am Oriental Soc, Vol 0112, 1992; auth, The Canaanites Peoples of the Old Testament World, 94. **CONTACT ADDRESS** 5689 County Hwy D, Oregon, WI 53575. **EMAIL** knschovi@facstaff.wisc.edu

SCHRADER, DAVID
PERSONAL Born 10/01/1947, Northfield, MN, m, 1980, 2 children **DISCIPLINE** PHILOSOPHY **EDUCATION** St Olaf Col, BA, 69; Harvard Univ, MTS, 71; Univ Mass, MA, 74; PhD, 75. **CAREER** Instr, Loras Col, 75-77; Asst Prof, Loras Col, 77-79; Asst Prof, Austin Col, 79-84, Assoc Prof, Austin Col, 84-89; Assoc Prof, Wash & Jefferson Col, 89-96; Prof, Wash & Jefferson Col, 96-. **HONORS AND AWARDS** Nat Endowment for the Humanities Grants, 77, 81, 85, 91. **MEMBERSHIPS** APA, Am Soc for Value Inquiry, Int Soc for Value Inquiry, Soc for Bus Ethics, Soc for Philos of Relig. **RESEARCH** Professional Ethics, philosophy of economics, relation between science and theology. **SELECTED PUBLICATIONS** Ed, Ethics and the Practice of Law, Prentice Hall (Englewood Cliffs, NJ), 88; auth, The Corporation as Anomaly, Cambridge Univ Pr (Cambridge), 93; auth, "Technology: Our Contemporary Snake," Res in Philos and Technol, vol X (90): 205-215; auth, "The Antinomy of Divine Necessity," Int J for Philos of Relig, vol 30 (91): 45-59; auth, "Libera Arts: Education for Leadership and Adaptability," A J of the Lib Arts, vol 43 (91): 9-17; auth, "The New Orleans Jazz: Basketball and Music," in The Relevance of the Philos of Sport (Sankt Augustic, GER: Academia Verlag, 93), 15-24; auth, "The Oddness of Corporate Ownership," J of Soc Philos, vol 27, no 2 (96); auth, "Simonizing James: Taking Demand Seriously," Transactions of the Charles S. Pierce Soc, vol XXXIV, no 4 (98): 1005-1028; auth, "Home Is Where The Heart Is: Homelessness and the Denial of Moral Personality," in The Ethics of Homelessness: A Philos Perspective (Amsterdam: Rodopi, 99), 63-78; auth, "Natural Law in the Constitutional Thought of Frederick Douglass," in Frederick Douglass: Philosopher (Cambridge: Basil Blackwell, 99). **CONTACT ADDRESS** Dept Philos, Washington and Jefferson Col, 60 S Lincoln St, Washington, PA 15301-4812. **EMAIL** dschrader@washjeff.edu

SCHRAG, CALVIN ORVILLE
PERSONAL Born 05/04/1928, Marion, SD, m, 1964, 1 child **DISCIPLINE** PHILOSOPHY **EDUCATION** Bethel Col, Kans, BA, 50; Yale Univ, BD, 53; Harvard Univ, PhD, 57. **CAREER** From asst prof to assoc prof, 57-63, interim head dept, 72-73, Res Found grants, 59 & 61, prof, 63-81, George Ade Distinguished Prof Philos to Prof Emer, Purdue Univ, West Lafayette, 82-, Vis lectr, Univ Ill, 59-60; Eli Lilly fel, 62; vis prof, Northwestern Univ, 63-64; Guggenheim fel, 65-66. **HONORS AND AWARDS** Fulbright Fel; Guggenheim Fel; NEH Gr (3). **MEMBERSHIPS** Am Philos Asn; Metaphys Soc Am; Soc Phenomenol & Existential Philos. **RESEARCH** Phenomenology; existentialism; philosophy of the human sciences. **SELECTED PUBLICATIONS** Contribr, Phenomenology: The Philosophy of Edmund Husserl and Its Interpretation, Doubleday, 57; coauth, Masterpieces of World Philosophy, Salem, 61; auth, Existence and Freedom, Northwest Univ, 61; contribr, Heidegger and the Quest for Truth, Quadrangle, 68; Experience and Being, 69 & co-ed & contribr, Patterns of the Life-World, 70, Northwest Univ; auth, Radical Reflection and the Origin of the Human Sciences, Purdue Univ, 80; auth, Communicative Praxis and the Space of Subjectivity, Indiana, 86; auth, The Resources of Rationality, Indiana, 92; auth, Philosophical Papers, SUNY, 94; auth, The Self After Postmodernity, Yale, 97. **CONTACT ADDRESS** Dept of Philos, Purdue Univ, West Lafayette, West Lafayette, IN 47907-1968. **EMAIL** cschrag@purdue.edu

SCHRAG, OSWALD O.
PERSONAL Born 06/04/1916, Parker, SD, m, 1945 **DISCIPLINE** PHILOSOPHY, RELIGION **EDUCATION** Bethel CAl, AB, 42; Hartford Theol Sem, BD, 45, STM, 48; Boston Univ, PhD, 52. **CAREER** Minister, Bolton Congregational Church, Conn, 45-48; trustee scholar, Boston Univ, 48-49, asst, 49-50; minister, W Congregational Church, 51; minister, Chicopee Congregational Church, Mass, 52; assoc prof, 52-58, chmn dept, 57-72 & 76-81, Prof Philos, PROF PHILOS & RELIG EMER, 86- , FISK UNIV, 58-. **HONORS AND AWARDS** Tyler Prize, Hartford Theol Sem, 43-44. **MEMBERSHIPS** Am Philos Asn; Am Theol Soc; Am Acad Relig; Metaphys Soc Am; Soc Philos Relig (vpres, 71-72, pres, 72-73); Jaspers Soc N Am (pres, 82-83); mem Hon Presidium elected by Jaspers Soc, Int Jaspers Conf, 88. **RESEARCH** Philosophy of religion; history of philosophy; contemporary philosophy and theology. **SELECTED PUBLICATIONS** Auth, Existentialist ethics and axiology, Southern J Philos, 63; Jaspers: Beyond traditional metaphysics and ontology, Int Philos Quart, 65; Philosophical, religious, and scientific symbols, Int J Philos Relig, Vol II, No 2; Existence, Existenz, and Transcendence, An Introduction to the Philosophy of Karl Jaspers, Duquesne Univ, 71; contrib auth Jaspers Today: Philosophy at the Threshold of the Future, Univ Press Am, 88; Karl Jaspers: Philosopher Among Philosophers, Wurtzberg, Konigshausen & Neuman, 93; Karl Jaspers Philosophy of the Way to World Philosophy, Wurtzburg, Konigshausen and Neuman, 98; A Companion to the Philosophers, Blackwell Publ, 98. **CONTACT ADDRESS** 3511 Echo Hill Rd, Nashville, TN 37215.

SCHRAG, PHILIP G.
PERSONAL Born 04/12/1943, Chicago, IL, m, 1985, 4 children **DISCIPLINE** LAW **EDUCATION** Harvard Col, AB, 64; Yale Law Sch, LLB, 67. **CAREER** Asst coun, NAACP Legal Defense and Educ Fund, 67-70; Consumer Advocate of the City of New York, 70-71; assoc prof, 71-73, prof of Law, Columbia Univ, 71-77; Deputy Gen Coun, US Arms Control and Disarmament Agency, 77-81; prof of Law and Dir, Center for Applied Legal Studies, 810. **HONORS AND AWARDS** AB, magna cum laude, Harvard Col, 64. **MEMBERSHIPS** Member of the Bar in New York and the District of Columbia, Am Bar Asn, Am Immigration Lawyers Asn. **RESEARCH** Public interest law; refugee law; legal education; civil litigation; immigration law. **SELECTED PUBLICATIONS** Auth, Counsel for the Deceived, Pantheon Books (72); auth, Cases and Materials on Consumer Protection, West Pub Co (73); coauth with Michael Meltsner, Public Interest Advocacy: Materials for Clinical Legal Education, Little, Brown and Co (74); coauth with Michael Meltsner, Toward Simulation in Legal Education: An Experimental Course in Pretrial Litigation, 2nd ed, Foundation Press (79); auth, Behind the Scenes: The Politics of a Constitutional Convention, Georgetown Univ Press (85); auth, Listening for the Bomb: A Study in Nuclear Arms Control Verification Policy, Westview Press (89); auth, Civil Procedure: A Simulation Supplement, Little, Brown and Co (90); auth, Global Action: Nuclear Test Ban Diplomacy at the End of the Cold War, Westview (92); coauth with Michael Meltsner, Reflections on Clinical Legal Education, Northeastern Univ Press (98); auth, A Well Founded Fear: The Congressional Battle to Save Political Asylum in Amercia, Routledge (2000). **CONTACT ADDRESS** The George Washington Univ, 600 New Jersey Ave, NW, Washington, DC 20001-2075. **EMAIL** schrag@law.georgetown.edu

SCHREIBER, MAE N.
PERSONAL Born 05/03/1941, Wahiawa, HI, m, 1964, 4 children **DISCIPLINE** GOVERNMENT INFORMATION SOURCES; INTERNATIONAL TRADE SOURCES **EDUCATION** Oh St Univ, BS, 63; Simmons Col, MLS, 88. **CAREER** Ref librn to asst prof to assoc prof, Univ Akron, 89-. **MEMBERSHIPS** Amer Libr Assoc, Assoc of Col & Res Libr; Amer Assoc of Univ Prof; Assoc for Bibliogr of Hist. **RESEARCH** Government infor sources; int trade sources; evacuation of Japanese Americans from the West coast. **SELECTED PUBLICATIONS** Auth, Big Emerging Markets: Best Prospects, Electonic Market Data Book, 96; Integrating and Advertising Government Publications Internally and Externally: A Guide for Documents Librarians, J of Interlibrary Loan, Document Delivery & Infor Supply, 97; Cataloging Government Publication, Technicalities, 98; International Trade Sources: A Research Guide, Garland Press, 97. **CONTACT ADDRESS** Bierce Library, Univ of Akron, Reference Dept, Akron, OH 44325-1709. **EMAIL** mae1@uakron.edu

SCHREINER, THOMAS R.
DISCIPLINE NEW TESTAMENT **EDUCATION** W Ore Univ, BS; W Conservative Baptist Sem, MDiv, ThM; Fuller Theol Sem, PhD. **CAREER** Instr, Bethel Theol Sem; Azusa Pacific Univ; prof, S Baptist Theol Sem. **HONORS AND AWARDS** Pauline Schol **SELECTED PUBLICATIONS** Auth, Interpreting the Pauline Letters; The Law and Its Fulfillment: A Pauline Theology of Law; co-auth, The Grace of God, The Bondage of the Will; Women in the Church: A Fresh Analysis of 1 Romans 2:9-15. **CONTACT ADDRESS** New Testament Dept, So Baptist Theol Sem, 2825 Lexington Rd, Louisville, KY 40280. **EMAIL** tschreiner@sbts.edu

SCHREITER, ROBERT JOHN
PERSONAL Born 12/14/1947, Nebraska City, NE **DISCIPLINE** RELIGION **EDUCATION** St Joseph's Col, BA, 68; Univ Nijmegen, Netherlands, Dr theol, 74. **CAREER** From Asst Prof to Assoc Prof, 74-85, Prof Theol, Cath Theol Union, Chicago, 85-, Dean, 77-86. **MEMBERSHIPS** Am Acad Relig; Cath Theol Soc Am; Am Soc Missiology. **RESEARCH** Contextual theology; Christology; hermeneutics. **SELECTED PUBLICATIONS** Auth, Constructing Local Theologies, 85; Faces of Jesus in Africa, 91; Reconciliation, 92; The New Catholicity, 97. **CONTACT ADDRESS** Catholic Theol Union at Chicago, 5401 S Cornell Ave, Chicago, IL 60615-6200. **EMAIL** rschreit@ctu.edu

SCHRIFT, ALAN D.
PERSONAL Born 03/02/1955, Brooklyn, NY, m, 1984 **DISCIPLINE** PHILOSOPHY **EDUCATION** Brown Univ, BA, 77; Purdue Univ, MA, 80, PhD, 83. **CAREER** Vis asst prof, Clarkson Univ, 85-87; from asst prof to prof, chemn, Grinnell Col, 87-. **HONORS AND AWARDS** Purdue Univ Fel, 78-79; David Ross Res Fel, 81-83, Purdue Univ; Travel Grant, 84; Fel Stud, 85-86, Am Council Learned Soc; Harris Fac Fel, 90-91, Grinnell Col; External Fel, 91, Univ Or, Eugene; Nat Endowment Hum, 92, 97. **MEMBERSHIPS** Am Philos Asn; Soc Phenomenology Existential Philos; Nietzsche Soc; N Am Nietzsche Soc; Fredrich Nietzsche Soc; Int Asn Philos Lit. **RESEARCH** 20th century European philosophy: existentialism, poststructuralism, hermeneutics, Nietzsche, Foucault, 19th century philosophy, philosophy of literature, aesthetics. **SELECTED PUBLICATIONS** Auth, Nietzsche and the Question of Interpretation: Between Hermeneutics and Deconstruction, 90; auth, Nietzsche's French Legacy: A Genealogy of Poststructuralism, 95; ed, The Logic of the Gift: Toward an Ethic of Generosity, 98; auth, art, Kofman, Nietzsche, and the Jews, 99; auth, art, Nietzsche's Contest: Nietzsche and the Culture Wars, 00; auth, art, Rethinking the Subject, or How One Becomes-other than What One Is, 00; ed, Why Nietzsche Still? Reflections on Drama, Culture, and Politics, 00. **CONTACT ADDRESS** Dept of Philosophy, Grinnell Col, Dept of Philos, Grinnell, IA 50112. **EMAIL** schrift@grinnell.edu

SCHROEDER, JEANNE L.
DISCIPLINE COMMERCIAL LAW **EDUCATION** Williams Col, BA, 75; Stanford Univ, JD, 75. **CAREER** Prof, Yeshiva Univ. **MEMBERSHIPS** Milgrim Thomajan & Lee, P.C. **RESEARCH** Feminist jurisprudence; Corporate finance, and securities law. **SELECTED PUBLICATIONS** Auth, Abduction From the Seraglio: Feminist Methodologies and the Logic of Imagination; Feminism Historicized; History's Challenge to Feminism; Security Interests Under Article 8 of the U.C.C. **CONTACT ADDRESS** Yeshiva Univ, 55 Fifth Ave, New York, NY 10003-4301. **EMAIL** schroedr@ymail.yu.edu

SCHROEDER, MILTON R.
PERSONAL Born Philadelphia, PA, 2 children **DISCIPLINE** LAW **EDUCATION** Wesleyan Univ, BA, 62; Univ Chicago, JD, 65. **CAREER** Law Clerk, Hon Carl McGowan, 65-66; Law Assoc, Sidley & Austin, 66-69; Prof, Ariz State Univ, 69-. **MEMBERSHIPS** Am Law Inst; Am Bar Asn; Am Soc of Intl Law. **RESEARCH** Banking Law; Commercial Law; International Business Transactions. **SELECTED PUBLICATIONS** Auth, The Law and Regulation of Financial Institutions, Sheshunoff Infor Serv; auth, Financial Services Reform: The Gramm-Leach-Bliley Act, Sheshunoff Infor Serv, 99. **CONTACT ADDRESS** Sch of Law, Arizona State Univ, Box 877906, Tempe, AZ 85287-7906. **EMAIL** Milton.Schroeder@asu.edu

SCHROEDER, STEVEN H.
PERSONAL Born 06/29/1954, Wichita Falls, TX **DISCIPLINE** RELIGION, PHILOSOPHY **EDUCATION** Valparaiso Univ, BA, 74; Univ Chicago, MA, 76; PhD, 82. **CAREER** Tchr, Roosevelt Univ, Univ N Iowa, & Calumet Col, 84-96; Assoc Prof, Capital Univ, 97-. **HONORS AND AWARDS** Emily Dickinson Poetry Awd, 96; Samuel Ostrowsky Humanities Awd, 95. **MEMBERSHIPS** APA; AAR; ASA; Intl Bonhoeffer Soc; Intl Virginia Woolf Soc; Soc for Philo in the Cont World **SELECTED PUBLICATIONS** It's the End of the World as We Know It (And I Feel Fine): The End of History, Marxist Eschatology and the New World Order, Jour of Soc Phil, 92; The End of History and Responsibility to Order the World: Dietrich Bonhoeffer and the New World Order, Union Sem Quart Rev, 92; A Community and a Perspective: Lutheran Peace Fellowship and the Edge of the Church, 1941-1991, Univ Press of Amer, 93; An Interview With Mairead Corrigan Maquire, The Christian Century, 94;The Imperialism of Our Little Senses: An Essay on the Southwest and Civilization, Cimarron Rev, 95; Eyes of Texas: Seven Songs Out of Lubbock, Jour Amer Stud Assn of TX, 95; No Goddess Was Your Mother: Western Philosophy's Abandonment of its Multicultural Matrix , Phil in Cont World, 95; The End of History and the New World Order, Theol and Prac of Res, Ess on Dietrich Bonhoeffer, Trinity Press, 94; Notes Towards a Poetics of Persons, Becoming Persons, App Theol Press, 95; Virginia Woolfs Subject and the Subject of Ethics: Notes Toward a Poetics of Persons, Ed Mellen Press, 96; Memo Re: God, Ram Rev, 93; On Measuring Coastlines, Mosaic, 94; It is Good for My Heart, Mosaic, 94; Why Sarah Laughed, Ram Rev, 94-95; Good Faith One Cannot Be Present Alone, Rhino, 95; River of My Childhood, Ram Rev, 95-96; Presence of Mind/Body of Thought, Ram Rev, 96-96; A Story About a Man I Think In New Jersey, Ram Rev, 96-97; Weather Report, Georgetown Rev, 96. **CONTACT ADDRESS** 5710 S. Kimbark #3, Chicago, IL 60637-1615. **EMAIL** sschroed@capital.edu

SCHROEDER, WILLIAM
DISCIPLINE PHILOSOPHY **EDUCATION** Univ Mich, PhD, 79. **CAREER** Assoc prof,Univ Ill Urbana Champaign. **RESEARCH** Recent Continental philosophy; philosophy in and of literature and film. **SELECTED PUBLICATIONS** Auth, Sartre and His Predecessors: The Self and the Other; ed, Blackwell Companion to Continental Philosophy. **CONTACT ADDRESS** Philosophy Dept, Univ of Illinois, Urbana-Champaign, 52 E Gregory Dr, Champaign, IL 61820. **EMAIL** wschroed@staff.uiuc.edu

SCHUBERT, E.
PERSONAL Born 03/29/1945, Glendale, CA, m, 1971, 4 children **DISCIPLINE** MEDICINE; PSYCHIATRY **EDUCATION** Asbury Col, BA 66; Indiana Univ Med Sch, MD 70; Meth Hosp IN, intern 70-72; Amer Bd Family Practice, Diplom, 76; Amer Bd Emerg 81, recert 90; Amer Bd Psychiatry and Neurology, 96. **CAREER** Family Practice, 72-73; Emergency Med, 73-89; Psychiatry, 89-; Indiana Univ, clinical asst psychiatry. **HONORS AND AWARDS** IN Psych Soc Res Awd; Who's Who of American Women; Who's Who in: Health and Med, Med and Healthcare, Sci and Engineering, the World, the Midwest; Mother of the Year; Outstanding Young Women of Amer; nominated for chief resident; dir of psychiatry class for occup ther students; fac-res educ retreat; examiner for oral bd rev. **MEMBERSHIPS** AAFP; ACEP; APA; CMDS. **RESEARCH** Cross Cultural and Missionary psychiatry. **SELECTED PUBLICATIONS** Auth, What Missionaries Need to Know About Burnout and Depression, New Castle IN, Olive Branch Pub, 93; Intl Bulletin of Missionary Research, rev, Cross-Cultural Conflict: Building Relationships for Effective Ministry, Elmer, Inter Varsity Press, 95; Even MK's Can Become Depressed, Interact, 95; MMPI As a Predictive Tool for Missionary Candidates, Jour Psychology and Theology, 96; Personality Disorders in Overseas Missions: Guidelines for the Mental health care Professional, Jour of Psychol and Theol, 93; Missionary Care: Counting the Cost, ed Kelly O'Donnell, Selection and Screening Challenges: Bruising Personality Disorders and the MMPI, Carey, Pasadena, 92. **CONTACT ADDRESS** 2239 N Cadiz Pike, New Castle, IN 47362. **EMAIL** abs@iquest.net

SCHUBERT, JUDITH
DISCIPLINE THEOLOGY **EDUCATION** Georgian Court Col, BA, 66; Providence Col, MA, 75; Ecole Biblique et Archeologique, Eleve Titulaire, 86; Fordham Univ, PhD, 92. **CAREER** Instr Music, Georgian Court Col, 78-80; instr Relig Studies, Georgian Court Col, 80-85; lectr Relig Studies, Georgian Court Col, 87-92; asst prof Relig Studies, Georgian Court Col, 92-95; prof Relig Studies, Georgian Court Col, 00; dir, master arts Theol, Georgian Court Col, 97-. **HONORS AND AWARDS** NEH Grant, Brown Univ; Grant, Ecole Biblique et Archeologique. **MEMBERSHIPS** Col Theol Soc; Cath Bibl Asn; Soc Bibl Lit; Cath Theol Soc Am; Mercy Asn Scripture Theol. **RESEARCH** Luke-Acts; Women and Bible. **SELECTED PUBLICATIONS** Auth, "Jesus as Prophet," Bible Today, 97; auth, "The Good Samaritan: A Reflection of the Compassion of God," Mast Jour, 97; auth, "Two Forgotten Disciples in John," Mast Jour, 95. **CONTACT ADDRESS** 900 Lakewood Ave., Lakewood, NJ 08701. **EMAIL** schubert@georgian.edu

SCHUCHARD, BRUCE G.
PERSONAL Born 11/30/1956, Corona, CA, m, 1990, 2 children **DISCIPLINE** EXEGETICAL THEOLOGY **EDUCATION** Univ Mich, BS, 79; Concordia Theol Sem, MDiv, 84, STM, 85; Union Theol Sem, PhD, 91. **CAREER** Pastor, St. James, Iowa, 90-97; asst prof, exegetical theol, Concordia Sem, 97- . **MEMBERSHIPS** Soc of Bibl Lit. **RESEARCH** Johannine literature; New Testament use of the Old Testament. **SELECTED PUBLICATIONS** Auth, Scripture within Scripture: The Interrelationship of Form and Function in the Explicit Old Testament Citations in the Gospel of John, Scholars Press, 92. **CONTACT ADDRESS** Concordia Sem, 801 DeMun Ave, Saint Louis, MO 63105. **EMAIL** schuchardb@csl.edu

SCHUCK, PETER H.
PERSONAL Born 04/26/1940, New York, NY, m, 1966, 2 children **DISCIPLINE** LAW **EDUCATION** Cornell Univ, BA, 62; Harvard Univ, JD, 65, MA, 69; NYork Univ, LLM, 66. **CAREER** Assoc, Cahill, Gordon, Reindel & Ohl, 65-67 & Wachtell, Lipton, Rosen & Katz, 67-68; teaching fel govt, Harvard Univ, 69-70; consult, Ctr Study Responsive Law, 71-72; dir, Wash Off, Consumers Union, 72-77; dep asst secy, US Dept Health, Educ & Welfare, 77-79; assoc prof Law, 78-81, Simeon E Baldwin Prof Law, 84, prof law, Yale Univ, 81-. **HONORS AND AWARDS** Guggenheim Fel, 84-85. **RESEARCH** Administrative law; tort law; regulation; immigration, citizenship, and refugee law. **SELECTED PUBLICATIONS** Auth & ed, The Judiciary Committees, Viking, 75; auth, Suing Government; Citizen Remedies for Official Wrongs, Yale Univ, 83; Citizenship Without Consent: Illegal Aliens in the American Party, Yale Univ, 85; Agent Orange on Trial: Mass Toxic Disasters in the Courts, Harvard Univ, 87; Tort Law and the Public Interest: Competition, Innovation, and Consumer Welfare, Norton, 91; ed, Foundations of Administrative Law, Oxford Univ, 94; Citizens, Strangers, and In-Betweens: Essays on Immigration and Citizenship, Westview Press, 98; Paths to Inclusion: The Integration of Migrants in the United States and Germany, Berghahn Books, 98; auth, The Limits of Law: Essays on Democratic Governance, Westview Press, 00. **CONTACT ADDRESS** Law Sch, Yale Univ, PO Box 208215, New Haven, CT 06520-8215. **EMAIL** peter.schuck@yale.edu

SCHUELER, G. FREDERICK
PERSONAL Born 08/09/1944, Columbus, OH, m, 1966, 2 children **DISCIPLINE** PHILOSOPHY **EDUCATION** Stanford Univ, BA, 66; Univ Calif, MA, 68; PhD, 73. **CAREER** Prof, Univ N Mex, 90-. **MEMBERSHIPS** Am Philos Asn. **RESEARCH** Ethics; Philosophy of Mind. **SELECTED PUBLICATIONS** Auth, Desire, MIT Press, 95; auth, The Idea of a Reason for Acting, Mellen, 89. **CONTACT ADDRESS** Dept Philos, Univ of New Mexico, Albuquerque, 1 Univ Campus, Albuquerque, NM 87131-0001. **EMAIL** schueler@unm.edu

SCHUFREIDER, GREGORY
DISCIPLINE HISTORY OF PHILOSOPHY, RECENT CONTINENTAL PHILOSOPHY, THE PHILOSOPHY OF ART **EDUCATION** Northwestern Univ, BA, 69; Univ Calif, Santa Barbara, MA, PhD, 75. **CAREER** Prof, La State Univ. **RESEARCH** Heidegger. **SELECTED PUBLICATIONS** Auth, An Introduction to Anselm's Argument, Temple UP, 78; The Metaphysician as Poet-Magician, in Metaphilosophy, 79; Art and the Problem of Truth, Man and World, 81; Heidegger on Community, Man and World, 81; The Logic of the Absurd, in Philos and Phenomenol Res, 83; Overpowering the Center: Three Compositions by Modrian, in JAAC, 85; Heidegger Contribution to a Phenomenology of Culture, 86; Confessions of a Rational Mystic: Anselm's Early Writings, Purdue Univ ser, in the Hist of Philos, 94. **CONTACT ADDRESS** Dept of Philos and Relig Stud, Louisiana State Univ and A&M Col, 106 Coates Hall, Baton Rouge, LA 70803.

SCHULTENOVER, DAVID, SJ
PERSONAL Born 08/19/1938, Sauk Rapids, MN, s **DISCIPLINE** HISTORICAL THEOLOGY **EDUCATION** Spring Hill Col, BS, 63; Loyola Univ, MS, 66; St. Louis Univ, PhD, 75 **CAREER** Prof, 94-pres, Assoc Prof, 85-94, Adj Asst Prof, 78-83, Creighton Univ; Asst Prof, 75-78, Marquette Univ; Book review editor for Theological Studies, 00. **HONORS AND AWARDS** Nat Endowm for the Humanities Fel; Alpha Sigma Nu Ntl Bk Awd; Deutscher Akademischer Austauschdienst Fel; Alpha Sigma Nu **MEMBERSHIPS** Am Acad of Relig; Am Soc Church History; Cath Theolog Soc of Am **RESEARCH** Christology; Roman Catholic Modernism; Models and Images of the Church **SELECTED PUBLICATIONS** Auth, George Tyrrell: In Search of Catholicism, Patmos Press, 81; Auth, A View from Rome: The Eve of the Modernist Crisis, Fordham University Press, 93. **CONTACT ADDRESS** Jesuit Community, Creighton Univ, 2500 California Plaza, #Jesuit, Omaha, NE 68178-0001. **EMAIL** dnover@creighton.edu

SCHULTZ, CARL
PERSONAL Born 09/15/1930, New Castle, PA, m, 1955, 3 children **DISCIPLINE** BIBLICAL STUDIES, OLD TESTAMENT **EDUCATION** Malone Cool, BRE, 52; Houghton Cool, BA, 53; Wheaton Cool, MA, 55; Brandeis Univ, PhD, 73. **CAREER** Asst Proof, Houghton Cool, 65-67; Adjunct Proof, United Theol Sem, 98-; From Assoc. Proof to Proof, Houghton Cool, 74--. **HONORS AND AWARDS** Student Senate Excellence Awd, Houghton Cool, 75-76, 83-84; Malone Cool Alumni Assoc. Cert of Merit, 88; Paul Harris Feel, Fillmore Rotary Club, 88; Independent Cool Fund of NY Teaching Excellence Awd, NY State Electric & Gas Co, 94. **MEMBERSHIPS** Soc of Bibl Lit, Am Acad of Relig, Nat Assoc. of Profs of Hebrew. **RESEARCH** Apocalyptic and wisdom literature. **SELECTED PUBLICATIONS** Auth, "Biblical Warrant for a Career," Wesleyan Advocate (86); auth, "The Enigma of Ecclesiastes," The Preacher's Mag (88); auth, "Responsible Reluctance or When a Quick Yes is Unwise," in A Greater Work to Do (Wesley Pr, 91); auth, "When Reading is Difficult," J for Case Teaching (92); auth, "A Biblical Warrant for Women in Leadership," Milieu (94); auth, "The Cohesive Issue of Mispat in Job," Go to the Land I will Show you, Brandeis Univ Pr (96); auth, "Introduction to Proverbs and Hebrew Poetry," Wesley Bibl Ser (98). **CONTACT ADDRESS** Dept For Lang, Houghton Col, PO Box 128, Houghton, NY 14744-0128. **EMAIL** cschultz@houghton.edu

SCHULTZ, JOSEPH P.
PERSONAL Born 12/02/1928, Chicago, IL, m, 1955, 3 children **DISCIPLINE** JEWISH STUDIES, RELIGION **EDUCATION** Yeshiva Univ, BA, 51; Jewish Theol Sem, MHL, 55; Brandeis Univ, PhD, 62. **CAREER** Lectr foreign lang, Boston Univ, 63-64, instr foreign lang, 64-68, asst prof relig, 68-73; assoc prof hist, 73-78, Oppenstein Bros Distinguished Prof Judaic Studies, Univ MO-Kansas City, 78-, Dir Judiac Studies Prog, 73-, dir Center for Relig Studies, 95; Res grant, Grad Sch Arts & Sci, Boston Univ, 71-72. **HONORS AND AWARDS** Hyman G Enelow Awd, Jewish Theol Sem, 76. **MEMBERSHIPS** Asn Jewish Studies; Am Acad Relig. **RESEARCH** Comparative religion; Jewish studies. **SELECTED PUBLICATIONS** Auth, Angelic opposition to the ascension of Moses and the revelation of the law, Jewish Quart Rev, 71; The religious psychology of Jonathan Edwards and the Hasidic Masters of Habad, J Ecumenical Studies, 73; The Lurianic strand in Jonathan Edwards' Concept of Progress, Judaica, 74; Reciprocity in confucian and Rabbinic ethics, J Relig Ethics, 74; contribr, Studies and Texts in Honor of Nahum Glatzer, Brill, 75; auth, From My Father's Vineyard, Vile-Goller, 78; co-ed, From Destruction to Rebirth: The Holocaust and the State of Israel, Univ Am, 78; auth, Judaism and The Gentile Faiths; Comparative Studies in Religion, Fairleigh Dickinson Univ, 78; Mid-America's Promise: A Profile of Kansas City Jewry, Am Jewish Hist Soc, 82; ed, Ze'enah U-Re'enah: Book of Genesis, Dropsie Col, 85; Sinai and Olympus: A Comarative Study with Lois S. Spatz, Univ Press of Am, 95. **CONTACT ADDRESS** Naropa Inst, 2130 Arapahoe Ave., Boulder, CO 80302.

SCHULTZ, NANCY L.
PERSONAL Born 04/24/1957, Detroit, MI, d, 2 children **DISCIPLINE** LAW **EDUCATION** Univ Wisc, BA, 78; Univ Pa, JD, 81. **CAREER** Instr, Villanova Univ, 86-89; dir, George Washington Univ, 89-96; adj prof, Howard Univ, 94-95; Chapman Univ, 96-. **MEMBERSHIPS** Assoc of Legal Writing Dir; ABA Law Student Div. **RESEARCH** Teaching and learning, lawyerint skills. **SELECTED PUBLICATIONS** Auth, "How Do Lawyers Really Think?", 42 J Legal Educ 57 (92); coauth, "Persuasive Writing for Lawyers and the Legal Profession", Matthew Bender, (April 95); coauth, "Legal Research", Casenotes, (96); coauth, "Civility, Responsibility, and Professionalism", Orange County Lawyer, (Nov 96); auth, "Building a Professional Community", 11 Geo J. Legal Ethics 1, (97); coauth, "Legal Writing and Other Lawyering Skills, Matthew Bender, third edition (Apr 98); auth, "Live(s) for the State?", NEXUS, (Fall 98); auth, "There's a New Test in Town: Preparing Students for the MPT", Perspectives: Teaching Legal Research and Writing (Fall 99): auth, "The Needs of the Many v. The Needs of the Few (Accommodating Students With ADD), UMKC Law Rev (forthcoming). **CONTACT ADDRESS** Sch of Law, Chapman Univ, One University Blvd, Orange, CA 92807. **EMAIL** nschultz@chapman.edu

SCHULTZ, REYNOLDS BARTON
PERSONAL Born 08/09/1951, Elmhurst, IL, m, 1985, 1 child **DISCIPLINE** PHILOSOPHY, POLITICAL SCIENCE **EDUCATION** Univ Chicago, PhD, 87. **CAREER** Lectr, Univ Chicago, 89- . **HONORS AND AWARDS** Dept nomination, Leo Strauss Awd for dissertation; vice-pres, Sidgwick Soc. **MEMBERSHIPS** APSA; Sidgwick Soc. **RESEARCH** Nineteenth and twentieth century Anglo-American ethics and political theory; Henry Sidgwick; John Addington Symonds; Gay Studies. **SELECTED PUBLICATIONS** Ed, Essays on Henry Sidgwick, Cambridge, 92; auth, The Social and Political Philosophy of Bertrand Russell, Philos of the Soc Sci, 96; ed, Complete Works & Select Correspondence of Henry Sidgwick, InteLex, 97; auth, "Henry Sidgwick in 2001", Utilitas, 00. **CONTACT ADDRESS** Social Sciences Collegiate Division, Univ of Chicago, 5845 South Ellis Ave, Chicago, IL 60637-1404. **EMAIL** rschultz@midway.uchicago.edu

SCHULTZ, WALTER
PERSONAL Born 01/23/1950, Chicago, IL, m, 1975, 2 children **DISCIPLINE** PHILOSOPHY **EDUCATION** Univ Minnesota, PhD, 97. **CAREER** Cedarville Col, 97-. **HONORS AND AWARDS** Univ Wisconsin - Eauclaire; Sigma Gamma Zeta, Scholastic Honor Soc; Winner Bertrand Russell Competition on Logic; Cedarville College Faculty Scholarship Grant, 98. **MEMBERSHIPS** Amer Phil Assoc; Soc of Christian Philosophers; Evangelical Philosophical Soc. **RESEARCH** Ethics; welfare economics; logic/epistemology and philosophy of religion **SELECTED PUBLICATIONS** Auth, Wittgenstein and Postmodern Epistemology, Wittgenstein's Philosophy of Mathematics, 93; Towards a Communitarian Liberalism, Kinesis, 94; What is Truth, Torch, 98; auth, The Moral Conditions of Economic Efficiency, 01. **CONTACT ADDRESS** Cedarville Col, Cedarville, OH 45314-0601. **EMAIL** schultz@cedarville.edu

SCHULTZ-ALDRICH, JANICE LEE
PERSONAL Born Cleveland, OH, m **DISCIPLINE** PHILOSOPHY **EDUCATION** John Carroll Univ, BA, 69; State Univ NYork Buffalo, MA, 72, PhD, 78. **CAREER** Asst prof & assoc prof, 79-88, Prof Philos, Canisius Col, 89-. **MEMBERSHIPS** Am Cath Philos Asn. **RESEARCH** Aquinas; business ethics; natural law and human rights. **SELECTED PUBLICATIONS** Auth, "Adam of St Victor," "Adelaid of Bath," "Richard of St Victor," "John of Salisbury," & "Honorius Augustodunensis," In: Dict of the Middle Ages, Scribner's, summer 82; many articles on Thomas Aquinas in The New Scholasticism, Proceedings of the PMR Conference, Am Cath Philos Quart (also articles on Abelard, Boethius), 82-01; co-transl, An Exposition of the 'On the Hebdomads' of Boethius, by Thomas Aquinas, Cath Univ Am, 01. **CONTACT ADDRESS** Dept of Philos, Canisius Col, 2001 Main St, Buffalo, NY 14208-1098. **EMAIL** SchultzJ@canisius.edu

SCHUTZ, SAMUEL R.
PERSONAL m, 1 child **DISCIPLINE** EVANGELISM AND MINISTRY **EDUCATION** Calif State Univ, BA, 66; Univ Calif, PhD, 69; Andover Newton Theol Sch, MDiv; postdoctoral stud, Gordon-Conwell Theol Sem; N Park Theol Sem; Fuller Theol Sem. **CAREER** Instr, Westmont Col; Gordon Col; prof, dir, DMin prog, assoc dean, Bethel Sem, 86-90; act dean, Bethel Sem, 89-90; prof, Gordon-Conwell Theol Sem, 90-. **HONORS AND AWARDS** Res grant, US Off Edu; Nat Inst Mental Health. **MEMBERSHIPS** Mem, Amer Psychol Assn. **SELECTED PUBLICATIONS** Contrib ed, Jour Psychol and Theol. **CONTACT ADDRESS** Gordon-Conwell Theol Sem, 130 Essex St, South Hamilton, MA 01982.

SCHWAB, PETER
PERSONAL Born 11/15/1940, New York, NY, s **DISCIPLINE** POLITICAL SCIENCE **EDUCATION** New School for Social Res, MA, 66, PhD, 69. **CAREER** Asst prof, 71-73, assoc prof, 73-80, prof, Political Sci, Purchase Col, SUNY, 80-. **HONORS AND AWARDS** Fulbright Scholar, 67; U.N. Commission on Human Right-authored book, Human Rights, selected as primary reference, 86. **RESEARCH** Cuba-the U.S. embargo, Human Rights. **SELECTED PUBLICATIONS** Auth, Cuba: Confronting the U.S. Embargo, St Martin's Press, 98; Ethiopia, Politics, Economics, and Society, Lynne Rienner Pub, 85; coauth, Toward a Human Rights Framwork, Praeger Pub, 82; Human Rights: Cultural & Ideological Perspectives, Praeger Pub, 79; auth, Human Rights = New Perspectives, New Realities, Lynne Rienner Publ, 00. **CONTACT ADDRESS** Dept of Political Sci, SUNY, Col at Purchase, Purchase, NY 10577. **EMAIL** schwabsuny@aol.com

SCHWAB, STEWART J.
DISCIPLINE LAW **EDUCATION** Swarthmore Col, BA, 75; Univ Mich, MA, 78, JD, 80, PhD, 81. **CAREER** Res Asst, Fed Reserve Bank Philadelphia, 75-76; Summer Assoc, Covington & Burling, 79; Law Clerk, US Court of Appeals, 81-82; Law Clerk, US Supreme Court, 82-83; Vis Prof, Univ Mich, 88; Vis Fel, Ctr Socio-Legal Studies, Wolfson Col, Oxford Univ, 90; Olin Vis Res Prof Law & Econ, Univ Va, 91; Chapman Tripp Vis Lectr, Victoria Univ Fac Law, Wellington, New Zealand, 97; Fulbright Sr. Schol, Ctr Law & Econ, Australian Nat Univ, 97-98; Asst Prof to Prof Law, Cornell Law Sch, 83-. **HONORS AND AWARDS** Nat Sci Found Grant, 85-87; Fund for Labor Relations Studies, 89-90. **MEMBERSHIPS** Am Bar Asn; DC Bar; Am Arbitration Asn. **SELECTED PUBLICATIONS** Auth, Employment Life Cycles and the Employment-At-Will Doctrine, Cornell Law Forum, 94; coauth, Property Rules and Liability Rules: The Cathedral in Another Light, NY Univ Law Rev, 95; auth, Wrongful Discharge Law and the Search for Third-Party Effects, Tex Law Rev, 96; Legal Positivism as an Empirical Proposition, Cornell Law Rev, 97; coauth, Employment Law: Cases and Materials, Lexis Law Publ, 93, 2nd ed, 98; Employment Law: Selected Federal and State Statutes, Lexis Law Publ, 93, 2nd ed, 98; Foundations of Labor and Employment Law, Oxford Univ Press (forthcoming 99); author of numerous other articles. **CONTACT ADDRESS** Law School, Cornell Univ, Myron Taylor Hall, Ithaca, NY 14853. **EMAIL** sjs15@cornell.edu

SCHWABACH, AARON
PERSONAL Born 03/03/1963, Chicago, IL, m **DISCIPLINE** LAW **EDUCATION** Antioch Col, BA, 85; Univ Calif Berkeley, JD, 89. **MEMBERSHIPS** State Bar of CA; State Bar of FL; Am Soc of Intl Law. **RESEARCH** International Environmental Law. **SELECTED PUBLICATIONS** Auth, "Thomas Jefferson as an Unsuccessful Advocate for Freedom in Howell

v. Netherland," Thomas Jefferson Law Review, 98; auth, "Using International Law to Prevent Environment Harm from Increased Use of Desalination," Texas Intl Law Journal, 99; auth, "Environmental Damage Resulting from the NATO Military Action Against Yugoslavia," Columbia Journal Environmental Law, 00; auth, "The Legality of the NATO Bombing Operation in the Federal Republic of Yugoslavia," Pace Intl Law Review, 99; auth, "Thomas Jefferson and Sally Hemings," Thomas Jefferson Law Review, 99; auth, "Yugoslavia v. NATO, Security Council Resolution 1244, and the Law of Humanitarian Intervention," Syracuse Journal Intl Law and Comm, 00; auth, "Humanitarian Intervention and Environmental Protection: The Effect of the Kosovo War on the Law of War,' Columbia Journal E Euro Law, forthcoming; auth, "From Schwizerhalle to Baia Mare: The Continuing Failure of International Law to Protect Europe's Rivers," VA Environmental Law Journal, forthcoming; auth, "The Tisza Cyanide Disaster and International Law," Environmental Law Report, 00; auth, "NATO's War in Kosovo and the Final Report to the Prosecutor of the International Criminal Tribunal for the Former Yugoslavia," Tulane Journal Intl Law, 01. **CONTACT ADDRESS** Thomas Jefferson Sch of Law, 2121 San Diego Ave, San Diego, CA 92110-2928. **EMAIL** aarons@tjsl.edu

SCHWANAUER, FRANCIS
DISCIPLINE PHILOSOPHY **EDUCATION** Univ Stuttgart, Ger, PhD, 59. **CAREER** Prof **RESEARCH** Semiotics; workings of the mind; role of the brain. **SELECTED PUBLICATIONS** Auth, Truth is a Neighborhood, transl into Ger; The Mind is a Fact; Those Fallacies by Slight of Reason. **CONTACT ADDRESS** Dept of Philosophy, Univ of So Maine, 96 Falmouth St, PO Box 9300, Portland, ME 04104-9300. **EMAIL** franz@usm.maine.edu

SCHWANDA, TOM
PERSONAL Born 10/23/1950, East Stroudsburg, PA, m, 1977, 2 children **DISCIPLINE** RELIGION **EDUCATION** Moravian Col, BA, 72; New Brunswick Theol Sem, M Div, 75; Fuller Theol Sem, D Min, 92. **CAREER** Pastor, Immanuel Reformed Church, 87-92; interim senior Pastor, Remembrance Reformed Church, 92-93; chemn, Reformed Spirituality Network, 92-; Co-dean, Lutheran Theological Seminary at Gettysburg, 96-98; Assoc, Reformed Church in America, 95-99; instr, Reformed Bible Col, 99-00; instr, Fuller Theological Seminary, 00; Instr, Tyndale Seminary, Toronto, 00. **HONORS AND AWARDS** Who's Who in Am Col and Univ, 72; Tringle Honor Soc, Moravian Col, 72; Who's Who in Am, 95-. **MEMBERSHIPS** Calvin Studies Soc, Czech Hist Conf, Czech Soc for Arts and Sci, Evangel Theol Soc, Soc for the Study of Christian Spirituality, Spiritual Dir Int. **RESEARCH** Reformed spirituality, worship as corporate spiritual formation, spirituality of leadership, history of spirituality. **SELECTED PUBLICATIONS** Auth, Reformed Spirituality, CRC Publ, 95: auth, Celebrating God's Presence: The Transforming Power of Public Worship, CRC Publ, 96; auth, "Closing the Gap: Recovering the Experiential Nature of reformed Spirituality," Reformed Review 49.2 (95-96): 109-125; auth, "The Unforced Rhythms of Grace, A Reformed Perspective on Sabbath," Perspectives 11.3 (96): 14-17; auth, "Praying the Scriptures with Head and Heart: Rediscovering Lectio Divina," Banner 133.23 (98): 24-26; auth, "Autobiographies of Giving: Dorcas," Reformed Review 53.1 (99): 54-59; auth, "Pilgrimage and Spiritual Maturity: Growing in Christ, Reformed Review (forthcoming): auth, "Jan Hus" and "Hussites," Encycl of Christianity 2 (forthcoming). **CONTACT ADDRESS** Dept Rel, Reformed Bible Col, 3333 E Beltline Ave NE, Grand Rapids, MI 49525-9781. **EMAIL** tschwanda@reformed.edu

SCHWARTZ, BRYAN
DISCIPLINE LAW **EDUCATION** Queen's Univ, LLB, 78; Yale Univ, LLM, 78, JSD, 86. **CAREER** Asst prof, 81-84; assoc prof, 84-87; prof, 87-. **HONORS AND AWARDS** Rh Institute Awd for Outstanding Scholarship in the Humanities, 89 **RESEARCH** Constitutional law; charter of rights; international law. **SELECTED PUBLICATIONS** Auth, Still Thinking, Voyageur, 92; Opting In? The New Federal Proposals on the Constitution, Voyageur, 92; First Principles, Second Thoughts, 86; Fathoming Meech Lake, 87. **CONTACT ADDRESS** Fac of Law, Univ of Manitoba, Robson Hall, Winnipeg, MB, Canada R3T 2N2. **EMAIL** bschwar@cc.umanitoba.ca

SCHWARTZ, ELI
PERSONAL Born 04/02/1921, New York, NY, m, 1948, 2 children **DISCIPLINE** ECONOMICS **EDUCATION** BS Acctg Univ of Denver, 43; U.S. Army, 43-46; Special Student,Univ of Manchester England, 45; MA Econ Univ of CO, 48; PhD in Econ, Brown Univ 52; Thesis: Studies in Distribution of Tax Burdens by Income Groups-A Critique. **CAREER** Named to Charles W MacFarlane Chair of Econ, Lehigh Univ 80,(Emeritus,91); Cam Econ Dept, Lehigh Univ, 78-84; Vis Prof, Tel Aviv Univ, 75; Fulbright Lecturer and Consulting Prof Autonomous, Univ of Madrid, Spain, 72; Lecturer London School of Econ, 66; Prof of ECON and Finance, Lehigh Univ, 62; Lehigh Univ, 54-, Retired active Prof emeritus, 91; Lecturer, Michigan State Univ 53-54; Chief Dis Econ(G11) Providence Dis of O.P.S, 51-53; Inst, Brown Univ, Providence Rhode Island, 48-51; Inst, Univ of Rhode Island, 47-48. **RESEARCH** Valuation of lifetime incomes; Money and Banking; Macro-economics; Finance. **SELECTED PUBLICATIONS** Ed,(with J.R. Aronson), Management Policies in Local Government Finance, Intl City Managers Assoc, Washington DC, 75(2nd ed 81,3rd ed 87,4th ed 96); Market Interest Rates and the Total Offset Method Re-visited, (forthcoming JFE); Life Insurance as an Offset in Wrongful Death Cases, Journal of Forensic Economics, 94; Capacity Planning in Public Utilities: An Inventory Theoretic Approach, Journal of Land Economics, 84; Reforming Public Pension Plans to Avoid Unfunded Liability, Management Information Service, ICMA (with J.R. Aronson and V.G. Munley), 83; The Economics of Lifetime Income, (with R.J. Thornton), The Forum (published by the Amer Bar Assoc), 83; Note on Stability Conditions Applied to Particular Market, (with Donald A. Moore), Southern Economic Journal, 55. **CONTACT ADDRESS** Dept of Econ, Lehigh Univ, Bethlehem, PA 18015.

SCHWARTZ, HERMAN
DISCIPLINE CONSTITUTIONAL LAW, CIVIL RIGHTS **EDUCATION** Harvard Univ, AB, 53; Harvard Law Sch, JD, 56; **CAREER** Prof, Am Univ. **HONORS AND AWARDS** ACLU-Niagara Frontier Awd, 72; William Conable Awd Civil Rights, 74; NY State Bar Asn Criminal Justice Section Awd Outstanding Work,76; Medgar Evers Awd, 76; Felicitation Humanitarian Work, 77; Citizens Counsel for Human Rights Awd,82. **MEMBERSHIPS** U.S./Israel Civil Liberties Law prog; Human Rights Watch Committee, 87; co-dir, Wash Col Law, Human Rights Ctr.; Found, Civil Soc; Congressional Human Rights Found; Helsinki Watch; Am Civil Liberties Union, 69. ACLU; U.S. Senate comt; Dept Treasury. **RESEARCH** Civil rights and liberties. **SELECTED PUBLICATIONS** Auth, Packing the Court: the Conservative Compaign to Rewrite the Constitution; The Burger Years, 78; contrib, Harvard Law Rev, Yale Law Jour, Mich Law Rev, Univ Chicago Law Rev, NY Times; auth, The Struggle for Constitutional Justice in Post-Communist Europe, 00. **CONTACT ADDRESS** American Univ, 4801 Massachusetts Ave, Washington, DC 20016. **EMAIL** hschwar@wcl.american.edu

SCHWARTZ, JUSTIN
PERSONAL Born 07/19/1957, Columbus, OH, m, 1983, 2 children **DISCIPLINE** LAW, PHILOSOPHY **EDUCATION** Princeton Univ, AB, 79; Cambridge Univ, Mphil, 82; Univ Mich, MA, 84, PhD, 89; Ohio State Univ, JD, 98. **CAREER** Asst prof, Kalamazoo Col, 88-89; Ohio State Univ, 89-94; Judicial law clerk, US Court of Appeals, 7th Cir, 98-99; US District Court, ND III, 99-. **HONORS AND AWARDS** Articles Editor, Ohio State Law J, 97-98; JD summa cum laude, Ohio State Univ, 98; Order of the Coif, 98; Berger Prize in Philosophy of Law of the American Philosophical Association (best published paper of the Previous two years, 99. **MEMBERSHIPS** Nat Lawyers Guild; Am Philos Asn; Radial Philos Asn; Illinois Bar, Seventh Circuit Bar, Northern District of Illinois Bar, Am Bar Ass, Seventh Circuit Bar Assoc. **RESEARCH** Philosophy of law; Political and social philosophy; Philosophy of social science; Labor and employment law; Constitutional law and theory; legislation; federal jurisdiction. **SELECTED PUBLICATIONS** Auth, "Money for Nothing: Business Location Incentives and the Law," 98; "A Not So Quite Color-Blind Constitution: Racial Discrimination and Racial Preference in Justice O'Connor's 'Newest' Equal Protection Jurisprudence" in Ohio State Law J, 97; "Relativism, Reflective Equilibrium, and Justice" in Legal Studies, 97; auth, "Investment by Consent: Business Location Incentives and the Law", coauth, in No More Candy Store: States and Cities Making Job Subsidies Accountable, 2nd ed., 98; auth, "Rights of Inequality: Rawlsian Justice, Equal Opportunity, and the Status of the Family," Legal Theory, 00. **CONTACT ADDRESS** Chambers of Judge Elaine E Bucklok, US District Court, ND, Ill, US Court House, 1764 Dirksen Bldg, Chicago, IL 60604. **EMAIL** justin_schwartz@ilnd.uscourts.gov

SCHWARTZ, MARTIN A.
DISCIPLINE LAW **EDUCATION** City Col, BBA, cum laude, 66; Brooklyn Law Sch, JD, magna cum laude, 68; NYork Univ, LLM, 73. **CAREER** Mng atty, Westchester Legal Serv; adj prof, NY Law Schl; prof Law, Touro Col. **MEMBERSHIPS** NY State Bar Asn comt on State Const Law. **SELECTED PUBLICATIONS** Auth, Public Interest Law, NY Law J; Section 1983 Litigation: Federal Evidence; coauth, Section 1983 Litigation: Claims, Defenses and Fees, 91. **CONTACT ADDRESS** Dept of Law, Touro Col, New York, Brooklyn, NY 11230. **EMAIL** MartinS@tourolaw.edu

SCHWARTZ, SHULY RUBIN
PERSONAL Born 03/26/1953, Brooklyn, NY, m, 1973, 4 children **DISCIPLINE** JEWISH HISTORY **EDUCATION** Barnard Col, BA; Jewish Theol Sem Am, MA, PhD. **CAREER** Rabbi Irving Lehrman Res Asst Prof Am Jewish Hist; dean, Albert A. List Col Jewish Studies. **HONORS AND AWARDS** Doctoral Dissertation Scholarship, 85-86; Doctoral Scholarship, 85-86, 82-83; Honorable Mention Awd, 99; Rabbi Levi A. Oln Memorial Fel, 99-00; Josoeph H. Fichter Res Awd, 99-00. **MEMBERSHIPS** Am Hist Asn; Am Jewish Hist Soc; Asn for Jewish Studies; Asn for the Sociology of Relig. **RESEARCH** Image and role of the Rebbetzin, (rabbi's wife), in American Jewish life, American Jewish Religious Movements; Jewish women. **SELECTED PUBLICATIONS** Auth, The Emergence of Jewish Scholarship in America: The Publication of the Jewish Encyclopedia, Hebrew Union Col Press, 91; Camp Ramah: The Early Years, 1947-1952, Conser Judaism, 87; Ramah Philosophy and the Newman Revolution, Studies in Jewish Education and Judaica in Honor of Louis Newman. **CONTACT ADDRESS** Jewish Theol Sem of America, 3080 Broadway, New York, NY 10027. **EMAIL** shschwartz@jtsa.edu

SCHWARTZ, WILLIAM
DISCIPLINE ESTATE PLANNING, PROPERTY, AND TORTS **EDUCATION** Boston Univ, JD, 55; Stanford Univ, AM, 60. **CAREER** Prof, Yeshiva Univ; vcprs, Acad Affairs. **HONORS AND AWARDS** Dir, Viacom, Inc.; vchmn, UST Corp. **MEMBERSHIPS** Asn Trial Lawyers Am; Legal Adv Comt NY Stock Exchange; Legal Adv Board; Nat Comn Medical Malpractice; NGO Section, UN. **RESEARCH** Estate planning, property, and torts. **SELECTED PUBLICATIONS** Areas of research. **CONTACT ADDRESS** Yeshiva Univ, 55 Fifth Ave, New York, NY 10003-4301.

SCHWARZ, MAY L.
PERSONAL Born 10/04/1945, Sandusky, OH, d, 2 children **DISCIPLINE** CHURCH MUSIC **EDUCATION** Oberlin Col, BM, 67; Ohio State Univ, MM, 68; Trinity Lutheran Sem, MTS, 89. **CAREER** Asst prof to prof, Trinity Lutheran Sem 89-. **HONORS AND AWARDS** Pi Kappa Lambda. **MEMBERSHIPS** ALCM; AGO; ACDA; Hymn Soc in Am and Can. **RESEARCH** Psalmody, including music, texts, performance practices in use in today's churches, Building Parish Music Programs, including the role and partnership of clergy and musicians, Organ chorale preludes of J.S. Bach compared to those of contemporary composers. **SELECTED PUBLICATIONS** Auth, "The Prelude: A Foretaste of the Feast to Come", Sursum Corda, Jan 89; auth, "The Psalms in Worship: Strategies for Congregational Use", Sursum Corda, Dec 89; auth, "Music During Distribution", Sursum Corda, July 91; auth, "Church Music at Trinity Seminary", Grace Notes, VII.2 (April 92); auth, "Partnership of Clergy and Musician", The Guilder, January 94. **CONTACT ADDRESS** Dept Pastoral Ministry, Trinity Lutheran Sem, 2199 E Main St, Columbus, OH 43209-3913. **EMAIL** mschwarz@trinity.capital.edu

SCHWEER, G. WILLIAM
PERSONAL Born Independence, MO, m, 3 children **DISCIPLINE** EVANGELISM **EDUCATION** Univ Mo, BS; Cent Baptist Theol Sem, BD, ThM, ThD; addn stud, Trinity Evangel Sem; SF State Univ; Fuller Sem; Oxford Univ. **CAREER** Instr, Baptist Sem Indonesia, 57-70; pres, Baptist Sem Indonesia, 70; fac, 75; E. Hermond Westmoreland prof, 96; sr prof, Golden Gate Baptist Theol Sem-, 96. **HONORS AND AWARDS** Pastor, First Baptist Church of Union Star; Calvary Baptist Church of Independence; First Baptist Church, Palatine, Ill. **SELECTED PUBLICATIONS** Auth, Personal Evangel for Today, Broadman; pub(s), Adult Teacher; Home Life; Open Windows mag(s). **CONTACT ADDRESS** Golden Gate Baptist Theol Sem, 578 Americans Way, Fairfield, CA 94533. **EMAIL** wschweer@aol.com

SCHWEICKART, DAVID
PERSONAL Born 02/11/1942, Cleveland, OH, m, 1966, 2 children **DISCIPLINE** PHILOSOPHY **EDUCATION** Univ Dayton, BS, 64; Univ Va, PhD in math, 69; Ohio State Univ, PhD in phil, 77. **CAREER** Prof, Loyola Univ, 75-; 3 times at Loyola Rome Center, 87-88, 94-95, 99-00; vis prof of Math, Univ Ky, 69-70 & vis prof of Philos, Univ NH, 86-87; lectr in, Spain, Cuba, El Salvador, Czech Republic, US, and Italy. **HONORS AND AWARDS** Fac Mem of the Year, 99. **MEMBERSHIPS** Am Philos Asn; Radical Philos Asn; Union for Radical Political Economics. **RESEARCH** Soc and Polit philosophy; theories of socialism and marxism; feminist philosophy; critical theory. **SELECTED PUBLICATIONS** Auth, Capitalism or Worker Control An Ethical and Economic Appraisal, Praeger, 80; auth, Against Capitalism, Cambridge UP, 93 & Westview Press, 96, publ in Spanish as, Masalla del capitalismo, 97; coauth, Market Socialism: The Debate Among Socialists, Routledge, 98; auth, After Capitalism, Rowman and Littlefield, forthcoming; articles in, Theoria, Rev of Radical Polit Econ, Can Journal of Philos, Econ and Philos, Critical Rev, Sci and Soc, Soc Theory and Practice, Praxis Int & The Nat Women's Stud Asn J. **CONTACT ADDRESS** Dept of Philosophy, Loyola Univ, Chicago, 6525 N. Sheridan Rd, Chicago, IL 60626. **EMAIL** dschwei@luc.edu

SCHWEITZER, DON
DISCIPLINE SYSTEMATIC THEOLOGY **EDUCATION** Princeton Theol Sem, PhD, 93. **CAREER** Sessional lectr, 97-99, SIAST Prince Albert SK. **MEMBERSHIPS** AAR; CCS. **RESEARCH** Contemporary Christian Theology. **SELECTED PUBLICATIONS** Auth, Douglas Hall's Critique of Jugen Moltmann's Eschatology of the Cross, in: Studies Religion Sciences Religieuses, 98; Gregory Baum on the revelatory work of the Holy Spirit, Horizons, 97; Gregory Baum on Secularization Evangelism and Social Change, Rel Studies and Theol, 96; Curse God and Die: Was Job's Wife Completely Wrong?,

Touchstone, 96; Marginality Status and Power in Asian-American Theology, The Ecumenist, 96; Interpreting Bishop Spong Literally, Touchstone, 95; Jurgen Moltmann's theology as a theology of the Cross, Stud In rel sci Religieuses, 95; The Consistency of Jurgen Moltmann's Theology, Stud Rel Sci, Religiuses, 93; Biblical Principles applied to native-white relationships, The Prince Albert Daily Herald, 93. **CONTACT ADDRESS** 65 11th St East, Prince Albert, SK, Canada S6V 0Z8.

SCHWEITZER, THOMAS A.

DISCIPLINE LAW **EDUCATION** Col Holy Cross, AB, cum laude, 66; Univ Wis, MA 68, PhD, 71; Yale Univ, JD, 77. **CAREER** Assoc, Davis Polk & Wardwell; trial atty, US Dept of Energy; assoc prof Law, Touro Col. **HONORS AND AWARDS** Ford Found fel, WI. **SELECTED PUBLICATIONS** Auth, The United Nations as a Source of Domestic Law: Can Security Council Resolutions be Enforced in American Courts?, Yale Stud in World Pub Order, 78; Federal Oil Price Controls in Bankruptcy Cases: Government Claims for Repayment of Illegal Overcharges Should Not Be Subordinated as 'Penalties' Under 11 USC 726, (a) (4), Okla Law Rev, 89; Student 'Academic Challenge' Cases: Should Judges Grade the Professors on Due Process and Respect for Students' Contract Rights?, Am Univ Law Rev, 91; Lee v. Weisman and the Establishment Clause: Are Invocations and Benedictions at Public School Graduations Constitutionally Unspeakable?, Unvi Detroit Mercy Law Rev, 92; Lee v. Weisman: Whither the Establishment Clause and the Lemon v. Kurtzman Three-Pronged Test?, Touro Law Rev, 93; The Progeny of Lee v. Weisman: Can Student-Initiated Prayer at Public School Graduations Still Be Constitutional?, Brigham Young Univ J of Pub Law, 95; Hate Speech and the First Amendment: Can They Be Reconciled?, Conn Law Rev, 95. **CONTACT ADDRESS** Dept of Law, Touro Col, New York, Brooklyn, NY 11230. **EMAIL** thomass@tourolaw.edu

SCHWERIN, ALAN

PERSONAL Born 03/16/1953, Johannesburg, South Africa, m, 1977, 2 children **DISCIPLINE** PHILOSOPHY **EDUCATION** Rhodes Univ, MA, 78; Rice Univ, PhD, 88. **CAREER** Sr Lectr, Univ of Transkei (South Africa), 80-85; Asst Prof, McNeese Univ, 88-95; Chr, Dept of Political Science and Philosophy, Monmouth Univ, 96-. **HONORS AND AWARDS** Rice Univ Fel; Stanley Travelling Fel; Human Sciences Research Grant (South Africa). **MEMBERSHIPS** Amer Phil Assoc; Hume Soc; Leibnig Soc; Soc for 18th Century Studies **RESEARCH** David Hume's philosophy; Betrand Russell's epistemology **SELECTED PUBLICATIONS** Auth, Some Thoughts on Introducing Young Minds to Science, Soaring Digest, 93; Ed, On the Assertation I am my Brain, Expanding the Universe: An Introduction to Philosophy, 93; The Expanding Universe: An Introduction to Philosophy, 93; Soaring to New Heights, The Science Teacher, 94; Auth, Hume's Paradoxical Thesis and His Critics: Some Comments, Southwest Philosophy Review, 95; The Rise of Modern Philosophy, Leibniz Society Review, 96; Some Thoughts on Thinking and Teaching Styles, Inquiry: Critical Thinking Across the Disciplines, 96; A Scorched Sole: Apartheid's Landscape and Ideas, The Mcneese Review, 97; Some Questions about Kant's Clear Question, Southwest Philosophy Review, forthcoming. **CONTACT ADDRESS** Dept of Political Science and Philosophy, Monmouth Univ, 400 Cedar Ave, West Long Branch, NJ 07764. **EMAIL** aschweri@monmouth.edu

SCHWITZGEBEL, ERIC

PERSONAL Born Boston, MA, m, 1997, 1 child **DISCIPLINE** PHILOSOPHY **EDUCATION** Stanford, BA, 91; Univ Calif, PhD, 97. **CAREER** Asst Prof, Univ Calif, 97-. **RESEARCH** Ancient Chinese philosophy, epistemology, metaphilosophy, philosophy of psychology, philosophy of mind, philosophy of science. **SELECTED PUBLICATIONS** Auth, "Zhuangzi's Attitude Toward Language and His Skepticism," in Essays on Skepticism, Relativism and Ethics in the Zhuangzi (Albany: St Univ NY Pr, 96), 68-96; auth, "Theories in Children and the Rest of Us," Philos of Sci, Supplemental Issue 63 (96): 202-210; coauth, "Whose Concepts are They Anyway? The Role of Philosophical Intuition in Empirical Psychology," in Rethinking Intuition (Lanham: Rowman and Littlefield, 98), 75-91; auth, "Representation and Desire: A Philosophical Error with Consequences for Theory-of-Mind Research," Philos Psychol 12 (99): 157-180; auth, "Reply to Commentators: Scientific and Everyday Theories are of a Piece," Sci & Educ 8 (99): 575-582; auth, "Children's Theories and the Drive to Explain," Sci & Educ 8 (99): 457-488; auth, "Gradual Belief Change in Children," Human Develop 42 (99): 283-296. **CONTACT ADDRESS** Dept Philosophy, Univ of California, Riverside, Riverside, CA 92521-0201. **EMAIL** eschwitz@citrus.ucr.edu

SCOLEDES, ARISTOTLE

PERSONAL Born 02/22/1929, New York, NY, m, 1977, 3 children **DISCIPLINE** PHILOSOPHY; AERONAUTICS; ASTRONAUTICS **EDUCATION** Syracuse Univ, BA, 51; Johns Hopkins Univ, MSE, 53; MIT, ScD, 57; Stanford Univ, PhD, 65. **CAREER** Res assoc, Johns Hopkins Univ, 51-53; res fel Univ Chicago, 53-54; res fel, MIT, 55-59; exec engr, project coord Apollo Mission program, Philco Western Develop Labs/Ford Aerospace, 60-62; asst prof, philos of sci, Alfred Univ, 62-63; assoc prof, philos of sci and theoretical biol, SUNY Buffalo, 63-68; prof philos sci and technol, Georgia Inst Technol, 68-72; sr consult, sponsored minorities prog Econ Opportunity Atlanta/CETA, 72-77; proj mgr, dir, Consulting Consortium, Stanford Univ, 77-95; MIT/Stanford Venture Lab. **HONORS AND AWARDS** Hon fel, AIAA, 71; Res Serv Recognition award, Offices of Naval Res and Chief of Naval Oper, 84; Who's Who in America, 99; Who's Who in World, 99; Who's Who in Science and Engineering, 99; and Dictionary Intern'l Biog, 00. **MEMBERSHIPS** Nat Space Soc; Planetary Soc; AAUP; Democritos Soc; Hist of Sci Soc; Air Force Asn; Philos of Sci Asn; APA; Sigma Xi; Tau Beta Pi. **CONTACT ADDRESS** 84 Roosevelt Cir, Palo Alto, CA 94306-4218. **EMAIL** variari@aol.com

SCOLES, EUGENE FRANCIS

PERSONAL Born 06/12/1921, Shelby, IA, m, 1942, 2 children **DISCIPLINE** LAW **EDUCATION** State Univ Iowa, AB, 43; JD, 45; Harvard Univ, LLM, 49; Columbia Univ, JSD, 55. **CAREER** Assoc Seyfarth, Shaw & Fairweather, Chicago, Ill, 45-46; from asst prof to assoc prof law, Northeastern Univ, 46-49; from assoc prof to prof, Univ Fla, 49-56; prof, Univ Ill, Champaign, 56-68; prof & dean, 68-74, distinguished prof, Univ Ore, 74-82, Prof Emer, Sch Law, Univ Ore, 82-. **MEMBERSHIPS** Asn Am Law Schs (pres, 78). **RESEARCH** Trusts and estates; conflict of laws. **SELECTED PUBLICATIONS** Coauth, Cases and materials on conflice of laws, 2nd ed, West Pub Co (St. Paul), 72; coauth, Problems and materials on future interests; coauth, Conflicts of laws, West Pub (St. Paul, Minn), 82; auth, Conflict of laws, 3rd ed, West Group (St. Paul, Minn), 00; coauth, Problems and materials on decedents' estates and trusts, 6th ed, Aspen Law and Business (Gaithersburg), 00. **CONTACT ADDRESS** Col of Law, Univ of Oregon, Eugene, OR 97403. **EMAIL** escoles@law.uoregon.edu

SCORGIE, GLEN G.

PERSONAL Born 03/29/1952, Vancouver, BC, Canada, m, 1978, 3 children **DISCIPLINE** HISTORICAL THEOLOGY **EDUCATION** Univ of St Andrews, Scotland, PhD, 86. **CAREER** Data-processing marketing asst, 74-76; IBM Canada, Toronto; adjunct prof of theology, 84-91, Canadian Theological Seminary; dir of admissions, 76-79, asst prof, 84-88, acting dean of faculty, Jan-May 89, assoc prof 88-91, Canadian Bible Col; academic dean and vice-pres, 91-96, prof 95-96, North Amer Baptist Col; prof, Bethel Theological Seminary, 96-. **HONORS AND AWARDS** Who's Who in America; British Government Overseas Research Student Scholarship; Regent College Church History Prize; Delta Epsilon Chi Honor Society. **MEMBERSHIPS** American Academy of Religion; Canadian Evangelical Theological Assn; Conference on Faith and History; Evangelical Theological Society. **RESEARCH** Key Determinants of Spirtual Resilience: An Interdisciplinary Perspective; Movie Theology: Thinking Christianly about Contemporary Film and Cinema; Asian theology and spirituality, Christology and pluralism. **SELECTED PUBLICATIONS** Auth, A Call for Continuity: The Theological Contribution of James Orr, 88; Directionary of Twentieth Century Christian Biography, 95; auth, A.B. Simpson, Holiness and Modernity, in Studies in Canadian Evangelical Renewal, Faith Today, 96; coauth, Human Life is Not Sheep: An Ethical Perspective on cloning, Journal of the Evangelical Theological Society, Dec 97; auth, Yearning for God: The Potential and Poverty of the Catholic Spirituality of Francis de Sales, Journal of the Evangelical Theological Society, Sept 98. **CONTACT ADDRESS** 6116 Arosa St, San Diego, CA 92115-3902. **EMAIL** gscourgie@bethel.edu

SCOTCHMER, SUZANNE ANDERSEN

PERSONAL Born 01/23/1950, Seattle, WA, s **DISCIPLINE** ECONOMICS **EDUCATION** Univ Wash, BA, 70; Univ Calif Berkeley, MA, 70; PhD, 80. **CAREER** Asst prof to assoc prof, Harvard Univ, 80-86; assoc prof to prof, Univ Calif, 86-. **HONORS AND AWARDS** Sloan Fel; Olin Fel; Phi Beta Kappa; NSF Principal Investigator; Hoover Nat Fel. **MEMBERSHIPS** Am Econ Asn; Econometric Soc. **RESEARCH** Law and economics; Intellectual property. **SELECTED PUBLICATIONS** Auth, "Standing on the Shoulders of Giants: Cumulative Research and the Patent Law," J of Econ Perspectives, (91): 29-41; auth, "On the Evolution of Optimizing Behavior," J of Econ Theory, (92): 392-406; co-auth, "Patent Breadth, Patent Life, and the Pace of Technological Improvement," J of Econ and Management Strategy, (98): 1-32; auth, "Rules of Evidence and Statistical Reasoning in Court," in New Palgrave Dictionary of Economics and the law, Macmillan Press, 98; auth, "On the Optimality of the Patent Renewal System," Rand J of Econ, (99): 181-196; co-auth, "On the Evolution of Attitudes toward Risk in Winner-Take-All Games," J of Econ Theory, (990: 125-143; co-auth, "Clubs and the Market," Econometrica, (99): 1185-1218; auth, "Local Public Goods and Clubs," in 2001 Handbook of Public Economics, Vol III, (forthcoming); co-auth, "Damages and Injunctions in the Protection of Intellectual Property," RAND J of Econ, 01. **CONTACT ADDRESS** Dept Econ, Univ of California, Berkeley, 549 Evans Hall, No 3880, Berkeley, CA 94720-3880. **EMAIL** scotch@socrates.berkeley.edu

SCOTT, CHARLES

PERSONAL Born 09/03/1935, Oklahoma, OK, m, 1994, 3 children **DISCIPLINE** PHILOSOPHY **EDUCATION** S. Methodist Univ, BA, 57; Eberhard-Karls Univ, Fulbright Fel, 57-58; Yale Div Sch, MDiv, 61; Yale Grad Sch, MA, 62, PhD, 65. **CAREER** Yale Berk Col, dean, inst, 63-66; Vanderbilt, asst prof, assoc prof, prof, 66-94; Mellon Regional Fac Devel Prog, dir, 79-87; Robert Penn Warren Center, dir, 87-93; Penn State Univ, E.E. Sparks prof, 94-. **HONORS AND AWARDS** Phi Beta Kappa, Fulbright Fel, Kent-Danforth Fel, Hooker Fel, Julia A. Archibald High Sch, Chancellor's Cup, NEH Fel, Vanderbilt sr res Fel. **MEMBERSHIPS** APA, SPEP, SSPP, AAUP, MSA, NEH reviewer. **RESEARCH** 19th and 20th cent Euro philos. **SELECTED PUBLICATIONS** Auth, Boundaries in Mind: A Study of Immediate Awareness Based in Psychotherapy, Scholars Press and Crossroads Press, 82; auth, The Language of Difference, Humanities Press Intl and MacMillan 87; auth, The Question of Ethics: Nietzsche, Foucault, Heidegger, Indiana Univ Press, 90; auth, On the Advantages and Disadvantages of Ethics and Politics, Indiana Univ Press, 96; auth, The Time of Memory, in: Contemporary Continental Philosophy, 98. **CONTACT ADDRESS** Dept of Philosophy, Pennsylvania State Univ, Univ Park, 240 Sparks Building, University Park, PA 16802. **EMAIL** ces11@psu.edu

SCOTT, DAVID ALLEN

DISCIPLINE SYSTEMATIC THEOLOGY **EDUCATION** Amherst Col, BA, 54-58; Episcopal Divinity Sch, MDiv, 59-61; Princeton Univ, MA, 63-65, PhD, 68; Goethe Inst, Ebersberg, Passed State Exam in Ger Lang, 66; Tubingen Univ, stud and res, 66-67. **CAREER** Part-time asst, part-time chaplain, Trinity Church, Princeton Univ, 63-65; grad asst, Princeton Theol Sem, 65; instr, Episcopal Divinity Sch, 68-70; asst prof, 70-73; assoc prof, 73-79; instr, Dartmouth Col, 76; prof, 79-89; William Meade prof, Va Theol Sem, 89-. **HONORS AND AWARDS** Order of the Holy Cross, missionary, Liberia, W Africa, 61-63; **SELECTED PUBLICATIONS** Auth, Episcopal Ethical Teaching: Case Study Abortion;The Crisis in Moral Teaching in the Episcopal Church, Morehouse, 92; Christian Character: Jeremy Taylor and Christian Ethics Today, Latimer House, 91; Creation as Christ: A Problematic Theme in Some Feminist Theology, Speaking the Christian God, The Holy Trinity and the Challenge of Feminism, William B. Eerdmanns Publ Comp, 91. **CONTACT ADDRESS** Virginia Theol Sem, 3737 Seminary Rd, Alexandria, VA 22304. **EMAIL** DAScott@vts.edu

SCOTT, GARY ALAN

PERSONAL Born Long Beach, CA, m, 1995 **DISCIPLINE** PHILOSOPHY **EDUCATION** Duquesne Univ, PhD, 95. **CAREER** Vis asst prof, Whittier Col, 95-96; vis asst prof, Siena Col, 96-97; asst prof, St Peter's Col, 97-. **HONORS AND AWARDS** Kenny Res Fel, 99, 00. **MEMBERSHIPS** Am Philos Assoc; Soc for Ancient Greek Philos; Int Assoc for Philos and Lit. **RESEARCH** History of Plato Interpretation, issues in Socratic pedagogy. **SELECTED PUBLICATIONS** Auth, "Setting Free the Boys: Limits and Liberation in Plato's Lysis", disClosure: J of Soc Theory 4, (94-5): 24-43; auth, "Irony and Inebriation in Plato's Symposium: The Disagreement Between Socrates and Alcibiades Over Truth-Telling", J of Neoplatonic Studies 3.2 (95): 25-60; auth, "Games of Truth: Foucault's Analysis of the Transformation from Political to Ethical Parrhesia", Southern J of Philos 34.1 (96): 97-114; coauth, "An Overlooked Motive in Alcibiades' Symposium Speech", Interpretation 24.1 (96): 67-84; auth, "Foucault's Analysis of Power's Methodologies", Auslegung 21.2 (96): 125-133; auth, "Plato's Immortalization of Socrates", Proceedings of the Fifth Conf of the Int Soc for the Study of European Ideas, eds, Frank Brinkhuis and Sasha Tamor, MIT Pr, 98; coauth, "Eros as Messenger in Diotima's Teaching", Who Speaks for Plato?: Studies in Platonic Anonymity, ed Gerald A. Pr, Rowman and Littlefield (00): 147-59; auth, "Plato's Socrates as Educator", SUNY Series in Ancient Greek Philos, ed Anthony Presud, SUNY Pr, 00; auth, "Plato and the Authorial Voice: On Gonzalez and Michelini", Plato as Author: The Rhetoric of Philosophy, eds Larry Host and Anne Michelini, (forthcoming); ed, Rethinking Socratic Method: Essays in dialogue with Gregory Vlastos's The Socratic Elenchus", Pa State Univ Pr, (forthcoming). **CONTACT ADDRESS** Dept Philos, Saint Peter's Col, 2641 Kennedy Blvd, Jersey City, NJ 07306-5943. **EMAIL** scott-g@spcvxa.spc.edu

SCOTT, GREGORY L.

PERSONAL Born Washington, DC **DISCIPLINE** PHILOSOPHY, DANCE EDUCATION **EDUCATION** Univ Of California, BA, 79; Columbia Univ, MA, 86; Univ of Toronto, PhD, 92. **CAREER** Adj, NYU/New School Univ, 95-; Dir of Doctoral Stud, 95-98, Dance Edu, NY Univ; Vis Res Fellow, Philo, 95-97, Princeton Univ; Asst Prof Philo, 93-95, Univ of Ottawa, Canada; Asst Prof, Philo, 92-93, St Mary's Univ, Halifax; Asst Prof Philo, 91-92, Texas Tech Univ, Lubbock. **MEMBERSHIPS** APA, Soc of Dance Hist Stud. **RESEARCH** Ancient Greek Philosophy; Aesthetics; Philosophy of Sex. **SELECTED PUBLICATIONS** Auth, Banes and Carroll on Defining Dance, Dance Research Journal, 97; The Poetics of Performance, The Necessity of Performance and Spectacle in Aristotelian Tragedy, eds, Salim Kemal and Ivan Gaskell, Cambridge Univ Press, 99; Empires, Egalitarianism and the International Dance Academy, Proceedings of the Society of Dance History Scholars Conference-Border Crossings, Dance and Boundaries in Society, Politics, Gender, Education and Technology, Ryerson Polytechnic Univ, Toronto, Ontario, 95. **CONTACT ADDRESS** 83 Park Terrace W #3A, New York, NY 10034. **EMAIL** gs30@is3.nyu.edu

SCOTT, HUGH B.
PERSONAL Born 04/29/1949, Buffalo, NY, m, 1973 **DISCIPLINE** LAW **EDUCATION** Niagara University, Lewiston, NYork, BA, 1967-71; State University of New York at Buffalo Law School, JD, 1971-74. **CAREER** County of Erie Dept of Law, assistant county attorney, 74-75; City of Buffalo Dept of Law, asst corporation counsel, 75-77; Dept of Justice, Buffalo, NY, asst US attorney, 77-79; New York State Dept of Law, Buffalo, NY, asst attorney general, 79-83; UB Law School, Amherst Campus, Lecturer, 80-; NY State Office of Court, Buffalo, City Court Judge, 83-. **MEMBERSHIPS** Board of managers, Buffalo Museum of Science, 1989-; board of directors, UB Law Alumni Association, 1988-; former vice chairman, Urban League of Buffalo, 1980; advisory council, TransAfrica Buffalo, 1990-; member, Alpha Kappa Boule, 1983-. **CONTACT ADDRESS** Buffalo City Court, 25 Delaware, Suite 600,, Buffalo, NY 14202.

SCOTT, JAMES
DISCIPLINE PHILOSOPHY OF CULTURE **EDUCATION** Columbia Univ, PhD. **CAREER** Philos, Univ Ark **SELECTED PUBLICATIONS** Area: philosophy of art, and American philosophy. **CONTACT ADDRESS** Univ of Arkansas, Fayetteville, Fayetteville, AR 72701. **EMAIL** jhscott@comp.uark.edu

SCOTT, KERMIT
DISCIPLINE MEDIEVAL PHILOSOPHY **EDUCATION** Columbia Univ, PhD. **CAREER** Assoc prof, Purdue Univ. **RESEARCH** Social and political philosophy; Marxism. **SELECTED PUBLICATIONS** Published articles, a translation, and a critical text on medieval philosophy. **CONTACT ADDRESS** Dept of Philos, Purdue Univ, West Lafayette, 1080 Schleman Hall, West Lafayette, IN 47907-1080.

SCOTT, KIERAN
PERSONAL Born 08/28/1942, County Cavan, Ireland, m, 1988 **DISCIPLINE** RELIGION, EDUCATION **EDUCATION** Columbia Univ, PhD, 78. **CAREER** Fordham Univ NY. **MEMBERSHIPS** AAR, CTS, APRRE, REA **RESEARCH** Church edu; ecclesiology; adult edu; youth ministry, ministerial theology. **SELECTED PUBLICATIONS** Coauth, Perspectives on Marriage, Oxford Press; auth, Perspectives on Marriage, Oxford Press, 00. **CONTACT ADDRESS** 115 Cornell Ave, Hawthorne, NJ 07506. **EMAIL** kieranscott@yahoo.com

SCOTT, NATHAN ALEXANDER, JR.
PERSONAL Born 04/24/1925, Cleveland, OH, m, 1946, 2 children **DISCIPLINE** THEOLOGY **EDUCATION** Univ Mich, BA, 44; Union Theol Sem, MDiv, 46; Columbia Univ, PhD, 49. **CAREER** Instr, asst prof, assoc prof Hum and Dir General Educ Prog in Hum, Howard Univ, 48-55; asst prof, assoc prof, prof, Theol and Lit, 55-72, Shailer Mathews Prof of Theol and Lit, 72-76, Univ Chicago; William R. Kenan Prof Relig Stud, Univ Va, 76-90, now William R. Kenan Prof Emer, Univ Va. **HONORS AND AWARDS** Hon LittD, Brown Univ, 81; hon LittD, Northwestern Univ; hon HumD, Univ Mich, 88; hon LHD, Wesleyan Univ, 89; hon DD, Bates Col, 90; hon STD, Univ of the South, 92; hon DD, Kenyon Col, 93; hon DD, Wabash Col, 96. **MEMBERSHIPS** Am Acad of Arts and Sci; MLA; Am Acad Relig. **RESEARCH** Modern American poetry; Victorian literature; modern literary theory; modern theology. **SELECTED PUBLICATIONS** Auth, The Broken Center: Studies in the Theological Horizon of Modern Literature, Yale, 66; auth, Negative Capability: Studies in the New Literature and the Religious Situation, Yale, 69; auth, The Wild Prayer of Longing: Poetry and the Sacred, Yale, 71; auth, The Poetics of Belief, Univ North Carolina, 85; auth, Visions of Presence in Modern Amrican Poetry, Johns Hopkins, 93. **CONTACT ADDRESS** Prof Relig Studies & English, Univ of Virginia, Charlottesville, VA 22903.

SCOTT, PETER DALE
PERSONAL Born 01/11/1929, Montreal, PQ, Canada, m, 1956, 3 children **DISCIPLINE** ENGLISH, POLITICAL SCIENCE **EDUCATION** McGill Univ, BA, 49, PhD(polit sci), 55. **CAREER** Lectr polit sci, McGill Univ, 55-56; foreign serv off, Can Foreign Serv, 56-61; lectr speech, 61-62, acting asst prof, 62-63, asst prof, 63-66, asst prof, 66-68, assoc prof, 68-80, PROF ENGLISH, UNIV CALIF, BERKELEY, 80-, Humanities res fel, Univ Calif, Berkeley, 68; Guggenheim fel, 69-70. **RESEARCH** Covert Politics; medieval Latin poetry; literature and politics. **SELECTED PUBLICATIONS** Auth, Mcnamara And Vietnam - Reply/, New York Rev Of Books, Vol 0042, 1995. **CONTACT ADDRESS** 2823 Ashby Ave, Berkeley, CA 94705.

SCOTT, TIMOTHY
PERSONAL Born 10/22/1957, Regina, SK, Canada, s **DISCIPLINE** NEW TESTAMENT **EDUCATION** SSL; STD. **CAREER** President, St Joseph's Col, Univ of Alberta. **MEMBERSHIPS** AAR-SBL; CBA; CSBS; CTSA. **RESEARCH** New Testament; Hermeneutics **CONTACT ADDRESS** St. Joseph's Col, Alberta, Univ of Alberta, Edmonton, AB, Canada T6G 2J5. **EMAIL** timscott@gpu.srv.ualberta.ca

SCOTT, WALTER GAYLORD
PERSONAL Born 12/22/1928, El Paso, TX, m, 1950, 2 children **DISCIPLINE** PHILOSOPHY **EDUCATION** Baylor Univ, BA, 49, MA, 58; Southwestern Baptist Theol Sem, BD, 52, ThM, 54; Johns Hopkins Univ, PhD(philos), 69. **CAREER** Instr philos, Baylor Univ, 55-56; asst prof & acting chmn philos, La Col, 56-57; jr instr philos, Johns Hopkins Univ, 59-60; asst prof philos, 60-69, acting chmn dept relig, 61-67, assoc prof philos & chmn dept, 70-76, assoc prof philos, Okla State Univ, 76-97, assoc prof emeritus, 97-. **MEMBERSHIPS** Central Div Am Philos Asn; Southwestern Philos Soc; Medieval Acad Am; Renaissance Soc Am; Soc Medieval & Renaissance Philos. **RESEARCH** Philosophy of William Ockham; medieval cosmology; medieval geomancy; oriental philosophy, philosophy of religion. **CONTACT ADDRESS** Dept of Philos, Oklahoma State Univ, Stillwater, Stillwater, OK 74078-0002. **EMAIL** wscott_osu@osu.net

SCOTT, WILLIAM
PERSONAL Born 02/04/1949, Grainger County, TN, m, 1973, 2 children **DISCIPLINE** THEOLOGY **EDUCATION** E Tex Baptist Univ, BA, 73; SW Baptist Theol Sem, MA, 77; New Orleans Baptist Theol Sem, EdD, 93. **CAREER** Asst Prof to Assoc Prof, Liberty Univ, 93-. **MEMBERSHIPS** Am Asn of Marriage and Family Therapy. **RESEARCH** Pastoral Counseling: Effective Treatments. **CONTACT ADDRESS** Dept Relig & Philos, Liberty Univ, PO Box 20000, Lynchburg, VA 24506. **EMAIL** wscott@liberty.edu

SCOTTO, DOMINIC
PERSONAL Born 12/03/1929, Brooklyn, NY, s **DISCIPLINE** THEOLOGY **EDUCATION** St. Francis Col, BA, 63; Cath Univ Am, STB, 67; STL, 68; Univ Notre Dame, MA, 72; Pontifical Univ, Italy, STL, 75; STD, 79. **CAREER** U.S. Air Force, 51-55; prof, St. Francis Sem, 69-80; prof, Franciscan Univ Steubenville, 97-. **MEMBERSHIPS** Cath Liturgical soc of Am; Societas Liturgica. **RESEARCH** History of Church Worship. **SELECTED PUBLICATIONS** Auth, The Liturgy of the Hours, St. Bede's Pr; auth, The Table of the Lord, St. Bede's Pr. **CONTACT ADDRESS** Dept Theol, Franciscan Univ of Steubenville, 1235 University Blvd, Steubenville, OH 43952-1763.

SEARLE, JOHN R.
PERSONAL Born 07/31/1932, Denver, CO, m, 1958, 2 children **DISCIPLINE** PHILOSOPHY **EDUCATION** Univ of Wisconsin; Oxford Univ, BA, 55, MA & DPhil, 59. **CAREER** Lectr philos, Christ Church Col, Oxford, Prof Philos, Univ Calif, Berkeley, 59-, vis posts at Universities in North and South America and in Europe, spec asst to chancellor, 65-67, panelist and moderator weekly prog, World Press, Nat Educ TV, 70-77; Reith Lectr, BBC, London, 84; Mass Inst Technol Vis Comt for Ling & Philos, 71-77; Guggenheim fel, 75-76; mem bd dirs, Coun Philos Studies, 75-80; mem bd trustees, Nat Humanities Ctr, 75-90; mem bd dirs, Am Coun Learned Soc, 79-87, mem Nat Coun, Nat Endowment of the Humanities 92-96, mem bd, Neurosciences Res Prog, 89-96, mem Am Acad of Arts and Sciences, 76-. **HONORS AND AWARDS** Adelphi, Wisconsin, Bucharest, Turin; Jovellanos, Jesn Nicod, Homer Smith. **MEMBERSHIPS** Aristotelin Soc; Am Acad Arts & Sci; Am Philos Asn. **RESEARCH** Philosophy of language; philosophy of mind; philosophy of society. **SELECTED PUBLICATIONS** Auth, Speech Acts, 69, auth, The Campus War, 71; auth, Expression and Meaning, 79; auth, Intentionality, 83; auth, Minds, Brains and Science, 84; coauth, Foundations of Illocutionary Logic, with D. Vanderveken, 85; auth, The Rediscovery of The Mind, 92; auth, The Construction of Social Reality, 95; auth, The Mystery of Consciousness, 97; auth, Mind, Language and Society, 98. **CONTACT ADDRESS** Dept of Philos, Univ of California, Berkeley, Berkeley, CA 94720.

SEARLS, EILEEN H.
PERSONAL Born 04/27/1925, Madison, WI **DISCIPLINE** LAW **EDUCATION** Univ Wi, BA, 48, JD, 50, MS, 51 **CAREER** Instr to asst prof to assoc prof, librn, St. Louis Univ, 52-53 **MEMBERSHIPS** ABA; ALA, Wi Bar Assoc; Bar Assoc Metrop St. Louis; Amer Assoc Law Librn; Mid Amer Assoc Law Librn; SW Assoc Law Librn. **CONTACT ADDRESS** 3700 Lindell Blvd, Saint Louis, MO 63108. **EMAIL** searlseh@slu.edu

SECADA, JORGE E. K.
PERSONAL Born 03/02/1951, Lima, Peru, s **DISCIPLINE** PHILOSOPHY **EDUCATION** Univ Catolica de Peru, BA, 75; Univ of York, England, B Phil, 77; Univ Cambridge, PhD, 83. **CAREER** Fel, St. John's Col, 80-84; assoc prof, Univ Va, 84-. **HONORS AND AWARDS** Brit Coun Scholar, 75-77; Title A fel, St. John's Col, 80-84; NEH distinguished visiting prof, State Univ NY at Potsdam, 98. **MEMBERSHIPS** APA; Soc Peruana de Filosofia; Soc for Medieval and Renaissance Philos. **RESEARCH** Late medieval and early modern philosophy; Metaphysics; Political philosophy. **SELECTED PUBLICATIONS** Auth, Berkeley y el idealismo, Del Renacimiento a la Ilustracion II, Madrid, 98; auth, Descartes y la escolastica, Arete, 96; auth, Cartesian Metaphysics, Cambridge Univ Press, 00; auth, "Berkeley, Descartes y los origenes del idealismo" in Giusti, ed., LA FILOSOFIA HOY, Lima, 00. **CONTACT ADDRESS** Dept. of Philosophy, Univ of Virginia, Cabell Hall 512, Charlottesville, VA 22903. **EMAIL** jes2f@virginia.edu

SECKINGER, DONALD SHERMAN
PERSONAL Born 02/01/1933, New York, NY, m, 1955, 3 children **DISCIPLINE** PHILOSOPHY & HISTORY OF EDUCATION **EDUCATION** Univ Calif, Los Angeles, AB, 54, MA, 56, EdD, 65. **CAREER** From asst prof to assoc prof educ, Calif State Univ, Los Angeles, 64-70; assoc prof educ found, 70-77, Prof Educ Found, Univ Wyo, 77-, Vis lectr educ, Univ Calif, Los Angeles, 68-69. **MEMBERSHIPS** Fel Philos Educ Soc; Am Educ Studies Asn; fel Far Western Philos Educ Soc(-secy-treas, 74-77, vpres, 77 & pres, 78-). **RESEARCH** Philosophical anthropology; existential philosophy. **SELECTED PUBLICATIONS** Auth, Tombaugh,Clyde - Discoverer Of The Planet Pluto - Levy,D/, J Of The W, Vol 0032, 1993. **CONTACT ADDRESS** Dept of Educ Founds, Univ of Wyoming, Laramie, WY 82070.

SEDGWICK, TIMOTHY F.
PERSONAL Born 12/06/1946, Melrose Park, IL, m, 1968, 2 children **DISCIPLINE** CHRISTIAN ETHICS **EDUCATION** Albion Col, AB, 69; Vanderbilt Univ, Grad Sch Rel, MA, 74, PhD, 75. **CAREER** Asst prof, Denison Univ, 75-76; Marshall Univ, 76-77; Blackburn Col, 77-78; asst prof to prof, Seabury-Western Theol Sem, 78-97; prof, Va Theol Sem, 97-. **SELECTED PUBLICATIONS** Auth, The Christian Moral Life, Eerdmans, 99; auth, The Making of Ministry, Cowley, 93; Sacramental Ethics: Paschal Identity and the Christian Life, Fortress, 87; coauth, Faithful Living Faithful Dying: Anglican Reflections on End of Life Care, Morehouse, 00; co-ed, The Crisis in Moral Teaching in the Episcopal Church, Morehouse, 92. **CONTACT ADDRESS** Virginia Theol Sem, 3737 Seminary Rd, Alexandria, VA 22304. **EMAIL** TSedgwick@vts.edu

SEDLER, ROBERT ALLEN
PERSONAL Born 09/11/1935, Pittsburgh, PA, m, 1960, 2 children **DISCIPLINE** LAW **EDUCATION** Univ Pittsburgh, BA, 56, JD, 59. **CAREER** Teaching assoc law, Rutgers Univ, 59-60, asst prof, 61; from asst prof to assoc prof, St Louis Univ, 61-65; from assoc prof to prof, Univ Ky, 66-77; Prof Law, Wayne State Univ, 77-, Assoc prof & asst dean, Haile Sellassic Univ, 63-66. **MEMBERSHIPS** Am Bar Asn; ACLU. **RESEARCH** Conflict of laws; civil rights; constitutional law. **SELECTED PUBLICATIONS** Auth, Across State Lines: Applying the Conflict of Law to Your Practice, 89; The Complex Litigation Projects Proposal For Federally-Mandated Choice Of Law In Mass Torts Cases - Another Assault On State Sovereignty/, Louisiana Law Rev, Vol 0054, 1994; auth, "Constitutional Law-United States," Encyclopedia of Laws, 94. **CONTACT ADDRESS** Law Sch, Wayne State Univ, 468 Ferry Mall, Detroit, MI 48202-3698. **EMAIL** 222396@wayne.edu

SEESKIN, KENNETH
DISCIPLINE PHILOSOPHY **EDUCATION** Yale Univ, PhD. **CAREER** Prof, Northwestern Univ. **RESEARCH** Ancient philosophy, Jewish philosophy, philosophy of religion, philosophy in literature. **SELECTED PUBLICATIONS** Auth, Dialogue and Discovery: A Study in Socratic Philosophy; Jewish Philosophy in a Secular Age. **CONTACT ADDRESS** Dept of Philosophy, Northwestern Univ, 1801 Hinman, Evanston, IL 60208.

SEGAL, ALAN FRANKLIN
PERSONAL Born 08/02/1945, Worcester, MA, m, 1970, 2 children **DISCIPLINE** JUDAICA, HISTORY OF RELIGION **EDUCATION** Amherst Col, BA, 67; Brandeis Univ, MA, 69; Hebrew Union Col, BHL, 70; Yale Univ, MPhil, 72, PhD(Judaica), 75. **CAREER** Asst prof Judaica, Princeton Univ, 74-78; assoc prof, Univ Toronto, 78-81; Assoc Prof Judaica, Barnard Col & Grad Fac, Columbia Univ, 81-, Woodrow Wilson fel, 67-68; Jewish Mem Found fel, 73 & 78; Guggenheim fel, 78; chairperson Judaica Sect IAHR, Winnipeg, 80; Mellon fel, Aspen Inst, 81; chmn relig dept, Barnard Col, 81; Ingeborg Rennert Prof of Judaic Studies. **HONORS AND AWARDS** Woodrow Wilson Fel; Guggenheim Fel; NEH Fel; NEH Grant; Jerome Malino Awd; Mellon Fel; Annenberg Fel. **MEMBERSHIPS** Soc Bibl Lit; SNTS, Asn Jewish Studies; Asn Sci Study Relig; Am Acad of Relig; CSBS; ATS. **RESEARCH** Judaica; early Christianity. **SELECTED PUBLICATIONS** Auth, Two Powers in Heaven: Rabbinic Polemics Against Christianity and Gnosticism, Brill, 77; coauth, Philo and the Rabbis on the name of God, J Study Judaism, 79; Heavenly ascent in Hellenistic Judaism, early Christianity and their environments, 23: 2 & Rabbinc Polemic and the radicalization of Gnosticism, 23:2, ANRW; Ruler of this world: Attitudes towards mediator figures and the problem of a sociology of Gnosticism, In: Jewish and

Christian Self-Definition II, Fortress, 81; Hellenistic magic: Some questions of definition, In: Studies in Gnosticism Presented to Gilles Quispel on the Occasion of his 65th Birthday, Brill, Leiden, 81; auth, Rebecca's Children, Harvard, 86; auth, Paul the Convert, Yale, 90. **CONTACT ADDRESS** Dept of Relig, Barnard Col, New York, NY 10027. **EMAIL** asegal@barnard.columbia.edu

SEIDEL, ASHER M.
PERSONAL Born 06/22/1943, Philadelphia, PA, m, 1977, 2 children **DISCIPLINE** METAPHYSICS, EPISTEMOLOGY, AND PHILOSOPHICAL ASPECTS OF COGNITIVE SCIENCE **EDUCATION** Rutgers Univ, AB, philos, 65; Univ Mich, philos, MA, 67, PhD, 70. **CAREER** Teaching fel, Univ Mich, 68-70; visiting asst prof, Mich State Univ, 70-71; asst prof, Miami Univ, 71-84; assoc prof, Miami Univ, 84-. **SELECTED PUBLICATIONS** Auth, Searle's New Argument, Dialogue, 97; rev, Thinking About Logic, Teaching Philosophy, Stephen Read, 96; auth, Plato, Wittgenstein, and Artificial Intelligence, Metaphilos, 91; auth, Chinese Rooms A, B, and C, Pacific Philos Quart, 89; auth, Searle on the Biological Basis of Cognition, Analysis, 88; auth, The Probability of Free Will, Philos, 85; auth, Numbers as Qualities, Philos, 84; auth, Anti Zero-Growth: Brief for Development, Philos and Soc Action, 81; auth, The Picture Theory of Meaning, Linguistics and Philos, 77; auth, Universals and the Coextension of Qualities, New Scholasticism, 76. **CONTACT ADDRESS** Philosophy Dept., Miami Univ, 10 Oakhill Dr, Oxford, OH 45056. **EMAIL** seidela@muohio.edu

SEIDEL, GEORGE J.
PERSONAL Born 04/25/1932, Tacoma, WA **DISCIPLINE** PHILOSOPHY **EDUCATION** St Martin's Col, BA, 55; Univ Toronto, MA, 60; PhD, 62. **CAREER** Prof, philos, St Martin's Col, 62- . **HONORS AND AWARDS** Fulbright fel, 61-62; Orgn Am States fel, 65. **MEMBERSHIPS** APA; N Am Fichte Soc; Northwest Conf on Philos. **RESEARCH** German idealism; twentieth century continental philosophy. **SELECTED PUBLICATIONS** Auth, Fichte's Wissenschaftslehre of 1794: A Commentary on Part I, Purdue, 93; auth, Minded Body/Embodied Mind, man and World, 94; auth, A Key to Heidegger's Beitrage, Gregorianum, 95; auth, The Atheism Controversy of 1799 and the Christology of Fichte's Anweisung zum seligen Leben of 1806, New Perspectives on Fichte, Humanities, 95; auth, Buddhism as Radical Religion, Darshana Int, 95; auth, Angels, Peter Lang, 95; auth, Fichte and German Idealism: The Heideggerian Reading, Idealistic Stud, 98; auth, Heidegger's Last God and the Schelling Connection, Laval Theologique et Philosophique, 99; auth, Knowledge as Sexual Metaphor, Susquehana, 00; auth, Toward a Hermeneutics of Spirit, Bucknell, 00; auth, Fate of Innate Ideas in Fichte, Idealistic Studies, 00. **CONTACT ADDRESS** Saint Martin's Col, 5300 Pacific Ave SE, Lacey, WA 98503. **EMAIL** gseidel@crc.stmartin.edu

SEIDENFELD, TEDDY
PERSONAL Born 05/15/1948, New York, NY, m, 1971, 2 children **DISCIPLINE** PHILOSOPHY **EDUCATION** Univ Rochester, AB, 69; Columbia Univ, PhD, 76. **CAREER** HA Simon prof Phil Stat, 97-, ch, fac sen, 95-96, head, dept Phil, 89-94, prof Phil and Stat, 87-, assoc prof, 86, assoc prof Phil, 85, Carnegie Mellon Univ; assoc prof Phil and Hea care res, 83, assoc prof Phil, 81, Washington Univ; asst prof Phil and Hist Phil of Sci, 77, asst prof Phil, 75, Univ Pittsburgh. **HONORS AND AWARDS** NSF Grant DMS-9801401; STICERD disting scholar, London sch Econ, 97; asst-PI in FIPSE awd; NSF grant; vis scholar, summer inst, Vaxjo Univ, Sweden, 92. **MEMBERSHIPS** Am Philosophical Asn; Am Statistical Asn; Asn for Symbolic Logic; Philosophy of Scie Asn; Phi Kappa Phi Honor Soc; Sigma Xi. **RESEARCH** Philosophy of Science. **SELECTED PUBLICATIONS** Coauth, A Representation of Partially Ordered Preferences, Ann Stat 23, 95, 2168-2217; Coauth, Reasoning to a Foregone Conclusion, J Am Stat Assoc 91, 96, 1228-1235; coauth, Divisive Conditioning: Further Results on Dilation, Phil Sci 64, 97, 411-444. **CONTACT ADDRESS** Dept of Philosophy, Carnegie Mellon Univ, Pittsburgh, PA 15213. **EMAIL** Teddy@stat.cmu.edu

SEIDMAN, ANN
PERSONAL Born 04/30/1926, New York, NY, m, 1946, 5 children **DISCIPLINE** LAW **EDUCATION** Smith Col, BA, 47; Columbia Univ, MA, 53; Univ Wisc, PhD, 68. **CAREER** Lectr, Univ Bridgeport, 58-62; lectr, Univ Ghana, 62-66; sen lectr, Univ Dar es Salaam Tanzania, 68-72; lectr, Univ Wisc, 70-72; prof, Univ Zambia, 72-74; vis assoc prof, Univ Mass, 74-75; vis aff prof, Clark Univ, 75-78; vis prof, Univ Mass Amherst, 76-78; prof, Brown Univ, 78-79; prof, Clark Univ, 79-80; prof, Univ Zimbabwe, 80-83; adj prof, Clark Univ, 83-85; vis prof, Brandeis Univ, 87-88; fulbright prof, Univ Beijing, 88-89; adj prof and co-dir, Boston Univ, 92-; adj prof, Clark Univ, 86-00; vis prof, Univ Witswatersrand, 98-. **HONORS AND AWARDS** Phi Beta Kappa. **MEMBERSHIPS** African Studies Asn; Am Asn of Univ Prof; am Econ Asn; Asn of Concerned African Scholars; Am Coun on Educ; Econ Develop Bureau; UN Develop Prog; Task Force for Sustainable Develop in Africa. **RESEARCH** Agricultural and industrial development, regional cooperation; The use of law to facilitate good governance democratic institutional change to foster development. **SELECTED PUBLICATIONS** Auth, Apartheid, Militarization, and the U.S. Southeast, Africa World Press, 90; co-ed, Twenty-first Century Africa: Towards a New Vision of Sustainable Development, Africa World Press, 92; co-auth, State and Law in the Development Process--Problem-solving and Institutional Change in the Third World, Macmillan, 94; co-ed, Making Development Work = Legislative Reform for Institutional Transformation and Good Governance, Kluwer Law, 99; co-auth, Legislative Theory, Methodology and Techniques: A Practical Manual for Drafters, Kluwer Law, (forthcoming). **CONTACT ADDRESS** Sch of Law, Boston Univ, 765 Commonwealth Ave, Boston, MA 02215. **EMAIL** aseidman@bu.edu

SEIDMAN, LOUIS MICHAEL
PERSONAL Born 02/16/1947, Washington, DC, m, 1977, 1 child **DISCIPLINE** LAW **EDUCATION** Univ Chicago, BA, 68; Harvard Univ, JD, 71. **CAREER** Law clerk, US Ct of Appeals, 71-72 & Supreme Ct Justice, 72-73; staff atty, DC Pub Defender Serv, 73-76; asst prof law, 76-79, assoc prof, 79-82, Prof Law, Georgetown Univ Law Ctr, 82- **RESEARCH** Criminal law; constitutional law. **SELECTED PUBLICATIONS** Auth, The Problems With Privacys Problem - Response/, Mich Law Rev, Vol 0093, 1995. **CONTACT ADDRESS** Law Ctr, Georgetown Univ, 600 New Jersey N W, Washington, DC 20001-2022.

SEIDMAN, ROBERT
PERSONAL m, 1946, 5 children **DISCIPLINE** LAW **EDUCATION** Harvard Col, AB, 41; Columbia, JD, 48. **CAREER** Lectr, Univ of Ghana, 62-66; prof, Univ of Wis, 66-72; prof, Boston Univ, 72-90; prof emeritus, 90-. **HONORS AND AWARDS** Fulbright Prof, China, 88-89. **RESEARCH** Legislative drafting, legislatures, law and development. **SELECTED PUBLICATIONS** Coauth, Law, Order and Power, Addison-Wesley, (Boston), 69; auth, State, Law and Development, Croom-Helm (London), 78; coauth, State and Law in the Development Process, Macmillan (London), 94; coauth, Legislative Drafting for Democratic Social Change: A Manual for Drafters, Kluwer Law International, (London), 00. **CONTACT ADDRESS** Sch of Law, Boston Univ, 765 Commonwealth Ave, Boston, MA 02215. **EMAIL** rseidman@bu.edu

SEIGEL, MICHAEL L.
DISCIPLINE LAW **EDUCATION** Princeton Univ, AB; Harvard Univ, JD. **CAREER** Prof, Univ Fla, 90-; vis prof, Univ BC, Can; past asst US atty, Philadelphia; spec atty, US Dept Justice, Organized Crime Racketeering Sect, Philadelphia Strike Force, 85-89; clerk, Judge Edward R. Becker, US Ct Appeals, 3rd Circuit. **MEMBERSHIPS** Pa Bar; Phi Beta Kappa. **RESEARCH** Evidence, criminal law, professional responsibility, federal criminal law. **CONTACT ADDRESS** School of Law, Univ of Florida, PO Box 117625, Gainesville, FL 32611-7625. **EMAIL** seigel@law.ufl.edu

SEIGFRIED, CHARLENE
DISCIPLINE CLASSICAL AMERICAN PHILOSOPHY, 19TH-CENTURY PHILOSOPHY, FEMINIST PHILOSOPHY **EDUCATION** Loyola Univ, Chicago, PhD. **CAREER** Prof, Purdue Univ. **RESEARCH** Pragmatism and feminism. **SELECTED PUBLICATIONS** Published works in the areas of social and political philosophy, metaphysics, and aesthetics. **CONTACT ADDRESS** Dept of Philos, Purdue Univ, West Lafayette, 1080 Schleman Hall, West Lafayette, IN 47907-1080.

SEIGFRIED, HANS
PERSONAL Born 12/18/1933, German Karavukovo, Yugoslavia, m, 1970, 1 child **DISCIPLINE** PHILOSOPHY **EDUCATION** St Rupert Gymnasium, Bischofshofen/Salzburg, 49-55; St Gabriel Academy, Moedling/Vienna, Grad Studies, 55-60; Univ Bonn/Germany; Philosophy Germanistik Canon Law, PhD, 66. **CAREER** Asst prof, 68-69, assoc prof, 72-81, prof, 82-, Dept of Philosophy, Loyola Univ of Chicago. **HONORS AND AWARDS** Yale Univ, Dept of Phil, Postdoctoral Fel, 66-67; Univ of TX at Austin, Postdoctoral Fel, 67-68. **MEMBERSHIPS** Amer Phil Asn; Soc for Phenomenology and Existential Phil; Intl Soc for Phil and Technology; Soc for the Advancement of Amer Phil; North Amer Nietzsche Soc; North Amer Kant Soc; Heidegger Conf; Soc for the Philosophic Study of Genocide and the Holocaust. **RESEARCH** Kantian and Post-Kantian transcendental phil, phenomenology esp Heidegger, 19th century phil esp Nietzsche & Marx, contemporary German phil, phil and science/technology, Amer phil esp Dewey, phil and literature, human rights. **SELECTED PUBLICATIONS** Auth, Heideggers Technikkritik, Lebenswelt und Wissenschaft Studien zum Verhaltnis von Phanomenologie und Wissenschaftstheorie, Bouvier Verlag, 91; art, On the Ambivalence of Progress in Nietzsche and Heidegger Science and Technology as Mediators, Allgemeine Zeitschrift fur Philosophie 16, 91; art, Nietzsche's Natural Morality, Jour of Value Inquiry 26, 92; art, Dewey's Critique of Kant's Copernican Revolution Revisited, Kant-Studien 83, 93; art, Art as Fetish in Nietzsche and Heidegger, Intl Stud in Phil 27, 95; auth, Heidegger at the Nuremberg Trails The Letter on Humanism Revisited, Martin Heidegger and the Holocaust, Humanities Press, 96; art, Human Rights Ends-in-view & Controlled Inquiry A Response to Paul Chevigny's Dialogue Rights, Jour of Speculative Phil 12, 98; auth, The Voices of the Victims, Contemporary Portrayals of Auschwitz an Genocide: Philosophical Challenges, Humanities Press, 98; auth, We the people/s Bloody universal principles and ethnic codes, Philosophy & Social Criticism 27, 01; auth, Truth & Use, Synthese, 01. **CONTACT ADDRESS** Philosophy Dept, Loyola Univ, Chicago, 6525 North Sheridan Road, Chicago, IL 60626-5385. **EMAIL** hseigfr@luc.edu

SEIPLE, DAVID I.
PERSONAL Born 06/03/1949, Columbus, OH, s **DISCIPLINE** PHILOSOPHY **EDUCATION** Col of Wooster, BA, 71; Drew Univ, MTS, 74; Columbia Univ, PhD, 93. **CAREER** Adj instr, Drew Univ, theol, 73-76; tchg asst, Columbia Univ, 79; adj lectr, relig, Wagner Col, 83; adj instr, philos, NY Inst Technol, 83; adj lectr, philos, LaGuardia Commun Col, 83-86; adj lectr, Drew Univ, 89; adj lectr, hum, NYU, 85-91, currently independent scholar. **HONORS AND AWARDS** Miller Prize, philos, 71; MacDaniel fel, 74; Magna Cum Laude, 74; SCE summer res grant, 90; Lina Kahn prize in metaphysics, 91. **MEMBERSHIPS** APA, Soc for the Advanc of Am Philos, Am Academy of Religion. **RESEARCH** Ethics, aesthetics, gay/lesbian philosophy, American philosophy/Dewey studies, Religious Studies, Reformation Theology. **SELECTED PUBLICATIONS** Auth, Exemplary Ethics in the History of Moral Theory, Punishment, War, in, Ethics Applied, McGraw-hill, 93; auth, Experience and the Organic Unity of Artworks, in Kelly, ed, Encyclopedia of Aesthetics, Oxford, 98; co-ed, Dewey Reconfigured, SUNY, 99; auth, Arthur C. Danto, in Dictionary of Literary Biography, Bruccoli Clark and Layman, forthcoming; auth, Philosophy's Labrynth, http://www.dseiple.com. **CONTACT ADDRESS** 204 W 108th St, No 44, New York, NY 10025. **EMAIL** dseiple@idt.net

SEIPP, DAVID J.
PERSONAL Born 10/19/1955, Dubuque, IA, m, 1994 **DISCIPLINE** LEGAL HISTORY **EDUCATION** Harvard Col, AB, 77; Merton Col Oxford, BA, 79; St. Johns' Col Cambridge, LLB, 80; Harvard Law Sch, JD, 82. **CAREER** Law clerk, U.S. Court of Appeals, 82-83; assoc, Foley, Hoag, and Eliot, 83-86; assoc prof, Boston Univ Sch Law, 86-92; prof, 92- . **MEMBERSHIPS** Selden Soc; Am Soc for Legal Hist; Am Law Inst. **RESEARCH** Legal history. **SELECTED PUBLICATIONS** Auth, The Concept of Property in the Early Common Law, Law and Hist Rev, 94; auth, Crime in the Year Books, Law Reporting in Britain: Proceedings of the Eleventh British Legal History Conference, 95; auth, The Distinction Between Crime and Tort in Early Common Law, Boston Univ Law Rev, 96; auth, Holmes's Path, Boston Univ Law Rev, 97; auth, The Mirror of Justices, Learning the Law: Proceedings of the Thirteenth British Legal History Conference, 99. **CONTACT ADDRESS** School of Law, Boston Univ, 765 Commonwealth Ave, Rm 934B, Boston, MA 02215. **EMAIL** dseipp@bu.edu

SEITZ, BRIAN
DISCIPLINE PHILOSOPHY **EDUCATION** PhD. **CAREER** From asst prof to assoc prof, Babson Col. **MEMBERSHIPS** APA, SPEP, IAPL, ASE, SBE. **RESEARCH** Social and Political Philosophy. **SELECTED PUBLICATIONS** Auth, The Trace of Political Representation, SUNY Press; co-ed, Eating Culture, SUNY Press. **CONTACT ADDRESS** Arts and Humanities, Babson Col, Babson Park, MD 02157-0310.

SELENGUT, CHARLES
PERSONAL Born New York, NY **DISCIPLINE** THEOLOGY **EDUCATION** Drew Univ, MA, 69, PhD, 83. **CAREER** Visiting Prof, Drew Univ, 85-; Prof, County Col of Morris, 70-. **HONORS AND AWARDS** Natl Endowment for the Humanities Awd, 88; Eastern Sociological Soc Merit Awd **MEMBERSHIPS** Soc for the Scientific Study of Religion; Amer Sociological Soc. **RESEARCH** Comparative fundamentalism; conversion to new religion **SELECTED PUBLICATIONS** Auth, Seeing Society, 92; Accounting for Fundamentalism; By Torah Alone: Yeshive Fundamentalism in Jewish Society, 94; Judaism in a Post Modern Age, 99. **CONTACT ADDRESS** 544 Rutland Ave., Teaneck, NJ 07666-2923. **EMAIL** cselengu@ccm.edu

SELIGMAN, ADAM
PERSONAL Born 01/18/1954, Rutland, VT, m, 1992, 2 children **DISCIPLINE** RELIGION **EDUCATION** Hebrew Univ Jerusalem, PhD, 88. **CAREER** Asst prof, Univ Colo, Boulder, 93-95, assoc prof, 95-96; assoc prof, Boston Univ, 96-. **HONORS AND AWARDS** Rothchild Fel, 88-89; Fulbright Fel, Hungary, 90-92. **RESEARCH** Religion, sociology, and politics. **SELECTED PUBLICATIONS** Coauth and ed with S. N. Eisenstadt and L. Roniger, Centre Formation, Protest Movements and Class Structure in Europe and the United State, New York Univ Press (87); coauth and ed with A. Seligman, ed, Order and Transcendence: The Role of Utopias and the Dynamics of Civilizations, Int Studies in Sociology and Social Anthropology, vol 50, E. J. Brill (89); auth, The Idea of Civil Society, The Free Press (92, many translations); auth, Innerwordly Individualism: Charismatic Community and its Institutionalization, Transaction Press (94); coauth and ed, The Transition from Socialism in Eastern Europe, A. Seligman, ed, Comparative Social Research, Vol 14, JAI Press (94); auth, The Problem of Trust, Princeton Univ Press (97, paperback, 2000); coauth and ed,with Mark Lichbach, Market and Community: The Bases of Social

Order, Revolution and Relegitimization, Penn State Univ Press (forthcoming fall 2000); auth, Modernity's Wager: Authority, the Self and Transcendence, Princeton Univ Press (forthcoming Oct 2000). **CONTACT ADDRESS** Dept relig, Boston Univ, 745 Commonwealth Ave, Boston, MA 02215-1401.

SELIGMAN, JOEL
PERSONAL Born 01/11/1950, New York, NY, m, 1982, 2 children **DISCIPLINE** LAW **EDUCATION** Univ Calif, AB, 71; Harvard Univ, JD, 74. **CAREER** Assoc Prof, Northeastern Univ, 77-83; Prof, George Wash Univ, 83-86; Vis Prof to Prof, Univ Mich, 86-95; Prof and Dean, Univ Ariz, 95-99; Prof and Dean, Wash Univ, 99-. **MEMBERSHIPS** State Bar of Calif; CPA; Am Law Inst; Am Bar Asn. **RESEARCH** Securities and Corporations. **SELECTED PUBLICATIONS** Co-auth, "Fundamentals of Securities Regulation," Aspen Law & Bus, 94; auth, "Corporations: Cases and Materials," Aspen Law & Bus, 95; auth, The Transformation of Wall Street: A History of the Securities and Exchange Commission and Modern Corporate Finance, Houghton Mifflin, 95; auth, "Goetterdammerung for the Securities Act?," Wash Univ L Rev, 97; auth, "A Mature Synthesis: O'Hagan Resolves 'Insider'," Del J Corp L, 98; auth, "In Memoriam: Louis Loss," Harvard L Rev, 98; auth, Securities Regulation, Foundation Press, 98; auth, "Securities Regulation and 2001 Annual Supplement," Aspen Law & Bus, 00. **CONTACT ADDRESS** Sch of Law, Washington Univ, 1 Brookings Dr, Campus Box 1120, Saint Louis, MO 63130. **EMAIL** seligman@wulaw.wustl.edu

SELINGER, CARL MARVIN
PERSONAL Born 12/28/1934, Los Angeles, CA, m, 1959, 2 children **DISCIPLINE** LAW **EDUCATION** Univ Calif, Berkeley, BA, 55; Harvard Univ, JD, 58. **CAREER** Prof law, Albany Law Sch, Union Univ, 61-63 & Univ NMex, 63-68; acad dean, Bard Col, 68-75; prof law, Univ Hawaii, 75-79; dean & prof law, Univ Detroit, 79-82; dean & prof law, WVa Univ, 82-; consult, Nat Endowment for Humanities, 68, Legal Serv Prog, Off Econ Opportunity, 70, Curric Study Proj Comt, Asn Am Law Schs, 71, Bryn Mawr Col, 74 & Hawaii Inst Mgt & Anal Gov, 77; NIH grant dir prof communicating ethical dimension of pub policy issues through the info media, 74-75; reporter, Devitt Comt Pilot prog US Dist Court, Eastern Dist Mich, 81. **MEMBERSHIPS** Asn Am Law Schs, Chemn, section on Comparative Law; Am Soc Political & Legal Philos; Inter-Am Bar Asn, Pres, Committee XII. **RESEARCH** Law and ethics; the legal profession; reform of undergraduate education. **SELECTED PUBLICATIONS** Auth, The Public's Interest in Preserving the Dignity and Unity of the Legal Profession, 32 Wake Forest L Rev 861, 97; Dramatizing on Film the Uneasy Role of the American Criminal Defense Lawyer: True Believer, 22 Okla. City U.L. REV. 223, 97; Public Interest Lawyering in Mexico and the United States, 27 U. Miami Inter-Am. L. Rev. 343, 96; The Retention of Limitations on the Out-of-Court Practice of Law By Independent Paralegals, 9 Geo J Legal Ethics 879, 96; Inventing Billable Hours: Contract vs Fairness in Charging Attorneys' Fees, 22 Hofstra L Rev, 671, 94; The Law on Lawyer Efforts to Discredit Truthful Testimony, 46 Okla L Rev 99, 93; Robinson Crusoe Torts, 96, W Va L Rev 169, 93. **CONTACT ADDRESS** Sch of Law, West Virginia Univ, Morgantown, PO Box 6130, Morgantown, WV 26506-6130. **EMAIL** cselinge@wvu.edu

SELJAK, DAVID
DISCIPLINE RELIGIOUS STUDIES **EDUCATION** Univ Toronto, BA, 82; MA, 87; McGill Univ, PhD, 96. **CAREER** Asst prof, St. Jerome's Univ. **MEMBERSHIPS** Am Academy of Relig; Canadian Soc for the study of Relig; Canadian Catholic Hist Asn; Canadian Soc of Church Hist. **SELECTED PUBLICATIONS** Auth, "Modernization Theory nad a New Look at the Hsitory of the Catholic Church in Quebec,"; auth, "The Jesuit Journal 'Relations,' 1959-1969: Modernity, Religion and Nationalism in Quebec,"; auth, "Why the Quiet Revolution was quiet": The Catholic Church's reaction to the secularization of nationalism in Quebec,". **CONTACT ADDRESS** Dept of Religious Studies, St. Jerome's Univ, Waterloo, ON, Canada N2L 3G3. **EMAIL** dseljak@watarts.uwaterloo.ca

SELLERS, MORTIMER
PERSONAL Born 04/21/1959, Philadelphia, PA, m, 1984, 1 child **DISCIPLINE** JURISPRUDENCE **EDUCATION** Harvard Univ, AB, 80, JD, 88; Oxford Univ, DPhil, 86, BCL, 88. **CAREER** Prof law and dir, center for Intl and Comparative Law, Univ Baltimore Sch Law, 89- . **HONORS AND AWARDS** Rhodes Scholar, 80. **MEMBERSHIPS** Amer soc Polit and Legal Philos; Selden soc; Amer Soc Intl Law. **RESEARCH** Political and legal philosophy; Constitutional Law. **SELECTED PUBLICATIONS** Auth, American Republicanism, Macmillan and NYU Press, 94; The Sacred Fire of Liberty, Macmillan and NYU Press, 98. **CONTACT ADDRESS** School of Law, Univ of Baltimore, 1420 North Charles St, Baltimore, MD 21201. **EMAIL** msellers@ubmail.ubalt.edu

SELNER-WRIGHT, SUSAN C.
DISCIPLINE PHILOSOPHY AND METAPHYSICS OF THOMAS AQUINAS **EDUCATION** Univ Notre Dame, BA, 83; Cath Univ Amin Wash, MA, 86, PhD, 92. **CAREER** Dept Philos, Mt Saint Mary's Col **HONORS AND AWARDS** Nat Endowment for the Humanities awd, 94. **RESEARCH** Metaphysics of the relation between charity toward God and toward neighbor. **SELECTED PUBLICATIONS** Auth, The Order of Charity in Thomas Aquinas. **CONTACT ADDRESS** Dept of Philosophy, Mount Saint Mary's Col and Sem, 16300 Old Emmitsburg Rd, Emmitsburg, MD 21727-7799. **EMAIL** selner@msmary.edu

SELVIDGE, MARLA J.
PERSONAL Born 11/11/1948, Gross Pt, MI, m, 1982 **DISCIPLINE** BIBLICAL LANGUAGES AND LITERATURE **EDUCATION** Taylor Univ, BA, 70; Wheaton Col, MA, 73; St. Louis Univ, PhD, 80. **CAREER** Asst prof, John Wesley Col, 73-74; pers dir, Thalhimers, 74-76; res asst, Cts for Reformation Res, 76-77; dir evening div, St Louis Univ, 77-80; lect, St. Louis Univ, 78-80; asst prof, Carthage Col, 80-81; asst prof, Univ Dayton, 81-84; asst prof, Converse Col, 84-87; chemn Relig and Philos, Converse Col, 84-85; coordr grant writing, Cheshire Public Sch, 87-89; asst prof, Marist Col, 89-90; dir, assoc prof, Central Missouri St Univ, 90-94; prof, dir, Center for Relig Stud, Central Missouri St Univ, 94- . **HONORS AND AWARDS** Tenney Awd, Best Thesis, 73; Fac of the Year, 74; nominated Outstanding Women in America, 80; res grant, William R. Kenan Fund and Natl Endowment for the Hum, 84-87; res grant CMSU, 91-92; Missouri Hum Council Grant, 92-94; Byler Awd for Outstanding Research and Teaching, 99. **MEMBERSHIPS** Soc Bibl Lit; Am Acad Relig; Missouri St Tchr Asn. **SELECTED PUBLICATIONS** Auth, "Chautauqua Revival Brings to Life Religious Figures," Relig Stud News, 93; "Mennonites and Amish," Women in American Religious History, Kathryn Kuhlman, Missouri Chautauqua, 93; "Magic and Menses," Explorations, 93; "Discovering Women," Teacher Created Materials, 95; "Notorious Voices," Continuum, 96; "Reflections on Violence and Pornography," A Feminist Companion to the Bible, Sheffield, 96; The New Testament, PrenticeHall, 99, 2nd ed, forthcoming. **CONTACT ADDRESS** Center For Religious Studies, Central Missouri State Univ, Martin 118, Warrensburg, MO 64093. **EMAIL** mjs85674@cmsu2.cmsu.edu

SENCERZ, STEFAN
PERSONAL Born 06/08/1954, Warsaw, Poland **DISCIPLINE** PHILOSOPHY **EDUCATION** Univ Rochester, PhD, 91. **MEMBERSHIPS** Am Philoso Asn. **RESEARCH** Ethical theory; Applied ethics; Metaphysics. **CONTACT ADDRESS** 9350 S Padre Island Dr, #11, Corpus Christi, TX 78418. **EMAIL** sencerz@falcon.tamucc.edu

SENNETT, JAMES
PERSONAL Born 08/04/1955, Norfolk, VA, m, 1978, 1 child **DISCIPLINE** PHILOSOPHY **EDUCATION** Atlanta Christian Col, BA, 77; Lincoln Christian Sem, MDiv, 81; Univ Nebraska, MA, 87, PhD, 90. **CAREER** Asst prof philos, Pacific Lutheran Univ, 90-92; asst prof philos, Palm Beach Atlantic Col, 92-95; asst prof philos, McNeese State Univ, 95- . **HONORS AND AWARDS** Exec Comm Soc of Christian Philos, 95-97; Pew scholar, 98. **MEMBERSHIPS** APA; Southern Soc of Philos and Psychol; Soc of Christian Philos. **RESEARCH** Philosophy of religion; philosophy of mind; religion and science. **SELECTED PUBLICATIONS** Auth, Modality, Probability, and Rationality: A Critical Examination of Alvin Plantinga's Philosophy, Peter Lang, 92; auth, Toward a Compatibility Theory for Internalist and Externalist Epistemologies, Philos and Phenomenological Res, 92; auth, The Inscrutable Evil Defense Against the Inductive Argument from Evil, Faith and Philos, 93; auth, Is God Essentially God? Relig Stud, 94; auth, Theism and Other Minds: On the Falsifiability of Non-Theories, Topoi, 95; auth, Christianity, Education, and the Image of God, Christianity, Humanism, Health: Proceedings from the First International Symposium, Ukraine, 95; auth, Requiem for an Android? A Response to Lillegard, Cross Currents, 96; auth, Direct Justification and Universal Sanction, J of Philos Rev, 98; ed, The Analytic Theist: A Collection of Alvin Plantinga's Works in Philosophy of Religion, Eerdmans, 98; auth, Is There Freedom in Heaven? Faith and Philos, forthcoming. **CONTACT ADDRESS** Dept of Social Sciences, McNeese State Univ, PO Box 92335, Lake Charles, LA 70809-2335. **EMAIL** jsennett@mail.mcneese.edu

SENOR, THOMAS
DISCIPLINE EPISTEMOLOGY **EDUCATION** Univ Ariz, PhD. **CAREER** English and Lit, Univ Ark. **SELECTED PUBLICATIONS** Ed, The Rationality of Belief and the Plurality of Faith, Cornell Univ Press, 96. **CONTACT ADDRESS** Univ of Arkansas, Fayetteville, Fayetteville, AR 72701. **EMAIL** senor@comp.uark.edu

SENT, ESTHER MIRJAM
PERSONAL Born 03/09/1967, the Netherlands, m, 1994 **DISCIPLINE** ECONOMICS **EDUCATION** Stanford Univ, PhD, 94. **CAREER** Prof. **HONORS AND AWARDS** Joseph Dorfman Best Dissertation Awd for the Best Dissertation in Hist of Econ Thought, 95; Gunnar Myrdal Prize, 99. **MEMBERSHIPS** Am Econ Asn, Asn for Evolutionary Political Economy, Committee on the Status of Women in the Economics Profession, European Asn for Evolutionary Political Economy, Hist of Econ Soc, Hist of Science Soc, International Network for Economic Methodology, Philosophy of Science Asn, Soc for the Social Stud of Science. **RESEARCH** Philosophy of economics; history of economic thought; economics of science; science studies. **SELECTED PUBLICATIONS** Auth, Convenience: The Mother of All Rationality in Sargent, 96; What an Economist Can Teach Nancy Cartwright, 96; Sargent versus Simon: Bounded Rationality Unbound, 97; auth, An Economist's Glance at Goldman's Economics, 97; rev, STS: A Reflexive Review, 97; auth, Sargent and the Unvearable Lightness of Symmetry, 98; auth, Engineering Dynamic Economics, 98; auth, Artificial Intelligence, 98; auth, Bounded Rationality, 98; auth, Economics of Science: Survey and Suggestions, 99; auth, John F. Muth: From Bounded Rationality to Rational Expectations and Back Again, 99. **CONTACT ADDRESS** History and Philosophy of Science Dept, Univ of Notre Dame, Notre Dame, IN 46556. **EMAIL** Sent.2@nd.edu

SEPLOWITZ, RENA C.
DISCIPLINE LAW **EDUCATION** Barnard Col, AB, summ cum laude, 73; Columbia Law Sch, JD, 75; **CAREER** Prof Law, Touro Col; articles ed, Columbia J of Law and Soc Prob; assoc ed, Real Property Probate & Trust J; pvt prac, Kay, Scholer, Fierman, Hayes & Handler. **HONORS AND AWARDS** Harlan Fiske Stone Scholar; Summa Cum Laude, Phi Beta Kappa, 73. **MEMBERSHIPS** Am Bar Asn; Asn of the Bar of the City of NY. **SELECTED PUBLICATIONS** Auth, Testamentary Substitutes: Retained Interests, Custodial Accounts, and Contractual Transactions A New Approach, Am Univ Law Rev, 88; coauth, Testamentary Substitutes - A Time for Statutory Clarification, Real Property and Probate J, 88; auth, Transfers Before Marriage and the Uniform Probate Code's Redesigned Elective Share Why the Partnership Is Not Yet Complete, Ind Law Rev, 91. **CONTACT ADDRESS** Touro Col, New York, Brooklyn, NY 11230. **EMAIL** RenaS@tourolaw.edu

SEPPER, DENNIS L.
PERSONAL Born 01/26/1951, Medina, OH, m, 1975, 2 children **DISCIPLINE** PHILOSOPHY, ETHICS **EDUCATION** Harvard Univ, BA; Univ Chicago, MA, PhD. **CAREER** Dept Philos, Univ Dallas **HONORS AND AWARDS** DAAD scholar, 77-79; Univ of WI Institute for res in Humanities, Fel, 88-89; NEH, Fel, 89-90; J Paul Getty Institute Scholar, 01-02. **MEMBERSHIPS** Am Philosophical Assoc, Metaphysical Soc of Am, Philosophy of Sci Assoc, Hist of Sci Soc. **SELECTED PUBLICATIONS** Auth, Showing, Doing, and the Ontology of Using Scientific Instruments, Proc Eleventh Intl Sci Instrument Symp, Bologna: Grafis Edizioni, 94; Newton's Optical Writings: A Guided Study, series Masterworks of Discovery, Rutgers Univ Press, 94; Newton's Optics as Classic: On Teaching the Texture of Science, PSA, 94; Descartes's Imagination: Proportion, Images, and the Activity of Thinking, Univ Calif Press, 96; auth, The Texture of thought: Why Descartes Meditationes is Meditational and Why it Matters," Descartes Nat Philos, London: Routledge, (00), 736-750. **CONTACT ADDRESS** Dept of Philos, Univ of Dallas, 1845 E Northgate Dr, Irving, TX 75062. **EMAIL** sepper@acad.udallas.edu

SERAFINI, ANTHONY
PERSONAL Born 05/31/1943, Paterson, NJ, m, 1970, 1 child **DISCIPLINE** PHILOSOPHY **EDUCATION** Cornell Univ, AB, 65; Syracuse, PhD, 72. **CAREER** Assoc Prof, Centenary Col. **MEMBERSHIPS** APA; PA Philos Asn. **RESEARCH** History of Philosophy of Science. **SELECTED PUBLICATIONS** Auth, Willenstein & Contemporary, Longwood Press, 93; auth, A History of Philosophy, Intl Scholars Press, 00. **CONTACT ADDRESS** Dept Humanities, Centenary Col, 400 Jefferson St, Hackettstown, NJ 07840-2184.

SERANO, J.
PERSONAL Born 02/02/1943, Philadelphia, PA, s **DISCIPLINE** THEOLOGY **EDUCATION** St. Norbert Col, BA, 65; Heythrop, STL, 70; Univ Penn, MA, 73; Catholic Univ Am, STD, 81. **CAREER** Priest, 69-; Lecturer, St Joseph's Univ, 74-. **MEMBERSHIPS** CTS. **CONTACT ADDRESS** Dept Theol, Saint Joseph's Univ, 5600 City Ave, Philadelphia, PA 19131-1308. **EMAIL** jserano@daylesford.org

SEREQUEBERHAN, TSENAY
PERSONAL Born 05/18/1952, Eritrea, m, 1979, 2 children **DISCIPLINE** PHILOSOPHY **EDUCATION** Univ Mass, BA, 79; Boston Col, MA, 82, PhD, 88. **CAREER** Instr, Boston Col, 82-83; Univ Mass at Boston, 83-88; Asst prof, Hampshire Col, 88-94; Assoc prof, Simmons Col, 94-96; Vis assoc prof, Simmons Col, 96-97; Brown Univ, 98-. **HONORS AND AWARDS** Res Grant, Simmons Col, 95; Hewlett-Mellon Fac Dev Grant, Hampshire Col, 90-92. **MEMBERSHIPS** APA; African Studies Asn. **RESEARCH** Philosophy, African-American Philosophy, African Philosophy, Ancient Philosophy. **SELECTED PUBLICATIONS** African Philosophy: The Essential Readings, 91; auth, The Hermeneutics of African Philosophy, 94; "Fanon and the Contemporary Discourse of African Philosophy: The Case of Immanuel Kant," 96; "Reflections on: In My Father's House, Research in African Literatures," 96; auth, Eurocentrism in Philosophy: The Case of Immanuel Kant," The Philosophical Forum, 96; auth, Frantz Fanon: A Critical Reader, ed. Lewis R. Gordon, Blackwell, 96; "The Cri-

tique of Eurocentrism and the Practice of African Philosophy," 97; "Africanity at the End of the 20th Century," 98; auth, Our Heritage, Rowman & Littlefield Pub Inc, 00. **CONTACT ADDRESS** Dept of Philos and Relig, Morgan State Univ, 1700 E Cold Spring Ln, Holmes Hall 309, Baltimore, MD 21251-0001.

SERGEEV, MIKHAIL
PERSONAL Born 04/29/1960, Moscow, Russia, m, 1980, 1 child **DISCIPLINE** PHILOSOPHY, RELIGION **EDUCATION** Moscow State Inst of Int Rel, BA, 82; Temple Univ, MA, 93; PhD, 97. **CAREER** Instr, Rowan Univ, 93-94; Instr, St Joseph's Univ, 94-95; Teaching Asst, Temple Univ, 91-94, 96; Examining Instr, Drexel Univ, 97; Instr, Albright Col, 98; Instr, Temple Univ, 98; Sen Lect, University of the Arts, 97-. **MEMBERSHIPS** Am Acad of Relig, APA, Am Assoc for the Advancement of Slavic Studies, Mid-Atlantic Slavic Conf, Soc for the Study of Russ Relig Thought, Assoc of Russ-Am Scholars in the USA, Russ Philos Soc. **RESEARCH** Comparative/world religions, philosophy of religion, modern Christian thought, religion and art. **SELECTED PUBLICATIONS** Auth, "Religious Nationalism in Russia: A Postmodern Identity?" J of the CAREE, vol XIV, no 2 (94): 31-35; auth, "Postmodern Themes in the Philosophy of Nikolai Berdiaev," J of the CAREE vol XIV, no 2 (94): 31-35; auth, "Russian Orthodoxy: Renewal or Revival?" J of Ecumenical Studies, vol XXXII, no 1(96): 36-43; auth, "Russian Orthodoxy: Renewal or Revival?" J of the Christians Associated for a Relationship with Eastern Eur (CAREE), vol XVI, no 3(96): 27-34; auth, "Sophiology of Nikolai Berdiaev," Transactions of the Assoc of Russ-Am Scholars in the USA, vol XXIX (98): 59-72; auth, "Three Sources and Three Components of Russian Sophiology," Soc for the Study of Russ Relig Thought Newsletter (SSRRT), vol V, no 1 (99): 23-24. **CONTACT ADDRESS** Dept Lib Arts, Univ of the Arts, 320 S Broad St, Philadelphia, PA 19102-4901. **EMAIL** msergeev@early.com

SEROKA, JAMES H.
PERSONAL Born 03/05/1950, Detroit, MI, m, 1970, 2 children **DISCIPLINE** PUBLIC ADMINISTRATION **EDUCATION** Univ Mich, BA, 70; Mich State Univ, MA, 72; PhD, 76. **CAREER** Vis Asst Prof, Univ NC, 76-77; Asst Prof, Appalachian State Univ, 77-79; Prof, S Ill Univ, 79-88; Prof and Dept Head, Penn State Univ., 88-90; Prof and Dir, Univ N Fla, 91-98; Prof and Dir, Auburn Univ, 98-. **HONORS AND AWARDS** Fulbright Fel, 80; Fel, NAS, 81; Fel, IREX, 86. **MEMBERSHIPS** Am Polit Sci Asn; S Polit Sci Asn; Midwest Polit Sci Asn; Intl Studies Asn; Am Soc for Pub Admin; Am Asn for the Advan of Slavic Studies; Comm Develop Soc; W Polit Sci Asn; Rural Sociol Asn; Intl City Management Asn. **RESEARCH** Democratization; Rural and Small Town Public Administration; East Central European Political Studies. **SELECTED PUBLICATIONS** Co-ed, Contemporary Political Systems: Classifications and Typologies, Lynne Rienner Press, 90; co-ed, The Failure of Democratic Transformation: The Tragedy of Yugoslavia, M.E. Sharpe, 93. **CONTACT ADDRESS** Center for Govt Serv, Auburn Univ, 2236 Haley Center, Auburn, AL 36849. **EMAIL** jseroka@auburn.edu

SESSIONS, ROBERT
DISCIPLINE PHILOSOPHY **EDUCATION** Drake Univ, BA, 67; Univ Mich, MA, 70, PhD, 75. **CAREER** Asst prof philos, 73-77, Univ Minn; asst prof philos, 77-79, Luther Col, Decoral; asst manager, 79-84, CETA reg office, Decorah; asst prof philos, 84-85, Grinnell Col; prof, 85-, Kirkwood Community Col, Rapid Cedars, IA. **HONORS AND AWARDS** Woodrow Wilson & Danforth Graduate fels; Master Tchr Awd, Nat Inst for Staff & Organ Devel, 88; Master Tchr Awd, Community Col Hum Asn, 89; Asn of Comm Col Trustees Tchr of Yr Awd for Midwest Reg, 91; Asn of Comm Col Trustees Nat Tchr of Yr Awd, 91; NEH grants, 90-97. **SELECTED PUBLICATIONS** Auth, Working in America: A Humanities Reader, Univ Notre Dame Press, 92; auth, Work and the Environment, Community Col Hum Rev, 94; auth, Teaching Humanities Courses on the Environment, Comm Col Hum Rev, 94; auth, An Annotated Bibliography on Humanities and the Environment, Comm Col Hum Rev, 94; auth, Ecofeminism and Work, Ecological Feminism: Multidisciplinary Perspectives, IN Univ Press, 95; auth, Work, Encycl of Ed, 95 ed; auth, Education is a Gift, Not a Commodity, Comm Col Hum Rev, 96; auth, Deep Ecology versus Ecofeminism: Healthy Differences or Incompatible Philosophies?, Ecological Feminist Philosophies, Ind Univ Press, 96; auth, Work and the Environment; Toward Reconciliation, Utopian Visions of Work & Commmunity, Obermann Ctr for Advanced Stud, Univ Iowa, 96; auth, Work and Peacemaking, Institutional Violence, Ind Univ Press. **CONTACT ADDRESS** Arts & Humanities, Kirkwood Comm Col, P.O. Box 2068, Cedar Rapids, IA 52406. **EMAIL** bsessio@kirkwood.cc.ia.us

SESSIONS, WILLIAM LAD
PERSONAL Born 12/03/1943, Somerville, NJ, m, 1965, 2 children **DISCIPLINE** PHILOSOPHY **EDUCATION** Univ Colo, Boulder, BA, 65; Columbia Univ, MA, 67; Yale Univ, PhD, 71. **CAREER** Teaching fel, Yale Univ, 69; instr philos, Univ Conn, Waterbury, 70-71; from Asst Prof to Assoc Prof, 71-83, Prof Philos, Washington & Lee Univ, 83-, Ballengee 250th Anniversary Prof, 99-; Assoc Dean of Col, 92-95, Actg Dean, 95-96. **MEMBERSHIPS** Am Philos Asn; Soc Philos Relig; Va Philos Asn; Soc Christian Philos. **RESEARCH** Philosophy of religion. **SELECTED PUBLICATIONS** Auth, Hartshorne's early philosophy, in Studies in religion, Am Acad Relig, 73; Charles Hartshorne and thirdness, summer 74 & On Inclusion: A response to Hartshorne, winter 79, Southern J Philos; Kant and Religious Belief, Kant-Studien, 4: 455-468; William James and the Right to Over-Believe, Philos Res Arch, 6: 1420; Rawls's Concept and Conception of Primary Good, Social Theory & Pract, fall 81; The Concept of Faith, Cornell Univ Press, 94. **CONTACT ADDRESS** Dept of Philos, Washington and Lee Univ, 116 N Main St, Lexington, VA 24450-2504. **EMAIL** sessionsl@wlu.edu

SETTLE, TOM
PERSONAL Born 08/30/1931, Manchester, England, m, 1956, 3 children **DISCIPLINE** PHILOSOPHY **EDUCATION** Univ Manchester, BSc, 52, cert educ, 58; Univ Leeds, BA, 55; Univ Hong Kong, PhD(philos), 65. **CAREER** Minister, Methodist Church Gt Brit, 55-57; chaplain & head sci, Methodist Col, Hong Kong, 58-65; minister, Methodist Church Gt Brit, 65-67; asst prof, 67-70, assoc prof, 70-75, dean, Col Arts, 75-80, Prof Philos to Prof Emer, Univ Guelph, 75-. **MEMBERSHIPS** Can Philos Asn; Philos Sci Asn; Can Soc Hist & Philos Sci. **RESEARCH** Philosophy of science and of religion; political economy; ethics. **CONTACT ADDRESS** Dept of Philos, Univ of Guelph, MacKinnon Bldg, 3rd Floor, Guelph, ON, Canada N1G 2W1.

SETZER, CLAUDIA
PERSONAL Born 03/11/1952, La Crosse, WI, m, 1998, 2 children **DISCIPLINE** BIBLICAL STUDIES **EDUCATION** Macalester Col, BA, 74; Jewish Theological Seminary, MA, 80; Columbia/Union, PhD, 90. **CAREER** ASST/ASSOC PROF OF RELIGIOUS STUDIES, MANHATTAN COL, 90-. **MEMBERSHIPS** AAR/SBL **RESEARCH** New Testament; Early Judaism & Christianity. **SELECTED PUBLICATIONS** Auth, Jewish Reactions to Early Christians, Fortress, 94; auth, Excellent Women: Female Witness to the Resurrection, JBL, 97. **CONTACT ADDRESS** Dept of Religious Studies, Manhattan Col, Manhattan College Pkwy, Bronx, NY 10471. **EMAIL** csefzer@manhattan.edu

SEUNG, THOMAS KAEHAO
PERSONAL Born 09/20/1930, Jungju, Korea, m, 1965, 3 children **DISCIPLINE** PHILOSOPHY **EDUCATION** Yale Univ, BA, 58, MA, 61, PhD, 65. **CAREER** From lectr to instr, Yale Univ, 63-65; asst prof, Fordham Univ, 65-66; from asst prof to assoc prof, 66-72, Prof Philos, Univ Tex, Austin, 72-; Soc Relig Higher Educ fel, 69-70; Am Coun Learned Soc fel, 70-71; NEH fel, 77-78. **RESEARCH** Continental philosophy; philosophy of culture; philosophy of values. **SELECTED PUBLICATIONS** Auth, The fragile leaves of the Sibyl: Dante's master plan, Newman, 62; Kant's Transcendental Logic, Yale Univ, 69; Cultural Thematics, Yale Univ, 76; Structuralism and Hermeneutics & Semiotics, Columbia Univ, 82; Thematics in Hermeneutics, Columbia Univ, 82; Institution and Construction: The Foundation of Normative Theory, Yale Univ, 93; Kant's Platonic Revolution in Moral and Political Philosophy, Johns Hopkins Univ, 94; Plato Rediscovered, Rowman and Littlefield, 96. **CONTACT ADDRESS** Dept Philos, Univ of Texas, Austin, Austin, TX 78712-1180. **EMAIL** t.k.seung@mail.utexas.edu

SEYMOUR, JACK L.
PERSONAL Born 10/27/1948, Kokomo, IN, m, 1997, 2 children **DISCIPLINE** HISTORY AND PHILOSOPHY OF EDUCATION **EDUCATION** Ball State Univ, BS; Vanderbilt Divinity School, DMin & MDiv; George Peabody Col of Vanderbilt, PhD. **CAREER** Asst prof Church & Ministry, Vanderbilt Univ 74-78; Dir Field Educ, Chicago Theol Sem, 78-82; prof Christian Educ, assoc prof, asst prof, Scarritt Grad School, 82-88; prof Relig Educ, 88-, acad dean, 96-, Garrett-Evangelical Theol Sem, 88-. **RESEARCH** Theology of people of God; Ethnographic Research in education; Theological education. **SELECTED PUBLICATIONS** Coauth Educating Christians: The Intersection of Meaning, Learning, and Vocation, Abdington Press, 93; For the Life of a Child: The 'Religious' in the Education of the Public, Relig Educ, 94; Contemporary Approaches to Christian Education, Theological Perspectives on Christian Formation, W B Eerdmans, 96; The Ethnographer as Minister: Ethnographic Research in the Context of Ministry Vocations, Relig Educ, 96; Temples of Meaning: Theology and the People of God, Lib Relig Educ, 96; rev Essays on Religion and Education: An Issue in Honor of William Bean Kennedy, Relig Educ, 96; The Cry for Theology: Laity Speak about the Church, and The Cry for Theology: Laity Speak about Theology, PACE: Professional Approaches for Christian Education, 96; auth Mapping Christian Education: Approaches to Congregational Learning, Abingdon Press, 97; Thrashing in the Night: Laity Speak about Religious Knowing, Relig Educ, 97. **CONTACT ADDRESS** Garrett-Evangelical Theol Sem, 2121 Sheridan Rd, Evanston, IL 60201. **EMAIL** Jack-Seymour@garrett.edu

SEYNAEVE, JAAK
DISCIPLINE NEW TESTAMENT STUDIES **EDUCATION** Univ Leuven/Louvain STD, 50, Magister in Theol, 55. **CAREER** Vis prof, prof Relig Stud, La State Univ. **SELECTED PUBLICATIONS** Auth, Cardinal Newman's Doctrine on Holy Scripture, Louvain, 53. **CONTACT ADDRESS** Dept of Philos and Relig Stud, Louisiana State Univ and A&M Col, 106 Coates Hall, Baton Rouge, LA 70803.

SHACKELFORD, DON
PERSONAL Born 07/18/1934, Joplin, MO, m, 1954, 5 children **DISCIPLINE** RELIGIOUS STUDIES **EDUCATION** Central Christian Col, AA, 54; David Lipscomb Univ, BA, 56; New Orleans Baptist Theol Sem, BD, 64, ThD, 77. **CAREER** Prof, Harding Univ, Searcy, 72-, Dean, Int Studies, 80-; Lubbock Christian Univ, chair, Bible dept, 75-77. **HONORS AND AWARDS** Distinguished Teacher Awd, Harding Univ, 82. **MEMBERSHIPS** Soc Biblical Lit, Am Soc of Oriental Res. **RESEARCH** Biblical studies. **SELECTED PUBLICATIONS** Ed, writer, New Testament Survey, Searcy, AR: Resource Pubs (87); auth, Critical Introduction to the Old Testament, private pub, rev ed (94). **CONTACT ADDRESS** Dept Relig & Philos, Harding Univ, 900 E Center Ave, Searcy, AR 72149-0002. **EMAIL** shackelford@harding.edu

SHAFER-LANDAU, RUSSELL
PERSONAL Born 02/18/1963, Paris, France, m, 1989, 2 children **DISCIPLINE** PHILOSOPHY **EDUCATION** Brown Univ, AB, 86; Oxford Univ, MS, 87; Univ Ariz, MA, 89; PhD, 92. **CAREER** Asst prof, Univ Kans, 92-97; assoc prof, Univ Calif-Berkeley, 97-98; assoc prof, Univ Kans, 97-. **MEMBERSHIPS** Am Philos Asn. **RESEARCH** Ethics; Philosophy of Law **SELECTED PUBLICATIONS** Auth, articles, Must Punishment Morally Educate?, lAward and Philosophy, 91; Health Care and Human Values, Health Care: Myths, Values and Expectations, 94; Vegetarianism, Causation and Ethical Theory, Pub Affairs Quart, 4; Ethical Disagreement, Ethical Objectivism and Moral Indeterminacy, Philos and Phenomenol Res, 94; Supervenience and Moral Realism, Ratio, 94; Specifying Absolute Rights, Ariz LAward Rev, 95; Vagueness, Borderline Cases and Moral Realism, Am Philos Quart, 95; The Failure of Retributivism, Philos Studies, 96; Moral Rules, Ethics, 97; Ethical Subjectivsm, Reason and Responsibility, 98; Moral Judgement and Moral Motivation, Philos Quart, 98. **CONTACT ADDRESS** Philosophy Dept, Univ of Kansas, Lawrence, Lawrence, KS 66045. **EMAIL** rsl@falcon.cc.ukans.edu

SHAFFER, JEROME A.
PERSONAL Born 04/02/1929, Brooklyn, NY **DISCIPLINE** PHILOSOPHY **EDUCATION** Cornell Univ, BA, 50; Princeton Univ, PhD, 52; Univ Conn, MA 66. **CAREER** Assoc prof, Swarthmore Col, 55-67; Dept Head, Univ Conn, 67-94; Marital & Family Therapist, 96-. **HONORS AND AWARDS** Senior Fel; Ntl Humanities Found Fel; Woodrow Wilson Fel; Fulbright Fel **MEMBERSHIPS** Amer Philos Assoc; Amer Assoc for Marital & Family Therapy **RESEARCH** Philosophy of Mind; Philosophical Psychology. **SELECTED PUBLICATIONS** Auth, Philosophy of Mind, Prentice Hall, 68; auth, Reality, Knowledge, and Value, Random House, 71; auth, "Dreaming," Amer Philos Quart, 84; "An assesment of emotion," Amer Philos Quart, 82; many articles. **CONTACT ADDRESS** Dept of Philosophy, Univ of Connecticut, Storrs, Philosophy/U-54, Storrs, CT 06269-2054. **EMAIL** jshaffer@uconn.edu

SHAFFER, NANCY E.
PERSONAL Born Los Angeles, CA **DISCIPLINE** THE HISTORY AND PHILOSOPHY OF SCIENCE **EDUCATION** Graceland Col, BS, 85; Rice Univ, MA, 87; Ariz State Univ, MA, 91; Univ Calif, Davis, PhD, 96. **CAREER** Instr, Concordia Univ, Montreal, Quebec; asst prof, Univ Nebr, Omaha. **MEMBERSHIPS** Philos of Sci Asn; Am Asn of Philos Tchr. **RESEARCH** Biased reasoning and error, Contextualism and Naturalism, Philosophy of the cognitive and social sciences. **SELECTED PUBLICATIONS** Auth, Bias in Scientific Practice, Philos of Sci; auth, "What is Bias," (forthcoming); auth, "Teaching Critical Thinking skills via the Internet," (forthcoming). **CONTACT ADDRESS** Dept of Philos and Relig, Univ of Nebraska, Omaha, Omaha, NE 68182-0265. **EMAIL** nshaffer@unomaha.edu

SHAFIQ, MUHAMMED
PERSONAL Born 11/01/1951, Pakistan, m, 1972, 6 children **DISCIPLINE** RELIGION **EDUCATION** Temple Univ, PhD, 82. **CAREER** Prof and Dept Chair, Peshawar Univ Pakistan, 95-97; Exec Dir, Islamic Center of Rochester, 97-; Adj Prof, St John Fisher Col, 97-. **HONORS AND AWARDS** President Awd, Pakistan, 94; Gold Medal, Pakistan, 74. **RESEARCH** Islamic; Islamic Thought and Issues. **CONTACT ADDRESS** Dept Relig Studies, St. John Fisher Col, 3690 E Ave, Rochester, NY 14618-3537. **EMAIL** lcrs@worldnet.att.net

SHAKOOR, ADAM ADIB
PERSONAL Born 08/06/1947, Detroit, MI, d, 8 children **DISCIPLINE** LAW **EDUCATION** Wayne State Univ, Univ of MI Labor Sch, certificate 1969; Wayne State Univ, BS 1971, MEd 1974, JD 1976; King Abdul Aziz Univ Saudi Arabia, certificate 1977. **CAREER** Wayne County Comm Coll, Detroit MI, prof bus law & black studies, 71-93; Marygrove Coll, Detroit MI, prof real estate law, 84; 36th Dist Court, Detroit MI, chief

judge, 81-89; City of Detroit, deputy mayor, chief administrative officer, 89-93; Reynolds, Beeby & Magnuson, partner, 94-97; Shakoor Grubba & Miller, PC, 97- ; chmn of bd, Black Legends of Professional Basketball Foundation,k Inc; vchmn of bd, Charity Motors, Inc. **HONORS AND AWARDS** Grnd Fellowship HUD 1971-73; Grad Fellow SE MI Council of Govt 1971-73; Wolverine Bar Assn Scholarship Natl Bar Assn 1975; Cert of Distinction Com for Student Rights 1979; Certificate of Merit for Exceptional Achievement in Govt Affairs MI State Legislature 1980; Resolution of Tribute MI State Legislature 1981; numerous others. **MEMBERSHIPS** Consult in comm affairs New Detroit Inc 1973-74; pres Black Legal Alliance 1975-76; founding mem Natl Conf of Black Lawyers Detroit Chap 1975-; com mem New Detroit Inc 1977-81; president of bd, Boysville, Inc, 1994; club pres Optimist Club of Renaissance Detroit 1982-83; pres Assoc of Black Judges of MI1985-86; life mem Kappa Alpha Phi. **CONTACT ADDRESS** Shakoor, Grubba & Miller, PC, 615 Griswold, Ste 1800, Detroit, MI 48226.

SHALLECK, ANN
DISCIPLINE FAMILY LAW. CHILD WELFARE **EDUCATION** Bryn Mawr Col, AB, 71; Harvard Law Sch, JD, 78. **CAREER** Prof, Am Univ. **MEMBERSHIPS** DC Task Force on Gener Bias in Courts; Asn Am Law Sch (AALS), Comt Curric & Res; Nat Women's Law Ctr; Prog Comt, AALS 88, 91; Planning Comt, Office Coun Child Abuse & Neglect Practice Manual, Child Protection Proceedings; Adv Comt; Coun Court Excellence. **RESEARCH** Women; Law Clinic Theories of state, family and socity. **SELECTED PUBLICATIONS** Articles, clinical education, child welfare, and women's rights. **CONTACT ADDRESS** American Univ, 4400 Massachusetts Ave, Washington, DC 20016.

SHAMAN, JEFFREY MARC
PERSONAL Born 06/29/1941, Pittsburgh, PA, m, 1966, 2 children **DISCIPLINE** LAW **EDUCATION** Pa State Univ, BA, 64; Univ Southern Calif, JD, 67; Georgetown Univ, Llm, 71. **CAREER** Asst prof, Univ Akron, 71-73; asst prof, 73-74, assoc prof, 74-79, prof Law, DePaul Univ, 79-, coop atty, Am Civil Liberties Union, 81-; Wechlander Chems for Prof Ethics, 94-95. **HONORS AND AWARDS** Outstanding Leadership Awd - ACLU of Illinois, 90-93; Excellence in Teaching Awd, DePaul Univ, 93; Outstand Fac Serv, DePaul Univ, Col of Law, 98. **MEMBERSHIPS** Am Law Inst; Am Soc Legal Hist. **RESEARCH** Constitutional law; federal courts; conflict of laws. **SELECTED PUBLICATIONS** Auth, The rule of reasonableness in constitutional adjudication, Hasting Const Law Quart, 75; coauth, Huffman v Pursue: The federal courthouse door closes further, Boston Univ Law Rev, 76; auth, Revitalizing the clear and present danger test: Toward a principled interpretation of the 1st Amendment, Villanova Law Rev, 76; Persons who are mentally retarded: Their right to marry and have children, Family Law Quart, 78; The First Amendment rule against overbreadth, Temple Law Quart, 79; Legal aspects of artificial insemination, J Family Law, 79; The choice of law process: Territorialism and functionalism, William & Mary Law Rev, 80; The Constitution, the Supreme Court and creativity, Hastings Const Law Quart, 82. **CONTACT ADDRESS** Col of Law, DePaul Univ, 25 E Jackson Blvd, Chicago, IL 60604-2287. **EMAIL** jshaman@condor.depaul.edu

SHANAB, ROBERT
PERSONAL Born 09/29/1939, Jerusalem, Palestine, s, 2 children **DISCIPLINE** PHILOSOPHY **EDUCATION** Ohio State Univ, PhD, 69. **CAREER** From Instr to Prof Philos, Cleveland State Univ, 69-70, Fla State Univ, 70-76, Univ Nev at Las Vegas, 77-87, Calif State Univ at Northridge, 88-92, Univ Nev at Las Vegas, 92-. **MEMBERSHIPS** Am Philos Asn; Amnesty Int; Libr Congress Assoc. **RESEARCH** Arabic culture; history of philosophy; logic. **SELECTED PUBLICATIONS** Co-ed and contribr, Readings in Philosophy and Literature, Kendall/Hunt, 71; Present Day Issues in Philosophy, Kendall/Hunt, 72; Social Philsophy: From Plato to Che, Kendall/Hunt, 72; auth, Misconceptions about Arabic Medieval Philosophy, Pakistan Philos J, 7/74; Historical Roots of Three Intellectual Movements, J Fac Arts, Univ Benghazi, 82; auth, "Ghazali and Aquinas on Causation," The Monist (74); auth of numerous other articles. **CONTACT ADDRESS** 4868 Benecia Way, Las Vegas, NV 89122. **EMAIL** reashanab@hotmail.com

SHANAHAN, THOMAS JOSEPH
PERSONAL Born 06/10/1936, Milwaukee, WI **DISCIPLINE** THEOLOGY **EDUCATION** St Louis Univ, AB, 60, AM, 61; Fordham Univ, PhD, 75. **CAREER** Eng tchr, Creighton Prep Sch, 61-64; instr theol, Marquette Univ, 69-70; Asst Prof Theol, Creighton Univ, 73. **MEMBERSHIPS** Cath Theol Soc Am; Am Acad Relig. **RESEARCH** Eccesiology; spirituality; death and dying. **SELECTED PUBLICATIONS** Auth, Negroes in nursing education: A report on Catholic schools, Hosp progress, 7/61 & Interracial Rev, 7/61; contribr, Theology Today, Bruce, 65; co-ed, Prose and Poetry of the World, 65 & Patterns of Literature, 67, L W Singer. **CONTACT ADDRESS** Creighton Univ, 2500 California Plz, Omaha, NE 68178-0001. **EMAIL** tshan@creighton.edu

SHANKS, HERSHEL
PERSONAL Born 03/08/1930, Sharon, PA, m, 1966, 2 children **DISCIPLINE** ENGLISH LITERATURE; SOCIOLOGY; LAW **EDUCATION** Haverford Col, BA, 52; Colombia Univ, MA, 56; Harvard Law Sch, LLB, 56. **CAREER** Founder and ed, Bibl Archaeol Rev, 74-; ed, Bible Rev, Archaeol Odyssey, and Moment. **MEMBERSHIPS** ASOR; SBL; AOS; NEAS; ABA. **RESEARCH** Archaeol; Bible; Judaism. **SELECTED PUBLICATIONS** Ed, Understanding the Dead Sea Scrolls, Random Hse, 92; co-auth, The Rise of Ancient Israel, Biblical Archaeol Soc, 92; ed, Christianity and Rabbinic Judaism: A Parallel History of Their Origins and Early Development, Biblical Archaeol Soc, 92; auth, Jerusalem: An Archaeological Biography, Random Hse, 95; auth, The Mystery and Meaning of the Dead Sea Scrolls, Random Hse, 98. **CONTACT ADDRESS** Biblical Archael Soc, 5208 38th St, NW, Washington, DC 20015. **EMAIL** shanks@clark.net

SHANKS, NIALL
DISCIPLINE PHILOSOPHY **EDUCATION** Univ Alberta, PhD. **CAREER** Assoc prof, E Tenn State Univ. **RESEARCH** Philosophy of biology; philosophy of science; philosophy of mind. **SELECTED PUBLICATIONS** Auth, Idealization in Contemporary Physics, Rodopi, 98; Biochemical Reductionism in Biological Context, Idealistic Studies, 97; co-auth, Mind Viruses and the Importance of Cultural Diversity, Rodopi, 98; Brute Science: The Dilemmas of AnimalExperimentation, Routledge, 97; Methodology and the Birth of Modern Cosmology, Studies Hist Philos Modern Physics, 97. **CONTACT ADDRESS** Philosophy Dept, East Tennessee State Univ, Box 70717, Johnson City, TN 37614- 0717. **EMAIL** shanksn@etsu.edu

SHANNON, DANIEL E.
PERSONAL Born 10/30/1955, Bethesda, MD, m, 1991, 2 children **DISCIPLINE** PHILOSOPHY **EDUCATION** Loyola Univ, BA 80; Univ Toronto, MA 82, PhD 89. **CAREER** Univ Toronto, inst 86-88; McGill Univ, asst prof 89-90; DePauw Univ, asst prof, assoc prof, 90 to 97-. **HONORS AND AWARDS** Faculty Fellow, 00-03. **MEMBERSHIPS** APA; CPA; HSA. **RESEARCH** German idealism; continental philosophy. **SELECTED PUBLICATIONS** Auth, The Journey of the Mind of God to Us, Clio, 98; Hegel: On modern Philosophy versus Faith, Philo and Theology, 96; A Criticism of a False Idealism and Onward to Hegel, The Owl of Minerva, 95. **CONTACT ADDRESS** Dept of Philosophy, DePauw Univ, 100 Center St, Greencastle, IN 46135. **EMAIL** deshan@depauw.edu

SHANNON, THOMAS A.
PERSONAL Born 09/28/1940, Indianapolis, IN, m, 1972, 2 children **DISCIPLINE** SOCIAL ETHICS; MEDICAL ETHICS **EDUCATION** Quincy Univ, BA, 64; St Joseph Sem, STB, 68; Boston Univ School Theol, STM, 70, PhD, 73. **CAREER** Prof, religion & social ethics, dept humanities, Worcester Polytechnic Inst; Paris Fletcher Distinguished Prof Hum, 88-90. **HONORS AND AWARDS** WPI Trustees Awd, 88; Dr Hum Letters Quincy Univ, 96. **MEMBERSHIPS** AAR; Hastings Ctr; AAAS; Amer Soc Bioethics & Hum; Soc Christian Ethics. **RESEARCH** Medical ethics; Fetal status; Genetics; Cloning. **SELECTED PUBLICATIONS** Ed, Bioethics: Selected Readings, Paulist Press, 93; auth, The Ethical Method of John Duns Scotus, Franciscan Univ Press, 95; coauth, The Context of Casuistry, Georgetown Univ Press, 95; auth, Made in Whose Image? Genetic Engineering and Christian Ethics, Hum Press, 97; auth, An Introduction to Bioethics, Paulist Press, 97. **CONTACT ADDRESS** Dept of Humanities & Arts, Worcester Polytech Inst, 100 Institute Rd, Worcester, MA 01609. **EMAIL** tshannon@wpi.edu

SHAPERE, DUDLEY
PERSONAL Born 05/17/1928, Harlingen, TX, m, 4 children **DISCIPLINE** PHILOSOPHY, HISTORY **EDUCATION** Harvard Univ, BA, 49; Ma, 54; PhD, 57. **CAREER** Instr, Ohio St Univ, 57-60; Asst Prof to Prof, Univ Chicago, 60-72; Prof, Univ Ill, 72-75; Prof, Univ Md, 75-84; Prof, Wake Forest Univ, 84-. **HONORS AND AWARDS** Fel, Am Asn for the Advan of Sci, 70; Nat Sci Found Grants, 70-72, 73, 74-75, 76-78, 85-86; Res Fel, Universidad Autonoma de Mexico, 81, 86; Otto G Neugebauer Fel, Inst for Advan Study, forthcoming. **MEMBERSHIPS** APA, PSA, Hist of Sci Soc, APA, Am Asn for the Advan of Sci. **CONTACT ADDRESS** Dept Philos & Hist, Wake Forest Univ, Drawer 7229, Reynolds Station, Winston-Salem, NC 27109. **EMAIL** shapere@wfu.edu

SHAPIRO, DANIEL
PERSONAL Born 05/02/1954, New York, NY **DISCIPLINE** PHILOSOPHY **EDUCATION** Vassar Col , BA, 76; Univ Minn, PhD, 84. **CAREER** Assoc prof philos, West Va Univ, 88-. **MEMBERSHIPS** Amer Philos Assn; Intl Econ Philos Assn. **RESEARCH** Social and political philosophy; public policy. **SELECTED PUBLICATIONS** Auth, "Can Old-Age Social Insurance Be Justified?" Social Philosophy and Policy, spring 97; auth, "Profits and Morality," Ethics, Jan 97; auth, "Why Even Egalitarians Should Favor Market Health Insurance," Social Philosophy and Policy, spring 98; auth, "A Pluralist Case for Social Security Privatization," Cato Policy Analysis, 98; auth, "Addiction and Drug Policy," Morality and Moral Controversies, 98. **CONTACT ADDRESS** Dept of Philosophy, West Virginia Univ, Morgantown, PO Box 6312, Morgantown, WV 26506-6312. **EMAIL** dshapiro@wvu.edu

SHAPIRO, DAVID L.
PERSONAL Born 10/12/1932, New York, NY, m, 1954, 1 child **DISCIPLINE** LAW **EDUCATION** Harvard Univ, BA, 54; LLB, 57. **CAREER** Atty, Covington & Burling, 57-62; law clerk, US Supreme Court, 62-63; asst prof to prof, Harvard Law Sch, 63-; Deputy Solicitor General, US Dept of Justice, 88-91. **MEMBERSHIPS** Am Law Inst. **RESEARCH** Federalism, Civil and Administrative Procedure, legal Profession, Statutory Interpretation. **SELECTED PUBLICATIONS** Auth, "The Choice of Rulemaking of Adjudication in the Development of Administrative Policy,' 78 Harvard Law Rev, 921, (65); auth, Hart & Wechsler's The Federal Courts and the Federal System, Foundation Pr, 73; auth, "Mr. Justice Rehnquist: A Preliminary View," 90 Harvard law Rev 293, (76); auth, "The Enigma of the Lawyer's Duty to Serve," 55 NYU Law Rev 735, (80); auth, "Jurisdiction and Discretion," 60 NYU Law Rev 543, (85); auth, "Courts, Legislatures, and Paternalism," 74 Va Law Rev 519, (88); auth, "Continuity and Change in Statutory Interpretation," 67 NYU Law Rev 921, (92); auth, Federalism: A Dialogue, Northwestern Univ Pr, 95; auth, "Class Actions: The Class as Party and Client," 73 Notre Dame Law Rev 913, (98); auth, Preclusion in Civil Actions, Foundation Pr, 01. **CONTACT ADDRESS** Law Sch, Harvard Univ, Cambridge, MA 02138.

SHAPIRO, GARY
PERSONAL Born 06/17/1941, St. Paul, MN, d, 3 children **DISCIPLINE** PHILOSOPHY **EDUCATION** Columbia Col, BA, 63; Columbia Univ, PhD, 70. **CAREER** Univ Kansas, asst prof, assoc prof, prof, 70-91; Univ Richmond, T-B prof in the human and prof philo, 91-. **HONORS AND AWARDS** School of Crit & Theol, fellow, 76-77; ACLS 78-79; NHC, 93-94 **MEMBERSHIPS** APA, SPEP, ASA **RESEARCH** Fr and Ger philo of 19th and 20th cen; philo of art. **SELECTED PUBLICATIONS** Auth, Nietzschean Narratives, IN Univ Press, 89; Alcyone: Nietzsche on Gifts, Noise and Women, State Univ NY Press, 91; Earthwards: Robert Smithson and Art After Babel, Univ Cal Press, 95; co-ed, Hermeneutis: Questions and Prospects, Univ Mass Press, 84; ed, After the Future: Postmodern Times and Places, State Univ of NY Press, 90. **CONTACT ADDRESS** Dept of Philosophy, Univ of Richmond, Richmond, VA 23173. **EMAIL** gshapiro@richmond.edu

SHAPIRO, HENRY L.
PERSONAL Born New York, NY **DISCIPLINE** ANCIENT PHILOSOPHY, AESTHETICS **EDUCATION** Univ Toronto, BA, 60; Columbia Univ, PhD, 69. **CAREER** Preceptor philos, Columbia Univ, 64-66; actg asst prof, Univ Calif, Riverside, 66-68; chmn dept, 70-73, Asst Prof Philos Univ Mo-St Louis, 68-. **RESEARCH** Greek philosophy; 19th century continental philosophy; philosophy of literature. **SELECTED PUBLICATIONS** **CONTACT ADDRESS** Dept of Philos, Univ of Missouri, St. Louis, 8001 Natural Bridge, Saint Louis, MO 63121-4499.

SHAPIRO, MICHAEL H.
PERSONAL Born 08/03/1938, Los Angeles, CA, d, 2 children **DISCIPLINE** CONSTITUTIONAL LAW; BIOETHICS AND LAW **EDUCATION** Univ Calif, Los Angeles, BA,59; MA,62; Univ Chicago, JD,64. **CAREER** Dorothy W. Nelson prof;Univ Southern Calif. **MEMBERSHIPS** Order of the Coif; Phi Beta Kappa; Institutional Review Board, Los Angeles County/USC Medical Center, since 1989; Member, Pacific Council for Health Policy and Ethics; Reviewer, U.S. Department of Energy (Proposals to Study the Human Genome Project), 1990-92; Advisory Panel to the Joint Committee on Surrogate Parenting of the California Legislature **RESEARCH** Constitutional Law, Constitutional Law II, Bioethics, and Healthcare Regulation. **SELECTED PUBLICATIONS** Auth, Law, Culpability and the Neural Sciences; Bioethics and Law: Cases, Materials and Problems & Who Merits Merit? Some Problems in Distributive Justice Posed by the New Biology. **CONTACT ADDRESS** School of Law, Univ of So California, University Park Campus, Los Angeles, CA 90089. **EMAIL** mshapiro@law.usc.edu

SHAPIRO, RAMI
DISCIPLINE AMERICAN JUDAISM **EDUCATION** Hebrew Union Col-Jewish Inst of Rel. **CAREER** Rabbi, Temple Beth Or, Miami, Fla; pres & sr rabbi, Metivta. **RESEARCH** Contemporary American Judaism. **SELECTED PUBLICATIONS** Auth, Wisdom of the Jewish Sages: A Modern Reading of Pirke Avot, Bell Tower/RandomHouse, 95; auth, Minyan: Ten Principles for Living a Life of Integrity, 97; auth, The Way of Solomon: Finding Joy and Contentment in the Wisdom of Ecclesiastes, 00; ed, Proverbs: The Wisdom of Solomon (Sacred Teachings), 01. **CONTACT ADDRESS** Temple Beth Or, 11715 SW 87th Ave, Miami, FL 33176-4305. **EMAIL** rabbirami@simplyjewish.com

SHAPIRO, SCOTT J.
DISCIPLINE LAW **EDUCATION** Columbia Col, Ba, 87; Yale Law School, JD, 90; Oxford Univ, Visiting Academic, 93; Columbia Univ, PhD, 96. **CAREER** Instr, Columbia Univ, 93-94; Asst to Assoc Prof, Benjamin N Cardozo School of Law, 96-. **HONORS AND AWARDS** Jonathan Lieberson Memorial Awd; Yale Law Journal, Sen Editor; Phi Beta Kappa; Visiting Jun Scholar, Univ BC, 00; Dissertion Grant, Nat Endowment for the Humanities, 94-95; Mellon Foundation Fac Fel, 91-93. **SELECTED PUBLICATIONS** Ed, Oxford Handbook of Jurisprudence and Philosophy of Law, Oxford, forthcoming; auth, "Authority," in Oxford Handbook of Jurisprudence and Philosophy of Law, Oxford, forthcoming; auth, "Judicial Can't," Nous, forthcoming; auth, "Hart, Herbert Lionel Aldophus," A companion to Analytical Philosophy, Oxford, forthcoming; auth, "Law, Morality and the Guidance of Conduct," 6 Legal Theor, forthcoming; auth, "The Bad Man and the Internal Point of View," in The Path of the Law and Beyond: The Legacy of Oliver Wendell Holmes, Cambridge, forthcoming; auth, "On Hart's Way Out," in Readings in the Philosophy of Law, Garland Press, 00; auth, "The Difference That Rules Make," in Analyzing Law: New Essays in Legal Theory, Clarendon Press, 98; auth, "Rule-Guided Behavior," in The New Palgrave Dictionary of Economics and the Law, 98. **CONTACT ADDRESS** School of Law, Yeshiva Univ, 55 5th Ave, New York, NY 10003-4301.

SHAPIRO, STEWART
PERSONAL Born 06/15/1951, Youngstown, OH, m, 1975, 3 children **DISCIPLINE** PHILOSOPHY, MATH **EDUCATION** Case Western Res Univ, BA, 73; SUNY, MA, 75, PhD, 78. **CAREER** Vis lect, 82, Hebrew Univ, Jerusalem; vis fel, 87-88, Ctr for Phil of Sci, Univ Pitts; prof, 96-97, dept of Logic & Metaphysics, Univ St Andrews, Scotland; instr, 78-91, prof, 91-, dept phil, Ohio St Univ, Newark. **HONORS AND AWARDS** OSUN, Scholar Achievements, 92, 97, res grants, 90, 92. **SELECTED PUBLICATIONS** Auth, Foundations Without Foundationalism: A Case for Second-Order Logic, Oxford Logic Guides 17, Oxford Univ Press, 91; auth, Reasoning, Logic, and Computation, Philos Math 3, 95; auth, Introduction, Philos Math 3, 96; coauth, Intuitionism, Pluralism, and Cognitive Command, J Phil, 96; ed, The Limits of Logic: Second-Order Logic and the Skolem Paradox, The International Research Library of Philosophy, Dartmouth Pub Co, 96; auth, Philosophy of Mathematics: Structure and Ontology, Oxford Univ Press, 97; auth, Induction and Indefinite Extensibility: the Godel Sentence in True, But Did Someone Change the Subject?, Mind 107, 98; auth, Logical Consequence: Models and Modality, Philos of Math Today; Proceed of Intl Conf in Munich, 98. **CONTACT ADDRESS** Dept of Philosophy, Ohio State Univ, Newark, Newark, OH 43055.

SHAPO, MARSHALL S.
PERSONAL Born 10/01/1936, Philadelphia, PA, m, 1959, 2 children **DISCIPLINE** LAW **EDUCATION** Univ Miami, AB, 58, Llb, 64; Harvard Univ, Am, 61. **CAREER** Instr hist, Univ Miami, 60-61; from asst prof to assoc prof law, Univ Tex, Austin, 65-70; prof law, 70-76, Joseph M Hartfield Prof, Law Sch, Univ Va, 76-78; Frederic P Vose Prof Law, Northwestern Univ, 78-, Mem torts round table coun Asn Am Law Sch, 67-69, chmn, 70, mem exec coun, torts-compensation syst round table, 73; vis prof, Sch of Law, Univ Va, 60-70, Univ Mich, summer 73 & Univ Gottingen, summer 76; Nat Endowment for Humanities sr fel, 74-75; sesquicentennial assoc, Univ Va, 74-75; vis fel, Ctr Socio-legal Studies, Welfson Col, Oxford Univ, 75; mem, Ctr Advan Studies, Univ Va, 76-77 & panel Food Safety Regulation & Societal Impact, Inst Med, Nat Acad Sci, 78; adv subcomt, Infringement Sci Freedom in US, Am Advan Sci, 77-78; consult, Med Malpractice & Tort Law Reform, US Dept Justice, 78-79; reporter spec comt, Tort Liability System, Am Bar Asn, 80-; consult, Pres Comn Study Ethical Prob Med & Biomed & Behavior Res, 80-81; exec comt, Torts-Compensation Systems Sect, 80-81, secy, 81-82 & chair-elect, 82-83. **MEMBERSHIPS** Am Law Inst. **RESEARCH** Legal control of products hazards and deceptive advertising; tort and compensation law; legal control of science and technology. **SELECTED PUBLICATIONS** Auth, Comparing Products-Liability - Concepts In Europ And Am Law/, Cornell Int Law J, Vol 0026, 1993; In The Looking-Glass - What Torts Scholarship Can Teach Us About The Am Experience/, Northwestern Univ Law Rev, Vol 0089, 1995; In Search Of The Law Of Products-Liability - The Ali Restatement Project/, Vanderbilt Law Rev, Vol 0048, 1995; Freud, Cocaine, And Products-Liability/, Boston Univ Law Rev, Vol 0077, 1997. **CONTACT ADDRESS** 1910 Orrington Ave, Evanston, IL 60201.

SHARF, ROBERT H.
PERSONAL Born Toronto, ON, Canada **DISCIPLINE** BUDDHIST STUDIES **EDUCATION** Univ Toronto, BA, 79; MA, 81; Univ Mich, PhD, 91. **CAREER** From asst prof to assoc prof, McMaster Univ, 89-95; assoc prof, Univ of Mich, 95-. **HONORS AND AWARDS** Res Grant, Soc Sci and Humanities Res Coun of Can; 92-95; Mich Humanities Awd, 99-00. **MEMBERSHIPS** Am Acad of Relig, Asn of Asian Studies, Int Asn for Buddhist Studies. **RESEARCH** Medieval Chinese Buddhism, Japanese Religion, Methodological Issues in the Study of Religion. **SELECTED PUBLICATIONS** Auth, "The Zen of Japanese Nationalism," in Curators of the Buddha: The Study of Buddhism under Colonialism (IL: Univ of Chicago Press, 95), 107-160; auth, "Sanbokyodan: Zen and the Way of the New Religions," Japanese J of Relig Studies 22.3-4 (95): 417-458; auth, "Whose Zen? Zen Nationalism Revisited," in Rude Awakenings: Zen, the Kyoto School, and the Question of Nationalism, (HI: Univ of Hawaii Press, 95), 40-51; auth, "Buddhist Modernism and the Rhetoric of Meditative Experience," Numen 42.3 (95): 228-283; transauth, "Experience," Critical Terms for Religious Studies," (NY: Univ of Chicago Press, 98), 94-116; auth, "On the Allue of Buddhist Relics," Representations 66 (99): 75-99; co-ed, The Living Image: Japanese Buddhist Icons in Their Monastic Contexts, Stanford Univ Press, forthcoming; auth, The 'Treasure Store Treatise': Issues in the Study of Medieval Chinese Buddhism, Univ of Hawaii press (Honolulu, HI), forthcoming. **CONTACT ADDRESS** Dept Asian Lang, Univ of Michigan, Ann Arbor, 105 S State St, Ann Arbor, MI 48109-1285. **EMAIL** rsharf@umich.edu

SHARKEY, PAUL
PERSONAL Born 03/25/1945, Oakland, CA, m, 1986, 1 child **DISCIPLINE** PHILOSOPHY; HEALTH **EDUCATION** Univ S Mississippi, MPH, 93; Univ Notre Dame, PhD, 73. **CAREER** Univ S Mississippi, prof emeritus, 96; Am Soc Philos Counseling & Psychotherapy, Am Philos Pract Assoc, vpres. **HONORS AND AWARDS** Two USM Excellence Awards, Sigma Xi, Eta Sigma Gamma, Realia Special Commendation. **MEMBERSHIPS** APA, ASPCP, APPA, APHA. **RESEARCH** Health ethics; law policy; Philosophical counseling; hypnotherapy. **SELECTED PUBLICATIONS** Auth, A Philosophical examination of the History and values of Western Medicine, Edwin Mellen Pr, 92; auth, Health Values and Professional Responsibility, Health Values, 95; auth, Bioclinical Ethics and the Mid-Level Practitioner, Advance for Physician Assistants, 95; auth, Individual Liberty vs. the Public Good: Coping with the Tuberculosis Epidemic, Clinician Rev, 93; auth, Can the Principle of Bioethics Work for Public Health, Abstracts of the American Public Health Association, 96. **CONTACT ADDRESS** Am Philos Pract Assoc, Univ of So Mississippi, PO Box 222, Lancaster, CA 93584. **EMAIL** pwsharkey@appa.edu

SHARMA, ARVIND
PERSONAL Born 01/13/1940, Varanasi, India **DISCIPLINE** RELIGION **EDUCATION** Allahabad Univ, BA, 58; Syracuse Univ, MA, 70; Harvard Divinity School, StM, 74; Harvard Univ, PhD, 78. **CAREER** Lectr, Univ of Queensland, 76-80; Lectr, Sr Lectr, Univ of Sydney, 80-87; Assoc Prof, 86-, Mcgill Univ. **HONORS AND AWARDS** Birks Chair Comparative Religion, McGill Univ, 94. **MEMBERSHIPS** Amer Acad of Religion; Amer Oriental Soc; Assoc of Asian Studies **RESEARCH** Comparative religion; religion and human rights **SELECTED PUBLICATIONS** Ed, Religion and Women, 94; Today's Women in World Religions, 94; Our Religions, 95; Auth, The Philosophy of Religion and Advaita Vedanta, 95; The Philosophy of Religions: A Buddhist Perspective, 95; Hinduism for Our Times, 96. **CONTACT ADDRESS** McGill Univ, 3520 University St., Montreal, QC, Canada H3A 2A7. **EMAIL** cxlj@musica.mcgill.ca

SHARMA, JAGDISH P.
PERSONAL Born 01/04/1934, m, 1962, 2 children **DISCIPLINE** ANCIENT HISTORY & RELIGION **EDUCATION** Agra Univ, BA, 55; Univ London, BA(hons), 59, PhD(ancient hist), 62. **CAREER** Vis asst prof Indian hist, Univ Va, 63-64; vis asst prof sch int serv, Am Univ, 64; asst prof, 64-68, assoc prof, 68-76, prof Indian hist, Univ Hawaii, Manoa, 76-; dir undergrad majors in Asian studies, Univ Hawaii, 69-71, chm hist forum, Hist Fac Res Sem, 69-75, 97-; adv, Jainas Am. **MEMBERSHIPS** Asn Asian Studies; life fel Royal Asiatic Soc; Am Orient Soc; AAUP. **RESEARCH** Ancient republics; ancient politics and democracy in the ancient world; Jainism; comparative religions. **SELECTED PUBLICATIONS** Auth, Republics in Ancient India, c 1500 BC-500 BC, E J Brill, Leiden, 68; coauth, Hinduism, Sarvodaya and Social Change, In: Religion and Political Modernization, Yale Univ, 74; auth, Jaina and Buddhist Traditions Regarding the Origins of Ajatasattu's War within Vajjians: A New Interpretation, Shramana, Vol 25, No 9 & 10; Hemacandra: The Life and Scholarship of a Jaina Monk, Asian Profile, Vol 3, No 2; Jainas as a Minority in Indian Society and History, Jain J, Vol 10, No 4; coauth, Dream-Symbolism in the Sramanic Tradition, Firma KLM-Calcutta, 80; ed & contribr, Individuals and Ideas in Modern India; auth, Nine Interpretative Studies, Firma KLM-Calcutta, 82; Time Perspective in the Study of Culture, J Soc Res, 3/79; Life-Pattern of the Jinas in Bibliography: East & West, ed by Carol Ramalb, Hon, 89; Jawaharlal Nehru--A Biographical Sketch, in Foreign Visitors to Congress: Speeches and History for US Capitol Society, Wash, DC, Millwood, NY, Karaus Int Pubs, 2 vols, 89; August 15 (1947)-India in Book of Days-1987: An Encyclopedia, Ann Arbor: The Reirian Press, 88; Japan as Seen From America and India: My First Impressions in Japanese with Eng Summary in Japan in the World Vol XIII Takushoku Univ, Tokyo, 94; Indian Thinking and Thinkers in Perspectives on History & Culture (in honor of Prof D P Singhal), ed by Arvind Sharma, Indian Books Centre, Delhi, 92; Individuals and Ideas in Traditional India, ed with contribution, MRML, New Delhi (in press); Jaina Yakshas, Kusumanjali, Meerut, India, 89, 93; The Jinasattvas: Class and Gender in the Social Origins of Jaina Heroes, ed by N. K. Wagle, Univ Toronto Press, (99): 72-85; Political History in the Historiography of Ancient India: New Trends and Prospects in Political History in a Changing World, ed by G C Pande, et al Kusumanjali, Jodhpur, 92; Ambapali's Vesali about 500 B C in City in Pre-Modern Asia, ed by Leslie Gunawardana (forthcoming). **CONTACT ADDRESS** Dept Hist, Univ of Hawaii, Manoa, 2530 Dole St, Honolulu, HI 96822-2383. **EMAIL** jpsharma@hawaii.edu

SHARP, MIKE
DISCIPLINE POLITICAL SCIENCE **EDUCATION** Northwest Mo State Univ, BA, 72; Univ Okla, MA, 89, PhD, 90. **CAREER** Vis asst prof, 87-88, asst prof, 88-94, ASSOC PROF, 94-, CHAIR POL SCI, 97-, NORTHEASTERN STATE UNIV. **CONTACT ADDRESS** Dept of Pol Sci, Northeastern State Univ, Tahlequah, OK 74464. **EMAIL** sharp@cherokee.nsuok.edu

SHARPE, CALVIN WILLIAM
PERSONAL Born 02/22/1945, Greensboro, NC, m **DISCIPLINE** LAW **EDUCATION** Clark Coll, BA 1967; Oberlin Coll, Post-Baccalaureate 1968; Chicago Theological Seminary, attended 1969-71, MA, 1996; Northwestern Univ Law Sch, JD 1974. **CAREER** Hon Hubert L Will US District Court, law clerk 1974-76; Cotton Watt Jones King & Bowlus Law Firm, assoc 1976-77; Natl Labor Relations Bd, trial attorney 1977-81; Univ of VA Law School, asst prof 1981-84; Case Western Reserve Univ, prof of law (tenured) 1984-; Arizona State University College of Law (Tempe), scholar-in-residence, 90; George Washington University National Law Center, DC, visiting professor, 91; Case Western Reserve University Law School, professor/associate dean, academic affairs, 91-92; De Paul Univ College of Law, Distinguished Visiting Professor, 95-96; Chicago-Kent Coll of Law, visiting scholar; Visiting Prof, Univ of Minnesota Law School, 98; Prof Law, John Deaver Drinko-Baker & Hostetler, 99. **MEMBERSHIPS** National Academy of Arbitrators 1991-; convener/first chair, Labor and Employment Law Section, IRRA, 1994-96; labor panel Amer Arbitration Assoc 1984-; bd of trustees Cleveland Hearing & Speech Ctr 1985-89; mem OH State Employment Relations Bd Panel of Neutrals 1985-; Phoenix Employment Relations Bd Panel of Neutrals; Los Angeles City Employee Relations Bd Panel of Neutrals; chair-evidence section Assn of Amer Law Schools 1987; Assn of Amer Law Schools Committee on Sections and Annual Meeting 1991-94; exec bd Public Sector Labor Relations Assoc 1987-89; Federal Mediation and Conciliation Serv Roster of Arbitrators 1987-; Permanent Arbitrator State of Ohio, OH Health Care Employees Assoc Dist 1199, 1987-92; AFSCME/OCSEA, 1987-92; State Council of Professional Educators OEA/NEA 1989-; Federation of Police 1988-92; Youth Services Subsidy Advisory Bd of Commissioners, Cuyahoga County Ohio 1989. **SELECTED PUBLICATIONS** Publications: "Two-Step Balancing and the Admissibility of Other Crimes Evidence, A Sliding Scale of Proof," 59 Notre Dame Law Review 556, 1984; "Proof of Non-Interest in Representation Disputes, A Burden Without Reason," 11 Univ Dayton Law Review 3, 1985; "Fact-Finding in Ohio, Advancing the Pole of Rationality in Public Sector Collective Bargaining," Univ of Toledo Law Review, 1987; "NLRB Deferral to Grievance-Arbitration, A General Theory," 48 Ohio St LJ No 3, 1987; Introduction, The Natl War Labor Bd and Critical Issues in the Development of Modern Grievance Arbitration, 39 Case W Res L Rev No 2, 1988; A Study of Coal Arbitration Under the National Bituminous Coal Wage Agreement-Between 1975 and 1991, vol 93, issue 3, National Coal Issue, West Virginia Law Review; "The Art of Being A Good Advocate," Dispute Resolution Journal, January 1995; "Judging in Good Faith -- Seeing Justice Marshall's Legacy Through A Labor Case," 26 Arizona State LJ 479 (1994); "From An Arbitrator's Point of View--The Art of Being a Good Advocate;" Dispute Resolution Journal, 1995; Book Review: Edward J Imwinkelreid, Evidentiary Distinction: Understanding the Federal Rules of Evidence, 1993; and Arthus Best, Evidence and Explanations, 1993; 46 J Legal Ed 150, 1996; auth, "Seniority," in Common Law of the Workplace, BNA, 98; auth, "By Any Means Necessary--Unprotected Conduct and Decisional Discretion Under the National Labor Relations Act," 20 Berkeley Journal of Employment and Labor Law, 99; auth, Understanding Labor Law, with Douglas E. Ray and Robert N. Strassfeld, Matthew-Bender, 99; auth, "Judicial Review of Labor Arbitration Awards: A View From The Bench," 52 Nat. Acad. Arb. Ann. Proc 126, BNA 99. **CONTACT ADDRESS** Prof of Law, Case Western Reserve Univ, 11075 East Boulevard, Cleveland, OH 44106.

SHARPE, KEVIN J.
DISCIPLINE RELIGIOUS STUDIES **EDUCATION** Univ Canterbury, BS; La Trobe Univ, PhD; Boston Univ, PhD. **CAREER** Prof. **RESEARCH** Philosophy of religion; systematic theology; philosophy of science; mathematics; science and religion; science and society. **SELECTED PUBLICATIONS** Auth, David Bohm's World: New Physics and New Religion, 93; Religion's Response to Change, 85; From Science to an Adequate Mythology, 84; Toward an Authentic New Zealand Theology, 83; Religion and New Zealand's Future, 82; co-auth, Religion and Nature, 83. **CONTACT ADDRESS** Religious Studies Dept, Union Inst, 440 E McMillan St, Cincinnati, OH 45206-1925.

SHARPE, VIRGINIA A.
DISCIPLINE PHILOSOPHY, MEDICAL ETHICS **EDUCATION** Smith Col, AB, 81; Georgetown Univ, MA, 86, PhD, 91. **CAREER** Asst prof, dept med, 92-96, vis asst prof, 96-97, Georgetown Univ; Deputy Dir, 99-, The Hastings Center. **HONORS AND AWARDS** Charles E. Culpeper Scholar in Med Hum. **MEMBERSHIPS** Am Philos Asn; Int Soc for Environmental Ethics; Am Soc for Bioethics and Humanities. **SELECTED PUBLICATIONS** Auth, Justice and Care: The Implications of the Kohlberg-Gillian Debate for Medical Ethics, Theoretical Med, 92; coauth, Appropriateness in Patient Care: A New Conceptual Framework, Milbank Quart, 96; coauth, Affiliations Between Catholic and Non-Catholic Health Care Providers and the Availability of Reproductive Health Services, Kaiser Family Found, 97; Why "Do No Harm"?, Theoretical Med, 97; coauth, Medical Ethics in the Courtroom: A Reappraisal, J of Med and Philos, 97; auth, The Politics, Economics, and Ethics of 'Appropriateness, Kennedy Inst of Ethics J, 97; coauth, Medical Harm: Historical, Conceptual and Ethical Dimensions of Iatrogenic Illness, Cambridge Univ Press, 98; auth, Taking Responsibility for Medical Mistakes, Margin of Error: The Necessity, Inevitability & Ethics of Mistakes in Med and Bioethics Consultation, Univ Pub Group, 00; coauth, Wolves and Human Communities, Washington, DC: Island Press, 00; Sharpe, VA, Norton, B, Donnelley, S. Wolves and Human Communities, Wash DC: Island Press, 00. **CONTACT ADDRESS** Hastings Ctr, 21 Malcom Gordon Dr., Garrison, NY 10524-5555. **EMAIL** sharpeva@thehastingscenter.org

SHAVELL, S.
PERSONAL Born 05/29/1946, Washington, DC **DISCIPLINE** ECONOMICS **EDUCATION** Univ Michigan, AB 68; MIT, PhD 73. **CAREER** Harvard Univ, asst prof, assoc prof, 74-80; Harvard Law school, asst prof 80-82, prof 82-. **HONORS AND AWARDS** Guggenheim Fel; Fel Econ Soc **MEMBERSHIPS** AEA; ALEA **RESEARCH** Law and economics **SELECTED PUBLICATIONS** Auth, Economic Analysis of Accident Law, Harvard Univ Press, Cam MA, 87; The Fundamental Divergence Between the Private and the Social Motive to Use the Legal System, Jour of Legal Stud, 97; Acquisition and Disclosure of Information Prior to Sale, Rand Jour of Econ, 94; The Optimal Structure of Law Enforcement, Jour of Law and Econ, 93. **CONTACT ADDRESS** School of Law, Harvard Univ, Cambridge, MA 02138. **EMAIL** shavell@law.harvard.edu

SHAVIRO, DANIEL N.
PERSONAL Born 05/11/1957, New York, NY, m, 1988, 2 children **DISCIPLINE** LEGAL STUDIES **EDUCATION** Princeton Univ, AB, 78; Yale Law Sch, JD, 81. **CAREER** Atty, US Congress, Joint Committee, 84-87; Caplin & Drysdale, taxation (Legislation Atty), 81-84; Asst Prof to Prof, Univ of Chicago Law Sch, 87-95; Prof, NYork Univ Law Sch, 95-. **MEMBERSHIPS** ABA, AALS, ALEA. **RESEARCH** Public Economics, Distributive Justice. **SELECTED PUBLICATIONS** Auth, "The Minimum Wage, the Earned Income Tax Credit, and Optimal Subsidy Policy," 64 Univ of Chicago Law Rev 405 (97); auth, Do Deficits Matter?, Univ of Chicago Press, 97; auth, "Effective Marginal tax Rates on Low-Income Households," 84 tax Notes 1191 (Aug 23, 99); auth, "Commentary: Inequality, Wealth, and Endowment," Tax Law Rev (forthcoming); coauth, "The Economics of Vouchers," in Vouchers and the Provision of Public Services (Brookings Inst Press, forthcoming); auth, "Endowment and Inequality," in Tax Justice Reconsidered: The Moral and Ethical Bases of Taxation, ed. Joseph Thorndike and Dennis Ventry (Urban Inst Press, forthcoming); auth, "Some Observations Concerning Multi-Jurisdictional Tax Competition," in Regulatory Competition and Economic Integration: Comparative Perspectives (Oxford Univ Press, forthcoming); coauth, Federal Income Taxation (12th Ed), Aspen Law & Bus, forthcoming; auth, When Rules Change: An Economic and Political Analysis of Transition Relief and Retroactivity, Univ of Chicago Press, forthcoming; auth, Making Sense of Social Security Reform, Univ of Chicago Press, forthcoming. **CONTACT ADDRESS** Sch of Law, New York Univ, 40 Washington Sq S, New York, NY 10012-1005. **EMAIL** shavirod@turing.law.nyu.edu

SHAW, CURTIS MITCHELL
PERSONAL Born 04/13/1944, Jacksonville, TX, d **DISCIPLINE** LAW **EDUCATION** Univ of NM, BS 1967; Loyola Univ of LA, JD 1975. **CAREER** Priv Prac, atty; Musical Entertainers & Motion Picture Personalities, rep; Denver Public Schools, educator; LA Unified School Dist Bd; Hollywood Chamber of Commerce; LA Co Bar Assn; Langston Law Club; Amer Bar Assn; Beverly Hills Bar Assn. **MEMBERSHIPS** Dir num motion picture & prod cos. **CONTACT ADDRESS** 433 N Camden Dr., Ste. 600, Beverly Hills, CA 90210-4410.

SHAW, DANIEL
PERSONAL Born 10/28/1951, Aurora, IL, m, 1992, 2 children **DISCIPLINE** AESTHETICS, 19TH AND 20TH CENTURY CONTINENTAL PHILOSOPHY **EDUCATION** Northern Ill Univ, BA, 72, MA, 75; Ohio State Univ, PhD, 81. **CAREER** Lectr, Ohio State Univ, 79-81; asst prof, Gettysburg Col, 81-86; assoc prof, 86-, Perf Arts comt, 88-90, treas, 92-94, Prof Develop Comt, 88-91, 92-94, fac adv, WLHU Radio Station, Philos Club, ch, APSCUF Presidential Eval Comt, 89, ch, APSCUF Honors Comt, 89-90, 90-91, APSCUF Gender Issues Comt, ch, APSCUF Comt to Revise the Prom Doc, Lock Haven Univ, 95. **HONORS AND AWARDS** NEH, summer sem, Univ Calif, Riverside, 85; Deut Academisches Austauschdienst (DAAD) scholar prog, 86; NEH summer sem, Yale Univ, 94. **SELECTED PUBLICATIONS** Auth, The Survival of Tragedy: Dostoevsky's The Idiot, Dialogue: J of the Nat Honor Soc for Philos, Oct, 75; Absurdity and Suicide: A Reexamination, Philos Res Arch, Mar, 86; A Kuhnian Metatheory for Aesthetics, J of Aesthet and Art Criticism, Fall, 86; Nietzsche as Sophist: A Polemic, Int Philos Quart, Dec, 86; Rorty and Nietzsche: Some Elective Affinities, Int Stud in Philos, Nov, 89; The American Democratic Ideology, The Lock Haven Int Rev, Fall, 90; Thelma and Louise: Liberating or Regressive? in Film, Individualism and Community, Ronald Dotterer, ed, Susquehanna UP, 94; Lang Contra Vengeance: The Big Heat, J of Value Inquiry, Dec 95; auth, "Existential Implications of 'Dead Ringers'," Film and Philos 3 (97); auth, "Nietzche's Sophistic Aesthetics," Jrnl of Nietzsche Stud, Special Nietzsche and Post-Analytic Philos Conf Ed (forthcoming); auth, book note on John Gedo's "The Artist and the Emotional Life," in Jrnl of Aesthetics and Art Crit (forthcoming). **CONTACT ADDRESS** Lock Haven Univ of Pennsylvania, R.D. 2, 190A, Mill Hall, PA 17751. **EMAIL** dshaw@eagle.1hup.edu

SHAW, GARY M.
DISCIPLINE LAW **EDUCATION** Univ IL, AB, 75; John Marshall Law Sch, JD, 79; Temple Univ, LLM, 83. **CAREER** Prof, Touro Col, counr, Govt of Belarus, 94, lectr, Conf on Const Law for mem of the Polish Parliament, Poland. **MEMBERSHIPS** Am Bar Assoc, Cent and E Europ Law Initiative, Assoc of Am Law Schls. **SELECTED PUBLICATIONS** Auth of the annual revisions of Evidence Laws of New York and has written sev law rev articles. **CONTACT ADDRESS** Touro Col, New York, 300 Nassau Rd, Huntington, NY 11743. **EMAIL** GaryS@tourolaw.edu

SHAW, MARVIN C.
PERSONAL Born 03/27/1937, Los Angeles, CA, m, 1959, 2 children **DISCIPLINE** PHILOSOPHY **EDUCATION** Occidental Col, BA 59; Union Theol Sem, MA, 62; Columbia Univ, PHD, 68 **CAREER** Prof of Relig Studies, Mont St Univ, 68-00. **HONORS AND AWARDS** Phi Kappi Phi Nat Scholastic Hon Soc; Danforth Assoc, Danforth Found; Fridley Distinguished Tch Awd, MT St Univ **MEMBERSHIPS** Am Acad of Relig; Highlands Inst; Soc for Buddhist-Christian Studies **RESEARCH** American Pragmatism and Naturalism; Process Theology; Buddhist-Christian Dialogue **SELECTED PUBLICATIONS** Auth, The Paradox of Intention: Reaching the goal by giving up the attempt to reach it, Atlanta Scholars Press, 1988; Auth, Nature's Grace: Essays on H.N. Weiman's Finite Theism, New York, Peter Lang, 1995 **CONTACT ADDRESS** 604 S Black Ave, Bozeman, MT 59715.

SHAW, SUSAN J.
PERSONAL Born 09/30/1943, New York, NY, s, 2 children **DISCIPLINE** THEOLOGICAL AND RELIGIOUS STUDIES, FEMINISM **EDUCATION** Syracuse Univ, BMusEd, 65; Alliance Theological Seminary, MDiv, 84; Drew Univ, MPhil, 89, PhD, 91. **CAREER** Music teacher, Westchester County NY Schools, 66-73; commun specialist, World Relief, 81-84; instr, Berkshire Christian Col, 87-90; instr, Pace Univ, 90-91; vP & dean, Trinity Col & Seminary, 93-96; asst vpres, distance ed, ed video conferencing, 97-. **HONORS AND AWARDS** Drew Merit Scholar; Who's Who in Am Women. **MEMBERSHIPS** Int Ministerial Fel; Am Acad of Rel/Soc of Biblical Lit; Am Asn of Univ Women; Nat Women's Studies Asn. **SELECTED PUBLICATIONS** Contribur, International Ministerial Fellowship Pastoral Letter, Women as Ministers, Int Ministerial Fel, 96-98; auth, The Theological Handbook of Misogynist Texts, Multiple Ministries Press, 96; auth, Doing More Than Any Man Has Ever Done, Multiple Ministries Press, 95; contribur, ed, The Consultant, 95-96; coauth, Smith, Abby Hadassah and Julia Evelina Smith, Am Nat Bio, Oxford Univ Press, 94. **CONTACT ADDRESS** 80 W Grand St., Apt C6, Mount Vernon, NY 10552-2131. **EMAIL** drsjshaw@hotmail.com

SHAW, THEODORE MICHAEL
PERSONAL Born 11/24/1954, New York, NY, m **DISCIPLINE** LAW **EDUCATION** Wesleyan Univ, BA, Honors, 1976; Columbia Univ School of Law, JD, 1979. **CAREER** US Dept of Justice, Civil Rights Div, trial attorney, 79-82; NAACP Legal Defense Fund, asst counsel, 82-87, western regional counsel, 87-90, assoc dir-counsel, 93-; Columbia Univ School of Law, anjunct prof, 93-; Univ of MI School of Law, asst prof of law, 90-93. **HONORS AND AWARDS** US Dept of Justice, Civil Rights Div, Special Commendation, 1981; Aspen Inst Fellowship on Law & Society, 1987; Twentyfirst Century Trust Fellowship on Global Interdependence, London Eng, 1989; Salzburg Seminars Fellowship, Salzburg, Austria, Summer, 1991; Langston Bar Assn, (Los Angeles, CA) Civil Trial Lawyer of the Year, 1991; Metropolitan Bar Association (Nyork) Outstanding Attorney of the Year, 98. **MEMBERSHIPS** Wesleyan Univ, bd of trustees, alumni elected trustee, 1986-89, charter mem, 1992-, sec of the bd, 1993-00; Poverty & Race Research Action Council, bd mem, 1990-; Archbishop's Leadership Proj, bd mem, 1994-98; Greater Brownsville Youth Council, bd mem, 1982-; Natl Bar Assn; Amer Bar Assn. **CONTACT ADDRESS** NAACP Legal Defense & Educational Fund Inc, 99 Hudson St, 16th Fl, New York, NY 10013. **EMAIL** eshaw@naacpldf.org

SHAW, WAYNE EUGENE
PERSONAL Born 05/23/1932, Covington, IN, m, 1957, 3 children **DISCIPLINE** HOMILETICS, SPEECH **EDUCATION** Lincoln Christian Col, AB, 54; Christian Theol Sem, BD, 60; Butler Univ, MS, 63; Ind Univ, PhD, 69. **CAREER** Prof preaching, Lincoln Christian Sem, 66-, acad dean, 74-, Mem chaplaincy endorsement comn, Christian Churches & Churches of Christ, 74-; academic dean, 74-00; Pres, North Am Christian Convention, 99. **MEMBERSHIPS** Acad Homiletics. **RESEARCH** Preaching; communication; Biblical studies. **SELECTED PUBLICATIONS** Auth, The historian's treatment of the Cane Ridge Revival, Filson Quart, 62; contribr, The Seer, The Savior, The Saved, Col Press, 63; coauth, Birth of a Revolution: How the Church Can Change the World, Standard, 74; auth, Designing the Sermon, Bicentennial Comt, 75; Love in the midst of crises, Christian Standard, 77; auth, Pastoral Epistles: Blueprint for 28 Messages Built on God's Word, 99; auth, "The Plymouth Pulpit: Henry Ward Beecher's Auction Block". **CONTACT ADDRESS** 100 Campus View Dr, Lincoln, IL 62656-2111. **EMAIL** shaw@lccs.edu

SHEA, EMMETT A.
PERSONAL Born 10/24/1931, Worchester, MA, m, 1961, 1 child **DISCIPLINE** POLITICAL SCIENCE, GOVERNMENT, HISTORY **EDUCATION** Boston Univ, BS, 55, Ed M, 56, AM, 61; Boston Col, AM, 71; Boston Col/Int Inst for Advanced Studies, PhD, 82. **CAREER** Prof, Worchester State Col, 62-, chair, Dept of Hist & Political Sci, 70-79, coordr, grad prog, 70-; lectr, Wellesley Col, 57-62; vis prof, Regis Col, 65-70; vis prof, Col of the Holy Cross, 63-73. **HONORS AND AWARDS** Pi Gamma Mu (Nat Soc Sci Honor Soc); Phi Alpha Theta (Nat Hist Honor Soc); Certificate of Meritorious Service, Commonwealth of Mass. **MEMBERSHIPS** Am Hist Asn, New England Hist Asn, Asn for the Advancement of Slavic Studies, N E Slavic Asn, Am Asn for Asian Studies. **RESEARCH** 19th and 20th century Russia, Soviet Union, Russian Federation, American-Russian/Soviet relations, U.S.-East Asia relations. **CONTACT ADDRESS** Dept Hist & Govt, Worcester State Col, 486 Chandler Sr, Worcester, MA 01602-2832.

SHEAR, JONATHAN
PERSONAL Born 08/17/1940, Washington, DC, m, 1990 **DISCIPLINE** PHILOSOPHY **EDUCATION** Brandeis Univ, BA, 62; Univ California-Berkeley, PhD, 72. **CAREER** Instr, Lone Mountain Col, 70-71; Prof, Maharishi Intl Univ, 72-83; Dir, Inst for Philosophy and Consciousness, 79-84; Asst Prof Col of William & Mary, 88-89; Affil Assoc Prof, Virginia Commonwealth Univ, 94-; Affil Asst Prof, 90-94, Adj Prof, 87-90, Managing Editor, J. of Consciousness Studies, 94-. **HONORS AND AWARDS** Fulbright Scholar in Phil of Science, London School of Economics; Woodrow Wilson Fel in Philosophy, Univ California-Berkeley; Distinct Adjunct Fac, Virginia Commonwealth Univ. **MEMBERSHIPS** Am Phil Asn. **RESEARCH** The significance of deep experiences of inner awareness, especially as produced by traditional Asian experimental methodologies for traditional questions of Western Philosophy and Psychology **SELECTED PUBLICATIONS** Auth, The Inner Dimension: Philosophy and the Experience of Consciousness, 90; On Mystical Experiences as Empirical Support for Perennial Philosophy, Journal of the American Academy of Religion, 94; Mystical Knowledge, Sufi, 95; The Hard Problem: Closing the Empirical Gap, J. of Consciousness Studies, 96; On a Culture-Independent Core Component of Self, East-West Encounters in Philosophy and Religion, 96; ed, Explaining Consciousness: The Hard Problem, 97; Ethics and the Experience of Happiness, Crossing Boundaries: Ethics, Antinomianism and the History of Mysticism, forthcoming; Scientific Exploration of Meditation Techniques, J. of Consciousness, forthcoming. **CONTACT ADDRESS** Dept of Philosophy, Virginia Commonwealth Univ, Richmond, VA 23284-2025. **EMAIL** jcs@richmond.infi.net

SHEARER, RODNEY H.
PERSONAL Born 09/21/1944, Reading, PA, m, 1966, 4 children **DISCIPLINE** BIBLICAL STUDIES, OLD TESTAMENT, HEBREW BIBLE **EDUCATION** Conrad Weiser Area Schools, high school diploma, 62; Lebanon Valley Col, BA, 66; Lutheran Theological Seminary in Gettysburg, 66-68; United Theological Seminary in Dayton, Ohio, MDiv, 69; Drew Univ, PhD, 85. **CAREER** Assoc Pastor, St. Paul's United Methodist Church, 69-72; pastor, Green Village United Methodist Church, 72-76; chaplain & adjunct asst prof of religion, Lebanon Valley Col, 76-80; pastor, Fritz Memorial UMC, 80-87; Pastor, Ono UMC, 87-; Dir of United Methodist Studies & Adjunct Lectr in Worship & United Methodist Polity, Evangelical School of Theology, 95-99; Academic Dean, Evangelical School of Theol, 99-. **HONORS AND AWARDS** Whos Who in Religion, 85; Who's Who in Biblical Studies and Archeol, 93; Eagle Scout Community Leaders and Noteworthy Americans. **MEMBERSHIPS** Soc of Biblical Lit; ordained elder in full connec-

tion, Eastern Pa Conf of The United Methodist Church. **RESEARCH** Biblical studies in ministry and worship. **SELECTED PUBLICATIONS** Auth, A Contextual Analysis of the Phrase "Al-tira" as it Occurs in the Hebrew Bible and in Selected Related Literature, Univ Microfilms Int, 86; the following articles in The Anchor Bible Dictionary, Doubleday, 92: Ashnah; Bakbuk; Barkos; Bazlith; Besai; Bishlam; Darkon; Gahar; Habaiah; Jahaziel; Jarib; Joiarib; Josiphiah; Juel; Mahli; Meremoth; Noadiah; Ono; Sherebiah; Uthai; Zarahiah. **CONTACT ADDRESS** 211 W Park Ave, Myerstown, PA 17067-1238. **EMAIL** rshearer@evangelical.edu

SHEEHAN, THOMAS
PERSONAL Born 06/25/1941, San Francisco, CA, m, 3 children **DISCIPLINE** PHILOSOPHY **EDUCATION** St Patrick's Col, BA, 63; Fordham Univ, MA, 68, PhD(philos theol), 71. **CAREER** Adj prof philos, Loyola Univ, Rome, 70-71; asst prof, St Mary's Col, Rome, 71-72; asst prof to prof Philos, Loyola Univ Chicago, 72-; freelance journ, El Salvador, 82-89; prof, Rel Studies, Stanford Univ, 99-. **HONORS AND AWARDS** Mellon Found grant teaching develop, 75; Am Cath Philos Asn publ subsidy, 77; dir philos, Col Phaenomenologicum, Perugia, Italy, 77-78; Fritz Thyssen Stiftung grant, 79-80; Nat Endowment for Humantities grant, 80; Ford Found grant, 83-85. **MEMBERSHIPS** Am Philos Asn; Soc for Phenomenol & Existential Philos. **RESEARCH** Metaphysics; philosophy of religion; continental philos; Marxism. **SELECTED PUBLICATIONS** Ed, Heidegger's, The Man and the Thinker, Precedent Press, 81; Karl Rahner: The Philosophical Foundations, Ohio Univ Press, 82; auth, The First Coming: How the Kingdom of God Became Christianity, Random House, 86; Heidegger and the Nazis, NY Rev of Books, 88; Das Gewesen, In: From Phenomenology to Thought, Errancy and Desire, Kluwer, 95; ed & transl, Edmund Husserl, Psychological and Transcendental Phenomenology, Kluwer, 97; auth, Friendly Fascism, In: Fascism's Return, Univ Nebr Press, 98; Nihilism in Phenomenology, Japanese and American Perspectives, Kluwer, 98; Martin Heidegger, Routledge Encyclopaedia of Philosophy, 98; ed & transl, Heidegger, Logic: The Question of Truth, Ind Univ Press (in prep); auth, "Nihilism and its Discontents," in Heidegger and Practical Philosophy SUNY Pr, forthcoming; auth, "Kehre and Ereignis" in A Companion to Martin Heidegger's Introduction to Metaphysics, Yale Univ Pr, 00; auth, "From Divinity to Infinity," in The Onve and Future Jesus, Polebridge Pr, 00; auth, "Choosing One's Fate: Sein und Zeit, 74," Research in Phenomenology, 99; auth, "Friendly Fascism: Business as Usual in America's Backyard," in Facism's Return, ed, J Richard Golson, Univ of Nebraska Pr, 98, pp 260-300. **CONTACT ADDRESS** Dept of Rel Studies, Stanford Univ, Stanford, CA 94305. **EMAIL** tsheehan@stanford.edu

SHEEHY, ELIZABETH A.
DISCIPLINE LAW **EDUCATION** Osgoode Hall Law Sch, LLB; Univ British Columbia, LLM. **CAREER** Prof. **MEMBERSHIPS** Can Asn Elizabeth Fry Soc. **SELECTED PUBLICATIONS** Auth, Criminal Law and Procedure: Cases, Context and Critique; auth, Criminal Law and Pricedure: Proof, Defences and Beyond. **CONTACT ADDRESS** Fac Common Law, Univ of Ottawa, 57 Louis Pasteur, Fauteux Hall Rm. 301, Ottawa, ON, Canada K1N 6N5. **EMAIL** esheehy@uottawa.ca

SHEEHY, JOHN
PERSONAL Born 06/18/1925, Allegan, MI, m, 1968, 6 children **DISCIPLINE** PHILOSOPHY, THEOLOGY, SOCIOLOGY **EDUCATION** St Mary's, BA, 46; Catholic Univ Am, STL, 50; Notre Dame Univ, MA, 70. **CAREER** Management Development, Beth Steel Corp, 69-86; prof, Purdue Univ N Central Campus, 86-00; Priest. **HONORS AND AWARDS** Part-time Teacher of the Year, Purdue Univ N Central Campus, 99. **SELECTED PUBLICATIONS** Auth, Church's History of Injustice and Why This Priest Left, Univ Pr of Am, 99. **CONTACT ADDRESS** Dept Soc Sci, Purdue Univ, No Central, 1401 S US Hwy 421, Westville, IN 4631-9542. **EMAIL** jsheehy@purduenc.edu

SHEELEY, STEVEN M.
PERSONAL Born 12/02/1956, Springfield, MO, m, 1992, 2 children **DISCIPLINE** RELIGION **EDUCATION** Southwest Montana State Univ, BSEd, 79; Southwestern Baptist Theol Sem, Mdiv, 83; IN Univ, Special Stud, 84; Southern Baptist Theol Sem, PhD, 87. **CAREER** Assoc Dean of the Col, Shorter Col, 97-; ch, Effectiveness Plan Coun, 97-; assoc prof, Shorter Col, 93-; ch, The Mrs Columbus Roberts Division Relig & Philos, Shorter Col, 92- & act ch, 92; sponsor: Theta Alpha Kappa Nat Relig & Theol Hon Soc, 96-; asst prof, Shorter Col, 88-93; ch, Self-Stud Comt on Conditions of Eligibility, 90-92; mem, Self-Stud Steering Comt, 89-92; ch, Self-Stud Comt on Intercollegiate Athletics, 89-92; adj prof, The Southern Baptist Theol Sem, 87-88. **HONORS AND AWARDS** Outstanding Young Men of Am, 96; Sigma Tau Delta Int Engl Hon Soc, 96; Theta Alpha Kappa Nat Rel and Theol Hon Soc, 96; Vulcan Materials Tchg Excellence & Campus Leadership Awd, Shorter Col, 94; Who's Who in Bibl Stud and Archaeol, 92-93; Argo Yearbk Dedication, Shorter Col, Class of 92; Who's Who Among Stud in Am Univ & Col, 85-86, 79-80, 77-78; Am Bibl Soc Awd, Southwestern Baptist Theol Sem, 83; Phi Kappa Phi Nat Scholastic Hon Soc, 79. **MEMBERSHIPS** Soc Bibl Lit; Nat Asn Baptist Prof Rel; Seven Hills Rotary Club. **SELECTED PUBLICATIONS** Auth, Narrative Asides in Luke-Acts, JSNTS, Sheffield: JSOT/Sheffield Acad Press, 92; Following everything closely: Narrative presence in Luke 1-2, Essays in Lit 20, 93; Lift Up Your Eyes: John 4:4-42, Rev and Expositor, 95; The Narrator in the Gospels: Developing a Model, Perspectives in Rel Stud 16, 89; Narrative Asides and Narrative Authority in Luke-Acts, Bibl Theol Bull 18, 88; The Politically Correct Church: Ephesians 2:11-22, Interpreting Ephesians for Preaching and Tchg, Macon, Smyth and Helwys Press, 96; Acts, Holman Bibl Handbk, Nashville, Broadman Press, 92; Demetrius the Chronographer 208, Elijah, Apocalypse of 244, Ezekiel the Tragedian 283, Jacob, Ladder of 425, Jacob, Prayer of 425, Jeremiah, Letter of 438, Persecution in the New Testament 668, Righteousness 765f, Shem, Treatise of 818, Shroud of Turin 822, Swine 864, Tobit 922, Zephaniah, Apocalypse of 983f, Mercer Dictionary of the Bibl, Macon, Mercer UP, 90; coauth, The Bible in English Translation: An Essential Guide Nashville, Abingdon Press, 97; rev(s), Engaging the New Testament: An Interdisciplinary Introduction. In JBL/CRBR Online Rev(s), 97; Moses or Jesus: An Essay in Johannine Christology; John, the Son of Zebedee: The Life of a Legend; John, the Maverick Gospel; and Scott Sinclair, The Road and the Truth: The Editing of John's Gospel, Perspectives in Rel Stud 23, 96; Windows on the World of Jesus: Time Travel to Ancient Judea, Bibl Archaeologist 58, 95; Our Journey With Jesus: Discipleship according to Luke-Acts, Critical Rev of Bk(s) in Rel 92, Atlanta, Scholars Press, 93; Paul, In Other Words, Bibl Archaeologist 55, 92; Host, Guest, Enemy, and Friend, Rev and Expositor 89, 92; coauth, Choosing a Bible, Abingdon Pr, 99. **CONTACT ADDRESS** Div of Relig and Philos, Shorter Col, Georgia, 315 Shorter Ave, Box 2007, Rome, GA 30165-4267. **EMAIL** ssheeley@shorter.edu

SHEETS-JOHNSTONE, MAXINE
PERSONAL Born 09/05/1930, San Francisco, CA, m, 1974, 2 children **DISCIPLINE** DANCE PHILOSOPHY **EDUCATION** Univ Calif, Berkeley, BA, 52; Univ Wisc, MS, 54, PhD, 63. **CAREER** Prof, dance, 68-84, prof, phil, 88-, Univ Ore; independent scholar, 98-. **MEMBERSHIPS** Husserl Cir; Soc for Phenomenology and Existential Philosophy. **RESEARCH** Interdisciplinary: phil of mind/body; evolutionary biology; psychol/psychiatry. **SELECTED PUBLICATIONS** Auth, The Phenomenology of Dance, Univ Wisc Press, 66, Arno Press, 80; auth, Illuminating Dance: Philosophical Explorations, Assoc Univ Press, 85; auth, The Roots of Thinking, Temple Univ Press, 90; auth, Giving the Body It's Due, SUNY Press, 92; auth, The Roots of Power: Animate form and Gendered Bodies, Open Court, 94; auth, The Primacy of Movement, John Benjamins Pub, 99; auth, Race and Other Miscalculations, Misconceptions, and Mismeasures: Essays in Honor of Ashley Montague, General Hall Pub, 95; art, Taking Evolution Seriously: A Matter of Primate Intelligence, Etica & Animali 8, 96; art, Tribal Lore in Present-Day Paleoanthropology: A Case Study, Anthropology of Consciousness 7/4, 96; art, On the Significance of Animate Form, Analecta Husserliana, Kluwer Acad, 98; art, Consciousness: A Natural History, J Consciousness Stud 5/3, 98; art, Binary Opposition as an Ordering Principle in (Male?) Human Thought, Phenomenology & Feminism, Kluwer Acad, 99; art, The Primacy of Movement, John Benjamins Pub, 98. **CONTACT ADDRESS** Dept of Philosophy, Univ of Oregon, Eugene, OR 97403. **EMAIL** msj@oregon.uoregon.edu

SHEHADI, FADLOU A.
PERSONAL Born 02/09/1926, Beiruit, Lebanon, m, 1954, 3 children **DISCIPLINE** PHILOSOPHY **EDUCATION** Am Univ Beirut, BA, 48; Princeton Univ, PhD, 59. **CAREER** Asst instr, Princeton Univ, 50-51; instr, Rutgers Univ, 53-57; asst prof, 57-63; assoc prof, 63-72; full prof, 72-94; prof emer, 94-. **HONORS AND AWARDS** Rockefeller fel; NEH grant. **MEMBERSHIPS** Am Philos Asn. **RESEARCH** Islamic philosophy. **SELECTED PUBLICATIONS** Auth, Philosophies of Music in Medieval Islam, 95; co-ed, Applied Ethics and Ethical Theory, 88; auth, Metaphysics in Islamic Philosophy, 82; auth, Ghazali's al-Maqsad al-Asna, 71; auth, Ghazali's Unique Unknowable God, 64. **CONTACT ADDRESS** 220 State Rd, Princeton, NJ 08540. **EMAIL** Fshehadi@aol.com

SHELLEY, BRUCE
DISCIPLINE HISTORICAL THEOLOGY **EDUCATION** Columbia Bible, BA; Fuller Sem, M.Div; Iowa Univ, Ph.D. **CAREER** Sr prof, Denver Sem. **HONORS AND AWARDS** Ed adv bd, Christian Hist; consult ed, InterVarsity's popular Dictionary of Christianity in Am. **SELECTED PUBLICATIONS** Auth, Church History in Plain Language; All the Saints Adore Thee; The Gospel; and the American Dream and The Consumer Church; corresponding ed, Christianity Today; pub(s), articles in Encycl Am; Evangel Dictionary of Theol; New Intl Dictionary of the Christian Church. **CONTACT ADDRESS** Denver Conservative Baptist Sem, PO Box 10000, Denver, CO 80250. **EMAIL** bruces@densem.edu

SHELP, EARL E.
PERSONAL Born 10/28/1947, Louisville, KY **DISCIPLINE** THEOLOGY **EDUCATION** Univ Louisville, 69; So Baptist Theol Sem, Theol, 72, Theol Ethics, 76. **CAREER** Res fel, , 76-88 Inst of Relig, asst prof, 77-88, Baylor Col of Med; vis prof, 85, 89, Dept of Relig, Dartmouth Col; pres, 88-, Found For Interfaith Res and Ministry **HONORS AND AWARDS** America's Awd, Postive Thinking Found at Kennedy Center, Wash, DC, 92. **MEMBERSHIPS** Soc of Christian Ethics. **RESEARCH** Medical ethics; theol ethics; pastoral theol. **SELECTED PUBLICATIONS** Co-ed, Competency: A Study of Informal Completency Determinations in Primary Care, Philos and Med Series, 36, Kluwer Acad Pubs, 91; contrib auth, The Social Impact of AIDS, Nat Acad Press, 93; ed, Secular Bioethics in Theological Perspective, Theol and Med Series, vol 8, Kluwer Acad Pubs, 96; co-auth, Prediction of Grief and HIV/AIDS-related Burnout in Volunteers, AIDS Care 8, no 2, 96; co-auth, Ministries of Sustaining Presence: Congregational Care Teams, Abingdon Press; ed, Pastoral Ministry Series, Pilgrim Press, 1 vol yr, 85-90; ed, Theology & Med Ser, Kluwer Academic Pubs, 92-97. **CONTACT ADDRESS** Interfaith Care Partners, 701 N Post Oak Rd, #330, Houston, TX 77024.

SHELTON, JIM D.
DISCIPLINE PHILOSOPHY **EDUCATION** Univ Kans, PhD, 72. **CAREER** Prof, Univ Central Ark. **RESEARCH** Twentieth-century analytic philosophy; philosophy of science; modern philosophy. **SELECTED PUBLICATIONS** Auth, The Role of Obbservation and Simplicity in Einstein's Epistemology, Studies in History and Philosophy of Science; auth, Schlick and Husserl on the Foundations of Phenomenology, Philosophy and Phenomelogical Research; auth, Responsibility and Freedom: A Revision of Schlick's Soft Determinism, Dialogos; auth, Contextualism: A Right Answer to the Wrong Question, Southwest Philosophical Studies; auth, Schlick's Theory of Knowledge, Synthese, 89; coauth, Husserl's Phenomenology and the Ontology of the Natural Sciences, Phenomenology of Natural Science, 92; Up From Poverty, Falling in Love With Wisdom, 93; auth, Seeing and Paradigms in the Chemical Revolution, Philosophy in Science, 94. **CONTACT ADDRESS** Univ of Central Arkansas, 201 Donaghey Ave, Conway, AR 72035-0001.

SHELTON, MARK
DISCIPLINE PHILOSOPHY **EDUCATION** Harvard Univ, PhD, 96 **CAREER** Visiting Instr, 94-96, Georgetown Univ; Asst Prof, 96-, Old Dominion Univ. **MEMBERSHIPS** Amer Phil Assoc **RESEARCH** Ethics; political philosophy; Hegel **CONTACT ADDRESS** Dept of Philosophy, Old Dominion Univ, 4100 Powhatan Ave, Norfolk, VA 23529-0083.

SHEN, RAPHAEL
PERSONAL Born 10/29/1937, Shanghai, China, s **DISCIPLINE** ECONOMICS **EDUCATION** Mich State, PhD, 75. **CAREER** Sr Research Scholar, The Kennedy Institute, Georgetown Univ, 76-77; Asst Prof of Economics, Univ of Detroit, 77; Assoc Prof of Economics, Univ of Detroit, 80-86; Prof of Economics, Univ of Detroit, 86-. **MEMBERSHIPS** American Economic Assn/Atlantic Economic Assn. **RESEARCH** Economics in transition (Eastern Europe and China), Resource Economics, Economic Development. **SELECTED PUBLICATIONS** Auth, The Polish Economy: Legacies from the Past, Prospects for the Future, Praeger Publishers, 92; auth, Economic Reform in Poland and Czechoslovakia: Lessons in Systemic Transformation, Praeger Publishers, 93, auth, "Lithuania's Economic Restructuring," in Lituanina Papers, Univ of Tasmania (Australia), 95; auth, Restructuring the Baltic Economies: Disengaging 50 Years of Integration with the U.S.S.R., Praeger Publishers, 94; auth, Ukraine's Economic Reform: Obstacles, Errors, Lessons, Praeger Publishers, 95; auth, The Restructuring of Romania's Economy: A Paradigm of Flexibility and Adaptability, Praeger Publishers, 97; auth, "Restructuring Ukraine's Economic system," Toward a New Ukraine II: Meeting the Next Century, ed. Theofil Kis and Irena Makaryk, Univ of Ottawa, 99; auth, China's Economic Reform: an Experiment in Pragmatic Socialism, Praeger Publishers, Greenwood Publishing Group, 00. **CONTACT ADDRESS** Dept Economics, Univ of Detroit Mercy, PO Box 19900, Detroit, MI 48219. **EMAIL** shznrs@udmercy.edu

SHENK, WILBERT
PERSONAL Born 01/16/1935, m, 1957, 3 children **DISCIPLINE** MISSION HISTORY, MISSION STUDIES **EDUCATION** Goshen Col, BA, 55; Univ Ore, MA, 64; Univ Aberdeen, PhD, 78. **CAREER** Mennonite Central Comt, 55-59; admin sec, Mennonite Central Comt, 63-65; vpres, Overseas Ministries of the Mennonite Board of Missions, 65-90; prof, Assoc Mennonite Bibl Sem, 90-95; prof, Fuller Theol Sem, 95-. **MEMBERSHIPS** Am Soc of Missiology, International Asn for Mission Studies. **RESEARCH** 19th and 20th century missions and theology, modern/postmodern culture. **SELECTED PUBLICATIONS** Auth, Write the Vision, Trinity Press, 95; auth, Changing Frontiers of Mission, Orbis Books, 99; auth, By Faith They Went Out, Inst of Mennonite Studies, 00. **CONTACT ADDRESS** Sch of World Mission, Fuller Theol Sem, 135 N Oakland Ave, Pasadena, CA 91182-0001.

SHEPPARD, ANTHONY
DISCIPLINE LAW **EDUCATION** Univ British Columbia, BA, 64; LLB, 67; LLM, 68. **CAREER** Asst prof, 69-72; assoc prof, 72-76; prof, 76-. **MEMBERSHIPS** UBC Fac Asn. **RESEARCH** Evidence; creditors remedies; equity law; taxation

law. **SELECTED PUBLICATIONS** Auth, pubs about creditors remedies, equitable remedies, evidence and taxation. **CONTACT ADDRESS** Fac of Law, Univ of British Columbia, 1822 East Mall, Vancouver, BC, Canada V6T 1Z1. **EMAIL** sheppard@law.ubc.ca

SHER, GEORGE
PERSONAL Born 11/10/1942, New York, NY, m, 1972, 1 child **DISCIPLINE** PHILOSOPHY **EDUCATION** Brandeis Univ, BA, 64; Columbia Univ, PhD, 72. **CAREER** Instr to asst prof, Fairleigh Dickinson Univ, 66-74; assoc prof to prof, Univ of Vt, 74-91; Herbert S. Autrey prof, Chair, Rice Univ, 91-. **HONORS AND AWARDS** NEH Grant, 77; Univ of Vt Res Fel, 82, 87, 90; Fel, Inst for Advanc Studies in the Humanities, 80; Fel, Nat Humanities Centre, 80-81; NEH Fel, 87-88; Univ Scholar Awd, Univ of Vt, 88-89; NEH Fel, 00-01. **MEMBERSHIPS** Am Philos Assoc. **RESEARCH** Ethics, Social Philosophy, Political Philosophy. **SELECTED PUBLICATIONS** Ed, Reason at Work: Introductory Readings in Philosophy, Harcourt Brace Jovanovich, 84; Auth, Desert, Princeton Univ Pr, 87; ed, Moral Philosophy: Selected Readings, Harcourt Brace Jovanovich, 87; auth, Beyond Neutrality: Perfectionism and Politics, Cambridge Univ Pr, 97; auth, Approximate Justice: Studies in Non-Ideal Theory, Towman and Littlefield, 97; auth, "Ethics, Character, and Action", Soc Philos and Policy, Winter 98; auth, "Diversity", Philos and Pub Aff, Spring 99; coed, Social and Political Philosophy: Contemporary Readings, Harcourt Brace, 99; auth, "But I Could Be Wrong", Social Philos and Policy, (forthcoming); auth, "Blame for Traits", Nous, (forthcoming). **CONTACT ADDRESS** Dept Philos, Rice Univ, 6100 Main St, Houston, TX 77005-1827. **EMAIL** gsher@ruf.rice.edu

SHER, GILA
DISCIPLINE PHILOSOPHY **EDUCATION** Columbia Univ, PhD, 89. **CAREER** Prof, Univ Calif, San Diego. **RESEARCH** Truth & philosophical method; Quine's epistemology; Logic & the mind. **SELECTED PUBLICATIONS** Auth, The Bounds of Logic: A Generalized Viewpoint, The MIT Press, 91; "Did Tarski Commit Tarski's Fallacy?," Jour of Symbolic Logic 61, 96; "Semantics and Logic," Handbk of Contemp Semantic Theory, 96; "Logical Consequence," The Encycl of Philos Supplement, Macmillan, 96; "Logical Terms," The Encycl of Philos Supplement, Macmillan, 96; Partially-Ordered (Branching) Generalized Quantifiers: A General Definition, Jour Philos Logic 26, 97; auth, "Is Logic a Theory of the Obvious?" European Review of Philosphy 4 (99); auth, "Is There a Place for Philosophy in Quine's Theory?" The Journal of Philosophy 96 (99); coed, Beetween Logic and Intuition: Essays in Honor of Charles Parsons, Cambridge Univ Press, 00; auth, "On the Possibility of a Substantive Theory of Truth," Syntese 117, 98-99; auth, "The Formal-Structural view of Logical Consequence," The Philosophical Review 110 (01). **CONTACT ADDRESS** Dept of Philos 0119, Univ of California, San Diego, 9500 Gilman Dr, La Jolla, CA 92093-0119. **EMAIL** gsher@acsd.edu

SHERIDAN, THOMAS L.
PERSONAL Born 12/17/1926, New York, NY **DISCIPLINE** THEOLOGY **EDUCATION** Woodstock Col, MD, AB, 50, MA, 52, STL, 58; Cath Inst Paris, STD, 65. **CAREER** Tchr, Xavier High Sch, 51-54; instr, 59-62, asst prof theol, Fordham Univ, 65-66; assoc prof, St. Peters Col, NJ, 66-75, chmn dept, 68-75, chmn, Faculty of Senate Comt, 86-88; chmn, Theol Dept, 86-88; prof Theol, St Peter's Col, NJ, 75-98 prof emer. **MEMBERSHIPS** Cath Theol Soc Am; Col Theol Soc. **RESEARCH** Systematics. **SELECTED PUBLICATIONS** Auth, Newman on Justification, Alba, 67; articles and reviews, In: Theol Studies; America; Spiritual Life & Homiletic & Pastoral Rev. **CONTACT ADDRESS** Dept of Theol, Jesuit Comt, 50 Glenwood Ave, Jersey City, NJ 07306-4606. **EMAIL** sheridan_t@spcvxa.spc.edu

SHERLINE, ED
PERSONAL Born 12/04/1959, Evanston, IL, s **DISCIPLINE** PHILOSOPHY **EDUCATION** Princeton Univ, BA, 82; Univ Chicago, MA, 83; Univ IL, PhD, 90. **CAREER** Univ Wyoming, lectr, asst prof, assoc prof, 89-. **MEMBERSHIPS** APA **RESEARCH** Ethics; Political philo **SELECTED PUBLICATIONS** Auth, Confirmation Theory and Moral Justification, Philo Stud, 94. **CONTACT ADDRESS** Dept of Philosophy, Univ of Wyoming, Laramie, WY 82071-3392. **EMAIL** sherline@uwyo.edu

SHERMAN, NANCY
DISCIPLINE PHILOSOPHY **EDUCATION** Harvard Univ, PhD. **CAREER** Prof. **MEMBERSHIPS** U.S. Naval Acad. **RESEARCH** Moral philosophy; history of moral philosophy; moral psychology and the emotions; ancient philosophy; ancient ethics; psychoanalysis; military ethics. **SELECTED PUBLICATIONS** Auth, Making a Necessity of Virtue, Cambridge, 97; The Fabric of Character, Oxford, 89; ed. Apostle's Ethics: Critical Essays, Rowenon and Littlefield, 99. **CONTACT ADDRESS** Dept of Philosophy, Georgetown Univ, 37th and O St, Washington, DC 20057.

SHERMAN, ROGER
PERSONAL Born 09/10/1930, Jamestown, NY, m, 2 children **DISCIPLINE** ECONOMICS **EDUCATION** Harvard Univ, MBA, 59; Carnegie-Mellon Univ, MS, 65, PhD, 66. **CAREER** Asst, assoc prof, and Brown-Forman prof of Economics, Univ VA, 65-99, economics dept chair, 82-90; prof of Economics, Univ Houston, 99-. **HONORS AND AWARDS** Fulbright lect, 72; Rockefeller Found vis scholar, 85; VA Soc Sci Asn Outstanding Scholar, 94; Pres, Southern Economic Asn, 00. **MEMBERSHIPS** Am Economic Asn; Economic Science Asn; Industrial Org Soc; Royal Economic Soc; Southern Economic Asn. **RESEARCH** Experimental economics; industrial org and regulation. **SELECTED PUBLICATIONS** Auth, A Private Ownership Bias in Transit Choice, Am Economic Rev, 67; Risk Attitude and Cost Variability in a Capacity Choice Experiment, Rev of Economic Studies, 69; Congestion Interdependence and Urban Transit Fares, Econometrica, 71; Oligopoly: An Empirical Approach, D C Heath, 72; The Psychological Difference between Ambiguity and Risk, Quart J of Economics, 74; Second-Best Pricing with Stochastic Demand, with Michael Visscher, Am Economic Rev, 78; Waiting-Line Auctions, with Charles A Holt, J of Political Economy, 82; Nonprice Rationing and Monopoly Price Structures when Demand is Stochastic, with Michael Visscher, Bell J of Economics, 82; The Regulation of Monopoly, Cambridge Univ Press, 89; The Loser's Curse, with Charles A Holt, Am Economic Rev, 94; auth, Optimal Work-sharing Discounts, J of Regulatory Economics, 01; auth, The Future of Market Regulation, Southern Economic J, 01. **CONTACT ADDRESS** Dept of Economics, Univ of Houston, Houston, TX 77204-5882. **EMAIL** rsherman@uh.edu

SHEROVER, CHARLES M.
PERSONAL Born 01/20/1922, New York, NY, s **DISCIPLINE** PHILOSOPHY **EDUCATION** Oberlin Col, AB, 43; Northwestern Univ, MA, 47; New York Univ, PhD, 66. **CAREER** Vis Prof, 69, Duquesne; grad fac, 70-74, The New School; instr to prof, 63-93, Prof Emeritus, Hunter Col/CUNY, 93; SUNY Stony Brook, 78; Emory Univ, 89. **MEMBERSHIPS** APA; Intl Soc for the Study of Time; Metaphysical Soc of Amer; Soc for Advancement of Amer Phil; The Heidegger Conf. **RESEARCH** Philosophy of time; democratic theory; Kant Rousseau **SELECTED PUBLICATIONS** Auth, Time Freedom and the Common Good, Suny Press, 89; auth, Heidegger, Kant and Time; auth, The Human Experience of Time. **CONTACT ADDRESS** PO Box 6604, Santa Fe, NM 87505.

SHERRY, JOHN E. H.
PERSONAL Born 03/17/1932, New York, NY, m, 1960, 3 children **DISCIPLINE** LAW **EDUCATION** Yale Univ, BA, 54; Columbia Law Sch, JD, 59; NYork Univ Law Sch, LLM, 68. **CAREER** Prof of Law, Cornell Univ, 72-97; Prof Emeritus, 97; Vis Prof at Canesius Col, 97-98. **HONORS AND AWARDS** US Diplomatic Representative to UNIDROIT, 79. **MEMBERSHIPS** External Collaborator to World Tourism Organization, Madrid, Spain. **RESEARCH** Business & Hotel Law. **SELECTED PUBLICATIONS** Auth, The Laws of Innkeepers, rev ed, Cornell Univ Press, 94; auth, Legal Aspects of Hospitality Management, 2nd ed, Educ Found of Nat restaurant Asn, 94. **CONTACT ADDRESS** Cornell Univ, 1100 Elizabeth Dr., Oak Island, NC 28465. **EMAIL** jes22@cornell.edu

SHERWIN, SUSAN
DISCIPLINE PHILOSOPHY **EDUCATION** Univ York, BA, 69; Stanford Univ, PhD, 74. **CAREER** Prof. **RESEARCH** Feminist theory, bioethics, ethics. **SELECTED PUBLICATIONS** Auth, Feminist and Medical Ethics, Hypatia, 89; No Longer Patient: Feminist Ethics and Health Care, 92; Theory vs Practice in Ethics, Philos Perspectives on Bioethics, 96; The Politics of Women's Health, Temple UP, 98. **CONTACT ADDRESS** Dept of Philos, Dalhousie Univ, Halifax, NS, Canada B3H 3J5. **EMAIL** susan.sherwin@dal.ca

SHERWOOD, O. PETER
PERSONAL Born 02/09/1945, Kingston, Jamaica, m **DISCIPLINE** LAW **EDUCATION** Brooklyn Coll, BA 1968; NYork Univ Sch of Law, JD 1971. **CAREER** NY Civil Court, law sec to Hon Fritz W Alexander II 1971-74; NAACP Legal Def & Educ Fund Inc, atty 1974-84; NY Univ School of Law, adj asst prof of law 1980-87; State of NY, solicitor general, 86-91; City of New York, corporation counsel, 91-93; Kalkines, Arky, Zall & Bernstein, partner, 94-; NYS Ethics Commission, commissioner, 98-2003. **MEMBERSHIPS** Trustee NY Univ Law Ctr Found; co-chmn Compliance & Enforcement Comm NY & St Bar Assn; Taskforce on NY St Div on Human Rights 1977-80; board of directors New York City Comm Action Legal Serv 1971-75; 100 Black Men; Metro Black Bar Assn; Natl Bar Assn; secretary, Bar of the City of New York Association, 1992-97. **CONTACT ADDRESS** Kalkines, Arky, Zall & Bernstein, 1675 Broadway, New York, NY 10019.

SHERWOOD, STEPHEN K.
PERSONAL Born 05/08/1943, Hollywood, CA, s **DISCIPLINE** BIBLICAL THEOLOGY **EDUCATION** Pontifical Gregorion Univ, STD, 90. **CAREER** Assoc prof, Oblate Sch of Theology, 91- . **MEMBERSHIPS** Catholic Biblical Assn; Soc of Biblical Lit. **RESEARCH** Narrative criticism of Hebrew Bible. **SELECTED PUBLICATIONS** Auth, Mad God Not Been on My Side, An Examination of the Narrative Technique of the Story of Jacob and Laban Genesis 29,1 -32,2, 90; auth, Psalm 112-A royal Wisdom Psalm?, CBQ, 89. **CONTACT ADDRESS** 285 Oblate Dr., San Antonio, TX 78216-6693. **EMAIL** sksherwood@earthlink.net

SHERWOOD, WALLACE WALTER
PERSONAL Born 10/06/1944, Nassau, Bahamas **DISCIPLINE** LAW **EDUCATION** St Vincent Coll, BA 1966; Harvard Univ, LLM 1971; George Washington Univ, JD 1969. **CAREER** Legal Svcs, staff atty 1969-71; MA Comm Against Discrimination, commnr 1971-73; Roxbury Pub Def, dir 1971-73; OEO, gen counsel 1973-74; Lawyers Comm for Civil Rights under Law, exec div 1974-76; Private Practice, Attorney 1976-; NE Univ Coll of Criminal Justice, assoc prof. **HONORS AND AWARDS** Dulles Fulbright Awd Natl Law Ctr 1969; Teacher of The Year, 1987 Coll of Criminal Justice. **MEMBERSHIPS** Mem MA Bar Assn 1969-; mem Boston Bar Assn 1969-; mem MA Council for Pub Justice. **CONTACT ADDRESS** Col of Criminal Justice, Northeastern Univ, 360 Huntington Ave, Boston, MS 02115. **EMAIL** w.sherwood@neu.edu

SHIBLES, WARREN ALTON
PERSONAL Born 07/10/1933, Hartford, CT, m, 1977, 3 children **DISCIPLINE** PHILOSOPHY **EDUCATION** Univ Conn, BA, 58; Univ Colo, MA, 63. **CAREER** Instr philos, NTex State Univ, 66; lectr, Parsons Col, 66-67; Asst Prof Philos, Univ Wis-Whitewater, 67-, Dir, Lang Press, 71-; Teach, Tuebingen Univ, Germany. **MEMBERSHIPS** Am Philos Asn; AAUP; Div Philos Psychol of Am Psychol Asn. **RESEARCH** Philosophy; psychology; poetry. **SELECTED PUBLICATIONS** Auth, Metaphor: An Annotated Bibliography and History, 71, Death: An Interdisciplinary Analysis, 74, Emotion: The Method of Philosophical Therapy, 74, Ethics for Children, 78, Emotion: A Critical Analysis for Children, 78, Humor: A Critical Analysis for Children, 78, Time: A Critical Analysis for Children, 78 & Rational Love, 78, Lang Press, auth Emotion in Aesthetics, Kluwer, 95, auth Unsere Gefuhlswelt, Lehrman Verlag, 95, auth Was it Zeit?, Lehrman Verlog, 97; auth, Ethik, 99; auth, Luegen und Luegen Lassen, 00. **CONTACT ADDRESS** PO Box 342, Whitewater, WI 53190-1790. **EMAIL** shiblesw@mail.uww.edu

SHIELDS, BRUCE E.
PERSONAL Born 08/09/1937, PA, m, 1957, 3 children **DISCIPLINE** NEW TESTAMENT AND HOMILETICS **EDUCATION** Milligan Col, BA, 59; Princeton Theol Sem, BD, 65; Eberhard-Karls Universitaet zu Tubingen, D Theol, 81. **CAREER** Prof, 77-83, Lincoln Christian Sem; prof , 83-, Emmanuel Sch Relig. **HONORS AND AWARDS** NEH sum grant, 91. **MEMBERSHIPS** Soc of Bibl Lit; Acad of Homiletics; Societas Homiletica. **RESEARCH** Preaching in the early church. **SELECTED PUBLICATIONS** Auth, Romans, Cincinnati: Standard Pub Co, 88; auth, Campbell on Language and Revelation and Modern Approaches to Language, Building Up the Church: Scripture, Hist, & Growth, A Festschrift in Honor of Henry E. Webb, Milligan Col, 93, TN; rev, Dale B. Martin, Slavery as Salvation: The Metaphor of Slavery in Pauline Christianity, Yale Univ Press, 90, Restor Quart vol 35, 93; rev, Sidney Greidanus, The Modern Preacher and the Ancient Text: Interpreting and Preaching Biblical Literature, Eerdmans Pub Co, 88, J for Christian Stud, 93; auth, The Areopagus Sermon as a Model for Apologetic Preaching, Faith in Pract: Stud in Bk of Acts, A Festschrift in Honor of Earl and Ottie Mearl Stuckenbruck, European Evangel Soc, 95; auth, John Henry Jowett, Concise Encycl of Preaching, Westminster/John Knox Press, 95; rev, Jeffrey T. Myers, Unfinished Errand into the Wilderness: Tendenzen und Schwerpunkte der Homilitic in den USA 1960-1985, doct diss, Johannes Gutenburg Univ, Mainz, Germany, in Homiletic, XXI/1, 96; rev, H. David Schuringa, Hearing the Word in a Visual Age in Encounter, 97; auth, Integrating Ministry and Theology: One Seminary's Story, Theological Ed, vol 33, no 2, 97; auth, Preaching and Culture, Homiletic vol XXII no 2, 97; auth, Readers Guide: Literary Resources for Worship, Leaven vol 6, no 1, 98. **CONTACT ADDRESS** Emmanuel Sch of Religion, One Walker Dr, Johnson City, TN 37601-9438. **EMAIL** shieldsb@esr.edu

SHIELDS, DONALD J.
PERSONAL Born 10/28/1937, Paris, IL, m, 1962, 2 children **DISCIPLINE** COMMUNICATION, POLITICAL SCIENCE **EDUCATION** Eastern IL Univ, BS, 59; Purdue Univ, MS, 61, PhD, 64. **CAREER** Staff asst speech, IN State Democratic Comt, 62; asst prof, Cornell Univ, 64-65; asst prof, 65-71, assoc prof, 71-79, prof speech, IN State Univ, Terre Haute, 79. **MEMBERSHIPS** Speech Commun Asn; Nat Soc Studies Commun; Am Forensic Asn; Am Asn Univ Prof. **RESEARCH** Polit persuasion and commun networks. **CONTACT ADDRESS** Dept of Speech, Indiana State Univ, 210 N 7th St, Terre Haute, IN 47809-0002. **EMAIL** cmshield@ruby.indstate.edu

SHIELDS, GEORGE W.
PERSONAL Born 04/22/1951, Louisville, KY, m, 1985, 1 child **DISCIPLINE** PHILOSOPHY **EDUCATION** Univ of Louisville, BA, 73, MA, 75; Univ of Chicago, PhD, 81; further study, Oxford Univ, 83. **CAREER** Lectr, Univ of Louisville,

75-55, 79-81; from asst professorial lectr to professorial lectr, Univ of Louisville, 81-; adj lectr, Ind Univ Southeast, 80-82, 83-85; vis asst prof, Ind Univ Southeast, 82-83; adj prof, Ky State Univ, 84-85; from asst prof to prof, Ky State Univ, 85-; chair, Div of Lit, Langs, and Philos, 94-. **HONORS AND AWARDS** Nat Defense/Col of Arts and Scis Scholar Awd, Univ of Louisville, 72-73; A. Flexner Honorarium for Grad Study, Univ of Louisville, 73; First Prize Awd, Ky Philos Asn Essay Contest, 73; R.C. Smith Mem Awd for Excellence in Philos, Univ of Louisville Honors Convocation, 74; Grad Teaching Apprentice Stipend, Univ of Louisville, 74; Phi Kappa Phi Nat Honor Soc, 76; Bingham Found Grant Awd, Univ of Louisville, 76; House Scholar, Disciples House of the Univ of Chicago, 77-79; Commonwealth of Ky Fac Incentive Fund Merit Salary Recipient, 86; President, Kentucky Philos Asn, 87-88; Nat Endowment for the Hums Travel Grant, 90; Hon Order of Ky Colonels, 92; U.S. Dept of Educ Title III Grant Awd, 95; Templeton Found Sci and Relig Course Prog Awd, 97; numerous Ky State Univ Fac Res Fund Comt Grant Awds; numerous biographical entries in Who's Who; Distinguished Prof Awd, 00-01. **MEMBERSHIPS** Am Acad of Relig; Am Philos Asn; Asn for Sci and Cult; Asn for Integrative Studies; Ctr for Process Studies; Ky Philos Asn; Soc of Christian Philos; Soc for Philos of Relig; Soc for the Study of Process Philos; Southeastern Sem in Early Modern Philos. **SELECTED PUBLICATIONS** Coed, Proceedings of the Institute for Liberal Studies, vols 1-10, 90-999; Foundations of Cultures: Readings, 92; The Convergence of Cultures: Readings, 93; The Search for New Forms of Culture, 94; coed and coauth, Faith and Creativity: Essays in Honor of Eugene H. Peters, 87; Science, Technology, and Religious Ideas, 94; auth, Preface, in Science, Technology, and Religious Ideas, 94; Introduction to Nietzsche, in The Search for New Forms of Culture, 94; Review of Lewis E. Hahn, ed. The Philosophy of Charles Hartshorne, Vol. 20, Library of Living Philosophers Series, in Int J for Philos of Relig 36/4, 94; Introduction, in Proceedings of the Inst for Liberal Studies 6, 95; Abstract: Donald Sherburne, 'Whitehead and Dewey on System and Experience' in Frontiers of American Philosophy, in Process Studies 24/3, 95; Design, Chance and Necessity, in Facets of Faith and Science: Vol 4, Interpreting God's Action in the World, 96; Abstract: Nicholas Rescher, 'The Promise of Process Philosophy' in Frontiers of American Philosophy, in Process Studies 24/3, 96; Introduction to Descartes: Discours de la methode and Le monde, in The Convergence of Cultures, 96; Introduction, in Proceedings of the Inst for Liberal Studies 7, 96; Critical Study: Nicholas Rescher, Process Metaphysics: An Introduction to Process Philosophy, in Process Studies 25, 96; Introduction: On the Interface of Analytic and Process Philosophy, in Process Studies 25, 96; auth, "Pragmatism, Interdisciplinarity, and Liberal Educ," Asn for Integrative Studies Newsletter 18 (Oct 96); Introduction, in Proceedings of the Institute for Liberal Studies 8, 97, Critical Study: Dorothy Emmet, The Passage of Nature, in Process Studies, 26/1-2, 97; rev, of The Zero Fallacy and Other Essays in Neoclassical Philos, by Charles Hartshorne and M. Valady, Int J for Philos of Religion 40 (Dec 98). **CONTACT ADDRESS** 4630 Shady View Dr, Floyds Knobs, IN 47119. **EMAIL** gshields@gwmail.kysu.edu

SHIELDS, MARY E.
PERSONAL Born 12/05/1960, Butler, PA **DISCIPLINE** RELIGION **EDUCATION** Westminster Col, BA, 82; Princeton Theol Sem, MDiv, 86; Emory Univ, PhD, 96. **CAREER** Tchg and res fel, Univ St Andrews, Scotland, 92-94; adj instr, Emory Univ, 94-95; instr, 95-96, asst prof, 96-99; Drury Col; assoc prof, Trinity Lutheran Sem, 99-. **HONORS AND AWARDS** Magna cum laude; Neumann Prize, 84; Kenneth Willis Clark Student Essay Awd, 91; Mellon Diss Fel, 92-93; Drury Fac Awd for Leadership, 98. **MEMBERSHIPS** Am Academy of Religion, Soc of Biblical Lit, Soc for Old Testament Study, Nat Asn of Presbyterian Clergywomen. **RESEARCH** The marriage metaphor in the Hebrew prophets; feminist criticism of the Hebrew Bible; literary criticism of the Hebrew Bible. **SELECTED PUBLICATIONS** Auth, "Subverting a Man of God, Elevating a Woman: Role and Power Reversals in 2 Kgs 4," Journal for the Study of the Old Testament 58, (93): 59-69; rev, of Fragmented Women: Feminist (Sub)versions of Biblical Narratives by J. Cheryl Exum, Theological Book Review 6 (June 94); rev, of Let the Oppressed Go Free: Feminist Perspectives on the New Testament by Luise Schottroff, Biblical Interpretation 2, (94); auth, "Circumcision of the Prostitute: Gender, Sexuality and the Call to Repentance in Jer. 3:1-4:4," Biblical Interpretation 3:1, (95): 61-74; rev, of Women in the Biliical Tradition ed. George Brooke, Bibical Interpretation 4, (96); auth, "Multiple Exposures: Body Rhetoric and Gender Characterization in Ezekiel 16," Journal of Feminist Studies in Religion 14, (98): 5-18; auth, "Haggai," Dictionary of Biblical Interpretation, ed. John H. Hayes, Nashville: Abingdon Press, (99): 478-80; auth, "A Self Response to 'Subverting a Man of God, Elevating a Woman: Role and Power Reversals in 2 Kings 4," Samuel and Kings: A Feminist Companion to the Bible (Second Series), ed. by Athalya Brenner, Sheffield: Sheffield Academic Press, (00): 125-128; auth, "Subverting a Man of God, Elevating a Woman: Role and Power Reversals in 2 Kings 4," Reprinted in Samuel and Kings: A Feminist Companion to the Bible (Second Series), ed by Athalya Brenner, Sheffield: Sheffield Academic Press, (00): 115-124; auth, "Revelation Meets Star Trek and X-Files or A New Twist on Ancient Traditions?: Teaching the Heaven'ss Gate Cult," Teaching Apocalypse, ed by Tina Pippin, Vol 1, AAR Teaching Series, (forthcoming). **CONTACT ADDRESS** Dept of Philosophy and Religion, Trinity Lutheran Sem, 2199 E Main St, Columbus, OH 43209-2334. **EMAIL** mshields@trinity.capital.edu

SHIELS, FREDERICK L.
PERSONAL Born 06/10/1949, Wilmington, DE, d, 2 children **DISCIPLINE** POLITICAL SCIENCE **EDUCATION** Vanderbilt Univ, BA, 71; Johns Hopkins Univ, MA, 73; Cornell Univ, PhD, 77. **CAREER** Teaching Asst, Cornell Univ, 73-75; Vis Asst Prof, Baruch Col, 77-78; Asst Prof to Prof, Mercy Col, 78-. **HONORS AND AWARDS** Fulbright Sen Lecturer, Japan, 85-86; Summer Fel, Intl Studies Asn, 75; Peace Studies Prog Res Grant, Cornell Univ, 75, 76; Program Grant, Cornell Univ, 76; Grant, Cornell Ctr for Intl Studies Grant, 75. **MEMBERSHIPS** APSA, ISA. **RESEARCH** Third World; US politics; Political economy. **SELECTED PUBLICATIONS** Auth, "Misperception at the Top," in Inadvertent Nuclear War, Pergamon, 93; auth, "The American Interlude in Okinawa: 1945-72," in Okinawa: Challenge and Adaptation at Japan's Periphery, Univ Hawaii Press, forthcoming; auth, Preventable Disasters: Why Governments Fail, Rowman and Littlefield, 91; auth, Ethnic Separatism and World Politics, Univ Press of Am, 83; auth, Tokyo and Washington: Dilemmas of a Mature Alliance, Lexington Books, 80; auth, America, Okinawa, and Japan, Univ Press of America, 80; auth, The New American Foreign Policy: A Primer for the 1980s, Collegium Books, 79. **CONTACT ADDRESS** Dept Cultural Studies, Mercy Col, 555 Broadway, Dobbs Ferry, NY 10522-1134. **EMAIL** fshiels@mercynet.edu

SHIELS, RICHARD DOUGLAS
PERSONAL Born 04/05/1947, Detroit, MI, m, 1972 **DISCIPLINE** AMERICAN AND RELIGIOUS HISTORY **EDUCATION** Hope Col, BA, 68; Yale Univ, MAR, 71; Boston Univ, PhD, 76. **CAREER** Asst prof, Boston Univ, 75-76; asst prof, 76-82, assoc orof hist, Ohio St Univ, Newark, 82-. **MEMBERSHIPS** Orgn Am Historians; AHA. **RESEARCH** American intellectual and social history. **SELECTED PUBLICATIONS** Auth, "Second Great Awakening in Connecticut," Church History, Vol 49, 80; Feminization of American congregationalists, 1730-1835, Am Quart, Vol 33, 81. **CONTACT ADDRESS** History Dept, Ohio State Univ, Newark, 1179 University Dr, Newark, OH 43055-1797. **EMAIL** shiels.1@osu.edu

SHIER, DAVID
PERSONAL Born 11/19/1958, Cleveland, OH, m, 1988, 2 children **DISCIPLINE** PHILOSOPHY **EDUCATION** Wayne State Univ, PhD, 93 **CAREER** Wash State Univ, asst prof, 94-. **MEMBERSHIPS** APA, BRS **RESEARCH** Philo of language; philo of mind. **SELECTED PUBLICATIONS** Auth, Why Kant Finds Nothing Ugly, Brit Jour of Aesthetics, 98; auth, How Can Pictures Be Propositions?, Ratio, 97; co-ed The Two Envelope Paradox Resolved, Analysis, 97; auth, Direct Reference for the Narrow Minded, Pac Philo Quart, 96. **CONTACT ADDRESS** Dept of Philosophy, Washington State Univ, Box 645130, Pullman, WA 99164-5130. **EMAIL** shier@wsu.edu

SHILLING, BURNETTE P.
DISCIPLINE CHRISTIAN MINISTRIES **EDUCATION** Taylor Univ, BA; Winebrenner Sem, MDiv; Trinity Evangel Divinity Sch, DMin; Bowling Green State Univ, PhD. **CAREER** Campus pastor, Bluffton Col; assoc prof, 86-; dir, DMin Dipl in Pastoral Stud, Wiinebrenner Theol Sem. **HONORS AND AWARDS** Interim writer/ed, Workman Quart; The Gem. **MEMBERSHIPS** Mem, Speech Commun Assn; Cent States Speech Commun Assn; Rel Speech Commun Assn. **SELECTED PUBLICATIONS** Pub(s), articles in The Church Advocate; Churches of God, General Conf; contrib, Life Application Bible, Tyndale House, 88. **CONTACT ADDRESS** Winebrenner Theol Sem, 701 E Melrose Ave, PO Box 478, Findlay, OH 45839.

SHILLINGTON, V. GEORGE
PERSONAL Born 05/23/1937, Porthdown, Northern Ireland, m, 1959, 2 children **DISCIPLINE** RELIGION **EDUCATION** Cent Baptist Col, BTh; Waterloo Lutheran Univ, BA, 70; Cent Baptist Sem, Mdiv, 72; Wilfred Laurier Univ, MA, 73; McMaster Univ, PhD, 85; **CAREER** Emmanuel Bib Col, asst prof, 73-81; Concord Col Univ of Winnipeg, asst prof, 81-85, assoc prof 85-96, prof 96-. **HONORS AND AWARDS** NT Studies Award **MEMBERSHIPS** SBL **RESEARCH** Rhetoric of Silence in the letters of Paul. **SELECTED PUBLICATIONS** Auth, A New Testament Perspective on Work, CGR 90; Jesus and His Parables, T&T Clarke 97; II Corinthians, Herald Press 98; Atonement Texture in I Corinthians 5:5, JSNT 98. **CONTACT ADDRESS** Dept of Biblical Studies, Concord Col, Manitoba, 169 Riverton Ave, Winnipeg, MB, Canada R2L 2E5. **EMAIL** georges@farlink.com

SHIMMYO, THEODORE T.
PERSONAL Born 08/13/1944, Japan, m, 1970, 4 children **DISCIPLINE** THEOLOGY **EDUCATION** Univ Tokyo, BS, 71; Drew Univ Madison, M.Phil, 81; PhD, 84. **CAREER** Asst prof, Unification Theol Sem, 84-96; asst dean, 87; asst acad dean, 87-94; pres, 94-; assoc prof, 96-. **MEMBERSHIPS** Karl Barth Soc N Amer; Soc Stud Process Philos. **RESEARCH** Christian theology. **SELECTED PUBLICATIONS** Auth, Explorations in Unificationism, 97. **CONTACT ADDRESS** Unification Theol Sem, 10 Dock Rd, Barrytown, NY 12507-5000.

SHIN, SUN JOO
DISCIPLINE PHILOSOPHY **EDUCATION** Seoul Nat Univ, BA, 79; Stanford Univ, MA, 81, PhD, 91. **CAREER** Assoc prof. **RESEARCH** Philosophy of logic; philosophy of language; logic. **SELECTED PUBLICATIONS** Auth, Peirce and the Logical Status of Diagrams, Hist Philos Logic, 93; A Semantic Analysis of Venn Diagrams, J Symbolic Logic, 93; The Logical Status of Diagrams, 94. **CONTACT ADDRESS** Philosophy Dept, Univ of Notre Dame, 336/7 O'Shaughnessy, Notre Dame, IN 46556. **EMAIL** shin.3@nd.edu

SHINER, LARRY
PERSONAL Born 05/06/1934, Oklahoma City, OK, m, 1980, 2 children **DISCIPLINE** PHILOSOPHY, HISTORY **EDUCATION** Northwestern Univ, BA, 56; Universite de Strasbourg, Doctorate, 61. **CAREER** Asst prof, Univ of Tampa, 61; assoc prof, Cornell Col, 62-71; prof, Univ of IL Springfield, 71-. **HONORS AND AWARDS** William S. Pilling Fel, 59; Danforth Cross-Disciplinary Fel, 67. **MEMBERSHIPS** Am Soc for Aesthetics. **RESEARCH** Philosophy of Art, 18th Century Studies. **SELECTED PUBLICATIONS** Auth, The Secularization of History, Abingdon Pr, 68; auth, The Secret Mirror: Literary Form and History in Tocqueville; Cornell Univ, 98. **CONTACT ADDRESS** Dept Hist, Univ of Illinois, Springfield, PO Box 19243, Springfield, IL 62794-9243. **EMAIL** shiner.larry@uis.edu

SHINER, ROGER ALFRED
PERSONAL Born 05/13/1940, Kidderminster, England **DISCIPLINE** PHILOSOPHY **EDUCATION** Cambridge, BA, 63, MA, 66, PhD(philos), 71; Univ Alta, MA, 65. **CAREER** Sessional lectr, 65-66, from asst prof to assoc prof, 66-77, Prof Philos, Univ Alta, 77- **MEMBERSHIPS** Mind Asn; Can Philos Asn; Class Asn Can; Royal Inst Philos; Aristotelian Soc. **RESEARCH** Greek philosophy; ethics; philosophy of religion. **SELECTED PUBLICATIONS** Auth, Norm and Nature: The movements of legal thought, Oxford: Clarendon Press, Claredon Law Series, 92; auth, 'Organizations and Agency,' Legal Theory 1, (94-95): 283-310; auth, 'Advertising and Freedom of Expression,' Univ of Toronto Law Journal 45, (95): 179-204, reprinted in Advertising Law Anthology 18, 96; auth, 'The Silent Majoritty Speaks: RJR MacDonald Inc v Canada,' Constitutional Forum 7.1, (95-96): 9-16; auth, 'Law and Morality,' in Dennis M. Patterson, ed, A Companion to the Philosophy of Law and Legal Theory, Oxford: Basil Blackwell, (96): 436-449; auth, 'The Causal Theory of Taste,' Journal of Aesthetics and Art Criticism 54, (96): 237-249; auth, 'Advertising, Free Expression and Public Goods,' in Rex Martin and Gerhard Springer, eds, Rights, Stuttgart: Franz Steiner Verlag, (97): 177-183; auth, 'Sparshott and the Philosophy of Philosophy,' Journal of Aesthetic Education 31.2, (97): 3-8; auth, 'Causes and Tastes: A Response,' Journal of Aesthetics and Art Criticism 55, (97): 320-324; auth, 'Jurisprudence,' The Canadian Encyclopedia Plus, Multimedia CD ROM edition, ed, James Marsh, Toronto: McLelland and Stewart, 97. **CONTACT ADDRESS** Dept of Philos, Univ of Alberta, Edmonton, AB, Canada T6G 2E5. **EMAIL** roger.shiner@ualberta.ca

SHIPKA, THOMAS A.
PERSONAL Born 02/17/1943, Youngstown, OH, m, 1967, 2 children **DISCIPLINE** PHILOSOPHY **EDUCATION** John Carroll Univ, AB, philos, 66; Boston Col, PhD, philos, 69. **CAREER** Asst prof, philos, Youngstown State Univ, 69-74; assoc prof, philos, Youngstown State Univ, 74-81; prof, philos, Youngstown State Univ, 81-; chair, dept of philos and relig, Youngstown State Univ, 86-. **HONORS AND AWARDS** Distinguished Prof award, Youngstown State Univ, 80, 84; Davenport award, Nat Educ Asn, 94; Watson Merit award, Youngstown State Univ, 91, 97. **MEMBERSHIPS** Amer Philos Asn; Nat Educ Asn. **RESEARCH** Social and political philosophy; Unions in higher education; Evaluation in higher education. **SELECTED PUBLICATIONS** Auth, Philosophy: Paradox and Discovery, 4th ed, McGraw-Hill, 96; auth, Organizing the Faculty at Youngstown State, Thought & Action, vol XII, no 2, 105-106, fall, 96; auth, Personnel Evaluation in American Higher Education: An Introduction, School Personnel Evaluation Manual, Wash, DC, Nat Educ Asn, 137-155, 87; auth, A Critique of Anarchism, Studies in Soviet Thought, 15, 219-224, 85. **CONTACT ADDRESS** Dept. of Philos, Youngstown State Univ, 1 University Plz, Youngstown, OH 44555. **EMAIL** tashipka@cc.ysu.edu

SHIPLEY, ANTHONY J.
PERSONAL Born 05/19/1939, New York, NY, m, 1960, 1 child **DISCIPLINE** THEOLOGY **EDUCATION** Drew University, BA 1961; Garrett Seminary, DMin 1964; Adrian College, DD 1974. **CAREER** Coun Dir, 71; United Methodist Church, supt Detroit West Dist 1982-; Scott Church, pastor, 87-; UMC, General Board of Global Ministry, deputy general secretary, 92; Christ United Methodist Church, sr pastor, 94. **MEMBERSHIPS** Consultant NCJ Urban Network; adjunct prof Garrett Evangelical Theol Sem; bd of dir Adrian Coll; Board of National Black United Fund; President's Assn of the Amer Mgmt Assn; delegate, Gen Conf of the United Methodist 1980; lecturer, Church Admin at N MS Pastors School; Inst for Adv Pastoral Studies; pres Natl Fellowship Conf Council; dir Detroit Council of Churches; MI State Council of Churches; MI

State United Ministries in Higher Educ; Natl Bd of Higher Educ & Min; mgmt consultant Charfoos Christenson Law Firm; bd dir Methodist Theol School in OH; founder, McKenzie High School/Adrian College Bound Program; bd of directors, Barton McFarland Neighborhood Assn; Cuvy Leadership Center, certified trainer, 7 Habits of Highly Effective People; U-Snap-Back Comm Development Corp, chair of bd; Phoenix District Boy Scouts of America, chair; Chandler Park Academy Charter Schl, founder. **SELECTED PUBLICATIONS** Author: "The Care & Feeding of Cliques in the Church" Interpreter Magazine 1975; "The Self Winding Congregation" Interpreter Magazine 1975; "The Council on Ministries as a Support System"; "Everybody Wants to Go to Heaven But Nobody Wants to Die" Christian Century 1976; "Long Range Planning in the Local Church" MI Christian Advocate; "Something for Nothing" MI Christian Advocate; "Fable of Disconnection" MI Christian Advocate. **CONTACT ADDRESS** Christ Methodist Church, 19505 Canterbury Rd., Detroit, MI 48221.

SHIRLEY, EDWARD S.
DISCIPLINE EPISTEMOLOGY **EDUCATION** Univ South, BA, 52; Va Theol Sem, MDiv, 56; Hartford Sem Found, STM; 60; Univ Mass, PhD, 69. **CAREER** Prof, La State Univ. **SELECTED PUBLICATIONS** Published articles on such topics as philosophy of language, mind-body problem, scepticism, truth, perception, and about such thinkers as Descartes, Kant, Santayana, James, Wittgenstein, Quine, Rorty, Ryle, Chisholm, Goodman, and Putnam in Philos Stud, Philos of Sci, J of Critical Anal, Erkenntnis, Southern J of Philos, J of Speculative Philos, and Philos Topics. **CONTACT ADDRESS** Dept of Philos and Relig Stud, Louisiana State Univ and A&M Col, 106 Coates Hall, Baton Rouge, LA 70803.

SHKOLNICK, RODNEY
DISCIPLINE CONTRACT LAW **EDUCATION** State Univ Iowa, BA, 53; Univ Iowa, JD, 55. **CAREER** Instr, Univ Mich Law Sch, 59 and 60; dean, Creighton Law Sch, 77-88; partner, McGrath, North, 65-71; prof, Creighton Univ. **SELECTED PUBLICATIONS** Coauth, Nebraska Uniform Commercial Code Forms; pub in, Nebr and Creighton Law Rev(s). **CONTACT ADDRESS** Sch of Law, Creighton Univ, 2500 California Plaza , Omaha, NE 68178. **EMAIL** shkolnic@Creighton.edu

SHOBEN, ELAINE W.
DISCIPLINE LAW **EDUCATION** Barnard Col, BA; Univ Calif Hastings, JD. **CAREER** Prof, Univ Ill Urbana Champaign. **HONORS AND AWARDS** Ed, Hastings Law J; fel, Am Bar Found; ed, J Legal Edu. **MEMBERSHIPS** Asn Am Law Sch. **RESEARCH** Torts; remedies; and employment discrimination; workplace law, tort policy, and the uses and abuses of the contempt power. **SELECTED PUBLICATIONS** Auth, pubs on employment discrimination and the legal application of quantitative methods; co-auth, Remedies: Cases and Problems, Foundation, 89; Employment Discrimination Cases and Materials, West, 90; Employment Law. **CONTACT ADDRESS** Law Dept, Univ of Illinois, Urbana-Champaign, 52 E Gregory Dr, Champaign, IL 61820. **EMAIL** eshoben@uiuc.edu

SHOEMAKER, DAVID W.
PERSONAL Born 07/24/1964, Ft. Wayne, IN, m, 1996, 2 children **DISCIPLINE** PHILOSOPHY **EDUCATION** Univ Cal Irvine, PhD, 96 **CAREER** Vis asst prof, Philosophy, Arkansas State Univ, 96-97; vis asst prof, Univ Memphis, 97-. **MEMBERSHIPS** Amer Philos Soc **RESEARCH** Personal identity; Ethical theory; Philosophy of law. **SELECTED PUBLICATIONS** Auth, Theoretical Persons and Practical Agents, Philos & Public Affairs, 96. **CONTACT ADDRESS** Dept of Philosophy, Univ of Memphis, Memphis, TN 38152. **EMAIL** dshoemkr@memphis.edu

SHOEMAKER, MELVIN H.
PERSONAL Born 02/11/1940, Jay County, IN, m, 1961, 3 children **DISCIPLINE** NEW TESTAMENT BIBLICAL LITERATURE; BIBLICAL THEOLOGY **EDUCATION** Indiana Wesleyan University, AB, 62; Hebrew Seminar in Israel, Univ of Wisconsin, Graduate Studies, 66; Asbury Theological Seminary, MDiv, 67; Drew Univ, MPhil, 88; Fuller theological seminary, Pasadena, CA, D Min, 97. **CAREER** Instr, Indiana Wesleyan Univ, 66-67; prof, Bartlesville Wesleyan Col, 79-84; prof, CP Haggard Sch of Theology, 86-, dir, honors program, Azusa Pacific Univ, 95-. **HONORS AND AWARDS** Biographical listings in Dictionary of International Biography, 79; Who's Who in Religion, 92; Alphi Chi Teacher of the Year at Azusa Pacific Univ, 93; Who's Who in the West, 97; Who's Who in America, 99. **MEMBERSHIPS** Wesleyan Theological Soc, 80-82, 91-present; APU Honors Program Council, 91-present; APU Education Council, 94-present; Soc of Biblical Lit, 87-present; International Soc of Theta Phi; Advisory Council for the Oxford Honors Semester of the Coalition for Christian Colleges & Universities, 97-2003; International Education Committee of the National Collegiate Honors Council 97-2003; Small College Honors Programs Committee of the National Collegiate Honors Council, 97-2003. **RESEARCH** NT Biblical Literature and theology; gospels. **SELECTED PUBLICATIONS** Auth, Good News to the Poor in Luke's Gospel, Connection, 94; King, Christ as, Lamb, Lamb of God, Life, Priest, Christ as, Baker BookHouse, 96; Discipling Generation X, Fuller Theological Seminary, 97; The Frusit that Jesus Seeks, Decision, Nov 98. **CONTACT ADDRESS** Azusa Pacific Univ, 901 E Alosta, Azusa, CA 91702-7000. **EMAIL** mshoemaker@apu.edu

SHOFNER, ROBERT DANCEY
PERSONAL Born 11/22/1933, Seattle, WA **DISCIPLINE** PHILOSOPHICAL THEOLOGY **EDUCATION** Univ Puget Sound, BA, 61; Yale Univ, BD, 64; Hartford Univ, PhD(theol), 72. **CAREER** Minister, Marlborough Congregational Church, 64-67; teaching fel theol, Hartford Sem Found, 67-70; from asst prof to assoc prof, 70-78, Prof Relig Studies, Calif State Univ, Northridge, 78-, Chmn Dept, 72- **MEMBERSHIPS** Am Acad Relig; Am Philos Asn; Soc Values Higher Educ. **RESEARCH** Systematic theology; theological ethics. **SELECTED PUBLICATIONS** Auth, Luther on The bondage of the will, Scottish J Theol, 2/73; Anselm Revisited, Brill, 74. **CONTACT ADDRESS** Dept of Relig Studies, California State Univ, Northridge, Northridge, CA 91330.

SHOPSHIRE, JAMES MAYNARD
PERSONAL Born 10/07/1942, Atlanta, GA, m **DISCIPLINE** THEOLOGY **EDUCATION** Clark Coll, BA 1963; Interdenominational Theological Ctr Gammon Seminary, BD 1966; Northwestern Univ, PhD 1975. **CAREER** Interdenominational Theol Ctr, asst prof 1975-80, chair of church & soc dept 1978-80; Wesley Theological Seminary, assoc prof 1980-83, assoc dean 1980-85, prof 1983-. **HONORS AND AWARDS** Rockefeller Doctoral Fellowship Fund for Theol Educ 1971-72; Crusade Scholarship United Methodist Church 1973-74. **MEMBERSHIPS** Minister Bethlehem United Methodist Church 1964-66, Burns United methodist Church 1966-71, Ingleside-Whitfield United Meth Church 1974-75. **CONTACT ADDRESS** Prof of Sociology of Religion, Wesley Theol Sem, 4500 Massachusetts Ave NW, Washington, VT 20016.

SHORES, DAVID FRANCIS
PERSONAL Born 08/28/1941, New Hampton, IA, m, 1964, 2 children **DISCIPLINE** LAW **EDUCATION** Univ Iowa, BBA, 65, JD, 67; Georgetown Univ, LLM, 69. **CAREER** Trial atty, Fed Trade Comn, Washington, DC, 67-69; assoc, Porter, Stanley, Platt and Arthur, Columbus, Ohio, 69-72; asst prof, 72-74, assoc prof, 74-77, Prof Law, Wake Forest Univ, 77-. **RESEARCH** Antitrust; taxation. **SELECTED PUBLICATIONS** Auth, Narrowing the Sherman Act Through an Extension of Colgate: The Matsushita Case, Tenn. Law Rev, 88; State Taxation of Gross Receipts and the Negative Commerce Clause, Mo Law Rev, 89; Closing the Open Transaction Loophole: Mandatory Installment Reporting, VA Tax Rev, 90; Recovery of Unconstitutional Taxes: A New Approach, VA. Tax Rev, 92; Repeal of General Utilities and the Triple Taxation of Corporate Income, Tax Lawyer, 92; Taxation of Interstate Commerce: Quill, Allied Signal and a Proposal, Neb L Rev, 93; Law, Facts, and Market Realities in Antitrust Cases After Brooke and Kodak, SMU Law Rev, 95; Deferential Review of Tax Court Decisions: Dobson Revisited, Tax Lawyer, 96; auth, Section 304 and the Limits of Statuatory Law, Tax Rev, 97; auth, Reexamining Continuity of Shareholder Interest in Corporate Reorganizations, 17 Virginia Tax Rev, 419 (98); auth, Reexamining Continuity of Shareholder Interest in Corporate Diversiona, 18 Virginia Tax Rev, 473 (99). **CONTACT ADDRESS** Sch of Law, Wake Forest Univ, PO Box 7206, Winston-Salem, NC 27109-7206. **EMAIL** dshores@law.wfu.edu

SHOSKY, JOHN
DISCIPLINE PHILOSOPHY **EDUCATION** American Univ, PhD, 92 **CAREER** Adjunct Prof, 90-94, George Mason Univ; Adjunct Prof, Philosophy, 87-, American Univ; Visiting Prof of Phil, Charles Univ, Prague, 98; Visiting Senior member, Linnerz Col, University of Oxford 97-98. **CONTACT ADDRESS** 1806 Rollins Dr., Alexandria, VA 22307.

SHRADER, DOUGLAS WALL, JR.
PERSONAL Born 05/22/1953, Grundy, VA, m, 1975, 2 children **DISCIPLINE** PHILOSOPHY **EDUCATION** Virginia Tech, BA, 74; Univ Illinois, MA, 75, PhD, 79. **CAREER** Asst prof, 79-85, assoc prof, 85-92, prof, 92-99, actng dean of human & fine arts, 91-93, chmn, philos, 88, 91, 93-, SUNY Oneonta. **HONORS AND AWARDS** Philosophy Educ Society Dissertation Awd, 79, NEH Awd, 80, 85, 89, 95,98, ASDP China Field Study, 99, Chancellor's Awd for Excellence in Teaching, 91, Alumni Commendation for Academic Excellence, 95, Foundation for Long Term Care, 98. **MEMBERSHIPS** Society ofr Ancient Greek Philosophy, Society for The Study of Islamic Philosophy and Science, NY Stat Foundations of Educ Asn, East-West Center Assoc. **RESEARCH** Epistemology & metaphysics, philos of sci & relig, philos of life and death. **SELECTED PUBLICATIONS** Auth, Ethics: Theory and Practice, Regents College, 96; auth, Pathways to Philosophy, Prentice Hall, 96; auth, Seed of Wisdom, Global, 97; auth, Language, Ethics, & Ontology, Global, 98; auth, Children of Athena, Global, 99; auth, The Fractal Self, Global, 00. **CONTACT ADDRESS** Dept of Philosophy, SUNY, Col at Oneonta, Oneonta, NY 13820-4015. **EMAIL** shradedw@oneonta.edu

SHREVE, GENE R.
PERSONAL Born 08/06/1943, San Diego, CA, m, 1973 **DISCIPLINE** LAW **EDUCATION** Univ Okla, AB, 65; Harvard Law Sch, LLB, 68; LLM, 75. **CAREER** Assoc prof, Vt Law Sch, 75-81; vis assoc prof, George Washington Univ, 81-83; assoc prof to prof, New York Law Sch, 83-87; prof, Indiana Univ Bloomington, 86-. **HONORS AND AWARDS** Leon H. Wallace Teaching Awd, 93-94; Gavel Awd, 95; Teaching Excellence Recognition Awd, 96-97. **MEMBERSHIPS** Am Law Inst; Am Soc for Polit and Legal Philos; Local Rules Advisory Comm; Assoc of Am Law Schl. **RESEARCH** Procedure, jurisprudence, constitutional law. **SELECTED PUBLICATIONS** Auth, "Conflicts Law - State or Federal?", 68 Ind LJ 907, (93): auth, "Civil Procedure: Other Disciplines, Globalization, and Simple Gifts", 92 Mich L Rev 1401 (94); auth, "Choice of Law and the Forgiving constitution", 71 Ind LJ 271 (96): auth, "The Odds Against Teaching Conflicts", 27 U Toledo L Rev 587 (96): auth, A Conflict-of-Laws Anthology, Anderson Pub, 97; auth, "Notes from the Eye of the Storm", 48 Mercer L Rev 823, (97): auth, "Rhetoric, Pragmatism and the Interdisciplinary Turn in Legal Criticism - A Study of Altruistic Judicial Argument", 46 Am J of Comparative L 41 (98): auth, "Every Conflicts Decision is a Promise Broken", La Law Rev (forthcoming). **CONTACT ADDRESS** Sch of Law, Indiana Univ, Bloomington, 211 S Ind Ave, Bloomington, IN 47405-7001.

SHRIVER, DONALD W.
PERSONAL Born 12/20/1927, Norfolk, VA, m, 1953, 3 children **DISCIPLINE** RELIGION **EDUCATION** Davidson College, AB 51; Union Seminary VA, BD 55; Yale Univ DS, STM 57; Harvard Univ, PhD 63. **CAREER** Presbyterian Church USA, minister, 55-; N Carolina State Univ, prof, 62-72; Emory Univ, prof 72-75; Union Theological Seminary NY, pres, Wm E Dodge Prof, Wm E Dodge Prof Emeritus, 75 to 98-; Columbia Univ schools of Bus, Journ, Law and Intl Affs, adj prof of ethics. **HONORS AND AWARDS** Six honorary degrees. **MEMBERSHIPS** SCE; CFR; SSSR. **RESEARCH** Religious ethics; influence of society and religion on each other; business ethics and intl peace, with emphasis on social recovery from massive violence. **SELECTED PUBLICATIONS** Auth, Spindlers and Spires: Religion and Social Change in Gastonia, 76; auth, Beyond Success: Corporations and Their Critics, 90; auth, An Ethic for Enemies: Forgiveness in Politics, 95. **CONTACT ADDRESS** 440 Riverside Dr., #58, New York, NY 10027-6830. **EMAIL** dwshriver@aol.com

SHRIVER, GEORGE HITE
PERSONAL Born 10/26/1931, Jacksonville, FL, m, 1986, 4 children **DISCIPLINE** WESTERN RELIGIOUS HISTORY **EDUCATION** Stetson Univ, AB, 53; Southeastern Baptist Theol Sem, NC, BD, 56; Duke Univ, PhD(hist & church hist), 61. **CAREER** Instr relig, Duke Univ, 58-59; assoc prof church hist, Southeastern Baptist Theol Sem, NC, 59-68, prof hist, 68-73; assoc prof, 73-76, Prof Hist, GA Southern Col, 76-99, Emer, 99; Am Asn Theol Schs fel & Swiss-Am exchange scholar, 65-66; consult, Choice, 70- **HONORS AND AWARDS** Prof of the Yr, GSU, 75; Ruffin Cup Awd, GSU, 98. **MEMBERSHIPS** Am Soc Church Historians; AHA; Am Acad Relig; AAUP. **RESEARCH** Philip Schaff and Mercersburg theology; American religious dissent; the ecumenical movement. **SELECTED PUBLICATIONS** Auth, The changed concept of religious liberty in Roman Catholics, Outlook, 8/66; Renewal and the dynamic of the provisional, Christian Century, 12/67; The Teilhardian tradition and the theological quest, Relig in Life, autumn 68; American Religious Heretics, 66, transl, From Science to Religion, 68 & The Humanness of John Calvin, 91, Abindon; contrib ed, Contemporary Reflections on the Medieval Christian Tradition, Duke Univ, 73; auth, Philip Schaff: Christian Schader and Ecumenical Prophet, Mercer Press, 87; auth, Dictionary of Henry Trials in American Christianity, Greenwood Press, 98; auth, Encyclopedia of Religious Controversier in the U.S., Greenwood Press, 98; auth, Pilgrims Through the Years, Providence House, 99. **CONTACT ADDRESS** 106 Benson Dr, Statesboro, GA 30458. **EMAIL** cshriver@frontiernet.net

SHUGRUE, RICHARD E.
DISCIPLINE CONSTITUTIONAL LAW **EDUCATION** Univ Nebr, BA, 59, JD,62, PhD, 68. **CAREER** Priv pract, Lincoln, Nebr, 62-64; spec asst dir, Nebr State Dept Agr, 64-66; asst prof and ch dept Polit Sci, Creighton Univ, 66- to assoc prof, 71-. **MEMBERSHIPS** Past ch, House Deleg, Nebr State Bar Asn; bd dir, Amer Judicature Soc. **SELECTED PUBLICATIONS** Pub(s) Creighton Law Rev; Prairie Barrister; Trial Lawyers Forum; Nebr Law Rev. **CONTACT ADDRESS** Sch of Law, Creighton Univ, 2500 California Plaza , Omaha, NE 68178. **EMAIL** shugrue@culaw.Creighton.edu

SHULER, PHILIP L.
PERSONAL Born 07/02/1938, Fort Worth, TX, m, 1991, 6 children **DISCIPLINE** RELIGION **EDUCATION** Calremont Grad Univ, MA, 67; McMaster Univ, PhD, 75 **CAREER** Prof, 79-pres, McMurry Univ **HONORS AND AWARDS** Societas Novi Testamentum Studiorum Member; Fulbright Res Lctr Scholar; Soc of Bibl Lit Pres, Southwest Region; Southwest Commission of Religious Studies Pres **MEMBERSHIPS** Soc of Bibl Lit; Societas Novi Testamentum Studiorum; Inst for the

Renewal of Gospel Studies **RESEARCH** Gospel Genre, Holocaust; Synoptic Problem; Canonical Gospels; Elie Wiesel **SELECTED PUBLICATIONS** Auth, A Genre for the Gospels: the Biographical Character of Matthew, Fortress, 82; Coauth, Beyond the Q Impasse: Luke's Use of Matthew, Trinity International, 97 **CONTACT ADDRESS** 2501 Darrell Dr, Abilene, TX 79606-3403. **EMAIL** pshuler@abilene.com

SHUMAN, DANIEL WAYNE
PERSONAL Born 05/04/1948, Philadelphia, PA, m, 1982, 2 children **DISCIPLINE** LAW **EDUCATION** Univ Ariz, BS, 69, JD, 72. **CAREER** Supv atty, Pima County Legal Aid Soc, 72-75; asst atty gen, State Ariz, 76-77; Assoc Prof Law, Southern Methodist Univ, 77- **MEMBERSHIPS** Am Judicature Soc; Asn Am Law Sch. **RESEARCH** Psychotherapist-patient privilege; civil commitment of mentally ill; psychological underpinnings of rules of evidence. **SELECTED PUBLICATIONS** Auth, The Problem With Empirical-Examination Of The Use Of Court-Appointed Experts - A Report Of Non-Findings/, Behavioral Scis & The Law, Vol 0014, 1996. **CONTACT ADDRESS** Sch of Law, So Methodist Univ, P O Box 750001, Dallas, TX 75275-0001.

SHUSTER, MARGUERITE
PERSONAL Born 09/10/1947, Oxnard, CA, s **DISCIPLINE** THEOLOGY **EDUCATION** Stanford Univ, BA, 68; Fuller Theol Sem, MDiv, 75; PhD, 77. **CAREER** Asst to assoc pastor, Arcadia Presbyterian Church, 80-86; pastor, Knox Presbyterian Church, 87-92; assoc prof, Fuller Theol Sem, 92-. **HONORS AND AWARDS** Phi Beta Kappa, 68; Rockefeller Fel, 71; Outstanding Young Women of Am, 79, 83; Lilly Technology Grant, 98. **MEMBERSHIPS** AAR; SBL; Presbytery of San Gabriel. **RESEARCH** Systematic theology, doctrine of humankind. **SELECTED PUBLICATIONS** Auth, Power, Pathology, Paradox: The Dynamics of Evil and Good, Zondervan, (Grand Rapids), 87; coed, Perspectives on Christology: Essays in Honor of Paul K. Jewett, Zondervan (Grand Rapids), 91; ed, Who We Are: Our Dignity as Human, Eerdmans (Grand Rapids), 96; auth, "The Preaching of the Resurrection of Christ in Augustine, Luther, Barth, and Thielicke", in The Resurrection, eds Stephen Davis, Daniel Kendall and Gerald O'Collins, Oxford Univ Pr, (97): 308-338; auth, "Preaching from Acts, the General Epistles, and Revelation", in Dictionary of the Later New Testament and Its Developments, eds R.P. Martin, P.H. Davids, D.G. Reid, InterVarsity Pr, 97; auth, "The Holy and Glorious Flesh", Living Pulpit 7.1 (98): 10-11; auth, "The Use and Misuse of the Idea of the Imitation of Christ", Ex Auditu 14 (98): 70-81; auth, "In the End, Hope", Living Pulpit 8.1 (99): 10-11; auth, "Struggling to Conceive God", Living Pulpit 8.2 (99): 6-7; auth, "Preaching on the Trinity: A Preliminary Investigation", in The Trinity, eds Stephen Davis, Daniel kendall, and Gerald O'Collins, Oxford Univ Pr, 99. **CONTACT ADDRESS** Fuller Theol Sem, 135 N Oakland Ave, Pasadena, CA 91182-0001. **EMAIL** shuster@fuller.edu

SHUSTERMAN, RICHARD
DISCIPLINE LIBERAL STUDIES, PHILOSOPHY **EDUCATION** Oxford Univ, PhD, 79. **CAREER** Fac, Pierre Bourdieu and Col Internationale de Philosophie, present; prof pholos, Temple Univ, present; vis sr lctr liberal sutdies, Eugene Lang Col. **RESEARCH** Am and French philos. **SELECTED PUBLICATIONS** Auth, Pragmatic Aesthetics; Practicing Philosophy; essays and books include studies of T.S. Eliot's poems and of the analytic philosophy of art. **CONTACT ADDRESS** Eugene Lang Col, New Sch for Social Research, 66 West 12th St, New York, NY 10011.

SHWAYDER, DAVID
DISCIPLINE PHILOSOPHY **EDUCATION** Oxford Univ, PhD, 54. **CAREER** Prof emer, Univ Ill Urbana Champaign. **RESEARCH** First philosophy; practical reason and philosophy of language; theory of knowledge; philosophy of mathematics. **SELECTED PUBLICATIONS** Auth, Modes of Referring and the Problem of Universals; The Stratification of Behavior; Statement and Referent: An Enquiry into the Foundations of Our Conceptual Order. **CONTACT ADDRESS** Philosophy Dept, Univ of Illinois, Urbana-Champaign, 105 Gregory Hall, 810 S Wright St, Champaign, IL 61820. **EMAIL** shwayder@uiuc.edu

SIA, SANTIAGO
DISCIPLINE PHILOSOPHY **EDUCATION** Divine Word Sem, BA, 69; MA, 71; St Patrick's Col, BD, 74; Univ Dublin, PhD, 80. **CAREER** Vis Asst Lectr, Milltown Inst of Theol and Philos, 77-82; From Lectr to Sen Lectr, Newman Col, 82-89; From Asst Prof to Prof, Loyola Marymount Univ, 89-. **HONORS AND AWARDS** Fel, Milltown Inst of Philos and Theol, Ireland; Grant, Deutscher Akademischer Austousdienst; Sen Res Fel, Katholieke Universiteit, Belgium. **MEMBERSHIPS** APA, Brit Soc for Philos of Relig, European Soc for Process Thought. **RESEARCH** Philosophy of religion, ethics, process thought, comparative philosophy, interdisciplinary studies. **SELECTED PUBLICATIONS** Auth, God in Process Thought: A Study in Charles Hartshorne's Concept of God, Martinus Nijhoff, 85; ed, Process Thought and the Christian Doctrine of God, St Bede's Publ, 86; ed, Charles Hartshorne's Concept of God: Philosophical and Theological Responses, Kluwer Acad Publ, 89; coauth, From Suffering to God: Exploring Our Images of God in the Light of Suffering, St Martin's Pr, Macmillan Pr, 94; coauth, The Fountain Arethuse: A Novel, The Book Guild, 97; co-ed, "Framing a Vision of the World: Essays in Philosophy, Religion and Science," Louvain Philos studies, 14 (99). **CONTACT ADDRESS** Dept Philos, Loyola Marymount Univ, 7900 Loyola Blvd, Los Angeles, CA 90045-2659. **EMAIL** ssia@lmumail.edu

SIBLEY, JACK RAYMOND
PERSONAL Born 06/17/1930, Arnett, OK, m, 1949, 2 children **DISCIPLINE** PHILOSOPHY, PHILOSOPHICAL THEOLOGY **EDUCATION** Phillips Univ, AB, 54; Phillips Grad Sem, DB, 57; Univ Chicago, Am, 63, PhD, 67. **CAREER** Assoc prof relig & philos, Bethany Col, WVa, 67-70; prof philos, Tex Woman's Univ, 70-. **MEMBERSHIPS** Am Acad Relig; Am Philos Assn; Southwestern Philos Soc; SCent Soc 28th Century Studies; Int Soc Metaphysics. **RESEARCH** Process philosophy; process theology; classical and humanist studies. **SELECTED PUBLICATIONS** Auth, An Effort at a Portrait & Precious Vien, Euthanaasia, Illness, Crisis & Loss, 94; art, An Ethic of Negotiability, Lamar Journal of Humanities, 94; art, The Absence of Ethics in Scriptural Religions, Encounter, 94. **CONTACT ADDRESS** PO Box 425470, Denton, TX 76204-5470.

SICHA, JEFFREY FRANKLIN
PERSONAL Born Cleveland, OH **DISCIPLINE** PHILOSOPHY **EDUCATION** Oberlin Col, AB, 62; Oxford Univ, DPhil, 66. **CAREER** Asst prof philos, Univ Ill, Chicago Circle, 66-68 & Amherst Col, 68-73; assoc prof, 73-79, Prof Philos, Calif State Univ, Northridge, 79-, Mellon fel philos, Univ Pittsburgh, 67-68; Nat Endowment Humanities fel, 73-74. **RESEARCH** Philosophy of language; epistemology; metaphysics. **SELECTED PUBLICATIONS** Auth, Counting and the natural numbers, Philos Sci, 9/70; A Metaphysics of Elementary Mathematics, Univ Mass, 74; Logic: The fundamentals of a Sellarsian theory, In: The Philosophy of Wilfrid Sellars: Queries & Extensions, Reidel, 78; ed, Introd to Pure Pragmatics & Possible Worlds: The Early Essays of Wilfrid Sellars, Ridgeview, 78. **CONTACT ADDRESS** Dept of Philos, California State Univ, Northridge, 18111 Nordhoff St, Northridge, CA 91330-8253.

SICHEL, WERNER
PERSONAL Born 09/23/1934, Munich, Germany, m, 1959, 2 children **DISCIPLINE** ECONOMICS **EDUCATION** Northwestern Univ, PhD, 64. **CAREER** Prof & chr, dept economics, W Mich Univ, 85-. **HONORS AND AWARDS** Fulbright sr lectr, Univ Belgrade, 68-69; vis schol Hoover Inst, Stanford Univ, 84-85. **MEMBERSHIPS** Midwst Bus Econ Asn; Midwst Econ Asn. **RESEARCH** Telecommunication industry **SELECTED PUBLICATIONS** auth Basic Economic Concepts, Chicago: Rand McNally, 74; Economics, Boston: Houghton Mifflin, 84; Economics Journals and Serials: An Analytical Guide, Westport: Greenwood Press, 86; coauth The State of Economic Science: The Views of Six Nobel Laureates, W E Upjohn Inst for Employment Res, 89; Networks, Infrastructure and the New Task for Regulation, Univ Mich Press, 96; Promoting Competition in Michigan Telecommunication Markets Through Innovative Legislation, Mich State Univ, 98. **CONTACT ADDRESS** Dept of Economics, Western Michigan Univ, Kalamazoo, MI 49008. **EMAIL** werner.sichel@wmich.edu

SIDER, MORRIS
PERSONAL Born 11/20/1928, Cheapside, ON, Canada, m, 1951, 2 children **DISCIPLINE** RELIGION **EDUCATION** Upland Col, BA, 52; ThB, 53; Univ Western Ont, MA, 55; SUNY, PhD, 66. **CAREER** Prof to Dept Chair, Messiah Col, 63-. **HONORS AND AWARDS** Can Coun Fel, 58-59; Alumnus of the Year Awd, Niagara Christian Col, 82; Excellence in Teaching Awd, Messiah Col, 87; Distinguished Alumnus Awd, Messiah Col, Sears Roebuck Foundation Teaching Excellence and Campus Leadership Awd. **MEMBERSHIPS** Am Hist Asn, Can Hist Asn. **RESEARCH** Church history. **CONTACT ADDRESS** Dept Relig & Philos, Messiah Col, Grantham, PA 17027. **EMAIL** msider@messiah.edu

SIDER, RONALD J.
PERSONAL Born 09/17/1939, Stevensville, ON, Canada, m, 1961, 3 children **DISCIPLINE** THEOLOGY **EDUCATION** Waterloo Lutheran Univ, BA, 62; Yale, MA, 63; Yale, BD, 67; Yale PhD, 69. **CAREER** Prof, E Baptist Theol Sem. **HONORS AND AWARDS** Pres, Evangelicals for Soc Action. **SELECTED PUBLICATIONS** Auth, Evangelical Faith and Social Ethics, China Graduate Graduate School of Theology (Hong Kong), 86; auth, Completely Pro-Life, Intervarsity, 87; auth, Preaching About Life in a Threatening World, Westminster, 88; auth, JustLife/88: A 1988 Election Study Guide for Justice, Life and Peace, Eerdmans, 88; auth, Testing the Limits of Nonviolence, Hodder and Stoughton, 88; One-Sided Christianity? Uniting the Church to Heal a Lost and Broken World, Zondervan/Harper, (Hodder and Stoughton, UK), 93, (Brendow, German), 95; auth, Cup of Water, Bread of Life: Inspiring Stories About Overcoming Lopsided Christianity, Zondervan/Harper, 94, (Triangle, UK), 95; Christianity and Economics in the Post-Cold War Era: The Oxford Declaration and Beyond, Eerdmans, 94; auth, Genuine Christianity, 96; Just Generosity: A New Vision for Overcoming Poverty in America, Baker, 99. **CONTACT ADDRESS** Eastern Baptist Theol Sem, 6 Lancaster Ave, Wynnewood, PA 19096. **EMAIL** ronsider@esa-online.org

SIDER, THEODORE
PERSONAL Born 04/20/1967, New Haven, CT, s **DISCIPLINE** PHILOSOPHY OF LANGUAGE **EDUCATION** Gordon Col, BS, 88; Univ Mass, PhD, 93. **CAREER** Asst Prof to Assoc Prof, Univ Rochester, 92-98; Assoc Prof, Syracuse Univ, 98-. **HONORS AND AWARDS** Prof of the Year, Univ Rochester, 98; Visiting fel, Princeton Univ, 96; Editorial board, Philosophical Studies. **SELECTED PUBLICATIONS** Auth, "Modal Constructionism," in The Oxford Handbook of Metaphysics, Oxford Univ Press, forthcoming; auth, "Recent Work on Identity Over Time," Philosophical Books, (00): 81-89; auth, "The Stage View and Temporary Intrinsics," Analysis, forthcoming; auth, "Simply Possible," Philosophy and Phenomenological Research, forthcoming; auth, "Global Supervenience and Identity across Times and Worlds," Philosophy and Phenomenological Research, (99): 913-937; auth, "Presentism and Ontological Commitment," The Journal of Philosophy, (99): 325-347; auth, "Four-Dimensionalism," The Philosophical Review, (97): 197-231; auth, "A New Grandfather Paradox?", Philosophy and Phenomenological Research, (97): 139-144; auth, "All the World's a Stage," Australasian Journal of Philosophy, (96): 433-453; auth, "In Defense of Global Supervenience," Philosophy and Phenomenological Research, (92): 833-854. **CONTACT ADDRESS** Dept Philos, Syracuse Univ, Syracuse, NY 13244-1170. **EMAIL** trsider@syr.edu

SIEBER, JOHN HAROLD
PERSONAL Born 09/19/1935, Janesville, WI, m, 1960, 2 children **DISCIPLINE** RELIGION, CLASSICS **EDUCATION** Luther Col, BA, 58; Luther Theol Sem, BD, 62; Claremont Grad Sch, PhD(relig), 66. **CAREER** Asst prof classics, 65-67, asst prof relig, 67-72, assoc prof, 72-78, Prof to Prof Emer Relig & Classics, Luther Col, 78-. **HONORS AND AWARDS** Am Philos Soc res grant, 72. **MEMBERSHIPS** Soc Bibl Lit. **RESEARCH** Theology of Rudolf Bultman; Gnostic library from Nag-Hammdi, Egypt. **SELECTED PUBLICATIONS** Auth, An introduction to the Tractate Zostrianos from Nag Hammadi, Novum Testamentum, 7/73. **CONTACT ADDRESS** Dept of Relig, Luther Col, 700 College Dr, Decorah, IA 52101-1045. **EMAIL** sieberjo@luther.edu

SIEG, WILFRIED
PERSONAL Born 07/01/1945, Lunen, Germany, m, 1979, 2 children **DISCIPLINE** PHILOSOPHY **EDUCATION** Univ Munster, Germany, 71; Stanford Univ, MA, 75, PhD, 77. **CAREER** Asst to assoc prof, Columbia Univ, 77-85; assoc prof to prof and dept head, philos, Carnegie Mellon Univ, 85- . **MEMBERSHIPS** Assoc of Symbolic Logic; Amer Philos Assoc; Amer Math Soc. **RESEARCH** Philos of math; math & logic; found of cognitive sci. **SELECTED PUBLICATIONS** Coauth, Iterated Inductive Definitions and Subsystems of Analysis, Berlin-Heidelberg-New York, 81; ed, Acting and Reflecting, Synthese Libr, 90, auth, "Relative Consistency and Accessible Domains, Synthese 84 (90): 259-297; Logic and Computation, Contemp Math, 90; auth, "Herbrand Analyses, Archive of Mathematical Logic 30 (91): 409-441; co-auth, "Searching for proofs," in Philosophy and the Computer, L. Burkholder ed. (Westview Press, 92), 137-159; auth, "Mechanical Procedures and Mathematical Experience," in Mathematics & Mind, A. George ed (Oxford Univ Press, 94); coed, Natural Deduction, Studia Logica, 98; auth, Step by Recursive Step: Church's analysis of effective calculability, Bull Symbolic Logic, 97. **CONTACT ADDRESS** Dept of Philosophy, Carnegie Mellon Univ, 135 Baker Hall, Pittsburgh, PA 15213. **EMAIL** ws15@andrew.cmu.edu

SIGLER, ROBERT T.
PERSONAL Born 09/13/1941, m, 2 children **DISCIPLINE** CRIMINAL JUSTICE **EDUCATION** S Ill Univ, BA, 64; MA, 69; Univ Mo, PhD, 74. **CAREER** Asst prof, Univ Ark, 74; prof and dir, Univ Ala, 88-92, 97-. **HONORS AND AWARDS** Plaque of appreciation, N Ala Criminal Justice Students, 83, 89, 94, 96, 97, 98; Outstanding advisor, Univ Ala, 89, 91; Outstanding Commitment to Teaching Award, Univ Ala, 90; Plaque in appreciation of serv, VIP Bd of Trustees, 96; Outstanding Fac Award, Alpha Phi Sigma, 01. **MEMBERSHIPS** ASA; ACA; ACJS; ASC; IAVCJ; SPSSI. **RESEARCH** Domestic violence; Courtship violence; Stress; Community corrections; Criminalization process. **SELECTED PUBLICATIONS** Co-auth, Forced Sexual Intercourse in Intimate Relationships, Dartmouth, 97; co-auth, "Forced Sexual Intercourse Among Intimates and quot," J of Family Violence, (00): 95-108; co-auth, "Public Perceptions: The stability of the Public's Endorsements of the Definition and Criminalization of the Abuse of Women," J of Criminal Justice, (000: 165-180; co-auth, "Use of the World Wide Web, Hyperlinks, and Managing the news by Criminal Justice Agencies," Policing, An Intl J of Police Strategies and Management, (000: 318-338; co-auth, "Forced Sexual Intercourse Among Intimates and quot," J of Family Violence, (00): 95-108; co-auth, "Public Perceptions: The Stability of the Public's Endorsements of the Definition and Criminalization of the

Abuse of Women," J of Criminal Justice, (00): 165-180; coauth, "Is It All About Money? The Orientation toward the Use of Assets Forfeiture by Drug Enforcement Officers. An Examination of the Application of federal Policy," Carolina Acad Press, 01. **CONTACT ADDRESS** Dept Criminal Justice, Univ of Alabama, Tuscaloosa, Tuscaloosa, AL 35487-0268. **EMAIL** rsigler@cj.as.ua.edu

SIGMAN, HILARY A.
DISCIPLINE ECONOMICS **EDUCATION** Yale Univ, BA, 86; Cambridge Univ, MPhil, 88; MIT, PhD, 93. **RESEARCH** Economics analysis of environmental policy. **CONTACT ADDRESS** Dept Econ, Rutgers, The State Univ of New Jersey, New Brunswick, 75 Hamilton St, New Brunswick, NJ 08901-1248. **EMAIL** sigman@econ.rutgers.edu

SIGMUND, PAUL EUGENE
PERSONAL Born 01/14/1929, Philadelphia, PA, w, 1964, 3 children **DISCIPLINE** POLITICAL SCIENCE **EDUCATION** Georgetown Univ, BA, 50; Harvard Univ, MA, 54, PhD 59. **CAREER** Instr, sr tutor, Harvard Univ, 59-63; assoc prof, Polit, 63-70; Prof, Polit, Princeton Univ, 70-. **HONORS AND AWARDS** Tappan Thesis Prize, Harvard. **MEMBERSHIPS** Am Polit Sci Asn, Latin Am Studies Asn, Conf for the Study of Polit Thought, Phi BetaKappa. **RESEARCH** History of Political Theory, 1200-1700; Latin American Politics; Religion and Politics **SELECTED PUBLICATIONS** auth, Liberation Theology at the Crossroads: Democracy or Revolution?, 90; auth, The United States and Democracy in Chile, 93; transl, Nicholas of Cusa, The Catholic Concordance, 96; ed, Evangelization and Religious Freedom in Latin America, 99. **CONTACT ADDRESS** Dept of Polit, Princeton Univ, Princeton, NJ 08540. **EMAIL** paulsig@princeton.edu

SILBAUGH, KATHARINE
PERSONAL Born 02/01/1963, Corning, NY, m, 1990, 2 children **DISCIPLINE** LAW **EDUCATION** Amherst Col, BA, 85; Univ Chicago Law Sch, JD, 92. **CAREER** Assoc prof of law, Boston Univ, 93-pres; Assoc prof, 93-99; prof 99-. **HONORS AND AWARDS** Order of the Cof **MEMBERSHIPS** Illinois Bar **RESEARCH** Women's household labor; family law. **SELECTED PUBLICATIONS** Auth, Miller V. Albright Problems of Constituionalization in Family Law, 79; auth, Turning Labor Into Love: Housework and the Law, 91 Northwestern L. Rev. 1-86, 96; Coauth, A Guide to America's Sex Laws, 96; auth, Commodification and Women's Household Labor, 9 Yale J. Law & Fem, 97; auth, The Polygamous Heart?, a review of Arlie Hochschild's 'The Time Bind', in 1 Green Bag 2d, 97; auth, Grounded Applications: Feminism and Law at the Millenium, 50 Maine L. Rev. 201-209, 98; auth, Marriage Contracts and the Family Economy, 93 Northwestern, rev. 65-143, 98; auth, B.U.L. Rev. 1139-1160, 99. **CONTACT ADDRESS** Sch of Law, Boston Univ, 765 Commonwealth Ave, Boston, MA 02215. **EMAIL** silbaugh@bu.edu

SILBER, DANIEL
DISCIPLINE PHILOSOPHY **EDUCATION** George Washington Univ, BA, 89; MA, 93, PhD, 94, Vanderbilt Univ. **CAREER** Asst Prof, Philosophy, Florida Southern Col. **CONTACT ADDRESS** 111 Lake Hollingsworth Dr., Lakeland, FL 33801. **EMAIL** dsilber@flsouthern

SILBER, JOHN
PERSONAL Born 08/15/1926, San Antonio, TX, m, 1947, 7 children **DISCIPLINE** PHILOSOPHY **EDUCATION** Trinity Univ, BA, 47; Yale Univ, MA, 52, PhD, 56. **CAREER** Instr philos, Yale Univ, 52-55; from asst prof to prof, Univ Tex, Austin, 55-70, chm dept philos, 62-67 & comp studies, 67, univ prof arts & lett & dean col arts & sci, 67-70; Univ Prof Philos & Law, Boston Univ, 71-, Fulbright res scholar, Ger, 59-60; guest prof, Univ Bonn, 60; Guggenheim fel, Univs London & Oxford, 63-64; assoc ed, Kant-Studies, 68-87; Lindley lectr, Univ Kans, 70; mem ed adv comt, New England Aquarium, 71; trustee, Col St Scholastica, 73; mem, Nat Comn United Methodist Higher Educ, 74-77; mem bd visitors, Air Univ, 74-80; mem exec bd, Nat Humanities Inst, 75-78. **HONORS AND AWARDS** Wilbur Lucius Cross Medal, Yale Grad Sch, 71; lhd, kalamazoo col, 70 & univ evansville, 75; lld, maryville col, 75, col st scholastics, 75 & colo col, 78; ded, southwestern at memphis, 78. **MEMBERSHIPS** Am Asn Higher Educ; Royal Inst Philos; Am Soc Polit & Legal Philos. **RESEARCH** Financing of higher education. **SELECTED PUBLICATIONS** Auth, The Ethical Significance of Kant's Religion, Harper, 60; auth, The Pollution of Time, Ctr Mag, 9-10/71; auth, Tenure in Context, In: The Tenure Debate, Jossey-Bass, 73; auth, Democracy: Its Counterfeits and Its Promise, Boston Univ, 76; auth, The Flight From Excellence, Harpers Mag, 6/77; auth, The Tuition Dilemma, Atlantic Mag, 7/78. **CONTACT ADDRESS** Off of the Chancellor, Boston Univ, 147 Bay State Road, Boston, MA 02215-2802.

SILK, WILLIAM
PERSONAL Born 07/25/1941, Chicago, IL, m, 1982, 2 children **DISCIPLINE** CRIMINAL JUSTICE, CORRECTIONS, SOCIOLOGY **EDUCATION** Depaul Univ, BA, 69; Depaul Univ, MA, 74; Chicago State Univ, MS, 89; Nova Southeastern Univ, Doctor Public Administration Degree, 83. **CAREER** Adjunct Instr, Sociology Dept, Moraine Valley Community Col; Adjunct Instr, Criminal Justice and Corrections, City of Chicago Police Department, Sergeant of Police. **HONORS AND AWARDS** The National Dean's List, Eleventh Annual Edition, Volume II, 87-88, Educational Communication Inc.; Dept Commendation, Chicago Police Dept. **MEMBERSHIPS** Amer Academy for Professional Law Enforcement, Chicago, Illinois Chapter. **RESEARCH** Juvenile Delinquency, Criminal Activity. **SELECTED PUBLICATIONS** Auth, "Reducing the Rate of Juvenile Delinquency, Nova Southeastern Univ, Ft. Lauderdale, FLA; auth, "Juvenile Delinquency as a Learned Behavior," DePaul Univ, Chicago, Illinois. **CONTACT ADDRESS** Dept Social Science, Moraine Valley Comm Col, 10900 S 88th Ave, Palos Hills, IL 60465.

SILLIMAN, MATTHEW R.
PERSONAL Born 08/28/1956, Hanover, NH, d **DISCIPLINE** PHILOSOPHY **EDUCATION** Purdue Univ, PhD, 86. **CAREER** Vis asst prof, Earlham Col, 85; asst prof, N Adams State Col, 86-93; assoc prof, NASC/Mass Col Lib Arts, 93-. **MEMBERSHIPS** Am Philos Asn; N Am Soc Soc Philos. **RESEARCH** Social and political philosophy; philosophy of law. **SELECTED PUBLICATIONS** Coauth, Critical Thinking and the Argumentative Essay, Inquiry: Critical Thinking Across the Disciplines, Summer, 98; auth, Law, Politics, and Tushnet's Epistemology, Rending & Renewing Soc Order, 96; auth, The Antioch Policy: A Community Experiment in Communicative Sexuality, Date Rape, Feminism, Philos & Law, 96; auth, Domestic Abuse: Locke's Liberal (mis)Treatment of Family, Is Feminist Philos Philos?, 97; auth, Freedom, Property and the Politics of Family, Freedom, Obligation and Rights, 93. **CONTACT ADDRESS** Dept of Philosophy, Mass Col of Liberal Arts, North Adams, MA 01247. **EMAIL** msillima@mcla.mass.edu

SILVA, MOISES
DISCIPLINE RELIGION **EDUCATION** Bob Jones Univ, BA; Westminster Theol Sem, BD, ThM; Dropsie Univ, grad stud; Univ Manchester, PhD. **CAREER** Instr, Westmont Col; instr, dept ch, Westminster Theol Sem; vis lectr, Fuller Theol Sem; Trinity Evangel Divinity Sch; E Baptist Theol Sem; Mary French Rockefeller Distinguished prof, Gordon-Conwell Theol Sem, 96-. **MEMBERSHIPS** Mem, Evangel Theol Soc; Intl Org Septuagint and Cognate Stud; Inst Biblical Res; Soc Biblical Lit; Studiorum Novi Testamenti Societas. **SELECTED PUBLICATIONS** Auth, Explorations in Exegetical Method: Galatians as a Test Case; An Introduction to Biblical Hermeneutics. **CONTACT ADDRESS** Gordon-Conwell Theol Sem, 130 Essex St, South Hamilton, MA 01982.

SILVER, BRUCE
PERSONAL Born 09/21/1944 **DISCIPLINE** PHILOSOPHY **EDUCATION** Univ Col, BA, 65; MA, 67; PhD, 71. **CAREER** Asst prof, Univ S Flor, 71-76; assoc prof, 77-83; prof, 84-. **RESEARCH** History of renaissance and modern philosophy; American philosophy. **SELECTED PUBLICATIONS** Auth, "The Conflicting Microscopic World's of Berkeley's Three Dialogues," J Hist Ideas 37 (76): 343-49; auth, "Clarke on the Quaker Background of William Bartram's Approach to Nature," J Hist Ideas 47 (86): 507-10; auth, "Boswell on Johnson's refutation of Berkeley," J Hist Ideas 54 (93): 437-47. **CONTACT ADDRESS** Dept Philosophy, Univ of So Florida, 4202 East Fowler Ave, FAO233, Tampa, FL 33620-9951. **EMAIL** bsilver@chuma1.cas.usf.edu

SILVER, MARJORIE A.
DISCIPLINE LAW **EDUCATION** Brandeis Unvi, BA, summa cum laude, 70; Univ Pa, JD, magna cum laude, Order of the Coif, 73. **CAREER** Ch reg civil rights atty, US Dept of Educ, 79-83; assoc prof, NY Law Schl, 83-91; arbitrator, Better Bus Bur of Metropolitan NY, 86-89; assoc prof, Touro Col. **MEMBERSHIPS** Mem, Civil Rights Comt, 88-91; 92-, Educ and Law Comt, 91-92, Asn of the Bar of the City of NY. **SELECTED PUBLICATIONS** Auth, The Uses and Abuses of Informal Procedures in Federal Civil Rights Enforcement, George Washington Law Rev, 87; Evening the Odds: The Case for Attorneys' Fee Awards for Administrative Resolution of Title VI and Title VII Disputes, NC Law Rev, 89; In Lieu of Preclusion: Reconciling Administrative Decisionmaking and Federal Civil Rights Claims, Ind Law J, 90; Giving Notice: An Argument for Notification of Putative Plaintiffs in Complex Litigation, Washington Law Rev, 91; Fairness and Finality: Third-Party Challenges to Employment Discrimination Consent Decrees After the 1991 Civil Rights Act, 62 Fordham Law Rev 321, 93; coauth, Dissent without Opinion: The Behavior of Justice William O. Douglas in Federal Tax Cases, 75. **CONTACT ADDRESS** Dept of Law, Touro Col, New York, Brooklyn, NY 11230. **EMAIL** MarjorieS@tourolaw.edu

SILVER, MITCHELL
PERSONAL Born 10/04/1950, New York, NY, m, 2 children **DISCIPLINE** PHILOSOPHY **EDUCATION** Univ of Connecticut, PhD, 80. **CAREER** Lectr, 17 yr, Philos, U MA, Boston. **HONORS AND AWARDS** Phi Beta Kappa. **MEMBERSHIPS** APA. **RESEARCH** Ethics; Political Philosophy. **SELECTED PUBLICATIONS** Auth, Respecting the Wicked Child, Univ of Mass Press, 98; A Philosophy of Secular Identity and Education. **CONTACT ADDRESS** Dept of Philos, Univ of Massachusetts, Boston, 100 Morrissey Blvd, Boston, MA 02125-3393. **EMAIL** mitchell.silver@umb.edu; silver@umbsky.cc.umb.edu

SILVERS, ANITA
PERSONAL Born 11/01/1940, New York, NY **DISCIPLINE** PHILOSOPHY, AESTHETICS **EDUCATION** Sarah Lawrence Col, BA, 62; Johns Hopkins Univ, PhD(philos), 67. **CAREER** Prof Philos, San Francisco State Univ, 67-, Vis lectr philos, Sussex Univ, 72-73; assoc ed, J Aesthetics & Art Criticism, 79-; mem, Nat Coun Humanities, 80-; Exec Secy, Coun Philos Studies, 79-82. **MEMBERSHIPS** Am Philos Asn; Am Soc Aesthetics; Asn Advan Humanities. **RESEARCH** Philosophy of the arts; ethics; journalism ethics. **SELECTED PUBLICATIONS** Auth, Vincent Story, The Importance Of Centextualism For Art Educ/, J Of Aesthetic Educ, Vol 0028, 1994. **CONTACT ADDRESS** 15 Otsego Ave, San Francisco, CA 94112.

SILVERSTEIN, JOSEF
PERSONAL Born 05/15/1922, Los Angeles, CA, m, 1954, 2 children **DISCIPLINE** GOVERNMENT, POLITICAL SCIENCE **EDUCATION** Univ Calif, LA, BA, 52; Cornell Univ, PhD, 60. **CAREER** Asst prof, Wesleyan Univ, 59-64; assoc prof, 64-67; prof, 67-78; chm, Polit Sci dept, Rutgers Col, 77-80; prof, Rutgers Col, 78-92; prof emer, Rutgers Univ, 92-98; Prof, Rutgers Univ, 98-. **HONORS AND AWARDS** Fulbright Sr Lectr, Univ Malaysia, 67-68, Mandalay Univ, Burma, 61-62. **MEMBERSHIPS** APSA; AAS. **RESEARCH** Comparative politics; Foreign policy; International relations. **SELECTED PUBLICATIONS** auth, "Change in Burma," Current Hist, 95; auth, "Federalism as a Solution to the Ethnic Problem in Burma," Verlag Rugler, 97; auth, "Burma's Uneven Struggle," Jour of Democracy, 96; auth, "The Civil War, the Minorities and Burma's New Politics," in Burma: the Challenge of Change in a Divided Society, St. Martin's Press, 97; auth, "Forty Years of Failure in Burma," in Government, Politics and Ethnic Relations in Asia and the Pacific, MIT Press, 97; auth, "The Idea of Freedom in Burma and the Political Thought of Daw Aing San Suc Ky" in Asian Freedoms: The Idea of Freedom in East and Southeast Asia, Cambridge Univ Press, 98; auth, "East Asia: A Year of Uneven Progress," in Freedom is the World 1997-1998, New York, 98; auth, "Evolution and Salience of Burma's National Culture," in Burma: Prospects for a Democratic Future, Wash Brookings Inst Press, 98. **CONTACT ADDRESS** 93 Overbrook Dr, Princeton, NJ 08540. **EMAIL** josefs@rci.rutgers.edu

SILVIA, STEPHEN J.
PERSONAL Born Buffalo, NY **DISCIPLINE** POLITICAL ECONOMICS **EDUCATION** Cornell Univ, BS; Yale Univ, MA, PhD. **CAREER** Prof, Am Univ. **HONORS AND AWARDS** Fulbright Res Fel; Nat Endowment Humanities grant; Robert Bosch Fel. **RESEARCH** Comparative industrial politics and comparative economic systems. **SELECTED PUBLICATIONS** Articles, Bus Contemp World; Comp Polit; German Polit; German Studies Rev; Gewerkschaftliche Monatshefte; Industrial & Labor Relations Rev; Int Joul Politl Econ; New German Critique and W European Polit. **CONTACT ADDRESS** American Univ, 4400 Massachusetts Ave, Washington, DC 20016. **EMAIL** ssilvia@american.edu

SIMCO, NANCY DAVIS
PERSONAL Born 05/09/1940, Rogers, AR, d **DISCIPLINE** PHILOSOPHY **EDUCATION** Univ Kans, BA, 62, MA, 65, MPhil & PhD(philos), 69. **CAREER** From instr to asst prof philos, 66-73, assoc prof, 73-78, Prof Philos, Univ Memphis, 78-, Assoc Dean Res & Grad Studies, Col Arts & Sci, 75-89, Ed, Southern J Philos, 74-, dept ch, 89- **MEMBERSHIPS** Am Philos Asn; Asn Symbolic Logic; Metaphys Soc Am; Southern Soc Philos & Psychol (pres, 85-86); Asn Philos Jour Ed (pres 93-); SW Phil Soc (pres, 88-); Soc of Phil in Am; Conf of Phil Soc. **RESEARCH** Contemporary metaphysics; philosophical logic. **SELECTED PUBLICATIONS** Auth, Strawson's ontology in individuals, 71 & Note on instances of invalid elementary argument forms, 73, Southern J Philos; Transcendental arguments and ontological commitment, Proc XVth World Cong Philos, 73; Logic and ontology as normative sciences, Fifth Int Cong Logic, Methodology & Philos Sci, 75; coauth, Elementary Logic, Dickenson, 76; auth, Elementary Logic, 2nd ed, Wadsworth, 83, 3rd ed, McGraw-Hill, 96; auth, Rationality, Sci Rationality, and Philos Questions, PROC XVIth World Cong Philos, 78; auth, The Linguistic Turn Afain, SW Phil Rev, 89; auth, On Avoiding Rejection by Journals, Am Philos Assoc, 97. **CONTACT ADDRESS** Dept of Philos, Univ of Memphis, Memphis, TN 38152-0001. **EMAIL** nsimco@memphis.edu

SIMMELKJAER, ROBERT T.
PERSONAL Born New York, NY, m **DISCIPLINE** LAW **EDUCATION** CCNY, BS Pol Sci 1962, MA Pol Sci 1964; Columbia Univ Teachers Coll, EdD Ed Admin 1972; Columbia Univ Business School, MBA Bus Admin 1977; Fordham Univ School of Law, JD 1978. **CAREER** Inst for Ed Devel, exec asst to pres 1969-71; NY City Bd of Ed, principal 1971-74; CCNY, prof ed admin 1974-79, dean of gen studies and vice provost for academic administration, 79-86; Attorney/arbitrator; Gover-

nor's Advisory Commission for Black Affairs, executive director 1986-88; New York City Transit Authority, administration law judge 1988-90; Joint Commission for Integrity in the Public Schools, deputy chief counsel 1989-90; Institute for Mediation and Conflict Resolution, president 1991-. **HONORS AND AWARDS** NY State Regents Scholarship 1957; US OE Ed Fellowship 1969-70; Great Cities Rsch Fel, 71; **MEMBERSHIPS** PERC, OCB 1977-; minority school fin network Urban League & NAACP 1980-83; bd of dir Inst for Mediation & Conflict Resolution 1980-84; consult Ford Found, Natl School Fin Proj, NY Task Force Equity & Excellence, Urban Coalition Local School Devel 1980-83; vice chmn Personnel Appeals Bd US Acctg Office 1981-84; speaker, consult US Info Agency 1981-84; consult NY Univ School of Bus 1982-83; board of directors, Institute for Mediation and Conflict Resolution, 1980-92; board of directors, National Academy of Arbitrators, 1988-. **SELECTED PUBLICATIONS** Chap in "A Quest for Ed Oppty in a Major Urban School District, The Case of Washington DC" 1975; author, "From Partnership to Renewal, Evolution of an Urban Ed Reform," The Ed Forum, 1979; author, "State Aid to Substantially Black School Districts," Crisis and Opportunity; "Finality of Arbitration Awards, The Arbitration Forum," Fall 1989; author chapters on Representation, Collective Bargaining Impasses in Federal Civil Service Law and Procedures, BNA, 1990; "State Aid to Substantially Black School Districts," in Crisis and Opportunity Report (NY, NY); Federal Civil Service Law and Procedure, Washington, DC (BNA) 1990: two chapters on collective bargaining and arbitration. **CONTACT ADDRESS** 160 W 97th St, New York, NY 10025.

SIMMONS, A. JOHN
PERSONAL Born 05/04/1950, Dover, NJ, m, 1986, 2 children **DISCIPLINE** PHILOSOPHY **EDUCATION** Princeton, AB, 72; Cornell Univ, MA, 75; PhD, 77. **CAREER** Asst prof to Commonwealth prof, Univ Va, 76-; vis prof, Johns Hopkins Univ, 81; vis prof, Univ Haw, 90. **HONORS AND AWARDS** Nat Merit Scholar, 68; Phi Beta Kappa, 72; summa cum laude, Princeton, 72; NEH Fel, 80-81; All-University Teaching Awd, 92-93. **MEMBERSHIPS** Am Philos Asn; Am Soc for Political and Legal Philos. **RESEARCH** Moral, political, legal philosophy. **SELECTED PUBLICATIONS** Auth, Moral Principles and Political Obligations, Princeton Univ Press (79), paperback (81); auth, The Lockean Theory of Rights (in the Series: "Studies in Moral Political, and Legal Philosophy," Princeton Univ Press (92), paperback (94); auth, On the Edge of Anarchy: Locke, Consent, and the Limits of Society (in the series: "Studies in Moral, Political, and Legal Philosophy," Princeton Univ Press (93), paperback (95); auth, "Makers' Rights," The J of Ethics 2, 1-22 (98); auth, "Justification and Legitimacy," Ethics 109, 739-771 (July 99); auth, "John Locke," Fairness," and "Political Obligation," in C. B. Gray, ed, The Philosophy of Law: An Encyclopedia, Garland Pub (99); auth, Justification and Legitimacy: Essays on Rights and Obligations, Cambridge Univ Press (forthcoming); auth, Social and Political Philosophy, in the series: "Fundamentals of Philosophy," under contract with Oxford Univ Press (in progress). **CONTACT ADDRESS** Dept Philos, Univ of Virginia, 512 Cabell Hall, Charlottesville, VA 22903-3125. **EMAIL** ajs7m@virginia.edu

SIMMONS, ESMERALDA
PERSONAL Born 12/16/1950, Brooklyn, NY **DISCIPLINE** LAW **EDUCATION** Hunter Coll CUNY, BA, 74; Brooklyn Law School, JD, 78. **CAREER** New York City Law Dept, honors attorney, civil rights employment unit, 78-79; US Dist Ct US Dist Judge Henry Bramwell, law clerk, 79-80; US Dept of Educ Office of Civil Rights, regional civil rights atty, 80-82; NY Dept of Law Atty General's Office, asst attorney general, 82-83; NY State Div of Human Rights, first deputy commissioner, 83-85; Medgar Evers Coll Ctr for Law and Social Justice, dir, 85-. **HONORS AND AWARDS** Partner in Educ Awd NY City Bd of Educ, 81; Appreciation Awd Central Brooklyn Mobilization, 82; Lawyer of the Year Bedford Stuyvesant Lawyers Assn Inc, 84; Imani Awd Weusi Shule Parents Council, 84; Professional of the Year Nat Assn of Negro Business and Professional Womens Clubs Inc, 86; Harriet Tubman Awd, Fannie Lou Hamer Collective, 87; Woman on the Move, Concerned Women of Brooklyn, 88; Leadership Awd, Asian Americans for Equality, 90; Leadership in Civil Rights Awd, United Negro College Fund, Brooklyn Chapter, 90; Women for Racial and Economic Equality, Fannie Lou Hamer Awd, 91; council member Annette M Robenson, Spirited Leadership Awd, 92; Community Service Society, Ellen Luriel Awd, 92; Magnolia Tree Earth Center, Magnolia Awd, 92. **MEMBERSHIPS** Natl Conf Black Lawyers, 75-; Natl Bar Assn; Fund for the City of New York. **CONTACT ADDRESS** Ctr for Law & Social Justice, Medgar Evers Col, CUNY, 1473 Fulton St, Brooklyn, NY 11216.

SIMMONS, JACK R.
PERSONAL Born 12/08/1964, San Diego, CA, m, 1993, 1 child **DISCIPLINE** PHILOSOPHY **EDUCATION** LSU BA 87, MA 90; Tulane Univ PhD, 97. **CAREER** Vis asst prof, Univ N Fla, 97-98; asst prof, Savannah St Univ, 98. **MEMBERSHIPS** Amer Philos Assoc **RESEARCH** Film Theory; Critical Theory; Hermeneutics. **SELECTED PUBLICATIONS** Auth, The Ontology of Perception in Cinema, Film and Philos, 98; auth, The Colonizing Power of The English Patient, Film and History on CD Rom, 99; auth, Truth and Method, Gadamer World Philosophy, 00; auth, Distance Learning: Education or Economics? The International Journal of Value-Based Management, 00; auth, Educational Technology and Academic Freedom, Techne, 00. **CONTACT ADDRESS** Dept of Humanities, Savannah State Univ, PO Box 20029, Savannah, GA 31404. **EMAIL** simmonsj@savstate.edu

SIMMONS, LANCE
DISCIPLINE PHILOSOPHY, ETHICS **EDUCATION** Univ Calif, AB; Univ Notre Dame, MA, PhD. **CAREER** Dept Philos, Univ Dallas **SELECTED PUBLICATIONS** Auth, Kant's Highest Good: Albatross, Keystone, Achilles Heel, Hist of Philos Quart, 93; auth, Abelardian Ethics Reconstructed, Proc Amer Cath Philos Assn, 93; Three Kinds of Incommesurability Thesis, Amer Philos Quart, 94. **CONTACT ADDRESS** Dept of Philos, Univ of Dallas, 1845 E Northgate Dr, Irving, TX 75062. **EMAIL** simmons@acad.udallas.edu

SIMMONS, PAUL D.
PERSONAL Born 07/18/1936, Troy, TN, m, 1963, 3 children **DISCIPLINE** THEOLOGICAL-PHILOSOPHICAL ETHICS **EDUCATION** Southeaster Theol Sem, ThM, 67; Southern Baptist Theol Sem, PhD, 70; post-graduate studies, Princeton Univ, 78 & Cambridge Univ, 84. **CAREER** Prof, Southern Baptist Theol Sem, 70-93; adj prof, Univ of Louisville, 94-; clinical prof, Univ of Louisville, 97-. **HONORS AND AWARDS** David Gunn Awd as champion of Women's Reproductive Rights, 94. **MEMBERSHIPS** Am Soc of Law, Medicine and Ethics, Am Acad of Relig, Nat Asn of Baptist Professors of Relig. **RESEARCH** Health Care Ethics, Genetics and Reproductive Ethics. **SELECTED PUBLICATIONS** Auth, "Baptist-Evangelical Biomedical Ethics," Bioethics Yearbook Vol III, D. Reidel (Boston, MA), 93; auth, "Personhood, the Bible and the Abortion Debate," The Ethics of Abortion: Pro-Life v. Pro-Choice, Prometheus Books (Buffalo, NY), 93; auth, "Biotechnical parenting: Biblical and Human issues," Reproductive Rights: Medical, Ethical, and Legal Perspectives, 95; auth, "The Narrative Ethics of Stanley Hauerwas: A Question of Method," Secular Bioethics in Theological perspective, Kluwer Press (Dordrect, the Netherlands), 96; auth, "Baptist-Evangelical Biomedical Ethics," Bioethics Yearbook Vol V, D. Reidel (Boston, MA), 97; auth, "Buchman, Frank N.D.," Religion in Geschichte und Gegenwart, 99; auth, "Religious Liberty: a Heritage at Stake," Christian Ethics Today 5.4 (99): 28-31; ed, Freedom of Conscience, Prometheus (Buffalo, NY), 00; auth, "Religious Liberty and Abortion Policy: Casy as 'Catch-22," J of Church and State 42.1 (00); coauth, "Ethics & Aging: Confronting Abuse and Self-Neglect," J of Elder Abuse and Neglect 11.2 (00). **CONTACT ADDRESS** Dept Philos, Univ of Louisville, 2301 S 3rd St, Louisville, KY 40292-0001. **EMAIL** pdsimm01@gwise.louisville.edu

SIMMONS, WILLIAM A.
PERSONAL Born Metairie, LA, m, 3 children **DISCIPLINE** THEOLOGY AND PHILOSOPHY **EDUCATION** Lee Univ, BA, 78; Princeton, MA, Phd; Univ St Andrews, PhD. **CAREER** Conn Comm Col; Assoc prof, Lee Univ, 97-. **HONORS AND AWARDS** Lee Univ Excellence Res Awd, 94. **RESEARCH** Galatians and Philippians; Karl Barth. **SELECTED PUBLICATIONS** Auth, Areas: Different aspects of the New Testament; auth, A Theology of Inclusion; auth, New Testament Survey. **CONTACT ADDRESS** Dept of Religion, Lee Col, Tennessee, 1120 N. Ocoee St, Cleveland, TN 37320-3450. **EMAIL** wsimmons@leeuniversity.edu

SIMON, JULIUS J.
PERSONAL m, 3 children **DISCIPLINE** PHILOSOPHY **EDUCATION** PhD **CAREER** Fac, Univ Tex at El Paso, over 4 yrs; Fulbright Scholar. **RESEARCH** Jewish Philosophy and 19th- and 20th-century German and French philosophy; philosophical roots of nationalist-inspired genocide. **SELECTED PUBLICATIONS** Ed, History, Religion, and Meaning: American Reflections on the Holocaust and Israel, Greenwood Press, 00. **CONTACT ADDRESS** Dept of Philosophy, Univ of Texas, El Paso, Worrell Hall, El Paso, TX 79968. **EMAIL** jsimon@utep.edu

SIMON, LARRY G.
DISCIPLINE CONSTITUTIONAL LAW **EDUCATION** Hobart Col, BA,63; Yale Univ, LLB,66. **CAREER** H.W. Armstrong prof, Univ Southern Calif; clerked for, Honorable Earl Warren, Ch Justice US; taught at, Yale Law Sch. **MEMBERSHIPS** Order of the Coif. **RESEARCH** Constitutional Law, Legal Profession, and Insurance. **SELECTED PUBLICATIONS** Auth, The Authority of the Framers of the Constitution & The Authority of the Constitution and its Meaning. **CONTACT ADDRESS** School of Law, Univ of So California, University Park Campus, Los Angeles, CA 90089.

SIMON, ROBERT L.
PERSONAL Born 05/12/1941, Brooklyn, NY, m, 1967, 2 children **DISCIPLINE** PHILOSOPHY **EDUCATION** Lafayette, Col, BA, 63; Univ Pa, PhD, 69. **CAREER** Prof, Hamilton Col. **HONORS AND AWARDS** Fel, NEH. **MEMBERSHIPS** Am Philos Assoc; Int Assoc for the Philos of Sports. **RESEARCH** Political and social philosophy, critical thinking. **SELECTED PUBLICATIONS** Auth, Fair Play, 91; auth, Neutrality and the Academic Ethic, 94; auth, The Individual and the Political Order, 98. **CONTACT ADDRESS** Dept Philos, Hamilton Col, New York, 198 College Hill Road, Clinton, NY 13323-1218.

SIMON, SHELDON W.
PERSONAL Born 01/31/1937, St. Paul, MN, m, 1962, 1 child **DISCIPLINE** POLITICAL SCIENCE **EDUCATION** Univ Minnesota, PhD 64. **CAREER** Arizona State Univ, prof 75-, dir Asian Stud 80-88, ch Poli Sci 75-79. **HONORS AND AWARDS** Phi Beta Kappa; Summa cum laude; Outstanding Fac Awd; Phi Kappa Phi. **MEMBERSHIPS** AAUP; APSA; ISA. **RESEARCH** Asian security; regionalism in Asia. **SELECTED PUBLICATIONS** Auth, Asian Political Economy and Security Toward the 21st Century: A Review Essay, Intl Politics, 98; auth, Security Prospects in Southeast Asia: Collaborative Efforts and the ASEAN Regional Forum, The Pacific Rev, 98; auth, The Limits of Defense and Security Cooperation in Southeast Asia, The Jour of Asian and African Studies, 98; auth, Alternative Visions of Security in Northeast Asia, The Jour of NE Asian Studies, 96; auth, Alternate Visions of Security in the Asia-Pacific, Pacific Affs, 96; auth, Security Economic Liberalism and Democracy: Asian Elite Perceptions of Post Cold War Foreign Policy Values, NBR Analysis, 96; auth, Southeast Asian Security in the New Millenium, co-ed, Armonk NY, M E Sharpe, 96; auth, " Asian Armed Forces: Internal and External Tasks and Capabilities," NBR Analysis, May 00; auth, " Is There a Strategy For East Asia?" Contemporary Southeast Asia, Dec 99; auth, " Multilateralism in Japan's Security Policy," The Korean Journal of Defence Analysis, Winter 00. **CONTACT ADDRESS** Political Science Dept, Arizona State Univ, Tempe, AZ 85287-2001. **EMAIL** shells@asu.edu

SIMON, WILLIAM HACKETT
PERSONAL Born 07/06/1947, Chicago, IL, m, 1981, 2 children **DISCIPLINE** LAW **EDUCATION** Princeton Univ, AB, 69; Harvard Univ, JD, 74. **CAREER** Assoc atty, Foley, Hoag & Eliot, 74-77; staff atty, Legal Serv Inst, 79-81; Asst Prof Law, Stanford Univ, 81- **RESEARCH** Social welfare; legal profession; jurisprudence. **SELECTED PUBLICATIONS** Auth, The Practice of Justice, Harvard U.P., 98; auth, The Community Economic Development Movement, Duke U.P., 01. **CONTACT ADDRESS** Law Sch, Stanford Univ, Stanford, CA 94305-1926. **EMAIL** wsimon@leland.stanford.edu

SIMPSON, DICK
PERSONAL Born 11/08/1940, Houston, TX, m, 1985, 2 children **DISCIPLINE** POLITICAL SCIENCE **EDUCATION** Univ Tex, BA, 63; Ind Univ, MA, 64, PhD, 68; McCormick Theol Sem, MDiv, 84. **CAREER** For Area Fel, Ford Found, Sierra Leone, 66-67; from instr, assist, assoc and full prof, 67- , Univ Illinois, Chicago; dir, Office of Chicago Studies, 87-90; dir Chicago Political Studies Project, 92-95; dir Graduate Stud Polit Sci, 95-96. **HONORS AND AWARDS** Silver Circle Awd for excellence in teaching, 71; Outstanding Young Men of America Awd, 72; Emmy nomination for documentary film, 89; Teaching Recognition Program Awd, 97. **MEMBERSHIPS** Am Polit Sci Asn; Midwest Polit Sci Asn; Ill Polit Sci Asn. **RESEARCH** Urban politics; American politics; religion and politics; electoral politics. **SELECTED PUBLICATIONS** Coauth, Political Action: The Key to Understanding Politics, Ohio Univ, 84; auth, The Politics of Compassion and Transformation, Ohio University, 89; ed, Blueprint of Chicago Government: 1989, Univ Illinois at Chicago, 89; co-ed, The Crazy Quilt of Government: Units of Government in Cook County, 1993, University of Illinois at Chicago, 94; auth, Winning Elections: A Handbook of Modern Participatory Politics, HarperCollins, 96; auth, Rogues, Rebels, and Rubberstamps, Westview, 00. **CONTACT ADDRESS** Dept of Political Science, Univ of Illinois, Chicago, PO Box 4348, Chicago, IL 60680. **EMAIL** simpson@uic.edu

SIMPSON, EVAN
DISCIPLINE PHILOSOPHY **EDUCATION** Duke Univ, PhD. **CAREER** Prof. **RESEARCH** Moral and political philos. **CONTACT ADDRESS** Philosophy Dept, McMaster Univ, 1280 Main St W, Hamilton, ON, Canada L8S 4L9.

SIMPSON, GARY M.
DISCIPLINE SYSTEMATIC THEOLOGY **EDUCATION** Concordia Sr Col, BA, 72; Christ Sem-Seminex, MDiv, 76, ThD, 83. **CAREER** Adj tchr, Warner Pacific Col; Pacific Lutheran Theol Sem; Lutheran Inst Theol Edu; assoc prof, 90-. **HONORS AND AWARDS** Pastor, Immanuel Lutheran Church; chaplain, Highland-Alameda County Hospital, Oakland, 76-81; minister of edu and youth, St. Charles Christian Church, 81-83; pastor, Resurrection Lutheran Church, 83-90; ch, Jewish-Christian Assn Ore; VP, Oregon Holocaust Resource Ctr; ch, Oregon Governor's Task Force on Hunger. **MEMBERSHIPS** Mem, Amer Acad Rel; Soc Christian Ethics; Gospel and Our Culture Network. **SELECTED PUBLICATIONS** Ed bd(s), Word & World; pub(s), essays on theology and public life, Eng and Ger lang collections. **CONTACT ADDRESS** Dept of Systematic Theology, Luther Sem, 2481 Como Ave, Saint Paul, MN 55108. **EMAIL** gsimpson@luthersem.edu

SIMPSON, MARK E.
PERSONAL Born 07/29/1958, Saginaw, MI, s **DISCIPLINE** CHRISTIAN EDUCATION **EDUCATION** Spring Arbor Col, BA; Denver Conservative Baptist Sem, MACE; DePauw Univ, MA; Trinity Evangel Divinity Sch, PhD. **CAREER** Acad Doctorate Prog(s) coord, Trinity Evangel Divinity Sch; assoc dean, Nontraditional Edu, Col Liberal Arts, Trinity Intl Univ; assoc prof; assoc dean, Sch Christian Edu and Leadership; Gaines S. Dobbins assoc prof; assoc dean for doctoral studies, sch. . . **HONORS AND AWARDS** North Am Prof of CE (NAPCE) Cert of Recognition; Trinity Evangelical Divinity School Christian Service Awd. **RESEARCH** North Am Prof of Christian Education; Leadership, web-based education, simulation and discovery learning. **SELECTED PUBLICATIONS** Ed, NAPCE Newsletter; contrib, With an Eye on the Future: Development and Mission in the 21st Century; pub(s), Christian Edu Jour; Key To Christian Edu. **CONTACT ADDRESS** Sch Christian Edu and Leadership, So Baptist Theol Sem, 2825 Lexington Rd, Louisville, KY 40280. **EMAIL** msimpson@sbts.edu

SIMPSON, PETER
DISCIPLINE PHILOSOPHY **EDUCATION** Univ Toronto, PhD. **RESEARCH** Philos of hist; phenomenology; empiricism. **SELECTED PUBLICATIONS** Auth, Hegel's Transcendental Induction, 98; art, Out of this World: Heidegger and the Problem of Phenomenology, Strategies of Critique, 91; auth, "Hegel's conscientious theodicy," in A postmodern ethics of glory, ed. by D. Goicoechea and M. Zlomisslic, (Ottawa, ON: Thoughthouse Publishing Group, 94): 3-13; auth, "On the history of medern philosophy, by F.W.J. Schelling," in Review of Metaphysics, 195, (96): 681-682. **CONTACT ADDRESS** Philosophy Dept, Laurentian Univ, 935 Ramsey Lake Rd, Sudbury, ON, Canada P3E 2C6.

SIMPSON, PETER P.
PERSONAL Born, England **DISCIPLINE** CLASSICS, PHILOSOPHY **EDUCATION** Victoria Univ Manchester, UK, PhD **CAREER** Asst prof, Univ Col Dublin, Ireland, 82-84; asst prof, Catholic Univ Am, DC, 84-88; Full prof, City Univ NY, 88- . **HONORS AND AWARDS** Earhart found fel, 95; Jr fel, Ctr Hellenic stud, 92. **MEMBERSHIPS** APA; ACPA; APSA; SAGP; APPA. **RESEARCH** Ancient and medieval philosophy; moral and political philosophy. **SELECTED PUBLICATIONS** Auth, The Politics of Aristotle, U of North Carolina P, 97; A Philosophical Commentary on the Politics of Aristotle, U of North Carolina P, 98. **CONTACT ADDRESS** Dept of Philosophy, Col of Staten Island, CUNY, 2800 Victory Blvd, 2N, Staten Island, NY 10314. **EMAIL** simpson@postbox.csi.cuny.edu

SIMPSON, STEPHEN WHITTINGTON
PERSONAL Born 03/14/1945, Philadelphia, PA, m **DISCIPLINE** LAW **EDUCATION** Harvard Univ, AB 1966; Univ of PA, JD 1969. **CAREER** Suns Co, Inc, chief counsel, 78-87; Goodrs Greenfield, atty 1973-77; Dechert, Price & Rhoades, atty 1970-73; PA Superior Ct, law clerk 1969-70; Vance, Jackson, Simpson & Overton, Attorney, currently. **MEMBERSHIPS** Amer Bar Assc; Philadelphia Bar Assc; Barristers Club. **CONTACT ADDRESS** Vance, Jackson, Simpson, & Overton, 1429 Walnut St, 8th Floor, Philadelphia, PA 19107.

SIMS, GENEVIEVE CONSTANCE
PERSONAL Born 11/04/1947, Baltimore, MD, s **DISCIPLINE** LAW **EDUCATION** North Carolina State Univ, BA, 1969; Univ of Southern California, MPA, 1976; North Carolina Central Univ, JD, 1986. **CAREER** Law Offices of Genevieve C. Sims, lawyer, 87-; Merit Sys Protection Bd, special asst, 79-81; US Civil Serv Commn, special asst commr, 77-78; Office of Mgmt & Budget Exec Office Pres, mgmt analyst, 76-77; US Civil Serv Commn, personnel mgmt spec, 72-76; Office of State Personnel, North Carolina State Govt, econ analyst 1969-72; North Carolina State Univ, Raleigh, NC, asst professor, 82-93; North Carolina Central Univ, Durham, NC, visiting instr, 82-92. **HONORS AND AWARDS** Awd, North Carolina Special Olympics, 1982. **MEMBERSHIPS** Former chairperson, bd of dir, Shelley School; bd of dir, North Carolina Assn Black Lawyers, 1989-92; board of directors, North Carolina Academy of Trial Lawyers, 1995-; North Carolina Bar Assn; board of directors, United Black Fund of Washington, 1976-81. **CONTACT ADDRESS** 313 S Blount St, Raleigh, NC 27601.

SIMSON, ROSALIND
PERSONAL Born 04/03/1952, New York, NY, m, 1971, 2 children **DISCIPLINE** PHILOSOPHY **EDUCATION** Yale Univ, BA, 73; PhD, 79. **CAREER** Asst Prof to Assoc Prof, Hobart William Smith Col, 79-. **MEMBERSHIPS** Am Philos Asn; Am Asn of Univ Prof. **RESEARCH** Epistemology; Feminist Philosophy. **CONTACT ADDRESS** Dept Philos, Hobart and William Smith Cols, Geneva, NY 14456-3304. **EMAIL** simson@hws.edu

SIMUNDSON, DANIEL J.
DISCIPLINE OLD TESTAMENT **EDUCATION** Stanford Univ, BA, 55; Lutheran Sch Theol, BD, 59; Harvard Univ, PhD, 71. **CAREER** Hospital chaplain, Wash Univ Med Sch, 61-67; asst prof, Appalachian State Univ, 71-72; tchg fel, Harvard Univ, 70-71; prof, 81-; dean of stud (s), 74-75; dean acad aff, 76-78, 88-93, 95-96. **HONORS AND AWARDS** Graduate Prize fel, Harvard Univ, 71; Fredrik A. Schiotz fel, Cambridge Univ, 78-79; pastor, salem lutheran church, 59-61. **SELECTED PUBLICATIONS** Auth, Faith Under Fire, 80, reprint, 91; Hope for All Seasons, 88; The Message of Job, 86; Where Is God in My Praying?, 86; Where Is God in My Suffering?, 83; coauth, Chosen: The Story of God and His People, 76. **CONTACT ADDRESS** Dept of Old Testament, Luther Sem, 2481 Como Ave, Saint Paul, MN 55108. **EMAIL** dsimunds@luthersem.edu

SINCLAIR, BARBARA
DISCIPLINE POLITICAL SCIENCE **CAREER** Lectr to assoc prof, Univ Calif Riverside, 70-. **HONORS AND AWARDS** Fel, Am Polit Sci Asn, 78-79; Richard F. Fenno Prize, Am Polit Sci Asn; D.B. Hardeman Prize, Lyndon B. Johnson Found; Pres Chair, Univ Calif, 90-92, 93-96. **MEMBERSHIPS** Am Polit Sci Asn; S Polit Sci Asn; Intl Polit Sci Asn. **RESEARCH** U.S. Congress; Legislature; Women in American Politics. **SELECTED PUBLICATIONS** Auth, Legislators, Leaders and Lawmaking, Johns Hopkins Univ Press, 95; auth, Unorthodox Lawmaking: New Legislative Processes in the U.S. Congress, CQ Press, 97. **CONTACT ADDRESS** Dept Polit Sci, Univ of California, Los Angeles, 4289 Bunche, PO Box 951472, Los Angeles, CA 90095-1472. **EMAIL** sinclair@polisci.ucla.edu

SINCLAIR, SCOTT
PERSONAL Born 03/29/1950, Baltimore, MD, s **DISCIPLINE** BIBLE: SPECIALIZATION-NEW TESTAMENT **EDUCATION** Johns Hopkins Univ, BA, 71, MA, 72; Church Div School of the Pac, MDiv, 76; Grad Theol Union, PhD, 86. **CAREER** Tutor, Codrington Col, Barbados, 87-91; instr, Dominican Univ, 92- . **MEMBERSHIPS** Soc Bibl Lit; Anglican Asn Bibl Schol. **RESEARCH** Gospels, Paul, Revelation. **SELECTED PUBLICATIONS** Auth, A Study Guide to Mark's Gospel, Bibal (96); auth, The Road and the Truth: The Editing of John's Gospel, Bibal, 94; auth, Revelation-A Book for the Rest of Us, Bibal, (92). **CONTACT ADDRESS** Dept Relig & Philos, Dominican Col of San Rafael, 50 Acacia Ave, San Rafael, CA 94901-2230.

SINGER, BETH J.
PERSONAL Born 10/27/1927, New York, NY, 2 children **DISCIPLINE** PHILOSOPHY **EDUCATION** Univ Wis, BA, 49; Columbia Univ, MA, 58, PhD, 67. **CAREER** From instr to asst prof, Manhattanville Col, 66-72; asst prof, 72-73, assoc prof social insts, ideas & philos, 74-80, prof philos, Chp, 91-95, prof emer, 96, Brooklyn Col, 80-96. **HONORS AND AWARDS** Herbert W Schneider Awd Distinguished Contrib Understanding Develop Am Philos, Soc Advan Am Philos, 94. **MEMBERSHIPS** Am Philos Asn; Soc Advan Am Philos; Metaphys Soc; Charles S Peirce Soc; Concerned Philos Peace; Alain Locke Soc. **RESEARCH** History of philosophy; American philosophy; metaphysics; philosophy of human rights. **SELECTED PUBLICATIONS** Auth, The rational society: A critical study of Santayana's social thought, Case West Reserve Univ, 70; ed, Philosophy After Darwin: Chapters for the Career of Philosophy, Vol III and Other Essays by John Herman Randall, Jr, Columbia Univ, 77; Ordinal Naturalism, An Introduction to the Philosophy of Justus Buchler, Bucknell Univ, 82; ed, Antifoundationalism Old and New, Temple Univ, 92; Operative Rights, SUNY, 93; Human Nature and Community, Open Times, 97; Pragmatism, Rights, and Democracy, Fordham Univ, 98. **CONTACT ADDRESS** Dept of Philos, Brooklyn Col, CUNY, 2900 Bedford Ave, Brooklyn, NY 11210-2889. **EMAIL** 105152.1772@compuserve.com

SINGER, IRVING
PERSONAL Born 12/24/1925, New York, NY, m, 1949, 4 children **DISCIPLINE** PHILOSOPHY **EDUCATION** Harvard Univ, AB, 48, MA, 49, PhD, 52. **CAREER** Instr philos, Sage Sch Philos, Cornell Univ, 53-56; asst prof, Univ Mich, 56-59; assoc prof, 59- 69,prof philos, Mass Inst Technol, 69-, Fulbright grant, Univ Paris, 55-56; vis lectr, Johns Hopkins Univ, 57-58; Am Coun Learned Soc award, 58, grant-in-aid, 66-67; vis lectr, Mass Inst Technol, 58- 59; Bollingen award, 58-59, grant-in-aid, 65-66 & fel, 66-67; Hudson Rev fel, 58-59; Guggenheim fel, 65-66; fel, Villa I Tatti, Harvard Ctr Ital Renaissance Studies, Florence, Italy, 65-67; Rockefeller Found res grant, 70-72; vis lectr philos, Harvard Univ, 77-81. **MEMBERSHIPS** Am Philos Asn; Am Soc Aesthetics. **RESEARCH** Aesthetics; moral philosophy; philosophy of life sciences. **SELECTED PUBLICATIONS** Auth, Santayana's Aesthetics, Harvard Univ, 57; The Nature of Love: Plato to Luther, Random, 66; The Goals of Human Sexuality, Norton, 73; Mozart & Beethoven: The Concept of Love in Their Operas, Johns Hopkins Univ, 77; The Nature of Love Trilogy, Chicago Univ, 84-87; Meaning in Life: The Creation of Value, Free Press, 92; Meaning in Life Trilogy, John Hopkins Univ, 94-96; Reality Transformed: Film as Meaning and Technique, MIT, 98. **CONTACT ADDRESS** Dept of Ling & Philos, Massachusetts Inst of Tech, 77 Massachusetts Ave, E 39-351, Cambridge, MA 02139-4307. **EMAIL** pis@mit.edu

SINGER, J. DAVID
PERSONAL Born 12/07/1925, New York, NY, m, 1991, 2 children **DISCIPLINE** POLITICAL SCIENCE **EDUCATION** Duke Univ, BA, 46; NYork Univ, PhD, 56; NWestern Univ, Hon Doctor of Laws, 83. **CAREER** NY Univ, Inst, 54-55; Vassar Coll, Inst, 55-57; Univ MI, Mental Health Res Inst, Sr Sc, 61-83; Univ of Oslo, Inst for Soc Res, Fullbright Fellow, 63-64; Univ MI, Assoc Prof, 65-65; Prof of Political Sci, 65-; Carnegie Endowment and Grad Inst of Intl Studies, Geneva, 67-68; ZUMA and the Univ of Mannheim, W Germany, 67-68; Graduate Inst of Intl Studies, Geneva, 83-84; Netherlands Inst for Advanced Studies, Wassenaar, 84; Intl Inst for Peace, Vienna; Polemological Inst, Univ of Groningen, 91-. **HONORS AND AWARDS** Ford Found Iowa Seninar in Intl Relations, 56; Ford Found Training Grant, Harvard Univ, 57-58; Fullbright Res Scholar, Univ of Oslo, 63-64; Natl Sci Found Res Grant, 78-83; Phoenix Memorial Fund Res Grant, 81-82; World Soc Found Res Grant, 88-90; Lifetime Achievement Awd, APSA Conflict Process Section, 90; Natl Sci Found Res Grant, 92-94; Chair Helen Dwight Reid Awd Comm APSA, 95-96; Fulbright Res Scholar, Nat Chengchi Vair Taipei, Taiwan, 97. **SELECTED PUBLICATIONS** Peace in the Global System: Displacement,Interregnum or Transformation?, in Kegley; ed, The Long Post-War Peace, NY Harper Collins, pp56-84, 91; Toward a Behavioral Science of World Politics, in Jessor; ed, Perspectives on Behavioral Science: The Colorado Lectures, Boulder CO Westview Press, pp131-147 91; Nuclear Confrontation: Ambivalence, Rationality and the Doomsday Machine, in Bornschier and Lengyes; Formations and Values in the World System: World Society Studies, New Brunswic NJ, Transaction Publ, pp257-281, 92; Conflict Research, the Security Divemma and Learning from History, in Behavior, Culture and Conflict in World Politics, William Zimmerman and Harold K. Jacobson, Univ MI Press, pp79-92, 93; Early Warning Indicators for Cultural Groups in Danger, Journal of Ethno-Development, pp105-110, 94; Armed Conflict in the Former-Colonial Regions: From Classification to Explanation, in van der Goor et al, ed Between Development and Destruction, pp35-49, NY St Martins, 96; auth, Nations at War, Cambridge Univ Press, 98. **CONTACT ADDRESS** Dept of Polit Sci, Univ of Michigan, Ann Arbor, Ann Arbor, MI 49104-3028. **EMAIL** jdsinger@umich.edu

SINGER, JOSEPH W.
PERSONAL Born 05/23/1954, Long Branch, NJ, m, 1986, 1 child **DISCIPLINE** LAW **EDUCATION** Williams Col, BA, 76; Harvard Univ, AM, 78; JD, 81. **CAREER** Law Clerk, NJ, 81-82; Assoc Atty, Palmer & Dodge, 82-83; Prof, Boston Univ, 84-92; Prof, Harvard Law Sch, 92-. **MEMBERSHIPS** Am Asn of Law Sch. **RESEARCH** Property Law; Conflict of Laws; American Indian Law. **SELECTED PUBLICATIONS** Auth, "Sovereignty and Property", Northwestern Univ L Rev, 91; auth, "No Right to Exclude: Public Accommodations and Private Property," Northwestern Univ L Rev, 96; auth, "Rent," Boston Col L Rev, 97; auth, "Property Law: Policies, Rules and Practices," Aspen L and Bus, 97; auth, The Edges of the Field: Lessons on the Obligations of Ownership, Beacon, 00; auth, Entitlement: The Paradoxes of Property, Yale Univ Press, 00; auth, "Introduction to Property," Aspen L and Bus, 01. **CONTACT ADDRESS** Sch of Law, Harvard Univ, Cambridge, MA 02138. **EMAIL** jsinger@law.harvard.edu

SINGER, MARCUS G.
PERSONAL Born 01/04/1926, New York, NY, m, 1947, 2 children **DISCIPLINE** PHILOSOPHY **EDUCATION** Univ Illinois, AB, 48; Cornell Univ, PhD, 52. **CAREER** Asst in Philosophy, 48-49, Instr, 51-52, Cornell Univ; Instr, 52-55, Asst Prof, 55-59, Assoc Prof, 59-63, Prof, 63-92, Prof Emer, 92-, Chr, Dept Phil, 63-, Univ Wisconsin (Madison). **HONORS AND AWARDS** Western Div Fel, Amer Phil Assoc, 56-57; Guggenheim Fel, 62-63; Inst for Resarch in the Humanities Fel, 84. **MEMBERSHIPS** Amer Phil Assoc (pres, 85-86); AAUP; Royal Inst Phil; Wisconsin Acad of Sciences Arts and Letters; Sidgwick Soc; Phi Betta Kappa; Phi Kappa Phi **RESEARCH** Ethics; moral philosphy; legal philosophy; political philosophy; practical logic; American philosophy, philosophy of culture; history of ethics **SELECTED PUBLICATIONS** Auth, Generalization in Ethics, 61, 63, 75; Nineteenth Century British Ethics, 92; Institutional Ethics, 93; Presuppositions of Inference, 98. **CONTACT ADDRESS** Dept of Philosophy, Univ of Wisconsin, Madison, 600 N. Park St., Madison, WI 53706.

SINGH, MANN GURINDER
PERSONAL Born 12/10/1949, Batala, India, m, 1977, 2 children **DISCIPLINE** RELIGION **EDUCATION** MTS, Harvard Divinity Sch, 87; PhD, Relig, Columbia Univ, 93. **CAREER** Assoc prof, relig, Columbia Univ, 97-99; Dir, Columbia-UCSB in Punjab Chandigarh, 97-; Kapany prof, sikh studies, Univ Calif Santa Barbara, 99-. **MEMBERSHIPS** Amer Acad of Relig. **RESEARCH** Early Sikh manuscripts; Religion and society in the Punjab; Punjabi literature; Sikhs in the USA. **SELECTED PUBLICATIONS** Co-ed, Studying the Sikhs issues for North America, Albany, SUNY Press, 93; auth, The Goindval Pothis, Cambridge, Harvard Series, 51, 96; auth, The Making of Sikh Scripture, New York, Oxford Univ Press, 01. **CONTACT ADDRESS** Religious Studies, Univ of California, Santa Barbara, Santa Barbara, CA 93106. **EMAIL** gm7@columbia.edu

SINKLER, GEORGETTE
DISCIPLINE PHILOSOPHY **EDUCATION** Princeton Univ, BS; Cornell Univ, PhD. **CAREER** Philos Dept, Univ IL at Chicago **RESEARCH** Medieval philos; philos of relig; early mod philos. **SELECTED PUBLICATIONS** Auth, Ockham and Ambiguity, Medieval Philosophy & Theology, 94; Causal Principles, Degrees of Reality, and the Priority of the Infinite, Can Jour Philos, 89. **CONTACT ADDRESS** Philos Dept, Univ of Illinois, Chicago, 601 S Morgan Street, Chicago, IL 60607.

SINNOT-ARMSTRONG, WALTER P.
PERSONAL Born 05/01/1955, Memphis, TN, m, 1977, 2 children **DISCIPLINE** PHILOSOPHY **EDUCATION** Amherst Col, BA, 77; Yale Univ, PhD, 82. **CAREER** Prof, Dartmouth Col, 81-. **HONORS AND AWARDS** Fels, Harvard Ethics Prog, 99; Fel, Australian Nat Univ, 96; Whiting Fel, 81. **MEMBERSHIPS** Am Philos Asn. **RESEARCH** Ethics, philosophy of law, informal logic. **SELECTED PUBLICATIONS** Auth, Moral Dilemmas, 88; coauth, Understanding Arguments, 91-00; coauth, Philosophy of Law, 96. **CONTACT ADDRESS** Dept Philos, Dartmouth Col, 6035 Thorton Hall, Hanover, NH 03755-3592. **EMAIL** wsa@dartmouth.edu

SINSHEIMER, ANN M.
DISCIPLINE LEGAL REASONRY AND WRITING **EDUCATION** Univ Mich, AB, 85; MA, 86; Univ Pittsburgh, JD, 94. **CAREER** Assoc prof, Univ of Pittsburgh. **MEMBERSHIPS** Pa Bar, ABA. **RESEARCH** Writing, English as a Second Language. **SELECTED PUBLICATIONS** Coauth, Legal English: An Introduction to the Legal Language and Culture of the US. **CONTACT ADDRESS** Sch of Law, Univ of Pittsburgh, 3900 Forbes Ave, Pittsburgh, PA 15260.

SIPFLE, DAVID A.
PERSONAL Born 08/29/1932, Pekin, IL, m, 1954, 2 children **DISCIPLINE** PHILOSOPHY **EDUCATION** Carleton Col, BA, 53; Yale Univ, MA, 56, PhD, 58. **CAREER** Mem fac philos, Robert Col, Turkey, 57-58, Am Col Girls, Turkey, 57-60; from asst prof to assoc prof, 60-70, chmn dept, 68-71, Prof Philos, Carleton Col, 70-92; William H Laird prof Philos & Lib Arts, 92-98; prof Emeritus, 98-; Nat Endowment for Humanities younger humanist fel, 71- 72; Nat Sci Found fac fel, 75-76. **HONORS AND AWARDS** Bush Fac Develop Awd, Carleton Col, 81. **MEMBERSHIPS** Western Div Am Philos Asn; Metaphys Soc Am; Philos of Sci Asn. **RESEARCH** Philosophy of science; philosophy of time and space; the problem of freedom. **SELECTED PUBLICATIONS** Auth, A wager on freedom, Int Philos Quart, 6/68; Henri Bergson and the epochal theory of time, In: Bergson and the Evolution of Physics, Univ Tenn, 69; Free action and determinism, Ratio, 6/69; On the intelligibility of the epochal theory of time, In: Basic Issues in the Philosophy of Time, Open Court, 71; trans with Mary-Alie Sipble of Emile Meyerson, The Relativistic Deduction, Boston Studies in the Philosophy of Science, D Reidel, 75; Emile Meyerson, Explanation in the Sciences, Boston Studies, Kluner Academic Publishers, 85. **CONTACT ADDRESS** Dept of Philosophy, Carleton Col, 1 N College St, Northfield, MN 55057-4044. **EMAIL** david.sipfle@carleton.edu

SIRICO, LOUIS J., JR.
DISCIPLINE ADVANCED LEGAL WRITING, PROPERTY, CONSTITUTIONAL HISTORY **EDUCATION** Yale Univ, BA, 67; Univ Tex Sch Law, JD, 72. **CAREER** Prof & dir, Legal Writing Prog;Villanova Univ, 81-. **HONORS AND AWARDS** Order of the Coif; founding ed-in-ch, amer j criminal law; assoc ed, texas law rev. **MEMBERSHIPS** Dist Columbia Bar Asn; Conn Bar; bd dir, Legal Writing Inst; Asn Legal Writing Directors; ed bd, Perspectives: Tchg Legal Res and Writing; ed bd, Casenotes Publ Co; adv bd, Villanova Univ Paralegal Prog. **RESEARCH** Legal writing, constitutional law. **SELECTED PUBLICATIONS** Coauth, Legal Research; Persuasive Legal Writing for Lawyers and the Legal Profession, 95; Introduction to Legal Writing and Oral Advocacy, 2d ed, 93 & How to Talk Back to the Telephone Company: Playing the Telephone Game to Win, 79. **CONTACT ADDRESS** Law School, Villanova Univ, 800 Lancaster Ave, Villanova, PA 19085-1692. **EMAIL** sirico@law.vill.edu

SIRRIDGE, MARY
DISCIPLINE ANCIENT AND MEDIEVAL PHILOSOPHY, PHILOSOPHY OF ART **EDUCATION** St Mary's Col, Notre Dame, BA, 67; Ohio State Univ, MA, PhD, 72. **CAREER** Prof, La State Univ. **RESEARCH** Philosophy of language in ancient and medieval thought. **SELECTED PUBLICATIONS** Auth, Donkeys, Stars and Illocutionary Acts, J of Aesthet and Art Criticism; The Moral of the Story: Exemplification and the Literary Work, The Brit J of Aesthet; Can Est' Be Used Impersonality?, in Sophisms in Medieval Logic and Grammar. **CONTACT ADDRESS** Dept of Philos and Relig Stud, Louisiana State Univ and A&M Col, 106 Coates Hall, Baton Rouge, LA 70803. **EMAIL** pisirr@lsu.edu

SISK, G. C.
PERSONAL Born 05/29/1960, Des Moines, IA, m, 1981, 1 child **DISCIPLINE** LAW **EDUCATION** Montana State Univ, BA, highest honors, 81; Univ Washington, JD, highest honors, 84. **CAREER** From asst prof to prof law, Drake Univ, 91-; appeal Att'y, Karr Tuttle Campbell, 89-91; appeal staff, US Dept of Justice, 86-89; clerk, Judge R R Breezer US Circ, 85-86; legis Asst, US Senator Slade Gorton, 84-85. **HONORS AND AWARDS** Order of the Coif. **MEMBERSHIPS** ABA; APSA. **RESEARCH** Judicial decision making, litigation with the Federal Govt, legal ethics. **SELECTED PUBLICATIONS** Auth, Questioning Dialogue by Judicial Decree: A Different Theory of Constitutional Review and Moral Discourse, Rutgers L Rev, 94; Comparative Fault and Common Sense, Gonzaga L Rev, 94/95; auth, The Balkanization of the Appellate Justice: The Proliferation of Local Rules in the Federal Circuits, U CO L Rev, 97; auth, The Essentials of the Equal Access to Justice Act: Court Awards of Attorney's Fees for Unreasonable Govt Conduct, part two, LA L Rev, 95, part one 94; coauth, The Sun Sets On Federal Common Law: Corporate Successor Liability Under CERCLA After O'Melveny and Myers, VA Environ L J, 97; auth, The Balkanization of the Appellate Justice: The Proliferation of Local Rules in the Federal Circuits, U CO L Rev, 97; coauth, Charting the Influences on the Judicial Mind: An empirical Study of Judicial Reasoning, NYU L Rev, 98; auth, Stating the Obvious: Protecting Religion for Religion's Sake, Drake L Rev, 98; auth, Litigation with the Federal Government, Foundation, 00. **CONTACT ADDRESS** Law School, Drake Univ, Cartwright Hill, Des Moines, IA 50311. **EMAIL** greg.sisk@drake.edu

SISMONDO, SERGIO
DISCIPLINE PHILOSOPHY **EDUCATION** Univ Toronto, BA; MA; Cornell Univ, PhD. **CAREER** Dept Philos, Queen's Univ, 93- **RESEARCH** Philosophy of science; history and philosophy of biology; metaphysics. **SELECTED PUBLICATIONS** Auth, "The Scientific Domains of Feminist Standpoints," Perspectives on Science 3, 95: 49-65; auth, Science without Myth: On Constructions, Reality and Social Knowledge, Albany, NY: SUNY Press, 96; auth, "Deflationary Metaphysics and the Construction of Laboratory Mice" Metaphilosophy, forthcoming, 97; auth, "Reality for Cybernauts," Postmodern Culture, forthcoming 97. **CONTACT ADDRESS** Philosophy Dept, Queen's Univ at Kingston, Kingston, ON, Canada K7L 3N6. **EMAIL** sismondo@post.queensu.ca

SISSON, RUSSELL
PERSONAL Born 08/15/1959, Memphis, TN, m, 1985, 1 child **DISCIPLINE** RELIGION; PHILOSOPHY **EDUCATION** Rhodes Col, BA, 81; Yale Univ, MDiv, 84, Emory Univ, 94. **CAREER** Instr, Memphis Theological Seminary, 92; adjunct prof, Murray State Univ, 96-97; assoc prof, Union Col, 97-. **HONORS AND AWARDS** Winner John Templeton Fdn Science-Religion Course Competition, 98. **MEMBERSHIPS** Soc Biblical Lit; Amer Acad of Religion. **RESEARCH** Rhetoric and the Bible; philos of language; religion and science. **CONTACT ADDRESS** Dept of Hist, Relig, Philos, Union Col, Kentucky, 310 College St., Barbourville, KY 40906. **EMAIL** rsisson@unionky.edu

SITTSER, GERALD L.
PERSONAL Born 06/14/1950, Milwaukee, WI, w, 1971, 4 children **DISCIPLINE** THEOLOGY **EDUCATION** Hope Col, BA, 72; Fuller Theol Sem, MDiv, 75; Univ Chicago, PhD, 89. **CAREER** Assoc pastor, 75-79, Emmanuel Reformed Church, CA; chaplain, 79-85, Northwestern Col, IA; asst, assoc, full prof, relig & philos, 89-, Whitworth Col. **HONORS AND AWARDS** Most Influential Professor Awd. **RESEARCH** Religion and WW II; relig and democracy in post war Amer. **SELECTED PUBLICATIONS** Auth, The Adventure, InterVarsity Press, 85; auth, Loving Across Our Differences, InterVarsity Press, 94; auth, A Grace Disguised: How the Soul Grows Through Loss, Zondervan, 96; auth, A Cautious Patriotism: The American Churches and the Second World War, Univ of NCar Press, 97. **CONTACT ADDRESS** Dept of Relig and Philos, Whitworth Col, 300 W Hawthorne Rd, Spokane, WA 99251. **EMAIL** gsittser@whitworth.edu

SKAGGS, JIMMY M.
PERSONAL Born 06/13/1940, Gorman, TX, 3 children **DISCIPLINE** AMERICAN STUDIES, ECONOMICS **EDUCATION** Sul Ross State Col, Tex, BS, 62; Tex Tech Univ, MA, 65, PhD(hist), 70. **CAREER** From asst prof to assoc prof econ, 70-77, assoc prof Am studies, 75-77, Chmn Dept Am Studies, Wichita State Univ, 75-, Prof Am Studies & Econ, 77-. **MEMBERSHIPS** Southwestern Soc Sci Asn; Mid-Continent Am Studies Asn. **SELECTED PUBLICATIONS** Auth, Chisholm,Jesse - Ambassador Of The Plains - Hoig,S/, J Of The W, Vol 0032, 1993; The Frontier World Of Fort-Griffin - The Life And Death Of A Western Town - Robinson,C/, Pac Hist Rev, Vol 0062, 1993; Tex Crossings - The Lone Star State And The Am Far W, 1836-1986 - Lamar,Hr/, Pac Hist Rev, Vol 0062, 1993; Imagining Development - Economic Ideas In Peru Fictitious Prosperity Of Guano, 1840-1880 - Gootenberg,P/, Agricultural Hist, Vol 0069, 1995. **CONTACT ADDRESS** Dept of Am Studies, Wichita State Univ, Wichita, KS 67208.

SKAGGS, REBECCA
PERSONAL Born 01/30/1950, Berkeley, CA, m, 1995 **DISCIPLINE** PHILOSOPHY **EDUCATION** Patten Coll, Oakland, BS, 69; Holy Names Coll, Oakland, BA, 70; Wheaton Coll, MA, 72; Drew Univ, Madison, PhD, 76; Dominican School of Philos and Theol, Berkeley, MA, 90. **CAREER** Prof of New Testament, 75-, Academic Dean, 78-, Patten Coll. **HONORS AND AWARDS** Fellowship at Kierkegaard Library, St Olaf's Coll. **SELECTED PUBLICATIONS** Auth, Before the Times, Strawberry Hill Press, 80; The World of the Early Church, Edwin Mellen Press, 90; co-auth, Pentecostal Hermeneutics and Post-Modern Literary Theory, Pneuma, 94; Critical Thinking and the Christian Perspective: A Response to Baird and Soden, Faculty Dialogue, 95; The Role of Reason in Faith, paper presented at European Pentecostal-Charismatic Res Assoc, 95; Knowledge of Things Unseen, Seminar paper at International Conference for Critical Thinking at Sonoma State Univ, 96. **CONTACT ADDRESS** 2433 Coolidge Ave, Oakland, CA 94601.

SKELLY, BRIAN
PERSONAL Born 03/25/1960, Stamford, CT, m, 1985, 2 children **DISCIPLINE** PHILOSOPHY **EDUCATION** Mich St Univ, BA, 81; Rome Gregorian Univ, PhL, 84; Univ of Mass/Amherst, PhD, 91. **CAREER** Univ of Hartford, 92-; St Joseph Col, 93-. **HONORS AND AWARDS** Phi Beta Kappa; Eta Sigma Phi Classics Honor Soc. **RESEARCH** Ethics, history of philos, natural theology. **CONTACT ADDRESS** 59 Crystal Brook Dr, Springfield, MA 01118-1907. **EMAIL** brianskelly@msn.com

SKEMP, V.
PERSONAL Born 08/08/1967, La Crosse, WI, m, 1997 **DISCIPLINE** BIBLICAL STUDIES **EDUCATION** St Johns Univ, BA, 90; Catholic Univ Am, MA, 95; PhD, 99. **CAREER** Adj lectr, Georgetown Univ, 94-99; lectr, The Catholic Univ of Am, 98; asst prof, The Col of St Catherine, 99-. **HONORS AND AWARDS** Graduated cum laude, St Johns Univ, 90. **MEMBERSHIPS** Soc of Biblical Lit, The Catholic Biblical Asn of Am. **RESEARCH** Septuagint, Narrative and Literary Criticism, Reader-Response Criticism, Hermeneutics, Translation, Vulgate, Book of Revelation, Epistle to Hebrews. **SELECTED PUBLICATIONS** Auth, "Adelphos and the Theme of Kinship in Tobit," Ephemerides Theologicae Lovanienses (99), 92-103. **CONTACT ADDRESS** Dept Theol, Col of St. Catherine, 2004 Randolph Ave, PO Box 4071, Saint Paul, MN 55105-1750.

SKERIS, ROBERT A.
PERSONAL Born 05/11/1935, Sheboygan, WI **DISCIPLINE** THEOLOGY **EDUCATION** Rheinische Friedrich-Wilhelms Univ Bonn, PhD, 75. **CAREER** Prof, Pontifical Inst Sacred Music, 86-90; prof, Christendom Col, 90-. **HONORS AND AWARDS** Ordem Nacional dos Bandeirantes, 83; Order of Merit, 89, Republic of Austria; Knight of the Holy Sepulchre of Jerusalem, 95; sec head, maria laach, 78-86; pres, music asn am, 98. **MEMBERSHIPS** Church Music Asn Am; Catholic Music Assocs; Fel Catholic Scholars. **RESEARCH** Hymnology; theology of worship and of it's music. **SELECTED PUBLICATIONS** Auth, Chroma Theou, 76; auth, Crux et Cithara, 83; auth, Divini Cultus Studium, 90; auth, Cum Angellis Canere, 90. **CONTACT ADDRESS** 722 Dilllingham Ave, Sheboygan, WI 53081-6028. **EMAIL** rskeris@christendom.edu

SKIBA, PAULETTE
DISCIPLINE THEOLOGY **EDUCATION** Marquette Univ, BVM. **CAREER** Asst prof, Clarke Col. **MEMBERSHIPS** Cath Theol Soc; AAR; Soc for Buddhist-Christian Stud. **RESEARCH** Karl Rahner; systematics; liberation theol; Christian-Buddhist Studies. **CONTACT ADDRESS** Dept of Religious Studies, Clark Col, 1550 Clarke Dr, Dubuque, IA 52001. **EMAIL** pskiba@clarke.edu

SKJOLDAL, NEIL O.
DISCIPLINE RELIGION **EDUCATION** Cedarville Col, BA, 85; Bibl Theol Sem, Mdiv, 88, STM, 91; Trinity Evangelical Div Sch, PhD, 95. **SELECTED PUBLICATIONS** Article, Jour Evangelical Theol Soc; Contrib, New Int Dictionary Old Testament Theol & Exegesis. **CONTACT ADDRESS** Trinity Intl Univ, So Florida, 500 NE 1st Ave, PO Box 109674, Miami, FL 33101-9674.

SKLAR, LAWRENCE
PERSONAL Born 06/25/1938, Baltimore, MD, m, 1962, 1 child **DISCIPLINE** PHILOSOPHY **EDUCATION** Oberlin Col, BA, 58; Princeton Univ, MA, 60, PhD(philos), 64. **CAREER** From instr to asst prof philos, Swarthmore Col, 62-66; asst prof, Princeton Univ, 66-68; assoc prof, 68-74, Prof Philos, Univ Mich, Ann Arbor, 74-, Am Coun Learned Soc Study fel, 65-66; Guggenheim Found fel, 74-75. **HONORS AND AWARDS** Franklin J Matchette Prize, Am Philos Asn, 75. **MEMBERSHIPS** Am Philos Asn; Philos Sci Asn. **RESEARCH** Philosophy of physics; philosophy of science; epistemology. **SELECTED PUBLICATIONS** Auth, Types of intertheoretic reduction, Brit J Philos Sci, 8/67; The conventionality of geometry, Am Philos Quart, 1/69; Statistical explanation and Ergodic theory, Philos Sci, 6/73; Space, Time and Spacetime, Univ Calif, 74; Methodological conservatism, Philos Rev, 7/75; Inertia, graviation and metaphysics, Philos Sci, 3/76; What

might be right about the causal theory of time, Synthese, 6/77; Facts, conventions and assumptions in the theory of spacetime, Minn Studies Philos Sci, 77. **CONTACT ADDRESS** Dept of Philos, Univ of Michigan, Ann Arbor, Ann Arbor, MI 48104.

SKLAR, RICHARD LAWRENCE
PERSONAL Born 03/22/1930, New York, NY, m, 1962, 2 children **DISCIPLINE** POLITICAL SCIENCE **EDUCATION** Univ of Utah, AB, 52; Princeton Univ, MA, 57, PhD, 61. **CAREER** Asst prof, Brandeis Univ, 61-63; lectr, univ of Ibadan, 63-65; sr lectr, Univ of Zambia, 66-68; PROF, 69-94, PROF EMERITUS, UCLA, 94-. **HONORS AND AWARDS** Past pres, African Studies Asn, 81-82; UCLA Distinguished Teaching Awd, 88. **MEMBERSHIPS** African Studies Asn; Am Political Sci Asn. **RESEARCH** Developmental democracy; postimperialism; politics in Africa. **SELECTED PUBLICATIONS** Auth, Nigerian Political Parties, 63, 83; auth, Corporate Power in an African State, 75; coauth, Postimperialism, 87; coauth, African Politics and Problems in Development, 91. **CONTACT ADDRESS** Dept of Political Sci, Univ of California, Los Angeles, Los Angeles, CA 90095-1472. **EMAIL** rsklar@ucla.edu

SKLOOT, ROBERT
PERSONAL Born 07/27/1942, Brooklyn, NY **DISCIPLINE** THEATRE, DRAMA, JEWISH STUDIES **EDUCATION** Union Col, NYork, AB, 63; Cornell Univ, MA, 65; Univ Minn, Minneapolis, PhD, 68. **CAREER** Prof theatre & drama & Jewish studies, Univ of Wis-Madison, 68-, Assoc Vice-Chancellor Acad Affairs, 96-, Dir Ctr Jewish Studies, 99-; Fulbright prof theatre, Hebrew Univ, Jerusalem, Israel, 80-81, Univ Austria, Vienna, 88, Cath Univ Valparaiso, Chile, 96. **RESEARCH** Holocaust drama; British, classical and American drama; directing. **SELECTED PUBLICATIONS** Ed, The Theatre of the Holocaust: Four Plays, Univ Wis Press, 82, vol 2, 99; auth, The Darkness We Carry: The Drama of the Holocaust, Univ Wis Press, 88. **CONTACT ADDRESS** Dept of Theatre & Drama, Univ of Wisconsin, Madison, 821 University Ave, Madison, WI 53706-1497. **EMAIL** rskloot@facstaff.wisc.edu

SKOLNIKOFF, EUGENE B.
PERSONAL Born 08/29/1928, Philadelphia, PA, m, 1957, 2 children **DISCIPLINE** POLITICAL SCIENCE **EDUCATION** M.I.T., SM/SB, 50; Oxford, BA/MA, 52; M.I.T., Phd, 65 **CAREER** White House staff, 58-63; prof, M.I.T., 65-; vis lectr, Yale Univ, 97; vis res scholar, Balliol Col, 89; dir, M.I.T. Center Intl Studies, 72-87; senior consultant, White House Office Sci & Tech, 77-81. **HONORS AND AWARDS** Rhodes Scholar; Rockefeller Found Scholar; Tau Beta Pi; Eta Kappa Nu; Sigma Xi; Amer Acad Arts Sci Fel; Amer Assoc Advancement Sci Fel; Carnegie Endowment Intl Peace; Commander's Cross of the Order of Merit of the Fed Repub Germany, 86; Order of the Rising Sun, Gold Rays, Neck Ribbon, Japanese Govt, 89 **MEMBERSHIPS** Amer Assoc Advan Sci; Amer Assoc Rhodes Scholars; Amer Pol Sci Assoc; Amer Acad Arts Sci; Amer Council Germany; Coun For Rel; Fed Amer Sci; Soc Social Studies Sci; United Nations Assoc; World Assoc Int Rel **RESEARCH** Science; Technology and International Affairs; Environment; Foreign Policy; Science Policy; International Organizations **SELECTED PUBLICATIONS** Coauth, The Implementation and Effectiveness of International Environmental Commitments: Theory and Practice, MIT, 98; auth, The Elusive Transformation: Science, Technology and the Evolution of International Politics, Princeton, 93; co-ed, Visions of Apocalypse: End or Rebirth?, Holmes & Meier, 85 **CONTACT ADDRESS** Building E53-473, Cambridge, MA 02139. **EMAIL** ebskol@mit.edu

SKOVER, DAVID
PERSONAL Born 12/04/1951, Racine, WI, s **DISCIPLINE** LAW **EDUCATION** Princeton Univ, AB 74; Yale Univ Sch of Law, JD, 78. **CAREER** Law Clerk, Judge Jon O. Newman, United States Court of Appeals, Newark NJ, 78-79; Trademark Atty, Levi-Strauss Co., 79-82; asst prof, 82-85, assoc prof, 85-90, prof, Univ Puget Sound Sch of Law, 90-94; Prof, Seattle Univ Sch of Law, 94-. **HONORS AND AWARDS** Consult, Advisory Comn on Inter-Governmental Relations, 88-90; Consult and Presenter, The Inquiring Mind Program, Wash Comn for the Humanities, 90-91; Consult and Presenter, Political Philosophy in Teaching Seminar, Nat Endowment for the Humanities, 91, 93. **MEMBERSHIPS** Am Asn of Law Schs. **RESEARCH** Constitutional law; mass media theory and free speech jurisprudence; law and sexuality; First Amendment & the Internet. **SELECTED PUBLICATIONS** Coauth, Tactics of Legal Reasoning, Carolina Academic Press, 86; coauth, The Future of Liberal Legal Scholarship, 87 Mich Law Rev 601, 88; coauth, The First Amendment in the Age of Paratroopers, 68 Tex Law Rev 1087, 90; coauth, Paratexts, 44 Stanford Law Rev 509, 92; coauth, Pissing in the Snow: A Cultural Approach to the First Amendment, 45 Stanford Law Rev 783, 93; coauth, Commerce & Communications, 40 Texas Law Rev 697; 93; coauth, The Pornographic State, 107 Harvard Law Rev 1374, 94; coauth, The Death of Discourse, Westview Press/ HarperCollins, 96; coauth, Speech & Power, The Nation, 97; coauth, Comedy on Trial: Lenny Bruce's struggles for Free Speech, forthcoming, (02). **CONTACT ADDRESS** Law Sch, Seattle Univ, 900 Broadway, Seattle, WA 98122-4077. **EMAIL** davidskover@seanet.com

SKRUPSKELIS, AGNAS K.
PERSONAL Born 03/15/1938, Kaunas, Lithuania, m, 1964, 2 children **DISCIPLINE** PHILOSOPHY **EDUCATION** Fordham Univ, BS, 59; Univ Toronto, MA, 61, PhD, 67. **CAREER** Instr, 64-67, asst prof, 67-71, assoc prof, 71-77, prof, Univ SC, 77-94, Prof Emeritus, 94-. **MEMBERSHIPS** Am Philos Asn, Peirce Soc, Asn for the Advancement of Baltic Studies. **RESEARCH** William James; American philosophy. **SELECTED PUBLICATIONS** Ed, The Correspondence of William James, Univ Press of Va (92-, projected 12 vols). **CONTACT ADDRESS** Dept Philos, Univ of So Carolina, Columbia, Columbia, SC 29225.

SKYRMS, BRIAN
PERSONAL Born 03/11/1938, Pittsburgh, PA **DISCIPLINE** PHILOSOPHY OF SCIENCE, ECONOMICS **EDUCATION** Lehigh Univ, BA (Econ), 60; BA (Philos), 61; Univ Pittsburgh, MA, 62; PhD (Philos), 64. **CAREER** Asst prof, Calif State Univ-Northridge, 64-65; asst prof, Univ Del, 65-66; vis asst prof, Univ Mich, 66-67; asst prof, 67-68, assoc prof, 68-70, prof, Univ of Ill-Chicago, 70-80; prof, Univ Calif-Irvine, 80-97; prof, Econ, 97- , prof, Philos, 97- , prof, Social Sci, 99- , Univ Calif-Irvine. **HONORS AND AWARDS** Andrew Mellon Fel, Univ Pitts, 61-64; Nat Sci Found Fel, Sums 68-69, Sum 80, Fall 80, Sums 84-86, Winter 87, Sums 88-90, Sums 93-95; Dist Alum Awd for Excel, Univ Pitts, 86; Hum Coun Sr Fel & Old Dom Fel, Princeton Univ, 87, Guggenheim Fel, 87-88, Pres's Res Fel in the Hum, 93-94, Fel, Ctr for Advan Studiy in the Behav Scis, 93-94, Elected, Am Acad of Arts& Scis, 94; Elected, Nat Acad of Scis, 99; Lakatos Prize, 99; Pres, Pac Div Am Philos Asn, 00-01. **MEMBERSHIPS** Am Philos Asn; Asn for Symbolic Logic; Philos of Sci Asn; Game Theory soc; Soc for Exact Philos; Am Asn for the Advance of Sci. **RESEARCH** Philosophy of science and language; epistemology. **SELECTED PUBLICATIONS** Auth, Causal Necessity, Yale Univ Pr (New Haven), 80; auth, Pragmatics and Empiricism, Yale Univ Pr (New Haven), 84; auth, The Dynamics of Rational Deliberation, Harvard Univ Pr (Cambridge, MA), 90; co-ed, Existence and Explanation, Kluwer (Dordrecht), 91; co-ed, Probability and Conditionals, Cambridge Univ Pr (Cambridge), 94; auth, Evolution of the Social Contract, Cambridge Univ Pr (Cambridge), 96; co-ed, The Dynamics of Norms, Cambridge Univ Pr (NYork, NY), 97; co-ed, The Logic of Strategy, Oxford Univ Pr (NYork, NY), 99; co-auth, "Bargaining with Neighbors: Is Justice Contagious?" J of Philos 96 (99): 588-598; auth, "Stability and Explanatory Significance of Some Simple Evolutionary Models," Philos of Sci (Mar 00): 94-113 **CONTACT ADDRESS** Dept of Logic & Philos of Sci, Univ of California, Irvine, Irvine, CA 92697-5100. **EMAIL** bskyrms@uci.edu

SLATE, PHILIP
PERSONAL Born 10/01/1935, Louisville, KY, m, 1957, 3 children **DISCIPLINE** EUROPEAN MISSIONS, COMMUNICATION, HISTORICAL MISSIOLOGY **EDUCATION** David Lipscomb Univ, BA, 57; Harding Grad Sch, MA, 61; Oxford Univ, England, 68-71, Fuller Theological Seminary , D. Miss, 76. **CAREER** Instr, Harding Grad Sch Rel, 72-93; prof, Missions and Homiletics; dean, Graduate School of Relig, 86-92; chm, prof, Abilene Christian Univ, Dept of Missions, 93-99. **HONORS AND AWARDS** Outstanding Teacher award from Harding; Outstanding Alumus from both Harding Univ and David Lipscomb Univ. **MEMBERSHIPS** Mem, Am Soc Missiology; Evangelical Missiological Soc; Evangelical Theol Soc. **SELECTED PUBLICATIONS** Auth, Perspectives on Worldwide Evangelism, Resource Publ, 88; co-auth, Reaching Russia, ACU Press, 94; articles, Culture Concept and Hermeneutics: Quest to Identify the Permanent in Early Christianity. Encounter 53, 92; The Deceiving Nature of Adaptation in E-1 Situations, J Applied Missiology 3, 95; Two Features of Irenasus' Missiology. Missiology 23, 96; auth, "Irenaeus" in Biographical Dictionary of Christian Missions; numerous articles. **CONTACT ADDRESS** Dept of Missions, Abilene Christian Univ, 822 Bradford Place, Murfreesboro, TN 37130. **EMAIL** slate@bible.acu.edu

SLATER, PETER
PERSONAL Born 03/24/1934, Newcastle-upon-Tyne, England **DISCIPLINE** THEOLOGY **EDUCATION** McGill Univ, BA, 54; Queen's Col Cambridge, BA, 57, MA, 61; Harvard Univ, PhD, 64. **CAREER** Asst prof relig, Haverford Col, Pa, 64-70; assoc prof relig, Sir George Williams Univ, Montreal, 70-71; assoc to full prof relig, Carleton Univ, 71-82; prof theol, Wycliffe Col, 82-85; prof theol, Toronto Sch Theol Grad Fac, 82-, prof, Centre Relig Stud, 83-, dean divinity, Trinity Col, 85-90, Prof Emer Systematic Theol, Trinity Col, Toronto Sch Theol, Univ Toronto; Adj Prof General Theol, Seminary New York 95-98. **HONORS AND AWARDS** Gold Medal Philos McGill, 54; Harvard Prize Fel, 57. **MEMBERSHIPS** Can Soc Stud Relig; Am Acad Relig; Soc Values Higher Educ; Am Theol Soc; N Am Paul Tillich Soc; Am Soc Stud Relig; Can Theol Soc. **SELECTED PUBLICATIONS** Auth, The Dynamics of Religion and Culture in Canada, 77; co-ed, Traditions in Contact and Change, 83; co-ed, Toronto Journal of Theology, 85-94. **CONTACT ADDRESS** General Theol Sem, 175 9th Ave, New York, NY 10011-4977.

SLATTERY, KENNETH F.
PERSONAL Born 06/12/1921, Brooklyn, NY **DISCIPLINE** PHILOSOPHY **EDUCATION** Cath Univ Am, MA, 50, PhD, 52. **CAREER** Instr Greek & Ger, St Joseph's Col, NJ, 48-49; instr Philos, Cath Univ Am, 49-52; assoc prof, Niagara Univ, 52-54; dean students, Mary Immaculate Sem, 54-56; asst prof Philos, St John's Univ, NY, 56-61; dean grad sch & sch educ, Niagara Univ, 61-65, pres, 65-76; vpres Commun, St John's Univ, 76-79, acad vpres, St John's Univ, Staten Island Campus, 79-,; mem bd trustees, Cardinal Newman Col, St Louis, 79-85, Molloy Col, Hempstead, NY, 81-99. **HONORS AND AWARDS** LLD, St John's Univ, NY, 69; DH, Cath Univ PR, 77. **MEMBERSHIPS** Am Cath Philos Asn; Fel Cath Scholars. **RESEARCH** Philosophical psychology. **SELECTED PUBLICATIONS** Auth, The Necessity for God for a Complete Psychological Understanding of the Nature of Man, 50 & The Virtue of Temperance & Its Relation to the Emotions, 52, Cath Univ Am Press. **CONTACT ADDRESS** St. John's Univ, 8150 Utopia Pky, Jamaica, NY 11439-0002. **EMAIL** slatterk@stjohns.edu

SLAVIN, STEPHEN L.
PERSONAL Born 07/29/1939, Brooklyn, NY, s **DISCIPLINE** ECONOMICS **EDUCATION** New York Univ, PhD 73. **CAREER** Dept Econ, Union Col **MEMBERSHIPS** AEA **SELECTED PUBLICATIONS** Auth, The Einstein Syndrome: Corporate Anti-Semitism in America Today, UP of America, 82; auth, Jelly Bean Economics, Phlisophical Library, 84; auth, Economics: A Self-Teaching Guide, Wiley, 88; coauth, Practical Algebra, with Peter Selby, Wiley, 91; Quick Algebra Review, with Peter Selby, Wiley, 92; auth, Chances Are: The Only Statistics Book You'll Ever Need, UP of Amer, 98; Math Essentials, Learning Express, Random House, 98; Math For Your First and Second Grader, Wiley, 95; Quick Business Math, Wiley, 95; coauth, Precalculus with Ginny Crisonino, Wiley, 01; auth, Economics, Mc-Graw-Hill, 6th ed, 01. **CONTACT ADDRESS** Dept of Economics, Union Col, New York, 564 Marlborough RD, Brooklyn, NY 11226.

SLAWSON, W. DAVID
DISCIPLINE ADMINISTRATIVE LAW **EDUCATION** Amherst Col, AB,53; Princeton Univ, MA,54; Harvard Univ, LLB,59. **CAREER** Torrey H. Webb prof;Univ Southern Calif; past asst coun, Presidential Comn on the Assassination of President Kennedy; gen coun, US Price Comn; private practice, Colo. **MEMBERSHIPS** Phi Beta Kappa; Sigma Xi; Order of the Coif; Chair, Section on Contracts, American Association of Law Schools (AALS), 1989; Member, Planning Committee, AALS Conference on the Teaching of Contracts, 1988. **RESEARCH** Antitrust Law, Contracts, and Insurance.. **SELECTED PUBLICATIONS** Auth, Binding Promises: The Late 20th Century Reformation of Contract Law; The New Inflation: The Collapse of Free Markets & The New Meaning of Contract: The Transformation of Contract Law by Standard Forms. **CONTACT ADDRESS** School of Law, Univ of So California, University Park Campus, Los Angeles, CA 90089-0071.

SLEIGH, ROBERT COLLINS
PERSONAL Born 11/30/1932, Marblehead, MA, m, 1953, 3 children **DISCIPLINE** PHILOSOPHY **EDUCATION** Dartmouth Col, BA, 54; Brown Univ, MA, 57, PhD, 63. **CAREER** From instr to assoc prof, Wayne State Univ, 58-69; prof, Univ of Mass, 69- ; vis prof, Univ of Mich, 73; Univ of Ariz, 84; Univ of Calif, 89; Univ of Notre Dame, 90; Amherst Col, 97; Harvard Univ, 97-98. **HONORS AND AWARDS** Fel, Ctr for Advan Study in the Behavioral Scis, 67-68; Inst for Advan Study, 82-83, 86-87; Am Coun of Learned Socs, 75-76, 67-68; NEH, 91-92. **MEMBERSHIPS** APA; AHA; Leibniz Soc of North Am. **RESEARCH** Early Modern Philos; Leibniz. **SELECTED PUBLICATIONS** On Quantifying into Epistemic Contexts, Nous I, 67; Restricted Range in Epistemic Logic, The Jour of Philos, 72; Truth and the Principle of Sufficient Reason in the Philosophy of Leibniz, Leibniz: Critical and Interpretive Essays, ed M. Hooker, 82; Leibniz on Malebranche on Causality, Central Themes in Early Modern Philos: Essays presented to J. Bennett, 90; Leibniz and Arnauld: A Commentary on their Correspondence, 90; Leibniz on Divine Foreknowledge, Faith and Philos, vol 11, 94; coauth, Determinism and Human Freedom, The Cambridge Hist of 17th Century Philos, ed V. Chappell, 98. **CONTACT ADDRESS** Dept of Philosophy, Univ of Massachusetts, Amherst, Amherst, MA 01003.

SLINGERLAND, DIXON
PERSONAL Born 11/05/1943, Nunda, NY, w, 3 children **DISCIPLINE** NEW TESTAMENT **EDUCATION** Tufts Univ, BA, 66; Lutheran Sch Theology Chicago, MDiv, 69; Union Theol Sem, PhD, 73. **CAREER** Tutor asst, Union Theol Sem, 70-72; pastor, St Jacobi Lutheran Ch, Brooklyn, 73-79; instr, Wagner col, 77-78; vis prof, Brite Div Sch, 85; prof, Hiram Col, 79-. **HONORS AND AWARDS** Summer res grant, Hiram Col, 87, 89, 94, 96; Middle Eastern Studies Res grant, Hiram Col, fall 93; Lilly Endowment Grant, Hiram Col, 91-92; res grant, Institutum Judaicum, Tubingen Univ, 72-73. **MEMBERSHIPS** Am Acad of Religion; Am Asn of Univ Profs; Evangelical Lutheran Church in Am; Garfield Soc of Hiram Col; Phi Beta Kappa Soc; Soc of Biblical Lit. **RESEARCH** Old Testament/ Hebrew Scriptures; Apocrypha and Pseudepigrapha; Hellenistic

Judaism; Greco-Roman Religiosity; New Testament and Christian origins. **SELECTED PUBLICATIONS** Auth, "Suetonius Claudius 25.4 and the Account in Cassius Dio," Jewish Quarterly Review 79 (89): 305-322; auth, Acts 18:1-17 and Luedemann's Pauline Chronology," Journal of Biblical Literature 109 (90): 687-691; auth, "Acts 18:1-18, the Gallio Inscription and Absolute Pauline Chronology," Journal of Biblical Literature 110 (91): 439-449; auth, "Suetonius Claudius 25.4, Acts 18 and Paulus Orosius' Historiarum adversum paganos libri VII: Dating the Claudian Expulsion(s) of Roman Jews," Jewish Quarterly Review 83 (92): 127-144; auth, review, "Jarl Henning Ulrichsen's Die Grundschrift der testamente der Zwolf Patriarchen: Eine Untersuchung zu Umfang, Inhalt und Eigenart der ursprunglichen Schrift," Critical Review of Books in Religion (93): 185-187; auth, review, "Maren Niehoff's The Figure of Joseph in Post-Biblical Jewish Literature," Ioudaios Review 3.011 (93); auth, Claudian Policymaking and the Early Imperial Repression of Judaism at Rome, South Florida Studies in the History of Judaism 140, Scholars Press (Atlanta), 97; auth, "Blaming the Victims: Modern Historiography on the Early Imperial Mistreatment of Roman Jews," forthcoming; auth, "Pagan Reconstruction of Judaism from 70 CE," in Judaism from Moses to Muhammed, ed. Jacob Neusner, et al. (The Brill Library of Ancient Judaism, Leiden, forthcoming). **CONTACT ADDRESS** Dept of Relig Stud, Hiram Col, PO Box 67, Hiram, OH 44234. **EMAIL** slingerlandh@hiram.edu

SLOBOGIN, CHRISTOPHER
DISCIPLINE LAW **EDUCATION** Princeton Univ, AB; Univ Va, JD, LLM. **CAREER** Stephen C. O' Connell ch, assoc dean for fac develop, aff prof psychiat, Univ Fla, 82-. **HONORS AND AWARDS** Alumni res scholar, 94-; Professional Excellence Award, 99. **MEMBERSHIPS** Ch, Asn Amer Law Schools Criminal Justice Sect; past ch, AALS Sect on Law Mental Disability. **RESEARCH** Law & psychiatry, criminal law & procedure, evidence, professional responsibility, social science & law. **SELECTED PUBLICATIONS** Auth, Regulation of Police Investigation and Criminal Procedure: An Analysis of Cases and Concepts; coauth, Psychological Evaluations for the Court; coauth, Law & the Mental Health System: Civil and Criminal Aspects, 3rd ed., 99; coauth, Criminal Procedure: An Analysis of Cases and Concepts, 4th ed., 00. **CONTACT ADDRESS** School of Law, Univ of Florida, PO Box 117625, Gainesville, FL 32611-7625. **EMAIL** slobogin@law.ufl.edu

SLOCUM, ROBERT B.
PERSONAL Born 05/21/1952, Macon, GA, m, 1982, 3 children **DISCIPLINE** THEOLOGY **EDUCATION** Vanderbilt Univ, BA, 74; JD, 77; Nashotah House Sem, MDiv, 86; Univ of the South, DMin, 92; Marquette Univ, PhD, 97. **CAREER** Judge Advocate, US Air Force, 78-83; Parish Ministry, 86-92; Rector, Lake Geneva, 93-; lectr, Marquette Univ, 97-. **MEMBERSHIPS** Am Acad of Relig; AAUP; Col Theol Soc; Soc of Anglican and Lutheran Theol; Soc for the Study of Christian Spirituality. **SELECTED PUBLICATIONS** Auth, "Reflections of a Peacetime Veteran", Mil Chaplains' Rev (88): 71-73; auth, "Justification: Stumbling Block for Anglican-Roman Catholic Unity?", St Luke's J of Theol 32.3 (89): 169-180; auth, "The Ark and the Rainbow, A Children's pageant for Holy Week", Living Church, (90): 12-13; coed, Documents of Witness, A History of the Episcopal Church, 1782-1985, Church Hymnal Corp, 94; auth, "Romantic Religion in Wisconsin: James DeKoven and Charles C Grafton", Anglican and Episcopal Hist 65.1 (96): 82-111; auth, "The Chicago-Lambeth Quadrilateral: Development in an Anglican approach to Christian Unity", J of Ecumenical Studies 33.4 (96): 471-486; ed, Prophet of Justice, Prophet of Life, Essays on William Stringfellow, Church Pub Inc, (NY), 97; ed, A New Conversations, Essays on the Future of Theology and the Episcopal Church, Church Pub Inc, (NY), 99; auth, "Finding Consensus", The Living Church, (99): 15-16; auth, The theology of William Porcher DuBose: Life, Movement, and Being, Univ of SC Pr, (forthcoming). **CONTACT ADDRESS** Dept Theol, Marquette Univ, PO Box 1881, Milwaukee, WI 53201-1881. **EMAIL** rbslocum@genevaonline.com

SLOYAN, GERARD
PERSONAL Born 12/13/1919, New York, NY, s **DISCIPLINE** RELIGION **EDUCATION** Seton Hall Univ, AB, 40; Cath Univ Am, STL, 44; PhD, 48. **CAREER** Instr, Cath Univ of Am, 50-67; prof, Temple Univ, 67-90; Distinguished Prof Lectr, Cath Univ of Am, 92-; Georgetown Univ, 97-. **HONORS AND AWARDS** John Courtney Murray Awd; Johannes Quastern Awd; Berakah Awd. **MEMBERSHIPS** Cath Bible Assoc of Am; Soc of Bible Lit; Cath Theol Soc of Am; Col Theol Soc; Am Theol Soc; N Am Acad of Liturgy. **RESEARCH** New Testament and Patristic Thought, A.D. 100-600. **SELECTED PUBLICATIONS** Auth, The Crucifixion of Jesus. History, Myth, Faith, Fortress (Minneapolis), 95; auth, Walking in the Truth, Perseverers and Deserters. 1, 2 and 3 Johns, Trinity Pr Int, (Valley Forge, PA), 95. **CONTACT ADDRESS** Dept Relig and Relig Educ, Catholic Univ of America, 620 Michigan Ave NE, Washington, DC 20064-0001. **EMAIL** cua-religed@cua.edu

SLUSSER, MICHAEL
DISCIPLINE THEOLOGY **EDUCATION** Catholic Univ Belgium, STB 66; Univ Oxford, D. Phil 75. **CAREER** Univ St. Thomas MN, 68-81, 85-87; Catholic Univ, 81-85; Duquesne Univ, 87-. **MEMBERSHIPS** SBL; CTSA; NAPS; AIEP; CTS. **SELECTED PUBLICATIONS** Auth, St. Gregory Thaumaturgus: Life and Works, WA, Catholic U of Amer Press 98. **CONTACT ADDRESS** Dept of Theology, Duquesne Univ, Pittsburgh, PA 15282. **EMAIL** slusser@duq.edu

SMALL, KENNETH ALAN
PERSONAL Born 02/09/1945, Sodus, NY, m, 1968, 1 child **DISCIPLINE** ECONOMICS **EDUCATION** Univ of Calif at Berkeley, PhD, 76. **CAREER** Asst prof, Princeton Univ, 76-83; ASSOC PROF TO PROF, UNIV OF CALIF AT IRVINE, 83-. **HONORS AND AWARDS** Gilbert White Fellow, Resources for the Future, 99-00; Distinguished Member Awd, Transportation and Public Utilities Group, American Economic Assoc, 99. **MEMBERSHIPS** Am Economic Asn; Econometric Soc; Royal Economic Soc; Transportation Res Board; Regional Sci Asn Int; Am Real Estate & Urban Economics Asn; Assoc of Environmental and Resource Economists. **RESEARCH** Urban economics; transportation economics; environmental economics. **SELECTED PUBLICATIONS** Auth, Approximate Generalized Extreme Value Models of Discrete Choice, J of Econometrics, 94; auth, Urban Transportation Economics, Harwood Acad Pub, 92; co-ed, Transport Economics: Selected Readings, Harwood Acad Pub, 97; coauth, Environment and Transport in Economic Modelling, Kluwer Acad Press, 98; coauth, The Economics of Traffic Congestion, Am Scientist, 94; coauth, Urban Spatial Structure, J of Economic Lit, 98; coauth, Urban Transportation, Handbook of Regional and Urban Economics, North-Holland, forthcoming. **CONTACT ADDRESS** Dept of Economics, Univ of California, Irvine, Irvine, CA 92697-5100. **EMAIL** ksmall@uci.edu

SMALL, LAWRENCE FARNSWORTH
PERSONAL Born 12/30/1925, Bangor, ME, m, 1947, 4 children **DISCIPLINE** HISTORY, POLITICAL SCIENCE **EDUCATION** Univ Maine, BA, 48, MA, 51; Bangor Theol Sem, BD, 48; Harvard Univ, PhD, 55. **CAREER** Asst minister, All Souls Church, Lowell, Mass, 50-52 & First Congregational Church, Winchester, Mass, 52-55; minister, Paramus Congregational Church, NJ, 55-59; assoc prof hist & polit sci, 59-61, dean & registr, 61-65, actg pres, 65-66, Prof Hist, Rocky Mountain Col, 61-, Pres, 66-75, retired, 90. **HONORS AND AWARDS** D.H.L. hon. Rocky Mountain Col. **MEMBERSHIPS** AHA; Am Polit Sci Asn. **RESEARCH** American intellectual and religious history, especially Unitarianism and Fundamentalism. **SELECTED PUBLICATIONS** Ed & contribr, History of Religion in Montana, 2 vols; Trails Revisited, The Story of the Montana/Northern Wyoming Conference, U.C.C.; A Century of Politics on the Yellowstone, Journey With the Law, the Life of Judge William J. Jameson; Montana Passage, A Homesteader's Heritage; Courageous Journey, the Road to Rocky Mountain College. **CONTACT ADDRESS** 7320 Sumatra Pla, Billings, MT 59102.

SMALLS, O'NEAL
PERSONAL Born 09/07/1941, Myrtle Beach, SC **DISCIPLINE** LAW **EDUCATION** Tuskegee Inst, BS 1964; Harvard Law Sch, JD 1967; Georgetown Univ, LLM 1975. **CAREER** Amer Univ, assoc prof 1969-76; Systems & Applied Sci Corp, bd of dirs, 74-85; George Washington Univ Sch of Law, prof law 1976-79; American Univ, prof of law 1979-88; Univ of SC School of Law, professor, 88-. **MEMBERSHIPS** Mem Harvard Law Sch Res Com 1966-67; asst dir Harvard Law Sch Summer Prog for Minority Students 1966; dir of admissions & chmn of Com Admissions & Scholarships Amer Univ 1970-74; mem DC, Natl, Amer Bar Assns; chmn bd dir Skyanchor Corp; exec bd DC Bapt Conv; Services Com & bd trustees Law Sch Admissions Coun Princeton 1972-76; adv com Leg Serv Plan Laborers' Dist coun of Washington DC 1973-75; bd dir Systems & Applied Sci Corp 1974-85; bd chmn, Frewood Foundation, 1987-; Freedoms Foundation, pres/chair of bd, Myrtle Beach, SC, currently. **SELECTED PUBLICATIONS** Articles "Class Actions Under Title VII" Amer Univ Law Review 1976; "The Path & The Promised Land" Amer Univ Law Review 1972; booklets "New Directions, An Urban Reclamation Program for the Dist of Columbia" July 1982; "Manhood Training An Introduction to Adulthood for Inner City Boys Ages 11-13" April 1985. **CONTACT ADDRESS** Professor of Law, Univ of So Carolina, Columbia, Columbia, SC 29208.

SMALLWOOD, JAMES MILTON
PERSONAL Born 07/10/1944, Terrell, TX, m, 2 children **DISCIPLINE** HISTORY, POLITICAL SCIENCE **EDUCATION** ETex State Univ, BS, 67, MA, 69; Tex Tech Univ, PhD(hist, polit sci), 74. **CAREER** Instr hist, ETex State Univ, 67-69, Southeastern Okla State Univ, 69-70 & Tex Tech Univ, 70-74; dir Will Rogers Res Proj, 76-81, Prof Hist, Okla State Univ, 75-, Consult, Okla Humanities Coun & Okla Heritage Asn, 77-. **MEMBERSHIPS** AHA; Orgn Am Historians; Southern Hist Asn; Western Hist Asn. **RESEARCH** Recent United States history; Southern United States history; Civil War, Reconstruction. **SELECTED PUBLICATIONS** Auth, And Gladly Teach, Univ Okla, 76; Blacks in Reconstruction Texas, ETex Hist J, 76; Disaffection in Confederate Texas, Civil War Hist, 76; Urban Builder: The Life and Times of Stanley Draper, Univ Okla, 77; Black self-help and education in Reconstruction Texas, Bull Negro Hist, 78; Banquo's ghost and the Paris Peace Conference, East Europ Quart, 78; Will Rogers's Daily Telegrams (4 vols), Okla State Univ, 78; Time of Hope, Time of Despair: Black Texans During Reconstruction, Kennikat Press, 81. **CONTACT ADDRESS** Dept of Hist, Oklahoma State Univ, Stillwater, Stillwater, OK 74074.

SMART, NINIAN
PERSONAL Born 05/06/1927, Cambridge, United Kingdom, m, 1954, 4 children **DISCIPLINE** HISTORY, PHILOSOPHY **EDUCATION** Oxford Univ, BA, 51, B Phil, 54. **CAREER** Univ of Wales, 52-55; Univ of London, 56-61; Chair, Univ of Birmingham, 61-67; Lancaster Univ, 67-89; Univ of Calif Santa Barbara, 77-99. **HONORS AND AWARDS** Honorary Doctorates from Chicago Loyola Univ, Glasgow Univ, Sterling Univ, Kelamya Univ, Lancaster Univ. **MEMBERSHIPS** AAR; ASSR; BSRS; Aristotelian Soc. **RESEARCH** Philosophy of Religion, Comparative Study of Religion, Indian Religions, Chinese Religions, Religion and Politics. **SELECTED PUBLICATIONS** Auth, Religions and Faith, 58, 00; auth, The World's Religions, 88, 97; auth, Dimensions of Religions, 97; auth, World Philosophies, 99. **CONTACT ADDRESS** Dept Relig Studies, Univ of California, Santa Barbara, 552 University Rd, Santa Barbara, CA 93106-0002.

SMAW, ERIC
PERSONAL Born 01/22/1971, Washington, DC, s **DISCIPLINE** PHILOSOPHY; ETHICS; LAW **EDUCATION** Penn State Univ, BA, 96; Univ KY, MA, 01. **CAREER** Logic instr, Phil of Law. **RESEARCH** Legal ethics; Intl law. **CONTACT ADDRESS** Philosophy Dept, 1415 Patterson Office Tower, Lexington, KY 40506-0027. **EMAIL** edsmaw0@pop.uky.edu

SMILLOV, MARIN S.
PERSONAL Born 01/27/1963, Targovishte, Bulgaria, m, 1997, 1 child **DISCIPLINE** PHILOSOPHY **EDUCATION** Univ FL, PhD, 97. **CAREER** Vis Prof, Univ Central FL, 96-; Vis Lect, Univ FL, 98-. **MEMBERSHIPS** Am Philos Asn; FL Philos Asn. **RESEARCH** Epistemology; metaphysics; philos of mind; ethics; social and political philos. **CONTACT ADDRESS** 6914 SW 80th Dr., Gainesville, FL 32608. **EMAIL** msmillov@aol.com

SMIT, HANS
PERSONAL Born 08/13/1927, Amsterdam, Netherlands, m, 1954, 2 children **DISCIPLINE** LAW **EDUCATION** Univ Amsterdam, LLB, 46, JD, 49; Columbia Univ, AM, 53, LLB, 58. **CAREER** Attorney, The Hague, Netherlands, 49-56, Sullivan & Cromwell, 59-60; prof law, 60-78, Stanley H Fuld Prof Law, Columbia Univ, 78-, Reporter, US Comt on Int Rules of Judicial Procedure, 60-68; dir proj in int procedure & proj on Europ legal insts, Columbia Univ Summer Prog in Am Law, Leyden & Amsterdam, 62-; adv, US Deleg to UN Comn on Int Trade Law, 71-; vis prof int-nat com law, Univ Paris I, Sorbonne-Pantheon, 76-77; dir, Parker Sch Foreign & Comparative Lang, 80- **MEMBERSHIPS** Am Foreign Law Asn; Int Bar Asn; Int Fiscal Asn; Neth Bar Asn. **RESEARCH** Civil Procedure; international law; international procedure. **SELECTED PUBLICATIONS** Coauth, International Cooperation in Litigation, M Nijhoff, The Hague, 65; Elements of Civil Procedure, Foundation, 70 & International Business Transaction in the Common Market, 72, Columbia Law Sch; auth, Smit & Herzog, Commentary on the EEC Treaty, (6 vols), Matthew Bender, 77; coauth, Henkin, Pugh, Schachter & Smit, Int Law, 81. **CONTACT ADDRESS** 435 W 116th St, Box 4435, New York, NY 10027-7201.

SMITH, BARDWELL L.
PERSONAL Born 07/28/1925, Springfield, MA, m, 1961, 5 children **DISCIPLINE** RELIGIOUS TRADITIONS OF ASIA **EDUCATION** Yale Univ, BA, BD, PhD. **CAREER** Religion, Carleton Univ. **HONORS AND AWARDS** Phi Beta Kappa; magna cum laude (Yale, BA; Yale, BD); fel, Am Coun of Learned Societies, 72-73; Fulbright fel, 86-87; collaborative res grant, Nat Endowment for the Humanities, 91-94. **MEMBERSHIPS** Am Academy of Religion; Asn of Asian Studies; Am Soc for the Study of Religion. **RESEARCH** Buddhism and soc in Sri Lanka and Japan; Buddhist pilgrimages; Japanese gardens; Japanese women and child loss. **SELECTED PUBLICATIONS** Auth, The Two Wheels of Dhamma, 72; auth, Unsui: A diary of Zen Monastic Life, 73; auth, The Tenure Sabare, 73; auth, Essays on T'ang Soc: The Interpaly of Social, Political and Economic Forces, 76; auth, Religion and the Legitimation of Power in Sri Lanka, 78; auth, Essays on Qupta Culture, 83; auth, ed, The City as a Sacred Complex, 87; auth, Warlords, Artists, Commoners: Japan in the Sixteenth Century, 81. **CONTACT ADDRESS** Carleton Col, 100 N College St., Northfield, MN 55057. **EMAIL** bsmith@carleton.edu

SMITH, BARRY
PERSONAL Born 06/04/1952, Bury, England **DISCIPLINE** MATHEMATICS & PHILOSOPHY **EDUCATION** Oxford Univ, BA, 73, MA, 77; Manchester Univ, PhD, 76. **CAREER**

Res fel, Univ Sheffield, 76-79; lectr, Univ Manchester, 79-89; prof, int acad philos, liechtenstein, 89-93; prof, SUNY Buffalo, 93-; Res Sci, Nat Ctr geog infor & anal, 96-. **HONORS AND AWARDS** Alexander von Humboldt fel, 84-85. **MEMBERSHIPS** Amer Philos Soc **RESEARCH** Metaphysics; Austrian philosophy; Husserl. **SELECTED PUBLICATIONS** Ed, Philosophy and Political Change in Eastern Europe, Hegeler Inst, 93; auth, Austrian Philosophy: The Legacy of Franz Brentano, Open Court, 94; ed, European Philosophy and the American Academy, The Hegeler Inst, 94; coed, The Cambridge Campanion to Husserl, Cambridge Univ Press, 95; auth, Formal Ontology, Common Sense, and Cognitive Science, Int Jour Human-Computer Studies, 95; auth, More Things in Heaven and Earth, Grazer Philos Studien, 95; Mereotopology: A Theory of Parts and Boundaries, Data and Knowledge Engineering, 96; On Substances, Accidents and Universals: In Defence of a Constituent Ontology, Philos Papers, 97. **CONTACT ADDRESS** Dept of Philosophy, SUNY, Buffalo, 607 Baldy Hall, Buffalo, NY 14260-1010. **EMAIL** phismith@buffalo.edu

SMITH, BRIAN H.
PERSONAL Born 08/01/1940, Freeport, NY, m, 1980, 2 children **DISCIPLINE** POLITICAL SCIENCE **EDUCATION** Fordham Univ, Ab, 64; Woodstock Col, Mdiv, 70; Union Theolog Sem, STM, 71; Yale Univ, PhD, 79. **CAREER** From asst prof to assoc prof, MIT, 80-87; prof, Ripon Col, 87-. **HONORS AND AWARDS** Outstanding Acad Book; Best Prof Book; Catholic Press Asn. **MEMBERSHIPS** Latin Am Stud Asn; Am Acad Relig. **RESEARCH** Religion and politics, NGO's and development in Latin Am. **SELECTED PUBLICATIONS** Auth, art, Non governmental Organisations in International Development: Trends and Future Research Priorities, 93; auth, art, Religion and Politics: A New Look Through an Old Prism, 95; coauth, The Catholic Church and Democracy in Chile and Peru, 97; auth, art, Nongovernmental Organizations, 98; auth, Religious Politics in Latin America, Pentecostal vs. Catholic, 98. **CONTACT ADDRESS** Dept of Religion, Ripon Col, Ripon, WI 54971-0248. **EMAIL** smithb@mail.ripon.edu

SMITH, CHARLES EDISON
DISCIPLINE LAW **EDUCATION** California Polytechnic, BS, 1965; Georgetown University, Washington, DC, JD, 1972; Duke University, LLM, 1983. **CAREER** US Patent and Trademark Office, Washington, DC, Patent Examiner, 67-69; Xerox Corp, Patent Attorney, 72-75; Bechtel Corp, Patent Attorney, 75-78; Golden Gate University, Assistant Professor of Law, 77-79; Con Edison, Consultant, 87-; North Carolina Central University School of Law, Durham, NC, Professor, currently. **HONORS AND AWARDS** Fellowship Grant, Duke University, 1982-83; American Jurisprudence Awd, Lawyers Cooperative Publishers. **MEMBERSHIPS** Arbitrator, American Bar Assn, 1979-, state reporter (NC), ABA Limited Partnership Laws, 1986-; member, Delta Theta Phi Law Fraternity, 1970-; commissioner, North Carolina Statutes Commission, 1987-; attorney volunteer, AIPLA Inventor Consulting Service, 1985-; state reporter (NC), ABA Limited Liability Company Act, 1993-. **CONTACT ADDRESS** Professor of Law, No Carolina Central Univ, 1512 S Alston Ave, Durham, NC 27707.

SMITH, CINDY J.
DISCIPLINE CRIMINOLOGY **CAREER** Program Coordinator, Ohio State Univ, 86-87; Teacher, Otto A Fischer School, 90-95; consultant, Rand, 93-96; Vis Lecturer, St Louis Mo, 96; Asst Prof, Univ Ill, 96-98; Asst Prof, Univ Baltimore, 98-. **HONORS AND AWARDS** Service Excellence Awd, Orange County Probation Dept, 93; Appreciation of Service, Orange County Probation Dept, 95; Certificate of Recognition Outstanding Efforts with Students with Disabilities, Univ Mo, 96. **MEMBERSHIPS** Am Soc of Criminol, Acad of Criminal Justice Sci, Asn for the Treatment of sexual Abusers, Am correctional Asn, Nat org for the Treatment of Abuser. **RESEARCH** Juvenile sex offender typology, treatment, and legal interventions; Program evaluation; implementation, process an outcome evaluation; Gender issues in juvenile justice. **SELECTED PUBLICATIONS** Auth, The Illinois Department of Corrections' Juvenile Sex Offender Treatment program: The Final Report of the Program Evaluation, in press; auth, A Juvenile Sex Offender Typology: Feasibility Study of File Data Collection, Washington, 99; auth, A Comprehensive Bibliography of Scholarly Research and Literature Relating to Juvenile Sex Offenders, Washington, 99; auth, An Implementation Evaluation of the Pretrial and Drug Intervention Programs in Illnois; Macon and Peoria Counties, Chicago, 98. **CONTACT ADDRESS** Dept Criminol, Univ of Baltimore, 1420 N Charles St, Baltimore, MD 21201. **EMAIL** cjsmith@ubmail.ubalt.edu

SMITH, D. MOODY
PERSONAL Born 11/21/1931, Murfreesboro, TN, m, 1954, 4 children **DISCIPLINE** RELIGION, NEW TESTAMENT **EDUCATION** Davidson Coll, BA, 54; Duke Univ, BD, 57; Yale Univ, MA, 58, PhD, 61. **CAREER** Asst prof, New Testament, Meth Theol Sch, 60-65; assoc prof New Testament, 65-70, prof New Testament, 70-87, dir grad stud rel, 74-80, George Washington Ivey Prof New Testament, 87-, Div Sch, Duke Univ; Pres, Soc bib Lit, 99. **HONORS AND AWARDS** Lilly fel, 63-64; Guggenheim fel, 70-71; Asn Theol Schs fel, 77-78; res mem, Ctr Theol Inquiry, 90, 91; Scholar/Teacher of the Year, Duke Univ, 93; Dist Alumni, Duke Div Sch, 93. **MEMBERSHIPS** Soc Bib Lit; Studiorum Novum Testamentum Soc, Am Theol Soc, Ctr Theol Inquiry. **RESEARCH** New Testament hist, exegesis, theol; gospels and letters of John; hist New Testament crit. **SELECTED PUBLICATIONS** Auth, The Composition and Order of the Fourth Gospel, Yale Univ Press, 65; coauth, Anatomy of the New Testament, Prentice- Hall, 69, 95; auth, Johannine Christianity, Univ SC Press, 84; auth, John Among the Gospels, Fortress, 92; auth, The Theology of the Gospel of John, Cambridge Univ Press, 95; auth, John (Abingdon New Testament Commentaries), Abingdon, 99. **CONTACT ADDRESS** Duke Univ, Box 33 Divinity, Durham, NC 27708. **EMAIL** dmsmith@mail.duke.edu

SMITH, DANIEL L.
DISCIPLINE LAW, LIBRARY SCIENCE, COMPARATIVE LITERATURE **EDUCATION** Univ Iowa, BS (biochemistry), 80, BA (Russian), 89, MFA (Comp lit), 93, JD, 93, MA (Libr, Info Sci), 94. **CAREER** Publisher, Canonymous Pr, 92-; ref librn, curator, Cornell Law Libr, 97-00; asst ed, Exchanges: A J of Translations, Univ Iowa, 89-93. **SELECTED PUBLICATIONS** Auth, "Postmodern [Sic]ness: Ecritique of Anesthetic Judgement," Ecritique 1 (92); auth, Minims, 93; auth, "Self-Determination in Tibet: The Politics of Remedies," Ecritique, 2 (96); auth, "The Legacy of Nuremberg: Sustaining Human Rights," Cornell Law Forum, 25 (99). **CONTACT ADDRESS** Canonymous Pr, P. O. Box 6613, Ithaca, NY 14851-6613. **EMAIL** smith@canonymous.com

SMITH, DAVID H.
PERSONAL Born 04/28/1939, Evanston, IL, m, 1961, 3 children **DISCIPLINE** RELIGIOUS STUDIES **EDUCATION** Carleton Col, BA, 61; Yale Div Sch, BD, 64; Princeton Univ, PhD, 67. **CAREER** Asst prof, Rel Stud, 67-70, assoc prof, 70-79, Indiana Univ; sr res scholar, Joseph and Rose Kennedy Inst for Bioethics, Georgetown Univ, 73-74; prof rel Stud, Indiana Univ, 79- ;dir, Poynter Ctr for the Stud Ehtics and Am Inst, 82; Sem dir, Liberal Education and Moral Criticism, at Workshop on the Liberal Arts, funded by Lilly Endow, 85-94; subj matter expert, Chaplain Corps, US Navy, 85-86; Ch, Exec Comm, Assn Practical and Prof Ethics, 91- . **HONORS AND AWARDS** Natl Endow human fel, Summer 69; Cross-Disciplinary fel, Soc Rel in Higher Ed, 73-74; Lilly Endow open fel, 80-81; fel, Hastings Ctr, 74-86; Amoco disting tchg awd, 78; Student Alumni Coun outstanding fac awd, 86. **RESEARCH** Professional ethics; ethics and governance; theological ethics; teaching ethics. **SELECTED PUBLICATIONS** On Being Queasy, IRB: A Review of Human Subjects Research 2, 4, April 80, 6-7; Deciding for the Death of a Baby, in Marc D. Basson, ed, Rights and Responsibilities in Modern Medicine, New York, Alan R. Liss, Inc, 81, 49-55; The American Way of Hospice, with Judith A. Granbois, Hastings Center Report, 12, 2, April 82, 8-10; A Theological Context for the Relationship Between Patient and Physician, in Earl L. Shelp, ed, The Clinical Encounter, Dordrecht, D. Reidel Publ Co, 83, 289-301; Who Counts? Jour of Rel Ethics, 12, 2, Fall 84, 240-255; Ed, Respect and Care in Medical Ethics, Lanham, MD, Univ Press Am, 84; Medical Loyalty: Dimensions and Problems of a Rich Idea, in Earl L. Shelp, ed, Theology and Bioethics, Dordrecht: D. Reidel Publ Co, 85, 267-282; Our Religious Traditions and the treatment of Infants, in Thomas H. Murray and Arthur L. Caplan, eds, Which Babies Shall Live? Humanistic Dimensions of the Care of Imperilled newborns, Clifton, NJ, Humana Press, 85; Care of the Sick, Fidelity, Hospitality, Loyalty, in The Westminster Dictionary of Christian Ehtics, Philadelphia, The Westminster Press, 86; The Limits of Narrative, in Joanne Trautmann Banks, ed, Literature and Medicine: Use and Abuse of Literary Co-Concepts in Medicine, Baltimore: Johns Hopkins UP, 86; The Moral Dimension to Teaching, in David D. Dill and Patricia K. Fullager, ed, The Knowledge Most Worth Having in Teacher Education, Proceedings of the Chancellor's Invitational Conference, Chapel Hill: Univ NC, 86; Health and Medicine in the Anglican Tradition: Conscience, Community and Compromise, New York: Crossroads Publ Co, 86; McCormick and Medicine, Rel Stud Rev, 13, 1, Jan 87, 42-44; Suffering, Medicine and Christian Theology, in Stephen E. Lammers and Allen Verhey, eds, On Moral Medicine: Theological Perspectives in Medical Ethics, Grand Rapids: William B. Eerdmans Publ Co, 87; On Paul Ramsey: A Covenant-Centered Ethic for Medicine, Second Opinion, 6, Nov 87, 107-127, Reprinted in Aleen Verhey and Stephen E. Lammers, eds, Theological Voices in Medical Ethics, Grand Rapids, William B. Eerdmans Publ Co, 93, 7-29; AIDS and Aid for Patient and Healer, with Robin Levin Penslar and Judith A. Granbois, rep submit to Task Force on AIDS Ethical/Legal Working Group, Pub Health Svc, US Dept Health and Human Svcs, Dec 2, 87; Teaching Ethics in a Professional Age, in Bruce A. Kimball, ed, Teaching Undergraduates: Essays from the Lilly Endowment Workshop on the Liberal Arts, New York: Prometheus Books, 88, 151-172; Wombs for Rent, Selves for Sale, Jour Contmep Hea Law and Policy, 4, Spring 88, 23-36; Using Human Fetal Tissue for Transplantation and Research: Selected Issues, in Report of the Human Fetal Tissue Transplantation and Research Panal, 2, F1-F43, Bethesda MD, Dept Hea and Human Svcs, Natl Inst Hea, Dec, 88; Called to Profess: Religion and Secular Theories of Vocation, The Centennial Rev, 34, 2, Spring 90, 275-294; The Anglican Communion, in Bioethics Yearbook-Vol I: Theological Developments in Bioethics, 1988-90, Dordrecht, Boston, London: Kluwer Acad Publ, 91; Quality, Not Mercy: Some Reflections on Recent Work in Medical Ethics, Medical Human Rev, 5, 2, July 91, 9-18; Trustees and Health Care Priorities, Trustee, 44, 11, Nov 91, 16-17; The Episcopal Church and Assisted Reproduction, in The Episcopal Church as Moral Teacher: A Critical Study, Harrisburg, PA, Morehouse-Barlow, 92; Seeing and Knowing Dementia, in Dementia and Aging: Ethics, Values, and Policy Choices, Baltimore, The Johns Hopkins Univ Press, 92, 44-54; Moral Responsibilities of Trustees, Jour of Non-Profit Mgt, 2, 4, 92, 351-362; The Anglical Tradition, in Bioethics Yearbook-Vol 3, Theological Developments in Bioethics, 1992-94, Dordrecht, Boston, London, Kluwer, 97; Religion and the Use of Animals in Research: Some First Thoughts, Ethics and Behavior, 72, 97, 137 Entrusted: The Moral Responsibilities of Trustees, Bloomington, Indiana UP, 95; The Social Face of Death: Confronting Mortality in Paoli, Indiana, Bloomington, Poynter Ctr, 98; Paul Ramsey, Love and Killing, in Smith and Johnson, Love and Society; Suicide, with Seymour Perlin and Warren T. Reich, ed, Encycl of Bioethics, vol 4, New York: Macmillan Publ Co, and the Free Press, 1618-1627; The Abortion of Defective Fetuses: Some Moral Considerations, in Smith, ed, No Rush to Judgment; **CONTACT ADDRESS** Poynter Center, Indiana Univ, Bloomington, 618 E 3rd St, Bloomington, IN 47405.

SMITH, DAVID R.
PERSONAL Born 09/27/1946, Loveland, OH, m, 1969 **DISCIPLINE** LAW **EDUCATION** Central State Univ, Wilberforce OH, BA, 1969; DePaul Univ Coll of Law, Chicago IL, JD, 1974. **CAREER** US Dept of Energy, asst chief counsel, 72-83; Cole & Smith, partner, 83-85; The MAXIMA Corp, corporate senior vp, gen counsel sec, 85-; Reed, Smith, Shaw & McClay, counsel; Alexander, Gebhardt, Aponte & Marks, partner, currently. **MEMBERSHIPS** Alpha Phi Alpha Frat, 1969; Amer Bar Assn; Maryland Bar Assn; Natl Bar Assn; Illinois Bar Assn; admitted to practice: US Supreme Court; US Claims Court; Federal Trial Bars: Illinois; Maryland; Virginia; District of Columbia. **SELECTED PUBLICATIONS** Author: "Contracting with The Federal Government: 10 Key Areas," Chicago Bar Association, 1984; Small Business and Technology Devel Contract Mgmt Magazine; Sphinx Magazine, 1983; "Exploring The Energy Frontier," Natl Bar Assn, 1982. **CONTACT ADDRESS** Alexander, Gebhardt, Aponte & Marks, 8601 Georgia Ave, Silver Spring, MD 20910.

SMITH, DAVID T.
PERSONAL Born 12/11/1935, Pawtucket, RI, m, 1958, 3 children **DISCIPLINE** LAW **EDUCATION** Yale Univ, BA; Boston Univ, JD. **CAREER** Prof, Univ Fla, 68-. **MEMBERSHIPS** Mass Bar; Amer Law Inst; Order of the Coif; Omicron Delta Kappa; Fla Blue Key; adv bd, HEIRS; Title Issues and Standards Com, Fla Bar Real Property, Probate and Trust Law Sect. **RESEARCH** Property, estates and trusts, fiduciary administration, future interests. **SELECTED PUBLICATIONS** Auth, Florida Probate Code Manual; Florida Estates Practice Guide. **CONTACT ADDRESS** School of Law, Univ of Florida, PO Box 117625, Gainesville, FL 32611-7625. **EMAIL** smithdt@law.ufl.edu

SMITH, DENNIS E.
PERSONAL Born 12/01/1944, Conroe, TX, m, 1966, 1 child **DISCIPLINE** NEW TESTAMENT **EDUCATION** Abilene Christian Univ, BA, 67; MA, 69; Princeton Theol Sem, MDiv, 72; Harvard Div Sch, ThD, 80. **CAREER** Asst prof, Princeton Theol Sem, 79-81; asst prof, Oklahoma State Univ, 81-86; from assoc prof to prof, Phillips Theol Sem, 86-. **MEMBERSHIPS** Soc of Bibl Lit; Westar Inst. **RESEARCH** Ancient meal customs; social history of the early Christian world. **SELECTED PUBLICATIONS** Coauth, Many Tables: The Eucharist in the New Testament and Liturgy Today, SCM & Trinity Press Int, 90; ed, "How Gospels Begin," Semeia 52 (90); auth, The Storyteller's Companion to the Bible, v.10: John, Abingdon, 96; ed, The Storyteller's Companion to the Bible, v.12: Acts, Abingdon, 99; ed, The Storyteller's Companion to the Bible, v.13: Women in the New Testament, Abingdon, 99; ed, The Chalice Introduction to the New Testament, Chalice (forthcoming). **CONTACT ADDRESS** Phillips Theol Sem, 539 S Gary Pl., Tulsa, OK 74104-3119. **EMAIL** demcsmith@aol.com

SMITH, EDWIN M.
DISCIPLINE INTERNATIONAL LAW **EDUCATION** Harvard Univ, AB,72; JD,76. **CAREER** Leon Benwell prof Law and Int Relations,Univ Southern Calif; past atty, National Oceanic Atmospheric Admin; past spec coun for policy, US Senator Daniel Patrick Moynihan; app by pres Clinton as a sci and policy adv, US Arms Control and Disarmament Agency. **MEMBERSHIPS** Coun For Relations; past VP, Amer Soc Int Law. **RESEARCH** International law; international relations theory; foreign relations law. **SELECTED PUBLICATIONS** Auth, The Endangered Species Act and Biological Conservation; Congressional Authorization of Nuclear First Use: Problems of Implementation; The United Nations in a New World Order & Understanding Dynamic Obligations: Arms Control Agreements. **CONTACT ADDRESS** School of Law, Univ of So California, University Park Campus, Los Angeles, CA 90089. **EMAIL** esmith@law.usc.edu.

SMITH, ELTON EDWARD
DISCIPLINE LITERATURE, RELIGIOUS STUDIES **EDUCATION** NYU, BS, 37; Andover Newton Theol Sch, MST, 40; Syracuse Univ, PhD, 56. **CAREER** Pastor in churches, Mass, Ore, NYork, Fla, 40-56; dist prof, Univ S Fla, 61-. **HONORS AND AWARDS** Distinguished Prof Brit Lit and Bible; Dr Div, Linfield Col; Fulbright Lectureships, Univ Algiers, Mod V Univ, Univ Paris, Univ London; Grad Tuition, Cambridge Univ. **MEMBERSHIPS** MLA; SAMLA; AAUP. **SELECTED PUBLICATIONS** Auth, Charles Reade; co-auth, William Godwin; auth, My Son, My Son, Pentland Pr; auth, Angry Young Men of the Thirties; auth, auth, The Two Voices: A Tennyson Study, Univ Nebr Pr, 64; Tennyson's 'Epic Drama', up Am (Lanham, Md), 97; co-ed, The Haunted Mind: The Supernatural in Victorian Literature (Lanham, Md: Scarecrow Pr, 99). **CONTACT ADDRESS** 14714 Oak Vine Dr, Lutz, FL 33549-3229.

SMITH, ERVIN
PERSONAL Born 12/15/1939, Augusta, GA, m, 1966, 1 child **DISCIPLINE** RELIGION **EDUCATION** Paine Col, Augusta, GA, BS, 60; Drew Univ Theological School, Madison, NJ, Master Divinity, 68; Northwestern Univ and Garrett Theological Seminary, Evanston, IL, PhD, 76. **CAREER** Prof of Christian Ethics, Methodist Theological School, Delaware, OH, 71-. **HONORS AND AWARDS** Rockefeller Fel, 65-68. **MEMBERSHIPS** Society of Christian Ethics. **RESEARCH** Martin Luther King, Jr.; Understanding Racism; Contemporary Moral Issues. **SELECTED PUBLICATIONS** Auth, "The Ethics of Martin Luther King Jr.," Mellon Press, Lewiston, NY, 81; auth, "Christian Ethics and Affirmative Action, United Theological Seminary and Methodist," Theological School in Ohio Theological Journal, Spring, 98. **CONTACT ADDRESS** Dept Religion, Methodist Theol Sch in Ohio, 3081 Columbus Pike, Delaware, OH 43015-3211. **EMAIL** esmith@mtso.edu/ esmithlove@aol.com

SMITH, F. LAGARD
DISCIPLINE LAW AND MORALITY SEMINAR **EDUCATION** Willamette Univ, BS, 66; Willamette Univ Sch Law, JD, 68. **CAREER** Dep dist atty, Malheur County, 68-70; dist atty, 70-71; dir, OR State Bar, 71-72; prof. **MEMBERSHIPS** Mem, OR State Bar; Am Bar Assn. **SELECTED PUBLICATIONS** Auth, Criminal Law Color Book; The Narrated Bible; The Daily Bible; ACLU-The Devil's Advocate, Marron Publ, 96; numerous Christian bk(s). **CONTACT ADDRESS** Sch of Law, Pepperdine Univ, 24255 Pacific Coast Hwy, Malibu, CA 90263.

SMITH, GEORGE P.
PERSONAL Born 09/01/1939, Wabash, IN, s **DISCIPLINE** LAW **EDUCATION** Ind Univ, BS, 61; JD, 64; LLD, 98; Columbia Univ, LLM, 75. **CAREER** Prof, Cath Univ of Am, 77-. **HONORS AND AWARDS** Cert of Merit, EPA, 74; Australian-Am Fulbright Found Awd, Univ New S Wales, 84; Citation of Hon, Ind Univ, 85; Distinguished Alumni Medallion, Ind Univ, 85. **MEMBERSHIPS** BFEHV, AALS, ILPHP, UNAS, ALI. **RESEARCH** Law, science, medicine and bioethics. **SELECTED PUBLICATIONS** Auth, "In the Beginning: A Tenth Anniversary History of the Journal of Contemporary Health Law and Policy," 10 J of Contemp Health Law and Policy 285 (94); auth, Family Values and the New Society: Dilemmas of the 21st Century, Praeger Publ (Westport, CT), 98; auth, "John L Garvey: A Tribute," 49 Cath Univ Law Rev 1 (99); auth, "The Elderly and Patient Dumping," 73 Fla Bar J 85 (99); auth, "Judicial Decisionmaking in the Age of Biotechnology,' 13 Notre Dame J of Law, Ethics and Public Policy 34 (99); auth, "Euphemistic Codes and Tell-Tale Hearts: Humane Assistance in End-of-Life Cases," 10 Health Matrix, J of Law-Med (00); auth, "Genetic Enhancement Technologies and the New Society," 4 Med Law Int 85 (00); auth, Human Rights and Biomedicine, Kluwer Int (The Hague, Netherlands), forthcoming; auth, "Cigarette Smoking as a Public Hazard: Crafting Common Law and Legislative Strategies for Abatement," forthcoming. **CONTACT ADDRESS** Dept Law, Catholic Univ of America, 620 Michigan Ave NE, Washington, DC 20064-0001.

SMITH, HAROLD TELIAFERRO, JR.
PERSONAL Born 04/10/1947, Miami, FL, d, 3 children **DISCIPLINE** LAW **EDUCATION** Fla A&M Univ, BS, 68; Univ of Miami, JD, 73. **CAREER** Dade County Public Defenders, Attorney; Dade County Attorneys Office, Long and Smith PA, H T Smith PA, president, currently. **HONORS AND AWARDS** Best Lawyers in America, 95-96; National Conference of Black Lawyers, Service Awd, 91; Miami Herald, Charles Whited Spirit of Excellence Awd, 93. **MEMBERSHIPS** National Bar Association, president, 1994-95; Miami Partners for Progress, co-chair, 1993-; Inroads/Miami, secretary, 1993-; Community Partnership for the Homeless, board, 1993-94; Kappa Alpha Psi Fraternity, 1983-; Miami Dade Branch, NAACP, executive committee, 1990-; Boyscott Miami Campaign, co-spokesperson, 1990-93; Coalition fo a Free South Africa, chair, 1985-90. **SELECTED PUBLICATIONS** Wrote numerous articles for publication and gave hundreds of speeches and seminars. **CONTACT ADDRESS** H T Smith, P A, 1017 NW 9th Ct, Miami, FL 33136.

SMITH, HEMAN BERNARD
PERSONAL Born 08/20/1929, Alexandria, LA, m, 1952 **DISCIPLINE** LAW **EDUCATION** Univ of Maryland (Far East Div), attended, 1958-60; Univ of Pacific, McGeorge School of Law, JD, 1971. **CAREER** Partner, sr attorney, Smith, Hanna, de Bruin & Yee, Sacto Calif, 71-78; partner, Smith & Yee, Sacto Calif, 78-84; sr attorney, Smith & Assoc, Sacto Calif, 84-; exec dean, Univ Northern California, LP Sch of Law, Sacto Calif, 84-88. **MEMBERSHIPS** Bd mem, Amer Red Cross, Sacto CA, 80-87; Minority Steering Comm California Youth Authority, 85-87; Sacto Urban League; Sacto NAACP; Zeta Beta Lambda; Wiley Man Bar Asn, 88-. **CONTACT ADDRESS** Smith & Associates, 6370 Havenside Dr., Sacramento, CA 95831.

SMITH, J. CLAY, JR.
PERSONAL Born 04/15/1942, Omaha, NE, m, 4 children **DISCIPLINE** LAW **EDUCATION** Creighton Univ Omaha, NE, AB 1964; Howard Law Sch Washington, DC, JD 1967; George Washington Law Sch Washington, DC, LLM, 1970, SJD 1977. **CAREER** US Army Judge Advocates Gen Corp, capt lyr 1967-71; Arent Fox Kintner Plotkin & Kahn Washington, DC, assc 1971-74; Fed Commctn Cmsn, deputy chf cable TV bureau 1974-76; Fed Communications Commission, assc gen cnsl 1976-77; Equal Emplymnt Opprtnty Cmsn, us cmsnr apptd by Jimmy Carter 1977-82, actng chrmn apptd by Ronald W Reagan 1981-82; Howard Univ Sch of Law, Prof of Law 1982-, dean & professor of law, 86-88. **HONORS AND AWARDS** First African American Governor of Boys State (NE) and Nation (1959); First African American elected as natl pres, Fed Bar Assn 1980-81; founder juris art movement Washington Bar Assn 1978; Am Bar Assn 1982-; order of the coif hon George Washington Law Sch 1978; Ollie May Cooper Awd, 1986; The C Francis Stradford Awd 1986; Outstanding Alumni Achievement Awds from Howard University, 1981, Creighton University, 1989, George Washington University, 1990. **MEMBERSHIPS** NE Bar Assoc 1967; mem Howard Law Sch Alumni Assc 1967-; Dist of Columbia Bar 1968; pres bd dir Washington Bar Assc 1970; US Supreme Court 1973; advsr pres Natl Bar Assc 1973-; mem NAACP 1975-; mem Urban League 1975-; natl pres mem Fed Bar Assc 1979; utlty spec Pblc Serv Cmsn 1982-84; editorial board ABA Compleat Lawyer 1984-87; Advisory Committee, DC Bar Exam; bd mem Natl Lawyers Club; planning committee for Task Force on Black Males, AM Psyh Assn 1986-90; mem Am Law Inst 1986-88; chair Natl Bar Assn Comm on History of Blk Lawyers; legal counsel for the Elderly Policy Bd 1986-88. **SELECTED PUBLICATIONS** Publications, Fed Bar Assn Natl Pres Messages, Fed Bar News, CIVICS LEAP, Law Reason & Creativity, Mgng Multi-ethnic Multi-racial Workforce Criminal, Chronic Alcoholism -- Lack of Mens Rea -- A Dfns Pblc Intoxication 13 Howard Law Journal, An Investment in a New Century, Wash Afro Am; The Black Bar Assn & Civil Rights; A Black Lawyer's Response to the Fairmont Papers; Memoriam: Clarence Clyde Ferguson, Jr, Harvard Law Rev; Forgotten Hero: Charles H Houston, Harvard Law Rev; Justice & Jurisprudence & The Black Lawyer, Notre Dame Law Rev; Emancipation: The Making of The Black Lawyer, 1844-1944; National Book Award of the Natl Conference of Black Political Scientist, 1995; Rebels in Law: Voices in History of Black Women Lawyers, 1998; Served on the transition team of President Clinton & Vice Pres Gore, 1992. **CONTACT ADDRESS** Sch of Law, Howard Univ, 2900 Van Ness St NW, Washington, DC 20008. **EMAIL** js@law.howard.edu

SMITH, JANET E.
DISCIPLINE BIOETHICS, PHILOSOPHY OF GOD **EDUCATION** Grinnell Col, BA; Univ NC, MA; Univ Toronto, PhD. **CAREER** Dept Philos, Univ Dallas **SELECTED PUBLICATIONS** Auth, Natural Law and Personalism in Veritatis Splendor, Veritatis Splendor: American Responses, Sheed and Ward, 95; Pope John Paul II, Feminists, Women, and the Church, Cath Dossier 1:4, 95; The Christian View of Sex: A Time for Apologetics, Not Apologies, The Family in America, Review of Turning Point, Corssroad Publ, 95; Homiletic and Pastoral Rev, 96; The Pre-Eminence of Autonomy in Bioethics, Human Lives: Critical Essays on Consequentialist Bioethics, McMillan Press, 97; Old Stuff, New Stuff, Dossier, 97; Rights, the Person and Conscience in the Catechism, Dossier, 97. **CONTACT ADDRESS** Dept of Philos, Univ of Dallas, 1845 E Northgate Dr, Irving, TX 75062.

SMITH, JERALDINE WILLIAMS
PERSONAL Born 01/14/1946, Tampa, FL, m **DISCIPLINE** LAW **EDUCATION** Univ of FL, BS Journalism 1967; Atlanta Univ, MBA 1970; FL State Law School, JD 1981. **CAREER** Freedom Savings, bank mgr 1973-75; Digital Equip Corp, admin mgr 1975-77; FL Dept of Ins, lawyer 1983-. **HONORS AND AWARDS** William Randolph Hearst Natl Newspaper Awds Winner 1967; Businesswoman of the Year Iota Phi Lambda 1971. **MEMBERSHIPS** Mem Amer Bar Assoc, FL Bar Assoc, Natl Newspaper Publ Assoc, FL Press Assoc. **SELECTED PUBLICATIONS** Capital Outlook Weekly Newspaper, publ 1983-. **CONTACT ADDRESS** Capitol Outlook Newspaper, PO Box 11335, Tallahassee, FL 32302.

SMITH, JESSE OWENS
PERSONAL Born 12/05/1942, Comer, AL, m, 1987 **DISCIPLINE** POLITICAL SCIENCE **EDUCATION** California State University, Los Angeles, CA, BA, 1971; University of Chicago, Chicago, IL, MA, 1973, PhD, 1976. **CAREER** University of Wisconsin, Oshkosh, WI, professor, 74-76; San Diego State University, San Diego, CA, professor, 77-84, California State University, Fullerton, CA, professor, 84-. **MEMBERSHIPS** California Black Faculty and Staff Association, 1978-; National Conference of Black Political Scientists, 1972-; National Council of Black Studies, 1976-; American Political Science Association, 1976-; National Association for the Advancement of Black Studies. **CONTACT ADDRESS** Professor of Political Science, California State Univ, Fullerton, 800 State College Dr, Fullerton, CA 92631.

SMITH, JOHN EDWIN
PERSONAL Born 05/27/1921, Brooklyn, NY, m, 1951, 2 children **DISCIPLINE** PHILOSOPHY **EDUCATION** Columbia Univ, BA, 42, PhD, 48; Union Theol Sem, MDiv, 45. **CAREER** Instr philos and relig, Vasar Col, 45-46; from instr and asst prof to prof philos, 46-72, Barnard Col, chemn dept, 61-64; Clark Prof Philos, Yale Univ, 72-91, Clark Prof Emer, 91- ; Gen.Ed., Yale Ed. The Works of Jonathan Edwards, 65-91; Gen.Ed., Emer. 91-. **HONORS AND AWARDS** Herbert W. Schneider Awd for contributions to American Thought over an entire career, 90; Founder's Medal, MSA, 96; named Honorary Alumnus, Harvard Div Sch, 60. **MEMBERSHIPS** APA; Metaphysical Soc Am; Charles S. Peirce Soc; Am Theol. Society, 67-68; APA, VP, 80, 81; Metaphysical Society of America, 70-71; Hegel Society of Am 71; Charles S. Peirce Society, 92 **RESEARCH** Metaphysics; philosophy of religion; American philosophy. **SELECTED PUBLICATIONS** Auth, Royce's Social Infinite, Liberal Art, 50; auth, Reason and God, Yale, 61; auth, The Spirit of American Philosophy, Oxford, 63, 2nd ed. SUNY Press, 83; auth, Religion and Empiricism, Marquette, 67; auth, Experience and God, Oxford, 68, 2nd. Ed. Fordham, 95; auth, Themes in American Philosophy, Harper, 70; auth, The Analogy of Experience, Harper, 73; auth, Purpose and Thought: The Meaning of Pragmatism, Yale, 78; auth, America's Philosophical Vision, Chicago, 92; auth, Jonathan Edwards: Puritan, Preacher, Philosopher, Notre Dame, 92; auth, Quasi-Religions, St Martin's, 95; auth, Reason, Experience, and God: John E. Smith in Dialogue, Fordham, 97. **CONTACT ADDRESS** Dept of Philosophy, Yale Univ, PO Box 201562, New Haven, CT 06520-1562. **EMAIL** john.smith@yale.edu

SMITH, JONATHAN ZITTELL
PERSONAL Born 11/21/1938, New York, NY, m, 1964, 2 children **DISCIPLINE** HISTORY OF RELIGION, HELLENISTIC RELIGIONS **EDUCATION** Haverford Col, BA, 60; Yale Univ, PhD(hist relig), 69. **CAREER** Instr relig, Dartmouth Col, 65-66; actg asst prof, Univ Calif, Santa Barbara, 66-68; asst prof, 68-73, William Benton prof relig & human sci, 74-82, dean col, 77-82, Robert O Anderson Distinguished Serv Prof Humanities, Univ Chicago, 82-, Co-ed, Hist Relig, 68-81. **HONORS AND AWARDS** McGill Univ, DD, (honoris causa), 96; Fellow, Am Acad of Arts & Sciences, 00; Pres, North Am Assoc for the Study of Religion, (1996-2002). **MEMBERSHIPS** Soc Bibl Lit; Am Acad Relig; Am Soc Study Relig; North Am Assoc for the Study of Religion. **RESEARCH** Hellenistic religions; anthropology of religion; method and theory of religion. **SELECTED PUBLICATIONS** Auth, Map is not Territory: Studies in the History of Religions, E J Brill, 78; Imagining Religion: From Babylon to Jonestown, Univ Chicago, 82; auth, To Take Place: Toward Theory in Ritual Univ Chicago, 87; auth, Drudgery Divine: On the Comparison of Early Christianities and the Religions of Late Antiquity, Univ Chicago, 90; gen.ed., The Harper Collins Dictionary of Religion, Harper Collins, 95. **CONTACT ADDRESS** Univ of Chicago, 1116 E 59th St, Chicago, IL 60637.

SMITH, KATHRYN
PERSONAL Born 08/20/1954, Orange, CA, m, 1974, 2 children **DISCIPLINE** RELIGION **EDUCATION** Claremont Grad Univ, PhD, 97. **CAREER** Adj prof, Univ Washington, 99-00; asst prof Of New Testament, Azusa Pac Univ., 00- . **HONORS AND AWARDS** Claremont tuition grants, 94-96. **MEMBERSHIPS** Soc of Bibl Lit. **RESEARCH** New Testament; Synoptic Gospels; early Jewish groups; early Jewish Christianity. **CONTACT ADDRESS** Azusa Pacific Univ, 701 E Alosta Avenue, Azusa, CA 91702-7000. **EMAIL** kjssmith@apu.edu

SMITH, KELLY C.
PERSONAL Born 01/18/1964, Atlanta, GA, m, 1985, 3 children **DISCIPLINE** PHILOSOPHY **EDUCATION** Duke Univ, MS, 92, PhD, 94. **CAREER** Vis asst prof, Ga State Univ, 93-94; asst prof, Col NJ, 94-98; asst prof, Clemson Univ, 98-. **MEMBERSHIPS** Am Philos Asn; Philos Sci Asn; Int Soc Hist, Philos, & Soc Studies Biol; Am Asn Advan Sci; Nat Ctr Sci Educ. **RESEARCH** Philosophy of science; philosophy of biology; bioethics; genetics; evolution. **SELECTED PUBLICATIONS** Auth, Equivocal Nations of Accuracy and Genetic Screening of the General Population, Mt Sinai Jour Med, 98; coauth, The Extended Replicator, Biol & Philos, 96; coauth, Sober on Brandon on Screening-Off and the Levels of Selec-

tion, Philos Sci, 94; auth, The Effects of Temperature and Daylength on the Rosa Polyphenism in the Buckeye Butterfly Precis Coenia (Nymphalidae), Jour Res Lepidoptera, 93; auth, Neo-rationalism Vs. Neo-Darwinism: Integrating Development and Evolution, Biol & Philos, 93; auth, Marketing Structuralism: Reflections on the Process Structuralist Critique of Neo-Darwinism, Rivista di Biologia/Biol Forum, 93; auth, The New Problem of Genetics: A Response to Gifford, Biol & Philos, 92; auth, "Genetic Disease, Genetic Testing and the Clinician, 01. **CONTACT ADDRESS** Dept of Philosophy and Religion, Clemson Univ, 101 Hardin Hall, Clemson, SC 29634-1508. **EMAIL** kcs@clemson.edu

SMITH, LARRY L.
PERSONAL Born 05/26/1945, Salt Lake City, UT, s **DISCIPLINE** POLITICAL SCIENCE **EDUCATION** Univ Utah, BS, 70; MSW, 72; DSW, 74. **CAREER** From Asst Prof to Prof, Univ of Utah, Sch of Soc Work, 74-. **HONORS AND AWARDS** Phi Kappa Phi, 70; Phi Beta Kappa, 70. **MEMBERSHIPS** Licensed Marriage and Family Therapist, Clinical Soc Worker and Certified Soc Worker, State of Utah. **RESEARCH** Marriage and Family Counseling, Corrections, and Mental Health. **SELECTED PUBLICATIONS** Auth, "How Couples Misuse Money," Family Therapy 19-2 (92): 35-40; coauth, "An Anger Management Workshop for Inmates in a Medium Security facility," J of Offender Rehabil 19-3/4 (93): 103-111; coauth, "An Anger-Management Workshop for Women Inmates," Families in Soc 75-3 (94): 172-175; coauth, "Women Inmates, Drug Abuse, and the Salt Lake County Jail," Am Jails 13-3 (July/Aug 99): 43-47; coauth, Introduction to Social Work 8th ed, Allyn and Bacon (Boston), 00. **CONTACT ADDRESS** Grad Sch of Soc Work, Univ of Utah, 201 S 1460 E 250 S, Salt Lake City, UT 84112. **EMAIL** lsmith@socwk.utah.edu

SMITH, LUTHER EDWARD, JR.
PERSONAL Born 05/29/1947, St. Louis, MO, m **DISCIPLINE** THEOLOGY **EDUCATION** WA Univ, AB, 69; Eden Theol Sem, Mdiv, 72; St Louis Univ, PhD, 79. **CAREER** E St Louis Welfare Rgts Org, coord 70-72; Educ for Blk Urban Mnstrs, exec coord 72-79; Lane Tabernacle CME Church, asst pstr 72-79; Black Church Ldrs Prog St Louis Univ, prog coord 75-79; Candler School of Theol, Emory Univ, prof of Church and Comm. **HONORS AND AWARDS** Distg srv awards St Louis and Mid St Louis Cty Jaycees, 75; member of Honor Society International Society of Theta Phi, 87; member, Omicron Delta Kappa, 91; Inducted into the Martin Luther King, Jr Collegium of Scholars, Morehouse Col. **MEMBERSHIPS** Bd chmn Northside Team Ministries, 73-79; 1st vice pres MO Assoc Soc Welfare St Louis Div, 73-79; prog coord Metropolitan Ministerial Alliance of St Louis, 75-79, Urban Churches in Community Dev Prog, 78-79; bd mem Urban Training Org of Atlanta, 80-; bd mem Inst for World Evangelism, 82-, Eden Theological Sem; Families First, 92. **SELECTED PUBLICATIONS** Auth, Howard Thurman: The Mystic as Prophet, 81; auth, Intimacy and Mission: Intentional Community as Crucible for Radical Discipleship, 94. **CONTACT ADDRESS** Candler School of Theol, Emory Univ, Bishops Hall, Atlanta, GA 30322. **EMAIL** lsmit03@emory.edu

SMITH, LYNN C.
DISCIPLINE LAW **EDUCATION** Calgary Univ, BA, 67; Univ British Columbia, LLB, 73. **CAREER** Dean, 91-; adj prof, 91-. **HONORS AND AWARDS** Dir, Women's Legal Edu Action Fund; dir, Nat Judicial Inst. **MEMBERSHIPS** Law Soc. **RESEARCH** Constitutional Law, civil litigation; evidence. **SELECTED PUBLICATIONS** Auth, Have the Equality Rights Made Any Difference?, Univ Toronto, 94; Beverly McLachlin, Greenwood, 96; co-auth, The Equality Rights, Wilson & Lafleur Ltee, 96. **CONTACT ADDRESS** Fac of Law, Univ of British Columbia, 1822 East Mall, Vancouver, BC, Canada V6T 1Z1. **EMAIL** lsmith@law.ubc.ca

SMITH, MARK STRATTON
PERSONAL Born 12/06/1955, Paris, France, m, 1982, 3 children **DISCIPLINE** HEBREW BIBLE, ANCIENT NEAR EAST **EDUCATION** Johns Hopkins Univ, BA, 75; Catholic Univ of Am, MA, 79; Harvard Div Sch, MTS, 80; Hebrew Univ, vis res, 83-84; Yale Univ, MA, 82; MPhil, 83; PhD, 85. **CAREER** Instr, Albertus Magnus Col, 81-82; instr, Yale Univ, 82-83; instr, Ecole Biblique et Archaeologique Francaise, 83-84; asst prof, Univ of St Thomas Saint Paul Sem, 84-86; asst prof, Yale Univ, 86-93; lectr, Univ of Penn, 94-95, 98-99; Lady Davis vis prof, Hebrew Univ, 97; assoc prof to prof, Saint Joseph's Univ, 93-00; Skirball Prof of Bible & Ancient Near Eastern Studies, NYork Univ, 00- . **HONORS AND AWARDS** Mary Cady Tew Prize, Mitchell Dahood Memorial Prize, Mellon Fell, Morse Fell, Dorot Dead Sea Scrolls Fel. **MEMBERSHIPS** CBA; OTC; SBL. **SELECTED PUBLICATIONS** Auth, Psalms: The Divine Journey, NY / Mahwah, NJ: Paulist Press, 87; The Early History of God: Yahweh and the Other Deities in Ancient Israel, San Fran/NY: Harper and Row, 90; auth, The Laments of Jeremiah and Their Context: A Literary and Redactional Study of Jeremiah 11-20, Society of Biblical Lit Monograph, Atlanta GA: Scholars, 90; auth, The Origins and Development of the Waw-Consecutive: Northwest Semitic Evidence From Ugarit to Qumran, Harvard Semitic Studies, Atlanta GA, Scholars Press, 91; auth, The Ugaritic Baal Cycle: vol 1, Introduction with Text, Translation and Commentary of KTU 1.1-1.2 Vetus Testamentum Supplements, Leiden: Brill, 94; auth, The Pilgrimage Pattern in Exodus, with Contributions by E. M. Bloch-Smith, Jour for the Soc of OT Supplements, Sheffield: Sheffield Acad Press, 97; ed., Probative Pontificating in Ugaritic and Biblical Studies: Collected Essays, by M. H. Pope, Munster: Ugarit-Verlag, 94; coauth, Qumran Cave 4Q XIV: Parabiblical Texts, Part 2, Discoveries in the Judaean Desert, Oxford: Clarendon, 95; auth, The Son of Man in Ugaritic, Catholic Bibl Quart, 83; auth, The Psalms as a Book for Pilgrims, Interpretation, 92; auth, Myth and Myth-making in Ugaritic and Israelite Literatures, Ugarit and the Bible: Proceedings of the International Symposium on Ugarit and the Bible, Manchester 92, Munster: Ugarit-Verlag, 94; auth, The Death of Dying and Rising Gods in the Biblical World: An Update, with Special Reference to Baal in the Baal Cycle, in: Scandinavian Jour of the OT, 99. **CONTACT ADDRESS** Dept of Hebrew & Judaic Studies, New York Univ, New York, NY 10003. **EMAIL** bloch.smith@erols.com

SMITH, MARSHA A. ELLIS
DISCIPLINE RELIGION **EDUCATION** Ouachita Baptist Univ, BME; Southwestern Baptist Theol Sem, MDiv, PhD. **CAREER** Instr, Baptist Theol Sem Zambia; adj prof, assoc VP, S Baptist Theol Sem. **SELECTED PUBLICATIONS** Gen ed, The Holman Book of Biblical Charts; Maps; Reconstructions; contrib, Holman Bible Dictionary; Holman Bible Handbook; The Woman's Study Bible; Biblical Illustrator. **CONTACT ADDRESS** So Baptist Theol Sem, 2825 Lexington Rd, Louisville, KY 40280. **EMAIL** mellissmith@sbts.edu

SMITH, PAMELA A.
PERSONAL Born 10/22/1947, New York, NY **DISCIPLINE** THEOLOGY **EDUCATION** Villanova Univ, MA, 71; St. Charles Borromeo Univ, MA, 83; Duquesne Univ, PhD, 95. **CAREER** Assoc dean, 96-. **MEMBERSHIPS** Col Theol Soc; Cath Theol Soc of Am; Am Acad of Relig; Soc of Christian Ethics. **RESEARCH** Environmental ethics; Creation theology; Lay spirituality. **SELECTED PUBLICATIONS** Auth, What Are They Saying About Environmental Ethics?, 97; Days of Dust and Ashes: Hope-filled Lenten Reflections, 97; Woman Gifts: Biblical Models for Forming Church, 94; Life After Waster: Mystagogia for Everyone, 93; "Sitting Still with Mark on a Non-Sick Day," 99; "The Ecospirituality of Alice Walker: Green Lap, Brown Embrace, Blue Body," 98; "Toward an Ecological Model of the Church," 98; "The Ecotheology of Annie Dillard: A Study in Ambivalence," 95. **CONTACT ADDRESS** SS Cyril & Methodius Sem, 3535 Indian Tr, Orchard Lake, MI 48324-0515. **EMAIL** au669@detroit.freenet.org

SMITH, PAUL
PERSONAL Born 09/20/1935, South Bend, IN, m **DISCIPLINE** THEOLOGY **EDUCATION** Talladega Clge, AB 1957; Hartford Sem, MDiv 1960; Eden Theological Sem, DMin 1977. **CAREER** WA Univ, assc vice chancellor 1974-78; Morehouse Coll, vice pres 1978-79; Columbia Theological Sem, adjunct prof 1979-; Candler School of Theology, Adjunct Prof 1979-; Hillside Presb Church, pastor. **HONORS AND AWARDS** NEH Recepient 1982; publ Unity, Diversity, Inclusiveness 1985; book J Knox Press Theology in a Computerized World 1985-86. **MEMBERSHIPS** Trustee Presby Schl of Christian Educ 1981-; consult Howard Thurman Educ Trust 1982; bd mem Child Srv Family Cnslng 1983-; Metro Fair Housing Srv Inc 1981-; Ldrshp Atlanta 1981; mem Council Atlanta Presb; former mem State Adv Comm US Civil Rights Comm 1977-1983. **CONTACT ADDRESS** Hillside Presb Church, 1879 Columbia Dr, Decatur, GA 30032.

SMITH, RANDALL BRIAN
PERSONAL Born 07/31/1959, Upper St. Clair, PA, s **DISCIPLINE** MEDIEVAL PHILOSOPHY; MEDIEVAL THEOLOGY **EDUCATION** Cornell Col, BA, 81; Univ Dallas, MA, 87; Univ Notre Dame, MMS, 91; PhD, 98. **CAREER** Post-Doctoral Res Assoc, Univ Notre Dame, 98-99. **HONORS AND AWARDS** Bradley Fel; Strake Found Grant. **MEMBERSHIPS** Amer Philos Assoc **RESEARCH** Thomas Aquinas; Medieval Philosophy & Theology; Natural Law; History of Biblical Exegesis. **CONTACT ADDRESS** Dept of Theology, Univ of Notre Dame, Notre Dame, IN 46556. **EMAIL** rsmith.11@nd.edu

SMITH, ROBERT HARRY
PERSONAL Born Holyoke, ME **DISCIPLINE** NEW TESTAMENT **EDUCATION** Concordia Sem, BA, MDiv, STM, ThD. **CAREER** Assoc prof, Concordia Sem; dean, Christ Sem-Seminex; prof, 83. **HONORS AND AWARDS** GTU Core Doctoral Fac. **MEMBERSHIPS** Memb, Bd of Dir(s), Berkeley Emergency Food Proj. **SELECTED PUBLICATIONS** Ed, Preaching Helps, Currents in Theology and Mission; auth, Easter Gospels: The Resurrection of Jesus According to the Four Evangelists, 83; Hebrews in The Augsburg Commentary Series, 84; Matthew in The Augsburg Commentary Series, 89; Easter: Proclamation 4, 92; Holy Week: Proclamations 5, 93; auth, Apocalypse: A Commentary on Revelation in Word and Image, 00. **CONTACT ADDRESS** Dept of New Testament, Pacific Lutheran Theol Sem, 2770 Marin Ave, Berkeley, CA 94708-1597. **EMAIL** rsmith@plts.edu

SMITH, ROBERT HOUSTON
PERSONAL Born 02/13/1931, McAlester, OK, m, 1969, 1 child **DISCIPLINE** RELIGION **EDUCATION** Univ Tulsa, BA, 52; Yale Univ, BD, 55, PhD(New Testament), 60. **CAREER** From instr to prof relig, 60-72, chmn humanities div lib studies prog, 68-69, Fox Prof Relig, Col Wooster, 72-, Chmn Dept Relig, 81-, Yale Two Bros fel, Am Sch Orient Res, Jerusalem, 58-59; mem staff, Univ Pa Mus archaeol exped, El Jib, Gibeon, 59, univ archaeol exped, Tell es-Saidiyeh, Jordan, 64; dir, Wooster exped, Pella, Jordan, 65-; lectr Digging up the Past ser on Educ Exchange, NBC-TV, 68; Nat Endowment for Humanities grant, 79- & Nat Geog Soc grant, 79- **HONORS AND AWARDS** Christian Res Found Prize, 60. **MEMBERSHIPS** Soc Bibl Lit; Am Orient Soc; Am Schs Orient Res; Archaeol Inst Am. **RESEARCH** Biblical studies; art and archaeology; business and professional ethics. **SELECTED PUBLICATIONS** Auth, Excavations in the Cemetery at Khirbet Kufin, Palestine, Colt Archaeol Inst, 62; Pella of the Decapolis, Col Wooster, 73; New directions for ethical codes, Asn & Soc Manager, 74; coauth, Atomic absorption for the archaeologist, J Field Archaeol, 76; Inclusions in ancient ceramics, Archaeometry, 76; Patches of Godlight: The Pattern of Thought of C S Lewis, Univ Ga Press, 81; Pella in Jordan, Report on the Seasons of 1979-81, Australian Nat Gallery, Canberra, 82. **CONTACT ADDRESS** The Col of Wooster, Wooster, OH 44691.

SMITH, ROBIN
PERSONAL Born 09/02/1946, TN, m, 1 child **DISCIPLINE** PHILOSOPHY **EDUCATION** Univ Chattanooga, BA, 68; Claremont Grad Sch, PhD, 74. **CAREER** Prof & dept head, Tex A&M Univ 94-. **HONORS AND AWARDS** Franklin J. Matchette Found Conf Grant, 91; NEH Fel for Col Teachers, 92-93. **MEMBERSHIPS** Sec, KSU Chap, AAUP, 91-94; APA Central Div Prog Comt, 88 and 94; sec/Treas, APA Central Div, 96-. **RESEARCH** Logic, ancient philosophy, hist of logic, medieval philosophy. **SELECTED PUBLICATIONS** Auth, Aristotle, Topics I, VIII, and Selections, Clarendon Aristotle Series, Oxford UUP, 97; chap 2, Logic, in The Cambridge Companion to Aristotle, Cambridge UP, 95 & Aristotle's Regress Argument, in Studies on the History of Logic, de Gruyter, 96; rev, The Origins of Aristotelian Science, Can Philos Reviews 13, 93. **CONTACT ADDRESS** Dept of Philosophy, Texas A&M Univ, Col Station, College Station, TX 77843-4237. **EMAIL** rasmith@aristotle.tamu.edu

SMITH, STANLEY G.
PERSONAL Born 07/21/1940, Brooklyn, NY, m **DISCIPLINE** LAW **EDUCATION** Seton Hall U, JD 1970; Rutgers U, BA Actg **CAREER** Urb Dev Res Inc, pres; Newark Hsng Dev & Rehab Corp, pres, chief exec ofcr 1980-; City Newark NJ, asst corp cncl 1972; Fed Prog Newark Hsng Dev Corp, att; Fidelity Union & Trust Co, fed asst, code enfor, fin analyst 1968-70; RCA, 64-68; Seton Hall Univ Sch of Law, prof 1972-; Lofton Lester & Smith, att law prtnr 1985. **HONORS AND AWARDS** On dean's list Rutgers Univ 1961-62; adjunct prof Seton Hall Univ 1972-; St Schlrshp (4 yrs) Rutgers Univ 1957; Hon Soc Seton Hall Law Sch 1967; Hon Schlrshp NJ Bell Elks Club. **MEMBERSHIPS** Mem Nat Bar Assn; concerned legal asso mem, bd dirs Nghbrhd Hlth Serv Corp 1972; bd dirs Voice Nwspr 1971-72; vice pres Phi Sigma Delta 1960; member, New Jersey State Bar Assn, 1990-91. **CONTACT ADDRESS** Smith & Forbes, 1032 South Ave, Plainfield, NJ 07062.

SMITH, STEVEN G.
PERSONAL Born 07/28/1953 **DISCIPLINE** PHILOSOPHY OF RELIGION; PHILOSOPHY OF HUMAN NATURE; GENDER; HISTORY OF PHILOSOPHY AND RELIGIOUS THOUGHT **EDUCATION** Fla State Univ, BA, 73; Vanderbilt Univ, MA, 78; Duke Univ, PhD, 80. **CAREER** Dept Philos, Millsaps Col **RESEARCH** Ethics, aesthetics, metaphysics. **SELECTED PUBLICATIONS** Auth, The Argument to the Other: Reason Beyond Thought in Karl Barth and Emmanuel Levinas, 83; The Concept of the Spiritual: An Essay in First Philosophy, 88 & Gender Thinking, 92; auth, "Sympathy, Scruple, and Piety: The Moral and Religious Valuation of Nonhumans," Journal of Religious Ethics, 21, (93): 319-342; auth, "Bowl Climbing: The Logic of Religious Question Rivalry," International Journal for Philosophy of Relig, 36, (94): 27-43; auth, "Greatness in Theism and Atheism: The Anselm-Feuerbach Conversation," Modern Theology, 12, (96): 385-403; auth, "Abraham's Family in Children of Gebelawi," Literature and Theology, 11, (97): 168-184; auth, "Can I Know Your IQ," Public Affairs Quarterly, 11, (97): 365-382; auth, "Kinds of Best World," International Journal for Philosophy of Religion, 44, (98): 145-162; auth, "Three Religious Attitudes," Philosophy and Theology, 11, (98): 3-24. **CONTACT ADDRESS** Dept of Philosophy, Millsaps Col, 1701 N State St, Jackson, MS 39210. **EMAIL** smithsg@millsaps.edu

SMITH, SUSAN WARRENER
PERSONAL Born 08/29/1944, Cincinnati, OH, m, 1982, 3 children **DISCIPLINE** THEOLOGICAL & RELIGIOUS STUDIES **EDUCATION** Boston Univ, BA, 66; Univ Mich, MA, 68; Drew Univ, PhD, 91. **CAREER** Adj Prof, Seton Hall Univ, 90-92; Dir, Christian Educ, 85-95; pastor, 95-. **HONORS AND AWARDS** Mead Hall Circle Study Prize; TA. **MEMBERSHIPS** AAR; Campus Min Asn Columbus **RESEARCH**

Cistercian Studies **SELECTED PUBLICATIONS** Auth, Bernard of Clairvaux and the Natural Realm: The Four Elements, Cistercian Stud Quart, 91; rev, The Things of Greater Importance: Bernard of Clairvaux Apologia and the Medieval Attitude Toward Art, Cistercian Stud Quart, 91; auth, Bernard of Clairvaux and the Nature of the Human Being: The Special Senses, Cistercian Stud Quart, 95; Bernard of Clairvaux and the Natural Realm: Images Related to the Elements, Cistercian Stud Quart, 96; The 1996 Institute of Cistercian Studies Conference, Cistercian Stud Quart, 96; The 1997 Institute of Cistercian Studies Conference, Cistercian Stud Quart, 97. **CONTACT ADDRESS** Indianola Presbyterian Church, 1970 Waldeck Ave, Columbus, OH 43201-1593. **EMAIL** abssws@aol.com

SMITH, TERRY
DISCIPLINE CIVIL PROCEDURE, EMPLOYMENT SECURITY, VOTING RIGHTS AND POLITICAL PARTICIPA AND LABOR LAW **EDUCATION** Brown Univ, AB, 86; NYork Univ Sch Law, JD, 89. **CAREER** Law clk, US Court of Appeals, Sixth Circuit, 89-90; assoc, Kirkland & Ellis, 90-93; assoc prof, 93-. **SELECTED PUBLICATIONS** Auth, Rediscovering the Sovereignty of the People: The Case for Senate Districts, 75 NC Law Rev 1, 96. **CONTACT ADDRESS** Law Sch, Fordham Univ, 113 W 60th St, New York, NY 10023. **EMAIL** tsmith@mail.lawnet.fordham.edu

SMITH, W. ALAN
PERSONAL Born 01/24/1949, Cleveland, TN, m, 1971, 2 children **DISCIPLINE** THEOLOGY; RELIGIOUS EDUCATION **EDUCATION** FL State Univ, BA, 72, additional grad study, 72-73; The Divinity School, Vanderbilt Univ, MDiv, 76, DMin, 83; additional grad study, School of Theology, Univ of the South, 83; School of Theology at Claremont, CA, PhD, 91. **CAREER** Pastor, First C. C. (Disciples of Christ), Greenville, KY, 76-79; Pastor, Fairhope Christian Church (Disciples of Christ), Fairhope, AL, 79-84; Assoc Minister, First Christian Church (Disciples of Christ), Pomona, CA, 84-87; asst prof relig, 87-95, assoc prof relig, 95-97, Prof Relig, 97-, Asst Dean for Academic Affairs, FL Southern Col, 98-00; acting ch, Education Dept, Florida Southern Col, 00-01. **HONORS AND AWARDS** Phi Eta Sigma Lover of Wisdom Awd, FSC, 92; Panhellenic Teacher of the Year Awd, FSC, 93; Grant recipient, Jessie Ball du Post summer seminars, 96; Fac/staff Volunteer of the Year Awd, FSC, 96. **MEMBERSHIPS** Amer Academy Relig; Soc Biblical Lit; Assoc Profs and Researchers in Relig Ed; Relig Ed Assoc; Disciples Assoc for The Academic Discussion of Christian Education; United Methodist Assoc for the Academic Study of Christian Education. **RESEARCH** Theology; religious ed; hermeneutical theory; Biblical studies; congregational studies; children in worship; youth ministry; Native Amer religions and philos. **SELECTED PUBLICATIONS** Auth, Children Belong in Worship: A Guide to the Children's Sermon, St Louis: CBP Press (Chalice Press), 84; Youth in the Local Congregation in Disciple Youth in the Church, St Louis: Christian Board of Pub, 85; Church Membership Curriculum, Called to Be Disciples: Worshiping, Witnessing, Serving, 4 vols, with cassette tape, St Louis: Christian Board of Pub, 88; Six articles in Harper's Encyclopedia of Religious Education, San Francisco: Harper & Row, 90; contrib, Discerning the Call: Advancing the Quality of Ordained Leadership, ed, John M. Imbler and Linda Plengemeier, St Louis: Chalice Press, 92; Intersubjectivity and Community: Some Implications from Gadamer's Philosophy for Religious Education, Relig Ed 88, no 3, summer 93; Naaman and Elisha: Healing, Wholeness, and the Task of Religious Education, Relig Ed 89, no 2, spring 94; A Cherokee Way of Knowing: Can Native American Spirituality Impact Religious Education?, Relig Ed 90, no 2, spring 95. **CONTACT ADDRESS** Florida So Col, 111 Lake Hollongsworth Dr., Lakeland, FL 33801-5698. **EMAIL** wsmith@flsouthern.edu

SMITH, WALLACE CHARLES
PERSONAL Born 11/06/1948, Philadelphia, PA, m, 1976, 1 child **DISCIPLINE** THEOLOGY **EDUCATION** Villanova U, BA 1970; Eastern Bapt Sem, MDiv 1974; Eastern Bapt Sem, DMin 1979. **CAREER** Eastern Bapt Sem, asst Prof-Pastorial Min, 79-85; Calvary Bapt Church, pastor, 74-85; Prof Practice of Ministry, Vanderbilt Divinity School, 85-91; Pastor, First Baptist Chapitol Hill, 85-91; Shiloh Baptist Church, pastor, 91. **HONORS AND AWARDS** President Washington Metropolitan Ministerium; Vice Chair Board of Directors, Eastern Seminary; 1996 Bnai Brith Man of The Year, DC. **MEMBERSHIPS** Exec bd Chester Br NAACP 1974-; pres Chester Clergy Assn 1977-79; pres Chester Community Improvement Project 1979-. **SELECTED PUBLICATIONS** Auth, The Church in The Life of The Black Family, Judson Press. **CONTACT ADDRESS** Pastor Shiloh Baptist Church, 1500 9th St, NW, Washington, DC 20001. **EMAIL** pastor@shilohbaptist.org

SMITH, WILLIAM A.
PERSONAL Born 12/12/1929, Newburgh, NY, m, 1958, 5 children **DISCIPLINE** PHILOSOPHY **EDUCATION** Gregorian Univ, Rome, PhD, 53; St John's Univ, PhD, 67. **CAREER** Instr, Col of New Rochelle, 56-57; from instr to prof, Seton Hall Univ, 58- . **HONORS AND AWARDS** McQuald Medal, 88. **RESEARCH** Ethics; American philosophy; philosophy of death. **SELECTED PUBLICATIONS** Auth, Ethical Reflections, Simon & Schuster, 97; auth, Readings in Ethics, 3d ed, Kendall Hunt, 98. **CONTACT ADDRESS** Dept of Philosophy, Seton Hall Univ, So Orange, 400 S Orange Ave, South Orange, NJ 07079. **EMAIL** smithwia@shu.edu

SMITH, YOLANDA Y.
PERSONAL Born 10/01/1957, San Antonio, TX, s **DISCIPLINE** RELIGIOUS STUDIES **EDUCATION** Ariz State Univ, BAE, 79; MEd, 84; Va Union Univ, MDiv, 90; Claremont Sch Theol, PhD, 97, 98. **CAREER** Instr, Alhambra High Sch, 79-83; Instr, Rio Salada Community Col, 92-93; Adj Instr, Claremont Sch Theol, 97; Vis Fac, Seattle Univ, 99; Vis Asst Prof, Iliff Sch Theol, 98-. **HONORS AND AWARDS** USA Doctoral Grant, Am Baptist Churches, 94-95; Theol Educ Black Doctoral Scholars Fel, 94-97; President's Awd for Acad Excellence, Claremont Sch of Theol, 98; Grant, Wabash Ctr for Teaching and Learning, 00. **MEMBERSHIPS** Am Acad Relig, Soc Bibl Lit, Relig Educ Asn, Asn Profs and Res in Relig Educ, Asn Pan African Doctoral Scholars, Asn Practical Theol. **RESEARCH** Theological perspectives of Christian religious education, history theory and methodology of Christian religious education, educational practice with particular attention to the role of the Arts, Christian education in the African-American experience, multicultural approaches to education in the church, womanist approaches to Christian religious education. **SELECTED PUBLICATIONS** Co-ed, Resources for Sacred Teaching, Allen J Moore Multicultural Resource and Res Ctr, 95; auth, "Sister to Sister: Women Sharing Christ One with Another," in Woman to Woman: Approaches to Witness and Outreach, Nat Ministries Pr (96); coauth, "Olivia Pearl Stokes: A Living Testimony of Faith," in Faith of our Foremothers: Women Changing Relig Educ, Westminster/John Knox Pr (97), 100-120; auth, "He Still Wid Us-Jesus: The Musical Theology of the Spirituals," Christian Hist, issue 62, vol XVII, no 2 (99): 18-19; auth, "The Spirit of Creativity," in Essays in Hon of Dr Grant S Shockley (forthcoming); auth, "A Womanist Approach to Teaching the Triple-Heritage Through the African-American Education" (forthcoming); auth, "Teaching Through the Spirituals: New Possibilities for African-American Christian Education" (forthcoming); **CONTACT ADDRESS** Dept Relig Studies, Iliff Sch Theol, 2201 S University Blvd, Denver, CO 80210-4707. **EMAIL** ysmith@iliff.edu

SMITHBURN, JOHN ERIC
PERSONAL Born 11/21/1944, Noblesville, IN, 1 child **DISCIPLINE** LAW **EDUCATION** IN Univ, BS, 66, MA, 69, JD, 73. **CAREER** Assoc prof law, 78-82, Prof Law, Notre Dame Law Sch, 82-, Fac, Ind Judicial Ctr, 77-, Nat Judicial Col, 78, Nat Inst Trial Advocacy, 79- & Nat Col Juvenile Justice, 79. **HONORS AND AWARDS** Tchg Serv Awd, Nat Judicial Col, 82. **RESEARCH** Family law; evidence; juvenile law **SELECTED PUBLICATIONS** Auth, Sentencing in Indiana: Appellate review of the trial court's discretion, Valparaiso Law Rev, winter 78; Perceived perjury as a factor in criminal sentencing, Res Gestae, 10/79; Review of Bellow and Moulton, The Lawyering Process: Materials for Clinical Instruction in Advocacy, Ariz Law J, No 1, 1980; coauth, Effective assistance of counsel: In quest of a uniform standard of review, Wake Forest Law Rev, 8/81; auth, Review of Nolan, Trial Practice: Cases and Materials, Univ Calif Los Angeles Law Rev, Vol 28, No 5; Judicial Discretion, Nat Judicial Col, 81, successor ed, 91; co-ed, Lizzie Borden: A Case Book of Family and Crime in the 1890s, Tichenor Inc, 81; auth, Criminal Trial Advocacy, NITA, 83, 2nd ed, 85; Indiana Family Law, vols 14-15, West, 91; Family Law: Problems and Documents, Aspen, 97. **CONTACT ADDRESS** Law Sch, Univ of Notre Dame, Notre Dame, IN 46556. **EMAIL** smithburn.1@nd.edu

SMITHERMAN, CAROLE
PERSONAL m **DISCIPLINE** LAW **EDUCATION** Spelman College, BA, political science; Miles Law School, JD, 1979. **CAREER** Miles Law School, professor, 82-; State of Alabama, circuit court judge, 91; private practice, attorney, currently. **HONORS AND AWARDS** Recipient of numerous honors and awards for public service. **SELECTED PUBLICATIONS** First African-American woman deputy district attorney, State of Alabama, 1982; first appointed woman judge, City of Birmingham, 1986; first appointed African-American woman circuit court judge, 1991. **CONTACT ADDRESS** Rodger & Carole Smitherman, 1919 Morris Ave, Suite 1550, Birmingham, AL 35203.

SMOKER, PAUL L.
DISCIPLINE PEACE STUDIES AND INTERNATIONAL RELATIONS **EDUCATION** Lancaster Univ, Eng, MSc, PhD. **CAREER** Lloyd Prof Peace Stud and World Law, Antioch Col. **MEMBERSHIPS** Int Peace Res Asn; World Future Soc; World Futures Stud Fedn. **RESEARCH** The evolution of holistic peace theory. **SELECTED PUBLICATIONS** Auth, Peacekeeping, in Encyclopedia of the Future, MacMillan, 96; coauth, A Reader n Peace Studies, Pergamon Press, 90; Collected Papers of Lewis Fry Richardson, Cambridge UP, 1993; Inadvertent Nuclear War: The Implications of the Changing Global Order, Pergamon Press, 93; Towards Global/Local Cultures of Peace, in UNESCO Readings in Peace and Conflict Stud, 96; Exploring the Foundations for Inner-Outer Peace in the Twenty-First Century, Int J of Peace Stud, 96. **CONTACT ADDRESS** Antioch Col, Yellow Springs, OH 45387.

SMURL, JAMES FREDERICK
PERSONAL Born 08/20/1934, Wilkes-Barre, PA, m, 1967, 4 children **DISCIPLINE** PHILOSOPHY, THEOLOGY **EDUCATION** St Mary's Univ, Md, BA, 55; Gregorian Univ, STL, 59; Cath Univ Am, STD, 63. **CAREER** Instr theol, Marywood Col, 59-61; asst prof, St Pius X Sem, Pa, 64-67; asst prof humanities & relig, Okla State Univ, 68-70, assoc prof, 70-73; assoc prof relig studies & chmn dept, 73-80, Prof Social & Comp Relig Ethics, Ind Univ, Indianapolis, 80-, Vis scholar, Kennedy Ctr Bioethics, 78-; vis prof, Ind Univ, Bloomington, 79; adj prof nursing, med genetics, Ind Univ, Indianapolis, 80-; Lilly open fac fel, 81. **MEMBERSHIPS** Am Acad Relig; Soc Christian Ethics; Soc Values Higher Educ. **RESEARCH** Thomistic ethics; social and comparative religious ethics; distributive justice in American culture. **SELECTED PUBLICATIONS** Auth, To Generate New Will, Cimarron Rev, 6/68; Willingness: Key To Freedom, J Thought, 69; Religious Ethics, Prentice-Hall, 72; Cross-cultural comparisons in ethics, J Relig Ethics, 76; Eligibility for legal aid: Whom to help when unable to help all, Int Law Rev, 79; Distributing the burden fairly: Ethics and national health policy, Man & Med, 80; Making ethical decisions systematically, Nursing Life, 82. **CONTACT ADDRESS** Dept Relig Studies, Indiana Univ-Purdue Univ, Indianapolis, 1100 W Michigan St, Indianapolis, IN 46202-2880.

SMYERS, KAREN A.
PERSONAL Born 10/31/1954, Annapolis, MD, d **DISCIPLINE** RELIGION **EDUCATION** Smith Col, BA, 76; Princeton Univ, MA, 89, PhD, 93. **CAREER** Lectr, Princeton Univ, 92; asst dir, prof anthrop, EAGLE Prog, Japan, 93; asst prof Wesleyan Univ, 93-. **HONORS AND AWARDS** Nat Rsrc Fel, 83-84; Coll Women's Asoc of Japan fel, 84-85; Princeton Univ Fel, 86-87, 87-88, 88-89, 91-92; Fulbright-Hays Diss Fel, 89-90; Japan Found Diss Fel, 90-91; A W Mellon Post-Enrollment Fel, 92; Fac Proj Grant, Wesleyan Univ, 94, 98; Pedag Develop Grant, Wesleyan Univ, 95, 96; Japan Soc for the Prom of Sci Postdoc Fel, 97-98; Japanese Ministry of Ed Grant, 97-98; cum laude, smith col, 76. **MEMBERSHIPS** Am Anthrop Asoc; Am Acad of Rel; Asoc of Asian Stud; C G Jung Found for Anal Psychol; Conn Asoc for Jungian Psychol. **RESEARCH** Anthropology of religion; religions of Japan, Jungian thought. **SELECTED PUBLICATIONS** Auth, "The Japanese Altar," in Dictionary of Art, Macmillan, 96; "My Own Inari: Personalization of the Deity in Inari Worship," Japanese Jrnl of Relig Stud, 96; "Encountering the Fox in Contemporary Japan: Thoughts of an American Anthropologist," in Etudes sur les Cultes Populaires de Japon, 98; Inari Pilgrimage, Japanese Jrnl of Relig Stud, 97; "The Fox and the Jewel: Shared and Private Meanings in Japanese Inari Worship," Univ Hawaii, forthcoming **CONTACT ADDRESS** Dept of Religion, Wesleyan Univ, Middletown, CT 06459. **EMAIL** ksmyers@wesleyan.edu

SMYLIE, JAMES HUTCHINSON
PERSONAL Born 10/20/1925, Huntington, WV, m, 1952, 3 children **DISCIPLINE** AMERICAN CHURCH HISTORY **EDUCATION** Washington Univ, BA, 46; Princeton Theol Sem, BD, 49, ThM, 50, PhD(church hist), 58. **CAREER** Asst minister, First Presby Church, St Louis, 50-52; instr church hist, Princeton Theol Sem, 56-59, asst prof, 59-62, dir studies, 60-62; alumni vis prof church hist, 62-64, assoc prof, 64-67, PROF AM CHURCH HIST, UNION THEOL SEM, VA, 67-95, Advan Relig Studies Found grant, 67; ed, J Presby Hist, 68-95. **MEMBERSHIPS** AHA; Am Cath Hist Asn; Am Studies Asn; Am Soc Church Historians (secy, 63-). **RESEARCH** Religion and politics; religion and culture. **SELECTED PUBLICATIONS** Auth, Into All the World, 65; auth, A Cloud of Witnesses, John Knox, 65; ed, Presbyterians and the American Revolution: A documentary account, 74; Presbyterians and the American Revolution: An interpretive account, J Presby Hist, 76; auth, A Brief History of Presbyterians, Geneva Press, 96. **CONTACT ADDRESS** 3211 Noble, Richmond, VA 23222.

SMYTHE, THOMAS W.
PERSONAL Born 02/03/1941, Buffalo, NY, m, 1969, 1 child **DISCIPLINE** PHILOSOPHY **EDUCATION** Univ Mich, PhD, 71; Univ Calif, MA, 65; State Univ NYork, BA, 63. **CAREER** Vis instr, NC Cent Univ, 96-97; vis asst prof, NC State Univ, 94-96; adj asst prof, Fayetteville State Univ, 92-94. **MEMBERSHIPS** Am Philos Asn; Triangle Ethics Discussion Group; Soc Christian Philos. **RESEARCH** Self-knowledge; problems of consciousness; philosophy of religion. **SELECTED PUBLICATIONS** Auth, The Reliability of Premise and Conclusion Indicators, Inquiry: Critical Thinking Across the Disciplines, Spring, 97; auth, Fawkes on Indicator Words, Inquiry: Critical Thinking Across the Disciplines, Fall, 96; coauth, Simplicity and Theology, Relig Studies, June, 96; coauth, Swinburne's Argument for Dualism, Faith & Philos, Jan, 94. **CONTACT ADDRESS** 213 Chesley Lane, Chapel Hill, NC 27514. **EMAIL** twsmythe@email.unc.edu

SNEED, JOSEPH DONALD
PERSONAL Born 09/23/1938, Durant, OK, m, 1998, 1 child **DISCIPLINE** PHILOSOPHY OF SCIENCE **EDUCATION** Rice Univ, BS, 60; Univ Ill, MS, 62; Stanford Univ, PhD(-philos), 64. **CAREER** Prof philos, Stanford Univ, 66-73; policy analyst, SRI Int, Menlo Park, Calif, 73-74; prof philos, Univ Munich, Ger, 74-76, Univ Calif, Santa Cruz, 76-77, Tech Univ

Eindhoven, Netherlands, 77-78 & State Univ NY Albany, 78-80; Prof Humanities, Colo Sch Mines, 80-, Vis prof, Univ Uppsala, Sweden, 69 & Heidelberg Univ, Ger, 76. **MEMBERSHIPS** Am Philos Asn. **RESEARCH** Logical structure of empirical theories; decision theory; distributive justice. **SELECTED PUBLICATIONS** Auth, Quantum mechanics and classical probability theory, Synthese, 20: 34-64; The Logical Structure of Mathematical Physics, Reidel, Dordrecht, Holland, 71; co-ed, Restructuring the Federal System: Approaches to Accountability in Post-Categorical Programs, Crane-Russak, 75; auth, John Rawls and the liberal theory of society, Erkenntnis, 4/76; coauth, Generalized net structures for empirical theories, Part I, Studia Logics, Vol XXXVI, No 3; Patrick Suppes' contribution to the foundations of physics, In: Profile of Contemporary Philosophers: Patrick Suppes, Reidel, Dordrecht, Holland, 78; auth, A utilitarian framework for policy analysis in food and food-related foreign aid, In: Food Policy: US Responsibility in the Life and Death Choices, Free Press, 78; Theoritization and invariance principles, In: The Logic and Epistemology of Scientific Change, Nonth-Halland, 79. **CONTACT ADDRESS** Humanities & Soc Sci Dept, Colorado Sch of Mines, 1500 Illinois St, Golden, CO 80401-1887. **EMAIL** jsneed@mines.edu

SNEIDERMAN, BARNEY
DISCIPLINE LAW **EDUCATION** Trinity Col, BA, 59; Univ Conn, LLB, 68; Univ NY, LLM, 67. **CAREER** Prof, Univ of Man. **RESEARCH** Criminal law; issues in law and biomedical ethics; issues in crime and punishment; the limits of law. **SELECTED PUBLICATIONS** Auth, Just Say No to the War on Drugs, Manitoba Law, 96; Euthanasia in the Netherlands, 96; co-auth, Canadian Medical Law: An Introduction for Physicians and Other Health Care Professionals, 96. **CONTACT ADDRESS** Fac of Law, Univ of Manitoba, Robson Hall, Winnipeg, MB, Canada R3T 2N2. **EMAIL** sneiderm@cc.umanitoba.ca

SNODGRASS, KLYNE RYLAND
PERSONAL Born 12/28/1944, Kingsport, TN, m, 1966, 2 children **DISCIPLINE** BIBLICAL STUDIES **EDUCATION** Columbia Bible Col, BA, 66; Trinity Evangel Divinity Sch, MDiv, 69; Univ St Andrews, Scotland, DPhil, 73. **CAREER** Lectr, bibl studies, Georgetown Col, 73-74; asst prof, 74-78, assoc prof bibl lit, N Park Theol Sem, 78-84, prof, 84-89, dean of faculty, North Park Theol Sem, 88-93, Paul W. Brandel Prof of New Testament Studies, 89-; ed, Ex Auditu, consulting ed, NIV Application Commentary, trans analysis, New Living Translation. **HONORS AND AWARDS** Recipient of Asn of Theological Schools grant for sabbatical research, 81; Honorary Alumnus of North Park Col for 94; Recipient of Pew Evangelical Scholars Program grant for 95-96; Listed in Who's Who in Am Education, Who's Who in Biblical Studies and Archaeology, and Who's Who in Religion. **MEMBERSHIPS** Soc Bibl Lit; Inst Bibl Res, ex sec, 89-93, pres, 93-95; Chicago Soc Bibl Research, ex sec, 82-86, vice pres, 89-90, pres, 90-91; Studiorum Novi Testamenti Societas. **RESEARCH** The parables of Jesus; the semitic background of the New Testament; Pauline studies. **SELECTED PUBLICATIONS** Auth, Western Non-Interpolations, J Bibl Lit, 73; The Parable of the Wicked Husbandmen: Is the Gospel of Thomas Version the Original, New Testament Studies, 75; Liberty or Legality?, The Pauline Dilemma, 75, Exegesis and Preaching: The Principles and Practice of Exegesis, 76 & Paul and Women, 76, Covenant Quart; I Peter 2.1-10: Its Formation and Literary Affirmities, New Testament Studies, 78; Streams of Tradition Emerging from Isaiah 40: 1-5 and Their Adaptation in the New Testament, J Study New Testament, Vol VIII, 80; The Parable of the Wicked Tenants, Tubingen: J. C. B. Mohr (Paul Siebeck), 83; A Biblical and Theological Basis for Women in Ministry: An Occasional Paper, Chicago: Covenant Pubs, 87; Between Two Truths: Living with Biblical Tensions, Grand Rapids: Zondervan Pub House, 90; Divorce and Remarriage: An Occasional Paper, Chicago: Covenant Pubs, 92; Ephesians in The NIV Application Commentary, Grand Rapids: Zondervan Pub House, 96; and numerous articles in : Journal of Biblical Literature, New Testament Studies, Covenant Companion, Seminary Review: North Park Theological Seminary, The Covenant Quarterly, Daughters of Sarah, Journal for the Study of the New Testament, Bulletin of Biblical Research, New Testament Backgrounds: A Sheffield Reader, Women, Authority and the Bible, Christianity Today, The Best in Theology, The Pauline Writings, SBL Seminar Papers, Treasures New and Old: Contributions to Matthean Studies, Baker Encyclopedia of the Bible, The Second Century, Mercer Dictionary of the Bible, Perspectives on John: Method and Interpretation in the Fourth Gospel, New Testament Criticism and Interpretation, The Right Doctrine From the Wrong Texts?, Biblical Research, Dictionary of Jesus and the Gospels, Chiasmus in the New Testament, Interpretation, Gospel Interpretation: Narrative-Critical and Social-scientific Approaches, Holman Bible Handbook, A Dictionary of Biblical Tradition in English Literature, Perspectives in Religious Studies, Gospel in Paul: Studies on Corinthians, Galations and Romans for Richard N. Longenecker, Theology, News and Notes; auth, Common Linfe in the Early Church: Essays Honoring Graydon F. Snyder; auth, Judgement Day at the White House; auth, Jesus and the Restoration of Israel; auth, The Challenge of Jesus Parables. **CONTACT ADDRESS** No Park Theol Sem, 3225 W Foster Ave, Chicago, IL 60625-4810. **EMAIL** ksnodgr@northpark.edu

SNOEYENBOS, MILTON
DISCIPLINE PHILOSOPHY OF ART, ORGANIZATIONAL AND BUSINESS ETHICS, INFORMAL LOGIC, PHIL **EDUCATION** Univ Minn, PhD, 75. **CAREER** Assoc prof, Ga State Univ. **HONORS AND AWARDS** Several teaching awards. **SELECTED PUBLICATIONS** Coed, Business Ethics; author of over sixty articles, primarily in business ethics and philosophy of art. **CONTACT ADDRESS** Georgia State Univ, Atlanta, GA 30303.

SNOOK, LEE E.
PERSONAL Born 03/14/1930, Lewistown, PA, m, 1952 **DISCIPLINE** SYSTEMATIC THEOLOGY **EDUCATION** Gettysburg Col, BA; Lutheran Theol Sem, MDiv, 56; Union Theol Sem, STM, 67, PhD, 70. **CAREER** Univ pastor, Cornell, 60-70; instr, United Theol Col; vis prof, Univ Zimbabwe, 87-89, 92-93; asst prof, 70; prof, 77-; Instituted Luther Sem Program in Zimbabwe, 92; prof emer, 99-. **HONORS AND AWARDS** Sr fel, Inst Advan Stud Rel, Univ Chicago, 84; sr pastor, chaplain, cornell univ, 62-70; pastor, good shepherd evangel lutheran church, 59-62; st luke evangel lutheran church, 55-59. **MEMBERSHIPS** Mem, ALC task force. **RESEARCH** Christianity and culture in Africa; hist and dev of doctrine of Trinity and of Holy Spirit. **SELECTED PUBLICATIONS** Auth, The Anonymous Christ, Jesus as Savior in Modern Theology, 86; Preaching on National Holidays, 76; O God..Pay Attention: A Journal for Lent, 70; auth, "What in the World Is God Doing?, Re-imagining Spirit and Power," Minneapolic: Fortress Press, 99. **CONTACT ADDRESS** Dept of Systematic Theology, Luther Sem, 2481 Como Ave, Saint Paul, MN 55108. **EMAIL** lsnook@luthersem.edu

SNOW, STEVEN GREGORY
DISCIPLINE POLITICAL SCIENCE **EDUCATION** Univ IA, BA, 86; Univ WA, MA, 89; PhD, 94. **CAREER** Prof, Wagner Col, 94-. **HONORS AND AWARDS** Fulbright Lecturer, Panama City, 96. **RESEARCH** Political economy; Comparative politics (W Europe). **SELECTED PUBLICATIONS** Auth, "Balancing on the Brink: Rationality, Radicalism and Military Insurrection in Spain and Chile," Journal of Political and Military Sociology, (98): 273-289; auth, "Reformers and Investors in Sweden and France: Crisis and Confidence during the Depression," Research in Political Economy, 99; auth, "Voices of Hostile Capital: Social Order and Investment Confidence during the Second Spanish Republic," South European society and Politics, 99; co-auth, "Pathways in the Periphery: Tourism to Indigenous Communities in Panama," Social Science Quarterly, forthcoming. **CONTACT ADDRESS** Dept Soc Sci, Wagner Col, 1 Campus Rd, Staten Island, NY 10301-4479. **EMAIL** sgsnow@wagner.edu

SNYDER, GLENN HERALD
PERSONAL Born 10/08/1924, Superior, WI, m, 1951, 3 children **DISCIPLINE** POLITICAL SCIENCE **EDUCATION** Univ Oregon, BS, 48; Columbia Univ, PhD, 56. **CAREER** Tchg fel, Wesleyan Univ, 53-55; lectr, res assoc, Columbia Univ, 55-58; res assoc, Princeton Univ, 58-60; assoc prof, Univ Denver, 60-62; vis assoc prof, Univ Calif, Berkeley, 62-64; assoc prof, prof, SUNY Buffalo, 64-84; prof, prof emer, Univ North Carolina, 84-. **HONORS AND AWARDS** Fel, Woodrow Wilson Ctr, 81-82; fel, Guggenheim Found, 90-91. **MEMBERSHIPS** Am Polit Sci Asn; Int Inst for Strategic Stud; Triangle Inst for Strategic Stud. **RESEARCH** International relations; military affairs. **SELECTED PUBLICATIONS** Auth, Deterrence and Defense, Princeton, 61; coauth, Strategy, Politics and Defense Budgets, Columbia, 62; auth, Stockpiling Strategic Materials, Chandler, 67; coauth, Conflict Among Nations, Princeton, 77; auth, Alliance Politics, Cornell, 97. **CONTACT ADDRESS** Dept of Political Science, Univ of No Carolina, Chapel Hill, 520 Morgan Creek Rd, Chapel Hill, NC 27514. **EMAIL** gsnyder1@email.unc.edu

SOBEL, LIONEL S.
DISCIPLINE LAW **EDUCATION** Univ Calif, Berkeley, BA, 66; Univ Calif, Los Angeles, JD, 69. **CAREER** Prof Loyola Univ, 82-; former partner, Freedman & Sobel, Beverly Hills; ed, Entertainment Law Reporter, 78-. **RESEARCH** Copyright; trademark; libel; privacy problems. **SELECTED PUBLICATIONS** Writes on, of copyright, entertainment and sports law. **CONTACT ADDRESS** Law School, Loyola Marymount Univ, 7900 Loyola Blvd, Burns 344, Los Angeles, CA 90045. **EMAIL** lsobel@lmulaw.lmu.edu

SOBER, ELLIOTT REUBEN
PERSONAL Born 06/06/1948, Baltimore, MD, m, 1969, 2 children **DISCIPLINE** PHILOSOPHY **EDUCATION** Univ Pa, BA, 69, MScEd, 70; Harvard Univ, PhD, 74. **CAREER** From Asst Prof to Assoc Prof, 74-84, Prof Philos, Univ Wis, Madison 84-. **HONORS AND AWARDS** Lakatos Prize, 89; Vilas Res Prof, 93-. **MEMBERSHIPS** Am Philos Asn (Pres Central Div, 98-99); Philos Sci Asn. **RESEARCH** Philosophy of biology and psychology; metaphysics; epistemology. **SELECTED PUBLICATIONS** Auth, The Nature of Selection: Evolutionary Theory in Philosophical Focus, MIT Press, 84, 2nd ed, Univ Chicago Press, 93; Reconstructing the Past: Parsimony, Evolution, and Inference, MIT Press, 88, Japanese ed, Souju Publ, 96; coauth, Reconstructing Marxism: Essays on Explanation and the Theory of History, Verso Press, 92, Portugese ed, 93; auth, Philosophy of Biology, Westview Press, 93, UK ed, Oxford Univ Press, 93, Span ed, Alianza, 96; From a Biological Point of View: Essays in Evolutionary Philosophy, Cambridge Univ Press, 94; coauth, Unto Others: The Evolution and Psychology of Unselfish Behavior, Harvard Univ Press, 98. **CONTACT ADDRESS** Dept of Philos, Univ of Wisconsin, Madison, 600 North Park St, Madison, WI 53706-1403. **EMAIL** ersober@facstaff.wisc.edu

SOBSTYL, EDRIE
DISCIPLINE PHILOSOPHY **EDUCATION** Univ Alberta, PhD, 95. **CAREER** Asst prof. **HONORS AND AWARDS** Ed asst, Acta Analytica. **RESEARCH** Philosophy of science; feminist theory; social and political philosophy; theory of knowledge. **SELECTED PUBLICATIONS** Coauth, Women, Madness and Special Defenses in the Law, Jour Soc Philos, 90. **CONTACT ADDRESS** Dept of History, Univ of Texas, Dallas, Richardson, TX 75083-0688. **EMAIL** esobstyl@utdallas.edu

SOCKNESS, BRENT
PERSONAL Born 03/02/1962, St. Paul, MN, m, 1989, 2 children **DISCIPLINE** THEOLOGY **EDUCATION** St Olaf Col, BA, 84; Univ Chicago, MA, 85, PhD, 96. **CAREER** Instr, relig, DePaul Univ, 88; res anal, City of Chicago Bd Ethics, 89-90; instr and tutor, relig, St Olaf Col, 92, 93-96; DAAD res grant, Germany, 92-93; asst prof relig stud, Stanford Univ, 96-. **HONORS AND AWARDS** Phi Beta Kappa, 83; Summa Cum Laude, 84; fel, Divinity Sch, Univ Chicago, 87-88, 88-89; Josephine De Karmen Fel, 88-89; jr fel, Inst for Advan Stud Relig, Univ Chicago, 89-90; Brown Fac Fel, Stanford Univ, 98-99; Benlin Prize fel, Am Academy - Berlin. **MEMBERSHIPS** Am Acad Relig; Ernst-Troeltsch-Gesellschaft; Schleiermacher-Gesellschaft, Soc of Christian Ethics. **RESEARCH** Nineteenth-century German theology and ethics. **SELECTED PUBLICATIONS** Auth, Luther's Two Kingdoms Revisited: A Response to Reinhold Niebuhr's Criticism of Luther, Jour of Relig Ethics, 92; auth, The Ideal and the Historical in the Christology of Wilhelm Herrmann: The Promise and Perils of Revisionary Christology, Jour of Relig, 92; auth, Ethics as Fundamental Theology: The Function of Ethics in the Theology of Wilhelm Herrmann, Annual of Soc of Christian Ethics, 92; auth, Looking Behind the Social Teachings: Troeltsch's Methodological Reflections in Grundprobleme der Ethik, Annual Soc of Christian Ethics, 95; auth, Troeltsch's Practical Christian Ethics: The Heidelberg Lectures, Annual of Soc of Christian Ethics, 97; auth, Against False Apologetics: Wilhelm Herrmann and Ernst Troeltsch in Conflict, JCB Mohr, 98. **CONTACT ADDRESS** Dept of Religious Studies, Stanford Univ, Stanford, CA 94305. **EMAIL** sockness@leland.stanford.edu

SODEN, RICHARD ALLAN
PERSONAL Born 02/16/1945, Brooklyn, NY, m, 1969 **DISCIPLINE** LAW **EDUCATION** Hamilton Coll, AB 1967; Boston Univ Sch of Law, JD 1970. **CAREER** Hon Geo Clifton Edwards Jr US Court of Appeals for the 6th Circuit, law clerk 1970-71; Boston Coll Sch of Law, faculty 1973-74; Goodwin Procter & Hoar LLP, assoc 1971-79, partner 1979-. **HONORS AND AWARDS** American Bar Foundation, Fellow; Boy Scouts of America, Silver Beaver Awd and Community Youth Svc Awd, Heritage District; Theodore L Storer Awd; Boston University School of Law, Silver Shingle Awd; Massachusetts Bar Association, Community Service Awd; UNICEF-Boston Local Hero Awd; Camille Cosby World of Children Medallion. **MEMBERSHIPS** Amer Natl MA & Boston Bar Assns, Boston Bar Association, president, 1994-95; MA Black Lawyers Assn, pres, 1980-81; chairman, emeritus, trustee Judge Baker Guidance Ctr 1974-; chairman, Boston Municipal Rsch Bureau 1996-98; pres United South End Settlements 1977-79; adv cncl Suffolk Univ Sch of Mgmt 1980-; faculty MA Continuing Legal Educ 1980-; pres Mass Black Lawyers Assn 1980-81; Adv Task Force on Securities Regulation Sec of State of the Commonwealth of MA 1982-; pres, Greater Boston Cncl Boy Scouts of Amer 1997-99; adv comm on Legal Educ Supreme Judicial Ct of MA 1984-; Mass Minority Business Devel Commn; bd of visitors Boston Univ Goldman School of Graduate Dentistry; trustee, Boston University, 1995-; co-chairman, 1991-93, Lawyers Committee for Civil Rights Under Law; Amer Bar Assn, House of Delegates, 1995-97, chair, Standing Comm on Bar Activities and Services 1998-. **CONTACT ADDRESS** Goodwin Procter & Hoar, LLP, Exchange Pl, Boston, MS 02109.

SOFFER, GAIL
DISCIPLINE PHILOSOPHY **EDUCATION** Columbia Univ, PhD, 89. **CAREER** Assoc prof, Eugene Lang Col. **RESEARCH** Phenomenology; hermeneutics; hist of philos; metaphysics; epistemology. **SELECTED PUBLICATIONS** Auth, Heidegger, Humanism, and the Destruction of History, Rev Metaphysics, 96; Husserl and the Question of Relativism, 91. **CONTACT ADDRESS** Eugene Lang Col, New Sch for Social Research, 66 West 12th St, New York, NY 10011.

SOFFER, WALTER
PERSONAL Born 09/22/1941, Philadelphia, PA, m, 1987 **DISCIPLINE** PHILOSOPHY **EDUCATION** Temple Univ,

BA, 65; New Sch Social Res, MA, 70, PhD, 77. **CAREER** Asst prof philos, George Washington Univ, 73-75; asst prof to Prof, Philos State Univ NY Col, Geneseo, 76-. **HONORS AND AWARDS** Chancellor's Awd for Excellence in Teaching, 82. **RESEARCH** Descartes; ancient philos; mod philos. **SELECTED PUBLICATIONS** Auth, The Methodological Achievement of Cartesian doubt, Southern J Philos, spring 78; Descartes, Rationality and God, Thomist, 10/78; Kant on the Tutelage of God and Nature, Thomist, 1/81; Husserl's Neo-Carteianism, Res in Phenemenology, winter, 81; Descartes's Rejection of the Aristotelian Soul, Int Studies in Philos, vol XVI, no 1, 84; co-ed, The Crisis of Liberal Democracy: A Straussian Perspective, SUNY Press, 87; auth, From Science to Subjectivity: An Interpretation of Descartes's Meditations, Greenwood Press, 87; Dreaming, hyperbole, & Dogmatism, Idealistic Studies, vol XVIII, no 2, 88; reprint of Descartes's Rejection of the Aristotelian Soul, in Moyal, ed, Descartes: Critical Assessments, vol III, London, 91; Modern Rationalism, Miracles, & Revelation: Strauss's Critique of Spinoza, in Deutsch & Nicgorski, eds, Leo Strauss: Political Philosopher and Jewish Thinker, Rowman & Little, 94; Descartes' Secular Paradise: The Discourse on Method as Biblical Criticism, Philos and Theol, vol 8, no 4, summer 94; Socrates's Proposals Concerning Women: Feminism or Fantasy?, Hist of Political Thought, vol XVI, issue 2, summer 95. **CONTACT ADDRESS** NY Col, SUNY, Col at Geneseo, 1 College Cir, Geneseo, NY 14454-1401. **EMAIL** soffer@geneseo.edu

SOHN, LOUIS BRUNO
PERSONAL Born 03/01/1914, Lwow, Poland **DISCIPLINE** LAW **EDUCATION** John Casimir Univ, dipl, ScM, LLB, 35; Harvard Univ, LLM, 40, SJD, 58. **CAREER** Lectr, Harvard Univ, 47-51, asst prof, 51-53, prof law, Law Sch, 53-81; Prof Emer, 81-; Prof Law, Law Sch, Ga Univ, 81-, Consult, Legal Dept, UN Secretariat, 48, 69, Legal Affairs Off, UN, 50-51, US Arms Control & Disarmament Agency, 61-70 & Off Int Security Affairs, US Dept Defense, 63-70; vchmn, Fed Am Scientists, 63-64; chmn, Comn Study Orgn Peace, 68-; consult int law, US Dept State, 70-71, counr law of the sea task force, 72-; dep deleg, US Deleg to UN Law of Sea Conf, 74-81; comnr-at-large, US Nat Comn Unesco. **HONORS AND AWARDS** Addison-Brown Prize Harvard Univ, 41; John Harvey Gregory Fel, 46; John Harvey Gregory Lectr on World Organization, 47. **MEMBERSHIPS** Am Soc Int Law; Int Law Asn. **RESEARCH** International law; United Nations; human rights. **SELECTED PUBLICATIONS** Auth, Cases on World Law, 50 & Cases on United Nations Law, 56, 2nd ed, 67, Found Press; coauth, World Peace Through World Law, Harvard Univ, 58, 2nd ed, 60, 3rd ed, 66; ed, Basic Documents of African Regional Organizations (4 vols), Oceans, 71-72; Managing The Law Of The Sea--Ambassador Pardos Forgotten 2nd Idea, Columbia J Of Transnational Law, Vol 36, 97; Important Improvements In The Functioning Of The Principal Organs Of The United-Nations That Can Be Made Without Charter-Revision, Am J Of Int Law, Vol 91, 97; coauth, International Protection of Human Rights, Bobbs, 73; auth, Bipartie Consultative Commissions for Preventing and Resolving Disputes Relating to International Trade Treaties, In El Derecho International en un Mundo en Transformacion, 94; auth, How American International Lawyers Prepared for the San Francisco Bill of Rights, American Journal of International Law, 95; auth, The Human Rights Movement: From Roosevelt's Four Freedoms to the Interdependence of Peace, Development and Human Rights, 95; auth, The Importance of the Peaceful Settlement of Disputes Provisions of the United Nations Convention on the Law of the Sea, In Entry into Force of the Law of the Sea Convention, 95; auth, Interpreting the Law, In United Nations Legal Order, 95; auth, "Settlement of Law of the Sea Disputes," International Journal of Marine and Coastal Law 10 (95): 205 **CONTACT ADDRESS** Law Sch, Harvard Univ, Cambridge, MA 02138.

SOKOLOWSKI, ROBERT S.
PERSONAL Born 05/03/1934, New Britain, CT **DISCIPLINE** PHILOSOPHY **EDUCATION** Cath Univ Am, BA, 56, MA, 57; Cath Univ Louvain, MA, 61, PhD, 63. **CAREER** From instr to assoc prof, 63-71, prof philos, 71-, Cath Univ Am; vis assoc prof philos, grad fac, 69-70, New Sch Social Res; NEH jr fel, 71-72; vis prof philos, 78, Univ Tex, Austin; NEH fel, independent study & res, 82-83; vis prof, 84, Villanova Univ; vis prof, 92, Yale Univ. **HONORS AND AWARDS** Pres, Metaphysical Soc, 89-90; mem, Polish Acad of Sci, 96; 26th Oppenheimer Lectr, Los Alamos, NM, 96; Festschrift: The Truthful and the Good. **MEMBERSHIPS** Soc Phenomenol & Existential Psychol; Am Philos Assn; Am Cath Philos Soc; Metaphys Soc Am. **RESEARCH** Phenomenology; Aristotle; philosophy of language. **SELECTED PUBLICATIONS** Auth, Pictures, Quotations, and Distinctions, Notre Dame Univ Press, 92; auth, Eucharistic Presence, CVA Press, 94; auth, Introduction to Phenomenology, Cambridge Univ Press, 00. **CONTACT ADDRESS** Sch of Philos, Catholic Univ of America, Washington, DC 20017. **EMAIL** sokolowski@cva.edu

SOKOLOWSKI, WILLIAM R.
DISCIPLINE PHILOSOPHY **EDUCATION** MDiv, MA, PhD. **CAREER** Central Connecticut State Univ, prof. **HONORS AND AWARDS** Fulbright Scholarship, CT State Elections Enforcement Commission **RESEARCH** Semiotics; Pragmatism; Science. **CONTACT ADDRESS** 1300 Woodstick Rd, Wolcott, CT 06716. **EMAIL** sokol@juno.com

SOKOLSKY, JOEL J.
PERSONAL Born 07/21/1953, Toronto, ON, Canada, m, 1981, 3 children **DISCIPLINE** POLITICAL SCIENCE **EDUCATION** Univ Toronto, BA, 76; Johns Hopkins Sch Adv Intl Studies, MA, 78; Harvard Univ, PhD, 86. **CAREER** Instr, Johns Hopkins Univ, 80-84; asst prof, Dalhousie Univ, 84-86; asst prof to prof and dept head and dean, Royal Military Col, 86-; adj assoc prof to prof, Queen's Univ. 88. **HONORS AND AWARDS** Teaching Excellence Honour List, RMC, 95; NATO Fel, 83-84, 95-97; Canada-U.S. Fulbright Fel, 95-96. **MEMBERSHIPS** Asn for Can Studies in the U.S.; Sen Fel, Queen's Univ Centre for Intl Relations; NATO Partnership for Peace Consortium of Defence Acad and Strategis Studies Inst. **RESEARCH** Canadian Foreign and Defence Policy; American Foreign and Defence Policy; Modern Naval Strategy. **SELECTED PUBLICATIONS** Auth, Seapower in the Nuclear Age: The United States Navy and NATO, 1948-1980, Routledge, 91; auth, Great Ideals and Uneasy Compromises: The U.S. Approach to Peacekeeping," Intl J 95; auth, The Americanization of Peacekeeping: Implications for Canada, Queen's Univ Press, 97; auth, Projecting Stability: NATO and Multilateral Naval Cooperation in the Post Cold War Era, Dalhousie Univ, 98; auth, "Over There with Uncle Sam: Peacekeeping, the 'Trans-European Bargain' and the Canadian Forces," in What NATO for Canada? Kingston, 00; auth, "The Bilateral Security Relationship: Will National Missile Defence Involve Canada?" The Am Rev of Can Studies, 00; auth, The Revolution in Military Affairs and the Future of Arms Control and Verification, Dept of For Affairs, 01. **CONTACT ADDRESS** Dept Polit and Econ, Royal Military Col, PO Box 1700, Stn Forces, Kingston, ON, Canada K7K 7B4. **EMAIL** sokolsky-j@rmc.ca

SOLAN, LAWRENCE
PERSONAL Born 05/07/1952, New York, NY, m, 1982, 2 children **DISCIPLINE** LAW, LINGUISTICS **EDUCATION** Brandeis Univ, BA, 74; Univ Massachusetts, PhD Linguistics, 78; Harvard Law School, JD, 82. **CAREER** Law Clerk, Supreme Ct of NJ, 83-86; assoc, Orans, Elsen & Lupert, 83-86; partner, Orans, Elsen & Lupert, 89-96; Assoc Prof, Brooklyn Law School ol, 96-. **HONORS AND AWARDS** Bd Dir, Int Acad of Law and Mental health, 98-. **MEMBERSHIPS** Ling Soc of Am; Asn of the Bar of the City of New York; Law and Soc Asn; Int Asn of Forensic Ling; Int Acad of Law and Mental Health. **RESEARCH** Law; Language; Cognition. **SELECTED PUBLICATIONS** Auth, The Language of Judges, 993; When Judges Use the Dictionary, Am Speech, 93; Chomsku and Cardozo: Linguistics and the Law, 94; When All is Lost: Why it is Difficult for Judges to Write About Concepts, Graven Images, 94; Judicial Decision and Linguistic Analysis: Is There a Linguist in the Court?, Wash Univ, 95; Learning Our Limits: The Decline of Textualism in Statutory Cases, Wisconsin L Rev, 97; rev, Making Sense in Law, Forensic Ling, 97; Law, Language, and Lenity, William & Mary Rev, forthcoming; coauth, Linguists on the Witness Stand: law, Language and Cognition, forthcoming. **CONTACT ADDRESS** Brooklyn Law Sch, 250 Joralemon St, Brooklyn, NY 11201. **EMAIL** lsolan@brooklaw.edu

SOLDAN, ANGELIKA
PERSONAL Born 02/10/1953, Hennigsdorf, m, 1987, 1 child **DISCIPLINE** PHILOSOPHY **EDUCATION** Humboldt Univ, MA, 75, PhD, 90; Martin Luther Univ, PhD, 82. **CAREER** Asst prof, philos, Martin Luther Univ, 75-80; asst prof, 81-89, assoc prof, philos, 89-91, Humboldt Univ; adj prof philos, 92-97, Univ Texas, Edinburgh; adj instr, English as a Second Lang, 97-98, adj prof, philos, 92-98, Univ Texas, Brownsville; sr lectr, German, English as a Second Lang, Univ Wisconsin, Eau Claire, 98- . **HONORS AND AWARDS** Scholar for Joint Sessions of Workshops, UK, 91. **MEMBERSHIPS** Int Fromm Soc; APA; Asn for Practical and Professional Ethics; Asn of Am Teachers of German. **RESEARCH** Ethical values; Kegel; Fromm; Marx; Nietzsche; cultural history; humor and society; eighteenth, nineteenth, twentieth century philosophy. **SELECTED PUBLICATIONS** Auth, Das Sozialismusbild Erich Fromms, Erich-Fromm-Archiv, 93; auth, Lotte in Weimar, oden eine Zwischenstation Thomas Manns auf dem Wege zu sich, Orbis Litterarum, 96; auth, To Live Together, but Laugh Apart? German-German Communication Problems as Mirrored by Jokes, Int J of Humor Res, 98; auth, Im Wahren Leben: Franz Kafka Zwischen Beruf und Berufung, Mississippi Lang Crusader, 98. **CONTACT ADDRESS** 404 Santa Ana Ave, Rancho Viejo, TX 78575. **EMAIL** asoldan@utb1.utb.edu

SOLHEIM, BARBARA P.
PERSONAL Born Evanston, IL **DISCIPLINE** PHILOSOPHY, ETHICS **EDUCATION** Univ Ill Chicago, PhD, 96. **CAREER** Adj prof, Lake Forest Col; Wm Rainey Harper Col. **HONORS AND AWARDS** Phi Beta Kappa; Phi Kappa Phi. **MEMBERSHIPS** Am Philos Soc. **RESEARCH** Ethics; Medical ethics; Business ethics; Environmental ethics. **SELECTED PUBLICATIONS** Auth, "The Possibility of a Duty to Love" in The Journal of Social Phlosophy, Spring 99. **CONTACT ADDRESS** 654 Warwick Rd, Deerfield, IL 60015. **EMAIL** bpsolheim@aol.com

SOLL, A. IVAN
PERSONAL Born 03/29/1938, Philadelphia, PA, m, 1988, 1 child **DISCIPLINE** PHILOSOPHY **EDUCATION** Princeton Univ, AB, 60; PhD, 64. **CAREER** Instr, 64-66; asst prof, 66-69; assoc prof, 69-73; prof, 73-, Univ Wisconsin; prof, Univ Michigan/Wisconsin, 83; dir, Univ Michigan/Wisconsin, 85-86; dir, Univ Wisconsin/Univ California, 89; vis prof, Justus-Liebig Univ, Ger, 89; prof, Univ Wisconsin/Univ Michigan, Italy, 91, 94; vis lectr, Univ Ack, Aust, 93; dir, Univ Wis/Cal, Hang, 93-94; prof, Univ, Wis/Cal, Italy, 97; prof, Univ Wis/Michigan/Duke, Italy, 01. **HONORS AND AWARDS** Warbecke Prize; Phi Beta Kappa; Woodrow Wilson Fel; Fulbright Fel; Spencer Found Gnt; Who's Who in Midwest, Am, Men Dist; Authors Writ, Intelle; NEH Gnt; ACLS Trv Gnt; CES Trv Gnt; IRHM Fel; DAAD Gnt. **SELECTED PUBLICATIONS** Auth, An Introduction to Hegel's Metaphysics, Univ Chic Press (Chicago and London), 69; auth, What Goes Around Comes Around, Tiramisu Press, 95; auth, 'Redeeming Life through Art: Nietzsche contra Schopenhauer" in Willingness & Nothingness: Schopenhauer as Nietzsche's Educator, ed. C Janaway (Ox Univ Press, 98); auth, "On the Purported Insignificance of Death: Whistling in the Dark?" in Death and Philosophy, eds. JE Malpas, Robert C Solomon (Routledge, London, 98); auth, "Walter Kaufinann," Am Nat Biog, Ox Univ Press, 99); auth, "Die Abschaffung der Arbeit: Ein irreefuhrender Traum von ein Scheinparadies," in Die Zukunfi des Wissens, ed. Jurgen Mittelstrass, UVK Univ Konstanz, 99); auth, "Das Ratsel der Grausamkeit, das Paradox der Askese und der Wille zur Macht," in Entdecken und Verraten: Zu Leben und Werk Friedrich Nietzsches, ed A Schirmer, R Schmidt (Verlag Hermann Bohlaus Nachfolger, Weimar, 99); auth, "Ten Momentous Events of the 20th Century," in World Book Millennium Project, 99; rev, Theories of Modern Art I: From Winckelmann to Baudelaire, by Moshe Barash, J Aesth Art Crit 50 (92); auth, "Nietzsche on the Illusions of Everyday Life," in Nietzsche 's Postmoralism (Camb Univ Press, forthcoming); auth, Nietzsche, Hegel und eine Aesthetik des Kunstlers," in Hegel Jahrbuch, J Intl Hegel Soc (forthcoming). **CONTACT ADDRESS** Dept Philosophy, Univ of Wisconsin, Madison, 600 North Park St, Madison, WI 53706. **EMAIL** aisoll@facstaff.wisc.edu

SOLOMON, ROBERT CHARLES
PERSONAL Born 09/14/1942, Detroit, MI **DISCIPLINE** PHILOSOPHY **EDUCATION** Univ Pa, BA, 63; Univ Mich, MA, 65, PhD(philos), 67. **CAREER** Instr philos, Princeton Univ, 66-68; vis asst prof, Univ Calif, Los Angeles, 68-69; asst prof, Univ Pittsburgh, 69-71; asst prof, City Univ New York, 71-72; assoc prof, 72-77, Prof Philos, Univ Tex, Austin, 77-, Vis asst prof, Univ Pa, 67-68; vis sr lectr, La Trobe Univ, Melbourne, 70-71; City Univ New York Res Found grant, 72; Nat Endowment for Humanities grant, 76; consult ed, J Theory Social Behav, 77-; Bus Eth Quarterly, 92-. **HONORS AND AWARDS** Standard Oil Outstanding Teaching Awd, 73; President's Associates Outstanding Teacher Awd, 85; President's Associates Outstanding Teacher Awd, 96; UT Dept of Philos Teaching Awd (multiple), Acad of Distinguished Teachers, UT, 97-05; Chad Oliver Plan II Teaching Awd, 98. **MEMBERSHIPS** Am Philos Asn; Soc Phenomenol & Existential Philos; President Int Soc for Res on Emotions; Chancellor's Council, 99-; Littlefield Soc, 01-; Plan II Parlin Fel, (as professor, 99-); Plan II Parlin Fel, (as donor, 99-); Pres, Int Soc for Res on Emotions, 00-04. **RESEARCH** Existentialism and Phenomenology; 19th century German philosophy; philosophy of psychology; Business Ethics; Emotions. **SELECTED PUBLICATIONS** Auth, From Rationalism to Existentialism, 72 & ed, Phenomenology and Existentialism, 72, Harper; Nietzsche, Doubleday, 73; Existentialism, Randon, 74; auth, The Passions, Doubleday, 76; Introducing Philosophy, Harcourt, 77; History & Human Nature, Harcourt, 79; Love: Emotion Myth & Metaphor, 81; auth, Introducing the Existentialists, (Indianapolis), Hackett, 81; auth, Introduction the German Idealist, (Indianapolis), Hackett, 81; auth, In the Spirit of Hegel, 83; auth, What is Emotion? With C, Calhoun, 84; auth, It's Good Business, 85; auth, From Hegel to Existentialism, 87; auth, About Love: Reinventing Romance for Our Times, 88; auth, Continental Philosophy Since 1750: The Rise and Fall of the Self, 88; auth, Reading Nietzsche, with Kathleen Higgins, 88; auth, A Passion for Justice, 90; auth, What is Justice? With Mark Murphy, 90; auth, The Philosophy of (Erotic) Love, with Kathleen Higgins, 91. **CONTACT ADDRESS** Dept of Philos, Univ of Texas, Austin, 0 Univ of Texas, Austin, TX 78712-1026.

SOLOMON, WILLIAM DAVID
DISCIPLINE PHILOSOPHY **EDUCATION** Baylor Univ, BA, 64; Univ Tex, PhD, 72. **CAREER** Assoc prof. **RESEARCH** Ethical theory; medical ethics. **SELECTED PUBLICATIONS** Auth, Moral Realism and Moral Dilemmas, 86; Moral Realism and the Amoralist, Midwest Studies Philos, 87; Internal Objections to Virtue Ethics, Midwest Studies Philos, 88. **CONTACT ADDRESS** Philosophy Dept, Univ of Notre Dame, 336/7 O'Shaughnessy, Notre Dame, IN 46556. **EMAIL** solomon.1@nd.edu

SOLTOW, LEE
PERSONAL Born Chicago, IL, m, 1949, 3 children **DISCIPLINE** ECONOMICS **EDUCATION** Univ Wisconsin, PhD **CAREER** Ohio Univ, prof econo, 50-98. **HONORS AND AWARDS** Distg prof. **MEMBERSHIPS** AEA; ASA. **RE-**

SEARCH Income and wealth distribution. **SELECTED PUBLICATIONS** Income and Wealth Inequality in the Netherlands, 16th to 20th Century, with Luiten van Zander, Amsterdam, Het Spinhuis, 98; Property and Inequality in Victorian Ontario: Structural patterns and Cultural Communities in the 1871 Census, with Gordon Darroch, Univ Toronto Press, 94. **CONTACT ADDRESS** Dept Economics, Ohio Univ, Athens, OH 45701. **EMAIL** soltow@ohio.edu

SOLUM, LAWRENCE B.
DISCIPLINE LAW **EDUCATION** Univ Calif, Los Angeles, BA, 81; Harvard Univ, JD, 84. **CAREER** Prof & William M. Rains fel; clerk, hon William Norris US Ct Appeals, 9th Circuit; ch jurisp sect, Asn Amer Law Sch(s) & ch-elect, Asn's Sect on Law & Interp; fac, Loyola Law Sch, 85-; assoc dean, Acad Aff, 93-96; vis prof, Univ Southern Calif, 92; vis prof, Boston Univ, 97-98. **SELECTED PUBLICATIONS** Publ on, civil procedure; Const theory; legal philosophy. **CONTACT ADDRESS** Law School, Loyola Marymount Univ, 7900 Loyola Blvd, Burns 334, Los Angeles, CA 90045. **EMAIL** lsolum@lmulaw.lmu.edu

SOMERVILLE, ROBERT
DISCIPLINE RELIGION **EDUCATION** Yale Univ, PhD. **CAREER** Prof of Relig, Hist, Columbia Univ. **RESEARCH** History of Christianity through the 16th century Reformation; Medieval Latin church; Medieval Latin manuscripts. **SELECTED PUBLICATIONS** Auth, Pope Alexander III and the Council of Tours; Scotia Pontifica: Papal Letters to Scotland before the Pontificate of Innocent III; Pope Urban II, the Collectio Britannica; Council of Melfi. **CONTACT ADDRESS** Dept of Religion, Columbia Col, New York, 2960 Broadway, New York, NY 10027-6902. **EMAIL** somervil@columbia.edu

SOMMER, BENJAMIN D.
PERSONAL Born 07/06/1964, New York, NY, m, 1995, 2 children **DISCIPLINE** RELIGION **EDUCATION** Yale, BA, 86; Brandeis, MA, 91; Univ Chicago, PhD, 94. **CAREER** Asst prof, Northwestern Univ, 94-00; assoc prof, Northwestern Univ, 00-. **HONORS AND AWARDS** ACLS, 98-99; Yad Hana Div Fel, 98-99; Salo Baron Prize by Am Academy for Jewish Res, 00. **MEMBERSHIPS** SBL; AOS; AJS **RESEARCH** History of Israelite religion; literary study of Bible; history of biblical exegesis **SELECTED PUBLICATIONS** Art, Did Prophecy Cease? Evaluating a Re-evaluation, Jour of Bible Lit, 96; art, The Scroll of Isaiah as Jewish Scripture, Or, Why Jews Don't Read Books, Soc of Bibl Lit 1996 Sem Papers, Scholars Press 96; art, Allusions and Illusion: The Unity of the Book of Isaiah in Light Of Deutero-Isaiah's Use of Prophetic Tradition, New Visions of Isaiah, Sheffield Acad Press, 96; art, Exegesis, Allusion and Intertextuality in the Hebrew Bible: A Response to Lyle Eslinger, Vetus Testamentum, 96; auth, A Prophet Reads Scripture: Allusion in Isaiah 40-66, Stanford Univ Press, 98; auth, Revelation at Sinai in the Hebrew Bible and Jewish Theology," The Journal of Religion 79; (99): 422-451; auth, "Refelcting on Moses: The Redaction of Numbers 11," The Joural of Biblical Literature 118, (99): 601-624; auth, "New Light on the Compsition of Jeremiah," The Catholic Bblical Quarterly 61, (99): 646-666; auth, "Translation as Commentary: The Case of the Septuagint to Exodus 32-33," accepted for publication in Textus: The Annual of the Hebrew Univ Bible Project, (forthcoming); auth, "Conflicting Constructions of Divine Presence in the Priestly Tabernacle," Biblical Interpretation: A Journal of Contemporary Approaches 9, (01): 41-64. **CONTACT ADDRESS** Dept of Religion, Northwestern Univ, 1940 Sheridan Rd, Evanston, IL 60208-4050. **EMAIL** b-sommer@northwestern.edu

SOMMER, JOHN D.
PERSONAL Born 01/19/1929, Peoria, IL, m, 1950, 3 children **DISCIPLINE** PHILOSOPHY **EDUCATION** Univ Chicago, PhD, 65. **CAREER** Assoc prof, Miami Univ, 62-90; prof, Western Col, 72-74; lect, Univ Md, overseas, 76-77. **MEMBERSHIPS** APA. **RESEARCH** History of philosophy. **SELECTED PUBLICATIONS** Auth, Moments of Soul, Peter Lang Publ, forthcoming. **CONTACT ADDRESS** PO Box 356, Oxford, OH 45056. **EMAIL** jnsommer@erinet.com

SONDEREGGER, KATHERINE
DISCIPLINE WESTERN RELIGIOUS THOUGHT **EDUCATION** Smith Col, AB; Yale Univ, MDiv, STM; Brown Univ, PhD. **CAREER** Prof, act, Women's Stud prog; Middlebury Col, 87-. **RESEARCH** Study of theology. **SELECTED PUBLICATIONS** Auth, That Jesus Christ was Born a Jew: Karl Barth's Doctrine of Israel. **CONTACT ADDRESS** Dept of Religion, Middlebury Col, Middlebury, VT 05753.

SONESON, JEROME P.
DISCIPLINE RELIGION **EDUCATION** North Pk Col, Ba, 76; Harvard Div Sch, MDiv, 80; Harvard Grad Sch, AM, 82; PhD, 90. **CAREER** Asst Prof to Assoc Prof, Univ N IA, 91-. **HONORS AND AWARDS** Outstanding Teaching Awd, 94; Charlotte Newcombe Dessertation Fel, 85-86; N Am Ministerial Fel, 77-80. **MEMBERSHIPS** Am Acad of Relig; Highlands Inst for Am Relig and Philos Thought. **RESEARCH** Theological and ethical reflection on public issues such as religious diversity in the south, the environment, and war. **SELECTED PUBLICATIONS** Auth, Pragmatism and Pluralism: John Dewey's Significance for Theology, Fortress Press, 93. **CONTACT ADDRESS** Dept Relig & Philos, Univ of No Iowa, Cedar Falls, IA 50614-0027. **EMAIL** soneson@uni.edu

SONTAG, FREDERICK EARL
PERSONAL Born 10/02/1924, Long Beach, CA, m, 1950, 2 children **DISCIPLINE** PHILOSOPHY **EDUCATION** Stanford Univ, Ba, 49; Yale Univ, MA, 51; PhD, 52; Col of Idaho, LLD, 71. **CAREER** Instr, Yale Univ, 51-52; prof to Denison Prof of Philos, Pomona Col, 52-; vis prof, Union Theol Sem, 59-60; vis prof, Collegio di Sant' Anselmo, 66-67; vis prof, Univ of Copenhagen, 72; Theologian-in-Residence, Am Church in Paris, 73; vis scholar, Center for the Study of Japanes Relig, 74; vis fel, The East-West Center, 74; vis lectr, Peoples Republic of China, 84; vis lectr, Chinese Univ of Hong Kong, 85; vis lectr, Univ of S Africa, 88; vis fel, Jesus Col at Cambridge Univ, 91-92. **HONORS AND AWARDS** Kent Fel, Soc on Relig in Higher Educ; Wig Distinguished Prof Awd, Pomona Col, 70, 76, & 93; listed in Who's Who in America, 96. **MEMBERSHIPS** Phi Beta Kappa, Am Philos Asn, Metaphysical Soc of Am, Int Soc for Metaphysics, Am Acad of Relig, Soc for the Sci Study of Relig, Asn for Humanistic Psychol, Soc for Philos and Psychol, Soc of Christian Philos, New Camaldoli Hermitage--Camaldoli Monks. **RESEARCH** Metaphysics, philosophy of Religion, Existentialism, Philosophical Psychology, and Philosophical Theology. **SELECTED PUBLICATIONS** Auth, The Return of the Gods, Peter Lang Pub (New York), 89; auth, Uncertain Truth, Univ Press of Am (Lanham, MD), 95; auth, Wittgenstein and the Mystical: Philosophy as an Ascetic Practice, Scholar's Press (Atlanta, GA), 95; auth, The Acts of the Trinity, Univ Press of Am (Lanham, MD), 96; auth, The Descent of Women, Paragon House (St Paul, MN), 97; auth, Truth and Imagination, Univ Press of Am (Lanham, MD), 98. **CONTACT ADDRESS** Dept Philos, Pomona Col, 333 N College Way, Claremont, CA 91711-4429.

SORENSEN, ROY
PERSONAL Born 02/25/1957, Brooklyn, NY, m, 1982, 2 children **DISCIPLINE** PHILOSOPHY **EDUCATION** Mich State Univ, PhD, 82. **CAREER** Asst prof, Univ Del, 84-87; asst prof, 87-90, assoc prof, 90-95, full prof, 95-, NY Univ; full prof, Dartmouth Col, 99. **MEMBERSHIPS** Amer Philos asn; Soc exact Philos. **RESEARCH** Philosophy of Language; Philosophy of Logic; Epistemology. **SELECTED PUBLICATIONS** Auth, Blindspots, Oxford: Clarendon Press, 88; Thought Experiments, NY, Oxford UP, 92; Pseudo-Problems, London: Routlege, 93. **CONTACT ADDRESS** Dept of Philosophy, Dartmouth Col, Hanover, NH 03755. **EMAIL** roy.sorensen@dartmouth.edu

SORKIN, DAVID E.
DISCIPLINE LAW **EDUCATION** Ind Univ, BS, 85; BA, 85; Harvard Univ, JD, 88; Ind Univ, MLS, 91. **CAREER** Visiting Lecturer, Ind Univ Sch of Law, 90-91; Asst Prof, John Marshall Law Sch, 91-; Visiting Scholar, Purdue Univ, 99-00. **RESEARCH** Information Technology Law **CONTACT ADDRESS** John Marshall Law Sch, 315 S Plymouth Court, Chicago, IL 60604-3969. **EMAIL** david@sork.com

SORRENSON, RICHARD J.
DISCIPLINE HISTORY OF PHILOSOPHY **EDUCATION** Auckland Univ, MS, 84; Princeton Univ, PhD, 93. **CAREER** Asst prof, Ind Univ. **HONORS AND AWARDS** Res fel, Nat Sci Found; res fel, Ind Univ; res fel, Am Philos Soc. **MEMBERSHIPS** Am Philos Soc. **RESEARCH** Voyages of scientific discovery, history of technology, science and gender, the chemical revolution, science and enlightenment. **SELECTED PUBLICATIONS** Auth, The ship as a scientific instrument in the eighteenth century, Osiris. 96; Towards a history of the Royal Society of London in the 18th century, 96. **CONTACT ADDRESS** Dept of Hist and Philos of Sci, Indiana Univ, Bloomington, Goodbody 130, Bloomington, IN 47405. **EMAIL** rjs@indiana.edu

SOSA, ERNEST
PERSONAL Born 06/17/1940, Cuba, m, 1961, 2 children **DISCIPLINE** PHILOSOPHY **EDUCATION** Univ Pittsburgh, PhD, 64. **CAREER** Postdoc Fel to Prof, Brown Univ, 64-; Distinguished Visiting Prof, Rutgers Univ, 98-. **HONORS AND AWARDS** Oxford Companion to Philos; Routledge Biographical Dictionary of 20th Century Philos. **MEMBERSHIPS** Am Philos Asn. **RESEARCH** Epistemology; Metaphysics; Moral Epistemology. **SELECTED PUBLICATIONS** Contrib, Knowledge in Perspective, Cambridge Univ Press, 91. **CONTACT ADDRESS** Dept Philos, Rutgers, The State Univ of New Jersey, New Brunswick, PO Box 270, New Brunswick, NJ 08903-0270.

SOUTHERLAND, PETER
PERSONAL Born 05/29/1947, England **DISCIPLINE** RELIGIOUS STUDIES, ANTHROPOLOGY **EDUCATION** Univ London Sch Oriental and African Studies, MA, 76; Polytech Central London, BA Photography, 86; Oxford Univ, PhD, 99. **CAREER** Instr, La State Univ. **MEMBERSHIPS** Am Anthrop Asn. **RESEARCH** Architecture, Religion, Colonialism, Globalization, India, Benin. **SELECTED PUBLICATIONS** Auth, "Khash-Kanait Architecture," in Encyclopedia of Vernacular Architecture of the World, ed. Paul Oliver (Cambridge Univ Press, 97); auth, "In Memory of the Slaves: An African View of the Diaspora in the Americas," in Representation of Blackness and the Performance of Identity, ed. Jean Muteba Rahier (Greenwood Press, 99). **CONTACT ADDRESS** La State Univ, 1529 Moreland Ave, Baton Rouge, LA 70808. **EMAIL** psuther@lsu.edu

SOVERN, JEFF
PERSONAL Born 12/26/1956, Minneapolis, MN, w, 2 children **DISCIPLINE** LAW **EDUCATION** Columbia Univ, AB, 77; JD, 80. **CAREER** Law Clerk, U S Dist Ct for the Dist of Md, 80-81; From Asst Prof to Prof, St Johns Univ Law Sch, 83-. **HONORS AND AWARDS** Man of the Year, 86. **RESEARCH** Consumer protection. **SELECTED PUBLICATIONS** Auth, "Toward the Regulation of Secret Warranties," Advancing the Consumer Interest, no 2 (95): 13-19; auth, "Creating a Private Cause of Action Under the New York Fair Debt Collection Practices Act," Record 345 (95); auth, "Good Will Adjustment Games: An Economic and Legal Analysis of Secret Warranty Regulation," Mo Law Rev, (95): 323-414; auth, "Implied Warranties of Quality in the Sale of New Homes," in Enycl of Housing (98): 307-309; auth, "Opting In, Opting Out or No Option at All: The Fight for Control of Personal Information," Wash Law Rev (99): 1033. **CONTACT ADDRESS** Dept Law, St. John's Univ, 8000 Utopia Pkwy, Jamaica, NY 11439-0001. **EMAIL** jsovern@sjulawfac.stjohns.edu

SOVERN, MICHAEL I.
PERSONAL Born 12/01/1931, New York, NY, m, 1952, 4 children **DISCIPLINE** LAW **EDUCATION** Columbia Univ, AB, 53, LLB 55. **CAREER** From asst prof to assoc prof law, Univ Minn Law Sch, 55-58; mem fac, Columbia Law Sch, 57-, prof law, 60-, Chancellor Kent Prof Law, Columbia Univ Law Sch, 81-, Dean, 70-79, chmn, Exec Comt Fac, 68-69, provost, exec vpres, 79-80, pres, 80-93, pres emer, 93-. **HONORS AND AWARDS** LLD (hon), Columbia Univ, 80; PhD (hon), Tel Aviv Univ, 82; LLD (hon), Univ South Calif, 89; Commendatore in the Order of Merit of the Republic of Italy, 91; Alexander Hamilton Medal, Columbia Col, 93; Citizens Union Civic Leadership awared, 93; Fel, Am Acad Arts and Sci. **MEMBERSHIPS** Bd dirs AT&T, Pfizer, Sequa, Asian Cultural Coun, Shubert Org, Stat WNET-TV, Freedom Forum Newseum; chmn, NYC Charter Rev Comn, 82-83; co-chmn, 2nd Cir Comn on Reduction of Burdens and Costs in Civil Litigation, 77-80; chmn, Comn on Integrity in Govt, 86; pres, Ital Acad Advanced Studies in Am, 91-93, Shubert Found, 96; chmn, Japan Soc, 93; Am Acad Rome, 93; chmn, Nat Adv Coun Freedom Forum Media Studies Ctr, 93-; Pulitzer Prize bd, 80-93, chmn pro-tem, 86-87; trustee Kaiser Family Found, Presdl Legal Expense Trust, 94-98; ABA; Counc Fgn Rels; Asn Bar City NY; Am Arbitration Asn (panel arbitrators); Am Law Int; Econ Club; Nat Acad Arbirtators, Am Philosophical Soc. **RESEARCH** Dir legal restraints on radical discrimination in employment, Twentieth Century Fund, 62-66; spl counsel to gov NJ, 74-77; cons Time mag, 65-80. **SELECTED PUBLICATIONS** Auth, Legal Restraints on Racial Discrimination in Employment, 66; Law and Poverty, 69; Of Boundless Domains, 94. **CONTACT ADDRESS** Sch of Law, Columbia Univ, 435 W 116th St, New York, NY 10027.

SPAETH, BARBETTE S.
PERSONAL Born 03/26/1956, Chicago, IL, s **DISCIPLINE** GREEK AND ROMAN RELIGION, MYTHOLOGY, LATIN LITERATURE **EDUCATION** John Hopkins Univ, PhD, 87. **CAREER** Class, Tulane Univ. **HONORS AND AWARDS** Phi Beta Kappa, 76; Lord fel,Amer Sch Class Stud at Athens, 83; Robinson travel fel, John Hopkins Univ, 86; fel, Am Sch Class Stud at Athens, 86-87; Broneer fel, Am Acad, Rome, 90-91. **MEMBERSHIPS** Am Philol Asn; Arch Inst. **RESEARCH** Witchcraft in antiquity, women's cults in antiquity, instructional technology in classics. **SELECTED PUBLICATIONS** Auth, The Goddess Ceres and the Death of Tiberius Gracchus, Hist, 90; Athenians and Eleusinians in the West Pediment of the Parthenon, Hesperia, 91; The Goddess Ceres and Roman Women, Newcomb Ctr for Res on Women Newsletter, 93; The Goddess Ceres in the Ara Pacis Augustae and the Carthage Relief, Amer Jour Archaeol 98, 94; auth, The Roman Goddess Ceres, Univ of TX Pr, Austin, 96; auth, The Pompeii Project and Issues in Multimedia Devleopment, Classical World, 91.6, 98, 503-512. **CONTACT ADDRESS** Dept of Class, Tulane Univ, 6823 St Charles Ave, New Orleans, LA 70118. **EMAIL** spaeth@mailhost.tcs.tulane.edu

SPAHT, KATHERINE S.
PERSONAL Born 01/20/1946, Shreveport, LA, m, 1971, 3 children **DISCIPLINE** LAW **EDUCATION** Univ Miss, BA, 68; La State Univ, JD, 71. **CAREER** La State Univ, 72-, Jules F. and Frances L. Landry Prof of Law, Vice Chancellor, 90-92. **HONORS AND AWARDS** Member, Governor's Task Force on Higher Educ, 96; Member, Academic Advisory Comt, Inst for Am Values, 98-; Hon Fel, La Col of Commentators, 99-. **MEMBERSHIPS** La Family Law Coun, Am Law Inst, Baton Rouge and La Bar Asns, **SELECTED PUBLICATIONS**

Coauth, Matrimonial Regimes, Vol 16, La Civil Law Treatise, West (89, 91, 92, 93, 94, 95, 96, 97, 98); coauth, Louisiana Matrimonial Regimes: Cases and Materials (92, 95, 98); auth, Family Law in Louisiana, Law Center Pubs Inst (94, 95, 98, 2000); auth, Successions and Donations: Cases and Reading Materials, with C. Samuel, Tulane Law Sch and C. Picou, Southern Law Sch (fall 96); auth, "New Pro-Family Policies: Covenant Marriage and the "Children-First" Principle," Communitarian Network Int Conf (Feb 99); auth, "Marriage: Why a Second Tier Called Covenant Marriage?," 12 Regent Univ Law Rev 1 (99-2000); auth, "The Family As Community: Implementing the 'Children-First' Principle," Strengthening As American Marriages: A Communitarian Perspective, ed by M. Whyte (2000). **CONTACT ADDRESS** Sch of Law, La State Univ, Baton Rouge, LA 70803. **EMAIL** kspaht@lsu.edu

SPALDING, CHRISTOPHER J.

PERSONAL Born 03/26/1964, Minneapolis, MN, m **DISCIPLINE** RELIGION **EDUCATION** Boston Univ, BA, 93; Univ Sheffield, UK, MA, 96. **CAREER** Asst head, relig, Cardigan Mountain Schl. **MEMBERSHIPS** AAR; SBL. **RESEARCH** Buddhist/Christian dialogue **CONTACT ADDRESS** 1825 Vine St. #1, Berkeley, CA 94703-1161.

SPALDING, JAMES COLWELL

PERSONAL Born 11/06/1921, Kansas City, MO, m, 1945, 5 children **DISCIPLINE** RELIGION **EDUCATION** Univ Ill, BA, 42; Hartford Theol Sem, BD, 45; Columbia Univ, PhD(relig), 50. **CAREER** Prof relig, Mo Valley Col, 48-53; assoc prof relig & philos, Trinity Univ, 53-56; from asst prof to assoc prof relig, 56-68, Prof Relig, Univ Iowa, 68-, Dir Sch Relig, 71-**MEMBERSHIPS** Am Acad Relig; Renaissance Soc Am; Coun Grad Studies Relig (sec-treas, 68-); Am Soc Reformation Res; Am Soc Church Hist. **RESEARCH** History of Christian thought. **SELECTED PUBLICATIONS** Auth, Ulster 1641--Aspects Of The Rising, Church Hist, Vol 66, 97; Predestination, Policy And Polemic--Conflict And Consensus In The English Church From The Reformation To The Civil-War, Sixteenth Century J, Vol 26, 95; Ulster 1641--Aspects Of The Rising, Church Hist, Vol 66, 97; Authority, Church, And Society In George Herbert--Return To The Middle-Way, Church Hist, Vol 63, 94; ed, Calvin And Calvinism, 14 Vols, Sixteenth Century J, Vol 24, 93. **CONTACT ADDRESS** Dept of Relig, Univ of Iowa, Iowa City, IA 52242.

SPALDING, PAUL S.

PERSONAL Born 05/18/1950, Kansas City, MS, m, 1978, 3 children **DISCIPLINE** RELIGIOUS STUDIES **EDUCATION** Univ Wis Madison, BA, 72, Yale Univ, M Div, 75; MA, 76; Univ Iowa, PhD, 81. **CAREER** Asst to assoc prof, IL Col, 88-. **MEMBERSHIPS** Am Soc for Eighteenth Century Studies; Am Soc of Church Hist; Ger Studies Assoc; Midwest Jewish Studies Assoc; Soc for the Hist of Authorship, Reading and Publishing. **RESEARCH** Religion and culture in early modern Europe; The Enlightenment; Censorship and toleration, Jewish and Christian relations. **SELECTED PUBLICATIONS** Auth, Seize the Book, Jail the Author: Johann Lorenz Schmidt and Censorship in Eighteenth-Century Germany, Purdue Univ Pr, (W Lafayette, IN), 98; auth, "Wenn Zwei: sich streiten", Europa in der Fruhen Neuzeit, ed Erich Donnert, (Cologne: Bohlau, 99), 341-49; auth, "Toward a Modern Torah: Moses Mendelssohn's Use of a Banned Bible", Modern Judaism 91.1 (Feb 99): 67-82; auth, "'Der Wertheimer' und sein Wertheimer Jahlouch", (forthcoming); auth, "Holy Roman Empire", Censorship: A World Encycl, ed Derek Jones (forthcoming). **CONTACT ADDRESS** Dept Relig and Philos, Illinois Col, 1101 W College Ave, Jacksonville, IL 62650-2212. **EMAIL** spalding@hilltop.ic.edu

SPANOS, WILLIAM

PERSONAL Born 01/01/1925, Newport, NH, d, 1954, 4 children **DISCIPLINE** ENGLISH, POSTMODERN THEORY **EDUCATION** Wesleyan Univ, BA, 50; Columbia Univ, MA, 54; Univ Wis, PhD (Eng), 64. **CAREER** Master Eng, Mt Hermon Sch, 51-53; asst ed, Encycl Americana, Grolier, 54-56; instr Eng, Univ KY, 60-62; asst prof, Knox Col, 62-66; Asst Prof Eng & Comp Lit, State Univ NY Binghamton, 66-, Fulbright prof Am lit, Nat Univ Athens, 69-70; founder & ed, boundary 2, 72-. **HONORS AND AWARDS** Hon degree, Univ of Athens, 87. **MEMBERSHIPS** MLA; Col Eng Asn; Mod Greek Studies Asn. **RESEARCH** Contemporary theory, postmodernism. **SELECTED PUBLICATIONS** Ed, A Casebook on Existentialism, Crowell, 66; auth, The Christian Tradition in Modern British Verse Drama: The Poetic of Sacramental Time, Rutgers Univ, 67; Modern drama and the Aristotelian tradition: The formal imperatives of absurd time, Contemp Lit, summer 71; The detective and the boundary: Some notes on the postmodern literary imagination, fall 72, Heidegger, Kierkegaard and the Hermenentic circle: Toward a postmodern theory of interpretation as dis-closure, winter 76 & Breaking the circle: Hermenentics as dis-closure, winter 77, boundary 2; ed, Existentialism 2, Random House, 77; Repititions: the Postmodern Occasion in Literature and Culture, Louisiana State Univ Press, 87; Heidegger and Criticism: Retrieving The Politics of Destruction, Univ of MN Press, 93, The End of Education, Univ of MN Press, 93; The Errant Art of Moby Dick: The Canon, the Cold War and the Struggle for American Studies, Duke Univ, 95; auth, America's Shadow: An Anatomy of Empire, Univ Minn Press, 00. **CONTACT ADDRESS** Dept of English, SUNY, Binghamton, Binghamton, NY 13901. **EMAIL** wspanos@binghamton.edu

SPARKS, KENTON L.

PERSONAL Born 07/11/1963, Flemingsburg, KY, m, 1988, 2 children **DISCIPLINE** BIBLICAL STUDIES **EDUCATION** Johnson Bible Col, Tenn, Ba, 85; Kennesaw State Univ, MBA, 87; Columbia Bibl Sem, MA, 90; Univ North Carolina, Chapel Hill, PhD, 96. **CAREER** Instr, relig, North Carolina Wesleyan Col, 92-94; tchg fel, Univ North Carolina, Chapel Hill, 93-95; resident scholar, Providence Baptist Church, Raleigh NC, 93-; Special Asst to Sr Pastor. **HONORS AND AWARDS** Cum laude, 85; Eta Beta Rho, 90. **MEMBERSHIPS** Soc of Bibl Lit; Inst for Bibl Res; Catholic Bibl Asn; Evangel Theol Soc. **RESEARCH** Hebrew law; Hebrew; Hebrew historiography; ethnicity. **SELECTED PUBLICATIONS** Auth, In the Footsteps of the Sages: Interpreting Wisdom for Preaching, Faith and Mission, 95; auth, Ethnicity and Identity in Ancient Israel, Eisenbrauns, 98; auth, Patriarchs, and, Semites, in Freedman, ed, Eerdmans Dictionary of the Bible, Eerdmans, forthcoming; coauth, Israelite Literature in Its Ancient Context: A Comparative Introduction to the Genres of the Hebrew Bible, Hendrickson, forthcoming. **CONTACT ADDRESS** Providence Baptist Church, 6339 Glenwood Ave, Raleigh, NC 27612. **EMAIL** kent@pray.org

SPEIDELL, TODD

PERSONAL Born 07/31/1957, Chicago, IL, m, 1990, 1 child **DISCIPLINE** THEOLOGY, ETHICS; PSYCHOLOGY **EDUCATION** Gordon Col, BA, 79; Fuller Theological Seminary, M Div, 83, PhD,86, Fuller Theological Seminary; New College Edinburgh, postdoctoral study, July 92, 95. **CAREER** Dir, of Extended Education and Adjunct prof, 87-89, Fuller Theological Seminary; assoc prof, 89-90, Knoxville Col; head of religious studies, 90- , Webb Sch of Knoxville. **MEMBERSHIPS** Karl Barth Soc of North America; Intl Bonhoeffer Soc. **RESEARCH** Theological ethics, theology and culture. **SELECTED PUBLICATIONS** Auth, The Incarnation as Theological Imperative for Human Reconciliation: A Christocentric Social Ethic, 86; Coed, Incarnational Ministry: The Presence of Christ in Church, Society, & Family, Essays in Honor of Ray S. Anderson, 90; auth, A Trinitarian Ontology of Persons in Society, Scottish Journal of Theology, 94; auth, I Want a Picture of God! The Chaplain's Craft, 94; auth, Confessions of a Lapsed Skeptic: acknowledging the Mystery and Manner of God, 00; auth, From Conduct to Character: A Primer in Ethical Theory, 00. **CONTACT ADDRESS** 1137 Farrington Dr., Knoxville, TN 37923. **EMAIL** todd_speidell@webbschool.org

SPELLMAN, LYNNE

DISCIPLINE ANCIENT GREEK PHILOSOPHY **EDUCATION** Unv Ill, PhD. **CAREER** Philos, Univ Ark **HONORS AND AWARDS** Vis fel, Cambridge Univ.s **SELECTED PUBLICATIONS** Auth, Substance and Separation in Aristotle, Cambridge Univ Press, 95. **CONTACT ADDRESS** Univ of Arkansas, Fayetteville, Fayetteville, AR 72701. **EMAIL** lspellm@comp.uark.edu

SPELLMAN, NORMAN WOODS

PERSONAL Born 05/17/1928, Robstown, TX, m, 1950, 4 children **DISCIPLINE** RELIGION **EDUCATION** Southwestern Univ, BA, 49; Perkins Sch Theol, Southern Methodist Univ, BD, 52; Yale Univ, PhD, 61. **CAREER** Instr relig, Southern Methodist Univ, 58-60; from asst prof to prof, 60-76, prof Relig & Philos, Southwestern Univ, 76-98; RETIRED 6/01/98. **MEMBERSHIPS** Am Soc Church Hist; Am Hist Asn; Am Acad Relig; Am Studies Asn. **RESEARCH** American church history; American Methodism. **SELECTED PUBLICATIONS** Coauth, History of American Methodism (3 vols), Abingdon, 64 & 66; Early Leaders in Texas Methodism, Am Methodism, 66; The early native Methodist preachers, Duke Div Sch Rev, autumn 69. **CONTACT ADDRESS** Dept of Relig & Philos, Southwestern Univ, 1001 E University, Georgetown, TX 78626-6100.

SPENCE, JOSEPH SAMUEL, SR.

PERSONAL Born 12/20/1950, m **DISCIPLINE** LAW **EDUCATION** Pikes Peak Coll, AA; Univ of MD, BSc; Webster Univ, MA; Washburn Univ Law School, JD; Faith Theological Seminary, Bdiv. **CAREER** Century 21 Real Estate, realtor assoc 1978-80; United States Army, capt 1980-86; Riley County District Attorney's Office, 87; City of Topeka Attorney's Office, 88-89; Kansas State Senate, 88-89; Milwaukee Area Technical Col, 91-; Spence Law Offices, Milwaukee, 92-; US Army Reserves (ret), major, 97. **HONORS AND AWARDS** Founder & chapter pres, Lambda Alpha Epsilon Criminal Justice Fraternity, 1974; Distinguish Mil Student 1979, Distinguish Mil Grad 1980 Howard Univ ROTC; Earl Warren Scholar NAACP Legal Defense Fund 1986-89; various awards for public speaking; Daughters of Am Revolution Awd; Distinguish Grad Air Assault Sch; Distinguish Grad Logistics Automated Mgt Sch; Expert Shooting Qualification; Jurcyk-Royle Oral Advocacy Competition; Cert of Merit, Washburn Law Clinic, 1988; Cert of Commendation, Am Bar Asn, 1989; Good Shepherd Awd, BSA, 01; various mil awards & commendations. **MEMBERSHIPS** Legal Counsel, Alpha Phi Alpha; Rep-at-large Frederick Douglass Ctr Manhattan KS 1986-87, WSBA Washburn Law Sch 1986-87; Kiwanis Int 1986-87; marshal Phi Alpha Delta Law Frat 1986-87; founder & charter pres NAACP Manhattan KS 1986; founder & legal advisor, Lex Explorer, Washburn Law Sch, 1988; chairperson Legal Redress Comm NAACP KS 1987-89; mem Manhattan Kansas Chamber of Commerce, Manhattan KS; Am Red Cross; Commissioner-at-large, Am Bar Asn, 1987-89; Christian Lawyers Asn, 1987-; Christian Legal Soc; Americans United for Seperation of Church & State; Am Bar Asn; Nat Bar Asn; Am Trial Lawyer Asn; Wis Acad of Trial Lawyers; Family Law Soc; Leander Fole Inns of Court. **CONTACT ADDRESS** PO Box 26342, Milwaukee, WI 53226. **EMAIL** josephal@execpc.com

SPENCER, AIDA BESANCON

PERSONAL Born 01/02/1947, Santo Domingo, Dominican Republic, m, 1972, 1 child **DISCIPLINE** NEW TESTAMENT **EDUCATION** Douglass Col, BA, 68; ThM, 75, MDiv, 73, Princeton Theological Seminary; Southern Baptist Theological Seminary, PhD, 82. **CAREER** Adjunct Prof, 74-76, New York Theological Seminary; Academic Dean, Prof, 76-78, Alpha-Omega Community Theological School; Asst/Assoc Prof, 82-92, Prof 92-, Gordon Conwell Theological Seminary. **HONORS AND AWARDS** Staley Distinguished Scholar, 94; Christianity Today Book Award, 96. **MEMBERSHIPS** Evangelical Theol Soc; Soc of Biblical Research; Christians for Biblical Equality; Asociacion para la educacion teologica hispana **RESEARCH** Paul's letters; Luke; Acts; Peter; James; women's concerns **SELECTED PUBLICATIONS** Auth, Paul's Literary Style, 84; auth, Beyond the Curse, 85; auth, The Prayer Life of Jesus, 90; The Goddess Revival, 95; God through the Looking Glass: Glimpses from the Arts, 98; The Global God: Multicultural Evangelical Views of God, 98. **CONTACT ADDRESS** 130 Essex St, South Hamilton, MA 01982.

SPENCER, JAMES CALVIN, SR.

PERSONAL Born 10/21/1941, Detroit, Mich, m, 1987, 2 children **DISCIPLINE** PHILOSOPHY, RELIGION **EDUCATION** Calif State Univ, Los Angeles, BA, 66; State Univ NY Buffalo, MA, 70; PhD(philos), 73. **CAREER** Asst to assoc prof, 71-81, Prof Philos, Cuyahoga Community Col, 81-; Consult continuing education division, Kansas Stave Univ, 86; Case Western Univ, 73; Ford Motor Co, Brookport, OH, 90; Campus Planning Inst, Cleveland, 91-94; PBS Nat Fac Referral Network, 96-; pres, Spencer Enterprises, Brecksville, OH, 91-. **MEMBERSHIPS** Am Philos Asn; Am Acad Relig; Int Phenomenol Soc. **RESEARCH** Phenomenology; pedagogy; film criticism. **SELECTED PUBLICATIONS** Auth, The Nightmare Never Ends, 92; coauth, Instructor's Manual for the Voyage of Discovery: A History of Western Philosophy, 96. **CONTACT ADDRESS** Dept of Philos, Cuyahoga Comm Col, Western, 11000 W Pleasant Val, Cleveland, OH 44130-5199.

SPENDER, ROBERT D.

PERSONAL Born 11/17/1945, Waterbury, CT, m, 1970, 3 children **DISCIPLINE** BIBLICAL STUDIES **EDUCATION** Barrington Col, BA, 67; Trinity Evangel Div Sch, MA, 70; Dropsie Univ, PhD, 76. **CAREER** Prin and found, West Woods Chr Acad, Hamden, Conn, 75-78; asst and assoc prof Bibl Stud, 78-85, dept chemn 82-85, Barrington Col; prof Bibl Stud, 85-95, chemn 89-95, Briarcliff Manor; actg vpres for Acad Aff, Kings Col, 88; prof Bibl Stud, 95- , dept chemn 98- , Lancaster Bible Col. **HONORS AND AWARDS** Prof of the Year, Barrington Col, 82; Prof of the Year, Kings Col, 91. **MEMBERSHIPS** Soc of Bibl Lit; Evangel Theol Soc. **RESEARCH** Old Testament Prophets; idols and idolatry. **SELECTED PUBLICATIONS** Contribur, Baker Encyclopedia of the Bible, Baker Book House, 88; contribur, Elwell, ed, Evangelical Dictionary of Biblical Theology, Baker Book House, 96; contribur, Van Geweren, ed, The New International Dictionary of Old Testament Theology and Exegesis, Zondervan, 97. **CONTACT ADDRESS** Lancaster Bible Col, 901 Eden Rd, Lancaster, PA 17601. **EMAIL** bspender@lbc.edu

SPIEGEL, JAMES S.

PERSONAL Born 07/26/1963, Pontiac, MI, m, 1998, 1 child **DISCIPLINE** PHILOSOPHY **EDUCATION** MI State Univ, PhD, 93. **CAREER** Assoc prof, Taylor Univ. **MEMBERSHIPS** APA; Intl Berkeley Soc and Soc of Christian Philosphers. **RESEARCH** Philosophy of Relig; Ethics; George Berkeley. **SELECTED PUBLICATIONS** Auth, The Theological Orthodoxy of Berkeley's Immaterialism, Faith and Philosophy, April 96; auth, A Berkeleyan Approach to the Problem of Induction, Science and Christian Belief, 98; auth, Hupocrisy: Moral Fraud and Other Vices, 99; auth, "Can a Christian be Coherently Morally Pro-Life and Politically Pro-Choice?," Christian Scholar's Review, 00. **CONTACT ADDRESS** Philosophy Dept, Taylor Univ, Upland, Upland, IN 46989. **EMAIL** jmspiegel@tayloru.edu

SPILLENGER, CLYDE

PERSONAL Born 03/24/1960, New York, NY, s **DISCIPLINE** LAW **EDUCATION** Princeton Univ, AB, 82; Yale Univ, JD, 87; Yale Univ, Mphil, 88. **CAREER** Lectr and res fel, Univ Wisconsin Law School, 90-92; acting prof law, UCLA, 92-98. **MEMBERSHIPS** Am Soc for Legal His; Law

& Soc Asn; Org of Am Historians. **RESEARCH** Am legal and constitutional his; law and lang. **SELECTED PUBLICATIONS** Auth, "Reading the Judicial Canon: Alexander Bickel and the Book of Brandeis", Jour of Am Hist 79, 92; auth, "Elusive Advocate: Reconsidering Brandeis as Public Interest Lawyer", Yale Law Jour 105, 96. **CONTACT ADDRESS** School of Law, Univ of California, Los Angeles, 405 Hilgard Ave., Los Angeles, CA 90095. **EMAIL** spilleng@mail.law.ucla.edu

SPILSBURY, PAUL
PERSONAL Born 01/29/1966, Port Shepstone, South Africa, m, 1988, 1 child **DISCIPLINE** NEW TESTAMENT STUDIES **EDUCATION** Regent Col, MCS; Univ of Cambridge, PhD. **CAREER** From Asst to assoc prof bibl stud, Canadian Bible Col, 94-. **MEMBERSHIPS** SBL; Can Soc Bibl Stud. **RESEARCH** Flavius Josephus; Christian origins; ancient use of scripture. **SELECTED PUBLICATIONS** Auth, Contra Apionem and Antiquitates Judaicae: Points of Contact, in Feldman, ed, Josephus' Contra Apionem: Studies in its Character and Context with a Latin Concordance to the Portion Missing In Greek, Brill, 96; auth, God and Israel in Josephus: A Patron-Client Relationship, in Mason, ed, Understanding Josephus, Sheffield, 98; auth, The Image of the Jew in Flavius Josephus' Paraphrase of the Bible, Mohr Siebeck, 98; auth, Josephus' Pattern of Religion, in Carson, ed, Justification and Variegated Nomism: A Fresh Appraisal of Paul and Second Temple Judaism, vol 1, Mohr Siebeck, 99. **CONTACT ADDRESS** 4400 4th Ave, Regina, SK, Canada S4T 0H8. **EMAIL** pspilsbu@cbccts.sk.ca

SPINA, FRANK ANTHONY
PERSONAL Born 09/30/1943, Long Beach, CA, m, 1994, 2 children **DISCIPLINE** OLD TESTAMENT STUDIES **EDUCATION** Greenville Col (Ill), BA, 65; Asbury Theological Seminary, MDiv, 68; MA, 70, PhD, 77, Univ Michigan **CAREER** Prof, Seattle Pacific Univ, 73-. **MEMBERSHIPS** Soc of Biblical Lit; Wesleyan Theological Soc; Scholarly Engagement with Anglican Doctrine **RESEARCH** Theological interpretation of Old Testament narrative; canon and hermeneutics **SELECTED PUBLICATIONS** Auth, Eli's Seat: The Transition from Priest to Prophet in Samuel 1-4, Journal for the Study of the Old Testament, 94; Wesleyan Faith Seeking Biblical Understanding, Wesleyan Theological Journal, 95; The Problematic of Faculty Remuneration in the Christian College, Christian Scholars Review, 96; The Face of God: Esau in Canonical Context, The Quest for Context & Meaning: Studies in Biblical Intertextuality in Honor of James A. Sanders, 97; Rahab (the Harlot), Dictionary of Old Testament Theology and Exegesis, 97; Rahab (the Monster), Dictionary of Old Testament Theology and Exegesis, 97. **CONTACT ADDRESS** Dept of Religion, Seattle Pacific Univ, Seattle, WA 98119. **EMAIL** fspina@spu.edu

SPITZ, ELLEN HANDLER
PERSONAL Born New York, NY, 3 children **DISCIPLINE** FINE ARTS; PHILOSOPHY **EDUCATION** Barnard Col, BA; Harvard Univ, MAT; Columbia Univ, PhD. **CAREER** Barnard Col; Columbia, CUNY; Hebrew Univ of Jerusalem; Rutgers Univ; Stanford Univ. **HONORS AND AWARDS** Getty scholar, 89-90; Bunting fel, 96-97; fel, Ctr for Adv Study in Behavioral Sci, Stanford Univ, 97-98. **MEMBERSHIPS** Col Art Asn; Amer Soc for Aesthetics; Amer Psychoanalytic Asn. **RESEARCH** Psychological perspectives on art and literature. **SELECTED PUBLICATIONS** Auth, Art and Psyche, Yale Univ Press, 85; auth, Image and Insight, Columbia Univ Press, 91; auth, Museum of the Mind, Yale Univ Press, 94; auth, Inside Picture Books, Yale Univ Press, 99. **CONTACT ADDRESS** Dept. of Art and Art History, Stanford Univ, Stanford, CA 94305.

SPITZER, MATTHEW L.
PERSONAL Born 06/23/1952, Los Angeles, CA, m, 1973, 1 child **DISCIPLINE** ADMINISTRATIVE LAW **EDUCATION** Univ Calif, Los Angeles, BA, 73; Univ Southern Calif, JD,77; Calif Inst Technol, PhD, 79. **CAREER** Dean of University of Southern California Law School, 00; William T. Dalessi Professor of Law,Univ Southern Calif; Director of the Communications Law and Policy Institute; and Director of Law and Economics Programs at the University of Southern California; taught at, Northwestern Univ. **HONORS AND AWARDS** Ronald H. Coase Prize in Law & Economics. **MEMBERSHIPS** Am Law Institute. **RESEARCH** Administrative Law, Broadcast Regulation, and Economic Analysis of Law. **SELECTED PUBLICATIONS** Auth, Seven Dirty Words and Six Other Stories: Controlling the Content of Print and Broadcast & Experimental Law and Economics; coauth, Public Policy Toward Cable Television. **CONTACT ADDRESS** School of Law, Univ of So California, University Park Campus, Los Angeles, CA 90089. **EMAIL** mspitzer@usc.edu

SPOHN, WILLIAM C.
PERSONAL Born 06/07/1944, Washington, DC, m, 1996 **DISCIPLINE** CHRISTIAN ETHICS **EDUCATION** Univ Chicago Divinity School, PhD, 78. **CAREER** Asst to assoc prof, Jesuit School of Theol Berkeley, 78-92; Dir Bannan Inst for Jesuit Educ & Christian Values, Santa Clara Univ, 92-. **HONORS AND AWARDS** Presidential Prof Ethics & Common Good, 96-98. **MEMBERSHIPS** Cath Theol Soc Am; Soc Christian Ethics; Am Acad Relig; Highlands Inst Am Relig Thought. **RESEARCH** Scripture and ethics; American religion; spirituality and ethics; moral psychology. **SELECTED PUBLICATIONS** Auth The Magisterium and Morality, Theol Studies, 93; William James on Religious Experience: An Elitist Account?, Am J Theol & Philos, 94; Jesus and Ethics, Proceedings of the Cath Theol Soc Am, 94; Jesus and Christian Ethics, Theol Studies, 95; What Are They Saying About Scripture and Ethics, Paulist Press, 95; Morality on the Way of Discipleship: The Use of Scripture in Veritatis Splendor, Veritatis Splendor: American Responses, Sheed and Ward, 95; coauth Knowledge of God and Knowledge of Self: An American Empiricist Approach, Christian Ethics: Problems and Prospects, Pilgrim Press, 96; Finding God in All Things: Jonathan Edwards and Ignatius Loyola, Finding God in All Things: Essays in Honor of Michael J. Buckley, Crossroad Press, 96; Spirituality and Ethics: Exploring the Connections, Theol Studies, 97; coauth, Rights of Passage: The Ethics of Immigration and Refugee Policy, Theol Studies, 98. **CONTACT ADDRESS** Dept of Religious Studies, Santa Clara Univ, Santa Clara, CA 95053. **EMAIL** wspohn@scu.edu

SPONHEIM, PAUL R.
PERSONAL Born 01/16/1930, Thier River Falls, MN, m, 1955, 3 children **DISCIPLINE** SYSTEMATIC THEOLOGY **EDUCATION** Concordia Col, BA, 52; Luther Sem, BTh, 57; Univ Chicago, MA, 60, PhD, 61. **CAREER** Prof, dept ch, Concordia Col; lectr, Univ Chicago, 60-61; vis prof, Lutheran Sem, Gettysburg, Pa, 66-67; vis lectr, Luther Sem, 64, 66, 69; from assoc prof to prof, Luther Sem, 69-; dean acad aff, Luther Sem, 74-76. **MEMBERSHIPS** Mem, Amer Acad Rel; Amer Theol Soc; Amer Philos Soc; Assn for the UN; Scandinavian Amer Soc. **SELECTED PUBLICATIONS** Coauth, Contemporary Forms of Faith, 67; auth, Faith and Process, 79; coauth, Christian Dogmatics, 84; auth, God: Question and Quest, 85; coauth, Suffering and Redemption: Exploring Christian Witness within a Buddhist Context, 88; coauth, ed, A Primer on Christian Prayer, 88; coauth, Lutherans and the Challenge of Religious Pluralism, 90; auth, Faith and the Other: A Relational Theology, 93; auth, The Pulse of Creation, 99. **CONTACT ADDRESS** Dept of Systematic Theology, Luther Sem, 2481 Como Ave, Saint Paul, MN 55108. **EMAIL** psponhei@luthersem.edu

SPRADLEY, GAREY B.
PERSONAL Born 01/27/1945, Corpus Christi, TX, m, 1975, 3 children **DISCIPLINE** THEOLOGY **EDUCATION** Univ Tex, BBA, 67; JD, 71; Southwestern Sem, MDiv, 83; Syracuse Univ, MA, 90; PhD, 91. **CAREER** Assoc Prof, Univ Houston, 78-83; Prof, Grove City Col, 91-. **HONORS AND AWARDS** Who's Who Among Am Teachers, 84, 96; Who's Who in the World, 00. **MEMBERSHIPS** Soc of Christian Philosophers. **RESEARCH** Epistemology; Philosophical Theology; Realisms/Antirealisms. **SELECTED PUBLICATIONS** Auth, "Richard Swinburne: Revelation," in Faith and Philosophy, (Oxford Univ Press, 920, 328; Auth, "Caroline Davis: The Evidential Force of Religious Experience," in Christian Scholar's Review, (92): 425. **CONTACT ADDRESS** Dept Relig & Philos, Grove City Col, 100 Campus Dr, Grove City, PA 16127-2101. **EMAIL** gbspradley@gcc.edu

SPRAGENS, JANET R.
DISCIPLINE FEDERAL PERSONAL INCOME TAX **EDUCATION** Wellesley Col, BA, 64; George Washington Univ, JD, 68. **CAREER** Prof, Am Univ. **HONORS AND AWARDS** Exec dir, Am Tax Policy Inst; Managing ed, The Tax Lawyer; Chair, Low Income Taxpayer Comt; Consult, U.S. Dept Labor 84-85, Dept Treasury, 84-86; Dept of Juestice, 97, pt. **MEMBERSHIPS** WCL Tax Clinic. Am Law Inst;, ABA Tax Section. Executive Committee, Teaching Tax Comt, ABA; Tax Clinic Modeling Project; depts tax issues;Asn Am Law Sch; Maxwell-Macmillan Fed Taxes Adv Board. **RESEARCH** Tax law **CONTACT ADDRESS** American Univ, 4400 Massachusetts Ave, Washington, DC 20016.

SPRAGUE, ELMER D., JR.
PERSONAL Born 08/14/1924, Havelock, NE, m, 1948, 4 children **DISCIPLINE** PHILOSOPHY **EDUCATION** Univ NE, Lincoln, BA, 48; Oxford Univ, BA, 50, D Phil, 53. **CAREER** Instr, , 48 Kearney State Tchrs Col; assoc prof, 53, AR Polytechnic Col; prof, 53-97, Brooklyn Col, prof of philos emeritus, Brooklyn Col, CUNY, 97-. **HONORS AND AWARDS** Phi Beta Kappa, NE Alpha, 48; Rhodes Scholar, Oxford Univ, 48-51; fac fel, CUNY, 64, 81; The Paul Robert and Jean Shuman Hanna Prof of Philos, Hamline Univ, 87; vis prof philos, The Col at New Paltz, SUNY, 88; Scholar Incentive Awd, CUNY, 93-94. **MEMBERSHIPS** Am Philos Asn; Mind Asn; Hume Soc. **RESEARCH** Metaphysics; philos of mind, Hume. **SELECTED PUBLICATIONS** Auth, Metaphysical Thinking, Oxford Univ Press, NY, 78; auth, Persons and Their Minds, Westview Press, 99. **CONTACT ADDRESS** PO Box 350, Cold Spring, NY 10516. **EMAIL** sprague@highlands.com

SPRAGUE, ROSAMOND KENT
PERSONAL Born 05/16/1922, Brookline, MA, w, 1946 **DISCIPLINE** PHILOSOPHY **EDUCATION** Bryn Mawr Col, BA, 45, MA, 48, PhD, 53. **CAREER** Lectr, Haverford Col, 53-54; pt-time lectr, Bryn Mawr Col, 54-55, 55-56; fel, Am Asoc Univ Women, Cambridge Univ, Princeton Univ, 56-57; vis fel, Princeton Univ, 56-57; instr, Bryn Mawr, 58-61, lectr, 61-62; asst lectr, Univ Birmingham, 64-65; assoc prof, Univ of South Carolina, 65-68, prof, 68-91; vis prof, Univ Toronto, 71-72; vis fel, Wolfson Col, 76; vis prof, Catholic Univ, 92-93. **HONORS AND AWARDS** Founder, Soc for Ancient Greek Philos, pres, 72-74; senior fel, Univ So Carolina, 74; hon Phi Beta Kappa, 75. **SELECTED PUBLICATIONS** Auth, Plato's Use of Fallacy, Routledge, 62; trans, Plato's Euthydemus, Bobbs-Merrill, 65; ed, The Older Sophists, USC, 72; ed, A Matter of Eternity, Eerdmans, 73; trans, Plato's Laches and Charmides, Bobbs-Merrill, 73; auth, Plato's Philosopher-King, USC, 76. **CONTACT ADDRESS** Dept of Philos, Univ of So Carolina, Columbia, Columbia, SC 29208.

SPRETNAK, CHARLENE
DISCIPLINE RELIGION **EDUCATION** St Louis Univ, BA, 68; Univ Calif, MA, 81. **CAREER** Lecturer, Univ Calif, 78-86; Prof, Calif Inst of Integral Studies, 93-. **HONORS AND AWARDS** Phi Beta Kappa. **MEMBERSHIPS** Am Acad of Relig, PEN. **RESEARCH** Ecological postmodernism; cultural history of the Modern Era. **SELECTED PUBLICATIONS** Auth, Lost Goddesses of Early Greece, 78; ed, The Politics of Women's Spirituality, 82; co-auth, Green Politics, 84; auth, The Spiritual Dimension of Green Politics, 86; auth, States of Grace, 91; auth, The Resurgence of the Real, 97. **CONTACT ADDRESS** Dept Philos & Relig, California Inst of Integral Studies, 1453 Mission St, San Francisco, CA 94103-2557.

SPRING, RAYMOND LEWIS
PERSONAL Born 08/05/1932, Warsaw, NY, m, 1955, 4 children **DISCIPLINE** LAW **EDUCATION** Washburn Univ Topeka, BA, 57, JD, 59. **CAREER** Atty, Crane, Martin, Claussen & Ashworth, 59-65; from asst prof to assoc prof law, 65-71, asst dean sch, 67-70, actg dean, 70-71, prof & dean sch, 71-78, Distinguished Prof Law, Washburn Univ Topeka, 78-, Vis prof, St Louis Univ, summer, 82. **HONORS AND AWARDS** Prof of Year, 80; Distinguished Serv Awd, 87. **MEMBERSHIPS** Am Bar Asn; KS Bar Asn; Topeka Bar Asn. **RESEARCH** Criminal law; law and mental health **SELECTED PUBLICATIONS** Coauth, Vernon's KSA Criminal Code, 71 & Vernon's KSA Code of Criminal Procedure, 73, West Publ; The End of Insanity, Baranski, 82; Patients, Psychiatrist & Lawyers: Law and the Mental Health System, Anderson, 89, 2nd ed, 97. **CONTACT ADDRESS** Law Sch, Washburn Univ of Topeka, 1700 S W College Ave, Topeka, KS 66621-0001. **EMAIL** zzspri@washburn.edu

SPRINKLE, JOE M.
PERSONAL Born 08/18/1953, Oklahoma City, OK, m, 1986, 2 children **DISCIPLINE** BIBLICAL STUDIES **EDUCATION** Univ Okla, BS, 76; Trinity Evangelical Divinity Sch, Masters Divinity, 81; Hebrew Union Col, MPhil, 87; PhD, 91. **CAREER** From instr to prof, Toccoa Falls Col, 88-. **HONORS AND AWARDS** Samuel Sandmel Scholar in Bible, 82-83; Workum Found Fel, 83-85; Dr. David Lefkowitz Interfaith Fel, 85-87; Erna & Julius Krouch Fund Scholar, 87-88; Ilse Hitchman Fel Tuition Scholar, 88-89; Kosberg Family Interfaith Scholar, 89-91; Fac Educ Scholar, Toccoa Falls, Col, 90-91; listed in Who's Who in Biblical Studies and Archaeology, 93; Fac Scholar of the Year, Toccoa Falls Col, 93-94; listed in Marquis Who's Who in the South and Southwest, 95-98; listed in Who's Who in Am Education, 96-97; listed in Who's Who Among America's Teachers, 00; listed in Strathmore's Who's Who, 00-01. **MEMBERSHIPS** Soc of Biblical Lit, Evangelical Theol Soc, Inst for Biblical Res. **RESEARCH** Biblical Laws, History. **SELECTED PUBLICATIONS** Auth, "Literary Approaches to the Old Testament: A Survey of Recent Scholarship," J of the Evangelical Tehol Soc 32.3 (89): 299-310; auth, "The Interpretation of Exodus 21:22-25 (Lex Talionis) and Abortion," Westminster Theol J 55 (93): 233-253; auth, The book of the Covenant: A Literary Approach, Sheffield Academic Press, 94; auth, " Clean, Unclean," "Command, commandment," "Decrees," "Law," and "Requirement," in Evangelical Dictionary of Biblical Theology, ed. W. Elwell (CO: Baker, 96); auth, "Old Testament Perspectives on Divorce and Remarriage," J of the Evangelical Theol Soc 40.4 (97): 529-550; auth, "2 Kings 3: History of Historical Fiction?" Bull for Biblical Res 9 (99): 247-270; auth, "Red Heifer," "Sexuality, Sexual Ethics," and "Theft" in Dictionary of the Pentateuch, eds. David Baker and T. Desomond Alexander (InterVarsity, forthcoming); auth, "The Laws of Clean and Unclean and their Relationship with the concept of Sacred Space," Alliance Academic Rev (forthcoming); auth, "You Shall not Bear False Witness," Decision 41 (forthcoming); auth, "Deuteronomic 'Just War' Theory (Deuteronomy 20) and 2 Kings 3:27," Zeitschrift fur Altorientalische und Biblische Rechtsgeschichte (forthcoming). **CONTACT ADDRESS** Sch of Bible and Theol, Toccoa Falls Col, PO Box 800236, Toccoa Falls, GA 30598-0236. **EMAIL** jsprinkl@toccoafalls.edu

SPROUL, BARBARA CHAMBERLAIN
PERSONAL Born 06/18/1945, New York, NY, 2 children **DISCIPLINE** COMPARATIVE RELIGION, HUMAN RIGHTS **EDUCATION** Sarah Lawrence Col, BA, 66; Columbia Univ, MA, 68, PhD, 72. **CAREER** Asst prof, 72-77, assoc

prof, 77-79, prof relig, 79, chmn prog in relig, 73-, Hunter Col; mem exec comt human rights, Amnesty Int USA, 70, gen secy, 78-. **MEMBERSHIPS** Am Acad Relig. **RESEARCH** Creation mythology; human rights. **SELECTED PUBLICATIONS** Ed, Primal Myths, Harper & Row, 79. **CONTACT ADDRESS** Dept of Relig, Hunter Col, CUNY, 695 Park Ave, New York, NY 10021-5085.

SPROUL, R. C.
PERSONAL Born 02/13/1939, Pittsburgh, PA, m, 1960 **DISCIPLINE** SYSTEMATIC THEOLOGY **EDUCATION** Westminster Col, BA, 61; Pittsburgh Theol Sem, BD, 64; Free Univ Amsterdam, Drs, 69; Geneva Col, LittD, 76; Grove City Col, LHD, 93. **CAREER** Instr, Westminster Col, 65-66; Asst prof, Gordon Col, 66-68; Asst prof, Conwell Sch of Theol, 68-69; Minister of Theol, Col Hill United Presbyterian Church, 69-71; Chairman and Pres, Ligonier Ministries, 71-; Vis prof, Gordon Conwell Theol Sem, 71-81; John Dyer Trimble, Sr. Chair of Systematic Theol, Reformed Theol Sem, 87-95; Prof, Reformed Theol Sem, 80-95; Distinguished prof, Knox Theol Sem, 95-; Dir, Coalition for Chr Outreach, 71-76, Evangelism Explosion Int, 80-81, Prison Fel, Inc, 79-84, Found for Reformation, 90-99, Serve Int, 82-. **HONORS AND AWARDS** Founder, ch, bd of Ligonier Ministries; principal spokesman, hist Christian theol; pres, Intl Coun of Bibl Inerrancy. **SELECTED PUBLICATIONS** Auth, The Invisible Hand, Word Publishing, 96; auth, Grace Unknown, Baker Publishing, 97; auth, Willing to Believe, Baker, 97; auth, The Priest with Dirty Clothes, Chariot Publishing, 97; auth, Holiness of God, Tyndale House Publishers, 98; auth, The Last Days According to Jesus, Baker, 98; auth, Getting the Gospel Right, Baker, 99; auth, In the Presence of God, Word, 99; auth, A Walk with Jesus, Christian Focus, 99; auth, The Consequences of Ideas, Crossway Books, 00. **CONTACT ADDRESS** Dept of Systematic Theol & Apologetics, Knox Theol Sem, 5554 N Federal Hwy, Fort Lauderdale, FL 33308.

SPRUNGER, MARY S.
DISCIPLINE THEOLOGY **EDUCATION** Bethel Col, BA; Univ IL, MA, PhD. **CAREER** Theol Dept, Eastern Mennonite Univ **SELECTED PUBLICATIONS** Articles: Conrad Grebel Rev. **CONTACT ADDRESS** Eastern Mennonite Univ, 1200 Park Road, Harrisonburg, VA 22802-2462.

SPRY, IRENE
PERSONAL Born Transvaal, South Africa **DISCIPLINE** ECONOMIC HISTORY **EDUCATION** London Sch Econ, 24-25; Girton Col, Cambridge, BA, 28; Bryn Mawr Col, MA, 29. **CAREER** Lectr, asst prof, Univ Toronto, 29-38; lectr, writer & reviewer, 45-67; assoc prof/prof, 68-73, Prof Emer, Univ Ottawa, 74-. **HONORS AND AWARDS** Res Fel, Can Plains Res Ctr; Can Coun Res Awd, 65; Distinguished Can Citizen Awd, Univ Regina, 87; Off, Order Can, 93; LLD Univ Toronto, 71; DU Univ Ottawa, 85. **SELECTED PUBLICATIONS** Auth, The Palliser Expedition, 64; auth, The Papers of the Palliser Expedition, 1857-1860, 68; auth, The Transition from a Nomadic to a Settled Society in Western Canada, 1856-1896, in Trans Royal Soc Can, 68. **CONTACT ADDRESS** Univ of Ottawa, Ottawa, ON, Canada K1N 6NS.

SQUADRITO, KATHLEEN MARIE
PERSONAL Born 01/11/1945, San Jose, CA **DISCIPLINE** PHILOSOPHY **EDUCATION** San Jose State Univ, BA, 68; Washington Univ, St Louis, MA, 72, PhD(philos), 73. **CAREER** Asst prof, 73-80, Assoc Prof Philos, Ind-Purdue Univ, Ft Wayne, 80-. **MEMBERSHIPS** Am Philos Asn. **RESEARCH** John Locke; seventeenth century philosophy; metaphysics. **SELECTED PUBLICATIONS** Auth, Locke, Quine and natural kinds, Mod Schoolman, 72; Locke's view of essence and its relation to racism, 75 & The Essay: 4.4.3, 78, Locke Newslett; Locke's Theory of Sensitive Knowledge, Univ Press Am, 78; John Locke, G K Hall, 79. **CONTACT ADDRESS** Indiana Univ-Purdue Univ, Fort Wayne, 2101 Coliseum Blvd E, Fort Wayne, IN 46805-1445.

SREEDHAR, SUSANNE
PERSONAL Born Washington, DC **DISCIPLINE** PHILOSOPHY **EDUCATION** Wesleyan Univ, Ba, 97; Univ North Carolina, 98-. **CAREER** Author **RESEARCH** Ethics; political philosophy. **CONTACT ADDRESS** 54 Hwy Bypass, Apt 29D, Chapel Hill, NC 27516. **EMAIL** sreedhar@email.unc.edu

SREENIVASAN, GOPAL
PERSONAL Born 07/10/1964, Munich, Germany **DISCIPLINE** PHILOSOPHY **EDUCATION** McGill, BA, 86; Oxford, BPhil, 88; Univ Calif Berkeley, PhD, 93. **CAREER** Asst Prof, Princeton Univ, 93-00-. **HONORS AND AWARDS** Laurance S. Rockefeller Univ Preceptor, Princeton Univ, 96-99; Senior Fellow, Dept of Clinical Bioethics, NIM, 00 **MEMBERSHIPS** Am Philos Asn. **RESEARCH** Moral and Political Philosophy. **SELECTED PUBLICATIONS** Auth, The Limits of Lockean Rights In Property, 95; Interpretation and Reason, Philos and Public Affairs, 98; auth, What is the General Will? Philosophical Review, 00; auth, Understanding alien moral, Philo and Phenomenological Research, 01. **CONTACT ADDRESS** Dept of Clinical Bioethics, National Institutes of Health, Magnuson Clincial Center, Building 10 Rm IC118, Bethesda, MD 20892-1156. **EMAIL** gopalsreenivasan@hotmail.com

STACK, GEORGE JOSEPH
PERSONAL Born 11/08/1932, New York, NY, m, 1962, 2 children **DISCIPLINE** PHILOSOPHY **EDUCATION** Pace Col, BA, 60; Pa State Univ, MA, 62, PhD(philos), 64. **CAREER** From instr to asst prof philos, C W Post Col, Long Island Univ, 63-67; from asst prof to assoc prof, 67-70, chmn dept, 70-77, Prof Philos, State Univ NY Col Brockport, 70-, State Univ NY grant-in-aid, 68-70; consult, Ctr Philos Exchange, 70- & Choice, 72- **MEMBERSHIPS** Eastern Div Am Philos Asn. **RESEARCH** History of philosophy; phenomenology and existentialism. **SELECTED PUBLICATIONS** Auth, Berkeley's Analysis of Perception, Mouton, The Hague, 70, 72; On Kierkegaard: Philosophical Fragments, Humanities, 76; Kierkegaard's Existential Ethics, Ala Univ, 77; Sartre's Philosophy of Social Existence, Warren Green, 77. **CONTACT ADDRESS** Dept of Philos, SUNY, Col at Brockport, Brockport, NY 14420.

STACK, STEVEN
PERSONAL Born 12/20/1947, Providence, RI, d, 3 children **DISCIPLINE** CRIMINOLOGY **EDUCATION** Univ Conn, BA, 69; MA, 70; MA, 73; PhD, 76. **CAREER** Asst prof, Alma Col, 76-79; asst prof, Ind Univ, 79-81; assoc prof, Pa State Univ, 81-85; assoc prof to prof, Auburn Univ, 85-90; prof, Wayne State Univ, 90-. **HONORS AND AWARDS** Candace Rogers Awd, 76; Edwin Shneidman Awd, 85; Guggenheim Found Grant, 98, 99; Who's Who in Am, 00; 2000 Outstanding Intellectuals of the 20th Century. **MEMBERSHIPS** ASA; ASC; SSSP; SSSR; MSS; SSS; NCFR; AAS. **RESEARCH** Criminology, suicidology, mental health. **SELECTED PUBLICATIONS** Coauth, "Spatial Autocorrelation with Regard to Suicide in the United States", Crime Analysis Through Computer Mapping, eds, Carolyn Block, Margaret Dabdoub, Suzanne Fregly, Police Exec Res Forum (95): 49-58; auth, "Sociological Analysis of Rational Suicide: An analysis of Attitudes", Contemporary Perspectives on Rational Suicide, ed James L. Werth, Taylor and Francis (99): 41-47; auth, "Publicized Executions and the Incidence of homicide: Methodological Sources of Contradictory Findings", Handbook of Criminal Justice Administration, eds Toni Dupont-Morales and Michael Hooper, Marcel Decker Pub, (99); auth, "Occupation and Suicide" and "Social Differences in Suicidal Behavior", Encyclopedia of Criminology and Deviant behavior, Vol 4, ed Clifton Bryant, Taylor and Francis, (00); coauth, "Confidence in the Police in Industrial Nations", International Criminal Justice Issues in global Perspective, ed Del Rounds, Allyn and Bacon, (00): 71-81; auth, "Work and Economy", Comprehensive Textbook of Suicidology, ed Ronald Maris, Guilford, (00): auth, "Sociological Research into Suicide", Suicide: Resources for the Millennium, ed David Lester, Taylor and Francis (00): coauth, "Race, Occupation, and Suicide Risk in Ohio, 1989-1991", Review of Suicidology, ed John McIntosh, Guilford Pr, (00): coauth, "Police Suicide: An Analysis", Am J of Police, ed Dennis Kenney, Praeger, (00). **CONTACT ADDRESS** Dept Criminal Justice, Wayne State Univ, 2305 FAB, Detroit, MI 48202. **EMAIL** aa1051@wayne.edu

STACKHOUSE, JOHN G., JR.
DISCIPLINE THEOLOGY; PHILOSOPHY OF RELIGION; CHURCH HISTORY **EDUCATION** Queen's Univ Kingston, BA, 80; Wheaton Col Grad Sch, 82; Univ Chicago, PhD, 87. **CAREER** Instr, Wheaton Col Grad Sch, 84-86; Asst Prof, NWestern Col, Iowa, 87-90; from Asst Prof to Prof Religion, Univ Manitoba, 90-98; Sangwoo Youtong Chee Prof Theology, Regent Col, Vancouver, 98-. **HONORS AND AWARDS** Prof of the Year (Awd for Teaching Excellence), NWestern Col, 89; Rh Found Awd for Outstanding Contributions to Schol and Res in the Humanities, Univ Manitoba, 93; Outreach Awd for Community Service, Univ Manitoba, 97; First Place for Editorial Writing, Canadian Church Press, 98. **MEMBERSHIPS** Am Acad Relig; Am Soc Church Hist; Canadian Soc Church History; Canadian Evangelical Theol Asn. **RESEARCH** Epistemology; philosophy of religion; religion in North America. **SELECTED PUBLICATIONS** Auth, Canadian Evangelicalism in the Twentieth Century: An Introduction to Its Character, Univ Toronto Press, 93; Can God Be Trusted? Faith and the Challenge of Evil, Oxford Univ Press, 98; author of over 200 journal articles and reviews. **CONTACT ADDRESS** Regent Col, 5800 University Blvd., Vancouver, BC, Canada V6T 2E4. **EMAIL** jgs@regent-college.edu

STACKHOUSE, MAX LYNN
PERSONAL Born 07/29/1935, Fort Wayne, IN, m, 1959, 3 children **DISCIPLINE** CHRISTIAN ETHICS **EDUCATION** De Pauw Univ, BA, 57; Harvard Univ, BD, 61, PhD, 64. **CAREER** Lectr Christian ethics, Divinity Sch, Harvard Univ, 64-66; from asst prof to Herbert Gezork Prof Christin Ethics, Andover-Newton Theol Sem, 66-93; vis prof, United Theol Col, Bangalore, India, 73; Stephen Colwell Prof of Christian Ethics, Princeton Theol Sem, 93- ; vis lectr, Episcopal Theol Sch, Boston Col, Bucknell Univ, Bluffton Col, Northeastern Univ, Tufts Univ, Ohio Wesleyan Univ & Dickinson Col. **HONORS AND AWARDS** Winner of Melchor Prize, 76; DHL honoris causa, DePauw, 94. **MEMBERSHIPS** Fel Soc Relig Higher Educ; fel Soc Europ Cult; Am Acad Social & Polit Philos; Soc Sci Studies Relig (past pres); Am Soc Christian Ethics; Am Theol Soc. **SELECTED PUBLICATIONS** Ed & auth introd, The Righteousness of the Kingdom, Abingdon, 68; coauth, The Death of Dialogue and Beyond, Friendship, 69; auth, The Ethics of Necropolis, 71 & Ethics and the Urban Ethos, 73, Beacon; The Hindu ethos and development, Relig & Soc, fall 73; ed & auth introd, On Being Human Religiously, Beacon, 76; auth, Creeds, Society, and Human Rights, Eerdmans, 84, Parthenon, 96; auth, Public Theology and Political Economy, Univ Press of America, 91; ed, contribur, On Moral Business, Eerdmans, 95; auth, Christian Social Ethics in a Global Era, Abingdon; auth, Covenant and Commitments: Faith, Family & Economic Life, Westminster, 97; ed, contribur, God and Globalization, Trinity Pr Int, 00. **CONTACT ADDRESS** Princeton Theol Sem, PO Box 821, Princeton, NJ 08542. **EMAIL** max.stackhouse@ptsem.edu

STACY, WAYNE
PERSONAL Born 10/19/1950, FL, m, 1970, 1 child **DISCIPLINE** RELIGIOUS STUDIES **EDUCATION** Beach Atlantic Col, BA; Southern Baptist Theol Seminary, PhD. **CAREER** Prof, Midwestern Baptist Theol Seminary, 86-91; prof, 91-; Prof of Religion, Gardner-Webb Univ, 95-97; Dean, School of Divinity, Gardner-Webb Univ, 97-. **SELECTED PUBLICATIONS** Auth, pubs on biblical studies; auth, A Baptist's Theology (Smyth & Helwys); The Search, Fields Publishing. **CONTACT ADDRESS** Dept of Religious Studies and Philosophy, Gardner-Webb Univ, PO Box 997, Boiling Springs, NC 28017. **EMAIL** wstacy@gardner-webb.edu

STADLER, INGRID
PERSONAL Born 07/06/1930, Vienna, Austria, m, 1952 **DISCIPLINE** PHILOSOPHY **EDUCATION** Vassar Col, BA, 52; Radcliffe Col, MA, 53, PhD, 59. **CAREER** From instr to assoc prof, 58-73, chmn dept, 72-78, Prof Philos, Wellesley Col, 73-, Mem regional selection comt, Woodrow Wilson Fel Found, 62-; Wellesley Col res grant, 63-64; Braitmayer Found fel, 68; consult, WGBH-TV, 72-; res scholar fel, Radcliffe Inst Independent Studies, 72-73; ed, Ethical Issues for our Time, 73; vis scholar philos, Sch Humanities & Soc Sci, Mass Inst Tech & mem bd overseers, Ctr Res Women Higher Educ & Prof, Wellesley Col & Fedn Prof Women's Orgn, 74-; consult, Ed Mgt Serv, Inc, 75-78; mem comt for reaccreditation of Trinity Col, 76 & Smith Col, 77; mem task force on energy, Am Asn Univ Women, 76-77; mem selection comt, Mellon Fac Develop Grants, 76; consult, Project Impact, TV ser, Mass Coun for Arts & Pub Policy & Mt Wachusetts Community Col & panelist, First Ann Conf Business Ethics, Bentley Col, 77; chmn task force for reaccreditation of Wellesley Col & consult-panelist, The Massachusetts Story, Mass Coun for Arts & Pub Policy, 78; prof, Boston Architectural Ctr, 98. **MEMBERSHIPS** Am Philos Asn; Mind Asn; Asn Aesthet. **RESEARCH** Kant; aesthetics; recent and yet outstanding problems in theory of perception; art law, theories of ownership, efficacy of int law and int conventions; cultural policy of Japam and the U.K.; and the trials of war criminals at Nuernberg: causes and consequences. **SELECTED PUBLICATIONS** Auth, Seeing As, Philos Rev, 59; coauth, Kant, Doubleday, 67; auth Contemporary Art and its Philosophical Problems; auth, Treasuring Treasure, forthcoming. **CONTACT ADDRESS** Dept of Philosophy, Wellesley Col, 106 Central St, Wellesley, MA 02181-8204. **EMAIL** finanz@compuserve.com

STAFFORD, GILBERT W.
PERSONAL Born 12/30/1938, Portageville, MO, m, 1962, 4 children **DISCIPLINE** SYSTEMATIC THEOLOGY **EDUCATION** Anderson Coll, BA, 61; Andover Newton Theol Sch, MDiv, 64; Boston Univ, ThD, 73. **CAREER** Assoc Dean, 80-89 & 98-, Dean of the Chapel, 84-89 & 96-, Prof of Christian Theol, 76-, Dir of the Dr Of Ministry Prog, 98-, Anderson Univ Sch Theol; Commn on Christian Unity of the Church of God, Member, 75-78 & 80-, Chr, 85-90, Member Commn on Faith and Order in the USA, 84; Staley Lectr, 94-. **HONORS AND AWARDS** Distinguished Ministries Awd, Distinguished Service Awd, Anderson Univ Alumni Assoc; Bethany Heritage Awd; Golden Mike Awd, Board of Mass Commun of the Church of God. **MEMBERSHIPS** AAR, North Amer Acad of Ecumenists. **RESEARCH** Good and Evil; The Kingdom of God and Eschatology. **SELECTED PUBLICATIONS** Auth, Theology for Disciples: Systematic Considerations About the Life of Christian Faith, Anderson, Warner, 96; The Life of Salvation, Anderson, Warner, 79; Beliefs That Guide Us, Anderson, Center for Pastoral Studies, 77; The People of God, Anderson, Center for Pastoral Studies, 77; The Seven Doctrinal Leaders of the Church of God Movement, Anderson, Center for Pastoral Studies, 77; Church of God, Anderson, Indiana, The Renewal of Sunday Worship, vol III in The Complete Library of Christian Worship series, Nashville, Star Song; Booklets, Pub by Mass Communications Board of the Church of God; Gifts Most Precious; Gratitude; Handle With Care, Life's Dreams, Christ Jesus, Our Everything, A Hope for All of Us, 96; auth, Church of God at the Crossroads, Anderson, Maine, 00. **CONTACT ADDRESS** School Theology, Anderson Univ, 1100 E 5th St, Anderson, IN 46012-3495. **EMAIL** stafford@anderson.edu

STAFFORD, SUE P.
DISCIPLINE PHILOSOPHY **EDUCATION** Wheaton Col, Norton, BA, 67; Univ IL, Chicago Circle, MA, 68; Univ CT, PhD, 72. **CAREER** Assoc prof & dept ch; coach, Simmons Col

Debate Club; co-convener, Coun Ch(s), mem, Comt on Tenure and App; work with, Camp Dresser & McKee, an environ consult firm & Mass Corp for Educ Telecommun, MCET; mem, proj team which develop a pollution forecasting comp syst for Mex City. **RESEARCH** Theory of knowledge; philos of mind; tech and ethics. **SELECTED PUBLICATIONS** auth, Taking Philosophy to the Trenches, Philos and Comput, 92; Pattern Detection: Software Answers and the Issues They Raise, Presentation to GTE Laboratories, Waltham, 90; Computers as Partners in Medical Decision Making,invited presentation APPSA, NS, Can, 96; Ethical Implications of Computer-Assisted Decision-Making in Health Care, invited presentation Amer Bar Asn, New Orleans, 94; Knowledge, Ignorance, and Responsibility, invited presentation AAAS, annual meeting, 93; Software for the Detection of Fraudulent Medical Insurance Claims, Proceedings of DIAC-90 Symp, Directions in Advanced Comput, Boston, 90; coauth, When Genetic Information is Not Enough, The Genetic Resource, vol 6, 92. **CONTACT ADDRESS** Dept of Philos, Simmons Col, 300 The Fenway, Boston, MA 02115. **EMAIL** sstafford@simmons.edu

STAFFORD, WILLIAM SUTHERLAND
PERSONAL Born 11/09/1947, San Francisco, CA, m, 1969, 4 children **DISCIPLINE** CHURCH HISTORY **EDUCATION** Stanford Univ, BA, 65-69; Yale Univ, MA, Mphil, 69-74, PhD, 75; Univ de Strasbourg: Fac de theol protestante, 73-74. **CAREER** Tchg fel, Yale Col, 71-73; vis asst prof, Brown Univ, 74-76; asst prof, 76-82; assoc prof, Va Theol Sem, 82-90; David J. Ely prof, 90-; associate dean for Acad Aff, VP. **MEMBERSHIPS** ASCH, ACHA **RESEARCH** Late Medieval-Reformation Church History. **SELECTED PUBLICATIONS** Auth, Disordered Loves: Healing the Seven Deadly Sins, Cowley Publ, 94; Sexual Norms in the Medieval Church, A Wholesome Example: Sexual Morality in the Episcopal Church, 91; The Eve of the Reformation: Bishop John Fisher, 1509, Hist Mag Protestant Episcopal Church, 85. **CONTACT ADDRESS** Virginia Theol Sem, 3737 Seminary Rd, Alexandria, VA 22304. **EMAIL** wstafford@vts.edu

STAGAMAN, DAVID
PERSONAL Born 07/29/1935, Cincinnati, OH **DISCIPLINE** PHILOSOPHY **EDUCATION** Loyola Univ, BA, 58 MA, 67; West Baden Col, PhL, 60; Bellarmine Sch of Theol, STL, 67; Inst Catholique de Paris, ThD, 75. **CAREER** Vis prof, 72-75, asst prof, 75-83, assoc prof, 84-, acad dean, 87-96,Jesuit School of Theol at Berkeley. **HONORS AND AWARDS** Asn of Theol Sch fel, 78-79; listed, Who's Who in the West; listed, Who's Who in Religion; listed, International Who's Who. **MEMBERSHIPS** Am Acad Relig; Catholic Theol Soc of Am; Pacific Coast Theol Soc. **RESEARCH** Ecclesiology, especially authority in the Church; Wittgenstein and the study of religion. **SELECTED PUBLICATIONS** Auth, Authority in the Church: A Central Issue and Some Other Issues, Tripod, 90; auth, What Authority is Not! Tripod, 90; auth, The Implications for Theology of The Acting Person, in McDermott, ed, The Thought of Pope John Paul II, Gregorain Univ, 93; auth, A Democratic Catholic Church, Christian Century, 93. **CONTACT ADDRESS** Jesuit Sch of Theol, Berkeley, 1735 LeRoy Ave, Berkeley, CA 94709. **EMAIL** dstagama@jstb.edu

STAINTON, ROBERT J. H.
PERSONAL Born 09/20/1964 **DISCIPLINE** PHILOSOPHY **EDUCATION** York Univ, BA, 87, 88; Mass Inst Tech, PhD, 93; postdoc stud, Ctr for Cognitive Sci, Rutgers Univ, 97; Univ Mass, 96; Inst de Investigaciones Filosoficas, Univ Nacional Autonoma de Mexico, 94. **CAREER** Res coordr, York Univ, 88-91; lect, Salem State Col, 91; postdoctoral fel and instr, Univ Nac Autonoma de Mex, Summer 94; vis scholar, Univ Mass at Amherst, Winter 96; asst prof, Carleton Univ, 93-97; assoc prof, Carleton Univ, 97-; vis researcher, Rutgers Univ, Winter 97; vis assoc prof, Univ Puerto Rico at Mayaguez, Winter 99. **HONORS AND AWARDS** York Univ Entrance scholar, 84; York Univ In-Course scholar, 85-87; Glendon Col Philos prize, 88; Mass Inst Technol grad fel, 88; Andrew W Mellon fel in Humanities, 88; doc fel, Soc Sci and Humanities Res Coun of Can, 90; Andrew W Mellon Dissertation Year fel, 92; Carleton Univ $15,000 Res Achievement Awd, 99. **RESEARCH** Philosophy of language, pragmatics and formal semantics of natural language, philosophy of mind/cognitive science. **SELECTED PUBLICATIONS** Coauth, "Fodor's New Theory of Computation and Information," in Proceedings of the Eighteenth Conference of the Cognitive Science Society, (New York: Lawrnece Erlbaum Assocs, 96), 86-91; auth, Philosophical Perspectives on Language, Broadview Press (Peterborough, ON), 96; auth, "Remarks on the Syntax and Semantic of Mixed Quotation," in Philosophy and Linguistics (Boulder, CO: Westview Press, 99), 259-278; coed, Philosophy and Linguistics, Westview Press (Boulder, CO), 99; ed, Perspectives in the Philosophy of Language: A Concise Anthology, Broadview Press (Peterborough, ON), 00; coed, Communication in Linguistics: Papers in Honour of Michael Gregory, Editions du GREF (Toronto, ON), 00; coauth, Knowledge and Mind, The Mass Inst Technol Press (Cambridge, MA), 00; coauth, "Quotation, Demonstration and Innocence," in Working Through Thought, ed. R. Manning, (forthcoming); coauth, "'Obviously Propositions are Nothing..': Russell and the Logical Form of Belief Reports," in Logical Form and Language, ed. G. Preyer and G. Peter (Oxford Univ Press, forthcoming); auth, "Communicative Events as Evidence in Linguistics," in Communication in Linguistics (Toronto: Editions du GREF, forthcoming). **CONTACT ADDRESS** Dept of Philos, Carleton Univ, 1125 Colonel By Drive, Ottawa, ON, Canada K1S 5B6. **EMAIL** rob_stainton@carleton.ca

STALANS, LORETTA
PERSONAL Born 01/04/1964, Sweetwater, TN, m, 1986, 1 child **DISCIPLINE** CRIMINAL JUSTICE **EDUCATION** E Tenn State Univ, BA, 85; Univ IL, MA, 88; PhD, 90. **CAREER** Asst prof, Ga State Univ, 91-94; asst prof, Loyola Univ, 94-97; grad fac to assoc prof, Univ of Chicago, 94-. **HONORS AND AWARDS** Leonard D. Eron Awd, 91; Grant, Stevens Committee, Am Bar Assoc, 90-92; Grant, Ford Found, 91-92; Grant, Ga State Univ, 93-94; Grant, IL Criminal Justice Info Authority; Fel, Ctr for Ethics, Loyola Univ; Phi Kappa Phi. **MEMBERSHIPS** Am Psychol Soc; Law and Soc Assoc; Law and Psychol Assoc. **RESEARCH** Domestic violence, public opinion about crime and justice, sex offender recidivism and treatment compliance, jury nullification, expectancy effects. **SELECTED PUBLICATIONS** Coauth, "Editors Introduction: Public opinion about the creation, enforcement and punishment of criminal offenses", Am Behav Sci, 39.4 (96): 369-378; auth, "Family harmony or individual protection?: Public recommendations about how police can handle domestic violence situations", Am Behav Sci 39.4, (96): 435-450; coauth, "the influence of gender and mental state on police decisions in domestic assault cases", Criminal Justice and Behav 24.2 (97): 157-176; coauth, "The meaning of procedural fairness: A comparison of taxpayers' and representatives' views of their tax audits", Soc Justice Res 10.3 (97): 311-331; coauth, Public Opinion, Crime, and Criminal Justice, Westview Pr, (Boulder, CO), 97; auth, "Gender Perspective and Policing", Contemporary Policing: Personnel, Issues, and Trends, ed M. Dantzker, Butterworth-Heinemann, (Newton, MA), (97): 1-29; coauth, "Crime, Criminal Justice and Public Opinion", The Handbook of Crime and Punishment, ed M. Tonry, Oxford Univ Pr, (Oxford, 98): 31-57; coauth, "Leveling the playing field: Prestige and Representation in regulatory enforcement", Law & Soc Rev 33.4 (99); rev, of "Inaccuracies in Children's Testimony; Memory, Suggestibility, or Obedience to Authority", by Jon Meyer, Criminal Justice Rev 23.2 (99): 244-246; coauth, "Gender and socialization: How women and men police officers handle domestic violence", Women and Criminal Justice, (forthcoming). **CONTACT ADDRESS** Dept Criminal Justice, Loyola Univ, Chicago, 820 N Michigan Ave, Chicago, IL 60611.

STALEY, JEFFREY L.
PERSONAL Born 12/22/1951, Kansas City, MO, m, 1985, 2 children **DISCIPLINE** RELIGION **EDUCATION** Wheaton Col, BA, 73; Fuller Theol Sem, MA, 79; PhD, 85. **CAREER** Asst Prof, Univ Portland, 85-92; Vis Prof, Univ Notre Dame, 92-93; Vis Prof, Seattle Univ, 94-95; Vis Prof, Pac Lutheran Univ, 98-. **MEMBERSHIPS** Am Acad of Relig, Soc of Bibl Lit, Cath Bibl Asn. **SELECTED PUBLICATIONS** Auth, The Print's First Kiss: A Rhetorical Investigation of the Implied Reader in the Fourth Gospel, Scholar Pr (Atlanta, GA), 88; auth, Reading with a Passion: Rhetonz Autobiography and the American West in the Gospel of John, Continuum (New York, NY), 95. **CONTACT ADDRESS** Dept Relig, Pacific Lutheran Univ, 12180 Park Ave S, Tacoma, WA 98447-0001. **EMAIL** staleyjl@plu.edu

STALLARD, MICHAEL D.
PERSONAL Born 10/13/1953, Ft. Bragg, NC, m, 1980, 3 children **DISCIPLINE** THEOLOGY **EDUCATION** Univ Ala, Huntsville, BS, 75; Liberty Baptist Sem, Mdiv, 80; Dallas Theol Sem, STM, 84; PhD, 93. **CAREER** Instr, Liberty Baptist Col, 79-81; avionics engineer, General Dynamics, 81-86; Sr. Pastor, Tabernacle Baptist Church, Arlington, TX, 86-92; adjunct instr, Arlington Baptist Col, 90-91; Urban Outreach and Church Planting, 92-94; assoc prof, Baptist Bible Sem, 94-. **MEMBERSHIPS** Evangelical Theol Soc; Evangelical Missiological Soc; Conservative Theol Soc; Majority Text Soc; Pre-Trib Study Group. **RESEARCH** Hermeneutics, theological method, eschatology, dispensationalism, church history. **SELECTED PUBLICATIONS** Auth, "Ironside, Henry Allen, Eschatology of" in Dictionary of Premillennial Theology, gen. ed mal Couch, Grand Rapids: Kregel, 183-84 (96); auth, "Theocratic Kingdom," in Dictionary of Premillennial Theology, gen. ed Mal Couch, Grand Rapids: Kregel, 405-406 (96); auth, "The Challenge of Progressive Dispensationalism," Baptist Bulletin, 23-26 (July 97); auth, "Literal Interpretation, Theological Method, and the Essence of Dispensationalism," The J of Ministry and Theol 1, 5-36 (spring 97); auth, "Emile Guers: An Early Darbyite Response to Irvingism and a Precursor to Charles Ryrie," The Conservative Theol J 1, 31-46 (April 97); auth, "Prophetic Hope in the Writings of Arno C. Gaebelein," The J of Ministry and Theol 2, 190-210 (fall 98); auth, "Communicating the Gospel to a Biblically Illiterate Culture," Baptist Bulletin, 23-26 (99); auth, "Justification by Faith or Justification by Faith Alone," The Conservative Theol J, 3, 53-73 (April 99); auth, "Inerrancy in the Major Prophets," The Conservative Theol J, 3, 160-181 (Aug. 99); ed, Ther History of Dispensationalism, Kregel Pubs (forthcoming). **CONTACT ADDRESS** Dept Relig, Baptist Bible Col of Pennsylvania, P.O. Box 800, Clarks Summit, PA 18411-0800.

STAM, JAMES H.
PERSONAL Born 12/29/1937, Paterson, NJ, m, 1991, 5 children **DISCIPLINE** PHILOSOPHY **EDUCATION** Upsala Col, BA, 58; Univ Vienna, Austria, 58-59; Brandeis Univ, MA, 61, PHD, 64. **CAREER** Prof philos, co-dir, Writing Across the Curriculum, assoc dean Wirths Campus, Upsala Col, 62-95; Millicent Fenwick Prof of Educ and Public Issues, Monmouth Univ, 95- . **HONORS AND AWARDS** Fel, Newberry Libr, 68; NEH Jr Fel, 69; Lindback Awd for Distinguished Tchg, 70; NEH summer sem and fel; NYU Assoc and Scholar in Residence, 83-90. **MEMBERSHIPS** Soc for Ancient Greek Philos; Philos of Educ Soc; Hegel Soc of Am; Soc for the Study of African Philos; Nat Asn for Sci, Soc and Technol; Nat Asn for Hum Educ; AAUP. **RESEARCH** History of philosophy; Greek philosophy; German philosophy; philosophy of language; philosophy of education. **SELECTED PUBLICATIONS** Auth, Inquiries into the Origin of Language: The Fate of a Question, in Chomsky, ed, Studies in Language, Harper & Row, 76; auth, Benjamin Lee Whorf, in Encyclopedia of Language and Linguistics, Pergamon, 94; auth, Leadership in the Teaching University, in Sarsar, ed, Education for Leadership and Social Responsibility, Center for the Study of Public Issues, 96; auth, The Courage of One's Words: Characters and Their Arguments in Plato's Laches, in Richardson, ed, Understanding Schleiermacher: From Translation to Interpretation, Edwin Mellen, 98. **CONTACT ADDRESS** Dept of Interdisciplinary Studies, Monmouth Univ, 400 Cedar Ave, West Long Branch, NJ 07764-1898. **EMAIL** jstam@mondec.monmouth.edu

STAMBAUGH, JOAN
PERSONAL Born 06/10/1932, Pittsburgh, PA **DISCIPLINE** PHILOSOPHY **EDUCATION** Vassar Col, BA, 53; Columbia Univ, MA, 55; Univ Freiburg, PhD(philos), 58. **CAREER** Lectr English, Univ Freiburg, 62-63; from instr to asst prof philos, Vassar Col, 64-69; Asst Prof Philos, Hunter Col, 69-, Ger Res Asn res fel, 60-62; Freiburg Sci Soc fel, 62-63; fel, Arnold Bergstraesser Inst, 63-64; instr, Dutchess Community Col, 66-67; Nat Endowment for Humanities fel, 73-74; co-ed, Heidegger Transl, Harper & Row. **MEMBERSHIPS** Am Philos Asn. **RESEARCH** Nineteenth century and contemporary German thought; problem of time; Buddhism. **SELECTED PUBLICATIONS** Auth, Unterschungen zum Problem der Zeit bei Nietzsche, M Nijhoff, The Hague, 59; Music as a temporal form, J Philos, 64; Das Gleiche in Nietzsches Gedanken der ewigen Wiederkunft des Gleichen, Rev Int Philos, 64; Geist und Welt, Acts XIV Int Cong Philos, 68; Nietzsche's Thought of Eternal Return, Hopkins, 72. **CONTACT ADDRESS** Dept of Philos, Hunter Col, CUNY, 695 Park Ave, New York, NY 10021-5085.

STAMEY, JOSEPH DONALD
PERSONAL Born 01/10/1934, Cisco, TX, m, 1955, 1 child **DISCIPLINE** PHILOSOPHY, RELIGION **EDUCATION** Southern Methodist Univ, BA, 55; BD, 59; MA, 61; Boston Univ, PhD, 68. **CAREER** From asst prof to assoc prof, 67-76, prof philos & relig, McMurry Univ, 76- ; adj prof, Hardin-Simmons Univ, 86- . **HONORS AND AWARDS** CASE Prof for TX, 91; Turner Distinguished Prof of Philos and t Mims, AL Rev, 1/76. **CONTACT ADDRESS** Dept of Philos, Hardin-Simmons Univ, 2200 Hickory, Abilene, TX 79698. **EMAIL** jstamey@mcm.edu

STANCELL, DOLORES WILSON PEGRAM
PERSONAL Born 10/26/1936, New York, NY, m **DISCIPLINE** LAW **EDUCATION** Rutgers U, BA 1970; Rutgers Sch of Law, JD 1974; MI State U, Annual Regulatory Studies Prog 1976. **CAREER** NJ Dept of Pub Adv Div of Rate Counsel, asst dep pub adv; Hon David D Furman Superior Ct Chan Div NJ, law sec 1974-75; Rutgers Univ Rutgers Jour of Comptrs & the Law, admin 1973; Jersey Shore Med Ctr, nurse 1972; Middlesex Cty Legal Svcs, legal intern 1970; Rutgers Urban Studies Ctr, rsch asst 1968; Head Start MCEOC, nurse 1967; Head Start, nurse 1966; Beth Israel Hosp, staff nurse 1958-62; Fordham Hosp, staff nurse 1957-58. **HONORS AND AWARDS** Human Rels Awrd Fordham Hosp 1957. **MEMBERSHIPS** Am Bar Assn Sect on Legal Educ & Admissions to the Bar 1977-78; Forum Comm on Hlth Law 1977-78; Gen Practice 1976-77; Natl Bar Assn 1st vp, Women's Div 1977-78; vice pres Civil Trial Advocacy Sect 1977-78; Legislation & Uniform & State Laws Comm 1977-78; nom com Women's Div 1976-77; Fed Bar Assn; Garden State Bar Assn; NJ State Bar Assn; Hlth Leg & Hlth Plng Serv Com 1976-78; Monmouth Bar Assn; Crmnl Pract Com 1976-78; treas Assn Black Women Lawyers NJ 1977-78; Rutgers Law Sch Alumni Assn; Rutgers Univ Alumni Assn; panelist MRC-TV NY Program, Medical Costs, The Breath of Life 1977; Am Nurses Assn; NJ State Nurses Assn; vol Ocean-Monmouth Legal Serv 1972; vol urban agt Rutgers Urban Studies Cen 1967-68; Pub Policy Forum on Civil Disorders & Forum on the Futureof NJ Rutgers Univ 1968; co Rutgers-Douglass Coll Elem Sch Tutorial Prog 1967-68; trustee Unitarian Soc 1970-72; Acad Adv Com 1977-78; bd Parents Assn Rutgers Prep Sch 1970-71; New Brunswick YWCA; Urban League; NAACP. **SELECTED PUBLICATIONS** Articles Wilson, Computerization of Welfare Recipients, Implications for the Individual & The Right to Privacy 4 Rutgers Journal of Computers and The Law 163 (1974); Minoritiy Workers 1 Womens Rights Law Reporter 71 (1972-73). **CONTACT ADDRESS** 10 Commerce Ct, Newark, NJ 07102.

STANDEN, JEFFERY A.
DISCIPLINE CRIMINAL JUSTICE, CRIMINAL PROCEDURE, JURISPRUDENCE, EVIDENCE **EDUCATION** Georgetown Univ, AB, 82; Univ Va, JD, 86. **CAREER** Clk, Hon Robert F Chapman, US Court of Appeals, 86-87; assoc, Hunton & Williams, Richmond, 86-90; dep gen couns, US Sentencing Comm, 89-90; asst prof, 90-94; assoc prof, 94-97; prof, 97-. **SELECTED PUBLICATIONS** Ed, Va Law Rev. **CONTACT ADDRESS** Sch of Law, Willamette Univ, 900 State St, Salem, OR 97301. **EMAIL** jstanden@willamette.edu

STANFORD, PRESTON K.
DISCIPLINE PHILOSOPHY **EDUCATION** Univ Calif San Diego, PhD, 97. **CAREER** Asst prof, Univ Calif Irvine, 97-. **MEMBERSHIPS** APA; PSA. **RESEARCH** Philosophy of science; Philosophy of biology; Metaphysics; History of modern philosophy. **SELECTED PUBLICATIONS** Auth, Reference and natural kind terms: The real essence of Locke's View, Pac Philos Quart 79: 78-97, 98; auth, For pluralism and against realism about species, Philos Sci 62: 70-91, 95; auth, Preaching to the Choir? Robert Klee and the Latest Face of Scientific Realism, Studies in the history and Philo of Sci 30: 367-375, 99; auth, Refining the casual theory of reference for natural kind terms, Philo Studies 97: 99-129, 00; auth, An Antirealist Explanation of the Success of Science, Philo Sci 67: 266-284, 00 (forthcoming); auth, Refusing the Devil's Bargain: What Kind of Underdetermination Should We Take Seriously?, Philo Sci Asn, (forthcoming); auth, The Manifest Connection: Causation, Meaning and David Hume, Jour fo the Hist of Philo, (forthcoming); auth, The Units of Selection and the Casual Structure of the World, Erkenntnis, (forthcoming). **CONTACT ADDRESS** Dept. of Philosophy, Univ of California, Irvine, Irvine, CA 92697-4555. **EMAIL** stanford@uci.edu

STANFORD, ROSEMARY
PERSONAL Born 05/12/1942, Portsmouth, VA, m, 1993, 2 children **DISCIPLINE** CRIMINAL JUSTICE **EDUCATION** Univ S Fla, BA, 76; MA, 79; Fla State Univ, PhD, 84. **CAREER** Asst prof, Pan Am Univ, 82-85; assoc prof, Univ of S Fla, 85-96; pres, Justice System Advocates, 93-96; assoc prof, Univ of Houston Victoria, 96-99; exec dir, Univ of Houston Victoria, 00. **HONORS AND AWARDS** Who's Who of Am Women 86-96; Who's who In the World, 96; Teaching Awd, Univ of S Fla, 92; Awd, State of Fla, 94. **MEMBERSHIPS** Am Criminal Justice System. **RESEARCH** Program Evaluation, Juvenile and Minority Researcher. **SELECTED PUBLICATIONS** Auth, "Disadvantaged Hispanic College Students and social Privation: Programming for Sophistication", J of Contemp Criminal Justice 5.2 (89): 40-50; coauth, "Domestic Disturbance Danger Rate", J of Police Sci and Admin 17.4 (90): 244-249; auth, "Judicial Response to Spouse Abuse", J of Police and Criminal Psychol, 71 (91): 24-29. **CONTACT ADDRESS** Dept Arts and Sci, Univ of Houston, Victoria, 3007 N Ben Wilson, Victoria, TX 77901. **EMAIL** stanfordr@vic.uh.edu

STANISLAWSKI, MICHAEL
DISCIPLINE JEWISH, RUSSIAN, AND EUROPEAN INTELLECTUAL HISTORY **EDUCATION** Harvard Univ, 73, PhD, 79. **CAREER** Nathan J Miller prof. **SELECTED PUBLICATIONS** Auth, Tsar Nicholas I and the Jews, 83; For Whom Do I Toil?, 88; Psalms for the Tsar, 88; co-auth, Heritage: Civilization and the Jews: Study Guide, 84; ed, Heritage: Civilization and the Jews: Source Reader, 84. **CONTACT ADDRESS** Dept of Hist, Columbia Col, New York, 2960 Broadway, New York, NY 10027-6902.

STANLEY, JOHN E.
PERSONAL Born 03/24/1943, Connelsville, PA, m, 1970, 2 children **DISCIPLINE** BIBLE **EDUCATION** Anderson Col, BA, 65; Anderson Sch Theol, MDiv, 69; Lutheran Theol Sem, STM; Univ Denver, Iliff Sch Theol, PhD, 86. **CAREER** Pastor, 69-80; prof, Warner Pacific Coll, 83-95; Prof Biblical & Rel Studies, Messiah Coll, 95-. **HONORS AND AWARDS** Louisville Inst grant, 98; NEH summer grant, 86. **MEMBERSHIPS** Soc Bibl Lit **RESEARCH** Bibl interpretation, psalms. **SELECTED PUBLICATIONS** various **CONTACT ADDRESS** 130 Sholly Dr, Mechanicsburg, PA 17055. **EMAIL** jstanley@messiah.edu

STANLEY, KATHRYN VELMA
PERSONAL Born 02/09/1967, Detroit, MI, s **DISCIPLINE** LAW **EDUCATION** Spellman College, BA, 1989; Univ of Virginia School of Law, JD, 1992. **CAREER** Children's Defense Fund, student intern, 88-89; Alabama Capitol Representation Resource Center, staff atty, 92-. **HONORS AND AWARDS** Black Law Student Assn, Member of the Year, 1992. **MEMBERSHIPS** Sigma Alpha Iota Music Fraternity, vp, 1988-89; Black Law Students Assn, UVA Chapter, pres, 1991-92; Youth Entrepreneurship System, board sec, 1995-. **SELECTED PUBLICATIONS** Essence Magazine, Back Talk, December 1994; Virginia Lawyer (Alumni Magazine), Winter 1995. **CONTACT ADDRESS** Alabama Capital Representation Resource Center, 114 N Hull St, Montgomery, AL 36105.

STANLEY, TOM
PERSONAL Born 07/14/1950, Canton, OH, m, 1982 **DISCIPLINE** BUSINESS, ECONOMIC STUDIES **EDUCATION** Univ Akron, BSIM, 72; Kent State Univ, MA, 73; Purdue Univ, MS, 80; Purdue Univ, PhD, 82. **CAREER** Asst Prof, Western Ky Univ, 80-82; Asst Prof, Ill State Univ, 82-86; Asst Prof, Western Ill Univ, 84-86; Prof, Hendrix Col, 86-. **HONORS AND AWARDS** Anbar Electronic Intelligence Citation of Excellence; Distinguished Paper Awd, Southern Soc of Economists, 92. **MEMBERSHIPS** AEA, Soc for the Advancement of Socio-Econ. **RESEARCH** Economic time series, meta-analysis, methodology of economics. **SELECTED PUBLICATIONS** Auth, "Empirical Economics? An Econometric Dilemma with only Methodological Solution," J of Econ Issues, 32 (98): 191-218; auth, "New Wine in Old Bottles: A Meta-Analysis of Ricardian Equivalence," Southern Econ J, 64 (98): 713-727; coauth, "Gender Wage Discrimination Bias? A Meta-Regression Analysis," J of Human Resources, 33 (98): 947-973; auth, Challenging Times Series: Limits to Knowledge, Inertia and Caprice, Edward Elgar Publ, 00. **CONTACT ADDRESS** Dept Bus & Econ Studies, Hendrix Col, 1600 Washington Ave, Conway, AR 72032-4115. **EMAIL** stanley@hendrix.edu

STANOVSKY, DEREK
DISCIPLINE PHILOSOPHY **EDUCATION** Univ of Tex Austin, BA, 85, PhD, 94. **CAREER** Appalachian State Univ, lectr, 95-. **RESEARCH** Feminist theory; 20th century continental philosophy. **SELECTED PUBLICATIONS** Auth, Fela and His Wives: The Import of a Postcolonial Masculinity, in: Jouvert: A Jour Postcolonial Stud, vol 2, no 1 98; auth, Speaking As, Speaking For and Speaking With: The Pitfalls and Possibilities of Men Teaching Feminism, Feminist Teacher, vol 11, no 1 97; auth, "Princess Diana, Mother Teresa, and the Value of Women's Work," Womens Studies Assoc J, vol 11, no 2: 146-151, (99). **CONTACT ADDRESS** Dept of Interdisciplinary Studies, Appalachian State Univ, Boonie, NC 28608. **EMAIL** stanovskydj@appstate.edu

STARBUCK, SCOTT R.
PERSONAL Born 11/12/1963, m, 2 children **DISCIPLINE** BIBLICAL STUDIES **EDUCATION** Whitworth Col, BA, 85; Princeton Theol Seminary, MDiv, 88, PhD, 95. **CAREER** Res Dir, 83-84, Teaching Asst, 84-85, Co-Dir Resident Chaplain Prog, Whitworth Col, 84-85; Teaching Asst, 87-88, Res Asst, 88-92, Sub-ed and contribr, PTS Int Dead Sea Scrolls Project, 86-87, Actg Dir, Office of Computer Assistance for Textual Res, Princeton Theol Seminary, 88-91; Res Theologian, 91-92, Sr Pastor and Head of Staff, Hopewell Presbyterian Church, 92-97; Sr Pastor and Head of Staff, Wellshire Presbyterian Church, 97-98; dir, SRASassociates: Scholarly Communication Consultants, 98. **HONORS AND AWARDS** National Deans List, 85; Outstanding Philos Student, Whitworth Col, 85; Princeton Doctoral Teaching Fel, 88-91; Princeton Doctoral Fel, 88-91; The George S. Green Doctoral Fel in Old Testament, 88-90; Guest Lectr, Princeton Theol Seminary, 91-92; Vis Lectr in Congregational Ministries, Princeton Theol Seminary, 94-95. **MEMBERSHIPS** Presbytery of Denver; Soc Bibl Lit; Cath Bibl Soc; Am Sch Oriental Res; Samaritan Inst. **SELECTED PUBLICATIONS** Auth, Like Dreamers Lying in Wait, We Lament: A New Reading of Psalm 126, Koinonia, 89; coauth, Graphic Concordance to the Dead Sea Scrolls, Westminster/John Knox, 91; auth, Ministerial Development and Spiritual Support Groups, Testament, Spring 95; And What Had Kings? The Reappropriation of Court Oracles Among the Royal Psalms of the Hebrew Psalter, Univ Mich Press, 96; Engaging the World With Christ: Participating in the Royal Office of Christ, Theol Matters, 98; Court Oracles in the Psalms: A New Examination of the So-Called Royal Psalms in their Ancient Near Eastern Context, Scholars Press (forthcoming). **CONTACT ADDRESS** Wellshire Presbyterian Church, 2999 S. Colorado Blvd., Denver, CO 80222-6607. **EMAIL** director@srasassociates.com

STARK, HERMAN E.
PERSONAL Born 10/04/1966, Elmhurst, m, 1990 **DISCIPLINE** PHILOSOPHY **EDUCATION** Northern IL Univ, BA, MA; Univ Memphis, PhD. **CAREER** Inst, 92-94, Univ of Memphis; inst, 93-94, Shelby State Comm Col; asst prof, 94-95, Northern Illinios Univ; coordinator of phil, 95-, South Suburban Col. **HONORS AND AWARDS** Magna Cum Laude, Deans Awd, Distinction on MA Logic Examinations, The Meritorious Grad Tchng Awd, Univ of Memphis; The Amer Phil Assoc Certificate for Tchng Excl. **MEMBERSHIPS** APA **RESEARCH** The nature of rationality **CONTACT ADDRESS** Dept of Humanities, So Suburban Col, 15800 State St., South Holland, IL 60473-1200. **EMAIL** hstark@acilan.ssc.cc.il.us

STARK, TRACEY
PERSONAL Born 02/10/1965, Minneapolis, MN, s **DISCIPLINE** PHILOSOPHY **EDUCATION** Boston Col, PhD. **CAREER** Asst prof, Univ Maine Orono; asst prof, St. John's Sem, Boston. **MEMBERSHIPS** APA; Soc for Phenomenol & Existential Philos. **RESEARCH** Phenomenology; critical theory; psychoanalysis. **SELECTED PUBLICATIONS** Auth, "Dignity of the Particular: Adorno on Kant's Aesthetics," Philos & Soc Critisicm; "Arendt & the White Rose," Budhi, forthcoming **CONTACT ADDRESS** 15 Gardner St., Apt. B, Allston, MA 02134. **EMAIL** starktr@bc.du

STARKEY, LAWRENCE H.
PERSONAL Born 07/10/1919, Minneapolis, MN, s, 3 children **DISCIPLINE** PHILOSOPHY **EDUCATION** Univ Louisville, BA, 42; Southern Baptist Theol Sem, MDiv, 45; Univ So Calif, MA, 51, PhD, 60. **CAREER** Asst prof Los Angeles Baptist Col and Sem, 47-51; writer, Moody Inst of Sci, 55-57; assoc prof philos, phys sci, Bethel Col, 58-62; assoc prof, philos and relig, chemn, Linfield Col, 62-63; eng writer, General Dynamics, 63-66; assoc prof philos & hum, Alma Col, 66-68; assoc ed and principal ed of philos, Encyclopedia Britannica, 68-72; assoc prof philos & hum, chemn, Jamestown Col, 73-75; lectr philos & relig, producer television studies, field coord, N Dakota State Univ, 76-79; mech des Concord Inc, 77-85; instr philos, Moorhead State Univ, 85-86; lectr philos Univ Missouri, 86-87; independent scholar, 88- . **HONORS AND AWARDS** Delegate, citizen ambassador program to Russia and Hungary; J.B. Speed Jr scholar; BA honors in biol. **MEMBERSHIPS** Am Sci Affiliation; APA; Metaphysical Soc of Am. **RESEARCH** Synoptic thinking; integrating philosophy, religion, science and literature; particle physics; relativity; cosmology; new archaeological findings on the patriarch Joseph. **SELECTED PUBLICATIONS** Auth, Particle and Astro-Physics Challenge Kant's Phenomenalism; auth, A Less Fantastic God: A Biologist Sees Him as Evolving from Matter; auth, The Inherence of Particles in Universe, of Force in Plenum: Leibniz vis-a-vis Relativistic Cosmology and Black-Hole Gravitation; auth, Kant's Cosmological Antinomies and Modern Physics; auth, Necessity and Purposiveness in the Cosmic Setting and History of Life; contribu to People Who Made America: Pictorial Encyclopedia; coauth, in "Eleaticism" and "Realism" article in Encyclopedia Britannica. **CONTACT ADDRESS** 1325 N 63rd St, Wauwatosa, WI 53213.

STATON, CECIL P.
PERSONAL Born 01/26/1958, Greenville, SC, m, 1986, 2 children **DISCIPLINE** BIBLICAL STUDIES **EDUCATION** Furman Univ, BA, 80; Southeastern Seminary, MDIU, 82; THM, 85; Univ of Oxford, PhD, 88. **CAREER** Asst prof to assoc prof, Mercer Univ, 91-96; assoc provost, Mercer Univ, 97-. **HONORS AND AWARDS** R.T. Daniel OT Southeastern Awd, 83; Baggot Awd, Furman Univ, 80; G. Henton Davies Prize for OT and Hebrew, Southeastern Seminar, 85; Overseas Research Student Awd, Univ of Oxford, 87; Richard Furman Heritage Awd, Furman Univ, 00. **MEMBERSHIPS** Nat Assoc of Baptist Prof of Relig; Am Acad of Relig; Soc of Bibl Lit. **RESEARCH** Theophany; Genesis; Pentateuch. **SELECTED PUBLICATIONS** Auth, How Long, O Yahweh?: The Complaint Prayer of Psalm 13, Faith and Mission, VII/2, Spring 90, 59-67; ed and auth, Interpreting Isaiah for Preaching and Teaching, Macon: Smyth & Helwys, 91; auth, "The Worship Experience", Formations Commentary, Macon: Smyth & Helwys, 92, 17-35; ed and author, Interpreting Hosea for Preaching and Teaching, Macon: Smyth & Helwys, 93; auth, "The History of Smyth & Helwys Publishing", The Struggle for the Soul of the SBC, Macon: Mercer University Press, 93; auth, Obadiah, Mercer Commentary on the Bible Macon: Mercer University Press, 94; ed and auth, Interpreting Amos for Preaching and Teaching, Macon: Smyth & Helwys, 95; ed and auth, Why Am I A Baptist: Reflections on Being Baptist in the 21st Century, Smyth & Helwys, 99; auth, "Theophany" Eerdmans Dictionary of the Bible, Grand Rapids: William B. Eerdmans Publishing (forthcoming); auth, "Genesis", Smyth & Helwys Bible Commentary, Macon: Smyth & Helwys (forthcoming). **CONTACT ADDRESS** Dept Christian Studies, Mercer Univ, Macon, 6316 Peake Rd, Macon, GA 31210. **EMAIL** cps@helwys.com

STAUB, JACOB J.
PERSONAL Born 05/04/1951, New York, NY, m, 1975, 3 children **DISCIPLINE** RELIGION, MEDIEVAL JEWISH PHILOSOPHY, CONTEMPORARY JEWISH THOUGHT **EDUCATION** Reconstructionist Rabbinical College, ordination, 77; Temple Univ, PhD, 80. **CAREER** Asst Prof, Dept Relig, Lafayette Col, 77-83; ACAD DEAN, RECONSTRUCTIONIST RABBINICAL COL, 83-. **HONORS AND AWARDS** Gladstone Prize Fine Teaching; 97; fel, Acad Jewish Philos, 99; Mellow Fel Jewish Philos, **MEMBERSHIPS** Asn Jewish Studies; Am Acad Relig; Reconstructionist Rabbinical Asn. **RESEARCH** Medieval Jewish Philos, Medieval Bible Commentaries. **SELECTED PUBLICATIONS** Coauth, "The Spiritualization of Peoplehood and the Reconstructionist Curriculum of the Future," in Windows on the Jewish Soul: Resources for Teaching the Values of Spiritual Peoplehood, 94, Hauvrot; auth, "Reconstructionism" and "Mordecai M. Kaplan," Encyclopedia Britannica, 99; auth, "Reconstructionist Judaism," The Encyclopedia of Judaism, The Religion, 99, E. J. Brill; auth, "Interpreting Jewish History in Light of Zionism," The Reconstructionist, Spring 98; auth, "How Are We Tested: The Binding of Isaac," Reconstructionism Today, Fall 97; auth, "From Slavery to Freedom," Creating Passover Memories, 97, Making Connections, Community Hebrew Schools; auth, "Mordecai M. Kaplan," "Reconstructionism," "Reconstructionist Rabbinical College," "Milton Steinberg," Oxford Dictionary of the Jewish Religion, 97, Oxford Univ Press; auth, "Evolving Definitions of Evolution," The Reconstructionist, Fall 96; auth, "How Can Reconstructionists Pray?" Reconstructionism Today, Spring 96, and Connecting Prayer and Spirituality: Kol Haneshamah as a Creative Teaching and Learning Text, 96, The Reconstructionist Press; auth, "Flexible Boundaries," The Re-

constructionist, Fall 94; "Submission as a Value," Reconstructionism Today, Fall 93; auth, "Theology and Community: A Response," in Imagining the Jewish Future, 92, State Univ NY Press; auth, "Idud Ha-Aliyah MiTzafron Amerika," in Si'ah Mesharim, 92; auth, "Reconstructionism," in Encyclopedia of Jewish-American History and Culture, 92, Garland Publishing; auth, "Reconstructionist Judaism," in Encyclopedia of Religions in the United States: One Hundred Religious Groups Speak for Themselves, 92, Crossroad/Continuum; coauth, "Jewish Philosophy: Medieval and Modern," in The Schocken Guide to Jewish Books, 92, Schocken Books; coauth, "Exploring Judaism: A Reconstructionist Approach," 00. **CONTACT ADDRESS** Acad Dean, Reconstructionist Rabbinical Col, 1299 Church Rd, Wyncote, PA 19095. **EMAIL** staub@rrc.edu

STEBENNE, DAVID
PERSONAL Born 07/04/1960, Providence, RI, s **DISCIPLINE** HISTORY, LAW **EDUCATION** Yale Univ, BA, 82; Columbia Univ, JD, MA, 86, PhD, 91. **CAREER** Lectr, Hist, Yale Univ, 91-93; asst prof, Hist, Ohio State Univ, 93-97; Assoc Prof, Hist, Ohio State Univ, 97-. **MEMBERSHIPS** Am Hist Asn; Org Am Hist; Bus Hist Conf; Md Bar **RESEARCH** Modern US history; politics, economics, labor & legal history **SELECTED PUBLICATIONS** Arthur J. Goldberg: New Deal Liberal, Oxford Univ Press, 96. **CONTACT ADDRESS** Hist Dept, Ohio State Univ, Columbus, 106 Dulles Hall, 230 w 17th, Columbus, OH 43210-1367. **EMAIL** stebenne.1@osu.edu

STECKEL, RICHARD H.
PERSONAL Born 06/28/1944, Milledgeville, GA, m, 1972, 2 children **DISCIPLINE** ECONOMICS **EDUCATION** Oberlin College, BA, 66; Univ OK, MA, 70; Univ Chicago, MA, 73, PhD, 77. **CAREER** Instr, Asst Prof, Assoc Prof, Prof, 74 to 89-, Ohio State Univ. **HONORS AND AWARDS** Charles Warren Fel; OSU Dist Lectr, . **MEMBERSHIPS** EHA; SSHA; PAA; AHA; EHA; AEA; AAPA. **RESEARCH** Long term trends in health care and nutrition. **SELECTED PUBLICATIONS** Coed, Health and Welfare During Industrialization, Univ Chicago Press, 97. **CONTACT ADDRESS** Economics Dept, Ohio State Univ, Columbus, 1945 N High St, Columbus, OH 43210. **EMAIL** steckel.1@osu.edu

STECKER, ROBERT
PERSONAL Born 10/04/1947, New York, NY, m, 2 children **DISCIPLINE** PHILOSOPHY **EDUCATION** Mass Inst Tech, PhD, 75. **CAREER** PROF, PHILOS, CENTRAL MICH UNIV. 83-, lectr, National Univ of Singapore, 77-83; asst prof, Univ Houston, 75-76. **HONORS AND AWARDS** MAGB Awd, 00; Research Prof, 99; President's Awd; Fon Outstanding Research, 98. **RESEARCH** APA; RSA; Aesthetics; Ethics; History of Modern Philosophy; Philosophy of Mind. **SELECTED PUBLICATIONS** Auth, "Artworks," Penn State Press, 97; auth, "John Locke Essay Concerning Human Understanding in Focus," Routledge, 00. **CONTACT ADDRESS** 4538 Comanche, Okemos, MI 40864. **EMAIL** robert.stecker@cmich.edu

STEEGER, WILLIAM P.
PERSONAL Born 05/26/1945, Brooklyn, NY, m, 1968, 4 children **DISCIPLINE** OLD TESTAMENT ARCHEOLOGY **EDUCATION** Univ Florida, BA, 67; Southern Baptist Theol Sem, Louisville, Mdiv 70, PhD, 83; Univ of Louisville, KY, MA, 72. **CAREER** Instr, 69-73, Univ of Louisville; Prof, 76-86, Baptist Theol of Southern Africa, Johannesburg, S Africa; Prof, 78-86, Die Theol Sem van die Baptist; Prof, 83-84, Oakland City Coll; Prof, 86, Ouachita Baptist Univ, Arkadelphia, AR, Chr Div of Rel and Philos, prof to retire prof, So Baptist Theol Sem. **HONORS AND AWARDS** Phi Kappa Phi; Phi Alpha Theta; Amer Ed, KY, South; Biblical Stud and Archaeol; Man of Achievement; Vis Prof of OT-Southern Baptist Theol Sem, KY. **MEMBERSHIPS** Soc of Biblical Lit; Evangelical Theol Soc; Inst of Biblical Res; Natl Assoc of Baptist Prof of Rel. **RESEARCH** Old Testament; Biblical Archaeology. **SELECTED PUBLICATIONS** Contrib auth, Anchor Bible Dictionary, Doubleday & Co; Contrib auth, Mercer Commentary of the Bible, Mercer Univ Press; auth, Joshua: An Exposition, Baptist Theological College of Southern Africa, Johannesburg, South Africa; Psalms: An Exposition, Old Testament Theology, Old Testament Introduction, Baptist Theo College of S Africa, Johannesburg, S Africa. **CONTACT ADDRESS** Dept Old Testament, So Baptist Theol Sem, 2825 Lexington Rd., Louisville, KY 40280. **EMAIL** steeger@alpha.edu

STEELE, RICHARD B.
PERSONAL Born 11/03/1952, Philadelphia, PA, m, 1978, 3 children **DISCIPLINE** CHRISTIAN THEOLOGY **EDUCATION** Haverford Col, BA, 74; Yale Divinity School, MDiv, 78; Marquette Univ, PhD, 90. **CAREER** Pastor, Trinity-Pilgrim United Methodist Church, Brookfield, WI, 85-95; instr Theol, Marquette Univ, Milwaukee, WI, 93-94; asst prof Theol, Milwaukee Theol Inst, Milwaukee, WI, 90-95; Assoc Prof Theol, Seattle Pacific Univ, Seattle, WA, 95-. **HONORS AND AWARDS** Arthur J. Schmitt fel, Marquette Univ, 86-87; Top Prof Ivy Honorary (Mortarboard), Seattle Pacific Univ, 96. **MEMBERSHIPS** Amer Acad Relig; Hist Soc of the United Methodist Church; Karl Barth Soc; Wesleyan Theol Soc. **RESEARCH** Jonathan Edwards; Eastern Orthodox theology; religion and disability; moral psychology and Christian formation. **SELECTED PUBLICATIONS** Auth, Review of Randy L. Maddox, ed, Aldersgate Reconsidered, Wesleyan Theol J, spring-fall 94; Gracious Affection and True Virtue according to Johnathan Edwards and John Wesley, PhD dissertation, Marquette Univ, 90, rev ed, Wesleyan and Pietist Studies Series, Scarecrow Press, 94; Why Church Growth is a Red Herring, Circuit Rider, March 94; review of Brett Webb-Mitchell, God Plays Piano, Too: The Spiritual Lives of Disabled Children, Medical Col of WI, Bioethics Bull, fall 95; Narrative Theology and the Religious Affections in Theology Without Foundations: Religious Practice and the Future of Theological Truth, ed Stanley Hauerwas, Nancy Murphy, and Mark Nation, Abingdon Press, 94; John Wesley's Synthesis of the Revival Practices of Jonathan Edwards, George Whitefield, and Nicholas von Zinzendorf, Wesleyan Theol J, spring 95; many other articles, and several publications forthcoming; auth, "Unremitting Compassion: The Moral Psychology of Parenting Children with Genetic Disorders," Theology Today, 00; auth, "Devoto Post-Moderna: On Using a Spiritual Classic as a Diagnostic Tool in a Freshman Christian Formation Course," Horizons: The Jouranl of the College Theology Society, 00; auth, Strangely Chilled: Heart Religion in the Wesleyan Theological Tradition, Scarecrow Press, forthcoming. **CONTACT ADDRESS** Seattle Pacific Univ, 3307 Third Ave W, Seattle, WA 98119-1997. **EMAIL** rsteele@spu.edu

STEEVES, PAUL DAVID
PERSONAL Born 06/20/1941, Attleboro, MA, m, 1962, 2 children **DISCIPLINE** RUSSIAN MODERN & ECCLESIASTICAL HISTORY **EDUCATION** Washington Univ, AB, 62; Univ Kans, MA, 72, PhD(Russ hist), 76. **CAREER** Asst instr Western civilization, Univ Kans, 66-68; vis lectr hist, Kans State Teachers Col, 71-72; asst prof, 72-78, PROF HIST, STETSON UNIV, 78-, DIR RUSS STUDIES, 76-, DIR HONORS PROG, 78-, Ed, Newsletter, Conf Faith & Hist, 79. **HONORS AND AWARDS** O P Backus Awd, Univ Kans, 76; W H McInery Awd, Stetson Univ, 79. **MEMBERSHIPS** AHA; Conf Faith & Hist; Am Asn Advan Slavic Studies; Soc Study Relig Under Communism; Southern Conf Slavic Studies. **RESEARCH** Evangelical Baptist movement in Russia. **SELECTED PUBLICATIONS** Auth, Baptists as subversives in the contemporary Soviet Union, In: God and Caesar, Conf Faith & Hist, 71; ed, Church and State in USSR, A sourcebook, Stetson Univ, 73; auth, Alexander Karev, evangelical in a Communist land, Fides et Historia, 76; Amendment of Soviet law concerning religious association, J Church & State, 77. **CONTACT ADDRESS** Dept of Hist, Stetson Univ, De Land, 421 N Woodland Blvd, Deland, FL 32720-3761.

STEFANOVIC, INGID LEMAN
PERSONAL Born, Canada, m, 4 children **DISCIPLINE** PHILOSOPHY **EDUCATION** Univ St Michael's Col, BA, 74; Univ Toronto, MA, 75; PhD, 79. **CAREER** Asst prof, Univ Victoria BC, 80-81; lectr and asst prof, York Univ, 81-91; asst prof, Brock Univ, 91-93; asst prof to assoc prof and assoc chair, , Univ Toronto, 93-. **HONORS AND AWARDS** Dean's Excellence Awd, Univ Toronto, 97. **MEMBERSHIPS** Intl Asn for Environ Philos; World Soc for Ekistics. **RESEARCH** Environmental and architectural phenomenology; Perceptions of place; Environmental ethics. **SELECTED PUBLICATIONS** Auth, "Encouraging Environmental Care," in Canadian Issues in Environmental Ethics, Broadview Press, 97; auth, "Phenomenological Encounters with Place: Cavtat to Square One," J of Environ Psychol, (98): 31-44; auth, "Phenomenological Reflections on Ecosystem Health," in Ethics and the Environment, Vol 5, (00): 253-269; auth, Safeguarding Our Common Future: Rethinking Sustainable Development, SUNY Press, 00. **CONTACT ADDRESS** Dept Philos, Univ of Toronto, 215 Huron St, Toronto, ON, Canada M5S 1A1. **EMAIL** ingrid.stefanovic@utoronto.ca

STEFFEN, LLOYD
PERSONAL Born 11/27/1951, Racine, WI, m, 1981, 3 children **DISCIPLINE** RELIGION STUDIES **EDUCATION** New Col, BA, 73; Andover Newton Theological School, MA (cum laude), 78; Yale Divinity School, MDiv (cum laude), 78; Brown Univ, PhD, 84. **CAREER** Teaching Fellow, Brown Univ, 79-82; Asst/Assoc Prof, Northland Col, 82-90; Chair, Dept Philosophy and Relgion, Northland Col, 84-90; Vis Assoc Prof, Temple Univ, 91; Prof and Univ Chaplain, Lehigh Univ, 90. **HONORS AND AWARDS** Faculty Research Awds, Lehigh Univ, 94, 8, NEH Summer Institute, 95, Harvard Univ 88, Summer Fac Development Awds, Northland College, 87, 90, Fellow, Coolidge Research Colloquium, 86, NEH Summer Stipend, 85, Title III-C Summer Stipend, 85, Univ Fel, Brown Univ, 87, Edward Ashley Walker Scholarship Prize, Yale Univ, 77, member, Phi Eta Sigma, Phi Alpha Theta. **MEMBERSHIPS** Am Academy of Religion, Am Philosophical Assoc, Society of Christian Ethics, Society for Values in Higher Educ, Society of Comparative and Asian Philosophy. **RESEARCH** Ethics (social, religions, axiological, medical/professional), personal disorders in contemporary life, emotions and self-deception, philosophy of religion and theology, religion and modern culture. **SELECTED PUBLICATIONS** Auth, Self-Deception and the Common Life, 84; auth, Life/Choice: The Theory of Just Abortion, 94, 99; auth, Abortion: A Reader, 96; auth, Executing Justice: The Moral Meaning of the Death Penalty, 99. **CONTACT ADDRESS** Dept Religion Studies, Lehigh Univ, 9 W Packer Ave, Unit 3, Bethlehem, PA 18015-3082. **EMAIL** lhsl@lehigh.edu

STEIGERWALD, DIANE
PERSONAL Born, PQ, Canada **DISCIPLINE** PHILOSOPHY **EDUCATION** McGill Univ Montreal, PhD, 94. **CAREER** Author **RESEARCH** Islamic philosophy; dialogue between Abrahamic faiths. **SELECTED PUBLICATIONS** Auth, La pensee philosophique et theologique de Shahrastani, Sainte-Foy: Laval Univ Press, 97; auth, Majlis Discours sur l'Ordre et la creation, Sainte-Foy: Laval Univ Press, 98; auth, L'islam et ses valeurs communes au judeo-christianisme, Laval Univ Press, forthcoming; Le role de la logique dans la reconciliation de la philosophie et de la religion chez Averroes, Laval Theologique et Philosophique, 96; auth, The Divine Word (Kalima) in Shahrastani's Majlis, Studies in Religion and Sciences religieuses, 97. **CONTACT ADDRESS** 161 Rue Saint-Aubin, Chateauguay, QC, Canada J6K 2S2. **EMAIL** alibaya@minet.ca

STEIKER, CAROL S.
PERSONAL Born 05/31/1961, Philadelphia, PA, m, 1990, 2 children **DISCIPLINE** LAW **EDUCATION** Harvard-Radcliffe Colleges, AB (hist and lit), 82; Harvard Law School, JD, 86. **CAREER** Law clerk to Judge J Skelly Wright, US Court of Appeals for the District of Columbia Circuit, 86-87; law clerk to Justice Thurgood Marshall, US Supreme Court, 87-88; staff attorney, DC Public Defender Service, 88-92. **RESEARCH** Criminal law; criminal procedure; capital punishment; legal ethics. **SELECTED PUBLICATIONS** Auth, Sober Second Thoughts: Reflections on Two Decades of Constitutional Regulation of Capital Punishment, 109 Harvard Law Rev 355, 95; Counter-Revolution in Constitutional Criminal Procedure? Two Audiences, Two Answers, 94 MI Law Rev 2466, 96; Foreword: Punishment and Procedure: Punishment Theory and the Criminal-Civil Procedural Divide, 85 Georgetown Law J 775, 97; with Jordan M Steiker, Judicial Developments in Capital Punishment Law, in America's Experiment with Capital Punishment: Reflections on the Past, Present, and Future of the Ultimate Penal Sanction, Acker, Bohm & Lanier, eds, Carolina Academic Press, 98. **CONTACT ADDRESS** Law School, Harvard Univ, Griswold 409, Cambridge, MA 02138. **EMAIL** steiker@law.harvard.edu

STEIN, ERIC
PERSONAL Born 07/08/1913, Czechoslovakia, m, 1955 **DISCIPLINE** LAW **EDUCATION** Charles Univ, Czech, Jud, 37; Univ Mich, JD, 42. **CAREER** With US Dept State, 46-55, adv, US Deleg, UN Gen Assembly, 47-55; Prof Law, Law Sch, Univ Mich, Ann Arbor, 55-, Vis prof int orgn, Law Sch, Stanford Univ, 56, 77; Guggenheim fel, 62-63; Soc Sci Res Coun award, 65; mem adv coun, Inst Europ Studies, Free Univ Brussels, 65-; adv panel, Bur Europ Affairs, Dept State & consult dept, 66-69; mem, Atlantic Coun, 66, vchmn comt Atlantic studies, 66-68; vis prof, Inst Advan Legal Studies, Univ London, 75. **HONORS AND AWARDS** Alexander von Humboldt Prize, 82; dr, free univ brussels, belgium, 78. **MEMBERSHIPS** Am Bar Asn; Coun Foreign Rels; Am Soc Int Law; Int Acad Comp Law; Brit Inst Int & Comp Law. **RESEARCH** International law and organization; European law; comparative law. **SELECTED PUBLICATIONS** Auth, International-Law In Internal Law--Toward Intization Of Central Eastern-European Constitutions, Am J Of Int Law, Vol 88, 94; Out Of The Ashes Of A Federation, 2 New Constitutions, Am J Of Comparative Law, Vol 45, 97; Peaceful Separation--A New Virus, Columbia J Of Transnational Law, Vol 36, 97; auth, Czecho-Slovakia: Ethnic Conflict, Constitutional Fissure, Negotiated Break-up, Univ of Michigan Press, 97; auth, Thoughts from a Bridge: A Retrospective of Writings on New Europe and American Federalism, 00. **CONTACT ADDRESS** Law Sch, Univ of Michigan, Ann Arbor, Ann Arbor, MI 48104. **EMAIL** steine@umich.edu

STEIN, HOWARD
PERSONAL Born 01/21/1929, New York, NY, d, 1948, 2 children **DISCIPLINE** PHILOSOPHY OF SCIENCE **EDUCATION** Columbia Univ, AB, 47; Univ Chicago, PhD(philos), 58; Univ MI, Ann Arbor, MS, 59. **CAREER** Prof philos, Case Western Reserve Univ, 67-73; prof philos, Columbia Univ, 73-80, prof philos, Univ Chicago, 80-; Nat Sci Found sci fac fel, 58-59 & sr fel, 65-66; mem US nat comt, Int Union Hist & Philos Sci, 72-74; mem sect comt VII of prog comt of 1975, Int Cong Logic, Methodology & Philos Sci, 72-75; Guggenheim fel, 74-75; adv comt hist philos sci, Nat Sci Found, 77-79; emer, 00. **HONORS AND AWARDS** Am Academy of Arts and Sciences, FEL, 89-. **MEMBERSHIPS** Am Philos Asn; Philos Sci Asn; Am Math Soc; AAUP; Fedn Am Sci. **RESEARCH** Foundations of physics; history of physics; Hist of philosophy, Hist and philosophy of mathematics. **SELECTED PUBLICATIONS** Auth, Newtonian space-time, In: The Annus Mirabilis of Sir Isaac Newton, Maxwell, and Beyond, In: Historical and Philosophical Perspectives of Science, Univ MN, 70; On the Conceptual Structure of Quantum Mechanics, In: Paradigms and Paradoxes, Univ Pittsburgh, 72; Some Philosophical Prehistory of General Relativity, In: Foundations of Space-Time Theories, Univ MN, 77. **CONTACT ADDRESS** Dept of Philos, Univ of Chicago, 1010 E 59th St, Chicago, IL 60637-1512. **EMAIL** h-stein@uchicago.edu

STEIN, JANICE GROSS
DISCIPLINE POLITICAL SCIENCE **EDUCATION** McGill Univ, BA, 64, PhD, 69; Yale Univ, MA, 65. **CAREER** Prof, Univ of Toronto **SELECTED PUBLICATIONS** Auth, Getting to the Table: Processes of International Prenegotiation; Choosing to Cooperate: How States Avoid Loss; We All Lost the Cold War. **CONTACT ADDRESS** Fac of Law, Univ of Toronto, 78 Queen's Park, Toronto, ON, Canada M5S 1A1.

STEIN, ROBERT H.
DISCIPLINE NEW TESTAMENT **EDUCATION** Rutgers Univ, BA; Fuller Theol Sem, BD; Andover Newton Theol Sch, STM; Princeton Theol Sem, PhD; addn stud, Univ Tubingen. **CAREER** Instr, Bethel Theol Sem, 69-97; Mildred and Ernest Hogan prof, 97. **SELECTED PUBLICATIONS** Auth, Luke in Broadman & Holman's New American Commentary; Playing by the Rules; The Method and Message of Jesus' Teachings; Jesus the Messiah. **CONTACT ADDRESS** New Testament Dept, So Baptist Theol Sem, 2825 Lexington Rd, Louisville, KY 40280. **EMAIL** rstein@sbts.edu

STEIN, STEPHEN J.
DISCIPLINE RELIGIOUS STUDIES **EDUCATION** Concordia Sen Col, BA, 62; Concordia Sem, BD, 66; Yale Univ, MA, 68, PhD, 70. **CAREER** Asst prof, 71-73, assoc prof, 73-81, prof, 81-95, Chancellor's Prof Rel Stud, Adj Prof Hist, 95-,Ind Univ. **RESEARCH** History of religions in America; early American history; sectarian studies. **SELECTED PUBLICATIONS** Auth, Transatlantic Extensions: Apocalyptic in Early New England, Manchester, 84; Letters from a Young Shaker: William S. Byrd at Pleasant Hill, Univ Ky, 85; The Shaker Experience in America: A History of the United Society of Believers, Yale, 92; ed, Jonthan Edwards's Writings: Text, Context, Interpretation, Univ Ind, 96; ed, The Works of Jonathan Edwards: Apocalyptic Writings, 97; ed, Notes on Scripture, 98; co-ed, The Encyclopedia of Apocalypticism, 98. **CONTACT ADDRESS** Dept of Religious Studies, Indiana Univ, Bloomington, Sycamore Hall 230, Bloomington, IN 47405. **EMAIL** stein@indiana.edu

STEINBERG, THEODORE LOUIS
PERSONAL Born 01/08/1947, Baltimore, MD, m, 3 children **DISCIPLINE** MEDIEVAL ENGLISH; JEWISH LITERATURE **EDUCATION** Johns Hopkins Univ, BA, 68; Univ Ill, AM, 69, PhD(English), 71. **CAREER** Asst prof, 71-75, assoc prof, 75-79, prof English, State Univ NY Col Fredonia, 79- **HONORS AND AWARDS** Chancellor's Awd for Excellence in Teaching, 96; **MEMBERSHIPS** Medieval Acad Am; Am Asn Prof Yiddish; Spenser Soc. **RESEARCH** Medieval and Renaissance literature; Jewish literature. **SELECTED PUBLICATIONS** Auth, Spenser's Shepherdes Calender and EK's, Mod Lang Studies, winter 73; The schoolmaster: Teaching sixteenth century literature, English Rec, 73; I B Singer: Responses to catastrophe, Yiddish, 75; The anatomy of Euphues, Studies English Lit, 77; Mendele Mocher Seforim, G K Hall, 77; The humanities and the Holocaust, Humanist Educators, 80; Poetry and the perpendicular style, J Aesthet & Art Criticism, 81; Piers Plowman and Prophecy, Garland, 91. **CONTACT ADDRESS** Dept of English, SUNY, Col at Fredonia, Fredonia, NY 14063. **EMAIL** theodore.steinberg@fredonia.edu

STEINBOCK, BONNIE
PERSONAL Born 02/06/1947, New York, NY, m, 1977, 3 children **DISCIPLINE** PHILOSOPHY **EDUCATION** Tufts Univ, BA, 68; Univ Calif, Berkeley, PhD(philos), 74. **CAREER** Asst prof philos, Col Wooster, 74-77; asst prof to prof Philos, State Univ NY, Albany, 77-; chair, Philos Dept, 91-94, 98-. **HONORS AND AWARDS** Phi Beta Kappa; Fel, Hastings Center **RESEARCH** Moral philosophy; philosophy of law; bioethics. **SELECTED PUBLICATIONS** Auth, numerous articles; ed, Killing and Letting Die, Prentice-Hall, 80, 2nd ed with Alastair Norcross, 94; auth, Life Before Birth, Oxford, 92; coauth, Ethical Issues in Modern Medicine, with John Arras, 95, 99; coauth, New Ethics for the Public's Health, with Dan Beauchamp, 99. **CONTACT ADDRESS** Dept of Philos, SUNY, Albany, 1400 Washington Ave, Albany, NY 12222-1000. **EMAIL** steinboc@albany.edu

STEINBOCK, DANIEL J.
PERSONAL m, 2 children **DISCIPLINE** LAW **EDUCATION** Yale Univ, BA, JD. **CAREER** Prof. **SELECTED PUBLICATIONS** Auth, Unaccompanied Refugee Children in Host Country Foster Families, Int J Refugee Law, 96; Refuge and Resistance, Georgetown, 93; The Admission of Unaccompanied Children Into the U.S., Yale Law Policy Rev, 89; co-auth, Unaccompanied Children, 88. **CONTACT ADDRESS** Col Law, Univ of Toledo, Toledo, OH 43606. **EMAIL** dsteinb@uoft02.utoledo.edu

STEINBUCH, THOMAS A.
PERSONAL Born 10/23/1949, Brooklyn, NY, s **DISCIPLINE** PHILOSOPHY **EDUCATION** Univ Mass Amherst, PhD, philos, 81. **CAREER** Independent scholar. **SELECTED PUBLICATIONS** Auth, A Commentary on Nietzsche's Ecce Homo, Univ Press of Am, 94. **CONTACT ADDRESS** 501 Brian St., Mount Horeb, WI 53572. **EMAIL** steinbuc@mailbag.com

STEINER, VERNON J.
PERSONAL Born 03/25/1950, Wooster, OH, m, 1971, 2 children **DISCIPLINE** THEOLOGICAL STUDIES; OLD TESTAMENT EXEGESIS **EDUCATION** Grace Univ, BA, 72; W Sem, MDiv, 96, ThM, 79; Trinity Evangelical Divinity School, PhD, 92. **CAREER** Sr Pastor, Oak Lake Bible Church Lincoln, NE, 77-86; tchg fel in Hebrew, Trinity Divinity School, 87-90; asst prof Bibl studies, Assc Can Theol School, Langley, BC, 90-95; dir & adj prof, free lance lectr, The Miqra Inst, 95-. **MEMBERSHIPS** SBL; ETS **RESEARCH** Canonical and compositional strategies; Hebrew and Greek exegesis; History of the Hebrew Bible. **CONTACT ADDRESS** 3201 Briarwood Ave, Lincoln, NE 68516. **EMAIL** VJSTEINER@aol.com

STEINHART, ERIC
DISCIPLINE PHILOSOPHY **EDUCATION** Penn State Univ, BS, 83; Boston Col, MA; SUNY at Stony Brook, PhD, 96. **CAREER** Prof **RESEARCH** Intersection of metaphysics, history of philosophy, and computation; making computational models of metaphysical systems, both historical and of my own invention; 19th century philosophy. **SELECTED PUBLICATIONS** Auth, Digital metaphysics, The Digital Phoenix: How Computers are Changing Philosophy. New York: Basil Blackwell, 98 ; Leibniz's palace of the fates: A 17th century virtual reality system, Presence: Teleoperators and Virtual Environments 6 1, 97; NETMET: A program for generating and interpreting metaphors, Computers and Humanities, 95; Structural idealism, Idealistic Stud, 94; Beyond proportional analogy: A structural model of analogy, Pragmatics and Cognition, 94; Analogical truth-conditions for metaphors, Metaphor and Symbolic Activity, 94; Metaphor, Encycl of Lang and Ling, Oxford: Pergamon Press, 93; coauth, Self-recognition and countermemory, Philos Today, 89; Generating metaphors from networks, Approaches to Metaphor, Synthese Lib, Dordrecht: Kluwer Acad, 94. **CONTACT ADDRESS** Dept of Philosophy, William Paterson Col of New Jersey, 300 Pompton Rd., Atrium 267, Wayne, NJ 07470.

STEINMAN, JOAN E.
PERSONAL Born 06/19/1947, Brooklyn, NY, d, 1974, 2 children **DISCIPLINE** LAW, PHILOSOPHY **EDUCATION** Univ Rochester, AB, 69; Harvard Law School, JD, 73. **CAREER** From asst prof law to distinguished prof law, Chicago-Kent Col Law, Illinois Inst Tech, 77-. **HONORS AND AWARDS** Ralph L Brill Awd, 77; Julia Beveridge Awd, 96; Dean's Prize for Excellence in Teaching, 95; served on bench NIU Moot Court Prize Argument, 96. **MEMBERSHIPS** Am Law Inst; Am Asn Univ Women Legal Advocacy Network; Am Bar Asn; Chicago Council Lawyers, Fed Courts Comm; Soc Am Law Teachers; Harvard Law School Women's Law Asn Mentor; CBA Alliance for Women; Bd, Pro Bono Advocates, 95-99; Chicago Lincoln Am Inn of Court; Am Law Inst; Fed Judicial Code Revision Project, 95; and consultative groups for Complex Litigation Project; Restatement of the Law, Torts, and Interanational Rules of Civil Procedure; NASD Board of Arbitrators; Ill Governor's Grievance Panel. **RESEARCH** Fed courts, fed civil procedure, complex litigation, appellate procedure. **SELECTED PUBLICATIONS** Auth, Reverse Removal, 78 Iowa Leg Rev, 93; auth, Supplemental Jurisdiction in 1441 Removed Cases: An Unsurveyed Frontier of Congress's Handiwork, 35 Ariz Leg Rev, 93; auth, The Effects of Case Consolidation on the Procedural Rights of Litigants: What They are, What They Might Be, Part I and Part II, 42 UCLA Leg Rev, 95; auth, Women, Medical Care, and Mass Tort Litigation, 68 Chicago-Ken Leg Rev, excerpted in A Products Liability Anthology, 95; auth, The Scope of Appellate Jurisdiction: Pendent Appellate Jurisdiction Before and After Swint, 49 Hastings Law Jour, 98; auth, Cross Currents: Supplemental Jurisdication, Removal, and the ALI Revision Project, 74 IND Law Jour, 99; auth, The Newest Frontier of Judicial Activism: Removal Under the All Writs Act, BUL Rev 80 (00). **CONTACT ADDRESS** Chicago Kent Col of Law, Illinois Inst of Tech, 565 W Adams St, Chicago, IL 60661. **EMAIL** jsteinma@kentlaw.edu

STEINMANN, ANDREW E.
PERSONAL Born 05/29/1954, Cincinnati, OH, m, 1976, 2 children **DISCIPLINE** RELIGIOUS STUDIES **EDUCATION** Univ Mich, PhD, 90. **CAREER** Instr, Concordia Col, 86-90; asst prof, 90-91; adjunct prof, Ashland Univ, 96-00; assoc prof, Concordia Univ, 00-. **MEMBERSHIPS** Soc of Bibl Lit; Cath Bibl Asn; Evangelical Theol Soc. **RESEARCH** Near Eastern studies; Biblical studies. **SELECTED PUBLICATIONS** Auth, Are My Prayers Falling on Dear Ears?, 97; ed, God's Word, 95; auth, "Bible (1) Translation," 99; "Response to Leslie Lanier 'On the Public Reading of Scripture'" in Logia: A J of Lutheran Theol, 98; "Communicating the Gospel Without Theological Jargon: Translating the Bible into Reader-Friendly Language" in Concordia Theol Quart, 97; "Jacob's Family Goes to Egypt: Varying Portraits of Unity and Disunity in the Textual Traditions of Exodus 1:1-5" in TC, 97; "When the Translations of Catechetical Proof Texts Don't Communicate" in Concordia J, 96. **CONTACT ADDRESS** Concordia Univ, Illinois, 7400 Augusta St, River Forest, IL 60305. **EMAIL** asteinmann@aol.com

STEINMETZ, DAVID CURTIS
PERSONAL Born 06/12/1936, Columbus, OH, m, 1959, 2 children **DISCIPLINE** CHURCH HISTORY **EDUCATION** Wheaton Col, Ill, AB, 58; Drew Univ, BD, 61; Harvard Univ, ThD(church hist), 67. **CAREER** From asst prof to assoc prof church hist, Lancaster Theol Sem, 66-71; assoc prof, 71-79, Prof Church Hist & Doctrine, Divinity Sch, Duke Univ, 79-, Am Asn Theol Schs fac fel, Oxford Univ, 70-71; vis prof church hist, Harvard Univ, 77; Guggenheim fel, Cambridge Univ, 77-78. **MEMBERSHIPS** Am Soc Church Hist; Am Soc Reformation Res; Mediaeval Acad Am; Renaissance Soc Am; Soc Bibl Lit. **RESEARCH** History of Christian thought in the late Middle Ages and Reformation. **SELECTED PUBLICATIONS** Auth, Misericordia Dei, The Theology of Johannes von Staupitz in Its late Medieval Setting, Brill, Leiden, 68; Reformers in the Wings, Fortress, 71 & Baker, 81; Libertas Christiana: Studies in the Theology of John Pupper of Goch (1475), Harvard Theol Rev, 72; Late Medieval Nominalism and the Clerk's Tale, Chaucer Rev, 77; The Baptism of John and the Baptim of Jesus in Huldrych Zwingli, Balthasar Hubmaier and Late Medieval Theology, In: Continuity and Discontinuity in Church History, Brill, Leiden, 79; The Superiority of Pre-Critical Exegesis, Theol Today, 80; Luther and Staupitz: An Essay in the Intellectual Origins of the Protestant Reformation, Duke, 80; Calvin on Isaiah 6: A Problem in the History of Exegeis, Interpretation, 82. **CONTACT ADDRESS** Divinity Sch, Duke Univ, Durham, NC 27706.

STEINMO, SVEN
PERSONAL Born 08/24/1953, Minneapolis, MN, m, 1980, 2 children **DISCIPLINE** POLITICAL SCIENCE **EDUCATION** Univ Calif Santa Cruz, BA, 74; Univ Calif Berk, MA, 78; MPH, 81; PhD, 87. **CAREER** Asst prof, dir, assoc prof, Univ Col Boulder, 87-; vis sci, Univ Gottenburg, 00. **HONORS AND AWARDS** Abe Fel, Abe Found Soc Sci Res Coun, 01-03; Ger Marshall Fund Fel 01; STINT Vis Sci, SFICRHE, 00; Edmond Keller Writ Prize Best Ess,1 st Amend, 99' Best Bk, Polit Econ, pub 91, 92, SAPE, 94; Gabriel Almond Awd, doct dis, APSA, 89; Dean's Writ Awd, 89; Henry Robert Braden Fel, 85; Dis Res Fel, ACLS, SSSRC, 84-85; Thord-Gray Mem Dis Res Fel, 84; Fulbright-Hays Dis Res Fel, 83-84; Teach Recog Awds, Univ Col, Mortar Bd Hon Soc, 99; Outs Professor Intern Affairs, Univ Col, 96, 97; Spec Recog Awd, Univ Col, Sigma Iota Rho, 95; Outs Undergrad Teach Recog Awd, Univ Col, Mortar Bd Hon Soc, 93; Ann Teach Recog Awd, Univ Col, SOAR, 89. **MEMBERSHIPS** APSA; CES. **RESEARCH** Political economy; American political development **SELECTED PUBLICATIONS** Auth, Taxation and Democracy: Swedish, British and American Approaches to Financing the Welfare State (Yale UP, 93); co-ed, Structuring Politics: Historical Institutionalism in Comparative Analysis (Cambridge UP, 92); co-auth, "Do Institutions Really Matter?," Comp Polit Stud 31 (98):165-187; co-auth, "It's the Institutions, Stupid!: Why the United States Can't Pass Comprehensive National Health Insurance," J Health Policy Law (95): 329-372; auth, "Why Is Government So Small in America?," Governance (95): 303-334; auth, "The End of Redistribution? International Pressures and Domestic Policy Choices," Challenge (94); " Political Institutions and Tax Policy in the United States, Sweden and Britain" World Politics (89): 500-535; auth, " Social Democracy vs. Socialism: Goal Adaptation in Social Democratic Sweden," Politics and Soc (88): 403-46. **CONTACT ADDRESS** Dept of Polit Sci, Univ of Colorado, Boulder, Ketchum 106, PO Box 333, Boulder, CO 80309-0333.

STEINWEIS, ALAN
DISCIPLINE EUROPEAN, JEWISH HISTORY **EDUCATION** Univ NC, Chapel Hill, PhD, 88. **CAREER** Hyman Rosenberg Assoc Prof Hist, dir, Judaic Stud, Univ Nebr, Lincoln. **HONORS AND AWARDS** Fulbright award, 96. **SELECTED PUBLICATIONS** Art, Ideology, and Economics in Nazi Germany, Univ NC Press, 93. **CONTACT ADDRESS** Univ of Nebraska, Lincoln, 637 Oldfat, Lincoln, NE 68588-0417. **EMAIL** aes@unlserve.unl.edu

STELTENKAMP, MICHAEL F.
PERSONAL Born 11/14/1947, Detroit, MI, s **DISCIPLINE** PHILOSOPHY, ANTHROPOLOGY **EDUCATION** Univ Detroit, BA, 70; Ind Univ, MA, 71; Loyola Univ Chicago, MDiv; Mich State Univ, PhD. **CAREER** Chair of Soc Sci Dept, Red Cloud Indian Sch, Pine Ridge SD, 71-74; Adj Prof, Saginaw Valley State Univ, Mich, 86-90; Mus Curator, Prof, Bay Mills Community Col, May Mills Reservation, Brimley, Mich; Assoc Prof, Wheeling Jesuit Univ, WVa. **HONORS AND AWARDS** Alpha Sigma Nu Nat Book Awd, 94. **MEMBERSHIPS** Soc of Jesus (Jesuits) of Cath Church, Am Anthrop Asn. **RESEARCH** Native North America, World Religions, Religious Movements Today. **SELECTED PUBLICATIONS** Auth, The Sacred Vision: Native-American Religion and Its Practice Today, Paulist Press, 83; auth, Black Elk: Holy Man of the Oglala, Univ of Okla Press, 93. **CONTACT ADDRESS** Dept Relig and Philos, Wheeling Jesuit Univ, 316 Washington Ave, Wheeling, WV 26003-6243. **EMAIL** mfs@wju.edu

STEMPSEY, WILLIAM EDWARD
PERSONAL Born 01/26/1952, Albany, NY **DISCIPLINE** PHILOSOPHY, BIOETHICS, PATHOLOGY **EDUCATION**

Boston Col, BS, 74; SUNY, Buffalo Sch of Med, MD, 78; Loyola Univ, MA, 88; Jesuit Sch of Theol, Berkeley, M Div, 91, STM, 92; Georgetown Univ, PhD, 96. **CAREER** Intern, Boston City Hosp, MA, 78-79; res, Univ Hospital, Boston, 80-82; tchng fel, Pathol, Boston Univ School of Med, 80-82; res, The Children's Hosp, Boston, 84-85; clin fel in Pathol, 84-85; ordained priest, Soc of Jesus (Jesuits), 92; clin scholar, Harvard Medical Sch, Ctr for Clin Bioethics, Georgetown Univ Med Ctr, 95-96; asst prof, dept of philos, Col Of The Holy Cross, 96-. **HONORS AND AWARDS** Alpha Epsilon Delta, IL Eta Chapter, 88. **MEMBERSHIPS** The Hastings Center; Kennedy Inst of Ethics; Soc for Health & Human Values; APA; Soc of Jesus (Jesuits), 82-; European Soc for Philos of Med & Healthcare, 98-. **RESEARCH** Philos of diagnosis; concepts of health and disease; ethical issues in death and dying; ethics of organ transplantation. **SELECTED PUBLICATIONS** Coauth, "Incommensurability: Its Implications for the Patient/Physician Relation," J of Medicine and Philos 20 (95): 253-269; auth, "Paying People to Give Up Their Organs: The Problem with Commodification of Body Parts," Medical Humanities Rev 10 (fall 96): 45-55; auth, "End-of-Life Decisions: Christian Perspectives," Christian Bioethics 3 (97): 249-261; auth, "The Battle for Medical Marijuana in the War on Drugs," America 12 (98): 14-16; auth, "Laying Down One's Life for Oneself," Christian Bioethics 4 (98): 202-224; auth, "The Quarantine of Philos in Medical Educ: Why Teaching the Humanities May Not Produce Humane Physicians," Medicine, Health Care, and Philos 2 (99): 3-9; auth, "No Biblical Warrant for Suicide," Ethics & Medics 6 (June 99): 1-2; auth, Disease and Diagnosis: Value-Dependent Realism, Kluwer Academic Publ (Dordrecht), 99; auth, "A Pathological View of Disease," Theoretical Medicine and Bioethics, forthcoming; auth, "Miracles and the Limits of Medical Knowledge," Medicine, Health Care and Philos, forthocoming. **CONTACT ADDRESS** Dept of Philosophy, Col of the Holy Cross, One College St, Worcester, MA 01610-2395. **EMAIL** wstempsey@holycross.edu

STENDAHL, KRISTER
PERSONAL Born 04/21/1921, Stockholm, Sweden, m, 1946, 3 children **DISCIPLINE** THEOLOGY **EDUCATION** Univ Uppsala, Teol kand, 44, Teol lic, 49, Teol, dr, 54. **CAREER** Student pastor, Univ Uppsala, 48-50, instr exeg, 51-54, docent, 54; from asst prof to assoc prof New Testament, 54-58, Morrison prof, 58-63, Frothingham prof Bibl studies, 63-68, John Lord prof & dean, 68-79, Andrew W Mellon Prof Divinity, Harvard Divinity Sch, 80-; bishop, Stockholm Church of Sweden, 84-88; Robert and Myra Kraft and Jacob Hiatt Distinguished Prof of Christian Studies, Brandeis Univ, 91-93. **MEMBERSHIPS** Studorum Novi Testamenti Soc; Nathan Soederblom Soc; Am Acad Arts & Sci; Soc Bibl Lit. **SELECTED PUBLICATIONS** Auth, The School of St. Matthew, 54, 2nd ed, 68; auth, The Bible and the Role of Women, 66; auth, Holy Week, 74; auth, Paul Among Jews and Gentiles, 76; auth, Meanings, 84; auth, Final Account, 95; auth, Energy for Life, 99. **CONTACT ADDRESS** Harvard Univ, 45 Francis Ave, Cambridge, MA 02138-1994. **EMAIL** krister_stendhal@harvard.edu

STENGER, ROBERT LEO
PERSONAL Born 09/19/1934, St. Paul, MN, m, 1971 **DISCIPLINE** CHRISTIAN ETHICS, LAW **EDUCATION** St Thomas Col, Ill, BA, 56, MA, 57; Cath Univ Am, STD, 63; Univ Iowa, JD, 74. **CAREER** Asst prof philos & theol & head dept, Dominican Col, 63-64; asst prof moral theol, Aquinas Inst Sch Theol, Iowa, 64-68; asst prof Christian ethics, Sch Relig, Univ Iowa, 68-74; asst prof, 74-77, assoc prof, 77-80, Prof Law, Univ Louisville, 80- **MEMBERSHIPS** Cath Theol Soc Am; Am Soc Christian Ethics; Am Bar Asn. **RESEARCH** Constitutional law; mediaeval Canon law; Christian social ethics; law and medicine. **SELECTED PUBLICATIONS** Auth, The episcopacy as an ordo according to the mediaeval Canonists, Mediaeval Studies, 67; Repertorium iuris religiosorum: Basel, Universitats bibliothek C V 13, Studies Gratiana, 67; The Supreme Court and illegitimacy, 1968-1977, Family Law Quart, winter 78; auth, Assisted Reproduction, J of Law & Health, 95; auth, Adolescents' Medical Decisions J of Law and Health, 01. **CONTACT ADDRESS** Sch of Law, Univ of Louisville, Louisville, KY 40292. **EMAIL** bob.stenger@louisville.edu

STENSTAD, GAIL
DISCIPLINE PHILOSOPHY **EDUCATION** Vanderbilt Univ, PhD. **CAREER** Assoc prof, E Tenn Stat Univ **MEMBERSHIPS** Heidegger; environmental ethics. **SELECTED PUBLICATIONS** Auth, The Turning in Ereignis and Transformation of Thinking, Heidegger Studies, 96; Thinking what is strange, Heidegger Studies, 94; The last God-A reading, Res Phenomenology, 93; Merleau Ponty's logos: The Sensing of the Flesh, Philos Today, 92; Singing the Earth, Thomas Jefferson Univ, 92; Attuning and Transformation, Heidegger Studies, 91; Thinking (beyond) Being, Heidegger Studies, 90. **CONTACT ADDRESS** Philosophy Dept, East Tennessee State Univ, Box 70717, Johnson City, TN 37614- 0717. **EMAIL** stenstad@etsu.edu

STENSVAAG, JOHN-MARK
PERSONAL Born 07/01/1947, Minneapolis, MN, m, 1970, 5 children **DISCIPLINE** LAW **EDUCATION** Augsburg Col, BA, 74; Harvard Law Sch, JD, 74. **CAREER** Law Clerk, US Dist Court, 74-76; Spec Asst Atty Gen, Minn State Atty Gen, 76-79; Asst Prof to Prof, Vanderbilt Univ, 79-88; Vis Prof to Prof, Univ Iowa, 87-. **HONORS AND AWARDS** Danforth Grad Fel, 69; Environ Protection Agency Fel, 73; Paul J. Hartman Teaching Awd, 85; Teaching Awd, Univ Iowa , 89; Dist Alumni Awd, Augsburg Col, 93. **RESEARCH** Environmental Law. **SELECTED PUBLICATIONS** Co-auth, Clean Air Act: Law & Practice, Aspen Pub, 91; auth, The Not So Fine Print of Environmental Law, Loy LA Law Rev, 94; auth, The Fine Print of State Environmental Audit Privileges, UCLA J Environ Law & Policy, 97; auth, Materials on Environmental Law, West Group, 99. **CONTACT ADDRESS** Col of Law, Univ Iowa, 462 Boyd Law Bldg, Iowa City, IA 52242-1113. **EMAIL** J-Stensvaag@uiowa.edu

STENT, MICHELLE DORENE
PERSONAL Born 02/04/1955, New York, NY, s **DISCIPLINE** LAW **EDUCATION** Univ of Puerto Rico, Certificate of Merit 1974; Univ of London, Certificate of Distinction 1975; Tufts Univ, BA 1976; Howard Univ School of Law, JD 1980. **CAREER** Senator Edward W Brooke, intern 1976; Office of Civil Rights, public info consultant 1979; Congressional Black Caucus, graduate student intern 1979; Congressman Charles Rangel, legislative intern 1980; Comm on Educ and Labor US House of Reps, legislative counsel 1980-85; United Negro Coll Fund, dir govt affairs, assoc general counsel, Washington Office, vice pres 1989-. **HONORS AND AWARDS** Articles published Black Issues in Higher Education, Point of View; honorary doctorate, Texas Coll, Tyler, TX, 1987; Title IX Awd, Natl Assn for Equal Opportunity in Higher Educ, 1987. **MEMBERSHIPS** Bd dirs Caribbean Action Lobby; consultant Natl Urban League; select comm Congressional Black Caucus Intern Program; mem Delta Theta Phi Law Fraternity, Natl Bar Assn; assn mem Congressional Black Assocs, NAACP, Natl Urban League, Natl Assn of Black Women Attorneys, Coalition of 100 Black Women; bd of dir, Natl Coalition Black Voter Participation 1985-; bd of dir, Capitol City Ballet, 1988-. **SELECTED PUBLICATIONS** Newspaper Articles, NY Voice, Mississippi Memo Digest, Tyler Courier Times, editor/writer, Government Affairs Reports UNCF, 1985-. **CONTACT ADDRESS** United Negro Col Fund Inc, 1025 Vermont Ave, #810 NE, Washington, DC 20005.

STEPHAN, PAUL BROOKE, III
PERSONAL Born 12/29/1950, Somerville, NJ, m, 1976, 3 children **DISCIPLINE** LAW **EDUCATION** Yale Univ, BA 73; MA 74; Univ Virginia, JD, 77. **CAREER** Judge L.H. Campbell us Cir App, law clerk, 77-78; Justice LF Powell Supreme Ct US, law clerk 78-79; asst prof, 79-83, assoc prof, 83-85, prof, 85-91, Hunton & Williams Res Prof, 92-95, Barron F Black Res Prof, 96-99, Percy Brown Jr Prof, 91- , E James Kelly, Jr--Class of 1965 Res Prof, Univ Virginia Sch of Law, 00-03. **HONORS AND AWARDS** Donahue Lec. **MEMBERSHIPS** ALI; ASIL; ASCL; DC BAR; VA BAR. **RESEARCH** Post Socialist Legal Development, Intl Law, Taxation. **SELECTED PUBLICATIONS** Auth, Constitutional Limitations on Privatization, coauth, Am Jour Comp L, 98; Creative Destruction-Idiosyncratic Claims of International Law and the Helms-Burton Legislation, Stetson L Rev, 98; Accountability and International Law Making: Rules Rents and Legitimacy, NW Jour Intl L & Bus, 97; The Fall-Understanding the Collapse of Soviet Communism, Suffolk U L Rev, 95; Barbarians Inside the Gates: Public Choice Theory and International Economic Law, Am U Jour Intl L & Pol'y, 95; Foreword and Westernization of the European East? In: Law Reform in Post-Communist Europe: The View From Within, coauth, 94; International Business and Economics-Law and Policy, 93, 2nd edition, 96 coauth. **CONTACT ADDRESS** Law School, Univ of Virginia, 580 Massie Rd, Charlottesville, VA 22903-1789. **EMAIL** pbs@virginia.edu

STEPHENS, CYNTHIA DIANE
PERSONAL Born 08/27/1951, Detroit, MI, m, 1 child **DISCIPLINE** LAW **EDUCATION** Univ of MI, BA 1971; Atlanta Univ, postgraduate 1971-72; Emory Law School, JD 1976; auth, Michigan Non-standard Jury Intructions, Lawyers Coop, 95. **CAREER** Natl Conf of Black Lawyers, so regional dir, 76-77; Natl League of Cities, coord, 77-78; Pan-African Orthodox Christian Church, genl counsel, 78-82; Michigan Senate, assoc general counsel, 79-82; Wayne County Charter Commn, vice-chmn, 80-81; Law Offices of Cynthia D Stephens, attorney, 81-82; 36th District Ct, judge, 82-85; Wayne County Community Coll, Faculty, 85-; Univ of Detroit Law School, Faculty, 88-; Wayne County Circuit Court, Judge, 85-; Detroit Coll of Law, faculty, 90-95; fac, Nat Judicial Col, 95-. **HONORS AND AWARDS** Outstanding Woman Awd Woodward Ave Presbyterian Ch 1982; Disting Serv Awd Region 5 Detroit Public Schools 1983; Wolverine Bar Member of the Yr 1984; Little Rock Baptist Ch Golden Heritage Awd for Judicial Excellence 1984; Outstanding Woman in Law Hartford Memorial Bapt Ch 1985; Disting Alumni Awd Cass Tech HS 1987; Susan B Anthony, Natl Organization of Women, 1988; Anita Hill Awd, Detroit Human Rights Commission, 1991. **MEMBERSHIPS** Mem Wolverine Bar Assoc 1979; bd mem Wayne Co Neighborhood Legal Serv 1980; mem New Detroit Inc 1981-; bd mem Assoc of Black Judges of MI 1982-89, MI Dist Judges Assoc 1982-85, Greater Detroit Health Care Cncl 1983-85; guest lecturer Southern Univ Women and Leadership Symposium Baton Rouge LA 1983, Western MI Univ Dept of Women Studies Kalamazoo 1983; Univ of MI Symposium series for the Ctr for African and Afro-Amer Studies 1984; mem adv bd African Diaspora Project of the Delta Inst 1984-88; mem City Wide Sch Comm Organization-at-Large 1984-86, Delta Manor LDHA 1984-, YMCA Downtown Detroit 1984; mem Amer Bar Assoc Comm on Judicial Evaluation 1984-85, Delta Sigma Theta Detroit Alumni 1984-85; mem adv bd MI Bar Journal 1985-; Amer Corporate Counsel Pro-Bono Adv Comm 1982-88; bd of commissioners, State Bar of MI 1986-94; mem Natl Conference of Black Lawyers, 1997-; Natl Assoc of Women Judges; MI Judges Assoc. **SELECTED PUBLICATIONS** Auth, "Judicial Selection and Diversity," MI Bar Journal Vol 64 No 6 1985. **CONTACT ADDRESS** 3rd Circuit Court, 1719 City-County Bldg, Detroit, MI 48226.

STEPHENS, LYNN
DISCIPLINE PHILOSOPHY **EDUCATION** Harvard Univ, MA; Univ Mass, PhD. **CAREER** Prof, Univ Ala Birmingham, 79-. **RESEARCH** Philosophical psychology, history of philosophy. **SELECTED PUBLICATIONS** Coauth, Seven Dilemmas in World Religions, Paragon House, 94; co-ed, Philosophical Psychopathology, MIT Press, 94. **CONTACT ADDRESS** Dept of Philosophy, Univ of Alabama, Birmingham, 1400 University Blvd, Birmingham, AL 35294-1150.

STEPHENS, R. EUGENE
PERSONAL Born 04/05/1940, Knoxville, TN, m, 1961, 2 children **DISCIPLINE** CRIMINAL JUSTICE **EDUCATION** Univ TN, BS, 61; GA State Univ, MCJ, 74; Emory Univ, PhD, 76. **CAREER** Journalist, Atlanta Constitution, UPI, Cincinnati Enquirer, etc, 60-71; asst to dean, School of Urban Life, GA State Univ, 72-75; prof, Col Criminal Justice, Univ SC, 76-. **HONORS AND AWARDS** Sigma Delta Chi Awd; Outstanding Paper Awd, Acad Criminal Justice; Ed of the Year, Southern Criminal Justice Asn. **MEMBERSHIPS** Acad Criminal Justice Sci, Am Soc Criminology, Police Futurists Int, World Future Soc. **RESEARCH** Futures research. **SELECTED PUBLICATIONS** Auth, "Technology, Crime & Civil Liberties," in R. L. Coster and A. E. Wiens, Technology and the Quality of Life, NY: Glencoe (96); auth, "Humanizing 21st Century Justice: Balancing 'Freedom To' and 'Freedom From'," in Kenneth W. Hunter and Timothy C. Mack, International Rights and Responsibilities for the Future, Westport, CN: Praeger (96); auth, "Youth at Risk: Saving the World's Most Precious Resource," The Futurist, 31 (2), 31-38 (97); auth, "Thinking Globally, Acting Locally: Bringing Peace to Everyone's 'Hood'," Crime & Justice Int, 14 (18 & 19), 9-10, 32-33 (98); auth, "Cyber-Biotech Terrorism: Going High Tech in the 21st Century," in Harrey W. Kushner, ed, The Future of Terrorism: Violence in the New Millenium, Thousand Oaks, CA: Sage Pubs (98); auth, "Preventing Crime: The Promising Road Ahead," The Futurist, 33(9), 29-34 (99); coauth with W. G. Doerner, "Do We Need a War on Crime or Peace in the 'Hood'," in James D. Sewell, ed, Controversial Issues in Policing, Boston: Allyn and Bacon (99); auth, "A Futures Perspective on Leadership Development," in Terry D. Anderson, ed, Every Officer is a Leader: Transforming Leadership in Police, Justice, and Public Safety, Boca Raton, FL: St. Lucie Press (2000). **CONTACT ADDRESS** Col Criminal Justice, Univ of So Carolina, Columbia, Columbia, SC 29225-0001.

STEPHENS, WILLIAM O.
PERSONAL Born 06/10/1962, Lafayette, IN, s **DISCIPLINE** PHILOSOPHY **EDUCATION** Earlham Col, BA, 84; Univ Pa, PhD, 90. **CAREER** From asst prof to assoc prof, Creighton Univ, 90-. **HONORS AND AWARDS** Phi Beta Kappa, 84; Georgia M. Watkins Scholar in Greek & Latin, 84; Teaching Fel, Univ Pa, 84-90; Summer Res Fel, Creighton Univ, 92, 98; Fel, US W Acad Dev and Technol Fel, 95; William F. Kelley SJ Outstanding Service Achievement Awd, 96; Summer Scholar, Ctr for Hellenic Studies, 97. **MEMBERSHIPS** Am Philos Asn, Phi Sigma Tau, Eta Sigma Phi, Soc for Ancient Greek Philos, Soc for Philos in the Contemporary World, Soc for the Study of Ethics and Animals, The Human Soc of the United States. **RESEARCH** Stoicism, Ethics and Animals, Environmental Ethics. **SELECTED PUBLICATIONS** Auth, "Stoic Naturalism, Rationalism, and Ecology," Environmental Ethics 16.3 (94): 275-286; auth, "Masks, Androids, and Primates: The Evolution of the Concept 'Person'," Etica & Animali 9 (98): 111-127; auth, "The Simile of the Talus in Cicero, De Finibus 3.54," Classical Philology 91.1 (96): 59-61; auth, "Epictetus on How the Stoic Sage Loves," Oxford Studies in Ancient Philos 14 (96): 193-210; auth, "Five Arguments for Vegetarianism," Environmental Ethics: Concepts, Policy, and Theory, ed. Joseph DesJardins (CA: Mayfield Publ Co., 99), 288-301; transl, "The Ethics of the Stoic Epictetus: An English Translation," by Adolf F. Bonhoffer, Peter Lang (New York), 96 & 00. **CONTACT ADDRESS** Dept Philos, Creighton Univ, 2500 California Plaza, Omaha, NE 68178-0001. **EMAIL** stphns@creighton.edu

STEPHENSON, KEN COOPER
DISCIPLINE LAW **EDUCATION** Univ London, LLB, 64; Cambridge Univ, LLM, 66. **CAREER** Founding fac member, Univ o Leicester, 66-71; asst dean, Univ of Leicester, 81-2, 91; teaching, Bond Univ, 94-95; chairperson of Graduate Studies,

Univ of Leicester. **HONORS AND AWARDS** Connought Fel in the Legal Theory and Public Policy Program, Univ of Toronto, 85-86. **SELECTED PUBLICATIONS** Auth, Personal Injury Damages in Canada, Carswell, 96, Tort Theory, Captus, 93; co-ed, Charter Damages Claims, Carswell, 90. **CONTACT ADDRESS** Col of Law, Univ of Saskatchewan, 15 Campus Dr, Saskatoon, SK, Canada S7N 5A6. **EMAIL** CooperSt@law.usask.ca

STERBA, JAMES P.
DISCIPLINE PHILOSOPHY **EDUCATION** LaSalle Col, BA, 66; Univ Pittsburgh, MA, 72, PhD, 73. **CAREER** Prof. **RESEARCH** Political philosophy; environmental ethics; philosophy of peace and justice. **SELECTED PUBLICATIONS** Auth, Feminist Justice and the Pursuit of Peace, Hypatia, 94; Contemporary Social and Political Philosophy, 94; From Liberty to Welfare, Ethics, 94; Justifying Morality and the Challenge of Cognitive Science, Ethics Cognitive Sci, 95; Understanding Evil: American Slavery, the Holocaust and the Conquest of the American Indians, 95; Racism and Sexism: The Common Ground, Comparing Sex Race, 96; Morality in Practice, 96; Is Feminism Good for Men and are Men Good for Feminism?, Men Doing Feminism, 97; Social and Political Philosophy: Classical Western Texts in Feminist and Multicultural Perspectives, 97; Feminist Philosophies, Second Edition, 98; Justice: Alternative Political Perspectives, 98; Justice for Here and Now, 98; Religion and Rawls, 98; A Biocentrist Strikes Back, 98. **CONTACT ADDRESS** Philosophy Dept, Univ of Notre Dame, 336/7 O'Shaughnessy, Notre Dame, IN 46556. **EMAIL** sterba.1@nd.edu

STERCKX, ROEL
PERSONAL Born 05/13/1969, Turnhout, Belgium, s **DISCIPLINE** CHINESE PHILOSOPHY, HISTORY **EDUCATION** Katholieke Univ Leuven, Lic Sinology, 91; Cambridge Univ, MPhil, 93; PhD, 97. **CAREER** Asst prof, Univ of Ariz, 01-. **HONORS AND AWARDS** Allen and Amy Mary Preston Read Scholar, Cambridge Univ, 93; Spalding Scholar, 95; Fel, Wolfson Col, Univ of Oxford, 97. **MEMBERSHIPS** Assoc for Asian Studies. **RESEARCH** Thought, religion and cultural history of China during the Warring States and early imperial periods. **SELECTED PUBLICATIONS** Auth, "An Ancient Chinese Horse Ritual," Early China 21 (96): 47-79; auth, "Transcending Habitats: Authority, Territory, and the Animal Realm in Warring States and Early Imperial China," Bull of the Brit Assc for Chinese Studies, (96): 9-19; auth, "Transforming the Beasts. Animals and Music in Early China," Toung Pao 86, 1-3, (00): 1-46; auth, The Animal and the Daemon in Early China, SUNY Pr, (Albany) in press. **CONTACT ADDRESS** Dept of E Asian Studies, Univ of Arizona, Franklin Bldg 404, Tucson, AZ 85721. **EMAIL** sterckx@email.arizona.edu

STERLING, GREGORY
PERSONAL Born 11/21/1954, San Jose, CA, m, 1975, 2 children **DISCIPLINE** RELIGION **EDUCATION** Fla Col, AA, 75; Houston Baptist Univ, BA, 78; Pepperdine Univ, MA, 72, Graduate Theol Union, PhD, 90. **CAREER** Vis asst prof, to assoc prof, Univ of Notre Dame, 89-. **HONORS AND AWARDS** Fel, Lilly Endowment, 91-92; Res Stipend, ISLA, 92, 93, 96, 98; Vis Scholar, Henkels, 94, 99; Presidential Awd, Univ of Notre Dame, 99; Grant, ISLA, 99-02; Fel, Hebrew Univ, 00-01; Who's Who in Am, 00. **MEMBERSHIPS** Chicago Soc of Bibl Res, NA Patristics Soc, Studiorum Novi Testamenti Societas, Cath Bibl Assoc, Soc of Bibl Lit. **RESEARCH** Second Temple Judaism and Christian Origins, Philo of Alexandria., Josephus, Luke-Acts, the Historical Jesus. **SELECTED PUBLICATIONS** Auth, "Historiography and Self-Definition: Josephos, Luke-Acts, and Apologetic Historiography," NovTSup 64, E.J. Brill, (92); coed, Wisdom and Logos: Studies in Jewish Thought in Honor of David Winston, Scholars Pr, (Atlanta), 97; coed, the Studia Philonica Annual 11, Scholars Pr, 99; coed, Hellenism in the Land of Israel, Univ of Notre Dame Pr, in press; auth, Hellenistic Philosophy in Greek-Speaking Judaism: Essays of David Winston, in press. **CONTACT ADDRESS** Dept Theol, Univ of Notre Dame, 327 O'Shaugnessy Hall, Notre Dame, IN 46556-5639. **EMAIL** gregory.e.sterling.1@nd.edu

STERN, CRAIG A.
PERSONAL Born 04/26/1954, Cleveland, OH, m, 1981, 3 children **DISCIPLINE** LAW **EDUCATION** Univ Va, BA, 75; JD, 78. **CAREER** Assoc atty, Fried, Frank, Harris, Shriver & Kampelman, 78-81; asst dep dir, Office of the President-Elect, 80-81; Counsel, US Senate Comm on the Judiciary, 81-83; assoc ed, center for Judicial Studies, 83-85; Counsel, Constitutional Law Center, 85; Lawyer, 85-89; adj prof, Regent Univ, 88-90; asst US atty, E Dist of Va, 89-90; asst prof to assoc prof, Regent Univ, 90-. **MEMBERSHIPS** Am Bar Assoc; Federalist Soc; Philadelphia Soc. **RESEARCH** Biblical sources and analysis of Anglo-American law. **SELECTED PUBLICATIONS** Auth, Church, State and Education: A Federal Circuit Manual, 85; auth, Judging the Judges: The First Two Years of the Reagan Bench, 85; auth, Foreign Judgments and the Freedom of Speech: Look Who's Talking, 60 Brook L, 94; auth, Things Not Nice: An Essay on Civil Government, Regent Univ Law Rev, 97; auth, What's a Constitution Among Friends? - Unbalancing Article III, Univ Pa Law Rev 1043, 98; auth, Justinian: Lieutenant of Christ, Legislator for Christendom, Regent Univ Law Rev, 99; auth, Crime, Moral Luck, and the Sermon on the Mount, 48, Cath Univ Law Rev, 99. **CONTACT ADDRESS** School of Law, Regent Univ, 1000 Regent Univ Dr, Virginia Beach, BA 32464-5037. **EMAIL** craiste@regent.edu

STERN, DAVID S.
DISCIPLINE PHILOSOPHY **EDUCATION** Louisiana St Univ, BA, 77; Univ CA, San Diego, PhD, 85. **CAREER** Asst prof, 85-89, Louisiana St Univ; vis asst prof, 89-90, Univ of CA, San Diego; asst prof, 90-93, assoc prof, 93-, Univ of Toledo. **MEMBERSHIPS** APA; Hegel Soc of Amer; Metaphysical Soc; Soc for Phenomenology and Existential Phil. **RESEARCH** 19th and 20th Century European phil; social and political phil. **SELECTED PUBLICATIONS** Rev, Michael Inwood, A Hegel Dictionary, Cambridge Blackwell, 92; rev, Thomas Nagel, Equality and Partiality, Oxford Univ Press, 91; rev, Will Kymlicka, Contemporary Political Philosophy An Introduction, Oxford Clarendon Press, 90; auth, Foundationalism Holism or Hegel, GWF Hegel Critical Assessments, Vol III, Routledge, 93; auth, Transcendental Apperception and Subjective Logic Kant and Hegel on the Role of the Subject, Hegel on the Modern World, SUNY Press, 95; auth, The Ties that Bind The Limits of Aesthetic Reflection in Kierkegaards Either/Or, The Intl Kierkegaard Comm Either/Or I, Mercer Univ Press, 95; art, Unending Modernity, Inquiry Vol 38 No 3, 95; auth, Kant and Hegel on the Logic of Being for Self, Proceedings of the Eighth Intl Kant Congress, Vol 1, Marquette Univ Press, 95; auth, State Sovereignty the Politics of Identity and the Place of the Political, Problems Without Borders Persp on the Third World Sov, St. Martins, 96. **CONTACT ADDRESS** Dept of Philosophy, Univ of Toledo, Toledo, OH 43606. **EMAIL** dstern@utoledo.edu

STERN, LAURENT
PERSONAL Born 03/22/1930, Budapest, Hungary **DISCIPLINE** PHILOSOPHY **EDUCATION** Univ Zurich, PhD, 52. **CAREER** Lectr Philos, City Col NY, 59-61; asst prof, Univ Wash, 61-66; assoc prof, 66-70, chmn dept, 68-71, chmn dept & dir grad prog philos, 76-79, prof Philos, Rutgers Univ, 70-. **MEMBERSHIPS** Am Soc Aesthet; Am Philos Asn; Aristotelian Soc; AAUP. **RESEARCH** Late 19th Century philosophy; Theories of interpretation; Philosophy of literature. **SELECTED PUBLICATIONS** Various articles. **CONTACT ADDRESS** Dept of Philosophy, Rutgers, The State Univ of New Jersey, New Brunswick, New Brunswick, NJ 08903. **EMAIL** lstern@rci.rutgers.edu

STEUBEN, NORTON L.
PERSONAL Born 02/14/1936, Milwaukee, WI, m, 2 children **DISCIPLINE** LAW **EDUCATION** Univ Mich, BA, 58; JD, 61. **CAREER** Lecturer, SUNY, 61-68; Asst prof to Prof, Univ Colo, 68-; vis Prof, Univ Seattle, 92093 **HONORS AND AWARDS** SI Goldberg Awd, Alpha Epsilon Pi, 57; Barristers Soc, Univ Mich, 60-61; Order of Coif, 61; Best Monograph, Duke Univ, Distinguished Service Awd, Buffalo Area Chamber of Commerce, 66; John W Reed Awd, Univ Colo, 70; Teaching recognition Awd, Univ Colo, 72; Teaching recognition Awd, Univ Colo, 82. **MEMBERSHIPS** am Bar Asn, Am Judicature Soc, NY State Bar Asn, Colo Bar Asn, Boulder county Bar Asn, am Asn of Univ Prof, Tau Epsilon Rho, Nat Tax Asn. **RESEARCH** Income Tax Aspects of real Estate Transactions; Income Tax Aspects o financing Techniques; General Concepts of Income Taxation. **SELECTED PUBLICATIONS** Auth, "Annual Problem and statutory supplement for Cases and Materials n Real Estate Planning," The Foundation Press, Inc, 90; auth, "Problems in the fundamentals of federal Income Taxation," the foundation Press, 94; auth, "Teacher's Manual for Problems in the fundamentals of federal Income Taxation," The foundation Press, 94; auth, "Problems in the Federal Income Taxation of Business Enterprises," foundation Press, 96; auth, "Teacher's Manual for Problems in the federal Income Taxation of Business Enterprises, " the foundation Press, 96; auth, "Drafting the Percentage Rent Clause," 26 Real Estate law Journal, 98; auth, "Tax considerations of Small Businesses," OCD Baltic Forum for Entrepreneurship and Enterprise Development, 98; auth, "Tax Reform in Ukraine," OECD Tax Reform Conf, 99; auth, "Choice of Entity for the Development and Operation of Real Estate," forthcoming. **CONTACT ADDRESS** School of Law, Univ of Colorado, Boulder, PO Box 401, Boulder, CO 80309-0401. **EMAIL** steuben@spot.colorado.edu

STEUSSY, MARTI J.
PERSONAL Born 09/07/1955, Dayton, OH, m, 1978, 2 children **DISCIPLINE** HEBREW BIBLE **EDUCATION** St Olaf Col, BA, 77; Earlham Sch of Relig, 82; Vanderbilt Univ, 92. **CAREER** Vis instr, Christian Theol Sem, 88-89, asst prof of O. T., 89-95, assoc prof of Biblical Interpretation, 96-. **HONORS AND AWARDS** Presidential Scholar, 73; Nat Sci Found Grad Fel, 79; Phi Beta Kappa; ATS Women's Fac Develop Grant, 93; Nat Relig Leadership Prog participant, 97-99. **MEMBERSHIPS** SBL, Network of Biblical Storytellers, Asn of Disciples for Theol Discussion, Forrest-Moss Inst. **RESEARCH** Psalms, biblical narrative, religion and science, Bible and ecology. **SELECTED PUBLICATIONS** Auth, Gardens in Babylon: Narrative Faith in the Greek Legends of Daniel, SBLDS, Atlanta: Scholar's Press (93); auth, David: Biblical Portraits of Power Studies on Personalities of the O. T., Columbia, SC: Univ of SC Press (99). **CONTACT ADDRESS** Dept Biblical Studies, Christian Theol Sem, PO Box 88267, Indianapolis, IN 46208-0267. **EMAIL** Mstreussy@cts.edu

STEVENS, JOHN PAUL
PERSONAL Born 04/20/1920, Chicago, IL, m, 1942, 4 children **DISCIPLINE** LAW **EDUCATION** Univ Chicago, AB, 41; Northwestern Univ, JD, 47. **CAREER** Law clerk, US Supreme Court Justice Wiley Rutledge, 47-48; assoc, Poppenhusen, Johnston, Thompson & Raymond, 48-50; assoc coun, Subcomt Study Monopoly Power, Judiciary Comt US House Rep, 51-52; partner, Rotschild, Hart, Stevens & Barry, 52-70; US circuit judge, Seventh Circuit, Assoc Justice, US Supreme Court, 75-, Mem, Atty General's Nat Comt Study Antitrust Laws, 53-55; The Freedom Of Speech, Yale Law J, Vol 102, 93; Is Justice Irrelevant, Northwestern Univ Law Rev, Vol 87, 93. **CONTACT ADDRESS** US Supreme Court, One First St NE, Washington, DC 20543.

STEVENS, PAUL W.
PERSONAL Born 11/25/1937, Fulton, MS, m, 1959, 2 children **DISCIPLINE** THEOLOGY **EDUCATION** Miss Col, BA, 60; New Orleans Baptist Theol Sem, BD, 64, PhD, 72. **CAREER** Dir Christian Trng, Southwest Baptist Col, 69-71; serv, New Orleans Baptist Theol Sem, 71-82; dir DMin prog, New Orleans Baptist Theol Sem; dir Cont Edu and Field Edu, New Orleans Baptist Theol Sem; VP Stud Aff, New Orleans Baptist Theol Sem; asst dir Field Mission prog, New Orleans Baptist Theol Sem; dir, Field Edu, 88-; assoc dean for the DMin Degree, 97-. **HONORS AND AWARDS** Pastor, McBee Baptist Church, 56-59; Ctr Hill Baptist Church, 59-62; Buckatunna Baptist Church, 63-65; Coteau Baptist Mission, 66-68; Ridgecrest Baptist Church, 82-88. **MEMBERSHIPS** Assn Theol Field Edu, In-Service Guidance Dir S Baptist Convention, Nat Coun Bivocational Ministry, SBC, Assn Case Tchg, Steering Comm Assoc of Doctor of Ministry Educs. **SELECTED PUBLICATIONS** Auth, The Supervisory Conference, Chapter in Experiencing Ministry Supervision, Broadman & Holman, 95; pub(s), Encycl S Baptists; Deacon; Jour Suprv and Trng in Ministry. **CONTACT ADDRESS** Sch Theol, Southwestern Baptist Theol Sem, PO Box 22720, Fort Worth, TX 76122-0418. **EMAIL** pws@swbts.edu

STEVENS-ARROYO, ANTONIO M.
DISCIPLINE COMPARATIVE RELIGION **EDUCATION** Passionist Monastic Sem, BA, 64; St Michael's Col, MA, 68; NYork Univ, MA, 75; Fordham Univ, PhD, 81. **CAREER** Dept Puerto Rican Stud, PROF, 89-, CUNY, BROOKLYN COL; fel, teach, Ctr Stud Am Rel, Woodrow Wilson Ctr, Princeton Univ, Union Theol Sem, Fordham Univ, Rutgers Univ, Ctr Adv Stud Puerto Rico and Caribbean, San Juan, Univ La Laguna, Spain; assoc ed, Encyclopedia Cont Religion, Macmillian Ref Libr; ed bd, Latino Studies Journal. **CONTACT ADDRESS** RISC, Brooklyn Col, CUNY, 2900 Bedford Ave, Brooklyn, NY 11210. **EMAIL** astevens@brooklyn.cuny.edu

STEVENSON-MOESSNER, JEANNE
PERSONAL Born 03/05/1948, Memphis, TN, m, 1975, 2 children **DISCIPLINE** THEOLOGY **EDUCATION** Vanderbilt Univ, BA, 70; Princeton Theol Sem, MA, Summa cum laude, 75; Univ of Basel, Switz, PhD, 86. **CAREER** Emory Univ, adj; Samford Univ, adj; Columbia Theol Sem, adj asst prof, 84-97; Univ of Dubuque Theol Sem, assoc prof, 97-, Presbyterian Minister, ordained, 96-. **MEMBERSHIPS** PCUSA, AAPC, AAR, SPT. **RESEARCH** Pastoral Care of women; multicultural developmental issues; cultural dissolution; maternal bonding. **SELECTED PUBLICATIONS** Mono, Through the Eyes of Women: Insights for Pastoral Care, The Handbook of Women Care, Fortress Press, 96; Women in Travail and Transition: A New Pastoral Care, co-ed, Fortress Press, 91; Theological Dimensions of Maturation in a Missionary Milieu, European Univ Studies Series 23, P. Lang Verlag, 89; auth, In Her Own Time: Women and Develop Issues in Pastoral Care, Fortress Press, 00. **CONTACT ADDRESS** Dept of Pastoral Theology, Univ of Dubuque, 2000 University Ave, Dubuque, IA 52001. **EMAIL** jmoessne@dbq.edu

STEWART, CARLYLE F., III
PERSONAL Born 09/23/1951, Detroit, MI, m, 1988, 3 children **DISCIPLINE** THEOLOGY **EDUCATION** Wilber Force Univ, BA, 73; Univ of Chicago, MA, 74; Chicago Theol Sem, MDiv, 77, DMin, 78; Northwestern Univ, PhD, 82. **CAREER** Garrett-evangelical Theol Sem, asst prof, 82-83; Wayne State Univ, lectr, 87; United Theol Sem, mentor, 95-97; Hope United Methodist Church, sr pastor, 83-. **HONORS AND AWARDS** Hull Univ, Eng, Will Wilber Force Scholar, 71-72; Alpha Kappa Mu Honor Soc, 72; Rockefeller sch, 78-80; Fulbright Fel, 73; Harvard Divinity School, Merrill Fel, 90; Circuit Rider Awd, 93 **MEMBERSHIPS** AAR, SBL, ACIL, WTS, BISC **RESEARCH** Ethics, black theology; African American religion; African religion; literature and philosophy. **SELECTED PUBLICATIONS** Auth, Was Abraham Lincoln of African Descent?, in: Transformer News, 95; Recognize Feelings to Help Defuse Anger, Southfield Eccentric, 95; Yes Beethoven Was a Brother!, Transformer News, 95; Justice Theologically Hinges on Justice Socially, Southfield Eccentric, 95; Divine Spirit Col-

ors Your Religious, Scientific Beliefs, Southfield Eccentric, 95; Who's Preaching This Sunday?, Circuit Rider Mag, 97; Street Corner Theology: Indigenous Reflections on the Reality of God in the African American Experience, John Winston Pub, 96; Joy Songs, Trumpet Blasts and Hallelujah Shouts: Sermons in the African - American Preaching Tradition, CSS Pub, 97; How Long Will You Limp?: Sermons on Pentecost, CSS Pub, 97; Soul Survivors, Westminster John Knox Pr (Louisville), 97; Sankofa: Celebrations for the African - American Church, United Church Press, 97; Black Spirituality and Black Consciousness: Soul Force, Culture, and Freedom in the African - American Experience, African World Press, 98; Deformed Disfigured & Despised, CSS Publ, 00; On Wings As Eagles, Abingdon Pr, 00. **CONTACT ADDRESS** Hope United Methodist Church, 26275 Northwestern Hwy., Southfield, MI 48076. **EMAIL** dstewarttii@aol.com

STEWART, CHARLES TODD
PERSONAL Born 05/13/1922, New York, NY, m, 1953, 3 children **DISCIPLINE** ECONOMICS **EDUCATION** George Wash Univ, BA, 46, MA, 48, PhD, 54. **CAREER** Asst prof, 47-49, Utah St Univ; Sr res analyst, 52-58, Georgetown Univ Grad School; Sr economist, 58-62, Dir of Economic Res, 62-63, US Chamber of Commerce; prof of econ, 63-92, prof emeritus, 92-, George Wash Univ **HONORS AND AWARDS** Ohira Memorial Prize for 1987. **MEMBERSHIPS** AAAS; Am Economic Asn. **RESEARCH** Discovery and invention; health care policy; inequality and its causes. **SELECTED PUBLICATIONS** Auth, Low Wage Workers in an Affluent Society, The Nelson Hall Co, 74; auth, Air Pollution, Human Health, and Public Policy, Lexington Bks, 79; coauth, Technology Transfer and Human Factors, Lexington Bks, 87; auth, Healthy, Wealthy, or Wise?, M. E. Sharpe, 95; auth, Inequality and Equity: Economics of Greed, Politics of Envy, Ethics of Equality, Greenwood Pubs, 98. **CONTACT ADDRESS** 5147 Macomb St NW, Washington, DC 20016.

STEWART, DANIEL LEWIS
PERSONAL Born 09/25/1937, New York, NY **DISCIPLINE** LAW, ECONOMICS **EDUCATION** Univ Calif, Los Angeles, BA, 58; Harvard Univ, JD, 61; Oxford Univ, MLitt, 63; Univ Wis, PhD(law & econ), 67. **CAREER** Fulbright scholar, Univ Chile, 63-64; proj assoc, Land Tenure Ctr, Univ Wis, 64-65; fel, Int Legal Ctr, Chile, 67-70; assoc atty, Gang, Tyre & Brown, 70; chief, Environ Law Sect, Health Probs Poor, Nat Legal Prog, 70-71; Prof Law, Loyola Law Sch, 71-, Assoc Dean, 81-, Vis prof law & econ; Univ Chile, 67-70; mem hearing bd, South Coast Air Quality Mgt Dist, 77-80, chmn, 78-80; The Law Of Prime-Numbers, Ny Univ Law Rev, Vol 68, 93. **RESEARCH** Theoretical rationale for judicial decisions dealing with natural resource allocation. **SELECTED PUBLICATIONS** Auth, El Derecho de Aguas en Chile, Ed Juridica, Santiago, Chile, 70. **CONTACT ADDRESS** Law Sch, Loyola Marymount Univ, 1441 W Olympic Blvd, Los Angeles, CA 90015.

STEWART, DAVID
PERSONAL Born 05/16/1938, Savannah, GA, m, 1959, 2 children **DISCIPLINE** PHILOSOPHY **EDUCATION** Abilene Christian Col, BA, 60, MA, 61; Rice Univ, PhD(philos), 65. **CAREER** Lectr philos, Rice Univ, 64-65; asst prof, NTex State Univ, 65-66; exec ed, R B Sweet Publ Co, Austin, Tex, 66-70; from asst prof to assoc prof, 70-78, Prof Philos, Ohio Univ, 78-, Res inst fel, Ohio Univ, 74, assoc provost, 81-93, provost 93-96, trustee prof, Phil, 96-. **MEMBERSHIPS** Am Philos Asn; Am Acad Relig. **SELECTED PUBLICATIONS** coauth, Exploring Phenomenology, Am Libr Asn, 74; co-ed, Social and political essays by Paul Ricoeur, Ohio Univ, 74; The Philosophy of Paul Ricoeur, Beacon, 78; The Meaning of Humanness in a Technological Era, Ohio Univ, 78; auth, Exploring the Philosophy of Religion, Prentice-Hall, 4th ed 98; Fundamentals of Philosophy, Macmillan 4th ed 98; auth, Business Ethics, McGraw Hill, 96. **CONTACT ADDRESS** Dept of Philosophy, Ohio Univ, Athens, OH 45701-2979. **EMAIL** dstewart1@ohiou.edu

STEWART, MELVILLE Y.
PERSONAL Born 06/19/1935, Boston, MA, m, 1958, 5 children **DISCIPLINE** PHILOSOPHY **EDUCATION** Gordon Col, BA, 58; Westminster Theol Sem, MDiv, 61; Andover Newton Theol Sch, STM, 68; Univ Conn, MA, 72; Univ Minn, PhD, 83. **CAREER** Asst prof, 72-75, assoc prof, 76-86, prof, 87- , Bethel Col; vis prof, St Petersburg State Univ, Russia, 92-93; vis prof, Peking Univ, 96-97. **HONORS AND AWARDS** Greene Prize in Apologetics, 61; dist scholar award, 95-96. **MEMBERSHIPS** MN Philos Assoc; APA. **RESEARCH** Philosophy of religion. **SELECTED PUBLICATIONS** Auth, The Greater-Good Defense, An Essay on the Rationality of Faith; co-ed, Problems in Christian Philosophy; ed, Philosophy of Religion, An Anthology of Contemporary Views; co-ed, East and West Religious Ethics and Other Essays; co-ed, The Symposium of Chinese-American Philosophy and Religious Studies. **CONTACT ADDRESS** Dept of Philosophy, Bethel Col, Minnesota, Saint Paul, MN 55112. **EMAIL** stemel@bethel.edu

STEWART, WILLIAM H.
PERSONAL Born 04/18/1935, Greensboro, NC **DISCIPLINE** THEOLOGY **EDUCATION** NC A&T State Univ, BS 1960; Central MI Univ, MA 1973; Blackstone School of Law, JD 1977; Western CO Univ, DBAdm 1980. **CAREER** Coop League of the USA, dir demonstration prog 1966-69; General Elect Co Chicago, training dir 1969-70; City of Ann Arbor, dir model cities prog 1970-71; US Dept of Housing Urban Dev, div dir 1971-75; Exec Seminar Ctr US Civil Serv Commiss, assoc dir 1975-78; TN Valley Authority Div of Energy Use, mgr Community Conserv Proj 1978-86; Mutual Housing Corp, exec dir, 87-90; Knoxville College, Div of Business & Social Sciences, dir, 87-91; Mother Love Baptist Church, pastor, 87-92; US Department of Energy, Southeastern Power Administration, Power Marketing Division, program manager, 91-94; Macedonia Outreach Ministries, pres, 94-96; Rochdale Institute, ceo, 96-. **HONORS AND AWARDS** Youth & Commun Serv Frederick Douglass Chapter Hamilton Co 1981; Serv Awd Lane Coll Jackson TN 1981; Distinguished Citizen City of Chattanooga TN 1981; Outstanding Mem Alpha Iota Alpha 1983; Distinguished Serv Sun Belt Assn Ind 1984; Humanitarian Awd, Jas B Dudley High School Alumni Assn, 1988; Distinguished Service Awd, Southeastern Power Admin, 1994; Doctorate of Divinity, Laurence Univ, 1968; Doctor of Laws, Buckner Univ, 1970. **MEMBERSHIPS** Alpha Phi Alpha Fraternity 1959-; pres bd of dir The Stewart-Candida Co 1978-85; dean Chattanooga Baptist Bible Coll 1981-84; pres bd of dir Chattanooga Area Minority Investment Forum 1981-87; chmn bd of dir Sun Belt Allied Industries 1985-86; chmn Seville-Benz Corp 1986-93; pres, Operation PUSH, Chattanooga, TN, 1986-88. **CONTACT ADDRESS** New Monumental Baptist Church, 715 E 8th Street, Chattanooga, TN 37403.

STICH, STEPHEN P.
PERSONAL Born 05/09/1943, New York, NY, m, 1971, 2 children **DISCIPLINE** PHILOSOPHY **EDUCATION** Univ Pa, BA, 64; Princeton Univ, PhD, 68. **CAREER** Teaching Asst, Princeton Univ, 65; From Asst Prof to Assoc Prof, Univ Mich, 68-78; From Assoc Prof to Prof, Univ Md, 78-86; Prof, Univ Calif, 86-89; Prof, Rutgers Univ, 89-. **HONORS AND AWARDS** Travel Grant, Nat Res Coun, 79; Res Grant, Nat Sci Found, 81-82; Fel, Stanford Univ, 83-84; Fel, Nat Endowment Humanities, 96. **MEMBERSHIPS** APA, SPP, PSA, Fulbright Alumni Asn. **RESEARCH** Standards and priorities in academic development, arts and humanities, cognitive science. **SELECTED PUBLICATIONS** Auth, From Folk Psychology to Cognitive Science: The Case Against Belief, Bradford Books/MIT Pr (Cambridge, MA), 83; auth, The Fragmentation of Reason: Preface to a Pragmatic Theory of Cognitive Evaluation, Bradford Books/MIT Pr (Cambridge, MA), 90; auth, Deconstructing the Mind, Oxford UP (New York, NY), 96; coauth, "The Varieties of Off-Line Simulation," in Theories of Theories of Mind (Cambridge: Cambridge UP, 96), 39-74; coauth, "Cognitive, Penetrability, Rationality and Restricted Simulation," Mind and Lang 12 3/4 (97): 297-326; auth, "Is Man A Rational Animal?" in Questioning Matters: An Introduction to Philos Inquiry (Mountain View, CA: Mayfield Publ Co, 99), 221-236; coauth, "A Cognitive Theory of Pretense," Cognition 74 2 (00): 115-147; auth, "Cognitive Pluralism," Routledge Encycl of Philos (forthcoming). **CONTACT ADDRESS** Dept Philos, Rutgers, The State Univ of New Jersey, New Brunswick, Davison Hall/Douglass Campus, New Brunswick, NJ 08901-2882. **EMAIL** stich@ruccs.rutgers.edu

STICHLER, RICHARD
PERSONAL Born 12/29/1942, Reading, PA, m, 1988 **DISCIPLINE** PHILOSOPHY **EDUCATION** Marlboro Coll, BA, 66; Georgetown Univ, MA, 72, PhD, 78; Drexel Univ, MS, 92 **CAREER** Asst prof/prof, 84-present, Alvernia Coll. **HONORS AND AWARDS** NDEA Title IV Fel:Georgetown Univ; Beta Phi Mu Award: Drexel Univ; Univ Fel: Univ of Maryland; Graduated with Honors: Marlboro Coll **MEMBERSHIPS** Amer Assoc of Univ Profs, member, Committee for Professional Ethics; President, Pennsylvania Division of AAUP (1998-2000); Vice President (96-98); member, Amer Philosophical Assn; Amer Catholic Philosophical Assn **RESEARCH** Ethics; Political Philosophy; Philosophical Psychology; Ancient Philosophy **SELECTED PUBLICATIONS** Auth, "The Right to Revolution: Locke or Marx?" Terrorism, Justice and Social Values, Mellon Press, 90; auth, " On Reforming the ALA Code of Ethics," American Libraries, 92; auth " Ethics in the Information Market," Journal of Information Ethics, 93; auth, Review of Kindly Inquisitors: The New Attacks on Free Thought, by Jonathan Rauch, in Journal of Information Ethics, Spring 95; Review of Only Words, by Catherine A. MacKinnon, in Journal of Information Ethics, Fall 96; Academic Freedom and Faculty Responsibility in Disciplinary Proceedings, Academe, 97; coed, Ethics, Information, and Technology: Readings, Mcfarland and Co., 98. **CONTACT ADDRESS** Dept of Philos, Alvernia Col, Reading, PA 19607. **EMAIL** stichri@alvernia.edu

STIEB, JAMES
PERSONAL Born 09/10/1970, Denver, CO, s **DISCIPLINE** LIBERAL ARTS, PHILOSOPHY **EDUCATION** Temple Univ, PA, 96; Univ of CO, BA, 93; St. Johns Col, MD, BA, 94. **CAREER** St. John's Col at Annapolis, MD Laboratory asst, 90-91; elect english dept, Temple Univ, 96-97; asst adj prof, Cheyney State Univ, 98-99; teaching asst, Temple Univ, 98-; asst adj prof, Widener Univ, Univ Col, 97-; asst adj prof, Drexel Univ, 97-; asst adj prof, Drexel Univ, 98-; asst adj prof, Villanova Univ, 99-. **MEMBERSHIPS** Am Philos Assoc; Soc for the Discussion of Realism and Antirealism. **RESEARCH** Metaphysics, Epistemology, Philosophy of Lang; Hist of Philosophy, Social & Political Philosophy, Logic, Critical Reasoning, Applied Ethics. **SELECTED PUBLICATIONS** Auth, "Philosophy Reflections on the Analytic Continental Divide," Sch, 98. **CONTACT ADDRESS** Dept of Philosophy, Temple Univ, 6350 Greene St., Duval Apt No 222, Philadelphia, PA 19144. **EMAIL** jsteib@nimbus.ocis.temple.edu

STILL, TODD
PERSONAL Born 02/22/1966, Wichita Falls, TX, m, 1990, 2 children **DISCIPLINE** BIBLICAL STUDIES **EDUCATION** Baylor Univ, BA, 88; Southwestern Baptist Theol Sem, MDiv, 91; Univ Glasgow, PhD, 96. **CAREER** Assoc prof, Dallas Baptist Univ, 95-. **HONORS AND AWARDS** Listed in Who's Who Among Teachers; listed in Int Dir of Distinguished Leadership. **MEMBERSHIPS** Soc of Biblical Lit, Nat Asn of Baptist Professors of Relig. **RESEARCH** Paul, Serial-scientific criticism of the New Testament. **SELECTED PUBLICATIONS** Auth, Conflict at Thessalonics, Sheffield Acad Pr, 99. **CONTACT ADDRESS** Dept Christian Studies, Dallas Baptist Univ, 3000 Mountain Creek Pkwy, Dallas, TX 75211-9209. **EMAIL** todd@dbu.edu

STINGL, MICHAEL
DISCIPLINE PHILOSOPHY **EDUCATION** Univ Wis, MA; Univ Toronto, PhD, 86. **CAREER** Prof, Univ of Lethbridge, 89-. **RESEARCH** Theoretical ethics; social and political philosophy; philosophy of language; contemporary analytic philosophy; early modern philosophy; formal and informal logic. **CONTACT ADDRESS** Dept of Philosophy, Univ of Lethbridge, 4401 University Dr W, Lethbridge, AB, Canada T1K 3M4. **EMAIL** stingl@uleth.ca

STITH, RICHARD T.
PERSONAL Born 11/17/1944, Corrallis, OR, m, 1970, 3 children **DISCIPLINE** LAW **EDUCATION** Harvard Univ, AB, 65; Univ Calif Berkeley, MA, 67; Yale Univ, MPhil, 71; PhD, 73; Yale Law Sch, JD, 73. **CAREER** Valparaiso Univ Sch of Law, 73-. **HONORS AND AWARDS** Fulbright Prof, 80-81; 88, 92, 96, 00-01. **MEMBERSHIPS** Nat Lawyers Assoc. **SELECTED PUBLICATIONS** Auth, The World as Reality, as Resource, and as Pretenses", 20 Am J of Jurisprudence (75): 141-53; auth, "The Problem of Public Pretense", Indian Philos Quarterly 8.1 (80): 13-29; auth, "A Critique of Fairness", 16 Valpairaiso Univ Law Rev, (82): 459-81; auth, "Toward Freedom From Value", On Moral Med (87): 127-43; auth, "New Constitutional and Penal Theory in Spanish Abortion Law", 35 Am J of Comp Law (87): 513-58; auth, "Will There Be a Science of Law in the Twenty-First Century?", 22 Revue Generale de Droit (91): 373-79; auth, "Images, Spirituality, and Law", 10 J of Law and Relig, (93): 33-47; auth, "Unconstitutional Constitutional Amendments: The Extraordinary Power of Nepal's Supreme Court", 11 Am Univ J of Int Law and Policy, (96): 47-77; auth, "On Death and Dworkin: A Critique of His Theory of Inviolability", 56 Md Law Rev 997): 289-383; auth, "The Rule of Law vs The Rule of Judges: A Plea for Legal Pluralism", Political Thought (97): 31-55. **CONTACT ADDRESS** Sch of Law, Valparaiso Univ, 651 College Ave, Valparaiso, IN 46383-6461. **EMAIL** richard.stith@valpo.edu

STITH-CABRANES, KATE
PERSONAL Born 03/16/1951, St. Louis, MO, m, 1984, 2 children **DISCIPLINE** ECONOMICS, LAW **EDUCATION** Dartmouth Univ, AB, 73; Harvard Univ Kennedy Sch Govt, MPP, 77; Harvard Law Sch, JD, 77. **CAREER** Assoc prof, 85-91, prof, 91-98, Lafayette S Foster Prof Law, Yale Law Sch, 98-. **MEMBERSHIPS** Phi Beta Kappa; Am Law Inst; Counc For Relations; Comt Law, Justice, Nat Acad Scis. **RESEARCH** Congress; constitutional law; criminal law. **SELECTED PUBLICATIONS** various **CONTACT ADDRESS** Law Sch, Yale Univ, PO Box 208215, New Haven, CT 06520-8215.

STITT, ALLAN J.
DISCIPLINE LAW **EDUCATION** Univ Toronto, BC, 84; Windsor Univ, LLB, 88; Univ Detroit, JD, 88; Harvard Univ, LLM, 92. **CAREER** Law clerk, Ontario Court of Appeal; prof, Univ Toronto; practices Alternative Dispute Resolution, Stitt Feld Handy Houston; teaching asst, Harvard, 94-95 Pres of the Arbitration and Mediation Institute of Ontario, 97-98. **SELECTED PUBLICATIONS** Co-auth, Understanding the Income Tax Act; co-ed, CCH ADR Practice Manual; auth, ADR For Organizations, 98. **CONTACT ADDRESS** Fac of Law, Univ of Toronto, 78 Queen's Park, Toronto, ON, Canada M5S 1A1.

STITT, B. GRANT
PERSONAL Born 06/10/1947, Chicago, IL, m, 1987, 1 child **DISCIPLINE** CRIMINAL JUSTICE **EDUCATION** Univ Ariz, BA, 69; MA, 76; PhD, 79. **CAREER** Teaching Asst, Univ Ariz, 70-76; Adj Instructor, Pima Cmty Col, 71-72; Asst Prof, Memphis State Univ, 76-84; Asst Prof, Univ Mich, 84-89; Assoc Prof to Prof and Dept Chair, Univ Nev, 89-. **MEMBERSHIPS** Am soc of Criminol, Acad of Criminal Justice Sci, Inst of criminal Justice Ethics, Midwestern Criminal Justice Asn, Western and pacific Asn of Criminal Justice Educators, Calif Homicide Investigators Asn. **RESEARCH** Ethical and Moral

Dilemmas in Criminal Justice, Legalized Gambling and Crime, The Sociology and Social Psychology of Law Enforcement, Theoretical Criminology, Law and Society, Deterrence and Juvenile Delinquency. **SELECTED PUBLICATIONS** Auth, "The Effect of Casino Gambling on Crime in New Casino Jurisdictions," Journal of Crime and Justice, forthcoming; auth, "Casino Gambling and Bankruptcy in New US Casino Jurisdictions," Journal of Socio-Economics, forthcoming; auth, "Attitudes of Community Leaders in New Casino Jurisdictions Regarding Gambling's effects on Crime and Quality of Life," Journal of Gambling Studies, forthcoming; auth, "A Minor Concern? Underage Gambling and the Law," The Social Science Journal, forthcoming; auth, "How Do Casinos Affect Communities," Business perspectives, (99): 23-27; auth, "an analysis of Casino Gambling and alcohol Consumption among University Students," Journal of Gambling Studies, (98): 135-150; auth, "Ethical Dilemmas in Community Oriented Policing and problem solving," Police Quarterly, (98): 19-34; auth, "Plea Bargaining: Myths and Realities," in Filling the Gap: Critical readings in Criminal Justice, Simon & Schuster, 98; auth, "Defining the Limits of social Science: Emerging Teaching Conflicts in Criminal Justice," American Association of Behavioral and Social Sciences perspectives Journal, (98): 12-38; auth, "Focus Groups and Criminal Justice program Evaluation," Journal of Criminal Justice Education, (98): 71-80. **CONTACT ADDRESS** Dept Criminal Justice, Univ of Nevada, Reno, N Virginia Ave, Reno, NV 89557-0001. **EMAIL** stitt@unr.edu

STIVERS, ROBERT L.

PERSONAL Born 04/25/1940, Cincinnati, OH, m, 1992, 2 children **DISCIPLINE** RELIGION; ETHICS **EDUCATION** Columbia Univ, PhD 73, MPhil 71' Union Theol Sem, MDiv 69; Yale Univ, BA 62. **CAREER** Pacific Lutheran Univ, prof, assoc prof, asst prof, 74 to 97-; Union Theol Sem, grad asst 71-73; US Navy, weapons off 62-66. **MEMBERSHIPS** AAR; SCE; ACT. **RESEARCH** Environmental ethics. **SELECTED PUBLICATIONS** Jour, The Case Method Inst, co-ed vol 5,6,7,8; Christian Ethics: A Case Method Approach, coauth, Orbis Books, 89, 2nd ed, 94; Reformed Faith and Economics, U Press of Amer, 89; The Public Vocation of Christian Ethics, co-ed, Pilgrim Press, 86. **CONTACT ADDRESS** Dept of Religion, Pacific Lutheran Univ, Tacoma, WA 98447. **EMAIL** stiverrl@plu.edu

STOCKMAN, ROBERT H.

PERSONAL Born 10/06/1953, Meriden, CT, m, 1992, 1 child **DISCIPLINE** HISTORY OF RELIGION **EDUCATION** Wesleyan Univ, BA, 75; Brown Univ, MSc, 77; Harvard Divinity School, MTS, 82, ThD, 90. **CAREER** Grad res asst, Brown Univ, 75-77; instr, Geology and Oceanography, Comm Col of RI, 77-80; instr, Geology, Boston State Col, 80-82; instr, Geology, Univ Lowell, 83-84; instr, Geology and Astronomy, Bentley Col, 83-90; teaching asst, Harvard Univ, 86-89; asst prof relig, DePaul Univ, 95-96; Instr Relig, DePaul Univ, 90-95, 96-98. **MEMBERSHIPS** Amer Academy Relig; Middle East Studies Assoc; Soc Iranian Studies; Assoc Baha i Studies, member, ex comm, 90-98, member and chair, Study of Religions Section, 89-. **RESEARCH** Amer Bahai hist; Amer relig hist. **SELECTED PUBLICATIONS** Auth, The Bahai Faith in America, vol 1, Origins, 1892-1900, Baha'i Pub Trust, 85, vol 2, Early Expansion, 1900-1912, George Ronald, 95; The Baha'i Faith in America: One Hundred Years, in World Order, vol 25, no 3, spring 94; Paul Johnson's Theosophical Influence in Baha'i History: Some Comments, in Theosophical Hist, vol 5, no 4, Oct 94; The Baha'i Faith: A Portrait, in Joel Beversluis, ed, A Sourcebook for the Earth's Community of Religions, 2nd ed, CoNexus Press, 95; The Baha i Faith in the 1990's, article in Dr Timothy Miller, ed, America's Alternative Religions, SUNY Press, 95; The Vision of the Baha' i Faith, in Martin Forward, Ultimate Visions: Reflections on the Religions We Choose, One World, 95; The Baha'i Faith in England and Germany, 1900-1913, in World Order, vol 27, no 3, spring 96; The Baha'i Faith section of the Pluralism Project, CD Rom, Columbia Univ Press, 97; many other articles, several forthcoming publications. **CONTACT ADDRESS** Institute for Baha'i Studies, 224 Swanson Cir, South Bend, IN 46615. **EMAIL** rstockman@usbnc.org

STOCKMEYER, NORMAN OTTO, SR

PERSONAL Born 05/24/1938, Detroit, MI, m, 1968, 3 children **DISCIPLINE** LAW **EDUCATION** Oberlin Col, AB, 60; Univ Mich, JD, 63. **CAREER** Law Clerk, 65; Res Dir, Appellate Court, 66-76; Prof, Thomas M Cooley Law Sch, 77-. **HONORS AND AWARDS** Delta Theta Phi Nat Teacher of the Year Awd; Stanley & Beattie Teaching Awd; Stud Bar Asn Barrister Awd. **MEMBERSHIPS** Am Bar Asn; State Bar of MI; Am Soc of Writers on Legal Subjects. **RESEARCH** Law of contracts; Law of remedies; Judicial administration. **SELECTED PUBLICATIONS** Auth, Michigan Law of Damages, 88. **CONTACT ADDRESS** Thomas M. Cooley Law Sch, PO Box 13038, Lansing, MI 48901. **EMAIL** stochmen@cooley.edu

STOEBER, MICHAEL

PERSONAL Born 11/06/1958, Calgary, AB, Canada, m, 1980, 2 children **DISCIPLINE** THEOLOGY **EDUCATION** Univ Toronto, PhD, 90. **CAREER** Assoc prof, Regis Col. **HONORS AND AWARDS** Fel, Res Counc of Can, 90-92. **MEMBERSHIPS** Soc of Hindu-Christian Studies; Can Soc of Christian Philos; Am Assoc of Relig; Catholic Theol Soc of Am. **RESEARCH** Philosophy of comparative spirituality. **SELECTED PUBLICATIONS** Auth, Evil and the Mystics' God: Towards A Mystical Theodicy, MacMillan Pr, (London), 92; auth, "Constructivisit Epistemologies of Mysticism: a Critique and a Revision", Relig Studies 29 (93): 169-184; auth, "From Proclamation to Interreligious Dialogue: The Parliaments of Religion", The Living Light 30.1 (93): 32-41; auth, "Dostoevsky's Devil: The Will to Power", J of Relig 74.1 (94): 26-44; auth, Theo-Monistic Mysticism: A Hindu-Christian Comparison, Macmillan Pr, (London), 94; auth, "Sri Ramakrishna, Swami Vivekananda, and Hindu-Christian Dialogue", Hindu-Christian Studies 8. (95): 23-35; auth, "World Parliament of Religions", New Catholic Encycl, Vol 19, ed Berard Marthaler, Jack Heraty and Assoc, (Palatine, IL), 96; coed, Critical Reflections on the Paranormal, State Univ of NY Pr, (Albany, NY), 96; auth, "Hell, Divine Love and Divine Justice", Logos 2.1, (99): 176-199. **CONTACT ADDRESS** School of Theol, Regis Col, Ontario, 15 St Mary St, Toronto, ON, Canada M4Y 2R5. **EMAIL** stoeber@cua.edu

STOEBUCK, WILLIAM BREES

PERSONAL Born 03/18/1929, Wichita, KS, m, 1951, 3 children **DISCIPLINE** LAW **EDUCATION** Wichita State Univ, BA, 51; Ind Univ Bloomington, MA, 53; Univ Wash, JD, 59; Harvard Univ, SJD, 73. **CAREER** Pvt pract law, Seattle, Wash, 59-64; asst prof, Univ Denver, 64-67; Prof Law, Univ Wash, 67-, Ford fel, Law Sch, Harvard Univ, 66-67. **MEMBERSHIPS** Order of the Coif; Am Asn Law Schs. **RESEARCH** Eminent domain; adverse possession; landlord and tenant. **SELECTED PUBLICATIONS** Auth, The property right of access versus the power of eminent domain, Tex Law Rev, 69; Condemnation of rights the condemnee holds in lands of another, Iowa Law Rev, 70; A general theory of eminent domain, Wash Law Rev, 72; Nontrespassory Takings in Eminent Domain, Bobbs, 77; Running covenants: An analytical primer, Wash Law Rev, 77; Police power, takings, and due process, Washington & Lee Law Rev, 80; Back To The Crib, Wash Law Rev, Vol 69, 94. **CONTACT ADDRESS** Sch of Law, Univ of Washington, 1100 N E Campus Pky, Seattle, WA 98105-6605.

STOEFFLER, FRED ERNEST

PERSONAL Born 09/27/1911, Happenbach, West Germany, m, 1941, 2 children **DISCIPLINE** RELIGION, HISTORY OF CHRISTIANITY **EDUCATION** Temple Univ, BS, 38, STM, 45, STD, 48; Yale Univ, BD, 41. **CAREER** Pastor, Methodist Church, 39-51; from asst prof to prof hist Christianity, 51-62, Prof Relig, Temple Univ, 62-, Mem coun, Am Soc Church Hist, 77-79. **MEMBERSHIPS** Am Soc Church Hist; Am Soc Reformation Res; AHA; Acad Polit Sci; Am Acad Relig. **RESEARCH** Reformation; mysticism; pietism. **SELECTED PUBLICATIONS** Auth, Mysticism in the Devotional Literature of Colonial Pennsylvania, Pa Ger Folklore Soc, 49; The Rise of Evangelical Pietism, Brill, Leiden, 65; transl, B Lohse, History of Doctrine, Fortress, 66; auth, German Pietism During the 18th Century, Brill, Leiden, 73; ed & contribr, Continental Pietism and Early American Christianity, Wm B Eerdmans, 76; Anton Wilhelm Bohme: Studies On The Ecumenical Thought And Dealings Of A Pietist From Halle, Church Hist, Vol 61, 92. **CONTACT ADDRESS** Dept of Relig, Temple Univ, Philadelphia, PA 19122.

STOEHR, KEVIN L.

PERSONAL Born 11/19/1967, Portland, ME **DISCIPLINE** PHILOSOPHY **EDUCATION** Bowdoin Col, BA, 90; Boston Univ, MA, 94, PhD, 96. **CAREER** Asst prof Rhetoric and Hum, Boston Univ. **HONORS AND AWARDS** James Bowdoin Scholar, 90; Fulbright Scholar, 93-94; Junior Fel, Inst of Human Sci, 93, 94. **MEMBERSHIPS** APA, Society for the Philosophical Study of the Contemporary Visual Arts (SPSCVA), Conference of Philosophical Societies (COPS). **RESEARCH** Philosophy; literature; politics; religion; film. **SELECTED PUBLICATIONS** Ed, Philosphies of Religion, Art, and Creativity: Volume IV of the Proceedings of the 20th World Congress of Philosophy, PDC; auth, "The Virtues of Circular Reasoning," in Epistemology: Vol. V of the Proceedings of the 20th WCP. **CONTACT ADDRESS** College of General Studies, Boston Univ, 871 Commonwealth Ave., Boston, ME 02215. **EMAIL** kstoehr@bu.edu

STOEVER, WILLIAM K. B.

PERSONAL Born 06/20/1941, Riverside, CA, m, 1971 **DISCIPLINE** HISTORY OF RELIGION **EDUCATION** Pomona Col, BA, 63; Yale Univ, MDiv, 66, MPhil, 69, PhD(relig studies), 70. **CAREER** Asst prof, 70-75, assoc prof, 76-80, prof humanities, Western Wash Univ, 80-, Chemn, Dept Lib Studies 78-, Nat Endowment for Humanities res fel, 74-75. **MEMBERSHIPS** AHA; Am Soc Church Hist; Am Acad Relig; Am Studies Asn. **RESEARCH** History and historiography of religion in Amica; 17th century Puritanism; Jonathan Edwards; religion and cultural change. **SELECTED PUBLICATIONS** Auth, Henry Boynton Smith and the German theology of history, Union Sem Quart Rev, fall 69; Nature, grace, and John Cotton: The theological dimension in the New England antinomian controversy, Church Hist, 3/75; A Faire and Easie Way to Heaven: Covenant Theology and Antinomianism in Early Massachusetts, Wesleyan Univ Press, 78; The Godly Will's Discerning: Shepard, Edwards, and the Identification of True Godliness, Jonathan Edwards's Writings: Text, Context, Interpretation, Ind Univ Press, 97. **CONTACT ADDRESS** Dept of Lib Studies, Western Washington Univ, M/S 9084, Bellingham, WA 98225-5996. **EMAIL** bristow@wwu.edu

STOKES, LOUIS

PERSONAL Born 02/23/1925, Cleveland, OH, m, 1960 **DISCIPLINE** LAW **EDUCATION** Case Western Reserve Univ, 1946-48; Cleveland Marshall Law School, JD, 1953. **CAREER** US House of Representatives, 11th Congressional District, Ohio, rep 1968-98, chairman, House Appropriations Subcommittee on VA-HUD-Independent Agencies, member, Appropriations Subcommittee on the District of Columbia, Subcommittee on Labor-Health and Human Services Education; private practice, attorney; Case Western Univ, visiting scholar, 98-. **HONORS AND AWARDS** Distinguished Serv Awd; Certificate of Appreciation, US Comm on Civil Rights; William L Dawson Awd, 1980; honorary degrees: Wilberforce Univ, Shaw Univ, Livingstone College, Ohio College of Podiatric Medicine, Oberlin College, Morehouse College, Meharry Medical College, Atlanta Univ, Howard Univ, Morehouse School of Medicine, Central State Univ, Xavier Univ. **MEMBERSHIPS** Bd of trustees Martin Luther King Jr Ctr for Social Change, Forest City Hosp, Cleveland State Univ; bd dirs Karamu House; vice chmn, trustee bd St Paul AME Zion Church; fellow OH State Bar Assn; mem Cleveland Cuyahoga Cty, Amer Bar Assn, Pythagoras Lodge #9; exec comm Cuyahoga Cty Dem Party; exec comm OH State Dem Party; mem Urban League, Citizens League, John Harlan Law Club, Kappa Alpha Psi, Amer Civil Liberties Union, Plus Club, Amer Legion, African-Amer Inst Intl Adv Council; vice pres NAACP Cleveland Branch 1965-66; vice chmn Cleveland Sub-Com of US Comm on Civil Rights 1966; guest lecturer Cleveland Branch NAACP. **CONTACT ADDRESS** Congressman, US House of Representatives, Rayburn Bldg, Rm 2365, Washington, DC 20515.

STOKES, MACK B.

PERSONAL Born 12/21/1911, Wonsan, Korea, m, 1942, 3 children **DISCIPLINE** PHILOSOPHICAL THEOLOGY **EDUCATION** Asbury Col, BA, 32; Duke Univ, BD, 35; Boston Univ, PhD, 40. **CAREER** Asst prof, 41, prof, Parker Prof, assoc dean, 43-72, Candler Sch Theol, Emory Univ; Bishop of the United Methodist Church, 72- . **HONORS AND AWARDS** Res fel theol, 36-38, Bowne fel philos, 38-39, Boston Univ; Lambuth Univ, LLS, 63; Millsaps Col, DD, 74. **MEMBERSHIPS** APA. **RESEARCH** Theology and philosophical theology; contemporary issues in these fields. **SELECTED PUBLICATIONS** Auth, The Epic of Revelation, McGraw Hill; auth, Talking with God: A Guide to Prayer, Abingdon, 89; auth, Theology for Preaching, Bristol House, 94; auth, Major United Methodist Beliefs. **CONTACT ADDRESS** 2637 Peachtree Rd NE, Atlanta, GA 30305.

STOLZENBERG, N. M.

PERSONAL Born 09/06/1961, Boston, MA, m, 1986, 2 children **DISCIPLINE** LAW **EDUCATION** Yale Col , BA, 84; Harvard Univ Law Sch, JD, 87. **CAREER** Asst prof of law, 88-91, assoc prof, 91-94, prof, 94 -, USC Law Sch; visiting prof of law, Columbia Univ Law Sch, 95. **RESEARCH** Legal theory; political theory; religion and law; cultural pluralism; law and literature. **SELECTED PUBLICATIONS** Auth, "He Drew a Circle That Shut Me Out: Assimilation, Indoctrination, and the Paradox of a Liberal Education," Harvard Review, v 106, n 581, 93; "Un-covering the Tradition of Jewish 'Dissimilation:' Frankfurter, Bickel, and Cover on Judicial Review," Southern California Interdisciplinary Law Jour, v 809, 94; "A Tale of Two Villages (or Legal Reform Comes to Town)," in NOMOS XXXIX: Ethnicity and Group Rights, 97; "The Puzzling Persistence of Community: The Cases of Airmont and Kiryas Joel," in From Ghetto to Emancipation, Univ Scranton Press, 97; "A Book of Laughter and Forgetting: Kalman's 'Strange Career' and the Marketing of Civic Republicanism," Harvard Law Review, v 111, n 1025, 98; "Jiminy Cricket: A Commentary on Professor Hill's Four Conceptions of Conscience," in NOMOS XL: Integrity and Conscience, NY Univ Press, 98. **CONTACT ADDRESS** Law Sch, Univ of So California, Univ Park, Los Angeles, CA 90089.

STONE, ALAN ABRAHAM

PERSONAL Born 08/15/1929, Boston, MA, m, 1952, 3 children **DISCIPLINE** LAW **EDUCATION** Harvard Univ, AB, 50; Yale Univ, MD, 55. **CAREER** Prof Law & Psychiat, Harvard Univ, 72-, Assoc attending psychiatrist, McLean Hosp, 69-; assoc psychiatrist, 69-75, consult psychiat, Mass Gen Hosp, 77-; fel, Ctr Advan Studies Behav Sci, 80-81; Tanner lectr, 82. **HONORS AND AWARDS** Guttmacher Prize, 76; Guggenheim Awd, 78-79; Isaac Ray Awd, 82. **MEMBERSHIPS** Fel Am Psychiat Asn (vice-pres, 77-78, pres-elect, 78-79, pres, 79-80); Group Advan Psychiat. **RESEARCH** Psychopathology. **SELECTED PUBLICATIONS** Coauth, Longitudianal Studies of Child Personality, Harvard Univ, 59; The Abnormal Personality Through Literature, Prentice, 66; auth, Legal education on the couch, Harvard Law Rev, 71; Suicide precipitated by psychotherapy, Am J Psychother, 71; Psychiatry kills: a critical evaluation of Dr Thomas Szasz, J Psychiat &

Law, 73; ed, Mental Health and Law: A System in Transition, Govt Printing Off, 75; auth, Revisiting The Parable--Truth Without Consequences, Int J Of Law And Psychiatry, Vol 17, 94. **CONTACT ADDRESS** Sch of Law, Harvard Univ, 1525 Massachusetts, Cambridge, MA 02138-2903. **EMAIL** stone@law.harvard.edu

STONE, CHRISTOPHER D.
DISCIPLINE LAW **EDUCATION** Harvard Univ, AB,59; Yale Univ, JD,62. **CAREER** Roy P. Crocker prof, Univ Southern Calif; US Dept Energy; counseled, US Sentencing Comn on corporate crime; prof, Yale Univ & Univ Mich. **RESEARCH** Business Organizations; International Environmental Law; Property; Law, Language, & Ethics; & Rights of Groups. **SELECTED PUBLICATIONS** Auth, Law, Language, & Ethics; Should Trees Have Standing--Toward Legal Rights for Natural Objects; Where the Law Ends; Earth & Other Ethics; The Gnat is Older than Man: Global Environment & Human Agenda; Should Trees Have Standing. **CONTACT ADDRESS** School of Law, Univ of So California, University Park Campus, Los Angeles, CA 90089.

STONE, DENNIS J.
DISCIPLINE LAW **EDUCATION** Univ Calif, Berkeley, BA, 70; MLS, 71; Univ Pac, JD, 77. **CAREER** Assoc Prof, Gonzaga Univ, 79-83; Prof, Univ Ct, 83-95; Prof, Fla Coastal Sch of Law, 95-. **MEMBERSHIPS** AALL, ABA, AALS, ASIL, CLLA, ALL. **SELECTED PUBLICATIONS** Co-ed, "Legal Resources and Legal Systems in Sub-Saharan Africa," in Doing Bus in Africa (90); auth, Law Library Design 1986-1995: University of Connecticut School of Law Library, a compilation, 94; auth, Library Design Technology: Technical Specifications for Library Design, forthcoming. **CONTACT ADDRESS** Dept Law, Fla Coastal Sch of Law, 7555 Beach Blvd, Jacksonville, FL 32216-3003. **EMAIL** dstone@fcsl.edu

STONE, JEROME ARTHUR
PERSONAL Born 04/29/1935, Holden, MA, m, 1953, 2 children **DISCIPLINE** PHILOSOPHY, RELIGIOUS STUDIES **EDUCATION** Univ Chicago, BA, 54; Andover Newton Theol Sch, MDiv, 58; Univ Chicago, MA, 64, PhD Philos Relig, 73. **CAREER** Teacher Philos & Relig, Kendall Col, 64-81, chmn, Philos Dept, 68-81, dir, Humanities Div, 74-75; prof Philos, William Rainey Harper Col, 81-, adj assoc prof, Christopher Newport Col, Col William St Mary, 75. **MEMBERSHIPS** Am Philos Asn; Am Acad Relig; NAm Paul Tillich Soc; Asn Develop Philos Teaching (pres, 82-83). **RESEARCH** Environmental Ethics; Cross-cultural philosophy of religion; philosophical hermeneutics; the logic of moral reasoning. **SELECTED PUBLICATIONS** Auth, Tillich and Schelling's later philosophy, In: Kairos and Logos, NAm Paul Tillich Soc, 78; contribr, Samuel Alexander, In: Twentieth-Century Thinkers, Gale Research press; coed, The Chicago School of Theology, 2 Vols, Edwin Mellen, 96. **CONTACT ADDRESS** Dept of Philosophy, William Rainey Harper Col, 1200 W Algonquin, Palatine, IL 60067-7398. **EMAIL** jstone@harper.cc.il.us

STONE, RONALD HENRY
PERSONAL Born 03/26/1939, Humboldt, IA, m, 1984, 2 children **DISCIPLINE** SOCIAL ETHICS, RELIGION **EDUCATION** Morningside Col, BA, 60; Union Theol Sem, BD, 63; Columbia Univ, PhD(relig, soc), 68. **CAREER** Instr ethics, Union Theol Sem, 67-68; asst prof relig, Columbia Univ, 68-69; assoc prof ethics, 69-72, John Witherspoon Prof, Christian Ethics, Pittsburgh Theol Sem, 72-; Adj prof relig, Univ Pittsburgh, 72-81; vis scholar, Cambridge Univ, 72 & Harvard Univ, 75; Trinity College, Oxford, 99. **HONORS AND AWARDS** Am Asn Theol Schs fac grant, 72 & 75. **MEMBERSHIPS** Am Acad Relig; Am Soc Christian Ethics; Am Theol Soc. **RESEARCH** Political ethics; religion and society; Christian political biography. **SELECTED PUBLICATIONS** Ed, Faith and Politics, Braziller, 68; auth, Reinhold Niebuhr: Prophet to Politicians, Abingdon, 72; Realism and Hope, Univ Press Am, 77; ed, Liberation and Change, 77 & Paul Tillich's Radical Social Thought, 80, John Knox; Profesor Reinhold Niebuhr, Westminster, 92; auth, The Ultimate Imperative, Pilgrim Press, 99. **CONTACT ADDRESS** 616 N Highland Ave, Pittsburgh, PA 15206-2525. **EMAIL** rstone@pts.edu

STONE, S. L.
PERSONAL Born 12/01/1952, New York, NY, m, 4 children **DISCIPLINE** RELIGION **EDUCATION** Princeton Univ, BA, 74; Yale Univ, 74-75; Columbia Univ Law Schl, JD, 78. **CAREER** Law clerk, 78-79, Judge John Minor Wisdom, 5th Circuit, US Court of Appeals; atty; 79-83, Paul, Weiss, Rifkind, Wharton & Garrison, NY Litigation Dept; assoc dean, 87-90, Acad Affairs, prof, 83-, Benjamin Cardozo Schl of Law. **HONORS AND AWARDS** Stone Scholar, Columbia Univ; Danforth Fel in Relig & Class Civilization, Yale Univ; BA summa cum laude; Phi Beta Kappa; Univ Scholar George Potts Prize; John Robinson Mem Prize, Princeton. **MEMBERSHIPS** Comm of Profes & Judical Ethics; Comm on Fed Courts; Comm on Legal Ed; Bar Assn of NY; Intl Assn Jewish Lawyers and Jurists. **SELECTED PUBLICATIONS** Art, The Preclusive Effect of State Court Judgments on Subsequent 1983 Actions, 78 Columbia Law Rev, 78; art, Sinaitic and Noahide Law: Legal Pluralism in Jewish Law, 12 Cardozo Law Rev 1157, 91; art, The Transformation of Prophecy, 4 Cardozo Stud in Law & Lit, 167, 92; art, Judaism and Postmodernism, 14 Cardozo Law Rev 98, 93; art, In Pursuit of the Countertext: The Turn to the Jewish Legal Model in Contemporary American Legal Theory, 106 Harvard Law Rev 813, 93; art, The Emergence of Jewish Law In Postmodernist Legal Theory, Harvard Law Schl Occas Paper Ser, 2/94; art, Justice, Mercy, and Gender in Rabbinic Thought, 8 Cardozo Stud in Law & Lit 139, 96; art, What Do American Jews Believe, Symposium, Comm Mag, 96. **CONTACT ADDRESS** Cardozo Sch of Law, 55 5th Ave, New York, NY 10003. **EMAIL** sstone@ymail.yu.edu

STONE, VICTOR J.
PERSONAL Born 03/11/1921, Chicago, IL, m, 3 children **DISCIPLINE** LAW **EDUCATION** Oberlin Col, AB, 42; Columbia Univ, LLB, 48. **CAREER** Assoc law, Sch Law, Columbia Univ, 48-49; res assoc, Sch Law, Univ Chicago, 53-55; from asst prof to assoc prof, 55-59, Prof Law, Col Law, Univ IL, Urbana-Champaign, 59-, Ford Found law fac fel int legal studies, 62-63; lectr comp law, Int Univ Comp Sci, Luxembourg, 63; vchmn, Ill State Appellate Defender Comn, 73-77 & 78-80; assoc vpres acad affairs, Univ IL, Urbana-Champaign, 75-78; Am Asn Univ Prof, gen coun 78-79, pres 82-84. **HONORS AND AWARDS** LL.D, Oberlin Col, 83. **MEMBERSHIPS** Am Bar Asn; Am Judicature Soc; AAUP (pres, 82-84). **RESEARCH** Judicial administration and procedure; American federalism; conflict of laws. **SELECTED PUBLICATIONS** Coauth, Illinois Pattern Instructions, West Publ, 2nd ed, 71; auth, Original process and appearance, In: Illinois Civil Practice Before Trial, Inst Continuing Educ of Bar, 73; ed, Civil Liberties and Civil Rights: The David C Bawn Memorial Lectures, Univ of IL, 77. **CONTACT ADDRESS** Col of Law, Univ of Illinois, Urbana-Champaign, 504 E Pennsylvania, Champaign, IL 61820-6909. **EMAIL** vstone@law.uiuc.edu

STORCH, STEVEN R.
DISCIPLINE PHILOSOPHY **EDUCATION** SUNY Buffalo, BA, 87; PhD, 97. **CAREER** Vis Prof, 98-, NC St Univ; Vis Prof, NC Weseley Col, 97-. **MEMBERSHIPS** APA; North Amer Sartre Soc. **RESEARCH** Sartre stud; ethics, continental philos. **CONTACT ADDRESS** 2716 Little River Dr, Hillsborough, NC 27278. **EMAIL** storchs@aol.com

STORTZ, MARTHA ELLEN
DISCIPLINE HISTORICAL THEOLOGY; ETHICS **EDUCATION** Carleton Col, BA; Univ Chicago, MA, PhD. **CAREER** Prof **HONORS AND AWARDS** Mem, convener, GTU Core Dr fac; adv comm, LCA Study on Issues Concerning Homosexuality, 86; bd mem,, Ctr for Women and Rel, GTU; ELCA rep, Intl Consult of Lutheran Women Theologians, Helsinki, 91. **MEMBERSHIPS** Mem, Ctr for Global Edu, Augsburg Col; ELCA Task Force on Theol Edu; ELCA Commn for Church in Soc Bd. **SELECTED PUBLICATIONS** Auth, PastorPower, Abingdon Press, 93. **CONTACT ADDRESS** Dept of Historical Theology and Ethics, Pacific Lutheran Theol Sem, 2770 Marin Ave, Berkeley, CA 94708-1597. **EMAIL** mstortz@autobahn.org

STORY, J. LYLE
DISCIPLINE BIBLICAL LANGUAGES; NEW TESTAMENT **EDUCATION** Sterling Col, BA; Fuller Theol Sem, MDiv, PhD. **CAREER** Assoc dean; prof, 84. **SELECTED PUBLICATIONS** Auth, Greek To Me; The Greek Memory System; contrib auth, The Spirit-Filled Life Bible. **CONTACT ADDRESS** Dept of Biblical Languages and New Testament, Regent Univ, 1000 Regent Univ Dr, Virginia Beach, VA 23464-9831.

STOWERS, STANLEY KENT
PERSONAL Born 02/24/1948, Munice, IN, m, 1968, 2 children **DISCIPLINE** HISTORY OF EARLY CHRISTIANITY **EDUCATION** Abilene Christian Univ, AB, 70; Princeton Theol Sem, MA, 74; Yale Univ, PhD(relig studies), 79. **CAREER** Asst prof relig studies, Phillips Univ, 79-80; Asst Prof Relig Studies, 81-91, PROF REL STUDIES, BROWN UNIV, 91-. **HONORS AND AWARDS** Sheridan Teaching Awd, 97; Woodrow Wilson fel, 92; NEH fel, 91; FIAT fel, 90. **MEMBERSHIPS** Am Acad Relig; Soc Bibl Lit. **RESEARCH** Early Christianity; Hellenistic philosophy; early Christian literature; Greek Religion. **SELECTED PUBLICATIONS** Auth, The Diatribe and Paul's Letter to the Romans, Scholars Press, 81; auth, A Rereading of Romans, Yal Univ Press, 94; auth, Letter Writing in Greco-Roman Anqiquity, Westminster Press, 86. **CONTACT ADDRESS** Dept of Relig Studies, Brown Univ, Box 1927, Providence, RI 02912-9127. **EMAIL** Stanley_Stowers@brown.edu

STRAMEL, JAMES
PERSONAL Born 04/05/1960, Salina, KS **DISCIPLINE** PHILOSOPHY **EDUCATION** Univ Southern Calif, MA, 85, PhD, 96. **CAREER** Adj fac, Santa Monica Col. **MEMBERSHIPS** APA. **RESEARCH** Ethics, gay studies. **SELECTED PUBLICATIONS** Auth, A New Verdict on the Jury Passage: Theaetetus 201a-c, Ancient Philos, 89; auth, How to Write a Philosophy Paper, Univ Press of Am, 94; auth, Outing, Ethics and Politics: A Reply to Mohr, in Corvino, ed, Same Sex: Debating the Ethics, Culture, and Science of Homosexuality, Rowman & Littlefield, 97. **CONTACT ADDRESS** 201 Ocean Park Blvd, #C, Santa Monica, CA 90405. **EMAIL** stramel_james@smc.edu

STRANG, J. V.
PERSONAL Born 10/14/1942, Kirtland, OH, s **DISCIPLINE** PHILOSOPHY **EDUCATION** Boston Univ, PhD, 84. **CAREER** Lctr, Plymouth State Col, 90-; Exec dir, Boston Conservative Soc, 87-94. **RESEARCH** Ancient Philosophy; Political Philosophy; Ethics. **CONTACT ADDRESS** Dept of Philosophy, Plymouth State Col, Univ System of New Hampshire, 17 Allston St, Dorchester, MA 02124. **EMAIL** jstrang@mail.plymouth.edu

STRANGE, JAMES F.
PERSONAL Born 02/02/1938, Pampa, TX, m, 1960, 4 children **DISCIPLINE** BIBLICAL STUDIES, ARCHEOLOGY **EDUCATION** Rice Univ, BA, 59; Yale Univ, MDiv, 64; Drew Univ, PhD, 70. **CAREER** Asst prof, 72-75, assoc prof, 75-80, prof relig studies, Univ S Fla, Tampa, 80-, dean col arts & lett, 81-89, Montgomery fel, William F Albright Inst Archaeol Res, Jerusalem, 70-71; fel Off Judeo-Christian Studies, Duke Univ, 71-72; asoc dir, Joint Exped to Khirbet Shema', Israel, 71-73; assoc dir, Meiron Excavation Proj, Israel, 73-78; vis lectr, Univ of the Orange Free State, Repub S Africa, 79; Nat Endowment for Humanities fel, Jerusalem, 80; dir, Survey in Galilee, 82; dir USF Excavations at Sepphoris, Israel, 83; dir, Excavations Qumran, 96; Benjamin Meaker vis prof Inst Advan Stud, Univ Bristol, 97. **HONORS AND AWARDS** Samuel Robinson Lect, Wake Forest Univ, 81; ; Herbert G. May Memorial Lecture, Oberlin Col, 88; The Parkhurst Lectures, Southwestern Col, 91; McMannis Lect, Wheaton Col, 96. **MEMBERSHIPS** Soc Bibl Lit; Israel Explor Soc; Am Schs Orient Res; NY Acad Sci; Soc Sci Explor. **RESEARCH** Archaeology of Israel in Roman to Arab times; Roman and Byzantine ceramics in the Eastern Mediterranean; computer models for Roman-Byzantine archaeology and historical geography. **SELECTED PUBLICATIONS** Coauth, Archaeology and rabbinic tradition at Khirbet Shema, the 1970 and 1971 campaigns, Bibl Archaeologist, 72; Excavations at Meiron in Upper Galilee--1971, 1972, 74 & auth, Late Hellenistic and Herodian ossuary tombs at French Hill, Jerusalem, 75, Bull of Am Schs of Orient Res; coauth, Ancient Synagogue Excavations at Khirbet Shema, Upper Galilee, Israel 1970-1972, Duke Univ, 76; auth, Capernaum, Crucifixion, Methods of, & Magdala, Interpreter's Dictionary of Bible, suppl vol, 76; Excavations at Meiron, in Upper Galilee--1974, 1975: A second preliminary report, 78 & coauth, Excavations at Meiron, 81, Am Schs of Orient Res; Archaeology and the religion of Judaism, Aufstieg und Niedergang der Roemischen Welt, 81; coauth, The Excavations at the Ancient Synagogue of Gush Halav, Israel, 90; co-ed, "Ancient Texts, Archaeology as Text, and the Problem of the First Century Synagogue," The Evolution of the Synagogue, Valley Forge: Trinity Press International, 00. **CONTACT ADDRESS** Dept Relig Studies, Univ of So Florida, 4202 Fowler Ave, CPR 107, Tampa, FL 33620-9951. **EMAIL** strange@chuma1.cas.usf.edu

STRANGE, STEVEN K.
DISCIPLINE ANCIENT PHILOSOPHY **EDUCATION** Univ TX, PhD, 81. **CAREER** Philos, Emory Univ. **RESEARCH** Ancient philos, especially Platonism and Hellenistic philosophy, the hist of Platonism, and the hist of ethics. **SELECTED PUBLICATIONS** Transl, Porphyry, On Aristotle's Categories. **CONTACT ADDRESS** Emory Univ, Atlanta, GA 30322-1950. **EMAIL** philsks@emory.edu

STRASSER, MARK
PERSONAL Born 06/15/1955, Bridgeport, CT **DISCIPLINE** PHILOSOPHY **EDUCATION** Harvard Col, BA, 77; Univ Chicago, MA, 80, PhD, 84; Stanford Law Schl, JD, 93. **CAREER** Asst prof, phil, 84-87, Univ Texas, Arlington; asst prof, phil, 87-90, Wash Univ, MO; asst prof, 93-96, assoc prof, law, 96-99, Capital Univ Law Schl; prof of Law, Capital Univ, 99-; vis prof, Univ of Maryland, 99-00. **HONORS AND AWARDS** NEH sum sem vis fel, ethics & med, Houston TX, 86; NEH sum Inst, Lincoln NE, 84. **RESEARCH** Constitutional law; bioethics & law. **SELECTED PUBLICATIONS** Auth, Francis Hutcheson's Moral Theory: Its Form and Utility, Longwood Academic/Hollowbrook Commun, 90; auth, The Moral Philosophy of John Stuart Mill: Toward Modifications of Contemporary Utilitarianism, Longwood Academic/Hollowbrook Commun, 91; auth, Agency, Free Will, and Moral Responsibility, Hollowbrook Pub, 92; auth, Legally Wed: Same-Sex Marriage and the Constitution, Cornell Univ Press, 97; auth, "Baker and Some Recipes for Disaster: On DOMA, Covenant Marriages, and Full Faith and Credit Jurisprudence," 64, (98): 307-351; auth, "Consstitutional limitations and Baehr Possibilities: On Retroactive Legislation, Reasonable Expectations, and Manifest Injustice," 29, Rutgers L.J, (98): 271-314; auth, The Challence of Same-Sex Marriage: Federalist Principles and Constitutional Protections, Prareger Publishers/Greenwood Publishing Group, 99; auth, "From Colorado to Alaska by Way of Cincinnati: On Romer, Equality Foundation, and the Constitutionality of Referenda, 36, Hous. L. Rev., (99): 1193-1250; auth, The Privileges of National Citizenship: On Saenz, Same-Sex Couples, and the right to Travel, 52, Rutgers L. Rev, (00): 553-588. **CONTACT ADDRESS** Law Sch, Capital Univ, 4334 Brookie Ct, Columbus, OH 43214. **EMAIL** mstrasser@law.capital.edu

STRAUMANIS, JOAN
PERSONAL Born 02/10/1937, New York, NY, w, 1969, 3 children **DISCIPLINE** PHILOSOPHY; MATHEMATICS **EDUCATION** Antioch Col, BA, 57; Univ Col, MA, 59; Univ Maryland, PhD, 74 **CAREER** Tchg asst, Dept of Philos, Univ Maryland, 69-71; Prog Off, Nat Sci Found, 77-78; vis res prof, Dept of Philos, Univ Bristol, 80; from asst prof, 71-76, to assoc prof, 76-82, to prof, 82, Dept of Philos, Denison Univ; prof of Philos, 82-86, Assoc Provost, 82-83, Acad Dean, 83-86, Kenyon Col; prof of Philos & Dean of Fac, 86-92, Rollins Col; Prog Off, 92-95, consult & adj, 95-, FIPSE US Dept of Educ; Herbert & Ann Siegel Dean, Col Arts & Sci, 95-97, dean emer & prof of philosophy, 97-99, Lehigh Univ; prog officer, FIPSE US Dept of Ed, 99-. **HONORS AND AWARDS** Univ Col Found Grad fel, 57-58; US Steel Found Grad fel, 67-69; Danforth Assoc, 76; Awd Excellence Tchg Univ Maryland, 70; Omicron Delta Kappa, 81; Fac Ldr Awd, Denison Univ, 81. **MEMBERSHIPS** Amer Civil Liberties Union; Proj Kalaeidoscope; W Asn Schools & Col; Amer Philos Soc. **RESEARCH** Philosophy of science; Logic; Reform of science education; Womens studies **SELECTED PUBLICATIONS** Auth, The Case Against Human Sociobiology, Amer Philos Asn, 83; Of Sissies and Spinsters: Shifts in Value of Sex-Marked Terms, Amer Philos Asn, Chicago, 83; A Laboratory Manual for the Philosophy of Biology, Philosophy of Biology in the Philosophy Cirriculum, San Fran Univ, 83; auth, Duties to Oneself: An Ethical Basis for Self-Liberation? Jour Soc Philos, 84; Explosive Freedom: Impressions of Glasnost, Rollins Alumni Rec, 88; Struggles with the Maxwell Demon, Rollins Col, 88; Support Issues, The Use of Symbolic Computation in Undergraduate Mathematics, Math Asn Amer, 92; rev, A Deans-Eye View: The Golden Age of Universities on the Make, Change, 92. **CONTACT ADDRESS** FIPSE, 1990 K St NW 8th Fl, Washington, DC 20006-8544. **EMAIL** joan_strausmanis@ed.gov

STRAUSBERG, STEPHEN FREDERICK
PERSONAL Born 09/03/1943, Brooklyn, NY **DISCIPLINE** ECONOMIC HISTORY **EDUCATION** Brooklyn Col, BA, 64; Cornell Univ, PhD(hist), 70. **CAREER** Res historian, US Pub Land Law Rev Comn, 66-67; asst prof, 68-82, ASSOC PROF HIST, UNIV ARK, FAYETTEVILLE, 82-, Proj planner, Ark Humanities Prog, 76-78. **HONORS AND AWARDS** Outstanding Humanist, Ark Humanities Prog, 76. **MEMBERSHIPS** AHA; Orgn Am Historians. **RESEARCH** Southern economic history; history of public lands; Arkansas history. **SELECTED PUBLICATIONS** Contribr, History of the Public Domain, US Govt Printing Off, 69; Historical Abstracts, 72-76 & America, 73-76, ABC-Clio; auth, Federal Stewardship on the Frontier, Arno, 78; Swamplands in Indiana, Ind J Hist, 78; The New Deal in Arkansas, The Depression in the Southwest, Kennikat Press, 80. **CONTACT ADDRESS** Dept of Hist, Univ of Arkansas, Fayetteville, Fayetteville, AR 72701-1202.

STRAUSS, MARCY
PERSONAL 2 children **DISCIPLINE** LAW **EDUCATION** Northwestern Univ, BS, 78; Georgetown Univ, JD, 81. **CAREER** Prof, Loyola Univ 84-; clerk, hon James B. Moran US Dist Ct, Northern Dist Ill, 81-83. **RESEARCH** Writes on, freedom of speech & other Const issues. **CONTACT ADDRESS** Law School, Loyola Marymount Univ, 919 S Albany, Burns 403, Los Angeles, CA 90015. **EMAIL** mstrauss@lmulaw.lmu.edu

STRAUSS, MARK
PERSONAL Born 11/16/1959, Fort Worth, TX, m, 1984, 3 children **DISCIPLINE** NEW TESTAMENT **EDUCATION** Westmont Coll, BA; Talbot School Theol, Mdiv, ThM; Univ Aberdeen, PhD. **CAREER** Prof, Christian Heritage Coll, 92-95; Prof, Bethel Sem San Diego, 93-. **MEMBERSHIPS** Soc of Bibl Lit; Evangel Theol Soc; Inst for Bibl Res. **RESEARCH** New Testament; Bible Translation; Hermeneutics. **SELECTED PUBLICATIONS** Mark L. Strauss, The Davidic Messiah in Luke-Acts (Sheffield: Sheffield Academic Press, 95); Distorting Scripture? The Challenge of Bible Translation and Gender Accuracy (Downers Grove, IL: InterVarsity), 98. **CONTACT ADDRESS** 1565 Avenida Ladera, El Cajon, CA 92020-1303. **EMAIL** m-strauss@bethel.edu

STRAUSS, PETER L.
PERSONAL Born 02/26/1940, New York, NY, m, 1964, 2 children **DISCIPLINE** ADMINISTRATIVE LAW **EDUCATION** Harvard Univ, AB, 61; Yale Univ, LLB, 64. **CAREER** Law clerk, US Ct Appeals, DC, 64-65 & US Supreme Ct, 65-66; lectr criminal law, Haile Sellassi I Univ, 66-68; asst to solicitor gen, US Dept Justice, 68-71; Prof, Admin, Const & Family Law, Columbia Law Sch, 71-; Consult admin law, US Admin conf, 71-74 & 77-80; gen coun, US Nuclear Regulatory Comn, 75-77; consult, ABA Coordr, Group on Regulatory Reform, 80-. **HONORS AND AWARDS** U S Dept of Justice 71; US NRC 77. **MEMBERSHIPS** Am Asn Law Sch; Soc Am Law Teachers; Am Bar Asn. **RESEARCH** Infrastructure of agency rulemaking; presidential participation in agency action; administrative law reform. **SELECTED PUBLICATIONS** Ed, Fetha Nagast, The Law of the Kings, Haile Sellassi I Univ, 68; auth, Gellhorn & Byse's Administrative Law: Cases and Comments, with Rakoff, Schotland, and Farina; Administrative Law Problems, Verkuil, 79 & 83; auth, An Introduction to Administrative Justice in the United States, Carolina Acad Pr, 89. **CONTACT ADDRESS** Law Sch, Columbia Univ, 435 W 116th St, New York, NY 10027-7201. **EMAIL** strauss@law.columbia.edu

STREETER, JARVIS
PERSONAL Born 07/06/1949, Oakland, CA, m, 1988, 2 children **DISCIPLINE** RELIGIOUS STUDIES **EDUCATION** Univ Southern Calif, Los Angeles BA, 71; Luther Sem St Paul, MD, 82; Yale Univ Divinity School, New Haven, STM, 82; Southern Methodist Univ, Dallas, PhD, 90. **CAREER** Teacher of Math and Sci, Kiriani Harambee High School, Kenya, 71-72; pastoral asst, Ascension Lutheran Church Thousand Oaks, 73-74; vicar and lectr, Gustavus Adolphus Coll, St Peter, 76-77; lec tr, Luther Sem St Paul, 76-77; pastor, St Andrew Lutheran Church and Church of the Christ the Redeemer, 78-79; lectr, Augsburg Coll, Minneapolis, 80; lectr, Southern Methodist Univ Perkins School Theol, 86-87; asst prof, calif Lutheran Univ, 88-93; assoc prof, Calif Lutheran Univ, 93-. **HONORS AND AWARDS** Res Fel, Yale Univ Divinity School, 82-83; Grad Program in Rel Studies Fel, Southern Methodist Univ, 83-88; Outstanding Prof of the Year, Calif Lutheran Univ, 91; Hewlett Foundation Sabbatical Fel, 94. **MEMBERSHIPS** Am Acad of Rel; Evangel Lutheran Church in Am. **RESEARCH** Religion. **SELECTED PUBLICATIONS** Auth, Human nature and Human Sinfulness: Ernest Becker's Anthropology and the Contemporary Western Erbsunde Debate, 90; The Development of Ernest Becker's Anthropology, Soundings: An Interdisciplinary J, forthcoming. **CONTACT ADDRESS** California Lutheran Univ, 60 W Olsen Rd, Thousand Oaks, CA 91360. **EMAIL** streeter@clunet.edu

STRICKLAND, HENRY C.
PERSONAL Born 10/04/1958, Atlanta, GA, m, 1987, 3 children **DISCIPLINE** LAW **EDUCATION** Presbyterian Col, BA, 80; Vanderbilt Univ, Sch Law, JD, 83. **CAREER** Asst prof, 88-92, assoc prof, 92-97, prof, Cumberland Sch of Law, Samford Univ, Birmingham, Ala, 97-. **HONORS AND AWARDS** Who's Who Among America's Teachers, 94-98. **MEMBERSHIPS** ABA (Section of Dispute Resolution), Asn of Am Law Schs (Section of Dispute Resolution). **RESEARCH** Arbitration law; U.S. Constitutional Law (14th Amendment). **SELECTED PUBLICATIONS** Coauth, "Modern Arbitration for Alabama: A Concept Whose Time Has Come," 25 Cumberland Law Rev, 59 (95); auth, "Allied-Bruce Terminix, Inc v Dobson: Widespread Enforcement of Arbitration Agreements Arrives in Alabama, " 56 Ala Lawyer, 238 (July 95); auth, "Does the Federal Arbitration Act Bar States from Requiring that Arbitration Provisions Be Conspicuous?," Preview of United States Supreme Court Cases, 1995-96 Term, Issue No 7 (April 4 96); auth, "Does the Due Process Clause Require Workers' Compensation Insurers to Give Notice to Employees Before Suspending Payment of Disputed Bills?," Preview of United States Supreme Court Cases, 1998-99 Term, Issue No 4 (Dec 31, 98). **CONTACT ADDRESS** Sch of Law, Samford Univ, 800 Lakeshore Dr, Birmingham, AL 35229-0001.

STRICKLAND, RUTH ANN
PERSONAL Born 09/23/1959, Goldsboro, NC, m, 1999, 1 child **DISCIPLINE** POLITICAL SCIENCE **EDUCATION** Univ of South Carolina, PhD, 89. **CAREER** Prof, Appalachian State Univ, 12 years. **HONORS AND AWARDS** Inducted into the Acad of Outstanding Teachers, Coll of Arts and Sciences, 98. **MEMBERSHIPS** Amer Political Science Assn; NC Political Sci Assn. **RESEARCH** Amer natl government; public policy analysis; judicial process. **SELECTED PUBLICATIONS** Auth, "The Incivility of Mandated Drug Treatment through Civil Commitments," Politics and Life Sciences, Mar 96; coauth, "North Carolina v. Robert Lee Carter: Good Faith Exceptions and New Judicial Federalism in North Carolina," Albany Law Review, v 59, n 5, 96; coauth, "The NAFTA(-ization) of Sexual Harassment: The Experiences of Canada, Mexico, and the United States," NAFTA: Law and Business Review Jour of the Americas, Spring 97; coauth, Contemporary World Issues: Campaign and Election Reform: A Reference Handbook, 1997; auth, "Abortion: Pro-choice versus Pro-life, " in Moral Controversies in American Politics: Cases in Social Regulatory Policy, 1998. **CONTACT ADDRESS** Dept of Political Sci & Criminal Justice, Appalachian State Univ, Boone, NC 28608. **EMAIL** strcklndra@appstate.edu

STRICKMAN, NORMAN
PERSONAL Born 03/09/1940, Brooklyn, NY, m, 1961, 2 children **DISCIPLINE** JUDAIC STUDIES **EDUCATION** Yeshiva Univ, BA, 61; Bernard Revel Grad School, MHL, 63; Dropsie Univ, PhD, 70. **CAREER** Assoc Prof and Chair, Touro Col, 75-; **HONORS AND AWARDS** Memorial Foundation for Jewish Studies, 70. **MEMBERSHIPS** Asn for Jewish Studies, Rabbinical Coun of Am, NY Board of Rabbis. **RESEARCH** Medieval Jewish Philosophy, Abraham Ibn Ezra **SELECTED PUBLICATIONS** Auth, Ibn Ezra's Commentary on the Pentateuch (NUMBERS), Menorah Press, 99; auth, Ibn Ezra's Commentary on the Pentateuch (EXODUS), Menorah Press, 96; auth, Ibn Ezra's Commentary on the Pentateuch (GENESIS), Menorah Press, 88; auth, "Rabbenu Zerachiah and His Work, Part III," Ha-Darom; auth, "Rabbenu Zerachiah Ha-Levi and His Work, Part II," Ha-Darom; auth, "Rabbenu Zerachiah Ha-Levi and His Work, Part I," Ha-Darom; auth, "A Note on the Text of the Babylonian Talmud Gittin 6a," Jewish Quarterly Review, 76; auth, "Rabbenu Zerachiah Ha-Levi and His Work The Ma'or," Bitzaron, 74 **CONTACT ADDRESS** Dept Judaic Studies, Touro Col, New York, 27 W 23rd St, New York, NY 10010-4202.

STRIEDER, LEON
PERSONAL Born 03/10/1950, Sealy, TX, s **DISCIPLINE** LITURGY, SACRAMENTS **EDUCATION** Univ St Thomas, BA, 72; Gregorian Univ, Rome, STB, 75; Pontifical Liturgical Inst, Rome, SLL, 80; SLD, 94. **CAREER** Hispanic Min, Dio Austen, 76-82; Campus Min, TX AM Univ, 82-90; Form Fac, St Mary's Sem, 90-; adj UST, Sch Theology. **MEMBERSHIPS** Southwest Lit Con Bd; NFLCB. **RESEARCH** All aspects of Liturgical life in the Roman Catholic Church. **SELECTED PUBLICATIONS** Auth, The Promise of Obedience in Ordination Rites. **CONTACT ADDRESS** Dept Theology, Univ of St. Thomas, Texas, 9845 Memorial Dr, Houston, TX 77024. **EMAIL** strieder@stthom.edu

STRIKWERDS, ROBERT A.
PERSONAL 3 children **DISCIPLINE** PHILOSOPHY **EDUCATION** Univ of Notre Dame, PhD, 82. **CAREER** Ind Univ **MEMBERSHIPS** Am Philosophical Asn, Philosophy of Science Asn, Asn for Practical and Professional Ethics, National Collegiate Honors Council. **RESEARCH** Ethics; philosophy of social sciences. **CONTACT ADDRESS** Indiana Univ, Kokomo, 2300 S Washington St, PO Box 9003, Kokomo, IN 48904-9003.

STROBLE, PAUL E., JR.
PERSONAL Born 01/02/1957, Vandalia, IL, m, 1984, 1 child **DISCIPLINE** RELIGION **EDUCATION** Greenville Col, BA, 79; Yale Divin School, MDiv, 82; Univ of Virginia, PhD, 91. **CAREER** Illinois Dept Conserv, researcher, historic sites, 78-79; Albertus Magnus Coll, ta, 81-82; Univ of Virginia, grad asst, 86-87; N Arizona Univ, p/t instr, 87-91; Linsey Wilson Col, p/t instr, 91; Spalding Univ, p/t instr, 91-95; Presbyterian Theol Sem, 92-, Univ of Louisville, adj instr, 97-99; Indiana Univ S/E, adj instr, 95-. **MEMBERSHIPS** AAR, ISHS, PAS, KBSNA **RESEARCH** Karl Barth and 20th Cent Philo; Antebellum Amer hist; teaching of philo and relig; creative writing. **SELECTED PUBLICATIONS** Auth, Advent Christmas 1997 Study Book: Scriptures for the Church Season, United Methodist Publishing House, 97; Journeys Home: Thoughts and Places, Self pub/illus, 95; The Social Ontology of Karl Barth, Intl Scholars Pub, 94; High on the Okaw's Western Bank: Vandalia, IL, 1819-1839, Univ of Illinois Press, 92; History of Methodism in Louisville and Jefferson County, Kentucky, Encycl of Louisville, f/c; Kentucky Council of Churches, 1947-1997, commis booklet, 97; Ferdinand Ernst and the German Colony at Vandalia, Illinois History Teacher, 97; Systems and Leadership in the Parish, The Quart Rev, 95; Destined in Love: Lectionary Texts By and About Paul, The Quart Rev, 96; Without Running Riot: Kant, Analogical Language and Theological Discourse, Sophia: Jour of Philo, 93. **CONTACT ADDRESS** Dept of Religious Studies, Indiana Univ, Southeast, 8919 Bingham Dr, Louisville, KY 40242-3366. **EMAIL** 103501.466@compuserve.com

STROH, GUY WESTON
PERSONAL Born 03/28/1931, Elizabeth, NJ, m, 1966 **DISCIPLINE** PHILOSOPHY **EDUCATION** Princeton Univ, AB, 53, Am, 55, PhD(Philos), 57. **CAREER** From asst prof to assoc prof, 56-66, prof Philos, Rider Col, 66-, chmn dept, 63-. **HONORS AND AWARDS** Lindback Found Awd, 66. **MEMBERSHIPS** Am Philos Asn; AAUP; C S Peirce Soc. **RESEARCH** American philosophy; ethics; philosophy of mind. **SELECTED PUBLICATIONS** Auth, Plato and Aristotle, An Introduction, Rider Col, 64; American Philosophy from Edwards to Dewey, Van Nostrand, 68; Professor Feibleman's philosophy in relation to currents of the twentieth century, Studium Gen, Heidelberg, 7/71; Mind and spirit in Feibleman's philosophy, Tulane Studies in Philos, 76; American Ethical Thought, Nelson Hall, 79; The Moral Vision of Diana Trilling, Explorations: 20th Century, 92. **CONTACT ADDRESS** Dept of Philosophy, Rider Univ, 2083 Lawrenceville Rd., Lawrenceville, NJ 08648-3099. **EMAIL** philosophy@rider.com

STROKER, WILLIAM DETTWILLER
PERSONAL Born 05/23/1938, Paris, KY, m, 1967, 1 child **DISCIPLINE** NEW TESTAMENT STUDIES, HELLENISTIC RELIGIONS, EARLY CHRISTIANITY **EDUCATION** Transylvania Univ, BA, 60; Yale Univ, BD, 63, MA, 66, PhD, 70. **CAREER** From instr to asst prof, 69-76, assoc prof Relig, 76-82, Prof Relig, Drew Univ, 82-. **HONORS AND AWARDS** Scholar-Teacher of the Year, Drew Univ, 89. **MEMBERSHIPS** Soc Bibl Lit. **RESEARCH** Non-Canonical traditions about Jesus; religious thought of the hellenistic period; Pauline theology and influence. **SELECTED PUBLICATIONS** Auth, "Extracanonical Sayings of Jesus," 89. **CONTACT ADDRESS** Dept of Relig, Drew Univ, 36 Madison Ave, Madison, NJ 07940-1493. **EMAIL** wstroker@drew.edu

STROLL, AVRUM
PERSONAL Born 02/15/1921, Oakland, CA, m, 1955, 2 children **DISCIPLINE** PHILOSOPHY **EDUCATION** Univ Calif, Berkeley, PhD, 51. **CAREER** Univ Oregon, 50-51; Univ British Columbia, 52-63; Univ Calif, San Diego, 63-. **HONORS AND AWARDS** All Univ Calif lectr, 65; Guggenheim fel, 73. **MEMBERSHIPS** APA. **RESEARCH** Philosophy of language; epistemology; history of modern philos. **SELECTED PUBLICATIONS** Auth, That Puzzle We Call the Mind, Grazer Philosophische Studien, 93; auth, Moore and Wittgenstein on Certainty, Oxford Univ, 94; ed, Epistemology: New Essays in the Theory of Knowledge, London, 94; auth, On Following a Rule, in Egidi, ed, Wittgenstein: Mind and Language, Kluwer, 95; auth, The Argument from Possibility, in Skepticism in the History of Philosophy, Kluwer, 96; auth, Ethics Without Principles, Proceedings of the 18th International Wittgenstein Symposium, 96; auth, Sketches of Landscapes: Philosophy by Example, MIT, 98; auth, Twentieth Century Analytic Philosophy, in, A History of Western Philosophy, Columbia, 98; auth, G.E. Moore, in Cambridge Companion to the Philosophers Series, Blackwell, 98; auth, G. E. Moore, in, The Encyclopedia of Empiricism, Greenwood, 98; auth, Twentieth Century Analytic Philos, Columbia, 00. **CONTACT ADDRESS** Dept of Philosophy, Univ of California, San Diego, La Jolla, CA 92093. **EMAIL** astroll@ucsd.edu

STROM, LYLE E.
DISCIPLINE LAW **EDUCATION** Creighton Univ, BA, JD. **CAREER** Clin prof & dir, Robert M. Spire Internship Prog; pvt pract, Omaha, 53-85; from mem US dist Ct dist Nebr, 85 to ch judge, 87-94 and sr judge, 95; ch, Gender Fairness Task Force for the 8th Circuit; co-ch, Fed Practice Comt US dist Ct dist Nebr; adj fac, Creighton Law Sch, tchg Munic Corp, 58-70 and Trial Pract, 74-95. **HONORS AND AWARDS** Highest Triennial Average awd, 53. **MEMBERSHIPS** Eighth Circuit Judicial Conf comt; exec comt and bd trustees, Mid-Am Coun Boy Scouts Am; past pres, Nebr State Bar Asn & Omaha Bar Asn; House Deleg, Nebr State Bar Asn; Nebr Supreme Ct Comt on Practice and Procedure. **SELECTED PUBLICATIONS** Auth, Nebraska Jury Instructions; Nebraska Rules of Evidence; pub(s) in, Creighton Law Rev & Nebr Law Rev. **CONTACT ADDRESS** School of Law, Creighton Univ, 2500 California Plaza, Omaha, NE 68178.

STROMBERG, JAMES S.
PERSONAL Born 09/06/1926, Chippewa Falls, WI **DISCIPLINE** PHILOSOPHY **EDUCATION** Col St Thomas, BA, 50; Laval Univ, MA, 57, PhL, 59, PhD(philos), 65. **CAREER** From instr to prof philos, Univ St Thomas, 56-; chmn dept, Univ St Thomas, 80-85. **MEMBERSHIPS** Am Philos Asn; Am Cath Philos Asn. **RESEARCH** Logic; ethical theory. **SELECTED PUBLICATIONS** Auth, Essay on Experimentum I, Laval Theol et Philos, 67, 68. **CONTACT ADDRESS** Dept of Philosophy, Univ of St. Thomas, Minnesota, 60 South Mississippi River Blvd., Saint Paul, MN 55105-1096. **EMAIL** strombergjames@uswest.net

STRONG, DOUGLAS M.
PERSONAL Born 09/27/1956, Buffalo, NY, m, 1986, 2 children **DISCIPLINE** HISTORY OF CHRISTIANITY **EDUCATION** Houghton Col, BA, 78; Princeton Theological Seminary, Mdiv, 81, PhD, 90. **CAREER** PROF OF HIST OF CHRISTIANITY, WESLEY THEOLOGICAL SEMINARY, 89-. **HONORS AND AWARDS** President, Wesleyan Theological Society, 97-99. **MEMBERSHIPS** Am Acad of Religion; Am Soc of Church Hist; Am Hist Asn; Wesleyan Theological Soc. **RESEARCH** 19th Century American religious history. **SELECTED PUBLICATIONS** Auth, Reading Christian Ethics: A Historical Sourcebook, Westminster John Knox, 96; auth, They Walked in the spirit: Personal Faith and Social Action in America, Westminster John Knox, 97; auth, Perfectionist Politics: Abolitionism and the Religious Tensions of American Democracy. **CONTACT ADDRESS** Wesley Theol Sem, 4500 Massachusetts Ave NW, Washington, DC 20016. **EMAIL** gnorts@erols.com

STRONG, JOHN S.
PERSONAL Born 08/28/1956, Philadelphia, PA **DISCIPLINE** ECONOMICS, FINANCE **EDUCATION** Wash & Lee Univ, BA, 78; Harvard Univ, MPP, 81; Phd, 86. **CAREER** Prof, School of Business, Col of William and Mary, 85-; vis prof, Harvard Univ, 89-90; vis scholar, Harvard Inst for Int Development, 93; vis economist, World Bank, 99-00. **HONORS AND AWARDS** Fulbright Scholar, 78-79; Phi Beta Kappa; Nat Sci Found Grad Fel, 79-82. **MEMBERSHIPS** Am Econ Asn; Am Fin Asn. **RESEARCH** Transport economics. **SELECTED PUBLICATIONS** Coauth, Moving to Market: Restructuring Transport in the Former Soviet Union, Harvard Univ Press, 96; coauth, Why Airplanes Crash: Aviation Safety in a Changing World, Oxford Univ Press, 92. **CONTACT ADDRESS** School of Business, Col of William and Mary, Williamsburg, VA 23187. **EMAIL** john.strong@business.wm.edu

STRONG, L. THOMAS, III
PERSONAL Born 05/20/1961, Nashville, TN, m, 1984, 2 children **DISCIPLINE** NEW TESTAMENT; GREEK **EDUCATION** New Orleans Baptist Theol Sem, PhD 93, MDiv 87; Union Univ, BA 83. **CAREER** New Orleans Baptist Theol Sem, assoc dean Undergrad stud, ch Theol Dept, assoc prof NT and Greek, 93-. **MEMBERSHIPS** SBL; AAR; ETS; ACS. **RESEARCH** Pauline studies; Textual Criticism; Spiritual Disciplines. **SELECTED PUBLICATIONS** Auth, Contrasts: Luke 18, Theol Educator; An Essential Unity, Theol Edu; Claudius, Biblical Illustrator. **CONTACT ADDRESS** 3939 Gentilly Blvd, New Orleans, LA 70126. **EMAIL** tstrong@nobts.edu

STRONKS, JULIA K.
DISCIPLINE LAW **EDUCATION** Univ Iowa Col of Law, JD, 85; Univ Maryland-College Park, PhD, 95. **HONORS AND AWARDS** Fulbright, the Netherlands, 92. **RESEARCH** Law and policy; constitutional law; comparative law **CONTACT ADDRESS** Dept of Political Studies, Whitworth Col, Spokane, WA 99251. **EMAIL** jstronks@whitworth.edu

STROUD, SARAH
DISCIPLINE PHILOSOPHY **EDUCATION** Harvard Univ, BA, 88; Princeton Univ, PhD, 94. **RESEARCH** Contemp analytic moral theory; contemp analytic meta-ethics; hist of moral philos; applied ethics; logic; analytic philos. **SELECTED PUBLICATIONS** Auth, Dworkin and Casey on Abortion, 96; auth, Moral Relativism and Quasi-Absolutism, 98; art, Moral Overridingness and Moral Theory, Pacific Philos Quarterly, 98; auth, Deontologisme et droits, Philosophique, vol. 26, no. 1, 99; auth, "The Aim of Affirmative Action," Social Theory and Practive, vol. 25, no. 3, 99; auth, "Moral Commitment and Moral Theory," Journal of Philosophical Res, 00. **CONTACT ADDRESS** Philosophy Dept, McGill Univ, 845 Sherbrooke St, Montreal, QC, Canada H3A 2T5. **EMAIL** sarah@philo.mcgill.ca

STRUCKHOFF, DAVID
PERSONAL Born 08/16/1942, St Louis, MO, m, 1999, 2 children **DISCIPLINE** CRIMINAL JUSTICE **EDUCATION** Quincy Col, BA, 66; Ill Inst Tech, MS, 69; S Ill Univ, PhD, 77. **CAREER** Corr soc, Ill Dept Corr, 68-77; prog dir, Joliet Corr Cen, 75-77; consult, Cook Cnty, 77-78; adj prof, Col St Francis, 77; consult, MRI, 77-80; asst prof, Loyola Univ, 77-80; assoc prof, 80-; pres, pres emer, dir, Just Res Cen, 86-; vis prof, Govs State Univ, 94; Intl Crim Just Edu, Moraine Valley Comm Col, 96; fac, Union Inst, 97. **HONORS AND AWARDS** US Dept Just, Grad Res Fel; Outstand Am Men and Women; Outstand Ser Awd; Crim Just Ser Cit; Deans Excell Teach Awd; Dist Ser, ICA, ACA; NCJ Hon Soc; Who's Who in Law, Edu, Intl Bus, Midwest, Worldwide; ICA Pres Awd; Morris J Wexler Awd; Sujack Teach Awd, 94, 97, 98; Top Ten, Loyola Univ. **MEMBERSHIPS** ACA; IAC; ACJS; ICA; MACJE; ACRIM. **SELECTED PUBLICATIONS** Ed, Encyclopedia of Criminal Justice, Greenwood Pub, 96; ed, Modernization of Police Scheduling, Shift Work and Resource Allocation, SL Pub (Joliet, IL), 96; ed, Juvenile Delinquency: Annual Editions, 99/00, Dushkin/McGraw Hill (Sluice Dock, CT), 99; coauth, "Diagnosing , Assessing and Tuning Your Shifts," in Modernization of Police Scheduling (SL Justice Research: Chicago, IL, 98); auth, "Community Policing and Property Values," in Property and Commerce Valuation, ed. J Lombardi (American Realtors: Washington, DC, 98); auth, "Wyatt Earp," Encyclopedia of Criminal Justice, Greenwood Pub (SC), 96 ; auth, "Sherrifs," Encyclopedia of Criminal Justice, Greenwood Pub (SC), 96 ; auth, "Posses," Encyclopedia of Criminal Justice, Greenwood Pub (SC), 96 ; auth, "Bat Masterson," Encyclopedia of Criminal Justice, Greenwood Pub (SC), 96 ; auth, "Sociological Theory of Crime," Encyclopedia of Criminal Justice, Greenwood Pub (SC), 96; auth, "Psychological Theory of Crime," Encyclopedia of Criminal Justice, Greenwood Pub (SC), 96; auth, "Biochemical Theory of Crime," Encyclopedia of Criminal Justice, Greenwood Pub (SC), 96; coauth, The American Jail in Western Civilization," American Jails (Hagerstown, MD), 98. **CONTACT ADDRESS** Dept Criminal Justice, Loyola Univ, Chicago, 820 N Michigan Ave, Chicago, IL 60611. **EMAIL** docdave@justiceresearch.com

STRUGNELL, JOHN
PERSONAL Born 05/25/1930, Barnet, England, d, 1957, 5 children **DISCIPLINE** BIBLICAL STUDIES, SEMITICS **EDUCATION** Oxford Univ, BA, 52, MA, 55. **CAREER** Epigraphist, Dead Sea Scrolls, Palestine Archaeol Mus, Jerusalem, 54-56; res, Orient Inst, Chicago, 57; epigraphist, Palestine Archaeol Mus, 57-60; asst prof Old Testament, divinity sch, Duke Univ, 60-66; assoc prof, 66-68, Prof Christian Origins, Divinity Sch, Harvard Univ, 68-, Mem, Brit Sch Archaeol, Jerusalem, 60-; Am Coun Learned Soc fel, 68-69. **RESEARCH** Northwest Semitic epigraphy; Qumran Scrolls; Near-Eastern history. **SELECTED PUBLICATIONS** Auth, Quelques inscriptions Samaritaines, Rev Bibl, 67; Notes en marge, Vol V, Discoveries in the Judean Desert of Jordan, Rev Qumran, 7:163-276; A Critical Note In Evaluation Of The 'Dead Sea Scrolls Uncovered By Robert Eisenman And Michael Wise, J Of Biblical Lit, Vol 112, 93; coauth, Discoveries in the Judean Desert X (with E. Qimron); coauth, Discoveries in the Judean Desert XXXIV (with D.J. Harrington). **CONTACT ADDRESS** Divinity Sch, Harvard Univ, 45 Francis Ave, Cambridge, MA 02138.

STRUM, PHILIPPA
PERSONAL Born 12/14/1938, New York, NY, 1 child **DISCIPLINE** POLITICAL SCIENCE **EDUCATION** Grad Facul of the New Sch, PhD, 64. **CAREER** Res fel, Harvard Univ, summer, 60; lectr to instr, Brooklyn Col, 62-64; lectr, The New Sch, summer 62 & 63; instr to assoc prof, Rutgers Univ, Newark, 64-72; assoc prof, Brooklyn Col, 72-75; acting chair, Brooklyn Col, 74-75; vis prof, Barnard Col, 78-79; vis scholar, NY Univ, 82-83; res fel, Truman Inst of Hebrew Univ, 85-86; Dubach Vis Distinguished Prof, Ore State Univ, Apr 11-15, 88; Fulbright sr lectr, Bogazici Univ, Istanbul, Spr, 95; Lyons Distinguished Vis Prof, Va Commonwealth Univ, Apr, 97; fel, Woodrow Wilson Intl Ctr for Scholars, 97-98; prof, City Univ of NY, Brooklyn Col and the Grad Ctr, 74-98; Broeklundian prof, polit sci, City Univ of NY, Brooklyn Col and the Grad Ctr, 98-; Walter Gibbs vis prof, Wayne State Univ Law School, 00-01. **HONORS AND AWARDS** Fel, Woodrow Wilson Ctr, 97-98; Scholar's Incentive Awd, Brooklyn Col, Spr 96-Aut 97; Fulbright Tchg Fel, Turkey, Spr, 95; Hughes-Gosset Awd for Hist Excellence, Jour of Supreme Ct Hist, 94; fel, Woodrow Wilson Ctr, Wash, DC, 97-98; City Univ of NY Facul Res Awd Prog, 94-95, 99-00. **MEMBERSHIPS** Am Polit Sci Asn; Am Civ Liberties Un; Board of Directors. **RESEARCH** Civil liberties and human rights; Am constitutional law and government; Women and politics. **SELECTED PUBLICATIONS** Auth, The Women Are Marching; The Second sex in the Palestinian Revolution, Lawrence Hill, 92; auth, Brandeis: Beyond Porgressivism, Univ Press of Kansas, 93; ed, Brandeis on Democracy, Univ Press of Kansas, 94; auth, The Road Not Taken: Constitutional Nondecision Making in 1948-1950 and its Impact on Civil Liberties in the Israeli Political Culture, ed Troen and Lucas, Israel: The First Decade of Independence, SUNY Press, 95; auth, Human Rights and Gender issues, Women's Studies Rev, Istanbul, 95; auth, West Bank Women an dthe Intifada, Ed, Suha Sabah, palestinian Women of Gaza nad the West Bank, Ind Univ Press, 98; auth, Privacy: The Debate in the United Staates Since 1945; Harcourt Brace, 98; auth, When the Nazis Came to Skokie: Freedom for the Speech We Hate, Univ Prerss of Kansas, 99; auth, The Innovative Lawyering of Louis D. Brandeis, American Lawyer, Dec 99; auth, Change and Continuity on the Supreme Court: Conversations with Justice Harry A. Blackmun, Univ of Richmond Law Review, Mar 00. **CONTACT ADDRESS** 124 W. 79th St., New York, NY 10024. **EMAIL** pstrum@mindspring.com

STUART, DOUGLAS KEITH
PERSONAL Born 02/08/1943, Concord, MA, m, 1971, 8 children **DISCIPLINE** OLD TESTAMENT, NEAR EASTERN LANGUAGES **EDUCATION** Harvard Univ, BA, 64, PhD, 71. **CAREER** Instr Near East hist, 68-69, Gordon Col; asst prof, 71-77, assoc prof, 78-81, prof Old Testament, 81-, Gordon-Conwell Theol Sem; pres, 74-, Boston area chap, Huxley Inst Biosocial Res; co-chmn, 75-, Boston Theol Inst; trustee, 80-, Mass Bible Soc; trustee, Boxford Acad, 96-. **MEMBERSHIPS** Am Schs Orient Res; Inst Bibl Res; Evangel Theol Soc; Soc Bibl Lit; Bibl Archeol Soc. **RESEARCH** Hebrew meter; minor prophets; exegesis techniques. **SELECTED PUBLICATIONS** Coauth, How to Read the Bible for All Its Worth, Zondervan Publ House, 82; auth, Hosea-Jonah, Word Biblical Comm, 87; auth, Hosea-Jonah, Word Biblical Themes, 88; auth, Favorite Old Testament Passages, Westminster Press, 89; auth, Malachi, Baker Bk House, 98. **CONTACT ADDRESS** Gordon-Conwell Theol Sem, 130 Essex St, South Hamilton, MA 01982-2395.

STUART, JAMES DONALD
PERSONAL Born 09/14/1939, Owensboro, KY, m, 1961, 2 children **DISCIPLINE** PHILOSOPHY **EDUCATION** Cincinnati Bible Col, BSL, 62, ThB, 63; Univ Cincinnati, MA, 67, PhD, 70. **CAREER** Instr philos, Univ Cincinnati, 66-68; from Asst Prof to Assoc Prof, 68-83, Prof Philos, Bowling Green State Univ, 83; Prof Emeritus, Bowling Green State Univ, 98. **MEMBERSHIPS** Am Philos Asn. **RESEARCH** Hist of mod philos; Kant; Berkeley; Descartes. **SELECTED PUBLICATIONS** Coauth, Review of G Buchdahl's Metaphysics and the philosophy of science, Philos Sci, 6/72; Kant's two refutations of idealism, 75 & Berkeley's appearance-reality distinction, 77, Southwestern J Philos; Bekeley on Dreaming & Perceiving, Proc Ohio Philos Asn, 76; Asst ed, The Philosopher's Index: A Retrospective Index to US Publications from 1940, 78; Ethical relativism and the teaching of values, Forum, 82; Imposing Values with Respect for Persons, Eastern Ed J, 83; The Role of Dreaming in Descartes' Meditations, Hist Philos Quart, 83; Frankfurt on Descartes Dream Argument, Philos Forum, 85; Descartes' Proof of the External World, Hist Philos Quart, 86; Retributive Justice and Prior Offenses, Philos Forum, 86; Deterrence, Desert, and Drunk Driving, Public Affairs Quart, 89; Logical Thinking, An Introduction to Logic, McGraw Hill, 85, 2nd ed, 97. **CONTACT ADDRESS** Dept of Philos, Bowling Green State Univ, 1001 E Wooster St, Bowling Green, OH 43403-0001. **EMAIL** jstuart@bgnet.bgsu.edu

STUBENBERG, LEOPOLD
DISCIPLINE PHILOSOPHY **EDUCATION** Univ Graz, BA, 84; Univ Ariz, MA, 88, PhD, 92. **CAREER** Assoc prof. **RESEARCH** Philosophy of mind; epistemology. **SELECTED PUBLICATIONS** Auth, Justifying Basic Belief Forming Processes, Knowledge Tchg Wisdom, 96; The Place of Qualia in

the World of Science, 96. **CONTACT ADDRESS** Philosophy Dept, Univ of Notre Dame, 336/7 O'Shaughnessy, Notre Dame, IN 46556. **EMAIL** stubenberg.1@nd.edu

STUCKEY, PRISCILLA F.
PERSONAL Born 03/21/1957, OH, s **DISCIPLINE** GENDER AND RELIGIOUS STUDIES **EDUCATION** Grad Theol Union, PhD, 97 **CAREER** Development Editor **HONORS AND AWARDS** Young Scholars Awd, 95. **MEMBERSHIPS** Natl Women's Studies Asn, Am Acad of Religion. **SELECTED PUBLICATIONS** Auth, Light Dispels Darkness: Gender, Ritual and Society in Mozart's The Magic Flute, 95. **CONTACT ADDRESS** 3060 Butters Dr, Oakland, CA 94602. **EMAIL** pstuckey@california.com

STUDZINSKI, RAYMOND JAMES
PERSONAL Born 04/18/1943, Detroit, MI **DISCIPLINE** RELIGION, PSYCHOLOGY **EDUCATION** St Meinrad Col, BA, 66; IN Univ, MA, 73; Fordham Univ, PhD(theol), 77. **CAREER** Asst prof theol, St Meinrad Sch Theol, 73-77; fel, Menninger Found, 79-81; asst prof relig, 81-85, assoc prof relig, Cath Univ Am, 85-. **MEMBERSHIPS** Soc Sci Study Relig; Relig Res Asn. **RESEARCH** Psychology of religion; contemporary spirituality; spiritual direction. **SELECTED PUBLICATIONS** Spiritual Direction and Midlife Development, Chicago: Loyola Univ Press, 85. **CONTACT ADDRESS** Relig Dept, Catholic Univ of America, 620 Michigan Ave N E, Washington, DC 20064-0002. **EMAIL** studzinski@cua.edu

STUESSER, LEE
DISCIPLINE LAW **EDUCATION** Winnipeg Univ, BA, 77; Brock Univ, BEd, 79; Guelph Univ, MA, 80; Univ Manitoba, LLB, 84; Harvard Univ, LLM, 86. **CAREER** Asst prof, Univ Ottawa, 86-88; prof, 88-. **RESEARCH** Criminal law; evidence; litigation; remedies. **SELECTED PUBLICATIONS** Auth, An Advocacy Primer, Carswell, 90; Introduction to Advocacy, 93; Essentials of Canadian Law: Evidence, 96. **CONTACT ADDRESS** Fac of Law, Univ of Manitoba, Robson Hall, Winnipeg, MB, Canada R3T 2N2. **EMAIL** lstuess@cc.umanitoba.ca

STUHLMUELLER, CARROLL
PERSONAL Born 04/02/1923, Hamilton, OH **DISCIPLINE** SCRIPTURE **EDUCATION** Cath Univ Am, STL, 52; Pontif Bibl Inst, Rome, SSL, 54, SSD, 69. **CAREER** Mem fac, St Meinrad Sch Theol, 65-68; Prof Scripture, Cath Theol Union, 68-, Asst prof, Viatorian Sem, Evanston, Ill, 55-58 & Loretto Jr Col, 59-61, 62-65 & Ursuline Col, 61-63; prof, St John's Univ, NY, 70-75; vis prof, Ecole Biblique & Archaeol, Jerusalem, 73; assoc ed, Cath Bibl Quart, 73-77; ed, The Bible Today, 80-; prof scripture, St John's Univ, NY, fall, 70-74. **HONORS AND AWARDS** DHL, St Benedict Col, 69. **MEMBERSHIPS** Cath Bibl Asn Am (vpres, 77-78, pres, 78-79); Soc Bibl Lit; Col Theol Soc; Theol Soc Am. **RESEARCH** Biblical foundations of mission; prophets Haggai & Zechariah; Biblical spirituality from the Psalms. **SELECTED PUBLICATIONS** Auth, Creative redemption in Deutero-Isaiah, Bibl Inst Press, Rome, 70; Thirsting for the Lord, Alba House, 77; Biblical Meditations for Lent, Paulist Press, 78; ed, Women and Priesthood: Future Directions, Liturgical Press, 78; Biblical Meditations for Easter Season, 79; Biblical Meditations for Advent and Christmas, 80; The Psalms, M Glazier Publ, (2 vols), 82; Biblical foundations of Mission, Orbis Press, 83. **CONTACT ADDRESS** Catholic Theol Union at Chicago, 5401 S Cornell Ave, Chicago, IL 60615.

STUHR, WALTER MARTIN
DISCIPLINE ETHICS **EDUCATION** Yale Univ, BA; Pacific Lutheran Theol Sem, BD; Univ Chicago, PhD. **CAREER** Acad dean; prof, 67; dir, MA, MTS, degree prog(s); pres, 78-88. **HONORS AND AWARDS** Co-dir, PLTS Ctr for Lutheran Church Growth and Mission. **MEMBERSHIPS** Mem, Candidacy Comm, ELCA Region I; Richmond Shimada, Japan, Sister City Prog; Soc of Christian Ethics; Bishop's Nuclear Deterrence Planning Comm. **CONTACT ADDRESS** Candidacy Committee, The Extraordinary Candidacy Project (ECP), 1320 Evelyn Avenue, Berkeley, CA 94702. **EMAIL** excp@dnai.com

STULMAN, LOUIS
PERSONAL Born 08/03/1953, Baltimore, MD, m, 1975, 4 children **DISCIPLINE** RELIGION **EDUCATION** Roberts Wesleyan Col, BA, 78; Drew Univ, MPhil, 81, PhD, 82; Univ Mich, Post Doct, 89. **CAREER** Tchng & res asst, 79-81, Bibl Stud Res fel, 80-81, instr, Hebrew, 81-82, Drew Univ; vis scholar, 88-89, Univ Mich; adj prof, 85-97, prof, 97-,Univ Findlay; asst prof, 82-86, assoc prof, 87-88, prof, 96-97, Gale and Harriette Ritz Prof, 96-97, Dist Scholar, 97-, Winebrenner Theol Sem **HONORS AND AWARDS** Who's Who in Midwest, 94-95; Outstanding Ed, Findlay OH, 89; Outstanding Young Men of Am, 86; Who's Who in Relig and Archaeol, 85-86, 92-93; Hebrew Bible Awd, Drew Univ, 81-82; Drew Grad Sch Res Fel, 80-81; Alpha Kappa Sigma Hon Soc, 77-78. **MEMBERSHIPS** Soc of Bibl Lit; Natl Assn of Prof of Hebrew. **SELECTED PUBLICATIONS** Auth, Four Remarkable Women in Matthew 1:1-17, Church Adv 156/7, 91; auth, Sex and Familial Crimes in the D Code: A Witness to Mores in Transition, J for Stud of OT 53, 92; auth, Dynamic Correspondence and Preaching, Homiletic 18/1, 93; auth, Insiders and Outsiders in the Book of Jeremiah: Shifts in Symbolic Arrangements, J for Stud of OT 66, 95, reprint, Sheffield Reader: The Prophets, Sheffield Acad Press, 96; auth, Order Amid Chaos: Jeremiah As Symbolic Tapestry, Sheffield Acad Press, 98; auth, Troubling Jeremiah: New Readings of the Book of Jeremiah, Sheffield Acad Press, 99. **CONTACT ADDRESS** Col of Liberal Arts, Univ of Findlay, 1000 N Main St, Findlay, OH 45840. **EMAIL** stulman@findlay.edu

STUMP, DAVID JAMES
PERSONAL Born 03/21/1955, Santa Monica, CA, m, 2 children **DISCIPLINE** PHILOSOPHY **EDUCATION** Northwestern Univ, PhD, 88. **CAREER** Assoc prof, Univ San Francisco. **MEMBERSHIPS** APA; PSA; HSS; HOPOS. **RESEARCH** Philosophy of Science. **SELECTED PUBLICATIONS** Auth, Afterword: New Directions in the Philosophy of Science Studies, Disunity of Sci: Boundaries, Contexts and Power, 96; From Epistemology and Metaphysics to Concrete Connections, , Disunity of Sci: Boundaries, Contexts and Power, 96; Poincare's Curious Role in the Formalization of Mathematics, henri Poincare: Sci and Philos, Int Congress Nancy France 94, 96; Reconstructing the Unity of Mathematics circa 1900, Perspectives on Sci, 97; Poincare Jules Henri, Routledge Encycl of Philos, 98; co-ed, The Disunity of Sci: Boundaries, Contexts and Power, 96. **CONTACT ADDRESS** Dept of Philosophy, Univ of San Francisco, San Francisco, CA 94117-1080. **EMAIL** stumpd@usfca.edu

STUNTZ, WILLIAM J.
PERSONAL Born 07/03/1958, Washington, DC, m, 1980, 3 children **DISCIPLINE** LEGAL STUDIES **EDUCATION** Col William & Mary, BA, 80; Univ Va, JD, 84. **CAREER** Notes Ed, Va Law Rev; Law Clerk, Eastern Dist Pa, 84-86; Law Clerk, US Supreme Court, 85-86; Asst Prof, Univ Va, 86-90; Prof, Univ Va, 90-00; Prof, Harvard Law Sch, 00-. **HONORS AND AWARDS** Roger and Madeline Traynor Prize, Alumni Asoc Awd for Acad Excellence. **RESEARCH** Criminal law and criminal procedure. **SELECTED PUBLICATIONS** Coauth, Constitutional Criminal Procedure, 3rd ed, Little, Brown & Co, 95; auth, "Privacy's Problem and the Law of Criminal Procedure, 93," Mich Law Rev 1016-1078 (95); auth, "The Substantive Origins of Criminal Procedure, 105," Yale Law J (95): 393-447; auth, "The Virtues and Vices of the Exclusionary Rule, 20," Harvard J of Law and Public Policy (97): 443-455; auth, "The Uneasy Relationship Between Criminal Procedure and Criminal Justice, 107," Yale Law J 1-76 (97); auth, "Law and the Christian Story," First Things (97): 26-29; auth, "Sin, Rights and Equality," in The Christian and Am Law (98), 225-246; auth, "Race, Class and Drugs, 98," Columbia Law Rev 1795-1842 (98); auth, "The Distribution of Fourth Amendment Privacy, 67," George Wash Law Rev 1265-1289 (99). **CONTACT ADDRESS** Legal Studies, Harvard Univ, Cambridge, MA 02138. **EMAIL** stuntz@law.harvard.edu

STURM, DOUGLAS EARL
PERSONAL Born 04/22/1929, Batavia, NY, m, 1953, 2 children **DISCIPLINE** RELIGION, POLITICAL THEORY **EDUCATION** Hiram Col, AB, 50; Univ Chicago, DB, 53, PhD(theol soc ethics), 59. **CAREER** Nat exec secy, Christian Action, 54-56; from asst prof to assoc prof relig, 59-67, assoc prof relig & polit sci, 67-70, actg chmn dept polit sci, 68-69, chmn dept relig, 69-74, 89-90, dir univ honors coun, 70-72, presidential prof, 74-80, Prof Relig & Polit Sci, 70-95, PROF EMERITUS, 95-, ADJ PROF, 96-, BUCKNELL UNIV; Am Coun Learned Soc fel, 64-65; Harvard Law Sch fel law & philos, 64-65; Soc Relig Higher Educ fel, 66 & cross-disciplinary studies fel, 67-68; dir, Inst Study Human Values, 66-67; consult ed, Bucknell Press, 71-83; vis prof social ethics, Andover Newton Theol Sch, Newton Centre, 72-73; vis prof ethics & soc, Univ Chicago, 76-77; res fel, Inst Adv Study Rel, Univ Chicago, 83-84; vis res prof, Univ Tenn, 91-92; bd consultants, J Rel, 72-83; edit bd, J Rel Ethics, 74-84; edit bd, J Law and Rel, 82-, edit bd, Soundings: An Interdisc j, 95-. **HONORS AND AWARDS** Lindback Awd, 66; Class of 1956 Lect Awd, Bucknell, 68; Univ Chicago Div Sch, Alumnus of the Year, 88; Lifetime Achievement, J Law & Rel, 95; Rainey Awd, Bucknell Univ, 94; Travis Lectureship Awd for Soc Just, 96. **MEMBERSHIPS** Soc Christian Ethics (exec secy, 68-72, vpres, 79-80, pres, 80-81); Soc Values Higher Educ; Am Soc Polit & Legal Philos; European Soc Cult; Am Polit Sci Asn. **RESEARCH** Religious ethics; social and political philosophy; legal philosophy. **SELECTED PUBLICATIONS** Lon Fuller's multidimensional natural law theory, Stanford Law Review, 5/65; Corporations, constitutions, and covenants: On forms of human relations and the problem of legitimacy, J Relig, 9/73; Politics and divinity: Three approaches in American political science, Thought: Am J Cult & Idea, 12/77; On meanings of public good: An exploration, J Relig, 1/78; Process thought and political theory: Implications of principle of internal relations, Rev Politics, 7/79, reprint, Process Thought and Social Theory, 81; American legal realism and the covenantal myth: Worldviews in the practice of law, Mercer Law Rev, winter 80; The prism of justice: E Pluribus Unum?, The Annual of Soc of Christian Ethics, 81; Praxis and promise: On the ethics of political theology, Ethics, 7/82; auth, Community and Alienation: Essays on Process Thought and Public LIfe, Univ Notre Dame, 88; auth, Solidarity and Suffering: Toward a Politics of Relationality, State Univ NY Press, 98; auth, Identity and Alterity: Summons to a New Axial Age, Forum on Religin and Ecology, 99. **CONTACT ADDRESS** Col of Arts & Sci, Bucknell Univ, Lewisburg, PA 17837. **EMAIL** sturm@bucknell.edu

STURM, FRED G.
PERSONAL Born 10/15/1925, Batavia, NY, m, 1971, 2 children **DISCIPLINE** PHILOSOPHY **EDUCATION** Allegheny Col, AB, 45; Union Theol Sem, MDiv, 48; Univ of Rochester, AM, 50; Columbia Univ, PhD, 61. **CAREER** Chair, Faculdade be Teologica de IBF, Brasil, 51-51; prof, Instituto Port Alegre, 52; prof, Western Col for Women, 54-74; adj assoc prof, SUNY, Buffalo, 74-75; prof, Univ of NMex, 75-. **HONORS AND AWARDS** Phi Beta Kappa; Fulbright Res, Taiwan, 62; Brazil, 65, 90; Soc Sci Res Counc, 66. **MEMBERSHIPS** Am Philos Assoc; Int Soc for Chinese Philos; Royal Asiatic Soc; Brasilian Acad of Philos; Soc for Iberian and Latin Am Thought. **RESEARCH** Chinese and East Asian Philosophical Tradition, Brasilian and Latin American Philosophical Tradition, Philosophy of Art and Aesthetics, Phenomenology. **SELECTED PUBLICATIONS** Auth, The Philosophy of Spirit of Raimundo de Faria Brito; coed, Pueblo Style and Regional Architecture; auth, Confucian Philosophy of Art: Aesthetic Norms in the Thought of Xunzi; auth, Leibniz, Jesuits, I Qing: Chinese Impact on Modern European Thought; auth, Beyond the "East-West" Dichotomy: The Philosophical Journey of Nisida Kitaro; auth, The Philosophical Ambiance of Brasilian Independence; auth, Dependence and Originality in Ibero-American Philosophy. **CONTACT ADDRESS** Dept Philos, Univ of New Mexico, Albuquerque, Albuquerque, NM 87131-0001. **EMAIL** kesfgs@aol.com

STURM, FRED GILLETTE
DISCIPLINE PHILOSOPHY **EDUCATION** Allegheny Col, AB, 46; Union Theological Seminary, MDiv, 48; Rochester, AM, 50; Columbia Univ, PhD, 61; Vanderbilt, cert, 49; Tunghai, cert, 63. **CAREER** Prof, Univ NMex. **MEMBERSHIPS** Int Ctr for Asian Stud; Royal Asiatic Soc; Int Sinological Comt; co-dir; REs Gp for Chinese & Comp Aesthet; Int Soc for Chinese Philos; Ctr de Estudos Luso-Brasileiros; Acad Brasileira de Filosofia; pres, Soc for Iberian and Lat Am Thought. **RESEARCH** Philos of Art and Aesthetics, Latin Am and Iberian Philos, Chinese and East Asian Philos, Phenomenology, C.S. Peirce. **SELECTED PUBLICATIONS** Auth, American Indians: Time in Outlook and Language, in Encycl of Time, Garland, 95; Radhakrishnan's Philosophy of Art, in New Essays in the Philosophy of Sarvepalli Radhakrishnan,Indian Bk Ctr, 95; Philosophy and the Intellectual Tradition, in Latin America: Its Problems and Its Promise, 3rd ed, Boulder & London, 97; Brazil, Philosophy, in Encycl of Philos, Routledge, 98. **CONTACT ADDRESS** Univ of New Mexico, Albuquerque, Albuquerque, NM 87131. **EMAIL** gillette@unm.edu

STUTTS, DEBORAH A.
PERSONAL Born 10/28/1949, Orlando, FL, d, 2 children **DISCIPLINE** NEW TESTAMENT STUDIES **EDUCATION** New Orleans Baptist Theol Sem, ThD, 89. **CAREER** Alabama Bd Of Pardons & Paroles, 90-. **MEMBERSHIPS** SBL. **RESEARCH** Textual criticism. **SELECTED PUBLICATIONS** Auth, Textual History of the Gospel of Matthew. **CONTACT ADDRESS** PO Box 611047, Birmingham, AL 35261-1047. **EMAIL** dwho@aol.com

STYLIANOPOULOS, THEODORE
PERSONAL Born 10/26/1937, Messinia, Greece, m, 1963, 4 children **DISCIPLINE** NEW TESTAMENT STUDIES **EDUCATION** Holy Cross Orthodox Sch of Theology, BA, 62; Boston Univ Sch of Theology, STM, 64; Harvard Divinity Sch, ThD, 72. **CAREER** Prof of New Testament, 67- , Holy Cross. **HONORS AND AWARDS** Lilly Found Fel; Archbishop Iakovos Faculty Prize; Protopresbyter of the Ecumenical Patriarchate of Constantinople. **MEMBERSHIPS** Soc of Biblical Literature; Orthodox Theological Soc in Amer. **RESEARCH** Matthew, John, Paul; Book of Revelation; Hermenentics; Patristics. **SELECTED PUBLICATIONS** Auth, Justin Martyr, Encyclopedia of Early Christianity, 97; auth, The New Testament: An Orthodox Perspective, 97; auth, Orthodox Biblical Interpretation, Dictionary of Biblical Interpretation, 98. **CONTACT ADDRESS** 15 Park Ave, Nutham, MA 02494. **EMAIL** stylianopoulos@msn.com

SUBER, PETER DAIN
PERSONAL Born 11/08/1951, Evanston, IL, m, 2 children **DISCIPLINE** PHILOSOPHY **EDUCATION** Earlham Col, BA, 73; Northwestern Univ, MA, 74, PhD, 78, JD, 82. **CAREER** Lectr philos, Northwestern Univ & Nat Col Educ, 74-79; asst prof, 82-88, assoc prof, 88-95, prof philos, Earlham Col, 95-; Gen ed, Hippias Search Engine; co-ed, NOESIS. **MEMBERSHIPS** Am Philos Asn; Hegel Soc Am. **RESEARCH** Hist of philos; skepticism; logic reflexivity ethics. **SELECTED PUBLICATIONS** Auth, Is Philsosphy Dead?, The Earlhamite, 112,2, 993): 12-14; auth, A Year of Teaching with Dialog, Newsletter on Teaching Philosophy, 93, 1, (94): 123-26; auth, Question-Begging Under a Non-Foundational Model of Argument, Argumentation, 8, (94): 241-50; auth, Legal Reasoning After Post-Modern Critiques of Reason, Legal Writing, 3, (97): 21-50; auth, Infinite Reflections, St. John's Re-

view, XLIV, 2, (98): 1-59; auth, The Case of the Speluncean Explorers: Nine New Opinions, Routledge, 98; auth, Amendment, in Christopher Berry Gray ed., Philosophy of Law: An Encyclopedia, Garland Pub Co, 99; auth, Civil Disobedience, in Christopher Berry Gray ed., Philosophy of Law: An Encyclopedia, Garland Pub Co, 99; auth, Parternalism, in Christopher Berry Gray ed., Philosophy of Law: An Encyclopedia, Garland Pub Co, 99; auth, Self-Reference in Law, in Christopher Berry Gray ed., Philosophy of Law: An Encyclopedia, Garland Pub Co, 99. **CONTACT ADDRESS** Dept Philos, Earlham Col, 801 National Rd W, Richmond, IN 47374-4095. **EMAIL** peters@earlham.edu

SUBOTNIK, DAN
DISCIPLINE LAW **EDUCATION** Columbia Univ, BA, 63; MBA, 66; JD, 66. **CAREER** Corp Fin Off, Birr, Wilson and Comp; lectr, Northwestern Univ; fac mem, Unvi Ill, Chicago; vis assoc prof, Univ Santa Clara; vis assoc prof, Seton Hall Law Schl; lectr Univ Chicago, 80-90; prof Law, Touro Col. **SELECTED PUBLICATIONS** He has written on a wide range of topics including taxation, accounting, and academic research. **CONTACT ADDRESS** Dept of Law, Touro Col, New York, Brooklyn, NY 11230. **EMAIL** DanS@tourolaw.edu

SUGGS, JON-CHRISTIAN
PERSONAL Born 12/28/1940, Shreveport, LA, m, 1983, 4 children **DISCIPLINE** CRIMINAL JUSTICE **EDUCATION** Baker Univ, BA, 62; Univ Kans, PhD, 78. **CAREER** Instr to prof and dept head, CUNY, 73-. **HONORS AND AWARDS** NEH Summer Fel, 84; Scholar in Residence, Schomburg Center, 94-95; Fel, CUNY, 88-91. **MEMBERSHIPS** MLA; Am Soc for Legal Hist; Am Studies Asn. **RESEARCH** Law and African American literature; American biography; Narrative theory; Working-class culture. **SELECTED PUBLICATIONS** Auth, American Proletarian Culture: The Twenties and the Thirties, Vol XI, Dictionary of Literary Biography, Gale, 93; auth, Whispered Consolations: Law and Narrative in African American Life, Univ Mich Press, 00. **CONTACT ADDRESS** John Jay Col of Criminal Justice, CUNY, 85 Bedford St, New York, NY 10014-3753. **EMAIL** jscjj@sprintmail.com

SUH, DAE-SUK
PERSONAL Born 11/22/1931, Korea, m, 1960, 2 children **DISCIPLINE** PUBLIC LAW AND GOVERNMENT **EDUCATION** Tex Christian Univ, BA, 56; Ind Univ, MA, 58; Columbia Univ, PhD, 64. **CAREER** Asst prof, Univ Houston, 65-66; assoc prof, 67-71; dir, Ctr for Korean Studies, Univ Hawaii at Manoa, 72-94; prof, 72- . **HONORS AND AWARDS** Honorary prf Yanbian Univ, Yanji, Jilin, China, 91; Korea Found Prof of Policy Studies, Univ Hawaii, 94- . **MEMBERSHIPS** Am Polit Sci Asoc; Asoc for Asian Studies. **RESEARCH** North and South Korea; East Asian security. **SELECTED PUBLICATIONS** Auth, Kim Il Sung: The North Korean Leader, 95; auth, Kin Nichisei to Kin Shonichi, 97; North Korea after Kim Il Sung, 98. **CONTACT ADDRESS** 7122 Niumalu Loop, Honolulu, HI 96825-1635. **EMAIL** daesook@hawaii.edu

SULEIMAN, MICHAEL W.
PERSONAL Born 02/26/1934, Tiberias, Palestine, m, 1963, 2 children **DISCIPLINE** POLITICAL SCIENCE **EDUCATION** Bradley Univ, BA 60; Univ Wis, MS 62, PhD 65. **CAREER** Kansas State Univ, Dept hd pol sci, AESF, prof, Dist Prof, 75 to 90-; Univ Calif Berk, vis sch, 79; KSU, assoc prof, 68-72; Univ London, vis sch, 69-70; KSU, asst prof, 65-68; Abbotsholme Sch, tchr, 55-56; Bishop's Sch Jordan, tchr, 53-55. **HONORS AND AWARDS** Princeton Inst Adv Stud; 2 NEH Fel; Fulbright-Hays Fel; Phi Kappa Phi; Dist Grad Fac Mem; MASUA Hon Mem; Smithsonian Inst Gnt; APS Fel; ARCE Fel; Ford Fac Res Fel; KSU Fac Res Fel; Phi Eta Sigma Schshp. **MEMBERSHIPS** APSA; MESA; MEI; IAMCR; AIMS; ASA; AISA. **RESEARCH** Comparative politics; Middle East politics; Political socialization in developing countries esp Middle East; Parties and political development; Amer images of Middle East Peoples; the Arab-American Community. **SELECTED PUBLICATIONS** Auth, Arabs in America: Building a New Future, ed, coauth, Philadelphia PA, Temple Univ Press, 99; US Policy on Palestine form Wilson to Clinton, ed, coauth, Belmont MA, AAUG Press, 95; auth, Arab Americans: Continuity and Change, co-ed, coauth, Belmont MA, AAUG Press, 89; The Arabs in the Mind of America, Brattleboro VT, Amana Books, 88; auth, American Images of Middle East Peoples: Impact of the High School, Middle East Studies Assoc, NY, 77; auth, Political Parties in Lebanon: The Challenge of a Fragmented Political Culture, Ithaca NY, Cornell U Press, 67; auth, "The Mokarzels' Contributions to the Arabic-Speaking Community in the United States," Arab Stud Qtly, 99; auth, "Islam, Muslims and Arabs in America: The Other of the Other of the Other . . ." Jrnl of Muslim Minority Affairs, 99; Tunisia and the World: Attitudes of Tunisian Youths Towards Other Countries, Maghreb Rev, 97; auth, Arab Immigration to America, 1880-1940, Awraq, Madrid, 96; auth, The Arab-American Left, in: Paul Buhle, Dan Geogakas, eds, The Immigrant Left, Albany NY, SUNY Pr, 96; auth, Arab Americans and the Political Process, Ernest Mccarus, ed, Arab-Americans: An Evolving Identity, Ann Arbor, U of Michigan Press, 94; auth, Political Orientation of Young Tunisians: The Impact of Gender, Arab Studies Quart, 93. **CONTACT ADDRESS** Dept of Political Science, Kansas State Univ, Manhattan, KS 66506. **EMAIL** suleiman@ksu.edu

SULLIVAN, JOHN G.
PERSONAL Born 12/12/1936, Newport, RI, m, 1987, 1 child **DISCIPLINE** PHILOSOPHY **EDUCATION** Cath Univ of Amer, BA, 58, MA, 59, Basselin fel, 56-59; Lateran Univ, Rome, JCD, 66; Univ NC Chapel Hill, PhD, philos, 82. **CAREER** Exec asst to the Bishop of Providence and asst chancellor for RI diocese, 66-68; admin asst to pres and general mgr of Gallagher Comm, 68-70; mem of fac, dept of philos, Elon Col, 70-; Maude Sharpe Powell prof of philos; co-designer and founding fac mem, SOPHIA, 87-. **HONORS AND AWARDS** Winner, Elon Col Daniel-Danieley award for excellence in teaching, 80; first recipient of Maude Sharpe Powell Professorship, 85; Fac inductee into Phi Kappa Phi, 97. **MEMBERSHIPS** NC Philos Asn; Amer Philos Asn; Omicron Delta Kappa; Phi Kappa Phi. **RESEARCH** Ethics and leadership; Transpersonal developmental psychology; Philosophy of religion; Ancient and medieval philosophy and Eastern philosophy. **SELECTED PUBLICATIONS** Auth, Going Down Our Own Well, Meridians, vol 4, 2, 97; auth, Small Mind, Big Mind, Meridians, vol 3, no 2, Spring, 96; auth, On Becoming an Elder, Meridians, vol 2, no 2, Winter, 94; auth, To Come To Life More Fully: An East West Journey, Traditional Acupuncture Inst, 91. **CONTACT ADDRESS** Dept. of Philosophy, Elon Col, Campus box 2102, Elon College, NC 27244. **EMAIL** sullivan@elon.edu

SULLIVAN, MARY C., RSM
PERSONAL Born 06/15/1931, Rochester, NY **DISCIPLINE** LITERATURE, RELIGION **EDUCATION** Nazareth Col Rochester, BA, 54; Univ Notre Dame, MA, 61, PhD(English), 64; Univ London, MTh, 88. **CAREER** Asst prof English, Catherine McAuley Col, 63-65, pres, 65-68; asst prof, Marymount Col, NY, 67-69; assoc prof lang & lit, 69-81, Prof Lang & Lit, Rochester Inst Technol, 81-, dean col liberal arts, 77-87, chair, acad senate, 96-99; Consult & evaluator, Comn Higher Educ, Mid States Asn, 68-90. **MEMBERSHIPS** MLA; Mercy Higher Ed Colloquium; Mercy Asn in Scripture and Theol. **RESEARCH** Nineteenth and 20th century English and American literature; religion and literature; biography. **SELECTED PUBLICATIONS** Auth, The function of setting in Howells' The Landlord at Lion's Head, Am Lit, 63; Moby Dick, CXXIX: The cabin, Nineteenth Century Fiction, 65; Caroline Gordon: A Reference Guide, G K Hall, 77; Conrad's Paralipsis in the narration of Lord Jim, Conradiana, 78; Catherine McAuley and the Tradition of Mercy, Univ Notre Dame Press, 95; auth, The Friendship of Florence Nightingale and Mary Clare Moore, Univ Pa Press, 99. **CONTACT ADDRESS** Col of Lib Arts, Rochester Inst of Tech, 1 Lomb Memorial Dr, Rochester, NY 14623-5603. **EMAIL** mxsgsl@atsrit.edu

SULLIVAN, RUTH
DISCIPLINE LAW **EDUCATION** Univ Minn, BA; Concord Univ, MA, LLB. **CAREER** Prof, Univ of Ottawa. **RESEARCH** Administrative law, statutory interpretation, linguistics, legal drafting, legal theory. **SELECTED PUBLICATIONS** Auth, pubs on legal drafting, language, law and interpretation. **CONTACT ADDRESS** Fac Common Law, Univ of Ottawa, Fauteux Hall, 57 Louis Pasteur, Ottawa, ON, Canada K1N 6N5. **EMAIL** resulliv@uottawa.ca

SULLIVAN, STEPHEN J.
PERSONAL Born 11/21/1956, New York, NY, d, 1 child **DISCIPLINE** PHILOSOPHY **EDUCATION** Cornell Univ, PhD, 90. **CAREER** Assoc prof Philos, Univ Southern Ind, 96- . **MEMBERSHIPS** APA; Ind Philos Asn. **RESEARCH** Ethics; epistemology; philosophy of religion. **SELECTED PUBLICATIONS** Coauth, "Harman on Relativism and Moral Diversity," Critica (98); auth, Rev of Robert L. Arrington, Rationalism, Realism, and Relativism: Perspectives in Contemporary Moral Epistemology, in Ethics, 91; Harman, Ethical Naturalism, and Token-Token Identity, Philos Papers, 91; Arbitrariness, Divine Commands, and Morality, Intl Jour Philos Rel, 93; Relativism, Evil, and Disagreement: A Reply to Hocutt, Philosophia, 93; Adams's Theistic Argument from the Nature of Morality, Jour Relig Ethics, 93; Why Adam's Needs to Modify His Divine-Command Theory One More Time, Faith and Philos, 94; Goldman's Early Causal Theory of Knowledge, Grazer Philos Stud, 95. **CONTACT ADDRESS** Dept of Philosophy, Univ of So Indiana, Evansville, IN 47712. **EMAIL** ssulliva@usi.edu

SULLIVAN, WILLIAM JOSEPH
PERSONAL Born 05/10/1931, Arlington, MA, m, 1965, 6 children **DISCIPLINE** RELIGIOUS STUDIES **EDUCATION** St Paul's Col, DC, BA, 53, MA, 57; Cath Inst Paris, STL, 63, STD, 67. **CAREER** Asst dir, Newman Ctr, Univ Calif, Berkeley, 57-61; asst dir, Newman Ctr, Mass Inst Technol, 61-62; mem staff, Faith & Order Secretariat, World Coun Churches, Geneva, Switz, 65-66; prog analyst, Off Econ Opportunity, 67-69; asst prof relig studies, 69-75, chmn dept, 70-73, Assoc Prof Relig Studies, St John Fisher Col, 75-, Mem adv coun, Off Permanent Diasonate Roman Cath Diocese, Rochester, 78-. **MEMBERSHIPS** Nat Newman Chaplains Asn (treas, 60-62); Col Theol Soc; Cath Theol Soc Am **RESEARCH** Early Christian interpretations of Biblical teachings on poverty and wealth; relationship between Israel and Christianity during the primitive Christian era. **SELECTED PUBLICATIONS** Contribr, The Capuchin Annual, Capuchin, Dublin, 67, Mixed Marriages, an Honest Appraisal, Abbey Press, 67; Why Priests Leave, Hawthorne, 69; coauth, chap, In: Beyond Survival: Bread and Justice in Christian Perspective, Friendship, 77; Crime and Community in Biblical Perspective, 81. **CONTACT ADDRESS** Dept of Relig Studies, St. John Fisher Col, 3690 East Ave, Rochester, NY 14618-3597. **EMAIL** wsullivan@sjfc.edu

SULLIVAN, WINNIFRED F.
PERSONAL Born 04/12/1950, London, England, m, 1975, 2 children **DISCIPLINE** RELIGIOUS STUDIES **EDUCATION** Cornell Univ, BA 71; Univ Chicago, JD 76, PhD 93. **CAREER** Washington & Lee univ, asst prof 94-; Dean of Students, Sr Lectr, Univ of Chicago Divinity School, 00-. **HONORS AND AWARDS** Charlotte Newcombe Diss Fell. **MEMBERSHIPS** AAR; ABA; LSA. **RESEARCH** Comparative Study of relig and law. **SELECTED PUBLICATIONS** Auth, Paying the Words Extra: Religious Discourse in the Supreme Court of the United States, Cambridge, Harv U Cen for the Stud of World Rel, 94; Religion and the Law, in: Philip Goff and Paul Harvey, eds, Themes in American religion and Culture, UCP, forthcoming; American Religion is Naturally Comparative, in: Kimberly C. Patton and Benjamin C. Ray, eds, A Magic Still Swells: The Case for Comparative Religion in the Post Modern Age, UCP, forthcoming; Judging Religion, Marquette Law Rev, 98; Finding a True Story of American Religion: Comments on L H LaRue's Constitutional Law as Fiction: Narrative in the Rhetoric of Authority, Wash and lee U Law Rev, 96; The Difference Religion Makes: Reflections On Rosenberger, The Christian Century, 96; auth, "Introduction" and "Competing Theories of Religion and Law in the Supreme Court of the United States: an Hasidic Case," in special voume entitled "Religion, Law and the Construction of Idnetities," Numen 43, 96; auth, "Exporting Religious Freedom," Commonweal, 99; reprinted in CSSR Bulletin 28:2, 99; Context 31:11, 99; auth, "A New Discourse and Practice," in Stephen Feldman, Law and Religion: A Critical Anthology, New York Univ Press, 00. **CONTACT ADDRESS** Dept of Religion, Univ of Chicago, The Divinity School, 1025 E 58th St, Chicago, IL 60637. **EMAIL** wsullivan@uchicago.edu

SUMLER-EDMOND, JANICE L.
PERSONAL Born 08/10/1948, New York, NY, s **DISCIPLINE** LAW **EDUCATION** UCLA, Los Angeles CA, BA, 1970, MA, 1971; Georgetown Univ, Washington DC, PhD, 1978; UCLA School of Law, Los Angeles CA, JD, 1985. **CAREER** Spelman Coll, Atlanta GA, visiting prof, 80-81; Reginald Heber Smith Fellowship, legal aid of Los Angeles, 85-86; Clark Atlanta Univ, Atlanta GA, assoc prof, 86-; Mack Haygood, McLean, Attorneys, Atlanta, GA, attorney, 89-95. **HONORS AND AWARDS** Lubic Memorial Law Scholarship, 1983-84; Southern Fellowship Fund Summer Research Awd, 1988; Judicine Fellow, US Supreme Court, Washington, DC, 1991-92; Panel of Neutrals, American Arbitration Association. **MEMBERSHIPS** Natl vice dir, Assn of Black Women Historians, 1986-88, natl dir, 1988-90; mem, Georgia Assn of Black Women Attorneys, 1987-; recruiter, Georgetown Univ, 1988-. **SELECTED PUBLICATIONS** "The Forten-Purvis Women and the Antislavery Crusade," Journal of Negro History, 1981; "Personhood and Citizenship: Black Women Litigants, 1867-1890," University of Massachusetts Press, 1997. **CONTACT ADDRESS** History Dept, Clark Atlanta Univ, Brawley Dr & Fair St, Atlanta, GA 30314.

SUMMERS, CLYDE W.
PERSONAL Born 11/21/1918, Grass Range, MT, m, 1947, 4 children **DISCIPLINE** LAW **EDUCATION** Univ Ill, BS, 39, JD, 42; Columbia Univ, LLM, 46, JSD, 52. **CAREER** From instr to assoc prof law, Univ Toledo, 42-49; assoc prof to prof, Univ Buffalo, 49-57; from vis prof to prof, Yale Univ, 56-75; Prof Law, Univ Pa, 75-, Guggenheim fel, 55; Ford Found fel, 63; Nat Endowment for the Humanities independent study fel, 77-78. **HONORS AND AWARDS** MA, Yale Univ, 57; LLD, Univ Louvain, 66; Dr, Univ Stockholm, 78. **MEMBERSHIPS** Am Bar Asn; Indust Relat Res Asn; Nat Acad Arbitrators; Int Soc Labor Law & Social Legis. **RESEARCH** Labor Law and the Law, 53 & Employment Relations and the Law, 58, Little; Frontiers of Collective Bargaining, Harper, 67; Labor Law: Cases and Materials, Foundation, 68. **SELECTED PUBLICATIONS CONTACT ADDRESS** 753 N 26th St, Philadelphia, PA 19130.

SUMMERS, ROBERT SAMUEL
PERSONAL Born 09/19/1933, Halfway, OR, m, 1955, 5 children **DISCIPLINE** LAW, JURISPRUDENCE **EDUCATION** Univ Ore, BS, 55; Harvard Univ, LLB, 59. **CAREER** Lawyer, Portland, Ore, 59-60; from asst prof to prof, Univ Ore, 60-68; Prof Law, Cornell Univ, 69-, Vis assoc prof law, Stanford Univ, 63-64; consult Coun Legal Educ Opportunity, 68-71; chmn, comt civic educ, Asn Am Law Schs, 72-74. **MEMBERSHIPS** Am Soc Polit & Legal Philos; Asn Am Law Schs. **RESEARCH** Contracts and commercial law. **SELECTED PUBLICATIONS** Gen ed & contribr, Essays in Legal Philosophy & More Essays in Legal Philosophy, Blackwells, Eng, 68 & Univ Calif, 71; coauth, Law, Its Nature, Functions and Limits, Prentice-Hall, 2nd ed, 72; Hornbook on the Uniform Commercial Code, 72 & Teaching Materials on Uniform Commercial Code, 2nd ed, 74, West Publ; auth, The American Legal System, 74 & Jus-

tice and Order Through Law, 74, Ginn; Instrumentalism and American Legal Theory, Cornell Univ Press, 82; H.L.A. Hart: The Concept-Of-Law--Estimations, Reflections, And A Personal Memorial, J Of Legal Education, Vol 45, 95. **CONTACT ADDRESS** Law Sch, Cornell Univ, Ithaca, NY 14850.

SUNDARAM, K.
PERSONAL Born 08/16/1947, Kumbakonam, India, m, 1974, 2 children **DISCIPLINE** PHILOSOPHY **EDUCATION** BS, 66, MA, Mlit, 68, Univ of Madras; SUNY/Buffalo, PhD, 74. **CAREER** Prof and Chr, Lake Mich College, 73-; Adjunct Grad Prof, Siena Heights Univ, 98-99. **HONORS AND AWARDS** Sr Fellow, Ctr for the Study of World Religions, Harvard; NEH grant **MEMBERSHIPS** Amer Phil Assoc; Phil of Science Assoc; Amer Assoc of Phil Teachers **RESEARCH** Philsophy of science; comparative philosophy **SELECTED PUBLICATIONS** Auth, Joseph Priestly and the Sciences in America, Michigan Academian, 99. **CONTACT ADDRESS** Dept of Philosophy, Lake Michigan Col, 2755 E Napier Ave, Benton Harbor, MI 49022-1899. **EMAIL** sundaram@lmc.cc.mi.us

SUNDBERG, WALTER
DISCIPLINE CHURCH HISTORY **EDUCATION** S.t Olaf Col, BA, 69; Princeton Theol Sem, MDiv, 73, PhD, 81; Univ Tubingen, Ger, 71-72. **CAREER** Vis instr, Augsburg Col, 80; instr, Augsburg Col, 81-84; US Army Chaplains prog, 77; Lutheran Theol Sem, Philadelphia, 76; vis prof, Col St. Catherine, 85-86; asst prof, 84; assoc prof, 86; prof, 94-; act ch, hist dept, 87-88. **HONORS AND AWARDS** Rockefeller Theol fel; grad fel; Amer Lutheran Church; asst minister, como park lutheran church; ed bd(s), lutheran quart; lutheran commentator; bd mem, great commn network; lutheran bible ministries; lutheran bible inst; alc inter-church relations comm. **MEMBERSHIPS** Mem adv coun, Interpretation. **SELECTED PUBLICATIONS** Contrib, Ministry in 19th Century European Lutheranism, Called and Ordained: Lutheran Perspectives on the Office of Ministry, 90; pub(s), articles in First Things, Lutheran Quart, Lutheran Forum; coauth, The Bible in Modern Culture: Theology and Historical Critical Method from Spinoza to Kasemann, 95. **CONTACT ADDRESS** Dept of Church History, Luther Sem, 2481 Como Ave, Saint Paul, MN 55108. **EMAIL** wsundber@luthersem.edu

SUNSHINE, EDWARD R.
PERSONAL Born 04/28/1939, Tiffin, OH, m, 1977, 1 child **DISCIPLINE** RELIGION, ETHICS **EDUCATION** Loyola Univ, Chicago, BA, 62, MA, 65; Grad Theol Union, PhD, 88. **CAREER** Lect, Theol, 72-76, Loyola Univ; fel, 83-84, Christian Ethics, Pacific Sch of Relig; instr, social ethics, 84, Univ San Fran; instr, moral theol, 84-85, Holy Family Col; instr, theol, 84-86, Roman Cath Diocese, Oakland; lect, relig stud, 86-87, Santa Clara Univ; asst prof, 88-91, assoc prof, 91-, Barry Univ. **HONORS AND AWARDS** Fel, Pacific Sch of Relig, Berkeley, 83-84; Lib travel grant, Ctr for Latin Amer Stud Univ Fla, 91. **MEMBERSHIPS** Cath Theol Soc of Am; AAR; Soc of Christian Ethics; Soc for the Study of Christian Ethics. **RESEARCH** Relation between rhetoric and ethic in Spanish colonial church documents. **SELECTED PUBLICATIONS** Coauth, Catholicism in America: A Moral-Theological Perspective, Chicago Stud, 91; ed, Proceed: First Global Village Conf, Barry Univ Ctr for Applied & Profes Ethics, 92; auth, Sexual Morality from a Social Perspective, Chicago Stud, 92; auth, Prophecy and Persuasion: The Use of Dominican Scholarship by Abolitionist Clerics in Late 17th-Century Cuba, in Human Rights and the Quincentary: Contributions of Dominican Scholars and Missionaries, Rosary Col, 93; auth, Veritatis Splendor et Rhetorica Morum: The Splendor of Truth and the Rhetoric of Morality, in Veritatis Splendor: Amer Responses, Sheed & Ward, 95; coauth, Speaking Morally: The Thirty Year Debate Between Richard A. McCormick and Stanley Hauerwas, Irish Theol Quart, 63:1, 98; auth, Catechisms in the Americas, in Christian Ethics and the New Catechism, Scranton Univ Press, forthcoming. **CONTACT ADDRESS** Dept of Theol and Philos, Barry Univ, 11300 NE Second Ave., Miami Shores, FL 33161-6695. **EMAIL** esunshine@mail.barry.edu

SUPPE, FREDERICK
PERSONAL Born 02/22/1940, Los Angeles, CA, s **DISCIPLINE** PHILOSOPHY **EDUCATION** Univ Calif, AB, 62; Univ Mich, MA, 64; PhD, 67. **CAREER** Instr to Asst Prof, Univ Ill, 64-73; Lecturer to Prof, Univ Md, 80-94; Assoc prof to Emeritus Prof and Dept Chair, 73-00; Prof and Chair, Tex Tech Univ, 00-. **HONORS AND AWARDS** Elected Sigma Xi, 75; Amicus Poloniae Badge, 75; ACLS grant; NSF grant; NEH grant; NSF Sen Fel. **MEMBERSHIPS** Am Philos Asn, Philos of Sci Asn, Soc for Christian Philos, Soc of Gay and Lesbian Philos, Am Geophysical Union **RESEARCH** Philosophy of Science, History of Science, History and Philosophy of the Planetary and Geosciences, Epistemology, Philosophy of Gender, Nursing Theory, HIV/AIDS Epidemiological modeling. **SELECTED PUBLICATIONS** Auth, The Structure of Scientific Theories, Univ Ill Press, 74; auth, The Semantic Conception of Theories and Scientific Realism, Univ Ill Press, 97; auth, "Explaining Homosexuality: Philosophical Issues, and Who Cares Anyhow/," in Gay Ethics: Outing, Civil Rights, and the Meaning of Science, 94; auth, "Science Without Induction," in The Cosmos of Science, Univ Pittsburgh Press, 97; auth, "Credentialing Scientific Claims," Perspectives on Science, (93): 153-203; auth, "The Structure of a Scientific Paper," Philosophy of Science, (98): 381-405; auth, "Middle-Range Theory of Unpleasant Symptoms: An Update," Advances in Nursing Science, (97): 14-27. **CONTACT ADDRESS** Dept Philos, Texas Tech Univ, Box 43012, Lubbock, TX 79409-3275. **EMAIL** frederick.suppe@ttu.edu

SUPPES, PATRICK
PERSONAL Born 03/17/1922, Tulsa, OK, m, 1979, 5 children **DISCIPLINE** PHILOSOPHY **EDUCATION** Univ Chicago, BS, 43; Columbia Univ, PhD, 50. **CAREER** Instr, 50-52, asst prof, 52-55, assoc prof, 55-59, prof, 59-92, prof emer, 92- , Stanford Univ. **HONORS AND AWARDS** Honory Doctor's degree, Univ Nijmegen, Netherlands, 79; Docteur Honoris Causa, Adacemie de Paris, Univ Rene Descartes, 82. **MEMBERSHIPS** Natl Acad of Sci; AAAS; Norwegian Acad of Sci and Lett; Chilean Acad of Sci; Finnish Acad of Sci and Lett. **RESEARCH** Mathematical psychology; neuropsychology; philosophy of science; educational psychology. **SELECTED PUBLICATIONS** Coauth, Foundations of Measurement, v.2: Geometrical, Threshold, and Probabilistic Representations, Academic, 89; coauth Foundations of Measurement, v.3: Representation, Axiomatization, and Invariance, Academic, 90; auth, Language for Humans and Robots, Blackwell, 91; auth, Models and Methods in the Philosophy of Science: Selected Essays, Kluwer Academic, 93. **CONTACT ADDRESS** 678 Miranda Ave, Stanford, CA 94306. **EMAIL** suppes@ockham.stanford.edu

SUR, CAROLYN WORMAN
PERSONAL Born 11/21/1942, Effingham, IL, s **DISCIPLINE** SYSTEMATIC THEOLOGY; MATHEMATICS **EDUCATION** Notre Dame Col, BS, 64; St. Louis Univ, MS, 74; PhD, 92. **CAREER** Teacher, math and biology, Rosary High, St. Louis Archdiocese, 64-66; teacher math, Teutopolis Comm High, Teutopolis, IL, 66-68; teacher math and biology, St. Francis de Sales High, St. Louis, MO, 68-74; teacher, math and biology, St. Paul High School, Highland, IL, 74-80; teacher art, math, and biology, Vincent Gray Alternative High, East St. Louis, IL, 80-83; teacher, math & computers, Aquinas High, Fort Madison, IA, 83-84; teaching asst, depts of math and theol, St. Louis Univ, St. Louis, MO, 84-91; adjunct teacher, math, Washington Univ Col, St. Louis, MO, 89-91; dir of residence, Mount Mary Col, Milwaukee, WI, 91-92; adjunct prof, math, Mount Mary Col, Milwaukee, WI, 94-95; prof, systematic theol, Sacred Heart School of Theol (sem), Hales Corner, WI, 92-94. **HONORS AND AWARDS** Cum laude graduate, 64; 3.805 grade point average, PhD program, 92; Theology: Theta Alpha Kappa National Honor Soc, 85; Mathematics: Pi Mu Epsilon National Honor Soc, 74, Kappa Mu Epsilon, 92; Nat Science Found grant, mathematics, 68-74; Nat Science Found grant, genetics, 77; Bogert Fund-$500 for res on Mysticism (Quaker sponsored), June, 90. **MEMBERSHIPS** Am Academy Relig, 90-. **RESEARCH** Medieval theology, especially writings of Medieval Women Mystics; illuminations; eco-spirituality and cosmology; Am theol issues. **SELECTED PUBLICATIONS** Auth, Feminine Images of God in the Visions of Hildegard of Bingen's Scivias, Edwin Mellon Press, 93; The Post-Abortion Syndrome: A Theological Reflection, America, Sept 28, 96; Unwanted Pregnancies, Abortions are Linked to Low Self-Esteem, Shreveport Times, May 96; The Spirituality of Gardening, Peacework, Jan 97; The Inner City (poetry), in Tracing Shadows, Nat Library of Poetry, 97; Religious Experience and Transcendence in Annie Dillard's Eco-Spirituality, in Wagering on Transcendence, Sheed & Ward, 97. **CONTACT ADDRESS** Greco Inst, 3500 Fairfield, Shreveport, LA 71104-4108. **EMAIL** csur@dioshpt.org

SURRENCY, ERWIN C.
PERSONAL Born 05/11/1924, Jesup, GA, m, 1945, 2 children **DISCIPLINE** LEGAL HISTORY **EDUCATION** Univ Ga, AB, 47, AM, 48, LLB, 49; George Peabody Col, MALS, 50. **CAREER** Librn, Charles Klein Law Libr, Temple Univ, 50-78, from asst prof to assoc prof law, 54-60, prof, 60-78; Prof Law & Dir Law Libr, Univ Ga, 79-, Ed, Am J Legal Hist, 57-; lectr, Queen's Univ, Belfast, 63-64; mem, Asn Am Law Schs; consult, Nigerian Govt on Law Libr, 75-76. **MEMBERSHIPS** Am Soc Legal Hist (pres, 57-59); Am Hist Asn; Stair Soc; Selden Soc; Am Asn Law Libr (pres, 73-74). **RESEARCH** History of the legal profession in America; history of the federal courts; legal history of Georgia. **SELECTED PUBLICATIONS** Auth, Marshall Reader, 55; How The United-States Perfects An International Agreement, Law Libr J, Vol 85, 93; coauth, Research in Pennsylvania Law, 55; Guide to Legal Research, 59, Oceana. **CONTACT ADDRESS** Dept of Law, Univ of Georgia, Athens, GA 30601.

SUTER, RONALD
PERSONAL Born 11/01/1930, Geneva, Switzerland, m, 1998, 2 children **DISCIPLINE** PHILOSOPHY **EDUCATION** Univ Chicago, AB, 53; Oxford Univ, BA, 59, MA, 62; Stanford Univ, PhD, 67. **CAREER** Instr, Middlebury Col, VT, 62-63; instr, 63-66, asst prof, 66-69, assoc prof, 69-74, Prof, MI State Univ, 74-. **HONORS AND AWARDS** Pres, Jowett Soc, Oxford, 57; co-chmn, Hume Soc, Stanford, 60-61; dir, 1968 Fall Isenberg Memorial Series on the Philosophy of Ludwig Wittgenstein; Nat Endowment for the Humanities summer stipend, 70; recipient, Col of Arts and Letters Distinguished Fac Res Awd, 88-89. **MEMBERSHIPS** APA **RESEARCH** Ethics; philos of art; philos of mind; Wittgenstein. **SELECTED PUBLICATIONS** Auth, The Isenberg Memorial Lecture Series, 1965-1966, ed and auth of the intro, East Lansing: MI State Univ Press, 69; Six Answers to the Problem of Taste, Univ Press Amer, 79; Are You Moral?, Univ Press Amer, 84, revised ed, 91; Interpreting Wittgenstein: A Cloud of Philosophy, a Drop of Grammar, Temple Univ Press, 89, paperback, 91, Korean trans, 98; What is This Thing Called Love?, forthcoming. **CONTACT ADDRESS** Dept of Philos, 955 Lilac Ave., East Lansing, MI 48823. **EMAIL** suteron@pilot.msu.edu

SUTHERLAND, GAIL HINICH
DISCIPLINE ASIAN RELIGIONS, HINDUISM AND BUDDHISM **EDUCATION** Univ Chicago, PhD, 88. **CAREER** Assoc prof, La State Univ. **RESEARCH** The body, sexuality, food, gender, and ethical reversals in Indian religions; Asian religions in the American South. **SELECTED PUBLICATIONS** Auth, The Disguises of the Demon: The Development of the Yaksa in Hinduism and Buddhism, SUNY, 91; Asvaghosa and Saigyo: A Comparison of Two Buddhist Poets, in Relig and Lit, 91. **CONTACT ADDRESS** Dept of Philos and Relig Stud, Louisiana State Univ and A&M Col, 106 Coates Hall, Baton Rouge, LA 70803.

SUTTER, LESLIE E.
PERSONAL Born 11/08/1960, Traverse City, MI, s **DISCIPLINE** PHILOSOPHY, EDUCATION **EDUCATION** CSUDH, MA, 86; Univ Berne, PhD, 91; Columbia Pacific Univ, D.A. (Hon.), 91, Univ Sarasota, EdD, 01. **CAREER** Adj prof, Edison Col, 94-; prof, Int Col, 97-; co-chair, Lib Arts, 00-, chair Lib Arts, 00; chair, Interdisciplinary studies; 00; asst dean, Social Sciences and Humanities, 01. **HONORS AND AWARDS** Non-resident scholar, Univ Berne, 93; prof of the year, Int col, 98, 00; Fulbright nominee to Republic of Moldova, 01. **MEMBERSHIPS** Am Hist Asn; APA; ASPCP; APPA. **RESEARCH** Existentialism; logical positivism; immigration questions. **SELECTED PUBLICATIONS** Auth, Joy of Catholic Paganism, Rustte Press, 87; auth, Swiss Emigration Agencies, UMI, 91; auth, Philosophy and Religion, McGraw-Hill, 97; auth, Logic for Beginners, Int. Press, 00. **CONTACT ADDRESS** Intl Col, 2655 Northbrooke Dr., Naples, FL 33919. **EMAIL** lsutter@internationalcollege.edu

SWAIN, CHARLES W.
PERSONAL Born 07/30/1937, Des Moines, IA, m, 1958, 2 children **DISCIPLINE** HISTORY OF RELIGION **EDUCATION** State Univ Iowa, AB, 59; Brown Univ, PhD(relig), 65. **CAREER** Instr relig, Oberlin Col, 63-65; from asst prof to assoc prof, 65-77, Prof Relig, Fla State Univ, 77-, Soc Relig Higher Educ Asian relig fel, 67-68; vis lectr, Ctr Study World Relig, Harvard Univ, 67-68; Helmsley lectr, Brandeis Univ, 68. **MEMBERSHIPS** Am Acad Relig; AAUP; Soc Values Higher Educ. **RESEARCH** History of western religious thought; history of western philosophy; phenomenology of religion. **SELECTED PUBLICATIONS CONTACT ADDRESS** Dept of Relig, Florida State Univ, 600 W College Ave, Tallahassee, FL 32306-1096.

SWAIN, JAMES H.
PERSONAL Born 07/04/1954, Philadelphia, PA, m, 1985 **DISCIPLINE** LAW **EDUCATION** Univ of Bridgeport, BA 1975; Temple Univ School of Law, JD 1978; Univ of Pennsylvania Law School, LLM 1986. **CAREER** US Atty So Dist of NY, summer intern 1977; Third Circuit Ct of Appeals, clerkship intern Hon A Leon Higginbotham 1978; US Dept of Labor, trial atty office of reg solicitor, 78-88; US Dept of Justice, Eastern PA, asst US atty, 89-94; US Dept of Justice, Southern FL, 94-. **HONORS AND AWARDS** Scholar of the Year Awd, Omega Psi Phi Frat Inc, Rho Upsilon Chap 1975-76; Distinguished Serv Awd, Black Amer Law Students Assn, 1977-78; Certificate of Appreciation, Barristers Assn of Philadelphia, 1978-79, 1979-80; Omega Psi Phi Frat Inc, Mu Omega Chap; US Department of Justice, John Marshall Awd, 1992. **MEMBERSHIPS** Barristers Assn of Philadelphia, executive committee, 1979-80, 1986-89, legislation revue committee, 1978-82; mem bd of dir, Community Legal Services, 1988-94; Wynnfield Residents Assn, board of directors, 1988-94, executive vp, 1992-93; mem, Federal Bar Assn Philadelphia Chapter, 1988-; Philadelphia Bar Assn, 1989-; Federal Bar Assn, 1979-; trustee, Mount Pleasant Baptist Church, Philadelphia, PA; Federal Bar Association Miami Chapter, 1996-; Inns of Court University of Miami's Chapter, 1996-; Dade County Black Lawyers Association, 1994-; National Bar Association, Florida State Chapter, 1996-. **SELECTED PUBLICATIONS** Auth, "Protecting Individual Employees: Is it Safe to Complain About Safety?," University of Bridgeport Law Review, 1988; auth, "Statutory Basics of Money Laundering Forfeiture", Global Media Alert, 01. **CONTACT ADDRESS** US Atty's Office, 99 NE 4th St, Miami Beach, FL 33140.

SWAN, KENNETH P.
DISCIPLINE LAW **EDUCATION** BEng, R.M.C., 64; LLB, Univ Alberta, 70. **CAREER** Prof, Queen's Univ, 73-82; private legal practice, Toronto, ON, 82-; Special Lectr, Fac of Law,

Univ Toronto, 84-. **SELECTED PUBLICATIONS** Auth, pubs on various aspects of labour law and labour relations. **CONTACT ADDRESS** Fac of Law, Univ of Toronto, 78 Queen's Park, Toronto, ON, Canada M5S 1A1.

SWANGER, DAVID
PERSONAL Born 08/01/1940, Newark, NJ, m, 1970, 3 children **DISCIPLINE** PHILOSOPHY, CREATIVE WRITING **EDUCATION** Swarthore Col, BA, 63; Harvard Univ, MAT, 64; EdD, 70. **CAREER** Prof, Univ Calif-Santa Crux, 87-. **HONORS AND AWARDS** NEA Poetry Fel; 'Golden Apple' UCSC Teaching Awd. **MEMBERSHIPS** Phi Delta Kappa, Philos of Educ Soc, Poets & Writers. **RESEARCH** Educational philosophy, poetry. **SELECTED PUBLICATIONS** Auth, Essays in Aesthetic Education, Mellen, 91; auth, This Waking Unafraid, Univ of Mo, 95. **CONTACT ADDRESS** Dept Educ, Univ of California, Santa Cruz, 1156 High St, Santa Cruz, CA 95064-1077. **EMAIL** dswanger@cats.ucsc.edu

SWANGER, EUGENE R.
DISCIPLINE JAPANESE, CHINESE, BUDDHIST, CONFUCIAN, TAOIST, AND ZEN TRADITIONS **EDUCATION** Capital Univ, BA, BD; Oberlin Col, STM, MA; Univ Iowa, PhD. **CAREER** Prof, 67-; former dept chair. **HONORS AND AWARDS** Alumni Asn Awd; lect, foreign service inst, u. s. state dept; distinguished vis lect, for service inst, 93; ndea fel, japan. **RESEARCH** Oriental religions. **SELECTED PUBLICATIONS** Areas: Buddhist Ecumenical Movement, the church-state controversy in Japan, the role of the Shaman in Japan, and omamori story tokens in Japanese culture. **CONTACT ADDRESS** Wittenberg Univ, Post Office Box, Springfield, OH 45501-0720.

SWANSON, BERT E.
PERSONAL Born 08/15/1924, Tacoma, WA, w, 1968 **DISCIPLINE** POLITICAL SCIENCE **EDUCATION** George Washington Univ, BA, 50; Univ Oregon, MA, 56; PhD, 59. **CAREER** Hunter Col, 59-61; Sarah Lawrence, 61-71; Univ Fla, 71-. **RESEARCH** Urban policy and politics. **SELECTED PUBLICATIONS** Auth, Dialogued Community, in, Commun Econ Develop, 81. **CONTACT ADDRESS** Dept of Political Science, Univ of Florida, Gainesville, FL 32601. **EMAIL** bes@nervm.nerdc.ufl.edu

SWANSON, CAROL B.
PERSONAL Born 12/01/1954, Cleveland, OH, m, 1978, 2 children **DISCIPLINE** LAW **EDUCATION** Bowdoin Col, AB, 77; Vanderbilt Univ Sch of Law, JD, 81. **CAREER** Assoc, Sullivan & Cromwell, NY, 81-84; asst US atty, US Atty Office, 84-86; assoc to partner/shareholder, Popham Haik Schnobrich & Kaufman Ltd, 86-89; prof, law, Hamline Univ Sch of Law, 89-. **HONORS AND AWARDS** Phi Beta Kappa, prof of the year award, 90-91. **MEMBERSHIPS** Amer Bar Asn; Minn State Bar Asn; Minn Continuing Legal Educ. **RESEARCH** Business law issues including corporate governance. **SELECTED PUBLICATIONS** Auth, Reinventing Insider Trading: The Supreme Court Misappropriates the Misappropriation Theory, 32, Wake Forest Law Rev, 1157, dec, 97; auth, The Turn in Takeovers: A Study in Public Appeasement and Unstoppable Capitalism, 30, Ga Law Rev, 943, 96; auth, Corporate Governance: Slipping Seamlessly into the Twenty-First Century, 21, J Corp Law, 417, 96; auth, Juggling Shareholder Rights and Strike Suits in Derivative Litigation: The ALI Drops the Ball, 77, Minn Law Rev, 1339, 93; auth, Anticompetitive Practices in Great Britain: Expanded Enforcement Under the Competition Act 1980, 15, V and J Transnational L, 65, 82. **CONTACT ADDRESS** Sch of Law, Hamline Univ, 1536 Hewitt Ave, MS-C2044, Saint Paul, MN 55104-1284. **EMAIL** cswanson@gw.hamline.edu

SWANSTROM, TODD F.
PERSONAL Born 02/12/1948, St Paul, MN, m, 1995, 3 children **DISCIPLINE** POLITICAL SCIENCE **EDUCATION** Macalester Col, BA, 70; Washington Univ, MA, 71; Princeton Univ, PhD, 81. **CAREER** Asst prof, 82-89; assoc prof, 89-87, SUNY Albany; prof, 97-. **HONORS AND AWARDS** Phi Beta Kappa; Woodrow Wilson Fel; Outstand Teach Year Awd; Pi Sigma Alpha Awd, Bst Paper; UAC, Bst Paper; ADSA, Bst Bk Awd. **MEMBERSHIPS** APSA; UAA. **RESEARCH** Urban politics; housing policy. **SELECTED PUBLICATIONS** Auth, The Crisis of Growth Politics: Cleveland. Kucinich and the Challenge of Urban Populism, Temple Univ Press (Philadelphia), 85; co-ed, Beyond the City Limits: Urban Policy and Economic Restructuring in Comparative Perspective, Temple Univ Press (Philadelphia), 90; coauth, City Politics: Private Power and Public Policy, Harper Collins (NY), 94; coauth, The Democratic Debate: An Introduction to American Politics, Houghton Mifflin (Boston), 95; auth, Semisovereign Cities: The Politics of Urban Development," Polity 21 (88): 83-110, reprinted, in Enduring Tensions in Urban Politics, ed. Dennis Judd, Paul Xantor (NY: Macmillan, 92): 512-531; and in Urban and Regional Policy, ed. Jon Pierre (Edward Elgar, 95): 400-427; auth, "Ideas Matter: Reflections on the New Regionalism," Cityscape 2 (96): 5-21; auth, "The Stubborn Persistence of Local Land Use Powers: A Comment on Morrill," Polit Geog 7 (98): 25-32; auth, "The Nonprofitization of United States Housing policy: Dilemmas of Community Development," Comm Devel J 34 (99): 28-37; coauth, "The Urban Electorate in Presidential Elections: 1920-1996," Urban Aff Rev 35 (99): 72-91. **CONTACT ADDRESS** Dept Political Science, SUNY at Albany, 1400 Washington Ave, Albany, NY 12222-1000. **EMAIL** t.swanstrom@albany.edu

SWARTLEY, WILLARD M.
PERSONAL Born 08/06/1936, Doylestown, PA, m, 1958, 2 children **DISCIPLINE** BIBLICAL STUDIES (NEW TESTAMENT) **EDUCATION** Eastern Mennonite Col, BA, 59; Goshen Bibl Sem, BD, 62; Princeton Theol Sem, PhD, 73. **CAREER** Prof, 78-, Acting Dir , 97, 99, Dir, 79-88, Sum Sch Dir, 90-93, 95-00, Dean, 95-00, Associated Mennonite Biblical Seminary. **HONORS AND AWARDS** Coed, Study of Peace and Scripture Series, 90; Ed, New Testament for Believers Church Bible Commentary Series, Herald Press, 89-. **MEMBERSHIPS** Soc of Bibl Lit; Chicago Soc for Bibl Res; Colloquium on Violence and Religion; Studiorum Novi Testament, Soicetas, 99-. **RESEARCH** New Testament, hemeneutics, peace theology. **SELECTED PUBLICATIONS** Auth, Slavery, Sabbath, War and Women, Herald Press, 88; ed, Love of Enemy and Nonretaliation in the New Testament, w/JK, 92; coed, The Meaning of Peace, w/JK, 92/00; ed, Violence Renounced: Rene Girard, Biblical Studies, and Peacemaking, Pandora US; Oxford Companion to the Bible, 93; Auth, Isreal's Scripture Traditionsand the Synoptic Gospels: Story Shaping Story, Hendrickson, 94; From High-Tech and Triage to Service and Shalom, Mennonite Med Mess, 94; The Anabaptist Use of Scripture: Contemporary Applications and Prospects, Anabaptist Current, 95; War and Peace in the New Testament, Aufstieg und Niedergang der Romischen Welt II 26.3 Wide Gruyter; 2298-21408, 96; Research Note: Sunday Syllabus Serendipity, Mennonite Quart Rev, 96; CoAuth, Blending Body and Soul: Sociological Study of the New Testament, Conrad Grebel Rev, 96; Auth, War , Encyclopedia of Early Christianity, Garland, 97; The Role of Women in Mark's Gospel: A Narrative Analysis, Bib Theol Bul, 97; A Temple In Time, The Mennonite, 97; Intertextuality in Early Chrisitian Literature, Dict of Later New Test and Its Dev, 97; the Banquet, Persp on the Parables, 97; CoEd Building Communities of Compassion, HeraldPress, 98; Mutual Aid Based in Jesus and Early Christianity, Building, 98; auth, Discipleship and Imitation of Jesus/Suffering Servant: The Mimesis of New Creation, Violence, 00 . **CONTACT ADDRESS** Associated Mennonite Biblical Sem, 3003 Benham Ave, Elkhart, IN 46517. **EMAIL** wswartley@ambs.edu

SWARTZ, ALICE M.
PERSONAL Born 11/07/1943, Scranton, PA **DISCIPLINE** LITURGICAL STUDIES **EDUCATION** Drew Univ, PhD, 97. **CAREER** Adj asst prof, religious studies, Col St Elizabeth, 98-. **MEMBERSHIPS** Cath Bibl Asn; Amer Acad Relig; Cath Theol Soc Am **RESEARCH** Liturgy; Spirituality **CONTACT ADDRESS** Col of Saint Elizabeth, 2 Convent Rd, Morristown, NJ 07960.

SWARTZ, BARBARA E.
DISCIPLINE LAW **EDUCATION** Temple Univ, BA, 66; Univ MI, MA, 67; NYork Univ, JD, 71; Columbia Univ, MPH, 91. **CAREER** Bruce K Gould Distinguished Prof Law, Touro Col; clin assoc prof, NY Univ; lectr, Columbia Univ. **HONORS AND AWARDS** Fulbright scholar, Univ Copenhagen, Denmark, 78-79. **MEMBERSHIPS** Consult, World Health Orgn. **RESEARCH** Law (criminal practice, health law, and family law) **SELECTED PUBLICATIONS** Auth, Responsibility for Drug Induced Injury. **CONTACT ADDRESS** Touro Col, New York, 300 Nassau Rd, Huntington, NY 11743. **EMAIL** BarbaraS@tourolaw.edu

SWAYNE, STEVEN ROBERT
PERSONAL Born 01/25/1957, Los Angeles, CA **DISCIPLINE** THEOLOGY **EDUCATION** Occidental Coll, BA (summa cum laude, phi beta kappa) 1978; Fuller Theological Seminary, MDiv 1983; Univ of CA, Berkeley, CA, PhD, 98. **CAREER** Lake Ave Congregational Church, adm Asst to sr pastor, 78-85; Seattle Pacific Univ, dir of campus ministries, 85-90; asst prof, Dartmouth Col. **HONORS AND AWARDS** recital appearances (piano) on West Coast; first prize, John Wesley Work III Composition Competition 1979; First Prize, Johana Hodges Piano Competition, 1981; Chancellor's Minority Pre-Doctoral Fellowship, Univ of CA-Berkeley, 1990-91. **MEMBERSHIPS** Ordained minister Conservative Congregational Christian Conf 1984-; lay pastor Westminster Chapel 1986-; member, executive committee, Alumni/ae Association, Fuller Theological Seminary 1987-; mem, alumini/ae council, Fuller Theological Seminary, 1989-. **SELECTED PUBLICATIONS** Music published Fred Bock Music Productions; articles published in various Christian periodicals. **CONTACT ADDRESS** Dept of Music, Dartmouth Col, Hinman Box 6187, Hanover, NH 03755. **EMAIL** Steven.R.Swayne@dartmouth.edu

SWEARER, DONALD K.
PERSONAL Born 08/02/1934, Wichita, KS, m, 1964, 2 children **DISCIPLINE** HISTORY OF RELIGION **EDUCATION** Princeton Univ, BA, cum laude 56, MA, 65, PhD, 67; Yale Univ, BD, 62, STM, 63. **CAREER** Assoc Prof 70-75, Prof 75-, Eugene M Lang Res Prof 87-92, Charles and Harriet Cox McDowell Prof of Religion 92-, Swarthmore College; Instr, Asst Prof 65-70, Oberlin College. **HONORS AND AWARDS** Phi Beta Kappa; Lent Fel; 3 NEH Fels; Fulbright Fel; Guggenheim Fel; 2 Fulbright Fels. **MEMBERSHIPS** AAAS; AAR; ASSR; SBCS; AAUP. **RESEARCH** Buddhism; Comparative Religious Ethics. **SELECTED PUBLICATIONS** Auth, Holism and the Fate of the Earth, Rel and Ecology: Forging an Ethic Across Traditions, forthcoming; Center and Periphery: Buddhism and Politics in Modern Thailand, Buddhism and Politics in Modern Asia, ed, Ian Harris, Cassell's 98; Buddhist Virtue Voluntary Poverty and Extensive Benevolence, J of Rel Ethics, 98; The Worldliness of Buddhism, Wilson Qtly, 97; Bhikkhu Buddhadasa's Interpretation of the Buddha, J of the American Acad of Religion, 96; Hypostasizing the Buddha: Buddha: Image Consecration in Northern Thailand, Hist of Religions, 95; coauth, The Legend of Queen Cama, Camadevivamsa, Albany NY, SUNY Press, 98; auth, The Buddhist World of Southeast Asia, Albany, SUNY Press, 95; Ethics Wealth and Salvation, A Study in Buddhist Social Ethics, coed, Columbia, Univ S Carolina Press, pbk ed, 92. **CONTACT ADDRESS** Dept of Religion, Swarthmore Col, Swarthmore, PA 19081. **EMAIL** dswearel@swarthmore.edu

SWEENEY, LEO
PERSONAL Born 09/22/1918, O'Connor, NE **DISCIPLINE** PHILOSOPHY **EDUCATION** St Louis Univ, PhL,-43, MA, 45, STL, 51; Univ Toronto, PhD, 54. **CAREER** From instr to prof philos, St Louis Univ, 54-68; res prof, Creighton Univ, 68-70; vis prof, Cath Univ Am, 70-72; vis prof, 72-74, res prof philos, Loyola Univ, Chicago, 74-, assoc ed, Mod Schoolman, 56-68, corresp ed, 68-. **HONORS AND AWARDS** Am Coun Learned Soc res fel, 63-64; res grant, Creighton Univ, 68-69. **MEMBERSHIPS** Jesuit Philos Asn (secy, 60-63, pres, 65- 66); Am Cath Philos Asn (vpres, 79-80, pres, 80-8 1); Soc Int l'Etude de Philos Medievale; Soc, Ancient Greek Philos; Am Maritain Asn; Fel Cath Schol; Nat Asn Schol; Soc for Medieval/Renaissance Philos; Cardinal Newman Soc; Jesuit Philos Asn. **RESEARCH** Greek philosophy up to Proclus; the problem of divine infinity in Greek, Mediaeval and Renaissance philosophy; metaphysics throughout history of philosophy. **SELECTED PUBLICATIONS** Auth, Metaphysics of Authentic Existentialism, Prentice-Hall, 65; Infinity in the Presocratics: A Bibliographical and Philosophical Study, Nijhoff, The Hague, 72; Bonaventure and Aquinas on Divine Being as Infinite, in Southwestern J Philos, 7/74; Henry Jackson's Interpretation of Plato, in J Hist Philos, 75; Ease in Albert the Great's Texts on Creation, in Albert the Great: Commemorative Essays, Univ Okla Press, 80; Participation and the Structure of Being in Proclus' Elements of Theology, in The Structure of Being: A Neoplatonic Approach, State Univ NY Press, 81; Can Aquinas Speak to the Modern World?, in One Hundred of Thomism: Aeterni Patris and Afterwards, Univ St Thomas Press, 81; ed, Infinity: Proc Am Cath Philos Asn, Vol 55, 81; auth, Greek and Medieval Studies in Honor of Leo Sweeney, SJ, Peter Lang, 94; Authentic Metaphysics in Age of Unreality, Peter Lang, 96; Christian Philosophy, in Greek, Medieval, Contemporary Reflections, Peter Lang, 97; Divine Infinity in Greek and Medieval Thought, Peter Lang, rev ed, 98. **CONTACT ADDRESS** Dept of Philos, Loyola Univ, Chicago, 6525 N Sheridan Rd, Chicago, IL 60626-5385.

SWEET, JUSTIN
PERSONAL Born Madison, WI **DISCIPLINE** LAW **EDUCATION** Univ Wis-Madison, BA, 51, LLB, 53. **CAREER** Atty, State of Wis, 53-54; atty pvt pract, 57-58; assoc prof law, 58-63, Prof Law, Univ Calif, Berkeley, 63-, Fulbright prof, Univ Rome, 65-66; vis prof, Hebrew Univ Jerusalem, 70 & Cath Univ Louvain, 73; lectr, Univ Oslo, 73, York Univ, Ont, 76 & Hebrew Univ, Jerusalem, 80; Delay In Construction Contracts--A Comparative-Study Of Legal Issues Under Swiss And Anglo-American Law, Am J Of Comparative Law, Vol 43, 95. **RESEARCH** Architectural and engineering law; basic contract law. **SELECTED PUBLICATIONS CONTACT ADDRESS** Sch of Law, Univ of California, Berkeley, Berkeley, CA 94720.

SWEETMAN, BRENDAN M.
PERSONAL Born 08/25/1962, Dublin, Ireland, m, 1984, 3 children **DISCIPLINE** PHILOSOPHY **EDUCATION** Univ Col Dublin, BA, 83, MA, 86; Cambridge Univ, Dir. R.S., 87; Univ S Cal, MA, 90, PhD, 92. **CAREER** Tutor Philos, Univ Col, 85-86; vis lectr, 92, Loyola Marymount Univ; asst prof, 92-97, Assoc Prof Philos, Rockhurst University; Chair of Department 00-. **HONORS AND AWARDS** Grad scholar, Univ Col, 84-86; Fulbright Travel Awd, Irish Govt, 87; Dean fel, Univ S Cal, 87-91; Pres Res grant, Rockhurst Univ, 94 & 96 & 98. **MEMBERSHIPS** Gabriel MarcelSoc; Am Cath Philos Asn; Soc Christian Philos; Am Soc Study Fr Philos; Am Philos Asn; Am Maritain Asn. **RESEARCH** Philosophy of religion; contemporary European philosophy. **SELECTED PUBLICATIONS** ed, Comtemporary Perspectives on Religious Epistemology, Oxford Univ Press, 92; coauth, Truth and Religious Belief: M. E. Sharpe, 1998; ed., The Failure of Modernism, Catholic University of America Press, 99; Non-conceptual knowledge in Jacques Maritain and Gabriel Marcel, in Freedom, Virtue, and the Common Good, Univ Notre Dame, 95; Gabriel Marcel and the Problem of Knowledge, Jour of Am Soc for Study of Fr Philos, 95; The Deconstruction of Western Metaphysics: Derrida and Maritain on Identity, in Postmodernism and Christian Philos, 97; Postmodernism, Derrida and Dif-

ferance: A Critique, Int Philos Quart, 99. **CONTACT ADDRESS** Dept of Philosophy, Rockhurst Col, 1100 Rockhurst Rd., Kansas City, MO 64110. **EMAIL** Sweetman@Vax1.Rockhurst.Edu

SWETLAND, KENNETH L.
PERSONAL m, 3 children **DISCIPLINE** MINISTRY **EDUCATION** Wheaton Col, AB, 59, MA, 62; Gordon Divinity Sch, MDiv; Andover Newton Theol Sch, Dmin, 76. **CAREER** Chaplain, Penn State Univ; acad dean, prof, Gordon-Conwell Theol Sem, 72-. **HONORS AND AWARDS** Pastor, Pigeon Cove Chapel, 64-72; Calvary Baptist Church, 68-72. **MEMBERSHIPS** Mem, Acad Homiletics; Assn for Case Tchg; Amer Assn of Christian Coun(s); Amer Assn Rel; Soc Biblical Lit. **SELECTED PUBLICATIONS** Auth, The Hidden World of the Pastor: Case Studies on Personal Issues of Real Pastors, Baker Bk House, 95; ed, Jour Case Tchg, 89-91. **CONTACT ADDRESS** Gordon-Conwell Theol Sem, 130 Essex St, South Hamilton, MA 01982.

SWIDLER, LEONARD
PERSONAL Born 01/06/1929, Sioux City, IA, m, 1957, 2 children **DISCIPLINE** RELIGION; HISTORY **EDUCATION** St Norbert Col, BA, 50; Marquette Univ, MA, 55; Univ Tubingen, STL, 59; Univ Wis, PhD(hist), 61. **CAREER** From asst prof to assoc prof hist, Duquesne Univ, 60-66; Prof Relig, Temple Univ, 66-, Founder & co-ed, J Ecumenical Studies, 64-; mem, Comt Educ for Ecumenism & Presby/ Reformed and Roman Cath Consultation, 65-; fel, Inst Ecumenical & Cult Res, 68-69; Fulbright res grant, Ger, 72-73; guest prof Cath & Protestant theol, Univ Tubingen, 72-73; guest prof Philos, Nankai, Tianjin, 87; Co-Founder/Dir, Global Dialogue Institute, 95-. **HONORS AND AWARDS** LLD, La Salle Col, 77. **MEMBERSHIPS** Am Soc Church Hist; Am Acad Relig; Cath Theol Soc, Am; Church Hist Soc. **RESEARCH** Inter-religious dialogue; modern church history; women in religion and society; global ethics. **SELECTED PUBLICATIONS** Ed, Ecumenism, the Spirit and Worship, 66; auth, The Ecumenical Vanguard, 66; Freedom in the Church, 69; coauth, Bishops and People, 71; Isj en Isjah, 73; auth, Women in Judaism, 76; Blood Witness for Peace and Unity, 77; coauth, Women Priests, 77; Yeshua: A Model for Moderns, 87; After the Absolute, 90; Toward a Catholic Constitution, 96; THEORIA-PRAXIS, 98; auth, The Study of Religion in the Age of Dialogue, 00. **CONTACT ADDRESS** Dept of Religion, Temple Univ, 1114 W Berks St, Philadelphia, PA 19122-6090. **EMAIL** dialogue@vm.temple.edu

SWINDLER, JAMES KENNETH
PERSONAL Born 09/17/1947, Pratt, KS, m, 1970, 2 children **DISCIPLINE** PHILOSOPHY **EDUCATION** Univ Kans, BA, 73, MA, 73, PhD(philos), 78. **CAREER** Prof and chmn dept of philos, Westminster Col, 77-95; vis assoc prof, Univ of Miami, 83; Prof and Chm, Dept of Philos, IL State Univ; consultant, Univ of Kansas, 82 NEH, 85, 96-, Baker Univ, 92, Utah State Univ, 93, Arkansas Dept of Higher Ed, 95-96, prof and chmn, dept of philos, Wittenberg Univ, 95-00; Davidson Col, 97, Wichita State Univ, 97, Mary Washington Col, 97. **HONORS AND AWARDS** Review of Metaphysics Dissertation Essay Prize, NEH fellowships, Univ of Utah Humanities Ctr Fellow, 91-92. **MEMBERSHIPS** Am Philos Asn; Southwestern Philos Soc; AAUP; Cent States Philos Asn;Phi Beta Kappa. **RESEARCH** Metaphysics; history of philosophy; social philosophy. **SELECTED PUBLICATIONS** Auth, Parmenides' Paradox: Negative Reference and Negative Existentials, The Review of Metaphysics, 80; Butchvaror on Existence, Southern Journal of Philosophy, 81; Material Identity and Sameness, Philosophical Topics, 85; MacIntyres' Republic, The Theorist, 90; Davidson';s Razor, Southwest Philosophy Rev, 91; The Permanant Heartland of Subjectivity, Idealistic Studies, 96; Social Intentions: Aggregate, Collective, and General, Philos of the Social Sciences, 96; Weaving: An Analysis of the Constitution of Objects, Construtivist Moral Realism: Intention and Invention in Social Reality, Southwest Philos Rev, 98. **CONTACT ADDRESS** Dept of Philos, Illinois State Univ, Normal, IL 61790. **EMAIL** jswindler@wittenberg.edu; philosophy.ilstu.edu

SWINTON, KATHERINE E.
PERSONAL Born 08/14/1950, East York, ON, Canada **DISCIPLINE** LAW, HISTORY **EDUCATION** Univ Alta, BA, 71; Osgoode Hall Law Sch, York Univ, LLB, 75; Yale Univ, LLM, 77. **CAREER** Parliamentary intern, House of Commons, 71-72; law clerk, Supreme Court Can, 75-76; asst prof, Osgoode Hall Law Sch, 77-79; asst prof, 79-82, assoc prof, 82-87, prof fac law, Univ Toronto, 88-97; JUSTICE, ONTARIO COURT (GENERAL DIVISION), 97-. **SELECTED PUBLICATIONS** Auth, The Supreme Court and Canadian Federalism: The Laskin-Dickson Years, 90; co-ed, Studies in Labour Law, 83; co-ed, Competing Constitutional Visions: The Meech Lake Accord, 88; co-ed, Rethinking Federalism, 95. **CONTACT ADDRESS** Ontario Court, 361 University Ave, Toronto, ON, Canada M5G 1T3.

SWITALA, KRISTIN
PERSONAL Born 08/07/1967, Pittsburgh, PA, m, 1996 **DISCIPLINE** PHILOSOPHY **EDUCATION** Villanova Univ, BA, 89; Vanderbilt Univ, PhD, 93. **CAREER** Asst prof, Univ Tenn Chattanooga, 93-. **HONORS AND AWARDS** Outstanding Prof Awd, 93; Excellence in Teaching Awd, Coll of Art and Sci, 95; Nat Alumni Asn Outstanding Teacher Awd 96; Women's Network Best Site Awd, 98. **MEMBERSHIPS** APA; SPEP; Phi Betta Kappa, Phi Sigma Tau. **RESEARCH** Continental Philosophy; Feminist Theory. **SELECTED PUBLICATIONS** Auth, Aristotelian History, Dialogue, 91; A Postmodern Musicological Approach to the Authentic Performance Debate, Selected Studies in Phenomenology and Existential Philos, 94; Foucault and the Mutation of Language, Philos Today, 97; Chantal Chawaf Talks About Her New Novel, The Chantal Chawaf Newsletter, 97; Chawaf Discusses Her Influences, The Chantal Chawaf Newsletter, 97; Feminist Theory website, 97; Taking Risks: Teaching Redemption to Freshmen Philosophy Students, The Chantal Chawaf Newsletter, 98. **CONTACT ADDRESS** Dept of Philosophy, Univ of Tennessee, Chattanooga, Chattanooga, TN 37403-2598. **EMAIL** kswitala@hotmail.com

SYLIOWICZ, JOSEPH S.
PERSONAL Born 12/07/1931, Belgium, m, 1960, 2 children **DISCIPLINE** INTERNATIONAL STUDIES **EDUCATION** BA Univ of Denver, 53; MA School of Adv Intl Studies, John Hopkins Univ, 55; PhD Columbia Univ, 61. **CAREER** Univ MD, Extension Div, 60; Hunter Col, 61-62; Brooklyn Col, 61-64; Long Island Univ, 66; Univ Mich 80; Univ Utah, 80; Oxford Univ, Michaelmas Term, 84; founder, Intermodal Trans Inst and Prof, Graduate School of Intl Studies, Univ Denver, present. **HONORS AND AWARDS** Outstanding Educator of the Year, Colo Transportation Comm, 99; Intl Awd for Dci and Ethics in Trans Res, Alliance for Trans Res, 97; Outstanding Scholar, Burlington Northern Found Awd, 86; Sr Assoc St Anthony's Col and Fel Dept of External Studies, Oxford Univ, 84-85; Fulbright Sr Res Fellowship, 83; Soc Sci Res Council, 68-69. **MEMBERSHIPS** Phi Beta Kappa; Pi Gamma Mu; Tau Kappa Alpha; Phi Delta Rho; Am Men of Sci; Who's Who in the West; Dictionary of Intl Bio; Intl Scholars Dir; Intl Auth; Writer Who's Who. **RESEARCH** Transportation and sustainable development; Middle East education. **SELECTED PUBLICATIONS** Denver International Airport: Lessons Learned, McGraw Hill,96, Co-auth; Politics, Technology and Development: Decision Making in the Turkish Iron and Steel Industry, NY: St Martins Press and London: The Manmillan Press Ltd/St Antony's College Series, 91; Education in L C Brown, ed, The Imperial Legacy: The Ottoman Imprint on the Balkans and the Middle East, NY, Coumbia Univ Press, 95; Education and Political Development in M Heper ed, Politics in the 3rd Turkish Republic, Westview, 93; Revisiting Transportation Planning and Decision Making Theory, co-auth, 74. **CONTACT ADDRESS** Graduate School of Intl Studies, Univ of Denver, Denver, CO 80210. **EMAIL** JSZYLIOW@DU.EDU

SYLLA, EDITH DUDLEY
PERSONAL Born 08/15/1941, Cleveland, OH, m, 1963, 2 children **DISCIPLINE** HISTORY OF SCIENCE, MEDIEVAL PHILOSOPHY **EDUCATION** Radcliffe Col, AB, 63; Harvard Univ, AM, 64, PhD(hist of sci), 71. **CAREER** Instr social studies, 68-70, asst prof hist, 70-75, assoc prof, 75-81, Prof Hist, NCar State Univ, 81-; Reviewer, Zentralblatt fur Math, 73. **HONORS AND AWARDS** NSF res grant, Oxford, Eng, 75-76; fel, Andrew D White Ctr for Humanities, Cornell Univ, 78-79, Inst Advan Studies, Princeton, 82-83. **MEMBERSHIPS** Hist Sci Soc; Mediaeval Acad Am; AAAS; AHA; Int Soc Study Mediaeval Philos. **RESEARCH** History of 14th century philosophy; medieval logic, mathematics and science. **SELECTED PUBLICATIONS** Auth, Medieval quantifications of qualities: The Merton School, Arch Hist Exact Sci, 71; Medieval concepts of the latitude of forms: The Oxford calculators, Arch Hist Doctrinale et Litteraire Moyen Age, 74; co-ed, The Cultural Context of Medieval Learning, Reidel, 75; auth, Autonomous and handmaiden science: St Thomas Aquinas and William of Ockham on the physics of the eucharist, In: The Cultural Context of Medieval Learning, Reidel, 75; coauth, Richard Swineshead, In: Dict of Scientific Biography (vol 13), Scribner's, 75; The science of motion, In: Science in the Middle Ages, Univ Chicago. **CONTACT ADDRESS** Dept of Hist, No Carolina State Univ, Box 8108, Raleigh, NC 27695. **EMAIL** edith_sylla@ncsu.edu

SYNAN, VINSON
PERSONAL Born 12/01/1934, Hopewell, VA, m, 1960, 4 children **DISCIPLINE** CHURCH HISTORY **EDUCATION** Univ Richmond, BA; Univ Ga, MA, PhD. **CAREER** Dean; prof, 94. **MEMBERSHIPS** Soc for Pentecostal Studies, Founder. **RESEARCH** Pentecostal/charismatic movements. **SELECTED PUBLICATIONS** Auth, Emmanuel Col:The First Fifty Years, MA thesis, N Wash Press, 68; The Holiness-Pentecostal Movement in the U.S., PhD dissertation, Eerdmans, 71; The Old-Time Power: History of the Pentecostal Holiness Church, Advocate Press, 73; Charismatic Bridges, Word of Life, 74; Aspects of Pencostal/Charismatic Origins, Logos, 75; Azusa Street, Bridge Publ, 80; In the Latter Days, Servant, 85; The Twentieth-Century Pentecostal Explosion, Creation House, 87; Launching the Decade of Evangelization, N Amer Renewal Srv Comm, 90; Under His Banner: A History of the FGBMFI, Gift Publ, 92; The Spirit Said Grow, MARC, World Vision, 92; auth, The Century of the Holy Spirit, Thomas Nelson, 01. **CONTACT ADDRESS** Sch of Divinity, Regent Univ, 1000 Regent Univ Dr, Virginia Beach, VA 23464-9831. **EMAIL** vinssyn@regent.edu

SYPNOWICH, CHRISTINE
DISCIPLINE PHILOSOPHY **EDUCATION** Univ Toronto, BA, 82; Oxford, Dphil, 87 **CAREER** Queen's, 90; tutorial teaching, Oxford, appointment, Univ of Leeds, 86-87; taught at Univ of Leiden in Holland, 88; vis position, Univ of California, San Diego, 89 **RESEARCH** Legal Theory and Socialism; Difference and Equality; The Self, Civility and Finitude. **SELECTED PUBLICATIONS** Auth, The Concept of Socialist Law, Oxford, 90; co-auth, The Social Self, Sage, 95. **CONTACT ADDRESS** Philos Dept, Queen's Univ at Kingston, Kingston, ON, Canada K7L 3N6. **EMAIL** cs4@post.queensu.ca

SYVERUD, K. D.
PERSONAL Born 10/23/1956, Rochester, NY, m, 1982, 3 children **DISCIPLINE** LAW **EDUCATION** Univ Michigan, JD, 81, MA, 83. **CAREER** Dean, Garner Anthony Prof, 97-, Vanderbilt Univ Law Sch; Prof, 87-97, Michigan Law Sch. **HONORS AND AWARDS** J Legal Edu, editor. **MEMBERSHIPS** ALI; ABA; LSA. **RESEARCH** Negotiation; Litigation; Insurance ; Risk; Class Actions; Complex Litigation. **SELECTED PUBLICATIONS** Auth, What Professional Responsibility Scholars Should Know About Insurance, Ct Ins L J, 98; Alternative Dispute Resolution and the Decline of the American Civil Jury, UCLA L Rev, 97; coauth, Why Civil Cases Go to Trial, Dispute Resolution, 97; coauth, Don't Try: Civil Jury Verdicts in a System Geared to Settlement, UCLA L Rev, 96; coauth, The Professional Responsibilities of Insurance Defense Lawyers, Duke L J, 95; On the Demand for Liability Ins, TX L Rev, 94; Taking Students Seriously: A guide for New Law Teachers, J Legal Edu, 93; coauth, Bargaining Impediments and Settlement Behavior, Ch 3 of Dispute Resolution: Bridging the Settlement Gap, ed, D Anderson, JAI Press 96. **CONTACT ADDRESS** Law Sch, Vanderbilt Univ, 21st Ave at Grand, Nashville, TN 37240. **EMAIL** k.syverud@vanderbilt.edu

SZABADOS, BELA
PERSONAL Born 08/10/1942, Hungary, m, 1966, 1 child **DISCIPLINE** PHILOSOPHY **EDUCATION** Sir George Williams Univ, BA, 66; Univ Calgary, MA, 68, PhD(philos), 72. **CAREER** Lectr philos, Univ Lethbridge, 71-72 & Univ Calgary, 72-73; asst prof, Simon Fraser Univ, 73-74; ASSOC PROF PHILOS, UNIV REGINA, 75-, Can Coun fel, 74-75. **MEMBERSHIPS** Can Philos Asn; Aristotelian Soc; Am Philos Asn. **RESEARCH** Philosophy of mind; philosophy of knowledge; ethics; Contemporary Analytical Philo, Philo of Lang, Wittgenstein, Aesthetics. **SELECTED PUBLICATIONS** Auth, 'On Irrationality' in Theodore Geraets, ed, Rationality Today/La Rationalite, Univ of Ottawa Press, 77; auth, 'The Self, Its Passions and Self-Deception' in M.W. Martin, ed, Self-Deception and Self-Understanding: New Essays in Philosophy and Psychology, Univ of Kansas, '85; auth, 'Moral Expertise,' in Wes Cragg, ed, Contemporary Moral Problems, First, Second and Third editions, McGraw-Hill/Ryerson, 87; auth, In Light of Chaos, Thistledown, 90; auth, 'Neither Nothing Nor Something' in Marlene Kadar, ed, Lifewriting, Oxford Univ Press, 92; coed, On The Track of Reason, Westview, 92; coauth, 'Hypocrisy, Change of Mind, Weakness of Will,' Metaphilosophy, (99): 60-78; auth, 'Was Wittgenstein an Anti-Semite?: The Significance of Anti-Semitism for Wittgenstein's Philosophy,' Canadian Journal of Philosophy, Vol 30, (99): 1-27; auth, 'Addiction and Authorship,' EA: Canadian Journal of Aesthetics, 99; coauth, 'Hypocrisy and Consequentialism,' Utilitas, (98): 168-194. **CONTACT ADDRESS** Dept of Philos, Univ of Regina, Regina, SK, Canada S4S 2A0. **EMAIL** bela.szabados@uregina.ca

SZASZ, PAUL CHARLES
PERSONAL Born 06/12/1929, Vienna, Austria, m, 1969, 2 children **DISCIPLINE** INTERNATIONAL LAW **EDUCATION** Cornell Univ, BS, EP, 52, LLB, 56. **CAREER** Law clerk, US Court Appeals, 5th Circuit, 56-57; legal officer, Int Atomic Energy Agency, 58-65, nuclear energy control safeguards officer, 65- 66; atty, Int Bank Reconstruct & Develop & Int Centre Settlement Investment Disputes, 66-71; sr legal officer, 71-77, Prin Legal Off, UN, 77-; dir, General Legal Div & Deputy to UN Legal Couns, 74-89;, Legal coun, Preparatory Comn Int Fund Agr Develop, 76-77, Conf Estab UN Indust Develop Org, 78-79 & Conf Inhumane Conventional Weapons, 78-80; Legal Adviser, UN Transitional Asst Group for Namibia, 89-90; Legal Adviser, Int Conf on the Former Yugoslavia, 92-95; Acting Dep to the UN Legal Council, 97; legal consult, Int Civil Serv Comm, 91-99; prof, NYU Sch of Law, 91-. **HONORS AND AWARDS** Ross Essay Prize, Am Bar Asn, 66. **MEMBERSHIPS** Am Soc Int Law; Am Judicature Soc. **RESEARCH** International judicial, administrative and legislative procedures, with special reference to the United Nations system, the environment and to the control of nuclear energy. **SELECTED PUBLICATIONS** Auth, The Law and Practices of the International Atomic Energy Agency, (IAEA), 70; ed, History of the International Convention on the Settlement of Investment Disputes, World Bank, 70; co-auth, International Environment Law: Basic Investments and Refernces, 91;

Peacekeeping in Operation--A Conflict Study of Bosnia, Cornell Int Law J, Vol 28, 95; The Protection of Human-Rights Through the Dayton/Paris Peace Agreement on Bosnia, Am J Int Law, Vol 90, 96; auth, International Environmental Law and Policy, 98; Complexifacation of the United Nations System, 3 Max Planck Yearbook of United Nations Law 1, 99. **CONTACT ADDRESS** New York Univ, 100 Sharp's Landing, PO Box 253, Germantown, NY 12526-0253. **EMAIL** szasz@valstar.net

T

TABBERNEE, WILLIAM
PERSONAL Born 04/21/1944, Rotterdam, Netherlands, m, 3 children **DISCIPLINE** EARLY CHURCH HISTORY **EDUCATION** Coburg Tchrs Col, TPTC, 65; Melbourne Col of Divinity, DipRE, 68, LTh, 68; Univ Melbourne, BA, 72, PhD, 79; Yale Divinity Sch, STM, 73. **CAREER** Lectr, Church history and systematic theol, 73-76, chemn Dept of Christian Thought and Hist, 77-80, Col of the Bible, Melbourne, Australia; dean, Evangelical Theol Asn, Melbourne, Australia, 79-80; prin, Col of the Bible of Churches of Christ in Australia, 81-91; pres, prof of Christian Thought and Hist, 91-94, Stephen J. England prof of Christian Thought and History, 95-, Phillips Theol Sem. **HONORS AND AWARDS** DDiv, Phillips Univ, 93. **MEMBERSHIPS** AAR; NAPS; Australian and New Zealand Soc for Theol Stud. **RESEARCH** Early Christianity; Montanism. **SELECTED PUBLICATIONS** Auth, Montanist Regional Bishops: New Evidence from Ancient Inscriptions, Jour of Early Christian Stud, 93; auth, Evangelism Beyond the Walls, Impact, 95; auth, Lamp-bearing Virgins: An Unusual Episode in the History of Early Christian Worship based on Mt25:1-13, Europ Evangel Soc, 95; auth, Paul of Tarsus: Church Planter Par Excellence, Australian Christian, 96; auth, 25 December, Christmas? Australian Christian, 96; auth, Unfencing the Table: Creeds, Councils, Communion and the Campbells, Mid-Stream, 96; auth, Augustine: Doctor of Love, Australian Christian, 97; auth, Archaeology; Revelation Revelations, Australian Christian, 97; auth, Athanasius: Champion of Orthodoxy, Australian Christian, 97; auth, Eusebius' Theology of Persecution: As Seen in the Various Editions of His Church History, Jour of Early Christian Stud, 97; auth, Ignatius, the Letter- Writing Martyr, Australian Christian, 97; auth, Learning to Handle the Gospel and the Fire Simultaneously: Ministerial Education for the Twenty-First Century, in Exploring Our Destiny, World Convention of Churches of Christ, 97; auth, Montanist Inscriptions and Testimonia: Epigraphic Sources Illustrating the History of Montanism, Patristic Monograph Ser, Mercer Univ, 97; auth, Our Trophies Are Better Than Your Trophies: The Appeal to Tombs and Reliquaries in Montanist- Orthodox Relations, Studia Patristica, 97; auth, Perpetua; The First Woman Journalist, Australian Christian, 97; auth, Eusebius: Chronicler of a Golden Age, Australian Christian, 98; auth, Francis of Assisi: Preacher to the Birds, Australian Christian, 98; auth, Mary Magdalene: A Saint with an Undeserved Reputation, Australian Christian, 98; auth, Restoring Normative Christianity: Episkope and the Christian Church, Mid-Stream, 98. **CONTACT ADDRESS** Phillips Theol Sem, 4242 S Sheridan Rd, Tulsa, OK 74145. **EMAIL** ptspres@fullnet.net

TABER, JOHN
DISCIPLINE CLASSICAL INDIAN PHILOSOPHY, 19TH CENTURY GERMAN PHILOSOPHY **EDUCATION** Univ Kans, BA, 71; Univ Hamburg, PhD, 79. **CAREER** Assoc prof, Univ NMex. **SELECTED PUBLICATIONS** Auth, Transformative Philosophy: A Study of Sankara, Fichte, and Heidegger, Univ Hawaii Press, 83; contribur, articles on Indian Philos, Routledge Encycl of Philos, 95. **CONTACT ADDRESS** Univ of New Mexico, Albuquerque, Albuquerque, NM 87131. **EMAIL** jataber@unm.edu

TAGGART, WALTER JOHN
DISCIPLINE MODERN LAND TRANSACTIONS, SECURED TRANSACTIONS, BANKRUPTCY, FEDERAL COURTS AND THE FEDERAL SYSTEM, NEGOTIABLE INSTRUMENTS AND PAYMENT LAW, REAL ESTATE DOCUMENTATION **EDUCATION** Belmont Abbey Col, AB, 65; Villanova Univ Sch Law, JD, 68. **CAREER** Prof, Villanova Univ. **MEMBERSHIPS** Order of the Coif; Trustee, Amatex Disease Trust and Nat Gypsum Settlement Trust; Trustees' Adv Comt Pacor Settlement Trust; Philadelphia Community Legal serv; Amer Asn Law Sch, Sect on Real Property, Subcomt on Commercial Real Estate, 74-77 & Sect on Creditors' Rights, 80; chp, ABA Sect Corp, Banking, and Bus Law, Comt on Railroad Reorganizations, 76-78; Adv bd, Practical Lawyer, ABA Sect Real Property, Probate and Trust Law, Comt on Creditors' Rights in Real Estate Financing; exec comt, Young Lawyers Sect, Pa Bar Asn. **RESEARCH** Real property, probat, trust law, bankruptcy and business law **SELECTED PUBLICATIONS** Auth, The New Bankruptcy Court System, 59 Bank L.J. 231, 85; The New Bankruptcy Rules, 7 ALI-ABA Course Materials J 7, 84; Collier on Bankruptcy, 15th ed, Vol 5, 1161-74; co-ed and contribur, Practicing Under the Bankruptcy Reform Act, 79 & Moore's Fed Practice, 72 Rev Rule 55, 77 Revision of Conflicts Jurisdiction, Vol 1A, Part 2. **CONTACT ADDRESS** Law School, Villanova Univ, 800 Lancaster Ave, Villanova, PA 19085-1692. **EMAIL** taggart@law.vill.edu

TAIWO, OLUFEMI
DISCIPLINE PHILOSOPHY **EDUCATION** Univ Ife, Obafemi Awolowo Univ, Ile-Ife, Osun State, Nigeria, BA, 78, MA, 81; Univ Toronto, MA, PhD, 86. **CAREER** Assoc prof, Loyola Univ, 91-; lectr, Obafemi Awolowo Univ, Ile-Ife, Nigeria, 86-90; staff develop fel, Can-Nigeria Linkage Prog Women's Stud Inst Study Women, Mount Saint Vincent Univ & Centre for Int Stud, Dalhousie Univ, Halifax, NS, Can, 88-89; Rockefeller postdr fel, Africana Stud and Res Center, Cornell Univ, Ithaca, NY, 90-91; co-founder, Int Soc African and African Diaspora Philos and Stud, ISAADPS & Int Soc Stud Africa, ISSA; served on, Comt Int Coop Am Philos Asn, 93-96; ed, APA Newsletter on Philos and Int Coop; organized, on behalf Amer Philos Asn, Fulbright 50th Anniversary Distinguished Fel Lect, 96. **RESEARCH** Marxism; philosophy of law; soc and political philosophy; ethics; feminism; African philosophy; nationalism; philosophy of the soc sciences. **SELECTED PUBLICATIONS** Auth,Legal Naturalism: A Marxist Theory of Law, Ithaca: Cornell UP, 96; publ in, The Nigerian J of Philos; Callalloo: J African and African-Amer Arts, Letters and Criticism; Can Rev of Stud in Nationalism; Philos Forum; Int Philos Quart; Tchg Philos; Issue: A J of Opinion. **CONTACT ADDRESS** Dept of Philosophy, Loyola Univ, Chicago, 820 N. Michigan Ave., Chicago, IL 60611.

TALAR, CHARLES J. T.
PERSONAL Born 12/02/1947, Port Chester, NY, s **DISCIPLINE** SYSTEMATIC THEOLOGY **EDUCATION** St. Mary's Seminary Col, AB, 70; Cath Univ, MA, 73; St. Mary's SOT, STM, 74; Cath Univ, PhD, 80; St. Mary's SOT, STL, 81; New Sch Soc Res, MA, 85; St. Mary's Sem, STD, 87. **CAREER** Assoc pastor, St. Thomas Aquinas Parish, Fairfield, Conn, 79-82; St. Mary's Sem SOT, 84-86; pastor, Church of Our Saviour, English Speaking Int Roman Cath Commun of the Hague, 86-90; vis asst prof, Fordham Univ, 90-91; assoc prof, Alvernia Col, 91-97; prof, St. Mary's Sem and Univ, 97- . **MEMBERSHIPS** Am Acad of Relig; Soc of Bibl Lit; Am Cath Hist Asoc; AIZEN; Soc for the Sociology of Relig. **RESEARCH** Roman Catholic modernism; nineteenth-century French Catholicism. **SELECTED PUBLICATIONS** Coed, Sanctity and Seculcrity During the Modernist Period, Subsidia hagiographica, 79; auth, Conspiracy to Commit Heresy: The Anti-Americanist Polemic of Canon Henri Delassus, U.S. Cath Hist, 93; auth, Tropics of Autobiographical Discorse: An Examination of Newman's Apologia, Religions of the Book, 96; auth, Saint of Authority and Saint of the Spirit: Paul Sebatier's Vie de saint Francois d'Assise, Cath Hist Rev, 96; auth, (Anti)hagiography and Mysticism in the Work of J.K. Huysmans, Excavatio, 97; auth, The Effective History of Tradition: Mohler, Le Roy, Schillebeeck, J Hist Modern Theol, 97; auth, (Re)reading, Reception and Rhetoric, Lang, 99; auth, Innovation and biblical inperpretation in Darrell Jodoch, ed. Catholicism Contending with Modernity, Cambridge, 00. **CONTACT ADDRESS** St. Mary's Sem and Univ, 5400 Roland Ave., Baltimore, MD 21210. **EMAIL** ctalar@stmarys.edu

TALBERT, CHARLES H.
PERSONAL Born 03/19/1934, Jackson, MS, m, 1961, 2 children **DISCIPLINE** RELIGIOUS STUDIES **EDUCATION** Samford Univ, BA, 56; The Southern Baptist Theol Sem, BD, 59; Vanderbilt Univ, PhD, 63. **CAREER** From prof to Wake Forest Prof, Wake Forest Univ, 63-96; Distinguished Prof of Relig, Baylor Univ. **HONORS AND AWARDS** Post-doctoral fel, Cooperative Prog in the Humanities, 68-69; Post-doctoral fel, Soc for Relig in Higher Educ, 71-72; Doctor of Letters, Samford Univ, 90. **MEMBERSHIPS** Soc of Biblical Lit, Nat Asn of Baptist Professors of Relig, Studiorum Nori Testamenti Societas, Catholic Biblical Asn, Phi Beta Kappa, Phi Kappa Phi, Omicron Delta Kappa. **RESEARCH** The Relation of Early Christianity to its Mediterranean Milieu. **SELECTED PUBLICATIONS** Auth, The Apocalypse: A Reading of the Revelation to John, 94; auth, Reading Acts, 97. **CONTACT ADDRESS** Dept Relig, Baylor Univ, Waco, PO Box 97284, Waco, TX 76798-7284. **EMAIL** charles_talbert@baylor.edu

TALBOTT, WILLIAM J.
PERSONAL Born 01/19/1949, Fort Belvoir, VA, d, 2 children **DISCIPLINE** PHILOSOPHY **EDUCATION** Princeton Univ, AB, 70; Harvard Univ, PhD, 76. **CAREER** Asst prof, Dept of Philos, 90-96, assoc prof Dept Pilos, 96-, Univ Wash; NEH fel, 96-97. **MEMBERSHIPS** Am Philos Asn; Soc Philos & Psychol. **RESEARCH** Epistemology; Ethics; Political philosophy; Rational choice theory. **SELECTED PUBLICATIONS** Auth The Reliability of the Cognitive Mechanism: A Mechanist Account of Empirical Justification, Garland Publ, 90; Intentional Self-Deception in a Single, Coherent Self, Philos and Phenomenol Res, 95; rev The Nature of Rationality, The Philos Rev, 95; Rules for Reasoning, in Philos & Psychol, 95; commentary Real Self-Deception, Behavioral and Brain Science, 97; coauth Games Lawyers Play: Legal Discovery and Social Epistemology, Legal Theory, 98. **CONTACT ADDRESS** Dept of Philosophy, Univ of Washington, Box 35 3350, Seattle, WA 98195-3350. **EMAIL** wtalbott@u.washington.edu

TALIAFERRO, CHARLES
PERSONAL Born 08/25/1952, New York, NY, m, 1987 **DISCIPLINE** PHILOSOPHY & LITERATURE **EDUCATION** Univ Rhode Island, MA; Harvard Univ, MTS; Brown, MA & PhD, 94. **CAREER** Instr, Univ Mass, 82-84; instr, Univ Notre Dame, 84-85; vis scholar, Univ Oxford, 91-92; vis fel, Princeton Univ, 98-99; prof, philos, St. Olaf Col, 85-. **HONORS AND AWARDS** NEH fel, 91. **MEMBERSHIPS** Amer Philos Asn. **RESEARCH** Philosophy of mind; Philosophy of religion; Ethics. **SELECTED PUBLICATIONS** Auth, Praying with C. S. Lewis, St. Mary's Press, 98; auth, Contemporary Philosophy of Religion, Blackwell, 98; co-ed, A Companion to Philosophy of Religion, Blackwell, 97; auth, Consciousness and the Mind of God, Cambridge Univ Press, 94. **CONTACT ADDRESS** Dept. of Philosophy, St. Olaf Col, Northfield, MN 55057. **EMAIL** taliafer@stolaf.edu

TALLEY, ERIC L.
DISCIPLINE LAW **EDUCATION** Univ Calif, San Diego, BA,88; Stanford Univ, JD,95; PhD,95. **CAREER** Assoc prof, Univ Southern Calif; John Olin Foundation fel; prof, Stanford Univ. **MEMBERSHIPS** Phi Beta Kappa. **RESEARCH** Business Organizations; Contracts, Quantitative Methods in the Law, & Law & Strategic Behavior. **SELECTED PUBLICATIONS** Auth, Investment Policy and Exit-Exchange Offers Within Financially Distressed Firms; Contract Renegotiation, Mechanism Design, and the Liquidated Damages Doctrine & Comparable Worth: Its Economic and Political Policy Dimensions. **CONTACT ADDRESS** School of Law, Univ of So California, University Park Campus, Los Angeles, CA 90089.

TANCREDI, LAURENCE RICHARD
PERSONAL Born 10/15/1940, Hershey, PA **DISCIPLINE** LAW AND MEDICINE; LAW AND PSYCHIATRY; PSYCHIATRIC ETHICS **EDUCATION** Franklin & Marshall Coll, AB, 62; Univ Pa Sch Medicine, MD, 66; Yale Univ Sch Law, JD, 72; Columbia Univ, resid, Psychiatry, 74-75; resid, Yale Univ Sch Med, Psychiatry, 75-77. **CAREER** Sr prof assoc, Inst Medicine, Nat Acad Sci, 72-74; assoc prof, New York Univ Med Sch, Psychiatry, 77-84; adj prof, New York Univ Law Sch, 81-84; med staff, Harris County Psych Center, 89-92; med dir, Regent Hosp, 92-93; CLIN PROF, NEW YORK UNIV MED SCH, 92-; CLIN PROF, UNIV CALIF-SAN DIEGO SCH MED, HEALTH CARE SCI, 93-; MED STAFF, BROOKHAVEN NAT LABS, 96-. **MEMBERSHIPS** Am Coll Psych; AmA cad Psych & Law; Am Psych Asn; Group Advance Psych **RESEARCH** Alternative systems for medical injury compensation; Conceptual foundations of what constitutes scientific fact as that knowledge affects legal decision-making; Implications of discoveries from the use of imaging technologies on understanding how the brain/mind works **SELECTED PUBLICATIONS** Dangerous Diagnostics: The Social Power of Biological Information, Univ Chicago Press, 94; The Anthropology of Medicine, Prager Publ, 97. **CONTACT ADDRESS** 22 Riverside Dr, No 14-A, New York, NY 10023. **EMAIL** lrt3@juno.com

TANDY, CHARLES
PERSONAL Born 04/04/1947, Princeton, KY, s **DISCIPLINE** PHILOSOPHY **EDUCATION** Univ Louisville, KY South Col, BA, 69; Western Maryland Col, MLA, 85; Univ MS, PhD, 93. **CAREER** Tchr, physics & math, 71-72, Central City HS KY; caseworker, 72-73, LaGrange Reformatory; caseworker, 73-84, Soc Sec Admin; Dir, 84-88, Life Extension Info Svcs, Tandys Dandys Info Computer & Library Based Res and Info Retrieval; independent consl, 93-, private practice; vis scholar, Philosophy Dept, 94-95, Stanford Univ; vis fac, Intl Programs, 95-97, Purdue Univ; vis fel, Phil & Ed, 97-98, consl asst prof, 98-, Ria Univ Inst for Advanced Study. **HONORS AND AWARDS** First Prize Natl Essay Contest, United Nations Asn of NY; Prof Presentation Travel Fel, Univ of MS; Biographical Listings; Comm Leaders and Noteworthy Amer; Dist of Intl Biography; Intl Who's Who in Com Svc; Intl Who's Who of Intellectuals. **MEMBERSHIPS** Amer Hist Asn; Amer Phil Asn; Intl Asn for Mathematical and Computer Modeling; Phil of Ed Soc. **RESEARCH** Biomedical ethics; English as a foreign language; foundations of education; futuristics; interrelation of the disciplines; metaphysics of personal identity; philosophy of education; philosophy of Kant; philosophy of Kenneth Boulding; world history. **SELECTED PUBLICATIONS** Auth, "Educational Philosophy For The 21st Century," 96; auth, ITTHO's Graduate Program in Education, vol 1, 2, 3, Purdue Univ: West Lafayette, IN, 96; auth, "Edautional Philosophy, Technical and Vocational Education, And Social-Economic Development: Toward The Creation And Flourishing Of Extraterrestrial Communities," in UNESCO UNEVOC Regional Conference Steering Committee, 96; auth, Development of a Graduate Program for the Department of Eduation and Humanities, Institut teknologi Tun Hussein Onn, Purdue Univ: West Lafayette, IN, 97; coauth, "Importing Curriculum to a Developing Country: A Case Study of the Issues and Strategies, Mathematical Modelling and Scientific Computing, vol. 8, 97; coauth, "Quantitative Research and the Preactice of Teaching," Mathematical Modelling and Scientific Computing, vol. 8, 97; auth, "Some Philosphic Questions For Systems Theorists And Model Builders: Do You See What I Hear?" Mathematical Modelling and Scientific Computing, vol. 8, 97; contrib, "Rickert, Heinrich" (German Neo-Kantian Philosopher), in Woold, D. R. ed., A Global Encyclopedia of Historical Writing, Garland publishing, Inc: New York, 98; auth, "MRQ Analysis of the Ria Univ Institute," A Scholarly Paper Presented in April 98 at St. Edmund

Hall, Univ of Oxford, England, 98; auth, "Is There A Postgraduate English and Linguistics Progran in Kung Shan University's Future?" Journal of Teacher Research, 99. **CONTACT ADDRESS** Stanford Univ, PO Box 20170, Palo Alto, CA 94309. **EMAIL** tandy@ria.edu

TANFORD, J. ALEXANDER
PERSONAL Born 01/23/1950, Iowa City, IA, m, 1992, 2 children **DISCIPLINE** LAW **EDUCATION** Princeton Univ, AB, 72; Duke Univ, JD, 76; Duke Univ, LLM, 79. **CAREER** Instr, Duke Univ School of Law, 77-79; asst prof, Ind Univ School of Law, Bloomington79-83; assoc prof, Ind Univ School of Law, Bloomington 83- 86; vis prof, Washington Univ School of Law, St. Louis, 85; prof, Ind Univ School of Law, Bloomington 86-; vis scholar, Univ of Iowa Col of Law, fall 86 and spring 89. **HONORS AND AWARDS** Teaching Excellence Recognition Awd; John S. Hastings Fac Fel; Indiana Supreme Court Rules of Evidence Committee; Harry T. Ice Fac Fel; ICLU Richard Zweig Coopeating Atty Awd; Ira C. Batman Fac Fel; Univ Nominee, Lilly Endowment Fac Open Fel; CIC Exchange Scholar; John S. Bradway Fel; Mordecai Soc Awd for Teaching. **MEMBERSHIPS** AAUP; Law & Soc Asn; Am Psychology-Law Soc. **RESEARCH** Trial law & procedure, especially interdisciplinary issues in psychology and law. **SELECTED PUBLICATIONS** Auth, "The Law and Psychology of Jury Instructions", in 68 Nebraska Law Review 71, 90; auth, "Racism in the Adversary System: Defense Use of Peremptory Challenges", in 63 Southern Calif Law Review 1015, 90; auth, "The Limits of a Scientific Jurisprudence: The Supreme Court and Psychology", in 66 Indiana Law Journal 137, 90; auth, "Law Reform by Courts, Legislatures and Commissions Following Empirical Research on Jury Instructions", in 25 Law and Soc Review 155, 91; auth, "Novel Scientific Evidence of Intoxication: Acoustic Analysis of Voice Tapes from the Exxon Valdez", in 82 Journal of Criminal Law and Criminology 579, 91; auth, Trial Practice Problems and Case Files 2nd ed, 92; auth„"Thinking About Elephants: Admonitions, Empirical Research and Legal Policy" in 60 UMKC Law Review 645, 92; auth, "Keeping Cross-Examination Under Control", in 18 Am Journal of Trial Advocacy 245, 94; auth, " The Death of Graduation Prayer: the Parrot Sketch Redux", in 24 Journal of Law & Educ 423, 95; auth, "The In/Into Controversy", in 91 Northwestern Univ Law Review 637, 97; auth, The Trial Process: Law, Tactics and Ethics 2nd ed, 93; auth, Indiana Trial Evidence Manual 4th ed, 99. **CONTACT ADDRESS** Sch of Law, Indiana Univ, Bloomington, 211 S. Indiana Ave., Bloomington, IN 47405. **EMAIL** tanford@indiana.edu

TANG, PAUL C. L.
PERSONAL Born 01/23/1944, Vancouver, Canada, s **DISCIPLINE** PHILOSOPHY **EDUCATION** Univ Toronto, ARCT, 62; Univ BC Canada, B.Sc, 66; Simon Fraser Univ Canada, MA, (ED), 71; Washington Univ, MA, 75, PhD, 82; Georgetown Univ, Kennedy Inst Ethics, Cert, Bioethics, 83; Harvard Univ, NEH Fel, 88. **CAREER** Res asst, biochemist, 68-70, Vancouver General Hosp, Vancouver; lectr, instr, 72-76, Washington Univ; vis lectr, 78-79, res develop officer & asst to grad dean, 80-82, So Illinois Univ Edwardsville; asst prof, 82-85, Grinnell Col; asst prof, assoc, 85-, prof, chmn, phil dept, 88-94, adj prof, Asian & Asian Amer Stud, 94-, prof, Univ Honors prog, acting chmn, phil dept, 98, grad adv, 98-, Calif St Univ, Long Beach. **HONORS AND AWARDS** Phi Beta Delta; Internationalizing the Curriculum Awd, 93; Fac Adv of the Year Awd, Asn Students, Inc. CSULB, 88, 89, 91, 95; Cert of Merit, Student Phil Asn (SPA), CSLUB, 88, 89, 90, 93, 94, 96, 97, 98; SPA Fac Mem of the Year Awd, 91; Special Awd, SPA, 92; Dist Fac Tchng Awd, CSULB, 95; Most Valuable Prof Awd, Col of Liberal Arts, CSULB, 95; Outstanding Grad Prof Awd, SPA, CSULB, 95; APA award for Excel in Tchng, 95, 97; CSULB Outstanding Prof Awd, 96-97; CSU System-wide Trustees' Outstanding Prof Awd, 96-97; Cert of Recogn, Continued Commitment to Education, CA St Senate, 97; CSULB Scholarly & Creative Act Awd, 95, 97; Nobel Laureate in Chem, CSULB, 86; Nobel Laureate in Physics, CSULB, 92; Phi Betta Kappa; Phi Kappa Phi. **MEMBERSHIPS** APA; Phil of Sci Asn; Hist of Sci Soc; The Hastings Ctr; Amer Soc for Aesthetics; Western Soc Sci Asn; NY Acad of Sci; Maison Internationale des Intellectuels and of L'Academie MIDI; Paris France & Rain am Lech, Germany. **RESEARCH** Phil of natural science; phil of social science; history & phil of biology; theory of knowledge; phil of lang; logic; Asian phil. **SELECTED PUBLICATIONS** Coauth, Anti-realism and the Complementarily Model of Mind-Brain, Boston Stud in the Phil of Science, Vol 169, 92, reprinted, Revue Roumaine De Philosophy, Vol 37, 93; auth, Representation and the Complementarity Model of Mind-Brain, Forms of Representations: An Interdisciplinary Theme for Cognitive Science, 96; auth, Ilya Prigogine, Biographical Encycl of Scientists, Marshall Cavendish Corp, 98; auth, " The Monoamine Hypothesis, Placebos, and Problems of Theory Construction In Psychology and Psychiatry," The Social Science Journal Vol 36, No 4, 99: 595-602; auth, " Was the Truth Ever Meant to Explain Much? A Critique of Nancy Cartwright," The Social Science Journal, Vol 39, No4 99: 615-621; auth, " A Review Essay: Recent Literature on Cognitive Science" The Social Science Journal" Vol 39 No 4, 99: 675-686; auth, ' Paul Churchland" In World Philosophers and Their Works, Pasadena, CA, Salem press, 00: 370-373; auth, " Overview of Paul Chruchland's The Engine of Reason, the Seat of Soul," World Philosophers and Their Works, Pasadena, CA, Salem Press, 00: 373-377; auth, " Stephen Toulmin," World Philosophers and Their Works, Pasadena, CA, Salem Press, 00: 1908-1911. **CONTACT ADDRESS** Dept of Philosophy, California State Univ, Long Beach, 1250 Bellflower Blvd, Long Beach, CA 90840. **EMAIL** pcltang@csulb.edu

TANNEHILL, ROBERT C.
PERSONAL Born 05/06/1934, Clay Center, KS, m, 1955, 3 children **DISCIPLINE** NEW TESTAMENT STUDIES **EDUCATION** Hamline Univ, BA, 56; Yale Divinity Sch, BD, 59; Yale Univ, MA, 60; Yale Univ, PhD, 63. **CAREER** Instr, new testament, Oberlin Grad Sch of Theol, 63-66; asst prof, 66-69, assoc prof, 69-74, prof, 74-, acad dean, 94-, new testament, Meth Theol Sch in Oh. **HONORS AND AWARDS** Danforth fel, 56-63; Tews prize, Yale Divinity Sch, 57; Two Brothers fel, Yale Univ, 60-61; Asn of Theol Sch Facul fel, 69-70; Asn of Theol Sch Basic Theol Scholar and Res Awd, 75-76; Asn of Theol Sch Theol Scholar and Res Awd, 82; Soc of Bibl Lite, Claremont fel, 82; assoc ed, Soc of Bibl Lite Monogr Series, 79-85; mem, ed board, Jour of Bibl Lit, 88-93; co-chair, lit aspects of the Gospels and Acts grp, Soc of Bibl Lit, 91-96; Asn of Theol Sch Theol Scholar and Res Awd, 94-95. **MEMBERSHIPS** Soc of Bibl Lit; Studiorum Novi Testamenti Soc. **RESEARCH** Luke and Acts; Literary methods in New Testament study. **SELECTED PUBLICATIONS** Auth, The Narrative Unity of Luke - Acts, 2 vols, Fortress Pr, 86, 90; auth, Should We Love Simon the Pharisee?, Hermeneutical Reflections on the Pharisees in Luke, Currents in Theol and Mission, 21, 424-433, 94; auth, Cornelius and Tabitha Encounter Luke's Jesus, Interpretation, 48, 347-56, 94; auth, The Gospels and Narrative Literature, The New Interpreter's Bible, vol VIII, 56-70, Abingdon Press, 95; auth, Luke, Abingdon New Testament Commentaries, Abingdon Press, 96; auth, Literature, the NT as, The Harper Collins Bible Dictionary, 611-614, Harper San Francisco, 96; auth, Freedom and Responsibility in Scripture Interpretation, with Application to Luke, Literary Studies in Luke-Acts: Essays in Honor of Joseph B. Tyson, 265-78, Mercer Univ Press, 98. **CONTACT ADDRESS** Methodist Theol Sch in Ohio, 3081 Columbus Pike, PO Box 8004, Delaware, OH 43015. **EMAIL** btannehill@mtso.edu

TARALA, JOSEPH J.
PERSONAL m **DISCIPLINE** PHILOSOPHY **EDUCATION** Temple Univ, PhD candidate, 96. **CAREER** Adj Inst, Seton Hall Univ, 4 yrs; Prof, Lincoln Univ, 2 yrs; Drew University 1 year. **MEMBERSHIPS** APA **RESEARCH** Biomedical ethics; practical ethics in general **SELECTED PUBLICATIONS** auth, Personal Identity, Pearson Custom Publishing, 00. **CONTACT ADDRESS** 1008 Seventh Ave, Toms River, NJ 08757.

TARAN, LEONARDO
PERSONAL Born 02/22/1933, Galarza, Argentina, m, 1971, 1 child **DISCIPLINE** CLASSICS, ANCIENT PHILOSOPHY **EDUCATION** Princeton Univ, PhD, 62. **CAREER** Fel res, Inst Res Humanities, Univ Wis, 62-63; jr fel res, Ctr Hellenic Studies, 63-64; asst prof classics, Univ Calif, Los Angeles, 64-67; assoc prof, 67-71, chmn dept, 76-79, Prof, 71-87, Jay Prof Greek & Latin Langs, Columbia Univ, 87-; Am Philos Soc grant, 63, 71 & 75; fel Am Coun Learned Soc, 66-67, 71-72; Guggenheim Found fel, 75; mem Inst Advan Study, Princeton, 66-67 & 78-79; NEH fee. 1986-87. **MEMBERSHIPS** Am Philol Asn; Soc Ancient Greek Philos. **RESEARCH** Ancient philosophy; Greek literature. **SELECTED PUBLICATIONS** Auth, Parmenides, Princeton Univ, 65; Asclepius of Tralles: Commentary to Nicomachus' introduction to arithmetic, Am Philos Soc, 69; The creation myth in Plato's Timaeus, in Essays in Greek Philosophy, State Univ NY, 71; coauth, Eraclito, testimonianze e imitazioni, La Nuova Italia Editrice, 72; auth, Academica: Plato, Philip of Opus and the Pseudo-Platonic Epinomis, Am Philos Soc Memoirs, 75; Anonymous Commentary on Aristotle's de Interpretatione, Anton Hain, 78; Speusippus and Aristotle on homonymy and synonymy, Hermes, 106: 73-99; Speusippus of Athens, Leiden, Brill, 81. **CONTACT ADDRESS** Dept of Classics, Columbia Univ, 2960 Broadway, New York, NY 10027-6900. **EMAIL** lt1@columbia.edu

TARLOCK, ANTHONY DAN
PERSONAL Born 06/02/1940, Oakland, CA, m, 1977, 3 children **DISCIPLINE** LAW **EDUCATION** Stanford Univ, AB, 62, LLB, 65. **CAREER** Asst prof law, Univ Ky, 66-68; from asst prof to assoc prof, Ind Univ, Bloomington, 68-72, prof, 72-81; PROF LAW, ITT CHICAGO KENT, 81-, Consult pesticide regulation, Nat Acad Sci, 73-75; vis prof law, Univ Pa, 74-75, Univ Chicago, 79 & Univ Mich, 82; Member, Water Science and Technology Board, National Academy of Sciences, 88-94; Chair, Committee on Western Water Management, 90-92; Visiting Prof Law, Univ PA, 74-75, Univ Chicago, 79, Univ MI, 82; Raymond A Rice Distinguished Visitor, Univ Kansas 85, Univ, Hawaii, 01. **RESEARCH** Water law; land use law; environmental law. **SELECTED PUBLICATIONS** Auth, Local-Government Protection of Biodiversity--What is Its Niche, Univ Chicago Law Rev, Vol 60, 93; auth, Law of Water Rights and Resources, West Group, 88; auth, Environmental Protection Law and Policy, Aspen Publishing Co., with Anderson, Glicksman and Mandelker, 99; auth, Can Cowboys Become Indians: Protecting Western Communities As Endangered Cultural Remnants, Arizona State L. Journal, Vol. 31, 539. **CONTACT ADDRESS** Col of Law, Illinois Inst of Tech, 565 W Adams, Chicago, IL 60661. **EMAIL** dtarlock@kentlaw.edu

TARR, NINA W.
DISCIPLINE LAW **EDUCATION** Southern Ill Univ, BA; Univ Wash, MA; Univ Iowa, PhD. **CAREER** Established and directs the College's Law Clinic, which opened in the spring of 96; Prof, Univ Ill Urbana Champaign. **RESEARCH** Family law; legal problems of the elderly poor. **SELECTED PUBLICATIONS** Auth, pubs on clinical education. **CONTACT ADDRESS** Law Dept, Univ of Illinois, Urbana-Champaign, 209 Law Bldg, Mc 594, 504 E. Pennsylvania, Champaign, IL 61820. **EMAIL** ntarr@law.uiuc.edu

TARTAGLIA, PHILIP
PERSONAL Born 07/02/1935, Albany, NY, m, 1960, 2 children **DISCIPLINE** PHILOSOPHY **EDUCATION** NYork Univ, BA, 60, MA, 64, PhD(philos), 66. **CAREER** Asst prof philos, Slippery Rock State Col, 67-68; asst prof, 68-72, assoc prof, 72-85, prof philos, Potsdam Col, 85-. **RESEARCH** Mathematical logic; linguistics; cybernetics; ethics; philos of lang. **SELECTED PUBLICATIONS** Auth, Problems in the Construction of a Theory of Natural Language, Mouton, The Hague, 72. **CONTACT ADDRESS** Dept Philos, SUNY, Col at Potsdam, 44 Pierrepont Ave, Potsdam, NY 13676-2299.

TARVER, LEON R., II
PERSONAL m **DISCIPLINE** POLITICAL SCIENCE **EDUCATION** Southern University, BA, political science; Harvard University, John F Kennedy School of Government, MA, public administration; Union Institute, PhD, public administration. **CAREER** Southern Univ System, Baton Rouge, LA, vice-chancellor for administration, prof of public administration, Prof of Public Policy and Urban Affairs, pres, currently. **CONTACT ADDRESS** So Univ and A&M Col, Baton Rouge, LA 70813.

TASHIRO, PAUL Y.
PERSONAL Born 09/21/1933, Tokyo, Japan, m, 1963, 1 child **DISCIPLINE** BIBLE **EDUCATION** HUC-JIR, Cincinnati, OH, PhD, 89, Bibl & Ancient Near Eastern Stud. **CAREER** Prof, 86-91, Lindsey Wilson Col; prof, 91-, Wesley Theol Sem. **MEMBERSHIPS** Wesleyan Theol Soc; Evangel Theol Soc; Amer Oriental Soc; Inst of Bibl Res; Soc for Bibl Lit; Natl Assn of Prof of Hebrew. **RESEARCH** TNK; Semitic lang; linguistics; comparative linguistics, assyriology. **SELECTED PUBLICATIONS** Auth, Comparative Study on Sumerian Culture and Ancient Japanese Culture; auth, Research Ecology for Ancient Culture and Languages. **CONTACT ADDRESS** Wesley Biblical Sem, 5980 Floral Dr, PO Box 9938, Jackson, MS 39206-0938. **EMAIL** ptashiro@aol.com

TASHJIAN, JIRAIR S.
PERSONAL Born 08/11/1939, Jordan, m, 1966, 2 children **DISCIPLINE** NEW TESTAMENT **EDUCATION** Claremont Grad Univ, PhD, 87. **CAREER** Prof, Southern Nazarene Univ, 83-. **MEMBERSHIPS** Soc of Biblical Lit. **RESEARCH** Gospels, Question of the Historical Jesus. **SELECTED PUBLICATIONS** Auth, Jesus Olivet Discourse in the Second Coming, ed, H. Ray Dunning, Beacon Hill Press, Kansas City, 95. **CONTACT ADDRESS** So Nazarene Univ, Bethany, OK 73008. **EMAIL** jtashjia@snu.edu

TASSI, ALDO
DISCIPLINE PHILOSOPHY **EDUCATION** Fordham Univ, PhD, 70; Marquette Univ, MA, 63; Iona Col, BA, 55. **CAREER** Prof, 72-present, Loyola Coll MD; Asst Prof, 66-72, Fordham Univ; Asst Prof, 63-66, Duquesne Univ. **HONORS AND AWARDS** Fulbright Scholar to Italy, 61-63. **MEMBERSHIPS** Amer Philos Assoc; Metaphysical Soc of Amer; Amer Catholic Philos Assoc. **RESEARCH** Philosophy and Theatre, Metaphysics, Performance Theory, Philosophy and the Arts, William James, Nietzsche, Aristotle. **SELECTED PUBLICATIONS** Auth, Philosophy and Theatre, International Philosophical Quarterly, 98; Impersonation and Performance, Playing Classical Greek Theatre, eds, S Patsalidis & E Sakellaridou, Univ Studio Press, 98; Philosophy and Theatre: An Essay on Contemplation and Catharsis, International Philosophical Quarterly, 95; Spirituality as a Stage of Being, Divine Representations, ed, A Astell, Paulist Press, 94; Person and the Mask of Being, Philosophy Today, 93. **CONTACT ADDRESS** Dept of Philosophy, Loyola Col, 4501 N Charles St, Baltimore, MD 21210. **EMAIL** tassi@vax.loyola.edu

TATE, PAUL DEAN
PERSONAL Born 11/22/1945, Fort Worth, TX, m, 1976 **DISCIPLINE** PHILOSOPHY, SANSKRIT **EDUCATION** Univ Tex, Austin, BA, 67; Yale Univ, MPhil, 74, PhD, 76. **CAREER** Dean of Grad Studies, Idaho State Univ **MEMBERSHIPS** Am Philos Assn. **RESEARCH** The philosophy of Martin Heidegger; the nature of language; Indian philosophy. **SELECTED PUBLICATIONS** Auth, His Holiness Gives an Example, Kite Bks, 73; auth, The Agivtic Hotel, Latitude Press, 87. **CONTACT ADDRESS** Idaho State Univ, 921 S 8th Ave, Box 8399, Pocatello, ID 83209-0001. **EMAIL** tatepaul@isu.edu

TATUM, W. BARNES
PERSONAL Born 04/24/1938, Mobile, AL, m, 2 children **DISCIPLINE** RELIGIOUS STUDIES **EDUCATION** Birmingham-Southern Col, BA, 60; Duke Univ, BD, 63, PhD, 66; Univ of North Carolina Greensboro, MLS, 91. **CAREER** Relig fac, Huntingdon Col, 66-73; relig fac, Greensboro Col, 73-. **HONORS AND AWARDS** NEH Summer Sem for Col Tchrs, 82, 87. **MEMBERSHIPS** Am Acad of Relig; Soc Bibl Lit; ALA. **RESEARCH** Christian origins; historical Jesus. **SELECTED PUBLICATIONS** Auth, "Did Jesus Heal Simon's Mother-in-Law of a Fever," Dialogue, 94; "The Resurrection & Historical Evidence," Foundations and Facets Forum, 94; John the Baptist and Jesus, Polebridge, 94; Jesus at the Movies, Polebridge, 97; "Jesus' So-Called Triumphal Entry," Foundations and Facets Forum, 98; In Quest of Jesus, rev ed, Abingdon, 99. **CONTACT ADDRESS** Greensboro Col, 815 W Market St, Greensboro, NC 27401. **EMAIL** tatumb@gborocollege.edu

TATZ, MARK
PERSONAL Born 02/05/1945, New York, NY, d, 2 children **DISCIPLINE** RELIGION **EDUCATION** Univ of Calif Berk, BA, 66; Univ of Wash, MA, 72; Univ British Columbia, PhD, 78. **CAREER** Univ Washington, instr, 74; Naropa Inst Core Faculty, acting chemn, Buddhist Stud, 79-81; Antioch Int, postdoc, instr, 82; Caifl Inst of Integral Stud, prof, 83-91; Inst of Buddhist Stud, adj prof, 91-96; Univ Calif Extension, instr, 92-, Calif Col of Arts & Crafts, sr instr, 96-98. **HONORS AND AWARDS** NDEA fel, Univ British Columbia, Killan fel, Shastri Indo-Can Inst, jr fel, Am Inst Indian Stud, sr fel, Am Acad of Relig, grant. **MEMBERSHIPS** AAR, AOS, AHA, IABS, IATS. **RESEARCH** Indo-Tibetan Buddhism; comparative religions. **SELECTED PUBLICATIONS** Auth, The Skill in Means (Upayakausalya) Sutra. Delhi, Motilal Banarsidass, Tibet House, 94; auth, The Complete Bodhisattva: Asanga's Chapter on Ethics with the Commentary by Tsong-kha-pa, The Basic Path to Awakening, Stud in Asian Thought and Religion, Lewiston NY, Edwin Mellen Press, Philosophic Systems According to Advayavajra and Vajrapani, Jour of Buddhist and Tibetan Studies, 94; auth, Brief Communication (On Thus Have I Heard), in: Indo-Iranian Jour, 93. **CONTACT ADDRESS** 5413 Claremont Ave, Oakland, CA 94618. **EMAIL** tatz@uclink4.berkeley.edu

TAUBER, ALFRED I.
PERSONAL Born 06/24/1947, Washington, DC, m, 2000, 4 children **DISCIPLINE** PHILOSOPHY; HISTORY OF SCIENCE **EDUCATION** BS, 69, Tufts Univ; MD, 73, Tufts Univ School of Medicine **CAREER** Instr, 78-80, Asst Prof, 80-82, Harvard Medical School; Assoc Prof Medicine, 82-86, Assoc Prof Biochemistry, 82-86; Assoc Prof Pathology, 84-87, Prof of Medicine, 86-, Prof of Pathology, 87-, Boston Univ School of Medicine; Prof Philosophy, 93-, College of Arts and Sciences, Boston Univ. **RESEARCH** Philosophy and the history of science **SELECTED PUBLICATIONS** Coauth, Metchnikoff and the Origins of Immunology: From Metaphor to Theory, 91; Auth, The Immune Self: Theory or Metaphor, 94; Coauth, The Generation of Diversity: Clonal Selection Theory and the Rise of Molecular Immunology, 97; Auth, Confessions of A Medicine Man: An Essay in Popular Philosophy, 99. **CONTACT ADDRESS** Center for Philosophy and History of Science, Boston Univ, Boston, MA 02115. **EMAIL** ait@bu.edu

TAVANI, HERMAN
PERSONAL m, 1 child **DISCIPLINE** PHILOSOPHY, PHILOSOPHY AND COMPUTERS **EDUCATION** West Chester Univ, BA, MA; Temple Univ, PhD. **CAREER** Assoc prof, ch, dept Philos, dir, Lib Stud prog, Rivier Col; Vis Sci in Occup Hea, Harvard Univ; vis scholar, assoc fel, Dartmouth Hum Inst; assoc ed, Comput and Soc; bk rev ed, Ethics and Infor Technol; software tech writer, publ supvr, Digital Equip Corp. **MEMBERSHIPS** Pres, Northern New Eng Philos Asn; Am Philos Asn. **SELECTED PUBLICATIONS** Auth, "Personal Privacy in the Information Age: An Ethical Dilemma," InSight vol 3, no 1 (Spring/Summer 96): 155-169; auth, "Selecting a Computer Ethics Coursebook," Computers & Soc vol 26, no 4 (Dec 96): 15-21; auth, "Journals and Periodicals on Computers, Ethics, and Society," Computers & Soc vol 27, no 2 (June 97): 20-26; auth, "Computer Ethics: Current Perspectives and Resources," APA Newsltr on Philos & Computers vol 99, (Spring 00): 166-170; auth, "Privacy and Security." Chap. 4 in Internet Ethics, ed D. Langford (London/New York: MacMillan Publishers/St. Martin's Press, 00); auth, "Defining the Boundaries of Computer Crime: Piracy, Break-Ins, and Sabotage in Cyberspace," Computers & Soc vol 30, no 3 (Sept 00): 3-9; auth, "Privacy-Enhancing Technologies as a Panacea for Online Privacy Concerns: Some Ethical Considerations," J of Info Ethics vol 9, no 2 (Winter 00); ed, Public Health Ethics: A Bibliography, Harvard Educ & Res Ctr, 01; co-ed, Readings in CyberEthics, Jones & Bartlett Pub (Sudbury, MA), 01; co-ed Computer Ethics: Philosophical Enquiry, Special Issue of Ethics and Information Technology (Vol 3 No 1), in press. **CONTACT ADDRESS** Philos Dept, Rivier Col, Nashua, NH 03060-5086. **EMAIL** htavani@rivier.edu

TAYLOR, ANGUS
DISCIPLINE PHILOSOPHY **EDUCATION** Queen's Univ, BA; Univ Toronto, MA; Univ Sussex, MSc; York Univ, PhD. **CAREER** Vis asst prof. **RESEARCH** Social and political thought; ethics; and the interrelations of science; nature and society. **SELECTED PUBLICATIONS** Auth, Magpies, Monkeys, and Morals: What Philosophers Say about Animal Liberation. **CONTACT ADDRESS** Dept of Philosophy, Univ of Victoria, PO Box 3045, Victoria, BC, Canada V8W 3P4.

TAYLOR, CHARLES
DISCIPLINE PHILOSOPHY **EDUCATION** Univ Oxford, PhD. **CAREER** Vis prof, Northwestern Univ. **RESEARCH** Ethics, Social and Political Philosophy, Modern European Philosophy. **SELECTED PUBLICATIONS** Auth, Hegel, Cambridge Univ Press, 75; auth, Philosophical Papers, Cambridge Univ Press, 85; auth, Sources of the Self: The Making of the Modern Identity, Harvard Univ Press, 89. **CONTACT ADDRESS** Dept of Philosophy, Northwestern Univ, 1818 Hinman, Evanston, IL 60208.

TAYLOR, CHARLES L.
PERSONAL Born 11/08/1935, SC, m, 1958, 2 children **DISCIPLINE** POLITICAL SCIENCE **EDUCATION** Yale Univ, PhD, 63. **CAREER** Asst prof, William and Mary, 62-66; dir Polit Sci res Libr, Yale Univ, 66-70; assoc prof and prof, Va Polytech Inst and State Univ, 70- . **HONORS AND AWARDS** John Marshall prof, Budapest Univ of Ec Sci; Distinguished Alumnus, Carson Newman Col. **MEMBERSHIPS** Am Polit Sci Asn; Int Stud Asn. **RESEARCH** European politics; cross-national political events measurement. **SELECTED PUBLICATIONS** Coauth, Partisanship, Candidates and Issues: Attitudinal Components of the Vote in German Federal Elections, in von Beyme, ed, German Political Studies III, Sage, 78; coauth, World Handbook of Political and Social Indicators, 3d ed, Yale, 83; coauth, Mapping Mass Political Conflict and Civil Society: Issues and Prospects for the Automated Development of Event Data, J of Conflict Resolution, 97. **CONTACT ADDRESS** Dept of Political Science, Virginia Polytech Inst and State Univ, Blacksburg, VA 24061-0130. **EMAIL** clt@vt.edu

TAYLOR, FELICIA MICHELLE
PERSONAL Born 02/14/1960, Concord, NC, s **DISCIPLINE** CRIMINAL LAW **EDUCATION** Cabarrus Community College, private pilot ground school, 1982; Univ of North Carolina, Chapel Hill, BA, sociology, 1982, Charlotte, MS, criminal justice, 1984; Florida State Univ, PhD, criminology, 1987. **CAREER** Univ of NC at Charlotte, admissions counselor, 83-84; Barber-Scotia Clg, administrative asst for financial planning and development, 84-85; Shaw Univ at Raleigh, prof, 85-87, CAPE Ctr at Wilmington, adj prof, 92; The Florida State Univ, instructor, 88-91, Academic Support Services, tutor, 89-91; Florida A&M Univ, adj profr, 90-91; Florida Department of Hlth and Rehabilitative Services, abuse registry counselor, 91; Univ of NC at Wilmington, guest lecturer, 92; Federal Bureau of Prisons, research analyst, 92-; Shaw Univ, Raleigh, NC, Prof of Criminal Justice, 93-. **HONORS AND AWARDS** Honor Court, UNC Chapel Hill, 1980-82; UNC Charlotte, First graduate of Masters of Science Degree in Criminal Justice/ Management Program, 1984; Patricia Roberts Harris Fellowship, 1987-. **MEMBERSHIPS** Sweet Carolines 1980-82; Young Democrats 1982-83, Cloud Cappers Ltd Assn 1982-; Delta Sigma Theta, Inc 1984-; CVAN, Volunteer Assn for Battered Women, 1985; intake counselor, Probation & Parole, 1983-84; counselor Mecklenburg Co Charlotte; chmn UNICEF; Hall Rep 1980-81; UNC-Ch sec of dorm 1981-82; UNC Chapel Hill co-chmn 1st UNCF Tennis Tourn in Cabarrus Co; Advisor, Society of Criminal Justice 1985-87; Cooperative Colleges Task Force, 1986; American Criminal Justice Society, 1987-; Criminology Association, 1987-; Academy Criminal Justice Sciences, 1989-90; Guardian Ad Litem, 1988-; mediator, Durham County Mediation Svcs, 1996-; mem, Supreme Court Historical Society, 1994-. **SELECTED PUBLICATIONS** Author, works presented: Conference for Social Problems, "Gender Bias Amongst State Institutional Drug Treatment Programs," April 1990; "Effects of Pornography on Women," April 1988; Assn of Criminal Justice Professionals, "History of Women's Prisons in the State of Florida"; Southern Conference, "Role Play," 1987. **CONTACT ADDRESS** PO Box 51751, Durham, NC 27717.

TAYLOR, G. H.
PERSONAL Born 06/15/1951, Cambridge, MA, m, 1989, 1 child **DISCIPLINE** LAW **EDUCATION** Brown Univ, AB, 73; Univ Chicago, MA, 76, PhD cand; Harvard Law Sch, JD, 88. **CAREER** Asst prof, 89-95, assoc prof, 95- , Univ Pittsburgh. **HONORS AND AWARDS** Phi Beta Kappa. **MEMBERSHIPS** Am Soc for Pol and Legal Philos. **RESEARCH** Hermeneutics; legal hermeneutics; statutory construction. **SELECTED PUBLICATIONS** Ed, Lectures on Ideology and Utopia, 86; auth, Structural Textualism, BU Law Rev, 95; auth, Textualism at Work, DePaul Law Rev, 95; coauth, Critical Hermeneutics, Chicago-Kent Law Review, 01. **CONTACT ADDRESS** School of Law, Univ of Pittsburgh, Pittsburgh, PA 15260. **EMAIL** taylor@law.pitt.edu

TAYLOR, GENE FRED
PERSONAL Born 07/13/1941, Florence, AL, m, 1964, 1 child **DISCIPLINE** PHILOSOPHY **EDUCATION** Florence State Col, BS, 65; FL State Univ, MME, 65, PhD, 69. **CAREER** Assoc prof, 69-76, Prof Philos, Ala A&M Univ, 76-, Evaluator, Comt for Hum in AL. **HONORS AND AWARDS** MA, St John's Col, NM, 75. **MEMBERSHIPS** Am Philos Asn. **RESEARCH** The cognitive status of aesthetic experience. **SELECTED PUBLICATIONS** Auth, The philosophical basis of scientific linguistics, Ala A&M Univ Fac Res J, 8/76. **CONTACT ADDRESS** Dept of Behavioral Sci, Alabama A&M Univ, PO Box 229, Normal, AL 35762-0285. **EMAIL** gtaylor@asnaam.aamu.edu

TAYLOR, GRACE W.
DISCIPLINE LAW **EDUCATION** Fla State Univ, AB, MA; Univ Fla, JD. **CAREER** Clarence J. TeSelle prof and dir, Legal Inf Ctr, Univ Fla, 62-. **HONORS AND AWARDS** Marian Gould Gallagher Distinguished Service awd, Amer Asn Law Libraries, 97; Marta Lange/Congressional Quart awd, Law and Polit Sci Sect of the Asn Col and Res Libraries, 97. **MEMBERSHIPS** NCAIR bd Trustees, 78-96; AALL; Beta Phi Mu; Phi Beta Kappa, UF chap pres. **RESEARCH** Computers & the law. **CONTACT ADDRESS** School of Law, Univ of Florida, PO Box 117625, Gainesville, FL 32611-7625. **EMAIL** lawbt@nervm.nerdc.ufl.edu

TAYLOR, JAMES
PERSONAL Born 06/28/1956, Portland, OR, m, 1981, 3 children **DISCIPLINE** PHILOSOPHY **EDUCATION** Westmont Col, BA, 78; Fuller Theol Sem, MA, 81; Univ Ariz, MA, 85; PhD, 87. **CAREER** Asst to assoc prof philos, Bowling Green Univ, 87-93; assoc to prof, Westmont Col, 94- . **HONORS AND AWARDS** Hum Teacher Yr, Westmont Col, 97. **MEMBERSHIPS** Am Philos Asn, Soc Christian Philos. **RESEARCH** Epistemology, Philosophy of religion. **SELECTED PUBLICATIONS** Auth, "Kelly on the Logic of Eternal Knowledge," The Mod Schoolman, 67, pp 141-147, (90); auth, "Epistemic Justification and Psychological Realism," Synthese, 85, pp 199-230, (90); auth, "Plantinga's Proper Functioning Analysis of Epistemic Warrant," Philos Stud, 64, pp 185-202, (91); auth, "Conceptual Analysis and the Essence of Knowledge," Am Philos Quart, 30, pp 15-26, (93); auth, "Scepticism and the Nature of Knowledge," Philos, 22, pp 3-27, (93); auth, "Plantinga on Epistemic Warrant, "Philo and Phenomenol Res, 55, pp 421-426, (95); auth, "Foley's Egocentric Epistemology," Nous, 32, pp 265-275, (98). **CONTACT ADDRESS** Dept Philos, Westmont Col, 955 La Paz Rd, Santa Barbara, CA 93108-1023. **EMAIL** taylor@westmont.edu

TAYLOR, JON
PERSONAL Born 06/30/1938, Gays Mills, WI, 1938 children **DISCIPLINE** HEBREW SCRIPTURES **EDUCATION** Pontifical Bibl Inst, SSL, 70. **CAREER** Prof Relig, Univ Great Falls, 85-. **MEMBERSHIPS** CBA; AAR; SBL; ASOR; HIART. **RESEARCH** Science and religion. **CONTACT ADDRESS** 1301 20th St S, Great Falls, MT 59405. **EMAIL** jtaylor01@ugf.edu

TAYLOR, LESTER D.
PERSONAL Born 03/08/1938, IA, d, 2 children **DISCIPLINE** ECONOMICS **EDUCATION** Univ Iowa, BA, 60; Harvard Univ, PhD, 63. **CAREER** Asst prof, Harvard Univ, 64-68; assoc prof, Univ Mich, 69-74; vis prof, Univ Ariz, 72-73; prof, Univ Ariz, 74-; vis prof, Charles Univ Prague, 96. **HONORS AND AWARDS** Phi Beta Kappa, 60; Woodrow Wilson Fel, 60. **MEMBERSHIPS** Am Econ Asn; Econometric Soc; Intl Schumpeter Soc. **RESEARCH** Capital and monetary economics; Consumption economics; Economics of regulated industry. **SELECTED PUBLICATIONS** Auth, Telecommunications Demand, 94; auth, Capital, Accumulation, and Money, 00. **CONTACT ADDRESS** Dept Econ, Univ of Arizona, 401 W McClelland Hall, PO Box 210108, Tucson, AZ 85721-0108. **EMAIL** ltaylor@bpa.arizona.edu

TAYLOR, MICHAEL JOSEPH
PERSONAL Born 01/05/1924, Tacoma, WA **DISCIPLINE** THEOLOGY **EDUCATION** Gonzaga Univ, BA, 47, MA, 49; Santa Clara Univ, STM, 55; Woodstock Col, STD, 61. **CAREER** Instr humanities, Bellarmine Prep Sch, 48-51; instr theol, Gonzaga Univ, 56-59; from asst prof to assoc prof, 61-72, Prof Relig Studies, Seattle Univ, 73-94, prof emer, 95-; Lilly fel, 64-65; consult, Idaho Ecumenical Conf, 68; vis prof, Seton Hall Univ, 69-71. **MEMBERSHIPS** Col Theol Soc. **RESEARCH** Sacramental theology; Pauline and Johannine scripture studies. **SELECTED PUBLICATIONS** Auth, Protestant Liturgical Renewal: A Catholic Viewpoint, Newman Press, 63; Liturgy and Christian Unity, with R P Marshall, Prentice-Hall, 65; ed, Liturgical Renewal in the Christian Churches, Helicon, 67; The Sacred and the Secular, Prentice, 68; The Mystery of Sin and Forgiveness, Alba House, 71; Sex: Thoughts for Contemporary Christians, Doubleday, 72; The Mystery of Suffering and Death, 73, A Companion to Paul: Readings in Pauline Theology, 75, A Companion to John: Readings in Johannine Theology, 77 & The Sacraments: Readings in Contemporary Sacramental Theology, 81, Alba House; John, the Different Gospel, Alba House, 83; The Sacraments as Encasement, Liturgical Press, 86; Paul: His Letters, Message and Heritage--A Reflective Commentary, Alba House, 97; auth, Purgatory, 98. **CONTACT ADDRESS** PO Box 80651, Seattle, WA 98108.

TAYLOR, PATRICIA E.
PERSONAL Born 02/17/1942, New Haven, m **DISCIPLINE** LAW **EDUCATION** IL Inst Tech, BS 1967; Yale Law School, JD, 1971. **CAREER** Commun Prog Inc, commun wrkr 1963-65; Onondaga Lega Svc, law clk 1971-73; Princeton U, vis lctr 1974-. **HONORS AND AWARDS** Reginald Herber Smith Fel, 71-73; Outst Yng Wmn Am 1974. **MEMBERSHIPS** Mem NJ Bar Assn; US Sup Ct Bar; Allan Guttmacher Institute, bd of dir, 1986-89; assoc Gen Couns Educ Testing Serv Princeton NJ; bd dir ARC 1972-73. **CONTACT ADDRESS** Educ Testing Serv, Rosedale Rd, Princeton, NJ 08541.

TAYLOR, RAYMOND HARGUS
PERSONAL Born 10/04/1913, Bell County, KY, m, 1954, 2 children **DISCIPLINE** RELIGION **EDUCATION** Cumberland Ky Col, AA, 51; Carson-Newman Col, BA, 53; Southern Baptist Theol Sem, BD, 56, ThD, 61. **CAREER** Pastor, Mt Carmel Baptist Church, Ky, 57-61; Min Christian educ, Temple Baptist Church, NC, 61-63; Chaplain Col, Chowan Col, 63-90; asst pres & dir, Denominational Rel(s), Chowan Col, 90-91; chemn, Dept Rel and Philos, Chowan Col, 91-; deacon, Murfreesboro Baptist Church; bd dir, Hertford County Habitat for Humanity; bd dir, NC Baptist Hist Soc; coord coun, CBF NC. **MEMBERSHIPS** Am Acad Rel; Am Soc of Church Hist; Nat Asn Baptist Prof Rel; NC Baptist Hist Soc; Soc Bibl Lit; Southern Baptist Hist Soc; VA Baptist Hist Soc; William H Whittsitt Baptist Heritage Soc. **RESEARCH** Hist Research & Writing; Drama; Music; Genealogical Research. **SELECTED PUBLICATIONS** Auth, The Baptist Church at Cashie, 1770-1970, 70; A Century and a Quarter of Service: A History of Murfreesboro Church, 1848-1973, 73; Seventy-Five Years of Loving, Sharing, Caring: A History of Winter Park Baptist Church, 1913-1988, 89; Partners in Missions and Ministry: A History of Flat River Baptist Association, 93; The Heritage of a Century: A History of Chadbourn Baptist Church, 1890-1990, 93; Remembering the Past-Renewing the Future: A History of North Rocky Mount Baptist Church, 1895-1995, 96; contrib articles for publ in, Dictionary NC Biog, Encycl Southern Baptists & Mercer Dictionary of the Bible. **CONTACT ADDRESS** Dept of Relig, Chowan Col, 200 Jones Dr, PO Box 1848, Murfreesboro, NC 27855.

TAYLOR, RICHARD STUART
PERSONAL Born 06/24/1942, Chicago, IL **DISCIPLINE** AMERICAN HISTORY, HISTORY OF RELIGION **EDUCATION** Wheaton Col, Ill, BA, 64; Northern Ill Univ, MA, 70, PhD(hist), 77. **CAREER** Publ ed, 78-80, Dir Off Res & Publ, Hist Sites Div, Ill Dept Conserv, 80- **MEMBERSHIPS** AHA; Am Soc Church Hist; Orgn Am Historians; Soc Historians Early Am Repub. **RESEARCH** Evangelicalism in 19th century America; antebellum reform; new thought in the 1920s. **SELECTED PUBLICATIONS** Auth, Preachers--Billy Sunday, and Big-Time American Evangelism, J Am Hist, Vol 80, 93; Between Memory and Reality--Family and Community in Rural Wisconsin, 1870-1970, J Interdisciplinary Hist, Vol 26, 95. **CONTACT ADDRESS** Illinois Historical Preservation Agency, 523 W Monroe Apt 1, Springfield, IL 62704.

TAYLOR, RODNEY
DISCIPLINE RELIGIOUS STUDIES **EDUCATION** Columbia Univ, PhD. **CAREER** Prof. **SELECTED PUBLICATIONS** Auth, The Religious Dimensions of Confucianism; The Confucian Way of Contemplation; co-auth, They Shall Not Hurt: Human Suffering and Human Caring; pubs on Confucianism as a religious tradition, Neo-Confucian spiritual cultivation, Confucian meditation, and Confucian autobiography. **CONTACT ADDRESS** Religious Studies Dept, Univ of Colorado, Boulder, Boulder, CO 80309. **EMAIL** Rodney.Taylor@Colorado.edu

TAYLOR, VELANDE P.
PERSONAL Born 09/10/1923, New York, NY, m, 1961 **DISCIPLINE** LITERATURE, PHILOSOPHY **EDUCATION** Hunter Col, BA, 44; Columbia Univ, MA, 45, PhD, 47. **CAREER** Instr, Paul Smiths Col, 46-47; asst prof, East Carolina Univ, 47-58; prof, head hum dept, Colorado Women's Col, 58-66; vis prof. St Mary's Univ, 66-69; prof, Middle Georgia Col, 69-72; prof, writer in residence and ed, Acad J, 74-84, Hong Kong Baptist Col; section ed, URAM J of Int Stud in the Philos of Understanding, 84-89; WordCraft by Lan, 93- ; ed, publ WordCraft Books, 96- . **HONORS AND AWARDS** Int Mark Twain Soc, 47, Order of the Dannebrog, 51; Freedom Found, 51, Bronze Medal, 52, Gold Medal, 53. **MEMBERSHIPS** APA; Acad of Am Poets; Grunewald Guild. **SELECTED PUBLICATIONS** Auth, Homilies in the Marketplace: Parables for Our Times, 96; Copper Flowers, 97, 99; Walking Songs, 97, 98; Tales from the Archetypal World, 98; Flowing Water, Singing Sand: The Metaphysics of Change, 99; Between the Lines, 99; auth, The Zodiac Affair, 00, gallery, 01. **CONTACT ADDRESS** #1008, Seattle, WA 98104-1273.

TAYLOR, WALTER F., JR.
PERSONAL Born 12/15/1946, Omaha, NE, m, 1969, 2 children **DISCIPLINE** NEW TESTAMENT **EDUCATION** Midland Lutheran Col, BA, 69; Lutheran Theol Sem, MDiv, 73; Claremont Grad Univ, PhD, 81. **CAREER** Greek instr, S Calif Sch Theol, 73-76; asst prof, 81-84; assoc prof, 84-91; prof, Trinity Lutheran Sem, 91-96; Ernest W. and Edith S. Ogram prof, 96-; vis prof, Univ Heidelberg, 88-89. **HONORS AND AWARDS** Alumni Honor Roll, 97-98; Master Teacher Awd, 96; Midland Lutheran College; ATS Theological Scholarship and Research Awd, 88-89; Fulbright Professor, 88-89. **MEMBERSHIPS** Society of Biblical Literature; Society for Antiquity and Christianiy; Catholic Biblical Association. **RESEARCH** Cultural anthropology as a tool for studying the New Testament; Pauline ethics; sociological exegesis; ministry in the Pastoral Epistles; leadership in the early church. **SELECTED PUBLICATIONS** Auth, Obligation: Foundation for Paul's Ethics, Trinity Sem Rev, 98, Josephinum Jour Theol, 98; Romans: New Life in Christ Jesus, Inspire, Augsburg, 98; Cultural Anthropology as a Tool for Studying the New Testament: Part II, Trinity Sem Rev, 97; Jesus Within His Social World: Insights from Archaeology, Sociology, and Cultural Anthropology, Word & World, Supplement 3, 97; Cultural Anthropology as a Tool for Studying the New Testament: Part I, Trinity Sem Rev, 96; Captive and Free: Insights From Galatians, Intersections, Augsburg, 95; Reclaiming Revelation, The Lutheran, 93-94; auth, "Ephesians," Dictionary of Biblical Interpretation, 99; auth, "New Quests for the Historical Jesus," Trinity Seminary Review, 93; auth, "1 and 2 Timothy, Titus," Te Deutero-Pauline Letters," 93; auth, "Unity/Unity of Humanity" and "Humanity, NT View of," Anchor Bible Dictionary, 92 Ephesians, Augsburg, 85. **CONTACT ADDRESS** Trinity Lutheran Sem, 2199 E Main St, Columbus, OH 43209-2334. **EMAIL** wtaylor@trinity.capital.edu

TAYLOR, WILLIAM B.
PERSONAL Born 07/23/1944, Milan, TN, m, 1999, 2 children **DISCIPLINE** CRIMINAL JUSTICE **EDUCATION** Univ Southern Miss, BA, 66; MA, 68; London Sch Economics, Univ London, PhD, 74. **CAREER** Prof of Criminal Justice, Univ of Southern Miss, 81-. **HONORS AND AWARDS** Founder and chief administrator of the Ctr for International Education in the University of Southern Miss, 79-86; Recipient of Awd for Outstanding Service in Criminal Justice Educ, Soc of Police and Criminal Psychol, 76; co-recipient (with Ernest B. Gurman) of the Annul Res Awd, Region III, Nat Univ Continuing Educ Asn, 87; Individual of the Year Awd, Prof Bail Agents of the United States, 98. **MEMBERSHIPS** Soc of Police and Criminal Psychology; Soc Sci Hist Asn; Southern Criminal Justice Educators Asn; Acad of Criminal Justice Scis. **RESEARCH** Penology; the economics of crime and punishment; 19th century Mississippi history. **SELECTED PUBLICATIONS** Auth, Brokered Justice: Race, Politics, and Mississippi Prisons, 1798-1992, Columbus, Oh: Ohio State Univ Press (93); co-ed with Kenneth Bourne, The Horner Papers: Selections From the Correspondence and Miscellaneous Writings of Francis Horner, M. P., 1795-1817, Edinburgh, Scotland: Edinburgh Univ Press (94); auth, Down on Parchman Farm: The Great Prison in the Mississippi Delta, Columbus, Ohio: Ohio State Univ Press (99). **CONTACT ADDRESS** Dept Criminal Justice, Univ of So Mississippi, 2805 Hardy St, Hattiesburg, MS 39406. **EMAIL** usmcjd@netdoor.com

TAYLOR, WILLIAMSON S.
PERSONAL Born 09/09/1942, m, 1970, 2 children **DISCIPLINE** THEOLOGY **EDUCATION** Boston Univ, School of Theology, ThD, 89. **CAREER** Assoc Dir Ministerial Studies, 86-92, Harvard Divinity School; Sr Pastor, St. Mark's UCC Church, Boston, 84-94; Adjunct Lectr, Florida Intl Univ, 98-; Rector/Priest, Episocal Churches of St. Anne and St. Andrew, 94-; Dean of Broward Deanery, Diocese of Southeast Fl, 98-. **MEMBERSHIPS** Amer Assoc Religion; Soc Biblical Lit. **RESEARCH** New Testament; comparative religions; personality and culture **CONTACT ADDRESS** 3102 Hollywood Blvd., Hollywood, FL 33021.

TEEHAN, JOHN
PERSONAL Born 03/12/1962, Brooklyn, NY, m, 1987, 2 children **DISCIPLINE** PHILOSOPHY **EDUCATION** Queens Col, MA, 87; Grad Ctr, PHD, 92 **CAREER** Asst Prof of Philos, 89-98, Hofstra Univ; Asst Prof of Philos, 98-pres, Sch for Univ Stud **MEMBERSHIPS** Am Philos Assoc; Am Psych Assoc; Soc of Humanist Philos **RESEARCH** Evolution & Theories of Self & Ethics; Philosophy of Religion. **SELECTED PUBLICATIONS** Auth, "What's a Philosopher to Do," Metaphilosophy, 94; auth, "In Defense of a Naturalism," Journal of Speculative Philos, 96; auth, "Character, Integrity and Dewey's Virtue Ethics," Transactions of CS Peirce Soc, (95); auth, "Noble Humanism: A Post-Davwinian Moval Ideal," in Possibility of the Impossible: Planetary Humanism for Russia and The World (Moscow: Russian Humanist Soc, 01). **CONTACT ADDRESS** Sch for Univ Studies, 130 Hofstra Univ, Hempstead, NY 11549. **EMAIL** nucjpt@hofstra.edu

TEGEDER, VINCENT GEORGE
PERSONAL Born 10/01/1910, La Crosse, WI **DISCIPLINE** HISTORY POLITICAL SCIENCE **EDUCATION** St John's Univ, Minn, BA, 33; Univ Wis, MA, 42, PhD, 49. **CAREER** Prof hist, 46-79, Emer Prof Hist, St John's Univ, Minn, 79-, Archivist, 75-96, Vis prof hist, Sacramento State Col, 65-66 & 67 & Int Div, Sophia Univ, Tokyo, 73-74. **HONORS AND AWARDS** NCAIS, India, 70. **MEMBERSHIPS** Am Cath Hist Asn. **RESEARCH** American West during the Civil War; culture on the frontier; colonization. **SELECTED PUBLICATIONS** Auth, "Lincoln," MVHR, Vol 35, 77; auth, Obituary (rev), Cath Hist Rev, Vol 80, 94. **CONTACT ADDRESS** St. John's Univ, Archives Collegeville, MN 56321. **EMAIL** vtegeder@csbsju.edu

TEISER, STEPHEN F.
DISCIPLINE RELIGIOUS STUDIES; EAST ASIAN STUDIES **EDUCATION** Oberlin Col, AB, 78; Princeton Univ, MA, 83; PhD, 86. **CAREER** Vis asst prof, Middlebury Col, 86-87; asst prof, Univ S Ccalif, 87-88; prof dept of religion, Princrton Univ, 88- ; **HONORS AND AWARDS** ACLS Awd Best Book Hist Relig, 88; AAS Joseph Levenson Awd Best Book Chinese Studies, 94. **MEMBERSHIPS** Asn Asian Studies; Am Acad Relig; Soc Study Chinese Relig; Am Asn Study Relig. **RESEARCH** Chinese Buddhism; manuscripts from Dunhuang. **SELECTED PUBLICATIONS** Auth, The Growth in Purgatory, Religion and Society in T'ang and Sung China, Univ Hawaii Press, 93; The Scripture on the Ten Kings and the Making of Purgatory in Medieval Chinese Buddhism, Univ Hawaii, 94; Popular Religion, Chinese Religion: The State of the Field, Jour Asian Studies, 95; Introduction: The Spirits of Chinese Religion, Religions of China in Practice, Princeton Univ Press, 96; The Ghost Festival in Medieval China, Princeton Univ Press 88. **CONTACT ADDRESS** Dept of Religion, Princeton Univ, Seventy-Nine Hall, Princeton, NJ 08544-1006. **EMAIL** sfteiser@princeton.edu

TELLER, PAUL
PERSONAL Born 02/10/1943, Chicago, IL, m, 1996, 2 children **DISCIPLINE** PHILOSOPHY **EDUCATION** Stanford, BS, 65; MIT, PhD, 69. **CAREER** Prof, Univ of Calif Davis. **HONORS AND AWARDS** Phi Beta Kappa; Woodrow Wilson Fel; Nat Sci Found Grad Fel. **MEMBERSHIPS** Am Philos Assoc; Philos of Sci Assoc; AAAS. **RESEARCH** Philosophy of Science. **SELECTED PUBLICATIONS** Auth, An Interpretive Introduction to Quantum Field Theory, Princeton Univ Pr, 95; auth, "Quantum Field Theory", Routledge Encyclop of Philos; auth, "Supervenience", A Companion to Metaphysics, eds J Kim and E Sosa, Blackwells, (Oxford, 95): 484-6; auth, "Field Theory", Cambridge Dict of Philos, ed Robert Audi, Cambridge Univ Pr, (96): 266-7; auth, "Reduction", Cambridge Dict of Philos, ed Robert Audi, Cambridge Univ Pr, (96): 679-80; auth, "Wave and Particle Concepts in Quantum Field Theory", Perspectives on Quantum Reality, ed R Clifton, Kluwer, (96): 143-154; auth, "Quantum Mechanics and Haecceities", Interpreting Bodies: Classical and Quantum Objects in Modern Physics, ed Elena Castellani, Princeton Univ Pr, (98): 114-141; auth, "The Ineliminable Classical Face of Quantum Field Theory", Conceptual Foundations of Quantum Field Theory, ed Tian Yu Cao, Cambridge Univ Pr, (99): 314-23; auth, "On Huggett and Weingard's Review of an Interpretive Introduction to Quantum Field Theory: Continuing the Discussion", Philos of Sci, (98): 151-161; auth, "Against Against Overlap and Endurance", Reality and Supervenience, eds Gerhard Preyer and Frank Siebelt, (forthcoming). **CONTACT ADDRESS** Dept Philos, Univ of California, Davis, 1 Shields Ave, Davis, CA 95616-5270. **EMAIL** prteller@ucdavis.edu

TENENBAUM, SERGIO
DISCIPLINE ETHICS, HISTORY OF MODERN PHILOSOPHY, PRACTICAL REASON **EDUCATION** Hebrew Univ Jerusalem, BA, 88; Univ Pittsburgh, MA, 93, PhD, 96. **CAREER** Asst prof, Univ NMex. **SELECTED PUBLICATIONS** Auth, Hegel's Critique of Kant in the Philosophy of Right, in Kant Studien; Realists without a Cause: Deflationary Theories of Truth and Ethical Realism, Can J of Philos. **CONTACT ADDRESS** Univ of New Mexico, Albuquerque, Albuquerque, NM 87131. **EMAIL** sergio@unm.edu

TEPLY, LARRY L.
DISCIPLINE LAW **EDUCATION** Univ Nebr, BA, 69; Univ Fla, JD, 72; Harvard Univ, LLM, 73. **CAREER** Prof, Creighton Univ; staff atty, US Fed Trade Comn, 76-77. **MEMBERSHIPS** Order of the Coif. **SELECTED PUBLICATIONS** Auth, Legal Research and Citation, 4th ed, West, 92; Legal Writing, Analysis, & Oral Argument, West, 90; Legal Negotiation in a Nutshell, West, 92; coauth, Civil Procedure, Foundation Press, 94; pub(s), Yale Law J; Creighton Law Rev; Tulane Law Rev; Univ Fla Law Rev; Univ Miami Law Rev; J Health Politics; Policy and Law; Hastings Int and Comp Law Rev & Trademark Reporter. **CONTACT ADDRESS** Sch of Law, Creighton Univ, 2500 California Plaza , Omaha, NE 68178. **EMAIL** teply@culaw.Creighton.edu

TERCHEK, RONALD JOHN
PERSONAL Born 07/29/1936, Cleveland, OH, m, 1998, 2 children **DISCIPLINE** POLITICAL SCIENCE **EDUCATION** Univ Chicago, BA, 58, MA, 60; Univ Maryland, PhD, 65. **CAREER** From Asst prof to prof, Univ Maryland, 65- . **HONORS AND AWARDS** Omicron Delta Kappa; Lilly Fel, 93-94; University Teaching Excellence Awds, 85, 89, 92; listed, Who's Who in the East, 98. **MEMBERSHIPS** Am Polit Sci Asn; Foundations on Polit Theory; Conf for the Study of Polit Theory; Pi Sigma Alpha; Phi Kappa Phi; Int Asn for Philos of Law and Social Philos. **RESEARCH** Classical liberalism: Locke, Smith, and J.S. Mill; liberal democratic theory; Gandhi's politi-

cal theory with special emphasis on his critique of modernity and modernization; civic realism. **SELECTED PUBLICATIONS** Ed, Interactions; Foreign Policy as Public Policy, Am Enterprise Inst, 83; auth, Republican Paradoxes and Liberal Anxieties: Retrieving Neglected Fragments in Political Theory, Rowman & Littlefield, 96; auth, Leo Strauss and the Republican Tradition, in Deutsch, ed, Leo Strauss, the Straussians, and the Study of the American Regime, Rowman & Littlefield, 97; auth, the Political Thought of Mahatma Gandhi, Rowman & Littlefield, 98. **CONTACT ADDRESS** Dept of Government and Politics, Univ of Maryland, Col Park, College Park, MD 20742-7215. **EMAIL** rterchek@gvpt.umd.edu

TEREZAKIS, KATIE
PERSONAL Born 01/08/1972, CT **DISCIPLINE** PHILOSOPHY **EDUCATION** New School for Social Research, PhD, in progress. **RESEARCH** Political philosophy, Neitzsche, Marx, Hegel, German Idealism. **SELECTED PUBLICATIONS** Auth, Ruthless Criticism/Relentless Creation, Marx, Neitzsche and the End of Modern Society. **CONTACT ADDRESS** Dept of Philosophy, New Sch for Social Research, 65 5th Ave, New York, NY 10011.

TERFA, SOLOMON
PERSONAL Born 04/21/1951, Addis Ababa, Ethiopia, m, 1993, 2 children **DISCIPLINE** INTERNATIONAL RELATIONS **EDUCATION** Univ Calif at Los Angeles, BA, 73; Atlanta Univ, MA, 75; PhD, 85. **CAREER** Asst prof & chair, Addis Ababa Univ, 89-93; asst prof, Alcorn State Univ, 94-. **MEMBERSHIPS** Am Pol Sci Asn, Miss Pol Sci Asn, Nat Geog Soc. **SELECTED PUBLICATIONS** Auth, "Pluralism as an Instrument of Political Stability and Development," Ethiopian J of Development Res 13.1 (91): auth, "Why Another Civil War in Ethiopia," Ethiopia Review (92)' auth, "Ethiopian Students," Reflections On Ethnic Politics (Chicago, IL: Nyala Publ Co, 93); auth, "Danger Lurks," Ethiopian Examiner (94); auth, "Before Ethiopia is Caught Off Guard," Moresh 2.6 (94); auth, "Frustration-Aggression or What?" Ethiopian Review (97); auth, "The Personality Dimension of the Ethio-Eritrean War," Ethiopian Register 6.11 (99). **CONTACT ADDRESS** Dept Soc Sci, Alcorn State Univ, 1000 Alcorn Dr, Alcorn State, MS 39096-7500. **EMAIL** sterfa@aol.com

TERMINI, ROSEANN B.
DISCIPLINE LAW **EDUCATION** Drexel Univ, BS, 75; Temple Univ, Med, 79; Temple Univ Sch Law, JD, 85. **CAREER** Temple Univ Sch of Pharmacy, Villanova Univ, Sch of Law; clerked, Honorable Donald E. Wieand, Superior Ct Pa; past regulatory aff atty, Pa Power and Light; past sr dep atty gen, Off Atty Gen, Commonwealth Pa; taught at, Dickinson Law Sch; adj prof, St Joseph's Univ; adj prof, Widener Univ Sch Law; **HONORS AND AWARDS** Pa Bar Asn, Plain Lang Awd. **SELECTED PUBLICATIONS** Publ on, consumer contract law, the envt, food pharmaceutical and med device law. **CONTACT ADDRESS** Law School, Villanova Univ, 800 Lancaster Ave, Villanova, PA 19085-1692. **EMAIL** termini@law.vill.edu

TERNES, HANS
PERSONAL Born 09/10/1937, Kogolniceanu, Romania, m, 1962, 2 children **DISCIPLINE** GERMAN LITERATURE, AESTHETICS, ROMANCE PHILOSOPHY **EDUCATION** Univ Il, BA, 61, MA, 63; Univ Pa, PhD, 68. **CAREER** Lectr English, Univ Freiburg, Ger, 65-66; instr Ger, Univ Pa, 66-68; asst prof, 68-75, from assoc prof to prof Ger, Lawrence Univ, 76-. **MEMBERSHIPS** Am Asn Teachers Ger; MLA. **RESEARCH** Twentieth century German literature, primarily Thomas Mann, Friedrich Durrenmatt, Franz Kafka; problems in aesthetics, the grotesque; genre studies, nature poetry. **SELECTED PUBLICATIONS** Auth, Das Problem der Gerechtigkeit in Durrenmatts Die Panne, Germanic Notes, 75; Das Groteske in den Werken Thomas Manns, Stuttgarter Arbeiten zur Germanistik, 75; Anmerkungen zur Zeitblomgestalt, Germanic Notes, 76; co-ed, Probleme der Komparatistik & Interpretation, Festschrift for Prof Andre von Gronicka, Bouvier Vlg, Bonn, 78; contribr, Franz Kafka's Hunter Gracchus: an interpretation, Festschrift for Prof Andre von Gronicka, 78; Das Bild des Helden in DDR Roman, Rocky Mtn Rev, 83; The fantastic in the works of Franz Kafha, The Scope of the Fantastic, Greenwood, Inc, 85; Wolfgang Ammon Ein Deutsch-Brasilianischer Schriftsteller, Hans Staden-Jahrbuch, Sao Paulo, 86; Franz Xaver Kroetz, Magill's Critical Survey of Drama: Foreign Languages, Salem Press Ca, 86. **CONTACT ADDRESS** Dept of German, Lawrence Univ, 115 S Drew St, Appleton, WI 54911-5798. **EMAIL** Hans.Ternes@Lawrence.edu

TERPSTRA, VERN
PERSONAL Born 08/20/1927, Grand Rapids, MI, m, 1950, 2 children **DISCIPLINE** INTERNATIONAL BUSINESS, MARKETING **EDUCATION** BA 50, MBA 51, PhD 65, all Univ of Michigan. **CAREER** Prof of International Business Univ of Michigan 66-92, Asst Prof Marketing Wharton School 64-66, Dir Mormal School Congo 53-61. **HONORS AND AWARDS** Fellow-Academy of International Business; Fellow -Marketing Sci Institute;Fellow-Ford Foundation. **MEMBERSHIPS** Academy of International Business-President 70-72, Amer Marketing Assoc **RESEARCH** International Marketing, International Business, Cross Cultural Issues **SELECTED PUBLICATIONS** International Marketing 7th ed, Dryden Press, 97; International Dimensions of Marketing Kent 3rd ed, 93; Cultural Enviornment of International Business 3rd ed, Southwestern, 91; Lectures in International Marketing(Chinese) National Center for Management Development Dalian China, 86: Univ Educ for International Business AEIB 69; Amer Marketing in the Common Market Praeger, 67; Co-auth Comparative Analysis for International Marketing, Allyn&Bacon, 67; Co-auth Marketing Development in the European Economic Community, McGraw-Hill, 64; Co-auth, Patents and Progress, Irwin, 65. **CONTACT ADDRESS** Graduate School of Business, Univ of Michigan, Ann Arbor, Ann Arbor, MI 48109. **EMAIL** vterp@umich.edu

TERRELL, FRANCIS D'ARCY
PERSONAL Born 05/13/1940, Caledonia, NY, m **DISCIPLINE** LAW **EDUCATION** Univ of Toledo, BS 1970; Columbia Law School, JD 1973. **CAREER** Shearman & Sterling, assoc Attorney 1973-75; Private Practice, Law 1975-77; Jones & Terrell, partner 1977-82; Bronx Comm Coll, deputy chmn/prof 1982-. **HONORS AND AWARDS** Lt col 20 yrs; Bronze Star; Air Medal; Meritorious Serv Medal; Commendation Medal; Combat Infantry Badge. **MEMBERSHIPS** Mem Amer Business Law Assocs 1984-. **CONTACT ADDRESS** Dept of Business, Bronx Comm Col, CUNY, W 181st & Univ Ave, Bronx, NY 10453.

TERRELL, HUNTINGTON
PERSONAL Born 10/07/1925, Syracuse, NY, m, 1950, 3 children **DISCIPLINE** PHILOSOPHY, PEACE STUDIES **EDUCATION** Colgate Univ, AB, 44; Harvard Univ, AM, 48, PhD, 56. **CAREER** From instr to assoc prof, 51-67, dir gen educ course in Philos & Relig, 58-63, prof Philos, Colgate Univ, 67-, spec auditor Govt & Philos, Harvard Univ, 68-69; vis fel, Princeton Univ, 64 & 76-77, ret 98. **MEMBERSHIPS** Am Philos Asn; Soc Philos & Pub Affairs. **RESEARCH** Political, international, ecomonic, environmental ethics. **SELECTED PUBLICATIONS** Auth, Moral objectivity and moral freedom, Ethics, 1/65; Are moral considerations always overriding?, Australasian J Philos, 5/69. **CONTACT ADDRESS** Colgate Univ, 13 Oak Dr, Hamilton, NY 13346 1379.

TERRELL, JOANNE M.
PERSONAL Born 04/18/1958, Springfield, MA, s **DISCIPLINE** THEOLOGY **EDUCATION** Rollins Cool, BA, 81; Union Theol Sem, MDiv, 90; MPhil, 94; PhD, 97. **CAREER** Asst Prof, Chicago Theol Sem, 97-. **HONORS AND AWARDS** Feel, Union Theol Sem; Feel, Fund for Theol Educ; Daniel Day Williams Prize for Outstanding Work in Theol, Union Theol Sem; Thomas P. Johnson Distinguished Visiting Scholar Awd, Rollins Col. **MEMBERSHIPS** Am Acad of Relig, Soc of Bibl Lit, Soc for the Study of Black Relig. **RESEARCH** African-American studies, women's studies, moral philosophy, world religions and spirituality, American civil religion. **SELECTED PUBLICATIONS** Auth, Power in the Blood? The Cross in the African-American Experience, Orbis Books, 98. **CONTACT ADDRESS** Dept Theol, Chicago Theol Sem, 5757 S University Ave, Chicago, IL 60637. **EMAIL** jterrell@chgosem.edu

TERRELL, TIMOTHY PRATER
PERSONAL Born 10/02/1949, Kyoto, Japan, m, 1969, 2 children **DISCIPLINE** LAW, LEGAL PHILOSOPHY **EDUCATION** Univ Md, BA, 71; Yale Univ, JD, 74; Oxford Univ, dipl, 80. **CAREER** Assoc, Kilpatrick & Cody, 74-76; asst prof property trusts & estates, 76-78, ASSOC PROF PROPERTY JURISPRUDENCE, SCH LAW, EMORY UNIV, 78-, Vis prof, Col Law, Univ Iowa, 79. **RESEARCH** Property rights and legal theory; moral philosophy; economic theory and its relation to law and ethics. **SELECTED PUBLICATIONS** Auth, Ethics with an Attitude--Comments on New Directions for Keck Philanthropy, Law Contemp Problems, Vol 58, 95. **CONTACT ADDRESS** Law Sch, Emory Univ, 1364 Clifton Rd N E, Atlanta, GA 30322-0001.

TERRY, CHARLES T.
DISCIPLINE LAW **EDUCATION** Stanford Univ, BA; SW Univ Sch Law, JD; NYork Univ, LLM. **CAREER** Instr, NY Univ; instr, SW Univ Sch Law; assoc dean, prof, Univ Ill, 90-. **SELECTED PUBLICATIONS** Auth, pubs on combining taxation, finance, and economics. **CONTACT ADDRESS** Law Dept, Univ of Illinois, Urbana-Champaign, 52 E Gregory Dr, Champaign, IL 61820. **EMAIL** cterry@law.uiuc.edu

TERRY, J. MARK
PERSONAL Born 08/11/1949, Siloam Springs, AR, m, 1971, 2 children **DISCIPLINE** CHRISTIAN MISSIONS AND EVANGELISM **EDUCATION** John Brown Univ, BS; Southwestern Baptist Theol Sem, MDiv, PhD. **CAREER** Prof, S Baptist Missionary, Philippines; A. P. and Faye Stone prof, 93; assoc dean, Billy Graham Sch Missions, Evangel and Church Growth; prof, South Baptist Theol Sem. **MEMBERSHIPS** Evangel Missiological Soc; Amer Soc Missiology; Acad for Evangel in Theol Edu. **SELECTED PUBLICATIONS** Auth, Evangelism: A Concise History; auth, Church Evangelism; ed, Missiology: An Introduction. **CONTACT ADDRESS** Billy Graham Sch Missions, Evangel and Church Growth, So Baptist Theol Sem, 2825 Lexington Rd, Louisville, KY 40280. **EMAIL** mterry@sbts.edu

TESCHNER, GEORGE A.
DISCIPLINE PHILOSOPHY **EDUCATION** Rutgers Univ, BA; NYork Univ, MA; grad fac, New Sch for Soc Res, MA, PhD. **CAREER** Philos, Christopher Newport Univ. **SELECTED PUBLICATIONS** Auth, The Concept of Justice in Computer Managed Telecommunications Featured in Horizons of Justice, Peter Lang Publ, 96. **CONTACT ADDRESS** Dept of Philos, Christopher Newport Univ, 1 University Place Newport News, Newport News, VA 23606. **EMAIL** teschner@cnu.edu

TESELLE, EUGENE A.
PERSONAL Born 08/08/1931, Ames, IA, m, 1978, 5 children **DISCIPLINE** THEOLOGY **EDUCATION** Univ of Colo, BA, 52; Princeton Theological Seminary, BD, 55; Yale Univ, MA, 60, PhD, 63. **CAREER** Asst minister, First Presbyterian Church of East Orange, 55-58; instr, 62-63; asst prof, Dept of Religious Studies, Yale Univ, 63-69; assoc prof, 69-74, prof, Vanderbilt Divinity School, 74-99; prof emeritus, Vanderbilt Divinity Sch, 99-. **HONORS AND AWARDS** Phi Beta Kappa, 52; Presbyterian Grad Fel, 58; Rockefeller Doctoral Fel, 60; Kent Fel, 61; Thomas Jefferson Awd, Vanderbilt Univ, 96. **MEMBERSHIPS** Am Acad of Religion; Am Soc of Church Hist; Soc for Early Christian Studies. **RESEARCH** History of doctrine; theology in the reformed tradition; religion in contemporary society. **SELECTED PUBLICATIONS** Auth, Augustine the Theologian, Herder & Herder, 70; Augustine's Strategy as an Apologist, Villanova Univ Press, 74; Christ in Context: Divine Purpose and Human Possibility, Fortress Press, 75; Thomas Aquinas: Faith and Reason, Graded Press, 88; Living in Two Cities: Augustinian Trajectories in Political Thought, Univ of Scranton Press, 99. **CONTACT ADDRESS** Divinity School, Vanderbilt Univ, Nashville, TN 37240. **EMAIL** eugene.a.teselle@vanderbilt.edu

TESKE, ROLAND JOHN
PERSONAL Born 10/29/1934, Milwaukee, WI **DISCIPLINE** PHILOSOPHY **EDUCATION** St Louis Univ, BA, 58, MA, 59, PhL, 59, STL, 66; Univ Toronto, PhD(philos), 73. **CAREER** Instr philos, Marquette Univ, 70-73; asst prof, St Louis Univ, 73-74; Asst PROF PHILOS, MARQUETTE UNIV, 74-, Actg dean, Col Philos & Lett, St Louis Univ, 73-74; ed, The Mod Schoolman, 74-76; dir honors prog, Marquette Univ, 78-81; assoc prof, Marguette Univ,83; prof, Marquette Univ, 85; ed, Medieval Philosophical Texts in Translation, 89-; vis prof, Santa Clara Univ, 90; vis prof, John Carrol Univ, 93-94. **MEMBERSHIPS** Am Cath Philos Asn; Jesuit Philos Asn. **RESEARCH** Metaphysics; St Augustine; history of philosophy. **SELECTED PUBLICATIONS** Transl, The William of Auvergne: The Immortality of the Soul Translated with Introduction and Notes, Mediaeval Philosophical Texts in Translation, vol 360 Milwaukee: Marquette Univ Press, 91; transl, Henry of Ghent: Disputed Questions on Free Will, Translated with an Introduction and Notes Mediaeval Texts in Translation , Vol 32 , Milwaukee, Marquette Univ Press, 93; coed, Augustine: Presbyter Factus Sum, New York: Peter Lang, 93; auth, St Augustine: Arianism and Other Heresies, Heresies, Memorandum to Augustine, To Orosius in Refutation of the Preiscillianists and Origenists, Arian Sermon, Answer to an Arian Sermon, Debate with Maximinus, Answer to Maximinus, Answer to an Enemy of the Law and the Prophets, Hyde Park, NY: New City Press, 95; auth, Paradoxes of Time in St Augustine: The 96 Aquinas Lecture, Milwaukee: Marquette Univ Press, 96; auth, St Augustine: Answer to the Pelagians: The Punishment and Forgiveness of Sins and the Baptism of Little Ones, The Spirit and the Letter, Nature and Grace, The Perfection of Human Righteousness, The Proceedings against Pelagius, The Grace of Christ and Original Sin, The Nature and Origin of the Soul I, 23, Hyde Park, NY: New City Press, 97; transl, William of Auvergne: The Universe of Creatures, Selections Translated with and Introduction and Notes, Mediaeval Philosophical Texts in Translation, 35, Milwaukee: Marquette Univ Press, 98; auth, St Augustine: Answer to the Pelegians II, Marriage and Desire, Answer to Two Letters of the Pelagians, Answer to Julian, I, 24, Hyde Park, NY, New City Press, 98; auth, St Augustine Answer to the Pelagians III, Unfinished Work in Answer to Julian, Hyde Park, NY, New City Press, 99; auth, St Augustine: Answer to the Pelagians IV, Grace and Free Choice, Rebuke and Grace, The Predestination of the Saints, and the Gift of Perseverance, Introduction, translation, and notes by Roland J Teske, S J I, 26, Hyde Park, NY, New City Press, 99. **CONTACT ADDRESS** Dept of Philos, Marquette Univ, Milwaukee, WI 53233. **EMAIL** roland.teske@marquette.edu

TESON, FERNANDO R.
PERSONAL Born 08/03/1950, Buenos Aires, Argentina, m, 1996, 3 children **DISCIPLINE** INTERNATIONAL LAW **EDUCATION** Univ de Buenos Aires, JD, 75; Univ Libre de Bruxelles, Lic droit international 82; Northwestern Univ, SJD, 87. **CAREER** Assoc prof, Univ de Buenos Aires, 78-80; prof, Ariz Stae Univ, 84-; vis prof, Univ Torcuato di Tella, Argentina, 96-. **HONORS AND AWARDS** James N Raymond Fel, North-

western Univ. **MEMBERSHIPS** Am Soc of Int Law; AMINTAPHIL; Comm for Intersocietal Relations. **RESEARCH** International Law Theory, Political Philosophy, Human Rights. **SELECTED PUBLICATIONS** Auth, "The Rawlsian Theory of International Law", 9 Ethics and Int Affairs 79, (95); auth, "Low-Intensity Conflict and State Sovereignty: a Philosophical Analysis", Legal and Moral Constraints on Low-Intensity Conflicts 87, eds A Coll, J Ord and S Rose, US Naval War Col Int Law Studies, (95); auth, "Changing Perceptions of Domestic Jurisdiction and Intervention", Beyond Sovereignty: Collectively Defending Democracy in the Americas 29, ed Tom Farer, Johns Hopkins Univ Pr, 96; auth, "Collective Humanitarian Intervention", 17 Mich J of Int Law, 323 (96); auth, Humanitarian Intervention; An Inquiry Into Law and Morality, transnational Pub, 97; auth, A Philosophy of International Law, Westview Pr, 98; auth, "Ethnicity, Human Rights, and Self-determination", Int Law and Ethnic Conflict 86, ed D Wippman, Cornell Univ Pr, 98; auth, "Kantian International Liberalism", International Society: Diverse Ethical Perspectives, eds T Nardin and D Mapel, Princeton Univ Pr, 98; auth, "Two Mistakes About Democracy", Int Legal Proceedings 126, 99; auth, "A Defense of Liberal Democracy for Africa", 12 Cambridge Rev of Int Affairs 29, (99). **CONTACT ADDRESS** Col of Law, Arizona State Univ, PO Box 877906, Tempe, AZ 85287-7906. **EMAIL** fernanco.teson@asu.edu

TEVES, RITA R.
DISCIPLINE PHILOSOPHY **EDUCATION** Univ Santo Tomas, BA, 55; MA, 68; Univ Southern Calif, MS, 79; PhD, 84. **CAREER** Prof, Mapua Inst of Technology, Philippines, 60-69; Adj lectr, Univ of Southern Calif, 84-89; Prof, Los Angeles Trade-Tech Col, 77-. **HONORS AND AWARDS** Phi Delta Kappa; Outstanding Scholar, USC Sch of Educ; Model Student - Outstanding Pianist, Secondary Hon Student, Educ Alumni Asn USC; Outstanding Achievement in Res, Educ Alumni Asn, USC. **MEMBERSHIPS** Am Educ Studies Asn, Alpha Um Gamma, Phi Delta Kappa, Far Western Philos of Educ Soc, St. John of God Nursing Hops Auxiliary, Mary Crest Manor Auxiliary Guild, Am Educ Res Asn, Comp and Int Educ Soc, Int Soc for Educ Biog, De Camera Soc, Good Shepherd Center Auxiliary Guild, **RESEARCH** Lifelong learning, Adult education, Existentialism, Thomism, Ancient Greek philosophy. **SELECTED PUBLICATIONS** Co-ed, Readings in the Western Thought I. From the Ancient Times to the Medieval Ages, Ken Publ Co (Quezon City, Philippines), 65; auth, "Karl Jaspers: His Idea of the Physician and Doctor-Patient Relationship," Nursing J, Col of Nursing, Univ of Santo Tomas Press (68); auth, "The Concept of Man in the Philosophy of Karl Jaspers," Unitas 44-4, Univ of Santo Tomas Press, Manila, Philippines (Dec 71). **CONTACT ADDRESS** Dept Soc Sci and Fine Arts, Los Angeles Trade-Tech Col, 400 W Wash Blvd, Los Angeles, CA 90015-4108.

THAGARD, PAUL
DISCIPLINE PHILOSOPHY **EDUCATION** Univ Toronto, PhD, 77. **RESEARCH** Philos of science; cognitive science; artificial intelligence. **SELECTED PUBLICATIONS** Auth, Conceptual Revolutions, Princeton, 92; Computational Philosophy of Science, MIT, 88; coauth, Induction: Processes of Inference, Learning, and Discovery, MIT, 86; Mental Leaps: Analogy in Creative Thought, MIT, 95. **CONTACT ADDRESS** Dept of Philosophy, Univ of Waterloo, 200 University Ave W, Waterloo, ON, Canada N2L 3G1. **EMAIL** pthagard@uwaterloo.ca

THAIN, GERALD JOHN
PERSONAL Born 10/14/1935, Galena, IL, m, 1965, 3 children **DISCIPLINE** LAW **EDUCATION** Univ Iowa, BA, 57, JD, 60. **CAREER** Vis asst prof, Col Human Ecol, Univ Md, 70-74; asst prof law, Univ Wis, 74-76 & Georgetown Univ, 76-77; assoc prof, 77-80, Prof Law, Univ Wis, 80-, Assoc Dean Law, 84-96, Chair, Consumer Law, 92-; Dir, Div Nat Advert Regulation, Fed Trade Comn, 70-73; lectr Food & Drug Law, New York Univ, 73-; co-dir, Ctr Pub Representation, Madison Wis, 77-84, Bd Dir, 98-; scholar in residence, Col Commun, Univ Ill, 80-; Bd Dir, Consumer Law Litigation Project, 95-; Vis Prof, Giessen Univ (Germany), 95; member of the Board of Directors of the Center for East Asian Legal Studies, 96-; Vis Prof, Chuo Univ (Japan), 97; member of the Board of Directors of the Center for East Asian Legal Studies, 99-. **HONORS AND AWARDS** N Burkan Copyright Law Contest, Am Soc Composers, Auth & Publ, 60; Distinguished Advert Scholar Awd, Univ Ill, 80. **MEMBERSHIPS** Law & Soc Asn. **RESEARCH** Advertising law; administrative law; trade regulation; cigarette litigation; e-commerce; first amendment and commercial speech. **SELECTED PUBLICATIONS** Auth, Advertising regulations and new FTC, Fordham Urban Law J, 73; Suffer the Hucksters?, Boston Univ Law Rev, 76; Credit advertising and law, Washington Univ Law Rev, 76; coauth, Public Interest Law, Univ Calif Press, 77; auth, Seven dirty words and FCC, Ky Law J, 79; contribr, White Collar Crime, Free Press, 80; Food Safety Council Final Report, Food Safety Coun, 82; Consumerism in the 1980's, Univ Md Law & Pub Policy Inst, 82; Consumer Law: U.S. & Asia, 96; Cigarette Advertising: Legal vs. Psychological; Constitutional Aspects of Cigarette Regulation, Proceedings of Nat Conf on so-called Tobacco Settlement, Inst for Legal Studies, 97; contrib, Law & Cinema(00); Wisconsin Consumer Act: Update, Lorman, 99. **CONTACT ADDRESS** Law Sch, Univ of Wisconsin, Madison, 975 Bascom Mall, Madison, WI 53706-1301. **EMAIL** gjthain@facstaff.wisc.edu

THALOS, MARIAM G.
PERSONAL Born 02/17/1962, Cairo, Egypt, m, 1991, 2 children **DISCIPLINE** PHILOSOPHY **EDUCATION** Univ Ill, Chicago, PhD, 93. **CAREER** Assoc prof, State Univ of New York, Buffalo; member of Cognitive Sci Center and Baldy Center for Law and Policy, Univ at Buffalo. **HONORS AND AWARDS** Vis res fel, Inst for Advanced Study, Australian Nat Univ; Nat Endowment of Humanities Fel. **MEMBERSHIPS** Am Philos Asn, Philos of Sci Asn, British Soc for the Philos of Sci. **SELECTED PUBLICATIONS** Rev, Rationality, Allocation and Reproduction by Vivian Walsh (Oxford Univ Press), Ethics, 109 (98): 222-223; auth, "In Favor of Being Only Human," Philos Studies, 93 (99): 265-98; auth, "Two Dogmas of Naturalized Epistemology," Dialectica, 53 (99): 111-138; auth, "Why We Believe," J for General Philos of Sci, 30 (99): 317-339; auth, "Units of Decision," Philos of Sci, 66 (99): proceedings vol, S324-@338; auth, "Degrees of Freedom in the Social World," J of Political Philos, 7 (99): 453-77; auth, "Searle's Foole: How a Constructionist Account of Society Cannot Substitute for a Causal One," Am J of Economics and Sociol (forthcoming 2000); auth, "Paradox and its Undoing: A Speech Manifesto," Logical Consequence: Rival Approaches, in Logic and Cognitive Systems Series, Oxford: Hermes Sci Pubs (forthcoming 2000); auth, "The Self," "Metaphysics," and "Ontology," in Routledge Encyclopedia of Feminist Theories, gen ed Lorraine Code (forthcoming); auth, "The Logic in Scientific Discovery: On Popper's analysis of the scientific enterprise," in The Classics of Western Philosophy, J. Garcia, G. Reichberg, and B. Schumacher, Blackwells (forthcoming 2002). **CONTACT ADDRESS** Dept Philos, SUNY, Buffalo, 135 Park Hall, Buffalo, NY 14260-4150. **EMAIL** thalos@acsu.buffalo.edu

THANDEKA, Null
PERSONAL Born 03/25/1946, Jersey City, NJ, p, 2000 **DISCIPLINE** RELIGION **EDUCATION** Univ Ill, BS, 67; Columbia Univ, MS, 68; Univ Calif Los Angeles, MA, 82; Claremont Grad Sch, PhD, 88. **CAREER** Assoc Prof, Calif State Univ, 73; Asst Prof, San Francisco State Univ, 87-91; Asst Prof, Williams Col, 91-97; Visiting Scholar, Union Theol Sem, 96-98; Meadville Lombard Theol Sch, 98-. **HONORS AND AWARDS** Kate Connolly-Weinert Awd, Am Acad of Relig, 98; Res Fel, San Francisco State Univ, 89; First Prize, Jean Fairfax-Muskiwinni Fel, 85; Goethe Inst Fel, 85; Who's Who in Am; Who's Who Among Black Americans; Ebony Success Library: 1000 Successful Blacks; Who's Who Among Students in Am Col and Univ. **MEMBERSHIPS** Am Acad of Relig; Soc for the Sci Study of Relig; Soc for the Study of Black Relig; Unitarian Universalist Ministers Asn; Directors Guild of Am. **RESEARCH** Systematic Theology (Schleiermacher); Philosophy of Religion (Kant); Post-Freudian Psychoanalytic Shame Theory; Cultural Studies (race, gender and class genealogies of the self). **SELECTED PUBLICATIONS** Auth, The Embodied Self: Friedrich Schleiermacher's Solution to Kant's Problem of the Empirical Self, SUNY Press, 95; auth, "The Self Between Feminist Theory and Theology," in Horizons in Feminist Theology: Identity, Tradition, and Norms, (Minneapolis: Fortress Press, 97), 79-98; auth, "The Whiting of Euro-Americans: A Divide and Conquer Strategy," The World XII, (98): 14-20; auth, Learning to be White: Money, Race and God in America, Continuum, 98; auth, "Middle-Class Poverty," The World XIII, (99): 16-23; auth, "The Cost of Whiteness," Tikkun: A Bimonthly Jewish Critique of Politics, Culture & Society, (99): 33-38; auth, "Why Anti-Racism will Fail," Journal of Liberal Religion, (99): 1-11; auth, "The Communitarian Self," The Responsive Community: Rights and Responsibilities, 00. **CONTACT ADDRESS** Dept Relig, Meadville/Lombard Theol Sch, 5701 S Woodlawn Ave, Chicago, IL 60637-1602. **EMAIL** thandeka@meadville.edu

THARP, LOUIS
PERSONAL Born 03/05/1938, Miami, FL, m, 1996, 1 child **DISCIPLINE** PSYCHOLOGY, PHILOSOPHY **EDUCATION** Yale Univ, BA, 60; Claremont Grad Univ, MA, 67; PhD, 74. **CAREER** Prof, Long Beach City Col, 67-; Dir of Online Learning, 99-. **HONORS AND AWARDS** Yale Debate Asn Excellence Awd. **RESEARCH** Online learning in the Third World. **SELECTED PUBLICATIONS** Coauth, Letters to an Unborn Child, Harper & Row, 74; auth, Winning by Quitting, Synergy Pr, 00. **CONTACT ADDRESS** Dept Soc Sci, Long Beach City Col, 4901 E Carson St, Long Beach, CA 90808-1706. **EMAIL** louistharp@earthlink.com

THATCHER, TOM
PERSONAL Born 03/23/1967, m, 1987, 1 child **DISCIPLINE** BIBLICAL LITERATURE **EDUCATION** Cincinnati Bible Col, BA, 89, MA, 92; Cincinnati Bible Sem, MDiv, 92; S Baptist Theol Sem, PhD, 96. **CAREER** Prof, Louisville Bible Col, 92-94; assoc prof, Cincinnati Bible Col & Seminary, 94- . **HONORS AND AWARDS** Salutatorian, Cincinnati Bible Col, 89; Baker Book House Award, Cincinnati Bible Col, 92; Metroversity Graduate Paper Award, 95; Midwest Bible Soc Grad Paper Award, 95. **MEMBERSHIPS** Soc of Biblical Lit; Inst for Biblical Res; **RESEARCH** Johannine lit; hist Jesus; Hermenatics; oral tradition. **SELECTED PUBLICATIONS** Auth, Mouth, Temperature, Travel Story, in The Dictionary of Biblical Imagery, IVP 98; Early Christianities and the Synoptic Eclipse: Problems in Situating the Gospel of Thomas, Biblical Inter, 99; John: The Gospel of Ambiguity, Scholars Press, 99; 1 2 3 John, in The Expositor's Bible Commentary, forthcoming; coed, Jesus in Johannine Tradition: New Directions, Fortress, forthcoming. **CONTACT ADDRESS** Cincinnati Bible Col and Sem, 2700 Glenway Ave, Cincinnati, OH 45204. **EMAIL** tom.thatcher@cincybible.edu

THAYER, H. S.
PERSONAL Born New York, NY, m, 1958, 3 children **DISCIPLINE** PHILOSOPHY **EDUCATION** Bard Col, BA, 45; Columbia Univ, MA, 47, PhD, 49. **CAREER** Instr, 49-54, asst prof, 54-61, philos, Columbia Univ; vis prof, NY Sch of Psychiat, 59-65; asst prof, 61-65, assoc prof & chemn, 65-68, prof, 68-90, philos, CUNY. **HONORS AND AWARDS** Bush Fel, 47, 48; Guggenheim Fel, 70; NEH Fel, 74. **MEMBERSHIPS** APA; Soc for Advanc of Am Philos. **RESEARCH** Ancient Greek philosophy; American philosophy. **SELECTED PUBLICATIONS** Auth, Introduction to Pragmatism & The Meaning of Truth, in, The Works of William James, Harvard, 75; auth, Meaning and Action: A Critical History of Pragmatism, rev ed, Hackett, 81; auth, Objects of Knowledge, in Stuhr, ed, Philosophy and the Reconstruction of Culture, SUNY, 93; auth, Peirce and Truth: Some Reflections, Trans of the C.S. Peirce Soc, 96; auth, Plato's Style: Temporal, Dramatic and Semantic Levels in the Dialogues, in Hart, ed, Plato's Dialogues: The Dialogical Approach, Edwin Mellon, 97. **CONTACT ADDRESS** 4 Salisbury Point, Apt 4B, Nyack, NY 10960.

THEILE, KARL H.
PERSONAL Born St. Louis, MO **DISCIPLINE** HISTORY; INTERNATIONAL RELATIONS **EDUCATION** Univ Rochester, BS, 61; Calif State Univ, LA, MA, 63; Univ Southern Calif, PhD, 81. **CAREER** Prof, dept chemn, LA T-TCC, 70-. **MEMBERSHIPS** Hum Asn Calif **RESEARCH** World War II **SELECTED PUBLICATIONS** Auth, Beyond Monsters and Clowns, 96. **CONTACT ADDRESS** 3940 Fairway Ave, Studio City, CA 91604.

THERIAULT, MICHEL
PERSONAL Born 12/02/1942, Toronto, ON, Canada **DISCIPLINE** CANON LAW, HISTORY **EDUCATION** Univ Montreal, Bphil, 62; McGill Univ, MLS, 76; Pontif Univ St Thomas (Rome), JCD, 71. **CAREER** Head acquisitions dept, Univ Montreal Libr, 69-75; chief, Retrospective Nat Biblio Div, Nat Libr Can, 75-85; asst prof, 85-92, Assoc Prof Canon Law, St Paul Univ, 92-. **MEMBERSHIPS** Can Canon Law Soc (secytreas, 88-90, vice-pres, 95-97); Soc Law Eastern Churches (deleg Can, 87-97); Bibliog Soc Can (assoc secy, 81-86). **SELECTED PUBLICATIONS** Auth, Neo-vagin et impuissance, 71; auth, Le livre religieux au Quebec depuis les debuts de l'imprimerie jusqu'a la Confederation 1764-1867, 77; auth, The Institutions of Consecrated Life in Canada from the Beginning of New France up to the Present, 80; ed, Choix et acquisition des documents au Quebec, vol 1, 77; co-ed, Proceedings of the 5th International Congress of Canon Law, 86; co-ed, Code de droit canonique, 90; co-ed, Canonical Studies Presented to Germain Lesage, 91; co-ed, Studia Canonica, Index 1-25 1967-1991, 92; co-ed, Code of Canon Law Annotated, 93; transl, A Manual for Bishops, 94. **CONTACT ADDRESS** Faculty of Canon Law, Saint Paul Univ, 223 Main St, Ottawa, ON, Canada K1S 1C4. **EMAIL** theriaul@fox.nstn.ca

THIBEAU, MATTHEW J.
PERSONAL Born 12/02/1957, Chicago, IL, m, 1990, 2 children **DISCIPLINE** RELIGION **EDUCATION** Loyola Univ, Chicago, BBA; Univ St Mary of the Lake, Mundelein, IL, M Divinity. **CAREER** Ed consultant, McGraw-Hill; dir, Private/Parochial Marketing, School Div, Macmillan, 89; CA District manager, Macmillan/McGraw-Hill, 90; Dir of Marketing, Wm H. Sadlier, 93; President, Harcourt Religion Publisher, 94-. **MEMBERSHIPS** Cath Book Pubs Assoc, brd of dirs; Nat Cath Educational Exhibitors, brd of dirs. **SELECTED PUBLICATIONS** Auth, McGraw-Hill's Reading Teachers Supplement for Faith and Values; coordinated the development of the Integrating Catholic Heritage supplement to The World Around Us (Social Studies prog; auth, "Character Development in Catholic Schools." **CONTACT ADDRESS** Harcourt Religion Publishers, 1665 Embassy West Dr., Suite 200, Dubuque, IA 52002-2259. **EMAIL** mthibeau@harcourt.com

THIGPEN, CALVIN HERRITAGE
PERSONAL Born 01/07/1924, Greenville, NC, m **DISCIPLINE** MEDICINE, LAW **EDUCATION** VA State Coll, BS 1953; Univ VA, MD 1962, JD 1974. **CAREER** Hopewell, VA, teacher 1953-58; Stuart Prod Co, cosmetics/chem plant mgr 1957-58; Med Coll VA, intern 1962-63; Petersburg General Hosp, staff mem 1963; private practice 1963; VA State Coll, assoc & physician 1964-71; Petersburg Gen Hosp, vice chief/general practice section 1969-70; Office Attorney General VA, intern 1972-73; Univ VA, rsrch asst legal adv 1973-74; Private Practice, Attorney 1975-. **HONORS AND AWARDS** pres, Natl Guardsmen Inc 1967-70; Library Human Resources Amer Bicentennial Rsch Inst 1973; Fellow Amer Coll Legal Med 1976; Mem Bd of Visitors VA State Univ 1978-82; VA Dele-

gate to the White House Conf on Library & Info Serv 1979; Chief of Staff Petersburg Gen Hosp 1980; Diplomate Amer Bd of Legal Med 1982. **MEMBERSHIPS** Mem, Sigma Pi Sigma Natl Physics Hon Soc; Beta Kappa Chi Natl Sci Hon Soc; Phi Delta Phi Legal Fraternity; Dem Com Hopewell 1965-75; bd dir Salvation Army; Hopewell Chamber of Commerce; Old Dominion Med Soc; exec com Old Dominion Med Soc 1965. **CONTACT ADDRESS** 734 South Sycamore St, Petersburg, VA 23803.

THIRUVENGADAM, RAJ
PERSONAL Born 02/03/1967, Baltimore, MD, s, 1 child **DISCIPLINE** PHILOSOPHY **EDUCATION** Purdue Univ, PhD, 94 **CAREER** Asst Prof, Simmons Col, 94-pres; Assoc Dir, 96-98 **MEMBERSHIPS** Am Philos Assoc; Radical Philos Assoc; Intl Assoc for Philos & Lit; Soc for Asian & Comparative Philos **RESEARCH** Aesthetics; Philosophy of Culture; Asian Philosophy & Religion; Multiculturalism; Social & Political Philosophy **SELECTED PUBLICATIONS** Auth, Getting Tipsy on the Border Between the Banal and the Bizarre: Negotiating Familiarity and Foreignness in Teaching Asian Religions, a presentation to ASIANetwork Conf, Chicago, 96; Democracy as Mass Communicative Action, a presentation to the Philos Dept, Purdue Univ, 94; A Question Before Discourse Ethics: The Problem of the Apostle, a presentation to the Midwest Critical Theory Roundtable, St Louis Univ, 93; How to Read Mass Culture?: A Read-Our-Response Theory, a presentation to the Cultural Studies Collective, Purdue Univ, 93; coauth, What is Enlightened Freedom? An Essay on What Kant Taught Us, in The Long Path to Nearness: A Corporeal Philosophy of Communication, Humanities Press, 97. **CONTACT ADDRESS** Dept of Philos, Simmons Col, 300 The Fenway, Boston, MA 02115. **EMAIL** rthiruvengad@vmsvax.simmons.edu

THOMAS, CHANTAL
PERSONAL Born 09/13/1971, Montreal, QC, Canada, s **DISCIPLINE** LAW **EDUCATION** McGill Univ, BA, 92; Harvard Univ, JD, 95. **CAREER** Assoc prof, Fordham Univ, 95-. **HONORS AND AWARDS** James McGill Outstanding Scholarship Awd. **MEMBERSHIPS** Am Soc of Int Law. **RESEARCH** International economic law; international law and development, critical theory. **SELECTED PUBLICATIONS** Auth, "Customary International Law and State Taxation of Corporate Income: The Case for the Separate Accounting Method", 14 Berkeley Int L J 99 (96); auth, "Transfer of Technology in the Contemporary International Order, 22 Fordham Int L J 2096 (99); auth, "Does the 'Good Governance' Policy of the Bretton Woods Institutions Privilege Markets at the Expense of Democracy?", 14 Conn J Int L 551 (99); auth, "Causes of Inequality in the International Economic Order: Critical Race Theory and Postcolonial Development, 9 Transnational L and Contemp Probls 1 (99); auth, "Comparing the '1990s -Style' and '1980s'Style' Debt Crises", 93 Am Soc Int L Proc (forthcoming); auth, "Critical Race Theory and Postcolonial Development Theory: Observations on Methodology", 44 Vill L Rev (forthcoming), auth, "Globalization and the Reproduction of Hierarchy", 32 UC Davis L Rev (forthcoming), auth, "International Debt Forgiveness and Global Poverty Reduction", 26 Fordham Urb L J. (forthcoming). **CONTACT ADDRESS** School of Law, Fordham Univ, 140 W 62nd St, New York, NY 10023-7407. **EMAIL** cthomas@mail.lawnet.fordham.edu

THOMAS, CLARENCE
PERSONAL Born 06/23/1948, Pin Point, GA, d **DISCIPLINE** LAW **EDUCATION** Immaculate Conception Seminary, 1967-68; Holy Cross College, BA, 1971; Yale University Law School, JD, 1974. **CAREER** Hill, Jones & Farrington, legal aid, summers, 71-74; Attorney General John Danforth, State of Missouri, staff member, 74-77; State of Missouri, asst attorney general, 74-77; Monsanto Corp, legal counsel, 77-80; Senator John Danforth, legislative asst, 79-81; US Federal Govt, Dept of Education, asst secretary for civil rights, 81-82; Equal Employment Opportunity Commission, chairman, 82-89; US Court of Appeals for District of Columbia Circuit, appointed circuit judge, 90-91; United States Supreme Court Justice, confirmed, 91-. **MEMBERSHIPS** Black Student Union, Holy Cross College, founder, 1971. **CONTACT ADDRESS** US Supreme Court, 1 1st St NE, Washington, DC 20543-0001.

THOMAS, CLAUDE RODERICK
PERSONAL Born 03/15/1943, Clarksdale, MS, s **DISCIPLINE** LAW **EDUCATION** MI State Univ, BA 1972; Thomas M Cooley Law School, JD 1976. **CAREER** Lansing Police Dept, police officer 69-75; Ingham Cty Pros Office, asst prosecutor 76-80; Lansing Community College, Lansing, MI, Adj Prof, 76-; Thomas M Cooley Law School, Lansing, MI, Adj Prof, 88-; 54A Dist Court, Dist Judge 81-. **HONORS AND AWARDS** Alumni of the Year Cooley Law School 1981. **MEMBERSHIPS** Mem State Bar Character & Fitness 1977-, Boys Club; bd dir Cooley Credit Union 1980-81; member, Phi Beta Sigma, 1983-. **CONTACT ADDRESS** Lansing City Hall #6, Lansing, MI 48933.

THOMAS, DAVID
DISCIPLINE RELIGION **EDUCATION** Notre Dame Univ, Doctorate. **CAREER** Instr, Loyola Univ, New Orleans; instr, Saint Louis Univ; instr, St Meinrad Sch Theol; instr, chp, Regis Univ, 81-; adv, Synod on Family Life, Rome; codir, Ctr for Families, Tabor Press. **SELECTED PUBLICATIONS** Auth, The Catholic Catechism: family Style, Tabor Press; We Are Family: Sharing food for the Soul, Tabor Press; In the Midst of Family, and Family Basics: Thriving in the Midst of Threat, Tabor Press. **CONTACT ADDRESS** Regis Univ, Denver, CO 80221-1099.

THOMAS, DOUGLAS L.
PERSONAL Born 02/28/1945, Jacksonville, FL, m **DISCIPLINE** LAW **EDUCATION** City Coll NYork, BA 1968; Columbia Univ Law Sch, JD 1971. **CAREER** Harvard Law School, teaching fellow faculty; RCA Corp, atty 1973-74; Dewey Ballantine Busby Palmer & Wood, assoc 1971-73; Youth Serv Agy, coord 1971; Youth Serv & Agy, dir 1970; NYC Dept Prob, investigator 1969-71; Harlem Consumer's Union, law asst 1969; Jamaica Comm Corp, dir summer prog 1968; Morningside Comm Center, group leader 1967-68; Prima RE Corp, re salesman 1965-67. **HONORS AND AWARDS** Outstanding achiev awards, goldman scholarship award City Coll Sch Social & Psychol Fndtns; Charles Evan Hughes Fellowship. **MEMBERSHIPS** Mem Assn Bar NYC; NY State Bar Assn Coun Concerned Black Execs; Emerging Black Profl; Intl Law Soc; Black Am Law Students Assn; Omega Psi Phi. **CONTACT ADDRESS** Law Sch, Harvard Univ, Cambridge, MA 02138.

THOMAS, DUNCAN
PERSONAL Born 03/03/1958, Zimbabwe **DISCIPLINE** ECONOMICS **EDUCATION** Bristol Univ, BS, 81; Princeton Univ, PhD, 86. **CAREER** Asst Prof to Assoc Prof, Yale Univ, 81-94; Assoc Prof to Prof, UCLA, 94-; Sen Econ, RAND, 93-01. **HONORS AND AWARDS** Alfred P. Sloan Pre-Doctoral Fel, 84-85; Fulbright Awd, 81-83. **MEMBERSHIPS** Am Econ Asn; Population Asn of Am. **RESEARCH** Economics of the household; Health; Poverty; Economic development. **SELECTED PUBLICATIONS** Auth, "Intra-Household Resource Allocation: An Inferential Approach," J of Human Resources, 90; co-auth, "The Demographic Transition in Southern Africa: Another Look at the Evidence form Botswana and Zimbabwe," Demography, 94; co-auth, "Human Resources: Empirical Models of Household Decisions," in Handbook of Development Economics, Vol 3, 95; co-auth, "Does Head Start Make a Difference," Am Econ Rev, 95; co-auth, "Health and Wages of Men and Women: Evidence for Men and Women in Urban Brazil," J of Econometrics, 97; co-auth, "Health, Nutrition, and Economic Development," J of Econ Lit, 98; co-auth, "On the Road: Marriage and Mobility in Malaysia,' J of Human Resources, 98; co-auth, "Lost But Not forgotten: Attrition and Follow-up in the Indonesian Family Life Survey," J of Human Res, 01; co-auth, "Women's Health and Pregnancy Outcomes: does Access to Services Make a Difference?" Demography, 01. **CONTACT ADDRESS** Dept Econ, Univ of California, Los Angeles, 405 Hilgard, Los Angeles, CA 90024. **EMAIL** dt@ucla.edu

THOMAS, HERMAN EDWARD
PERSONAL Born 12/12/1941, Bryson City, NC, m **DISCIPLINE** THEOLOGY **EDUCATION** Hartford Sem Fdn, PhD 1978; Duke Univ Divinity Schl, ThM (honors) 1969; Duke Univ Divinity Schl, BD 1966; NCA&T State Univ, BS (cum laude)1963. **CAREER** Berkley HS, Aberdeen, NC, HS teacher 1966-67; Student Affrs, Morris Coll, Sumter, SC, 68-69; Religion & Phil, Springfield Col, Sprg, MA, instr 1969-74; Black Studies, Springfield Coll, Sprg, MA, coord 1971-74; Rel Stud, asst prof, assoc prof, currently; AAA Studies UNCC, asst dir 1974-86; UTOP, director, 86-. **HONORS AND AWARDS** Mary Reynolds Babcock Schlrshp Duke Divinity Schl 1963-66; coord-Humanist Afro-Am Hist Project in Charlotte, NC Humanities Comm 1983-83; Religion & Slavery in JWC Pennington Jrnl of ITC 1979. **MEMBERSHIPS** Mem Am Acdmy of Religion 1973-; chair steer commit NC Cncl of Black studies 1975-76; assoc Mnstr First Baptist Church-West 1975-; fdng mem Natl Cncl for Black Studies 1975-; chrmn brd of dir Afro-Amer Cultural Cntr 1979-84; mem Soc for the Study of Black Religion 1980-, recording sec and historian, 1994-97; brd mem Charl-Merk Arts & Science Cncl 1984-. **SELECTED PUBLICATIONS** Author, "A Summary and Critical Analysis of the 'Color of God: the Concept of God in Afro American Thought'," Amez Quarterly, v 102, n 1, pp 38-41, 1990; "Revisioning the American Dream: Individualism and Community in African American Perspective," Star of Zion, v 14, n 21, January 21, 1993; James WC Pennington: African American Churchman and Abolitionist, Garland Publishing, 1995. **CONTACT ADDRESS** Univ of No Carolina, Charlotte, 121 Garinger Bldg, 9201 University City Blvd, Charlotte, NC 28223.

THOMAS, JOHN JOSEPH
PERSONAL Born 07/02/1942, Pittsburgh, PA, m, 1984, 2 children **DISCIPLINE** PHILOSOPHY **EDUCATION** La Salle Univ, BA, 65; Univ Miami, MA, 72, PhD(philos), 73. **CAREER** Teaching asst philos, Univ Miami,68-72; instr, Univ Ga, 73-74; Assoc Prof Philos, Columbus Col, 74-77; assoc prof, Columbus Col, 77-93; prof, Col St Univ, 93-98. **MEMBERSHIPS** Am Philos Asn. **RESEARCH** History of philosophy; physical theories and ontology; social-political philosophy. **SELECTED PUBLICATIONS** Auth, A First Study of Philosophical Thought. **CONTACT ADDRESS** Columbus State Univ, 4225 University Ave, Columbus, GA 31907-5645. **EMAIL** thomas_john@colstate.edu

THOMAS, KENDALL
PERSONAL Born 02/22/1957, East Chicago, IN **DISCIPLINE** LAW **EDUCATION** Yale College, New Haven, CT, BA, 1978; Yale Law School, New Haven, CT, JD, 1982. **CAREER** Columbia University in the City of New York, New York, NY, asst/associate professor, 84-92, prof, 92-. **CONTACT ADDRESS** School of Law, Columbia Univ, 435 W 116th St, New York, NY 10027.

THOMAS, M. CAROLYN
PERSONAL Born 01/29/1936, KY, s **DISCIPLINE** BIBLICAL STUDIES **EDUCATION** Brescia Col, BA; Loyola Univ, MA; Union Theol Sem, STM, 81; Fordham Univ, PhD, 85. **CAREER** Teacher, Trinity Lutheran Sem, 86-87; teacher, Brescia Col, 90-91; teacher, Pontifical Col, 91-. **HONORS AND AWARDS** Teaching Fel, Fordham Univ. **MEMBERSHIPS** Catholic Bibl Asn, Soc of Bibl Lit. **RESEARCH** Gospel of John, Philippiano. **SELECTED PUBLICATIONS** Auth, Will the Real God Please Stand Up, Paulist Press, 91; auth, Gift and Response, Paulist Press, 94; auth, Journey Into John, St Anthony Messenger Press, 98. **CONTACT ADDRESS** Dept Theol, Pontifical Col Josephinum, 7625 N High St, Columbus, OH 43235-1499. **EMAIL** cthomas@pcj.edu

THOMAS, MAXINE SUZANNE
PERSONAL Born 01/23/1948, Junction City, KS, m **DISCIPLINE** LAW **EDUCATION** Univ of WA, BA 1970, JD 1973. **CAREER** Univ of OR Schl of Law, asst prof 1976-89; Univ of OR, asst dean 1976-79; WA, asst atty gen 1973-76; assoc dean and assoc prof Univ of Georgia 1989-. **HONORS AND AWARDS** Nominated OR Outst Young Women 1978, Kellogg Natl Fellow 1985-1988, Fulbright lecturer 1988. **MEMBERSHIPS** Mem Natl Assc of Clge & Univ Attys 1974-76; standing com on environmental law Amer Bar Assc 1979-; honorary mem Phi Delta Phi 1977-; mem OR Amer Counc on Educ Com to Promote Women to Higher Educ Admin 1978-. **CONTACT ADDRESS** Sch of Law, Univ of Georgia, Athens, GA 30602.

THOMAS, NIGEL J. T.
PERSONAL Born 02/07/1952, Rochester, United Kingdom, m, 1992, 2 children **DISCIPLINE** HISTORY AND PHILOSOPHY OF SCIENCE **EDUCATION** Leeds Univ, PhD, 87. **CAREER** Instr, Calif Inst Techol, 90-92; instr, Rio Hondo Coll, 96-97; adj asst prof Calif State Univ, 95-. **MEMBERSHIPS** Am Philos Asn; Soc for Philos and Psychol; Cognitive Sci Soc; Hist of Sci Soc; Soc for Machines and Mentality; Cheiron; Am Psychol Asn; Asn for the Scientific Study of Consciousness, Soc for the Multidisciplinary Study of Consciousness. **RESEARCH** Philosophy of Mind; Imagination; Cognitive Science; History of Psychology. **SELECTED PUBLICATIONS** Rev, The Imagery Debate, 94; auth, Imagery and the coherence of Imagination: a Critique of White, J of Philos Res, 97; A Stimulus to the Imagination, Psyche, 97; Mental Imagery, the Stanford Encycl of Philos, 97; entries on Sir Frederick Gowland Hopkins and Marshall W Nirenberg, The Biographical Encycl of Sci, 98; auth, "Experience and Theory as Determinants of Attitudes Towards Mental Representation," American J of Psychology, 102, (89), 395-412; auth, Imagery and the Coherence of Imagination: a Critique of White, J of Philosophical Res, 22, (97), 95-127; auth, A Stimulus to the Imagination, Psyche 3, 97; auth, Enries on Sir Frederick Gowland Hopkins, and Marshall W. Nirenberg-in Richard Olson & Roger Smith, eds. The Biographical Encyclopedia of Scientists, New York: Marshall Cavendish Corp., 98; auth, Zombie Killer--in S.R. Hameroff, A.W. Kaszniak, & A.C. Scott eds., Toward a Science of Consciousness II, Cambridge, MA: MIT Press, 98; auth, Zombie Killer--in S.R. Hameroff, A.W. Kaszniak, & A.C. Scott, eds., Toward a Science of Consciousness II, Cambridge, MA: MIT Press, 98; auth, Mental Imagery in E. Zalta, ed. The Stanford Encyclopedia of Philosophy, 99; auth, Imagination in C. Eliasmith, ed. Dictionary of Philosophy of Mind, 99; auth, Are Theories of Imagery Theories of Imagination? An Active Perception Approach to Conscious Mental Content,--Cognitive Science, 23, (99), 207-245; auth, Mental Imagery, Philosophical Issues About, forthcoming in Encyclopedia of Cognitive Science, Macmillan: London; Auth, Are Theories of Imagery Theories of Imagination? An Active perception Approach to Conscious Mental Content, Cognitive Sci, forthcoming. **CONTACT ADDRESS** 86 South Sierra Madre Blvd #5, Pasadena, CA 91107. **EMAIL** n.j.thomas70@members.leeds.ac.uk

THOMAS, NORMAN C.
PERSONAL Born 02/16/1932, Sioux Falls, SD, m, 1953, 4 children **DISCIPLINE** POLITICAL SCIENCE **EDUCATION** Univ Michigan, BA 53; Princeton Univ, MA 58, PhD 59. **CAREER** Univ Cincinnati, Charles Phelps Taft Prof, Prof Emeritus, 71 to 98-; Duke Univ, prof 69-71; Univ Mich, inst, asst prof ,assoc prof, 59-69. **HONORS AND AWARDS** Phi Beta Kappa; U of Cin, Grad Fel, Dist Tchg Prof **MEMBERSHIPS** APSA; MPSA; SPSA; ASPA **RESEARCH** Amer polit institution; Us Presidency; Amer pub policy and admin. **SELECTED PUBLICATIONS** Auth, The Politics of the Presidency, coauth, 4th ed, C Q Press, 97; Education in National Politics,

75; Rule 9: Politics Administration and Civil Rights, 66. **CONTACT ADDRESS** 510 Oliver Court, Cincinnati, OH 45215-2505. **EMAIL** normcthom@aol.com

THOMAS, OWEN CLARK

PERSONAL Born 10/11/1922, New York, NY, m, 1981, 3 children **DISCIPLINE** THEOLOGY **EDUCATION** Hamilton Col, AB, 44; Episcopal Theol Sch, BD, 49; Columbia Univ, PhD, 56. **CAREER** Dir col work, Diocese, NY, 51-52; from instr to assoc prof, 52-65, PROF THEOL, EPISCOPAL THEOL SCH, 65-, Vis prof Pontiff Gregorian Univ, 73-74. **HONORS AND AWARDS** DDiv, Hamilton Col, 70. **MEMBERSHIPS** Soc Values Higher Educ; Am Theol Soc; Am Acad Relig. **RESEARCH** Philosophy of religion; systematic theology; history of Christian thought. **SELECTED PUBLICATIONS** Auth, Religious Plurality and Contemporary Philosophy--An Examination of Varieties of Inclusivism and the Myth of Christian Uniqueness--A Critical Survey, Harvard Theol Rev, Vol 87, 94; Public Theology and Counter-Public Spheres--David Tracy, Distinction Between Fundamental and Systematic Christian Theology, a Reconsideration of His Thesis on Religious Pluralism, Harvard Theol Rev, Vol 85, 92. **CONTACT ADDRESS** 10 St John's Rd, Cambridge, MA 02138.

THOMAS, RANDALL S.

DISCIPLINE LAW, ECONOMICS **EDUCATION** Haverford Col, PA, BA (honors), 77; Univ MI, Ann Arbor, PhD (economics), 83; Univ MI Law School, JD (Order of the Coif, honors), 85. **CAREER** Economist, USAID/Univ MI, Center for Res on Economic Development, Niger, West Africa, and Ann Arbor, MI, 79-82; economist/financial analyst to the World Bank in Malawai, East Africa with Bookers Agriculture Int, Ltd, London, England, Sept to Dec, 82; economic consult to USAID, Somalia, East Africa, May 83; summer law clerk, Piper & Marbury, Baltimore, MD, May-Aug 84; law clerk to the Honorable Charles W Joiner, Fed District Court for the Eastern District of MI, Ann Arbor, MI, 85-86; assoc, Potter Anderson & Corroon, Wilmington, DE, 86-87; Corporate and Securities Law Assoc, Skadden, Arps, Slate, Meagher, & Flom, Wilmington, DE, 87-90; prof, Univ of IA College of Law, Iowa City, 90-95, 96-; vis prof of Law, Univ Washington School of Law, Seattle, March 95, March 96; vis prof of Law, Boston Univ School of Law, 95; vis prof of Law, Univ MI School of Law, 96. **HONORS AND AWARDS** Rackham Grad School fel, Univ MI, Ann Arbor; Nat Health Inst fel, Univ MI, Ann Arbor. **MEMBERSHIPS** DE Bar, 87. **SELECTED PUBLICATIONS** Auth, Improving Shareholder Monitoring of Corporate Management By Expanding Statutory Access to Information, 38 AZ Law Rev, 331, 96, reprinted in Coprorate Practice Commentator 563, 96; Encouraging Relational Investment and Controlling Portfolio Investment in Developing Countries in the Aftermath of the Mexican Financial Crisis, with Entique Carrasco, 34 Columbia J of Transactional Law 539, 96; Using State Inspection Statutes for Discovery in Federal Securities Actions, with Kennneth J Martin, 77 Boston Univ Law Rev 69, 97; reprinted in Corporate Practice Commentator, 523, 97; Reinventing Corporate Governance: Shareholder Activism by Labor Unions, with Stewart Schwab, 96 MI Law Rev 1018, 98; Auctions in Bankruptcy: Theoretical Analysis and Practical Guidance, with Robert G, Hansen, 18 Int Rev of Law and Economics 159, 98; When Should Labor be Allowed to Submit Shareholder Proposals?, with Kenneth J Martin, 73 Washington Law Rev, 41, 98; Firm Committment Underwriting Risk and the Over-Allotment Option: Do We Need Better Legal Regulation?, with James F Cotter, Securities Regulation Law J, fall 98; The Efficiency of Sharing Liability for Hazardous Waste: Effects of Uncertainty Over Damages, with Robert G Hansen, Working Paper, 98; Improving Corporate Bankruptcy Law Through Venue Reform, with Robert Rasmussen, Working Paper, 98; several other publications. **CONTACT ADDRESS** College of Law, Univ of Iowa Col of Law, Melrose and Bylington, Iowa City, IA 52242. **EMAIL** randall-thomas@uiowa.edu

THOMAS, TIMOTHY

PERSONAL Born 06/01/1961, New Haven, CT, m, 1993 **DISCIPLINE** CRIMINAL JUSTICE **EDUCATION** Univ S C, BS, 84; MCJ, 88. **CAREER** Coordinator Criminal Justice Prog, Piedmont Community Col, 92-. **MEMBERSHIPS** NC Criminal Justice Asn, Southern Criminal Justice Asn, Acad of Criminal Justice Sci. **CONTACT ADDRESS** Dept Criminal Justice, Piedmont Comm Col, PO Box 1197, Roxboro, NC 27573.

THOMASMA, DAVID C.

PERSONAL Born 10/31/1939, Chicago, IL, m, 1992, 4 children **DISCIPLINE** PHILOSOPHY, THEOLOGY **EDUCATION** B.S., 61; B.A., PhB., 63; M.A., Ph.L., 65; STC, 67; STL, 68; Ph.D., 72 (CUA). **CAREER** Dir, Prog on Human Vlaues and Med, VTCHS, Mephis, 73-81; Medical Humanities Prog, Loyola, 81-01. **HONORS AND AWARDS** Fulbright Senior Fel, 84; Netherlands English Chair of Medical Ethics, 84-. **MEMBERSHIPS** ASBH; ESPMH; APA; ACPA; IAB; ACCP (guest). **RESEARCH** Philosophy of medicine; bioethics; clinical ethics. **SELECTED PUBLICATIONS** 315 articles and 25 books. **CONTACT ADDRESS** Neiswanger Institute for Bioethics and Health Policy, Loyola Univ, Chicago, 2160 S First Ave, Maywood, IL 60153. **EMAIL** DThoma1@lumc.edu

THOMASSON, GORDON C.

PERSONAL Born 12/28/1942, Santa Monica, CA, m, 1975, 4 children **DISCIPLINE** HISTORY, RELIGION **EDUCATION** UCLA, AB, 66; UCSB, AM, 72; Cornell Univ, PhD, 87. **CAREER** Asst prof, 80-82, Cuttington Univ; world stud fac, 88-93, Marlboro Col & Schl for Intl Training; asst prof, 93-, Broome Com Col (SUNY); intl stud adj, 96-98, CCNY **RESEARCH** Globval hist, world relig, anthropology of development, Liberia, Southeast Asia, Mormonism. **CONTACT ADDRESS** 280 Academy Dr., Vestal, NY 13850. **EMAIL** thomasson_g@mail.sunybroome.edu

THOMPSON, ALMOSE ALPHONSE, II

PERSONAL Born 02/12/1942, Shawnee, OK, m **DISCIPLINE** LAW **EDUCATION** UCLA, BS 1962, Teaching Credential 1965, EdD 1972; Cal State Univ Long Beach, MA 1970; Vanderbilt Univ Law School, JD 1988. **CAREER** LA Unified school Dist, secondary teacher 1965-68; CA State Univ, dir project upward bound & asst prof 1968-70; UCLA, part time instructor 1970-71; Holman &Thompson Inc, educ consul 1970-72; Univ of CA Santa Barbara, assoc dean of students; Portland State Univ, asst prof of curriculum & instruction 1972-74; Moorhead State Univ, asst prof of secondary educ 1974-75; CA State Univ, assoc prof & dir; Martin Luther King Jr Genl Hosp & Charles R Drew Post Grad Med School, educ eval specialist 1976-78; City of LA, prog dir 1978-79; Curatron Systems Inc, vice pres & Head of educ div 1978-79; Metropolitan Weekly, staff writer 1980-84; TN State Univ, prof of educ admin; syndicated columnist, Metropolitan Weekly; The Legal Clinic, Nashville, TN, sr partner, 89-. **HONORS AND AWARDS** Awd for article "Blacks in America before Columbus" Negro History Bulletin 1975; 2 Grad Fellowships UCLA 1964 1970; Awd from The Black Caucus TN Genl Assembly 1982; Awd from the Mayor of Memphis 1982; passed written examination for Tennessee Bar, Tennessee Board of Bar Examiners, 1989. **MEMBERSHIPS** Bd mem Walden Univ Bd of Rsch Advisors & Readers 1984-; rsch fellow selected 3 consecutive yrs Southern Educ Found 1980-83; mem ASPA, Natl Assn of Black, State of TN Pol Sci Assn; State's Media Corp; TN Prof Educational Admin Assn; Natl Assn of Social & Behavorial Scientists. **SELECTED PUBLICATIONS** "Black Studies is Down to This" Black Times 1976; "Albina & Educational Reform" Portland Observer Special Issue Feb 15 1974; "The Student's Guide to Better Grades" NDS 1983; contributor "On Being Black, An In-Group Analysis" edited by David Pilgrim, published by Wyndham Hall Press 1986. **CONTACT ADDRESS** Legal Clinic, 939 Jefferson St, Ste 100, Nashville, TN 37200.

THOMPSON, CYNTHIA L.

PERSONAL Born 06/03/1943, Buffalo, NY **DISCIPLINE** CLASSICS IN GREEK NEW TESTAMENT **EDUCATION** Yale Univ, PhD, 73, MA, 68; Wellesley Col, BA, 66. **CAREER** Res, 73-75, Harvard Divinity School; Asst Prof of Classics & Religion, 75-80, Denison Univ, Granville, DH; Editor, 80-94, 97-, Westminster John Knox Press; Editor, 94-97, Fortress Press, Minneapolis, Philadelphia, Louisville. **HONORS AND AWARDS** Phi Beta Kappa **MEMBERSHIPS** APA, SBL. **RESEARCH** Women's Adornment in Greek-Roman World; Classical and Biblical Heritage. **SELECTED PUBLICATIONS** Auth, Hairstyles, Head Coverings and St Paul's Portraits From Roman Corinth, Biblical Archaeologist, 88; Rings of Gold-Neither Modest Nor Sensible, Bible Review, 93. **CONTACT ADDRESS** 39 Roslin St, #3, Dorchester, MA 02124. **EMAIL** cynthom@aol.com

THOMPSON, DAVID L.

PERSONAL Born 05/17/1940, Austin, MN, m, 1962, 3 children **DISCIPLINE** BIBLICAL STUDIES **EDUCATION** IN Wesleyan Univ, BA, 62; Asbury Theol Sem, BD, 65, ThM, 67; John Hopkins Univ, PhD, 73. **CAREER** Asbury Theol Sem, 76-82, Prof 86-; Teaching, 73-76, Wesleyan Univ. **HONORS AND AWARDS** Woodrow Wilson Fel. **MEMBERSHIPS** SBL; CBA; IBR; WTS. **RESEARCH** Scriptural Intertexuality; Hermeneutics. **SELECTED PUBLICATIONS** Auth, Holiness for Hurting People: Discipleship as Recovery, Indianapolis IN, Wesleyan Pub House, 98; Bible Study That Works, revised edition, IN, Evangel Press, 94. **CONTACT ADDRESS** Asbury Theol Sem, 204 N Lexington Ave, Wilmore, KY 40390-1199. **EMAIL** david_thompson@asburyseminary.edu

THOMPSON, EARL A.

PERSONAL Born 10/15/1938, Los Angeles, CA, m, 1961, 1 child **DISCIPLINE** ECONOMICS **EDUCATION** UCLA, BA; Harvard Univ, MA; PhD. **CAREER** Asst Prof, Stanford Univ; Asst Prof to Full Prof, UCLA. **MEMBERSHIPS** AEA. **RESEARCH** The welfare properties of evolutionary equilibria under various information-generating processes. **CONTACT ADDRESS** Dept Econ, Univ of California, Los Angeles, 405 Hilgard Ave, Los Angeles, CA 90095-147703. **EMAIL** thompson@econ.ucla.edu

THOMPSON, GEORGE, JR.

PERSONAL Born 10/12/1931, Richmond, VA, w, 1955, 1 child **DISCIPLINE** THEOLOGY **EDUCATION** Va Union Univ, BA, 54; Southern Baptist Theological Seminary, 57; Univ of Chicago, MA, 62, PhD, 74. **CAREER** Assoc prof, Bluefield State Col, 62-62; coord for higher ed rel studies, 65-72, assoc prof, Payne Theological Seminary, 63-72; Prof, E Stroudsburg Univ, 72-; vis prof, Harvard Univ, 75-77; Vis Prof, Lutheran Theological Seminary at Philadelphia, 81-. **HONORS AND AWARDS** Doctor of Divinity, Martha Vineyard Theological Seminary, 94; Martin Luther King Jr. Faculty Awd, E Stroudsburg Univ, 00; Distinguished Prof and Scholar Awd, Lutheran Theological Seminary at Philadelphia, 00. **MEMBERSHIPS** Am Acad of Rel; Am Philos Asn; Soc for the Study of Black Philosophy; Soc for the Scientific Study of Rel. **CONTACT ADDRESS** PO Box 945, Glenside, PA 19038-0945. **EMAIL** gthomp@esu.edu

THOMPSON, KENNETH F.

DISCIPLINE PHILOSOPHY **EDUCATION** Yale Univ, BA; Union Theol Sem, BD; Columbia Univ, PhD. **CAREER** Assoc prof, Loyola Univ,67-; lectr, DePauw Univ, Ind & Loyola's Rome Center; dept chp & dir, grad stud. **RESEARCH** Early modern philosophy, especially Descartes and Hume; Whitehead; philosophy of mind; philosophy of religion. **SELECTED PUBLICATIONS** Auth, Whitehead's Philosophy of Religion; articles on, philos topics. **CONTACT ADDRESS** Dept of Philosophy, Loyola Univ, Chicago, 820 N Michigan Ave, Chicago, IL 60611.

THOMPSON, LEONARD LEROY

PERSONAL Born 09/24/1934, IN **DISCIPLINE** RELIGIOUS STUDIES **EDUCATION** DePauw Univ, BA, 56; Drew Univ, BD, 60; Univ Chicago, MA, 63, PhD(New Testament), 68. **CAREER** Instr relig, Lawrence Univ, 65-66 & Wright State Univ, 66-68; asst prof, 68-71, assoc prof, 72-80, PROF RELIG, LAWRENCE UNIV, 80-, Nat Endowment for Humanities fel, 81-82. **MEMBERSHIPS** Am Acad Relig; Soc Bibl Lit. **RESEARCH** Biblical studies; Greco-Roman religions. **SELECTED PUBLICATIONS** Auth, Regnum-Caelorum--Patterns of Future Hope in Early Christianity, J Relig, Vol 74, 94; Revelation--Vision of a Just World, Cath Biblical Quart, Vol 55, 93. **CONTACT ADDRESS** 902 E. Eldorado, Appleton, WI 64911.

THOMPSON, M. T., JR.

PERSONAL Born 04/15/1951, Saginaw, MI, m **DISCIPLINE** LAW **EDUCATION** Oakland Univ, BA 1973; Northeastern Univ Sch of Law, JD 1977. **CAREER** Michigan Bell Telephone Co, mgr 1973-74; Natl Labor Relations Bd, Attorney 1977-79; Lewis White & Clay PC, Attorney 1979-83; MT Thompson Jr PC, Attorney 1983-. **MEMBERSHIPS** Admitted to practice MI Supreme Court 1977, US Sixth Circuit Court of Appeals 1980, US Supreme Court 1984. **SELECTED PUBLICATIONS** Author "Institutional Employment Discrimination as a Legal Concept," 1981. **CONTACT ADDRESS** MT Thompson Jr, PC, 330 South Washington Ave, Saginaw, MI 48607.

THOMPSON, MARGARET SUSAN

PERSONAL Born 01/25/1949, Brooklyn, NY **DISCIPLINE** HISTORY, POLITICAL SCIENCE **EDUCATION** Smith Col, AB, 70; Univ Wis-Madison, MA, 72, PhD(hist), 79. **CAREER** Instr, Knox Col, 77-78, asst prof, 79-81; Asst Prof Hist, Syracuse Univ, 81-, Nat Endowment for Humanities res grant, summer, 80; J Franklin Jameson fel, AHA, 80-81. **HONORS AND AWARDS** Ford Foundation Graduate Fel, 72-74; Newberry Library (Chicago) Res Fel, 75; Alice Smith Fel, Wisconsin State Historical Soc, 75-76; Russell Sage Foundation Postdoctoral Fel in the Social Sciences, 83-84; Cushwa Center for Study of American Catholicism, Univ of Notre Dame, Res Grant, 84; Rockefeller Foundation Humanities Fel, 85-86. **MEMBERSHIPS** Orgn Am Historians; Am Polit Sci Asn; Soc Sci Hist Asn; AHA. **RESEARCH** American political history; Civil War and Reconstruction; 20th century politics. **SELECTED PUBLICATIONS** Auth, Cultural Conundrum--Sisters, Ethnicity, and the Adaptation of American-Catholicism, Mid Am Hist Rev, Vol 74, 92; Rose Hawthorne Lathrop--Selected-Writings, Cath Hist Rev, Vol 81, 95; auth, "The Ministry of Women and the Transformation of Catholicism in the 19th-Century America," History of European Ideas, 95; auth, Concentric Circles of Sisterhood," Claiming Our Roots: Sesquecentennial History of the IHM Sisters, 95. **CONTACT ADDRESS** Syracuse Univ, 145 Eggers Hall, Syracuse, NY 13244-1090. **EMAIL** msthomps@syr.edu

THOMPSON, O.

PERSONAL Born 03/20/1942, Tulsa, OK, m, 1976, 4 children **DISCIPLINE** CRIMINOLOGY **EDUCATION** Calif State Univ, BA, 70; Univ S Calif, MA, 73; PhD, 88. **CAREER** Deputy Sheriff to Chief Deputy, Riverside County, Calif,65-92; Chief of Police, Inglewood, 92-97. **MEMBERSHIPS** NOBLE, IACP, ASIS, PERF, Police Foundation. **RESEARCH** Death penalty, Sentencing laws, Police practices, The internet and its impact on criminal justice education, Criminal law, Criminal procedure, Criminal investigations, Executive and dignitary protection, Law in American Society. **CONTACT ADDRESS** Dept Criminal Justice, Riverside Comm Col, 4800 Magnolia Ave, Riverside, CA 92506. **EMAIL** thompson@rccd.cc.ca.us

THOMPSON, PAUL B.
PERSONAL Born 07/22/1951, Springfield, MO, m, 1975, 2 children **DISCIPLINE** PHILOSOPHY **EDUCATION** State Univ NYork at Stony Brook, PhD. **CAREER** Texas A&M Univ, vis asst prof, asst prof, 81-86; US Agency Intl Devel, vis prof, 86-87; Texas A&M Univ, assoc prof, prof, 87-97; Inst for Biosciences & Tech, A&M Univ, dir, 92-97, Purdue Univ, dist prof, 97-. **HONORS AND AWARDS** Nat Center Food & Agri, res fel, 86-87; Texas A&M, Maria Julia & George R. Jordan, jr prof Awd, AAEA Awd, 92; AAEA Awd, 93; New Mex State Univ, vis dist prof, 93-94; Yale Univ, Post doc Fel, 94-95; Purdue Univ, Joyce & Edward E. Brewer, prof of Appl Ethics, 97-. **MEMBERSHIPS** APA, AAEA, SAFHV, SRA, ISEE, IS for Ecolo & Econ **RESEARCH** Philo of techn; ecolo; econom. **SELECTED PUBLICATIONS** Auth, Agricultural Ethics: Research, Teaching and Public Policy, Iowa State Univ Press, 98; Food Biotechnology in Ethical Perspective, Chapman and Hall, 97; The Spirit of the Soil: Agriculture and Environmental Ethics, Routledge Pub Co, 95; co-ed, Ethics, Public Policy, and Agriculture, Macmillan, 94; Arctic, Sustainability: What It Is and What It Is Not, in: Agro-ecology, 98; Ethics and Food Safety, in: Social Construct of Safe Food: Health, Ethics and Safety in Late Modernity, Workshop Report, 98; Toward a Discourse Ethics for Animal Biotechnology, Biotechnology International, 97; The Cloning Debate, Cent for Sc & Tech Policy Newsletter, 97. **CONTACT ADDRESS** Dept of Philosophy, Purdue Univ, West Lafayette, West Lafayette, IN 47907. **EMAIL** pault@purdue.edu

THOMPSON, WILLIAM M.
PERSONAL Born 12/06/1943, Boise, ID, m, 1976, 2 children **DISCIPLINE** PHILOSOPHICAL AND SYSTEMATIC THEOLOGY **EDUCATION** St. Thomas Col, BA, 65; M Div, 69; St. Mary's Sem and Univ, STM; Univ of St. Michael's Col, PhD, 73. **CAREER** Asst/assoc prof, Carroll Col, 76-85; assoc prof, Duquesne Univ, 85-87; prof, 87- . **MEMBERSHIPS** Eric Voegelin Soc; Karl Rahner Soc; Cath Theol Soc of Am. **RESEARCH** Theology and philosophy in dialogue; religion and political philosophy; spirituality and theology/religion in dialogue. **SELECTED PUBLICATIONS** Auth, Christology and Spirituality, 91; The Struggle for Theology's Soul, 96. **CONTACT ADDRESS** Dept. of Theology, Duquesne Univ, Pittsburgh, PA 15282. **EMAIL** thompsonw@duq.edu

THOMSEN, MARK
PERSONAL Born 02/24/1931, m, 1952, 4 children **DISCIPLINE** SYSTEMATIC THEOLOGY **EDUCATION** Dana Col, BA, 53; Trinity Theological Seminary, BD, 56; Princeton Theological Seminary, Th.M, 67; Northwestern Univ and Garrett Theological Seminary, PhD, 71. **CAREER** Academic dean,Theol Col N Nigeria, 59-67; assoc prof, Dana Col, 67-72; assoc prof, Luther Seminary, 80-82; dir, Grad Stud, 82-88; exec dir, division for Global Mission, ELCA, 88-96. **HONORS AND AWARDS** Exec dir, Div for Global Mission. **MEMBERSHIPS** Am Soc of Missiology. **SELECTED PUBLICATIONS** Auth, "A Three -Dimensional Approach to Neo-Supenaturalism," Dialog, Spring, 77; auth, "A Christology of the Spirit and the Nicene Creed," Spring, 77; auth, "A Parabolic Theology of Preaching," Dialog, Summer, 80; auth, "Dialog as a Mark of Out Christian Mission," World Encounter, Spring, 87; auth, "Jesus Crucified and the Mission of the Church," International review of Mission, April, 88; auth, "Toward the 21st Century: The ELCA Looks Forward in Mission," World Encounter, No 1, 88; auth, "The Finality of the Crucified and the Global Mission of the Church," Word and World, Summer, 89; auth, "The Christian Mission in the Muslim World," Word and World, Spring, (96): 194-202; auth, "Living form the Table: The Future of Ecumenism," Word and World, Summer, (98): 315-317; auth, "In the Spirit of Jesus: A Vision Paper on Christian Service and Mission," In Mission at the Dawn of the 21st Century: A Vision for the Church, ed, Paul Varo Martinson, Minneapolis, Kirk House Publishers, (99): 255-267. **CONTACT ADDRESS** Dept of Systematic Theology, Lutheran Sch of Theol at Chicago, 1100 E 55th St, Chicago, IL 60615. **EMAIL** mthomsen@lstc.edu

THOMSON, GARRETT
PERSONAL Born 06/03/1956, m, 4 children **DISCIPLINE** PHILOSOPHY **EDUCATION** Newcastle on Tyne, Eng, BA, 78; Oxford, Balliol Col, Eng, PhD, 84. **CAREER** Instr, Univ Bogota; National Univ; assoc prof & Compton chair of Philos, Col of Wooster, 94-. **SELECTED PUBLICATIONS** Auth, Needs, Routledge, 87; auth, Introduction to Modern Philosophy, Wadsworth, 93; auth, Descartes to Kant, 97; auth, On Descartes, Wadsworth, 99; auth, On Kant, Wadsworth, 99; co-auth, On Aristotle, Wadsworth, 99. **CONTACT ADDRESS** Dept of Philos, The Col of Wooster, Wooster, OH 44691. **EMAIL** gthomson@acs.wooster.edu

THOMSON, KATHRYN
DISCIPLINE LAW **EDUCATION** Univ Victoria, BA; Univ British Columbia, LLB; Ottawa Univ, LLM. **CAREER** Law, Univ Victoria. **HONORS AND AWARDS** Dir, Law Found British Columbia. **SELECTED PUBLICATIONS** Auth, pubs on feminist legal theory and equality litigation. **CONTACT ADDRESS** Fac of Law, Univ of Victoria, PO Box 2400, Victoria, BC, Canada V8W 3H7. **EMAIL** ket@uvic.ca

THOMSON, WILLIAM
PERSONAL Born 05/24/1927, Ft Worth, TX, m, 1948, 4 children **DISCIPLINE** MUSIC THEORY; PHILOSOPHY **EDUCATION** N Texas State Col, BM, 48, MM, 49; Ind Univ, PhD, 52. **CAREER** SUL Ross State Col, 51-60; prof music theory, Ind Univ, 61-69; scholar in resident, Univ Hawaii, 67-68; Kulas prof music, Case W Res Univ, 69-73; prof music, univ arizona, 73-75; Ziegle prof music & dept chr music, SUNY Buffalo, 75-80; Dean School of Music, USC, 80-95. **HONORS AND AWARDS** Outstanding Tchr Awds, Case W Res Univ, 71 & Univ Arizona, 75; Choice Outstanding Acad Book, 92. **MEMBERSHIPS** Soc Mus Theory; Col Mus Soc; Am Musicol Soc. **RESEARCH** Perceptual basis of musical experience. **SELECTED PUBLICATIONS** Coauth, Materials and Structure of Music, 65; auth, Introduction to Ear Training; auth Introduction to Music as Structure, 69; Music for Listeners, 71; Introduction to Music Reading, 75; Sound, musical, Encycl Britannica, 78; Advanced Music Reading, 81; Schoenbergs Error, 91; trans Consonance and Dissonance in Music, 93; auth, Tonality in Music: A General Theory, 99. **CONTACT ADDRESS** 3333 E California Blvd., Pasadena, CA 91107. **EMAIL** sansptom@aol.com

THORELLI, HANS BIRGER
PERSONAL Born 09/18/1921, Newark, NJ, m, 1948, 2 children **DISCIPLINE** POLITICAL ECONOMY **EDUCATION** Univ Stockholm, Swe, MA, 44, LLB, 45, PhD, 54; Northwestern Univ, 46-47. **CAREER** Prof, Bus Admin, Univ Chicago, 59-64; vis prof, IMD, Lausanne, 64-65; vis prof, London Grad Sch Bus, 69-70; Prof, Bus Admin, Ind Univ, 64-. **MEMBERSHIPS** Am Econ Asn; Am Mktg Asn; Acad Mgt **RESEARCH** International Business Strategy, Public Policy; Marketing; Management **SELECTED PUBLICATIONS** International Operations Simulation Mark 2000 Administrator's Compendium, Prentice-Hall, 94; edr, Integral Strategy: Concepts and Dynamics, JAI Press, 95; edr, Integral Strategy: Integration as Focus, JAI Press, 95. **CONTACT ADDRESS** Kelley Sch Bus, Indiana Univ, Bloomington, Marketing 328L, Bloomington, IN 47401. **EMAIL** thorelli@indiana.edu

THORNBURG, E. G.
PERSONAL Born 05/03/1954, Norwalk, CT, m, 1976, 1 child **DISCIPLINE** LAW **EDUCATION** Col of William and Mary, BA, 76; S Methodist Univ, JD, 79. **CAREER** SMU, dir, asst prof, assoc prof, prof, 84-. **HONORS AND AWARDS** Dr. Don M. Smart tchg Awd; Phi Beta Kappa. **MEMBERSHIPS** ALI; AALS; ABA; State Bar TX. **RESEARCH** Civil procedure; discovery; juries; comparative procedure; judicial discretion; internet ADR. **SELECTED PUBLICATIONS** Auth, Going Private: Technology, Due Process, and Internet Dispute Resolution, 34 UC Davis L Rev 151; auth, Giving the Haves a Little More: Considering the 1998 Discovery Proposals, SMUL, 98; auth,The Power and the Process: Instructions and the Civil Jury, Fordham L Rev, 98; auth, Ch 10&11 in 1997 and 1998 Supplements, Dorsano & Crump, TX; auth, Civil Procedure: Pretrial Litigation, 89; auth, Metaphors Matter: How Images of Battle, Sports and Sex Shape the Adversary System, Wis Women's L. J., 95; auth, The Costs of Attorney-Client Privilege, Brief, 94. **CONTACT ADDRESS** School of Law, So Methodist Univ, PO Box 0116, Dallas, TX 75275. **EMAIL** ethornbu@mail.smu.edu

THORNELL, RICHARD PAUL
PERSONAL Born 10/19/1936, New York, NY, m **DISCIPLINE** LAW **EDUCATION** Fisk Univ, magna cum laude, 1956; Pomona Coll, 1955; Woodrow Wilson Sch, MPA, 1958; Yale Law Sch, JD, 1971. **CAREER** Howard Univ Sch of Law, prof of Law, currently, vice pres, general counsel, 84-88, Univ Faculty Senate, immediate past chair; Rosenman Colin Freund Lewis & Cohen NYC, assoc litigation dept 1975-76; US Comm Relations Serv Dept of Justice, chief fed progms staff 1965-66; Africa Reg Ofc US Peace Corps, chief program staff; US Dept of State Agency for Intl Develop, econ & intl rel ofcr 1958-61. **HONORS AND AWARDS** Fisk Univ, Africare Distinguished Serv Awd; Fisk Univ Gen Alumni Assn 1978; Grad Fellowship Princeton U; Fellowship Grant Yale Law Sch; Intl Achievement Awd William S Thompson Intl Law Soc dir com Nat Bd of YMCA'S of USA; exec com m1980. **MEMBERSHIPS** Bars of NY/DC/Fed Cts/US Supreme Ct; bd of advisors, Smithonian Environmental Res Ctr; bd of dir YMCA of Wash DC 1977-83; bd of dir Africare 1977-83; trustee Phelps Stoke Fund 1980-85; lay mem bd of dir, com Nat Bd of YMCA'S of USA; exec com & gen counsel Fisk Univ Gen Alumni Assn 1977-79; Phi Beta Kappa, Delta Chap, Fisk Univ 1956-; elected Council on Foreign Relations. **CONTACT ADDRESS** Howard Univ, 2400 Van Ness St NW, Washington, VT 20008.

THORNTON, DAVID
PERSONAL Born 10/16/1957, Austin, TX, m, 1992, 1 child **DISCIPLINE** INTERNATIONAL RELATIONS **EDUCATION** Univ NC at Greensboro, BA, 79; MA, 86; Univ SC, PhD, 93. **CAREER** From asst to assoc prof, Campbell Univ. **HONORS AND AWARDS** NEH Summer Inst, 99. **RESEARCH** International Economic Relations, International Political Economy, Commercial Aeronautics and Civil Aviation. **SELECTED PUBLICATIONS** Auth, Airbus Industrie: The Politics of an International Industrial Collaboration, St Martin's Press, 95. **CONTACT ADDRESS** Dept Govt & Hist, Campbell Univ, PO Box 356, Buies Creek, NC 27506-0356. **EMAIL** thornton@camel.campbell.edu

THORP, JOHN
DISCIPLINE PHILOSOPHY **EDUCATION** Trent Univ, BA, 70; Oxford Univ, BPhil, 72; DPhil, 76. **CAREER** Asst prof, Univ of Ottawa, 76; assoc prof, Univ of Ottawa, 81; assoc prof, Univ of Western Ontario, 92; ch of Philos, Univ of Western Ontario. **RESEARCH** Ancient Greek and Roman thought and in modern metaphysics and epistemology. **SELECTED PUBLICATIONS** Auth, Free Will, a defence against neurophysiologicl determinism, Routledge & Kegan Paul, London & Boston, (80): 162; auth, El libre albedrio, Editorial Herder, Barcelona, (85): 153; auth, La figure d'Achille chez Aristote Melanges Pascal, Cahiers d'Etudes Anciennes, XXIV-II, (90): 357-363; auth, Aristotle's Horror Vacui, Canadian Journal of Philosophy, XX, (90): 149-166; auth, "The Social Construction of Homosexuality," Phoenix, 46, (92): 54-61; auth, Asterix et les quiaia: la derniere poche de resistance, in Dialogue, XXII, (93): 461-73; auth, "Aristotle's Rehabilitation of Rhetoric, in Propaganda and the Ethics of Rhetoric, vol. III, (93): 13-30; auth, Aristotle on Probalilistic Reasoning, Canadian Journal of Rhetorical Studies, IV, (94): 157-172; auth, "Le couteau de Delphes: reflexions sur un legs nocif d'Aristote," in Cahiers d'etudes anciennes, XXXII, (96): 115-121. **CONTACT ADDRESS** Dept of Philosophy, Univ of Western Ontario, London, ON, Canada N6A 5B8. **EMAIL** jthorp@julian.uwo.ca

THORPE, SAMUEL
DISCIPLINE PHILOSOPHY **EDUCATION** Univ Arkansas, BA, 71; Oral Roberts Univ, MA, 81; Univ Tulsa, PhD, 89. **CAREER** Asst Prof, 91-96, Assoc Prof, 96-, Oral Roberts Univ. **CONTACT ADDRESS** Dept of Theology, Oral Roberts Univ, Tulsa, OK 74171. **EMAIL** srthorpe@oru.edu

THORSON, NORM
DISCIPLINE LAW **EDUCATION** Univ Nebr, BS; MS; JD; PhD. **CAREER** Prof **HONORS AND AWARDS** Pres, Am Agricultural Law Asn. **RESEARCH** Agricultural law; public lands and natural resources; oil and gas; water law; international environmental law. **SELECTED PUBLICATIONS** Auth, Cases and Materials on Agricultural Law, W; co-auth, Agricultural Law; Nebraska Water Law and Administration. **CONTACT ADDRESS** Law Dept, Univ of Nebraska, Lincoln, 103 Ross McCollum Hall, PO Box 830902, Lincoln, NE 68588-0420. **EMAIL** nthorson@unlinfo.unl.edu

THRO, LINUS J.
PERSONAL Born 01/15/1913, St. Charles, MO **DISCIPLINE** MEDIEVAL PHILOSOPHY **EDUCATION** St Louis Univ, AB, 34, lic theol, 45; Col Immaculate Conception, lic phil, 38; Univ Montreal, MA, 38; Univ Toronto, PhD, 48. **CAREER** Instr, Regis Col, 38-41; from instr to assoc prof, 49-72, chmn dept, 68-74, PROF MEDIAEVAL PHILOS, ST LOUIS UNIV, 72- **MEMBERSHIPS** Am Philos Asn; Metaphys Soc Am; Am Cath Philos Asn. **RESEARCH** Thought and influence of John Duns Scotus; philosophy and religion in relation to science. **SELECTED PUBLICATIONS** Auth, A Note on Universals, Mod Schoolman: Gilson and Duns Scotus, New Scholasticism; Questions on Aristotle 'Metaphysics X and Xii' by Dymsdale,John in Latin Text and Analysis of 13th-Century Philosophical Work, Manuscripta, Vol 0036, 1992. **CONTACT ADDRESS** Dept of Philos, Saint Louis Univ, Saint Louis, MO 63103.

THRONVEIT, MARK A.
DISCIPLINE OLD TESTAMENT **EDUCATION** St. Olaf Col, BA, 71; Luther Sem, MDiv, GM; Union Theol Sem, PhD, 82. **CAREER** Tchg fel, Union Theol Sem, 979-81; tchg asst, Presbyterian Sch for Christian Educ, 79-80; adj prof, Augsburg Col, 91; St. Thomas Univ, 91; instr, 81; assoc prof, 87-. **HONORS AND AWARDS** AAL scholar; Minnie Bruce awd in New Testament, Luther Sem, 75; James A. Jones Memorial fel; assoc pastor, first eng lutheran church, 78. **MEMBERSHIPS** Mem, Soc Bibl Lit; member of the steering comm for the Chronicles, Ezra-Nehemiah consultation, 84-86, group, 86-91, section, 91-. **SELECTED PUBLICATIONS** Auth, Ezra-Nehemiah, Interpretation Commentaries, 92; Exploring the Yearly Lectionary Series A, 91; When Kings Speak: Royal Speech and Royal Prayer in Chronicles, 87. **CONTACT ADDRESS** Dept of Old Testament, Luther Sem, 2481 Como Ave, Saint Paul, MN 55108. **EMAIL** mthrontv@luthersem.edu

THURSBY, GENE ROBERT
PERSONAL Born 05/08/1939, Akron, OH, m, 1963 **DISCIPLINE** INDIC RELIGION, HISTORY OF RELIGIONS **EDUCATION** Oberlin Col, BA, 61, BDiv, 64; Duke Univ, PhD(-relig), 72. **CAREER** Asst prof, 70-76, ASSOC PROF RELIG, UNIV FLA, 76-, CONSULT, CHOICE: J ASN COL AND RES LIBR, 70-; scholar-diplomat, US Dept State Sem SAsia, 72 and Sem Pop Matters, 73. **MEMBERSHIPS** Am Acad Relig; Am Orient Soc; Royal Asiatic Soc Gt Brit and Ireland; Asn Asian Studies; Soc Asian and Comp Philos. **RESEARCH** Inter-religious relations in South Asia; history of Hindu religious and social movements in the 20th century; philosophical analysis

for religious uses of language. **SELECTED PUBLICATIONS** Auth, Some Resources for History of Religions, Bull Am Acad Relig, 67; coauth, South Asian Proscribed Publications, 1907-1947, Indian Arch, 69; Hindu-Muslim Relations in British India, Brill, 75; Religious Nationalism in Hindus And Muslims In India, J Asian Hist, Vol 0030, 96. **CONTACT ADDRESS** Dept of Relig, Univ of Florida, P O Box 117410, Gainesville, FL 32611-7410.

THURSTON, BONNIE BOWMAN
PERSONAL Born 10/05/1952, Bluefield, WV, w, 1980 **DISCIPLINE** NEW TESTAMENT **EDUCATION** Bethany Col, BA, 74; Univ Va, MA, 75, PhD, 79. **CAREER** Grad inst, Eng, 76-79, asst dean, Col Arts and Sci, inst, Eng and Rel stud, 79-80, Univ Va; adj, Eng Theol, Wheeling Jesuit Univ, 80-81; asst prof, Eng, Human, Bethany Col, 81-83; tutor, inst stud Christian Origins, Tuebingen, Ger, 83-85; assoc prof Theol, dir, ch, dept Theol, Wheeling Jesuit Univ, 85-95; prof New Test, Pittsburgh Theol Sem, 95-. **HONORS AND AWARDS** Valedictorian, first hon lit, hon soc in Drama, Eng, Jour, Bethany Col , 74; Philip Francis du Pont fel, Univ Va, 76; Who's Who in Bibl studs and Archeol, 87; Who's Who in the World, 87; Who's Who in Rel, 91; schol-in-res, Wheeling Jesuit Univ, 92; Alpha Sigma Nu; Alum Achiev Awd in Rel. **MEMBERSHIPS** Amer Sch Oriental Res; Catholic Bibl Asn; Intl Thomas Merton Soc; Soc Bibl Lit; Soc Buddhist-Christian Stud. **RESEARCH** New Testament; Christian Origins; Christian Spirituality. **SELECTED PUBLICATIONS** Auth, The Conquered Self: Emptiness and God in Buddhist-Christian Dialogue, Japanese Jour Rel Studs, 12/4, 85; Matt 5:43-45: You, Therefore, must be perfect, Interpretation, 41/2, 87; The Gospel of John and Japanese Buddhism, Japanese Rel, 15/2, 88; Thomas Merton: Pioneer of Buddhist-Christian Dialogue, Cath World, May/June, 89; Wait Here and Watch: A Eucharistic Commentary on Matt 26-28, Chalice, 89; The Windows: A Women's Ministry in the Early Church, Fortress, 89; Language, Gender and Prayer, Lexington Theol Quart, 27/1, 92; Spiritual Life in the Early Church, Fortress, 93; Proclamation 5, Series C: Holy Week, Fortress, 94; Reading Colossians, Ephesians, and II Thessalonians, Crossroad, 95; Women in the New Testament, Crossroad, 98; auth, For Everything a Season, Crossroad, 99; auth, Fruit of the Spirit Growth of the Heart, Liturgical Press, 00. **CONTACT ADDRESS** Dept of New Testament, Pittsburgh Theol Sem, 616 N Highland Ave, Pittsburgh, PA 15206. **EMAIL** BThurston@pts.edu

TIBBETTS, PAUL E.
DISCIPLINE PHILOSOPHY **EDUCATION** Univ Ill, PhD, 86. **CAREER** Dept Philos, Univ Dayton **RESEARCH** Epistemology; philosophy of mind; philosophy of science. **SELECTED PUBLICATIONS** Auth, Threading-the-Needle: The Case for and against Common-Sense Realism, Hum Stud 13, 90; Residual Dualism in Computational Theories of Mind, Dialectica, 96; Neurobioloy and the Homoculous Thesis, Man and World, 96. **CONTACT ADDRESS** Dept of Philos, Univ of Dayton, 300 Col Park, Dayton, OH 75062. **EMAIL** tibbetts@checkov.hm.udayton.edu

TIBERIUS, VALERIE
PERSONAL Born 05/28/1967, Toronto, Canada **DISCIPLINE** PHILOSOPHY **EDUCATION** Univ of Toronto, BA, 90; UNC-Chapel Hill, MA, 92; PhD, 97. **CAREER** Asst Prof, Univ of Minnesota, 98-; Asst Prof, Franklin & Marshall Coll, 97-98 **HONORS AND AWARDS** McKnight Summer Fellowship, Univ of Minnesota, 99; Mellon Fellowship in the Humanities, 90-92, 95-96. **MEMBERSHIPS** Amer Philosophical Assoc; British Society for Ethical Theory; Central States Philosophical Assoc. **RESEARCH** Ethics, Practical Reason, Moral Psychology. **SELECTED PUBLICATIONS** Auth, "Humean Heroism: Value Commitments and the Source of Normativity," Pacific Philosophical Quarterly, forthcoming; auth, "Deliberation about the Good: Justifying What We Value," forthcoming from Garland Publishing in the series Dissertations in Ethics; auth, "Full Information and Ideal Deliberation," Journal of Value inquiry, Volume 31, No. 3, Sept 97, pp 329-338; auth, Arrogance", with John Walker, American Philosophical Quarterly, Volume 35, No. 4, Oct 98, pp 379-390; auth, "Justifying Reasons for Valuing: An Argument Against the Social Account," The Southern Journal of Philosophy, Volume XXXVII, No. 1, Spring 99, pp 141-158. **CONTACT ADDRESS** Dept Philosophy, Univ of Minnesota, Twin Cities, 271 19th Ave S, 831 Heller Hall, Minneapolis, MN 55455-0430. **EMAIL** tiber001@tc.umn.edu

TIDMAN, PAUL
DISCIPLINE LOGIC, APPLIED PHILOSOPHY **EDUCATION** Asbury Col, Wilmore, BA, 78; Univ Notre Dame, PhD, 90. **CAREER** Dept Philos, Mt Union Col **RESEARCH** Epistemology/Metaphysics. **SELECTED PUBLICATIONS** Auth, The Justification of A Priori Intuitions, Philos and Phenomenol Res, 56, 96; Logic and Modal Intuitions, The Monist, 77, 94; Conceivability as a Test of Possibility, Amer Philos Quart, 31, 94; Lehrer on a Premise of Epistemic Cogency, Philos Stud, 67, 92 & The Epistemology of Evil Possibilities, Faith and Philos, 10, 93; coauth, Logic and Philosophy, 7th ed, Belmont, Calif: Wadsworth Press, 94;. Instructor's Manual for Logic and Philosophy, 7th ed, Belmont, Calif: Wadsworth Press, 94; contribur, Conceivability, Cambridge Dictionary Philos, Cambridge UP, 95 & Review: Review of Reinhard Grossman's The Fourth Way: A Theory of Knowledge, Mind, 101, 92. **CONTACT ADDRESS** Dept of Philosophy, Mount Union Col, 1972 Clark Ave, Alliance, OH 44601. **EMAIL** tidmanpa@muc.edu

TIEDE, DAVID L.
DISCIPLINE NEW TESTAMENT **EDUCATION** St. Olaf Col, BA, 62; Luther Sem, BD, 66; Harvard Univ, PhD, 71. **CAREER** Summer instr, Harvard Divinity Sch, 67; tchg fel, Harvard Univ, 69; part time instr, Northeastern Univ, 70; asst prof, Scripps Col; Claremont Col, 70-71; vis prof, Claremont Col, 78-79; vis prof, Yale Divinity Sch, 86-87; prof, 71; pres, 87-. **HONORS AND AWARDS** Assoc pastor, Trinity Lutheran Church, 72-75; bd mem, Tentmakers Ministries; Lutheran Leadership Inst; co-ch, LukeActs Semr of the Soc Bibl Lit; ch of bd of publ, Evangel Lutheran Church Am, ELCA. **SELECTED PUBLICATIONS** Auth, Jesus and the Future, 90; Holy Week: Proclamation 4, 89; Luke: Augsburg Commentary on the New Testament, 88; Search Bible Studies, Units I and II, 83; Prophecy and History, LukeActs, 80. **CONTACT ADDRESS** Dept of New Testament, Luther Sem, 2481 Como Ave, Saint Paul, MN 55108. **EMAIL** dtiede@luthersem.edu

TIEFER, CHARLES
PERSONAL Born 01/21/1954, New York, NY, m, 1995, 1 child **DISCIPLINE** LAW **EDUCATION** Columbia Col, BA, 74; Harvard Law Sch, JD, 77. **CAREER** Deputy Gen Coun, House of Rep, 84-95; Assoc Prof, Univ Baltimore, 95-. **MEMBERSHIPS** NCMA, ASIL. **RESEARCH** Legislation, government contracts, international law. **SELECTED PUBLICATIONS** Auth, Congressional Practice and Procedure, 89; auth, The Semi-Sovereign President, 92; auth, Government Contract Law, 99. **CONTACT ADDRESS** Dept Law, Univ of Baltimore, 1420 N Charles St, Baltimore, MD 21201-5720. **EMAIL** ctiefer@usmail.us.lt.edu

TIERNEY, JAMES E.
DISCIPLINE LAW **EDUCATION** Rutgers Col, BA; NY Univ, JD, LLM. **CAREER** Prof. **RESEARCH** Contract and Commercial Law, Federal Taxation. **SELECTED PUBLICATIONS** Auth, Equitable Recoupment Revised, Ky Law J, 92; Reassessing Sales and Liquidations of Partnership Interests, Fla Tax Rev, 94. **CONTACT ADDRESS** Col Law, Univ of Toledo, Toledo, OH 43606. **EMAIL** jtierne@pop3-utoledo.edu

TIERNEY, KEVIN H.
PERSONAL Born 09/22/1942, Bristol, England **DISCIPLINE** LAW **EDUCATION** St John's Col, Cambridge Univ, BA, 64; MA, 68; LLB, 65; Yale Law School, LLM, 67. **CAREER** Assoc Lawyer, Donovan Leisure Newton & Irvine, 69-70; Assoc Prof and Prof, Wayne State Univ, 71-79; Prof, Univ Calif, 79-. **HONORS AND AWARDS** Fel, Ransom Center, 92, 95. **MEMBERSHIPS** State Bar of Mich. **RESEARCH** History, Biography. **SELECTED PUBLICATIONS** Auth, Courtroom Testimony: A Policeman's Guide, 70; auth, How to be a Witness, 71; auth, Darrow: A Biography, 79. **CONTACT ADDRESS** Col of Law, Univ of California, San Francisco, 198 McAllister St, San Francisco, CA 94102-4907. **EMAIL** tierneyk@uchastings.edu

TIERNEY, NATHAN
PERSONAL Born 03/16/1953, Swansea, UK, m, 1985, 2 children **DISCIPLINE** PHILOSOPHY **EDUCATION** Univ Melbourne, BA, 75; Columbia Univ, PhD, 89. **CAREER** Assoc prof, Cal Luth Univ, 90-; dept ch, 00-. **MEMBERSHIPS** APA; SCP; NAS; SCAS. **RESEARCH** Ethics (Moral psychology, metaphysics of morals, professional ethics). **SELECTED PUBLICATIONS** Auth, Imagination and Ethical Ideas, SUNY Press (Albany, NY), 94. **CONTACT ADDRESS** Dept Philosophy, California Lutheran Univ, 60 West Olsen Rd, Thousand Oaks, CA 91360-2700. **EMAIL** tierney@clunet.edu

TIERSMA, PETER M.
PERSONAL Born, Netherlands, m **DISCIPLINE** LAW **EDUCATION** Stanford Univ, BA, 74; Univ Calif, San Diego, PhD, 80; Univ Calif, Berkeley, JD, 86. **CAREER** Prof & Joseph Scott fel; Fulbright fel, Neth; lectr, Univ Calif, San Diego & Miami Univ Ohio; clerk, Justice Stanley Mosk, Calif Supreme Ct; private practice, Pettit & Martin, San Francisco & Price, Postel & Parma, Santa Barbara fac, Loyola Law Sch, 90-. **SELECTED PUBLICATIONS** Writes on, relationship between language and the law. **CONTACT ADDRESS** Law School, Loyola Marymount Univ, 919 S Albany St, Los Angeles, CA 90015. **EMAIL** peter.tiersma@lls.edu

TIESSEN, TERRANCE
PERSONAL Born 02/18/1944, Hamilton, ON, Canada, m, 1965, 4 children **DISCIPLINE** THEOLOGY **EDUCATION** Ontario Bible Col, BTh, 64; Sir Wilfred Laurier Univ, BA, 66; Wheaton Col, MA, 68; Westminster Theol Sem, ThM, 75; Ateneo de Manila Loyola Sch Theol, PhD, 84. **CAREER** Asian Theol Sem Manila, prof, 75-86; Ontario Bible Col, vpres acad & student affairs, 86-89; Providence Col, prof, 93-96; Providence Theol Sem, prof, 93-. **MEMBERSHIPS** AAP, ACT, CETA, CTS, ETS, SCE. **RESEARCH** Divine providence; theology of religion; theology of petitionary prayer. **SELECTED PUBLICATIONS** Auth, Gnosticism as Heresy: The Response of Irenaeus, in: Hellenization Revisited: Shaping a Christian Response within the Greco-Roman World, ed., W.E. Helleman, NY: Univ Press Am, 94; auth, Irenaeus on the Salvation of the Unevangelized, ATLA Monograph Series, Metuchen NJ: Scarecrow Press, 93; auth, Divine Justice and Universal Grace: A Calvinistic Proposal, in: Evangel Rev Theol, 97; auth, Irenaeus and Modern Responses to the Challenge of Religious Pluralism, ATA Jour, 96; auth, Can the Unevangelism Be Saved?: A Review Article, Didaskalia, 93. **CONTACT ADDRESS** Dept of Theology, Providence Col and Theol Sem, Otterburne, MB, Canada R0A 1G0. **EMAIL** ttiessen@providence.mb.ca

TIGAY, JEFFREY HOWARD
PERSONAL Born 12/25/1941, Detroit, MI, m, 1965, 4 children **DISCIPLINE** BIBLICAL STUDIES, ANCIENT NEAR EASTERN LITERATURE **EDUCATION** Columbia Col, BA, 63; Jewish Theol Sem, Am, MHL, 66; Yale Univ, PhD(comp Blbl & Ancient Near East Studies), 71. **CAREER** From A.M Ellis asst prof to prof, Hebrew & Semitic Lang & Lit, Univ Pa, 71-; chair, Jewish Studies Program, Univ Pa, 95-98; vis assoc prof, Bible Jewish Theol Sem Am. **HONORS AND AWARDS** Lindback Awd for disting teaching, Univ of Pennsylvania; grantee, Nat Sci Found, 72; assoc, Univ Sem on Studies Hebrew Bible, Columbia Univ, 72; Am Coun Learned Soc fel, 75-76; fel, inst Advan Studies, Hebrew Univ, Jerusalem, 78-79; grant, Am Philos Soc, 80 & Am Coun Learned Soc, 80-81; Nat Endowment for Humanities summer res fel, 80; fel, Am Acad for Jewish Research, 80, 86; Mem Fedn Jewish Cult fel, 81-82; scholar-in-residence, Jewish Publication Soc of Am, 86-87; fel, Annenberg Res Institute, 91-92. **MEMBERSHIPS** Am Acad for Jewish Research, Am Schools of Oriental Res; Assoc for Jewish Studies; The Biblical Colloquium; Soc of Biblical Lit. **RESEARCH** Biblical literature and exegesis; comparative Biblical and ancient Near Eastern studies; ancient Judaism. **SELECTED PUBLICATIONS** Auth, The Evolution of the Gilgamesh Epic, Univ Pa Pr (Philadelphia), 82; auth/ed, Empirical Models for Biblical Criticism, Univ Pa Pr (Philadelphia), 85; auth, "You Shall Have No Other Gods," Israelite Religion in the Light of Hebrew Inscriptions, in Harvard Semitic Studies 31 (Atlanta: Scholars Pr, 86); co-ed, Studies in Midrash and Related Lit, Jewish Publication Soc (Philadelphia), 88; auth, The JPS Torah Commentary: Deuteronomy, Jewish Publication Soc of Am (Philadelphia), 96; co-ed, Tehilla le-Moshe, Biblical and Judaic Studies in Honor of Moshe Greenberg, Eisenbraun's (Winona Lake, Indiana), 97. **CONTACT ADDRESS** Dept Asian & Middle Eastern Studies, Univ of Pennsylvania, 847 Williams Hall, Philadelphia, PA 19104-6305. **EMAIL** jtigay@sas.upenn.edu

TILES, J. E.
PERSONAL Born 01/16/1944, Racine, WI, m, 1969 **DISCIPLINE** PHILOSOPHY **EDUCATION** Carleton Col, BA, 66; Univ Bristol, BA, 68; Univ Bristol, MS, 70; Oxford Univ, D. Phil., 78 **CAREER** Lectr, Univ Reading, 74-89; prof, Univ Hawaii, 89- **RESEARCH** Ancient Philosophy, Ethics and Social Philosophy **SELECTED PUBLICATIONS** Dewey, Routledge, 88; co-auth, An Introduction to Historical Epistemology, Blackwell, 93; ed, John Dewey: Critical Assessments, Routledge, 92; Moral Measures, Routledge, 00. **CONTACT ADDRESS** Dept Philos, Univ of Hawaii, Manoa, 2530 Dole St., Honolulu, HI 96822. **EMAIL** jtiles@hawaii.edu

TILLERS, PETER
DISCIPLINE LAW OF EVIDENCE **EDUCATION** Yale Col, AB, 66; Harvard Law Sch, JD, 69; LLM, 72. **CAREER** Vis assoc prof, Boston Col Law Sch, 75-76; asst to assoc prof, Univ Puget Sound sch of Law, 72-77; assoc prof, Rutgers/Camden Law Sch, 77-78; vis assoc prof, Univ Colo Law Sch, 80-81, Summer 81; assoc prof, New England Law Sch, 81-86; prof, Benjamin N Cardozo Sch of Law, Yeshiva Univ. **HONORS AND AWARDS** Sr Max Rheinstein Fel, Univ of Munich, 83-84; dist vis, Fac of Law, Queen's Univ of Belfast, Northern Ireland, 87; vis mem, Oxford Univ Law Fac, 88; Huber Dist Vis Prof, Boston Col Law Sch, 89; adj prof, NYork Univ Sch of Law, 94; sr res assoc, Yale Law Sch, 00-01; vis prof, Harvard Law Sc, 02; former chemn, secy,evidence secn asn am law schs; fel law & hum, harvard univ; senior max rheinstein fel, univ munich; legal adv latvian mission, un. **RESEARCH** The process of fact investigation, and the logic of inductive inference. **SELECTED PUBLICATIONS** Auth, modern Theories of Relevancy, Little, Brown & Co, 83; auth, Prejudice, Politics, and Proof, 86 Mich Law Rev 768, 88; auth, The Value of Evidence in Law, 39 Northern Ireland Legal Q 167, 88; auth, Webs of Thinkgs in the Mind: A New Science of Evidence, 87 Mich Law Rev 1225, 89; co-auth, A Theory of Prelim,inary Fact Investigation, 24 Univ Calif-Davis Law Rev 931, 91; auth, Marshalling Evidence in Adversary Litigation, 13 Cardozo Law Rev 657, 91; co-auth, Hearsay Logic, 76 Minn Law Rev 1601, 92; auth, Intellectual History, Probablility, and the Law of Evidence, 91 Mich Law Rev 1465, 93; auth, Exaggerated and Misleading Repoirts of the Death of Conditional Relevance, 93 Mich Law Rev 478, 94; auth, What Is Wrong with Character Evidence?, 49 Hastings Law J 781, 98; **CONTACT ADDRESS** Yeshiva Univ, 55 Fifth Ave, New York, NY 10003-4301. **EMAIL** tillers@tiac.net

TILLES, GERALD EMERSON
PERSONAL Born 07/15/1942, Detroit, MI, m **DISCIPLINE** LAW **EDUCATION** Wayne State U, BSED 1964, MA 1970, JD 1971. **CAREER** Detroit Bd Educ, tchr 1964-70; prv prctc law 1972-75; Cty Wayne, asst corp cnsl 1975-84; Bureau Wrkrs Dsblty Comp State Of MI, admn law judge 1984-, funds administrator 1987, magistrate 1987. **HONORS AND AWARDS** Robbins Awrd Wayne State Law Sch 1971. **MEMBERSHIPS** Pstr/fndr Chapel Savior Ann Arbor, MI 1980-; wrtr MI Chronicle 1971-74; bd review chrmn Superior Twp 1984-; mem Wolverine Bar Assc, State Bar MI; minister United Methodist Church. **CONTACT ADDRESS** State of Michigan, 1200 Sixth St, Detroit, MI 48226.

TILLEY, JOHN
PERSONAL Born 02/15/1952, Omaha, NE **DISCIPLINE** PHILOSOPHY **EDUCATION** USMA, BS, 75; Univ Ga, MA, 83; Univ Wis, PhD, 88. **CAREER** Asst prof, 88-94, assoc prof, Ind Univ Perdue Univ Indianapolis (IUPUI), 94- . **HONORS AND AWARDS** FACET awd for excellence in tchg, 93; Ind Univ press awd for disting tchg, 97. **MEMBERSHIPS** Amer Philos Assn; S Soc Philos and Phsychol; Soc for Ethics. **RESEARCH** Ethics; Ethical Theory. **SELECTED PUBLICATIONS** Auth, Inner Judgements and Moral Relativism, Philos 18, 88, 171-190; Moral Relativism, Internalism, and the Humean View of Practical Reason, Mod Schoolman 69, 92, 81-109; Accounting for the Tragedy in the Prisoner's Dilemma, synthese 99, 94, 251-276; Two Kinds of Moral Relativism, Jour Value Inquiry 29, 95, 187-192; Motivation and Practical Reasons, Erkenntnis 47, 97, 105-127; Hedonism, in Encycl of Applied Ethics, San Diego, Academic Press Inc, 88, vol 2, 551-559; The Problem for Normative Cultural Relativism, Ratio Juris 11(3), 98, 272-290; Cultural Relativism, Universalism, and the Burden of Proof, Millennium 27(2), 275-297. **CONTACT ADDRESS** Dept of Philosophy, Indiana Univ-Purdue Univ, Indianapolis, 425 University Blvd, Indianapolis, IN 46202. **EMAIL** jtilley@iupui.edu

TILLEY, TERRENCE W.
PERSONAL Born 04/19/1947, Milwaukee, WI, m, 1969, 2 children **DISCIPLINE** PHILOSOPHY OF RELIGION, SYSTEMATIC THEOLOGY **EDUCATION** Univ of San Francisco, AB, 70; Graduate Theol Union at Berkeley, PhD, 76. **CAREER** Teaching Fel, Church Divinity Sch of the Pacific, 72-74; asst prof, Georgetown Univ, 76-79; from asst prof to prof, St Michael's Col, 79-89; assoc prof to prof, Fla State Univ, 89-94; Dir of Grad Studies, Univ of Dayton, 9496; prof and Chemn of Relig Studies, Univ of Dayton, 94-. **HONORS AND AWARDS** Fel, State of Calif, 70-72; Fel for Col Teachers, NEH; Gerald E. Dupont Awd, St Michael's Col, 83; Book of the Year Awd, Col Theol Soc, 86; Edmundite Lectureship, St Michael's Col, 89; Col of Arts & Sci Awd, Fla State Univ, 90-91; Teaching Incentive Prog Awd, Fla State Univ, 94. **MEMBERSHIPS** Am Acad of Relig, Col Theol Soc, Soc for Philos of Relig, Soc of Christian Philos, Catholic Theol Soc of Am, Karl Rahner Soc, Am Asn of Univ Professors. **RESEARCH** Topics in philosophy of religion (problem of evil, multiple religious traditions, rationality of religious belief and practice; practice based theology; narrative theology; Christology). **SELECTED PUBLICATIONS** Auth, Postmodern Theologies: The Challenge of Religious Diversity, Orbis, 95; auth, The Wisdom of Religious Commitment, Georgetown Univ Press, 95; co-ed, The Exercise of the Primacy: Continuing the Dialogue, Crossroad Pub Co., 98; co-ed, Things New and Old: Essays on the Theology of Elizabeth A. Johnson, Crossroad/Herder, 99; auth, "A Recent Vatican Document on 'Christianity and the World Religions'," Theol Studies 60.3 (99): 318-337; auth, "Displacements," Horizons 26.1 (99): 325-329; auth, "The Philosophy of Religion and the Concept of Religion: D.Z. Phillips on Religion and Superstition," J of the Am Acad of Relig, 68.2, (forthcoming); auth, "Foreword," Suffering, Society, and Scripture, Paulist Press (Mahwah, NJ), forthcoming; auth, Inventing Catholic Tradition, Orbis, forthcoming. **CONTACT ADDRESS** Dept Relig Studies, Univ of Dayton, 300 College Park, Dayton, OH 45469-1530. **EMAIL** terrence.tilley@notes.udayton.edu

TIMBIE, JANET ANN
PERSONAL Born 10/17/1948, San Francisco, CA, m, 1969, 2 children **DISCIPLINE** HISTORY OF CHRISTIANITY, COPTIC LANGUAGE **EDUCATION** Stanford Univ, AB, 70; Univ Pa, PhD(relig studies), 79. **CAREER** Reader hist and relig, Am Univ, 71-72 and prof lectr relig, 80-81; Dumbarton Oaks Ctr for Byzantine Studies fel, 78-79; Mellon fel, Cath Univ, 79-80; Catholic Univ 93-; RES AND WRITING, 82-, Ed and transl, US Cath Conf Bishops, 79-82. **MEMBERSHIPS** Cath Bibl Asn; Soc Bibl Lit; Am Acad Relig; Int Asn Coptic Studies; N Amer Patristic Soc. **RESEARCH** Christianity in Egypt through 5th century; development of early Christian monasticism; Coptic language and literature. **SELECTED PUBLICATIONS** Auth, The dating of a Coptic-Sahidic Psalter codex from the University Museum in Philadelphia, Le Museon, 75; Dualism and the Concept of Orthodoxy in the Thought of the Monks of Upper Egypt, Edwin Mellen P; The Status of Women and Gnosticism in Irenaeus and Tertullian, Cath Biblical Quart, Vol 0058, 96; coauth, The Nag Hammadi library in English, Religious Studies Rev, 82; co-ed, The Testament of Job, Scholars Press, 75. **CONTACT ADDRESS** 4608 Merivale Rd, Chevy Chase, MD 20815. **EMAIL** jtimbie@worldnet.att.net

TIMMERMAN, JOAN H.
PERSONAL Born 11/14/1938, Dickeyville, WI, s **DISCIPLINE** RELIGIOUS STUDIES **EDUCATION** Marquette Univ, PhD. **CAREER** Prof Theol; Prof Leadership Studies, Col St. Catherine. **HONORS AND AWARDS** Sr. Mona Riley Prof Humanities, 93-96; Ann O'Hare Graff Awd, Cath Theol Soc Am, 97. **MEMBERSHIPS** CTSA; SSSS; AAUP **RESEARCH** Sacramental theory; sexuality; Clare Boothe Luce - politics and spirituality. **SELECTED PUBLICATIONS** Auth, Sexuality and Spiritual Growth, Crossroad, 92; co-ed, Walking in Two Worlds. Women's Spiritual Paths, North Star Press, 92; auth, Rethinking Christian Sexuality, The Spiral Path, Yes Int Publ, 93; Religion and Violence. The Persistence of Ambivalence, Transforming a Rape Culture, Milkweed Press, 93; Sex: Sacred or Profane?, Readings in Moral Theology, No. 8. Dialogue About Catholic Sexual Teaching, Paulist, 93; The Sexuality of Jesus and the Human Vocation, Sexuality and the Sacred. Sources for Theological Reflection, Westminster/John Knox, 94. **CONTACT ADDRESS** Col of St. Catherine, 2004 Randolph Ave., #4240, Saint Paul, MN 55105. **EMAIL** defcanary@aol.com

TINSLEY, FRED LELAND, JR.
PERSONAL Born 08/30/1944, Detroit, MI, m **DISCIPLINE** LAW **EDUCATION** So U, BA 1969; So U, JD 1972. **CAREER** Champman Tinsley & Reese, prtnr present; Lone Star Gas Co, regulatory atty 1975-77; US Secur & Exchange Commn, trial atty 1973-75; LA Constl Conv, resrch asst 1973; Reginald Heber Smith Fellow Legal Serv 1972. **MEMBERSHIPS** Bd of dir Mental Hlth Assn of Dallas 1976-78; mem adv coun TX Employ Commn 1977-79; bd of dir Dallas Legal Serv Found Inc 1979-; mem exec com Dallas Co Dem Party 1980-; bd of dir Jr Black Acad of Arts & Letters Inc 1980-; asso judge Dallas Muncpl Cts 1978-. **CONTACT ADDRESS** Chapman Tinsley & Reese, One Brookriver Pl, Ste 370, Dallas, TX 75247.

TISO, FRANCIS V.
PERSONAL Born 09/19/1950, Mount Vernon, NY **DISCIPLINE** THEOLOGY **EDUCATION** Columbia Univ and Union Theol Seminary, NYork, Mphil, 86; PhD, 89; Harvard Univ, Cambridge, MA, Mdiv, 75-78; Cornell Univ Col of Arts and Sci, Ithaca, NYork, AB, 68-72. **CAREER** Docente, 96-97, Univ della Terza Eta, Isernia; Le Rel dell'India Medioevale, 97-98; docente Invitato, Buddhist and Christian Soteriologh, 95-96, Studio Teologico Fiorentino; Direttore to Docente, 86-93, Istituto di Sci Rel, Isernia, Italy; Teaching Asst, 84-85, Columbia Univ; Lectr, Dept of Rel and Philos, 78-83, Mercer Coll; Ed and Admin, 80-83, The Seabury Press, NY. **HONORS AND AWARDS** Am Philos Soc Res Fellowship, 97-; Am Acad of Rel Res Fellowship, 97; Pres Fellow, Columbia Univ, 85-87; Field Examinations; Comprehensive Examinations. **MEMBERSHIPS** AOS; AAR. **RESEARCH** Life, songs and teaching of Milanesa; Theology and spirituality of Evagrius Ponticus. **SELECTED PUBLICATIONS** Auth, The Voice of Milarepa: Redaction-critical Research on the Songs and Oral Teachings, The VIIIth Intl Seminar of the IATS, Bloomington, IN, 98; auth, The Sign Beyond All Signs: Christian Monasticism in Dialogue with India, Bangalore Asirvanam Benedictine Monastery, 97; auth, A Catholic Priest Takes a Look at Tibetan Buddhism and Inter-religious Dialogue, Lecture at Library of Tibetan Works and Archives, Dharamasala, HP, India, 97; auth, Resurrection and Transformation in Early Christianity and in the Trajectory of Evagrius Ponticus, at the Museum of Science, Brescia, 96. **CONTACT ADDRESS** St. Bernard Church, 615 H St., Box 169, Eureka, CA 95502. **EMAIL** tiso@northcoast.com

TITIEV, ROBERT JAY
PERSONAL Born 07/01/1941, Ann Arbor, MI, m, 1970 **DISCIPLINE** PHILOSOPHY OF SCIENCE **EDUCATION** Harvard Univ, AB, 64; Stanford Univ, MS, 66, PhD(philos), 69. **CAREER** Asst prof, 69-77, assoc prof philos, Wayne State Univ, 77-. **HONORS AND AWARDS** Res grant-in-aid, 72-73. **MEMBERSHIPS** Asn of Symbolic Logic. **RESEARCH** Logic; measurement theory. **SELECTED PUBLICATIONS** Computer Presentation of Topics in Measurement Theory, J Educ Data Processing, 74; Sentences, Semantics, Stimuli, and Quine, Theoria, 75; The Coherence Condition, Journal of the International Society for Computer Research in Philosophy, 75-76; On Capturing Intuitive Notions Within Formal Systems, Metaphilosophy, 77; On Self-Sustenance in Systems of Epistemic Logic, Notre Dame, Journal of Formal Logic, 80; A Locus Problem Involving the Three-Dimensional City-Block Metric, J Math Psychol, 80; Diagnosis of Ailing Belief Systems, J Philos Res, 93; Causal Troubles, J Philos Res, 95; Arbitrage and the Dutch Book Theorem, J Philos Res, 97; Finiteness, Perception, and two Contrasting Cases of Mathematical Idealization, J Philos Res, 98. **CONTACT ADDRESS** Dept Philos, Wayne State Univ, 51 W Warren Ave, Detroit, MI 48202-3919.

TM, KING
PERSONAL Born 05/09/1929, Pittsburgh, PA, s **DISCIPLINE** RELIGIOUS STUDIES; THEOLOGY; ENGLISH **EDUCATION** Univ Pitts, BA, 51; Fordham Univ, MA, 59; Univ Strasbourg, DSR, 68. **CAREER** Asst prof, 68-74, assoc prof, 74-89, full prof, 89-, Georgetown Univ. **MEMBERSHIPS** Cosmos & Creation; Univ Fac for Life. **RESEARCH** Science and religion; Psychology and religion; History of spirituality. **SELECTED PUBLICATIONS** Auth, Sartre and the Sacred, Univ Chicago Press, 74; Teilhard's Mysticism of Knowing, Seabury, 81; Teilhard de Chardin, Glazier, 88; Enchantments, Religion and the Power of the Word, Sheed & Ward, 89; Merton: Mystic at the Center of America, Liturgical, 92; Jung's Four & Some Philosophers, Univ Notre Dame Press, 98; coed, Letters of Teilhard de Chardin and Lucile Swan, Georgetown Univ Press, 93. **CONTACT ADDRESS** Dept of Theology, Georgetown Univ, Washington, DC 20057. **EMAIL** kingt@gunet.georgetown.edu

TOADVINE, TED
PERSONAL Born 03/12/1968, Salisbury, MD, s **DISCIPLINE** PHILOSOPHY **EDUCATION** Salisbury State Univ, BA, philos, 90; Univ Memphis, philos, MA, 95; PhD, 96. **CAREER** William F. Dietrich res fel, Fla Atlantic Univ, 96-97; visiting prof, philos, Kalamazoo Col, 97-98; asst prof, philos, Emporia State Univ, 98-. **MEMBERSHIPS** The Merleau-Ponty Circle; Soc for Phenomenol and Existential Philos; Amer Philos Asn; Southern Soc for Philos & Psychol. **RESEARCH** Phenomenology; Existentialism; Post-structuralism; Environmental philosophy; Aesthetics; Philosophy of nature; History of philosophy. **SELECTED PUBLICATIONS** Auth, The Art of Doubting: Merleau-Ponty and Cezanne, Philos Today, 41, Winter, 97; auth, Absolution of Finitude in Hegel's Phenomenology of Spirit, Southwest Philos Rev, 12, Jul, 96; auth, Hermeneutics and the Principle of Explicability, Auslegung, 20, Summer, 95. **CONTACT ADDRESS** Div. of Social Sciences, Emporia State Univ, Box 4032, Emporia, KS 66801-5087. **EMAIL** toadvint@emporia.edu

TOBIAS, CARL WILLIAM
PERSONAL Born 01/28/1947, Petersburg, VA, m **DISCIPLINE** ADMINISTRATIVE LAW, CONSTITUTIONAL LAW **EDUCATION** Univ Va, LLB. **CAREER** Prof, Univ Montana; vis fac, Georgetown Univ, Temple Univ, Univ NC, Univ Pittsburgh, Rutgers Univ-Camden and Seton Hall; prof, Univ Nev, Las Vegas. **MEMBERSHIPS** Am Law Inst; Dist Ct Local Rules Rev Comt; 9th Circuit Judicial Coun and the Civil Justice Reform Act Adv Gp; US Dist Ct for the Dist of Mont. **SELECTED PUBLICATIONS** Wrote extensively in the areas of federal civil procedure and federal courts, publishing articles in numerous journals, including Cornell Law Rev, Stanford Law Rev, Columbia Law Rev, and Harvard J on Legis. **CONTACT ADDRESS** Univ of Nevada, Las Vegas, Las Vegas, NV 89154.

TOBIN, FRANK J.
DISCIPLINE MEDIEVAL LITERATURE AND PHILOSOPHY, GERMAN **EDUCATION** Stanford Univ, PhD. **CAREER** Prof Ger, Univ Nev, Reno; ed bd, Studia Mystica and Mystic Quart. **RESEARCH** Translation of Mechthild von Magdeburg. **SELECTED PUBLICATIONS** Published major books on Meister Eckhart and on Mechthild von Magdeburg, numerous articles on the German Middle Ages, and a co-authored two-volume anthology of German literature. **CONTACT ADDRESS** Univ of Nevada, Reno, Reno, NV 89557. **EMAIL** tobinf@scs.unr.edu

TOBIN, THOMAS HERBERT
PERSONAL Born 11/08/1945, Chicago, IL **DISCIPLINE** NEW TESTAMENT, CHRISTIAN ORIGINS **EDUCATION** Xavier Univ, Ohio, LittB, 67; Loyola Univ Chicago, AM, 73; Harvard Univ, PhD(relig studies), 80. **CAREER** Instr, Xavier Univ, Ohio, 69-70; grad asst, Harvard Univ, 77-80; ASST PROF THEOL, LOYOLA UNIV CHICAGO, 80- **MEMBERSHIPS** Studiorum Novi Testamenti Societas Catholic; Biblical Asn of Am Soc of Biblical Lit; Chicago Soc of Biblical Res; Midwest Patristic Seminar; Midwest Patristic Seminar; North Am Patrisic Soc; Philo Institute. **RESEARCH** Letters of Paul, Helenistic Judaism: Philo of Alexadria, Hellenstic Philosophy Middle Platonism, Gnosticsm. **SELECTED PUBLICATIONS** Auth, Philo and the Sibyl: Interpreting Philo's Escatology," in The Studia Philonica Annual, 9, 97; rev, "What Shall We Say That Abraham Found? The Controversy behind Romans 4," in Harvard Theological Rev, 88:4, (95): 437-52; auth, "Was Philo a Middle Platonist? Some Suggestions," in The Studia Philonica Annual 5, (93): 147-50; auth, "Controversy and Continuity in Rom, 1:18-3:20," in CBQ 55, (93): 298-318; auth, Of Scribes and Scrolls: Essays In Honor of the Sixtieth Birthday of John Sturgnell, Washington, DC: Univ Press of Am/Col Theol Soc, 90; auth, The Spirituality of Paul, Message of Biblical Spirituality 12, Wilmington, DE, Michael Glazier, 87. **CONTACT ADDRESS** Dept of Theology, Loyola Univ, Chicago, 1331 W Albion Ave, Chicago, IL 60626. **EMAIL** ttobin@luc.edu

TODD, DONALD DAVID
PERSONAL Born 10/26/1930, Pine Bluff, AR, m, 1951, 2 children **DISCIPLINE** PHILOSOPHY **EDUCATION** San Francisco State Col, BA, 58; Univ BC, PhD(philos), 67. **CAREER** Instr philos, Golden State Col, 60-61; lectr, Univ BC,

64-67; asst prof, 67-73, ASSOC PROF PHILOS, SIMON FRASER UNIV, 73- **MEMBERSHIPS** Can Philos Asn. **RESEARCH** Epistemology; history of British Empiricism; aesthetics. **SELECTED PUBLICATIONS** Auth, Reid Redivivus?, Tex Studies Lit Lang 72; Direct Perception, Philos Phenomenol Res, 3/75; Henry James and the Theory of Literary Realism, Philos Lit, fall 76; coauth, Adjusters and Sense Data, Am Philos Quart, 1/72; ed, The Philosophical Orations of Thomas Reid, Philos Res Archives, 6/77. **CONTACT ADDRESS** Dept of Philos, Simon Fraser Univ, Burnaby, BC, Canada V5A 1S6. **EMAIL** donald_todd@sfu.ca

TODD, VIRGIL H.
PERSONAL Born 06/22/1921, Davidson Co, TN, m, 1941, 1 child **DISCIPLINE** RELIGION **EDUCATION** Bethel Col, BA, 45; Cumberland Presby Theol Sem, BD, 47; Scarritt Col, MA, 48; Vanderbilt Univ, PhD(Old Testament), 56. **CAREER** Instr, Bethel Col, 46-47, assoc, prof Bible & Relig, 52-54, prof Old Testament, Memphis Theol Sem, 54-, minister, Cumberland Presby Churches, Tenn & Ky, asst moderator, Gen Assembly, 64-65 & 79-80, moderator, Tenn Synod, 67-68; moderator, Gen Assembly, 85-86. **MEMBERSHIPS** Soc Bibl Lit. **RESEARCH** Prophetic Eschatology; the prophecy of Ezekiel. **SELECTED PUBLICATIONS** Auth, The Eschatology of Second Isaiah & Prophet Without Portfolio, Christopher, 72. **CONTACT ADDRESS** Memphis Theol Sem, 168 E Parkway S, Memphis, TN 38104-4340.

TOENJES, RICHARD H.
DISCIPLINE PHILOSOPHY, BUSINESS ETHICS **EDUCATION** St Louis Univ, BA, 66, MA, 67; Univ Southern CA, PhD, 77. **CAREER** Assoc prof, Univ NC, Charlotte. **MEMBERSHIPS** Phi Kappa Phi. **RESEARCH** Moral motivation in business ethics; existentialist notions of freedom and commitment. **SELECTED PUBLICATIONS** Auth, Toward A Critical Habit of Mind: The Course in Critical Thinking at UNC-Charlotte, APA Newsl on Tchg Philos, 87; coauth, Integrating Liberal Learning into Technical Education, Thought and Action, Vol V, No 2, 89; The Engineer and The Societal Dilemma: A Team Taught Interdisciplinary Approach, 1990 ASEE-SE Sect Proc, Apr, 90; auth, Virtue and Ethics in Business: Seminar Case Studies, Kendall/Hunt, 97. **CONTACT ADDRESS** Dept of Philosophy, Univ of No Carolina, Charlotte, Charlotte, NC 28223-0001. **EMAIL** rhtoenje@email.uncc.edu

TOLCHIN, SUSAN JANE
PERSONAL Born 01/14/1941, New York, NY, m, 1965, 2 children **DISCIPLINE** POLITICAL SCIENCE **EDUCATION** Bryn Mawr Col, BA, 61; Univ Chicago, MA, 62; New York Univ, PhD, 68. **CAREER** Asst prof to prof, Public Administration, 78-98, prof Public Policy, George Washington Univ, 98-. **HONORS AND AWARDS** Marshall Dimock Awd, Am Soc for Public Administration, 97. **MEMBERSHIPS** Nat Academy of Public Administration; Am Soc for Public Administration; Am Political Science Asn. **RESEARCH** US competiveness and trade policy; US government; Congress. **SELECTED PUBLICATIONS** Co-auth, Buying Into America-How Foreign Money is Changing the Face of Our Nation, Times Books/ Random House, 88, Berkeley paperback ed, 89, new paperback ed, Farragut Pubs, 93, Taiwan & Japan eds, 89, Korean ed, 90; co-auth, Selling Our Security-The Erosion of America's Assets, Alfred A Knopf, 92, Penguin paperback, 93; auth, Halting the Erosion of America's Critical Assets, Issues in Science and Technology, J of the Nat Academy of Sciences, vol IX, no 3, spring 93; Women in the US Congress and Jeanette Rankin, published in The Encyclopedia of the United States Congress, Simon & Schuster, 94; The Angry American-How Voter Rage is Changing the Nation, Westview/HarperCollins, 96; Missles to Plowshares: The Switch from War to Peace, J of Socio-Economics, vol 25, no 4, 96; The Globalist from Nowhere: Making Governance Competitive in the International Environment, Public Administration Rev, Jan/Feb 96, vol 56, no 1 (Received the Marshall Dimock award for the best lead article of the Public Administration Review for 1996, annual convention, Am Soc Public Admin, Philadelphia, PA, July 97). **CONTACT ADDRESS** Inst of Public Policy, George Mason Univ, Fairfax, Fairfax, VA 22030. **EMAIL** stolchi1@gmu.edu

TOLLEFSON, CHRIS
DISCIPLINE LAW **EDUCATION** Queen's Univ, BA, 82; Univ Victoria, LLB, 85; Osgoode Hall Law Sch, LLM, 93. **CAREER** Law, Univ Victoria **HONORS AND AWARDS** Exec dir, Univ Victoria Environ Law Centre. **MEMBERSHIPS** Chair, Sierra Legal Defense Fund **SELECTED PUBLICATIONS** Auth, The Wealth of Forests: Markets, Regulation and Sustainable Forestry, Univ British Columbia, 89; pubs on environmental law. **CONTACT ADDRESS** Fac of Law, Univ of Victoria, Begbie Bldg, Rm 235, PO Box 2400, Victoria, BC, Canada V8W 3H7. **EMAIL** ctollef@uvic.ca

TOLLIVER, RICHARD LAMAR
PERSONAL Born 06/26/1945, Springfield, OH, d **DISCIPLINE** THEOLOGY **EDUCATION** Miami Univ, Oxford, OH, BA, religion, 1967; Boston Univ, Boston, MA, MA, Afro-American Studies, 1971; Episcopal Divinity School, Cambridge, MA, Master of Divinity, 1971; Howard Univ, Washington, DC, PhD, political science, 1982; Boston Univ, Boston, MA, political science, 1986. **CAREER** St Cyprian's Church, Boston, MA, rector, 72-77; St Timothy's Church, Washington, DC, rector, 77-84; US Peace Corps, Kenya, assoc country dir, 84-86; US Peace Corps, Mauritania, country dir, 86-88; Howard Univ, Washington, DC, prof, 88-89; St Edmund's Episcopal Church, Chicago, IL, rector, 89-. **HONORS AND AWARDS** Fellowship for Doctoral Studies, Natl Science Foundation, 1979-82; Distinguished Service Awd, St Augustine's Coll, 1983; Regional Finalist, White House Fellowship, 1983; Distinguished Achievement Medal, Miami University, 1996. **MEMBERSHIPS** Natl Conference of Black Political Scientists, 1982-; Beta Boule, Sigma Pi Phi Fraternity, 1991-; Omega Psi Phi Fraternity, 1968-; pres, St Edmund's Redevt Corp, 1989-; natl bd of dir, Union of Black Episcopalians; vice pres, board of directors, St Edmund's Academy; board of directors of trustees, Bennett College. **CONTACT ADDRESS** Priest, St. Edmund's Episcopal Church, 6105 South Michigan Avenue, Chicago, IL 60637.

TOMARCHIO, JOHN
PERSONAL Born 08/08/1962, Brooklyn, NY **DISCIPLINE** PHILOSOPHY **EDUCATION** Columbia Univ, BA, 84; MA, 94, PhD, 96, Catholic Univ of Amer. **CAREER** NEH Fel, 96-98, Core Curriculum, Boston Univ; Asst Prof, 98-, Villanova Univ. **HONORS AND AWARDS** Natl Fulbright Fel, Milan-Rome, 94-95. **MEMBERSHIPS** Amer Phil Assoc; Amer Catholic Phil Assoc; Societe Intl Pour L'Etude De la Philosophie Medievale; Soc for Medieval & Renaissance Phil; Soc for Ancient Greek Phil. **RESEARCH** Classical Metaphysics; Thomas Acquinas; History of philosophy **SELECTED PUBLICATIONS** Auth, Four Indices for the Thomistic Axiom: Omne quod recipitur in aliquo recipitur in eo secundum modum recipientis, Medieval Studies 60 (98); Thomistic Axiomatics in an Age of Computers, History of Philosphy Quarterly 16 (99); auth, "Aquinas's Division of Being According to Modes of Existing," Rev of Metaphysics, forthcoming. **CONTACT ADDRESS** Dept of Philosophy, Villanova Univ, 800 Lancaster Ave., Villanova, PA 19085-1699. **EMAIL** john.tomarchio@villanova.edu

TOMINAGA, THOMAS T.
PERSONAL Born Pago Pago, American Samoa **DISCIPLINE** PHILOSOPHY **EDUCATION** San Francisco State Univ, BA, 63; Fisk Univ, MA, 65; Georgetown Univ, PhD(philos), 73. **CAREER** Asst prof, 71-79, ASSOC PROF PHILOS, UNIV NEV, LAS VEGAS, 79-, Vis prof East-West comp philos, Univ Orient Studies, Los Angeles, 73-74. **MEMBERSHIPS** Am Philos, Asn; Aristotelian Soc; Asn Asian Studies; Mind Asn; Soc Asian and Comp Philos. **RESEARCH** Analytic philosophy of language, logic, and mind; Wittgenstein-Zen Buddhism; East-West comparative philosophy. **SELECTED PUBLICATIONS** Auth, Wittgensteinian Approach to the Problem of Other Minds, Viewpoint, Winter 69; Auth, Symbols and Referents in Symbolic Logic, Int Logic Rev, 12/76; Reference and Meaning in The Language of Sensation, Lektos, Fall 77; Wittgenstein's Tractatus and Buddhist Four-Fold Logic, Proc Second Int Wittgenstein Symp, 78; Possibility of a Taoist-Like Wittgensteinian Environmental Ethics, J Chinese Philosophy, Vol 21, 94; Coauth, Iris Murdoch and Muriel Spark: A Bibliography, Scarecrow, 76. **CONTACT ADDRESS** Dept of Philos, Univ of Nevada, Las Vegas, 4505 Maryland Pkwy, Las Vegas, NV 89154.

TOMLINS, CHRISTOPHER L.
PERSONAL Born 04/02/1951, Beaconsfield, England, m, 1980, 2 children **DISCIPLINE** HISTORY; LEGAL STUDIES **EDUCATION** Oxford Univ, BA, 73; Sussex Univ, MA, 74; Oxford Univ, MA, 77; Jonhs Hopkins Univ, MA, 77; PhD, 81. **CAREER** La Trobe Univ, lectr, 80-85; sr lectr, 86-88; reader, 89-94; res fel, Am Bar Found, 92-96; sr res fel, 96- . **HONORS AND AWARDS** Fulbrigh Fel, 75; Am Bar Found Legal Hist Fel, 84; Am Hist Asoc Littleton-Griswold Fund Fel, 88; Erwin W. Surrency Prize, Am Soc for Legal Hist, 89; James willard Hurst Pirze of the Law and Soc Asoc, 94; Littleton-Griswold Prize of the Am Hist Asoc and the Am Soc for Legal Hist, 94. **MEMBERSHIPS** Am Hist Asoc; Orgn of Am Hist; Econ Hist Asoc; Am Soc for Legal Hist. **RESEARCH** American legal history and the history of legal culture, 16th-20th centuries; history of work and labor. **SELECTED PUBLICATIONS** Auth, Law, Labor, and Ideology in the Early American Republic, 93; auth, How Who Rides Whom: Recent 'New' Histories of American Labor Law and What They May Signify, Social Hist, 95; auth, Subordination, Authority, Law: Subjects in Labor History, Int Labor and Working Class Hist, 95; auth, Why Wait for Industrialism? An Historiographical Argument, Labor Hist, 99; co-ed with Bruce H. Mann, The Many Legalities of Early American, forthcoming. **CONTACT ADDRESS** American Bar Foundation, 750 N Lake Shore Dr, Chicago, IL 60611. **EMAIL** clt@abfn.org

TOMLINSON, JOHN G.
DISCIPLINE LAW **EDUCATION** Univ Redlands, BA, 66; Univ Calif, Irvine, MA, 68; Univ Southern Calif, PhD, 74. **CAREER** Assoc dean, Univ Southern Calif. **RESEARCH** Graduate relations, development, and activities central to the "Campaign for the Second Century." **SELECTED PUBLICATIONS** Auth, "James Brown Scott, Intelligent Minds, and the Founding of a Law School of Permanent Character," USC Law 2 (95); auth, "From the Beginning . . . USC Law School: Largely a Student's School: The Idea of Association," USC Law 2 (96); auth, "The Origins of the Hale Moot Court," USC Law 10 (96); auth, "Shoulder to Shoulder: Litta Belle Hibben Campbell and Women of the USC Law School During the Early Years," USC Law 6 (97); auth, "Surmounting the Prejudices: Four Lives in Legal Education, Community Lawyering, and Philanthropy," USC Law 11, (97); auth, "Four Lives," USC Trojan Family Magazine 34 (98); auth, "Benchmarks: The USC Law School and Its Judicial Relationships," USC Law 6 (98); auth, "Frank Monroe Porter and a Law School of Permanence," USC Law 4 (99); auth, "Intellectual Adventures: A Century of Faculty Thought and a Law School Permanent in Nature," USC Law 4 (00) **CONTACT ADDRESS** School of Law, Univ of So California, University Park Campus, Los Angeles, CA 90089. **EMAIL** ttomlins@law.usc.edu

TONG, LIK KUEN
PERSONAL Born 10/26/1935, Hong Kong, m, 1969, 3 children **DISCIPLINE** PHILOSOPHY, RELIGION **EDUCATION** NYork Univ, BS, 58; New Sch Social Res, PhD, 69. **CAREER** Asst prof, 67-74, assoc prof, 74-80, Prof Philos, Fairfield Univ, 80 -. **HONORS AND AWARDS** Outstanding Educator of America, Outstanding Educrs Am, 75. **MEMBERSHIPS** Am Philos Asn; Soc Asian & comp Philos; Asn Asian Studies; Soc Study Process Philos; Int Soc Chinese Philos; Int Inst for Field-Being. **RESEARCH** Metaphysics; comparative culture and philsophy; history of thought. **SELECTED PUBLICATIONS** Auth, The word and other poems, China Cult Enterprise Co, 69; Confucian jen and platonic eros: A comparative study, 9/73 & Care, wonder, and the polarization of being: An essay on human destiny, 9/74, Chinese Cult, Taipei; The concept of time in Whitehead and the I Ching, 9/74 & The meaning of philosophical silence: Some reflections on the use of language in Chinese thought, 3/76, J Chinese Philos; Context and reality: A critical interpretation of Whitehead's philosophy of organism (Chinese), China Soc Sci Press, 98. **CONTACT ADDRESS** Dept of Philos, Fairfield Univ, 1073 N Benson Rd, Fairfield, CT 06430-5195. **EMAIL** lktong@fair1.fairfield.edu

TONG, ROSEMARIE
PERSONAL Born 07/19/1947, Chicago, IL, m, 1992, 2 children **DISCIPLINE** PHILOSOPHY **EDUCATION** Marygrove Col, BA, 70; Catholic Univ, MA, 71; Temple Univ, PhD, 78. **CAREER** Asst, assoc prof, philos, Williams Col, 78-88; vis prof, hum, 88-89, prof medical hum and philos, 89-98, Davidson Col ; vis prof philos and women's stud, Lafayette Col, 93; prof, liberal arts dept, Univ Miss, 98; dist prof health care ethics, Univ NCar, Charlotte, 99-. **HONORS AND AWARDS** Teacher of the year, Williams Col, 82; Carnegie Found Prof of the Year, 86; hon DLaws, Marygrove Col, 87; hon DHL, SUNY Oneonta, 93; listed, Who's Who in American Education, Who's Who in the South and Southwest, Who's Who in America. **MEMBERSHIPS** Bioethics Resource Group; North Am Soc for Social Philos; Soc for Health and Human Values; North Am Soc for Social Philos; APA; Am Asn of Bioethics; Am Asn of Philos Tchrs; Am Asn of Univ Women; Am Legal Stud Asn; Am Soc of Law, Medicine, and Ethics; Am Soc for Polit and Legal Philos; Am Soc for Value Inquiry; Asn for Practical and Prof Ethics; Nat Coun for Res on Women; Nat Inst for Healthcare Res; Nat Women Stud Asn; Int Asn of Bioethics; Int Asn for Philos of Law and Social Philos; Int Soc for Value Inquiry. **RESEARCH** Feminist thought; bioethics; healthcare policy; professional and applied ethics. **SELECTED PUBLICATIONS** Auth, Feminine and Feminist Ethics, Wadsworth, 93; coauth, Controlling Our Reproductive Destiny: A Technological and Philosophical Perspective, MIT, 94; co-ed, Feminist Philosophy: Essential Readings in Theory, Reinterpretation, and Application, Westview, 94; auth, Unity in Diversity, Knowledge Products, 95; auth, Feminist Approaches to Bioethics, Westview, 96; co-ed, Feminist Philosophies: Problems, Theories, and Applications, Prentice-Hall, 2d ed, 97; auth, Feminist Thought: A More Comprehensive Introduction, Westview, 98. **CONTACT ADDRESS** Ctr for Prof and Appl Ethics, Dept of Philos, Univ of No Carolina, Charlotte, 9201 Univ City Blvd, Charlotte, NC 28223-0001. **EMAIL** rotong@email.uncc.edu

TOOLEY, MICHAEL J.
PERSONAL Born 03/17/1941, Toronto, ON, Canada, m, 1976, 2 children **DISCIPLINE** PHILOSOPHY **EDUCATION** Univ Toronto, BA, 64; Princeton Univ, PhD, 67. **CAREER** Asst Prof, Stanford Univ, 67-74; Res Fel, Australian Nat Univ, 74-79; Vis Assoc Prof, Univ Ut, 77; Sen Res Fel, Australian Nat Univ, 79-80; Vis Assoc Prof, Wichita State Univ, 80-81; Assoc Prof to Prof, Univ Miami, 81-83; Prof, Univ W Australia, 83-88; Sen Res Fel, Australian Nat Univ, 88-92; Prof, Univ Colo, 92-. **HONORS AND AWARDS** Woodrow Wilson Fel, 64-65; Woodrow Wilson Dissertation Fel, 66-67; Fel, Japan Soc for the Promotion of Sci, 99; Fel, Australian Acad of the Humanities; Excellence in Res Awd, Boulder, 98-99. **MEMBERSHIPS** Am Philos Asn; Australian Acad of the Humanities, Australasian Asn of Philos. **RESEARCH** My primary research interests are in the areas of metaphysics, epistemology, philosophy of religion, and ethics. In metaphysics, my work has been focused upon the nature of time, causation, and laws of nature. In epistemology, I am interested in problems connected with our knowledge of the physical world and other minds, and in

the classical problem of induction. In philosophy of religion, my primary focus is upon the rationality of theistic belief. In ethics, my research is concerned with issues in the areas of medical ethics, and sexual morality. **SELECTED PUBLICATIONS** Auth, "The Nature of Causation: A Singularist Account," Can J of Philos, (90): 271-232; auth, "Causation: Reductionism Versus Realism," Philos and Phenomenol Res, (90): 215-236; co-ed, Causation, Oxford Univ Press, 93; auth, Time, Tense, and Causation, Oxford Univ Press, 97; ed, Analytical Metaphysics, Garland Pub, 99; auth, La natura del tempo, McGraw-Hill, 99. **CONTACT ADDRESS** Dept Philos, Univ of Colorado, Boulder, 2595 Univ Heights Ave, Boulder, CO 80302. **EMAIL** Michael.Tooley@colorado.edu

TOOTE, GLORIA E. A.
PERSONAL Born 11/08/1931, New York, NY **DISCIPLINE** LAW **EDUCATION** Howard Univ School Law, JD 1954; Columbia Univ Graduate School Law, LLM, 1956. **CAREER** Natl Affairs Section Time Magazine, former mem; NYC, Prac law 1954-71; Toote Town Publs Inc, pres; Action Agency Off Volunteer Action Liaison, asst director 1971-73; Dept Housing & Urban Devel, asst sec 1973-75; author & lecturer; NYC, presently engaged in practice of law; Trea Estates & Enter Inc, pres, currently. **HONORS AND AWARDS** Newsmakers Awd, Nat Assn of Black Women Atty, NY Fed of Civil Serv Org, Navajo Tribe, Nat Assn of Real Estate Brokers, Nat Citizens Participation Counc, Nat Bar Assn; YMCA World Serv Awd, Women's Nat Rep Club, New York City Housing Auth, Res Adv Counc MA-CT-NY-NJ, Pol Ldrshp Awd, NNPA. **MEMBERSHIPS** Bd mem, Arbitrator Assn, Consumer Alert, Council of Economic Affairs for the Republic/Natl Black United Fund; cited by the following organizations, Natl Business League, Alpha Kappa Alpha Sorority, US Chamber of Commerce, Natl Newspaper Publication Assn; member, Hoover Institution on War, Revolution and Peace; Fannie Mae, bd of dirs, 1992-. **CONTACT ADDRESS** Trea Estates & Enterprises Ins, 282 W 137th St, New York, NY 10030-2407.

TOPEL, BERNADETTE
PERSONAL Born 09/16/1947, Minneapolis, MN, s **DISCIPLINE** SYSTEMATIC THEOLOGY **EDUCATION** Univ St. Michael's Col, PhD, 88. **CAREER** Instr, College St. Catherine, 77-78; instr, Fairfield Univ, 86-88; asst prof, Providence Col, 88- 97. **MEMBERSHIPS** Am Acad of Relig. **RESEARCH** Feminist theology. **CONTACT ADDRESS** 7549 E Christmas Cholla Dr., Scottsdale, AZ 85255-2731. **EMAIL** btopel@aol.com

TORELL, KURT CHARLES
PERSONAL Born 08/04/1962, Stockton, CA, m, 1991, 2 children **DISCIPLINE** PHILOSOPHY **EDUCATION** Boston Univ, BA, 83; Duquesne Univ, MA, 85, PhD, 92; Univ Pitt, MA, 87. **CAREER** Asst Prof, Assoc Prof, Dir, 94-, Lewis Clark State College. **HONORS AND AWARDS** Eugene Baldeck Awd; SAS Awd Teaching Excellence. **MEMBERSHIPS** Hume Soc; APA. **RESEARCH** Modern Philosophy, Native American Philosophy, Environmental Ethics. **SELECTED PUBLICATIONS** Auth, Socrates Meets Two Coyotes, J of Philo Res, 00. **CONTACT ADDRESS** Lewis-Clark State Col, 500 8th Ave, Lewiston, ID 83501. **EMAIL** ktorell@lcsc.edu

TORIBIO, JOSEFA
PERSONAL Born 10/07/1961, Spain, m, 1991 **DISCIPLINE** PHILOSOPHY **EDUCATION** Complutense Univ, Madrid Spain, BA, 84, Pedagogical Qual, 85, MA, 85, PhD cum laude, 88. **CAREER** GAT, 85-88, asst prof, 89-93, Compulutense Univ; asst prof Washington Univ, St. Louis, MO, 93-. **HONORS AND AWARDS** Fellowship DAAD, Dusseldorf, Ger; Fleming Fel, Univ Sussex, Brighton UK **MEMBERSHIPS** APA, SSLMPS **RESEARCH** Philo Mind; Cog Science. **SELECTED PUBLICATIONS** Auth, Meaning and Other Non-Biological Categories, Philo Papers, 88; Language in the World, A Philosophical Inquiry Max J. Cresswell, Philo Psychology, 95; Ruritania and Ecology: Reply to Ned Block, Philo Issues, 95; Pulp Naturalism, Il Cannocchiale Rivista di Studi Filosofici, Twin Pleas: Probing Content and Compositionally Philo and Pheno Research, 97; Ecological Content Prag and Cog, 97; auth, "Pulp Naturaloism," Invited Contrubution to a special issue on Philosophy of Mind and Cognitive Science of Il Cannocchiale, Rivista di Studi Filosofici, 2, (97), 185-195; auth, "The Implicit Conception of Implicit Conceptions: Reply to Christopher Peacocke," Philosophical Issues, 9, (98), 115-120; auth, "Meaning, Dispostions, and Normativity," Minds and Machines, 9, (99), 399-413; auth, "Extruding Intentionality from the Metaphysical Flux," Journal of Experimental and theoretical Ai, 11, (99), 501-518; auth, "Modularity, Relativism, and Neural Constructivism," Cognitive Science Quarterly, vol. 3, (01), forthcoming. **CONTACT ADDRESS** Dept of Philosophy, Washington Univ, One Brookings Dr, Campus PO Box 1073, Saint Louis, MO 63130. **EMAIL** pepa@twinearth.wustl.edu

TORJESEN, KAREN JO
PERSONAL Born 10/10/1945, San Francisco, CA, d, 1 child **DISCIPLINE** RELIGION **EDUCATION** Claremont Grad Sch, PhD, 82. **CAREER** George August Gottingen Germany, asst prof, 78-82; Mary Washington Col, asst prof, 82-85; Fuller Theol Sem, assoc prof, 85-87; Claremont Grad Univ, prof, 87-. **MEMBERSHIPS** ASCH, AAR. **RESEARCH** Hist Christianity; gender sexuality; women's hist. **SELECTED PUBLICATIONS** Auth, Hermeneutical Procedure and Theological Structure in Origen's Exegesis, Patristische Texte and Untersuchungen, Deutsche Akademie der Wissenschaft, Berlin: de Gruyter, 85; auth, When Women Were Priests: Women's leadership in the Early Church and the Scandal of their Subordination in the Rise of Christianity, Harper/Collins: San Francisco, 93; auth, Als Frauen noch Priesterinnen waren, Frankfurt: Zweitausendeins Verlag, 95; auth, In Praise of Noble Women: Gender and Honor in Ascetic Texts, in: Discursive Formations, Ascetic Piety and the Interpretation of Early Christian Literature, ed., V.Wimbush, Atlanta Press, 92; auth, Martyrs, Ascetics and Gnostics: Gender Crossing in Early Christianity, in: Gender Reversals, ed., S. Ramet, NY: Routledge, forthcoming. **CONTACT ADDRESS** Dept of Religion, Claremont Graduate Sch, Claremont, CA 91711. **EMAIL** karen.torjesen@cgu.edu

TORNELL, AARON
PERSONAL Born, Mexico **DISCIPLINE** ECONOMICS **EDUCATION** ITAM, BA; MIT, PhD. **CAREER** Assoc prof, Harvard Univ; assoc prof, UCLA. **MEMBERSHIPS** NBER; AEA. **CONTACT ADDRESS** Dept Econ, Univ of California, Los Angeles, 8283 Bunche, Box 951477, Los Angeles, CA 90095-1477. **EMAIL** tornell@econ.ucla.edu

TORNQUIST, LEROY J.
DISCIPLINE CIVIL PROCEDURE, EVIDENCE, NEGOTIATION, TRIAL & APPELLATE PRACTICE **EDUCATION** Northwestern Univ, BS, 62; JD, 65. **CAREER** Assoc, Williams, McCarthy & Kinley, Rockford, Ill, 65-66; partner, King, Robin, Gale & Pillinger, Chicago, 66-71; assoc dean, Loyola Univ, 71-77; vis prof, McGeorge Univ, 77-78; prof, 78-; dean, 78-87. **HONORS AND AWARDS** Ch, Proc & Reg Comm, Park Ridge, Ill, 71; officer, Ore Symphony of Salem, 91- 94. **MEMBERSHIPS** Member & Speakers Comm, Salem City Club, 93-. **SELECTED PUBLICATIONS** Co-auth, Trial Diplomacy. **CONTACT ADDRESS** Sch of Law, Willamette Univ, 900 State St, Salem, OR 97301. **EMAIL** ltornqui@willamette.edu

TORRAGO, LORETTA
DISCIPLINE PHILOSOPHY **EDUCATION** New York Univ, BA, 89; Cornell Univ, PhD, 96. **CAREER** Asst Prof, 96-, Univ Utah **CONTACT ADDRESS** Dept of Philosophy, Univ of Utah, 341 Orson, Salt Lake City, UT 84112. **EMAIL** l.torrago@m.cc.utah.edu

TORRES, SAM
PERSONAL Born 01/07/1946, TX, m, 1975, 1 child **DISCIPLINE** CRIMINAL JUSTICE **EDUCATION** Claremont Grad Sch, PhD, 83. **CAREER** US Probation Off, 73-95; prof, Cal State Univ, 95-. **MEMBERSHIPS** ASS; ACJS; ACA; APPA. **RESEARCH** Probation; parole; drug abuse; corrections; drug courts. **SELECTED PUBLICATIONS** Co auth, Encyclopedic Dictionary of Criminology, Copperhouse Pub (97); auth, "Has the Privatization Concept been Successful?", in Controversial Issues in Corrections, by Charles Fields (Allyn and Bacon Pub, 99); auth, "Drug-Involved Adult Offenders: Community Supervision Strategies and Considerations, Am Probation & Parole Asn (99); auth, "Hate Crimes Against African-Americans: Extent of Problem," J Contem Crim Just 15 (99); auth, "Early Termination: Outdated Concept in an Era of Punitiveness," Fed Prob (99); coauth, "Choosing the Probation & Parole Officer Substance-Abuse Specialist," J Offender Monitoring (00); coauth, "Probation and Parole Officer Style and Substance Abusing Offenders," Offender Prog Rep (00); coauth, "Selecting the Substance-Abuse Specialist," Fed Prob J (00); auth, "Monitoring Prescription Medication Use Among Substance-Abusing Offenders," Fed Prob J (98); coauth, "An Evaluation of Operation Roundup: An Experiment in the Control of Gangs to Reduce Crime, Fear of Crime, and Improve Police Community Relations," Policing: Intl J Police Strategies & Manage 21 (98); coauth, "A Process Evaluation of Drug Courts in Los Angeles County." Just Sys J 19 (98); coauth, "A Comparative Analysis of Community Policing and Crime Reduction in a Vietnamese and Latino Neighborhood," Policing: Intl J Police Strat Manage (pending); coauth, "Pre and Posttest Differences Between Vietnamese and Latino Residents Involved in a Community Policing Experiment," Policing: An Intl J Police Strat Manage (pending); coauth, "Training the Substance-Abuse Specialist," Fed Prob J (pending). **CONTACT ADDRESS** Criminal Justice, California State Univ, Long Beach, 1250 Bellflower Blvd, Long Beach, CA 90840-0001. **EMAIL** storres@csulb.edu

TORRES-GREGORY, WANDA
DISCIPLINE PHILOSOPHY **EDUCATION** Univ PR, BA, MA; Boston Univ, PhD. **CAREER** Part-time asst prof; tchr of the Yr Nomination, Suffolk Univ, 96. **RESEARCH** Latin Am philos; philos of lang; logic; 20th century philos. **SELECTED PUBLICATIONS** Auth, Traditional Language and Technological Language, a translations of Uberlieferte Sprache und Technische Sprache, 96; Heidegger y Quine: La posibilidad de un dialogo, in Dialogos 64, 94; Indeterminacy of Translation/Subdeterminacy of Theory: A Critique, in Dialogos 53, 89; The Question in Latin American Philosophy, a presentation to the Philos Dept, Simmons Col, 96; Martin Heidegger: Language and Technology, a presentation to the Philos Soc, Suffolk Univ, 95. **CONTACT ADDRESS** Dept of Philos, Simmons Col, 300 The Fenway, Boston, MA 02115.

TOULOUSE, MARK G.
PERSONAL Born 02/01/1952, Des Moines, IA, m, 1976, 3 children **DISCIPLINE** AMERICAN RELIGIOUS HISTORY **EDUCATION** Howard Payne Univ, BA, 74; Southwestern Baptist Theol Sem, MDiv, 77; Univ Chicago, PhD, 84. **CAREER** Instr, relig stud, Ill Benedictine Col, 80-82, asst prof, 82-84; asst prof of hist, Phillips Univ Grad Sem, 84-86; asst prof, Brite Divinity Sch, Texas Chr Univ,86-89, assoc prof, 89-91, assoc dean, 91-94, prof, 94- 99; Prof and Dean, 99-. **HONORS AND AWARDS** Henry Luce III Fel, 97-98; Who's Who in Relig, 89-90, 92-93; Men of Achievement, 93; Who's Who in Am Educ, 96-97. **MEMBERSHIPS** Am Acad Relig; Am Soc of Church Hist; Disciples of Christ Hist Soc. **RESEARCH** American theology; American religion and culture; history of Christian Church (Disciples of Christ). **SELECTED PUBLICATIONS** Auth, The Christian Century and American Public Life: The Crucial Years,1956-1968, in New Dimensions in Modern American Religious History, 93; auth, A Case Study: Christianity Today and American Public Life, in J of Church and State, 93; auth, W.A. Criswell, in Dictionary of Baptists in America, 94; auth, The Braunschweiger-Bibfeldts: the Metaphysical Incarnation of Wo/Man, in The Unrelieved Paradox, 94; auth, The Christian Church (Disciples of Christ), in Encyclopedia Americana, 94; auth, What is the Role of a Denomination in a Post-Denominational Age, in Lexington Theol Q, 94; auth, Sojourners, in Popular Religious Magazines of the United States, 95; auth, several entries in Encylopedia of Religious Controversies in the United States, 97; auth, The Problem and Promise of Denominational History, in Discipliana, 97; auth, Joined in Discipleship: The Shaping of Contemporary Disciples Identity, Chalice, rev ed, 97; coed, Makers of Christian Theology in America, Abingdon, 97; auth, "The Transformation of John Foster Dulles," Mercer University Press, 85; coed, "Sources of Christian Theology in America," Abingdon, 99; ed, "Walter Scott: A Nineteenh-Century Evangelical, Chalice," 99. **CONTACT ADDRESS** Brite Divinity School, Texas Christian Univ, TCU Box 298130, Fort Worth, TX 76129. **EMAIL** m.toulouse@tcu.edu

TOWNER, WAYNE SIBLEY
PERSONAL Born 01/10/1933, Scottsbluff, NE, m, 1956, 2 children **DISCIPLINE** RELIGION, PHILOLOGY **EDUCATION** Yale Univ, BA, 54, BD, 60, MA, 61, PhD, 65. **CAREER** Eng tchr, Gerard Inst, Sidon, Lebanon, 54-57; instr Old Testament, Princeton Theol Sem, 63-64; lectr, divinity sch, Yale Univ, 64-65, asst prof 65-69, assoc prof Old Testament, 69-71; prof & dean Theol Sem, Univ Dubuque, 71-75; Prof Old Testament, Union Theol Sem, Richmond, Va, 75-, Dean, 85-88. **HONORS AND AWARDS** First Prize, Theology Category, Harper Collins Annual Best Sermons Awd, 87; Second Prize, Christian Ministry, Alfred P Klausner Sermon Awd, 97; Doctor of Div, Coe College, 00. **MEMBERSHIPS** Soc Bibl Lit. **RESEARCH** Old Testament; rabbinic lit. **SELECTED PUBLICATIONS** Auth, The Rabbinic Enumeration of Scriptural Examples, Brill, Leiden, 73; How God Deals with Evil, Westminster, 76; Daniel, Westminster John Knox, 84; Genesis, Westminster Bible Companion, 01. **CONTACT ADDRESS** 3401 Brook Rd, Richmond, VA 23227-4514. **EMAIL** stowner@union-psc.edu

TOWNES, EMILIE M.
PERSONAL Born 08/01/1955, Durham, NC, s **DISCIPLINE** CHRISTIAN ETHICS **EDUCATION** Univ Chicago, BA, 77; AM, 79; D Min, 82; Northwestern Univ, PhD, 89. **CAREER** Instr, DePaul Univ, 88-89; asst prof, St. Paul Sch Theol, 89-94; assoc prof, 94-98; prof, 98-99; prof, Union Theol Sem, 99- . **HONORS AND AWARDS** ATS Younger Scholars Awd. **MEMBERSHIPS** Am Acad of Relig; Soc of Christian Ethics; Soc for the Study of Black Relig; Soc for the Study of Higher Values in Educ. **RESEARCH** Christian Ethics; Womanist Ethics; Critical Social Theory; Cultural theory and studies; Postmodernism and social postmodernism. **SELECTED PUBLICATIONS** Auth, Womanist Justice, Womanist Hope, 93; auth, A Troubling in My Soul: Womanist Perspectives of Evil and Suffering, 93; auth, In a Blaze of Glory: Womanist Spirituality as Social Witness, 95; ed, Embracing the Spirit: Womanist Perspectives on Hope, Salvation, and Transformation, 97; auth, Breaking the Fine Rain of Death: African American Health Care and a Womanist Ethic of Care, forthcoming. **CONTACT ADDRESS** Union Theol Sem, New York, 3041 Broadway, New York, NY 10027. **EMAIL** emtownes@uts.columbia.edu

TOWNS, ELMER
PERSONAL Born 10/21/1932, Savannah, GA, m, 1953, 3 children **DISCIPLINE** RELIGION **EDUCATION** Northwestern Col, Minneapolis, Minn, BA; Southern Meth Univ, Dallas, Tex, MA; Dallas Theol Sem, Dallas, Tex, THM; Garrett Theol Sem, Evanston, Ill, MRE; Fuller Theol Sem, Pasadena, Calif, D min. **CAREER** Distinguished prof, Systematic Theol, 71-; dean, Sch of Relig, Liberty Univ, Lynchburg, Va, 71-. **HONORS AND AWARDS** Dr of Literature, Calif Grad Sch of Theol; Dr. of Divinity, Bapt Bible Col, Springfield, Mo, Gold Medallion, Evang

Publ Asn, 95. **MEMBERSHIPS** Evang Theol Soc; N Amer Soc of Church Growth. **RESEARCH** Evangelism; Spirituality. **SELECTED PUBLICATIONS** Auth, Rivers Of Revival, Regal Books, 97; Stories On The Front Porch, Regal Books, 97; Worship Wars, Broadman-Holman, 96; A Journey Through the Old Testament, Harcourt Brace, 96; A Journey Through the New Testament, Harcourt Brace, 96; A Practical Encyclopedia: Evangelism & Church Growth, Regal Books, 95; The Eight Laws of Leadership, Church Growth Inst, 94; Ten Sunday Schools That Dared to Change, Regal Books, 93; Town's Sunday School Encyclopedia, Tyndale House, 93. **CONTACT ADDRESS** Liberty Univ, 1971 University Blvd., Lynchburg, VA 24502. **EMAIL** eltowns@liberty.edu

TOWNSEND, DABNEY W., JR.
DISCIPLINE PHILOSOPHY **EDUCATION** Emory Univ, PhD, 70. **CAREER** Asst prof, eng and philos, Catawba Col, 69-73; asst, assoc, prof, philos, Univ Texas, Arlington, 73-97; dean, Col of Arts and Sciences, Armstrong Atlantic State Univ, 97- . **HONORS AND AWARDS** Phi Beta Kappa. **MEMBERSHIPS** Am Soc for Aesthet; Int Aesthet Soc; APA. **RESEARCH** Aesthetics; eighteenth century British philosophy; philosophy of language. **SELECTED PUBLICATIONS** Auth, Hutcheson and Complex Ideas: A Reply to Peter Kivy, J of Aesthet and Art Criticism, 93; auth, The Aesthetics of Joseph Priestley, J of Aesthet and Art Criticism, 93; auth, Metaphor, Hermeneutics, and Situations, in Hahn, ed, Philos of Paul Ricoeur, Open Court, 95; auth, Beauty, in Barbanell, ed, Encyclopedia of Empiricism, Greenwood, 97; auth, The Picturesque, J of Aesthet and Art Criticism, 97; auth, Aesthetics: Classic Readings from the Western Tradition, Wadsworth, 97; auth, An Introduction to Aesthetics, Basil Blackwell, 97; contribur, Kelly, ed, Encyclopedia of Aesthetics, Oxford, 98; contribur, Budd, ed, Routledge Encyclopedia of Philosophy: Aesthetics, Routledge, 98; contribur, Haldane, ed, Routledge Encyclopedia of Philosophy: Modern Philosophers II (Eighteenth Century), Routledge, 98; auth, Eighteenth-Century British Aesthetics, Baywood, 98; auth, Hume's Aesthetic Theory, Routledge, 00. **CONTACT ADDRESS** College of Arts and Sciences, Armstrong Atlantic State Univ, Savannah, GA 31419. **EMAIL** townseda@pirates.armstrong.edu

TRACTENBERG, PAUL L.
PERSONAL Born 06/03/1938, Newark, NJ, m, 1978, 3 children **DISCIPLINE** LAW **EDUCATION** Wesleyan Univ, BA, 60; Univ Mich Law Sch, JD, 63. **CAREER** Atty, Sullivan and Cromwell, NY, 64-65; assoc gen coun, Peace Corps, Washington, DC, 65-67; coun, Governor's Comt Rev Civil Rights Laws, NY, 67-68; atty, Fried, Frank et al, NY, 68-70; assoc prof law, 70-78, Prof Law, Rutgers Law Sch, 78-, Spec coun, New York City Bd Educ, 68-70 and Comn Human Rights, 70-71; dir, Educ Law Ctr Inc, Newark, 73-76; consult official field reader, Nat Inst Educ, 74-79; consult, Chicano Educ Proj 79- and Israeli Ministry Educ and Cult, 81-82; vis prof, Law Fac, Hebrew Univ, Jerusalem, 81-82; CHMN BD, EDUC LAW CTR, 82- **RESEARCH** Impact of courts on educational reform; use of competency testing in public education; education of the handicapped and disadvantaged. **SELECTED PUBLICATIONS** Auth, Current School Problems, Practising Law Inst, 70; Selection of Teachers and Supervisors in Urban School Systems, 72 and Testing the Teacher, 73, Agathon Press; Reforming School Finance Through State Constitutions: Robinson V Cahill Points The Way, Rutgers Law Rev, 27: 365; Ne Role Of The Courts And Teacher Certification in Legal Issues in Teacher Preparation and Certification, Eric Clearing House Teacher Educ, 6/77; Testing for Minimum Competency: A Legal Analysis in Minimum Competency Achievement Testing: Motives, Models, Measures and Consequences, McCutchan P, 80; Legal Implications of Performance Testing in Vocational Education: An Overview--Performance Testing: Issues Facing Vocational Education, Nat Ctr Res Voc Educ, 80; A Clear and Powerful Voice for Poor Urban Students--Chief-Justice Wilentz, Robert Role, Rutgers Law Rev, Vol 49, 97; coauth, Pupil testing: A legal view, Phi Delta Kappan, 59: 249. **CONTACT ADDRESS** Law Sch, Rutgers, The State Univ of New Jersey, Newark, 123 Washington St, Newark, NJ 07102-3192. **EMAIL** tractnbg@andromeda.rutgers.edu

TRAMMELL, RICHARD LOUIS
PERSONAL Born 05/26/1942, Shelbyville, KY, m, 1962, 3 children **DISCIPLINE** AMERICAN PHILOSOPHY, PHILOSOPHY OF RELIGION **EDUCATION** Berea Col, BA, 64; Union theol Sem, NYork, BD, 67; Columbia Univ, PhD, 71. **CAREER** Instr philos, Morehead State Univ, 67; asst prof, 71-77, assoc prof, 77-97, Prof Philos, Grove City Col, 97-, Am Philos Soc res grant, 71. **RESEARCH** Charles Peirce. **SELECTED PUBLICATIONS** Auth, Review of Paul Ramsey's Fabricated Man, Union Sem Quart, summer 71; Religion, reason and instinct in the philosophy of C S Peirce, Transactions Charles S Peirce Soc, winter 72; Peirce's final opinion, Transactions XVth World Cong Philos; Saving life and taking time, J Philos, 3/75; Mathematics and the conventionalist assumption, Southwestern J Philos, fall 76; Tooley's moral symmetry principle, Philos Pub Affairs, spring 76; coauth, Fairness, utility and survival, Philosophy, 10/77; auth, Euthanasia and the law, J Soc Philos, 1/78. **CONTACT ADDRESS** Dept of Philos, Grove City Col, 100 Campus Dr, Grove City, PA 16127-2104.

TRAUB, GEORGE WILLIAM
PERSONAL Born 01/30/1936, Chicago, IL, s **DISCIPLINE** THEOLOGY & LITERATURE, SPIRITUALITY **EDUCATION** Xavier Univ, BLitt, 58; West Baden Col, PhL, 61; Loyola Univ Chicago, MA, 68; Cornell Univ, PhD, 73. **CAREER** Instr English, Greek & Latin, Loyola Acad, Ill, 61-64; from Asst Prof to Assoc Prof English, 72-80; Dir Formation & Continuing Educ, Chicago Prov Soc of Jesus, 80-85; Jesuit Prof Theology & Dir Ignatian Programs, Xavier Univ, 87-; **MEMBERSHIPS** Coordrs for Mission & Identity, Assoc of Jesuit Cols and Univs. **RESEARCH** Ignatian sprituality; Jesuit history & education; theology and literature. **SELECTED PUBLICATIONS** Coauth, The Desert and the City: An Interpretation of the History of Christian Spirituality, Loyola Univ Press, 84; Do You Speak Ignatian? A Glossary. . . .Jesuit Circles: 5th ed, Xavier Univ, 00. **CONTACT ADDRESS** Xavier Univ, Ohio, 3800 Victory Pky, Cincinnati, OH 45207-5185. **EMAIL** traub@xu.edu

TRAUTMAN, DONALD T.
PERSONAL Born 06/06/1924, Cleveland, OH, m, 1954, 3 children **DISCIPLINE** LAW **EDUCATION** Harvard Univ, AB and LLB, 51. **CAREER** Law clerk, 52-53; asst prof, 53-56, Prof Law, Harvard Univ, 56-, Adv to reporter, restatement second, Conflict of Laws, 55-71; Guggenheim fel, 69; MEM, US DEPT ADVISORY COMT ON PVT INT LAW, 75- **MEMBERSHIPS** Am Soc Int Law; Am Foreign Law Asn. **RESEARCH** Conflict of laws; admiralty; contracts, federal courts, computers and law. **SELECTED PUBLICATIONS** Auth, 4 Models For International Bankruptcy/, American Journal Of Comparative Law, Vol 41, 93; Some Thoughts on Choice of Law, Judicial Discretion, and the Alis Complex Litigation Project, La Law Rev, Vol 54, 94; coauth, Materials on Accounting, Found, 59; Law of Multistate Problems, Little, 65. **CONTACT ADDRESS** Law Sch, Harvard Univ, Cambridge, MA 02138.

TRAVERS, ARTHUR HOPKINS
PERSONAL Born 07/29/1936, Gary, IN, m, 1963, 2 children **DISCIPLINE** LAW **EDUCATION** Grinnel Col, BA, 57; Harvard Univ, LLB, 62. **CAREER** Asst prof law, Univ Kans, 65-68, assoc prof, 68-69, prof, 69-71; vis prof, 70-71, prof law, Univ Colo, 71-, actg dean, Law Sch, Univ Colo, 73-74, assoc dean, 74-75; fel law & econ, Law Sch, Univ Colo, 78-79. **MEMBERSHIPS** Am Bar Asn; Am Econ Asn; Selden Soc. **RESEARCH** Antitrust; law and economics; trade regulation, intellectual property. **SELECTED PUBLICATIONS** auth, articles in various law journals, 68-. **CONTACT ADDRESS** Sch of Law, Univ of Colorado, Boulder, PO Box 401, Boulder, CO 80309-0401. **EMAIL** Arthur.Travers@spot.Colorado.edu

TRAYNOR, MICHAEL
PERSONAL Born 10/25/1934, Oakland, CA, m, 1956, 3 children **DISCIPLINE** ECONOMICS; LAW **EDUCATION** Univ Calif, Berkeley, BA, 55; Harvard Law, JD, 60 **CAREER** Lctr, Univ Calif, 82-89, 96-98; partner, Cooley Godward, LLP, San Francisco, CA. **HONORS AND AWARDS** Amer Assoc for the Advance Sci Fel; Amer Bar Found Fel **MEMBERSHIPS** Am Law Inst, 00-; Bar Asn of San Fran, 73. **RESEARCH** Conflict of Laws; Intellectual Property; First Amendment. **SELECTED PUBLICATIONS** Auth, "Countering the Excessive Subpoena for Scholarly Research, Law and Contemporary Problems, Law & Contemporary Problems, 97; co-chair, "Unifying Environmental Protection in California," California EPA Unified Environmental Statute Commission, 97; auth, "Clinical Trials: Products Liability and Informed Consent," Ntl L.J., 96; auth, "The Pursuit of Happiness," 52 Vand. L. Rev. 1025, 99; auth, "An Introductory Framework for Analyzing the Proposed Hague Convention on Jurisdiction and Foreign Judgements in Civil and Commercial Matters: U.S. and European Perspectives," 6 Ann. Surv. Int'l & Comp. L., 00; auth, "Public Sanctions, Pricate Liability, and Judicial Responsibility," Willamette L. Rev., 01, (forthcoming); auth, "Some Open Questions About Attorney-Client Privilege and Work Product in a Multidisciplinary Practice," 36 Wake Forest L. Rev., 01, (forthcoming). **CONTACT ADDRESS** 1 Maritime Plaza, Ste. 2000, San Francisco, CA 94111-3580. **EMAIL** traynormt@cooley.com

TREAT, JAMES
PERSONAL Born 09/13/1962, Anadarko, OK, m, 1997 **DISCIPLINE** RELIGIOUS STUDIES **EDUCATION** Grad Theol Union, PhD, 93 **CAREER** Asst prof, Univ Calif Santa Cruz, 92-95; asst prof, Univ New Mex, 95-00. **SELECTED PUBLICATIONS** Auth, Native and Christian: Indigenous Voices on Religious Identity in the United States and Canada, Routledge, 96; auth, For this land: Writings on Religion in America by Vine Deloria, Jr., Routledge, 99. **CONTACT ADDRESS** Honors Col, Univ of Oklahoma, Norman, OK 73019.

TREDWAY, JOHN THOMAS
PERSONAL Born 09/04/1935, North Tonawanda, NY, m, 1950, 2 children **DISCIPLINE** CHURCH & INTELLECTUAL HISTORY **EDUCATION** Augustana Col, BA, 57; Univ Ill, MA, 58; Garrett Theol Sem, BD, 61; Northwestern Univ, PhD, 64. **CAREER** From asst prof to prof hist, 64-75, dean col, 70-75, pres, 75-, Augustana Col, Ill; vis prof, Waterloo Lutheran Sem, 67-68; chmn, Nat Lutheran-Methodist Theol Dialogs, 77-. **MEMBERSHIPS** Am Soc Church Historians; AHA. **RESEARCH** Nineteenth century American and British church history; modern European intellectual history. **SELECTED PUBLICATIONS** Auth, Newman: Patristics, ecumenics and liberalism, Christian Century, 65; co-ed, The Immigration of Ideas, Augustana Hist Soc, 68. **CONTACT ADDRESS** Augustana Col, Illinois, Rock Island, IL 61201.

TRESS, DARYL MCGOWAN
PERSONAL Born New York, NY, m **DISCIPLINE** PHILOSOPHY **EDUCATION** Queens Col, CUNY, BA, 74; SUNY Buffalo, PhD, 83. **CAREER** Assoc prof, philos, Fordham Univ, 94- . **HONORS AND AWARDS** Cum Laude, 74; Bunting Fellowship at The Radcliffe Institute for Advanced Studies, Harvard Univ, 00-01. **MEMBERSHIPS** Soc for Ancient Greek Philos; APA. **RESEARCH** Ancient philosophy. **SELECTED PUBLICATIONS** Auth, Relations in Plato's Timaeus, J of Neoplatonic Stud, 94; coauth, Liabilities of the Feminist Use of Narrative: A Study of Sara Ruddick's Story in Maternal Thinking, Public Affairs Q, 95; auth, The Metaphysical Science of Aristotle's Generation of Animals and Its Feminist Critics, in Ward, ed, Feminism and Ancient Philosophy, Routledge, 96; auth, Aristotle's Child: Formation Through Genesis, Oikos and Polis, Ancient Philos, 97; auth, The Philosophical Genesis of Ecology and Environmentalism, in Robinson, ed, The Greeks and the Environment, Rowman & Littlefield, 97; auth, Environmentalism's Relation to the History of Philosophy, Global Bioethics, 98; auth, "Aristotle Against the Hippocratics on sexual Generation: A Reply to Coles" Phronesis, 99; auth, "Relations and Intermediates in Plato's Timaeus" in Plato and Platonism, van Ophuisen, ed, 99; auth, Bioethics: Ancient Themes in Contemporary Issues, "Ancient and modern Reflections on medical ethics and the best interests of the sick child", Polansky, ed, 00. **CONTACT ADDRESS** Dept of Philosophy, Fordham Univ, Bronx, NY 10458. **EMAIL** tress@fordham.edu

TRESS, DARYL MCGOWEN
DISCIPLINE PHILOSOPHY **EDUCATION** SUNY/Buffalo, PhD. **CAREER** Asst prof, Fordham Univ. **RESEARCH** Ancient philos, sci and med theories of generation. **SELECTED PUBLICATIONS** Auth, The Metaphysical Science of Aristotle's Generation of Animals and Its Feminist Critics, Rev of Metaphysics, 92; Relations in Plato's Timeaeus, Jour Neoplatonic Stud, 94; co-auth, Liabilities of the Feminist Use of Narrative: A Study of Sara Ruddick's Story in Maternal Thinking, Pub Aff Quart, 95. **CONTACT ADDRESS** Dept of Philos, Fordham Univ, 113 W 60th St, New York, NY 10023.

TREUSCH, PAUL E.
PERSONAL Born Chicago, IL, 1 child **DISCIPLINE** LAW **EDUCATION** Univ Chicago, PhB, 32, JD, 35. **CAREER** Atty, pvt practice, 35-37; law fac legal res & writing, Law Sch, La State Univ, 37-38; asst chief coun, Off Chief Coun, Internal Revenue Serv, 38-70; prof law, 65-73 & 76-79, prof emeritus, 79-, Law Sch, Howard Univ; prof 73-76, prof emeritus, 76-, Sch of Law, Boston Univ; Prof Law, Sch of Law, Southwestern Univ, 79-, Prof lectr law, Law ctr, George Washington Univ, 66-72; prof lectr law, Law Ctr, George Washington, 66-72; nat pres Feb Bar Asn, 69-70; mem, House of Deligates, Am Bar Asn, 70-72; Fed Bar Found Bd, 70-; head, law firm of Winston & Strawn-DC office, 70-72; tax adv comt, Am Law Inst, 79-; special counsel to Sec of US Senate, 70-72. **MEMBERSHIPS** Am Law Inst; Am Judicature Soc; Asn Am Law Sch. **SELECTED PUBLICATIONS** Auth, Tax Exempt Charitable Organizations, Am Law Inst, 88. **CONTACT ADDRESS** 675 S Westmoreland, Los Angeles, CA 90005-3905. **EMAIL** ptreusch@swlaw.edu

TRIBE, LAURENCE HENRY
PERSONAL Born 10/10/1941, Shanghai, China, m, 1964, 2 children **DISCIPLINE** LAW, PHILOSOPHY **EDUCATION** Harvard Univ, AB, 62, JD, 66. **CAREER** Law clerk, Supreme Court Calif, 66-67 and US Supreme Court, 67-68; exec dir Technol Assessment Panel, Nat Acad Sci, 68-69; asst prof, 69-72, PROF LAW, HARVARD UNIV, 72-, Consult and mem, President's Sci Adv Comt Panel Chemicals and Health, 71-73; mem, Nat Sci Found Adv Comt Computing Activities, 71-74; mem, Nat Sci Found-Nat Endowment Humanities Adv Comt Human Value Implications of Sci and Technol, 73-; consult and mem, US Senate Comt Pub Works, 70-72; mem, Task Force Develop Regulations for Psychosurgery, 73-; chief appellate coun, Calif Energy Comn, Nuclear Moratorium Case, 79- **HONORS AND AWARDS** Coif Awd, 78; Scribe Awd, 79. **RESEARCH** Legal, constitutional and jurisprudential theory; the role of law in shaping technological development; uses and abuses of mathematical methods in policy and systems analysis. **SELECTED PUBLICATIONS** Auth, Channeling Technology Through Law, Bracton, 73; Technology assessment and the fourth discontinuity: The limits of instrumental rationality, Southern Calif Law Rev, 6/73; Foreword: Toward a model of roles in the due process of life and law, Harvard Law Rev, 11/73; The emerging reconnection of individual rights and institutional design: federalism, bureaucracy, and due process of law making, Creighton Law Rev, 3/77; Unraveling National League of Cities; The new federalism and affirmative rights to essential government services, Harvard Law Rev, 4/77; American Constitutional Law, Foundation Press, 78; Jurisdictional gerrymandering: Zoning disfavored rights out of the federal courts, 16

Harvard Law Rev 129, summer 81; coauth (with Jesse Choper & Yale Kamisar), The Supreme Court: Trends and Developments, 1980-81, Vol III, Nat Pract Inst Inc, 82. **CONTACT ADDRESS** Law Sch, Harvard Univ, 1525 Massachusetts, Cambridge, MA 02138-2903.

TRIGILIO, JO
DISCIPLINE PHILOSOPHY; WOMEN'S STUDIES **EDUCATION** Marietta Col, BA, 83; Univ Oregon, MA, 93, PhD, 96. **CAREER** Vis instr, 97-98, Calif St Univ, Chico; asst prof, 98-, Bentley Col. **HONORS AND AWARDS** Phi Beta Kappa **MEMBERSHIPS** Soc for Women in Phil; Soc for Advan of Am Phil; Nat Women' s Studies Asn. **RESEARCH** Feminist theory; feminist epistemology; Amer phil. **CONTACT ADDRESS** 15 Bay State Ave., #1, Somerville, MA 02144-2114. **EMAIL** jtrigilio@bentley.edu

TRIPLETT, TIM
PERSONAL Born 06/28/1949, OH **DISCIPLINE** EPISTEMOLOGY **EDUCATION** Univ of Massachusetts, Amherst, PhD, 82, MA, 80, Philos; John Hopkins Univ, Baltimore, MD, Grad Courses and Seminars in Philos; Antioch Coll, Yellow Springs, OH, BA, 72; Univ of East Anlia, Norwich, England, Undergrad Philos Curriculum, 69-70. **CAREER** Assoc Prof of Philos, 88-, Lectr, 80-81, Instr, 81-83, Asst Prof, 83-88, Univ of New Hampshire. **HONORS AND AWARDS** Amer Coun of Learned Soc; New Hampshire Coll of Lib Art Faculty Summer Res Stipend; Discretionary Res Support Prog Grant; Sr Faculty Fellowship, Center of Hum, Univ of New Hampshire; Fellowship, Univ of New Hampshire Grad Sch. **MEMBERSHIPS** Amer Philos Assoc. **RESEARCH** Philosophy of Mind; 20th Century Analytic Philosophy; Applied Ethics; Sociology of Knowledge; Formal and Informal Logic; East Asian Philosophy. **SELECTED PUBLICATIONS** Auth, Is There Anthropological Evidence that Logic is Culturally Relative?, British Journal for the Philosophy of Science 45, 94; Review of Knowledge and Evidence, Paul Moser, Cambridge Univ Press, Philosophy and Phenomenological Research 51, pp 945-949, 91; Azande Logic Versus Western Logic? British Journal for the Philosophy of Science 39, pp 361-366, 88; Rescher's Metaphilosophy, in progress; The Viability of Strong Foundationalism, in progress; The Later Sellars: Defender of the Given, in progress; many other pubs. **CONTACT ADDRESS** Dept Philosophy, Univ of New Hampshire, Durham, Durham, NH 03824. **EMAIL** tat@cisunix.unh.edu

TRISCO, ROBERT FREDERICK
PERSONAL Born 11/11/1929, Chicago, IL, s **DISCIPLINE** HISTORY & RELIGION **EDUCATION** St. Mary of the Lake Seminary, BA, 51; Pontifical Gregorian Univ, STL, 55, Hist. Eccl.D, 62. **CAREER** Inst, 59-63, Asst Prof, 63-65, Assoc Prof, 65-75, Prof, 75-96, Vice-Rector for Academic Affairs, 66-68, Chemn, Dept of Church Hist, 75-78, Prof, Dept of Church Hist, Kelly-Quinn Distinguished Professor of Church Hist, 99-; The Catholic Univ of Am, 76-. **HONORS AND AWARDS** Honorary degree, Doctor of Humane Letters, Belmont Abbey Col, 92; Honorary Prelate of His Holiness (Monsignor), 92. **MEMBERSHIPS** Am Catholic Hist Asn, Sec 1961-, Sec and Treas 1983-; Am Soc of Church Hist; Pontifical Commt for Hist Sci. **RESEARCH** History of the Catholic Church in the United States and in the British Isles; history of the modern Papacy. **SELECTED PUBLICATIONS** Ed, The Catholic Hist Rev, 63-. **CONTACT ADDRESS** Catholic Univ of America, Curley Hall, Washington, DC 20064. **EMAIL** TRISCO@cua.edu

TRISTAN, J.
PERSONAL Born 06/29/1952, Toronto, ON, Canada, w, 1976, 1 child **DISCIPLINE** PHILOSOPHY **EDUCATION** Univ Oregon, BS, 89, MA, 92; Southern Ill Univ, Carbondale, PhD, 96. **CAREER** Instr, Southern Ill Univ Carbondale, 92-96; instr, Auburn Univ, 97-98; lectr, Univ North Carolina, Charlotte, 98-99. **HONORS AND AWARDS** Doctoral fel 94-95; Morris Eames Scholar Awd, 94-95. **MEMBERSHIPS** APA; Soc for Advancement of Am Philos; Midwest Prgamatist Prog Comm. **RESEARCH** John Dewey's theory of inquiry; history and philosopy of technology; educational practices; inovative, creative and critical thinking technique. **SELECTED PUBLICATIONS** coauth, "Signs Against Trees," Am J of Semiotics, 94; "Warrant and the End of Inquiry," Hester, ed, New Essays on Dewey's Logical Theory, Oxford, 99; "Experiment, Bias, and the Establishment of Standards," Tuana, ed, Feminist Perspectives on John Dewey, Penn State, 99. **CONTACT ADDRESS** Dept of Philos, Univ of No Carolina, Charlotte, 9201 University City, Charlotte, NC 28223-0002. **EMAIL** jtristan@concentric.net

TROBISCH, DAVID
PERSONAL Born 08/18/1958, Ebolowa, Cameroon, m **DISCIPLINE** THEOLOGY OF NEW TESTAMENT **EDUCATION** Magister theol, 81; Dr theol, 89; Dr theol habil, 95. **CAREER** Hochschulassistent Universitat Heidelberg, GER, 89-95; vis assoc prof, Yale Divinity School, New Haven, 96-97; assoc prof of New Testament, Bangor Theol Sem, 97-00; Throckmorton-Hayes Prof of New Testament Language and Literature, 00-. **MEMBERSHIPS** AAR/SBL. **RESEARCH** Letters of Paul; Biblical manuscripts; Biblical theology; canon. **SELECTED PUBLICATIONS** Ed, with H J Dorn, V. Rosenberger, Zu dem Septuagintapapyrus VBP IV 56, Zeitschrift fur Papyrologie und Epigraphik 61, 85; auth, Die Entstehung der Paulusbriefsammlung: Studien zu den Anfangen der christlichen Publizistik, NTOA, 10, Freiburg, Schweiz: Universitatsverlag, Gottingen: Vandenhoeck, 89; Paul's Collection of Letters: Exploring the Origins, Fortress Press, 94, German trans, Kaiser, 94; Die Endredaktion des Neuen Testaments: Eine Untersuchung zur Entstehung der christlichen Bibel, NTOA 31, Vanderhoek, 96; Die Mormonen, Konstanz/Neukirchen-Vluyn, 98; The Council of Jerusalem in Acts 15 and Paul's Letter to the Galatians, Christopher Seitz and Kathryn Greene-McCreight ed., Theological Exegesis: Essays in Honor of Brevard S. Childs Grand Rapids: Eerdmans, 99; auth, Uber die Kunst, zwischen den Zeilen zu lesen: Gedanken zu 1Kor 4, 6: Nicht uber das hinaus, was geschrieben steht, Dielheimer Blatter zur Archaologie und Textuberlieferung der Antike und Spatantike, 30, 99, 193-195; auth, The First Edition of the New Testament, New York: Oxford University Press, 00. **CONTACT ADDRESS** Bangor Theol Sem, 300 Union St, Bangor, ME 04401. **EMAIL** DTrobisch@BTS.edu

TROEGER, THOMAS
PERSONAL Born 01/30/1945, Suffern, NY, m **DISCIPLINE** HOMILETICS **EDUCATION** Yale Univ, BA, 67; Colgate Rochester Divinity Sch, BD, 70; STD, Dickinson Col, 93. **CAREER** Assoc Pator, New Hartford Presbyterian Church, 70-77; from assoc prof to prof, Colgate Rochester Divinity School/Bexley Hall/Crozer Theol Sem, 77-91; Ralph E. and Norma E. Peck Prof of Preaching and Commun, The Iliff Sch of Theol, 91-. **HONORS AND AWARDS** Ecumenical Scholar, Colgate Rochester Divinity Sch, 67-68; Scriven Found Scholar, 63-67. **MEMBERSHIPS** Acad of Homiletics, Hymn Soc, N Am Acad of Liturgy. **RESEARCH** Homiletics, Worship, and Congregational Song. **SELECTED PUBLICATIONS** Auth, Ten Strategies for Preaching in a MultiMedia Culture, Abingdon Press (Nashville, TN), 96; coauth, Wrestling with the Patriarchs. Retrieving Women's Voices in Preaching, Abingdon Press (Nashville, TN), 96; contribur, New Proclamation Series A 1999, Easter Through Pentecost, Fortress Press (Minneapolis, MN), 99; auth, Preaching While the Church is Under Reconstruction. The Visionary Role of Preachers in a Fragmented World, Abingdon Press (Nashville, TN), 99; auth, the words to "Make Our Church One Joyful Choir," Oxford Univ Press--Oxford Church Music (Oxford Univ Press, NY), 00; auth, the words to "Direct Us, Lord, Through Darkness: for Mixed Choir (SATB) Unaccompanied," Oxford Univ Press--Oxford Church Music (Oxford Univ Press, NY), 00; auth, the words to "The Faith That We Have Sown. An Anthem for Mixed Choir (SATB), Brass, Timpani, Percussion, and Organ," Oxford Univ Press--Oxford Church Music (Oxford Univ Press, NY), 00. **CONTACT ADDRESS** Dept Theol, Iliff Sch of Theol, 2201 S Univ Blvd, Denver, CO 80210-4707. **EMAIL** ttroeger@iliff.edu

TROTTER, A. H., JR.
PERSONAL Born 10/10/1950, Maryville, TN, m, 1972, 3 children **DISCIPLINE** BIBLICAL STUDIES, FILM AND CULTURE **EDUCATION** Univ Virginia, BA, 72; Gordon-Conwell Theol Sem, MDiv, 75; Univ Cambridge, PhD, 87. **CAREER** Tchr, Westminster Schs, Atlanta, 75-78; exec dir, Elmbrook Christian Study Ctr, 81-87; exec dir, Center for Christian Study, 87- . **RESEARCH** Life of Jesus; Biblical interpretation, New Testament studies; systematic theology; film and culture. **SELECTED PUBLICATIONS** Auth, Interpreting the Epistle to the Hebrews, Baker Book House, 97. **CONTACT ADDRESS** Ctr for Christian Study, 128 Chancellor St, Charlottesville, VA 22903. **EMAIL** drew@studycenter.net

TROTTER, GARY
DISCIPLINE LAW **EDUCATION** Univ Toronto, LLB, 85; Osgoode Hall Law Sch, LLM, 90; Cambridge Univ, MPhill, 91. **CAREER** Counsel, Crown Law Office-Criminal, Ministry of the Attorney General for Ontario **HONORS AND AWARDS** Ed, Criminal Law Quarterly. **SELECTED PUBLICATIONS** Auth, The Law of Bail in Canada; pubs on criminal law. **CONTACT ADDRESS** Fac of Law, Univ of Toronto, 78 Queen's Park, Toronto, ON, Canada M5S 1A1.

TROTTER, GRIFFIN
PERSONAL Born 12/30/1957, Missoula, MT, m, 1985, 3 children **DISCIPLINE** PHILOSOPHY & MEDICINE **EDUCATION** St Louis Univ, MD, 85; Vanderbilt Univ, PhD, 95. **CAREER** Asst prof Ethics & asst prof Surgery, St Louis Univ. **MEMBERSHIPS** AMA; APA; Soc for the Advan of Am Philos; Asn for Practical and Prof Ethics. **RESEARCH** Healthcare ethics; classical American philosophy. **SELECTED PUBLICATIONS** Auth, The Loyal Physician, Vanderbilt Univ, 97. **CONTACT ADDRESS** Saint Louis Univ, 6975 Delmar Blvd, University City, MO 63130. **EMAIL** trotterr@slu.edu

TROUT, J. D.
PERSONAL Born 12/28/1959, Cleveland, OH, m, 1992, 1 child **DISCIPLINE** PHILOSOPHY, COGNITIVE SCIENCE AND HISTORY **EDUCATION** Bucknell Univ, philos and history BA, 82; Cornell Univ, MA, 86; Cornell Univ, Philos and cognitive sci PhD, 88. **CAREER** Mellon postdoctoral fel, Bryn Mawr Col, 88-89; visiting asst prof, Va Tech, 91-92; asst prof, 92-, assoc prof, 95-, Loyola Univ. **HONORS AND AWARDS** NSF Predoctoral fel; Mellon postdoctoral fel. **MEMBERSHIPS** Am Philos Asn; Philos of Sci Asn; Acoustical Soc of Am; Psychonomic Soc. **RESEARCH** Philosophy of science; Philosophy of mind; Speech perception. **SELECTED PUBLICATIONS** Auth, Measuring the Intentional World: Realism, Naturalism, and Quantitative Methods in the Behavioral Sciences, NY, Oxford Univ Press, 98; coauth, with Paul Moser and Dwayne Mulder, The Theory of Knowledge: A Thematic Introduction, NY, Oxford Univ Press, 98; with Paul Moser, Contemporary Materialism: A Reader, London and NY, Routledge, 95; with Richard Boyd and Philip Gasper, The Philos of Sci, Cambridge, MA, Bradford Books, The MIT Press, 91; articles, Entries on Alchemy and Uniformity of Nature, ed R. Audi, The Cambridge Dict of Philos, Cambridge, Cambridge Univ Press, 95; Diverse Tests on an Independent World, Studies in History and Philosophy of Science, 26, 3, 407-429, 95; with R. Burian, Ontological Progress in Science, Can Jour of Philos, 25, 2, 177-201, 95; with P. K. Moser, Physicalism, Supervenience, and Dependence, ed U. D. Yalcin and E. E. Savellos, Supervenience: New Essays, Cambridge, Cambridge Univ Press, 95; Auster Realism and the Worldly Assumptions of Inferential Statistics, ed M. Forbes, D. Hull and R. Burian, PSA 1994, vol 1, Lansing, Mich, Philos of Sci Asn, 190-199, 94; A Realistic Look Backward, Studies in History and Philosophy of Science, 25, 1, 37-64, 94. **CONTACT ADDRESS** Dept. of Philosophy, Loyola Univ, Chicago, 6525 N Sheridan Rd, Chicago, IL 60626. **EMAIL** jtrout@orion.it.luc.edu

TROWBRIDGE, JOHN
PERSONAL Born 07/02/1970, Glen Cove, NY, m, 1996, 2 children **DISCIPLINE** PHILOSOPHY **EDUCATION** Washington Univ, AB, 93; MA, Phil, 96, MA, East Asian Lang and Lit, 96, Ohio State Univ; PhD Student, Univ Hawaii at Manoa **CAREER** Grad Teaching Assoc, 94-98, OH State Univ. **HONORS AND AWARDS** Graduate Degree Fel, East-West Center, 98-; Foreign Lang and Area Studies Fel, 95-96, 96-97. **MEMBERSHIPS** Soc for Asian and Comparative Phil; Am Phil Assoc; Asn for Asian Studies. **RESEARCH** Classical Chinese and comparative philosophy; epistemology; ancient Greek philosophy; Asian religions. **SELECTED PUBLICATIONS** The Relationship Between Skepticism and Epistemological Relativism in the Qi Wu Lun, Chapter of the Zhuang Zi, 96. **CONTACT ADDRESS** Dept of Philosophy, Univ of Hawaii, Manoa, 2530 Dole St., Sakamaki H, Honolulu, HI 96822-2383. **EMAIL** trowbrid@hawaii.edu

TROYER, JOHN G.
PERSONAL Born 12/02/1943, Detroit, MI, m, 1992, 2 children **DISCIPLINE** PHILOSOPHY **EDUCATION** Swarthmore Coll, BA, 65; Harvard Univ, MA, 67; PhD, 71. **CAREER** asst prof, Univ Conn, 70-77; assoc prof, 77-. **HONORS AND AWARDS** Phi Beta Kappa; Frank Knox Mem Fel; NEH Fel; Mem Common Rm. **MEMBERSHIPS** APA; IBS; HS; SPP; OBS. **RESEARCH** Early modern philosophy; Wittgenstein; normative theory. **SELECTED PUBLICATIONS** Auth, "Locke on the Names of Substances," in Theory of Knowledge, ed. John Locke (Chappell, 92); ed, "The Existence of Simples," in Wittgenstein and Impact Contemporary Thought (Leinfellner, 80); auth, "Bioethics," in Collier's Encyclopedia, vol IV (86); ed, In Defense of Radical Empiricism: Essays and Lectures by Roderick Firth, Rowman Littlefield (Lanham, MD), 97; auth, "Roderick Firth," in American National Biography (Oxford Univ Press, 99). **CONTACT ADDRESS** Dept Philosophy, Univ of Connecticut, Storrs, 840 Mansfield Rd, Storrs, CT 06268. **EMAIL** john.troyer@vconn.edu

TRUEMPER, DAVID GEORGE
PERSONAL Born 02/01/1939, Aurora, IL, m, 1963, 2 children **DISCIPLINE** SYSTEMIC THEOLOGY **EDUCATION** Concordia Sr Col, BA, 61; Concordia Sem, MDiv, 65, STM, 69; Lutheran Sch Theol, PhD, 74. **CAREER** Instr, 67-72, asst prof, 72-77, assoc prof, Theol, Valparaiso Univ, 77-84, prof Theol, 84-; chmn Theol, 93-; dir coun on Study of Rel, 93-; vis prof, Concordia Sem, 73-74, Concordia Sem-in-Exile, 74 & Univ Notre Dame, 77-78; dir, Study Ctr, Valparaiso Univ, Reutlingen, Germany, 74-76; pastor, St John Lutheran Church, La Crosse, Ind, 79-84. **MEMBERSHIPS** Am Acad Relig; NAm Acad Liturgy; Societas Liturgica. **RESEARCH** Sixteenth-century theological controversy; contemporary Christology; ecumenical theology and interconfessional dialogue. **SELECTED PUBLICATIONS** Coauth, Review essay of A Statement of Scriptural and Confessional Principles, Cresset, 5 & 10/73; ed & contribr, Confession and Congregation, Occasional Paper No 3, Cresset, 78; auth, (Lutheran Churches) Doctrine and theology, nature and function of the church, In: Profiles in Belief, II, Harper & Row, 78; contribr & ed, Promise and Faith, Valparaiso Univ Press, 2nd ed, 80; auth, The myth/truth of Christological arguments, Currents in Theol & Mission, 78; coauth, Keeping the Faith: A Guide to the Christian Message, Fortress Press, 81; auth, The Catholicity of the Augsburg confession, 16th Cent J, 80; man ed, Proceedings of the North American Academy of Liturgy, 86-97; man ed, Religious Studies Review, 93-; man ed, Bulletin of the CSSR, 93-; ed, CSSR Directory of Departments and Programs of Religious Studies in North America, 93-. **CONTACT ADDRESS** Dept Theol, Valparaiso Univ, 651 College Ave, Valparaiso, IN 46383-6493. **EMAIL** david.truemper@valpo.edu

TRULEAR, HAROLD DEAN
DISCIPLINE RELIGION **EDUCATION** Morehouse Col, BA, 75; MPhil, 79, PhD, 83, Drew Univ. **CAREER** Instr, 77-78, Jersey City State Col; Instr, 78-83, Asst Prof, 83-86, Drew Univ, Theol Sch; Dir, Black Church Studies, 87-90, Eastern Baptist Theol Sem; Dean, 90-96, Prof, 96-98, New York Theol Sem; VP, Church Collaborative Initiatives, 98-, Public/Private Ventures. **CONTACT ADDRESS** Public/Private Ventures, One Commerce Sq., 2005 Market St., Philadelphia, PA 19103. **EMAIL** dtrulear@ppv.org

TRULL, JOE
PERSONAL Born 12/02/1935, Oklahoma City, OK, m, 1955, 3 children **DISCIPLINE** RELIGION **EDUCATION** Okla Bapt Univ, BA, 57; Southwestern Bapt Theol Sem, MDiv, 58; ThD, 60. **CAREER** Assoc Prof, Carson Newman Col, 64-65; Pastor, Churches in Tex and Va, 65-85; Prof , New Orleans Bapt Theol Sem, 85-99; Adj Teacher, Logsdon Theol Sem, 00-. **MEMBERSHIPS** Soc of Christian Ethics, Nat Asn of Baptist Prof of Relig, Christians for Biblical Equality. **RESEARCH** Ministerial Ethics, Clergy Sexual Abuse, Gender Equality. **SELECTED PUBLICATIONS** Auth, Ministerial Ethics: Being a Good Minister, 93; auth, Walking in the Way: An Introduction to Christian Ethics, 97. **CONTACT ADDRESS** Logsdon Theol Sem, 101 Mount View Rd, Wimberley, TX 78676. **EMAIL** jtrull@eudoramail.com

TRUMBOWER, JEFFREY A.
PERSONAL Born 06/19/1960, Orlando, FL **DISCIPLINE** RELIGION **EDUCATION** Vanderbilt Univ, BA, 82; Univ Chicago Div Sch, MA, 84; PhD, 89. **CAREER** Asst Prof to Assoc Prof, St Michael's Col, 89-. **MEMBERSHIPS** Soc of Biblical Lit; N Am Patristics Soc; AAUP. **RESEARCH** Early Christianity. **SELECTED PUBLICATIONS** Auth, "Editor's Bookshelf: Recent Literature on Philemon," Journal of Religion, (88); 203; auth, "Origen's Exegesis of John 8: 19-53: the Struggle with Heracleon over the Idea of Fixed Natures," Vigiliae Christianae, (89): 138-154; auth, Born From Above: The Anthropology of the Gospel of John, Paul Siebeck, 92; auth, "Hermes Trismegistos," in The Anchor Bible dictionary, (Doubleday, 92), 156-157; auth, "The Historical Jesus and the Speech of Gamaliel (Acts 5:35-39)," New Testament Studies, (93): 500-517; auth, "The Role of Malachi in the Career of John the Baptist," in The gospels and the Scriptures of Israel, (JSOT Press, 94), 28-41; auth, "Traditions Common to the Primary Adam and Eve Books and On the Origin of the World," Journal for the Study of the Pseudepigrapha, (96): 43-54; auth, "Acts of Paul and Thecla 28-31," in Prayer from Alexander to Constantine: A Critical anthology, (Routledge press, 97), 280-284; auth, "Augustine's Rejection of Posthumous Salvation: Social Contexts and Implications," in Social Constructions of the Afterlife, SBL Pub, forthcoming; auth, Rescue for the Dead: The Posthumous Salvation of Non-Christians in Early Christianity, Oxford Univ Press, forthcoming. **CONTACT ADDRESS** Dept Relig, Saint Michael's Col, 1 Winooski Park, Colchester, VT 05439-0002. **EMAIL** jtrumbower@smcvt.edu

TRUNDLE, ROBERT
PERSONAL Born 07/07/1943, Washington, DC, m, 1985 **DISCIPLINE** PHILOSOPHY **EDUCATION** Ohio State Univ, BA, 72; Univ Toledo, MA, 74; Univ Colo, PhD, 84. **CAREER** Asst teach, Univ Tol, 72-74; grad fel, Rice Univ, 75; instr, Univ Col, 81-83; adj instr, Regis Col, 82-84; adj asst prof, 84-86; asst prof, N Ken Univ, 87-91; assoc prof, 91-98; prof, 98-. **HONORS AND AWARDS** Grad Teach asst; Grad Fel; Outstand Asst Prof. **MEMBERSHIPS** US Army Res Off Asn; NYAS; SRSSX; SMP; APA; Phi Kappa Phi. **RESEARCH** History of philosophy; philosophy of science; a relationship of science to ethics and politics. **SELECTED PUBLICATIONS** Auth, Ancient Greek Philosophy, 94; auth, Beyond Absurdity, 86; auth, From Physics to Politics: The Metaphysical Foundations of Modern Philosophy, 99; auth, Medieval Modal Logic and Science: Augustine on Scientific Truth and Thomas on its Impossibility Without a First Cause, 99. **CONTACT ADDRESS** Dept Sociology, Anthropology, No Kentucky Univ, Newport, KY 41099-0001. **EMAIL** trundle@nku.edu

TRYMAN, MFANYA DONALD
PERSONAL Born 01/26/1948, Montclair, NJ, m **DISCIPLINE** POLITICAL SCIENCE **EDUCATION** Pasadena City Coll, AA Liberal Art 1969; CA State Polytechnic Univ, BS Political Science 1971; FL State Univ, MA 1972, MSPA 1974, PhD 1975. **CAREER** TX Southern Univ, assoc prof 75-81; Univ of Houston, prof 81-82; Jackson State Univ, assoc prof 81-85, dir MPPA program 81-; Prairie View A&M Univ, Assoc Prof, 85-. **HONORS AND AWARDS** CA State Polytechnic Univ Magna Cum Laude 1971; Outstanding Black Sr Scholar Awd 1971; Outstanding Educator Legislative Black Caucus of TX Awd 1979; fellow, Dept of Labor & Howard Univ 1980; Scholar Spotlight on Scholars Awd 1983; Cert of Merit NASA Johnson Space Center 1986. **MEMBERSHIPS** Mem conf of minority Public Admin 1976-; mem Natl conf of Black Political Scientists 1976-; natl campaign adv St Rep El Franco Lee 1978; bd mem advbd Congressman Mickey Leland 1978-80; voluntary boxing dir Hester House Comm Org 1979; vice pres Demographic Environs Rsch Inc 1980-85; project mgr Comm & Economic Develop Work Study Prog 1983-; dir Master of Public Policy & Admin Prog Jackson State Univ 1983-85; mem Natl Forum of Black Public Admins 1983-85, natl Conf of Black Studies 1985-87. **SELECTED PUBLICATIONS** l of over 40 articles & two books on Black Politics Affirmative Action Public Policy and Econ Devel in professional journals & mags. **CONTACT ADDRESS** Political Science, Prairie View A&M Univ, 14543 Leacrest Dr, Houston, TX 77049.

TSCHEMPLIK, ANDREA
PERSONAL Born 08/16/1961, Darmstadt, Germany, m, 1991 **DISCIPLINE** PHILOSOPHY **EDUCATION** Upsala Col, BA, 82; Bryn mawr Col, MA, 85; CUNY, PhD, 97. **CAREER** Adj prof, Hunter Col, CUNY, 87-91; asst prof philos, Upsala Col, 91-95; adj prof philos, Drew Univ, 95-98; asst prof philos, George Washington Univ, 98- . **HONORS AND AWARDS** Tchr of the year award, 94. **MEMBERSHIPS** APA; Soc for Ancient Greek Philos; Soc for the Stud of Africana Philos; AAUP. **RESEARCH** History of philosophy; Greek philosophy; German philosophy. **SELECTED PUBLICATIONS** Auth, Framing the Question of Knowledge: Beginning Plato's Theaetetus, in press; ed, Plato's Dialogues: New Studies and Interpretations, Rowman & Littlefield, 93. **CONTACT ADDRESS** 17 Deckertown Tpke, Sussex, NJ 07461. **EMAIL** atschemp@gwu.edu

TSEBELIS, GEORGE
PERSONAL Born 07/11/1952, Athens, Greece, m, 1991, 2 children **DISCIPLINE** POLITICAL SCIENCE **EDUCATION** Nat Tech Univ Athens, BS, 75; Inst d'Etudes Polit Paris, BA, 79; Pierre et Marie Curie Univ Paris, PhD, 79; Wash Univ, PhD, 85. **CAREER** Wash Univ, 84-85; Stanford Univ, 85-86; Duke Univ, 86-87; UCLA, 87-. **HONORS AND AWARDS** Russell Sage Fel, 00-01; Simon Guggenheim Fel, 95-96; Hoover Inst Nat Fel, 92-93; NSF Grant; Gregory Luebbert Awd, 94; Pi Sigma Alpha Awd, 92. **MEMBERSHIPS** APSA. **RESEARCH** Comparative Politics; Political Institutions; Political Parties; European Union Politics. **SELECTED PUBLICATIONS** Auth, Nested Games, Univ Calif Press; co-auth, Bicameralism, Cambridge Univ Press; auth, "The Power of the European Parliament as a Conditional Agenda-Setter," Am Polit Sci Rev, (94): 128-142; auth, "Decision Making in Political Systems: Veto Players in Presidentialism, Parliamentarism, Multicameralism, and Multipartyism,: Brit J of Polit Sci, (95): 289-326; auth, "An Institutional Critique of Intergovernmentalism," Intl Org, (96): 269-299; auth, "Veto Players and Institutional Analysis," Governance, (00): 441-474; auth, "Veto Players and Law Production in Parliamentary Democracies: An Empirical Analysis," Am Polit Sci Rev, (99): 591-608; auth, "Legislative Procedures in the EU: An Empirical Analysis," Brit J of Polit Sci, (forthcoming). **CONTACT ADDRESS** Dept Polit Sci, Univ of California, Los Angeles, 4289 Bunche, Box 951472, Los Angeles, CA 90095-1472. **EMAIL** tsebelis@ucla.edu

TSIRPANLIS, CONSTANTINE NICHOLAS
PERSONAL Born 03/18/1935, Cos, Greece **DISCIPLINE** HISTORY, PHILOSOPHY **EDUCATION** Greek Theol Sch Halki, Istanbul, Lic theol, 57; Harvard Univ, STM, 62; Columbia Univ, AM, 66; Fordham Univ, PhD(hist), 73. **CAREER** Instr mod Greek, NY Univ, 64-70; teacher classics and chmn dept, Collegiate Sch, NY, 67-69; instr mod Greek, New Sch Social Res, 68-70; res and writing, 70-72; adj prof world hist, NY Inst Technol, 72-75; Assoc Prof Church Hist and Greek Studies, Unification Theol Sem, 76-, Lectr class philol, Hunter Col, 66-67; lectr medieval and ancient hist, Mercy Col, 72; adj prof Western civilization, Delaware County Community Col, 75, Dutchess County Community Col, 76. **HONORS AND AWARDS** Nat Medal Greek Rebirth, Greek Govt, 72. **MEMBERSHIPS** NAm Acad Ecumenists; Am Soc Neo-Hellenic Studies (exec vpres, 67-69); Am Philol Asn; Medieval Acad Am; NAm Patristic Soc. **RESEARCH** Late Byzantine intellectual history and theology; early Byzantine theology and philosophy; Greek patristics. **SELECTED PUBLICATIONS** Auth, The Incarnation in St Athanasius' Thought, 63 & The Theology of History in Clement of Alexandria, 64, Athens; The imperial administration in John Lydus, Byzantinische Zeitschrift, Ger, 73; Mark Eugenicus and the Council of Florence, Salonica, 74; The Liturgical and Mystical Theology of N Cabasilas, Athens, 76; A Modern Greek Idiom and Phrase Book, Barrons, 78; Greek Patristic Theology, 79; Studies in Byzantine History, 80. **CONTACT ADDRESS** Unification Theol Sem, 10 Dock Rd, Barrytown, NY 12507.

TU, WEI-MING
PERSONAL Born 02/26/1940, Kunming, China, m, 1963, 1 child **DISCIPLINE** HISTORY, RELIGIOUS PHILOSOPHY **EDUCATION** Tunghai Univ, Taiwan, BA, 61; Harvard Univ, MA, 63, PhD(hist), 68. **CAREER** Vis lectr humanities, Tunghai Univ, Taiwan, 66-67; lectr EAsian studies, Princeton Univ, 67-68, asst prof, 68-71; from asst prof to assoc prof hist, Univ Calif, Berkeley, 71-77, prof, 77-81; Prof Chinese Hist and Philos, Harvard Univ, 81-, Consult-panelist, Nat Endowment for Humanities, 75; Am Coun Learned Soc fel, 77; mem bd dirs, Chinese Cult Found San Francisco, 79- **MEMBERSHIPS** Asn Asian Studies; Soc Asian and Comp Philos; Am Acad Polit Sci. **RESEARCH** Chinese intellectual history; Confucianism in East Asia; religious philosophy. **SELECTED PUBLICATIONS** Auth, Introduction--Cultural Perspectives, Daedalus, Vol 0122, 93; Destructive Will and Ideological Holocaust--Maoism as a Source of Social Suffering in China, Daedalus, Vol 0125, 96. **CONTACT ADDRESS** Dept of EAsian Lang and Civilizations, Harvard Univ, Cambridge, MA 02138.

TUBB, GARY
DISCIPLINE RELIGION **EDUCATION** Harvard Univ, BA, 73, MA, 76, PhD, 79. **CAREER** Prof. **RESEARCH** Sanskrit literary theory. **SELECTED PUBLICATIONS** Auth, pubs on Sanskrit poetry and poetics. **CONTACT ADDRESS** Dept of Religion, Columbia Col, New York, 2960 Broadway, New York, NY 10027-6902. **EMAIL** gat4@columbia.edu

TUBBS, JAMES B.
PERSONAL Born 07/21/1953, Florence, SC, s **DISCIPLINE** RELIGIOUS STUDIES **EDUCATION** Hampden-Sydney Col, BS; Univ VA, MA, PhD. **CAREER** Assoc prof, Univ Detroit Mercy, 86-. **HONORS AND AWARDS** President's awd for Fac Excellence, Col Liberal Arts, 96. **MEMBERSHIPS** Med Ethics Resource Network Mich, Soc of Christian Ethics, Am Acad of Relig. **RESEARCH** Christian theology and the moral issues in biomedicine and health care policy. **SELECTED PUBLICATIONS** Auth, Christian Theol and Med Ethics: Four Contemporary Approaches, Kluwer, 96. **CONTACT ADDRESS** Dept of Religious Studies, Univ of Detroit Mercy, 8200 W. Outer Dr., PO Box 19900, Detroit, MI 48219-0900. **EMAIL** tubbsjb@udmercy.edu

TUCHLER, DENNIS JOHN
PERSONAL Born 12/25/1938, Berlin, Germany, m, 1961, 2 children **DISCIPLINE** LAW **EDUCATION** Reed Col, BA, 60; Univ Chicago, JD, 63. **CAREER** From asst prof to assoc prof law, 65-71, Prof Law, St Louis Univ Sch Law, 71-, Consult, Codification of Ord, City of Dellwood, Mo, 67 & City of Maplewood, Mo, 68-. **RESEARCH** Conflict of laws; legal ethics. **SELECTED PUBLICATIONS** Auth, Boundaries to party autonomy in the UCC: A radical view, St Louis Univ Law J, 67; Oregon conflicts: Toward an analysis of governmental interests?, Ore Law Rev, 68; Some Thoughts about the Rules of Professional Conduct, S Publ Law Forum 25, 86; A Short Summary of American Conflict Law: Choice of Law, St Louis Univ Law J 37, 93. **CONTACT ADDRESS** School of Law, Saint Louis Univ, 3700 Lindell Blvd, Saint Louis, MO 63108-3412.

TUCK, DONALD RICHARD
PERSONAL Born 04/24/1935, Albany, NY, m, 1957, 2 children **DISCIPLINE** HISTORY OF RELIGIONS, ASIAN STUDIES **EDUCATION** Nyack Col, BS, 57; Wheaton Col, MA, 65; Univ Iowa, PhD(relig and cult), 70. **CAREER** Minister of youth, Presby Church, Ill, 63-65; interim minister, Methodist Church, Fed Church and United Church of Christ, Iowa, 65-69; teaching and res asst, Sch Relig, Univ Iowa, 67-68; from instr to assoc prof relig, 69-78, PROF RELIG, WESTERN KY UNIV, 78-, Fac res grant, Radhakrishnan and Tagore, 70; fac res grant, Tagore, 72; consult, Choice, 76-, Nat Endowment Humanities, 77- and South Asia in Rev, 78-; fac res grant, Santal Relig, 76 and soc aspects, Bhagavata, Purana, 78. **MEMBERSHIPS** Am Acad Relig; Asn Asian Studies. **RESEARCH** Religion and culture of Modern India; Sarvepalli Radhakrishnan and Rabindranath Tagore; Bengal Vaisnavism-Caitanya. **SELECTED PUBLICATIONS** Auth, Lacuna in Sankara Studies--A Thousand Teachings Upadesasahasri, Asian Philos, Vol 0006, 96. **CONTACT ADDRESS** Dept of Relig and Philos, Western Kentucky Univ, 1 Big Red Way St, Bowling Green, KY 42101-3576.

TUCKER, BONNIE
PERSONAL Born 08/04/1939, New York, NY, d, 3 children **DISCIPLINE** LAW **EDUCATION** Syracuse Univ, BS, 61; Univ Colo, JD, 80. **CAREER** Law clerk, U.S. Court of Appeals, 80-81; atty, Pa, 81-87; prof, Ariz State Univ, 87-; vis prof, Monash Univ, 94; vis prof, Cornell Law Sch, 93; vis prof, Roger Williams Univ, 98; vis prof, Univ Colo, 90; vis prof, Univ San Diego, 87. **HONORS AND AWARDS** Outstanding Alumni Award, Univ Colo, 96; Outstanding Alumni Award, Syracuse Univ, 96; Phoenix Mayors Award, 96; Outstanding Serv Award, Ariz Center for Disability Law; Reynolds Soc Award, 98; Ariz Woman of Distinction Award, 98. **MEMBERSHIPS** Order of the Coif. **RESEARCH** Disability Law. **SELECTED PUBLICATIONS** Auth, Legal Rights of Persons with Disabilities: An Analysis of Federal Law, LRP Pub, 90; auth, "Discrimination on the Basis of Disability: The Need for a Third Wave Movement," Cornell J of L and Pub Policy, 94; auth, The Feel of Silence, Temple Univ Press, 95; auth, IDEA Advocacy for Children who are Deaf or Hard of Hearing: A Question and Answer Book for Parents and Professionals, Sing Pub, 97; auth, Federal Disability Law in a Nutshell, West Pub, 98; auth, Cochlear Implants: A Handbook, McFarland, 98; co-auth, The Law of Disability Discrimination, Anderson Pub Co, 99; auth, "The Supreme Court's Definition of Disability Under the ADA: A Return to the Dark Ages," Ala L Rev, (00): 321-374; auth, "Access to Health Care for Individuals with Hearing Impairments," Houston L Rev, (00): 1101-1162; auth, "The ADA's Revolving Poor: Inherent Flaws in the Civil Rights Paradigm," Ohio State L J, 01. **CONTACT ADDRESS** Col Law, Arizona State Univ, McAllister and Orange St, PO Box 877906, Tempe, AZ 85287. **EMAIL** bonnie.tucker@asu.edu

TUCKER, GENE M.
PERSONAL Born 01/08/1935, Albany, TX, m, 1957, 2 children **DISCIPLINE** RELIGION; OLD TESTAMENT **EDUCATION** McMurry Col, BA, 57; Yale Divinity School, MD, 60; Yale Univ, MA, 61; PhD, 63. **CAREER** Asst prof Relig, Grad School Relig, Univ S Cal, 63-66; asst prof , Divinity School, Duke Univ, 66-70; assoc prof, 70-77, prof, 77-95, assoc Dean, 78-83, actg dir grad studies relig, 87-88, prof Old Testament, Emer 95- , Candler School Theol, Emory Univ. **MEMBERSHIPS** Soc Bibl Lit (pres 96); Am Schools Oriental Res; Int Orgn Study Old Testament; Colloquium Bibl Res; Am Asn Univ Prof. **SELECTED PUBLICATIONS** Ed, Cultural Anthropology and the Old Testament, Guides to Biblical Scholarship, Fortress Press, 96; coed Marvin A Sweeney, Isaiah 1-39, Forms of the OT Lit, Wm Eerdmans, 96; auth Old Testament, HarperCollins Bible Dictionary, 96; auth Rain on a Land Where No One Lives: Hebrew Bible on the Environ, Jour Bibl Lit, 97; For Everything There is a Season, Reflections on Aging and Spiritual Growth, Abingdon Press, 98; ed The Forms of the Old Testament Literature: A Commentary, Wm Eerdmans, 98; auth of some sixty articles in journals, reference works or volumes of essays including: Jour Bibl Lit, Cath Bibl Quart; Vetus Testamentum; Interpretation; Harpers Dictionary of Bible, Interpreters Dictionary of Bible, Supplementary Volume, Oxford Study Edition: New English Bible. **CONTACT ADDRESS** 234 S Madison, Unit H, Denver, CO 80209. **EMAIL** gtucker@du.edu

TUCKER, GORDON
PERSONAL m, 3 children **DISCIPLINE** RELIGION **EDUCATION** Harvard Univ, BA; Princeton Univ, PhD. **CAREER** Adj asst prof, Jewish Theol Sem Am. **MEMBERSHIPS** Comt Jewish Law Standards; UJA Fedn NY. **SELECTED PUBLICATIONS** Auth, pubs on Jewish philosophy and law; Jewish affairs. **CONTACT ADDRESS** Dept of Jewish Philos, Jewish Theol Sem of America, 3080 Broadway, PO Box 3080, New York, NY 10027. **EMAIL** gotucker@jtsa.edu

TUCKER, MARY EVELYN
PERSONAL Born 06/24/1949, New York, NY, m, 1978 **DISCIPLINE** RELIGION, HISTORY **EDUCATION** Trinity Col, BA, 71; SUNY, Fredonia, MA, 72; Fordham Univ, MA, 77; Columbia Univ, PhD, 85. **CAREER** Lectr, Eng, Erie Commun Col, 72; lectr Eng, Notre Dame Seishin Univ, Japan, 73-75; lectr relig, Elizabeth Seton Col, 76-78; preceptor, Columbia Univ, 79-80, 83; asst prof hist, Iona Col, 84-89; assoc prof relig, Bucknell Univ, 89-98; prof religion, Bucknell Univ, 99- . **HONORS AND AWARDS** Phi Beta Kappa; HEW fel, 71-72; NEH fel, 77; Columbia Pres fel, 80-81, 81-82; Japan Found fel, 83-84; Mellon fel, 85-86; Columbia Univ postdoctoral res fel, 87-88; Person of the Year Awd, Bucknellian, 92; NEH Chair in the Hum, 93-96; sr fel, Center for the Study of World Relig, Harvard Univ, 95-96; Trinity Col Centennial Alumnae Awd for Academic Excellence, 97; assoc in res, Reischaur Inst of Japanese Stud, Harvard Univ, 95-00. **MEMBERSHIPS** Neo-Confucian Stud, Columbia Univ. Regional Sem on Japan, Columbia Univ; Am Teilhard Asn; Environ Sabbath, UN Environ Prog; AAR; Asn Asian Stud; Soc for Values in Higher Educ; Asn for Relig and Intellectual Life. **SELECTED PUBLICATIONS** Auth, Moral and Spiritual Cultivation in Japanese Neo-Confucianism: The Life and Thought of Kaibara Ekken (1630-1714), SUNY, 89; co-ed, Worldviews and Ecology, Bucknell Univ, 93; co-ed, Buddhism and Ecology: The Interaction of Dharma and Deeds, Harvard Univ, 97; co-ed, Confucianism and Ecology: The Interrelation of Heaven, Earth, and Humans, Harvard Univ, 98; Hinduism and Ecology:The Intersection of Earth, Sky, and Water, Harvard Univ, 99. **CONTACT ADDRESS** Dept of Religion, Bucknell Univ, Lewisburg, PA 17837. **EMAIL** mtucker@bucknell.edu

TUCKER, WILLIAM E.
PERSONAL Born 06/22/1932, Charlotte, NC, m, 1955, 3 children **DISCIPLINE** AMERICAN RELIGIOUS & CHURCH HISTORY **EDUCATION** Atlantic Christian Col, BA, 53, LLD, 78; Tex Christian Univ, BD, 56; Yale Univ, MA, 58, PhD(relig), 60. **CAREER** From assoc prof to prof relig & philos, Atlantic Christian Col, 59-66, chmn dept, 62-66; assoc prof church hist & asst dean, Brite Divinity Sch, Tex Christian Univ, 66-69, prof church hist, 69-76, assoc dean, 69-71, dean, 71-76; pres, Bethany Col, 76-79; chancellor, Tex Christian Univ, 79-98, trustee, Disciples of Christ Hist Soc, 69-; mem bd, Christian Church (Disciples of Christ), 71-, dir bd higher educ, 73-, chmn bd, 75-77; pres, Coun Southwestern Theol Schs, 75-76; vpres, WVa Found Independent Cols, 77-. **HONORS AND AWARDS** LLD, Atlantic Christian Col, 78; DHL, Chapman Col, 81; DHu, Bethany Col, 82. **RESEARCH** American church history since 1865; history and thought of the Christian Church (Disciples of Christ) and related religious groups; Fundamentalism and the Church in America. **SELECTED PUBLICATIONS** Auth, J H Garrison and Disciples of Christ, Bethany, 64; contribr, The Word We Preach, Tex Christian Univ, 70; Westminster Dictionary of Church History, Westminster, 71; Dictionary of American Biography, suppl 3, Scribner's, 73; coauth, Journey in Faith: A History of the Christian Church (Disciples of Christ), Bethany, 75; contribr, Encycl of Southern History, La State Univ Press, 79. **CONTACT ADDRESS** Chancellor Emeritus, 100 Throckmorton St, Ste 416, Fort Worth, TX 76102-2870. **EMAIL** w.tucker@tcu.edu

TUELL, STEVEN SHAWN
PERSONAL Born 10/03/1956, Liverpool, OH, m, 1981, 3 children **DISCIPLINE** RELIGIOUS STUDIES AND HEBREW BIBLE **EDUCATION** W VA Wesleyan Col, BA, 78; Princeton Theol Sem, Mdiv, 81; Union Theol Sem, PhD, 89. **CAREER** Pastor, Jacob Albright Meth Chur, WV, 81-85; Asst Prof , Erskine Col, 89-92; Asst Prof, 92-97, Assoc Prof, 97- , Randolph Macon Col; interim pastor, Woodlake United Meth Chur, Midlothian, VA, adj prof, Presbyterian School of Christ Edu, Richmond, VA, 94; adult Bible studies instr, United Methodist Publishing House, Nashville, TN, 97. **HONORS AND AWARDS** Who's Who in Bibl Studies & Archeol, 92; Tchr Awrd, United Methodist Brd of Higher Edu and Ministry, 95; Thomas Branch Excel in Tchng, 94 & 96; Who's Who Amer Tchrs, 98; nominated State Coumcil of Higher Edu in VA Outstanding Fac Awd. **MEMBERSHIPS** Soc Bibl Lit; SE Comm for Stud Religion **RESEARCH** Hebrew Bible, Second Temple Period; Ezekiel; Chronicles; ANE Myth & Religion **SELECTED PUBLICATIONS** Auth, The Law of the Temple in Ezekiel 40-48, Harvard Semitic Monographs Series 49; Atlanta: Scholars, 92; Auth, A Riddle Resolved by an Enigma, Jour of Bibl Lit 112, 93; auth, Interpretation, Louisville: Westminster-John Knox, 01; auth, The Rivers of Paradise: Ezek 47:1-12 and Gen 2:10-14; God Who Creates: Essays in Honor of W. Sibley Towner, Eerdmans, (00), 171-189; auth, "Divine Presence and Absence in Ezekiel's Prophecy," in Theology and Anthropology in Ezekiel, forthcoming. **CONTACT ADDRESS** 100 Slash Drive, Ashland, VA 23005. **EMAIL** Stuell@rmc.edu

TUERKHEIMER, FRANK M.
PERSONAL Born 07/27/1938, New York, NY, m, 1968, 2 children **DISCIPLINE** LAW **EDUCATION** Columbia Univ, BA, 60; Law Sch Univ NYork, LLB, 63. **CAREER** Legal coun to Atty Gen of Switz, 64-65; asst US atty, Southern Dist of NY, 65-70; vis assoc prof, 70-73, Prof Law, Sch of Law, Univ Wis-Madison, 73-, Assoc special prosecutor, Watergate Special Prosecuting Force, 73-75, consult, 75-77; US atty, Western Dist of Wis, 77-81. **HONORS AND AWARDS** Man in the News, NY Times, 4/75; Habush-Bascom Professor of Law, Univ Wis. **SELECTED PUBLICATIONS** Auth, Service of process in New York City: A proposed end to unregulated community, Columbia Law Rev, 72; coauth, Judge Weinfield and the criminal law, NY Univ Law Rev, 75; auth, The executive investigates itself, Calif Law Rev, 77; Prosecution of Criminal Cases: Where Executive and Judicial Power Meet, Am Criminal Law Rev 251, 87; Convictions Through Hearsay in Child Sexual Abuse Cases: A Logical Progression Back to Square One, Marq Law Rev 47, 88; Rape Shield Laws: A Revisit and Proposed Revision, Ohio State Law J 1245, 90; coauth, Clomazone Damage to Off-Site Vegetation: Test Results are Negative But Plants Wither and Die, Whittier Law Rev 749, 93; auth, A More Realistic Approach to Teaching Appellate Advocacy, J Legal Educ 113, 95; United States v. Martinez on Appeal: The Disturbing Anatomy of Harmless Error, Am J Trial Advocacy 269, 97; Evidence: Theory and Practice, Lexis-Nexis, 97 (electronic text). **CONTACT ADDRESS** Law Sch, Univ of Wisconsin, Madison, 975 Bascom Mall, Madison, WI 53706-1301. **EMAIL** frankt@cs.wisc.edu

TULIS, JEFFREY K.
PERSONAL Born 10/01/1950, Long Branch, NJ, m, 1978, 2 children **DISCIPLINE** POLITICAL SCIENCE **EDUCATION** Bates Col, BA, 72; Brown Univ, MA, 74; Univ Chicago, PhD, 82. **CAREER** Asst prof polit, Princeton Univ, 81-87; Asn prof of govt, Univ Tex at Austin, 88-. **HONORS AND AWARDS** Claire E Turner Awd, Bates Col; Fellow, Am Coun of Learned Stud; Asn Teaching Awd; Phi Beta Kappa. **MEMBERSHIPS** Am Polit Sci Asn. **RESEARCH** American politics; Constitutional theory; political philosophy. **SELECTED PUBLICATIONS** Co-ed, The Presidency in the Constitutional Order, La State Univ Press, 81; auth, The Rhetorical Presidency, Princeton Univ Press, 87; auth, The Constitutional Presidency and American Political Development, The Constitution and the American Presidency, SUNY Press, 91; auth, Riker's Rhetoric of Ratification, Stud in Am Polit Dev, 5, 2, Fall 91; auth, Revising the Rhetorical Presidency, Beyond the Rhetorical Presidency, Tex AM Press, 96; auth, Constitutional Abdication: The Senate, the President, and Appointments to the Supreme Court, Case West Law Rev, 47, 4, Sum 97; auth, Reflections on the Rheetorical Presidency in American Political Development, Speaking to the People: The Rhetorical Presidency in Historical Perspective, Univ Mass Press, 98. **CONTACT ADDRESS** 7105 Running Rope, Austin, TX 78731. **EMAIL** jtulis@gov.utexas.edu

TULL, HERMAN
PERSONAL Born 10/27/1955, Philadelphia, PA, m, 1978, 2 children **DISCIPLINE** HISTORY AND LITERATURE OF RELIGIONS **EDUCATION** Hobart Col, BA, 78; Northwestern Univ, PhD, 85. **CAREER** Asst prof, Rutgers Univ; lectr, Princeton Univ. **HONORS AND AWARDS** Univ fel, Northwestern Univ; Getty Postdoctoral fel. **RESEARCH** Vedic ritual; Gnomic literature in Sanskrit. **SELECTED PUBLICATIONS** Auth, Hinduism, Harper's Dictionary of Religious Education, 90; auth, F. Max Muller and A.B. Keith: 'Twaddle,' the 'Stupid' Myth, and the Disease of Indology, NUMEN, 91; auth, The Tale of 'The Bride and the Monkey': Female Insatiability, Male Impotence, and Simian Virility in Indian Literature, J Hist of Sexuality, 93; auth, The Killing That Is Not Killing: Men, Cattle, and the Origins of Non-Violence (ahimsa) in the Vedic Sacrifice, Indo-Iranian J, 96; auth, The Veduic Origins of Karma: Cosmos as Man in Ancient Indian Myth and Ritual. **CONTACT ADDRESS** 228 Terhune Rd., Princeton, NJ 08540. **EMAIL** hwtull@msn.com

TUMLIN, JOHN S.
DISCIPLINE PHILOSOPHY **EDUCATION** Emroy Univ; PhD. **CAREER** Tchr lit, Southern Polytech State Univ. **RESEARCH** Sci fiction. **SELECTED PUBLICATIONS** Auth, publ(s) on Herman Melville; ed, to Joel Chandler. **CONTACT ADDRESS** Hum and Tech Commun Dept, So Polytech State Univ, S Marietta Pkwy, PO Box 1100, Marietta, GA 30060. **EMAIL** jtumlin@spsu.edu

TUMPKIN, MARY A.
PERSONAL Born 11/13/1949, Detroit, MI, m, 1970, 1 child **DISCIPLINE** BIBLICAL STUDIES **EDUCATION** South FL Center for Theol Studies, Doctor of Ministry, 98. **CAREER** Senior Minister, Universal Truth Center. **RESEARCH** Soc of Biblical Lit; Westar Inst; Am Academy of Relig. **CONTACT ADDRESS** 21310 NW 37th Ave, Carol City, FL 33056. **EMAIL** mtumpkin@aol.com

TUNICK, DAVID C.
DISCIPLINE LAW **EDUCATION** Univ Calif, Los Angeles, BA, 63; Univ Calif, Los Angeles, JD, 71. **CAREER** Prof & J. Howard Ziemann fel; clerk, hon Malcolm M. Lucas US Dist Ct, Central Dist Calif; practiced, Mori & Katayama, Los Angeles; fac, Loyola Univ, 74-; vis prof, Univ Bridgeport, 83. **SELECTED PUBLICATIONS** Writes on, Computers, the Law & Civil Procedure. **CONTACT ADDRESS** Law School, Loyola Marymount Univ, 7900 Loyola Blvd, Burns 418, Los Angeles, CA 90045. **EMAIL** dtunick@lmulaw.lmu.edu

TURETZKY, NACHUM
PERSONAL Born 06/04/1961, Israel, m, 1997, 2 children **DISCIPLINE** PHILOSOPHY **EDUCATION** Cuny, BA, 89; CUNY, presently in graduate sch. **CAREER** Adjunct, 98, FH LaGuardia Community Col/CUNY. **MEMBERSHIPS** APA **RESEARCH** Philosophy of sci; Social and political philosophy **CONTACT ADDRESS** 149 W. 117 Street, #1, New York, NY 10026. **EMAIL** turetzky@bway.net

TURKINGTON, RICHARD C.
DISCIPLINE LAW **EDUCATION** Wayne State Univ, BA, 63; Wayne State Univ Sch Law, JD, 66; NYork Univ Sch Law, LLM, 67. **CAREER** Prof, Villanova Univ. **MEMBERSHIPS** Interdisciplinary Comt, Health Law Pa Bar Asn; chemn, Amer Asn Law Sch Sect on Defamation and Privacy. **RESEARCH** Privacy; confidentiality; AIDS and HIV related information policy. **SELECTED PUBLICATIONS** Coauth, Privacy: Cases and Materials, 92; contrib ed, AIDS, A Medical-Legal Handbook, 91 & AIDS, Law and Society, Report of the Pennsylvania Bar Association Task Force on Acquired Immune Deficiency Syndrome, 88. **CONTACT ADDRESS** Law School, Villanova Univ, 800 Lancaster Ave, Villanova, PA 19085-1692. **EMAIL** turk@law.vill.edu

TURNBULL, ROBERT GEORGE
PERSONAL Born 07/01/1918, Scotland, SD, m, 1939, 1 child **DISCIPLINE** PHILOSOPHY **EDUCATION** Univ Minn, BA, 39, PhD(philos), 52; Oberlin Col, BD, 43. **CAREER** Instr humanities, Univ Minn, 48-50; from instr to prof philos, Univ Iowa, 50-64, chmn dept, 53-64; prof, Oberlin Col, 64-65; chmn dept, 68-80, PROF PHILOS, OHIO STATE UNIV, 65-, Mem, Coun Philos Studies, 67-70; ed, Philos Res Archives, 81-. **MEMBERSHIPS** Am Philos Asn (exec secy, 66-69, pres, 77-78). **RESEARCH** Ancient and medieval philosophy; ethics; metaphysics. **SELECTED PUBLICATIONS** Coauth, Essays in Ontology, M Nijhoff, The Hague, 63; contritir & co-ed, Space, Matter and Motion, 73 & Perception, 78, Ohio State Univ; coauth, Empirical and A Priori elements in Broad's epistemology, In: The Philosophy of C D Broad; Knowledge and the forms in the later platonic dialogues, Proceedings & Addresses of Am Philos Asn, 78; The Later Concept of Scientific Explanation, In: Science and the Sciences in Plato, Eidos, 80. **CONTACT ADDRESS** Dept of Philos, Ohio State Univ, Columbus, Columbus, OH 43210.

TURNER, DONALD A.
PERSONAL Born 03/03/1962, Tuscaloosa, AL, s **DISCIPLINE** PHILOSOPHY **EDUCATION** Knox Col, BA, 84; Univ Pittsburgh, MA, 88; PhD, 94. **CAREER** Vis Asst Prof, Univ of Notre Dame, 94-94; vis asst prof, W Va Univ, 95-98; vis asst prof, Hillsdale Col, 98-99; asst. prof, Hillsdale Col, 99-. **HONORS AND AWARDS** Mellon Pre-Doctoral Fel, Univ of Pittsburgh; Teaching Fel, Univ of Pittsburgh; Sen Teaching Fel, Univ of Notre Dame. **MEMBERSHIPS** Am Philos Asn, Soc of Christian Philos. **RESEARCH** Philosophy of Religion, Metaphysics. **SELECTED PUBLICATIONS** Auth, "The Many Universes Solution to the Problem of Evil," in Richard M. Gale and Alexander Pruss (eds); auth, The Existence of God, Ashgate Publishing (Aldershot, England), (forthcoming). **CONTACT ADDRESS** Dept Relig & Philos, Hillsdale Col, 33 E College St, Hillsdale, MI 49242-1205. **EMAIL** donald.turner@hillsdale.edu

TURNER, JOHN D.
PERSONAL Born 07/15/1938, Glen Ridge, NJ, m, 1992, 2 children **DISCIPLINE** HISTORY OF RELIGION **EDUCATION** Dartmouth Col, AB, 60; Union Theol Sem, BD, 65, ThM, 66; Duke Univ, PhD, 70. **CAREER** Asst prof, Univ Montana, 71-75; Cotner Col Prof Relig, 76- , Assoc prof History, 76-83, Chr, Prog Relig Stud, 78- , Prof Classics & History, 84- , Univ Nebraska-Lincoln. **HONORS AND AWARDS** Rockefeller Doctoral fel, 68, Phi Beta Kappa, 69, Duke Univ; Am Soc Learned Soc fel, 76. **MEMBERSHIPS** Soc Bibl Lit; Studiorum Novi Testamenti Soc; Int Soc Neoplatonic Stud; Int Asn Coptic Stud; Corresp Inst Antiq & Christianity. **RESEARCH** Biblical studies; History of Hellenistic/Graeco-Roman Religion and Philosophy; Gnosticism; History of Later Greek Philosophy; Codicology and Papyrology; Greek, Coptic, Egyptian and Hebrew language and literature. **SELECTED PUBLICATIONS** Auth, Typologies of the Sethian Gnostic Treatises from Nag Hammadi, Les textes de Nag Hammadi et le probleme de leur classification: Actes du colloque tenu a Quebec du 15 au 22 Septembre, 1993, Peeters and Univ Laval, 95; ed, The Nag Hammadi Library After Fifty Years: Proceedings of the 1995 Society of Biblical Literature Commemoration, E.J. Brill, 97; auth, To See The Light: A Gnostic Appropriation of Jewish Priestly Practice and Sapiential and Apocalyptic Visionary Lore, Mediators of the Divine: Horizons of Prophecy and Divination on Mediterranean Antiquity, Scholars Press, 98; The Gnostic Seth, Biblical Figures Outside the Bible, Trinity Int Press, 98; Introduction & Commentaire, Zostrien, Presses de l'Universite Laval/Editions Peeters, 99; ed, Gnosticism and Later Platonism: Themes, Figures, Texts, Society of Biblical Literature, 00; auth, Marsanes (NHX,1), Presses de l'Universite Laval, edition peeters, 00; auth, Gnosticism and the Platonic Tradition, Presses de l'Universite Laval, editions peeters, 00. **CONTACT ADDRESS** Dept of Classics, Univ of Nebraska, Lincoln, 238 Andrews Hall, Lincoln, NE 68588-0337. **EMAIL** jturner2@unl.edu

TURNER, ROBERT FOSTER
PERSONAL Born 02/14/1944, Atlanta, GA, m, 1 child **DISCIPLINE** NATIONAL SECURITY LAW, INTERATIONAL LAW, CONSTITUTIONAL LAW, U.S. FOREIGN P **EDUCATION** IN Univ, BA Gov't ,68; Law School, JD 81; SJD, 96; Univ VA, Law School. **CAREER** Co founder and Assoc Dir, Center for Natl Sec Law, Univ of VA, School of Law, 81; Special Asst, Under Sec of Defense for Policy, 81-82; Cousel Pres, Intelligence Oversight Board The White House, 82-84; Principal Deputy Asst, Sec of State for Legislative and Intergovernmental Affair, US Dep of State, 84-85; Pres, US Inst of Peace, Washington DC, 86-87; Assoc Dir, Center for Natl Security Law, Univ VA, School of Law, 87-present. **HONORS AND AWARDS** Distinguished Lectures US Military Academy(West Point); Chm ABA Standing Comm on Executive-Congressional Rlations ABA Section of International Law & Practive, Trustee, Intercollegiate Studies Inst; Dir, Thomas Jefferson Inst for Public Policy; Expert witness before more than a dozen Comm of US Senate and House. **MEMBERSHIPS** Council on Foreign Affairs; Academy of Political Sci; Amer Soc of International Law. **RESEARCH** Natl Security and the Constitution; War Powers; Separation of Powers; Intl Law and the Use of Force; Origins of and Solutions to War; US Foreign Policy and Diplomatic Hist. **SELECTED PUBLICATIONS** Author or editor of: Vietnamese Communism: Its Origins and Development; The Qar Powers Resolution: Its Implementation in Theory and Practice; Nicaragua v. United States: A Look at the Facts; Repealing the War Powers Resolution: Restoring the Rule of Law in US Foreign Policy; National Security Law, Contibutor to major US and foreign newspapers; NT Times, Wall Street Journal ,Washington Post ,Jerusalem Post. **CONTACT ADDRESS** Univ of Virginia, Charlottesville, VA 22901. **EMAIL** rft3m@virginia.edu

TURQUETTE, ATWELL R.
PERSONAL Born 07/14/1914, Texarkana, TX, m, 1998, 5 children **DISCIPLINE** PHILOSOPHY **EDUCATION** Univ Arkansas, BA, 36; Duke Univ, MA, 37; Cornell Univ, PhD, 43. **CAREER** Asst prof, 37-38, assoc prof, 39-40, Florida Southern Col; fel, Univ Chicago, 38-39; asst teaching asst, 40-43, instr, 43-45, Cornell Univ; asst prof, 45-48, assoc prof, 48-52, prof, 52-75, prof emer, 75- , Univ Ill, Urbana-Champaign. **HONORS AND AWARDS** Duke Univ scholar; fel, Univ Chicago; fel, Cornell Univ; Rockefeller Gen Educ Board grant; NSF grants. **MEMBERSHIPS** APA; Am Math Soc; Landan Math Soc; Calcutta Math Soc; Symbolic Logic Asn; Charles S Peirce Soc; Bertrand Russell Soc; Soc for Indust and Appl Math; AAAS; NY Acad Sci; IEEE Computer Soc. **RESEARCH** Logic; philosophy of science; history of ideas. **SELECTED PUBLICATIONS** Auth, Many-valued Logics, with J.B. Rasser, North Holland, 52; auth, An Alternative Minimal and Intuitive Axiomatic System for M-Valued Logic, Int Cong of Math, Zurich, 94; auth, Explanation as the Converse of Applications, 10th Int Congress of Logic, Methodology, and Philos of Sci, Florence, 95; auth, A Generalization of Tarski's Moglichkeit, Auckland, 97. **CONTACT ADDRESS** 914 W Clark, Champaign, IL 61821-3328. **EMAIL** aturquette1@iopener.net

TUSAN, GAIL S.
PERSONAL Born 08/03/1956, Los Angeles, CA, d **DISCIPLINE** LAW **EDUCATION** University of California, Los Angeles, BA, 1978; George Washington University, JD, 1981; University of Nevada/National Judicial College, 1992. **CAREER** U.S. Department of Justice, intern, 80-81; Kilpatrick & Cody, associate, 81-84; Asbill, Porter, associate, 84-86; Joyner & Joyner, partner, 86-90; City Court of Atlanta, judge, 90-92; State Court of Fulton County, judge, 92-95; Institute of Continuing Judicial Education, faculty member; Georgia State University Law School, faculty member; Superior Court of Fulton County, judge, 95-. **HONORS AND AWARDS** YWCA of Greater Atlanta's Academy of Women Achievers, Inductee, 1995; Cited by Georgia Informer as one of Georgia's 50 Most Influential Black Women, 1994; Justice Robert Benham, Law Related Supporter of the Year Awd, 1992; Martin Luther King Jr Center for Nonviolence and Social Change Community Service Peace and Justice Awd, 1991; Ebony, Thirty Leaders of the Future, 1985. **MEMBERSHIPS** Georgia State Bar, 1981-; Georgia Association of Black Women Attorneys, president, 1983, executive committee; Gate City Bar Association; Atlanta Bar Association; Judicial Procedure and Administration Advisory Committee; Committee on Professionalism. **CONTACT ADDRESS** Judge, Superior Court of Fulton County, 185 Central Ave SW, Rm T8955, Atlanta, GA 30303.

TUSHNET, MARK VICTOR
PERSONAL Born 11/18/1945, Newark, NJ, m, 1969, 2 children **DISCIPLINE** LAW, AMERICAN LEGAL HISTORY **EDUCATION** Harvard Col, BA, 67; Yale Univ JD & MA, 71. **CAREER** Asst prof, 73-76, assoc prof, 76-79, prof law, Univ Wis, 79-; prof law, Georgetown Univ Law Ctr, 81-. **MEMBERSHIPS** Orgn Am Historians; Am Soc Legal Hist; Am Hist Assn; Conf Critical Legal Studies. **RESEARCH** Constitutional law; federal jurisdiction; American legal history. **SELECTED PUBLICATIONS** Auth, The Warren Court in Historical Perspective, ec, University of Press of Virginia, 93; auth, Making Civil Rights Law: Thurgood Marshall and the Supreme Court, 1936-1961, Oxford University Press, 94; auth, Brown v Board of Education, Franklin Watts, 95; coauth, Remnants of Belief: Contemporary Constitutional Issues, Oxford University Press, 96; auth, Making Constitutional Law: Thurgood Marshall and the Supreme Court, 1961-1991, Oxford University Press, 97; auth, Taking the Constitution Away from the Courts, Princeton Univ Press, 99. **CONTACT ADDRESS** Law Ctr, Georgetown Univ, 600 New Jersey NW, Washington, DC 20001-2022. **EMAIL** tushnet@law.georgetown.edu

TUTTLE, HOWARD N.
PERSONAL Born 12/15/1935, Salt Lake City, UT, m, 1963, 2 children **DISCIPLINE** PHILOSOPHY **EDUCATION** Univ Utah, BA, 58, MA, 59; Harvard Univ, MA, 63; Brandeis Univ, PhD, 67. **CAREER** Prof philos, Univ New Mexico. **RESEARCH** Philosophy of history; philosophy of life. **SELECTED PUBLICATIONS** Auth, Wilhelm Dilthey's Philosophy of History; auth, The Dawn of Historical Reason; auth, The Crowd is Untruth. **CONTACT ADDRESS** 939 Donner Way, Apt 108, Salt Lake City, UT 84108.

TWADDELL, GERALD E.
PERSONAL Born 03/23/1943, Dayton, KY, s **DISCIPLINE** PHILOSOPHY **EDUCATION** Sem of St. Pius X, BA, 63; Univ Strasbourg, Diploma d'E F M, 65; Catholic Univ Paris, STB, 67; Univ Cincinnati, MA, 74; Catholic Univ Paris, PhL, 74, D Phil, 77. **CAREER** Prof, Sem of St. Pius X, 67-77, dean, 70-77; asst prof philos, 77-87, assoc prof, 88-92, prof philos, Thomas More Col, 93-, asst academic dean, 77-81, dir Institutional Res, 81-84, College Marshall, Thomas More Col, Crestview Hills, KY, 85-97. **HONORS AND AWARDS** Mina Shaughnessy Scholar, FIPSE, US Dept of Ed, 83. **MEMBERSHIPS** Am Philos Asn; Am Cath Philos Asn; KY Philos Asn (pres, 82-83); Gabriel Marcel Soc; Am Asn Philos Teachers. **RESEARCH** Theory of value; applied ethics. **CONTACT ADDRESS** Thomas More Col, 333 Thomas More Parkway, Crestview Hills, KY 41017-3428. **EMAIL** Gerald.Twaddell@thomasmore.edu

TWEED, THOMAS A.
PERSONAL Born 12/28/1954, Philadelphia, PA **DISCIPLINE** RELIGIOUS, AMERICAN STUDIES **EDUCATION** Pa State Univ, BS, 77; Harvard Univ, MTS, 79; Stanford Univ, MA, 83; PhD, 89. **CAREER** Asst prof, Univ of Miami, 88-93; asst prof to prof, Univ of NC, 93-. **HONORS AND AWARDS** NEH Fel, 94-95; Am Acad of Relig Awd for Excellence, 98. **MEMBERSHIPS** Am Soc for the Study of Relig. **RESEARCH** Religion in North America. **SELECTED PUBLICATIONS** Auth, The American Encounter with Buddhism, 1844-1912: Victorian Culture and the Limits of Dissent, Ind Univ Pr (Bloomington), 92; auth, Our Lady of the Exile: Diasporic Religion at a Cuban Catholic Shrine in Miami, Oxford Univ Pr, (NY), 97; ed, Retelling U.S. Religious History, Univ of Calif Pr (Berkeley), 97; coed, Asian Religions in America: A Documentary History, Oxford Univ Pr, (NY), 99. **CONTACT ADDRESS** Dept Relig Studies, Univ of No Carolina, Chapel Hill, CB #3225, 101 Saunders Hall, Chapel Hill, NC 27599-3225.

TWESIGYE, EMMANUEL
PERSONAL Born 05/25/1948, Rukungiri, Uganda, m, 1976, 4 children **DISCIPLINE** THEOLOGY **EDUCATION** EAU, DipTh, 70; MUK, BA, 73, DipEd, 73; Wheaton Grad Sch, MA, 78; Univ of the South, STM, 79; Vanderbilt Univ, MA, 82, VU, PhD, 83. **CAREER** Chaplain, head, dept of rel stud, Uganda Nat Tchrs Col, 73-77; assoc prof, chemn relig and philos, Fisk Univ, 83-89; prof, dir BWS, Ohio Wesleyan Univ, 89-98. **HONORS AND AWARDS** Honors degrees; listed, Who's Who in the World, Who's Who in the Mid- West, International Who's Who of Intellectuals, 5000 Personalities, Men of Achievement. **MEMBERSHIPS** Am Acad Relig; Soc of Bibl Lit; Am Asn of Philos; Ohio Acad of Relig. **RESEARCH** African theology and philosophy; evolutionary ethics. **SELECTED PUBLICATIONS** Auth, Common Ground: African Religion and Philosophy, 87; auth, The Global Human Problem, 88; Auth, God, Race, Myth and Power, 91; auth, African Religion, Philosophy, and Christianity in Logos-Christ, 96. **CONTACT ADDRESS** Dept of Religion and Philosophy, Ohio Wesleyan Univ, Delaware, OH 43015. **EMAIL** ektwesig@cc.owu.edu

TWETTEN, DAVID B.
PERSONAL Born 07/06/1957, Spencer, IA, m, 1982, 3 children **DISCIPLINE** PHILOSOPHY **EDUCATION** Univ Toronto, Pontifical Inst of Mediaeval Stud, MSL, 87, PhD, phil and medieval stud, 93. **CAREER** Asst prof, 91-99, Marquette Univ. **HONORS AND AWARDS** Dist Scholar Recognition, Marquette Univ, 97; Phi Beta Kappa. **MEMBERSHIPS** APA; ACPA; Soc for Medieval and Renaissance Phil; Soc Intl d'Histoire des Sciences et de la Philosophie Arabes et Islamiques; Soc Intl pour l'Etude de la Philosophie Medievale; Intl Comm for the History of Medieval and Renaissance Natural Phil. **RESEARCH** Ancient and medieval philosophy **SELECTED PUBLICATIONS** Auth, Why Motion Requires a Cause: The Foundation for a Prime Mover in Aristotle and Aquinas, Phil & the God of Abraham: Essays in Mem of James A Weisheipl, O P, Pontifical Inst of Mediaeval Stud, 91; auth, Averroes on the Prime Mover Proved in the Physics, Viator: Medieval & Renaissance Stud 26, 95; auth, Clearing A Way for Aquinas: How the Proof from Motion Concludes to God, Proc of the Amer Cath Phil Asn 70, 96; auth, Back to Nature in Aquinas, Medieval Phil & Theology 5.2, 96; auth, Albert the Great on Whether Natural Philosophy Proves God's Existence, Archives d'histoire doctrinale et litteraire du moyen age 64, 97. **CONTACT ADDRESS** Dept of Philosophy, Marquette Univ, Coughlin 234, PO Box 1881, Milwaukee, WI 53201-1881. **EMAIL** david.twettend@marquette.edu

TWISS, SUMNER BARNES
PERSONAL Born 12/02/1944, Baltimore, MD, m, 1967, 2 children **DISCIPLINE** PHILOSOPHY OF RELIGION, RELIGIOUS ETHICS **EDUCATION** Johns Hopkins Univ, BA, 66; Yale Univ, MA and MPhil, 71, PhD(relig studies), 74. **CAREER** Teaching fel ethics, Divinity Sch, Yale Univ, 69-70, teaching assoc, 70-71; from instr to asst prof relig studies, 71-76, assoc prof, 76-80, Prof Relig Studies, Brown Univ, 80-, Consult ethics, Inst Soc, Ethics and Life Sci, 72, fel, 73; Soc Values Higher Educ fel, 72. **HONORS AND AWARDS** AM, Brown Univ, 77. **MEMBERSHIPS** Am Acad of Relig; Soc for Asian and Comparative Philos; Soc of Christian Ethics; Asn for Asian Studies. **RESEARCH** Comparative Religious Ethics; Comparative Moral and Religious Thought; Philosophy and Theory of Religion; Contemporary Moral Problems: Human Rights. **SELECTED PUBLICATIONS** Auth, Comparative Religious Ethics: A New Method, Harper & Row, 78; auth, Genetic Counseling, Facts, Values and Norms, 79; auth, Experience of the Sacred: Readings in the Phenomenology of Religion, Brown Univ/Univ Press of New England, 92; auth, Religion and Human Rights, Project on Religion & Human Rights, 94; auth, Religious Diversity and American Religious History: Studies in Traditions and Cultures, Univ Georgia Press, 97; auth, Explorations in Global Ethics: Comparative Religious Ethics and Interreligious Dialogue, Westview Press, 00. **CONTACT ADDRESS** Dept of Relig Studies, Brown Univ, Box 1927, Providence, RI 02912.

TWITCHELL, MARY POE
DISCIPLINE LAW **EDUCATION** Hollins Col, BA; Univ NC, Chapel Hill, MA; Univ Fla, JD; Yale Law Sch, LLM. **CAREER** Prof, Univ Fla, 82-. **MEMBERSHIPS** Civil Justice Reform Adv Gp, US Dist Ct, Middle Dist Fla, 91-93; Fla Bar; Order of the Coif. **RESEARCH** Civil procedure, federal practice. **SELECTED PUBLICATIONS** Auth, "The Myth of General Jurisdiction," 101 Harv. L. Rev. 610, 88. **CONTACT ADDRESS** School of Law, Univ of Florida, PO Box 117625, Gainesville, FL 32611-7625. **EMAIL** twitchell@law.ufl.edu

TYLENDA, JOSEPH N.
PERSONAL Born 06/26/1928, Dickson City, PA **DISCIPLINE** THEOLOGY **EDUCATION** Univ Scranton, AB, 48; Boston Col, STL, 60; Pontif Gregorian Univ, STD, 64. **CAREER** Asst prof hist theol, Woodstock Col, Md, 64-73, dir libr, 68-70; lectr, Pontif Gregorian Univ, 70-73; assoc prof theol, Loyola Col, Md, 73-74; ASST ED, THEOL STUDIES, 74-. **MEMBERSHIPS** Theol Soc Am; Polish Inst Arts and Sci Am; Am Soc Church Hist. **RESEARCH** John Calvin and reformed theology. **SELECTED PUBLICATIONS CONTACT ADDRESS** Georgetown Univ, Washington, DC 20057.

TYLER, RONALD
PERSONAL Born 04/30/1938, St. Joseph, MO, m, 1963, 1 child **DISCIPLINE** NEW TESTAMENT **EDUCATION** E NM Univ, BA, 61, MA, 64; Baylor Univ, PhD, 73; Vancouver Sch Theol, 77. **CAREER** Instr, Kilgore Col, 62-68; ch, Kilgore Col, 66-68; min, Church of Christ, 68-72; prof, Pepperdine Univ, 72-01 **HONORS AND AWARDS** Vis fel, Princeton theol sem, 86. **MEMBERSHIPS** Soc Bibl Lit; Gamma Theta Upsilon; The Cath Bibl Asst Am. **SELECTED PUBLICATIONS** Auth, "The Source and Function of Isaiah 6:9-10 in John 12:40," in Johannine Studies: Essays in Honor of Frank Pack, 89; rev, Gerd Theissen, Psychological Aspects of Pauline Theology in The Princeton Seminary Bulletin, 90; rev, Leon Morris, The Epistle to the Romans in interpretation, July, 90; rev, Jerry Sumney, Identifying Paul's Opponents in 2 Corinthians, in CBQ, Oct. 91; rev, James Dunn, Romans 1-8 and Romans 9-16 in Restoration Quarterly, 93; rev, Raymond Martin, Studies in the Life and Ministry of Paul and Related Issues, in Critical Review of Books in Religion, V.8 (1995); rev, auth, "First Corinthians 4:6 and Hellenistic Pedagogy," CBQ, Jan. 98; auth, "Not Going Beyond What Is Written: 1 Corinthians 4:6 in the History of Interpretation," Forthcoming in Restoration Quarterly; rev, Odette Mainville, Un Plaidoyer en Faveur De L'Unite: La Lettre Aux Romains, CBS, Oct. 00. **CONTACT ADDRESS** Dept of Relig, Pepperdine Univ, 24255 Pacific Coast Hwy, Malibu, CA 90263. **EMAIL** rtyler@pepperdine.edu

TYRRELL, BERNARD JAMES
PERSONAL Born 05/10/1933, Yakima, WA **DISCIPLINE** PHILOSOPHY, RELIGIOUS STUDIES **EDUCATION** Gonzaga Univ, AB, 57, MA, 58; Santa Clara Univ, MA, 66; Fordham Univ, PhD, 72. **CAREER** Asst prof, 72-77, assoc prof, 77-81, Prof to Prof Emeritus, Philos & Relig Studies, Gonzaga Univ, 82-. **HONORS AND AWARDS** Phi Beta Kappa, Fordham Univ, 72. **MEMBERSHIPS** Am Acad Relig; Cath Theol Soc; Nat Guild Cath Psychiatrists. **RESEARCH** Religion and psychology. **SELECTED PUBLICATIONS** Auth, The dynamics of conversion, Homiletic & Pastoral Rev, 6/72; Christotherapy, In: Wisdom and Knowledge, Vol II, Abbey Press, 72; New Context of the Philosophy of God, In: Language, Truth and Meaning, Gill & Macmillan, 73; Bernard Lonergan's Philosophy of God, Notre Dame, 74; Christotherapy, Seabury, 75; Christotherapy and the Healing of Communal Consciousness, The Thomist, 10/76; Christotheraphy: A Concrete Instance of a Christian Psychotherapy, Bull Nat Guild Cath Psychiatrists, 77; Christotherapy II: A New Horizon for Counselors, Spiritual Directors and Seekers of Healing and Growth in Christ, Paulist Press, 82; Christointegration, Paulist Press, 89; Affectional Conversation, Method J of Lonergan Studies, Vol 14, No 1, spring 96. **CONTACT ADDRESS** Jesuit House, Gonzaga Univ, 502 E Boone Ave, Spokane, WA 99258-0001. **EMAIL** btyrrell@gonzaga.edu

TYSON, JOHN R.
DISCIPLINE THEOLOGY **EDUCATION** Grove City Col, AB, 74; Asbury Theol Sem, Mdiv, 77; Grad Sch Drew Univ, MPhil,80, PhD, 83. **CAREER** Prof; Houghton Col, 79; past assoc pastor, First United Methodist Church, Cocoa, Fla. **HONORS AND AWARDS** Founding mem & bd dir, Charles Wesley Soc. **MEMBERSHIPS** Oxford Inst Methodist Theol; Wesleyan Theol Soc, Wesley Stud Sect Amer Acad Rel; Amer Soc Church Historians. **SELECTED PUBLICATIONS** Publ on, theological topics, 3 bk(s). **CONTACT ADDRESS** Dept of Religion and Philosophy, Houghton Col, PO Box 128, Houghton, NY 14744.

TYSON, JOSEPH B.
PERSONAL Born 08/30/1928, Charlotte, NC, m, 1954, 1 child **DISCIPLINE** RELIGION **EDUCATION** Duke Univ, AB, 50, BD, 53; Union Theol Sem, NYork, STM, 55, PhD, 59. **CAREER** From asst prof to assoc prof, 58-74, chmn dept, 65-75, 87-95; PROF RELIG, SOUTHERN METHODIST UNIV, 74-98; Prof emeritus, 98. **MEMBERSHIPS** Soc Bibl Lit; Am Acad Relig; Studiorum Nova Testamenti Soc. **RESEARCH** New Testament. **SELECTED PUBLICATIONS** Auth, "The New Testament and Early Christianity," 84; auth, "The Death of Jesus in Luke-Acts, 88; auth, "Images of Judaism in Luke-Acts," 92; "Luke, Judaism, and the Scholars," 99. **CONTACT ADDRESS** Dept of Relig Studies, So Methodist Univ, P O Box 750202, Dallas, TX 75275-0202. **EMAIL** jtyson@mail.smu.edu

U

UDDO, BASILE JOSEPH
PERSONAL Born 04/22/1949, New Orleans, LA, m, 1971, 3 children **DISCIPLINE** CONSTITUTIONAL LAW **EDUCATION** Loyola Univ, New Orleans, BBA, 70; Tulane Univ, JD, 73; Harvard Univ, 74. **CAREER** Instr legal process, Boston Univ, 73-74; asst prof const law, 75-77, assoc prof, 77-81, PROF CONST LAW, LOYOLA UNIV LAW SCH, NEW ORLEANS, 81-, Nat comt, Human Life Found, 79-; consult, Prog Values in Educ, Asn Cath Col and Univ, 80-; Prolife adv comt, US Cath Conf, 80-; adv comt, Am Family Inst, 80- **RESEARCH** Constitutional law--especially relating to issues concerning the right to life; family law--impact of law on families; law and ethics--professional responsibility. **SELECTED PUBLICATIONS** Auth, Federal-Policy on Forgoing Treatment or Care--Contradictions or Consistency, Issues in Law and Medicine, Vol 0008, 92. **CONTACT ADDRESS** Law Sch, Loyola Univ, New Orleans, 6333 Loyola Ave, New Orleans, LA 70118.

UDOH, FABIAN E.
PERSONAL Born 11/06/1954, Nigeria, m, 1993, 2 children **DISCIPLINE** THEOLOGY **EDUCATION** Duke Univ, PhD, 96. **CAREER** Asst Prof, 96-98, Hobart & William Smith College; Asst Prof, 98-, Humanities, Univ of Notre Dame. **MEMBERSHIPS** AAR/SBL, CBA. **RESEARCH** New Testament interpretation, Second Temple Jewish history, African theology. **CONTACT ADDRESS** Program of Liberal Studies, Univ of Notre Dame, 215 O'Shaughnessey, Notre Dame, IN 46556. **EMAIL** udoh.1@nd.edu

UEDA, MAKOTO
PERSONAL Born 05/20/1931, Ono, Japan, m, 1962, 2 children **DISCIPLINE** LITERATURE, AESTHETICS **EDUCATION** Kobe Univ, BLitt, 54; Univ Nebr, MA, 56; Univ Wash, PhD(comp lit), 61. **CAREER** Lectr Japanese, Univ Toronto, 61-62, from asst prof to prof, 62-71; PROF JAPANESE, STANFORD UNIV, 71-96. **RESEARCH** Japanese literature, including theatre; comparative literature, especially Japanese and Western; literary theory and criticism. **SELECTED PUBLICATIONS** Auth, Modern Japanese Poets and the Nature of Literature, Stanford Univ Press, 83; auth, The Mother of Dreams, Kodansha International, 86; auth, Basho and His Inerpreters, Stanford Univ Press, 92; auth, Modern Japanese Tanka, Columbia Univ Press, 96; auth, The Path of Flowering Thorn, Stanford Univ Press, 98; auth, Light Verse from the Floating World, Columbia Univ Press, 99. **CONTACT ADDRESS** 160 Formway Ct., Los Altos, CA 94022.

UITTI, ROGER W.
PERSONAL Born 10/29/1934, Chicago, IL, m, 1959, 4 children **DISCIPLINE** THEOLOGY **EDUCATION** Northwestern Coll, BA, 56; Wisc Evangel Lutheran Sem, BD, Ordained, 59; Luther Sem St Paul, MTh, 64; Lutheran School of Theo Chicago, PhD, 73. **CAREER** Instr, 62-66, Asst Prof, 66-80, theology, Concordia Coll, River Forest; adj Asst Prof, 77-79, Rosary Coll, River Forest; vis Asst Prof, 79, Mundelein Coll; Assoc Prof, 80-87, Prof, Old Testament, 87-, Dean of stud, 92-98, Lutheran Theo Sem, Saskatoon SK; sessional Lectr, 80-94, Univ of Saskatoon, SK. **HONORS AND AWARDS** LSTC Grad Scholarship, Univ of Chicago, AAL Concordia Coll Fac Scholarship. **MEMBERSHIPS** SBL, EES, AOS. **RESEARCH** Old Testament & the Arts, Old Testament Synoptic study, Old Testament Law/Law Collations. **SELECTED PUBLICATIONS** Auth, The Imagery Behind Luther's Ein feste Burg, in: Church Music, 75; A New Lectionary for a New Church? in: Currents in Theology and Mission, 88; Christian Disunity and Unity, Consensus, 91; Health and Wholeness in the Old Testament, Consensus, 91; co-auth, Duplicate Histories, A New Study Instrument for the Hebrew Bible, in: The Fourth R, 90; co-auth, The Arts and the Church, in: Consensus, 99. **CONTACT ADDRESS** Lutheran Theol Sem, Saskatoon, 114 Seminary Cres, Saskatoon, SK, Canada S7N 0X3. **EMAIL** roger.uitti@usask.ca

ULANOV, ANN BELFORD
PERSONAL Born 01/01/1938, Princeton, NJ, m, 1968, 4 children **DISCIPLINE** DEPTH PSYCHOLOGY, CHRISTIAN THEOLOGY **EDUCATION** Radcliffe Col, BA, 59; Union Theol Sem, MDiv, 62, PhD, 67. **CAREER** From instr to assoc prof psychiat and relig, Union Theol Sem, 66-74; Psycho-Therapist, 65-; prof psychiat and relig, union theol sem, 74-, Res psychotherapist, Inst Relig and Health, 62-65; bd mem, C G Jung Training Ctr, 71 **MEMBERSHIPS** Am Asn Pastoral Counr; C G Jung Found Anal Psychol; Int Asn Anal Psychol; Nat Accreditation Asn and Exam Bd Psychoanal; Am Theol Soc. **RESEARCH** Feminine psychology; religion and the unconscious; the witch archetype. **SELECTED PUBLICATIONS** Auth, The Golden Ass of Apuleius--the Liberation of the Feminine in Man, Parabola-Myth Tradition Search for Meaning, Vol 0018, 93; Exploring Sacred Landscapes--Religious and Spiritual Experiences in Psychotherapy, Jour Rel and Health, Vol 0033, 94; The Work of Loewald, Hans, an Introduction and Commentary, Jour Rel and Health, Vol 0033, 94; Leaving My Fathers House-- A Journey to Conscious Femininity, Jour Rel and Health, Vol 0033, 94; A Womans Identity, Jour Rel and Health, Vol 0033, 94; Object Relations Therapy, Jour Rel and Health, Vol 0033, 94; Projective and Introjective Identification and the Use of the Therapists Self, Jour of Rel and Health, Vol 0033, 94; Envy--Further Thoughts, Jour Rel and Health, Vol 0034, 95; Sacred Chaos--Reflections on God Shadow and the Dark Self, Jour Rel and Health, Vol 0034, 95; The Mystery of the Conjunctio--Alchemical Images of Individuation, Jour Rel and Health, Vol 0034, 95; In Gods Shadow--The Collaboration of White, Victor and Jung,C.G., Jour Rel and Health, Vol 0034, 95; Protestantism and Jungian Psychology, Jour of Rel and Health, Vol 0035, 96; A Meeting of Minds--Mutuality in Psychoanalysis, Jour of Rel and Health, Vol 0035, 96; Tillich, Paul First--A Memoir of the Harvard Years, Jour Rel and Health, Vol 0036, 97; Always Becoming--An Autobiography, Jour Rel and Health, Vol 0036, 97; Practicing Wholeness, Jour of Rel and Health, Vol 0036, 97. **CONTACT ADDRESS** Union Theol Sem, New York, 3041 Broadway at 121st St, New York, NY 10027.

ULEN, THOMAS S.
DISCIPLINE LAW **EDUCATION** Dartmouth Col, BA; Oxford Univ, MA; Stanford Univ, PhD. **CAREER** Prof, Univ Ill Urban Champaign; Dir of the University's master's degree program in public policy and public administration, 99- **HONORS AND AWARDS** Ed, Int Rev Law Economics. **MEMBERSHIPS** Am Law Economics Asn. **RESEARCH** Law, economics; including quantitative methods of legal decision-making. **SELECTED PUBLICATIONS** Co-auth, Law and Economics. **CONTACT ADDRESS** Law Dept, Univ of Illinois, Urbana-Champaign, 228 Law Bldg, Mc 594, 504 E Pennsylvania, Champaign, IL 61820. **EMAIL** tulen@law.uiuc.edu

ULIAN, JOSEPH
PERSONAL Born 11/09/1930, Ann Arbor, MI, 2 children **DISCIPLINE** PHILOSOPHY **EDUCATION** Harvard Univ, AB, 52; AM, 53, PhD, 57. **CAREER** Instr, Stanford Univ, 57-58; asst prof, Johns Hopkins Univ, 58-60; vis asst prof, Univ Pa, 59-60; res assoc, Univ Pa, 61-62; vis asst prof, Univ Chicago, 62-63; asst prof, Univ Calif at Santa Barbara, 64-66; from assoc prof to prof, Washington Univ, 65-; lectr, Univ Calif at Berkeley, 61; consult, Res Directorate System Development Corp., 62-70. **HONORS AND AWARDS** Phi Beta Kappa. **MEMBERSHIPS** Am Philos Asn, Asn for Symbolic Logic, Am Soc for Aesthetics. **RESEARCH** Sports, Theatre, Music. **SELECTED PUBLICATIONS** Coauth, The Web of Belief, Random House, 70 & 78; auth, "Quine and the Field of Mathematical Logic," in The Philosophy of W. V. Quine, ed. Hahn and Schilpp (Open Court, 86); coauth, "Truth About Jones," J of Philos 74 (77). **CONTACT ADDRESS** Dept Philos, Washington Univ, 1 Brookings Dr, Campus Box 1073, Saint Louis, MO 63130-4862.

ULRICH, DOLPH
DISCIPLINE LOGIC, LOGICAL THEORY, PHILOSOPHY OF MATHEMATICS **EDUCATION** Wayne State Univ, PhD. **CAREER** Prof, Purdue Univ. **RESEARCH** Many-valued logics; modal logic. **SELECTED PUBLICATIONS** Coauth, Elementary Symbolic Logic. **CONTACT ADDRESS** Dept of Philos, Purdue Univ, West Lafayette, 1080 Schleman Hall, West Lafayette, IN 47907-1080.

ULRICH, LAWRENCE P.
DISCIPLINE PHILOSOPHY **EDUCATION** Catholic Univ of Am, BA, 61; MA, 62; Xavier Univ, MEd, 64; Univ of Toronto, PhD, 72; Univ of Dayton, MS, 85. **CAREER** From asst prof to prof, Univ Dayton, 64- ; vis prof, Antioch Col, 68; adj assoc prof, Wilminton Col, 78-84; clinical assoc, Wright State Univ, Sc of Med, 80-; vis prof, Georgetown Univ Med Sch, 83; ch, dept of philos, Univ Dayton, 85-93; vis prof, Col of Mt St Joseph, 87; adj prof, Ohio Univ Col of Osteopathic Med, 96-. **RESEARCH** Meidcal ethics; social philosophy; business ethics. **SELECTED PUBLICATIONS** Auth, The Patient Self-Determination Act: A Training Program for Health Care Professionals, Breckenridge Bioethics, 91; The Patient Self-Determination Act and Cultural Diversity, Cambridge Quart of Healthcare Ethics, 94; Ethical Issues in Medical Practice: Á Healthcare Education Course for Medical Students, Ohio Univ, 96. **CONTACT ADDRESS** Dept of Philos, Univ of Dayton, 300 Col Park, Dayton, OH 45469-1546. **EMAIL** lawrence.ulrich@notes.udayton.edu

UMIDI, JOSEPH L.
DISCIPLINE PRACTICAL THEOLOGY **EDUCATION** Kalamazoo Col, BA; Acadia Divinity Col, MDiv; Trinity Evangel Divinity Sch, DMin. **CAREER** Instr, Discipleship Training Sem, YWAM; prof, 85. **HONORS AND AWARDS** Founding bd mem, Hampton Rd(s) United Christians, 90-95; co-founder, consult, Can Christian Commun, Inc; founding bd mem, Leadership Training Intl, 92-96; bd mem, Missions S Am, 94-96; founding bd mem, Operation Breaking Through, 96. **SELECTED PUBLICATIONS** Auth, Avoiding Leadership Snares, Youth Ministries Mag, Sonlife Ministries, Elburn, 95; Leadership Land Mines, Regent Univ Sch of Divinity Rev, vol 1; In the Beginning; Breathe, Canada, Breathe; Ministry By The Book, Living By The Book, Christian Broadcasting Network, Inc, CBN Publ, 93; Surveys of regional prayer strategies, Strategic Intercession for the 90's, Umidi Publ, 94; auth, rel columnist, Can Newspaper. **CONTACT ADDRESS** Dept of Practical Theology, Regent Univ, 1000 Regent Univ Dr, Virginia Beach, VA 23464-9831.

UNDERWOOD, HARRY
DISCIPLINE LAW **EDUCATION** Oxford Univ, BA, 76; Univ Toronto, LLB, 79. **CAREER** Lawyer, McCarthy Tetrault **RESEARCH** Civil litigation. **SELECTED PUBLICATIONS** Auth, pubs on legal subjects. **CONTACT ADDRESS** Fac of Law, Univ of Toronto, 78 Queen's Park, Toronto, ON, Canada M5S 1A1.

UNDERWOOD, JAMES L.
DISCIPLINE CONST LAW, FEDERAL PRACTICE, AND CIVIL AND POLITICAL RIGHTS **EDUCATION** Emory Univ, AB, 59, JD, 62; Yale Univ, LLM, 66. **CAREER** Strom Thurmond prof, Univ of SC. **SELECTED PUBLICATIONS** Auth, leading treatises on civil litigation in fed courts. **CONTACT ADDRESS** School of Law, Univ of So Carolina, Columbia, Law Center, Columbia, SC 29208-. **EMAIL** JimU@law.law.sc.edu

UNGAR, ANTHONY
DISCIPLINE PHILOSOPHY **EDUCATION** Stanford Univ, PhD. **CAREER** Assoc prof, Univ Albany, State Univ NY. **RESEARCH** Logic, philosophy of logic, philosophy and foundations of mathematics. **SELECTED PUBLICATIONS** Auth, Normalization, Cut-Elimination, and the Theory of Proofs, 92. **CONTACT ADDRESS** Dept of Philosophy, SUNY, Albany, Albany, NY 12222. **EMAIL** amu78@cnsunix.albany.edu

UNNO, MARK
DISCIPLINE EAST ASIAN RELIGIONS **EDUCATION** Oberlin, BA, Stanford, MA, PhD. **CAREER** Religion, Carleton Univ. **MEMBERSHIPS** Auth, Japanese Pure Land Buddhism. **CONTACT ADDRESS** Carleton Col, 100 S College St., Northfield, MN 55057-4016.

UNNO, TAITETSU
PERSONAL Born 02/05/1929, Japan, m, 1958, 1 child **DISCIPLINE** BUDDHIST STUDIES **EDUCATION** Univ Calif, Berkeley, BA, 51; Univ Tokyo, MA, 56, PhD(Buddhist studies), 68. **CAREER** Instr Orient lang, Univ Calif, Los Angeles, 59-61; vis lectr hist, Univ Ill, 68-69, asst prof hist & Asian studies, 69-70, assoc prof, 70-71; Prof World Relig,Smith Col, 71-88, Jill Ker Conway Prof Relig, 88-. **HONORS AND AWARDS** Mellon Fel, 85; Ernest Pon Awd for Civil and Human Rights, 88; Japan Found Fel, 94. **MEMBERSHIPS** Asn Asian Studies; Am Acad Relig; Am Orient Soc; NAm Soc Buddhist Studies. **RESEARCH** Buddhist studies; comparative religion; East Asian history. **SELECTED PUBLICATIONS** Auth, The Religious Philosophy of Tanabe Hajime, Asian Humanities Press, 90; The Religious Philosophy of Nishitani Keiji, Asian Humanities Press, 90; Tannisho: A Shin Buddhist Classic, Buddhist Study Ctr, 2nd rev ed, 96; River of Fire, River of Water, Doubleday, 98. **CONTACT ADDRESS** Dept of Relig, Smith Col, 98 Green St, Northampton, MA 01063-0001. **EMAIL** tunno@smith.edu

UPTON, JULIA A.
PERSONAL Born 09/15/1946, New York, NY **DISCIPLINE** THEOLOGY **EDUCATION** Ohio Dominican Col, BA, 67; St Johns Univ, MA, 75; Fordham Univ, PhD, 81. **CAREER** Assoc Prof, St Johns Univ, 80-. **MEMBERSHIPS** NAAL, CTSA. **RESEARCH** Liturgy, liturgical architecture. **SELECTED PUBLICATIONS** Auth, A Time for Embracing and Reclaiming Reconciliation, Liturgical Pr, 99. **CONTACT ADDRESS** Dept Theol, St. John's Univ, 8150 Utopia Pkwy, Jamaica, NY 11439-0001. **EMAIL** uptonj@stjohns,edu

UPTON, THOMAS VERNON
PERSONAL Born 04/27/1948, Antigo, WI, m, 1977 **DISCIPLINE** PHILOSOPHY, THEOLOGY **EDUCATION** Cath Univ Am, BA, 70, MA, 72, PhD, 77. **CAREER** Asst prof, 77-81, assoc prof philos, 81-, Gannon Univ. **HONORS AND AWARDS** NEH, summer sem grant, 80, 83, 86, 88. **MEMBERSHIPS** Am Philos Assn; Ancient Greek Philos; Am Cath Philos Assn. **RESEARCH** Aristotle and Greek philosophy and science; medical ethics. **SELECTED PUBLICATIONS** Auth, "Aristotle on Hypothesis and the Unhypothesized First Principle," Rev of Metaphysics 39 (85); auth, "Excluded Middle and Casuality: Aristotle's Reply to the Determinist," Hist of Philos Quarterly 4 (87); auth, "Rorty's Epistemological Nihilism," Personalist Forum III (87); auth, "Aristotle on Existence: Escaping the Snare of Ontology?" The New Scholasticism LXII, (88); auth, "The If-It-Is Question in Aristotle," Ancient Philos 11 (91). **CONTACT ADDRESS** Dept of Philos, Gannon Univ, University Square, Erie, PA 16541. **EMAIL** t.upton@velocity.net

URBAN, MICHAEL
PERSONAL Born 05/28/1947, Los Angeles, CA, m, 1971, 2 children **DISCIPLINE** POLITICAL SCIENCE **EDUCATION** Univ Kansas, PhD 76. **CAREER** Univ Cal SC, prof. **HONORS AND AWARDS** NCEEES Gnt; NEH; NSF. **MEMBERSHIPS** AAASS. **RESEARCH** Russian Politics and Culture. **SELECTED PUBLICATIONS** Auth, The Rebirth of Politics in Russia, Cambridge Univ Press, 97; auth, Ideology and System Change in the USSR and East Europe, ed, St Martins, 92; More Power to the Soviets, Edward Elgar, 90; **CONTACT ADDRESS** Stevenson College, Univ of California, Santa Cruz, Santa Cruz, CA 95064. **EMAIL** urban47@cats.ucsc.edu

URBROCK, WILLIAM JOSEPH
PERSONAL Born 09/14/1938, Chicago, IL, m, 2 children **DISCIPLINE** RELIGIOUS STUDIES **EDUCATION** Concordia Sr Col, BA, 60; Concordia Sem, MDiv, 64; Harvard Univ, PhD, 75. **CAREER** Asst prof relig, Lycoming Col, 69-71; from Asst Prof to Assoc Prof, 72-80, Prof Relig, Univ Wisc-Oshkosh, 80-; ed, Transactions, Wisc Acad Sci, Arts, & Letters, 92-. **MEMBERSHIPS** Soc Bibl Lit; Am Sch Orient Res; Soc Antiquity & Christianity; Cath Bibl Asn Am; Conf Christianity & Lit. **RESEARCH** Biblical studies, Old Testament. **SELECTED PUBLICATIONS** Auth, 'Em Sisera beShirat Devorah, Beit Mikra 131, 92; Blessings and Curses in Anchor Bible Dictionary, 92; The Book of Amos, The Sounds and the Silences, Currents in Theol & Mission, 96; Psalm 90: Moses, Mortality and.. the Morning, Currents in Theol & Mission, 98; author of numerous other articles. **CONTACT ADDRESS** Dept of Relig, Univ of Wisconsin, Oshkosh, 800 Algoma Blvd, Oshkosh, WI 54901-8601. **EMAIL** urbrock@uwosh.edu

URY, M. WILLIAM
PERSONAL Born 04/05/1956, Cleveland, OH, m, 1984, 4 children **DISCIPLINE** SYSTEMIC & HISTORICAL THEOLOGY **EDUCATION** Asbury Col, BA, 78; Asbury/Theolog Seminary, M.Div, 83; Drew Univ, PhD, 91. **CAREER** Prof, Wesley Theolog Seminary, 89-00, **HONORS AND AWARDS** Tchr of the Year, 94-95; Who's Who in Amer Univ & Col; Phi Alpha Theta; Theta Phi. **MEMBERSHIPS** Amer Acad Relig; Evangel Theolog Seminary; Wesley Theolog Soc. **RESEARCH** Theology; Historical Theology; Philosophy; Languages. **SELECTED PUBLICATIONS** Coauth, Loving Jesus: A Guidebook for Mature Discipleship, Discipleship Manual Vol III, 98; coauth, Following: A Guidebook for Mature Discipleship Vol II, Discipleship Manual, 97; The World is Still Our Parish, Good News Mag, 96. **CONTACT ADDRESS** Wesley Biblical Sem, Box 9928, Jackson, MS 39286. **EMAIL** bury@wbs.edu

UTTON, ALBERT E.
PERSONAL Born 07/06/1931, Aztec, NM, m, 1959, 2 children **DISCIPLINE** LAW **EDUCATION** Univ NMex, BA, 53; Oxford Univ, BA, 56, MA, 59. **CAREER** Assoc, John Simms Jr, Law Off, Albuquerque, 59-60; partner, Simms and Robinson, 60-61; from asst prof to assoc prof, 61-68, PROF LAW, UNIV NMEX, 68-, Mem, Inner Temple, Inns of Court, London; mem, Univs Comt Water Resources; mem, Comn Environ Policy, Law and Admin. **MEMBERSHIPS** Int Law Asn; Am Soc Int Law; Int Union Conserv Nature and Natural Resources. **RESEARCH** Law of the continental shelf, planning for the conservation, development and use of natural resources; international resources and environmental law. **SELECTED PUBLICATIONS** Auth, Managing North-American Transboundary Water-Resources .1.--Introduction, Natural Resources Jour, Vol 0033, 93; Assessing North-America Management of Its Transboundary Waters/, Natural Resources Jour, Vol 0033, 93; Water and the Arid Southwest--An International Region Under Stress, Natural Resources Jour, Vol 0034, 94; Which Rule Should Prevail in International Water Disputes--That of Reasonableness or That of No Harm, Natural Resources Jour, Vol 0036, 96; Cuixmala Model Draft Treaty for the Protection of the Environment and the Natural-Resources of North-America, Natural Resources Jour, Vol 0036, 96; Regional Cooperation--The Example of International Waters Systems in the 20th-Century, Natural Resources Jour, Vol 0036, 96. **CONTACT ADDRESS** Sch of Law, Univ of New Mexico, Albuquerque, Albuquerque, NM 87131.

UVILLER, H. RICHARD
PERSONAL Born 07/03/1929, New York, NY, m, 1964, 1 child **DISCIPLINE** LAW **EDUCATION** Harvard Univ, AB, 51; Yale Law Sch, LLB, 53. **CAREER** Atty, Off Legal Counsel, US Dept Justice, 53-54; asst dist atty, Off Dist Atty, NYC, 54-68; Arthur Levitt Prof Law, Columbia Univ, 68-. **MEMBERSHIPS** Am Law Inst; Lawyer's Comt on Violence. **RESEARCH** Criminal process. **SELECTED PUBLICATIONS** Auth, The Processes of Criminal Justice, 2d ed, West, 79; auth, Tempered Zeal, Contemp Bks, 88; auth, "Client Taint: the Embarrassment of Rudolph Giuliani," 9 Crim J Ethics 3 (90); auth, "Self Incrimination by Inference," 81 J Crim Law & Crimin 37 (90); auth, "Acquitting the Guilty," 2 Crim Law Forum 1 (90); auth, "Credence, Character, and the Rules of Evidence," 42 Duke Law J 776 (93); auth, Virtual Justice: The Flawed Prosecution of Crime in America, Yale Univ Pr, 96; auth, "Unconvinced, Unreconstructed, & Unrepentant," 43 Duke Law J 834 (94); auth, "The Lawyer as Liar," 13 Crim J Ethics 2 (94); auth, The Tileted Playing Field: Is Criminal Justice Unfair?, Yale Univ Pr, 99. **CONTACT ADDRESS** Law Sch, Columbia Univ, 435 W 116th St, New York, NY 10027-7201. **EMAIL** uviller@law.columbia.edu

UZGALIS, WILLIAM
DISCIPLINE PHILOSOPHIES OF CHINA **EDUCATION** Univ Calif, Irving, BA; Calif State Univ, Long Beach, MA; Stanford Univ, PhD. **CAREER** Philos, Oregon St Univ. **SELECTED PUBLICATIONS** Auth, The Anti-Essential Locke and Natural Kinds; The Same Tyrannical Principle: The Lockean Legacy on Slavery. **CONTACT ADDRESS** Dept Philos, Oregon State Univ, Corvallis, OR 97331-4501. **EMAIL** wuzgalis@orst.edu

V

VACEK, EDWARD VICTOR
PERSONAL Born 05/12/1942, Omaha, NE, s **DISCIPLINE** PHILOSOPHY, CHRISTIAN ETHICS **EDUCATION** St Louis Univ, BA, 66, MA, 67, PhL, 68; Weston Sch Theol, MDiv, 73; Northwestern Univ, PhD(philos), 78; Loyola Univ Chicago, STL, 81. **CAREER** Instr math, Campion High Sch, 66-68; instr philos, Creighton Univ, 69-70 & 72-73 & Seattle Univ, 77-78; asst prof ethics, Jesuit Sch Theol, Chicago, 78-81; Prof Ethics, Weston Sch Theol, 81-. **MEMBERSHIPS** Soc Philos Sex & Love; Soc Christian Ethicists; Cath Theol Soc Am. **RESEARCH** Ethics; phenomenology; Max Scheler; love; sexuality. **SELECTED PUBLICATIONS** Auth, Love, Human and Divine: the Heart of Christian Life, Georgetown Univ Press, 94; The Eclipse of Love for God, America, 3/96; Love, Christian and Diverse: A Response to Colin Grant, J Relig Ethics, Spring 96; Love for God -- Is It Obligatory?, The Annual of the Soc Christian Ethics, 96; Divine-Command, Natural-Law, and Mutual-Love Ethics, Theol Studies, 12/96; Religious Life and the Eclipse of Love for God, Rev for Religious, March/April 98; author of numerous other articles. **CONTACT ADDRESS** Weston Jesuit Sch of Theol, 3 Phillips Place, Cambridge, MA 02138-3495. **EMAIL** edvacek@aol.com

VAGTS, DETLEV F.
PERSONAL Born 02/13/1929, Washington, DC, m, 1954, 2 children **DISCIPLINE** LAW **EDUCATION** Harvard Univ, AB, 48, LLB, 51. **CAREER** Asst prof, 59-62, Prof Law, Law Sch, Harvard Univ, 62-, Counr Int Law, US Dept of State, 76-77; assoc reporter, Restatement Foreign Relations Law 79-87. **HONORS AND AWARDS** Max Planck Research Awd, 91. **MEMBERSHIPS** Am Bar Asn; Am Soc Int Law; AAAS. **RESEARCH** Corporations and international transactions. **SELECTED PUBLICATIONS** Coauth, Transnational Legal Problems, 68, 2nd ed, 76 & ed, Basic Corporation Law, 73, 2nd ed, 79, Foundation. **CONTACT ADDRESS** Dept of Law, Harvard Univ, Cambridge, MA 02138. **EMAIL** vagts@law.harvard.edu

VAILLANCOURT, DANIEL
DISCIPLINE PHILOSOPHY **EDUCATION** St Francis Col, Biddeford, Maine, BA; DePaul Univ Chicago, PhD, 76. **CAREER** Prof; Loyola Univ, 90-; 18 yrs fac, 5 yrs chp Humanities, Mundelein Col; 3 yrs dean, Masters Lib Stud Prog; Fulbright grant, Paris,71-72. **RESEARCH** Philosophy of human nature; contemporary French philosophy; philosophy of religion. **SELECTED PUBLICATIONS** Coauth, Lenin to Gorbachev: Three Generations of Soviet Communists, Harlan-Davidson, 89-rev ed 94; articles in, philos, lit, Marxism & Communism, soc & econ philos; transl several works in, soc philos from Fr to Engl. **CONTACT ADDRESS** Dept of Philosophy, Loyola Univ, Chicago, 820 N Michigan Ave, Chicago, IL 60611.

VAIRO, GEORGENE M.
PERSONAL Born 05/14/1950, New York, NY **DISCIPLINE** LAW **EDUCATION** Sweet Briar Col, BA, 72; Univ Va, MEd, 75; Fordham Univ, JD, 79. **CAREER** Prof; clerk, hon Joseph M. McLaughlin, US Dist Ct Eastern Dist NY; assoc spec in Antitrust Law, Skadden, Arps, Slate, Meagher & Flom, NY; Fordham Law Sch, fac, 82-95 & assoc dean, 87-95; ch, Leonard F. Manning Distinguished Ch, 94; chp, Dalkon Shield Claimants Trust; ed bd, Moore's Fed Practice; Loyola Law School, fac, 95-. **HONORS AND AWARDS** Fordham Law School Dean's Medal of Recognition, 95; Sweet Briar Col Distinguished Alumna, 97. **MEMBERSHIPS** Am Law Inst. **RESEARCH** Resolution of mass tort claims; Federal jurisdiction and procedure. **SELECTED PUBLICATIONS** Publ on, federal procedure and jurisdiction. **CONTACT ADDRESS** Law School, Loyola Marymount Univ, 919 Albany St, Los Angeles, CA 90015. **EMAIL** geogene.vairo@lls.edu

VALERI, MARK
DISCIPLINE RELIGIOUS STUDIES **EDUCATION** Whitworth, BA, 76; Yale Univ, MDiv, 79; Princeton, PhD, 85. **CAREER** Asst prof Religious Studies, Lewis and Clark; prof Church History, Union Theological Seminary. **HONORS AND AWARDS** Francis Makemie Prize, 95. **MEMBERSHIPS** Am Antiquarian Soc. **RESEARCH** 18th century religion in New England. **SELECTED PUBLICATIONS** Fel Publ, The Economic Thought of Jonathan Edwards, Church Hist 60, 91; auth, The New Divinity and the American Revolution, William and Mary Quart 46, 89; Law and Providence in Joseph Bellamy's New England: The Origins of the New Divinity in Revolutionary America, Oxford Univ, 94; Religious Discipline and the Market: Puritans and the Issue of Usury, William and Mary Quart, 97; auth, The Works of Jonathan Edwards, vol. 17, Sermons and Discourses 1730-1733. **CONTACT ADDRESS** Union Theol Sem, Virginia, 3401 Brook Rd., Richmond, VA 23227. **EMAIL** mvaleri@utsva.edu

VALL, GREGORY
PERSONAL Born 07/27/1961, Cleveland, OH, m, 1996, 2 children **DISCIPLINE** BIBLICAL STUDIES **EDUCATION**

Franciscan Univ Stenberville, BA, 84; Cath Univ Am, MA, 90; PhD, 93. **CAREER** Fel, Cath Univ of Am, Wash DC, 89-92; Prof, Notre Dame Sem, New Orleans, 92-00; Asst Prof, Franciscan Univ of Stenberville, 00-. **HONORS AND AWARDS** Cath Univ of Am Fel, 89-92; Cath Bibl Asn of Am Mem Stipend, 89-92. **MEMBERSHIPS** Cath Bibl Asn Am, 89-, Soc Bibl Lit, 93-. **RESEARCH** Old Testament, Biblical Hebrew. **SELECTED PUBLICATIONS** Auth, "What was Isaac Doing in the Field? (Gen 24:63)," Vetus Testamentum 44 (94): 513-523; auth, "Enigma of Job 1:21a," Biblica 76 (95): 325-342; auth, "From Whose Womb Did the Ice Come Forth? Procreation Images in Job 38:28-19," Cath Bibl Quart 57 (95): 504-513; auth, "Psalm 22-17b: The Old Guess," J of Bibl Lit 116 (97): 45-56; auth, "The Feast of Weeks," The Bible Today 36/1 (Jan/Feb 98): 24-28; auth, "Psalm 132: Praying in the Messianic Spirit," The Bible Today 38/3 (May/June 00). **CONTACT ADDRESS** Dept of Theol, Franciscan Univ of Steubenville, 1235 University Blvd, Stenberville, OH 43952.

VALLEGA-NEU, DANIELA
PERSONAL Born 06/13/1966, Vorese, Italy, m, 1998 **DISCIPLINE** PHILOSOPHY **EDUCATION** Albert-Ludwigs-Universitat, Freiburg, Ger, MA, 92; PhD, 95. **CAREER** Instr, Freidrich-Schiller-Universitat Jena, Ger, summer sem, 97; lectr, dept of philos, Pa State Univ, 98-99; vis lectr, Calif State Univ, Stanislaus, 99-. **HONORS AND AWARDS** Fel, Landesgraduierten foerderung von Baden Wuerttemberg, for doctoral these, 93-95; Res fel, DAAD (German Academic Exchange Service), PA State Univ, 97-98. **MEMBERSHIPS** Amer Philos Assoc; Soc for Phenomenology and Existential Philos; Heidegger Conf of Am; Allgemeine Gesellschaft fuer Philosophie in Deutschland; Deutsche Gesellschaft fur Phaenomenologische Forschung; Martin Heidegger Gesellschaft. **RESEARCH** Contemporary continental philos; phenomenology; hermeneutics; deconstruction. **SELECTED PUBLICATIONS** Auth, Die Notwendigkeit der Grundung im Zeitalter der Dekonstruktion, Zur Grundung in Heideggers Beitragen zur Philosophie: unter Hinzuziehung der Derridaschen Dekonstruktion, Berlin: Duncker & Humblot, 97; La Questione del Corpo nei Beitrage zur Philosophie, in Giornale di Metafisica, 98; Overcoming the Ontological Difference in Heidigger's Contributions to Philosophy, in Proceedings of the 32nd Annual Heiddegger Conf, Villanova Univ, 98; Gerard Ruff, Am Ursprung der Zeit, Berlin: Duncker & Humblot, 97, in Theologische Literaturzeitung, 98; auth, "The Question of the Body in Heidegger's 'Contributions to Philosophy,'" in Proceedings of the 34th Annual Heidegger Conference (Huntington Univ, 00); auth, "Poietic Saying," in A Companion to Heidegger's 'Contributions to Philosophy' (Ind Univ Press, 01); coed, A Companion to Heidegger's 'Contributions to Philosophy,' Ind Univ Press, 01. **CONTACT ADDRESS** Dept of Philos, California State Univ, Stanislaus, 801 W Monte Vista Ave, Turlock, CA 95382. **EMAIL** dvallega@toto.csustan.edu

VALLENTYNE, PETER
PERSONAL Born 03/25/1952, New Haven, CT, m, 1983 **DISCIPLINE** PHILOSOPHY **EDUCATION** Fellow of the Soc Actuaries, 76; McGill Univ, BA, 78; Univ Pittsburgh, MA, 81; Univ Pittsburgh, PhD, 84. **CAREER** Actuarial Supervisor, Financial Forecasting Dept, Great West Life Assurance Co, Winnipeg, 73-75; admin assoc to the pres, Va Commonwealth Univ, Fall 92; Harvard Mgt Development Prog, 94; ch, Philos Rel stud, Va Commonwealth Univ, 88- ; asst prof, Univ Western Ontario, 84-88; asst prof, Va Commonwealth Univ, 88-90, assoc prof, 90- . **HONORS AND AWARDS** Amer Coun Learned Soc fel, 97; NEH, Ed Div grant, for fac workshops tchg ethics across the curriculum 96-98; Who's Who Among America's Tchrs, 96, and Who's Who in the South and Southwest; Va Found Human pub lect grants, 95-96; Va Commonwealth Univ Res Grant-in-Aid, 90; Res Coun Canada grant for conf on contractarian thought, 87; Canada Coun Doc Fel, 81-83. **MEMBERSHIPS** Amer Philos Assn; Can Philos Assn; S Soc Philos and Psychol; Va Philos Asn. **RESEARCH** Ethical theory; political philosophy. **SELECTED PUBLICATIONS** Auth, Gauthier on Morality and Rationality, Eidos 5, 86, 79-95, reprinted with revisions as Gauthier's Three Projects, in Contractarianism and Rational Choice: Essays on David Gauthier's Morals by Agreement, ed Peter Vallentyne, Cambridge UP, 91, 1-12; The Teleological/Deontological Distinction, The Jour Value Inquiry, 21, 87, 21-32; Utilitarianism and the Outcomes of Action, The Pacific Philosophical Quart, 68, 87, 57-70; Prohibition Dilemmas and Deontic Logic, Logique et Analyse, 18, 87, 113-122; Teleology, Consequentialism, and the Past, The Jour Value Inquiry, 22, 88, 89-101; Rights Based Paretianism, The Canadian Jour Philos, 18, 88, 527-544; Gimmicky Representations of Moral Theories, Metaphilosophy, 19, 88, 253-263; Explicating Lawhood, Philos Sci, 55, 88, 598-613; Critical Review of J. L. Mackie's Persons and Values and Ted Honderich's Morality and Objectivity, The Can Jour Philos, 18, 88, 595-607; Two Types of moral Dilemmas, Erkenntnis, 30, 89, 301-318; how to combine Pareto Optimality with Liberty Considerations, Theory and Decision, 27, 89, 217-240; Equal Opportunity and the Family, Publ Affairs Quart, 3, 89, 29-47, reprinted in Children's Rights Revisioned: Philosophical Readings, ed Rosalind Ladd, Wadsworth Press, 96, 82-97; Contractarianism and the Assumption of Mutual Unconcern, Philos Stud, 56, 89, 187-192, reprinted in Contractarianism and Rational Choice: Essays on David Gauthier's Moral by Agreement, ed Peter Vallentyne, Cambridge UP, 91, 71-75; ed, Contractarianism and Rational Choice: Essays on David Gauthier's Morals by Agreement, Cambridge UPs, 91; The Problem of Unauthorized Welfare, Nous 25, 91, 295-321; Motivational Ties and Doing What One Wants Most, Jour Philos Res, XVI, 91, 437-439; Libertarianism, Autonomy, and Children, Publ Affairs Quart, 5, 91, 333-352; Moral Dilemmas and Comparative Conceptions of Morality, S Jour Philos, XXX, 92, 117-124; Child Liberationism and Legitimate Interference, Jour Soc Philos, 23, 92, 5-15; Utilitarianism and Infinite Utility, Australasian Jour Philos, 71, 93, 212-217; The Connection Between Prudential Goodness and moral Permissibility, Jour Soc Phil, 24, 93, 105-128; Infinite Utility: Anonymity and Person-Centeredness, Australasian jour Philos, 73, 95, 413-420; Taking Justice too Seriously, Utilitas, 7, 95, 207-216; Response-Dependence, Rigidification, and Objectivity, Erkenntnis 44, 95, 101-112; Self-Ownership and Equality: Brute Luck, Gifts, Universal Domination, and Leximin, Ethics 107, 97, 321-343; Infinite Utility and Finitely Additive Value theory, Jour Philos, 94, 97, 5-26; Intrinsic Properties Defined, Philos Stud, 88, 97, 209-219. **CONTACT ADDRESS** Dept of Philosophy, Virginia Commonwealth Univ, Richmond, VA 23284-2025. **EMAIL** peter.vallentyne@vcu.edu

VALLICELLA, WILLIAM F.
DISCIPLINE PHILOSOPHY **EDUCATION** Boston Col, PhD, 78. **CAREER** 78-89, Univ of Dayton, Oh; 89-91, Case Western Reserve Univ; 91-, independent scholar. **HONORS AND AWARDS** Various NEH Grants **MEMBERSHIPS** APA **RESEARCH** Metaphysics, philosophy of religion, German philosophy. **SELECTED PUBLICATIONS** Auth, "Bundles and Indiscernibility, A Reply to O'Leary-Hawthorne," Analysis, 97; auth, On an Insufficient Argument Against Sufficient Reason, Ratio, 97; auth, "Could a Classical Theist be a Physicalist?," Faith & Philos, 98; auth, "God Causation and Occasionalism," Religious Stud, 99; auth, "Three Conceptions of States of Affairs," Nous 2 (00): 237-259; auth, "Does the Cosmological Argument Depend on the Ontological?," Faith and Philos 4 (Oct, 00); auth, "Could the Universe Cause Itself to Exist?," Philos 75 (00): 604-612; auth, "From Facts to God: An Onto-Cosmological Argument," Int J for Philos of Relig 3 (Dec, 00); auth, "Brentano on Existence," Hist of Philos Quart (forthcoming); auth, "Relations, Monism, and the Vindication of Bradley's Regress," Dialectica (forthcoming). **CONTACT ADDRESS** 5172 S. Marble Dr., Gold Canyon, AZ 85219-3387. **EMAIL** billvallicella@compuserve.com

VALLIERE, PAUL R.
PERSONAL Born 11/27/1943, Buffalo, NY, m, 1966, 3 children **DISCIPLINE** RELIGION **EDUCATION** Williams Col, BA,, 65; Columbia Univ, MA, 68, PhD, 74. **CAREER** Asst prof, Columbia Univ, 73-82; assoc prof to full prof, McGregor Prof in Humanities, Butler Univ, 82-. **MEMBERSHIPS** Am Acad of Relig, Am Asn for Advancement of Slavic Studies. **RESEARCH** Orthodox Christianity, Russian religious philosophy. **SELECTED PUBLICATIONS** Auth, Modern Russian Theology: Bukharev, Soloviev, Bulgakov, Edinburgh: T & T Clark (2000). **CONTACT ADDRESS** Dept Relig & Philos, Butler Univ, 4600 Sunset Ave, Indianapolis, IN 46208-3443. **EMAIL** pvallier@butler.edu

VAN BUREN, JOHN
DISCIPLINE PHILOSOPHY **EDUCATION** McMaster Univ, PhD. **CAREER** Assoc prof, Fordham Univ. **RESEARCH** Continental Philosophy, environmental ethics. **SELECTED PUBLICATIONS** Auth, The Young Heidegger: Rumor of the Hidden King, Ind UP, 94; Reading Heidegger From the Start, SUNY Press, 94; Critical Environmental Hermeneutics, Env Ethics, Oxford UP, 95. **CONTACT ADDRESS** Dept of Philos, Fordham Univ, 441 E Fordham Rd, Bronx, NY 10458. **EMAIL** evanburen@fordham.edu

VAN CAMP, JULIE C.
PERSONAL Born 06/05/1947, Davenport, IA **DISCIPLINE** PHILOSOPHY **EDUCATION** Mount Holyoke Col MA, 69; Georgetown Univ, JD, 80; Temple Univ, MA, 75, PhD, 82. **CAREER** Temple Univ & Tyler S of A, ta, 70-71; Manor Jr Col, lectr, 71; Black Hawk Col, lectr, 72; Comm Col of Phil, lectr, 72-74; Georgetown Univ Law Cen, law fel, 77-78; G. Mason Univ, lect, 84; Univ of Cal, lectr, 90; Cal State Univ Long Beach, asst prof, assoc prof, full prof, 90-. **HONORS AND AWARDS** Distinguished Teaching Awd, CSULB, 1999. **MEMBERSHIPS** AAUP, APA, ASA, BSA, CHA, CRD, DCA, DC Bar, Cal State Bar. **RESEARCH** Philo probs art law; free speech for artists; philo and dance. **SELECTED PUBLICATIONS** Auth, Non-Verbal Metaphor: A Non-Explanation of Meaning in Dance, in: Brit Jour of Aesthetics, 96; The Colorization Controversy, in: Jour of Value Inquiry, 95; Creating Works of Art From Works of Art: The problem of Derivative Works, Jour of Arts Mgmt, Law and Soc, 94; The Philosophy of Art Law, in: Metaphilo, 94; Indecency on the Internet: Lessons from the Art World, in: Enter, Pub & Arts Handbook, Clark Boardman Callaghan, 96; Judging Aesthetic Value: @ Live Crew, Pretty Woman, and the Supreme Court, in: Enter, Pub & Arts Handbook, 95; Copyright of Choreographic Works, in: Enter, Pub and Arts Handbook, 94; Ethical Issues in the Courts (Wadsworth, 2000). **CONTACT ADDRESS** Dept of Philosophy, California State Univ, Long Beach, 1250 Bellflower Blvd, Long Beach, CA 90840-2408. **EMAIL** jvancamp@csulb.edu

VAN CLEVE, JAMES
PERSONAL Born 05/19/1948, Mankato, MN, m, 1974, 2 children **DISCIPLINE** PHILOSOPHY **EDUCATION** Univ Iowa, BA, 69; Univ Rochester, MA, 72, PhD, 74. **CAREER** Asst, assoc, prof, philos, Brown Univ, 73- ; Fubright vis prof Jadavpur Univ, Calcutta, 80; vis prof philos, Duke Univ, 93. **HONORS AND AWARDS** Fulbright Awd, 80; ACLS fel, 81; Nat Hum Ctr Fel, 90-91. **MEMBERSHIPS** APA; N Am Kant Soc. **RESEARCH** Epistemology; metaphysics; history of modern philosophy. **SELECTED PUBLICATIONS** Auth, Foundationalism, Epistemic Principles, and the Cartesian Circle, Philos Rev, 79; auth, Three Versions of the Bundle Theory, Philos Stud, 85; auth, Right, Left, and the Fourth Dimension, Philos Rev, 87; auth, Semantic Supervenience and Referential Indeterminacy, J of Philos, 92; auth, If Meinong Is Wrong, Is McTaggart Right? Philos Topics, 96; auth, Problems from Kant, Oxford Univ, 99. **CONTACT ADDRESS** Dept of Philosophy, Brown Univ, Providence, RI 02912. **EMAIL** jvc@brown.edu

VAN DE MORTEL, JOSEPH A.
PERSONAL Born 07/04/1952, Deurne, Netherlands, m, 1978, 3 children **DISCIPLINE** PHILOSOPHICAL THEOLOGY **EDUCATION** Univ San Francisco, MA 77. **CAREER** Cerritos Col, dept ch, 92-98, prof, 88- . **HONORS AND AWARDS** Templeton Prize Science and Religion, 98 **MEMBERSHIPS** APA, AAR **RESEARCH** Philo of relig; process philo; technology. **SELECTED PUBLICATIONS** Auth, The Thinkers Dictionary: a Handbook for Philosophy, McGraw Hill Press, 95. **CONTACT ADDRESS** 4642 Hazelbrook Ave, Long Beach, CA 90808.

VAN DER LINDEN, HARRY
PERSONAL Born 07/03/1950, Eindhoven, Netherlands, m **DISCIPLINE** PHILOSOPHY **EDUCATION** Univ of Utrecht, BS, 72; Univ of Groningen, MA, 78; Wash Univ, PhD, 85. **CAREER** Vis asst prof, Colgate Univ, 85-88; vis asst prof, Univ of NC Chapel Hill, 88-90; asst prof to prof, Butler Univ, 90-. **HONORS AND AWARDS** Johnsonian Prize, Columbia Univ, 85. **MEMBERSHIPS** Am Philos Assoc; NW Kant Soc; Radical Philos Assoc. **RESEARCH** Kantian Ethics, Global Justice, International Ethics, Ethics of Consumption. **SELECTED PUBLICATIONS** Auth, Kantian Ethics and Socialism, Hackett, (Indianapolis), 88; auth, "Cohen, Collective Responsibility, and Economic Democracy", Il Cannocchiale: Rivista di Studi Filosofici 1-2, (91): 345-361; auth, "Cohens sozialistische Rekonstruktion der Ethik Kants", in ethischer Sozialismus: Zur politischen Philosophie des Neukantianismus, ed Helmut Holzhey, (Frankfurt am Main: Suhrkamp, 94), 146-165; auth, "La philosophie politique de Hermann Cohen et la critique communautarienne du liberalisme", Cahiers de philosophie politique et juridique, Vol 26, Presses Univ de Caen, (94): 93-118; auth, Kant, The Duty to Promote International Peace, and Political Intervention" in Proceedings of the Eighth Int Kant Congress, ed Hoke Robinson, Marquette Univ Pr, (95): 71-81; auth, "Marx's Political Universalism", Topoi 15 (Sept 96): 235-245; auth, "A Kantian Defense of Enterprise Democracy", in Autonomy and Community: Readings in Contemporary Kantian Social Philos, ed Sidney Axinn and Jane Kneller, State Univ of NY Pr, 98, 213-237. **CONTACT ADDRESS** Dept Relig and Philos, Butler Univ, 4600 Sunset Ave, Indianapolis, IN 46208-3443. **EMAIL** hvanderl@butler.edu

VAN DER VYVER, JOHAN D.
PERSONAL Born 02/21/1934, South Africa, m, 1960, 4 children **DISCIPLINE** LAW **EDUCATION** Potchefstroom Univ, BComm, 54; LLB, 56; BA, 65; Univ Pretoria, LLD, 74; Univ Zululand, LLD, 93. **CAREER** Lectr to prof, Potchefstroom Univ, 58-78; dean, 72-74; prof, Univ of the Witwatersrand, 79-95; IT Cohen Prof of Int Law, Emory Univ, 95-. **HONORS AND AWARDS** Toon van den Heever Prize, 78; Alexander von Humboldt Stipendium 86; Distinguished Alumni Awd, Potchefstroom Univ, 95; Honorary Medallion of the Soc of Univ Teachers of Law of S Africa, 97; Essays in Honor of JD van der Vyver, 99. **MEMBERSHIPS** Am Soc of Int Law; Advocate of the High Court of S Africa. **RESEARCH** Human Rights Law, International Criminal Law, Church-State Relations. **SELECTED PUBLICATIONS** Coauth, Introduction to Legal Science, Butterworths, (Durban), 72; auth, The Juridical Function of State and Church: A Critical Analysis of the Doctrime of Sphere Sovereigny, Butterworths, (Durban), 72; auth, Human Rights, Potchefstroom: Inst for the Advan of Calvinism 74; auth, The Protection of Human Rights in South Africa, Juta & Co, 75; auth, Seven Lectures on Human Rifhts, Juta & Co, 76; coauth, The Law of Persons and Family Law, Juta & Co, 80; auth, The Republic of South Africa Constitution Act, Lex Patria, (Johannesburg/Cape Town), 84; auth, Reformed Christians and Social Justice, Dordt Col Pr, (Sioux Center, IA), 88. **CONTACT ADDRESS** Sch of Law, Emory Univ, 1364 Clifton Rd NE, Atlanta, GA 30322-1061.

VAN DYKE, BRIAN D.
PERSONAL Born 08/19/1962, Auburn, WA, m, 1992, 3 children **DISCIPLINE** THEOLOGY **EDUCATION** Multnomah Bible Col, AA, 87, BSC, 88; Simon Greenleaf Univ, MA, 91; Univ Aberdeen, UK, MTh, 95, PhD, 98. **CAREER** Adj prof, Dominion Col, 97; chaplain, US Army, 98- . **MEMBERSHIPS** APA; British Soc for Phil of Relig. **RESEARCH** Hegel; British

idealism;Systematic theology; Philosophy of religion. **SELECTED PUBLICATIONS** Auth, Hegel and Evolution: A Reappraisal, Contemp Philos, 96. rev of A.P.F. Sell's Philosophical Idealism and Christian Belief, Scottish J of Theol. **CONTACT ADDRESS** 3809 Water Oak Dr, Kileen, TX 76542. **EMAIL** brianvandyke@netscape.net

VAN EVRA, JAMES
DISCIPLINE PHILOSOPHY **EDUCATION** Mich State Univ, PhD, 66. **RESEARCH** Logic; philos of science. **SELECTED PUBLICATIONS** Auth, pub(s) on logic and philos of science. **CONTACT ADDRESS** Univ of Waterloo, 200 University Ave W, Waterloo, ON, Canada N2L 3G1. **EMAIL** vanevra@uwaterloo.ca

VAN HOOK, JAY M.
PERSONAL Born 01/09/1939, Clifton, NJ, m, 1960, 4 children **DISCIPLINE** PHILOSOPHY **EDUCATION** Calvin Col, BA, 60; Columbia Univ, PhD, 66. **CAREER** From asst prof to assoc prof Philos, Hood Col, 66-74; from assoc prof to prof Philos, Northwestern Col, 74-. **HONORS AND AWARDS** Woodrow Wilson Fel, 60-61. **MEMBERSHIPS** Am Philos Asn; Int Soc African & African Diaspora Philos & Studies; Soc Christian Philos. **RESEARCH** African philosophy; postmodernism; philosophy of religion. **SELECTED PUBLICATIONS** Auth, African Philosophy and the Universalist Thesis, Metaphilosophy, Oct, 97; auth, Kenyan Sage Philosophy: A Review and Critique, The Philos Forum, Fall, 95; auth, African Philosophy: Its Quest for Identity, Quest: Philos Discussions, June, 93; auth, Caves, Canons, and the Ironic Teacher in Richard Rorty's Philosophy of Education, Metaphilosophy, Jan/April, 93; co-ed, Jacques Ellul: Interpretive Essays, 81. **CONTACT ADDRESS** Dept of Philosophy, Northwestern Col, Iowa, 101 7th St. SW, Orange City, IA 51041. **EMAIL** vanhook@nwciowa.edu

VAN INWAGEN, PETER
PERSONAL Born 09/21/1942, Rochester, NY, m, 1989, 1 child **DISCIPLINE** PHILOSOPHY **EDUCATION** Rensselner Polytechnic Inst, BS, 65; Univ of Rochester, PhD, 69. **CAREER** Asst Prof to Prof, 71-95, Syracuse Univ; John Cardinal O'Hara Prof of Philo, 95-, Univ of Notre Dame. **HONORS AND AWARDS** NEH, Res Fellowships. **MEMBERSHIPS** APA, Soc of Christian Philos. **RESEARCH** Metaphysics. **SELECTED PUBLICATIONS** Co-ed, Metaphysics, The Big Questions, Oxford, Basil Blackwell, 98; Auth, Material Beings, Ithaca, NY, Cornell Univ Press, 90 and 95; Metaphysics, Boulder; Westview Press and London, Oxford Univ Press, 93; God, Knowledge, and Mystery, Essays in Philosophical Theology, Ithaca, Cornell Univ Press, 95; The Possibility of Resurrection and Other Essays in Christian Apologetics, Boulder, Westview Press, 97; Being, A Study in Ontology, Oxford at the Clarendon Press, forthcoming; auth, Ontology, Identity, and Modality: Essays in Ontology, Cambridge, Cambridge Univ Press, 01. **CONTACT ADDRESS** Dept of Philosophy, Univ of Notre Dame, Notre Dame, IN 46556-5639. **EMAIL** peter.vaninwagen.1@nd.edu

VAN NORDEN, BRYAN W.
DISCIPLINE PHILOSOPHY **EDUCATION** Univ Pa, BA, 85; Stanford Univ, PhD, 91. **CAREER** Asst prof, Vassar Col, 95-; vis asst prof, Univ Northern Iowa, 94-95; Univ Vt, 91-93; lectr, Stanford Univ, 90-91; Chiang Ching-kuo fel, 93; Stanford Center for E Asian Stud For Lang & Area Stud fel, 89; Mellon fel, 85. **RESEARCH** Ethics; Chinese Philosophy. **SELECTED PUBLICATIONS** Auth, Mencius on Courage, in Midwest Stud in Philos, The Philosophy of Religion, Univ Notre Dame Press, 97; Competing Interpretations of the Inner Chapters, Philos East & West, :2, Apr 96; What Should Western Philosophy Learn from Chinese Philosophy, Chinese Language, Thought and Culture: Nivison and His Critics, Open Ct Press, 96; Mencius & Lao Tzu, Cambridge Dictionary of Philososphy, Cambridge Univ Press, 95; ed, The Ways of Confucianism: Investigations in Chinese Philosophy, Open Ct Press, 96; rev(s), Confucian Traditions in East Asian Modernity, Pac Aff, 97; Confucian Moral Self Cultivation, J Asian Stud, 96; A Daoist Theory of Chinese Thought, Ethics, 95; Nature and Heaven in the Xunzi, J Asian Stud, 94; Knowing Words, J Chinese Rel, 93; Tai Chen on Mencius, J Chinese Rel, 93; John Dewey and American Democracy, Philos Eeast & West, 93. **CONTACT ADDRESS** Dept of Philosophy, Vassar Col, 124 Raymond Ave., Poughkeepsie, NY 12604-0310. **EMAIL** brvannorden@vassar.edu

VAN PATTEN, JAMES J.
PERSONAL Born 09/09/1925, North Rose, NY, m, 1961 **DISCIPLINE** HISTORY, PHILOSOPHY **CAREER** Asst, assoc prof, 62-69, Cent Mo St Univ; assoc, Soc for Hist/Philos of Educ; prof, 69-71, Univ Okla; assoc, prof, 71-99, Univ Ark; Adj Prof, Fla Atlantic Univ, 00; Emer Prof, Univ of Arkansas, 00-. **MEMBERSHIPS** APA, Amer Ed Res Assn, Ed Law Assn, Phil of Ed Soc, Amer Ed Stud Assn, Am Philos Soc, World Future Soc. **RESEARCH** Futurism, history of Amer educ, global educ, phil/history. **SELECTED PUBLICATIONS** Auth, What's Really Happening in Education, Univ Press Amer, 97; auth, The Culture of Higher Education, Univ Press Amer, 96; auth, Watersheds in Higher Education, Mellon Press NY, 97; coauth, History of Education in America, Prentice Hall/Merrill, 99; auth, A New Century in Retrospect and Prospect, Univ Pr of Am, 00; auth, Higher Education Culture, Case Studies and a New Century, Univ Pr of Am, 00. **CONTACT ADDRESS** Education Leadership, Univ of Arkansas, Fayetteville, GE 303 Education, Fayetteville, AR 72701. **EMAIL** jvanpatt@aol.com

VAN RHEENEN, GAILYN
PERSONAL Born 01/04/1946, Runnells, IA, m, 1968, 4 children **DISCIPLINE** CHURCH PLANTING AND DEVELOPMENT, MISSIOLOGY **EDUCATION** Harding Univ, BA, 68; ACU, MS, 74; Trinity Evangelical Divinity Sch, Dmiss, 90. **CAREER** Vis missionary, Harding Univ, 77-78, 82-83; prof, Abilene Christian Univ, 86-00. **HONORS AND AWARDS** African mission fel; distinguished alumnus award, Crowley's Ridge Acad, 77; distinguished alumnus in Bible, Harding Univ, 82; grad tchr yr, ACU, 92; VP, Southwest region Evangelical Missiological Soc, 93-96; VP for Publications, Evan, Miss Soc, 96-99.; vp, southwest region evangelical theol soc. **MEMBERSHIPS** Mem, Am Soc Missiology; Evangelical Missiological Soc; Intl Soc Frontier Missiology. **RESEARCH** Church planting and development; anthropology, animism, evangelism, theology of mission. **SELECTED PUBLICATIONS** Auth, Missions Alive! Revitalizing Missions in Churches of Christ, ACU Press, 94; Missions: Biblical Foundations and Contemporary Strategies, Zondervan, 96; Cultural Conceptions of Power in Biblical Perspective, Missiology 21, 93; The Impact of Animistic and Western Perspectives of Illness Upon Medical Missions, Siloam Notes 9, 93; Animism, Secularism, and Theism, Intl Jour Frontier, Missions 10, 93; A Theology of Culture: Desecularizing Anthropology, Intl Bulletin Frontier Missions 14, 97. **CONTACT ADDRESS** Graduate School of Theology, Abilene Christian Univ, Abilene, TX 79699-9000. **EMAIL** rheenen@bible.acu.edu

VAN ROOJEN, MARK
PERSONAL Born, IL **DISCIPLINE** ETHICS AND POLITICAL PHILOSOPHY **EDUCATION** Princeton Univ, PhD, 93. **CAREER** Assoc prof, Univ Nebr, Lincoln; vis asst prof, Brown Univ, 93-94; vis assoc prof, Univ of Arizona, 00. **RESEARCH** Metaethics. **SELECTED PUBLICATIONS** Auth, Humean Motivation and Humean Rationality, Philos Stud 79, 95; Moral Functionalism and Moral Reductionism, Philos Quart 46, 96; auth, Expressivism and Irrationality, Philos Review 105, 96; auth, Affirmative Action, Non-Consequentialism, on Responsibility for the Effects of Past Discrimination, Public Affairs Quarterly 11, 97; auth, Reflective Moral Equilibrium and Psychological Theory, Ethics, 109, 99; auth, Motivational internalism: A Somewhat Less Idealized Account, Philos Quarterly 50, 00. **CONTACT ADDRESS** Univ of Nebraska, Lincoln, 1010 Oldfather Hall, Lincoln, NE 68588-0321.

VAN SETERS, JOHN
PERSONAL Born 05/02/1935, Hamilton, ON, Canada, m, 1960, 2 children **DISCIPLINE** OLD TESTAMENT, NEAR EASTERN STUDIES **EDUCATION** Univ Toronto, BA, 58; Yale Univ, MA, 59, PhD(Near Eastern studies), 65; Princeton Theol Sem, BD, 62. **CAREER** Asst prof Near Eastern studies, Waterloo Lutheran Univ, 65-67; assoc prof Old Testament, Andover Newton Theol Sch, 67-70; assoc prof Near Eastern studies, Univ Toronto, 70-76, prof Near Eastern studies, 76-77; James A Gray Prof Bibl Lit, Dept Of Relig, Univ NC, Chapel Hill, 77- & Chmn Dept, 80-88, 93-95; emer distinguished Univ prof, 00-. **HONORS AND AWARDS** Woodrow Wilson fel, 58; Princeton fel Old Testament, 62; Obermann fel Yale, 62, 63; Agusta-Hazard Fel, 64; Canada Council res grant, 73; Guggenheim Mem Awd; 79-80; NEH sem, 84, 89; NEH res fel, 85-86; ACLS res fel, 91-92; sen res fel, Katholiek Univ Leuven, 97; AHA Breasted Prize, 85; Am Acad Rel bok award, 86; Canadian Hist Asn Ferguson Prize, hon men, 86; Th.D (honoris causa), The Univ of Lausanne, Switzerland, 99; assoc dir wadi tumilat archaeol expedition to tell el maskhuta, egypt, 78,81. **MEMBERSHIPS** Am Schs Orient Res; Soc Bibl Lit; Soc Study Egyptian Antiq; Am Orient Soc; Catholic Biblical Asn; Canadian Soc of Biblical Studies, 00. **RESEARCH** Book of Genesis; Pentateuch; historical books: Joshua to II Kings; Hebrew Law; Near Eastern Historiography. **SELECTED PUBLICATIONS** Auth, The Hyksos: A New Investigation, Yale Univ, 66; auth, Abraham in History and Tradition, Yale Univ, 75; Histories and historians of the Ancient Near East: The Israelite, Orientalia, 81; auth, In Search of History, Historiography in the Ancient World and the Origins of Biblical History, Yale Press, 83; auth, Prologue to History: The Yahwist as Historian in Genesis, Westminster/John Knox Press and Theologischer Verlag (Zurich), 92; auth, The Life of Moses: The Yawhist as Historian in Exodus-Numbers, Westminster/John Knox Press and Kok-Pharos:Lampen, Netherlands, 94; auth, From Faithful Prophet to Villain: Observations on the Tradition History of the Balaam Story, in a Biblical Itinerary: In Search of Method, Form and Content. Essays in Honor of George W. Coats, 97; auth, "Solomon's Temple: Fact and Ideology in Biblical and Near Eastern Historiography," Catholic Bibl Quart 59 (97); auth, "The Deuteronomistic Reaction to the Pentateuch: The Case Against it," in Deuteronomy and Deuteronomic Literature: Festscrift for C Brekelmans, Leuven Univ Press, 97; auth, The Pentateuch: A Social-Science Commentary, Sheffield Acad Press, 99. **CONTACT ADDRESS** Dept of Relig, Univ of No Carolina, Chapel Hill, 600 Maple Forest Place, Waterloo, ON, Canada N2T 2S8. **EMAIL** jvansete@wlu.ca

VANALLEN, RODGER
PERSONAL Born 04/13/1938, Philadelphia, PA, m, 1963, 5 children **DISCIPLINE** RELIGIOUS STUDIES, THEOLOGY **EDUCATION** Villanova Univ, BS, 59, MA, 64; Temple Univ, PhD(relig), 73. **CAREER** PROF RELIG STUDIES, VILLANOVA UNIV, 64-, Co-ed, Horizons, 73-79, assoc ed, 79-. **MEMBERSHIPS** Col Theol Soc; Am Acad Relig; Cath Theol Soc Am; Am Cath Hist Asn; AAUP. **RESEARCH** American Catholicism; Christian ethics. **SELECTED PUBLICATIONS** Auth, Morality of artificial insemination revisited, Homiletic & Pastoral Rev, 70; John Calvin on clerical celibacy, Am Benedictine Rev, 71; Religious life and Christian vocation, 72 & American Catholicism, 74, Cross Currents; Sexual morality, In: New Cath Encycl, 74; The Commonweal and American Catholicism, Fortress, 74; The American Catholic, Cross Currents, 77; ed, American Religious Values and the Future of America, Fortress, 78. **CONTACT ADDRESS** Dept of Relig Studies, Villanova Univ, 845 E Lancaster Ave, Villanova, PA 19085.

VANCE, DONALD RICHARD
PERSONAL Born 07/18/1957, Mobile, AL, m, 1987, 1 child **DISCIPLINE** BIBLICAL INTERPRETATION **EDUCATION** Oral Roberts Univ, BA, 80; Inst Holy Land Stud, Israel, MA, 82; Univ Denver, Iliff Schl Theol, PhD, 87. **CAREER** Adj prof, 86-87, Oral Roberts Univ; adj prof, 89-92, Hebrew & Ugaritic lang, Iliff Schl Theol; adj prof, 90-93, class Hebrew, consort: Colo Christian Univ, Denver Sem, St Thomas Sem, Iliff Schl Theol, Univ of Den, Ctr Judaic Stud; asst prof, 94- Oral Roberts Univ. **HONORS AND AWARDS** Dept Fac Mem of Year, 95-96; Who's Who in Bible Stud & Archaeol; Who's Who Among Amer Col & Univ, 90-92, 91-92, 92-93; Grad Fel, Oral Roberts Schl Theol, 79-80. **MEMBERSHIPS** ASOR; SBL; ALSC; NAPH; NAS; SPS. **RESEARCH** Phoenician lang; NW Semitics; Bibl hermeneutics; Bibl poetry. **SELECTED PUBLICATIONS** Art, The Book of Abraham, Ex-Mormons & Christians Und Newsl 3:4, 92; art, Literary Sources for the History of Palestine and Syria: The Phoenician Inscriptions, Part 2, Bibl Archaeol 57:2, 94; art, Literary Sources for the History of Palestine and Syria: The Phoenician Inscriptions, Part 1, Bibl Archaeol 57:1, 94; art, Toward a Poetics of Biblical Hebrew Poetry: The Question of Meter, PhD Dis, Univ Denver & Iliff Schl Theol, 97. **CONTACT ADDRESS** Oral Roberts Univ, 7777 S Lewis Ave., Tulsa, OK 74171. **EMAIL** drvance@oru.edu

VANDALE, ROBERT
DISCIPLINE RELIGION **EDUCATION** Univ Iowa, PhD. **CAREER** Relig, Westminister Col. **RESEARCH** Relig in Am; theol; christian ethics; Mid E rel. **SELECTED PUBLICATIONS** Publ on, relig issues in public edu. **CONTACT ADDRESS** Rel, Hist, Philos, Classics Dept, Westminster Col, Pennsylvania, New Wilmington, PA 16172-0001. **EMAIL** vandalrl@westminster.edu

VANDENAKKER, JOHN
PERSONAL Born 11/02/1959, Ottawa, ON, Canada **DISCIPLINE** THEOLOGY **EDUCATION** Gregorian Univ (Rome), ThD, 93. **CAREER** Lectr Theol, Dominican Col, Ottawa. **MEMBERSHIPS** AAR. **SELECTED PUBLICATIONS** Auth Small Christian Communities and the Parish, Sheed & Ward, 94. **CONTACT ADDRESS** 126 Young St, Ottawa, ON, Canada KI4 3P9. **EMAIL** frjohnv@home.com

VANDER KAM, JAMES C.
PERSONAL Born 02/15/1946, Cadillac, MI, m, 1967, 3 children **DISCIPLINE** BIBLICAL STUDIES **EDUCATION** Calvin Col, BA 68; Calvin Theol Sem, BD 71; Harvard Univ, PhD 76. **CAREER** N Carolina State Univ, asst prof, assoc prof, prof, 76-91; Univ Notre Dame, prof, John A O'Brien Prof, 91 to 98-. **HONORS AND AWARDS** Fulbright Fel; Outstanding Tchg Awd; Outstanding Res Awd; 6 NEH Gnts. **MEMBERSHIPS** SBL; ASOR; CBA; Assoc for Jewish Studies. **RESEARCH** Dead Sea Scrolls; Second-Temple Jewish Hist and Lit; Hebrew Bible. **SELECTED PUBLICATIONS** The Dead Sea Scrolls Today, Grand Rapids, Eerdmans, 94; The Community of the Renewed Covenant: The Notre Dame Symposium on the Dead Sea Scrolls, Notre Dame, Univ of Notre Dame, 94; Enoch: A Man for All Generations, Columbia, U of S Carolina Press, 95; The Jewish Apocalyptic Heritage in Early Christianity, co-ed, Minneapolis, Fortress Press, 96; Auth, Calendars in the Dead Sea Scrolls: Measuring Time, London, Routledge, 98; Qumran Cave 4 VI: Poetical and Liturgical Texts, part 1, co-ed, DJD 11, Oxford, Clarendon 98; translated into six other lang; Qumran Cave 4, Parabiblical texts, VIII part 1=DJD 13 94, XIV part 2=DJD 19 95, XVII part 3=DJD 2296, consult ed, Oxford, Clarendon Press; auth, Qumran Grotte 4 XVIII Textes Hebreux (4Q521-4Q528, 4Q,576-4Q579), volume editor DJD 25, 98; auth, Qumran Cave 4 XX Poetical and Liturgical Texts, Part 2, DJD 29, 99; auth, From Revelation to Canon: Studies in the Hebrew Bible and Second Temple Literature, Leiden: Brill, 00; coed, Encyclopedia of the Dead Sea Scrolls, New York/Oxford, 00. **CONTACT ADDRESS** Dept of Theology, Univ of Notre Dame, 327 O'Shaughnessy Hall, Notre Dame, IN 46556. **EMAIL** vanderkam.1@nd.edu

VANDER VLIET, MARVIN J.
PERSONAL Born 12/26/1944, Grand Rapids, MI, m, 1969, 5 children **DISCIPLINE** RELIGION **EDUCATION** Calvin Col, Grand Rapids, BA, 67; Calvin Theol Sem, BD, 72, MTh, 75; Calvin Sem, MDiv, 79, N Amer Bapt Sem, DMin, 93. **CAREER** Christian Reform Church, pastor, 73-. **MEMBERSHIPS** Society of Biblical Literature; Calvinist Cadet Corps. **RESEARCH** Old Test; Talmud; Qumran. **CONTACT ADDRESS** First Jenison Christian Reformed Church, 8355 Tenth Ave, Jenison, MI 49428-9232. **EMAIL** mvvliet@aol.com

VANDERGRIFF, KEN
PERSONAL Born 11/12/1954, Knoxville, TN, m, 1976, 2 children **DISCIPLINE** OLD TESTAMENT **EDUCATION** Fla St Univ, BS, 76; SW Baptist Theol Sem, MA, 81; SW Baptist Theol Sem, PhD, 88 **CAREER** Adj Prof of Relig, 88-95, Wayland Baptist Univ; Adj Prof of Relig, 96-pres, Campbell Univ **HONORS AND AWARDS** Stella Ross Awd, 81 **MEMBERSHIPS** Soc of Bibl Equality; Interfaith Alliance; Christians for Bibl Equality **RESEARCH** Intertextuality in the Bible; Use of Bible in Art and Literature **CONTACT ADDRESS** 212 Forest Brook Dr, Apex, NC 27502. **EMAIL** kenv2@mindspring.com

VANDERPOOL, HAROLD YOUNG
PERSONAL Born 06/28/1936, Port Arthur, TX, m, 1960, 3 children **DISCIPLINE** AMERICAN HISTORY, ETHICS **EDUCATION** Harding Col, BA, 58; Abilene Christian Univ, MA, 60; Harvard Univ, BD, 63, PhD(relig & hist), 71, ThM, 76. **CAREER** From instr to asst prof relig & Am studies, Wellesey Col, 66-75; Harvard Univ Interfac Prof Med Ethics fel, 75-76; Assoc Prof Hist Med & Med Ethics, Univ Tex Med BR, Galveston, 76- **HONORS AND AWARDS** Kennedy Fnd Fel; Outstand Acad Bk, Assn of Col and Res Lib; Special Govt Emp for the NIH and US FDA **MEMBERSHIPS** Am Asn for Hist Med; AHA; Am Soc Church Hist; Soc Health & Human Values; Am Studies Asn. **RESEARCH** Ethics of reseach with Human Subjects; medical ethics; hisoty of medicine in American society; religion and society. **SELECTED PUBLICATIONS** Auth, The ethics of terminal care, JAMA, 78; auth, Responsibility of Physicians Toward Dying Patients, Medical Complications in Cancer Patients, Raven, 81; auth, Medicine and Religion: How Are They Related? J Relig & Health, 90; auth, Death and Dying: Euthanasia and Sustaining Life: Historical Perspective, Ency of Bioethics, Simon & Schuster MacMillan, 95; coauth, The Ethics of Research Involving Human Subjects, U Pub Group, 96; auth, Doctors and the Dying of Patients in American History, Physician Assisted Suicide, Indiana Univ, 97; auth, Critical Ethical Issues in Clinical Trials with Xenotransplants, The Lancet, 98. **CONTACT ADDRESS** Inst of Med Humanities, Univ of Texas, Med Branch at Galveston, 301 University Blvd, Galveston, TX 77555-1311. **EMAIL** hvanderp@utmb.edu

VANDERVORT, LUCINDA
DISCIPLINE LAW **EDUCATION** Bryn Mawr Col, BA, 68; McGill Univ, MA, 70, PhD, 73; Queen's Univ, LLB, 77; Yale Univ, LLM, 80. **CAREER** Assoc prof, 82-. **MEMBERSHIPS** Law Soc of Upper Canada. **RESEARCH** Legal theory with an emphasis on criminal and administrative law and on issues related to access to legal representation and the implications of equality and democratic political theory for law and legal institutions under conditions of social diversity. **SELECTED PUBLICATIONS** Auth, Consent and the Criminal Law, 90; Mistake of Law and Sexual Assault: Consent and Mens Rea, 88; Political Control of Independent Administrative Agencies, 80; Blumberg on 'Moral Criticism', 75. **CONTACT ADDRESS** Col of Law, Univ of Saskatchewan, 15 Campus Dr, Saskatoon, SK, Canada S7N 5A6. **EMAIL** vandervort@law.usask.ca

VANDERWILT, JEFFERY T.
DISCIPLINE THEOLOGY **EDUCATION** Univ Notre Dame, PhD 96. **CAREER** Loyola Marymont Univ, asst prof 98. **MEMBERSHIPS** NAAL; AAR; NAAE. **RESEARCH** Liturgy; Worship; Sacramental Theology; Liturgical Music. **SELECTED PUBLICATIONS** Auth, A Church Without Borders: The Eucharist and the Church in Ecumenical Context, Collegeville, Michael Glazier Books, 98. **CONTACT ADDRESS** Dept of Theology, Loyola Marymount Univ, 7900 Loyola Blvd, Los Angeles, CA 90045. **EMAIL** jvanderw@lmumail.lmu.edu

VANDOORN-HARDER, NELLY
PERSONAL Born, Netherlands, m, 2 children **DISCIPLINE** THEOLOGY **EDUCATION** Univ Amsterdam, MA, 82; BA, 86; PhD, 93. **CAREER** Instr, Leiden Univ, 84-86; Dir, Cairo Refugee Agency, 86-91; Asst Prof, Dura Wacana Univ, 93-99; Asst Prof, Valparaiso Univ, 99-. **HONORS AND AWARDS** Grant, Dutch Reformed Church, 92-93; Ford Found Grant, 99-00. **MEMBERSHIPS** AAR, MESA, KITLV, Asn for Asian Studies. **RESEARCH** Christians in the Middle East, Islam in Southeast Asia, gender studies. **SELECTED PUBLICATIONS** auth, Contemporary Coptic Nuns, Univ SC Pr, 95; coed, Between Desert and City: The Coptic Orthodox Church Today, Nouns Forlag (Oslo, Norway), 97. **CONTACT ADDRESS** Dept Theol, Valparaiso Univ, 651 College Ave, Valparaiso, IN 46383-6461.

VANDUZER, ANTHONY J.
DISCIPLINE LAW **EDUCATION** Queen's Univ, BA, LLB; Univ British Columbia, LLM. **CAREER** Assoc prof, Univ Ottawa, 89-. **MEMBERSHIPS** Can Bar Asn. **SELECTED PUBLICATIONS** Auth, pubs on corporate law, merger notification under the Canadian Competition Act and business and trade law issues. **CONTACT ADDRESS** Fac Common Law, Univ of Ottawa, 57 Louis Pasteur, Fauteux Hall Rm. 354, Ottawa, ON, Canada K1N 6N5. **EMAIL** vanduzer@uottawa.ca

VANNOY, J. ROBERT
PERSONAL Born 03/03/1937, Wilmington, DE, m, 1965, 4 children **DISCIPLINE** OLD TESTAMENT **EDUCATION** Shelton Col, BA, 57; Faith Theol Sem, M Div, STM, 92; Free Univ Amsterdam, The Netherlands, ThD, 77. **CAREER** Instr, Shelton Col, 61-62; instr, Faith Theol Sem, 65-68; asst prof of Old Testament, Faith Theol Sem, 68-71; assoc prof of Old Testament, 71-77, Prof of Old Testament, Biblical Theological Sem, 77-. **MEMBERSHIPS** Evangelical Theol Soc; Soc of Biblical Lit. **RESEARCH** Historical books of the Old Testament; Old Testament Theology. **SELECTED PUBLICATIONS** Contrib, New International Version Study Bible, ed by Kenneth Barker, Zondervan, 85; ed, Interpretation & History: Essays in Honour of Allan A. Macrae, ed by R. Laird Harris, Swee-Hwa Quek, and J. Robert Vannoy, Christian Life Pub, 86; contrib, Baker Encyclopedia of the Bible, ed Walter A. Elwell, Baker Book House, 88; contrib, New Geneva Study Bible, R. C. Sproul, gen ed, Thomas Nelson Pubs, 95; contrib, Evangelical Dictionary of Biblical Theology, ed Walter A. Elwell. Baker, 95; contrib, The New International Dictionary of Old Testament Theology, Willem A. VanGemeren, gen ed, Zondervan, 97. **CONTACT ADDRESS** Biblical Theol Sem, 200 N Main St, Hatfield, PA 19440. **EMAIL** RVannoy@biblical.edu

VARNADO, DOUGLAS
PERSONAL Born 04/25/1953, Pensacola, FL, m, 1976, 2 children **DISCIPLINE** THEOLOGY; MISSIOLOGY **EDUCATION** Middle Tn St Univ, BS, 76; Tn St Univ, MA Ed, 83; Lipscomb Univ, MAR, 85; Vanderbilt Univ, M.Div, 87; Trinity Evangelical Divinity School, D.Miss, 96. **CAREER** Senior pastor community church. **HONORS AND AWARDS** Sears Roebuck Tchg Awd of Excellence; Tchr of Year, Lipscomb Univ **MEMBERSHIPS** Evangelical Missiological Soc; Soc Bibl Lit; Amer Acad Relig. **RESEARCH** Theology of Spirituality **CONTACT ADDRESS** Community Church, 381 West Main St., Hendersonville, TN 37075. **EMAIL** doug_varnado@communitychurchville.org

VARNER, GARY EDWARD
PERSONAL Born 03/10/1957, Newark, OH **DISCIPLINE** PHILOSOPHY **EDUCATION** Ariz State Univ, BA, 80; Univ Ga, MA, 83; Univ Wis, PhD, 88 **CAREER** Asst prof, Tex A&M, 90-96; assoc prof, Tex A&M, 96-. **RESEARCH** Environmental ethics, animal welfare and rights philosophies, philos issues in environmental law. **SELECTED PUBLICATIONS** Auth, In Nature's Interests? Interests, Animal Rights and Environmental Ethics, Oxford, 98; auth, "Environmental Law and the Eclipse of Land as Private Proper-ty," Ethics and Environmental Policy: Theory Meets Practice, Univ Ga, 94; auth, "What's Wrong with Animal Byproducts?" Jrnl Agricultural Environ Ethics, 94; auth, "Should You Clone Your Dog?" Animal Welfare, Britain, 8, (99): 407-420; auth, "Pets, Companion Animals, an dDomesticated Partners," in Ethics for Everyday, David Benatar, ed., McGraw-Hill, (forthcoming). **CONTACT ADDRESS** Philosophy Dept, Texas A&M Univ, Col Station, College Station, TX 77843. **EMAIL** g-varner@tamu.edu

VARNER, WILLAIM
PERSONAL Born 05/26/1947, Spartanburg, SC, m, 1972, 3 children **DISCIPLINE** JUDAICA **EDUCATION** Bob Jones Univ, BA, 69; Biblical Theol Sem, M Div; ThM; Dropsie Col, MA; Temple Univ, EdD. **CAREER** Dean, Bible Inst, 86-96; prof, Master's Col, 96-00. **HONORS AND AWARDS** Valedict, Dropsie Coll. **MEMBERSHIPS** ETS. **RESEARCH** Judaica. **SELECTED PUBLICATIONS** Auth, Jacobs Dozen; auth, Chariot of Israel. **CONTACT ADDRESS** Dept Bible Studies, The Masters Col, 21726 Placertia Canyon, Newhall, CA 91321. **EMAIL** dribex@yahoo.com

VARZI, ACHILLE C.
PERSONAL Born 05/08/1958, Italy, m, 1986, 2 children **DISCIPLINE** PHILOSOPHY **EDUCATION** BA, Sociol, Univ Trento, Italy, 82; MA, PhD, Philos, Univ Toronto, Can, 83, 94. **CAREER** Res, Inst for Sci and Tech Res, Trento, Italy, 88-95; asst prof, 95-00, assoc prof, 00-, Columbia Univ. **MEMBERSHIPS** Amer Philos Asn; Asn for Symbolic Logic; Euro Soc for Analytic Philos. **RESEARCH** Logic; Formal semantics; Metaphysics. **SELECTED PUBLICATIONS** Coauth, "The Niche," Nous 33 (99): 214-238; ed, The Nature of Logic, CSLI Publ/Cambridge Univ Press, 99; coauth, Parts and Places: The Structures of Spatial Representation, MIT Press, 99; auth, An Essay in Universal Semantics, Kluwer Acad Publ, 99; coed, Speaking of Events, Oxford Univ Press, 00; coauth, "Fiat and Bona Fide Boundaries," Philos and Phenomenol Res 60 (00): 401-420; coauth, "Some Pictures are Worth 2_aleph_null Sentences," Philos 75 (00): 377-381; coauth, "Topological Essentialism," Philos Studies 100 (00): 217-236; auth, "Mereological Commitments," Dialectica 54 (00): 283-305; auth, "Vagueness in Geography," Philos and Geog 4 (01): 49-65. **CONTACT ADDRESS** Dept of Philos, Columbia Univ, 1150 Amsterdam Ave, MC 4971 Philos Hall, New York, NY 10027. **EMAIL** achille.varzi@columbia.edu

VAUGHAN, FREDERICK
PERSONAL Born 04/19/1935, Dartmouth, NS, Canada, m, 1967, 2 children **DISCIPLINE** CONSTITUTIONAL LAW, POLITICAL PHILOSOPHY **EDUCATION** St Mary's Univ, BA, 56; Gonzaga Univ, MA, 61; Univ Chicago, MA, 64, PhD(polit sci), 67. **CAREER** Lectr polit sci, Royal Mil Col Can, 65-66; from asst prof to assoc prof, 66-76, chmn dept, 71-76, PROF POLIT SCI, UNIV GUELPH, 76-, Vis fel, Wolfson Col, Oxford, 70-71. **MEMBERSHIPS** Can Polit Sci Asn; Am Polit Sci Asn. **RESEARCH** Influence of Epicureanism; judicial biography of Justice E M Hall; Supreme Court of Canada. **SELECTED PUBLICATIONS** Auth, The Rhetoric of Morality and Philosophy, Plato Gorgias and Phaedrus, Philos and Rhet, Vol 0028, 95. **CONTACT ADDRESS** Dept of Polit Studies, Univ of Guelph, Guelph, ON, Canada N1G 2W1.

VAUGHN, BARRY
PERSONAL Born 10/29/1955, Mobile, AL, s **DISCIPLINE** CHURCH HISTORY **EDUCATION** Harvard Univ, BA, 78; Yale Univ, MDiv, 82; Univ of St Andrews, UK, PhD, 90. **CAREER** Asst prof, Samford Univ, 88-90; asst prof, 90-91, adj prof, 93-98, Univ Alabama. **HONORS AND AWARDS** Day fel, 82; Rotary Grad Fel, 84-85. **MEMBERSHIPS** AAR; AHA. **SELECTED PUBLICATIONS** Auth, Benjamin Keach's The Gospel Minister's Maintenance Vindicated and the Status of Ministers among Late Seventeenth Century Baptists, Baptist Rev of Theol, 93; auth, Reluctant Revivalist: Isaac Watts and the Evangelical Revival, Southeastern Comn on the Study of Relig, 93; auth, Resurrection and Grace: The Sermons of Austin Farrer, Preaching, 94; auth, Sermon, Sacrament, and Symbol in the Theology of Karl Rahner, Paradigms, 95; auth, The Glory of a True Church: Benjamin Keach and Church Order among Late Seventeenth Century Particular Baptists, Baptist Hist and Heritage, 95; auth, The Pilgrim Way: A Short History of the Episcopal Church in Alabama, in, Our Church: The Diocese of Alabama in history and Photographs, 96; auth, Gospel Songs and Evangelical Hymnody: Evaluation and Reconsideration, Am Organist, 96; auth, When Men Were Numbered, Anglican Dig, 97; auth, Sermons for Advent and Christmas, Clergy J, forthcoming. **CONTACT ADDRESS** 4041 Ridge Ave, #4-303, Philadelphia, PA 19129-1550. **EMAIL** anglcan@aol.com

VAUGHN, LEA B.
PERSONAL Born 07/18/1953, Seattle, WA, m, 1978, 2 children **DISCIPLINE** LAW **EDUCATION** Radcliffe Col, 71-72; Princeton Univ, AB, 75; Univ Mich, JD, 78. **CAREER** Asst Prof to Prof, Univ Washington, 84-. **MEMBERSHIPS** Mich Bar Asn, Am Bar Asn. **RESEARCH** Labor and Employment Law; Civil Procedure; ADR. **CONTACT ADDRESS** School of Law, Univ of Washington, 1100 NE Campus Pkwy, Seattle, WA 98105-6605. **EMAIL** lvaughn@u.washington.edu

VAUGHN, MICHAEL S.
PERSONAL Born 05/24/1962, Springfield, MO, m, 1989, 1 child **DISCIPLINE** CRIMINAL JUSTICE **EDUCATION** Sam Houston State Univ, PhD, 93 **CAREER** Assoc prof, dept of criminal justice, georgia state univ, 93-. **HONORS AND AWARDS** Phi Kappa Phi **MEMBERSHIPS** Acad Criminal Justice Sci; Amer Soc Criminol; Amer Judicature Soc **RESEARCH** Legal issues in criminal justice; Cross-cultural crime and social control. **SELECTED PUBLICATIONS** Auth, Prison Civil Liability for Inmate-Against-Inmate Assault and Breakdown/Disorganization Theory, Jour Criminal Justice, 96; coauth, Drug Crime in Taiwan: A Time-Series Analysis From 1965 to 1994, Deviant Behavior, 96; auth, Prison Officials Liability for Inmate-to-Inmate Assault: A Review of Case Law, Jour Offender Rehabil, 97; Civil Liability Against Prison Officials for Prescribing and Dispensing Medication and Drugs to Prison Inmates, Jour Legal Med, 97; First Amendments Civil Liability Against Law Enforcement Supervisors for Violating their Subordinates Rights to Engage in Overt Political Expression, Policing: An Int Jour of Police Strategies and Mgt, 97; Political Patronage in Law Enforcement: Civil Liability Against Police Supervisors for Violating their Subordinates First Amendment Rights, Jour Criminal Justice, 97; auth, "Practicing Penal Harm Medicine in the United States: Prisoners' Voices From Jail, Justice Quart," 99; auth, "Law Enforcement: Pissing Off the Police Civil Liability Under the First Amendment and the Fighting Words Docrine, Criminal Law Bulletin," 99; auth, "Penal Harm Medicine: State Tort Remedies fro Delaying and Denying Correctional Health Care to Prisoners, Crime, Law, and Social Change," 99; Police Sexual Violence: Civil Liability Under State Tort Law," Crime and Delinquency, 99; coauth, Drugs in Thailand: Assessing Police Attitudes, Int Jour Offender Ther & Comp Criminol, 98; Separate and Unequal: Prison Versus Free-World Medical Care, Justice Quart, 98; coauth, "Incompetent Jail and Prison Doctors, Prison Jour, 00. **CONTACT ADDRESS** Dept of Criminal Justice, Georgia State Univ, Box 4018, Atlanta, GA 30302-4018. **EMAIL** mvaughn@gsu.edu

VAUGHN, ROBERT GENE
PERSONAL Born 03/10/1944, Chickasha, OK, m, 1969, 3 children **DISCIPLINE** PUBLIC LAW, JUDICIAL PROCESS **EDUCATION** Univ Okla, BA, 66, JD, 69; Harvard Univ, LLM, 70. **CAREER** Assoc atty, Pub Interest Res Group, 70-72; asst prof, 72-74, assoc prof, 74-77, PROF LAW, THE AM UNIV, 77-, Consult, Nat Ctr Admin Justice, 76-; vchmn, Ethics Comt, Am Bar Asn, 77-79; scholar in residence, Kings Col, Univ London, 79-80; spec adv selection comn on treas and the civil serv, House of Commons, 80. **RESEARCH** Public employment law; government in formation laws and policy. **SELECTED PUBLICATIONS** Auth, The Spoiled System: A Call for Civil Service Reform, 75; auth, Principles of Civil Service Law, 76, Supp 77, 78; auth, Conflict of Interest Regulation in the Federal Executive Branch, 79; auth, The Merit Systems Protection Board: Rights and Remedies, 84; rev ed, 95; auth, South American Consumer Protection Laws, 96; auth, "Normative Controversies Underlying Contemporary Debates About Civil Justice Reform: A Way of Talking About Bureaucracy and the Future of the Federal Courts," 76 Denver Univ. L. Rev. 217, (98); auth, A Documentary Companion to a Civil Action, 99; auth, "State Whistleblower Statutes and the Future of Whistleblower Protection," 51 Ad. L. Rev. 581 (99); ed, Freedom of Information, 00. **CONTACT ADDRESS** Sch Law, American Univ, 4400 Mass Ave N W, Washington, DC 20016-8200. **EMAIL** vaughn@wci.american.edu

VEATCH, ROBERT M.
PERSONAL Born 01/22/1939, Utica, NY, m, 1987, 2 children **DISCIPLINE** PHILOSOPHY **EDUCATION** Purdue Univ, BA, 61; Univ Ca, MA, 62; Harvard Univ, BD 67; MA, 70; PhD, 71. **CAREER** Prof. **HONORS AND AWARDS** D Hum, Creighton U, 99. **SELECTED PUBLICATIONS** Auth, Medical Ehics, Second ed, Sudbury, MA, Jones and Bartlett, 97; auth, The Journal of Medicine and Philosophy: The Chaos of Care and Care Theory, 23 (2) Dorecht: The Netherlands, Swets & Zeitlinger Publishers, 98; auth, Source Rook in Medical Ethics: A Documentary History, Washington, DC, Georgetown Univ Press, 98; auth, Advance Directives and Surrogate Decision Making in Health Care, Balitmore, MD, Johns Hopkins Univ Press, 98; coauth, Ehics Applies, Needham Heights, MA, Simon & Schuster, 99; coauth, Case Studies in Pharmacy Ethics , New York, Oxford Univ Press, 99; auth, The Basics of Bioehtics, Upper Saddle River , NJ, Prentice-Hall, 00; auth, Cross Cultural Perspectives in Medical Ethics, Second ed, Sudbury, MA, Jones and Bartlett. 00; auth, The Ethics of Organ Transplantation, Washington DC, Georgetown Univ Press, forthcoming; coauth, Cast Studies in Nursing Ethics, Second ed, Sudbury, MA, Jones & Bartlett, 00. **CONTACT ADDRESS** Dept of Philosophy, Georgetown Univ, 37th and O St, Washington, DC 20057.

VECSEY, CHRISTOPHER
PERSONAL Born 12/07/1948, New York City, NY, m, 1980, 1 child **DISCIPLINE** RELIGION, NATVE AMERICAN STUDIES **EDUCATION** PhD, 77, Northwestern Univ. **CAREER** Prof, Colgate Univ. **RESEARCH** American Indian Religions. **SELECTED PUBLICATIONS** Auth, American Indian Environments, Syracuse Univ, 80, auth, Traditional Ojibwa Religion and Its Historical Changes, American Philosophical Society, 83; auth, Imagine Ourselves Richly, Corssroad/Continuum, 88; auth, Where the Two Roads Meet, The paths of Kateri's Kin, Iroquois Land Claims, Syracuse Univ, 88; auth, auth, American Indian Catholics, Padres' Trail, Univ Notre Dame Press, 96, 97, 99; ed, Religion in Native North America, Idaho Press, 90; Handbook of American Indian Religious Freedom, Crossroad/Continuum, 91. **CONTACT ADDRESS** Dept of Philos and Relig, Colgate Univ, 13 Oak Drive, Hamilton, NY 13346. **EMAIL** wkelly@mail.colgate.edu

VEENKER, RONALD ALLEN
PERSONAL Born 05/13/1937, Huntington Park, CA, m, 1960, 1 child **DISCIPLINE** OLD TESTAMENT; ANCIENT NEAR-EASTERN STUDIES **EDUCATION** Bethel Col, Minn, BA, 59; Bethel Theol Sem, BDiv, 63; Hebrew Union Col, PhD(Ancient NE), 68. **CAREER** Asst prof, Univ Miami, 67-68; assoc prof, 68-76, Prof Bibl Studies, Western KY Univ, 76-, Fel, Hebrew Union Col, Jewish Inst Relig, 77-78. **MEMBERSHIPS** Am Orient Soc; Soc Bibl Lit. **RESEARCH** Old Babylonian economic and legal texts; computer assisted analysis of Old Babylonian economic texts. **SELECTED PUBLICATIONS** Auth, Stages in the Old Babylonical legal process, Hebrew Union Col Annual, 76; contribr, Interpreter's Dictionary of the Bible: Supplement, Abingdon, 76; auth, Gilgamesh and the Magic Plant, Bibl Archaeol, Fall 81; A Response to W.G. Lambert, Bibl Archaeol, Spring 82; Noah, Herald of Righteousness, Proceedings of the Eastern Great Lakes and Midwest Bibl Soc, vol VI, 86; coauth, Me m, the First Ur III Ensi of Ebla, In: Ebla 1975-1985: Dieci anni di studi linguistici e fililogici, Atti del Convegno Internazionale, Napoli, 10/85; auth, Texts and Fragments: The Johnstone Collection, J of Cuneiform Studies, vol 40, no 1, 88; A critical review of Karl van Lerberghe, Old Babylonian Legal and Administrative Texts from Philadelphia, Orientalia Lovaniensia Analecta 21, Uitgeverij Peeters, 86, for the J of the Am Orient Soc, 92; Texts and Fragments: Collection of the Erie Historical Museum, J of Cuneiform Studies, vol 43, no 1, 93. **CONTACT ADDRESS** Dept of Philos & Relig, Western Kentucky Univ, 1 Big Red Way St, Bowling Green, KY 42101-3576. **EMAIL** ronald.veenker@wku.edu

VEHSE, CHARLES T.
PERSONAL Born 03/07/1961, Huntington, WV, m, 1984, 1 child **DISCIPLINE** HISTORY OF RELIGIONS **EDUCATION** Univ of Chicago, PhD, 98, MA, 85; Brown Univ, AB, 83. **CAREER** Vis Asst Prof, 96-, West VA Univ; lectr, 88-91, Dept of Theo, Loyola Univ Chicago; Tutor for German Lang, 82-83, Brown Univ. **HONORS AND AWARDS** Dean's Prof Travel Grant; Solomon Goldman Lecture; Vis Res Fellow; Fellow, Interuniversity Prog for Jewish Stud; Arie and Ida Crown Mem Res Grant; Lucius N. Littauer Found Res Grant; Bernard H. and Blanche E. Jacobson Found Res Grant; Stipendium des Landes Baden-Wurtemberg. **RESEARCH** Religious and Judaic Studies, German Judaism of the modern era, History and Methods in the History of Religion, Ritual Studies and Comp Liturgy, History and Interpretaion of the Hebrew Bible; Humanities and Social Sciences, German Language and Literature. **SELECTED PUBLICATIONS** Auth, Religious Practice and Consciousness, A Case Study of Time from the 19th century, Consciousness Research Abstracts, Thorverton, UK, J of Consci Stud, 98; Were the Jews of Modern Germany as Emancipated and Assimilated as We Think?, The Solomon Goldman Lectures, 96-97, Spertus Institute of Jewish Studies; Long Live the King, Historical Fact and Narrative Fiction in 1 Samuel 9-10, The Pitcher Is Broken, Memorial Essays for Gosta WW. Ahlstrom, Sheffield Academic Press, 95. **CONTACT ADDRESS** 252 Stansbury, PO Box 6312, Morgantown, WV 26506. **EMAIL** cvehse@wvu.edu

VELKLEY, RICHARD L.
PERSONAL Born 03/17/1949, Cincinnati, OH, s **DISCIPLINE** PHILOSOPHY **EDUCATION** Cornell Univ, BA, 71; Pa State Univ, 78. **CAREER** Asst & Assoc Prof, Stonehill Col, 87-96; Assoc Prof, Catholic Univ of Am, 97-. **HONORS AND AWARDS** Vis Schol, Harvard Univ, 96; NEH Fellow, Univ Iowa, 92; Bradley Fellow, Univ Toronto, 86-87. **MEMBERSHIPS** Am Catholic Philos Asn; N Am Kant Soc; Hegel Soc. **RESEARCH** European philosophy, 18th century; Kant; Rousseau; German idealism; Heidegger; political philosophy; metaphysics; philosophy of art, culture, education, history. **SELECTED PUBLICATIONS** Auth, Freedom and the End of Reason: On the Moral Foundation of Kant's Critical Philosophy, Univ Chicago Press, 89; ed, D. Henrich, The Unity of Reason: Essays on Kant's Philosophy, Harvard Univ, Press, 94. **CONTACT ADDRESS** Sch of Philos, Catholic Univ of America, 112A McMahon Hall, Washington, DC 20064. **EMAIL** velkley@cua.edu

VELTRI, STEPHEN
PERSONAL Born 03/29/1955, Pittsburgh, PA, m, 1984, 3 children **DISCIPLINE** LAW **EDUCATION** Univ Pittsburgh, BA, 77; Georgetown Univ, JD, 81; Columbia Univ, LLM, 86. **CAREER** Information specialist, Library of Congress, 78-81; assoc attorney, Berkman Ruslander Pohl Lieber & Engel, 81-85; prof, Ohio N Univ Col Law, 86-. **HONORS AND AWARDS** Fowler V. Harper Awd, Teaching Awd. **MEMBERSHIPS** Am Bar Asn, Asn of Am Law Schools. **RESEARCH** Commercial paper, Secured transactions & property. **SELECTED PUBLICATIONS** Auth, The ABCs of the UCC, Article 3: Negotiable Instruments - Article 4: Bank Deposits and Collection, American Bar Association, 97; auth, "Should Foreign Exchange Be 'Foreign' to Article two of the Uniform Commercial code?," Cornell Intl L.J, 94. **CONTACT ADDRESS** Col of Law, Ohio No Univ, 525 S Main St, Ada, OH 45810-6000. **EMAIL** s-veltri@onu.edu

VENEZIANO, CAROL
PERSONAL Born 02/02/1952, Quincy, IL, m, 1978, 2 children **DISCIPLINE** CRIMINAL JUSTICE **EDUCATION** DePauw Univ, BA, 74; Auburn Univ, MS, 77; Sam Houston State Univ, PhD, 82. **CAREER** Asst prof to assoc prof, Memphis State Univ, 81-88; prof, Southeast Missouri State Univ, 88-98. **HONORS AND AWARDS** Two teaching awards; three research awards. **MEMBERSHIPS** Acad of Criminal Justice Sci; Am Soc of Criminol; Am Correctional Asn; Midwestern Criminal Justice Asn; Southern Criminal Justice Asn. **RESEARCH** Criminological theory; correlates of delinquency; correctional institutions. **SELECTED PUBLICATIONS** Coauth, Evaluating Investigator Job Performance: An Analysis of Practitioner Opinions, in The Justice Prof, 93; coauth, Psychosocial and Sociodemographic Characteristics of DWI Offenders, in J of Addictions & Offender Counseling, 93; coauth, Are Victimless Crimes Actually Harmful?, in J of Contemp Criminal Justice, 93; coauth, Project REACH: A Therapeutic Club Model, in New Designs for Youth Development, 94; coauth, Stress-related Factors Associated with Driving While Intoxicated, in J of Alcohol and Drug Educ, 94; coauth, The Development of an Exit Exam in Criminal Justice for Graduating Seniors: A Case Study, in J of Criminal Justice Ed, 94; coauth, Attitudes Toward Community Based Corrections as an Alternative to Incarceration, in Corrections Today, 95; coauth, A Survey of Inmates with Disabilities, in Encyclopedia of American Prisons, Garland, 95; coauth, A Comparison of the Dispositions of Juvenile Offenders Certified as Adults with Juvenile Offenders Not Certified, in Juvenile and Family Court J, 95; coauth, Reasons for Refraining from Criminal Activity, in Am J of Criminal Justice, 96; coauth, Factors Accounting for Not Engaging in Illegal Acts in Relationship to Type of Crime, in J of Crime and Justice, 96; coauth, Correlates of Assertiveness among Institutionalized Juvenile Delinquents, in J of Crime and Justice, 97; coauth, The Academic Achievement of Juvenile Delinquents Relative to Intellectual Ability: Implications for Research and Educational Program Development, in Practical Applications for Criminal Justice Statistics, Butterworth-Heinemann, 98; coauth, "The relationship between adolescent sex offender behaviors and victim characteristics with prior victimization," in Journal of Interpersonal Violence, 00. **CONTACT ADDRESS** Dept of Criminal Justice, Southeast Missouri State Univ, MS 8200, Cape Girardeau, MO 63701. **EMAIL** cveneziano@semovm.semo.edu

VER EECKE, WILFRIED
PERSONAL Born 08/22/1938, Tielt, Belgium, m, 1967, 4 children **DISCIPLINE** PHILOSOPHY **EDUCATION** Leuven, Belgium, Lic Thomistic Philos, 61, Lic Philos in Fac of Arts, 62, PhD, 66; Georgetown Univ, MA in Economics, 71. **CAREER** High school tchr, Heule, Belgium, 62-63, Kortrijl, Belgium, 63-65; instr Nursing School, Kortrijl, Belgium, 64-65; res, Nat Sci Found of Belgium, 65-69; asst prof, 67-72, assoc prof, 72-80, chr, 80-83, Prof Dept of Philos, Georgetown Univ, 80- . **SELECTED PUBLICATIONS** Auth, Hamlet: Doubting, Wholesomeness, Acting, and Forgiveness, Manuscript, 96; The Law of the Heart and Its Disappointment. Hegel on Law. Lacan on Paranoia, Manuscript, 96; Peirce and Freud: The Tole of Telling the Truth in Therapeutic Speech, 96; The Super-Ego and the Moral Vision of the World, 96; Depletable Resources, Requested Manuscript, 96; The Limits of Both Socialist and Capitalist Economics, Inst for Refromational Studies, Potchefstroomse Univ, 96; A Refundable Tax Credit for Children: Self-Interest-Based and Morally Based Arguments, The Jour of Socio-Economics, 96; The Concept Merit Good, The Ethical Dimension in Economic Theory and the History of Economic Thought, Jour Socio-Economics, 98. **CONTACT ADDRESS** Dept Philos, Georgetown Univ, Washington, DC 20057. **EMAIL** vereeckw@gunet.georgetown.edu

VERCHICK, ROBERT R.
PERSONAL Born Las Vegas, NV **DISCIPLINE** LAW **EDUCATION** Stanford Univ, BA; Harvard Univ, JD. **CAREER** Asst prof **HONORS AND AWARDS** Ed, Harvard Civil Rights-Civil Liberties Law Rev. **RESEARCH** Environmental law. **SELECTED PUBLICATIONS** Auth, pubs on environmental law and land use. **CONTACT ADDRESS** Law Dept, Univ of Missouri, Kansas City, 5100 Rockhill Rd, Kansas City, MO 64110-2499. **EMAIL** verchickr@umkc.edu

VERENE, DONALD P.
PERSONAL Born 10/24/1937, Galesburg, IL, m, 1960, 1 child **DISCIPLINE** PHILOSOPHY **EDUCATION** Knox Col, AB, 59; Wash Univ, AM, 64; PhD, 64. **CAREER** Asst to assoc prof, N Ill Univ, 64-71; assoc prof to prof, Pa State Univ, 71-82; prof and Chair, Emory Univ, 82-; vis fel, Pembroke Col, Oxford, 88; Dir Inst for Vico Studies, Emory Univ, 82-. **HONORS AND AWARDS** LHD Honoris causa, Knox Col, 90; Galileo Prize for Philos, Italy, 98. **MEMBERSHIPS** Am Philos Assoc, E Div; Hegel Soc of Am. **RESEARCH** German Idealism; Italian Humanism; metaphysics; philosophy of culture; and philosophy of imagination; with emphasis on the thought of Hegel; Cassirer; and Vico **SELECTED PUBLICATIONS** Ed, Symbol, Myth and Culture: Essays and Lectures of Ernst Cassirer 1935-1945, 79; auth, Vico's Science of Imagination, 81; auth, The New Art of Autobiography, 91; auth, Hegel's Recollection, 85; auth, Philosophy and the Return to Self-Knowledge, 97. **CONTACT ADDRESS** Dept Philos, Emory Univ, 1364 Clifton Road NE, Atlanta, GA 30322-1061. **EMAIL** dverene@emory.edu

VERHAEGH, MARCUS
PERSONAL Born Los Angeles, CA **DISCIPLINE** PHILOSOPHY **EDUCATION** Free Univ Amsterdam, Doctorandus, 97. **CAREER** Tchng asst, 97-, Emory Univ. **HONORS AND AWARDS** Natl Merit Scholar, 89. **MEMBERSHIPS** APA. **RESEARCH** Ethics; aesthetics; hist of philos. **SELECTED PUBLICATIONS** Auth, Hypothetical and Psychoanalytic Interpretation, J of Philos Res, 99. **CONTACT ADDRESS** 551 Dorset St, Cambry, CA 93428. **EMAIL** mverhae@emory.edu

VERHEY, ALLEN DALE
PERSONAL Born 05/14/1945, Grand Rapids, MI, m, 1965, 3 children **DISCIPLINE** CHRISTIAN ETHICS, NEW TESTAMENT STUDIES **EDUCATION** Calvin Col, BA, 66; Calvin Theol Sem, BD, 69; Yale Univ, PhD(relig ethics), 75. **CAREER** Guest lectr Christian ethics, Calvin Theol Sem, 72-75; asst prof, 75-80, ASSOC PROF RELIG, HOPE COL, 80-, Ordained minister, Christian Reformed Church, 75-; Lilly Found fel, 77. **MEMBERSHIPS** Soc Ethics, Soc Life Sci; Am Soc Christian Ethics; Soc Bibl Lit. **RESEARCH** The use of scripture in ethics; biblical ethics; the ethics of John Calvin. **SELECTED PUBLICATIONS** Auth, The Holy-Bible and Sanctified Sexuality--An Evangelical Approach to Scripture and Sexual Ethics, Interpretation-Jour Bible and Theol, Vol 0049, 95. **CONTACT ADDRESS** Dept of Philos, Hope Col, 137 E 12th St, Holland, MI 49423-3698.

VERKAMP, BERNARD
PERSONAL Born 02/20/1938, Huntingburg, IN, s **DISCIPLINE** THEOLOGY **EDUCATION** St. Louis Univ, PhD, 72. **CAREER** Prof of Philosophy, Vincennes Univ, 72-00. **HONORS AND AWARDS** Phi Beta Kappa. **MEMBERSHIPS** AAVP; APA. **RESEARCH** Philosophy of Religion. **SELECTED PUBLICATIONS** Auth, "The Indifferent Mean," Athens and Detroit: Ohio and Wayne State University Press, 77; auth, "The Moral Treatment of Returning Warriors: Medieval and Modern Times, London and Toronto: Associate University Presses, 93; auth, "The Evolution of Religion: A Reexamination, Scranton: University of Scranton Press, 95; auth, "The Senses of Mystery: Religious and Non-Religious, Scranton: University of Scranton Press, 97. **CONTACT ADDRESS** Dept Philosophy, Vincennes Univ, 1002 North 1st St., Vincennes, IN 47591-1504. **EMAIL** bvarkamp@vunet.vinu.edu

VERKRUYSE, PETER
PERSONAL Born 12/07/1959, Kewanee, IL, m, 1979, 4 children **DISCIPLINE** RELIGION, COMMUNICATION **EDUCATION** Lincoln Christian Col, BA, 82; Lincoln Christian Sem, MA, 87; Lincoln Christian Sem, MDiv, 88; Univ Ill, MA, 90; Univ Ill, PhD, 95. **CAREER** Grad Teaching Asst, Lincoln Christian Col, 82-85; Res Asst, Univ Ill, 90-91; Adj Fac, Danville Area Community Col, 90-91; Adj Fac, Millikin Univ, 93-94; Grad Teaching Asst, Univ Ill, 88-94; Assoc Prof, Ky Christian Col, 94-00; Asst Prof, Ill Col, 00-. **HONORS AND AWARDS** Marie Hochman Nichols Awd, Univ Ill, 92; Stafford H Thomas Awd, Univ Ill, 93; Fel, Univ Ill, 93; Who's Who Among Am Teachers. **MEMBERSHIPS** Nat Commun Asn, Relig Commun Asn, Int Soc for the Hist of Rhetoric, Acad of Homiletics. **RESEARCH** American public address, history of rhetoric, Alexander Campbell, classical Greek rhetoric. **SELECTED PUBLICATIONS** Auth, "African-American Preachers in the Restoration Tradition," Christian Standard (96); auth, "Discovering the Restoration's African-American History," Christian Chronicle (96); auth, Building Blocks for Bible Study, Col Pr (Joplin, MO), 97; auth, The College Press NIV Commentary: Hebrews, Col Pr (Joplin, MO), 97; auth, "Rebekah, Bride of Isaac," Preaching On-Line (99). **CONTACT ADDRESS** Dept Relig & Commun, Illinois Col, Jacksonville, IL 62650.

VERMAZEN, BRUCE JAMES
PERSONAL Born 06/06/1940, Cedar Rapids, IA, d **DISCIPLINE** PHILOSOPHY **EDUCATION** Univ Chicago, AB, 61, MA, 62; Stanford Univ, PhD, 67. **CAREER** Instr English, Univ Ky, 62-64; asst prof, 67-76, assoc prof, prof philos, 85-, Univ Calif, Berkeley, 76-; dept ch, 92-93 & 95-98. **MEMBERSHIPS** Am Philos Asn; Am Soc Aesthet. **RESEARCH** Philosophy of language; ethics; philosophy of mind; American popular music. **SELECTED PUBLICATIONS** Auth, Consistency and underdetermination, Philos & Phenomenol Res, 3/68; auth, Information theory and musical value, J Aesthet & Art Criticism, spring 71; auth, Semantics and semantics, Found Lang, 8/71. **CONTACT ADDRESS** Dept Philos, Univ of California, Berkeley, 314 Moses Hall, Berkeley, CA 94720-2391.

VERNEZZE, PETER J.
DISCIPLINE PHILOSOPHY **EDUCATION** Univ Wis, BA, 82, PhD, 88. **CAREER** Assoc prof, Waynesburg Univ. **RESEARCH** Ancient philosophy, history of ideas, critical thinking. **SELECTED PUBLICATIONS** Auth, Reason and the World: A Critical Thinking Textbook, Kendall/Hunt: Dubuque, Iowa, 92, sec ed, 95 **CONTACT ADDRESS** Dept of Political Science, Waynesburg Col, 51 W College St, Waynesburg, PA 15370. **EMAIL** pvernezze@weber.edu

VERNOFF, CHARLES ELLIOTT
PERSONAL Born 02/11/1942, Miami, FL **DISCIPLINE** COMPARATIVE PHILOSOPHY OF RELIGION **EDUCATION** Univ Chicago, BA, 63; Univ Calif, Santa Barbara, MA, 72, PhD(relig studies), 79. **CAREER** Prof Relig, Cornell Col, 78-. **MEMBERSHIPS** Am Acad Relig; Asn Jewish Studies. **RESEARCH** Theory and method in the study of religion; modern Jewish thought; Holocaust studies; Judaism; American civil religion. **SELECTED PUBLICATIONS** Auth, Towards a transnatural Judaic theology of Halakhah, In: Jewish Essays and Studies, Vol II, Reconstructionist Rabbinical Col Press, 81. **CONTACT ADDRESS** Dept of Relig, Cornell Col, 600 First St W, Mount Vernon, IA 52314-1098. **EMAIL** cvernoff@cornell-iowa.edu

VERTIN, MICHAEL
PERSONAL Born 09/25/1939, Breckenridge, MN **DISCIPLINE** PHILOSOPHY, RELIGION **EDUCATION** St John's Univ, BA, 62; Cath Univ Am, STL, 72; Univ Toronto, PhD(philos), 73. **CAREER** Spec lectr philos, 70-71, asst prof philos and relig studies, 72-78, ASSOC PROF PHILOS AND RELIG STUDIES, ST MICHAEL'S COL, UNIV TORONTO, 78-, Counr, Coun Scholarly Proj, Bernard Lonergan Trust Dund, 75-82. **MEMBERSHIPS** Am Cath Philos Asn; Can Philos Asn; Cath Theol Soc Am; Metaphys Soc Am. **RESEARCH** The philosophical foundations of interdisciplinary studies; philosophy of theology; God and evil. **SELECTED PUBLICATIONS** Auth, "Philosophy of God, Theology, and the Problems of Evil,"; auth, "Marechal, Lonergan, and the Phenomenology of Knowing,"; auth, "Is God in Process?"; ed, Appropriating the Lonergan Idea, by F.E. Crowe; auth, "Science, and Cognitional Conversion,". **CONTACT ADDRESS** Dept of Philos, Univ of Toronto, 215 Huron St, Toronto, ON, Canada M5S 1A1. **EMAIL** mvertin@chass.utoronto.ca

VIDAL, JAIME R.
PERSONAL Born 11/28/1943, Ponce, Puerto Rico **DISCIPLINE** THEOLOGY **EDUCATION** Fordham Univ, PhD, 84. **CAREER** Asst prof rel stud, Seton Hall Univ, 85-90; asst dir, Cushwa Ctr Stud Amer Cath, Univ Notre Dame, 90-94; Dir Hispanic Stud, Pontifical Col Josephinum, 94-97; Msgr James Supple Ch of Cath Stud, Dept Philos/Rel Stud, Iowa State Univ, 97-; Managing Dir/Ed, Franciscan Press, Quincy Univ, 99-. **MEMBERSHIPS** Medieval Acad Amer; PARAL: Project for the Analysis of Religion Among Latinos; Amer Acad Rel; Am Soc Church Hist; US Cath Hist Soc. **RESEARCH** Medieval Catholicism; Franciscanism; Hispanic Popular Catholicism. **SELECTED PUBLICATIONS** Auth, Citizens, Yet Strangers: The Puerto Rican Experience, in Puerto Rican and Cuban Catholics in the US: 1900-1965 ed Jay P. Dolan and Jaime R. Vidal, vol 2 of Notre Dame History of US Hispanic Catholics, Notre Dame, IN, U of Notre Dame P, 94; Towards an Understanding of Synthesis in Iberian and Hispanic-American Popular Religiosity, in An Enduring Flame: Studies in Latino Popular Religiosity, ed Anthony Stevens Arroyo and Ana Maria Diaz-Stevens. New York, Bildner Ctr W Hemisphere Stud, CUNY, 95, 69-95; Christopher Columbus, Bartolome de Las Casas, Santeria, Magic and Voodoo in The Harper Encycl of Catholicism, ed Richard McBrien, San Francisco, 95; Pilgrimage in the Christian Tradition, in Concilium: Rev Intl de Theologie, Aug 96; Hispanic Catholics in America, in The Encycl of US Cath Hist, ed Michael Glazier and Thomas Shelley, Collegeville, MN, The Liturgical Press, Michael Glazier bks, 97. **CONTACT ADDRESS** Quincy Univ, 915 N 18th, Quincy, IL 62301. **EMAIL** jvidal@iastate.edu

VIELKIND, JOHN N.
PERSONAL Born 06/29/1945, Neptune, NJ **DISCIPLINE** PHILOSOPHY **EDUCATION** St Mary's Sem and Univ, BA, 67; Duquesne Univ, MA, 70; PhD, 74. **CAREER** Instr, Duquesne Univ, 70-74; Asst Prof, Midwestern State Univ, 74-81; Assoc Prof to Prof and Dept Chair, Marshall Univ, 81-. **HONORS AND AWARDS** Merit Awd, Marshall Univ, 98; Dean's Merit Awd, Marshall Univ, 96. **MEMBERSHIPS** Soc for Phenomenology and Existential Philos, Am Philos Asn, N Am Nietzsche Soc, Heidegger Circle, Colloquium on Violence and Relig, W Va Philos Soc, W Va Humanities Coun. **RESEARCH** Platonic Dialogues; Kant, Nietzsche, Heidegger; Philosophy of Art; Philosophy of Religion; Interdisciplinary Study of Language and Literature. **SELECTED PUBLICATIONS** Auth, "The Pathology of a Genealogist," a review of Infectious Nietzsche by David Farrell Krell, Research in Phenomenology, (97): 226-233. **CONTACT ADDRESS** Dept Philos, Marshall Univ, 400 Hal Greer Blvd, Huntington, WV 25755-0001. **EMAIL** vielkind@marshall.edu

VIGILANTI, JOHN A.
PERSONAL Born 08/11/1946, New York, NY, s **DISCIPLINE** THEOLOGY **EDUCATION** St Joseph's Sem, Yonkers, BA, 68, MDiv, 72; Inst for Relig Studies, MA, 79; Fordham, MA, 82; Cath Univ Am, JCL, 84; Iona, MS, 87; Fordham, EdD, 91. **CAREER** Assoc pastor, St Thomas, 72-75; assoc pastor, St Bartholomew, 75-82; Canonical consult and defender of the bond, Metropolitan Tribunal, 84-87; teacher, Mt St Ursula High School, Bronx, NY, 86-; adjunct asst prof, Iona Col, 94; adjunct asst prof, Fordham Univ, 94; adjunct asst prof, Col of Mt St Vincent, Bronx, NY, 95-96; Judge, Promoter of Justice, New York Archdiocese, Metropolitan Tribunal, 87-94; pastor, O. L. Assumption, Bronx, NY, 94-95. **HONORS AND AWARDS** Chaplain Officer Basic Course, 81, Advanced Course, 84; Chaplain Res Component General Staff Course, 94; Battalion Chaplain, 102D Combat Engineers, 42D Infantry Div, New York Nat Guard, 81-90; Sr Chaplain, 107th Brigade, 42D Infantry Div, NY Nat Guard, 90-93; Chaplain, 107th Support Group NYARNG, 93-98; Chaplain, 53rd Troop Command, 98-. **MEMBERSHIPS** Canon Law Soc Am, Nat Guard Assoc, New York Militia Asn. **RESEARCH** Relationships, contemporary ethical problems, academic freedom. **SELECTED PUBLICATIONS** Auth, Academic Freedom and the Adult Student in Catholic Higher Education, Krieger (92). **CONTACT ADDRESS** Dept Humanities, Col of Mount Saint Vincent, 6301 Riverdale Ave, Bronx, NY 10471-1046.

VILLAFANE, ELDIN
PERSONAL Born Santa Isabel, Puerto Rico, m, 3 children **DISCIPLINE** CHRISTIAN SOCIAL ETHICS **EDUCATION** Hartwick Col; Cent Bible Col, BA; Wheaton Grad Sch Theol, MA; Boston Univ, PhD. **CAREER** Founding dir, Gordon-Conwell's Ctr for Urban Ministerial Edu, 76-90; prof, Gordon-Conwell Theol Sem, 76-; assoc dean, Urban and Multicult Aff, 90-93; exec dir, Contextualized Urban Theol Edu Enablement Prog. **HONORS AND AWARDS** One of the nation's 10 most influential Hispanic leaders and scholars, Nat Cath Reporter, 92; pres, soc pentecostal stud; la communidad of hisp amer scholars of theol and rel; co-ch, greater boston develop coalition; emmanuel gospel center. **SELECTED PUBLICATIONS** Auth, The Liberating Spirit: Toward an Hispanic American Pentecostal Social Ethic, Eerdman's Publ Co, 93; Seek the Peace of the City: Reflections on Urban Ministry, Eerdmans Publ Co. **CONTACT ADDRESS** Gordon-Conwell Theol Sem, 130 Essex St, South Hamilton, MA 01982.

VIMINITZ, PAUL
DISCIPLINE PHILOSOPHY **EDUCATION** Dalhousie Univ, BA; Univ Regina, MA; Univ Alberta, PhD. **CAREER** Prof, Univ fo Lethbridge. **RESEARCH** Applications of Game Theory to ethics and political philosophy. **SELECTED PUBLICATIONS** Auth, pubs on ethics and political philosophy. **CONTACT ADDRESS** Dept of Philosophy, Univ of Lethbridge, 4401 University Dr W, Lethbridge, AB, Canada T1K 3M4.

VINCENT, DAVID
PERSONAL Born 04/24/1938, Dayton, OH, s **DISCIPLINE** PHILOSOPHY **EDUCATION** OSU, MA, 63; Cath Univ of Am, MA, 60; Cath Univ of Am, BA **CAREER** Tchr of Classics, 64-69, Ath of OH; Tchr of Classics, 69-73, Elder HS, Past Assign, 64-pres, Archdiocese of Cincinnati **CONTACT ADDRESS** St. Mary Church, Springfield, OH 45506-1306. **EMAIL** dvincent@dnaco.net

VINCI, THOMAS
DISCIPLINE PHILOSOPHY **EDUCATION** Univ Toronto, BA, 71; Univ Pittsburgh, PhD, 77. **CAREER** Assoc prof. **RESEARCH** Epistemology, philosophy. of science, history of modern philosophy. **SELECTED PUBLICATIONS** Co-auth, "Novel Confirmation," Brit Jour Phil Sci, 83; auth, Objective Chance, Indicative Conditionals and Decision Theory, Synthese, 88; various entries in the Cambridge Dictionary of Philos, 95; Cartesian Truth, Cambridge UP, 98. **CONTACT ADDRESS** Dept of Philos, Dalhousie Univ, Halifax, NS, Canada B3H 3J5. **EMAIL** thomas.vinci@dal.ca

VINING, JOSEPH
PERSONAL Born 03/03/1938, Fulton, MO, m, 1965, 2 children **DISCIPLINE** LAW AND JURISPRUDENCE **EDUCATION** Yale Univ, BA, 59; Cambridge Univ, MA, 61; Harvard Univ, JD, 64. **CAREER** Atty, Dept Justice, 64-65; asst to exec dir, Nat Crime Comn, 65-66; Prof Law, Univ Mich, Ann Arbor, 69-; Consult, Off Econ Opportunity, 68 & Admin Conf US, 69-72; res assoc, Clare Hall, Cambridge Univ, 73, vis mem, Fac Law, 73. **HONORS AND AWARDS** NEH sr fel, 82-; Rockefeller Found Bellagio Fel, 97. **MEMBERSHIPS** Am Law Inst; Am Acad Arts & Sci. **RESEARCH** Administrative law; legal method and theology; corporate law. **SELECTED PUBLICATIONS** Auth, Legal Identity, Yale Univ Press, 78; The Authoritative and the Authoritarian, Univ Chicago Press, 86; From Newton's Sleep, Princeton Univ Press, 95. **CONTACT ADDRESS** Law Sch, Univ of Michigan, Ann Arbor, 625 S State St, Ann Arbor, MI 48109-1215.

VISION, GERALD
DISCIPLINE PHILOSOPHY **EDUCATION** Univ Mich, PhD, 67. **CAREER** Prof of Philos, Temple Univ **MEMBERSHIPS** Am Philos Asn; Aristotelian Soc; Soc Philos & Psychol. **RESEARCH** Philosophy of language; philosophy of mind; analytic metaphysics; history of philosophy. **SELECTED PUBLICATIONS** Rev RoyBhaskar, Philosophy and the Idea of Freedom, Philos Books, 93; auth, Fictionalism and Fictional Utterance, Pacific Philos Quart, 93; Adimadversions on the Causal Theory of Perception, Philos Quart, 93; The Rule-Following Paradox and Dispositions, Philos and the Cognitive Sci: Papers of the Sixteenth Int Wittgenstein Symp, 93; Problems of Vision: Rethinking the Causal Theory of Perception, Oxford Univ Press, 96; Michael Dummett, The Seas of Language, Philos Books, 95; Disquotational Truth Theories, Proceedings of the Tenth Mtg of Congress for Logic, Method and the Philos Sci, 95; Why Correspondence Truth Will Not Go Away, Notre Dame Jour Formal Logic, 97; Believing Sentences, Philos Studies, 97; Perceptual Content, Philos, 98; Blindsight and Philosophy, Philos Psychol, 98. **CONTACT ADDRESS** Dept of Philosophy, Temple Univ, Philadelphia, PA 19122. **EMAIL** vision@vm.temple.edu

VISOTZKY, BURTON L.
PERSONAL Born 10/19/1951, Chicago, IL, m, 2 children **DISCIPLINE** TALMUD AND RABBINICS **EDUCATION** Univ Ill, BA; Harvard Univ, MA; Jewish Theol Sem Am, MA, PhD. **CAREER** Fac, 77-; assoc and acting dean grad schl, 92-96; Nathan and Janet Appleman Chair Midrash and Interreligious Studies; dir, Louis Finkelstein Inst Relig Soc Studies 96-98; adm prof, Union Theol Sem NY. **HONORS AND AWARDS** Vis Fac,Hebrew Union Col, NY; vis scholar, oxford univ; vis fel and life mem clare hall, univ cambridge; vis fac, princeton theol sem; vis fac, russ state univ hum; consult and participant in genesis: a living conversation, pbs, 96; consult prince of egypt, dreamworks skg, 98. **MEMBERSHIPS** Society of Bib Lit, Assoc of Jewish Studies, Rabbinical Assembly **SELECTED PUBLICATIONS** Auth, Midrash Mishle, Hebrew, NY, JTSA, 90; auth, Reading the Book, Anchor 91; auth, Reading the Book: Making the Bible a Timeless Text, Doubleday/Anchor, 91; The Genesis of Ethics, Crown; Schocken, 96; auth, Midrash on Proverbs, Yale, 92; auth, Fathers of the World,

Tubinaer, 95; auth, Genesis of Ethics, 96; auth, Road to Redemption, Crown, 98; auth, From Mesopotamia to Modernity: Ten Intro's to Jewish History and Lit, 99. **CONTACT ADDRESS** Jewish Theol Sem of America, 3080 Broadway, New York, NY 10027. **EMAIL** buvisotzky@jtsa.edu

VIVAS, ELISEO
PERSONAL Born 07/13/1901, m, 1925, 1 child **DISCIPLINE** PHILOSOPHY **EDUCATION** Univ Wis, PhD, 35. **CAREER** Asst prof philos, Univ Wis, 36-44; assoc prof, Univ Chicago, 44-47; prof philos and English, Ohio State Univ, 47-51; John Evans prof moral and intellectual philos, 51-69, EMER PROF PHILOS, NORTHWESTERN UNIV, EVANSTON, 69-; Guggenheim Found fel, 39-40; vis distinguished prof philos and English, Rockford Col, 69-71. **MEMBERSHIPS** Am Soc Aesthet; Metaphys Soc Am. **RESEARCH** Value theory. **SELECTED PUBLICATIONS** Auth, Effects of Story Reading on Language, Language Learning, Vol 46, 96. **CONTACT ADDRESS** PO Box 414, Wilmette, IL 60091.

VIVIAN, CORDY TINDELL
PERSONAL Born 07/30/1924, Howard County, MO, m **DISCIPLINE** THEOLOGY **EDUCATION** Western IL Univ, BA 1948; Amer Baptist Theol Sem, BD 1958; New School for Social Rsch, Doctorate 1984; Western IL Univ, Doctorate 1987. **CAREER** Natl Bapt Conv USA Inc, natl dir 1955-61; 1st Comm Church, pastor 1956-61; Cosmo Comm Church, pastor 1961-63; SCLC, natl dir 1962-67; Shaw Univ, minister 1972-73; natl dir sem without walls 1974-; Black Action Strategies & Info Center Inc (BASIC), bd chmn. **MEMBERSHIPS** Chmn Natl Anti-Klan Network; mem Natl Black Leadership Roundtable; chmn Southern Organizing Comm Educ Fund; bd mem Inst of the Black World; bd mem Intl United Black Fund; co-dir Southern Reg Twentieth Anniversary March on Washington For Jobs Peace & Freedom; bd mem Southern Christian Leadership Conf, Souther Organizing Comm, Natl Council of Black Churchmen, The African Inst for the Study of Human Values; mem Racial Justice Working Group Natl Council Churches; vstg prof Wartburg Theol Sem; intl lecture & consult tours Africa, Tokyo, Isreal, Holland, Manila, Japan. **SELECTED PUBLICATIONS** Auth, Black Power & The Amer Myth, Amer Joseph, Date & Fact Book of Black Amer; editor the Baptist, Layman Mag for Baptist Men; listed in 1000 Successful Blacks, The Ebony Success Library, Odyssey, A Journey Through Black Amer, From Montgomery to Memphis, Clergy in Action Training, Unearthing Seeds of Fire, The Idea of Highlander, The Trouble I've Seen. **CONTACT ADDRESS** BASIC, 595 Parsons St, Atlanta, GA 30314.

VOELZ, JAMES W.
PERSONAL Born 06/18/1945, Milwaukee, WI, m, 1977, 1 child **DISCIPLINE** EXEGETICAL THEOLOGY **EDUCATION** Concordia Sr Col, BA, 67; Concordia Sem, MDiv, 71; Cambridge Univ, England, PhD, 78. **CAREER** Asst prof, 75-76, Concordia Theol Sem, Ill; asst prof, to assoc prof, 82-89, Concordia Theol Sem, Ind; pastoral asst, Zion Lutheran Church, Ind, 84-88; guest instr, 83, assof prof, 89-93, prof exegetical theol, 93- , dean grad sch, 96- , Concordia Sem, Missouri. **HONORS AND AWARDS** John W. Behnken Fel, 82-83. **MEMBERSHIPS** Studiorum Novi Testamenti Soc; Soc of Bibl Lit; Int Org of Septuagint Cognate Stud. **RESEARCH** Greek grammar; hermeneutics; Mark; narrative and parable interpretation. **SELECTED PUBLICATIONS** Auth, "The Language of the New Testament," ANRW, 25, 84; auth, Fundamental Greek Grammar, Concordia, 86, 2d ed, 93; auth, Present and Aorist Verbal Aspect: A New Proposal, Neotestamentica, 93; auth, Multiple Signs, Levels of Meaning and Self as Text; Elements of Intertextuality in Intertextuality and the Bible, Semeia: An Experimental J for Bibl Criticism, 95; auth, What Does This Mean? Principles of Biblical Interpretation in the Post-Modern World, CPH, 95, 2d ed, 97. **CONTACT ADDRESS** Concordia Sem, 801 DeMun Ave, Saint Louis, MO 63105. **EMAIL** voelzj@csl.edu

VOGEL, MANFRED H.
PERSONAL Born 09/15/1930, Tel Aviv, Israel, m, 1962 **DISCIPLINE** PHILOSOPHY OF RELIGION **EDUCATION** Wayne State Univ, BA, 53; Columbia Univ, MA, 55, PhD, 64. **CAREER** From asst prof to assoc prof, 63-71, Prof Philos Relig, Northwestern Univ, Evanston, 71, CHMN DEPT, 72-. **MEMBERSHIPS** Am Acad Relig; Am Theol Soc. **SELECTED PUBLICATIONS** Auth, Historicism, the Holocaust and Zionism, Mod Judaism, Vol 14, 94; An Interview with Vogel, Marcia, Wide Angle Quart J Film Hist Theory Criticism Practice, Vol , 97. **CONTACT ADDRESS** Dept of Relig, Northwestern Univ, 1940 Sheridan Rd., Evanston, IL 60208-0850.

VOGELAAR, HAROLD STANTON
DISCIPLINE MISSIONS, WORLD RELIGIONS **EDUCATION** New Brunswick Theol Sem; Columbia Univ. **CAREER** Adj prof **HONORS AND AWARDS** Ch, Christian-Muslim Working Group of NCCC's Interfaith Relations; co-ch, Conf for Improved Muslim-Christian Relations of Greater Chicago. **SELECTED PUBLICATIONS** Coauth, Activities of the Immigrant Muslim Communities in Chicago, Muslim Communities in N Am, State U of New York P, 94. **CONTACT ADDRESS** Dept of Missions and World Religions, Lutheran Sch of Theol at Chicago, 1100 E 55th St, Chicago, IL 60615. **EMAIL** hvogelaa@lstc.edu

VOGELS, WALTER A.
PERSONAL Born 10/14/1932, Antwerp, Belgium, s **DISCIPLINE** BIBLICAL STUDIES **EDUCATION** Pontifical Biblical Inst, Rome, LLS, 60; Univ Ottawa, PhD (Th), 68; St Paul Univ, DTh, 70; Gregorian Univ, Rome, LTh, 88. **CAREER** Prof Biblical studies, Int School of Theology of the Missionaries of Africa, Ottawa, 60-68; Full Prof Biblical Studies (Hebrew Bible), Faculty of Theology, St Paul Univ, 66-. **MEMBERSHIPS** Assoc Catholique oles studes bibliques en Canada; Cath Biblical Assoc Amer; Cath Biblical Assoc Can; Soc of Biblical Lit; Soc Catholique de la Bible. **RESEARCH** Torah. **SELECTED PUBLICATIONS** Auth, Interpreting Scripture in the Third Millenium, 95; Job: L'homme qui e bien parle de Dieu, 95; Abraham et se legende: Genese 12, 1-25, 11, 96; Moise eux multiples visaper: Der l'Exode eu Deutironome, 97; and 25 articles in the last 5 years. **CONTACT ADDRESS** Saint Paul Univ, 223 Main St., Ottawa, ON, Canada K1S 1C4. **EMAIL** wvogels@ustpaul.uottawa.ca

VOLKMER, RONALD R.
DISCIPLINE LAW **EDUCATION** Creighton Univ, BA, 66, JD, 68; Univ Ill, LLM, 73. **CAREER** Prof, Creighton Univ, 69-; tchg fel, Univ Ill, 68-69; Cook grad fel, Univ Mich, 75-76. **MEMBERSHIPS** Alpha Sigma Nu; House Deleg, Nebr State Bar Asn; bd dir, Nebr State Bar Found; bd mem, Fam Hous Adv Serv, Inc; ch, Nebr Supreme Ct Adv Coun on Dispute Resolution. **SELECTED PUBLICATIONS** Pub(s), Creighton Law Rev & Iowa Law Rev. **CONTACT ADDRESS** Sch of Law, Creighton Univ, 2500 California Plaza , Omaha, NE 68178. **EMAIL** volkmer@culaw.Creighton.edu

VOLLMAR, VALERIE J.
PERSONAL Born 10/21/1946, Corvallis, OR **DISCIPLINE** ESTATE & GIFT TAXATION, ESTATE PLANNING, TRUSTS & ESTATES **EDUCATION** Univ Ore, BA, 68; Willamette Univ, JD, 75. **CAREER** Clk, US District Court, Portland, Ore, 75-77; assoc, clk, Marsh & Lindauer, 77-80; partner, Clark, Marsh, Lindauer, McClinton & Vollmar, Salem, Ore, 81-84; vis prof, 84-85; asst prof, 85-87; assoc prof, 87-93; prof, 93-. **HONORS AND AWARDS** Oregon State Bar President's Membership Service Awd, 89; Jerry E. Hudson Awd for Distinguished Teaching, 99; exec comm, ore state bar, 84-90; ch, 88-89; exec comm, am assn law sch(s), 88-94; ch, 92. **MEMBERSHIPS** Mem, Phi Beta Kappa; Willamette Valley Estate Planning Coun; Amer Col Trust & Estate Couns. **RESEARCH** Trusts and estates, physician-assisted suicide. **SELECTED PUBLICATIONS** Comment ed, Willamette Law Jour. **CONTACT ADDRESS** Sch of Law, Willamette Univ, 900 State St, Salem, OR 97301. **EMAIL** vvollmar@willamette.edu

VOLLRATH, JOHN F.
PERSONAL Born 06/22/1941, OH, m, 1971, 1 child **DISCIPLINE** PHILOSOPHY **EDUCATION** Valparaiso Univ, BA, 63; Indiana Univ, PhD, 67. **CAREER** Prof, philos, Univ Wisc Stevens Point, 71-. **HONORS AND AWARDS** Woodrow Wilson fel, 63-64. **MEMBERSHIPS** Philos of Sci Asn; Amer Philos Asn. **RESEARCH** Philosophy of science. **SELECTED PUBLICATIONS** Auth, Science and Moral Values. **CONTACT ADDRESS** Dept of Philosophy, 2100 Main St., Stevens Point, WI 54481. **EMAIL** jvollrat@uwsp.edu

VOLOKH, EUGENE
PERSONAL Born 02/29/1968, Kiev, USSR **DISCIPLINE** LAW **EDUCATION** UCLA, BS (math-computer science), 83, JD, 92. **CAREER** Law clerk to Judge Alex Kozinski, US Court of Appeals for the Ninth Circuit, 92-93; law clerk to Justice Sandra Day O'Connor, US Supreme Court, 93-94; acting prof, UCLA Law School, 94-99, prof, 99-. **RESEARCH** Constitutional law; free speech; religious freedom; gun control; cyberspace law; equal protection; sexual harassment. **SELECTED PUBLICATIONS** Auth, Computer Media for the Legal Profession, 94 MI Law Rev 2058, 96; Freedom of Speech, Permissible Tailoring and Transcending Strict Scrutiny, 144 Univ PA Law Rev 2417, 96; Material on Free Speech Defense to Sexual Harassmenrt Claims, in Barbara Lindermann & David Kadue, Sexual Harassment in Employment Law, ch 27, BNA Supp 97; The California Civil Rights Initiative: An Interpretive Guide, 44 UCLA Law Rev 1335, 97; What Speech Does "Hostile Work Environment" Harassment law Restrict?, 85 Georgetown Law J, 97, excerpted in Women's Freedom Network, Rethinking Sexual Harassment, Cathy Young, ed, 88; Freedom of Speech, Shielding Children, and Transcending Balancing, 1997 Supreme Court Rev 141; Written Testimony Regarding the Constitutionality of Federal Transportation Contract Set-Asides, Senate Subcommittee on the Constitution, Federalism and Property Rights, Oct 1, 1997; The Commonplace Second Amendment, 73 NYU Law Rev 793, 98; The Amazing Vanishing Second Amendment, 73 NYU Law Rev 831, 98; Freedom of Speech and Independent Judgment Review in Copyright Cases, 107 Yale Law J 2431, 98; Written testimony Regarding the Property of Amending RICO to Exempt Political Protest, House Subcommittee on Crime, July 17, 98; numerous other scholarly articles and other publications. **CONTACT ADDRESS** School of Law, Univ of California, Los Angeles, 405 Hilgard Ave, Los Angeles, CA 90095. **EMAIL** volokh@law.ucla.edu

VON DEHSEN, CHRISTIAN D.
DISCIPLINE PENTATEUCH, CHRISTOLOGIES OF THE NEW TESTAMENT **EDUCATION** CUNY, BA; Lutheran Theol Sem, MDiv; at Union Theol Sem, MA; PhD. **CAREER** Carthage Col. **MEMBERSHIPS** Phi Beta Kappa **SELECTED PUBLICATIONS** Auth, Policy and Politics: The Genesis and Theology of Social Statements in the Lutheran Church in America. **CONTACT ADDRESS** Carthage Col, 2001 Alford Dr., Kenosha, WI 53140.

VON ECKARDT, BARBARA
DISCIPLINE PHILOSOPHY OF SCIENCE AND PHILOSOPHY OF PSYCHOLOGY **EDUCATION** Case Western Reserve Univ, PhD, 74. **CAREER** Prof, assoc dean, Col of Arts and Sci, Univ Nebr, Lincoln. **RESEARCH** The foundations of cognitive science. **SELECTED PUBLICATIONS** Auth, Cognitive Psychology and Principled Skepticism, J of Philos 81, 84; What is Cognitive Science?, Cambridge, 93; The Empirical Naivete of the Current Philosophical Conception of Folk Psychology, in P Machamer and M Carrier, eds, Philosophy and the Sciences of Mind, Pittsburgh, 96. **CONTACT ADDRESS** Univ of Nebraska, Lincoln, Lincoln, NE 68588-0417.

VON KELLENBACH, KATHARINE
PERSONAL Born 05/18/1960, Stuttgart, Germany, m, 1991, 2 children **DISCIPLINE** FEMINISM AND RELIGION **EDUCATION** Gymnasium Munich, Abitur, 79; Kirchliche Hochschule Berlin, Colloquiuum, 81; Georg August Univ Gottingen; Temple Univ, MA, 84, PhD, 90. **CAREER** Teaching Asst to Instr, Temple Univ, 85-88; Vis Lectr, Lehigh Univ, Spring 89; Vis Asst Prof, Lehigh Univ/Muhlenberg Col/Moravian Col (joint appointment), 90-91; Asst Prof Religion, St. Mary's Col of Md, 91-; Assoc Prof Religion, St. Mary's College, 00-. **HONORS AND AWARDS** DAAD Schol, Ger Acad Exchange Service, 83-84; Coolidge Colloquium, Cambridge, Mass, 86; Charlotte W. Newcombe Fel, 89-90; Fac Development Grants, St. Mary's Col, 91-98; ACLS Fellowship, 00-01; DAAD Study Visit Grant. **MEMBERSHIPS** Am Acad Relig; Soc Values in Higher Educ; Europ Soc Women Theol Res. **RESEARCH** Women and religion; Holocaust studies; Jewish-Christian relations. **SELECTED PUBLICATIONS** Auth, Anti-Judaism in Feminist Religious Writings, Schol Press, 94; God Does Not Oppress Any Human Being: The Life and Thought of Rabbi Regina Jonas, Leo Baeck Institute: Yearbook XXXIX, 94; Overcoming the Teaching of Contempt, Feminist Companion to the Bible, Sheffield Acad Press, 97; Reproduction and Resistance During the Holocaust, Women and the Holocaust, Univ Am Press (forthcoming); co-ed, Zwischen-Rame: Deutsche Feministische Theologinnen im Ausland, 00; author of numerous articles and other publications. **CONTACT ADDRESS** Dept Philosophy and Religious Studies, St. Mary's Col of Maryland, Saint Mary's City, MD 20686-0000. **EMAIL** kvonkellenbach@osprey.smcm.edu

VON WAHLDE, URBAN C.
PERSONAL Born 10/28/1941, Covington, KY, m, 2 children **DISCIPLINE** NEW TESTAMENT STUDIES **EDUCATION** Loyola Univ, BA, 65; MA, 66; Marquette Univ, PhD, 75. **CAREER** Asst prof, St Mary of the Plains Col, 74-76; asst to assoc prof, Univ of Scranton, 76-81; assoc prof to prof, Loyola Univ of Chicago, 81-. **HONORS AND AWARDS** Alpha Sigma Nu; Alpha Sigma Lambda; Excellence in Teaching Awd, Univ of Scranton, 79; Who's Who in Relig; 2000 Outstanding Relig Leaders of the Twentieth Century, 00. **MEMBERSHIPS** Cath Bibl Assoc; Soc of Bibl Lit; Chicago Soc of Bibl Res; Studiorum Novi Testamenti Societas. **RESEARCH** New Testament, especially the Johannine Literature. **SELECTED PUBLICATIONS** Auth, "The Gospel of John and the Presentation of Jews and Judaism", Within Context, eds L. Klenicki, D. Efroymson, E. Fisher, Liturgical Pr, (Collegeville, 93); auth, "Community in Conflict: The History and Social Context of the Johannine Community", Interpretation 49.4 (95): 379-89; auth, "The Problems of Acts 4:251: A New Proposal", Zeitschri ft fur die neutestamentliche Wissenshaft Bd 86 (95): 265-267; auth, "The Theological Assessment of the First Christian Persecution: The Apostles' Prayer and Its Consequences in Acts 4,24-31", Biblica 76.4 (95): 523-531; auth, "Acts 4,24-31: The Prayer of the Apostles in Response to the Persecution of Peter and john - And Its Consequences", Biblica 77.2 (96): 237-244; auth, "The Relationships Between Pharisees and Chief Priests: Some Observations on the Texts in Matthew, John, and Josephus", New Testament Studies 42.4 (96): 506-522; auth, "Community in Conflict", Gospel Interpretation: Narrative-Critical and Social-Scientific Approaches, Trinity Int, (Harrisburg, 97): 222-233; auth, "Das Johannesevangelium und die Juden un Judaismus", Studien zur neutestamentichen Hermeneutik nach Auschwitz, ed P Fiedler and G. Dautzenberg, (99): 89-114; auth, "You Are of Your Father the Devil in Its Context: Stereotyped Polemic in Jn 8;38-47", Anti-Judaism in the Fourth Gospel and Jewish-Christian Dialogue, Katholieke Univ Leuven, (Leuven, 99): 359-379; auth, "The Jews in John's Gospel: Fifteen Years of Research (1983-1998)", Ephemerides Theologicae Lovanienses (Belgium), LXXVI, Fasciculus 1 (00): 30-55. **CONTACT ADDRESS** Dept Theol, Loyola Univ, Chicago, 6525 N Sheridan Rd, Chicago, IL 60626-5344. **EMAIL** uvonwah@luc.edu

VORSPAN, RACHEL
PERSONAL Born 08/15/1945, New York, NY, m, 1982, 1 child **DISCIPLINE** LAW **EDUCATION** Univ Calif, AB, 67; Columbia Univ, MA, 68; PhD, 75; Harvard Law Sch, JD, 79. **CAREER** Assoc Prof, Fordham Univ Sch of Law, 94-. **HONORS AND AWARDS** Fulbright Renewal Awd, United Kingdom, 72-73; Res Coun Fel, Univ Mo, 75; Grant APA, 76; Grant, ACLS, 75-76; Summer Res Grants, Fordham Law Sch, 89-91, 97-98. **MEMBERSHIPS** ASLH, ALWD, AALS, ABCNY, ABA. **RESEARCH** Legal history. **SELECTED PUBLICATIONS** Auth, Industrialization and the Working Classes: Selected Documents, Columbia UP, 76; auth, "Vagrancy and the new Poor Law in Late-Victorian and Edwardian England," 92 English Hist Rev 59 (77); auth, "Post-Discharge Coercion of Bankrupts by Private Creditors," 91 Harvard Law Rev 1336 (78); auth, "Freedom of Assembly and the Right of Passage in Modern English Legal History," 34 San Diego Law Rev 921 (97); auth, "The Political Power of Nuisance Law: Labor Picketing and the Courts in Modern England, 1871-Present," 46 Buffalo Law Rev 593 (98); auth, "Rational Recreation and the Law: The Transformation of Urban Popular Leisure in Victorian England," 44 McGill Law J (forthcoming). **CONTACT ADDRESS** Dept Law, Fordham Univ, 140 W 62nd St, New York, NY 10023-7407. **EMAIL** rvorspan@mail.lawnet.fordham.edu

VOS, ARVIN G.
PERSONAL Born 07/28/1942, Taintor, IA, m, 1967, 5 children **DISCIPLINE** MEDIEVAL PHILOSOPHY **EDUCATION** Calvin Col, AB, 64; Univ Toronto, MA, 66, PhD(philos), 70. **CAREER** Asst prof, 70-75, assoc prof, 75-80, Prof Philos, Western KY Univ, 81-, Adj prof, Sch Theol, Fuller Theol Sem, 78-79; vis prof philos, Calvin Col, 80-81. **MEMBERSHIPS** Soc Christian Philosophers. **RESEARCH** Thomas Aquinas; Augustine; Dante **SELECTED PUBLICATIONS** Auth, Aquinas, Calvin & Contemporary Protestant Thought, 85. **CONTACT ADDRESS** Dept of Philos & Relig, Western Kentucky Univ, 1 Big Red Way, Bowling Green, KY 42101-3576. **EMAIL** arvin.vos@wku.edu

VOS, NELVIN LEROY
PERSONAL Born 07/11/1932, Edgerton, MN, m, 1958, 3 children **DISCIPLINE** ENGLISH, THEOLOGY **EDUCATION** Calvin Col, AB, 54; Univ Chicago, AM, 55 PhD(theol & lit), 64. **CAREER** Instr English, Univ Chicago, AM; instr English, Unity Christian High Sch, 55-57; instr English, Calvin Col, 57-59; asst prof, Trinity Christian Col, 63-65; from assoc prof to prof English, Muhlenberg Col, 65-00; head dept, Muhlenberg Col, 76-87; VP and dean, Muhlenberg Col, 87-93; pres, Muhlenberg Col, 95-99; ex dir, Muhlenberg Col, 99-. **MEMBERSHIPS** MLA; Conf Christianity & Lit (secy, 65-67, pres, 68-70); Phi Beta Kap; Soc for Arts, Religion, and Contemp Culture. **RESEARCH** Comic theory; contemporary drama; theology and culture. **SELECTED PUBLICATIONS** Auth, The Drama of Comedy: Victim and Victor, 66; auth, For God's Sake Laugh, John Knox, 67; Versions of the Absurd Theater: Ionesco and Albee, Eerdmans, 68; The process of dying in the plays of Edward Albee, Educ Theatre J, 3/73; Monday's Ministries, Fortress, 79; The Great Pendulum of Becoming: Images in Modern drama, Eerdmans, 80; auth, Seven Days a Week: Faith in Action, Fortress, 85; auth, Connections: Faith and Life, Fortress, 86, 97; auth, Where in the World Are You? Connecting Faith and Daily Life, Alban, 96; The Maestro: Giuseppi Hoschetti's Story, Nacci, 00. **CONTACT ADDRESS** Dept of English, Muhlenberg Col, 2400 W Chew St, Allentown, PA 18104-5586. **EMAIL** hlvos@gateway.net

VOSPER, JIM M.
PERSONAL Born 03/29/1947, Centralia, WA, s **DISCIPLINE** HISTORY, EDUCATION, PHILOSOPHY **EDUCATION** Saint Martin's Col, BA, 68; Univ Nebr, Lincoln, MA, 73, PhD, 76. **CAREER** Part-time instr, Centralia Col, 77-; part-time instr, South Puget Sound Community Col, 84-. **HONORS AND AWARDS** McNair Scholar Mentor, 96. **MEMBERSHIPS** Am Fedn of Teachers, Nat Educ Asn. **RESEARCH** Pacific Northwest history, educational history, religion in history. **SELECTED PUBLICATIONS** 19 biographical sketches for the three volume Biographical Dictionary of American Educators, 78. **CONTACT ADDRESS** Dept Humanities & Soc Sci, Centralia Col, 600 W Locust St, Centralia, WA 98531-4035. **EMAIL** jvosper@centralia.ctc.edu

VRAME, ANTON C.
PERSONAL Born 04/16/1959, Chicago, IL **DISCIPLINE** THEOLOGY **EDUCATION** DePaul Univ, BA, 81; Univ Chicago, MA, 83; Holy Cross Greek Ortho, Sch Theol, MDiv, 89; Boston Coll, PhD, 97. **CAREER** Managing ed, Holy Cross Orthodox Press, 96-. **MEMBERSHIPS** AAR; APRRE; REA; OTSA. **RESEARCH** Educational theory. **SELECTED PUBLICATIONS** Auth, "The Educating Icon: Teaching Wisdom and Holiness in the Orthodox Way (99); auth, The Educating Icon, Brookline MA, HCO Press, 99. **CONTACT ADDRESS** Dept Theology, Hellenic Col, 50 Goddard Ave, Boston, MA 02131. **EMAIL** tony_vrame@hchc.edu

VUKOWICH, WILLIAM T.
PERSONAL Born 10/31/1943, East Chicago, IN **DISCIPLINE** LAW **EDUCATION** Ind Univ, AB, 65; Univ Calif, Berkeley, JD, 68; Columbia Univ, JSD, 76. **CAREER** Asst prof law, Willamette Univ, 68-70; assoc prof, 70-73, prof law, Georgetown Univ, 73-; Ford urban law fel, Columbia Univ, 69-70; visiting prof, LUISS (Rome), 99; visiting prof, Univ of Heidelberg, 00. **MEMBERSHIPS** Order of Coif. **RESEARCH** Commercial law; creditor and debtor rights; life sciences and the law. **SELECTED PUBLICATIONS** Auth, Insurable Interest: When it Must Exist, Willamette Law J, 3/71; art, The Dawning of the Brave New World-Legal, Ethical and Social Issues of Eugenics, Univ Ill Law Forum, 71; art, Debtor's Exemption Rights, Georgetown Law J, 2/74; auth, "Lawyers and the Standard Form Contract System," Geo J. L. Ethics (93): 799; auth, "Civil Remedies in Bankruptcy for Corporate Fraud," Am B. Inst L. Rev. (98): 439. **CONTACT ADDRESS** Law Ctr, Georgetown Univ, 600 New Jersey NW, Washington, DC 20001-2022. **EMAIL** vukowich@law.georgetown.edu

VYHMEISTER, NANCY JEAN
PERSONAL Born 08/31/1937, Portland, OR, m, 1959, 2 children **DISCIPLINE** MISSIONS; BIBLICAL STUDIES **EDUCATION** Andrews Univ, EdD, 78. **CAREER** Instr Bibl Lang, River Plate Univ, Argentina, 64-71; asst and assoc prof Mission, 79-84, prof Mission, 91-, Andrews Univ; Prof Bibl Stud (s), Adventist Intl Inst Adv Stud (s), 85-91. **HONORS AND AWARDS** Ed, Andrews Univ Sem Stud (s), 91- . **MEMBERSHIPS** SBL **RESEARCH** Teaching Religion in College; Women in Ministry; Research writing. **SELECTED PUBLICATIONS** Auth, Gramatica Elemental del Griega del Nuevo Testamento, Libertador San Martin, Argentina: Publ SALT, 81; Handbook for Research: Guidelines for Theology Students, Silang, Philippines, AIIAS Publ, 89; transl, ed, Comentario biblico Adventista, vol 7, Boise, Pacific Press, 78-90; Manual de investigacion, Libertador San Martin, Argentina, Publ SALT, 94; The Rich Man in James 2: Does Ancient Patronate Illumine the Text?, Andrews Univ Sem Stud (s), 33, 95, 265-283; Handbook for Research: Guidelines for Theology Students, rev ed, Berrien Springs, MI, SDA Theol Sem, 98; Proper Church Behavior in 1 Timothy 2:8-15, in Women in Ministry: Biblical and Historical Perspectives, ed, Nancy Vyhmeister, 333-354, Berrien Springs, MI, Andrews UP, 98; ed, Women in Ministry: Biblical and Historical Perspectives, Berrien Springs, MI, Andrews UP, 98. **CONTACT ADDRESS** Dept of Mission, Andrews Univ, 4525 Timberland Dr, Berrien Springs, MI 49103. **EMAIL** vyhmeist@andrews.edu

W

WACHSMUTH, WAYNE R.
PERSONAL Born 06/08/1958, WI, m, 1990, 3 children **DISCIPLINE** THEOLOGY **EDUCATION** Bethany Bible Col, BS, 81; Trinity Evangelical Div School, MA, 90. **CAREER** Academic dean, Christian Life Col, 96- **HONORS AND AWARDS** Registr, dir, student svc **RESEARCH** Contemporary theology. **CONTACT ADDRESS** 301 N Emerson, Mount Prospect, IL 60056. **EMAIL** WWachs@concentric.net

WADDELL, JAMES
PERSONAL Born, WV, m **DISCIPLINE** HISTORY, PHILOSOPHY **EDUCATION** Duke Univ, AB, 60; BD, 63; Oxford Univ, PhD, 65. **CAREER** Instructor, Princeton Univ, 65-68; Prof and Assoc Dean, Stephens Col, 72-79; Prof, Dean and Vice Pres, Col of Santa Fe, 79-82; Prof and Dean, Western N Mex Univ, 82-85; Prof, Dean and Assoc Vice Pres, Univ Redlands, 85-93; Academic Dean to President, Menlo Col, 94-. **HONORS AND AWARDS** NEH Grant, 84; Roswell Messing Fel, Oxford Univ, 74; Woodrow Wilson Fac Fel, Princeton Univ, 66068; Scholarship, Duke Univ, 56-60. **MEMBERSHIPS** Am Asn of Higher Educ, Am Asn of Univ Prof, Am Philos Soc, Am Acad of Relig, N Mex Coun of Art Educ, Inst for Adv Philos Res, Royal Inst of Philos. **RESEARCH** Philosophy and sexuality; History and philosophy of education, Relation of philosophy, religion and literature. **SELECTED PUBLICATIONS** Auth, "Philosophies Make Philosophers," Falling in Love with Wisdom: American Philosophers Talk About their calling, Oxford Univ Press, 93; auth, "Serious Educators and Self-directed Adults: an alliance for Success," Journal of Self-directed Education, (88): 7-10; auth, "Keble and the Reader's Imagination," Christianity and Literature, (85): 39-56; auth, "The Abandonment of Authority," Research Bulletin, (83): 2-3; co-ed, Art and Religion as Communication, John Knox Press, 74; auth, **CONTACT ADDRESS** President, Menlo Col, 1000 El Camino Real, Atherton, CA 94027-4300. **EMAIL** jwaddell@menlo.edu

WADE, JEFFRY
PERSONAL Born 07/30/1950, Jackson, MS, m **DISCIPLINE** LAW **EDUCATION** Univ Fla, JD, 85 **CAREER** Dir, Environmental Div Ctr for Governmental Responsibility, Univ Fla Col of Law, 85-. **RESEARCH** Environmental law; land use planning and regulation; growth management; water law; wetlands protection; coastal zone management; sustainable development; ecosystem management; trade and the environment; international environmental law. **SELECTED PUBLICATIONS** Auth, Hurricane Mitigation and Post-Disaster Redevelopment: Principles and Practices Vols. 1 & 2, Fla Coastal Management Prog, Fla Dept of Community Affairs, 96; auth, Current and Emerging Issues in Florida Water Policy, Fla Ctr for Environmental Studies, Fla Atlantic Univ, 96; auth, "The Brazilian Pantanal and Florida Everglades: A Comparison of Ecosystems, Uses and Management", in Proceedings of the Second Pantanal Symposium, corumba, Mato Graosso do Sul, Brazil, 96; auth, "Minimum Flows and Levels: Analysis of Florida Programs", a report to the Fla Dept of Environmental Protection, Office of Water Policy, 96; co-ed, Protecao de Direitos Ambientais e Sociais: Manual para Operadores Juridicos, United States Information Agency, 98. **CONTACT ADDRESS** Ctr for Governmental Responsibility, 230 Bruton Geer Hall, PO Box 117629, Gainesville, FL 32611. **EMAIL** wade@law.ufl.edu

WADE, ROBERT J.
DISCIPLINE LAW, TAXATION **EDUCATION** Ind Univ, BS, 60; Univ Mich, JD, 63; Southern Methodist Univ, LLM, 68. **CAREER** Asst prof, Tex Tech Univ, 64-68; assoc prof, Wright State Univ, 68-71; prof & dir of Inst for Int Legal Educ, Capital Univ Law Sch, 71-. **HONORS AND AWARDS** Fel, Southwestern Legal Found, 63-64. **MEMBERSHIPS** Ohio State Bar Asn, Am Bar Asn, Ind State Bar Asn. **RESEARCH** Taxation, International Law. **CONTACT ADDRESS** Sch of Law, Capital Univ, 303 E Broad St, Columbus, OH 43215-3201. **EMAIL** rjwj@aol.com

WADELL, PAUL J.
PERSONAL Born 03/01/1951, Louisville, KY, s **DISCIPLINE** THEOLOGY **EDUCATION** Univ Notre Dame, PhD, 85. **CAREER** Prof of Theol, Catholic Theol Uniion, 84-87; Vis Prof in Theol, Univ Scranton, 97-98; Assoc Prof in Theol, St Norbert Col, 98. **MEMBERSHIPS** Am Acad of Relig; Soc of Christian Ethics; Catholic Theol Soc of Am. **RESEARCH** Virtues; ethics of St Thomas Aquinas; role of friendship in the Moral Life. **SELECTED PUBLICATIONS** Auth, Taming An Unruly Family Member: Ethics and the Ecological Crisis, The Ecological Challenge: Ethical, Liturgical, and Spiritual Responses, The Liturgical Press, 52-64, 94; auth, Pondering the Anomaly of God's Love: Ethical Reflections on Access to the Sacraments, Developmental Disabilities and Sacramental Access: New Paradigms for Sacramental Encounters, The Liturgical Press, 53-72, 94; auth, The Human Way Out: The Friendship of Charity as a Countercultural Practice, The Merton Annual, vol 8, 38-58, 95; auth, Ethics and the Narrative of Hispanic Americans: Conquest, Community, and the Fragility of Life, Dialogue Rejoined: Theology and Ministry in the United States Hispanic Reality, The Liturgical Press, 125-144, 95; auth, Redeeming the Things We Can Never Undo: The Role of Forgiveness in Anne Tyler's Saint Maybe, New Theol Rev, vol 8, no 2, 34-48, 5/95; auth, Confronting the Sin of Racism: How God's Dream for the World Can Be Redeemed, New Theol Rev, vol 9, no 2, 6-19, 5/96; auth, Morality: A Course on Catholic Living, William H Sadler, Inc, 98. **CONTACT ADDRESS** Relig Stud Dept, St. Norbert Col, 100 Grant St, De Pere, WI 54115-2099. **EMAIL** wadepj@mail.snc.edu

WADLINGTON, WALTER JAMES
PERSONAL Born 01/17/1931, Biloxi, MS, m, 1955, 4 children **DISCIPLINE** LAW **EDUCATION** Duke Univ, AB, 51; Tulane Univ, LLB, 54. **CAREER** Asst prof law, Tulane Univ, 60-62; assoc prof, 62-64, Prof Law, Univ VA, 64-, James Madison Prof, 69- ; PROF OF LEGAL MEDICINE, UNIV VA SCHOOL MEDICINE, 79- . **RESEARCH** Family breakdown; adoption and child care; state intervention in medical decision making. **SELECTED PUBLICATIONS** Coauth, Cases and Materials on Domestic Relations, 4th ed; & Statutory Materials on Family Law, 71, 74, 2nd ed, 78, Foundation; auth, Divorce without fault without perjury, 52: 32 & The Loving Case: Virginia's anti-miscegenation statute in historical perspective, 52: 1189, Va Law Rev; coauth, Caser and Materials on Law and Medicine, Foundation, 80; Children in the Legal System, 2nd ed, 97. **CONTACT ADDRESS** Law School, Univ of Virginia, Charlottesville, VA 22903. **EMAIL** wjw@virginia.edu

WAETJEN, HERMAN C.
PERSONAL Born 06/16/1929, Bremen, Germany, m, 1960, 3 children **DISCIPLINE** NEW TESTAMENT **EDUCATION** Concordia Theol Sem, BA, 50, BD, 53; Univ Tubingen, Dr theol(New Testament), 58. **CAREER** Instr philos, Concordia Theol Sem, 57; asst prof New Testament, Univ Southern Calif, 59-62; assoc prof, 62-74, ROBERT S DOLLAR PROF NEW TESTAMENT, SAN FRANCISCO THEOL SEM, 74-; PROF NEW TESTAMENT, GRAD THEOL UNION, 62-; Am Asn Theol Schs res grant, Ger, 65-66; vis prof, Univ Nairobi, 73-74; Am Asn Theol Schs res grant, SAfrica, 79-80; prof, Fed Theol Sem, Pietermaritzburg, SAfrica. **MEMBERSHIPS** Soc Bibl Lit. **RESEARCH** New Testament scholarship; history of religions; Hellenistic culture. **SELECTED PUBLICATIONS** Auth, the Gospel and the Sacred in Poetics of Violence in Mark, Interp J Bible Theol, Vol 50, 96; The Corinthian Body, Theol Today, Vol 53, 97; auth, The Origin & Destiny of Humanness: Gospel of Matthew; auth, A Reordering of Power A Socio-political Reading of Mark's Gospel; auth, Praying the Lord's Prayer. **CONTACT ADDRESS** San Francisco Theol Sem, San Anselmo, CA 94960. **EMAIL** mwaetjen@marin.k12.ca.us

WAGGONER, LAWRENCE W.
PERSONAL Born 07/02/1937, Sidney, OH, m, 1963, 2 children **DISCIPLINE** LAW **EDUCATION** Univ Cincinnati, BBA, 60; Univ MI, JD, 63; Oxford Univ, DPhil, 66. **CAREER** Atty, Cravath, Swaine & Moore, 63; prof, Col of Law, Univ IL, 68- 72 & Sch of Law, Univ VA, 72-73; Prof Law, Law Sch, Univ MI, 73. **MEMBERSHIPS** Am Law Inst; Acad fel, Am Col Trust & Estate Coun. **RESEARCH** Property law; federal taxation; estate planning. **SELECTED PUBLICATIONS** Auth, Future Interests in a Nutshell, West Publ Co, 81; coauth, Federal Taxation of Gifts, Trusts, and Estates, West Publ Co, 3rd ed, 97; Family Property Law: Wills, Trusts, and Future Interests, Found Press, 2nd ed, 97. **CONTACT ADDRESS** Law Sch, Univ of Michigan, Ann Arbor, 625 S State St, Ann Arbor, MI 48109-1215. **EMAIL** waggoner@umich.edu

WAGNER, ANNICE
DISCIPLINE LAW **EDUCATION** Wayne State Univ, BA, JD. **CAREER** National Capital Housing Authority, general counsel; Superior Court D.C., assoc judge, 77-90; DC Ct Appeals, assoc judge, beginning 90; DC Supreme Ct, Chief Judge, currently; Harvard Univ, Instructor, currently. **CONTACT ADDRESS** District of Columbia Supreme Court, 500 Indiana Ave NW, Rm 600, Washington, DC 20001.

WAGNER, MICHAEL FRANK
PERSONAL Born 09/29/1952, Victoria, TX, s **DISCIPLINE** MEDIEVAL & ANCIENT PHILOSOPHY **EDUCATION** TX A&M Univ, BA, 74; OH State Univ, MA, 76, PhD(philos), 79. **CAREER** Teaching asst, OH State Univ, 75-79, lectr, 79-80; asst prof Philos, 80-84, assoc prof, 84-88, prof philos, Univ San Diego, 89-; lectr, Capital Univ, 79-80. **MEMBERSHIPS** Am Philos Asn; Int Soc Neoplatonic Studies (US secy, 80-); Soc Medieval & Renaissance Philos; Medieval Asn Pac; Am Cath Philos Asn. **RESEARCH** Medieval neoplatonism and its foundations in ancient thought; history of metaphysics, epistemology and theology and their relation to the development of Western science; informal logic and its relation to formal logic. **SELECTED PUBLICATIONS** Contribr, The Structure of Being: A Neoplatonic Approach, State Univ NY, 82; An Historical Intro to Moral Philos, Prentice-Hall, 90; contrib, Cambridge Companion to Plotinus, 97; misc journals. **CONTACT ADDRESS** Dept Philos, Univ of San Diego, 5998 Alcala Park, San Diego, CA 92110-2492. **EMAIL** mwagner@acusd.edu

WAGNER, PAUL ANTHONY
PERSONAL Born 08/28/1947, Pittsburgh, PA, m, 1970, 3 children **DISCIPLINE** PHILOSOPHY **EDUCATION** Truman State Univ, BS, 69; Univ Mo-Columbia, MEd, 72, MA, 76; PhD, 78. **CAREER** Instr philos, Moberly Area Jr Col, 74-75; instr philos educ, Univ Mo, 75-79; from asst prof philos & philos educ to prof and director, proj in Professional Ethics, Univ Houston, Clear Lake City, 79-; consult, Dept Corrections, State of Mo, 77-81 & Clear Creek Independent Sch Dist, 79-82; vis scholar, Dept Philos & Inst Math Study Soc Sci, 81; vis scholar, Harvard Univ, 85-86. **HONORS AND AWARDS** Chancellor's Distinguished Service prof, 84; Atrium Circle Distinguished prof, 82; Who's Who is America; Who's Who in American Education; Who's Who is the World; Who's Who in the South and Southwest. **MEMBERSHIPS** Am Philos Asn; Philos Sci Asn; Brit Philos Sci Asn; fel, Philos Educ Soc. **RESEARCH** Philosophy of science; ethics; philosophy of education; total quality management **SELECTED PUBLICATIONS** Auth, Policy studies, Hobbs and Normative Prescriptions for Organizations, J Thought, 1/81; auth, The Aristotlean Notion of Nomos and Policy Studies, Rev J Philos & Soc Sci, 1/81; auth, Rationality, Conceptual Change and Philosophy of Education, Scientia, winter 81; auth, A Philosophical Approach to Mathematics Education, Proc Philos Educ Soc, 1/81; auth, Philosophy in Mathematics Education, Metaphilos, 1/82; åuth, Moral Education, Indoctrination and the Principle of Minimizing Substantive Moral Error, Proc Philos Educ Soc, 3/82; auth, The Ethical Legal and Multicultural Foundations of Teaching, Brown/Benchmark Pub, 92; auth, Understanding Professional Ethics, Phi Delt Kappan Fastback, 96. **CONTACT ADDRESS** School of Education, Univ of Houston, 2700 Bay Area Blvd, Houston, TX 77058-1025. **EMAIL** wagner@cl.uh.edu

WAGNER, STEVEN
DISCIPLINE PHILOSOPHY **EDUCATION** Princeton Univ, PhD, 78. **CAREER** Assoc prof,Univ Ill Urbana Champaign. **RESEARCH** Metaphysics; philosophy of mind; epistemology; philosophy of mathematics; philosophy of logic; philosophy of language. **SELECTED PUBLICATIONS** Auth, The Rationalist Conception of Logic; Truth, Physicalism and Ultimate Theory; co-ed, Naturalism: A Critical Appraisal. **CONTACT ADDRESS** Philosophy Dept, Univ of Illinois, Urbana-Champaign, 52 E Gregory Dr, Champaign, IL 61820. **EMAIL** shwayder@staff.uiuc.edu

WAGNER, WENCESLAS JOSEPH
PERSONAL Born 12/12/1917, Poland, m, 1979, 3 children **DISCIPLINE** LAW, POLITICAL SCIENCES **EDUCATION** Univ Warsaw, LLM, 39; Univ Paris, Dr en Droit, 47; Northwestern Univ, JD, 50, LLM, 53, SJD, 57. **CAREER** Jr judge, Warsaw, Poland, 41-44; res assoc, French Inst Air Transp, 47-48; vis prof Slavic lit, Fordham Univ, 48-49; teaching fel law, Northwestern Univ, 50-53; From instr to prof, Univ Notre Dame, 53-62; prof, Ind Univ, 62-71; PROF LAW, UNIV DETROIT, 71-; Fulbright grant and vis prof, Law Schs, Paris and Rennes, France, 59-60; consult, Law Principles of Civilized Nations Proj, Cornell Univ, 60, vis prof law sch, 61-62; US Dept State lectr, Senegal, Morocco and Algeria, 60, world tour, 62; lectr, Int Fac Comp Law, Luxembourg, 60 and 63; legal coun, Ger Consulate Gen, Ind, 67-68; Fulbright lectr, Latin am, 68; Kosciuszko Found lectr, Poland, 71; vis prof, Univ Clermont-Ferrand, 73; vis prof, Warsaw, 80-81. **MEMBERSHIPS** Am Asn Comp Study Law; Am Foreign Law Asn (vpres, 70-72); Am Soc Legal Hist (treas, 62-64); Polish Inst Arts and Sci Am; Int Asn Cath Jurists (vpres, 73-). **RESEARCH** Comparative law; torts; federalism. **SELECTED PUBLICATIONS** Auth, Supremacy and Integrity in Member State Law as a Limiting Principle in the United States and the European Union, Soundings, Vol 79, 96. **CONTACT ADDRESS** Law Sch, Univ of Detroit Mercy, Detroit, MI 48226.

WAHL, RUSSELL
PERSONAL Born 09/02/1952, Oslo, Norway, m, 1984, 2 children **DISCIPLINE** PHILOSOPHY **EDUCATION** Colby Col, BA, 74; Ind Univ, MA, 77; PhD, 82. **CAREER** Instr to asst prof, Wabash Col, 80-85; asst prof to prof, Idaho State Univ, 85-; dir of philos, Idaho State Univ, 95-; faculty senate chemn, Idaho State Univ, 96-97; prof, Harvard Univ Summer School, 98-00. **HONORS AND AWARDS** Phi Beta Kappa, 74; NEH Summer Fel, 83, 86, 91; Outstanding Researcher, Idaho State Univ, 94. **MEMBERSHIPS** Am Philos Asn, Burtrand Russell Society **RESEARCH** Early modern philosophy, Bertrand Russell, philosophy of languages. **SELECTED PUBLICATIONS** Auth, "The Arnauld-Malebranche Controversy and Descartes' Ideas," Monist (88); auth, "Russell's Theory of Meaning and Denotation and 'On Denoting,'" J of the Hist of Philos (93); auth, "Impossible Propositions and the Forms of Objects in Wittgenstein's Tractatus," Philos Quart (95); auth, "How Can What I Perceive Be True?" Hist of Philos Quart (95); auth, "The Port-Royal Logic," Hist Antecedents to Informal Logic (97); coauth, "Colour: Physical or Phenomenal," Philos (98). **CONTACT ADDRESS** Dept English & Philos, Idaho State Univ, 921 S 8th Ave, PO Box 8056, Pocatello, ID 83209-0002. **EMAIL** wahlruss@isu.edu

WAINWRIGHT, GEOFFREY
PERSONAL Born 07/16/1939, England, m, 1965, 3 children **DISCIPLINE** THEOLOGY **EDUCATION** Univ Cambridge, BA, 60; MA, 64; BD, 72; DD, 87; Univ Geneva, PhD, 69. **CAREER** Ordained, Methodist Ministry, 67; prof, Yabunde, Cameroon, 67-73; lectr, Queen's Col, 73-79; prof, Union Theol Sem, 79-83; prof, Duke Univ, 83-; vis prof, Univ of Notre Dame, 93, 97; vis prof, Univ of Melbourne, Australia, 91; vis prof, Pontifical Gregorian Univ, Rome, 95. **HONORS AND AWARDS** Leverhulme Europ Fel, 66-67; Ger Acad Exchange Ser, 82; Pew Evangelical Scholars Prog, 96-97; Honored by Festschrift, Oxford Univ Pr, 99. **MEMBERSHIPS** Am Theol Soc; Societas Liturgica; Joint Comm for Dialogue between the World Methodist Council and the Roman Cath Church. **RESEARCH** Theology. **SELECTED PUBLICATIONS** Auth, Doxology, 80; Methodists in Dialogue, 95; For Our Salvation, 97; Worship with One Accord, 97; Lesslie Newbigin: A Theological Life, 00. **CONTACT ADDRESS** Divinity School, Duke Univ, PO Box 90967, Durham, NC 27708-0967. **EMAIL** gwain@duke.edu

WAINWRIGHT, SUE
PERSONAL Born 01/18/1966, PA, m, 1996, 1 child **DISCIPLINE** PHILOSOPHY **EDUCATION** Allentown Col of St. Francis de Sales, BA, 94; Westchester Univ, MA, 95. **CAREER** Adjunct prof, Northampton Community Col. **MEMBERSHIPS** Am Philos Asn. **RESEARCH** Morality; Buddhism. **CONTACT ADDRESS** 4730 Main Rd W, Emmaus, PA 18049.

WAINWRIGHT, WILLIAM J.
PERSONAL Born 02/14/1935, Kokomo, IN, m, 1958, 2 children **DISCIPLINE** PHILOSOPHY **EDUCATION** Kenyon Coll, BA, 57; Univ of Michigan, MA, 59, PhD, 61. **CAREER** Inst, Asst Prof, 60-62, Univ of Illinois-Urbana; Assoc to Prof, 62-98, Univ of Wisconsin, Milwaukee; Distinguished Prof, 98-. **HONORS AND AWARDS** Woodrow Wilson Fellowship; Horace H. Rackham Fellowship; 3 NEH Summer Fellowship; Distinguished Tchr; Res Awd, Univ of Wisconsin; Phi Beta Kappa; Phi Kappa Phi. **MEMBERSHIPS** Amer Philos Assoc; Amer Acad Rel; Soc of Christian Philos; Soc Philos Rel. **RESEARCH** Philosophy of Religion, Ethics, History of Modern Philosophy. **SELECTED PUBLICATIONS** Co-ed, Philosophy of Religion, Selected Readings, William Rowe, Harcourt Brace, 98; auth, Philosophy of Religion, An Annotated Bibliography, Garland Press, 78; Mysticism, Univ of Wisconsin Press. 81; Philosophy of Religion, Wadsworth, 98; Reason and the Heart, Cornell Univ Press, 95; God, Philosophy and Academic Culture, Scholar's Press, 96. **CONTACT ADDRESS** Dept Philosophy, Univ of Wisconsin, Milwaukee, Milwaukee, WI 53201. **EMAIL** wjwain@csd.uwm.edu

WAKIN, MALHAM M.
PERSONAL Born 03/31/1931, Oneonta, NY, m, 1976, 8 children **DISCIPLINE** PHILOSOPHY **EDUCATION** Univ Notre Dame, AB, 52; State Univ NYork, Am, 53; Univ Southern Calif, PhD(philos), 59. **CAREER** Res asst, Capitol Area Sch Develop Asn, Albany, NY, 52-53; from instr to prof Philos, 59-64, asst dean Soc Sci & Humanities, 64-65, grad prog, 65-67, head dept Fine Arts & Philos, 67-73, head dept Polit Sci & Philos, 73-77, prof Philos, US Air Force Acad, 67-95, head Dept Philos & Fine Arts & assoc dean Acad, 77-95; Lyon chair in Philos, 95-97; prof Emeritus, 97-. **MEMBERSHIPS** Mountain Plains Philos Conf; Am Cath Philos Asn; Inter-Univ Sem Armed Forces & Soc; Joint Services Conf Prof Ethics. **RESEARCH** Ethics; military philosophy; medical ethics; legal ethics; ethics & leadership. **SELECTED PUBLICATIONS** Auth, Communities look at their school principals, Capitol Areas Sch Develop Asn, 53; coauth, The vocation of arms, Space Dig, 7/63; auth, Dynamism and discipline, New Scholasticism, Summer 67; The Viet Cong Political Infrastructure, Dept Defense, 68; The American military-theirs to reason why, Air Force Mag, 3/71; The ethics of leadership, Am Behav Scientist, 5-6/76; ed & contribr, War, Morality, and the Military Profession, Westview Press, 79, 86; coauth, The Teaching of Ethics in the Military, Hastings Ctr, 82; auth, Integrity First: Reflections of a Military Philosopher, Lexington Press, 00. **CONTACT ADDRESS** Dept of Philos, United States Air Force Acad, United States Air Force Academy, CO 80840.

WALD, PATRICIA M.
PERSONAL Born 09/16/1928, Torrington, CT, m, 1952, 5 children **DISCIPLINE** LAW **EDUCATION** Conn Col for Women, BA, 48; Yale Law Sch, LLB, 51. **CAREER** Law clerk, U.S. Court of Appeals for the Second Circuit, 51-52; assoc, Arnold, Fortas & Porter, 52-53; mem, Nat Conf on Bail & Criminal Justice, 63-64; consult, Nat Conf on Law & Poverty, 65; mem, President's Comn on Crime in the District of Columbia, 65-66; consult, President's Comn on Law Enforcement and Administration of Criminal Justice, 66-67; atty, Office of Criminal Justice, Dept Justice, 67-68; atty, Neighborhood Legal Services Prog, 68-70; consult, Nat Advisory Comt on Civil Disorder, 68; consult, Nat Comn on the Causes & Prevention of Violence, 69; co-Dir, For Found Drug Abuse Res Project, 70; atty, Ctr for Law & Soc Policy, 71-72; dir of Office of Policy & Issues, Sargent Shriver Vice Presidential Campaign, 72; atty, Mental Health Law Project (Litigation Dir 75-77), 72-77; asst atty gen for legislative affairs, 77-79; circuit judge, 79-, chief judge, 86-91, U.S. Court of Appeals for the District of Columbia Circuit. **HONORS AND AWARDS** Distinguished Alumnae Awd, Conn Col, 72; August Voelmer Awd, Am Soc Criminology, 76; Woman Lawyer of the Year, Women's Bar Asn of D.C., 84; Annual Merit Awd, Nat Asn Women Judges (Division 4), 86; Annual Awd, NY Women's Bar Asn, 87; Merit Awd, Yale Law Sch, 87; Honorary Order of the Coif, Univ Md Law Sch, 91; Sandra Day O'Connor Medal of Honor, Seton Hall Law Sch, 93; Margaret Brent Women Lawyers of Achievement Awd, Am Bar Asn Comn on Women in the Professsion, 94; Nat Asn Women Judges Annual Awd, 94; Juvenile Ctr Awd, 95; Trial Lawyers Asn of Metropolitan Washington Awd for Judicial Excellence, 98; The District of Columbia Bar Thurgood Marshall Awd, 98; recipient of numerous Doctor Laws. **SELECTED PUBLICATIONS** Auth, Doing Right by Our Kids: A Case Study in the Perils of Making Policy on Television Violence, Univ Minn, 94; auth, Whose Public Interest Is It Anyway?: Advice for Altruistic Young Lawyers, Me. Law Rev 4, 95; auth, Judicial Review - Fiftieth Anniversary of the Administrative Procedure Act, Admin Law Rev 350, 96; auth, Judicial Review in Midpasage: The Uneasy Partnership Between Courts and Agencies Plays On, Tulsa Law J 221, 96; auth, Judicial Review in the Time of Cholera, Admin Law Rev 659, 97; auth, ADR and the Courts: An Update, Duke Law J 1445, 97; author of numerous other articles. **CONTACT ADDRESS** 333 Constitution Ave., NW, Rm. 3832, Washington, DC 20001. **EMAIL** Patricia_M._Wald@cadc.uscourts.gov

WALDAU, PAUL
PERSONAL Born 01/16/1950, CA **DISCIPLINE** ETHICS; RELIGIOUS STUDIES; PHILOSOPHY **EDUCATION** Univ Oxford, PhD 98; Harvard Univ, sr fel 97; Claremont Grad Sch, 86-92; Univ Cal LA, JD 78; Stanford Univ, MA 72-74; Univ Chicago, 71-72; Univ Cal Santa Barb, BA summa cum laude, 71. **CAREER** Asst Clinical prof, Tufts Univ School of Veterinary Medicine; adj, positions at Boston Col Law School and Episcopal Divinity School. **HONORS AND AWARDS** Phi Beta Kappa. **MEMBERSHIPS** APA; AAR; CBA; IIC; ISEE; Pali Text Soc; L'Chaim Soc; Intl Interfaith Cen; Interdisc Res Netw on the Environ and Soc **RESEARCH** Ethics; philosophical and religious traditions; environ and other animals; environ ethics; applied ethics. **SELECTED PUBLICATIONS** Auth, Buddhism and Ecology: Balancing Convergence Dissonance and the Risk of Anachronism, eds, Mary Evelyn Tucker Duncan Williams, Jour of Bud Ethics, Cambridge MA, Harv Univ Cen for Stud of World Rel, 97; Inclusivist Ethics: Prospects in the Next Millennium, in: Humans and Great Apes at an Ethical Frontier, Smithsonian Inst, 98; Shortcomings in Isolated Traditions of Ethical Discourse: The Case of Andrew Linzey's Animal Theology, Between the Species, 98; Hinduism Buddhism, Judaism and Sacrifice, and Islam, Factory Farming, Specieism, Bushmeat, articles in: The Encycl of Animal Rights and Animal

Welfare, eds, Marc Bekoff, Carron A Meany, Greenwood Pub, 97; Buddhism and Animal Rights, in: Buddhism and Contemporary Issues, ed, Damien Keown, Goldsmith Col, Univ London, 97; Farming, Zoos and Specieism, coauth, in: Dict of Ethics Theology and Soc, London, NY, Routledge Press, 96; auth, Inclusivist Ethics, in: Humans and Great Apes at an Ethical Frontier, Smithsonian Inst, 01; auth, The Specter of Speciesism, Oxford Univ Press, 01. **CONTACT ADDRESS** 23 Hartford Ave N, Upton, MA 01568. **EMAIL** paulwaldau@aol.com

WALDRON, MARY ANNE
DISCIPLINE LAW **EDUCATION** Brandon Col, BA, 69; Univ Manitoba, LLB, 73; Univ British Columbia, LLM, 75. **CAREER** Asst prof, 72-92; prof, 92-. **RESEARCH** Real estate law; plain language research. **SELECTED PUBLICATIONS** Auth, The Law of Interest in Canada; co-auth, Cases and Materials on Contracts. **CONTACT ADDRESS** Fac of Law, Univ of Victoria, PO Box 2400, Victoria, BC, Canada V8W 3H7. **EMAIL** mwaldron@uvic.ca

WALDRON, WILLIAM S.
DISCIPLINE ASIAN RELIGIOUS TRADITIONS **EDUCATION** Univ Wis, BA, PhD. **CAREER** Prof; Middlebury Col, 96-. **RESEARCH** Indigenous psychological systems of Indian Buddhism and their dialogue with modern psychology. **SELECTED PUBLICATIONS** Publ on, res interest. **CONTACT ADDRESS** Dept of Religion, Middlebury Col, Middlebury, VT 05753. **EMAIL** wwaldron@middlebury.edu

WALDROP, RICHARD E.
PERSONAL Born 09/04/1950, Pasadena, TX, m, 1972, 4 children **DISCIPLINE** MISSIOLOGY **EDUCATION** Northwest Bibl Col, BA, 72; Bethel Theol Sem, MATS, 75; Fuller Theol Sem, MA, 84; Fuller Theol sem, Dmiss, 93. **CAREER** Dir., Facultad Teologica Pentecostal, 88-94; Assoc Prof World Missions, Church of God Theol Sem, 94-00. **HONORS AND AWARDS** ASM, SPS, IAMS, Latin Am. Pentecostalism. **MEMBERSHIPS** Soc for Pentecostal Studies, Int Assoc for Mission Studies, Am Soc of Missiology, Fraternidad Teologica Latinoamericana. **RESEARCH** Latin American Pentecostalism **SELECTED PUBLICATIONS** Auth, "The Social Consciousness and Involvement of the Full Gospel Church of God of Guatemala," in CyberJ for Pentecostal-Charismatic Res, no 2 (97); auth, "Jesus the Missionary," in The Pentecostal Minister Sermon Resource Manual, vol 6 (Cleveland, TN: Pathway Pr, 99). **CONTACT ADDRESS** Church of God Sch of Theol, 900 Walker St NE, PO Box 3330, Cleveland, TN 37320. **EMAIL** rewaldrop@aol.com

WALEN, ALEC D.
PERSONAL Born 03/09/1965, Washington, DC, s **DISCIPLINE** LAW & PHILOSOPHY **EDUCATION** Harvard, JD, 98; Univ of Pittsburgh, PhD, 93 **CAREER** Kennedy Sch of Gov; asst prof, 93-94; Fed Dist Ct of MA, lect, 97; Lafayette Col; law clerk, 98-99, Fed Dist Ct of MA; assoc at Mayer, Brown, & Platt in Washington DC, 99-00; asst prof, Division of Legal & Ethical Studies, Univ of Baltimore, 00-. **MEMBERSHIPS** Am Philos Assoc **RESEARCH** Moral, Political, Legal Theory **SELECTED PUBLICATIONS** Auth, Consensual Sex Without Assuming the Risk of Carrying an Unwanted Fetus, Brooklyn Law Review, 97, 1051-1140; Auth, The Defense of marriage Act and Moral Auth, The William & Mary Bill of Rights Journal, 97, 619-642 **CONTACT ADDRESS** 132 Roberts Ln, Apt. 401, Alexandria, VA 22314-4609. **EMAIL** walen@banet.net

WALGREN, KENT
PERSONAL Born 02/17/1947, m, 2 children **DISCIPLINE** LAW **EDUCATION** Brigham Young, BA, 71; Utah Col Law, JD, 74. **CAREER** Asst atty gen, Utah **HONORS AND AWARDS** PetersonFellowship; American Antiquarian Society, Worchester, MA, 95; Recipient Harry E. Pratt Memorial Awd by the Illinois Historical Society for article adjudged as best-written and researched contribution to Illinois History for 1981 (Kent L. Walgren, "James Adams: Early Springfield Mormon and Freemason," in Journal of The Illinois State Historical Society, Vol. 75, No. 2 (Summer 1982), pp., 121-136. **RESEARCH** Early U.S. Freemasonry **SELECTED PUBLICATIONS** Fel Publ, A Bibliography of Pre-1851 Louisiana Scottish Rite Imprints, In: Heredom: Jour Scottish Rite Res Soc 4, 96; auth, A Bibliography of Pre-1851 American Scottish Rite Imprints (non-Louisiana), In: Heredom: J Scottish Rite Res Soc 3, 95; Inside the Salt Lake Temple: Gisbert Bossard's 1911 Photographs, In: Dialogue: A Journal of Mormon Thought 29, No 3, 96. **CONTACT ADDRESS** PO Box 2441, Salt Lake City, UT 84110. **EMAIL** scallywags@earthlink.net

WALHOUT, DONALD
PERSONAL Born 08/09/1927, Muskegon, MI, m, 1958, 4 children **DISCIPLINE** PHILOSOPHY **EDUCATION** Adrian Col, BA, 49; Yale Univ, MA, 50, PhD, 52. **CAREER** Instr, Yale Univ, 52-53; prof, 53-92, emer prof, philos, 92-, Rockford Col. **HONORS AND AWARDS** Phi Beta Kappa; Adrian Col alumni award, 59; Hackley Distinguished lectr, 88. **MEMBERSHIPS** Amer Philos Asn; Amer Asn of Univ Prof; The Hopkins Soc. **RESEARCH** Ethics and history of philosophy; Philosophy of religion. **SELECTED PUBLICATIONS** Auth, A Comparative Study of Three Aesthetic Philosophies, Hist of Philos Quart, 98; auth, Grading Across a Career, Col Teaching, 97; auth, Hermeneutics and the Teaching of Philosophy, Teaching Philos, 84; auth, Send My Roots Rain, A Study of Religious Experience in the Poetry of Gerard Manley Hopkins, Oh Univ Press, 81; auth, Human Nature and Value Theory, The Thomist, 80; auth, Festival of Aesthetics, Univ Press of Amer, 78; auth, The Good and the Realm of Values, Univ Notre Dame Press, 78. **CONTACT ADDRESS** 320 N. Rockford Av., Rockford, IL 61107. **EMAIL** donwal@hughestech.net

WALIGORE, JOSEPH
PERSONAL m, 3 children **DISCIPLINE** PHILOSOPHY **EDUCATION** Syracuse Univ, PhD, 95. **CAREER** Lectr;prof, UWSP, 94-. **RESEARCH** New Age Movement and its relationship to other movements in Western cultural history. **SELECTED PUBLICATIONS** Auth, Nagarjuna: Emptiness, Taxes and Tweezers, J Theta Alpha Kappa, 95. **CONTACT ADDRESS** Dept of Philosophy, Univ of Wisconsin, Stevens Point, Stevens Point, WI 54481. **EMAIL** jwaligor@uwsp.edu

WALKER, CHARLES EDWARD, JR.
PERSONAL Born 05/01/1951, Anchorage, AK, m, 1983 **DISCIPLINE** LAW **EDUCATION** University of California Santa Barbara, BA (magna cum laude), 1973; London School of Economics, 1977; Boston College Law School, JD, 1978. **CAREER** Oxnard Union High School District, teacher, 74-75; U.S. Department of Agriculture Office of the General Counsel, Attorney, 78-79; Boston Superior Court, law clerk, (Hon. James Lynch, chief justice) 79-80; Suffolk University Law School Council on Legal Education Opportunity, teaching fellow, 80-82, 87-89; University of Massachusetts, instructor, 80-82; Massachusetts Court of Appeals, law clerk, 80-81; Commonwealth of Massachusetts, (Hon. Frederick L. Brown, Associate Justice) Assistant Attorney General, 81-87; New England School of Law, assistant professor, 87-; Executive of Elder Affairs, general counsel, currently; Massachusetts Commission Against Discrimination, chmn. **HONORS AND AWARDS** Project Commitment Inc, Distinguished Service Awd, 1988; New England School of Law, Charles Hamilton Houston Distinguished Service Awd, 1990; Governor of Massachusetts, Excellence in Legal Education Citation; Boston College Law School, William Kenneally Alumnus of Year, 1995. **MEMBERSHIPS** Massachusetts Bar Association Committee for Admissions, chair; Roxbury Defenders Committee Inc, acting president, 1982-; Boston College Law School Black Alumni Network, President co-founder, 1981-; Cambridge Economic Opportunity Commission, Board of Directors, 1982-86; Massachusetts Black Lawyers Association Executive Board, president, 1993-95; NAACP National Urban League, 1985-; Good Shepherd Church of God in Christ Trustee Board, Chairman, 1985-; Wheelock College Family Theatre, Board of Directors; Massachusetts Law Review, editorial board, 1990-96. **SELECTED PUBLICATIONS** Author, "Liquor Control Act: Alcoholic Beverages Control Commission," 1986, "Violation of Injunctions: Criminal and Civil Contempt," MBA - Restraining Orders and Injunctions, pages 1-15; Massachusetts Bar Association speaker, "Obedience is Better than Sacrifice," 1988; "The History and Impact of Black Lawyers in Massachusetts," Massachusetts Supreme Judicial Work, Historical Law Society Law Journal. **CONTACT ADDRESS** One Ashburton Place, Boston, MS 02108. **EMAIL** walksanfarm@aol.com

WALKER, GEORGE KONTZ
PERSONAL Born 07/08/1938, Tuscaloosa, AL, m, 1966, 2 children **DISCIPLINE** LAW, HISTORY **EDUCATION** Univ AL, BA, 59; Vanderbilt Univ, LLB, 66; Duke Univ, MA, 68; Univ VA, LLM, 72. **CAREER** From asst prof to assoc prof, 72-76, Prof Law, Wake Forest Univ, 77-, Woodrow Wilson fel, Duke Univ, 62-63; Sterling fel, Yale Law Sch, 75-76; vis prof law, Marshall-Wythe Sch Law, Col William & Mary, 79-80; vis prof Law, Univ Ala Sch Law, 85; Charles H Stockton Prof Intl Law, Naval War Col, 92-93. **HONORS AND AWARDS** Phi Beta kappa, Order of Barristers (hon), Order of the Coif (hon), Am Law Inst. **MEMBERSHIPS** Virginia, North Carolina Bars; Am Soc Int law; Int law Asn, Am Bar Asn; Maritime Law assoc, VA, NC Bar Asns; admitted to practice in federal courts. **RESEARCH** International law; federal jurisdiction; admiralty; conflict of laws; civil procedure; alternative dispute resolution. **SELECTED PUBLICATIONS** Ed, of 10 bks, over 40 bk chpts, articles. **CONTACT ADDRESS** Sch of Law, Wake Forest Univ, PO Box 7206, Winston-Salem, NC 27109-7206.

WALKER, JAMES SILAS
PERSONAL Born 08/21/1933, LaFollette, TN, m, 1954, 4 children **DISCIPLINE** RELIGION, PHILOSOPHY **EDUCATION** Univ Ariz, BA, 54; McCormick Theol Sem, BD, 56; Claremont Grad Sch, PhD (relig), 63. **CAREER** Asst pastor, Cent Presby Church, Denver, Colo, 57-60; assoc prof philos and relig, Huron Col, SDak, 63-66; assoc prof, 66-70, PROF PHILOS AND RELIG AND CHMN DEPT, HASTINGS COL, 70, DEAN, 79-. **MEMBERSHIPS** Am Acad Relig; Soc Bibl Lit; Am Philos Asn; Am Schs Orient Res. **RESEARCH** Contemporary continental theology, especially early Barthian theology; contemporary semantic analysis. **SELECTED PUBLICATIONS CONTACT ADDRESS** Dept of Philos and Relig, Hastings Col, Hastings, NE 68901.

WALKER, JEFF T.
PERSONAL Born 01/27/1962, Mena, AR, m, 1990, 2 children **DISCIPLINE** CRIMINOLOGY **EDUCATION** Univ Ark, BS, 84; MA, 88; Sam Houston State Univ, PhD, 92. **CAREER** Asst Prof to Prof, Univ Ark, 90-. **HONORS AND AWARDS** Frederick M. Thrasher Awd, 95; Fac Excellence Awd, Univ AR, 97. **MEMBERSHIPS** Acad of Criminal Justice Sci; Am Soc of Criminol; SW Asn of Criminal Justice; Justice Res and Statistical Asn; AR Law Enforcement and Criminal Justice Asn. **RESEARCH** Criminal behavior; Neighborhood change; Complex systems science; Police use of force. **SELECTED PUBLICATIONS** Co-auth, "Community Policing and Patrol Cars: Oil and Water or a Well Oiled Machine?," Police Forum, (93): 1-9; auth, "Computers in Criminal Justice: Issues and Applications," Criminal Justice Review, (93): 308-309; auth, "Shaw and McKay Revisit Little Rock," in Varieties of Criminology, Pegmon Press, 93; auth, "The Virtual Visiting Professor," The Criminologist, (94): 6-7; auth, "Fax Machines and Social Surveys: Teaching an Old Dog New Tricks," Journal of Quantitative Criminology, (94): 181-188; auth, "Police and Correctional Use of Force: Legal and Policy Standards and Implications," Crime and Delinquency, (96): 144-156; auth, "Computer Crime," in Encyclopedia of Modern Social Issues, Salem Press, 96; auth, "Crime," in Encyclopedia of Modern Social Issues, Salem Press, 96; co-auth, "Yes, The Police Are in Chaos," Police Forum, 99; auth, Statistics in Criminal Justice: Analysis and Interpretation, Aspen Pub, 99 **CONTACT ADDRESS** Dept Criminal Justice, Univ of Arkansas, Little Rock, 2801 S University Ave, Little Rock, AR 72204. **EMAIL** jtwalker@ualr.edu

WALKER, MARGARET
PERSONAL Born 08/08/1948, Evergreen Park, IL **DISCIPLINE** PHILOSOPHY **EDUCATION** Univ of Illinois at Chicago, BA, 69; Northwestern Univ, MA, 71, PhD, 75. **CAREER** Prof to Full Prof of Philo, 74-, Fordham Univ; Vis Sr Scholar, 97, Univ of South FL, St Petersburg; Vis Assoc Prof, Dept of Philo, 94, Washington Univ; Instr, 91, NEH Simmer Inst, Bethany Coll; Guest Prof, 81, Catholic Univ of Leuven, Belgium. **HONORS AND AWARDS** Frances Elvidge Fellow; Fordham Univ Faculty Fellowships, 82, 86, 92, 96. **MEMBERSHIPS** APA, Society for Women in Philosophy. **RESEARCH** Anglo-American Ethics, Feminist Theory, Wittgenstein. **SELECTED PUBLICATIONS** Auth, Moral Understandings, A Feminist Study in Ethics, NY, Routledge, 98; ed, Mothertime: Women, Aging, & Ethics, Hankam, MD, Ronman & Withlefield, 99; Ineluctable Feelings and Moral Recognition, Midwest Studies in Philosophy, Vol XXII, eds, PA French, TE Uehling, Jr. and HK Wettstein, Notre Dame, Indiana. Univ of Notre Dame Press, 98; Moral Epistemology in: A Companion to Feminist Philosophy, eds, A Jaggar and I Young, Oxford Blackwell Pub, 98; Geographies of Responsibility, New York, The Hastings Center Report, 97; Picking Up Pieces, Lives, Stories and Integrity, in: Feminists Rethink the Self, ed, DT Meyers, Boulder, Colorado, Westview Press, 97. **CONTACT ADDRESS** Dept of Philosophy, Fordham Univ, 441 E Fordham Road, Bronx, NY 10458. **EMAIL** mwalker@fordham.edu

WALKER, MARGARET URBAN
DISCIPLINE PHILOSOPHY **EDUCATION** Northwestern Univ, PhD. **CAREER** Assoc prof, Fordham Univ. **RESEARCH** Moral theory, moral psych, moral epistemology. **SELECTED PUBLICATIONS** Auth, Partial Consideration, Ethics, 92; Feminism, Ethics, and the Question of theory, Hypatia, 92; Keeping Moral Space Open: New Images of Ethics Consulting, Hastings Ctr Rpt, 93; Where Do Moral Theories Come From? Philos Forum, 95; Feminist Skepticism, Authority, and Transparency, Moral Epistemology, Oxford UP, 95. **CONTACT ADDRESS** Dept of Philos, Fordham Univ, 113 W 60th St, New York, NY 10023.

WALKER, REBECCA
PERSONAL Born 06/19/1969, Stanford, CA **DISCIPLINE** PHILOSOPHY **EDUCATION** Stanford Univ, AB, 91, PhD, 98. **CAREER** Post-Doctoral Fel in Bioethics, Johns Hopkins Univ, Bioethics Inst. **MEMBERSHIPS** Am Philoso Asn. **RESEARCH** Ethical theory and bioethics. **CONTACT ADDRESS** 637 3rd Street, NE, #405, Washington, DC 20002. **EMAIL** rwalker@jhsph.edu

WALKER, STANLEY M.
PERSONAL Born 07/15/1942, Chicago, IL, m **DISCIPLINE** LAW **EDUCATION** Harvard Coll, AB 1964; Yale Univ Law School, JD, 1967. **CAREER** Judge A Leon Higginbotham US Dist Ct, law clerk, 67-69; Dechert Price & Rhoads, assoc, 69-70; Pepper, Hamilton & Scheetz, Assoc, 70-71; Pennsylvania St Bd of Law Exam's, examiner, 71-74; Comm Legal Services, staff & mng atty, 71-72; Greater Philadelphia Comm Devel Corp, exec vice pres, 72-73; The Rouse Co, sr atty, 73-79; Univ of Texas School of Law, assoc prof, 79-89; Exxon Co, USA, counsel, 89-95; Friendswood Development Company, gen counsel, 95-. **MEMBERSHIPS** Mem, Amer Bar Assn & Natl Bar Assn; mem, of Bars of US Supreme Court, District of Columbia, Pennsylvania, Maryland, & Texas; mem, Austin Econ Devel Comm, 1985-89; alt mem, City of Austin Bd of Adjustment 1985-86; mem, Action for Metropolitan Govt Comm, 1988-89. **CONTACT ADDRESS** General Counsel, Friendswood Development Company, 550 Greens Pkwy, #100, Houston, TX 77067-4538.

WALKER, STEPHEN G.
PERSONAL Born 08/12/1942, Jefferson, IA, m **DISCIPLINE** POLITICAL SCIENCE **EDUCATION** Creighton Univ, AB, 64; Univ Fla, MA, 65; PhD, 71. **CAREER** Asst prof to prof, Ariz State Univ, 69-. **MEMBERSHIPS** Am Polit Sci Assoc, Int Studies Assoc, Int Soc of Polit Psychol. **RESEARCH** Foreign Policy Analysis and Decision-Making, Belief Systems of Political Elites, Strategic Interaction and Conflict Resolution, Personality Assessment of Political Leaders. **SELECTED PUBLICATIONS** Auth, "The Interface Between Beliefs and Behavior: Henry Kissinger's Operational Code and the Vietnam War," Jour of Conflict Resolution 21, (77): 129-167; auth, "Bargaining Over Berlin: A Re-Analysis of the First and Second Berlin Crises," Jour of Politics 44 (82): 152-164; auth, "The Motivational Foundations of Political Belief Systems: A Re-Analysis of the Operational Code Construction," Int Studies Quart 27, (83): 179-202; coauth, "Integrative Complexity and British Decisions During the Munich and Polish Crisis," Jour of Conflict Resolution 38, (94): 3-23; coauth, "Systematic Procedures for Operational Code Analysis: Measuring and Modeling Jimmy Carter's Operational Code," Int Studies Quart 43 (98): 173-188; coauth, "Presidential Operational Codes and Foreign Policy Conflicts in the Post-Cold War World," Jour of Conflict Resolution 43, (99): 610-625. **CONTACT ADDRESS** Dept of Polit Sci, Arizona State Univ, MC2001, Tempe, AZ 85287. **EMAIL** stephen.walker@asu.edu

WALKER, T. B.
PERSONAL Born 05/21/1940, Utica, NY, m, 1988, 5 children **DISCIPLINE** LAW, SOCIOLOGY **EDUCATION** Princeton Univ, BA, 62; Univ Denver, JD, 67, MA, 69. **CAREER** Asst prof of Law, McGeorge Sch Law, Univ of the Pacific, 69-70; vis assoc prof of law, Univ of Toledo, 69-70; assoc prof of law, Indiana Univ, 70-71; Assoc prof to prof of law, Univ Denver, 71- . **HONORS AND AWARDS** Magna Cum Laude, 62, 67; Order of St. Ives; listed Who's Who in Am and Best Lawyers in Am Since 1987; ed-in-chief, family law q, 83-92. **MEMBERSHIPS** Fel, Am Acad of Matrimonial Lawyers; founding fel, Int Acad of Matrimonial Lawyers; ABA. **RESEARCH** Legal rights of children and the lawyer's role. **SELECTED PUBLICATIONS** Co-auth, Family Law in the Fifty States: An Overview, in Family Law Q, 85-93; auth, Family Law From A to Z: A Primer on Divorce, in Family Advocate, 90. **CONTACT ADDRESS** 6601 S University Blvd, Ste 200, Littleton, CO 80121. **EMAIL** TBWalker10@aol.com

WALKER, WILLIAM O., JR.
PERSONAL Born 12/06/1930, Sweetwater, TX, d, 3 children **DISCIPLINE** RELIGIOUS STUDIES **EDUCATION** Austin Col, BA, 53; Austin Presbyterian Theol Sem, MDiv, 57; Univ Tex-Austin, MA, 58; Duke Univ, PhD, 62. **CAREER** Inst Greek and Bible, Austin Col, 54-55; inst rel, Duke Univ, 60-62; asst prof, 62-66, assoc prof, 66-75, prof, 75, Rel, Trinity Univ . **HONORS AND AWARDS** Alpha Chi Natl Hon Soc, 52; Who's Who among studs in Amer Univ and Col, 52; James Battle Grad fel, Classics, 57; James B. Duke grad fel, 58; Rockefeller Brothers grad fel, 59-60; outstanding ed awd, 83. **MEMBERSHIPS** Studiorum Novi Test Soc; Soc Bibl Lit; Catholic Bibl Asn Amer; Amer Asn Univ Prof. **RESEARCH** Interpolations in the Pauline Letts; Relation between Luke-Acts and the Pauline Letts; Son of Man; Synoptic Problem. **SELECTED PUBLICATIONS** Ed, The HarperCollins Bible Pronunciation Guide, San Francisco, Harper San Fran, 94; ed, The HarperCollins Bible Dictionary, San Francisco, HarperSanFrancisco, 96; Transl, Translation and Interpretation of Eav Mn in Galatians 2:16, Journal of Biblical Literature 116, 3 (97): 515-520; auth, Acts and the Pauline Corpus Revisited: Peter's Speech at the Jerusalem Conference, in Literary Studies in Luke-Acts: Essays in Honor of Joseph B. Tyson, Mercer UP (98): 77-86; auth, Is First Corinthians 13 a Non-Pauline Interpolation?, The Catholic Biblical Quarterly 60, 3 (99): 533-552. **CONTACT ADDRESS** Dept of Religion, Trinity Univ, San Antonio, TX 78212-7200. **EMAIL** wwalker@trinity.edu

WALKER, WYATT TEE
PERSONAL Born 08/16/1929, Brockton, MA, m **DISCIPLINE** THEOLOGY **EDUCATION** VA Union Univ, BS (magna cum laude) 1950, MDiv (summa cum laude) 1953, LHD 1967; Rochester Theological Ctr, Omin 1975; graduate work at the Univ of Ife in Nigeria and Univ of Ghana. **CAREER** Historic Gillfield Baptist Church, Petersburg VA, minister, 53-60; Dr Martin Luther King Jr, chief of staff; SCLC, Atlanta, vice pres, bd exec dir, 60-64; Abyssinian Baptist Church, NYC, pulpit minister, 65-66; Governor NYC, special asst on urban affairs; Cannan Baptist Church of Christ NYC, minister, CEO, 67-; Church Housing Development Fund Inc, president/ CEO, 75-. **HONORS AND AWARDS** Received numerous human rights awards including the Elks Human Rights Awd, 1963; Natl Alpha Awds in Civil Rights, 1965; Shriners Natl Civil Rights Awd, 1974; Civil Rights Awd, ADA, 1975; Honorary LHD, Virginia Union University, 1967; Honorary DD, Edward Waters College, 1985; Honorary D Litt, Gettysburg College, 1988; Top Fifteen Greatest African American Preacher In the US, Ebony Magazine, 1993; roles in "Mama, I Wanna Sing," & "Malcolm X." **MEMBERSHIPS** mem, World Peace Council, 1971-; Programme to Combat Racism of the World Council of Churches, world commissioner; Consortium for Central Harlem Development, chairman; Religious Action Network of the American Committee on Africa, secretary general, president; Natl Action Network, chairman of the board. **SELECTED PUBLICATIONS** Auth, Black Church Looks at the Bicentennial, Somebody's Calling My Name, Soul of Black Worship, Road to Damascus, The Harvard paper, Soweto Diary, Del World Conf on Religion and Peace, Japan, China Diary, Common Thieves, The Harvard Paper, Soweto Diary, Occasional Papers of a Revolutionary, Spirits that Dwell in Deep Woods. **CONTACT ADDRESS** Canaan Baptist Church, 132 West 116th St, New York, NY 10026.

WALL, BARBARA E.
DISCIPLINE PHILOSOPHY **EDUCATION** Fordham Univ, BA, 68; Marquette Univ, MA, 70, PhD, 79. **CAREER** Assoc prof & dir, Villanova Univ. **SELECTED PUBLICATIONS** Auth, Love and Death in the Philosophy of Gabriel Marcel, Wash, DC: UP Am, 77; Rerum Novarum and Its Critics on Social and Secual Hierarchies, Four Revolutions: Catholic Social Teaching's Unfinished Agenda, Lanham, MD: UP Am, 93; The Concept of Death in the Philosophy of Gabriel Marcel, Philos Aspects of Thanatol, Vol 2 & Marx's Analysis of the Relationship between Private Property and the State in His Early Writings, Philos Today, 87; co-ed, Journal for Peace and Justice Studies, Vols 1-6. **CONTACT ADDRESS** Dept of Philosophy, Villanova Univ, 800 Lancaster Ave, Villanova, PA 19085-1692.

WALLACE, B. ALAN
PERSONAL Born 04/17/1950, Pasadena, CA, m, 1989, 1 child **DISCIPLINE** RELIGIOUS STUDIES **EDUCATION** Amherst Col, BA, 87; Stanford Univ, PhD, 95 **CAREER** Lectr, Univ CA, Santa Barbara **HONORS AND AWARDS** Summa Cum Laude, 87; Phi Beta Kappa, Amherst Col; Jacob Javits Fel, Stanford Univ. **MEMBERSHIPS** Amer Acad of Religion **RESEARCH** Tibetan Buddhism; religion and science interface **SELECTED PUBLICATIONS** Auth, Choosing Reality: A Buddhist View of Physics and the Mind, 96; co-translator, A Guide to the Bodhisattva Way of Life, 97; auth, Dreaming, and Dying: An Exploration of Consciousness with the Dalai Lama, 97; auth, Healing Emotions: Conversations with the Dalai Lama on Mindfulness, Emotions, and Health, 97; auth, translator and ed, Natural Liberation: Padmasambhava's Teaching on the Six Bardos, 98; auth, A Spacious Path to Freedom: Practical Instructions on the Union of Mahamudra and Atiyoga, Karma Chagme, 98; Auth, The Bridge of Quiescence: Experiencing Tibetan Buddhist Meditation, 98; auth, The Buddhist Tradition of Samatha: Methods for Refining and Examing Consciousness, Journal of Consciousness Studies, 99; auth, "The Taboo of Subjectivity: Toward a New Science of Consciousness," 00. **CONTACT ADDRESS** Dept of Religious Studies, Univ of California, Santa Barbara, Santa Barbara, CA 93106. **EMAIL** bwallace@humanitas.ucsb.edu

WALLACE, CATHERINE MILES
PERSONAL Born 02/08/1950, Chicago, IL, m, 3 children **DISCIPLINE** ENGLISH, LITERATURE, RELIGION **EDUCATION** Northwestern Univ, MA, 73; Univ Mich, PhD, 77. **CAREER** Asst prof, Northwestern Univ, 76-82; writer in residence, Seabury-Western Theol Seminary. **HONORS AND AWARDS** Bk rev ed, Anglican Theol Rev; Lilly Found, Writer in Residence, 01-05. **MEMBERSHIPS** MLA; SBL; AAR; SCE; SSCS; The Authors Guild. **RESEARCH** Social ethics; social policy. **SELECTED PUBLICATIONS** Auth, The Design of Biographia Literaria, Allen/Unwin, 83; auth, For Fidelity: How Intimacy and Commitment Enrich Our Lives, Knopf, 98; auth, Dance Lessons, Moorehouse, 99. **CONTACT ADDRESS** Writer in Residence, Seabury-Western Theol Sem, 2122 Sheridan Rd, Evanston, IL 60201-2938. **EMAIL** books.atr@seabury.edu

WALLACE, DANIEL B.
PERSONAL Born 06/05/1952, Pasadena, CA, m, 1974, 4 children **DISCIPLINE** NEW TESTAMENT STUDIES **EDUCATION** Dallas Theol Sem, PhD, 95. **CAREER** Assoc prof, Dallas Theol Sem. **HONORS AND AWARDS** Gold Medallion finalist for Exegetical Syntax; Who's Who in Religion; Int Man of Year. **MEMBERSHIPS** Soc of Bibl Lit; Evangelical Theol Soc; Inst for Bibl Res; Soc of New Testament Studies. **RESEARCH** New Testament. **SELECTED PUBLICATIONS** Auth, Greek Grammar Beyond the Basics: An Exegetical Syntax of the New Testament, 96; auth, The Basics of New Testament Syntax: An Intermediate Greek Grammar, 00. **CONTACT ADDRESS** Dallas Theol Sem, 3903 Swiss Ave., Dallas, TX 75204. **EMAIL** danb@flash.net

WALLACE, DEWEY D., JR.
PERSONAL Born 01/08/1936, Chicago, IL, m, 1956, 2 children **DISCIPLINE** RELIGION **EDUCATION** Witworth College, BA 57; Princeton Theol Sem, BD 60; Princeton Univ, MA 62, PhD 65. **CAREER** George Washington Univ, asst prof, assoc prof, prof, 63 to 98-. **HONORS AND AWARDS** Rockefeller Doctoral Fel. **MEMBERSHIPS** AAR; ASCH; PHS. **RESEARCH** English Reformation; religion in 17th century England; Puritanism; religion in the US **SELECTED PUBLICATIONS** Editor, The Pioneer Preacher, by Sherlock Bristol, Urbana, Univ IL Press, 89; editor, The Spirituality of the Later English Puritans: An Anthology , Macon, Mercer Univ Press, 89; Socinianism Justification by Faith and the Sources of John Locke's , The Reasonableness of Christianity, Jour Hist Ideas, 84. **CONTACT ADDRESS** Dept of Religion, The George Washington Univ, Washington, DC 20052. **EMAIL** dwallace@gwis2.circ.gwu.edu

WALLACE, JAMES DONALD
PERSONAL Born 05/21/1937, Troy, NY, m, 1960, 2 children **DISCIPLINE** PHILOSOPHY **EDUCATION** Amherst Col, BA, 59; Cornell Univ, PhD(philos), 63. **CAREER** From instr to assoc prof, 62-70, Prof Philos, Univ Ill, Urbana, 70-. **HONORS AND AWARDS** Am Coun Learned Soc Fel, 83-84; James H. Becker Lectr, Cornell Univ, 90. **MEMBERSHIPS** Am Philos Soc; Am Asn Univ Prof; Asn for Practical and Prof Ethics; Ill Philos Asn. **RESEARCH** Ethical theory, practical ethics, social philosophy. **SELECTED PUBLICATIONS** Auth, Virtues and Vices, Cornell Univ Press, 78; Moral Relevance and Moral Conflict, Cornell Univ Press, 88; Ethical Norms, Particular Cases, Cornell Univ Press, 96. **CONTACT ADDRESS** Dept of Philosophy, Univ of Illinois, Urbana-Champaign, 810 S Wright St, Urbana, IL 61801-3611. **EMAIL** jwallace@uiuc.edu

WALLACE, JOHN
DISCIPLINE PHILOSOPHY **EDUCATION** Stanford Univ, PhD. **RESEARCH** Philosophy of language; political philosophy; philosophy of education. **SELECTED PUBLICATIONS** Auth, Translation Theories and the Decipherment of Linear B, Theory Decision, Assoc Univ, 84; Positive, Comparative, Superlative, J Philos, 72; On the Frame of Reference, Synthese, 70; Sortal Predicates and Quantification, J Philos, 65; co-auth, Some Thought Experiments about Mind and Meaning, Stanford, 90. **CONTACT ADDRESS** Philosophy Dept, Univ of Minnesota, Twin Cities, 355 Ford Hall, 224 Church St SE, Minneapolis, MN 55455. **EMAIL** walla003@tc.umn.edu

WALLACE, KATHLEEN
PERSONAL Born, NY **DISCIPLINE** PHILOSOPHY **EDUCATION** SUNY Stony Brook, PhD, 83. **CAREER** Visiting Asst Prof, 84-85, Hunter Coll; Asst Prof, 85-90, Assoc Prof, 90-, Chmn philosophy, Hofstra Univ. **HONORS AND AWARDS** DAAD stipendium, 2 NEH Awds. **MEMBERSHIPS** APA, SWP, SAAP, AAPP, Hume Society. **SELECTED PUBLICATIONS** Co-ed with introduction for, Metaphysics of Natural Complexes, SUNY Press, 89; co-ed, Nature's Perspectives, Prospects for Ordinal Metaphysics, SUNY Press, 90; auth, General Education and the Modern University, in: Liberal Education, 83; Making Categories or Making Worlds II, in: Texas A&M Studies in American Philosophy, 91; Reconstructing Judgement, Emotion and Moral Judgement, in: Hypatia, J of Feminist Philo, 93; Incarnation Difference and Identity, Materialism Self and the Life of Spirit in the Work of George Santayana, in: Metaphysics in Experience, American Philosophy in Transition, ed, D Anderson & R Hart, Fordham Univ Press, 97; auth, "Anonymity", Ethics & Information Technology 1, No 1, (99): 23-35; auth, "Outological Parity &/or Orrdinabity", Metaphilosophy, 30, No 4, (99): 302-318. **CONTACT ADDRESS** Dept of Philosophy Heger Hall 115, Hofstra Univ, Hempstead, NY 11549. **EMAIL** phikaw@hofstra.edu

WALLACE, PAUL
PERSONAL Born 07/21/1931, Los Angeles, CA, m, 1976, 2 children **DISCIPLINE** POLITICAL SCIENCE **EDUCATION** Univ CA, Berkeley, AB, 53, MA, 57, PhD, 66. **CAREER** Univ MO-Columbia, asst to full prof 64, ch 81-82, 84-85, dir 79-80, ch intl affs 87-88, lectr 81, 83, CA State Univ, vis lectr 61, 63; Asia Found, superv ref scvs 57-60. **HONORS AND AWARDS** MiddleBush Prof; Facul Alumni Awd; 5 Smithsonian funded stud; Ford Found Gnt; Provost Gnt; Sr RES Fell; AIIS Fell; Fulbright Fell; Smithsonian and Ford bk project. **MEMBERSHIPS** APSA; MPSA; AAS. **RESEARCH** Politics of South Asia. **SELECTED PUBLICATIONS** Region and Nation in India, ed Paul Wallace, New Delhi, Oxford &IBH, 85; General Elections, 1996, Economic and Political Weekly, India, 97; Sikh Nationalist Terrorism in India, NY, M E Sharpe, 97; Problems of Partitions in Europe and South Asia, Slavic Rev, 96; Political Violence and Terrorism in India, in: Martha Crenshaw, ed, Terrorism in Context, PA State Univ Press, 95. **CONTACT ADDRESS** Univ of Missouri, Columbia, 203 Professional Building, Columbia, MO 65211-6030. **EMAIL** wallacep@missouri.edu

WALLACE, PAUL STARETT, JR.
PERSONAL Born 01/22/1941, Wilmington, m, 1966, 1 child **DISCIPLINE** LAW **EDUCATION** North Carolina Central Univ, BS, 1962, JD, 1966. **CAREER** US Copyright Office Library of Congress, copyright examiner, 66-71; Congressional Research Serv, Library of Congress, former senior legislative atty, head of the Congress section, amer law div, Washington, DC, 84-86, coord of multidis programs, 86-96; Specialist in American Public Law, American Law Division, 96-. **HONORS AND AWARDS** Mem, Pi Gamma Mu Natl Soc Science Honor Soc; Commendation Awd Outstanding Qualities of Leadership & Dedicated Serv, 1980; Distinguished Serv Awd, 1984; Fed Bar Assn Longstanding and Dedicated Serv Awd, 1986; Omega Psi Phi Fraternity, Alpha Omega Chapter, Scroll of Honor, 1991. **MEMBERSHIPS** Advisory bd, Comm Action for

Human Serv Inc, 1983-; Fed Bar Assn News & Jrnl, 1980-81; sec, Cncl of Crct; vice pres, Fed Bar Assn, 1981-82; pres, Capitol Hill Chapter Fed Bar Assn, 1979-80; adv bd mem, Federal Bar News & Journal, 1980-82; natl vice pres, District of Columbia Circuit Fed Bar Assn, 1981-82; chairperson, co-chair, Federal Bar Assn, natl mem committee, 1982-83; Section on the Admin of Justice, Washington, DC, 1984-89; mem, Dist of Columbia Bar Assn, US Supreme Court; continuing educ bd, Fed Bar Assn, 1985-; vice-chairperson, Library of Congress US Savings Bond Campaign, 1985; mem, Omega Psi Phi, US Dist Ct for District of Columbia; mem, US Court of Appeals for the DC Circuit; special editor Fed Bar Assn News & Journal, 1984, 1986; mem US Dist Court for the 8th Circuit, Phiha Delta Law Fraternity Intl; mem, Natl & Amer Bar Assoc; 33 Degree Mason; chairperson continuing educ bd, Fed Bar Assn, 1987-89; bd of trustees, Peoples Congregational Church, Washington, DC, 1985-90; Peoples Congregational Church, church council, 1990-; Foundation of the Federal Bar Association, board of directors, 1991-; Foundation of the Federal Bar Association, advisor, 1991; chairman, Diaconate Board, Peoples Congregational Church, 1993-95; chairman, Church Council, Peoples Congregational Church, 1996-; treasurer, Foundation of the Federal Bar Association, 1993-. **CONTACT ADDRESS** Library of Congress, Independence Ave SE, Washington, DC 20540. **EMAIL** pwallace@crs.loc.gov

WALLACE, ROBERT M.
PERSONAL Born 05/15/1947, CA, s, 4 children **DISCIPLINE** PHILOSOPHY **EDUCATION** Oxford Univ BA 68; Cornell Univ PhD 94. **CAREER** Univ Wisconsin-Milwaukee, assist prof 94-97; Univ Penn, lectr 98-99-; Colgate University, assist prof 99-. **HONORS AND AWARDS** NEH; ACLS Fel **MEMBERSHIPS** APA; Hegel Soc Amer **RESEARCH** Ethical theory; social and political philo; German philo. **SELECTED PUBLICATIONS** Auth, Hegel on Ethical Life and Social Criticism, How Hegel Reconciles Private Freedom and Citizenship, forthcoming in Jourl of Philosophical Research; Mutual Recognition and Ethics: A Hegelian Reformulation of the Kantian/Argument for the Rationality of Morality, Amer Phil Quart, 95; Blumenberg's Third Way between Habamas and Gadamer, eds T. Flynn and D. Judowitz, SUNY Press, 93. **CONTACT ADDRESS** Dept of Philosophy & Religion, Colgate Univ, 4333 Oakland Ave, Apt 303, Milwaukee, WI 53211-1672. **EMAIL** rwallace@mail.colgate.edu

WALLACE, WILLIAM A.
PERSONAL Born 11/05/1918, New York, NY, s **DISCIPLINE** PHILOSOPHY OF SCIENCE, MEDIEVAL, RENAISSANCE **EDUCATION** Manhattan Col, BEE, 40; Catholic Univ Am, MS, 52; Dominican House Studies, STB, 52; STL, 54; Univ Feiburg, PhD, 59; ThD, 62. **CAREER** Lect philos, Dominican House Studies, 54-62; lectr philos & ed, New Cath Encycl, Cath Univ Am, 62-65; research assoc, hist of sci, Harvard Univ, 65-67; prof, 70-88; emeritus, 88-; sr fel, Folger Inst, 75-76; vis prof, West Vir Univ, 80; vis prof, Univ Padua, 83-84; prof, Univ Maryland, 88-; assoc mem, Grad Fac Philo, 91-; assoc ed, Encyl of Renaissance, 97-00. **HONORS AND AWARDS** Woodrow Wilson Fel; Princeton IAS Mem; Who's Who in Am; Sigma Xi; Phi Beta Kappa; Alum Achiev Awd; ACP Aquinas Medal; CUAS Awd; Hon DSc, Providence Col, 73; Hon Dlitt, Molloy Col, 74; Hon LHD, Manhattan Col, 75; Hon LHD, Fairfield Univ, 86. **MEMBERSHIPS** ACPA; HSS; PSA; NSF. **RESEARCH** Systematic studies in methodology; early modern philosophy; Renaissance; Medieval; philosophy of science. **SELECTED PUBLICATIONS** Auth, Prelude to Galileo: Essays on Medieval and Sixteenth-Century Sources of Galileo's Thought, Studies in the Philosophy of Science (Dordrecht-Boston: D Reidel Pub, 81); auth, Galileo and His Sources: The Heritage of the Collegio Romano in Galileo's Science, Princeton Univ Press, 84; ed, Reinterpreting Galileo, Studies in Philo and Hist of Philo (Washington: Catholic Univ Am Press, 86); co-ed, auth of intro, notes, commentary, Galileo Galilei, Tractatio de praecognitlonibus et praecognitis and Tractatio de demonstratione, Editrice Antenore (Padua), 88; auth, Galileo, the Jesuits and the Medieval Aristotle, Variorum Pub (Aldershot, UK), 91; auth, Galileo's Logic of Discovery and Proof The Background, Content, and Use of His Appropriated Treatises on Aristotle's Posterior Analytics, Boston Studies in the Philosophy of Science (Dordrecht Boston-London: Kluwer Academic Pub, 92); auth The Modeling of Nature: Philosophy of Science and Philosophy of Nature in Synthesis, Catholic Univ Am Press (Washington, DC), 96; ed, Albertus Magnus, Am Cath Philo Quart; "Foreword," 1-6; "Albert the Great's Inventive Logic: His Exposition of the Topic of Aristotle," 11-39, 96; ed, Encyclopedia of the Renaissance, Charles Scribner's Sons (NY), 99. **CONTACT ADDRESS** Dept Philosophy, Univ of Maryland, Col Park, 1125 Skinner Bldg A, College Park, MD 20742-7615. **EMAIL** wallacew@wam.umd.edu

WALLIS, JAMES
DISCIPLINE PHILOSOPHY, RELIGION **EDUCATION** Claremont Grad Sch, PhD, 93. **CAREER** Prof, 96-, Comm Col So Nev. **HONORS AND AWARDS** Fel, Nat Conf of Christians & Jews, sem in Jerusalem. **MEMBERSHIPS** AAR/SBL; Ctr for Process Stud. **RESEARCH** Jewish-Christian relations; Holocaust studies; Theodicy. **SELECTED PUBLICATIONS** Auth, Post-Holocaust Christianity, Univ Press Am, 97. **CONTACT ADDRESS** Comm Col of So Nevada, 7300 Pirates Cove, # 1057, Las Vegas, NV 89146-1124. **EMAIL** jim_wallis@ccsn.nevada.edu

WALLWORK, ERNEST
PERSONAL Born 10/06/1937, Orange, NJ, m, 1973, 2 children **DISCIPLINE** ETHICS **EDUCATION** Harvard Univ, PhD 71; Yale Univ, Mdiv 64; Harvard Business Sch, MBA 61; Bucknell Univ, BS 59. **CAREER** Syracuse Univ, prof 83 to 99-; National Inst Health, bioethicist 87-89; SUNY Health Sci Cen, adj prof, 84-99; Yale Univ, assoc prof, 74-79. **HONORS AND AWARDS** Woodrow Wilson Fel; Who's Who in the World; D R Sharpe lectr; Phi Beta Kappa; NEH; Major Figure for SSSR. **MEMBERSHIPS** APA; APA; AAR; SCE; WPS. **RESEARCH** Psychoanalysis and Ethics; ethical theory and confidentiality. **SELECTED PUBLICATIONS** Auth, Psychoanalysis and Ethics, Yale Univ Press, 91; Critical Issues in Modern Religion, coauth, 2nd ed, Prentice Hall 90; Durkheim: Morality and Milieu, Harvard Press, 72. **CONTACT ADDRESS** Dept of religion, Syracuse Univ, 3021 Davenport St N W, Washington, DC 20008. **EMAIL** ewallwork@att.net

WALSH, ANDREW
PERSONAL Born 09/13/1957, Louisville, KY, m, 1990, 1 child **DISCIPLINE** RELIGION **EDUCATION** Trinity Col, BA, 79; Yale Div Sch, MAR, 87; Harvard Univ, AM, 89; PhD, 96. **CAREER** Visiting Asst Prof, Trinity Col, 93-. **MEMBERSHIPS** Am Acad of Relig; Am Hist Asn; Orthodox Theol Soc of Am. **RESEARCH** Religion and American Culture, especially urban life. **CONTACT ADDRESS** Dept Relig, Trinity Col, Connecticut, 300 Summit St, Hartford, CT 06106-3100. **EMAIL** andrew.walsh@trincoll.edu

WALSH, CAREY ELLEN
PERSONAL Born 04/03/1960, Troy, NY **DISCIPLINE** HEBREW BIBLE **EDUCATION** Allegeury Col, BA, 82; Yale Divinity Sch, M Div, 85; Univ Chicago, AM, 89; Harvard, ThD, 96. **CAREER** Asst prof, Hebrew Bible, Rhodes Col. **MEMBERSHIPS** CBA; SBL. **RESEARCH** Archaelogy, Social hist of ancient Israel; Ancient Agriculture. **SELECTED PUBLICATIONS** Auth, Fruit of the Vine: Viticulture in Ancient Israel and the Hebrew Bible, HSM, in press; auth, Gods's Vineyard, BR, 98. **CONTACT ADDRESS** Rhodes Col, 2000 N Parkway, Memphis, TN 38104. **EMAIL** walsh@rhodes.edu

WALSH, DAVID JOHN
PERSONAL Born 07/29/1950, Clonmel, Ireland, m, 1976, 2 children **DISCIPLINE** MODERN AND POLITICAL PHILOSOPHY **EDUCATION** Univ Col Dublin, BA, 72, MA, 74; Univ Va, PhD (govt), 78. **CAREER** Vis asst prof humanities, Univ Fla, 78-79; ASST PROF GOVT AND PHILOS, UNIV SC, SUMTER, 79-. **MEMBERSHIPS** Am Polit Sci Asn; Southern Polit Sci Asn; Hegel Soc Am. **RESEARCH** Relationship between religious experiences and political symbols and movements; Hegel and modern ideological movements; Jacob Boehme and esoteric religious movements of Renaissance. **SELECTED PUBLICATIONS** Auth, State Common Law Wrongful Discharge Doctrines in Update, Refinement, and Rationales, Am Bus Law J, Vol 33, 96; On the Meaning and Pattern of Legal Citations in Evidence from State Wrongful Discharge Precedent Cases, Law Soc Rev, Vol 31, 97. **CONTACT ADDRESS** Dept of Govt and Philos, Univ of So Carolina, Sumter, Sumter, SC 29150.

WALSH, JAMES JEROME
PERSONAL Born 05/23/1924, Seattle, WA, m, 1946, 2 children **DISCIPLINE** PHILOSOPHY **EDUCATION** Reed Col, BA, 49; Oxford Univ, AB, 51, MA, 56; Columbia Univ, PhD, 60. **CAREER** From instr to asst prof, 54-62, assoc prof, 63-66, dir grad studies, 63-66, chmn dept, 67-73, Prof Philos, Columbia Univ, 67, DIR GRAD STUDIES, 73-; Am Coun Learned Soc res fel, 62-63; ED, J PHILOS, 64-; Guggenheim fel, 66-67. **MEMBERSHIPS** Am Philos Asn. **RESEARCH** History of philosophy; ethics; mediaeval philosoph. **SELECTED PUBLICATIONS** Auth, Bones of Contention and the Plight of Refugees and Exiles as Determined by the Policies of Rome and the Aetolian League Pharsalus, Phthiotic Thebes, Larisa Cremaste, Echinus, Clas Philol, Vol 88, 93; Flamininus And the Propaganda of Liberation and Rome Relations with Greece at the Beginning of the 2nd Century Bc, Hist Zeitschrift Alte Geschichte, Vol 45, 96. **CONTACT ADDRESS** Dept of Philos, Columbia Univ, New York, NY 10027.

WALSH, JEROME T.
PERSONAL Born 06/14/1942, Detroit, MI **DISCIPLINE** HEBREW BIBLE **EDUCATION** Pontifical Bible Inst, SSL, 75; Univ Mich, PhD, 82. **CAREER** Assoc prof, 89-95, St John's Univ, NY; prof, 96-, dept head, theol & relig stud, 97-, Univ Botswana. **MEMBERSHIPS** Soc of Biblical Lit; Catholic Biblical Assn Amer. **RESEARCH** Literary analysis of Hebrew Bible. **SELECTED PUBLICATIONS** Auth, 1 Kings, Collegeville, Litur, 96. **CONTACT ADDRESS** 32-23 88th St, Apt 404, Jackson Heights, NY 11369. **EMAIL** jwalsh3000@cs.com

WALSH, JOHN H.
PERSONAL Born 09/14/1927, Pittsburgh, PA, m, 1953, 4 children **DISCIPLINE** PHILOSOPHY **EDUCATION** Duquesne Univ, BA, 52, MA, 58; Georgetown Univ, PhD (philos), 68. **CAREER** PROF PHILOS, CALIF STATE COL, PA, 61-. **RESEARCH** Philosophy of play and leisure; philosophical psychology; metaphysics. **SELECTED PUBLICATIONS** Auth, Compliance Inspections and Examinations by the Securities and Exchange Commission, Bus Lawyer, Vol 52, 96. **CONTACT ADDRESS** Dept of Philos, California Univ of Pennsylvania, California, PA 15419.

WALSH, THOMAS
PERSONAL Born 11/08/1949, Louisville, KY, m, 1982, 2 children **DISCIPLINE** RELIGION **EDUCATION** Vanderbilt Univ, PhD **CAREER** Exec Dir, 86-pres, Internatl Relig Found **MEMBERSHIPS** AAR; Intl Coalition for Relig Freedom **RESEARCH** Ethics; Interreligious Dialogue **SELECTED PUBLICATIONS** Auth, "Liberalism and Communitarianism: The Global Duel Between the Right and the Good, Sage, 99; Auth, "Ethics in Christianity and Islam," in Muslim Christian Dialogue, Paragon House, 98; **CONTACT ADDRESS** 941 Audubon Pkwy, Louisville, KY 40213-1109. **EMAIL** tgw@mindspring.com

WALTER, EDWARD F.
PERSONAL Born 10/31/1932, New York, NY, m, 1960, 2 children **DISCIPLINE** PHILOSOPHY **EDUCATION** St John's Univ, BA, 54; NYork Univ, MA, 65, PhD, 68. **CAREER** Prof Philos, Univ MO-Kansas City, 66, prof emer of Philos. **MEMBERSHIPS** Western Philos Asn; Am Soc Value Inquiry. **RESEARCH** Soc ethics; polit philos. **SELECTED PUBLICATIONS** Auth, Margolis, the emotive theory, and cognitivism, J Value Inquiry, spring 76; Liberalism and morality and the future, Philos Forum, 76; William James' chance, Midwest J Philos, spring 77; Is libertarianism logically coherent?, Philos & Phenomenol Res, fall 78; Rationality: Minimal and maximal, Reason Papers, winter 78; Personal consent and moral obligation, J Value Inquiry, 15: 19-33; Revising Mill's Utilitarianism, J Social Philos, 5/81; The Immorality of Limiting Growth, State Univ NY, 81. **CONTACT ADDRESS** Dept Philos, Univ of Missouri, Kansas City, 5100 Rockhill Rd, Kansas City, MO 64110-2499. **EMAIL** ewalter@umkc.edu

WALTER, JAMES J.
PERSONAL Born 01/01/1947, Indianapolis, IN, m **DISCIPLINE** BIOETHICS, CHRISTIAN ETHICS **EDUCATION** St. Meinrad Col, BA, 69; Katholieke Univ te Leuven, BA, 70; STB, 71; MA, 71, PhD, 74; Hoger Inst Voor Wijsbegeerte, PhB, 72. **CAREER** Lectr, Mangrove Col, 71; instr to asst prof of Christian Ethics, Catholic Univ of Am, 72-75; assoc prof of Christian Ethics, St. Meinrad Sch of Theol, 75-85; assoc prof to prof of Christian Ethics, Loyola Univ of Chicago, 85-99; Austin & Ann O'Malley Chair in Bioethics and Prof of Christian Ethics, Loyola Marymount Univ, 99-. **HONORS AND AWARDS** Post-Doctoral Fel, Loyola Univ of Chicago's Stritch School of Medicine, 89; Grad Fac Member of the Year Awd, Loyola Univ of Chicago, 92. **MEMBERSHIPS** Catholic Theol Soc of Am, Soc of Christian Ethics, Am Soc for Bioethics and Humanities. **RESEARCH** Issues in bioethics, methodological issues in Christian and philosophical ethics, professional ethics. **SELECTED PUBLICATIONS** Auth, Conversion and Discipleship: A Christian Foundation for Ethics and Doctrine, Fortress Press (Philadelphia, PA), 86; co-ed, Quality of Life: The New Medical Dilemma, Paulist Press (New York, NY), 90; auth, "'Playing God' or Properly Exercising Human Responsibility?: Some Theological Reflections on Human Germ-Line Therapy," New Theol Rev 10 (97): 39-59; auth, "Notes on Moral Theology: Theological Issues in Genetics," Theol Studies 60 (99): 124-134. **CONTACT ADDRESS** Dept Theol, Loyola Univ, Chicago, 6525 N Sheridan Rd, Chicago, IL 60626-5385. **EMAIL** jwalter@lmu.edu

WALTERS, GWENFAIR
DISCIPLINE CHURCH HISTORY **EDUCATION** Wellesley Col, BA; Gordon-Conwell Theol Sem, MDiv; Cambridge Univ, PhD. **CAREER** Consult, hist archv proj, Cambridge Univ; asst prof, 93-; adv to Women; dir, Edu Tech Develop, Gordon-Conwell Theol Sem, 93-. **RESEARCH** History of worship, spirituality, media, technology, and the arts in the Church. **SELECTED PUBLICATIONS** Ed, Towards Healthy Preaching. **CONTACT ADDRESS** Gordon-Conwell Theol Sem, 130 Essex St, South Hamilton, MA 01982.

WALTERS, JOHN R.
PERSONAL Born 09/03/1952, Pontiac, MI, m **DISCIPLINE** NEW TESTAMENT **EDUCATION** Univ Mich, BA, 75; Asbury Theol Sem, Mdiv, 79; Univ Oxford, DPhil, 86. **CAREER** Instr, 82-83, Asbury Col; lib, adj prof, 91-, Asbury Theol Sem. **HONORS AND AWARDS** John Wesley Fel, 79-82; Theta Phi, 77. **MEMBERSHIPS** Soc Bibl Lit, 77-; Inst for Bibl Res, 91-. **RESEARCH** Ancient Jewish piety; ancient gnostic piety; ancient Christian piety. **SELECTED PUBLICATIONS** Art, Hebrews, Asbury Bible Comm, 92; auth, Perfection in New Testament Theology, Mellen, 95; art, The Rhetorical Arrangement of Hebrews, Asbury Theol J, 96; auth, Perfection, Purity, Power: Redefining the Spirit-Led Life for the 21st Century, Soc

of Pentecostal Stud, 27th annual mtg, 98. **CONTACT ADDRESS** Asbury Theol Sem, 204 N Lexington Ave, Wilmore, KY 40390-1199. **EMAIL** john_walters@ats.wilmore.ky.us

WALTERS, STANLEY D.
PERSONAL Born 07/30/1937, Lawrence, KS **DISCIPLINE** RELIGION **EDUCATION** Princeton Theol Sem, ThM, 60; Yale Univ, PhD, 62. **CAREER** Greenville Col IL, prof, 61-68; Central Mich Univ, prof, 70-76; Univ Toronto Knox Col, prof, 76-92; Rosedale Presbyterian Church Toronto, minister, 92-. **MEMBERSHIPS** SBL **RESEARCH** Old testament; Hist Biblical Interpretation. **SELECTED PUBLICATIONS** Auth, After Drinking 1 Samuel 1:9, Crossing Boundaries and Linking Horizons: Studies in Honor of Michael C.Astour, 97. **CONTACT ADDRESS** Rosedale Presbyterian Church, 39 Whitney Ave, Toronto, ON, Canada M4W 2A7. **EMAIL** manthano@internet.com

WALTKE, BRUCE K.
DISCIPLINE OLD TESTAMENT **EDUCATION** Dallas Theol Sem, ThD; Harvard Univ, PhD. **CAREER** Instr, Dallas Theol Sem; Regent Col; Westminster Theol Sem; prof of Old Testament, Reformed Theol Sem. **SELECTED PUBLICATIONS** Auth, Intermediate Hebrew Grammar; auth, Introduction to Biblical Hebrew Syntax; auth, Understanding the Will of God; ed, New Geneva Study Bible; coed, Theological Wordbook of the Old Testament. **CONTACT ADDRESS** Dept of Old Testament, Reformed Theol Sem, Florida, 1231 Reformation Dr, Oviedo, FL 32765. **EMAIL** bwaltke@rts.edu

WALTMAN, JEROLD LLOYD
PERSONAL Born 07/26/1945, Monroe, LA, m, 1986, 3 children **DISCIPLINE** POLITICAL SCIENCE **EDUCATION** La Tech, BA; Denver Univ, MA; Ind Univ, PhD. **CAREER** Kenkaker Community Col, 69-72; La Col, 76-78; Univ Southern Miss, 78-. **RESEARCH** Comparative public administration; labor market policy. **SELECTED PUBLICATIONS** Auth, The Politics of the Minimum Wage, Univ of Ill Pr, 00; American Government: Politics and Citizenship, Am Press, 98; The Political Origins of the U.S. Income Tax, Univ Press of Miss, 85; Copying Other Nations' Policies, Schenkman, 80; coauth, Minimum Wage Increases and the Business Failure Rate, J of Economic Issues, Spring 98. **CONTACT ADDRESS** Dept of Political Sci, Univ of So Mississippi, Box 5108, Hattiesburg, MS 39406. **EMAIL** jerold.waltman@usm.edu

WALTON, CRAIG
PERSONAL Born 12/06/1934, Los Angeles, CA, m, 1980, 6 children **DISCIPLINE** PHILOSOPHY **EDUCATION** Claremont Grad Univ, PhD, 65. **CAREER** Univ S Cal, instr, asst prof, 64-68; N Illinois Univ, asst prof, 68-71; Emory Univ, vis asst prof, 71; N Illinois Univ, assoc prof, 71-72; Univ of Nev, assoc prof, prof, chmn philo, dir/prog coord, Ethics & policy studies, 72-. **HONORS AND AWARDS** Phi Beta Kappa; Barrick Dist Sch; NDEA fell; UNLV Res Sabbatical; 6 eds, Who's Who in the West; Intl Who's Who in Edu; Who's Who in Amer Edu. **MEMBERSHIPS** SSHP, BSHP, APA, Intl Hume Society, Intl Hobbes Society, ISEE, MSA, AAUP, CSPT, SAAP. **RESEARCH** Renaissance and early mod philo: Ramus, Montaigne, Hobbes, Pascal, and Hume; hist of ethics; crit thinking and prac reasoning; moral psycology and edu. **SELECTED PUBLICATIONS** Auth, Treatise on Ethics 1684, by Nicolas Malebranche, in: Intl Archives of the History of Ideas, Kluwer Acad Pub, 93; Hobbes Science of Natural Justice, co-ed, Intl Archives of the Hist of Ideas, Martinus Nijhoff pub, 87; High Level Ethical Risk: Unsound Practices at Yucca Mountain, in: Science Technology and the American West, ed, Stephen Tchudi, Reno, Univ Nev Press, 97. **CONTACT ADDRESS** Inst for Ethics and Policy Studies, Univ of Nevada, Las Vegas, Las Vegas, NV 89154-5049. **EMAIL** cwalton@nevada.edu

WALTON, DOUGLAS
PERSONAL Born Hamilton, ON **DISCIPLINE** PHILOSOPHY **EDUCATION** Univ Waterloo, BA, 64; Univ Toronto, PhD, 72. **CAREER** Prof, 69. **HONORS AND AWARDS** Killam res fel, 87-89; fel-in-residence, Netherlands Inst for Advanced Stud in the Hum and Soc Sci, 89-90; ISSA prize, 91. **RESEARCH** Argumentational informal logic. **SELECTED PUBLICATIONS** Auth, Slippery Slope Arguments, Oxford, Clarendon Press, (92): 296; auth, Plausible Argument in Everyday Conversation, (SUNY Speech Communication Series), Albany State Univ of New Yrok Press, (92): 320; auth, The Place of Emotion in Argument, Univ Park, Pa, Penn State Press, (92): 294; auth, Commitment in Dialogue: Basic Concepts of Interpersonal Reasoning (SUNY Series in Logic and Language), with Erik C.W.Krabbe, Albany State Univ of New York Press, (95): 223; auth, A Pragmatic Theory of Fallacy, Tuscaloosa, Univ of Alabama Press, (95): 324; auth, Arguments form Ignoranec, Univ Park, Pa, Penn State Pres, (96): 313; auth, Argument Structure: A Pragmatic Theory, Univ of Toronto Press, (96): 304; auth, Argumentation Schemes for Presumptive Reasoning, Mahwah, N.J., Erlbaum, (96): 218; auth, Fallacies Arising from Ambiguity, Dordrecht, Kluwer Academic Publishers, (96): 293; auth, Appeal to Pity: Argumentum ad Misericordiam, SUNY Press, (97): 225. **CONTACT ADDRESS** Dept of Philosophy, Univ of Winnipeg, 515 Portage Ave, Winnipeg, MB, Canada R3B 2E9. **EMAIL** douglas.walton@uwinnipeg.ca

WALTON, KENDALL
DISCIPLINE PHILOSOPHY **EDUCATION** Univ of Calif Berkley, BA, 61; Cornell Univ, PhD, 67. **CAREER** Lectr to prof, Univ of Mich, 65-. **HONORS AND AWARDS** Fel, Rockefeller Found; fel, Am Acad of Arts and Sci; Charles L Stevenson Collegiate Prof of Philos, Univ of Mich. **RESEARCH** Aesthetics, Philosophy of Music, Philosophy of Mind, Philosophy of Language. **SELECTED PUBLICATIONS** Auth, "Categories of Art", Philos Rev 79, (July 70): 334-367; auth, "Transparent Pictures: On the Nature of Photographic Realism", Critical Inquiry 11/2 (Dec 84): 246-277; auth, "What is Abstract About the Art of Music?", J of Aesthetics and Art Criticism, 46/3 (Spring 88): 351-364; auth, Mimesis As Make-Believe: On the Foundations of the Representational Arts, Harvard Univ Pr, 90; auth, "Metaphor and Prop Oriented Make-Believe", Europ J of Philos, 1.1 (Apr 93): 39-57; auth, How Marvelous!: Toward a Theory of Aesthetic Value", J of Aesthetics and Art Criticism, 51.3 (Summer 93): 499-510; auth, "Listening with Imagination: Is Music Representational?", J of Aesthetics and Art Criticism, 52.1 (Winter 94): 47-61; auth, "Projectivism, Empathy, and Musical Tension", Philos Topics, 00. **CONTACT ADDRESS** Dept Philos, Univ of Michigan, Ann Arbor, 435 S State St, Ann Arbor, MI 48109-1003. **EMAIL** klwalton@umich.edu

WALTON, R. KEITH
PERSONAL Born Birmingham, AL, m **DISCIPLINE** LAW **EDUCATION** Yale College, BA; Harvard Law School, JD. **CAREER** US District Ct, Northern District of AL, law clerk, 90-91; King & Spalding, assoc, 91-93; White House Security Review, deputy dir, 94-95; US Dept of the Treasury, chief of staff, enforcement, 93-96; Columbia Univ, Univ Scy, 96-. **MEMBERSHIPS** Enterprise Foundation, NY advisory bd, 1996-; Council on Foreign Relations, NY advisory bd, 1996-; Wilberforce Univ, trustee, 1997-; Alpha Phi Alpha; Sigma Pi Phi. **CONTACT ADDRESS** Columbia Univ, 535 W 116 St, 211 L, New York, NY 10027.

WALTON, WOODROW E.
PERSONAL Born 11/04/1935, Washington, DC, m, 1959, 2 children **DISCIPLINE** RELIGION **EDUCATION** TX Christn Univ, BA, 57; Duke Univ, BD, Mdiv, 60; Univ of OK, MA, 70; Sch of Theol and Missions-Oral Roberts Univ, Dmin, 93 **CAREER** Pastor, 60-75, Christn Church Disciples of Christ; Evangelist, 81-, Assemblies of Pastoral God **HONORS AND AWARDS** Cert, Inst for Adult Edu, IN Univ; b honor roll **MEMBERSHIPS** Am Asn of Christian Counrs **RESEARCH** Biblical studies, US Hist **CONTACT ADDRESS** Dir Inst Res, Amber Bible Col and Sem, 4300 Highline No 202, Oklahoma City, OK 73108-1843.

WALTZ, KENNETH NEAL
PERSONAL Born 06/08/1924, Ann Arbor, MI, m, 1949, 3 children **DISCIPLINE** POLITICAL SCIENCE **CAREER** Ford Prof, Univ CA, Berkeley, 71-94, Emeritus, 94-; res assoc, inst of War and Peace Studies and adjunct prof, Columbia Univ, 97-; vis appointments at various institutions, including Columbia, Harvard, the London School of Economics, Australian Nat Univ, Kings Col (London), the Woodrow Wilson Center, Peking and Fudan Universities. **HONORS AND AWARDS** James Madison Awd, distinguished contribution to political science; Pres, American Political Science Association, 87-88; Gloalization and American Power, National Interest, Spring 00; Structural International Security, Summer 00; Realism after the Cold War. **SELECTED PUBLICATIONS** Auth, Man, the State, and War, 59; Foreign Policy and Democratic Politics, 67, 92; co-ed and co-auth, Conflict in World Politics, 71; co-ed, The Use of Force, 71, 4th ed 93; auth, Theory of International Politics, 79; The Spread of Nuclear Weapons, Adelphi Paper No 171, 81; Nuclear Myths and Political Realities, Am Political Science Rev, Sept 90, Heinz Eulau award for best article in the Review; The Emerging Structure of International Politics, Int Security, fall 93; co-auth, The Spread of Nuclear Weapons: A Debate, 95; auth, Evaluating Theories, Am Political Science Rev 91, Dec 97; Thoughts About Virtual Nuclear Arsenals, in Michael J Mazarr, ed, Nuclear Weapons in a Transformed World: The Challenge of Virtual Nuclear Arsenals, St Martin's, 97; Kant, la democratie et la paix, in Pierre Laberge, Guy Lafrance, and Denis Dumas, eds, L'annee 1795-Kant: Essai sur la Paix, Paris: Librarie Philosophique J Vrin, 97; Intimations of Multipolarity, Copenhagen: DUPI, 00; several translations into Chinese, Spanish, and Italian. **CONTACT ADDRESS** Inst of War and Peace Studies, Columbia Univ, 420 W 118th St, New York, NY 10027.

WALZER, MICHAEL
PERSONAL Born 03/03/1935, m, 2 children **DISCIPLINE** POLITICAL SCIENCE **EDUCATION** Brandeis Univ, BA, 56; Harvard Univ, PhD, 61. **CAREER** Prof Government, Harvard Univ, 66-80; Prof Social Science, Inst Advan Study, 80-. **RESEARCH** Politics; Political theory; Moral philosopht. **SELECTED PUBLICATIONS** On Toleration, Yale Univ Press, 87. **CONTACT ADDRESS** School of Social Science, Inst for Advanced Studies, Princeton, NJ 08540.

WAN, ENOCH
DISCIPLINE MISSIONS **EDUCATION** State Univ NYork, PhD. **CAREER** Instr, Can Theol Sem; Alan Hayes Belcher prof. **HONORS AND AWARDS** Founder, dir, Ctr for Intercult Stud. **SELECTED PUBLICATIONS** Auth, Mission Resource Manual and A Devotional Commentary on Mark. **CONTACT ADDRESS** Dept of Missions, Reformed Theol Sem, Mississippi, 5422 Clinton Blvd, Jackson, MS 39209-3099.

WAN, SZE-KAR
PERSONAL Born 04/23/1954, Changsha, China, m, 1996 **DISCIPLINE** RELIGION **EDUCATION** Brandeis Univ, AB, 75; Gordon-Conwell Theol Sem, MDiv, 82; Harvard Univ, ThD, 92. **CAREER** Assoc prof New Testament, Andover Newton Theol Sch, 96-. **HONORS AND AWARDS** Lilly Fac Res Grant, 97-98; Lady Davis Post-Doc Fel, 93-94; Sinclair Kennedy Fel Harvard Univ, 89-90; NWO Fel, 90. **MEMBERSHIPS** SBL/AAR; CBA; Ethnic Chinese Bibl Colloquium. **RESEARCH** Pauline studies; Chinese Christian hermeneutics; New Testament. **SELECTED PUBLICATIONS** Auth, Allegorical Interpretation East and West: A Methodological Enquiry into Comparative Hermeneutics, Text & Experience, 95; auth, Abraham and the Promise of the Spirit: Galatians and the Hellenistic-Jewish Mysticism of Philo, Soc of Bibl Lit 95 Seminar Papers, 95; auth, Charismatic Exegesis: Philo and Paul Compared, Studia Philonica Annual, 94; auth, The Quaestiones et Solutiones in Genesim et in Exodum of Philo Judaeus: A Synoptic Approach, Soc Bibl Lit 93 Seminar Papers, 93. **CONTACT ADDRESS** Dept of New Testament, Andover Newton Theol Sch, 42 Browning Rd, Somerville, MA 02145. **EMAIL** Szekar@worldnet.att.net

WANG, ENBAO
PERSONAL Born 10/25/1953, China, m, 1 child **DISCIPLINE** POLITICAL SCIENCE **EDUCATION** Shaanxi Normal Univ, China, BA, 82; Univ Alabama, MA, 87; PhD, 93. **CAREER** Vis asst prof, Lewis-Clark State Univ, 93-96; asst prof, Univ Hawaii, 97-. **HONORS AND AWARDS** Joseph Eugene Baldeck Mem Awd. **MEMBERSHIPS** ACPSS **RESEARCH** Political economy of Greater China (mainland China, Hong Kong, Taiwan, and Macao.) **SELECTED PUBLICATIONS** Auth, Hong Kong, 1997: The Politics of Transition (Lynne Rienner Pub, 95) **CONTACT ADDRESS** Dept Social Science, Univ of Hawaii, Hilo, 200 West Kawili St, Hilo, HI 96720-4075. **EMAIL** enbao@hawaii.edu

WANG, HAO
PERSONAL Born 05/20/1931, Tsinan, China, d, 3 children **DISCIPLINE** LOGIC **EDUCATION** Southwestern Asn Univ, China, AB, 43; Tsing Hua Univ, AM, 45; Harvard Univ, PhD, 48. **CAREER** Teacher math, China, 43-46; asst prof philos, Harvard Univ, 51-56; reader in philos math, Oxford Univ, 56-61; PROF, ROCKEFELLER UNIV, 67-; Gordon McKay prof math logic and appl math, Harvard Univ, 61-67; John Locke lectr philos, Univ Oxford, 54-55. **MEMBERSHIPS** Asn Symbolic Logic; Am Acad Arts and Sci; Brit Acad. **RESEARCH** Mathematical logic; general philosophy. **SELECTED PUBLICATIONS** Auth, Time in Philosophy and in Physics in from Kant and Einstein to Godel, Synthese, Vol 102, 95; Tianjin Surveys of 1,000 Urban Households, 1983-1992 in Introduction, Chinese Law and Government, Vol 29, 96. **CONTACT ADDRESS** Rockefeller Univ, New York, NY 10021.

WANG, HSIAO-MING
PERSONAL Born 08/08/1955, Taiwan **DISCIPLINE** CRIMINAL JUSTICE **EDUCATION** Univ Feng-Chia, Bachelor Commerce, 77; Univ St Thomas, MBA, 92; Sam Houston State Univ, PhD, 98. **CAREER** Asst prof, Univ of La at Lafayette, 98-. **MEMBERSHIPS** Acad of Criminal Justice Sci (Policing Section). **RESEARCH** Comparative Criminal Justice System, White-Collar Crime, Research Methods, Statistics, and Policing. **SELECTED PUBLICATIONS** Coauth, "Japanese Management and policing in the Context of Japanese Culture," policing: An Int J of Police Strategies and Management 20.4 (97): 600-608; coauth, "The War Drugs in Taiwan: An American Model," Drug War, American Style: the Internationalization of Failed Policy and its Alternatives, Garland, forthcoming; coauth, "Cultural Influences on Taiwanese Police Management and Control Practices: An Exploratory Investigation of Ouchi"s Theory Z," Int J of the Sociol of Law 28.2 (forthcoming). **CONTACT ADDRESS** Dept Criminal Justice, Univ of Louisiana, Lafayette, PO Box 42810, Lafayette, LA 70504-0001. **EMAIL** hxw0282@louisiana.edu

WANG, WILLIAM KAI-SHENG
PERSONAL Born 02/28/1946, New York, NY, m, 1972, 1 child **DISCIPLINE** LAW, ECONOMICS **EDUCATION** Amherst Col, BA, 67; Yale Univ, JD, 71. **CAREER** Asst to mgr partner risk arbitrage, Gruss & Co, 71-72; from asst prof to assoc prof law, Univ San Diego, 72-77, prof, 77-81; prof law, Law Sch, Hastings Col, 81-, vis prof, Villanova Univ Law Sch, spring 99, UCLA Law Sch, spring 90, Univ Calif, Davis, 75-76 & Law Sch, Hastings Col, spring 80; consult, White House Domestic Policy staff, spring 79. **SELECTED PUBLICATIONS** Auth, Booting the professors, Washington Star, 1/9/78; A tightwad's guide to Las Vegas, New West, 1/29/79 & Moneysworth, 6/79; A chicken in every pot, and forty-one channels for every

television set, I Commun & the Law 97, 79; Toilet paper--it's good as gold, San Francisco Chronicle, 4/26/80; The dismantling of higher education, Part 1, 29 Improving Col & Univ Teaching 55 & 29 Improving Col & Univ Teaching 115, 82; Trading on material non-public information on impersonal stock markets: Who is harmed, and who can sue whom under Sec Rule 10b-5?, 54 Southern Calif Law Rev 1217, 81; Reflections on convenience translations: A reply to Professor Brooks, 17 San Diego Law Rev 209, 80 & Corp Coun Annual, 81; Insider Trading, supp, co-auth with Marc Steinberg, Aspen Law and Business, 96, 00. **CONTACT ADDRESS** Law Sch, Hastings Col, 200 Mc Allister St, San Francisco, CA 94102-4978. **EMAIL** wangw@uchastings.edu

WANG, XINLI
PERSONAL Born 08/14/1957, China, m, 1987, 1 child **DISCIPLINE** PHILOSOPHY **EDUCATION** Changcun Inst Geology PR China, BS, 82; Huazhong Univ Sci and Technology PR China, MA, 88; Univ Conn, PhD, 99. **CAREER** Instr, Xian Col of Geology PR China, 82-85; Asst Prof, Huazhong Univ PR China, 88-90; Teaching Asst, Univ of Conn, 90-92; Lectr, Univ of Conn, 92-97; Vis Asst Prof, Trinity Col, Conn, 97-99; Asst Prof, Juanita Col Pa, 99-. **HONORS AND AWARDS** Excellent MA Thesis Awd, Huazong Univ PR China, 88; Phi Kappa Phi, 92-97; Grad Teaching Assistantship, Univ of Conn, 90-92; Lectureship, Univ of Conn, 92-97; Dissertation Fel, Univ of Conn, 94; Excellence in Teaching Awd, Univ of Conn, 96. **MEMBERSHIPS** Am Philos Asn, The Philos of Sci Asn, Brit Soc for the Philos of Sci, Asoc of Chinese Philosophers in Am. **RESEARCH** Philosophy of Language, Philosophy of Science, Contemporary Analytical Philosophy. **SELECTED PUBLICATIONS** Auth, "Truth-value Gaps and Ontological gaps," in Proceedings of 10th Int Congress of Logic, Methodology and Philos of Sci (Florence, Italy, Aug 95); auth, "A Critique of the Translational Approach to Incommensurability," Prima Philos 11-3 (98): 293-306; auth, "Is the Notion of Semantic Prresupposition Empty?," Dialogues 73 (99): 61-91. **CONTACT ADDRESS** Dept Philos, Juniata Col, 1700 Moore St, Huntingdon, PA 16652-2119. **EMAIL** Wang@Juanita.com

WANGU, MADHU BAZAZ
PERSONAL Born 08/29/1947, Srinagar, India, m, 1971, 2 children **DISCIPLINE** PHENOMENOLOGY OF RELIGION **EDUCATION** Univ Pittsburgh, PA, PhD. **CAREER** Idependent scholar, writer, & teacher. **MEMBERSHIPS** Am Academy of Relig; Asn for Asian Studies. **RESEARCH** Hindu Goddesser; Indian art and aesthetics. **SELECTED PUBLICATIONS** Auth, Hermeneutics of a Kashmiri Mahatmya Text in Context, in Texts in Context: Traditional Hermeneutics in South Asia, ed Jeffrey Timm, SUNY Press, 92; Budhism: World Religions, Facts on File, 93; Buddha's Meditation Images: Compassion in Stone, and The Temple: Microcosm of Hindu Sel-Understanding, sem papers, Pitt Informal Prof, Univ Pittsburgh, Oct 94; Jain Creativity: Ethics in Art and Indo-Islamic Painting: Portraits of Acculturation, sem papers, Pitt Informal Prog, Univ Pittsburgh, Nov 95; Iconography and Symbology: The Body of the Goddess, sem paper, Pitt Informal Prog, Univ Pittsburgh, Oct 96; Kamala's Final Ascent, unpublished manuscript, 97; A Slice of My Life: A Travelogue, unpublished manuscript, 98; Sacred Femininity: female Images in Indian Art: Past to Present, forthcoming 99. **CONTACT ADDRESS** 301 High Oaks Court, Wexford, PA 15090. **EMAIL** zoonw@aol.com

WANNER, DIETER
PERSONAL Born 08/08/1943, Bern, Switzerland **DISCIPLINE** ROMANCE AND GENERAL LINGUISTICS **EDUCATION** Univ Zurich, DPhil(Romance ling), 68. **CAREER** Asst pro, 70-75, ASSOC PROF SPAN, ITAL AND LING, UNIV ILL, URBANA-CHAMPAIGN, 75-87, prof 87-88. **HONORS AND AWARDS** Humsoldt Research Prize, 94-95; NEH Fellowship, 1983-84. **MEMBERSHIPS** Ling Soc Am; Spanish. **RESEARCH** Italian linguistics; Romance linguistics; historical linguistics, syntex. **SELECTED PUBLICATIONS** Auth, Romance Language Pronouns Which Express Identity, Romance Philol, Vol 46, 93; Motives for Linguistic Change in the Formation of the Spanish Object Pronouns, Hispanic Rev, Vol 62, 94; Grammatical Research on the Characteristics of Rhaeto Romance as Spoken in Graubunden Grisons, Romance Philol, Vol 49, 95; Syntax of Spoken Raeto Romance, Romance Philology, Vol 49, 96. **CONTACT ADDRESS** Dept of Span and Port, Ohio State Univ, Columbus, 266 Cunz Hall, 1841 Millikin Rd., Columbus, OH 43210-1229. **EMAIL** wanner.2@osu.edu

WANTLAND, BURDETT L.
PERSONAL Born 10/30/1933, Decatur, IL, m, 1956, 3 children **DISCIPLINE** RELIGION AND PHILOSOPHY **EDUCATION** Lincoln Chris College, BA; Christian Theol Sem, MDiv; Butler Univ, MA; Univ Missouri, MA. **CAREER** Asst Prof, 68-, Univ West Georgia. **HONORS AND AWARDS** Honors in Hebrew Greek **MEMBERSHIPS** AAR; SSSR; SBL; WSTSTAR. **RESEARCH** Historical Jews; Nature of Belief. **CONTACT ADDRESS** Dept of Philo and English, State Univ of West Georgia, Maple St, Carrollton, GA 30118. **EMAIL** bwantland@wstga.edu

WAPNER, PAUL
DISCIPLINE GLOBAL ENVIRONMENTAL POLITICS **EDUCATION** Univ Colo, BA, Univ Chicago, MA, Princeton Univ, PhD. **CAREER** Assoc prof, Dir of Environmental Policy Prog, Am Univ. **RESEARCH** Environmental politics and ethics; Social movements and international relations theory. **SELECTED PUBLICATIONS** Auth, Environmental Activism and World Civic Politics, Albany: State Univ NY, 96; ed, Principled World Politics: The Challenge of Normative International Relations, Lanham, MD: Rowman and Littlefield, 00. **CONTACT ADDRESS** American Univ, 4400 Massachusetts Ave, Washington, DC 20016.

WARD, BENJAMIN F.
DISCIPLINE PHILOSOPHY **EDUCATION** Yale Univ; PhD, 72. **CAREER** Prof, 80-, Duke Univ. **RESEARCH** Aesthetics; philos of music; Frankfurt School; process philos; philos of sport. **SELECTED PUBLICATIONS** Auth, publ(s) on metaphysics; comp lit. **CONTACT ADDRESS** Philos Dept, Duke Univ, West Duke Bldg, Durham, NC 27706.

WARD, BRUCE
DISCIPLINE RELIGIOUS STUDIES **EDUCATION** McMaster Univ, PhD; Univ Toronto, BA. **CAREER** Prof, Relig Studies, Laurentian Univ. **RESEARCH** Modern philosophy of religion; religion and literature. **SELECTED PUBLICATIONS** Auth, Dostoevsky and the Hermeneutics of Suspicion, 97; art, The Absent 'Finger of Providence' in The Brothers Karamazov, Lonergan Rev, 96; art, Christianity and the Modern Eclipse of Nature, Jour Am Acad Relig, 95; auth, Prometheus or Cain? Albert Camus's Account of the Western Quest for Justice, 91; auth, The Recovery of Helen: Albert Camus's Attempt to Restore the Greek Idea of Nature, 90. **CONTACT ADDRESS** Religious Studies Dept, Laurentian Univ, 935 Ramsey Lake Rd, Sudbury, ON, Canada P3E 2C6. **EMAIL** bward@nickel.laurentian.ca

WARD, JULE D.
PERSONAL Born 09/08/1942, Detroit, MI, m, 1964, 4 children **DISCIPLINE** PRACTICAL THEOLOGY **EDUCATION** Univ of Chicago, Divinity Schl, PhD, theol, 96. **CAREER** Asst Vis Prof, De Paul Univ, 9 yrs. **MEMBERSHIPS** AAR, CTS, SCE, CTSA **RESEARCH** Marriage and family. **SELECTED PUBLICATIONS** Auth, LaLeche League: At the Crossroads of Medicine, Feminism, Religion, Univ of NC Press, 00. **CONTACT ADDRESS** Religious Studies, DePaul Univ, 2320 N Kenmore Ave, Chicago, IL 60614. **EMAIL** jward1@ppost.depaul.edu

WARD, JULIE
DISCIPLINE PHILOSOPHY **EDUCATION** Univ Calif, San Diego, PhD, 84. **CAREER** Assoc prof, Loyola Univ, 90-; former fac, Univ Ore, Mt Holyoke & Stanford; involved in, Women's Stud Comt & its Steering Comt; member, Acad Coun & Core Curric; undergrad adv, philos majors. **RESEARCH** Ancient philosophy, especially Plato, Aristotle; Hellenistic philosophy; feminism. **SELECTED PUBLICATIONS** Auth, Feminism and Ancient Philosophy, Routledge, 96. **CONTACT ADDRESS** Dept of Philosophy, Loyola Univ, Chicago, 820 N Michigan Ave, Chicago, IL 60611.

WARD, ROY BOWEN
PERSONAL Born 10/10/1934, Jacksonville, FL **DISCIPLINE** RELIGION **EDUCATION** Abilene Christian Col, BA, 56; Harvard Univ, Stb, 59, ThD (New Testament studies), 67. **CAREER** Instr relig, Conn Col, 63-64; From asst prof to assoc prof, 64-77, chmn dept, 71-78, assoc provost, 78-80, PROF RELIG, MIAMI UNIV, 77-; DANFORTH ASSOC, DANFORTH FOUND, 69-; lects, New Testament, Sch Relig, Earlham Col, 70; vis assoc prof relig, Rice Univ, 70-71; admin fel, Am Coun Educ, 76-77. **MEMBERSHIPS** Soc Bible Lit; Am Acad Relig; Studiorum Novi Testamenti Societas. **RESEARCH** New Testament studies; Judaism of the Second Commonwealth; religions of the Hellenistic world. **SELECTED PUBLICATIONS** Auth, the works of Abraham, 68 & Partiality in the assembly, 69, Harvard Theol Rev; James of Jerusalem, Restoration Quart, 74; Letter of James, Interpreter's Dict Bibl, 76; Abraham traditions in early Christianity, Studies Testament Abraham, 76; coauth, Is Christology inherently antisemitic?, J Am Acad Relig, 77. **CONTACT ADDRESS** Miami Univ, 500 E High St, Oxford, OH 45056-1602.

WARD, THOMAS M.
PERSONAL Born Pittsburgh, PA, m, 1967, 3 children **DISCIPLINE** LAW **EDUCATION** Univ Pa, BA; Univ of Notre Dame, LLB; Univ Ill, LLM. **CAREER** Prof; pvt prac, Burlington, Vermont; taught, Univ SC; Univ. Ill.; Univ Maine, 76-; past vis prof, Jefferson Smurfit vis prof, Notre Dame, Univ Ill, Univ College Gallway, 84-85; adj prof, Franklin Pierce Law Ctr in Concord, NH. **MEMBERSHIPS** Consultant, Licensing Executives Soc; Reporter, USPYO Study of the Recording Requirements for Sec interests in Intellectual Property. **RESEARCH** Intellectual property. **SELECTED PUBLICATIONS** Auth, Intellectual Property in Commerce, 00. **CONTACT ADDRESS** School of Law, Univ of So Maine, 246 Deering Ave., Portland, ME 04102. **EMAIL** tward@usm.maine.edu

WARDEN, DUANE
PERSONAL Born 10/16/1942, Franklin, AK, m, 1962, 1 child **DISCIPLINE** RELIGION, NEW TESTAMENT STUDIES **EDUCATION** Harding Univ, BA, 65; Harding Grad School, MA, 78; Duke Univ, PhD, 86. **CAREER** Prof, chair of dept, Ohio Valley Coll, 84-93; prof, asst dean, Harding Univ, 93-. **HONORS AND AWARDS** Teacher of the Year, Ohio valley Coll, 89-90; NEH Grants, 87, 91. **MEMBERSHIPS** Soc of Bibl; Evangel and Theol Soc. **RESEARCH** NT World; I Peter; Hermeneutics. **SELECTED PUBLICATIONS** Auth, Alienation and Communityin 1 Peter, 86; the Forty Thousand Citizens of Ephesus, Classical Philol, 88; Imperail Persecution and the Dating 1 Peter and Revelation, J of the Evangel Theol Soc, 91; The Words of Jesus on Divorce, Restoration Quart, 97. **CONTACT ADDRESS** Harding Univ, Box 2280, Searcy, AR 72149. **EMAIL** dwarden@harding.edu

WARE, BRUCE A.
DISCIPLINE CHRISTIAN THEOLOGY **CAREER** Asst prof, W Conservative Baptist Sem; asst prof, Bethel Theol Sem; assoc prof, ch dept Biblical and Systematic Theol, Trinity Evangel Divinity Sch; assoc dean, prof, S Baptist Theol Sem. **SELECTED PUBLICATIONS** Co-ed, The Grace of God and the Bondage of the Will. **CONTACT ADDRESS** Christian Theology Dept, So Baptist Theol Sem, 2825 Lexington Rd, Louisville, KY 40280. **EMAIL** bware@sbts.edu

WARE, CORINNE
PERSONAL Born 05/16/1932, Harlingen, TX, d, 3 children **DISCIPLINE** RELIGIOUS STUDIES **EDUCATION** Tex Christian Univ, BS, 52; Episcopal Theol Sem Southwest, MAR, 89; Southern Baptist Theol Sem, DMin, 92. **CAREER** Pastoral Coun, The Samaritan Coun Ctr, 90-97; Asst Prof, Episcopal Theol Sem Southwest, 97-. **HONORS AND AWARDS** Fel, Am Asn of Pastoral Counrs. **MEMBERSHIPS** AAPC, LMFT **RESEARCH** Spirituality. **SELECTED PUBLICATIONS** Auth, Discover Your Spiritual Type, The Alban Inst, 95; auth, Connecting to God: Nurturing Spirituality in Small Groups, The Alban Inst, 97. **CONTACT ADDRESS** Dept Relig Studies, Episcopal Theol Sem of the Southwest, PO Box 2247, Austin, TX 78768-2247.

WARFIELD, TED A.
DISCIPLINE PHILOSOPHY **EDUCATION** Univ Ark, BA, 91; Rutgers Univ, PhD, 95. **CAREER** Asst prof. **RESEARCH** Philosophy of mind; epistemology; metaphysics. **SELECTED PUBLICATIONS** Auth, Determinism and Moral Responsibility are Incompatible, Philos Topics, 96; Divine Foreknowledge and Human Freedom are Compatible, Nous, 97; co-ed, Mental Representation: A Reader, 94. **CONTACT ADDRESS** Philosophy Dept, Univ of Notre Dame, 336/7 O'Shaughnessy, Notre Dame, IN 46556. **EMAIL** warfield.3@nd.edu

WARK, WESLEY K.
PERSONAL Born 12/31/1952, Edmonton, AB, Canada **DISCIPLINE** INTERNATIONAL RELATIONS **EDUCATION** Carlton Univ, BA, 75; Cambridge Univ, MA, 77; London Sch Econ, PhD, 84. **CAREER** Vis prof, McGill Univ, 83-84; assoc prof, Univ Calgary, 84-88; assoc prof international relations, Univ Toronto, 88-. **HONORS AND AWARDS** Alta Heritage Scholar, 79-83 **MEMBERSHIPS** Founding mem, Can Asn for Security & Intelligence Studies; mem, Brit Stud Group on Intelligence. **RESEARCH** Intelligence studies; popular culture of espionage during the Cold War. **SELECTED PUBLICATIONS** Auth, The Ultimate Enemy, 85; auth, Spy Fiction, Spy Films and Real Intelligence, 91; auth, Espionage Past, Present, Future?, 93; ed, Intelligence Nat Security J, 86-. **CONTACT ADDRESS** Trinity Col, Univ of Toronto, Toronto, ON, Canada M5S 1H8. **EMAIL** wesley.wark@sympatico.ca

WARNKE, GEORGE C.
PERSONAL Born 08/27/1951, Washington, DC, m, 2 children **DISCIPLINE** PHILOSOPHY **EDUCATION** Reed Col, BA, 73; Boston Univ, MA, 78; PhD, 82. **CAREER** From asst prof to assoc prof, Yale Univ, 82-91; prof, Univ of Calif Riverside, 91-. **HONORS AND AWARDS** Fel, Bunkny Institute, 85-87; Member, Inst for Advanced Study, 91-92 **MEMBERSHIPS** Am Philos Asn, Soc for Women in Philos. **RESEARCH** Contemporary German philosophy, feminist philosophy, ethics, political philosophy. **SELECTED PUBLICATIONS** Auth, Justice and Interpretation, MIT Press, 93; auth, Legitimate Differences: Interpretation in the Abortion Controversy and Other Public Debates, Univ of Calif, 99. **CONTACT ADDRESS** Dept Philos, Univ of California, Riverside, 1604 HMIVSS Bldg., Riverside, CA 92521-0209. **EMAIL** warnke@ucrac1.ucr.edu

WARREN, ALVIN C., JR.
PERSONAL Born 05/14/1944, Daytona Beach, FL, m, 1966, 2 children **DISCIPLINE** LAW **EDUCATION** Yale Univ, BA, 66; Univ Chicago, JD, 69. **CAREER** Asst prof, Univ Conn, 69-73; assoc prof, Duke Univ, 73-74; assoc prof and prof, Univ Penn, 74-79; Ropes & Gray Prof Law, Harvard Univ, 79- . **HONORS AND AWARDS** Phi Beta Kappa; Guggenheim Fel. **MEMBERSHIPS** ABA. **RESEARCH** Tax law and policy. **SELECTED PUBLICATIONS** Auth, Integration of Individu-

al and Corporate Income Taxes, American Law Institute, 93; auth, Financial Contract Innovation and Income Tax Policy, Harvard Law Rev, 93; auth, Alternatives for Corporate Tax Reform, in Shapiro, ed, Enterprise Economics and Tax Reform, Progressive Foundation, 94; auth, Alternatives for International Corporate Tax Reform, Tax Law Rev, 94; auth, The Proposal for an Unlimited Savings Allowance, Tax Notes, 95; auth, How Much Capital Income Taxed under an Income Tax is Exempt under a Cash-Flow Tax?, Tax Law Rev, 96; auth, Three Versions of Tax Reform, William and Mary Law Review, 97; coauth, Integration of Corporate and Individual Income Taxes: An Introduction to the Issues, Tax Notes, 98; coauth, Integration of the U.S. Corporate and Individual Income Taxes: The Treasury Department and American Law Institute Reports, Tax Analysts, 98. **CONTACT ADDRESS** Dept of Law, Harvard Univ, Cambridge, MA 02138. **EMAIL** warren@law.harvard.edu

WARREN, ANN KOSSER
PERSONAL Born 04/13/1928, Jersey City, NJ, m, 1949, 5 children **DISCIPLINE** MEDIEVAL AND RELIGIOUS HISTORY **EDUCATION** City Univ New York, BA, 49; Case Western Reserve Univ, MA, 76, PhD (hist), 80. **CAREER** Lectr Hist, Case Western Reserve Unvi, 80-; Vis asst prof, Hiram Col, fall, 80. **MEMBERSHIPS** Mediaeval Acad Am; AHA; Soc Church Hist; Midwest Medieval Asn. **RESEARCH** Medieval English recluses: anchorites and hermits; medieval spirituality: pilgrimage phenomena; medieval social history: will studies and family history. **SELECTED PUBLICATIONS** Auth, the Black Death and Pastoral Leadership in the Diocese of Hereford in the 14th Century, Church Hist, Vol 65, 96; A History of Canterbury Cathedral, Albion, Vol 28, 96; Contemplation and Action in the Other Monasticism, Cath Hist Rev, Vol 83, 97. **CONTACT ADDRESS** Dept of Hist, Case Western Reserve Univ, Cleveland, OH 44106.

WARREN, DONA
PERSONAL Born 03/01/1965, Fargo, ND **DISCIPLINE** PHILOSOPHY **EDUCATION** Univ Minn, PhD, 95. **CAREER** Asst prof philos, Univ Wisc, Stevens Pt, 95- . **HONORS AND AWARDS** Excellence in Tchg Awd, 95. **MEMBERSHIPS** APA. **RESEARCH** Philosophy of mind; philosophy of religion. **SELECTED PUBLICATIONS** Auth, Those Who Can, Do: A Response to Sidney Gendin's Am I Wicked? Tchg Philos, 96; auth, How Many Angels Can Dance on the Head of a Pin? The Many Kinds of Questions in Philosophy, Tchg Philos, forthcoming; auth, Externalism and Causality: Simulation and the prospects for a Reconciliation, Mind & Lang, forthcoming. **CONTACT ADDRESS** Philosophy Dept, Univ of Wisconsin, Stevens Point, Rm 489 CCC, Stevens Point, WI 54481-3897. **EMAIL** dwarren@uwsp.edu

WARREN, EDWARD W.
PERSONAL Born 01/20/1929, San Francisco, CA, m, 1955, 3 children **DISCIPLINE** PHILOSOPHY, GREEK **EDUCATION** Stanford Univ, BA, 50; Johns Hopkins Univ, PhD (philos), 61. **CAREER** Asst prof philos, Syracuse Univ, 59-63; From asst prof to prof, 63-70, PROF CLASSICS AND PHILOS, SAN DIEGO STATE UNIV, 70-. **MEMBERSHIPS** Am Philol Asn; Soc Greek Philos; AAUP; Int Soc Neo-Platonic Studies. **RESEARCH** Greek philosophy; Plotinus; metaphysics. **SELECTED PUBLICATIONS CONTACT ADDRESS** Dept of Class and Orient Lang and Lit, San Diego State Univ, San Diego, CA 92182.

WARREN, ELIZABETH
PERSONAL Born 06/22/1949, OK, m, 1980, 2 children **DISCIPLINE** LAW **EDUCATION** Univ Houston, BS, 70; Rutgers Univ, JD, 76. **CAREER** Lectr, Rutgers Univ, 77-78; asst prof to assoc prof and assoc dean, Univ Houston, 78-83; res assoc to prof, Univ Tex Austin, 83-87; vis prof, Univ Mich, 85; prof, Univ Pa, 87-95; prof, Harvard Law Sch, 95-. **HONORS AND AWARDS** Am Col of Consumer Financial Services Lawyers 2000 Award; Brown Award, Fed Judicial Center, 98; Commendation for Serv, Am Bankruptcy Bd of Cert, 98; Outstanding Pub Serv, Am Col of Bankruptcy, 98; Albert A. Sacks-Paul Freund Award, Harvard Law Sch, 97; Lindback Award, 94; Fel, Am Col of Bankruptcy, 93; Finalist, Distinguished Scholar Pub Award, Am Sociol Asn, 89-92; Silver Gavel Award, Am Bar Asn, 90; Harvey Levin Award, Univ Pa, 89, 92; L. Hart Wright Teaching Excellence Award, Univ Mich, 86; Frankel Pub Award for Outstanding Writing, 82; Outstanding Teacher Award, Univ Houston, 81. **MEMBERSHIPS** Coun of the Am Law Inst; Nat Bankruptcy Rev Commission; Am Bankruptcy Bd of Cert; Nat Sci Found; Am Asn of Law Sch; Asn of Am Law Sch. **RESEARCH** Empirical research on families in financial distress and on failing businesses. **SELECTED PUBLICATIONS** Auth, Business Bankruptcy, Fed Judicial Cent, 93; co-auth, Secured Transactions: A Systems Approach, Little, Brown & Co, 95; auth, Report of the National Bankruptcy Review Commissions, 97; co-auth, Commercial Law: A Systems Approach, Little, Brown & Co, 98; co-auth, Financial Difficulties of Small Businesses and Reasons for Their Failures, Small Bus Admin, 98; co-auth, "Financial Characteristics of Businesses in Bankruptcy," Am Bankruptcy L J, 99; co-auth, "Rethinking the Debates over Health Care Financing: Evidence from the Bankruptcy Courts," NYU L Rev, 01. **CONTACT ADDRESS** Sch of Law, Harvard Univ, 200 Hausser Hall, Cambridge, MA 02138. **EMAIL** ewarren@law.harvard.edu

WARREN, LINDA
PERSONAL Born 05/30/1947, s, 1 child **DISCIPLINE** PHILOSOPHY **EDUCATION** Univ Wash, MSc, 82; SUNY, MA, 95; SUNY, Binghamton, PhD, Candidate **CAREER** SUNY Bing, adj prof, 96-97; Edmonds CC and Seattle Cent CC, Seattle WA, 97-. **HONORS AND AWARDS** TA Awd **MEMBERSHIPS** IAPH, SWIP, APA **RESEARCH** Feminist Ethics; Women and Poverty; Global Politics. **SELECTED PUBLICATIONS** Auth, Out of the Class Closet, in: Feminist Teacher. **CONTACT ADDRESS** Dept of Philosophy, Edmonds Comm Col, 6204 24th Ave NE, Seattle, WA 98115-7011.

WARREN, MANNING G., III
PERSONAL Born 08/20/1958, Dothan, AL, s, 5 children **DISCIPLINE** LAW **EDUCATION** Univ Ala, BA, 70; George Wash Univ, JD, 73. **CAREER** Prof, Univ Ala, 83-90; vis prof, Geo Wash Univ, 84-85; vis prof, Emory Univ, 87; H Edward Harter Ch Comm Law, Univ Louisville, 90-. **HONORS AND AWARDS** Fulbright Scholar; Outstand Scholar Awd; Outstand Teach Awd. **MEMBERSHIPS** ALI; AJS; DC Bar Asn. **RESEARCH** International corporate finance; securities regulation; legal ethics. **SELECTED PUBLICATIONS** auth, "Federalism and Investor Protection," Duke J Law Contemp Prob (98); auth, "European Union's Investment Services Directive," Penn J Intl Bus Law (94); auth, " The Global Harmonization of Securities Laws," Harvard Intl Law J (90). **CONTACT ADDRESS** Sch Law, Univ of Louisville, 2301 S 3rd St, Louisville, KY 40292-0001.

WARREN, PAUL R.
PERSONAL Born 06/18/1957, Albany, NY, s **DISCIPLINE** PHILOSOPHY **EDUCATION** Alfred Univ, BA, 79; Univ Wisconsin, PhD, 88. **CAREER** TA, 80-85, Univ Wisconsin; instr, 86-88,Rice Univ; asst prof, 88-94, assoc prof, 94- , FL Intl Univ. **RESEARCH** Social political philosophy; Ancient philosophy. **SELECTED PUBLICATIONS** Auth, Should Marxists Be Liberal Egalitarians, Journal of Political Philosophy; auth, Self-Ownership, Reciprocity and Exploitation, Canadian Journal of Philosophy. **CONTACT ADDRESS** Dept of Philosophy, Florida Intl Univ, Miami, FL 33199. **EMAIL** warrenp@fiu.edu

WARREN, SCOTT
DISCIPLINE POLITICAL SCIENCE AND PHILOSOPHY **EDUCATION** Univ VA, BA; Claremont Grad Sch, MA, PhD. **CAREER** Assoc prof, Dean of Stud, Antioch Col. **RESEARCH** Contemp critical theory. **SELECTED PUBLICATIONS** Auth, The Successful College Student and The Emergence of Dialectical Theory, Univ Chicago Press. **CONTACT ADDRESS** Antioch Col, Yellow Springs, OH 45387.

WARTLUFT, DAVID J.
PERSONAL Born 09/22/1938, Stouchsbung, PA, d, 4 children **DISCIPLINE** AMERICAN LUTHERAN HISTORY **EDUCATION** BA, Muhlenberg Col, 1960; MDiv, LTSP, 1964; MA, Univ Pa, 1964; MS in Library Science, Drexel Univ, 1968; Pastorate in Pa, 1964-65. **CAREER** Dir of the Library; cord, Formation Group prog. **HONORS AND AWARDS** Bd of dir(s), treasurer, Lutheran Hist Conf; exec sec, Amer Theol Library Assn. **RESEARCH** Exploring the Lutheran heritage. **SELECTED PUBLICATIONS** Pub(s), on American Lutheranism. **CONTACT ADDRESS** Dept of Practical Theology, Lutheran Theol Sem at Philadelphia, 7301 Germantown Ave, Philadelphia, PA 19119-1794. **EMAIL** Dwartluft@ltsp.edu

WASHINGTON, JAMES MELVIN
PERSONAL Born 04/24/1948, Knoxville, TN, m **DISCIPLINE** THEOLOGY **EDUCATION** Univ of TN Knoxville, BA 1970; Harvard Divinity School, MTS 1970-72; Yale Univ, MPhil 1972-75, PhD 1975-79. **CAREER** Yale Divinity School, instr 1974-76; Union Theol Sem, assoc prof 1976-86, prof, currently; Haverford Coll, vstg assoc prof 1983-84; Columbia Univ, visiting assoc prof 1984-85; Oberlin Coll, vstg assoc prof 1985-86; Union Theol Sem, prof of Modern & American Church History 1986; visiting lecturer Princeton Theological Seminary Princeton, NJ l989-90; visiting prof Princeton Univ Princeton, NJ l989-90. **HONORS AND AWARDS** Fellow Woodrow Wilson Found 1970-71; Protestant Fellow Fund for Theol Ed 1971-72; Rockefeller Doctoral Fellow Fund for Theol Ed 1972-74; Teaching Fellow Harvard Univ 1971-72; book Frustrated Fellowship 1985; Christopher Awd for editing A Testament of Hope, The Essential Writings of Martin Luther King, Jr 1987. **MEMBERSHIPS** Bd mem Amer Baptist Churches USA 1982-85, Natl Council of Churches 1985-87, Amer Baptist Historical Soc 1977-82; mem, exec comm Faith & Order Commissof the Natl Council of Churches 1985-87; consult Religious Affairs Dept, NAACP; Publications, A Testament of Hope, The Essential Writing of Martin Luther King,Jr (Harper & Row 1986); Frustrated Fellowship, The Black Baptist Quest for Social Power (Mercer Univ Press 1986); assoc editor American Natl Biography l989-. **CONTACT ADDRESS** Professor Church Hist, Union Theol Sem, New York, 3041 Broadway, New York, NY 10027.

WASHINGTON, ROBERT BENJAMIN, JR.
PERSONAL Born 10/11/1942, Blakeley, GA, m, 1969 **DISCIPLINE** LAW **EDUCATION** St Peter's College, BS, econ/political sci, 1967; Howard Law School, JD, 1970; Harvard University Law School, LLM, 1972. **CAREER** Harvard Law School, teaching fellow, 70-72; US Senate Comm on the District of Columbia, Attorney, 71-72; Howard Univ Law School, assoc prof of law and director of communication skills, 72-73; Christopher Columbus College of Law, lecturer, 72-73; US House of Representatives Comm on the District of Columbia, Attorney, 73-75; George Washington Univ Law Center, lecturer, 75, assoc prof of law, 78; Danzansky, Dickey, Tydings, Quint & Gordon, senior partner, 75-81; Georgetown Law Center, associate professor, 78-82; Finley, Kumble, Wagner, senior partner and member of the National Management Committee, 81-87, managing partner, Washington office, 86-88; Finley, Kumble, Wagner, Heine, Underberg, Manley, Myerson & Casey, Washington, DC, co-managing partner, 86-88; Laxalt, Washington, Perito, & Dubuc, managing partner, 88-91; Washington & Christian, managing partner, 91-; Washington Strategic Consulting Group, Inc, chairman/chief executive officer, currently. **HONORS AND AWARDS** Cobb Fellowship, Howard Law School, 1969; Harvard Law School, teaching fellowships, 1970-72. **MEMBERSHIPS** District of Columbia Bar Assn; American Bar Assn; Natl Bar Assn; Washington Bar Assn; Federal Bar Assn; American Judicature Society; Supreme Court Historical Society; Phi Alpha Delta Legal Fraternity; board member, Natl Bank of Washington, 1981-89; board member, Medlantic Healthcare Group; board member, Medlantic Management Corp; board member, Healthcare Partners; board member, AVW Electronic Systems Inc; adivsory board, The Home Group (AmBase); board of trustees, Corcoran Gallery of Art; board member, Natl Symphony Orchestra Assn; Metropolitan AME Church. **CONTACT ADDRESS** Washington & Christian, 805 15th St, NW, Washington, DC 20005.

WASSERMAN, RHONDA S.
PERSONAL Born 07/08/1958, Newark, NJ, m, 1991, 3 children **DISCIPLINE** LEGAL STUDIES **EDUCATION** Cornell Univ, AB, 80; Yale Law Sch, JD, 83. **CAREER** Asst prof law, Univ Pittsburgh Sch of Law, 86-90, assoc prof, 90-94, prof, 94-. **HONORS AND AWARDS** Phi Beta Kappa; grad with distinction in all subjects, Cornell; Clyde Dunnaway Prize in Govt, Cornell; Benjamin N. Cardozo Prize, Yale; Student Bar Asn Excellence in Teaching Awd, 90; Chancellor's Distinguished Teacher Awd, 2000. **MEMBERSHIPS** ABA, Allegheny County Bar Asn, Soc of Am Law Teachers, Women's Bar Asn of Western Pa. **RESEARCH** Class actions, remedies, jurisdiction, due process, family law. **SELECTED PUBLICATIONS** Auth, "The Subpoena Power: Pennoyer's Last Vestige, " 74 Minn Law Rev 37 (89); auth, "Equity Transformed: Preliminary Injunctions to Require the Payment of Money," 70 B. U. L. Rev, 623 (90); auth, "Equity Renewed: Preliminary Injunctions to Secure Potential Money Judgements," 67 Wash Law Rev, 257 (92), quoted in Grupo Mexicano de Descarrollo, S.A. v Alliance Bond Fund, 119 S CCt (99); auth, "Rethinking Review of Remands: Proposed Amendments to the Federal Removal Statute, 43 Emory Law J 83 (94); auth, "Parents, Partners and Personal Jurisdiction," Univ Ill Law Rev, 813 (95); auth, Divorce and Domicile: Time to Sever the Knot," 39 William & Mary Law Rev, 1 (97); auth, "Dueling Class Actions," 80 B. U. Law Rev (2000). **CONTACT ADDRESS** Sch of Law, Univ of Pittsburgh, 219 Law Bldg, Pittsburgh, PA 15260-7102. **EMAIL** wasserman@law.pitt.edu

WATANABE, MORIMICHI
PERSONAL Born 08/08/1926, Yamagata, Japan, m, 1954, 1 child **DISCIPLINE** LATE MEDIEVAL HISTORY, POLITICAL SCIENCE **EDUCATION** Univ Tokyo, LLB, 48; Columbia Univ, MA, 56, PhD (polit theory), 61. **CAREER** Lectr polit sci, Meiji Gakuin Jr Col, Tokyo, 48-50, prof, 50; instr, Meiji Gakuin Col, 49-51, lectr, 51-54; vis asst prof, Kans State Col Pittsburg, 60-61; instr, Queens Col, NY, 61-63; From asst prof to assoc prof, 63-71, Prof Hist and Polit Sci, C W Post Ctr, Long Island Univ, 71-; Am Philos Soc res grants, 64, 70 and 77; Am Coun Learned Soc res grant, 66; Found Reformation Res grant-in-aid, 70; vis prof, Fac Law, Univ Tokyo, 76 and Fac Law, Keio Univ, 76. **MEMBERSHIPS** AHA; Mediaeval Acad Am; Renaissance Soc Am; Am Cath Hist Asn; Am Soc Church Hist. **RESEARCH** History of legal and political thought; Conciliar Movement; Nicholas of Cusa. **SELECTED PUBLICATIONS** Auth, The Political Ideas of Nicholas of Cusa, with Special Reference to his De Concordantia Catholica, Libr Droz, Geneva, Switz, 63; The Episcopal election of 1430 in Trier and Nicholas of Cusa, Church Hist, 39: 229-316; Nicholas of Cusa and the idea of tolerance, In: Nicolo' Cusano agli inizi del Mondo Moderno, Sansoni Ed, Florence, 70; Authority and consent in church government: Panormitanus, Aeneas Sylvius, Cusanus, J Hist Ideas, 33: 217-236; Humanism in the Tyrol: Aeneas Sylvius, Duke Sigmund and Gregor Heimburg, J Medieval & Renaissance Studies, 4: 177-202; Gregor Heimburg and early humanism in Germany, In: Philosophy & Humanism: Renaissance Essays in Honor of Paul O Kristeller, Brill, Leiden, 76; translr (into Japanese), Paul O Kristeller, Renaissance Thought, Univ Tokyo, 77; auth, Imperial reform in the mid-fifteenth century: Gregor Heimburg and Martin Mair, J Medieval & Renaissance Studies, 9: 209-235. **CONTACT ADDRESS** C W Post Ctr, Long Island Univ, C.W. Post, 720 Northern Blvd, Greenvale, NY 11548-1300.

WATERS, C. KENNETH
DISCIPLINE PHILOSOPHY OF SCIENCE **EDUCATION** Univ Va, BA, 79; Ind Univ, MA, 84; PhD, 85. **CAREER** Asst prof, John Carroll Univ, 84-87; vis prof, Rice Univ, 89; asst prof, 87-91; vis scholar, Cambridge Univ, 94-95; asst prof, Univ Minn, 91-94; assoc prof, 94-; cen dir, 96-. **HONORS AND AWARDS** NSF, 89, 94. **MEMBERSHIPS** APA; PSA; HSS. **RESEARCH** Philosophy of biology; genetics; molecular structure; evolution; epistemology. **SELECTED PUBLICATIONS** Co-ed, Julian Huxley: Biologist and Statesman of Science, Rice UP (Houston, TX), 93; auth, "Causal Regularities in the Biological World of Contingent Distributions," Biol and Philo 13 (98): 5-36; auth, "Genes Made Molecular," Philo Sci 61 (94): 163-85; auth, "Tempered Realism about the Force of Selection," Philo Sci 58 (91): 553-73; auth, "Why the Anti-reductionist Consensus Won't Survive: The Case of Classical Mendelian Genetics," in PSA 1990 (90): 125-39, reprinted in Conceptual Issues in Evolutionary Biology, ed. Elliott Sober (Cambridge, MA: MIT Press, 93) 2nd ed; auth, "Rosenberg's Rebellion," Biology Philo 5 (90): 225-39; coauth, "The Illusory Riches of Sober's Monism," J Philo 85 (90): 158-161; auth, "Relevance Logic Brings Hope to Hypothetico-deductivism," Philo Sci 54 (87): 453-64; auth, "Taking Analogical Inference Seriously: Darwin's Argument from Artificial Selection," PSA 1986 1(86): 502-13. **CONTACT ADDRESS** Dept Philosophy, Univ of Minnesota, Twin Cities, 271 19th Ave S, Minneapolis, MN 55455. **EMAIL** ckwaters@tc.umn.edu

WATERS, DONOVAN W. M.
DISCIPLINE LAW **EDUCATION** Oxon Univ, BA, 52, BCL, 53, MA, 58, DCL, 90; London Univ, PhD, 63; Univ Victoria, LLD, 95. **CAREER** Prof emer, 96-. **HONORS AND AWARDS** Pres, Int Acad Estate Trust Law. **SELECTED PUBLICATIONS** Auth, The Constructive Trust; The Law of Trusts in Canada. **CONTACT ADDRESS** Fac of Law, Univ of Victoria, PO Box 2400, Victoria, BC, Canada V8W 3H7. **EMAIL** dwwaters@uvic.ca

WATERS, JOHN W.
PERSONAL Born 02/05/1936, Atlanta, GA, s **DISCIPLINE** THEOLOGY **EDUCATION** Atlanta Univ Summer School, 1955-58; Fisk Univ, BA 1957; Univ of Geneva Switzerland, Cert 1962; GA State Univ, 1964, 1984; Boston Univ, STB 1967, PhD 1970; Univ of Detroit, 1974-75. **CAREER** Army Ed Ctr Ulm W Germany, admin 1960-63; Atlanta Bd of Ed, instr 1957-60, 63-64; Myrtle Baptist Church W Newton MA, minister 1969; Ctr for Black Studies Univ of Detroit, dir, assoc prof 1970-76; Interdenom Theol Ctr, prof 1976-86; The Gr Solid Rock Baptist Church Riverdale, minister 1981-; senior vice pres 1984-; Primerica Financial Services, College Park, GA, senior vice president, 84-. **HONORS AND AWARDS** The Nat Fel Fund Fel in Relig 1968-70; Fel The Rockefeller Doctoral Fel in Relig 1969-70; Disting Lectr Inst for Christian Thought John Courtney Murray Newman Ctr MI 1975; first fac lectr, Interdenominational Theological Ctr, 1979. **MEMBERSHIPS** Mem bd dir Habitat for Humanity in Atlanta 1983; mem bd of trustees Interdenom Theol Ctr 1980-84; vice pres Coll Park Ministers Fel; chair South Atlanta Joint Urban Ministry 1984-94; Prison Ministries with Women, 1988-96; Am Acad Relig, 1969-; Soc of Bibl Lit, 1969-; Am Asn of Univ Professors (AAUP), 1971-. **CONTACT ADDRESS** 6280 Camp Rd., Riverdale, GA 30296.

WATERS, RAPHAEL THOMAS
PERSONAL Born 01/16/1924, Sydney, Australia, d, 1955 **DISCIPLINE** PHILOSOPHY, PHARMACY **EDUCATION** Univ Sydney, PhC, 45; Univ Montreal, BPh, 59, LPh, 60, DPh, 61. **CAREER** Sr lectr philos, Aquinas Acad, 62-64; lectr, Univ Ottawa, 69-70, asst prof, 70-76; asst prof, 76-81, assoc prof philos, 81-91, prof philos, Niagara Univ, 91-; Niagara Univ; exec dir, Int Mother's Day Walk for Life; Nat Chair, Scholars for Social Justice. **MEMBERSHIPS** Am Cath Philos Asn; Austrailian Maritain Asn; Thomas Aquinas Int Soc NAm. **RESEARCH** Epistemology; social and political philosophy; medical ethics. **SELECTED PUBLICATIONS** Auth, Some Epistemological Questions Concerning the Non-medical Use of Drugs, Rev Univ Ottawa, 10-11/75; The Moral Justification of Capital Punishment: Soc Justice Rev, 82; The Relationship of Moral Philosophy to Moral Theology, Listening, 83; The Nature of Man: A Philosopher's Viewpoint, Linacre Quart, 82, 85; The Two Faces of Capitalism, Soc Justice Rev, July/August 84; Two Ethical Traditions and Their Effects on Human Rights, Proceedings of the Fellowship of Catholic Scholars, 85; Capital Punishment and the Principle of Double Effect, in Philos and Culture, Montreal, ed Montmorency, 5 vols, 86; The Basis for Traditional Rights and Responsibilities Parents, in Parental Rights: The Contemporary Assault on Traditional Liberties, ed Stephen Krason and D'Agostino, Front Royal Christiandom Col Press, 88; Values and Rights in Education, in The Recovery of American Education: Reclaiming a Vision, Lanham, MD, Univ Press Am, 91; Capital Punishment: An Act of Murder, Revenge, or Justice?, Contemp Philos, vol XVI, Nov/Dec 94; Capital Punishment: An Evil Act or An Act of Justice?, Soc Justice Rev, Jan 96; The Structure of the Model Family, Soc Justice Rev, Nov/Dec 96; The Ethics of Eugenics, Soc Justice Rev, Nov/Dec 97; The Common Good: Its Nature and Properties, Soc Justice Rev, July, 98; auth, The Principle of Double Effect: Its Use and Misuse, Social Justice Review, Nov.-Dec., 99. **CONTACT ADDRESS** Niagara Univ, Niagara University, NY 14109. **EMAIL** rwaters@niagara.edu

WATKINS, JOHN C.
PERSONAL Born 04/02/1935, Mobile, AL, m, 1972, 4 children **DISCIPLINE** CRIMINAL JUSTICE **EDUCATION** Univ of Ala, BS, 57; JD, 62; Fla State Univ, MS, 64; Northwestern Univ, LLM, 68. **CAREER** Asst Prof, Univ of Ala, 65-69; Acting Chair Dept of Bus Law, Culverhouse Col of Commerce and Bus Admin, Univ of Ala, 66-67; Assoc Prof, Sam Houston Stat Univ, Huntsville Tex, 69-71; Prof, Univ of Ala, 71-. **HONORS AND AWARDS** NIMH Fel of Criminol, Fla State Univ, 63-64; Delta Tau Kappa; Omicron Delta Kappa. **MEMBERSHIPS** Ala State Bar Asn, Alpha Kappa Psi (bus), Phi Alpha Delta (law), Alpha Kappa Delta (sociol). **RESEARCH** Juvenile Justice, International Criminal Law, War Crimes. **SELECTED PUBLICATIONS** Auth, "War Crimes: Nuremberg-My Lai - Bosnia," in Magill's Encylopedia of Social Issues vol 6 (Passadena, CA: Salem Press, 96), 1675-1679; auth, "World War II: German Propoganda," in Magill's Encylopedia of Propoganda (Passadena, CA: Salem Press, 98), 893-897; auth, The Juvenile Justice Century: A Sociolegal Commentary on American Juvenile Courts, Carolina Acad Press (Durham, NC), 98; auth, Selected Cases on Juvenile Justice in the Twentieth Century, The Edwin Mellen Press Inc (Lewiston, NY), forthcoming; auth, "The Criminal Insanity Defense," and "The Juvenile Justice System," in Encyclopedia of Criminology and Deviant Behavior (Philadelphia, PA: Taylor & Francis Inc, forthcoming). **CONTACT ADDRESS** Dept Criminal Justice, Univ of Alabama, Tuscaloosa, PO Box 870320, Tuscaloosa, AL 35487-0001.

WATSON, CLETUS CLAUDE, T.O.R.
PERSONAL Born 11/03/1938, Philadelphia, PA, s **DISCIPLINE** THEOLOGY **EDUCATION** St Francis College, Loretto, PA, BA, 1962; St Francis Seminary, Loretto, PA, ordained, 1966; LaSalle University, Philadelphia, PA, MA, 1974; St Charles Seminary, Philadelphia, PA, MDiv, 1976. **CAREER** Bishop Egan High School, Fairless Hills, PA, chairman, teacher, 66-76; St Francis Prep School, Spring Grove, PA, chairman, dean of students, 77-81; University of Florida Med School, Gainesville, FL, teacher, med ethics, 81-85; Holy Faith Catholic Church, Gainesville, FL, assoc pastor, teacher, 81-85; San Jose Catholic Church, Jacksonville, FL, assoc pastor, teacher, 85-88; St Joseph Academy, St Augustine, FL, teacher, chairman, 86-89; Church of the Crucifixion, Jacksonville, FL, pastor, teacher, 88-. **HONORS AND AWARDS** Black History Month Awd, Jacksonville Naval Base, 1987; commissioned in Afro-American ministry, Jacksonville, FL, 1990; One Church/One Child Awd, Jacksonville, FL, 1990; Citizens Awd, Jacksonville, FL, 1991; Alumni Awd in Humanities, St Francis College, 1992; International Biographical Assn Man of the Year Awd, 1993; Amer Biographical Inst Man of the Year Awd, 1994. **MEMBERSHIPS** Advisory bd member, Presbyteral Council of the Diocese of St Augustine, 1988-95; advisory board member, Afro-American Office (Diocese), 1987-; advisory board member, Catholic Charities Office (Diocese), 1991-97; advisory board member, Ministry Formation Board, 1991-92; member, National Black Catholic Clergy Caucus, 1966-; member, Black Catholic Congress, 1987-. **SELECTED PUBLICATIONS** Author, The Concept of Love: An Ongoing Perspective, Brentwood Christian Press; author, The Concept of God and the Afro-American, Brentwood Christian Press; poems include "A Man Called Black"; "Fifty Plus Five". **CONTACT ADDRESS** Pastor, Church of the Crucifixion Rectory, 6079 Bagley Road, Jacksonville, FL 32209-1800.

WATSON, D. F.
PERSONAL Born 05/15/1956, Watertown, NY, m, 1984, 1 child **DISCIPLINE** NEW TESTAMENT AND CHRISTIAN ORIGINS **EDUCATION** Houghton Col, BA, 78; Princeton Theol Sem, Master of Divinity, 81; Duke Univ, Dr of Philos, 86. **CAREER** Asst prof of bibl studies, Ashland Theol Sem, 84-86; pastor, Tri-Church Parish United Meth Churches, Steuben, North Western, and Westernville, NY, 87-89; asst prof, 89-92, assoc prof, 92-96, prof, 96-, New Testament studies, chair, dept relig and philos, 93-98, Malone Col, Canton, Oh. **HONORS AND AWARDS** Dict of Intl Bio, 25th ed, 97; 26th ed, 98; 27th ed, 99; 28th ed, 00Outstanding People of the 20th Cent, 99; Who's Who in Amer Educ, 5th ed, 96-97; Who's Who in the Midwest, 25th ed, 96-97; 26th ed, 98-99; Who's Who in Bibl Studies and Archaeol, 2nd ed, 93; Malone Col first Distinguished Facul Awd for Scholar, 97-98; Malone Col Facul Forum Showcase of Res Awd for Res on Ancient Educ: Greek, Roman and Jewish, fall 97; ; Malone Col Facul Forum Showcase of Res Awd for Res on The New Testament Tchg on the Antichrist, fall 95; ; Malone Col Facul Forum Showcase of Res Awd for Res on A Socio-Rhetorical Commentary on Paul's Epistle to the Philippians, fall 94; Malone Col Facul Forum prize, Developing a Personal Publishing Program, spring, 92; Amer Bible Soc Scholarly Achievement Awd for Excellence in Bibl Studies, Houghton, 78; summa cum laude graduate, Houghton, 78; Comprehensive Examination Honors, Houghton, 7; Dean's list, Houghton, 74-78. **MEMBERSHIPS** Studiorum Novi Testamenti Soc, 95-; Soc of Bibl Lit, 81-; Cath Bibl Asn of Amer, 83-; Eastern Great Lakes Bibl Soc, 84-; Inst for Bibl Res, 93-; Intl Soc for the Hist of Rhetoric, 86-; John Wesley Fel, 82-. **RESEARCH** New Testament; Rhetorical criticism; Biblical interpretation **SELECTED PUBLICATIONS** Auth, "The Letter of Jude" and "The Second Letter of Peter" in The New Interpreter's (12 Vols, Nashville, Abindon, 98) 12.321-61; 12. 471-500; auth, Rhetorical Criticism of the Bible: A Comprehensive Bibliography with notes on history and method, Bibl Interpretation Series 4, Leiden, E. J. Brill, 94; ed, Persuasive Artistry: Studies in New Testament Rhetoric in Honor of George A. Kennedy, Jour for the Study of the New Testament Supplement series 50, Sheffield, Sheffield Acad Press, 91; articles, ed, Vernon Robbins's Socio-Rhetorical Criticism: A Review, Jour for the Study of the New Testament, 70, 69-115, 98; Rhetorical Criticism of Hebrews and the Catholic Epistles Since 1978, Currents in Res: Bibl Studies 5, 175-207, 97; Rhetorical Criticism of the Pauline Epistles Since 1975, Currents in Res: Bibl Studies 3, 219-48, 95; Building a New Testament Library: James-Revelation, Catalyst: Contemporary Evangelical Perspectives for United Methodist Seminarians 20/4, 3, 94. **CONTACT ADDRESS** Prof. of New Testament Studies, Malone Col, 515 25th St. NW, Canton, OH 44709. **EMAIL** jwatson@ashland.edu

WATSON, DAIVD LOWES
PERSONAL Born 03/31/1938, Newcastle upon Tyne, England, m, 1961, 2 children **DISCIPLINE** THEOLOGY **EDUCATION** Merton Col. Oxford Univ, BA, 61, MA, 65; Eden Theol Sem, MDiv, 74; Duke Univ, PhD, 78. **CAREER** Asst master, Duke's Sch, 61-64; overseas rep, Am Field Service Int Scholarships, 64-68; West Slough commun dir, 68-71; pastor, Prospect Park United Meth Churches, 71-75; pastor, Holly Springs Un Meth Church, 75-78; McCreless prof evangelism, Perkins Sch Theol, So Meth Univ, 78-84; staff, General Bd Discipleship, Un Meth Church, 84-92; prof theol & congregational life & mission, Wesley Theol Sem, 92-98; Dir, Offic Pastoral Formation, Nashville Episcopal Area, Un Meth Church, 98-. **MEMBERSHIPS** Acad Evangelism in Theol Educ; Am Acad Rel; Am Soc Church Hist; Am Soc Missiology; Asn Profs Missions; Wesleyan Theol Soc; World Meth Hist Soc. **SELECTED PUBLICATIONS** Auth, Accountable Discipleship, Discipleship Resources, 84, 85, 87-90, German ed, 90; auth, Covenant Discipleship: Christian Formation through Mutual Accountability, Discipleship Resources, 91, 95; auth, Forming Christian Disciples: The Role of Covenant Discipleship and Class Leaders in the Congregation, Discipleship Resources, 91, 95; auth, Proclaiming Christ in All His Offices: Priest, Prophet, Potentate, in The Portion of the Poor: Good News to the Poor in the Wesleyan Tradition, Kingswood Books, 95; auth, Response to Creation Theology as a Basis for Global Witness, in Evangelization, The Heart of Mission: A Wesleyan Imperative, General Board of Global Ministries, 95; auth, God's New Household, in The Upper Room 1997 Disciplines, The Upper Room, 96. **CONTACT ADDRESS** Office Pastoral Formation, 149 Smotherman Ct, Murfreesboro, TN 37129. **EMAIL** DavidLowes@aol.com

WATSON, H. JUSTIN
PERSONAL Born 06/06/1957, VanBuren, AK **DISCIPLINE** RELIGIOUS STUDIES **EDUCATION** Florida State Univ, PhD, 96, MA, 92, Rel; Univ of the South, Polit Sci, BA, 79. **CAREER** Lectr, 97-99, Inst, 96-97, Tchg Asst, 92-95, FSU Dept Rel. **HONORS AND AWARDS** FSU Dissertation Fellowship; FSU Univ Fellowship; Tchg Assoc, FSU Prof for Instr Excellence; Natl Merit Scholar. **MEMBERSHIPS** Amer Acad Rel; Amer Stud Assoc; Amer Soc of Church Hist; Soc for the Sci Stud of Rel; Amer Polit Sci Assoc. **RESEARCH** Contemporary American Social and Political Movements, Christian Right, Evangelicalism and Fundamentalism, New of Alternative Religious Movements; Religious Ethics. **SELECTED PUBLICATIONS** Auth, The Christian Coalition: Dreams of Restoration and Demands for Recognition, NY, St Martin's Press, Scholarly and Reference Division, 97; What the Christian Coalition Really Wants, Louvain Studies, 98. **CONTACT ADDRESS** Dept Religion, Florida State Univ, Tallahassee, FL 32306-1029. **EMAIL** jwtson@mailer.fsu.edu

WATSON, JAMES R.
PERSONAL Born 07/29/1938, Blue Island, IL, m, 1969 **DISCIPLINE** PHILOSOPHY **EDUCATION** Southern Ill Univ Carbondale, PhD, 73. **CAREER** Prof Philos, Loyola Univ New Orleans, 73-. **HONORS AND AWARDS** Loyola Univ Alumni Teaching Awd, 91. **MEMBERSHIPS** APA; Friedrich Nietzsche Soc; Heidegger Conference; IAPL; ISSEI; IPS, SPEP, SPSGH; SPSCVA. **RESEARCH** Continental Philosophy; Visual Imagery; Postmodernism; Holocaust and Genocide; Ethics. **SELECTED PUBLICATIONS** Auth, Between Auschwitz and Tradition: Postmodern Reflections of the task of Thinking, 94; Die Auschwitz Galaxy, 97; Kontinental Philosophie aus Amerika: 22 Photogrammische Portrate, 98; Contemporary Portrayals of Auschwitz and Genocide, 98; Portraits of Continental Philosophers in America, 99. **CONTACT ADDRESS** Dept of Philosophy, Loyola Univ, New Orleans, New Orleans, LA 70118. **EMAIL** jrwatson@datastar.net

WATSON, JAMES SHAND
PERSONAL Born 07/05/1946, Scotland **DISCIPLINE** INTERNATIONAL LAW **EDUCATION** Edinburgh Univ, LLB, 69; Univ Ill, LLM, 72. **CAREER** Teaching asst, Univ Ill, 70-71; asst prof, 71-74, assoc prof, 74-77, PROF LAW, COL

LAW, MERCER UNIV, 77-; Vis prof, Law Sch, Baylor Univ, summer 82, Emory, 83. **MEMBERSHIPS** London Inst World Affairs; Am Soc Int Law; Am Soc Polit and Legal Philos. **RESEARCH** Theory of international law and customary legal systems; the law of the sea; human rights. **SELECTED PUBLICATIONS** Auth, Theory and Reality in the International Enforcement of Human Rights, Transnational, 99. **CONTACT ADDRESS** Col Law, Mercer Univ, Macon, Macon, GA 31210.

WATSON, JOANN FORD
DISCIPLINE THEOLOGY **EDUCATION** DePaul Univ, BA, 78; Princeton Theol Sem, M Div, 81; Northwestern Univ, PhD, 84. **CAREER** Prof, theol, Ashland Theol Sem, Ashland, Oh. **HONORS AND AWARDS** Phi Beta Kappa. **MEMBERSHIPS** AAR; SBL. **RESEARCH** Theology; Women's studies. **SELECTED PUBLICATIONS** Auth, Manna for Sisters in Christ; auth, Mutuality in Christ; auth, Meditations in Suffering; auth, Sister to Sister; auth, Karl Barth's Doctrice of Man and Woman. **CONTACT ADDRESS** 910 Center St., Ashland, OH 44805.

WATSON, RICHARD A.
PERSONAL Born 02/23/1931, New Market, IA, m, 1955, 1 child **DISCIPLINE** PHILOSOPHY **EDUCATION** Univ Iowa, BA, 53; MA, 57; PhD, 61; Univ Minn, MS, 59. **CAREER** Instr, Univ Mich, 61-64; From asst prof to prof, Wash Univ, 64-. **MEMBERSHIPS** Am Philos Asn. **RESEARCH** Descartes, Cartesians, Early Modern Philosophy. **SELECTED PUBLICATIONS** Auth, Good Teaching: A Guide for Students, Southern Ill Univ Press, 97; auth, Representational Ideas From Plato to Patricia Churchland, Kluwer Academic Pub, 95; auth, Writing Philosophy: A Professional Guide, Southern Ill Univ Press, 92; auth, The Breakdown of Cartesian Metaphysics, Humanities Press Intl, 87. **CONTACT ADDRESS** Philos, Washington Univ, 1 Brookings Dr, Campus Box 1073, Saint Louis, MO 63130-4862. **EMAIL** rawatson@artsci.wustl.edu

WATSON, STEPHEN
DISCIPLINE PHILOSOPHY **EDUCATION** Carroll Col, BA, 72; Duquesne Univ, MA, 75, PhD, 79. **CAREER** Prof. **RESEARCH** Contemporary continental thought; 19th century philosophy; aesthetics. **SELECTED PUBLICATIONS** Auth, Between Tradition and Oblivion: Foucault, the Complication of Form, the Literatures of Reason, and the Aesthetics of Existence, Cambridge, 94; Phenomenology, Interpretation, and Community, 95; Interpretation, Dialogue, and Friendship: On the Remainder of Community, Res Phenomenology, 97; Tradition(s): Refiguring Community and Virtue in Classical German Thought, 97; Reinterpreting the Political: Continental Philosophy and Political Theory, 98. **CONTACT ADDRESS** Philosophy Dept, Univ of Notre Dame, 336/7 O'Shaughnessy, Notre Dame, IN 46556.

WATSON, WALTER
PERSONAL Born 12/31/1925, New York, NY, m, 1953, 2 children **DISCIPLINE** PHILOSOPHY **EDUCATION** Instr to asst prof, Univ Chicago, 51-59; NSF Sci Fac Fel, Cal Inst Technol, 58-59; assoc prof t o prof, 59-92, EMER, 93-, SUNY-Stony Brook; vis app, Univ PR, 63-64 and Univ HI, 82. **MEMBERSHIPS** Am Philos Asn. **RESEARCH** Pluralism. **SELECTED PUBLICATIONS** Auth Principles for Dealing with Disorder, Jour Chinese Philos, 81; The Architectonics of Meaning: Foundations of the New Pluralism, Univ Chicago Pressm 93; Types of Pluralism, The Monist, 90; Systematic Pluralism and The Foundationalist Controversy, Reason Papers, 91; McKeons Semantic Schema, Philos and Rhetoric, 94; Dogma, Skepticism, and Dialogue, The Third Way: New Directions in Platonic Studies, Rowman and Littlefield, 95; Rembrandts Aristotle, Hypotheses, 96. **CONTACT ADDRESS** 6 Bobs Ln, Setauket, NY 11733. **EMAIL** Watsonwalt@aol.com

WATTS, JAMES W.
PERSONAL Born 08/24/1960, Zurich, Switzerland, m, 1985, 1 child **DISCIPLINE** HEBREW BIBLE AND THE OLD TESTAMENT **EDUCATION** Pomona Col, BA, 82; Southern Sem, M Div, 85; Th M, 86; Yale Univ, PhD, 90. **CAREER** Instr, Yale Div Sch, 89; vis asst prof, Stetson Univ, 90-91; asst prof, Hastings Col, 93-98; assoc prof, Hastings Col, 98-99; assoc prof, Syracuse Univ 99- . **HONORS AND AWARDS** Phi Beta Kappa, Hastings Col Facul Achievement award. **MEMBERSHIPS** Soc of Bibl Lit; Nat Asn of Prof of Hebrew. **RESEARCH** Biblical Narrative; Mixed genres; Law, ritual and rhetoric in the Hebrew bible. **SELECTED PUBLICATIONS** Auth, Reading Law: The Rhetoricl Shaping of the Pentateuch, Th ebiblical Seminar, Sheffield: Sheffield Academic Press, 99; art, Reader Identification and Alienation in the Legal Rhetoric of the Pentateuch, Bilblical Interpretation 7/1, 99; ed, Forming Prophetic Literature: Essays on Isaiah and the Twelve in Honor of John D. W. Watts, JSOT suppl series 235, Sheffield Acad Press, 96; auth, Psalm and Story: Inset Hymns in Hebrew Narrative, JSOT suppl series 139, JSOT Press, 92; article, The Legal Characterization of Moses in the Rhetoric of the Pentateuch, Jour of Bibl Lit, 117, 415-26, 98; article, The Legal Characterization of God in the Pentateuch, Hebrew Union Col Annual, 67, 1-14, 97; article, Psalmody in Prophecy: Habakkuk 3 in Context, Forming Prophetic Literature, 209-223; article, Public Readings and Pentateuchal Law, Vetus Testamentum, 45, 4, 540-57, 95; article, Rhetorical Strategy in the Composition of the Pentateuch, Jour for the Study of the Old Testament, 68, 3-22, 95; article, Song and the Ancient Reader, Perspectives in Relig Studies, 22, 2, 135-47, 95; article, Leviticus, Mercer Commentary on the Bible, Mercer Univ Press, 157-74, 94; article, This Song: Conspicuous Poetry in Hebrew Prose, Verse in Ancient Near Eastern Prose, Neukirchener Verlag, 345-58, 93. **CONTACT ADDRESS** Dept of Religion, Syracuse Univ, Syracuse, NY 13244. **EMAIL** jwwatts@syr.edu

WAUGH, EARLE HOWARD
PERSONAL Born 11/06/1936, Regina, SK, Canada, m, 1970, 3 children **DISCIPLINE** HISTORY OF RELIGION **EDUCATION** McMaster Univ, BA, 59, MA, 65; Univ Chicago, MA, 68, PhD(hist relig), 72. **CAREER** Lectr, Indiana Univ, 70-71; Asst Prof, Univ of Alberta, 74-76; Assoc Prof, Univ of Alberta, 76-85; Prof, Univ of Alberta, 86-; Guest Prof, St. Thomas Univ, 92-93; Acting Chair, Univ of Alberta, 97-98. **HONORS AND AWARDS** Alberta Film Awd, 78; Gold Medal, Houston International Film Festival, 79; Silver Medal, Educational Houston International Film Festival, 79. **MEMBERSHIPS** Am Acad of Relig; Mid East Studies Asn; Can Soc Study Relig; Boreal Circle Soc; Am Res Center in Egypt; Soc for Medieval Studies; International Soc for the Study of Non-Traditional Medicine; Asn for Canadian Studies; Canadian Mediterranean Institute. **RESEARCH** Islam in North Am; Middle Eastern Sufism, Alberta Cree Traditions, Religious Interaction in Alberta. **SELECTED PUBLICATIONS** Auth, The Munshidin of Egypt, Their World and Their Song, Univ of South Carolina Press, Columbia, South Carolina, 89; auth, Dissonant Worlds: Rogier Vandersteene; auth, Among the Cree Wilfrid Laurier Univ Press, Waterloo, 96; coed, The Muslim Family in North America, Univ of Alberta Press, Edmonton, 91; coed, The Shaping of an American Islamic Discourse: A Memorial to Fazlur Rahman, Scholar's Press, Istanbul, (94): 129-143; auth, "Alexander in Islam: the Sacred Persona in Muslim Rulership adab," in Subject and Ruler: The Cult of the Ruler in Classical Antiquity, Alastair Small, ed, Journal of Roman Archeology, Supplementary Series 17, (96): 237-253; auth, "Wach and the Double Truth," in Teaching Theology and Religion, Vol 1, (97): 20-25; transl, "In Praise of the Prophet, Muhammad," Trans. & comm in Windows on the House of Islam, Univ of California Press, Berkeley, CA, (98): 120-123; auth, "Introduction," and "Beyond Scylla and Kharybdis: The Discourses of Isalmic Idenity in Fazlur Rahman," in The Shaping of an American Islamic Discourse: A Memorial to Fazlur Rahman, Earle H. Waugh and Frederic M Den, ed, Scholar's Press, Atlanta, Gerogia, (99): 1-; auth, "Dead Men in sultry Darkness': Western Theory the Problematic of a Baseline Cultural Motif in Islamic Ascetic Tradition," in Journal of Asian and African Studies, Vol 34, 1, (99): 1-20. **CONTACT ADDRESS** Dept of Comp Lit, Relig, & Film/Media Stud, Univ of Alberta, 347 Arts, Edmonton, AB, Canada T6G 2E6. **EMAIL** earle.waugh@ualberta.ca

WAUTISCHER, HELMUT
PERSONAL Born 06/15/1954, Klagenfurt, Austria **DISCIPLINE** PHILOSOPHY, PSYCHOLOGY **EDUCATION** Karl-Franzens Univ, Graz Austria, PhD, 85. **CAREER** Concurrent lectr, San Diego State Univ, 88-91; CSU Long Beach, 89-92; vis asst prof, Humboldt State Univ, 92-94; Universitatslektor, Univ Klagenfurt Austria, 95-97; concurrent lectr, Sonoma State Univ 95-. **HONORS AND AWARDS** Fulbright, 81; Executive Bd SAC, 91-; Executive Bd COPS, 97-. **MEMBERSHIPS** Am Philos Asn; Amer Anthropol Asn; Soc for the A nthropol of Consciousness; Council of Philos Soc; Karl Jasper Soc; Osterreichische Gesellschaft Fur Philosophie. **RESEARCH** Consciousness Studies; Philosophical Anthropology. **SELECTED PUBLICATIONS** Auth, Dreaming 'On Love and Awareness' Dialogue and Humanism, 94; ed, Anthropology of Consciousness, 94; Tribal Epistemologies: Essays in the Philosophy of Anthropology, 98; auth, "Tribal Epistemlogies: Essays in the Philosophy of Anthropology," Ashgate Publishing, 98; auth, "Ontology of Consciousness: A Modern Synthesis," forthcoming; auth, "The Path to Knowledge, in V.M. Pivojev, ed. Bachtin and the Problem of Methodology for Humanitarian Knowledge," forthcoming; auth, "Bewufstseinsforschung in interkultureller Diskussion," Polylog 3, 99, 111-112; auth, "Pathways to Knowledge," in H. Wautischer, ed. Tribal Epistemologies, 3-14, Ashgate Publ., 98; auth, "Reason and Awareness in Ethics," Querying the Philosphers Desire for Safety through Reasoning," Journal of Ethical Studies, 95, 2-17; auth, "Dreaming and the Cognitive Revolution," Guest Editorial, Anthropology of Consciousness, 5/3 94, 1-2; auth, "On Love and Awareness," Dialogue and Humanism IV/2-3 94, 31-40. **CONTACT ADDRESS** Dept of Philosophy, Sonoma State Univ, 1801 E Cotati Ave, Rohnert Park, CA 94928-3609. **EMAIL** wautisch@sonoma.edu

WAUZZINSKI, ROBERT
PERSONAL Born 04/18/1950, Farrell, PA, m, 1975, 2 children **DISCIPLINE** PHILOSOPHY, RELIGION **EDUCATION** Clarion Univ, BS; Pittsburgh Theol Sem, MDiv; Univ Pittsburgh, PhD. **CAREER** Edward B. Lindaman Endowed Chair of Commun, Tech and Change, 86-92; sr scholar, Ind Univ Purdue, 92-94; prof, Ball State UNiv, 94-. **HONORS AND AWARDS** Distinguished Scholar, Thomas Staley Found, 93; Chavane Vis Scholar, Baylor Univ, 87. **MEMBERSHIPS** SHOT; Am Acad of Relig. **RESEARCH** Philosophy of Technology, Religion and Economics, Philosophy of Economics. **SELECTED PUBLICATIONS** Auth, Between God and Gold: Protestant Evangelicalism and the Industrial Revolution, 1824-1914; auth, Discerning Prometheus: The Cry for Wisdom in an Age of Technology; auth, More Than Money: The Story of Dwelling House Savings and Loan, (forthcoming). **CONTACT ADDRESS** Dept Philos & Religious Studies, Ball State Univ, Muncie, IN 47306. **EMAIL** wabber15@aol.com

WAY, GARY DARRYL
PERSONAL Born 02/25/1958, Newark, NJ, m, 1987 **DISCIPLINE** LAW **EDUCATION** Rutgers Coll, New Brunswick, NJ, BA 1980; New York Univ School of Law, New York City, JD 1983. **CAREER** Haight, Gardner, Poor & Havens, New York City, associate, 83-86; National Basketball Assn, New York City, staff Attorney, 86-88; NBA Properties Inc, New York City, asst general counsel, 88-. **SELECTED PUBLICATIONS** Author of "Japanese Employers and Title VII," 1983. **CONTACT ADDRESS** NBA Properties Inc, 645 Fifth Ave, New York, NY 10022.

WAY, ROSEMARY CAIRNS
DISCIPLINE LAW **EDUCATION** Queen's Univ, BM, LLM; Univ Western Ontario, LLB, MM. **CAREER** Assoc prof. **RESEARCH** Criminal law theory and the impact of the Charter of Rights on the substantive response to violence against women and law reform initiatives in this area. **SELECTED PUBLICATIONS** Auth, pubs on criminal law theory and impact of the Charter of Right; co-auth, Dimensions of Criminal Law. **CONTACT ADDRESS** Fac Common Law, Univ of Ottawa, Fauteux Hall, 57 Louis Pasteur, Ottawa, ON, Canada K1N 6N5. **EMAIL** rmcairns@uottawa.ca

WAYMACK, MARK H.
DISCIPLINE PHILOSOPHY **EDUCATION** Johns Hopkins Univ, PhD, 87. **CAREER** Assoc prof; co-dir, philos dept's grad prog in Health Care Ethics; Buehler Center on Aging fel; adj asst prof Med, Northwestern Univ Med Sch for its Prog on Med Ethics and Humanities in Med; former fac, Col William and Mary, Univ Md Baltimore County & Univ Md Sch Med. **MEMBERSHIPS** Chicago Clin Ethics Prog; Soc for Health and Human Values & Amer Soc on Aging. **RESEARCH** Health care ethics; ancient Greek ethics, especially Plato; early modern philosophy, especially Hutcheson, Hume; Scottish moral philosophy. **SELECTED PUBLICATIONS** Coauth, Medical Ethics and the Elderly, Health Admin Press, 88; Single-Malt Whiskeys of Scotland, Open Ct, 92; The Book of Classic American Whiskeys, Open Ct, 95. **CONTACT ADDRESS** Dept of Philosophy, Loyola Univ, Chicago, 820 N Michigan Ave, Chicago, IL 60611.

WAYNE, ANDREW
DISCIPLINE PHILOSOPHY OF SCIENCE **EDUCATION** Univ Toronto, BS, 89; Univ Calif, San Diego, PhD, 94. **CAREER** Ass prof; dir, Sci and Hum Aff Prog, Concordia Univ. **RESEARCH** History of physics, philosophy of physics, philosophy of science, epistemology, logic, and science and technology studies. **SELECTED PUBLICATIONS** Auth, "Bayesianism and Diverse Evidence," Philosophy of Science, (95), 111-21; auth, "Theoetical Unity: The Case of the Standard Mode," Perspectives on Science 4, (96), 391-407; auth, "Degrees of Freedom and the Interpretation of Quantum Field Theory," Erkenntnis 46, (97) 165-73; **CONTACT ADDRESS** Dept of Philos, Concordia Univ, Montreal, 1455 de Maisonneuve W, Montreal, QC, Canada H3G 1M8. **EMAIL** awayne@alcor.concordia.ca

WAYSDORF, SUSAN L.
DISCIPLINE FAMILY LAW AND HEALTH LAW **EDUCATION** Univ Chicago, AB, 72; Univ MD, JD, 91. **CAREER** Assoc prof, tchr & co-dir, HIV-AIDS/Publ Entitlements Clin; Skadden Arps fel & staff atty, Whitman-Walker Legal Serv Dept, Wash DC; adj prof, Howard Univ Sch Law & Am Univ WAsh Col Law; consulted, White House Off of Nat AIDS Policy & Domestic Policy Coun. **HONORS AND AWARDS** Helped to draft legislation affecting women and parents with AIDS, kinship care providers, and prisoners with AIDS. **MEMBERSHIPS** Expert on the issues of women, families and AIDS, and access to health care for the poor; served on the fac for, DC Bar training in family law, child custody, and AIDS advocacy. **SELECTED PUBLICATIONS** Publ on, issues of women, families and AIDS, and access to health care for the poor. **CONTACT ADDRESS** School of Law, Univ of District of Columbia, 4200 Connecticut Ave Northwest, Washington, DC 20008.

WEATHERFORD, ROY C.
PERSONAL Born 05/30/1943, Middlebrook, AK, m, 1966, 1 child **DISCIPLINE** PHILOSOPHY **EDUCATION** Harvard Univ, PhD, 72. **CAREER** Prof, Univ of South Florida, 72-. **HONORS AND AWARDS** Danforth Grad Fel; Bechtel Prize in Philos. **MEMBERSHIPS** Fla Philos Asn; APA. **RESEARCH** Ethics; Epistemology. **SELECTED PUBLICATIONS** Auth, Philosophical Foundations of Probability Theory; The Implications of Determinism; World Peace and the Human Family. **CONTACT ADDRESS** Dept of Philosophy, Univ of So Florida, Tampa, FL 33620. **EMAIL** Roy_Weatherford_PhD72@post.harvard.edu

WEATHERLY, JON A.
PERSONAL Born 11/29/1958, Indianapolis, IN, m, 1979, 2 children **DISCIPLINE** THEOLOGY **EDUCATION** Cincinnati Bible Col, BA, 81, MA, 82; Trinity Evangelical Divinity Sch, Mdiv, 84; Univ Aberdeen, PhD, 92. **CAREER** Assoc Min, Southside Christian Church, 84-87; from assoc prof to prof to chemn, 90-, Cincinnati Bible Col and Sem. **HONORS AND AWARDS** Excellence in Tchg Awd; Greater Cincinnati Consortium of Colleges and Universities; valedictorian, 81, cincinnati bible col. **MEMBERSHIPS** Society of Biblical Literature; Evangelical Theological Society; Tyndale Fel. **RESEARCH** Theology of Luke-Acts; early Jewish-Christian relations. **SELECTED PUBLICATIONS** Auth, Monk, Mercenary or Missionary: How Do You Pay Your Preacher, 87; auth, The Jews in Luke-Acts, 89; auth, The Authenticity of 1 Thessalonians 2. 13-16: Additional Evidence, 91; auth, Anti-Semitism, 92; rev, History, Literature and Society in the Books of Acts, 98. **CONTACT ADDRESS** Cincinnati Bible Col and Sem, 2700 Glenway Ave, Cincinnati, OH 45204. **EMAIL** jon.weatherly@cincybible.edu

WEATHERSTON, MARTIN B.
PERSONAL Born 05/16/1956, Hamilton, ON, Canada, m, 1998, 3 children **DISCIPLINE** PHILOSPHY **EDUCATION** Univ Toronto, BA, 79; MA, 82; PhD, 88. **CAREER** Asst Prof, John Carroll Univ, 88-89; Asst Prof, Univ Toronto, 89-91; From Asst Prof to Assoc. Prof, E Stroudsburg Univ, 92-. **MEMBERSHIPS** Heidegger Conf of N Am. **RESEARCH** Heidegger, Kant. **SELECTED PUBLICATIONS** Rev, basic Questions of Philosophy: Selected "Problems" of "Logic," Ind Univ Pr (Bloomington, IN), 94; auth, "Heidegger on Assertion and Kantian Intuition," J of Speculative Philos, vol 5, no 4: 276-297; auth, "The Rigor of Heidegger's Thought," Man and World, vol 25, no 2: 181-198; auth, "Formal Intuitions and the Categories," Int Studies in Philos, XXV/3: 75-86; auth, "Kant's Assessment of Music in the 'Critique of Judgement'," The Brit J of Aesthetics, vol 36, no 1 (96); rev, Phenomenological Interpretation of Kant's Critique of Pure Reason, Ind Univ Pr (Bloomington, IN), 97; auth, "Technology and Teleology in Heidegger," Tekhnehma (forthcoming). **CONTACT ADDRESS** Dept Philos, East Stroudsburg Univ of Pennsylvania, 200 Prospect St, East Stroudsburg, PA 18301-2991. **EMAIL** mweather@po-box.esu.edu

WEAVER, DOROTHY JEAN
PERSONAL Born 01/21/1950, Harrisonburg, VA, s **DISCIPLINE** NEW TESTAMENT **EDUCATION** Union Theological Sem VA, PhD 87; Univ Berne Switzerland Ex Fel 81-82. **CAREER** Eastern Mennonite Seminary, prof 96-; Tantur Ecumenical Inst Jerusalem, vis sch 96; Near East Sch Theology Lebanon, vis prof, 95-96; Eastern Mennonite Sem, asst prof. assoc prof, 87-96; Assoc Biblical Seminaries, vis lect 86-87; Eastern Mennonite Sem, instr 84-86. **HONORS AND AWARDS** Berne Exch fel; union Theo Sem VA; Women's Lectshp; Assoc Menn Bib Sem. **MEMBERSHIPS** CBA; SBL; Matthew Gp mem. **RESEARCH** Gospel of Matthew; Narrative Criticism. **SELECTED PUBLICATIONS** Auth, Matthew's Missionary Discourse: A Literary Critical Analysis, Sheffield Eng, Sheffield Acad Press, 90; Between text and Sermon: John 18:1-19:42, Interpretation, 95; AIDS in the Congregation: Biblical Perspectives, Conrad Grebal Rev, 95; Power and Powerlessness: Matthew's Use of Irony in the Portrayal of Political Leaders, in: Treasures New and Old: Recent Contributions to Matthean Studies, eds, David R. Bauer and Mark Allen Powell, Atl GA, Sch Press, 96; rev, Households and Discipleship: A Study of Matthew, by Warren Carter, Sheffield JSOT Press, 94, and What They are Saying About Matthew's Sermon on the Mount? by Warren Carter, NY/Mahwah NJ, Paulist Press, 94, in: Crit Rev of Books In Religion, 96. **CONTACT ADDRESS** Dept of New Testament, Eastern Mennonite Univ, Eastern Mennonite Seminary, Harrisonburg, VA 22802-2462. **EMAIL** weaverdj@emu.edu

WEAVER, DOUG
PERSONAL Born 04/22/1956, Fredericksburg, VA, m, 1979, 2 children **DISCIPLINE** CHURCH HISTORY **EDUCATION** Miss Col, BA, 78; Southern Baptist Theol Sem, M Div, 81; PhD, 85. **CAREER** Asst prof, Bluefield Col, 86-88; prof, Chair, Brewton-Parker Col, 89-. **HONORS AND AWARDS** Jordan Teacher Excellence Awd, Brewton Parker Col **MEMBERSHIPS** AAR; ASCH; NABPR. **RESEARCH** American Religion: Pentecostalism, Baptist History. **SELECTED PUBLICATIONS** Auth, The Healer Prophet: William Marrion Branham, Mercer Univ Pr, 87; auth, A Cloud of Witnesses, Smyth & Helwyn Publ, 93; auth, From Our Christian Heritage, Smyth & Helwys Publ, 98; ed, The Whitsitt Journal; auth, Every Town Needs a Downtown Church: A Hist of FBC Gainesville, Fl, Southern Baptist Hist Soc, 00. **CONTACT ADDRESS** Dept Relig and Philos, Brewton-Parker Col, PO Box 2120, Mount Vernon, GA 30445-0197. **EMAIL** dweaver@cybersouth.com

WEAVER, J. DENNY
PERSONAL Born 03/20/1941, Kansas City, KS, m, 1965, 3 children **DISCIPLINE** RELIGION **EDUCATION** Goshen Col, BA, 63; Goshen Bibl Sem, MDiv, 70; Duke Univ, PhD, 75. **CAREER** Asst prof, 74-75, asst prof relig, 75-78, assoc prof relig, 78-83, prof relig, 83- , chemn dept of hist and relig, 93- , Bluffton College; vis prof of theol, Canadian Mennonite Bible Col, 90-91. **MEMBERSHIPS** Am Soc of Church Hist; Am Acad of Relig; Conf on Faith and Hist; Mennonite Hist Soc. **RESEARCH** Contextual theologies; nonviolent theology; issues in Christology and atonement. **SELECTED PUBLICATIONS** Auth, The Socially Active Community: An Alternative Ecclesiology, in Sawatsky, ed, The Limits of Perfectionism: Conversations with J Lawrence Burkholder, Pandora, 93; auth, Christus Victor, Ecclesiology, and Christology, Mennonite Q Rev, 94; auth, Some Theological Implications of Christus Victor, Mennonite Q Rev, 94; auth, Narrative Theology in an Anabaptist-Mennonite Context, Conrad Grebel Rev, 94; auth, Understandings of Salvation: The Church, Pietistic Experience, and Non-Resistance, in Bowman, ed, Anabaptist Currents: History in Conversation with the Present, Bridgewater Col, 95; auth, The Anabaptist Vision: A Historical or a Theological Future, Conrad Grebel Rev, 95; auth, Amish and Mennonite Soteriology: Revivalism and Free Church Theologizing in the Nineteenth Century, Fides et Historia, 95; auth, Pacifism, in Hillerbrand, ed, The Oxford Encyclopedia of the Reformation, Oxford, 96; auth, Christus Victor, Nonviolence, and Other Religions, in, Weaver, ed, Mennonite Theology in Face of Modernity: Essays in Honor of Gordon D. Kaufman, Bethel Col, 96; auth, Peace-Shaped Theology, Faith and Freedom : A J of Christian Ethics, 96; auth, Keeping Salvation Ethical: Mennonite and Amish Atonement theology in the Late Nineteenth Century, Herald, 97; auth, Teaching for Peace, in Huebner, ed, Mennonite Education in a Post-Christian World: Essays Presented at the Consultation on Higher Education, Winnnipeg, June 1997, CMBC Pub, 98; auth, Reading Sixteenth-Century Anabaptism Theologically: Implications for Modern Mennonites as a Peace Church, Conrad Grebel Rev, 98; auth, Making Yahweh's Rule Visible in Grimsrud and Johns, ed, Peace and Justice Shall Embrace: Power and Theopolitics in the Bible: Essays in Honor of Millard Lind, Pandora Press US, 99; auth, Theology in the Mirror of the Martyred and Oppressed: Reflections on the Intersections of Yoder and Cone, in Hanerwas, efal. Ed., The Wisdom of the Cross: Essays in Honor of John Howard Yoder, Eerdmans, 99; auth, Nicaez, Womanist Theology, and Anabaptist Particularity, in, Biesecker-Mast and Biesecker-Mast, ed., Anabaptists and Postmodernity, Pandora Press US, 00; auth, Anabaptist Theology in Face of Postmodernity: A Proposal for the Thrid Millenium, Pandora Press US, 00; auth, Reading the Past, Present, and Future in Revelation, in Johns, ed, Apocalypticism and Millenialism: Shaping a Believers Church Eschatology for the 21st Century, Pandora Press Canada, 00. **CONTACT ADDRESS** Bluffton Col, 280 W College Ave, Bluffton, OH 45817-1196. **EMAIL** weaverjd@bluffton.edu

WEAVER, MARY JO
DISCIPLINE RELIGIOUS STUDIES **EDUCATION** Univ Notre Dame, PhD, 73. **CAREER** Prof, Ind Univ, Bloomington. **RESEARCH** Roman Catholicism; contemporary Christianity; feminism and Christianity. **SELECTED PUBLICATIONS** Auth, New Catholic Women, 95; Springs of Water in a Dry Land, 92; auth, Being Right: Conservative American Catholics, 95; Introduction to Christianity, 97; auth, What's Left?: Liberal American Catholics, 99. **CONTACT ADDRESS** Dept of Religious Studies, Indiana Univ, Bloomington, Sycamore Hall 230, Bloomington, IN 47405. **EMAIL** weaverm@indiana.edu

WEAVER, RUSSELL L.
PERSONAL Born 10/24/1952, Kansas City, MO, m, 1995, 2 children **DISCIPLINE** LAW, POLITICAL SCIENCE **EDUCATION** Univ of Mo, BA, 74; JD, 78. **CAREER** Herbert Heff Chair of Excellence, Cecil C. Humphreys Sch of Law at Univ of Memphis, 92; distinguished vis prof, S Tex Col of Law, 98-99; prof, Louis D. Brandeis Sch of Law at the Univ of Louisville, 82-. **HONORS AND AWARDS** Res Awd for Outstanding Res, Scholar and Creative Activity, 93; award for scholar, Louis D. Brandeis Sch of Law, 92 & 93; teaching award, Louis D. Brandeis Sch of Law, 95; Brown, Todd & Heyburn Fel, 95-97 & 98-99; service award, Louis D. Brandeis Sch of Law, 98; Pres Awd for Distinguished Service, Univ of Louisville, 98; Distinguished Univ Scholar, Univ of Louisville, 99-; career achievement award, Louis D. Brandeis Sch of Law, 00. **RESEARCH** Constitutional Law, Defamation, Free Speech, Administrative Law. **SELECTED PUBLICATIONS** Coauth, The Constitutional Law Anthology, Anderson, 97; coauth, Communications Law: Media, Entertainment & Regulation, Anderson, 97; coauth, Administrative Law and Practice: Problems and Cases, West, 97; coauth, Modern Remedies: Cases, Problems & Exercises, West, 97; coauth, Readings in Criminal Law, Anderson, 98; coauth, Selected Federal and State Administrative and Regulatory Laws, West, 99; coauth, Constitutional Law: Cases, History & Dialogues 2nd edition, Anderson, 99. **CONTACT ADDRESS** Sch of Law, Univ of Louisville, 2301 S 3rd St, Louisville, KY 40292-0001.

WEBB, EUGENE
PERSONAL Born 11/10/1938, Santa Monica, CA, m, 1964 **DISCIPLINE** COMPARATIVE LITERATURE, RELIGION **EDUCATION** Univ Calif, Los Angeles, BA, 60; Columbia Univ, MA, 26, PhD(comp lit), 65. **CAREER** Asst prof English, Simon Fraser Univ, 65-66; asst prof, 66-76, Prof Comp Relig & Comp Lit, Univ Wash, 76-. **MEMBERSHIPS** Am Acad Relig. **RESEARCH** Twentieth century English, German and French literature; 18th century English; philosophy of history. **SELECTED PUBLICATIONS** Auth, Samuel Beckett: A Study of His Novels, 70 & The Plays of Samuel Beckett, 72 Univ Wash; Peter Owen, London; The Dark Dove: The Sacred and Secular in Modern Lit, 75 & Eric Voegelin: Philosopher of History, 81, Univ Wash. **CONTACT ADDRESS** Dept of English, Univ of Washington, Seattle, WA 98195.

WEBB, GISELA
PERSONAL Born 07/15/1949, San Juan, Puerto Rico, m, 2 children **DISCIPLINE** ISLAMIC STUDIES, COMPARATIVE RELIGION STUDIES, PHILOSOPHY OF MYSTICISM **EDUCATION** Temple Univ, PhD, 89. **CAREER** Assoc prof Dept Relig Stud, Seton Hall Univ, 89-; Phi Beta Kappa; NEH award. **MEMBERSHIPS** AAR; MESA; ACSIS. **RESEARCH** Medieval and contemporary developments of mysticism, esp Sufism womens studies. **SELECTED PUBLICATIONS** Tradition and Innovation in Contemporary American Islamic Spirituality, Muslim Communities in North America, SUNY Press, 94; Islam, Sufism, & Subud, An Alternative Relig, SUNY Press, 95. **CONTACT ADDRESS** 125 Union Ave, Bala-Cynwyd, PA 19004. **EMAIL** webbgise@shu.edu

WEBBER, GEORGE WILLIAMS
PERSONAL Born 05/02/1920, Des Moines, IA, m, 1943, 5 children **DISCIPLINE** CHRISTIAN ETHICS **EDUCATION** Harvard Col, AB, 42; Union Theol Sem, MDiv, 48; Columbia Univ, PhD, 63. **CAREER** Mem fac, Union Theol Sem, 48-73; Pres, NY Theol Sem, 69-, Group ministry, E Harlem Protestant Parish, 48-65; dir, Metrop Urban Serv Tr, 65-69. **HONORS AND AWARDS** STD, Gen Theol Sem, 69; DD, Yale Univ, 81. **SELECTED PUBLICATIONS** Auth, God's Colony in Man's World, 60, Congregation in Mission, 64 & Today's Church, 79, Abingdon; Led by the Spirit, Pilgrim Books, 90. **CONTACT ADDRESS** New York Theol Sem, 5 W 29th St, New York, NY 10001-4501.

WEBBER, RANDALL C.
PERSONAL Born 11/28/1961, Oak Ridge, TN, s **DISCIPLINE** HISTORY; RELIGIOUS STUDIES, SOCIOLOGY **EDUCATION** Furman Univ, BA, 82; Southern Baptist Theological Seminary, MDiv, 85, PhD, 89. **CAREER** Manuscript editor, 87-89, Paradigms; asst ed, 89-92, Univ MI; dir, emergency housing, Salvation Army, 92- ; proprietor, Webber Church Consulting, 97- . **HONORS AND AWARDS** Who's Who in Bibl Studies and Archaeol, 93. **MEMBERSHIPS** Soc of Bibl Lit; Am Acad of Bereavement; Nat Bd of Cognitive Behavioral Therapists. **RESEARCH** Early Christianity; Grief; Politics. **SELECTED PUBLICATIONS** Auth, Successful Grief and Chronic Homelessness: Is There a Relationship? Grief Work, 95; auth, Kentucky Reader Proposes Ethics Code for Churches, Baptist Today, 95; auth, Reader-Response Analysis of the Epistle of James, 96; auth, An Idealistic Reading of the Apocalype, 99. **CONTACT ADDRESS** 325 E Kentucky St, Louisville, KY 40203-2709. **EMAIL** rcwbbb@juno.com

WEBER, LEONARD J.
DISCIPLINE ETHICS **EDUCATION** Josephinum Col, BA; Marquette Univ, MA; McMaster Univ, PhD. **CAREER** Prof,dir, Univ Detroit Mercy, 72-. **RESEARCH** Practical ethical issues in health care, management, and public service. **CONTACT ADDRESS** Dept of Philosophy, Univ of Detroit Mercy, 4001 W McNichols Rd, PO Box 19900, Detroit, MI 48219-0900. **EMAIL** WEBERLJ@udmercy.edu

WEBER, MARK E.
PERSONAL Born 09/26/1960, Rapid City, SD, m, 1982, 2 children **DISCIPLINE** PHILOSOPHY **EDUCATION** Whenton Col , BA, 82; Yale Univ, MA, 85; Boston Univ, PhD, 92. **CAREER** Adj asst prof, Univ Conn; Quinnipiac Coll; Sacred Heart Univ; Univ New Haven. **MEMBERSHIPS** Am Philos Asn; Soc for Philos and Psychol. **RESEARCH** Wittgenstein; Philosophy of Mind. **SELECTED PUBLICATIONS** Wittgenstein on Language: Games of Visual Sensation and Language - Games of Visual Objects, Southern J of Philos, 93; Representation and Intention: Wittgenstein on what makes a picture of a target, Southern J of Philos, 98. **CONTACT ADDRESS** 198 Foster St., New Haven, CT 06511. **EMAIL** weberme@aol.com

WEBER, MICHAEL
PERSONAL Born 03/27/1965, Toronto, ON, Canada **DISCIPLINE** PHILOSOPHY **EDUCATION** Williams Col, BA, 87; Oxford Univ, BA, 90; Univ Mich, PhD, 98. **CAREER** Asst prof, Yale Univ, 98- . **HONORS AND AWARDS** Mellon Fel, 90. **MEMBERSHIPS** APA. **RESEARCH** Ethics, political philosophy. **SELECTED PUBLICATIONS** Auth, The Resilience of the Atlais Paradox, Ethics, 98. **CONTACT ADDRESS** Dept of Philosophy, Yale Univ, New Haven, CT 06520. **EMAIL** michael.weber@yale.edu

WEBER, SAMUEL F.
PERSONAL Born 06/13/1947, Chicago, IL, s **DISCIPLINE** RELIGION **EDUCATION** St Meinrad Col, BA, 70; MDiv, 90; Pontifical Athenaeum Saint Anselm, Rome, STL, 75; Univ

Colo, MA, 91. **CAREER** Fac mem, Saint Meinrad Sch of Theol, 76-97; fac mem, Saint Meinrad Col, 84-97; assoc prof, Wake Forest Univ, 98-. **MEMBERSHIPS** N Am Acad of Litugy, Archeol Inst of Am; Class Assoc of the Midwest and South, Am Guild of Organists; Hymn Soc of am; Soc for Cath Liturgy. **SELECTED PUBLICATIONS** Coed, Hymnal for the Hours, GIA, 89; auth, "Taking Up the Psalter", Reformed Liturgy and Music 23, (89); auth, "The Carthusians", Dictionary of Christian Spirituality, Liturgical Pr, (Collegeville), 93. **CONTACT ADDRESS** Dept Relig, Wake Forest Univ, PO Box 7719, Winston-Salem, NC 27109.

WEBER, THEODORE R.
PERSONAL Born 06/07/1928, New Orleans, LA, m, 1955, 2 children **DISCIPLINE** THEOLOGY **EDUCATION** Louisana St Univ, BA, 47; Yale Univ, BD, 50, MA, 56, PhD, 58. **CAREER** Pastor, Louisana & Conn, 45-56; prof, soc ethics, 58-97, Candler Schl of Theol, Emory Univ; ministeral staff, 92-93, St Giles Cathedral, Edinburgh; vis prof, Chinese Univ, Hong Kong, 99. **HONORS AND AWARDS** Pres, Soc of Christian Ethics, U.S. & Can, 88; Emory Williams Dist Tchr Awd, 87; hon vis scholar, New Col Edinburgh Univ, 92-93. **MEMBERSHIPS** Soc of Christian Ehics, Societas Ethica; Soc for the Stud of Christian Ethics; Am Acad of Relig. **RESEARCH** Christian political thought; John Wesley's ethics; Reinhold Niebuhr; just war theory. **SELECTED PUBLICATIONS** Auth, Truth & Political Leadership, Pres Address to Soc of Christian Ethics in the U. S. & Can, Ann of Soc of Christian Ethics, 89; auth, Christian Realism, Power, & Peace, Theo Pol & Peace, Orbis Books, 89; auth, Thinking Theologically about International Development, Making of an Economic Vision: John Paul II's On Soc Concern, Univ Press of Amer, 91; art, Political Order in Ordo Sahutis; A Wesleyan Theory of Political Institutions, J of Church & State 3T, 95; auth, Politics in the Order of Salvation, Abingdon Press, 01 **CONTACT ADDRESS** 1641 Ridgewood Dr NE, Atlanta, GA 30307-1250. **EMAIL** reltrw@emory.edu

WEBER, TIMOTHY P.
PERSONAL Born 05/25/1947, Los Angeles, LA, m, 1968, 2 children **DISCIPLINE** CHURCH HISTORY **EDUCATION** UCLA, BA, 69; Fuller Theol Sem, M Div, 72; Univ Chicago, MA, 74, PhD, 76. **CAREER** Asst, assoc, prof, 76-92, Denver Sem; David T Porter Prof, Church hist, 92-96, S Baptist Theol Sem; vice pres, acad affairs, dean of sem, prof, 97-, N Baptist Theol Sem. **RESEARCH** General hist of Christianity; Amer relig hist, evangelicalism, fundamentalism, millennial movements. **SELECTED PUBLICATIONS** Auth, "Living in the Shadow of the Second Coming," U of Chicago Press, 87. **CONTACT ADDRESS** No Baptist Theol Sem, 660 # Butterfield Rd, Lombard, IL 60148. **EMAIL** tpweber@seminary.edu

WEBERMAN, DAVID
PERSONAL Born 07/02/1955, Detroit, MI, s **DISCIPLINE** LAW **EDUCATION** Univ of Munich, MA, 82; Columbia Univ, M Phil, 87, PhD, 90. **CAREER** Asst prof, Univ Wis, 90-98; asst prof, Ga State Univ, 99-. **HONORS AND AWARDS** Pres fel, Columbia Univ, 83-85; fel, Law & Philosophy, Harvard Univ, 98-99. **MEMBERSHIPS** Amer Philos Asn; Soc Phenomenol & Existential Philos; N Am Sarte Soc. **RESEARCH** 20th Century European philosophy; Philosophy of history; Law interpretation. **SELECTED PUBLICATIONS** Auth, Historische Objektivitat, Peter Lang, 91; Foucault's Reconception of Power, Philos Forum, 95; Heidegger and the Disclosive Character of the Emotions, The S Jour of Philos, 96; Sartre, Emotions and Wallowing, Amer Philos Quart, 96; Liberal Democracy, Autonomy and Ideology Critique, Soc Theory and Practice, 97; The Non-Fixity of the Historical Past, Rev of Metaphysics, 97; coauth, "Heidegger and the Source(s) of Intelligibility," Continental Philosophy Rev 3 (98): 369-386. **CONTACT ADDRESS** Dept of Philos, Georgia State Univ, PO Box 4089, Atlanta, GA 30302-4089. **EMAIL** dweberman@gsu.edu

WEBSTER, WILLIAM H.
PERSONAL Born 10/26/1946, New York, NY, m, 1967, 1 child **DISCIPLINE** LAW **EDUCATION** New York Univ, BA (cum laude), 1972; Univ of California, Berkeley, School of Law, JD, 1975. **CAREER** Black Law Journal, UCLA & Univ of California at Berkeley, research assoc, 73; Natl Economic Devel & Law Project, post-grad, 74-76; Natl Economic Devel & Law Center, Berkeley, CA, atty, 76-82; Hunter & Anderson, partner, 83-; Webster & Anderson, managing partner, 93-. **HONORS AND AWARDS** Martin Luther King Fellowship; New York State Regents Incentive Awds; Howard Memorial Fund Scholarship; Alpha Phi Alpha Scholarship. **MEMBERSHIPS** Past mem bd of dirs, Natl Training Inst for Comm Economic Devel, Artisans Cooperative Inc; past mem, Mayor's Housing Task Force Berkeley; mem, State Bar of California, US Dist Ct No Dist of California, US Tax Ct, Natl Assoc of Bond Lawyers, Natl Bar Assoc, Charles Houston Bar Assn; past mem, City of Berkeley Citizens Comm on Responsible Investments; Kappa Alpha Psi. **SELECTED PUBLICATIONS** "Tax Savings through Intercorporate Billing," Economic Devel Law Center Report, 1980; pub, "Housing, Structuring a Housing Development," Economic Devel Law Center Report, 1978; various other publications. **CONTACT ADDRESS** Webster & Anderson Law Office, 469 Ninth St, Ste 240, Oakland, CA 94607. **EMAIL** bwebster@websteranderson.com

WECHSLER, BURTON D.
DISCIPLINE CONSTITUTIONAL LAW **EDUCATION** Univ Mich, AB, 47; Harvard Law Sch, JD, 49 **CAREER** Prof, Am Univ. **HONORS AND AWARDS** Alumni Distinguished Tchr Awd; Outstanding Tchr Awd Am Univ, Wash Col Law, 92, 90, 89, 88, 84, 80, 79; Burton Wechsler Moot Court Competition, 93; Third-year class Outstanding Teacher Awd, 96, 94; Outstanding Fac Awd for Outstanding Teaching, 95. **RESEARCH** Constitutional Law; Federal Courts; First Amendment. **SELECTED PUBLICATIONS** Auth, "Inter vivos Estate Trust," 103 Trusts and Estates 1192, 64; rev, The Petitioners: The Story of the Supreme Court of the United States and the Negro 1, Valparaiso Law Review 179, 66; auth, "Federal Courts, State Criminal Law and the First Amendment," 49 New York Univ Law Review 740, 74; auth, "A Tribute to Justice Douglas," 1 Antioch Law Journal 1, 81. **CONTACT ADDRESS** American Univ, 4400 Massachusetts Ave, Washington, DC 20016.

WECKMAN, GEORGE
PERSONAL Born 03/20/1939, Philadelphia, PA **DISCIPLINE** HISTORY OF RELIGION **EDUCATION** Philadelphia Lutheran Sem, BD, 63; Univ Chicago, PhD, 69. **CAREER** Asst prof Philos, 68-72, assoc prof, 72- , Ohio Univ. **MEMBERSHIPS** AAR. **RESEARCH** Monasticism. **SELECTED PUBLICATIONS** Auth, My Brothers' Place: An American Lutheran Monastery, Lawrenceville, VA, Brunswick Publ Corp, 92; Reduction in the Classroom, in Religion and Reductionism: essays on Eliade, Segal, and the Challenge of the Social Sciences for the Study of Religion, ed, Thomas A. Idinopulos and Edward Yonan, Leiden, E.J. Brill, 94, 211-219; Respect of Others' Sacreds, in The Sacred and its Scholars, ed Thomas A. Idinopulos and Edward Yonan, Leiden, E.J. Brill, 96. **CONTACT ADDRESS** Dept of Philosophy, Ohio Univ, 19 Park Pl, Athens, OH 45701. **EMAIL** weckman@ohio.edu

WECKSTEIN, DONALD THEODORE
PERSONAL Born 03/15/1932, Newark, NJ, m, 1993, 4 children **DISCIPLINE** LAW **EDUCATION** Univ Wis-Madison, BBA, 54; Univ TX, Austin, JD, 58; Yale Univ, LLM, 59. **CAREER** Asst prof law, Sch Law, Univ CT, 59-62; assoc prof, Col Law, Univ TN, 62-67; prof, Sch Law, Univ CT, 67-72; dean, 72-81, Prof Law, Sch Law, Univ San Diego, 72-; consult, Admin Conf US, 69-72; chmn, San Diego County Employee Rels Panel, 73-75; arbitrator labor, Fed Mediation Conciliation Serv, 77. **HONORS AND AWARDS** Phi Delta Phi (Honors) Legal Fraternity, Univ TX, 56-58; First Prize, Nathan Burkan Copyright Competition, Univ TX, 57; Am Jurisprudence Awd, Public Utilities, Univ TX, 57. **MEMBERSHIPS** Am Arbit Asn; Indust Rel Res Asn; SPIDR; Nat Acad Arbitrators; Asn Am Law Sch; CA Dispute Resolution Coun; Southern Calif Mediation Asn; Int Soc for Labor Law & Social Security; Dispute Resolution Forum of San Diego; Am Bar Asn; San Diego County Bar Asn; Calif State Bar; TX Bar Asn; served as Ch, mem Bd Dir, Pres, and other numerous positions in many of these and other past orgs. **RESEARCH** Fed court jurisdiction; legal profession and ethics; labor law and arbitration; alternative dispute resolution. **SELECTED PUBLICATIONS** Ed, Education in the Professional Responsibilities of the Lawyer, Univ Va, 70; coauth, Moore's Federal Practice, Matthew Bender, 2nd ed, 64; coauth, Professional Responsibility in a Nutshell, West Publ Co, 80, 2nd ed, 91; author of numerous articles. **CONTACT ADDRESS** Sch of Law, Univ of San Diego, 5998 Alcala Park, San Diego, CA 92110-2492. **EMAIL** donaldw@acusd.edu

WEDDLE, DAVID L.
PERSONAL Born 01/27/1942, m, 2 children **DISCIPLINE** RELIGION **EDUCATION** Grace Bible Col, Grand Rapids, Mich, BRE, 64; Hope Col, Holland Mich, BA, 66; Harvard Univ, MA, 70, PhD, 73. **CAREER** Asst prof relig stud, Westmont Col, 70-72; lectr relig stud, Univ Calif, 73; asst prof, 73-78, assoc prof, 78-84, prof of religion, 84- , Cornell Col. **HONORS AND AWARDS** Summa Cum Laude, 66; res scholar reading prog of Cedar Rapids Public Lib, funded by US Inst for Peace, 94-95; Norman & Richard Small Senior Faculty Chair, Cornell Col, 98-00. **MEMBERSHIPS** Am Acad Relig; Am Soc of Church Hist; Am Theol Soc; Middle East Stud Asn. **RESEARCH** American religion; Christian theology; Islam. **SELECTED PUBLICATIONS** Auth, Jonathan Edwards on Men and Trees and the Problem of Solidarity, Harvard Theol Rev, 74; auth, The Image of the Self in Jonathan Edwards: A Study of Autobiography and Theology, J of the Am Acad of Relig, 75; auth, The Beauty of Faith in Jonathan Edwards, Ohio J of Relig Stud, 76; auth, The Democracy of Grace: Political Reflections on the Evangelical Theology of Jonathan Edwards, Dialog, 76; auth, The Law and the Revival: A new Divinity for the Settlements, Church Hist, 78; auth, The Liberator as Exorcist: James Cone and the Classic Doctrine of the Atonement, Relig in Life, 80; auth, Christians in Liberal Education, Relig Educ, 85; auth, The Law as Gospel: Revival and Reform in the Theology of Charles G. Finney, Scarecrow, 85; auth, The Melancholy Saint: Jonathan Edwards' Interpretation of David Brainerd as a Model of Evangelical Spirituality, Harvard Theol Rev, 88; auth, The Christian Science Textbook: An Analysis of the Religious Authority of Science and Health by Mary Baker Eddy, Harvard Theol Rev, 91. **CONTACT ADDRESS** 1181 Abbe Creek Rd, Mount Vernon, IA 52314-9726. **EMAIL** weddle@cornell-iowa.edu

WEDGWOOD, RALPH N.
PERSONAL Born 12/10/1964, Vancouver, BC, Canada, s **DISCIPLINE** PHILOSOPHY **EDUCATION** Oxford Univ, BA, 87; King's Col London, MA, 89; Cornell Univ, PhD, 94. **CAREER** UCLA, vis asst prof, 93-94; Univ of Stirling Scotland, lectr, 94-95; MIT, asst prof, 95-; assoc prof, 99-. **HONORS AND AWARDS** NHC fel. **MEMBERSHIPS** APA, BSET. **RESEARCH** Ethics; metaphysics; epistemology. **SELECTED PUBLICATIONS** Auth, The A Priori Rules of Rationality, Philosophy and Phenomenological Research, 99; auth, The Essence of Response-Dependence, Euro Rev Philos, 98; auth, The Fundamental Principle of Practical Reasoning, Intl Jour Philos Stud, 99; auth, Same-Sex Marriage: A Philosophical Defense, Philosophy and Sex, rev ed. 98; auth, Non-Cognitivism, Truth and Logic, Philos Stud, 97; auth, Theories of Content and Theories of Motivation, Euro Jour Philos, 98; auth, Conceptual Role Semantics for Moral Terms, Philosophical Review, (forthcoming); auth, The Price of Non-reductive Moral Realism, Ethical Theory and Moral Practice, 99; auth, The Price of Non-reductive Physicalism, Nous, 00. **CONTACT ADDRESS** Dept of Philosophy and Linguistics, Massachusetts Inst of Tech, Cambridge, MA 02139. **EMAIL** wedgwood@mit.edu

WEEKES, MARTIN EDWARD
PERSONAL Born 06/06/1933, New York, NY, m, 1984 **DISCIPLINE** LAW **EDUCATION** Manhattan Coll NYork, BS 1954; Univ of So CA, JD 1961. **CAREER** Douglas Aircraft Santa Monica CA, engr draftsman 1956-60; Charles Meram Co Los Angeles, engr 1960-62; Deputy District Atty 1962-63; Div Chief; Co Counsel 1963-. **HONORS AND AWARDS** Rector's Awd Episcopal Ch of the Advent 1967; Finished Second in All-Army Talent Contest 1956. **MEMBERSHIPS** First pres Frederick Douglass Child Devel Cntr 1963; mem bd dir Rose Brooks Sch of Performing Arts 1974-; mem Reserve Faculty EPA; Lectured on Environmental Law; guest lecturer USC; **SELECTED PUBLICATIONS** Twenty publications Library of Congress; contrib author CA Adminstr Agency Practice CEB. **CONTACT ADDRESS** County Counsel, LA County, 648 Hall of Administration, Los Angeles, CA 90012.

WEEMS, VERNON EUGENE, JR.
PERSONAL Born 04/27/1948, Waterloo, IA, s **DISCIPLINE** LAW **EDUCATION** Univ of IA, BA 1970; Univ of Miami Sch of Law, JD 1974. **CAREER** US Small Business Admin, atty/advisor 1977-78, 79-81; A Nation United Inc, pres/ceo/chmn bd 1982-85; Weems Law Office, Attorney 1978-; Weems Productions and Enterprises, ceo/consultant 1987-. **HONORS AND AWARDS** Recognition of Excellence 1986. **MEMBERSHIPS** Mem Amer Bar Assoc 1977-82, IA State Bar Assoc 1977-82, St Johns Lodge Prince Hall Affil 1977-86, Federal Bar Assoc 1979-82; mem bd of dirs Black Hawk County Iowa Branch NAACP. **SELECTED PUBLICATIONS** Publication "Tax Amnesty Blueprint for Economic Development," 1981; Leadership Awd OIC/Iowa 1982; Service Appreciation Awd Job Service of Iowa 1985; article "Chapter 11 Tax Subsidies," 1986. **CONTACT ADDRESS** Weems Productions/Enterprises, PO Box 72, Waterloo, IA 50704-0072.

WEIBE, PHILLIP H.
PERSONAL Born 08/23/1945, MB, Canada, m, 1968, 2 children **DISCIPLINE** PHILOSOPHY **EDUCATION** Univ Adelaide (philos), PhD, 73. **CAREER** Asst prof philos, Brandon Univ, Manitoba, 73-78; assoc prof philos, 78-88, Full Prof, Trinity Western Univ, Langley, BC, 88-. **HONORS AND AWARDS** Commonwealth Scholarship to Australia, 70-73. **MEMBERSHIPS** Can Philos Asn; Am Academy Relig. **RESEARCH** Philosophical theology; philosophy of science. **SELECTED PUBLICATIONS** Auth, Hempel and Instantial Confirmation, Philos Res Archives, 2, 76; Criteria of Strengthening Evidence, Philos Res Archives, 4, 78; Theism in an Age of Science, Univ Press Am, 88; Jesus' Divorce Exception, The J of the Evangelical Theol Soc, 32, 89; Existential Assumptions for Aristotelian Logic, The J of Philos Res, 16, 91; Authenticating Biblical Reports of Miracles, The J of Philos Res, 17, 92; Visions of Jesus: Direct Encounters from the New Testament to Today, Oxford Univ Press, 97. **CONTACT ADDRESS** Dept of Philos, Trinity Western Univ, 7600 Glover Rd., Langley, BC, Canada V2Y 1Y1. **EMAIL** pweibe@twu.ca

WEIDMANN, FREDERICK W.
PERSONAL Born 12/31/1961, Watford, Herfordshire, United Kingdom, m, 1984, 2 children **DISCIPLINE** RELIGION, THEOLOGY **EDUCATION** Muhlenberg Col, BA, 83; Yale Univ Divinity Sch, MDiv, 88; Yale Univ Grad Sch Arts and Scis, PhD, 93. **CAREER** Lectr, Yale Univ Divinity Sch, 94-95; asst prof of New Testament, Union Theol Sem, New York, 95-. **HONORS AND AWARDS** John F. Endors Res Grant, 92; Soc of Biblical Lit Res Grant, 96-97. **MEMBERSHIPS** Am Acad of Relig, Int Asn for Coptic Studies, North Am Patristic Soc, Soc for Biblical Lit. **RESEARCH** New Testament and other early Christian literature, particularly martyr literature; the social-historical and socio-rhetorical contexts of early Christians and their writings. **SELECTED PUBLICATIONS** Auth, Polycarp and John: The Harris Fragments and their Challenge to the Literary Tradition, Christianity and Judaism Series, no 12, Notre Dame: Univ Notre Dame Press (99); auth, "Paul (Saul of

Tarsus)," and "Jesus of Nazareth," in Chris von Dehsen, ed, Lives and Legacies: A Biographical Encyclopedia of People who Have Changed the World, vol 2: Philosophers and Religious Leaders, Phoenix: Oryx Press (99): auth, " 'Rushing Judgement'?: Willfulness and Martydom in Early Christianity," Union Sem Quart Rev, 53 (99): 61-69; auth, " 'To Sojourn' or 'To Dwell'?: Scripture and Identity in the Martyrdom of Polycarp," in Charles Bobertz and David Brakke, ed, Interpretation and (Early Christian Identity, Christianity and Judaism in Antiquity Series, Notre Dame: Univ of Notre Dame Press (forthcoming); auth, "Response to Walter Brueggemann, 'Vision for a New Church and a New Century Part II: Holiness Become Generosity," Union Sem Quart Rev (forthcoming); of intro and transl, "The Martyrs of Lyons," in Richard Valentasis, ed, Religions of Late Antiquity in Practice, Princeton: Princeton Univ Press (forthcoming). **CONTACT ADDRESS** Dept Bible Studies, Union Theol Sem, New York, 3041 Broadway, New York, NY 10027-5710.

WEIDNER, DONALD JOHN
PERSONAL Born 06/15/1945, Brooklyn, NY, m, 1976, 1 child **DISCIPLINE** LAW **EDUCATION** Fordham Univ, BS, 66; Univ Tex, Austin, JD, 69. **CAREER** Assoc, Willkie, Farr & Gallagher, New York, 69-70; Bigelow fel, Univ Chicago, 70-71; asst prof, Univ SC, 71-74; assoc prof, Cleveland State Univ, 74-76; vis prof, Univ Tex, Sch of Law, 78; vis prof, Univ NMex, Sch of Law, 79; vis prof, Stanford Law Sc, 81; vis prof, Univ NCar, Sch of Law, 91; assoc prof, 76-78, assoc dean, 84-85, dean, 91-97, prof, 78- , interim dean, 98-00, dean, 00- , Fla State Univ, Col of Law. **HONORS AND AWARDS** Prof of the Yr, FLa State Univ Col of Law, 79. **MEMBERSHIPS** Amer Law Inst; ABA. **RESEARCH** Partnership taxation; tax policy; property. **SELECTED PUBLICATIONS** Co-auth, Real Estate: Taxation and Bankruptcy, West, 79; auth, "Special Allocations and Capital Accounts," in Symposia on Federal Taxation (Res Inst Amer, 81), chap 5; auth, "RUPA and Fiduciary Duty: The Texture of Relationship," 58 Duke J Law & Contemp Probs 81 (95); co-auth, General and Limited Liability Partnerships Under the Revised Uniform Partnership Act, West, 96; auth, "The Crises of Legal Education: A Wake-Up Call for Faculty," 47 J Legal Ed (97); auth, "Foreword to Freedom of Contract and Fiduciary Duty: Organizing the Internal Relations of the Unincorporated Firm," 54 Wash & Lee Law Rev 389 (97); auth, "The Florida Supreme Court Commission on Professionalism and the Crises of Legal Education," 71-5 Fla Bar J 64 (97); auth, "Cadwalader, RUPA and Fiduciary Duty," 54 Wash & Lee Law Rev 877 (97); auth, "Law School Engagement in Professionalism and Improved Bar Relations," 72-7 Fla Bar J 40 (98); auth, "Synthetic Leases: Structured Finance, Financial Accounting and Tax Ownership," 25 J Corp Law 445 (00). **CONTACT ADDRESS** Col of Law, Florida State Univ, 425 W Jefferson St, Tallahassee, FL 32306-1601. **EMAIL** dweidner@law.fsu.edu

WEIL, LOUIS
PERSONAL Born 05/10/1935, Houston, TX, s **DISCIPLINE** LITURGICS **EDUCATION** S Methodist Univ, BMus; Harvard Univ, AM; Gen Theol Sem, Magister Sacrae Liturgiae, STB; Inst Cath de Paris, STD. **CAREER** James F. Hodges prof, Church Divinity Sch Pacific. **MEMBERSHIPS** Sacramental Theology, Societas Liturgica, North, American Academy of Liturgy, International Anglican Liturgical Consultation. **SELECTED PUBLICATIONS** Auth, Shape and Focus in Eucharistic Celebration, A Prayer Book for the Twenty-first Century, Church Hymnal Corp, 96; The Place of the Liturgy in Michael Ramsey's Theology, Michael Ramsey as Theologian, Darton, Longman and Todd, 95; The Contribution of the Anglican Theological Review in Recent Liturgical Perspective, Anglican Theol Rev, 94; Reclaiming the Larger Trinitarian Framework of Baptism, Creation and Liturgy, Pastoral Press, 93; Baptism and Mission, Growing in Newness of Life, Anglican Bk Ctr, 93; A Larger Vision of Apostolicity: The End of an Anglo-Catholic Illusion, Fountain of Life, Pastoral Press, 91. **CONTACT ADDRESS** Church Divinity Sch of the Pacific, 2451 Ridge Rd, Berkeley, CA 94709-1217. **EMAIL** lweil@cdsp.edu

WEIL, VIVIAN
PERSONAL Born Cincinnati, OH **DISCIPLINE** PHILOSOPHY **EDUCATION** Univ Chicago, AB, 49, MA, 53; Univ Ill, Chicago, PhD, 72. **CAREER** Asst prof, Ill Inst of Technol, 72-78, Sr res assoc, 78-87, assoc prof, 87-95, Dir, Center for the Study of Ethics in the Professions, 87-. **HONORS AND AWARDS** Fel, Am Asn for the Advancement of Sci; Phi Beta Kappa. **MEMBERSHIPS** Am Philos Asn, Am Asn for the Advancement of Sci, Asn for Practical and Professional Ethics, Society for the Soc Studies of Sci. **RESEARCH** Professional ethics, responsibility in organizations, scientific research ethics, engineering ethics, science studies, theoretical issues of responsibility. **SELECTED PUBLICATIONS** Auth, "Scientific Research Ethics," The Encyclopedia of Philosophy Supplement, Macmillan: New York (96): 519-520; auth, "Whistleblowing: What Have We Learned Since the Challenger?," Engineering Ethics Update, Vol 6, No 2 (Aug 96): 1-3; coauth with Tom Calero and Michael Davis, "Responsible Communication Between Engineers and Managers," in Responsible Communication, Creskill, NJ: Hampton Press (96); auth, "Owning and Controlling Technical Information," in Responsible Commmunication: Ethical Issues in Business, Industry, and the Professions, eds Michael Pritchard and James Jaksa, Creskill, NJ: Hampton Press (96); auth, "Engineering and Business Ethics," A Dictionary of Business Ethics, eds P. H. Werhane and R. E. Freeman, Blackwell Pubs: Cambridge, MA (97); auth, Case Commentaries in Research Ethics: Fifteen Cases and Commentaries, ed Brian Schrag, Asn for Practical and Prof Ethics: Bloomington, IN, Vol 1 (Feb 97): 20-21, 56-57, 125-126, (Feb 98): 7-8, 31-33, 154-156, (Feb 99): 19-21, 57-59, 122-124; auth, "Learning How to Identify Ethical Problems in the Workplace and Acquiring the Skills to Deal With These Problems," in Engineering Ethics: History, Context, and Significance, eds Irina Alexeyeva, Alexei Sidorov, Vadim Rozin, Moscow Acad of Innovations Management, Moscow, Russia (Dec 97): 19-23; auth, "Comments on 'The Psychology of Whistleblowing' and 'The Voice of Experience'," Science and Engineering Ethics, Vol 4, No 1 (98): 29-31; auth, "Professional Standards: Can They Shape Practice in an International Context?" Science and Engineering Ethics, Vol 4, No 3 (98): 1-12; auth, "The Information Revolution: A Dose of Reality," Science Communication, Vol 20, No 1 (98): 135-140; coauth with Robert Arzbaecher, "Ethics and Relationships in Laboratories and Research Communities," Professional Ethics, 4:3 & 4, 83-125. **CONTACT ADDRESS** Center for the Study of Ethics in the Professions, Illinois Inst of Tech, 10 W 31st St, Stuart Bldg, Rm 102, Chicago, IL 60616. **EMAIL** Vivian.weil@iit.edu

WEILER, JOSEPH
DISCIPLINE LAW **EDUCATION** Univ Toronto, BA, 69; Osgoode Univ, LLB, 72; Univ Calif, LLM, 74. **CAREER** Asst prof, 74-79; assoc prof, 79-87; prof, 87-. **HONORS AND AWARDS** Dir, Pacific Inst Law Pub Policy; dir, Asia Pacific Bus Inst, 85-87. **MEMBERSHIPS** Can Bar Asn. **RESEARCH** Labour law; conflict resolution. **SELECTED PUBLICATIONS** Auth, pubs about labour law, criminal law, and sports and entertainment law. **CONTACT ADDRESS** Fac of Law, Univ of British Columbia, 1822 East Mall, Vancouver, BC, Canada V6T 1Z1. **EMAIL** weiler@law.ubc.ca

WEILER, PAUL C.
PERSONAL Born 01/29/1939, Port Arthur, ON, Canada, m, 1988, 4 children **DISCIPLINE** LAW **EDUCATION** Univ Toronto, BA, 60; MA, 61; Osgood Hall Law Sch, LLB, 64; Harvard, LLM, 65. **CAREER** Prof, York Univ, 65-73; chairman, Labor Relations Board, 74-78; prof, Harvard Univ, 79-. **HONORS AND AWARDS** Honorary Doctorate, Univ of Toronto, 00. **MEMBERSHIPS** Am Bar Assoc, Law Soc of Upper Can, Nat Acad of Sci. **RESEARCH** Canadian Judicial Process, Personal Injury and Torts, Labor and Employment Law, Sports and the Law, Entertainment, Media, and the Law. **SELECTED PUBLICATIONS** Auth, In the Last Resort: A Critical Study of the Supreme Court of Canada; auth, Reconcilable Differences: New Directions in Canadian Labor Law; auth, Legal Policy for Workplace Injuries; auth, Governing the Workplace: The Future of Labor and Employment; auth, Medical Malpractice on Trial; auth, Enterprise Responsibility for Personal Injury; auth, The Measure of Malpractice; auth, Sports and the Law; auth, Entertainment, Media and the Law; auth, Leveling the Playing Field: How the Law Can Make Sports Better for Fans. **CONTACT ADDRESS** Harvard Univ, Langdell West 323, Cambridge, MA 02138. **EMAIL** pweiler@law.harvard.edu

WEIMA, JEFFREY A. D.
PERSONAL Born 07/16/1960, m, 1983, 5 children **DISCIPLINE** THEOLOGY **EDUCATION** Brock Univ, BA, 83; Calvin Theol Sem, M Div, 86; Th M, 87; St. Michael's Col, Univ Toronto, PhD, 92. **CAREER** Instr, relig & theol, Redeemer Col, 88-92; asst prof, 92-94, assoc prof, 94-, new testament, Calvin Theol Sem. **HONORS AND AWARDS** Grant, Fac Heritage Fund, Calvin Theol Sem, 96, 98; Developing Your Role As A Scholar, 95; grant, Calvin Alumni Asn, 95; doctoral fel, Social Sci and Humanities Res Coun, Canada, 91; Founders' prize, 90; doctoral fel, Wycliffe Col, Univ Toronto, 87-90; Ontario Grad Scholar, Govt of Ontario, 87-90. **MEMBERSHIPS** Soc of Bibl Lit; Chicago Soc of Bibl Res; Inst for Bibl Res; Evangel Theol Soc. **SELECTED PUBLICATIONS** Monogr, co-auth, An Annotated Bibliography of 1 and 2 Thessalonians, New Testament Tools and Studies, 26, Leiden, Brill, 98; monogr, Neglected Endings: The Significance of the Pauline Letter Closings, Jour for the Study of the New Testament suppl series 101, Sheffield, JSOT Press, 94; article, An Apology for the Apologetic Function of 1 Thessalonians 2:1-12, Jour for the Study of the New Testament, 68.4, 73-99, 97; rev, First and Second Thessalonians, Jour of Bibl Lit, 116.4, 761-763, 97; article, The Letter to Diognetus, Dict of the Later New Testament & Its Developments, InterVarsity, 302-304, 97; article, What Does Aristotle Have to Do with Paul? An Evaluation of Rhetorical Criticism, Calvin Theol Jour, 32.2, 458-468, 97; rev, Comfort One Another. Reconstructing the Rhetoric and Audience of 1 Thessaloanians, Jour of the Evangel Theol Soc 39, 482-483, 96; article, How You Must Walk to Please God: Holiness and Discipleship in 1 Thessalonians, Patterns of Discipleship in the New Testament, 98-119, Eerdmans, 96; article, Two Challenges to Our Reformed Heritage, Calvin Sem Forum 3, 1-2, 96; article, 30 Meditations, Today, 45.2, 95; article, The Pauline Letter Closings: Analysis and Hermeneutical Significance, Bull for Bibl Res, 5, 177-198, 95; article, Preaching the Gospel in Rome: A Study of the Epistolary Framework of Romans, Gospel in Paul Studies in Galatians, Corinthians and Romans for Richard N. Longenecker, JSOT Press, 350-380, 94. **CONTACT ADDRESS** Calvin Theol Sem, 3233 Burton St. SE, Grand Rapids, MI 49546. **EMAIL** weimje@calvin.edu

WEINBERG, HAROLD R.
PERSONAL Born 11/15/1943, Louisville, KY **DISCIPLINE** LAW **EDUCATION** Case Western Reserve Univ, AB, 66, JD, 69; Univ Ill, LLM, 75. **CAREER** Assoc, Ulmer, Berne, Laronge, Glickman & Curtis, 69-71; grad teaching asst, Col Law, Ill, 71-72; asst prof, 72-76, assoc prof, 76-80, Prof Law, Col Law, Univ KY, 80-, Univ Chicago fel law & econ, 78-79; consult, Ky Legis Res Comn, 79-80. **MEMBERSHIPS** Am Soc Legal Hist; Asn Am Law Sch. **RESEARCH** Commercial law; antitrust law; American legal history. **SELECTED PUBLICATIONS** Auth, Tort claims as intangible property: An exploration from an assignee's perspective, 64 Ky Law J 49, 75; Secured party's right to sue third persons for damage to or defects in collateral, 81 Commun Law J 445, 76; Toward maximum facilitation or intent to create enforceable article nine security interests, 18 BC Ind & Commun Law Rev 1, 76; The New law and economics, Rev, 79; Sales law, economics, and the negotiability of goods, 9 J Legis Studies 569, 80; Markets overt, voidable titles, and feckless agents: Judges and efficiency in the antebellum doctrine of good faith purchase, 56 Tulane Law Rev 1, 81; Commerical paper in economic theory and legal history, 70 Ky Law J 1, 81; Legislative-Process And Commercial-Law - Lessons From The Copyright Act Of 1976 And The Uniform-Commercial-Code, Business Lawyer, Vol 0048, 1993. **CONTACT ADDRESS** Sch Law, Temple Univ, Philadelphia, PA 19122. **EMAIL** hweinber@service1.ukky.edu

WEINBERG, STEVEN
PERSONAL Born 05/03/1933, New York, NY, m, 1 child **DISCIPLINE** THEORETICAL PHYSICS **EDUCATION** AB, Cornell Univ, 54; PhD, Princeton Univ, 57. **CAREER** Josey Regental Prof Sci, Univ TX, 82-; Morris Loeb Vis Prof Physics, Harvard Univ, 83-; Harvard Univ, Higgns Prof Physics, 73-83; Smithsonian Astrophysical Observatory, Sr Sci, 73-83. **HONORS AND AWARDS** Andrew Gemant Awd; Natl Medal Of Sci; Nobel Prize in Physics; Dannie Heinemann Prize; James Madison Medal; Lewis Thomas Prize. **MEMBERSHIPS** Matl Acad of Sci; Royal Soc; Am Philos Soc; Amer Acad Arts & Sciences. **RESEARCH** Theoretical Physics. **SELECTED PUBLICATIONS** The Quantum Theory of Fields, Vol 1, 2,3: Foundations, Cambridge Univ Press, 95, 96,00; Dreams of a Final Theory, Pantheon, NY, 93; auth, First Three Minutes, Basic Books, 77; auth, "Discovery of Subatomic Particles," Scientific American/Freeman, 82. **CONTACT ADDRESS** Univ of Texas, Austin, Austin, TX 78712. **EMAIL** weinberg@physics.utexas.edu

WEINBERGER, LEON JUDAH
PERSONAL Born 08/23/1926, Przemysl, Poland, m, 1954, 3 children **DISCIPLINE** PHILOSOPHY, RELIGION **EDUCATION** Clark Univ, BA, 57; Brandeis Univ, MA, 59, PhD(Near E), 63; Jewish Theol Sem, MHL, 64. **CAREER** From asst prof to assoc prof relig, 64-72, acting head dept relig, 70-71, res grants, 66 & 69, Prof Relig Studies, Univ Ala, 72-, Resource consult teacher educ, Nat Coun Relig & Pub Educ, 72; proj dir, Nat Endowment Humanities grant, 72-73; assoc, Danforth Found, 73; chmn, New Col Rev Bd, Univ Ala, 73-76; gen ed Judaic studies, Univ Ala Press, 74-; Am Acad Jewish Res publ grants, 75 & 78; emer, Clark Univ. **HONORS AND AWARDS** Algernon Sydney Sullivan Awd, 78; Awded the Friedman Prize, 95; Burnum Distinguished Fac award, 96. **MEMBERSHIPS** Am Orient Soc; Am Acad Relig. **RESEARCH** Hebrew language and literature; Middle East; comparative religion. **SELECTED PUBLICATIONS** Auth, The Death of Moses in the Synagogue Liturgy, Ann Arbor Publ, 63; Hebrew Poetry in Byzantium, Part I (Hebrew), Hebrew Union Col Annual, 68; On the Provenance of Benjamin B Samuel Qushtani, Jewish Quart Rev, 79; Some beliefs and opinions in the Romaniote liturgy, Hebrew studies, 79; A New Source on the Return to Zion Movement in 13th Century Kastoria (Hebrew), Hadoar, 79; Romaniote Penitential Poetry, Am Acad Jewish Res, 80; Themes in Jewish mysticism in the Romaniote Liturgy (Hebrew), Bitzaron, 80; Mesianic Expectations in Kastoria on the Eve of Sabbatianism, In: Go and Study, Essays and Studies in Honor of Alfred Jospe, Ktav, 80; Karaite Piyyut In Southeastern Europe + Evidence Of Karaite Liturgical Poetic Influence From Rabbanite Neoplatonist Form, Language, And Rhetoric, Jewish Quarterly Review, Vol 0083, 1992; Dari,Moses Moses-Ben-Abraham-Ben-Saadia-Ha-Rofe-Dari, Karaite Poet And Physician + A Study On 13th-Century Medieval Karaism And The Writings Of The Hispanic-Hebrew Rabbanites, Jewish Quarterly Review, Vol 0084, 1994; auth, Jewish Hymnography: A Literary History. **CONTACT ADDRESS** Dept of Relig Studies, Univ of Alabama, Tuscaloosa, PO Box 6173, University, AL 35486. **EMAIL** lweinber@woodsquad.as.ua.edu

WEINER, NEAL O.
PERSONAL Born 07/24/1942, Baltimore, MD, 2 children **DISCIPLINE** PHILOSOPHY, CLASSICS **EDUCATION** St John's Col, Md, BA, 64; Univ Tex, PhD, 68. **CAREER** Asst prof philos, State Univ NY Col Old Westbury, 68-70; Assoc Prof Philos, Marlboro Col, 70-, Vis assoc prof philos, St Mary's Col, Notre Dame, IN, 77-78; tutor, Grad Inst St John's Col,

NM, 78. **HONORS AND AWARDS** Wilson Fellow; Danforth Fellow. **MEMBERSHIPS** Am Philos Asn; Northern New Eng Philos Asn. **RESEARCH** Class philos; psychiatry and ethics. **SELECTED PUBLICATIONS** Auth, The Articulation of Thought, Marlboro Col, 86; The Harmony of the Soul, SUNY, 93 **CONTACT ADDRESS** Dept of Philos, Marlboro Col, General Delivery, Marlboro, VT 05344-9999.

WEINER, ROBERT
PERSONAL Born 07/30/1950, New Haven, CT, m, 1990, 2 children **DISCIPLINE** PHILOSOPHY, RELIGION **EDUCATION** Johns Hopkins Univ, BA, 72; Georgetown Univ, MA, 73; Yale Univ, MA, 75; Univ Cologne, PhD, 81. **CAREER** Editor, Global Digest Intl News Services, 81-84; lect, Calif State Univ, Sonoma, 88-92; lect, coord Lib Stud, Saint Mary's Col, 85-96; chair lib arts, John F. Kennedy Univ, 97-99, consult on creativity and education, 99-. **MEMBERSHIPS** Am Phil Asn; Asn Integrative Stud; Mod Lang Asn; Nat Coun Teach Eng. **RESEARCH** Creativity, interdisciplinary curricular design, global social change, Leonardo da Vinci. **SELECTED PUBLICATIONS** Auth, "Western & Contemporary Global Conceptions of Creativity in Relief Against Approaches from So-Called 'Traditional' Cultures," in Issues in Integrative Stud, 15, 97; auth, "The Interdisciplinary Tree Exercise," in Developing Adult Learners, 99; auth, Creativity and Beyond, Suny Press, 00. **CONTACT ADDRESS** 5439 Carlton St, Oakland, CA 94618. **EMAIL** rob.weiner@aya.yale.edu

WEINREB, LLOYD L.
PERSONAL Born 10/09/1936, New York, NY, m, 1963, 3 children **DISCIPLINE** LAW, PHILOSOPHY **EDUCATION** Dartmouth Col, BA, 57; Univ Oxford, BA, 59, MA, 63; Harvard Law Sch, LLB, 62. **CAREER** Asst prof law, 65-68, prof law, 68-93, dane prof law, Harvard Law Sch 93-. **RESEARCH** Law; political philosophy; legal philosophy. **SELECTED PUBLICATIONS** Auth, Denial of Justice, Free Pr, 77; auth, Natural Law and Justice, Harvard Univ Pr, 87; auth, Oedipus at Fenway Park: What Rights Are and Why There Are Any, Harvard Univ Pr, 94; auth, Criminal Law (6th ed), Foundation Pr, 98; auth, Criminal Process (6th ed), Foundation Pr, 98; auth, "Copyright for Functional Expression," 111 Harvard Law Rev 1149, 98; auth, "Fair Use and How It Got That Way," 45 J Copyright Soc 634, 98; auth, "Your Place or Mine: Privacy of Presence under the Fourth Amendment," Sup Ct Rev 252, 99; auth, "The Right to Privcacy," 17 Soc Phil & Policy (No 2) 25 (Summer 00); auth, Leading Constitutional Cases on Criminal Justice, Foundation Pr, annual. **CONTACT ADDRESS** Dept of Law, Harvard Univ, Cambridge, MA 02138. **EMAIL** weinreb@law.harvard.edu

WEINRIB, ERNEST JOSEPH
PERSONAL Born 04/08/1943, Toronto, ON, Canada, m, 1970 **DISCIPLINE** LAW, ANCIENT HISTORY **EDUCATION** Univ Toronto, BA, 65, LLB, 72; Harvard Univ, PhD(classics), 68. **CAREER** Asst prof classics, 68-70, asst prof law, 72-75, assoc prof, 75-81, Prof Law, Fac Law, Univ Toronto, 81-. **HONORS AND AWARDS** Killam Res Fel, 86-88; Connaught Sr Fel, 90-91; Fel of the Royal Soc of Canada. **MEMBERSHIPS** Class Can Asn; Asn Can Law Teachers. **RESEARCH** Tort law; Roman law; jurisprudence; legal theory. **SELECTED PUBLICATIONS** Auth, Judiciary law of M Livius Drusus, Historia, 70; Obnuntiatio: two problems, Z Savigny-Stuftung, 70; A step forward in factual causation, Mod Law Rev, 75; The fiduciary obligation, 75 & Illegality as a tort defense, 76, Univ Toronto; Contribution in a contractual setting, Can Bar Rev, 76; Utilitarianism, Economics, and Legal Theory, Univ Toronto Law J, 80; The Case for a Duty to Rescue, Yale Law J, 80; Obedience to the Law in Plato's Crito, Am J Jurisprudence, 82; The Jurisprudence Of Legal Formalism, Harvard Journal Of Law And Public Policy, Vol 0016, 1993; auth, The Idea of Private Law, Harvard Univ Press, 95. **CONTACT ADDRESS** Fac of Law, Univ of Toronto, Toronto, ON, Canada M5S 1A1. **EMAIL** e.weinrib@utoronto.ca

WEINSTEIN, JACK B.
PERSONAL Born 08/10/1921, KS, m, 1945, 3 children **DISCIPLINE** LAW **EDUCATION** Brooklyn Col, BA, 43; Columbia Univ, LLB, 48. **CAREER** George Washington Univ Law, adj prof 92-93; Brooklyn Law Sch, adj prof 87-98; NY Univ Law, adj prof 84-85; NYS Constitutional Conv, advisor 67; NYS Temp Comm, commissioner 66; Columbia Univ Law, 67-98, prof 56-67, assoc prof 52-56; Harvard Univ Law, adj prof, 82; and others; Fed State civil proced, evid, admin, acc, bus law, crim law. **HONORS AND AWARDS** Fuld Awd; NYork State Bar Assoc; St. Frances Col Hon Doctorate Degree; Gold Medal NYork State Bar; Hon Doctorate Long Island Univ; Distinguished Serv Medal Awd; Judicial Recognition Awd; Edward J. Devitt Distinguished Serv Awd; Yale Hon Doctorate Laws; Hon William J. Brennan Awd; NLJ Lawyer of the Year; Albany Law Sch Hon Doctorate Law; Yeshiva Univ Doctorate Law; Columbia Law Sch AA Excellence Awd; FBC Excellence in Jurisp; NYork Law Sch Medal of Hon; Allard k. Lowenstein Mem Awd; Charles W. Froessel Awd; Brooklyn Law Sch Hon Doctorate Law; BCAA Alumnus of the Year; Am Jewish Community Human Relations Awd. **MEMBERSHIPS** AAAS; AJS; ALI; AAUP; ABA; ABCNY; BANC; IJA; IAJLJ; NLADA; SALT; ISPT; USJC; SCJC. **SELECTED PUBLICATIONS** Auth, Essays on the NYork Constitution, 66; auth, A NYork Constitution Meeting Today's Needs and Tomorrow's Challenges, 67; co-auth, Manual of NYork Civil Procedure, 67; auth, Reform of the Federal Rule-Making Process, Ohio State Univ Press, 77; auth, "Rule-making by the Courts," in The Judicial Admin Div Handbook, Am Bar Assoc, The Improvement of the Admin of Justice, 81; co-auth, Materials on Science and Law, 92 **CONTACT ADDRESS** U.S. District Court, Eastern District of NY, 225 Cadman Plaza East, Brooklyn, NY 11021. **EMAIL** Jack_Weinstein@NYED.USCourts.gov

WEINSTEIN, STANLEY
PERSONAL Born 11/13/1929, Brooklyn, NY, m, 1952, 1 child **DISCIPLINE** BUDDHIST & EAST ASIAN STUDIES **EDUCATION** Komazawa Univ, Japan, BA, 58; Univ Tokyo, MA, 60; Harvard Univ, PhD(Far Eastern lang), 66. **CAREER** Lectr Far Eastern Buddhism, Univ London, 62-68; assoc prof Buddhist studies, 68-74, Prof Buddhist Studies, Yale Univ, 74-; NEH sr fel, 74-75. **MEMBERSHIPS** Am Orient Soc; Asn Asian Studies **RESEARCH** Buddhist studies; East Asian languages and history. **SELECTED PUBLICATIONS** Auth, The Kanjin kakumusho: A Compendium of the Teachings of the Hosso Sect, Komazawa Daigaku Kenkyu Kiyo, 60; contr ed, Japanese-English Buddhist Dictionary, Tokyo, 65; Buddhism, In: The Cambridge Encyclopedia of China, Cambridge Univ Press, 82; 38 medium length and 82 short articles In: The Encyclopedia of Japan, Kodansha, Tokyo, 82; Alayavijnana and Buddhism, Schools of: Chinese Buddhism, In: The Encyclopedia of Religion, Macmillang Publ Co, 87; Buddhism Under the T'ang, Cambridge Univ Press, 87; Nihon Bukkyo to ichi Amerikajin Bukkyo kenkyuka no setten: Todai no Bukkyo no hakkan ni chinande, Komazawa Daigaku Bukkyo gakubu ronshu, 88; tangdae Pulgyo chongp'a hyongsong e issoso hwangsil ui huwon (in Korean)(Imperial Patronage in the Formation of the Tang Buddhist Schools), Chonggyo wa munhwa (Relgion and Culture), 12/95; Rennyo shiso ni okeru renzokusei to henka (Continuity and Change the Thought of Rennyo Shonin [1415-1499], In: rennyo no sekai (The World of Rennyo), Bun'eido, Kyoto, Japan, 98; auth, "Aristocratic Buddhism," in The Cambridge History of Japan, vol. 2, ed. Donald H. Shively and William H. McCollough (Cambridge Univ Press, 99); transl, Tangdai fojiao, Foguang Wenhua Shiye (Taipei, Japan), 99. **CONTACT ADDRESS** Dept of Relig Studies, Yale Univ, PO Box 208287, New Haven, CT 06520-8287. **EMAIL** stanley.weinstein@yale.edu

WEINTRAUB, RUSSELL JAY
PERSONAL Born 12/20/1929, New York, NY, m, 1953, 3 children **DISCIPLINE** LAW **EDUCATION** NYork Univ, BA, 50; Harvard Univ, JD, 53. **CAREER** Teaching fel law, Law Sch, Harvard Univ, 55-57; prof, Univ Iowa, 57-65; Prof Law, Law Sch, Univ Tex, Austin, 65-. **HONORS AND AWARDS** Ronald Graveson Memorial lectr, 00; Hague lectr; Carl Fulda Awd in Int Law. **MEMBERSHIPS** Am Law Inst; Am Bar Found; Tex Bar Found; Int Litigation and Arbitration. **RESEARCH** Conflict of laws; contracts. **SELECTED PUBLICATIONS** Auth, Commentary on the Conflict of Laws, Found Press, 71, 4th ed, 01; Admiralty Choice-Of-Law Rules For Damages, Journal Of Maritime Law And Commerce, Vol 0028, 1997; coauth, Cases and Materials on Conflict of Laws, Foundation 11th ed, 00; auth, International Litigation and Arbitration, Carolina Academic Press, 3rd ed. 01. **CONTACT ADDRESS** Sch of Law, Univ of Texas, Austin, 727 E 26th St, Austin, TX 78705-3224. **EMAIL** rweintraub@mail.law.utexas.edu

WEIR, JOHN P.
DISCIPLINE LAW **EDUCATION** McMaster, BComm; Queen's Univ, LLB; Osgoode, York, LLM. **CAREER** Prof; Osgoode Hall, Barrister-at-Law; past supt, Insurance & asst Dep Minister, Ministry of Financial Institutions, Ont. **RESEARCH** Insurance; taxation; administrative and government regulation; medico-legal; and evidence law. **SELECTED PUBLICATIONS** Auth, Structured Settlements and The Annotated Insurance Act of Ontario; coauth, Norwood on Life Insurance Law in Canada. **CONTACT ADDRESS** Col of Business Administration, Education and Law, Univ of Windsor, 401 Sunset Ave, Windsor, ON, Canada N9B 3P4. **EMAIL** jweir@uwindsor.ca

WEIRICH, PAUL
PERSONAL Born 09/30/1946, Chicago, IL, m, 1968, 2 children **DISCIPLINE** PHILOSOPHY **EDUCATION** St Louis Univ, BA, 68; Univ Calif at Los Angeles, PhD, 77. **CAREER** Vis asst prof, Univ New Orleans, 77-78; postdoctoral fel & instr, Univ Rochester, 78-80; asst prof, Univ Rochester, 80-87; asst prof, Cal Poly at Pomona, 87-88; asst prof, Univ Mo at Columbia, 88-97. **HONORS AND AWARDS** NSF Summer Fel, 88. **MEMBERSHIPS** Am Philos Asn. **RESEARCH** Practical Reasoning. **SELECTED PUBLICATIONS** Auth, Equilibrium and Rationality: Game Theory Revised by Decision Rules, Cambridge Univ Press, 98; auth, Decision Space: Multidimensional Utility Analysis, Cambridge Univ Press, forthcoming. **CONTACT ADDRESS** Dept Philos, Univ of Missouri, Columbia, 438 General Classroom Bldg, Columbia, MO 65211-4160. **EMAIL** pweirich@missouri.edu

WEISBERG, RICHARD H.
PERSONAL Born 05/24/1944, New York, NY, m, 1968, 3 children **DISCIPLINE** LAW **EDUCATION** Brandeis Univ, AB, 65; Cornell Univ, MA, 67, PhD(comp lit), 70; Columbia Univ, JD, 74. **CAREER** Asst prof French & comp lit, Univ Chicago, 71-75; assoc prof, 77-79, Prof Law, Cardozo Law Sch, Yeshiva Univ, 79-, Nat Endowment for Humanities younger humanist fel, 72-73; Cornell Soc for Humanities jr fel, 75-76; vis prof, Eng Lit, Brandeis Univ, 89; vis prof, Schl Law UCLA, 90, 99; Floersheimer prof, Constitutional Law, Yeshiva Univ, 95- . **HONORS AND AWARDS** Rockefeller/Bellagio fel, 96; Guggenheim fel, 98-99. **MEMBERSHIPS** MLA, AALS, Law & Humanities Institute. **RESEARCH** Lit and the law; torts; trusts and estates. **SELECTED PUBLICATIONS** Auth, "An example not to follow: Ressentiment in notes from underground," Mod Fiction Studies, 75-76; auth, "Comparative law in comparative literature: Examining magistrate in Dostoyevski and Camus," Rutgers Law Rev, 76; auth, "Wigmore's legal novels revisited: New resources for the expansive lawyer," Northwestern Law Rev, 76; auth, "Hamlet and un coup de des: Mallarme's emerging constellation," Mod Lang Notes, 77; auth, 'Law, Literature and Cardozo's Judicial Poetics," Cardozo Law Rev, 79; auth, How Judges Speak: Some Lessons on adjudication in Billy Budd, Sailor with an Application to Justice Rehnquist, New York Univ Law Rev, 82; auth, The Failure of the Word, Yale U Press, 84; auth, When Lawyers Write, Little Brown, 87; auth, Poethics, Columbia Univ Press, 92; auth, Vichy Law and the Holocaust in France, NYU Press, 96. **CONTACT ADDRESS** Cardozo Law Sch, Yeshiva Univ, 55 Fifth Ave, New York, NY 10028. **EMAIL** rhweisbg@aol.com

WEISBERG, RICHARD H.
DISCIPLINE CONSTITUTIONAL LAW **EDUCATION** Boston Univ, JD, 55; Stanford Univ, AM, 60. **CAREER** Prof, Yeshiva Univ; **HONORS AND AWARDS** Asso, Cleary, Gottlieb, Steen & Hamilton; Fel, NEH, 72-73, Soc Hum Cornell Univ, 75-76; pres, Law & Hum Inst, 79-86, chair, 87; chair; Law & Hum Sect, Am Asn Law Schs; fel, Am Coun Learned Socs, 89-90. **SELECTED PUBLICATIONS** Auth, The Failure of the Word, Yale, 84, 89, 90; When Lawyers Write, Little, Brown, 87; Poethics: And Other Strategies of Law and Literature, Columbia Univ Press, 92; gen ed, Cardoza Studies in Law and Lit. **CONTACT ADDRESS** Yeshiva Univ, 55 Fifth Ave, New York, NY 10003-4301.

WEISBURD, ARTHUR M.
PERSONAL Born 07/10/1948, Memphis, TN, m, 1989 **DISCIPLINE** LAW **EDUCATION** Princeton Univ, AB, 70; Univ Mich, JD, 76. **CAREER** Asst prof to prof, Univ of NC, 81-. **MEMBERSHIPS** Am Soc of International Law, ABA. **RESEARCH** Sources of international law, international law of human rights, international law regarding use of force. **SELECTED PUBLICATIONS** Auth, Use of Force: The Practice of States Since World War II, Penn State Press, 97. **CONTACT ADDRESS** School of Law, Univ of No Carolina, Chapel Hill, Chapel Hill, NC 27599. **EMAIL** amw@email.unc.edu

WEISENFELD, JUDITH
DISCIPLINE RELIGION **EDUCATION** Princeton Univ, PhD. **CAREER** Asst prof. **SELECTED PUBLICATIONS** Auth, African American Women and Christian Activism in the New York City YWCA 1905-1945, Harvard, 97; co-ed, This Far by Faith: Readings in African American Women's Religious Biography, Routledge, 96. **CONTACT ADDRESS** Dept of Religion, Columbia Col, New York, 2960 Broadway, New York, NY 10027-6902. **EMAIL** jweisenfeld@barnard.columbia.edu

WEISS, HEROLD D.
PERSONAL Born 09/05/1934, Montevideo, Uruguay, m, 1962, 2 children **DISCIPLINE** RELIGION **EDUCATION** Andrews Univ, MA, 57, BD, 60; Duke Univ, PhD, 64. **CAREER** Instr rclig, Andrews Univ, 61-62, asst prof New Testament, Andrews Univ, 65-69; assoc prof relig studies, 69-72, Prof Relig Studies, St Mary's Col, Ind, 72-; Adj prof, Univ Notre Dame; McCormick Theol Sem, Chicago & Northern Baptist Theol Sem. **MEMBERSHIPS** Soc Bibl Lit; Am Acad Relig; fel Inst Antiquity & Christianity. **RESEARCH** The religious world of the first century; Biblical studies. **SELECTED PUBLICATIONS** Auth, Paul Tarsues: His Gospel and Life, Andrews Univ Press, 89; auth, The pagani among the contemporaries of the first Christians, J Bibl Lit, 86: 42-52; History and a gospel, Novum Testamentum, 10: 81-94; The law in the Epistle to the Colossians, Cath Bibl Quart, 34: 294-314; Footwashing in the Johannine community, Novum Testamentum, 21: 298-325; The Sabbath in the synoptic gospels, JSNT, 90, reprinted, in New Testament Backgrounds: A Sheffield Reader, Sheffield Acad Press, 97; The Sabbath in the fourth Gospel, JBL, 91; Philo on the Sabbath, in Heirs of the Septuagint: Philo, Hellenistic Judaism and Early Christianity, Studia Philonica Annual, 91; The Sabbath among the Samaratins, JSJ, 94; Paul and the judging of days, ZNW, 95; Sabbatismos in the Epistle to the Hebrews, CBQ, 96; The Sabbath in the Pauline corpus, in Wisdom and Logos: Studies in Jewish Thought in Honor of David Winston, Studia Philonica Annual, 97; The Sabbath in the writings of Josephus, JSJ,99. **CONTACT ADDRESS** Saint Mary's Col, Indiana, Box 78, Notre Dame, IN 46556. **EMAIL** hweiss@saintmarys.edu

WEISS, RAYMOND L.
PERSONAL Born 02/12/1930, Cleveland, OH **DISCIPLINE** PHILOSOPHY **EDUCATION** Univ Cincinnati, BA, 51; Hebrew Union Col-Jewish Inst Relig, BHL & MHL, 56; Univ Chicago, PhD, 66. **CAREER** From instr to asst prof, 65-72, assoc prof, 72-80, Prof Philos, Univ Wis-Milwaukee, 80- **MEMBERSHIPS** Am Philos Asn. **RESEARCH** Maimonides; existentialism; ethics. **SELECTED PUBLICATIONS** Auth, Kierkegaard's return to Socrates, New Scholasticism, autumn 71; Language and ethics: Reflections on Maimonides' ethics, J Hist Philos, 10/71; Hermann Cohen's Religion of Reason, Cent Conf Am Rabbis J, winter 74; Historicism and science: Thoughts on Quine, Dialectica, summer 75; coauth, Ethical Writings of Maimonides, NY Univ, 75; Maimonides' Ethics: The Encounter of Philosophic and Religious Morality, Univ Chicago Press, 91. **CONTACT ADDRESS** Dept of Philos, Univ of Wisconsin, Milwaukee, PO Box 413, Milwaukee, WI 53201-0413.

WEISS, ROSLYN
PERSONAL Born 10/21/1952, Brooklyn, NY, m, 1973, 2 children **DISCIPLINE** PHILOSOPHY **EDUCATION** Columbia Univ, PHD, 82 **CAREER** 91-present, Lehigh Univ; 88-91 Univ of Delaware; 81-88, Hood col **HONORS AND AWARDS** Earhart Found Fel; NEH Fel; Center for Hellenic Studies Fel **MEMBERSHIPS** Am Philos Assoc; Int Plato Soc; Assoc for Jewish Studies **RESEARCH** Philosophy **SELECTED PUBLICATIONS** Auth, Socrates Dissatisfied, Oxford Univ Press, 98; Auth, From Freedom to Formalism:Maimonides on Prayer, Journal of the Central Conf of Am Rabbis, Fall 97, 29-43; Auth, Hedonism in the Protagoras and the Sophist's Guarantee, Ancient Philos 10, 1990, 17-39 **CONTACT ADDRESS** Dept of Philosophy, Lehigh Univ, 15 University Dr, Bethlehem, PA 18015. **EMAIL** rwp3@lehigh.edu

WEISS, T. G.
PERSONAL Born 02/26/1946, Detroit, MI, m, 1975, 2 children **DISCIPLINE** POLITICAL SCIENCE **EDUCATION** Harvard Univ, BA; Princeton Univ, MA, PhD. **CAREER** Res Prof, 90-98, Brown's Univ; exec Dir, 85-89, Intl Peace Acad; Sr Econ Affs Officer, 75-85, United Nations Conf Switz; Pres Prof, 98-; CUNY Graduate Center . **HONORS AND AWARDS** Council of Foreign Relations Member; Chairs Intl Org Section of the Intl Studies Assoc; Intl Inst for Strategic Studies Mem; External Research Advisory Bd of the UN High Commissioner for Refugees in Geneva; Trustee of Moses Brown Friends Sch RI. **SELECTED PUBLICATIONS** Coauth, Humanitarian Challenger and intreventions, 00; auth, Military-Civilian Interventions, 99; ed, UN Subcontracting: Task-sharing with Regional Security Arrangements and Service-providing NGOs, 98; coed, Collective Conflict Mgmt and Changing World Politics, 98; coauth, The United Nations and Changing World Politics, 00; coed, Political Gain and Civilian Pain: Humanitarian Impacts of Economic Sanctions, 97; coauth, The News Media Civil War and Humanitarian Action, 96; coed, NGOs the UN and Global Governance, 96; coed, Volunteers Against Conflict, 96; coed, From Massacres to Genocide: The Media Public Policy and the Humanitarian Crises, 96; ed, The United Nations and Civil Wars, 95; coauth, Humanitarian Politics, 95; coauth, Humanitarian Action in Times of War: A Handbook for Practitioners, 93. **CONTACT ADDRESS** Graduate Sch & Univ Center, Graduate Sch and Univ Ctr, CUNY, 365 Fifth Ave, New York, NY 10016. **EMAIL** tweiss@gc.cuny.edu

WEISSBRODT, DAVID SAMUEL
PERSONAL Born 10/13/1944, Washington, DC, m, 1970, 2 children **DISCIPLINE** LAW **EDUCATION** Univ CA, Berkeley, JD, 69. **CAREER** Assoc prof, 75-78, Prof Law, Sch of Law, Univ MN, 78-, Co-dir, Univ MN Human Rights Center; co-dir, Univ Mn Human Rights Library (http://www.umn.edu/humanrts); Chair, Int Human Rights Internship Prog, 76-90. **HONORS AND AWARDS** Briggs & Morgan Prof, 89-97; Fredrickson & Byron Prof, 98-; Member, UN Sub-committee on Prevention of Discrimination and Protection of Minorities, 96-99. **MEMBERSHIPS** Am Soc Int Law; Am Law Inst. **RESEARCH** International human rights law; immigration law; administrative law. **SELECTED PUBLICATIONS** Coauth, The Death Penalty Cases, CA Law Rev, 68; The Role of Nongovernmental Organization in the Implementation of Human Rights, Tex Int Law J, 77; Human rights legislation and United States Foreign Policy, Ga J Int & Comp Law, 77; United States Ratification of the Human Rights Covenants, Minn Law Rev, 78; coauth (with McCarthy), Human Rights Fact-finding by Nongovernmental Organizations, Va J Int Law, 81; auth, A New United Nations Mechanism for Encouraging the Ratification of Treaties, Am J Int Law, 82; International Trial Observers, Stanford J Int Law, 82; Strategies for the Selection and Pursuit of International Human Rights Matters, Yale J World Pub Order, 82; coauth, with Parker, Orientation Manual: The UN Commission on Human Rights, its Sub-commission, and Related Procedures, 92; co-ed, with Wolfrum, The Right to a Fair Trial, 97; coauth, with Newman, International Human Rights, 2nd ed, 96; auth, Immigration Law and Procedure, 4th ed, 98; and 90 other articles. **CONTACT ADDRESS** Law Sch, Univ of Minnesota, Twin Cities, 229 19th Ave S, Minneapolis, MN 55455-0401. **EMAIL** weiss001@tc.umn.edu

WEITHMAN, PAUL J.
DISCIPLINE PHILOSOPHY **EDUCATION** Univ Notre Dame, BA, 81; Harvard Univ, MA, 86, PhD, 88. **CAREER** Assoc prof. **RESEARCH** Ethics; contemporary political philosophy; medieval political philosophy. **SELECTED PUBLICATIONS** Auth, Of Assisted Suicide and 'The Philosophers' Brief', Ethics, 98; Equality and Complementarity in the Political Thought of Aquinas, Theological Studies, 98; ed, Religion and Contemporary Liberalism, 97. **CONTACT ADDRESS** Philosophy Dept, Univ of Notre Dame, 336/7 O'Shaughnessy, Notre Dame, IN 46556. **EMAIL** weithman.1@nd.edu

WELBORN, L. L.
PERSONAL Born 10/04/1954, Memphis, TN, m, 1976, 2 children **DISCIPLINE** RELIGION, NEW TESTAMENT AND EARLY CHRISTIAN LITERATURE **EDUCATION** Harding Col, BA, 76; Yale Divinity School, MAR, 79; Univ Chicago, MA, 83; Vanderbilt Univ, MA, 84, PhD, 93. **CAREER** Asst prof, McCormick Theol Sem, 85-91; assoc prof, United Theol Sem, 91-98. **HONORS AND AWARDS** National Merit scholarship; Tew Prize; Rotary fel; Harold Stirling Vanderbilt fel. **MEMBERSHIPS** Soc of Biblical Lit. **RESEARCH** Pauline Epistles; Apostolic Fathers; Greco-Roman World. **SELECTED PUBLICATIONS** Auth, "On the Date of First Clement," Biblical Research, 85; auth, "First Clement," The Anchor Bible Dictionary, 92; auth, Politics and Rhetoric in the Corinthian Epistles, Mercer, 97; auth, "Primum tirocinium Pauli," Biblische Zeitschrift, 99; auth, "The Runaway Paul: A Character in the Fool's Speech, 2 Cor. 11:1-12:10," Harvard Theological Review, 99. **CONTACT ADDRESS** United Theol Sem, 1810 Harvard Blvd, Dayton, OH 45406. **EMAIL** llwelborn@united.edu

WELCH, EDWARD L.
PERSONAL Born 03/10/1928, Helena, AR, m **DISCIPLINE** LAW **EDUCATION** St Louis Univ, BS, Commerce, 1957; Washington Univ, St Louis, MO, JD, Order of Coif, 1960. **CAREER** Stockham Roth Buder & Martin, assoc atty; Univ of Wisconsin, Milwaukee, lecturer; Allis-Chalmers Mfg Co, Milwaukee, WI, & Springfield, IL, labor law atty, 61-67; Natl Labor Relations Bd 14th Region; staff atty, 67-69; atty. **MEMBERSHIPS** Gen counsel, Natl Alliance of Postal & Fed Employees, Washington, DC, 1971-90; senior litigation specialist 1990-; adj prof, Southern Illinois Univ, Carbondale, 1974-; school bd atty, East St Louis School Dist, 189, 1978-; mem, Amer Bar Assn, Illinois State Bar Assn, Madison City Bar Assn; life mem, NAACP. **CONTACT ADDRESS** PO Box 93, Edwardsville, IL 62025.

WELCH, JOHN
PERSONAL Born 08/23/1942, Cumberland, MD, s **DISCIPLINE** PHILOSOPHY **EDUCATION** Univ Pittsburgh, MLS. **CAREER** Assoc Prof to Asst Prof, 73-. **MEMBERSHIPS** Am Library Asn. **RESEARCH** Library usage instruction; Teaching basic philosophy. **CONTACT ADDRESS** Dept Humanities, Virginia Western Comm Col, PO Box 14007, Roanoke, VA 24038-4007. **EMAIL** jwelch@vw.cc.va.us

WELCH, ROBERT H.
PERSONAL Born 05/14/1938, Elizabethtown, TN, m, 1961, 3 children **DISCIPLINE** CHURCH ADMINISTRATION **EDUCATION** E Tenn State Univ, BS, 60; Naval Post-Grad Sch, MS, 67; Southwestern Baptist Theol Sem, MARE, 85, PhD, 89. **CAREER** US Navy, Retired; Assoc prof, Univ Okla, 77-82; adj prof, 87-88; asst prof, Liberty Univ Theol Sem, 87-88; assoc prof, Southwestern Baptist Theol Sem, 91-; assoc dean, Ph.D Stud. **HONORS AND AWARDS** Who's Who in Professionals, 98; SWBTS Pres Merit Scholar 86 and Marsh Outstanding Ph.D. Scholar., 88; church bus admin, trinity baptist church, 82-85. **SELECTED PUBLICATIONS** Auth, The Church Organization Manual, NACBA, 99; Contribution Leadership Handbook of Practical Theology, Vol III, Leadership and Admin, Baker Bk(s), 94; co-auth, A Maintenance Management Manual for Southern Baptist Churches, Convention Press, 90; auth, Advisory Board Your Church Magazine, CTI. **CONTACT ADDRESS** Sch Edu Ministries, Southwestern Baptist Theol Sem, PO Box 22366, Fort Worth, TX 76122-0366. **EMAIL** bobw@swbts.swbts.edu

WELKER, DAVID DALE
PERSONAL Born 12/18/1938, St. Louis, MO **DISCIPLINE** PHILOSOPHY **EDUCATION** Univ Mich, AB, 60, PhD(philos), 68; Univ Calif, Berkeley, MA, 62. **CAREER** Asst prof, 64-80, Assoc Prof Philos, Temple Univ, 80-. **RESEARCH** Philosophy of language; metaphysics. **SELECTED PUBLICATIONS** Auth, Existential statements, J Philos, 70; A difficulty in Ziffs theory of meaning, Philos Studies, 70; Locutionary Acts and Meaning, Philos Forum, 73; Subjects, Predicates, and Features, Mind, 79. **CONTACT ADDRESS** Dept of Philos, Temple Univ, 1114 W Berks St, Philadelphia, PA 19122-6029.

WELLER, ERIC JOHN
PERSONAL Born 01/10/1938, Colchester, England, m, 1959, 4 children **DISCIPLINE** PHILOSOPHY **EDUCATION** Hofstra Univ, BA, 60; Univ Rochester, PhD, 64. **CAREER** From instr to asst prof, 63-69, assoc prof Philos, 69-, Fac Coordr Curric, 67-70, Dean of Studies, 70-76, Acting Dean of Fac, 76-77, Dean Fac, 77-90, Chair, Dept of Philos & Relig, Skidmore Col, 92-; dean of the Fac Emer. **MEMBERSHIPS** Am Philos Asn. **RESEARCH** Philosophy of the social sciences; philosophical psychology; epistemology. **CONTACT ADDRESS** Dept of Philos, Skidmore Col, 33 fifth Ave., Saratoga Springs, NY 12866-3524. **EMAIL** eweller@skidmore.edu

WELLIVER, KENNETH BRUCE
PERSONAL Born 10/07/1929, Baltimore, MD, m, 1953, 3 children **DISCIPLINE** BIBLE, RELIGION **EDUCATION** DePauw Univ, BA, 51; Yale Univ, BD, 54, MA, 56, PhD(relig), 61. **CAREER** Assoc prof philos & relig, Nat Col, 59-64; instr philos, Jr Col Kansas City, 61-63; assoc prof Bible & relig, 64-68, chmn dept, 65-75, assoc dean, 77-79, Prof Bible & Relig, WVA Wesleyan Col, 68-97, prof emeritus, 97-, Vpres Acad Affairs & Dean Col, 79-87, Vis prof, Grad Sch, Ecumenical Inst, World Coun Churches, 70-71. **MEMBERSHIPS** AAUP; Soc Bibl Lit; Am Acad Relig. **RESEARCH** New Testament history; early Christian Biblical exegesis; Japanese religions. **CONTACT ADDRESS** West Virginia Wesleyan Col, 59 College Ave, Buckhannon, WV 26201-2699. **EMAIL** welliver@wvwc.edu

WELLMAN, CARL
PERSONAL Born 09/03/1926, Lynn, MA, m, 1953, 4 children **DISCIPLINE** PHILOSOPHY **EDUCATION** Univ Ariz, BA, 49; Harvard Univ, MA, 51, PhD, 54. **CAREER** From instr to prof philos, Lawrence Univ, 53-68; prof philos, 68-, Wash Univ; Am Coun Learned Soc res fel, Univ Mich, 65-66; Nat Endowment Humanities fel, 72-73; Nat Humanities Ctr fel, 82-83. **MEMBERSHIPS** Am Philos Asn; Int Asn Philos Law & Social Philos (secy-gen, 75-79). **RESEARCH** Moral philosophy; philosophy of law; theory of rights. **SELECTED PUBLICATIONS** Auth, Real Rights, Oxford, 95; auth, An Approach to Rights, Kluwer, 97; auth, The Proliferation of Rights, Westview, 98. **CONTACT ADDRESS** Dept of Philosophy, Washington Univ, 1 Brookings Dr, Saint Louis, MO 63130-4899. **EMAIL** wellman@twinearth.wustl.edu

WELLMAN, JAMES K., JR.
PERSONAL Born 08/20/1958, Portland, OR, m, 1985, 2 children **DISCIPLINE** AMERICAN RELIGION **EDUCATION** Univ Wash, BA, 81; Princeton Sem, MDiv, 85; Univ Chicago, PhD, 95. **CAREER** Lectr, Univ Wash, Pacific Lutheran Univ. **HONORS AND AWARDS** Louisville Dis Fel, Louisville Inst Grant; SSR Student Paper Awd. **MEMBERSHIPS** AAR; RRA; SSSR. **RESEARCH** Amer relig; 20th cent; business ethics; contemp Amer spirituality. **SELECTED PUBLICATIONS** Auth, The Gold Coast Church and the Ghetto: Christ and Culture in Mainline Protestantism, Univ Ill Press, 99; auth, The Power of Religious Public: Staking Claims in American Society, Praeger Press, 99. **CONTACT ADDRESS** 8527 Hansen Rd., Bainbridge Island, WA 98110. **EMAIL** jkwamw@uswest.net

WELLS, DAVID FALCONER
PERSONAL Born 05/11/1939, Bulawayo, Zimbabwe, m, 1965, 2 children **DISCIPLINE** SYSTEMATIC THEOLOGY, CHURCH HISTORY **EDUCATION** Univ London, EngL, BD, 66; Trinity Evangel Divinity Sch, ThM, 67; Univ Manchester, PhD, 69. **CAREER** From asst prof to prof church hist, Trinity Evangel Divinity Sch, 69-77, prof syst theol, 78-79; Prof Syst Theol, Gordon-Conwell Theol Sem, 79-, Acad dean, Gordon-Conwell Theol Sem, Charlotte, 98-; Res fel, Divinity Sch, Yale Univ, 73-74; mem, Int Evangel Roman Cath Dialog Missions, 81-; chmn, Task Force Roman Cath, World Evangel Fel Theol Comn, 81-84. **HONORS AND AWARDS** Distinguished lectr, London Inst for Contemp Christianity, London, 85. **RESEARCH** Contextualization; Christology; Roman Cath modernism. **SELECTED PUBLICATIONS** Ed, Toward a Theology for the Future, Creation House, 71; auth, Revolution in Rome, Inter-Varsity Press, 73; ed, The Evangelicals, Abingdon Press, 75; auth, Search for Salvation, Inter-Varsity Press, 78; The Prophetic Theology of George Tywell, Scholars Press, 81; ed, The Eerdmans Handbook of American Christianity, Eerdmans, 83; auth, The Person of Christ: A Biblical and Historical Analysis of the Incarnation, Crossway, 84; ed, Reformed Theology in America: A History of Its Modern Development, Eerdmans, 85; ed, God the Evangelist: How the Holy Spirit Words to Bring Men and Women to Faith, Eerdmans, 87; ed, Christian Faith and Practice in the Modern World: Theology from an Evangelical Point of View, Eerdmans, 88; ed, Turning to God: Biblical Conversion in the Modern World, Baker, 89; ed, The Gospel in the Modern World: A Tribute to John Stott, InterVarsity, 91; auth, No Place for Truth, Or, Whatever Happened to Evangelical Theology, Eerdmans, 93; auth, God in the Wasteland: The Reality of Truth in a World of Fading Dreams, Eerdmans, 94; auth, Losing Our Virtue: Why the Church Must Recover Its Moral Vision, Eerdmans, 98. **CONTACT ADDRESS** Gordon-Conwell Theol Sem, 130 Essex St, South Hamilton, MA 01982-2395.

WELLS, DONALD A.
PERSONAL Born 04/17/1917, St. Paul, MN, m, 1940, 2 children **DISCIPLINE** PHILOSOPHY **EDUCATION** Hamline Univ, BA, 40; Boston Univ, STB, 43, PhD, 46. **CAREER** Asst

prof, philos, Oregon State Univ, 46-48; asst, assoc, prof, chemn, philos, Washington State Univ, 48-69; prof philos, chemn, Univ Ill, Chicago Cir, 69-71; prof philos, chemn, Univ Hawaii, 71-92. **HONORS AND AWARDS** Sleeper fel, Boston Univ, 44-46; Kent fel, Danforth Found, 42; Ford Found fel, UCLA, 52-53; Rockefeller Found fel, 80; founder, int philos for the prevention of nuclear omnicide. **MEMBERSHIPS** APA; Philos for Peace; Int Philos for the Prevention of Nuclear Omnicide. **RESEARCH** War and moral issues; war crimes; laws of war; just war theory. **SELECTED PUBLICATIONS** Auth, The Law of Land Warfare: A Guide to the US Army Manuals, Greenwood, 92; ed, An Encyclopedia of War and Morality, Greenwood, 96. **CONTACT ADDRESS** 1200 Miramar Ave, #210, Medford, OR 97504. **EMAIL** donwells@grrtech.com

WELLS, JEROME C.
PERSONAL Born 05/08/1936, Detroit, MI, m, 1963, 1 child **DISCIPLINE** ECONOMICS **EDUCATION** Univ Mich, BA, 58; John Hopins Univ, MA, 61; Univ Mich, PhD, econo, 64. **CAREER** Univ Pittsburg, Prof, econo, pub admin, 90-; Ahmadu Bello Univ, Nigeria, vis prof, econ, 75-76; Univ Pittsburg, Assoc Prof, econo, 69-90; Univ Ibadan, Nigeria, Research Assoc, vis lectr, econ, 65-67; Univ Pitts, Asst Prof, econo, 64-69; Univ Ibadan, Nigeria, vis asst lectr, 61-62. **HONORS AND AWARDS** Am Farm Eco Dissert Awd, 65. **MEMBERSHIPS** AEA; AAEA; African Studies Asn; Intl Asn Agri Econ. **RESEARCH** Agri performance, econ devel; cross sec charac econo growth; measuring agri output; media econo; macroecono behavior. **SELECTED PUBLICATIONS** Structural Analysis of Manufacturers-led Growth in Asia, with James H Cassing, Ru-Zhong Wang, Paper, conf Eastern Economic Asn, Washington DC, 97; African Economic Growth-Lack Of it-Revisited, Univ Pittsburg, Dept Econ, 96. **CONTACT ADDRESS** Univ of Pittsburgh, Dept Economics, Pittsburgh, PA 15213. **EMAIL** wells01+@pitt.edu

WELLS, JONATHAN
PERSONAL Born New York, NY, m, 1982, 2 children **DISCIPLINE** BIOLOGY, THEOLOGY **EDUCATION** Yale Univ, PhD , 86; Univ CA, Berkeley, PhD, 94. **CAREER** Post-Doct, res biolog, Univ Calif, Berkeley; sr fel, The Discovery Inst, Seattle, Wash; assoc ed, Origins & Design, Evanston, Ill. **MEMBERSHIPS** AAR; Am Asn for the Advancement of Sci; Am Sci Affil; Am Soc for Cell Biology; Int Soc for the Hist, Philos, and Social Studies of Biology; Soc for Develop Biology. **SELECTED PUBLICATIONS** Auth, Marriage and the Family in Unification Theology, Dialogue & Alliance, 9, 95; auth, Issues in the Creation-Evolution Controversies, The World & I, 96; auth, Confocal Microscopy Analysis of Living Xenopus Eggs and the Mechanism of Cortical Rotation, Development, 122, 96; Microtubule-mediated organelle transport and localization of beta-catenin to the future dorsal side of Xenopus eggs, Proc Natl Acad Sci USA, 94, 97; auth, Homology: A Concept in Crisis, Origins and Design 18, 97; auth, Theological Witch-Hunt: The NCC Critique of the Unification Church, J of Unification Stud 1, 97; auth, Evolution by Design, The World & I, 98; auth, Abusing Theology: Howard Van Till's Forgotten Doctrine of Creation's Functional Integrity, Origins & Design 19, 98; Haeckel's Embryos and Evolution: Setting the Record Straight, Amer Biology Tchr, 99. **CONTACT ADDRESS** 1402 Third Ave., #400, Seattle, WA 98101. **EMAIL** jonwells1@compuserve.com

WELLS, WILLIAM W.
DISCIPLINE LAW **EDUCATION** Eastern Oregon Col, BS; Univ Puget Sound; JD; Univ Wash, MLL. **CAREER** Prof and dir, Garbrecht Law Libr, 86-; past asst dir, Burns Law Libr, George Wash Univ; past sr ref librn, Univ Va Law Sch; assoc provost for Technol, Inf Syst, and Libr, USM, 90; past app to, State Ct Libr Comt. **SELECTED PUBLICATIONS** Auth, Maine's Legal Research Guide. **CONTACT ADDRESS** School of Law, Univ of So Maine, 96 Falmouth St, PO Box 9300, Portland, ME 04104-9300.

WELTON, WILLIAM A.
PERSONAL Born 01/31/1961, Lakewood, OH, s **DISCIPLINE** PHILOSOPHY **EDUCATION** Duquesne Univ, PhD, 93. **CAREER** Instr, philos, Xavier Univ, 97-98; vis fac, Xavier Univ. **MEMBERSHIPS** Amer Philos Asn; Soc for Ancient Greek Philos. **RESEARCH** Plato; Aristotle. **SELECTED PUBLICATIONS** Auth, Divine Inspiration and the Origins of the Laws in Plato's Laws, Polis, 14, no 1 and 2, 53-83, 97; co-auth, An Overlooked Motive in Alcibiades' Symposium Speech, Interpretation, 24, 1, 67-84, 96; co-auth, The Viability of Virtue in the Mean, Apeiron, 28, 4, 79-102, 96; auth, Incantation and Expectation in Laws II, Philos and Rhetoric, 29, 3, 211-224, 96. **CONTACT ADDRESS** Philos Dept, Xavier Univ, Ohio, 3800 Victory Pkwy, Cincinnati, OH 45207. **EMAIL** wawel@xu.campus.mci.net

WENDEROTH, CHRISTINE
PERSONAL Born 10/12/1949, Passiaic, NJ, 2 children **DISCIPLINE** THEOLOGICAL STUDIES & LIBRARIANSHIP **EDUCATION** Oberlin Col, BA, 71; Univ NC, MSLS, 73; Emory Univ, MA, 78, PhD, 82. **CAREER** Assoc dir of Library & asst prof of Practical Theology, Columbia Theol Sem, Decatur, GA, 80-93; dir of The Library & asst prof of Ministry, Colgate Rochester Divinity School, 94-. **MEMBERSHIPS** Am Theol Library Asn; AAR/SBL. **RESEARCH** Practical theology; gender studies. **CONTACT ADDRESS** Ambrose Swasey Library, Colgate Rochester Divinity Sch/Bexley Hall/Crozer Theol Sem, 1100 S Goodman, Rochester, NY 14620. **EMAIL** cwenderoth@crds.edu

WENGERT, ROBERT
DISCIPLINE PHILOSOPHY **EDUCATION** Univ Toronto, PhD. **CAREER** Assoc prof, Univ Ill Urbana Champaign. **RESEARCH** Medieval philosophy; history and philosophy of logic; logic programming; applied ethics. **SELECTED PUBLICATIONS** Auth, The Sources of Intuitive Cognition in William of Ockham; The Paradox of the Midwife; Necessity of the Past: What is Ockham's Model?. **CONTACT ADDRESS** Philosophy Dept, Univ of Illinois, Urbana-Champaign, 105 Gregory Hall, 810 S Wright St, Champaign, IL 61820. **EMAIL** wengert@ntx1.cso.uiuc.edu

WENINGER, ROBERT
DISCIPLINE PHILOSOPHY **EDUCATION** Frankfurt Univ, PhD. **CAREER** Asst, assoc, Wash Univ, 88-97; PROF, GERM, COMP LIT, CHAIR, DEPT GER, WASH UNIV, 97-. **CONTACT ADDRESS** Dept of Germanic Languages & Literatures, Washington Univ, 1 Brookings Dr., Saint Louis, MO 63130. **EMAIL** rkwening@artsci.wustl.edu

WENNBERG, ROBERT N.
DISCIPLINE PHILOSOPHY **EDUCATION** Univ Calif, Santa Barbara, PhD, 73. **CAREER** Prof philos, 70-. **HONORS AND AWARDS** Tchr yr, 73, 82, 89, 94; fac res award, 86. **RESEARCH** Ethics. **SELECTED PUBLICATIONS** Auth, Terminal Choices: Euthanasia, Suicide and the Right to Die, Eerdmans, 89; Life in the Balance: Exploring the Abortion Controversy, Eerdmans, 85; Animal Suffering and the Problem of Evil, Christian Scholar's Rev, XXI, 91; The Right to Life: Reflections on Three Theories, Christian Scholar's Rev, XIV, 85. **CONTACT ADDRESS** Dept of Philos, Westmont Col, 955 La Paz Rd, Santa Barbara, CA 93108-1099.

WENNEMYR, SUSAN E.
PERSONAL Born 04/16/1964, Tulsa, OK, m, 1991 **DISCIPLINE** THEOLOGY; CULTURE **EDUCATION** Harvard Univ, BA (Philos), 86; Univ Chicago, PhD (Theol), 95. **CAREER** Asst prof relig, Manchester Col, asst dir of Brethren Colleges Abroad, 93-96; Dean of Davenport Col and Instr of Relig Studies, Yale Univ, 97-. **HONORS AND AWARDS** Mellon fel for graduate study; Mellon dissertation grant. **MEMBERSHIPS** Am Academy Relig; Soc for Values in Higher Ed; Asn on Relig and Intellectual Life. **RESEARCH** Global Christian theology; psychology and relig; deconstructionism and Christian tradition. **SELECTED PUBLICATIONS** Auth, Dancing in the Dark: Deconstructive A/ Theology Leaps with Faith, J of the Am Academy of Relig, 66:3, fall 98; Feminist Christian Ethics, in Encyclopedia of Feminism, Routledge, forthcoming. **CONTACT ADDRESS** Box 200018 Yale, New Haven, CT 06520. **EMAIL** magnus.wennemyr@yale.edu

WENTZ, RICHARD E.
PERSONAL Born 01/10/1928, Palmerton, PA, m, 1991, 4 children **DISCIPLINE** RELIGION **EDUCATION** Ursinus Col, AB, 48; Lancaster Theol Seminary, BD, 51; George Washington Univ, M Phil, 70; PhD, 71. **CAREER** Master, Mercersburg Acad, 55-62; asst prof & educ dir of rel studies, PSU, 62-72; prof, Ariz State Univ, 72-99, prof emeritus, PSU, 99-. **HONORS AND AWARDS** Lilly Endowment Grant; Danforth Found Awd; Vis Fel, Nanzen Inst for Rel and Culture, Japan, 87; Bell Distinguished Vis Prof, Univ of Tulsa, 91. **MEMBERSHIPS** Am Acad of Rel, Am Soc of Church Hist, Pa German Soc. **RESEARCH** Pennsylvania German religion & culture, the Mercersburg movement in American religion, twentieth century American religious thought, American public religion, the privatization of the divine. **SELECTED PUBLICATIONS** Auth, Religion in the New World: The Shaping of Religious Traditions in the United States, Fortress, 90; auth, Pennsylvania Dutch Folk Spirituality, Paulist, 93; auth, Why People Do Bad Things in the Name of Religion, Mercer, 93; auth, John William Nevin, American Theologian, Oxford, 97; auth, The Culture of Religious Pluralism, Westview, 98. **CONTACT ADDRESS** Dept Rel, Arizona State Univ, PO Box 873104, Tempe, AZ 85287-3104. **EMAIL** richard.wentz@asu.edu

WERNER, RICHARD W.
PERSONAL Born 04/23/1947, Chester, PA, m, 1968, 2 children **DISCIPLINE** PHILOSOPHY **EDUCATION** Rutgers Univ, BA, 70; Univ Rochester, MA, 73; PhD, 74. **CAREER** Instr of Philosophy, Westfield Col, 74-75; Asst Prof, Kirkland Col, 75-78; Asst Prof Hamilton Col, 78-81; Assoc Prof, Hamilton Col 81-88; Prof, Hamilton Col, 88-; John Stuart Kennedy Prof, Hamilton Col, 94. **HONORS AND AWARDS** First Prize John Dewey Essay Contest, 74, NEH Summer Seminar on Contemporary Moral Issues, 79, John Dewey Research Fel, 83-84, Tennent Caledonian Fellow, Univ of St. Andrews, 89 **MEMBERSHIPS** APA, Concerned Philosophers for Peace. **RESEARCH** Ethics, Pragmatism. **SELECTED PUBLICATIONS** Auth, "John Dewey: Pragmatism and Justification in Ethics-A Reconstruction," The Personalist, 60 (79): 273-289; auth, "Ethical Realism," Ethics, 93 (83): 653-679; auth, "Abortion: The Outological and Moral Status of the Unborn, selections, Ethics: Theory and Practice, ed. Manuel Velasquez and Cynthia Rostankowski (Englewood Cliffs, NJ: Prentice Hall, 85), 252-260; auth, "The Immorality of Nuclear Deterrence, Political Realism and International Morality, ed. Diana Meyers and Kenneth Kipnis (Boulder, CO, Westview Press, 87), 158-178; auth, "Nuclear Deterrence and the Limits of Moral Theory," The Monist 70 (87): 355-376; auth, "Animal Use for Human Organ Transplant," Biomedical Ethics Review, ed, James Humder and Robert Almeder (Clifton, NJ: The Humana Press, 88), 65-87; auth, "South Africa: University Neutrality and Divestment," Neutrality and Academuc Ethics, ed. Robert Simon (Totowa, NJ: Roman and Littlefield, 94), 161-171; auth, "Various Entries for Encyclopedia on War and Ethics, ed. Donald Wells (Westport CT: Greenwood Press, 96). **CONTACT ADDRESS** Dept Philosophy, Hamilton Col, New York, 198 College Hill Rd, Clinton, NY 13323-1218. **EMAIL** rwerner@hamilton.edu

WERT, NEWELL JOHN
PERSONAL Born 10/10/1926, West Lawn, PA, m, 1947, 3 children **DISCIPLINE** SOCIAL ETHICS **EDUCATION** Albright Col, AB, 47; United Theol Sem, BD, 50; Boston Univ, PhD, 58. **CAREER** Asst prof sociol, Otterbein Col, 54-57; from asst prof to assoc prof, 57-63, prof Christian ethics & dean, United Theol Sem, 63-; mem, study comn on church & state, Nat Coun Churches, 62-64; deleg, World Conf Church & Soc, Geneva, Switz, Aug 66. **HONORS AND AWARDS** Am Assn Theol Schs fac fel studies ecumenical social ethics, Geneva, 66-67. **MEMBERSHIPS** Soc Christian Ethics; Am Acad Relig. **RESEARCH** Sociological writing of Roman Catholic scholars; institutional aspects of Christian churches; professional ethics. **SELECTED PUBLICATIONS** Auth, Dimensions of Decision, Graded Press, 68. **CONTACT ADDRESS** United Theol Sem, 1810 Harvard Blvd, Dayton, OH 45406-4599.

WERTH, LEE FREDERICK
PERSONAL Born 02/09/1941, York, PA, m, 1967, 2 children **DISCIPLINE** PHILOSOPHY **EDUCATION** Case Western Reserve Univ, BA, 62; Univ Waterloo, PhD, 72. **CAREER** Instr philos, Althouse Col Educ, Univ Western Ont, 69-70; asst prof, 72-78, assoc prof philos, Cleveland State Univ, 79-**MEMBERSHIPS** Philos Sci Asn; Am Philos Asn; Can Philos Asn; Int Soc Study Time. **RESEARCH** Philosophy of space and time; metaphysics; early modern philosophy. **SELECTED PUBLICATIONS** Auth, Annihilating nihilism, 74, Some Second Thoughts on First Principles, 75, A Declaration of Interdependence 76, Philosophy in Context; Normalizing the Paranormal, Am Philos Quart, 1/78; The Untenability of Whitehead's Theory of Extensive Connection, Process Studies, spring 78; On again, Off again, Philosophers Speak on Science Fiction, Nelson-Hall (in press); Siddhartha and Slaughterhouse Five, The Intersection of Science Fiction & Philosophy, Greenwood (in press); ed, Science fiction & philosophy, Philos Context, Vol 11, 81; Clarifying Concrecence in Whitehead's Process Philosophy, Chap 12-The Study of Time VII: Time and Process, Int Univ, 93; Evolutionary Epistemology and Pragmatism, in Living Doubt (Essays concerning the epistemology of Charles Sanders Peirce), Kluwer Acad Publ, 94; The Anthropocentric Predicaments and the Search for Extraterrestrial Intelligence, J Appl Philos, 98. **CONTACT ADDRESS** Dept of Philos, Cleveland State Univ, 1983 E 24th St, Cleveland, OH 44115-2440. **EMAIL** l.werth@csuohio.edu

WERTHEIMER, ELLEN
DISCIPLINE CONTRACTS, PRODUCTS LIABILITY, MEDICAL MALPRACTICE, THE SUPREME COURT **EDUCATION** Yale Univ, BA, 75; Yale Law Sch, JD, 79. **CAREER** Prof, Villanova Univ; clerked to, Honorable Frank A. Kaufman, US Dist Judge, US Dist Ct Dist Md & to Honorable James Hunter III, US Circuit Judge, US Ct Appeals Third Circuit;past assoc, Pepper, Hamilton & Scheetz; past ch, Villanova Curric Comt and Clerkship Comt. **MEMBERSHIPS** Order Coif; Phi Beta Kappa. **RESEARCH** Products liability; medical malpract, law and medicine, torts. **SELECTED PUBLICATIONS** Auth, Unavoidably Unsafe Products: A Modest Proposal, Chi- Kent L Rev, 96; The Third Restatement of Torts: An Unreasonably Dangerous Doctrine, Suffolk U L. Rev, 95; The Smoke Gets in Their Eyes: Product Category Liability and Alternative Feasible Designs in the Third Restatement, Tenn L Rev, 94; Azzarello Agonistes: Bucking the Strict Products Liability Tide, Temple L Rev, 93 & Unknowable Dangers and The Death of Strict Products Liability: The Empire Strikes Back, Cinc L Rev, 92. **CONTACT ADDRESS** Law School, Villanova Univ, 800 Lancaster Ave, Villanova, PA 19085-1692. **EMAIL** wertheim@law.vill.edu

WERTHEIMER, JACK
DISCIPLINE JEWISH HISTORY **EDUCATION** Queens Col CUNY, BA, MA; Columbia Univ, MPhil; PhD, 78. **CAREER** Adj lectr, City Col and Queens Col CUNY; vis asst prof, Vassar College; adj assoc prof, US Mil Acad West Point; dir, Joseph and Miriam Ratner Ctr Study Conser Judaism; provost/chief acad off, Jewish Theol Sem Am; Joseph and Martha Mendelson Prof Am Jewish Hist. **HONORS AND AWARDS** Grant, Pew

Charitable Trusts; Nat Jewish Bk Awd, 93-94. **RESEARCH** History and the contemporary state of Conservative Judaism. **SELECTED PUBLICATIONS** Auth, Unwelcome Strangers East European Jews in Imperial Germany, Oxford Univ Press, 87; A People Divided: Judaism in Contemporary America, Basic Bks and Univ Press New England, 97; ed, The American Synagogue--A Sanctuary Transformed, Cambridge Univ Press, 87; The Uses of Tradition: Jewish Continuity in the Modern Era, JTS/Harvard,93; The Modern Jewish Experience--A Reader's Guide, NYU Press, 93. **CONTACT ADDRESS** Jewish Theol Sem of America, 3080 Broadway, New York, NY 10027. **EMAIL** jawertheimer@jtsa.edu

WERTHEIMER, ROGER
PERSONAL Born 04/10/1942, Buffalo, NY, d **DISCIPLINE** PHILOSOPHY **EDUCATION** Brandeis Univ, BA, 63; Harvard Univ, MA, 67; Harvard Univ, 69; Portland Metro Police Acad, OPOC, 70; Boston Univ, Psych Coun Train, 76. **CAREER** AGREE Co, Pres, 84-98; Cal State Univ, lectr, 95; L B State Univ, CA, assoc prof, 89-94; Univ Houston, vis assoc prof, 83-84; Carnegie Mell Univ, assoc prof, 77-83; Univ Houston, vis assoc prof, 77; Univ Cincinnati, v assoc prof, 76; Boston State Hosp, researcher; therapist, 75-77; Tuffs Univ, vis assoc prof, 74-75; Guggenheim Fel 73-74. **HONORS AND AWARDS** Harvard Univ Grad Scholarships, 64 - 65; NYS Regents Fel, 66; Kent Fel, 67; Harvard Univ, CAR Prize, 69; Guggenheim Fel, 73; Mellon Gnt, 78; CSULB Inter Edu Awd, 91; NEH Grant, 94; APA Rockefeller Prize, 98 **MEMBERSHIPS** MPPS, APA, AAAE **RESEARCH** Ethics; philosophy; epistemology. **SELECTED PUBLICATIONS** Auth, The Significance of Sense: Meaning, Modality and Morality, Cornell UP, 72; Socratic Skepticism, in: Metaphilosophy, 93; Synonymy Without Analyticity, in: Inter Philo Pre Exchange, 94; Constraining Condemning, in: Ethics, 98; Identity: Logic, Ontology, Epistemology, in: Philo 98. **CONTACT ADDRESS** 1327 North Olive Dr #A, North Hollywood, CA 90069. **EMAIL** rwertheim@juno.com

WERTZ, S. K.
PERSONAL Born 10/27/1941, Amarillo, TX, M, 1967 **DISCIPLINE** PHILOSOPHY **EDUCATION** Univ OK, PhD, 70; Univ Kent at Canterbury, post grad, 65; Rice Univ, post grad, 88. **CAREER** Texas Christian Univ, Ft Worth, inst, asst prof, assoc prof, prof, 30 yr. **HONORS AND AWARDS** Fel Amer Acad of Kinesi and Phys Edu, 95-, Phi Beta Delta (NHSIS), Alumni mem Phi Beta Kappa, TCU Chap **MEMBERSHIPS** APA, ASA, PSSS, Hume Society, Collingwood Society, SPS, AAKPE **RESEARCH** Hist mod philo; philo of hist; aesth and sport. **SELECTED PUBLICATIONS** Auth, Talking a Good Game: Inquiries into the Principles of Sport, S Meth Univ Press, 91; Sports Inside Out: Readings in Literature and Philosophy, Tex Christ Univ Press, 85, Human Nature and Art: From Descartes and Hume to Tolstoy, Jour Aesth Edu, 98; Mill on Mathematics: The Ayer-Quinton Interpretations, SW Philo Rev, 97; Moral Judgements in History: Humes Position, Hume Studies, 96; Sport Conundrum (Its Massive Appeal): Bernard Jeu's Semiotic Solution, Aethlon: Jour of Sport Lit, 96; Is Sport Unique? A Question of Definability, Jour Philo of Sport, 95; The Role of Practice in Collingwood's Theory of Art, SW Philo Review, 95; Hume and the Historiography of Science, Jour Hist of Ideas, 93; auth, Between Hume's Philosophy and History, Univ Press of America, 00. **CONTACT ADDRESS** Dept of Philosophy, Texas Christian Univ, PO Box 297250, Fort Worth, TX 76219. **EMAIL** swertz@gamma.is.tuc.edu

WESS, ROBERT C.
DISCIPLINE PHILOSOPHY **EDUCATION** Scotus Col, BA, 62; Xavior Univ, MA, 66; Univ Notre Dame; PhD, 70. **CAREER** Tchr, OH Dominican Col, 72-79; tchr, Pembroke State Univ, 79-84; tchr, S Polytech State Univ, 84-. **MEMBERSHIPS** MLA; GA SC Col Asn. **RESEARCH** Compos studies. **SELECTED PUBLICATIONS** Auth, publ(s) on Puritan lit; work of Washington Irving; res and tchg compos. **CONTACT ADDRESS** Hum and Tech Commun Dept, So Polytech State Univ, S Marietta Pkwy, PO Box 1100, Marietta, GA 30060. **EMAIL** rwess@spsu.edu

WESSELSCHMIDT, QUENTIN F.
PERSONAL Born 02/03/1937, Washington, MD, m, 1963 **DISCIPLINE** THEOLOGY, CLASSICS (GREEK AND LATIN) **EDUCATION** St Paul's Jr Coll, Concordia, MO, 57; Concordia Sr Coll, BA, 59; Concordia Sem, BD, 63; Marquette Univ, MA, 69, Univ Iowa, PhD, 79. **CAREER** Pastor, Our Savior Lutheran Church, IL, 63-65; prof, Concordia Coll, WI, 65-73; instr, Milwaukee Lutheran High Schhol, WI, 74-77; prof, Concordia Sem, Mo, 77-. **MEMBERSHIPS** North Am Patristic Soc; Am Philol Asn; Class Asn of the Mid w and s. **RESEARCH** Patristics. **SELECTED PUBLICATIONS** Auth, chapter, Heritage, Motion; Chapter, Light from Above; articles, Concordia J. **CONTACT ADDRESS** 801 De Mun Ave, Saint Louis, MO 63105.

WEST, CHARLES CONVERSE
PERSONAL Born 02/03/1921, Plainfield, NJ, m, 1944, 3 children **DISCIPLINE** THEOLOGY, ETHICS **EDUCATION** Columbia Univ, BA, 42; Union Theol Sem, NYork, BD, 45; Yale Univ, PhD, 55. **CAREER** Instr hist, Peking Nat Univ, 48; soc sci, Cheeloo Univ, 48-49; Christian ethics, Nanking Theol Sem, 49-50; dozent, Kirchliche Hochsch, Berlin, Ger, 51-53; assoc dir, Ecumenical Inst, Bessey World Council Churches, 56-61; charge de cours theol, Inst Hautes Etudes Oecumeniques, Univ Geneva, 56-61; assoc prof, 61-63, Prof Christian Ethics, Princeton Theol Sem, 63-91, Acad Dean, 79-84, EMERITUS, 91-, Mem comt on confession of 1967, United Presby Church USA, 61-67; chmn, US Asn Christian Peace Conf, 65-72; mem int affairs comn, Nat Coun Churches, 67-69; working comt, dept church & soc, World Coun Churches, 68-83; John Courtney Murray fel, Woodstock Theol Ctr, 76-77. **MEMBERSHIPS** Am Soc Christian Ethics (vpres, 72-73, pres, 73-74); Am Theol Soc (vpres, 82-83, pres, 83-84). **RESEARCH** Christian theology and action in an East Asian environment; Christianity and Marxism; theology and ethics of politics. **SELECTED PUBLICATIONS** Auth, Communism and The Theologians, SCM Press, London, 58, Westminster & McMillan, 63; Outside the Camp, Doubleday, 59; coauth, The Sufficiency of God: Essays in Honor of Dr W A Visser 't Hooft, SCM Press & Westminister, 63; Community, Christian and secular, In: Man in Community, Asn Press, 66; Act and being in Christian and Marxist perspective, In: Openings for Marxist-Christian Dialogue, Abingdon, 69; auth, Ethics, Violence and Revolution, Coun Relig & Int Affairs, 70; The Power to be Human, Macmillan, 71; Facts, morals and the bomb, In: To Avoid Catastrophe, Eerdmans, 79; auth, "Power, Truth, and Community in Modern Culture," Trinity Press International, 99. **CONTACT ADDRESS** Princeton Theol Sem, PO Box 821, Princeton, NJ 08542. **EMAIL** ccwrcw@bellatlantic.net

WEST, FREDERICK S.
PERSONAL Born 11/10/1944, St. Paul, MN, m, 1973, 4 children **DISCIPLINE** THEOLOGY **EDUCATION** Grinnell Col, BA, 67; Chicago Theol Sem, MDiv, 74; Univ Notre Dame, PhD, 88. **CAREER** Adjunct instr, United Theol Sem, 99-. **MEMBERSHIPS** Am Acad of Relig; North Am Acad of Liturgy; Mercersburg Soc. **RESEARCH** Liturgical methodology. **SELECTED PUBLICATIONS** Auth, Scripture and Memory: The Ecumenical Hermeneutic of the Three-Year Lectionaries, 97; The Comparative Liturgy of Anton Baumstark, 95; "An Annotated Bibliography of the Three-Year Lectionaries," 93; "Models of Renewing Worship: United Church of Christ Worship," 93. **CONTACT ADDRESS** 200 Oak Knoll Dr, Marine on Saint Croix, MN 55047.

WEST, GEORGE FERDINAND, JR.
PERSONAL Born 10/25/1940, Adams Co, MS, m **DISCIPLINE** LAW **EDUCATION** Tougaloo Coll, BA 1962; So Univ Sch of Law, JD 1966; Univ MS, JD 1968. **CAREER** Natchez Adams Co Sch Bd, appt/co-atty 1967-95; State Adv Bd for Voc Edn, appt 1968; Natchez-Adams Co C of C, appt/dir 1974; Jeff Co Sch Sys, atty 1974; MS Sch Bd Assn, dir/atty; Radio Pgm "Fact-Finding", modrtr; Copiah-Lincoln Jr Coll Natchez Br, bus law prof; Natchez News Leader, mg edtr;Private Practice Natchez, MS, **HONORS AND AWARDS** Outstand Yng Men in Am 1967-; Comm Ldr of Am 1972; Lifetime Rosco Pound Fel, 72; Most Distinguished Black Attorney Travelers Coalition, 1988; Doctor of Humane Letters, Natchez Coll, 1989; Man of the Year, Natchez, MS, NAACP, 1990; Man of the Year, Natchez Business & Civic League, 1991; Most Outstanding Attorney, NAACP, 1992; Recorded first music album entitled "Ole Time Way," 1993; Outstanding Attorney for the African Methodist Episcopal Southern District & Man of the Year, Zion Chapel AME Church, 1995; recognized by the Magnolia Bar Assn and recipient of the "Pioneer and Leadership Awd" 1997-98. **MEMBERSHIPS** Mem MS Bar Assn 1968; rsrchr/procter MS State Univ 1973; NAACP; Natchez Bus & Civ Lgue; vice pres Gov Com Hire the Hndcp; trust/sunday sch tchr Zion Chap AME Ch; contributing editor, Bluff City Post, 1978-; chmn, Natchez-Adams School Bd, 1988-. **CONTACT ADDRESS** PO Box 1202, Natchez, MS 39120.

WEST, HENRY ROBISON
PERSONAL Born 12/16/1933, Athens, GA, m, 1955, 2 children **DISCIPLINE** PHILOSOPHY **EDUCATION** Emory Univ, AB, 54; Duke Univ, MA, 58; Union Theol Sem, MDiv, 59; Harvard Univ, PhD(philos), 65. **CAREER** Instr hist philos & sociol, Spelman Col, 57-60; instr humanities, Mass Inst Technol, 61- 65; from asst prof to assoc prof, 65-76, prof philos, Macalester Col, 76-, Old Dominion fel, 65; vis asst prof, Univ Minn, 68; Ford Found grant, Oxford, 70-71; vis prof, Univ Chicago, 78-79; vis prof, Univ of North Carolina, Chapel Hill, 80. **MEMBERSHIPS** Soc Philos & Pub Affairs; Am Philos Asn; Am Soc Polit & Legal Philos; Southern Soc Philos & Psychol. **RESEARCH** Utilitarian ethics; the philosphy of John Stuart Mill; political philosophy. **SELECTED PUBLICATIONS** Auth, Reconstructing Mill's proof of the principle of utility, Mind, 4/72; Utilitarianism, Encyclopedia Britannica, 15th ed, Encycl Brit, 74; Mill's naturalism, J Value Inquiry, 75; Mill's qualitative hedonism, Philos, 76; Comparing utilitarianism, Philos Res Arch, 76; Mill's moral conservatism, Midwest Studies Philos, 76; co-ed, Moral Philosophy: Classic Texts and Contemporary Problems, Dickenson, 77; Mill's proof of the principle of utility, In: The Limits of Utilitarianism, Univ Minn Press, 81; auth, Mill, John Stazrt, Encyclopedia of Ethics, 00. **CONTACT ADDRESS** Dept of Philosophy, Macalester Col, 1600 Grand Ave, Saint Paul, MN 55105-1899. **EMAIL** west@macalester.edu

WEST, JAMES E.
PERSONAL Born 08/29/1960, Oceanside, CA, m, 1983, 1 child **DISCIPLINE** THEOLOGY **EDUCATION** Carson-Newman Col, BA, 85; Southern Baptist Theol Sem, MDiv, 88, ThM, 91; Andersonville Baptist Sem, ThD, 94. **CAREER** Browns Baptist Church, Norlina NC, pastor, 86-90; Vance-Granville Comm Col, inst, 87-91; Tabbs Creek Baptist Church, pastor, 90-93; First Baptist Church Petros TN, pastor, 93-, Quartz Hill Sch of Theol, adj prof, 96-; adj prof of Ancient Near Eastern Stud, Hudson Col, 00-. **HONORS AND AWARDS** Ordained Baptist Minister. **MEMBERSHIPS** SBL, ASOR, CBAA, IOTS, FJS. **RESEARCH** New testament; Hebrew literature; historical Jesus. **SELECTED PUBLICATIONS** Auth, The Eerdman's Dictionary of the Bible, entries; Abaddon, Apollyon, Hades, Sheol, Eerdman's Pub, 00; auth, Biblical Studies, A Beginner's Guide, Quartz Hill Pub, 98; auth, essays, Quartz Hill Jour of Theol; abstracts in: Old Testament Abstracts. **CONTACT ADDRESS** First Baptist Church, 321 Main St, Petros, TN 37845-0300. **EMAIL** Jwest@highland.net

WEST, MARTHA S.
PERSONAL Born 02/05/1946, Pomona, CA, 3 children **DISCIPLINE** HISTORY; LAW **EDUCATION** Brandeis Univ, BA, 67; Indiana Univ, JD, 74. **CAREER** Atty, 74-82; asst prof, Univ Calif Davis Law Sch, 82-88; prof and assoc dean, 88-92; prof, 92- . **HONORS AND AWARDS** The 1981 Redding Scholar, Indianapolis Chamber of Com, Lacy Exec Leadership Series, 81-82; The Ruth E. Anderson Awd from Women's Res and Resources Ctr and Women's Studies Prog, UC Davis, for outstanding service on behalf of campus women, 90; Sacramento YWCA Outstanding Woman of the Year in Educ, 91; The Deanna Falge Awd for diversity and affirmative action, UC Davis, 96; The William & Sally Rutte Distinguished Teaching Awd, UCD Law Sch, 97. **MEMBERSHIPS** AAUP; NLG; ABA. **RESEARCH** Women's legal rights; sex discrimination in higher education. **SELECTED PUBLICATIONS** Auth, Gender Bias in Academic Robes: The Law's Failure to Protect Women Faculty, Temple Law Rev, 94; auth, Women Faculty: Frozen in Time, Academe, 95; auth, History Lessons: Affirmative Action, The Women's Rev of Books, 96; auth, The Historical Roots of Affirmative Action, La Raza Law J, 96; co-auth with H.H. Kay, Sex-Based Discrimination: Text, Cases, and Materials, 96; auth, Equitable Funding of Public Schools under State Constitutional Law, J Gender, Race, and Justice, 98. **CONTACT ADDRESS** School of Law, Univ of California, Davis, Davis, CA 95616. **EMAIL** mswest@ucdavis.edu

WESTACOTT, EMRYS
PERSONAL Born 10/22/1956, Nottingham, England, m, 1986, 2 children **DISCIPLINE** PHILOSOPHY **EDUCATION** Sheffield, BA, 79; McGill, MA, 84; Univ Texas, PhD, 95. **CAREER** Vis asst prof, Southwestern Univ, 95-96; asst prof, Alfred Univ, 96- . **MEMBERSHIPS** APA. **RESEARCH** Relativism; ethics; continental philosophy. **SELECTED PUBLICATIONS** Auth, On the Motivations for Relativism, Cogito; auth, Relativism: An Allegorical Elucidation, Philos Now; auth, Relativism and Autonomy, The Philos Forum; auth, Teaching Mills On Liberty, Tchg Philos. **CONTACT ADDRESS** Division of Human Studies, Alfred Univ, Alfred, NY 14802. **EMAIL** westacott@bigvax.alfred.edu

WESTBLADE, DONALD
PERSONAL Born 03/11/1953, Denver, CO, m, 1983, 3 children **DISCIPLINE** NEW TESTAMENT **EDUCATION** Williams Col, BA, 74; Fuller Sem, MDiv, 78; Yale Univ, 83, MPhil, 87. **CAREER** ASST PROF REL, 88-00, HILLSDALE COL. **MEMBERSHIPS** SBL, AAR, IBR, ETS **RESEARCH** New Testament ethics and rhetoric; New Testament theology. **SELECTED PUBLICATIONS** Auth, Divine Election in the Pauline Literature, in The Grace of God, The Bondage of the Will, vol 1, Baker, 95. **CONTACT ADDRESS** Hillsdale Col, 33 E College, Hillsdale, MI 49242. **EMAIL** westblade@hillsdale.edu

WESTERMEYER, PAUL
PERSONAL Born 03/28/1940, Cincinnati, OH, m, 1963, 4 children **DISCIPLINE** CHURCH MUSIC **EDUCATION** Univ Elmhurst, BA, 62; Lancaster Theol Sem, 65; Sch Sacred Mus, Union Theol Sem, SMM, 66; Univ Chicago, MA, 74, PhD, 78; additional study, Sch Cantorum; Concordia Theol Sem, 66; liturgical stud prog, Notre Dame, 69; Lutheran Gen Hospital, 83. **CAREER** Cantor, Ascension Lutheran Church, 82-90; ast pastor, Ascension Lutheran Church, 86-90; Vis prof, Yale Univ Inst Sacred Mus, 89-90; prof, dept ch, choir dir, organist, Elmhurst Col, 68-90; prof, 90-. **HONORS AND AWARDS** Pres, Hymn Society in the US & Canada, 98-00; National Chairman, Amer Guild of Organists, 91-98; Sears--Roebuck Awd Elmhurst College, for Teaching Excellence & Campus leadership, 90; Schaff Prize in church History, Lancaster Seminary, 65. **MEMBERSHIPS** Mem, Amer Choral Dir(s) Assn; Amer Guild of Organists; Amer Soc of Church Hist; Evangel and Reformed Hist Soc; Hymn Soc Am; Intl Arbeitsgemeinschaft fur Hymnologie; Liturgical Conf; Mercersburg Soc; N Amer Acad of Liturgy. **RESEARCH** Theology Music; Hymnody; Liturgy; 19th Century. **SELECTED PUBLICATIONS** Auth, With Tongues of Fire, 95; The Church Musician, 88. **CONTACT ADDRESS** Dept of Music, Luther Sem, 2481 Como Ave, Saint Paul, MN 55108. **EMAIL** pwesterm@luthersem.edu

WESTLEY, RICHARD J.
DISCIPLINE PHILOSOPHY **EDUCATION** Marquette University, BA; Univ Toronto, MA; LMS Bontifical Inst Mediaeval Stud, Toronto;Univ Toronto, PhD, 54. **CAREER** Prof; Loyola Univ, part-time 57 & full-time 68-; lectr, Loyola's Inst Pastoral Stud, Chicago & Barat Col, Lake Forest, Ill. **RESEARCH** Aristotle's ethics; medieval philosophy, especially Aquinas; Kant's ethics; Kierkegaard; Feuerbach; Marx; philosophy of religion; ethical theory; Christian ethics; health care ethics. **SELECTED PUBLICATIONS** Auth, When It's Right to Die: Conflicting Voices, Difficult Choices, 94; Good Things Happen: Experiencing Community in Small Groups, 92; Life, Death and Science, 59; A Theology of Presence, 88; Morality and Its Beyond, 84; Redemptive Intimacy, 81; The Right to Die, 80; What a Modern Catholic Believes About the Right to Life, 73 & I Believe - You Believe, 73. **CONTACT ADDRESS** Dept of Philosophy, Loyola Univ, Chicago, 820 N Michigan Ave, Chicago, IL 60611.

WESTMORELAND, ROBERT B.
DISCIPLINE ETHICS, POLITICAL PHILOSOPHY, PHILOSOPHY OF LAW **EDUCATION** Davidson Col, BA; Univ NC, Chapel Hill, MA, PhD. **CAREER** Asst prof, Univ MS, 89-. **RESEARCH** The problem of moral objectivity. **SELECTED PUBLICATIONS** Auth, Liberalism and the AIDS Crisis, Clin Res and Regulatory Aff, 95. **CONTACT ADDRESS** Univ of Mississippi, Oxford, MS 38677. **EMAIL** prrbw@vm.cc.olemiss.edu

WESTON, BURNS H.
PERSONAL Born 11/05/1933, Cleveland, OH, d, 2 children **DISCIPLINE** INTERNATIONAL LAW, JURISPRUDENCE. **EDUCATION** Oberlin Col, BA, 56; Yale Univ, LLB, 61, JSD, 70. **CAREER** Assoc atty, Paul, Weiss, Rifkind, Wharton & Garrison, NY, 61-64; from asst prof to assoc prof law, 66-69, dir, Ctr World Order Studies, 72-76, prof Law, Univ Iowa, 69-, res fel, Procedural Aspects of Int Law Inst, 67-; consult Naval War Col, 68-69; vis lectr, Grinnell Col, 74-; Inst for World Order sr fel, 76-78, mem exec comt, Consortium on Peace Res, Educ & Develop, 76-; consult, Club Rome Proj on Global Learning, 77-; mem bd trustees, Global Educ Assocs, 78-. **MEMBERSHIPS** Am Soc Int Law; Int Studies Asn; Consortium on Peace Res, Educ & Develop; Int Peace Res Asn; World Future Studies Fedn. **RESEARCH** Third World development; international claims; peace and world order education. **SELECTED PUBLICATIONS** Auth, International Law and the Deprivation of Foreign Wealth: a Framework for Future Inquiry, in: The Future of the International Legal Order--Wealth and Resources, 70; coauth, Valuation upon the Deprivation of Foreign Enterprise: A Policy-Oriented Approach to the Problem of Compensation Under International Law, In: The Valuation of Nationalized Property in International Law, 71; auth, International Claims: Postwar French Practice, Syracuse Univ, 71; coauth, International Claims: Their Settlement by Lump Sum Agreements, Univ Va, 75; auth, Constructive Takings Under International Law: A Modest Foray into the Problem of Creeping Expropriation, Va J Int Law, 75; contribr & co-ed, Toward World Order and Human Dignity: Essays in Honor Myres S McDougal, Free Press, 76; auth, Contending with a Planet in Peril and Change: The Rationale and Meaning of World Order Education, Inst for World Order, 78. **CONTACT ADDRESS** College of Law, Univ of Iowa, Melrose and Bylington, Iowa City, IA 52242. **EMAIL** burns-weston@uiowa.edu

WESTON, THOMAS SPENGLER
PERSONAL Born 03/14/1944, Abilene, TX, m, 1977, 5 children **DISCIPLINE** PHILOSOPHY OF SCIENCE, LOGIC **EDUCATION** Mass Inst Tech, BS, 66, PhD(philos), 74. **CAREER** Instr philos, Mass Inst Tech, 69-70; from instr to asst prof, Univ Southern Calif, 70-74; asst prof to prof philos, San Diego State Univ, 74-. **MEMBERSHIPS** Asn Symbolic Logic. **RESEARCH** Philosophy of science; logic. **SELECTED PUBLICATIONS** Auth, Theories whose quantification cannot be substitutional, Nous, 11/74; Kreisel, the continuum hypothesis and second-order set theory, J Philos Logic, 76; The continuum hypothesis is independent of second-order set theory, Notre Dame J Formal Logic, 77; Approximate Truth, J of Philos Logic, vol 16, 87; Approximate Truth and Scientific Realism, Philos of Sci, vol 59, 92. **CONTACT ADDRESS** Dept of Philos, San Diego State Univ, 5500 Campanile Dr, San Diego, CA 92182-8142. **EMAIL** tweston@mail.sdsu.edu

WESTPHAL, JONATHAN
PERSONAL Born 01/14/1951, Sussex, England, m, 1973, 4 children **DISCIPLINE** PHILOSOPHY **EDUCATION** Univ London, PhD, 81. **CAREER** Assoc prof. **HONORS AND AWARDS** Humboldt Fel. **RESEARCH** Philosophy of mind, vector logic. **SELECTED PUBLICATIONS** Auth, Colour: A Philosophical Introduction; Colour: Some Philosophical Problems From Wittgenstein; Philosophical Propositions; ed, Certainty and Justice; co-ed, Reality of Time and of Life and Death. **CONTACT ADDRESS** Dept of English and Philosophy, Idaho State Univ, Pocatello, ID 83209. **EMAIL** westjona@isu.edu

WESTPHAL, MEROLD
DISCIPLINE PHILOSOPHY **EDUCATION** Yale Univ, PhD. **CAREER** Distinguished prof, Fordham Univ. **RESEARCH** Philos of relig and polit theology. **SELECTED PUBLICATIONS** Auth, History and Truth in Hegel's Phenomenology, Hum Press, 79, 90; God, Guilt, and Death: An Existential Phenomenology of Religion, Ind UP, 87; Kierkegaard's Critique of Reason and Society, Mercer UP, 87, Penn State UP, 91; Suspicion and Faith: The Religious Uses of Modern Atheism, Eerdmans Press, 1993; Becoming a Self: A Reading of Kierkegaard's Concluding Unscientific Postscript, Purdue UP, 96. **CONTACT ADDRESS** Dept of Philos, Fordham Univ, 113 W 60th St, Bronx, NY 10458.

WETTSTEIN, HOWARD K.
PERSONAL Born 08/11/1943, Richmond, VA, m, 1969, 2 children **DISCIPLINE** PHILOSOPHY **EDUCATION** Yeshiva Col, BA, 65; CUNY, PhD, 76. **CAREER** Asst prof, Univ Minn, Morris, 74-81; vis assoc prof, Stanford Univ, 81-83; assoc prof, Univ Notre Dame, 83-89; prof, chemn dept 92-98, philos, Univ Calif, Riverside, 89- . **HONORS AND AWARDS** NEH, 81-82; ACLS, 81-82. **MEMBERSHIPS** APA. **RESEARCH** Philosophy of language; philosophy of religion. **SELECTED PUBLICATIONS** Co-ed, Midwest Stud in Philos, 75- ; auth, Has Semantics Rested Upon A Mistake: And Other Essays, Stanford, 91; auth, Terra Firma: Wittgenstein's Naturalism, The Monist, 95; auth, Doctrine, Faith and Philos, 97; auth, Awe and the Religious Life: A Naturalistic Perspective, in Wettstein, ed, Midwest Studies in Philosophy: The Philosophy of Religion, 98; auth, Against Theodicy, in Dawson, ed, Proceedings of the 20th World Congress of Philosophy, Philosophy Documentation Center, forthcoming. **CONTACT ADDRESS** Dept of Philosophy, Univ of California, Riverside, Riverside, CA 92521. **EMAIL** Howard.Wettstein@ucr.edu

WETZEL, JAMES RICHARED
PERSONAL Born 12/02/1959, Baltimore, MD **DISCIPLINE** RELIGION **EDUCATION** Princeton Univ, BA, 82; Columbia Univ, MA, 84, PhD, 90. **CAREER** Assoc prof, Colgate Univ, 88-. **HONORS AND AWARDS** Charlotte Newcombe, 87; postdoctoral fel, Center for Philos of Rel, Notre Dame, 91-92; Phi Eta Sigma Prof of the Year, 97, Panhellenic Awd for Excellence in Teaching, 00. **MEMBERSHIPS** AAR, APA, Soc for the Philosophy of Relig, Soc for Medieval and Renaissance Philosophy. **RESEARCH** Medieval philosophy; philosophy of religion; Augustine; mysticism. **SELECTED PUBLICATIONS** Auth, Augustine and the Limits of Virtue, Cambridge Univ Press, 92; Infinite Return: Two Ways of Wagering with Pascal, Relig Studies, 93; auth, Moral Personality, Perversity, and Original Sin, J of Relig Ethics, 95; auth, The Missing Adam: A Reply to Gilbert Meilander, J of Relig Ethics, 95; auth, Time After Augustine, Relig Studies, 95; auth, Some Thoughts on the Anachronism of Forgiveness, Journal of Religious Ethics, 99, auth, Crisis Mentalities: Augustine After Descartes American Catholic Philosophical Quarterly, 00. **CONTACT ADDRESS** Dept of Philos & Relig, Colgate Univ, 13 Oak Dr, Hamilton, NY 13346-1398. **EMAIL** jwetzel@mail.colgate.edu

WEXLER, DAVID BARRY
PERSONAL Born 04/04/1941, Brooklyn, NY, m, 1963, 2 children **DISCIPLINE** LAW **EDUCATION** State Univ NYork, BA, 61; NYork Univ, JD, 64. **CAREER** Assoc prof, 67-70, John D. Lyons Prof Law and prof psychology, Univ Ariz, 70-, Lectr, Law Ctr, Georgetown Univ, 66-67; consult, President's Comn Law Enforcement and Admin Justice, 67, Nat Comn Marihuana & Drug Abuse, 72 & Courts Task Force, Nat Adv Comt Criminal Justice Standards & Goals, 72; assoc ed, Criminology; prof law ans dir, Int Network on Therapeutic Jurisprudence, Univ Puerto Rico. **HONORS AND AWARDS** Manfred S Guttmacher Forensic Phychiat Awd, Am Psychiat Asn, 72; New York Univ School of Law Distinguished Alumnus Legal Scholarship/Teaching Award; Distinguished Service Award from the National Center for State Courts. **RESEARCH** Criminal law and procedure; law and psychiatric justice; law and psychiatry. **SELECTED PUBLICATIONS** Auth, Mental Health Law: Major Issues, Plenum Press, 81; auth, Therapeutic Jurisprudence: The Law as a Therapeutic Agent, Carolina Academic Press, 90; auth, Essays in Therapeutic Jurisprudence, Carolina Academic Press, 91; auth, Law in a Therapeutic Key: Developments in Therapeutic Jurisprudence, Carolina Academic Press, 96; coauth, Practicing Therapeutic Jurisprudence: Law as a Helping Profession, Carolina Academic Press, 00. **CONTACT ADDRESS** Univ of Arizona, College of Law, Tucson, AZ 85721-0001. **EMAIL** dwexler@compuserve.com

WEXLER, STEPHEN
DISCIPLINE LAW **EDUCATION** Columbia Univ, BA, 64; Univ NY, LLB, 67; LLM, 68. **CAREER** Prof. **HONORS AND AWARDS** Grad, Professional Baseball Umpires School **RESEARCH** Legal philosophy; consumer protection. **SELECTED PUBLICATIONS** Auth, pubs about burden of proof. **CONTACT ADDRESS** Fac of Law, Univ of British Columbia, 1822 East Mall, Vancouver, BC, Canada V6T 1Z1. **EMAIL** wexler@law.ubc.ca

WEYER, ROBERT A.
PERSONAL Born 12/29/1948, Hoboken, NJ, m, 1974, 2 children **DISCIPLINE** CRIMINAL JUSTICE **EDUCATION** Central Col, BA, 70; Jersey Cty State Col, MA, 75; New School Soc Res, Ment Hlth Admin, 85; Rutgers Univ, PhD, 93. **CAREER** Prof, County Col Morris, 75-. **HONORS AND AWARDS** Who's Who Am Teach, 98. **MEMBERSHIPS** E Socio Soc; ASA. **RESEARCH** Social policy; medical sociology; sociology of organizations. **SELECTED PUBLICATIONS** Auth, "Block Grants at the Local Level: New Jersey's Experience with New Federalism," New Eng j Human Ser (85) vol 5, no 3; co-ed, Seeing Society: Perspectives of Social Life, Allyn and Bacon (Boston), 94; coauth, "Changing Trends in Mental Health Legislation: Anatomy of Reforming a Civil Commitment Law," J Health Politics, Policy, Law (96) vol 21, no 4. **CONTACT ADDRESS** Dept Criminal Justice, County Col of Morris, 214 Center grove Rd, Randolph, NJ 07869. **EMAIL** rweyer@ccm.edu

WEYRAUCH, WALTER OTTO
PERSONAL Born 08/27/1919, Lindau, Germany, m, 1952, 3 children **DISCIPLINE** LAW **EDUCATION** Univ Frankfurt, Dr jur, 51; Georgetown Univ, Llb, 55; Harvard Univ, Llm, 56; Yale Univ, JSD, 62. **CAREER** Asst instr law, Yale Univ Law Sch, 56-57; from Assoc Prof to Prof, 57-98, Prof Law, Col Law, Univ Fla, 98-; Mem, Ger Bar, Frankfurt, 49-52; US Court of Appeals, Allied High Comn, 51; vis consult soc sci, Space Sci Lab, Univ Calif, Berkeley, 65-66; chmn, comt studies beyond first degree in law, Asn Am Law Sch, 65-67; vis prof law, Rutgers Univ Sch Law, 68; polit sci, Univ Calif, Berkeley, 68-69; consult, Comn Experts Problems Succession of Hague Conf Pvt Int Law, US State Dept, 69-72; vis prof law, Univ Frankfurt, Ger, 75; Stephen C. O'Connell Chair; Honorary Prof of Law, Johann Wolfgang Goethe Univ, Frankfurt Main, Ger, 80-; Distinguished Prof of Law, Univ of Florida, 98. **MEMBERSHIPS** Int Soc of Family Law; Law and Soc Asn. **RESEARCH** Law and the social sciences; family law; comparative law. **SELECTED PUBLICATIONS** Auth, The Personality of Lawyers, Yale Univ, 64; Dual systems of family law, Calif Law Rev, 5/66; Zum Gesellschaftsbild des Juristen, Luchterhand, Neuwied, Ger, 70; The basic law or constitution of a small group, J Social Issues, 71; Taboo and magic in law, Stanford Law Rev, 73; coauth, Autonomous Lawmaking: The Case of the Gypsies, Yale Law J 103, 93; auth, Romaniya: An Introduction to Gypsy Law, Am J of Comparative Law 45, 97; Oral Legal Traditions of Gypsies and Some American Equivalents, Am J Comparative Law 45, 97; ed, Gypsy Law Symposium, Am J Comparative Law, Spring 97. **CONTACT ADDRESS** Col of Law, Univ of Florida, Gainesville, FL 32611-9500. **EMAIL** weyrauch@law.ufl.edu

WHALEY, DOUGLAS JOHN
PERSONAL Born 09/25/1943, Huntingburg, IN, d, 1 child **DISCIPLINE** LAW **EDUCATION** Univ Md, BA, 65; Univ Tex, JD, 68. **CAREER** Assoc law firm, Chapman & Culter, 68-70; from asst prof to prof law, Law Sch, Ind Univ, Indianapolis, 70-76; Prof Law, Col Law, Ohio State Univ, 76-; Vis prof, Sch Law, Univ NC, 73-74 & Univ Calif, Hastings, 82-83; Vist Prof, Boston College, 99-00. **RESEARCH** Commercial law; consumer problems. **SELECTED PUBLICATIONS** Auth, Warranties & the Practitioner, Practicing Law Inst, 81; contribr, Couse's Ohio Legal Forms, Anderson Publ Co, 82; Problems & Materials on Commercial Law, Aspen, 97; Problems & Materials on Consumer Law, Aspen, 98. **CONTACT ADDRESS** Law Sch, Ohio State Univ, Columbus, 55 W 12th Ave, Columbus, OH 43210-1306. **EMAIL** dglswhaley@aol.com

WHARTON, A. C., JR.
PERSONAL Born 08/17/1944, Lebanon, TN, m **DISCIPLINE** LAW **EDUCATION** TSU, BA 1966; Univ MS, JD 1971. **CAREER** EEOC, decision drafter 1967-68; trial attorney, 71-73; Lawyers Com for Civil Rights Under Law, proj dir 1973; Univ MS, adj prof; Shelby Co TN, pub defender 1980; Private Practice, Wharton & Wharton. **HONORS AND AWARDS** US Atty Gen Honor Law Grad Prog 1971. **MEMBERSHIPS** Past exec dir Memphis Area Leagl Serv Inc; mem Amer Bar Assn; Natl Legal Aid & Defender Assn; Natl Bar Assn; TN Bar Assn; NAACP; pres Leadership Memphis Alumni Assn 1979; Operation PUSH; Urban League. **CONTACT ADDRESS** 161 Jefferson Ave, Ste 402, Memphis, TN 38103.

WHEELER, ARTHUR M.
PERSONAL Born 11/20/1928, Toledo, OH, d, 3 children **DISCIPLINE** PHILOSOPHY; ENGLISH **EDUCATION** Bowling Green State Univ, BA, 51; Univ Chicago, MA, 53; Univ Wis, Madison, PhD, 58. **CAREER** Instr, 58-62, asst prof, 62-66, assoc prof, 66-70, prof, 70-91, Kent State Univ, Ohio; Retired. **HONORS AND AWARDS** Summer res grants, 66, 79; Sigma Tau Delta (English). **MEMBERSHIPS** AAUP; Amer Philos Assoc; Ohio Philos Assoc; Tri-State Philos Assoc; Soc for the Philos Study of Relig; Southern Soc for Philos and Psychol; Ohio Academy of Relig. **RESEARCH** Ethics; philos of relig; free will. **SELECTED PUBLICATIONS** Auth, On Lewis' Imperatives of Right, Phil Studies, 61; God and Myth, Hibbert Journal, 64; Are Theological Utterances Assertions?, Sophia, 69; Bliks as Assertions and as Attackable, Phil Studies, 74; Prima Facie and Actual Duty, Analysis, 77; On Moral Nose, Phil Quart, 77; Fiat Justitia, ruat Caelum, Ethics, 86. **CONTACT ADDRESS** 7686 Diagonal Rd., Kent, OH 44240.

WHEELER, DAVID L.
PERSONAL Born 12/08/1946, Louisville, KY, m, 1990, 2 children **DISCIPLINE** THEOLOGY **EDUCATION** Georgetown Col, BA, 68; Yale Divinity Sch, MDiv, 71, Grad Theol Union, ThD, 84. **CAREER** Adj prof, Montclair St Univ, 84-85; prof, Cent Baptist Theol Sem, 85- . **HONORS AND AWARDS** Luther Wesley Smith Citation, Amer Baptist Churches, 89 **MEMBERSHIPS** Amer Acad of Relig; Amer Philos Assoc; Baptist Assoc of Philos Teachers; Nat Assoc of Baptist Prof of Relig; Soc of Christian Philos. **RESEARCH** Evangelical faith & process; relational thought; atonement; religious lang. **SELECTED PUBLICATIONS** Auth, Renewal Through the Classics, Christian Ministry, 96; Renewal Ecclesiology, Renew, 96; The Cosmic Christ and the Man of Sorrows, Explorations: J for Adventurous Thought, 96; Quine and the Religious Uses of Language, Perspectives in Relig Stud, 97; Central Thoughts for Ministry in the Twenty-First Century, Smyth & Helwys, 98. **CONTACT ADDRESS** Central Baptist Theol Sem, 741 N 31 St, Kansas City, KS 66102. **EMAIL** wheels@cbts.edu

WHEELER, SAMUEL C., III
PERSONAL Born 02/05/1944 **DISCIPLINE** PHILOSOPHY **EDUCATION** Carleton Col, BA, 66; Princeton Univ, PhD, 70. **CAREER** Asst Prof to Prof, Univ Conn, 70-; Dir of Grad Studies, Univ Conn. **HONORS AND AWARDS** Chancellor's Res Fel, Univ Conn, 01. **MEMBERSHIPS** APA; Acad for the Second Amendment; Willington Hill Fire Dept. **RESEARCH** Metaphysics, ethics, ancient philosophy, deconstruction. **SELECTED PUBLICATIONS** Auth, "Plato's Enlightenment," in Hist of Phil Quart, vol 14, 2, 97; auth, "Reparations Reconstructed," in Am Phil Quart, vol 34, 3, 97; auth, "Self-Defense and Coerced Risk- Acceptance," in Pub Aff Quart, vol 11, 4, 97; auth, "Arms as Insurance," Pub Aff Quart, 99; auth, Deconstruction as Analytic Philosophy, Standford Univ Press, 00. **CONTACT ADDRESS** Univ of Connecticut, Storrs, U-54, 103 Manchester Hall, 344 Mansfield Rd, Storrs, CT 06269. **EMAIL** swheeler@uconnvm.uconn.edu

WHEELER, SONDRA E.
PERSONAL Born 01/30/1956, Bridgeport, CT, m, 1977, 3 children **DISCIPLINE** RELIGIOUS STUDIES **EDUCATION** Wesleyan Univ, BA, 79; Yale Divinity Sch, MAR, 87; Yale Univ, PhD, 92. **CAREER** Asst Prof, Duquesne Univ, 92-93; Assoc Prof, Wesley Theol Sem, 93-. **MEMBERSHIPS** Soc Bibl Lit, Soc Christian Ethics. **SELECTED PUBLICATIONS** Auth, Wealth as Peril and Obligation: New Testament on Possessions, 95; auth, Stewards of Life: Bioethics and Pastoral Care, 96. **CONTACT ADDRESS** Dept Relig Studies, Wesley Theol Sem, 4500 Mass Ave NW, Washington, DC 20016. **EMAIL** swheeler@wesleysem.org

WHEELER, STANTON
PERSONAL Born 09/27/1930, Pomona, CA, m, 1951, 3 children **DISCIPLINE** SOCIOLOGY OF LAW **EDUCATION** Pomona Col, BA, 52; Univ Wash, MA, 56, PhD(sociol), 58. **CAREER** Acting instr, Univ Wash, 56-58; instr social rel, Harvard Univ, 58-60; Fulbright res scholar, Insts Sociol & Criminol, Univ Oslo, 60-61; asst prof social rel, Harvard Univ, 61-63; assoc prof sociol, Univ Wash, 63-64; sociologist, Russell Sage Found, 64-68; adj assoc prof sociol & law, 66-68, Prof Sociol & Law, Yale Law Sch, 68-, Mem, Russell Sage Found, 68-; fel, Ctr Advan Studies Behav Sci, 70-71; mem, Comt on Incarceration, 71-. **MEMBERSHIPS** Am Sociol Asn; Soc Studies Social Probs (pres-elect); Law & Soc Asn. **RESEARCH** Sociology of crime, deviance and incarceration; sociology of sport and leisure. **SELECTED PUBLICATIONS** Coauth, Socialization After Childhood: Two Essays, 66, auth, Deviant behavior, In: Sociology: An Introduction, 67, rev ed, 73 & coauth, Controlling Delinquents, 68, Wiley; auth, On Record: Files and Dossiers in American Life, Russell Sage Found, 69; Socialization in correctional institutions, In: Handbook of Socialization Theory and Research, Rand McNally, 69; The Prospects For Large-Scale Collaborative Research - Revisiting The Yale White-Collar Crime Research-Program, Law And Social Inquiry-Journal Of The American Bar Foundation, Vol 0018, 1993. **CONTACT ADDRESS** Russell Sage Prog, Yale Univ, PO Box 208215, New Haven, CT 06520-8215.

WHELAN, STEPHEN T.
PERSONAL Born 07/28/1947, Philadelphia, PA, m, 1971, 1 child **DISCIPLINE** LAW, HISTORY **EDUCATION** Princeton Univ, BA, 68; Harvard Univ, JD, 71. **CAREER** Atty, 75-, partner, 78, Thacher Proffitt & Wood, Mudge Rose Guthrie & Alexander. **HONORS AND AWARDS** Magna cum laude, Princeton Univ; Outstanding Sr, student pol org, Princeton Univ. **MEMBERSHIPS** Amer Bar Asn; Fel, Amer Col of Investment Counsel; The Economic Club, NY. **RESEARCH** Financial law; econ history **SELECTED PUBLICATIONS** Auth, New York's Uniform Commercial Code New Article 2A, Matthew Bender & Co., 94; art, American Bar Association Annual Survey: Leases, Bus Lawyer, Vol 49, 94 & Vol 50, 95 & Vol 51, 96 & Vol 52, 97; art, Securitization of Medical Equipment Finance Contracts, Med Finance & Tech Yearbook, Euromoney Pub, 95; art, Securitization of Medical Equipment Finance Contracts, World Leasing Yearbook, Euromoney Pub, 96; coauth, The ABC's of the UCC: Article 2A (Leases), Amer Bar Asn, 97; art, Asset Securitization, Comm Finance Guide, Matthew Bender, 98. **CONTACT ADDRESS** Thacher Proffitt & Wood, 2 World Trade Ctr, New York, NY 10048. **EMAIL** swhelan@thacherproffitt.com

WHELAN, WINIFRED
PERSONAL Born Chicago, IL **DISCIPLINE** THEOLOGY **EDUCATION** Marquette, MA, 68; Northwestern Univ, PhD, 85. **CAREER** Prof, St Bonaventure Univ. **MEMBERSHIPS** Am Acad Rel; Asn Prof Res Rel Educ. **RESEARCH** Religious education; epistemology. **SELECTED PUBLICATIONS** Auth, art, 1209: Founding of the Franciscans, 97; auth, art, 1009: The Church of the Holy Sepulchre is Destroyed, 97; auth, art, Theologians and Women's Theology, 97; auth, art, Roman Catholic Church, 98; auth, art, Chicago, 98. **CONTACT ADDRESS** St. Bonaventure Univ, Box 144, Saint Bonaventure, NY 14778-0144. **EMAIL** whelan@sbu.edu

WHIDDEN, WOODROW W., II
PERSONAL Born 10/15/1944, Orlando, FL, m, 1969, 3 children **DISCIPLINE** THEOLOGY **EDUCATION** Southern Adventist Univ, BA, 67; Seventh-day Adventist Theol Sem, BDiv, 69; Drew Univ, MA, 87, PhD, 89. **CAREER** Prof, 90-. **MEMBERSHIPS** Adventist Soc for Religious Studies; Wesleyan Theol Soc; Am Acad of Relig. **RESEARCH** Adventism; Theology; American religion and culture. **SELECTED PUBLICATIONS** Auth, Ellen White on the Humanity of Christ, 97; Ellen G. White on Salvation, 95; auth, "Salvation Pilgrimage: The Adventist Journey into Justification by Faith and Trinitarianism," in Ministry, 98; "Ellen White and the Basics of Salvation," in Ministry, 97; "Wesleyan on Imputation: A Truly Reckoned Reality or Antinomian Polemical Wreckage?", in The Asbury Theol J, 97; "Adventist Soteriology: The Wesleyan Connection," in Wesleyan Theol J, 95; "The Vindication of God and the Harvest Principle," in Ministry, 94; "Eschatology, Soteriology, and Social Activism in Four Mid-Nineteenth Century Holiness Methodists," in Wesleyan Theol J, 1994; "Essential Adventism or Historic Adventism?", in Ministry, 93. **CONTACT ADDRESS** Religion Dept, Andrews Univ, 208 Griggs Hall, Berrien Springs, MI 49104. **EMAIL** whiddenw@andrews.edu

WHIPPS, JUDY
PERSONAL Born 10/12/1951, Muskegon, MI, m, 1987 **DISCIPLINE** PHILOSOPHY **EDUCATION** Grand Valley State Univ, BA, 92; Univ Chicago, MA, 95; The Union Inst, PhD, 98. **CAREER** Vis prof, Philos, Grand Valley State Univ, 95-99; Asst Prof of Philosopy Coordinator, Liberal Studies Program, GVSU . **HONORS AND AWARDS** Outstanding stud awd, Mich Asn Gov Boards of State Univ, 92; Liberal stud (s) dept Outstanding studies awd, 92. **MEMBERSHIPS** Amer Philos Asn; Soc Advance Amer Philos. **RESEARCH** Pragmatism; social and political philosophy; feminism. **SELECTED PUBLICATIONS** Auth, Rev, Needleman, Money and the Meaning of Life, Grand Rapids Press, Oct 92. **CONTACT ADDRESS** Dept of Philosophy, Grand Valley State Univ, 3154 Pine Meadow, Grandville, MI 49418. **EMAIL** Whippsj.@gvsu.edu

WHITACRE, RODNEY A.
PERSONAL Born 12/28/1949, Des Moines, IA, m, 1972, 2 children **DISCIPLINE** BIBLICAL STUDIES **EDUCATION** Gordon Col, AB, 73; Gordon-Conwell Theol Seminary, MATS, 76; Univ Cambridge, PhD, 81. **CAREER** Dir Greek Prog, Gordon-Conwell Theol Seminary, 81-83; Prof Bibl Studies, Trinity Episcopal Sch Ministry, 83-. **MEMBERSHIPS** Soc Bibl Studies; Inst Bibl Res. **RESEARCH** New Testament; Hellenistic Greek. **SELECTED PUBLICATIONS** Auth, Johannine Polemic: The Role of Tradition and Theology, Schol Press, 82; The Moon of Our Darkness [: Unity and Diversity in Scripture], Mission & Ministry, 91; The Biblical Vision [Regarding Women's Ordination], The Evangelical Cath, 94; Studying the Scriptures, The Evangelical Cath, 94; John, IVP New Testament Commentary, InterVarsity Press (forthcoming 99). **CONTACT ADDRESS** Trinity Episcopal Sch for Ministry, 311 Eleventh St., Ambridge, PA 15003. **EMAIL** RodWhitacre@TESM.edu

WHITBECK, CAROLINE
PERSONAL m, 1995, 3 children **DISCIPLINE** PHILOSOPHY **EDUCATION** Wellesley Col, BA, 62; Boston Univ, MA, 65; Massachusetts Inst Technology, PhD, 70. **CAREER** Teach asst, math, 63-65, The Mitre Corp; Lectr, 68-70, asst prof, 70-71, res assoc in psychiatry, 71-73, Yale Univ; asst prof, 73-78, SUNY Albany, post dr fel, 77-78, The Hastings Center; assoc prof, 78-82, Dept of Preventative Med and Comm Health, Univ of TX Med School Galveston; res fel, Center for Policy Alt, 9/82-8/83, vis assoc prof, School of Engineering, 9/83-8/86, lectr, mech eng & res scholar, 9/86-1/88, sr lectr in mech eng, 1/88-6/97, Mass Inst of Tech; prof, Dept of Mech and Aerospace Eng & Philosophy & Elmer G. Beamer-Hubert H Schneider Prof in Ethics, 97-, Case Western Reserve Univ. **HONORS AND AWARDS** Hastings Center Fel, 77-78; NSF Vis Professorship of Women, 83-85; Amer Asn for the Advancement of Science Fel, 89; Phi Beta Kappa; Vis Scholar, 94-95. **MEMBERSHIPS** Amer Asn of Bioethics; Amer Asn for the Advancement of Univ Prof; Amer Phil Asn; Asn for Practical and Prof Ethics; Asn of MIT Alumnae; Hastings Center; Inst of Electrical and Electronic Eng; Phil of Science Asn; Sigma Xi; Soc for Women in Phil; Soc of Women Eng. **RESEARCH** Practical ethics; professional ethics in eng, science, health care and education; research ethics; bioethics (incl ethical issues in genetics; phil of science, technology, & med; the education development of women and minorities in eng and other scientific professions; feminist phil. **SELECTED PUBLICATIONS** Auth, Imaging Technologies, Encycl of Childbearing, Oryx Press, 93; auth, Virtual Environments: Ethical issues and Significant Confusions, Presence: Teleoperators and Virtual Environments, 93; auth, Ought We Blame Technology for the Failings of Medical Ethics? A Response to Daniel Callahan's How Technology Seduced the Sanctity of Life, First Things, 94; auth, Teaching Ethics to Scientist and Engineers: Moral Agents and Moral Problems, Science & Engineering Ethics, 95; auth, Biomedical Engineering, 2nd Ed of Encycl of Bioethics, Macmillan, 95; auth, Trust, 2nd Ed of Encycl of Bioethics, Macmillan, 95; auth, Trustworthy Research, and Editorial Introduction, Science & Eng Ethics, 95; auth, Ethics as Design: Doing Justice to Moral Problems, Hastings Center Report, 96; art, Problems and Cases: New Directions in Ethics 1980-1996, Jour of Prof Ethics, 97; coauth, Science, Scientist and Human Rights Education, Human Rights Education in the 21st Century: Conceptual and Practical Challenges, Univ of PA Press, 97; auth, Using Problems and Cases in Teaching Professional Ethics: Theory and Practice, Tchng Criminal Justice Ethics: Strategic Issues, Anderson Pub Co, 97; auth, Research Ethics, Encycl of Applied Ethics, Academic Press, 98; auth, Ethics in Engineering Practice and Research, Cambridge Univ Press, 98. **CONTACT ADDRESS** Philosophy Dept, Case Western Reserve Univ, 10900 Euclid Ave, Cleveland, OH 44106-7199. **EMAIL** cwhitbeck@onlineethics.org

WHITE, ALFRED LOE
PERSONAL Born 10/19/1957, Framingham, MA, m, 1993, 2 children **DISCIPLINE** PHILOSOPHY **EDUCATION** Catholic Univ of Amer, PhD, 97. **CAREER** Asst Prof, 98-, Univ of Baltimore. **HONORS AND AWARDS** Full Fel at Catholic Univ. **MEMBERSHIPS** ACPA **RESEARCH** Philosophy of mind, Thomas Aquinas, Phenomenology. **SELECTED PUBLICATIONS** Auth, Why the Cognitive Power?, Proceedings of the 1998 Amer Cath Philo Assoc, 98. **CONTACT ADDRESS** 10092 Hatbrim Terrace, Columbia, MD 21046. **EMAIL** awhite@ubmail.ubalt.edu

WHITE, CHARLES SIDNEY JOHN
PERSONAL Born 09/25/1929, New Richmond, WI **DISCIPLINE** HIST OF RELIGIONS, HINDUISM & MEDIEVAL & MODERN HINDI POETRY **EDUCATION** Univ Wis, BA, 51; Univ of the Am, MA, 57; Univ Chicago, MA, 62, PhD, 64. **CAREER** Asst prof Indian studies, Univ WI, 65-66; asst prof, relig thought & S Asian studies, Univ PA, 66-71; coordr, ctr Asian Studies, 73-76, assoc prof, Am Univ, 71-78, Dir Ctr Asian Studies, 76-78, Prof Philos & Relig, Am Univ 78-94, Prof Emer Philos & Relig, 95-, chmn dept philos & relig, 84-87 & 88-94, Dir Inst Vaishnava Studies, 71-; Vis lectr Hist Relig, Princeton Univ, 68; Vis prof world relig, Lakehead Univ, Thunder Bay, Ontario, 74, 77, 80, 82, 84 & 88 (summers); Vis prof, Wesley Sem, Fall 85; Jr fel, Am Inst Indian Studies, Poona, India, 64-65 & res fel, Agra, 68-69, trustee, 73-; Kern Found Fel, 72. **HONORS AND AWARDS** Inst Int Educ graduate award, Span lang and lit, Universidad nacional de Mexico; Rockefeller Doctoral fel, relig, hon, Univ Chicago, 61; NDEA fel, Hindu-Urdu, Univ Chicago 61-64; Am Philos Soc fel, 66-67; Summer res grant, Univ PA, India, 70; Col Arts & Sci travel res grant, summer 74; Am Univ travel grant, India, summer 76; Center for Asian Studies, Am Univ, summer grant, 78; Smithsonian Grant, prin investigator, India, 82-83; Am Univ Col Arts & Sci Awd fro Outstanding Scholar, 84; Am Univ Senate Comt Res, India, summer 87; CAS Mellon Awd; Am Inst Indian Studies fac res fel, India, 95, spring 97. **MEMBERSHIPS** Am Asn Asian Studies; Am Acad Relig; Am Orient Soc; Soc Sci Study Relig. **RESEARCH** Hist of relig methodology; Hindu lit; Islam. **SELECTED PUBLICATIONS** Auth, Sufism in Hindi literature, 64 & Krishna as divine child, 70, Hist Relig; Heaven, In: The Encyclopedia Britannica, 65; Resources for the study of Medieval Hindu devotional religion,, Am Philos Soc Yearbk 67; A Note Toward Understanding in Field Method, In: Understanding in History of Relition, Univ Chicago Press, 67; Bhakti, In: The Encyclopedia Britannica, 68; Devi, Dharma, Dayanand Saraswati, Durga, Diwali, The Encyclopedia Americana, 68; Krsna as divine child, Hist Relig, 70; The Sai Baba movement, J Asian Studies, 72; Henry S Olcott: A Buddhist apostle, Theosophist, 4/73; co-auth, Responses to Jay J Bim on Bernard Meland, Jour Relig, 4/73; Swami Muktananda, Hist Relig, 74; Caurasi Pad of Sri Hit Harivams (transl), Univ Hawaii, 77; Structure in history of religions, Hist Relig, 78; Ramayana, Ramanuja, Ram Mohan Roy, Ramakrishna, Encyclopedia Americana, 79; Ramakrishna's Americans, Yugantar Prakashan, 79; Madhva, Mahavira, Mantra, Mandala, Manu, Encyclopedia Americana, 79; Mother Guru: Jnanananda of Madras, India, In: Unspoken Worlds: Women's Religious Lives, Harper and Row, 80, 2nd ed, Wadsworth, 88; The Hindu Holy Person, Ramakrishna, Satya Sai Baba, J Krishnamurti, Ramana Maharshi, Sadhu, Guru, Rsi, Acarya, Meher Baba, In: Abingdon Dictionary of Living Religions, 81, Perennial Dictionary of World Religions, Harper and Row, 89; Untouchables, Parsis, Encyclopedia Americana, 81; Kuan Yin, Juggernaut, Kali, Kama Sutra, Karma, Kautilya, Krishna, Jiddu Krishnamurti, Kshatriya,

Kumbha Mela, Lakshmi, In: Encyclopedia Americana, 82; co-auth, The Religious Quest, Univ Md. 83, 2nd ed, 85; Religion in Asia, In: Funk and Wagnall's Yearbook, 85-93, and Collier's International Yearbook; Almsgiving, Gift Giving, Jiddu Krishnamurti: A Biograhy, In: Encyclopedia of Religion, Macmillan Co, 86; Inwardness and privacy: Last bastions of religious life, Theosophis, 86 & Holistic Human Concern for World Welfare, 87; Indian developments: Sainthood in Hinduism, In: Sainthood: Its Manifestations in World Religions, Univ Calif Press, 88, paperbk, 8/90; co-auth, Joseph Campbell: Transformations of Myth Through Time, and An Anthology of Readings, Harcourt Brace Jovanovich, 89; co-ath (with David Haberman), rev, Sonic Theology: Hinduism and Sacred Sound by Guy L Beck, Jour Vaisnava Studies, spring 94; Nimbarka Sampradaya, Anandamayi Ma, Ramana Marsi, Sadhu, Swami, svamin, In: HarperCollins Dictionary of Religion, 95; The remaining Hindi works of Sri Hit Harivams, Jour Vaisnava Studies, fall 96; Mircea Eliade, Bengal Nights .. Maitreyi Devi, It Does Not Die, rev, Love and Politics for Eliade, Annals of Scholarship, summer 97; Muhammad as Spiritual Master, In: The Quest, 8/98. **CONTACT ADDRESS** Dept of Philos & Relig, American Univ, 4400 Massachusetts Ave NW, 123 McCabe Hall, Washington, DC 20016-8056.

WHITE, DAVID
PERSONAL Born 01/08/1948, Tulsa, OK, m, 1972, 1 child **DISCIPLINE** RELIGION **EDUCATION** Nebr State Univ, BS, 71; SW Baptist Theol Sem, Masters Relig Educ; PhD. **CAREER** Childrens minister, First Baptist Church, Roanoke VA, 74-76; supvr, SW Baptist Theol Sem, 76-83; prof, relig, E Texas Baptist Univ, 83- . **HONORS AND AWARDS** SW Baptist Theol Sem fel; Outstanding Young Men Am. **MEMBERSHIPS** S Baptist Relg Educ Asn; SW Baptist Relig Educ Asn; Texas Baptist Hist Soc. **RESEARCH** Religious education and New Testament. **SELECTED PUBLICATIONS** Auth, article on outreach, Outreach Magazine, May 79; auth, article for parents, Living with Children, June 88. **CONTACT ADDRESS** Dept Relig, East Texas Baptist Univ, 1209 N Grove St, Marshall, TX 75670-1423. **EMAIL** dwhite@etbu.edu

WHITE, DAVID A.
PERSONAL Born 03/23/1942, South Bend, IN, m, 1973, 2 children **DISCIPLINE** PHILOSOPHY **EDUCATION** Univ Toronto, PhD, 73. **CAREER** Instr, Christian Bros Univ, 66-67; Marian Col, 67-68, 69-70, 72-73; asst prof, Mankato State Univ, 73-75; mem fac, New School for Soc Res, 78; adj asoc prof, DePaul Univ, 82- ; instr, Northwestern Univ, 93- . **HONORS AND AWARDS** NEH Summer Stipend, Case Western Reserve Univ, 74; ACLS Fel, 85-86. **MEMBERSHIPS** Amer Philos Assoc **RESEARCH** Ancient philosophy; philosophy and literature; aesthetics; philosophy and children. **SELECTED PUBLICATIONS** Auth, Heidegger and the Language of Poetry, Nebraska, 78; auth, The Grand Contimumm, Reflections on Joyce and Metaphysics, Pittsburgh, 83; auth, Logic and Ontology in Heidegger, Ohio State, 85; auth, The Turning Wheel, Susquehanna, 88; Myth and Metaphysics in Plato's Phaedo, Susquehanna, 89; Rhetoric and Reality in Plato's Phaedrus, SUNY, 93; auth, Philosophy for Kids, Prufrock Press, 01; 45 articles. **CONTACT ADDRESS** 6608 N Bosworth, Chicago, IL 60626-4224. **EMAIL** dwhite6886@aol.com

WHITE, DONALD WALLACE
PERSONAL Born Summit, NJ **DISCIPLINE** AMERICAN HISTORY, INTERNATIONAL RELATIONS **EDUCATION** Hartwick Col, BA, 69; City Col, City Univ New York, MS, 72; NYork Univ, MA, 72, PhD(hist), 79. **CAREER** Asst res scientist, 76-80, Assoc Res Scientist, NY Univ, 80-87, Instr NY Univ, 72-73 & 79, asst ed, Papers William Livingston, 76-79, assoc ed, 79-80, asst to McGeorge Bundy, nuclear weapons hist, 79-87, adj asst prof and instructor, 82-. **HONORS AND AWARDS** Outstanding Teaching Awd, New York Univ, Postdoctoral res grants from the Dept of Hist; NEH; Res Grant from the New Jersey Historical Commission; Service Awd of the Morris County Historical Soc. **MEMBERSHIPS** Am Historical Asn. **RESEARCH** Culture and ideas of post-World War II United State foreign affairs; global history patterns of the rise and decline of civilizations; local history. **SELECTED PUBLICATIONS** Auth, "A Local History Approach to the American Revolution: Chatham, New Jersey," New Jersey History 96 Spring-Summer (78): 49-64; assoc ed, The Paper of William Livingston, Trenton, NJ: Rutgers University Press and the New Jersey Historical Commission, vol 1, 79, vol 2, 80; auth, "A Local History Approach to the American Revolution: Chatham, New Jersey, New Jersey History 96 (78): 49-64; auth, A Village at War: Chatham, New Jersey, and the American Revolution, Fairleigh Dickinson Univ Press (Rutherford, NJ), 79; auth, "Census-Making and Local History: In Quest of the People of a Revolutionary Village," Prologue: Journal of the National Archives 14 (82): 157-68; auth, "Census-Making and Local History: In Quest of the People of a Revolutionary Village," Prologue: Journal of the National Archives 14 (82): 157-68; auth, "It's a Big Country: Writers on Internarionalism and the American Landscape after World War II," Journal of the West 26 (87): 80-86; auth, "The Nature of World Power in American History: An Evaluation at the End of World War, Diplomatic History 11 (87): 181-202; auth, "History and American Internationalism: The Formulation from the Past after World War II," Pacific Historical Review 58 (89): 145-72; auth, "The American Century in World History," Journal of World History 3 (92): 105-27; auth, The American Century: The Rise and Decline of the United States As a World Power Yale Univ Press (New Haven and London), paperback ed, 99, Chinese language edition, forthcoming; auth, "Mutuable Destiny: The End of the American Century?" Harvard International Review 20 (97/98): 42-47; **CONTACT ADDRESS** Gallatin School, New York Univ, 715 Broadway, New York, NY 10003.

WHITE, FRANKIE WALTON
PERSONAL Born 09/08/1945, Yazoo City, MS **DISCIPLINE** LAW **EDUCATION** Wellesley College, 1964-65; Tougaloo Coll, BA (magna cum laude) 1966; Univ of CA at Los Angeles, MA 1967; Syracuse University, Syracuse, NYork, 1972-73; Univ of MS, JD 1975. **CAREER** Fisk Univ, instructor of English 1967-69; Wellesley Coll, lecturer in English 1969-70; Tougaloo Coll, asst prof of English 1970-71; Syracuse Univ, asst dir of financial aid 1971-72; Central MS Legal Svcs, staff atty 1975-77; State of MS, spec asst atty general 1977; TX Southern Univ, student legal counselor 1977-79; State of MS, asst atty general 1979-. **HONORS AND AWARDS** Woodrow Wilson Fellow; Reginald Heber Smith Comm Lawyer Fellow; Women of Achievement Awd in Law & Govt Women for Progress of Mississippi Inc 1981; Distinguished Alumni Citation NAFEO 1986. **MEMBERSHIPS** Alpha Kappa Alpha Sor Inc 1964-; mem Magnolia, Mississippi Bar Assn 1975-; The Links Inc 1977-; Commission of Colleges Southern Assn of Colls & Schools 1982-; bd of trustees, Southern Assn of Colleges & Schools, 1988-91; Leadership Jackson, 1989-; chairman, Council of State Education Attorneys, 1990-91; bd of dirs, Natl Assn of State Boards of Education, 1991. **CONTACT ADDRESS** State of Mississippi, P O Box 220, Jackson, MS 39205.

WHITE, FREDERIC PAUL, JR.
PERSONAL Born 02/12/1948, Cleveland, OH, m **DISCIPLINE** LAW **EDUCATION** Columbia Coll New York, BA, 1970; Columbia Law School New York, JD, 1973. **CAREER** Squire Sanders & Dempsey, assoc attny, 73-78; Cleveland State Univ, asst professor, 78-81, assoc prof, 81-86, prof, 86-, assoc dean, 94-. **MEMBERSHIPS** Mem, bd of trustees, Cleveland Legal Aid Soc, 1981-84, Trinity Cathedral Comm Devel Fund, 1981-89; pres, Norman S Minor Bar Assn, 1984; acting judge & referee, Shaker Heights Municipal Court, 1984-90; mem, Omega Psi Phi Fraternity Inc, Zeta Omega Chapter; host, CSU City Focus radio show, 1981-85; bd of advisors, African-Amer Museum, 1986-90. **SELECTED PUBLICATIONS** Book, "Ohio Landlord Tenant Law," Banks-Baldwin Law Publ Co, 1984, 2nd ed, 1990, 3rd ed, 1995; 2 law review articles, "Cleveland Housing Ct," "Ohio Open Meeting Law"; Contrib Author Antieau's Local Govt Law; co-author chapts "Criminal Procedure Rules for Cleveland Housing Ct"; Frequent guest on local TV/radio landlord-tenant law subjects; contributing editor, Powell on Real Property; Thompson on Real Property. **CONTACT ADDRESS** Cleveland State Univ, 1801 Euclid Ave, Cleveland, OH 44115.

WHITE, G. EDWARD
PERSONAL Born 03/19/1941, Northampton, MA, m, 1966, 2 children **DISCIPLINE** LAW, HISTORY **EDUCATION** Amherst Coll, BA, 63; Yale Univ, MA, 64; PhD, 67; Harvard Univ, JD, 70. **CAREER** Prof, Univ Virginia, 72-. **HONORS AND AWARDS** AAAS Fel; Tri Coif Awd, Dist Schl; SAH Fel. **MEMBERSHIPS** ALI; ASLH. **RESEARCH** Constitutional history; legal history; constitutional law. **SELECTED PUBLICATIONS** Auth, Earl Warren: A Public Life, Oxford, 82; auth, The Marshall Court and Cultural Change, Oxford, 91; auth, Justice Oliver Wendell Holmes: Law and the Inner Self, Oxford, 93; auth, Creating the National Pastime: Baseball Transforms Itself, Princeton, 96; auth, Intervention and Detachment: Essays on Legal History and Jurisprudence, Oxford, 94; auth, The Constitution and the New Deal, Harvard, 00. **CONTACT ADDRESS** School of Law, Univ of Virginia, 580 Massie Rd, Charlottesville, VA 22903-3244. **EMAIL** gewhite@law5.law.virginia.edu

WHITE, HOWARD A.
PERSONAL Born 10/06/1927, New York, NY, m, 1968 **DISCIPLINE** LAW **EDUCATION** City College (CCNY), BEE, 1949; St Johns Univ, JD, 1954; New York Univ, MPA, 1959. **CAREER** Powsner, Katz & Powsner, associate, 53-62; Federal Communications Comm, general atty, (public utilities), 62-66; Communications Satellite Corp, general atty, 66-68; ITT Communications, general counsel & exec vp, 68-87; St Johns Univ School of Law, prof of law, 88-. **MEMBERSHIPS** Federal Communications Bar Assn; American Bar Assn; NY State Bar Assn. **SELECTED PUBLICATIONS** "Five Tuning The Federal Govt Role in Public Broadcasting," 46 Fed Comm LJ 491, 1994. **CONTACT ADDRESS** Professor of Law, St. John's Univ, 8000 Utopia Parkway, Jamaica, NY 11439.

WHITE, HUGH
PERSONAL Born 12/02/1936, Columbus, GA, m, 1960, 2 children **DISCIPLINE** HEBREW BIBLE **EDUCATION** Asbury Col, AB, 58; Candl Sch of Theol, BD, 61; Drew Univ, Phd, 67 **CAREER** Assoc Prof, 65-70 TN Wesleyan Col; asst prof to prof, 70-99, Rutgers Univ; emeritus prof, 99-, Rutgers Univ. **HONORS AND AWARDS** Outst Tch Awd, 70; RJ Dept of Higher Educ Awd, 85 **MEMBERSHIPS** Am Acad of Relig; Soc of Bibl Lit; Soc for Study of Narrative; Walker Percy Soc **RESEARCH** Ancient Narrative **SELECTED PUBLICATIONS** Auth, Narration & Discourse in the Book of Genesis, Cambridge, 91 **CONTACT ADDRESS** 47 Truman Ave, Haddonfield, NJ 08033. **EMAIL** hwhite@crab.rutgers.edu

WHITE, JAMES F.
PERSONAL Born 01/23/1932, Boston, MA, m, 1997, 5 children **DISCIPLINE** THEOLOGY **EDUCATION** Harvard Univ, AB, 53; Union Theol Sem, BD, 56; Duke Univ, PhD, 60. **CAREER** Instr, Ohio Wesleyan Univ, 59-61; prof, Southern Methodist Univ, 61-83; prof, Univ Notre Dame, 83-99; chaired prof, Drew Univ, 00-. **HONORS AND AWARDS** Danforth Fel; Fulbright Fel; Fels, Associated Theol Schs. **MEMBERSHIPS** N Am Acad of Liturgy, Liturgical Confr, Soc Liturgica, Am Soc Church Hist. **RESEARCH** Christian Worship in the West Since 1500, Architectural Setting of Christian Worship, Sacramental Theology. **SELECTED PUBLICATIONS** Auth, Protestant Worship, 89; auth, Roman Catholic Worship, 95; auth, Christian Worship in North America, 97; auth, The Sacraments in Protestant Practice and Faith, 99. **CONTACT ADDRESS** Dept Theol, Univ of Notre Dame, 327 O'Shaugnessy Hall, Notre Dame, IN 46556-5639.

WHITE, JAMES JUSTESEN
PERSONAL Born 02/19/1934, Omaha, NE, m, 1956, 3 children **DISCIPLINE** LAW **EDUCATION** Amherst Col, BA, 56; Univ Mich, JD, 62. **CAREER** From asst prof to assoc prof, 64-70, Prof Law, Univ Mich, Ann Arbor, 70-. **RESEARCH** Commercial law; consumer credit. **SELECTED PUBLICATIONS** Coauth, Teaching Materials on Commercial Transactions, 69 & Handbook on the Uniform Commercial Code, 72, West. **CONTACT ADDRESS** Law Sch, Univ of Michigan, Ann Arbor, Ann Arbor, MI 48104.

WHITE, JANICE G.
PERSONAL Born 08/21/1938, Cincinnati, OH, m, 1962 **DISCIPLINE** LAW **EDUCATION** Western Reserve University, BA, 1963; Capital University Law School, JD, 1977. **CAREER** Legal Aid Society of Columbus, Reginald Heber Smith Community, Law Fellow, 77-79; Franklin County Public Defender, juvenile unit, public defender, 79-80; Ohio State Legal Services Association, legislative counsel, 80-84; State Employment Relations Board, labor relations specialist, 84, administrative law judge, 84-88; Capital Univ Law & Graduate Center, Alumni Relations & Multi-Cultural Affairs Director, 88-. **HONORS AND AWARDS** United Church of Christ, Outstanding Woman in the Ohio Conference, 1985; Columbus Alumnae Chapter, Outstanding Delta, 1986; United Negro College Fund Inc, Meritorious Service Awd, 1989. Reginald Heber Smith, Community Law Fellow, 1977-79; assisted in the negotiations for release of hostages from Teheran, 1980. **MEMBERSHIPS** American Bar Association; Ohio Bar Association; Central Community House; Links Inc; National Conference of Black Lawyers; Women Lawyers of Franklin County Inc; Columbus Commission on Community Relations; Delta Sigma Theta Sorority Inc; United Negro College Fund. **CONTACT ADDRESS** Alumni Relations & Minority Affairs, Capital Univ, 303 E Broad St, Columbus, OH 43215-3200.

WHITE, JOHN D.
PERSONAL Born 07/23/1948, Benham, KY **DISCIPLINE** MUSIC; PHILOSOPHY **EDUCATION** Univ Ky, BM, 70; Univ Idaho, MM, 72; Univ Iowa, PhD, 77. **CAREER** Sabbatical replacement, Willamette Univ, spring, 74; asst prof, 76-78, interim chair, 78-79, assoc prof, 78-80, dept chair, fall, 80, Western Wy Community Col, driver, Webb's Trucking, spring, 81; assoc prof, Benedict Col, 81-82; assoc prof, Chattahoochee Valley State Community Col, 82-83; grad study in philos, Univ Ky, spring, 84; lectr, Okla State Univ, 84-85; grad asst, Univ Tex Austin, 85-86; grad study in philos, Univ Iowa, spring, 87; assoc prof, Col of the Ozarks, 87-88; pianist, Univ Iowa, 88-89; prof, philos/humanities, Talladega Col, 89-. **SELECTED PUBLICATIONS** Auth, The Pythagorean Derivation and Theories of Truth, 96; auth, The Substance Argument, 95; auth, The Confluence of Deism, African Creation Myth, and Thomas Hobbes, 94; auth, Philosophy of Law, 94; auth, The Origin of Number, 93; auth, The Antigone Effect, 92; auth, Belief System Internal Inconsistency, 91; auth, The Maker's Mind Model in Aesthetics, 91; auth, The Analysis of Law and the Nesting of the Philosophy of History in the History of Empiricism, 88; auth, Some Remarks on Some Remarks on Logical Form, 87; auth, Considerations on Infinity Derived from Spinozist Theory, 87; auth, Empiricism, Hume, Quantum Mechanics, and Universe Models, 86. **CONTACT ADDRESS** Dept. of Philosophy, Talladega Col, Campus Box 165, Talladega, AL 35160.

WHITE, JOHN L.
PERSONAL Born 05/31/1940, Washington, MO, m, 1961, 3 children **DISCIPLINE** NEW TESTAMENT, CHRISTIAN ORIGINS **EDUCATION** William Jewell Coll, BA, 62; Vanderbilt Univ, MA, 68; PhD, 70. **CAREER** Asst prof, Mo School Rel, 69-75; assoc prof, 76-81; assoc prof, Loyola Univ Chicago, 81-87; prof, Loyola Univ Chicago, 87-. **HONORS AND AWARDS** Chairman of Soc of Bibl Lit Ancient Epistography Group, 74-79; Assoc in Council Soc of Bibl Lit, 79-81;

bd of Dir of Polebridge Puss, 87-; Pres, Chicago Soc of Bibl Res. **MEMBERSHIPS** Am Soc of Papyrology; cath Bibl Asn; Chicago Soc of Bibl Res; Soc of Bibl Lit. **RESEARCH** Ancient letterwriting; First generation Christianity; St Paul; Influence of Greco-Roman culture on Christianity. **SELECTED PUBLICATIONS** Auth, Apostolic Mission and Apostolic Message, Origins and Method, 93; auth, Light From Ancient Letters, 86; auth, The Apostle of God, 99. **CONTACT ADDRESS** 6545 N Bosworth, Chicago, IL 60626. **EMAIL** Jwhite@luc.edu

WHITE, JONATHAN
PERSONAL Born 04/06/1951, South Charleston, WV, m, 1972, 2 children **DISCIPLINE** CRIMINAL JUSTICE **EDUCATION** West Mich Univ, BA, 71; MA, 74; West Theol Sem, MDiv, 92; Mich State Univ, PhD, 82. **CAREER** Prof, Grand Valley State Univ, 83-. **HONORS AND AWARDS** Outstanding Teacher, 96; Outstanding Educator, 95; Vanderploeg Awd in Church History. **RESEARCH** Terrorism, Religion and Violence, International Conflict. **SELECTED PUBLICATIONS** Auth, Terrorism: An Introduction. 3rd Edition, (forthcoming); auth, Terrorism: An Introduction. 2nd Edition, Wadsworth Pub (Belmont, CA) 97; auth, The Prussian Army: 1640 to 1871, Univ Press of Am (Landham, MD) 96; auth, "The Fog of Limited War," Freeman Magazine, (99); auth, "The Law Enforcement Role in National Defense: An Analysis of the American Response to Low-Intensity Conflict," Criminology: Special International Issue on Terrorism, (98). **CONTACT ADDRESS** Dept Criminal Justice, Grand Valley State Univ, 256 AuSable Hall, Allendale, MI 49401. **EMAIL** whitej@gvsu.edu

WHITE, KEVIN
DISCIPLINE AQUINAS, MEDIEVAL PHILOSOPHY **EDUCATION** Univ Ottawa, PhD. **CAREER** Philos, Catholic Univ Am. **RESEARCH** Thomistic psychology; Aquinas; Augustine. **SELECTED PUBLICATIONS** Auth, The Meaning of Phantasia in Aristotle's De anima, III, 3-8, Dialogue 24, 85; St Thomas Aquinas and the Prologue to Peter of Auvergne's Quaestiones super De sensu et sensato, Documenti e studi sulla tradizione filosofica medievale 1, 90; three previously unpublished chapters from St Thomas Aquinas's Commentary on Aristotle's Meteora: Sentencia super Meteora 2;13-15, Mediaeval Studies 54 , 92; The Virtues of Man the Animal sociale: Affabilitas and Veritas in Aquinas, The Thomist 57, 93; Individuation in Aquinas's Super Boetium De Trinitate, Q;4, American Catholic Philosophical Quarterly 69, 95; Aquinas on the Immediacy of the Union of Soul and Body, in Paul Lockey, ed;, Studies in Thomistic Theology, Houston: Center for Thomistic Studies, 96; Ed, Hispanic Philosophy in the Age of Discovery, Catholic Univ Am Press, 97; Coed, Jean Capreolus et son temps, Cerf, 97. **CONTACT ADDRESS** Catholic Univ of America, 620 Michigan Ave Northeast, Washington, DC 20064. **EMAIL** whitek@cua.edu

WHITE, LELAND J.
PERSONAL Born Charleston, SC **DISCIPLINE** RELIGION **EDUCATION** St Mary's Sem & Univ, BA, 62; Pontif Univ Gregoriana, Rome, STL, 66; Univ Mich, Ann Arbor, MA, 72; Duke Univ, PhD(relig), 74, Seton Hall Univ Law Sch, JD, 92. **CAREER** Instr theol, Sulpician Sem of the Northwest, 68-69 & St John Provincial Sem, 69-70; asst prof relig studies, Nazareth Col, Kalamazoo, 74-76; asst prof, Siena Col, 76-82, chmn relig studies dept, 79-82; Prof Theol, St John's Univ, Jamaica NY, 82-, Nat Endowment for Humanities fel relig, Yale Univ, 76; dir, Reinhold Niebuhr Inst Relig & Cult, 77-79; mem, bd of assoc ed, Bibl Theol Bull, 80-; Nat Endowment for Humanities fel, Princeton Univ, 81; Leo John Dehon fel theol, 82. **MEMBERSHIPS** Am Bar Assoc, SC Bar Assoc, AM Acad Relig; Cath Theol Soc Am; Col Theol Soc; AAUP. **RESEARCH** Theology; religion and culture; political theology. **SELECTED PUBLICATIONS** Auth, Religion and Law in America, 98; auth, Bible, Church and Culture, 97; auth, Jesus the Christ: A Bibliography, 88; auth, Christ and the Christian Movement: Jesus in the New Testament, the Creeds and Modern Theology, 85; auth, Theology and Authority: A Cross-Cultural Analysis of Theological Scripts, Theology and Authority **CONTACT ADDRESS** Dept of Theol and Relig Stu, St. John's Univ, 8000 Utopia Pky, Jamaica, NY 11439-0001. **EMAIL** whitelel@shu.edu

WHITE, M. CHRIS
PERSONAL Born 10/16/1943, SC, m, 1965, 2 children **DISCIPLINE** RELIGION **EDUCATION** Emory Univ, PhD, 72. **CAREER** Prof relig, 72-80, Exec Vice-Pres, Elon Col, 80-86; pres, Gardner-Webb Univ, 86- . **HONORS AND AWARDS** Woodrow Wilson Fel. **MEMBERSHIPS** AAR; SBL. **RESEARCH** New Testament studies. **CONTACT ADDRESS** Gardner-Webb Univ, PO Box 897, Boiling Springs, NC 28017. **EMAIL** mcwhite@gardner-webb.edu

WHITE, MARSHA
PERSONAL Born 04/02/1950, Boston, MA **DISCIPLINE** HEBREW BIBLE **EDUCATION** Harvard Univ, PhD, 94. **CAREER** Instr, Phillips Exeter Academy, 84-85; teaching fel, Harvard Col, 88, 90, 91; instr, Harvard Divinity School, fall 91; lect, Col of the Holy Cross, 93-94; instr, Hebrew Col, Brookline, MA, 94-95; lect, Univ MA, spring 95; instr, Classical Asn of New England Summer Inst, 94-98; instr, Temple Bethel, 95-96; vis asst prof, Wesleyan Univ, fall 96; lect, Andover Newton Theol School, 95-97; vis lect in Judaic Studies, Brown Univ, fall 97; instr, Havurat Shalom, Sommerville, MA, 97-98. **HONORS AND AWARDS** Listed in Who's Who in Biblical Studies and Archaeology, 2nd ed (1992-93), Washington, DC: Biblical Archaeology Soc, 93; Soc Biblical Literature Regional Scholar. **MEMBERSHIPS** Soc Biblical Lit; Asn for Jewish Studies. **RESEARCH** Ancient Israelite historiography. **SELECTED PUBLICATIONS** Auth, The Elohistic Depiction of Aaron: A Study in the Levite-Zadokite Controversy, in Studies in the Pentateuch, ed, J. A. Emerton, supplemental to Vetus Testamentum 41, Leiden: Brill, 90; Jonah, in The Women's Bible Commentary, eds Carol Newsom and Sharon Ringe, Louisville: Westminster/John Knox, 92; Naboth's Vineyard and Jehu's Coup: The Legitimation, of a Dynastic Extermination, Vetus Testamentum 44, 94; The Elijah Legends and Jehu's Coup, Brown Judaic Studies 311, Atlanta: Scholars, 97; Review of Diversity in Pre-Exilic Hebrew by Ian Young, JBL 116, 97; Bathsheba, Elisha, Nathan, Uriah, in Eerdmans Dictionary of the Bible, eds, David Noel Freedman, Allen C. Myers, Astrid B. Beck, Grand Rapids: Eerdmans, forthcoming. **CONTACT ADDRESS** 16 Mountain Ave., Somerville, MA 02143-1309. **EMAIL** mesh33@aol.com

WHITE, MICHAEL J.
PERSONAL Born 02/25/1948, Canton, IL **DISCIPLINE** ANCIENT PHILOSOPHY **EDUCATION** Ariz State Univ, BA, 70; Univ Calif, San Diego, MA, 73, PhD(philos), 74. **CAREER** Asst prof, 74-79, Assoc Prof Philos, Ariz State Univ, 79-, Vis asst prof, Univ Tex, Austin, 76-77; vis assoc prof, Univ Ariz, fall, 81. **MEMBERSHIPS** Am Philos Asn. **RESEARCH** Ancient philosophy; mathematical logic; philosophy of language. **SELECTED PUBLICATIONS CONTACT ADDRESS** Dept of Philosophy, Arizona State Univ, MC 2004, Tempe, AZ 85287. **EMAIL** mjwhite@asu.edu

WHITE, MORTON G.
PERSONAL Born 04/29/1917, New York, NY, m, 1997, 2 children **DISCIPLINE** PHILOSOPHY **EDUCATION** City Col New York, BS, 36; Columbia Univ, AM, 38, PhD, 42. **CAREER** Instr physics, City Col New York, 43; instr philos, Columbia Univ, 42-46; asst prof, Univ Pa, 46-48, Harvard Univ, 48-50, assoc prof, 50-53, prof, 53-70, chmn dept, 54-57, acting chmn dept, 67-69; Prof Philos, Sch Hist Studies, Inst Advan Study, 70-87, PROF EMERITUS, 87-, Woodbridge prize, Columbia Univ, 42; Guggenheim fel, 50-51; vis prof, Univ Tokyo, Summers 52 & 60 & spring 66; mem, Inst Advan Study, 53-54, 62-63, 67-68 & 68-69; fel, Ctr Advan Studies Behav Sci, 59-60; Am Coun Learned Socs, 62-63; vis prof, City Univ New York, 68-69. **HONORS AND AWARDS** Butler Medal, Columbia Univ 61; lhd, city univ new york, 75. **MEMBERSHIPS** Fel Am Acad Arts & Sci; Am Philos Soc; Am Antiquarian Soc; Am Philos Asn. **RESEARCH** Epistemology; ethics; philosophy of history; history of American thought. **SELECTED PUBLICATIONS** Auth, The Origin of Dewey's Instrumentalism, 43, Columbia Univ; auth, Social Thought in America, 49, Viking; ed, The Age of Analysis, 55, Houghton Mifflin; auth, Toward Reunion in Philosophy, 56, Harvard Univ; auth, Religion, Politics and The Higher Learning, 59 & coauth, The Intellectual Versus The City, 62, Harvard Univ; auth, Foundations of Historical Knowledge, Harper, 65; Science and Sentiment in America, 72 ed, Documents in The History of American Philosophy, 72, auth, Pragmatism and the American Mind, 73, Philosophy of the American Revolution, 78 & What Is and What Ought to Be Done, 81, Oxford Univ; co-auth, Journeys to the Japanese, Univ British Columbia, 86; auth, Philosophy, The Federalist, and the Constitution, Oxford Univ, 87; auth, The Question of Free Will, Princeton Univ, 93; A Philosopher's Story, Penn State Press, 99. **CONTACT ADDRESS** Inst for Advanced Study, Princeton, NJ 08540.

WHITE, NICHOLAS P.
PERSONAL Born 07/17/1942, New York, NY, d, 3 children **DISCIPLINE** PHILOSOPHY **EDUCATION** Harvard, BA, 63, MA, 65, PhD, 70. **CAREER** Univ of Mich, asst prof, assoc prof, prof, 68-94; Univ of Utah, Pres prof, 94-. **HONORS AND AWARDS** ACLS, NEH, Guggenheim Fel. **RESEARCH** Greek philo; Metaphysics; ethics. **CONTACT ADDRESS** Dept of Philosophy, Univ of Utah, Salt Lake City, UT 84112.

WHITE, PATRICIA D.
PERSONAL Born 07/08/1949, Syracuse, NY, d, 2 children **DISCIPLINE** INCOME TAX **EDUCATION** Univ Mich, BA, 71; MA, 74; JD, 74. **CAREER** Vis asst prof, Univ of Toledo, 76-77; vis assoc prof to assoc prof, Georgetown Univ, 79-88; vis prof, Univ of Mich, 88-94; prof, Univ of Utah, 94-98; prof, dean, Ariz State Univ, 99-. **HONORS AND AWARDS** L. Hart Wright Outstanding Teaching Awd, Univ of Mich. **MEMBERSHIPS** Am Col of Tax Counsel, Am Philos Assoc. **RESEARCH** Income Tax, Medical Ethics, Philosophy of Law. **SELECTED PUBLICATIONS** Auth, "Philosophy and Law: Some Observations on MacCormick's Legal Reasoning and Legal Theory," 78 Mich Law Rev 737, (80); rev, "Law and Moral Obligation" and "The Authority of Law" by Joseph Roz, 49 Chicago Law Rev 249, (82); auth, "The Concept of Person, the Law, and the Use of the Fetus in Biomedicine," Abortion and the Status of the Fetus, ed W. Bondeson, D. Reidel Publ Co, (83); auth, "An Essay on the Conceptual Foundations of the Tax Benefit Rule," 82 Mich Law Rev 486, (83); auth, "The Teachings of Jurisprudence and Legal Philosophy in Law Schools: Special Problems of Pedagogy," 36 Jour of Legal Educ 563, (86); auth, "Should the Law Define Death? A Genuine Question," in Death: Beyond Whole Brain Criteria, ed, R.M. Zaner, D. Reidel Pub Co, (88); auth, "Pain and Suffering and the Law," BioLaw, (88); auth, "Realization, Recognition, Reconciliation, Rationality and the Structure of the Federal Income Tax System," 88 Mich Law Rev 2034, (90); auth, "Appointing a Proxy Under the Best of Circumstances," 92 Utah Law Rev 842, (92); auth, Tax Law Vols I and II, Int Libr of Essays in Law and Legal Theory, Dartmouth Publ Co and NY Univ Pr, (London, NY), 95; auth, "Reflections on the Enterprise," Toledo Law Rev, (00). **CONTACT ADDRESS** Col of Law, Arizona State Univ, McAllister and Orange Sts, PO Box 877906, Tempe, AZ 85287-7906. **EMAIL** patricia.white@asu.edu

WHITE, R. FOWLER
DISCIPLINE NEW TESTAMENT AND BIBLICAL LANGUAGES **EDUCATION** Vanderbilt Univ, BA, MA; Dallas Theol Sem, ThM; Westminster Theol Sem, PhD. **CAREER** Dean, Knox Theol Sem. **RESEARCH** Biblical theology and hermeneutics. **CONTACT ADDRESS** Knox Theol Sem, 5554 N Federal Hwy, Fort Lauderdale, FL 33308.

WHITE, RONALD C.
PERSONAL Born 05/22/1939, Minneapolis, MN, m, 1991, 2 children **DISCIPLINE** HISTORY, RELIGIOUS STUDIES **EDUCATION** Univ Calif at Los Angeles, BA, 61; Princeton Theol Sem, M Div, 64; Princeton Univ, MA, 70; PhD, 72. **CAREER** Lectr, Colo Col, 65-66; Instr, Princeton Univ, 70-71; Asst Prof, Rider Col, 72-74; Asst/Assoc Prof, Whitworth Col, 74-81; Vis Prof, San Francisco Theol Sem, Grad Theol Union, 79; Vis Lectr/Lectr, Princeton Theol Sem, 81-88; Ed, Princeton Sem Bul, 83-88; Reader, Huntington Libr, 88-; Prof, Fuller Theol Sem, 89-93; Vis Prof, The Sch of Theol at Claremont, 90-91; Vis Prof, Occidental Col, 91-92; Lectr, Univ Calif, Los Angeles, 91-95; Vice-Pres for Acad Affairs, Dean, Prof, San Francisco Theol Sem, 96-. **HONORS AND AWARDS** World Coun of Churches Scholar, Lincoln, Eng, 66-67; Princeton Univ Fel, 68-70; Ford Found Fel in Ethnic Studies, 70-72; Rider Col Fac Fel, 73; Princeton Univ Vis Fel, 86; Haynes Fel, Huntington Libr, 89; Louisville Inst Fel, 92-94; Lilly Endowment Fel, 94-95. **MEMBERSHIPS** Am Acad of Rel, AHA, Am Soc of Church Hist, Asn of Case Teaching. **RESEARCH** African-American Religious History, Abraham Lincoln, The Social Gospel, Youth Ministry. **SELECTED PUBLICATIONS** Coauth, The Social Gospel: Religion and Reform in Changing America, Temple Univ Press (Philadelphia), 76; coauth, American Christianity: A Case Approach, Eerdmans (Grand Rapids), 86; co-ed, Partners in Peace and Education, (Grand Rapids), 88; co-ed, An Unsettled Arena: Religion and the Bill of Rights, Eerdmans (Grand Rapids), 90; auth, Liberty and Justice for All: Racial Reform and the Social Gospel, Harper and Row (San Francisco), 90; auth, "Youth Ministry at the Center: A Case Study of Young Life," in Reforming the Center: American Protestantism, 1900 to the Present (Grand Rapids: Eerdmans, 98); auth, "Lincoln's Sermon on the Mount: The Second Inaugural," in Religion and the American Civil War, ed. Randall M. Miller, Harry S. Stout, and Charles Reagan Wilson (NY: Oxford Univ Press, 98). **CONTACT ADDRESS** Vice-Pres Acad Affairs, Dean Church Hist, San Francisco Theol Sem, 2 Kensington Rd, San Anselmo, CA 94960-2905.

WHITE, STEPHEN W.
PERSONAL Born 11/01/1941, Atlanta, GA, m, 1963, 2 children **DISCIPLINE** PHILOSOPHY **EDUCATION** Oglethorpe Univ, BA, 66; Univ Ga, Ma, 69, PhD, 71. **CAREER** From asst prof to assoc prof to prof, 70-85, E Tenn State Univ; assoc prof, Auburn Univ, 85-98; ed, Natl Forum, 78-93; ed, Child & Adolescent Newsletter, 93-94. **HONORS AND AWARDS** Phi Kappa Phi; Phi Beta Kappa. **MEMBERSHIPS** Amintaphil; Southern Society Philos Psychol; Am Philos Asn; Society Scholar Publ. **RESEARCH** Social-political philosophy; applied ethics. **CONTACT ADDRESS** 698 Queens Way, Auburn, AL 36830. **EMAIL** whitesw@mail.auburn.edu

WHITE, V. ALAN
PERSONAL Born 04/03/1953, Florence, AL **DISCIPLINE** PHILOSOPHY **EDUCATION** Univ of Tennessee, PhD, 82. **CAREER** Asst Prof, Assoc Prof to Prof Philos, 81-, Univ of Wisconsin-Manitowoc. **HONORS AND AWARDS** Carnegie CASE, Wisconsin Prof Yr, 96-97. **MEMBERSHIPS** APA, Aristotelian Soc. **RESEARCH** Metaphysics; Philosophy of Science. **SELECTED PUBLICATIONS** Auth, Frankfurt, Failure and Finding Fault, Sorites, 98; co-auth, Introductory Philosophy-A Restricted Tipic Approach, In The Socratic Tradition, Essays on Teaching Philosophy, ed, Tziporah Kasachkoff, pub by Rowman and Littlefield, 98; Ray on the Twin Paradox, Metaphysical Review: Essays on the Foundations of Physics, 97; Picturing Einstein's Train of Thought, Philosophy, 96; Single-Topic Introductory Philosophy-An Update, Teaching Philosophy, 96. **CONTACT ADDRESS** Dept Philosophy, Univ of Wisconsin Ctr, Manitowoc County, Manitowoc, WI 54220. **EMAIL** awhite@uwc.edu

WHITEBOOK, JOEL
DISCIPLINE PHILOSOPHY **EDUCATION** New Sch Soc Res, PhD, 78; CUNY, PhD, 84. **CAREER** Adj prof, Eugene Lang Col. **RESEARCH** Psychoanalysis and psychotherapy; Foucault. **SELECTED PUBLICATIONS** Auth, articles on psych, philos, and economics; Perversion and Utopia: A Study in Psychoanalysis and Critical Theory, 95. **CONTACT ADDRESS** Eugene Lang Col, New Sch for Social Research, 66 West 12th St, New York, NY 10011.

WHITEBREAD, CHARLES H.
PERSONAL Born 04/02/1943, Washington, DC **DISCIPLINE** CRIMINAL PROCEDURE, JUVENILE LAW **EDUCATION** Princeton Univ, BA, 65; Yale Univ, LLB, 68. **CAREER** Prof Law, Univ Va Law Sch, 68-81; George T Pfleger prof Law, Univ Southern Calif Law Sch, 81-, Legal staff mem, Forensic Psychiat Clinic, Univ Va Hospital, 68-81; consult, Nat Comn Causes & Prev Violence, 68-69 & Nat Comn Marijuana & Drug Abuse, 71-72; fac mem, Fed Bur Invest Nat Acad, 72-; lectr, Am Acad Judicial Educ Conf, 72- & Nat Asn Dist Attys, 81-. **HONORS AND AWARDS** Israel Peres Prize, Yale Univ Law Sch, 68; FBI's Edwin E. Erickson Awd, 85, 91; Natl Judicial Fnd and Am Judges Assoc, Glenn R. Winters Awd, 85; elected to Am Law Inst, 86. **MEMBERSHIPS** Am Bar Asn. **RESEARCH** Criminal procedure; juvenile law and procedure. **SELECTED PUBLICATIONS** Auth, Interrogations in New Haven: The impact of Miranda, Yale Law J, 76: 1519; ed, Mass Production Justice and the Constitutional Ideal, Univ Va Press, 69; auth, 2 chaps in Educational Perspectives in the Drug Abuse Crisis, 71; coauth, The Marijuana Conviction, Univ Va Press, 74; Juvenile Law & Procedure, Nat Coun Juvenile Ct Judges, 74; auth, Constitutional Criminal Procedure, Am Acad Judicial Educ, 78; coauth, Criminal Procedure, 4th ed, 00; coauth, Cases & Materials on Children in the Legal System 2nd ed, Found Press, 97; auth, Recent Decisions of the United States Supreme Court, American Acad of Judicial Education, annual. **CONTACT ADDRESS** Law Sch, Univ of So California, 699 Exposition Blvd, Los Angeles, CA 90089-0071. **EMAIL** cwhitebr@law.usc.edu

WHITEHEAD, BRADY, JR.
DISCIPLINE NEW TESTAMENT **EDUCATION** Rhodes Col, BA, 52; Candler Sch of Theol, MDiv, 55; Grad Sch of Arts & Sci, MA, 57; Boston Univ Sch of Theol, ThD, 72 **CAREER** Prof, 67-98, Lambuth Univ **MEMBERSHIPS** Soc of Bibl Lit **SELECTED PUBLICATIONS** Auth, What Goes Around Comes Around: An Essay on the Unity of the Book of Isaiah; How Methodists Interpret the Bible **CONTACT ADDRESS** 4600 Bells Hwy, Jackson, TN 38305.

WHITEHOUSE, GEORGE
DISCIPLINE COMMUNICATIONS LAW **EDUCATION** Univ Southern MS, BS, 71, MS, 72, PhD, 74; Cath Univ Am, WA, JD, 85. **CAREER** Prof & dir, Grad Study, Dept Mass Commun; Legal asst to Comnr, Fed Commun Comn, WA, 84-85; legal asst to ch counsel & VP for Congressional-Govt Relations of the Nat Asn of Broadcasters, WA, 83-84; asst prof & dir, Div Broadcasting & Jour, Mass Commun Dept, Univ Tex, 80-82; assoc prof & dir, Div Mass Commun, Univ N Ala, 78-80; prof, Stephens Col; Columbia, 74-78; commun adv, governments Saudi Arabia & Iran, US State Dept in Jeddah, SA & Teheran; Supt, US Air Force Sch Commun Adminr & Sch Commun, US Air Force Tehn Training Command; res & develop engineer. **MEMBERSHIPS** Fed Commun Bar Asn; Am Bar Asn; ABA Forum Comt on Commun Law; DC Bar Asn; DC Ct of Appeals Bar; Pa Bar Asn; Asn Educ in Jour and Mass Commun; Broadcast Educ Asn; Radio-TV News Directors Asn; Soc Prof Jour; Broadcast Educ Asn; Sioux City, IA Press Club; Soc Motion Picture and TV Engineers; Soc Broadcast Engineers; Am Consult League. **RESEARCH** Effects of the newly legislated Telecommunications Act of 96. **SELECTED PUBLICATIONS** Auth, High Definition Television (HDTV): A Primer, Commun Lawyer, 89; The Professionalization of Journalists, keynote address to Sioux City Press Club, 89; The Professionalization of Journalism, for Commun Lawyer, 86; Understanding the New Technologies of the Mass Media, textbk, Prentice-Hall, 86; The Berwick Doctrine: Suburban Community Policy, Fed Commun Comn, Wash, 84; coauth, Broadcasting and Government, contributing author, Nat Asn Broadcasters, Wash, 84; reviewer-consult, For Houghton Mifflin, prepubl manuscript of textbk, Introd to Telecommun, McGregor, 96; For McGraw-Hill, prepubl manuscript of textbk, Media Law, 3rd ed, Holsinger, 95; For Focal Press, prepubl manuscript of textbk, Winning The Global TV News Game, Johnston, 95; For Focal Press, prepubl manuscript of workbk, Cases and Exercises in Electronic Media Mgt, 94; For McGraw-Hill, prepubl manuscript for textbk, The Int World of Electronic Media, 93 & For Prentice-Hall, prepubl manuscript for Mng the Electronic Media, 91. **CONTACT ADDRESS** Dept of Mass Commun, Univ of So Dakota, Vermillion, 414 E Clark St, Vermillion, SD 57069. **EMAIL** gwhiteho@sundance.usd.edu

WHITFORD, WILLIAM C.
PERSONAL Born 01/16/1940, Madison, WI, m, 1965, 4 children **DISCIPLINE** LAW **EDUCATION** Univ Wis, BA, 61; Yale Univ, LLB, 64. **CAREER** Law clerk, US Ct Appeals, Washington, DC circuit, 64-65; asst prof, 65-69, assoc prof, 69-71, Prof Law, Univ Wis, Madison, 71-; Young-Bascom Prof Bus Law, 86-; Vis sr lectr, Univ Col, Dar es Salaam, Tanzania, 67-69; vis prof law, Stanford Univ, 72-73; Fulbright vis prof, Univ Nairobi, 75-76; vis prof, Boston Univ Sch Law, 87. **MEMBERSHIPS** Law & Soc Asn; Conf Critical Legal Studies. **RESEARCH** Consumer law; taxation. **SELECTED PUBLICATIONS** Auth, Strict products liability and the auto industry, Vol 1968, 68, Law and the consumer transaction: A case study of the auto warranty, Vol 1968, 69, The functions of disclosure regulation of consumer transactions, Vol 1973, 73, coauth, Why process consumer complaints, Vol 1974, 74, The impact of denying self-help repossession of automobiles, Vol 1975, 75, auth, A critique of the consumer credit collection system, Vol 1979, 79 & Structuring consumer protection legislation to maximize effectiveness, Vol 1981, 82, Wis Law Rev; Comment on a theory of consumer product warranty, Yale Law J, Vol 91, 82; The small case procedure of the United States Tax Court: A successful small claims court, ABFRJ, 85; Ian Macneil's contribution to contracts scholarship, Wis Law Rev, 85; The appropriate role of security interests in consumer transactions, Cardozo Law Rev, 86; Lowered horizons: Implementation research in a post-CLS world, Wis Law Rev, 86; Has the time come to repeal chapter 13, Ind Law J, 89; co-auth, Bargaining over equity's share in the bankruptcy reorganization of large, publicly held companies, Univ Pa Law Rev, 90; co-auth, Venue choice and forum shopping in the bankruptcy reorganization of large publicly held companies, Wis Law Rev, 91; co-auth, Preemptive cramdown, Am Bank Law J, 91; Corporate governance in the bankruptcy reorganization of large publicly held companies, Univ Pa Law Rev, 93; Patterns in the bankruptcy reorganization of large, publicly held companies, Cornell Law Rev, 93; co-auth, Compensating unsecured creditors for extraordinary bankruptcy reorganization risks, Wash Univ Law Rev, 94; What's right about chapter 11, Wash Univ Law Rev, 94; The ideal of individualized justice: Consumer bankruptcy as consumer protection, and consumer protection in consumer bankruptcy, Am Bank Law J, 94; What's right about chapter 11?, Wash Univ Law Rev, 94; co-auth, Compensating unsecured creditors for extraordinary bankruptcy reorganization risks, Wash Univ Law Rev, 94; Contract law and the control of standardized terms in consumer contracts: An American report, European Rev of Private Law, 95; co-auth, Contracts: Law in Action, Michie, 95; co-auth, A black critique of the Internal Revenue Code, Wis Law Rev, 96; Changing definitions of fresh start in American bankruptcy law, J Consumer Policy, 97; Remarkable, NC Law Rev, 98; auth, Secured Creditors and Consumer Bankruptcy, York Law J, 99; The Rule of Law, Wis Law Rev, 00. **CONTACT ADDRESS** Law Sch, Univ of Wisconsin, Madison, 975 Bascom Mall, Madison, WI 53706-1301. **EMAIL** whitford@lawmail.law.wisc.edu

WHITLOCK, LUDER
PERSONAL Born 06/06/1940, Jacksonville, FL, m, 1959, 3 children **DISCIPLINE** PASTORAL MINISTRY **EDUCATION** Univ Fla; Westminster Theol Sem; Vanderbilt Univ, DMin. **CAREER** Prof, 75; actg pres, 78; pres, 79-. **HONORS AND AWARDS** Pres, Found for Reformation; dir, Key Life Network, Inc; Pres and Exec Commn Assoc Theol Sch(s), USA, Can; dir, Nat Assn of Evangel; co-pres, Intl Reformed fel; dir, Natl Commn on Higher Educ; adv bd(s), Found for Thought and Ethics; Amer Acad of Ministry; Ed Adv Bd of Leadership; Intl Inst for Christian Stud; ed adv bd, Reformed Mind: A Jour for the Spiritual and Intellectual Develop of Church Leaders; Christian Assn of PrimeTimers; Bibl Manhood and Womanhood; Christian Coun; New Heritage USA; Mission Amer Nat Comm; Outstanding Young Men of Am. He is also on the Board of Reference, Patkai Ministries, India and Belhaven Col; Pres, Foundation for Reformation; Pres and Ex Committee Assoc of Theol Schools in US & Canada. **MEMBERSHIPS** Mem, Fel of Evangel Sem Pres(s); Mission Am Natl Comm. **RESEARCH** Ministry; Sprituality. **SELECTED PUBLICATIONS** Contrib, The Evangel Dictionary of Theol; Baker Encycl of the Bible; Reformed Theol in Am; The Changing of the Evangel Mind; The Dictionary of Twentieth Century Christian Biography; contrib, A Mighty Long Journey, The Practice of Confessing Subscription; auth, The Sprituality Quest. **CONTACT ADDRESS** Dept of Pastoral Ministry, Reformed Theol Sem, Mississippi, 5422 Clinton Blvd, Jackson, MS 39209-3099. **EMAIL** lwhitlock@rts.edu

WHITMAN, JEFFREY P.
PERSONAL Born 04/25/1955, Scanton, PA, m, 1978, 2 children **DISCIPLINE** PHILOSOPHY **EDUCATION** US Military Acad, BS, 77; Brown Univ, PhD, 91. **CAREER** Commissioned Officer, US Army, 77-95; asst and assoc prof, US Military Acad, West Point, NY, 87-95; asst and assoc prof Philos, Susquehanna Univ, PA, 95- . **MEMBERSHIPS** Amer Philos asn; Asn Practical prof Ethics; Amer Asn Philos tchrs. **RESEARCH** Applied Ethics; Ethics; Epistemology; Just War Theory. **SELECTED PUBLICATIONS** Auth, Utilitarianism and the Laws of Land Warfare, Publ Affairs Quart, July 93; The Many Guises of the Slippery Slope Argument, Soc Theory and Practice, Spring 94; Citizens and Soldiers: Teaching Just War Theory at the US Military Academy, Tchg Philos, March 94; The Soldier as Conscientous Objector, Publ Affairs Quart, Jan 95; Reclaiming the Medical Profession, Prof Ehtics, Spring 95; An End to Sovereignty?, The Jour of Soc Philos, Fall 96; auth, The Power and Value of Philosophical Skepticism, Lanham, MD, Rowman and Littlefield, 96; Exploring Moral Character in the Philosophy Class, Tchg Philos, June 98. **CONTACT ADDRESS** Dept of Philosophy, Susquehanna Univ, Selinsgrove, PA 17870. **EMAIL** whitman@susqu.edu

WHITMAN, ROBERT
PERSONAL Born 05/18/1936, New York, NY, m, 1961, 2 children **DISCIPLINE** LAW **EDUCATION** City Col NY, BBA, 56; Columbia Univ Law Sch, JD, 59; NY Univ Law Sch, LLM 71. **CAREER** Assoc in Law, Columbia Law Sch, 59-60; asst prof, Univ Md Law Sch, 60-62; private practice, 66-; prof of law, Univ Conn Law Sch, 66-. **HONORS AND AWARDS** Harlan Fisk Stone Scholar; Order of the Coif; B. Jaffin Prize in Socio-Legal Res. **MEMBERSHIPS** Am Bar Asn, Conn Bar Asn, Am Law Inst, Am Col of Trust & Estate Counsel, Law Prof Advisory Group For Trusts & Estates, Soc For Trusts & Estates Practitioners. **SELECTED PUBLICATIONS** Coauth, After Death Tax Planning, ALI-ABA, 90 & 99; coauth, Counseling Older Clients, ALI-ABA, 97; auth, Basic Estate Planning & Administration for Benefactors & Beneficiaries, 98; auth, Fiduciary Accounting Guide, ALI-ABA, 98; coauth, Basic Accounting for Lawyer, ALI-ABA, 99; auth, Estate Planning and Administration for Estate and Trust Benefactors and Beneficiaries, The Graduate Group, 99. **CONTACT ADDRESS** Sch of Law, Univ of Connecticut, Hartford, 55 Elizabeth St, Hartford, CT 06105-2213. **EMAIL** rwhitman@law.uconn.edu

WHITNEY, BARRY L.
PERSONAL Born 12/10/1947, Cornwall, ON, Canada, 3 children **DISCIPLINE** PHILOSOPHY **EDUCATION** McMaster Univ, BA, 71, PhD, 77. **CAREER** Prof, 76-. **HONORS AND AWARDS** Research Prof, Univ of Windsor, Process Studies, 96 ff. **MEMBERSHIPS** AAR; Am Philos Asn. **RESEARCH** Process philosophy; Philosophy of religion and theodicy. **SELECTED PUBLICATIONS** Auth, Theodicy: An Annotated Bibliography, 1960-1991, 98; Theodicy, 93; What Are They Saying About God and Evil?, 89; Evil and the Process God, 85. **CONTACT ADDRESS** Dept of Classics, Univ of Windsor, PO Box 33830, Detroit, MI 48232. **EMAIL** whitney@uwindsor.com

WHITNEY, RUTH
PERSONAL Born 03/08/1938, Quincy, IL, d **DISCIPLINE** RELIGION; WOMEN'S STUDIES **EDUCATION** Marquette Univ, BS; Catholic Univ Am, MA, PhD. **CAREER** Asst prof, relig, Rutgers Univ, 73-79; Adj fac, Women's Studies, Univ So Fla, 89- . **HONORS AND AWARDS** Alpha Sigma Nu. **MEMBERSHIPS** Am Acad Relig; Natl Women's Stud Asn. **RESEARCH** Women; religion; spirituality; psychology; politics. **SELECTED PUBLICATIONS** Auth, Feminism and Love: Transforming Ourselves and Our World, Cross Cultural, 98. **CONTACT ADDRESS** 700 14th Ave N, Saint Petersburg, FL 33701-1018. **EMAIL** whitneyra@aol.com

WHITT, LAURIE A.
PERSONAL Born 08/03/1952, San Diego, CA, m, 1994 **DISCIPLINE** PHILOSOPHY **EDUCATION** Col of William & Mary, BA, 75; Queen's Univ, MA, 76; Univ Western Ontario, PhD, 85. **CAREER** Instr, Univ Western Ontario, 81-83; asst prof, Southern Methodist Univ, 84-86; asst prof, Mich Technol Univ, 86-92, assoc prof, 92-. **HONORS AND AWARDS** Citation for Teaching Excellence and Teaching Excellence Honor Roll, Mich Tech Univ, 93, 98; Humanities Res Ctr Fel, Australian Nat Univ, 96; Howard Found Fel, 2000-2001. **MEMBERSHIPS** Am Philos Asn, Soc for the Soc Study of Sci, Radical Philos Asn, Soc for Women in Philos, Law and Soc Asn, Am Indian Sci and Engineering Soc. **RESEARCH** Science studies, indigenous studies, legal studies. **SELECTED PUBLICATIONS** Auth, "Thaw," The Spoon River Poetry Rev, Vol XXI, No 2 (winter 96): 25; auth, "Ghost Pain: 1840," The Spoon River Poetry Rev, Vol XXI, No 2 (summer/fall 96): 23-24; auth, "An Amphibian," Absinthe, Vol 9, Issue 2 (96): 46; auth, "metis," Absinthe, Vol 9, Issue 2 (96): 44-45 (reprint); auth, "Song of Return," the Kerf (May 97): 34-35; auth, "Penelope Waits," Porcupine Literary Arts Mag, Vol 3, Issue 2 (98): 18-19; auth, "My-Lady-In-The-Cage," Porcupine Literary Arts Mg, Vol 3, Issue 2 (98): 16-17; auth, "Biocolonialism and the Commodification of Knowledge," Science as Culture, 7, No 1 (98): 33-67; auth, "Resisting Value-Bifurcation: Indigenist Critiques of the Human Genome Diversity Project," Daring To Be Good: Feminist Essays in Ethico-Politics, eds, Ann Ferguson & Bat Ami Bar-On," Great Britain: Routledge, Chapman and Hall (98): 70-86; auth, "Indigenous Peoples, Intellectual Property Law and the New Imperial Science, " Oklahoma City Univ Law Rev, 23, No 1 & 2 (98): 211-259; coauth with Alan W. Clark, "University Senates and the Law: A Case Study," Thought and Action, XV, No 2 (fall 99): 119-130; auth, "Cultural Imperialism and the Marketing of Native America," Native American Cultural Issues, ed by Dine Champagne, Walnut Creek, Calif: AltaMir Press (99): 169-192; coauth, "Indigenous Perspectives," A Companion to Environmental Philosophy, ed Dale Jamieson, Great Britain: Basil Blackwell (00): 3-20. **CONTACT ADDRESS** Dept Humanities, Michigan Tech Univ, 1400 Townsend Dr, Houghton, MI 49931-1200. **EMAIL** lawhitt@mtu.edu

WHITTAKER, JOHN
DISCIPLINE PSYCHOLOGY OF RELIGION, THEORIES OF RELIGION, PHILOSOPHY OF RELIGION **EDUCATION** Yale Univ, PhD, 74. **CAREER** Prof Relig Stud, dir, Relig Stud prog, La State Univ. **RESEARCH** The philosophy of religion; D.Z. Phillips; Wittgenstein; Kierkegaard. **SELECTED PUBLICATIONS** Auth, Matters of Faith and Matters of Principle, Trinity UP, 81; The Logic of Religious Persuasion, Peter Lang, 91. **CONTACT ADDRESS** Dept of Philos & Relig Stud, Louisiana State Univ and A&M Col, 106 Coates Hall, Baton Rouge, LA 70803. **EMAIL** jwhitt1@lsu.edu

WHITTEN, RALPH U.
DISCIPLINE LAW **EDUCATION** Univ Texas, BBA, 66, JD, 69; Harvard Univ, LLM, 72. **CAREER** Prof, Creighton Univ; law clerk, US Ct Appeals 4th Circuit, 69-70; tchg fel, Harvard Law Sch, 70-72; prof, Univ SC Sch Law, 72-77. **MEMBERSHIPS** Order of the Coif. **SELECTED PUBLICATIONS** Coauth, The Constitution and the Common Law, DC Health, 77; Cases and Problems on Civil Procedure: Basic and Advanced, Rothman, 97; Civil Procedure, Found Press, 94; pub(s), Amer J Comp Law; Maine Law Rev; Hastings Constitutional Law Quart; Memphis State Law Rev; Creighton Law Rev; NC Law Rev; Duke Law J. **CONTACT ADDRESS** Sch of Law, Creighton Univ, 2500 California Plaza , Omaha, NE 68178. **EMAIL** rwhitten@culaw.Creighton.edu

WHITTIER, DUANE HAPGOOD
PERSONAL Born 09/15/1928, Hanover, NH, m, 1960 **DISCIPLINE** PHILOSOPHY **EDUCATION** Univ NH, BA, 50; Univ IL, MA, 52, PhD, 61. **CAREER** From instr to asst prof philos, PA State Univ, 61-67; assoc prof, 67-78, Prof Philos, Univ NH, 78-, Vis prof, Univ IL, 63-64. **RESEARCH** Aesthetics; hist Am philos; metaphysics. **SELECTED PUBLICATIONS** Auth, Basic assumption and argument in philosophy, 10/64 & Causality and the self, 4/65, Monist; contribr, Studies in Philosophy and the History of Science, Coronado, 70; auth, Metaphor as aesthetic meaning, New Scholasticism, 78; The Frankenstein axiom, Int Philos Quart, 79; Akrasia: The Absence of Which Virtue?, Logos, 87. **CONTACT ADDRESS** Dept of Philos, Univ of New Hampshire, Durham, 125 Technology Dr, Durham, NH 03824-4724.

WHITTLESEY, WELLINGTON W.
PERSONAL Born 03/17/1920, Los Angeles, CA, m, 1947 **DISCIPLINE** THEOLOGY **EDUCATION** Wm Penn Col, AB, 41; Drake Univ, AM, 55; Northgate Grad Sch, PhD, 64. **CAREER** Prof, Kingswood Col, 46-47; Asst Prof, Wm Penn Col, 54-63; Prof to Pres and Chancellor, St Petersburg Theol Sem, 83-. **HONORS AND AWARDS** Life Member, YMCA; Life Member, Asn of Evangelical Theol. **RESEARCH** Friends (Quaker) Theological Scholars; The Anglican Separated Communicats (since 1873). **CONTACT ADDRESS** President/Chancellor, St Petersburg Theol Sem, 10830 Navajo Dr, Saint Petersburg, FL 33708-3116. **EMAIL** wwwpres@aol.com

WICCLAIR, MARK ROBERT
PERSONAL Born 01/06/1944, Los Angeles, CA, m, 1973, 1 child **DISCIPLINE** PHILOSOPHY **EDUCATION** Reed Col, BA, 66; Columbia Univ, MPhil, 74, PhD, 76. **CAREER** Fulbright fel, 66-67; from instr to asst prof philos, Lafayette Col, 75-78; from asst prof to prof phil, adjunct prof community med, 90-, WVa Univ, 78-, 79-81 adjunct prof med, Univ Pittsburgh, 91-. **HONORS AND AWARDS** Phi Beta Kappa, 66; Woodrow Wilson fel, 67-68; Hum Found WVA Fel, 80 & 87; NEH fel, 88; Outstanding Teacher Awd, WVA Univ, 87-88, 88-89; Outstanding Res Awd WVA Univ, 94-95; Benedum Distinguished Schol Awd WVA Univ, 95-96; Outstanding Pub Serv Awd, 96-97. **MEMBERSHIPS** Am Philos Asn; Am Soc Bioethics Hum. **RESEARCH** Ethics; medical ethics; ethics and aging. **SELECTED PUBLICATIONS** Auth, Film and mental processes, 3/77 & The principle of nonintervention: A critical examination of a contractarian justification, 2/78, Proc & Add Am Philos Asn; Film theory and Hugo Muensterberg's The Film: A Psychological Study, J Aesthet Ed, 7/78; Human rights and intervention, Human Rights and United States Foreign Policy: Principles and Applications, Lexington Books, 79; Rawls and the principle of nonintervention, John Rawls' Theory of Social Justice, Ohio Univ, 80; The abortion controversy and the claim that this body is mine, Social Theory & Prac, fall 81; Is prostitution morally wrong?, Philos Res Archives, 81; Ethics and the Elderly, Oxford Univ, 93; Medical ethics in the United States, Marmara Med J, 95; Mandatory Retirement: An ethical analysis, SW J on Aging, 95; Futility: A conceptual and ethical analysis, McGraw-Hill, 96; auth, "Conscientious Objection in Medicine," Bioethics, Vol 14, No 3, (00); auth, "Ethics, Community, and the Elderly: Health Care Decision-Making for Incompetent Elderly Patients," in Ethics and Community in the Health Care Professions (London: Routledge, 99); auth, "What Can Be Learned About the Ethical Soundness of Medicare HMOs From Studies Comparing Them to Fee-For-Service Medicare?" Jrnl of Ethics, Law, and Aging, Vol 5, No1, (Spring/Summer 99); auth, "The Continuing Debate Over Risk-Related Standards of Competence," Bioethics, Vol 13, No 2, (99). **CONTACT ADDRESS** Dept of Philos, West Virginia Univ, Morgantown, PO Box 6312, Morgantown, WV 26506-6312. **EMAIL** wicclair@pitt.edu

WICKER, KATHLEEN O'BRIEN
PERSONAL Born 05/24/1937, Buffalo, NY **DISCIPLINE** NEW TESTAMENT, CLASSICAL LANGUAGES **EDUCATION** Mundelein Col, BA, 59; Loyola Univ, Chicago, PhD(hist western origins), 66. **CAREER** From instr to asst prof hist & classics, Mundelein Col, 65-71; asst prof, 71-77, assoc prof, 76-84, prof, 84- , New Testament, Mary W Johnson and J Stanley Johnson prof in Hum, 96- , Scripps Col. **HONORS AND AWARDS** Lectr classics, Loyola Univ Chicago, 70-71; partic, Corpus Hellenisticum Novi Testamenti Proj, 71-77; actg dean fac, Scripps Col, 79-81. **MEMBERSHIPS** Am Acad of Relig. **RESEARCH** NT and ECL; African Christianity. **SELECTED PUBLICATIONS** Auth, Plutarch: Mulierum Virtutes, In: Plutarch's Ethical Writings and the Early Christian Literature, E J Brill, Leiden, 78; auth, Porphyry, Letter to Marcella, Scholars, 87; auth, "Conversion and Culture: A Comparative Study of the Conversions of Paul and Christians," In: Ancient and Modern Perspectives on the Bible and Culture, Scholars (98); auth, "Mami Water in African Religion and Spirituality, In: African Spirituality forms, Meanings and Expressions, Crossroad (00). **CONTACT ADDRESS** Dept of Religion, Scripps Col, 1030 Columbia Ave, Claremont, CA 91711-3948. **EMAIL** kwicker@scripps@ol.edu

WICKS, ANDREW C.
PERSONAL Born 09/19/1963, Oak Ridge, TN, m, 1987, 2 children **DISCIPLINE** RELIGIOUS ETHICS **EDUCATION** Univ Tenn Knoxville, BA, 86; Univ Va, MA, 89; Univ Va, PhD, 92. **CAREER** Asst ed, Ctr for Biomedical Ethics, Univ Va, Charlottesville, Va, 90-92; trainee consult, Ethics Consult Svc, Univ Va Health Sci Ctr, Charlottesville, Va, 91-92; adjunct facul, Germanna Comm Col, Locust Grove, Va, 89; tchg asst, dept of relig studies and health sci ctr, Univ Va, Charlottesville, Va, Basic Clinical Ethics and Helth Care Law, 89-92, Amer Relig Hist, 1850-Present, 90, theol, ethics, and med, 87-89, relig ethics and moral prob, 87-89; visg prof, Pacific Coast Banking Sch, Seattle, Wash, 8/96, 8/97; visg prof, Helsinki Sch of Econ and Bus Admin, Helsinki, Finland, 9/96, 9/97; Asst to assoc prof, Univ Wash, grad bus sch, 92-. **HONORS AND AWARDS** Phi Beta Kappa; Omicron Delta Kappa; Phi Kappa Phi. **MEMBERSHIPS** Soc for Bus Ethics; Acad of Mgt. **RESEARCH** Business ethics; corporate social responsibility. **SELECTED PUBLICATIONS** Coauth, Organization Studies and the New Pragmatism, Orgn Sci, 98; auth, In Search of Experts: A Conception of Expertise for Business Ethics, Bus Ethics Quart, 98; Health Care Ethics/Business Ethics, entry in Dict of Bus Ethics, Oxford Univ Press, 97; On Macintrye, Modernity and the Virtues: A Response to Dobson, Bus Ethics Quart, 97; Reflections on The Practical Relevance of Feminist Thought to Business, Bus Ethics Quart, 96; coauth, An Evaluation of Journal Quality: The Perspective of Business Ethics Researchers, Bus Ethics Quart, 96; coauth, Integrating Strategic Decision-Making and Business Ethics: A Cognitive Approach, Acad of Mgt Best Paper Proceed for 1996; auth, Overcoming the Separation Thesis: The Need for Reconsideration of SIM Research, Bus and Soc, 96; coauth, Is Pharmacy a Profession?, Ethical Issues in Pharmacy, Applied Therapeutics, 96; **CONTACT ADDRESS** School of Business, Univ of Washington, Box 353200, Seattle, WA 98195-3200. **EMAIL** acwekw@u.washington.edu

WIDER, KATHLEEN V.
DISCIPLINE PHILOSOPHY **EDUCATION** Wayne State Univ, PhD, 78. **CAREER** Assoc to Asst Prof, 88-00, Prof, 00-, Univ of Michigan-Dearborn; Adjunct Assoc Prof Philo, 87-88, Hunter Coll, CUNY; Adj Prof Philo and Eng, 80-87, Center for Creative Stud. **MEMBERSHIPS** APA, SPEP, SSP&P, Sartre Soc of North Amer. **RESEARCH** Philosophy of mind, Sartre, Existential Philosophy, bridges between continental and analytic Philosophy. **SELECTED PUBLICATIONS** Auth, The Bodily Nature of Consciousness, Sartre and Contemporary Philosophy of Mind, Ithaca, NY, Cornell Univ Press, 97; Truth and Existence, The Idealism in Sartre's Theory of Truth, International Journal of Philosophical Studies, 95; Sartre and the Long-Distance Truck Driver, The Journal of the British Society for Phenomenology, 93; auth, "The Self and Others: Imitation in Infants and Sartre's Analysis of the Look," Continental Philos Rev 32, (99): 195-210. **CONTACT ADDRESS** Humanities Dept, Univ of Michigan, Dearborn, Dearborn, MI 48128. **EMAIL** kwider@umd.umich.edu

WIDISS, ALAN I.
DISCIPLINE LAW **EDUCATION** Univ Southern Calif, BS, 60, BL, 63; Harvard Univ, ML, 64. **CAREER** Vis prof, Univ San Diego, summers 74, 75, 77; Dir, Mass No-Fault Automobile Insurance Study, 72-77; asst prof, Univ of Iowa, 65-68, assoc prof, 68-69, prof, 69-. **MEMBERSHIPS** Am Bar Asn, Asn of Trial Lawyer of Am, Iowa City Youth Orchestra Bd, Iowa City/Johnson Co Arts Coun, Am Law Inst, Am Arbitration Asn Panels, Calif Bar Asn. **RESEARCH** The insurance system, insurance law, and regulation of the insurance industry; non-judicial dispute resolution (especially arbitration law and practice); interaction of law, the legal system, and societal changes. **SELECTED PUBLICATIONS** Auth, "Uninsured Motorist Coverage," in Automoblie Liability Insurance, Bobbs-Merrill (71); ed, "Introduction and Uninsured Motorist Claims," in Arbitration: Commercial Disputes, Insurance, and Tort Claims, NY: Practicing Law Inst (79); auth, Teachers Manual (for use with Insurance and the Course Supplements for Insurance Law), West Pub Co, St Paul, Minn (90); auth, Uninsured and Underinsured Motorist Insurance, 2nd ed, Vol 1, 85, 90, Vol II, 87, 92, Vol III, 90, 95, Anderson Pub Co, Cincinnati, Ohio (98); auth, "Uninsured and Underinsured Motorist Insurance Dispute Claims," in The Arbitration Asn Insurance ADR Manual, Shepard's/McGraw-Hill (93); auth, "Obligating Insurers to inform insured's about the existence of rights and duties regarding coverage for losses," 1 Conn Insurance Law J, 67-95 (95); auth, "Bad Faith in Fact and Fiction: Ruminations on John Grisham's Tale About Insurance Coverages, Punitive Damages, and The Great Benefit Life Insurance Company," 26 Univ of Memphis Law Rev, 1377-1403 (96); auth, "Underinsured Motorist Coverage for Amounts Awarded as Punitive Damages in a Suit Against the Tortfeasor: Delving Into the Dilemma Created by Diverging Public Policies and Private Interests," 43 Drake Law Rev 780-811 (95). **CONTACT ADDRESS** College of Law, Univ of Iowa, Melrose and Bylington, Iowa City, IA 52242. **EMAIL** alan-widiss@uiowa.edu

WIEDMANN, SALLY N.
PERSONAL Born 10/27/1949, Fargo, ND, m, 1971, 1 child **DISCIPLINE** PHILOSOPHY **EDUCATION** Univ Northern Iowa, BA, 90; MPhil, 92; Univ Miami, PhD, 96. **CAREER** From vis instr to adj instr, Univ Central Fla, 96-98; asst prof, N Ga Col & State Univ, 98-. **HONORS AND AWARDS** Master's Thesis Awd (2nd Place), Univ N Iowa, 92; Univ Fel, Univ Miami, 93-96. **MEMBERSHIPS** Am Philos Asn. **RESEARCH** Environmental Ethics, Kant's Moral Philosophy. **CONTACT ADDRESS** Dept Hist & Sociol, No Georgia Col, Dunlap 207, Dahlonega, GA 30597. **EMAIL** snwiedmann@ngcsu.edu

WIEGERS, WANDA
DISCIPLINE LAW **EDUCATION** Univ Saskatchewan, LLB, 78, BA, 83; Univ Toronto, LLM, 87. **CAREER** Assoc prof, 87-. **MEMBERSHIPS** Law Soc Saskatchewan. **RESEARCH** Economic analysis of law; feminist and critical legal theory; women and the welfare state; poverty law. **SELECTED PUBLICATIONS** Auth, Compensation for Wife Abuse: Empowering Victims?, Law Rev, 94; Economic Analysis of Law and 'Private Ordering': A Feminist Critique, 92; The Use of Age, Sex, and Marital Status as Rating Variables in Automobile Insurance, 89. **CONTACT ADDRESS** Col of Law, Univ of Saskatchewan, 15 Campus Dr, Saskatoon, SK, Canada S7N 5A6. **EMAIL** Wiegers@law.usask.ca

WIERENGA, EDWARD RAY
PERSONAL Born 10/14/1947, Chicago, IL, m, 1971, 2 children **DISCIPLINE** PHILOSOPHY & RELIGIOUS STUDIES **EDUCATION** Calvin Col, AB, 69; Univ Mass, Amherst, MA & PhD, 74. **CAREER** Asst prof philos, IL State Univ, 74-75 & Calvin Col, 75-77; Asst Prof Philos Relig, Univ Rochester, 77-94, prof relig, univ rochester, 94. **HONORS AND AWARDS** Dedalus Fel, 00; Clark Art Institute Res, Fel, 00-01. **MEMBERSHIPS** Am Philos Asn. **RESEARCH** Philos of relig; metaphysics; epistemology. **SELECTED PUBLICATIONS** Auth, The Nature of God, cornell, 89. **CONTACT ADDRESS** Prog of Relig Studies, Univ of Rochester, 500 Joseph C Wilson, Rochester, NY 14627-9000. **EMAIL** edwd@troi.cc.rochester.edu

WIGAL, DONALD
PERSONAL Born 01/16/1933, Indianapolis, IN, s **DISCIPLINE** RELIGION **EDUCATION** Univ Dayton, BS, 55; Univ Notre Dame, MA, 65; Columbia Pac Univ, PhD, 85. **CAREER** Educr, Marianists, 51-69; Researcher, Grey Advert, 70-75; Ed, Dell Publ, 75-80; Ed, Lakewood Books, 80-85; Writer, Wigal Works, 85-. **HONORS AND AWARDS** Distinguished Alumni Awd, Univ Dayton, 85. **MEMBERSHIPS** ASCAP **RESEARCH** Paranormal phenomena, mystical theology, scriptural allusions in English literature, ecumenical comparisons of scriptures. **SELECTED PUBLICATIONS** Auth, Questions About the Bible, Coleco, 85; auth, General Knowledge, Coleco, 85; auth, Guide to Personality, Cosmopolitan, 98; auth, Guide to the Unexplained, Renaissance Books, 99; auth, Visions of Nostradamus and Other Prophets, Random House, 99. **CONTACT ADDRESS** Dept Alternative Res, Inst for Independent Studies, PO Box 432, New York, NY 10156. **EMAIL** donwigal@ix.nctcom.com

WIGAL, GRACE J.
DISCIPLINE LEGAL RESEARCH AND WRITING **EDUCATION** Marshall Univ, BA, 72, MA, 76; W Va Univ Col Law, JD, 89. **CAREER** Instr, Col Law, 90; dir, Legal Res and Wrtg Prog, 92; dir, Acad Support Prog, 93; dir, Appellate Advocacy Prog; act dir, -. **HONORS AND AWARDS** W Va Law Rev Lit award, 89. **MEMBERSHIPS** Order of the Coif. **SELECTED PUBLICATIONS** Ed, W V Law Rev; Auth, bk(s), articles, on legal issues that arise in the medical and construction settings. **CONTACT ADDRESS** Law Sch, West Virginia Univ, Morgantown, PO Box 6009, Morgantown, WV 26506-6009.

WIGALL, STEVE R.
PERSONAL Born 04/15/1951, Lindsay, CA, m, 1973, 1 child **DISCIPLINE** SPIRITUAL DIRECTIONAL THEOLOGY

EDUCATION Boston Univ School Theol, ThD, 98. **MEMBERSHIPS** Presby N N England **RESEARCH** Spiritual direction - Protestant and Reformed. **SELECTED PUBLICATIONS** Auth What is a Spiritual Directors Authority, Rev for Relig, 97; Historys Role in Defining Spiritual Direction, Rev for Relig, 98; A Sacramental Paradigm Employing the Lords Supper in Calvin as a Theological Rationale for Spiritual Direction, Boston School Theol, 98. **CONTACT ADDRESS** 296 Lowell St, Lawrence, MA 01841. **EMAIL** uncwig@aol.com

WIGGINS, JAMES BRYAN
PERSONAL Born 08/24/1935, Mexia, TX, m, 1956, 2 children **DISCIPLINE** RELIGION; HISTORY **EDUCATION** Tex Wesleyan Col, BA, 57; Southern Methodist Univ, BD, 59; Drew Univ, PhD(hist theol), 63. **CAREER** Instr English, Union Jr Col, 60-63; from asst prof to assoc prof relig, 63-75, Prof Relig, Syracuse Univ, 75-, Eliaphalet Remington Prof of Rel, 98, Chmn, 81-, Soc Relig Higher Educ fel; Found Arts, Relig & Cult fel; AAUP. **MEMBERSHIPS** Am Acad Relig; Am Soc Church Hist. **RESEARCH** Interaction of theology with other strands of intellectual history, particularly since Reformation; Narrative language in religious discourse; religion and Culture studies. **SELECTED PUBLICATIONS** Auth, The Methodist episcopacy: 1784-1900, Drew Gateway, 63; John Fletcher: The embattled saint, Wesleyan Col, 65; coauth, The foundations of Christianity, Ronald, 69; auth, Theological reflections on reflecting on the future, Crosscurrents, winter 71; Story, In: Echoes of the Wordless Word, Am Acad Relig, fall 73; ed, Religion as Story, Harper & Row, 75; auth, Re-visioning psycho-history, Theology Today, 76; contribr, Death and Eschatology, In: Introduction to Study of Religion, Harper & Row, 78; Christianity: A Cultural Perspective, Prentice Hall, 84; In Praise of Religion Diversity, Routledge, 96. **CONTACT ADDRESS** Dept of Religion, Syracuse Univ, 501 HL, Syracuse, NY 13244. **EMAIL** jbwiggru@syr.edu

WIGGINS, OSBORNE P., JR.
DISCIPLINE PHILOSOPHY **EDUCATION** New Sch for Soc Res, PhD. **CAREER** Dept Philos, Univ Louisville **HONORS AND AWARDS** Egner prize, Univ Zurich. **RESEARCH** Philos of psychiatry. **SELECTED PUBLICATIONS** Auth, articles on Husserl and other phenomenological figures; ed, Philos Perspectives on Psychiatric Diagnostic Classification, The Johns Hopkins UP, 94. **CONTACT ADDRESS** Dept of Philos, Univ of Louisville, 2301 S 3rd St, Louisville, KY 40292. **EMAIL** opwigg01@ulkyvm.louisville.edu

WIGGINS, WILLIAM H., JR.
PERSONAL Born 05/30/1934, Port Allen, LA, m **DISCIPLINE** THEOLOGY **EDUCATION** OH Wesleyan U, BA 1956; Phillips' Sch of Theol, BD 1961; Louisville Prebyn Theol Sem, MTh 1965; IN U, PhD 1974. **CAREER** IN Univ, asso prof 1980-, asst prof 1974-79, grad teaching asst & lecturer 1969-73; TX Coll, dir rel life 1965-69; Freeman Chapel CME Church, pastor 1962-65; Lane Coll, prof 1961-62. **HONORS AND AWARDS** Num grants & flwhps; num publ; doc film "In the Rapture" anthologized wks appear in num publ & jour. **MEMBERSHIPS** Fellow of the Folklore Inst IN U; founder dir Afro-Am Folk Archive IN U; so reg dir IN Chap Assn for the Study of Afro-Am Life & History; mem Smithsonian Inst African Diaspora Adv Gr Com; exec bd Hoosier Folklore Soc; ed bd The Jour of the Folklore Inst; prestr Am Folklife Fest 1975-76; field wk Smithsonian Inst 1975-76; pres Assn of African -Am Folklorists Minister Christian Meth Epis Ch; mem Am Folklore Soc; Nat Cncl for Blk Studies; Assn for the Study of Afro-Am Life & History; Assn of African & African-Am Folklorists; Hoosier Folklore Soc; Pop Cult Assn;Num Grants **CONTACT ADDRESS** Dept of Folklore, Indiana Univ, Bloomington, Bloomington, IN 47401.

WIKE, VICTORIA S.
DISCIPLINE PHILOSOPHY **EDUCATION** MacMurray Col, BA ; Univ de Paris Sorbonne, LL; Pa State Univ, MA, PhD. **CAREER** Prof, Loyola Univ Chicago, 79-; 1 yr lectr, Univ Rome Campus. **RESEARCH** Kant's moral philosophy, health care ethics, professional ethics. **SELECTED PUBLICATIONS** Auth, Kant on Happiness in Ethics, 94; Kant's Antinomies of Reason, 82; articles in, J Value Inquiry, Idealistic Stud, The Southern J Philos; coauth, Morality and The Professional Life, 00. **CONTACT ADDRESS** Dept of Philosophy, Loyola Univ, Chicago, 6525 N Sheridan Rd., Chicago, IL 60626. **EMAIL** vwike@luc.edu

WILCOX, JOEL
PERSONAL Born 03/22/1951, Grand rapids, MI, m, 1984 **DISCIPLINE** PHILOSOPHY **EDUCATION** Univ Minnesota, PhD 90; John Hopkins Univ, MA 84. **CAREER** Providence College, dir, assoc prof, asst prof, 93 to 97-; Xavier Univ LA, asst prof 90-93. **MEMBERSHIPS** APA; IAGP; RIPS; SAGP; SIPR **RESEARCH** Greek Philos and Asian Philos. **SELECTED PUBLICATIONS** Auth, Whole-Natured Forms in Empedocles' Cosmic Cycle, Stud in Ancient Greek Philos, SUNY Press, 98; Empedocles, Dictionary of Literary Biography: Greek Authors, Gale Research Co, 95; The Origins of Epistemology in Early Greek Thought, Edwin Mellen Press, 94, anthologized in: The Philosophical Yearbook, Inst for Philos, 95; Invted rev of K. H. Volkman-Schluck, Die Philosophie der Vorsokratiker: Der Anfang der abendlandischen Metaphysik, Ancient Philos, 94; On the Distinction Between Thought and Perception in Heraclitus, Apeiron, 93. **CONTACT ADDRESS** Dept of Philosophy, Providence Col, Providence, RI 02918. **EMAIL** wilcoxjs@providence.edu

WILCOX, JOHN R.
PERSONAL Born New York City, NY, m, 1974, 3 children **DISCIPLINE** RELIGION **EDUCATION** Marist Col, BA, 61; Fordham Univ, MA, 66; Union Theological Seminary, PhD, 77. **CAREER** High Sch Teacher, Marist high Schs, 62-67; instr, Marist Col, 67-68; adjunct instr, Fordham Univ, 70-74; prof, Manhattan Col, 74-. **HONORS AND AWARDS** Fulbright Fellow, MAGNA cum LAUDE. **MEMBERSHIPS** Collegium; Am Asn of Univ Admin; Asn for Practical and Prof Ethics; Col Theology Society; Hastings Ctr; Society for Bus Ethics; Society of Christian Ethics; Society for the Values in Higher Educ. **SELECTED PUBLICATIONS** Coauth, Promoting an Ethical Campus Culture: The Values Audit, NASPA Jour, Vol 29 No 4, 92; coauth, The Leadership Compass: Values and Ethics in Higher Education, Higher Educ Repot, No 1, 92; ed, The Internationalization of American Business: Ethical Issues and Cases, McGraw-Hill, 92; auth, A Report on the Mandate: Ethics Training in the Futures Industry, Ethikos: Examining Ethical Issues in Bus, Vol 9 No 1, 95; co-ed, Enhancing Religious Identity: Best Practices From Catholic Colleges, Georgetown Univ Press, 00. **CONTACT ADDRESS** Religious Studies Dept, Manhattan Col, Bronx, NY 10471. **EMAIL** jwilcox@manhattan.edu

WILDBERG, CHRISTIAN
PERSONAL Born 02/12/1957, Flensburg, Germany, m, 1997, 1 child **DISCIPLINE** CLASSICS, ANCIENT PHILOSOPHY **EDUCATION** Cambridge Univ, PhD, 84; Marburg Univ, MTh, 85. **CAREER** Res Fellow, 84-87, Caius Coll Cambridge; Vis Lectr, 87-88, Univ of TX at Austin; Asst Prof, 88-94, Freie Univ Berlin; Res Fellow, 95-96, Center for Hellenic Studies, Washington; Assoc Prof of Classics 96-, Princeton Univ. **HONORS AND AWARDS** Res Grant-DFG; Res grant, Howard Found. **MEMBERSHIPS** Amer Philos Assoc; Amer Philo Assoc; **RESEARCH** Aristotle, Neoplatonism, Tragedy. **SELECTED PUBLICATIONS** Auth, Philoponus against Aristotle on the Eternity of the World, London, Duckworth, 87; John Philoponus Criticism of Aristotle's Theory of Aether, Peripatio vol 6, pp 274, Berlin, NY, 88; Simplicius against Philpopnus on the Eternity of the World, London, Duckworth, pp 95-135, 91; Hyperesie und Epiphanie, Zur Bedeutung und Funkiton der Gotter in den Dramen des Euripdes, in prog; Aristoteles, DeCaelo, Translation, into German and Commentary, in prog. **CONTACT ADDRESS** Dept of Classics, Princeton Univ, 108 East Pyne, Princeton, NJ 08544. **EMAIL** wildberg@princeton.edu

WILEY, GEORGE
PERSONAL Born 11/26/1946, Jackson, TN, m, 1993, 3 children **DISCIPLINE** RELIGION **EDUCATION** Univ NC Chapel Hill, BA, 68; Emory Univ, MDiv, 71; PhD, 78. **CAREER** Prof, Baker Univ, 77-. **HONORS AND AWARDS** Morehead Scholar; Phi Beta Kappa; Osborne Chair of Rel. **MEMBERSHIPS** Am Acad of Rel. **RESEARCH** Early Christianity; Christian Ethics. **CONTACT ADDRESS** Baker Univ, Box 65, Baldwin City, KS 66006-0065. **EMAIL** wiley@harvey.bakeru.edu

WILHELM, ROBERT
PERSONAL Born 06/22/1936, St Louis, MO, m, 1986, 1 child **DISCIPLINE** POLITICAL SCIENCE **EDUCATION** St Louis Univ, PhD, 86. **CAREER** Prof, Imperial Valley Col, 62-. **HONORS AND AWARDS** Nat Hon Soc for Polit Sci; Pi Sigma Alpha; Outstanding Educr of Am, 73. **MEMBERSHIPS** Assoc for Borderlands Studies. **RESEARCH** International crime, terrorism and national security issues, intergovernmental relations. **SELECTED PUBLICATIONS** Auth, The Transnational Relations of U S Law Enforcement Agencies in the Imperial County-Baja, California Border Region, U S Dept of Justice, 87. **CONTACT ADDRESS** Dept Polit Sci, Imperial Valley Col, PO Box 1831, El Centro, CA 92244-1831. **EMAIL** wilhelm@imperial.cc.ca.us

WILHITE, DENNIS
PERSONAL Born 10/27/1951, MI, m, 1972, 4 children **DISCIPLINE** RELIGION **EDUCATION** Bapt Bible Col, BRE, 73; Grand Rapids Bapt Sem, MRE, 89. **CAREER** Youth Pastor, New York, 73-81; Youth Pastor, Grand Rapids MI, 81-91; Prof, Bapt Bible Col Sem, 91-. **HONORS AND AWARDS** Who's Who Am Educ, 99-00. **RESEARCH** Experiential learning; Cross-cultural education. **CONTACT ADDRESS** Dept Relig, Baptist Bible Col of Pennsylvania, PO Box 800, Clarks Summit, PA 18411-0800. **EMAIL** dwiilhite@bbc.edu

WILIAMS, RON G.
DISCIPLINE PHILOSOPHY **EDUCATION** Stanford Univ, PhD, 75. **CAREER** Prof. **RESEARCH** Logic philosophy of language; philosophy of science; aesthetics. **SELECTED PUBLICATIONS** Co-auth, Philosophical Analysis, 65; Ritual Art and Knowledge, 93. **CONTACT ADDRESS** Philosophy Dept, Colorado State Univ, Fort Collins, CO 80523.

WILKINS, DAVID BRIAN
DISCIPLINE LAW **EDUCATION** Harvard University; Harvard Law School, JD. **CAREER** Clerk, US Supreme Court Justice Thurgood Marshall; Kirkland & Ellis prof of law, Harvard Law School; dir, Program on the Legal Profession. **SELECTED PUBLICATIONS** Sixth African-American tenured professor at Harvard University. **CONTACT ADDRESS** Law Sch, Harvard Univ, Hauser Hall 312, Cambridge, MA 02138. **EMAIL** dwilkins@law.harvard.edu

WILKINS, MIRA
PERSONAL Born 06/01/1931, New York, NY **DISCIPLINE** BUSINESS HISTORY **EDUCATION** Radcliffe Col/Harvard Univ, AB, 53; Cambridge Univ England, PhD, 57. **CAREER** Res assoc, Weyerhaeuser Enterprises Hist, Columbia Univ, 57-58, res assoc, Ford Motor Co Hist, 58-60, co-dir, Ford Overseas Hist Proj, 60-62, proj dir Hist Am Bus Abroad, Grad Sch Bus, 62-66, adj asst prof, 64-66; assoc prof Hist & Indust Admin, Union Col, 66-68; vis lectr Hist, Smith Col, 68-70; prof Econ, Fla Int Univ, 74-, supvr, Corpus Christi Col, Cambridge Univ, 56-57; instr, Wayne State Univ, 58-59; lectr Econ Hist, Univ Mass, Amherst, 72; dir, Foreign Investment Fla Proj, 75-80; Guggenheim fel, 81-82. **HONORS AND AWARDS** Fla Int Univ Prof Exc Awd, 94; 93 Cass Prize for best article in Business History, 92. **MEMBERSHIPS** Am Econ Asn; AHA; Acad Int Bus; Bus Hist Conf; Econ Hist Assn. **RESEARCH** International business history; economic history; history of foreign investment in the United States. **SELECTED PUBLICATIONS** Auth, American Business Abroad: Ford on Six Continents, Wayne State Univ, 64; The Emergence of Multinational Enterprise: American Business Abroad from the Colonial Era to 1914, Harvard Univ, 70; The role of private business in the international diffusion of technology, J Econ Hist, 3/74; Multinational oil companies in South America in the 1920s: In Argentina, Bolivia, Brazil, Chile, Colombia, Ecuador, Peru, Bus Hist Rev, Fall 74; The Maturing of Multinational Enterprise: American Business Abroad from 1914 to 1970, Harvard Univ, 74; The oil companies in perspective, In: Daedalus, Fall 75; Modern European economic history and the multinationals, J Europ Econ Hist, Winter 77; Multinational automobile enterprises and regulation: An historical overview, In: Government, Technology, and the Future of the Automobile, McGraw-Hill, 80; The History of Foreign Investment in the United States to 1914, Cambridge, Mass: Harvard Univ Press, 1989. **CONTACT ADDRESS** Dept of Economics, Florida Intl Univ, Miami, FL 33199-0001. **EMAIL** Wilkinsm@fiu.edu

WILKINSON, D.
PERSONAL Born Capron, IL **DISCIPLINE** CRIMINAL JUSTICE **EDUCATION** Cornell Univ, BA, 90; Univ Illinois, MA, 92; State Univ New Jersey, PhD, 98. **CAREER** Leg int, Pub Def Off, 89; res asst, Cornell Col, 89-90; res asst, Univ IL, 90-91; proj coord, 91-93; cen mgr, 9293; res assoc, Harvard Univ, 92-93; adj instr, Rutgers Univ, 94-95; proj mgr, 95; co invest, Univ IL, 95-98; staff assoc, proj dir, Columbia Univ, 95-98; asst prof, Temple, 98-. **HONORS AND AWARDS** Deans Diss Awd, 98; Res Excell Awd, 97; Univ Fel, SUNJ; Teach Res Asstshp; Grad Res asstshp; Chic Bar, 91; Dean's List, 88-90. **MEMBERSHIPS** ACJS; ASC; TAUP; HWG; AWSD. **SELECTED PUBLICATIONS** Coauth, "The Effect of Organizational Structure and Climate on Police Reform: A Comparison of Two Cities," in The Challenge of Community Policing: Testing the Promises," ed. DP Rosenbaum (Newbury Park, CA: Sage Pub, 94):110- 126; coauth, "Cops in the Classroom: A Randomized Impact Evaluation of D.A.R.E." J Res Crime Delinq 31(94): 1-40; coauth, "Community Responses to Drug Abuse: A Program Evaluation." Nat Inst Justice Res Report, U.S. Department of Justice, Nat Inst Just, Wash, DC, 94); coauth, "The Role of Firearms in Violence 'Scripts': The Dynamics of Gun Events Among Adolescent Males," Law and Contemp Prob 59 (96): 55-90; coauth, "Firearms and Youth Violence." in Handbook of Adolescent Violence, eds. D Stoff, J Belinger, J Maser (NY: Wiley): 551-567; coauth, "The Social Contexts and Functions of Adolescent Violence," in Violence in American Schools, eds. Delbert S Elliott, Beatrix A Hamburg, Kirk Williams (Cambridge Univ Press, 98); coauth, "Situational Contexts of Adolescent Violence in New York City." Revue Europeenne des Migrations Intl 14 (98): 63-76; coauth, "Guns, Youth Violence and Social Identity in Inner Cities," in Crime and Justice, eds. M Tonry, M Moore (Chicago: Univ Chic Press, 98); coauth, "A Theory of Violent Events," in Advances in Criminology Theory: The Criminal Event, eds. Robert Meier, Leslie Kennedy (New Brunswick, NJ: Transaction, 00). **CONTACT ADDRESS** Dept Criminal Justice, Temple Univ, 1115 West Berks St, Gladfelter Hall 5th Fl, Rm 528, Philadelphia, PA 19122. **EMAIL** dwilki02@astro.ocis.temple.edu

WILKS, DUFFY J.
PERSONAL Born 02/15/1936, Spur, TX, m, 4 children **DISCIPLINE** PHILOSOPHY **EDUCATION** Tex Tech Univ, BA, 81; M Ed, 84; EdD, 94. **CAREER** Asst prof, W. Texas Col. **HONORS AND AWARDS** Distinguished Service, Tex Counseling Asn. **MEMBERSHIPS** Tex Counseling Assoc; Am Counseling Assoc; Tex Comm Col Teachers Assoc; Int Assoc of Addictions and Offender Counseling; **RESEARCH** Philosophy, Theory-Etiology. **SELECTED PUBLICATIONS** Auth, Closing of the American Mind, 89; auth, An Unquiet Mind, Jamison, 97; auth, Free Will: Readings in Philosophy, Pere-

boom, 98. **CONTACT ADDRESS** Dept Social Science, W Tex Col, 5400 Col Ave, #119, Snyder, TX 79549. **EMAIL** duffywilks@hotmail.com

WILL, JAMES EDWARD
PERSONAL Born 01/18/1928, Palatine, IL, m, 1954, 7 children **DISCIPLINE** SYSTEMATIC THEOLOGY **EDUCATION** NCent Col, BA, 49; Evangel Theol Sem, BD, 52; Columbia Univ & Union Theol Sem, PhD, 62. **CAREER** Asst prof relig, NCent Col, 55-59; from assoc prof to prof philos theol, Evangel Theol Sent, 59-73; prof Syst Theol, Garrett-Evangelical Theol Sem, 73-98 (retired), Fac adv, Nat Intersem Coun Intersem Movement, 66-67 & 68-69; mem comn faith & order, Nat Coun Churches, 70-78; deleg, Democratic Nat Convention, 72; dir, Peace and Justice Center, Garrett Evangel Theol Sem, 75-85; mem, Interunit Comt on Int Concerns, Nat Coun Churches, 79-85; mem, Working Comt Churches' Human Rights Prog, 79-86; mem, Continuation Comt Warsaw Europ Christian Forum, 79-82; chemn, Corsortium for Int Theol Educ, 79-81; Ecumenical Inst, Tantur, 86, Univ Zimbabwe, 89-90. **HONORS AND AWARDS** Am Asn Theol Schs fac studies fel, Free Univ Berlin, 67-68; Am Asn Theol Schs fac studies fel, Univ Vienna, 74-75. **MEMBERSHIPS** Am Theol Soc; Am Soc Christian Ethics; Am Acad of Relig. **RESEARCH** Marxist-Christian dialogue; philosophical theol; peace and justice; Inter-relig dialogue. **SELECTED PUBLICATIONS** Auth, "Understanding the impact of world-wide inequities," Christian Century, 5: 75; auth, "Local congregations: Reluctant peacemakers," Explor, fall 77; auth, "The place of ideology in theology," J Ecumenical Studies, winter 77; auth, Must Walls Divide?, Friendship Press, 81; auth, Philosophy and Social Thought, Congregatio Sanctissimi Redemptoris, 81; auth, "Christian-Marxist ethical dialogue from a process perspective," Encounter, autumn 81; auth, "Promise and Peril in Poland, The Christian Century, 1: 81; auth, "European peace and American churches," The Christian Century, 3: 82; auth, The Moral Reflection of Nuclear Deterrance, Friendship Pr, 85; auth, Christology of Peace, Westminster/John Knox, 89; auth, The Universal God, Westminster/John Knox, 94. **CONTACT ADDRESS** 1010 Lake Ave, Wilmette, IL 60091. **EMAIL** james.will@nwu.edu

WILL, W. MARVIN
PERSONAL Born 03/25/1937, Peace Valley, MO, m, 1962 **DISCIPLINE** POLITICAL SCIENCE **EDUCATION** McPherson Col, BA, 60; Univ Missouri, Columbia, MA, 64, PhD, 72. **CAREER** Instr, Univ Missouri, Columbia, 62-64, 67-69; instr, Florissant Valley Commun Col, 64-69; asst prof, 69-79, assoc prof, 79- , Univ Tulsa; dir, Civic Educ Ctr, St Louis, 76-78; adj prof, Washington Univ, 76-78; vis prof, Univ of the West Indies, 91-92; vis prof Col of Micronesia, 99-2000. **HONORS AND AWARDS** Fel, US Dept of State, 81; Fulbright res scholar, 91-92; Oklahoma Polit Sci Scholar of the Year, 92; Citation of Merit, Bd of Trustees, McPherson Col, 95; Rotary Int Fel, 98; NEH grant; Ford Found grant; Mellon grant. **MEMBERSHIPS** Int Studies Asn; Caribbean Stud Asn; Midwest LA Stud Asn; Latin Am Stud Asn; Am Polit Stud Asn; Am Prof for Peace in the Middle East; Okla Polit Sci Asn; UNAU. **RESEARCH** Authoritarianism and democracy in the Caribbean Basin; non-governmental and international organizations as promoters of democracy and human rights. **SELECTED PUBLICATIONS** Co-ed, The Restless Caribbean, Praeger, 79; coauth, The Caribbean in the Pacific Century, Lynne Rienner, 93; auth, Seizing the Moment: Caribbean Integration and the Role of Economic Crisis, in Sullivan, ed, The Caribbean Basin, Congressional Research Service, GPO, 93; auth, Beyond the Cold War: Security and Policy Projections from the Pacific and Caribbean Basins, in Crotty, ed, Post-Cold War Policy, Nelson-Hall, 95; auth, NGOs and IGOs as Promoters of Liberal Democracy: Cases from Nicaragua and Guyana, in Griffith, ed, Democracy and Human Rights in the Caribbean, Westview, 97; auth, From Rebellion to Institutional Development and Democracy in the Caribbean, in Kelly, ed, Assessing Democracy in Latin America, Westview, 98. **CONTACT ADDRESS** 1136 S Pittsburg Ave, Tulsa, OK 74112-5104. **EMAIL** wmwill@utulsa.edu

WILLACY, HAZEL M.
PERSONAL Born 04/20/1946, MS, m, 2 children **DISCIPLINE** LAW **EDUCATION** Smith Clg, BA 1967; Case Western Reserve U, JD 1976. **CAREER** Bureau of Labor Stats, lbr ecnmst 1967-72; Baker Hostetter, atty 1976-80; Sherwin Williams, labor rel atty 1980-82, asst dir labor relations, 83-87, dir Labor Relations, 87-93; dir, Empl Policies/Labor Relations, 93-. **HONORS AND AWARDS** Order of Coif 1976. **MEMBERSHIPS** Mem ABA OH St Bar Asso 1976-; mem, Exec Bd Greater Cleveland Coun, Boy Scouts of America; mem, bd of trustees, Meridia Physician Network, 1995-. **SELECTED PUBLICATIONS** articles publ 1970, 76, 80. **CONTACT ADDRESS** Sherwin Williams Co, 101 Prospect Ave, Cleveland, OH 44115. **EMAIL** cyberion12@aol.com

WILLEMS, ELIZABETH
PERSONAL Born 05/22/1937, Cologne, MN **DISCIPLINE** MORAL THEOLOGY; PSYCHOLOGY **EDUCATION** Univ Chicago, MA, 81; Marquette Univ, PhD, 86. **CAREER** Prof, Moral Theology & Dir MA Prog, 94-, Notre Dame Sem, 85-. **HONORS AND AWARDS** Ats fel; Nat Cath Press Asn Awd **MEMBERSHIPS** CTSA; CTS; SCE **RESEARCH** Moral theology: Social ethics, principles, sexual ethics. **SELECTED PUBLICATIONS** Auth, Understanding Catholic Morality, Crossroad, 97. **CONTACT ADDRESS** 2901 S Carrollton, New Orleans, LA 70118. **EMAIL** EWILL74623@aol.com

WILLETT, CYNTHIA
DISCIPLINE CONTEMPORARY CONTINENTAL PHILOSOPHY **EDUCATION** PA State Univ, PhD, 88. **CAREER** Philos, Emory Univ. **HONORS AND AWARDS** Winship Distinguished Res School. **RESEARCH** Social theory; philosophy of literature. **SELECTED PUBLICATIONS** Auth, Maternal Ethics and Other Slave Moralities; auth, The Soul of Justice, Theorizing Multiculturalism. **CONTACT ADDRESS** Emory Univ, Atlanta, GA 30322-1950. **EMAIL** cwillet@emory.edu

WILLIAMS, CHRISTOPHER
PERSONAL Born 09/23/1960, Oak Hill, OH **DISCIPLINE** PHILOSOPHY **EDUCATION** Furman Univ, BA, 82; Univ Pitts, MA, 88, PhD, 93. **CAREER** Vis asst prof, 90-91, asst prof, 91-98, assoc prof, 98- Univ Nevada, Reno. **HONORS AND AWARDS** Fel, Soc for Hum, Cornell Univ, 98-99. **MEMBERSHIPS** APA; Amer Soc for Aesthetics; British Soc for Aesthetics; Hume Soc. **RESEARCH** Aesthetics; ethics; philosophy of mind. **SELECTED PUBLICATIONS** Art, Is Tragedy Paradoxical?, British J of Aesthetics 38, 98; art, Modern Art Theories, J of Aesthetics & Art Criticism 56, 98; auth, A Cultivated Reason: An Essay on Hume and Humeanism, Pa State, 99. **CONTACT ADDRESS** Dept of Philosophy, Univ of Nevada, Reno, Mail Stop 102, Reno, NV 89557. **EMAIL** ctw@unr.edu

WILLIAMS, CLIFFORD E.
PERSONAL Born 12/07/1943, Chicago, IL, m, 1965, 1 child **DISCIPLINE** PHILOSOPHY **EDUCATION** Wheaton Col, BA, 64; Ind Univ, PhD, 72. **CAREER** From instr to assoc prof, St John Fisher Col, 68-82; vis assoc prof, Houghton Col, 80; vis prof, Wheaton Col, 89-99; from assoc prof to prof, Trinity Col, 82-. **HONORS AND AWARDS** Awd for Teaching Excellence and Campus Leadership, Sears Robuck Found, 89. **MEMBERSHIPS** Philos of Time Soc, Soc of Christian Philos. **RESEARCH** Philosophy of time, Kierkegaard. **SELECTED PUBLICATIONS** Auth, Free Will and Determinism: A Dialogue, Hackett Publ Co (Indianapolis, IN), 80; auth, "Indeterminism and the Theory of Agency," Philo and Phenomen Res XLV (84): 111-119; auth, "The Date-Analysis of Tensed Sentences," The Australasian J of Philos 70 (92): 198-203; auth, "The Phenomenology of B-Time," S J of Philos XXX (92): 123-137; auth, "Kierekegaardian Suspicion and Properly Basic Beliefs," Rel Studies 30 (94): 261-267; auth, "Christian Materialism and the Parity Thesis," Int J for Philos of Rel 39 (96): 1-14; auth, "The Metaphysics of A- and B-Time," Philos Quart 46 (96): 371-381; auth, Singleness of Heart: Restoring the Divided Soul, Eerdmans Publ Co (Grand Rapids, MI), 94 & Regent Col Publ (Vancouver, Can), 00; auth, On Love and Friendship: Philosophical Readings, Jones and Bartlett Publ (Boston), 95 & Wadsworth Publ Co (Belmont, CA), 97. **CONTACT ADDRESS** Dept Philos, Trinity Christian Col, 2065 Half Day Rd, Deerfield, IL 60015-1241. **EMAIL** cwilliams@trin.edu

WILLIAMS, CYNTHIA A.
DISCIPLINE LAW **EDUCATION** Univ Calif Berkeley, BA; Univ NYork, JD. **CAREER** Law clerk, Judge Milton L. Schwartz, US District Court; asst prof, Univ Ill Urbana Champaign. **HONORS AND AWARDS** Am Jurisprudence Awd; ed, ny univ law rev. **RESEARCH** Torts; business organizations; securities regulation; and a seminar on corporate social responsibility. **SELECTED PUBLICATIONS** Auth, pubs on voter registration. **CONTACT ADDRESS** Law Dept, Univ of Illinois, Urbana-Champaign, 52 E Gregory Dr, Champaign, IL 61820. **EMAIL** cwilliam@law.uiuc.edu

WILLIAMS, DANIEL
PERSONAL Born 05/11/1955, St Louis, MO, m **DISCIPLINE** THEOLOGY, HISTORICAL THEOLOGY, PATRISTICS **EDUCATION** Northeastern Col, BA, 78; Trinity Evangelical Divinity Sch, MDiv, 81; Princeton Theol Sem, ThM, 85; Univ Toronto, MA, 86. **CAREER** Asst prof, Loyola Univ, Chicago, 94-2000, assoc prof, 2000-. **HONORS AND AWARDS** NEH Fel for Univ Teachers, 200-01. **MEMBERSHIPS** Am Soc of Church Hist, Ecclesiastical Hist Soc, Groupe Suisse d'Etudes Partristiques, Int Asn for Patristic Studies, Midwest Patristics Sem, North Am Patristic Soc. **RESEARCH** Latin early fathers; orthodoxy and heresy; doctrinal development of Trinity. **SELECTED PUBLICATIONS** Co-ed and contribur, Arianism After Arius: Essays on the Development of the Fourth Century Trinitarian Conflicts, Edinburgh: T & T Clark (93); auth, Ambrose of Milan and the End of the Nicene-Arian Conflicts, Oxford Univ Press (95); auth, "Another Exception to Later Fourth Century 'Arian' Typologies: The Case of Germinius of Sirmium," The J of Early Christian Studies, 4 (96): 335-357; auth, "Historical Portrait or Polemical Portrayal?: The Alignment between Pagans and Arians in the Later Fourth Century," Studia Patristica XXIX (97): 178-194; auth, "Politically Correct in Milan: A Response to P. Kaufman's 'Diehard Homoians and the Election of Ambrose'," J of Early Christian Studies, 5 (97): 441-46; auth, "Constantine, Nicaea and the 'Fall' of the Church," in Christian Origins: Theology, Rhetoric and Community, eds, L. Ayres and G. Jones, London: Routledge Press (98): 117-136; auth, "The Search for Sola Scriptura in the Early Church," Interpretation, 52 (98): 338-350. **CONTACT ADDRESS** Dept Theol, Loyola Univ, Chicago, 6525 N Sheridan Rd, Chicago, IL 60626-5344. **EMAIL** dwilli1@orion.it.luc.edu

WILLIAMS, DENNIS E.
PERSONAL Born 07/22/1934, Toledo, OH, m, 1956, 2 children **DISCIPLINE** CHRISTIAN EDUCATION **EDUCATION** Bob Jones Univ, BS, MA; N Ariz Univ, MA; Southwestern Baptist Theol Sem, MRE, PhD. **CAREER** Exec dir, Christian Ministries Convention, 84-94; prof, ch dept Edu Ministries and Admin, Denver Sem, 71-94; instr, King of Kings Col, Tel Aviv; Providence Theol Sem, Can; Caribbean Grad Sch Theol; Asian Grad Sch Theol; Asian Theol Sem, Philippines; dean, Sch Christian Edu and Leadership, prof, S Baptist Theol Sem, 94-. **HONORS AND AWARDS** Distinguished Educator award, Southwestern Baptist Rel Edu Assn. **SELECTED PUBLICATIONS** Auth, Volunteers For Today's Church: How To Recruit and Retain Workers; contrib, Leadership Handbook of Practical Theol; Christian Edu:Foundations For The Future; pub(s), Christian Edu Today; Christian Edu Jour; Key To Christian Edu; Leader Idea Bank; Small Gp Letter; Super Sunday Sch Sourcebook. **CONTACT ADDRESS** Sch Christian Edu and Leadership, So Baptist Theol Sem, 2825 Lexington Rd, Louisville, KY 40280. **EMAIL** celead@sbts.edu

WILLIAMS, DONALD T.
PERSONAL Born 01/10/1951, Norfolk, VA, m, 1972, 2 children **DISCIPLINE** THEOLOGY **EDUCATION** Taylor Univ, BA, 73; Trinity Evangel Div School, MDiv, 76; Univ Georgia, PhD, 85. **CAREER** Pastor, First Evangel Free Church, Marietta, GA, 82-87; vis lectr and tutor, Centre for Medieval and Renaissance Stud of Keble Col, Oxford Univ, 94, 97; pastor, Trinity Fel, Toccoa, GA, 92- ; assoc prof English, Toccoa Falls Col, 87- . **HONORS AND AWARDS** Faculty Scholar of the Year, Toccoa Falls Col, 97. **MEMBERSHIPS** Ministerial Asn, Evangel Free Church of Am; Evangel Theol Soc; Evangel Philos Soc; Southeastern Renaissance Conf; Mythopoeic Soc. **RESEARCH** Theology; Medieval and Renaissance literature; philosophy; theology and literature. **SELECTED PUBLICATIONS** Auth, The Person and the Work of the Holy Spirit, Broadman & Holman, 94; auth, The Candle Rekindled: Hugh Latimer on the Temporal Order, in Bauman, ed, Evangelical Renderings: To God and Caesar, Christian Publ, 94; auth, Christian Poetics, Past and Present, in, Barratt, ed, The Discerning Reader: Christian Perspectives on Literature and Theory, Baker, 95; auth, John Foxe, in, Bauman, ed, Historians of the Christian Tradition: Their Methodology and Influence on Western Thought, Broadman & Holman, 95; auth, Apologetic Responses to Post-Modernism: Panel Discussion, Philosophia Christi, 96; auth, Apologetic Responses to Post-Modernism: A Symposium, in, Bauman, ed, Evangelical Apologetics: Selected Essays from the 1995 Evangelical Theological Society Convention, Christian Publ, 96; auth, Inklings of Reality: Essays Toward A Christian Philosophy of Letters, Toccoa Falls Press, 96; auth, Reflections from Plato's Cave: Musings on the History of Philosophy, Philosophia Christi, 97; auth, The Disciple's Prayer, Christian Publ, 99. **CONTACT ADDRESS** PO Box 800807, Toccoa Falls, GA 30598. **EMAIL** dtw@toccoafalls.edu

WILLIAMS, FRANKLIN P.
PERSONAL Born 06/04/1946, Marianna, FL, m, 1989, 1 child **DISCIPLINE** JUVENILE JUSTICE **EDUCATION** Fla State Univ, BS, 68; MA, 73; PhD, 76. **CAREER** Asst Prof, Rochester Inst Tech, 76-79; Assoc Prof, Sam Houston State Univ, 79-88; ch, Calif State Univ, 88-00; Prof, Prairie View A&M Univ, 00-. **HONORS AND AWARDS** ALA Best Ref Works, Encycl of Am Prisons, 96; Trustee, Acad of Criminal Justice Sci. **RESEARCH** Criminology, juvenile justice, corrections, drug abuse. **SELECTED PUBLICATIONS** ed, Encyclopedia of American Prisons, Garland Publ (New York, NY), 96; auth, "There's Still a Lot of Folks Grateful to the Lone Ranger," Social Pathology, 3(1) (97): 16-23; auth, Law Enforcement Operations and Management: Contemporary Literature in Theory and Practice, Garland Publ (New York, NY), 97; auth, Victims of Crime and the Victimization Process: Contemporary Literature in Theory and Practice, Garland Publ (New York, NY), 97; auth, The American Court System: Contemporary Literature in Theory and Practice," Garland Publ (New York, NY), 97; auth, Criminology Theory: Contemporary Literature in Theory and Practice, Garland Publ (New York, NY), 97; auth, Drug Use and Drug Policy: Contemporary Literature in Theory and Practice, Garland Publ (New York, NY), 97; auth, Criminology Theory: Selected Classic Readings, 2nd ed, Anderson (Cincinnati, OH), 98; auth, Imagining Criminology: An Alternative Orienting Perspective, Garland Publ (New York, NY), 99; auth, Criminological Theory, 3rd ed, Princeton-Hall (Englewood Cliffs, NJ), 99. **CONTACT ADDRESS** Dept Juv Justice, Prairie View A&M Univ, PO Box 4017, Prairie View, TX 77446. **EMAIL** Frank_Williams@pvamu.edu

WILLIAMS, GARY C.
PERSONAL Born 01/07/1952, Santa Monica, CA, m, 1980 **DISCIPLINE** LAW **EDUCATION** UCLA, BA, 1973; Stanford Law School, JD, 1976. **CAREER** California Agricultural Labor Relations Board, staff attorney; ACLU Foundation of Southern California, asst legal dir, staff attorney; Loyola University School of Law, professor, currently. **MEMBERSHIPS** Southern Christian Leadership Conference/LA, bd of dir; ACLU of Southern California, bd of dir; Mount Hebron Baptist Church, chairman; Stanford Law School Board of Visitors. **SELECTED PUBLICATIONS** Hastings Constitutional Law Quarterly, "The Wrong Side of the Tracks," p 845, 1992; Southwestern University Law Review, "Can Government Limit Tenant Blacklisting?," vol 24, p 1077, 1995; auth, "On the Q.T. and Very Hush Hush: Should California's Constitutional Right to Privacy Protect Public Figures From Publication of Confidential Personal Information?", Loyola Entertainment Law Journal 19 (99): 337; auth, "The Right of Privacy versus the Right to Know: The War Continues," Loyola Entertainment Law Journal 19 (99): 215; auth, "Don't Try to Adjust Your Television-I'm Black," Ruminations on the Recurrent Controversy over the Whiteness of TV, Iowa Journal of Gender, Race and Justice 4 (00): 99; auth, "Incubating Monsters? Prosecutorial Responsibility for the Rampart Scandal," Loyola Law Review, forthcoming. **CONTACT ADDRESS** Professor, Loyola Marymount Univ, 919 S Albany St, Los Angeles, CA 90015. **EMAIL** gary.williams@lls.edu

WILLIAMS, GARY G. COHEN
DISCIPLINE RELIGION **EDUCATION** Temple Univ, BSed, 56; Faith Theol Sem, Mdiv, 61, STM, 64; Grace Theol Sem, ThD, 66. **SELECTED PUBLICATIONS** Contib ed, Kirban Prophecy Bible; Red Letter Bible; Christian Life Bible. **CONTACT ADDRESS** Trinity Intl Univ, So Florida, 500 NE 1st Ave, PO Box 109674, Miami, FL 33101-9674.

WILLIAMS, GREGORY HOWARD
PERSONAL Born 11/12/1943, Muncie, IN, m **DISCIPLINE** LAW **EDUCATION** Ball St U, BA 1966; Univ of MD, MA 1969; George Washington U, JD 1971, MPhil 1977, PhD 1982. **CAREER** Delaware Co, IN, deputy sheriff 1963-66; US Senate, legal aide 1971-73; GW Washington Project Washington DC, coord 1973-77; Univ of IA, assoc dean law prof 1977-87, professor of law, 87-93; Ohio State University, College of Law, dean and Carter C Kissell prof of law, 93- **MEMBERSHIPS** Consultant Foreign Lawyer Training Prog Wash DC 1975-77; consultant Nat Inst (Minority Ment Health Prog) 1975; mem IA Adv Comm US Civil Rights Commn 1978-88; mem IA Law Enforcement Acad Coun 1979-85; pres-, Asn of American Law Schs, 1999. **SELECTED PUBLICATIONS** Book, Law and Politics of Police Discretion 1984; article "Police Rulemaking Revisited" Journal Laws & Cont Problems 1984; article "Police Discretion" IA Law Review 1983; book The Iowa Guide to Search & Seizure 1986; Author, Life on the Color Line, The True Story of a White Boy Who Discovered He Was Black, 1995. **CONTACT ADDRESS** Col of Law, Ohio State Univ, Columbus, 55 W 12th Avenue, Columbus, OH 43210. **EMAIL** williams.604@osu.edu

WILLIAMS, J. RODMAN
PERSONAL Born 08/21/1918, m, 1949, 3 children **DISCIPLINE** SYSTEMATIC THEOLOGY **EDUCATION** Davidson Col, AB; Union Theol Sem, BD, ThM; Columbia Univ, PhD. **CAREER** Chaplain, US Marine Corps; Chaplain/prof. Beloit College; Pastor, First Presbyterian Church Rockford, IL; prof, Austin Presbyterian Seminary; pres, prof, Melodyland School of Theology; prof, Regent University School of Divinity. **HONORS AND AWARDS** Phi Beta Kappa; chaplain, us marine corps; pastor, first presbyterian church; pres, intl presbyterian charismatic communion; organizer, leader, first europ charismatic leaders conf(s); pres, soc pentecostal stud. **SELECTED PUBLICATIONS** Auth, Contemporary Existentialism and Christian Faith, 65; The Era of the Spirit, 71; The Pentecostal Reality, 72; Ten Teachings, 74; The Gift of the Holy Spirit Today, 80; Renewal Theology, vol 1, God, the World, and Redemption, Zondervan, 88; Renewal Theology, vol 2, Salvation, the Holy Spirit, and Christian Living, Zondervan, 90; The Gifts of the Holy Spirit, Charisma, 92; Biblical Truth and Experience: A Reply to Charismatic Chaos by John F. MacArthur, Jr, Paraclete 27/3, 93; What Catholics Should Know about Protestants, Charisma, 95; Renewal Theology, vol 3, The Church, the Kingdom, and Last Things, Zondervan, 92; Renewal Theology 3 vols in one, Zondervan, 96. **CONTACT ADDRESS** Regent Univ, 1000 Regent Univ Dr, Virginia Beach, VA 23464-9831. **EMAIL** rodmwill@regent.edu

WILLIAMS, JAY G.
PERSONAL Born 12/18/1932, Rome, NY, m, 1956, 4 children **DISCIPLINE** RELIGION **EDUCATION** Hamilton Col, BA, 54; Union Theol Semi NYork, M(Div), 57; Columbia Univ, PhD(philos relig), 64. **CAREER** Assoc dir, A Christian Ministry in Nat Parks, Nat Coun Churches, 57-60; from instr to prof relig, 60-76, Walcott-Barlett Prof Ethics & Christian Evidences, Hamilton Col, 76-. **HONORS AND AWARDS** Ford humanities grants, 70-72. **MEMBERSHIPS** Am Acad Relig; Hermetic Studies; Buddhist-Christian Studies; Thomas Nast Soc; Soc for the Study of Chinese Relig. **RESEARCH** Philos rel. East and West. **SELECTED PUBLICATIONS** Auth, Ten Words of Freedom, Fortress, 71; Understanding the Old Testament, Barron's, 73; Yeshua Buddha, Quest, 78; Judaism, Quest, 80; Spiritual Approach to Male/Female Relations, Quest, 84; Riddle of the Sphyx, UPA, 90; Angels and Mortals, Quest, 90; Along the Silk Route, GSP, 91; Matters of Life and Death, GSP, 93; Dark Trees and Empty Sky, GSP, 94; A Reassessment of Absolute Skepticism and Religious Faith, Mellen, 96; Education of Edward Robinson, UTS, 97; auth, The Times and Life of Edward Robinson, SBL, 99. **CONTACT ADDRESS** Dept of Relig Studies, Hamilton Col, New York, 198 College Hill Rd., Clinton, NY 13323-1292. **EMAIL** jwilliam@Hamilton.edu

WILLIAMS, JUNIUS W.
PERSONAL Born 12/23/1943, Suffolk, VA **DISCIPLINE** LAW **EDUCATION** Amherst Coll, BA 1965; Yale Law Sch, JD 1968; Inst of Pol Kennedy Sch of Gov Harvard Univ, fellow 1980. **CAREER** Newark Comm Devel Admin & Model Cities Prog, dir 1970-73; Essex Newark Legal Svcs, exec dir 1983-85; City of Newark, candidate for mayor 1982; Private Practice, Attorney 1973-83, 85-; "Return to the Source," New Jersey, business manager, vocalist, instrumentalist, 85-; real estate developer, Newark, NJ, 87-; Town of Irvington, Irvington, NJ, legislative counsel, 90-94, town Attorney, 94-. **HONORS AND AWARDS** Distinguished Service Awd Newark Jaycees 1974; Concerned Citizens Awd Bd of Concerned Citizens Coll of Med & Dentistry of NJ; Fellow MARC 1967-68, 1973. **MEMBERSHIPS** 3rd vice pres Natl Bar Assn; 2nd vice pres 1976; pres Natl Bar Assn 1978-79; mem bd of dirs Agricultural Missions Inc; mem Natl, Amer, NJ, Essex Co Bar Assn; mem Critical Minorities Problems Comm; Natl Assn Housing & Redevel Officials; mem Equal Oppor Fund Bd 1980; Essex Co Ethics Comm 1980; fndr & dir Newark Area Planning Assn 1967-70; co-chmn Comm Negotiating Team NJ Coll Med & Dentistry Controversey 1967; guest spkr/lecturer Yale Univ, Harvard Law Sch, Rutgers Univ, Cornell Univ, Univ NC; pres Yale Law Sch Assoc of NJ 1981-82; fndr/pres Leadership Development Group 1980-; consultant Council of Higher Educ in Newark; bd of trustees Essex Co Coll 1980-84; mem & former sec Newark Collaboration Group; founder/first chmn Ad Hoc Comm of Univ Heights 1984-86; UniversityHeights Neighborhood Develent Corp., consultant, developer, 1986-93. **CONTACT ADDRESS** 132 Harper Ave, Irvington, NJ 07111.

WILLIAMS, KAREN HASTIE
PERSONAL Born 09/30/1944, Washington, DC, m, 3 children **DISCIPLINE** LAW **EDUCATION** Univ of Neuchatel Switzerland, Cert 1965; Bates Coll, BA 1966; Fletcher School of Law & Diplomacy Tufts Univ, MA 1967; Columbus Law School Catholic Univ of Amer, JD 1973. **CAREER** Fried Frank Harris Shriver & Kampelman, assoc atty 1975-77; US Senate Comm on Budget, chief counsel 1977-80; Office of Fed Procurement Policy Office of Mgmt & Budget, admin 1980-81; Crowell & Moring, of counsel 1982, sr partner. **HONORS AND AWARDS** Director's Choice Awd, 1993; National Women's Economic Alliance; Breast Cancer Awareness Awd, Columbia Hospital for Women, 1994; Judge Learned Hand Awd, 1995, American Jewish Committee. **MEMBERSHIPS** Past chmn, Amer Bar Assoc Publ Contract Law Sect; bd of dir Crestar Bank Washington DC; Lawyers Comm for Civil Rights Under Law; board of directors Federal National Mortgage Association; board of directors Washington Gas Light Co; chair Black Student Fund; bd of dir exec comm DC Chap Amer Red Cross; chair, bd of dir Greater Washington Rsch Ctr; bd of dir NAACP Legal Defense Fund; former mem Trilateral Commission; Continental Airlines Inc, bd of directors. **CONTACT ADDRESS** Crowell and Moring, 1001 Pennsylvania Ave, NW, Washington, DC 20004.

WILLIAMS, KYLE
PERSONAL Born 01/25/1963, Denver, CO **DISCIPLINE** RELIGION **EDUCATION** Hunter Coll, BA; SUNY Albany, MA. **CAREER** Admin, Lincoln Center/Institute; admin, New York Open Center; Prof religion, Hunter Coll. **MEMBERSHIPS** AAR **RESEARCH** Religion & the Arts **CONTACT ADDRESS** 611 W 158th St, #6E, New York, NY 10032.

WILLIAMS, MARCUS DOYLE
PERSONAL Born 10/24/1952, Nashville, TN, m **DISCIPLINE** LAW **EDUCATION** Fisk Univ, BA, 1973 (university honors); Catholic Univ of Amer, School of Law, JD, 1977. **CAREER** Office of the Commonwealth Atty, asst commonwealth atty, 78-80; George Mason Univ, lecturer in business legal studies, 80-95; Office of the County Atty, asst county atty, 80-87; Gen Dist Court, judge, 87-90; Circuit Court, Judge, 90-; National Judicial College, faculty, 92. **HONORS AND AWARDS** Beta Kappa Chi, Scientific Honor Soc, Fisk Univ Chapter, 1973; Distinguished Youth Awd, Office of the Army, Judge Advocate Gen, 1976; Thomas J Watson Fellow, 1977-78; Fairfax County Bd of Supvr, Serv Commendation, 1987; Serv Appreciation Awd, Burke-Fairfax Jack & Jill, 1989; Service Appreciation Awd, Black Law Students Assn of Catholic University, 1990; Otis Smith Alumnus Awd, 1997; American Participant Program Lectures, Liberia, Zambia, Botswana, sponsored by USIA, 1990; **MEMBERSHIPS** Bd mem, Fairfax-Falls Church, Criminal Justice Adv Bd, 1980-81; freelance writer and reviewer, 1981-; mem, Amer Business Law Assn, 1984-; bd of assocs, St Paul's Coll, 1986-87; vice chmn, Continuing Legal Educ Comm, Fairfax Bar Assn, 1986-87; Virginia delegate, National Conference of Special Court Judges, 1990; Omega Psi Phi Fraternity, 1971. **SELECTED PUBLICATIONS** Articles: "Arbitration of Intl Commercial Contracts: Securities and Antitrust Claims," Virginia Lawyer, 1989, "European Antitrust Law and its Application to Amer Corp," Whittier Law Review, 1987, "Judicial Review: The Guardian of Civil Liberties and Civil Rights," George Mason University Civil Rights Law Journ 1991, "Lawyer, Judge, Solicitor, General Education: A Tribute to Wade H McCree, Jr," National Black Law Journal, 1990. **CONTACT ADDRESS** Circuit Court, 4110 Chain Bridge Rd, Fairfax, VA 22030. **EMAIL** marcar@erols.com

WILLIAMS, MEREDITH
PERSONAL Born 07/29/1947, Anniston, AL, m, 1973, 1 child **DISCIPLINE** PHILOSOPHY **EDUCATION** NY Univ, BA, 69, PhD, 74; Univ of Chicago, MA, 70. **CAREER** Asst prof to assoc prof, Wesleyan Univ, 74-85; assoc prof, Northwestern Univ, 85-00; prof, Johns Hopkins Univ, 00. **HONORS AND AWARDS** Rockefeller Fel, 69; Woodrow Wilson Diss Fel, 73-74. **MEMBERSHIPS** Am Philos Assoc; AAUP; Soc for Philos of Psychol. **RESEARCH** Wittgenstein, philosophy of mind, philosophy of psychology. **SELECTED PUBLICATIONS** Auth, Wittgenstein, Kang, and the 'Metaphysics of Experience', Kang-Studien, 90; auth, "Narrow Content, Norms, and the Individual" in Midwest Studies in Philosophy XV, ed Ted Uehling, 90; auth, "Rules, Community, and the Individual", in Meaning-Scepticism, ed. Klaus Puhl (Berlin/NY: de Gruyter, 91); auth, "Private States, Public Practices" Intl Philos Quarterly, 94; auth, "The Philosophical Significance of Learning in the Later Wittgenstein", Can Jour of Philos, 94; auth, "The Implicit Intricacy of Thought and Action" in Language Beyond Post-Modernism, ed. David M. Levin (Northwestern Univ Pr, 97); auth, Wittgenstein, Mind and Meaning: Toward a Social Conception of Mind, Routledge (London), 98; auth, "The Etiology of the Obvious, in Wittgenstein in America, ed. Tim McCarthy (Cambridge: Oxford Univ Pr) (forthcoming); auth, "Wittgenstein and the Problem of Normativity", Studi Perugini (forthcoming). **CONTACT ADDRESS** Dept Philos, Northwestern Univ, 1818 Hinman Ave, Evanston, IL 60208-1315. **EMAIL** mwill@northwestern.edu

WILLIAMS, MICHAEL J.
DISCIPLINE PHILOSOPHY **EDUCATION** Princeton Univ, PhD. **CAREER** Charles and Emma Morrison prof Humanities, Northwestern Univ. **RESEARCH** Epistemology, history of modern philosophy. **SELECTED PUBLICATIONS** Auth, Groundless Belief; Unnatural Doubts. **CONTACT ADDRESS** Dept of Philosophy, Northwestern Univ, 1801 Hinman, Evanston, IL 60208. **EMAIL** m-williams@northwestern.edu

WILLIAMS, NANCY M.
PERSONAL Born 06/15/1967, LaRochelle, France, s **DISCIPLINE** PHILOSOPHY, WOMEN'S STUDIES **EDUCATION** Winthrope Univ, BS, 89; Univ NC, Charlotte, BA, 93; Univ S Fla, MA, 97. **CAREER** Lectr, UNC Charlotte; lectr, Queens Coll. **MEMBERSHIPS** APA; NCPS; Feminist Ethics and Soc Theory; Intl Netwk Fem Appro Bioethics. **RESEARCH** Feminist Theory; feminism; 20th Cent continental philosophy; existentialism; history of philosophy; ancient and modern philosophy. **SELECTED PUBLICATIONS** Rev, "Justice for Here and Now, James Sterba (Cambridge, CUP, 98), Concerned Philos for Peace NL 19 (99): 18-20; auth, "Epilogue," in Globalizing Feminist Bioethics: Woman's Health Concerns Worldwide, in print. **CONTACT ADDRESS** Dept Philosophy, Univ of No Carolina, Charlotte, 9201 University City Blvd, Charlotte, NC 28223-0001. **EMAIL** nwilliam@email.uncc.edu

WILLIAMS, PAUL R.
DISCIPLINE LAW AND INTERNATIONAL RELATIONS **EDUCATION** Univ Calif Davis, BA, Stanford Univ, JD; Univ of Cambridge, Phd. **CAREER** Asst prof, Am Univ. **HONORS AND AWARDS** Exec dir, Public Int Law & Policy Gp; dir, Public Inst Law Policy Prog, Carnegie Endowment. **MEMBERSHIPS** CA; OC Bars. **RESEARCH** Public International Law. **SELECTED PUBLICATIONS** Auth, Water Marketing and Instream Flows: the Next Step in Protecting California's Instream Values, 9, Stanford Environmental Law Journal 132, 90; auth, The Politics and Policy of Deep Seabed Mining, Book Review 40, American Journal Comparative Law 376, 92; auth, State Succession and the International Financial Institutions: Political Criteria or Sound Management?, 43 International and Compartive Law Quarterly 776, 94; auth, International Environmental Dispute Resolution: The Dispute Between Slovakia and Hungary Concerning Construction of the Gaboikovo and Nagymaros Dams, 19, Columbia Journal of Environmental Law 1, 94; auth, Treaty Succession: Conflicting State Practice, 23, Denver Journal of International Law and Polity 1, 94; auth, Bankruptcy in Russia: The Evolution of a Comprehensive Russian Bankruptcy Code, 21 Review of Central and East European Law 511, 95; auth, UN Mandates: The Letter of the Law, in With No Peace to Keep: United Nations Peacekeeping and the War in the Former Yugoslavia, 95; auth, Can International Legal Principles Promote the Resolution of Central and East European Transboundary Environmental Disputes?, 7 George-

town International and Environmental Law Review 421, 95. **CONTACT ADDRESS** American Univ, 4400 Massachusetts Ave, Washington, DC 20016.

WILLIAMS, PETER W.
PERSONAL Born 08/08/1944, Hollywood, FL, m, 1980, 2 children **DISCIPLINE** RELIGIOUS STUDIES **EDUCATION** Harvard Univ, AB, 65; Yale Univ, AM, 67, MPhil, 68, PhD, 70. **CAREER** Distinguished Prof of Relig and Am Studies, Miami Univ, 70-. **HONORS AND AWARDS** Pres, Amer Soc of Church Hist. **MEMBERSHIPS** Amer Studies Assoc; Amer Academy Relig; Hist Soc of the Episcopal Church; Soc of Architectural Historians; Vernacular Architecture Forum. **RESEARCH** Amer religious architecture. **SELECTED PUBLICATIONS** Auth, Houses of God: Region, Religion and Architecture in the United States, Univ IL Press, 97. **CONTACT ADDRESS** Dept of Comparative Relig, Miami Univ, Oxford, OH 45056. **EMAIL** williapw@muohio.edu

WILLIAMS, PRESTON N.
PERSONAL Born 05/23/1926, Alcolu, SC, m **DISCIPLINE** THEOLOGY **EDUCATION** Washington & Jefferson Coll, AB 1947, MA 1948; Johnson C Smith Univ, BD 1950; Yale Univ, STM 1954; Harvard Univ, PhD 1967. **CAREER** Boston Univ School Theol, Martin Luther King Jr prof social ethics 1970-71; Harvard Div School, acting dean 1974-75, Houghton prof theol & contemporary change 1971-. **HONORS AND AWARDS** Ordained to ministry Presb Church 1950. **MEMBERSHIPS** Acting dir WEB DuBois Inst 1975-77; editor-at-large Christian Century 1972-; mem, pres Amer Acad Religion 1975-; dir, pres Amer Soc Christian Ethics 1974-75; mem Phi Beta Kappa. **SELECTED PUBLICATIONS** Contrib articles to professional jrnls. **CONTACT ADDRESS** Divinity Sch, Harvard Univ, 45 Francis Ave, Cambridge, MA 02138.

WILLIAMS, SAMUEL KEEL
PERSONAL Born 03/18/1940, Rocky Mount, NC, m, 1962, 3 children **DISCIPLINE** RELIGION **EDUCATION** Wake Forest Univ, BA, 62; Southeastern Baptist Theol Sem, BD, 66; Harvard Univ, PhD(relig), 72. **CAREER** Instr relig, Wake Forest Univ, 69-70; instr relig & actg chaplain, 71-72, asst prof to prof Relig, Colo Col, 73-. **HONORS AND AWARDS** Fulbright Schol, 62-63; Woodrow Wilson Fel, 66-67; Sears-Roebuck Found Awd for Excellence in Teaching, 90. **MEMBERSHIPS** Soc Bibl Lit; Catholic Bibl Asn. **RESEARCH** Early Christian soteriology; Pauline theology. **SELECTED PUBLICATIONS** Auth, Jesus' Death as Saving Event: The Background and Origin of a Concept, Scholars, 75; Galatians, Abingdon, 97. **CONTACT ADDRESS** Dept of Relig, Colorado Col, 14 E Cache La Poudre, Colorado Springs, CO 80903-3294. **EMAIL** swilliams@ColoradoCollege.edu

WILLIAMS, WILBERT LEE
PERSONAL Born 08/25/1938, Corsicana, TX, m, 1961 **DISCIPLINE** LAW **EDUCATION** Prairie View A&M Coll, BS 1960; Howard Univ School of Law, JD 1971; Inst for New Govt Attys 1971; Howard Univ School of Divinity, 1987-90 M Div. **CAREER** US Dept of Agr, farm mgmt supr 1965-68; United Planning Org Wash DC, exec ofcr 1968-71; US Dept of Agr Office of Gen Counsel Wash DC, atty 1971-84; US Dept of Agr, equal opportunity officer; pastor, The First New Horizon Baptist Church, currently. **HONORS AND AWARDS** Recip 1st Annual Achievement Awd OEO Natl Advisory Comm for Legal Serv Program 1968. **MEMBERSHIPS** Past vice pres & founding mem CHASE Inc; former mem DC Neighborhood Reinvestment Commission; past mem bd dir Neighborhood Legal Serv Program Washington DC; past mem bd trustee United Planning Org Washington DC. **SELECTED PUBLICATIONS** President and founder, The First New Horizon Community Development Corp. **CONTACT ADDRESS** Pastor, First New Horizon Baptist Church, PO Box 176, Clinton, MD 20735.

WILLIAMS, WILLIAM C.
PERSONAL Born 07/12/1937, Wilkes-Barre, PA, m, 1959, 1 child **DISCIPLINE** BIBLICAL STUDIES **EDUCATION** Central Bible Col, BA, 63, MA, 64; New York Univ, MA, 66, PhD, 75. **CAREER** Reference Librarian, Hebraic Section, Library of Congress, Washington, DC, 67-69; Prof of Old Testament, Col Vanguard Univ, Southern CA Col, Costa Mesa, 69-; vis prof: Singapore, Malaysia, Belgium, Great Britain, 85; Israel, 86; Regent Univ, Virginia Beach, VA, 92, Belgium 00. **HONORS AND AWARDS** Nat Defense Educ Act Title VI fel, NYU, 64-67; NEH Scholar, summer 92; Marquis' Who's Who in America, 94-; Delta Sigma, 96; Delta Alpha, Distinguished Educator Awd, 97; Sigma Chi Pi, 97; Distinguished Educator Awd, Assemblies of God, 98; postdoctoral study: hebrew univ, jerusalem, israel, semitic langs, 77-78; inst of holyland studies, jerusalem, israel, archaeology and geography of israel, spring 86. **MEMBERSHIPS** Soc of Biblical Lit; Evangelical Theol Soc; Inst of Biblical Res. **RESEARCH** Hebrew lang and related Biblical theology. **SELECTED PUBLICATIONS** Auth, Greek word studies for The Complete Biblical Library, The New Testament Greek-English Dictionary, The Complete Biblical Library, 90; Hebrew I: A Study Guide, 80, 86, & Hebrew II: A Study Guide, 86, Int Correspondence Inst; articles for Evangelical Dictionary of Biblical Theology, ed Walter Elwell, Baker, 96; Commentary on Hosea for Pentecostal Commentary Series, Sheffield Academic Press, forthcoming; They Spoke From God, a textbook for Old Testament Survey, Logion, forthcoming; articles for the New International Dictionary of Old Testament Theology, Zondervan, 98; numerous other articles and publications; translation and revision consultant for several publications. **CONTACT ADDRESS** Vanguard Univ, 55 Fair Dr., Costa Mesa, CA 92627. **EMAIL** wwilliams@vanguard.edu

WILLIAMS, WILLIAM J.
PERSONAL Born 12/25/1935, Montgomery, AL, s **DISCIPLINE** LAW **EDUCATION** Morehouse Col, AB, 52; NYork Univ, MPA, 54; Univ of So Calif, PhD, 66. **CAREER** NY State Com/Govtl Operations NY City, admin adv 59-60; Bldg Serv Union, rsch dir joint council #8, 60-61; Calif State Legislature, consult 61-62; US Congressman Augustus F Hawkins, congressional field dir, 62-66; US Equal Employment Oppor Comm, dep staff dir, 66-67; US Commn on Civil Rights, dir western progs, 67-68; LA Co/LA City, employee relations bd mediator, 74; from asst prof to prof, Univ So Calif, 80- . **HONORS AND AWARDS** Teaching Excellence Awd, School of Public Admin, USC, 1978; Man of the Year, Alpha Phi Omega; Distinguished Prof Awd, USC Graduate Student Assn, 1989. **MEMBERSHIPS** Pub Personnel Asn; Am Humanist Soc; Am Soc for Pub Admin; Int Soc for Gen Semantics; Am Poli Sci Asn; Soc of Equal Employment Consult; Inst for Gen Semantics; Am Asn of Univ Profs; Am Acad of Poli & Soc Sci; Am Asn for the Advan of Sci; Am Fed of Radio & TV Artists. **RESEARCH** Applied epistemology; thinking about thinking; creative thinking; general semantics; epistemics-decision making. **SELECTED PUBLICATIONS** Auth, General Semantics and the Social Sciences, Philos Lib (NYork), 72; auth, Uncommon Sense and Dimensional Awareness, Univ Pubs (Los Angeles), 73; auth, Epistemics: Personalizing the Process of Change, Univ Pubs (Los Angeles), 75; auth, Selections from Semantic Behavior and Decision Making, Univ So Calif Pr (Los Angeles), 75; auth, Semantic Behavior and Decision Making, Monograph Pub, Univ Microfilms Int (Ann Arbor), 78; auth, The Miracle of Abduction, Epistemics Inst Pr (Los Angeles), 85; auth, New Thnking for a New Millenium, 00. **CONTACT ADDRESS** Univ of So California, University Park, Los Angeles, CA 90007. **EMAIL** willw@usc.edu

WILLIAMS, WINTON E.
DISCIPLINE LAW **EDUCATION** Tulane Univ, BBA; Univ Miss, LLB; Yale Univ, LLM. **CAREER** Prof, Univ Fla, 69-. **MEMBERSHIPS** Miss Bar; Phi Delta Phi; Omicron Delta Kappa; Phi Kappa Phi. **RESEARCH** Creditors' remedies and bankruptcy, secured transactions in personal property, sales. **SELECTED PUBLICATIONS** Auth, Games Creditors Play: Collecting from Overextended Consumers. **CONTACT ADDRESS** School of Law, Univ of Florida, PO Box 117625, Gainesville, FL 32611-7625. **EMAIL** williams.win@law.ufl.edu

WILLIAMS, YVONNE LAVERNE
PERSONAL Born 01/07/1938, Washington, DC, s **DISCIPLINE** LAW **EDUCATION** Barnard Coll, BA, 1959; Boston Univ, MA, 1961; Georgetown Univ, JD, 1977. **CAREER** US Info Agency, foreign serv officer, 61-65; African-Amer Inst New York, dir womens Africa comm, 66-68; Benedict Coll, Columbia, SC, assc prof African American studies, 68-70; US Congress Washington, DC, press sec Hon Walter Fauntroy, 70-72; African-Amer Scholars Council Washington, DC, dir 1972-73; Leva Hawes Symington Martin, Washington, DC, assoc atty, 77-79; Brimmer & Co Washington, DC, asst vice pres, 80-82; Tuskegee University, vice pres for Fed & Intl Rel & Legal Counsel 1983-1996; Academy for Educational Development Public Policy & Intl Affairs Fellowship Program, natl dir, 96-. **HONORS AND AWARDS** Boston University, African Research & Studies Program Fellowship, 1959-60. **MEMBERSHIPS** Mem Oper Crossroads Africa, 1960-, Barnard-in-Washington, 1960-; mem Amer Bar Assoc, 1980-, Natl Bar Assoc, 1980-, Dist of Columbia Bar, 1980-; alumnae trustee, Barnard Coll, New York, NY, 1988-92; mem, Overseas Devel Council, Washington, DC, 1988-; bd of dir, Golden Rule Apartments, Inc, Washington, DC, 1986-. **SELECTED PUBLICATIONS** Author, "William Monroe Trotter, (1872-1934)"; in Reid "The Black Prism," New York, 1969. **CONTACT ADDRESS** Public Policy and Intl Affairs Fellowship Prog, 1875 Conn Ave NW, Washington, DC 20009.

WILLIAMSON, CLARK M.
PERSONAL Born 11/03/1935, Memphis, TN, m, 1960, 1 child **DISCIPLINE** THEOLOGY **EDUCATION** Transylvania Univ, BA, Univ Chicago, BD, MA, PhD, 69. **CAREER** Christian Theol Sem, prof; Sch of Theol Claremont, vis prof; Chateau de Bossey Ecumenical Inst, vis prof. **MEMBERSHIPS** CSGJ, ATS, AAR, ADTD, TCCC. **SELECTED PUBLICATIONS** Auth, A Mutual Witness: Toward Critical Solidarity Between Jews and Christians, ed. St. Louis: Chalice Press, 92; auth, The Church and the Jewish People, ed., St Louis: Chalice Press, 94; auth, A Guest in the House of Israel, Louisville: Westminster/John Knox Press, 93; auth, Mark, Mahwah NJ: Paulist Press, forthcoming; Adventures of the Spirit: A Guide to Worship from the Perspective of Process Theology, coauth, Lanham MD: Univ Press Am, 97; The Vital Church, coauth, St Louis MO: Chalis Press, 98. **CONTACT ADDRESS** Christian Theol Sem, PO Box 88267, Indianapolis, IN 46208.

WILLIAMSON, LAMAR
PERSONAL Born 07/24/1926, Monticello, AR, m, 1949, 4 children **DISCIPLINE** BIBLICAL THEOLOGY **EDUCATION** Davidson Col, BA, 47; Union Theol Seminary in Virginia, BD, 51; Fac Theol Protestante, Montpellier, France, BTheol, 52; Yale Univ, PhD, 63. **CAREER** Pastor, Harveyton and Hall Memorial Presbyterian Churches, 52-56; Prof New Testament, Inst Superieur de Theol, Kananga, Zaire, 57-66; Vis Prof New Testament, Union Theol Seminary, 66-68; Prof Bibl Studies, Presbyterian Sch Christian Educ, 69-91; Prof New Testament, Fac Theol Reformee au Kasai, Zaire/Congo, 92-94. **HONORS AND AWARDS** Phi Beta Kappa; Omega Delta Kappa. **MEMBERSHIPS** Soc Bibl Lit. **RESEARCH** Fourth gospel. **SELECTED PUBLICATIONS** Auth, Mark, Interpretation: A Bible Commentary for Teaching and Preaching, John Knox Press, 83; Ishaku: An African Christian Between Two Worlds, Fairway Press, 92; transl, Prayers for My Village, Upper Room Bks, 94; co-ed, A Book of Reformed Prayers, Westminster John Knox Press, 98. **CONTACT ADDRESS** PO Box 224, Montreat, NC 28757. **EMAIL** lamar@buncombe.main.nc.us

WILLIAMSON, WILLIAM B.
PERSONAL Born 01/27/1918, Amsterdam, NY, m, 1941, 2 children **DISCIPLINE** PHILOSOPHY **EDUCATION** Temple Univ, BS, 40, STB, 42, EdD, 66; Lutheran Theo Sem, STM, 45; Lehigh Univ, MA, 50. **CAREER** Instructor Chaplain School, WW II, US Army; Asst Prof, 45-50, Lehigh Univ; Assoc Prof, Cheyney State Coll; Prof, Ursinus Coll. **HONORS AND AWARDS** Episcopal Church Fel, Hon DD, National Univ; Hon Fel, Oriel College Oxford Univ; Hon DHL, Lindbeck Awd for Distinguished Teaching, Ursinus Coll. **RESEARCH** The question of the historical Jesus, who wrote the New Testament? **SELECTED PUBLICATIONS** Auth, A Handbook for Episcopalians, Morehouse-Barlow, 60; Ian Ramsey, Hendrickson Pub, 92; An Encyclopedia of Religions in the United States, Crossroads, 91; Night Thoughts About God, in: The Unitarian Universalist Christian, 91; Is the USA a Christian Nation? in: Free Inquiry, 93; Evangelism for Today, in: The Living Church, 93; A New Look at Primary Focus, in: Episcopal Life, The Penn Episcopalian, 94. **CONTACT ADDRESS** Pine Run Community, 12 Golden Rain Cluster, Doylestown, PA 18901.

WILLIMON, WILLIAM HENRY
PERSONAL Born 05/15/1946, Greenville, SC, m, 1969, 2 children **DISCIPLINE** PASTORAL THEOLOGY **EDUCATION** Wofford Col, BA, 68; Yale Univ, MDiv, 71; Emory Univ, STD, 73. **CAREER** ASSOC PROF LITURGY & WORSHIP, DUKE UNIV, 76-, Pastor, Northside United Methodist Church, 80. **MEMBERSHIPS** NAm Acad Liturgy; Am Acad Relig. **RESEARCH** Liturgy and ethics; Christian worship. **CONTACT ADDRESS** Sch Divin, Duke Univ, Durham, NC 27706. **EMAIL** will@duke.edu

WILLIS, ROBERT E.
PERSONAL Born Scottsbluff, NE, m, 1950, 4 children **DISCIPLINE** CHRISTIAN ETHICS, MODERN RELIGIOUS THOUGHT **EDUCATION** Occidental Col, AB, 55; San Francisco Theol Sem, BD, 58, ThD(ethics & theol), 66. **CAREER** Asst prof relig, Col Emporia, 60-62; ASSOC PROF RELIG, HAMLINE UNIV, 62-, Vis asst prof, Macalester Col, 68-69. **MEMBERSHIPS** Am Acad Relig; Am Soc Christian Ethics; AAUP; fel Soc Values Higher Educ. **RESEARCH** Jewish-Christian relations. **SELECTED PUBLICATIONS** Auth, Auschwitz and the Good + National-Socialism and Morality, a Radical Challenge Towards a Reconfiguring of the Nazi Ethic, Holocaust and Genocide Stud, Vol 0008, 94. **CONTACT ADDRESS** Dept of Relig, Hamline Univ, 1536 Hewitt Ave, Saint Paul, MN 55104.

WILLIS, STEVEN J.
DISCIPLINE LAW **EDUCATION** La State Univ, BS, JD; NYork Univ, LLM. **CAREER** Prof, Univ Fla, 81-. **MEMBERSHIPS** La Bar; Fla Bar; La Soc Certified Public Accountants; Order of the Coif. **RESEARCH** Partnership taxation, tax exempt organizations and income taxation. **CONTACT ADDRESS** School of Law, Univ of Florida, PO Box 117625, Gainesville, FL 32611-7625. **EMAIL** willis@law.ufl.edu

WILLIS, TIM
PERSONAL Born 11/03/1959, Nashville, TN, m, 1982, 3 children **DISCIPLINE** RELIGION **EDUCATION** Abilene Christian Univ, BA, 81, MA, Mdiv, 84; Harvard Univ, 90. **CAREER** Vis instr, Abilene Christian Univ , 87; teaching asst, Abilene Christian Univ 87-88; vis prof, 89-90; asst prof, 90-94; assoc prof, 94-00; prof, 00-. **HONORS AND AWARDS** Hon Bible Student, 81; grants, Christian Scholar Found, 86-88; teaching fel, Harvard Univ, 86-88. **MEMBERSHIPS** Soc of BibLit; Catholic Bib Assoc. **RESEARCH** Hebrew Bible; Sociology of Israel. **SELECTED PUBLICATIONS** Auth, Mate, Mother, and Metaphor: Gomer and Israel in Hosea 1-3, Essays on Women in Earliest Christianity, Vol Two, MO: Col Press, 95; His Steadfast Love Endures Forever: General Remarks on the Book of Psalms, Leaven, 96; The Nature of Jephthah's Authority, Catholic Biblical Quart 57, 96; rev, Review of Charisma and Authority in Israelite Society, by Rodney R. Hutton, Restoration Quart 38, 96. **CONTACT ADDRESS** Religion Div., Pepperdine Univ, 24255 Pacific Coast Hwy, Malibu, CA 90263. **EMAIL** twillis@peperdine.edu

WILLS, DAVID WOOD
PERSONAL Born 01/25/1942, Portland, IN, m, 1964, 3 children **DISCIPLINE** RELIGION **EDUCATION** Yale Univ, BA, 62; Princeton Theol Sem, BD, 66; Harvard Univ, PhD(relig & soc), 75. **CAREER** Asst prof, Univ Southern Calif, 70-72; from Asst Prof to Prof Relig, 72-94, Winthop H. Smith Prof Relig, Amherst Col, 94-. **MEMBERSHIPS** Am Acad Relig; Am Soc Church Hist; Am Hist Asn; Am Studies Asn. **RESEARCH** African-American religious history; religious history of the Atlantic world; American religious history. **SELECTED PUBLICATIONS** Contribr, Black Apostles: Afro-American Churchmen Confront the Twentieth Century, 78 & co-ed (with Richard Newman) & contribr, Black Apostles at Home and Abroad: Afro-Americans and the Christian Mission from the Revolution to Reconstruction, 82, G.K. Hall; contribr, Between the Times: The Travail of the Protestant Establishment in America, 1900-1960, 89; Religion and American Politics: From the Colonial Period to the 1980's, 90; Dictionary of Christianity in America, 90; Blackwell Dictionary of Evangelical Biography: 1730-1860, 95; Minority Faiths and the Protestant Mainstream, 97. **CONTACT ADDRESS** Dept of Relig, Amherst Col, Amherst, MA 01002-5003. **EMAIL** dwwills@amherst.edu

WILLS, GREGORY A.
PERSONAL 3 children **DISCIPLINE** CHURCH HISTORY **EDUCATION** Duke Univ, BS; Gordon-Conwell Theol Sem, MDiv; Duke Univ, ThM; Emory Univ, PhD. **CAREER** Archives and spec coll(s) libn, Boyce Centennial Lib, Assoc Prof, S Baptist Theol Sem. **SELECTED PUBLICATIONS** Auth, dissertation, Democratic Religion: Freedom, Authority, and Church Discipline in the Baptist South, 1785-1900, Oxford UP; entries on Basil Manly, Jr. and Jesse Mercer, Amer Nat Biography. **CONTACT ADDRESS** Dept of Church History, So Baptist Theol Sem, 2825 Lexington Rd, Louisville, KY 40280. **EMAIL** gwills@sbts.edu

WILLS, LAWRENCE M.
PERSONAL Born 04/10/1954, Calhoun, KY, m, 1982, 2 children **DISCIPLINE** NEW TESTAMENT **EDUCATION** Harvard Col, BA, 76; Harvard Divinity Schl, MTS, 80, ThD, 87. **CAREER** Dir, lang stud, 85-93, asst prof, N Test, 93-94, Harvard Divinity Schl; assoc prof, bibl stud, 94-99; Prof, 99-; Episcopal Divinity Schl. **HONORS AND AWARDS** Jewish Novel in the Ancient World, awarded Outstanding Acad Bk 1995, Choice Mag. **MEMBERSHIPS** Soc of Biblical Lit; Assn for Jewish Stud. **RESEARCH** Ancient Judaism; New Testament; Hebrew Bible **SELECTED PUBLICATIONS** Auth, Quest of the Historical Gospel, Routledge, 97; auth, Jewish Novel in the Ancient World, Cornell, 95. **CONTACT ADDRESS** Episcopal Divinity Sch, 99 Brattle St, Cambridge, MA 02138. **EMAIL** lwills@episdivschool.org

WILMOT, DAVID WINSTON
PERSONAL Born 04/26/1944, Panama, m **DISCIPLINE** LAW **EDUCATION** Univ of AR, BA 1970; Georgetown Univ Law Ctr, JD 1973. **CAREER** Little Rock, asst city mgr 1968-70; Dolphin Branton Stafford & Webber, legal asst 1970-72; Georgetown Univ Law Ctr, rsch asst; OEO Legal Svcs, intern; DC Proj on Comm Legal Asst, dep dir 1972-73; DC Convention Ctr Bd of Dirs, general counsel; Hotel Assoc Washington DC, general counsel; Georgetown Univ, asst dean, dir 1973-92; Harmon & Wilmot, partner, 92-. **HONORS AND AWARDS** Dean's List 1967-70; Dean's Counselor Awd Univ of AR 1969; Outstanding Serv Awd Georgetown Univ Stud Bar Assoc 1971; Cert of Merit DC Citz for Better Ed 1972; Jeffrey Crandall Awd 1972; WA Law Reptr Prize 1973; Robert D L'Heureux Scholarship. **MEMBERSHIPS** Pres Stud for Equality 1967-68; vice pres GULC Legal Aid Soc 1972-73; pres Black Amer Law Stud Assoc 1972-73; adv bd DC Bds & Comms Adv Bd Georgetown Today 1973-76; mem DC Bar, PA Bar;, US Supreme Court of Appeals, DC Ct of Appeals, Supreme Ct of PA, Assoc of Amer Law Schools, Law School Admin Council, Amer Bar Assoc, Trial Lawyers Assoc, Natl Bar Assoc, Natl Conf of Black Lawyers, Alpha Kappa Psi, Lawyers Study Group, Potomac Fiscal Soc; public employees relations bd Wash DC; mem Firemens & Policement Retirement Bd; mem bd of dirs Federal City Natl Bank, Washington Waterfront Restaurant Corp; mem bd of governors Georgetown Univ Alumni Assoc; mem bd of dirs District Cablevision Inc. **CONTACT ADDRESS** Harmon & Wilmot, 1010 Vermont Ave NW, Washington, DC 20005.

WILSHIRE, BRUCE W.
PERSONAL Born 02/08/1932, Los Angeles, CA **DISCIPLINE** PHILOSOPHY **EDUCATION** New York Univ, PhD, 66. **CAREER** Prof, Rutgers Univ. **MEMBERSHIPS** APA. **SELECTED PUBLICATIONS** Auth, Role Playing and Identity: The Limits of Theater as Metaphor, Ind Univ Press, 91; auth, The Moral Collapse of the University: Professionalism, Purity, Alienation, SUNY Press, 90; auth, Wild Hunger: The Primal Roots of Modern Addiction, Rowman and Littlefield, 98; auth, The Primal Roots of American Philosophy: Pragmatism, Phenomenology, and Native American Thought, Penn St Press, 00. **CONTACT ADDRESS** Dept Philosophy, Rutgers, The State Univ of New Jersey, New Brunswick, PO Box 270, New Brunswick, NJ 08903-0270. **EMAIL** brucewilsh@juno.com

WILSON, BRADLEY E.
PERSONAL Born 07/01/1961, Detroit, MI, m, 1997 **DISCIPLINE** PHILOSOPHY **EDUCATION** Purdue Univ, BA, 82; Univ of N Carolina, 85, PhD, 91. **CAREER** Univ of Pittsburgh, vis asst prof, 91-96; Slippery Rock Univ, asst prof, 97-. **HONORS AND AWARDS** Phi Beta Kappa **MEMBERSHIPS** APA, PSA **RESEARCH** Hist and philo of biology; med ethics; philo of med. **SELECTED PUBLICATIONS** Auth, Changing Conceptions of Species, in: Bio & Philo, 96; Futility and the Obligations of Physicians, in: Bioethics, 97; Fitting the Picture to the Frame: Comments for Ruth Millikan, in: Mindscapes: Philo, Sc and the Mind, Univ of Pitt Press, 97; A (Not-So-Radical) Solution to the Species Problem, in Bio & Philo, 95; Comments on Ruse's The Species Problem, in: Concepts, Theol 7 Rationality in the Bio Sc, Univ of Pitt Press, 95; Are Species Sets?, in: Bio & Philo, 91. **CONTACT ADDRESS** Dept of Philosophy, Slippery Rock Univ of Pennsylvania, Slippery Rock, PA 16057. **EMAIL** Bradley.Wilson@sru.edu

WILSON, CHARLES REAGAN
PERSONAL Born 02/02/1948, Nashville, TN **DISCIPLINE** AMERICAN HISTORY, RELIGION **EDUCATION** Univ Tex, El Paso, BA, 70, MA, 72; Univ Tex, Austin, PhD(hist), 77. **CAREER** Vis prof Am studies, Univ Wuerzburg, West Ger, 77-78; lectr, Univ Tex, El Paso, 78-80; vis prof, Tex Tech Univ, 80-81; Asst Prof Am Hist, Univ Miss, 81-, Co-ed, Encycl Southern Cult, 81- **RESEARCH** Southern culture; American religion; popular culture. **SELECTED PUBLICATIONS** Auth, Bishop Thomas Frank Gailor: Celebrant of Southern tradition, Tenn Hist Quart, fall 79; The religion of the lost cause: Southern civil religion, J Southern Hist, 5/80; Baptized in Blood: The Religion of the Lost Cause, 1865-1920, Univ Ga Press, 80; Robert Lewis Dabney: Religion and the Southern holocaust, Va Mag Hist & Biog, 1/81; Southern funerals, cemeteries, the lost cause, Thomas Frank Gailor and Charles Todd Quintard, Encycl Southern Relig (in prep). **CONTACT ADDRESS** Univ of Mississippi, Box 6640, University, MS 38655.

WILSON, CLARENCE S., JR.
PERSONAL Born 10/22/1945, Brooklyn, NY, m, 1972 **DISCIPLINE** LAW **EDUCATION** Williams College, BA, 1967; Foreign Service Institute of the United States, 1969; Northwestern University, School of Law, JD, 1974. **CAREER** US Department of State, Caracas, Venezuela, third secretary, vice counsel, 69-71; Friedman and Koven, associate Attorney, 74-76; United States Gypsum Company, legal department, 76-79; sole practitioner, 79-81; Law Offices of Jewel S Lafontant, partner, 81-83; Chicago-Kent College of Law, adjunct professor, 81-94; Boodell, Sears, Sugrue, Giambalvo and Crowley, associate Attorney, 83-84; sole practitioner and counsel, 84-; Columbia College, adjunct professor, 96-97. **MEMBERSHIPS** Trustee, Chicago Symphony Orchestra, 1987-96; Art Institute of Chicago, bd mbr, Cmte on Twentieth Century Painting, Sculpture, Development, 1989-, trustee, 1990-; director, 1974-83, advisory board member, 1983-, Citizens Information Service of Illinois; bd mbr, The Harold Washington Foundation, 1989-92; bd mbr, Implementation Cmsn of The Lawyers Trust Fund of Illinois, 1983-85; bd mbr, Northwestern Univ School of Law Alumni Assn, 1979-84; project manager, Dept of Justice Task Force, The President's Private Sector Survey on Cost Control in the Federal Government, "The Grace Commission," 1982-84; governing bd, Illinois Arts Cncl, 1984-89, panel, Established Regional Organizations, 1998-; Illinois representative, Arts Midwest, 1985-89; Chicago and Cook County Bar Associations; trustee, Merit Music Program, 1991-96; Chicago Department of Cultural Affairs, Mayor's Advsry Bd, 1988-97; School of the Art Institute of Chicago, mem bd of governors, 1994-; Dept of Music at the Univ of Chicago, visiting committee mem, 1992-; Ministry of Culture, Republic of Venezuela, special counsel, 1989-90; DuSable Museum of African American History Inc, outside counsel, 1988-; Jazz Museum of Chicago, vice chair, 1994-97. **SELECTED PUBLICATIONS** Author, "Visual Arts and the Law," in Law and the Arts--Art and the Law, 1979; author of several copyright/art law articles. **CONTACT ADDRESS** 25 E Washington St, Ste 1515, Chicago, IL 60602-1804. **EMAIL** hcwilson@ix.netcom.com

WILSON, DANNY K.
PERSONAL Born 03/24/1959, Corinth, MS, m, 1987, 2 children **DISCIPLINE** THEOLOGY; NEW TESTAMENT STUDIES **EDUCATION** Union Univ, BA, 80; MDiv, 84, PhD, 95, Southwestern Theological Seminary **CAREER** Minister of Youth Activities, First Baptist Church, AR, 85-88; Minister of Youth Activities, Eastern Hills Baptist Church, AL, 88-90; Teaching Fel, Southwestern Baptist Theological Seminary, TX, 92-95; Adj Prof of New Testament, Southwestern Bapt Theol Sem, TXm 96; Assoc Prof of Christian Stud, Calif Bapt Univ, CA, 96-. **HONORS AND AWARDS** Faculty of the Year, 97 and 98. **MEMBERSHIPS** AAR/SBL; Inst for Biblical Research; In Service Guidance Assoc. **RESEARCH** Messianic Secrecy **CONTACT ADDRESS** California Baptist Col, 8432 Magnolia Ave, Riverside, CA 92504. **EMAIL** dwilson@calbaptist.edu

WILSON, DONALD E.
PERSONAL Born 01/04/1931, Corbin, KY, m, 1953, 3 children **DISCIPLINE** HISTORY, POLITICAL SCIENCE **EDUCATION** Univ Louisville, BA, 53; WVa Univ, MA, 61; Univ Denver, PhD, 79. **CAREER** Off, US Air Force, 53-79; From Fac to Prof, Samford Univ, 79-. **HONORS AND AWARDS** Phi Kappa Phi; Phi Alpha Theta; Pi Gamma Mu. **MEMBERSHIPS** SHA, Ala Asn Historians, NAS. **RESEARCH** Military history, World War II, the air war, Vietnam. **SELECTED PUBLICATIONS** Auth, In Search of Patriots in World War II Britain, Samford UP, 98. **CONTACT ADDRESS** Dept Hist & Polit Sci, Samford Univ, 800 Lakeshore Dr, Birmingham, AL 35229-0001. **EMAIL** dewilson@samford.edu

WILSON, EVELYN
PERSONAL Born 07/07/1949, Packersburg, WV, m, 1983, 2 children **DISCIPLINE** LAW **EDUCATION** Oberlin Col, AB, 71; Univ Utah, MS, 75; Paul M Hebert Law Center, JD, 83. **CAREER** Vesting Asst Prof, Washington and Lee Univ Law School, 88-89; Asst Prof to Assoc Prof, Southern Univ, 86-. **MEMBERSHIPS** La State Bar Asn, Am Bar Asn **RESEARCH** Federal Court Jurisdiction; Civil Rights History. **SELECTED PUBLICATIONS** Auth, "Finding Our Way Through the affirmative Action Debate, 96; auth, "Black men Killing Black Men," B.R. Pos, 95; auth, "The Right to Institute Proceedings," in due Process of Law, 94; auth, "Time out; Give Black Men a Break!," B.R. Post, 94 **CONTACT ADDRESS** School of Law, So Univ and A&M Col, PO Box 9294, Baton Rouge, LA 70813-5000.

WILSON, HOLLY
DISCIPLINE PHILOSOPHY **EDUCATION** Vanderbilt Univ, BA, 79; Pa State Univ, MA, 84; PhD, 89. **CAREER** Asst prof, Marquette Univ, 88-96; adj prof, Mundelein Sem, 96-97; asst prof, Northeast LA Univ, 97-. **HONORS AND AWARDS** PBK. **MEMBERSHIPS** Am Philos Asn; N Am Kant Soc; Soc for Women in Philos; Soc for Phenomenol and Existential Philos. **RESEARCH** Kant; Hermeneutics; Feminist Philosophy; Ethics. **SELECTED PUBLICATIONS** Auth, Gadamer's Alleged Conservatism, Selected Studies in Phenomenol and Existential Philos, 96; Kant's Integration and Morality, Kantstudien, 97; Kant and Ecofeminism, Ecofeminism: Women, Culture, Nature, 97; Rethinking Kant from the Perspective of Ecofeminism, Feminist Interpretation of Kant, 97; Kant's Evolutionary Theory of Marriage, Autonomy and Community: readings in Contemporary Kantian Soc Philos, forthcoming. **CONTACT ADDRESS** Dept of History & Govt, Univ of Louisiana, Monroe, Monroe, LA 71209. **EMAIL** hiwilson@ulm.edu

WILSON, JACK HOWARD
PERSONAL Born 02/11/1935, Lenoir City, TN **DISCIPLINE** NEW TESTAMENT **EDUCATION** Univ Tenn, BA, 56; Emory Univ, BD, 58, PhD, 62. **CAREER** ASSOC PROF RELIG, TENN WESLEYAN COL, 62-65, PROF, 65-80. **MEMBERSHIPS** Soc Bibl Lit; Am Acad Relig. **SELECTED PUBLICATIONS** Auth, The Corinthians who say there is no resurrection of the dead, Z Neutestamentliche Wiss, 68. **CONTACT ADDRESS** Virtue Rd, Lenoir City, TN 37771.

WILSON, JEFFREY R.
PERSONAL 3 children **DISCIPLINE** ECONOMICS **EDUCATION** University of West Indies, St Augustine, W.I., BA, Mathematics, 1977; Iowa State University, Ames, IA, MS, Statistics 1980, PhD, Statistics, 1984. **CAREER** Iowa State Univ, Ames, IA, graduate research asst, 80-83; Oklahoma State Univ, Stillwater, OK, visiting asst prof of statistics, 83-84; Arizona State Univ, Tempe, AZ, asst prof of statistics, 85-91, assoc prof of statistics, Dir of Interdisciplinary Program in Statistics, Prof of Economics, currently. **HONORS AND AWARDS** Teaching Awd, Golden Key Honor Society, Arizona State University; Faculty Research Development Awd, College of Business, AZ, 1990; Outstanding Graduate Teaching Awd, College of Business, AZ, 1986; Distinguished Service Awd, Minority Student Affairs, Ames, IA, Iowa State Univ, 1983, Final Year Book Prize, Math & Econ, Univ of West Indies, 1977; Mathematics Scholarship, Univ of West Indies, 1974-77; George Washington Carver Achievement Awd, Iowa State Alumni Assn, 1995. **MEMBERSHIPS** American Statistical Association, 1980; Royal Statistical Society, 1985. **CONTACT ADDRESS** Economics, Col of Bus, Arizona State Univ, Tempe, AZ 85287-3806. **EMAIL** jeffrey.wilson@asu.edu

WILSON, JOE BRANSFORD, JR.
DISCIPLINE SOUTH ASIAN STUDIES, RELIGIOUS STUDIES **EDUCATION** Univ Wis, Madison, BA, MA; Univ Va, PhD. **CAREER** Assoc prof Philos and Relig, asst ch and chair-elect, dept Philos and Relig, Univ NC, Wilmington. **RESEARCH** Yogacara School of Buddhism. **SELECTED PUBLICATIONS** Auth, Translating Buddhism from Tibetan: An Introduction to the Language of Literary Tibetan and the Study of Philosophy in Tibetan, Snow Lion, 92; Problems and Methods in the Translation of Buddhist Texts from Tibetan, in Buddhist Translations: Problems and Perspectives, Tibet House, 95; Tibetan Commentaries on Indian Shastras, in Jose Cabezon and Roger Jackson, eds, Tibetan Literature: Studies in Genre, Snow Lion, 96; Persons, Minds, and Actions: Indo-Tibetan Analyses of the Person in Anglo-American Perspective, in Ninian Smart and B Srinivasa Murthy, eds, East-West Encounters in Philosophy and Religion, Popular Prakashan, 96; The Monk as Bodhisattva: a Tibetan Integration of Buddhist Moral Points of View,

J of Relig Ethics 24.2, 96. **CONTACT ADDRESS** Univ of No Carolina, Wilmington, Bear Hall, Wilmington, NC 28403-3297. **EMAIL** wilsonj@uncwil.edu

WILSON, JOHN ELBERT
PERSONAL m, 3 children **DISCIPLINE** CHURCH HISTORY **EDUCATION** Emory Univ, BA, 64; Drew Univ, MDiv, 67; Claremont Grad Univ, PhD, 75. **CAREER** PD, church hist, Univ of Basel, Switzerland, 83-84; PROF OF CHURCH HIST, PITTSBURGH THEOLOGICAL SEMINARY, 84-. **MEMBERSHIPS** Am Acad of Relig; Am Soc of Church Hist; Int Schelling Soc. **SELECTED PUBLICATIONS** Auth, Schellings Mythologie. Zur Auslegung der Philosophie der Mythologie und der Offenbarung, Frommann-Holzboog, 93; auth, Schelling und Nietzsche. Zur Auslegung der freuhen Werke Friedrich Nietzsches, W. de Gruyter, 96. **CONTACT ADDRESS** Pittsburgh Theol Sem, 616 N Highland Ave, Pittsburgh, PA 15206-2596. **EMAIL** jwilson@pts.edu

WILSON, JOHN FREDERICK
PERSONAL Born 04/01/1933, Ipswich, MA, m, 1954, 4 children **DISCIPLINE** AMERICAN RELIGIOUS HISTORY **EDUCATION** Harvard Col, AB, 54; Union Theol Sem, NYork, MDiv, 57, PhD, 62. **CAREER** Lectr relig, Barnard Col, 57-58; from instrto prof, 60-77,asst dean, 65-72, chmn dept, 74-81, COLLORD PROF RELIG, PRINCETON UNIV, 77-, dean of graduate school, 94-; Mem bd dirs, Union Theol Sem, NY, 77-. **HONORS AND AWARDS** Guggenheim Fellowship, 99. **MEMBERSHIPS** AHA; Am Soc Church Hist (pres, 76); Soc Values Higher Educ; Asn Document Editing; Am Studies Asn. **RESEARCH** Puritan studies; religion in American history; Jonathan Edwards. **SELECTED PUBLICATIONS** Auth, Pulpit in Parliament, 69; auth, Public Religion in American Culture, 79; ed, Jonathan Edwards: A History of the Work of Redemption, 89; auth, The Churching of America, 1776-1990, J Church and State, Vol 0035, 93; When Time Shall be no More, J Interdisciplinary Hist, Vol 0024, 94; A New Denominational Historiography + The Importance of Continuing Study of Denominations for American Religious History, Relig and Amer Culture J of Int, Vol 0005, 95; Cosmos in the Chaos, Theol Today, Vol 0053, 96; Religious Melancholy and Protestant Experience in America, J Interdisciplinary Hist, Vol 0026, 96; The Politics of Revelation and Reason, J Interdisciplinary Hist, Vol 0028, 97. **CONTACT ADDRESS** Dept of Relig, Princeton Univ, 13 1879 Hall, Princeton, NJ 08544. **EMAIL** jfwilson@princeton.edu

WILSON, JONATAN R.
DISCIPLINE BIBLICAL AND CONTEMPORARY THEOLOGY **EDUCATION** Duke Univ, PhD, 89. **CAREER** Sr pastor, Edmonds Baptist Church, 80-86; lectr, Duke Univ, 87; adj asst, Fuller Theol Sem Extension, 91, 94; assoc prof, Westmont Col, 89-. **HONORS AND AWARDS** Tchr yr, 93. **RESEARCH** Ethics. **SELECTED PUBLICATIONS** Auth, Living Faithfully in a Fragmented World. Trinity Press International, 97; Theology as Cultural Critique: The Achievement of Julian Hartt, Mercer UP, 96; Toward a Trinitarian Rule of Worship, CRUX 29/2, 93. **CONTACT ADDRESS** Dept of Rel, Westmont Col, 955 La Paz Rd, Santa Barbara, CA 93108-1099.

WILSON, JOSEPH F.
PERSONAL Born 12/02/1951, Chicago, IL, m, 1984 **DISCIPLINE** POLITICAL SCIENCE **EDUCATION** Columbia College, New York, NYork, BA, 1973; Columbia University, New York, NYork, MA, 1975, MPh, 1978, PhD, 1980. **CAREER** Rutgers University, New Brunswick, NJ, assistant professor, 80-86; Brooklyn College, Brooklyn, NY, associate professor, 86-94, prof, 94-; Brooklyn Coll Center for Diversity and Multicultural Education, currently. **HONORS AND AWARDS** Distinguished Tow Professor of Political Science, 1993-95. **MEMBERSHIPS** Director, Brooklyn College Multicultural Center, 1990-95; appoints committee, Political Sceince Dept, 1989-95; executive committee, Black Faculty & Staff Association, 1987-95. **SELECTED PUBLICATIONS** Author, Tearing Down the Color Bar, Columbia University Press, 1989, The Re-education of The American Working Class, Greenwood Press, 1990, Black Labor in America, Greenwood Press, 1986. **CONTACT ADDRESS** Political Science Dept, Brooklyn Col, CUNY, James Hall, Brooklyn, NY 11210.

WILSON, KENT
DISCIPLINE PHILOSOPHY **EDUCATION** Univ Pittsburgh, PhD, 69. **CAREER** Assoc prof, Univ IL at Chicago . **RESEARCH** Philos of lang; metaphysics; lang and mind; linguistic theory; philosophical logic; epistemology. **SELECTED PUBLICATIONS** Auth, Some Reflections on the Prosentential Theory of Truth, D. Reidel, 90; Comment on Jim Mackenzie, Peter of Spain, and Begging the Question, Jour Philos Logic, 92; co-auth, The Intentional Fallacy: Defending Beardsley, Jour Aesthet Art Criticism, 95; co-ed, Philosophical Logic, D. Reidel, 69. **CONTACT ADDRESS** Philos Dept, Univ of Illinois, Chicago, S Halsted St, PO Box 705, Chicago, IL 60607. **EMAIL** kentw@uic.edu

WILSON, KIM ADAIR
PERSONAL Born 09/04/1956, New York, NY, d **DISCIPLINE** LAW **EDUCATION** Boston College, BA cum laude, 1978; Hofstra University School of Law, JD, 82. **CAREER** New York City Department of Investigation, investigative attorney, 86-89; New York State Supreme Court, Court Attorney, 89-. **HONORS AND AWARDS** New York Association of Black Psychologists, The Nelson Mandela International Citizen of the Year Awd, 94; National Bar Association, Outstanding Bar Association Affiliate Chapter Awd, 95; The Judicial Friends, The Jane Matilda Bolin Awd, 96. **MEMBERSHIPS** National Bar Association, bd of governors, 95-99; New York State Bar Association, house of delegates, 94-97; Metropolitan Black Bar Association, 94-96. **SELECTED PUBLICATIONS** Co-author: "Affirmative Action Can Help Create Tradition of Excellence," New York Law Journal, May 95; "US Constitution and its Meaning to the African-American Community," National Bar Association Magazine, Volume 10, No 4, pp 3 & 30; Author of book review, Affirmative Action, Race & American Values, published my book review, New York Law Journal, Jan 10, 97. **CONTACT ADDRESS** New York State Supreme Court, Bronx County, 851 Grand Concourse, Ste 217, Bronx, NY 10451.

WILSON, ROBERT
DISCIPLINE PHILOSOPHY **EDUCATION** Cornell Univ, PhD, 92. **CAREER** Asst Prof, Univ Ill Urbana Champaign. **HONORS AND AWARDS** Am Assoc of Pub, Psychology Prize, 99. **RESEARCH** Philosophy of mind; philosophy of science; cognitive science. **SELECTED PUBLICATIONS** Auth, Cartesian Psychology and Physical Minds, Cambridge, 95; auth, The Induvidual in Biology and Psychology, Cambridge, MA: MIT Press, 99; ed, Species: New Interdisciplinary Essays, Cambridge, MA: MIT Press, 99; ed, The MIT Encyclopedia of the Cognitive Sciences, Cambridge, MA: MIT Press, 99, auth, "The Mind Beyond Itself," Metarepresentation, New York: Oxford Univ Press, (00); ed, Explanation and Cognition, Cambridge, MA: MIT Press, (00). **CONTACT ADDRESS** Philosophy Dept, Univ of Illinois, Urbana-Champaign, 52 E Gregory Dr, Champaign, IL 61820. **EMAIL** rwilson@uiuc.edu

WILSON, SAMUEL S.
PERSONAL Born 08/11/1924, Cincinnati, OH, 4 children **DISCIPLINE** LAW **EDUCATION** Princeton Univ, AB, 47; Univ Cincinnati, JD, 61. **CAREER** Reporter, Cincinnati Times-Star, 47-52, Washington corresp, 52-56, asst city ed, 56-57, assoc ed, 57-58; atty, Nieman, Aug, Elder & Jacobs, Ohio, 61-65; assoc prof law, 65-68, actg dean col law, 69-70, prof to prof emer, Univ of Cincinnati, 68-, dean, Col of Law, 74-. **MEMBERSHIPS** Am Bar Asn. **RESEARCH** Constitutional law; civil procedure; real property. **SELECTED PUBLICATIONS** Auth, Rutter, Irvin, C.--in Memoriam, Univ Cincinnati Law Rev, Vol 0061, 93. **CONTACT ADDRESS** Col of Law, Univ of Cincinnati, PO Box 210040, Cincinnati, OH 45221-0040.

WILSON, VICTOR M.
PERSONAL Born 07/27/1946, Padhlam, England, m, 1973, 2 children **DISCIPLINE** BIBLICAL STUDIES AND RHETORICAL CRITICISM **EDUCATION** Barton Col, BA (summa cum laude), 76; Princeton Theol Seminary, MDiv, 79; Emory Univ, DMin, 92. **CAREER** Adjunct prof, Barton Col, 82-83; lectr, Eastern Theological Seminary, 93-94; PASTOR, ST. JOHN'S PRESBYTERIAN CHURCH, 92-. **HONORS AND AWARDS** Friar Alumni Awd, Princeton Seminary; Nat Acad Honor Soc; Who's Who in Am Col and Univ; Nat Soc Sci Honor Soc; Am Bible Soc Awd. **MEMBERSHIPS** Soc of Biblical Lit; Catholic Biblical Asn. **RESEARCH** Rhetorical Criticism of Biblical and Ancient Classical Literature. **SELECTED PUBLICATIONS** Auth, Divine Symmetries: The Art of Biblical Rhetoric, 97. **CONTACT ADDRESS** St. John's Presbyterian Church, PO Box 399, Devon, PA 19333-0399. **EMAIL** vmwswd@aol.com

WILSON, WILLIE FREDERICK
PERSONAL Born 03/08/1944, Newport News, VA, m, 1973 **DISCIPLINE** THEOLOGY **EDUCATION** Ohio Univ, BS, 1966; Howard Univ, Divinity School, MDiv, 1969; Doctoral Studies, 1969-71. **CAREER** Union Temple Baptist Church, pastor, 73-. **HONORS AND AWARDS** USA Today, Top 10 Most Valuable People in USA, 1985; US Presidential Svc Awd, 1997; Natl Congress of Black Churchmen, One of 100 Model African American Churches in America. **MEMBERSHIPS** Brd of Trustees, Univ of the District of Columbia. **SELECTED PUBLICATIONS** Auth, Releasing the Power Within Through Spiritual Dynamics -- The Genius of Jesus Revealed. Publication, "The African American Wedding Manual"; Ordained as WOLOF priest in Gambia, West Africa, 1980; enstated as Ashanti subchief in Ghana, 1993. **CONTACT ADDRESS** Pastor, Union Temple Baptist Church, 1225 W Street SE, Washington, VT 20020.

WIMBERLY, EDWARD P.
PERSONAL Born 10/22/1943, THE, PA, m, 1966 **DISCIPLINE** THEOLOGY **EDUCATION** Univ of Arizona, BA, 1965; Boston Univ, School of Theology, STB, 1968, STM, 1971; Boston Univ Graduate School, PhD, 1976. **CAREER** Emmanuel Church, pastor, 66-68; St Andrews United Methodist Church, pastor, 68-74; Worcester Council of Churches, urban minister, 69-72; Solomon Carter Fuller Mental Health Center, pastoral consultant, 73-75; Interdenominational Theological Center, Atlanta, assoc professor, 75-83; Oral Roberts Univ, School of Theology, Tulsa, assoc professor, assoc dean, doctoral studies, 83-85; Garrett Evangelical Theological Seminary, Evanston, IL, assoc professor, pastoral care, 85-. **HONORS AND AWARDS** Serv award, United Methodist Children's Home, 1983. **MEMBERSHIPS** Bd of dirs, United Methodist Children's Home, 1977-83, Interdenominational Theological Center, 1982-83; mem, Amer Assn of Pastoral Counselors, 1976-, Amer Assn of Marriage & Family Therapists, 1976-, Friends of Wesley Comm Center, 1983-; mem & bd of dirs, Destination Discovery, 1983-. **SELECTED PUBLICATIONS** Auth, "Pastoral Counseling and Spiritual Values," 1982; co-author with Anne Wimberly, "Liberation and Human Wholeness," 1986; co-author with wife, "One House One Hope," 1989. **CONTACT ADDRESS** Dept Relig, Interdenominational Theol Ctr, 700 MLK Jr Dr SW, Atlanta, GA 30314-4143.

WIMBUSH, VINCENT L.
DISCIPLINE RELIGION **EDUCATION** Harvard Univ, MA, PhD. **CAREER** Prof. **SELECTED PUBLICATIONS** Ed, Ascetic Behavior in Greco-Roman Antiquity: A Sourcebook, 90; Discursive Formations, Ascetic Piety, and the Interpretation of Early Christian Literature, 92; co-ed, Asceticism. **CONTACT ADDRESS** Dept of Religion, Columbia Col, New York, 2960 Broadway, New York, NY 10027-6902. **EMAIL** vw7@columbia.edu

WINDLEY-DAOUST, SUSAN M.
DISCIPLINE RELIGION **EDUCATION** MA, 91, PhD, 98, Vanderbilt Univ. **CAREER** Asst Prof, Theology, Univ of St. Thomas **MEMBERSHIPS** Am Academy of Religion, Catholic Theological Society of Am **CONTACT ADDRESS** Univ of St. Thomas, Minnesota, 2115 Summit Ave., Saint Paul, MN 55105. **EMAIL** smwindley@stthomas.edu

WINFREE, L. THOMAS, JR
PERSONAL Born 12/02/1946, Wytheville, VA, m, 1969, 1 child **DISCIPLINE** SOCIOLOGY, CRIMINAL JUSTICE **EDUCATION** Univ Richmond, BA, 68; Va Commonwealth Univ, MS, 74; Univ Mont, PhD, 76. **CAREER** Vis instr, Univ NMex, 75-76; asst prof, East Tex State Univ, 76-79; asst prof to assoc prof, La State Univ, 79-87; assoc prof to prof, NMex State Univ, 87-. **HONORS AND AWARDS** Alpha Kappa Delta; Fel in Criminology and Deviant Behavior, Nat Inst of Mental Health; Who's Who in the South and Southwest; Who's Who in Am Law. **MEMBERSHIPS** Am Soc of Criminology, Acad of Criminal Justice Scis, Am Sociol Asn. **RESEARCH** Juvenile delinquency, youth gangs, American prison and jails. **SELECTED PUBLICATIONS** Co-ed, Expert Witnesses: Criminologists in the Courtroom, Albany, NY: State Univ of NY Press (87); coauth, Crime and Justice: An Introduction, 2nd ed, Chicago: Nelson Hall, Inc (92); coauth, Understanding Crime: Theory and Practice, Chicago: Nelson Hall, Inc (96); coauth, Contemporary Corrections: California: ITP/West/Wadsworth (98); coauth, Juvenile Justice, NY: McGraw-Hill (2000); coauth, "On classifying driving-whole-intoxicated offenders: The experiences of a city-wide D.W.I. Drug court," J of Criminal Justice, 28, 1 (2000): 1-9; coauth, "Exploring gang membership between Hispanic & youth in two southwestern cities," The Soc Sci J (forthcoming); coauth, "Drunk drivers, DWI 'drug court' treatment and recidivism: Who fails?," Justice Res and Policy (forthcoming). **CONTACT ADDRESS** Dept Criminal Justice, New Mexico State Univ, msc 3487, Las Cruces, NM 88003. **EMAIL** twinfree@nmsu.edu

WING, ADRIEN KATHERINE
PERSONAL Born 08/07/1956, Oceanside, CA, d **DISCIPLINE** LAW **EDUCATION** Newark Academy, HS, 1974; Princeton, AB, 1978; UCLA, MA, 1979; Stanford Law School, JD, 1982. **CAREER** Upward Bound, UCLA, teacher/counselor, 79; Rosenfeld, Meyer & Susman, law clerk, 80; United Nations, intern, 81; Curtis, Mallet, et al, lawyer, 82-86; Rabinowitz, Boudin, et al, lawyer, 86-87; University of Iowa Law School, professor of law, 87-. **HONORS AND AWARDS** Haywood Burns-Shanara Gilbert Award, 1997; National Conference of Black Lawyers, Hope Stevens Award, 1988; numerous others. **MEMBERSHIPS** Natl Conf of Black Lawyers, intl chair, 1985-95; Transafrica Forum Scholars Council, 1993-95; Assn of Black Princeton Alumni Bd, 1982-87; Stanford Law School , bd of visitors, 1993-96; American Soc of Intl Law, Southern Africa interest group chair, 1994-95; Council on Foreign Relations, life member, 1993-; Natl Black Law Students Assn, bd of directors, 1981-82, American Friends Service Comm, Middle East Programs Bd 1998-2000; American Assn of Law Schools Minority Section Executive Comm 1997-; Intl Third World Legal Studies Assn Bd 1996-, Princeton Comm to Nominate Trustees 1997-00, Princeton Alumni Council 1996-2000, Iowa Peace Institute Bd 1993-95; Iowa City Foreign Relations Council Bd 1989-94; Palestine Human Rights Campaigns Bd 1986-91; American Soc of Intl Law Executive Council 1986-89, 1996-99, Executive Comm 1998-99; American Bar Assn, American Branch Intl Law Assn, Natl Bar Assn, Soc of

American Law Teachers; Bd of editors' American Journal of Comparative Law. **SELECTED PUBLICATIONS** Over 40 publications including: Democracy, Constitutionalism & Future State of Palestine, Jerusalem, 1994; "Rape, Ethnicity, Culture", Critical Race Theory Reader, Temple Univ, 1995; "Weep Not Little Ones", in African Americans & the Living Constitution, Smithsonian, 1995; Editor of Critical Race Feminism: A Reader, NYU, 1997; Languages: French, Swahili, Portuguese; auth, Global Critical Race Feminism: An International Reader, NYU Press, 00. **CONTACT ADDRESS** College of Law, The Univ of Iowa, Melrose and Bylington, Iowa City, IA 52242. **EMAIL** adrien-wing@uiowa.edu

WININGER, KATHLEEN J.
PERSONAL Born 10/19/1953, Bridgeport, CT, 1 child **DISCIPLINE** PHILOSOPHY **EDUCATION** Southern Conn State Univ, BA, 77; Temple Univ, PhD, 88. **CAREER** Asst Prof, Univ S Maine, 89-. **MEMBERSHIPS** RPA, APA, NANS, SWP, ASA, AAWS. **RESEARCH** Philosophy of culture. **SELECTED PUBLICATIONS** Auth, Nietzsche's Reclamation of Philosophy, Rodopi Pr (Amsterdam), 97; auth, Philosophy and Sex, Prometheus Books (Amherst, NY), 98; auth, "Friedrich Nietzsche," Makers of Western Cult 1800-1914: A Biog Dict of Lit Influences, Greenwood Pr (99); auth, "Ida B Wells," Makers of Western Cult 1800-1914: A Biog Dict of Lit Influences, Greenwood Pr (99); auth, "Women Appropriating, Women Appropriated: A Neo-Colonial Encounter," Beyond Poetry: Ways and Means Out of the Current Stalemate (99); auth, "Following African Identity in Bessie Head: An Exiles Philosophical Journey," Int Conf on Women in Higher Educ Proceedings (00). **CONTACT ADDRESS** Dept Philos, Univ of So Maine, PO Box 9300, Portland, ME 04104-9300. **EMAIL** wininger@maine.edu

WININGS, KATHY
PERSONAL Born 04/04/1953, Indianapolis, IN, s **DISCIPLINE** RELIGION & EDUCATION **EDUCATION** Fordham Univ, BA, 86; Unification Theol Seminary, MRE/MDiv, 87; Teachers Col, EdD, 96. **CAREER** Asst Prof. Unification Theol Seminary, 90-, Dir DMin Prog, 97-; Exec Dir, Int Relief Friendship Found, 94-; Dir, Nat Youth Ministry, 97-; Pres, Educare. **HONORS AND AWARDS** Kappa Delta Pi. **MEMBERSHIPS** APRRE; REA; Natl Asn Ecumenical Staff. **RESEARCH** Education - curriculum & teaching; ministry; service learning. **SELECTED PUBLICATIONS** Ed, contrib, Understanding the Church of the Latter-Day Saints, Christian Traditions in America; The Role of Religion in Promoting World Peace, World Univ Times; auth, "Campus Ministry and New Paradigms for Educating Religiously," Relig Educ J; auth, Building Character Through Service Learning (forthcoming). **CONTACT ADDRESS** 177 White Plains Rd., Tarrytown, NY 10591. **EMAIL** IRFFint@aol.com

WINK, WALTER
PERSONAL Born 05/21/1935, Dallas, TX, m, 1979, 3 children **DISCIPLINE** NEW TESTAMENT STUDIES **EDUCATION** Southern Methodist Univ, BA, 56; Union Theol Sem, MDiv, 59, PhD, 63. **CAREER** Pastor, United Methodist Church, Hitchcock, Tex, 62-67; asst prof New Testament, 67-70, assoc prof New Testament, 70-76, Union Theol Sem, NYC; prof bibl interpretation, Auburn Theol Sem, 76- . **HONORS AND AWARDS** Magna Cum Laude, 56; Peace fel, US Inst of Peace, 89. **MEMBERSHIPS** Am Acad Relig; Soc for Bibl Lit; Studiorum Novi Testamenti Societas. **SELECTED PUBLICATIONS** Auth, Naming the Powers, Fortress, 84; auth, Unmasking the Powers, Fortress, 86; auth, Violence and Nonviolence in South Africa, Fortress, 87; auth, Engaging the Powers, Fortress, 92; auth, Cracking the Gnostic Code: The Powers in Gnosticism, Scholars, 93; auth, Proclamation 5: Holy Week, Year B, Fortress, 93; auth, Healing a Nation's Wounds: Reconciliation on the Road to Democracy, Sweden, Life and Peace Inst, 97; auth, The Third Way: Reclaiming Jesus' Nonviolent Alternative, Netherlands, Int Fel of Reconciliation, 97; auth, The Powers That Be, Doubleday, 98; auth, When the Powers Fall: Reconciliation on the Road to Democracy, Fortress, 98; ed, Homosexuality and Christian Faith, Fortress, 99; ed, Peace is the Way, Orbis, 00. **CONTACT ADDRESS** Auburn Theol Sem, 3041 Broadway, New York, NY 10027. **EMAIL** wwink@bcn.net

WINKLER, KENNETH P.
PERSONAL Born 10/25/1950, Rockville Center, NY, m, 1997, 2 children **DISCIPLINE** PHILOSOPHY **EDUCATION** Trinity Col, BA, 71; Univ Texas, PhD, 77. **CAREER** Prof Philos, Wellesley Col, 78-; vis prof Philos, Brown Univ, 01, Harvard Summer School, 92, 95, 96; vis lctr, MIT, 94; vis prof, Brandeis Univ, 92; lctr, Harvard Univ Extension, 91-92, 83-85; lctr, UCLA, 80; vis asst prof, UCLA, 78; asst prof, Kalamazoo Col, 77-78; inst, SUNY Gereseo, 75-77. **HONORS AND AWARDS** NEH Fel, 94-95; ACLS Fel, 89-90; Andrew W. Mellon Fac Fel, Harvard Univ, 82-83; Phi Beta Kappa, 71. **MEMBERSHIPS** Amer Philos Assoc **RESEARCH** Early Modern Philosophy **SELECTED PUBLICATIONS** Ed, John Locke, An Essay Concerning Human Understanding, Hackett, 96; Locks on Personal Identity, Jour History of Philos, 91; auth, "The New Home," Phil Rev (91); auth, Berkeley: An Interpretation, Oxford Pr, 89. **CONTACT ADDRESS** Dept of Philosophy, Wellesley Col, Wellesley, MA 02481. **EMAIL** kwinkler@wellesley.edu

WINSTON, DIANE
DISCIPLINE RELIGION **EDUCATION** Princeton Univ, PhD, 96. **CAREER** Prog Off, Relig Pew Charitable Trusts. **MEMBERSHIPS** AAR; SSSR; ASCH; OAH; ASA. **RESEARCH** American religious history; religion and media; religion and higher education. **SELECTED PUBLICATIONS** Auth, Red Hot and Righteous: The Urban Religion of the Salvation Army, Harvard University Press, 99. **CONTACT ADDRESS** Pew Charitable Trusts, 2005 Market Street, 1 Commerce Square, Philadelphia, PA 19103. **EMAIL** dwinston@pewtrusts.com

WINSTON, KENNETH IRWIN
PERSONAL Born 06/17/1940, Boston, MA, m, 1975 **DISCIPLINE** LEGAL PHILOSOPHY **EDUCATION** Harvard Univ, BA, 62; Columbia Univ, MA, 68, PhD(philos), 70. **CAREER** Instr philos, Columbia Univ, 68-69; asst prof, 69-76, assoc prof, 76-82, prof Philos, Wheaton Col, MA, 82-98; LECTURER IN ETHICS, HARVARD UNIV, 98-; Am Coun Learned Soc study fel & res fel, Ctr Study Law & Soc, Berkeley, CA, 72-73; vis asst prof, Brown Univ, 75; lectr educ, Harvard Univ, 78-79; Nat Endowment for Humanities fel & vis scholar, Harvard Law Sch, 80-81. **HONORS AND AWARDS** John Dewey Sr Fel, 84-85; A. Howard Meneely Prof, Wheaton Col, 96-98. **MEMBERSHIPS** Eastern Div Am Philos Asn; Conf Study Polit Thought; Soc Philos & Pub Affairs; Am Soc Polit & Legal Philos. **RESEARCH** Philosophy of law; practical ethics. **SELECTED PUBLICATIONS** Auth, On Treating Like Cases Alike, CA Law Rev, 1/74; Self-incrimination in Context, Southern CA Law Rev, 3/75; Taking Dworkin Seriously, Harvard Civil Rights/Civil Lib Law Rev, 4/78; ed, The Principles of Social Order: Selected Essays of Lon L Fuller, Duke Univ, 81; auth, Toward a Liberal Conception of Legislation, In: Liberal Democracy, New York Univ Press, 82; ed, The Responsible Judge: Readings in Judicial Ethics, with John T. Noonan, Jr, Praeger, 93; ed, Gender and Public Policy: Cases and Comments, with Mary Jo Bane, Westview, 93; auth, Teaching With Cases, in Teaching Criminal Justice Ethics, ed, J. Kleinig and M. L. Smith, Anderson, 97; Moral Opportunism: A Case Study, in Integrity and Conscience, ed, I. Shapiro and R. M. Adams, NYU, 98; auth, Three Models for the Study of Law, in Rediscovering Fuller, ed. W. Witteveen and W. van der Burg, Amsterdam Univ, 99; auth, Constructing Law's Mandate, in Recrafting the Rule of Law, ed. D. Dyzenhaus, Hart Pub, 99. **CONTACT ADDRESS** Kennedy School of Government, Harvard Univ, 79 J. F. K. Street, Cambridge, MA 02138. **EMAIL** kenneth_winston@harvard.edu

WINSTON, MORTON E.
PERSONAL Born 01/16/1949, Philadelphia, PA, m, 1971, 3 children **DISCIPLINE** PHILOSPHY **EDUCATION** Swarthmore College, BA 70; Univ IL, MA 72; Phd 78. **CAREER** Dept of Philosophy and Religion, College of New Jersey. **HONORS AND AWARDS** Co-dir, Core Course: Soc, Ethics, Tech; Adv, TCNJ Amnesty Int; Former Ch, Fac Res Leave Comt; Dept Philos & Relig; Ch, Board dir, Amnesty Intl USA; Fulbright Fel S Africa; Fulbright Senior Scholar, Thailand 99-00; Fulbright Senior Scholar, South Africa, 92-93; Chair, Board of Directors, Amnesty International USA; Phi Beta Kappa; Phi Kappa Phi. **MEMBERSHIPS** Am Philosophical Assoc. **RESEARCH** Human rights theory; biomedical ethics; business and professional ethics; philosophy of technology. **SELECTED PUBLICATIONS** Auth, Prospects for a Revaluation of Academic Values, in Joseph Moxley, ed, The Processes and Politics of Scholarly Publication, NY: Greenwood Press, 95; An Emergency Response System for the International Community: Commentary on The Politics of Rescue, Ethics and International Affairs, vol 11, 97; The Prevention of Institutionalized Intergroup Violence, Health and Human Rights, vol 2, no 3, July 97; ed, with Ralph Edelbach, Society, Ethics, and Technology, Belmont, CA: Wadsworth Pub Co, 00. **CONTACT ADDRESS** Dept of Philosophy and Religion, The Col of New Jersey, PO Box 7718, Ewing, NJ 08628-0718. **EMAIL** mwinston@tcnj.edu

WINSTON SUTER, DAVID
PERSONAL Born 03/01/1942, Staunton, VA, m, 1978, 1 child **DISCIPLINE** NEW TESTAMENT **EDUCATION** Davidson Col, BA, 64; Univ Chicago, BD, 67; MA, 70, PhD, 77. **CAREER** Asst prof, Wichita State Univ, 74-81; Vis Asst prof, Pacific Lutheran Univ, 81-83; Assoc prof, Saint Martin's Col, 83-89; Prof, Saint Martin's Col, 89-. **HONORS AND AWARDS** Burlington Northern Found Awd , 90-91; The Commander's Certificate, 94; Nat Endowment Hum Summer Sem Col Tchrs: The Adam and Eve Narrative in Christian and Jewish Tradition, 96; dean, hum div, 91-97. **RESEARCH** Society of Biblical Lit, Antcient Judism. **SELECTED PUBLICATIONS** Auth, The Drama of Christian Theology in the Gospel of John, Jour Relig, 69; Apocalyptic Patterns in the Similitudes of Enoch, Scholars Press, 78; Fallen Angel, Fallen Priest: The Problem of Family Purity in 1 Enoch 6-16, Hebrew Union Col Annual, 79; Tradition and Composition, Scholars Press, 79; Masal in the Similitudes of Enoch, Jour Biblical Lit, 81; Weighed in the Balance: The Similitudes of Enoch in Recent Discussion, Relig Studies Rev, 81; The Measure of Redemption: The Similitudes of Enoch, Nonviolence, and National Integrity, Scholars Press, 83; Apocrypha, Old Testament, Baruch, the Book of, Bel and the Dragon, Daniel, the Additions to, Ecclesiasticus, Esdras, the First Book of, Esdras, the Second Book of, Esther, the Rest of the Book of, Gentile, Judith, The Letter of Jeremiah, Maccabees, the First Book of the, Maccabees, the Second Book of the, The Prayer of Manasseh, Pseudonym, The Song of the Three Children, Susanna, Theophany, Tobit, Vengeance, and The Wisdom of Solomon, Harper & Row, 85; Atmosphere as Antagonist: The Symbolism of Evil in Mark, Explorations: Jour Adventurous Thought, 89; Of the Devil's Party: The Marriage of Heaven and Hell in Satanic Verses, S Asian Rev, 92; Apocrypha, Old Testament, Baruch, the Book of, Bel and the Dragon, Daniel, the Additions to, Ecclesiasticus, Esdras, the First Book of, Esdras, the Second Book of, Esther, the Rest of the Book of, Gentile, Judith, The Letter of Jeremiah, Maccabees, the First Book of the, Maccabees, the Second Book of the, Maccabees, the Third Book of the, Maccabees, the Fourth Book of the, The Prayer of Manasseh, Psalm 151, Pseudonym, The Song of the Three Children, Susanna, Theophany, Tobit, Vengeance, and The Wisdom of Solomon, Harper San Francisco, 96. **CONTACT ADDRESS** Saint Martin's Col, 5300 Pacific Ave, Lacey, WA 98503-1297. **EMAIL** dsuter@stmartin.edu

WINT, ARTHUR VALENTINE NORIS
PERSONAL Born 10/26/1950, Kingston, Jamaica, m, 1971, 4 children **DISCIPLINE** CRIMINAL JUSTICE **EDUCATION** Washington State University, Pullman, WA, BA, 1973; University of Washington School of Law, Seattle, WA, JD, 1976; Harvard University, Institute for Educational Management, 1993. **CAREER** Evergreen Legal Services, Seattle, WA, legal asst, 76-77; City of Seattle, Seattle, WA, eo investigator, 77-79; Washington State Univ, Pullman, WA, dir of aff action, 79-86; California State Univ, Fresno, Fresno, CA, asst to the pres, dir of affirmative action, 86-92; Calif State Univ, Fresno, Exec Asst to Pres, 92-; Assoc Prof of Criminology, 91-; Prof, 00-. **HONORS AND AWARDS** Teaching Leadership Awd, NAACP, Fresno, 1989; Pew Teaching Awd, University of Washington, 1989; Senate Intern, Washington State Senate, 1972; Certificate, Harvard Univ, IEM, 93. **MEMBERSHIPS** Academy of Criminal Justice Sciences, American Association for Affirmative Action, director Region IX, 1990-91; Public Info Committee, 1988-90, director Region X, 1985-86; California Association of AA Officers, 1986-; board member, Golden Valley Girl Scouts, 1987-90; NAACP, 1976-; Church of Christ, 1975-; Central California Employment, round table, 1989-. **RESEARCH** Ethical consideration in restorative justice; child molestation and abuse: the service providers perspective; community assessment: alternative detention facility for juveniles; star children: class, caste and delinquency in Kingston, Jamaica. **SELECTED PUBLICATIONS** Coed, "Promoting Racial Harmony in Academe©For The Common Good," CSUF, 89; coauth, "The Status of Police Officers' Liability For Negligence Involving The Use Of Firearms," American Criminal Justice Association-Lambda Alpha Epsilon Journal, (94); auth, "Criminal Victimization and Its Effect on Fear of Crime and Justice Attitudes," Journal of Interpersonal Violence 12 (97): 748-58; auth, "There Is Power In The Blood," The Journal of Criminal Justice Education, (98); coauth, "Are Restorative Justice Processes Too Lenient toward Offenders?" in Fuller, J.R., and Hickey, E.W., Controversial Issues In Criminology (Boston: Allyn & Bacon), 99. **CONTACT ADDRESS** Dept of Criminology, California State Univ, Fresno, 2225 E San Ramon Ave m/s mc 104, Fresno, CA 93740-8029. **EMAIL** arthurw@csufresno.edu

WINTER, DOUGLAS E.
PERSONAL Born 10/30/1950, St. Louis, MO, m, 1977, 2 children **DISCIPLINE** LAW **EDUCATION** Univ Ill, BS, 71, MS, 72; Harvard Law Sch, JD, 75; US Army Judge Advocate General's Sch, Honor Grad, 77. **CAREER** Lieutenant, Military Intelligence, US Army, 73-76; Law Clerk, US Court Appeals 8th Circuit, 75-76; Assoc Atty, Covington & Burling, 76-77, 78-80, 81-84; Captain, Judge Advocate General Corps, US Army, 77; Vis Prof, Univ Iowa Col Law, 80-81; Assoc Atty, Bryan Cave McPheeters & McRoberts, 85-86; Partner Atty, 87-97, Bryan Cave LLP, Retired Partner Atty (Of Counsel), Bryan Cave LLP, 98-; Self-employed professional writer, 76-. **HONORS AND AWARDS** Nothern Va Festival of the Lit Arts Prize, 79; World Fantasy Awd winner, 86; Int Horror Awd winner, 95, 96, 98; Whitman-Walker Clinic Public Service Awd, 97. **MEMBERSHIPS** Am Bar Asn; member of bar associations of Mo, Ill, and DC; Nat Bk Critics Circle; Horror Writers Asn. **RESEARCH** Literature, film, popular culture. **SELECTED PUBLICATIONS** Auth, Stephen King, Starmont House, 82; Shadowings: The Reader's Guide to Horror Fiction, Starmont House, 83; Stephen King: The Art of Darkness, New Am Libr, 84; Faces of Fear, Berkeley, 85; ed, Black Wine, Dark Harvest, 86; auth, Splatter: A Cautionary Tale, Footsteps Press, 87; ed, Prime Evil, New Am Libr, 88; auth, Darkness Absolute, Pulphouse Press, 91; Black Sun, One Eyed Dog, 94; ed, Revelations, HarperCollins, 97; auth, Run, Alfred A Knopf, 00; auth, American Zombie, Borderlands Press (forthcoming 00); Clive Barker: The Dark Fantastic. HarperCollins (forthcoming 01); author of numerous articles and short fiction. **CONTACT ADDRESS** Bryan Cave LLP, 700 13th St. NW, Washington, DC 20005. **EMAIL** dewinter@bryancavellp.com

WINTER, JOHN ELLSWORTH
PERSONAL Born 10/26/1926, York, PA, m, 1982 **DISCIPLINE** PHILOSOPHY AND SOCIOLOGY **EDUCATION**

Juniata Col, BA, 50; Villanova Univ, MA, 63; Temple Univ, 69. **CAREER** York Col, PA, 58-63; Clarion Univ, PA, 63-64; Millersville Univ, PA, 64-77, 78-94; Univ of Vienna, Austria, 77-78; prof emer, Millersville Univ, 95- . **HONORS AND AWARDS** Coleman Awd; Outstanding Tchr of Amer. **MEMBERSHIPS** AAUP; Foundation of Thanatology; APSCUF; PA Phil Assn; Am Phil Assn; Hobbes Assn; Kierkegaard Soc **RESEARCH** Philosophical anthropology; humor; political theory. **SELECTED PUBLICATIONS** The New American Scholar, Oregon St Univ, 63; A New Theory of Election to Public Office in America, Chicago, 98. **CONTACT ADDRESS** Millersville Univ of Pennsylvania, PO Box 1002, Millersville, PA 17551-0302.

WINTER, RALPH A.
DISCIPLINE LAW **EDUCATION** Univ British Columbia, BA, 74; Univ Ca, MA, PhD, 79; B.Sc. From the Univ of British Columbia. **CAREER** Prof **SELECTED PUBLICATIONS** Auth, pubs on economics of competition policy, the theory of contracts, industrial organization and the interaction between the tort system and liability insurance markets; co-auth, Competition Policy and Vertical Exchange. **CONTACT ADDRESS** Fac of Law, Univ of Toronto, 78 Queen's Park, Toronto, ON, Canada M5S 1A1. **EMAIL** rwinter@chass.utoronto.ca

WINTERS, FRANCIS XAVIER
PERSONAL Born 10/12/1933, Roaring Spring, PA **DISCIPLINE** POLITICAL ETHICS, THEOLOGY **EDUCATION** Fordham Univ, AB, 58, MAT, 59, PhD, 73; Woodstock Col, PhL, 58, STB, 63, STL, 65. **CAREER** Instr Latin, English & Fr, Loyola High Sch, Baltimore, 58-61; instr philos, Loyola Col, Md, 66-67; instr Christian ethics, 70, asst prof & dean fac, 71-72, asst prof theol, 72-77, Woodstock Col; assoc prof theol, Sch Foreign Serv, Georgetown Univ, 77-, prof, 98; Trustee, Coun Relig & Int Affairs, 71-; mem bd dir, Wheeling Col, 72; trustee, Gonzaga High Sch, Washington, DC, 72-; consult ethics, Comn Orgn Govt Conduct Foreign Policy, 75-76; lectr ethics, Army War Col, Carlisle, Penn, 76-78, Foreign Serv Inst, US Dept State, 77. **HONORS AND AWARDS** Teacher of Year Awd, Sch Foreign Serv, Georgetown Univ, 78 & 82. **RESEARCH** Ethics and international relations; ethical theory; religion in America. **SELECTED PUBLICATIONS** Auth, Nuclear Deterrence Morality: Atlantic Community Bishops in Tension, Theol Studies, 9/82; auth, The Year of the Hare: America in Vietnam, 1/63-2/64, University of Georgia Press, 97. **CONTACT ADDRESS** Sch of Foreign Serv, Georgetown Univ, Washington, DC 20057-0001. **EMAIL** wintersf@gunet.georgetown.edu

WINTLE, THOMAS
DISCIPLINE CHURCH HISTORY **EDUCATION** Chicago Theol Sem, DMN, 75 **CAREER** Par Minist, 75-95, Par Minist, 95-pres **MEMBERSHIPS** AAR; ASCH **RESEARCH** New England Church Hist **SELECTED PUBLICATIONS** Auth, A New England Village Church, 85 **CONTACT ADDRESS** 3 Conant Rd, Weston, MA 02193-1625.

WIPPEL, JOHN F.
PERSONAL Born 08/21/1933, Pomeroy, OH, s **DISCIPLINE** PHILOSOPHY **EDUCATION** Catholic Univ Am, BA, 55; MA, 56; STL, 60; Louvain Univ, PhD, 65; Maitre-Agrege de l'Ecole Saint Thomas d'Aquin, Louvain-la-Neuve, 81. **CAREER** Instr to prof, Catholic Univ 60-. **HONORS AND AWARDS** Basselin Scholarship, Catholic Univ, 53-56; Pennfield Scholarship, Catholic Univ, 61-63; NEH Fel, 70-71, 85; Aquinas Medal, Catholic Philos Assoc, 99. **MEMBERSHIPS** Am Philos Assoc; Am Catholic Philos Assoc; Soc for Medieval and Renaissance Philos. Med Acad of Am. **SELECTED PUBLICATIONS** Coauth, coed, Medieval Philosophy: From St. Augustine to Nicholas of Cusa, Free Press, (NY), 69; cotrans, St Thomas Aquinas and Radical Aristotelianism by F. Van Steenberghen, Catholic Univ of Am Pr, 80; auth, The Metaphysical Thought of Godfrey of Fontaines, Catholic Univ of Am Pr, (Washington, DC), 81; auth, Metaphysical Themes in Thomas Aquinas, Catholic Univ of Am Pr, (Washington, DC), 84; coauth, "Les questions disputees et les questions quodlibetiques dan les facultes de theologie, de droit et de medecine, in Quodlibetal Questions, Chiefly in Theology Faculties, Brepols (Belgium, 85): 153-222; trans, Boethius of Dacia: 'On the Supreme Good,' 'On the Eternity of the World,' 'On Dreams', Pontifical Inst of Mediaeval Studies (Toronto), 87; ed, Studies in Medieval Philosophy, Catholic Univ of Am Pr, (Washington, DC), 87; auth, Mediaeval Reactions to the Encounter between Faith and Reason: The Aquinas Lecture, Marquette Univ Pr, (Milwaukee), 95; auth, The Metaphysical Thought of Thomas Aquinas, Catholic Univ of Am Pr, (Washington, DC), (forthcoming). **CONTACT ADDRESS** Dept Philos, Catholic Univ of America, 620 Michigan Ave NE, Washington, DC 20064-0001. **EMAIL** wippel@cua.edu

WIRTH, JASON M.
PERSONAL Born 02/03/1963, San Francisco, CA, s **DISCIPLINE** PHILOSOPHY **EDUCATION** Holy Cross, Worcester, MA, BA, 85; Villanova Univ, MA, 90; Binghamton Univ, PhD, 94. **CAREER** Asst Prof of Philo, Oglethorpe Univ, Atlanta, 94-00; to assoc prof of philo, 00-. **HONORS AND AWARDS** Fellowship of Amer Assoc of Coll and Univ; Polished Apple Awd; Fulbright Fellowship; Univ Fellowship; Edge Awd; DAAD Fellowship; John Tich Awd; Phi Beta Kappa; Alpha Sigma Nu; Phi Sigma Tau. **MEMBERSHIPS** GCPC, GPS, SPEP, APA, IAPL. **RESEARCH** German Philosophers from Kant to present; Contemporary French Philosophy; Aesthetics, Comparat. **SELECTED PUBLICATIONS** Transl, Martin Heidegger's Letters on His Political Involvement, The Graduate Journal Of Philosophy: Special Issue: Heidegger and Politics, 91; auth, It Has, Like you, No Name, Paul Celan and the Question of Address, in: Encountering the Other, Studies in Literature, History and Culture, ed, G Brinker-Gabler, Albany: The State Univ of NY Press, 95; auth, "The Souls of Kinds and Kinds of Souls: W.E.B. Du Bois and the Soul of Race," Int Studies in Philos, XXVII:1, 96; auth, "Exhilarated Depair and Optimism in Nothing: Francis Bacon and the question of Representation," Int Studies in Philos, XXXI:1, 99; auth, "Schelling and the Force of Nature," in Interrogating the Tradition, The State Univ NYork Press, 99; auth, "Beyond 'Black Orpheus': Thoughts on the Good of African Philos," in Race and Racism in Continental Philos, Ind Univ Press, forthcoming; auth, "Wretched Desire: Bataille and Kristeva on Abjection," Philos Today, forthcoming. **CONTACT ADDRESS** Dept of Philosophy, Oglethorpe Univ, 4484 Peachtree Road NE, Atlanta, GA 30319. **EMAIL** jsirth@oglethorpe.edu

WIRZBA, NORMAN
PERSONAL Born 02/07/1964, Lethbridge, AB, Can **DISCIPLINE** PHILOSOPHY **EDUCATION** Univ Lethbridge, BA, 86; Yale Univ Divinity School, MAR, 88; Loyola Univ, MA, 91; PhD, 94. **CAREER** Lecturer, Northern Ill Univ, 92-93; asst prof, St. Thomas More Col, 93-95; asst prof, Georgetown Col, 95-. **HONORS AND AWARDS** Christian Faith & Life Sabbatical Grant, Louisville Inst. **MEMBERSHIPS** Am Philos Asn, Baptist Asn of Philos Teachers, Society for Continental Philos & Theol. **RESEARCH** Environmental Philosophy, Continental Philosophy, Philosophy of Religion. **SELECTED PUBLICATIONS** Auth, "Becoming a Culture of Creation: The Difference Agrarianism Makes," (under review), First Things; auth, "Soil-cultivating Citizens: An Agrarian Contribution to Political Life,: (forthcoming), The Land Report; auth, "Caring and Working: An Agrarian Perspective," The Christian Century (99): 898-901; auth, "Thinking with the Stomach in Mind: Agrarianism and the Future of Philosophy," Contemporary Philosophy (99): 42-47; auth, "The Apostle Paul and the Transformation of Minds," Christian Scholars Review; auth, "An Ethical Turn in Philosophy: The Work of Emmanuel Levinas," Books & Culture (forthcoming); auth, "Grace at Work: A Review of Wendell Berry's 'A Timbered Choir'," The Christian Century (98): 1090-91. **CONTACT ADDRESS** Dept Philos, Georgetown Col, 400 E College St, Georgetown, KY 40324-1628. **EMAIL** nwirzba0@georgetowncollege.edu

WISE, EDWARD MARTIN
PERSONAL Born 08/08/1938, New York, NY, 2 children **DISCIPLINE** LAW, LEGAL HISTORY **EDUCATION** Univ Chicago, BA, 56; Cornell Univ, LLB, 59; NYork Univ, LLM, 60. **CAREER** Res assoc, Comparative Criminal Law Proj, 63-64; res fel, Inst Judicial Admin, 64-65; assoc prof, 65-68, prof Law, Wayne State Univ, 68-; assoc dean 86-92; Vis prof, NY Univ Sch Law, 68; gen coun, Am Civil Liberties Union Mich, 77-86; vis prof, Univ Utrecht, 79-98. **MEMBERSHIPS** Am Soc Legal Hist; Am Soc Int Asn Penal Law (pres, 89-); Am Soc Int Law; Selden Soc; Am Law Inst; Int Acad of Comparative Law; Int Law Assoc. **RESEARCH** International and comparative criminal law; legal history. **SELECTED PUBLICATIONS** Auth, International Criminal Law, 65; auth, Anglo-American Criminal Justice, 67; Studies in Comprative Criminal Law, 75; auth, The Italian Penal Code, 78; auth, Criminal Science in a Global Society, 94; auth, Art Dedere Art Judicare, 95; Comparative Law-Cases-Text-Materials, 98. **CONTACT ADDRESS** Law Sch, Wayne State Univ, 468 Ferry Mall, Detroit, MI 48202-3698. **EMAIL** E.M.Wise@Wayne.edu

WISE, PHILIP D.
PERSONAL Born 01/03/1949, Andalusia, AL, m, 1968, 3 children **DISCIPLINE** THEOLOGY **EDUCATION** Samford Univ, BA, 70; MA, 73, PhD, 80, New Orleans Baptist Theological Seminary. **CAREER** Lctr, Culham Col, Abingdon, England, 74-76; Lectr, United National Baptist Theology Seminary, New Orleans, 70-71; Guest Lctr, Baptist Seminary, Ogbomosho, Nigeria, 84; Guest Lctr, Intl Baptist Seminary, Singapore, 90; Guest Lctr, Cetown Baptist Col, South Africa, 92; Lectr, 77-78, Adjunct Lctr, 97, New Orleans Baptist Theological Seminary; Pastor, First Baptist Church, Dothan, Alabama, 89-. **HONORS AND AWARDS** Recipient Samford Univ Alabama Minister of the Year, 94; Paul Harris Fel, 97. **MEMBERSHIPS** Selma Ministers Assoc; Blue-Gray Football Assoc; Central Alabama Fellowship of Christian Athletes; Amer Cancer Soc of Montgomery; Dothan Ministerial Union; Dothan Area Chamber of Commerce; Dothan Area United Way; Brd Trustees, Samford Univ. **RESEARCH** Baptist World Alliance Commission on Doctrine and Interchurch Cooperation **SELECTED PUBLICATIONS** Coauth, A Dictionary of Doctrinal Terms, 83; Auth, Theology and the Pastorate, Proclaim, 84; Biblical Inerrancy: Pro or Con, Theological Educator, 88; Is Anyone for Divorce, Alabama Baptist Ethics Commission Magazine, 98. **CONTACT ADDRESS** 300 W Main St, Dothan, AL 36301. **EMAIL** philip@fbcdothan.org

WISEMAN, JAMES A.
PERSONAL Born 02/19/1942, Louisville, KY, s **DISCIPLINE** THEOLOGY **EDUCATION** Georgetown Univ, BA 63; Cath Univ Amer, MA 70, STD 79. **CAREER** Cath Univ Amer, asst prof, assoc prof, ch, 95 to 98-. **HONORS AND AWARDS** Alumni Achievement Awd in education, Catholic Univ of Amer, 99. **MEMBERSHIPS** CTSA; SSCS. **RESEARCH** Christian Spirituality; Interreligious Dialogue; Science and Religion. **SELECTED PUBLICATIONS** Auth, Mystical Literature and Modern Unbelief, Christian Spirituality and the Culture of Modernity: The Thought of Louis Dupre, Peter J. Casarella, George P. Schner, eds, Grand Rapids, Eerdmans, 98; The Spirituality of St. Therese of Lisieux as Seen in Her Poetry, Comm: Intl Catholic Rev, 97; The Kingdom of God in Monastic Interreligious Dialogue, Stud Missionalia, 97; The Interfaith Conf of Metro Washington, Jour of Ecumen Stud, 97; auth, "Learning to Love and Learning the Price: Thomas Merton and the Challenge of Celibacy," The Merton Annual, (99). **CONTACT ADDRESS** Dept of Theology, Catholic Univ of America, Washington, DC 20064. **EMAIL** jameswiseman@erols.com

WISHART, LYNN
DISCIPLINE LEGAL RESEARCH **EDUCATION** W Va Univ, BA, 69; Univ Mich, AMLS, 71; Wash Univ, JD, 77. **CAREER** Assoc dir, law libraries, Georgetown Univ, 81-84, Washington and Lee Univ, 78-81; Prof, Yeshiva Univ; Dir Law Library, Yeshiva Univ. **HONORS AND AWARDS** West Excellence Acad Law Librarianship Awd, 96. **MEMBERSHIPS** Am Library Asn; Am Asn Law Libraries. **SELECTED PUBLICATIONS** Area: library literature. **CONTACT ADDRESS** Yeshiva Univ, 55 Fifth Ave, New York, NY 10003-4301. **EMAIL** wishart@ymail.yu.edu

WISSLER, ROBERT W.
PERSONAL Born 03/01/1917, Richmond, IN, m, 1940, 4 children **DISCIPLINE** PATHOLOGY, IMMUNOPATHOLOGY, NUTRITIONAL PATHOLOGY **EDUCATION** Earlham Col, AB, 39; Univ Chicago, MS, 43, PhD, 46, MD, 48. **CAREER** Instr, 43-48, asst prof, 49-54, assoc prof, 55-60, prof, 61-, pathology, Donald N. Pritzker Distinguished Service Prof of Pathology, Univ Chicago, emeritus. **HONORS AND AWARDS** Keynote speaker, 27th Hugh Lofland Conf, 94; Donald S. Frederickson Career Achievement Awd, Xth Intl. Atherosclerosis Symposium, Montreal, Canada, 94; election to AAAS fellowship, 95; Emperor's Rising Sun award and medal from Japanese colleagues, 95; co-organizer, 29th Hugh Lofland Conf, 97. **MEMBERSHIPS** Amer Heart Assn, Coun on Arteriosclerosis, 55-; Intl Soc Cardiology, 67-; Lankenau Hospital, Scientific Advisory Bd, Div of Research, 70- ; Intl Cardiology Found, 72-; Amer Medical Assn, sr mem, 95-. **RESEARCH** Immune reaction to neoplasia; pathogenesis of atherosclerosis. **SELECTED PUBLICATIONS** Coauth, "A Study of the Development of Atherosclerosis in Childhood and Young Adults: Risk Factors and the Prevention of Progression in Japan and the USA," Path Intl, vol 46, 96; coauth, "Pathomorphological Findings of Lp(a) Deposition in Arterial Intima," Current Therapy (Japan), suppl, 96; coauth, "Microscopic Findings Associated with Blood Pressure Indices in Postmortem Human Aorta Samples from Young People (Ages 15-34)," Cardiovasc Path, vol 5, 96; coauth, "Effects of Serum Lipoproteins and Smoking on Atherosclerosis in Young Men and Women," Arterioscler Thromb Vasc Biol, vol 17, 97; auth, comments on the article, "Lipids and Atherosclerosis: An Impossible Causal Relationship," Am Clin Lab, vol 17, 98. **CONTACT ADDRESS** 5550 S. Shore Dr., No. 515, Chicago, IL 60637-1904.

WITHERINGTON, BEN
PERSONAL Born 12/30/1951, High Point, NC, m, 1977, 2 children **DISCIPLINE** RELIGION **EDUCATION** Univ N Carolina, BA, 74; Gordon-Conwell Theol Sem, MDiv, 77; Univ Durham, England, PhD, 81. **CAREER** Ashland Theo Sem, prof NT, 84-95; Asbury Theol Sem, prof NT, 95-. **HONORS AND AWARDS** Top Biblical Studies bk, Christianity Today, 95, 99; John Wesley fel for Life; resh fel, Cambridge Univ. **MEMBERSHIPS** SBL; Soc for Study of the New testament; Inst for Biblical Res. **RESEARCH** New Testament; Women in the New Testament; the historical Jesus. **SELECTED PUBLICATIONS** Auth, The Jesus Quest: The Third Search for the Jew of Nazareth, Intervaristy Press, 95; auth, Conflict and Community in Corinth: A Socio-Rhetorical Commentary on I and II Corinthians, Will B. Eerdmans, 95; auth, John's Wisdom: A Commentary on the Fourth Gospel, Westmin/John Knox Press, 95; auth, The Acts of the Apostles, 97; auth, The Many Faces of Christ: The Christologies of the New Testament and Beyond, Crossroads, 98; auth, Grace in Galatia: A Commentary on Paul's Letter to the Galatians, T&T Clark, 98; auth, Paul Quest: The Search for the Jew from Tarsus, Intervar Press, 98. **CONTACT ADDRESS** Dept of New Testament, Asbury Theol Sem, 204 N. Lexington Ave., Wilmore, KY 40390. **EMAIL** ben_witherington@wilmore.ky.us

WITHERSPOON, EDWARD, JR.
DISCIPLINE RELIGION; PHILOSOPHY **EDUCATION** Vanderbilt Univ, BS, 85; Univ Pittsburgh, PhD, 96. **CAREER** Vis asst prof, Univ Il Urbana-Champaign, 97-98; asst prof, Colgate Univ, 98- . **MEMBERSHIPS** Amer Philos Assoc **CONTACT ADDRESS** Dept of Philos & Relig, Colgate Univ, Hamilton, NY 13346. **EMAIL** ewitherspoon@mail.colgate.edu

WITMAN, EDWARD PAUL
PERSONAL Born 01/27/1945, Baldwin, NY, m, 1969, 2 children **DISCIPLINE** PHILOSOPHY **EDUCATION** Georgetown Univ, AB, 67; Fordham Univ, MA, 69, PhD(philos), 78; Cert in Bioethics and Medical Humanities, Columbia Univ Col of Physicians and Surgeons and Albert Einstein Col of Medicine-Mountefiore Medical Center, 97. **CAREER** Teaching fel philos, Fordham Univ, 69-71; vis lectr, Cathedral Col, NY, 71-72, 72-73; from instr to asst prof, 72-78, assoc prof Philos, 78-86, Full Prof, Georgian Court Col, 87-, chairman, dept of philos, 86, elected CEO of Faculty Assembly, 95-96. **MEMBERSHIPS** Soc Adv Process Studies; Am Philos Asn; Am Cath Philos Asn; Am Soc for Bioethics and the Humanities. **RESEARCH** Alfred N Whitehead; process philosophy; social & political philosophy; medical ethics. **CONTACT ADDRESS** Dept of Philos, Georgian Court Col, 900 Lakewood Ave, Lakewood, NJ 08701-2697. **EMAIL** witman@georgian.edu

WITMER, DONALD G.
PERSONAL Born, PA **DISCIPLINE** PHILOSOPHY **EDUCATION** New Col of the Univ of So Fla, BA, 90; Rutgers Univ, PhD, 97. **CAREER** Asst prof, 97-, Univ of Fla. **MEMBERSHIPS** APA. **RESEARCH** Metaphysics; philos of mind; language; ethics. **SELECTED PUBLICATIONS** Auth, Is Natural Kindness a Natural Kind?, co-auth, Philos Stud, 98; auth, What is Wrong with the Manifestability Argument for Supervenience, Australian J of Philos, 98; auth, Sufficiency Claims and Physicalism: A Formulation, Physicalism and Its Discontents, Cambridge Univ Press, forthcoming; auth, Supervenience Physicalism and the Problem of Extras, The So J of Philos, forthcoming; auth, Ontology, 98, dict entry, online Dict of Philos of Mind; auth, Identity Theories, 98, dict entry, online Dict of Philos of Mind. **CONTACT ADDRESS** Philos Dept, Univ of Florida, Gainesville, FL 32611-8545. **EMAIL** gwitmer@phil.ufl.edu

WITT, CHARLOTTE
DISCIPLINE PHILOSOPHY **EDUCATION** Georgetown Univ, PhD, 80. **CAREER** Assoc prof. **RESEARCH** Ancient philosophy; feminism; metaphysics. **SELECTED PUBLICATIONS** Auth, Substance and Essence in Aristotle, Cornell, 89; co-ed, A Mind of One's Own: Feminist Essays on Reason and Objectivity, Westview, 92. **CONTACT ADDRESS** Philosophy Dept, Univ of New Hampshire, Durham, Hamilton Smith Hall, Durham, NH 03824.

WITTE, ANN DRYDEN
PERSONAL Born 08/28/1942, Oceanside, NY, d, 1969, 1 child **DISCIPLINE** ECONOMICS **EDUCATION** Univ Fla, BA, 63; Columbia Univ, MA, 65; North Carolina State Univ, PhD, 71. **CAREER** Instr, econ, Tougaloo Col, 67-68; instr, econ, 70-72, vis asst prof, econ, 72-73, vis asst prof, public law and govt, 73-74; asst prof, 74-79, assoc prof, 79-83, prof, 83-95, Univ North Carolina, Chapel Hill; fel law and econ, Harvard Law School, 87-88; res assoc, Natl Bur Econ Res, 84- ; prof, econ, Wellesley Col, 85- ; prof econ, Fla Int Univ, 92- 00. **HONORS AND AWARDS** Fel, Am Statistic Asn; fel, Royal Statistic Soc; Dist scholar, Ariz State Univ; fel Am Soc of Criminol; Phi Beta Kappa. **MEMBERSHIPS** Am Econ Asn; Am Statistical Asn; Int Inst Public Finance; Europ Asn of Law and Econ; Am Law and Econ Asn. **RESEARCH** International taxation;Regulation; Effects of information; Welfare reform; Child care and well-being; Crime and criminal justice. **SELECTED PUBLICATIONS** Coauth, Provision of Child Care: Cost Functions for Profit- Making and Not-for-Profit Day Care Centers, J of Productivity Anal, 93; coauth, Tax Compliance: An Investigation Using Individual Tax Compliance Measurement Program Data, J of Quantitative Criminol, 93; coauth, Work and Crime: An Exploration Using Panel Data, Pub Finance, 94; coauth, Criminal Deterrence: Revisiting the Issues with a Birth Cohort, Rev of Econ and Statist, 94; coauth, Economic Effects of Quality Regulations in the Day Care Industry, Am Econ Rev, 95; coauth, Childcare in Massachusetts: Where the Supply Is and Isn't, Wellesley Res Center, 97. **CONTACT ADDRESS** Dept of Economics, Wellesley Col, Wellesley, MA 02181-8260. **EMAIL** awitte@wellesley.edu

WITTE, JOHN, JR.
PERSONAL Born 08/14/1959, St. Catharines, ON, Canada, m, 1995, 2 children **DISCIPLINE** LAW **EDUCATION** Calvin Col, BA, 82; Harvard Law Sch, JD, 85. **CAREER** Dir Law & Relig Prog, Emory Law Sch. **SELECTED PUBLICATIONS** Ed, Christianity and Democracy in Global Context, Westview Press, 93; co-ed, Religious Human Rights in Global Perspective: Legal Perspectives, Nijhoff, 96; co-ed, Religious Human Rights in Global Perspective: Religious Perspectives, Nijhoff, 96; co-ed, Human Rights in Judaism: Cultural, Religious and Political Perspectives, Aronson, 97; co-ed, From Sacrament to Contract: Marriage, Religion, and Law in the Western Tradition, John Knox Press, 97; co-ed, Proselytism and Orthodoxy in Russia: The New Wars for Souls, Orbis Books, 99; co-ed, Sharing the Book: Religious Perspectives on the Rights and Wrongs of Mission, Orbis Books, 99; auth, Religion and the American constitutional Experiment: Essential Rights and Liberties, Perseus Book Group, 00; auth, John Calin on Sex, Marriage, and Family Life, Eerdmans Pub Co, forthcomig; auth, Law and Protestantism: The Leal Teachins of the Lutheran Reformation, Cambridge Univ Press, forthcoming. **CONTACT ADDRESS** Sch of Law, Emory Univ, 1364 Clifton Rd NE, Atlanta, GA 30322-1061. **EMAIL** jwitte@law.emory.edu

WITTRUP, ELEANOR
DISCIPLINE PHILOSOPHY **EDUCATION** Harvard Div Sch, MTS, 89; Univ Calif, San Diego, PhD, 92. **CAREER** Univ Mass, Lowell, 92-95; Univ of the Pacific, 95- . **MEMBERSHIPS** APA; Hume Soc; Concerned Philos for Peace. **RESEARCH** Ethics; philosophy of mind; Hume; Kant. **CONTACT ADDRESS** Philosophy Dept, Univ of the Pacific, Stockton, 3601 Pacific Ave, Stockton, CA 95211. **EMAIL** ewittrup@uop.edu

WOGAMAN, JOHN PHILIP
PERSONAL Born 03/18/1932, Toledo, OH, m, 1956, 4 children **DISCIPLINE** SOCIAL ETHICS **EDUCATION** Col of the Pac, BA, 54; Boston Univ, STB, 57, PhD(social ethics), 60. **CAREER** From asst prof to assoc prof Bible & social ethics, Univ of the Pac, 61-66, dir Pac ctr student social issues, 61-66; assoc prof, 66-69, PROF CHRISTIAN SOCIAL ETHICS, WESLEY THEOL SEM, 69- DEAN, 72-, Fac res fel, Asn Theol Schs US & Can, 75. **MEMBERSHIPS** Am Soc Christian ethics (pres, 76-77); Am Acad Relig; Am Theol Soc. **RESEARCH** Church-state relations; theological ethics; economic ethics. **SELECTED PUBLICATIONS** Auth, Methodism's Challenge in Race Relations: A Study of Strategy, Boston Univ & Pub Affairs, 60; Protestant Faith and Religious Liberty, 67 & Guaranteed Annual Income: The Moral Issue, 68; Abingdon; The dilemma of Christian social strategy, In: Toward a Discipline of Social Ethics, Boston Univ, 72; ed, The Population Crisis and Moral Responsibility, Pub Affairs, 73; auth, A Christian Method of Moral Judgment, 76 & The Great Economic Debate: An Ethical Analysis, 77, SCM & Westminster; coauth, Quality of Life in a Global Society, Friendship, 78. **CONTACT ADDRESS** Wesley Theol Sem, 4400 Massachusetts Ave NW, Washington, DC 20016.

WOJCIK, MARK E.
PERSONAL Born 11/07/1961, Evergreen Park, IL, s **DISCIPLINE** LEGAL STUDIES **EDUCATION** Bradley Univ, BA, 83; John Marshall Law School, JD, 86; New York Univ School Law, LLM, 91. **CAREER** Asst Prof of Law, The John Marshall Law Sch, 92-; Court Counsel, Supreme Court of the Republic of Palau, 94-95. **HONORS AND AWARDS** Maurice Weigel Awd for Outstanding Service to the Legal Profession; Teacher of the Year Elected by First Year Law Students; John Marshall Alumni Asn Distinguished Service Awd. **MEMBERSHIPS** Amer Bar Assoc; Amer Anthrological Assoc; Legal Writing Institute; Scribes; National Lesbian and Gay Law Assoc; Chicago Bar Assoc; Illinois State Bar Assoc; Nebraska State Bar Assoc; Society of Amer Law Teachers. **RESEARCH** International Human Rights and Corporate Responsibility; Legal Issues of Sexual Orientation and Gender Identity. **SELECTED PUBLICATIONS** Auth, "Introduction to Legal English," International Law Institute, 98. **CONTACT ADDRESS** Dept Law, John Marshall Law Sch, 315 S Plymouth Ct, Chicago, IL 60604-3969. **EMAIL** 7wojcik@jmls.edu

WOLF, ARNOLD J.
PERSONAL Born 03/19/1924, Chicago, IL, m, 1987, 6 children **DISCIPLINE** JEWISH THEOLOGY; SOCIAL RESPONSIBILITY **EDUCATION** Univ CA, AA, 42; HUC-JIR, MHL, 48, DD, 73. **CAREER** USNR (decorated), 51-53; cong s., 57-72; Yale Univ, 72-80; Hzm Isamm Israel, 80-. **HONORS AND AWARDS** Ed, Judaism; First Jewish delegate to WCC, Nairobi, 75. **MEMBERSHIPS** CCAR; JCUA; JPF; Chair of Breira, 76-78. **RESEARCH** Modern Jewish thought. **SELECTED PUBLICATIONS** Auth, with L. Huffman, Jewish Spiritual Journeys; Unfinished Rabbi; Challenge to Confirmands; What is Man?; Rediscovering Judaism. **CONTACT ADDRESS** 1100 East Hyde Park Blvd., Chicago, IL 60615.

WOLF, HERBERT CHRISTIAN
PERSONAL Born 04/06/1923, Baltimore, MD, m, 1947, 5 children **DISCIPLINE** RELIGION **EDUCATION** Johns Hopkins Univ, AB, 43; Capital Univ, BD, 47; Univ Chicago, MA, 59; Harvard Univ, ThD, 68. **CAREER** Instr relig, Capital Univ, 45-47; lectr & Nat Lutheran Coun campus pastor, Mich State Univ, 48-57; from asst prof to assoc prof relig, 57-69, chmn dept, 69-79, PROF RELIG, WITTENBERG UNIV, 69-, Vis prof relig, Hood Col, 71-72, United Theol Col, Bangalore, India, 74. **MEMBERSHIPS** Am Acad Relig; Am Theol Asn; AAUP; Conf Relig SIndia. **RESEARCH** Lingayat movement in South India; the quest of the historical Jesus; concept of God as person. **SELECTED PUBLICATIONS** Auth, The responsibility of the church in higher education, 2/51 & Kierkegaard and the quest of the historical Jesus, 2/64, Lutheran Quart; An introduction to the idea of God as person, J Bibl & Relig, 1/64; Kierkegaard and Bultmann: The Quest of the Historical Jesus, Augsburg, 64. **CONTACT ADDRESS** Dept of Relig, Wittenberg Univ, Springfield, OH 45501.

WOLF, KENNETH BAXTER
PERSONAL Born 06/01/1957, Santa Barbara, CA, 2 children **DISCIPLINE** HISTORY, RELIGIOUS STUDIES **EDUCATION** Stanford, BA (Religious Studies), 79, PhD (History), 85. **CAREER** Asst prof, 85-92, Assoc Prof, Pomona Col, 92-, chair, Hist Dept, 95-98. **HONORS AND AWARDS** Phi Beta Kappa; Inst for Advanced Study, member 89-91; Wig Distinguished Prof, Pomona Col, 88, 93, 98. **MEMBERSHIPS** Medieval Academy; Medieval Asn of the Pacific; Assoc Members of the Inst for Advanced Study. **RESEARCH** Medieval Mediterranean hist; late antique/medieval Christianity; saints. **SELECTED PUBLICATIONS** Auth, The Earliest Spanish Christian Views of Islam, Church Hist 55, 86; Conquerors and Chroniclers of Early Medieval Spain, Liverpool Univ Press, 90, revised ed, forthcoming; The Earliest Latin Lives of Muhammad, in Michael Gervers and Ramzi Jibran Bikhazi, eds, Conversion and Continuity: Indigenous Christian Communities in Islamic Lands, Eighth to Eighteenth Centuries, Pontifical Inst of Mediaeval Studies, 90; Crusade and Narrative: Bohemond and the Gesta Francorum, J of Medieval Hist, 17, 91; The 'Moors' of West Africa and the Beginnings of the Portuguese Slave Trade, J of Medieval and Renaissance Studies 24, 94; Making History: The Normans and Their Historians in Eleventh-century Italy, Univ PA Press, 95; Christian Views of Islam in Early Medieval Spain, in John Tolan, ed, Medieval Christian Perspectives of Islam: A Collection of Essays, Garland, 96; Christian Martyrs in Muslim Spain, Cambridge Univ Press, 88, Japanese ed, K. Hayashi, trans, Tosui Shobou Press, 98; Muhammad as Antichrist in Ninth-century Cordoba, in Mark Meyerson, ed, Christians, Muslims and Jews in Medieval and Early Modern Spain: Interaction and Cultural Change, Univ Notre Dame Press, forthcoming. **CONTACT ADDRESS** 551 N. College Ave., Claremont, CA 91711. **EMAIL** kwolf@pomona.edu

WOLF, SUSAN R.
PERSONAL Born 07/23/1952, Chicago, IL, m, 1978, 2 children **DISCIPLINE** MATH AND PHILOSOPHY; PHILOSOPHY **EDUCATION** Yale Univ, BA, 74; Princeton Univ, PhD, 78. **CAREER** Asst prof, 78-81, Harvard Univ; asst prof, 81-86, Univ of Maryland; assoc prof, 86-90, prof, 90-98, Duane Peterson prof of ethics, 98, Johns Hopkins Univ. **HONORS AND AWARDS** Amer Council of Learned Societies fel, 81-82; Amer Assn of Univ Women Postdoctoral fel, 81-82; John Simon Guggenheim Memorial fel, 93-94; elected to Am Acad of Arts and Sci, 99. **MEMBERSHIPS** Amer Philosophical Assn; Amer Soc for Political and Legal Philosophy; AAUP. **RESEARCH** Ethics; Philosophy of Mind. **SELECTED PUBLICATIONS** Auth, Freedom Within Reason, 90; auth, Two Levels of Pluralism, Ethics, July 92; auth, Morality and Partiality, Philosophical Perspectives, 92; auth, Meaning and Morality, Proceedings of the Aristotelian Society, 97; auth, Happiness and Meaning: Two Aspect of the Good Life, Social Philosophy & Policy; 97. **CONTACT ADDRESS** Dept of Philosophy, Johns Hopkins Univ, Baltimore, Baltimore, MD 21218. **EMAIL** swolf@jhv.edu

WOLF, THOMAS PHILLIP
PERSONAL Born 09/27/1933, Norton County, KS, m, 1953, 3 children **DISCIPLINE** POLITICAL SCIENCE **EDUCATION** Wichita State Univ, AB, 59; MA, 61, PhD, 67, Stanford Univ. **CAREER** Asst Prof, 63-70, Assoc Prof, 70, Univ New Mexico; Assoc Prof, 70-75, Prof, Chr, 71-80, Prof Emeritys, 99-; Dean Social Sciences, Indiana Univ Southeast,92-98. **HONORS AND AWARDS** Woodrow Wilson Fel, 59-60; NEH Col Faculty in Residence, 76-77; Joseph J. Malone Fel, 86. **MEMBERSHIPS** Amer Political Science Assoc; Amer Assoc of Univ Prof; Hansard Soc for Parliamentary Govt; British Politics Group; Western Social Science Assoc; Midwest Political Science Assoc; North Amer Conference on British Studies; English speaking Union; Indiana Consortium on International Programs; Southwest Political Science Assoc; Louisville Committee on Foreign Reltions; Indiana Acad of Social Sciences; Indiana Political Science Assoc; Kentucky Political Science Assoc. **RESEARCH** British politics; American presidency; public opinion **SELECTED PUBLICATIONS** Auth, Winston Leonard Spencer Churchill, Statesman Who Changed the World, 93; auth, Harold Macmillan, Leaders of Contemporary Europe, 95; auth, The Cold War, Events that Changed the World in the 20th Century, 95. **CONTACT ADDRESS** Division of Social Sciences, Indiana Univ, Southeast, New Albany, IN 47150-2158. **EMAIL** tpwolf@ius.edu

WOLFE, ALAN
PERSONAL Born 06/10/1942, Philadelphia, PA, m, 1981, 3 children **DISCIPLINE** POLITICAL SCIENCE **EDUCATION** Temple Univ, BS, 63; Univ Pa, PhD, 67. **CAREER** Asst to Assoc Prof, Richmond Col, 70-78; Vis Assoc Prof, Univ Calif Santa Cruz, 77-79; Vis Scholar, Univ Calif Berkeley, 78-80; Vis Scholar, Harvard Univ, 82; Vis Prof, Univ Aarhus, 87-88; Adj Prof, Columbia Univ, 89; Assoc to Full Prof, Queens Col, 79-89; Dean, New Sch for Soc Res, 91-93; Prof, Boston Univ, 93-99; Prof, Boston Col, 99-. **HONORS AND AWARDS** Smith Richardson Found Fel, 00; Templeton Found, 00; NEH Summer Sem Series, 99, 96, 94; Lilly Endowment, 98; Russell Sage Found, 94; NY Times Notable Book of the Year; Robert Ezra Park Awd; Who's Who in the East; Who's Who in the World; contemporary Authors. **MEMBERSHIPS** Am Polit Sci Asn **RESEARCH** Lived Religion in America. **SELECTED PUBLICATIONS** Ed, American at Century's End, Univ Calif Press, 91; auth, The Human Difference, Univ Calif Press; auth,

Marginalized in the Middle, Univ Chicago Press, 96; auth, One Nation, After All, Viking Penguin, 98; auth, Moral Freedom, W.W. Norton, 01. **CONTACT ADDRESS** Boisi Center for Relig and Am Pub Life, Boston Col, Chestnut Hill, 24 Quincy Rd, Chestnut Hill, MA 02467. **EMAIL** wolfe@bc.edu

WOLFE, CHRISTOPHER
PERSONAL Born 03/11/1949, Boston, MA, m, 1972, 10 children **DISCIPLINE** POLITICAL SCIENCE **EDUCATION** Univ Notre Dame, BA, 71; Boston Col, PhD, 78. **CAREER** Instr, 75-78, Assumption Col; Asst prof, 78-85, assoc prof, 85-92, Prof 92- & Chr 97-, Marquette Univ, 78-; Woodrow Wilson Fel, 71; Phi Beta Kappa, 71; NEH Fel, 94. **HONORS AND AWARDS** Benchmark Book Year Awd, 87; Templeton Honor Rolls Educ Free Soc, 97. **MEMBERSHIPS** Am Polit Sci Assoc; Fel Cath Scholars; Federalist Soc. **RESEARCH** Constitutional law and judicial politics; Liberal Legal Theory; Natural Law. **SELECTED PUBLICATIONS** auth, "Liberalism and Paternalism: A Critique of Ronald Dworkin," Rev of Politics, 94; The Rise of Modern Judicial Review: From Constitutional Interpretation to Judge-Made Law, Rowman & Littlefield, 94; Liberalism at the Crossroads: An Introduction to Contemporary Liberal Political Theory and Its Critics, Rowman and Littlefield, 94; Being Worthy of Trust: A Response to Joseph Raz in Natural Law, Liberalism, and Morality, Oxford Univ Press, 96; How to Interpret the Constitution: Originalist Essays on Constitutional Interpretation and Judicial Review, Rowman & Littlefield, 96; "Natural Law and Liberal Public Reason," Am Jour of Jurisprudence, 97; Judicial Activism: Bulward of Freedom or Precarious Security?, Rowman & Littlefield, 97; Natural Law and Judicial Review in Natural Law and Contemporary Public Policy, Georgetown Univ Press, 98; **CONTACT ADDRESS** Dept of Political Science, Marquette Univ, Box 1881, Milwaukee, WI 53201-1881. **EMAIL** christopher.wolfe@marquette.edu

WOLFE, DAVID L.
PERSONAL Born 03/07/1939, Lock Haven, PA, m, 1962, 3 children **DISCIPLINE** ANTHROPOLOGY, THEOLOGY, PHILOSOPHY, PHILOSOPHY OF EDUCATION **EDUCATION** Wheaton Col, BA, 61, MA, 64; NYork Univ, PhD, 69. **CAREER** Inst to assoc prof of Philos, The Kings Col, NY, 63-70; asst to assoc prof of Philos, Wheaton Col, 70-74; assoc to prof of Philos, Gordon Col, 74-87; pastor, The Tunbridge Church, Tunbridge, VT, 87-. **MEMBERSHIPS** Am Philos Asn **RESEARCH** Religious epistemology' Philosophy of education; Philosophy of science. **SELECTED PUBLICATIONS** Auth Epistemology: The Justification of Belief, InterVarsity Press, 82; coed The Reality of Christian Learning, Christian Univ Press, 87; coed Slogans or Distinctives: Reforming Christian Education, Univ Press Am, 93. **CONTACT ADDRESS** Rivendell, 6 Wolfe Dr, Tunbridge, VT 05077. **EMAIL** rivendell5@juno.com

WOLFE, DEBORAH CANNON PARTRIDGE
PERSONAL Born Cranford, NJ, d **DISCIPLINE** THEOLOGY **EDUCATION** Columbia Univ, EdD, MA; Jersey City State Coll, BS; Postdoctoral Study, Vassar Coll, Union Theological Seminary, Jewish Theological Seminary of Amer. **CAREER** Tuskegee Univ, prof & dir grad work 1938-50; Queens College of CUNY, prof of education, 50-86; vstg prof, NY Univ 1951-54, Univ of MI 1952, Fordham Univ 1952-53, Columbia Univ 1953-54, TX Coll 1955, Univ of IL 1956-57, Wayne State Univ 1961, Grambling Univ; US House of Reps, ed chief comm on ed & labor 1962-65; Macmillan Publ Co, ed consult 1964; NSF, consult 1967-70; City Univ Ctr for African & Afro-Amer Studies and African Study Abroad, dir 1968-77; Natl Leadership Training Inst US Ofc of Ed, cons, vocational & tech ed 1968-71; First Baptist Church Cranford NJ, assoc minister, 75; Queens Coll, prof ed 1950-86; New Jersey State Board of Education, 63-93. **HONORS AND AWARDS** Bldgs named in honor of Deborah Wolfe: Trenton State Coll 1970, Macon County, AL ; Awd Hon Mem, Natl Soc for Prevention of Juvenile Delinquency; Women of Courage Radcliffe Coll; Special Honors Natl Alliance of Black School Educators, Northeastern Region Natl Assn of Colored Women's Clubs, Shrewsbury AME Zion Church; Citizen of the Year B'nai B'rith 1986; Citation Serv Omega Psi Phi Fraternity; Sojourner Truth Awd Natl Ann of Business & Professional Women; Top Ladies of Distinction Hon Mem, 1986; Medal for Comm Serv Queens Coll of CUNY, 1986; Distinguished Service Awd, Univ of Medicine & Dentistry of New Jersey and Seton Hall Univ; Honorary Doctorates: Stockton State Coll, Kean Coll of New Jersey, Jersey City State Coll Monmouth Coll, Centenary Coll, Bloomfield Coll, William Pater Coll, and numerous other educational institutions, 26 in all; Medal of Honor, Daughters of American Revolution; Women of Achievement, National YMCA; visiting scholar, Princeton Theological Seminary. **MEMBERSHIPS** Chair NJ State Bd of Higher Educ 1988-93; chmn admiss comm Queens Coll CUNY, UN Rep for Ch Women United 1971-; chmn AAUW Legis Prog Comm 1973-77; Commn on Fed Rel Amer Council on Ed 1972-77; trustee bd science serv AAAS; mem trustee bd Seton Hall Univ; adv comm Bd of Educ Cranford NJ; grand basileus, Zeta Phi Beta Sorority, 1954-65, chair, 1975-, Zeta Pi Beta Educ Found; sec Kappa Delta Pi Educ Foundation; vice pres, Natl Council of Negro Women; bd of dirs, Home Mission Council, Progressive Natl Baptist Convention; Resolutions Comm, Natl Assn of State Boards of Education; board of trustees: Science Service; Education Development Center; former pres, National Alliance of Black School Educators; chair, Monroe Human Relations Commission; pres, Rossmoor Interfaith Council. **CONTACT ADDRESS** First Baptist Church, 100 High St, Cranford, NJ 07016.

WOLFE, ROBERT F.
PERSONAL Born Independence, MO **DISCIPLINE** THEOLOGY **EDUCATION** Calvin Col, BA, 78; Westminster Sem, MA, 81; Calvin Sem, MDiv, 87; Southwestern Theol Sem, PhD, 96. **CAREER** Hosp chap, 87-88, Parkland Mem Hospital; tchng fel, res asst, 90-91; pastor/intern, pastor, 85-87. **HONORS AND AWARDS** Grad with honors, Westminster Sem & Calvin Sem. **MEMBERSHIPS** AAR; Soc of Bibl Lit; Inst for Bibl Res. **RESEARCH** The historical Jesus; early Christianity; philosophy of religion **SELECTED PUBLICATIONS** Art, Rhetorical Elements in the Speeches of Acts 7 and 17, J Transl & Text-Ling, vol 6 no 3, 93; auth, Pursuing ordination with Presbyterian Church (USA) to chaplaincy, independent research, translation, 96-. **CONTACT ADDRESS** 102 Blackfoot Trail N, Lake Kiowa, TX 76240. **EMAIL** safe-bwolfe@flash.net

WOLFENSTEIN, E. VICTOR
PERSONAL Born 07/09/1940, Cleveland, OH, m, 1969, 4 children **DISCIPLINE** POLITICAL SCIENCE **EDUCATION** Columbia Col, BA, 62; Princeton Univ, MA, 64; PhD, 65; S Calif Psychoanalytic Inst, PhD, 84. **CAREER** Asst prof to prof, UCLA, 65-; fac, S Calif Psychoanalytic Inst, 88-. **HONORS AND AWARDS** UCLA Mortar Board Fac Excellence Awd, 91; Outstanding Teacher Awd, S Calif Psychoanalytic Inst, 92-93; Distinguished Teaching Awd, UCLA; Guggenheim Fel, 74-75. **MEMBERSHIPS** Am Polit Sci Asn; S Calif Psychoanalytic Inst. **RESEARCH** Critical theory; Psychoanalytic-Marxism, Psychoanalytic Theory and Practice; African-American Culture and Politics; Feminist Theory. **SELECTED PUBLICATIONS** Auth, The Victims of Democracy: Malcolm X and the Black Revolution, Guilford Pub, 93; auth, Psychoanalytic-Marxism: Groundwork, Builford Pub, 93; auth, "Black Liberation and the Jewish Question," in Blacks and Jews on the Couch, Praeger-Greenwood Pub, 99; auth, Inside/Outside Nietzsche: Psychoanalytic Explorations,' Cornell Univ Press, 00; auth, "On the Road Not Taken: 'Revolt and Revenge'," in The Souls of Black Folk, 00; auth, "New Souls for Old?: Race, Gender, and the Transformational Effects of Social Movements," in Studies in Gender and Sexuality, 00. **CONTACT ADDRESS** Dept Polit Sci, Univ of California, Los Angeles, 4289 Bunche, Box 951472, Los Angeles, CA 90095-1472. **EMAIL** evw@ucla.edu

WOLFF, ROBERT PAUL
PERSONAL Born 12/27/1933, New York, NY, m, 1962 **DISCIPLINE** PHILOSOPHY **EDUCATION** Harvard Univ, AB, 53, AM, 54, PhD(philos), 57. **CAREER** Instr philos, Harvard Univ, 58-61; asst prof philos & soc sci, Univ Chicago, 61-64; from assoc prof to prof philos, Columbia Univ, 64-71; prof Philos, 71-91, Prof Afro-Am Studies, Univ MA, 92-; Soc Sci Res Coun fel, 57-58. **MEMBERSHIPS** Am Soc Polit & Legal Philos; Am Philos Asn. **RESEARCH** History of modern philosophy; social and political philosophy; philosophy of education. **SELECTED PUBLICATIONS** Ed, The Essential Hume, New Am Libr, 69; In Defense of Anarchism, Harper, 70; Philosophy: A Modern Encounter, Prentice-Hall, 71; The Rule of Law, Simon & Schuster, 71; Styles of Political Action in America, Random, 72;The Autonomy of Reason, Harper, 73; auth, About Philosophy, Prentice-Hall, 76; Understanding Rawls, Princeton Univ, 77. **CONTACT ADDRESS** Dept of Afro-Am Studies, Univ of Massachusetts, Amherst, Amherst, MA 01002. **EMAIL** rwolff@afroam.umass.edu

WOLFMAN, BERNARD
PERSONAL Born 07/08/1924, Philadelphia, PA, 3 children **DISCIPLINE** LAW **EDUCATION** Univ Pa, AB, 46, JD, 48. **CAREER** Part-time instr polit sci, Univ Pa, 46-49, part-time lectr, Law Sch, 59-62, part-time prof, 62-63, prof law, 63-76, chmn univ senate & chmn task force on univ governance 69-70, dean, 70-75; Gemmill prof tax law & tax policy, Univ Pa Law Sch, 73-76; Fessenden Prof Law (Taxation), Harvard Law Sch, 76-, Consult, US Treasury Dept, 63-68, 77-80; vis prof, Harvard Law Sch, 64-65; Adv Group Comnr Internal Revenue 66-67; gen counsel, AAUP, 66-68; consult, Am Law Inst-Income Tax Proj, 74-; exec comt, Fed Tax Inst New England, 76-. **HONORS AND AWARDS** Fel, Cent Adv Study Behav Sci, 75-76; Irvine lectr, Law Sch, Cornell Univ, 80; Fel, Am Col of Tax Counsel, Regent for 1st Circuit; lld, jewish theol sem, 71. **MEMBERSHIPS** Am Bar Asn; Am Law Inst; Order Coif. **RESEARCH** Tax law. **SELECTED PUBLICATIONS** Auth, Professors and the ordinary and necessary business expense, Univ Pa Law Rev, 64; Federal tax policy and the support of science, In: Law and the Social Role of Science, Rockefeller Univ, 66; Bosch, its implications and aftermath: The effect of state court adjudications on federal tax ligitation, Univ Miami Ann Inst Estate Planning 69; Federal Income Taxation of Corporate Enterprise, Aspen Law & Bus, 3rd ed, 90; The Behavior of Justice Douglas in Federal Tax Cases, Univ Pa Law Rev, 12/73; sr auth, Dissent Without Opinion: The Behavior of Justice William O Douglas in Federal Tax Cases, Univ Pa, 75; The supreme court in the Lyon's den: A failure of judicial process, Cornell Law Rev, 81; coauth, Ethical problems in federal tax practice, Aspen Law & Bus, 3d ed, 85; coauth, Standards of Tax Practice, Aspen Law & Bus, 5th ed, 99. **CONTACT ADDRESS** Dept of Law, Harvard Univ, Cambridge, MA 02138. **EMAIL** wolfman@law.harvard.edu

WOLFRAM, CHARLES W.
PERSONAL Born 02/28/1937, Cleveland, OH, m, 1965, 2 children **DISCIPLINE** CIVIL PROCEDURE, LEGAL ETHICS **EDUCATION** Univ Notre Dame, AB, 59; Univ Tex Law Sch, LLB, 62. **CAREER** Asst prof law, Univ Minn Law Sch, 65-67, assoc prof, 67-70, prof, 70-82; PROF LAW, CORNELL LAW SCH, 82-, Vis prof law, Southern Calif Law Ctr, 76-77 & Cornell Law Sch, 81-82. **MEMBERSHIPS** Am Law Inst. **RESEARCH** American civil procedure; legal ethics; federal jurisdiction. **SELECTED PUBLICATIONS** Auth, Mass Torts--Messy Ethics, Cornell Law Rev, Vol 0080, 95. **CONTACT ADDRESS** Law Sch, Cornell Univ, Myron Taylor Hall, Ithaca, NY 14853-4901.

WOLGAST, ELIZ H.
PERSONAL Born 02/27/1929, NJ, m, 1949, 2 children **DISCIPLINE** ENGLISH; PHILOSOPHY **EDUCATION** Cornell Univ, BA, 50, MA, 52; Univ Wash, PhD, 55. **CAREER** Univ Calif Davis, 66-67; Calif State Hayward, 68-97; visiting prof, Dartmouth Col, 75-76; Univ Wales, Lampeter, 95, 96. **HONORS AND AWARDS** AAUW fel, 58; ACLS fel, 70; NEH fel, 78, 88; Finnish Acad fel, 92; Rockefeller Bellagio fel, 88. **MEMBERSHIPS** APA. **RESEARCH** Wittgenstein; Ethics; Epistemology. **SELECTED PUBLICATIONS** Auth, "Personal Identity", Philos Invest, 99; auth, Democracy: The Message from Athens, Consequences of Modernity in Contemporary Legal Theory, Dunker & Humbolt, 98; auth, Mental Causes and the Will, Philos Investigations, Winter, 97; auth, Moral Paradigms, Philos, Spring, 95; auth, Individualism and Democratic Citizenship, Democrazia e Diritto, Summer, 94; auth, The Demands of Public Reason, Columbia Law Rev, Oct, 94; auth, Primitive Reactions, Philos Investigations, Oct, 94; auth, Ethics of an Artificial Person: Lost Responsibility in Professions and Organizations, Stanford Univ Press, 92; auth, La Grammatica della Giustizia, Riuniti, Italy, 91; auth, The Grammar of Justice, Cornell Univ Press, 87; auth, Equality and the Rights of Women, Cornell Univ Press, 80; auth, Paradoxes of Knowledge, Cornell Univ Press, 77. **CONTACT ADDRESS** 1536 Olympus Av., Berkeley, CA 94708. **EMAIL** ewolgast@csuhayward.edu

WOLLENBERG, BRUCE
PERSONAL Born 10/12/1943, IN, m, 1969, 1 child **DISCIPLINE** RELIGIOUS STUDIES **EDUCATION** Univ Cal SB, PhD 86. **CAREER** St. Mark Lutheran Church, pastor, 98-. **MEMBERSHIPS** AAR **RESEARCH** American Religion; Post Modern Theology. **SELECTED PUBLICATIONS** Auth, Christian Social Thought in Great Britain Between the Wars, Univ Press of Amer, 97. **CONTACT ADDRESS** St. Mark Lutheran Church, 100 Alderman Rd, Charlottesville, VA 22903-1782. **EMAIL** brucew@stmarklutheran.org

WOOD, BRYANT G.
PERSONAL Born 10/07/1936, Endicott, NY, m, 1958, 4 children **DISCIPLINE** NEAR EASTERN STUDIES, BIBLICAL HISTORY, AND SYRO-PALESTINIAN ARCHAEOLOGY **EDUCATION** Univ Mich, MA, 74; Univ Toronto, PhD, 85. **CAREER** Visitng Prof, Dept of Near Eastern Studies, Univ Toronto, 89-90; Res Analysit, 90-94, Dir, Assoc for Biblical Res, 95-. **HONORS AND AWARDS** Endowment for Biblical Res Grant, 81; Travel Grant, 81, Summer Stipend, Nat Endowment for the Humanities, 92. **MEMBERSHIPS** Near East Archaeol Soc; Inst for Biblical Res. **RESEARCH** Archaeology of the Bronze Age and Iron Age Periods in Palestine. **SELECTED PUBLICATIONS** Auth, Pottery Making in Bible Times, By the Sweat of Thy Brow: Labor and Laborers in the Biblical World, Sheffield Academic Press, forthcoming; Cisterns and Reservoirs, Encyclo of the Dead Sea Scrolls, Oxford Univ Press, forthcoming; Water Systems, Encyclo of the Dead Sea Scrolls, Oxford Univ Press, forthcoming; The Role of Shechem in the Conquest of Canaan, To Understand the Scriptures: Essays in Honor of William H. Shea, Inst of Archeaol/Siegfried H. Horn Archaeol Museum, Andrews Univ, 97; Kh. Nisya, 94, Israel Exploration J, 95; Biblical Archaeology's Greatest Achievement, Failure and Challenge, Biblical Archaeol Rev, 95; Rev of Excavations at Tell Deir Alla, Bullet of the Am Schools of Oriental Res, 94; coauth, Kh. Nisya, 93, Israel Exploration J, 94. **CONTACT ADDRESS** Associates for Biblical Res, 4328 Crestview Rd., Harrisburg, PA 17112-2005. **EMAIL** bryantwood@email.msn.com

WOOD, CHARLES M.
PERSONAL Born 11/22/1944, Salida, CO, m, 1966, 1 child **DISCIPLINE** THEOLOGY **EDUCATION** Univ Denver, BA, 66; Boston Univ Sch of Theology, ThM, 69; Yale Univ, Mphilo, 71, PhD, 72. **CAREER** Unit Meth Chrch, Rocky Mtn Ann Con, Pastoral Minis, 72-76; Perkins School of Theology, SO Meth Univ, Asst Prof to Prof, theol, 76-92, Assoc Dean for Acad Affs, 90-93, Lehman Prof, Christ Doct, 92-. **HONORS AND AWARDS** Phi Beta Kappa; Omicron Delta Kappa. **MEMBERSHIPS** Am Acad Rel; Am Theo Soc. **RESEARCH**

Philos and Systema Theolo. **SELECTED PUBLICATIONS** Auth, Scripture Authenticity and Truth, J Rel, 96; The Question of the Doctrine of Providence, Theology Today, 92; Vision and Discernment, Scholars Press, 85; The Formation of Christian Understanding, Westminster Press, 81, 2d ed, Trinity Press, 93; Theory and Religious Understanding, Scholars Press, 75; auth, An Invitation to Theological Study, Trinity Press, 94. **CONTACT ADDRESS** Perkins School of Theology, So Methodist Univ, Dallas, TX 75275-0133. **EMAIL** cwood@mail.smu.edu

WOOD, DAVID C.
PERSONAL Born 12/21/1946, Oxford, United Kingdom, d, 2 children **DISCIPLINE** PHILOSOPHY **EDUCATION** Manchester Univ, BA, 68; Univ Warwick, PhD, 85. **CAREER** Lectr, Univ Warwick, 71-88; Sen Lectr, Univ Warwick, 88-92; Prof, Univ Warwick, 92-94; Prof, Vanderbilt Univ, 94-. **HONORS AND AWARDS** Jacque Voegeli Fel, Vanderbilt Univ, 96, 99. **MEMBERSHIPS** SPEP, IAEP, APA, Heidegger Circle. **RESEARCH** Deconstruction, phenomenology, time, Twentieth-Century European philosophy, Heidegger. **SELECTED PUBLICATIONS** Auth, Philosophy at the Limit, Routledge, 90; auth, The Deconstruction of Time, Humanities, 88; auth, The Deconstruction of Time, Northwestern UP, 00; **CONTACT ADDRESS** Dept Philos, Vanderbilt Univ, 2201 West End Ave, Nashville, TN 37235-0001. **EMAIL** david.c.wood@vanderbilt.edu

WOOD, FORREST E., JR.
PERSONAL Born 08/20/1937, Fairfield, TX, m, 1962, 2 children **DISCIPLINE** PHILOSOPHY **EDUCATION** Baylor Univ, BA, 58; Southwestern Baptist Theol Sem, ThD, 64; Southwestern Baptist Theol Sem, PhD, 74. **CAREER** Instr philos, Texas Wesleyan Col, 63-64; asst prof philos, Louisiana Col, 64-66; assoc prof philos, 66-86, prof, 87- , chemn Philos and Relig Dept, Univ So Mississippi. **HONORS AND AWARDS** Mem, Assoc of Philos of Relig, 85- ; evaluator, NEH; ed review board, Philos in the Contemporary World, 94- ; evaluator, Miss Humanities Coun; pres, Soc for Philos of Relig, 77-78; Danforth Assoc, 79-86. **MEMBERSHIPS** Soc for Philos of Relig; Miss Philos Soc; APA; Southern Soc for Philos and Psychol; Southwestern Philos Soc; Metaphysical Soc; Center for Process Stud. **SELECTED PUBLICATIONS** Auth, Whiteheadian Thought As A Basis for A Philosophy of Religion, University Press of Am, 86; auth, Henry David Thoreau: Vegetarian Hunter and Fisherman, Southwest Philos Rev, 93; auth, A Natural Philosophy of Our Time, Contemporary Philosophy, 95; auth, The Delights and Dilemmas of Hunting: The Hunting Versus Anti-Hunting Debate, University Press of America, 97. **CONTACT ADDRESS** Univ of So Mississippi, Southern Sta, PO Box 5015, Hattiesburg, MS 39406. **EMAIL** fwood@usm.edu

WOOD, FORREST GLEN
PERSONAL Born 03/15/1931, Oak Park, IL, m, 1978, 2 children **DISCIPLINE** AMERICAN NEGRO AND ECONOMIC HISTORY **EDUCATION** Sacramento State Col, AB, 57, MA, 58; Univ Calif, Berkeley, PhD(hist), 63. **CAREER** Asst prof hist, Bakersfield Ctr, 63-70, found res grant, 68, assoc prof, 70-80, Prof Hist, Calif State Col, Bakersfield, 80-, Vis prof Univ Iowa, summer 68 & Univ Calif, Santa Cruz, 71; Nat Endowment for Humanities, Brown, 76, Harvard, 81; consult, Nat Endowment for Humanities, 77-79. **MEMBERSHIPS** AHA; Orgn Am Historians; Southern Hist Asn; Asn Studies Negro Life & Cult. **RESEARCH** History of racism in America; Negro history; Civil War and Reconstruction. **SELECTED PUBLICATIONS** Auth, On revising reconstruction history, J Negro Hist, 4/66; Black Scare: The Racist Response to Emancipation and Reconstruction, Univ Calif, 68; Aspects of anti-Negro prejudice in mid-19th century America, Proc Afro-Am Conf, 69; On revising reconstruction history, White Power & Black Community, 69; The Era of Reconstruction, 1863-1877, Thomas Y Crowell, 75. **CONTACT ADDRESS** Dept of Hist, California State Univ, Bakersfield, Bakersfield, CA 93309.

WOOD, JOHN A.
DISCIPLINE CHRISTIAN ETHICS **EDUCATION** Columbia Bible Col, BA, 60; Southwestern Baptist Theol Sem, BD, 66; Baylor Univ, PhD, 75. **CAREER** Prof Relig, Baylor Univ, 81-. **MEMBERSHIPS** Amer Academy Relig; Soc of Christian Ethics. **RESEARCH** Peace issues; business ethics; analysis of films from an ethical perspective. **CONTACT ADDRESS** Dept of Relig, Baylor Univ, Waco, Waco, TX 76798. **EMAIL** John_Wood@Baylor.edu

WOOD, REGA
PERSONAL Born 12/08/1944, Pasadena, CA, m, 1965, 2 children **DISCIPLINE** PHILOSOPHY **EDUCATION** Reed Col, BA, 68; Cornell Univ, MA, 71, PhD, 75. **CAREER** Asst prof, St. Bonaventure Univ, 76-87, assoc prof, 87-89, full prof, 89-96; adjunct prof, Yale Divinity Sch; vis lect, Univ Calif San Diego, 86; senior res scholar, Yale Univ, 96-. **HONORS AND AWARDS** Am Philos Soc res grant, 97; Nat Endow for the Humanities fel, 97, archival res grant, 93; Alexander von Humboldt res fel, 91-92 & 83-84. **MEMBERSHIPS** Soc for Medieval and Renaissance Philos. **RESEARCH** Philosophy; History. **SELECTED PUBLICATIONS** Auth, Ockham on the Virtues, 97; "Richard Rufus and the Classical Tradition," 97; "Causality and Demonstration: An Early Scholastic Posterior Analytics Commentary," 96; "Individual Forms: Richard Rufus and John Duns Scotus," 96; "Richard Rufus and English Scholastic Discussion of Individuation," 96; "Angelic Individuation: According to Richard Rufus, St. Bonaventure and St. Thomas Aquinas," 96. **CONTACT ADDRESS** Philosophy Dept, Yale Univ, New Haven, CT 06520-8306. **EMAIL** Rufus@Pantheon.Yale.edu

WOOD, ROBERT
DISCIPLINE PHILOSOPHY **EDUCATION** Marquette Univ, BA, MA, PhD. **CAREER** Dept Philos, Univ Dallas **SELECTED PUBLICATIONS** Auth, Plato's Line Revisited: The Pedagogy of Complete Reflection, Rev of Metaphysics, 91; Six Heideggerian Figures, Amer Cath Philos Quart, 95; Being and Manifestness, Intl Philos Quart, 95; Recovery of the Aesthetic Center, Proc of the Amer Cath Philos Assn, 95. **CONTACT ADDRESS** Dept of Philos, Univ of Dallas, 1845 E Northgate Dr, Irving, TX 75062. **EMAIL** rwood@acad.udallas.edu

WOOD, WILLIAM L., JR.
PERSONAL Born 12/04/1940, Cleveland, OH, m **DISCIPLINE** LAW **EDUCATION** Brown U, BA 1962; Yale Law Sch, JD 1965. **CAREER** Untd Ch of Christ, 64; Mandell & Wright Houston TX, assoc 1965-68; Intl Nickel Co N Y & Pfizer Inc NY atty 1968-71; Union Carbide Corp NY atty 1971-74; City of N Y, gen cnsl & controller 1974-79; NY S Atty Gen, chief ed bureau 1979-81; NY St Office of Prof Disc, exec dir 1981-85; Wood & Scher, Attys, partner 1985-. **HONORS AND AWARDS** Black Achvrs in Industry Awd 1974 (Nom by Union Carbine Corp). **MEMBERSHIPS** Contributing editor, Discipline, natl journla covering prof discipline, 1982-84; Information Please Almanac, editor, 1981-82; NY St Dental Journal, What Every Dentist Should know about Prof Misconduct, June/July 1982 (vol 48 no 6 pp 378-380); NY St Dental Journal, an interview on prof dicipline Oct 1982 (vol 48 no 8 p 538); NY St Pharmacist, recent changes in prof dicipline (vol 57 no 1, Fall 1982, p v); NY St Dental Journal, Record retentiona professional responsibility even after the patient has gone, Feb 1984 (vol 50, no 2, p 98); NY St Pharmacist, To the new Supvr Pharmacist Congratulations & a word of Warning, summer 1983, vol 57, no 4; NY St Pharmacist, The violations comm vol 58, no 3, Spring 1984; Veterinary News, Legal Remedies for Unpaid Fees, May 1984; admtd to TX 1965, NY Bar 1969; NY St Bar Asso, Am Arbitration Asso, One Hundred Black Men Inc, Am Pub Hlth Asso, Natl Clearinghouse on Licensure, Enfrcmnt & Regulation. **CONTACT ADDRESS** Wood & Scher Attys at Law, One Chase Rd, Scarsdale, NY 10583.

WOODHOUSE, EDWARD JAMES
PERSONAL Born 12/25/1946, Durham, NC, 4 children **DISCIPLINE** POLITICAL SCIENCE **EDUCATION** Yale Univ, PhD, 83. **CAREER** Assoc Prof, Rensselaer Polytechnic Institute, 18 years. **HONORS AND AWARDS** Woodrow Wilson Fel; Int Studies; Assoc Sprout Awd in Int Ecology. **MEMBERSHIPS** Am Pol Sci; Soc for Soc Studies of Sci. **RESEARCH** Green Chemistry, Assistive Technologies, Envisioning a Commendable Civilization. **SELECTED PUBLICATIONS** Coed, Too Hot to Handle?: Social and Policy Issues in the Management of Radioactive Wastes, Yale Univ Press (New Haven, CT), 83; coauth, Averting Catastrophe: Strategies for Regulating Risky Technologies, Univ of Calif Press (Berkeley, CA), 86; coauth, The Demise of Nuclear Energy?: Lessons for Democratic Control of Technology, Yale Univ Press (New Haven, CT), 89; coauth, The Policy-Making Process, 3rd ed, Englewood Cliffs Prentice Hall, 93; coauth, "Incrementalism, Intelligent Trial-and-Error and the Future of Political Decision Theory," in A Heretical Heir of the Enlightenment, ed. H. Redner (Westview, 93); coauth, "Science, Government and the Politics of Knowledge," in Handbook of Science and Technology Studies (Sage, 95), 533-553; auth, "Can Science Be More Useful In Politics? The Case of Ecological Risk Assessment," Human and Ecological Risk Assessment 1 (95): 395-406; coauth, "When Expert Advice Works and When it Does Not," IEEE Technol and Soc Mag (97): 23-29; coauth, "Democratic Expertise: Integrating Knowledge, Power, and Participation," in Policy Studies Annual, ed. R. Hoppe et al (99); auth, "Reconstruction of a Technoscience?: The Greening of Chemistry and Chemical Engineering." **CONTACT ADDRESS** Dept of Sci & Technol Studies, Rensselaer Polytech Inst, 110 8th St, Troy, NY 12180-3590. **EMAIL** woodhouse@rpi.edu

WOODHOUSE, MARK B.
DISCIPLINE METAPHYSICS, PHILOSOPHY OF TIME, PHILOSOPHY OF MIND, EASTERN PHILOSOPHY AND **EDUCATION** Univ Miami, PhD, 70. **CAREER** Assoc prof, Ga State Univ. **SELECTED PUBLICATIONS** Auth, A Preface to Philosophy, 5th ed. **CONTACT ADDRESS** Georgia State Univ, Atlanta, GA 30303. **EMAIL** phlmbw@panther.gsu.edu

WOODRING, ANDREW N.
PERSONAL Born 04/10/1954, Defiance, OH, m, 1976, 3 children **DISCIPLINE** THEOLOGY **EDUCATION** Harvard Univ, BA, 76; Gordon-Conwell Theol Sem, M.Div, 80; Trinity Int Univ, PhD, 99. **CAREER** Pastor, Hope Evangelical Free Church, 84-92; adj prof, John Brown Univ, 92-93, 96-97; asst prof, LeTourneau Univ, 98-01; assoc prof, LeTourneau Univ, 01-. **MEMBERSHIPS** Evangelical Theol Soc; Soc Biblical Lit; Am Asn Relig. **RESEARCH** Church history; 18th century Evangelical revivals. **CONTACT ADDRESS** PO Box 7001, Longview, TX 75607-7001. **EMAIL** woodrina@letu.edu

WOODRUFF, PAUL
PERSONAL Born 08/28/1943, Summit, NJ, m, 1973, 2 children **DISCIPLINE** PHILOSOPHY **EDUCATION** Princeton Univ, PhD, 73. **CAREER** Prof, Univ Tex Austin, 73-. **MEMBERSHIPS** Am Philos Asn. **RESEARCH** Ancient Greek Philosophy. **SELECTED PUBLICATIONS** Auth, articles on philosophical topics; coauth, Plato: Phaedrus, 95; Early Greek Political Thought from Homer to the Sophists, 95. **CONTACT ADDRESS** Dept of Philosophy, Univ of Texas, Austin, Austin, TX 78712. **EMAIL** pbw@mail.utexas.edu

WOODWARD, J.
PERSONAL Born 09/17/1946, Chicago, IL, m, 1978, 1 child **DISCIPLINE** PHILOSOPHY **EDUCATION** Carelton Col, BA, 68; Univ Texas, PhD, 77. **CAREER** Prof, phil, 92-, Calif Inst Tech. **RESEARCH** Philosophy of science **SELECTED PUBLICATIONS** Auth, Supervenience and Singular Causal Claims, Explan & Its Limits, Cambridge Univ Press, 90; auth, Liberalism and Migration, Free Movement: Ethical Issues in the Transnational Migration of People and Money, Harvester-Wheatsheaf, 92; art, Realism About Laws, Erkenntnis 36, 92; auth, Capacities and Invariance, Phil Problems of the Internal & External Worlds: Essays Concerning the Phil of Adolph Grunbaum, Univ Pitts Press, 93; auth, Causality and Explanation in Econometrics, On the Reliability of Economic Models: Essays in the Phil of Economics, Kluwer, 95; coauth, Conduct, Misconduct and the Structure of Science, Amer Scientist, 96; art, Explanation, Invariance and Intervention, PSA 96; auth, Causal Modeling, Probabilities and Invariance, Causality in Crisis? Statistical Methods and the Search for Causal Knowledge in the Social Sciences, Univ Notre Dame Press, 97. **CONTACT ADDRESS** Div of Humanities and Social Sciences, California Inst of Tech, Pasadena, CA 91175. **EMAIL** jfw@hss.caltech.edu

WOODYARD, DAVID O.
PERSONAL Born 04/27/1932, Oak Park, IL, m, 1955, 2 children **DISCIPLINE** RELIGION **EDUCATION** Denison Univ, BA, 54; Union Theol Sem, NYork, MDiv, 58; Oberlin Col, DMin, 65. **CAREER** Dir univ Christian fel, Univ Conn, 58-60; asst prof relig & dean chapel, 60-77, assoc prof, 78-81, Prof Relig & Chmn Dept, Denison Univ, 81-, Danforth Intern Prog, 56-57. **MEMBERSHIPS** Nat asn Col & Univ Chaplains; Am Acad Religion. **RESEARCH** The doctrine of God; liberation theology; social ethics. **SELECTED PUBLICATIONS** Auth, Happenings in higher education, Foundations: J Baptist Hist & Theol, 7/67; Living Without God--Before God, 68, To Be Human Now!, 69, The Opaqueness of God, 70, Beyond Cynicism: The Practice of Hope, 73 & Strangers and Exiles: Living by Promises, 74, Westminster; coauth, Journey Toward Freedom: Economic Structures and Theological Perspectives, Fairleigh Dickinson Univ Press, 82; Risking Liberation: Middle Class Powerlessness and Social Heroism, John Knox Press, 88; Liberating Nature: Theology and Economics in the New Order, Pilgrim Press, 99. **CONTACT ADDRESS** Dept of Relig, Denison Univ, 1 Denison University, Granville, OH 43023-1359. **EMAIL** MAX:woodyard@denison.edu

WOOLDREDGE, JOHN
PERSONAL Born 08/19/1959, Bristol, PA, m, 1994, 2 children **DISCIPLINE** CRIMINAL JUSTICE **EDUCATION** Univ Illinois, PhD, 86. **CAREER** Asst prof, New Mex State Univ; asst prof, Univ Cincinnati; assoc prof. **HONORS AND AWARDS** FDC Gnt: NIJ Gnt, 95, 98. **SELECTED PUBLICATIONS** Coauth, "Parental Support and Juvenile Delinquency: Empirical Evidence from an Emerging Paradigm," in Contemporary Perspectives on Family Research, eds. G Fox, M Benson (eds.) forthcoming; coauth, "Predicting the Likelihood of Faculty Victimization: Individual Demographics and Routine Activities," in Legal, Social, and Policy Aspects of Campus Crime, eds. J Sloan, B Fisher (Orlando: Charles C. Thomas Pub, 95); auth, "The American Correctional Association," in Encyclopedia of American Prisons, eds. MD McShane, FP Williams III (San Bernardino: Garland Pub, 95); coauth, "High School Students' Adherence to Rape Myths and the Effectiveness of High School Rape Awareness Programs," Viol Again Wom 4 (97): 308-328; coauth, "Predicting the Estimated Use of Alternatives to Incarceration," J Quant Crim 13 (97):121-142; coauth, "Explaining Variation in Perceptions of Inmate Crowding," Prison J 77 (97): 27-40; coauth, "Severity of Dispositions and the Likelihood of Domestic Violence Recidivism," Crime Delinq 44 (98): 388-398; coauth, "Inmate Lifestyles and Opportunities for Victimization," J Res Crime Delinq 35 (98): 480-502; coauth, "Inmate Routines and Adjustment," Crim Just Behav 26 (99): 235-250. **CONTACT ADDRESS** Dept Criminal Justice, Univ of Cincinnati, 2600 Clifton Ave, Cincinnati, OH 45220. **EMAIL** john.wooldredge@uc.edu

WOOLLEY, PETER J.
PERSONAL Born 02/23/1960, New York, NY, m, 1994 **DISCIPLINE** COMPARATIVE POLITICS, HISTORY **EDUCA-**

TION St. Joseph's Univ, BA, 81; Univ Pittsburgh, MA, 83, PhD, 89. **CAREER** Book review editor, Journal of Conflict Studies, 97-; Chair, Dept of Social Sciences and History, Prof of Comparative Politics, Fairleigh Dickinson Univ, Madison, NJ, 98-. **HONORS AND AWARDS** Edwin Miller History Prize, US Naval War College. **MEMBERSHIPS** APSA. **RESEARCH** Japanese defense policy, maritime powers and decline. **SELECTED PUBLICATIONS** Auth, Geography and the Limits of US Military Intervention, in Conflict Quart, vol XI, no 4, fall 91; Japan's Security Policies: Into the Twenty-First Century, Jour East and West Studies, vol 22, no 2, Oct 92; Low-Level Military Conflict and the Future of Japan's Armed Forces, Conflict Quart, vol XIII, no 4, fall 93; Geography Revisited: Expectations of US Military Intervention in the Post-Cold War Era, in Peacemaking, Peacekeeping and Coalition Warfare, Fariborz L. Mokhtari, ed, Nat Defense Univ Press, 94; The Role of War and Strategy in the Transformation and Decline of Great Powers, Naval War Col Rev, Vol XLIX, no 1, winter 96; with Cdr. Mark S. Woolley, USN, The Kata of Japan's Naval Forces, Naval War Col Rev, Vol XLIX, no 2, spring 96; Japan's Minesweeping Decision 1991: An Organizational Response, Asian Survey, Vol XXXVI, no 8, Aug 96, reprinted in Edward R. Beauchamp, ed, Dimensions of Contemporary Japan, Vol II, Garland Pub, 99; Japan's Sealane Defense Revisited, Strategic Rev, Vol XXIV, no IV, fall 96; Arguing From the Same Premises: the Ideology is Intact, American Politics: Core Argument and Current Controversy, P. J. Woolley and A. R. Papa, eds, Prentice Hall Pubs, 98; In Defense of Pacific Rim Democracies: the US-Japan Alliance, Aiding Democracies Under Seige, Gabriel Marcela and Anthony Joes, eds, Praeger Pubs, 99; Japan's Navy: Politics and Paradox, 1971-2000, Lynne-Reinner Pubs, 00. **CONTACT ADDRESS** Dept of Social Sciences and History, Fairleigh Dickinson Univ, Florham-Madison, Madison, NJ 07940. **EMAIL** Woolley@alpha.fdu.edu

WOOLSEY, ROBERT
PERSONAL Born 10/31/1936, Fort Worth, TX, m, 1958, 2 children **DISCIPLINE** BUSINESS ADMINISTRATION **EDUCATION** Univ Tex, BS, 59; MS, 67; PhD, 69. **CAREER** Prof, Colo School of Mines, 69-. **HONORS AND AWARDS** Commander's Medal; Outstanding Civilian Service Medal; Distinguished Civilian Service Medal, US Army; Harold Lardor Prize. **MEMBERSHIPS** INFORMS, APICS. **RESEARCH** Acceptance of change in a technological culture. **CONTACT ADDRESS** Dept Bus & Econ Studies, Colorado Sch of Mines, 1500 Illinois St, Golden, CO 80401.

WORKS, ROBERT G.
DISCIPLINE LAW **EDUCATION** Kans State Univ, BA; St Louis Univ, JD. **CAREER** Prof **RESEARCH** Contracts; insurance. **SELECTED PUBLICATIONS** Auth, Nebraska Property and Liability Insurance Law, 85. **CONTACT ADDRESS** Law Dept, Univ of Nebraska, Lincoln, 103 Ross McCollum Hall, PO Box 830902, Lincoln, NE 68588-0420. **EMAIL** rworks@unlinfo.unl.edu

WORTH, SARAH ELIZABETH
PERSONAL Born 03/12/1970, Ann Arbor, MI **DISCIPLINE** PHILOSOPHY **EDUCATION** Furman Univ, BA, 92; Univ of Louisville, MA, 94; SUNY Buffalo, PhD, 97. **CAREER** Asst prof, Allegheny Col, 97-98; asst prof, Miami Univ, 98-99; asst prof, Furman Univ, 99-. **RESEARCH** Aesthetics; ancient philosophy, biomedical ethics. **SELECTED PUBLICATIONS** "Wittgenstein's Musical Understanding," British J of Aesthet, v 37, no 2. **CONTACT ADDRESS** Dept of Philosophy, Furman Univ, Greenville, SC 29613.

WREN, DANIEL ALAN
PERSONAL Born 01/08/1932, Columbia, MO, w, 1962, 3 children **DISCIPLINE** MANAGEMENT **EDUCATION** Univ Mo, BS, 54, MS, 60; Univ Ill, PhD, 64. **CAREER** Asst prof to prof, Fla State Univ, 63-73; Prof, Mgt, Univ Okla, 73-; David Ross Boyd prof mgt and McCasland Prof Am Free Enterprise. **HONORS AND AWARDS** Educator of the Year, Acad of Mgt, 91; Outstanding Educators of Am Awd; Merrick Found Awd for Teaching Excellence. **MEMBERSHIPS** Acad Mgt; Southern Mgt Asn; Bus Hist Conf. **RESEARCH** Management history; Business history; Business strategy. **SELECTED PUBLICATIONS** auth, "Learning from Experience: Henri Fayol", Jour of Mgt hist; auth, The Evolution of Management Thought, John Wiley & Sons, 94; ed, Early Managment Thought, Dartmouth Publ Ltd, 97; coauth, Management Innovators: The People and Ideas That Shaped Modern Business, Oxford Univ Pr, 98. **CONTACT ADDRESS** Univ of Oklahoma, Adams Hall, Rm 206, Norman, OK 73019-0450. **EMAIL** dwren@ou.edu

WREN, THOMAS
PERSONAL Born Kansas City, MO, m, 2 children **DISCIPLINE** PHILOSOPHY **EDUCATION** St. Marys Col, BA, 59; DePaul Univ, MA, 62; St. Marys Col, MED, 65; Loyola Univ Chicago, MA, 65; Northwstrn Univ, PhD, 69. **CAREER** Prof, 66-pres, Loyola Univ Chicago **SELECTED PUBLICATIONS** Auth, Moral Sensibilities, 2 vols; auth, Caring about Morality; Philosophy of Development; The Moral Domain; The Moral Self, The Personal Universe **CONTACT ADDRESS** Loyola Univ, Chicago, 6525 Sheridan Rd., Chicago, IL 60626.

WRIGGINS, JENNIFER
DISCIPLINE LAW **EDUCATION** Yale Univ, AB; Harvard Univ, JD. **CAREER** Prof; taught in, Trial Advocacy Workshop, Harvard Law Sch, 94, 95; clerked, Hon Edward T. Gignoux, US Dist Judge, Portland, Maine; past asst atty gen, Civil Rights Div Mass Atty Generals' Off in Boston; past Articles and Exec Ed, Harvard Women's Law J; past partner, Pressman, Kruskal & Wriggins in Cambridge, Mass. **MEMBERSHIPS** Bd Cambridge-Somerville Legal Serv; bd, Maine Civil Liberties Union and Civil Liberties Union Mass. **SELECTED PUBLICATIONS** Auth, Rape, Racism and the Law; Genetics, IQ, Determinism, and Torts: The Example of Discovery in Lead Exposure Litigation, Boston Univ Law Rev, 97; sect on Rape, in The Reader's Companion to US Women's Hist, 97; coauth, Supreme Ct amicus brief in the case of UAW v. Johnson Controls; Parental Rights Termination Jurisprudence: Questioning the Framework. **CONTACT ADDRESS** School of Law, Univ of So Maine, 246 Deering Ave., PO Box 9300, Portland, ME 04104-9300. **EMAIL** jwriggin@usm.maine.edu

WRIGHT, CHARLES ALAN
PERSONAL Born 09/03/1927, Philadelphia, PA, m, 1950, 5 children **DISCIPLINE** LAW **EDUCATION** Wesleyan Univ, AB, 47; Yale Univ, LLB, 49. **CAREER** From asst prof to assoc prof law, Univ Minn, 50-55; from assoc prof to prof, 55-65, Charles T McCormick Prof Law, 65-80, William B Bates Chair for the Admin of Justice, Univ Tex, Austin, 80-97, Charles Alan Wright chair in Federal Courts, 97-00; Vinson & Elkins Chair in Law, 95, Hayden W Head Regents Chair for Fac Excellence, 91; Consult, Ala Comn Procedural Reform, 56-57; vis prof, Univ Pa, 59-60; mem adv comt rules of civil procedure, Judicial Conf US, 61-64, standing comt rules practice & procedure, 64-76; reporter, Am Law Inst Studies Div Jurisdiction Between State & Fed Courts, 63-69; vis prof, Univ Pa Law School, 59-60, vis prof, Harvard Univ, 64-65, law, Yale Univ, 68-69, vis fel, Wolfson Col, Cambridge, Engl, 84; Arthur Goodhart vis prof, Legal Sci, Univ Cambridge, Cambridge, Engl, 90-91, vis scholar, Victoria Univ Wellington, New Zealand, 93; consult to counsel for President of US, 73-74; mem, Permanent Comt Oliver Wendell Holmes Devise, 75-. **HONORS AND AWARDS** Student Bar Asn Teaching Excellence Awd, 80; fel, Am Acad Arts & Sci, 84; Fel Res Awd, Fel of Am Bar Found, 89; Doctor of Humane Letters, honoris causa, Episcopal Theol Sem of Southwest, Austin, Tex, 92; Leon Green Awd, Tex Law Rev, 93; Distinguished Alum Awd, Wesleyan Univ, Middletown, CT, 93; Robert B McKay Prof Awd, Tort & Insurance Sect, Am Bar Asn, 95; Clarity Awd for Clear Legal Writing, Plain English Comt, State Bar Mich, 97; Fordham-Stein Prize, Fordham Univ, 97; Learned Hand Medal, Fed Bar Counc, 98; Lifetime Acheivement Awd, UT Law Sch, 00. **MEMBERSHIPS** Am Bar Asn; Am Law Inst; Am Judicature Soc; Inst Judicial Admin. **RESEARCH** Federal courts; judicial procedure; constitutional law. **SELECTED PUBLICATIONS** Auth, Wright's Minnesota Rules, 54; Cases on Remedies, 55; ed, Barron & Holtzoff, Federal Practice & Procedure, 58-61; co-auth, Cases on Federal Courts, 4th-9th ed, 62-92; Wright on Federal Courts, 1st-5th ed, 63-94; co-auth, Procedure -- The Handmaid of Justice, 65; co-auth, The American Law Institute Study of the Division of Jurisdiction between State and Federal Courts, 69; Federal Practice and Procedure, Criminal, Civil, Evidence, Jurisdiction and Related Matters, 69-97. **CONTACT ADDRESS** Law Sch, Univ of Texas, Austin, 727 E Dean Keeton, Austin, TX 78705-3224. **EMAIL** ckieke@mail.law.utexas.edu

WRIGHT, DANAYA C.
DISCIPLINE LAW **EDUCATION** Cornell Univ, BA; Univ Ariz, MA; Cornell Univ, JD; Johns Hopkins Univ, PhD. **CAREER** Asst prof, Univ Fla, 98-; past adj prof, Ind Univ; past vis asst prof, Ariz State Univ. **MEMBERSHIPS** Law and Soc Asn; Amer Soc for Legal Hist. **RESEARCH** Estates &trusts, feminist theory, urisprudence, legal history, and property. **CONTACT ADDRESS** School of Law, Univ of Florida, PO Box 117625, Gainesville, FL 32611-7625. **EMAIL** wrightdc@law.ufl.edu

WRIGHT, JOHN
PERSONAL Born 05/03/1942, Toronto, ON, Canada, m, 1997, 2 children **DISCIPLINE** PHILOSOPHY **EDUCATION** Univ Toronto, BA, 64; MA, 67; York Univ, PhD, 75. **HONORS AND AWARDS** Can Coun Fel, 76-78; Rockefeller Foundation Fel, Univ TX, 91. **MEMBERSHIPS** Am Philos Asn; Am Soc for 18th Cent Studies; Hume Soc; Eighteenth Cent Scottish Studies Soc; British Soc for the Hist of Philos. **RESEARCH** Early Modern Philosophy, especially Descartes, Locke, Hume; Early Modern Medicine & Science. **SELECTED PUBLICATIONS** Auth, "Metaphysics and Physiology: Mind, Body and the Animal Economy in 18th Century Scotland," in Studies in the Philosophy of the Scottish Enlightenment, (Oxford Univ Press, 90), 251-301; co-ed, Hume and Hume's Connexions, Edinburgh Univ Press, 94; co-ed, Psyche and Soma: Physicians and Metaphysicians in the History of Thought from Antiquity to Enlightenment, Oxford Univ Press, 00; co-ed, John Locke's An Essay Concerning Human Understanding In Focus, Routledge Press, 00; auth, "Hume's Causal Realism: Recovering a traditional Interpretation," in The New Hume: Interpretations for and Against Realist Readings of Hume on Causation, Routledge, 00; auth, "Materialism and the Life Soul in Eighteenth-Century Scotland," in The Scottish Enlightenment: Essays in Re-interpretation, Univ Rochester Press, 00. **CONTACT ADDRESS** Dept Relig & Philos, Central Michigan Univ, 100 W Preston Rd, Mount Pleasant, MI 48859-0001. **EMAIL** John.P.Wright@cmich.edu

WRIGHT, JOHN H.
PERSONAL Born 02/13/1922, San Francisco, CA **DISCIPLINE** THEOLOGY **EDUCATION** Mt St Michael's Sem, PhL, 46; Gonzaga Univ, MA, 46; Alma Col, STL, 53; Gregorian Univ, STD, 57. **CAREER** Instr philos, Gonzaga Univ, 46-49; prof extraordinarius theol, Gregorian Univ, 56-60; PROF THEOL, JESUIT SCH THEOL, BERKELEY, 60-; Prof Syst Theol, Grad Theol Union, 66-, Am Asn Theol Schs grant, 71-72; Bernard Hanley theol, Santa Clara Univ, 79-80. **MEMBERSHIPS** Cath Theol Soc Am (vpres, 71-72, pres, 72-73). **RESEARCH** Divine providence; theological method; ecumenism. **SELECTED PUBLICATIONS CONTACT ADDRESS** Jesuit Sch of Theol, Berkeley, 1735 LeRoy Ave, Berkeley, CA 94709.

WRIGHT, JOHN ROBERT
PERSONAL Born 10/20/1936, Carbondale, IL, s **DISCIPLINE** PATRISTIC & MEDIEVAL CHURCH HISTORY **EDUCATION** Univ of the South, BA, 58; Emory Univ, MA, 59; Gen Theol Sem, MDiv, 63; Oxford Univ, DPhil, 67. **CAREER** Instr church hist, Episcopal Theol Sch, MA, 66-68; asst prof ecclesiastical hist, 68-72, prof church hist, Gen Theol Sem, 72-, res assoc, Pontifical Inst Mediaeval Studies, Toronto, 76 & 81; mem, Comn Faith & Order, World Coun Churches & Standing Ecumenical Comn of Episcopal Church, 77-; mem, Anglican/Roman Cath Consult in US, 70-; res scholar, Huntington Libr, 77; Canon Theologian to the Bishop of New York; Theological Consultant to Ecumenical Office of the Episcopal Church. **HONORS AND AWARDS** Honorary DD Episcopal Theological Seminary of the Southwest, Austin, TX; Honorary DD, Trinity Lutheran Seminary, Columbus, OH; Honorary D. Cn.L. The University of the South, Sewanee, TN; Patriarchal crosses of distinction from the Ecumenical Patriarch of Constantinople, the Russian Orthodox Patriarch of Moscow, the Armenian Patriarch of Jerusalem, and the Syrian Orthodox Patriarch of Antioch, also from the Catholics of the Malankara Orthodox Church of India; Life Fellow of the Royal Historical Society, London; Chaplain of the Royal Order of St. John of Jerusalem. **MEMBERSHIPS** AHA; Mediaeval Acad Am; Am Soc Church Hist; Church Hist Soc; Royal Historical Society; Anglican Society (Pres.); North American Academy of Ecumenists (Pres.) **RESEARCH** Fourteenth century church-state and Anglo-Papal relations; Walter Reynolds, Archbishop of Canterbury 1314-1327; Lambert of Auxerre, mid-thirteenth century Dominican commentator on Aristotle. **SELECTED PUBLICATIONS** Ed, Handbook of American Orthodoxy, Forward Movement, 72; co-ed, Episcopalians and Roman Catholics: Can They Ever Get Together?, Dimension, 72; coauth, A Pope for All Christians?, Paulist, 76 & SPCK, 77; auth, A Communion of Communions: One Eucharistic Fellowship, Seabury, 79; The Church and The English Crown 1305-1334, Pontifical Inst Mediaeval Studies, Toronto, 80; The Canterbury Statement and the Five Priesthoods, One in Christ, Vol 11: 3 & Anglican Theol Rev, Vol 57: 4; Anglicans and the Papacy, J Ecumenical Studies, Vol 13: 3; The Accounts of the Constables of Bordeaux 1381-1390, with Particular Notes on their Ecclesiastical and Liturgical Significance, Mediaeval Studies, 42: 238-307; An Anglican Commentary on Selected Documents of Vatican II, Ecumenical Trends, Vol 9: 8 & 9; Quadrilateral at One Hundred, Mowbray, 88; Prayer Book Spirituality, Church Publishing, 89; The Anglican Tradition, SPCK/Fortress, 91; Readings for the Daily Office from the Early Church, Church Publishing, 91; They Still Speak: Readings for the Lesser Feasts, Church Publishing, 93. **CONTACT ADDRESS** General Theol Sem, 175 9th Ave, New York, NY 10011-4924. **EMAIL** wright@gts.edu

WRIGHT, LARRY
PERSONAL Born 08/24/1937, m, 1968, 1 child **DISCIPLINE** PHILOSOPHY OF SCIENCE **EDUCATION** Ind Univ, PhD. **CAREER** Prof, Univ Calif, Riverside. **RESEARCH** Basic reasoning; Wittgenstein; Philosophy of science. **SELECTED PUBLICATIONS** Auth, Teleological Explanation, Univ Calif Press, 76; Practical Reasoning, Harcourt Brace Jovanovich, 88; Argument and Deliberation: A Plea for understanding, The Jour of Philos, Vol 92, No 11, 95. **CONTACT ADDRESS** Dept of Philos, Univ of California, Riverside, 1156 Hinderaker Hall, Riverside, CA 92521-0209. **EMAIL** lwright@citrus.ucr.edu

WRIGHT, NICHOLAS THOMAS
PERSONAL Born 12/01/1948, Morpeth, England, m, 1971, 4 children **DISCIPLINE** NEW TESTAMENT **EDUCATION** Oxford Univ, BA, 71, BA, 73, MA, 75, DPhil, 81; Cambridge Univ, PhD(theol), 81. **CAREER** Res fel theol, Merton Col, Oxford, 75-78; fel & chaplain, Downing Col, Cambridge, 78-81; asst prof New Testament, McGill Univ, 81-; dean of Lichfield Cathedral, Staffordshire, England, 99. **RESEARCH** Pauline theology; christology, New Testament and modern; hermeneutics. **SELECTED PUBLICATIONS** Co-ed, The Glory of Christ in the New Testament: Studies in Christology in Memory of George Bradford Caird, Clarendon Pr, Oxford, 87; auth, Who Was Jesus?, Eerdmans, 92; auth, The Climax of the Covenant, Fortress, 93; auth, Jesus and the Victory of God, Fortress, 93;

auth, The Crown and the Fire, Eerdmans, 95; auth, The Lord and His Prayer, Eerdmans, 97; auth, For All God's Worth, Eerdmans, 97; auth, What St. Paul Really Said, Eerdmans, 97; auth, The Millinium Myth: Hope for a Postmodern World, Westminister John Knox Pr, 99; coauth, The Meaning of Jesus: Two Visions, Harper-SanFrancisco, 99. **CONTACT ADDRESS** Fac of Relig Studies, 3520 University St, Montreal, QC, Canada H3A 2A7.

WRIGHT, ROBERTA V. HUGHES
PERSONAL Born Detroit, MI, m, 1989 **DISCIPLINE** LAW **EDUCATION** Univ of MI, PhD 1973; Wayne State Univ Law Sch, JD; Wayne State U, MEd. **CAREER** Detroit Pub Sch, past sch social worker; Detroit Comm on Children & Youth, past dir; Shaw Coll, past vice pres for Academic Affairs; County Public Admin, practicing lawyer Michigan Courts & admitted to practice bar, District of Columbia and Supreme Court of USA; Lawrence, former prof; First Independence Nat Bank, inst organizer & dir; Charro Book Co, Inc, vice pres, currently. **HONORS AND AWARDS** Recipient NAACP Freedom Awd; MI Chronicle Newspaper Cit of Yr; Harriet Tubman Awd; Alpha Kappa Alpha Sorority Recognition Awd; Quality Quintet Awd Detroit Skyliner Mag. **MEMBERSHIPS** Mem Am Bar Assn; mem MI Bar Assn; past mem Am & MI Trial Lawyers Assn; mem Oakland Co Bar Assn; mem Detroit Bar Assn; Wayne State Univ Law Alumni; Univ of MI Alumni Assn; AKA Sorority; life mem NAACP; mem Renaissance Club; million dollar mem Museum of African American History. **CONTACT ADDRESS** Charro Book Co Inc, 29777 Telegraph Rd #2500, Southfield, MI 48034.

WRIGHT, TERRENCE C.
DISCIPLINE PHENOMENOLOGY AND CONTEMPORARY PHILOSOPHIES OF LITERATURE AND AESTHETICS **EDUCATION** St Vincent Col, BA; Villanova Univ, MA; Bryn Mawr Col, PhD. **CAREER** Fac, Mt Saint Mary's Col, 89-. **RESEARCH** Theories of interpretation in art and literature and the nature of poetic expression. **SELECTED PUBLICATIONS** Publ on, relationship between poetry and philos. **CONTACT ADDRESS** Dept of Philosophy, Mount Saint Mary's Col and Sem, 16300 Old Emmitsburg Rd, Emmitsburg, MD 21727-7799. **EMAIL** wright@msmary.edu

WRIGHT-BOTCHWEY, ROBERTA YVONNE
PERSONAL Born 10/09/1946, York, SC **DISCIPLINE** LAW **EDUCATION** Fisk U, BA 1967; Yale U, ISSP cert 1966; Univ MI Sch of Andrew Iii, JD. **CAREER** Private Practice; NC Central Univ School of Law, asst prof corp counsel Tanzania Legal Corp Dar es Salaam Tanzania; Zambia Ltd Lusaka Zambia, sr legal asst rural devel corp. **HONORS AND AWARDS** Outstdg Young Women of Am 1976; Sydney P Raymond lectr Jackson State Univ 1977. **MEMBERSHIPS** Mem NC Assn of Blck Lawyers; Nat Bar Assn; Nat Conf of Black Lawyers; SC & DC Bar Assn; hon mem Delta Theta Phi; consult EPA 1976; lectr Sci Jury Sel & Evidence Workshop; legal adv Zambian Corp Del to Tel Aviv, Israel 1971; Atty Gen of Zambia Select Com to Investigate Railways 1972; Delta Sigma Theta Sor; consult Women's Prison Group 1975; consult EPA Environmental Litigation Workshop 1976; NCBL Commn to Invest Discrim Prac in Law Schs 1977; dir Councon Legal Educ Oppor Summer Inst 1977; Phi Beta Kappa 1967. **CONTACT ADDRESS** 339 E Main, PO Box 10646, Rock Hill, SC 29730.

WU, FRANK H.
PERSONAL Born 08/20/1967, Cleveland, OH, m, 1998 **DISCIPLINE** LEGAL STUDIES **EDUCATION** Johns Hopkins, BA, 88; Univ Mich, JD, 91. **CAREER** Asst/Assoc Prof, Howard Univ, 95-. **HONORS AND AWARDS** Fel, Stanford, 94-99; Grant, Civil Liberties; Public Educ Fund. **MEMBERSHIPS** DC Bar Asn. **RESEARCH** Civil rights, race, immigration. **SELECTED PUBLICATIONS** Auth, "Neither Black Nor White: Asian American and Affirmative Action," 15 BC Third World L J 225 (95); coauth, chapt in The Affirmative Action Debate, ed. George Curry (96); auth, chapt in Illegal Immigration: Opposing Viewpoints," ed. Charles Cozic (96); coauth, Beyond Self-Interest: Asian Pacific Americans Toward a Community of Justice, A Politic Analysis of Affirmative Action, 96; coauth, "The Evolution of Race in the Law: The Supreme Court Moves from Approving Internment of Japanese Americans to Disapproving Affirmative Action for African American," 1 Mich J of Law and Race 165 (96); auth, "The Limits of Borders: A Moderate Proposal for Immigration Reform," 7 Stanford Law and Policy Rev 35 (96); coauth, "Have You No Decency? An Analysis of Racial Respects of Media Coverage on the John Huang Matter," 7 Asian Am Policy Rev 1 (97); auth, "Political Movements," 18 SAIS Rev 179 (98); auth, "New Paradigms of Civil Rights," 66 George Washington Law Rev 698 (98); coauth, "'People from China Crossing the River': Asian Americans and Foreign Influence," in book ed. Gordon Chang (Stanford Press, forthcoming). **CONTACT ADDRESS** Sch of Law, Howard Univ, 2900 Van Ness St NW, Washington, DC 20008-1106. **EMAIL** fwu@law.howard.edu

WU, JOSEPH SEN
PERSONAL Born 09/10/1934, Canton, China, m, 1982, 3 children **DISCIPLINE** PHILOSOPHY, CHINESE CLASSICS **EDUCATION** Taiwan Norm Univ, BA, 59; Wash Univ, MA, 62; Southern Ill Univ, PhD(philos), 67. **CAREER** From instr to asst prof philos Univ Mo-St Louis, 63-67; asst prof, Northern Ill Univ, 67-70; assoc prof, 70-73, prof philos, Calif State Univ Sacramento 73-, vis prof, Loyola Univ, Ill, 69-70 & Nat Taiwan Univ, 76-77. **MEMBERSHIPS** Am Philos Asn; Soc Comp & Asian Philos. **RESEARCH** American philosophy; Far Eastern philosophy; philosophy of culture. **SELECTED PUBLICATIONS** Auth, Contemporary Western Philosophy from an Eastern viewpoint, Int Philos Quart, 68; The Paradoxical Situation of Western Philosophy and the Search for Chinese Wisdom, Inquiry, 71; Understanding Maoism, Studies Soviet Thought, 74; Comparative Philosophy and Culture (in Chinese), Tung Ta, Taiwan, 78; Clarification and Enlightenment: Essays in Comparative Philosophy, Univ Am, 78; many articles in contemporary philosophy and comparative philosophy in 1980's and 1990's. **CONTACT ADDRESS** Dept of Philos, California State Univ, Sacramento, 6000 J St, Sacramento, CA 95819-6033.

WU, JULIE L.
PERSONAL Born 08/20/1949, Hong Kong, m, 1983 **DISCIPLINE** NEW TESTAMENT **EDUCATION** Fuller Theol Sem, PhD, 92. **CAREER** Assoc Prof of New Testament, Dir of Masters Degree Prog, 93-, Logos Evangelical Sem. **HONORS AND AWARDS** Women in Leadership Awd, ATS, 99. **MEMBERSHIPS** Soc of Biblical Lit. **RESEARCH** Pauline Lit and Theol. **SELECTED PUBLICATIONS** Auth, Liturgical Elements, in: Dictionary of Paul and his Letters, IVP, 93; Hymns, Liturgical Elements, Mary in: Dictionary of the Later New Testament and Its Development, IVP, 97, Galations in Zondervan Illustrated Bible Background Commentary, 00. **CONTACT ADDRESS** 9358 Telstar Ave, El Monte, CA 91731. **EMAIL** jleewu@les.edu

WU, KUANG-MING
PERSONAL Born 07/24/1933, Tainan, China, m, 1961, 4 children **DISCIPLINE** PHILOSOPHY, RELIGION, COMPARATIVE CULTURE, COMPARATIVE RELIGION, COMPARATIVE PHILOSOPHY **EDUCATION** Yale Univ, BD, 62, STM, 63, PhD(philos), 65. **CAREER** Instr philos, Yale Univ, 65-68; asst prof, 68-71, assoc prof, 71-80, PROF PHILOS, UNIV WIS-OSHKOSH, 80-, Vis prof philos, Univ Tex, El Paso, 81-82; Nat Taiwan Univ, 88-90, Nat Ching-Chong Univ, 92-96, Univ Pratoria, 92. **HONORS AND AWARDS** Distinguished Awd for On Chinese Body Thinking, Taiwan, 94; John McN Rosebush Univ Prof Univ of Wisconsin-OshKosh. **MEMBERSHIPS** Int Soc Chinese Philos. **RESEARCH** Oriental studies; existentialism and phenomenology; comparative culture; comparative philosophy. **SELECTED PUBLICATIONS** Coed, Thinking Through Death, 88; auth, Chuang Tzu (in Chinese), Tung Ta, Taipei, 88; auth, History and Thinking (in Chinese), Leng Ching, Taipei, 89; auth, The Butterfly as Companion, State Univ of NY Press, 90; auth, History, Thinking, and Literature in Chinese Philosophy, Academia Sinica, Taipei, 91; auth, On Chinese Body Thinking, Brill, Leiden, 97; auth, On the Logic of Togetherness, Brill, Leiden, 98; auth, On Metaphoring, Brill, Leiden, forthcoming. **CONTACT ADDRESS** Dept of Philos, Univ of Wisconsin, Oshkosh, Box 30791, Columbia, MO 65205. **EMAIL** kuang_wu@hotmail.com

WUBNIG, JUDY
PERSONAL Born Brooklyn, NY **DISCIPLINE** PHILOSOPHY **EDUCATION** Swathmore Col, BA, 55; Yale Univ, MA, 58, PhD, 63. **CAREER** Instr, hum, Col Basic Studs, Boston Univ, 60-62; instr, dept philos, Tufts Univ, 62-63; lectr, Univ Col, Northern Univ, 63-66; Asst Prof Philosophy, Univ Waterloo, 65-. **MEMBERSHIPS** Nat Asn Scholars; Am Philos Asn; Can Asn Univ Tchrs; Kant Ges; Metaphysical Soc N Am; Univ Ctrs Rational Alternatives. **SELECTED PUBLICATIONS** Auth, The Merit Criterion of Employment: An Examination of some Current Arguments Against Its Use, 76; auth, What Happened to Merit?, in Kitchener-Waterloo Record, 85; auth, The Rule of Ignorance in the United States and Canada, in Measure, 91. **CONTACT ADDRESS** Dept of Philosophy, Univ of Waterloo, Waterloo, ON, Canada N2L 3G1. **EMAIL** jwubnig@watarts.uwaterloo.ca

WUNSCH, JAMES STEVENSON
PERSONAL Born 09/27/1946, Detroit, MI, m, 1983, 3 children **DISCIPLINE** POLITICAL SCIENCE, AFRICAN STUDIES **EDUCATION** Duke Univ, Hist, BA, 68; Ind Univ, Polit Sci, MA, 70, African Stud/Polit Sci, PhD, 74. **CAREER** Assoc instr, Polit Sci, Ind Univ, 69-70; res fel, Inst African Stud, Univ Ghana, 71-72; fac, Creighton Univ, 73; to asst prof 73-78; to assoc prof 78-86; to prof 81-; vis sch, Univ Mich, 74; assoc investr, Nat Inst Mental Health Res Proj, 75-76; eval spec, US Dept Agric, Off Int Prog, 78-79; soc sci anal, Off Rural Develop & Develop Admin, US Agency Int Develop, 78-80; assoc investr, Nat Sci Found, 86; sr fel, Ind Univ, 85-86; vis assoc prof, Polit Sci, Ind Univ, 85-86; chr, Dept Polit Sci, Creighton Univ, 83-92; act ch, Creighton Univ, 96-97; act dir, Dept Polit Sci & Int Stud, Creighton Univ, 96-97; chr, Polit Sci/Int Stud, Creighton Univ, 97-; dir, African Stud Prog, Creighton Univ, 98-. **HONORS AND AWARDS** Phi Beta Kappa, Duke Univ; Fulbright Fel, Ghana, 71-72; Council on For Rel Fel, 78-79; NEH Fel, 78, 82; Senior Fel, Am Philo Soc, 00-01. **MEMBERSHIPS** Am Polit Sci Asn; Midwest Polit Sci Asn; African Stud Asn; Policy Stud Org **SELECTED PUBLICATIONS** "Review Essay: Public Administration and Local Government," African Stud Rev, 97; coauth, "Regime Transformation from Below: Decentralization, Local Governance and Democratic Reform in Nigeria," Studies in Comp Develop, Winter, 96; coauth, "Decentralization, Local Government and Primary Health Care in Nigeria: An Analytical Study," Jour of African Policy Stud, 95; coauth, The Failure of the Centralized State: Institutions and Self Governance in Africa, Inst Contemp Stud, 95; "African Political Reforms and International Assistance: What Can and Should Be Done?", Africa: Develop & Publ Policy, Macmillan Press, 94. **CONTACT ADDRESS** Dept Polit Sci, Creighton Univ, Omaha, NE 68178. **EMAIL** jwunsch@creighton.edu

WURZBURGER, WALTER S.
PERSONAL Born 03/29/1920, Munich, German, m, 1947, 3 children **DISCIPLINE** ETHICS, RELIGION **EDUCATION** Yeshiva Col, BA, 43; Harvard Univ, MA, 46; PhD, 51. **CAREER** Adj assoc prof, Yeshiva Univ, 67-80; adj prof, 80-. **HONORS AND AWARDS** Samuel Belkin Lit Awd. **MEMBERSHIPS** APA; AAR; AJS. **RESEARCH** Ethics; religion. **SELECTED PUBLICATIONS** Auth, Ethics of Responsibility, Jewish Pub Soc Am, 94; auth, "Imitatio Dei in the Philosophy of Rau Josef B Soloveitchik," in Hazon Nahun, Yeshiva Univ Press, 97; auth, God is Proof Enough, forthcoming. **CONTACT ADDRESS** Dept Humanities, Yeshiva Univ, 500 West 185th St, New York, NY 10033-3201. **EMAIL** wurzbur@ymail.yu.edu

WYDRZYNSKI, CHRISTOPHER J.
DISCIPLINE LAW **EDUCATION** Univ Windsor, BA, LLB; Osgoode, LLM. **CAREER** Prof, Univ of Windsor; Osgoode Hall, Barrister-at-Law; res dir, Legal Prof Res Prog. **SELECTED PUBLICATIONS** Auth, Immigration Law & Procedure. **CONTACT ADDRESS** Col of Business Administration, Education and Law, Univ of Windsor, 401 Sunset Ave, Windsor, ON, Canada N9B 3P4. **EMAIL** cwydrzy@uwindsor.ca

WYLIE, A.
PERSONAL Born Swindon, England **DISCIPLINE** PHILOSOPHY **EDUCATION** Mt Allison Univ, BA, 76; State Univ NY, Binghamton, MA, 78, PhD, 82. **CAREER** Vis postdoc fel, Calgary Inst Hum, 81-82; Mellon postdoc fel & instr, dept phil, Washington Univ, St. Louis, 83-84; instr, Univ Calgary, 84-85; asst prof, 85-89, fac arts res prof, 87-88, assoc prof, 89-93, Prof Philosophy, Univ Western Ont, 93-. **MEMBERSHIPS** Ctr Archaeol Public Interest; Am Philos Asn; Philos Sci Asn; Can Soc Hist Philos Sci; Can Soc Women Philos; Can Philos Asn. **SELECTED PUBLICATIONS** Auth, The Disunity of Science, 96; co-ed, Ethics in American Archaeology: Challenge for the 1990s, 95; co-ed, Equity Issues for Women in Archaeology, 94; co-ed, Critical Traditions in Contemporary Archaeology: Essays in the Philosophy, History and Socio-Politics of Archaeology, 89. **CONTACT ADDRESS** Dept Philos, Univ of Western Ontario, 1151 Richmond St, London, ON, Canada N6A 3K7. **EMAIL** awyllie@julian.uwo.ca

WYMA, KEITH D.
PERSONAL Born 09/24/1967, Beaver Falls, PA, m, 1991 **DISCIPLINE** PHILOSOPHY **EDUCATION** Calvin Col, BA, 90; Notre Dame, MA, 94, PhD, 97. **CAREER** Adj asst prof, 97-98, Notre Dame; adj instr, 97-98, Indiana Univ; asst prof, 98-, Whitworth Col. **RESEARCH** Moral responsibility, weakness of will, moral rational, justification. **CONTACT ADDRESS** Religion/Philosophy Dept, Whitworth Col, 300 W Hawthorne, Spokane, WA 99251. **EMAIL** kwyma@whitworth.edu

WYRE, STANLEY MARCEL
PERSONAL Born 03/31/1953, Detroit, MI, m, 1988 **DISCIPLINE** LAW **EDUCATION** Lawrence Institute of Technology, BS, 1976; Detroit College of Law, JD, 1984. **CAREER** Walbridge Aldinger Co, project estimator, 76-78; Palmer Smith Co., senior construction estimator/director, 79-83; Charfoos, Christensen & Archer PC, attorney-at-law, 84; Barton-Malow Co, construction manager, 84-87; professional photographer; Detroit Col of Law, adjunct professor, 85-; Lawrence Institute of Technology, assistant professor, 85-; Detroit Public Schools, assistant superintendent, 92-. **MEMBERSHIPS** American Arbitrator Association, arbitrator. **CONTACT ADDRESS** Assistant Superintendent, Physical Plant, Detroit Public Schools, 5057 Woodward Ave, School Center Bldg, Ste 520, Detroit, MI 48202.

WYRICK, STEPHEN VON
PERSONAL Born Dallas, TX, 2 children **DISCIPLINE** HEBREW BIBLE **EDUCATION** SW Baptist Theol Sem, M Div, 76, PhD, 81. **CAREER** Prof & Religion Dept Chr, Calif Baptist Col, 86-94; PRrof& Relig Dept Chr, Univ Mary Hardin-Baylor, 94- **HONORS AND AWARDS** NEH; Sr Res fel Wm F Albright Inst. **MEMBERSHIPS** SBL; ASOR; NABPR; NAPH; IES **RESEARCH** Iron I & Late Bronze Age **CONTACT ADDRESS** Univ of Mary Hardin-Baylor, 900 College St., UMHB Station Box 8356, Belton, TX 76513. **EMAIL** swyrick@umhb.edu

WYSCHOGROD, MICHAEL
PERSONAL Born 09/28/1928, Berlin, Germany, m, 1955, 2 children **DISCIPLINE** PHILOSOPHY **EDUCATION** City Col New York, BSS, 49; Columbia Univ, PhD, 53. **CAREER** Asst prof philos, City Col New York, 56-63, from asst prof to assoc prof, 63-68; assoc prof, 68-71, prof Philos, Baruch Col, 71, chmn dept, 76-92; PROF RELIGIOUS STUDIES, UNIV HOUSTON, 92-; Ed, Tradition, 60-; vis lectr, Jewish Theol Sem, NY, 67-68; vis assoc prof, Dropsie Univ, 68-70; vis prof, Heidelberg Col, 80. **MEMBERSHIPS** Asn Jewish Studies; Am Philos Asn. **RESEARCH** Philosophical psychology; philosophy of religion; Jewish thought, Jewish - Christian relations. **SELECTED PUBLICATIONS** Auth, Kierkegaard and Heidegger--the Ontology of Existence; Faith and the Holocaust, Judaism, summer 71; The Law, Jews and Gentiles--a Jewish Perspective, Lutheran Quart, Vol 21, No 4; coauth (with David Berger), Jews and Jewish Christianity, 78; The Body of Faith: God and the People Israel, 80. **CONTACT ADDRESS** Religious Studies, Univ of Houston, Houston, TX 77204-3784.

WYSONG, EARL
PERSONAL Born 06/25/1944, Kokomo, IN, m, 1966, 2 children **DISCIPLINE** SOCIOLOGY, POLITICAL SCIENCE **EDUCATION** Indiana Univ, BS, 67; Ball State Univ, MA, 71; Purdue Univ, PhD, 90. **CAREER** Prof, Ind State Univ, Kokomo, 90-. **HONORS AND AWARDS** Claude Rich Teach Awd, 96; Teach Excell, 97, 98; IN Univ Fac Awd, 93; Co-nom, C Wright Mills Awd, 00; co-nom, NCSA Schol Achiev Awd, 00. **MEMBERSHIPS** IASS; SSSP; ASA; NCSA; MSS; SSSP. **RESEARCH** Social inequalities; class; work; organizations; healthcare; drug policies. **SELECTED PUBLICATIONS** Coauth, "Evaluating DARE: Drug Education and the Multiple Meanings of Success," Policy Studies Review 9 (90):727-747; coauth, "Truth and DARE: Tracking Drug Education to Graduation and As Symbolic Politics," Social Problems 41 (94): 501-25; coauth, "A Decade of DARE: Efficacy, Politics, and Drug Education," Sociological Focus 28 (95): 283-311; auth, "Professional Societies, Interorganizational Linkages and Occupational Health Policy Reform," Social Problems 39 (92): 201-218; auth, "Conflicting Agendas, Interests, and Actors in Disease Prevention Policy-Making: Business, Labor and The High Risk Act," Intern J Health Ser 23 (93): 301-322; coauth, "Influence Networks, Professional Societies, and occupational Health Policy," in Research in Politics and Society: The Political Consequences of Social Network, ed. Gwen Moore, J Allen Whitt (Greenwich, CT, JAI Press, 92), 189-218; auth, High Risk and High Stakes: Health Professionals, Politics, and Policy, Greenwood Press, (Westport, CT), 92; coauth, "Family Friendly Workplace Benefits: Policy Mirage, Organizational Contexts, and Worker Power," Critical Sociology 24 (98): 244-276; coauth, The New Class Society, Rowan and Littlefield (Lanham, MD), 99. **CONTACT ADDRESS** Dept Social and Behavioral Sci, Indiana Univ, Kokomo, PO Box 9003, Kokomo, IN 46904. **EMAIL** ewysong@iuk.edu

Y

YAFFE, MARTIN DAVID
PERSONAL Born 02/19/1942, Hamilton, ON, Canada, m, 1963, 2 children **DISCIPLINE** PHILOSOPHY **EDUCATION** Univ Toronto, BA, 63; Claremont Grad Sch, PhD(philos), 68 **CAREER** Prof Philos, N Tex State Univ, 68-, Lectr philos, Tel-Aviv Univ, 71-72; vis prof relig studies, Southern Methodist Univ, 78-. **HONORS AND AWARDS** Nat Endowment for Humanities transl grant, 81-82; Bradley fel, 91; Earhart Fellow, 99. **MEMBERSHIPS** Acad Jewish Philos; Am Acad Relig; Am Polit Sci Asn; Nat Asn Scholars; North Am Spinoza Soc **RESEARCH** Classical political philosophy; Jewish thought. **SELECTED PUBLICATIONS** Coauth, Saint Thomas Aquinas, The Literal Expostion on the Book of Job: A Scriptural Commentary Concerning Providence; Scholars Press, 88; On Leo Strauss's Philosophy and Law: A Review Essay, Modern Judaism, 89; Autonomy, Community, Authority: Hermann Cohen, Carl Schmitt, Leo Strauss, In: Autonomy and Community, SUNY Press, 91; Leo Strauss as Judaic Thinker: Some First Notions, Relig Studies Rev, 1/91; One-Sided Platonism: Hermann Cohen on the Social Ideal in Plato and the Prophets, Il cannocchiale, 91; The Case Against the Great books--And Its Refutation, In: The Core and the Canon: A National Debate, Univ North Tex Press, 93; Two Recent Treatments of Spinoza's Theologico-Politico Treatise: A Review Essay, Modern Judaism, 93; Biblical Religion and Liberal Democracy: Comments on Spinoza's Theologico-Political Treatise and Sack's Commentary on the Book of Genesis, Polit Sci Rev, 94; On Beginning to Translate Spinoza's Tractatus Theologico-Politicus, Il cannocchiale, Rome, 94; The Histories and Successes of the Hebrews: The Demise of the Biblical Polity in Spinoza's Theologico-Political Treatise, Jewish Polit Studies Rev, 95; An Unsung Appreciation of the Musical-Erotic in Mozart's Don Giovanni: Hermann Cohen's Nod Toward Kierkegaard's Either/Or, In: International Kierkegaard Commentary on Either/Or I, Mercer Univ Press, 95; Spinoza's Theologico-Political Treatise--A First Inside Look, In: Piety and Humanity: Essays on Religion and Early Modern Political Philosophy, Rowman & Littlefield, 97; Shylock and the Jewish Question, Johns Hopkins Univ Press, 97. **CONTACT ADDRESS** Dept of Philos, Univ of No Texas, PO Box 310920, Denton, TX 76203-0920. **EMAIL** yaffe@unt.edu

YAGISAWA, TAKASI
PERSONAL Born Nagano, Japan **DISCIPLINE** PHILOSOPHY **EDUCATION** Univ London, BA, 77; Princeton Univ, PhD, 81. **CAREER** Teaching asst, Princeton Univ, 78-80; asst prof, Case Western Reserve Univ, 81-83; vis asst prof, Univ Minn, 84-85; vis asst prof, NYork Univ, 85-86; vis asst prof, Univ NC at Chapel Hill, 86-87; from asst prof to prof, Calif State Univ at Northridge, 87-. **HONORS AND AWARDS** Dawes Hicks Awd, Univ Col, 76; Grad Fel, Princeton Univ, 77-81; NEH Sem, Univ Md, 83; Charles Phelps Taft Postdoctoral Fel, Univ Cincinnati, 83-84; Res Release Grant, Calif State Univ at Northridge, 87, 89, 93 & 99; Affirmative Action Faculty Res Grant, Calif State Univ at Northridge, 88 & 89; Meritorious Performance and Professional Promise Awd, Calif State Univ at Northridge, 88; NEH Summer Stipend, 90; Summer Fel, Calif State Univ at Northridge, 90; NEH Summer Sem, Rutgers Univ, 92; NEH Summer Inst, Rutgers Univ, 93. **MEMBERSHIPS** Am Philos Asn. **RESEARCH** Philosophy of Language, Metaphysics. **SELECTED PUBLICATIONS** Auth, "Thinking in Neurons: Comments on Schiffer," Philos Studies (94): 287-296; auth, "Reference Ex Machina," in Reference and Meaning, eds. J. Hill and P. Kotatko (Prague: FILOSOPHIA Pub, 95), 215-242; auth, "Salmon Trapping," Philos and Phenomenological Res 57.2 (97): 351-370; auth, "A Somewhat Russellian Theory of Intensional Contexts," in Philosophical Perspectives 11: Mind, Causation, and World 1997, ed. J.E. Tomberlin (CA: Ridgeview Pub Co., 97), 43-82; auth, "Knocked Out Senseless: Naturalism and Analyticity," in The Maribor Papers: Essays on Semantic Naturalism, ed. Dunja Jutric (Slovenia: Univ of Maribor Press, 97), 82-95; auth, "Essentialism," "Saul Kripke," "Modal Logic," "Montague Grammar," and "Naming and Necessity," in Iwanami Dictionary of Philosophy, eds. K. Mishima et al (Tokyo: Iwanami Shoten, 97); auth, "Naming and Its Place in Reference," Lingua e Stile (98): 445-458; auth, "Partee Verbs," Philos Studies, forthcoming. **CONTACT ADDRESS** Dept Philos, California State Univ, Northridge, 18111 Nordhoff St, Northridge, CA 91330-0001. **EMAIL** tagashi.yagisawa@csun.edu

YALDEN, ROBERT
DISCIPLINE LAW **EDUCATION** Queen's Univ, BA, 84; Oxon Univ, MA, 86; Univ Toronto, LLM, 88. **CAREER** Law clerk, Madame Justice Wilson, Supreme Court Can, 89-90. **RESEARCH** Corporate and securities law. **SELECTED PUBLICATIONS** Auth, pubs on issues in corporate, administrative and constitutional law; co-auth, Corporations: Principles and Policies. **CONTACT ADDRESS** Fac of Law, Univ of Toronto, 78 Queen's Park, Toronto, ON, Canada M5S 1A1.

YALOWITZ, STEVEN
DISCIPLINE PHILOSOPHY **EDUCATION** Columbia Univ,PhD, 91. **CAREER** Prof, Philos, Univ Calif, San Diego. **RESEARCH** Intersection of semantics and psychology. **SELECTED PUBLICATIONS** Auth, Rationality and the Argument for Anomalous Monism, Philos Stud. **CONTACT ADDRESS** Dept of Philos, Univ of California, San Diego, 9500 Gilman Dr, La Jolla, CA 92093.

YAMADA, DAVID C.
DISCIPLINE LAW **EDUCATION** Valparaiso Univ, BA, 81; Empire State Col, MA, 99; NY Univ, JD, 85. **CAREER** Asst Atty Gen, NY State, 88-91; Sen Instr, NY Univ Sch of Law, 91-94; Asst Prof to Prof, Suffolk Univ, 94-. **MEMBERSHIPS** am Bar Asn; Nat Lawyers Guild; Nat Employment Lawyers Asn; Campaign Against Workplace Bullying; United Asn for Labor Educ; Scholars, Artists, and Writers for Soc Justice; Industrial Relations Res Asn. **RESEARCH** Employment law and policy; Workplace bullying and discrimination; Public interest law; Public intellectualism; Non-traditional higher education; Lifelong learning. **SELECTED PUBLICATIONS** Aut? "The Regulation of Pre-Employment Honest Testing: Striking a Temporary (?) Balance Between Self-Regulation and Prohibition," Wayne L Rev, 93; auth, "Same Old, Same Old: Law School Rankings and the Affirmation of Hierarchy," Suffolk Univ L Rev, 97; co-auth, "Beyond 'Economic Realities': The Case for Amending Federal Employment Discrimination Laws to Include Independent contractors," Boston Col L Rev, 97; auth, "Voices From the Cubicle: Protecting and Encouraging Private Employee speech in the Post-Industrial Workplace," Berkeley J of Employment & Labor L, 98; auth, "The Phenomenon of 'Workplace Bullying' and the Need for Status-Blind Hostile Work Environment Protection," Georgetown L J, 00; auth, "Brainstorming About Workplace Bullying: Potential Litigation Approaches for Representing Abused Employees," Employee Advocate, 00. **CONTACT ADDRESS** Sch of Law, Suffolk Univ, 120 Tremont St, Boston, MA 02108. **EMAIL** dyamada@acad.suffolk.edu

YAMASHITA, TADANORI
PERSONAL Born 12/23/1929, Tokyo, Japan, m, 1954 **DISCIPLINE** RELIGION **EDUCATION** Yale Univ, BD, 59, PhD(Near East lang & lit), 64. **CAREER** From instr to asst prof, 63-73, assoc prof, 73-80, prof relig, Mt Holyoke Col, 80-. **MEMBERSHIPS** Am Orient Soc; Asn Asian Studies; Soc Bibl Lit. **RESEARCH** Mythology of ancient Near East; myths and legends in Mahayana Buddhist Scriptures. **CONTACT ADDRESS** Dept Relig, Mount Holyoke Col, 50 College St, South Hadley, MA 01075-1461. **EMAIL** tyamashi@mtholyoke.edu

YANAL, ROBERT J.
PERSONAL Born 02/03/1948, Shenandoah, PA **DISCIPLINE** PHILOSOPHY **EDUCATION** Univ Pittsburgh, BA, 69; Univ Ill, MA, 70; PhD, 75. **CAREER** Prof, Wayne State Univ, 74- **MEMBERSHIPS** Am Philos Asn, Am Soc Aesthet, Am Asn of Univ Profs. **RESEARCH** Aesthetics, Philosophy of Law, Logic, Film. **SELECTED PUBLICATIONS** Auth, "Institutions of Art: Reconsiderations of George Dickie's Philosophy," (94); Auth, "The Danto-Wollheim Meaning Theory of Art, Ratio IX (96); Auth, "The Paradox of Suspense," Brit J of Aesthet, 36 (96);Auth, Paradoxes of Emotion and Fiction, Pa St Pr, 99; Auth, "Rebecca's Deceivers," Philos and Lit (00) 24. **CONTACT ADDRESS** Dept Philosophy, Wayne State Univ, 51 W Warren, Detroit, MI 48202. **EMAIL** Robert.Yanal@wayne.edu

YANCY, DOROTHY COWSER
PERSONAL Born 04/18/1944, Cherokee Cty, AL, s **DISCIPLINE** POLITICAL SCIENCE **EDUCATION** Johnson C Smith Univ, AB History 1964; Univ of MA Amherst, MA 1965; Atlanta Univ, PhD Polit 1978. **CAREER** Albany State Coll Albany GA, instr history 1965-67; Hampton Inst Hampton VA, instr history 1967-69; Evanston Twp HS, teacher 1969-71; Barat Coll Lake Forest IL, dir black studies 1971-72; Georgia Inst of Tech, assistant professor, 72-78, associate professor, 78-88, professor, 88-94; Johnson C. Smith Univ, prof, president, 94-. **HONORS AND AWARDS** Fulbright-Hayes Scholar 1968; collaborating author, The Fed Gov Policy & Black Enterprise 1974; mem: Omicron Delta Kappa, Phi Kappa Phi Honor Soc, Leadership Atlanta Class, 1984; Distinguished Alumnus, Johnson C Smith Univ, 1981; Outstanding Teacher of the Year, Georgia Institute of Technology, 1985; mem, People to People Delegation of Labor Experts, to Soviet Union & Europe, 1988, to London, Berlin, & Moscow, 1990; The Academy of Political and Social Sciences of the Small Hural, Ulan Bator, Mongolia, Lecturer and Consultant, 1991. **MEMBERSHIPS** Mem: Assn for the Study of Afro-Amer Life & History, Industrial Relations Res Assn, Soc of Professionals in Dispute Resolutions; mem, labor panel Amer Arbitration Assn 1980; mem exec comm Assn of Soc & Behavioral Sci; mem So Pol Sci Assn; spec master, FL Public Employees Relations Commn; bd mem Assn for the Study of Afro-Amer Life & History; mem Labor Arbitration Panel Fed Mediation & Conciliation Serv; mediator, Mediation Res & Educ Proj, Northwestern Univ, 1988-; mem, Arbitration Panel, Bd of Regents State Univ System of FL & AFSCME, 1988-; chw, Woman Power Commission, The Links, Inc, 1990-94; Johnson C Smith Univ, board of trustees, 1991-94; bd, Charlotte Chamber of Commerce, Charlotte Urban League, Metro Charlotte YMCA. **CONTACT ADDRESS** President, Johnson C. Smith Univ, 100 Beatties Ford Rd, Charlotte, NC 28216.

YANDELL, K. DAVID
DISCIPLINE PHILOSOPHY **EDUCATION** Univ Wis, Madison, PhD. **CAREER** Asst prof & asst chp, dept Philos at Loyola Univ Chicago, 93-. **RESEARCH** Early modern philosophy, especially Descartes; metaphysics; social and political philosophy. **SELECTED PUBLICATIONS** Articles in, Hist Philos Quart & Brit J Hist Philos. **CONTACT ADDRESS** Dept of Philosophy, Loyola Univ, Chicago, 820 N. Michigan Ave., Chicago, IL 60611.

YANDELL, KEITH E.
PERSONAL Born 07/16/1938, Davenport, IA, m, 1959, 4 children **DISCIPLINE** PHILOSOPHY **EDUCATION** Wayne State Univ, BA & MA, 60; Ohio State Univ, PhD(philos), 66. **CAREER** Instr philos, Ohio State Univ, 65-66; from asst prof to prof, Univ Wis-Madison, 66-74, Nat Endowment for Humanities younger humanist grant, 72-73. **MEMBERSHIPS** Am Philos Asn; Soc of Christian Philosophers. **RESEARCH** Philosophy of religion; history of philosophy; metaphysics; Indian philosophy. **SELECTED PUBLICATIONS** Auth, Basic Issues in the Philosophy of Religion, 71; auth, Christianity and Philosophy, 84; auth, Home's Inexplicable Myster, 90; auth, The Epistemology of Religions Experience, 93; auth, Philosophy of Religion, 99. **CONTACT ADDRESS** Univ of Wisconsin, Madison, 414 S Segoe Rd, Madison, WI 53711. **EMAIL** yandell@facstaff.wisc.edu

YANG, FENGGANG
PERSONAL Born 06/28/1962, Cangzhou, China, m, 1988, 2 children **DISCIPLINE** SOCIOLOGY; RELIGION; ETHNICITY **EDUCATION** Hebei Normal Univ, Shijiazhuang, China, BA, 82; Nankai Univ, Tianjin, China; MA, 92, PhD, 97, Catholic Univ of Amer. **CAREER** Lectr, Cangzhou Education Col, Hebei, China, 82-84; Asst Prof, People's Univ of China, 87-89; Research Assoc, Center for Immigration Research, Univ Houston, 97-. **HONORS AND AWARDS** Thomas V. Moore Doctoral Scholarship, 89-92; Research Awd for the Scientific Study of Religion, 93; Outstanding Graduate Student, Catholic Univ of Amer, 93 & 95; Teaching and Research Fel, People's Univ China, 94; Dissertation Fel, Univ of Illinois at Chicago, 94-95; Dissertation Fel, Louisville Inst of Protestantism and American Culture, 95-96; Postdoctoral Fel, Center for Immigration Research, 97-98; Research Fel, Center for Immigration Research, 99. **MEMBERSHIPS** Amer Sociological Assoc; Assoc for Sociology of Religion; Soc for the Scientific Study of Religion;

Assoc for Asian Amer Studies; Assoc for Asian Studies; Amer Acad of Religion. **RESEARCH** Chinese American religions and cultures; Chinese religions and cultures; Diasporic identities; Immigrant assimilation and ethnic groups. **SELECTED PUBLICATIONS** Auth, Decree and Covenant: Different Notions of Law in Chinese and Western Societies, Cultural China, 96; A Sociological Comparison of Christianity and the Chinese Traditional Value System, Christian Culture Review, 96; Tension and the Healthy Development of Society, Economic Ethics and Chinese Culture, 97; auth, "The Chinese Gospel Church: The Sinicization of Christianity," pp. 89-107 in Religion and The New Immigrants: Continuities and Adaptions in Immigrant Congregation, edited by Helen Rose Ebaugh and Janet S. Chafetz, Walnut Creek, CA: AltaMira Press, 00; auth, "Hsi Nan Buddhist Temple: Seeking to Americanize," pp. 67-87 in Religion and The New Immigrants: Continuities and Adaptions in Immigrant Congregations, edited by Helen Rose Ebaugh and Janet S. Chafetz, Walnut Creek, CA: AltaMira Press, 00; "Chinese American Religions," pp. 113-115 in Encyclopedia of Contemporary American Religion, edited by Wade Clark Roof, New York: Macmillan Reference USA, 00; auth, Fengang Yang, "The Growing Literature of Asian American Religions: A Review of the Field," Journal of Asian American Studies, 00; auth, Fenggang Yang and Helen Rose Ebaugh, "Religion and Ethnicity among New Immigrants: The Impact of Majority/ Minority Status in Home and Host Countries," Journal for the Scientific Study of Religion, 01; auth, Fenggang Yang and Helen Rose Ebaugh, "Transformations in New Immigrant Religions and Their Global Implications," American Sociological Review, 01; auth, PRC Immigrants in the US: A Demographic Profile and an Assessment of their Integration in the Chinese American Community, The Chines Triangle of Mainland-Taiwan-Hong Kong: Comparate Institutional Analyses, 01. **CONTACT ADDRESS** Dept of Sociology, Univ of So Maine, Portland, ME 04104-9300. **EMAIL** fyang@usm.maine.edu

YANG, XIAOSI
PERSONAL Born 03/31/1953, Shuzhou, China, m, 2 children **DISCIPLINE** PHILOSOPHY **EDUCATION** Johns Hopkins Univ, PhD, 98. **CAREER** Instr, Univ of Chicago, 98- . **MEMBERSHIPS** APA. **RESEARCH** Philosophy of family; epistemology. **CONTACT ADDRESS** 5547 S Dorchester, Apt 2, Chicago, IL 60637.

YAQUB, ALADDIN M.
DISCIPLINE LOGIC **EDUCATION** Univ Baghdad, BS, 78; Univ Wis, MA, 88, 90, PhD, 91. **CAREER** Asst prof, Univ NMex. **SELECTED PUBLICATIONS** Auth, The Liar Speaks the Truth: A Defense of the Revision Theory of Truth, Oxford, 93. **CONTACT ADDRESS** Univ of New Mexico, Albuquerque, Albuquerque, NM 87131. **EMAIL** ayaqub@unm.edu

YARBROUGH, MARILYN VIRGINIA
PERSONAL Born 08/31/1945, Bowling Green, KY, m, 1987 **DISCIPLINE** LAW **EDUCATION** Virginia State Univ, BA 1966; UCLA, JD 1973. **CAREER** IBM, systms eng 66-68; Westinghouse, systms eng, 69-70; Catonsville Community College, instr data proc, 70; Boston College Law School, teaching fellow, 75-76; Duke Law School, visting prof, 83-84; Univ of Kansas, law prof, 76-87 & assoc vice chancellor 83-87; Univ of Tennessee-Knoxville, law dean, 87-91; University of North Carolina Law School, prof of law, 92-. **HONORS AND AWARDS** Kansas Univ Women's Hall of Fame; Doctor of Laws, Univ of Puget Sound School of Law 1989; Frank D Reeves Awd, Natl Conference of Black Lawyers 1988; Society of American Law Teachers Awd, 1991; YWCA Tribute to Women Awd for Education, 1989; Distinguished Alumni Awd, Virginia State University, 1988; ABA, Women Lawyers of Achievement Awd, 1991. **MEMBERSHIPS** Pres bd cmt wrk Law Sch Admsn Cncl 1976-89; bd mem Accrediting Cncl Ed Journalism Mass Communications 1976-83; chmn KS Crime Victims Reparations Bd, 1980-83; Lawrence Housing Auth 1984-86; council member Am Bar Assc Sect Legal Ed Admsn to the Bar 1984-85; pres United Way of Lawrence, KS, 1985; KS Commission on Civil Rights, 1986-; NCAA Conf on Infractions, 1986-88, chairman, 1986-87; Rotary International, 1988-90; Pulitzer Prize board, 1990-; Poynter Institute for Media Studies, board of directors, 1990-92; First American Bank of Knoxville, board of directors, 1987-; United Way of Knoxville, board of directors, 1990-91. **CONTACT ADDRESS** Law Sch, Univ of No Carolina, Chapel Hill, Chapel Hill, NC 27599.

YARBROUGH, O. LARRY
DISCIPLINE BIBLICAL STUDIES (BOTH JEWISH AND CHRISTIAN SCRIPTURES) **EDUCATION** Birmingham-Southern Col, AB; Cambridge Univ, MA; Emory Univ, MDiv; Yale Univ, PhD. **CAREER** Prof; Middlebury Col, 83-. **SELECTED PUBLICATIONS** Auth, Not Like the Gentiles: Marriage Rules in the Letters of Paul; co-ed, The Social World of the Earliest Christians. **CONTACT ADDRESS** Dept of Religion, Middlebury Col, Middlebury, VT 05753.

YARTZ, FRANK
PERSONAL Born 02/05/1938, Cleveland, OH, s **DISCIPLINE** PHILOSOPHY **EDUCATION** St Louis Univ, MA, 64; PhD, 68. **CAREER** Fac member, Loyola Univ at Chicago, 65-. **HONORS AND AWARDS** Teaching Fel, St Louis Univ, 61-64. **MEMBERSHIPS** Am Philos Asn. **RESEARCH** History of Philosophy with an emphasis on Plato, Aristotle, Aquinas, and early modern thinkers. **SELECTED PUBLICATIONS** Auth, Introduction to Modern Philosophy, 95; auth, " Aristotle on Monsters," The Ancient World 28 (97): 1-7; auth, "The Importance of Theophrastus' Metaphysics in Ancient Greek Intellectual History," The Ancient World 29 (98): 151-160; rev, of "Method and Politics in Plato's Statesman," by M. S. Lane, The Ancient World 30 (99): 80-83; rev, of "The Order of Nature in Aristotle's Physics," by H. Lang, The Ancient World 30 (99). **CONTACT ADDRESS** Dept Philos, Loyola Univ, Chicago, 6525 N Sheridan Rd, Chicago, IL 60626-5344. **EMAIL** fyartz@luc.edu

YATES, JENNY
PERSONAL Born 10/19/1943, Greenville, SC **DISCIPLINE** RELIGION & PHILOSOPHY **EDUCATION** Furman Univ, BA, 65; Yale Div School, MAR, 67; Syracuse Univ, PhD, 73; C. G. Jung Inst, PG Dipl, 92. **CAREER** Calif tchr, vis assoc prof, 84; Yale Univ, res fel, 96-97; Wells Col, prof, Religion & Philosophy, 75-. **HONORS AND AWARDS** Wells Col, Tchg excellence Awd; Atkinson Endowed chair in Humanities. **MEMBERSHIPS** AAR, APA, Intl. AAP, IRSJA. **RESEARCH** Archetypical Psychology and the Female Self. **SELECTED PUBLICATIONS** Auth, forthcoming, Encountering Jung on Death and Immortality, Princeton Univ Press, 99; coauth, The Near Death Experience, Routledge Press, 96; auth, Psyche and the Split-Brain, Univ Press of Am, 94. **CONTACT ADDRESS** Dept of Religion and Philosophy, Wells Col, Aurora, NY 13026. **EMAIL** jyates@wells.edu

YATES, WILSON
PERSONAL Born 03/09/1937, Matthews, MO, m, 1961, 2 children **DISCIPLINE** THEOLOGY AND THE ARTS; ETHICS; RELIGION **EDUCATION** Southeast Mo State Univ, AB, 60; Vanderbilt Divinity Sch MDiv, 62; Harvard Univ, PhD(relig & sociol), 68. **CAREER** Asst prof, 67-70, assoc prof, 71-78, prof church & soc, United Theol Sem Twin Cities, 77-; prof rel, soc, & arts, 88; Dean of Sem, 88; Pres of Sem, 96. **MEMBERSHIPS** Soc Christian Ethics; Europ Cult Soc; Am Academy Relig. **RESEARCH** Social ethics and the social sciences; ethics; sexuality and the family; religion and art. **SELECTED PUBLICATIONS** Art, The Future of the Arts in Theological Education, British Journal of Theological Education, Winter 91-92; contributing ed, Theological Education, Sacred Imagination: The Arts and Theological Education, ATS Vol XXXI, No 1, Autumn, 94; co-ed, Theological Reflection on the Grotesque in Art and Literature, Eerdmans Publishing Co, 97. **CONTACT ADDRESS** United Theol Sem of the Twin Cities, 3000 5th St NW, New Brighton, MN 55112-2598. **EMAIL** wyates@ uniedseminary-mn.org

YEE, GALE A.
PERSONAL Born 04/09/1949, OH, s **DISCIPLINE** HEBREW BIBLE; OLD TESTAMENT **EDUCATION** Univ St Michael's Col, PhD, 85. **CAREER** Prof, Univ St Thomas, 84-98; Prof and dir, Studies in Feminist Liberation Theologies; Episcopal Divinity School, 98-; **HONORS AND AWARDS** Aquinas Found Fel; Cath Bibl Asn Your Scholars Fel. **MEMBERSHIPS** Cath Bibl Asn; Soc Bibl Lit; Ethnic Chinese Bibl Colloquium **RESEARCH** Hebrew Bible; Feminist Theory; Literary Theory. **SELECTED PUBLICATIONS** Auth, Composition & Tradition in the Book of Moses; Judges and Method; Jewish Feasts and the Gospel of John; Moses, New Interpreters Bible. **CONTACT ADDRESS** Episcopal Divinity Sch, 99 Brattle St, Cambridge, MA 02138. **EMAIL** gyee@ episdivschool.org

YEGGE, ROBERT BERNARD
PERSONAL Born 06/17/1934, Denver, CO **DISCIPLINE** LAW **EDUCATION** Princeton Univ, AB, 56; Univ Denver, MA, 58, JD, 59. **CAREER** Instr law, 59-63, adj assoc prof, 63-65, actg dean col, 65, dean col, 66-77, Prof Law, Col Law, Univ Denver, 66, Emer Dean Col, 77-, Assoc, Yegge, Hall & Evans, Attorneys-at-Law, 59-62, partner, 62-78; chmn adv comt, dept sociol, Princeton Univ, 62-69; chmn, Colo Coun Migrant & Seasonal Agr Workers & Families, 65-70; chmn, Colo Coun Arts St Humanities, 68-79; asst to pres, Denver Post, 71-73, managing trustee, Denver Ctr Performing Arts, 72-76; chmn law, sci & techol comt, Nat Sci Found, 77-; partner, Nelson & Harding, 78-; dean & prof law, Univ San Francisco, 80. **HONORS AND AWARDS** Educ Awd, Latin Am Educ Found, 76. **MEMBERSHIPS** Law & Soc Asn; Am Bar Asn; Am Sociol Asn; Am Acad Polit & Soc Sci; Am Law Inst. **RESEARCH** Relationships of law to society; legal change; legal relationships within the university. **SELECTED PUBLICATIONS** Auth, Divorce Litigants Without Lawyers, Family Law Quart, Vol 0028, 94. **CONTACT ADDRESS** Col of Law, Univ of Denver, 7039 E 18th Ave, Denver, CO 80220.

YELLEN, JANET L.
PERSONAL Born 08/13/1946, Brooklyn, NY, m, 1978, 1 child **DISCIPLINE** ECONOMICS **EDUCATION** Brown Univ, BA, 67; Yale Univ, PhD, 71. **CAREER** Asst Prof, Harvard Univ, 71-76; Econ, Bd of Gov Fed Reserve System, 77-78; Lectr, London Sch of Econ and Polit Sci, 78-80; Gov, Bd of Gov Fed Reserve System, 94-97; Chair, Coun of Econ Advisors, 97-99; Prof, Univ Calif at Berkeley, 80-. **HONORS AND AWARDS** Guggenheim Fel, 86; Fel, Nat Sci Found, 90-94; Maria and Sidney Rolfe Awd, Nat Econ Service, 97; Wilbur Lucius Cross Medal, Yale Univ, 97; Hon Doc of Laws degree, Brown Univ, 98; Hon Doc of Human Letters degree, Bard Col, 00 **MEMBERSHIPS** W Econ Asn; Am Econ Asn; Nat Bur of Econ Res; Brookings Panel on Econ Activity; Center for Intl Polit Econ. **RESEARCH** Macroeconomic policy; International economics; Labor markets. **SELECTED PUBLICATIONS** Co-auth, "The Fair Wage/Effort Hypothesis and Unemployment," Quart J of Econ, 90; co-auth, "East Germany in from the Cold: The Economic Aftermath of Currency Union," Brookings Papers on Economic Activity, 91; co-auth, "An Analysis of Out-of-Wedlock Childbearing in the United States," Quart Jl of Econ, 96. **CONTACT ADDRESS** Haas Sch of Bus, Univ of California, Berkeley, Berkeley, CA 94720-1900. **EMAIL** yellen@haas.berkeley.edu

YEO, KHIOK-KHNG
PERSONAL Born 06/01/1960, Malaysia, m, 1984, 3 children **DISCIPLINE** RELIGION **EDUCATION** St. Paul Bibl Col, BA, 87; Garrett-Evangel Theol Sem, MDiv, 90; Northwestern Univ, PhD, 92. **CAREER** Prof, Alliance Sem, Hong Kong, 93-96; prof New Testament Interpretation, Garrett-Evangel Sem, 96-. **HONORS AND AWARDS** Alliance Ward Fel, 96-97; Dempster Fel, 90-92; John Wesley Fel, 90-92; Lilly Faculty Res Grant, 99-00. **MEMBERSHIPS** Am Acad Relig; Soc Bibl Lit; Cath Bibl Lit; Soc of New Testament Studies. **RESEARCH** New Testament; Hermeneutics; cross-cultural studies. **SELECTED PUBLICATIONS** Auth, Rhetorical Interaction in 1 Corinthians 8 and 10: A Formal Analysis with Implications for a Cross-Cultural, Chinese Hermeneutic, 95; auth, Cross-Cultural Rhetorical Hermeneutics, 95; auth, Truth and Life, 95; auth, Lucan Wisdom: A Literary and Theological Reading of Luke, 95; auth, Between Female and Male: Feminist Theology and Hermeneutic, 95; auth, Ancestor Worship: Rhetorical and Cross-Cultural Hermeneutical Response, 96; auth, Spirituality, 96; auth, What Has Jerusalem to Do with Beijing? Biblical Interpretation from a Chinese Perspective, 98; auth, A Rhetorical Study of Acts 17:22-31: What Has Jerusalem to Do with Athens and Beijing?, Jian Dao: Jour Bibl Theol, 94; auth, Revelation 5 in the Light of Pannenberg's Christology: Christ the End of History and the Hope of the Suffering, Asian Jour Theol, Oct, 94; auth, Isaiah 5:1-7 and 27:2-6: Let's Hear the Whole Song of Rejection and Restoration, Jian Dao: Jour Bibl Theol, 95; auth, The Yin and Yang of God (Exodus 3:14) and Humanity (Genesis 1:27), Zeitschrift fur Religions und Geistesgeschichte, 94; auth, The Rhetorical Hermeneutic of 1 Corinthians 8 and Chinese Ancestor Worship, Bibl Interpretation, 94; auth, A Relational Theology of Worship: Wholeness from Creation of God to Recreation in Christ, Asia Jour Theol, 95; auth, A Confucian Reading of Romans 7:14-25: Nomos (Law) and Li (Propriety), Jian Dao: Jour Bibl Theol, 96; auth, The Christocentricness of Multi-Cultural Hermeneutics, Jian Dao: Jour Bibl Theol, 96; transl, Nag Hammadi Codices, vol 1, 00. **CONTACT ADDRESS** Dept of New Testament Interp, Garrett-Evangelical Theol Sem, 2121 Sheridan Rd., Evanston, IL 60201. **EMAIL** kkyeo@nwu.edu

YEZZI, RONALD D.
PERSONAL Born 04/26/1938, Erie, PA, m, 1960, 2 children **DISCIPLINE** PHILOSOPHY **EDUCATION** Univ Chicago, SB, 60; S Ill Univ, MA, 63, PhD, 68. **CAREER** Instr to asst prof Philos, Univ Tenn, 65-69; asst prof, 69-71, assoc prof, 71-79, prof Philosophy, 79-, Mankato State Univ. **MEMBERSHIPS** Am Philos Asn; Minn Philos Soc. **RESEARCH** Social and political philosophy; Business ethics; Medical ethics; Ethics; Philosophy of science. **SELECTED PUBLICATIONS** Auth Practical Ethics, G Bruno & Co, 93; Philosophical Problems: God, Free Will, and Determinism, G Bruno & Co, 93; Philosophical Problems: The Good Life, G Bruno & Co, 94; PhilosophyFirst Business Ethics: An Internet Course, 98. **CONTACT ADDRESS** 201 Chancery Ln, Mankato, MN 56001. **EMAIL** yezzi@mankato.msus.edu

YIANNOPOULOS, A. N.
PERSONAL Born 03/13/1928, Thessaloniki, Greece, m, 1967, 2 children **DISCIPLINE** LAW **EDUCATION** Univ Thessaloniki, LLB, 50; Univ Chicago, MCL, 54; Univ Calif, Berkeley, LLM, 55, JSD, 56; Univ Cologne, JD, 61. **CAREER** Prof law, La State Univ, Baton Rouge, 58-79; W R IRBY PROF LAW, TULANE UNIV, NEW ORLEANS, 79-, Reporter, La State Law Inst, 62- **RESEARCH** Civil law; comparative law; admirality. **SELECTED PUBLICATIONS** Auth, Civil Liability for Abuse of Right--Something Old, Something New, La Law Rev, Vol 0054, 94. **CONTACT ADDRESS** Tulane Univ, 662 Sunset Blvd, Baton Rouge, LA 70808.

YIZAR, MARVIN
PERSONAL Born 09/06/1950, Atlanta, GA, d, 4 children **DISCIPLINE** CRIMINAL JUSTICE AND PHILOSOPHY **EDUCATION** GA State Univ, BS, 77; CA State Univ, MA, 91; Univ SAfrica, PhD, 98. **CAREER** Res consul & tchr, 72-80, Fulton County; City of Atlanta, 80-88; State Of Ga, 88-98. **HONORS AND AWARDS** Who's Who in Am; Key to City of Atlanta; Lt Colonel GA Natl Guard. **MEMBERSHIPS** APA; Ancient and Accepted Free Masons Scottish Rite. **RE-**

SEARCH Artificial intelligence; logic programming; metaphysics; philos of mind; epistemology; phenomenology; theory of knowledge. **SELECTED PUBLICATIONS** Auth, What Black Muslims Under Farakhan Believe, 96; auth, Goedel's Incompleteness versus the Skolem-Lowenheim Theory, 97; auth, An Analysis of the Religious Philosophy of Free Masonry, 98. **CONTACT ADDRESS** HCO1-EF302048, Reidsville, GA 30453-9802.

YOCUM, GLENN E.
PERSONAL Born 07/14/1943, Hershey, PA, m, 1979, 3 children **DISCIPLINE** RELIGIOUS STUDIES **EDUCATION** Franklin & Marshall Col, BA, 65; Univ Oxford, DTh, 67; Union Theol Sem, MDiv, 69; Univ Penn, PhD, 76. **CAREER** C milo connick prof, religious studies, Whittier Col, 83-; ed. jour of amer acad relig, 94-. **HONORS AND AWARDS** Phi Beta Kappa; Amer Inst Indian Studies sr res fel, 81-82 & 89-90; Fulbright-Hays res fel, 89-90. **MEMBERSHIPS** Amer Acad Relig; Amer Oriental Soc; Asn Asian Studies; Mid E Studies Asn. **RESEARCH** Religion in South India; Religion in Turkey. **SELECTED PUBLICATIONS** Auth, The Ripening of Tamil Bhakti, Jour of Am Acad Relig, 94; Burning Widows, Sacred Prostitutes, and Perfect Wives: Recent Studies of Hindu Women, Relig Studies Rev, 94; Islam and Gender in Turkey, Relig Studies Rev, 95; auth,Techniques for Teaching the Advanced Religious Studies Course on Islam, CCHA Rev, 97. **CONTACT ADDRESS** Dept of Religious Studies, Whittier Col, Whittier, CA 90608. **EMAIL** gyocum@whittier.edu

YOCUM, SANDRA MIZE
DISCIPLINE RELIGIOUS STUDIES **EDUCATION** Marquette Univ, PhD. **CAREER** Assoc prof; dir, Grad Stud, Univ Dayton. **RESEARCH** American catholicism. **SELECTED PUBLICATIONS** Pubs, co-ed, American Catholic Traditions: Resources for Renewal, 97. **CONTACT ADDRESS** Dept of Religious Studies, Univ of Dayton, 300 College Park, 347 Humanities, Dayton, OH 45469-1679. **EMAIL** smize@notes.udayton.edu

YODER, JOHN
PERSONAL Born 02/12/1942, Iowa City, IA, m, 1966, 2 children **DISCIPLINE** INTERNATIONAL POLITICS AND PEACE STUDIES, AFRICAN STUDIES; AFRICAN HISTORY AND POLITICS **EDUCATION** Mennonite Sem, Mdiv; Northwestern Univ, PhD. **CAREER** Prof. **HONORS AND AWARDS** Fulbright grant, 87-88; Fulbright grant, 98; Pew Evangelical Scholars Prog grant, 97, 99; fulbright nat selection comm for africa. **RESEARCH** Relationship between the political values of ordinary citizens and the collapse of the Liberian state. **SELECTED PUBLICATIONS** Publ, articles on Dahomey, Uganda, Zaire, and colonial America; ed, Zaire, Dictionary of African Biography, Reference Publ, 79; auth, The Kanyok of Zaire, Cambridge, 92. **CONTACT ADDRESS** Dept of Hist, Whitworth Col, 300 West Hawthorne Rd, Spokane, WA 99251. **EMAIL** johnyoder@whitworth.edu

YOLTON, JOHN W.
PERSONAL Born 11/10/1921, Birmingham, AL, m, 1945, 2 children **DISCIPLINE** PHILOSOPHY **EDUCATION** McMaster Univ, D Litt, 76; York Univ, LLD, 74; Oxford Univ, Dphil, 52; Univ Cincinnati, BA, 45. MA, 46. **CAREER** Prof Emeritus, Rutgers Univ, 92; John Locke Prof of History of Philos, Rutgers Univ, 89-92; prof Philos, Rutgers Univ, 78-92; chair Philos Dept, Rutgers Univ, 87-88; Dean Rutgers Col, Rutgers Univ, 78-85; prof Philos, York Univ, 63-78; chair Philos Dept, York Univ, 63-73; prof Philos, Univ Maryland, 61-63. **HONORS AND AWARDS** Fulbright Grantee, Balliol Col, 50-52; Univ Fel, Univ Calif Berkeley, 49-50; Ntl Endowment Humanities Fel, 88-89; dir of seminar, Space and Time, Matter and Mind, Folger Shakespeare Libr, 81; FCS Schiller Essay Prize, Univ Calif Berkeley, 48; AS Eddington Essay First Prize, Institut International des Sciences Theoriques, Brussels, 56. **MEMBERSHIPS** Amer Philos Quart Ed Brd, 64-83; History of Philos Quart Ed Brd, 84-90; Studies in History of Philos & Sci Ed Brd; Jour History of Philos Ed Brd; Philos of Soc Sci Ed Brd; Jour of History of Ideas Ed Brd; Studi Internazionali di Filosofia Ed Brd; Eighteenth Century Studies Ed Brd, 82-85; Brit Jour History of Philos Ed Brd. **RESEARCH** Epistemology, metaphysics, 17th and 18th century British and continental philosophy, John Locke. **SELECTED PUBLICATIONS** Perception and Reality: A History from Descartes to Kant, Cornell Univ Pr, 96; A Locke Dictionary, Blackwell, 93; The Blackwell Companion to the Enlightenment, Blackwell Reference, 92; Ed, Philosophy, Religion and Science in the 17th and 18th Centuries, Univ Rochester Pr, 90; auth, Realism and Aooearances, Cambridge Univ Press, 00. **CONTACT ADDRESS** Dept of Philosophy, Rutgers, The State Univ of New Jersey, New Brunswick, 39 Wakefield Ln, Piscataway, NJ 08854.

YORK, ANTHONY DELANO
PERSONAL Born 08/23/1934, Winston-Salem, NC, m, 1957, 4 children **DISCIPLINE** BIBLICAL LITERATURE, SEMITIC LANGUAGES **EDUCATION** Cornell Univ, PhD(Semitic lang), 73. **CAREER** Fel Hebrew, Oxford Ctr for Post-Grad Hebrew, 73-75; lectr Hebrew, Leeds Univ, 75-78; asst prof, 78-81, Assoc Prof Bible, Univ Cincinnati, 81-; Prof Bible, Univ Cincinnati, 99. **MEMBERSHIPS** Soc Old Testament Study. **RESEARCH** Targum; Book of Job; ancient versions of the bible. **SELECTED PUBLICATIONS** Auth of articles in J Study Judaism, 73 & 78, J Bibl Lit, 74, Rev de Qumran, 75, Bibliotheca Orientalis, 75 & Vetus Testamentum 76; auth, The Bible as Literature Adam in The Dictionary of Biblical Tradition in English Literature; "Festacjroftem e.g. Studied in Honor of Dwight Young," and in The University of Dayton Review. **CONTACT ADDRESS** Univ of Cincinnati, 3343 Sherlock Ave, Cincinnati, OH 45220. **EMAIL** anthony.york@uc.edu

YOUNG, DAVID
PERSONAL Born 12/29/1960, Nashville, TN, m, 1983, 2 children **DISCIPLINE** RELIGION; NEW TESTAMENT **EDUCATION** Harding Graduate Sch of Relig, MA, 87; Vanderbilt Univ, MA, 91, PhD, 94. **CAREER** Minister, North Boulevard Church of Christ. **MEMBERSHIPS** AAR; SBL. **RESEARCH** New Testament **CONTACT ADDRESS** 1112 N Rutherford Blvd, Murfreesboro, TN 37130-1372.

YOUNG, ERNEST A.
DISCIPLINE CONSTITUTIONAL LAW **EDUCATION** Dartmouth Col, BA, 90; Harvard Law Sch, JD, 93. **CAREER** Vis Asst Prof, Villanova Univ, Past Res Asst to, Prof Laurence Tribe, Clerk, Hon Michael Boudin US Ct Appeals 1st Circuit, Clerk, Hon David Souter, US Supreme Ct, , assoc Covington & Burling (Wash, DC), adj prof, Georgetown Univ Law Ct, assoc, Cohan, Simpson, Cowlishaw & Wulff (Dallas, TX) 99. **HONORS AND AWARDS** Sears prize, 92, Best Brief award. **RESEARCH** Administrative law, admiralty law, constitutional law, fed courts. **SELECTED PUBLICATIONS** Auth, Recent Developments: Regulation of Racist Speech, Harv J Law Pub Pol"y, 91; auth, The Supreme Court 1991: Term--Leading Cases, Harv L Rev 163, 92; auth, rediscoverring Conseratism: Burkean Political Theory & constitutional Interpretation, 72 NC L Rev 619, 94; auth, Preemption at Sea, GW L Rev, 99. **CONTACT ADDRESS** Law School, Univ of Texas, Austin, Campus Mail Code: D1800, Austin, TX 78712. **EMAIL** eyoung@mail.law.utexas.edu

YOUNG, JAMES O.
DISCIPLINE PHILOSOPHY **EDUCATION** Simon Fraser Univ, BA; Univ Waterloo, MA; Univ Boston, PhD. **CAREER** Instr, Univ Calgary; res fel, Melbourne Univ; assoc prof, 85. **RESEARCH** Philosophy of language; epistemology; metaphysics and aesthetics. **SELECTED PUBLICATIONS** Auth, Global Anti-realism, 95; pub(s), Brit Jour of Aesthet; Can Jour of Philos; Erkenntnis; Jour Aesthet and Art Critcism; Metaphilosophy; Philos and Phenomen Res; Synthese. **CONTACT ADDRESS** Dept of Philosophy, Univ of Victoria, PO Box 3045, Victoria, BC, Canada V8W 3P4. **EMAIL** joy@uvic.ca

YOUNG, JAMES VAN
PERSONAL Born 06/12/1936, Waterloo, IA, m, 1959, 2 children **DISCIPLINE** POLITICAL SCIENCE **EDUCATION** Univ Iowa, BA, 58, JD, 60, PhD, 64. **CAREER** Instr, 64, Univ Iowa; asst prof, polit sci, 64-68, chmn, dept polit sci, 65-68, St Olaf Col; asst prof, 68-71, assoc prof, 71-75, chmn, dept polit sci, 71-82, prof, 75-98, prof emer, 98-, Central Mo St Univ. **HONORS AND AWARDS** Byler Dist Fac Awd, 98; Cert Amer Polit Sci Assn & Pi Sigma Alpha, dist tchng, 98; All-Amer Masters, Track & Field, USA Track & Field, 91-98. Big Ten Honor Medal, Scholar & Athletics, 59; Nile Kinnick Scholar, 54-58; Univ Fel, 63; Phi Beta Kappa, 59; Order of the Coif, 60; BA, Summa cum Laude, 58; JD, Magna cum Laude, 60. **MEMBERSHIPS** Amer Polit Sci Assn; Midwest Polit Sci Assn; Mo Polit Sci Assn; Supreme Court Hist Soc; Johnson County Hist Soc. **RESEARCH** Amer Constitutional law; civil rights & liberties; judicial process & politics; state government & politics; federalism & intergovernmental relations; national government **SELECTED PUBLICATIONS** Art, Venue-Transfer of Case Laying Venue in Wrong Federal District Court, Iowa Law Rev, vol 44, 59; coauth, Remembering Their Glory: Sports Heroes of the 1940s, Barnes & Co, 77; art, Freedom of the Press in the Public Schools: A Legal-Political Analysis, Persp in Schl Censorship, 77; coauth, Liberty Versus Authority: The Supreme Court 1951-1961, McCap J, CMSU, 97; auth, Judges and Science: The Case Law on Atomic Energy, Arno Press, 79; auth, Landmark Constitutional Law Decisions: Briefs and Analyses, Univ Press Amer, 93; art, Types of Law in Missouri, Govt & Polit of Mo, 95. **CONTACT ADDRESS** 320 Goodrich Drive, Warrensburg, MO 64093-2219. **EMAIL** jyoung@inet-hwy.com

YOUNG, JOHN TERRY
PERSONAL Born 09/22/1929, Houston, TX, m, 1954, 2 children **DISCIPLINE** THEOLOGY **EDUCATION** Baylor Univ, BA, 51; Southwestern Baptist Theol Sem, BD, 55, ThD, 62. **CAREER** Pastor, First Southern Baptist Church, Chula Vista, Calif, 57-62, Village Baptist Church, San Lorenzo, 62-63; ed, Calif Southern Baptist, 63-71; Prof Theol, New Orleans Baptist Theol Sem, 71-98, Mem, Baptist Joint Comt Pub Affairs, 65-72; Resolutions Comt of Southern Baptist Convention, 70 & 72. **MEMBERSHIPS** Am Acad Relig; Evangelical Theol Soc; Nat Asn of Baptist Professors of Relig; Conf on Faith and Hist. **SELECTED PUBLICATIONS** Auth, The Spirit Within You, 77 & The Church-Alive and Growing, 78, Broadman; A living church in a dying world, Theol Educ, 78; Compelled By The Cross, Broadman, 80. **CONTACT ADDRESS** 14839 N 22nd Ln, Phoenix, AZ 85023. **EMAIL** terryyoung@uswest.net

YOUNG, MICHAEL K.
PERSONAL Born 11/04/1949, Sacramento, CA, m, 1972, 3 children **DISCIPLINE** LAW **EDUCATION** Brigham Young Univ, BA, 73; Harvard Law School, JD, 76. **CAREER** Law cler, Judicial Court Mass, 76-77; law clerk, US Supreme Court, 77-78; deputy legal adviser, US Dept of State, 89-91; deputy undersecretary, US Dept of State, 91=93; fuyo prof, Columbia Univ, 78-98; dean and prof, George Wash Univ Law School, 98-. **HONORS AND AWARDS** Fel, POSCO Res Inst, 96; Alternate Head of Delegation, UN Conf on environment and Development, Rio de Janiero, 92; Head of Delegation, Conf on Security and Cooperation Negotiations for a Multilateral Pacific Settlement of Disputes Mechanism, Malta, 90; Chief counsel, US Delegation, 89; Nat Defense for Lang Fel, Title VI, 75. **MEMBERSHIPS** Japan Soc, Professional Fel Selection Committee, Advisory committee, Am Bar foundation, doing Business in Japan. **RESEARCH** International trade law and policy, international environmental law, Japanese law, dispute resolution, industrial policy, international commercial transactions, administrative process and procedure, the legal profession, traditional and modern Asian law, constitutional law and practice, corporate governance and international and foreign relations, in a variety of English, Japanese and Korean language publications. **SELECTED PUBLICATIONS** Auth, International Environmental Law, Michie Pub, (forthcoming), auth, "Lessons from the Battle front: US-Japan Trade Wars and Their Impact on the Multilateral Trading System," in The Multilateral Trade Regime in the 21st Century, (99); auth, An Overview of the Fundamentals of US Trade Law and Policy, 98; auth, Trilateral Perspectives on International Legal Issues: Relevance of Domestic Law & Policy, 96; auth, "Religious Liberties and Religious tolerance: An Agenda for the Future," Brigham Young University Law Review, 96; auth, "The Constitution Ignored: Review of The Constitutional Case Law of Japan, 1970 through 1990," Monumenta Nipponica, 97; auth, "International Dispute Resolution: Lessons from Malta," Trilateral Perspectives on International Legal Issues, 96; auth, "Dispute Resolution in the Uruguay round: Lawyers Triumph over Diplomats," The International Lawyer, 95; auth, " Introduction to Japanese Law," Japan Business Law Guide, 95; auth, "Structural Adjustment of Mature Industries in Japan: Legal Institutions, Industry Associations and Bargaining," The Promotion and Regulation of Industry in Japan, 91; auth, Ho wa Nichibel wo Hedateru Ka? (Does Law Create a Separation Between Japan and the United States?), 90. **CONTACT ADDRESS** Dept Law, The George Washington Univ, 2000 H Streets, NW, Washington, DC 20052. **EMAIL** myoung@main.nlc.gwu.edu

YOUNG, PAMELA DICKEY
PERSONAL Born 12/16/1955, NS, Canada **DISCIPLINE** RELIGIOUS STUDIES **EDUCATION** Southern Methodist Univ, PhD, 83. **CAREER** Asst prof, assoc prof, prof, Queen's Univ Dept of Relig Stud, 85- ; chemn, 96- . **MEMBERSHIPS** Am Acad Relig; Am Theol Soc; Canadian Soc for Stud of Relig; Canadian Theol Soc. **RESEARCH** Women and religion; feminine and theology; twentieth century theology; religion and culture. **SELECTED PUBLICATIONS** Ed, Theological Reflections on Ministry and Sexual Orientation, Trinity, 90; auth, Feminist Theology/Christian Theology: In Search of Method, Fortress, 90; auth, Teologia Feminista--Teologia Christiana: En Gusqueda de un Metodo, Demac, 93; auth, Theology and Committment, Toronto J of Theol, 93; auth, Ubi Christus Ibi Ecclesia: Some Christological Themes Relevant in Formulating New Ecclesiologies, in Wilson, ed, New Wine: The Challenge of the Emerging Ecclesiologies to Church Renewal, World Alliance of Reformed Churches, 94; auth, Christ in a Post-Christian World: How Can We Believe in Jesus Christ When Those Around Us Believe Differently or Not at All? Fortress, 95; auth, Feminist Theology: From Past to Future, in Joy, ed, Gender, Genre and Religion: Feminist Reflections, Wilfrid Laurier, 95; auth, Beyond Moral Influence to an Atoning Life, Theol Today, 95; auth, Experience, and, Norm, in Isherwood, ed, An A to Z of Feminist Theology, Sheffield Acad, 96; auth, Encountering Jesus Through the Earliest Witnesses, Theol Stud, 96; auth, Theme and Variation: The Social Gospel in a New Key, Toronto J of Theol, 96; auth, The Resurrection of Whose Body: A Feminist Look at the Question of Transcendence, in Downing, ed, Psychoanalysis, Feminism and Religion, forthcoming; **CONTACT ADDRESS** Dept of Religious Studies, Queen's Univ at Kingston, Theological Hall, Rm 414, Kingston, ON, Canada K7L 3N6. **EMAIL** youngpd@post.queensu.ca

YOUNG, PHILLIPS EDWARD
PERSONAL Born 06/08/1961, North Lewisburgh, OH, m, 1998 **DISCIPLINE** PHILOSOPHY **EDUCATION** Kent State Univ, BA, 84; Pa State Univ, MA, 95; PhD, expected 2000. **CAREER** Adjunct prof at: Rutgers Univ, Gwynned Mercy Col, La Salle Univ, and St Joseph's Univ; vis asst prof, Villanova Univ, 00-. **HONORS AND AWARDS** Designed and developed distance education courses in philosophy for Penn State; Interdisciplinary Fel in the Humanities, Penn State Univ, 88-89. **MEMBERSHIPS** APA, IAPL, Merleau-Ponty Circle, SPEP. **RESEARCH** Performing arts, political philosophy. **SELECTED PUBLICATIONS** Auth, Medical Ethics: A Study Guide,

The Penn State Univ, Dept of Distance Educ (94, revised, 96); auth, Ethics and Social Issues: Procedure Guide, The Penn State Univ, Dept of Distance Educ (95, revised 98); auth, Critical Thinking and Argument: Study Guide, The Penn State Univ, Dept of Distance Educ (96, revised 98); auth, "The Irony of Ironic Liberalism," Int Studies in Philos, vol 29, 1 (97); auth, Social and Political Philosophy: Study Guide, The Penn State Univ, Dept of Distance Educ (97, revised 98); auth, "Dance and the Problem of Postmodern Politics," Int Studies in Philos, vol 30, 1 (98); auth, "Music, Sedimentation, and Reversibility: Towards an Account of Authenticity," Merleau-Ponty Circle, The North East Wales Inst, Wales, UK (99); auth, "Legitimation and the Site of Chiasmatic Resistance: Merleau-Ponty and the Ethics of Discourse," Int Asn of Philos and Lit (99); auth, "Music and the Political: An Essay on Postmodern Judgement," Philosophy, Interpretation, and Culture (99); auth, "Ambiguity and Critique: Ethics and the Ch(i)asm of Political Life," The Dehiscence of Responsibility, Humanities Press, Dr. Duane Davis, ed (forthcoming). **CONTACT ADDRESS** Dept Philos, Villanova Univ, 800 Lancaster Ave, Villanova, PA 19085-1699. **EMAIL** phillips.edward.young@villanova.edu

YOUNGBLOOD, RONALD F.
PERSONAL Born 08/10/1931, Chicago, IL, m, 1952, 2 children **DISCIPLINE** OLD TESTAMENT **EDUCATION** Valparaiso Univ, BA, 52; Fuller Theol Sem, BD, 55; Dropsie Col, PhD, 61. **CAREER** Asst hist, Valparaiso Univ, 51-52; student instr Hebrew, Fuller Theol Sem, 54-55; Semitic lang, Dropsie Col, 58-61; asst prof Old Testament lang, Bethel Theol Sem, 61-65; assoc prof Old Testament interpretation, 65-70, prof Old Testament, 70-78; prof Old Testament & assoc dean, Wheaton Col Grad Sch, 78-80, dean, grad sch, 80-81; prof Old Testament & Semitic lang, Trinity Evangel Divinity Sch, 81-82; Prof Old Testament & Hebrew, Bethel Sem San Diego, 82-; Grant, Land of Bible Workshop, NY Univ, 66; fel archaeol, Hebrew Union Col, Jerusalem, 67-68; ed, Evangel Theol Soc, 76-98; mem exec comt on Bible transl, New Int Version, 78-. **MEMBERSHIPS** Evangel Theol Soc; Near E Archaeol Soc. **RESEARCH** Old Testament literature; Hebrew; Amarna correspondence. **SELECTED PUBLICATIONS** Auth, Amorite influence in a Canaanite Amarna letter, Bull Am Schs Orient Res, 12/62; Lqr't in Amos 4:12, J Bibl Lit, 3/71; The Heart of the Old Testament, 71, 2nd ed, 98 & Special Day Sermons, 73, Baker Bk; Faith of Our Fathers, Regal, 76; How It All Began, Regal, 80; Exodus, Moody, 83; Themes from Isaiah, Regal, 83; assoc ed, NIV Study Bible, Zondervan, 85; ed, The Genesis Debate, Thomas Nelson, 86; Nelson's Quick Reference Bible Concordance, Thomas Nelson, 93; gen ed, Nelson's New Illustrated Bible Dictionary, 95; exec ed, New International Reader's Version, Zondevwan, 98. **CONTACT ADDRESS** Bethel Sem, San Diego, 6116 Arosa St, San Diego, CA 92115-3999. **EMAIL** r-youngblood@bethel.edu

YOVEL, YIRMIYAHU
PERSONAL Born 10/20/1935, Haifa, Israel, m, 1960, 2 children **DISCIPLINE** PHILOSOPHY **EDUCATION** The Hebrew Univ of Jerusalem, BA, 61, MA, 64, PhD, 68. **CAREER** Hebrew Univ, Chair, Dept of Philos, Dir, S. H. Bergman Center for Philos Studies, Schulman Prof of Philos, Foder-Chiar, the Jerusalem Spinoza Inst; vis prof, Sorbonne, Hamburg, Milan, Princeton, Columbia, New School, etc.; Werner Marx Vis Prof of Philos, 93-96, Hans Jonas Prof of Philos, 96-. **HONORS AND AWARDS** The Israel Prize in Philosophy, 2000. **RESEARCH** Kant, Spinoza, Nietzsche, current theologies of the will and the rise of modernity, Jewish rationalism, the Marranos. **SELECTED PUBLICATIONS** Auth, Kant and the Renewal of Metaphysics, Jerusalem: The Bialik Inst (73, 87); auth, Kant and the Philosophy of History, Princeton Univ Press (80); auth, Spinoza and Other Heretics, Col 1: The Marrano of Reason, Vol II: The Adventure of Immanence, Princeton Univ Press (89); auth, Dark Riddle: Hegel, Nietzsch, and the Jews, Tel Aviv: Shocken Books (96); auth, Commentary to Hegel's Preface to the Phenomenology of Spirit, Heb., Jerusalem, Magnes Press (96); ed, The Affects: Spinoza as Psychologist, The New Sch of Philos J Pubs, NY (forthcoming); auth, "The Will in the Era of Revolution," in the Proceedings of the Hegel Congress held at Stuttgart (June 99). **CONTACT ADDRESS** Dept Philos, New Sch for Social Research, 65 5th Ave, New York, NY 10003-3003. **EMAIL** yovel@hz.hmm.hmji.ac.il

YU, ANTHONY C.
PERSONAL Born 10/06/1938, Hong Kong, m, 1963, 1 child **DISCIPLINE** RELIGION, WESTERN & CHINESE LITERATURE **EDUCATION** Houghton Col, BA, 60; Fuller Theol Sem, STB, 63; Univ Chicago, PhD(relig & lit), 69. **CAREER** Instr English, Univ Ill Chicago Circle, 67-68; from instr to asst prof relig & lit, 68-74, assoc prof, 74-78, Prof Relig & Lit, Divinity Sch & Prof Dept Far Eastern Lang & Civilizations, Comt Social Thought, English & Comp Lit, Univ Chicago, 78-90, Asst ed, J Asian Studies, 75-77, co-ed, Monogr Ser, 77-; Guggenheim Mem Found fel Chinese Lit, 76-77; Nat Endowment for Humanities special grant, 77-80 & 81-82; co-ed, J Relig, 80-90; Carl Darling Buck Distinguished Service Prof Humanities, 90; Sr Fel, Am Coun of Learned Soc, 86-87; Master Texts Study Grant, Seminar for Public Sch Teachers, NEH, 92; Phi Beta Kappa vis scholar, 01-02. **HONORS AND AWARDS** Gordon J Laing Prize, Univ of Chicago Press, 83. **MEMBERSHIPS** Asn Asian Studies, Elec Mem, China & Inner Asia Coun, 79-82; Am Acad Relig; Milton Soc of Am, Life Mem; MLA, Elec Mem, Exec Council, 98-01; Mem, Board of Dir, Illinois Hum Coun, 95-98; Elec Academician, Academia Sinica, 98; Elc Fel, Am academy of Arts and Sciences, 00. **RESEARCH** Religious approaches to classical literatures, western and non-western; comparative literature; translation. **SELECTED PUBLICATIONS** Auth, New Gods and old order: Tragic theology in the Prometheus Bound, J Am Acad Relig, 71; ed, Parnasus Revisited: Modern Criticism and The Epic Tradition, Am Libr Asn, 73; auth, Problems and prospects in Chinese-Western literary relations, In: Yearbook of General and Comparative Literature, 74; Chapter nine and the problem of narrative structure, J Asian Studies, 75; On translating the Hsi-yu chi, In: The Art and Profession of Translation, Hong Kong Transl Soc, 76; translr & ed, The Journey to the West, Vol I-IV, Univ Chicago, 77-83; Self and family in the Hung-lou meng, Chinese Lit: Essays, Articles, Rev, 80; Life in the garden: Freedom and the image of God in Paradise Lost, J Relig, 80; Order of Temptations in Paradis Regained, in Perspectives on Christology, ed, Marguerite Shuster & Richard Muller, Zondervan, 91; Rereading the Stone: Desire and the Making of Fiction in Honglou-meng, Princeton, 97. **CONTACT ADDRESS** Divinity Sch, Univ of Chicago, 1025-35 E 58th St, Chicago, IL 60637-1577. **EMAIL** acyu@midway.uchicago.edu

YUN, SAMUEL
PERSONAL Born 06/19/1958, Seoul, Korea, m, 1984, 4 children **DISCIPLINE** BIBLICAL STUDIES **EDUCATION** Univ of Dubuque Theol Sch, MAR, 85; Harvard Divinity Sch, ThM, 87. **CAREER** Assoc prof, Presbyterian Theol Sem in Am, 85- ; adj prof, New Brunswick Theol Sem, 94- ; pastor, Princeton Korean Presbyterian Church, 93- . **MEMBERSHIPS** SBL; AAR. **RESEARCH** Biblical spirituality. **SELECTED PUBLICATIONS** Auth, Living the Word, 90; auth, Living the Prayer, 94; auth, Living the Faith, 97. **CONTACT ADDRESS** 9 Sayre Dr, Princeton, NJ 08540. **EMAIL** samuelyun@hotmail.com

YURA, MICHAEL T.
PERSONAL Born 07/02/1945, Hazelton, PA, m, 1977, 3 children **DISCIPLINE** CRIMINOLOGY **EDUCATION** Ohio State Univ, PhD, 71. **CAREER** Prof, WVa Univ, 71-. **HONORS AND AWARDS** Col Sen Awd, 99; Golden Key Awd, 99. **MEMBERSHIPS** WVCA, MS2000, PICA, MCHD. **RESEARCH** Forensic science, children. **SELECTED PUBLICATIONS** Coauth, "A Comparative Study of the Interest Patterns of Black and White Athletes," Career Planning and Adult Develop Network, vol 7, no 1 (91); coauth, "Mentoring and Career Counseling Among University Faculty," J of Educ 177, 2 (95): 31-45; coauth, "The Effects of Goal Setting and Imagery Training on Free-Throw Performance of Female Collegiate Basketball Players," The Sports Psychol, 10, 4 (96): 182-197; coauth, "Ethics in Assessment and Testing," in Assessment and Testing in Applied Sport Psychol (forthcoming). **CONTACT ADDRESS** Dept Criminol, West Virginia Univ, Morgantown, PO Box 6121, Morgantown, WV 26506. **EMAIL** myura@wvu.edu

YUSA, M.
DISCIPLINE PHILOSOPHY OF RELIGION; BUDDHIST-CHRISTIAN DIALOGUE, NISHIDAN THOUGHT **EDUCATION** Univ CA at Santa Barbara, PhD, 83. **CAREER** From asst prof to prof, Western Washington Univ, 94-. **HONORS AND AWARDS** Japan Found Research Fel, 93-94. **MEMBERSHIPS** Amer Acad Rel; Assoc for Asian Studies; Amer Oriental Soc **RESEARCH** Cross-cultural hist of ideas **SELECTED PUBLICATIONS** Auth, Religion and Women, Women in Shinto: Images Remembered, State Univ of NY Press, Albany, 94; auth, Rude Awakenings: The Kyoto School, Zen, and the Question of Nationalism, Nishida and Totalitarianism: A Philosopher's Resistance, Univ of Hawaii Press, Honolulu, 95; auth, Eastern Buddhist, Nishida Kitaro Mem Issue, Reflections on Nishida Studies, 95; auth, Shiso No. 857 special issue commemorating 50th aniv of death of Nishida Kitaro, A Reflection on the Study of Nishida Philosophy in America, 95; auth, Rude Awakenings: The Kyoto School, Zen, and the Question of Nationalism, Nishida and Totalitarianism: A Philosopher's Resistance, Univ of Hawaii Press, Honolulu, 95; auth, A Companion to World Philosophies, Contemporary Buddhist Philosophy, Blackwell Publishers, Oxford, 97; auth, Denki Nishida Kitaro, Kyoto, Toeisha, 98; auth, Intl Encyclopedia of Philosophy, Zeami, 98; auth, Monumenta Nipponica, Philosophy and Inflation, Miki Kiyoshi in Weimar Germany 1922-24, 98, Nishida and Hearn, 96. **CONTACT ADDRESS** Dept of Modern and Classical Languages, Western Washington Univ, Bellingham, WA 98225.

Z

ZAAS, PETER S.
DISCIPLINE RELIGIOUS STUDIES **EDUCATION** Oberlin Col, AB, 74; Univ Chicago, MA, 77, PhD, 82. **CAREER** Vis scholar, Duke Univ, 78-79; instr, Hamilton Col, 79-81; asst prof, Hamilton Col, 81-82 and Siena College, 82-89 & 89-95; prof, Siena Col, 95; ch, Dept Rel Stud, Siena Col, 92-95; serv to other inst(s), St Bernard's Inst, Empire State Col, Yale Divinity Sch, Skidmore Col & New Brunswick Theol Sem; mem, SBL Pauline Ethics Sem, 79-81; charter bd mem, Siena Inst Jewish Christian Stud & coordr, 89-92; actg dir, Siena Ins Jewish-Christian Stud, 91-92 & dir, 92-; ch, dept Rel Stud, Siena Col, 92-95; Convener, SBL Bibl Ethics and Exegesis Consultation, 85-86 & SBL Exegesis of Texts on Bibl Ethics Gp, 87-93; instr, Chautauqua Inst, 91-93; Siena Comt(s), Col Conduct, Long Range Plan, on Admis, Acad Comp Adv, Fac & ch Comparability. **MEMBERSHIPS** SBL, AAR, NAm Patristics Soc. **RESEARCH** Moral thought in Jewish and early Christian lit; The Church Fathers as Evidence for Jewish Life in Late Antiquity Hist and lit of Hellenistic Judaism; Christian origins; Historiography of early Christianity. **SELECTED PUBLICATIONS** Auth, Prophecy in Contemporary Jewish Religious Thought, Original essays on critical concepts, movements, and beliefs, NY, Scribner's Press, 87, paperback ed, Free Press, 89; Catalogues and Context: I Corinthians 5 and 6, New Testament Stud 34, 88; John Boswell and Pauline Sexual Ethics, Voices, 87; Protology and Eschatology in the Jewish-Christian Dialogue, in Torah and Revelation, Lewiston, NY, The Edwin Mellen Press, 92; Forward to J O Holloway, III, Peripetew as a Thematic Marker for Pauline Ethics, San Francisco: Mellen Res UP, 92; Paul and the hklh: Dietary Laws for Gentiles in I Corinthians 8-10, Jewish Law Asn Stud VII, Paris Conf Vol, Atlanta, Scholars Press, 94; What Comes out of a Person is What Makes a Person Impure: Jesus as Sadducee, Jewish Law Asn Stud VIII, Jerusalem 94 Conf Vol, Atlanta: Scholars Press, 96; rev(s), A Hidden Revolution, Bibl Archeol, 81; The Lord's Table: Eucharist and Passover in Early Christianity, 2nd Century, 82. **CONTACT ADDRESS** Dept of Relig Studies, Siena Col, 515 Loudon Rd., Loudonville, NY 12211-1462. **EMAIL** ZAAS@SIENA.EDU

ZABLOTSKY, PETER A.
DISCIPLINE LAW **EDUCATION** PA State Univ, BA, summa cum laude, 77; Columbia Univ, JD, 80. **CAREER** Assoc prof, Touro Col; writing and res ed, Columbia J of Law and Soc Prob; coordr, legal writing and Res prog, NY Law Schl. **HONORS AND AWARDS** Harlan Fiske Stone scholar. **SELECTED PUBLICATIONS** Publ in the areas of products liability, torts, civil rights, criminal procedure, and domestic rel(s). **CONTACT ADDRESS** Dept of Law, Touro Col, New York, Brooklyn, NY 11230. **EMAIL** peterz@tourolaw.edu

ZACHARIAS, RAVI
DISCIPLINE CULTURE AND RELIGION **EDUCATION** Univ New Delhi, BA; Ontario Bible Col, BTh; Trinity Evangel Theol Sem, MDiv; Houghton Col, DD; Asbury Col, LLD; post grad stud, Ridley Hall, Cambridge Univ. **CAREER** Distinguished vis prof. **SELECTED PUBLICATIONS** Auth, Can Man Live Without God; A Shattered Visage: The Real Face of Atheism; Deliver Us From Evil; Cries of the Heart. **CONTACT ADDRESS** So Evangelical Sem, 4298 McKee Rd, Charlotte, NC 28270.

ZACHARY, STEVEN W.
PERSONAL Born 04/24/1958, St Paul, MN, d **DISCIPLINE** LAW **EDUCATION** Mankato State University, BS, 1981; University of Minnesota School of Law, JD, 1984. **CAREER** City of St Paul, human rights specialist, 84-92; William Mitchell Col of Law, adjunct professor, 89-92; State of Minnesota, diversity and equal opportunity director, 92-97. **HONORS AND AWARDS** William Mitchell College of Law, Haines Distinguished Service Awd, 1992. **MEMBERSHIPS** NAACP St Paul Branch, president, 1990-93; MCLU, board member, 1990-93; MN Minority Lawyer's Association, 1987-93; JRLC, criminal justice taskforce chairperson, 1991-92; St Peter Claver School, school board president, 1987-88. **SELECTED PUBLICATIONS** What's In Store for Civil Rights in 1990. **CONTACT ADDRESS** Diversity & Equal Opportunity Director, State of Minnesota, Department of Employee Relations, 200 Centennial Office Bldg, 658 Cedar St, Saint Paul, MN 55155.

ZACK, ARNOLD MARSHALL
PERSONAL Born 10/07/1931, Lynn, MA, m, 1969, 2 children **DISCIPLINE** GOVERNMENT, ECONOMICS **EDUCATION** Tufts Col, BA, 53; Yale Univ, LLB, 56; Harvard Univ, MPA, 61. **CAREER** Labor management arbitrator/mediator, 60; fac, visiting prof, Cornell Univ, 82-83; Harvard Univ, Trade Union Prog, 84; visiting lectr, Yale Law School, 94-96. **HONORS AND AWARDS** Distinguished Service Award of Am Arbitration Asn; Cuslying Gavin Award of Archdiocese of Boston; Whitney North Seymour Medal. **MEMBERSHIPS** Am Bar Asn; Am Arbitration Asn; Nat Acad of Arbitrators, 94-95; Chmn Rev Panel, International Monetary Fund, 00-01. **RESEARCH** International labor dispute settlement systems. **SELECTED PUBLICATIONS** Coauth, Mediation and Arbitration of Labor Disputes, 97; auth, The Agreement in Negotiations and Arbitration, 2nd edition, 96; auth, Labor Arbitration Cases on the Merits, 89; auth, Labor Arbitration Procedural Issues, 91; auth, Arbitrating Discipline and Discharge Cases, Labor Relations Press, 00. **CONTACT ADDRESS** 170 W Canton St, Boston, MA 02118. **EMAIL** zack@post.harvard.edu

ZACK, NAOMI
PERSONAL Born 07/21/1944, Brooklyn, NY, d, 2 children **DISCIPLINE** PHILOSOPHY **EDUCATION** NYork Univ, BA, 66; Columbia Univ, PhD, 70. **CAREER** Assoc Prof, 90-, SUNY at Albany. **HONORS AND AWARDS** Woodrow Wilson Fel, NEH Fel, Woodrow Wilson Dissertation Fel, Pres ASVI 98. **MEMBERSHIPS** APA, CCSWP, ISVI. **RESEARCH** Racial theory, 17th century Philosophy. **SELECTED PUBLICATIONS** Auth, Bachelors of Science, Seventeenth Century Identity, Then and Now, Temple Univ Press, 96; Race and Mixed Race, Temple Univ Press, 93; Thinking About Race, Wadsworth Pub Co, 98; ed intro & art, Descartes' Realist Awake-Asleep Distinction and Naturalism in Women of Glos Philosophy, Blackwell Publishers, 00; ed intro & art, The American Sexualization of Race, in: Race/Sex, Their Sameness, Difference and Interplay, Routledge, 97; auth, Life After Race, in: American Mixed Race, Constructing Microdiversity, Rowman & Littlefield, 95. **CONTACT ADDRESS** Dept of Philosophy HU 257, Univ at Albany, SUNY, Albany, NY 12222. **EMAIL** nzack@cnsunix.albany.edu

ZAFERSON, WILLIAM S.
PERSONAL Born 02/10/1925, Greece, m, 1955 **DISCIPLINE** PHILOSOPHY; CLASSICAL LANGUAGES & LITTERATURE **EDUCATION** Univ Athens, BA, 52, PhD, 76; Univ Chicago, MA, 65. **CAREER** Asst prof, philos, Univ Upper Iowa, Fayette, 66-68; prof philos, marymount Col, 68-70; prof philos, St Mary's Univ, 70-72. **HONORS AND AWARDS** Magna Cum Laude, 76; A. Daniel Shorey fel, Univ Chicago. **MEMBERSHIPS** Am Asn Learned Soc; APA; AAUP; NRTA; Univ of Chicago Alumni Asn; National Asn of Scholars Who's Who in Am; Who Who in the World 18th Edition, 01; Goethe-Institut Chicago; The Swedish Cultural Society in Am-Chicago Chapter; Center for Scandinavian Studies. **RESEARCH** Ancient Greek mythology; original Greek texts of Hesiod, Homer, Pindar; the Greek tragedians; Plato; Aristotle; Plotimes; he Bible; Epictetus; Heraclitus. **SELECTED PUBLICATIONS** Auth, The Meaning of Metempsychosis, 65; auth, The Universe, Its Elements and Justice, 74; auth, A Hymn to Health, 75; auth, The Platonic View of Moral Law and the Influence of the Tragedians on Plato's Thoughts, 76; auth, The Songs of the Muses for Gods and Men, 97; Auth, Poem & Music Hephaetus, 99, 00. **CONTACT ADDRESS** PO Box 1551, Chicago, IL 60690.

ZAGANO, PHYLLIS
PERSONAL Born New York, NY **DISCIPLINE** RELIGION; LITERATURE **EDUCATION** Marymount Col, BA, 69; Boston Univ, MS, 70; C.W. Post Center of Long Island Univ, MA, 72; St. John's Univ, MA, 90; State Univ New York Stony Brook, PhD **CAREER** Boston Univ, 88-99. **MEMBERSHIPS** Am Acad Rel, co-chair, Roman Catholic Studies; Am Cath Philos Assoc; Am Jour Historians Assoc; Col Theol Soc; Soc Study Christian Spirituality; Spiritual Directors Int **SELECTED PUBLICATIONS** Ed, The Nuclear Arms Debate, New York: The Hudson River Press, 83; ed, Religion and Public Policy: A Directory of Organizations and People, The Rockford Institute (Rockford, Illinois), 87; coed, The Social Impact of the Mass Media, Ginn Press (Needham, MA), 91; ed, Woman to Woman: An Anthology of Women's Spiritualities, The Liturgical Press (Collegeville, MN), 93; auth, On Prayer, Paulist Press (Mahwah, NJ), 94; auth, Ita Ford: Missionary Martyr, Paulist Press (Mahwah, NJ), 96; co-ed, The Exercise of the Primacy: Continuing the Dialogue, Crossroad/Herder (New York), 98; co-ed, Things New and Old: Essays on the Theology of Elizabeth A. Johnson, New York: Crossroad/Herder, 98; ed, Twentieth-Century Apostles: Christian Spirituality in Action, The Liturgical Press (Collegiate, MN), 99; auth, Holy Saturday: An Argument for the Restoration of the Female Diaconate in the Catholic Church, Herder & Herder (New York), 00. **CONTACT ADDRESS** 250 E 63rd St, New York, NY 10021. **EMAIL** pzagano@interport.net

ZAHAVY, TZVEE
PERSONAL Born 11/23/1949, New York, NY, m, 1974, 2 children **DISCIPLINE** JEWISH AND RELIGIOUS STUDIES **EDUCATION** Yeshiva Univ, BA, 70, MS, 73; Brown Univ, PhD, 76. **CAREER** Teaching asst relig studies, Brown Univ, 74-76; asst prof, 76-80, Assoc prof Jewish Studies & Grad Fac Relig Studies & Ancient Studies, Univ MN, 80-88; prof 88-95; prof, Fairleigh Dickinson Univ, 97-; Am Coun Learned Soc fel, 82-83. **HONORS AND AWARDS** China Center and Off of Int Educ Travel Grants, 91; Col of Lib Arts Conf Grant, 89; 9-Wexner Foundation Institutional Grant, 88-9; National Endowment for the Humanities Summer Stipend, 88; Distinguished Teaching Award, Univ of MN, 84-85; Memorial Foundation for Jewish Culture Fellowship, 83-84; American Council of Learned Societies Fellowship, 83; American Council of Learned Societies, Grant-in-aid, 78; Award for Distinguished Contribution to Scholarship, Yeshiva University, 78; Tisch Foundation Fellowship, Brown University, 74; University Fellowship, Brown University, 73-74. **MEMBERSHIPS** Asn Jewish Studies; Soc Bibl; Lit; Am Acad Relig. **RESEARCH** Judaism in late antiquity; Rabbinics; Jewish prayer. **SELECTED PUBLICATIONS** Auth, The Mishnaic Law of Blessings and Players: Tractate Berakhot, Brown Univ Judaic Studies, 87; auth, The Talmud of the Land of Israel: Tractate Berkahot, Univ of Chicago Press, 89; auth, Studies in Jewish Prayer, Studies in Judaism, Univ Press of America, 90; auth, The Talmud of Babylonia: An American Translation, 92; auth, The Talmud of Babylonia: An American Translation, Scholars Press, 93; auth, The Talmud of Babylonia: An American Translation, Scholars Press, 94; auth, "Biblical Theory and Criticism: Midrash and Medieval Commentary," (Johns Hopkins Guide to Literary Theory and Criticism), 94, 81-84; auth, "The Predicament of the Postmodern American Jew," in Charles Selengut, (Jewish Identity in the Postmodern Age, St. Paul), 99; auth, "Piety" in The Encyclopedia of Judaism, (Leiden and New York), 99. **CONTACT ADDRESS** Dept Philosophy and Religion, Fairleigh Dickinson Univ, Teaneck-Hackensack, Teaneck, NJ 07666. **EMAIL** zahavy@andromeda.rutgers.edu

ZAKI, MAMOON
PERSONAL Born 08/01/1934, Baghdad, Iraq, m, 1980, 3 children **DISCIPLINE** POLITICAL SCIENCE **EDUCATION** Univ Baghdad, BA, 62; Howard Univ, MA, 76; Univ Calgary, PhD, 81. **CAREER** Asst Prof to Prof, Le Moyne-Owen Col; prof, Univ of Memphis; dean of academic affairs, Univ of Ajman, United Arab Emorates, 96-98. **MEMBERSHIPS** Am Polit Sci Asn, Tenn Polit Sci Asn. **RESEARCH** The Middle East and 3rd world countries. **SELECTED PUBLICATIONS** Auth, "Future Looks Brighter," The Commercial Appeal (94); auth, "Pragmatism carries the Day," The Commercial Appeal (94); contribur, "Encyclopedia of Politics and Religion," Congressional Quart (95); contribur, Encyclopedia of the Middle East, Simon & Schuster, 96; auth, "Iraqi File: A Documentary and Political Review," (98): 38-40; auth, "America and the Hashenite Union," File: A Documentary and Polit Rev, no 85 (99): 62-63. **CONTACT ADDRESS** Dept Soc Sci, LeMoyne-Owen Col, 807 Walker Ave, Memphis, TN 38126.

ZANER, RICHARD
PERSONAL Born 09/20/1933, Duncan, AZ, m, 1956, 2 children **DISCIPLINE** PHILOSOPHY & BIOETHICS **EDUCATION** Univ Houston, BS, 57; New Sch for Social Res, Grad Facul of Social and Polit Sci, PhD, 61. **CAREER** Instr, The New Sch, 60; Asst prof, Lamar State Col, 61-63; assoc prof, chair, Trinity Univ, 64-67; assoc prof, chair, Univ Tex Austin, 67-71; dir & prof, social sci and humanities in med, State Univ NY Stony Brook, 71-73; Easterwood prof & chair, Southern Methodist Univ, 73-81; A. G. Stahlman prof, med ethics, med, prof philos, prof ethics relig studies, Vanderbilt Univ. **HONORS AND AWARDS** Schutz mem award, PhD dissertation, 61; univ scholar, Univ Ctr of Ga, 75; Dotterer lectr, Pa State Univ, 81; prin speaker, 200th anniv celeb, Georgetown Univ, 89; Kegley lectr, Calif State Univ Bakersfield, 91; Leys lectr, Southern Ill Univ, 95; Inaugural Christine Martin lectr, Aust Bioethics Asn, 97; Inaugural lectr, Univ Melbourne Ctr for Bioethics, 97; Alfred Schutz mem lectr, Univ Ky, 97. **MEMBERSHIPS** Amer Philos Asn; Soc Phenomenol & Existential Philos; Soc Health & Human Values; Amer Soc Law & Ethics; Inst Soc, Ethics & Life Sci; Amer Psychol Asn; Amer Asn Univ Prof. **RESEARCH** Ethics in health care; Research ethics; Philosophy of medicine; Philosophical anthropology; Bioethics; Professional ethics. **SELECTED PUBLICATIONS** Auth, Ethical Issues in Cancer Pain Management, Cancer Pain Mgt: Principles and Practice, Butterworth-Heineman Publ, 97; auth, Phenomenology of Medicine, Encycl of Phenomenol, Kluwer Acad Publ, 97; foreward, Nursing Ethics: Therapeutic Caring Presence, Jones & Bartlett Publ, 95; auth, Reflection on Pain and Embodiment, Politics and the Human Body: Assault on Dignity, Vanderbilt Univ Press, 95; auth, Interpretation and Dialogue: Medicine as a Moral Discipline, Essays in Honor of Maurice Natanson, The Prism of Self, Kluwer Acad Publ, 95; auth, Phenomenology and the Clinical Event, Phenomenol of the Cultural Disciplines, Kluwer Acad Publ, vol 16, contrib to phenomenol, 94; auth, Experience and Moral Life: A Phenomenological Approach to Bioethics, A Matter of Principles? Ferment in U.S. Bioethics, The Park Ridge Ctr for the Study of Health, Faith and Ethics, Trinity Press Intl, 94; auth, Encountering the Other, Duties in Others, Theol and Med Series, Kluwer Acad Publ, 94; auth, Body: Embodiment: The Phenomenological Tradition, Encycl of Bioethics, The Kennedy Inst of Bioethics, new ed, 94; auth, Illness and the Other, Theol Analyses of the Clinical Encounter, Theol and Med Series, Kluwer Acad Publ, 94. **CONTACT ADDRESS** Center for Clinical and Research Ethics, Vanderbilt Univ, 319 Oxford House, Nashville, TN 37232-4350. **EMAIL** richard.zaner@mcmail.vanderbilt.edu

ZANK, MICHAEL
PERSONAL Born 04/09/1958, Bad Duerkheim, Germany, m, 1988, 2 children **DISCIPLINE** RELIGION **EDUCATION** Evangelical Church of the Palatine, MDiv, 86; Brandeis Univ, PhD, 94. **CAREER** Asst prof, Boston Univ. **MEMBERSHIPS** AAR; APA; AJS. **RESEARCH** Continental Philosophy; Modern Jewish Thought; Bible and Interpretation; German Jewish History and Culture. **SELECTED PUBLICATIONS** Auth, The Idea of Atonement in the Philosophy of Hermann Cohen, Brown Judaic Studies, 00. **CONTACT ADDRESS** Dept Relig, Boston Univ, 745 Commonwealth Ave, Boston, MA 02215. **EMAIL** mzank@bu.edu

ZAREMBKA, PAUL
PERSONAL Born 04/17/1942, St Louis, MO, m, 1980, 1 child **DISCIPLINE** ECONOMICS **EDUCATION** Univ Wis Madison, MS, 67; PhD, 67. **CAREER** Asst prof, Univ Calif-Berkeley, 67-72; assc to prof, SUNY-Buffalo, 76- . **HONORS AND AWARDS** Fulbright-Hayes lectr, 79; Who's Who in Economics; Who's Who in Am. **RESEARCH** Marxist economic theory. **SELECTED PUBLICATIONS** Auth, Toward a Theory of Economic Development, Holden-Day, San Fran, 72; ed, Frontiers in Econometrics, Acad Press, NY, 74; co-ed, Essays in Modern Capital Theory, N. Holland, Amsterdam, 76; ed, "The Development of State Capitalism in the Soviet System," Res in Polit Econ, JAI Press, Greenwich, Conn, 92, p. 123-161; auth, "Poland-The Deepening Crisis in Summer 1992," Monthly Rev, Jan 93, Vol 44:8. **CONTACT ADDRESS** Dept Econ, SUNY, Buffalo, PO Box 600001, Buffalo, NY 14260-0001. **EMAIL** Zarembka@acsu.buffalo.edu

ZAVODNY, JOHN
DISCIPLINE PHILOSOPHY **EDUCATION** Univ Tennessee, PhD. **CAREER** Adj prof, E Tenn State Univ. **SELECTED PUBLICATIONS** Auth, This Isn't About Shoes, Is It? A Response to Heidegger, Derrida and Shoes; The Therapeutic Philosophy of Richard Rorty. **CONTACT ADDRESS** Philosophy Dept, East Tennessee State Univ, Box 70717, Johnson City, TN 37614- 0717. **EMAIL** zavodnyj@etsu.edu

ZAX, JEFFREY S.
PERSONAL Born 12/07/1954, Gulfport, MS, m, 1988, 2 children **DISCIPLINE** ECONOMICS **EDUCATION** Harvard Col, BA, 76; Harvard Univ, PhD, 84. **CAREER** Assoc Prof, Queens Col, 84-90; Prof, Univ Colo at Boulder, 90-. **HONORS AND AWARDS** Fulbright Fel, 90. **MEMBERSHIPS** Am Econ Asn; Soc of Labor Econ; Chinese Econ Soc. **RESEARCH** Discrimination in labor, housing and credit markets; The Chinese economy; Applied microeconomics. **SELECTED PUBLICATIONS** Co-auth, "Today's associations, tomorrow's unions," Industrial and Labor Relations Rev, 90; co-auth, "Excludability and the effects of free riders: Right-to-work laws and local public sector unionization," Pub Finance Quart, 91; co-auth, "When is a move a migration?" Regional Sci and Urban Econ, 94; co-auth, "Property tax rate changes and the rate of development," J of Urban Econ, 94; co-auth, "Moving to the suburbs: Do relocating companies leave their black workers behind?" J of Labor Econ, 96; auth, "Immigration, race and space," in Help or Hindrance? The Economic Implications of Immigration for African Americans, 98; auth, "Housing reform in urban China," in How Far Across the River? Chinese Policy Reform at the Millenium, forthcoming. **CONTACT ADDRESS** Dept Econ, Univ of Colorado, Boulder, Dept Econ, Boulder, CO 80309-0256. **EMAIL** zax@colorado.edu

ZELLNER, HAROLD MARCELLARS
PERSONAL Born 05/06/1943, Macon, GA **DISCIPLINE** PHILOSOPHY **EDUCATION** Univ Miami, BA, 64, PhD(-philos), 71. **CAREER** Asst prof, 72-80, ASSOC PROF PHILOS, KENT STATE UNIV, 80- **MEMBERSHIPS** Am Philos Asn. **RESEARCH** Metaphysics; epistemology. **SELECTED PUBLICATIONS** Auth, Skepticism in Homer, Class Quart, Vol 0044, 1994; Antigone and the Wife of Intaphrenes--Sophocles, Class World, Vol 0090, 97. **CONTACT ADDRESS** Dept of Philos, Kent State Univ, Kent, OH 44240.

ZEMAN, JAROLD K.
PERSONAL Born 02/27/1926, Czechoslovakia **DISCIPLINE** CHURCH HISTORY **EDUCATION** Knox Col, Univ Toronto, BD, 52; Univ Zurich, DTheol, 66; McMaster Univ, DD, 85; Acadia Univ, DD, 94. **CAREER** Dir, Cont Theol Educ, 70-81, 85-91, dir confs, 81-85, Prof Church History, Acadia Univ & Acadia Divinity Col, 68-91; dir, Acadia Ctr Baptist Anabaptist Stud, Acadia Univ, 91-97. **MEMBERSHIPS** Pres, Baptist Fed Can, 79-82; mem, Rel Adv Comt CBC, 79-84; mem, Can Soc Ch Hist; Am Soc Ch Hist; Am Acad Relig. **SELECTED PUBLICATIONS** Auth, God's Mission and Ours, 63; auth, The Whole World at Our Door, 64; auth, Historical Topography of Moravian Anabaptism, 67; auth, The Anabaptists and the Czech Brethren, 69; auth, Baptists in Canada and Co-operative Christianity, 72; auth, The Hussite Movement and the Reformation, 77; auth, Baptist Roots and Identity, 78; auth, Renewal of Church and Society in the Hussite Reformation, 84; coauth, Baptists in Canada 1760-1990: A Bibliography, 89; ed, Baptists in Canada, 80. **CONTACT ADDRESS** PO Box 164, Wolfville, NS, Canada BOP 1XO.

ZEMAN, VLADIMIR
DISCIPLINE PHILOSOPHY **EDUCATION** Charles Univ, dipl in philos, 60; Charles Univ, Prague, PhD, 67; add stud and res, Austria and Ger. **CAREER** Dept Philos, Concordia Univ **RESEARCH** Kant's philos, philos aspects of science and technology. **SELECTED PUBLICATIONS** Auth, Can Eco- and Techno-Philosophies replace Humanism?, Advances in Ecosystems Research; co-ed, coauth, Transcendental Philosophy and Everyday Experience, Hermann Cohen's Concept of Transcendental Method, Hum Press, 97; auth, "Erazim Kohak - vivere per philosophare," Introduction to a selection from E. Kohak's works, D. Reidel Publ. Co, 98. **CONTACT ADDRESS** Dept of Philos, Concordia Univ, Montreal, Sir George William Campus, 2100 Mackay St., Montreal, QC, Canada H3G 1M8. **EMAIL** zemvlad@alcor.concordia.ca

ZHAO, QUANSHENG
DISCIPLINE COMPARATIVE POLITICS AND INTERNATIONAL RELATIONS **EDUCATION** Peking Univ, BA; UC Berkeley, MA, PhD. **CAREER** Prof, Am Univ. **HONORS AND AWARDS** Grants, Japan Found, Asia Found, Pacific Cult Found; Harvard Univ; chair, apsa's conf gp on china stud, 92-; ed bd, am asian rev. **MEMBERSHIPS** APSA, AAS, ISA. **RESEARCH** Comparative policymaking in East Asia; Political development and democratization; International relations theory and international security and political economy. **SELECTED PUBLICATIONS** Auth, Interpreting Chinese Foreign Policy, Oxford Univ Press, 96; Japanese Policymaking, Oxford Univ Press/Praeger, 93; co-ed, Politics of Divided Nations: China, Korea, Germany and Vietnam. **CONTACT ADDRESS** American Univ, 4400 Massachusetts Ave, Washington, DC 20016-8071. **EMAIL** qugzhao@american.edu

ZHENG, YIWEI
PERSONAL Born 08/16/1972, Shanghai, China, m, 1998 **DISCIPLINE** PHILOSOPHY **EDUCATION** Shanghai Jiao Tong Univ, BS, 87; Cleveland State Univ, MA, 93; Indiana Univ, PhD, 98. **CAREER** Asst prof, Philos, St Cloud St Univ, 99- . **HONORS AND AWARDS** Fel, Univ Iowa, 94-95; Larry Taylor Essay Prize, New Mexico and West Texas Philos Soc, 96; grad acad excellence awd, Indiana Univ, 97; Oscar R. Ewing Essay Prize, Indiana Univ, 98; APA grad stud travel stipend, APA, 98; Starr Fel, Off of Int Progs, Ind Univ, 99. **MEMBERSHIPS** APA; Radical Philos Asn; Southwestern Philos Soc. **RESEARCH** History of analytical philosophy; phenomenology and existentialism; history of philosophy. **SELECTED PUBLICATIONS** Auth, "On Hume's Theory of Self," Southwest Philos Stud, 97; "On the Self-destructive Nature of Consciousness," Philos, 97; "Ontology and Ethics in Sartre's Being and Nothingness," Southern J of Philos, 97; "On the Picture Theory in Wittgenstein's Tractatus," Kampits, ed, "Applied Ethics," Kirchberg, 98; "Metaphysical Simplicity and Semantical Complexity of Connotative Terms in ockham's Mental Language," Modern Schoolman, forthcoming; "Ockham's Connotation Theory and Ontological Elimination," J of Philos Res, forthcoming; "Configurations and Properties of Objects in Wittgenstein's Tractatus," Philos Investigations, forthcoming. **CONTACT ADDRESS** Dept of Philosophy, St. Cloud State Univ, 123 Brown Hall, 720 S 4th Ave, Saint Cloud, MN 56301.

ZIETLOW, REBECCA
PERSONAL m, 1 child **DISCIPLINE** LAW **EDUCATION** Barnard Col, BA; Yale Law Sch, JD. **CAREER** Asst prof. **MEMBERSHIPS** Law & Society Asn. **SELECTED PUBLICATIONS** Auth, Two Wrongs Don't Add up to Rights: The Importance of Perserving Due Process In Light of Recent Welfare Reform Measures, 45 The AM U L REV 1111, 96; auth, In the Supreme Court: Can a lack of funds bar an indigent mothe from appealing the termination of her parental rights? West's Legal News, 96; auth, Supreme Court Finds Right to Waiver of Appelate Fees in Parental Rights Termination Cases, Public Interest L REV, 97; auth, Giving Substance to Process: Countering the Due Process Conuterevolution, 75 Denver U L REV, 97; auth, Writing Scholarship While You Practice Law, 3 Mich J of Race & Law 589, 98; auth, Exploring a Substansive Approach to Equal Justice Under Law 28. New Mexico L REV 411, 98; auth, Beyond the Pronoun: Toward and Anti-Subordinating Method of Process, 10 Tes J Women & L forthcoming, 00. **CONTACT ADDRESS** Col Law, Univ of Toledo, Toledo, OH 43606. **EMAIL** rzietlo@uoft02.utoledo.edu

ZIFFER, WALTER
PERSONAL Born 03/05/1927, Czech, m, 4 children **DISCIPLINE** BIBLICAL STUDIES, LITERATURE, THEOLOGY **EDUCATION** Vanderbilt Univ, BE, 54; Oberlin Col, MA, 63; M Theol, 64; Univ de Strasbourg, France, Theol Dr, 71. **CAREER** Sr prof engineer, Inland Mfg Div of GMC, 54-60; prof, Fac de Theol Protestante Montpellier, 64-72; prof, Intermet Theol Sem, 72-77; pastor, Am Protestant Church of Brussels, 77-82; prof, Univ of Maine at Orono, 87-92, adj prof, Univ of NC at Asheville, 95-. **HONORS AND AWARDS** Thomas Kepler Awd, Oberlin Col, 64; Monroe Doctoral Fel, Oberlin Col, 64. **RESEARCH** 1st & 2nd century Jewish & Christian history, origins and development of anti-Semitism, Jewish-Christian relations. **SELECTED PUBLICATIONS** Auth, The Teaching of Disdain: An Examination of Christology and New Testament Attitudes Toward Jews; auth, The Birth of Christianity from the Matrix of Judaism. **CONTACT ADDRESS** Dept Classics, Univ of No Carolina, Asheville, 1 Univ Heights, Asheville, NC 28804-3251. **EMAIL** waziff@aol.com

ZILE, ZIGURDS LAIMONS
PERSONAL Born 07/24/1927, Riga, Latvia **DISCIPLINE** LAW **EDUCATION** Univ Wis-Madison, BA, 56, LLB, 58, LLM, 59; Harvard Univ, SJD, 67. **CAREER** From asst prof to assoc prof, 61-66, PROF LAW, UNIV WIS-MADISON, 66-, Vis prof law, Univ Helsinki, Finland, 77-78; Emer Prof, 90-. **MEMBERSHIPS** Asn Advan Baltic Studies. **RESEARCH** Comparative, environmental and international law. **SELECTED PUBLICATIONS** Auth, Constitutional Adjudication in Latvia; auth, J of Baltic Studies, 80,89; auth, Wisconsin Law Rev, 82,92; auth, Ideas and Forces in Soviet Legal History, Oxford Univ Pr, 92; auth, Toward the Rule of Law in Russia--Political and Legal Reform in the Transition Period, Slavic Rev, Vol 0053, 94; Rev of East and Cent. Eur. Law, 99; auth, Likums un Tiesibas, Riga, 00, 01. **CONTACT ADDRESS** Law Sch, Univ of Wisconsin, Madison, Madison, WI 53706-1399.

ZILFI, MADELINE CAROL
PERSONAL Born Norwood, MA, m, 1979, 1 child **DISCIPLINE** MIDDLE EAST, OTTOMAN EMPIRE, ISLAM, GENDER ISSUES **EDUCATION** Mt Holyoke Col, AB, 64; Univ Chicago, MA, 71, PhD(hist), 76. **CAREER** Asst prof Hist, Univ MD, Col Park, 76- **HONORS AND AWARDS** Recipent of grants and awards from Fulbright, the Social Sci Res Coun, and the Am Res Institute in Turkey as well as the University's Graduate Res Bd. **MEMBERSHIPS** AHA; Mid East Studies Asn; Turkish Studies Asn; Mid East Inst. **RESEARCH** Ottoman institutional history; Islamic law; Islamic fundamentalism. **SELECTED PUBLICATIONS** Auth, "The Kadizadelis: Discordant Revivalism in Seventh-Cenury Istanbul," Journal of Near Eastern Studies 45, 86; auth, The Politics of Piety: The Ottoman Ulema in the Post-Classical Age; ed, Women in the Ottaman Empire: Middle Eastern Women in the Early Modern Era, 97; auth, "We Don't Get Along: Women and Hul Divorce in the Eighteenth Century," 97. **CONTACT ADDRESS** Dept of Hist, Univ of Maryland, Col Park, College Park, MD 20742-0001. **EMAIL** mz11@umail.umd.edu

ZILLMAN, DONALD N.
DISCIPLINE LAW **EDUCATION** Univ Wis, BS, JD; Univ Va, LLM. **CAREER** Godfrey prof; Maine's first Godfrey prof Law; dean Law Sch, 91-98; past distinguished vis prof, US Mil Acad at West Point; prof, Univ Utah and dir, University's Energy Law Ctr, 79-86; dir, Univ Utah Col Law's Grad Stud, 86; past mem, US Army Judge Advocate General's Corps; past spec asst atty gen, Ariz; past vis prof, Univ Southampton, Engl. **HONORS AND AWARDS** American Law Institute. **RESEARCH** Government tort liability; military law and natural resources law. **SELECTED PUBLICATIONS** Auth or coauth, Foundation Press text on Energy Law; Maine Tort Law; Constitutional Law for the Citizen Soldier; auth, Energy Law and Policy for the 21st Century. **CONTACT ADDRESS** School of Law, Univ of So Maine, 96 Falmouth St, PO Box 9300, Portland, ME 04104-9300. **EMAIL** zillman@usm.maine.edu

ZIMANY, ROLAND DANIEL
PERSONAL Born 08/05/1936, East Orange, NJ, m, 1976 **DISCIPLINE** CHRISTIAN THEOLOGY, MODERN PHILOSOPHY **EDUCATION** Princeton Univ, AB, 58; NYork Univ, MBA, 65; Union Theol Sem, NYork, MDiv, 74; Duke Univ, PhD(relig), 80. **CAREER** ASST PROF PHILOS & RELIG, BLACKBURN COL, 80- **MEMBERSHIPS** Am Acad Relig. **RESEARCH** Hermeneutics; theology; Heidegger. **SELECTED PUBLICATIONS** Auth, Not Every Spirit--A Dogmatics of Christian Disbelief, Jour Amer Acad Rel, Vol 0064, 96. **CONTACT ADDRESS** 413 Morgan St, Carlinville, IL 62626.

ZIMMERMAN, DEAN
DISCIPLINE PHILOSOPHY **EDUCATION** Mankato State Univ, BA, 86; Brown Univ, MA, 90, PhD, 92. **CAREER** Assoc prof. **RESEARCH** Metaphysics; epistemology. **SELECTED PUBLICATIONS** Auth, Immanent Causation, Philos Perspectives, 97; Coincident Objects: Could a 'Stuff Ontology' Help?, Analysis, 97; Distinct Indiscernibles and the Bundle Theory, Mind, 97; Temporal Parts and Supervenient Causation: The Incompatibility of Two Humean Doctrines, Australasian J Philos, 98; co-ed, Metaphysics: The Big Questions, 98. **CONTACT ADDRESS** Philosophy Dept, Univ of Notre Dame, 336/7 O'Shaughnessy, Notre Dame, IN 46556. **EMAIL** zimmerman.4@nd.edu

ZIMMERMAN, DIANE L.
PERSONAL Born 04/16/1941, Newton, NJ, m, 1984 **DISCIPLINE** LAW **EDUCATION** Beaver Col, BA, 63; Columbia Univ, JD, 76. **CAREER** Journalist, Newsweek, 63-73; prof, NYork Univ School of Law77-. **HONORS AND AWARDS** Phi Kappa Phi; am Law Inst; Law clerk, jack B Weinstein, USD Ct, EDNY. **MEMBERSHIPS** Asn for the Bar of City of NY, Am Bar Asn, copyright Soc of USA. **RESEARCH** Intellectual property, Freedom of speech and press, Gender studies. **SELECTED PUBLICATIONS** Auth, Fitting Publicity rights into Intellectual Property and Free Speech Theory: Sam, You Made the Pants Too Long!, DePaul Arts & Enter, (in press); co-ed, Expanding the bounds of Intellectual Property, (forthcoming); auth, I Spy: The News-Gatherer Under Cover, Allen Chair Symposium Issue, 00; auth, The More Things Change, the Less They Seem 'Transformed': some Reflections of fair Use, J. Copyright Soc, of USA, 98; auth, "Who Put the right in the right of Publicity?" symposium volume, 98; auth, Report of the working committees to the Second Circuit Task Force on Gender, Racial, and Ethnic Fairness in the Courts of the Second Circuit, 97; auth, Am I Caught in a Time Warp or What? Reflections on Pornography and Purity, 93; auth, Information as speech, Information as Goods: some Thoughts on Marketplaces and the First Amendment, 92; auth, Book Review: Secrets and Secretiveness: Patterns in the Fabric of the Law?, 90; auth, False Light Invasion of Privacy: The Light That Failed, 89. **CONTACT ADDRESS** School of Law, New York Univ, 40 Wash Sq S, New York, NY 10012-1005.

ZIMMERMAN, EARL
PERSONAL Born Lebanon, PA, m, 1972, 3 children **DISCIPLINE** RELIGIOUS STUDIES **EDUCATION** E Mennonite Univ, BA, 85; MA, 87, Associated Mennonite Biblical Sem; M Div, 96. **CAREER** Prog Dir, E Mennonite Missions, 87-93; adj prof, E Mennonite Univ, 99-00. **MEMBERSHIPS** AAR; Soc of Christian Ethics. **SELECTED PUBLICATIONS** Auth, "Mission in a Neo-Colonial Context", Mission Focus 14, 86; auth, "Mission Reconsidered", Missionary Messenger, 90, 91; auth, "The Church that Meets in Damka", Gospel Herald, 92; auth, "A Visit to Mongolia", Missionary Messenger 70, 94; auth, "Renewing the Conversation: Mennonite Responses to Vatican II", Mennonite Quarterly Rev 73, (99):61-73; auth, "Fleeting Babylon: Menno's True Church in a Corrupt World", Conrad Grebel Rev, (forthcoming). **CONTACT ADDRESS** Dept Bible and Regli, Eastern Mennonite Univ, 1200 Park Rd, Harrisonburg, VA 22802-2404. **EMAIL** eszimerman@aol.com

ZIMMERMAN, JOSEPH F.
PERSONAL Born 06/29/1928, Keene, NH, m, 1998, 1 child **DISCIPLINE** POLITICAL SCIENCE AND ECONOMICS **EDUCATION** Univ of NH, BA, 50; Syracuse Univ, MA, 51, PhD, 54. **CAREER** Instr to prof, Worcester Polytechnic Inst, 54-65; prof, State Univ of NY at Albany, 65-. **HONORS AND AWARDS** Distinguished Citizen Awd, Nat Civic League, 86; Outstanding Academician, Section On Intergovernmental Admin and Management of the Am Soc for Public Admin, 97; Distinguished Federalism Scholar, Section on Federalism and Intergovernmental Relations, The Am Political Sci Assoc, 99. **MEMBERSHIPS** Am Political Sci Asn; Am Soc for Public Admin. **RESEARCH** Federalism; representation and electoral systems; state and local government, comparative local government with emphasis on the Republic of Ireland. **SELECTED PUBLICATIONS** Auth, The Recall: Tribunal of the People, 97; Interstate Relations: The Neglected Dimension of Federalism, 96; State-Local Relations: A Partnership Approach, 95; Curbing Unethical Behavior in Government, 94; Contemporary American Federalism, 92. **CONTACT ADDRESS** Grad School of Public Affairs, SUNY, Albany, 135 Western Ave., Albany, NY 12222. **EMAIL** zimmer@csc.albany.edu

ZIMMERMAN, JOYCE ANN
PERSONAL Born 04/13/1945, Dayton, OH **DISCIPLINE** THEOLOGY **EDUCATION** Univ Dayton, BS, 68; Athenaeum Ohio, MA, 73; St. John's Univ, MA, 81; Univ Ottawa, MA, 82, PhD, 87; St. Paul Univ, STL, 83, STD, 87. **CAREER** Ed, CPPS Newsl, 97-; adv, Nat Conf Cath Bishops Comm Liturgy, 95-; adj prof, Athenaeum Ohio, 94-; prof liturgy & dir sem liturgy, Conception Sem Col, 93-96; ed, Liturgical Ministry, 92-; dir, Inst Liturgical Ministry, 91-, fac, Summer Inst Pastoral Liturgy, St. Paul Univ, 90-92. **MEMBERSHIPS** N Am Acad Liturgy; Am Acad Relig. **RESEARCH** Liturgical theology; hermeneutics; methodology. **SELECTED PUBLICATIONS** Auth, Liturgy and Hermeneutics, 99; auth, Liturgy and Music: Lifetime Learning, 98; auth, Pray without Ceasing: Prayer for Morning and Evening, 93; auth, Liturgy as Living Faith: A Liturgical Spirituality, 93; auth, Theology of Liturgical Assembly: Saints, Relics & Rites, Liturgy, 98; coauth, Penance: Some Critical Issues, liturgical ministry, 95; auth, Liturgical Assembly: Who is the Subject of Liturgy?, liturgical ministry, 94; auth, A Blessing in Disguise? On Adoration of the Blessed Sacrament, Nat Bull Liturgy, Summer, 97; auth, When Do We Pray What? On the Relationship of Liturgical and Devotional Prayer, Nat Bull Liturgy, Summer, 97; auth, Making Sense of Time, Assembly, Nov, 96; coauth, Morning and Evening: Order of Service for Presider, Cantor, and Accompanist, 96; auth, A New Commandment: Eucharist as Loving, Eating and Drinking, and Serving, The Wine Cellar, Feb, 95; auth, Stop Decorating and Start Enhancing Your Worship, Today's Parish, Oct, 94; auth, Your Worship Space and the Liturgical Year, Today's Parish, Oct, 94. **CONTACT ADDRESS** 721 Hallworth Pl, Dayton, OH 45426-4817. **EMAIL** ilm@vandcom.com

ZIMMERMAN, MICHAEL E.
PERSONAL Born 07/07/1946, Akron, OH, m, 1986, 1 child **DISCIPLINE** PHILOSOPHY **EDUCATION** La State Univ, BA, 68; Tulane Univ, MA, 71, PhD, 74. **CAREER** Asst prof, Denison Univ, 74-75; Assoc Prof, 75-83, Prof, Tulane Univ, 83-. **HONORS AND AWARDS** NEH Fel, 88-89 **MEMBERSHIPS** AAR; APA; SPEP; ISEE; ISEP. **RESEARCH** Heidegger; environ philos; Buddhism; philos & gender; transpersonal philos. **SELECTED PUBLICATIONS** Auth, Heidegger's Confrontation with Modernity, Indiana Univ Press, 90; auth, Contesting Earth's Future: Radical Ecology and Postmodernity, Univ of Calif Press, 94; Martin heidegger: Anti-Naturalistic Critic of Technological Modernity, Ecological Thinkers, Guilford, 95; The Threat of Ecofascism, Soc Theory and Practice, 95; A Transpersonal Diagnosis of the Ecological Crisis, ReVision, 96; Environmental Philosophy: From Animal Rights to Radical Ecology, Prentice-Hall, 93, 97, 00; auth, Ron Wilber's Critique of Ecological Spirituality, in Beneath the Surface, MIT Press, 00. **CONTACT ADDRESS** Dept of Philos, Tulane Univ, New Orleans, LA 70118. **EMAIL** michaelz@tcs.tulane.edu

ZINKIN, MELISSA R.
PERSONAL Born 10/13/1967, New York, NY, s **DISCIPLINE** PHILOSOPHY **EDUCATION** Northwestern Univ, PhD, 99. **CAREER** Asst prof 98- **HONORS AND AWARDS** DAAD fel; Humanities teaching fel, Northwestern Univ; Research Semester Awd. **MEMBERSHIPS** APA **RESEARCH** Kant; modern philos; philos of science; political philos; feminist theory; aesthetics. **SELECTED PUBLICATIONS** Auth, Habermas on Intelligibility, Southern J of Philos, fall 98; review of Women, Property and Politics, by Donna Dickenson, Ethics, forthcoming. **CONTACT ADDRESS** Philosophy Dept, SUNY, Binghamton, PO Box 600, Binghamton, NY 13902-6000. **EMAIL** mzinkin@binghamton.edu

ZINN, GROVER A.
PERSONAL Born 06/18/1937, El Dorado, AR, m, 1962, 2 children **DISCIPLINE** EUROPEAN CHRISTIAN HISTORY **EDUCATION** Rice Inst, BA, 59; Duke Univ, BD, 62; PhD, 69. **CAREER** William H. Danforth prof, 66. **HONORS AND AWARDS** NEH Younger Humanist Fellowship and Research States, Oberlin College, 72-73; Research State, Oberlin College, 97-98. **RESEARCH** Medieval Christian thought, mysticism, iconography. **SELECTED PUBLICATIONS** Auth, Richard of St. Victor: The Twelve Patriarchs, The Mystical Ark; Book Three of the Trinity; Medieval France: An Encyclopedia. **CONTACT ADDRESS** Dept of Relig, Oberlin Col, Oberlin, OH 44074. **EMAIL** grover.zinn@oberlin.edu

ZIOLKOWSKI, ERIC JOZEF
PERSONAL Born 12/28/1958 **DISCIPLINE** RELIGION; LITERATURE **EDUCATION** Dartmouth Col, BA, 80; Univ Chicago, MA, 81; Univ Chicago, PhD, 87 **CAREER** Asst prof Comparative Literature, Univ Wisconsin Madison, 87-88; asst prof Religion, Lafayette Col, 88-94; assoc prof Religion, Lafayette Col, 94-. **HONORS AND AWARDS** Fel, Soc Arts Relig Cult, 97-; Thomas Roy and Lura Forrest Jones Awd for Superior Teaching, 98 **MEMBERSHIPS** Amer Acad Relig; Amer Assoc Univ Prof; Amnesty Int **RESEARCH** Religion and Literature, History of Religion, Philosophy of Religion **SELECTED PUBLICATIONS** Ed, A Museum of Faiths: Histories and Legacies of the 1893 World's Parliament of Religions, Scholars Press, 93; auth, The Sanctification of Don Quixote: From Hidalgo to Priest, Penn St Univ, 91; "Religion and Literature and the History of Religions: Grounds for Alliance." Jour Lit Theol, 98; "Sancho Panza and Nemi's Priest: Reflections on Myth and Literature." Myth and Method, 96; auth, Evil Children in Religion, Literature, and Art: The Bad Boys of Bethel, Macmillan Press, 00. **CONTACT ADDRESS** Dept Relig, Lafayette Col, Easton, PA 18042. **EMAIL** ziolkowe@lafayette.edu

ZIRING, LAWRENCE
PERSONAL Born 12/11/1928, Brooklyn, NY, m, 1962, 2 children **DISCIPLINE** POLITICAL SCIENCE **EDUCATION** Columbia Univ, PhD 62, MIA 57, BS 55. **CAREER** Western MI Univ, Arnold E Schneider Prof 98-, prof 73-98, assoc 67-73; Syracuse Univ, asst prof 64-67; Lafayette Col, asst prof 61-64; Dacca Univ :now Bangladesh:, vis asst prof 59-60. **HONORS AND AWARDS** Arnold E Schneider Prof; Distg Facul Schl; Jones Facul Teach Awd. **MEMBERSHIPS** Am Inst Pakistan Stud, trustee. **RESEARCH** Comp polit, Intl Rel, for policy. **SELECTED PUBLICATIONS** Coauth, Pakistan's Foreign Policy, Oxford Univ Press, 2d ed, 90; auth, Bangladesh: From Mujib to Ershad, Oxford Univ Press, 92; auth, The New Europe and the New World, New Issues Press, 93; auth, International Relations: A Political Dictionary, ABC-Clio, 95; auth, Pakistan in the Twentieth Century, Oxford Univ Press, 97; coauth, The United Nations, 3d ed, Harcourt Brace, 00. **CONTACT ADDRESS** Dept of Polit Sci, Western Michigan Univ, Kalamazoo, MI 49008. **EMAIL** ziring@wmich.edu

ZIRINSKY, MICHAEL PAUL
PERSONAL Born 11/25/1942, Brooklyn, NY, m, 1965 **DISCIPLINE** HISTORY, GOVERNMENT **EDUCATION** Oberlin Col, AB, 64; Am Univ, MA, 68; Univ NC, Chapel Hill, PhD(hist), 76. **CAREER** Instr hist, Randolph Macon Col, 65-67; asst prof, 73-79, Prof, 79-86; assoc prof, 79-86, prof, 86-, Boise State Univ. **MEMBERSHIPS** AHA; Mid East Inst; Brit Soc M.E. Studies; Mid East Studies Asn; Society for Iranian Studies. **RESEARCH** Modern Middle Eastern history (20th century); 20th century Iran. **SELECTED PUBLICATIONS** Auth, American Presbyterian Missionaries at Urmia during the Great War, Persia and the Great War, Okiver Bast, ed, Tehran: Institut Francais de Recherche en Iran, in press; auth," Blood, Power, and Hypocrisy: The Murder of Robert Imbrie and American Relations with Pahlavi Iran, 1924," International Journal of Middle East Studies 18 (86): 275-292; auth, "Presbyterian Missionaries and American Relations with Pahlavi Iran," The Iranian Journal of International Affairs, (89): 71-86; auth, "Harbingers of Change: Presbyterian Women in Iran," 1883-1949, American Presbyterians: Journal of Presbyterian History 70:3 (92):173-86; auth, "Imperial Power and Dictatorship: Britain and the Rise of Reza Shah, 1921-1926," International Journal of Middle East Studies 24 (92): 639-94; auth, "Presbyterian Missionary Women in Late Nineteenth and Early Twentieth Century Iran," translated into Persian by Manijeh Badiozamani, Nimeye-Diagar: Persian Language Feminist Journal 17 (93): 38-63; auth, "A Panacea for the Ills of the Country: American Presbyterian Education in Inter-War Iran," Iranian Studies vol 26, (93):: 119-137; auth, "Render Therefore unto Caesar That Which is Caesar's: American Presbyterian Educators and Reza Shah," Iranian Studies, vol 26 (93): 337-56; auth, "The Rise of Reza Khan, in John Foran, ed Social Movements in Iran: Historical and Theoretical Perspectives (Minneapolis: Univ of MN Press, 94), 44-77; auth, A Panacea for the Ills of the Country, American Presbyterian Education in Interwar Iran, Amer Presbyterians-Jour Presbyterian Hist, Vol 0072, 94; auth, "The Presbyterian Who Introduced Soccer to Iran," Presbyterian Outlook, 98. **CONTACT ADDRESS** Dept of Hist, Boise State Univ, Boise, ID 83725. **EMAIL** mzirins@boisestate.edu

ZIRKEL, PATRICIA MCCORMICK
PERSONAL Born 11/02/1943, m, 1968, 1 child **DISCIPLINE** HISTORICAL THEOLOGY **EDUCATION** St Thomas Aquinas Col, Sparkill, NYork, BS Ed, 66; St John's Univ, MA, 78; Fordham Univ, PhD, 89. **CAREER** Assoc prof, Coll. Of Professional Studies, St John's Univ, 90-. **HONORS AND AWARDS** Faculty Merit award, 97, 98. **MEMBERSHIPS** Am Academy of Relig; Am Asn of Univ Profs; Col Theol Soc. **RESEARCH** Christian theol-Medieval Europe; Christian Liturgy; Theodicy-Holocaust Studies. **SELECTED PUBLICATIONS** Auth, The Ninth Century Eucharistic Controversy: A Context for the Beginnnings of Eucharistic Doctrine in the West, Worship, vol 68, no 1, Jan 94; Why Should It Be Neccessary That Christ Be Immolated Daily?, Paschasius Radbertus on Daily Eucharist, Am Benedictine Rev, Sept 96; The Body of Christ and the Future of Liturgy, Anglican Theol Rev., vol. 81, no. 3, Summer 99. **CONTACT ADDRESS** St. John's Univ, 8000 Utopia Pkwy, Jamaica, NY 11439. **EMAIL** zirkelp@stjohns.edu

ZITO, ANGELA
DISCIPLINE RELIGION **EDUCATION** Univ Chicago, PhD, 89. **CAREER** Asst prof. **RESEARCH** History of Chinese religion and philosophy; history of ritual in China; history of the Chinese monarchy. **SELECTED PUBLICATIONS** Auth, Body, Subject and Power in China, Univ Chicago, 94; Of Body and Bush: Grand Sacrifice as Text Performance in 18th Century China, Univ Chicago, 97. **CONTACT ADDRESS** Dept of Religion, Columbia Col, New York, 2960 Broadway, New York, NY 10027-6902. **EMAIL** azito@barnard.columbia.edu

ZITTRAIN, JONATHAN L.
DISCIPLINE LAW **EDUCATION** Yale Univ, BS, 91; Harvard Law Sch, JD, 95; JFK Sch Govt, MPA, 95. **CAREER** Asst Prof, Harvard Law Sch, 00-. **CONTACT ADDRESS** Sch of Law, Harvard Univ, Cambridge, MA 02138.

ZLOTKIN, NORMAN
DISCIPLINE LAW **EDUCATION** Univ Toronto, LLB, 69; London Univ, LLM, 70. **CAREER** Assoc prof, 81-; assoc dean, 96-97. **HONORS AND AWARDS** Res dir, Native Law Centre, 82-86. **MEMBERSHIPS** Law Soc Saskatchewan; Law Soc Upper Can. **RESEARCH** Aboriginal law. **SELECTED PUBLICATIONS** Auth, Judicial Recognition of Aboriginal Customary Law in Canada, 84; co-auth, Affirming Aboriginal Title: A New Basis for Comprehensive Negotiations, 96. **CONTACT ADDRESS** Col of Law, Univ of Saskatchewan, 15 Campus Dr, Saskatoon, SK, Canada S7N 5A6. **EMAIL** norman.zlotkin@usask.ca

ZONG, DESHENG
PERSONAL Born 05/11/1961, Dali, China, m, 1989, 1 child **DISCIPLINE** PHILOSOPHY **EDUCATION** Tulane Univ, PhD, 98. **MEMBERSHIPS** APA. **RESEARCH** Ethics; Chinese philos. **SELECTED PUBLICATIONS** Auth, Epistemic Logic in Mohist Works, Philosphy East and West 50:2 (Epistemic); auth, "Agent-Neutrality is the Exclusive Feature of Consequentialism," Southern Journal of Philosophy, Vo. XXXVIII, 00; auth, "Studies of Intensional Contexts in Mohist Writings," Philosophy East and West 50:2, 00. **CONTACT ADDRESS** 83 Hudson St, Somerville, MA 02143. **EMAIL** d_zong@yahoo.com

ZUCK, LOWELL H.
PERSONAL Born 06/24/1926, Ephrata, PA, m, 1950, 1 child **DISCIPLINE** CHURCH HISTORY **EDUCATION** Elizabethtown Col, BA, 47; Bethany Bibl Sem, BD, 50; Yale Univ, STM, 51, MA, 52, PhD(Reformation church hist), 55. **CAREER** Vis prof philos & relig, Col Idaho, 54-55; from asst prof to assoc prof, 55-62, PROF CHURCH HIST, EDEN THEOL SEM, 62-, Teacher univ col, Washington Univ, 57-; Am Asn Theol Schs grants, 64-65 & 75-76; Am Philos Soc grant, 80; Nat Endowment for Humanities summer seminar, Johns Hopkins Univ, 82. **HONORS AND AWARDS** Fulbright Scholar Lecturer: Religious Studies, Romania, 1st sem. 00-01. **MEMBERSHIPS** AHA; Am Soc Church Hist; Am Soc Reformation Res (treas, 69-78); 16th Century Studies Conf (treas, 69-71, pres, 71-72). **RESEARCH** Anabaptist research; Reformation church history; Puritan church history. **SELECTED PUBLICATIONS** "Consolidation & Expansion", Vol. IV of "Living Theological Heritage of the United Church of Christ" (Cleveland: Pilgrim, 1999, 666pp.) "Socially Responsible Believers", 1986, "European Roots of the United Church of Christ", 1976, "Christianity and Revolution," 300 pp. Sourcebook, 1975; Auth, From Reformation Orthodoxy to the Enlightenment--Geneva 1670-1737--French, Church Hist, Vol 0063, 94; Ingdoms--The Church and Culture Through the Ages, Sixteenth Century Jour, Vol 0025, 94; Sin and the Calvinists--Morals Control and the Consistory in the Reformed Tradition, Church Hist, Vol 0065, 96; Hochstift and Reformation--Studies in the History of the Imperial Church Between 1517 and 1648--German, Sixteenth Century Jour, Vol 0027, 96; Calvinism in Europe, 1540-1620, Church Hist, Vol 0065, 96; Adultery and Divorce in Calvin, John Geneva, Church Hist, Vol 0065, 96; Poverty and Deviance in Early-Modern Europe, Sixteenth Century Jour, Vol 0027, 96; A Short History of Renaissance and Reformation Europe--Dances Over Fire and Water, Sixteenth Century Jour, Vol 0027, 96; The Oxford Encyclopedia of the Reformation, 4 Vols, Sixteenth Century Jour, Vol 0028, 97; Documents on the Continental Reformation, Sixteenth Century Jour, Vol 0028, 97. **CONTACT ADDRESS** Eden Theol Sem, 475 E Lockwood Ave, Saint Louis, MO 63119. **EMAIL** lzuck@eden.edu

ZUIDERVAART, LAMBERT P.
PERSONAL Born 08/01/1950, Modesto, CA, m, 1977 **DISCIPLINE** PHILOSOPHY **EDUCATION** Dordt Col, BA, 72; Inst Christian Studies, MPhil, 75; Univ Amsterdam, PhD, 81. **CAREER** Asst Prof, King's Univ Col, 81-85; Assoc Prof, Calvin Col, 85-89; Prof, Calvin Col, 89-. **HONORS AND AWARDS** CCCS Fel, Calvin Col, 95-96; REs Fel, Calvin Col, 96; Alumni Asn Fac Res Grants, Calvin Col, 96, 97; McGregor Summer Fel, 99; Summer Res Fel, Calvin Col, 98, 99, 00; Interim Res Leaves, Calvin Col, 98, 99, 00. **MEMBERSHIPS** APA, ASA, Can Soc for Aesthetics, Can Philos Asn, Int Asn of Aesthetics, Soc for Phenomenol and Existential Philos. **RESEARCH** The arts and public policy, Adorno and the Frankfurt School, the epistemology and hermeneutics of culture. **SELECTED PUBLICATIONS** Co-ed, Pledges of Jubilee: Essays on the Arts and Culture, Eerdmans Pr (Grand Rapids, MI), 95;auth, "Fantastic Things: Critical Notes Toward a Social Ontology of the Arts," Philosophia Reformata, 60 (95): 37-54; co-ed, "The Semblance of Subjectivity: Essays in Adorno's Aesthetic Theory," MIT Pr (Cambridge, MA), 97; auth, "Adorno, Theodore Wiesengrund: Survey of Thought," in Encycl of Aesthetics, vol 1 (New York: Oxford UP, 98), 16-20; auth, "Creative Border Crossing: Authenticity and Responsibility in New Public Culture," in Lit and the Renewal of the Public Sphere (London: Macmillan Pr; New York: St Martin's Pr, 00); ed, The Arts, Community and Cultural Democracy, Macmillan Pr, St Martin's Pr (London, UK; New York, NY), 00. **CONTACT ADDRESS** Dept Philos, Calvin Col, 3201 Burton St SE, Grand Rapids, MI 49546-4301. **EMAIL** zuid@calvin.edu

ZUKOWSKI, EDWARD, JR.
PERSONAL Born 12/25/1946, South River, NJ, m, 1991, 1 child **DISCIPLINE** THEOLOGY **EDUCATION** Fordham, PhD, 84. **CAREER** Assoc prof and chair, Religious Studies, Col of Mount St Vincent, Riverdale, NY, 87-. **HONORS AND AWARDS** Teacher of the Year, 89, 96; Science and Religion Course Competition Awd, Templeton Found, 98. **MEMBERSHIPS** Cath Theol Soc of Am; Col Theol Soc; Soc of Christian Ethics; Karl Rahner Soc; Am Academy of Relig; Am Soc for Psychol Res. **RESEARCH** Conscience; theology. **SELECTED PUBLICATIONS** Auth, Dimensions of Faith in History, Acton, MA: Cogley Press, 92; The Good Conscience of Nazi Doctors, Annal of Soc of Christian Ethics, 94. **CONTACT ADDRESS** Col of Mount Saint Vincent, 6301 Riverdale Ave, Riverdale, NY 10471. **EMAIL** MeZukowski@aol.com

ZUPKO, JACK
DISCIPLINE MEDIEVAL PHILOSOPHY **EDUCATION** Cornell Univ, PhD, 89. **CAREER** Philos, Emory Univ. **SELECTED PUBLICATIONS** Articles, Jour His Philos, Medieval Philos & Theol, Mediaeval Studies, Rev Metaphysics. **CONTACT ADDRESS** Emory Univ, Atlanta, GA 30322-1950.

ZVI, EHUD BEN
PERSONAL Born 03/12/1951, Argentina, m, 3 children **DISCIPLINE** BIBLICAL STUDIES **EDUCATION** The Hebrew Univ, BS, 74; Open Univ Israel, BS, 87; Tel Aviv Univ, MA, 84; Emory Univ, PhD, 90. **CAREER** Prof, Univ Alberta, 94-. **MEMBERSHIPS** SBL; ASOR; CBA; CSBS; AAR. **RESEARCH** Hebrew Bible and its historical context. **SELECTED PUBLICATIONS** Coauth, A Historical-Critical Study of The Book of Zephaniah, BZAW 19, Berlin/New York: de Gruyter, 91; auth, Readings in Biblical Hebrew, An Intermediate Textbook, New Haven: Yale Univ Press, 93; coauth, Readings in Biblical Hebrwe, An Intermediate Textbook, New Haven: Yale Univ Press, 93; auth, A Historical-Critical Study of The Book of Obadiah, BZAW 242, Berlin/New York: de Gruyter, 96; auth, "Geiger Abraham," Dictionary of Biblical Interpretation, Nashville, TN; Abingdon, vol. 1, (99): 435a-435b; auth, "Zephaniah, book of," Dictionary of Biblical Interpretation, Nashville, TN; Abingdon, vol. 2, (99): 669b-673a; auth, "Wrongdoers, Wrongdoing and Righting Wrongs in Micah 2," BibInt 7, (99): 87-100; auth, "A Deuteronomistic Redaction in/among The Twelve," A Contribution from the Standpoint of the Books of Mich, Aephaniah and Obadiah," Those Elusive Deuteronomists: The Phenomenon of Pan-Deuteronomism, Shef-

field: Sheffield Univ Press, (99): 232-61; co-ed, "When a Foreign Kings Speaks," Sheffield: Sheffield Academic Press, (99): 209-28; auth, "Israel, Assyrian Hegemony, and Some Considerations About Virtual Israelite History," Leiden: E.J. Brill, (00): 70-87; auth, Micah, Grand Rapids, Michigan/Cambridge, UK: Eerdmans, 00. **CONTACT ADDRESS** Religious Studies Dept, Univ of Alberta, Edmonton, AB, Canada T6G 2E6. **EMAIL** ehud.ben.zvi@ualberta.ca

ZWEIBEL, ELLEN
DISCIPLINE LAW **EDUCATION** Univ NY, BA; Brooklyn Law Sch, JD; Denver Univ, LLM. **CAREER** Prof, Univ of Ottawa. **SELECTED PUBLICATIONS** Auth, pubs on income tax policy issues relating to women and children, and alternative dispute resolution and mediation training. **CONTACT ADDRESS** Fac Common Law, Univ of Ottawa, Fauteux Hall, 57 Louis Pasteur, Ottawa, ON, Canada K1N 6N5. **EMAIL** ezweibel@uottawa.ca

ZWEIG, ARNULF
PERSONAL Born 11/11/1930, Essen, Germany, m, 1957, 2 children **DISCIPLINE** PHILOSOPHY **EDUCATION** Univ of Rochester, BA, 52; Stanford Univ, PhD, 60. **CAREER** Univ of Oregon, asst prof, assoc prof, prof, prof emeritus, assoc dean, Dept head; MIT vis prof, 64-65; Harvard, vis prof, 67-68; Tufts, vis prof, 70; adj prof, Baruch College. **HONORS AND AWARDS** Yale Univ Fel, ACLS Fel, NEH grants, Stanford Hum Prog Fel. **MEMBERSHIPS** APA, NAKS, IAP **RESEARCH** Kant; ethics; philo of law; aesthetics. **SELECTED PUBLICATIONS** Auth, trans & ed, Kant: Correspondence, Cambridge; auth, The Essential Kant; Wittgensteins Silence; Kant's Children. **CONTACT ADDRESS** 20 East 9th St, Apt 10-O, New York, NY 10003-5944. **EMAIL** azweig@nyc.rr.com

ZWICKY, JAN
PERSONAL Born, AB, Canada **DISCIPLINE** PHILOSOPHY **EDUCATION** Univ Calgary, BA, 76; Univ Toronto, MA, 77, PhD, 81. **CAREER** Prof, Univ Waterloo, 81-82, 85-86; prof, Princeton Univ, 82-83; prof, Univ Western Ont, 89-90; prof, Univ Alta, 92-93; prof, Univ NB, 94-96; Prof, Univ Victoria 96-. **RESEARCH** History of ideas; metaphilosophy; and ancient Greek philosophy. **SELECTED PUBLICATIONS** Auth, Wittgenstein Elegies, 86; auth, The New Room, 89; auth, Lyric Philosophy, 92; auth, Songs for Relinquishing the Earth, 96. **CONTACT ADDRESS** PO Box 1149, Mayerthorpe, AB, Canada T0E 1N0. **EMAIL** cashion@uvic.ca

ZWIEBACH, BURTON
PERSONAL Born 09/17/1933, New York, NY, m, 1962, 2 children **DISCIPLINE** POLITICS **EDUCATION** City Col of NYork, BA, 54; Columbia Law School, LLB, 57; Columbia Univ, PhD, 57. **CAREER** Assoc, 58, Stillman & Stillman; res Asst, 58-61, Advisory Comm on Prac & Proc, NY State Legislature; lect-Prof Poli-Sci, 63-, Queen's College, CUNY. **HONORS AND AWARDS** ABA Gavel Awd Cert of Merit. **MEMBERSHIPS** APA, ASPLP, Amintaphil, CSPT. **RESEARCH** Political theory, ethics. **SELECTED PUBLICATIONS** Auth, The Common Life, Temple Univ Press, 88; Civility and Disobedience, Cambridge Univ Press, 75. **CONTACT ADDRESS** Dept of Political Science, Queens Col, CUNY, 6530 Kissena Blvd, Flushing, NY 11367. **EMAIL** BZwiebach@aol.com

Geographic Index

McFadden, Daniel L.
McNulty, John K.
Merchant, Carolyn
Milgrom, Jacob
Millner, Dianne Maxine
Morgan, Donn F.
Muir, William Ker, Jr.
Nasu, Eisho
Olney, Martha L.
Osborne, Kenan Bernard
Peters, Theodore Frank
Quigley, John M.
Ramshaw, Elaine Julian
Roland, Gerard
Rose, Leo E.
Sanks, T. Howland
Sax, Joseph L.
Schneiders, Sandra Marie
Scotchmer, Suzanne Andersen
Scott, Peter Dale
Searle, John R.
Smith, Robert Harry
Spalding, Christopher J.
Stagaman, David
Stortz, Martha Ellen
Stuhr, Walter Martin
Sweet, Justin
Vermazen, Bruce James
Weil, Louis
Wolgast, Eliz H.
Wright, John H.
Yellen, Janet L.

Beverly Hills
Adams, John Oscar
Shaw, Curtis Mitchell

Burbank
Holmes, Robert Ernest

Camarillo
Fischer, Mark F.
Ford, Paul F.

Cambry
Verhaegh, Marcus

Canyon Country
MacArthur, John

Carson
Garber, Marilyn

Chico
Grelle, Bruce
Jollimore, Troy
Karman, James
Moore, Brooke N.

Claremont
Atlas, Jay David
Camp, Roderic A.
Cobb, John Boswell
Davis, Nathaniel
Dornish, Margaret Hammond
Easton, Patricia Ann
Elliott, Ward Edward Yandell
Erickson, Stephen Anthony
Frazee, Charles Aaron
Hutchison, John A.
Jaffa, Harry Victor
Kassam, Zayn
Kim, Chan-Hie
Kind, Amy L.
Kucheman, Clark Arthur
Louch, Alfred
Marler, Grant A.
McKirahan, Richard D.
Moss, Myra Ellen
Neumann, Harry
Parrott, Rod
Phillips, Dewi Zephaniah
Sanders, James Alvin
Sontag, Frederick Earl
Torjesen, Karen Jo
Wicker, Kathleen O'Brien
Wolf, Kenneth Baxter

Compton
Clegg, Legrand H., II

Corona
Kwon, Kyeong-Seog

Costa Mesa
Baldwin, Donald E.
Clark, David
Hoggatt, Jerry Camery

Ochoa, Tyler T.
Reich, Peter L.
Rose, I. Nelson
Williams, William C.

Cupertino
Rappaport, Steven D.

Cypress
Ricci, Paul O.

Daly City
Low, Roy

Davis
Bruch, C. S.
Byrd, James David, Jr.
Dundon, Stanislaus
Fleischer, Manfred Paul
Grossman, George S.
Groth, Alexander J.
Imwinkelried, Edward
Johnson, Kevin R.
Merlino, Scott A.
Oakley, John Bilyeu
Schaeffer, Peter Moritz-Friedrich
Teller, Paul
West, Martha S.

El Cajon
Strauss, Mark

El Centro
Wilhelm, Robert

El Monte
Hwang, Tzu-Yang
Wu, Julie L.

Elk Court
Peitz-Hillenbrand, Darlene

Encinitas
Farrell, Warren Thomas

Escalm
Pearson, Birger Albert

Eureka
Tiso, Francis V.

Fairfax
Leighton, Taigen Daniel

Fairfield
Schweer, G. William

Fontana
Maticich, Karen K.

Fremont
Nakasone, Ronald

Fresno
Benko, Stephen
Boyd, Robert
Geddert, Tim J.
Jackson, Jerome E.
Martens, Elmer Arthur
Pitt, Jack
Wint, Arthur Valentine Noris

Fullerton
Bakken, Gordon Morris
Brown, Daniel Aloysius
Hanson, Bruce
Koppel, Glenn
Levesque, Paul J.
Santucci, James A.
Smith, Jesse Owens

Gilroy
Hargis, Jeffrey W.

Glendale
Pressman, H. Mark

Glendora
Dingilian, Der Stepanos

Gold River
Loewy, Roberta S.

Goleta
Nogales, Patti

Hayward
Eagan, Jennifer
Neithercutt, Marc G.
Sapontzis, Steve Frederic

Huntington Beach
Mason, Jeffrey A.

Irvine
Antonelli, Gian Aldo
Bachman, James V.
Grofman, Bernard N.
Johnson, Ben
Maddy, Penelope
Malament, David Baruch
Monroe, Kristen R.
Munevar, Gonzalo
Saadoun, Mohamed
Santas, Gerasimos
Skyrms, Brian
Small, Kenneth Alan
Stanford, Preston K.

Kensington
Kohn, Richard

La Crescenta
O'Sullivan, Michael

La Jolla
Arneson, Richard J.
Brink, David O.
Churchland, Paul M.
Doppelt, Gerald D.
Friedman, Richard Elliott
Glymour, Clark
Hardimon, Michael O.
Jolley, Nicholas
Martin, Wayne M.
Reynolds, Edward
Sher, Gila
Stroll, Avrum
Yalowitz, Steven

La Mesa
Ruja, Harry

La Mirada
Bloom, John A.
Finley, Thomas John
Hayward, Douglas
Rhee, Victor

Lake Arrowhead
Morris, Paul

Lancaster
Loofbourrow, Richard C.
Sharkey, Paul

Livermore
Girill, T. R.
Porter, Andrew P.

Long Beach
Battenfield, James R.
Burke, Albie
Guerriere, Daniel
Jones, F. Stanley
Tang, Paul C. L.
Tharp, Louis
Torres, Sam
Van Camp, Julie C.
Van De Mortel, Joseph A.

Los Alamitos
Piar, Carlos R.

Los Altos
Ueda, Makoto

Los Altos Hills
Roth, Jean

Los Angeles
Aberbach, Joel D.
Abou El Fadl, Khaled M.
Altman, Scott A.
Araiza, William
Arlen, Jennifer H.
Armour, Jody D.
Aronson, Jonathan David
Barnes, Willie R.
Benson, Robert W.
Berenbaum, Michael
Bergman, Paul
Bernstein, Jerry

Berton, Peter
Bice, Scott H.
Binder, David A.
Binder, Leonard
Blumberg, Grace Ganz
Borsch, Frederick Houk
Brecht, Albert O.
Brown, Jonathan Charles
Bruno, James Edward
Bussel, Daniel J.
Caiden, Gerald E.
Campbell, Lee W.
Capron, Alexander M.
Chang, Howard F.
Chapple, C. K.
Chemerinsky, Erwin
Christol, Carl Quimby
Chyet, Stanley F.
Cohen, Stephen Marshall
Collins, Kenneth L.
Crossley, John P.
Cruz, David B.
Currie, Janet
Cutter, William
Darden, Christopher A.
Doepke, Matthias
Dudziak, Mary L.
Dukeminier, Jesse
Ellwood, Robert S.
Estrich, Susan
Finegan, Edward J.
Franklin, Carl M.
Franklin, Floyd
Freeman, Jody L.
Friedman, Philip Allan
Fry, Michael G.
Garet, Ronald R.
Garry, Ann
Gordon, Walter Lear, III
Griffith, Thomas D.
Hahn, Harlan
Handler, Joel F.
Hansen, Gary
Harberger, Arnold C.
Harris, Jimmie
Hieronymi, Pamela
Hill, Jacqueline R.
Hirsch, Werner Z.
Hossein, Ziai
Intrilligator, Michael D.
Jacoby, Sanford M.
James, Scott C.
Johnson, Chas Floyd
Just, Felix, S. J.
Karst, Kenneth L.
Katada, Saori
Keating, Gregory C.
Kelsey, Sean
Klein, Benjamin
Klerman, Daniel M.
Knoll, Michael S.
Kushner, James Alan
Lancaster, Herman Burtram
Lawrence, Lary
Lazaroff, Daniel E.
Lefcoe, George
Lester, Gillian
Levine, Martin L.
Lovett, Leonard
Lowenstein, Daniel H.
Lyon, Thomas D.
Marder, Nancy S.
May, Christopher N.
Maynard, Therese H.
McCaffery, Edward J.
McCann, Edwin
McGovern, William M.
Mead, Lisa M.
Michael, Aloysius
Miller, Donald
Munzer, Stephen Roger
Myers, Charles Edward
Naim, Elissa Ben
Peters, Aulana Louise
Popiden, John Robert
Pugsley, Robert Adrian
Rapoport, David C.
Rausch, Thomas P.
Resnik, Judith
Rubenstein, William
Ryan, Herbert Joseph
Saks, Elyn R.
Saltzman, Robert M.
Schmidhauser, John Richard
Shapiro, Michael H.
Sia, Santiago
Simon, Larry G.
Sinclair, Barbara
Sklar, Richard Lawrence

Slawson, W. David
Smith, Edwin M.
Sobel, Lionel S.
Solum, Lawrence B.
Spillenger, Clyde
Spitzer, Matthew L.
Stewart, Daniel Lewis
Stolzenberg, N. M.
Stone, Christopher D.
Strauss, Marcy
Talley, Eric L.
Teves, Rita R.
Thomas, Duncan
Thompson, Earl A.
Tiersma, Peter M.
Tomlinson, John G.
Tornell, Aaron
Treusch, Paul E.
Tsebelis, George
Tunick, David C.
Vairo, Georgene M.
Vanderwilt, Jeffery T.
Volokh, Eugene
Weekes, Martin Edward
Whitebread, Charles H.
Williams, Gary C.
Williams, William J.
Wolfenstein, E. Victor

Malibu
Caldwell, Harry M.
Carver, Marc
Chesnutt, Randall D.
Clark, W. Royce
Cochran, Robert F., Jr.
Colson, Darrel D.
Dunaway, Baxter
Durham, Ken R.
Gough, Russell W.
Henslee, William D.
Highfield, Ronald Curtis
Hughes, Richard T.
James, Bernard
Kmiec, Douglas William
Lynn, Richardson R.
Marrs, Riock R.
McDowell, Markus
Mendosa, Antonio
Miller, Anthony
Ogden, Gregory L.
Paniccia, Patricia L.
Rowland, Rick
Smith, F. Lagard
Tyler, Ronald
Willis, Tim

Marina del Rey
Moore, Max

Menlo Park
Holleran, John Warren
Patzia, Arthur G.

Merced
Hallman, Max

Mill Valley
Arbino, Gary P.
Harrop, Clayton Keith
Honeycutt, Dwight A.
Hornecker, Ronald L.
Martin, D. Michael
McCoy, Gary W.

Moorpark
Daurio, Janice

Moraga
Lu, Matthias

Mount View
Brennan, Mary Alethea

Newhall
Halstead, Thomas
Varner, Willaim

North Hollywood
Wertheimer, Roger

Northridge
Crittenden, Charles
Goss, James
Kellenberger, Bertram James
McHenry, Leemon
McIntyre, Ronald Treadwell
Saunders, Kurt M.
Shofner, Robert Dancey

COLORADO

Johnson, Frederick A.
Jordan, Robert Welsh
Kitchener, Richard F.
Kneller, Jane E.
Lee, Grant S.
Losonsky, Michael
Lyons, Daniel D.
Maffie, James
McKee, Patrick M.
Rollin, Bernard E.
Rolston, Holmes
Wiliams, Ron G.

Golden
Sneed, Joseph Donald
Woolsey, Robert

Greeley
Hodapp, Paul F.
Reichel, Phillip

Littleton
Walker, T. B.

Pueblo
Keller, Robert L.

Sterling
Elliott, Susan Elli

Trinidad
Durland, William

United States Air Force Academy
Wakin, Malham M.

Westminster
Ogden, Schubert Miles

CONNECTICUT

Avon
Kalvoda, Josef

Bethany
Martyn, James Louis

Bethel
Dobsevage, Alvin P.
Gorman, Rosemarie E.

Bridgeport
Rubenstein, Richard Lowell

Cromwell
Olczak, Joseph M.

Danbury
Roman, Eric

Fairfield
Dykeman, King John
Lang, Martin Andrew
Long, R. James
Manning, Christel
Naser, Curtis R.
Newton, Lisa Haenlein
Rouse, John Jay
Tong, Lik Kuen

Fairlfield
Grigg, Richard M.

Hamden
Bix, Brian
Davis, Richard
Glassner, Martin
Page, Benjamin Bakewell

Hartford
Arnold, Rudolph P.
Bijlefeld, Willem A.
Cobb, Kelton
Cohn, Henry S.
Desmangles, Leslie Gerald
Green, Clifford James
Hoyt, Thomas L., Jr.
Hyland, Drew Alan
Kirkpatrick, Frank Gloyd
Lang, Berel
Peters, Ellen Ash
Walsh, Andrew
Whitman, Robert

Middletown
Crites, Stephen Decatur
Horst, Steven
Long, Jerome Herbert
McAlister, Elizabeth
Smyers, Karen A.

New Britain
Iannone, A. Pablo

New Haven
Adams, Marilyn M.
Adams, Robert Merrihew
Blodgett, Barbara
Bond, Gilbert I.
Breyer, Stephen Gerald
Burt, Robert Amsterdam
Calabresi, The Honorable Guido
Childs, Brevard Springs
Dittes, James Edward
Duke, Steven Barry
Ellickson, Robert Chester
Farley, Margaret Ann
Fiss, Owen M.
Fraade, Steven D.
Goldstein, Abraham Samuel
Graetz, Michael J.
Harries, Karsten
Hein, Norvin
Kavanagh, Aidan
Keck, Leander E.
Lee, Sukjae
Marcus, Ruth Borcan
Meeks, Wayne Atherton
Outka, Gene Harold
Reisman, W. Michael
Rose-Ackerman, Susan
Schuck, Peter H.
Smith, John Edwin
Stith-Cabranes, Kate
Weber, Mark E.
Weber, Michael
Weinstein, Stanley
Wennemyr, Susan E.
Wheeler, Stanton
Wood, Rega

New London
Ankeny, Rachel A.
Green, Garrett
Lynch, Michael P.
Myers, Gerald E.

Niantic
Jackson, Joseph Hollister

Northampton
Aldrich, Mark

Stamford
Anderson, Susan Leigh
Gray, Sherman W., Jr.

Storrs
Baxter, Donald
Clark, Austen
Creevey, Lucy
Gilbert, Margaret
Hiskes, Anne L.
Jacobus, Lee Andre
Krimerman, Leonard I.
Kupperman, Joel J.
Lehmann, Scott K.
Luyster, Robert W.
McHugh, Michael P.
Meyers, Diana Tietjens
Millikan, Ruth G.
Shaffer, Jerome A.
Troyer, John G.
Wheeler, Samuel C., III

Torrington
Grover, Robinson Allen

West Hartford
Blumberg, Phillip Irvin
Dalton, Stuart
den Ouden, Bernard
Phillips, Robert L.
Rollins, Wayne Gilbert

West Haven
Marks, Joel Howard
Rafalko, Robert J.

Willimantic
Fitz, Hope K.

Wolcott
Sokolowski, William R.

DELAWARE

Dover
Hoff, Samuel B.
Mask, E. Jefferey

Lewes
McCagney, Nancy

Newark
Adams, Frederick R., Jr.
Brown, Robert Fath
Callahan, Daniel Francis
Dilley, Frank B.
Grubb, Farley
Heggen, Bruce A.
Rea, Michael C.

Wilmington
Alford, Haile Lorraine
Brame, Grace Adolphsen
Finkelstein, Rona G.
Malinowski, Michael J.
Ray, Douglas E.

DISTRICT OF COLUMBIA

Washington
Abu-Nimer, Mohammed
Adelman, Martin Jerome
Allen, Anita
Ambrosio, Francis J.
Anderson, David M.
Antoci, Peter
Argrett, Loretta Collins
Arnold, Steven H.
Banks, Sharon P.
Barbieri, William A., Jr.
Beauchamp, Tom
Becker, William Henry
Beckerman, Paul
Berkman, John
Birch, Bruce Charles
Blattner, William
Blecker, Robert A.
Borelli, John
Bork, Robert Heron
Boykin, Keith
Bradley, Denis J. M.
Brautigam, Deborah
Broad, Robin
Bub, Jeffrey
Buchanan, George Wesley
Bullock, Alice G.
Burgdorf, Robert L., Jr.
Burke, John
Bush, Nathaniel
Byrd, Jerry Stewart
Cahn, Edgar S.
Campbell, Ted A.
Capizzi, Joseph E.
Carroll, Raoul Lord
Carter, Barry Edward
Caws, Peter James
Cenkner, William
Chambers, John Curry, Jr.
Chandler, James P.
Cheek, King Virgil, Jr.
Childs, Winston
Clark, Leroy D.
Cohen, Stephen P.
Cohn, Sherman Louis
Cole, Basil
Collins, Mary
Condit, Richard E.
Cooper, Clement Theodore
Cotman, John W.
Cromwell, William C.
Crooms, Lisa A.
Cruise, Warren Michael
Crysdale, Cynthia S. W.
Cua, Antonio S.
Dalley, George Albert
Davis, John Wesley
Davis, Wayne
Dechert, Charles Richard
Delio, Ilia
Dellums, Leola M. Roscoe
Deng, Francis M.
Dienes, C. Thomas
Dinges, William
Dionne, E. J.
Donegan, Charles Edward
Donohoo, Lawrence
Dougherty, Jude Patrick
Downs, Anthony
Drinan, Robert Frederick
Druart, Therese-Anne
Dubay, Thomas E.
Echols, Marsha A.
Edwards, Harry T.
Eno, Robert Bryan
Everett, Ralph B.
Fields, Stephen M.
Fink, Beatrice
Finlayson, Arnold Robert
Fisher, Eugene J.
Fisher, Louis
Fitzmyer, Joseph A.
Ford, John T.
Fuller, Alfredia Y.
Galston, M.
Garthoff, Raymond L.
Garvey, John Leo
Gavil, Andrew I.
Gellhorn, Gay
Gignac, Francis Thomas
Gillis, Chester
Gilson, Anne Bathurst
Ginsburg, Martin D.
Goldfarb, Ronald L.
Goldstein, Joshua S.
Goodman, Louis
Gostin, Lo
Gravelle, Jane Gibson
Greenberg, Gershon
Gregg, Robert
Gros, Jeffrey
Groves, Harry Edward
Guttman, Egon
Haines, Diana
Halal, William E.
Hamilton, Eugene Nolan
Happel, Stephen P.
Harris, Charles Wesley
Hart, Christopher Alvin
Hassing, Richard F.
Hayden, John Carleton
Hayes, Diana L.
Heelan, Patrick Aidan
Heffron, Paul Thayer
Henry, Brent Lee
Hicks, H. Beecher, Jr.
Hoge, Dean R.
Horn, John Stephen
Hunter, Jerry L.
Jamar, Steven D.
Johnson, Jacob Edwards, III
Johnson, Johnnie L., Jr.
Jones, Charles B.
Jordan, Emma Coleman
Kellogg, Frederic R.
King, Patricia Ann
Kotler, Neil G.
Kotz, Samuel
Kramer, Robert
Krattenmaker, Thomas George
Kress, Robert Lee
Kuhn, Steven Thomas
Kurland, Adam H.
Lamm, Julia A.
Lance, Mark
Langan, John P.
Latham, Weldon Hurd
Lee, K. Samuel
Lee, Milton C., Jr.
Leonard, Walter J.
Lerman, Lisa G.
Lewis, Bradley
Lewis, Neil
Lewis, Peter
Lewis, William A., Jr.
Lobo, Alfonso Gomez
Loewe, William Patrick
Lubbers, Jeffrey S.
Lubic, Robert B.
Ludwikowski, Rett R.
Maloney, Francis J.
Marcin, Raymond B.
Mardin, Serif
Marlin-Bennett, Renee
Marthaler, Berard Lawrence
McCurdy, Howard Earl
McDonald, Peter J. T.
McEleney, Neil Joseph
McIntosh, Simeon Charles
McLean, George Francis
McManus, Frederick Richard
Mendelson, Johanna
Mitchell, Alan C.
Mittelman, James H.
Mohan, Robert Paul
Murphy, Mark Christopher
Musgrove, Philip
Mutchler, David Edward
Nasr, Sayed H.
Newsome, Clarence Geno
Norton, Eleanor Holmes
Orr, Janice
Page, Joseph Anthony
Parker, Vernon B.
Pasha, Mustapha
Patterson, Elizabeth Hayes
Payne, Steven
Pellegrino, Edmund Daniel
Pitofsky, Robert
Powers, Madison
Pozzo, Riccardo
Pritzl, Kurt
Quander, Rohulamin
Queen, Evelyn E. Crawford
Quitslund, Sonya Antoinette
Raskin, Jamin
Raven-Hansen, Peter
Rehnquist, William Hubbs
Reich, Warren T.
Reid, Inez Smith
Reuscher, John
Rice, Paul R.
Richardson, Henry
Richardson, John
Robbins, Ira Paul
Robinson, Reginald L.
Rossi, Christopher
Rothstein, Paul Frederick
Said, Abdul Aziz
Salla, Michael
Salzman, Jim
Sanders, Cheryl J.
Sargentich, Thomas O.
Schall, James Vincent
Schlagel, Richard H.
Schneider, Cathy
Schooner, Steven L.
Schrag, Philip G.
Schwartz, Herman
Seidman, Louis Michael
Shalleck, Ann
Shanks, Hershel
Sherman, Nancy
Silvia, Stephen J.
Sloyan, Gerard
Smith, George P.
Smith, J. Clay, Jr.
Smith, Wallace Charles
Sokolowski, Robert S.
Spragens, Janet R.
Stent, Michelle Dorene
Stevens, John Paul
Stewart, Charles Todd
Stokes, Louis
Straumanis, Joan
Strong, Douglas M.
Studzinski, Raymond James
Thomas, Clarence
Tm, King
Trisco, Robert Frederick
Tushnet, Mark Victor
Tylenda, Joseph N.
Vaughn, Robert Gene
Veatch, Robert M.
Velkley, Richard L.
Ver Eecke, Wilfried
Vukowich, William T.
Wagner, Annice
Wald, Patricia M.
Walker, Rebecca
Wallace, Dewey D., Jr.
Wallace, Paul Starett, Jr.
Wallwork, Ernest
Wapner, Paul
Washington, Robert Benjamin, Jr.
Waysdorf, Susan L.
Wechsler, Burton D.
Wheeler, Sondra E.
White, Charles Sidney John
White, Kevin
Williams, Karen Hastie
Williams, Paul R.
Williams, Yvonne LaVerne
Wilmot, David Winston
Winter, Douglas E.
Winters, Francis Xavier
Wippel, John F.
Wiseman, James A.
Wogaman, John Philip
Wu, Frank H.

Johnson, E. Elizabeth
Magee, Glenn A.
Marion, Laurie Cowan
Parry, Richard D.
Pippin, Tina
Smith, Paul

Demorest
Lytle, Timothy F.

Fort Valley
Bellamy, Donnie Duglie
Demenchonok, Edward V.

Franklin Springs
Bobic, Michael

Gainesville
Barlow, Brian C.

Macon
Bell, Nora Kizer
Hester, D. Micah
Staton, Cecil P.
Watson, James Shand

Marietta
Craig, William Lane
Gladson, Jerry A.
Tumlin, John S.
Wess, Robert C.

Milledgeville
Sallstrom, John Emery

Mount Berry
Carl, Harold F.
Hill, Harvey

Mount Vernon
Boomer, Dennis
Cheek, H. Lee, Jr.
Weaver, Doug

Oxford
Gowler, David B.

Reidsville
Yizar, Marvin

Riverdale
Waters, John W.

Rome
Nash, Robert N.
Papazian, Michael
Sheeley, Steven M.

Savannah
Nordenhaug, Erik
Simmons, Jack R.
Townsend, Dabney W., Jr.

Statesboro
Shriver, George Hite

Toccoa
Atkinson, Harley

Toccoa Falls
Sprinkle, Joe M.
Williams, Donald T.

Watkinsville
Hoeffner, Kent

HAWAII

Hilo
Wang, Enbao

Honolulu
Bloom, Alfred
Bontekoe, Ron
Callies, David Lee
Cheng, Chung-Ying
Ferguson, Kathy E.
Lamb, Ramdas
Richards, Leon
Roberts, Rodney C.
Sharma, Jagdish P.
Suh, Dae-Suk
Tiles, J. E.
Trowbridge, John

Kailua
Deutsch, Eliot

Mililani
Mamo, Nathan

IDAHO

Boise
Zirinsky, Michael Paul

Jerome
Feiss, Hugh

Lewiston
Torell, Kurt Charles

Moscow
George, Kathryn Paxton
Gier, Nicholas F.

Pocatello
Baergen, Ralph
Tate, Paul Dean
Wahl, Russell
Westphal, Jonathan

ILLINOIS

Bloomington
Gillett, Carl
Liechty, Daniel
Lord, Timothy C.
Mead, Walter Bruce

Carbondale
Alexander, Thomas
Eames, Elizabeth R.
Elsamahi, Mohamed
Gillan, Garth J.
Howie, John
Schedler, George Edward

Carlinville
Zimany, Roland Daniel

Champaign
Beckett, Steven J.
Boyle, Francis
Chandler, Hugh
Colombo, John D.
Cribbet, John E.
Cuffey, Kenneth H.
Davey, William J.
Ebbs, Gary
Feinberg, Walter
Finkin, Matthew W.
Freyfogle, Eric T.
Harris, Fred O.
Kaplan, Richard L.
Kesan, Jay P.
LaFave, Wayne R.
Maggs, Peter B.
McCarthy, Timothy
McConnaughay, Philip J.
McKim, Robert
Melnick, Atrhur
Mohr, Richard
Neely, Wright
Nowak, John E.
Painter, Richard W.
Reynolds, Laurie A.
Ross, Stephen F.
Rotunda, Ronald Daniel
Schacht, Richard
Schack, Haimo
Schroeder, William
Shoben, Elaine W.
Shwayder, David
Stone, Victor J.
Tarr, Nina W.
Terry, Charles T.
Turquette, Atwell R.
Ulen, Thomas S.
Wagner, Steven
Wengert, Robert
Williams, Cynthia A.
Wilson, Robert

Charleston
Lee, Young Sook

Chicago
Abadinsky, Howard
Abela, Paul R.
Adkins, Arthur William Hope
Ahlstrom, Gosta Werner
Alaimo, Kathleen
Alschuler, Albert W.
Amaker, Norman Carey
Ascough, Richard S.
Aydede, Murat
Ball, William Batten
Bangert, Mark Paul
Bannan, John F.
Barry, Robert M.
Bartky, Sandra
Bateman, Paul E.
Bergant, Dianne
Beschle, D. L.
Betz, Hans Dieter
Bevans, Stephen
Blachowicz, James
Blackman, Rodney J.
Blum, John D.
Boling, Robert Gordon
Bramer, Paul G.
Brauer, Jerald
Broniak, Christopher
Broudy, Harry S.
Browning, Don S.
Burkhart, John E.
Butler, Lee Hayward, Jr.
Carr, Anne E.
Carson, Thomas L.
Chastain, Charles
Cohen, Ted
Collins, Ardis B.
Costigan, Richard F.
Cronce, Philip
Cumings, Bruce
Cunningham, Suzanne M.
Currie, David P.
Cutrofello, Andrew
Dale, Walter R.
Dam, Kenneth W.
Davis, Michael
Decker, John F.
Derdak, Thomas J.
Dickie, George T.
Dworkin, Gerald
Echols, James Kenneth
Edelberg, Walter
Elsbernd, Mary
Engel, J. Ronald
Epstein, Richard Allen
Erwin, James Otis
Fiscella, Joan B.
Fischel, Daniel R.
Fish, Stanley E.
Fleischacker, Sam
French, Louise
French, William
Frohlich, Mary
Frymer-Kensky, Tikva
Fuerst, Wesley J.
Garber, Daniel Elliot
Gill, David W.
Gilmour, Peter
Gilpin, W. Clark
Gini, Alfred
Gittins, Anthony
Golb, Norman
Gomberg, Paul
Goroff, David B.
Graber, Doris A.
Graham, Stephen R.
Greeley, Andrew M.
Green, Michael J.
Grossman, Neal
Grover, Dorothy
Halwani, Raja
Handy, Lowell
Harrill, J. Albert
Hart, Bill
Hart, W. D.
Hartman, Laura Pincus
Haugeland, John Christian
Hayes, Zachary Jerome
Heinz, John P.
Helmholz, R. H.
Hiebert, Theodore
Hilbert, David
Hilliard, David C.
Hogenson, George B.
Homans, Peter
Hopkins, Dwight N.
Hoppe, E. A.
Hoppe, Leslie John
Huggett, Nick
Hughes, Joyce A.
Hylton, Peter
Ingram, David B.
Jarrett, Jon
Jones, Peter D. A.
Jung, Patricia Beattie
Jurisson, Cynthia
Kajevich, Steven N.
Kaufman, George G.
Klein, Ralph W.
Koptak, Paul E.
Krause, Joan H.
Krentz, Edgar
Laden, Anthony
Ladenson, Robert
Lane, Marc J.
Larrabee, Mary Jane
Lauer, Eugene F.
Lee, Johng O.
Lee, Mi Kyoung
Leroy Conrad, Robert
Lewis, Cary B., Jr.
Lichtenbert, Robert H.
Lincoln, Bruce K.
Linss, Wilhelm Camill
Lipson, Charles
Livezey, Lowell W.
Lorek, Robert
Lundbom, Jack R.
Macneil, Ian Roderick
Malm, Heidi
Manning, Blanche Marie
Marshall, Robert J.
Martin, Troy W.
McCulloh, Gerald William
McGinn, Bernard John
McGinty, Mary Peter
Meinwald, Constance
Michel, Walter L.
Mikva, A. J.
Mills, Charles
Morris, Calvin S.
Morris, Norval
Moser, Paul K.
Mosha, Raymond S.
Neely, David E.
Nilson, Jon
Notz, John K., Jr.
Nuzzo, Angelica
Nystrom, David P.
Oliker, Michael A.
Olken, Samuel R.
Ottley, Bruce L.
Overbeck, T. Jerome
Ozar, David T.
Park, Kyeong-Sook
Parks, Jennifer A.
Pawlikowski, John
Pennick, Aurie Alma
Peperzak, Adriaan Theodoor
Perelmuter, Hayim Goren
Pero, Albert
Perritt, Henry H., Jr.
Perry, Richard J., Jr.
Pintchman, Tracy
Porter, Kwame John R.
Postlewaite, Philip F.
Power, Margaret
Price, Daniel
Reisch, George
Reynolds, Frank E.
Rhoads, David
Ricoeur, Paul
Rodriguez, Jose David
Rosenblum, Victor Gregory
Rowan, Bernard
Samar, Vincent J.
Sassen, Saskia
Schechtman, Marya
Schmaus, Warren Stanley
Schneider, Laurel
Schreiter, Robert John
Schroeder, Steven H.
Schultz, Reynolds Barton
Schwartz, Justin
Schweickart, David
Seigfried, Hans
Shaman, Jeffrey Marc
Simpson, Dick
Sinkler, Georgette
Smith, Jonathan Zittell
Snodgrass, Klyne Ryland
Sorkin, David E.
Stalans, Loretta
Stein, Howard
Steinman, Joan E.
Struckhoff, David
Stuhlmueller, Carroll
Sullivan, Winnifred F.
Sweeney, Leo
Taiwo, Olufemi
Tarlock, Anthony Dan
Terrell, JoAnne M.
Thandeka
Thompson, Kenneth F.
Thomsen, Mark
Tobin, Thomas Herbert
Tolliver, Richard Lamar
Tomlins, Christopher L.
Trout, J. D.
Vaillancourt, Daniel
Vogelaar, Harold Stanton
von Wahlde, Urban C.
Walter, James J.
Ward, Jule D.
Ward, Julie
Waymack, Mark H.
Weil, Vivian
Westley, Richard J.
White, David A.
White, John L.
Wike, Victoria S.
Williams, Daniel
Wilson, Clarence S., Jr.
Wilson, Kent
Wissler, Robert W.
Wojcik, Mark E.
Wolf, Arnold J.
Wren, Thomas
Yandell, K. David
Yang, Xiaosi
Yartz, Frank
Yu, Anthony C.
Zaferson, William S.

De Kalb
Dye, James Wayne
Kisiel, Theodore Joseph
Michael, Colette Verger
Norris, James D.
Parot, Joseph John

Decatur
Jacobs, Jo Ellen
Mittal, Sushil

Deerfield
Alexanian, Joseph M.
de S. Cameron, Nigel M.
Harrold, Jeffery Deland
Lunde, Jonathan M.
Mitchell, C. Ben
Moulder, William J.
Schnabel, Eckhard J.
Solheim, Barbara P.
Williams, Clifford E.

Dekalb
Brown, Harold I.
Hudson, James L.
Michael, Colette

Edwardsville
Corr, Charles A.
Danley, John Robert
Hill, Jason D.
Pearson, Samuel C.
Welch, Edward L.

Elgin
Ferguson, Paul

Elmhurst
Parker, Paul P.

Elsah
Follis, Elaine R.

Eureka
McCoy, Jerry

Evanston
Darby, Derrick
Deigh, John
Fine, Arthur
Frisch, Mathias F.
Gooding-Williams, Robert
Goodnight, G. Thomas
Harley, Philip A.
Hill, Randolph K.
Hull, David L.
Kalantzis, George
Kieckhefer, Richard
Kraut, Richard
Lafont, Cristina
Levin, David M.
Lowe, Eugene Y., Jr.
McCarthy, Thomas A.

INDIANA

Shields, Donald J.

Upland
Charles, J. Daryl
Corduan, Winfried
Harbin, Michael A.
Helyer, Larry R.
Spiegel, James S.

Valparaiso
Bass, Dorothy C.
Brant, Dale
Brietzke, Paul H.
Conison, Jay
Geiman, Kevin
Greene, Martha D.
Hatcher, Richard Gordon
Herrera, Enrique
Klein, Kenneth
Krodel, Gottfried G.
Leeb, Carolyn
Ludwig, Theodore Mark
Meilaender, Gilbert
Niedner, Frederick A.
Rast, Walter Emil
Stith, Richard T.
Truemper, David George
Vandoorn-Harder, Nelly

Valparalso
Kennedy, Thomas

Vincennes
Rinderle, Walter
Verkamp, Bernard

West Lafayette
Bartlett, Robert V.
Bergmann, Michael
Bertolet, Rod
Cover, Jan
Curd, Martin Vincent
Curd, Patricia
Gill, Michael
Gustason, William
Kuehn, Manfred
Marina, Jacqueline
Matustik, Martin J. Beck
McBride, William Leon
Mitchell, Donald
Mumby, Dennis K.
Rowe, William L.
Russow, Lilly-Marlene
Scerri, Eric R.
Schrag, Calvin Orville
Scott, Kermit
Seigfried, Charlene
Thompson, Paul B.
Ulrich, Dolph

Westville
Sheehy, John

Winona Lake
Bateman, Herbert W.

IOWA

Ames
Bishop, Michael
Donaghy, John A.
Hollenbach, Paul William
Klemke, Elmer Daniel
Robinson, William Spencer
Sawyer, Mary R.

Burlington
Benjamin, Paul

Cedar Falls
Boedeker, Edgar
Brod, Harry
Crownfield, David R.
Holland, Margaret G.
Robinson, James Burnell
Soneson, Jerome P.

Cedar Rapids
Carroll, Rosemary F.
Lemos, John P.
Martin, Charlotte Joy
Robinson, Mary Elizabeth
Sessions, Robert

Davenport
Jacobson, Paul Kenneth
Johnson, Geraldine Ross

Decorah
Bailey, Storm M.
Bunge, Wilfred F.
Hanson, Bradley
Sieber, John Harold

Des Moines
Baker, Thomas E.
Begleitor, Martin D.
Dore, Laurie Kratky
Frank, Sally
Kniker, Charles R.
Patrick, Dale
Sisk, G. C.

Dubuque
Ashley, Benedict M.
Bailey, James L.
Bloesch, Donald G.
Colyer, Elmer M.
Freund, Norm
Healey, Robert Mathieu
Jung, L. Shannon
Martin, Raymond Albert
McDermott, John J.
Nessan, Craig L.
Platt, Elizabeth Ellan
Priebe, Duane A.
Quere, Ralph Walter
Skiba, Paulette
Stevenson-Moessner, Jeanne
Thibeau, Matthew J.

Forest City
Hamre, James S.

Grinnell
Burkle, Howard R.
Cummins, W. Joseph
Goldberg, Sanford C.
Meehan, M. Johanna
Rosenthal, Michael A.
Schrift, Alan D.

Iowa City
Adamek, Wendi
Addis, Laird Clark
Baird, Robert Dahlen
Beaudoin, John M.
Bezanson, Randall P.
Boyd, Willard L.
Boyle, John Phillips
Bozeman, Theodore D.
Butchvarov, Panayot K.
David, Marcella
Duerlinger, James
Fales, Evan Michael
Forell, George Wolfgang
Fumerton, Richard
Hines, N. William
Horwitz, Henry Gluck
Hovenkamp, Herb
Keen, Ralph
Knight, W. H.
Kuntz, J. Kenneth
Landini, Gregory
McCloskey, Deirdre
McPherson, James Alan
Nickelsburg, George William Elmer
Spalding, James Colwell
Stensvaag, John-Mark
Thomas, Randall S.
Weston, Burns H.
Widiss, Alan I.
Wing, Adrien Katherine

Janesville
Hallberg, Fred William

Lamoni
Mesle, C. Robert

Mount Vernon
Allin, Craig Willard
Ihlan, Amy
Vernoff, Charles Elliott
Weddle, David L.

Orange City
Rohrer, James
Van Hook, Jay M.

Oskaloosa
Porter, David L.

Sioux City
Cooney, William
Lawrence, John Shelton

Waterloo
Weems, Vernon Eugene, Jr.

Waverly
Bouzard, Walter

KANSAS

Atchison
Macierowski, E. M.
Meade, Denis
Nowell, Irene

Baldwin City
Hatcher, Donald L.
Wiley, George

Emporia
Roark, Dallas Morgan
Toadvine, Ted

Hillsboro
Miller, Douglas B.

Hutchinson
Chalfant, William Y.

Kansas City
Hutton, Chane
Keeney, Donald E.
May, David M.
Wheeler, David L.

Lawrence
Coggins, George Cameron
Cole, Richard
Cudd, Ann E.
DeGeorge, Richard
Genova, Anthony Charles
Head, John W.
Hoeflich, Michael H.
Marquis, Donald Bagley
Martin, Rex
Minor, Robert Neil
Mirecki, Paul A.
Piekalkiewicz, Jaroslaw
Robertson, Teresa
Saul, Norman E.
Shafer-Landau, Russell

Manhattan
Linder, Robert Dean
Nafziger, E. Wayne
Suleiman, Michael W.

North Newton
Friesen, Duane K.

Ottawa
Discher, Mark

Overland Park
Olson, Richard P.

Sterling
MacArthur, Steven D.

Topeka
Concannon, James M.
Elrod, Linda Diane Henry
Elrod, Linda Henry
Griffin, Ronald Charles
Spring, Raymond Lewis

Wichita
Chang, Dae Hong
Dooley, Patricia
Duram, James C.
Keel, Vernon
Mandt, Almer J., III
Pyles, John E.
Skaggs, Jimmy M.

Winfield
Gray, Wallace
Rankin, Steve

KENTUCKY

Ashland
D'Aoust, Jean-Jacques

Barbourville
Sisson, Russell

Berea
Hoag, Robert W.
Pearson, Eric
Schneider, Robert J.

Bowling Green
Ardrey, Saundra Curry
Casey, Kenneth
Curtis-Howe, E. Margaret
Long, John Edward
Schoen, Edward Lloyd
Tuck, Donald Richard
Veenker, Ronald Allen
Vos, Arvin G.

Burgin
Huddleston, Tobianna W.

Campbellsville
Medley, Mark S.

Covington
Blair, George Alfred

Crestview Hills
Twaddell, Gerald E.

Danville
Cooney, Brian Patrick
Glazier-McDonald, Beth
McCollough, C. Thomas
Mount, Eric, Jr.
Scarborough, Milton R.

Georgetown
Lunceford, Joe E.
Redditt, Paul L.
Wirzba, Norman

Grayson
Fiensy, David A.
Pickens, George F.

Highland Heights
Bell, Sheila Trice
Richards, Jerald H.

Lexington
Daniel, E. Randolph
Dowd, Sharyn
Dunnavant, Anthony L.
Fakhrid-Deen, Nashid Abdullah
Faupel, William
Fosl, Peter S.
Frank, Daniel H.
High, Dallas Milton
Jones, Paul Henry
Krislov, Joseph
Manns, James William
McAvoy, Jane
Moseley, James G.
Nugent, Donald Christopher
Olshewsky, Thomas Mack
Paulsell, William O.
Perreiah, Alan Richard
Pickens, Rupert Tarpley
Smaw, Eric

Louisville
Akin, Daniel L.
Alperson, Philip A.
Barnette, Henlee Hulix
Beougher, Timothy K.
Blaising, Craig A.
Blevins, James Lowell
Burnett, Donald L.
Cabal, Theodore James
Chancellor, James D.
Conver, Leigh E.
Cook, E. David
Cooper, Burton
Cruz, Virgil
Cunningham, Jack R.
Deering, Ronald F.
Drinkard, Joel F., Jr.
Fuller, Russell T.
Gentry, Peter J.
Grossi, Elizabeth L.
Hausman, Carl R.
Henry, Gray
Hoyt-O'Connor, Paul E.
Hughes, Robert Don
John, Eileen
Kimball, Robert
Lawless, Charles E.
Maloney, Thomas
March, Wallace Eugene
Martin, Janice R.
Martos, Joseph
Masolo, D. A.
Mobley, Tommy W.
Mohler, R. Albert, Jr.
Mueller, David L.
Mulder, John Mark
Poethig, Eunice Blanchard
Polhill, John B.
Potter, Nancy
Powell, Cedric Merlin
Rainer, Thom S.
Richardson, Brian C.
Rothenbusch, Esther H.
Schreiner, Thomas R.
Simmons, Paul D.
Simpson, Mark E.
Smith, Marsha A. Ellis
Steeger, William P.
Stein, Robert H.
Stenger, Robert Leo
Stroble, Paul E., Jr.
Terry, J. Mark
Walsh, Thomas
Ware, Bruce A.
Warren, Manning G., III
Weaver, Russell L.
Webber, Randall C.
Wiggins, Osborne P., Jr.
Williams, Dennis E.
Wills, Gregory A.

Morehead
Mangrum, Franklin M.

Murray
Foreman, Terry Hancock

Newport
Richards, Stephen C.
Trundle, Robert

Owensboro
Alexander, James
Fager, Jeff

Prestonburg
McAninch, Robert D.

Richmond
Fox, James Walker
Gray, Bonnie Jean
Harris, Bond
Minor, Kevin I.
Omatseye, Jim

Williamsburg
Ramey, George

Wilmore
Anderson, Neil D.
Arnold, Bill T.
Collins, Kenneth J.
Demaray, Donald E.
Green, Joel B.
Hamilton, Victor Paul
Kinghorn, Kenneth Cain
Lyon, Robert William
Peterson, Michael Lynn
Thompson, David L.
Walters, John R.
Witherington, Ben

LOUISIANA

Alexandria
Sanson, Jerry P.

Baton Rouge
Baker, John R.
Blakesley, Christopher L.
Bowers, J. W.
Buehler, Arthur
Buehler, Arthur F.
Burkett, Delbert Royce
Christian, Ollie
Crawford, William Edward
Day, Louis A.

Cambridge
Abe, Nobuhiko
Appel, Frederick
Appiah, Kwame Anthony
Barron, David J.
Bartholet, Elizabeth
Benhabib, Seyla
Berlin, Charles
Bok, Derek Curtis
Bovon, Francois
Cederman, Lars-Erik
Clifford, Richard J.
Cox, Archibald
Daley, Brian Edward
Dershowitz, Alan Morton
Dominguez, Jorge Ignacio
Dyck, Arthur James
Fallon, Richard H.
Fideler, Paul Arthur
Fisher, Roger
Foerst, Anne
Fried, Charles
Frug, Gerald E.
Gerken, Heather K.
Goldin, Claudia
Graham, William
Guinier, (Carol) Lani
Haar, Charles Monroe
Halperin, Daniel
Hanson, Paul David
Harrington, Daniel Joseph
Harris, Errol E.
Heck, Richard
Henrich, Dieter
Herwitz, David Richard
Hoffmann, Stanley
Horovitz, Amir
Hullett, James N.
Jasanoff, Sheila S.
Jolls, C.
Jones-Correa, Michael
Kane, Thomas Anthony
Kaplow, Louis
Katz, Milton
Kaufman, Andrew L.
Kaufman, Gordon Dester
Keenan, J. F.
Keeton, Robert Ernest
Kelman, Steven
Koester, Helmut
Korsgaard, Christine M.
Kujawa, Sheryl A.
LaMothe, Kimerer L.
Letts, Christine Webb
MacFarquhar, Roderick
Mack, Kenneth W.
Marrow, Stanley Behjet
Martin, Jane Roland
Martin, Joan M.
Martin, Michael Lou
Mazlish, Bruce
McGowan, Andrew
Minow, Martha
Moran, Richard
Nesson, Charles Rothwell
Nozick, Robert
Ogletree, Charles J., Jr.
Parsons, Charles D.
Perkins, Dwight Heald
Posen, Barry R.
Putnam, Hilary
Rawls, John
Reibetanz, S. Sophia
Rorty, Amelie Oksenberg
Roush, Sherrilyn
Sachs, John R.
Sander, Frank E. A.
Scanlon, T. M.
Scheffler, Israel
Shapiro, David L.
Shavell, S.
Singer, Irving
Singer, Joseph W.
Skolnikoff, Eugene B.
Sohn, Louis Bruno
Steiker, Carol S.
Stendahl, Krister
Stone, Alan Abraham
Strugnell, John
Stuntz, William J.
Thomas, Douglas L.
Thomas, Owen Clark
Trautman, Donald T.
Tribe, Laurence Henry
Tu, Wei-Ming
Vacek, Edward Victor
Vagts, Detlev F.
Warren, Alvin C., Jr.
Warren, Elizabeth
Wedgwood, Ralph N.
Weiler, Paul C.
Weinreb, Lloyd L.
Wilkins, David Brian
Williams, Preston N.
Wills, Lawrence M.
Winston, Kenneth Irwin
Wolfman, Bernard
Yee, Gale A.
Zittrain, Jonathan L.

Carlisle
Russell, C. Allyn

Charlestown
Schiavona, Christopher F.

Chesnut Hill
Langer, Ruth

Chestnut Hill
Belsley, David A.
Blanchette, Oliva
Byrne, Patrick Hugh
Cahill, Lisa Sowle
Cleary, John J.
Deleeuw, Patricia Allwin
Egan, Harvey Daniel
Garcia, Laura
Groome, Thomas H.
Gurtler, Gary M.
Himes, Michael J.
Hinsdale, Mary Ann
Kearney, Richard
Monan, James Donald
Morrill, Bruce T.
Pope, Stephen J.
Raelin, Joseph A.
Wolfe, Alan

Dorchester
Strang, J. V.
Thompson, Cynthia L.

Easton
Coogan, Michael
Goddu, Andre

Essex
Buckley, Thomas W.

Fall River
Kaufman, William E.

Framingham
Joseph, Stephen

Holden
Johnson, Donald Ellis

Jamaica Plain
Abrahamsen, Valerie
Sands, Kathleen M.

Lawrence
Wigall, Steve R.

Lynn
Fox, Samuel

Marlborough
Burris, John, Jr.

Medford
Bauer, Nancy
Bedau, Hugo Adam
Cartwright, Helen Morris
Conklin, John E.
Daniels, Norman
Dennett, Daniel C.
Krimsky, Sheldon
McConnell, Jeff
McLennan, Scotty
Meagher, Robert Francis
Rubin, Alfred P.

Milton
Hunter, Allan

Newton
Anderson, Alexis J.
Baron, Charles Hillel
Bloom, Robert M.
Brodin, Mark S.
Carlston, Charles E.
Coquillette, Daniel R.
Everett, William J.
Fontaine, Carole R.
Holladay, William Lee
Howe, Ruth-Arlene W.
Hurwitz, Ilana
Katz, Sanford Noah
Pazmino, Robert W.

North Adams
Silliman, Matthew R.

North Andover
Kitts, Margo
Ledoux, Arthur O'brien

Northampton
Ackelsberg, Martha A.
Connolly, John M.
Derr, Thomas S.
Donfried, Karl P.
Moulton, Janice
Unno, Taitetsu

Northhampton
Boyd, J. Wesley

Norton
Ladd, Rosalind Ekman

Nutham
Stylianopoulos, Theodore

Paxton
Bilodeau, Lorraine

Quincy
Braaten, Laurie
Phillips, Thomas

Roxbury
Enos, V. Pualani

Salem
Denby, David A.

Sherborn
Chung, Chai-sik

Somerville
Race, Jeffrey
Trigilio, Jo
Wan, Sze-Kar
White, Marsha
Zong, Desheng

South Hadley
Berkey, Robert Fred
Crosthwaite, Jane Freeman
Ferm, Deane William
Yamashita, Tadanori

South Hamilton
Beale, Gregory
Davis, John Jefferson
Gibson, Scott M.
Gruenler, Royce Gordon
Isaac, Gordon L.
Kaiser, Walter C., Jr.
Kline, Meredith George
Lints, Richard
Mounce, William D.
Niehaus, Jeffrey J.
Padilla, Alvin
Polischuk, Pablo
Pratico, Gary D.
Richardson, Kurt A.
Robinson, Haddon W.
Rosell, Garth M.
Schutz, Samuel R.
Silva, Moises
Spencer, Aida Besancon
Stuart, Douglas Keith
Swetland, Kenneth L.
Villafane, Eldin
Walters, Gwenfair
Wells, David Falconer

South Lancaster
Kennedy, D. Robert

Southbridge
Pentiuc, Eugene

Springfield
Baynes, Leonard M.
Bock, Robert L.
Cohen, Amy B.
Goldstein, Anne B.
Gouvin, Eric J.
Habermehl, Lawrence L.
Porter, Burton F.
Skelly, Brian

Upton
Waldau, Paul

Waltham
Jick, Leon Allen
Nemzoff, Ruth
Sarna, Jonathan D.
Sarna, Nahum M.

Watertown
Schagrin, Morton L.

Wellesley
Congelton, Ann
Johnson, Roger A.
Malino, Frances
Piper, Adrian Margaret Smith
Stadler, Ingrid
Winkler, Kenneth P.
Witte, Ann Dryden

Westfield
John, PM

Weston
Barry, William Anthony
Wintle, Thomas

Williamstown
O'Connor, Daniel D.

Worcester
Avery-Peck, Alan
Bashir, Shahzad
Burkett, Randall Keith
DeCew, Judith Wagner
Gottlieb, Roger Samuel
Hamilton, John Daniel Burgoyne
Janack, Marianne
Laffey, Alice L.
Lapomarda, Vincent Anthony
Manfra, Jo Ann
Murphy, Frederick J.
Saeed, Khalid
Shannon, Thomas A.
Shea, Emmett A.
Stempsey, William Edward

MICHIGAN

Adrian
Aichele, George

Albion
Davis, Ralph
Frick, Frank Smith
Horstman, Allen

Allendale
Hoitenga, Dewey J.
Parker, Kelly A.
Pestana, Mark
Rowe, Stephen C.
White, Jonathan

Alma
Massanari, Ronald Lee

Ann Arbor
Allen, Layman E.
Anderson, Elizabeth S.
Brehm, H. Alan
Burks, Arthur Walter
Conard, Alfred Fletcher
Crawford, Clan, Jr.
Darwall, Stephen L.
Dejnozka, Jan
Endelman, Todd Michael
Gibbard, Allan Fletcher
Green, Thomas Andrew
Kahn, Douglas A.
Kamisar, Yale
Krier, James Edward
Lempert, Richard O.
Lewis, David Lanier
Loeb, Louis Edward
Proops, Ian
Sandalow, Terrance
Schneider, Carl E.
Sharf, Robert H.
Singer, J. David
Sklar, Lawrence
Stein, Eric
Terpstra, Vern
Vining, Joseph
Waggoner, Lawrence W.
Walton, Kendall
White, James Justesen

Benton Harbor
Sundaram, K.

Berrien Springs
Bacchiocchi, Samuele
Burrill, Russell C.
Douglas, Walter
Economou, Elly Helen
Gane, A. Barry
Geraty, Lawrence Thomas
Greig, Alexander Josef
Kis, Miroslav M.
Merling, David
Paulien, Jon
Roche, Mark W.
Sabes, Jane
Vyhmeister, Nancy Jean
Whidden, Woodrow W., II

Big Rapids
Griffin, Richard W.
Hanford, Jack
Roy, Donald H.

Bloomfield Village
Meyer, George H.

Brighton
Browne, Gregory M.

Dearborn
Baumgarten, Elias
Hughes, Paul
Linker, Maureen
Procter, Harvey Thornton, Jr.
Wider, Kathleen V.

Dearborn Heights
Phillips, Randall R.

Detroit
Albrecht, Gloria H.
Anchustegui, Ann-Marie
Cook, Julian Abele, Jr.
Corvino, John F.
Crawford, David R.
Crenshaw, Ronald Willis
Dunne, Tad
Edwards, Abiyah, Jr.
Evans, Warren Cleage
Feaster, Bruce Sullivan
Goldfield, Michael
Granger, Herbert
Hertz, Richard C.
Hetzel, Otto J.
Holley, Jim
Hutchison, Harry Greene, IV
Koegel, Lynne
Lewis, David Baker
Littlejohn, Edward J.
Lombard, Lawrence B.
McGinnis, James W.
McGovern, Arthur F.
McKinsey, Michael
Morton, Charles E.
Muller, Earl
Pickering, George W.
Reed, Gregory J.
Reide, Jerome L.
Rike, Jennifer L.
Russell, Bruce Alan
Saliba, John A.
Schaberg, Jane D.
Sedler, Robert Allen
Shakoor, Adam Adib
Shen, Raphael
Shipley, Anthony J.
Stack, Steven
Stephens, Cynthia Diane
Tilles, Gerald Emerson
Titiev, Robert Jay
Tubbs, James B.
Wagner, Wenceslas Joseph
Weber, Leonard J.
Whitney, Barry L.
Wise, Edward Martin
Wyre, Stanley Marcel
Yanal, Robert J.

MINNESOTA

MISSISSIPPI

MISSOURI

Fulton
Mattingly, Richard Edward

Hannibal
Bergen, Robert D.
Pelletier, Samuel R.

Jefferson City
Mattingly, Susan Shotliff

Joplin
Bowland, Terry

Kansas City
Alarid, Leanne F.
Bangs, Carl
Berger, Mark
Berman, Jeffrey B.
Brady, Jules M.
Bredeck, Martin James
Carter, Warren
Cogdill, James
Cooper, Corinne
Deasley, Alex R. G.
Dunlap, Elden Dale
Feagin, Susan Louise
Ferguson, Kenneth D.
Gall, Robert
Hood, Edwin T.
Howell, John C.
Hoyt, Christopher R.
Jones, William Paul
Knight, Henry H., III
Kobach, Kris W.
Lambert, Jean Christine
Levit, Nancy
Martin, Robert K.
Matthaei, Sondra
McCarty, Doran Chester
Miles, Delos
Moenssens, Andre A.
Popper, Robert
Powell, Burnele Venable
Raser, Harold E.
Reitz, Charles
Richards, Edward P.
Sweetman, Brendan M.
Verchick, Robert R.
Walter, Edward F.

Kirksville
Hsieh, Dinghwa Evelyn
Jesse, Jennifer G.

Lees Summit
Nanos, Mark D.

Liberty
Chance, J. Bradley
David, Keith R.
Horne, Milton P.

Maryville
Field, Richard

Nevada
Byer, Inez

Saint Louis
Aiken, Jane Harris
Anderson, Vinton Randolph
Arand, Charles P.
Arp, Robert
Barmann, Lawrence F.
Bartelt, Andrew H.
Bayer, Hans F.
Bechtel, William
Benton, Catherine
Berman, Scott
Berquist, Jon L.
Blackwell, Richard Joseph
Blessing, Kamila
Brauer, James L.
Brickey, Kathleen F.
Brown, Eric
Buickerood, James G.
Carey, John M.
Charron, William C.
Clarke, Anne-Marie
Danker, Frederick W.
Davis, Lawrence H.
Dorsey, Elbert
Doyle, James F.
DuBois, James M.
Epstein, Lee
Feuerhahn, Ronald R.
Finney, Paul Corby
Friedman, Marilyn A.
Fuss, Peter L.
Gaffney, John Patrick
Gass, William Howard
Gerard, Jules Bernard
Gibbs, Jeffrey A.
Gordon, Robert Morris
Greenfield, Michael M.
Greenhaw, David M.
Heidenheimer, Arnold J.
Heil, John P.
Jackson, Carol E.
Jones, David Clyde
Joy, Peter
Karamustafa, Ahmet T.
Klass, Dennis
Kleingeld, Pauline
Konig, David Thomas
Leonard, Kimberly K.
Leven, Charles Louis
Levie, Howard Sidney
Levin, Ronald Mark
Lowry, William R.
Magill, Gerard
Mandelker, Daniel Robert
McGlone, Mary M.
McLeod, Frederick G.
Modras, Ronald E.
Munson, Ronald
Nagel, Norman E.
Nelson, Lynn Hankinson
Nicholson, L.
Norwood, Kimberly Jade
Ordower, Henry M.
Parr, Chris
Paulson, Stanley Lowell
Peter, David J.
Raabe, Paul R.
Raj, Victor A. R.
Rawling, J. Piers
Rosin, Robert L.
Roth, Paul A.
Rowold, Henry
Sale, Mary
Salisbury, Robert H.
Schlafly, Phyllis Stewart
Schuchard, Bruce G.
Searls, Eileen H.
Seligman, Joel
Shapiro, Henry L.
Thro, Linus J.
Toribio, Josefa
Tuchler, Dennis John
Ulian, Joseph
Voelz, James W.
Watson, Richard A.
Wellman, Carl
Weninger, Robert
Wesselschmidt, Quentin F.
Zuck, Lowell H.

Springfield
Browning, Peter
Burgess, Stanley M.
Cotton, Roger D.
Ess, Charles
Hedrick, Charles W.
Luckert, Karl Wilhelm
Moran, Jon S.
Moyer, James Carroll

University City
Trotter, Griffin

Warrensburg
Adams, Louis Jerold
Cust, Kenneth F. T.
Selvidge, Marla J.
Young, James Van

Webster Groves
Barker, William Shirmer, II

MONTANA

Billings
Small, Lawrence Farnsworth

Bozeman
Shaw, Marvin C.

Great Falls
Furdell, Ellzabeth Lane
Taylor, Jon

Helena
Ferst, Barry Joel
Hart, John
Lambert, Richard Thomas

Missoula
Dozier, Robert R.
Elliott, Deni
Grieves, Forest L.
Harrington, Henry R.
Kende, Mark
Lopach, James Joseph

NEBRASKA

Blair
Madsen, Charles Clifford

Fremont
Russell, William R.

Hastings
O'Connell, Robert H.
Walker, James Silas

Kearney
Counts, M. Reid
Glazier, Stephen D.
Martin, Thomas

Lincoln
Audi, Robert
Becker, Edward
Berger, Lawrence
Burnett, Stephen G.
Cahan, Jean
Casullo, Albert
Crawford, Dan
Crump, Arthel Eugene
Denicola, Robert C.
Edler, Frank H. W.
Eskridge, Chris W.
Heckman, Peter
Hoffman, Peter Toll
Hugly, Philip
Ide, Harry
Lepard, Brian
Lu, Suping
Mendola, Joseph
Perlman, Harvey
Pitt, David
Potter, Nelson
Potuto, Josephine R.
Sayward, Charles
Steiner, Vernon J.
Steinweis, Alan
Thorson, Norm
Turner, John D.
van Roojen, Mark
Von Eckardt, Barbara
Works, Robert G.

Norfolk
Donaldson, Daniel J.
Huddleston, Mark

Omaha
Andrus, Kay L.
Arav, Rami
Blizek, William L.
Brooks, Catherine M.
Burke, Ronald R.
Cederblom, Jerry
Conces, Rory
Culhane, Marianne B.
Fenner, G. Michael
Freund, Richard A.
Friedlander, Walter J.
Green, Barbara S.
Green, J. Patrick
Greenspoon, Leonard Jay
Hamm, Michael Dennis, S. J.
Hauser, Richard Joseph
Jensen, Tim
Kuo, Lenore
Lawson Mack, Raneta
Mahern, Catherine
Mangrum, R. Collin
Morse, Edward A.
Newman, Andrew
Okhamafe, Imafedia
Palmer, Russ
Pieck, Manfred
Roddy, Nicolae
Santoni, Roland J.
Schultenover, David, SJ
Shaffer, Nancy E.
Shanahan, Thomas Joseph
Shkolnick, Rodney
Shugrue, Richard E.
Stephens, William O.
Strom, Lyle E.
Teply, Larry L.
Volkmer, Ronald R.
Whitten, Ralph U.
Wunsch, James Stevenson

NEVADA

Las Vegas
Appell, Annette Ruth
Bybee, Jay S.
Finocchiaro, Maurice A.
McAffee, Thomas B.
Sarri, Samuel
Shanab, Robert
Tobias, Carl William
Tominaga, Thomas T.
Wallis, James
Walton, Craig

Reno
Achtenberg, Deborah
Axtell, G. S.
Hoffman, Piotr
Leone, Matthew C.
Lucash, Frank S.
Marschall, John Peter
Nickles, Thomas
Rusco, Elmer R.
Stitt, B. Grant
Tobin, Frank J.
Williams, Christopher

NEW HAMPSHIRE

Concord
Field, Thomas G., Jr.

Dover
Phelan, Jim

Durham
Brettschneider, Marla
Brockelman, Paul
Christie, Drew
De Vries, Willem A.
Dusek, Rudolph Valentine
Frankfurter, David
McNamara, Paul
Sample, Ruth
Triplett, Tim
Whittier, Duane Hapgood
Witt, Charlotte

Hanover
Breeden, James Pleasant
Doney, Willis
Gert, Bernard
Green, Ronald Michael
Masters, Roger D.
Moor, James H.
Ohnuma, Reiko
Penner, Hans Henry
Sinnot-Armstrong, Walter P.
Sorensen, Roy
Swayne, Steven Robert

Keene
Lee, Sander H.

Manchester
Berthold, George Charles
Huff, Peter A.

Nashua
Tavani, Herman

Peterborough
Donelan, James

Plymouth
Haight, David F.
Leibowitz, Constance

NEW JERSEY

Bloomfield
Hart, Richard E.
Price, Robert M.

Caldwell
Krug, Barbara C.

Camden
Carter, Theodore Ulysses
Cottrol, Robert James
Eichelberger, William L.
Feinman, Jay M.
Hull, N. E. H.
Klinghoffer, Arthur Jay
Kludze, A. Kodzo Paaku

Chatham
Kim, Younglae

Cranford
Wolfe, Deborah Cannon Partridge

Douglass
Bunzl, Martin

Dumont
Dorn, Louis

East Orange
Boraas, Roger Stuart
Chethimattam, John Britto

Ewing
Barnes, Gerald
Gotthelf, Allan
Omole-Odubekun, Omolola E.
Roberts, Melinda
Winston, Morton E.

Glassboro
Ashton, Dianne C.
Clough, Sharon
Jiao, Allan

Hackettstown
Serafini, Anthony

Haddonfield
Clouser, Roy A.
White, Hugh

Hawthorne
Scott, Kieran

Hoboken
Bennett, Philip W.
Linsenbard, Gail E.

Irvington
Williams, Junius W.

Jamesburg
Kramer-Mills, Hartmut

Jersey City
Carter, Guy C.
Cassidy, Laurence Lavelle
Giles, Thomas Ransom
Kennedy, Robert E.
Loughran, James N.
Schmidt, William John
Scott, Gary Alan
Sheridan, Thomas L.

Lakewood
Schubert, Judith
Witman, Edward Paul

Lawrenceville
Brown, Jerry Wayne
Good, Robert C.
Iorio, Dominick Anthony
Stroh, Guy Weston

Leonia
Barlow, J. Stanley

Linwood
Lacy, Allen

Lodi
Burnor, Richard N.

Pecorino, Philip Anthony
Rivera, Jenny
Zwiebach, Burton

Fly Creek
Kuzminski, Adrian

Fredonia
Belliotti, Raymond A.
Kohl, Marvin
Steinberg, Theodore Louis

Garden City
Ferrara, Louis F.
James, Marquita L.

Garrison
Sharpe, Virginia A.

Geneseo
Cook, William Robert
Deutsch, Kenneth L.
Edgar, William John
Soffer, Walter

Geneva
Baer, Eugen Silas
Daise, Benjamin
Gerhart, Mary
Lee, Steven Peyton
Simson, Rosalind

Germantown
Szasz, Paul Charles

Greenvale
Brier, Bob
Watanabe, Morimichi

Hamilton
Carter, John Ross
Glazebrook, Patricia
Irwin, Joyce Louise
Jacobs, Jonathan
Kepnes, Steven D.
McCabe, David
McIntyre, Lee C.
Olcott, Martha
Rubenstein, Eric M.
Terrell, Huntington
Vecsey, Christopher
Wetzel, James Richared
Witherspoon, Edward, Jr.

Harrison
Pepper, George B.

Hastings on Hudson
Forman, Robert

Hemlock
Eberle, Rolf A.

Hempstead
Holland, Robert A.
Teehan, John
Wallace, Kathleen

Houghton
Eckley, Richard K.
Schultz, Carl
Tyson, John R.

Huntington
Abramson, Harold I.
Hochberg, Stephen
Klein, Richard
Shaw, Gary M.
Swartz, Barbara E.

Ithaca
Bailey, Lee
Bensel, Richard F.
Benson, LeGrace
Carmichael, Calum MacNeill
Clermont, Kevin Michael
Cramton, Roger C.
Hodes, Harold T.
Hutcheson, Richard E.
Kates, Carol A.
MacDonald, Scott C.
McClain, John O.
McKenna, Michael S.
Mieczkowski, Bogdon
Neuhouser, Frederick
Palmer, Larry Isaac
Powers, David Stephen
Rachlinski, J. J.
Schwab, Stewart J.
Smith, Daniel L.
Summers, Robert Samuel
Wolfram, Charles W.

Jackson Heights
Walsh, Jerome T.

Jamaica
Boyle, Robin A.
Dolling, Lisa M.
Gregory, David L.
McKenna, John H., C.M.
Primeaux, Patrick
Satterfield, Patricia Polson
Slattery, Kenneth F.
Sovern, Jeff
Upton, Julia A.
White, Howard A.
White, Leland J.
Zirkel, Patricia McCormick

Katonah
Nnoruka, Sylvanos I.

Loudonville
Boisvert, Raymond
Dick, Michael B.
Fesmire, Steven A.
Meany, Mary Walsh
Zaas, Peter S.

Louisville
Burkey, John

Lynbrook
Langiulli, Nino Francis

Mount Vernon
Shaw, Susan J.

New Paltz
Garlick, Peter C.
Heath, Eugene

New Rochelle
Cutney, Barbara
Deignan, Kathleen P., CND
Jonas, Hans
Morgan, Joseph
O'Neill, William George

New York
Addams, Robert David
Alexakis, Alexander
Amsterdam, Anthony G.
Arkway, Angela
Awn, Peter
Babich, Babette E.
Balmer, Randall
Barnes, Joseph Nathan
Baumbach, Gerard
Baumrin, Bernard Herbert
Bayer, Richard C.
Bell, Derrick Albert, Jr.
Benson, Lenni B.
Berger, Vivian O.
Bernstein, Richard J.
Berofsky, Bernard A.
Betts, Richard Kevin
Blasius, Mark
Bleich, J. David
Block, Ned
Bloom, Irene
Boddewyn, Jean J.
Boghossian, Paul
Borg, Dorothy
Botein, Michael
Boyle, Ashby D., II
Brabant, Jozef M.
Braxton, Edward Kenneth
Brickman, Lester
Bristow, Edward
Brown, Steven M.
Cantor, Norman Frank
Capra, Daniel J.
Carman, Taylor
Carpenter, James Anderson
Castelli, Elizabeth
Chapman, Robert L.
Christopher, Russell L.
Cohen, Burton I.
Cohen, Martin Aaron
Cone, James H.
Cunningham, L. A.
Cunningham, Sarah Gardner
Davies, Brian
de Grazia, Edward
Deutsch, Celia
Devitt, Michael
deVries, Paul
Diller, Matthew
Dinkins, David N.
Donohue, John Waldron
Dorsen, Norman
Dougherty, Ray Cordell
Driver, Tom Faw
Eustice, James S.
Farnsworth, E. Allan
Feerick, John David
Feinberg, Barbara Jane
Feingold, Henry L.
Feldman, Yael S.
Felsenfeld, Carl
Field, Hartry
Fine, Kit
Fisher, Saul
Fishman, David E.
Fleming, James E.
Fletcher, Anthony Q.
Fletcher, George Philip
Fletcher, Robert E.
Fogelman, Martin
Fox, Eleanor M.
Franck, Thomas M.
Franklin, Naomi P.
Freeman, James B.
Fritsche, Johannes
Gallagher, David M.
Ganz, David L.
Gardner, Richard Newton
Garfinkel, Stephen Paul
Garro, A. M.
Geistfeld, Mark
Gelb, Joyce
Gerber, Jane Satlow
Gillman, Neil
Gluck, Andrew L.
Godfrey, Mary F.
Goldfarb, Jeffrey C.
Gottschalk, Alfred
Gottwald, Norman Karol
Gourevitch, Victor
Govan, Reginald C.
Gowans, Christopher W.
Grad, Frank P.
Gray, Ronald A.
Greco, John
Green, Judith
Greenawalt, Robert Kent
Greenbaum, Michael B.
Gross, Karen
Halberstam, Malvina
Halivni, David
Hamilton, Charles Vernon
Han, Jin Hee
Hardy, Michael A.
Hauser, Thomas
Hawley, John Stratton
Heidt, Sarah L.
Heller, Agnes
Henkin, Louis
Hoeflin, Ronald K.
Holtz, Avraham
Holtz, Barry
Hoxie, Ralph Gordon
Iannuzzi, John N.
Irvin, Dale T.
Isasi-Diaz, Ada Maria
Jackson, Janice Tudy
Jacobson, Arthur J.
Jervis, Robert
Johnson, John W.
Johnson, Patricia L.
Jones, Judith A.
Jones, William K.
Joseph, Weiler H. H.
Kahan, Marcel
Kamm, Frances Myrna
Kasachkoff, Tziporah
Katsoris, Constantine N.
Kaufmann, Frank
Kelbley, Charles A.
Kennedy-Day, Kiki
Kenny, Alfreida B.
Kitcher, Patricia
Kitcher, Philip
Korn, Harold Leon
Kovaleff, Theodore Philip
Kraemer, David
Kristeller, Paul Oskar
Kuhns, Richard
Lackey, Douglas Paul
Lamm, Norman
Landes, George Miller
Landesman, Charles
Lerner, Anne Lapidus
Levi, Isaac
Libo, Kenneth Harold
Lieberman, Jethro K.
Lienhard, Joseph T.
Lindt, Gillian
Lipsey, Robert E.
Lotz, David Walter
Lowenfeld, Andreas F.
Lubetski, Edith
Mann, Gurinder Singh
Marcus, David
Marsh, James L.
Martel, Leon C.
Martin, Randy
Martinez, H. Salvador
Marx, Anthony W.
Matasar, Richard
McGuckin, John A.
McLaughlin, Joseph M.
Menke, Christoph
Meron, Theodor
Miller, Danna R.
Miller, James
Millstein, Ira M.
Mockler, Robert J.
Mothersill, Mary
Muller, Ralf
Mullin, Robert Bruce
Murphy, Liam Beresford
Myers, Robert
Nagel, Thomas
Nikulin, Dmitri
Ostertag, Gary
Patry, William F.
Patterson, Mark R.
Pearce, Russell G.
Penrod, Steven D.
Perillo, Joseph M.
Peters, Francis Edward
Petit, Philip
Prager, Jonas
Press, Gerald
Price, Monroe E.
Proudfoot, Wayne
Purcell, E. A.
Quinn, Thomas Michael
Rabinowitz, Mayer E.
Reese, Thomas
Reichberg, Gregory M.
Reid, John P.
Reidenberg, Joel R.
Riggins, Thomas
Roe, Mark J.
Rosenfeld, Michel
Rosenthal, David M.
Rubinstein, Ernest
Rudenstine, David
Sachs, William L.
Santa Maria, Dario Atehortua
Schneider, Samuel
Schorsch, Ismar
Schroeder, Jeanne L.
Schwartz, Shuly Rubin
Schwartz, William
Scott, Gregory L.
Segal, Alan Franklin
Seiple, David I.
Shapiro, Scott J.
Shaviro, Daniel N.
Shaw, Theodore Michael
Sherwood, O. Peter
Shriver, Donald W.
Shusterman, Richard
Simmelkjaer, Robert T.
Slater, Peter
Smit, Hans
Smith, Mark Stratton
Smith, Terry
Soffer, Gail
Somerville, Robert
Sovern, Michael I.
Sproul, Barbara Chamberlain
Stambaugh, Joan
Stanislawski, Michael
Stone, S. L.
Strauss, Peter L.
Strickman, Norman
Strum, Philippa
Suggs, Jon-Christian
Tancredi, Laurence Richard
Taran, Leonardo
Terezakis, Katie
Thomas, Chantal
Thomas, Kendall
Tillers, Peter
Toote, Gloria E. A.
Townes, Emilie M.
Tress, Daryl McGowen
Tubb, Gary
Tucker, Gordon
Turetzky, Nachum
Ulanov, Ann Belford
Uviller, H. Richard
Varzi, Achille C.
Visotzky, Burton L.
Vorspan, Rachel
Walker, Margaret Urban
Walker, Wyatt Tee
Walsh, James Jerome
Walton, R. Keith
Waltz, Kenneth Neal
Wang, Hao
Washington, James Melvin
Way, Gary Darryl
Webber, George Williams
Weidmann, Frederick W.
Weisberg, Richard H.
Weisberg, Richard H.
Weisenfeld, Judith
Weiss, T. G.
Wertheimer, Jack
Whelan, Stephen T.
White, Donald Wallace
Whitebook, Joel
Wigal, Donald
Williams, Kyle
Wimbush, Vincent L.
Wink, Walter
Wishart, Lynn
Wright, John Robert
Wurzburger, Walter S.
Yovel, Yirmiyahu
Zagano, Phyllis
Zimmerman, Diane L.
Zito, Angela
Zweig, Arnulf

Newburgh
Cotter, James Finn

Niagara University
Bonnette, Dennis
Waters, Raphael Thomas

Nyack
Crockett, William
Danaher, James
Poston, Larry A.
Ruegsegger, Ronald W.
Thayer, H. S.

Oakland Gardens
Altman, Ira

Ogdensburg
Rocker, Stephen

Oneonta
Burrington, Dale E.
Green, Michael
Koch, Michael
Koddermann, Achim D.
Malhotra, Ashok Kumar
Roda, Anthony
Shrader, Douglas Wall, Jr.

Orangeburg
Lounibos, John

Oswego
Echelbarger, Charles G.

Pleasantville
Leiser, Burton

Pobdam
Mamary, Anne

Pomona
Kolak, Daniel

Port Jefferson
Schievella, P. S.

Potsdam
Hinchman, Lewis P.
Tartaglia, Philip

Poughkeepsie
Amaru-Halpern, Betsy
Borradori, Giovanna
Brakas, Jurgis George
Church, Jennifer
Cladis, Mark
Doherty, John F.

Canton
Dymale, Herbert Richard
Watson, D. F.

Cedarville
Schultz, Walter

Cincinnati
Al'Uqdah, William Mujahid
Atkins, Robert
Bracken, J. A.
Callan, T.
Cook, Michael J.
Cottrell, Jack Warren
Eagleson, Ian
Edwards, Ruth McCalla
Evans, William
Gauker, Christopher P.
Giblin, Marie J.
Harris, Norman
Kaufman, Stephen Allan
Kirshbaum, Hal
Knitter, Paul Francis
Kraut, Benny
Krome, Frederic
Lillie, Betty Jane
Meyer, Michael Albert
Minnich, Elizabeth
Moustakas, Clark
Petuchowski, Jakob Josef
Richardson, Robert Calvin
Rind, Miles
Rivers, Clarence Joseph
Rura, Svetlana
Rutter, Irvin C.
Sarason, Richard Samuel
Sharpe, Kevin J.
Thatcher, Tom
Thomas, Norman C.
Traub, George William
Weatherly, Jon A.
Welton, William A.
Wilson, Samuel S.
Wooldredge, John
York, Anthony Delano

Cleveland
Agich, George J.
Chandler, Everett A.
Epp, Eldon Jay
Fox, Richard Milan
Gensler, Harry J.
Gibbs, Lee Wayland
Gibbs, Paul J.
Grundy, Kenneth William
Haas, Peter J.
Johnson, Steven D.
Kadish, Mortimer R.
Katz, Lewis Robert
Kelly, Joseph F.
Ledford, Kenneth F.
Mason, David Raymond
McCoy, Patricia A.
McElhaney, James Willson
McHale, Vincent Edward
Mehlman, Maxwell
Murphy, Tim
Murray, J. Glenn
Pole, Nelson
Robertson, Heidi Gorovitz
Rooks, Charles Shelby
Rowan, Albert T.
Sharpe, Calvin William
Spencer, James Calvin, Sr.
Warren, Ann Kosser
Werth, Lee Frederick
Whitbeck, Caroline
White, Frederic Paul, Jr.
Willacy, Hazel M.

Columbus
Anderson, Dennis A.
Beatty, Otto, Jr.
Binau, Brad A.
Boh, Ivan
Bouman, Walter R.
Brand, Eugene L.
Brown, Lee Bateman
Carter, Percy A., Jr.
Childs, James M., Jr.
Doermann, Ralph W.
Elhard, Leland E.
Friedman, Harvey Martin
Gibbs, Jack Gilbert, Jr.
Hahm, David Edgar
Harms, Paul W. F.
Hoops, Merlin Henry
Huber, Donald L.
Huffman, Gordon, Jr.
Hutton, Rodney R.
Irwin, Raymond D.
Jost, Timothy Stolzfus
Kevern, John
Kielkopf, Charles F.
Kozyris, Phaedon John
Luck, Donald G.
Lynch, Joseph Howard
Makau, Josina M.
Nakamura, C. Lynn
Pappas, George Sotiros
Parks, Edward Y.
Patterson, Samuel C.
Pessin, Sarah
Powell, Mark Allan
Redenbarger, Wayne Jacob
Root, Michael
Sager, Allan Henry
Scanlan, James P.
Schwarz, May L.
Shields, Mary E.
Smith, Susan Warrener
Stebenne, David
Steckel, Richard H.
Strasser, Mark
Taylor, Walter F., Jr.
Thomas, M. Carolyn
Turnbull, Robert George
Wade, Robert J.
Wanner, Dieter
Whaley, Douglas John
White, Janice G.
Williams, Gregory Howard

Dayton
Anderson, William P.
Barnes, Michael Horton
Barr, David Lawrence
Benson, Paul H.
Branick, Vincent P.
Chinchar, Gerald T.
Doyle, Dennis M.
Fischer, Marilyn R.
Fouke, Daniel C.
Gorrell, Donald Kenneth
Hagel, Thomas L.
Heft, James L.
Herbenick, Raymond M.
Hertig, Paul
Hertig, Young Lee
Inbody, Tyron Lee
Inglis, John
Jablonski, Leanne M.
Johnson, Patricia Altenbernd
Kim, Ai Ra
Kozar, Joseph F.
Kunkel, Joseph C.
Lockwood, Kimberly Mosher
Luke, Brian A.
Lysaught, M. Therese
Martin, Judith G.
Moore, Cecilia
Mosser, Kurt
Nelson, James David
Preisser, Thomas
Quinn, John F.
Richards, William M.
Tibbetts, Paul E.
Tilley, Terrence W.
Ulrich, Lawrence P.
Welborn, L. L.
Wert, Newell John
Yocum, Sandra Mize
Zimmerman, Joyce Ann

Delaware
Easton, Loyd D.
Mercadante, Linda A.
Michael, Randall Blake
Smith, Ervin
Tannehill, Robert C.
Twesigye, Emmanuel

Findlay
Cecire, Robert C.
Draper, David E.
Kern, Gilbert Richard
Resseguie, James L.
Shilling, Burnette P.
Stulman, Louis

Gambier
Adler, Joseph A.
DePascuale, Juan E.

Granville
Ball, David T.
Cort, John E.
Lisska, Anthony Joseph
Martin, James Luther
Santoni, Ronald Ernest
Woodyard, David O.

Hiram
Slingerland, Dixon

Huber Heights
Puckett, Pauline N.

Kent
Barnbaum, Deborah
Culbertson, Diana
Fischer, Norman Arthuf
Nantambu, Kwame
Ryan, Frank X.
Wheeler, Arthur M.
Zellner, Harold Marcellars

Lima
Asuagbor, Greg

Marietta
Machaffie, Barbara J.

Marion
Handwerk-Noragon, Patricia

Middletown
Domino, Brian

Milford
Oppenheim, Frank M.

Mount Vernon
Cubie, David Livingston

Munroe Falls
DiPuccio, William

New Concord
Barrett, J. Edward
McClelland, William Lester
Nutt, R.

Newark
Shapiro, Stewart
Shiels, Richard Douglas

North Canton
Norton-Smith, Thomas M.

Oberlin
Krassen, Miles
McInerney, Peter K.
Merrill, Daniel Davy
Richman, Paula
Zinn, Grover A.

Oxford
Forshey, Harold Odes
Kane, Stanley G.
Kelly, Jim Kelly
McKenna, William R.
Momeyer, Rick
Newell, William H.
Pappu, Rama Rao
Rejai, Mostafa
Seidel, Asher M.
Sommer, John D.
Ward, Roy Bowen
Williams, Peter W.

Painesville
McQuaid, Kim
Miller, Benjamin

Pepper Pike
Gromada, Conrad T.
Matejka, George

Reynoldsburg
Rolwing, Richard J.

Rio Grande
Barton, Marcella Biro

Shaker Heights
Giannelli, Paul Clark

Springfield
Copeland, Warren R.
Levy, Robert J.
Millen, Rochelle L.
Nelson, Paul T.
Swanger, Eugene R.
Vincent, David
Wolf, Herbert Christian

Stenberville
Vall, Gregory

Steubenville
Miletic, Stephen F.
Scotto, Dominic

Stow
Ophardt, Michael

Toledo
Al-Marayati, Abid Amin
Andersen, Roger William
Barrett, John A.
Bourguignon, Henry J.
Bullock, Joan R.
Chapman, Douglas K.
Closius, Phillip J.
Edwards, Richard W.
Eisler, Beth A.
Friedman, Howard M.
Harris, David A.
Hopperton, Robert J.
Jan, George Pokung
Kadens, Michael G.
Kennedy, Bruce
Kennedy, Robin M.
Kirtland, Robert
Martyn, Susan
Merritt, Frank S.
Moran, Gerald P.
Mostaghel, Deborah M.
Puligandla, Ramakrishna
Quick, Albert T.
Raitt, Ronald D.
Richman, William M.
Steinbock, Daniel J.
Stern, David S.
Tierney, James E.
Zietlow, Rebecca

University Heights
McGinn, Sheila E.

Warren
Eminhizer, Earl Eugene

Westerville
Cooper, Allan D.
Halbert, Debora

Wickliffe
Hunter, Frederick Douglas
Latcovich, Mark A.

Wilberforce
Garland, John William

Wilmington
Jones, Thomas Canby

Wooster
Bell, Richard H.
Bucher, Glenn R.
Harris, Ishwar C.
Hustwit, Ronald E.
Plestina, Dijana
Scholz, Susanne
Smith, Robert Houston
Thomson, Garrett

Worthington
Josephson, Susan G.

Yellow Springs
Patel, Ramesh
Smoker, Paul L.
Warren, Scott

Youngstown
Leck, Glorianne Mae
Minogue, Brendan Patrick
Shipka, Thomas A.

OKLAHOMA

Bethany
Tashjian, Jirair S.

Edmond
Jackson, Joe C.

Norman
Barker, Peter
Cohen, Andrew I.
De Bolt, Darian C.
Doty, Ralph
Forman, Jonathan Barry
Hambrick, A. Fred
Hester, Lee
Merrill, Kenneth Rogers
Perkins, Edward Joseph
Scaperlanda, Michael
Treat, James
Wren, Daniel Alan

Oklahoma City
Arrow, Dennis Wayne
Brophy, Alfred L.
Emler, Donald
Faltyn, Tim
Gigger, Helen C.
Miller, John Douglas
Walton, Woodrow E.

Shawnee
Roberts, Victor William

Stillwater
Cain, James
Converse, Hyla Stuntz
Lawry, Edward George
Luebke, Neil Robert
Scott, Walter Gaylord
Smallwood, James Milton

Tahlequah
Sharp, Mike

Tishomingo
Rodden, Kirk A.

Tulsa
Blankemeyer, Kenneth Joseph
Brown, Paul Llewellyn
Clark, David S.
Goodwin, James Osby
Lederle, Henry
Mansfield, Mecklin Robert
Smith, Dennis E.
Tabbernee, William
Thorpe, Samuel
Vance, Donald Richard
Will, W. Marvin

OREGON

Corvallis
Campbell, Courtney S.
Clinton, Richard Lee
Hosoi, Y. Tim
Leibowitz, Flora L.
List, Peter C.
Moore, Kathleen D.
Ramsey, Jeff
Roberts, Lani
Scanlan, Michael
Uzgalis, William

Eugene
Baskin, Judith R.
Brownmiller, Sara N.
Epps, Garrett
Forell, Caroline
Hildreth, Richard George
Krawiec, Kimberly D.
Porter, Samuel C.
Sanders, Jack Thomas
Scoles, Eugene Francis
Sheets-Johnstone, Maxine

Forest Grove
Marenco, Marc

Gresham
Alexander, Ralph H.

Hammond
Lambert, J. Karel

Medford
Wells, Donald A.

Monmouth
Cannon, Dale W.
Perlman, Mark

Geographic Index

Scranton
Baker, Thomas E.
Casey, Timothy
Frein, Brigid Curtin
Friedrichs, David
Klonoski, Richard
Kopas, Jane
Mathews, Edward G., Jr.
McGinley, John Willard
Parente, William
Pinches, Charles R.
Sable, Thomas F.

Selinsgrove
Bohmbach, Karla G.
Whitman, Jeffrey P.

Slippery Rock
Larsen, Allan W.
Wilson, Bradley E.

Swarthmore
Frost, Jerry William
Meyer, Milton Wachsberg
Oberdiek, Hans Fredrick
Swearer, Donald K.

Uniontown
Pluhar, Evelyn Begley
Pluhar, Werner S.

Unionville
Grassie, William

University Park
Anderson, Douglas R.
Bodian, Miriam
Covert, Henry
Foti, Veronique M.
LaPorte, Robert, Jr.
Lingis, Alphonso
Ng, On-cho
Prebish, Charles Stuart
Price, Robert George
Russon, John E.
Sallis, John C.
Scott, Charles

Villanova
Abraham, Gerald
Anderson, Michelle J.
Becker, Lewis
Bersoff, Donald N.
Betz, Joseph M.
Brakman, Sarah-Vaughan
Brogan, Doris DelTosto
Brogan, Walter A.
Burt, Donald X.
Busch, Thomas W.
Cannon, John J.
Caputo, John D.
Carvalho, John
Cohen, Arnold B.
Colwell, Chauncey
Conn, Walter Eugene
Crabtree, Arthur Bamford
Dellapenna, Joseph W.
Dobbyn, John Francis
Doody, John A.
Doorley, Mark J.
Edelman, Diane Penneys
Eigo, Francis Augustine
Fielder, John H.
Flannery, Michael T.
Gafni, Abraham J.
Goff, Edwin L.
Gordon, Ruth E.
Gotanda, John Yukio
Hughes, Kevin L.
Hyson, John M.
Immerwahr, John
James, William
Johannes, John R.
Juliano, Ann Carey
Lanctot, Catherine J.
Llewellyn, Don W.
Losoncy, Thomas A.
Lurie, Howard R.
Magid, Laurie
Makowski, Lee
Malik, Hafeez
Maule, James Edward
McCartney, James J.
Miles, Kevin Thomas
Mulroney, Michael
Murphy, John F.
O'Brien, J. Willard
Packel, Leonard
Paffenroth, Kim
Pohlhaus, Gaile
Poulin, Anne Bowen
Prince, John R.
Rothman, Frederick P.
Schmidt, Dennis
Schoenfeld, Marcus
Scholz, Sally J.
Sirico, Louis J., Jr.
Taggart, Walter John
Termini, Roseann B.
Tomarchio, John
Turkington, Richard C.
Vanallen, Rodger
Wall, Barbara E.
Wertheimer, Ellen
Young, Phillips Edward

Washington
Mitchell, R. Lloyd
Schrader, David

Waynesburg
Glidden, Jock
Vernezze, Peter J.

West Brandywine
Dougherty, James E.

Wexford
Wangu, Madhu Bazaz

Wilkes-Barre
Irwin, William T.

Williamsport
Griffith, Stephen R.
Hughes, Richard Allan

Wyncote
Kamionkowski, Susan T.
Staub, Jacob J.

Wynnewood
Brauch, Manfred T.
Gross, Nancy Lammers
Keener, Craig S.
Koch, Glenn A.
McDaniel, Thomas F.
McNally, Michael J.
Sider, Ronald J.

York
Diener, Paul W.

RHODE ISLAND

Bristol
Bogus, Carl T.
Conley, Patrick Thomas

Kingston
Kim, Yong Choon

Middletown
Demy, Timothy J.

Newport
Croke, Prudence Mary
Liotta, Peter H.

Pautucket
Brodsky, Garry

Providence
Ackerman, Felicia
Almeida, Onesimo
Boss, Judith A.
Brock, Dan W.
Chambers, Timothy
Devine, Philip E.
Dreier, James
Estlund, David
Frerichs, Ernest S.
Gill, Mary Louise
Keating, James
Keefer, Donald R.
Reeder, John P., Jr.
Regnister, Bernard
Schmitt, Richard George
Stowers, Stanley Kent
Twiss, Sumner Barnes
Van Cleve, James
Wilcox, Joel

SOUTH CAROLINA

Central
Bross, James Beverley
Johnson, Dale

Charleston
Moore, Fred Henderson

Clemson
Hardesty, Nancy A.
McLean, Edward L.
Satris, Stephen A.
Smith, Kelly C.

Clinton
Presseau, Jack R.

Columbia
Adams, Gregory B.
Baird, Davis
Beyer, Bryan E.
Boyle, F. Ladson
Bridwell, R. Randal
Carter, Jeffrey D. R.
Costa, Michael J.
Crystal, Nathan M.
Day, Richard E.
Farley, Benjamin Wirt
Felix, Robert E.
Flanagan, James F.
Fowler, Vivia
Grigsby, Marshall C.
Hackett, Jeremiah M.
Haggard, Thomas R.
Halberstam, Michael
Harvey, John D.
Hubbard, F. Patrick
Johanson, Herbert A.
Johnson, Herbert A.
Jones, Donald L.
Kegley, Charles W.
Khushf, George
Lacy, Philip T.
Lewis, Kevin
Long, Eugene T.
Mather, Henry S.
Mathias, William J.
McAninch, William S.
McCabe, Kimberly A.
McCullough, Ralph C., II
Medlin, S. Alan
Miller, J. Mitchell
Montgomery, John E.
Mulholland, Kenneth B.
Owen, David G.
Patterson, Elizabeth G.
Peterson, Brian
Quirk, William J.
Skrupskelis, Agnas K.
Smalls, O'Neal
Sprague, Rosamond Kent
Stephens, R. Eugene
Underwood, James L.

Conway
DeWitt, Franklin Roosevelt
Rauhut, Nils

Due West
Johnson, Merwyn S.

Greenville
Beale, David Otis
Block, John Martin
Buford, Thomas O.
McKnight, Edgar Vernon
Schnaiter, Samuel E.
Worth, Sarah Elizabeth

Greenwood
Archie, Lee C.

Hartsville
Doubles, Malcolm Carroll

Inman
Combes, Richard E.

Okatie
Fitzgerald, John Joseph

Orangeburg
Gore, Blinzy L.

Pawleys Island
Comfort, Philip W.

Rock Hill
Craighead, Houston Archer
Wright-Botchwey, Roberta Yvonne

Spartanburg
Bullard, John Moore
Dunn, Joe Pender
Keller, James Albert
Michelman, Stephen A.

Sumter
Coyne, Anthony M.
Safford, John L.
Walsh, David John

SOUTH DAKOTA

Sioux Falls
Harris, J. Gordon
Leslie, Benjamin C.

Spearfish
Salomon, David A.

Vermillion
Meyer, Leroy N.
Whitehouse, George

Yankton
Frigge, S. Marielle
Kessler, Ann Verona

TENNESSEE

Athens
McDonald, William

Blountville
Charlton, Charles Hayes

Bristol
Fulop, Timothy E.

Chattanooga
Eskildsen, Stephen E.
Giffin, Phillip E.
Hall, Thor
Jacobs, David C.
Lippy, Charles
Resnick, Irven M.
Stewart, William H.
Switala, Kristin

Clarksville
Gildric, Richard P.
Muir, Malcolm, Jr

Cleveland
Beaty, James M.
Bowdle, Donald N.
Hoffman, Daniel
McMahan, Oliver
Moore, Rickie D.
Simmons, William A.
Waldrop, Richard E.

Collegedale
Coombs, Robert Stephen
Morris, Derek

Dayton
Ingolfsland, Dennis E.

Germantown
Cox, Steven L.
Miller, Stephen R.

Gullatin
Butler, Trent C.

Hendersonville
Varnado, Douglas

Hermitage
Albin, Thomas R.

Jackson
Davenport, Gene Looney
Dockery, David S.
Gushee, David P.
Patterson, James A.
Whitehead, Brady, Jr.

Jefferson City
Hawkins, Merrill M.

Johnson City
Gold, Jeff
Keith, Heather
LaFollette, Hugh
Rogers, W. Kim
Shanks, Niall
Shields, Bruce E.
Stenstad, Gail
Zavodny, John

Knoxville
Alexakos, Panos D.
Aquila, Richard E.
Bennett, James O.
Cohen, Sheldon M.
Edwards, Rem B.
Freeman, Edward C.
Galligan, Thomas C. Thomas C
Hardwig, John R.
Hodges, John O.
Speidell, Todd

Lenoir City
Wilson, Jack Howard

Martin
Maness, Lonnie E.

Memphis
Batey, Richard A.
Bufford, Edward Eugene
Chambliss, Prince C., Jr.
Dekar, Paul R.
Favazza, Joseph A.
Lacy, William Larry
Lewis, Jack Pearl
Limper, Peter Frederick
McKim, Donald K.
Muesse, Mark William
Nenon, Thomas J.
Prince, Arthur
Reed, Ross Channing
Robinson, Hoke
Russell, Irma S.
Shoemaker, David W.
Simco, Nancy Davis
Todd, Virgil H.
Walsh, Carey Ellen
Wharton, A. C., Jr.
Zaki, Mamoon

Milligan College
Farmer, Craig S.
Kenneson, Philip D.

Murfreesboro
Bombardi, Ronald Jude
Slate, Philip
Watson, Daivd Lowes
Young, David

Nashville
Arai, Paula K. R.
Baldwin, Lewis V.
Belton, Robert
Birch, Adolpho A., Jr.
Blumstein, James Franklin
Brown, R. L.
Burns, J. Patout, Jr.
Charney, Jonathan I.
Cloud, Fred
Compton, John J.
Cooper, Almeta E.
Covington, Robert N.
DeHart, Paul
Dickerson, Dennis Clark
Fisher, Eli D.
Froment-Meurice, Marc
Goodman, Lenn Evan
Graham, George Jackson
Handy, William Talbot, Jr.
Harrelson, Walter
Harrod, Howard L.
Haynes, William J., Jr.
Hodges, Michael P.
Hodgson, Peter C.
Hooks, Benjamin Lawson
Johnson, Dale Arthur
Lachs, John
Maier, Harold Geistweit
McCoy, Thomas Raymond

Putney
Halpern, Beth

Tunbridge
Wolfe, David L.

Washington
Felder, Cain Hope
Harvey, Louis-Charles
Miller, Tedd
Shopshire, James Maynard
Thornell, Richard Paul
Wilson, Willie Frederick

White River Junction
Madden, Edward H.

VIRGINIA

Alexandria
Bochnowski, Michael
Cook, Stephen L.
Davis, Ellen F.
Delacre, Georges
Dyer, James Mark
Eversley, Walter V. L.
Fuller, Reginald H.
Gearey, Amelia J.
Hanchey, Howard
Horne, Martha J.
Jones, Richard J.
McDaniel, Judith M.
Newman, Murray L.
Parrent, Allan Mitchell
Prichard, Robert W.
Ross, James F.
Scott, David Allen
Sedgwick, Timothy F.
Shosky, John
Stafford, William Sutherland
Walen, Alec D.

Arlington
Boylan, Michael A.
Byrne, James E.
Cohen, Lloyd R.
Hollander, Rachelle D.
Moss, Alfred A., Jr.

Ashland
Beatty, Joseph
Tuell, Steven Shawn

Blacksburg
Britt, Brian M.
Burian, Richard M.
Fitzpatrick, William J.
Hammond, Guy Bowers
Hattab, Helen
Klagge, James C.
Malbon, Elizabeth Struthers
Pitt, Joseph C.
Taylor, Charles L.

Bluefield
Crawford, Timothy G.
Lyle, Kenneth

Bridgewater
Phenix, Philip Henry

Buena Vista
Armstrong, John M.

Charlottesville
Bonnie, Richard J.
Casey, John Dudley
Childress, James Franklin
Cohen, George M.
Green, Mitchell S.
Hartt, Julian Norris
Howard, A. E. Dick
Leaman, George R.
Mathewes, Charles
Meador, Daniel John
Merrill, Richard Austin
Moore, John Norton
Nohrnberg, James Carson
Sabato, Larry J.
Scharlemann, Robert Paul
Scott, Nathan Alexander, Jr.
Secada, Jorge E. K.
Simmons, A. John
Stephan, Paul Brooke, III
Trotter, A. H., Jr.
Turner, Robert Foster
Wadlington, Walter James
White, G. Edward
Wollenberg, Bruce

Danville
Charity, Ruth Harvey
Laughlin, John C. H.

Dunn Loring
Mickolus, Edward F.

Fairfax
Kinnaman, Theodore J.
Pfund, Peter H.
Rothbart, Daniel
Tolchin, Susan Jane
Williams, Marcus Doyle

Fredericksburg
Aminrazavi, Mehdi

Front Royal
Carroll, Warren Hasty
Flippen, Douglas

Hampton
Duncan, John C., Jr.
Jefferson, M. Ivory
Jones, Bonnie Louise
Locke, Mamie Evelyn

Harrisburg
Fawkes, Don

Harrisonburg
Engle, James R.
Finger, Thomas
Gingerich, Ray C.
Grimsrud, Theodore G.
Keim, Albert N.
King, Sallie B.
Maclean, Iain Stewart
McKinney, Lauren D.
Morey, Ann-Janine
Sprunger, Mary S.
Weaver, Dorothy Jean
Zimmerman, Earl

Keswick
Bates, George Albert

Lexington
Brown, Alexandra
Davis, Winston
Hodges, Louis Wendell
Kirgis, Frederic Lee
LaRue, Lewis Henry
Martin, Joseph Ramsey
Partlett, David Frederick
Richter, Duncan J.
Sessions, William Lad

Lynchburg
Beck, W. David
Brindle, Wayne
Deibler, Timothy
Friedman, Lesley
Quillian, William F.
Scott, William
Towns, Elmer

Manassas
Ackley, John B.

Mechanicsville
Davis, Ronald E.

Natural Bridge
Cavanaugh, Maureen B.

Newport News
Beauchamp, Richard A.
Hoaglund, John Arthur
Powell, Jouett L.
Rose, Kenneth
Teschner, George A.

Norfolk
Brenner, William H.
Chen, Jie
Eckenwiler, Lisa A.
Evans, Rod L.
Ford, Lewis S.
Gainey, Randy R.
Hatab, Lawrence J.
Jones, William B.
Matthews, A. Warren
Putney, David P.
Shelton, Mark

Petersburg
Hill, Renee Afanan
Thigpen, Calvin Herritage

Radford
Lindberg, Debra
Martin, Glen T.

Reston
Myricks, Noel

Richmond
Achtemeier, Paul John
Bagby, Daniel G.
Brennen, Bonnie S.
Brown, William P.
Bryson, William Hamilton
Bugg, Charles B.
Cannon, Katie Geneva
Carroll, John T.
Ciulla, Joanne B.
Cobb, John Hunter, Jr.
Dawe, Donald Gilbert
DeVries, Dawn A.
Eakin, Frank Edwin
Edwards, Clifford Walter
Ellis, Anthony John
Farmer, David
Friedman, William Hillel
Gibson, William M.
Glover, Raymond F.
Gunlicks, Arthur B.
Hall, James
Hinson, E. Glenn
Hirsch, Herbert
James, Allix Bledsoe
Leary, David E.
Leith, John Haddon
Ottati, Douglas Fernando
Phipps, William Eugene
Polaski, Sandra Hack
Rissi, Mathias
Roberts, Samuel Kelton
Robertson, Benjamin W.
Rogers, Isabel Wood
Ross, Jerome C.
Schauber, Nancy Ellen
Shapiro, Gary
Shear, Jonathan
Smylie, James Hutchinson
Towner, Wayne Sibley
Valeri, Mark
Vallentyne, Peter

Roanoke
Delaney, David K.
Downey, James Patrick
Welch, John

Salem
Hartley, Roger
McDermott, Gerald D.

Stanardsville
Carpenter, Elizabeth S.

Virginia Beach
Foltz, Howard L.
Holman, Charles L.
Prosser, Peter E.
Story, J. Lyle
Synan, Vinson
Umidi, Joseph L.
Williams, J. Rodman

Williamsburg
Becker, Lawrence C.
Dwyer, James G.
Finn, Thomas M.
Furrow, Dwight
Kevelson, Roberta
Livingston, James Craig
Strong, John S.

Winchester
Copenhaver, John
Gladwin, Lee Allan

WASHINGTON

Bainbridge Island
Wellman, James K., Jr.

Bellingham
Feit, Neil
Hoover, Kenneth R.
Purtill, Richard L.
Stoever, William K. B.
Yusa, M.

Centralia
Vosper, Jim M.

Cheney
Kenney, Garrett C.

Clinton
Parks, Sharon Daloz

College Place
Maynard-Reid, Pedrito U.

Edmonds
Charette, Blaine
Payne, Philip B.

Ellensburg
Brennan, James Franklin
Keller, Chester

Issaquah
Harrisville, Roy A., III

Lacey
Langill, Richard L.
Seidel, George J.
Winston Suter, David

Mount Rainier
Andrew, Scott

Port Angeles
Machle, Edward Johnstone

Pullman
Broyles, James Earl
Keim-Campbell, Joseph
Myers, Michael W.
Shier, David

Seattle
Applegate, Judith K.
Burke, William Thomas
Chamberlain, Gary L.
Coburn, Robert C.
Cosway, Richard
Dombrowski, Daniel A.
Jay, Stewart
Keegan, John E.
Keyt, David
Kosrovani, Emilio M.
Leitich, Keith A.
Levi, Margaret
Mayerfeld, Jamie
McGee, Henry W., Jr.
Moore, Ronald
Palm, Craig W.
Potter, Karl Harrington
Prosterman, Roy L.
Reichmann, James B.
Risser, James C.
Rodriguez-Holguin, Jeanette
Scalise, Charles J.
Schoening, Jeffrey D.
Skover, David
Spina, Frank Anthony
Steele, Richard B.
Stoebuck, William Brees
Talbott, William J.
Taylor, Michael Joseph
Taylor, Velande P.
Vaughn, Lea B.
Warren, Linda
Webb, Eugene
Wells, Jonathan
Wicks, Andrew C.

Spokane
Baird, Forrest
Bynagle, Hans Edward
Cook, Michael L.
Dallen, James
Doohan, Helen
Downey, John
Edwards, James
Graham, J. Michele
Hartin, Patrick
Hunt, James
Mohrlang, Roger L.
Pomerleau, Wayne Paul
Sanford, Daniel
Sittser, Gerald L.
Stronks, Julia K.
Tyrrell, Bernard James
Wyma, Keith D.
Yoder, John

Tacoma
Alward, Lori L.
Arbaugh, George E.
Edwards, Douglas R.
Eklund, Emmet Elvin
Govig, Stewart D.
Ives, Christopher
Kay, Judith Webb
Killen, Patricia O'Connell
Nordby, Jon Jorgen
Oakman, Douglas E.
Pilgrim, Walter
Pinzino, Jane M.
Reigstad, Ruth
Staley, Jeffrey L.
Stivers, Robert L.

Vancouver
Dawn, Marva J.

Vashon Island
Lone, Jana Mohr

Yakima
Fike, Lawrence Udell, Jr.
Matsen, Herbert S.

WEST VIRGINIA

Buckhannon
Welliver, Kenneth Bruce

Fairmont
Pudsell, F. David

Huntington
Henderson, Herbert H.
Vielkind, John N.

Morgantown
Basu, Ananyo
Cohen, Debra R.
Drange, Theodore Michael
Eichorn, Lisa
Elkins, James R.
Jokic, Aleksander
Labys, Walter Carl
Maxey, B. Ann
Morris, William O.
Potesta, Woodrow A.
Selinger, Carl Marvin
Shapiro, Daniel
Vehse, Charles T.
Wicclair, Mark Robert
Wigal, Grace J.
Yura, Michael T.

Parkersburg
Allen, Bernard Lee

Philippi
Maddox, Timothy D. M.

West Liberty
Gold, Jonathan

Wheeling
Steltenkamp, Michael F.

WISCONSIN

Appleton
Boardman, William Smith
Dreher, John Paul
Ternes, Hans
Thompson, Leonard Leroy

De Pere
Abel, Donald C.
Duquette, David A.
Kersten, Frederick Irving
Patterson, Wayne Kief
Wadell, Paul J.

Geographic Index

Gray, Patrick T. R.
Maidman, Maynard Paul

Ottawa
Abell, Jennie
Anglin, Douglas G.
Baycroft, John A.
Bazan, Carlos
Benidickson, Jamie
Bonneau, Normand
Brook, Andrew
Coyle, J. Kevin
Currie, John H.
Dourley, John Patrick
Dray, William Herbert
Geraets, Theodore F.
Gourgues, Michel
Granger, Christopher
Gualtieri, Antonio Roberto
Kaplan, William
Korp, Maureen
Krawchuk, Andrii
Krishna, Vern
Kymlicka, Will
Lafrance, Yvon
Lamirande, Emilien
Magnet, Joseph E.
McRae, Donald M.
Mendes, Errol
Morse, Bradford W.
Osborne, Robert E.
Paciocco, David
Payne, Julien
Perrin, David
Petersen, Cynthia
Potvin, Thomas R.
Ratushny, Edward J.
Rodgers, Sanda
Sheehy, Elizabeth A.
Spry, Irene
Stainton, Robert J. H.
Sullivan, Ruth
Theriault, Michel
Vandenakker, John
VanDuzer, Anthony J.
Vogels, Walter A.
Way, Rosemary Cairns
Zweibel, Ellen

Peterborough
Burbidge, John William
Carter, Robert Edgar

Saint Catharines
Miles, Murray Lewis

Scarborough
Davies, Gordon F.
Ruthven, Jon M.

Sudbury
di Norcia, Vincent
Gagnon, Carolle
Giroux, Michel
Ketchen, Jim
Nash, Roger
Organ, Barbara
Pallard, Henri
Pelletier, Lucien
Sahadat, John
Simpson, Peter
Ward, Bruce

Toronto
Adams, George
Airhart, Phyllis
Ambrozic, Aloysius M.
Bazan, Bernardo C.
Bessner, Ronda
Best, Ernest E.
Bilaniuk, Petro Borys T.
Borrows, John
Boyle, Joseph
Braithwaite, John
Brown, James R.
Cameron, Donald M.
Ching, Julia
Chornenki, Genevieve A.
Code, Michael
Cole, Kenneth
Coop, Jack
Crowe, Frederick E.
Davies, Alan T.
De Sousa, Ronald B.
Dewart, Leslie
Dicenso, James
Dutcher-Walls, Patricia
Dyzenhaus, David
Eberts, Mary
Ellsworth, Randall
Evans, Donald D.
Fish, Arthur
Forguson, Lynd W.
Gannage, Mark
Gooch, Paul W.
Goodman, Susanne R.
Grant, John W.
Greenspan, Edward L.
Gupta, Neena
Hacking, Ian
Halperin, Stephen H.
Haney, Mary-Ann
Harris, Henry Silton
Hayes, Alan L.
Heath, Joseph
Hoffman, John C.
Hughes, Pamela S.
Hutchinson, Douglas S.
Hutchinson, Roger Charles
Irwin, William Henery
Jackman, Barbara
Jarvie, Ian Charles
Kennedy, David
Khan, Abrahim H.
Lawee, Eric J.
Leland, Charles Wallace
Leonard, Ellen M.
Lepofsky, David M.
Makuch, Stanley M.
Maniates, Maria Rika
Marmura, Michael Elias
Mason, Steve
McAuliffe, J. D.
Mcintire, Carl Thomas
McKague, Carla A.
McLellan, Bradley N.
Merkur, Dan
Morgan, Edward M.
Mullin, Amy M.
Nigosian, Solomon Alexander
Normore, Calvin Gerard
Norris, John
Northey, Rodney
Novak, David
Owens, Richard C.
Radomski, Harry B.
Rae, Bob
Richardson, Peter
Richardson, Stephen R.
Rosenthal, Peter
Sarra, Janis
Scarlett, James D.
Scharper, Stephen B.
Schner, George
Stefanovic, Ingid Leman
Stein, Janice Gross
Stitt, Allan J.
Stoeber, Michael
Swan, Kenneth P.
Swinton, Katherine E.
Trotter, Gary
Underwood, Harry
Vertin, Michael
Walters, Stanley D.
Wark, Wesley K.
Weinrib, Ernest Joseph
Winter, Ralph A.
Yalden, Robert

Trenton
Bonisteel, Roy

Waterloo
Abbott, W. R.
Ashworth, E. Jennifer
Brunk, Conrad
Campbell, Gerry
Centore, Floyd
Demarco, Don
DeVidi, Dave
George, Rolf A.
Grimes, Ronald L.
Groarke, Leo A.
Haworth, Lawrence L.
Hendley, Brian
Holmes, Richard H.
Horne, James R.
Klaassen, Walter
Lawson, Angus Kerr
Minas, Anne C.
Moore, Margaret
Novak, Joseph A.
Nutbrown, Richard A.
Orend, Brian
Reimer, James A.
Roberts, Don
Ross, Christopher F. J.
Seljak, David
Thagard, Paul
Van Evra, James
Van Seters, John
Wubnig, Judy

Windsor
Amore, Roy C.
Conklin, William E.
Manzig, John G. W.
Marasinghe, M. Lakshman
Mehta, Mahesh Maganlal
Nielsen, Harry A.
Weir, John P.
Wydrzynski, Christopher J.

QUEBEC

Chateauguay
Steigerwald, Diane

Laval
Ponton, Lionel
Roberge, Rene-Michel

Montreal
Bernier, Paul
Bird, Frederick
Boisvert, Mathieu
Boulad-Ayoub, Josiane
Bunge, Mario
Cauchy, Venant
Chausse, Gilles
Clarke, Murray
Davies, David
Deslauriers, Marguerite
Despland, Michel
DiGiovanni, George
Drage-Hale, Rosemary
Dwyer, Susan
Elkayam, Moshe
Gauthier, Yvon
Gravel, Pierre
Gray, Christopher
Hallett, Michael
Hamelin, Leonce
Hofbeck, Josef
Hori, G. Victor Sogen
Hudson, Robert
Joos, Ernest
Joseph, Norma Baumel
Kirby, Torrance W.
Klibansky, Raymond
Laywine, Alison
Lemieux, Lucien
Lewis, Eric
Lightstone, Jack
Mason, Sheila
McCall, Storrs
McDonough, Sheila
McGilvray, James
McLelland, Joseph Cumming
Menn, Stephen
Miller, David
Nielsen, Kai
Norton, David Fate
O'Connor, Dennis
Oppenheim, Michael
Ornstein, Jack
Orr, Leslie
Prades, Jose Albert
Ravvin, Norman
Rukmani, T. S.
Sharma, Arvind
Stroud, Sarah
Wayne, Andrew
Wright, Nicholas Thomas
Zeman, Vladimir

Quebec
de Koninck, Thomas
Pelchat, Marc

Rimouski
Dumais, Monique

Ste. Foy
Kempf, Stephen W.
Page, Jean-Guy
Painchaud, Louis

SASKATCHEWAN

Prince Albert
Schweitzer, Don

Regina
Krantz, Arthur A.
Spilsbury, Paul
Szabados, Bela

Saskatoon
Bilson, Beth
Bowden, Marie Ann
Buckingham, Don
Buckwold, Tamara
Cairns, Alan
Clark, Don
Corrigan, Kevin
Cuming, Ron
Flannigan, Rob
Foster, John
Fritz, Ron
Gosse, Richard
Greschner, Donna
Ish, Daniel
Jobling, David
Mackinnon, Peter
McConnell, William Howard
Norman, Ken
Quigley, Tim
Roach, Kent
Stephenson, Ken Cooper
Uitti, Roger W.
Vandervort, Lucinda
Wiegers, Wanda
Zlotkin, Norman

OTHER COUNTRIES

AUSTRALIA
Rothenberg, Gunther Eric

ENGLAND
Heilbron, John L.
Betz, Mark W.
Martines, Lauro
Pagel, Ulrich

SCOTLAND
Graham, Joyce